PASSENGER AND IMMIGRATION LISTS INDEX

1996 Supplement

Passenger and Immigration Lists Series

ISSN 0736-8267

PASSENGER AND IMMIGRATION LISTS INDEX

A Guide to Published Records
of More Than 2,540,000 Immigrants Who Came
to the New World between the Sixteenth
and the Mid-Twentieth Centuries

1996 Supplement

Edited by P. William Filby
and Paula K. Byers

GALE

an International Thomson Publishing company I(T)P®

Staff

Editors: P. William Filby, Paula K. Byers
Managing Editor: Neil E. Walker
Associate Editor: Frank V. Castronova
Proofreader: Sheri L. Chewning
Researcher: Margaret Johnson

Production Manager: Mary Beth Trimper
Production Assistant: Deborah Milliken
Graphic Services Manager: Barbara J. Yarrow
Desktop Publisher/Typesetter: C. J. Jonik

Manager, Data Entry Services: Benita L. Spight
Data Entry Supervisor: Gwendolyn S. Tucker
Data Entry Associates: Maleka Imrana, Kweli K. Jomo

Manager, Technical Support Services: Theresa Rocklin
Programmer: Ida M. Wright
Program Designers: Donald G. Dillaman, Al Fernandez, Jr.

Copyright ©1996
Gale Research Inc.
835 Penobscot Bldg.
Detroit, MI 48226-4094

Library of Congress Catalog Card Number 84-15404
ISBN 0-8103-9329-8
ISSN 0736-8267
Printed in the United States of America

I⊤P™   Gale Research, an ITP Information/Reference Group Company.
ITP logo is a trademark under license.

Passenger and Immigration Lists Index
Advisory Board

Arlene H. Eakle, PhD
President and Founder
The Genealogical Institute, Salt Lake City

Dorothy M. Lower
Former Head, History and Genealogy
Allen County Public Library, Fort Wayne, Indiana

Blair S. Poelman
Reference Consultant, U.S./Canada Reference
Family History Library, Salt Lake City

Curt B. Witcher
Manager, Genealogy Department
Allen County Public Library, Fort Wayne, Indiana

Contents

Foreword to
Passenger and Immigration Lists Index: 1996 Supplement

Passenger and Immigration Lists Index: 1996 Supplement brings together in one alphabet more than 131,000 citations found in over 110 published passenger, naturalization, and other immigration lists.

This book is the fifteenth supplement to the three-volume base set of *Passenger and Immigration Lists Index (PILI)*, published in 1981, which indexed over 300 published lists covering about 500,000 persons. *PILI* and its fifteen supplements now cover over 2,540,000 persons—still only a small fraction of the over 35,000,000 immigrants who came to the New World. For the user's convenience, all material in the first four annual supplements to the *PILI* base set is also available in one alphabet in *PILI 1982-85 Cumulated Supplements.* The material indexed in the *PILI 1986* through *1990* and *1991* through *1995 Supplements* is also available in one alphabet in *PILI 1986-90 Cumulated Supplements* and *PILI 1991-95 Cumulated Supplements*, respectively. At this time publication plans include a cumulation of annual supplements every five years.

For information on how to use *PILI,* please see the section entitled "How to Read a Citation," which begins on page xiii. **Complete bibliographic citations to the sources indexed in *PILI 1996 Supplement*, and the codes used to refer to them, may be found in the "Bibliography of Sources Indexed" section, beginning on page xvii.** Information as to where to find the sources indexed in *PILI* may be found in the "How to Locate Sources Indexed" section beginning on page xv.

Acknowledgments

In addition to the people acknowledged in the three-volume base set of *PILI,* the editors wish to thank the following individuals for their assistance with this supplement:

Ann Alder of Santa Clara, California

Judith P. Austin, Judith P. Reid, and Virginia S. Wood of the Library of Congress, Washington, D.C.

Orlo L. Jones and Terrence M. Punch for many of the Canadian sources

David F. Putnam and Yvette Longstaff, Reference Consultant, International Reference (for all French sources), of the Family History Library, The Church of Jesus Christ of Latter-day Saints, Salt Lake City, Utah

Ernest Thode of the Washington County Public Library, Marietta, Ohio

Special thanks are due to the Ontario Genealogical Society *(Families).*

Our appreciation, also, to the Advisory Board members, Arlene H. Eakle, Dorothy M. Lower, Blair S. Poelman, and Curt B. Witcher for their advice, encouragement, and recommendation of sources for this supplement of *Passenger and Immigration Lists Index.*

Last, but not least, my gratitude must go to Margaret Johnson of my immediate staff and the Gale Research editorial and data entry staffs, who have done so much to bring the whole project to fruition.

P. William Filby, F.S.G., F.N.G.S.
Former Director, Maryland Historical Society
January 1996

Introduction to
Passenger and Immigration Lists Index

Passenger and Immigration Lists Index (PILI) brings together in one alphabet citations to information about immigrants who arrived in the New World between the sixteenth and the mid-twentieth centuries. These names appear in a broad collection of published passenger lists, naturalization records, church records, family and local histories, voter and land registrations, etc.

Concept and Scope

Such lists are primary sources for genealogists, since, in the case of passenger lists, almost all passengers arriving in the New World during the period covered were not casual travelers but immigrants intending to remain in America as permanent residents. Information which documents a specific time and location of an immigrant in the New World is an invaluable aid to research on the history of a family in America. In addition, any of the lists that furnish this information may also furnish clues to the country of origin and other crucial bits of genealogical information. This is true of all the lists indexed in *PILI,* and researchers will want to make certain to consult the sources themselves for additional information.

It should be noted that in some cases variant versions of lists have been indexed in *PILI,* since copying is notoriously inaccurate and it is not unusual to note variations from list to list. Likewise, different information is frequently given about the circumstances of the immigration. Since no library holds all of the lists, the researcher will have a better opportunity to locate one of the versions.

Most of the sources indexed in the three-volume base set of *PILI* (1981) were identified by Harold Lancour's *Bibliography of Ship Passenger Lists, 1538-1825: Being a Guide to Published Lists of Early Immigrants to North America* (third edition revised by Richard J. Wolfe, New York: New York Public Library, 1963). In 1981, P.W. Filby edited a revised and updated edition of the Lancour bibliography, *Passenger and Immigration Lists Bibliography, 1538-1900: Being a Guide to Published Lists of Arrivals in the United States and Canada* (Detroit: Gale Research, 1981). Now in its second edition (published 1988), this bibliography identifies more than 2,550 published passenger and immigration lists, completely superseding Lancour's work. Many of the sources indexed in the earlier volumes of *PILI* are listed in *Passenger and Immigration Lists Bibliography,* 2nd edition.

Editorial Practices

All names listed in *PILI* have been compiled directly from published sources; unpublished sources are never indexed. The information given in a source about each immigrant and those accompanying him or her was edited to a standard format. Cross-references were made for each of those individuals who accompanied the primary listee since, without those cross-references, much valuable information would be lost.

PILI does not index passenger lists only. Naturalization lists and other publications where immigration to the New World can be determined to have occurred are indexed as well. Early in the project, the editors decided that all names, including alternate forms of the surname, in a given source would be indexed unless there was a definite reason for omission. Examples of names that would not be indexed are those whose data reflects birth in America or those with no listed surname.

The date and place appearing in *PILI* do *not* necessarily equate to the date and port of *arrival.* Locations referred to in some sources are in fact sometimes destinations, locations of settlement, or the particular location of the immigrant on the date cited. Dates may reflect the date of death, the date the listee requested permission to emigrate, or the point in time when documents place that person in the New World at the location specified. Although they are not ports and dates of arrival, these references are retained because the editors feel that when someone is searching for an elusive ancestor, all information is helpful. It is felt that no researcher will object to the inclusion of her or his ancestor even if the person did not arrive precisely on the date listed in *PILI*. By consulting the complete bibliographic citation for the source cited in a *PILI* entry, researchers can determine exactly what information the listed date and place represent.

While every attempt has been made to ensure accuracy, it has been impossible to search for corrections or errata in articles published after the ones indexed. Similarly, all names have been copied exactly as printed, even in cases where they might appear to be erroneous. Abbreviations, such as "Jno.," have been retained. Van, Van der, De, De La, von, van, etc. have been left as given in the source. Letters sometimes umlauted (¨) in German names (u, a, o) have not been spelled out (ue, ae, oe) unless they are spelled out in the source document.

It should be remembered that names of emigrants were often recorded as they were heard, that many emigrants could not spell their own names, and that authorities were not as literate as one would wish. Thus, variations in spelling of names occur and members of the same family arriving at different times or places may be found under more than one spelling. In using *PILI,* the researcher should search for every conceivable spelling of the name sought as well as adaptations of the surname based on the customs of the ancestor's country of origin. (For example, if the ancestor is a female of German extraction, the surname may be listed with an "in" appended at the end. Thus, "Mayer" is listed as "Mayerin.")

When ages given in the source books contain fractions of years, these fractions have been dropped. (For example, 14 1/2 will appear in *PILI* as 14.) Ages of children of less than a year have been shown in months, weeks, or days.

Suggestions Are Welcome

PILI, which indexes only published material, has had an effect on genealogical publishing. Researchers have responded to *PILI* by increasing their efforts to have new lists published. Librarians and researchers are encouraged to inform the editors of further lists that could be indexed in the future. Questions, comments, and suggestions may be sent to either Mr. P.W. Filby, Box 413, Savage, MD, 20763 or The Editors, *Passenger and Immigration Lists Index,* 835 Penobscot Bldg., Detroit, MI 48226-4094 [phone: (313)961-2242, fax: (313)961-6741].

How to Read a Citation

Citations in *Passenger and Immigration Lists Index (PILI)* can be of two types. The first type, the main entry, may read as follows:

```
     (1)         (2) (3)       (4) (5) (6)
Horan, Michael 38; New York, N.Y., 1848 9144 p47
          Wife: Anne 34
(7)       Son: Michael 6
          Son: Thomas 2
          Daughter: Catherine 4
```

The numbers in parentheses appearing in the above entry refer to the following explanations:

(1)   Name of the immigrant, as spelled in the original published source
(2)   Immigrant's age, when given
(3)   Place of arrival, naturalization, or other record of immigration
(4)   Year of arrival, naturalization, or other record of immigration
(5)   Code that refers to the source in which the particular list can be found. **Complete bibliographic citations to the sources indexed which include an explanation as to what information is provided by the place and year cited, and the codes used to refer to them, may be found in the "Bibliography of Sources Indexed" section, beginning on page xvii.**
(6)   Page number on which that particular name is listed in the source cited
(7)   Accompanying family members, if there are any, together with each person's relationship to the primary listee, and his or her age.

Occasionally a published list will not indicate a year of arrival or other reference year. In those instances the abbreviation *n.d.* (no date) is inserted:

Browne, John; Virginia, n.d. **6220** *p332*

Some immigration lists note that the main listee was accompanied by other persons, with only the relationships being indicated, and possibly the ages. Such information is included in the *PILI* listing:

Jacobs, Jan; New Netherland(s), 1659 **9143** *p174*
With wife & mother
With child 2
With child 4

The second type of citation found in *PILI* is the cross-reference. Cross-references have been generated by the computer for every accompanying relative whose name is found in the source. The only exception would be those lists where a relationship seemed obvious, but was not specified. Cross-references may read as follows:

```
    (1)       (2)           (3)
Rose, Maria 58 SEE Rose, Anton
```

The numbers in parentheses appearing in the above entry refer to the following explanations:

(1) Name of accompanying family member
(2) Family member's age, when given
(3) Name of the primary listee

Since cross-references are generated each time an accompanying individual is listed, duplicate cross-references will appear in *PILI* for names listed in more than one source or page:

> **Allerton,** Mary *SEE* Allerton, Isaack
> **Allerton,** Mary *SEE* Allerton, Isaack
> **Allerton,** Mary *SEE* Allerton, Isaack
> **Allerton,** Mary *SEE* Allerton, Isaack

This indicates to the researcher that there are four separate listings for Isaack Allerton in which Mary is given as someone who accompanied him.

A wife whose maiden name is supplied in a source document may appear in three places in *PILI*: a) in the husband's main listing, b) under the maiden name, and c) as a cross-reference under the married name:

> a) **Martine,** Malcolm; New York, 1738 **9760** *p9*
> *Wife:* Florence Anderson
>
> b) **Anderson,** Florence; New York, 1738 **9760** *p9*
>
> c) **Martine,** Florence Anderson *SEE* Martine, Malcolm

For information concerning how names are selected and indexed in *PILI*, see the "Editorial Practices" section of the Introduction beginning on page xi.

Annotations in the **"Bibliography of Sources Indexed"** section may consist of the following information:

> English translation of the title if source indexed was in a foreign language
> Statement denoting what the date and place cited in the *PILI* citation represent
> What other data (not indexed in *PILI*) is provided in the source that has been indexed
> Where the compiler or author of the source indexed found his or her information
> The location of the original records
> Additional information the staff of *PILI* felt would aid in the interpretation of the *PILI* citations.

How to Locate Sources Indexed

Large public libraries, state libraries, libraries with genealogical or history collections, and libraries of family associations and genealogical or historical societies are excellent places to check for the sources listed in the "Bibliography of Sources Indexed" section of *PILI*. It should be noted that while many libraries do not have the staff to research sources, librarians can provide guidance to assist researchers in their own investigations. Some libraries may provide lists of researchers for hire. The publisher of the magazine or book indexed can also be contacted; magazine publishers often offer reprints of articles they publish. Also, the bibliographic citation in *PILI* may provide information as to the location of the original records (if given in the source indexed).

Many of the books and periodicals containing articles indexed in *PILI* are among the holdings of some of the institutions listed below. The *Bibliography of Genealogy and Local History Periodicals with Union List of Major U.S. Collections* edited by Michael Barren Clegg and published by the Allen County Public Library Foundation in Fort Wayne, Indiana, is helpful in determining which of the major genealogical libraries hold a specific periodical (those libraries surveyed by Clegg are indicated below by an asterisk).

A sampling of institutions and organizations with major holdings of genealogical publications follows:

*Allen County Public Library**
Genealogy Department
900 Webster Street
P.O. Box 2270
Fort Wayne, IN 46801

*Atlanta-Fulton Public Library**
Special Collections Department
1 Margaret Mitchell Square
Corner of Carnegie Way and Forsythe
Atlanta, GA 30303-1089

Berkshire Athenaeum
Local History and Literature Services
1 Wendell Avenue
Pittsfield, MA 01201

California State Library
Sutro Library Branch
480 Winston Drive
San Francisco, CA 94132

*The Church of Jesus Christ of Latter-day Saints
Family History Library**
35 N.W. Temple
Salt Lake City, UT 84150

The Connecticut Historical Society
1 Elizabeth Street
Hartford, CT 06105

*Dallas Public Library**
Genealogy Collection
1515 Young Street
Dallas, TX 75201-9987

Denver Public Library
Genealogy Division
1357 Broadway
Denver, CO 80203-2165

Detroit Public Library
Burton Historical Collection
5201 Woodward Avenue
Detroit, MI 48202

The Filson Club Historical Society
1310 South Third Street
Louisville, KY 40208

Houston Public Library
Clayton Library
Center for Genealogical Research
5300 Caroline Street
Houston, TX 77004-6896

*Library of Congress**
Local History and Genealogy Reading Room
Humanities and Social Sciences Division
Thomas Jefferson Building, Room LJ20
10 First Street, S.E.
Washington, D.C. 20540

Library of Michigan
717 W. Allegan Street
P.O. Box 30007
Lansing, MI 48909

Los Angeles Public Library*
History and Genealogy Department
630 West Fifth Street
Los Angeles, CA 90071

National Society, Daughters of the
American Revolution Library
1776 D Street, N.W.
Washington, D.C. 20006-5392

New England Historic Genealogical Society*
99-101 Newbury Street
Boston, MA 02116-3087

The New York Public Library*
The Research Libraries
U.S. History, Local History
 and Genealogy Division
Fifth Avenue and 42nd Sts., Room 315S
New York, NY 10018

Newberry Library*
Local & Family History Room
60 West Walton Street
Chicago, IL 60610-3394

Onondaga County Public Library
Local History and Special Collections
447 South Salina Street
Syracuse, NY 13202-2494

Orange County Library System
Genealogy Department
101 East Central Blvd.
Orlando, FL 32801

Public Library of Cincinnati and Hamilton County*
History Department
800 Vine Street
Library Square
Cincinnati, OH 45202-2071

The State Historical Society of Wisconsin*
816 State Street
Madison, WI 53706-1482

Western Reserve Historical Society
Ohio Network of American History
 Research Centers
10825 East Boulevard
Cleveland, OH 44106-1778

Bibliography of Sources Indexed

★*Source Number*

★**53.26**

    ADAMS, RAYMOND D. *An Alphabetical Index to Ulster Emigration to Philadelphia, 1803-1850.* Baltimore, MD: Clearfield Co., 1992. 102p.

        Port and date of arrival. Author also includes address and county of origin as well as the name of the ship. Originally extracted from a townland index first printed in Dublin in 1861, Customs and Passenger lists located in the National Archives, passenger lists recorded by the Cunard and Cooke shipping lines, and civil parish emigration lists from the Public Record Office of Northern Ireland. Title on spine is *Ulster Emigration to Philadelphia, 1803-1850.*

★**95.2**

    ALLEN, DESMOND WALLS. *1918 Camp Pike, Arkansas, Index to Soldiers' Naturalizations.* Conway, AR: Arkansas Research, 1988. 134p.

        Date and place of naturalization. Source also provides birthdate or age, unit, country of birth or nationality, marital status, and volume and certificate number of the original record. Copies of the original record can be obtained from the Arkansas Historical Commission, Pulaski County World War I Naturalization Records Collection, One Capitol Mall, Little Rock, AR 72201. Source can be obtained from Arkansas Research, P.O. Box 303, Conway, AR 72032.

★**123.54**

    APPANOOSE COUNTY GENEALOGY SOCIETY. *Index to Naturalization Records of Appanoose County, Iowa.* Centerville, IA: Appanoose County Genealogy Society, [1985. 86p.]

        Date and place of naturalization. Pages added by indexer; title page is on page one; first section of data begins on page three, and second section on page 55. Source also provides volume and page numbers of the naturalization records at the office of the Appanoose County Clerk of Court in Centerville, Iowa for volumes 1-11. Volume, page, and certificate numbers are provided for volumes 12-17 where the volume and certificate number (vols. 13-17) or page number (vol. 12) should be cited for the Clerk of Court. Copies of the original records for vols. 13-17 can also be located in the genealogy section of the Drake Public Library, Des Moines, Iowa.

★**543.30**

    BIENVENU, LIONEL, and ALICE D. FORSYTH. "Ledger Giving Enlistments of Union Soldiers During the Civil War." In *New Orleans Genesis,* vol. 28:110 (Apr 1989), pp. 233-238 (A); vol. 28:111 (Jul 1989), pp. 322-327 (A,B); vol. 28:112 (Oct 1989), pp. 479-484 (B); vol. 29:113 (Jan 1990), pp. 108-117 (B); vol. 29:114 (Apr 1990), pp. 242-249 (B); vol. 29:115 (Jul 1990), pp. 362-370 (B); vol. 29:116 (Oct 1990), pp. 450-465 (C); vol. 30:117 (Jan 1991), pp. 54-62 (D); vol. 31:118 (Apr 1991), pp. 214-222 (D); vol. 30:119 (Jul 1991), pp. 372-380 (D); vol. 30:120 (Oct 1991), pp. 480-485 (E); vol. 31:121 (Jan 1992), pp. 27-32 (F); vol. 31:122 (Apr 1992), pp. 222-232 (F); vol. 31:123 (Jul 1992), pp. 373-384 (G).

        Date and place of enlistment. Source also provides regiment, company, birth place, height, and other information. Extracted from two ledgers located among the Confederate material held by the Jackson Barracks Military Library in New Orleans. Articles were to be continued after July 1992 but, to date, have not appeared. In this index, page numbers followed by an *A, B,* or *C* refer to vols. 30:120, 31:122, and 31:123, respectively.

★**778.5**

    BRASSEAUX, CARL A. *The "Foreign French:" Nineteenth-Century French Immigration into Louisiana.* Vol. 1: 1820-1839. Lafayette, LA: The Center for Louisiana Studies, University of Southwestern Louisiana, 1990. 569p.

        Date and port of arrival; a few (pp. 555-556) are date and place of first mention of residence in the New World. Author also provides sex, occupation, country of nativity (or, pp. 555-556, French hometown or province), name of ship, and port of departure. Extracted from passenger manifests of the New Orleans federal port authorities and Catholic church records.

★**1034.18**

    BURGERT, ANNETTE K. *York County Pioneers from Friedelsheim and Goennheim in the Palatinate.* Worthington, Ohio: AKB Publications, 1984. 28p.

        Date and port of arrival; a few are date and place of naturalization or first mention of residence in the New World. Surnames with no date indicate possible name variations. Spouses and children were assumed by indexer to have immigrated with main listee. Publisher's address is 691 Weavertown Road, Myerstown, PA 17067.

★**1219.7**

    COLDHAM, PETER WILSON. *The Complete Book of Emigrants, 1751-1776.* A comprehensive listing compiled from English public records of those who took ship to the Americas for political, religious, and economic reasons; of those who were deported for vagrancy, roguery, or non-conformity; and of those who were sold to labour in the new colonies. Baltimore: Genealogical Publishing Co., 1993. 349p.

        Date bound and intended destination; some are date and place of first mention of residence in the New World or date and place of death. Data was extracted from several sources. Dates prior to 1752 were rendered according to the modern calendar. Listings from 1607-1750 were indexed in *PILI* 1992, 1993, and 1994.

★**1450.2**

    DARLINGTON, JANE E. *Marion County, Indiana, Records Miscellanea.* Indianapolis: Indiana Historical Society, Family History Section, 1986. Parts A and B: pp. 1a-164a, 1b-43b.

> Port and date of arrival, a few are place and date of first mention of residence in the New World. Source also provides age, nativity, address in U.S., witnesses, etc. Indexer incorporated corrections listed on page 164a into the individual entries of those listees affected. Extracted from naturalization papers filed in Marion County, Indiana, 1832-1906, and held by the Indiana State Archives.

★1639.20

DOBSON, DAVID. *Directory of Scots in the Carolinas, 1680-1830.* Baltimore: Genealogical Publishing Co., 1986. 322p.

> Date of emigration with intended destination, date and place of naturalization, or date and place of first mention of residence in the New World.

★1641

DOLLINGER, MARION DEUTER. "The Seventh Day Adventist Church of Bowdle, South Dakota." In *Clues,* 1980, pt. 2, pp. 41-43.

> Date and place of the church's formation or date and place of settlement.

★1728.4—1728.5

DURBIN, LINDA L. "Pierce County [Washington] Voter Registration Surfaces at Swap Meet." In *Bulletin of the Seattle Genealogical Society.*
    ★1728.4
        Vol. 30:4 (Summer 1981), pp. 251-256.
    ★1728.5
        Vol. 31:1 (Fall 1981), pp. 10-17.

> Date and place of registration. Covers the years 1916-1920. Source includes residence; age; occupation; birthplace; time in state, county, and precinct; court name, state, county; and year of naturalization.

★1763

EBELING, JAKOB. "In der Neuen Welt verstorbene Auswanderer." In *Heimat im Bild,* nr. 40 and 48 (1972), unpaginated.

> "Emigrants who died in the New World." Placement of individual words in the title varies. Date and place of death. Also may provide town of origin, occupation and cause of death. Extracted from records in the city archives of Bensheim (Bergstrasse). In *PILI,* the page number indicates the volume number of the publication and the letter following the page number (*A, B, C,* and *D*) refers to the four quadrants of the page cited.

★2090

FLOM, GEORGE T. "The First Swedes in Burlington. Other Early Settlements in the State down to 1855: Swede Point, Bergholm, Swede Bend, Mineral Ridge. The Founders of These Settlements. Two Early Settlements in Northeastern Iowa." In *The Iowa Journal of History and Politics,* vol. 3:4 (Oct. 1905), pp. 607-615.

> Date and place of settlement; a few are date and port of arrival.

★2155

"THE FOUNDERS OF GERMANTOWN." In *Krefeld Immigrants and Their Descendants* (Links Genealogy Publications, Sacramento, CA), vol. 1:1 (1984), pp. 1-2.

> Date and port of arrival for the *Concord.*

★2212

FRENCH, ELIZABETH. *List of Emigrants to America from Liverpool, 1697-1707.* Boston: New England His-

toric Genealogical Society, 1913. 55p. Reprint. Genealogical Publishing Co., Baltimore, 1962, 1983.

> Date of emigration with intended destination. Originally appeared in *The New England Historical and Genealogical Register,* vols. 64-65. Also in source no. 9151, pp. 173-220 (indexed in *PILI,* first edition).

★2444

GERBER, ADOLF. "Emigrants from Wuerttemberg: The Adolf Gerber Lists." Edited by Donald Herbert Yoder. In *The Pennsylvania German Folklore Society [Yearbook],* vol. 10 (1945), pp. 132-237.

> Date of emigration and intended destination. This is an English-language edition which combines the original and supplementary Gerber lists. See also source nos. 4445 and 9964 (indexed in *PILI* 1989 and 1983, respectively).

★2467.7

"THE GERMAN SETTLERS WHO ARRIVED IN 1684." In *Krefeld Immigrants and Their Descendants* (Links Genealogy Publications, Sacramento, CA), vol. 1:1 (1984), p. 5.

> Date and place of settlement. Extracted from *250th Anniversary of the Settlement of Germantown* (Germantown [PA] Historical Society, 1933) and *The River's Source was a Small Stream Named Germantown* (David J. Smucker and Robert F. Ulle).

★2557.1—2557.2

GISLASON, DONALD E. "Icelandic Emigration from Glasgow. . ., S.S. *Waldensian.*" In *The Icelandic Canadian.*
    ★2557.1
        Vol. 43.1 (Sept. 1984), pp. 18-22; vol. 43:3 (Spring 1985), pp. 38-39; vol. 43:4 (Summer 1985), pp. 37-39 (these pages are indicated in this index by the code *A*).
    ★2557.2
        Vol. 44:2 (Winter 1985), pp. 36-38.

> Date and port of arrival in Quebec or Toronto. Title varies. Lists occupation and final destination. Many were going on to Minnesota.

★2691.4

GOELZER, BERND. "Amerikaauswanderer in den Lebenserinnerungen von Friedrich Daniel Vogelgesang." In *Saarlaendische Familienkunde,* Band 6, 22. Jahrgang, Heft 86 (1989), pp. 166-172.

> "Immigrants to America in the Memoirs of Friedrich Daniel Vogelsang." Date of emigration with intended destination or date and place of first mention of residence in New World. Also provides date and place of birth, marriage information, and/or spouse's birth information.

★2764.35

GREAT REGISTER OF VOTERS, County of Cochise, Territory of Arizona, 1890. Tucson, AZ: Arizona State Genealogical Society, 1986. 76p.

> Date and place of naturalization or registration. Age, country of birth, occupation, and local residence also provided. Consolidation of source nos. 1213.1-1213.3 (indexed in *PILI* 1988).

★2769.1—2769.10

"THE GREAT REGISTER, TULARE COUNTY, California, 1872." In *Sequoia Genealogical Society Newsletter* (Visalia, CA).
    ★2769.1
        Vol. 9:3 (Nov. 1982), pp. 3-6 (A-B).
    ★2769.2
        Vol. 9:4 (Jan. 1983), pp. 3-6 (B-C).
    ★2769.3
        Vol. 9:5 (Feb. 1983), pp. 3-6 (C-E).

★2769.4

Vol. 9:6 (Mar. 1983), pp. 3-6 (F-H).

★2769.5

Vol. 9:7 (Apr. 1983), pp. 3-6 (H-K).

★2769.6

Vol. 9:8 (May 1983), pp. 3-6 (K-M).

★2769.7

Vol. 10:1 (Sept. 1983), pp. 3-6 (M-R).

★2769.8

Vol. 10:2 (Oct. 1983), pp. 3-6 (R-S).

★2769.9

Vol. 10:3 (Nov. 1983), pp. 3-6 (S-Y).

★2769.10

Vol. 10:4 (Dec. 1983), pp. 3-6 (Y-Z and supplement, A-W).

Date and place of naturalization or registration. Also includes number on register, age, place of birth, occupation, and location of residence. For Great Register listings in Tulare County in the year 1888, see source nos. 2765-2768 (indexed in *PILI* 1987).

★2853.7

HAAS, FRANZ. "Rund um die Auswanderungswelle, 1851/53." In *Viernheimer Auswandererbuch,* Hans Knapp, editor. Viernheim: pr. pr., 1975, pp. 107-109.

"A quick look at the emigration wave of 1851-1853." Date of emigration and intended destination.

★2854

HACKER, WERNER. "American Emigrants from the Territories of the Bishopric of Speyer." Translated and edited by Don Yoder. In *Pennsylvania Folklife,* vol. 21:4 (Summer 1972), pp. 43-45.

Date of emigration with intended destination. Data abstracted from source no. 2856 (indexed in *PILI* 1993). Also in no. 9968, pp. 69-71 (indexed in *PILI* 1991). The original documents are located in the Karlsruhe State Archives.

★2859.11

HACKETT, J. DOMINICK, and CHARLES MONTAGUE EARLY. *Passenger Lists from Ireland.* Baltimore: Genealogical Publishing Co., 1981. 46p.

Date and port of arrival. Port of departure and name of ship also provided. Extracted from *The Journal of the American Irish Historical Society,* vols. 28 and 29 (1929-1931).

★2872.1

HAGLE, CHARLOTTE TADLOCK. *Cowlitz County, Washington Naturalizations, Comprehensive Index: Cowlitz County, Territory and State of Washington, 1859-1920, Naturalization Records.* Longview, WA: Lower Columbia Genealogical Society, P.O. Box 472, Longview 98632, 1990. 53p.

Place of naturalization. Source provides the page numbers of the naturalization documents in the records of the Cowlitz County clerk.

★2896.5

HANNABARGER, LINDA, and JEFF MEYER. *Naturalization Records of Fayette County, Illinois, 1838-1906.* Ramsey, IL: The Authors, 1988. 51p.

Date and port of arrival or date and place of declaration of intention or final oath. Also provides country of origin and names of sponsors.

★3377.6

"IMMIGRANT PASSENGER INFORMATION." In *Family Ties* (Holland Genealogical Society, Michigan), vol. 10:1 (Spring 1984), pp. 11-16.

Date and port of arrival of the *Audubon.* Includes occupation, country of origin, and final destination (most were bound for Syracuse, New York, and, ultimately, to Overisel, Michigan). Extracted from lists at Fort Wayne, Indiana, and Washington, D.C.

★3455.1—3455.5

"[IROQUOIS COUNTY ILLINOIS] NATURALIZATION RECORDS." In *The Iroquois Stalker* (Iroquois County Genealogical Society).

★3455.1

Vol. 4:1 (Winter 1974), pp. 9-14; vol. 4:2 (Spring 1974), pp. 40-55.

★3455.2

Vol. 5:2 (Spring 1975), pp. 43-53; vol. 5:3 (Summer 1975), pp. 71-80; vol. 5:4 (Fall 1975), pp. 94-106.

★3455.3

Vol. 6:1 (Winter 1976), pp. 16-26; vol. 6:2 (Spring 1976), pp. 45-55; vol. 6:3 (Summer 1976), pp. 78-86; vol. 6:4 (Fall 1976), pp. 104-115.

★3455.4

Vol. 7:1 (Winter 1977), pp. 24-29; vol. 7:2 (Spring 1977), pp. 50-56; vol. 7:3 (Summer 1976), pp. 78-83; vol. 7:4 (Fall 1977), pp. 92-94.

★3455.5

Vol. 11:1 (Winter 1981), p. 7.

Date of emigration and port of entry; a few are date and place of naturalization. Country of origin, place of residence, occupation, date and place of birth, port of emigration, ship, witnesses, spouse, and place of birth of spouse may also be provided. Assumed spouse, if also foreign-born, accompanied main entry.

★3627

JONES, HENRY Z., JR., and ANNETTE K. BURGERT. "A New Emigrant List: Bonfeld, 1710-1738." In *Der Reggeboge: Quarterly of the Pennsylvania German Society* (Breinigsville, PA), vol. 14:4 (Oct. 1980), pp. 3-20.

Date of emigration and place of settlement. Extracted from the last page of a Lutheran churchbook in Bonfeld (part of the city 6927 Bad Rappenau, Landkreis Heilbronn, Baden-Wurtemberg).

★3652

JORDAN, JOHN W. "Moravian Immigration to Pennsylvania, 1734-1767." In *Transactions of the Moravian Historical Society,* vol. 5 (1899), pp. 51-90.

Date and port of arrival. Also includes ship name and port of departure. See also source nos. 3650 (indexed in *PILI* 1983); 3654 (*PILI* 1982); and 3660 and 3661 (*PILI* 1987).

★3688

JUSTUS, NORMA MIZE. *A Compilation of Persons Drawing Pensions. . . with Some Naturalization and Pardon Records from Lawrence County, AR.* Powhatan, Arkansas: the author, [1983]. 8p.

Date and place of naturalization. Country of origin also provided. Extracted from records at the Powhatan Courthouse, Powhatan, AR, 72458. Page numbers provided by indexer; only the naturalizations listed on the next to the last page (ascribed as page 7 in *PILI*) were indexed.

★3689.17

KAISER, HORACE. "Immigrant List." In *Lexington Genealogical Exchange* (Lexington County, SC), vol. 2:1 (1983), pp. 21-23.

Date and port of arrival of German immigrants on the ship *Elizabeth* who petitioned for bounty grants as listed in Journal of Minutes of Colonial Council, South Carolina, Council Journal No. 21.

★3690.1

KAMINKOW, JACK, and MARION KAMINKOW. *A List of Emigrants from England to America, 1718-1759.* Baltimore: Magna Carta Book Co., 1984. Reprinted, with additional records originally incorporated in the "new edition" of 1981, Genealogical Publishing Co., 1989. 292p.

Date of indenture and colony to which bound. An *A* has been inserted by indexer to indicate that page number appears as a roman numeral in the introductory material of the source indexed. Additionally, additions and corrections listed on page xxvii in the source were incorporated into and indexed as part of the affected immigrant's main listing. Parish and county, occupation, initials of agent, years of service, whether signed or marked, and page number of the record in "Agreements to Serve in America" which is located at the Guildhall in London, England, are also provided.

★3702.7

KAMPHOEFNER, WALTER D., WOLFGANG HELBICH, and ULRIKE SOMMER. *News from the Land of Freedom: German Immigrants Write Home.* Ithaca, NY: Cornell University Press, 1991. 645p.

Date and port of arrival or date and place of settlement. Extracted from the Bochum Immigrant Letter Collection (BABS) at Ruhr University — Bochum, Germany.

★3840.1—3840.3

"KLAMATH COUNTY [California] GREAT REGISTER — 1869." In *Redwood Researcher* (Redwood Genealogical Society, Fortuna, CA).

★3840.1

Vol. 15:4 (May 1983), pp. 14-19.

★3840.2

Vol. 16:1 (Aug. 1983), pp. 14-19.

★3840.3

Vol. 16:2 (Nov. 1983), pp. 8-13.

Date and place of naturalization or registration. Information in source includes country of origin, occupation, and local residence. Klamath County was dissolved in 1874. Extracted from list housed at the Humboldt State University in Arcata, CA.

★4349

KREBS, FRIEDRICH. "Emigrants to America from the Duchy of Zweibruecken." Translated and edited by Don Yoder. In *Pennsylvania Folklife* (Collegeville, PA), vol.21:4 (Summer 1972), pp. 46-48.

Date and port of arrival, a few are date of emigration and intended destination. See also source nos. 4145 and 9968, pp. 72-74 (indexed in *PILI* 1984 and 1991, respectively). Extracted from documents in the Palatine State Archives in Speyer, Germany.

★4480

KUHNS, OSCAR. "A Genealogical Trip to Switzerland." In *The Pennsylvania-German,* vol. 7:6 (Oct. 1906), pp. 311-312.

Date of emigration and final destination. Extracted from *Die Bernischen Taufer* (written by Pastor Muller of Langnau, Switzerland) and a description of a journey from Zurich to America by Ludwig Weber.

★4525

LANGGUTH, OTTO. "Pennsylvania German Pioneers from the County of Wertheim." Translated and edited by Don Yoder. In *The Pennsylvania German Folklore Society [Yearbook],* vol. 12 (1947), pp. 196-289.

Date of emigration and intended destination or date and port of arrival. Extracted from manuscripts in the princely archive of Lowenstein-Wertheim-Rosenberg. Also in source nos. 4517 and 9964 (indexed in *PILI* 1991 and 1983, respectively).

★4533

LARIN, ROBERT. "L'emigration Montmorillonaise Vers la Vallee du Saint-Laurent aux XVIIieme et Debut du XVIIIieme Siecles." In *Memoires de la Societe Genealogique Canadienne-Francaise,* vol. 42:2 (Summer 1991), pp. 125-132.

"The Montmorillonaise Emigration to the Valley of Saint Laurent in the 17th and the Beginning of the 18th Centuries." Date of emigration and intended destination.

★4535.10—4535.12

LAWES, EDWARD. "Assisted Emigration." In *The Hampshire Family Historian.*

★4535.10

Pt. 1, vol. 10:4 (Feb. 1984), pp. 195-199.

★4535.11

Pt. 2, vol. 11:1 (May 1984), pp. 51-54.

★4535.12

Pt. 3, vol. 11:2 (Aug. 1984), pp. 113-115.

Date of emigration and intended destination. Extracted from the letter books of the Poor Law Commission Board (MH12 group) at Kew.

★4537.30

LAWSON, BILL *A Register of Emigrant Families from the Western Isles of Scotland to the Eastern Townships of Quebec, Canada.* Eaton Corner, Quebec: Comption County Historical Museum Society, 1988. 120p.

Date and place of settlement. Spouses and children of foreign birth were assumed to have immigrated with main listee. Extracted from census returns and parish registers held in the General Register House in Edinburgh or available on microfilm in the Public Library in Stornoway, Scotland.

★4606

LERSKI, JERZY JAN. "List of the Polish Exiles in the United States of North America." In *A Polish Chapter in Jacksonian America: The United States and the Polish Exiles of 1831.* Madison, MI: University of Wisconsin Press, 1958, pp. 172-180.

Date and port of arrival. Polish exiles who came from Trieste to New York on the frigates *Guerriera* and *Hebe;* on the corvettes *Lipsia* and *Adria;* and to Boston on the merchant vessel *Cherokee.*

★4610.10

LET'S GO TO AMERICA! The Path of Emigrants from Eastern Westphalia to the USA. Loehne: Heimatverein of the town of Loehne; Study Group for Local Culture, Bad Oeynhausen; and Hermann Brackmann KG, 1985. 169p.

Date and place of first mention of residence in the New World; most are date of emigration and intended destination. Extracted from *Beitraege zur Heimatkunde der Staedte Loehne und Bad Oeynhausen,* Sonderheft 4.

★4626.16

LINDSAY, JOICEY HAW. "Henrico County, Virginia, Naturalizations, 1844-1858." In *Magazine of Virginia Genealogy,* vol. 22:4 (Nov. 1984), pp. 12-17.

Date and place of naturalization. Includes country of origin. Compiled from the Henrico County Court Minute Books.

★4719.7

**["LIST OF PASSENGERS ON BOARD THE BRIG
JESSIE,. . .Belfast to Quebec."]** In *Ottawa Branch
News,* vol. 16:2 (Mar.-Apr. 1983), p. 21.

Date and port of arrival. The list originally appeared
in the *Quebec Mercury,* 5 June 1830.

★4719.17

"LIST OF PASSENGERS ON THE *ANN.*" In *The Genie*
(Ark-La-Tex Genealogical Association, Shreveport,
LA), vol. 17:4 (Oct. 1983), pp. 310-313.

Date and port of arrival. Also includes occupation,
Savannah lot number, and disposition by 1754. This
ship also covered in source nos. 1312/1322 and 3388/
6494 (indexed in *PILI* first edition and 1982, respectively).

★4719.30

**"LIST OF PASSENGERS, S.S. *SCHILLER* — 7 May
1875."** In *Milwaukee County Genealogical Society Re-
porter (M.C.G.S.),* vol. 17:3 (Nov. 1986), pp. 257-259.

Date and port of arrival. Much of the information was
extracted from the *Milwaukee Sentinel.*

★4778.1—4778.2

LITTLE, BARBARA V. "Petersburg Naturalizations,
1808-1812." In *The Southside Virginian.*
★4778.1
Vol. 4:4 (July 1986), p. 150.
★4778.2
Vol. 5:3 (July 1987), pp. 141-143.

Date and place of declaration of intention or of
first mention of residence in the New World. Abstracted from Petersburg Hustings Court Minute
Book.

★4779.3

LIVENGOOD, CANDY. "The 1786 Tax List for
Hempfield Twp., South District, Westmoreland County,
Pennsylvania." In *The Lost Palatine,* no. 27 (1985), pp.
13-14, 14A.

Date and port of arrival or date and place of naturalization.

★4814

LOGAN, ROBERT ARCHIBALD. "Highlanders from
Skye, in North Carolina and Nova Scotia: 1771-1818."
In *The Scottish Genealogist,* vol. 12:4 (Feb. 1966), pp.
92-107.

Date and port of arrival or date and place of first
mention of residence in the New World.

★4815.7

LOHMEYER, [FRITZ]. "Auswanderer aus dem
Kirchspiel Barnstorf." In *Heimat-Blaetter fuer die
Grafschaft Diepholz,* 7 Jahrgang, nr. 12 (26 July 1941),
p. 92.

"Emigrants from the church parish of Barnstorf."
Date of emigration with intended destination. Includes town of origin, year of birth.

★4914.15

MacCALLUM, STEPHEN. "The Voyage of the *Fanny.*"
Irene L. Rogers, editor. In *The Island Magazine* (Prince
Edward Island Heritage Foundation), no. 4 (Spring-Sum-
mer 1978), pp. 9-14.

Date and port of arrival. Originally published serially
in the *Evening Patriot,* beginning 5 September 1892.

★4915.24

McCARTHY, MICHAEL J. *The Irish in Newfoundland,
1623-1800.* St. John's, Newfoundland: Harry Cuff Publications, 1982, pp. 55-58.

"Convicts Landed in Newfoundland, 1789." Date
and port of arrival. Place of birth, crime, and sentence
also provided.

★4960—4963

McCRACKEN, GEORGE E. *"Welcome* Notes." In the
American Genealogist.
★4960
Vol. 38:3 (July 1962), pp. 152-163.
★4961
Vol. 39:1 (Jan. 1963), pp. 4-15; vol. 39:3 (July 1963),
pp. 164-169; vol. 39:4 (Oct. 1963), pp. 239-243.
★4962
Vol. 40:3 (July 1964), pp. 148-157.
★4963
Vol. 41:1 (Jan. 1965), pp. 38-40 (additions and corrections).

Date and port of arrival. For other references to the
Welcome, see source numbers 242, 1342, 4752
(indexed in *PILI* first edition); 6610, 8370 (*PILI*
1983); and 9143, vol. 1 (*PILI* 1984).

★4971

McDONNELL, FRANCES. *Emigrants from Ireland to
America, 1735-1743: A Transcription of the Report of
the Irish House of Commons into Enforced Emigration to
America.* Baltimore: Genealogical Publishing Co., 1992.
134p.

Date transportation ordered and intended destination.
Includes crime and county where order was enacted.
Extracted from *Journal of the House of Commons of
the Kingdom of Ireland,* vol. 7 (1796).

★5012.37

McNABB, MICHELE. "Naturalization Records — Mi-
nors — Volume 'C' (1866-1896)." In *Champaign
County [Illinois] Genealogical Society Quarterly,* vol.
5:3 (1983), pp. 59-63.

Date and place of application for naturalization. Also
provides page number in volume "C," birthplace,
length of residence in the U.S. and Illinois, and names
of sponsers. Compiled from microfilm roll 1026-928
in the Champaign County Historical Archives.

★5012.38—5012.40

McNABB, MICHELE. "Naturalization Records (1858-
1906)." In *Champaign County [Illinois] Genealogical
Society Quarterly.*
★5012.38
Vol. 5:4 (Mar. 1984), pp. 97-99 (nos. 1-51).
★5012.39
Vol. 6:1 (June 1984), pp. 25-26 (nos. 52-91); vol. 6:2
(Sept. 1984), pp. 52-54 (nos. 92-132, 269-283); vol.
6:3 (Dec. 1984), pp. 89-91 (nos. 284-307, 441-455,
75-94); vol. 6:4 (Mar. 1985), pp. 120-122 (nos. 95-
155).
★5012.40
Vol. 7:1 (June 1985), pp. 25-27 (nos. 156-206); vol.
7:2 (Sept. 1985), pp. 53-56 (nos. 207-268); vol. 7:3
(Dec. 1985), pp. 76-80 (nos. 269-295, 1-27).

Date and place of statement of intent or final
application. Place where intent was previously
filed, sponsor, and country to which allegiance is
being foresworn may also be provided. Extracted
from microfilm 1026-928 at the Champaign
County Historical Archives.

★5240.1

MARSH, BARBARA R. *Sedgwick County, Kansas, Naturalizations and Declaration of Intentions, 1870 to September 26, 1906.* Wichita, KS: Midwest Historical and
Genealogical Society, P.O. Box 1121, Wichita 67201-
1121, 1987. 93p.

Date and place of declaration of intention. May also include native country and date and place of naturalization. Extracted from records at the Clerk of the District Court, Civil Department, Wichita, KS.

★5262

MARTHALLER, AUBREY B. "Early German-Russian Settlers in Faith, Alberta, 1909-1950." In *Der Stammbaum (1988)/Heritage Review* (Germans from Russia Heritage Society), vol. 18:1 (Feb. 1988), p. 58.

Date and place of settlement. Settler's, spouse's, and ancestor's name; and Russian or German village or district of origin may be provided.

★5647.5

MILLER, JEANNE ROESNER. *German Immigrants in Posey County, Indiana.* Owensboro, KY: Cook-Mc-Dowell Publications, 719 East 6th Street, Owensboro 42301, 1981. 130p.

Date and place of first mention of residence in the New World; a few are date and port of arrival.

★5704.8

MITCHELL, BRIAN. *Irish Passenger Lists, 1847-1871.* Lists of passengers sailing from Londonderry to America on ships of the J. & J. Cooke line and the McCorkell line. Baltimore: Genealogical Publishing Co., 1992. 333p.

Date of departure and intended destination. Place of origin and name of ship are also provided.

★5881.1

MUNROE, J.B. *List of Alien Passengers, Bonded from January 1, 1847, to January 1, 1851, for the Use of the Overseers of the Poor, in the Commonwealth.* Boston: 1851. Reprint. Baltimore, MD: Genealogical Publishing Co., 1971; Clearfield Co., 1991. 99p.

Date and port of arrival. Country of birth and name of ship also provided.

★6013.19

"NATURALIZATION PAPERS ON MICROFILM at San Bruno, CA, Archives." In *Santa Clara County Historical and Genealogical Society Quarterly,* vol. 19:2 (Fall 1982), pp. 29-30; vol. 19:3 (Winter 1982), pp. 73-74; vol. 19:4 (Spring 1983), pp. 88-90.

Date and place of declaration of intention or naturalization; a few are date and port of arrival. May also provide country of origin.

★6013.40

"NATURALIZATION PROCEDURES: MONTGOMERY COUNTY Records at Independence, KS." In *The Descender,* vol. 16:4 (Nov. 1983), pp. 15-17.

Date and place of naturalization. Includes country of origin.

★6014.1—6014.2

"NATURALIZATION RECORDS — [Wyandot County, Ohio] PROBATE COURT." In *Wyandot Tracers.*

★6014.1

Vol. 1:2 (Summer 1983), pp. 1-3, "Vol. 1, 1842-1880."

★6014.2

Vol. 2:1 (Spring 1984), p. 7, "Vol. 2, 1860-."

Date and port of arrival or date and place of declaration. Also includes country of nativity, age, and/or date of application.

★6219

NUGENT, NELL M. *Cavaliers and Pioneers: A Calendar of Virginia Land Grants, 1623-1800.* Vol. 1:1-6. Richmond, VA: Dietz Printing Co., [1929-1931. Although vol. 6 ends with the year 1695, no other volumes were published.]

Date and place where land was patented and record was created listing those transported/imported. Only the names of those to be transported were indexed. Abstracted from Land Office records located at the Virginia State Library. See also source numbers 6220, 6223 (indexed in *PILI* 1984); and 6221 (*PILI* 1995).

★6251

"THE OATH OF ALLEGIANCE." In *The Bulletin of the Northumberland County [VA] Historical Society,* vol. 3:1 (July 1966), pp. 19-20.

Date and place of oath of allegiance to the Commonwealth of England.

★6254

"OATHS OF ALLEGIANCE, HARRIS COUNTY, TEXAS, Vol. 2, Oct. 1896." In *The Roadrunner* (Chaparral Genealogical Society, Tomball, TX), vol. 8:3 (1982), pp. 3-6.

Date and place where oath was sworn. Also includes native country.

★6410.22

OLSSON, NILS WILLIAM. "Naturalizations of Scandinavians in Penobscot Co., ME, 1840-1900." In *Swedish American Genealogist,* vol. 9:3 (Sept 1989), pp. 114-128.

Time span between arrival in U.S. and admittance to citizenship and place of residence at the time of admittance. Nationality, birth date, and date of declaration of intent also may be provided. Original record located at the Maine State Archives in Augusta.

★6410.32

OLSSON, NILS WILLIAM. "Swedes in the 1860 Census of Suffolk Co., MA." In *Swedish American Genealogist,* vol. 10:3 (Sept 1990), pp. 97-126.

Date and place of census (pp. 97-121); date and port of arrival or date and place of naturalization (pp. 122-126). Also provides occupation, country of nativity, etc. Extracted from the "Eighth Census for Massachusetts," microcopy 653, roll 520.

★6410.35

OLSSON, NILS WILLIAM. "The Swedish Brothers of Minneapolis: An Early Mutual Aid Society." In *Swedish American Genealogist,* vol. 1:2 (June 1981), pp. 45-67.

Timespan between arrival in U.S. and admittance to The Swedish Brothers or date and place of admittance. Also provides address, occupation, and date and place of birth.

★6508.3—6508.7

"PASSENGER LISTS." In *Gaelic Gleanings.*

★6508.3

Vol. 1:3 (May 1982), pp. 100-101.

Date and port of arrival of the brig *Leander.* Occupation, county of nativity, and final destination also provided. Extracted from National Archives microfilm 575-16.

★6508.4

Vol. 1:4 (Aug. 1982), p. 143.

Date and port of Scottish arrivals on the brig *Shakespeare.* Occupation also provided. Extracted from National Archives microfilm 237-12.

★6508.5

Vol. 2:1 (Nov. 1982), pp. 19-20.

Date and port of Irish arrivals on the brig *Paragon.* Extracted from National Archives microfilm 575-6.

★6508.6

Vol. 2:3 (May 1983), p. 115.

Date and port of Irish and Scottish arrivals on the *Stephen Baldwin* and the brig *Sophia*. Occupation also provided. Extracted from National Archives microfilms 425-62 and 255-19.

★**6508.7**
Vol. 2:4 (Aug. 1983), pp. 160-161.

Date and port of arrival for the brig *Pleiades*. Place of origin and occupation also provided. Extracted from National Archives microfilm 575-16.

★**7036**
PUNCH, TERRENCE M. "Irish Ancestors in the 'Lost and Found' of *The Boston Pilot*, 1840-1841." In *The Irish Ancestor*, vol. 10:2 (1978), pp. 116-127.

Date and place of mention of first residence in the New World or date of emigration with intended destination. Often provides place of origin.

★**7074.6**
PUNCH, TERRENCE M. *Les Montbeliardais en Nouvelle Ecosse: Une colonisation par des protestants etrangers au XVIIIe siecle (1750-1815).* Extracted from *Societe d'Emulation de Montbeliard*, vol. 81:108 (1985-1986), pp. 195-233 (extract published separately).

"The Montbeliardais in Nova Scotia: A colonization by the foreign Protestants in the 18th century." Date and port of arrival. Occupation, name of ship, and, sometimes, place of origin also provided. See also 7074.5 (indexed in *PILI* 1995).

★**7085.4**
PUNCH, TERRENCE M. "Scots from the Isle of Skye [Scotland] to Cape Breton, Nova Scotia, 1830." In *The Nova Scotia Genealogist*, vol. 4:1 (1986), pp. 44-45.

Date of emigration with intended destination. Extracted from P.A.N.S., record group 1, volume 67, documents 19 and 20.

★**7119**
QUATTLEBAUM, PAUL. "German Protestants in South Carolina in 1788." A petition for the incorporation of their churches. In *The South Carolina Historical and Genealogical Magazine*, vol. 47:4 (Oct. 1946), pp. 195-204.

Date of petition and place where signed. Extracted from a document in the Office of the Historical Commission of South Carolina. Supplements Bernheim's *History of the German Settlements and of the Lutheran Church in North and South Carolina*, 1872, pp. 288-311.

★**7129**
RACINE, JUANITA. "Caddo Parish Courthouse, Shreveport, LA." In *The Genie* (Ark-La-Tex Genealogical Association, Shreveport), vol. 15:1 (Jan. 1981), pp. 44-46.

Date and place of naturalization. Also provides suit, book, and page numbers of original records. Extracted from judicial records of probate and civil suit records filed 1867 through 1882.

★**7137**
RAPP, ALICE R. "Persons from Austria, Hungary, Prussia & Russia: From the 1900 Census, Carroll Township, Cambria County, Pennsylvania." In *Eastern & Central European Genealogist*, no. 4 (1980), pp. 168-171.

Date and port of arrival. Also provides number of years married, and date and place of birth.

★**7603**
ROBERT, NORMAND, and MICHEL THIBAULT. *Catalogue des Immigrants Catholiques des Iles Britanniques avant 1825.* Montreal: Society de Recherche Historique Archivo-Histo, 1988. 122p.

"Catalog of Catholic Immigrants from the British Isles before 1825." Date and place of first mention of residence in New World. Also provides names of parents, date and place of marriage, name of spouse, and place of origin.

★**7829**
S., A.L. "From Pfullingen." In *The Pennsylvania Dutchman*, vol. 5:14 (Mar. 15, 1954), p. 8.

Date of emigration and intended destination of persons from Pfullingen, Wuerttemberg. Extracted from *The History of Pfullingen* by Wilhelm Kinkelin, 1937.

★**7846**
SADOWSKY, LORRAINE. "Passenger Lists." In *Heritage Review*, vol. 12:1 (Feb. 1982), pp. 39-40.

Date and port of arrival for the S.S. *Kaiser Wilhelm der Grosse* and the S.F. *Fulda*. Also provides occupation, last residence, and final destination.

★**7857**
SALMELA, JOAN. "Index to Ogle County [Illinois] Naturalization Papers, 1839-1887." In *Illinois State Genealogical Society Quarterly*, vol. 17:1 (Spring 1985), pp. 2-8.

Date and place of declaration of intent or naturalization. Also specifies folder wherein documents are located.

★**8125.6**
SCHROEDER, HENNING. "Emigrants from Urbach/Westerwald, 1744, 1748/49, 1752." In *The Palatine Immigrant*, vol. 13:1 (Mar. 1988), pp. 22-24.

Date of emigration and intended destination or date and port of arrival.

★**8125.8**
SCHROEDER, HENNING. "German Emigrants from the Area of Wuppertal." In *Germanic Genealogist*, no. 27 (1984), pp. 435-438.

Date and port of arrival, date of emigration and intended destination, or date and place of first mention of residence in the New World. Date and place of birth, occupation, date and place of death, and other information also provided. Extracted and arranged alphabetically from source no. 2918.3 (indexed in *PILI* 1991).

★**8137**
SCHWALM, MARK A. "A Composite List of German Prisoners of War Held by the Americans, 1779-1782." In *Journal of Johannes Schwalm Historical Association* (Lyndhurst, OH), vol. 2:1 (1981), pp. 4-15.

Date and place of first mention of residence in the New World. Regiment, company, place of birth, and other information provided. Extracted from records found among the Bradford papers in the archives of the Pennsylvania Historical Society.

★**8208.4**
SCOTT, KENNETH. *Naturalizations in the Marine Court, New York City, 1834-1840.* Collections of the New York Genealogical and Biographical Society. Volume 15. New York: New York Genealogical and Biographical Society, 1991. 187p.

Date and place of naturalization. Name of recorder and, sometimes, country of prior allegiance provided. Extracted from records at the Municipal Archives in New York City, volumes 17, 18, and 19.

★**8365.25—8365.27**
SHELBY COUNTY GENEALOGICAL SOCIETY [Ohio]. "Declarations of Intent — from Minute Books, Shelby Co. Clerk of Courts Office." In *Shelbyana*.

★8365.25
No. 7 (Apr. 1981), p. 12. Books 4 and 5.

★8365.26
No. 9 (Oct. 1981), p. 12. Book 5.

★8365.27
No. 10 (Jan. 1982), p. 12. Books 6 and 7.

Date and place of declaration of intention. Country of nativity also provided.

★8582—8582.3
SMITH, CLIFFORD NEAL. *Early Nineteenth-Century German Settlers in Ohio (Mainly Cincinnati and Environs), Kentucky, and Other States.* German-American Genealogical Research Monograph, 20. McNeal, AZ: Westland Publications.

★8582
Part 1. 1984. 36p.

★8582.1
Part 2. 1988. 56p.

★8582.2
Part 3. 1988. 69p.

★8582.3
Part 4, Fascicles A (surnames A-J, pp. 1-34), B (K-Z, pp. 35-73), and C (appendices, pp. 75-101). 1991. 101p.

Date and port of arrival, date of emigration and intended destination, or date and place of first mention of residence in New World. Place of origin and other biographical data may also be provided. Listees were assumed to be immigrants unless source material proved otherwise. Extracted from issues of *Der Deutsche Pioniere,* a monthly magazine published by the Deutsche Pioniereverein (Union of German Pioneers) in Cincinnati, Ohio. Part I covers vols. 1-3; part 2, vols. 4-6; part 3, vol. 7; and part 4, vols. 8-9.

★8893—8894.2
SPERRY, KIP. "Some North Americans in the Old Parochial Registers of Scotland." In *National Genealogical Society Quarterly.*

★8893
Vol. 69:4 (Dec. 1981), pp. 261-267.

★8894.1
Vol. 72:3 (Sept. 1984), pp. 191-192.

★8894.2
Vol. 75:1 (Mar. 1987), pp. 55-58.

Date and place of first mention of residence in New World. Extracted from the Old Parochial Registers of the Church of Scotland housed at the New Register House in Edinburgh in the custody of the Registrar General for Scotland. Also on microfilm at the Family History Library in Salt Lake City, UT.

★9026.4
STIENS, ROBERT E. "Passenger List." In *Italian Genealogist,* no. 2 (1981), pp. 41-42.

Date and port of arrival for the steamship *Fulda.* Includes native country and last place of residence.

★9117
TENBARGE, ELEANOR. "Naturalization Records — Vanderburgh County, Indiana." In *The Tri-State Packet* (Tri-State Genealogical Society), vol. 4:2 (Dec. 1980), pp. 14-20.

Date and place of declaration of intention or swearing of oath. Also provides country of origin. Extracted from Vanderburgh County Circuit Records of Citizenship Intentions and Oaths of Allegiance in Order Books A (1 May 1820—9 November 1828), B (1

September 1829—1 April 1837), and G (22 March 1847—24 Sept. 1850).

★9162.6—9162.8
THRUSH, LILLIAN. "German Immigrants." In *The Bulletin: The Genealogical Society of South Brevard, Melbourne, Florida.*

★9162.6
Part 1: vol. 12:4 (Nov. 1986), pp. 104-105.

★9162.7
Part 2: vol. 13:1 (Feb. 1987), pp. 14-15.

★9162.8
Part 3: vol. 13:2 (May 1987), pp. 36-38.

Date of emigration and intended destination. Includes place of origin. Extracted from *Genealogie,* Oct. 1969.

★9228.30
TURK, LOUISE. *Permits to Enter Yavapai County Hospital & Poor Farm, 1897-1898.* Tucson, AZ: Arizona State Genealogical Society, 1988. [13p. Page numbers have been added by indexers; only recto pages were numbered with page 1 denoting the first page of data.]

Date and place of admittance. Place of birth and name(s) of relative(s) also included. Only listees of foreign birth were indexed.

★9228.40
TURK, LOUISE. *Yavapai County Hospital Deaths from 1885-1942.* Tucson, AZ: Arizona State Genealogical Society, 1988. [62p. Page numbers have been added by indexers; only recto pages were numbered with page 1 denoting the first page of data.]

Date and place of death. Country of birth also included. Only listees of foreign birth were indexed.

★9229.18
TURNER, THOMAS. "Ship Passengers to Quebec, 1815." In *Lost in Canada?* (Canadian-American Genealogical Journal), vol 15:2 (May 1989), pp. 74-82.

Date and port of arrival. Also includes port of embarkation, sailing date or number of days at sea, type and name of craft, and ship-master's name. Extracted from Quebec Harbour Master's *Arrivals Book.*

★9253
ULMER, ERWIN. "Passenger Lists." In *Heritage Review,* vol. 17:2 (May 1987), pp. 45-48.

Date and port of arrival. Name of ship, port of debarkation, and some occupations provided.

★9332
URLSPERGER, SAMUEL. *Detailed Reports on the Salzburger Emigrants Who Settled in America.* Wormsloe Foundation Publications. Athens, GA: University of Georgia Press.
[Reports on the Emigrants at Ebenezer, Georgia, 1738.] Vol. 5. 1980, pp. 316-323 (page 323 was indexed in *PILI* as page 323A).
Appendices II, III, and IV. Vol. 6. 1981, pp. 323-334.

Date and place of settlement or of first mention of residence in New World.

★9420.1—9420.2
VERGES, MRS. LOUIS P. "The Stephanite Migration to Missouri, 1839-1841." In *New Orleans Genesis* (New Orleans Genealogical Research Society).

★9420.1
Vol. 15:60 (Sept. 1976), parts. 1-2, pp. 373-378.

★9420.2
Vol. 16:61 (Jan. 1977), part 2, pp. 67-72; vol. 16:62 (Mar. 1977), part 3, pp. 165-170; vol. 16:63 (June 1977), part 4, pp. 357-362; vol. 16:64 (Sept. 1977), part 5, pp. 483-487.

Date and port of arrival of the *Olbers,* the *Johann Georg,* the *Copernicus,* the *Republik,* and the *Amalia.* Includes final destination, occupation, country of origin or last dwelling place, and miscellaneous notes. Adapted from source no. 2095 (indexed in *PILI* 1989).

★9460—9461

VOELKER, FRIEDRICH. "Die amerikanische Nachkommenschaft der Familie Gutmann-Klungler." In *Genealogie.*

★9460

Vol. 9:7 (July 1969), pp. 646-649.

★9461

Nach einmal ("Once more"). Vol. 11:2 (Feb. 1972), p. 47.

"The American Descendants of the Gutmann/ Klungler Family." Date and place of first mention of residence in New World. Place of origin (even of many German-American individuals who married into these two families) with age, places of settlement, and other information provided.

★9555.10

WALL, BETTY. "New York Passenger Lists: June 11-30, 1851, People Bound for Pittsburgh." In *Western Pennsylvania Genealogical Society Quarterly,* vol. 13:1 (Summer 1986), p. 26.

Date and port of arrival of the *Guy Mannering.* Occupation also provided. Most of those setting sail from Liverpool were born in Wales. Extracted from National Archives New York Passenger Lists (June 11-30, 1851), reel 100.

★9675.4—9675.8

WENDT, ALICE. "Index to the Ozaukee County [Wisconsin] Declarations of Intention and Naturalizations." In *Wisconsin State Genealogical Society Newsletter.*

★9675.4

Vol. 31:3 (Jan. 1985), pp. 193-194 (A-BE); vol. 31:4 (Apr. 1985), pp. 265-266 (BE-BR).

★9675.5

Vol. 32:1 (June 1985), pp. 49-50 (BR-DI); vol. 32:2 (Sept. 1985), pp. 121-122 (DI-FO); vol. 32:3 (Jan. 1986), pp. 189-190 (FO-GO); vol. 32:4 (Apr. 1986), pp. 263-264 (GO-HE).

★9675.6

Vol. 33:1 (June 1986), pp. 51-52 (HE-KA); vol. 33:2 (Sept. 1986), pp. 131-132 (KA-KO); vol. 33:3 (Jan. 1987), pp. 199-200 (KO-LE); vol. 33:4 (Apr. 1987), pp. 267-268 (LE-MA).

★9675.7

Vol. 34:1 (June 1987), pp. 51-52 (MA-NE); vol. 34:2 (Sept. 1987), pp. 129-130 (NE-PI); vol. 34:3 (Jan. 1988), pp. 199-200 (PI-RO); vol. 34:4 (Apr. 1988), pp. 269-270 (RO-SC).

★9675.8

Vol. 35:1 (Jun. 1988), pp. 65-66 (SC-SI); vol. 35:2 (Sept. 1988), pp. 121-126 (SI-Z).

Place where declaration of intention or naturalization was filed. Volume and page number where original record appears is also provided. Extracted from records housed in the Register of Deeds Office in Port Washington, Wisconsin. Microfilm copies are among the holdings of the University of Wisconsin Milwaukee Area Research Center.

★9678.1—9678.3

WESTCOTT, LOIS. "Boulder County [Colorado] Naturalization Records." In *Boulder Genealogical Society Quarterly.*

★9678.1

Vol. 13:4 (Nov. 1981), pp. 149-159 (A-C).

★9678.2

Vol. 14:1 (Feb. 1982), pp. 15-25 (D-I); vol. 14:2 (May 1982), pp. 58-62 (J-K); vol. 14:3 (Aug. 1982), pp. 122-131 (K-P); vol. 14:4 (Nov. 1982), pp. 163-168 (P-S).

★9678.3

Vol. 15:1 (Feb. 1983), pp. 13-19 (S-Z).

Date and place of naturalization; a few are date and port of arrival. Also provides country of origin, names of witnesses, and volume and page numbers of original record.

★9775.5

WHYTE, DONALD. "Scottish Emigration to Canada before Confederation." In *Families,* vol 21:4 (1982), pp. 197-222.

Date and place of first mention of residence in New World or date of emigration with intended destination. Other genealogical information provided. Indexers transcribed two lists in source and have indicated the transcription by adding an *A* after the affected page numbers.

★9777

WHYTE, DONALD. "Scottish Stone-Masons in Texas." In *The Scottish Genealogist* (Scottish Genealogy Society), vol. 13:2 (Oct. 1966), pp. 4-6.

Date of emigration with intended destination; a few are date and place of first mention of residence in New World.

★9786

WILHELMY, JEAN-PIERRE. *German Mercenaries in Canada.* Beloeil, Quebec: Maison des Mots, 1985. 332p.

Date and place of first mention of residence in New World, date and port of arrival, or date of emigration with intended destination. Includes much genealogical information. Indexers transcribed two lists in source and have indicated the transcription by adding an *A* after the affected page numbers.

★9788.3

WILLIAMS, MARY K. *Monongalia County, West Virginia, Naturalization Records, 1776-1906.* Morgantown, WV: the author (912 Hawthorne Avenue, Morgantown 26505), 1986. 22p.

Date and place of declaration of intention or admittance to citizenship. Native country, occupation, names of witnesses, and other information provided.

★9831.14

"WISCONSIN-BOUND PASSENGERS ON THE *TRIS.*" By Michael Cassady. In *Wisconsin State Genealogical Society Newsletter,* vol. 32:2 (Oct. 1985), p. 86; vol. 32:3 (Jan. 1986), pp. 153-154.

Date and port of arrival. Also includes occupation and place of origin. Extracted from National Archives microfilm series M237, item 704, reel 175.

★9831.18

"WISCONSIN-BOUND PASSENGERS ON THE *TRUSKO,* Arrived New York from Bremen, 19 June 1862." By Michael Cassady. In *Wisconsin State Genealogical Society Newsletter,* vol. 31:1 (July 1984), p. 16.

Date and port of arrival. Also includes occupation. Extracted from National Archives microfilm series M237, item 575, reel 220.

★9892.11

WOODBURN, CHARLES, and ELMER GERLACH. *Genealogical Extracts from Naturalization Records, Morgan County, Ohio.* McConnelsville, OH: Morgan County Historical Society, 1982. 50p. Reprint. 1983.

Timespan between date of arrival and date when filed declaration of intent or naturalization papers and place where papers were filed. Age, former allegiance, location of original record, and residence also provided. See also source no. 9892.4 (indexed in *PILI* 1988).

★9898

WUST, KLAUS. "The Emigration Season of 1738 — Year of the Destroying Angels." In *The Report: A Journal of German-American History* (Society for the History of the Germans in Maryland), vol. 40 (1986), pp. 21-56.

Date and port of arrival; a few are date of request to emigrate with intended destination or date and place of first mention of residence in the New World.

★9973.7—9973.8

"YORK COUNTY [Pennsylvania] NATURALIZA-TIONS, 1749-1773." In *Codorus Chronicles: The History and Genealogy of York County, Pennsylvania.*
    ★9973.7
    Vol. 4:2 (Aug. 1986), pp. 31-40.
    ★9973.8
    Vol. 4:3 (Nov. 1986), pp. 32-33.

        Date and place of naturalization. Also includes court where naturalized.

★9980.20

ZACHARIAS, PETER D. "Gemeinde Buch der Kolonien Reinland." In *Reinland: An Experience in Community.* N.p.: Reinland Centennial Committee, 1976, pp. 48-49.

"Common Book of the Reinland Colonists." Date and port of arrival. Name of ship, date of birth and place of origin also provided. Source is among the holdings of the Family History Library in Salt Lake City, UT.

★9980.29

ZALESKI, JAN S. "Polish Immigrants on S.S. *Nieuw Amsterdam,* 29 April 1912." In *The Eaglet: Polish Genealogical Society of Michigan,* vol. 11:2 (May 1991), pp. 48-75.

Date and port of arrival; a few are date and place of first mention of residence in New World. Place born, nationality, last residence, and other information also provided. If passenger was "going to" husband, wife, or parent, indexers assumed that husband, wife, or parent immigrated previously. Extracted from ship list on LDS film number 1400649.

★9982

ZIMMER, KLAUS. "Emigrants from the Ostertal." In *Der Reggeboge: Journal of the Pennsylvania German Society* (Breinigsville, PA), vol. 16 (1982), pp. 24-27.

Date and port of arrival or date and place of first mention of residence in the New World. Other genealogical information included. Transcribed from the German language article that appeared in vol. 9:9 (Dec. 1980) of *Mitteilungen zur Wanderungsgeschichte der Pfaelzer.*

PASSENGER AND IMMIGRATION LISTS INDEX

1996 Supplement

A

A La Toro, Bracila; Arizona, 1918 *9228.40* p21
Aadriaansen, Francis; New York, NY, 1851 *6013.19* p89
Aaken, H. J. van; Germantown, PA, 1684 *2467.7* p5
Aarhus, Gullick 24; Arkansas, 1918 *95.2* p11
Aaron, Simon; Baltimore, 1852 *2764.35* p2
Aase, Carl; Arkansas, 1918 *95.2* p11
Aase, Iver; Arkansas, 1918 *95.2* p11
Abadie, Batiste 21; New Orleans, 1862 *543.30* p233
Abadie, Bernard 22; New Orleans, 1836 *778.5* p1
Abadie, Jacques 39; America, 1838 *778.5* p1
Abadie, Jean 19; America, 1838 *778.5* p1
Abadie, Jean 22; New Orleans, 1836 *778.5* p1
Abadie, Jean 29; America, 1835 *778.5* p1
Abadie, Julien 28; New Orleans, 1839 *778.5* p1
Abadie, Louis 24; New Orleans, 1862 *543.30* p237
Abba, Elizabeth 20; Nova Scotia, 1774 *1219.7* p194
Abbate, Bemigia 17; New York, NY, 1893 *9026.4* p41
Abberley, John, Jr.; New York, NY, 1835 *8208.4* p6
Abberly, Thomas; New York, NY, 1839 *8208.4* p93
Abberlyn, Richard; Virginia, 1636 *6219* p19
Abbert, Peter 40; Maryland, 1739 *3690.1* p1
Abbert, Robert 15; Baltimore, 1775 *1219.7* p270
Abbeste, . . .; Canada, 1776-1783 *9786* p16
Abbeys, William; Virginia, 1638 *6219* p11
Abbin, James; Virginia, 1638 *6219* p153
Abbitt, Abraham 19; Jamaica, 1724 *3690.1* p1
Abbney, John 24; Maryland, 1724 *3690.1* p1
Abbot, John 20; Philadelphia, 1775 *1219.7* p255
Abbott, Bryan; Virginia, 1642 *6219* p194
Abbott, Christopher; Virginia, 1635 *6219* p69
Abbott, James; Virginia, 1636 *6219* p11
Abbott, Nicholas; Virginia, 1621 *6219* p15
Abbott, Peter 24; Jamaica, 1733 *3690.1* p1
Abbott, Samll.; Virginia, 1643 *6219* p199
Abbott, Symon; Virginia, 1636 *6219* p74
Abbott, Thomas; New York, NY, 1816 *2859.11* p24
Abbott, William; Ohio, 1840 *9892.11* p1
Abdelnour, Elias 28; Indianapolis, 1905 *1450.2* p1B
Abdey, Nicholas; Virginia, 1637 *6219* p85
Abdon, Allie 27; Arkansas, 1918 *95.2* p11
Abdullah, James; Arkansas, 1918 *95.2* p11
Abel, Charles; America, 1848 *1450.2* p1A
Abel, Frederick; America, 1850 *1450.2* p1A
Abel, Frederick 25; Kansas, 1892 *5240.1* p3
Abel, Frederick 25; Kansas, 1892 *5240.1* p77
Abel, John B.; New York, NY, 1838 *8208.4* p82
Abel, Joseph-Abel; Quebec, 1699 *7603* p25
Abel, Leonard; Philadelphia, 1760 *9973.7* p34
Abel, Michael; Wisconsin, n.d. *9675.4* p193
Abel, Peter; New York, NY, 1838 *8208.4* p82
Abele, Friederich; America, 1849 *8582.2* p1
Abeling, Sophie Margarete; America, 1841 *4815.7* p92
Abendroth, Peter; Illinois, 1887 *2896.5* p1
Abendroth, William; Illinois, 1887 *2896.5* p1
Abercrombie, James; Boston, 1775 *1219.7* p279
Abercrombie, Mary 27; Maryland, 1775 *1219.7* p266
Abercromby, James; New York, NY, 1816 *2859.11* p24
Abercromby, Robert; New York, NY, 1816 *2859.11* p24
Abercromby, William; North Carolina, 1723-1741 *1639.20* p1
Aberdeen, Charles 20; Tortola, 1773 *1219.7* p172
Aberg, Carl W. 38; Massachusetts, 1860 *6410.32* p107
Abernathy, Thomas; New York, NY, 1872 *9678.1* p149
Aberson, Joe Lucas; Arkansas, 1918 *95.2* p11
Abiet, Joseph 19; America, 1837 *778.5* p1
Abke, Anne Marie Charlotte; America, 1844 *4610.10* p138

Abke, Carl Friedrich Gottlieb; America, 1858 *4610.10* p140
Abke, Christine Louise; America, 1844 *4610.10* p119
Abkiewitch, Abraham; Arkansas, 1918 *95.2* p11
Ablesome, Isabell; Virginia, 1638 *6219* p116
Ably, Jacob 45; New Orleans, 1862 *543.30* p236
Abney, Thomas 48; Maryland, 1774 *1219.7* p220
Abodeely, Frank; Arkansas, 1918 *95.2* p11
Aboge, Richard; Virginia, 1637 *6219* p24
Abood, Abraham; Arkansas, 1918 *95.2* p11
Abott, Jon.; Virginia, 1635 *6219* p71
Abraham, . . .; Canada, 1776-1783 *9786* p16
Abraham, Barbara; Quebec, 1852 *5704.8* p94
Abraham, Geo.; Virginia, 1642 *6219* p186
Abraham, Leopold 29; Kansas, 1879 *5240.1* p60
Abraham, Levy; Virginia, 1851 *4626.16* p14
Abraham, Margaret; Quebec, 1853 *5704.8* p104
Abraham, Richard 20; Virginia, 1700 *2212* p32
Abraham, Robert 3; Quebec, 1852 *5704.8* p94
Abraham, Tony; Arkansas, 1918 *95.2* p11
Abraham, William; Quebec, 1852 *5704.8* p94
Abrahams, Alexander 23; Philadelphia, 1774 *1219.7* p233
Abrahams, Sarah; America, 1832-1833 *4535.12* p113
Abrahamsen, Swan 15; Arizona, 1918 *9228.40* p27
Abrahamsohn, Miriane 32; New York, NY, 1878 *9253* p46
Abrahamson, August; Shreveport, LA, 1878 *7129* p44
Abrahamson, Lars; Maine, 1871-1873 *6410.22* p118
Abrahamson, Magnus; Maine, 1871-1882 *6410.22* p118
Abrall, John; Virginia, 1638 *6219* p11
Abram, Ellis; Virginia, 1855 *4626.16* p15
Abram, Jobon 28; America, 1836 *778.5* p1
Abram, John; Virginia, 1635 *6219* p20
Abram, L. T. 18; America, 1832 *778.5* p1
Abram, Levi 26; America, 1836 *778.5* p1
Abram, Thomas; Quebec, 1851 *5704.8* p74
Abram, William; Quebec, 1851 *5704.8* p74
Abramowicz, Dominik; New York, 1831 *4606* p172
Abrams, Agatha; Quebec, 1878 *9980.20* p49
Abrams, Cathariena; Quebec, 1878 *9980.20* p49
Abrams, James 36; California, 1869 *3840.1* p14
Abrams, Peter; Quebec, 1878 *9980.20* p49
Abrams, Sara; Quebec, 1878 *9980.20* p49
Abrams, Susana; Quebec, 1878 *9980.20* p49
Abrams, Willhelm; Quebec, 1878 *9980.20* p49
Abramsohn, Isaac 26; Arkansas, 1918 *95.2* p11
Abramson, John; Wisconsin, n.d. *9675.4* p193
Abrisy, . . . 20; New Orleans, 1862 *543.30* p235
Abromet, Adolph; Indiana, 1863-1868 *1450.2* p1A
Abruzzo, Joe; Arkansas, 1918 *95.2* p11
Abshere, Lewis; Virginia, 1637 *6219* p83
Abt, . . .; Canada, 1776-1783 *9786* p16
Abtercrume, John; Virginia, 1639 *6219* p157
Accarie, Nicholas; New York, NY, 1835 *8208.4* p38
Aceto, Raffael; Arkansas, 1918 *95.2* p11
Achard, Auguste 24; America, 1837 *778.5* p1
Ache, Pierre; Louisiana, 1789-1819 *778.5* p555
Achenson, Adam 14; Massachusetts, 1849 *5881.1* p5
Achenson, Francis 10; Massachusetts, 1850 *5881.1* p5
Achenson, George 24; Massachusetts, 1850 *5881.1* p5
Achenson, William 17; Massachusetts, 1849 *5881.1* p6
Acher, Emilie 37; New Orleans, 1836 *778.5* p1
Acherson, Wm.; Virginia, 1638 *6219* p181
Acheson, Alex 30; Quebec, 1853 *5704.8* p105
Acheson, Ann 60; Quebec, 1853 *5704.8* p105
Acheson, Charles; Quebec, 1849 *5704.8* p51

Acheson, Daniel, Sr.; Philadelphia, 1816 *2859.11* p24
Acheson, David, Jr.; Philadelphia, 1816 *2859.11* p24
Acheson, Elizabeth; Philadelphia, 1850 *5704.8* p64
Acheson, Elizabeth 20; Philadelphia, 1853 *5704.8* p108
Acheson, Fanny; Quebec, 1849 *5704.8* p51
Acheson, James; Philadelphia, 1851 *5704.8* p76
Acheson, James; Philadelphia, 1864 *5704.8* p174
Acheson, James 24; St. John, N.B., 1858 *5704.8* p137
Acheson, Jane; Quebec, 1849 *5704.8* p57
Acheson, John; St. John, N.B., 1847 *5704.8* p24
Acheson, Johnston; Quebec, 1853 *5704.8* p104
Acheson, Mary; Philadelphia, 1816 *2859.11* p24
Acheson, Mary; Philadelphia, 1851 *5704.8* p76
Acheson, Mary; Quebec, 1849 *5704.8* p56
Acheson, Mary 3; Quebec, 1849 *5704.8* p51
Acheson, Mary 44; Philadelphia, 1864 *5704.8* p160
Acheson, Mary 60; Philadelphia, 1853 *5704.8* p108
Acheson, Mary Ann; Philadelphia, 1850 *5704.8* p64
Acheson, Mary Ann; Philadelphia, 1864 *5704.8* p174
Acheson, Nancy; Philadelphia, 1852 *5704.8* p84
Acheson, Sarah; Philadelphia, 1850 *53.26* p1
Acheson, Sarah; Philadelphia, 1850 *5704.8* p59
Acheson, Sarah; St. John, N.B., 1847 *5704.8* p24
Achgell, Anthony Henry; America, 1846 *1450.2* p1A
Achgell, Christian Frederick; America, 1844 *1450.2* p1A
Achille, Fanaga 25; Kansas, 1893 *5240.1* p79
Achilles, . . .; Canada, 1776-1783 *9786* p16
Achills, Frederick William; America, 1835 *1450.2* p1A
Achteres, Berend 4; New York, NY, 1847 *3377.6* p16
Achteres, Berendina 24; New York, NY, 1847 *3377.6* p16
Achteres, Derk John 54; New York, NY, 1847 *3377.6* p16
Achteres, Dinah 30; New York, NY, 1847 *3377.6* p16
Achteres, Elizabeth 53; New York, NY, 1847 *3377.6* p16
Achteres, Jan Willem 32; New York, NY, 1847 *3377.6* p16
Achteres, John 1; New York, NY, 1847 *3377.6* p16
Achyohn, Antoine 1; America, 1831 *778.5* p1
Achyohn, Frances 3; America, 1831 *778.5* p1
Achyohn, Francis 31; America, 1831 *778.5* p1
Achyohn, Magdlean 28; America, 1831 *778.5* p2
Ackelow, Curt Herrmann; Philadelphia Co., PA, 1878 *1450.2* p1A
Acker, Fritz; America, 1847 *1450.2* p2A
Acker, Jacob; Wisconsin, n.d. *9675.4* p193
Ackerman, Albert 23; Kansas, 1886 *5240.1* p69
Ackerman, Eilert; Illinois, 1894 *5012.37* p63
Ackerman, George 39; New Orleans, 1862 *543.30* p234
Ackerman, Henry; Illinois, 1894 *5012.40* p53
Ackerman, Herman; Illinois, 1894 *5012.37* p63
Ackerman, Jerry; Illinois, 1894 *5012.37* p63
Ackerman, John; Wisconsin, n.d. *9675.4* p193
Ackerman, Margaret 59; Kansas, 1879 *5240.1* p61
Ackerman, Max 33; Harris Co., TX, 1900 *6254* p6
Ackerman, Robert; Virginia, 1635 *6219* p71
Ackermann, . . .; Canada, 1776-1783 *9786* p16
Ackermann, Bernard; Wisconsin, n.d. *9675.4* p193
Ackermann, Carl Johann; Canada, 1776-1783 *9786* p242
Ackermann, Conrad; America, 1848 *8582.3* p1
Ackermann, Georg; America, 1839 *8582.1* p1
Ackermann, Heinrich; Kentucky, 1840 *8582.3* p99
Ackermann, Hermann E.; Illinois, 1888 *5012.37* p61
Ackermann, Johann Th.; Cincinnati, 1869-1887 *8582* p1
Ackerson, Nels; Illinois, 1896 *5012.40* p55
Ackerstrom, Carl L.; Maine, 1871-1882 *6410.22* p119
Ackland, Georg; Virginia, 1638 *6219* p120

Ackland, Mary; Virginia, 1638 ***6219*** *p120*
Acklen, Thomas; Boston, 1846 ***6410.32*** *p125*
Ackley, David 11; Massachusetts, 1848 ***5881.1*** *p5*
Ackley, Rose 22; Massachusetts, 1849 ***5881.1*** *p6*
Ackley, Thomas 24; Maryland, 1774 ***1219.7*** *p220*
Acklin, Bridgit 22; Massachusetts, 1860 ***6410.32*** *p114*
Acklin, Ths. 30; Massachusetts, 1860 ***6410.32*** *p114*
Ackmann, Heinrich; Kentucky, 1844 ***8582.3*** *p99*
Acone, Thomas; Virginia, 1642 ***6219*** *p15*
Acone, Thomas; Virginia, 1642 ***6219*** *p190*
Acoro, Pedro 28; New Orleans, 1862 ***543.30*** *p238*
Acosader, G.; Austin, TX, 1886 ***9777*** *p5*
Acosta, Guadalupe; Arizona, 1890 ***2764.35*** *p3*
Acourt, John; Virginia, 1753 ***1219.7*** *p17*
Acreland, Tho.; Virginia, 1648 ***6219*** *p251*
Acrelius, Isaac; Philadelphia, 1759 ***8582.3*** *p84*
Acres, Ellin 22; Pennsylvania, Virginia or Maryland, 1699 ***2212*** *p19*
Actin, Eliz 18; America, 1704 ***2212*** *p41*
Acton, John 24; Philadelphia, 1774 ***1219.7*** *p216*
Acton, John Whittaker; New York, NY, 1837 ***8208.4*** *p55*
Acton, Jon.; Virginia, 1642 ***6219*** *p197*
Actor, Elizabeth; Quebec, 1850 ***5704.8*** *p66*
Actor, Elizabeth; Quebec, 1851 ***5704.8*** *p74*
Actor, James; Quebec, 1850 ***5704.8*** *p66*
Actor, John; Quebec, 1847 ***5704.8*** *p17*
Acurio, Michele; Washington, 1859-1920 ***2872.1*** *p1*
Adae, C. F.; America, 1833 ***8582*** *p1*
Adair, A.; New York, NY, 1816 ***2859.11*** *p24*
Adair, Ann; St. John, N.B., 1848 ***5704.8*** *p45*
Adair, Daniel W.; Illinois, 1876 ***5012.39*** *p26*
Adair, Elizabeth *SEE* Adair, Joanna
Adair, Elizabeth; Philadelphia, 1849 ***5704.8*** *p53*
Adair, James *SEE* Adair, Joanna
Adair, James; Philadelphia, 1849 ***5704.8*** *p53*
Adair, Joanna; Philadelphia, 1849 ***53.26*** *p1*
*Relative:*James
*Relative:*William 11
*Relative:*Elizabeth
Adair, Joanna; Philadelphia, 1849 ***5704.8*** *p53*
Adair, John; Quebec, 1818 ***7603*** *p42*
Adair, John; St. John, N.B., 1848 ***5704.8*** *p45*
Adair, Robert 19; Quebec, 1863 ***5704.8*** *p153*
Adair, Robert 30; St. John, N.B., 1863 ***5704.8*** *p153*
Adair, Thomas; St. John, N.B., 1848 ***5704.8*** *p45*
Adair, William 11 *SEE* Adair, Joanna
Adair, William 11; Philadelphia, 1849 ***5704.8*** *p53*
Adair, Wm.; Philadelphia, 1816 ***2859.11*** *p24*
Adam, . . .; Canada, 1776-1783 ***9786*** *p41*
Adam, Mr.; Minnesota, 1855 ***8582.3*** *p82*
Adam, Anna Barbara *SEE* Adam, Jacob
Adam, Anna Barbara; Pennsylvania, 1753 ***2444*** *p181*
Adam, Anna Kummerlin *SEE* Adam, Johann Jacob
Adam, Anna Magdalena *SEE* Adam, Johann Jacob
Adam, Barbara *SEE* Adam, Johann Jacob
Adam, Fredrick 25; Kansas, 1884 ***5240.1*** *p65*
Adam, Fritz Theodore; Arkansas, 1918 ***95.2*** *p11*
Adam, Geo. 20; Canada, 1838 ***4535.12*** *p113*
Adam, Hans Jacob; Pennsylvania, 1753 ***2444*** *p132*
Adam, Isaac 22; Canada, 1838 ***4535.12*** *p113*
Adam, Jacob; Pennsylvania, 1753 ***2444*** *p181*
*Daughter:*Anna Barbara
Adam, James 20; Canada, 1838 ***4535.12*** *p113*
Adam, Johann Jacob; Port uncertain, 1754 ***2444*** *p132*
*Wife:*Anna Kummerlin
*Child:*Anna Magdalena
*Child:*Margaretha
*Child:*Maria
*Child:*Barbara
Adam, Johann Nicolaus; Cincinnati, 1829 ***8582.3*** *p87*
Adam, John; Wisconsin, n.d. ***9675.4*** *p193*
Adam, Louis 22; America, 1838 ***778.5*** *p2*
Adam, Margaretha *SEE* Adam, Johann Jacob
Adam, Maria *SEE* Adam, Johann Jacob
Adam, Marie 36; America, 1839 ***778.5*** *p2*
Adam, Robert; North Carolina, 1759-1801 ***1639.20*** *p1*
Adam, William 16; Philadelphia, 1775 ***1219.7*** *p248*
Adamec, Frank; Wisconsin, n.d. ***9675.4*** *p193*
Adamkewicz, Narcyz; Arkansas, 1918 ***95.2*** *p11*
Adamo, Michalangelo; Iowa, 1866-1943 ***123.54*** *p55*
Adamopoulos, Tom; Arkansas, 1918 ***95.2*** *p11*
Adams, Miss; Philadelphia, 1865 ***5704.8*** *p200*
Adams, Mr.; Quebec, 1815 ***9229.18*** *p74*
Adams, Mr. 38; New Orleans, 1831 ***778.5*** *p2*
Adams, Andrew; Carolina, 1726-1744 ***1639.20*** *p1*
Adams, Andrew; Philadelphia, 1853 ***5704.8*** *p102*
Adams, Andrew; Virginia, 1637 ***6219*** *p10*
Adams, Ann; New York, NY, 1864 ***5704.8*** *p172*
Adams, B. 11; New Orleans, 1830 ***778.5*** *p2*
Adams, B. 50; New Orleans, 1830 ***778.5*** *p2*
Adams, Calvin; New York, NY, 1839 ***8208.4*** *p97*
Adams, Cassy 20; Philadelphia, 1854 ***5704.8*** *p120*
Adams, Charles; Baltimore, 1811 ***2859.11*** *p8*
Adams, Clementi; Iowa, 1866-1943 ***123.54*** *p5*
Adams, D. 14; New Orleans, 1830 ***778.5*** *p2*
Adams, Daniel 12; St. John, N.B., 1850 ***5704.8*** *p65*
Adams, David; St. John, N.B., 1847 ***5704.8*** *p26*
Adams, David 6 mos; Quebec, 1847 ***5704.8*** *p16*
Adams, David 20; Quebec, 1862 ***5704.8*** *p151*
Adams, Eacy 17; Philadelphia, 1853 ***5704.8*** *p113*
Adams, Eade; Virginia, 1638 ***6219*** *p124*
Adams, Eliz.; Virginia, 1635 ***6219*** *p26*
Adams, Eliza; St. John, N.B., 1848 ***5704.8*** *p47*
Adams, Fanny; St. John, N.B., 1848 ***5704.8*** *p47*
Adams, Franz; Ohio, 1825-1829 ***8582.1*** *p46*
Adams, George 25; Virginia, 1774 ***1219.7*** *p185*
Adams, Hamilton 11; Quebec, 1847 ***5704.8*** *p16*
Adams, Heinrich; America, 1847 ***8582.3*** *p1*
Adams, Henry 23; St. John, N.B., 1854 ***5704.8*** *p122*
Adams, J. 13; New Orleans, 1830 ***778.5*** *p2*
Adams, Jacob; Iroquois Co., IL, 1892 ***3455.1*** *p9*
Adams, James; North Carolina, 1711 ***1639.20*** *p1*
Adams, James; St. John, N.B., 1866 ***5704.8*** *p166*
Adams, James 11; St. John, N.B., 1866 ***5704.8*** *p166*
Adams, James 16; Quebec, 1862 ***5704.8*** *p151*
Adams, James 20; Philadelphia, 1854 ***5704.8*** *p120*
Adams, James 23; Quebec, 1857 ***5704.8*** *p135*
Adams, Jane 4; Quebec, 1850 ***5704.8*** *p63*
Adams, Jane 55 *SEE* Adams, Robert
Adams, Jennette 23 *SEE* Adams, Robert
Adams, Joe 28; Kansas, 1889 ***5240.1*** *p3*
Adams, John; Colorado, 1894 ***9678.1*** *p149*
Adams, John; New York, NY, 1816 ***2859.11*** *p24*
Adams, John; New York, NY, 1838 ***8208.4*** *p86*
Adams, John; Virginia, 1645 ***6219*** *p240*
Adams, John; Virginia, 1698 ***2212*** *p17*
Adams, John 20; Pennsylvania, Virginia or Maryland, 1719 ***3690.1*** *p1*
Adams, John 37; Massachusetts, 1860 ***6410.32*** *p119*
Adams, John 40; Massachusetts, 1860 ***6410.32*** *p114*
Adams, John 40; North Carolina, 1850 ***1639.20*** *p1*
*Relative:*Mary 40
Adams, John B.; New York, NY, 1839 ***8208.4*** *p102*
Adams, Jon.; Virginia, 1642 ***6219*** *p192*
Adams, Joseph 28; Kansas, 1889 ***5240.1*** *p73*
Adams, Joseph 34; New Orleans, 1862 ***543.30*** *p235*
Adams, Lydia 21; Maryland, 1774 ***1219.7*** *p208*
Adams, Margaret; Philadelphia, 1853 ***5704.8*** *p102*
Adams, Margaret 7; Quebec, 1850 ***5704.8*** *p63*
Adams, Margaret Ann; Philadelphia, 1853 ***5704.8*** *p102*
Adams, Martha; Quebec, 1847 ***5704.8*** *p16*
Adams, Mary; St. John, N.B., 1866 ***5704.8*** *p166*
Adams, Mary 40 *SEE* Adams, John
Adams, Mary Jane 6; Quebec, 1847 ***5704.8*** *p16*
Adams, Matilda 2; Quebec, 1847 ***5704.8*** *p16*
Adams, Nancy; St. John, N.B., 1853 ***5704.8*** *p98*
Adams, Nathaniel 35; Virginia, 1774 ***1219.7*** *p243*
Adams, Philip 21; Jamaica, 1736 ***3690.1*** *p1*
Adams, Philip 30; Philadelphia, 1774 ***1219.7*** *p190*
With wife 26
Adams, Porter; New York, NY, 1865 ***5704.8*** *p194*
Adams, Q. 6; New Orleans, 1830 ***778.5*** *p2*
Adams, Rachell; Virginia, 1636 ***6219*** *p34*
Adams, Robert; Quebec, 1847 ***5704.8*** *p16*
Adams, Robert; St. John, N.B., 1850 ***5704.8*** *p67*
Adams, Robert 10; Quebec, 1847 ***5704.8*** *p16*
Adams, Robert 55; North Carolina, 1850 ***1639.20*** *p1*
*Relative:*Jane 55
*Relative:*Jennette 23
Adams, Robert L.; Illinois, 1860 ***7857*** *p2*
Adams, Ross; St. John, N.B., 1847 ***5704.8*** *p35*
Adams, S. 16; New Orleans, 1830 ***778.5*** *p2*
Adams, Sarah; Quebec, 1847 ***5704.8*** *p17*
Adams, Sarah; Quebec, 1850 ***5704.8*** *p63*
Adams, Sarah 8; St. John, N.B., 1850 ***5704.8*** *p65*
Adams, Semfiterna Palma Guzzi; Iowa, 1866-1943 ***123.54*** *p55*
Adams, Susana; St. John, N.B., 1847 ***5704.8*** *p26*
Adams, T. 40; New Orleans, 1830 ***778.5*** *p2*
Adams, T. H.; Washington, 1859-1920 ***2872.1*** *p1*
Adams, Tho.; Virginia, 1648 ***6219*** *p246*
Adams, Thomas; America, 1741 ***4971*** *p41*
Adams, Thomas; Philadelphia, 1851 ***5704.8*** *p70*
Adams, Thomas; Philadelphia, 1864 ***5704.8*** *p184*
Adams, Thomas; Virginia, 1637 ***6219*** *p114*
Adams, Thomas 8; St. John, N.B., 1866 ***5704.8*** *p166*
Adams, Thomas 32; Maryland, 1775 ***1219.7*** *p272*
Adams, William; Philadelphia, 1756 ***1219.7*** *p46*
Adams, William; Philadelphia, 1853 ***5704.8*** *p102*
Adams, William; Wisconsin, n.d. ***9675.4*** *p193*
Adams, William 8; Quebec, 1847 ***5704.8*** *p16*
Adams, William 22; Maryland, 1775 ***1219.7*** *p255*
Adams, William 23; Maryland, 1775 ***1219.7*** *p255*
Adams, William 35; Philadelphia, 1864 ***5704.8*** *p161*
Adams, William 39; New Orleans, 1862 ***543.30*** *p237*
Adams, William 45; Maryland, 1774 ***1219.7*** *p192*
Adams, Winand 33; Kansas, 1894 ***5240.1*** *p79*
Adams, Wm. 23; Canada, 1835 ***4535.10*** *p196*
Adamson, Anders; Iowa, 1850-1855 ***2090*** *p613*
Adamson, Andrew; Iowa, 1846 ***2090*** *p610*
With wife
Adamson, Charles; Colorado, 1904 ***9678.1*** *p149*
Adamson, Eliza; America, 1867 ***5704.8*** *p221*
Adamson, Hugh; America, 1867 ***5704.8*** *p221*
Adamson, James; America, 1867 ***5704.8*** *p221*
Adamson, John; America, 1867 ***5704.8*** *p221*
Adamson, John 18; Maryland, 1723 ***3690.1*** *p1*
Adamson, Martha J.; America, 1867 ***5704.8*** *p221*
Adamson, Mary A.; America, 1867 ***5704.8*** *p221*
Adamson, Thomas; New York, 1835 ***8208.4*** *p29*
Adamson, Thomas 21; Maryland, 1775 ***1219.7*** *p272*
Adarmann, Christ; Illinois, 1884 ***2896.5*** *p1*
Adaun, Mrs. 20; Louisiana, 1829 ***778.5*** *p2*
Adaun, P. 28; Louisiana, 1829 ***778.5*** *p2*
Adcock, John 18; Pennsylvania, 1733 ***3690.1*** *p1*
Adcock, John 21; Jamaica, 1737 ***3690.1*** *p1*
Addams, Geo.; Virginia, 1629 ***6219*** *p8*
Addams, Richard; Virginia, 1643 ***6219*** *p201*
Addams, Robert 17; Pennsylvania, 1725 ***3690.1*** *p1*
Addams, Tho.; Virginia, 1636 ***6219*** *p21*
Adde, John 3 *SEE* Adde, Solomon
Adde, Margaret 32 *SEE* Adde, Solomon
Adde, Solomon 30; Georgia, 1738 ***9332*** *p330*
*Wife:*Margaret 32
*Son:*John 3
Adderby, Thomas; Virginia, 1637 ***6219*** *p114*
Adderly, Ralph 16; Maryland, 1730 ***3690.1*** *p2*
Addey, William 18; Virginia, 1720 ***3690.1*** *p2*
Adding, Thomas 40; Maryland, 1774 ***1219.7*** *p244*
Addington, Jonathan; Virginia, 1639 ***6219*** *p151*
Addis, Abe Bettercat 21; Kansas, 1903 ***5240.1*** *p82*
Addis, Elizabeth 24; Philadelphia, 1774 ***1219.7*** *p182*
Addison, Elizabeth 24; Virginia, 1699 ***2212*** *p26*
Addison, Tho.; Virginia, 1636 ***6219*** *p115*
Addison, Tho.; Virginia, 1637 ***6219*** *p13*
Adea, Gabriel; Virginia, 1637 ***6219*** *p113*
Adege, L. 54; America, 1837 ***778.5*** *p2*
Adel, . . .; Canada, 1776-1783 ***9786*** *p16*
Adelaide, Adelaide 3; America, 1837 ***778.5*** *p2*
Adelbert, Francois 30; New Orleans, 1835 ***778.5*** *p3*
Adele Saunier, Miss; Port uncertain, 1839 ***778.5*** *p379*
Adelmann, Miss; New England, 1773 ***4525*** *p197*
Adelmann, Miss; Pennsylvania, 1773 ***4525*** *p197*
Adelmann, Barbara; Pennsylvania, 1752-1754 ***4525*** *p197*
Adelmann, Michel; Pennsylvania, 1752 ***4525*** *p197*
Adelmann, Wilhelm; Pennsylvania, 1750 ***4525*** *p233*
Adelsheim, . . .; Canada, 1776-1783 ***9786*** *p16*
Adelsheim, Carl Friedrich Christian; Quebec, 1776 ***9786*** *p255*
Adelsheim, F. v.; Quebec, 1776 ***9786*** *p105*
Aden, Hugh; Virginia, 1645 ***6219*** *p232*
Aden, Luke; Virginia, 1637 ***6219*** *p110*
Ader, Jr. 10; Port uncertain, 1839 ***778.5*** *p3*
Ader, Pere 35; Port uncertain, 1839 ***778.5*** *p3*
Adermann, August F.; Illinois, 1892 ***2896.5*** *p1*
Aderson, Roger; Virginia, 1638 ***6219*** *p120*
Adey, Simon; South Carolina, 1788 ***7119*** *p201*
Adge, Henry 73; Montreal, 1775 ***1219.7*** *p258*
Adge, Margaret 5 *SEE* Adge, Mary
Adge, Mary 14 *SEE* Adge, Mary
Adge, Mary 44; Montreal, 1775 ***1219.7*** *p258*
*Child:*Samuel 16
*Child:*Mary 14
*Child:*William 9
*Child:*Margaret 5
Adge, Samuel 16 *SEE* Adge, Mary
Adge, William 9 *SEE* Adge, Mary
Adi, Peter; Wisconsin, n.d. ***9675.4*** *p193*
Adkin, Christopher *SEE* Adkin, Tho.
Adkin, Tho.; Virginia, 1642 ***6219*** *p190*
*Relative:*Christopher
Adkinks, John 41; Philadelphia, 1774 ***1219.7*** *p219*
Adkins, Christ.; Virginia, 1635 ***6219*** *p26*
Adkins, David 22; Carolina, 1774 ***1219.7*** *p227*
Adkins, Richard; Virginia, 1642 ***6219*** *p189*
Adkins, Tho.; Virginia, 1643 ***6219*** *p23*
Adkinson, Matt.; Virginia, 1645 ***6219*** *p232*
Adkinson, Tho.; Virginia, 1645 ***6219*** *p232*
Adlam, Patrick; New York, NY, 1840 ***8208.4*** *p107*
Adler, Francis; America, 1846 ***1450.2*** *p2A*
Adler, Henry; America, 1848 ***8582.1*** *p1*
Adler, Herman; Wisconsin, n.d. ***9675.4*** *p193*
Adler, Hermann; Wisconsin, n.d. ***9675.4*** *p193*
Adler, Joseph; South Carolina, 1775 ***1219.7*** *p275*
Adleta, Martin; America, 1849 ***8582.1*** *p1*
Adlon, . . .; Canada, 1776-1783 ***9786*** *p16*
Adlum, Margaret 25; Massachusetts, 1847 ***5881.1*** *p5*
Adnet, Jean 24; America, 1839 ***778.5*** *p3*
Adney, George 18; Maryland, 1733 ***3690.1*** *p2*

2 *FOR A COMPLETE EXPLANATION OF ENTRY, SEE "HOW TO READ A CITATION" SECTION*

Adolf, Henry 26; Kansas, 1886 ***5240.1*** *p69*
Adolph, . . .; Canada, 1776-1783 ***9786*** *p16*
Adolph, Alpert; Colorado, 1900 ***9678.1*** *p150*
Adolphe, Peter 23; New Orleans, 1838 ***778.5*** *p3*
Adoue, Francois 32; New Orleans, 1839 ***778.5*** *p3*
Adrain, John; Ohio, 1883-1899 ***9892.11*** *p1*
Adrian, . . .; Canada, 1776-1783 ***9786*** *p41*
Adrick, Mary 21; America, 1702 ***2212*** *p39*
Adrien, Jean-Nicolas 38; America, 1838 ***778.5*** *p3*
Adrien, Nicolas 10; America, 1838 ***778.5*** *p3*
Adronio, Pablo 40; New Orleans, 1862 ***543.30*** *p234*
Adwell, Charles; Virginia, 1642 ***6219*** *p195*
Adwell, Katherin; Virginia, 1638 ***6219*** *p124*
Adye, John; Virginia, 1639 ***6219*** *p159*
Aebersold, Christian 30; Kansas, 1884 ***5240.1*** *p65*
Aeby, Rudolph; New York, NY, 1830 ***8208.4*** *p79*
Aeggs, Hugh; New York, NY, 1816 ***2859.11*** *p24*
Aegidia, Sister M.; Wisconsin, n.d. ***9675.4*** *p193*
Aepker, William; America, 1866 ***1450.2*** *p2A*
Aepker, William; America, 1891 ***1450.2*** *p2A*
Aerssn, Michal; Wisconsin, n.d. ***9675.4*** *p193*
Aeschlimann, Verena; Pennsylvania, 1709-1710 ***4480*** *p311*
Aesterlein, Jeremias; Pennsylvania, 1752-1753 ***4525*** *p235*
Aetorphn, J.C. 26; Harris Co., TX, 1898 ***6254*** *p5*
Afantakis, Nick Emm; Arkansas, 1918 ***95.2*** *p11*
Affal, Michael; Cincinnati, 1830-1835 ***8582.3*** *p98*
Affleck, John; New York, NY, 1836 ***8208.4*** *p23*
Affleck, Thomas; South Carolina, 1758 ***1639.20*** *p1*
Afflick, James 35; Jamaica, 1774 ***1219.7*** *p237*
Afterhider, Henry; Indiana, 1849 ***9117*** *p15*
Aftoora, Joseph 22; Kansas, 1896 ***5240.1*** *p80*
Aga, Isaac; Arkansas, 1918 ***95.2*** *p11*
Agace, Alexis 37; America, 1838 ***778.5*** *p3*
Agar, Benjamin 27; Virginia, 1774 ***1219.7*** *p241*
Agar, Edward; Virginia, 1635 ***6219*** *p73*
Agard, Edward; Virginia, 1640 ***6219*** *p160*
Agasse, Felicite 5; America, 1838 ***778.5*** *p3*
Agasse, Lucie 2; America, 1838 ***778.5*** *p3*
Agasse, Simon. 33; America, 1838 ***778.5*** *p3*
Agazzi, Israel; Iowa, 1866-1943 ***123.54*** *p5*
Agazzi, Pompeo; Iowa, 1866-1943 ***123.54*** *p5*
Agbort, Henry; Ohio, 1848 ***8365.27*** *p12*
Age, Hugh; Virginia, 1647 ***6219*** *p247*
Ager, John; Illinois, 1860 ***5012.39*** *p90*
Ageret, Jean 27; New Orleans, 1838 ***778.5*** *p3*
Agez, Henry; Wisconsin, n.d. ***9675.4*** *p193*
Agherine, James; America, 1737 ***4971*** *p55*
Agidio, Tibire; Wisconsin, n.d. ***9675.4*** *p193*
Agile, Ann 22; Quebec, 1853 ***5704.8*** *p105*
Agile, Christopher 18; Quebec, 1853 ***5704.8*** *p105*
Agile, Ellen 20; Quebec, 1853 ***5704.8*** *p105*
Agnaze, Magdalina 25; America, 1838 ***778.5*** *p4*
Agnaze, Philip 4; America, 1838 ***778.5*** *p4*
Agnessen, Grancois; Iowa, 1866-1943 ***123.54*** *p5*
Agnew, Ann; St. John, N.B., 1847 ***5704.8*** *p35*
Agnew, Deckey; New York, NY, 1815 ***2859.11*** *p24*
Agnew, James; New York, NY, 1840 ***8208.4*** *p109*
Agnew, Margaret 29; Massachusetts, 1849 ***5881.1*** *p5*
Agnostino, Nassi 33; West Virginia, 1904 ***9788.3*** *p4*
Agreeni, Henrick; Washington, 1859-1920 ***2872.1*** *p1*
Agren, Aleck E.; Washington, 1859-1920 ***2872.1*** *p1*
Agren, John; Minneapolis, 1882-1885 ***6410.35*** *p47*
Agren, John E.; Washington, 1859-1920 ***2872.1*** *p1*
Agueri, Benito 80; Arizona, 1926 ***9228.40*** *p30*
Ah Kee, Moy; New York, NY, 1880 ***1450.2*** *p2A*
Ahdenstel, . . .; Canada, 1776-1783 ***9786*** *p16*
Ahern, Charles 30; Massachusetts, 1850 ***5881.1*** *p5*
Ahern, Ellen 30; Massachusetts, 1850 ***5881.1*** *p5*
Ahern, Ellen 50; Massachusetts, 1850 ***5881.1*** *p5*
Ahern, James 25; Massachusetts, 1847 ***5881.1*** *p5*
Ahern, John 22; Massachusetts, 1849 ***5881.1*** *p5*
Ahern, Mary 31; Massachusetts, 1849 ***5881.1*** *p5*
Ahern, Owen 45; Massachusetts, 1850 ***5881.1*** *p5*
Ahern, Patrick 13; Massachusetts, 1850 ***5881.1*** *p6*
Ahern, Thomas 1; Massachusetts, 1850 ***5881.1*** *p6*
Ahier, Gedeon; New Brunswick, 1807 ***7603*** *p49*
Ahl, . . .; Canada, 1776-1783 ***9786*** *p41*
Ahlberg, Charlotte 38; Massachusetts, 1860 ***6410.32*** *p118*
Ahlberg, Charlotte A. 39; Massachusetts, 1860 ***6410.32*** *p118*
Ahlberg, H. P.; Washington, 1859-1920 ***2872.1*** *p1*
Ahlberg, Miles 42; Massachusetts, 1860 ***6410.32*** *p118*
Ahlberg, Nils A.; Boston, 1853 ***6410.32*** *p126*
Ahlberg, Nilson A. 36; Massachusetts, 1860 ***6410.32*** *p118*
Ahlborn, Wilhelm; Cincinnati, 1869-1887 ***8582*** *p1*
Ahlbrecht, Conrad 28; New Orleans, 1863 ***543.30*** *p238*
Ahle, Richard; Ohio, 1852-1875 ***9892.11*** *p1*
Ahle, William; Ohio, 1852-1875 ***9892.11*** *p1*
Ahlering, Heinrich; Kentucky, 1876-1877 ***8582.3*** *p1*
Ahlering, Hermann H.; Baltimore, 1838 ***8582.1*** *p1*
Ahlering, Herrmann H.; Cincinnati, 1869-1887 ***8582*** *p1*
Ahlering, J. F.; Cincinnati, 1869-1887 ***8582*** *p1*
Ahlering, Johann F. 20; Baltimore, 1836 ***8582.1*** *p1*
Ahlers, Conrad; America, 1848 ***8582.1*** *p1*
Ahlers, Franz; Cincinnati, 1838 ***8582.1*** *p1*
Ahlers, John; Cincinnati, 1846 ***8582.1*** *p1*
Ahlers, John; Wisconsin, n.d. ***9675.4*** *p193*
Ahlers, Karl; America, 1848 ***8582.3*** *p1*
Ahlersmeyer, Anne Marie 28; America, 1850 ***4610.10*** *p142*
Ahlersmeyer, Johann Friedrich Wilhelm; America, 1850 ***4610.10*** *p142*
Ahlf, George 26; Kansas, 1883 ***5240.1*** *p64*
Ahlf, Henry 37; Kansas, 1882 ***5240.1*** *p64*
Ahlhauser, Anthony; Wisconsin, n.d. ***9675.4*** *p193*
Ahlhauser, William; Wisconsin, n.d. ***9675.4*** *p193*
Ahlin, John; Colorado, 1904 ***9678.1*** *p150*
Ahlmark, Raul 45; Massachusetts, 1860 ***6410.32*** *p103*
Ahner, Michael; Wisconsin, n.d. ***9675.4*** *p193*
Ahnerich, John; Indiana, 1850 ***9117*** *p20*
Ahnert, Adolph Friedr. 34; New Orleans, 1839 ***9420.2*** *p69*
Ahnert, Amalia Theresia 2; Died enroute, 1839 ***9420.2*** *p69*
Ahnert, August Fredr. 27; New Orleans, 1839 ***9420.2*** *p69*
Ahnert, Fredhr. Dorothea 33; New Orleans, 1839 ***9420.2*** *p69*
Ahnert, Fredr. August 3; New Orleans, 1839 ***9420.2*** *p69*
Ahnert, Gotthild Fraugott 1 mo; New Orleans, 1839 ***9420.2*** *p69*
Ahnert, Johanne Christne. 31; New Orleans, 1839 ***9420.2*** *p69*
Aho, Annie; Washington, 1859-1920 ***2872.1*** *p1*
Aho, Arne; Washington, 1859-1920 ***2872.1*** *p1*
Aho, Artturi; Washington, 1859-1920 ***2872.1*** *p1*
Aho, Dan; Washington, 1859-1920 ***2872.1*** *p1*
Aho, Emma; Washington, 1859-1920 ***2872.1*** *p1*
Aho, Henry; Washington, 1859-1920 ***2872.1*** *p1*
Aho, Kalle; Washington, 1859-1920 ***2872.1*** *p1*
Aho, Lizzie; Washington, 1859-1920 ***2872.1*** *p1*
Aho, Matt F.; Washington, 1859-1920 ***2872.1*** *p1*
Aho, Waino; Washington, 1859-1920 ***2872.1*** *p1*
Ahoshew, James; Virginia, 1643 ***6219*** *p206*
Ahrends, George; Iroquois Co., IL, 1892 ***3455.1*** *p9*
Ahrendt, Christian J.; Wisconsin, n.d. ***9675.4*** *p193*
Ahrenholz, Dietrich; America, 1868 ***4610.10*** *p149*
*Child:*Louise
*Child:*Hermann
Ahrenholz, Hermann *SEE* Ahrenholz, Dietrich
Ahrenholz, Louise *SEE* Ahrenholz, Dietrich
Ahrenns, . . .; Canada, 1776-1783 ***9786*** *p16*
Ahrens, August; Kansas, 1900 ***5240.1*** *p3*
Ahrens, August 25; New Orleans, 1863 ***543.30*** *p323*
Ahrens, John; Illinois, 1888 ***5012.39*** *p52*
Ahrens, John G.; Cincinnati, 1869-1887 ***8582*** *p1*
Ahrens, Philip 40; New Orleans, 1862 ***543.30*** *p235*
Ahrestoph, Jques. 42; New Orleans, 1839 ***778.5*** *p4*
Ahsior, Mr. 19; New Orleans, 1839 ***778.5*** *p4*
Aichele, Anna Barbara Vellnagel *SEE* Aichele, Jacob
Aichele, Anna Maria; Pennsylvania, 1743-1800 ***2444*** *p132*
*Child:*Maria Margaretha
Aichele, Jacob; America, 1754 ***2444*** *p132*
*Wife:*Anna Barbara Vellnagel
*Child:*Johann Jacob
*Child:*Johannes
Aichele, Johann Jacob *SEE* Aichele, Jacob
Aichele, Johannes *SEE* Aichele, Jacob
Aichele, Maria Margaretha *SEE* Aichele, Anna Maria
Aicher, Thomas; Kansas, 1894 ***5240.1*** *p3*
Aiello, Tommaso; Iowa, 1866-1943 ***123.54*** *p55*
Aikan, James; St. John, N.B., 1847 ***5704.8*** *p21*
Aiken, Anne; New York, NY, 1811 ***2859.11*** *p8*
Aiken, Jane; New York, NY, 1811 ***2859.11*** *p8*
Aiken, Margaret A.; New York, NY, 1868 ***5704.8*** *p228*
Aiken, Samuel; Philadelphia, 1851 ***5704.8*** *p80*
Aiken, Sarah; New York, NY, 1866 ***5704.8*** *p213*
Aikenhoad, Patrick 20; Jamaica, 1731 ***3690.1*** *p2*
Aikens, Betty 30; Massachusetts, 1849 ***5881.1*** *p5*
Aikens, James 6; Massachusetts, 1849 ***5881.1*** *p5*
Aikens, John; New York, NY, 1811 ***2859.11*** *p8*
Aikin, Hugh R.; Philadelphia, 1868 ***5704.8*** *p230*
Aikin, James 41; New York, 1774 ***1219.7*** *p218*
Aikin, John; New York, NY, 1816 ***2859.11*** *p24*
Aikins, Bronte M.; America, 1893 ***1450.2*** *p2A*
Aikman, Francoise; Montreal, 1805 ***7603*** *p36*
Aima, Bresac 30; New Orleans, 1835 ***778.5*** *p4*
Aime, Anthony 27; New Orleans, 1836 ***778.5*** *p4*
Aime, Pierre D.; Halifax, N.S., 1752 ***7074.6*** *p216*
Ainley, Samuel 4; Massachusetts, 1848 ***5881.1*** *p6*
Ainley, Sarah 34; Massachusetts, 1848 ***5881.1*** *p6*
Ainley, Susan 12; Massachusetts, 1848 ***5881.1*** *p6*
Ainley, William 1; Massachusetts, 1848 ***5881.1*** *p6*
Ainscough, Abel; Iowa, 1866-1943 ***123.54*** *p55*
Ainsley, Alexander; South Carolina, 1804 ***1639.20*** *p1*
Ainsley, John; South Carolina, 1762 ***1639.20*** *p1*
Ainslicstead, James; Arkansas, 1918 ***95.2*** *p11*
Ainsly, Thomas 19; Maryland, 1720 ***3690.1*** *p2*
Ainson, Mary 1 *SEE* Ainson, Miles
Ainson, Mary 30 *SEE* Ainson, Miles
Ainson, Miles 6 *SEE* Ainson, Miles
Ainson, Miles 42; North America, 1774 ***1219.7*** *p200*
*Wife:*Mary 30
*Child:*Miles 6
*Child:*Thomas 3
*Child:*Mary 1
Ainson, Thomas 3 *SEE* Ainson, Miles
Aiot, . . .; Canada, 1776-1783 ***9786*** *p41*
Air, Charles James; South Carolina, 1803 ***1639.20*** *p1*
Aird, Andrew; New York, NY, 1839 ***8208.4*** *p91*
Aird, Robert; Quebec, 1770 ***7603*** *p36*
Aird, Thomas 25; St. John, N.B., 1866 ***5704.8*** *p167*
Aire, Robert; New York, NY, 1771 ***1219.7*** *p151*
Airls, Ann *SEE* Airls, William
Airls, Ann; Philadelphia, 1847 ***5704.8*** *p22*
Airls, Robert 6 mos *SEE* Airls, William
Airls, Robert 6 mos; Philadelphia, 1847 ***5704.8*** *p22*
Airls, William; Philadelphia, 1847 ***53.26*** *p1*
*Relative:*Ann
*Relative:*Robert 6 mos
Airls, William; Philadelphia, 1847 ***5704.8*** *p22*
Aisenbrey, Peter; America, 1752-1800 ***2444*** *p132*
With wife
With son
With stepchild
Aitchison, Robert; Charleston, SC, 1813 ***1639.20*** *p2*
Aitchison, William; Charleston, SC, 1806 ***1639.20*** *p2*
Aitkan, Dennis; Quebec, 1847 ***5704.8*** *p8*
Aitken, Ann Malcomsen; Newfoundland, 1851 ***8893*** *p264*
Aitken, James; Quebec, 1852 ***5704.8*** *p87*
Aitken, Peter; Iowa, 1866-1943 ***123.54*** *p5*
Aitken, William; Ontario, 1864 ***9775.5*** *p204*
Aitkins, James; Quebec, 1852 ***5704.8*** *p90*
Ajazzi, Dionigio 25; New York, NY, 1893 ***9026.4*** *p41*
Ajgl, Vladimir; Arkansas, 1918 ***95.2*** *p11*
Akerson, Peter; Colorado, 1894 ***9678.1*** *p150*
Akerstrom, John; Maine, 1871-1882 ***6410.22*** *p117*
Akesson, Nils; Minneapolis, 1882-1887 ***6410.35*** *p47*
Akin, Joseph; New York, NY, 1811 ***2859.11*** *p8*
Akin, Margaret; New York, NY, 1811 ***2859.11*** *p8*
Akin, Mary; New York, NY, 1811 ***2859.11*** *p8*
Akin, William; New York, NY, 1811 ***2859.11*** *p8*
Alain, . . .; Canada, 1776-1783 ***9786*** *p41*
Alander, Alexandra; Washington, 1859-1920 ***2872.1*** *p1*
Alander, Axel; Washington, 1859-1920 ***2872.1*** *p1*
Alander, Emil; Washington, 1859-1920 ***2872.1*** *p1*
Alander, Eva; Washington, 1859-1920 ***2872.1*** *p1*
Alander, Gustof Viktor; Washington, 1859-1920 ***2872.1*** *p1*
Alander, Haunes; Washington, 1859-1920 ***2872.1*** *p1*
Alander, Sylvia; Washington, 1859-1920 ***2872.1*** *p1*
Alando, August Constans; Iowa, 1866-1943 ***123.54*** *p5*
Alaux, Charles; Colorado, 1894 ***9678.1*** *p150*
Alba, Peter 18; Maryland, 1718 ***3690.1*** *p2*
Albaignac, M. 33; America, 1829 ***778.5*** *p4*
Alban, Frank 40; New Orleans, 1862 ***543.30*** *p236*
Albanowski, Waclow; Arkansas, 1918 ***95.2*** *p11*
Albate, Frank Joseph; Arkansas, 1918 ***95.2*** *p11*
Alber, Mathis; Philadelphia, 1764 ***9973.7*** *p39*
Alberda, Gert; Iroquois Co., IL, 1892 ***3455.1*** *p9*
Alberg, . . .; Canada, 1776-1783 ***9786*** *p41*
Albers, Anne Marie; America, 1852 ***4610.10*** *p151*
Albers, Antje; Baltimore, 1900 ***3455.1*** *p44*
Albers, Claus Henry 35; California, 1868 ***3840.1*** *p14*
Albers, Joseph Maria; Wisconsin, n.d. ***9675.4*** *p193*
Albers, Wilhelm; Cincinnati, 1788-1848 ***8582.3*** *p91*
Albert, . . .; Canada, 1776-1783 ***9786*** *p16*
Albert, Mr. 48; New Orleans, 1839 ***778.5*** *p4*
Albert, Mrs. Peter; Pennsylvania, 1785 ***4525*** *p198*
With 3 children
Albert, Alphonse; Illinois, 1880 ***2896.5*** *p1*
Albert, Andreas *SEE* Albert, Lorentz
Albert, Anna Barbara Wolff *SEE* Albert, Lorentz
Albert, Anne Marie Wilhelmine E.; America, 1856 ***4610.10*** *p157*
Albert, Christof; Pennsylvania, 1751 ***4525*** *p197*
With wife & children
Albert, Christr 69; Pennsylvania, 1787 ***4525*** *p197*
Albert, Friedrich Wilhelm Gottlieb; America, 1854 ***4610.10*** *p151*
Albert, J. 24; New Orleans, 1837 ***778.5*** *p4*
Albert, Jn.-Baptiste 19; America, 1838 ***778.5*** *p4*

Albert, Lorentz; Philadelphia, 1754 4525 p270
*Wife:*Anna Barbara Wolff
*Daughter:*Maria Apolonia
*Son:*Andreas
Albert, Lorenz; Pennsylvania, 1754 4525 p197
With wife children & sister-in-law
Albert, Maria Apolonia *SEE* Albert, Lorentz
Albert, Meyer; Arkansas, 1918 95.2 p11
Albert, Nicolas; Louisiana, 1789-1819 778.5 p555
Albert, Nicolaus; Pennsylvania, 1754 4525 p198
Albert, Peter; Pennsylvania, 1778 4525 p198
Albert, S. F.; Washington, 1859-1920 2872.1 p1
Albert, Susanna; Died enroute, 1754 4525 p272
Albert, Wilhelm; Pennsylvania, 1754 4525 p197
Albert, William 39; New Orleans, 1862 543.30 p234
Alberth, Johannes; Pennsylvania, 1754 4525 p197
Alberth, Lorentz; Pennsylvania, 1754 4525 p197
Alberti, . . .; Canada, 1776-1783 9786 p16
Alberti, Bartholomew; Washington, 1859-1920 2872.1 p1
Alberts, Dirk Flohr; Iroquois Co., IL, 1892 3455.1 p9
Alberts, Heinrich; New Netherland, 1630-1646 8582.2 p51
Alberts, John; Illinois, 1871 7857 p2
Albertsen, Mads Jakob; Arkansas, 1918 95.2 p12
Albertsmeier, Henry; America, 1854 1450.2 p99A
Albin, C. F.; Minneapolis, 1876-1877 6410.35 p47
Albin, John; Minneapolis, 1869-1878 6410.35 p47
Albony, Adele 28; America, 1835 778.5 p4
Albrandt, J. H.; Ohio, 1869-1887 8582 p1
Albrecht, . . .; Canada, 1776-1783 9786 p16
Albrecht, Andreas; Ohio, 1832 8582.1 p46
Albrecht, Christian; Illinois, 1901 5012.40 p79
Albrecht, George A.; Baltimore, 1848 1450.2 p2A
Albrecht, Jacob; Philadelphia, 1749-1773 9973.7 p40
Albrecht, John Andrew; New York, 1750 3652 p74
Albrecht, Joseph; Wisconsin, n.d. 9675.4 p193
Albrecht, W.L.A.; Wisconsin, n.d. 9675.4 p193
Albrette, Laure 20; New Orleans, 1836 778.5 p4
Albright, Chas 63; Arizona, 1911 9228.40 p15
Albright, George Heinrich; Iowa, 1866-1943 123.54 p55
Albright, Maria Cath.; Philadelphia, 1760 9973.7 p34
Albrinck, Georg Johann; America, 1845 8582.3 p1
Albrink, J. C.; America, 1836 8582.2 p1
Albsmeyer, Louise 25; America, 1881 4610.10 p159
Albus, . . .; Canada, 1776-1783 9786 p16
Albus, Georg; Halifax, N.S., 1778 9786 p270
Albus, Georg; New York, 1776 9786 p270
Alcich, Steve; Wisconsin, n.d. 9675.4 p193
Alcock, Richd; America, 1697-1707 2212 p9
Alcorn, Andrew 20; Philadelphia, 1833-1834 53.26 p1
*Relative:*Martha 20
Alcorn, Ann; New York, NY, 1867 5704.8 p223
Alcorn, Ann; Philadelphia, 1850 53.26 p1
*Relative:*Robert
Alcorn, Ann; Philadelphia, 1850 5704.8 p68
Alcorn, Bessy; America, 1868 5704.8 p227
Alcorn, Fanny 25; Philadelphia, 1864 5704.8 p160
Alcorn, Francis; Philadelphia, 1811 53.26 p1
With wife
Alcorn, Francis; Philadelphia, 1811 2859.11 p8
With wife
Alcorn, George 21; Philadelphia, 1857 5704.8 p133
Alcorn, Henry; New York, 1810 1450.2 p3A
Alcorn, James; Philadelphia, 1811 53.26 p1
Alcorn, James; Philadelphia, 1811 2859.11 p8
Alcorn, James; Philadelphia, 1866 5704.8 p215
Alcorn, James 11; St. John, N.B., 1859 5704.8 p140
Alcorn, Jane; Philadelphia, 1868 5704.8 p225
Alcorn, Jane; Quebec, 1848 5704.8 p42
Alcorn, Jane 30; St. John, N.B., 1859 5704.8 p140
Alcorn, John; Philadelphia, 1811 53.26 p1
With family
Alcorn, John; Philadelphia, 1811 2859.11 p8
With family
Alcorn, John; Quebec, 1848 5704.8 p42
Alcorn, Joseph; Philadelphia, 1811 53.26 p1
Alcorn, Joseph; Philadelphia, 1811 2859.11 p8
Alcorn, Margaret; Philadelphia, 1866 5704.8 p215
Alcorn, Martha; America, 1869 5704.8 p232
Alcorn, Martha; Philadelphia, 1866 5704.8 p215
Alcorn, Martha; Philadelphia, 1868 5704.8 p226
Alcorn, Martha 20 *SEE* Alcorn, Andrew
Alcorn, Mary; New York, NY, 1864 5704.8 p179
Alcorn, Robert *SEE* Alcorn, Ann
Alcorn, Robert; Philadelphia, 1850 5704.8 p68
Alcorn, William; Quebec, 1848 5704.8 p42
Alcorn, William 19; Philadelphia, 1860 5704.8 p145
Alcott, Alice; Virginia, 1636 6219 p79
Alcutt, Eliza.; Virginia, 1637 6219 p85
Aldag, Charles; America, 1848 1450.2 p3A
Aldag, Charles August; America, 1854 1450.2 p3A
Aldag, Louis; America, 1852 1450.2 p3A
Aldebert, F. 34; America, 1839 778.5 p4
Aldebert, Francois 30; America, 1836 778.5 p4
Alderbert, Joseph 30; Louisiana, 1827 778.5 p4
Alderbert, Marguerite 21; Louisiana, 1827 778.5 p5
Alderdice, George; Montreal, 1822 7603 p38
Aldersey, Grace; Virginia, 1646 6219 p240
Alderson, John; Colorado, 1894 9678.1 p150
Alderton, John 22; Maryland, 1774 1219.7 p221
Alderton, William 16; Maryland, 1724 3690.1 p2
Aldfield, Elizabeth 25; Nova Scotia, 1775 1219.7 p263
Aldham, Daniel 27; Maryland, 1775 1219.7 p257
Aldin, Thomas 21; Philadelphia, 1774 1219.7 p175
Aldinger, Gottlieb; Colorado, 1894 9678.1 p150
Aldorfer, Jacques Jean 28; New Orleans, 1862 543.30 p236
Aldorson, James 22; America, 1702 2212 p38
Aldred, Hannah 41; Massachusetts, 1850 5881.1 p5
Aldridg, Michaell 40; America, 1701 2212 p34
Aldridge, Christopher 24; Maryland, 1775 1219.7 p252
Aldridge, Randall 20; Pennsylvania, 1725 3690.1 p2
Aldridge, Thomas 21; Maryland, 1774 1219.7 p208
Aldridge, Thomas 24; Maryland, 1774 1219.7 p187
Aldrige, Fr.; Virginia, 1635 6219 p10
Aldrige, Margerie; Virginia, 1642 6219 p188
Aldwell, Samuel; New York, NY, 1816 2859.11 p24
Aleaume, Charles 36; New Orleans, 1838 778.5 p5
Alec, Speras; Arkansas, 1918 95.2 p12
Aleccia, Melchiore; Iowa, 1866-1943 123.54 p5
Alekares, John; Arkansas, 1918 95.2 p12
Alermio, Bridget 5; Massachusetts, 1849 5881.1 p5
Alermio, Ellen 11; Massachusetts, 1849 5881.1 p5
Alermio, James 7; Massachusetts, 1849 5881.1 p5
Alermio, Pat 9; Massachusetts, 1849 5881.1 p5
Alers, Conrad Anton; Quebec, 1776 9786 p259
Aleson, Andrew; Iowa, 1866-1943 123.54 p5
Alex, James; Arkansas, 1918 95.2 p12
Alex, John 28; Kansas, 1872 5240.1 p53
Alex, Mike; Arkansas, 1918 95.2 p12
Alexander, Ambrose 22; Barbados or Jamaica, 1733 3690.1 p2
Alexander, Andrew; Philadelphia, 1852 5704.8 p87
Alexander, Anne; New York, NY, 1816 2859.11 p24
Alexander, Anne; Philadelphia, 1853 5704.8 p112
Alexander, Anne Jane; New York, NY, 1816 2859.11 p24
Alexander, Annebell; Quebec, 1852 5704.8 p87
Alexander, Annebell; Quebec, 1852 5704.8 p90
Alexander, David; Maryland, 1757 1219.7 p53
Alexander, David; Philadelphia, 1852 5704.8 p91
Alexander, David; Quebec, 1848 5704.8 p42
Alexander, E.; Philadelphia, 1816 2859.11 p24
Alexander, Edward; San Francisco, 1865 2764.35 p2
Alexander, Eliza 3; St. John, N.B., 1851 5704.8 p78
Alexander, George; America, 1847 8582.1 p1
Alexander, George; New York, NY, 1816 2859.11 p24
Alexander, George 9; Quebec, 1847 5704.8 p13
Alexander, H. 18; Port uncertain, 1838 778.5 p5
Alexander, Harriet; New York, NY, 1816 2859.11 p24
Alexander, Heinrich; Cincinnati, 1869-1887 8582 p1
Alexander, Hugh Small; New York, NY, 1816 2859.11 p24
Alexander, Isabella; New York, NY, 1815 2859.11 p24
Alexander, Isabella; Philadelphia, 1847 53.26 p1
Alexander, Isabella; Philadelphia, 1847 5704.8 p31
Alexander, Jacob; Ohio, 1800-1885 8582.2 p58
Alexander, James; New York, NY, 1816 2859.11 p24
Alexander, James 11 *SEE* Alexander, William
Alexander, James 11; Quebec, 1847 5704.8 p13
Alexander, Jane; New York, NY, 1816 2859.11 p24
Alexander, Jane; Philadelphia, 1847 53.26 p1
Alexander, Jane; Philadelphia, 1847 5704.8 p14
Alexander, Jane 13; Quebec, 1848 5704.8 p42
Alexander, Jane 30 *SEE* Alexander, William
Alexander, Janet; Georgia, 1775 1219.7 p274
Alexander, John; Carolina, 1699 1639.20 p2
Alexander, John; Quebec, 1847 5704.8 p12
Alexander, John; Quebec, 1848 5704.8 p41
Alexander, John; Quebec, 1848 5704.8 p42
Alexander, John 6; Quebec, 1852 5704.8 p97
Alexander, John 20; Philadelphia, 1853 5704.8 p112
Alexander, John 23; Philadelphia, 1774 1219.7 p233
Alexander, Jonas 24; Kansas, 1888 5240.1 p72
Alexander, Joseph; Philadelphia, 1852 5704.8 p91
Alexander, Marg.; New York, NY, 1811 2859.11 p8
Alexander, Margaret; New York, NY, 1816 2859.11 p24
Alexander, Mark; New York, NY, 1837 8208.4 p54
Alexander, Martha 10 *SEE* Alexander, William
Alexander, Mary; Philadelphia, 1852 5704.8 p95
Alexander, Mary 18; Jamaica, 1735 3690.1 p2
Alexander, Mary Small; New York, NY, 1816 2859.11 p24
Alexander, Patrick; Virginia, 1638 6219 p160
Alexander, Robert; New York, NY, 1816 2859.11 p24
Alexander, Robert; Quebec, 1851 5704.8 p75
Alexander, Robert; Virginia, 1642 6219 p194
Alexander, Sarah; Quebec, 1848 5704.8 p42
Alexander, Sarah Jane; New York, NY, 1816 2859.11 p24
Alexander, Thomas; New York, NY, 1816 2859.11 p24
Alexander, William; New York, NY, 1840 8208.4 p106
Alexander, William; North Carolina, 1715-1766 1639.20 p2
Alexander, William; Nova Scotia, 1629 9775.5 p205
Alexander, William; Pennsylvania, 1821 9788.3 p4
Alexander, William; Quebec, 1848 5704.8 p42
Alexander, William; Savannah, GA, 1774 1219.7 p227
With wife
With 3 children
Alexander, William 32; Philadelphia, 1803 53.26 p1
*Relative:*Jane 30
*Relative:*James 11
*Relative:*Martha 10
Alexander, William 32; Savannah, GA, 1774 1219.7 p226
Alexanderson, Carl; Iowa, 1866-1943 123.54 p5
Alexanderson, Carl John Alfred; Iowa, 1866-1943 123.54 p5
Alexandratos, Peter; Wisconsin, n.d. 9675.4 p193
Alexandre, Mme. 22; New Orleans, 1826 778.5 p5
Alexandre, Jean 25; New Orleans, 1826 778.5 p5
Alexanian, Mugurdich G.; New York, 1891 1450.2 p3A
Alexopulos, Stanros 22; Kansas, 1905 5240.1 p83
Alf, Wilhelm; America, 1843 8582.2 p1
Alfano, Frank; Arkansas, 1918 95.2 p12
Alford, Mary 21; Maryland, 1774 1219.7 p235
Alford, William 26; Maryland, 1774 1219.7 p235
Alfred, Robert 22; Virginia, 1773 1219.7 p171
Alfreda, Laura 23; Massachusetts, 1860 6410.32 p112
Algeo, Catherine; St. John, N.B., 1847 5704.8 p26
Alges, John; New York, NY, 1811 2859.11 p8
Algir, Christian; Charleston, SC, 1775-1781 8582.2 p52
Algive, James 22; Philadelphia, 1854 5704.8 p118
Algive, Ramsey 20; Philadelphia, 1854 5704.8 p118
Algo, Samuel 18; Massachusetts, 1850 5881.1 p6
Alhers, Joseph Maria; Wisconsin, n.d. 9675.4 p193
Alice, Ellen; Virginia, 1635 6219 p70
Alice, Ellen; Virginia, 1637 6219 p180
Alicer, Jno 21; America, 1699 2212 p28
Alich, John Adam; Cincinnati, 1869-1887 8582 p1
Alicot, Ceasar 27; America, 1838 778.5 p5
Alimong, Nicholas; Pennsylvania, 1765 4779.3 p13
Alin, . . .; Canada, 1776-1783 9786 p41
Aliquot, F. 23; America, 1826 778.5 p5
Alison, Anne-Charlotte *SEE* Alison, George-Frederic
Alison, Catherine-Elisabeth *SEE* Alison, George-Frederic
Alison, Gabriel *SEE* Alison, George-Frederic
Alison, George-Frederic 40; Halifax, N.S., 1752 7074.6 p208
*Wife:*Catherine-Elisabeth
*Child:*Gabriel
*Child:*Marie-Elisabeth
*Child:*Anne-Charlotte
Alison, Marie-Elisabeth *SEE* Alison, George-Frederic
Alison, Patrick; Carolina, 1684 1639.20 p2
Aliszewski, Anton; Illinois, 1896 2896.5 p1
Alivaica, Jesus 40; Arizona, 1904 9228.40 p5
Alix, Joseph 23; New Orleans, 1831 778.5 p5
Aljovin, Gertrude; Washington, 1859-1920 2872.1 p1
Aljovin, James; Washington, 1859-1920 2872.1 p1
All, . . .; Canada, 1776-1783 9786 p41
All, Jacob; Ohio, 1800 8582.2 p55
Allam, George 17; Jamaica, 1723 3690.1 p2
Allam, Mary 20; America, 1701 2212 p35
Allan, Andrew; South Carolina, 1680-1830 1639.20 p2
Allan, Catherine 28; St. John, N.B., 1854 5704.8 p115
Allan, Charles 23; St. John, N.B., 1854 5704.8 p115
Allan, Christopher; Georgia, 1775 1219.7 p274
Allan, Hugh; Montreal, 1871 9775.5 p203
Allan, James; Quebec, 1848 5704.8 p41
Allan, James; Wilmington, NC, 1765-1811 1639.20 p2
Allan, John; Charleston, SC, 1797 1639.20 p2
Allan, John; Quebec, 1848 5704.8 p41
Allan, Jonathan 19; Philadelphia, 1774 1219.7 p234
Allan, Sarah; Quebec, 1848 5704.8 p41
Allan, Unfty; Philadelphia, 1847 53.26 p1
Allan, Unity; Philadelphia, 1847 5704.8 p22
Allan, William; Charleston, SC, 1798 1639.20 p2
Allan, Wilson; Quebec, 1848 5704.8 p41
Allard, Felix 50; America, 1838 778.5 p5
Allard, J.B. 30; America, 1832 778.5 p5
Allard, Josephe 22; America, 1827 778.5 p5
Allardyce, Alexander; Iowa, 1866-1943 123.54 p55
Allardyce, Jessie Gillespie; Iowa, 1866-1943 123.54 p55
Allardyce, William; Iowa, 1866-1943 123.54 p55
Allaway, Stephen 17; Maryland, 1723 3690.1 p2
Allbone, Isaac 21; Jamaica, 1736 3690.1 p3
Allbury, John 19; Antigua (Antego), 1738 3690.1 p3

Alle, . . .; Canada, 1776-1783 ***9786*** *p16*
Alleman, Nicholas; Pennsylvania, 1765 ***4779.3*** *p13*
Alleman, William 15; Virginia, 1774 ***1219.7*** *p241*
Allen, Mr.; New York, NY, 1815 ***2859.11*** *p24*
Allen, Agnes; New York, NY, 1816 ***2859.11*** *p24*
Allen, Alexander; North Carolina, 1803 ***1639.20*** *p2*
Allen, Andrew; Philadelphia, 1850 ***53.26*** *p1*
Allen, Andrew; Philadelphia, 1850 ***5704.8*** *p65*
Allen, Andrew 10; Philadelphia, 1853 ***5704.8*** *p102*
Allen, Ann 16; Canada, 1838 ***4535.12*** *p113*
Allen, Archibald Smyth; North Carolina, 1815 ***1639.20*** *p2*
Allen, Charles *SEE* Allen, Hugh
Allen, Charles *SEE* Allen, Hugh
Allen, Charles; Illinois, 1868 ***7857*** *p2*
Allen, Charles; Philadelphia, 1852 ***5704.8*** *p85*
Allen, Charles; Virginia, 1638 ***6219*** *p150*
Allen, Edward; Virginia, 1644 ***6219*** *p229*
Allen, Edward 19; Philadelphia, 1853 ***5704.8*** *p108*
Allen, Edwd.; Virginia, 1635 ***6219*** *p69*
Allen, Eliz.; New York, NY, 1816 ***2859.11*** *p24*
Allen, Ellen; America, 1863-1871 ***5704.8*** *p240*
Allen, Etham; Boston, 1776 ***1219.7*** *p277*
Allen, Francis; Virginia, 1643 ***6219*** *p203*
Allen, George; Montreal, 1805 ***7603*** *p40*
Allen, George; New York, NY, 1816 ***2859.11*** *p24*
Allen, George; New York, NY, 1834 ***8208.4*** *p4*
Allen, George 26; Philadelphia, 1833-1834 ***53.26*** *p1*
Allen, Grego.; Virginia, 1648 ***6219*** *p241*
Allen, H.; Washington, 1859-1920 ***2872.1*** *p1*
Allen, Hamilton 8; Philadelphia, 1853 ***5704.8*** *p102*
Allen, Hannah; Philadelphia, 1816 ***2859.11*** *p24*
Allen, Helena; Montreal, 1823 ***7603*** *p97*
Allen, Henry; America, 1740 ***4971*** *p73*
Allen, Henry; Philadelphia, 1851 ***5704.8*** *p81*
Allen, Henry 40; Harris Co., TX, 1898 ***6254*** *p5*
Allen, Henry S.; Philadelphia, 1816 ***2859.11*** *p24*
Allen, Hugh; Virginia, 1638 ***6219*** *p2*
Allen, Hugh; Virginia, 1638 ***6219*** *p2*
*Son:*Charles
Allen, Hugh; Virginia, 1638 ***6219*** *p150*
*Son:*Charles
Allen, Hugh; Virginia, 1638 ***6219*** *p150*
Allen, Isabella; New York, NY, 1865 ***5704.8*** *p194*
Allen, James; New York, NY, 1816 ***2859.11*** *p24*
Allen, James; New York, NY, 1833 ***8208.4*** *p60*
Allen, James; Philadelphia, 1853 ***5704.8*** *p102*
Allen, James; Quebec, 1849 ***5704.8*** *p57*
Allen, James; Virginia, 1643 ***6219*** *p203*
Allen, James; Virginia, 1646 ***6219*** *p238*
Allen, James 19; Pennsylvania, 1728 ***3690.1*** *p3*
Allen, James 21; Jamaica, 1736 ***3690.1*** *p3*
Allen, James 33; Harris Co., TX, 1898 ***6254*** *p5*
Allen, Jane; New York, NY, 1816 ***2859.11*** *p24*
Allen, John; Arizona, 1890 ***2764.35*** *p2*
Allen, John; Arkansas, 1918 ***95.2*** *p12*
Allen, John; Austin, TX, 1886 ***9777*** *p5*
Allen, John; New York, NY, 1839 ***8208.4*** *p102*
Allen, John; Virginia, 1636 ***6219*** *p28*
Allen, John; Virginia, 1639 ***6219*** *p159*
Allen, John; Virginia, 1643 ***6219*** *p206*
Allen, John 20; Jamaica, 1730 ***3690.1*** *p3*
Allen, John 21; Philadelphia, 1774 ***1219.7*** *p233*
Allen, John 25; Antigua (Antego), 1722 ***3690.1*** *p3*
Allen, John 32; New Orleans, 1862 ***543.30*** *p234*
Allen, John F.; Virginia, 1852 ***4626.16*** *p14*
Allen, Joseph; New York, NY, 1816 ***2859.11*** *p24*
Allen, Joseph; New York, NY, 1870 ***5704.8*** *p237*
Allen, Levi 69; Kansas, 1877 ***5240.1*** *p58*
Allen, Margaret; Philadelphia, 1853 ***5704.8*** *p103*
Allen, Mary; New York, NY, 1816 ***2859.11*** *p24*
Allen, Mary; Virginia, 1636 ***6219*** *p75*
Allen, Mary; Virginia, 1648 ***6219*** *p253*
Allen, Mary 12; Massachusetts, 1849 ***5881.1*** *p5*
Allen, Mary A.; New York, NY, 1867 ***5704.8*** *p218*
Allen, Mary Ann 19; Quebec, 1864 ***5704.8*** *p160*
Allen, Me. 28; New Orleans, 1839 ***778.5*** *p5*
Allen, Michael 17; Massachusetts, 1850 ***5881.1*** *p5*
Allen, Oliver; Virginia, 1635 ***6219*** *p74*
Allen, Pat. 24; Massachusetts, 1849 ***5881.1*** *p5*
Allen, Patrick 25; Maryland, 1773 ***1219.7*** *p172*
Allen, Peter; Philadelphia, 1816 ***2859.11*** *p24*
Allen, Peter H.; Philadelphia, 1816 ***2859.11*** *p24*
Allen, Rebecca; America, 1863-1871 ***5704.8*** *p240*
Allen, Robert; Philadelphia, 1868 ***5704.8*** *p226*
Allen, Robert; Virginia, 1638 ***6219*** *p122*
Allen, Robert 16; Virginia, 1774 ***1219.7*** *p240*
Allen, Samuel; New York, NY, 1816 ***2859.11*** *p24*
Allen, Samuel; New York, NY, 1834 ***8208.4*** *p59*
Allen, Samuel; Philadelphia, 1853 ***5704.8*** *p102*
Allen, Samuel 17; Jamaica, 1730 ***3690.1*** *p3*
Allen, Samuel 26; New Orleans, 1862 ***543.30*** *p236*
Allen, Samuel J.; Illinois, 1888 ***2896.5*** *p1*
Allen, Sanders; Virginia, 1643 ***6219*** *p204*
Allen, Sarah; Philadelphia, 1853 ***5704.8*** *p102*
Allen, Susan 22; Philadelphia, 1853 ***5704.8*** *p108*
Allen, Thomas; Illinois, 1853 ***7857*** *p2*
Allen, Thomas; New York, NY, 1816 ***2859.11*** *p24*
Allen, Thomas 22; Virginia, 1774 ***1219.7*** *p242*
Allen, Thomas 26; New Orleans, 1862 ***543.30*** *p237*
Allen, Thomas J.; Illinois, 1888 ***5012.39*** *p122*
Allen, William; New York, NY, 1833 ***8208.4*** *p42*
Allen, William; Virginia, 1638 ***6219*** *p119*
Allen, William 14; Maryland, 1719 ***3690.1*** *p3*
Allen, William 21; St. Christopher, 1722 ***3690.1*** *p3*
Allen, William 22; New Orleans, 1862 ***543.30*** *p235*
Allen, William 22; Philadelphia, 1775 ***1219.7*** *p274*
Allen, William John 16; Quebec, 1864 ***5704.8*** *p160*
Allenby, Wm.; Virginia, 1647 ***6219*** *p247*
Allendar, William 39; Maryland, 1775 ***1219.7*** *p248*
Allender, Gus; Washington, 1859-1920 ***2872.1*** *p1*
Allender, Mary Ann 27; St. John, N.B., 1866 ***5704.8*** *p166*
Allene, Jean Paul 21; New Orleans, 1836 ***778.5*** *p5*
Allengen, B. 12; New Orleans, 1830 ***778.5*** *p6*
Allengen, J. 10; New Orleans, 1830 ***778.5*** *p6*
Allengen, S. 7; New Orleans, 1830 ***778.5*** *p6*
Allenton, Elizabeth 21; Virginia, 1774 ***1219.7*** *p244*
Allera, John; Colorado, 1903 ***9678.1*** *p150*
Allerdyer, George 22; Jamaica, 1774 ***1219.7*** *p232*
Allerentia, Peter; Virginia, 1640 ***6219*** *p183*
Alleret, Madame 18; Port uncertain, 1838 ***778.5*** *p6*
Alleret, Peter 29; Port uncertain, 1838 ***778.5*** *p6*
Allerson, Ann; Virginia, 1633 ***6219*** *p31*
Allerson, William; Virginia, 1652 ***6251*** *p20*
Alleson, Wm.; Virginia, 1646 ***6219*** *p246*
Alley, Stephen 24; Philadelphia, 1803 ***53.26*** *p1*
Allford, Susannah 19; Virginia, 1720 ***3690.1*** *p3*
Allgaier, Michael; Kentucky, 1839-1840 ***8582.3*** *p98*
Allgen, J. 40; New Orleans, 1830 ***778.5*** *p6*
Allgen, S. 30; New Orleans, 1830 ***778.5*** *p6*
Alliat, Mr. 23; New Orleans, 1837 ***778.5*** *p6*
Allier, Gilbert 41; America, 1837 ***778.5*** *p6*
Allier, Gilbert 42; America, 1838 ***778.5*** *p6*
Allier, Gilbert, Mme. 35; America, 1838 ***778.5*** *p6*
Allietto, Battisto; Arkansas, 1918 ***95.2*** *p12*
Alligot, Thomas 36; Massachusetts, 1849 ***5881.1*** *p6*
Allin, August; Minneapolis, 1873-1881 ***6410.35*** *p47*
Allin, Robert; America, 1738 ***4971*** *p66*
Allin, Wm.; Virginia, 1635 ***6219*** *p26*
Allin, Wm.; Virginia, 1638 ***6219*** *p148*
Allinan, Oth.; America, 1741 ***4971*** *p61*
Alling, Anton; Iowa, 1866-1943 ***123.54*** *p5*
Allingham, Ann; Quebec, 1852 ***5704.8*** *p90*
Allingham, Anne; Quebec, 1852 ***5704.8*** *p87*
Allingham, Elisa; St. John, N.B., 1853 ***5704.8*** *p99*
Allingham, Mary Jane 13; St. John, N.B., 1858 ***5704.8*** *p137*
Allinghan, James 14; Philadelphia, 1853 ***5704.8*** *p112*
Allington, John 21; Maryland, 1775 ***1219.7*** *p259*
Allinsworth, John; Virginia, 1646 ***6219*** *p236*
Allis, James 14 *SEE* Allis, Tera
Allis, Tera 30; Philadelphia, 1804 ***53.26*** *p1*
*Relative:*James 14
Alliscon, Georges Frederick 40; Halifax, N.S., 1752 ***7074.6*** *p207*
With family of 4
Allison, Ann Jane; Philadelphia, 1851 ***5704.8*** *p77*
Allison, Charles; Quebec, 1815 ***7603*** *p25*
Allison, Jacques; Quebec, 1817 ***7603*** *p25*
Allison, Jane 43; Philadelphia, 1854 ***5704.8*** *p122*
Allison, John; Philadelphia, 1852 ***5704.8*** *p92*
Allison, Sarah; Virginia, 1642 ***6219*** *p198*
Allison, Sarah 24; Virginia, 1699 ***2212*** *p26*
Allison, Thomas; Arizona, 1887 ***2764.35*** *p1*
Allison, William; Virginia, 1636 ***6219*** *p7*
Allison, William 18; Virginia, 1773 ***1219.7*** *p169*
Alliton, Lydia 29 *SEE* Alliton, Thomas
Alliton, Thomas 35; Maryland, 1775 ***1219.7*** *p250*
*Wife:*Lydia 29
Allman, Charles; Boston, 1859 ***9678.1*** *p150*
Allom, S. 23; Philadelphia, 1775 ***1219.7*** *p255*
Allouay, John 38; New Orleans, 1830 ***778.5*** *p6*
Allpp, Bernhart; Pennsylvania, 1752 ***2444*** *p198*
Alls, Matilda; St. John, N.B., 1847 ***5704.8*** *p2*
Allsop, William; West Indies, 1765 ***1219.7*** *p112*
Allumbly, Wm.; Virginia, 1637 ***6219*** *p115*
Alm, Henry; Indiana, 1848 ***9117*** *p19*
Alman, Peter; Wisconsin, n.d. ***9675.4*** *p193*
Almand, Jacob; Pennsylvania, 1765 ***4779.3*** *p13*
Almand, Nicholas; Pennsylvania, 1765 ***4779.3*** *p13*
Almers, Henry; Philadelphia, 1742 ***3652*** *p55*
*Wife:*Rosina
Almers, Rosina *SEE* Almers, Henry
Almis, . . .; Canada, 1776-1783 ***9786*** *p16*
Almond, Samuel; Virginia, 1639 ***6219*** *p2*
Almquist, Charles; Iowa, 1866-1943 ***123.54*** *p5*
Alms, August; Cincinnati, 1869-1887 ***8582*** *p1*
Alms, Henry; Indiana, 1848 ***9117*** *p15*
Almstrom, A.; Minneapolis, 1875-1888 ***6410.35*** *p47*
Alounoron, Camila 12; New Orleans, 1838 ***778.5*** *p6*
Alpert, Adolph; Colorado, 1906 ***9678.1*** *p150*
Alphonse, J. 21; New Orleans, 1822 ***778.5*** *p6*
Alport, Ann; Virginia, 1636 ***6219*** *p21*
Alporte, Jon; Virginia, 1634 ***6219*** *p32*
Alreau, C. 25; Port uncertain, 1837 ***778.5*** *p6*
Alrus, Henry; Indiana, 1848 ***9117*** *p15*
Alsanson, John Michael 37; California, 1872 ***2769.1*** *p3*
Alsdorff, . . .; Canada, 1776-1783 ***9786*** *p16*
Alsebrook, John 15; Antigua (Antego), 1775 ***1219.7*** *p249*
Alsebrook, Samuel 17; Antigua (Antego), 1775 ***1219.7*** *p249*
Alsmeyer, Karl Friedrich Wilhelm; America, 1857 ***4610.10*** *p109*
Alson, Anne 23; Massachusetts, 1860 ***6410.32*** *p111*
Alson, Cristia 23; Massachusetts, 1860 ***6410.32*** *p111*
Alsop, John 15; Philadelphia, 1774 ***1219.7*** *p233*
Alsop, Nathaniel; New York, NY, 1811 ***2859.11*** *p8*
With wife
Alsopp, Henry; Virginia, 1648 ***6219*** *p250*
Alston, George; North Carolina, 1811 ***1639.20*** *p3*
Alt, Johann Gerhard; Ohio, 1869-1887 ***8582*** *p1*
Alt, John Gerhard; New York, NY, 1841-1845 ***8582.1*** *p1*
Alt, Louis; Wisconsin, n.d. ***9675.4*** *p193*
Alt, Nicklaus; Iroquois Co., IL, 1892 ***3455.1*** *p9*
Altane, Severnio; Arkansas, 1918 ***95.2*** *p12*
Altemann, Cath. Roth 73; America, 1895 ***1763*** *p40D*
Altenbockum, Ernst Eberhard von; Canada, 1780 ***9786*** *p268*
Altenbockum, Ernst Eberhard von; New York, 1776 ***9786*** *p268*
Altendorf, A. 18; America, 1853 ***9162.7*** *p14*
Altendorf, Hilarius; Wisconsin, n.d. ***9675.4*** *p193*
Altendorf, Joseph; Wisconsin, n.d. ***9675.4*** *p193*
Alter, . . .; Canada, 1776-1783 ***9786*** *p16*
Alter, Abraham; Ohio, 1798-1818 ***8582.2*** *p54*
Altgeld, John Peter; Illinois, 1892 ***3702.7*** *p20*
Althage, A. M. Christine; America, 1838 ***4610.10*** *p104*
Althaus, Mr.; Died enroute, 1738 ***9898*** *p31*
Althaus, Mrs.; Pennsylvania, 1738 ***9898*** *p31*
With 2 sons
Althaus, Julius 75; America, 1912 ***1763*** *p40C*
Althof, Anna Marie Mouise 53; America, 1871 ***4610.10*** *p113*
Althoff, Anton Friedrich; America, 1854 ***4610.10*** *p108*
Althouse, Jacob 34; Kansas, 1879 ***5240.1*** *p3*
Althouse, Jacob 34; Kansas, 1879 ***5240.1*** *p60*
Althschwager, William; Wisconsin, n.d. ***9675.4*** *p193*
Altman, Mrs.; Died enroute, 1875 ***4719.30*** *p258*
Altman, Andrew; Pennsylvania, 1749 ***4779.3*** *p13*
Altman, Anthony; Pennsylvania, 1749 ***4779.3*** *p13*
Altman, Anthony; Pennsylvania, 1765 ***4779.3*** *p13*
Altman, B. Peter; Pennsylvania, 1749 ***4779.3*** *p13*
Altman, Casper; Pennsylvania, 1765 ***4779.3*** *p13*
Altman, Gasper; Pennsylvania, 1749 ***4779.3*** *p13*
Altman, George Peter; Pennsylvania, 1749 ***4779.3*** *p13*
Altman, Hance Peter; Pennsylvania, 1749 ***4779.3*** *p13*
Altman, John; Wisconsin, n.d. ***9675.4*** *p193*
Altman, John Peter; Pennsylvania, 1765 ***4779.3*** *p13*
Altman, Joseph 21; Kansas, 1903 ***5240.1*** *p82*
Altman, Joseph M.; Ohio, 1851 ***1450.2*** *p3A*
Altman, Philip; Pennsylvania, 1749 ***4779.3*** *p13*
Altman, William; Pennsylvania, 1749 ***4779.3*** *p13*
Altman, William, Jr.; Pennsylvania, 1749 ***4779.3*** *p13*
Altmann, Claus H.; Wisconsin, n.d. ***9675.4*** *p193*
Altmeyer, Jakob 32; America, 1853 ***9162.8*** *p36*
Altomasi, Samuel 23; Arkansas, 1918 ***95.2*** *p12*
Altoven, Alfred 9; America, 1838 ***778.5*** *p7*
Altoven, Francois 29; America, 1838 ***778.5*** *p7*
Altoven, Suzanne 2; America, 1838 ***778.5*** *p7*
Altschaffl, Frank; Wisconsin, n.d. ***9675.4*** *p193*
Altschu, Kaspar; New York, NY, 1840 ***8208.4*** *p106*
Altstadt, John; Wisconsin, n.d. ***9675.4*** *p193*
Altz, Frederick; New York, NY, 1836 ***8208.4*** *p9*
Alvadj, Joso; Wisconsin, n.d. ***9675.4*** *p193*
Alvana, Pasquale; Arkansas, 1918 ***95.2*** *p12*
Alvin, John; America, 1698 ***2212*** *p8*
Alward, Andrew 23; Massachusetts, 1849 ***5881.1*** *p5*
Alwic, Jurges; Wisconsin, n.d. ***9675.4*** *p193*
Amact, John; New York, NY, 1816 ***2859.11*** *p24*
Aman, Jean 30; America, 1837 ***778.5*** *p7*
Amann, Johann Felix; Ohio, 1869-1887 ***8582*** *p1*
Amans, Mr. 34; America, 1836 ***778.5*** *p7*
Amar, J. A. 24; New Orleans, 1839 ***778.5*** *p7*
Amart, Mr. 22; New Orleans, 1821 ***778.5*** *p7*
Amat, J. 27; America, 1838 ***778.5*** *p7*
Amatis, Paul; Savannah, GA, 1733 ***4719.17*** *p310*
Amato, Giosepe; Arkansas, 1918 ***95.2*** *p12*

FOR A COMPLETE EXPLANATION OF ENTRY, SEE "HOW TO READ A CITATION" SECTION

Anderson, Hans 30; Arizona, 1927 ***9228.40*** *p31*
Anderson, Harold; Arkansas, 1918 ***95.2*** *p13*
Anderson, Harry; Maine, 1879-1886 ***6410.22*** *p120*
Anderson, Helene; Quebec, 1820 ***7603*** *p63*
Anderson, Henning; Colorado, 1905 ***9678.1*** *p151*
Anderson, Henry; Iroquois Co., IL, 1894 ***3455.1*** *p9*
Anderson, Henry 34; Kansas, 1886 ***5240.1*** *p69*
Anderson, Henry 46; Philadelphia, 1804 ***53.26*** *p1*
Anderson, Holver; Wisconsin, n.d. ***9675.4*** *p193*
Anderson, Hugh; Georgia, 1737 ***1639.20*** *p3*
*Wife:*Elizabeth
*Child:*Catherine
*Child:*Moira
*Child:*Alexander
Anderson, Hugh; Philadelphia, 1811 ***53.26*** *p1*
*Relative:*Ann
*Relative:*James
Anderson, Hugh; Philadelphia, 1811 ***2859.11*** *p8*
Anderson, Hugh; South Carolina, 1821 ***1639.20*** *p3*
Anderson, Irwin 9; Philadelphia, 1851 ***5704.8*** *p80*
Anderson, Isabella; Quebec, 1848 ***5704.8*** *p42*
Anderson, Isabella 11; Philadelphia, 1851 ***5704.8*** *p80*
Anderson, Isabella 50; Philadelphia, 1854 ***5704.8*** *p122*
Anderson, J. P.; Minneapolis, 1882-1886 ***6410.35*** *p49*
Anderson, Jacob; Washington, 1859-1920 ***2872.1*** *p1*
Anderson, James *SEE* Anderson, Hugh
Anderson, James; Colorado, 1904 ***9678.1*** *p151*
Anderson, James; New Orleans, 1849 ***5704.8*** *p58*
Anderson, James; New York, 1816 ***9892.11*** *p1*
Anderson, James; New York, NY, 1811 ***2859.11*** *p8*
Anderson, James; New York, NY, 1816 ***2859.11*** *p24*
Anderson, James; New York, NY, 1836 ***8208.4*** *p17*
Anderson, James; North Carolina, 1796-1874 ***1639.20*** *p3*
Anderson, James; North Carolina, 1813 ***1639.20*** *p3*
Anderson, James; Philadelphia, 1811 ***53.26*** *p1*
Anderson, James; Philadelphia, 1811 ***2859.11*** *p8*
Anderson, James; Philadelphia, 1847 ***53.26*** *p1*
Anderson, James; Philadelphia, 1847 ***5704.8*** *p23*
Anderson, James; Philadelphia, 1865 ***5704.8*** *p202*
Anderson, James; Washington, 1859-1920 ***2872.1*** *p2*
Anderson, James 8; Quebec, 1852 ***5704.8*** *p86*
Anderson, James 8; Quebec, 1852 ***5704.8*** *p91*
Anderson, James 10; Philadelphia, 1851 ***5704.8*** *p80*
Anderson, James 17; Philadelphia, 1854 ***5704.8*** *p122*
Anderson, James 35; New Orleans, 1863 ***543.30*** *p322*
Anderson, James 38; America, 1838 ***778.5*** *p8*
Anderson, James 54; North Carolina, 1850 ***1639.20*** *p4*
Anderson, Jane; New York, NY, 1815 ***2859.11*** *p24*
Anderson, Jane; Philadelphia, 1865 ***5704.8*** *p202*
Anderson, Jane; Quebec, 1847 ***5704.8*** *p13*
Anderson, Jane; St. John, N.B., 1847 ***5704.8*** *p18*
Anderson, Jane 7 *SEE* Anderson, Elizabeth
Anderson, Jane 11 *SEE* Anderson, Margaret
Anderson, Jane 11; Philadelphia, 1849 ***5704.8*** *p54*
Anderson, Jane 31; Massachusetts, 1860 ***6410.32*** *p115*
Anderson, Jennet; New York, NY, 1811 ***2859.11*** *p8*
Anderson, Jens Peter; Arkansas, 1918 ***95.2*** *p13*
Anderson, Johan B.; Colorado, 1895 ***9678.1*** *p151*
Anderson, Johan H.; Minneapolis, 1870-1876 ***6410.35*** *p49*
Anderson, Johana E. 30; Massachusetts, 1860 ***6410.32*** *p109*
Anderson, John; America, 1802 ***1639.20*** *p4*
Anderson, John; America, 1835 ***8893*** *p264*
Anderson, John; Boston, 1846 ***6410.32*** *p122*
Anderson, John; Boston, 1853 ***2896.5*** *p1*
Anderson, John; Illinois, 1876 ***5012.39*** *p52*
Anderson, John; Iowa, 1866-1943 ***123.54*** *p5*
Anderson, John; Iroquois Co., IL, 1896 ***3455.1*** *p9*
Anderson, John; Minneapolis, 1880-1885 ***6410.35*** *p49*
Anderson, John; Minneapolis, 1882-1883 ***6410.35*** *p49*
Anderson, John; Minneapolis, 1885-1886 ***6410.35*** *p49*
Anderson, John; New Orleans, 1849 ***5704.8*** *p59*
Anderson, John; New York, NY, 1815 ***2859.11*** *p24*
Anderson, John; Ohio, 1845 ***9892.11*** *p1*
Anderson, John; Ohio, 1847 ***9892.11*** *p1*
Anderson, John; Philadelphia, 1851 ***5704.8*** *p76*
Anderson, John; Philadelphia, 1865 ***5704.8*** *p202*
Anderson, John; St. John, N.B., 1847 ***5704.8*** *p15*
Anderson, John; St. John, N.B., 1852 ***5704.8*** *p94*
Anderson, John; San Francisco, 1851 ***6013.19*** *p89*
Anderson, John; Virginia, 1639 ***6219*** *p153*
Anderson, John; Virginia, 1649 ***6219*** *p252*
Anderson, John; Washington, 1859-1920 ***2872.1*** *p2*
Anderson, John 6 mos; Philadelphia, 1851 ***5704.8*** *p80*
Anderson, John 1 *SEE* Anderson, Elizabeth
Anderson, John 1; Quebec, 1852 ***5704.8*** *p86*
Anderson, John 1; Quebec, 1852 ***5704.8*** *p91*
Anderson, John 7; St. John, N.B., 1850 ***5704.8*** *p61*
Anderson, John 10 *SEE* Anderson, Margaret
Anderson, John 10; Philadelphia, 1849 ***5704.8*** *p54*
Anderson, John 12; Quebec, 1852 ***5704.8*** *p98*
Anderson, John 19; Virginia, 1722 ***3690.1*** *p4*
Anderson, John 20; Massachusetts, 1850 ***5881.1*** *p5*
Anderson, John 23; Kansas, 1892 ***5240.1*** *p76*
Anderson, John 26; Jamaica, 1724 ***3690.1*** *p4*
Anderson, John 28; New Orleans, 1862 ***543.30*** *p235*
Anderson, John 28; Philadelphia, 1804 ***53.26*** *p1*
Anderson, John 31; Massachusetts, 1860 ***6410.32*** *p102*
Anderson, John 43; California, 1869 ***3840.1*** *p14*
Anderson, John A.; Iowa, 1866-1943 ***123.54*** *p5*
Anderson, John Alfred; Illinois, 1894 ***5012.40*** *p53*
Anderson, John Alfred; Iroquois Co., IL, 1896 ***3455.1*** *p9*
Anderson, John Alvin; Arkansas, 1918 ***95.2*** *p13*
Anderson, John B.; Iroquois Co., IL, 1896 ***3455.1*** *p9*
Anderson, John C.; Illinois, 1888 ***5012.39*** *p122*
Anderson, John E.; Maine, 1889-1896 ***6410.22*** *p122*
Anderson, John Efraim; Arkansas, 1918 ***95.2*** *p13*
Anderson, John O.; Iowa, 1866-1943 ***123.54*** *p5*
Anderson, Johnston 13; Philadelphia, 1851 ***5704.8*** *p80*
Anderson, Joseph; Illinois, 1863 ***2896.5*** *p1*
Anderson, Joseph; New York, NY, 1835 ***8208.4*** *p51*
Anderson, Joseph; Philadelphia, 1816 ***2859.11*** *p24*
Anderson, Joseph 11; Philadelphia, 1865 ***5704.8*** *p202*
Anderson, Julius; Arkansas, 1918 ***95.2*** *p13*
Anderson, Karl Joh.; Iowa, 1866-1943 ***123.54*** *p5*
Anderson, Karl Jon; Iowa, 1866-1943 ***123.54*** *p5*
Anderson, Lars.; Iowa, 1849-1860 ***2090*** *p613*
Anderson, Lars Christian; Bangor, ME, 1891-1900 ***6410.22*** *p123*
Anderson, Lars Christian; Bangor, ME, 1895 ***6410.22*** *p127*
Anderson, Lars O.; Maine, 1881-1896 ***6410.22*** *p122*
Anderson, Lavina; Philadelphia, 1866 ***5704.8*** *p206*
Anderson, Lawerence; Wisconsin, n.d. ***9675.4*** *p193*
Anderson, Lawrence 85; Arizona, 1917 ***9228.40*** *p21*
Anderson, Letitia; Quebec, 1852 ***5704.8*** *p98*
Anderson, Letitia 3 *SEE* Anderson, Mary
Anderson, Louis; Iowa, 1866-1943 ***123.54*** *p5*
Anderson, Louren; Wisconsin, n.d. ***9675.4*** *p193*
Anderson, Madge 25; Philadelphia, 1861 ***5704.8*** *p148*
Anderson, Magnus; Iowa, 1846 ***2090*** *p610*
With 6 children
Anderson, Magnus; Maine, 1887 ***6410.22*** *p125*
Anderson, Magnus Christian 32; Arkansas, 1918 ***95.2*** *p13*
Anderson, Margaret; Philadelphia, 1816 ***2859.11*** *p24*
Anderson, Margaret; Philadelphia, 1849 ***53.26*** *p1*
*Relative:*Robert
*Relative:*Mary Ann
*Relative:*George
*Relative:*Rachel
*Relative:*Jane 11
*Relative:*John 10
Anderson, Margaret; Philadelphia, 1849 ***5704.8*** *p54*
Anderson, Margaret; Philadelphia, 1851 ***5704.8*** *p76*
Anderson, Margaret; Philadelphia, 1851 ***5704.8*** *p80*
Anderson, Margaret; Philadelphia, 1852 ***5704.8*** *p87*
Anderson, Margaret; Philadelphia, 1854 ***5704.8*** *p117*
Anderson, Margaret 13; Massachusetts, 1849 ***5881.1*** *p5*
Anderson, Margaret 36; Philadelphia, 1804 ***53.26*** *p2*
Anderson, Margaret J.; Quebec, 1847 ***5704.8*** *p28*
Anderson, Martha; New Orleans, 1849 ***5704.8*** *p58*
Anderson, Martin 30; Arkansas, 1918 ***95.2*** *p13*
Anderson, Mary; America, 1742 ***4971*** *p22*
Anderson, Mary; America, 1742 ***4971*** *p86*
Anderson, Mary; America, 1742 ***4971*** *p95*
Anderson, Mary; Maryland, 1742 ***4971*** *p107*
Anderson, Mary; New York, 1791 ***8894.1*** *p192*
Anderson, Mary; Quebec, 1849 ***5704.8*** *p52*
Anderson, Mary 2 *SEE* Anderson, Mary
Anderson, Mary 9 *SEE* Anderson, Elizabeth
Anderson, Mary 24; Philadelphia, 1803 ***53.26*** *p2*
*Relative:*Mary 2
Anderson, Mary 28; Massachusetts, 1860 ***6410.32*** *p104*
Anderson, Mary 30; Kansas, 1873 ***5240.1*** *p54*
Anderson, Mary 54; Virginia, 1775 ***1219.7*** *p258*
*Child:*George 12
*Child:*Ann 5
*Child:*Letitia 3
*Child:*Robert John 11
Anderson, Mary 64; Kansas, 1906 ***5240.1*** *p84*
Anderson, Mary Ann *SEE* Anderson, Margaret
Anderson, Mary Ann; Philadelphia, 1849 ***5704.8*** *p54*
Anderson, Mary Jane 30; St. John, N.B., 1853 ***5704.8*** *p109*
Anderson, Matilda 12; Quebec, 1848 ***5704.8*** *p42*
Anderson, Michael; Illinois, 1881 ***5012.39*** *p52*
Anderson, Moira *SEE* Anderson, Hugh
Anderson, Molly 45; St. John, N.B., 1861 ***5704.8*** *p146*
Anderson, Moses 5 *SEE* Anderson, Elizabeth
Anderson, N. P.; Washington, 1859-1920 ***2872.1*** *p2*
Anderson, Nancy 12; St. John, N.B., 1861 ***5704.8*** *p146*
Anderson, Nancy 50; Massachusetts, 1849 ***5881.1*** *p5*
Anderson, Nels; Iowa, 1866-1943 ***123.54*** *p5*
Anderson, Niels Christian 25; Arkansas, 1918 ***95.2*** *p13*
Anderson, Nils Alfred; Colorado, 1902 ***9678.1*** *p151*
Anderson, Nils P.; Minneapolis, 1869-1877 ***6410.35*** *p49*
Anderson, Olaf; Arkansas, 1918 ***95.2*** *p13*
Anderson, Olaf; Washington, 1859-1920 ***2872.1*** *p2*
Anderson, Ole; Colorado, 1904 ***9678.1*** *p151*
Anderson, Ole; Washington, 1859-1920 ***2872.1*** *p2*
Anderson, Ole G.; Iowa, 1852 ***2090*** *p615*
Anderson, Oscar; Illinois, 1895 ***5012.40*** *p54*
Anderson, P. Otto; Washington, 1859-1920 ***2872.1*** *p2*
Anderson, Peggy 10; Massachusetts, 1849 ***5881.1*** *p5*
Anderson, Penelope 23; Maryland, 1774 ***1219.7*** *p235*
Anderson, Per; Maine, 1872-1882 ***6410.22*** *p119*
Anderson, Per G.; Maine, 1871-1873 ***6410.22*** *p118*
Anderson, Per Gustaf; Iowa, 1851 ***2090*** *p611*
With wife
Anderson, Peter; Colorado, 1900 ***9678.1*** *p151*
Anderson, Peter; Illinois, 1860 ***5012.38*** *p98*
Anderson, Peter; Iowa, 1847 ***2090*** *p611*
With wife
Anderson, Peter; Washington, 1859-1920 ***2872.1*** *p2*
Anderson, Peter 36; Massachusetts, 1860 ***6410.32*** *p115*
Anderson, Peter A.; New York, 1884 ***2764.35*** *p75*
Anderson, Peter M.; Boston, 1843 ***6410.32*** *p125*
Anderson, Peter M.; Iroquois Co., IL, 1892 ***3455.1*** *p9*
Anderson, Rachel *SEE* Anderson, Margaret
Anderson, Rachel; Philadelphia, 1849 ***5704.8*** *p54*
Anderson, Robert *SEE* Anderson, Margaret
Anderson, Robert; Austin, TX, 1886 ***9777*** *p5*
Anderson, Robert; New Orleans, 1849 ***5704.8*** *p59*
Anderson, Robert; New York, NY, 1840 ***8208.4*** *p107*
Anderson, Robert; Philadelphia, 1849 ***5704.8*** *p54*
Anderson, Robert; Philadelphia, 1851 ***5704.8*** *p80*
Anderson, Robert; Philadelphia, 1865 ***5704.8*** *p189*
Anderson, Robert; Philadelphia, 1865 ***5704.8*** *p198*
Anderson, Robert; Quebec, 1849 ***5704.8*** *p57*
Anderson, Robert; Quebec, 1851 ***5704.8*** *p74*
Anderson, Robert 4; Wilmington, DE, 1831 ***6508.3*** *p101*
Anderson, Robert 16; Antigua (Antego), 1774 ***1219.7*** *p239*
Anderson, Robert 20; St. John, N.B., 1855 ***5704.8*** *p127*
Anderson, Robert 22; Quebec, 1854 ***5704.8*** *p119*
Anderson, Robert John 11 *SEE* Anderson, Mary
Anderson, Roger; Virginia, 1638 ***6219*** *p159*
Anderson, Roger; Virginia, 1640 ***6219*** *p184*
Anderson, Rose 13; St. John, N.B., 1852 ***5704.8*** *p94*
Anderson, Sally; St. John, N.B., 1850 ***5704.8*** *p61*
Anderson, Samuel; New York, NY, 1811 ***2859.11*** *p8*
Anderson, Samuel 5; St. John, N.B., 1850 ***5704.8*** *p61*
Anderson, Samuel 46; Philadelphia, 1804 ***53.26*** *p2*
Anderson, Samuel G.; Illinois, 1902 ***5012.40*** *p77*
Anderson, Sarah 16; Philadelphia, 1854 ***5704.8*** *p122*
Anderson, Sarah 19; St. John, N.B., 1856 ***5704.8*** *p132*
Anderson, Sarah A. 8; Philadelphia, 1865 ***5704.8*** *p202*
Anderson, Sarah Jane 9; St. John, N.B., 1850 ***5704.8*** *p61*
Anderson, Stephen 29; Kansas, 1878 ***5240.1*** *p3*
Anderson, Stephen 29; Kansas, 1878 ***5240.1*** *p59*
Anderson, Swan J.; Bangor, ME, 1885-1893 ***6410.22*** *p123*
Anderson, Swan J.; Bangor, ME, 1893 ***6410.22*** *p126*
Anderson, Swen; Iroquois Co., IL, 1896 ***3455.1*** *p9*
Anderson, T.; New York, NY, 1811 ***2859.11*** *p8*
Anderson, Tho.; Virginia, 1643 ***6219*** *p229*
Anderson, Thomas; Kansas, 1892 ***5240.1*** *p3*
Anderson, Thomas 20; Pennsylvania, 1738 ***3690.1*** *p4*
Anderson, Thomas 22; Maryland, 1774 ***1219.7*** *p235*
Anderson, Thompson 45; St. John, N.B., 1861 ***5704.8*** *p147*
Anderson, Thorwald 23; Arkansas, 1918 ***95.2*** *p13*
Anderson, Victor Fredenand; Arkansas, 1918 ***95.2*** *p13*
Anderson, William; America, 1785 ***8894.2*** *p57*
Anderson, William; Baltimore, 1811 ***2859.11*** *p8*
Anderson, William; Illinois, 1866 ***2896.5*** *p1*
Anderson, William; Iowa, 1866-1943 ***123.54*** *p3*
Anderson, William; New York, NY, 1811 ***2859.11*** *p8*
Anderson, William; New York, NY, 1815 ***2859.11*** *p24*
Anderson, William; New York, NY, 1816 ***2859.11*** *p24*
Anderson, William; Ohio, 1840 ***9892.11*** *p1*
Anderson, William; Philadelphia, 1816 ***2859.11*** *p24*
With mother & brother
Anderson, William; Philadelphia, 1852 ***5704.8*** *p88*
Anderson, William; Philadelphia, 1865 ***5704.8*** *p198*
Anderson, William; Quebec, 1850 ***5704.8*** *p63*
Anderson, William; Quebec, 1852 ***5704.8*** *p86*
Anderson, William; Quebec, 1852 ***5704.8*** *p91*
Anderson, William 1; St. John, N.B., 1853 ***5704.8*** *p109*
Anderson, William 3; St. John, N.B., 1850 ***5704.8*** *p61*
Anderson, William 4 *SEE* Anderson, Elizabeth
Anderson, William 4; Quebec, 1852 ***5704.8*** *p86*
Anderson, William 4; Quebec, 1852 ***5704.8*** *p91*
Anderson, William 16; St. John, N.B., 1861 ***5704.8*** *p147*
Anderson, William 18; Maryland, 1718 ***3690.1*** *p4*
Anderson, William 19; Philadelphia, 1864 ***5704.8*** *p157*
Anderson, William 20; Philadelphia, 1857 ***5704.8*** *p134*

Anderson, William 20; Virginia, 1724 *3690.1 p4*
Anderson, William 22; Philadelphia, 1854 *5704.8 p117*
Anderson, William 29; Massachusetts, 1860 *6410.32 p119*
Anderson, William 34; Maryland, 1775 *1219.7 p250*
Anderson, William 34; Maryland, 1775 *1219.7 p253*
Anderson, William 50; St. John, N.B., 1853 *5704.8 p109*
Anderson, William 53; Philadelphia, 1804 *53.26 p2*
Anderson, William Andrew; America, 1847 *1450.2 p3A*
Anderson, William Cooper; New York, NY, 1840 *8208.4 p112*
Anderson, William Richard; Arkansas, 1918 *95.2 p13*
Anderson, William Robert 23; Arkansas, 1918 *95.2 p13*
Anderson, Willoughby; Washington, 1859-1920 *2872.1 p2*
Andersson, Anders; Minneapolis, 1873-1878 *6410.35 p51*
Andersson, Anders; Minneapolis, 1873-1887 *6410.35 p47*
Andersson, Anders M.; Minneapolis, 1881-1887 *6410.35 p47*
Andersson, Anders Magnus; Minneapolis, 1873-1886 *6410.35 p47*
Andersson, Anders Petter; Minneapolis, 1866-1888 *6410.35 p47*
Andersson, Anders Petter; Minneapolis, 1873-1883 *6410.35 p47*
Andersson, Andrew M.; Minneapolis, 1881-1887 *6410.35 p47*
Andersson, Axel Wilhelm; Minneapolis, 1880-1884 *6410.35 p47*
Andersson, Carl; Colorado, 1897 *9678.1 p151*
Andersson, Carl; Minneapolis, 1876-1881 *6410.35 p51*
Andersson, Carl Johan; Minneapolis, 1884-1887 *6410.35 p60*
Andersson, Gustaf Alfred; Minneapolis, 1879-1885 *6410.35 p49*
Andersson, Johan Emil; Minneapolis, 1880-1885 *6410.35 p49*
Andersson, Johannes; Minneapolis, 1882-1883 *6410.35 p49*
Andersson, Joseph P.; Minneapolis, 1882-1886 *6410.35 p49*
Andersson, Nils; Minneapolis, 1854-1881 *6410.35 p50*
Andersson, Nils; Minneapolis, 1869-1877 *6410.35 p49*
Andersson, Pehr; America, 1860 *6410.35 p47*
Anderton, Mary 20; Maryland or Virginia, 1699 *2212 p22*
Anderton, Richard 13; Maryland, 1702 *2212 p36*
Anderton, William 18; Maryland, 1775 *1219.7 p273*
Andoe, James; New York, NY, 1816 *2859.11 p24*
Andrade, Abraham 24; Philadelphia, 1774 *1219.7 p183*
Andrae, . . .; Quebec, 1776 *9786 p105*
Andrain, Hilmer 37; Washington, 1916 *1728.4 p251*
Andre, . . .; Canada, 1776-1783 *9786 p41*
Andre, Francois; Louisiana, 1789-1819 *778.5 p555*
Andre, Jacome; Colorado, 1903 *9678.1 p151*
Andre, Jacques; Halifax, N.S., 1753 *7074.6 p216*
Andre, Joe; Arkansas, 1918 *95.2 p13*
Andre, Johannes; Saratoga, NY, 1777 *8137 p6*
Andre, L. 27; Louisiana, 1829 *778.5 p8*
Andreae, Peter; America, 1873 *1450.2 p4A*
Andreas, Jacob 29; New Orleans, 1862 *543.30 p234*
Andreasdottir, Jon 16; Quebec, 1879 *2557.1 p39A*
Andreasdottir, Jonatan 10; Quebec, 1879 *2557.1 p39A*
Andreasdottir, Kristiana 38; Quebec, 1879 *2557.1 p39A*
Andreasdottir, Kristinn 6 mos; Quebec, 1879 *2557.1 p39A*
Andreasdottir, Kristjan 6; Quebec, 1879 *2557.1 p39A*
Andreasdottir, Nina 3; Quebec, 1879 *2557.1 p39A*
Andreasdottir, Sesselia 20; Quebec, 1879 *2557.1 p39A*
Andreasdottir, Sigurdur 13; Quebec, 1879 *2557.1 p39A*
Andreasson, Jon 16; Quebec, 1879 *2557.1 p39A*
Andreasson, Kristinn 6 mos; Quebec, 1879 *2557.1 p39A*
Andreasson, Kristjan 6; Quebec, 1879 *2557.1 p39A*
Andreasson, Sigurdur 13; Quebec, 1879 *2557.1 p39A*
Andree, Carl Conrad; Quebec, 1776 *9786 p257*
Andrees, Carl Friedrich; America, 1849 *4610.10 p155*
*Son:*Justus Joseph Carl
*Wife:*Marie C. Wilmsmeyer
Andrees, Justus Joseph Carl *SEE* Andrees, Carl Friedrich
Andrees, Marie C. Wilmsmeyer *SEE* Andrees, Carl Friedrich
Andregg, Johann; America, 1828 *8582.2 p61*
Andren, J. E.; Minneapolis, 1880-1885 *6410.35 p49*
Andrepont, Joseph; Louisiana, 1789-1819 *778.5 p555*
Andres, John P.; Colorado, 1883 *5240.1 p3*
Andres, Wilhelm; Illinois, 1876 *2896.5 p1*
Andresen, Jacob; Wisconsin, n.d. *9675.4 p193*
Andress, Robert; New York, NY, 1834 *8208.4 p2*
Andreu, Antoine 22; America, 1839 *778.5 p8*
Andreu, Elisabeth 23; America, 1839 *778.5 p8*
Andreu, Jean 28; America, 1839 *778.5 p8*
Andreu, Joseph 20; America, 1839 *778.5 p8*
Andreu, Ludwig 11; America, 1839 *778.5 p8*
Andreu, Magd. 17; America, 1839 *778.5 p8*
Andrew, A. 25; New Orleans, 1831 *778.5 p8*
Andrew, Alexander 29; Virginia, 1774 *1219.7 p239*
Andrew, E.J.; Colorado, 1904 *9678.1 p151*
Andrew, John; America, 1853 *1450.2 p4A*
Andrew, John; St. John, N.B., 1847 *5704.8 p15*
Andrew, John 22; Virginia, 1699 *2212 p20*
Andrew, Moses 34; Nova Scotia, 1774 *1219.7 p209*
Andrew, Muade 31; New Orleans, 1862 *543.30 p233*
Andrew, Richard; Virginia, 1643 *6219 p230*
Andrew, Robert; Virginia, 1643 *6219 p204*
Andrew, William; Carolina, 1684 *1639.20 p4*
Andrewes, Edmund; Virginia, 1637 *6219 p113*
*Wife:*Eliza
Andrewes, Edward; Virginia, 1639 *6219 p161*
Andrewes, Eliza *SEE* Andrewes, Edmund
Andrewes, John; Virginia, 1639 *6219 p161*
Andrewes, John; Virginia, 1648 *6219 p252*
Andrewes, Rich.; Virginia, 1648 *6219 p241*
Andrewes, Roger; Virginia, 1637 *6219 p83*
Andrewes, Susan; Virginia, 1636 *6219 p76*
Andrewes, Wm.; Virginia, 1635 *6219 p27*
Andrews, Lt.; Quebec, 1815 *9229.18 p79*
Andrews, Dorothy; Virginia, 1637 *6219 p107*
Andrews, Elizabeth; New York, NY, 1864 *5704.8 p184*
Andrews, Ernest P. 51; Kansas, 1904 *5240.1 p83*
Andrews, Gabriel; Philadelphia, 1811 *53.26 p2*
Andrews, Gabriel; Philadelphia, 1811 *2859.11 p8*
Andrews, George; New York, NY, 1816 *2859.11 p24*
Andrews, Georges; Quebec, 1788 *7603 p69*
Andrews, Hannah 1 *SEE* Andrews, Thomas
Andrews, Israell; Virginia, 1642 *6219 p197*
Andrews, James 15; Wilmington, DE, 1831 *6508.7 p161*
Andrews, John; New York, NY, 1811 *2859.11 p8*
Andrews, John; New York, NY, 1833 *8208.4 p47*
Andrews, John 5 *SEE* Andrews, Thomas
Andrews, John 15; Maryland, 1718 *3690.1 p4*
Andrews, John 15; Pennsylvania, 1739 *3690.1 p4*
Andrews, John 17; Maryland, 1719 *3690.1 p4*
Andrews, Jon.; Virginia, 1636 *6219 p80*
Andrews, Joseph 18; Maryland or Virginia, 1720 *3690.1 p4*
Andrews, Joshua 23; Maryland, 1774 *1219.7 p180*
Andrews, Kurt; New York, NY, 1923 *3455.4 p26*
Andrews, Lilley 37 *SEE* Andrews, Thomas
Andrews, Mary 3 *SEE* Andrews, Thomas
Andrews, Mary 7 *SEE* Andrews, Thomas
Andrews, Mary 18; Virginia, 1720 *3690.1 p4*
Andrews, Nich.; Virginia, 1638 *6219 p159*
Andrews, Richard; Virginia, 1638 *6219 p147*
Andrews, Robert; New York, NY, 1815 *2859.11 p24*
Andrews, Robt., Jr.; New York, NY, 1815 *2859.11 p24*
Andrews, Roger; Virginia, 1643 *6219 p204*
Andrews, Susan; Virginia, 1638 *6219 p146*
Andrews, Susanna *SEE* Andrews, Wm.
Andrews, Thomas; New York, NY, 1815 *2859.11 p24*
Andrews, Thomas; Virginia, 1635 *6219 p20*
Andrews, Thomas; Virginia, 1639 *6219 p157*
Andrews, Thomas 20; Jamaica, 1737 *3690.1 p4*
Andrews, Thomas 35; Carolina, 1774 *1219.7 p225*
Andrews, Thomas 37; Nova Scotia, 1774 *1219.7 p195*
*Wife:*Lilley 37
*Child:*Mary 7
*Child:*John 5
*Child:*Mary 3
*Child:*Hannah 1
Andrews, William; Virginia, 1639 *6219 p159*
Andrews, William; Virginia, 1643 *6219 p204*
Andrews, William 23; Philadelphia, 1774 *1219.7 p205*
Andrews, William 31; North Carolina, 1774 *1219.7 p215*
Andrews, Willoughby; Washington, 1859-1920 *2872.1 p2*
Andrews, Wm.; Virginia, 1635 *6219 p1*
*Wife:*Susanna
Andrews, Wm.; Virginia, 1638 *6219 p145*
Andrews, Wm., Jr.; New York, NY, 1815 *2859.11 p24*
Andrews, Wm., Sr.; New York, NY, 1815 *2859.11 p24*
Andriessen, Arnold; New Netherland, 1630-1646 *8582.2 p51*
Andriessen, Hugo; America, 1861 *8125.8 p435*
Andrieux, . . .; Port uncertain, 1839 *778.5 p8*
Andrieux, Mme.; Port uncertain, 1839 *778.5 p9*
Andrieux, Mr.; Port uncertain, 1839 *778.5 p8*
Andriola, C.; Shreveport, LA, 1877 *7129 p44*
Andro, Anton 47; New Orleans, 1862 *543.30 p234*
Androhan, John; New York, NY, 1811 *2859.11 p8*
Andruilis, Sindurk; Wisconsin, n.d. *9675.4 p193*
Anduil, J. 52; New Orleans, 1836 *778.5 p9*
Andukowicz, Eleanora 28 *SEE* Andukowicz, Wiktoria
Andukowicz, Wiktoria 18; New York, 1912 *9980.29 p73*
*Sister:*Eleanora 28
Andur, Morris; Arkansas, 1918 *95.2 p14*
Aneloose, Castal 25; Texas, 1839 *778.5 p9*
Anesac, E. 29; New Orleans, 1831 *778.5 p9*
Anet, Antti; Washington, 1859-1920 *2872.1 p2*
Anet, Eljas; Washington, 1859-1920 *2872.1 p2*
Anfang, Joseph; Colorado, 1904 *9678.1 p152*
Angalka, John; Illinois, 1861 *2896.5 p1*
Angaran, Eugenie; Iowa, 1866-1943 *123.54 p3*
Angaran, Francesco; Iowa, 1866-1943 *123.54 p55*
Angaran, Giacobbe; Iowa, 1866-1943 *123.54 p3*
Angaran, Giovonni; Iowa, 1866-1943 *123.54 p3*
Angaran, Giuseppe; Iowa, 1866-1943 *123.54 p55*
Angaran, Joseph John; Iowa, 1866-1943 *123.54 p55*
Angaran, Luis; Iowa, 1866-1943 *123.54 p3*
Angaran, Maria; Iowa, 1866-1943 *123.54 p55*
Angel, Abraham 27; Maryland, 1774 *1219.7 p179*
Angel, William; New York, 1754 *3652 p79*
Angelas, Peter; Arkansas, 1918 *95.2 p14*
Angell, N. P.; Washington, 1859-1920 *2872.1 p2*
Angell, Stephen; New York, NY, 1833 *8208.4 p29*
Angelo, Anthony; Arkansas, 1918 *95.2 p14*
Angelo, Luigi; Arkansas, 1918 *95.2 p14*
Angelopoulous, James; Arkansas, 1918 *95.2 p14*
Angelos, Nick; Arkansas, 1918 *95.2 p14*
Angelot, Victor 25; Mobile, AL, 1837 *778.5 p9*
Angenant, . . .; Canada, 1776-1783 *9786 p16*
Angerer, . . .; Canada, 1776-1783 *9786 p16*
Angeretti, Nemo; Arkansas, 1918 *95.2 p14*
Angerman, John; New York, 1761 *3652 p87*
Angersbach, Johann Henrich; Philadelphia, 1779 *8137 p6*
Angever, . . .; Canada, 1776-1783 *9786 p16*
Angier, John 21; Maryland, 1724 *3690.1 p5*
Angius, John B.; Nevada, 1880 *2764.35 p1*
Anglade, A. 20; America, 1838 *778.5 p9*
Anglade, J. 26; Port uncertain, 1839 *778.5 p9*
Anglaise, J. 30; New Orleans, 1829 *778.5 p9*
Anglaise, J. B. 20; New Orleans, 1829 *778.5 p9*
Anglaise, Joseph 40; America, 1838 *778.5 p9*
Anglandere, Mr. 26; New Orleans, 1836 *778.5 p9*
Angle, Tonney D. 45; Kansas, 1897 *5240.1 p80*
Angley, Laurence; America, 1739 *4971 p38*
Angoran, Bartolo; Iowa, 1866-1943 *123.54 p3*
Angot, Adele 23; America, 1837 *778.5 p9*
Angove, William; Colorado, 1894 *9678.1 p152*
Angue, Peter; New York, NY, 1835 *8208.4 p39*
Angus, James; New York, NY, 1837 *8208.4 p48*
Angus, Thomas 21; United States or West Indies, 1736 *3690.1 p5*
Anicangiolo, Crescenzo 46; New York, NY, 1893 *9026.4 p41*
Anjet, L. 30; America, 1826 *778.5 p9*
Ankers, John; New York, NY, 1835 *8208.4 p43*
Annaberg, Dietsch von; Evansville, IN, 1854 *8582.1 p30*
Annacito, Emidio; Colorado, 1903 *9678.1 p152*
Anne Marie, Ms. 28; Port uncertain, 1836 *778.5 p9*
Annes, William; Wisconsin, n.d. *9675.4 p193*
Annice, John; Virginia, 1638 *6219 p122*
Anniers, Heinrich Daniel, I; Quebec, 1776 *9786 p258*
Annis, Mrs.; New York, NY, 1816 *2859.11 p24*
Annis, Robert; Virginia, 1636 *6219 p8*
Annis, Thomas; Virginia, 1638 *6219 p148*
Annis, William; Virginia, 1639 *6219 p153*
Annis, William; Virginia, 1639 *6219 p162*
Annone, Domenick; Iowa, 1866-1943 *123.54 p3*
Ansbro, John; Kansas, 1882 *5240.1 p3*
Ansbrow, Thomas; Quebec, 1825 *7603 p99*
Anschuetz, Carl; New York, NY, 1857 *8582 p1*
Anschutz, Anna 16; New York, NY, 1878 *9253 p47*
Anschutz, Carl 20; New York, NY, 1878 *9253 p47*
Anschutz, Christian 39; New York, NY, 1878 *9253 p47*
Anschutz, David 9; New York, NY, 1878 *9253 p47*
Anschutz, Dorthea 10 mos; New York, NY, 1878 *9253 p47*
Anschutz, Heinrich 7; New York, NY, 1878 *9253 p47*
Anschutz, Heinrich 22; New York, NY, 1878 *9253 p47*
Anschutz, Marie 39; New York, NY, 1878 *9253 p47*
Anschutz, Nicolaus 4; New York, NY, 1878 *9253 p47*
Ansell, Matthew 18; Maryland, 1718 *3690.1 p5*
Ansell, Thomas 20; Jamaica, 1736 *3690.1 p5*
Anselm, B. 27; America, 1838 *778.5 p9*
Ansey, Joseph; Wisconsin, n.d. *9675.4 p193*
Anshling, Michel 29; New Orleans, 1838 *778.5 p10*
Ansley, James 21; Port uncertain, 1774 *1219.7 p176*
Ansley, Thomas; Iowa, 1866-1943 *123.54 p3*
Anslinger, C. 25; Kansas, 1887 *5240.1 p70*
Anson, George; America, 1846-1847 *1450.2 p4A*
Anson, George 21; Maryland, 1775 *1219.7 p257*
Anspach, Nicholas; New York, 1754 *3652 p79*
Anssemann, Marguerite 22; America, 1835 *778.5 p10*
Anssemann, Nicolas 9 mos; America, 1835 *778.5 p10*
Anssemann, Nicolas 25; America, 1835 *778.5 p10*
Anstetz, Peter; Wisconsin, n.d. *9675.4 p193*
Ansup, Henry 18; Jamaica, 1725 *3690.1 p5*

Antanaitis, John; Wisconsin, n.d. 9675.4 p193
Antecetto, Gionotti; Arkansas, 1918 95.2 p14
Antee, Cormick; New York, NY, 1836 8208.4 p11
Antelle, Marie SEE Antelle, Pierre
Antelle, Pierre; Halifax, N.S., 1753 7074.6 p216
Relative:Marie
Antenson, Peter 28; New Orleans, 1862 543.30 p238
Antes, Kath. 17; America, 1853 9162.8 p36
Antes, Niklaus 52; America, 1853 9162.8 p36
Antes, Ph. 22; America, 1853 9162.8 p36
Antherson, Wm.; Virginia, 1636 6219 p75
Anthonissen, John; New York, NY, 1902 3455.3 p18
Anthony, James 24; Massachusetts, 1849 5881.1 p5
Anthony, John 21; Carolina, 1774 1219.7 p227
Anthony, Joseph; New York, NY, 1835 8208.4 p37
Anthony, William; Baltimore, 1811 2859.11 p8
Anticeaara, John T.; Washington, 1859-1920 2872.1 p2
Antinkaapo, Peter Abram; Washington, 1859-1920 2872.1 p2
Antiny, John; South Carolina, 1788 7119 p199
Antley, Mike; Arkansas, 1918 95.2 p14
Antoine, Adolph; Wisconsin, n.d. 9675.4 p193
Antoine, Cebestian; Wisconsin, n.d. 9675.4 p193
Antoine, Eugene 34; Kansas, 1897 5240.1 p81
Antoine, Frank X.; Wisconsin, n.d. 9675.4 p193
Antone, Jose M. 20; New Orleans, 1829 778.5 p10
Antoneikeika, Neik; Arkansas, 1918 95.2 p14
Antonetti, Antonio 43; Harris Co., TX, 1898 6254 p5
Antoni, Mrs. 29; Port uncertain, 1838 778.5 p10
Antoni, Adolf; Wisconsin, n.d. 9675.4 p193
Antoni, C. 22; Port uncertain, 1838 778.5 p10
Antoni, Hilda; Wisconsin, n.d. 9675.4 p193
Antoni, Johann; Wisconsin, n.d. 9675.4 p193
Antoni, N. 28; Port uncertain, 1838 778.5 p10
Antoni, Robert; Wisconsin, n.d. 9675.4 p193
Antonina, Antonio 25; West Virginia, 1903 9788.3 p4
Antonio, Mr. 45; New Orleans, 1836 778.5 p10
Antonio, Andreazza; Iowa, 1866-1943 123.54 p3
Antonio, Antonelly; Arkansas, 1918 95.2 p14
Antonio, Giognorio; Arkansas, 1918 95.2 p14
Antonio, Nicholas 20; New Orleans, 1862 543.30 p236
Antonio, P. 34; Port uncertain, 1838 778.5 p10
Antoniotti, Armando; Arkansas, 1918 95.2 p14
Antony, Mme.; America, 1839 778.5 p10
Antony, Mr.; America, 1839 778.5 p10
Antram, William; South Carolina, 1752 1219.7 p10
Antrin, Charles 30; Massachusetts, 1860 6410.32 p110
Antroutsopoulas, Gost; Arkansas, 1918 95.2 p14
Antrum, John 15; Maryland, 1719 3690.1 p5
Anttilla, Hilda; Washington, 1859-1920 2872.1 p2
Anttilla, John William; Washington, 1859-1920 2872.1 p2
Anttilla, Sylvia Iva; Washington, 1859-1920 2872.1 p2
Anttilla, William; Washington, 1859-1920 2872.1 p2
Anttonen, Jacki; Washington, 1859-1920 2872.1 p2
Antweiler, John 35; New Orleans, 1862 543.30 p236
Anwyle, Kenrick 27; Maryland, 1775 1219.7 p261
Anzia, Mike; Wisconsin, n.d. 9675.4 p193
Anzmann, Jean 33; Port uncertain, 1839 778.5 p10
Anzmann, Marie 42; Port uncertain, 1839 778.5 p10
Apel, Julius; Wisconsin, n.d. 9675.4 p193
Apfel, Salo; America, 1840 8582.3 p1
Apleton, Alice; Virginia, 1643 6219 p204
Apmann, Meta; New York, NY, 1922 3455.4 p26
Apolinski, John; Arkansas, 1918 95.2 p14
Aponik, Alexandra 6; New York, 1912 9980.29 p58
Aponik, Leonarda 10 mos; New York, 1912 9980.29 p58
Aponik, Marya 26; New York, 1912 9980.29 p58
Apostalopulas, Gus George; Arkansas, 1918 95.2 p14
Apostle, Constantine John; Arkansas, 1918 95.2 p14
Appel, . . .; Canada, 1776-1783 9786 p16
Appel, Anton; Minnesota, 1881 5240.1 p3
Appel, Arthur; Arkansas, 1918 95.2 p14
Appel, Conrad 18; New Orleans, 1862 543.30 p237
Appel, Henry; Illinois, 1856 7857 p2
Appel, Henry 22; New Orleans, 1862 543.30 p238
Appel, Martin 30; Arkansas, 1918 95.2 p14
Appel, Peter; New York, NY, 1923 3455.3 p84
Appel, Peter; New York, NY, 1923 3455.4 p29
Appelins, Frederick; Virginia, 1855 4626.16 p15
Appelius, Albrecht; Virginia, 1844 4626.16 p13
Appenroth, Christian; New York, NY, 1839 8208.4 p92
Appleby, Jane; America, 1736 4971 p12
Appleby, Robert 21; Nova Scotia, 1774 1219.7 p194
Appleby, William 18; New York, 1774 1219.7 p202
Appleford, . . . 28; Canada, 1835 4535.10 p196
Appleford, David; Illinois, 1859 7857 p2
Appleford, Isaac; Illinois, 1863 7857 p2
Applegate, George 24; Kansas, 1876 5240.1 p57
Applegate, John H. 21; Kansas, 1876 5240.1 p57
Appleman, John; Philadelphia, 1761 9973.7 p35
Applequest, Clarence 34; Massachusetts, 1860 6410.32 p121
Applequest, Fritz F. 8; Massachusetts, 1860 6410.32 p121
Applequest, Isaac F. 34; Massachusetts, 1860 6410.32 p121
Applequist, Isaac; Boston, 1888 6410.32 p126
Appleton, Francis 22; Maryland, 1774 1219.7 p191
Appleton, John; Boston, 1775 1219.7 p272
Appleton, John; New York, NY, 1836 8208.4 p23
Appleton, Jonathan 17; Pennsylvania, 1728 3690.1 p5
Appleton, Joseph; Iowa, 1866-1943 123.54 p3
Appleton, Joseph; Wisconsin, n.d. 9675.4 p193
Appleton, Rich.; Virginia, 1635 6219 p20
Appleton, Robert 24; North America, 1774 1219.7 p199
Appleton, Robert E.; New York, NY, 1839 8208.4 p91
Appleton, William; Iowa, 1866-1943 123.54 p3
Appletree, Joseph 15; West Indies, 1722 3690.1 p5
Appman, Eliesabeth; New York, NY, 1923 3455.4 p29
Approlonia, Dominick; Arkansas, 1918 95.2 p14
Appy, John; North America, 1763 1219.7 p93
ap Rich, Rich.; Virginia, 1643 6219 p207
Aptey, Thomas 19; Maryland, 1720 3690.1 p5
ap Thomas, Wm.; Virginia, 1648 6219 p249
Aragon, Louis 24; New Orleans, 1836 778.5 p10
Aram, John; Virginia, 1635 6219 p16
Aranburg, John 26; New Orleans, 1837 778.5 p11
Aranda, Ezequiel; Illinois, 1893 5012.37 p63
Arapakis, George; Arkansas, 1918 95.2 p14
Arasim, John; Arkansas, 1918 95.2 p14
Arbach, Jacob; Minnesota, 1879 5240.1 p3
Arbo, John; New York, 1761 3652 p87
Arbogart, Philip; New York, NY, 1837 8208.4 p41
Arbort, Christopher; Pennsylvania, 1785 4525 p229
Arbort, Christopher; Pennsylvania, 1785 4525 p245
Arbort, Christopher; Philadelphia, 1785 4525 p199
Arbour, Louis; Louisiana, 1789-1819 778.5 p555
Arbourt, Christoph; Philadelphia, 1785 4525 p198
Arbuckle, Angus W.; Nevada, 1880 2764.35 p2
Arbuckle, Ann 7; Quebec, 1847 5704.8 p15
Arbuckle, Catherine; Quebec, 1847 5704.8 p6
Arbuckle, Catherine 14; Quebec, 1847 5704.8 p6
Arbuckle, Eliza 4; Quebec, 1847 5704.8 p6
Arbuckle, Eliza Jane 11; Quebec, 1847 5704.8 p15
Arbuckle, Hanna 4; Quebec, 1847 5704.8 p15
Arbuckle, Isaac 5; Quebec, 1847 5704.8 p6
Arbuckle, Isabella; Quebec, 1847 5704.8 p6
Arbuckle, James 13; Quebec, 1847 5704.8 p6
Arbuckle, Jane 3 mos; Quebec, 1847 5704.8 p6
Arbuckle, John; New York, NY, 1838 8208.4 p62
Arbuckle, John; Quebec, 1847 5704.8 p6
Arbuckle, John; South Carolina, 1767 1639.20 p4
Arbuckle, John 2; Quebec, 1847 5704.8 p15
Arbuckle, Joseph 8; Quebec, 1847 5704.8 p6
Arbuckle, Mary; Quebec, 1847 5704.8 p15
Arbuckle, Mary 7; Quebec, 1847 5704.8 p6
Arbuckle, Mary 9; Quebec, 1847 5704.8 p15
Arbuckle, Matty 9 mos; Quebec, 1847 5704.8 p15
Arbuckle, Robert 18; Quebec, 1853 5704.8 p104
Arbuckle, Samuel; Quebec, 1847 5704.8 p15
Arbuckle, Samuel 4; Quebec, 1847 5704.8 p15
Arbuckle, Samuel 20; Quebec, 1858 5704.8 p137
Arbuckle, Thomas; Quebec, 1847 5704.8 p6
Arbuckle, Thomas 11; Quebec, 1847 5704.8 p6
Arbuckle, William 3; Quebec, 1847 5704.8 p6
Arbuckle, William 13; Quebec, 1847 5704.8 p15
Arburth, Andreas; Philadelphia, 1759 4525 p199
Arcaste, Marie-Anne; Quebec, 1752 7603 p36
Arch-Deacon, Kath 19; America, 1704 2212 p41
Archable, James; New Orleans, 1848 5704.8 p48
Archbold, Elizabeth; St. John, N.B., 1847 5704.8 p25
Archdale, Thomas 40; Maryland, 1774 1219.7 p230
Archdeacon, Tom; Illinois, 1888 5012.39 p122
Archellon, Marga; Virginia, 1632 6219 p180
Archer, Geo.; Virginia, 1629 6219 p8
Archer, Geo.; Virginia, 1636 6219 p77
Archer, Georg; Virginia, 1642 6219 p199
Archer, John; Virginia, 1645 6219 p239
Archer, John 18; Virginia, 1727 3690.1 p5
Archer, John 23; Maryland, 1775 1219.7 p249
Archer, Richard; Iowa, 1866-1943 123.54 p3
Archer, Theodorus 18; Jamaica, 1729 3690.1 p5
Archer, William 23; Maryland, 1774 1219.7 p229
Archer, Wm.; Virginia, 1642 6219 p196
Archerday, Tho.; Virginia, 1643 6219 p204
Archibald, Eliza Jane 18; Philadelphia, 1854 5704.8 p123
Archibald, Ellen Jane 19; St. John, N.B., 1856 5704.8 p131
Archibald, James 25; Kansas, 1884 5240.1 p66
Archibald, Margaret; Philadelphia, 1850 5704.8 p64
Archibald, Robert; Charleston, SC, 1799 1639.20 p4
Arckey, Martha 24; Philadelphia, 1854 5704.8 p123
Arckhoff, Henry; Buffalo, NY, 1847 1450.2 p2A
Arcy, Patrick D.; New York, NY, 1816 2859.11 p24
Ardecki, Stanislaw 28; New York, 1912 9980.29 p64
With niece
Arden, Henry; Virginia, 1638 6219 p124
Arden, Robert; Virginia, 1642 6219 p192
Ardin, Abraham 19; Pennsylvania, 1728 3690.1 p5
Ardin, John; Ohio, 1839 9892.11 p1
Ardin, John; Ohio, 1844 9892.11 p1
Ardington, Henry 14; Maryland, 1719 3690.1 p5
Ardis, Alexander; New York, NY, 1816 2859.11 p25
Ardouins, Mr. 35; Mexico, 1829 778.5 p11
Arduino, Pietro; Iowa, 1866-1943 123.54 p3
Aregon, Ellen 21; Massachusetts, 1847 5881.1 p5
Arenas, Ramone; California, 1869 2769.1 p3
Arend, George Philipp; Quebec, 1776 9786 p259
Arendall, Benjamin; South Carolina, 1788 7119 p202
Arends, Arend; Illinois, 1849 7857 p2
Arends, John; Illinois, 1888 5012.39 p52
Arenner, Bernard; New York, NY, 1811 2859.11 p8
Arens, . . .; Canada, 1776-1783 9786 p16
Arents, Agnes Streyper SEE Arents, Lenart
Arents, John Adam; Wisconsin, n.d. 9675.4 p193
Arents, Lenart; Pennsylvania, 1683 2155 p1
Wife:Agnes Streyper
Arents, Peter; Wisconsin, n.d. 9675.4 p193
Arenz, Franz; Illinois, 1805-1930 8125.8 p435
Arets, Agnes Streyper SEE Arets, Leonard
Arets, Leonard; Pennsylvania, 1683 2155 p1
Wife:Agnes Streyper
Arey, Robert; Virginia, 1646 6219 p240
Arfons, Tom; Arkansas, 1918 95.2 p14
Argan, Lawrence; Quebec, 1809 7603 p64
Argebrecht, Philipp; Ohio, 1800-1812 8582.2 p57
Argent, Adam 22; Maryland, 1774 1219.7 p181
Argent, George 17; North Carolina, 1736 3690.1 p6
Argenta, Angelo; Iowa, 1866-1943 123.54 p3
Argenta, Bortolo; Iowa, 1866-1943 123.54 p3
Argenta, Emilio; Iowa, 1866-1943 123.54 p3
Argenta, Luigi; Iowa, 1866-1943 123.54 p3
Argento, Sesar; Iowa, 1866-1943 123.54 p3
Argenton, A. 26; Port uncertain, 1837 778.5 p11
Argors, Richard 16; Georgia, 1774 1219.7 p188
Argue, Betrune 21; New Orleans, 1862 543.30 p235
Argue, George; Colorado, 1889 9678.1 p152
Arguse, Rich.; Virginia, 1637 6219 p24
Arin, Alice M. 31; Quebec, 1857 5704.8 p136
Arin, Eliza 6 mos; Quebec, 1857 5704.8 p136
Aring, Georg H.; America, 1837 8582.2 p1
Arionbar, Alexandre 35; America, 1821 778.5 p11
Arkane, Isaac; St. John, N.B., 1847 5704.8 p11
Arlinghaus, Herman; America, 1849 8582.3 p1
Armand, Mr. 22; New Orleans, 1839 778.5 p11
Armand, Mr. 30; America, 1822 778.5 p11
Armand, Mrs. 20; America, 1822 778.5 p11
Armand, Elizabeth 15; America, 1822 778.5 p11
Armand, Josef 50; America, 1831 778.5 p11
Armand, L. 20; New Orleans, 1823 778.5 p11
Armands, Mr. 50; Port uncertain, 1836 778.5 p11
Armant, Mme. 30; America, 1825 778.5 p11
Armant, J. Bte. 25; New Orleans, 1838 778.5 p11
Armant, John B. 15; New Orleans, 1836 778.5 p11
Armas, Salvatovae; Wisconsin, n.d. 9675.4 p193
Armatage, William 30; Maryland, 1773 1219.7 p173
Armbrecht, . . .; Canada, 1776-1783 9786 p16
Armbruster, Agnes SEE Armbruster, Martin
Armbruster, Andrew; Wisconsin, n.d. 9675.4 p193
Armbruster, Anna Maria Voeglin SEE Armbruster, Friedrich
Armbruster, Barbara SEE Armbruster, Martin
Armbruster, Bernhard; Wisconsin, n.d. 9675.4 p193
Armbruster, Christian; Colorado, 1900 9678.1 p152
Armbruster, Friedrich; Port uncertain, 1749-1800 2444 p133
Wife:Anna Maria Voeglin
Child:Johann Jacob
Child:Jacob Friedrich
Armbruster, Jacob Friedrich SEE Armbruster, Friedrich
Armbruster, Johann Jacob SEE Armbruster, Friedrich
Armbruster, John; Wisconsin, n.d. 9675.4 p193
Armbruster, Martin; Port uncertain, 1743-1800 2444 p133
Wife:Agnes
Child:Barbara
Armbruster, Robert; Colorado, 1902 9678.1 p152
Armburster, John; Wisconsin, n.d. 9675.4 p193
Armegnon, Pierre; New England, 1753 2444 p133
Armella, Martin; Iowa, 1866-1943 123.54 p3
Armellini, Domenius; Arkansas, 1918 95.2 p14
Armenaki, Ashella; Arkansas, 1918 95.2 p14
Armendrop, Peter; Ohio, 1840 9892.11 p1
Armenshon, Peter 40; Pennsylvania, 1753 2444 p133
Armeshon, Peter 40; Pennsylvania, 1753 2444 p133
Armeson, Pierre 40; Pennsylvania, 1753 2444 p133
Armestead, Ann SEE Armestead, William

Armestead, William; Virginia, 1636 ***6219*** *p1*
*Wife:*Ann
Armestrong, Geo.; Virginia, 1639 ***6219*** *p152*
Armetrading, Hen.; Virginia, 1635 ***6219*** *p69*
Armgrimsson, Sigurjon 1; Quebec, 1879 ***2557.1*** *p20*
Arminas, Josef 22; New York, NY, 1878 ***9253*** *p47*
Armingeon, Godefroy *SEE* Armingeon, Pierre
Armingeon, Jaques *SEE* Armingeon, Pierre
Armingeon, Jean Daniel *SEE* Armingeon, Pierre
Armingeon, Madeleine Vincent *SEE* Armingeon, Pierre
Armingeon, Pierre *SEE* Armingeon, Pierre
Armingeon, Pierre; New England, 1753 ***2444*** *p133*
*Wife:*Madeleine Vincent
*Child:*Pierre
*Child:*Jaques
*Child:*Godefroy
*Child:*Jean Daniel
Armingeon, Pierre 40; Pennsylvania, 1753 ***2444*** *p133*
Arminion, Peter 40; Pennsylvania, 1753 ***2444*** *p133*
Armistead, Joseph 17; Savannah, GA, 1775 ***1219.7*** *p274*
Armitage, John; New York, NY, 1811 ***2859.11*** *p8*
Armong, Jean 7; New Orleans, 1838 ***778.5*** *p12*
Armong, M. Bottu 34; New Orleans, 1838 ***778.5*** *p12*
Armour, Mr.; Quebec, 1815 ***9229.18*** *p78*
Armour, Janet; New York, NY, 1830 ***8894.2*** *p57*
Armour, Mary; Canada, 1832 ***8893*** *p263*
Arms, Friedrich; Vermont, 1777 ***8137*** *p6*
Armstead, Charity 21; Maryland, 1774 ***1219.7*** *p230*
Armstead, Joseph; Georgia, 1775 ***1219.7*** *p274*
Armstrong, Mr.; New York, NY, 1815 ***2859.11*** *p25*
With family
Armstrong, Alex; New York, NY, 1811 ***2859.11*** *p8*
Armstrong, Alexander 29; Philadelphia, 1803 ***53.26*** *p2*
Armstrong, Alice; St. John, N.B., 1853 ***5704.8*** *p99*
Armstrong, Andrew; Quebec, 1847 ***5704.8*** *p16*
Armstrong, Andrew 13; Quebec, 1847 ***5704.8*** *p16*
Armstrong, Ann; St. John, N.B., 1852 ***5704.8*** *p93*
Armstrong, Ann; St. John, N.B., 1853 ***5704.8*** *p98*
Armstrong, Arabella; New York, NY, 1811 ***2859.11*** *p8*
Armstrong, Arm.; New York, NY, 1811 ***2859.11*** *p8*
Armstrong, Arthur John 24; Arkansas, 1918 ***95.2*** *p15*
Armstrong, Bessey; St. John, N.B., 1851 ***5704.8*** *p79*
Armstrong, Bridget; Philadelphia, 1868 ***5704.8*** *p229*
Armstrong, Catherine; St. John, N.B., 1847 ***5704.8*** *p21*
Armstrong, Charles; Quebec, 1853 ***5704.8*** *p103*
Armstrong, Charles; St. John, N.B., 1851 ***5704.8*** *p80*
Armstrong, Christianna; St. John, N.B., 1847 ***5704.8*** *p19*
Armstrong, Christopher; St. John, N.B., 1847 ***5704.8*** *p19*
Armstrong, Christopher 9; St. John, N.B., 1847 ***5704.8*** *p19*
Armstrong, David; St. John, N.B., 1847 ***5704.8*** *p33*
Armstrong, Edish; Quebec, 1851 ***5704.8*** *p82*
Armstrong, Edward; Philadelphia, 1847 ***53.26*** *p2*
Armstrong, Edward; Philadelphia, 1847 ***5704.8*** *p22*
Armstrong, Edward; St. John, N.B., 1847 ***5704.8*** *p19*
Armstrong, Elen 8; Philadelphia, 1851 ***5704.8*** *p76*
Armstrong, Eliz.; New York, NY, 1811 ***2859.11*** *p8*
Armstrong, Eliza; New York, NY, 1811 ***2859.11*** *p8*
Armstrong, Eliza 13; St. John, N.B., 1853 ***5704.8*** *p99*
Armstrong, Elizabeth; Quebec, 1847 ***5704.8*** *p16*
Armstrong, Elizabeth; Quebec, 1851 ***5704.8*** *p75*
Armstrong, Ellen; New York, NY, 1858 ***3455.2*** *p77*
Armstrong, Ellen; New York, NY, 1858 ***3455.3*** *p51*
Armstrong, Fanny; New York, NY, 1816 ***2859.11*** *p25*
With 4 children
Armstrong, George; America, 1739 ***4971*** *p47*
Armstrong, George; America, 1741 ***4971*** *p49*
Armstrong, Henry 25; Massachusetts, 1849 ***5881.1*** *p5*
Armstrong, Henry 51; Massachusetts, 1849 ***5881.1*** *p5*
Armstrong, Hugh; New York, NY, 1815 ***2859.11*** *p25*
Armstrong, Hugh; Philadelphia, 1851 ***5704.8*** *p76*
Armstrong, Irvin; St. John, N.B., 1847 ***5704.8*** *p19*
Armstrong, Irvine 9; Quebec, 1853 ***5704.8*** *p103*
Armstrong, Irwin 9 mos; Quebec, 1851 ***5704.8*** *p82*
Armstrong, Isaac; New York, NY, 1811 ***2859.11*** *p8*
Armstrong, Isabella; Quebec, 1853 ***5704.8*** *p103*
Armstrong, Isabella 13; Quebec, 1853 ***5704.8*** *p103*
Armstrong, Isabella 20; St. John, N.B., 1854 ***5704.8*** *p121*
Armstrong, Isabella 25; St. John, N.B., 1861 ***5704.8*** *p146*
Armstrong, Isabella 50; St. John, N.B., 1861 ***5704.8*** *p146*
Armstrong, James; New York, NY, 1815 ***2859.11*** *p25*
Armstrong, James; Petersburg, VA, 1811 ***4778.2*** *p142*
Armstrong, James; Philadelphia, 1816 ***2859.11*** *p25*
Armstrong, James; Quebec, 1847 ***5704.8*** *p16*
Armstrong, James 6; Quebec, 1851 ***5704.8*** *p82*
Armstrong, James 20; St. John, N.B., 1861 ***5704.8*** *p146*
Armstrong, James 21; St. John, N.B., 1856 ***5704.8*** *p131*
Armstrong, James 50; St. John, N.B., 1861 ***5704.8*** *p146*
Armstrong, Jane; Philadelphia, 1849 ***53.26*** *p2*
Armstrong, Jane; Philadelphia, 1849 ***5704.8*** *p49*
Armstrong, Jane; Quebec, 1853 ***5704.8*** *p104*
Armstrong, Jane; St. John, N.B., 1847 ***5704.8*** *p19*
Armstrong, Jane 8; Quebec, 1851 ***5704.8*** *p82*
Armstrong, Jane 10; St. John, N.B., 1852 ***5704.8*** *p93*
Armstrong, Jane 40; Philadelphia, 1853 ***5704.8*** *p114*
Armstrong, John; America, 1737 ***4971*** *p63*
Armstrong, John; America, 1738 ***4971*** *p72*
Armstrong, John; America, 1741 ***4971*** *p76*
Armstrong, John; Iroquois Co., IL, 1892 ***3455.1*** *p9*
Armstrong, John; New York, NY, 1811 ***2859.11*** *p8*
Armstrong, John; New York, NY, 1816 ***2859.11*** *p25*
Armstrong, John; Quebec, 1850 ***5704.8*** *p67*
Armstrong, John; Quebec, 1851 ***5704.8*** *p82*
Armstrong, John; St. John, N.B., 1847 ***5704.8*** *p21*
Armstrong, John; St. John, N.B., 1848 ***5704.8*** *p44*
Armstrong, John; St. John, N.B., 1853 ***5704.8*** *p98*
Armstrong, John; St. John, N.B., 1853 ***5704.8*** *p107*
Armstrong, John 8; St. John, N.B., 1852 ***5704.8*** *p93*
Armstrong, John 20; St. John, N.B., 1856 ***5704.8*** *p131*
Armstrong, John 23; St. John, N.B., 1861 ***5704.8*** *p146*
Armstrong, John 25; New York, 1775 ***1219.7*** *p268*
With wife
Armstrong, John 25; Philadelphia, 1856 ***5704.8*** *p128*
Armstrong, John 29; Philadelphia, 1803 ***53.26*** *p2*
Armstrong, John James 12; St. John, N.B., 1847 ***5704.8*** *p33*
Armstrong, Letitia; St. John, N.B., 1847 ***5704.8*** *p33*
Armstrong, Letitia 9; St. John, N.B., 1847 ***5704.8*** *p33*
Armstrong, Marg.; New York, NY, 1811 ***2859.11*** *p8*
With child
Armstrong, Margaret; Philadelphia, 1850 ***53.26*** *p2*
Armstrong, Margaret; Philadelphia, 1850 ***5704.8*** *p69*
Armstrong, Margaret; St. John, N.B., 1853 ***5704.8*** *p106*
Armstrong, Martha; Quebec, 1851 ***5704.8*** *p82*
Armstrong, Mary; Quebec, 1853 ***5704.8*** *p104*
Armstrong, Mary; St. John, N.B., 1847 ***5704.8*** *p19*
Armstrong, Mary; St. John, N.B., 1851 ***5704.8*** *p79*
Armstrong, Mary 11; Quebec, 1851 ***5704.8*** *p82*
Armstrong, Mary 17; St. John, N.B., 1858 ***5704.8*** *p137*
Armstrong, Mary 27 *SEE* Armstrong, Thomas
Armstrong, Mary Ann 20; St. John, N.B., 1854 ***5704.8*** *p120*
Armstrong, Mary J.; Philadelphia, 1865 ***5704.8*** *p199*
Armstrong, Mary J.; St. John, N.B., 1847 ***5704.8*** *p21*
Armstrong, Mary Jane 10; St. John, N.B., 1861 ***5704.8*** *p146*
Armstrong, Mathew 23; Philadelphia, 1803 ***53.26*** *p2*
Armstrong, R.; New York, NY, 1811 ***2859.11*** *p8*
Armstrong, Rachael 25; Philadelphia, 1861 ***5704.8*** *p147*
Armstrong, Richard; Quebec, 1847 ***5704.8*** *p16*
Armstrong, Robert; Indiana, 1824 ***9117*** *p14*
Armstrong, Robert; Montreal, 1824 ***7603*** *p53*
Armstrong, Robert; Quebec, 1849 ***5704.8*** *p57*
Armstrong, Robert; St. John, N.B., 1847 ***5704.8*** *p19*
Armstrong, Robert 4; St. John, N.B., 1852 ***5704.8*** *p93*
Armstrong, Robert 18; Philadelphia, 1860 ***5704.8*** *p145*
Armstrong, Sally; Quebec, 1850 ***5704.8*** *p66*
Armstrong, Samuel; Philadelphia, 1816 ***2859.11*** *p25*
Armstrong, Samuel; Philadelphia, 1847 ***53.26*** *p2*
Armstrong, Samuel; Philadelphia, 1847 ***5704.8*** *p21*
Armstrong, Samuel; St. John, N.B., 1852 ***5704.8*** *p93*
Armstrong, Sarah; Philadelphia, 1851 ***5704.8*** *p76*
Armstrong, Sarah; St. John, N.B., 1849 ***5704.8*** *p56*
Armstrong, Sarah; St. John, N.B., 1851 ***5704.8*** *p80*
Armstrong, Sarah 6; St. John, N.B., 1847 ***5704.8*** *p19*
Armstrong, Sarah 10; Philadelphia, 1851 ***5704.8*** *p76*
Armstrong, Sarah 14; St. John, N.B., 1861 ***5704.8*** *p146*
Armstrong, Sarah 20; St. John, N.B., 1861 ***5704.8*** *p147*
Armstrong, Stewart; New York, NY, 1837 ***8208.4*** *p34*
Armstrong, Thomas; America, 1738 ***4971*** *p72*
Armstrong, Thomas; Brunswick, NC, 1739 ***1639.20*** *p4*
Armstrong, Thomas; New York, NY, 1838 ***8208.4*** *p65*
Armstrong, Thomas; Philadelphia, 1769 ***1219.7*** *p140*
Armstrong, Thomas; Quebec, 1847 ***5704.8*** *p16*
Armstrong, Thomas; St. John, N.B., 1851 ***5704.8*** *p72*
Armstrong, Thomas 2; St. John, N.B., 1851 ***5704.8*** *p79*
Armstrong, Thomas 11; St. John, N.B., 1847 ***5704.8*** *p19*
Armstrong, Thomas 20; St. Christopher, 1722 ***3690.1*** *p6*
Armstrong, Thomas 31; Philadelphia, 1803 ***53.26*** *p2*
*Relative:*Mary 27
Armstrong, William; America, 1736-1743 ***4971*** *p57*
Armstrong, William; New York, NY, 1834 ***8208.4*** *p26*
Armstrong, William; Ohio, 1867-1871 ***9892.11*** *p1*
Armstrong, William; Ohio, 1878 ***9892.11*** *p1*
Armstrong, William; Philadelphia, 1851 ***5704.8*** *p80*
Armstrong, William; St. John, N.B., 1847 ***5704.8*** *p19*
Armstrong, William; St. John, N.B., 1853 ***5704.8*** *p106*
Armstrong, William 9; St. John, N.B., 1853 ***5704.8*** *p106*
Armstrong, William 30; New York, 1775 ***1219.7*** *p269*
Armstrong, Wm.; New York, NY, 1811 ***2859.11*** *p8*
Armuth, Peter Heinrich; America, 1856 ***4610.10*** *p139*
Armye, Thomas; Virginia, 1638 ***6219*** *p150*
Arnack, Christopher; New York, NY, 1839 ***8208.4*** *p100*
Arnadottir, Ingibjorg 15; Quebec, 1879 ***2557.1*** *p20*
Arnadottir, Olafia 20; Quebec, 1879 ***2557.1*** *p20*
Arnadottir, Sigurbjorg 13; Quebec, 1879 ***2557.1*** *p20*
Arnadottir, Stefania 18; Quebec, 1879 ***2557.1*** *p20*
Arnadottir, Thuridur 60; Quebec, 1879 ***2557.1*** *p38*
Arnall, Robt.; Virginia, 1635 ***6219*** *p70*
Arnall, William; Virginia, 1621 ***6219*** *p34*
Arnason, Matusalem 22; Quebec, 1879 ***2557.1*** *p20*
Arnason, Sigurjon 1; Quebec, 1879 ***2557.1*** *p20*
Arnaud, Mr. 8; America, 1826 ***778.5*** *p12*
Arnaud, Mr. 30; New Orleans, 1839 ***778.5*** *p12*
Arnaud, D. 33; New Orleans, 1832 ***778.5*** *p12*
Arnaud, H.; New Orleans, 1839 ***778.5*** *p12*
Arnaud, H. 20; New Orleans, 1822 ***778.5*** *p12*
Arnaud, J. 27; New Orleans, 1835 ***778.5*** *p12*
Arnaud, J. C. 30; America, 1826 ***778.5*** *p12*
Arnaud, J. D. 25; New Orleans, 1822 ***778.5*** *p12*
Arnaud, J. P. 30; New Orleans, 1823 ***778.5*** *p12*
Arnaud, Joseph 22; New Orleans, 1835 ***778.5*** *p12*
Arnaud, Laurent 17; America, 1839 ***778.5*** *p12*
Arnaud, Louis 25; Mexico, 1827 ***778.5*** *p12*
Arnaud, Louis 25; New Orleans, 1826 ***778.5*** *p12*
Arnaud, Pierre 45; Quebec, 1667 ***4533*** *p126*
Arnaud, V. 18; New Orleans, 1839 ***778.5*** *p13*
Arnd, Charles Frederick 15 *SEE* Arnd, Charles Fredr.
Arnd, Charles Fredr. 36; New Orleans, 1839 ***9420.2*** *p484*
*Wife:*Jane Dorothea 36
*Son:*Charles Frederick 15
*Daughter:*Wilhelmine 7
Arnd, Jane Dorothea 36 *SEE* Arnd, Charles Fredr.
Arnd, Wilhelmine 7 *SEE* Arnd, Charles Fredr.
Arndall, Kath.; Virginia, 1639 ***6219*** *p154*
Arndt, Carl Hermann; Wisconsin, n.d. ***9675.4*** *p193*
Arndt, Mary; Minnesota, 1901 ***5240.1*** *p3*
Arndt, Rosina; New York, 1749 ***3652*** *p72*
Arndur, Samuel; Arkansas, 1918 ***95.2*** *p15*
Arneill, James; Philadelphia, 1852 ***5704.8*** *p85*
Arneill, Margaret; Philadelphia, 1852 ***5704.8*** *p85*
Arneill, Mary; Philadelphia, 1852 ***5704.8*** *p85*
Arnelius, J. P.; Washington, 1859-1920 ***2872.1*** *p2*
Arnelius, John P.; Washington, 1859-1920 ***2872.1*** *p2*
Arnell, William 18; Jamaica, 1725 ***3690.1*** *p6*
Arneson, John; Arkansas, 1918 ***95.2*** *p15*
Arneson, Martin; Washington, 1859-1920 ***2872.1*** *p2*
Arnett, John 20; Virginia, 1775 ***1219.7*** *p247*
Arngrimsdottir, Ingibjorg 15; Quebec, 1879 ***2557.1*** *p20*
Arngrimsdottir, Olafia 20; Quebec, 1879 ***2557.1*** *p20*
Arngrimsdottir, Sigurbjorg 13; Quebec, 1879 ***2557.1*** *p20*
Arngrimsdottir, Stefania 18; Quebec, 1879 ***2557.1*** *p20*
Arngrimsson, Matusalem 22; Quebec, 1879 ***2557.1*** *p20*
Arngusson, Ingibjorg 15; Quebec, 1879 ***2557.1*** *p20*
Arngusson, Matusalem 22; Quebec, 1879 ***2557.1*** *p20*
Arngusson, Olafia 20; Quebec, 1879 ***2557.1*** *p20*
Arngusson, Sigurbjorg 13; Quebec, 1879 ***2557.1*** *p20*
Arngusson, Sigurjon 1; Quebec, 1879 ***2557.1*** *p20*
Arngusson, Stefania 18; Quebec, 1879 ***2557.1*** *p20*
Arnhold, Carl 16 *SEE* Arnhold, Wilhelm
Arnhold, Heinrich 13 *SEE* Arnhold, Wilhelm
Arnhold, Louise 53 *SEE* Arnhold, Wilhelm
Arnhold, Wilhelm 58; America, 1869 ***4610.10*** *p149*
*Wife:*Louise 53
*Child:*Carl 16
*Child:*Heinrich 13
Arnholter, Carl 16 *SEE* Arnholter, Wilhelm
Arnholter, Carl Friedrich Wilhelm; America, 1868 ***4610.10*** *p149*
Arnholter, Heinrich 13 *SEE* Arnholter, Wilhelm
Arnholter, Louise 53 *SEE* Arnholter, Wilhelm
Arnholter, Wilhelm 58; America, 1869 ***4610.10*** *p149*
*Wife:*Louise 53
*Child:*Carl 16
*Child:*Heinrich 13
Arnice, John; Virginia, 1635 ***6219*** *p1*
*Wife:*Marie
*Son:*William
Arnice, Marie *SEE* Arnice, John
Arnice, William *SEE* Arnice, John
Arnidt, Johan; Wisconsin, n.d. ***9675.4*** *p193*
Arnold, . . .; Canada, 1776-1783 ***9786*** *p16*
Arnold, Mr. 26; New Orleans, 1822 ***778.5*** *p13*
Arnold, Mr. 38; New Orleans, 1822 ***778.5*** *p13*
Arnold, Andrew 68; Arizona, 1926 ***9228.40*** *p30*
Arnold, Anna Catharina *SEE* Arnold, Maria
Arnold, Anna Catharina; Pennsylvania, 1754 ***2444*** *p220*
Arnold, Anna Kathr. 3; America, 1854-1855 ***9162.6*** *p105*
Arnold, Anna Ottilia; America, 1754 ***4349*** *p46*
Arnold, Barbara *SEE* Arnold, Maria
Arnold, Carl; Wisconsin, n.d. ***9675.4*** *p193*
Arnold, Catherine 21; Philadelphia, 1855 ***5704.8*** *p124*
Arnold, Charles; New York, NY, 1832 ***1450.2*** *p4A*
Arnold, Edward 16; Philadelphia, 1774 ***1219.7*** *p232*

Arnold, Elizabeth 20; Jamaica, 1736 ***3690.1*** *p6*
Arnold, Florent; Illinois, 1892 ***5012.40*** *p26*
Arnold, Francis; New York, NY, 1838 ***8208.4*** *p75*
Arnold, Franziska 25; America, 1854-1855 ***9162.6*** *p105*
Arnold, George 20; America, 1835 ***778.5*** *p13*
Arnold, J.; New York, NY, 1816 ***2859.11*** *p25*
Arnold, James; New York, NY, 1815 ***2859.11*** *p25*
Arnold, James; New York, NY, 1816 ***2859.11*** *p25*
Arnold, James Henry; California, 1872 ***2769.1*** *p4*
Arnold, Johann; America, 1847 ***8582.3*** *p1*
Arnold, Joyce; Virginia, 1640 ***6219*** *p184*
Arnold, Louis; Wisconsin, n.d. ***9675.4*** *p193*
Arnold, Margarett; Virginia, 1641 ***6219*** *p184*
Arnold, Maria; Pennsylvania, 1754 ***2444*** *p194*
*Sister:*Anna Catharina
*Sister:*Barbara
Arnold, Peter 71; Arizona, 1914 ***9228.40*** *p18*
Arnold, Philip; America, 1848 ***1450.2*** *p4A*
Arnold, Richard Jackson; California, 1872 ***2769.1*** *p4*
Arnold, Robert 18; Maryland, 1723 ***3690.1*** *p6*
Arnold, Robt.; Virginia, 1637 ***6219*** *p180*
Arnold, Rosina Barbara; New York, 1749 ***3652*** *p72*
Arnold, Thomas 27; Maryland, 1774 ***1219.7*** *p187*
Arnold, Willi.; Virginia, 1638 ***6219*** *p11*
Arnold, William; New York, NY, 1816 ***2859.11*** *p25*
Arnold, William 21; Maryland, 1774 ***1219.7*** *p181*
Arnold, Wm.; Virginia, 1647 ***6219*** *p239*
Arnoldi, . . .; Canada, 1776-1783 ***9786*** *p41*
Arnoll, Robert; Virginia, 1638 ***6219*** *p121*
Arnot, William; South Carolina, 1790 ***1639.20*** *p4*
Arnott, David 20; Georgia, 1775 ***1219.7*** *p276*
Arnott, James 19; Philadelphia, 1854 ***5704.8*** *p117*
Arnott, Jane; Philadelphia, 1853 ***5704.8*** *p101*
Arnott, Mary; Philadelphia, 1853 ***5704.8*** *p101*
Arnoud, Jean 1; Port uncertain, 1836 ***778.5*** *p13*
Arnoud, Jeanne 30; Port uncertain, 1836 ***778.5*** *p13*
Arnoud, Lewis 28; New Orleans, 1831 ***778.5*** *p13*
Arnoult, Francois 32; America, 1836 ***778.5*** *p13*
Arnoult, Marie 32; New Orleans, 1838 ***778.5*** *p13*
Arns, Valentine; New Orleans, 1848-1856 ***1450.2*** *p4A*
Arnscough, Abel; Iowa, 1866-1943 ***123.54*** *p3*
Arnsdorf, Andr. Lorentz; Georgia, 1734 ***9332*** *p328*
Arnsdorf, Dorothea; Georgia, 1739 ***9332*** *p327*
*Son:*Peter 16
*Daughter:*Sophia 14
*Daughter:*Margaretha 12
*Daughter:*Dorothea 9
Arnsdorf, Dorothea 9 *SEE* Arnsdorf, Dorothea
Arnsdorf, Margaretha 12 *SEE* Arnsdorf, Dorothea
Arnsdorf, Peter 16 *SEE* Arnsdorf, Dorothea
Arnsdorf, Sophia 14 *SEE* Arnsdorf, Dorothea
Arnsley, John 46; Maryland, 1774 ***1219.7*** *p193*
Arntz, Albert; Wisconsin, n.d. ***9675.4*** *p193*
Arntzen, Juris Bernard; Illinois, 1849 ***8582.2*** *p51*
Arnvig, Svend 22; Arkansas, 1918 ***95.2*** *p15*
Arnwood, Roger; Virginia, 1635 ***6219*** *p71*
Arnwood, Roger; Virginia, 1638 ***6219*** *p121*
Aro, Evert; Arkansas, 1918 ***95.2*** *p15*
Arobbio, Joseph; Arkansas, 1918 ***95.2*** *p15*
Aron, Rich.; Virginia, 1643 ***6219*** *p202*
Aronne, Andrew; Arkansas, 1918 ***95.2*** *p15*
Aronson, Bengt; Minneapolis, 1867-1877 ***6410.35*** *p49*
Aronson, Fritz; Colorado, 1903 ***9678.1*** *p152*
Aronsson, Bengt; Minneapolis, 1867-1877 ***6410.35*** *p49*
Arpe, Peter; Virginia, 1638 ***6219*** *p159*
Arpene, Peter 26; Louisiana, 1863 ***543.30*** *p323*
Arpin, Mr. 29; America, 1839 ***778.5*** *p13*
Arquilla, Franco; Wisconsin, n.d. ***9675.4*** *p193*
Arrene, LeProne 35; America, 1835 ***778.5*** *p13*
Arridson, John A.; Iowa, 1866-1943 ***123.54*** *p3*
Arrigo, August; Arkansas, 1918 ***95.2*** *p15*
Arris, Jon.; Virginia, 1642 ***6219*** *p191*
Arrol, Jane 46; Quebec, 1853 ***5704.8*** *p105*
Arron, Jean 31; Port uncertain, 1839 ***778.5*** *p13*
Arrore, Alex 21; Kansas, 1901 ***5240.1*** *p82*
Arrye, Daniel; Virginia, 1638 ***6219*** *p14*
Arsement, Guillaume; Louisiana, 1789-1819 ***778.5*** *p555*
Arskine, Joseph 56; Philadelphia, 1804 ***53.26*** *p2*
Arson, Joe; Arkansas, 1918 ***95.2*** *p15*
Arson, John; Iowa, 1866-1943 ***123.54*** *p3*
Artale, Joe 25; Arkansas, 1918 ***95.2*** *p15*
Artaux, P. 32; America, 1835 ***778.5*** *p13*
Arte, Nick; Arkansas, 1918 ***95.2*** *p15*
Arteine, Roger; Virginia, 1642 ***6219*** *p189*
Arthur, . . .; Virginia, 1635 ***6219*** *p3*
Arthur, Alexander; West Virginia, 1821 ***9788.3*** *p4*
Arthur, Armstrong 9 mos; Philadelphia, 1854 ***5704.8*** *p118*
Arthur, Catherine; Quebec, 1847 ***5704.8*** *p29*
Arthur, Catherine 7; Quebec, 1847 ***5704.8*** *p29*
Arthur, Edward; Quebec, 1847 ***5704.8*** *p29*
Arthur, Eliza Jane 3; Quebec, 1859 ***5704.8*** *p143*
Arthur, Elizabeth; Quebec, 1847 ***5704.8*** *p29*
Arthur, Elizabeth 5; Quebec, 1847 ***5704.8*** *p29*
Arthur, Elizabeth Letitia 20; Philadelphia, 1858 ***5704.8*** *p138*
Arthur, Ellan; Quebec, 1847 ***5704.8*** *p29*
Arthur, Ellan 10; Quebec, 1847 ***5704.8*** *p29*
Arthur, Gaby; Quebec, 1847 ***5704.8*** *p29*
Arthur, Gryffith 21; Maryland or Virginia, 1699 ***2212*** *p24*
Arthur, Henry 5; Quebec, 1863 ***5704.8*** *p154*
Arthur, James; America, 1786 ***8893*** *p264*
Arthur, James; Philadelphia, 1811 ***53.26*** *p2*
Arthur, James; Philadelphia, 1811 ***2859.11*** *p8*
Arthur, James; Quebec, 1847 ***5704.8*** *p29*
Arthur, James; Virginia, 1642 ***6219*** *p197*
Arthur, James 12; Quebec, 1847 ***5704.8*** *p17*
Arthur, John; Philadelphia, 1849 ***53.26*** *p2*
Arthur, John; Philadelphia, 1849 ***5704.8*** *p52*
Arthur, John; Philadelphia, 1853 ***5704.8*** *p102*
Arthur, John; Quebec, 1847 ***5704.8*** *p29*
Arthur, John; Washington, 1859-1920 ***2872.1*** *p2*
Arthur, John 9 mos; Quebec, 1847 ***5704.8*** *p29*
Arthur, John 30; Quebec, 1863 ***5704.8*** *p154*
Arthur, Joseph; New York, NY, 1816 ***2859.11*** *p25*
Arthur, Margaret 20; St. John, N.B., 1857 ***5704.8*** *p135*
Arthur, Margaret 28; Quebec, 1859 ***5704.8*** *p143*
Arthur, Mary; Quebec, 1847 ***5704.8*** *p29*
Arthur, Mary 3; Quebec, 1847 ***5704.8*** *p29*
Arthur, Mary Ann; Quebec, 1847 ***5704.8*** *p29*
Arthur, Nancy; Philadelphia, 1848 ***53.26*** *p2*
Arthur, Nancy; Philadelphia, 1848 ***5704.8*** *p46*
Arthur, Rebecca; New York, NY, 1816 ***2859.11*** *p25*
Arthur, Richard 3; Quebec, 1863 ***5704.8*** *p154*
Arthur, Robert 20; Quebec, 1854 ***5704.8*** *p121*
Arthur, Rosanna 20; Philadelphia, 1854 ***5704.8*** *p118*
Arthur, Samuel 5; Quebec, 1859 ***5704.8*** *p143*
Arthur, Sarah 30; Quebec, 1863 ***5704.8*** *p154*
Arthur, Thomas 1; Quebec, 1859 ***5704.8*** *p143*
Arthur, Thomas 13; Quebec, 1847 ***5704.8*** *p29*
Arthur, William 9 mos; Quebec, 1847 ***5704.8*** *p17*
Arthur, William 7; Quebec, 1863 ***5704.8*** *p154*
Arthur, William 18; Quebec, 1854 ***5704.8*** *p121*
Arthurs, Alice; Virginia, 1642 ***6219*** *p34*
Arthurs, Alice; Virginia, 1642 ***6219*** *p195*
Arthurs, Christ.; Virginia, 1642 ***6219*** *p34*
Arthurs, Christ.; Virginia, 1642 ***6219*** *p195*
Arthurs, James; Virginia, 1642 ***6219*** *p34*
Arthurs, James; Virginia, 1642 ***6219*** *p195*
Arthurs, Martha; Montreal, 1821 ***7603*** *p53*
Arthurs, Mary 36; Maryland, 1775 ***1219.7*** *p257*
Arthurs, Thomas 35; Maryland, 1775 ***1219.7*** *p257*
Artiga, Jean 26; New Orleans, 1838 ***778.5*** *p13*
Artiguenave, Mme. 27; Port uncertain, 1839 ***778.5*** *p14*
Artiguenave, Ms.; Port uncertain, 1839 ***778.5*** *p13*
Artiguenave, Aline 6; Port uncertain, 1839 ***778.5*** *p14*
Artiquenave, Jean 28; New Orleans, 1838 ***778.5*** *p14*
Artmann, Franz; Cincinnati, 1869-1887 ***8582*** *p1*
Arundel, Peter; Virginia, 1623-1632 ***6219*** *p67*
Arundell, James; Virginia, 1637 ***6219*** *p82*
Arvidson, Charles; Maine, 1886-1896 ***6410.22*** *p122*
Arvidson, John; Maine, 1888-1896 ***6410.22*** *p123*
Arvidsson, Carl Gustaf; Minneapolis, 1880-1887 ***6410.35*** *p53*
Arvince, Ferdinand 35; America, 1839 ***778.5*** *p14*
Asacks, James 18; America, 1836 ***778.5*** *p14*
Asareto, Aurore 17; New Orleans, 1829 ***778.5*** *p14*
Asareto, Clotilde 13; New Orleans, 1829 ***778.5*** *p14*
Asareto, Ernest 8; New Orleans, 1829 ***778.5*** *p14*
Asbjornsson, Bjorn 30; Quebec, 1879 ***2557.1*** *p20*
Asbjornsson, Josef 28; Quebec, 1879 ***2557.1*** *p20*
Aschan, Ernst; Washington, 1859-1920 ***2872.1*** *p2*
Aschenbrener, Joseph 54; Kansas, 1894 ***5240.1*** *p79*
Aschenbrenner, Joe F.; Arkansas, 1918 ***95.2*** *p15*
Aschenbrenner, Joseph 54; Kansas, 1894 ***5240.1*** *p4*
Aschenbrenner, Peter; Washington, 1859-1920 ***2872.1*** *p2*
Aschert, Gustav; Wisconsin, n.d. ***9675.4*** *p193*
Ascke, Fredrick; Wisconsin, n.d. ***9675.4*** *p193*
Ascome, Tho 12; America, 1699 ***2212*** *p28*
Ascough, Richard; Virginia, 1635 ***6219*** *p32*
Ascroft, Henry 20; Virginia, 1699 ***2212*** *p26*
Asemissen, William; America, 1894 ***1450.2*** *p4A*
Asendorf, Dietrich 34; Kansas, 1888 ***5240.1*** *p4*
Asendorf, Dietrich 34; Kansas, 1888 ***5240.1*** *p72*
Asendorf, Henry; Iroquois Co., IL, 1895 ***3455.1*** *p9*
Asfendianos, John George; Arkansas, 1918 ***95.2*** *p15*
Ash, Alexander 1; St. John, N.B., 1848 ***5704.8*** *p43*
Ash, Anne; St. John, N.B., 1848 ***5704.8*** *p43*
Ash, Cath.; New York, NY, 1816 ***2859.11*** *p25*
Ash, Catharine 25; Massachusetts, 1849 ***5881.1*** *p5*
Ash, David; Philadelphia, 1848 ***53.26*** *p2*
Ash, David; Philadelphia, 1848 ***5704.8*** *p40*
Ash, Gottlieb; America, 1868 ***6014.1*** *p1*
Ash, Jacob; America, 1857 ***6014.1*** *p1*
Ash, Jane 23; Philadelphia, 1855 ***5704.8*** *p124*
Ash, Joseph; Iowa, 1866-1943 ***123.54*** *p3*
Ash, Robert 17; Maryland, 1719 ***3690.1*** *p6*
Ash, Robert 20; Wilmington, DE, 1831 ***6508.3*** *p100*
Ash, Thomas 29; Massachusetts, 1850 ***5881.1*** *p6*
Ashall, Georg; Virginia, 1641 ***6219*** *p184*
Ashbgarndottir, Bjorg 4; Quebec, 1879 ***2557.1*** *p20*
Ashbifoote, John; Virginia, 1646 ***6219*** *p236*
Ashbjarnsson, Bjorn 30; Quebec, 1879 ***2557.1*** *p20*
Ashbjarnsson, Josef 28; Quebec, 1879 ***2557.1*** *p20*
Ashburn, George; Maryland, 1742 ***4971*** *p106*
Ashburne, William 28; Virginia, 1773 ***1219.7*** *p170*
Ashcomb, John; Virginia, 1646 ***6219*** *p240*
Ashcomb, John, Jr.; Virginia, 1646 ***6219*** *p240*
Ashcomb, Winifrid; Virginia, 1646 ***6219*** *p240*
Ashe, John; Virginia, 1642 ***6219*** *p187*
Asheley, Peter; Virginia, 1622 ***6219*** *p27*
Ashenhurst, Martha; Quebec, 1852 ***5704.8*** *p94*
Asher, John 28; Virginia, 1773 ***1219.7*** *p169*
Ashers, John 22; Jamaica, 1738 ***3690.1*** *p6*
Ashfeild, James; Virginia, 1636 ***6219*** *p27*
Ashfield, Betty; St. John, N.B., 1848 ***5704.8*** *p39*
Ashfield, Hanson; St. John, N.B., 1848 ***5704.8*** *p39*
Ashfield, James 5; St. John, N.B., 1848 ***5704.8*** *p39*
Ashfield, John 13; St. John, N.B., 1848 ***5704.8*** *p39*
Ashfield, Lea; St. John, N.B., 1848 ***5704.8*** *p39*
Ashfield, Lea 1; St. John, N.B., 1848 ***5704.8*** *p39*
Ashfield, Rachel 9; St. John, N.B., 1848 ***5704.8*** *p39*
Ashfield, William 6; St. John, N.B., 1848 ***5704.8*** *p39*
Ashinhurst, Anne; Quebec, 1852 ***5704.8*** *p94*
Ashinhurst, Eliza Margaret 8; Quebec, 1852 ***5704.8*** *p94*
Ashinhurst, George; Quebec, 1852 ***5704.8*** *p94*
Ashinhurst, John; Quebec, 1852 ***5704.8*** *p94*
Ashinhurst, Mary; Quebec, 1852 ***5704.8*** *p94*
Ashinhurst, Matilda 13; Quebec, 1852 ***5704.8*** *p94*
Ashinhurst, Robert; Quebec, 1852 ***5704.8*** *p94*
Ashinhurst, Robert 10; Quebec, 1852 ***5704.8*** *p94*
Ashinhurst, Sarah Jane 12; Quebec, 1852 ***5704.8*** *p94*
Ashinhurst, William; Quebec, 1851 ***5704.8*** *p82*
Ashjian, Karopp; Connecticut, 1895 ***1450.2*** *p5A*
Ashjian, Seraph; America, 1892 ***1450.2*** *p5A*
Ashley, Ann 20; Virginia, 1699 ***2212*** *p27*
Ashley, Charles; Virginia, 1769 ***1219.7*** *p140*
Ashley, Daniel; New York, NY, 1816 ***2859.11*** *p25*
Ashley, John; Barbados, 1751 ***1219.7*** *p7*
Ashley, Nicholas; New York, NY, 1839 ***8208.4*** *p100*
Ashley, Samuel; Kingston, Jamaica, 1762 ***1219.7*** *p90*
Ashling, George 35; Philadelphia, 1774 ***1219.7*** *p216*
Ashly, Robert; Virginia, 1639 ***6219*** *p162*
Ashly, Tho.; Virginia, 1635 ***6219*** *p69*
Ashman, Alfred; Arizona, 1889 ***2764.35*** *p1*
Ashman, Joseph Wolfe; Philadelphia, 1832 ***8208.4*** *p38*
Ashton, Albert E.; Boston, 1920 ***3455.4*** *p82*
Ashton, Albert Ernest; Boston, 1920 ***3455.4*** *p81*
Ashton, Charles; Virginia, 1652 ***6251*** *p20*
Ashton, Edwd 21; America, 1705 ***2212*** *p43*
Ashton, Elizabeth; Virginia, 1698 ***2212*** *p12*
Ashton, H.H.; Iowa, 1866-1943 ***123.54*** *p3*
Ashton, Jno 20; America, 1703 ***2212*** *p38*
Ashton, Joane; Virginia, 1638 ***6219*** *p123*
Ashton, John 27; Maryland, 1775 ***1219.7*** *p257*
Ashton, John 29; Jamaica, 1730 ***3690.1*** *p289*
Ashton, Thomas; Virginia, 1635 ***6219*** *p23*
Ashton, Walter; Virginia, 1638 ***6219*** *p2*
*Wife:*Warbowe
Ashton, Warbowe *SEE* Ashton, Walter
Ashton, William 26; Virginia, 1775 ***1219.7*** *p246*
Ashwell, Henry; Virginia, 1639 ***6219*** *p161*
Ashworth, Jno 30; America, 1699 ***2212*** *p28*
Asimackipoulas, George; Arkansas, 1918 ***95.2*** *p15*
Asimackipoulos, George; Arkansas, 1918 ***95.2*** *p15*
Askansas, Abraham Leib; Colorado, 1893 ***9678.1*** *p152*
Askeland, Albert Johan 31; Arkansas, 1918 ***95.2*** *p15*
Asken, Mary Anne 5; Quebec, 1851 ***5704.8*** *p75*
Askew, William Addison; Arkansas, 1918 ***95.2*** *p15*
Askie, John 14; America, 1701 ***2212*** *p35*
Askin, Elizabeth; Philadelphia, 1849 ***53.26*** *p2*
Askin, Elizabeth; Philadelphia, 1849 ***5704.8*** *p53*
Askin, Mary; Philadelphia, 1852 ***5704.8*** *p85*
Askin, William; New York, NY, 1840 ***8208.4*** *p107*
Aslein, John; New York, NY, 1811 ***2859.11*** *p8*
Asley, John 23; Arkansas, 1918 ***95.2*** *p15*
Asley, Jon.; Virginia, 1635 ***6219*** *p27*
Asley, Mary 18; Antigua (Antego), 1756 ***1219.7*** *p48*
Asley, Mary 18; Antigua (Antego), 1756 ***3690.1*** *p6*
Asmann, Karl; America, 1852 ***8582.3*** *p1*
Asmundsdottir, Anna 11; Quebec, 1879 ***2557.1*** *p39*
Asmundsdottir, Geirmundur 10; Quebec, 1879 ***2557.1*** *p39*
Asmundsdottir, Gudrun 48; Quebec, 1879 ***2557.1*** *p39*
Asmundsdottir, Gunnar 9; Quebec, 1879 ***2557.1*** *p39*
Asmus, . . .; Canada, 1776-1783 ***9786*** *p16*
Asmus, Christian; New York, 1852 ***1450.2*** *p5A*

Asp, Carl 30; Massachusetts, 1860 6410.32 p112
Asp, Carl Johan; America, 1848 6410.32 p124
Asp, Margaret 23; Massachusetts, 1860 6410.32 p112
Aspen, Fred; Arkansas, 1918 95.2 p15
Asperkin, John 2 SEE Asperkin, William
Asperkin, Mary 26 SEE Asperkin, William
Asperkin, William 45; Philadelphia, 1774 1219.7 p214
Wife:Mary 26
Child:John 2
Aspinall, Thomas 35; Maryland, 1737 3690.1 p6
Aspinwall, Jno 17; St. Christopher, 1705 2212 p42
Aspitall, William; Mobile, AL, 1766 1219.7 p122
Asple, Pierce; New York, NY, 1816 2859.11 p25
Aspley, John 21; Virginia, 1774 1219.7 p225
Assan, Francois 36; Port uncertain, 1839 778.5 p14
Assargeut, Mr. 24; New Orleans, 1829 778.5 p14
Asse, Andrew; Virginia, 1643 6219 p202
Asselbie, Eliza.; Virginia, 1646 6219 p236
Assenquet, John 25; Port uncertain, 1836 778.5 p14
Asserguet Tiailhe, J. 22; New Orleans, 1839 778.5 p14
Assey, Francis; Virginia, 1639 6219 p151
Assick, Richard 20; Maryland, 1774 1219.7 p229
Assine, Alice; Virginia, 1638 6219 p186
Assman, Adolph; Philadelphia, 1779 8137 p6
Assman, Johannes; Philadelphia, 1780 8137 p6
Assman, Martin; Philadelphia, 1779 8137 p6
Assmer, . . .; Canada, 1776-1783 9786 p16
Assnie, Alice; Virginia, 1638 6219 p186
Astelme, Guillaume 23; Quebec, 1749 7603 p25
Asten, Robt.; Virginia, 1637 6219 p83
Astin, John; Virginia, 1643 6219 p201
Astly, Melicent 12; America, 1701 2212 p35
Astmann, . . .; Canada, 1776-1783 9786 p16
Aston, Richard 21; Maryland, 1774 1219.7 p181
Aston, Richard 24; Maryland, 1774 1219.7 p244
Aston, Robert 18; Maryland, 1774 1219.7 p236
Aston, Sarah; Philadelphia, 1849 53.26 p2
Aston, Sarah; Philadelphia, 1849 5704.8 p54
Aston, Thomas; Virginia, 1647 6219 p241
Aston, Walter; Virginia, 1643 6219 p204
Aston, Walter; Virginia, 1646 6219 p240
Wife:Warbowe
Aston, Warbowe SEE Aston, Walter
Astre, Andrew; Arkansas, 1918 95.2 p15
Astroth, August H.; Iowa, 1866-1943 123.54 p3
Astwood, Abraham 19; Windward Islands, 1722 3690.1 p6
Atcheson, Adam; New York, NY, 1816 2859.11 p25
Atcheson, Hugh; New York, NY, 1811 2859.11 p8
With wife
Atcheson, Thomas 25; St. John, N.B., 1854 5704.8 p114
Atchison, Elizabeth 3 mos; St. John, N.B., 1847 5704.8 p15
Atchison, George; Charleston, SC, 1728 1639.20 p4
Atchison, Hugh 4; St. John, N.B., 1847 5704.8 p15
Atchison, Jane; St. John, N.B., 1847 5704.8 p15
Atchison, John 12; St. John, N.B., 1847 5704.8 p15
Atchison, Joseph; St. John, N.B., 1847 5704.8 p15
Atchison, Joseph 8; St. John, N.B., 1847 5704.8 p15
Atchison, Mary; St. John, N.B., 1850 5704.8 p66
Atchison, Mary J. 6; St. John, N.B., 1847 5704.8 p15
Atchison, Mitchell 10; St. John, N.B., 1847 5704.8 p15
Atfield, Job 22; Kansas, 1877 5240.1 p58
Athanasia, Sister M.; Wisconsin, n.d. 9675.5 p121
Athas, Andrew George 30; Arkansas, 1918 95.2 p15
Athenaion, Stylianos Erotocritas 30; Arkansas, 1918 95.2 p15
Atheridge, John 37; Virginia, 1774 1219.7 p243
Atherton, Edmund 20; America, 1706 2212 p48
Atherton, Peter 10?; America, 1697-1707 2212 p18
Athor, James; Virginia, 1643 6219 p205
Athron, Bertram; New York, NY, 1908 3455.3 p25
Athron, William 29; Jamaica, 1729 3690.1 p6
Atken, John H.; New York, NY, 1831 8208.4 p29
Atkin, Jno.; Virginia, 1645 6219 p232
Atkin, John H.; New York, NY, 1831 8208.4 p29
Atkin, William; Colorado, 1898 9678.1 p152
Atkins, Abraham 22; Pennsylvania, 1735 3690.1 p6
Atkins, Agnes 7; Massachusetts, 1848 5881.1 p5
Atkins, Ann 39 SEE Atkins, John
Atkins, Anne; Charleston, SC, 1764 1639.20 p4
Atkins, Anth.; Virginia, 1643 6219 p205
Atkins, Antho.; Virginia, 1648 6219 p246
Atkins, David 4; Massachusetts, 1848 5881.1 p5
Atkins, Elizabeth 2; Massachusetts, 1848 5881.1 p5
Atkins, Fanny 29 SEE Atkins, John
Atkins, Henry 21; United States or West Indies, 1736 3690.1 p6
Atkins, Mrs. Hugh 26; Massachusetts, 1848 5881.1 p5
Atkins, Hugh 27; Massachusetts, 1848 5881.1 p5
Atkins, James 5; Massachusetts, 1848 5881.1 p5
Atkins, John 23; Maryland, 1775 1219.7 p254
Wife:Fanny 29
Atkins, John 60; Philadelphia, 1774 1219.7 p214
Wife:Ann 39
Atkins, Joseph; New York, NY, 1836 8208.4 p12
Atkins, Mary; New York, NY, 1811 2859.11 p8
Atkins, Mary 9 mos; Massachusetts, 1848 5881.1 p5
Atkins, R.J.; Iowa, 1866-1943 123.54 p3
Atkins, Richard; New York, NY, 1851 2896.5 p1
Atkins, Richard; Virginia, 1621 6219 p67
Atkins, Richard 22; Maryland, 1775 1219.7 p254
Atkins, Robert 9; Massachusetts, 1848 5881.1 p6
Atkins, Silvester; Virginia, 1629 6219 p8
Atkins, Thomas 19; Virginia, 1775 1219.7 p261
Atkins, Thomas 24; Virginia, 1774 1219.7 p225
Atkins, Thomas 27; Kansas, 1884 5240.1 p67
Atkins, William; Jamaica, 1752 1219.7 p15
Atkins, William; Jamaica, 1752 3690.1 p7
Atkins, William; Virginia, 1640 6219 p183
Atkins, William; Virginia, 1642 6219 p188
Atkins, William 21; Jamaica, 1736 3690.1 p6
Atkins, Wm.; Virginia, 1635 6219 p32
Atkinson, Mr.; Quebec, 1815 9229.18 p80
With wife
Atkinson, Mr.; Quebec, 1815 9229.18 p82
Atkinson, Alice 7; Massachusetts, 1848 5881.1 p5
Atkinson, Andrew; Philadelphia, 1864 5704.8 p172
Atkinson, Ann 19; North America, 1774 1219.7 p198
Atkinson, Ann 21 SEE Atkinson, Robert
Atkinson, Charles 6 SEE Atkinson, John
Atkinson, Charles Evelyn; Illinois, 1898 5012.39 p53
Atkinson, David; New York, NY, 1816 2859.11 p25
Atkinson, Edward; Petersburg, VA, 1805 4778.2 p141
Atkinson, Eliza; New York, NY, 1811 2859.11 p8
Atkinson, English 28; Boston, 1774 1219.7 p210
Atkinson, Frances 30 SEE Atkinson, John
Atkinson, Francis; New York, NY, 1815 2859.11 p25
Atkinson, Francis 30; Massachusetts, 1848 5881.1 p5
Atkinson, George; America, 1736 4971 p12
Atkinson, Henry; New York, NY, 1811 2859.11 p8
Atkinson, Henry; Virginia, 1639 6219 p156
Atkinson, James; New York, NY, 1811 2859.11 p8
Atkinson, Jane; New York, NY, 1811 2859.11 p8
Atkinson, Jas.; New York, NY, 1816 2859.11 p25
Atkinson, John; Iowa, 1866-1943 123.54 p3
Atkinson, John; Jamaica, 1753 1219.7 p23
Atkinson, John; Jamaica, 1753 3690.1 p7
Atkinson, John 1 SEE Atkinson, John
Atkinson, John 26; Maryland, 1775 1219.7 p268
Wife:Mary 21
Atkinson, John 45; North America, 1774 1219.7 p198
Wife:Frances 30
Child:Charles 6
Child:Martha 4
Child:Michael 3
Child:John 1
Atkinson, Joseph; Ohio, 1837 9892.11 p2
Atkinson, Joseph; Ohio, 1840 9892.11 p2
Atkinson, Lewis 3; America, 1829 9788.3 p4
Atkinson, Marg.; Virginia, 1643 6219 p207
Atkinson, Margaret; New York, NY, 1841 7036 p120
Atkinson, Marmaduke; Virginia, 1642 6219 p198
Atkinson, Martha 4 SEE Atkinson, John
Atkinson, Mary 21 SEE Atkinson, John
Atkinson, Mary 21; America, 1699 2212 p20
Atkinson, Mathew; Virginia, 1637 6219 p2
Atkinson, Mathew, Jr.; Virginia, 1637 6219 p2
Atkinson, Michael 3 SEE Atkinson, John
Atkinson, P. H. 21; New Orleans, 1862 543.30 p237
Atkinson, Richard 20; Barbados, 1718-1759 3690.1 p289
Atkinson, Robert 28; North America, 1774 1219.7 p200
Wife:Ann 21
Atkinson, Stephen 19; Massachusetts, 1849 5881.1 p6
Atkinson, Thomas; Virginia, 1637 6219 p2
Atkinson, William 16; North America, 1774 1219.7 p199
Atkinson, William 18; Maryland, 1775 1219.7 p272
Atkinson, William 31; St. John, N.B., 1866 5704.8 p166
Atkocz, Kazimis; Wisconsin, n.d. 9675.4 p193
Atkoezius, Anton; Wisconsin, n.d. 9675.4 p193
Atle-Anne, Olaf Berger; Arkansas, 1918 95.2 p15
Atmer, Edward 25; Maryland, 1774 1219.7 p192
Atmore, Thomas; Virginia, 1634 6219 p32
Attales, Mr. 35; Port uncertain, 1839 778.5 p14
Attaway, William; Virginia, 1637 6219 p8
Attema, Henry; Arkansas, 1918 95.2 p15
Attenbourough, William M.; Arizona, 1890 2764.35 p2
Atter, John; Virginia, 1642 6219 p189
Attera, Thomas; Virginia, 1637 6219 p85
Atteriodge, Patrick; Montreal, 1804 7603 p60
Attermeier, Henry; Ohio, 1869-1887 8582 p1
Attinger, Joh; Charleston, SC, 1775-1781 8582.2 p52
Attingsworth, John; Virginia, 1646 6219 p236
Attocke, Nazar.; Virginia, 1645 6219 p240
Attuard, Charles 29; Port uncertain, 1836 778.5 p14
Atwack, Jacob; Virginia, 1648 6219 p253
Atwell, Israell; Virginia, 1635 6219 p72
Atwell, Nicholas; Virginia, 1637 6219 p180
Atwell, Robert; Philadelphia, 1847 53.26 p2
Atwell, Robert; Philadelphia, 1847 5704.8 p13
Atwell, Symon; Virginia, 1648 6219 p249
Atwill, James; Quebec, 1847 5704.8 p29
Atwill, Mary; Quebec, 1847 5704.8 p29
Atwill, Mary Jane 3 mos; Quebec, 1847 5704.8 p29
Atwill, Nicholas; Virginia, 1635 6219 p70
Atwood, Ann; Virginia, 1635 6219 p3
Atwood, John 21; Maryland, 1735 3690.1 p7
Atyeo, Thomas 23; Kansas, 1892 5240.1 p76
Aub, Abraham; America, 1837 8582.3 p2
Auber, Peter 26; Virginia, 1773 1219.7 p169
Auberdiac, Pierre 22; America, 1838 778.5 p14
Auberpin, Mme. 36; Port uncertain, 1838 778.5 p15
Aubert, Mlle. 41; New Orleans, 1838 778.5 p15
Aubert, Christian Friedrich Wilhelm; America, 1882 4610.10 p101
Aubert, J. Joseph 40; New Orleans, 1839 778.5 p15
Aubert, Jean 33; New Orleans, 1838 778.5 p15
Aubert Courit, J. 30; New Orleans, 1839 778.5 p15
Aubert Couvit, J. 30; New Orleans, 1839 778.5 p15
Aubert Gontier, Pierre 53; New Orleans, 1826 778.5 p15
Aubic, Mr. 31; New Orleans, 1839 778.5 p15
Aubic, Laurent 24; New Orleans, 1839 778.5 p15
Aubin, F. C. B. de 47; America, 1832 778.5 p15
Aubinet, Anna 35; America, 1831 778.5 p15
Aubinet, Charles 3; America, 1831 778.5 p15
Aubinet, Francis 13; America, 1831 778.5 p15
Aubinet, Francis 35; America, 1831 778.5 p15
Aubinet, Jacques 2; America, 1831 778.5 p15
Aubinet, Joseph 5; America, 1831 778.5 p15
Aubinet, Moxanne 9; America, 1831 778.5 p16
Aubony, Thomas 22; Virginia, 1774 1219.7 p244
Aubourg, Augustine 4; New Orleans, 1822 778.5 p16
Aubourg, Heloise 29; New Orleans, 1822 778.5 p16
Aubre, Pierre 40; New Orleans, 1837 778.5 p16
Aubry, A. 18; America, 1832 778.5 p16
Aubry, Rion 22; New Orleans, 1862 543.30 p233
Aubry, Thecle-Cornelius; Quebec, 1670 7603 p94
Auburtin, Mr. 21; New Orleans, 1836 778.5 p16
Auchanan, John; Philadelphia, 1816 2859.11 p25
Auda, Bert; Iowa, 1866-1943 123.54 p3
Audare, Mrs. 26; Louisiana, 1821 778.5 p7
Audegou, Mr. 45; New Orleans, 1822 778.5 p16
Audet, Nicolas; Canada, 1663 4533 p127
Audibert, Mr. 28; America, 1839 778.5 p16
Audick, Daniell; Virginia, 1637 6219 p113
Audier, Marcellus A.; Wisconsin, n.d. 9675.4 p193
Audier, Victor; Wisconsin, n.d. 9675.4 p193
Audige, J. P. 35; New Orleans, 1827 778.5 p16
Audigio, Mr. 24; New Orleans, 1822 778.5 p16
Audinet, J. A.; Washington, 1859-1920 2872.1 p2
Audit, . . .; Quebec, 1776 9786 p105
Audley, Teg.; Virginia, 1639 6219 p158
Audoire, Guillaume; Quebec, 1777 7603 p70
Audrain, Master 9; America, 1839 778.5 p16
Audre, Frances Adreen 40; Harris Co., TX, 1898 6254 p5
Audry, Ellin; Virginia, 1642 6219 p193
Auduraudagy, John 34; New Orleans, 1822 778.5 p16
Auer, Tho.; Virginia, 1642 6219 p191
Auerbach, John; Washington, 1859-1920 2872.1 p2
Auerbach, Nathan; Arkansas, 1918 95.2 p15
Auerine, Jon.; Virginia, 1638 6219 p11
Auestad, Lars 23; Arkansas, 1918 95.2 p16
Auf Dem Kamp, Karl; Ohio, 1869-1887 8582 p1
Aufdemkamp, John F.; Illinois, 1892 5012.37 p62
Aufdemkampe, Louis; Illinois, 1892 5012.40 p26
Aufossy, Eugene 32; New Orleans, 1839 778.5 p16
Augaud, Miss 26; America, 1838 778.5 p16
Augent, M. 30; America, 1835 778.5 p16
Auger, Adam 12; America, 1699 2212 p28
Auger, Charles Rene Gatien; Louisiana, 1789-1819 778.5 p555
Auger, Jon.; Virginia, 1637 6219 p115
Augerle, Caspar; Pennsylvania, 1709 2444 p133
With wife
With 3 children
Augeron, Louis; Louisiana, 1789-1819 778.5 p555
Aughnalisk, Alexander; Philadelphia, 1852 5704.8 p91
Augrand, Mr. 22; America, 1838 778.5 p17
August, Anna 20; America, 1838 778.5 p17
August, Henry 20; America, 1838 778.5 p17
August, Johannes; Minneapolis, 1880-1883 6410.35 p60
August, Joseph 27; New Orleans, 1862 543.30 p237
Auguste, Mr. 18; New Orleans, 1827 778.5 p17
Auguste, G. 25; New Orleans, 1838 778.5 p17
Augustin, Mr. 25; Port uncertain, 1836 778.5 p17
Augustin, Chr. Gottl. 19; New Orleans, 1839 9420.2 p168

Augustin, Marg. 18; America, 1839 *778.5 p17*
Augustin, S. 22; New Orleans, 1839 *778.5 p17*
Augustine, Fracis; Wisconsin, n.d. *9675.4 p193*
Augustine, Henry F.; Illinois, 1870 *5012.38 p99*
Augustson, Carl Johan; Arkansas, 1918 *95.2 p16*
Augustsson, Carl Fritiof Albin; Minneapolis, 1876-1877
  6410.35 p47
Augustus, Prince; Quebec, 1778 *9786 p167*
Aukamp, Conrad; Illinois, 1890 *2896.5 p1*
Aukamp, Frederick; Illinois, 1892 *2896.5 p2*
Aukamp, William; Illinois, 1888 *2896.5 p2*
Aukamp, William; Illinois, 1889 *2896.5 p2*
Aul, . . .; Canada, 1776-1783 *9786 p16*
Aul, Edmot 32; Mexico, 1836 *778.5 p17*
Aul, Jacob; Ohio, 1800 *8582.2 p55*
Auld, James; New York, NY, 1811 *2859.11 p8*
Auld, Margaret; New York, NY, 1811 *2859.11 p8*
Auld, Mary; New York, NY, 1811 *2859.11 p8*
Auldjo, Alexander 16; Carolina, 1774 *1219.7 p231*
Auldjo, John 15; Carolina, 1774 *1219.7 p231*
Auleb, Catherine 20; America, 1835 *778.5 p17*
Auliff, Julia 30; Massachusetts, 1847 *5881.1 p5*
Aulig, C. E.; Milwaukee, 1875 *4719.30 p257*
Aull, Jacob; Cincinnati, 1869-1887 *8582 p1*
Aull, Jakob; Philadelphia, 1805 *8125.8 p435*
Aull, James; Philadelphia, 1849 *53.26 p2*
Aull, James; Philadelphia, 1849 *5704.8 p58*
Aull, Robert, Jr.; New York, NY, 1836 *8208.4 p15*
Aulman, Phillip; Iowa, 1855 *2769.1 p3*
Aultman, Andrew; Pennsylvania, 1749 *4779.3 p13*
Aultman, Anthony; Pennsylvania, 1749 *4779.3 p13*
Aultman, B. Peter; Pennsylvania, 1749 *4779.3 p13*
Aultman, Gasper; Pennsylvania, 1749 *4779.3 p13*
Aultman, George Peter; Pennsylvania, 1749 *4779.3 p13*
Aultman, Hance Peter; Pennsylvania, 1749 *4779.3 p13*
Aultman, Philip; Pennsylvania, 1749 *4779.3 p13*
Aultman, William; Pennsylvania, 1749 *4779.3 p13*
Aultman, William, Jr.; Pennsylvania, 1749 *4779.3 p13*
Aunes, Emil; Washington, 1859-1920 *2872.1 p2*
Aunes, Hulda; Washington, 1859-1920 *2872.1 p2*
Aunley, Robert; Virginia, 1639 *6219 p157*
Aunt, Phillipp; Virginia, 1635 *6219 p72*
Auperle, Caspar; Pennsylvania, 1709 *2444 p133*
  With wife
  With 3 children
Aupperle, David; Cincinnati, 1830 *8582.1 p51*
Aurianne, Jean 23; Port uncertain, 1838 *778.5 p17*
Auriel, John 27; New Orleans, 1838 *778.5 p17*
Aurillon, Jean 23; New Orleans, 1838 *778.5 p17*
Ausenig, Johan; Washington, 1859-1920 *2872.1 p2*
Ausmus, Johann; Illinois, 1800-1874 *8582.1 p55*
Austen, Charles 20; Quebec, 1853 *5704.8 p105*
Austen, George; America, 1741 *4971 p48*
Austen, George; America, 1742 *4971 p49*
Austin, Adam; Charleston, SC, 1782 *1639.20 p4*
Austin, Ann 17 *SEE* Austin, Thomas

Austin, Edward 28; Jamaica, 1731 *3690.1 p7*
Austin, Geo.; Virginia, 1643 *6219 p200*
Austin, Georg; Virginia, 1643 *6219 p200*
Austin, George I.; Virginia, 1856 *4626.16 p16*
Austin, Henry 56; Kansas, 1879 *5240.1 p60*
Austin, James 18; Philadelphia, 1853 *5704.8 p108*
Austin, Joel Spencer 41; California, 1872 *2769.1 p3*
Austin, John; Illinois, 1842 *7857 p2*
Austin, John; New York, NY, 1833 *8208.4 p59*
Austin, John; Quebec, 1847 *5704.8 p7*
Austin, Joseph 18; Maryland, 1774 *1219.7 p220*
Austin, Martha 18 *SEE* Austin, Thomas
Austin, Rebecca; New York, NY, 1816 *2859.11 p25*
Austin, Rich.; Virginia, 1635 *6219 p16*
Austin, Richard; Virginia, 1638 *6219 p148*
Austin, Sally Ann; Quebec, 1849 *5704.8 p51*
Austin, Sarah 12; Massachusetts, 1850 *5881.1 p6*
Austin, Sarah 25; Baltimore, 1775 *1219.7 p269*
Austin, Tho.; Virginia, 1600-1642 *6219 p192*
  With wife & 2 children
Austin, Thomas; New York, NY, 1816 *2859.11 p25*
Austin, Thomas 20; Jamaica, 1774 *1219.7 p243*
  *Sister:*Martha 18
  *Sister:*Ann 17
Austin, William 19; Maryland, 1735 *3690.1 p7*
Auston, Joseph 22; Quebec, 1856 *5704.8 p130*
Auston, Richd.; Virginia, 1648 *6219 p250*
Auston, Wm.; Virginia, 1637 *6219 p24*
Aut, . . .; Canada, 1776-1783 *9786 p16*
Autel, Marc 26; New Orleans, 1830 *778.5 p17*
Autenheimer, Mr.; Cincinnati, 1831 *8582.1 p51*
Autenheimer, Friederich; Cincinnati, 1859 *8582.3 p86*
Autenheimer, Friedrich; Cincinnati, 1828 *8582.1 p51*
Autere, Pierre 28; America, 1838 *778.5 p17*
Auth, Jacob 21; New Orleans, 1862 *543.30 p235*
Auth, Nicolaus; Cincinnati, 1869-1887 *8582 p1*
Authement, Jerome; Louisiana, 1789-1819 *778.5 p555*
Authement, Joseph; Louisiana, 1789-1819 *778.5 p555*
Authwaite, Thomas 22; New York, 1774 *1219.7 p203*
Autin, Francois 17; New Orleans, 1838 *778.5 p18*
Autoile, James 28; Port uncertain, 1838 *778.5 p18*
Autzel, Michel 22; America, 1835 *778.5 p18*
Avakias, Nerses Materon; Arkansas, 1918 *95.2 p16*
Avalardo, Perfirio 53; Arizona, 1923 *9228.40 p27*
Avarado, Marialdo 30; Arizona, 1914 *9228.40 p18*
Avel, Henry; America, 1842 *1450.2 p5A*
Avequin, D. 48; America, 1838 *778.5 p18*
Averbeck, Fr; Cincinnati, 1849 *8582.1 p1*
Averitt, Christo.; Virginia, 1636 *6219 p109*
Averon, Mr. 30; America, 1838 *778.5 p18*
Averry, Jon.; Virginia, 1642 *6219 p198*
Avery, Ann *SEE* Avery, Hen.
Avery, Charles 38; Virginia, 1774 *1219.7 p186*
Avery, Eliz.; Virginia, 1641 *6219 p184*
Avery, Hen.; Virginia, 1642 *6219 p199*
  *Wife:*Ann

Avery, Marke; Virginia, 1600-1643 *6219 p200*
Avey, William 21; Philadelphia, 1775 *1219.7 p258*
Avgenackes, Nickolas; Arkansas, 1918 *95.2 p16*
Aviet, H. 23; New Orleans, 1839 *778.5 p18*
Avinene, Lady 30; America, 1839 *778.5 p18*
Avinene, Candide 24; New Orleans, 1831 *778.5 p18*
Avinene, Candide 37; America, 1839 *778.5 p18*
Avinene, Fernando 20; New Orleans, 1831 *778.5 p18*
Avint, Phillip; Virginia, 1636 *6219 p109*
Avis, Robert 45; Jamaica, 1774 *1219.7 p243*
Avisson, Thomas 18; America, 1839 *778.5 p7*
Avril, Mr.; Port uncertain, 1839 *778.5 p18*
Awl, Jacob; Ohio, 1800 *8582.2 p55*
Awl, Margaret; Philadelphia, 1847 *53.26 p2*
  *Relative:*Martha
Awl, Margaret; Philadelphia, 1847 *5704.8 p14*
Awl, Martha *SEE* Awl, Margaret
Awl, Martha; Philadelphia, 1847 *5704.8 p14*
Axelsen, Emanuel; Arkansas, 1918 *95.2 p16*
Axelson, Ernest Henry; Boston, 1903 *3455.2 p74*
Axelson, Ernest Henry; Boston, 1903 *3455.3 p21*
Axelson, Ernest Henry; Boston, 1903 *3455.3 p45*
Axen, Paul; Wisconsin, n.d. *9675.4 p193*
Axen, Paula; Wisconsin, n.d. *9675.4 p193*
Axford, E.B.; Colorado, 1904 *9678.1 p152*
Ayala, Alfonso; California, 1876 *2764.35 p1*
Aycard, Lucien 37; America, 1831 *778.5 p18*
Ayers, John 27; Jamaica, 1739 *3690.1 p7*
Ayliffe, John 17; Maryland, 1774 *1219.7 p234*
Aylward, Henry 28; Jamaica, 1734 *3690.1 p7*
Ayne, Michel; New York, NY, 1838 *8208.4 p90*
Ayotte, . . .; Canada, 1776-1783 *9786 p41*
Ayre, William 24; Maryland, 1775 *1219.7 p265*
Ayrer, Anna M. Woehrle *SEE* Ayrer, Jacob Heinrich
Ayrer, Jacob Heinrich; New England, 1744-1800 *2444
  p134*
  *Wife:*Anna M. Woehrle
  *Child:*Johann Friedrich
Ayrer, Johann Friedrich *SEE* Ayrer, Jacob Heinrich
Ayres, Alexander; Washington, 1859-1920 *2872.1 p2*
Ayres, E. D.; Washington, 1859-1920 *2872.1 p2*
Ayres, William 25; Maryland, 1774 *1219.7 p181*
Ayrivie, A. 34; New Orleans, 1839 *778.5 p18*
Ayrivier, Guillaume 44; America, 1838 *778.5 p18*
Azereki, Powel; Wisconsin, n.d. *9675.4 p193*
Azerzkis, Wladislaus; Wisconsin, n.d. *9675.4 p193*
Azno, Henry; Illinois, 1861 *7857 p2*
Aznoe, Thomas; Illinois, 1876 *7857 p2*
Azzolin, Frank; Iowa, 1866-1943 *123.54 p3*
Azzolin, John; Iowa, 1866-1943 *123.54 p3*
Azzolin, Joseph; Iowa, 1866-1943 *123.54 p55*
Azzolin, Juseppi; Iowa, 1866-1943 *123.54 p55*
Azzolin, Kathryn; Iowa, 1866-1943 *123.54 p55*
Azzolin, Marco; Iowa, 1866-1943 *123.54 p3*

B

Baacke, . . .; Canada, 1776-1783 **9786** *p16*
Baader, Martin; Ohio, 1834 **8582.2** *p59*
Baaer, Nes L. 25; Kansas, 1880 **5240.1** *p62*
Baar, Gerhard Leo; America, 1850 **1450.2** *p6A*
Baardson, Bernedl; Wisconsin, n.d. **9675.4** *p193*
Baaske, Charles; Baltimore, 1881 **1450.2** *p1B*
Baatz, August; Wisconsin, n.d. **9675.4** *p193*
Babb, Edward; Virginia, 1639 **6219** *p155*
Babb, Jeffery; Illinois, 1893 **5012.40** *p53*
Babb, Joseph; Illinois, 1892 **5012.40** *p27*
Babb, Thomas; Illinois, 1905 **5012.37** *p63*
Babb, Thomas; Virginia, 1640 **6219** *p185*
Babbington, Michaell; Virginia, 1635 **6219** *p4*
Babbinton, John; Virginia, 1639 **6219** *p156*
Babecz, Stanley; Iowa, 1866-1943 **123.54** *p7*
Babela, Josef 46; New York, 1912 **9980.29** *p70*
Baber, Otto Karl Alexander; Wisconsin, n.d. **9675.4** *p193*
Baber, Rosa; Wisconsin, n.d. **9675.4** *p193*
Babiak, Catharine *SEE* Babiak, Paul
Babiak, Paul; America, 1899 **7137** *p168*
  *Wife:*Catharine
Babicz, Pawel; Iowa, 1866-1943 **123.54** *p7*
Babik, Catharine *SEE* Babik, Paul
Babik, Paul; America, 1899 **7137** *p168*
  *Wife:*Catharine
Babin, Mr. 15; America, 1830 **778.5** *p19*
Babin, F. 30; New Orleans, 1835 **778.5** *p19*
Babin, J. 25; New Orleans, 1835 **778.5** *p19*
Babin, J. 25; New Orleans, 1836 **778.5** *p19*
Babinelle, Mr. 35; Port uncertain, 1836 **778.5** *p19*
Babington, Tho; America, 1697 **2212** *p7*
Babister, Richard; Virginia, 1643 **6219** *p206*
Babiuk, Fiodor 24; New York, 1912 **9980.29** *p62*
Babka, Frank; Arkansas, 1918 **95.2** *p16*
Babyak, Catharine *SEE* Babyak, Paul
Babyak, Paul; America, 1899 **7137** *p168*
  *Wife:*Catharine
Bacanoia, Jesus 43; Arizona, 1923 **9228.40** *p27*
Bacar, Joseph; America, 1901 **1450.2** *p1B*
Bacarisse, Mr. 22; New Orleans, 1839 **778.5** *p19*
Bach, . . .; Canada, 1776-1783 **9786** *p16*
Bach, Elisabeth; Michigan, 1911 **2691.4** *p166*
Bach, Elisabeth; Minnesota, 1911 **2691.4** *p166*
Bach, Gabriel; Georgia, 1739 **9332** *p326*
Bach, Georg; Cincinnati, 1869-1887 **8582** *p1*
Bach, Georg; New York, NY, 1839 **8582.1** *p1*
Bach, George; Wisconsin, n.d. **9675.4** *p193*
Bach, Joseph; Kentucky, 1840 **8582.3** *p99*
Bach, Ott.; Georgia, 1738 **9332** *p321*
Bach, Philipp; Iowa, 1903 **2691.4** *p166*
Bachana, Adolphe 27; New Orleans, 1839 **778.5** *p19*
Bachelais, Francois 28; New Orleans, 1838 **778.5** *p19*
Bachelet, Mr. 30; Louisiana, 1820 **778.5** *p19*
Bachelier, Mr. 28; Port uncertain, 1838 **778.5** *p19*
Bachelor, Jane; Pennsylvania, 1682 **4963** *p40*
Bachelour, Jane; Pennsylvania, 1682-1684 **4960** *p152*
Bacher, Apollonia 10 *SEE* Bacher, Thomas
Bacher, Maria *SEE* Bacher, Thomas
Bacher, Maria 12 *SEE* Bacher, Thomas
Bacher, Maria Schweiger *SEE* Bacher, Thomas
Bacher, Matthew; New York, 1754 **3652** *p79*
Bacher, Matthias; Georgia, 1738 **9332** *p319*
Bacher, Thomas; Georgia, 1738 **9332** *p323*
Bacher, Thomas; Georgia, 1739 **9332** *p323*
  *Wife:*Maria Schweiger

Bacher, Thomas; Georgia, 1739 **9332** *p326*
  *Wife:*Maria
  *Daughter:*Maria 12
  *Daughter:*Apollonia 10
Bachere, Martin J. 22; New Orleans, 1862 **543.30** *p112*
Bachert, John; Illinois, 1882 **5012.39** *p52*
Bachia, Wm 39; New Orleans, 1862 **543.30** *p479*
Bachman, Abraham; Ohio, 1819 **8582.1** *p47*
Bachman, Bagette; Pittsburgh, 1943 **9892.11** *p2*
Bachman, George; New York, NY, 1834 **8208.4** *p36*
Bachman, H.; Milwaukee, 1875 **4719.30** *p257*
Bachman, Herman; Illinois, 1854 **7857** *p2*
Bachman, Joseph L. 23; New Orleans, 1862 **543.30** *p480*
Bachmann, Abraham; Ohio, 1819 **8582.1** *p2*
Bachmann, August 42; New Orleans, 1862 **543.30** *p115*
Bachmann, Franz; Lancaster, PA, 1777-1782 **8137** *p6*
Bachmann, John 29; New Orleans, 1862 **543.30** *p111*
Bachmann, Marie 63; America, 1895 **1763** *p40C*
Bachop, William; North Carolina, 1792 **1639.20** *p5*
Bachora, Stanislaw 17; New York, 1912 **9980.29** *p57*
Bachs, Martin Veisz; Virginia, 1775 **1219.7** *p275*
Bachs, Ottelia Veisz; Virginia, 1775 **1219.7** *p275*
Bachus, Henry 19; Philadelphia, 1774 **1219.7** *p217*
Bacigalupi, Charles 41; Arizona, 1890 **2764.35** *p9*
Back, Clemens; New Orleans, 1852 **1450.2** *p6A*
Back, Henry; America, 1850 **1450.2** *p6A*
Backas, John 19; Antigua (Antego), 1728 **3690.1** *p7*
Backenberg, C.F.; Wisconsin, n.d. **9675.4** *p193*
Backer, Chaplain; Quebec, 1778 **9786** *p267*
Backer, Benjamin; New York, 1856 **1450.2** *p1B*
Backhaus, Carl; Cincinnati, 1788-1848 **8582.3** *p89*
Backhaus, Carl 44; America, 1853 **4610.10** *p148*
  *Son:*Carl Heinrich
Backhaus, Carl Heinrich *SEE* Backhaus, Carl
Backhaus, Heinrich Wilhelm; America, 1850 **4610.10** *p142*
Backhaus, Karl Friedrich Wilhelm 30; America, 1852 **4610.10** *p147*
Backhof, Ludolph Gottlieb; New York, 1753 **3652** *p77*
Backman, Abraham; Pittsburgh, 1943 **9892.11** *p2*
Backman, J. L.; Iowa, 1866-1943 **123.54** *p7*
Backmann, Bernard; Baltimore, 1856 **1450.2** *p6A*
Backofmann, Herman; New York, NY, 1836 **8208.4** *p15*
Backs, Anne Marie Engel; America, 1856 **4610.10** *p140*
Backs, Carl Friedrich Gottlieb; America, 1882 **4610.10** *p110*
Backs, Carl Heinrich Hermann; America, 1885 **4610.10** *p110*
Backs, Charlotte Caroline Louise; America, 1857 **4610.10** *p105*
Backs, Heinr. Friedrich August; America, 1882 **4610.10** *p110*
Backster, Wm.; Virginia, 1637 **6219** *p108*
Backstrom, Simon; Minneapolis, 1880-1884 **6410.35** *p49*
Backwell, John; Virginia, 1642 **6219** *p188*
Bacock, Thomas; Virginia, 1646 **6219** *p239*
Bacon, Eliza; Philadelphia, 1865 **5704.8** *p200*
Bacon, Eliza.; Virginia, 1647 **6219** *p245*
Bacon, Elizabeth; St. John, N.B., 1848 **5704.8** *p45*
Bacon, Elizabeth 27 *SEE* Bacon, William
Bacon, John; New York, NY, 1811 **2859.11** *p8*
  With family
Bacon, John; St. John, N.B., 1848 **5704.8** *p45*
Bacon, Thomas; New York, NY, 1816 **2859.11** *p25*
Bacon, William; Montreal, 1818 **7603** *p53*
Bacon, William; St. John, N.B., 1848 **5704.8** *p44*
Bacon, William 7; America, 1843 **1450.2** *p6A*

Bacon, William 12 *SEE* Bacon, William
Bacon, William 28; Philadelphia, 1803 **53.26** *p2*
  *Relative:*Elizabeth 27
  *Relative:*William 12
Bacun, John; Wisconsin, n.d. **9675.4** *p193*
Bacus, Joseph 20; Port uncertain, 1839 **778.5** *p19*
Baczenas, Stanislaus; Wisconsin, n.d. **9675.4** *p193*
Baczko, G.; Wheeling, WV, 1852 **8582.3** *p78*
Baczynski, Teodor; Boston, 1834 **4606** *p179*
Bada, Michele; Arkansas, 1918 **95.2** *p16*
Badberger, Louis 35; Kansas, 1880 **5240.1** *p61*
Badcock, John 19; America, 1728 **3690.1** *p7*
Badden, John; Virginia, 1639 **6219** *p154*
Baddison, John 19; Maryland, 1729 **3690.1** *p7*
Baddoe, Georg; America, 1697 **2212** *p7*
Bade, Anton; America, 1835 **1450.2** *p6A*
Bade, Carl Frederich; Baltimore, 1838 **1450.2** *p6A*
Bade, Clemt.; Virginia, 1641 **6219** *p184*
Badechvic, Vinc; Iowa, 1866-1943 **123.54** *p7*
Baden, Frederick; Kansas, 1907 **6013.40** *p15*
Badendoerfer, Magdalena 46; America, 1839 **778.5** *p19*
Bader, . . .; Canada, 1776-1783 **9786** *p16*
Bader, Anna M. Marquard *SEE* Bader, Johann Georg
Bader, Anna Margaretha *SEE* Bader, Matthaeus
Bader, Anna Maria *SEE* Bader, Johann Georg
Bader, Anna Maria *SEE* Bader, Matthaeus
Bader, Eva Catharina *SEE* Bader, Johann Georg
Bader, George 33; New Orleans, 1862 **543.30** *p110*
Bader, Hans Martin *SEE* Bader, Matthaeus
Bader, Hansz Adam; America, 1747 **2444** *p134*
  *Brother:*Peter
  *Brother:*Matheus
Bader, James 26; New Orleans, 1862 **543.30** *p109*
Bader, Johan Gerg; Pennsylvania, 1750 **2444** *p134*
Bader, Johan Gerg; Pennsylvania, 1752 **2444** *p134*
Bader, Johan Gerg; Pennsylvania, 1754 **2444** *p134*
Bader, Johann Georg *SEE* Bader, Matthaeus
Bader, Johann Georg; New England, 1749 **2444** *p134*
  *Wife:*Anna M. Marquard
  *Child:*Eva Catharina
  *Granddaughter:*Anna Maria
Bader, Matheus *SEE* Bader, Hansz Adam
Bader, Matthaeus; America, 1752 **2444** *p134*
  *Wife:*Anna Maria
  *Child:*Johann Georg
  *Child:*Hans Martin
  *Child:*Anna Margaretha
  *Child:*Matthaus
  *Child:*Michael
Bader, Matthaus *SEE* Bader, Matthaeus
Bader, Michael *SEE* Bader, Matthaeus
Bader, Peter *SEE* Bader, Hansz Adam
Bader, Philip Christian; New York, 1752 **3652** *p76*
Badge, John; Virginia, 1642 **6219** *p197*
Badger, Ann; Virginia, 1639 **6219** *p156*
Badger, Ann; Virginia, 1649 **6219** *p252*
Badger, Benjamin 22; Virginia, 1774 **1219.7** *p185*
Badger, John 22; Philadelphia, 1775 **1219.7** *p274*
Badger, Thomas 25; Philadelphia, 1864 **5704.8** *p161*
Badham, John; Virginia, 1639 **6219** *p156*
Badham, Jon.; Virginia, 1639 **6219** *p149*
Badham, Margarett; Virginia, 1639 **6219** *p151*
Badie, P. 38; New Orleans, 1835 **778.5** *p19*
Badin, Stephan Theodor; Cincinnati, 1788-1848 **8582.3** *p89*
Badine, J.B. 24; Louisiana, 1820 **778.5** *p19*
Badiniskas, Antonas; Arkansas, 1918 **95.2** *p16*

Badley, Thomas; Virginia, 1642 6219 p196
Badnall, Jon.; Virginia, 1642 6219 p198
Badoin, S. 40; America, 1838 778.5 p19
Badtke, Louis Edward; Arkansas, 1918 95.2 p16
Badworth, James; Virginia, 1639 6219 p24
Baeckman, Henry; Virginia, 1856 4626.16 p16
Baeder, Mr.; South Carolina, 1736-1760 2444 p134
Baeder, Anna Margaretha Schaal *SEE* Baeder, Matthaeus
Baeder, August 28; Kansas, 1890 5240.1 p74
Baeder, Catharina Margaretha *SEE* Baeder, Matthaeus
Baeder, Matthaeus; South Carolina, 1760 2444 p134
*Wife:*Anna Margaretha Schaal
*Child:*Matthaus
*Child:*Catharina Margaretha
Baeder, Matthaus *SEE* Baeder, Matthaeus
Baehr, . . .; Canada, 1776-1783 9786 p16
Baehrmeyer, Christopher Henry; New York, 1753 3652 p77
Baemeister, Julius Carl Cornelius; America, 1881 4610.10 p124
Baenninger, Salomon; New York, NY, 1847 8582.1 p2
Baenziger, Conrad; Cincinnati, 1848 8582.1 p53
Baer, Anna 3; America, 1838 778.5 p20
Baer, Christine 35; America, 1838 778.5 p20
Baer, Frederick 30; New Orleans, 1862 543.30 p243
Baer, Henry; America, 1871 6014.1 p1
Baer, Jacob, Children; America, 1859 3702.7 p214
Baer, Jochen; Wisconsin, n.d. 9675.4 p194
Baer, Johann 1; America, 1838 778.5 p20
Baer, Johannes; America, 1855 3702.7 p214
Baer, John; New York, NY, 1922 3455.2 p80
Baer, Leopold 22; Kansas, 1888 5240.1 p72
Baer, Maa 5; America, 1838 778.5 p20
Baer, Peter 6; America, 1838 778.5 p20
Baer, Peter 36; America, 1838 778.5 p20
Baer, Samuel; America, 1869 6014.1 p1
Baerenz, Heinrich; Wisconsin, n.d. 9675.4 p194
Baerle, Caspar; New York, 1750 2444 p134
*Wife:*Sara
*Child:*Justina Magdalena
*Child:*Johann Caspar
*Child:*Sophia Catharina
Baerle, Johann Caspar *SEE* Baerle, Caspar
Baerle, Justina Magdalena *SEE* Baerle, Caspar
Baerle, Sara *SEE* Baerle, Caspar
Baerle, Sophia Catharina *SEE* Baerle, Caspar
Baermann, Fridolin; Ohio, 1800-1885 8582.2 p59
Baermann, Georg; Ohio, 1800-1885 8582.2 p59
Baertling, v., Jr.; Quebec, 1776 9786 p105
Baertling, v., Sr.; Quebec, 1776 9786 p104
Baertsch, Jacob; Philadelphia, 1776 8582.3 p84
Baetz, Konrad; Philadelphia, 1779 8137 p6
Baeumer, Friedrich Heinrich; America, 1854 4610.10 p116
Baeumler, Joseph Martin; Ohio, 1817 8582.3 p81
Baeurlin, Anna Maria; Pennsylvania, 1751 2444 p214
Baeuschlein, Andreas; America, 1754 4525 p199
With wife & child
Baeuschlein, Caspar; Pennsylvania, 1752 4525 p199
With wife
With 2 children
Baga, Giuseppe; Arkansas, 1918 95.2 p16
Bagalrer, Charles; Indiana, 1847 9117 p19
Bagan, James; New York, NY, 1836 8208.4 p12
Bagas, Gust; Arkansas, 1918 95.2 p16
Bagdonas, Frank; Wisconsin, n.d. 9675.4 p194
Bagel, Augustine 33; America, 1838 778.5 p20
Bagemihl, Caroline Louise 21; New York, NY, 1857 9831.14 p154
Bagemihl, Michael Gottfr. 27; New York, NY, 1857 9831.14 p154
Bager, Christian G.; Wisconsin, n.d. 9675.4 p194
Bager, John George; Pennsylvania, 1752 2444 p186
Bager, John George; Pennsylvania, 1753 2444 p155
Bagge, Andrew 23; Maryland, 1774 1219.7 p228
Bagge, Lorenz; New York, 1754 3652 p79
Baggeley, John; America, 1697 2212 p7
Baggot, Ann 20; Maryland, 1719 3690.1 p7
Bagham, Joan; Died enroute, 1682 4960 p155
Baghane, John; America, 1742 4971 p83
Baginsky, Martin; Washington, 1859-1920 2872.1 p2
Bagley, Dennis 24; Massachusetts, 1847 5881.1 p7
Bagley, Eliz.; Virginia, 1638 6219 p123
Bagley, Mary 30; Massachusetts, 1849 5881.1 p10
Baglini, Amelia; Washington, 1859-1920 2872.1 p2
Baglini, Ferdinando; Washington, 1859-1920 2872.1 p2
Baglini, Ivo; Washington, 1859-1920 2872.1 p2
Baglini, Varese; Washington, 1859-1920 2872.1 p2
Bagly, Hen.; Virginia, 1637 6219 p81
Bagly, James; Virginia, 1639 6219 p157
Bagly, Jon.; Virginia, 1642 6219 p194
Bagly, Thomas; Virginia, 1641 6219 p187
Bagnall, Lawrence 28; Virginia, 1774 1219.7 p186
Bagnanno, Mariano; Iowa, 1866-1943 123.54 p7
Bagnol, Roger; Virginia, 1635 6219 p33
Bagnoli, Leonardo; New York, 1898 1450.2 p1B
Bagott, Ann 20; Maryland, 1719 3690.1 p7
Bagshaw, Benjamin 12; Maryland or Virginia, 1699 2212 p23
Bagwell, Frederick W. 28; Kansas, 1879 5240.1 p61
Bagwell, John 20; Jamaica, 1736 3690.1 p8
Bagwell, Robert 23; Virginia, 1773 1219.7 p168
Bagwortth, John; Virginia, 1637 6219 p82
Bahan, Margaret 13; Massachusetts, 1849 5881.1 p10
Bahan, Peter 35; Massachusetts, 1849 5881.1 p11
Bahi, Joseph; Louisiana, 1789-1819 778.5 p555
Bahlul, Daniel; Shreveport, LA, 1879 7129 p44
Bahmann, Friedrich; America, 1849 8582.1 p2
Bahne, Andreas; America, 1848 8582.3 p2
Bahnmaier, Johann Christian; Port uncertain, 1794 2444 p135
Bahoig, Mr. 35; America, 1838 778.5 p20
Bahr, . . .; Canada, 1776-1783 9786 p16
Bahr, Mr.; Quebec, 1776 9786 p259
Bahr, Andrew; California, 1865 3840.1 p14
Bahwell, Adam; California, 1867 2769.1 p6
Baier, . . .; Canada, 1776-1783 9786 p16
Baier, Charles; Illinois, 1866 5012.38 p98
Baihler, Jean 29; America, 1838 778.5 p20
Bail, . . .; Canada, 1776-1783 9786 p16
Bailes, John; Virginia, 1652 6251 p20
Bailes, Thomas; Virginia, 1652 6251 p20
Bailey, Mr.; Quebec, 1815 9229.18 p77
With wife
With child
Bailey, Bernhard; Kentucky, 1839-1840 8582.3 p98
Bailey, Catherine; St. John, N.B., 1849 5704.8 p56
Bailey, Daniel; St. John, N.B., 1848 5704.8 p45
Bailey, David 5 *SEE* Bailey, George
Bailey, David 5; Philadelphia, 1850 5704.8 p60
Bailey, Edward 21; Maryland, 1774 1219.7 p204
Bailey, Elam C.; Ohio, 1841 9892.11 p2
Bailey, Eliza 21; Massachusetts, 1849 5881.1 p7
Bailey, Esther; Philadelphia, 1811 53.26 p2
Bailey, Esther; Philadelphia, 1811 2859.11 p8
Bailey, George; Philadelphia, 1850 53.26 p2
*Relative:*Sarah
*Relative:*George 7
*Relative:*David 5
*Relative:*Stewart 3
*Relative:*Matty Jane 9 mos
Bailey, George; Philadelphia, 1850 5704.8 p60
Bailey, George 7 *SEE* Bailey, George
Bailey, George 7; Philadelphia, 1850 5704.8 p60
Bailey, Henry L. 43; Massachusetts, 1860 6410.32 p120
Bailey, Henry Lawrence; New Orleans, 1837 6410.32 p126
Bailey, Hugh; Philadelphia, 1851 5704.8 p71
Bailey, Isaac 30; Maryland, 1775 1219.7 p252
Bailey, James; Philadelphia, 1850 5704.8 p64
Bailey, James; Washington, 1859-1920 2872.1 p2
Bailey, James 22; Philadelphia, 1774 1219.7 p183
Bailey, James 31; Maryland, 1774 1219.7 p178
Bailey, John; Virginia, 1858 4626.16 p17
Bailey, John 15; Philadelphia, 1774 1219.7 p233
Bailey, John 21; Virginia, 1774 1219.7 p238
Bailey, John 23; Maryland, 1774 1219.7 p187
Bailey, Jonathan 18; Jamaica, 1739 3690.1 p8
Bailey, Joseph 15; New Orleans, 1863 543.30 p248
Bailey, Josiah 22; Virginia, 1775 1219.7 p247
Bailey, Margaret; Philadelphia, 1850 5704.8 p64
Bailey, Matty Jane 9 mos *SEE* Bailey, George
Bailey, Matty Jane 9 mos; Philadelphia, 1850 5704.8 p60
Bailey, R. H.; Washington, 1859-1920 2872.1 p3
Bailey, Robert; New York, NY, 1836 8208.4 p59
Bailey, Sarah *SEE* Bailey, George
Bailey, Sarah; Maryland, 1751 1219.7 p1
Bailey, Sarah; Philadelphia, 1850 5704.8 p60
Bailey, Seth 21; Maryland, 1774 1219.7 p223
Bailey, Seth 21; Maryland, 1774 1219.7 p228
Bailey, Stewart 3 *SEE* Bailey, George
Bailey, Stewart 3; Philadelphia, 1850 5704.8 p60
Bailey, Thomas; Philadelphia, 1850 53.26 p3
Bailey, Thomas 17; Maryland, 1774 1219.7 p225
Bailey, Tim 22; Massachusetts, 1849 5881.1 p12
Bailey, William; Iowa, 1866-1943 123.54 p7
Bailey, William; Philadelphia, 1851 5704.8 p71
Bailey, William; South Carolina, 1791 1639.20 p5
Bailey, William 6; Massachusetts, 1850 5881.1 p12
Bailie, David; New York, NY, 1816 2859.11 p25
Bailie, Elizabeth 46 *SEE* Bailie, Mathew
Bailie, Evan 28; St. Vincent, 1775 1219.7 p251
Bailie, Isabella; New York, NY, 1816 2859.11 p25
Bailie, James; New York, NY, 1816 2859.11 p25
Bailie, John; New York, NY, 1816 2859.11 p25
Bailie, Mary Anne; New York, NY, 1816 2859.11 p25
Bailie, Mathew 48; Philadelphia, 1804 53.26 p3
*Relative:*Elizabeth 46
*Relative:*Stewart 20
*Relative:*Matty 18
Bailie, Matty 18 *SEE* Bailie, Mathew
Bailie, Robert; New York, NY, 1816 2859.11 p25
Bailie, Stewart 20 *SEE* Bailie, Mathew
Bailie, Thomas; New York, NY, 1816 2859.11 p25
Bailie, William; New York, NY, 1816 2859.11 p25
Bailleres, Mr.; Port uncertain, 1839 778.5 p20
Bailley, Martin; New York, NY, 1833 8208.4 p30
Baillie, Emily 18; St. John, N.B., 1862 5704.8 p151
Baillie, Hugh; New Brunswick, 1773 9775.5 p204
Baillie, John 1; St. John, N.B., 1862 5704.8 p151
Baillie, William; North America, 1759 1219.7 p70
Bailliet, Paul; Philadelphia, 1759 9973.7 p33
Baillon, A. J. 40; New Orleans, 1829 778.5 p20
Bailly, Frederique *SEE* Bailly, George-Frederic
Bailly, Frederique-Sybille R. *SEE* Bailly, George-Frederic
Bailly, George-Frederic 25; Halifax, N.S., 1752 7074.6 p208
*Wife:*Frederique
*Son:*Jean
Bailly, George-Frederic 25; Halifax, N.S., 1752 7074.6 p220
*Wife:*Frederique-Sybille R.
With child
Bailly, Jean *SEE* Bailly, George-Frederic
Bailly, Martin; New York, NY, 1833 8208.4 p30
Baily, Richard 15; Maryland, 1722 3690.1 p8
Baily, Wm. 22; New Orleans, 1862 543.30 p242
Baimbrick, Martin; New York, NY, 1811 2859.11 p8
With family
Bain, Alexander 26; Maryland, 1774 1219.7 p215
Bain, Alexander 27; Maryland, 1774 1219.7 p180
Bain, Catherine 25; Quebec, 1863 5704.8 p153
Bain, John 7; Quebec, 1863 5704.8 p153
Bain, John 27; Quebec, 1863 5704.8 p153
Bain, Margaret 9 mos; Quebec, 1863 5704.8 p153
Bain, Patrick; Boston, 1892 1450.2 p1B
Bain, Patrick; Philadelphia, 1850 53.26 p3
Bain, Patrick; Philadelphia, 1850 5704.8 p68
Bain, Thomas George; Arkansas, 1918 95.2 p16
Bain, William; Georgia, 1775 1219.7 p275
Bain, William 37; Wilmington, NC, 1774 1639.20 p5
Bainham, John; Virginia, 1621 6219 p2
Bainham, Thomas; Virginia, 1643 6219 p202
Bainier, Julien 30; America, 1839 778.5 p20
Bair, Marie Ann 16; America, 1831 778.5 p20
Baird, . . . 4; Philadelphia, 1854 5704.8 p123
Baird, . . . 6; Philadelphia, 1854 5704.8 p123
Baird, Agnes 7; Quebec, 1864 5704.8 p163
Baird, Agnes 30; Quebec, 1864 5704.8 p163
Baird, Andrew 11; Quebec, 1862 5704.8 p151
Baird, Ann 11; Philadelphia, 1854 5704.8 p123
Baird, Ann 30 *SEE* Baird, James
Baird, Anne 8; Quebec, 1862 5704.8 p151
Baird, Archibald; South Carolina, 1777 1639.20 p5
Baird, Catherine 8; Philadelphia, 1854 5704.8 p123
Baird, Catherine 16; Quebec, 1862 5704.8 p151
Baird, Catherine 48; Philadelphia, 1854 5704.8 p123
Baird, David; Philadelphia, 1847 53.26 p3
Baird, David; Philadelphia, 1847 5704.8 p30
Baird, Elenor 17 *SEE* Baird, James
Baird, George; New York, NY, 1816 2859.11 p25
Baird, George 18; Quebec, 1862 5704.8 p151
Baird, Hamilton 21; Quebec, 1862 5704.8 p151
Baird, James; Carolina, 1684 1639.20 p5
Baird, James; Philadelphia, 1852 5704.8 p88
Baird, James 13; Philadelphia, 1854 5704.8 p123
Baird, James 14; Quebec, 1862 5704.8 p151
Baird, James 18; Jamaica, 1749 3690.1 p8
Baird, James 19; Philadelphia, 1861 5704.8 p148
Baird, James 50; Quebec, 1862 5704.8 p151
Baird, James 58; Philadelphia, 1833-1834 53.26 p3
*Relative:*William 28
*Relative:*James, Jr. 23
*Relative:*John 9
*Relative:*Ann 30
*Relative:*Elenor 17
*Relative:*Mary Ann 14
*Relative:*Martha 7
Baird, James, Jr. 23 *SEE* Baird, James
Baird, Jane 20; Philadelphia, 1854 5704.8 p118
Baird, John 9 *SEE* Baird, James
Baird, John 20; Quebec, 1862 5704.8 p151
Baird, Joseph; New York, NY, 1837 8208.4 p53
Baird, Martha 7 *SEE* Baird, James
Baird, Mary 4; Quebec, 1864 5704.8 p163
Baird, Mary Ann 14 *SEE* Baird, James
Baird, Nancy 40; Quebec, 1862 5704.8 p151
Baird, Pat; Philadelphia, 1853 5704.8 p101
Baird, Samuel; New York, NY, 1816 2859.11 p25

Baird, Samuel 9; Quebec, 1862 ***5704.8*** *p151*
Baird, Samuel 20; St. John, N.B., 1857 ***5704.8*** *p135*
Baird, Susan; Quebec, 1851 ***5704.8*** *p73*
Baird, Thomas; Quebec, 1850 ***5704.8*** *p67*
Baird, Thomas 5; Quebec, 1862 ***5704.8*** *p151*
Baird, Thomas 30; Philadelphia, 1854 ***5704.8*** *p118*
Baird, Thomas 32; Quebec, 1864 ***5704.8*** *p163*
Baird, Washington; New York, NY, 1816 ***2859.11*** *p25*
Baird, William 6; Quebec, 1862 ***5704.8*** *p151*
Baird, William 28 *SEE* Baird, James
Baird, Winifred Irving; South Carolina, 1779 ***1639.20*** *p99*
Bairn, James; Quebec, 1847 ***5704.8*** *p13*
Bairn, John; St. John, N.B., 1852 ***5704.8*** *p84*
Bairst, John; Wisconsin, n.d. ***9675.4*** *p194*
Baiser, Chatrune 26; America, 1838 ***778.5*** *p20*
Baiser, Joseph 18; America, 1838 ***778.5*** *p20*
Baisley, Robert 39; Maryland, 1774 ***1219.7*** *p207*
Baitenmann, Georg Friedrich *SEE* Baitenmann, Johann Georg
Baitenmann, Johann Georg; America, 1735-1800 ***2444*** *p135*
*Wife:*Margaretha Eulenfuss
*Child:*Georg Friedrich
*Child:*Rosina
Baitenmann, Margaretha Eulenfuss *SEE* Baitenmann, Johann Georg
Baitenmann, Rosina *SEE* Baitenmann, Johann Georg
Baitsovitch, Sam; Iowa, 1866-1943 ***123.54*** *p7*
Baiz, Mr. 34; New Orleans, 1827 ***778.5*** *p21*
Bajat, P.; New Orleans, 1839 ***778.5*** *p36*
Bakar, Alexander; South Carolina, 1788 ***7119*** *p202*
Bakehaus, Henry; America, 1843 ***1450.2*** *p7A*
Bakemeir, Charles; America, 1851 ***1450.2*** *p7A*
Bakemeir, Frederick; America, 1849 ***1450.2*** *p7A*
Baker, . . .; Canada, 1776-1783 ***9786*** *p16*
Baker, Mr. 25; New Orleans, 1838 ***778.5*** *p21*
Baker, Abraham 17; Maryland, 1774 ***1219.7*** *p208*
Baker, Adam; New York, NY, 1837 ***8208.4*** *p52*
Baker, Adam 26; Kansas, 1873 ***5240.1*** *p54*
Baker, Alfred W.; Kansas, 1875 ***5240.1*** *p4*
Baker, Alice; Virginia, 1637 ***6219*** *p111*
Baker, Alice; Virginia, 1642 ***6219*** *p188*
Baker, Ann 16; Maryland, 1774 ***1219.7*** *p229*
Baker, Ann Pringle; Charleston, SC, 1680-1830 ***1639.20*** *p264*
Baker, Ann Sharp *SEE* Baker, Jon.
Baker, Bateman; Nova Scotia, 1771 ***1219.7*** *p150*
Baker, Catherine 35 *SEE* Baker, Mary
Baker, Charlie; Illinois, 1873 ***5012.39*** *p26*
Baker, Christian; New York, NY, 1835 ***8208.4*** *p29*
Baker, Daniel; Virginia, 1635 ***6219*** *p36*
Baker, Daniell; Virginia, 1637 ***6219*** *p83*
Baker, David; Cincinnati, 1869-1887 ***8582*** *p1*
Baker, Dorothy *SEE* Baker, John
Baker, Duncan 55; North Carolina, 1850 ***1639.20*** *p5*
Baker, Eliza.; Virginia, 1643 ***6219*** *p201*
Baker, Ellis; Virginia, 1635 ***6219*** *p10*
Baker, Ernest; Arkansas, 1918 ***95.2*** *p16*
Baker, Francis; Virginia, 1646 ***6219*** *p246*
Baker, Frank; Washington, 1859-1920 ***2872.1*** *p2*
Baker, Geo.; Virginia, 1637 ***6219*** *p113*
Baker, Georg; America, 1851 ***8582.3*** *p2*
Baker, George; Washington, 1859-1920 ***2872.1*** *p2*
Baker, George 29; Maryland, 1774 ***1219.7*** *p180*
Baker, George Jacob; America, 1817 ***1450.2*** *p7A*
Baker, Harry; Arkansas, 1918 ***95.2*** *p16*
Baker, Helgor; Philadelphia, 1780 ***8137*** *p6*
Baker, Henry; Indiana, 1836 ***9117*** *p15*
Baker, Henry 19; Maryland, 1754 ***1219.7*** *p28*
Baker, Henry 19; Maryland, 1754 ***3690.1*** *p8*
Baker, Herbert W. 24; Kansas, 1888 ***5240.1*** *p72*
Baker, Hugh; Virginia, 1637 ***6219*** *p111*
Baker, Humpherey 18; Maryland, 1729 ***3690.1*** *p8*
Baker, Isaac; Antigua (Antego), 1768 ***1219.7*** *p136*
Baker, James 22; Maryland, 1774 ***1219.7*** *p180*
Baker, James Fowler; Charleston, SC, 1680-1830 ***1639.20*** *p5*
Baker, Jesse; Washington, 1859-1920 ***2872.1*** *p2*
Baker, Jno; Virginia, 1698 ***2212*** *p15*
Baker, John; New York, NY, 1838 ***8208.4*** *p61*
Baker, John; Virginia, 1636 ***6219*** *p79*
Baker, John; Virginia, 1637 ***6219*** *p111*
*Wife:*Dorothy
Baker, John; Virginia, 1642 ***6219*** *p195*
Baker, John; Virginia, 1645 ***6219*** *p233*
Baker, John 17; Jamaica, 1720 ***3690.1*** *p8*
Baker, John 19; Jamaica, 1733 ***3690.1*** *p8*
Baker, John Ludwig; New York, NY, 1836 ***8208.4*** *p11*
Baker, Jon.; Virginia, 1629 ***6219*** *p8*
Baker, Jon.; Virginia, 1635 ***6219*** *p20*
Baker, Jon.; Virginia, 1636 ***6219*** *p32*
Baker, Jon.; Virginia, 1636 ***6219*** *p75*
*Wife:*Ann Sharp
Baker, Jon.; Virginia, 1637 ***6219*** *p11*
Baker, Jon.; Virginia, 1638 ***6219*** *p122*
Baker, Joseph; Indiana, 1847 ***9117*** *p19*
Baker, Joseph 16; Maryland, 1723 ***3690.1*** *p8*
Baker, Lewis; Virginia, 1638 ***6219*** *p150*
Baker, Martin; Virginia, 1643 ***6219*** *p201*
Baker, Mary 80; North Carolina, 1850 ***1639.20*** *p5*
*Relative:*Catherine 35
Baker, Michael 50; Kansas, 1888 ***5240.1*** *p4*
Baker, Michael 50; Kansas, 1888 ***5240.1*** *p72*
Baker, Nicholas; New York, NY, 1834 ***8208.4*** *p57*
Baker, Nicholas 19; Maryland, 1722 ***3690.1*** *p8*
Baker, Parker 29; Maryland, 1774 ***1219.7*** *p187*
Baker, Philip; Indiana, 1855 ***1450.2*** *p11A*
Baker, Ray; Washington, 1859-1920 ***2872.1*** *p2*
Baker, Richard; Virginia, 1636 ***6219*** *p74*
Baker, Richard; Virginia, 1639 ***6219*** *p24*
Baker, Richard; Virginia, 1639 ***6219*** *p151*
Baker, Richard 11; Philadelphia, 1775 ***1219.7*** *p248*
Baker, Sarah 19; St. Christopher, 1736 ***3690.1*** *p8*
Baker, Silvester; Virginia, 1643 ***6219*** *p206*
Baker, Solomon 21; Maryland, 1774 ***1219.7*** *p187*
Baker, Thomas 24; Jamaica, 1738 ***3690.1*** *p8*
Baker, William; Virginia, 1635 ***6219*** *p34*
Baker, William; Virginia, 1637 ***6219*** *p110*
Baker, William; Virginia, 1638 ***6219*** *p125*
Baker, William 18; Maryland, 1720 ***3690.1*** *p9*
Baker, William 19; Maryland, 1721 ***3690.1*** *p9*
Baker, Wm.; Virginia, 1637 ***6219*** *p11*
Baker, Wm.; Virginia, 1637 ***6219*** *p83*
Bakeson, Margaret 18; St. Christopher, 1733 ***3690.1*** *p9*
Bakkala, Andrew; Washington, 1859-1920 ***2872.1*** *p2*
Bakke, Lorents; Arkansas, 1918 ***95.2*** *p16*
Bakolis, George 38; Kansas, 1905 ***5240.1*** *p83*
Bakovnik, Jerney; Wisconsin, n.d. ***9675.4*** *p194*
Bakutis, Izidorus; Arkansas, 1918 ***95.2*** *p16*
Bakwell, John Henry; Philadelphia, 1868 ***5704.8*** *p230*
Baladimas, Pete; Arkansas, 1918 ***95.2*** *p16*
Balakirowa, Zofia 24; New York, 1912 ***9980.29*** *p58*
Balamel, B. 50; America, 1820 ***778.5*** *p21*
Baland, Thomas; New York, NY, 1816 ***2859.11*** *p25*
Balanis, Karmus Adam; Arkansas, 1918 ***95.2*** *p16*
Balbach, George; Wisconsin, n.d. ***9675.4*** *p194*
Balbee, Anthony 20; Jamaica, 1733 ***3690.1*** *p9*
Balbi, Antone 20; Jamaica, 1733 ***3690.1*** *p9*
Balciukonis, Joseph; Wisconsin, n.d. ***9675.4*** *p194*
Balcke, . . .; Quebec, 1776 ***9786*** *p104*
Bald, Jacob 35; Pennsylvania, 1753 ***2444*** *p135*
Baldarie, Antonio; Arkansas, 1918 ***95.2*** *p16*
Baldau, . . .; Canada, 1776-1783 ***9786*** *p16*
Balde, Henry; America, 1852 ***1450.2*** *p7A*
Balderon, G.; New Orleans, 1839 ***778.5*** *p21*
Baldet, Mr. 30; America, 1838 ***778.5*** *p21*
Baldigo, John; Arkansas, 1918 ***95.2*** *p16*
Balding, Francis; Virginia, 1642 ***6219*** *p197*
Balding, Gerda; Ohio, 1819-1899 ***9892.11*** *p2*
Baldini, Alesandro; Wisconsin, n.d. ***9675.4*** *p194*
Baldini, Dominick; Wisconsin, n.d. ***9675.4*** *p194*
Baldini, Fco. 21; New York, NY, 1893 ***9026.4*** *p41*
Baldini, P.; Wisconsin, n.d. ***9675.4*** *p194*
Baldini, Tony; Wisconsin, n.d. ***9675.4*** *p194*
Baldino, Lorenzo; Arkansas, 1918 ***95.2*** *p16*
Baldock, Dasey; Virginia, 1638 ***6219*** *p122*
Baldock, James 48; Kansas, 1872 ***5240.1*** *p52*
Baldock, James, Jr. 22; Kansas, 1872 ***5240.1*** *p52*
Baldock, Sarah 23; Maryland, 1773 ***1219.7*** *p173*
Baldoni, Guisippe; Iowa, 1866-1943 ***123.54*** *p7*
Baldrick, John 20; Quebec, 1859 ***5704.8*** *p143*
Baldridge, Ira; Washington, 1859-1920 ***2872.1*** *p2*
Baldry, John 22; Philadelphia, 1774 ***1219.7*** *p233*
Baldvinsdottir, Asta 6; Quebec, 1879 ***2557.1*** *p39*
Baldvinsson, Jon 12; Quebec, 1879 ***2557.1*** *p39*
Baldvinsson, Thorsteinn 11; Quebec, 1879 ***2557.1*** *p39*
Baldwin, Charles; Virginia, 1647 ***6219*** *p245*
Baldwin, Ellen 23; Massachusetts, 1849 ***5881.1*** *p7*
Baldwin, John; Virginia, 1648 ***6219*** *p253*
Baldwin, John 5; Massachusetts, 1850 ***5881.1*** *p9*
Baldwin, John 17; Maryland, 1718 ***3690.1*** *p9*
Baldwin, John 19; Jamaica, 1722 ***3690.1*** *p9*
Baldwin, John 20; Barbados, 1721 ***3690.1*** *p9*
Baldwin, Mary 3; Massachusetts, 1850 ***5881.1*** *p11*
Baldwin, Rola 2; Massachusetts, 1850 ***5881.1*** *p12*
Baldwin, William 22; Virginia, 1773 ***1219.7*** *p171*
Baldwin, William 24; Maryland, 1775 ***1219.7*** *p262*
Baldwin, William Thomas 40; California, 1872 ***2769.2*** *p4*
Baldwin, Wm.; Virginia, 1635 ***6219*** *p12*
Baldwyn, John; Virginia, 1636 ***6219*** *p74*
Baldzikowski, Walenty; Arkansas, 1918 ***95.2*** *p16*
Bale, Adam 24; Maryland, 1775 ***1219.7*** *p257*
Bale, John 25; Maryland, 1774 ***1219.7*** *p187*
Bale, Thomas, Jr.; New York, NY, 1834 ***8208.4*** *p2*
Bale, William; Philadelphia, 1868 ***5704.8*** *p225*
Balen, Isabella; St. John, N.B., 1847 ***5704.8*** *p35*
Balen, John; St. John, N.B., 1847 ***5704.8*** *p35*
Balen, Thomas 12; St. John, N.B., 1847 ***5704.8*** *p35*
Balen, William 10; St. John, N.B., 1847 ***5704.8*** *p35*
Bales, Tho.; Virginia, 1632 ***6219*** *p180*
Balestrere, Sam; Arkansas, 1918 ***95.2*** *p16*
Balfe, Oliver; Virginia, 1643 ***6219*** *p205*
Balfe, Oliver; Virginia, 1648 ***6219*** *p246*
Balffs, Marcus; New York, 1750 ***3652*** *p74*
Balfour, Andrew; Boston, 1772 ***1639.20*** *p6*
*Child:*Tibbie
Balfour, Andrew; South Carolina, 1741 ***1639.20*** *p5*
Balfour, Charles; America, 1793 ***1639.20*** *p6*
With wife & 6 children
Balfour, Edmund 9 mos; Quebec, 1847 ***5704.8*** *p17*
Balfour, George 4; Quebec, 1847 ***5704.8*** *p17*
Balfour, Henry; Charleston, SC, 1794 ***1639.20*** *p6*
Balfour, Isabella 11; Quebec, 1847 ***5704.8*** *p17*
Balfour, James 13; Quebec, 1847 ***5704.8*** *p17*
Balfour, Jane; Quebec, 1847 ***5704.8*** *p17*
Balfour, John; Charleston, SC, 1737-1781 ***1639.20*** *p6*
Balfour, Margaret 6; Quebec, 1847 ***5704.8*** *p17*
Balfour, Mary Jane 10; Quebec, 1847 ***5704.8*** *p17*
Balfour, Robert 7; Quebec, 1847 ***5704.8*** *p17*
Balfour, Tibbie *SEE* Balfour, Andrew
Balfour, William; Quebec, 1847 ***5704.8*** *p17*
Balfour, William 8; Quebec, 1847 ***5704.8*** *p17*
Balie, John 20; Virginia, 1700 ***2212*** *p30*
Balinsky, Peter; America, 1900 ***7137*** *p168*
Balis, Jean 26; New Orleans, 1838 ***778.5*** *p21*
Balissa, John Solomon 31; Maryland, 1774 ***1219.7*** *p222*
Balistocke, Rich.; Virginia, 1642 ***6219*** *p197*
Balivet, . . .; America, 1837 ***778.5*** *p21*
Balivet, Mme. 38; America, 1837 ***778.5*** *p21*
Balivet, Emile 25; America, 1837 ***778.5*** *p21*
Balke, Charles; America, 1851 ***1450.2*** *p7A*
Balke, Johann Casper; Quebec, 1776 ***9786*** *p262*
Balke, Julius; America, 1851 ***8582.3*** *p2*
Ball, Adam; Ohio, 1843 ***8582.1*** *p51*
Ball, Andrew; New York, NY, 1839 ***8208.4*** *p92*
Ball, Charles; Iowa, 1866-1943 ***123.54*** *p7*
Ball, Georg; Virginia, 1639 ***6219*** *p152*
Ball, James; New York, NY, 1815 ***2859.11*** *p25*
Ball, James 13; St. John, N.B., 1847 ***5704.8*** *p35*
Ball, Jane; America, 1741 ***4971*** *p16*
Ball, Jane; Annapolis, MD, 1742 ***4971*** *p93*
Ball, Jane; Maryland, 1742 ***4971*** *p107*
Ball, Joane; Virginia, 1643 ***6219*** *p230*
Ball, John; America, 1736 ***4971*** *p12*
Ball, John; Iowa, 1866-1943 ***123.54*** *p7*
Ball, Richard; Quebec, 1823 ***7603*** *p29*
Ball, Richard; Virginia, 1638 ***6219*** *p120*
Ball, Robert; America, 1741 ***4971*** *p23*
Ball, Sarah 17; Maryland or Virginia, 1720 ***3690.1*** *p9*
Ball, Silvanus 22; Virginia, 1774 ***1219.7*** *p241*
Ball, Thomas 20; Maryland, 1722 ***3690.1*** *p9*
Ball, Thomas 33; Virginia, 1774 ***1219.7*** *p227*
Ball, Wilhelm; Ohio, 1811 ***8582.1*** *p48*
Ball, William; New York, 1852 ***1450.2*** *p7A*
Balla, L. 30; America, 1838 ***778.5*** *p21*
Ballagh, James; New York, NY, 1816 ***2859.11*** *p25*
Ballagh, Robert; New York, NY, 1816 ***2859.11*** *p25*
Ballagh, Robert E.; New York, NY, 1816 ***2859.11*** *p25*
Ballah, William; New York, NY, 1811 ***2859.11*** *p8*
Ballain, Luis 65; New Orleans, 1826 ***778.5*** *p21*
Ballantine, Daniel; St. John, N.B., 1853 ***5704.8*** *p99*
Ballantine, David; Charleston, SC, 1798 ***1639.20*** *p6*
Ballantine, Jane; St. John, N.B., 1853 ***5704.8*** *p99*
Ballantine, John; Charleston, SC, 1830 ***1639.20*** *p6*
Ballantine, John; Philadelphia, 1852 ***5704.8*** *p91*
Ballantine, John 28; St. John, N.B., 1866 ***5704.8*** *p167*
Ballantine, Margaret; Philadelphia, 1852 ***5704.8*** *p91*
Ballantine, Matilda 3 mos; St. John, N.B., 1853 ***5704.8*** *p99*
Ballantine, William; Philadelphia, 1847 ***53.26*** *p3*
Ballantine, William; Philadelphia, 1847 ***5704.8*** *p2*
Ballantyne, Susan Stewart; Charleston, SC, 1820-1830 ***1639.20*** *p6*
Ballard, Cleston; Illinois, 1892 ***2896.5*** *p2*
Ballard, George 21; Virginia, 1774 ***1219.7*** *p225*
Ballard, Joseph 22; Jamaica, 1731 ***3690.1*** *p9*
Ballard, William; Illinois, 1894 ***2896.5*** *p2*
Ballars, John 20; New Orleans, 1829 ***778.5*** *p21*
Ballauf, Louis; Cincinnati, 1837 ***8582.1*** *p2*
Ballaver, George; Indiana, 1848 ***9117*** *p16*
Ballaves, John 30; Mexico, 1836 ***778.5*** *p22*
Ballaz, Peter 30; New Orleans, 1864 ***543.30*** *p246*
Balldwin, Thomas 17; Barbados, 1721 ***3690.1*** *p9*
Ballenganti, James; Iowa, 1866-1943 ***123.54*** *p7*
Ballenhorst, Margaret; New York, 1749 ***3652*** *p72*
Ballentine, James; Philadelphia, 1865 ***5704.8*** *p190*

Ballentine, Robert W.; Texas, 1836 **9777** *p4*
Ballentine, William 29; Kansas, 1888 **5240.1** *p72*
Baller, Andrew; Colorado, 1891 **9678.1** *p152*
Baller, Ole; Colorado, 1891 **9678.1** *p152*
Ballet, Mr. 32; America, 1839 **778.5** *p22*
Ballett, Samuel 27; Jamaica, 1737 **3690.1** *p9*
Ballhorn, Henry; Washington, 1859-1920 **2872.1** *p2*
Balli, Elizabeth; Wisconsin, n.d. **9675.4** *p194*
Balliache, . . .; Port uncertain, 1839 **778.5** *p22*
Balliache, Mr.; Port uncertain, 1839 **778.5** *p22*
Ballie, Frederique-Sybille R. *SEE* Ballie, George-Frederic
Ballie, George-Frederic 25; Halifax, N.S., 1752 **7074.6** *p220*
*Wife:*Frederique-Sybille R.
With child
Ballin, Carl 63; Denver, CO, 1897 **1763** *p40C*
Balling, Thomas 25; Jamaica, 1736 **3690.1** *p10*
Ballinger, Johann; Kentucky, 1840 **8582.3** *p99*
Balliset, M. 33; New Orleans, 1835 **778.5** *p22*
Ballmer, Michael 23; Jamaica, 1731 **3690.1** *p10*
Ballo, Anton; Wisconsin, n.d. **9675.4** *p194*
Ballo, Elizabeth; Wisconsin, n.d. **9675.4** *p194*
Ballot, Mrs. 30; New Orleans, 1829 **778.5** *p22*
Balls, Charles H.; New York, NY, 1849 **1450.2** *p7A*
Ballweck, Frederick; America, 1851 **1450.2** *p8A*
Ballweg, Ambrose; America, 1849 **1450.2** *p8A*
Balm, Jno. 35; Pennsylvania, 1753 **2444** *p135*
Balme, Catherine *SEE* Balme, Jaques
Balme, Jaques; Port uncertain, 1753 **2444** *p135*
*Wife:*Marie Costebel
*Child:*Susanne Maria
*Child:*Catherine
Balme, Marie Costebel *SEE* Balme, Jaques
Balme, Susanne Maria *SEE* Balme, Jaques
Balmer, Jakob; Ohio, 1815 **8582.1** *p48*
Balmer, Joseph 25; Kansas, 1875 **5240.1** *p56*
Balmert, Johann 26; America, 1854-1855 **9162.6** *p105*
Balsamo, Antonio; Arkansas, 1918 **95.2** *p16*
Balshaw, Richard 35; New Orleans, 1862 **543.30** *p108*
Balskewicz, Anna 17; New York, 1912 **9980.29** *p74*
Balsmeyer, Anne Cath.; America, 1838 **4610.10** *p133*
Balsomo, Salvatore; Arkansas, 1918 **95.2** *p16*
Baltakis, Miedas; Arkansas, 1918 **95.2** *p17*
Balthasar, Jenny; New York, NY, 1836 **8208.4** *p8*
Balton, Michael 13; Massachusetts, 1850 **5881.1** *p11*
Baltutis, Albion; America, 1886 **1450.2** *p8A*
Balut, Joachim M.; Arkansas, 1918 **95.2** *p17*
Balver, Beves; Virginia, 1642 **6219** *p197*
Balverd, James; South Carolina, 1729 **1639.20** *p6*
Baly, Richard; Virginia, 1636 **6219** *p75*
Balzano, Filippo 22; New York, NY, 1893 **9026.4** *p41*
Balzer, Valentine 54; Kansas, 1880 **5240.1** *p62*
Bamber, George; New York, NY, 1836 **8208.4** *p15*
Bamber, James; New York, NY, 1833 **8208.4** *p58*
Bamber, John; New York, NY, 1833 **8208.4** *p58*
Bamber, John; New York, NY, 1836 **8208.4** *p14*
Bamberg, J.G.; South Carolina, 1788 **7119** *p199*
Bamberg, J.G.; South Carolina, 1788 **7119** *p201*
Bamberger, Herman; America, 1853 **1450.2** *p8A*
Bamberger, Philipp; America, 1840 **8582.3** *p2*
Bambergy, Mme. 22; America, 1838 **778.5** *p22*
Bambergy, Mr. 30; America, 1838 **778.5** *p22*
Bambrick, Hugh; America, 1741 **4971** *p31*
Bambrick, Thomas; New York, NY, 1816 **2859.11** *p25*
Bambridge, Christopher; Virginia, 1638 **6219** *p159*
Bambridge, Christopher; Virginia, 1639 **6219** *p158*
Bamfeild, John; Virginia, 1649 **6219** *p252*
Bamfield, Albert; Ohio, 1854 **9892.11** *p2*
Bamford, Anthony; New York, NY, 1913 **3455.4** *p28*
Bamford, James 27; Kansas, 1889 **5240.1** *p73*
Bamford, William 22; Jamaica, 1730 **3690.1** *p10*
Bamforth, John; Virginia, 1642 **6219** *p191*
Bamour, M. 25; America, 1835 **778.5** *p22*
Bampf, . . .; Canada, 1776-1783 **9786** *p41*
Bampton, William; New York, NY, 1834 **8208.4** *p38*
Banas, James 20; St. John, N.B., 1866 **5704.8** *p166*
Banasjzak, Joseph; Arkansas, 1918 **95.2** *p17*
Banaszak, Steve; Arkansas, 1918 **95.2** *p17*
Banchetti, Floria; Arkansas, 1918 **95.2** *p17*
Banchetti, Florio; Arkansas, 1918 **95.2** *p17*
Banckes, Jon.; Virginia, 1635 **6219** *p12*
Banckes, Ralph 14; America, 1705 **2212** *p45*
Bancks, John; Virginia, 1638 **6219** *p149*
Bancks, Jon.; Virginia, 1637 **6219** *p110*
Bancroft, William; Virginia, 1640 **6219** *p181*
Banczakiewicz, Ludwik; New York, 1831 **4606** *p172*
Band, Isabella 35; Quebec, 1855 **5704.8** *p125*
Band, John 6; Quebec, 1855 **5704.8** *p125*
Band, Nathaniel 20; New England, 1721 **3690.1** *p10*
Band, William 8; Quebec, 1855 **5704.8** *p125*
Bandalow, Gottfried; Illinois, 1868 **2896.5** *p2*
Bandara, Geovani; Arkansas, 1918 **95.2** *p17*
Bandel, Friedrich; Quebec, 1776 **9786** *p260*
Bandell, Barbara 5; New Orleans, 1838 **778.5** *p22*
Bandemann, Johannes; Ohio, 1800 **8582.2** *p58*
Bandermann, . . .; America, 1869-1885 **8582.2** *p1*
Bandin, Paul; Iowa, 1866-1943 **123.54** *p7*
Bandle, Jacob Christian; America, 1848 **8582.3** *p2*
Bands, Mary 35; Maryland, 1774 **1219.7** *p215*
Bandush, Frank; Washington, 1859-1920 **2872.1** *p3*
Bandwick, John; Virginia, 1645 **6219** *p252*
Bane, Daniel; America, 1737-1738 **4971** *p59*
Bane, Garret; America, 1740 **4971** *p48*
Bane, John; Ohio, 1852 **9892.11** *p2*
Bane, Roger; Colorado, 1904 **9678.1** *p152*
Banecan, Christopher; New York, NY, 1811 **2859.11** *p8*
Banedios, Rosine 70; New Orleans, 1839 **9420.2** *p71*
Banen, Rich.; Virginia, 1635 **6219** *p20*
Baner, . . .; Canada, 1776-1783 **9786** *p41*
Banes, Thomas 20; Maryland, 1721 **3690.1** *p10*
Banfen, P. 31; New Orleans, 1822 **778.5** *p22*
Banfield, Charles; America, 1741 **4971** *p61*
Banfield, James 33; Jamaica, 1725 **3690.1** *p10*
Banfield, William 18; Antigua (Antego), 1728 **3690.1** *p10*
Bang, Christian; New York, NY, 1838 **8208.4** *p86*
Bange, Heinrich; America, 1850 **3702.7** *p322*
Bange, Heinrich; New Orleans, 1852 **3702.7** *p322*
Bangert, . . .; Canada, 1776-1783 **9786** *p16*
Bangert, Barbara 18; America, 1853 **9162.7** *p14*
Bangert, Christina 16; America, 1853 **9162.7** *p14*
Bangert, Elizabetha 25; America, 1853 **9162.7** *p14*
Bangert, Franz 21; America, 1853 **9162.7** *p14*
Bangert, Jacob; New York, NY, 1839 **8208.4** *p92*
Bangert, Katharina 4; America, 1853 **9162.7** *p14*
Bangert, Wilhelm; Illinois, 1845 **8582.2** *p51*
Banghel, Jacob 28; America, 1837 **778.5** *p22*
Bangson, Peter; Bangor, ME, 1872-1877 **6410.22** *p116*
Bangson, Peter; Maine, 1877 **6410.22** *p125*
Banick, Daniel; South Dakota, 1889 **1641** *p41*
Banick, Elizabeth; South Dakota, 1889 **1641** *p41*
Banick, Karl; South Dakota, 1889 **1641** *p41*
Banick, Karolina; South Dakota, 1889 **1641** *p41*
Baning, William; America, 1737 **4971** *p85*
Banister, Elizabeth; New York, 1743 **3652** *p60*
Banister, John; Virginia, 1636 **6219** *p80*
Banister, Nathaniel 15; Philadelphia, 1774 **1219.7** *p175*
Banister, Thomas; Virginia, 1639 **6219** *p159*
Banister, Thomas 19; Jamaica, 1774 **1219.7** *p237*
Banister, Wm.; Virginia, 1645 **6219** *p233*
Bank, Friedrich; Wisconsin, n.d. **9675.4** *p194*
Bankerhie, James 21; Maryland, 1774 **1219.7** *p224*
Bankhead, . . .; New York, NY, 1816 **2859.11** *p25*
Bankhead, Fanny; Quebec, 1848 **5704.8** *p42*
Bankhead, Robert 9 mos; Quebec, 1848 **5704.8** *p42*
Banki, Henry; America, 1850 **1450.2** *p8A*
Banks, Ann; Virginia, 1637 **6219** *p29*
Banks, Bridget; St. John, N.B., 1850 **5704.8** *p67*
Banks, Charles; Charleston, SC, 1788 **1639.20** *p7*
Banks, David 15; Maryland, 1774 **1219.7** *p208*
Banks, Henry; New York, NY, 1839 **8208.4** *p100*
Banks, Henry 17; West Indies, 1722 **3690.1** *p10*
Banks, Honora 20; Massachusetts, 1850 **5881.1** *p8*
Banks, Jane; Virginia, 1698 **2212** *p14*
Banks, John; Iowa, 1866-1943 **123.54** *p7*
Banks, John 43; Wilmington, NC, 1850 **1639.20** *p7*
Banks, Joseph 20; Jamaica, 1721 **3690.1** *p10*
Banks, Moses 21; Maryland, 1774 **1219.7** *p211*
Banks, Rich.; Virginia, 1635 **6219** *p72*
Banks, Rich.; Virginia, 1636 **6219** *p1*
Banks, Richard; Virginia, 1636 **6219** *p109*
Banks, Samuel; South Carolina, 1808 **1639.20** *p7*
Banks, Thomas; New York, NY, 1816 **2859.11** *p25*
Banks, Thomas 19; Virginia, 1720 **3690.1** *p10*
Banks, William; Philadelphia, 1767 **1219.7** *p129*
Banks, William 19; Pennsylvania, Virginia or Maryland, 1719 **3690.1** *p10*
Banks, William 24; Maryland, 1774 **1219.7** *p235*
Banmann, Elisabeth; Quebec, 1875 **9980.20** *p49*
Bannam, John; Annapolis, MD, 1742 **4971** *p93*
Bannan, Michael; Virginia, 1852 **4626.16** *p14*
Bannan, Peter; New York, NY, 1815 **2859.11** *p25*
Bannan, Peter; New York, NY, 1838 **8208.4** *p64*
Bannatyne, Thomas; Charleston, SC, 1804 **1639.20** *p7*
Bannel, Aeriol 15; America, 1836 **778.5** *p22*
Bannel, Alexander 8; America, 1836 **778.5** *p22*
Bannel, Etienne 41; America, 1836 **778.5** *p23*
Bannel, Francois 12; America, 1836 **778.5** *p23*
Bannel, Francoise 34; America, 1836 **778.5** *p23*
Bannel, Isidor 3; America, 1836 **778.5** *p23*
Bannel, Josephine 5; America, 1836 **778.5** *p23*
Bannel, Louis 14; America, 1836 **778.5** *p23*
Bannerm, Marzellus; Colorado, 1904 **9678.1** *p152*
Bannesten, John 24; Maryland, 1738 **3690.1** *p10*
Bannier, John G.; Wisconsin, n.d. **9675.4** *p194*
Bannin, John; New York, NY, 1816 **2859.11** *p25*
Bannin, Michael; Philadelphia, 1849 **53.26** *p3*
Bannin, Michael; Philadelphia, 1849 **5704.8** *p54*
Banning, Alexander A. 60; Arizona, 1890 **2764.35** *p4*
Banning, James 21; Maryland, 1774 **1219.7** *p179*
Banning, William; America, 1743 **4971** *p10*
Bannister, Edmund; New York, NY, 1840 **8208.4** *p105*
Bannister, Nicholas; Virginia, 1642 **6219** *p187*
Bannister, Stephen; Virginia, 1635 **6219** *p69*
Bannister, William; Virginia, 1638 **6219** *p122*
Bannister, Wm.; Virginia, 1636 **6219** *p77*
Bannon, John; America, 1741 **4971** *p23*
Bannon, John; Illinois, 1868 **2896.5** *p2*
Bannon, John; Maryland, 1742 **4971** *p107*
Bannon, Mary 45; Massachusetts, 1849 **5881.1** *p10*
Bannon, Michael; America, 1864 **2896.5** *p2*
Bannon, Owen; America, 1737 **4971** *p72*
Bannon, Rose 20; Massachusetts, 1847 **5881.1** *p11*
Bannon, Thomas; America, 1737 **4971** *p72*
Bannor, John; America, 1742 **4971** *p17*
Banord, James 20; St. John, N.B., 1854 **5704.8** *p119*
Banord, John 20; St. John, N.B., 1854 **5704.8** *p119*
Banse, Mary 25; Maryland, 1775 **1219.7** *p267*
Banson, Peter; Virginia, 1648 **6219** *p246*
Banton, Carrington; Virginia, 1642 **6219** *p193*
Banton, Tho.; Virginia, 1635 **6219** *p25*
Banton, William; Virginia, 1637 **6219** *p114*
Bantum, Margt; Virginia, 1698 **2212** *p16*
Banvard Family ; New York, 1752-1763 **7074.6** *p213*
Banvard, David 23 *SEE* Banvard, Pierre
Banvard, David 23; Halifax, N.S., 1752 **7074.6** *p207*
With family of 1
Banvard, Eve *SEE* Banvard, Pierre
Banvard, Francoise; Died enroute, 1752 **7074.6** *p208*
Banvard, Marie Elisabeth *SEE* Banvard, Pierre
Banvard, Pierre 50; Halifax, N.S., 1752 **7074.6** *p207*
With family of 2
Banvard, Pierre 50; Halifax, N.S., 1752 **7074.6** *p208*
*Daughter:*Marie Elisabeth
*Son:*David 23
*Daughter-in-law:*Eve
Banz, Gabriel 38; Port uncertain, 1836 **778.5** *p23*
Bapp, Conrad; Philadelphia, 1757 **9973.7** *p32*
Bapp, Maria Barbara; Pennsylvania, 1750 **2444** *p205*
Bapp, Maria Margaretha; Pennsylvania, 1750 **2444** *p135*
Baprens, Lucien 20; America, 1836 **778.5** *p23*
Baptist, John; America, 1896 **1450.2** *p8A*
Baptist, John 26; Virginia, 1774 **1219.7** *p240*
Baptiste, Mr.; New Orleans, 1820 **778.5** *p23*
Baptiste, George 40; Massachusetts, 1850 **5881.1** *p8*
Baptiste, Jean 57; Port uncertain, 1827 **778.5** *p23*
Baptiste, M. 30; New Orleans, 1837 **778.5** *p23*
Bar, Jacob, Children; America, 1859 **3702.7** *p214*
Bar, Johannes; America, 1855 **3702.7** *p214*
Bara, Mr. 16; New Orleans, 1835 **778.5** *p23*
Barach, Anna; Iowa, 1866-1943 **123.54** *p55*
Barach, Milos; Iowa, 1866-1943 **123.54** *p7*
Barach, Milos; Iowa, 1866-1943 **123.54** *p55*
Barada, Mr. 35; New Orleans, 1839 **778.5** *p23*
Baradat, J. 22; New Orleans, 1838 **778.5** *p24*
Baradere, P. 40; Port uncertain, 1835 **778.5** *p24*
Baraga, Friedrich; Cincinnati, 1788-1848 **8582.3** *p89*
Baraga, Friedrich; New York, NY, 1830 **8582** *p1*
Baraigne, John 38; Port uncertain, 1820 **778.5** *p24*
Baramus, Thomas; Virginia, 1643 **6219** *p204*
Barange, Jean; America, 1839 **778.5** *p24*
Baranowski, Josef 21 *SEE* Baranowski, Wladyslaw
Baranowski, Jozef; New York, 1835 **4606** *p179*
Baranowski, Pawel 22; New York, 1912 **9980.29** *p59*
Baranowski, Wladyslaw 19; New York, 1912 **9980.29** *p65*
*Brother:*Josef 21
Barattia, Carlo; Iowa, 1866-1943 **123.54** *p7*
Barauger, Desire 63; Arizona, 1908 **9228.40** *p10*
Baraza, Petro 30?; Arizona, 1890 **2764.35** *p7*
Barb, Mr. 20; New Orleans, 1835 **778.5** *p24*
Barbadge, Thomas; New York, NY, 1816 **2859.11** *p25*
Barbaglia, Frank; Iowa, 1866-1943 **123.54** *p7*
Barbaglia, Guiseppe; Iowa, 1866-1943 **123.54** *p7*
Barbaglia, Marco; Iowa, 1866-1943 **123.54** *p7*
Barbaglia, Maria Rosa; Iowa, 1866-1943 **123.54** *p55*
Barban, . . .; Canada, 1776-1783 **9786** *p16*
Barbancey, T. 25; New Orleans, 1837 **778.5** *p24*
Barbancey, Theophile 26; New Orleans, 1838 **778.5** *p24*
Barbar, Fra.; Virginia, 1647 **6219** *p247*
Barbarot, F. 14; America, 1839 **778.5** *p24*
Barbe, Frances 19; Port uncertain, 1838 **778.5** *p24*
Barbe, George 15; Port uncertain, 1838 **778.5** *p24*
Barbe, Jean 41; New Orleans, 1835 **778.5** *p24*
Barbe, John 48; Port uncertain, 1838 **778.5** *p24*
Barbe, Joseph 22; Port uncertain, 1838 **778.5** *p24*
Barbe, Joseph-Abel; Quebec, 1699 **7603** *p25*
Barbe, Margaret 48; Port uncertain, 1838 **778.5** *p24*
Barbe, Marie 33; Port uncertain, 1831 **778.5** *p25*

Barbe, Mary 17; Port uncertain, 1838 778.5 p25
Barbe, Nicholas 8; Port uncertain, 1838 778.5 p25
Barbe, Rachelle 13; Port uncertain, 1838 778.5 p25
Barbeard, William; Virginia, 1647 6219 p244
Barber, Andrew; Quebec, 1848 5704.8 p41
Barber, Charles; Virginia, 1698 2212 p16
Barber, Chesheave 24; Georgia, 1774 1219.7 p188
Barber, Elizabeth Songhurst *SEE* Barber, John
Barber, Elizabeth Songhurst *SEE* Barber, John
Barber, Ernest Alfred 33; Kansas, 1891 5240.1 p76
Barber, F. L.; Washington, 1859-1920 2872.1 p3
Barber, Frank; Wisconsin, n.d. 9675.4 p194
Barber, Georg; Virginia, 1638 6219 p24
Barber, Georg; Virginia, 1638 6219 p119
Barber, Georg; Virginia, 1639 6219 p151
Barber, Henry; New York, NY, 1839 8208.4 p102
Barber, Hugh; Virginia, 1639 6219 p154
Barber, James; Quebec, 1848 5704.8 p41
Barber, James 4 *SEE* Barber, Rebecca
Barber, James 4; Philadelphia, 1849 5704.8 p50
Barber, Jerimiah; Virginia, 1638 6219 p146
Barber, John; Pennsylvania, 1682 4960 p152
*Wife:*Elizabeth Songhurst
Barber, John; Pennsylvania, 1682 4960 p159
Barber, John; Pennsylvania, 1682 4961 p241
*Wife:*Elizabeth Songhurst
Barber, John 8 *SEE* Barber, Rebecca
Barber, John 8; Philadelphia, 1849 5704.8 p50
Barber, John 28; Jamaica, 1727 3690.1 p10
Barber, Joseph 21; Quebec, 1859 5704.8 p143
Barber, Margaret; Quebec, 1848 5704.8 p41
Barber, Rebecca 10; Philadelphia, 1849 53.26 p3
*Relative:*John 8
*Relative:*Thomas 6
*Relative:*James 4
Barber, Rebecca 10; Philadelphia, 1849 5704.8 p50
Barber, Richard; Virginia, 1639 6219 p154
Barber, Robert; Virginia, 1638 6219 p11
Barber, Samuel 50; Massachusetts, 1847 5881.1 p12
Barber, Thomas 6 *SEE* Barber, Rebecca
Barber, Thomas 6; Philadelphia, 1849 5704.8 p50
Barber, Vito; Arkansas, 1918 95.2 p17
Barberieo, Carmine 24; West Virginia, 1904 9788.3 p4
Barberos, Pierre 23; Port uncertain, 1838 778.5 p25
Barbet, John 21; Virginia, 1775 1219.7 p252
Barbet, L.; New Orleans, 1839 778.5 p24
Barbier, . . .; Port uncertain, 1839 778.5 p25
Barbier, Mme.; Port uncertain, 1839 778.5 p25
Barbier, Mr.; New Orleans, 1821 778.5 p25
Barbier, Alexandre 15; America, 1838 778.5 p25
Barbier, Alexandre 53; America, 1838 778.5 p25
Barbier, John 29; New Orleans, 1863 543.30 p248
Barbier, Sebastien 36; America, 1838 778.5 p25
Barbin, John 26; New Orleans, 1864 543.30 p249
Barbot, Caroline 10; New Orleans, 1826 778.5 p25
Barbot, Lewis 44; New Orleans, 1829 778.5 p26
Barbot, M. 12; New Orleans, 1826 778.5 p26
Barbour, Matthew; New York, NY, 1816 2859.11 p25
Barbur, James; Virginia, 1698 2212 p16
Barca, Joe; Arkansas, 1918 95.2 p17
Barclay, Agnes 64 *SEE* Barclay, William
Barclay, John; Buffalo, NY, 1832 9892.11 p2
Barclay, Robert; Colorado, 1904 9678.1 p153
Barclay, Thomas 16; Maryland, 1775 1219.7 p260
Barclay, William 68; South Carolina, 1850 1639.20 p7
*Relative:*Agnes 64
Barcroft, Cha.; Virginia, 1647 6219 p241
Barcroft, Char.; Virginia, 1647 6219 p241
Barcroft, Charles; Virginia, 1647 6219 p241
Barcroft, Jane *SEE* Barcroft, Jon.
Barcroft, Jon.; Virginia, 1637 6219 p115
*Wife:*Jane
Barczewski, Henryk; New York, 1831 4606 p172
Bard, Miss; America, n.d. 5647.5 p3
Bard, Antoine 17; New Orleans, 1827 778.5 p26
Bard, Christine; America, 1847 5647.5 p23
Bard, Robt.; Virginia, 1635 6219 p20
Bardau, Catharina Widmayer *SEE* Bardau, Johann Georg
Bardau, Johann Georg; Pennsylvania, 1752 2444 p135
*Wife:*Catharina Widmayer
Bardeil, Julie 20; America, 1838 778.5 p26
Bardeleben, Arthur de; South Carolina, 1788 7119 p198
Barden, Samuel 18; Maryland, 1727 3690.1 p11
Bardenave, A.; New Orleans, 1839 778.5 p26
Bardes, Christian; America, 1852 8582.3 p2
Bardes, Henry; America, 1847 8582.1 p2
Bardesono, Peter; Iowa, 1866-1943 123.54 p7
Bardeu, James A.; Illinois, 1870 7857 p2
Bardon, Smallwill 18; Maryland, 1727 3690.1 p11
Bardstrup, C.; Arizona, 1898 9228.30 p8
Barduca, Antonio; Iowa, 1866-1943 123.54 p7
Barduca, Florindo; Iowa, 1866-1943 123.54 p7
Bare, Richard 26; Nova Scotia, 1774 1219.7 p194
Bare, Samuel; New York, NY, 1816 2859.11 p25
Barefoot, Joan; America, 1743 4971 p22
Barefoot, Joan; America, 1743 4971 p95
Barefoot, Thomas 25; Maryland, 1775 1219.7 p249
Bareford, Thomas 26; Virginia, 1775 1219.7 p261
Bareille, Jean 27; America, 1838 778.5 p26
Barell, P. 28; America, 1835 778.5 p26
Barenz, Heinrich; Wisconsin, n.d. 9675.4 p194
Bares, Mr. 25; America, 1839 778.5 p26
Bares, Jacob; Wisconsin, n.d. 9675.4 p194
Bares, Jean 18; America, 1837 778.5 p26
Baret, Charles; Quebec, 1819 7603 p64
Baret, Johannes; Pennsylvania, 1744 2444 p135
Bareth, Johannes; Pennsylvania, 1744 2444 p135
Baretic, Vinko; Iowa, 1866-1943 123.54 p7
Baretich, Vjekoslav; Iowa, 1866-1943 123.54 p7
Barett, Edward 50; St. John, N.B., 1859 5704.8 p143
Bareville, Mrs. 40; Port uncertain, 1838 778.5 p26
Barfeild, Tho.; Virginia, 1643 6219 p206
Barfknecht, August; Illinois, 1877 2896.5 p2
Barfoot, Henry 25; Jamaica, 1730 3690.1 p11
Barfoote, Ann; Virginia, 1636 6219 p80
Barg, Arnold A.; Wisconsin, n.d. 9675.4 p194
Barg, Charles; Wisconsin, n.d. 9675.4 p194
Barge, Mr. 28; New Orleans, 1835 778.5 p26
Barge, Jacob; Philadelphia, 1760 9973.7 p34
Barget, Thomas 26; Virginia, 1773 1219.7 p171
Bargmann, Johann; Wisconsin, n.d. 9675.4 p194
Barham, James; Ohio, 1844 3840.1 p14
Baric, Charles 40; New Orleans, 1829 778.5 p26
Barichello, Bruno; Arkansas, 1918 95.2 p17
Barido, Catharina 4; America, 1836 778.5 p26
Barido, Catharina 29; America, 1836 778.5 p26
Barido, Pierre 2; America, 1836 778.5 p26
Barincou, Mr. 30; Port uncertain, 1838 778.5 p27
Barincourt, V.; New Orleans, 1839 778.5 p27
Barington, Fra.; Virginia, 1648 6219 p246
Bario, Edward 24; New Orleans, 1823 778.5 p27
Barios, Bte. 25; Louisiana, 1822 778.5 p27
Barke, Henry; Virginia, 1647 6219 p239
Barkeley, Jane; Virginia, 1639 6219 p162
Barkeley, Mary; Virginia, 1648 6219 p241
Barker, Mr.; Quebec, 1815 9229.18 p74
Barker, Bartholomew 29; New York, 1774 1219.7 p222
*Wife:*Sarah 30
Barker, Benjamin 18; Jamaica, 1739 3690.1 p11
Barker, Bernard; Montreal, 1822 7603 p89
Barker, Charles; Illinois, 1903 5012.40 p77
Barker, Charles 21; Maryland, 1775 1219.7 p273
Barker, Christopher; Virginia, 1640 6219 p18
Barker, Christopher; Virginia, 1648 6219 p250
Barker, Daniel 15; Maryland, 1723 3690.1 p11
Barker, Edward 24; Maryland, 1774 1219.7 p208
Barker, Elizabeth 19; Carolina, 1775 1219.7 p278
Barker, Elizabeth 20; Virginia, 1721 3690.1 p11
Barker, George; Virginia, 1636 6219 p26
Barker, Herbert; Illinois, 1904 5012.37 p63
Barker, James; Montreal, 1824 7603 p89
Barker, James; Virginia, 1636 6219 p32
Barker, James 23; Maryland, 1774 1219.7 p228
Barker, John; Illinois, 1903 5012.40 p77
Barker, John; New York, NY, 1811 2859.11 p8
Barker, John; Virginia, 1623 6219 p7
Barker, John; Virginia, 1636 6219 p22
Barker, John; Virginia, 1639 6219 p154
Barker, John; Virginia, 1648 6219 p252
Barker, Jon.; Virginia, 1637 6219 p84
Barker, Mary 31; Baltimore, 1775 1219.7 p269
Barker, Nicholas; Virginia, 1640 6219 p185
Barker, Patrick; Montreal, 1821 7603 p89
Barker, Sarah 30 *SEE* Barker, Bartholomew
Barker, Silvester; Virginia, 1638 6219 p146
Barker, Thomas; New York, NY, 1816 2859.11 p25
Barker, Thomas 16; Virginia, 1720 3690.1 p11
Barker, William; Virginia, 1635 6219 p72
Barker, William 18; Jamaica, 1725 3690.1 p11
Barker, William 22; Port uncertain, 1774 1219.7 p176
Barker, William 29; Jamaica, 1736 3690.1 p11
Barker, William 30; Jamaica, 1774 1219.7 p238
Barker, Wm.; Virginia, 1637 6219 p113
Barker, Wm.; Virginia, 1638 6219 p2
Barkhamen, August; Wisconsin, n.d. 9675.4 p194
Barking, Sophie Leonore; America, 1831 4815.7 p92
Barkley, Agnes 13; St. John, N.B., 1858 5704.8 p140
Barkley, Andrew 25; Philadelphia, 1856 5704.8 p128
Barkley, Anna Maria 16; St. John, N.B., 1858 5704.8 p140
Barkley, Eliza Jane 21; St. John, N.B., 1858 5704.8 p140
Barkley, John; Ohio, 1840 9892.11 p2
Barkley, John 15; St. John, N.B., 1858 5704.8 p140
Barkley, Margaret 18; St. John, N.B., 1858 5704.8 p140
Barkley, Mary 40; St. John, N.B., 1858 5704.8 p140
Barkley, Matthew 9; St. John, N.B., 1858 5704.8 p140
Barklie, L.; New York, NY, 1811 2859.11 p8
With family
Barkwith, Robt.; Virginia, 1635 6219 p35
Barlage, Joseph; America, 1849 8582.3 p2
Barlen, Joe; Arkansas, 1918 95.2 p17
Barlen, John; Iowa, 1866-1943 123.54 p7
Barlo, John; Virginia, 1648 6219 p251
Barloe, Tymothy; Virginia, 1635 6219 p35
Barlor, Charity; America, 1698 2212 p6
Barlow, Adam; Jamaica, 1756 1219.7 p48
Barlow, August; Wisconsin, n.d. 9675.4 p194
Barlow, Eliz; America, 1698 2212 p7
Barlow, Ellin; Virginia, 1698 2212 p17
Barlow, John 21; Maryland, 1775 1219.7 p259
Barlow, John 24; Jamaica, 1731 3690.1 p11
Barlow, Jon.; Virginia, 1642 6219 p198
Barlow, Jonathan 24; Nova Scotia, 1774 1219.7 p209
Barlow, Richard 20; Maryland or Virginia, 1699 2212 p24
Barlow, Stafford; Virginia, 1642 6219 p188
Barlow, Thomas 19; Maryland or Virginia, 1699 2212 p23
Barlow, William; Iowa, 1866-1943 123.54 p7
Barlow, William; Philadelphia, 1850 53.26 p3
Barlow, William; Philadelphia, 1850 5704.8 p59
Barly, Roger; Virginia, 1643 6219 p202
Barn, Joseph 68; Philadelphia, 1774 1219.7 p214
Barnaby, James; Virginia, 1623-1700 6219 p182
Barnaby, Sarah; Virginia, 1623-1700 6219 p182
Barnard, F. 35; Port uncertain, 1835 778.5 p27
Barnard, Jabez; San Francisco, 1850 4914.15 p10
Barnard, Jeremiah 23; Jamaica, 1758 1219.7 p59
Barnard, Jeremiah 23; Jamaica, 1758 3690.1 p11
Barnard, John 24; Maryland, 1774 1219.7 p192
Barnard, John 24; Maryland, 1774 1219.7 p235
Barnard, Margaret 48; America, 1838 778.5 p27
Barnard, Richard; Charles Town, SC, 1765 1219.7 p110
Barnard, William; Virginia, 1642 6219 p189
Barnard, William 20; Virginia, 1774 1219.7 p244
Barnard, William 22; Baltimore, 1775 1219.7 p270
Barnard, Wm.; Virginia, 1642 6219 p194
Barnarde, Joseph; Wisconsin, n.d. 9675.4 p194
Barnards, Jon.; Virginia, 1628 6219 p31
Barnau, Charles 8; Port uncertain, 1838 778.5 p27
Barnau, Francis 12; Port uncertain, 1838 778.5 p27
Barnbridge, George; Iowa, 1866-1943 123.54 p7
Barne, Antoine 17; New Orleans, 1838 778.5 p27
Barne, Barbary; Virginia, 1636 6219 p21
Barne, Thomas 25; Maryland, 1775 1219.7 p264
Barner, von; Canada, 1776 9786 p110
Barner, von; Canada, 1776-1783 9786 p169
Barner, Andrew; Pennsylvania, 1748-1800 2444 p137
Barner, Ferdinand Albrecht; Quebec, 1776 9786 p262
Barner, John Niss; Arkansas, 1918 95.2 p17
Barnes, Ann; America, 1741 4971 p16
Barnes, Ann; Virginia, 1646 6219 p240
Barnes, Bar.; Virginia, 1642 6219 p189
Barnes, Baraby; Virginia, 1637 6219 p85
Barnes, Edward; Virginia, 1639 6219 p158
Barnes, Edward 27; Philadelphia, 1775 1219.7 p248
Barnes, Elizabeth 18; Maryland, 1775 1219.7 p260
Barnes, F. G.; Washington, 1859-1920 2872.1 p3
Barnes, Henry; Virginia, 1639 6219 p156
Barnes, Henry; Virginia, 1652 6251 p20
Barnes, James; New York, NY, 1837 8208.4 p32
Barnes, James; Ohio, 1840 9892.11 p2
Barnes, James; Virginia, 1637 6219 p8
Barnes, James; Virginia, 1637 6219 p107
Barnes, James; Virginia, 1640 6219 p184
Barnes, James 14; Maryland, 1729 3690.1 p11
Barnes, James 28; Virginia, 1699 2212 p27
Barnes, James Ebenezer; Arkansas, 1918 95.2 p17
Barnes, John; Virginia, 1642 6219 p193
Barnes, John; Virginia, 1643 6219 p204
Barnes, John 15; Newfoundland, 1699-1700 2212 p18
Barnes, Joseph 17; Pennsylvania, 1725 3690.1 p11
Barnes, Martin; Virginia, 1600-1642 6219 p199
Barnes, Mary 28; Massachusetts, 1849 5881.1 p10
Barnes, Mathias; Wisconsin, n.d. 9675.4 p194
Barnes, Thomas 16; Virginia, 1751 1219.7 p4
Barnes, Thomas 16; Virginia, 1751 3690.1 p12
Barnes, Thomas 19; Maryland, 1729 3690.1 p12
Barnes, William 18; Jamaica, 1750 3690.1 p12
Barnet, Mme. 35; America, 1838 778.5 p27
Barnet, Mr. 3; America, 1838 778.5 p27
Barnet, Mr. 5; America, 1838 778.5 p27
Barnet, Bridget; Quebec, 1823 7603 p60
Barnet, John 22; Jamaica, 1730 3690.1 p12
Barnet, Thomas 22; Maryland, 1775 1219.7 p257
Barnett, Andrew 24; Philadelphia, 1803 53.26 p3
*Relative:*Annabella 20
Barnett, Annabella 20 *SEE* Barnett, Andrew
Barnett, Eliza Ann; St. John, N.B., 1847 5704.8 p10

Barnett, Elizabeth 16; Philadelphia, 1803 ***53.26*** *p3*
*Relative:*Jane 12
Barnett, Francis; Virginia, 1637 ***6219*** *p11*
Barnett, Frederick; New York, NY, 1840 ***8208.4*** *p113*
Barnett, Isaac 19; Maryland, 1724 ***3690.1*** *p12*
Barnett, Isabella; Quebec, 1847 ***5704.8*** *p12*
Barnett, James; New Orleans, 1849 ***5704.8*** *p58*
Barnett, James; New Orleans, 1849 ***5704.8*** *p59*
Barnett, James; New York, NY, 1815 ***2859.11*** *p25*
Barnett, James; Virginia, 1639 ***6219*** *p152*
Barnett, James R.; New York, NY, 1815 ***2859.11*** *p25*
Barnett, Jane 12 *SEE* Barnett, Elizabeth
Barnett, John; New Orleans, 1849 ***5704.8*** *p59*
Barnett, John 38; Philadelphia, 1803 ***53.26*** *p3*
*Relative:*Margaret 34
Barnett, Joseph; Virginia, 1642 ***6219*** *p199*
Barnett, Margaret 34 *SEE* Barnett, John
Barnett, Mary Ann; St. John, N.B., 1847 ***5704.8*** *p10*
Barnett, Nich.; Virginia, 1635 ***6219*** *p71*
Barnett, Nicho.; Virginia, 1638 ***6219*** *p181*
Barnett, Ogilby; St. John, N.B., 1847 ***5704.8*** *p10*
Barnett, Samuel; New Orleans, 1849 ***5704.8*** *p59*
Barnett, Sarah; New Orleans, 1849 ***5704.8*** *p58*
Barnett, Sarah 6 mos; St. John, N.B., 1847 ***5704.8*** *p10*
Barnett, Sarah Jane 8; New Orleans, 1849 ***5704.8*** *p59*
Barnett, Stephen; Virginia, 1636 ***6219*** *p77*
Barnett, Thomas; New York, 1870 ***1450.2*** *p1B*
Barnett, William; New Orleans, 1849 ***5704.8*** *p58*
Barnett, William; New York, NY, 1836 ***8208.4*** *p21*
Barnett, William; Quebec, 1847 ***5704.8*** *p12*
Barney, Catharine 26; Massachusetts, 1849 ***5881.1*** *p7*
Barney, Owen; Montreal, 1823 ***7603*** *p70*
Barney, Patrick; New York, NY, 1811 ***2859.11*** *p8*
Barnfield, Herbert 22; Jamaica, 1734 ***3690.1*** *p12*
Barnfield, John 20; Jamaica, 1731 ***3690.1*** *p12*
Barnham, Levi; Boston, 1776 ***1219.7*** *p277*
Barnheart, William; Indiana, 1848 ***9117*** *p19*
Barnhill, Alice; New York, NY, 1864 ***5704.8*** *p186*
Barnhill, David 26; Philadelphia, 1864 ***5704.8*** *p155*
Barnhill, Jane 18; Philadelphia, 1859 ***5704.8*** *p142*
Barnhill, Joseph; St. John, N.B., 1848 ***5704.8*** *p48*
Barnhill, Margaret 24; Philadelphia, 1864 ***5704.8*** *p155*
Barnhill, Martha 20; Philadelphia, 1859 ***5704.8*** *p142*
Barnich, John; Wisconsin, n.d. ***9675.4*** *p194*
Barnickel, . . .; Canada, 1776-1783 ***9786*** *p17*
Barnier, Peter; Philadelphia, 1770 ***1219.7*** *p145*
Barns, Mrs.; Quebec, 1815 ***9229.18*** *p79*
With family
Barns, Francis 19; Jamaica, 1730 ***3690.1*** *p289*
Barns, William; Baltimore, 1811 ***2859.11*** *p8*
Barns, William 17; Maryland, 1724 ***3690.1*** *p12*
Barnstow, John 42; Philadelphia, 1774 ***1219.7*** *p214*
Barnum, Alvin 37; Kansas, 1893 ***5240.1*** *p79*
Barobard, Mr. 53; America, 1839 ***778.5*** *p27*
Barois, J.P. 23; New Orleans, 1839 ***778.5*** *p27*
Baron, Mr. 29; New Orleans, 1839 ***778.5*** *p27*
Baron, Mr. 36; Ohio, 1837 ***778.5*** *p28*
Baron, Alexander; Charleston, SC, 1768-1819 ***1639.20*** *p7*
Baron, Alexander; South Carolina, 1748 ***1639.20*** *p7*
Baron, Ann; South Carolina, 1788 ***1639.20*** *p322*
Baron, August; Arizona, 1889 ***2764.35*** *p8*
Baron, Dominique 28; New Orleans, 1862 ***543.30*** *p110*
Baron, Jean 33; New Orleans, 1863 ***543.30*** *p247*
Baron, John 45; New Orleans, 1839 ***778.5*** *p28*
Baron, Pierre 18; New Orleans, 1839 ***778.5*** *p28*
Baron, Richard; St. Kitts, 1775 ***1219.7*** *p279*
Baron, William 31; Arizona, 1890 ***2764.35*** *p4*
Barone, Raffaele 35; West Virginia, 1898 ***9788.3*** *p4*
Barot, Ms. 41; New Orleans, 1836 ***778.5*** *p28*
Barousse, Etienne 18; New Orleans, 1839 ***778.5*** *p28*
Barousse, Germain 24; Louisiana, 1839 ***778.5*** *p28*
Barousse, Jean 18; New Orleans, 1839 ***778.5*** *p28*
Barousse, Joseph 20; America, 1838 ***778.5*** *p28*
Barousse, Prosper 24; Louisiana, 1839 ***778.5*** *p28*
Barr, Ann; Philadelphia, 1852 ***5704.8*** *p97*
Barr, Anne; New York, NY, 1869 ***5704.8*** *p232*
Barr, Anne 23; St. John, N.B., 1861 ***5704.8*** *p147*
Barr, Archibald; Virginia, 1847 ***4626.16*** *p13*
Barr, Biddy 9; St. John, N.B., 1861 ***5704.8*** *p147*
Barr, Catherine; Philadelphia, 1852 ***5704.8*** *p88*
Barr, Catherine 15; Philadelphia, 1858 ***5704.8*** *p139*
Barr, Daniel; St. John, N.B., 1849 ***5704.8*** *p56*
Barr, Daniel; St. John, N.B., 1851 ***5704.8*** *p78*
Barr, Edward; Philadelphia, 1866 ***5704.8*** *p205*
Barr, Elizabeth; Philadelphia, 1852 ***5704.8*** *p97*
Barr, Elizabeth 9; Philadelphia, 1857 ***5704.8*** *p132*
Barr, Elizabeth 21; Philadelphia, 1864 ***5704.8*** *p160*
Barr, Ellen 16; St. John, N.B., 1861 ***5704.8*** *p147*
Barr, George; Iowa, 1866-1943 ***123.54*** *p7*
Barr, George 3; Philadelphia, 1857 ***5704.8*** *p132*
Barr, Henry 8; St. John, N.B., 1861 ***5704.8*** *p147*
Barr, Hugh; Philadelphia, 1852 ***5704.8*** *p97*
Barr, James; Philadelphia, 1851 ***5704.8*** *p78*
Barr, James; Philadelphia, 1857 ***5704.8*** *p132*
Barr, James 19; St. John, N.B., 1863 ***5704.8*** *p152*
Barr, James 20; St. John, N.B., 1854 ***5704.8*** *p120*
Barr, James 32; Maryland, 1775 ***1219.7*** *p252*
Barr, Jane; Philadelphia, 1852 ***5704.8*** *p88*
Barr, John; New York, NY, 1811 ***2859.11*** *p8*
With family
Barr, John; New York, NY, 1816 ***2859.11*** *p25*
Barr, John; New York, NY, 1839 ***8208.4*** *p101*
Barr, John; New York, NY, 1868 ***5704.8*** *p231*
Barr, John; New York, NY, 1869 ***5704.8*** *p232*
Barr, John; Philadelphia, 1851 ***5704.8*** *p80*
Barr, John; Philadelphia, 1852 ***5704.8*** *p92*
Barr, John 3 mos; Philadelphia, 1853 ***5704.8*** *p114*
Barr, John 24; St. John, N.B., 1861 ***5704.8*** *p147*
Barr, John 43; Philadelphia, 1853 ***5704.8*** *p112*
Barr, Margaret; Philadelphia, 1849 ***53.26*** *p3*
*Relative:*Martha Jane
*Relative:*Sarah
Barr, Margaret; Philadelphia, 1849 ***5704.8*** *p53*
Barr, Margaret 7; Philadelphia, 1857 ***5704.8*** *p132*
Barr, Margaret 27; St. John, N.B., 1859 ***5704.8*** *p140*
Barr, Margaret Ann; Philadelphia, 1852 ***5704.8*** *p97*
Barr, Martha Jane *SEE* Barr, Margaret
Barr, Martha Jane; Philadelphia, 1849 ***5704.8*** *p53*
Barr, Mary; St. John, N.B., 1848 ***5704.8*** *p44*
Barr, Mary 11; St. John, N.B., 1861 ***5704.8*** *p147*
Barr, Mary 25; Philadelphia, 1857 ***5704.8*** *p132*
Barr, Mary Ann; Philadelphia, 1852 ***5704.8*** *p84*
Barr, Mary Jane 3; Philadelphia, 1857 ***5704.8*** *p132*
Barr, Patrick; Philadelphia, 1853 ***5704.8*** *p102*
Barr, Patrick; St. John, N.B., 1851 ***5704.8*** *p77*
Barr, R. H.; Washington, 1859-1920 ***2872.1*** *p3*
Barr, Robert; Philadelphia, 1865 ***5704.8*** *p193*
Barr, Robert 19; St. John, N.B., 1859 ***5704.8*** *p140*
Barr, Robert 26; Philadelphia, 1864 ***5704.8*** *p155*
Barr, Sarah *SEE* Barr, Margaret
Barr, Sarah; New York, NY, 1866 ***5704.8*** *p211*
Barr, Sarah; Philadelphia, 1849 ***5704.8*** *p53*
Barr, Sarah 18; St. John, N.B., 1861 ***5704.8*** *p147*
Barr, Sarah 21; North America, 1774 ***1219.7*** *p199*
Barr, Sarah Ann 30; Philadelphia, 1857 ***5704.8*** *p132*
Barr, Susan 22; Philadelphia, 1865 ***5704.8*** *p164*
Barr, T. S.; Washington, 1859-1920 ***2872.1*** *p3*
Barr, Thomas 22; Virginia, 1775 ***1219.7*** *p261*
Barr, William; New Orleans, 1852 ***5704.8*** *p98*
Barr, William; Philadelphia, 1852 ***5704.8*** *p88*
Barr, William 38; Philadelphia, 1857 ***5704.8*** *p132*
Barragan, John; America, 1743 ***4971*** *p54*
Barranco, Joe; Arkansas, 1918 ***95.2*** *p17*
Barrary, Michael; Illinois, 1866 ***2896.5*** *p2*
Barratt, James 25; Maryland, 1774 ***1219.7*** *p202*
Barratt, Thomas; New York, NY, 1836 ***8208.4*** *p11*
Barrau, Mr. 80; America, 1839 ***778.5*** *p28*
Barrau, J.J. 26; New Orleans, 1822 ***778.5*** *p28*
Barre, Mr. 19; New Orleans, 1829 ***778.5*** *p28*
Barre, Guillaume 48; New Orleans, 1838 ***778.5*** *p28*
Barre, Richard; Quebec, 1759 ***7603*** *p64*
Barrel, . . .; America, 1839 ***778.5*** *p28*
Barrel, Mme. 30; America, 1839 ***778.5*** *p29*
Barrel, P. 45; America, 1839 ***778.5*** *p29*
Barren, Mr. 21; New Orleans, 1837 ***778.5*** *p29*
Barres, Mr. 32; America, 1835 ***778.5*** *p28*
Barres, Jean 21; America, 1838 ***778.5*** *p29*
Barret, John; Wisconsin, n.d. ***9675.4*** *p194*
Barret, William; San Francisco, 1850 ***4914.15*** *p10*
Barret, William 19; Jamaica, 1729 ***3690.1*** *p12*
Barret, William 27; Jamaica, 1738 ***3690.1*** *p12*
Barret, William 28; Maryland, 1775 ***1219.7*** *p260*
Barret, Wm.; Virginia, 1648 ***6219*** *p250*
Barrett, Ann 11; Massachusetts, 1850 ***5881.1*** *p6*
Barrett, Anna; Philadelphia, 1852 ***5704.8*** *p88*
Barrett, Chatherine; America, 1741 ***4971*** *p41*
Barrett, Ellen 24; Massachusetts, 1849 ***5881.1*** *p7*
Barrett, Francis; Virginia, 1638 ***6219*** *p123*
With wife
Barrett, Isaac R. 22; Kansas, 1896 ***5240.1*** *p80*
Barrett, James; America, 1736 ***4971*** *p43*
Barrett, James 32; New Orleans, 1862 ***543.30*** *p245*
Barrett, James 33; Massachusetts, 1847 ***5881.1*** *p8*
Barrett, Joan; America, 1743 ***4971*** *p50*
Barrett, John 18; Massachusetts, 1849 ***5881.1*** *p8*
Barrett, John 20; Massachusetts, 1849 ***5881.1*** *p9*
Barrett, John 23; Massachusetts, 1850 ***5881.1*** *p9*
Barrett, Margaret 26; Massachusetts, 1849 ***5881.1*** *p10*
Barrett, Margaret Middleton; America, 1742 ***4971*** *p50*
Barrett, Mary 16; Massachusetts, 1849 ***5881.1*** *p10*
Barrett, Michael 39; Kansas, 1893 ***5240.1*** *p77*
Barrett, Owen 32; Massachusetts, 1847 ***5881.1*** *p11*
Barrett, Patrick; America, 1840 ***1450.2*** *p8A*
Barrett, Patrick 33; New Orleans, 1862 ***543.30*** *p113*
Barrett, Samuel 26; Kansas, 1893 ***5240.1*** *p4*
Barrett, Samuel 26; Kansas, 1893 ***5240.1*** *p79*
Barrett, William; New York, 1841 ***7036*** *p119*
Barrett, William 16; Philadelphia, 1774 ***1219.7*** *p183*
Barrett, William 21; Massachusetts, 1849 ***5881.1*** *p12*
Barrett, William 27; Jamaica, 1738 ***3690.1*** *p12*
Barria, Francisco 63; New Orleans, 1829 ***778.5*** *p29*
Barrial, Antonio 29; Arkansas, 1918 ***95.2*** *p17*
Barrieas, V. 30; Arizona, 1926 ***9228.40*** *p30*
Barrier, P. 26; Port uncertain, 1839 ***778.5*** *p29*
Barriere, Felix 25; Port uncertain, 1822 ***778.5*** *p29*
Barriere, Michel Bernard; Louisiana, 1789-1819 ***778.5*** *p555*
Barrington, Wm.; Virginia, 1643 ***6219*** *p229*
Barroms, John 16; Virginia, 1700 ***2212*** *p31*
Barron, Adolph; Illinois, 1878 ***2896.5*** *p2*
Barron, James; America, 1737 ***4971*** *p45*
Barron, James; America, 1738 ***4971*** *p46*
Barron, Patrick 22; St. John, N.B., 1856 ***5704.8*** *p131*
Barron, Susan; Philadelphia, 1864 ***5704.8*** *p185*
Barron, Thomas 20; St. John, N.B., 1856 ***5704.8*** *p131*
Barron, William; Philadelphia, 1852 ***5704.8*** *p92*
Barrot, James; America, 1736 ***4971*** *p45*
Barrow, Mr.; New York, NY, 1815 ***2859.11*** *p25*
Barrow, Edwin 6; Massachusetts, 1850 ***5881.1*** *p7*
Barrow, Fanny 40; Massachusetts, 1850 ***5881.1*** *p8*
Barrow, John; Virginia, 1642 ***6219*** *p197*
Barrow, John 33; Georgia, 1774 ***1219.7*** *p188*
Barrow, Joseph; New Jersey, 1818 ***9892.11*** *p2*
Barrow, Joseph; Ohio, 1835 ***9892.11*** *p2*
Barrow, Meta 4; Massachusetts, 1850 ***5881.1*** *p11*
Barrow, Robert 20; Maryland, 1735 ***3690.1*** *p12*
Barrow, Robert 40; Massachusetts, 1850 ***5881.1*** *p12*
Barrow, Thomas 20; Pennsylvania, 1723 ***3690.1*** *p12*
Barrow, Walter 6 mos; Massachusetts, 1850 ***5881.1*** *p12*
Barrow, William 3; Massachusetts, 1850 ***5881.1*** *p12*
Barry, Ann; South Carolina, 1767 ***1639.20*** *p7*
Barry, Bridget 12; Massachusetts, 1850 ***5881.1*** *p6*
Barry, Catharine 8; Massachusetts, 1849 ***5881.1*** *p7*
Barry, Charles 3; New Orleans, 1837 ***778.5*** *p29*
Barry, Charlotte 19; New Orleans, 1837 ***778.5*** *p29*
Barry, Christopher; America, 1742 ***4971*** *p71*
Barry, Edward; New York, NY, 1815 ***2859.11*** *p25*
Barry, Eliza 30; Massachusetts, 1849 ***5881.1*** *p7*
Barry, Ellen 22; Massachusetts, 1849 ***5881.1*** *p7*
Barry, Ellen 35; Massachusetts, 1849 ***5881.1*** *p7*
Barry, Fromais 11; New Orleans, 1837 ***778.5*** *p29*
Barry, Gabriel 43; New Orleans, 1837 ***778.5*** *p29*
Barry, James; California, 1851 ***6013.19*** *p29*
Barry, James; New York, NY, 1811 ***2859.11*** *p8*
Barry, James; Ohio, 1849 ***1450.2*** *p8A*
Barry, James 5; Massachusetts, 1849 ***5881.1*** *p8*
Barry, James 30; Kansas, 1879 ***5240.1*** *p60*
Barry, James, Jr.; Savannah, GA, 1774 ***1219.7*** *p227*
Barry, James, Sr.; Savannah, GA, 1774 ***1219.7*** *p227*
Barry, James Casey; New York, NY, 1816 ***2859.11*** *p25*
Barry, Joan; America, 1739 ***4971*** *p52*
Barry, Johanna 41; Massachusetts, 1849 ***5881.1*** *p9*
Barry, John; America, 1743 ***4971*** *p42*
Barry, John; America, 1857 ***1450.2*** *p9A*
Barry, John; Illinois, 1866 ***2896.5*** *p2*
Barry, John; New York, NY, 1811 ***2859.11*** *p8*
Barry, John 11; Massachusetts, 1850 ***5881.1*** *p9*
Barry, John 38; Massachusetts, 1849 ***5881.1*** *p9*
Barry, John 39; Massachusetts, 1848 ***5881.1*** *p8*
Barry, Julia; Montreal, 1825 ***7603*** *p65*
Barry, Julia 7; Massachusetts, 1849 ***5881.1*** *p8*
Barry, Julie 13; New Orleans, 1837 ***778.5*** *p29*
Barry, Justine 3; New Orleans, 1837 ***778.5*** *p29*
Barry, Madelaine 37; New Orleans, 1837 ***778.5*** *p29*
Barry, Margaret 45; Massachusetts, 1847 ***5881.1*** *p9*
Barry, Mary 2; Massachusetts, 1849 ***5881.1*** *p9*
Barry, Mary 5; Massachusetts, 1849 ***5881.1*** *p10*
Barry, Mary 8; Massachusetts, 1850 ***5881.1*** *p11*
Barry, Mary 17; Massachusetts, 1849 ***5881.1*** *p10*
Barry, Mary 18; Massachusetts, 1849 ***5881.1*** *p10*
Barry, Mary 24; Massachusetts, 1849 ***5881.1*** *p10*
Barry, Patrick; America, 1739 ***4971*** *p33*
Barry, Patrick; Massachusetts, 1849 ***5881.1*** *p11*
Barry, Patrick; New York, 1854 ***3840.1*** *p14*
Barry, Patrick; New York, NY, 1836 ***8208.4*** *p21*
Barry, Patrick 40; Massachusetts, 1850 ***5881.1*** *p11*
Barry, Philip; America, 1737 ***4971*** *p71*
Barry, Richard 1; Massachusetts, 1849 ***5881.1*** *p12*
Barry, Richard 20; Massachusetts, 1847 ***5881.1*** *p11*
Barry, Rose 45; Massachusetts, 1849 ***5881.1*** *p11*
Barry, Victorine 9; New Orleans, 1837 ***778.5*** *p29*
Barry, William 25; Maryland, 1774 ***1219.7*** *p244*
Barryciff, John 16; Maryland, 1724 ***3690.1*** *p13*
Barrycliff, John 16; Maryland, 1724 ***3690.1*** *p13*
Barsara, Mark; Iowa, 1866-1943 ***123.54*** *p7*
Barshall, Jon.; Virginia, 1642 ***6219*** *p198*
Barsley, Pat 20; Massachusetts, 1849 ***5881.1*** *p11*
Barstad, Carl Anton; Arkansas, 1918 ***95.2*** *p17*

20 *FOR A COMPLETE EXPLANATION OF ENTRY, SEE "HOW TO READ A CITATION" SECTION*

Barszcz, . . .; New York, 1831 ***4606*** *p172*
Bartee, Francis; Virginia, 1643 ***6219*** *p33*
Bartel, Adam; Ohio, 1869-1887 ***8582*** *p2*
Bartel, Henry 34; Kansas, 1887 ***5240.1*** *p70*
Bartel, Jean; Louisiana, 1826 ***778.5*** *p30*
Bartel, Johann; Kentucky, 1795 ***8582.3*** *p95*
Bartel, Johannes; Kentucky, 1796 ***8582.3*** *p95*
Bartel, John; Wisconsin, n.d. ***9675.4*** *p194*
Bartel, Peter H. 27; Kansas, 1893 ***5240.1*** *p79*
Bartelme, Ferdinand; Illinois, 1886 ***2896.5*** *p2*
Bartelns, Christian; Canada, 1783 ***9786*** *p38A*
Bartels, Albert F.; New York, NY, 1840 ***8208.4*** *p113*
Bartels, Frederick; America, 1837 ***1450.2*** *p9A*
Bartels, Henry; America, 1825 ***1450.2*** *p9A*
Bartels, Jacob; New York, NY, 1833 ***8208.4*** *p41*
Bartelsmeyer, Christian Friedrich; America, 1852 ***4610.10*** *p116*
Barten, Catherine 17; Quebec, 1856 ***5704.8*** *p130*
Barten, Edward 51; Quebec, 1853 ***5704.8*** *p105*
Barten, Gusty 21; Quebec, 1856 ***5704.8*** *p130*
Barten, James 50; Quebec, 1856 ***5704.8*** *p130*
Barten, Jane 18; Quebec, 1853 ***5704.8*** *p105*
Barten, Margaret 13; Quebec, 1853 ***5704.8*** *p105*
Barten, Margaret 46; Quebec, 1856 ***5704.8*** *p130*
Barten, Susan 56; Quebec, 1853 ***5704.8*** *p105*
Barter, William 41; Virginia, 1774 ***1219.7*** *p201*
Bartesch, Gottlieb; Wisconsin, n.d. ***9675.4*** *p194*
Barth, . . .; Canada, 1776-1783 ***9786*** *p17*
Barth, Albert; Wisconsin, n.d. ***9675.4*** *p194*
Barth, Carl Paul; Wisconsin, n.d. ***9675.4*** *p194*
Barth, Christina 28; America, 1838 ***778.5*** *p30*
Barth, Claudius; Wisconsin, n.d. ***9675.4*** *p194*
Barth, Eliza 2; America, 1838 ***778.5*** *p30*
Barth, Ernest; Wisconsin, n.d. ***9675.4*** *p194*
Barth, Frederick; New York, NY, 1836 ***8208.4*** *p17*
Barth, G.; Wisconsin, n.d. ***9675.4*** *p194*
Barth, Heinrich; America, 1849 ***8582.1*** *p2*
Barth, Jacob; Wisconsin, n.d. ***9675.4*** *p194*
Barth, Jean 30; America, 1838 ***778.5*** *p30*
Barth, Johan; Alberta, n.d. ***5262*** *p58*
Barth, John; Wisconsin, n.d. ***9675.4*** *p194*
Barth, Mathias; Wisconsin, n.d. ***9675.4*** *p194*
Barth, Peter; Wisconsin, n.d. ***9675.4*** *p194*
Barthau, Catharina Widmayer *SEE* Barthau, Johann Georg
Barthau, Johann Georg; Pennsylvania, 1752 ***2444*** *p135*
*Wife:*Catharina Widmayer
Barthe, Mme. 23; Port uncertain, 1838 ***778.5*** *p30*
Barthe, F. 35; New Orleans, 1836 ***778.5*** *p30*
Barthe, J. 28; Port uncertain, 1838 ***778.5*** *p30*
Barthe, John; New York, NY, 1838 ***8208.4*** *p65*
Barthel, . . .; Canada, 1776-1783 ***9786*** *p17*
Barthel, Amelia Augusta 13 *SEE* Barthel, Chris. Lovegod
Barthel, Caroline Juliane 34 *SEE* Barthel, Fr. Wm.
Barthel, Chris. Lovegod 43; New Orleans, 1839 ***9420.2*** *p484*
*Wife:*Jane Gilian 35
*Daughter:*Amelia Augusta 13
*Son:*Frederick Ralph 9
Barthel, Christ. Sophie 76; New Orleans, 1839 ***9420.2*** *p166*
Barthel, Fr. Wm. 47; New Orleans, 1839 ***9420.2*** *p165*
*Wife:*Caroline Juliane 34
*Child:*Richard 11
*Child:*Mathilde 9
*Child:*Theodor 7
*Child:*Maria 5
*Child:*Martin 9 mos
Barthel, Frederick Ralph 9 *SEE* Barthel, Chris. Lovegod
Barthel, Frederke Augusta 6 mos; Died enroute, 1839 ***9420.2*** *p484*
Barthel, Jane Gilian 35 *SEE* Barthel, Chris. Lovegod
Barthel, Maria 5 *SEE* Barthel, Fr. Wm.
Barthel, Martin 9 mos *SEE* Barthel, Fr. Wm.
Barthel, Mathilde 9 *SEE* Barthel, Fr. Wm.
Barthel, Richard 11 *SEE* Barthel, Fr. Wm.
Barthel, Theodor 7 *SEE* Barthel, Fr. Wm.
Barthelemy, Mme. 45; America, 1838 ***778.5*** *p30*
Barthelemy, M. 30; New Orleans, 1836 ***778.5*** *p30*
Barthelmus, Ferdenand; America, 1849 ***1450.2*** *p9A*
Barthes, Angelique 34; New Orleans, 1838 ***778.5*** *p30*
Barthes, Auguste 6; New Orleans, 1838 ***778.5*** *p30*
Barthes, Jean 35; New Orleans, 1838 ***778.5*** *p30*
Barthet, Francois 20; New Orleans, 1835 ***778.5*** *p30*
Bartho, George; Pennsylvania, 1752 ***2444*** *p135*
Barthol, Anton; Wisconsin, n.d. ***9675.4*** *p194*
Bartholi, Mr. 38; New Orleans, 1827 ***778.5*** *p30*
Bartholmew, Hen.; Virginia, 1643 ***6219*** *p206*
Bartholmew, John; America, 1859 ***6014.1*** *p1*
Bartholomae, . . .; Canada, 1776-1783 ***9786*** *p17*
Bartholomaeus, George 22; New Orleans, 1862 ***543.30*** *p243*
Bartholomai, . . .; Canada, 1776-1783 ***9786*** *p17*
Bartholomew, John W.; Arizona, 1890 ***2764.35*** *p3*
Bartholomew, William 21; Virginia, 1774 ***1219.7*** *p201*
Bartian, Mary 32; New Orleans, 1838 ***778.5*** *p30*
Bartian, Peter 52; New Orleans, 1838 ***778.5*** *p31*
Bartier, Antoine 26; New Orleans, 1838 ***778.5*** *p31*
Bartier, John; Quebec, 1853 ***5704.8*** *p104*
Bartin, Tho.; Virginia, 1637 ***6219*** *p24*
Bartke, August; Wisconsin, n.d. ***9675.4*** *p194*
Bartkowski, . . .; New York, 1831 ***4606*** *p172*
Bartkus, Jer.; Wisconsin, n.d. ***9675.4*** *p194*
Bartl, Andrew; Wisconsin, n.d. ***9675.4*** *p194*
Bartlan, Jose 25; America, 1835 ***778.5*** *p31*
Bartlau, Jose 25; America, 1835 ***778.5*** *p31*
Bartle, Richard 20; America, 1728 ***3690.1*** *p13*
Bartlet, Mrs. 30; Grenada, 1776 ***1219.7*** *p282*
Bartlet, James 30; Grenada, 1776 ***1219.7*** *p282*
Bartlet, John 17; Jamaica, 1736 ***3690.1*** *p13*
Bartlett, Benjamin; Arizona, 1877 ***2764.35*** *p9*
Bartlett, Christo.; Virginia, 1639 ***6219*** *p156*
Bartlett, John 12; Philadelphia, 1774 ***1219.7*** *p197*
Bartlett, John 19; Pennsylvania, 1722 ***3690.1*** *p13*
Bartlett, John 20; Maryland or Virginia, 1736 ***3690.1*** *p13*
Bartlett, Jos W. 34; New Orleans, 1862 ***543.30*** *p245*
Bartlett, Michaell; Virginia, 1638 ***6219*** *p147*
Bartlett, Richard; Virginia, 1645 ***6219*** *p235*
Bartlett, Richard 47?; California, 1867 ***3840.1*** *p16*
Bartlett, Thomas; New York, NY, 1837 ***8208.4*** *p53*
Bartley, Isabella; Philadelphia, 1865 ***5704.8*** *p188*
Bartley, Jacob; Ohio, 1840 ***9892.11*** *p2*
Bartley, James; New York, NY, 1839 ***8208.4*** *p102*
Bartley, John; America, 1743 ***4971*** *p69*
Bartley, John; Philadelphia, 1868 ***5704.8*** *p231*
Bartley, Margaret 40; Massachusetts, 1849 ***5881.1*** *p10*
Bartley, Michael; Illinois, 1868 ***5240.1*** *p4*
Bartley, Peter 28; New Orleans, 1862 ***543.30*** *p112*
Bartley, Thomas 18; Jamaica, 1725 ***3690.1*** *p13*
Bartley, Thomas 20; Massachusetts, 1849 ***5881.1*** *p12*
Bartley, William; Quebec, 1851 ***5704.8*** *p73*
Bartling, Mr.; America, 1879-1893 ***4610.10*** *p114*
With sister
Bartling, Carl Friedrich, II; Quebec, 1776 ***9786*** *p256*
Bartling, Charlotte; America, 1881 ***4610.10*** *p106*
Bartling, Ernst August, I; Quebec, 1776 ***9786*** *p261*
Bartling, Ernst Heinrich Ludwig; America, 1881 ***4610.10*** *p101*
Bartling, Friedrich Wilhelm Ludwig; America, 1884 ***4610.10*** *p113*
Bartling, Heinrich Friedrich; America, 1893 ***4610.10*** *p114*
With father
Bartling, Henriette 16; America, 1893 ***4610.10*** *p114*
Bartling, Wilhelm; Illinois, 1840-1890 ***4610.10*** *p59*
Bartlon, F. Henry; America, 1833 ***1450.2*** *p9A*
Bartol, John; Wisconsin, n.d. ***9675.4*** *p194*
Bartolmew, Nicholas; America, 1866 ***6014.1*** *p1*
Barton, Ann; Quebec, 1850 ***5704.8*** *p66*
Barton, Ann 12; St. John, N.B., 1864 ***5704.8*** *p159*
Barton, Belle; Arizona, 1898 ***9228.30*** *p6*
Barton, Catherine 9 mos; St. John, N.B., 1852 ***5704.8*** *p93*
Barton, Christian; Quebec, 1851 ***5704.8*** *p82*
Barton, Christopher; Quebec, 1851 ***5704.8*** *p75*
Barton, Edward; Quebec, 1850 ***5704.8*** *p66*
Barton, Elias; Virginia, 1642 ***6219*** *p195*
Barton, Eliza; St. John, N.B., 1852 ***5704.8*** *p93*
Barton, Elizabeth; St. John, N.B., 1852 ***5704.8*** *p93*
Barton, George; St. John, N.B., 1852 ***5704.8*** *p84*
Barton, George 36; Jamaica, 1739 ***3690.1*** *p13*
Barton, Gerard; St. John, N.B., 1852 ***5704.8*** *p84*
Barton, Germain 25; America, 1825 ***778.5*** *p31*
Barton, Ja; Virginia, 1698 ***2212*** *p11*
Barton, James; New York, NY, 1839 ***8208.4*** *p103*
Barton, James 6 mos; Quebec, 1851 ***5704.8*** *p82*
Barton, James 18; New York, 1775 ***1219.7*** *p246*
Barton, James 37; Quebec, 1858 ***5704.8*** *p138*
Barton, James 45; Quebec, 1855 ***5704.8*** *p126*
Barton, Jas.; South Carolina, 1788 ***7119*** *p198*
Barton, John 17; Quebec, 1855 ***5704.8*** *p126*
Barton, John 20; Quebec, 1857 ***5704.8*** *p136*
Barton, Joseph 12; St. John, N.B., 1852 ***5704.8*** *p93*
Barton, Margaret Jane 8; St. John, N.B., 1852 ***5704.8*** *p93*
Barton, Mary; St. John, N.B., 1852 ***5704.8*** *p84*
Barton, Mary 6; St. John, N.B., 1852 ***5704.8*** *p93*
Barton, Oliver; St. John, N.B., 1852 ***5704.8*** *p93*
Barton, Robert; Quebec, 1851 ***5704.8*** *p75*
Barton, Robert 13; St. John, N.B., 1852 ***5704.8*** *p93*
Barton, Robert John; Quebec, 1851 ***5704.8*** *p75*
Barton, Robt.; Virginia, 1637 ***6219*** *p11*
Barton, Sarah Ann; Quebec, 1849 ***5704.8*** *p57*
Barton, William; Quebec, 1851 ***5704.8*** *p82*
Barton, William; Virginia, 1636 ***6219*** *p8*
Barton, William; Virginia, 1639 ***6219*** *p152*
Barton, William 35; Virginia, 1775 ***1219.7*** *p275*
Barton, Wm 28; Maryland or Virginia, 1699 ***2212*** *p23*
Bartram, . . .; Canada, 1776-1783 ***9786*** *p17*
Bartsch, Ernst; Wisconsin, n.d. ***9675.4*** *p194*
Bartsch, George; Wisconsin, n.d. ***9675.4*** *p194*
Bartsch, Joseph 37; New Orleans, 1862 ***543.30*** *p481*
Bartz, John; Wisconsin, n.d. ***9675.4*** *p194*
Bartz, Peter; Arkansas, 1918 ***95.2*** *p17*
Baruch, David 25; America, 1853 ***9162.8*** *p36*
Baruch, Dorothee 19; America, 1853 ***9162.8*** *p36*
Baruch, Spring L. 22; America, 1853 ***9162.8*** *p36*
Barus, Jean 18; New Orleans, 1839 ***778.5*** *p31*
Barus, Karl; America, 1849 ***8582.2*** *p2*
Barusta, Bernard 33; America, 1839 ***778.5*** *p31*
Barusta, Jean 35; America, 1839 ***778.5*** *p31*
Barwell, Elizabeth 21; Maryland, 1774 ***1219.7*** *p210*
Barwick, Andrew 16; Jamaica, 1730 ***3690.1*** *p13*
Barwick, Martin; Charleston, SC, 1839 ***8582*** *p2*
Barwick, Thomas 26; Dominica, 1773 ***1219.7*** *p172*
Barwick, William; Arkansas, 1918 ***95.2*** *p17*
Barwick, William; Virginia, 1639 ***6219*** *p151*
Barwick, Wm.; Virginia, 1643 ***6219*** *p203*
Barwig, Martin; Charleston, SC, 1839 ***8582*** *p2*
Barwood, Robert; Virginia, 1642 ***6219*** *p186*
Basack, John; Iowa, 1866-1943 ***123.54*** *p7*
Basal, Jacques 33; America, 1838 ***778.5*** *p31*
Basby, James; Virginia, 1639 ***6219*** *p151*
Basch, Henry; Shreveport, LA, 1878 ***7129*** *p44*
Basdefer, M. 45; New Orleans, 1835 ***778.5*** *p31*
Baseley, Edmond; Ohio, 1860 ***6014.2*** *p7*
Baserque, Adolphe 22; New Orleans, 1837 ***778.5*** *p31*
Basford, Mary 18; Virginia, 1720 ***3690.1*** *p13*
Bashaw, Andrew; Virginia, 1639 ***6219*** *p155*
Bashaw, Giles; Virginia, 1648 ***6219*** *p245*
Bashor, C. L.; Washington, 1859-1920 ***2872.1*** *p3*
Basiks, Charles; Wisconsin, n.d. ***9675.4*** *p194*
Basiks, Klementina; Wisconsin, n.d. ***9675.4*** *p194*
Basiks, Michael; Wisconsin, n.d. ***9675.4*** *p194*
Basil, Winnefred 30; Massachusetts, 1849 ***5881.1*** *p12*
Basile, Mr. 33; Louisiana, 1820 ***778.5*** *p31*
Basin, Mr. 28; America, 1830 ***778.5*** *p31*
Baskarvill, Thomas 22; St. Christopher, 1730 ***3690.1*** *p289*
Baskervile, Robert; Virginia, 1642 ***6219*** *p193*
Baskevill, Richard; Virginia, 1639 ***6219*** *p156*
Baskin, Richard; Virginia, 1639 ***6219*** *p151*
Baslay, William 23; Philadelphia, 1775 ***1219.7*** *p259*
Basler, Karl 23; Kansas, 1884 ***5240.1*** *p66*
Basley, Julia Forbes 49; Kansas, 1893 ***5240.1*** *p78*
Basnar, Martin; Arkansas, 1918 ***95.2*** *p17*
Basnett, Willi.; Virginia, 1637 ***6219*** *p85*
Basnett, Wm.; Virginia, 1636 ***6219*** *p79*
Basquer, Antoine 20; New Orleans, 1862 ***543.30*** *p481*
Basqufil, Thomas 28; Philadelphia, 1735 ***3690.1*** *p13*
Bass, Abraham 25; Maryland, 1774 ***1219.7*** *p229*
Bass, Gregory; Virginia, 1642 ***6219*** *p189*
Bass, James 51; North Carolina, 1850 ***1639.20*** *p7*
Bass, John; Virginia, 1637 ***6219*** *p82*
Bassauce, Jacq. 36; Port uncertain, 1839 ***778.5*** *p31*
Bassault, Jacq. 36; Port uncertain, 1839 ***778.5*** *p31*
Basse, Francis 1; America, 1835 ***778.5*** *p31*
Basse, John 5; America, 1835 ***778.5*** *p31*
Basse, Joseph 3; America, 1835 ***778.5*** *p32*
Basse, Margareth 27; America, 1835 ***778.5*** *p32*
Basse, Michael 4; America, 1835 ***778.5*** *p32*
Basse, Thomas; New York, NY, 1850 ***6013.19*** *p29*
Basset, Casimir 30; New Orleans, 1831 ***778.5*** *p32*
Bassett, Georg; Virginia, 1637 ***6219*** *p108*
Bassett, Iszabella *SEE* Bassett, William
Bassett, Math.; Virginia, 1637 ***6219*** *p112*
Bassett, Mathew; Virginia, 1638 ***6219*** *p146*
Bassett, Thomas; Virginia, 1646 ***6219*** *p236*
Bassett, William; Virginia, 1639 ***6219*** *p151*
*Wife:*Iszabella
Bassewitz, Joachim Hieronymus von; Halifax, N.S., 1780 ***9786*** *p269*
Bassewitz, Joachim Hieronymus von; New York, 1776 ***9786*** *p269*
Bassler, George 22; Kansas, 1892 ***5240.1*** *p77*
Bassnett, Jon.; Virginia, 1637 ***6219*** *p110*
Basso, Ugo; Arkansas, 1918 ***95.2*** *p17*
Bassot, B. 20; New Orleans, 1830 ***778.5*** *p32*
Bast, Johann; Cincinnati, 1869-1887 ***8582*** *p2*
Bastard, Mr. 24; New Orleans, 1839 ***778.5*** *p32*
Bastard, George Victorian Felix; Arkansas, 1918 ***95.2*** *p17*
Bastard, Mary; America, 1736 ***4971*** *p44*
Bastard, Mary; America, 1736 ***4971*** *p45*
Bastel, Anton; Wisconsin, n.d. ***9675.4*** *p194*
Basterreche, Hyppolite 33; Port uncertain, 1839 ***778.5*** *p32*

Bastett, Francis; Virginia, 1643 6219 p204
Bastian, D.V. 35; America, 1829 778.5 p32
Bastian, William; Washington, 1859-1920 2872.1 p3
Bastien, F.; Port uncertain, 1839 778.5 p32
Bastien, Victor 22; New Orleans, 1823 778.5 p32
Bastien, Victor 25; New Orleans, 1822 778.5 p32
Bastien, Victor 32; America, 1831 778.5 p32
Bastier, Antoine 26; New Orleans, 1838 778.5 p31
Bastoloni, Joseph; Arkansas, 1918 95.2 p17
Bastow, Angelo 33; Kansas, 1874 5240.1 p55
Bastran, Saul 28; New Orleans, 1826 778.5 p32
Bastrizkey, Jim; Arkansas, 1918 95.2 p17
Bastus, Francisco 32; Arizona, 1910 9228.40 p15
Basup, Pete; Arkansas, 1918 95.2 p17
Bataille, Aime 28; America, 1822 778.5 p32
Batard, Gabriel 36; New Orleans, 1837 778.5 p32
Batcha, George; Wisconsin, n.d. 9675.4 p194
Batchelor, Jane; Pennsylvania, 1682-1684 4960 p152
Batchelor, Thomas 22; Maryland, 1774 1219.7 p235
Batchelor, Wm.; Virginia, 1623-1648 6219 p252
Bate, Ralph 22; America, 1702 2212 p37
Bate, Richard; Virginia, 1770 1219.7 p142
Bateman, Augusta 23; Massachusetts, 1860 6410.32 p116
Bateman, Benjamin 35; Maryland, 1775 1219.7 p260
Bateman, Henry 32; New Orleans, 1862 543.30 p481
Bateman, John 23; Virginia, 1774 1219.7 p186
Bateman, John 26; Jamaica, 1731 3690.1 p13
Bateman, Miles; Iowa, 1866-1943 123.54 p7
Bateman, Pershiphall; Virginia, 1647 6219 p239
Bateman, Robert; Virginia, 1637 6219 p85
Bateman, Robert; Virginia, 1643 6219 p199
Bateman, Sarah 21; Maryland, 1775 1219.7 p264
Bateman, Tho.; Virginia, 1635 6219 p23
Bateman, Thomas 22; Maryland or Virginia, 1737 3690.1 p13
Bateman, William 23; Philadelphia, 1774 1219.7 p183
Bater, Charles; Virginia, 1642 6219 p190
Bates, Anton; Iowa, 1866-1943 123.54 p7
Bates, John; Ohio, 1850-1871 9892.11 p2
Bates, John; Ohio, 1873 9892.11 p2
Bates, John 21; Philadelphia, 1803 53.26 p3
Bates, John 21; Virginia, 1774 1219.7 p238
Bates, John 27; Philadelphia, 1775 1219.7 p274
Bates, Joseph; Boston, 1776 1219.7 p283
Bates, Joseph; Quebec, 1851 5704.8 p75
Bates, Michael; Illinois, 1871 5012.39 p25
Bates, Nicholas; Virginia, 1637 6219 p112
Bates, Richard; Jamaica, 1749 3690.1 p14
Bates, Thomas 31; Kansas, 1884 5240.1 p65
Bates, William; Boston, 1828 8893 p262
Bates, William; Illinois, 1871 5012.39 p25
Bates, William Austin; Illinois, 1893 5012.40 p53
Bateson, Henry 23; Maryland, 1774 1219.7 p180
Batez, James; Iowa, 1866-1943 123.54 p7
Bath, Henry; New York, 1884 1450.2 p9A
Bath, John 23; Annapolis, N.S., 1775 1219.7 p262
Bath, Nicolaus; America, 1853 8582.3 p2
Bath, Patrick; America, 1743 4971 p11
Bath, Peter; America, 1742 4971 p94
Bath, Peter; America, 1743 4971 p86
Bath, Samuel 19; Maryland, 1719 3690.1 p14
Bath, Thos.; Virginia, 1637 6219 p115
Bath, William; New York, NY, 1838 8208.4 p64
Bathell, Peter 17; Windward Islands, 1722 3690.1 p14
Bathke, Herman; Wisconsin, n.d. 9675.4 p194
Bathke, Herman, Jr.; Wisconsin, n.d. 9675.4 p194
Bathke, Johann; Wisconsin, n.d. 9675.4 p194
Bathke, John; Wisconsin, n.d. 9675.4 p194
Bathmann, Christopf 25; New York, NY, 1857 9831.14 p153
Batho, John; Virginia, 1642 6219 p190
Bathropp, Jon.; Virginia, 1643 6219 p200
Batiste, Mme. 46; America, 1838 778.5 p33
Batiste, Mr. 40; New Orleans, 1823 778.5 p33
Batiste, Jean 26; America, 1831 778.5 p33
Batiste, Juan 53; America, 1838 778.5 p33
Batiste, Manuel R. 28; New Orleans, 1862 543.30 p480
Batiste, S. 20; Port uncertain, 1835 778.5 p33
Batowski, . . .; New York, 1831 4606 p172
Batro, Miss 5; New Orleans, 1837 778.5 p33
Batro, Mrs. 40; New Orleans, 1837 778.5 p33
Batrum, Lawr.; Virginia, 1643 6219 p200
Batt, Dorothy; Virginia, 1643 6219 p207
Batt, Henry *SEE* Batt, Thomas
Batt, Michael; Virginia, 1638 6219 p18
Batt, Robert 17; Windward Islands, 1722 3690.1 p14
Batt, Robert 18; Pennsylvania, Virginia or Maryland, 1723 3690.1 p14
Batt, Samuel 22; Maryland, 1774 1219.7 p180
Batt, Thomas; Virginia, 1639 6219 p157
*Brother:*Henry
Batt, Thomas 25; Virginia, 1774 1219.7 p241
Batte, Captain; Virginia, 1667 8582.3 p93
Battelli, Augusto; Wisconsin, n.d. 9675.4 p194
Batteman, John 26; Jamaica, 1731 3690.1 p13
Batten, Albert Edward; Arkansas, 1918 95.2 p18
Batten, Robert; New York, NY, 1834 8208.4 p39
Battest, John 23; New Orleans, 1837 778.5 p33
Battey, Richard 25; Jamaica, 1773 1219.7 p172
Battey, Thomas 30; Jamaica, 1730 3690.1 p14
Battigan, Catharine 20; Massachusetts, 1847 5881.1 p6
Battista, Gallina John; Arkansas, 1918 95.2 p18
Battistello, Francesco; Iowa, 1866-1943 123.54 p8
Battistello, John; Iowa, 1866-1943 123.54 p8
Battistello, Marco; Iowa, 1866-1943 123.54 p8
Battle, Mathew; Virginia, 1647 6219 p245
Battoclatte, George; Colorado, 1904 9678.1 p153
Battraminelli, Angelo 70; Arizona, 1922 9228.40 p26
Batts, John; Virginia, 1639 6219 p150
Batts, Joseph; Virginia, 1639 6219 p151
Batts, Wm.; Virginia, 1648 6219 p250
Battuello, Dominick; Iowa, 1866-1943 123.54 p8
Batty, Abraham; America, 1844 1450.2 p9A
Batty, John; America, 1844 1450.2 p9A
Batut, Jean 25; America, 1837 778.5 p33
Batvel, Daniel 40; Maryland, 1774 1219.7 p177
*Wife:*Rachel 30
With 3 children & mother-in-law
Batvel, Rachel 30 *SEE* Batvel, Daniel
Baty, John; Ohio, 1860 9892.11 p3
Batz, . . .; Canada, 1776-1783 9786 p17
Batz, Barbara; Pennsylvania, 1751 2444 p135
Batzig, Carl H.; Wisconsin, n.d. 9675.4 p194
Bau, A. 49; Louisiana, 1820 778.5 p33
Bauche, Dominico 34?; Arizona, 1890 2764.35 p9
Bauchen, Leonare 23; America, 1827 778.5 p33
Bauchon, Felix 38; New Orleans, 1863 543.30 p326
Baude, Jacob 24; America, 1838 778.5 p33
Baudin, Jean-Baptiste 37; Port uncertain, 1838 778.5 p33
Baudoin, Charles 25; Port uncertain, 1838 778.5 p33
Baudoin, Marie 45; New Orleans, 1823 778.5 p33
Baudoin, P. 34; New Orleans, 1820 778.5 p34
Baudot, Marie 27; New Orleans, 1837 778.5 p34
Baudouin, Mr. 34; New Orleans, 1829 778.5 p34
Baudouin, Cas...; Port uncertain, 1839 778.5 p34
Baudry, Pierre 35; New Orleans, 1837 778.5 p34
Baudwin, D. 40; New Orleans, 1835 778.5 p34
Bauer, . . .; America, 1869-1885 8582.2 p2
Bauer, . . .; Canada, 1776-1783 9786 p17
Bauer, Dr.; Cincinnati, 1788-1848 8582.3 p90
Bauer, Mr.; Michigan, 1867-1877 8582.3 p50
Bauer, Ad. 22; America, 1853 9162.8 p36
Bauer, Andreas; Georgia, 1734 9332 p327
Bauer, Andreas; Wisconsin, n.d. 9675.4 p194
Bauer, Andreas 4; America, 1853 9162.7 p14
Bauer, Anna 10; America, 1838 778.5 p34
Bauer, Anton 5; America, 1838 778.5 p34
Bauer, Apolinaur; Denver, CO, 1869 2764.35 p7
Bauer, Barbara; Ohio, 1860 5647.5 p63
Bauer, Bernhard; New England, 1752 4525 p199
With wife
With 6 children
Bauer, Carl Herman; Wisconsin, n.d. 9675.4 p194
Bauer, Catherine 4; America, 1838 778.5 p34
Bauer, Christina *SEE* Bauer, Emil
Bauer, David 38; Kansas, 1882 5240.1 p63
Bauer, Diel; Philadelphia, 1760 9973.7 p34
Bauer, Eliza 1; America, 1838 778.5 p34
Bauer, Emil; New York, NY, 1889 3455.2 p98
*Wife:*Christina
Bauer, Eva; New England, 1745-1800 2444 p135
*Child:*Johann Georg
Bauer, Frederick; America, 1832 1450.2 p10A
Bauer, G. 31; New York, NY, 1839 5647.5 p45
Bauer, Georg; Albany, NY, 1830-1854 3702.7 p150
Bauer, Georg; Ohio, 1836 8582.1 p47
Bauer, Mrs. Georg; Pennsylvania, 1773 4525 p199
With son
Bauer, George; Iroquois Co., IL, 1896 3455.1 p9
Bauer, George 22; New York, NY, 1853 3702.7 p153
Bauer, Herman; Illinois, 1881 2896.5 p2
Bauer, Jacob; America, 1832 8582.2 p60
Bauer, Jacob, Jr.; Wisconsin, n.d. 9675.4 p194
Bauer, Joh. 11 mos; America, 1853 9162.7 p14
Bauer, Johann; Cincinnati, 1869-1887 8582 p2
Bauer, Johann 26; New York, 1854 3702.7 p149
Bauer, Johann Bernhard; Pennsylvania, 1752 4525 p199
Bauer, Johann C.; New York, NY, 1848 8582.3 p2
Bauer, Johann Conrad; Baltimore, 1846 8582.1 p2
With parents
Bauer, Johann Conrad; Cincinnati, 1869-1887 8582 p2
Bauer, Johann Georg *SEE* Bauer, Eva
Bauer, John; America, 1848 8582.1 p2
Bauer, John 41; New Orleans, 1862 543.30 p482
Bauer, John George; Illinois, 1859 2896.5 p2
Bauer, John George 27; Philadelphia, 1848 1450.2 p10A
Bauer, John George 42; Kansas, 1887 5240.1 p4
Bauer, John George 42; Kansas, 1887 5240.1 p70
Bauer, John Gottfried; Ohio, 1869-1887 8582 p2
Bauer, John Jacob; Indiana, 1836 9117 p15
Bauer, Johs. 36; America, 1853 9162.7 p14
Bauer, Joseph 43; America, 1838 778.5 p34
Bauer, Kathr. 50; America, 1854-1855 9162.6 p104
Bauer, Marguerite 43; America, 1838 778.5 p34
Bauer, Maria Christina Ursula; Maryland, 1865-1869 3702.7 p206
Bauer, Maria Cristina; Maryland, 1869 3702.7 p214
Bauer, Marie 26; America, 1853 9162.7 p14
Bauer, Martin 44; Pennsylvania, 1752-1753 2444 p136
Bauer, Michael; America, 1840 8582.1 p2
Bauer, Nickolaus; New York, NY, 1909 3455.2 p100
Bauer, Peter 28; America, 1853 9162.8 p36
Bauernfeind, . . .; Canada, 1776-1783 9786 p17
Bauernfreund, . . .; Canada, 1776-1783 9786 p17
Baufen, Mr. 5; New Orleans, 1822 778.5 p34
Baufen, Mrs. 35; New Orleans, 1822 778.5 p34
Baugert, . . .; Canada, 1776-1783 9786 p17
Baugert, Martin; Illinois, 1896 5012.40 p55
Baughman, Abraham; Ohio, 1819 8582.1 p47
Baughmann, Abraham; Ohio, 1819 8582.1 p2
Baught, Stephen 16; Maryland, 1719 3690.1 p14
Baugle, Ferdinand; Ohio, 1840 9892.11 p3
Bauguon, Mr. 45; New Orleans, 1821 778.5 p34
Bauknecht, Georg; South Carolina, 1788 7119 p201
Bauknecht, George; South Carolina, 1788 7119 p199
Bauknecht, Johann Georg *SEE* Bauknecht, Michael
Bauknecht, Maria M. Stocklin *SEE* Bauknecht, Michael
Bauknecht, Michael; Port uncertain, 1749 2444 p136
*Wife:*Maria M. Stocklin
*Child:*Johann Georg
Baules, Jr. 16; New Orleans, 1825 778.5 p35
Baulet, Jacques 16; New Orleans, 1836 778.5 p35
Baulke, Thomas; Virginia, 1642 6219 p194
Baum, Lieut.-Col.; Quebec, 1776 9786 p104
Baum, F.; Quebec, 1776 9786 p102
Baum, Frederick W. 35; Kansas, 1874 5240.1 p56
Baum, Friedrich; Canada, 1776-1783 9786 p148
Baum, Friedrich; Quebec, 1776 9786 p252
Baum, Georg; Cincinnati, 1869-1887 8582 p2
Baum, George; Ohio, 1839 5647.5 p4
*Wife:*Sophia M. Donner
Baum, Henry; Philadelphia, 1762 9973.7 p37
Baum, J. C.; America, 1830 8582.2 p61
Baum, Jacob; Halifax, N.S., 1780 9786 p269
Baum, Jacob; New York, 1776 9786 p269
Baum, John; Wisconsin, n.d. 9675.4 p194
Baum, John 35; New Orleans, 1862 543.30 p483
Baum, John C.; Cincinnati, 1869-1887 8582 p2
Baum, Martin; Cincinnati, 1812 8582.2 p52
Baum, Sophia M. Donner *SEE* Baum, George
Bauman, August 33; Kansas, 1876 5240.1 p57
Bauman, Caroline 25; America, 1841 5647.5 p59
Bauman, David; Colorado, 1904 9678.1 p153
Bauman, Friedrich Johan *SEE* Bauman, George
Bauman, George; Indiana, 1844 5647.5 p59
Bauman, George; Ohio, 1837-1839 5647.5 p59
*Wife:*Sophia M. Donner
*Child:*Friedrich Johan
Bauman, Henrich; Philadelphia, 1779 8137 p6
Bauman, Joseph 28; New Orleans, 1864 5647.5 p67
Bauman, Peter; Illinois, 1870 5012.38 p99
Bauman, Sophia M. Donner *SEE* Bauman, George
Bauman, Walter; America, 1887 5647.5 p67
Bauman, William; Philadelphia, 1758 9973.7 p33
Baumann, . . .; Canada, 1776-1783 9786 p17
Baumann, A. 30; New York, NY, 1839 5647.5 p45
Baumann, Albert 26; New Orleans, 1862 543.30 p327
Baumann, Andrew; America, 1855 1450.2 p10A
Baumann, Anne Marie C. Engel *SEE* Baumann, Karl Heinrich
Baumann, Annette 26; New Orleans, 1838 778.5 p35
Baumann, Barbara; New York, NY, 1839 5647.5 p45
Baumann, Barbara 23; New York, NY, 1839 5647.5 p45
Baumann, Caspar H. Gottlieb *SEE* Baumann, Otto Heinrich
Baumann, Catharina Barbara *SEE* Baumann, Daniel
Baumann, Catharina Knodlin *SEE* Baumann, Daniel
Baumann, Daniel; Pennsylvania, 1751 2444 p136
*Child:*Johann Daniel
*Child:*Catharina Barbara
*Child:*Eva Maria
*Wife:*Catharina Knodlin
Baumann, Eva Maria *SEE* Baumann, Daniel
Baumann, Friedrich Johan *SEE* Baumann, George
Baumann, Fritz; Illinois, 1890 5012.39 p53
Baumann, Fritz; Illinois, 1892 5012.40 p26
Baumann, G. 27; New York, NY, 1839 5647.5 p45

Baumann, Georg; Virginia, 1732 ***8582.3*** *p96*
With father-in-law
Baumann, George; Indiana, 1844 ***5647.5*** *p59*
Baumann, George; New York, NY, 1839 ***5647.5*** *p45*
Baumann, George; Ohio, 1837-1839 ***5647.5*** *p59*
*Wife:*Sophia M. Donner
*Child:*Friedrich Johan
Baumann, J. 1; New York, NY, 1839 ***5647.5*** *p45*
Baumann, J. G. 24; New York, NY, 1839 ***5647.5*** *p45*
Baumann, Johann; Ohio, 1869-1885 ***8582.2*** *p56*
Baumann, Johann Daniel *SEE* Baumann, Daniel
Baumann, Karl Friedrich *SEE* Baumann, Karl Heinrich
Baumann, Karl Heinrich 33; America, 1852 ***4610.10*** *p147*
With wife
*Child:*Anne Marie C. Engel
*Child:*Karl Friedrich
Baumann, M.; Illinois, 1837 ***8582.2*** *p50*
Baumann, Margarete; Philadelphia, 1756 ***4525*** *p261*
Baumann, Margaretha; Ohio, 1732-1832 ***8582*** *p2*
Baumann, Margaretha; Pennsylvania, 1751 ***2444*** *p201*
Baumann, Martin; Ohio, 1798-1818 ***8582.2*** *p54*
Baumann, Matthias; Illinois, 1872 ***5012.39*** *p25*
Baumann, Michael; Illinois, 1837 ***8582.1*** *p55*
Baumann, Otto Heinrich; America, 1843 ***4610.10*** *p133*
*Wife:*Sophie L. Steinmann
*Son:*Caspar H. Gottlieb
Baumann, Rosina Barbara; Pennsylvania, 1753 ***2444*** *p136*
Baumann, Sophia M. Donner *SEE* Baumann, George
Baumann, Sophie; New York, NY, 1839 ***5647.5*** *p45*
Baumann, Sophie 22; New York, NY, 1839 ***5647.5*** *p45*
Baumann, Sophie L. Steinmann *SEE* Baumann, Otto Heinrich
Baumann, Tony; America, 1895 ***1450.2*** *p10A*
Baume, Lewis 25; Port uncertain, 1839 ***778.5*** *p35*
Baumeyer, A.M. Louise Bunermann *SEE* Baumeyer, Johann Christoph
Baumeyer, Anne Marie F. L. Henriette; America, 1844 ***4610.10*** *p111*
Baumeyer, Johann C. Ludwig *SEE* Baumeyer, Johann Christoph
Baumeyer, Johann Christoph; America, 1843-1844 ***4610.10*** *p111*
*Wife:*A.M. Louise Bunermann
*Son:*Johann C. Ludwig
Baumgaertner, Friedrich; Cincinnati, 1826 ***8582.1*** *p51*
Baumgaertner, Karl; New York, NY, 1849 ***8582.3*** *p3*
Baumgarten, George; New York, 1750 ***3652*** *p74*
Baumgartner, Baptist 21; New Orleans, 1862 ***543.30*** *p327*
Baumgartner, Carl; America, 1849 ***8582.2*** *p2*
Baumgartner, Nikolas; Pennsylvania, 1709-1710 ***4480*** *p311*
Baumgartner, Wolffgang; Georgia, 1738 ***9332*** *p319*
Baumier, Augustin 30; Louisiana, 1830 ***778.5*** *p35*
Baumstark, Hermann; Cincinnati, 1788-1848 ***8582.3*** *p90*
Baun, Ann; Philadelphia, 1847 ***53.26*** *p3*
Baun, Ann 8; Philadelphia, 1847 ***5704.8*** *p23*
Baun, Christian Jacob; Colorado, 1895 ***9678.1*** *p153*
Baun, F.; New York, NY, 1854 ***3702.7*** *p547*
Bauney, Timothy; America, 1850 ***1450.2*** *p10A*
Bauny, Mary; Montreal, 1824 ***7603*** *p81*
Baur, Anna *SEE* Baur, Martin
Baur, Anna Barbara *SEE* Baur, Martin
Baur, Anna Maria *SEE* Baur, Martin
Baur, Georg Heinrich *SEE* Baur, Martin
Baur, Johann Gottlieb *SEE* Baur, Martin
Baur, Ludwig Herman; America, 1851 ***8582.3*** *p3*
Baur, Martin; Pennsylvania, 1752-1753 ***2444*** *p136*
*Wife:*Anna Barbara
*Child:*Michael
*Child:*Anna
*Child:*Georg Heinrich
*Child:*Johann Gottlieb
*Child:*Anna Maria
Baur, Michael *SEE* Baur, Martin
Baures, J. 30; Port uncertain, 1839 ***778.5*** *p35*
Baurichter, Carl Friedrich *SEE* Baurichter, Carl Friedrich
Baurichter, Carl Friedrich 41; America, 1850 ***4610.10*** *p142*
*Wife:*Mathilde Sander
*Child:*Caroline Engel
*Child:*Carl Friedrich
*Child:*Hermann Heinrich
*Child:*Caroline Friederike
*Child:*Christine Wilhelmine
*Child:*Friedrich Wilhelm
Baurichter, Carl Heinrich; America, 1850 ***4610.10*** *p138*
Baurichter, Caroline Engel *SEE* Baurichter, Carl Friedrich
Baurichter, Caroline Friederike *SEE* Baurichter, Carl Friedrich
Baurichter, Christine Wilhelmine *SEE* Baurichter, Carl Friedrich
Baurichter, Friedrich Wilhelm *SEE* Baurichter, Carl Friedrich
Baurichter, Hermann Heinrich *SEE* Baurichter, Carl Friedrich
Baurichter, Mathilde Sander *SEE* Baurichter, Carl Friedrich
Baurlin, Henry 17; New Orleans, 1862 ***543.30*** *p246*
Baurlin, Wm 18; New Orleans, 1862 ***543.30*** *p246*
Baurmeister, Major; Canada, 1776-1783 ***9786*** *p201*
Baus, Nicholas; Wisconsin, n.d. ***9675.4*** *p194*
Bausbacker, Anna Maria 38; New Orleans, 1837 ***778.5*** *p35*
Bausbacker, Eliza 6 mos; New Orleans, 1837 ***778.5*** *p35*
Bausbacker, Frederic 10; New Orleans, 1837 ***778.5*** *p35*
Bausbacker, Maria 7; New Orleans, 1837 ***778.5*** *p35*
Bausbacker, Michel 2; New Orleans, 1837 ***778.5*** *p35*
Bausbacker, Nicolas 5; New Orleans, 1837 ***778.5*** *p35*
Bausbacker, Philip 84; New Orleans, 1837 ***778.5*** *p35*
Bausch, Wilh. 24; America, 1853 ***9162.7*** *p14*
Bausch, Wilhelm; Philadelphia, 1779 ***8137*** *p6*
Bauschet, John; Illinois, 1881 ***2896.5*** *p2*
Bause, Johann Carl; Quebec, 1776 ***9786*** *p259*
Bauser, Jacob; Illinois, 1858 ***2896.5*** *p2*
Baussager, Remis 25; Port uncertain, 1825 ***778.5*** *p35*
Baussan, J. 28; Louisiana, 1820 ***778.5*** *p35*
Bausson, . . .; Louisiana, 1820 ***778.5*** *p36*
Bausson, Mme. 24; Louisiana, 1820 ***778.5*** *p36*
Bausson, Mr. 15; Louisiana, 1820 ***778.5*** *p36*
Baut, Louis 25; America, 1839 ***778.5*** *p36*
Bavadat, J. 22; New Orleans, 1838 ***778.5*** *p24*
Bavard, Mr. 21; New Orleans, 1839 ***778.5*** *p36*
Bavel, Z. 30; New Orleans, 1835 ***778.5*** *p36*
Baverdez, F. 42; Port uncertain, 1839 ***778.5*** *p36*
Bawcock, William 19; Pennsylvania, 1719 ***3690.1*** *p14*
Bawcocke, Tho.; Virginia, 1600-1642 ***6219*** *p192*
Bawdler, Thomas 21; Maryland, 1774 ***1219.7*** *p221*
Baxter, Mr.; Quebec, 1815 ***9229.18*** *p77*
Baxter, Ann; Philadelphia, 1865 ***5704.8*** *p201*
Baxter, Barnaby 30; Maryland, 1774 ***1219.7*** *p181*
Baxter, Daniel; Washington, 1859-1920 ***2872.1*** *p3*
Baxter, Denis; Quebec, 1824 ***7603*** *p80*
Baxter, Elianor; Virginia, 1642 ***6219*** *p196*
Baxter, Eliza; St. John, N.B., 1847 ***5704.8*** *p9*
Baxter, George 21; Philadelphia, 1856 ***5704.8*** *p128*
Baxter, Hannah; New York, NY, 1866 ***5704.8*** *p204*
Baxter, Henry 17; Jamaica, 1725 ***3690.1*** *p14*
Baxter, James; New York, NY, 1866 ***5704.8*** *p211*
Baxter, Jane; Virginia, 1636 ***6219*** *p28*
Baxter, John; America, 1802 ***1639.20*** *p8*
Baxter, John; Philadelphia, 1864 ***5704.8*** *p183*
Baxter, John; St. John, N.B., 1847 ***5704.8*** *p9*
Baxter, John 3 mos; St. John, N.B., 1847 ***5704.8*** *p9*
Baxter, John 22; Kansas, 1871 ***5240.1*** *p52*
Baxter, Letty; St. John, N.B., 1847 ***5704.8*** *p9*
Baxter, Margaret 9; St. John, N.B., 1847 ***5704.8*** *p33*
Baxter, Mary; Quebec, 1822 ***7603*** *p97*
Baxter, Mathew; New York, NY, 1868 ***5704.8*** *p227*
Baxter, Matthew 17; Philadelphia, 1860 ***5704.8*** *p146*
Baxter, Nancy; St. John, N.B., 1847 ***5704.8*** *p9*
Baxter, Richard; Virginia, 1638 ***6219*** *p125*
Baxter, Robert; America, 1868 ***5704.8*** *p227*
Baxter, Robert; Illinois, 1864 ***5012.38*** *p98*
Baxter, Robert; St. John, N.B., 1847 ***5704.8*** *p9*
Baxter, Samuel; St. John, N.B., 1847 ***5704.8*** *p9*
Baxter, Samuel 2; St. John, N.B., 1847 ***5704.8*** *p9*
Baxter, Thomas; St. John, N.B., 1847 ***5704.8*** *p33*
Baxter, William; Philadelphia, 1849 ***53.26*** *p3*
Baxter, William; Philadelphia, 1849 ***5704.8*** *p54*
Baxter, William; St. John, N.B., 1847 ***5704.8*** *p9*
Baxter, Wm.; Virginia, 1636 ***6219*** *p74*
Baxton, J. J.; Iowa, 1866-1943 ***123.54*** *p8*
Bay, Aloia; Wisconsin, n.d. ***9675.4*** *p194*
Bay, Charles 26; Maryland, 1774 ***1219.7*** *p179*
Bay, John; Virginia, 1642 ***6219*** *p186*
Bay, John 24; Maryland, 1774 ***1219.7*** *p179*
Bayant, John; Virginia, 1635 ***6219*** *p26*
Bayard, A. 30; Port uncertain, 1835 ***778.5*** *p36*
Bayard, C.; New Orleans, 1839 ***778.5*** *p36*
Bayard, J.; New Orleans, 1839 ***778.5*** *p36*
Bayard, P.; New Orleans, 1839 ***778.5*** *p36*
Bayard, S.; New Orleans, 1839 ***778.5*** *p36*
Bayer, George; Colorado, 1884 ***9678.1*** *p153*
Bayer, Herman; Illinois, 1895 ***2896.5*** *p2*
Bayer, Jacob; New York, NY, 1838 ***8208.4*** *p87*
Bayer, John George 25; Kansas, 1893 ***5240.1*** *p78*
Bayer, Maria 76; Pennsylvania, 1911 ***1763*** *p40D*
Bayerley, John Michel; Pennsylvania, 1753 ***4779.3*** *p13*
Bayerly, Johann Michael; Pennsylvania, 1753 ***4779.3*** *p13*
Bayersdorfer, John 23; Kansas, 1891 ***5240.1*** *p76*
Bayet, Jean-Francois 29; Louisiana, 1820 ***778.5*** *p36*
Bayford, Hanna; Virginia, 1639 ***6219*** *p158*
Bayha, Anna Maria Schweizer *SEE* Bayha, Georg
Bayha, Barbara Arnold *SEE* Bayha, George, Jr.
Bayha, Catharina; Pennsylvania, 1754 ***2444*** *p207*
Bayha, Catharine *SEE* Bayha, Georg
Bayha, Georg; New York, 1754 ***2444*** *p136*
*Wife:*Anna Maria Schweizer
*Child:*Catharine
*Child:*George
*Child:*Johann Martin
Bayha, George *SEE* Bayha, Georg
Bayha, George, Jr.; Pennsylvania, 1754 ***2444*** *p194*
*Wife:*Barbara Arnold
Bayha, Johann Martin *SEE* Bayha, Georg
Bayhi, Joseph; Louisiana, 1789-1819 ***778.5*** *p555*
Baylac, Felix 33; Port uncertain, 1836 ***778.5*** *p37*
Bayland, William; Quebec, 1817 ***7603*** *p73*
Bayle, Mr.; New Orleans, 1839 ***778.5*** *p37*
Bayle, Darby 24; Philadelphia, 1803 ***53.26*** *p3*
*Relative:*Jean 21
Bayle, Jean 21 *SEE* Bayle, Darby
Baylen, Stephen; New Brunswick, 1823 ***7603*** *p96*
Bayley, John; New York, NY, 1816 ***2859.11*** *p25*
Bayley, Tho.; Virginia, 1645 ***6219*** *p235*
Bayley, Thomas; Jamaica, 1755 ***1219.7*** *p36*
Baylis, John 21; Maryland, 1774 ***1219.7*** *p211*
Bayliss, John 19; Virginia, 1731 ***3690.1*** *p14*
Bayliss, John 19; Virginia, 1751 ***1219.7*** *p4*
Bayliss, Joseph; Boston, 1776 ***1219.7*** *p282*
Bayly, . . .; Virginia, 1643 ***6219*** *p230*
Bayly, Arthur; Virginia, 1637 ***6219*** *p113*
Bayly, Joane; Virginia, 1632 ***6219*** *p180*
Bayly, John; Maryland, 1753 ***1219.7*** *p22*
Bayly, John; Maryland, 1753 ***3690.1*** *p14*
Bayly, Jone; Virginia, 1639 ***6219*** *p158*
Bayly, Lewis; Virginia, 1621 ***6219*** *p25*
Bayly, Margarett; Virginia, 1639 ***6219*** *p161*
Bayly, Peter; Virginia, 1635 ***6219*** *p3*
Bayly, Phillip; Virginia, 1639 ***6219*** *p22*
Bayly, Rebecca; Virginia, 1643 ***6219*** *p206*
Bayly, Rebena; Virginia, 1637 ***6219*** *p110*
Bayly, Richard; Virginia, 1638 ***6219*** *p122*
Bayly, Richard; Virginia, 1638 ***6219*** *p147*
Bayly, Richard; Virginia, 1643 ***6219*** *p33*
Bayly, Rob.; Virginia, 1648 ***6219*** *p253*
Baylye, Henry; Virginia, 1637 ***6219*** *p17*
Baylye, Jon.; Virginia, 1638 ***6219*** *p119*
Baylye, Richard; Virginia, 1638 ***6219*** *p33*
Baylye, Thomas; Virginia, 1637 ***6219*** *p24*
Bayne, Catharine; Philadelphia, 1864 ***5704.8*** *p177*
Baynes, John 24; Massachusetts, 1847 ***5881.1*** *p8*
Baynham, Richard 22; Maryland, 1774 ***1219.7*** *p220*
Bayol, Francois 20; New Orleans, 1831 ***778.5*** *p37*
Bayrett, Charles; Ohio, 1860 ***6014.2*** *p7*
Baysen, Johann; Wisconsin, n.d. ***9675.4*** *p194*
Baytes, Peter; Virginia, 1642 ***6219*** *p193*
Baywell, Thomas; Virginia, 1635 ***6219*** *p71*
With wife
Baz, Barbara; Pennsylvania, 1751 ***2444*** *p135*
Bazant, Josef 2 *SEE* Bazant, Jozefa Gite
Bazant, Jozefa Gite 28; New York, 1912 ***9980.29*** *p55*
*Daughter:*Marianna 8
*Son:*Josef 2
Bazant, Marianna 8 *SEE* Bazant, Jozefa Gite
Bazet, Mr. 23; America, 1838 ***778.5*** *p37*
Bazire, A. 24; Guatemala, 1827 ***778.5*** *p37*
Bazler, John Gootlip; Philadelphia, 1820 ***9892.11*** *p3*
Bazuqui, Jacques 38; New Orleans, 1862 ***543.30*** *p326*
Bazzo, Frank; Iowa, 1866-1943 ***123.54*** *p8*
Bazzo, Jiovanni; Iowa, 1866-1943 ***123.54*** *p8*
Bazzocco, Vittore; Iowa, 1866-1943 ***123.54*** *p8*
Bddr, Liby; New York, NY, 1895 ***1450.2*** *p1B*
Bea, Conrad 28; Washington Co., MD, 1838 ***1450.2*** *p10A*
Beach, Stephen; Virginia, 1639 ***6219*** *p158*
Beacom, Eliza; Quebec, 1850 ***5704.8*** *p63*
Beacom, George 8; Quebec, 1850 ***5704.8*** *p63*
Beacom, Robert 6; Quebec, 1850 ***5704.8*** *p63*
Beacon, Jane; St. John, N.B., 1853 ***5704.8*** *p107*
Beacon, John; America, 1741-1742 ***4971*** *p60*
Beacon, Robert; St. John, N.B., 1853 ***5704.8*** *p107*
Beadell, John; Virginia, 1636 ***6219*** *p80*
Beadle, Jon.; Virginia, 1636 ***6219*** *p80*
Beaghon, Stephen 15; Maryland, 1729 ***3690.1*** *p14*
Beagler, Michael; Pennsylvania, 1772 ***9973.8*** *p33*
Beal, Edward 19; Jamaica, 1723 ***3690.1*** *p15*
Beal, Frederick Lawrense 22; Arkansas, 1918 ***95.2*** *p18*
Beale, Benjamin 21; Maryland, 1773 ***1219.7*** *p173*
Beale, Edward 19; Jamaica, 1723 ***3690.1*** *p15*
Beale, George 37; Kansas, 1895 ***5240.1*** *p80*
Beale, Susan; Virginia, 1637 ***6219*** *p114*
Beall, J. W.; Washington, 1859-1920 ***2872.1*** *p3*
Beall, John 18; Maryland or Virginia, 1719 ***3690.1*** *p15*
Bealle, George 17; Jamaica, 1730 ***3690.1*** *p15*

Beamont, George 21; New York, 1774 *1219.7 p218*
Beamont, James; Maryland, 1775 *1219.7 p265*
Bean, Alexander 23; Georgia, 1775 *1219.7 p276*
 *Wife:*Christiana 18
Bean, Alfred J. 41?; Arizona, 1890 *2764.35 p7*
Bean, Christiana 18 *SEE* Bean, Alexander
Bean, Cornelius; Quebec, 1713 *7603 p87*
Bean, Daniel 22; Massachusetts, 1849 *5881.1 p7*
Bean, John 16; Maryland, 1775 *1219.7 p273*
Bean, Thomas 45; Maryland, 1775 *1219.7 p250*
Beane, Stephen; Virginia, 1638 *6219 p148*
Beanmont, John; St. John, N.B., 1852 *5704.8 p83*
Beans, William 17; Maryland, 1750 *3690.1 p15*
Bear, G. Henry; Illinois, 1859 *5012.38 p97*
Bear, John 25; New Orleans, 1838 *778.5 p37*
Bear, L. 32; New Orleans, 1835 *778.5 p37*
Bear, Thomas 21; Maryland, 1775 *1219.7 p257*
Bear, Thomas Whittle; Antigua (Antego), 1766 *1219.7
 p123*
Bearbaum, Henry; Illinois, 1879 *5012.39 p120*
Beard, Alice 27 *SEE* Beard, Thomas
Beard, Andrew; America, 1741 *4971 p67*
Beard, Eleanor; Philadelphia, 1864 *5704.8 p180*
Beard, Joane *SEE* Beard, William
Beard, Joane; Virginia, 1638 *6219 p116*
Beard, Jon.; Virginia, 1637 *6219 p24*
Beard, M. 20; America, 1826 *778.5 p37*
Beard, Margaret; Philadelphia, 1864 *5704.8 p180*
Beard, Mary; Virginia, 1647 *6219 p245*
Beard, Robert; Charleston, SC, 1775-1781 *8582.2 p52*
Beard, Robert 21; Maryland, 1774 *1219.7 p220*
Beard, Thomas; New York, NY, 1865 *5704.8 p203*
Beard, Thomas 28; Philadelphia, 1774 *1219.7 p182*
 *Wife:*Alice 27
Beard, Thomas 39; Maryland, 1775 *1219.7 p247*
Beard, William; Virginia, 1635 *6219 p70*
 *Wife:*Joane
Beard, William; Virginia, 1638 *6219 p116*
Beard, William 24; Maryland, 1774 *1219.7 p196*
Beardmore, John 23; Maryland, 1773 *1219.7 p173*
Beardsty, Elizabeth; Virginia, 1637 *6219 p107*
Beare, Christ.; Virginia, 1637 *6219 p86*
Beare, Wm.; Virginia, 1647 *6219 p245*
Bearing, John 24; Massachusetts, 1860 *6410.32 p113*
Bearne, Jon.; Virginia, 1637 *6219 p113*
Bearner, Georges; Quebec, 1816 *7603 p74*
Beason, John 32; New York, NY, 1828 *6508.4 p143*
Beason, Mary 28; New York, NY, 1828 *6508.4 p143*
Beast, Mary *SEE* Beast, Thomas
Beast, Richard *SEE* Beast, Thomas
Beast, Thomas; Virginia, 1636 *6219 p77*
 *Wife:*Mary
 *Son:*Richard
Beata, Emilo; Arkansas, 1918 *95.2 p18*
Beatall, Robert; Virginia, 1637 *6219 p112*
Beates, William; Virginia, 1637 *6219 p81*
Beathey, Richard 21; New Orleans, 1864 *543.30 p249*
Beatin, Christina 35; Kansas, 1878 *5240.1 p59*
Beatina, Sister M.; Wisconsin, n.d. *9675.4 p194*
Beatina, Sister M.; Wisconsin, n.d. *9675.8 p66*
Beaton, Alex *SEE* Beaton, John
Beaton, Alexander; Nova Scotia, 1830 *7085.4 p44*
 *Wife:*Mary
 *Child:*Anne
 *Child:*Ket
 *Child:*Donald
 *Child:*Isabel
 *Child:*John
Beaton, Angus *SEE* Beaton, John
Beaton, Ann *SEE* Beaton, John
Beaton, Ann *SEE* Beaton, Neil
Beaton, Ann MacAulay *SEE* Beaton, John
Beaton, Ann MacDonald *SEE* Beaton, Murdo
Beaton, Ann MacLean *SEE* Beaton, Neil
Beaton, Ann MacLeod *SEE* Beaton, Norman
Beaton, Anne *SEE* Beaton, Alexander
Beaton, Anne *SEE* Beaton, John
Beaton, Betsy *SEE* Beaton, John
Beaton, Catherine *SEE* Beaton, John
Beaton, Catherine *SEE* Beaton, John
Beaton, David 28; Wilmington, NC, 1774 *1639.20 p8*
 *Wife:*Flora McBride
Beaton, Donald *SEE* Beaton, Alexander
Beaton, Donald *SEE* Beaton, John
Beaton, Donald *SEE* Beaton, John
Beaton, Donald *SEE* Beaton, John
Beaton, Donald *SEE* Beaton, Neil
Beaton, Donald *SEE* Beaton, Samuel
Beaton, Donald *SEE* Beaton, William
Beaton, Donald; Nova Scotia, 1830 *7085.4 p45*
 *Wife:*Jannet
 *Child:*Malcolm
Beaton, Edward 20; Philadelphia, 1775 *1219.7 p258*

Beaton, Flora McBride *SEE* Beaton, David
Beaton, George; Quebec, 1851 *4537.30 p1*
 *Wife:*Janet MacDonald
 *Child:*Kirsty
 *Child:*Malcolm
Beaton, Isabel *SEE* Beaton, Alexander
Beaton, Isabel *SEE* Beaton, John
Beaton, Isabella *SEE* Beaton, John
Beaton, Janet Cameron *SEE* Beaton, John
Beaton, Janet MacDonald *SEE* Beaton, George
Beaton, Jannet *SEE* Beaton, Donald
Beaton, Jannet *SEE* Beaton, William
Beaton, John *SEE* Beaton, Alexander
Beaton, John *SEE* Beaton, John
Beaton, John; Nova Scotia, 1830 *7085.4 p44*
 *Wife:*Margaret
 *Child:*Mary
Beaton, John; Nova Scotia, 1830 *7085.4 p44*
 *Child:*Anne
 *Child:*John
 *Child:*Betsy
 *Child:*Isabel
 *Child:*Donald
Beaton, John; Quebec, 1843 *4537.30 p1*
 *Wife:*Janet Cameron
 *Child:*Catherine
 *Child:*Margaret
 *Child:*Alex
 *Child:*Donald
 *Child:*Isabella
Beaton, John; Quebec, 1851 *4537.30 p2*
 *Wife:*Ann MacAulay
 *Child:*Donald
 *Child:*Norman
 *Child:*Angus
 *Child:*Kirsty
 *Child:*Ann
 *Child:*Neil
 *Child:*Murdo
 *Child:*Catherine
Beaton, Ket *SEE* Beaton, Alexander
Beaton, Ket *SEE* Beaton, Samuel
Beaton, Kirsty *SEE* Beaton, George
Beaton, Kirsty *SEE* Beaton, John
Beaton, Malcolm *SEE* Beaton, Donald
Beaton, Malcolm *SEE* Beaton, George
Beaton, Malcolm; Nova Scotia, 1830 *7085.4 p44*
 *Wife:*Mary
Beaton, Malcolm; Quebec, 1838 *4537.30 p3*
Beaton, Margaret *SEE* Beaton, John
Beaton, Margaret *SEE* Beaton, John
Beaton, Mary *SEE* Beaton, Alexander
Beaton, Mary *SEE* Beaton, John
Beaton, Mary *SEE* Beaton, John
Beaton, Mary *SEE* Beaton, Malcolm
Beaton, Mary *SEE* Beaton, Samuel
Beaton, Mary *SEE* Beaton, William
Beaton, Mary; Quebec, 1854 *4537.30 p44*
Beaton, Murdo *SEE* Beaton, John
Beaton, Murdo; Quebec, 1840 *4537.30 p2*
 *Wife:*Ann MacDonald
Beaton, Neil *SEE* Beaton, John
Beaton, Neil *SEE* Beaton, William
Beaton, Neil; Quebec, 1838 *4537.30 p2*
 *Wife:*Ann MacLean
 *Child:*Donald
 *Child:*Ann
Beaton, Norman *SEE* Beaton, John
Beaton, Norman; Quebec, 1838 *4537.30 p3*
 *Wife:*Ann MacLeod
Beaton, Samuel; Nova Scotia, 1830 *7085.4 p44*
 *Wife:*Ket
 *Child:*Mary
 *Child:*Donald
Beaton, Thomas; Virginia, 1638 *6219 p24*
Beaton, William; Nova Scotia, 1830 *7085.4 p44*
 *Wife:*Mary
 *Child:*Donald
 *Child:*Neil
 *Child:*Jannet
Beattie, Andrew; New York, NY, 1816 *2859.11 p25*
Beattie, Francis 22; Charleston, SC, 1774 *1639.20 p8*
Beattie, Margaret 17; Philadelphia, 1860 *5704.8 p146*
Beattie, Rebecca *SEE* Beattie, William
Beattie, Rebecca; Philadelphia, 1848 *5704.8 p40*
Beattie, Thomas 18; St. John, N.B., 1862 *5704.8 p150*
Beattie, William; Philadelphia, 1848 *53.26 p3*
 *Relative:*Rebecca
Beattie, William; Philadelphia, 1848 *5704.8 p40*
Beatty, Adam; Quebec, 1853 *5704.8 p103*
Beatty, Alex; New York, NY, 1811 *2859.11 p8*
 With family
Beatty, Alexander; Quebec, 1847 *5704.8 p6*
Beatty, Ann 23; Philadelphia, 1856 *5704.8 p128*

Beatty, Anne; New York, NY, 1869 *5704.8 p233*
Beatty, Anne; Quebec, 1847 *5704.8 p7*
Beatty, Anne; Quebec, 1852 *5704.8 p94*
Beatty, Archibald; New York, NY, 1864 *5704.8 p180*
Beatty, Archy; St. John, N.B., 1847 *5704.8 p34*
Beatty, Catharine; Philadelphia, 1865 *5704.8 p198*
Beatty, Catherine; Philadelphia, 1850 *53.26 p3*
Beatty, Catherine; Philadelphia, 1850 *5704.8 p60*
Beatty, Con; Quebec, 1851 *5704.8 p74*
Beatty, David; New York, NY, 1816 *2859.11 p25*
Beatty, Eliza; New York, NY, 1816 *2859.11 p25*
Beatty, Eliza; New York, NY, 1864 *5704.8 p170*
Beatty, Eliza 6 mos; Philadelphia, 1853 *5704.8 p112*
Beatty, Eliza 6; Quebec, 1847 *5704.8 p6*
Beatty, Elizabeth; Quebec, 1847 *5704.8 p6*
Beatty, Elizabeth 10; Quebec, 1852 *5704.8 p94*
Beatty, Ellen 20; Quebec, 1855 *5704.8 p124*
Beatty, Faith; Philadelphia, 1867 *5704.8 p222*
Beatty, Fanny 22; St. John, N.B., 1855 *5704.8 p127*
Beatty, Florenda 50; St. John, N.B., 1859 *5704.8 p143*
Beatty, George *SEE* Beatty, William
Beatty, George; Philadelphia, 1811 *2859.11 p8*
Beatty, George 9; Quebec, 1847 *5704.8 p6*
Beatty, George 10; Quebec, 1847 *5704.8 p36*
Beatty, George 13; Quebec, 1847 *5704.8 p7*
Beatty, Isabella; Quebec, 1851 *5704.8 p74*
Beatty, Isabella; Quebec, 1851 *5704.8 p75*
Beatty, James; Quebec, 1847 *5704.8 p6*
Beatty, James; Quebec, 1847 *5704.8 p7*
Beatty, James 9; Quebec, 1847 *5704.8 p7*
Beatty, Jane *SEE* Beatty, William
Beatty, Jane; Philadelphia, 1811 *2859.11 p8*
Beatty, Jane; Philadelphia, 1847 *53.26 p3*
Beatty, Jane; Philadelphia, 1847 *5704.8 p5*
Beatty, Jane; Philadelphia, 1852 *5704.8 p85*
Beatty, Jane; Quebec, 1851 *5704.8 p74*
Beatty, Jane 11; Quebec, 1847 *5704.8 p7*
Beatty, Jas.; New York, NY, 1816 *2859.11 p25*
Beatty, John; Quebec, 1847 *5704.8 p27*
Beatty, John; St. John, N.B., 1847 *5704.8 p32*
Beatty, John; St. John, N.B., 1847 *5704.8 p34*
Beatty, Margaret *SEE* Beatty, Thomas
Beatty, Margaret; Philadelphia, 1848 *5704.8 p45*
Beatty, Margaret; Philadelphia, 1848 *5704.8 p46*
Beatty, Margaret; Quebec, 1850 *5704.8 p70*
Beatty, Margaret; Quebec, 1851 *5704.8 p75*
Beatty, Margaret 12; Quebec, 1847 *5704.8 p36*
Beatty, Martha; New York, NY, 1870 *5704.8 p237*
Beatty, Mary; New York, NY, 1870 *5704.8 p237*
Beatty, Mary; New York, NY, 1870 *5704.8 p238*
Beatty, Mary; Quebec, 1847 *5704.8 p7*
Beatty, Mary 6; Quebec, 1847 *5704.8 p36*
Beatty, Mary 20; Philadelphia, 1853 *5704.8 p112*
Beatty, Mary Ann 19; Philadelphia, 1864 *5704.8 p161*
Beatty, Oliver; New York, NY, 1811 *2859.11 p8*
Beatty, Patrick; Philadelphia, 1849 *53.26 p3*
Beatty, Patrick; Philadelphia, 1849 *5704.8 p50*
Beatty, Rachael; Quebec, 1852 *5704.8 p86*
Beatty, Rachel; Quebec, 1852 *5704.8 p90*
Beatty, Rachel 17; Philadelphia, 1864 *5704.8 p161*
Beatty, Rawlin; Quebec, 1852 *5704.8 p94*
Beatty, Rhoda; Quebec, 1847 *5704.8 p7*
Beatty, Robert; Philadelphia, 1851 *5704.8 p79*
Beatty, Thomas; Ohio, 1882 *5240.1 p4*
Beatty, Thomas; Philadelphia, 1848 *53.26 p3*
 *Relative:*Margaret
Beatty, Thomas; Quebec, 1847 *5704.8 p36*
Beatty, Thomas H.; Philadelphia, 1848 *5704.8 p45*
Beatty, William; New York, NY, 1816 *2859.11 p25*
Beatty, William; Ohio, 1874 *9892.11 p3*
Beatty, William; Philadelphia, 1811 *53.26 p3*
 *Relative:*Jane
 *Relative:*George
Beatty, William; Quebec, 1847 *5704.8 p7*
Beatty, William; Quebec, 1850 *5704.8 p69*
Beatty, William 6 mos; Quebec, 1847 *5704.8 p6*
Beatty, Wm.; Philadelphia, 1811 *2859.11 p8*
Beaty, Edward 50; Massachusetts, 1850 *5881.1 p7*
Beaty, Elizabeth 20; Philadelphia, 1854 *5704.8 p116*
Beau, Gabriel 55; America, 1823 *778.5 p37*
Beau, M. 20; Port uncertain, 1838 *778.5 p37*
Beaubien, Mr.; Quebec, 1815 *9229.18 p76*
Beauchery, Jules Eugene 32; New Orleans, 1838 *778.5
 p37*
Beaucire, Stanislas 24; New Orleans, 1838 *778.5 p37*
Beauclair, . . .; Canada, 1776-1783 *9786 p17*
Beaudet, Jean 16; Quebec, 1664 *4533 p130*
Beaudouin, Miss; New Orleans, 1839 *778.5 p37*
Beaudouin, E.; New Orleans, 1839 *778.5 p37*
Beaufeu, H. Maria Rosina 40; America, 1827 *778.5 p38*
Beaufeu, James Peter 9; America, 1827 *778.5 p38*
Beauford, John J. 25; New Orleans, 1862 *543.30 p111*
Beaulieu, Claude; Quebec, 1706 *7603 p23*

Beaumont, Richard 16; Maryland, 1727 ***3690.1*** *p15*
Beauregard, L.; New Orleans, 1839 ***778.5*** *p38*
Beaustrom, A.T.; Illinois, 1880 ***5012.39*** *p52*
Beautel, John G.; Wisconsin, n.d. ***9675.4*** *p194*
Beaver, Elizabeth 30; Nova Scotia, 1775 ***1219.7*** *p263*
Beaver, John 22; New England, 1699 ***2212*** *p19*
Beaver, Mathew; Virginia, 1638 ***6219*** *p121*
Beavour, Benjamin 15; Maryland, 1733 ***3690.1*** *p15*
Beazley, Thomas 25; Jamaica, 1739 ***3690.1*** *p15*
Bebb, John 26; Maryland, 1775 ***1219.7*** *p251*
Bebbee, Elizabeth; Quebec, 1788 ***7603*** *p35*
Bebber, Jacob Isaac van; Germantown, PA, 1684 ***2467.7*** *p5*
Bebber, Jacobs Isaacs Van; Pennsylvania, 1683-1783 ***2155*** *p1*
Bebber, Lisbet Isaac van; Pennsylvania, 1683 ***2155*** *p1*
Bebber, Mathias van; Germantown, PA, 1684 ***2467.7*** *p5*
Bebe, Peder G.; Washington, 1859-1920 ***2872.1*** *p3*
Bebee, John; Virginia, 1638 ***6219*** *p150*
Bebendorff, . . .; Canada, 1776-1783 ***9786*** *p17*
Bebie, Alfred; Illinois, 1900 ***2896.5*** *p2*
Bebie, John; Illinois, 1905 ***2896.5*** *p3*
Bebinger, Killian; Philadelphia, 1764 ***9973.7*** *p39*
Beblat, Friedrich; Philadelphia, 1779 ***8137*** *p6*
Beble, John 26; Maryland, 1775 ***1219.7*** *p249*
Becc, Andreas *SEE* Becc, Andreas
Becc, Andreas; Pennsylvania, 1753 ***2444*** *p136*
*Wife:*Christina D. Krimmel
*Child:*Andreas
*Child:*Johannes
Becc, Christina D. Krimmel *SEE* Becc, Andreas
Becc, Johannes *SEE* Becc, Andreas
Beccue, William; Illinois, 1868 ***2896.5*** *p3*
Bech, Karl F.; Charleston, SC, 1775-1781 ***8582.2*** *p52*
Bech, Simon 17; New Orleans, 1862 ***543.30*** *p483*
Becham, William; Virginia, 1641 ***6219*** *p185*
Bechard, . . .; Canada, 1776-1783 ***9786*** *p41*
Bechart, John; America, 1854 ***1450.2*** *p10A*
Becheher, L.; Shreveport, LA, 1874 ***7129*** *p44*
Becherer, Constantine H.; New York, 1886 ***1450.2*** *p2B*
Becherer, Julius; New York, 1881 ***1450.2*** *p2B*
Bechman, George; Illinois, 1858 ***7857*** *p2*
Bechman, John; Illinois, 1858 ***7857*** *p2*
Bechstein, Johannes; Philadelphia, 1779 ***8137*** *p6*
Bechtel, Mr.; Kentucky, 1797 ***8582.3*** *p94*
With wife
*Son:*Johannes 11
*Daughter:*Sarah 9
*Child:*Maria 14
*Child:*Barbara 5
With son 16
Bechtel, Barbara 5 *SEE* Bechtel, Mr.
Bechtel, Henrich; Philadelphia, 1779 ***8137*** *p6*
Bechtel, Johannes 11 *SEE* Bechtel, Mr.
Bechtel, Maria; New York, 1761 ***3652*** *p88*
Bechtel, Maria 14 *SEE* Bechtel, Mr.
Bechtel, Sarah 9 *SEE* Bechtel, Mr.
Bechtell, Johannes; Philadelphia, 1779 ***8137*** *p6*
Bechtol, Anna Maria; New Orleans, 1803-1847 ***5647.5*** *p91*
Bechtold, A.C. 69; America, 1895 ***1763*** *p40D*
Bechtold, Anna Maria; New Orleans, 1803-1847 ***5647.5*** *p91*
Bechtold, Conrad 44; Kansas, 1889 ***5240.1*** *p4*
Bechtold, Conrad 44; Kansas, 1889 ***5240.1*** *p74*
Bechtold, Jacob; Indiana, 1874 ***5647.5*** *p129*
Bechtold, Nicholas; New Orleans, 1852 ***5647.5*** *p129*
Beck, . . .; Canada, 1776-1783 ***9786*** *p41*
Beck, Mme. 32; America, 1838 ***778.5*** *p38*
Beck, Amos 28; Virginia, 1774 ***1219.7*** *p238*
Beck, Andre 10; America, 1838 ***778.5*** *p38*
Beck, Andreas *SEE* Beck, Andreas
Beck, Andreas; Pennsylvania, 1753 ***2444*** *p136*
*Wife:*Christina D. Krimmel
*Child:*Andreas
*Child:*Johannes
Beck, Anton; Illinois, 1856 ***7857*** *p2*
Beck, August; Wisconsin, n.d. ***9675.4*** *p194*
Beck, Bernhardt; Pennsylvania, 1753 ***2444*** *p136*
Beck, Charles; Galveston, TX, 1853 ***2896.5*** *p3*
Beck, Christina D. Krimmel *SEE* Beck, Andreas
Beck, Christopher 20; Maryland, 1738 ***3690.1*** *p15*
Beck, Christopher 21; Maryland, 1775 ***1219.7*** *p247*
Beck, Cosmann 22; Port uncertain, 1839 ***778.5*** *p38*
Beck, Crist; Illinois, 1903 ***5012.40*** *p79*
Beck, David 29; Pennsylvania, 1848 ***1450.2*** *p10A*
Beck, Edward; America, 1848 ***1450.2*** *p11A*
Beck, Frederick; America, 1838 ***1450.2*** *p11A*
Beck, Frederick William 38; Kansas, 1902 ***5240.1*** *p4*
Beck, Frederick William 38; Kansas, 1902 ***5240.1*** *p82*
Beck, George; Canada, 1783 ***9786*** *p38A*
Beck, George; Philadelphia, 1761 ***9973.7*** *p35*
Beck, Gottlob; Wisconsin, n.d. ***9675.4*** *p194*
Beck, Hakon 31; Arkansas, 1918 ***95.2*** *p18*
Beck, Hans Michel; Pennsylvania, 1752 ***4525*** *p200*
Beck, Henry; Wisconsin, n.d. ***9675.4*** *p194*
Beck, Henry 40; New Orleans, 1837 ***778.5*** *p38*
Beck, Hugh; New York, NY, 1838 ***8208.4*** *p76*
Beck, Jacob; Cincinnati, 1800 ***8582.3*** *p87*
Beck, Jacob; Illinois, 1856 ***7857*** *p2*
Beck, Jacob; South Carolina, 1788 ***7119*** *p198*
Beck, James 30; Philadelphia, 1804 ***53.26*** *p4*
*Relative:*John 25
*Relative:*Mararet 24
Beck, Jean 3; America, 1838 ***778.5*** *p38*
Beck, Johan Marcus; Pennsylvania, 1751 ***4525*** *p201*
Beck, Johann; Cincinnati, 1869-1887 ***8582*** *p2*
Beck, Johann Bernhard; Pennsylvania, 1753 ***2444*** *p137*
Beck, Johann Jacob; Pennsylvania, 1753 ***2444*** *p136*
Beck, Johannes *SEE* Beck, Andreas
Beck, Johannes 16?; Pennsylvania, 1754 ***4525*** *p200*
Beck, John; Cincinnati, 1834 ***8582.1*** *p52*
Beck, John 25 *SEE* Beck, James
Beck, John H. 27; New Orleans, 1862 ***543.30*** *p482*
Beck, John Valentine; New York, 1761 ***3652*** *p87*
Beck, Laurent 38; America, 1838 ***778.5*** *p38*
Beck, Leonard 38; America, 1838 ***778.5*** *p38*
Beck, Louis Joseph 5; America, 1838 ***778.5*** *p38*
Beck, Mararet 24 *SEE* Beck, James
Beck, Margaret 1; Massachusetts, 1849 ***5881.1*** *p10*
Beck, Margaretha; Pennsylvania, 1742-1800 ***2444*** *p204*
Beck, Marguerite 7; America, 1838 ***778.5*** *p38*
Beck, Maria Agnes; Pennsylvania, 1742-1800 ***2444*** *p189*
Beck, Marie 2; America, 1838 ***778.5*** *p38*
Beck, Marie 8; America, 1838 ***778.5*** *p38*
Beck, Michael; New York, NY, 1836 ***8208.4*** *p23*
Beck, Richard; Virginia, 1639 ***6219*** *p156*
Beck, Vetter; South Carolina, 1788 ***7119*** *p198*
Beck, Wilhelm B. H.; America, 1852 ***8582.3*** *p3*
Beck, William; St. John, N.B., 1853 ***5704.8*** *p99*
Beck, William; Virginia, 1698 ***2212*** *p16*
Beck, William 17; Virginia, 1737 ***3690.1*** *p15*
Beckard, Sebastian 27; New Orleans, 1862 ***543.30*** *p108*
Beckel, Anna Catharina *SEE* Beckel, Georg Valentin
Beckel, Anna Elisabetha; Philadelphia, 1742 ***1034.18*** *p21*
Beckel, Anna Maria Rheinhard *SEE* Beckel, Georg Valentin
Beckel, Fredrick 19; America, 1837 ***778.5*** *p39*
Beckel, Georg Valentin 32; Pennsylvania, 1732 ***1034.18*** *p5*
*Wife:*Anna Maria Rheinhard
*Child:*Maria Margaretha
*Child:*Anna Catharina
*Child:*Joh. Michael
Beckel, Joh. Michael *SEE* Beckel, Georg Valentin
Beckel, Maria Margaretha *SEE* Beckel, Georg Valentin
Beckemeyer, W. 35; America, 1884 ***4610.10*** *p153*
Beckenhaupt, Johann; America, 1840 ***8582.1*** *p2*
Becker, . . .; Canada, 1776-1783 ***9786*** *p17*
Becker Family ; New York, 1882 ***3702.7*** *p476*
Becker, Miss; America, 1838 ***8582.3*** *p4*
Becker, Mr.; America, 1885 ***4610.10*** *p113*
Becker, A M Christine Althage *SEE* Becker, Anton Heinrich Gottlieb
Becker, Anna Marie Cath.; America, 1837 ***4610.10*** *p146*
Becker, Antoine 33; America, 1838 ***778.5*** *p39*
Becker, Anton Heinrich Gottlieb; America, 1838 ***4610.10*** *p104*
*Wife:*A M Christine Althage
*Son:*Karl Ludwig
Becker, August; America, 1852 ***8582.1*** *p2*
Becker, August; America, 1852 ***8582*** *p2*
Becker, Carl Dietrich; America, 1850 ***4610.10*** *p147*
Becker, Catharina 27; New York, NY, 1857 ***9831.14*** *p86*
Becker, Charles; Illinois, 1890 ***2896.5*** *p3*
Becker, Christian F.; Cincinnati, 1869-1887 ***8582*** *p2*
Becker, David 17; New York, NY, 1878 ***9253*** *p45*
Becker, Dorette Minna *SEE* Becker, Mathilde Eickhoff
Becker, Ernestine W. Henriette Heper; America, 1881 ***4610.10*** *p137*
Becker, Fred; Wisconsin, n.d. ***9675.4*** *p194*
Becker, Frederick; America, 1888 ***1450.2*** *p2B*
Becker, Frederick 39; New Orleans, 1862 ***543.30*** *p110*
Becker, Friedrich *SEE* Becker, Samuel
Becker, Friedrich; Philadelphia, 1779 ***8137*** *p6*
Becker, Friedrich A. Heinrich *SEE* Becker, Mathilde Eickhoff
Becker, Friedrich Carl Wilhelm *SEE* Becker, Johann Heinrich
Becker, Georg; Pennsylvania, 1759 ***4525*** *p200*
Becker, George; Philadelphia, 1760 ***9973.7*** *p35*
Becker, George; Wisconsin, n.d. ***9675.4*** *p194*
Becker, George 29; New Orleans, 1862 ***543.30*** *p115*
Becker, H.; Illinois, 1860 ***5012.38*** *p98*
Becker, Heinrich; America, 1840 ***8582.1*** *p2*
Becker, Henrich; Philadelphia, 1780 ***8137*** *p6*
Becker, Henry; Wisconsin, n.d. ***9675.4*** *p194*
Becker, Henry 38; California, 1867 ***3840.1*** *p16*
Becker, Hermann Martin; New York, NY, 1840 ***8208.4*** *p104*
Becker, Jacob 20; America, 1838 ***778.5*** *p39*
Becker, Jacob 40; New Orleans, 1862 ***543.30*** *p242*
Becker, Joh. 67; America, 1895 ***1763*** *p40C*
Becker, Johann C.; Cincinnati, 1869-1887 ***8582*** *p2*
Becker, Johann Christian; New York, NY, 1837 ***8582.3*** *p3*
Becker, Johann Friedrich 54; America, 1854 ***4610.10*** *p148*
With daughter
Becker, Johann Heinrich; America, 1886 ***4610.10*** *p113*
*Brother:*Friedrich Carl Wilhelm
Becker, John; Canada, 1783 ***9786*** *p38A*
Becker, John; Cincinnati, 1869-1887 ***8582*** *p2*
Becker, John; Washington, 1859-1920 ***2872.1*** *p3*
Becker, John; Wisconsin, n.d. ***9675.4*** *p194*
Becker, Joseph; America, 1864 ***1450.2*** *p11A*
Becker, Joseph; Cincinnati, 1869-1887 ***8582*** *p2*
Becker, Joseph; Wisconsin, n.d. ***9675.4*** *p194*
Becker, Karl; America, 1851 ***8582.3*** *p4*
Becker, Karl Ludwig *SEE* Becker, Anton Heinrich Gottlieb
Becker, Karoline; America, 1857 ***4610.10*** *p105*
Becker, Mrs. L.; Milwaukee, 1875 ***4719.30*** *p257*
Becker, Marie; America, 1848 ***4610.10*** *p120*
Becker, Marie Dorette Mathilde *SEE* Becker, Mathilde Eickhoff
Becker, Martin; Philadelphia, 1760 ***9973.7*** *p35*
Becker, Mathilde Eickhoff; America, 1887 ***4610.10*** *p114*
*Child:*Friedrich A. Heinrich
*Child:*Dorette Minna
*Child:*Marie Dorette Mathilde
Becker, Melchior; Philadelphia, 1779 ***8137*** *p6*
Becker, Michael; Ohio, 1838 ***8582.1*** *p48*
Becker, N.; Milwaukee, 1875 ***4719.30*** *p257*
Becker, Nicholas; Wisconsin, n.d. ***9675.4*** *p194*
Becker, Nicholaus Edward; Wisconsin, n.d. ***9675.4*** *p194*
Becker, Peter; Indiana, 1848 ***9117*** *p19*
Becker, Peter; Wisconsin, n.d. ***9675.4*** *p194*
Becker, Peter 29; New Orleans, 1862 ***543.30*** *p110*
Becker, Peter 40; New Orleans, 1862 ***543.30*** *p243*
Becker, Philip H.; Ohio, 1851 ***9892.11*** *p3*
Becker, Sam; Arkansas, 1918 ***95.2*** *p18*
Becker, Samuel; America, 1771 ***4349*** *p48*
*Brother:*Friedrich
Becker, Theo W.; Washington, 1859-1920 ***2872.1*** *p3*
Becker, Theodore; Wisconsin, n.d. ***9675.4*** *p194*
Becker, Thomas W.; Washington, 1859-1920 ***2872.1*** *p3*
Becker, Wilhelm; America, 1840 ***8582.1*** *p2*
Becker, Wilhelm; America, 1865 ***4610.10*** *p123*
Becker, William; Illinois, 1869 ***5012.38*** *p99*
Becker, William; Virginia, 1844 ***4626.16*** *p13*
Beckerle, Mathias 30; America, 1838 ***778.5*** *p39*
Beckermann, Anna; New York, NY, 1884 ***3702.7*** *p592*
Becket, William 21; New Orleans, 1862 ***543.30*** *p112*
Beckett, Jno 30; America, 1699 ***2212*** *p29*
Beckett, John 23; Maryland or Virginia, 1737 ***3690.1*** *p15*
Beckford, Mr.; Jamaica, 1774 ***1219.7*** *p237*
With family
Beckh, Andreas *SEE* Beckh, Johann Bernhard
Beckh, Andreas; Pennsylvania, 1753 ***2444*** *p136*
Beckh, Anna Maria *SEE* Beckh, Johann Bernhard
Beckh, Anna Maria Rothweiler *SEE* Beckh, Johann Bernhard
Beckh, Johann Bernhard; Pennsylvania, 1753 ***2444*** *p137*
*Wife:*Anna Maria Rothweiler
*Child:*Johannes
*Child:*Rosina Barbara
*Child:*Andreas
*Child:*Anna Maria
*Child:*Ursula
Beckh, Johannes *SEE* Beckh, Johann Bernhard
Beckh, Rosina Barbara *SEE* Beckh, Johann Bernhard
Beckh, Ursula *SEE* Beckh, Johann Bernhard
Beckius, Peter; Wisconsin, n.d. ***9675.4*** *p194*
Beckley, Edward 21; Jamaica, 1737 ***3690.1*** *p15*
Beckley, William 15; Pennsylvania, 1728 ***3690.1*** *p15*
Becklon, Joanna 44; Massachusetts, 1860 ***6410.32*** *p108*
Becklon, Mary C. 12; Massachusetts, 1860 ***6410.32*** *p108*
Beckman, Frank H.; Maryland, 1873 ***1450.2*** *p2B*
Beckman, Fred; Wisconsin, n.d. ***9675.4*** *p194*
Beckman, Fred 22; New Orleans, 1862 ***543.30*** *p245*
Beckman, Herman 32; New Orleans, 1862 ***543.30*** *p110*
Beckman, William; America, 1839 ***1450.2*** *p11A*
Beckmann, August; Cincinnati, 1869-1887 ***8582*** *p2*
Beckmann, Carl; Wisconsin, n.d. ***9675.4*** *p194*
Beckmann, Heinrich; America, 1848 ***8582.1*** *p2*

Beckmann, Johann Diedrich; America, 1854 ***4610.10*** *p139*
With wife
With daughter
Beckmann, Karl Friedrich; America, 1848 ***4610.10*** *p120*
*Father:*Karl Ludwig Meierotte
*Mother:*Marie Becker
Beckmann, Karl Ludwig Meierotte *SEE* Beckmann, Karl Friedrich
Beckmann, Marie Becker *SEE* Beckmann, Karl Friedrich
Becks, Henry 33; New Orleans, 1862 ***543.30*** *p117*
Beckstein, Frederick; New York, 1835 ***8208.4*** *p40*
Beckweth, Jarret; Virginia, 1636 ***6219*** *p10*
Beckwith, Daniel; Washington, 1859-1920 ***2872.1*** *p3*
Becraft, Thomas 33; Montreal, 1712 ***7603*** *p28*
Bectell, John; Philadelphia, 1759 ***9973.7*** *p33*
Bedall, Getrude; Virginia, 1642 ***6219*** *p198*
Bedder, Joseph; Ohio, 1869-1887 ***8582*** *p2*
Bedder, Joseph; Ohio, 1869-1887 ***8582*** *p33*
Beddiger, . . .; Canada, 1776-1783 ***9786*** *p17*
Beddow, John 36; West Virginia, 1895 ***9788.3*** *p4*
Bedegaruy, Jean 28; America, 1837 ***778.5*** *p39*
Bedel, David; America, 1777-1778 ***8582.2*** *p69*
Bedell, David; Philadelphia, 1783 ***8582.2*** *p66*
Beder, Frederick; Illinois, 1871 ***5012.39*** *p25*
Bedford, David; New York, NY, 1833 ***8208.4*** *p44*
Bedford, Franklin; Illinois, 1869 ***7857*** *p2*
Bedford, George 21; Barbados or Antigua, 1735 ***3690.1*** *p16*
Bedford, George 38; Jamaica, 1735 ***3690.1*** *p15*
Bedford, Jane; Virginia, 1638 ***6219*** *p153*
Bedford, Thomas 35; Maryland, 1775 ***1219.7*** *p255*
Bedinger, Benjamin F.; Kentucky, 1840 ***8582.3*** *p99*
Bedinger, Nicholas; Philadelphia, 1760 ***9973.7*** *p34*
Bedini, Guiseppe; Arkansas, 1918 ***95.2*** *p18*
Bedle, Tho.; Virginia, 1643 ***6219*** *p200*
Bedman, Thomas 19; New England, 1721 ***3690.1*** *p16*
Bednall, Thomas 18; West Indies, 1722 ***3690.1*** *p16*
Bednard, William; New York, NY, 1816 ***2859.11*** *p25*
Bedon, Stephen; Charles Town, SC, 1752 ***1219.7*** *p10*
Bedout, Mr. 52; New Orleans, 1839 ***778.5*** *p39*
Bedovar, Adolf; Minneapolis, 1880-1887 ***6410.35*** *p63*
Bedra, James; Arkansas, 1918 ***95.2*** *p18*
Bedsted, Thomas Martinus; Arkansas, 1918 ***95.2*** *p18*
Beeber, John; Philadelphia, 1760 ***9973.7*** *p34*
Beech, James; Jamaica, 1754 ***1219.7*** *p30*
Beecham, John; America, 1698 ***2212*** *p10*
Beecham, John; Virginia, 1698 ***2212*** *p11*
Beeching, George; New York, NY, 1836 ***8208.4*** *p19*
Beechler, Joseph; America, 1835 ***1450.2*** *p11A*
Beechum, George; Richmond, VA, 1841 ***7036*** *p127*
Beede, Tho.; Virginia, 1642 ***6219*** *p195*
Beedham, Rich.; Virginia, 1638 ***6219*** *p147*
Beeding, Henry 12; Maryland, 1719 ***3690.1*** *p16*
Beedle, Mercy 21; Maryland, 1775 ***1219.7*** *p253*
Beedler, Elizabeth 22; Maryland, 1775 ***1219.7*** *p253*
Beek, Elisabeth 37; New Orleans, 1838 ***778.5*** *p39*
Beeke, Thomas; Virginia, 1638 ***6219*** *p147*
Beeker, Frederick; America, 1833 ***1450.2*** *p11A*
Beeker, George 45; New Orleans, 1838 ***778.5*** *p39*
Beeker, Pierre 25; New Orleans, 1837 ***778.5*** *p39*
Beekman, Albert 43; New Orleans, 1862 ***543.30*** *p111*
Beekmann, . . .; Ohio, 1832 ***8582.2*** *p49*
With family
Beeman, Henry; New York, NY, 1836 ***8208.4*** *p17*
Beene, John 20; Jamaica, 1730 ***3690.1*** *p16*
Beener, Lawerence; Wisconsin, n.d. ***9675.4*** *p194*
Beer, Andreas; Wisconsin, n.d. ***9675.4*** *p194*
Beer, Gottlieb; Wisconsin, n.d. ***9675.4*** *p194*
Beer, John; Wisconsin, n.d. ***9675.4*** *p194*
Beer, Lorenz 23; America, 1853 ***9162.7*** *p14*
Beerman, Louis; New York, 1866 ***1450.2*** *p11A*
Beerman, Thomas; New York, NY, 1816 ***2859.11*** *p25*
Beermann, August; America, 1883 ***1450.2*** *p2B*
Beers, Hugh; Philadelphia, 1849 ***53.26*** *p4*
Beers, Hugh; Philadelphia, 1849 ***5704.8*** *p53*
Beers, Samuel; St. John, N.B., 1852 ***5704.8*** *p93*
Beesely, Peter; Virginia, 1636 ***6219*** *p26*
Beesten, Joseph; America, 1846 ***8582.1*** *p2*
Beeston, John 19; St. Christopher, 1722 ***3690.1*** *p16*
Beeth, Matilda; Quebec, 1847 ***5704.8*** *p8*
Beetz, Konrad; Philadelphia, 1779 ***8137*** *p6*
Begbie, Elizabeth; Carolina, 1829 ***1639.20*** *p8*
Begbie, Thomas; North Carolina, 1827 ***1639.20*** *p8*
Begemann, Anne Marie C. Charlotte; America, 1850 ***4610.10*** *p147*
Begemann, Anne Marie Henriette 1 *SEE* Begemann, Johann Friedrich
Begemann, Anne Marie Louise 10 *SEE* Begemann, Johann Friedrich
Begemann, Carl Friedrich *SEE* Begemann, Johann Friedrich
Begemann, Dorothee Friederike; America, 1844 ***4610.10*** *p147*
Begemann, Friedrich Wilhelm *SEE* Begemann, Johann Friedrich
Begemann, Johann Friedrich 42; America, 1854 ***4610.10*** *p148*
With wife
*Child:*Carl Friedrich
*Child:*Friedrich Wilhelm
*Child:*Anne Marie Louise 10
*Child:*Anne Marie Henriette 1
Beger, Franz Hermann; Illinois, 1894 ***1450.2*** *p12A*
Beger, Johann; America, 1853 ***2853.7*** *p109*
Beger, William; Wisconsin, n.d. ***9675.4*** *p194*
Begert, Johann; Quebec, 1776 ***9786*** *p263*
Begg, Richard; America, 1735-1743 ***4971*** *p8*
Beggs, Elenora; Savannah, GA, 1821 ***8893*** *p264*
Beggs, James; New York, NY, 1815 ***2859.11*** *p25*
Begin, . . .; Halifax, N.S., 1752 ***7074.6*** *p232*
Begin, Celestine 13; Port uncertain, 1839 ***778.5*** *p39*
Begin, Chatrine 45; Port uncertain, 1839 ***778.5*** *p39*
Begin, Francoise 20; Port uncertain, 1839 ***778.5*** *p39*
Begin, Jacques 25; Halifax, N.S., 1752 ***7074.6*** *p208*
*Wife:*Marie-Madeleine
Begin, Jean 45; Port uncertain, 1839 ***778.5*** *p39*
Begin, Joseph 9; Port uncertain, 1839 ***778.5*** *p39*
Begin, Marie 15; Port uncertain, 1839 ***778.5*** *p39*
Begin, Marie-Madeleine *SEE* Begin, Jacques
Begley, Andrew 17; St. John, N.B., 1854 ***5704.8*** *p119*
Begley, Andrew 21; Quebec, 1859 ***5704.8*** *p143*
Begley, Ann; Philadelphia, 1868 ***5704.8*** *p229*
Begley, Anthony 45; St. John, N.B., 1857 ***5704.8*** *p134*
Begley, Arthur; Philadelphia, 1867 ***5704.8*** *p221*
Begley, Bridget 22; Philadelphia, 1859 ***5704.8*** *p141*
Begley, Catherine; St. John, N.B., 1850 ***5704.8*** *p65*
Begley, Charles 18; St. John, N.B., 1857 ***5704.8*** *p134*
Begley, Christina 6; Philadelphia, 1864 ***5704.8*** *p161*
Begley, Elizabeth 11; Quebec, 1852 ***5704.8*** *p87*
Begley, Elizabeth 11; Quebec, 1852 ***5704.8*** *p90*
Begley, Elizabeth 53; Philadelphia, 1864 ***5704.8*** *p161*
Begley, Fanny; St. John, N.B., 1847 ***5704.8*** *p33*
Begley, George 7; Philadelphia, 1864 ***5704.8*** *p161*
Begley, Hugh 9; Philadelphia, 1864 ***5704.8*** *p161*
Begley, James; Quebec, 1852 ***5704.8*** *p90*
Begley, James 13; Quebec, 1852 ***5704.8*** *p87*
Begley, James 13; Quebec, 1852 ***5704.8*** *p90*
Begley, James 30; Quebec, 1859 ***5704.8*** *p143*
Begley, Jane; Quebec, 1852 ***5704.8*** *p87*
Begley, John 24; Philadelphia, 1855 ***5704.8*** *p124*
Begley, Joseph 20; St. John, N.B., 1857 ***5704.8*** *p134*
Begley, Margaret; Quebec, 1852 ***5704.8*** *p87*
Begley, Margaret; Quebec, 1852 ***5704.8*** *p90*
Begley, Mary; Philadelphia, 1851 ***5704.8*** *p79*
Begley, Mary; Quebec, 1852 ***5704.8*** *p87*
Begley, Mary; Quebec, 1852 ***5704.8*** *p90*
Begley, Mary Jane 22; Quebec, 1859 ***5704.8*** *p143*
Begley, Michael 25; St. John, N.B., 1857 ***5704.8*** *p134*
Begley, Nancy; Philadelphia, 1867 ***5704.8*** *p220*
Begley, Pat; Quebec, 1852 ***5704.8*** *p98*
Begley, Sarah Jane 9; Quebec, 1852 ***5704.8*** *p87*
Begley, Sarah Jane 9; Quebec, 1852 ***5704.8*** *p90*
Begley, William 19; St. John, N.B., 1857 ***5704.8*** *p134*
Begon, Luciano 30; New Orleans, 1838 ***778.5*** *p40*
Begoundau, O.; Port uncertain, 1829 ***778.5*** *p40*
Begtol, Jacob; Philadelphia, 1759 ***9973.7*** *p34*
Beguin, John Louis; New York, NY, 1834 ***8208.4*** *p78*
Begus, Johan; Wisconsin, n.d. ***9675.4*** *p194*
Begush, August; Wisconsin, n.d. ***9675.4*** *p194*
Behaim, Martin; America, n.d. ***8582.3*** *p79*
Behan, James; New York, NY, 1815 ***2859.11*** *p25*
Behle, Bernhard; Kentucky, 1839-1840 ***8582.3*** *p98*
Behlen, Karl; America, 1848 ***8582.3*** *p5*
Behling, Frank; Wisconsin, n.d. ***9675.4*** *p194*
Behling, Henry; Wisconsin, n.d. ***9675.4*** *p194*
Behling, Herbert Carl Reinhold; Wisconsin, n.d. ***9675.4*** *p194*
Behling, Herman; Wisconsin, n.d. ***9675.4*** *p194*
Behm, Ernest; Kansas, 1881 ***5240.1*** *p4*
Behme, Francis; Indiana, 1844 ***9117*** *p15*
Behme, Frederick; Indiana, 1848 ***9117*** *p16*
Behnan, Frederick 32; New Orleans, 1862 ***543.30*** *p243*
Behnke, Albert; Illinois, 1899 ***5012.40*** *p76*
Behnke, Carl; Wisconsin, n.d. ***9675.4*** *p194*
Behnke, Carl Welhelm 22; Kansas, 1872 ***5240.1*** *p53*
Behnke, Hans; New York, NY, 1921 ***3455.2*** *p80*
Behr, . . .; Canada, 1776-1783 ***9786*** *p17*
Behr, Charles 47; New Orleans, 1838 ***778.5*** *p40*
Behr, Joseph 17; New Orleans, 1862 ***543.30*** *p117*
Behrbom, . . .; Canada, 1776-1783 ***9786*** *p17*
Behrend, Peter; Illinois, 1896 ***5012.37*** *p63*
Behrends, Freiderich Johnson; Baltimore, 1891 ***3455.3*** *p113*
Behrends, Friedrich Johnson; Baltimore, 1891 ***3455.2*** *p53*
Behrends, John; Washington, 1859-1920 ***2872.1*** *p3*
Behrendt, Albert; America, 1868 ***1450.2*** *p12A*
Behrens, . . .; Canada, 1776-1783 ***9786*** *p17*
Behrens, Ahrend; Wisconsin, n.d. ***9675.4*** *p194*
Behrens, Carl 23; Kansas, 1904 ***5240.1*** *p83*
Behrens, Ernest; New York, 1875 ***1450.2*** *p12A*
Behrens, Frederic; Wisconsin, n.d. ***9675.4*** *p265*
Behrens, Heinrich; America, 1850 ***8582.3*** *p5*
Behrens, Henry; Kansas, 1892 ***5240.1*** *p4*
Behrens, Henry 36; Kansas, 1872 ***5240.1*** *p53*
Behrens, Herman; America, 1892 ***1450.2*** *p12A*
Behrens, Herman; Wisconsin, n.d. ***9675.4*** *p265*
Behrens, Jacob Johnson; Iroquois Co., IL, 1896 ***3455.1*** *p9*
Behrens, Johann Heinrich; America, 1842 ***4815.7*** *p92*
*Wife:*Margarete S. Schroder
With 4 children
Behrens, Margarete S. Schroder *SEE* Behrens, Johann Heinrich
Behrens, Martha; New York, NY, 1926 ***3455.4*** *p80*
Behrensmeier, Karl Friedr. Adolph; America, 1856 ***4610.10*** *p108*
Behrensmeyer, A. M. Louise Karoline; America, 1857 ***4610.10*** *p105*
Behrensmeyer, Carl Dietrich *SEE* Behrensmeyer, Karoline Schuster
Behrensmeyer, Caroline L. Charlotte *SEE* Behrensmeyer, Friedrich Wilh.
Behrensmeyer, Dorothea K. Charlotte 6 mos *SEE* Behrensmeyer, Friedrich Wilh.
Behrensmeyer, Friederike *SEE* Behrensmeyer, Karoline Schuster
Behrensmeyer, Friedrich Wilh. 36; America, 1857 ***4610.10*** *p105*
*Wife:*Louise Korsmeier 26
*Child:*Caroline L. Charlotte
*Child:*Heinr. F. W. Christine
*Child:*Dorothea K. Charlotte 6 mos
Behrensmeyer, Heinr. F. W. Christine *SEE* Behrensmeyer, Friedrich Wilh.
Behrensmeyer, Karoline Schuster; America, 1857 ***4610.10*** *p105*
*Child:*Friederike
*Child:*Carl Dietrich
Behrensmeyer, Louise Korsmeier 26 *SEE* Behrensmeyer, Friedrich Wilh.
Behringer, Peter; Pennsylvania, 1754 ***4525*** *p200*
With wife son & child
Behrmann, John; America, 1849 ***1450.2*** *p12A*
Beiar, Casper; New York, 1853 ***1450.2*** *p12A*
Beichert, . . .; Canada, 1776-1783 ***9786*** *p17*
Beid, Michael; America, 1847 ***8582.1*** *p34*
Beiderman, John; America, 1848 ***1450.2*** *p12A*
Beidleman, D. O.; Washington, 1859-1920 ***2872.1*** *p3*
Beier, Henry; Kansas, 1874 ***5240.1*** *p56*
Beig, George; Arizona, 1898 ***9228.30*** *p8*
Beige, Carl; Wisconsin, n.d. ***9675.4*** *p265*
Beighle, I. N.; Washington, 1859-1920 ***2872.1*** *p3*
Beignols, Ph. 42; America, 1835 ***778.5*** *p40*
Beil, Georg; Charleston, SC, 1775-1781 ***8582.2*** *p52*
Beile, C. F.; America, 1845 ***8582.1*** *p3*
Beinbied, Joseph 25; Port uncertain, 1839 ***778.5*** *p40*
Beinbrecht, Friedrich Wilhelm; Cincinnati, 1815 ***8582.1*** *p51*
Beinburn, John Gust; Wisconsin, n.d. ***9675.4*** *p265*
Beinhardt, Fettke 45; Kansas, 1879 ***5240.1*** *p60*
Beischlein, Andrew; America, 1754 ***4525*** *p199*
With wife & child
Beiser, Andreas; Cincinnati, 1869-1887 ***8582*** *p3*
Beisser, George; Ohio, 1851 ***9892.11*** *p3*
Beisser, John; Philadelphia, 1760 ***9973.7*** *p34*
Beisser, John George; Ohio, 1848 ***9892.11*** *p3*
Beitenman, George; Pennsylvania, 1750 ***2444*** *p135*
Beitenman, Johann Jacob; Pennsylvania, 1750 ***2444*** *p135*
Beith, James; California, 1866 ***3840.3*** *p12*
Beithnitz, . . .; Canada, 1776-1783 ***9786*** *p17*
Beitmann, Carl; Cincinnati, 1869-1887 ***8582*** *p3*
Beittenman, Georg Friederigh; Pennsylvania, 1750 ***2444*** *p135*
Beitz, Wilhelm; Philadelphia, 1779 ***8137*** *p6*
Beitzell, Jonathan; Philadelphia, 1761 ***9973.7*** *p36*
Bekemeyer, Christian 67; America, 1880 ***4610.10*** *p159*
Bekker, Balthasar 51; New York, 1902 ***1763*** *p40D*
Belair, Frank; Kansas, 1876 ***5240.1*** *p4*
Belaney, Joseph 49; Kansas, 1879 ***5240.1*** *p60*
Belanger, Mr.; Quebec, 1815 ***9229.18*** *p76*
Belany, William; Newfoundland, 1768 ***1219.7*** *p136*
Belcher, Tho.; Virginia, 1636 ***6219*** *p108*
Belcher, Walt.; Virginia, 1645 ***6219*** *p234*
Belcourt, Mr. 30; Cuba, 1829 ***778.5*** *p40*
Beldam, Jon.; Virginia, 1637 ***6219*** *p113*

Beldon, John 19; St. John, N.B., 1854 5704.8 p114
Beldy, Adam; America, 1886 1450.2 p12A
Bele, Martin; America, 1901 1450.2 p2B
Belet, Jacques 40; New Orleans, 1864 543.30 p247
Belfelt, John Christopher 26; North Carolina, 1736 3690.1 p16
Belfiglio, Camillo; Arkansas, 1918 95.2 p18
Belford, Ann J. 22; Philadelphia, 1854 5704.8 p120
Belgarrie, Antoine 24; New Orleans, 1821 778.5 p40
Belhooke, Jeremiah 16; Maryland, 1719 3690.1 p16
Belich, Mike; Iowa, 1866-1943 123.54 p8
Belinder, John 45; Antigua (Antego), 1774 1219.7 p237
Belker, Joseph; New York, 1848 1450.2 p13A
Bell, Andrew; Charleston, SC, 1807 1639.20 p8
Bell, Andrew; Georgia, 1734 1639.20 p8
Bell, Ann 5; New York, NY, 1828 6508.4 p143
Bell, Catherine 16; St. John, N.B., 1854 5704.8 p120
Bell, Christian; Wisconsin, n.d. 9675.4 p265
Bell, David; Jamaica, 1756 1219.7 p41
Bell, David; Jamaica, 1756 3690.1 p16
Bell, David; New York, NY, 1811 2859.11 p8
Bell, David; New York, NY, 1815 2859.11 p25
Bell, Eliza 21; Philadelphia, 1858 5704.8 p139
Bell, Elizabeth; South Carolina, 1769 1639.20 p8
Bell, Fanny 45; Philadelphia, 1853 5704.8 p108
Bell, Francis 58; Quebec, 1864 5704.8 p159
Bell, Geo.; Virginia, 1638 6219 p11
Bell, George; New York, NY, 1815 2859.11 p25
Bell, George 71; St. John, N.B., 1854 5704.8 p120
Bell, Guido; America, 1865 1450.2 p13A
Bell, H.; New York, NY, 1816 2859.11 p25
Bell, Henry; America, 1698 2212 p6
Bell, Henry; Virginia, 1698 2212 p11
Bell, Henry 24; Philadelphia, 1853 5704.8 p108
Bell, Henry 27; Maryland, 1774 1219.7 p215
Bell, Hugh; Ohio, 1844 9892.11 p3
Bell, Isabella 2; Quebec, 1849 5704.8 p51
Bell, Isabella Dempster; Charleston, SC, 1815 8894.2 p56
Bell, Isabella Jane 21; Philadelphia, 1856 5704.8 p128
Bell, Jacob; New York, NY, 1811 2859.11 p8
Bell, James; New York, NY, 1811 2859.11 p8
Bell, James 6; New York, NY, 1828 6508.4 p143
Bell, James 8; Quebec, 1850 5704.8 p63
Bell, James 24; Jamaica, 1773 1219.7 p171
Bell, James 24; Port uncertain, 1774 1219.7 p177
Bell, James 30; Kansas, 1884 5240.1 p66
Bell, James 40; Maryland, 1774 1219.7 p221
Bell, James 45; Philadelphia, 1853 5704.8 p108
Bell, James Albert; Chicago, 1898 3455.1 p43
Bell, Jane; Philadelphia, 1851 5704.8 p70
Bell, Jane 18; St. John, N.B., 1854 5704.8 p120
Bell, Jane 25; Maryland, 1775 1219.7 p265
Bell, Jane 36; St. John, N.B., 1854 5704.8 p120
Bell, Janet 28; New York, NY, 1828 6508.4 p143
Bell, Javis; Virginia, 1643 6219 p230
Bell, Joe Even; Arkansas, 1918 95.2 p18
Bell, John; Colorado, 1904 9678.1 p153
Bell, John; New York, NY, 1811 2859.11 p8
Bell, John; New York, NY, 1816 2859.11 p25
Bell, John; Ohio, 1840 9892.11 p3
Bell, John; Ohio, 1841 9892.11 p3
Bell, John; Virginia, 1638 6219 p181
Bell, John; Virginia, 1642 6219 p197
Bell, John; Virginia, 1648 6219 p246
Bell, John 6; Quebec, 1850 5704.8 p63
Bell, John 19; Maryland, 1719 3690.1 p16
Bell, John 19; Maryland, 1728 3690.1 p16
Bell, John 29; America, 1836 778.5 p40
Bell, John 35; New York, NY, 1828 6508.4 p143
Bell, John 36; Philadelphia, 1774 1219.7 p237
Bell, John 40; Arizona, 1890 2764.35 p7
Bell, John G.; Wisconsin, n.d. 9675.4 p265
Bell, John N.; Wisconsin, n.d. 9675.4 p265
Bell, John Peter; Wisconsin, n.d. 9675.4 p265
Bell, Joseph; Wisconsin, n.d. 9675.4 p265
Bell, Joseph 23; New England, 1699 2212 p19
Bell, Lewis 15; Maryland, 1724 3690.1 p16
Bell, Margaret; New York, NY, 1811 2859.11 p8
Bell, Margaret; Philadelphia, 1851 5704.8 p70
Bell, Margaret 17; St. John, N.B., 1859 5704.8 p140
Bell, Margt 4 mos; New York, NY, 1828 6508.4 p143
Bell, Mary; New York, NY, 1811 2859.11 p8
Bell, Mary; Philadelphia, 1866 5704.8 p211
Bell, Mary; Quebec, 1849 5704.8 p51
Bell, Mary; Quebec, 1850 5704.8 p63
Bell, Mary; St. John, N.B., 1850 5704.8 p65
Bell, Mary C.; New York, NY, 1816 2859.11 p25
Bell, Mary Jane; Quebec, 1850 5704.8 p63
Bell, Mathew; Quebec, 1815 9229.18 p75
Bell, Moses; America, 1834 1450.2 p13A
Bell, Nancy 15; Massachusetts, 1848 5881.1 p11
Bell, Nathan; Quebec, 1850 5704.8 p63
Bell, Rebecca H.; New York, NY, 1816 2859.11 p25
Bell, Richard; Virginia, 1638 6219 p148
Bell, Richard; Virginia, 1648 6219 p250
Bell, Robert; New York, 1828 9892.11 p3
Bell, Robert; Ohio, 1839 9892.11 p3
Bell, Robert; Philadelphia, 1866 5704.8 p209
Bell, Robert; South Carolina, 1737 1639.20 p8
Bell, Robert 19; St. John, N.B., 1859 5704.8 p140
Bell, Samuel; New York, NY, 1816 2859.11 p25
Bell, Samuel 10; Quebec, 1850 5704.8 p63
Bell, Samuel L.; Ohio, 1843 9892.11 p3
Bell, Sarah; Philadelphia, 1852 5704.8 p88
Bell, Tho; Virginia, 1638 6219 p115
Bell, Thomas; Colorado, 1903 9678.1 p153
Bell, Thomas; New York, NY, 1816 2859.11 p25
Bell, Thomas 19; Quebec, 1857 5704.8 p135
Bell, Thomas 25; St. John, N.B., 1854 5704.8 p122
Bell, Thomas 56; Kansas, 1882 5240.1 p63
Bell, Thomas C.; New York, NY, 1816 2859.11 p25
Bell, William; Illinois, 1892 5012.40 p27
Bell, William; New York, NY, 1811 2859.11 p8
Bell, William; Ontario, 1817 9775.5 p213
With wife
With 6 children
Bell, William; Quebec, 1850 5704.8 p63
Bell, William; South Carolina, 1827 1639.20 p8
Bell, William; Virginia, 1640 6219 p187
Bell, William 10; Philadelphia, 1856 5704.8 p128
Bell, William 12; Quebec, 1850 5704.8 p63
Bell, William 18; Maryland, 1728 3690.1 p17
Bell, William 29; New York, 1774 1219.7 p223
Bell, William 40; Virginia, 1774 1219.7 p190
Bell, Wm.; New York, NY, 1816 2859.11 p25
Bell, Wm.; Virginia, 1635 6219 p69
Bellais, Victor 30; Port uncertain, 1825 778.5 p40
Bellasyse, Thomas; Bermuda, 1751 1219.7 p6
Bellau, Mr.; Port uncertain, 1839 778.5 p40
Bellchambers, John; Illinois, 1860 5012.39 p90
Belleff, Vladimir Lane; Arkansas, 1918 95.2 p18
Bellegante, Bartolo; Iowa, 1866-1943 123.54 p8
Bellegante, Sebastian; Iowa, 1866-1943 123.54 p8
Bellenchio, Guenno; Wisconsin, n.d. 9675.4 p265
Bellerose, Jean; Quebec, 1672 7603 p70
Bellew, John; Wisconsin, n.d. 9675.4 p265
Bellford, Joseph 15; Pennsylvania, 1733 3690.1 p17
Bellingsly, William J. 21; Philadelphia, 1860 5704.8 p146
Bellitt, James; Colorado, 1904 9678.1 p153
Bellman, John 35; Philadelphia, 1804 53.26 p4
Bellman, Samuel 33; Philadelphia, 1804 53.26 p4
Bellmin, Leurs Orsa; Shreveport, LA, 1879 7129 p44
Belloc, Mr. 31; America, 1838 778.5 p40
Belloc, J. 21; New Orleans, 1837 778.5 p40
Belloc, P. 32; New Orleans, 1837 778.5 p40
Bellomo, Frank; Iowa, 1866-1943 123.54 p55
Bellomo, Frank; Iowa, 1866-1943 123.54 p57
Bellon, Henry 24; America, 1831 778.5 p40
Bellon, Honore 18; New Orleans, 1864 543.30 p362
Bellona, Joseph 25; West Virginia, 1892 9788.3 p4
Bellonzi, L. 31; Kansas, 1887 5240.1 p70
Bellos, Robert; Montreal, 1816 7603 p24
Bellow, Laurence; America, 1739 4971 p14
Bellowes, Thos.; Virginia, 1635 6219 p26
Belly, James; Virginia, 1634 6219 p32
Belman, Adam; Indiana, 1844 9117 p16
Belman, Charles 30; Massachusetts, 1860 6410.32 p103
Belman, Margaret 25; Massachusetts, 1860 6410.32 p103
Belock, Earnest 26; Ohio, 1877 6014.1 p1
Belot, Charles 28; Louisiana, 1826 778.5 p41
Belser, Carl; Cincinnati, 1831 8582.1 p51
Belser, Carl Friederich; America, 1831 8582.2 p60
Belser, Friederika; Cincinnati, 1835-1887 8582 p35
Belser, John; Cincinnati, 1831 8582.1 p51
Belser, Karl Friedrich; Cincinnati, 1869-1887 8582 p3
Belser, Wilhelm F.; Indiana, 1869-1887 8582 p3
Belsome, Ann; Virginia, 1637 6219 p83
Belt, Humphrey; Virginia, 1636 6219 p78
Belt, John C. 33; New Orleans, 1862 543.30 p484
Beltman, Hendrika 26; New York, NY, 1847 3377.6 p15
Beltman, Joseph; Indiana, 1844 9117 p16
Belton, Janet 20; Carolina, 1774 1219.7 p211
Beltram, Jas. 29; Port uncertain, 1838 778.5 p41
Beltz, Andrew 38; New Orleans, 1862 543.30 p117
Beltzhuber, Anna Maria SEE Beltzhuber, Christian Melchior
Beltzhuber, Anna Maria Dorothea SEE Beltzhuber, Christian Melchior
Beltzhuber, Christian Melchior; Port uncertain, 1752 2444 p137
*Wife:*Anna Maria
*Child:*Melchior
*Child:*Georg Eduard
*Child:*Johann Jacob
*Child:*Johann Martin
*Child:*Thomas
*Child:*Anna Maria Dorothea
Beltzhuber, Georg Eduard SEE Beltzhuber, Christian Melchior
Beltzhuber, Johann Jacob SEE Beltzhuber, Christian Melchior
Beltzhuber, Johann Martin SEE Beltzhuber, Christian Melchior
Beltzhuber, Melchior SEE Beltzhuber, Christian Melchior
Beltzhuber, Thomas SEE Beltzhuber, Christian Melchior
Belusiak, Martin; Arkansas, 1918 95.2 p18
Belver, Bevis; Virginia, 1643 6219 p205
Belz, George Andrew; California, 1866 2769.1 p4
Belzecki, . . .; New York, 1831 4606 p172
Belzhuber, Melcher; Pennsylvania, 1752 2444 p137
Belzhuber, Melcher; Pennsylvania, 1752 2444 p201
Bem, Conrad; Philadelphia, 1758 9973.7 p33
Beman, Carl; Iroquois Co., IL, 1894 3455.1 p9
Beman, William 39; Virginia, 1774 1219.7 p243
Bemanne, . . .; Canada, 1776-1783 9786 p17
Bemberry, John; Virginia, 1646 6219 p239
Bembrick, Jane; Virginia, 1656 6219 p22
Bembridge, Hen.; Virginia, 1642 6219 p195
Bembridge, John; Virginia, 1624 6219 p31
Bembridge, Tho.; Virginia, 1637 6219 p113
Bembridge, William; Virginia, 1638 6219 p123
Bemison, Thomas 32; Maryland, 1774 1219.7 p184
Bemulis, Joseph; Wisconsin, n.d. 9675.4 p265
Bena, Saturnin 45; Kansas, 1880 5240.1 p62
Benaben, Augustin 36; America, 1835 778.5 p41
Benabeu, J. 40; America, 1837 778.5 p41
Benac, Anna; Iowa, 1866-1943 123.54 p8
Benac, Anton; Iowa, 1866-1943 123.54 p8
Benac, Anton; Iowa, 1866-1943 123.54 p57
Benac, Filipina; Iowa, 1866-1943 123.54 p57
Benac, Franjo; Iowa, 1866-1943 123.54 p8
Benac, Ignace 31; New Orleans, 1839 778.5 p37
Benac, Stino; Iowa, 1866-1943 123.54 p8
Benac, Vinko; Iowa, 1866-1943 123.54 p8
Benand, Mlle. 23; New Orleans, 1839 778.5 p41
Benard, Mr. 22; New Orleans, 1838 778.5 p41
Benard, John Claude 24; New Orleans, 1836 778.5 p41
Benard, Joseph 29; New Orleans, 1836 778.5 p41
Benard, Julie 18; New Orleans, 1836 778.5 p41
Benard, Lucy 25; New Orleans, 1836 778.5 p41
Benard, Marian 64; New Orleans, 1836 778.5 p41
Benard, Michel 64; New Orleans, 1836 778.5 p41
Benaud, Mlle. 23; New Orleans, 1839 778.5 p41
Bence, Annie 59; Washington, 1916-1919 1728.4 p251
Bence, H. J. 58; Washington, 1916 1728.4 p251
Bence, Willie 32; Washington, 1916-1919 1728.4 p251
Bencroft, James 27; Maryland, 1774 1219.7 p235
Benczinczan, Nick; Arkansas, 1918 95.2 p18
Bend, John 21; Maryland, 1775 1219.7 p273
Benda, Frank; Wisconsin, n.d. 9675.4 p265
Bendal, Josiah 35; Maryland, 1775 1219.7 p251
Bendar, George; New York, NY, 1835 8208.4 p20
Bendel, Charles; Illinois, 1887 2896.5 p3
Bendell, Eliz. 6 SEE Bendell, Mria
Bendell, Geo. 10 SEE Bendell, Mria
Bendell, Hannah 19 SEE Bendell, Mria
Bendell, James 12 SEE Bendell, Mria
Bendell, John 17 SEE Bendell, Mria
Bendell, Mria 44; Montreal, 1855 4535.11 p52
*Child:*Hannah 19
*Child:*John 17
*Child:*James 12
*Child:*Geo. 10
*Child:*Eliz. 6
Bender, . . .; Canada, 1776-1783 9786 p17
Bender, Mrs.; Lancaster, PA, 1874 8582.1 p3
Bender, Ben 22; Arkansas, 1918 95.2 p18
Bender, Christopher 46; Savannah, GA, 1738 9332 p332
*Niece:*Elizabeth 24
Bender, Eberhard; New York, NY, 1838 8208.4 p87
Bender, Elizabeth 24 SEE Bender, Christopher
Bender, James; Iowa, 1866-1943 123.54 p8
Bender, Kath. 85; Washington, D.C., 1912 1763 p40C
Bender, Tobias; America, 1854 1450.2 p13A
Bender, Wilhelm; Cincinnati, 1869-1887 8582 p3
Bender, Xavier; Canada, 1776-1783 9786 p230
Bendikas, Stephen; Wisconsin, n.d. 9675.4 p265
Bendixen, Benjamin; Chicago, 1920 3455.2 p78
Bene, . . .; Cincinnati, 1840-1845 8582.3 p90
Benecke, . . .; Canada, 1776-1783 9786 p17
Benecke, August; Wisconsin, n.d. 9675.4 p265
Benecke, William; Wisconsin, n.d. 9675.4 p265
Benedeth, Tioravante 16; New York, NY, 1893 9026.4 p41
Benedetta, James Valentine; Arkansas, 1918 95.2 p18
Benedict, . . .; Canada, 1776-1783 9786 p17
Benediksdottir, Jacobina 2; Quebec, 1879 2557.1 p21

Benediktsdottir PASSENGER AND IMMIGRATION LISTS INDEX: 1996 SUPPLEMENT

Benediktsdottir, Benedikt 6 mos; Quebec, 1879 ***2557.1*** *p21*
Benediktsdottir, Thuridur 21; Quebec, 1879 ***2557.1*** *p21*
Benediktsson, Kristjan 12; Quebec, 1879 ***2557.1*** *p39A*
Benediktsson, Sigurbjorn 4; Quebec, 1879 ***2557.1*** *p39A*
Benefold, John 29; Maryland, 1774 ***1219.7*** *p229*
Benetone, Giovanni; Colorado, 1903 ***9678.1*** *p153*
Beney, Louis 26; America, 1838 ***778.5*** *p41*
Bengel, Anna Catharina; Port uncertain, 1717 ***3627*** *p15*
Benger, Else; Wisconsin, n.d. ***9675.4*** *p265*
Benger, Siegfried; Wisconsin, n.d. ***9675.4*** *p265*
Bengert, Nicolas 33; New Orleans, 1862 ***543.30*** *p115*
Bengillie, Marie; Quebec, 1782 ***7603*** *p24*
Bengle, . . .; Canada, 1776-1783 ***9786*** *p17*
Bengtson, John 66; Kansas, 1874 ***5240.1*** *p55*
Bengtson, Sophia 57; Kansas, 1876 ***5240.1*** *p57*
Bengtsson, Bengt H.; Colorado, 1904 ***9678.1*** *p153*
Benham, James; New York, NY, 1838 ***8208.4*** *p66*
Benich, . . .; New York, 1831 ***4606*** *p172*
Benie, Alexander; St. John, N.B., 1866 ***5704.8*** *p167*
Beniford, Wm 15; America, 1701 ***2212*** *p35*
Benike, Arnold; Kentucky, 1840-1845 ***8582.3*** *p100*
Benike, August; Wisconsin, n.d. ***9675.4*** *p265*
Benington, Jon.; Virginia, 1642 ***6219*** *p192*
Benit, Roman; New York, 1831 ***4606*** *p172*
Benitt, Henry; West Virginia, 1855 ***9788.3*** *p4*
Benjamin, J. A. 18; Guadeloupe, 1832 ***778.5*** *p41*
Benjamin, John 40; Maryland, 1775 ***1219.7*** *p250*
Benjamin, Morris; America, 1894 ***1450.2*** *p13A*
Benkel, Abraham; Iroquois Co., IL, 1894 ***3455.1*** *p9*
Benken, Heinrich; Kentucky, 1843 ***8582.3*** *p100*
Benkendorff, Oswald von; Missouri, 1869-1887 ***8582*** *p3*
Benkert, Hermann August Ludwig; America, 1882 ***4610.10*** *p124*
Benn, Anton; Arkansas, 1918 ***95.2*** *p18*
Benn, John; America, 1738 ***4971*** *p9*
Benn, Stephen; Virginia, 1637 ***6219*** *p85*
Bennard, J. 28; America, 1839 ***778.5*** *p41*
Benner, Bastian; Philadelphia, 1759 ***9973.7*** *p33*
Benner, Christian; Ohio, 1798-1818 ***8582.2*** *p54*
*Brother:*Heinrich
Benner, Heinrich *SEE* Benner, Christian
Benner, Michael; Ohio, 1798-1818 ***8582.2*** *p54*
Bennet, Mr.; Quebec, 1815 ***9229.18*** *p78*
With wife
With family
Bennet, Basile; New York, NY, 1833 ***8208.4*** *p47*
Bennet, George; Charleston, SC, 1783 ***1639.20*** *p9*
Bennet, James; New York, NY, 1761 ***1219.7*** *p81*
Bennet, James; New York, NY, 1811 ***2859.11*** *p8*
Bennet, James 20; Jamaica, 1729 ***3690.1*** *p17*
Bennet, Jane 23; Maryland or Virginia, 1699 ***2212*** *p24*
Bennet, John; America, 1738 ***4971*** *p40*
Bennet, John; America, 1741 ***4971*** *p69*
Bennet, John 15; Pennsylvania, 1728 ***3690.1*** *p17*
Bennet, Patrick; New York, NY, 1811 ***2859.11*** *p8*
With family
Bennet, Robert; Charleston, SC, 1805 ***1639.20*** *p9*
Bennet, Sarah 15; Virginia, 1720 ***3690.1*** *p17*
Bennet, Wm; America, 1697 ***2212*** *p7*
Bennett, Mr.; Quebec, 1815 ***9229.18*** *p81*
Bennett, Adam 30; Georgia, 1774 ***1219.7*** *p188*
Bennett, Ambro.; Virginia, 1635 ***6219*** *p3*
Bennett, David 30; North America, 1774 ***1219.7*** *p200*
*Wife:*Mary 30
Bennett, Edward 27; Maryland, 1774 ***1219.7*** *p236*
Bennett, Eliz.; Virginia, 1635 ***6219*** *p69*
Bennett, Eliz.; Virginia, 1637 ***6219*** *p112*
Bennett, Gilbert; Virginia, 1636 ***6219*** *p21*
Bennett, Henry 23; Philadelphia, 1774 ***1219.7*** *p183*
Bennett, Henry C.; Arkansas, 1918 ***95.2*** *p18*
Bennett, Joane; Virginia, 1636 ***6219*** *p74*
Bennett, John; Antigua (Antego), 1755 ***1219.7*** *p36*
Bennett, John; Antigua (Antego), 1755 ***3690.1*** *p17*
Bennett, John; Georgia, 1834 ***8208.4*** *p39*
Bennett, John; New York, NY, 1835 ***8208.4*** *p37*
Bennett, John; Virginia, 1637 ***6219*** *p112*
Bennett, John; Virginia, 1638 ***6219*** *p2*
Bennett, John; Virginia, 1652 ***6251*** *p20*
Bennett, John 18; Jamaica, 1736 ***3690.1*** *p17*
Bennett, Jon.; Virginia, 1635 ***6219*** *p20*
Bennett, Jon.; Virginia, 1637 ***6219*** *p113*
Bennett, Joseph; Arkansas, 1918 ***95.2*** *p18*
Bennett, Joseph 22; Virginia, 1774 ***1219.7*** *p240*
Bennett, Mary 30 *SEE* Bennett, David
Bennett, Maudlin; Virginia, 1642 ***6219*** *p191*
Bennett, Morris; Virginia, 1638 ***6219*** *p115*
Bennett, Nich.; Virginia, 1635 ***6219*** *p72*
Bennett, Noble; New York, NY, 1835 ***8208.4*** *p40*
Bennett, R. R. 32; Kansas, 1887 ***5240.1*** *p70*
Bennett, Rich.; Virginia, 1635 ***6219*** *p3*
Bennett, Rich.; Virginia, 1642 ***6219*** *p197*
Bennett, Richard 15; New York, 1775 ***1219.7*** *p246*
Bennett, Robert; Charleston, SC, 1752-1816 ***1639.20*** *p9*
Bennett, Robert; Virginia, 1635 ***6219*** *p73*
Bennett, Robert; Virginia, 1637 ***6219*** *p113*
Bennett, Robert 24; Port uncertain, 1774 ***1219.7*** *p176*
Bennett, Robt.; Virginia, 1635 ***6219*** *p68*
Bennett, Sarah; Virginia, 1642 ***6219*** *p196*
Bennett, Sarah 18; Pennsylvania, 1723 ***3690.1*** *p17*
Bennett, Sarah 22; Maryland, 1775 ***1219.7*** *p266*
Bennett, Tho.; Virginia, 1636 ***6219*** *p76*
Bennett, Thomas; New York, NY, 1816 ***2859.11*** *p25*
Bennett, Thomas 15; Philadelphia, 1774 ***1219.7*** *p212*
Bennett, Thomas 19; Maryland, 1774 ***1219.7*** *p206*
Bennett, Thomas 24; New York, 1774 ***1219.7*** *p197*
Bennett, Thomas 29; Maryland or Virginia, 1736 ***3690.1*** *p17*
Bennett, William 20; St. Vincent, 1774 ***1219.7*** *p175*
Bennett, William 20; St. Vincent, 1774 ***1219.7*** *p177*
Bennett, William James; Arkansas, 1918 ***95.2*** *p18*
Bennett, Z.; Philadelphia, 1811 ***53.26*** *p4*
Bennett, Z.; Philadelphia, 1811 ***2859.11*** *p8*
Benning, Friedrich Wilhelm von; Canada, 1780 ***9786*** *p268*
Benning, Friedrich Wilhelm von; New York, 1776 ***9786*** *p268*
Benning, Herman; Wisconsin, n.d. ***9675.4*** *p265*
Benning, James 25; Maryland, 1773 ***1219.7*** *p172*
Benninger, Frederick; New York, 1883 ***1450.2*** *p2B*
Benninger, Fried; America, 1849 ***8582.2*** *p2*
Benningham, Eliza; New York, NY, 1816 ***2859.11*** *p25*
Benningham, Thomas; New York, NY, 1816 ***2859.11*** *p25*
Bennington, George 32; Savannah, GA, 1775 ***1219.7*** *p274*
Bennison, Eliza.; Virginia, 1648 ***6219*** *p246*
Bennitt, Henry; West Virginia, 1855 ***9788.3*** *p4*
Bennon, John 22; St. John, N.B., 1862 ***5704.8*** *p150*
Bennoud, Charles; America, 1852 ***1450.2*** *p13A*
Benoger, Mr. 40; New Orleans, 1839 ***778.5*** *p42*
Benoist, Aloys 19; America, 1838 ***778.5*** *p42*
Benoit, David 44; America, 1836 ***778.5*** *p42*
Benoit, Emile 30; New Orleans, 1838 ***778.5*** *p42*
Benoit, Marie Louise 23; America, 1835 ***778.5*** *p42*
Benoit, Merentine 3; America, 1835 ***778.5*** *p42*
Benot, Auguste; Colorado, 1904 ***9678.1*** *p153*
Benoth, . . .; Canada, 1776-1783 ***9786*** *p17*
Benowitz, Bras 11 mos; New York, NY, 1878 ***9253*** *p46*
Benowitz, Jente 22; New York, NY, 1878 ***9253*** *p46*
Benowitz, Leise 1 mo; New York, NY, 1878 ***9253*** *p46*
Bensch, Martin; Wisconsin, n.d. ***9675.4*** *p265*
Benschoden, Cornelius; Ohio, 1823 ***8582.1*** *p46*
Bensen, Chris; Arizona, 1898 ***9228.30*** *p10*
Benson, A.; Washington, 1859-1920 ***2872.1*** *p3*
Benson, Alfred Herbert; Wisconsin, n.d. ***9675.4*** *p265*
Benson, Andrew; Washington, 1859-1920 ***2872.1*** *p3*
Benson, Arvid L.; Maine, 1884 ***6410.22*** *p125*
Benson, Arvid S.; Bangor, ME, 1881-1884 ***6410.22*** *p120*
Benson, August; Iowa, 1866-1943 ***123.54*** *p8*
Benson, Catherine; Philadelphia, 1852 ***5704.8*** *p89*
Benson, Charles J.; Colorado, 1905 ***9678.1*** *p153*
Benson, E.; Iowa, 1866-1943 ***123.54*** *p8*
Benson, Elizabeth; Philadelphia, 1847 ***53.26*** *p4*
Benson, Elizabeth; Philadelphia, 1847 ***5704.8*** *p24*
Benson, Fanny Ann 17; Philadelphia, 1854 ***5704.8*** *p117*
Benson, George; Ohio, 1849 ***9892.11*** *p3*
Benson, J. M.; Minneapolis, 1861-1888 ***6410.35*** *p49*
Benson, James; Philadelphia, 1852 ***5704.8*** *p85*
Benson, James 50; St. John, N.B., 1864 ***5704.8*** *p158*
Benson, John; Kansas, 1869 ***5240.1*** *p4*
Benson, John; Philadelphia, 1852 ***5704.8*** *p89*
Benson, John; Washington, 1859-1920 ***2872.1*** *p3*
Benson, John A.; Washington, 1859-1920 ***2872.1*** *p3*
Benson, Margaret 18; St. John, N.B., 1864 ***5704.8*** *p158*
Benson, Margaret 19; Philadelphia, 1854 ***5704.8*** *p117*
Benson, Mary; America, 1742 ***4971*** *p49*
Benson, Mary; America, 1742 ***4971*** *p50*
Benson, Mary; Philadelphia, 1852 ***5704.8*** *p85*
Benson, Mary 50; St. John, N.B., 1864 ***5704.8*** *p158*
Benson, Michael; Philadelphia, 1853 ***5704.8*** *p101*
Benson, Patrick; Canada, 1841 ***7036*** *p120*
Benson, Perry; Maine, 1871-1882 ***6410.22*** *p116*
Benson, Peter; Iowa, 1866-1943 ***123.54*** *p8*
Benson, Peter O.; Colorado, 1902 ***9678.1*** *p153*
Benson, Richard; Philadelphia, 1850 ***53.26*** *p4*
Benson, Richard; Philadelphia, 1850 ***5704.8*** *p60*
Benson, Robert; America, 1705 ***2212*** *p45*
Benson, Stephen Henry; New York, NY, 1835 ***8208.4*** *p29*
Benson, Thomas 29; Maryland, 1775 ***1219.7*** *p256*
Benson, William 19; St. John, N.B., 1864 ***5704.8*** *p158*
Benson, William 23; Virginia, 1775 ***1219.7*** *p246*
Benson, William 34; Kansas, 1878 ***5240.1*** *p59*
Benst, Mathias Joseph; Wisconsin, n.d. ***9675.4*** *p265*
Benstead, Mary *SEE* Benstead, Thomas
Benstead, Thomas; Virginia, 1636 ***6219*** *p79*
*Wife:*Mary
Bensteed, Mary *SEE* Bensteed, Thomas
Bensteed, Thomas; Virginia, 1636 ***6219*** *p79*
*Wife:*Mary
Benston, John; Washington, 1859-1920 ***2872.1*** *p3*
Bent, Joseph 19; Antigua (Antego), 1728 ***3690.1*** *p17*
Bentall, Robert; Virginia, 1636 ***6219*** *p80*
Bentenvegna, John 24; Arkansas, 1918 ***95.2*** *p18*
Benth, . . .; Canada, 1776-1783 ***9786*** *p41*
Benther, . . .; Canada, 1776-1783 ***9786*** *p41*
Bentinegno, Ignazio; Arkansas, 1918 ***95.2*** *p18*
Benting, Herman R.; Illinois, 1888 ***5012.37*** *p61*
Bentleg, William; Virginia, 1639 ***6219*** *p154*
Bentley, Benjamin 19; Maryland, 1739 ***3690.1*** *p17*
Bentley, George 30; Jamaica, 1734 ***3690.1*** *p17*
Bentley, Joe; Wisconsin, n.d. ***9675.4*** *p265*
Bentley, John; New York, NY, 1838 ***8208.4*** *p89*
Bentley, Mary 65; Halifax, N.S., 1774 ***1219.7*** *p213*
Bentley, Phoebe 51; Tortola, 1773 ***1219.7*** *p172*
Bentley, Thomas; New York, NY, 1838 ***8208.4*** *p73*
Bentley, William 15; Jamaica, 1774 ***1219.7*** *p189*
Bently, Eliza.; Virginia, 1635 ***6219*** *p22*
Bently, Hen.; Virginia, 1638 ***6219*** *p14*
Bently, Mary; America, 1735-1743 ***4971*** *p8*
Bento, John; New York, NY, 1839 ***8208.4*** *p96*
Benton, Abigall; Virginia, 1642 ***6219*** *p194*
Benton, Alice; Virginia, 1642 ***6219*** *p194*
Benton, Eliza. *SEE* Benton, John
Benton, Isabell; Virginia, 1642 ***6219*** *p194*
Benton, Joane *SEE* Benton, Jon.
Benton, John; Virginia, 1642 ***6219*** *p194*
*Wife:*Eliza.
Benton, Jon.; Virginia, 1642 ***6219*** *p194*
*Wife:*Joane
Benton, Jon.; Virginia, 1642 ***6219*** *p194*
Benton, Sam'l; New York, NY, 1816 ***2859.11*** *p25*
Benton, Tho.; Virginia, 1635 ***6219*** *p6*
Benton, Wm 42; New Orleans, 1862 ***543.30*** *p245*
Bentz, . . .; Canada, 1776-1783 ***9786*** *p17*
Bentz, August; Wisconsin, n.d. ***9675.4*** *p265*
Bentz, Catharina *SEE* Bentz, Hans
Bentz, Christina Barbara *SEE* Bentz, Hans
Bentz, Hans; Pennsylvania, 1711-1800 ***2444*** *p137*
*Wife:*Catharina
*Child:*Christina Barbara
Bentz, John; Philadelphia, 1761 ***9973.7*** *p36*
Benz, Jochem; Wisconsin, n.d. ***9675.4*** *p265*
Benz, Johanna; Pennsylvania, 1752 ***2444*** *p164*
Benz, John; Wisconsin, n.d. ***9675.4*** *p265*
Benzen, Christian; New Orleans, 1862 ***543.30*** *p481*
Benzer, Barbara; Pennsylvania, 1749 ***2444*** *p197*
Benzien, Anna Benigna; New York, 1754 ***3652*** *p79*
Benzien, Anna Maria; New York, 1754 ***3652*** *p78*
Benzien, C. T.; New York, 1754 ***3652*** *p78*
Benzien, Christel; New York, 1754 ***3652*** *p79*
Benzinger, J. G. 45; America, 1836 ***778.5*** *p42*
Bepler, Eduard; America, 1840 ***8582.1*** *p3*
Beppert, Frederick; Wisconsin, n.d. ***9675.4*** *p265*
Beppler, Wilh. 48; San Francisco, 1911 ***1763*** *p40C*
Berandt, Carl 27; Kansas, 1886 ***5240.1*** *p4*
Berandt, Carl 27; Kansas, 1886 ***5240.1*** *p68*
Berans, James; New Orleans, 1849 ***5704.8*** *p59*
Beraud, J. M. 18; Louisiana, 1820 ***778.5*** *p42*
Berberich, Michael Frank; Kansas, 1885 ***5240.1*** *p4*
Berck, . . .; Canada, 1776-1783 ***9786*** *p17*
Berckle, Eberhard; Pennsylvania, 1750-1776 ***2444*** *p144*
Berd, Johann; Wisconsin, n.d. ***9675.4*** *p265*
Bere, Theodore; Virginia, 1757 ***1219.7*** *p58*
Berens, Engel; Indianapolis, 1870 ***3702.7*** *p586*
Berens, Heinrich; New York, NY, 1923 ***3455.4*** *p94*
Berensmeyer, Anne M. W. Charlotte *SEE* Berensmeyer, Heinrich F. Gottlieb
Berensmeyer, Anne M.W.E. Poggemeyer *SEE* Berensmeyer, Heinrich F. Gottlieb
Berensmeyer, Anne Marie C. Louise *SEE* Berensmeyer, Heinrich F. Gottlieb
Berensmeyer, Carl Friedrich *SEE* Berensmeyer, Johann Carl August
Berensmeyer, Caspar Ernst Friedrich *SEE* Berensmeyer, Heinrich F. Gottlieb
Berensmeyer, Ernst F. Wilhelm *SEE* Berensmeyer, Heinrich F. Gottlieb
Berensmeyer, Ernst H. Christian *SEE* Berensmeyer, Johann Carl August
Berensmeyer, Heinrich F. Gottlieb; America, 1857 ***4610.10*** *p157*
*Wife:*Anne M.W.E. Poggemeyer
*Child:*Anne Marie C. Louise
*Child:*Caspar Ernst Friedrich
*Child:*Louise Caroline F.
*Child:*Anne M. W. Charlotte
*Child:*Ernst F. Wilhelm

28 *FOR A COMPLETE EXPLANATION OF ENTRY, SEE "HOW TO READ A CITATION" SECTION*

Berensmeyer, Heinrich P. Wilhelm *SEE* Berensmeyer, Johann Carl August
Berensmeyer, Johann Carl August; America, 1844 4610.10 p150
*Wife:*Marie S. M. Ilsabein
*Child:*Ernst H. Christian
*Child:*Heinrich P. Wilhelm
*Child:*Carl Friedrich
Berensmeyer, Louise Caroline F. *SEE* Berensmeyer, Heinrich F. Gottlieb
Berensmeyer, Marie S. M. Ilsabein *SEE* Berensmeyer, Johann Carl August
Berer, Michael; Wisconsin, n.d. 9675.4 p265
Beretta, Guseppe; Iowa, 1866-1943 123.54 p8
Beretta, Teresa; Iowa, 1866-1943 123.54 p57
Bereus, Karol; New York, 1831 4606 p172
Berg, . . .; Canada, 1776-1783 9786 p17
Berg, A.; Minneapolis, 1880-1884 6410.35 p49
Berg, Adam 43; Arizona, 1890 2764.35 p6
Berg, Alfrid; Minneapolis, 1872-1885 6410.35 p49
Berg, Allena; Washington, 1859-1920 2872.1 p3
Berg, Andreas; New York, 1717 3627 p11
*Wife:*Maria A. Lammingern
*Child:*Maria Apollonia
*Child:*Johann Andreas
*Child:*Johann Michael
With child
Berg, Anton; Washington, 1859-1920 2872.1 p3
Berg, August; America, 1851 8582.3 p5
Berg, Barbara 44; America, 1853 9162.8 p36
Berg, C. A.; Iowa, 1866-1943 123.54 p8
Berg, Carl D.; America, 1844 1450.2 p13A
Berg, Charles; Washington, 1859-1920 2872.1 p3
Berg, Charly; Iowa, 1866-1943 123.54 p8
Berg, Elene; Washington, 1859-1920 2872.1 p3
Berg, Elisabeth Ruffer 76; Canada, 1901 1763 p40D
Berg, Ella; Washington, 1859-1920 2872.1 p3
Berg, Franz 19; America, 1853 9162.7 p14
Berg, Gabrel; Washington, 1859-1920 2872.1 p3
Berg, George 38; Arizona, 1890 2764.35 p6
Berg, Gunner; Washington, 1859-1920 2872.1 p3
Berg, Hans; Washington, 1859-1920 2872.1 p3
Berg, Jacob; America, 1896 5240.1 p4
Berg, Jennie; Washington, 1859-1920 2872.1 p3
Berg, Johann Andreas *SEE* Berg, Andreas
Berg, Johann Michael *SEE* Berg, Andreas
Berg, Joseph 13; New Orleans, 1863 543.30 p363
Berg, Maria A. Lammingern *SEE* Berg, Andreas
Berg, Maria Apollonia *SEE* Berg, Andreas
Berg, Marie 55; Pennsylvania, 1909 1763 p40D
Berg, P. S.; Minneapolis, 1872-1880 6410.35 p50
Berg, P. S.; Minneapolis, 1879-1888 6410.35 p49
Berg, William; Illinois, 1892 5012.37 p62
Bergan, Mrs. 15; Port uncertain, 1826 778.5 p42
Bergan, Antoine 36; Port uncertain, 1826 778.5 p42
Bergan, Michael; New York, NY, 1838 8208.4 p66
Bergeard, Mr. 23; Port uncertain, 1838 778.5 p42
Bergen, Eleonore Brean; Quebec, 1763 7603 p94
Bergen, Marguerite; Montreal, 1823 7603 p84
Bergenmeyer, Cath Mgt; South Carolina, 1752-1753 3689.17 p22
With daughter
With son-in-law
Berger, . . .; Canada, 1776-1783 9786 p17
Berger, Andreas; New York, 1717 3627 p11
*Wife:*Maria A. Lammingern
*Child:*Maria Apollonia
*Child:*Johann Andreas
*Child:*Johann Michael
With child
Berger, Anette 26; America, 1836 778.5 p42
Berger, Anna Ottilia Arnold; America, 1754 4349 p46
*Child:*Wilhelm
*Child:*Johann Georg
*Child:*Maria Catharina
*Child:*Johannes
Berger, Anna Sophia; Pennsylvania, 1717 3627 p15
Berger, Celestin 26; America, 1836 778.5 p42
Berger, Christian 26; Kansas, 1891 5240.1 p5
Berger, Christian 26; Kansas, 1891 5240.1 p76
Berger, Elise; Wisconsin, n.d. 9675.4 p265
Berger, Emil; Wisconsin, n.d. 9675.4 p265
Berger, Frank; New York, 1882 1450.2 p2B
Berger, Frederick; America, 1869 1450.2 p13A
Berger, G. 18; America, 1835 778.5 p42
Berger, Gustave 24; Kansas, 1901 5240.1 p82
Berger, Hjalmer 22; Arkansas, 1918 95.2 p18
Berger, Jean 6 mos; America, 1836 778.5 p43
Berger, Johann Andreas *SEE* Berger, Andreas
Berger, Johann Georg *SEE* Berger, Anna Ottilia Arnold
Berger, Johann Michael *SEE* Berger, Andreas
Berger, Johannes *SEE* Berger, Anna Ottilia Arnold
Berger, Karl Edward 23; Kansas, 1896 5240.1 p5
Berger, Karl Edward 23; Kansas, 1896 5240.1 p80
Berger, Leopold Dobritz; Wisconsin, n.d. 9675.4 p265
Berger, Maria A. Lammingern *SEE* Berger, Andreas
Berger, Maria Apollonia *SEE* Berger, Andreas
Berger, Maria Catharina *SEE* Berger, Anna Ottilia Arnold
Berger, Peter; America, 1830 8582.2 p61
Berger, Peter; Ohio, 1869-1887 8582 p3
Berger, Philip 34; New Orleans, 1839 778.5 p42
Berger, Philipp; Wisconsin, n.d. 9675.4 p265
Berger, Pierre Joseph 17; New Orleans, 1836 778.5 p43
Berger, Wilhelm *SEE* Berger, Anna Ottilia Arnold
Berger, William; Wisconsin, n.d. 9675.4 p265
Bergerand, Mr. 36; New Orleans, 1839 778.5 p43
Bergeron, Antoine Marie 42; St. Louis, 1835 778.5 p43
Bergeron, Claude 38; New Orleans, 1839 778.5 p43
Bergerot, Mr. 30; New Orleans, 1839 778.5 p43
Bergerot, Auguste; Port uncertain, 1839 778.5 p43
Bergfeld, Anna 29; New Orleans, 1839 9420.2 p68
Bergfeld, Johann Gotthilf 34; New Orleans, 1839 9420.2 p68
Bergfeld, Marie 7; New Orleans, 1839 9420.2 p68
Bergfeld, Robert 5; New Orleans, 1839 9420.2 p68
Bergfeldt, Edwin 23; New Orleans, 1862 543.30 p480
Bergh, Laurance 21; Maryland, 1773 1219.7 p173
Berghalser, . . .; Canada, 1776-1783 9786 p17
Bergin, Daniel; New York, NY, 1816 2859.11 p25
Bergin, Jerry 33; Massachusetts, 1849 5881.1 p8
Bergin, Johanna 45; Massachusetts, 1849 5881.1 p8
Bergin, Laughlin; America, 1737 4971 p85
Bergin, Malachi; America, 1743 4971 p11
Bergin, Marie; Quebec, 1784 7603 p71
Bergin, Michael; New York, NY, 1838 8208.4 p66
Bergin, Thomas 11; Massachusetts, 1849 5881.1 p12
Bergis, Mr.; Port uncertain, 1839 778.5 p43
Bergis, Mr. 28; Port uncertain, 1838 778.5 p43
Bergland, Berdines Michael; Arkansas, 1918 95.2 p18
Berglasen, . . .; Canada, 1776-1783 9786 p17
Berglund, A. P.; Minneapolis, 1879-1880 6410.35 p50
Berglund, Carl; Washington, 1859-1920 2872.1 p3
Berglund, Frank Algot; Washington, 1859-1920 2872.1 p3
Bergman, Adolf; Minneapolis, 1854-1881 6410.35 p50
Bergman, Francis H.; Ohio, 1844 8365.27 p12
Bergman, John F.; Illinois, 1881 2896.5 p3
Bergman, Leopold; Washington, 1859-1920 2872.1 p3
Bergman, Uffe Klassen; Illinois, 1888 5012.39 p122
Bergman, William; Minneapolis, 1881-1883 6410.35 p50
Bergmann, Albert; Illinois, 1888 5012.37 p61
Bergmann, Anna; Quebec, 1876 9980.20 p48
Bergmann, Anna Wieb; Quebec, 1877 9980.20 p48
Bergmann, Bernh.; Quebec, 1876 9980.20 p48
Bergmann, Bernhard; Quebec, 1877 9980.20 p48
Bergmann, Bruno Christoph August; America, 1895 4610.10 p103
Bergmann, Cathariena; Quebec, 1877 9980.20 p48
Bergmann, Cornelius 15; Quebec, 1877 9980.20 p48
Bergmann, Cornl.; Quebec, 1877 9980.20 p49
Bergmann, Friedrich; Wisconsin, n.d. 9675.4 p265
Bergmann, Gertrude; Quebec, 1877 9980.20 p48
Bergmann, Heinrich; Quebec, 1877 9980.20 p48
Bergmann, Helena; Quebec, 1876 9980.20 p48
Bergmann, Helena 1; Quebec, 1876 9980.20 p48
Bergmann, Helena Huebert; Quebec, 1876 9980.20 p48
Bergmann, Henry; New York, 1750 3652 p74
Bergmann, Jacob; Kansas, 1884 5240.1 p5
Bergmann, Jacob; Kentucky, 1797 8582.3 p95
Bergmann, Jacob 16; Quebec, 1877 9980.20 p48
Bergmann, Johann; Quebec, 1877 9980.20 p48
Bergmann, Johann Ahrend 86; Baltimore, 1871 8582 p3
Bergmann, Maria 20; Quebec, 1877 9980.20 p48
Bergmann, Mary; America, 1879 5240.1 p5
Bergmann, Mary 33; Kansas, 1906 5240.1 p84
Bergmann, Peter; Quebec, 1877 9980.20 p49
Bergmann, Peter 18; Quebec, 1877 9980.20 p48
Bergmann, Sarah 24; Quebec, 1877 9980.20 p48
Bergmann, Susanna 42; Quebec, 1876 9980.20 p48
Bergner, Ernest; America, 1842 1450.2 p14A
Bergner, Peter; New York, NY, 1832 8208.4 p37
Bergnitz, Philip; Indiana, 1844 9117 p16
Bergogne de Fournier, Maurice de; Louisiana, 1789-1819 778.5 p555
Bergquist, Petter; Minneapolis, 1882-1886 6410.35 p50
Bergqvist, John; Iowa, 1849-1860 2090 p613
Bergstraeser, . . .; Canada, 1776-1783 9786 p17
Bergstrand, Charles William; America, 1879 1450.2 p14A
Bergstrand, Nicholas; Nevada, 1869 2764.35 p76
Bergstrom, Ben; Washington, 1859-1920 2872.1 p3
Bergstrom, Ed.; Minneapolis, 1884-1888 6410.35 p50
Bergstrom, Elena; Washington, 1859-1920 2872.1 p3
Bergstrom, Ellen Marie; Washington, 1859-1920 2872.1 p3
Bergstrom, Everett Nels 22; Arkansas, 1918 95.2 p18
Bergstrom, Isaac; Maine, 1890 6410.22 p126
Bergstrom, John; New York, NY, 1882 9678.1 p153
Bergt, Adolph Wm. 27; New Orleans, 1839 9420.2 p68
Bergt, Carl Adolph 22; New Orleans, 1839 9420.2 p68
Bergt, Christian Adolph 23; New Orleans, 1839 9420.2 p68
Bergtold, Anton; New Orleans, 1858 2896.5 p3
Bergwahl, Elizabeth 31; Massachusetts, 1860 6410.32 p118
Beriaud, Jean; Quebec, 1654 4533 p128
Beridon, Laurent 35; New Orleans, 1836 778.5 p43
Beridon, Louis 13; New Orleans, 1836 778.5 p43
Berieren, Wendelen; Illinois, 1857 7857 p2
Berilla, Andrew; Washington, 1859-1920 2872.1 p3
Beringer, Peter; Pennsylvania, 1754 4525 p200
Beringhele, Joe; Arkansas, 1918 95.2 p19
Beringhele, Joe 27; Arkansas, 1918 95.2 p19
Berinkel, John; Indiana, 1845 9117 p15
Berjerot, Mr. 18; New Orleans, 1837 778.5 p43
Berk, . . .; Canada, 1776-1783 9786 p17
Berke, Rudolph; Arkansas, 1918 95.2 p19
Berkel, Derk 38; New York, NY, 1847 3377.6 p15
Berkel, Jennie 23; New York, NY, 1847 3377.6 p15
Berkel, John 7; New York, NY, 1847 3377.6 p15
Berkemeier, Christoph Heinrich; America, 1857 4610.10 p109
Berkemeier, Karl Friedrich Wilhelm; America, 1854 4610.10 p108
Berkenbasch, Christian Frederick Henry; Illinois, 1860 5012.39 p90
Berkerlin, George 15; America, 1838 778.5 p43
Berkerlin, Henriette 24; America, 1838 778.5 p43
Berkerlin, Jean 33; America, 1838 778.5 p43
Berkerlin, Jean 33; America, 1838 778.5 p44
Berkes, George H.; Wisconsin, n.d. 9675.4 p265
Berkett, Thomas 17; Maryland or Virginia, 1699 2212 p22
Berkholz, Johan G.; Wisconsin, n.d. 9675.4 p265
Berkin, Thomas 18; Quebec, 1856 5704.8 p130
Berkly, Eberhard; Pennsylvania, 1750-1776 2444 p144
Berkowitz, H.; Arizona, 1884 2764.35 p7
Berkowitz, S.; New York, NY, 1876 2764.35 p8
Berle, Louis 31; New Orleans, 1862 543.30 p481
Berlen, Johann Caspar; America, 1750 2444 p134
Berlie, L. 20; America, 1832 778.5 p44
Berlincourt, Eleonore 24; America, 1836 778.5 p44
Berling, . . .; Canada, 1776-1783 9786 p17
Berling, Hermann Heinrich; New Orleans, 1846 8582.1 p3
Berlisk, Jonas; Wisconsin, n.d. 9675.4 p265
Berlotsky, Max; Arkansas, 1918 95.2 p19
Berlucchi, Bortolo; Arkansas, 1918 95.2 p19
Berman, Benjmain H.; Arkansas, 1918 95.2 p19
Berman, Peter; Wisconsin, n.d. 9675.4 p265
Bermann, Anton; Cincinnati, 1788-1848 8582.3 p89
Bermann, Isaak 20; New York, NY, 1878 9253 p46
Bermetti, Frank; Iowa, 1866-1943 123.54 p8
Bermingham, James; America, 1738-1743 4971 p91
Bermingham, James; Illinois, 1901 5012.40 p80
Bermingham, Thomas; Illinois, 1903 5012.40 p80
Bermingham, William; Illinois, 1898 5012.40 p55
Bermon, Mrs. 20; New Orleans, 1823 778.5 p44
Bermon, Adele 2; New Orleans, 1823 778.5 p44
Bermon, Auguste 28; New Orleans, 1823 778.5 p44
Bermudes, A. 8; Port uncertain, 1839 778.5 p44
Bernadae, Paul 34; Mexico, 1838 778.5 p44
Bernadet, Jean 22; New Orleans, 1839 778.5 p44
Bernadotte, Mr.; New Orleans, 1839 778.5 p44
Bernard, . . .; Canada, 1776-1783 9786 p41
Bernard, Mr.; Port uncertain, 1836 778.5 p44
Bernard, Mr. 15; America, 1836 778.5 p44
Bernard, Mr. 18; Louisiana, 1820 778.5 p44
Bernard, Mr. 37; New Orleans, 1825 778.5 p45
Bernard, Mr. 45; America, 1838 778.5 p44
Bernard, Mrs. 27; Port uncertain, 1838 778.5 p45
Bernard, Mrs. 28; Port uncertain, 1836 778.5 p45
Bernard, A. 22; America, 1836 778.5 p44
Bernard, Ant.; Port uncertain, 1839 778.5 p45
Bernard, Francis; New York, NY, 1836 8208.4 p23
Bernard, Jack; Washington, 1859-1920 2872.1 p3
Bernard, Jacques; New York, NY, 1835 8208.4 p37
Bernard, James 25; New Orleans, 1821 778.5 p45
Bernard, Jean Fouga 25; New Orleans, 1835 778.5 p45
Bernard, John 20; New Orleans, 1862 543.30 p116
Bernard, L. 23; New Orleans, 1831 778.5 p45
Bernard, Leon E. 38; New Orleans, 1822 778.5 p45
Bernard, Loubiere 28; New Orleans, 1864 543.30 p362
Bernard, P. 56; New Orleans, 1820 778.5 p45
Bernard, Peter 25; New Orleans, 1829 778.5 p45
Bernard, Richard; New York, NY, 1816 2859.11 p25
Bernard, Stephen; Virginia, 1628 6219 p31
Bernard, Thomas; Virginia, 1638 6219 p122

Bernard, Tony; Washington, 1859-1920 ***2872.1*** *p3*
Bernardi, Tony; Washington, 1859-1920 ***2872.1*** *p3*
Bernards, William; Illinois, 1891 ***5012.39*** *p53*
Bernards, William; Illinois, 1893 ***5012.40*** *p53*
Bernas, Karl Johan; Arkansas, 1918 ***95.2*** *p19*
Berndt, Albert; Wisconsin, n.d. ***9675.4*** *p265*
Berndt, Gottlieb; New York, 1749 ***3652*** *p71*
Berndt, Reinhold; Iroquois Co., IL, 1892 ***3455.1*** *p9*
Berner, . . .; Canada, 1776-1783 ***9786*** *p17*
Berner, Andreas *SEE* Berner, Andreas
Berner, Andreas; Pennsylvania, 1748-1800 ***2444*** *p137*
*Wife:*Barbara
*Child:*Andreas
Berner, Barbara *SEE* Berner, Andreas
Berner, John 24; Philadelphia, 1774 ***1219.7*** *p175*
Berner, William J. 51; Arizona, 1890 ***2764.35*** *p9*
Berners, Jane 29; Virginia, 1775 ***1219.7*** *p246*
Bernes, Richard; Virginia, 1646 ***6219*** *p240*
Bernet, C.; New Orleans, 1839 ***778.5*** *p45*
Bernet, M.; New Orleans, 1839 ***778.5*** *p45*
Bernet, Rodolph 25; Kansas, 1877 ***5240.1*** *p58*
Bernewitz, Johann Heinrich Carl; Quebec, 1776 ***9786*** *p258*
Berney, Ellen; New York, NY, 1816 ***2859.11*** *p25*
Berney, Thomas; New York, NY, 1816 ***2859.11*** *p25*
Bernhammer, Christian; America, 1848 ***1450.2*** *p14A*
Bernhard, . . .; Canada, 1776-1783 ***9786*** *p41*
Bernhard, Ad. 11; America, 1853 ***9162.7*** *p14*
Bernhard, Bernhard 16; America, 1853 ***9162.7*** *p14*
Bernhard, Frederick; America, 1867 ***2769.2*** *p3*
Bernhard, Georg; America, 1828-1877 ***8582.3*** *p5*
Bernhard, Johannes; Philadelphia, 1779 ***8137*** *p6*
Bernhard, Wenzel; New York, 1749 ***3652*** *p71*
Bernhardt, Fettke 45; Kansas, 1879 ***5240.1*** *p5*
Bernhardt, Frederick; New York, 1885 ***1450.2*** *p14A*
Bernhardt, Georg; Kentucky, 1830 ***8582.3*** *p99*
Bernhardt, James; Indiana, 1848 ***9117*** *p15*
Bernhardt, Lorenz; America, 1864 ***1450.2*** *p14A*
Bernhart, Nick; Wisconsin, n.d. ***9675.4*** *p265*
Bernheim, Jacob 17; New Orleans, 1837 ***778.5*** *p45*
Bernhose, John 23; Jamaica, 1738 ***3690.1*** *p17*
Berniard, Miss 7; New Orleans, 1836 ***778.5*** *p46*
Berniard, Charles 9; New Orleans, 1836 ***778.5*** *p45*
Berniard, Jeanne 31; New Orleans, 1836 ***778.5*** *p46*
Berniard, John 33; New Orleans, 1836 ***778.5*** *p46*
Bernick, Frank; Wisconsin, n.d. ***9675.4*** *p265*
Bernie, William; Charleston, SC, 1806 ***1639.20*** *p9*
Bernier, Miss 7; New Orleans, 1836 ***778.5*** *p46*
Bernier, C. 40; Port uncertain, 1839 ***778.5*** *p46*
Bernier, Charles 9; New Orleans, 1836 ***778.5*** *p45*
Bernier, Chas.; Port uncertain, 1839 ***778.5*** *p46*
Bernier, G. 24; New Orleans, 1838 ***778.5*** *p46*
Bernier, Jean 16; America, 1838 ***778.5*** *p46*
Bernier, Jean 33; America, 1838 ***778.5*** *p46*
Bernier, Jeanne 31; New Orleans, 1836 ***778.5*** *p46*
Bernier, John 33; New Orleans, 1836 ***778.5*** *p46*
Berningham, John 20; Philadelphia, 1774 ***1219.7*** *p224*
Bernloehr, Christ; New York, NY, 1872 ***1450.2*** *p3B*
Bernloehr, George; America, 1893 ***1450.2*** *p14A*
Bernloehr, John; America, 1872 ***1450.2*** *p3B*
Bernoth, . . .; Canada, 1776-1783 ***9786*** *p17*
Bernoth, Elisabetha Sullinger *SEE* Bernoth, Martin
Bernoth, Martin; New England, 1749 ***2444*** *p137*
*Wife:*Elisabetha Sullinger
Berns, Regiments-Feldscheer; Quebec, 1776 ***9786*** *p105*
Berns, Nicholas; Wisconsin, n.d. ***9675.4*** *p265*
Bernstein, Charles; Iowa, 1866-1943 ***123.54*** *p8*
Bernstein, Harry 25; Kansas, 1906 ***5240.1*** *p84*
Bernstein, Jacob; Arkansas, 1918 ***95.2*** *p19*
Bernstein, Joseph; Iowa, 1866-1943 ***123.54*** *p8*
Bernstein, Nathan A.; Philadelphia, 1875 ***1450.2*** *p3B*
Bernstein, Wolf; Iowa, 1866-1943 ***123.54*** *p8*
Bernsteni, Joseph; Iowa, 1866-1943 ***123.54*** *p8*
Bernstien, Jake; Arkansas, 1918 ***95.2*** *p19*
Bernt, Johann August; Quebec, 1776 ***9786*** *p255*
Berntson, Ole; Washington, 1859-1920 ***2872.1*** *p3*
Berny, Francois 38; America, 1836 ***778.5*** *p46*
Berolatti, Guiseppe; Arkansas, 1918 ***95.2*** *p19*
Berot, Frantz Ludwick; Philadelphia, 1761 ***9973.7*** *p36*
Berquerant, Amede 22; Mobile, AL, 1836 ***778.5*** *p46*
Berra, Ant. 20; New York, NY, 1893 ***9026.4*** *p41*
Berra, Joe; Arkansas, 1918 ***95.2*** *p19*
Berrane, Catharine 13; Massachusetts, 1849 ***5881.1*** *p7*
Berrane, John 9; Massachusetts, 1849 ***5881.1*** *p9*
Berrell, Bridget; New York, NY, 1868 ***5704.8*** *p227*
Berrell, Jane; New York, NY, 1868 ***5704.8*** *p227*
Berrell, Mary; New York, NY, 1868 ***5704.8*** *p227*
Berrey, Richard 16; America, 1704 ***2212*** *p41*
Berrey, Saml 13; America, 1705 ***2212*** *p43*
Berridge, Joseph; Indiana, 1847 ***9117*** *p18*
Berridge, Joseph 20; Jamaica, 1735 ***3690.1*** *p18*
Berridge, Margaret Sophia; Jamaica, 1756 ***1219.7*** *p41*
Berridge, Margrett Sophia; Jamaica, 1756 ***3690.1*** *p18*
Berrie, James; Charleston, SC, 1745 ***1639.20*** *p9*
Berrill, James; America, 1737 ***4971*** *p24*
Berriman, William; Virginia, 1635 ***6219*** *p70*
Berriman, Wm.; Virginia, 1648 ***6219*** *p245*
Berringer, Peter; Pennsylvania, 1754 ***4525*** *p200*
Berry, Barbara 18; Massachusetts, 1849 ***5881.1*** *p6*
Berry, David; Illinois, 1869 ***5012.38*** *p99*
Berry, Elizabeth *SEE* Berry, James
Berry, Elizabeth *SEE* Berry, James
Berry, Francis; New York, NY, 1816 ***2859.11*** *p25*
Berry, Francis; Virginia, 1643 ***6219*** *p204*
Berry, James; South Carolina, 1788 ***7119*** *p197*
Berry, James; Virginia, 1636 ***6219*** *p76*
*Wife:*Elizabeth
Berry, James; Virginia, 1637 ***6219*** *p107*
*Wife:*Elizabeth
Berry, James; Virginia, 1642 ***6219*** *p188*
Berry, James 15; Salem, MA, 1774 ***1219.7*** *p234*
Berry, James 31; Savannah, GA, 1774 ***1219.7*** *p226*
With child
Berry, James J. 54; Washington, 1916-1919 ***1728.4*** *p251*
Berry, John; America, 1736 ***4971*** *p39*
Berry, John; Boston, 1848 ***6410.32*** *p124*
Berry, John; New Brunswick, 1821 ***7603*** *p64*
Berry, John; New York, NY, 1864 ***5704.8*** *p184*
Berry, John; Virginia, 1642 ***6219*** *p197*
Berry, John 15; West Indies, 1722 ***3690.1*** *p18*
Berry, John 24; Maryland, 1735 ***3690.1*** *p18*
Berry, John 26; Philadelphia, 1775 ***1219.7*** *p255*
Berry, John B. 42; Massachusetts, 1860 ***6410.32*** *p109*
Berry, Joseph; Ohio, 1845 ***9892.11*** *p3*
Berry, Louis; Quebec, 1712 ***4533*** *p128*
Berry, Lydia; Virginia, 1645 ***6219*** *p252*
Berry, Marie 32; New Orleans, 1837 ***778.5*** *p46*
Berry, Martha; Quebec, 1852 ***5704.8*** *p94*
Berry, Michael; Illinois, 1856 ***7857*** *p2*
Berry, Michael; New York, NY, 1816 ***2859.11*** *p25*
Berry, Michael; New York, NY, 1840 ***8208.4*** *p106*
Berry, Noah 60; Massachusetts, 1860 ***6410.32*** *p101*
Berry, Peter 20; Maryland, 1729 ***3690.1*** *p18*
Berry, Robert; Virginia, 1641 ***6219*** *p187*
Berry, Rose 32; New Orleans, 1826 ***778.5*** *p46*
Berry, Teel; St. John, N.B., 1847 ***5704.8*** *p25*
Berry, Thomas 16; Maryland, 1775 ***1219.7*** *p252*
Berry, Thomas 17; Carolina, 1718 ***3690.1*** *p18*
Berry, Victor 36; New Orleans, 1837 ***778.5*** *p46*
Berry, William; Virginia, 1634 ***6219*** *p84*
Berry, William; Virginia, 1636 ***6219*** *p15*
Berrye, Nicholas; Virginia, 1636 ***6219*** *p27*
Berryman, Patrick; Philadelphia, 1867 ***5704.8*** *p217*
Berryman, William; Virginia, 1638 ***6219*** *p146*
Bersenas, Julius; Wisconsin, n.d. ***9675.4*** *p265*
Bersey, Jon.; Virginia, 1642 ***6219*** *p191*
Bersin, Joseph 25; America, 1837 ***778.5*** *p46*
Berson, Meyer Israel; Arkansas, 1918 ***95.2*** *p19*
Berstecher, George; Illinois, 1876 ***2896.5*** *p3*
Berstein, Isaak; Wisconsin, n.d. ***9675.4*** *p265*
Bert, M. 25; America, 1830 ***778.5*** *p46*
Bert, Michael; Wisconsin, n.d. ***9675.4*** *p265*
Bert, Pierre 30; New Orleans, 1829 ***778.5*** *p47*
Bertaud, Francois 27; New Orleans, 1839 ***778.5*** *p47*
Bertault, Rene; Quebec, 1712 ***4533*** *p128*
Bertchinger, Gottlieb; Wisconsin, n.d. ***9675.4*** *p265*
Berte, Heinrich; America, 1837 ***8582.3*** *p5*
Berte, Heinrich; Kentucky, 1837 ***8582.3*** *p99*
Bertel, John; New York, 1885 ***1450.2*** *p3B*
Bertel Ange, Joseph 20; Mississippi, 1829 ***778.5*** *p47*
Bertelle, Abramo; Iowa, 1866-1943 ***123.54*** *p8*
Bertelle, Giovanni; Iowa, 1866-1943 ***123.54*** *p8*
Bertelle, Josephine; Iowa, 1866-1943 ***123.54*** *p57*
Bertelli, Louigi; Iowa, 1866-1943 ***123.54*** *p57*
Bertelsen, Adelie Ann; Washington, 1859-1920 ***2872.1*** *p3*
Bertelsen, Bertel Kline; Washington, 1859-1920 ***2872.1*** *p4*
Bertelsen, Fay; Washington, 1859-1920 ***2872.1*** *p4*
Bertelsen, James 29; Kansas, 1886 ***5240.1*** *p68*
Berteram Family ; New York, 1765 ***8125.8*** *p436*
Bertet, Francois 22; New Orleans, 1836 ***778.5*** *p47*
Bertha, Dominique 27; New Orleans, 1835 ***778.5*** *p47*
Berthand, Abraham 21; Maryland, 1774 ***1219.7*** *p181*
Berthau, D. 36; New Orleans, 1839 ***778.5*** *p47*
Berthe, Charles 29; New Orleans, 1862 ***543.30*** *p114*
Berthlesen, James C. W. 28; Arkansas, 1918 ***95.2*** *p19*
Berthley, Bernard; Quebec, 1825 ***7603*** *p74*
Berthlot, Mr. 21; Port uncertain, 1838 ***778.5*** *p47*
Berthold, Carl 24; America, 1852 ***3702.7*** *p319*
Berthold, Gebhart; Philadelphia, 1760 ***9973.7*** *p34*
Berthold, Jacob 43; America, 1836 ***778.5*** *p47*
Berthold, Johannette; America, 1845-1847 ***3702.7*** *p320*
Berthold, Wilhelmine 26; New Orleans, 1852 ***3702.7*** *p322*
Bertholdy, Francois 35; America, 1837 ***778.5*** *p47*
Bertholemewe, Hen.; Virginia, 1647 ***6219*** *p241*
Berthonet, Mr. 35; New Orleans, 1839 ***778.5*** *p47*
Berthoud, Mr. 8; New Orleans, 1823 ***778.5*** *p47*
Berti, George; Arkansas, 1918 ***95.2*** *p19*
Bertin, Jules 21; New Orleans, 1839 ***778.5*** *p47*
Bertino, Joe, Jr.; Arkansas, 1918 ***95.2*** *p19*
Bertinsh, Alice 21; America, 1703 ***2212*** *p40*
Bertlinger, Bernard; Kentucky, 1840 ***8582.3*** *p99*
Bertly, James 22; Jamaica, 1735 ***3690.1*** *p18*
Bertman, A. 45; Kansas, 1891 ***5240.1*** *p76*
Bertoin, Vencenzo 37; New York, NY, 1893 ***9026.4*** *p41*
Bertolame, M. 25; America, 1836 ***778.5*** *p47*
Bertold, Frank; Illinois, 1862 ***2896.5*** *p3*
Bertoldo, Girolamo; Iowa, 1866-1943 ***123.54*** *p8*
Berton, William; Virginia, 1646 ***6219*** *p239*
Bertram, Alford 1; America, 1837 ***778.5*** *p48*
Bertram, Charles 27; New Orleans, 1862 ***543.30*** *p327*
Bertram, Charles W. C. A.; New York, NY, 1885 ***2896.5*** *p3*
Bertram, Charlotte 10; America, 1837 ***778.5*** *p48*
Bertram, Charlotte 27; America, 1837 ***778.5*** *p48*
Bertram, Chris Larsen; Arkansas, 1918 ***95.2*** *p19*
Bertram, Johannes; South Carolina, n.d. ***8582.3*** *p79*
Bertram, Marie Anne 6; America, 1837 ***778.5*** *p48*
Bertrand, Mr. 20; New Orleans, 1837 ***778.5*** *p48*
Bertrand, Mr. 23; New Orleans, 1823 ***778.5*** *p48*
Bertrand, D. W.; Washington, 1859-1920 ***2872.1*** *p4*
Bertrand, Etienne 21; America, 1838 ***778.5*** *p50*
Bertrand, J. 25; America, 1829 ***778.5*** *p48*
Bertrand, J. 28; America, 1829 ***778.5*** *p48*
Bertrand, J. P. 27; America, 1829 ***778.5*** *p48*
Bertrand, Jean; Montreal, 1690 ***4533*** *p129*
Bertrand, Jean 45; America, 1820 ***778.5*** *p48*
Bertrand, Joseph; Iroquois Co., IL, 1894 ***3455.1*** *p9*
Bertrand, Joseph 28; America, 1826 ***778.5*** *p48*
Bertrand, Joseph 39; Ohio, 1820 ***778.5*** *p48*
Bertrand, Joseph Hyacinthe 13; Ohio, 1820 ***778.5*** *p48*
Bertrand, Joseph S.; Washington, 1859-1920 ***2872.1*** *p4*
Bertrand, M. Louise 11; Port uncertain, 1839 ***778.5*** *p48*
Bertrand, Madeline 38; Port uncertain, 1839 ***778.5*** *p48*
Bertrand, Mary Hudson; Washington, 1859-1920 ***2872.1*** *p4*
Bertrand, Parfoit D. 17; America, 1838 ***778.5*** *p49*
Bertrand, Zenon; Washington, 1859-1920 ***2872.1*** *p4*
Bertrand-Comte, Mr. 21; New Orleans, 1835 ***778.5*** *p49*
Bertrand-Comte, Mr. 23; New Orleans, 1835 ***778.5*** *p49*
Bertsch, Johannes; Baltimore, 1839 ***8582.3*** *p5*
Bertsch, John; Cincinnati, 1869-1887 ***8582*** *p3*
Bertschinger, Carl; Wisconsin, n.d. ***9675.4*** *p265*
Bertus, Zelia 22; New Orleans, 1827 ***778.5*** *p49*
Berwick, Andrew 16; Jamaica, 1730 ***3690.1*** *p13*
Berwicke, Wm.; Virginia, 1648 ***6219*** *p250*
Bery, Michel 22; America, 1838 ***778.5*** *p49*
Beryshoin, C.; Iowa, 1866-1943 ***123.54*** *p8*
Berzenas, Julius; Wisconsin, n.d. ***9675.4*** *p265*
Besafe, Joseph Hassen; Iowa, 1866-1943 ***123.54*** *p8*
Besafe, Joseph Hassen; Iowa, 1866-1943 ***123.54*** *p57*
Besairdier, Peeter; Virginia, 1640 ***6219*** *p183*
Besairdier, Reene; Virginia, 1640 ***6219*** *p183*
Besancon, . . .; Halifax, N.S., 1752 ***7074.6*** *p232*
Besancon, David *SEE* Besancon, Jean-George
Besancon, Jean-George 44; Halifax, N.S., 1752 ***7074.6*** *p208*
*Wife:*Jeanne
*Child:*Marie
*Child:*Nicolas
*Child:*David
*Child:*Marie-Catherine
*Child:*Marie-Elisabeth
Besancon, Jean George 46; Halifax, N.S., 1752 ***7074.6*** *p207*
With family of 5
Besancon, Jeanne *SEE* Besancon, Jean-George
Besancon, Marie *SEE* Besancon, Jean-George
Besancon, Marie-Catherine *SEE* Besancon, Jean-George
Besancon, Marie-Elisabeth *SEE* Besancon, Jean-George
Besancon, Nicolas *SEE* Besancon, Jean-George
Besch, John; Wisconsin, n.d. ***9675.4*** *p265*
Besch, John Baptist; Wisconsin, n.d. ***9675.4*** *p265*
Besch, Peter; Wisconsin, n.d. ***9675.4*** *p265*
Beschard, . . .; Canada, 1776-1783 ***9786*** *p41*
Bescher, Philipp; Cincinnati, 1869-1887 ***8582*** *p3*
Beschler, . . .; Pennsylvania, 1769 ***4525*** *p265*
Beschler, Christian Ernst; Pennsylvania, 1764 ***4525*** *p200*
Beschong, Johannes; Ohio, 1801-1802 ***8582.2*** *p55*
Bese, J. 31; New Orleans, 1832 ***778.5*** *p49*
Besersen, Otto; New York, NY, 1836 ***8208.4*** *p14*
Besette, . . .; Canada, 1776-1783 ***9786*** *p17*
Beshler, Christian Ernst; Pennsylvania, 1764 ***4525*** *p201*
Besler, Christian Ernst; Pennsylvania, 1764 ***4525*** *p201*
Besler, J. B.; New Orleans, 1839 ***778.5*** *p49*
Besley, Joseph 23; Jamaica, 1774 ***1219.7*** *p184*
Besley, Oliver 26; Jamaica, 1774 ***1219.7*** *p184*

Besley, Walter; Virginia, 1642 ***6219*** *p186*
Besmer, Johann Christoph; Pennsylvania, 1749 ***2444*** *p140*
Besmer, Johann Christoph; Pennsylvania, 1749 ***2444*** *p163*
Besner, . . .; Canada, 1776-1783 ***9786*** *p17*
Besouth, James; Virginia, 1643 ***6219*** *p201*
Besouth, James; Virginia, 1643 ***6219*** *p201*
*Brother:*Samuell
Besouth, Samuell *SEE* Besouth, James
Besre, . . .; Canada, 1776-1783 ***9786*** *p17*
Bessayre, Victor 29; Port uncertain, 1838 ***778.5*** *p49*
Besselmann, . . .; Canada, 1776-1783 ***9786*** *p17*
Bessen, Tho.; Virginia, 1640 ***6219*** *p160*
Besserer, . . .; Canada, 1776-1783 ***9786*** *p17*
Besserer, Mr.; Quebec, 1815 ***9229.18*** *p82*
Besserer, Theodore; Canada, 1776-1783 ***9786*** *p231*
Besseres, Mr.; Canada, 1776-1783 ***9786*** *p232*
Bessett, William; Virginia, 1638 ***6219*** *p122*
Bessey, Joseph Hassen; Iowa, 1866-1943 ***123.54*** *p8*
Bessiere, Mr. 35; New Orleans, 1838 ***778.5*** *p49*
Bessmer, Anna Barbara *SEE* Bessmer, Hans Jerg
Bessmer, Christina *SEE* Bessmer, Hans Jerg
Bessmer, Cordula *SEE* Bessmer, Hans Jerg
Bessmer, Dorothea *SEE* Bessmer, Hans Jerg
Bessmer, Hans Jerg; Pennsylvania, 1750 ***2444*** *p140*
*Wife:*Anna Barbara
*Child:*Johann Caspar
*Child:*Maria Elisabetha
*Child:*Dorothea
*Child:*Christina
*Child:*Cordula
Bessmer, Johann Caspar *SEE* Bessmer, Hans Jerg
Bessmer, Maria Elisabetha *SEE* Bessmer, Hans Jerg
Besson, Mlle. 27; America, 1830 ***778.5*** *p49*
Besson, Mme. 65; America, 1830 ***778.5*** *p49*
Besson, Eleonor 32; Mobile, AL, 1835 ***778.5*** *p49*
Besson, Josef 25; America, 1837 ***778.5*** *p49*
Besson, Louis 50; New Orleans, 1839 ***778.5*** *p49*
Besson, Pierre 17; America, 1837 ***778.5*** *p49*
Besson, Tho.; Virginia, 1638 ***6219*** *p124*
Best, Adam; America, 1848 ***8582.1*** *p3*
Best, Anna Maria 9 mos; America, 1853 ***9162.8*** *p36*
Best, Anton 9; America, 1853 ***9162.8*** *p36*
Best, Dynes; Arkansas, 1918 ***95.2*** *p19*
Best, Georg; Virginia, 1639 ***6219*** *p156*
Best, George; New York, NY, 1811 ***2859.11*** *p8*
Best, Henry; Pennsylvania, 1765 ***4779.3*** *p13*
Best, James 22; Maryland, 1774 ***1219.7*** *p179*
Best, John *SEE* Best, Thomas
Best, John; Philadelphia, 1811 ***2859.11*** *p8*
With family
Best, Margaretha 33; America, 1853 ***9162.8*** *p36*
Best, Maria 7; America, 1853 ***9162.8*** *p36*
Best, Mary *SEE* Best, Thomas
Best, Sebastian 39; America, 1853 ***9162.8*** *p36*
Best, Seragh; New York, NY, 1811 ***2859.11*** *p8*
Best, Simon 11; America, 1853 ***9162.8*** *p36*
Best, Theodor 4; America, 1853 ***9162.8*** *p36*
Best, Thomas *SEE* Best, Thomas
Best, Thomas; Virginia, 1640 ***6219*** *p184*
*Wife:*Mary
*Child:*Thomas
*Child:*John
Best, Wilhelm 26; Pennsylvania, 1738 ***4779.3*** *p13*
Best, William; Pennsylvania, 1765 ***4779.3*** *p13*
Best, Wm.; Virginia, 1643 ***6219*** *p23*
Bestram, Martin; Wisconsin, n.d. ***9675.4*** *p265*
Bestwicke, Attwell; Virginia, 1644 ***6219*** *p232*
Beswick, Geo. G.; Ohio, 1840 ***9892.11*** *p3*
Betasso, Stephen; Colorado, 1889 ***9678.1*** *p154*
Betat, P. 28; America, 1835 ***778.5*** *p50*
Beteilhe, John 30; Jamaica, 1733 ***3690.1*** *p18*
Beteler, Gregory 18; Jamaica, 1729 ***3690.1*** *p18*
Betelier, Teofil; New York, 1831 ***4606*** *p172*
Betfer, Suzanne; Quebec, 1649 ***7603*** *p24*
Beth, Conrad; America, 1853 ***8582.3*** *p5*
Bethake, Dr.; Ohio, 1826 ***8582.2*** *p59*
Bethel, Mary Jane 26; Quebec, 1864 ***5704.8*** *p162*
Bethel, Thomas 26; Quebec, 1864 ***5704.8*** *p162*
Bethell, Peter 17; Windward Islands, 1722 ***3690.1*** *p14*
Bethge, . . .; Canada, 1776-1783 ***9786*** *p17*
Bethke, Frederick; Arkansas, 1918 ***95.2*** *p19*
Bethke, William; Wisconsin, n.d. ***9675.4*** *p265*
Bethone, Jon.; Virginia, 1637 ***6219*** *p8*
Bethune, Mr.; Quebec, 1815 ***9229.18*** *p74*
Bethune, Annabella Jones; Prince Edward Island, 1854 ***8893*** *p266*
Bethune, Catherine 70; North Carolina, 1850 ***1639.20*** *p9*
*Relative:*Sarah 65
Bethune, Colin; Wilmington, NC, 1772 ***1639.20*** *p9*
Bethune, John; Montreal, 1786 ***9775.5*** *p202*
Bethune, John; North Carolina, 1754-1854 ***1639.20*** *p9*
With father
Bethune, John 77; North Carolina, 1850 ***1639.20*** *p9*
Bethune, Murdoch; North Carolina, 1814 ***1639.20*** *p9*
Bethune, Sarah 65 *SEE* Bethune, Catherine
Betram, Etienne 21; America, 1838 ***778.5*** *p50*
Betrik, Anton; Kansas, 1887 ***5240.1*** *p5*
Betteley, Ann 22; Jamaica, 1733 ***3690.1*** *p18*
Bettendorf, William; Wisconsin, n.d. ***9675.4*** *p265*
Betteridge, John 56; Philadelphia, 1774 ***1219.7*** *p217*
Betterson, Christopher 33; Pennsylvania, 1728 ***3690.1*** *p18*
Betterton, Thomas 16; Maryland, 1729 ***3690.1*** *p18*
Bettiason, James 25; Maryland, 1774 ***1219.7*** *p182*
Bettin, Antonio; Iowa, 1866-1943 ***123.54*** *p8*
Bettinger, . . .; America, 1842 ***2691.4*** *p167*
Bettinger, Andreas *SEE* Bettinger, Andreas
Bettinger, Andreas; America, 1750 ***2444*** *p137*
*Wife:*Dorothea Gottschall
*Child:*Maria Dorothea
*Child:*Johann Jacob
*Child:*Andreas
*Child:*Johann Michael
*Child:*Georg Heinrich
Bettinger, Andreas; America, 1750 ***2444*** *p158*
Bettinger, Anna 22; America, 1839 ***778.5*** *p50*
Bettinger, Dorothea Gottschall *SEE* Bettinger, Andreas
Bettinger, Elisabetha V. Seegmuller; North America, 1792-1922 ***2691.4*** *p170*
With 2 sons
Bettinger, Georg Heinrich *SEE* Bettinger, Andreas
Bettinger, Johann Jacob *SEE* Bettinger, Andreas
Bettinger, Johann Michael *SEE* Bettinger, Andreas
Bettinger, Maria Dorothea *SEE* Bettinger, Andreas
Bettinger, Vernard 36; New Orleans, 1864 ***543.30*** *p246*
Bettmann, Frederick; New York, NY, 1840 ***8208.4*** *p103*
Bettmann, Moritz; America, 1840 ***8582.1*** *p3*
Bettmann, Peter; Ohio, 1843 ***8582.1*** *p51*
Bettner, Johann Philipp; Wisconsin, n.d. ***9675.4*** *p265*
Bettner, John; Wisconsin, n.d. ***9675.4*** *p265*
Betts, George; South Carolina, 1752-1753 ***3689.17*** *p21*
With wife
*Relative:*John Michael 9
Betts, James 15; Maryland, 1774 ***1219.7*** *p187*
Betts, John Michael 9 *SEE* Betts, George
Betts, Joseph 15; Maryland, 1720 ***3690.1*** *p19*
Betts, Joshua Ferguson 46; California, 1872 ***2769.2*** *p5*
Betts, Newman 24; Maryland, 1775 ***1219.7*** *p252*
Betty, John 29; Virginia, 1774 ***1219.7*** *p227*
Betz, Andreas; Pennsylvania, 1730-1779 ***2444*** *p140*
Betz, Barbara 3; New Orleans, 1838 ***778.5*** *p50*
Betz, Chatrine 11; New Orleans, 1838 ***778.5*** *p50*
Betz, Franz; America, 1838 ***8582.3*** *p5*
Betz, Heinrich; Ohio, 1801-1802 ***8582.2*** *p55*
Betz, Jean 17; New Orleans, 1838 ***778.5*** *p50*
Betz, Jean Nicolas 48; New Orleans, 1838 ***778.5*** *p50*
Betz, Johannes; Pennsylvania, 1752 ***4525*** *p201*
With family
Betz, John; Wisconsin, n.d. ***9675.4*** *p265*
Betz, Margurite 44; New Orleans, 1838 ***778.5*** *p50*
Betz, Marie 7; New Orleans, 1838 ***778.5*** *p50*
Betz, Matthias; Kentucky, 1869-1887 ***8582*** *p3*
Betz, Nic.; Wisconsin, n.d. ***9675.4*** *p265*
Betz, Nicholas Peter; Wisconsin, n.d. ***9675.4*** *p265*
Betz, Stephen; America, 1832 ***6014.1*** *p1*
Betzen, Barthol 34; Kansas, 1882 ***5240.1*** *p5*
Betzen, Barthol 34; Kansas, 1882 ***5240.1*** *p63*
Betzen, John; Minnesota, 1873 ***5240.1*** *p5*
Betzen, Peter; Minnesota, 1876 ***5240.1*** *p5*
Betzer, Conrad; Ohio, 1798-1818 ***8582.2*** *p53*
Betzner, Anton; Ohio, 1798-1818 ***8582.2*** *p53*
Beukert, . . .; Canada, 1776-1783 ***9786*** *p17*
Beulaygue, Etienne 28; New Orleans, 1838 ***778.5*** *p50*
Beurer, Euphrosina; Pennsylvania, 1752 ***2444*** *p186*
Beuschill, . . .; Canada, 1776-1783 ***9786*** *p17*
Beuschlein, Andreas; America, 1754 ***4525*** *p199*
With wife & child
Beuschlein, Andres; Pennsylvania, 1749 ***4525*** *p199*
Beuschlein, Caspar; Pennsylvania, 1752 ***4525*** *p199*
Beush, W. J.; Kansas, 1873 ***5240.1*** *p5*
Beust, . . .; Canada, 1776-1783 ***9786*** *p17*
Beutel, Elisabetha 3 mos; America, 1853 ***9162.7*** *p14*
Beutel, Elisabetha 30; America, 1853 ***9162.7*** *p14*
Beutel, Frz. Joseph 33; America, 1853 ***9162.7*** *p14*
Beutel, Leonh. 7; America, 1853 ***9162.7*** *p14*
Beutel, Wilhelm; Illinois, 1845 ***8582.2*** *p51*
Beuter, . . .; Canada, 1776-1783 ***9786*** *p17*
Beuth, Runer; Wisconsin, n.d. ***9675.4*** *p265*
Beutin, Charles; Illinois, 1866 ***5012.38*** *p98*
Beuting, Engelbart; Illinois, 1903 ***5012.40*** *p79*
Beuttler, Fred; Iroquois Co., IL, 1896 ***3455.1*** *p9*
Bevan, William; Arkansas, 1918 ***95.2*** *p19*
Bevel, Joseph 32; New Orleans, 1837 ***778.5*** *p50*
Beveridge, Mary 17; Maryland, 1774 ***1219.7*** *p207*
Beverly, Eliza; New York, NY, 1816 ***2859.11*** *p25*
Bevers, John 27; Maryland, 1727 ***3690.1*** *p19*
Beversdorf, Ernest August; Washington, 1859-1920 ***2872.1*** *p4*
Bevins, Patrick; Illinois, 1861 ***2896.5*** *p3*
Bevis, David; America, 1698 ***2212*** *p13*
Bevlan, John; America, 1742 ***4971*** *p83*
Bevsek, Anton; Wisconsin, n.d. ***9675.4*** *p265*
Bewes, William; Georgia, 1775 ***1219.7*** *p274*
With wife
Bewley, Wm.; Indiana, 1850 ***9117*** *p20*
Bewly, Ambrose; Virginia, 1642 ***6219*** *p196*
Bews, Isabel; Savannah, GA, 1774 ***1219.7*** *p227*
Bews, John; Savannah, GA, 1774 ***1219.7*** *p227*
Beyer, . . .; Canada, 1776-1783 ***9786*** *p17*
Beyer, Anna *SEE* Beyer, Johann Jakob
Beyer, Anna Maria; New York, 1752 ***3652*** *p76*
Beyer, Anna Rosina; New York, 1749 ***3652*** *p72*
Beyer, Anthony; California, 1872 ***2769.2*** *p5*
Beyer, Carl; Illinois, 1867 ***2896.5*** *p3*
Beyer, Charles; Illinois, 1866 ***5012.38*** *p98*
Beyer, Conrad Christophe; Canada, 1776-1783 ***9786*** *p243*
Beyer, Elisabeth *SEE* Beyer, Johann Jakob
Beyer, Eva *SEE* Beyer, Johann Jakob
Beyer, Frederick; New York, 1753 ***3652*** *p77*
Beyer, Frederick; Wisconsin, n.d. ***9675.4*** *p265*
Beyer, Friederich *SEE* Beyer, Johann Jakob
Beyer, Geo. Albt.; Canada, 1776-1783 ***9786*** *p207A*
Beyer, George Frederick; Philadelphia, 1758 ***9973.7*** *p33*
Beyer, Jakob *SEE* Beyer, Johann Jakob
Beyer, Johann Jakob; Philadelphia, 1752 ***8582.2*** *p67*
With wife & 12 children
*Child:*Jakob
*Child:*Katharina
*Child:*Anna
*Child:*Elisabeth
*Child:*Eva
*Child:*Friederich
*Child:*Margaretha
Beyer, Mrs. Joseph; Milwaukee, 1875 ***4719.30*** *p257*
Beyer, Katharina *SEE* Beyer, Johann Jakob
Beyer, Margaretha *SEE* Beyer, Johann Jakob
Beyer, Maria; New York, 1749 ***3652*** *p72*
Beyerink, Bernard Albert; Arkansas, 1918 ***95.2*** *p19*
Beyerle, Johann Michael; Pennsylvania, 1730 ***4779.3*** *p13*
Beyersdorfer, John; America, 1888 ***1450.2*** *p3B*
Beyle, . . .; America, 1800-1849 ***8582.3*** *p3*
Beyot, Victor 28; Port uncertain, 1839 ***778.5*** *p50*
Beyreis, Gottfried; Colorado, 1891 ***9678.1*** *p154*
Beys, John 24; North America, 1774 ***1219.7*** *p199*
Beyssert, . . .; Canada, 1776-1783 ***9786*** *p17*
Beytenman, Hans Jerg; Pennsylvania, 1750 ***2444*** *p135*
Bezanson, . . .; Halifax, N.S., 1752 ***7074.6*** *p232*
Bezar, John 60; New Orleans, 1839 ***778.5*** *p50*
Bezard, Jean P. 31; America, 1831 ***778.5*** *p50*
Bezaud, Fs. 18; America, 1837 ***778.5*** *p50*
Bezens, Peter; Wisconsin, n.d. ***9675.4*** *p265*
Bezy, Chery 34; New Orleans, 1836 ***778.5*** *p51*
Bezy, Prosper 37; America, 1838 ***778.5*** *p51*
Bezzak, Josef 24; New York, NY, 1893 ***9026.4*** *p41*
Bialkowski, . . .; New York, 1831 ***4606*** *p172*
Bialoglowski, . . .; New York, 1831 ***4606*** *p172*
Bialozynski, John Frank; Arkansas, 1918 ***95.2*** *p19*
Biamonte, Aimee 12; New Orleans, 1832 ***778.5*** *p51*
Biamonte, Amelia 32; New Orleans, 1832 ***778.5*** *p51*
Biamonte, Antoinette 10; New Orleans, 1832 ***778.5*** *p51*
Bianco-Nino, Luigi 28; New York, NY, 1893 ***9026.4*** *p41*
Bianishi, Nicola 34; West Virginia, 1903 ***9788.3*** *p4*
Biaty, William; Ohio, 1867 ***9892.11*** *p4*
Bibbie, George; South Carolina, 1785 ***1639.20*** *p9*
Bibby, John; Iowa, 1866-1943 ***123.54*** *p9*
Bibby, Mary *SEE* Bibby, William
Bibby, William; Virginia, 1636 ***6219*** *p76*
*Wife:*Mary
Bibend, Franziska; Costa Rica, 1853 ***8582.3*** *p30*
With uncle
Bibend, Franziska; New York, NY, 1857 ***8582.3*** *p31*
Biberon, Mlle.; Port uncertain, 1839 ***778.5*** *p51*
Biberon, Mme.; Port uncertain, 1839 ***778.5*** *p51*
Biberon, M.; Port uncertain, 1839 ***778.5*** *p51*
Biberon, M., Jr.; Port uncertain, 1839 ***778.5*** *p51*
Bibian, Jacob 33; New Orleans, 1862 ***543.30*** *p114*
Bibik, Stefania 17; New York, 1912 ***9980.29*** *p62*
Bichler, Dominic; Wisconsin, n.d. ***9675.4*** *p265*
Bichler, Michael; Wisconsin, n.d. ***9675.4*** *p265*
Bick, Bernard; Baltimore, 1839 ***8582.3*** *p6*
Bick, Bernhard; Cincinnati, 1869-1887 ***8582*** *p3*
Bick, Fr.; Virginia, 1636 ***6219*** *p75*
Bick, Fr.; Virginia, 1638 ***6219*** *p181*
Bick, Richard; Virginia, 1638 ***6219*** *p181*
Bickel, Eduard A.; America, 1849 ***8582.3*** *p6*
Bickel, Friedrich Wilhelm; America, 1854 ***4610.10*** *p121*

Bickel, Marg. Elis. 22; America, 1853 ***9162.7*** *p14*
Bickeler, Anna Maria *SEE* Bickeler, Thomas
Bickeler, Johann Friedrich *SEE* Bickeler, Thomas
Bickeler, Thomas; Carolina, 1752 ***2444*** *p137*
*Wife:*Anna Maria
*Child:*Johann Friedrich
Bickelhaupt, Peter 17; America, 1853 ***9162.7*** *p14*
Bickell, . . .; Canada, 1776-1783 ***9786*** *p17*
Bickenheuser, Philipp; America, 1850 ***8582.2*** *p3*
Bicker, . . .; Canada, 1776-1783 ***9786*** *p17*
Bickert, Nikolaus; Philadelphia, 1779 ***8137*** *p6*
Bickerton, Thomas; New York, NY, 1838 ***8208.4*** *p72*
Bickh, Hans Marx; Pennsylvania, 1750 ***4525*** *p201*
Bicknall, Edward 40; Maryland, 1774 ***1219.7*** *p204*
Bicknell, John 16; St. Christopher, 1720 ***3690.1*** *p19*
Biconnais, Mr. 20; New Orleans, 1837 ***778.5*** *p51*
Bics, John; Arkansas, 1918 ***95.2*** *p19*
Bictou, Mantilly 39; America, 1825 ***778.5*** *p51*
Bidal, A. 35; America, 1832 ***778.5*** *p51*
Biddle, John 25; Philadelphia, 1775 ***1219.7*** *p274*
Biddulph, George; New York, NY, 1836 ***8208.4*** *p19*
Bidemann, George; Pennsylvania, 1750 ***2444*** *p135*
Bidinger, Michael; Wisconsin, n.d. ***9675.4*** *p265*
Bidleman, Leonard; Philadelphia, 1760 ***9973.7*** *p35*
Bidos, Laurent 25; New Orleans, 1836 ***778.5*** *p51*
Bidos, May 28; New Orleans, 1836 ***778.5*** *p51*
Bidot, G. 55; New Orleans, 1827 ***778.5*** *p51*
Bidwell, Richard; New York, NY, 1834 ***8208.4*** *p1*
Bie, Joseph; Wisconsin, n.d. ***9675.4*** *p265*
Bieber, Nicolaus; Cincinnati, 1869-1887 ***8582*** *p3*
Bieber, Nikolaus 28; Port uncertain, 1839 ***778.5*** *p52*
Biech, Peter; Pennsylvania, 1854-1855 ***3702.7*** *p395*
Biedebach, Philip; Philadelphia, 1779 ***8137*** *p6*
Biedenharn, Heinrich; America, 1844 ***8582.2*** *p3*
Biedermann, Gottlieb; Wisconsin, n.d. ***9675.4*** *p265*
Biedermann, Julius; Wisconsin, n.d. ***9675.4*** *p265*
Biedinger, Peter; Cincinnati, 1869-1887 ***8582*** *p3*
Biefel, John Henry; New York, 1743 ***3652*** *p59*
*Wife:*Rosina
Biefel, Rosina *SEE* Biefel, John Henry
Bieg, Elizabeth; New York, 1749 ***3652*** *p72*
Bieg, Peter; Pennsylvania, 1854-1855 ***3702.7*** *p401*
Biehle, Auguste Carol 11 *SEE* Biehle, John Fredk.
Biehle, Fredk. Christopl. 6 *SEE* Biehle, John Fredk.
Biehle, Fredk. Wm. 12 *SEE* Biehle, John Fredk.
Biehle, Henry Ferdinand 2 *SEE* Biehle, John Fredk.
Biehle, Joha. Friederica 6 mos *SEE* Biehle, John Fredk.
Biehle, Johe. Fredke. 36 *SEE* Biehle, John Fredk.
Biehle, John Fredk. 35; New Orleans, 1839 ***9420.2*** *p361*
*Wife:*Johe. Fredke. 36
*Son:*Fredk. Wm. 12
*Daughter:*Auguste Carol 11
*Son:*Fredk. Christopl. 6
*Son:*Henry Ferdinand 2
*Daughter:*Joha. Friederica 6 mos
Biehler, . . .; Canada, 1776-1783 ***9786*** *p17*
Biehler, Johann Gottlieb 17; Halifax, N.S., 1752 ***7074.6*** *p207*
Bielefeld, . . .; Canada, 1776-1783 ***9786*** *p17*
Bielefeld, Johann; Wisconsin, n.d. ***9675.4*** *p265*
Bieler, Heinrich; America, 1828 ***8582.2*** *p61*
Bieler, Heinrich; Cincinnati, 1869-1887 ***8582*** *p3*
Bielfeld, John Christopher 26; North Carolina, 1736 ***3690.1*** *p16*
Bielinky, Abraham; Arkansas, 1918 ***95.2*** *p19*
Biella, John; Colorado, 1904 ***9678.1*** *p154*
Biella, Joseph; Colorado, 1904 ***9678.1*** *p154*
Biella, Peter; Colorado, 1903 ***9678.1*** *p154*
Bielstein, . . .; Canada, 1776-1783 ***9786*** *p17*
Bielstein, Thedel Wilhelm; Quebec, 1776 ***9786*** *p260*
Biemer, Heinrich; Cincinnati, 1829 ***8582.1*** *p51*
Bien, . . .; Pittsburgh, 1882 ***3702.7*** *p475*
Bien, Antoni 20; New York, 1912 ***9980.29*** *p55*
Bien Aime, Mrs. 33; Port uncertain, 1838 ***778.5*** *p52*
Bien Aime, F. 31; Port uncertain, 1838 ***778.5*** *p52*
Biendenbander, Henry; Wisconsin, n.d. ***9675.4*** *p265*
Bienias, . . .; New York, 1831 ***4606*** *p172*
Bienkowska, Michalina; New York, 1912 ***9980.29*** *p48*
Bienkowska, Michalina 19; New York, 1912 ***9980.29*** *p64*
Bienlien, Jacob; Wisconsin, n.d. ***9675.4*** *p265*
Biennomme, . . .; Canada, 1776-1783 ***9786*** *p17*
Bienvigned, Maurice 25; New Orleans, 1862 ***543.30*** *p111*
Bier, I.H.; Indiana, 1849 ***9117*** *p16*
Bierbaum, Ernst; Cincinnati, 1836-1843 ***3702.7*** *p79*
Bierbrod, Johann; Ohio, 1881 ***3702.7*** *p441*
Bierbroth, Mrs. Johann; Ohio, 1881 ***3702.7*** *p436*
Bierbroth, Johann; Ohio, 1881 ***3702.7*** *p436*
Bierchem, Martin; Wisconsin, n.d. ***9675.4*** *p265*
Biere, . . .; America, n.d. ***8582.3*** *p79*
Biere, Fr. W.; America, 1847 ***8582.1*** *p3*
Bieren, Anna Catherine; South Carolina, 1752-1753 ***3689.17*** *p21*
Biermacher, Peter, Family; America, 1818-1923 ***2691.4*** *p172*
Biermann, August; Cincinnati, 1869-1887 ***8582*** *p3*
Biernacki, . . .; New York, 1831 ***4606*** *p172*
Biernartos, Mr.; Port uncertain, 1836 ***778.5*** *p44*
Bierstadt, Albert; New Bedford, MA, 1833 ***8125.8*** *p435*
Bierstadt, Albert 2; New Bedford, MA, 1832 ***8582*** *p3*
With father & family
Biese, Philipp; Philadelphia, 1779 ***8137*** *p6*
Biesehke, Frank; Wisconsin, n.d. ***9675.4*** *p265*
Biesserner, Peter; Wisconsin, n.d. ***9675.4*** *p265*
Bietner, Daniel; Ohio, 1800 ***8582.2*** *p55*
Biever, John; Wisconsin, n.d. ***9675.4*** *p265*
Biever, Nicholas; Wisconsin, n.d. ***9675.4*** *p265*
Biever, Peter; Wisconsin, n.d. ***9675.4*** *p265*
Biezer, Lucia; Pennsylvania, 1750 ***2444*** *p139*
Biezer, Lucia; Pennsylvania, 1750 ***2444*** *p219*
Bifeld, Mr. 41; America, 1837 ***778.5*** *p52*
Biffeild, Sarah; Virginia, 1640 ***6219*** *p185*
Bigby, Thomas 28; Tobago, W. Indies, 1775 ***1219.7*** *p251*
Bigelow, Daniel; New York, NY, 1840 ***8208.4*** *p106*
Bigey, A. 30; America, 1839 ***778.5*** *p52*
Bigg, DeWitt Clinton 35; California, 1872 ***2769.1*** *p5*
Bigg, Elinor; Virginia, 1648 ***6219*** *p252*
Bigg, Sarah 19; Pennsylvania, 1739 ***3690.1*** *p19*
Bigg, William 20; Maryland, 1774 ***1219.7*** *p192*
Biggart, Robert; Philadelphia, 1852 ***5704.8*** *p96*
Bigger, John; America, 1849 ***1450.2*** *p14A*
Biggs, Alexander 15; Philadelphia, 1775 ***1219.7*** *p248*
Biggs, Francis; Virginia, 1638 ***6219*** *p122*
Biggs, John 18; Windward Islands, 1722 ***3690.1*** *p19*
Biggs, Rich.; Virginia, 1637 ***6219*** *p115*
Biggs, Richard 21; Maryland, 1775 ***1219.7*** *p262*
Biggs, Sarah 19; Pennsylvania, 1739 ***3690.1*** *p19*
Bighill, John; Virginia, 1647 ***6219*** *p241*
Bigley, Billy; St. John, N.B., 1849 ***5704.8*** *p55*
Biglow, John; Washington, 1859-1920 ***2872.1*** *p4*
Bignall, Grace 17; Virginia, 1719 ***3690.1*** *p19*
Bignall, Robert; Virginia, 1754 ***1219.7*** *p27*
Bignell, Christine; Quebec, 1753 ***7603*** *p26*
Bignell, Jane 47; Carolina, 1774 ***1219.7*** *p231*
Bigney, . . .; Halifax, N.S., 1752 ***7074.6*** *p232*
Bignon, Joseph N.; Michigan, 1873 ***2764.35*** *p4*
Bigourdan, Mr. 22; America, 1837 ***778.5*** *p52*
Bigsby, Robert 25; Virginia, 1730 ***3690.1*** *p289*
Bigue, Mr. 30; Port uncertain, 1838 ***778.5*** *p52*
Biguenet, . . .; Halifax, N.S., 1752 ***7074.6*** *p232*
Biguenet, Jacques 22; Halifax, N.S., 1752 ***7074.6*** *p208*
Bijo, Moise Joseph; Arkansas, 1918 ***95.2*** *p19*
Bikakis, Myron; Arkansas, 1918 ***95.2*** *p19*
Biker, Ann; Virginia, 1643 ***6219*** *p200*
Bilbey, Jon.; Virginia, 1647 ***6219*** *p241*
Bilbie, Margaret; Virginia, 1628 ***6219*** *p31*
Bilcliffe, Richard; Virginia, 1637 ***6219*** *p112*
Bilecki, Anton 20; New York, 1912 ***9980.29*** *p64*
Bilello, Joe; Arkansas, 1918 ***95.2*** *p20*
Biles, William 18; Maryland, 1774 ***1219.7*** *p207*
Bileskie, Charles; Illinois, 1867 ***5012.38*** *p98*
Bilesnaskiy, Andreas; Colorado, 1891 ***9678.1*** *p154*
Bilger, Felix; Illinois, 1896 ***5012.40*** *p54*
Bilier, Margaretha 33; America, 1838 ***778.5*** *p52*
Bilinski, . . .; New York, 1831 ***4606*** *p172*
Bilinsky, Theodore; Wisconsin, n.d. ***9675.4*** *p265*
Bill, Johann; America, 1846 ***8582.2*** *p3*
Bill, Walter; Virginia, 1636 ***6219*** *p79*
Bill, Walter; Virginia, 1637 ***6219*** *p116*
Billac, Jean-Pierre 31; Port uncertain, 1838 ***778.5*** *p52*
Billahea, Neale; Virginia, 1642 ***6219*** *p192*
Billan, Mary; Virginia, 1638 ***6219*** *p8*
Billau, Adam; New York, NY, 1844 ***8582*** *p3*
Billberg, Henning; Iowa, 1866-1943 ***123.54*** *p9*
Billbrough, John; New York, NY, 1834 ***8208.4*** *p27*
Billbrough, Will.; Virginia, 1634 ***6219*** *p84*
Billen, E.gene 22; Ohio, 1837 ***778.5*** *p52*
Biller, . . .; Canada, 1776-1783 ***9786*** *p17*
Biller, George; Arizona, 1898 ***9228.30*** *p6*
Billesimo, John; Iowa, 1866-1943 ***123.54*** *p9*
Billeskov, Anna; Wisconsin, n.d. ***9675.4*** *p265*
Billeskov, Carl Hed Nielsen; Wisconsin, n.d. ***9675.4*** *p265*
Billhard, . . .; Canada, 1776-1783 ***9786*** *p17*
Billiaud, Antoinesse 12; America, 1839 ***778.5*** *p52*
Billiaud, Maria 10; America, 1839 ***778.5*** *p52*
Billiaud, Maria 33; America, 1839 ***778.5*** *p52*
Billigheimer, Joseph; Cincinnati, 1869-1887 ***8582*** *p3*
Billigheimer, Joseph; New York, NY, 1841-1845 ***8582.1*** *p3*
Billin, Michaell; Virginia, 1642 ***6219*** *p192*
Billing, Adolphus E.; Boston, 1853 ***6410.32*** *p124*
Billing, John Goerg Fr.; Wisconsin, n.d. ***9675.4*** *p265*
Billing, Michael; Louisville, KY, 1869-1887 ***8582*** *p3*
Billinge, James; New York, NY, 1834 ***8208.4*** *p77*
Billinghurst, Matthew 26; Jamaica, 1735 ***3690.1*** *p19*
Billings, Adolph 28; Massachusetts, 1860 ***6410.32*** *p111*
Billings, August 24; Massachusetts, 1860 ***6410.32*** *p112*
Billings, Caroline 23; Massachusetts, 1860 ***6410.32*** *p111*
Billings, Jon.; Virginia, 1636 ***6219*** *p32*
Billings, M. E.; Washington, 1859-1920 ***2872.1*** *p4*
Billings, Sophia 32; Massachusetts, 1860 ***6410.32*** *p116*
Billings, William; Pensacola, FL, 1767 ***1219.7*** *p129*
Billingsleley, Alexander; Philadelphia, 1864 ***5704.8*** *p178*
Billington, Charles; Colorado, 1894 ***9678.1*** *p154*
Billins, John; Virginia, 1638 ***6219*** *p181*
Billiods, Friedrich; New York, NY, 1822 ***8582.1*** *p41*
Billiods, Friedrich; Ohio, 1843 ***8582.1*** *p51*
Billion, . . .; Canada, 1776-1783 ***9786*** *p17*
Billisfeld, Frank J.; Illinois, 1891 ***5012.37*** *p62*
Billman, Henry L.; Kansas, 1886 ***5240.1*** *p5*
Billmann, Henry L. 21; Kansas, 1886 ***5240.1*** *p69*
Billmyer, Jacob; Philadelphia, 1750 ***9973.7*** *p31*
Billtstein, Herm; Ohio, 1881 ***3702.7*** *p438*
Billus, Samuel; Virginia, 1775 ***1219.7*** *p275*
Bilou, Louis 16; New Orleans, 1863 ***543.30*** *p247*
Bilsborrow, Robert; New York, NY, 1834 ***8208.4*** *p31*
Bilsland, Thomas 36; Quebec, 1857 ***5704.8*** *p136*
Binaud, Joseph 40; New Orleans, 1837 ***778.5*** *p52*
Binck, Michael; Wisconsin, n.d. ***9675.4*** *p265*
Binder, . . .; Canada, 1776-1783 ***9786*** *p17*
Binder, Albert; Wisconsin, n.d. ***9675.4*** *p265*
Binder, Anna Barbara; Pennsylvania, 1740-1800 ***2444*** *p170*
Binder, Catherine; New York, 1749 ***3652*** *p72*
Binder, Dorothea; South Dakota, 1889 ***1641*** *p41*
Binder, Jakob; South Dakota, 1889 ***1641*** *p41*
Binder, Martin; Philadelphia, 1763 ***9973.7*** *p39*
Bindgi, F. 39; Port uncertain, 1838 ***778.5*** *p52*
Bindler, Jacob, Jr.; South Carolina, 1788 ***7119*** *p204*
Bindler, Jacob, Sr.; South Carolina, 1788 ***7119*** *p204*
Bindner, Franz 26; America, 1839 ***778.5*** *p53*
Bineker, Christiana 10 *SEE* Bineker, John Frederick
Bineker, John Frederick 35; Georgia, 1738 ***9332*** *p331*
*Daughter:*Christiana 10
*Son:*John Urich 7
Bineker, John Urich 7 *SEE* Bineker, John Frederick
Bing, Jon.; Virginia, 1635 ***6219*** *p10*
Bingham, Charles 22; Jamaica, 1734 ***3690.1*** *p19*
Bingham, James 22; Kansas, 1875 ***5240.1*** *p56*
Bingham, Samuell 28; Jamaica, 1736 ***3690.1*** *p19*
Bingham, Solomon 21; Kansas, 1875 ***5240.1*** *p5*
Bingham, Solomon 21; Kansas, 1875 ***5240.1*** *p56*
Bingham, Thomas 21; Kansas, 1876 ***5240.1*** *p57*
Bingham, Thomas 54; Kansas, 1875 ***5240.1*** *p56*
Bingham, William; America, 1742 ***4971*** *p69*
Bingham, William 14; Philadelphia, 1803 ***53.26*** *p4*
Bingham, William J.; Colorado, 1906 ***9678.1*** *p154*
Binghart, Catherine 6 *SEE* Binghart, John Adam
Binghart, George 9 mos *SEE* Binghart, John Adam
Binghart, George Michael 9 *SEE* Binghart, John Adam
Binghart, John Adam; South Carolina, 1752-1753 ***3689.17*** *p21*
*Relative:*John Matthew 18
*Relative:*Mary Margaret 11
*Relative:*George Michael 9
*Relative:*Catherine 6
*Relative:*George 9 mos
Binghart, John Matthew 18 *SEE* Binghart, John Adam
Binghart, Mary Margaret 11 *SEE* Binghart, John Adam
Bingle, Joseph 26; Jamaica, 1736 ***3690.1*** *p19*
Bingler, Konrad 82; Buffalo, NY, 1904 ***3763*** *p40C*
Bingley, Edward; Boston, 1757 ***1219.7*** *p55*
Bingley, William 18; New York, 1775 ***1219.7*** *p246*
Bink, Michael; Wisconsin, n.d. ***9675.4*** *p265*
Binker, Anton; Illinois, 1875 ***8582.2*** *p51*
Binki, Christian; Wisconsin, n.d. ***9675.4*** *p265*
Binks, George 22; Virginia, 1774 ***1219.7*** *p193*
Binley, Mr.; Quebec, 1815 ***9229.18*** *p82*
Binly, John; St. John, N.B., 1852 ***5704.8*** *p93*
Binnage, Moses; Indiana, 1848 ***9117*** *p15*
Binne, Thomas; New York, NY, 1816 ***2859.11*** *p25*
Binnel, Felix 36; America, 1825 ***778.5*** *p53*
Binney, Bridget; America, 1868 ***5704.8*** *p231*
Binney, Catharine; America, 1868 ***5704.8*** *p231*
Binnicker, Charles; South Carolina, 1788 ***7119*** *p202*
Binnicker, Charles; South Carolina, 1788 ***7119*** *p203*
Binnz, Joseph; Wisconsin, n.d. ***9675.4*** *p265*
Binoche, Mr. 38; New Orleans, 1839 ***778.5*** *p53*
Binoche, Mr. 40; America, 1838 ***778.5*** *p53*
Binot, Chatrine 18; Port uncertain, 1839 ***778.5*** *p53*
Binot, Marie 27; Port uncertain, 1839 ***778.5*** *p53*
Binquet, Claude 22; Louisiana, 1820 ***778.5*** *p53*
Bins, Valentin 24; America, 1838 ***778.5*** *p53*
Binsteed, John; Virginia, 1600-1642 ***6219*** *p193*
Biosiui, Torindo; Arkansas, 1918 ***95.2*** *p20*
Biot, Mr. 24; New Orleans, 1821 ***778.5*** *p53*
Biot, P. 46; America, 1835 ***778.5*** *p53*

32 *FOR A COMPLETE EXPLANATION OF ENTRY, SEE "HOW TO READ A CITATION" SECTION*

Biot, Pierre 31; America, 1838 *778.5 p53*
Biot, Pierre 36; America, 1823 *778.5 p53*
Birabon, Mr. 22; Louisiana, 1820 *778.5 p53*
Birac, Jean Desire 26; America, 1838 *778.5 p53*
Birbeck, William 16; Jamaica, 1774 *1219.7 p236*
Birch, Anne 20; Virginia, 1700 *2212 p32*
Birch, Geo.; Virginia, 1638 *6219 p117*
Birch, John; Jamaica, 1773 *1219.7 p167*
Birch, William 27; Maryland, 1775 *1219.7 p257*
Birchard, G. W.; Washington, 1859-1920 *2872.1 p4*
Birchard, G. W.; Washington, 1859-1920 *2872.1 p5*
Birchem, Jacob; Wisconsin, n.d. *9675.4 p265*
Birchenough, James 25; Virginia, 1699 *2212 p26*
Birckmayer, Maria Catharina; Pennsylvania, 1749 *2444 p138*
   With 8 children
Bird, Andrew 18; Virginia, 1700 *2212 p32*
Bird, Ashwell; Virginia, 1642 *6219 p198*
Bird, Charles 22; Massachusetts, 1848 *5881.1 p6*
Bird, Edward 26; Philadelphia, 1775 *1219.7 p274*
Bird, Hannah 20; St. Christopher, 1722 *3690.1 p19*
Bird, James 24; Maryland, 1774 *1219.7 p192*
Bird, Jno; America, 1698 *2212 p6*
Bird, John 16; Philadelphia, 1774 *1219.7 p175*
Bird, John 20; Maryland, 1735 *3690.1 p19*
Bird, John 29; Grenada, 1774 *1219.7 p180*
Bird, M. F.; Washington, 1859-1920 *2872.1 p4*
Bird, Mary; New York, NY, 1811 *2859.11 p8*
Bird, Mary 26; Maryland, 1774 *1219.7 p213*
Bird, Oliver; America, 1741 *4971 p99*
Bird, Peter 32; New Orleans, 1864 *543.30 p249*
Bird, Peter 50; Massachusetts, 1850 *5881.1 p11*
Bird, Richard; Virginia, 1636 *6219 p79*
Bird, Richard; Virginia, 1642 *6219 p194*
Bird, Samuel 20; Philadelphia, 1775 *1219.7 p255*
Bird, Stephen 18; Jamaica, 1734 *3690.1 p19*
Bird, Susan; Virginia, 1642 *6219 p186*
Bird, Thomas; New York, NY, 1811 *2859.11 p8*
Bird, Thomas 35; Antigua (Antego), 1734 *3690.1 p20*
Bird, William; Virginia, 1635 *6219 p71*
Bird, William 29; Virginia, 1774 *1219.7 p243*
Bird, Wm.; Virginia, 1635 *6219 p20*
Birdon, Mr. 30; America, 1838 *778.5 p53*
Bireley, Johann Michael; Pennsylvania, 1753 *4779.3 p13*
Birillion, Clode 46; Port uncertain, 1837 *778.5 p54*
Birk, Eliza; New York, NY, 1811 *2859.11 p8*
Birk, John; New York, NY, 1811 *2859.11 p8*
Birk, John; Philadelphia, 1815 *2859.11 p25*
Birkel, Johann; Kentucky, 1844 *8582.3 p101*
Birkel, John 18; Kansas, 1906 *5240.1 p84*
Birkett, John; Colorado, 1900 *9678.1 p154*
Birkhead, George 18; Jamaica, 1719 *3690.1 p20*
Birkhold, Lorenz August 38; New Orleans, 1862 *543.30 p115*
Birkholz, John; Wisconsin, n.d. *9675.4 p265*
Birkle, Joseph; America, 1849 *8582.3 p6*
Birkle, Mathias; Kentucky, 1840-1845 *8582.3 p100*
Birkleoff, R.; Washington, 1859-1920 *2872.1 p4*
Birkmaier, Anna Catharina SEE Birkmaier, Ludwig
Birkmaier, Anna Maria SEE Birkmaier, Ludwig
Birkmaier, Catharina Barbara SEE Birkmaier, Ludwig
Birkmaier, Johann Daniel; Pennsylvania, 1749 *2444 p138*
Birkmaier, Ludwig; Pennsylvania, 1749 *2444 p138*
   Sister:Catharina Barbara
   Sister:Anna Catharina
   Sister:Anna Maria
Birleck, P.W. 18; St. Kitts, 1774 *1219.7 p184*
Birley, Michael; Pennsylvania, 1730 *4779.3 p13*
Birmingham, Biddy 13; Massachusetts, 1849 *5881.1 p6*
Birmingham, Bridget 20; Massachusetts, 1849 *5881.1 p6*
Birmingham, Margaret 10; Massachusetts, 1849 *5881.1 p10*
Birmingham, Mary 1; Massachusetts, 1849 *5881.1 p10*
Birmingham, Michael 25; Massachusetts, 1850 *5881.1 p11*
Birmingham, Pat 12; Massachusetts, 1849 *5881.1 p11*
Birmingham, Thomas; New York, NY, 1838 *8208.4 p84*
Birn, Laughlin 21; Philadelphia, 1774 *1219.7 p233*
Birnbaum, Joachim; New York, 1749 *3652 p71*
Birnbaum, Joseph; New York, 1851 *1450.2 p14A*
Birnbryer, Adolph; America, 1849 *8582.3 p6*
Birner, Michael; Wisconsin, n.d. *9675.4 p265*
Birney, Margaret; St. John, N.B., 1853 *5704.8 p106*
Birney, Patrick; America, 1866 *5704.8 p209*
Birnie, George; Charleston, SC, 1818 *1639.20 p10*
Birnie, George 36; New York, NY, 1828 *6508.4 p143*
Birnie, John; Charleston, SC, 1828 *1639.20 p10*
Birnie, William 48; Charleston, SC, 1850 *1639.20 p10*
Birns, Barney; Baltimore, 1811 *2859.11 p8*
Birns, Rose Ann 18; Philadelphia, 1854 *5704.8 p120*
Biron, Pierre 21; New Orleans, 1822 *778.5 p54*
Birritella, Salvatore; Arkansas, 1918 *95.2 p20*

Birscher, . . .; Canada, 1776-1783 *9786 p17*
Birsinger, Frank Joseph 30; Kansas, 1884 *5240.1 p65*
Birt, Joseph 17; Jamaica, 1736 *3690.1 p20*
Birth, Martha; Wisconsin, n.d. *9675.4 p265*
Bisaker, Ambrose; Florida, 1766 *1219.7 p120*
Bisancon, Josephine 28; America, 1837 *778.5 p54*
Bisch, Chas. Joseph; Wisconsin, n.d. *9675.4 p265*
Bischel, Henry; Illinois, 1875 *2896.5 p3*
Bischhausen, E. von; New York, 1776 *9786 p278*
Bischof, Heinrich; Georgia, 1739 *9332 p326*
Bischof, Ludwig, Family; America, 1812-1923 *2691.4 p171*
Bischoff, . . .; Canada, 1776-1783 *9786 p17*
Bischoff, Mrs. 39; America, 1875 *4610.10 p124*
   Child:Adolf 9
   Child:Marie 6
Bischoff, Adolf 9 SEE Bischoff, Mrs.
Bischoff, Anna Catherine SEE Bischoff, David
Bischoff, David; Philadelphia, 1742 *3652 p55*
   Wife:Anna Catherine
Bischoff, Marie 6 SEE Bischoff, Mrs.
Bisckoft, George 31; Kansas, 1876 *5240.1 p56*
Biscoe, Mathew; Virginia, 1643 *6219 p200*
Bise, August 30; New Orleans, 1862 *543.30 p481*
Bisette, Claudine; Halifax, N.S., 1752 *7074.6 p216*
Bishline, Casper; Pennsylvania, 1752 *4525 p199*
Bishoffen, Mrs. 39; Georgia, 1738 *9332 p333*
Bishop, . . .; Canada, 1776-1783 *9786 p17*
Bishop, Ann 21; Maryland, 1775 *1219.7 p267*
Bishop, Francis Michael; Philadelphia, 1760 *9973.7 p35*
Bishop, Henry; Virginia, 1646 *6219 p240*
Bishop, J.H. 63; Arizona, 1925 *9228.40 p29*
Bishop, Jane Elizabeth Ogilvie; America, 1847 *8893 p264*
Bishop, John; New York, NY, 1811 *2859.11 p8*
   With wife
Bishop, John; Philadelphia, 1759 *9973.7 p34*
Bishop, John 21; Jamaica, 1736 *3690.1 p20*
Bishop, Joseph; California, 1886 *2764.35 p7*
Bishop, Margt 25; New England, 1699 *2212 p19*
Bishop, Robert; Illinois, 1905 *5012.37 p63*
Bishop, Sebone; Virginia, 1652 *6251 p20*
Bishop, Thomas 19; Philadelphia, 1775 *1219.7 p255*
Bishop, Thomas 21; Maryland, 1774 *1219.7 p181*
Bishopp, Ferdinando; Virginia, 1643 *6219 p204*
Bishopp, John; Virginia, 1643 *6219 p204*
   With wife
Bishopp, Jon.; Virginia, 1638 *6219 p149*
Bishopp, Oliver; Virginia, 1636 *6219 p74*
Bishopp, Walter; Virginia, 1643 *6219 p207*
Bishopp, William; Virginia, 1641 *6219 p184*
Bishoppe, Oliver; Virginia, 1637 *6219 p108*
Bisinger, Anna Magdalena SEE Bisinger, Hans Jerg
Bisinger, Anna Weiss SEE Bisinger, Hans Jerg
Bisinger, Hans Jerg; Pennsylvania, 1748-1800 *2444 p138*
   Wife:Anna Weiss
   Child:Anna Magdalena
   Child:Johann Jacob
Bisinger, Johann Jacob SEE Bisinger, Hans Jerg
Bisley, Franc.; Virginia, 1635 *6219 p17*
Bisley, Wm.; Virginia, 1642 *6219 p199*
Bisole, James; Virginia, 1647 *6219 p245*
Bissantz, G. Fred 26; Kansas, 1889 *5240.1 p5*
Bissantz, G. Fred 26; Kansas, 1889 *5240.1 p74*
Bissantz, Jacob 25; Kansas, 1872 *5240.1 p5*
Bissantz, Jacob 25; Kansas, 1872 *5240.1 p52*
Bissantz, Louis 23; Kansas, 1882 *5240.1 p5*
Bissell, Thomas 17; Philadelphia, 1774 *1219.7 p233*
Bisseron, A. 30; Port uncertain, 1836 *778.5 p54*
Bisseron, J. 32; Port uncertain, 1836 *778.5 p54*
Bisset, Catharine Munro SEE Bisset, Donald
Bisset, Donald; America, 1840 *8893 p266*
   Wife:Catharine Munro
Bissett, Eliza; New York, NY, 1864 *5704.8 p169*
Bissett, James; Illinois, 1846 *7857 p2*
Bissett, William; Charleston, SC, 1754 *1639.20 p10*
Bissey, Anthony 18; Pennsylvania, 1728 *3690.1 p20*
Bissikunor, Mr. 18; America, 1838 *778.5 p54*
Bisson, Philippe; Quebec, 1821 *7603 p48*
Biste, Jacinthe 31; Louisiana, 1839 *778.5 p54*
Biste, Rose 40; Louisiana, 1839 *778.5 p54*
Bisterfeld, Anna 5; New York, NY, 1878 *9253 p47*
Bisterfeld, Carl 10 mos; New York, NY, 1878 *9253 p47*
Bisterfeld, Carl 31; New York, NY, 1878 *9253 p47*
Bisterfeld, Christian 4; New York, NY, 1878 *9253 p47*
Bisterfeld, Marie 10 mos; New York, NY, 1878 *9253 p47*
Bisterfeld, Marie 25; New York, NY, 1878 *9253 p47*
Bistournel, John; New York, NY, 1836 *8208.4 p15*
Bitar, Abdo; Washington, 1859-1920 *2872.1 p4*
Bitar, Saleem A.; Washington, 1859-1920 *2872.1 p4*
Bithin, Mary 18; Virginia, 1720 *3690.1 p20*
Bitinger, Andreas; Pennsylvania, 1751 *2444 p137*

Bitinger, Andreas; Pennsylvania, 1751 *2444 p196*
Bitsch, Leonard; New York, NY, 1837 *8208.4 p53*
Bitsch, Wilhelm 18; America, 1853 *9162.7 p14*
Bittel, Jacob; New York, NY, 1838 *8208.4 p61*
Bitter, Peter; America, 1849 *8582.3 p6*
Bitterlich, J. G.; New York, 1748 *3652 p68*
Bitterwolf, George 42; New Orleans, 1862 *543.30 p108*
Bittick, John 38; California, 1872 *2769.1 p5*
Bitting, John; Philadelphia, 1760 *9973.7 p35*
Bittinger, Henry; Pennsylvania, 1769 *9973.8 p32*
Bittinger, Nicholas; Pennsylvania, 1768 *9973.8 p32*
Bittle, George; Pennsylvania, 1752 *4525 p204*
Bittner, John; Wisconsin, n.d. *9675.4 p265*
Bittner, Martha; Wisconsin, n.d. *9675.4 p265*
Bitzer, Agnes SEE Bitzer, Ludwig
Bitzer, Anna SEE Bitzer, Ludwig
Bitzer, Anna Maria SEE Bitzer, Hans Baltes
Bitzer, Anna Maria SEE Bitzer, Ludwig
Bitzer, Anna Maria SEE Bitzer, Ludwig
Bitzer, Dorothea SEE Bitzer, Hans Baltes
Bitzer, Dorothea Haerter SEE Bitzer, Hans Baltes
Bitzer, Friedrich SEE Bitzer, Ludwig
Bitzer, Hans Baltes; Pennsylvania, 1746 *2444 p138*
   Wife:Dorothea Haerter
   Child:Anna Maria
   Child:Sibylla
   Child:Dorothea
   Child:Ursula
Bitzer, Hans Balthass; Pennsylvania, 1746 *2444 p138*
Bitzer, Jakob, Sr.; South Dakota, 1889 *1641 p41*
Bitzer, Johann Jacob; Port uncertain, 1750-1800 *2444 p138*
Bitzer, Johanna; South Dakota, 1889 *1641 p41*
Bitzer, Johannes SEE Bitzer, Ludwig
Bitzer, Johannes; Pennsylvania, 1750 *2444 p139*
Bitzer, Lucia; Pennsylvania, 1750 *2444 p139*
Bitzer, Ludwig SEE Bitzer, Ludwig
Bitzer, Ludwig; Pennsylvania, 1750 *2444 p139*
   Wife:Anna Maria
   Child:Agnes
   Child:Ludwig
   Child:Johannes
   Child:Friedrich
   Child:Anna Maria
   Child:Anna
Bitzer, Sibylla SEE Bitzer, Hans Baltes
Bitzer, Simeon; South Dakota, 1889 *1641 p41*
Bitzer, Ursula SEE Bitzer, Hans Baltes
Bivins, Margarett; Virginia, 1642 *6219 p198*
Bix, Johannes; America, 1727-1800 *2444 p139*
Bixby, Mathias, Jr.; Washington, 1859-1920 *2872.1 p4*
Bize, Mathieu 25; America, 1837 *778.5 p54*
Bizer, Anna Maria SEE Bizer, Hans Baltes
Bizer, Dorothea SEE Bizer, Hans Baltes
Bizer, Dorothea Hearter SEE Bizer, Hans Baltes
Bizer, Hans Baltes; Pennsylvania, 1746 *2444 p138*
   Wife:Dorothea Hearter
   Child:Anna Maria
   Child:Sibylla
   Child:Dorothea
   Child:Ursula
Bizer, Sibylla SEE Bizer, Hans Baltes
Bizer, Ursula SEE Bizer, Hans Baltes
Bizet, Anne-Catherine SEE Bizet, Jacques
Bizet, Claudine SEE Bizet, Jacques
Bizet, Eleonore SEE Bizet, Jacques
Bizet, Jacques 43; Halifax, N.S., 1752 *7074.6 p208*
   Wife:Anne-Catherine
   Daughter:Eleonore
   With daughter
   Son:Jean-George 17
   Daughter:Claudine
Bizet, Jean 28; Montreal, 1697 *7603 p26*
Bizet, Jean-George 17 SEE Bizet, Jacques
Bizewski, Adolph 19; New York, 1912 *9980.29 p51*
Bizotat, A. 39; New Orleans, 1835 *778.5 p54*
Bjaring, Fridrikka 29 SEE Bjaring, Hans
Bjaring, Hans 6 SEE Bjaring, Hans
Bjaring, Hans 33; Quebec, 1879 *2557.1 p22*
   Relative:Fridrikka 29
   Relative:Hans 6
   Relative:Malfridur 4
   Relative:Sveinn
Bjaring, Malfridur 4 SEE Bjaring, Hans
Bjaring, Sveinn SEE Bjaring, Hans
Bjarn, . . .; Newfoundland, n.d. *8582.3 p79*
Bjarnadottir, Anna 11; Quebec, 1879 *2557.1 p39*
Bjarnason, Geirmundur 10; Quebec, 1879 *2557.1 p39*
Bjarnason, Gunnar 9; Quebec, 1879 *2557.1 p39*
Bjarnason, Halldor 1; Quebec, 1879 *2557.1 p38A*
Bjarnason, Jon 47; Quebec, 1879 *2557.1 p38A*
Bjarnason, Kristinn 17; Quebec, 1879 *2557.1 p38A*

Bjarnason, Tomas 9; Quebec, 1879 ***2557.1*** *p39A*
Bjelland, Hans Ottosan; Washington, 1859-1920 ***2872.1*** *p4*
Bjelland, Knut; Arkansas, 1918 ***95.2*** *p20*
Bjelland, Martin; Washington, 1859-1920 ***2872.1*** *p4*
Bjening, Wilhelm Ludvig; Arkansas, 1918 ***95.2*** *p20*
Bjerga, Bernhart; Arkansas, 1918 ***95.2*** *p20*
Bjerkness, Martin; Arkansas, 1918 ***95.2*** *p20*
Bjerring, Fridrikka 29 *SEE* Bjerring, Hans
Bjerring, Hans 6 *SEE* Bjerring, Hans
Bjerring, Hans 33; Quebec, 1879 ***2557.1*** *p22*
*Relative:*Fridrikka 29
*Relative:*Hans 6
*Relative:*Malfridur 4
*Relative:*Sveinn
Bjerring, Hans Peter; Arkansas, 1918 ***95.2*** *p20*
Bjerring, Malfridur 4 *SEE* Bjerring, Hans
Bjerring, Sveinn *SEE* Bjerring, Hans
Bjonstrom, Z.; Washington, 1859-1920 ***2872.1*** *p4*
Bjorck, John; Maine, 1887-1892 ***6410.22*** *p120*
Bjork, Andrew; Minneapolis, 1869-1884 ***6410.35*** *p50*
Bjorklund, Peter; Illinois, 1882 ***5012.39*** *p52*
Bjorkquist, Otto D.; Wisconsin, n.d. ***9675.4*** *p265*
Bjornker, Arne; Arkansas, 1918 ***95.2*** *p20*
Bjornsdottir, Bjorg 4; Quebec, 1879 ***2557.1*** *p20*
Bjornsdottir, Gudrun 30; Quebec, 1879 ***2557.1*** *p38A*
Bjornsdottir, Ingibjorg 6 *SEE* Bjornsdottir, Olof
Bjornsdottir, Olof 12; Quebec, 1879 ***2557.1*** *p22*
*Sister:*Ingibjorg 6
Bjornsdottir, Sigridur; Quebec, 1879 ***2557.1*** *p20*
Bjornsdottir, Stefan 5; Quebec, 1879 ***2557.1*** *p38A*
Bjornson, S.; Minneapolis, 1884-1885 ***6410.35*** *p50*
Bjornsson, Arni *SEE* Bjornsson, Thorvaldur
Bjornsson, Bjorn 5 *SEE* Bjornsson, Thorvaldur
Bjornsson, Gudvin 30; Quebec, 1879 ***2557.1*** *p38A*
Bjornsson, Halldor 3 *SEE* Bjornsson, Thorvaldur
Bjornsson, Jon 7 *SEE* Bjornsson, Thorvaldur
Bjornsson, Sven; Minneapolis, 1884-1885 ***6410.35*** *p50*
Bjornsson, Thorvaldur 9; Quebec, 1879 ***2557.1*** *p22*
*Brother:*Jon 7
*Brother:*Bjorn 5
*Brother:*Halldor 3
*Brother:*Arni
Bjornstrom, Z.; Washington, 1859-1920 ***2872.1*** *p4*
Bjurstrom, A.T.; Illinois, 1880 ***5012.39*** *p52*
Blaas, Claus; Illinois, 1886 ***5012.39*** *p120*
Blaase, Mathias; Cincinnati, 1869-1887 ***8582*** *p3*
Blach, Charlotte Emilie 30; New York, NY, 1857 ***9831.14*** *p153*
Blach, Ernestine Emilie 3; New York, NY, 1857 ***9831.14*** *p153*
Blach, Ernst Ludwig 10 mos; New York, NY, 1857 ***9831.14*** *p153*
Blach, Johann 40; New York, NY, 1857 ***9831.14*** *p153*
Blacius, Nicholas 28; Kansas, 1888 ***5240.1*** *p5*
Blacius, Nicholas 28; Kansas, 1888 ***5240.1*** *p71*
Black, Alexander; Ohio, 1851 ***9892.11*** *p4*
Black, Alexander; Quebec, 1849 ***5704.8*** *p57*
Black, Alexander 2; Quebec, 1849 ***5704.8*** *p57*
Black, Alexander 59; North Carolina, 1850 ***1639.20*** *p10*
Black, Allen; Ohio, 1828-1863 ***9892.11*** *p4*
Black, Allen; Ohio, 1865 ***9892.11*** *p4*
Black, Andrew; Philadelphia, 1847 ***53.26*** *p4*
Black, Andrew; Philadelphia, 1847 ***5704.8*** *p5*
Black, Ann; Philadelphia, 1867 ***5704.8*** *p219*
Black, Ann 4 *SEE* Black, Donald
Black, Anne Jane 14; Philadelphia, 1868 ***5704.8*** *p225*
Black, Archibald; New York, NY, 1815 ***2859.11*** *p25*
Black, Archy; St. John, N.B., 1847 ***5704.8*** *p21*
Black, Bell; St. John, N.B., 1847 ***5704.8*** *p9*
Black, Charles; Arkansas, 1918 ***95.2*** *p20*
Black, Charles 21; Philadelphia, 1857 ***5704.8*** *p133*
Black, Christian 8 *SEE* Black, Donald
Black, David; St. John, N.B., 1847 ***5704.8*** *p34*
Black, David 19; Savannah, GA, 1774 ***1219.7*** *p226*
Black, Denis 20; St. John, N.B., 1866 ***5704.8*** *p166*
Black, Donald 45; Wilmington, NC, 1775 ***1639.20*** *p10*
*Wife:*Janet 34
*Child:*Christian 8
*Child:*Ann 4
*Child:*Ewen 4
*Child:*Duncan 2
Black, Donaldson; New York, NY, 1811 ***2859.11*** *p8*
With family
Black, Duncan 2 *SEE* Black, Donald
Black, Edward; Virginia, 1637 ***6219*** *p113*
Black, Eliza 14; Philadelphia, 1868 ***5704.8*** *p225*
Black, Eliza Jane 5; Quebec, 1848 ***5704.8*** *p42*
Black, Elizabeth 36 *SEE* Black, William
Black, Elizabeth A. 20; Philadelphia, 1868 ***5704.8*** *p225*
Black, Ewen 4 *SEE* Black, Donald
Black, Flora 75; North Carolina, 1850 ***1639.20*** *p10*
Black, Francis; Quebec, 1863 ***5704.8*** *p154*
Black, G.; Carolina, 1745 ***1639.20*** *p10*
Black, George; New York, NY, 1811 ***2859.11*** *p8*
Black, George; St. John, N.B., 1847 ***5704.8*** *p34*
Black, Gustavus; Philadelphia, 1852 ***5704.8*** *p91*
Black, Hannah 7; Quebec, 1848 ***5704.8*** *p42*
Black, Isabel 65; North Carolina, 1850 ***1639.20*** *p10*
Black, James; Illinois, 1859 ***5012.39*** *p89*
Black, James; Philadelphia, 1867 ***5704.8*** *p221*
Black, James; St. John, N.B., 1847 ***5704.8*** *p11*
Black, James; St. John, N.B., 1848 ***5704.8*** *p44*
Black, James 2; Quebec, 1863 ***5704.8*** *p154*
Black, James 7; St. John, N.B., 1858 ***5704.8*** *p137*
Black, James 11; Philadelphia, 1868 ***5704.8*** *p230*
Black, James 12; St. John, N.B., 1847 ***5704.8*** *p21*
Black, James 22; Quebec, 1857 ***5704.8*** *p136*
Black, James M.; Ohio, 1843 ***8365.26*** *p12*
Black, Jane 22; Quebec, 1853 ***5704.8*** *p105*
Black, Jane 30; St. John, N.B., 1858 ***5704.8*** *p137*
Black, Janet 34 *SEE* Black, Donald
Black, John; America, 1790 ***1639.20*** *p10*
Black, John; Georgia, 1799 ***1639.20*** *p11*
Black, John; New York, NY, 1816 ***2859.11*** *p25*
Black, John; New York, NY, 1869 ***5704.8*** *p234*
Black, John; Quebec, 1848 ***5704.8*** *p42*
Black, John 11; Quebec, 1848 ***5704.8*** *p42*
Black, John 14; Wilmington, NC, 1775 ***1639.20*** *p10*
Black, John 15 *SEE* Black, William
Black, John 19; Pennsylvania, 1725 ***3690.1*** *p20*
Black, John 35; Quebec, 1863 ***5704.8*** *p154*
Black, John 39; West Virginia, 1901 ***9788.3*** *p4*
Black, John, Jr.; New York, NY, 1883 ***1450.2*** *p3B*
Black, Joseph; North Carolina, 1806 ***1639.20*** *p11*
Black, Joseph; Ohio, 1848 ***9892.11*** *p4*
Black, Joseph; Ohio, 1850 ***9892.11*** *p4*
Black, Joseph; Philadelphia, 1851 ***5704.8*** *p81*
Black, Keatty; St. John, N.B., 1847 ***5704.8*** *p21*
Black, Margaret 52; Quebec, 1853 ***5704.8*** *p105*
Black, Margaret J.; Philadelphia, 1864 ***5704.8*** *p170*
Black, Mary; Philadelphia, 1864 ***5704.8*** *p170*
Black, Mary; Quebec, 1849 ***5704.8*** *p57*
Black, Mary; St. John, N.B., 1847 ***5704.8*** *p11*
Black, Mary; St. John, N.B., 1847 ***5704.8*** *p21*
Black, Mary 3; Quebec, 1848 ***5704.8*** *p42*
Black, Mary 16; North Carolina, 1775 ***1639.20*** *p11*
Black, Mary 20; Massachusetts, 1849 ***5881.1*** *p10*
Black, Mary 65; North Carolina, 1850 ***1639.20*** *p11*
Black, Mary 70; North Carolina, 1850 ***1639.20*** *p11*
Black, Mary Ann 5; St. John, N.B., 1858 ***5704.8*** *p137*
Black, Michael; Charleston, SC, 1775-1779 ***8582.2*** *p3*
Black, Moses; New York, NY, 1816 ***2859.11*** *p25*
Black, Nancy; St. John, N.B., 1847 ***5704.8*** *p11*
Black, Nancy 9; Quebec, 1848 ***5704.8*** *p42*
Black, Nancy 16; Philadelphia, 1854 ***5704.8*** *p120*
Black, Peggy Jane; Quebec, 1848 ***5704.8*** *p42*
Black, Peter; Baltimore, 1816 ***2859.11*** *p25*
Black, Peter Paul; Ohio, 1869-1887 ***8582*** *p3*
Black, Prudence 15; Philadelphia, 1857 ***5704.8*** *p133*
Black, Rebecca 4; Quebec, 1849 ***5704.8*** *p57*
Black, Richard 11 *SEE* Black, William
Black, Robert; Quebec, 1848 ***5704.8*** *p42*
Black, Robert T.; Ohio, 1846 ***9892.11*** *p4*
Black, Samuel; Northwest Terr., 1823-1825 ***9775.5*** *p219*
Black, Samuel; Philadelphia, 1851 ***5704.8*** *p81*
Black, Sarah 7 *SEE* Black, William
Black, Sophia 30; Massachusetts, 1849 ***5881.1*** *p12*
Black, Stewart; Philadelphia, 1849 ***53.26*** *p4*
Black, Stewart; Philadelphia, 1849 ***5704.8*** *p54*
Black, Thomas; New York, NY, 1838 ***8208.4*** *p70*
Black, Thomas 9 *SEE* Black, William
Black, Thomas H. 32; Kansas, 1878 ***5240.1*** *p59*
Black, Wallace; Illinois, 1859 ***5012.39*** *p90*
Black, William; America, 1796 ***8894.1*** *p192*
Black, William; Charleston, SC, 1803 ***1639.20*** *p11*
Black, William; Charleston, SC, 1828 ***1639.20*** *p11*
Black, William; Illinois, 1860 ***5012.38*** *p97*
Black, William; Illinois, 1879 ***2896.5*** *p3*
Black, William; North Carolina, 1793-1877 ***1639.20*** *p11*
Black, William 13; Quebec, 1848 ***5704.8*** *p42*
Black, William 14 *SEE* Black, William
Black, William 16; St. John, N.B., 1867 ***5704.8*** *p167*
Black, William 43; Kansas, 1878 ***5240.1*** *p59*
Black, William 43; Nova Scotia, 1775 ***1219.7*** *p263*
*Wife:*Elizabeth 36
*Child:*William 14
*Child:*Richard 11
*Child:*John 15
*Child:*Thomas 9
*Child:*Sarah 7
Black, William 55; North Carolina, 1850 ***1639.20*** *p11*
Black, William, Jr.; South Carolina, 1759 ***1639.20*** *p11*
Blackaby, John 36; Virginia, 1731 ***3690.1*** *p20*
Blackburn, Alexander 11; Quebec, 1847 ***5704.8*** *p28*
Blackburn, Andrew; New York, NY, 1864 ***5704.8*** *p170*
Blackburn, Arthur 8; Quebec, 1847 ***5704.8*** *p28*
Blackburn, Benjamin 28; Carolina, 1774 ***1219.7*** *p179*
Blackburn, Eliza; Quebec, 1847 ***5704.8*** *p28*
Blackburn, Ester 20; Philadelphia, 1854 ***5704.8*** *p116*
Blackburn, George 22; Virginia, 1774 ***1219.7*** *p228*
Blackburn, Hugh; Quebec, 1847 ***5704.8*** *p6*
Blackburn, Hugh 9; Quebec, 1847 ***5704.8*** *p6*
Blackburn, Jacob 27; North America, 1774 ***1219.7*** *p200*
Blackburn, James; New York, NY, 1867 ***5704.8*** *p219*
Blackburn, James 5; Quebec, 1847 ***5704.8*** *p28*
Blackburn, Jane; Quebec, 1847 ***5704.8*** *p6*
Blackburn, Jane; Quebec, 1852 ***5704.8*** *p94*
Blackburn, John; Quebec, 1847 ***5704.8*** *p28*
Blackburn, John 7; New York, NY, 1864 ***5704.8*** *p170*
Blackburn, John 13; Quebec, 1847 ***5704.8*** *p28*
Blackburn, Martha; Quebec, 1847 ***5704.8*** *p28*
Blackburn, Mary; New York, NY, 1864 ***5704.8*** *p170*
Blackburn, Mary Ann; Philadelphia, 1853 ***5704.8*** *p101*
Blackburn, Patrick 11; Quebec, 1847 ***5704.8*** *p6*
Blackburn, Robert; Quebec, 1847 ***5704.8*** *p6*
Blackburn, Robert; Quebec, 1847 ***5704.8*** *p28*
Blackburn, Sarah; New York, NY, 1867 ***5704.8*** *p219*
Blackburn, Thomas 28; Nova Scotia, 1774 ***1219.7*** *p208*
With wife
With 2 children
Blackburn, William; Washington, 1859-1920 ***2872.1*** *p4*
Blackburn, William 6; Quebec, 1847 ***5704.8*** *p6*
Blackburne, John; Virginia, 1642 ***6219*** *p186*
Blackburne, Letitia; Philadelphia, 1850 ***53.26*** *p4*
Blackburne, Letitia; Philadelphia, 1850 ***5704.8*** *p60*
Blacke, Francis; Virginia, 1639 ***6219*** *p161*
Blacker, Eliza; Virginia, 1638 ***6219*** *p116*
Blackerby, William 40; Jamaica, 1731 ***3690.1*** *p21*
Blackett, Jane 20; Georgia, 1775 ***1219.7*** *p277*
Blackett, Tobiah 25; Carolina, 1774 ***1219.7*** *p211*
Blackey, Wm.; Virginia, 1647 ***6219*** *p244*
Blackford, William H.; New York, NY, 1838 ***8208.4*** *p73*
Blackham, George 21; Maryland, 1774 ***1219.7*** *p181*
Blackhaws, Sanders; Virginia, 1642 ***6219*** *p187*
Blacklin, Thomas; New York, NY, 1840 ***8208.4*** *p112*
Blacklock, William 23; Charleston, SC, 1774 ***1639.20*** *p12*
Blackly, Eliz.; Virginia, 1635 ***6219*** *p22*
Blackman, Eliza.; Virginia, 1648 ***6219*** *p252*
Blackman, Humphry; Virginia, 1638 ***6219*** *p124*
Blackman, Phillis; Virginia, 1639 ***6219*** *p155*
Blackman, Robert 22; Jamaica, 1731 ***3690.1*** *p20*
Blackman, Thomas; New York, NY, 1835 ***8208.4*** *p46*
Blackmore, Benjamin; New York, NY, 1839 ***8208.4*** *p96*
Blackmore, George 35; Jamaica, 1774 ***1219.7*** *p184*
Blackmore, John 27; Maryland, 1774 ***1219.7*** *p181*
Blackmore, William; Washington, 1859-1920 ***2872.1*** *p4*
Blackmore, William 16; Philadelphia, 1774 ***1219.7*** *p185*
Blackston, Thomas; Virginia, 1642 ***6219*** *p194*
Blackstone, Jon.; Virginia, 1635 ***6219*** *p69*
Blackwell, Amos 43; Maryland, 1774 ***1219.7*** *p235*
Blackwell, Andrew; Virginia, 1638 ***6219*** *p148*
Blackwell, Ayley; Virginia, 1698 ***2212*** *p14*
Blackwell, Edward 23; Massachusetts, 1849 ***5881.1*** *p7*
Blackwell, Henry 5; Massachusetts, 1849 ***5881.1*** *p8*
Blackwell, Honora 12; Massachusetts, 1849 ***5881.1*** *p8*
Blackwell, James 12; Massachusetts, 1849 ***5881.1*** *p8*
Blackwell, James 21; Jamaica, 1736 ***3690.1*** *p20*
Blackwell, John 10; Massachusetts, 1849 ***5881.1*** *p8*
Blackwell, John 33; Virginia, 1774 ***1219.7*** *p244*
Blackwell, John 39; Maryland, 1774 ***1219.7*** *p221*
Blackwell, Mary 8; Massachusetts, 1849 ***5881.1*** *p10*
Blackwell, Robert 7; Massachusetts, 1849 ***5881.1*** *p11*
Blackwell, Roger; Virginia, 1636 ***6219*** *p74*
Blackwell, Thomas 10 mos; Massachusetts, 1849 ***5881.1*** *p12*
Blackwood, Mr.; Quebec, 1815 ***9229.18*** *p74*
Blackwood, Mr.; Quebec, 1815 ***9229.18*** *p81*
Blackwood, Archibald; Iowa, 1866-1943 ***123.54*** *p9*
Blackwood, Elizabeth Murray Aitkenhead; Iowa, 1866-1943 ***123.54*** *p57*
Blackwood, John 18; Jamaica, 1733 ***3690.1*** *p20*
Blacock, Patrick; Virginia, 1634 ***6219*** *p32*
Blade, Anton; Arkansas, 1918 ***95.2*** *p20*
Bladen, William 16; Virginia, 1774 ***1219.7*** *p243*
Blades, Margret 19; Pennsylvania, 1731 ***3690.1*** *p20*
Blaenckle, Anna Maria *SEE* Blaenckle, Michael
Blaenckle, Anna Maria Hipp *SEE* Blaenckle, Michael
Blaenckle, Michael; America, 1770-1809 ***2444*** *p139*
*Wife:*Anna Maria Hipp
*Child:*Anna Maria
Blaeser, Johann Peter; America, 1845 ***8582.1*** *p3*
Blaha, Joe 31; Harris Co., TX, 1898 ***6254*** *p4*
Blaich, Jacob; Ohio, 1848 ***9892.11*** *p4*
Blaich, Johann Leonhard; Port uncertain, 1754 ***2444*** *p139*
*Wife:*Magdalena Mann
Blaich, Magdalen; Pennsylvania, 1752 ***2444*** *p147*
Blaich, Magdalena Mann *SEE* Blaich, Johann Leonhard

34 *FOR A COMPLETE EXPLANATION OF ENTRY, SEE "HOW TO READ A CITATION" SECTION*

Blain, Andrew; Charleston, SC, 1813 ***1639.20*** *p12*
Blain, Zachary; Iroquois Co., IL, 1894 ***3455.1*** *p9*
Blaine, Arthur; Washington, 1859-1920 ***2872.1*** *p4*
Blaine, Blanche; Washington, 1859-1920 ***2872.1*** *p4*
Blaine, Cora; Washington, 1859-1920 ***2872.1*** *p4*
Blaine, Dewey; Washington, 1859-1920 ***2872.1*** *p4*
Blaine, Edna; Washington, 1859-1920 ***2872.1*** *p4*
Blaine, Etta; Washington, 1859-1920 ***2872.1*** *p4*
Blaine, Florence; Washington, 1859-1920 ***2872.1*** *p4*
Blaine, Horace; Washington, 1859-1920 ***2872.1*** *p4*
Blaine, Joseph 26; Quebec, 1797 ***7603*** *p21*
Blaine, Mable; Washington, 1859-1920 ***2872.1*** *p4*
Blaine, Mamie; Washington, 1859-1920 ***2872.1*** *p4*
Blaine, Ray; Washington, 1859-1920 ***2872.1*** *p4*
Blaine, Vincent; Washington, 1859-1920 ***2872.1*** *p4*
Blaine, William; Washington, 1859-1920 ***2872.1*** *p4*
Blair, Andrew; Philadelphia, 1849 ***53.26*** *p4*
Blair, Andrew; Philadelphia, 1849 ***5704.8*** *p52*
Blair, Andrew 33; Philadelphia, 1859 ***5704.8*** *p142*
Blair, Ann; New York, NY, 1811 ***2859.11*** *p8*
Blair, Ann 19; St. John, N.B., 1864 ***5704.8*** *p158*
Blair, Ann Faichney; South Carolina, 1797 ***1639.20*** *p66*
Blair, Benjamin 30; Quebec, 1853 ***5704.8*** *p105*
Blair, Bernard 54; Kansas, 1872 ***5240.1*** *p53*
Blair, Catherine *SEE* Blair, George
Blair, Catherine; Philadelphia, 1811 ***2859.11*** *p9*
Blair, Cochran 1; Quebec, 1852 ***5704.8*** *p94*
Blair, Eliza; New York, NY, 1811 ***2859.11*** *p9*
Blair, Eliza; Philadelphia, 1811 ***2859.11*** *p9*
Blair, Elizabeth *SEE* Blair, James
Blair, Elizabeth; New York, NY, 1864 ***5704.8*** *p187*
Blair, Elizabeth; Philadelphia, 1851 ***5704.8*** *p76*
Blair, George; Philadelphia, 1811 ***53.26*** *p4*
*Relative:*Jane
*Relative:*Catherine
*Relative:*William
Blair, George; Philadelphia, 1811 ***2859.11*** *p9*
Blair, Hugh; Charleston, SC, 1830 ***1639.20*** *p12*
Blair, Isabella 20; Quebec, 1853 ***5704.8*** *p105*
Blair, James; Charleston, SC, 1794 ***1639.20*** *p12*
Blair, James; New York, NY, 1816 ***2859.11*** *p25*
Blair, James; Philadelphia, 1811 ***53.26*** *p4*
Blair, James; Philadelphia, 1811 ***53.26*** *p4*
*Relative:*Elizabeth
Blair, James; Philadelphia, 1811 ***2859.11*** *p9*
Blair, James; Philadelphia, 1852 ***5704.8*** *p96*
Blair, James; Philadelphia, 1853 ***5704.8*** *p101*
Blair, James; Quebec, 1847 ***5704.8*** *p28*
Blair, James 5; Quebec, 1852 ***5704.8*** *p94*
Blair, James 22; Philadelphia, 1834 ***53.26*** *p4*
Blair, James, Sr. 26; Philadelphia, 1833 ***53.26*** *p4*
*Relative:*Mary 20
Blair, Jane *SEE* Blair, George
Blair, Jane; Philadelphia, 1811 ***2859.11*** *p9*
Blair, Jane; Philadelphia, 1865 ***5704.8*** *p189*
Blair, Jane 13; Quebec, 1852 ***5704.8*** *p94*
Blair, Jane 30; Quebec, 1853 ***5704.8*** *p105*
Blair, John; Charleston, SC, 1797 ***1639.20*** *p12*
Blair, John; Iowa, 1866-1943 ***123.54*** *p9*
Blair, John; New York, NY, 1839 ***8208.4*** *p95*
Blair, John; Philadelphia, 1811 ***2859.11*** *p9*
Blair, John 1; St. John, N.B., 1848 ***5704.8*** *p39*
Blair, John 11; Quebec, 1852 ***5704.8*** *p94*
Blair, John 18; Philadelphia, 1853 ***5704.8*** *p112*
Blair, John 26; Kansas, 1872 ***5240.1*** *p53*
Blair, John 29; Philadelphia, 1803 ***53.26*** *p4*
Blair, Joseph C.; Illinois, 1900 ***5012.40*** *p76*
Blair, Joseph Cullon; Illinois, 1897 ***5012.39*** *p53*
Blair, Lewis William; St. John, N.B., 1848 ***5704.8*** *p39*
Blair, Margaret; Philadelphia, 1867 ***5704.8*** *p219*
Blair, Margaret; Quebec, 1852 ***5704.8*** *p94*
Blair, Martha 25; Quebec, 1853 ***5704.8*** *p105*
Blair, Mary 20 *SEE* Blair, James, Sr.
Blair, Mary Jane 21; St. John, N.B., 1864 ***5704.8*** *p158*
Blair, Nancy; St. John, N.B., 1848 ***5704.8*** *p39*
Blair, Richard; New York, NY, 1811 ***2859.11*** *p9*
Blair, Robert 19; Philadelphia, 1853 ***5704.8*** *p111*
Blair, Samuel; New York, NY, 1811 ***2859.11*** *p9*
Blair, Samuel; New York, NY, 1815 ***2859.11*** *p25*
Blair, Thomas; New York, NY, 1816 ***2859.11*** *p25*
Blair, Thomas; New York, NY, 1865 ***5704.8*** *p193*
Blair, Thomas; Philadelphia, 1851 ***5704.8*** *p76*
Blair, Wade; South Carolina, 1763 ***1639.20*** *p12*
Blair, William *SEE* Blair, George
Blair, William; Charleston, SC, 1828 ***1639.20*** *p12*
Blair, William; Quebec, 1852 ***5704.8*** *p94*
Blair, William; St. John, N.B., 1847 ***5704.8*** *p34*
Blair, William 9; Quebec, 1852 ***5704.8*** *p94*
Blair, William James; New York, NY, 1865 ***5704.8*** *p193*
Blair, Wm.; Philadelphia, 1811 ***2859.11*** *p9*
Blaise, Joseph 59; Kansas, 1881 ***5240.1*** *p63*
Blaising, Nicolas 23; New Orleans, 1836 ***778.5*** *p55*
Blaka, Martin; Wisconsin, n.d. ***9675.4*** *p265*
Blakbole, Henry; Indiana, 1848 ***9117*** *p15*
Blake, Andrew 40; Massachusetts, 1849 ***5881.1*** *p6*
Blake, Charles; Canada, 1776-1783 ***9786*** *p220*
Blake, Charles Frederick; America, 1836 ***1450.2*** *p15A*
Blake, Charles Frederick; New York, 1836 ***1450.2*** *p15A*
Blake, Edward; Virginia, 1635 ***6219*** *p73*
Blake, Edward 60; Arizona, 1885 ***9228.40*** *p1*
Blake, James; America, 1736-1743 ***4971*** *p57*
Blake, James; Savannah, GA, 1774 ***1219.7*** *p227*
Blake, James; Virginia, 1856 ***4626.16*** *p16*
Blake, James William; California, 1871 ***2769.2*** *p4*
Blake, John; New York, NY, 1811 ***2859.11*** *p9*
Blake, John 22; Maryland, 1733 ***3690.1*** *p20*
Blake, Margarett; America, 1698 ***2212*** *p5*
Blake, Mary 21; Massachusetts, 1849 ***5881.1*** *p10*
Blake, Nicholas; America, 1736-1743 ***4971*** *p57*
Blake, Roger 17; Jamaica, 1730 ***3690.1*** *p21*
Blake, Walter; Virginia, 1637 ***6219*** *p17*
Blake, William 19; Maryland, 1775 ***1219.7*** *p254*
Blake, Winne 20; Massachusetts, 1849 ***5881.1*** *p12*
Blakeley, James; New York, NY, 1870 ***5704.8*** *p237*
Blakeley, Mary; New York, NY, 1870 ***5704.8*** *p237*
Blakeley, Thomas; New York, NY, 1870 ***5704.8*** *p237*
Blakeley, William; New York, NY, 1870 ***5704.8*** *p237*
Blakely, Charles; Ohio, 1843 ***8365.25*** *p12*
Blakely, Joseph; Quebec, 1847 ***5704.8*** *p16*
Blakemore, William; Antigua (Antego), 1768 ***1219.7*** *p135*
Blakey, Mabell 32; Maryland, 1722 ***3690.1*** *p21*
Blakin, Ralph; Virginia, 1640 ***6219*** *p182*
Blakswik, James 21; North Carolina, 1774 ***1219.7*** *p189*
Blakswik, James 21; North Carolina, 1774 ***1639.20*** *p12*
Blame, William; New York, NY, 1815 ***2859.11*** *p25*
Blamire, Anthony; Virginia, 1752 ***1219.7*** *p15*
Blamter, Tho.; Virginia, 1637 ***6219*** *p11*
Blan, Mathias; Wisconsin, n.d. ***9675.4*** *p265*
Blanc, Mr. 22; New Orleans, 1822 ***778.5*** *p55*
Blanc, Mr. 30; Port uncertain, 1825 ***778.5*** *p55*
Blanc, Jean 35; America, 1837 ***778.5*** *p55*
Blanc, Joseph 24; America, 1838 ***778.5*** *p55*
Blanc, P. 25; New Orleans, 1829 ***778.5*** *p55*
Blanc, P. 36; New Orleans, 1825 ***778.5*** *p55*
Blancar, Mr. 52; Port uncertain, 1836 ***778.5*** *p55*
Blancaud, Mr. 50; New Orleans, 1839 ***778.5*** *p55*
Blanch, Alice 28; Massachusetts, 1849 ***5881.1*** *p6*
Blanch, John 6; Massachusetts, 1849 ***5881.1*** *p9*
Blanch, Martin 45; New Orleans, 1862 ***543.30*** *p244*
Blanch, Michael 4; Massachusetts, 1849 ***5881.1*** *p11*
Blanch, Roger; Virginia, 1637 ***6219*** *p13*
Blanch, Thomas; Virginia, 1648 ***6219*** *p246*
Blanchard, Mr. 23; America, 1839 ***778.5*** *p55*
Blanchard, Charles William; New York, NY, 1839 ***8208.4*** *p96*
Blanchard, James 20; Canada, 1838 ***4535.12*** *p113*
Blanchard, Victor; Port uncertain, 1839 ***778.5*** *p55*
Blanchfield, John 22; Massachusetts, 1849 ***5881.1*** *p8*
Blanchfield, Stephen; New York, NY, 1815 ***2859.11*** *p25*
Blancho, George; Iowa, 1866-1943 ***123.54*** *p9*
Blanchot, Victoire 26; Port uncertain, 1839 ***778.5*** *p55*
Blancks, Thomas; Virginia, 1637 ***6219*** *p86*
Blanco, B. 69; Port uncertain, 1836 ***778.5*** *p55*
Blanco, Santiago 37; New Orleans, 1822 ***778.5*** *p55*
Blancy, John 29; Maryland, 1774 ***1219.7*** *p181*
Bland, Mr.; Quebec, 1815 ***9229.18*** *p79*
Bland, Arthur 26; New York, 1774 ***1219.7*** *p218*
Bland, Edward; Virginia, 1636 ***6219*** *p75*
Bland, Edward; Virginia, 1638 ***6219*** *p181*
Bland, Edward; Virginia, 1647 ***6219*** *p245*
Bland, Eliza.; Virginia, 1647 ***6219*** *p245*
Bland, Ja.; Virginia, 1647 ***6219*** *p245*
Bland, John; New York, NY, 1838 ***8208.4*** *p71*
Bland, Ralph; Georgia, 1775 ***1219.7*** *p274*
Bland, Ralph 18; Savannah, GA, 1775 ***1219.7*** *p274*
Blandain, Peter 48; New Orleans, 1822 ***778.5*** *p56*
Blande, Augustine 27; America, 1839 ***778.5*** *p56*
Blande, Desire 37; America, 1839 ***778.5*** *p56*
Blandford, Alexand 22; America, 1699 ***2212*** *p28*
Blandin, Miss 10; New Orleans, 1837 ***778.5*** *p56*
Blandin, Mrs. 40; New Orleans, 1837 ***778.5*** *p56*
Blandin, Ms. 12; New Orleans, 1837 ***778.5*** *p56*
Blandin, Ms. 14; New Orleans, 1837 ***778.5*** *p56*
Blandin, Ms. 18; New Orleans, 1837 ***778.5*** *p56*
Blandin, M. 35; Port uncertain, 1836 ***778.5*** *p56*
Blandin, Manuel 32; New Orleans, 1832 ***778.5*** *p56*
Blandin, Manuel 42; Port uncertain, 1835 ***778.5*** *p56*
Blandow, Adolf; Illinois, 1892 ***5012.40*** *p26*
Blaney, Charles 39; New Orleans, 1862 ***543.30*** *p113*
Blaney, Hugh 7; Philadelphia, 1857 ***5704.8*** *p133*
Blaney, Isabella 50; Philadelphia, 1857 ***5704.8*** *p133*
Blaney, Joseph; New York, NY, 1866 ***5704.8*** *p213*
Blaney, Patrick; Philadelphia, 1848 ***53.26*** *p4*
*Relative:*Susan
Blaney, Patrick; Philadelphia, 1848 ***5704.8*** *p46*
Blaney, Susan *SEE* Blaney, Patrick
Blaney, Susan; Philadelphia, 1848 ***5704.8*** *p46*
Blank, Anthony 17; New York, 1775 ***1219.7*** *p246*
Blank, Jacob; Wisconsin, n.d. ***9675.4*** *p265*
Blank, Jacob 27; Kansas, 1879 ***5240.1*** *p60*
Blank, Martin; Wisconsin, n.d. ***9675.4*** *p265*
Blank, Peter; Wisconsin, n.d. ***9675.4*** *p265*
Blankenbuehler, Johann; America, 1844 ***8582.3*** *p6*
Blankenbuehler, Johann; America, 1844 ***8582.3*** *p86*
Blankenhorn, Chas. Henry; Wisconsin, n.d. ***9675.4*** *p265*
Blankenhorn, Heinrich; Charleston, SC, 1775-1781 ***8582.2*** *p52*
Blanker, Tho.; Virginia, 1637 ***6219*** *p114*
Blankes, Georg; Virginia, 1639 ***6219*** *p159*
Blankner, Joseph; Wisconsin, n.d. ***9675.4*** *p265*
Blannan, John; Arizona, 1898 ***9228.30*** *p7*
Blanque, B. 19; New Orleans, 1835 ***778.5*** *p56*
Blany, Eleanor; New York, NY, 1811 ***2859.11*** *p9*
Blany, Fanny; Philadelphia, 1847 ***53.26*** *p4*
*Relative:*Henry
*Relative:*John 11
*Relative:*Robert 7
*Relative:*Jane 5
Blany, Fanny; Philadelphia, 1847 ***5704.8*** *p31*
Blany, Henry *SEE* Blany, Fanny
Blany, Henry; Philadelphia, 1847 ***5704.8*** *p31*
Blany, Jane 5 *SEE* Blany, Fanny
Blany, Jane 5; Philadelphia, 1847 ***5704.8*** *p31*
Blany, John 11 *SEE* Blany, Fanny
Blany, John 11; Philadelphia, 1847 ***5704.8*** *p31*
Blany, Robert 7 *SEE* Blany, Fanny
Blany, Robert 7; Philadelphia, 1847 ***5704.8*** *p31*
Blare, Wm.; Virginia, 1643 ***6219*** *p204*
Blarevic, Ivan; Iowa, 1866-1943 ***123.54*** *p9*
Blase, Anne Marie Ilsabein; America, 1877 ***4610.10*** *p122*
Blaser, Friedrich; Kansas, 1891 ***5240.1*** *p5*
Blaser, Simon 23; Kansas, 1877 ***5240.1*** *p58*
Blashell, Francis 29; Nova Scotia, 1774 ***1219.7*** *p209*
Blaskovic, Twan; Iowa, 1866-1943 ***123.54*** *p9*
Blatch, Charles; San Francisco, 1850 ***4914.15*** *p10*
Blatt, Thomas; Virginia, 1642 ***6219*** *p198*
Blatter, Max 33; Kansas, 1905 ***5240.1*** *p83*
Blatter, Theophil; Iroquois Co., IL, 1896 ***3455.1*** *p9*
Blatzheim, Henry; Colorado, 1890 ***9678.1*** *p154*
Blau, Johann Hermann; America, 1857 ***8582.3*** *p6*
Blau, Mathias; America, 1843 ***8582.3*** *p6*
Blau, Mathias; Wisconsin, n.d. ***9675.4*** *p265*
Blaubach, Gottfried; Wisconsin, n.d. ***9675.4*** *p266*
Blaverwich, John; Iowa, 1866-1943 ***123.54*** *p9*
Blaye, Wm.; Virginia, 1632 ***6219*** *p180*
Blayney, Bridget 8; St. John, N.B., 1847 ***5704.8*** *p25*
Blayney, Elleanor; St. John, N.B., 1847 ***5704.8*** *p25*
Blayney, Jean; Quebec, 1816 ***7603*** *p85*
Blayney, John; St. John, N.B., 1847 ***5704.8*** *p25*
Blayney, Pat 5; St. John, N.B., 1847 ***5704.8*** *p25*
Blayney, William 10; St. John, N.B., 1847 ***5704.8*** *p25*
Blazek, Joseph; Arizona, 1897 ***9228.30*** *p1*
Blazek, Joseph 37; Arizona, 1897 ***9228.40*** *p2*
Blazer, U. Z.; America, 1883 ***5240.1*** *p5*
Blazevic, . . .; Iowa, 1866-1943 ***123.54*** *p9*
Blazevich, Ivan; Iowa, 1866-1943 ***123.54*** *p9*
Blazick, John; Arkansas, 1918 ***95.2*** *p20*
Blazina, Antonija; Iowa, 1866-1943 ***123.54*** *p57*
Blazina, Buna; Iowa, 1866-1943 ***123.54*** *p9*
Blazina, Martin; Iowa, 1866-1943 ***123.54*** *p9*
Blazina, Mate; Iowa, 1866-1943 ***123.54*** *p9*
Blazonia, Martin; Iowa, 1866-1943 ***123.54*** *p9*
Blazovic, Andres; Iowa, 1866-1943 ***123.54*** *p9*
Blea, Betty; St. John, N.B., 1848 ***5704.8*** *p47*
Blea, Catherine; St. John, N.B., 1848 ***5704.8*** *p47*
Blea, David; St. John, N.B., 1847 ***5704.8*** *p4*
Blea, Edward; St. John, N.B., 1848 ***5704.8*** *p47*
Blea, Eliza Jane; Philadelphia, 1851 ***5704.8*** *p70*
Blea, Hugh; St. John, N.B., 1847 ***5704.8*** *p4*
Blea, James; St. John, N.B., 1847 ***5704.8*** *p4*
Blea, John 9; St. John, N.B., 1848 ***5704.8*** *p47*
Blea, Mary; St. John, N.B., 1847 ***5704.8*** *p4*
Blea, Matilda 10; St. John, N.B., 1847 ***5704.8*** *p4*
Bleakley, Jane; New York, NY, 1815 ***2859.11*** *p25*
Bleakley, John; New York, NY, 1815 ***2859.11*** *p25*
Bleakley, John; Philadelphia, 1833-1834 ***53.26*** *p4*
Bleakley, William; New York, NY, 1815 ***2859.11*** *p25*
Bleakly, William; New York, NY, 1811 ***2859.11*** *p9*
Bleakney, Guillaume; Quebec, 1763 ***7603*** *p95*
Blear, Samll.; Virginia, 1643 ***6219*** *p202*
Blech, . . .; Canada, 1776-1783 ***9786*** *p17*
Blecha, Frank; Wisconsin, n.d. ***9675.4*** *p266*
Blechinger, Joseph; New Orleans, 1848 ***8582.1*** *p3*
Blechynden, Charles 20; Virginia, 1774 ***1219.7*** *p193*
Bleck, . . .; Canada, 1776-1783 ***9786*** *p17*
Blee, Hugh; Philadelphia, 1852 ***5704.8*** *p88*
Blee, Isabella; Philadelphia, 1852 ***5704.8*** *p88*
Bleese, James; Virginia, 1637 ***6219*** *p33*

Blei, Jacob; Illinois, 1870 ***2896.5*** *p3*
Blei, Nic; Wisconsin, n.d. ***9675.4*** *p266*
Bleich, . . .; Canada, 1776-1783 ***9786*** *p17*
Bleier, Julius; Wisconsin, n.d. ***9675.4*** *p266*
Bleikers, Johannes; Pennsylvania, 1683 ***2155*** *p2*
With wife
*Son:*Pieter
Bleikers, Pieter *SEE* Bleikers, Johannes
Bleimyer, Abraham; Philadelphia, 1768 ***9973.7*** *p40*
Bleiner, Anton; Illinois, 1887 ***5012.39*** *p52*
Bleker, Johann; New Netherland, 1630-1646 ***8582.2*** *p51*
Blencowe, Richard 25; Boston, 1774 ***1219.7*** *p189*
Blend, John; Virginia, 1646 ***6219*** *p243*
Blendinger, Johannes; America, 1851 ***8582.3*** *p6*
Bleneau, . . .; Canada, 1776-1783 ***9786*** *p41*
Blener, Anna *SEE* Blener, Fred
Blener, Fred; New York, NY, 1886 ***3455.1*** *p50*
*Wife:*Anna
Blenker, Ludwig; America, 1861-1865 ***8582.3*** *p91*
Blenkner, Joseph; Wisconsin, n.d. ***9675.4*** *p266*
Blesch, Philipp; America, 1842 ***8582.3*** *p6*
Bleschmidt, Herman; Wisconsin, n.d. ***9675.4*** *p266*
Blessing, Ann Marie 7 *SEE* Blessing, Leuhart
Blessing, Anna Catharina; Pennsylvania, 1750 ***2444*** *p216*
Blessing, Jacob 13 *SEE* Blessing, Leuhart
Blessing, Jakob; Ohio, 1798-1818 ***8582.2*** *p54*
Blessing, Leuhart; Frederick Co., MD, 1822 ***9892.11*** *p4*
*Child:*Leuhart 15
*Child:*Jacob 13
*Child:*Ann Marie 7
*Child:*Samuel 1
Blessing, Leuhart 15 *SEE* Blessing, Leuhart
Blessing, Michael; Maryland, 1820-1829 ***8582.1*** *p46*
Blessing, Samuel 1 *SEE* Blessing, Leuhart
Blesson, Elizabeth; Quebec, 1824 ***7603*** *p69*
Blest, Samuel; America, 1845 ***8582.1*** *p3*
Bletler, Moriz; America, 1865 ***1450.2*** *p15A*
Bletry, Antoine 32; America, 1836 ***778.5*** *p56*
Bletry, Benoite 30; America, 1836 ***778.5*** *p56*
Bletsoe, William; Virginia, 1639 ***6219*** *p157*
Bletstowe, Mathew; Virginia, 1641 ***6219*** *p186*
Blettner, Hans Henrich; Philadelphia, 1779 ***8137*** *p6*
Blettry, Catherine 25; America, 1836 ***778.5*** *p56*
Bletzger, Christoph Heinrich *SEE* Bletzger, Johann Georg
Bletzger, Christoph Heinrich; Pennsylvania, 1752 ***2444*** *p200*
With parents
Bletzger, Johann Georg; Port uncertain, 1752 ***2444*** *p200*
*Wife:*Magdalena Catharina
*Child:*Christoph Heinrich
Bletzger, Magdalena Catharina *SEE* Bletzger, Johann Georg
Bleuler, Adolph; Cincinnati, 1848 ***8582.1*** *p53*
Blew, Edward; Virginia, 1600-1642 ***6219*** *p193*
Blew, Richard 15; Pennsylvania, Virginia or Maryland, 1728 ***3690.1*** *p21*
Blewett, John; Nevada, 1878 ***2764.35*** *p6*
Blewitt, Bennett; Virginia, 1635 ***6219*** *p73*
*Wife:*Elizabeth
Blewitt, Elizabeth *SEE* Blewitt, Bennett
Bley, Mr.; Ohio, 1816 ***8582.1*** *p47*
Bley, Anton *SEE* Bley, Karl Wilhelm
Bley, Anton; America, 1847 ***8582.1*** *p3*
Bley, Karl Wilhelm 18; Baltimore, 1847 ***8582.3*** *p6*
*Brother:*Anton
Bley, Wilhelm; America, 1847 ***8582.1*** *p3*
Bleyer, Moritz; America, 1848 ***8582.3*** *p7*
Blick, Nicholas; Wisconsin, n.d. ***9675.4*** *p266*
Blickle, Joseph; America, 1837 ***1450.2*** *p15A*
Blieninger, Catharina Hohlscheit *SEE* Blieninger, Matthaeus
Blieninger, Matthaeus; Pennsylvania, 1749 ***2444*** *p201*
*Wife:*Catharina Hohlscheit
Bliesath, Gustav; Wisconsin, n.d. ***9675.4*** *p266*
Blight, Jacob; Virginia, 1637 ***6219*** *p110*
Bligneure, Mr. 17; Louisiana, 1838 ***778.5*** *p57*
Bligny, Miss; Port uncertain, 1839 ***778.5*** *p337*
Blikosch, Ignac; Wisconsin, n.d. ***9675.4*** *p266*
Blimmer, Angus; Baltimore, 1832 ***3702.7*** *p98*
Blin, Mr.; Quebec, 1815 ***9229.18*** *p78*
Blind, Joseph 25; Maryland, 1774 ***1219.7*** *p221*
Blineau, Mr. 48; Port uncertain, 1836 ***778.5*** *p57*
Blineau, Martin 42; America, 1837 ***778.5*** *p57*
Blings, Nicalaus; Wisconsin, n.d. ***9675.4*** *p266*
Blinkey, Charles 33; North America, 1774 ***1219.7*** *p199*
*Wife:*Sarah 33
*Child:*Jane 6
*Child:*Mary 1
Blinkey, Jane 6 *SEE* Blinkey, Charles
Blinkey, Mary 1 *SEE* Blinkey, Charles
Blinkey, Sarah 33 *SEE* Blinkey, Charles
Blinkhorn, Ann 3 *SEE* Blinkhorn, William
Blinkhorn, Ann 29 *SEE* Blinkhorn, William
Blinkhorn, Eleanor 1 *SEE* Blinkhorn, William
Blinkhorn, John 4 *SEE* Blinkhorn, William
Blinkhorn, William 7 *SEE* Blinkhorn, William
Blinkhorn, William 33; Nova Scotia, 1774 ***1219.7*** *p194*
*Wife:*Ann 29
*Child:*William 7
*Child:*John 4
*Child:*Ann 3
*Child:*Eleanor 1
Blinkinsops, James 16; Massachusetts, 1848 ***5881.1*** *p8*
Blinn, John Adam; Indiana, 1845 ***1450.2*** *p15A*
Bliskun, John; Arkansas, 1918 ***95.2*** *p20*
Bliss, Ann 17; Jamaica, 1730 ***3690.1*** *p21*
Bliss, Mary 14; Jamaica, 1730 ***3690.1*** *p21*
Bliss, Rachel 15; Jamaica, 1730 ***3690.1*** *p21*
Blithe, James; Virginia, 1638 ***6219*** *p115*
Blizard, John 16; Maryland, 1719 ***3690.1*** *p21*
Blobaum, Anne Marie; America, 1839 ***4610.10*** *p154*
Blobaum, Friedrich Wilhelm August; America, 1853 ***4610.10*** *p156*
Blobaum, Hermann Christian Friedrich; America, 1857 ***4610.10*** *p158*
Blobaum, Wilhelmine; America, 1841 ***4610.10*** *p154*
Bloch, Leopold; America, 1844 ***8582.3*** *p7*
Bloche, Frances 5; Port uncertain, 1838 ***778.5*** *p57*
Bloche, George 3; Port uncertain, 1838 ***778.5*** *p57*
Bloche, Margareth 27; Port uncertain, 1838 ***778.5*** *p57*
Bloche, Pierre 30; Port uncertain, 1838 ***778.5*** *p57*
Blocher, Michael; Pennsylvania, 1753 ***2444*** *p139*
Blociszewski, Floryan; America, n.d. ***4606*** *p180*
Block, . . .; Canada, 1776-1783 ***9786*** *p17*
Block, Albert; Illinois, 1876 ***5012.37*** *p59*
Block, Anna Marg. 25; America, 1853 ***9162.8*** *p36*
Block, Charles 32; New Orleans, 1862 ***543.30*** *p480*
Block, Christina 6 mos; America, 1853 ***9162.8*** *p36*
Block, Frederick; Illinois, 1859 ***5012.39*** *p54*
Block, Isaac 27; America, 1835 ***778.5*** *p57*
Block, Jacob; Wisconsin, n.d. ***9675.4*** *p266*
Block, John; Illinois, 1863 ***5012.38*** *p98*
Block, Nels Christian; Arkansas, 1918 ***95.2*** *p20*
Block, Rosina 36; New Orleans, 1839 ***9420.2*** *p358*
Block, Simon 25; Port uncertain, 1839 ***778.5*** *p57*
Blocker, Michael; Pennsylvania, 1753 ***2444*** *p139*
Blocki, Leon; Arkansas, 1918 ***95.2*** *p20*
Blodecker, . . .; Canada, 1776-1783 ***9786*** *p17*
Bloebaum, Carl F.; Baltimore, 1840 ***8582.1*** *p3*
Bloebaum, Carl Friedrich; Cincinnati, 1869-1887 ***8582*** *p3*
Bloebaum, Wilhelm; America, 1851 ***4610.10*** *p147*
Bloemhof, Wiebren Dories; New York, NY, 1893 ***1450.2*** *p3B*
Bloemker, Ernest Fred; America, 1890 ***1450.2*** *p15A*
Bloise, Abraham 20; Maryland, 1774 ***1219.7*** *p179*
Blok, James; Wisconsin, n.d. ***9675.4*** *p266*
Blom, John Harding; New York, NY, 1833 ***8208.4*** *p41*
Blomberg, Charles J.; Maine, 1895 ***6410.22*** *p127*
Blomberg, Lewis 31; Arizona, 1890 ***2764.35*** *p4*
Blomdahl, John; Minneapolis, 1868-1877 ***6410.35*** *p50*
Blomquist, Charles; Minneapolis, 1879-1880 ***6410.35*** *p50*
Blomquist, Charles; Minneapolis, 1882-1883 ***6410.35*** *p50*
Blomquist, Jordan; Minneapolis, 1882-1887 ***6410.35*** *p50*
Blondeau, C. 40; New Orleans, 1836 ***778.5*** *p57*
Blondet, Joseph 40; New Orleans, 1838 ***778.5*** *p57*
Blondet, Marie 30; New Orleans, 1838 ***778.5*** *p57*
Blondin, Ant. 22; New Orleans, 1831 ***778.5*** *p57*
Blonie, V. J.; Wisconsin, n.d. ***9675.4*** *p266*
Blonien, John; Wisconsin, n.d. ***9675.4*** *p266*
Blonn, . . .; Ohio, 1865 ***6014.2*** *p7*
Blood, David R.; New York, NY, 1815 ***2859.11*** *p25*
Blood, Richard 15; Pennsylvania, Virginia or Maryland, 1728 ***3690.1*** *p21*
Bloom, Axel 30; Massachusetts, 1860 ***6410.32*** *p112*
Bloom, Axel Emanuel; Boston, 1854 ***6410.32*** *p125*
Bloom, Charles; Colorado, 1904 ***9678.1*** *p154*
Bloom, Charles; Illinois, 1866 ***2896.5*** *p3*
Bloom, Esrel; Iowa, 1866-1943 ***123.54*** *p9*
Bloom, Frederick; Ohio, 1842 ***8365.25*** *p12*
Bloom, Jenette 31; Massachusetts, 1860 ***6410.32*** *p112*
Bloom, John 45; Kansas, 1886 ***5240.1*** *p68*
Bloom, John A.; New York, NY, 1838 ***8208.4*** *p84*
Bloom, Julius 20; Massachusetts, 1860 ***6410.32*** *p113*
Bloom, Julius Rudolph; New York, NY, 1856 ***6410.32*** *p125*
Bloom, Max 22; Kansas, 1906 ***5240.1*** *p83*
Bloom, Robert; Illinois, 1865 ***2896.5*** *p3*
Bloom, Sigmond; Illinois, 1866 ***2896.5*** *p3*
Bloomer, Eliza; Philadelphia, 1847 ***5704.8*** *p14*
Bloomer, Elizabeth *SEE* Bloomer, Thomas
Bloomer, Thomas; Philadelphia, 1847 ***53.26*** *p4*
*Relative:*Elizabeth
Bloomer, Thomas; Philadelphia, 1847 ***5704.8*** *p14*
Bloomfield, A.P.; Colorado, 1904 ***9678.1*** *p154*
Bloomfield, Saml; New York, NY, 1816 ***2859.11*** *p25*
Bloomquist, Alfred Theodore; New York, NY, 1889 ***3455.2*** *p96*
Bloomquist, Erik; Colorado, 1890 ***9678.1*** *p154*
Bloomquist, Ludwig; Colorado, 1894 ***9678.1*** *p154*
Blosevich, Joseph; Iowa, 1866-1943 ***123.54*** *p9*
Blosezevick, Peter; Iowa, 1866-1943 ***123.54*** *p9*
Bloss, John Frederick; New York, NY, 1838 ***8208.4*** *p62*
Blossell, Joseph 26; New Orleans, 1863 ***543.30*** *p246*
Blot, Mme.; America, 1838 ***778.5*** *p58*
Blot, Mr. 40; America, 1838 ***778.5*** *p57*
Blot, Jacob 21; America, 1839 ***778.5*** *p57*
Blott, Jacob 32; America, 1838 ***778.5*** *p58*
Blount, John 28; Maryland, 1775 ***1219.7*** *p259*
Bloussau, Mr. 18; New Orleans, 1839 ***778.5*** *p58*
Blouth, Jacob; Indiana, 1849 ***9117*** *p16*
Blow, Sarah 22; Canada, 1838 ***4535.12*** *p113*
Blowe, Georg; Virginia, 1638 ***6219*** *p146*
Blowers, Samson 19; Boston, 1776 ***1219.7*** *p282*
Bloyd, W. H.; Washington, 1859-1920 ***2872.1*** *p4*
Bloys, Daniel 18; Maryland, 1774 ***1219.7*** *p208*
Bloyse, Tho.; Virginia, 1632 ***6219*** *p180*
Blozina, Anton; Iowa, 1866-1943 ***123.54*** *p9*
Blozina, Matt; Iowa, 1866-1943 ***123.54*** *p9*
Blozina, Winko; Iowa, 1866-1943 ***123.54*** *p9*
Blozlurchi, Thomas; Iowa, 1866-1943 ***123.54*** *p9*
Blozlvich, Thomas; Iowa, 1866-1943 ***123.54*** *p9*
Blozza, P. O.; Iowa, 1866-1943 ***123.54*** *p9*
Blucher, Jacob; Wisconsin, n.d. ***9675.4*** *p266*
Blucklin, James; Philadelphia, 1853 ***5704.8*** *p101*
Blue, Mrs.; North Carolina, 1712-1814 ***1639.20*** *p13*
Blue, Ann Campbell 26; Quebec, 1862 ***5704.8*** *p151*
Blue, Catherine 80 *SEE* Blue, Christian
Blue, Christian 45 *SEE* Blue, John
Blue, Christian 45; North Carolina, 1850 ***1639.20*** *p12*
*Relative:*Catherine 80
Blue, Daniel 65; North Carolina, 1850 ***1639.20*** *p12*
Blue, Duncan; America, 1748 ***1639.20*** *p13*
Blue, Duncan; America, 1767 ***1639.20*** *p13*
Blue, John; America, 1803 ***1639.20*** *p13*
With wife & 5 children
Blue, John; North Carolina, 1745-1781 ***1639.20*** *p13*
Blue, John 31; Quebec, 1862 ***5704.8*** *p151*
Blue, John 50; North Carolina, 1850 ***1639.20*** *p13*
*Relative:*Christian 45
*Relative:*Mary 52
Blue, John 54; North Carolina, 1850 ***1639.20*** *p13*
*Relative:*Margaret 45
Blue, Malcolm; North Carolina, 1748 ***1639.20*** *p13*
Blue, Margaret 45 *SEE* Blue, John
Blue, Mary 1; Quebec, 1862 ***5704.8*** *p151*
Blue, Mary 52 *SEE* Blue, John
Blue, William; America, 1768 ***1639.20*** *p13*
Bluff, Henry 30; New Orleans, 1862 ***543.30*** *p114*
Bluhme, Sophie; America, 1839 ***3702.7*** *p312*
With parents
Blum, . . .; Canada, 1776-1783 ***9786*** *p17*
Blum, Adam 22; America, 1838 ***778.5*** *p58*
Blum, Carl; Baltimore, 1832 ***3702.7*** *p101*
Blum, Charles; Illinois, 1866 ***2896.5*** *p3*
Blum, Friedrich; Cincinnati, 1869-1887 ***8582*** *p3*
Blum, Gittel 4; New York, NY, 1878 ***9253*** *p47*
Blum, Hinde 24; New York, NY, 1878 ***9253*** *p47*
Blum, Johannes; Philadelphia, 1779 ***8137*** *p6*
Blum, Joseph Anton; Illinois, 1882 ***2896.5*** *p3*
Blum, Rachel 10 mos; New York, NY, 1878 ***9253*** *p47*
Blum, Raphael 28; America, 1853 ***9162.7*** *p14*
Blum, Regina 24; America, 1853 ***9162.7*** *p14*
Blum, Robert; Illinois, 1865 ***2896.5*** *p3*
Blum, Samuel; New York, NY, 1883 ***1450.2*** *p3B*
Blum, Sigmond; Illinois, 1866 ***2896.5*** *p3*
Blum, Simon 52; Kansas, 1885 ***5240.1*** *p67*
Blumbach Family ; New York, 1765 ***8125.8*** *p436*
Blumberg, . . .; Canada, 1776-1783 ***9786*** *p17*
Blumberg, Werner Henry 33; California, 1872 ***2769.2*** *p4*
Blumchen, . . .; Canada, 1776-1783 ***9786*** *p17*
Blume, . . .; America, 1869-1885 ***8582.2*** *p3*
Blume, . . .; Canada, 1776-1783 ***9786*** *p17*
Blume, Carl Gottlieb Wilhelm; America, 1865 ***4610.10*** *p158*
Blume, Frederick Wilhelm; West Virginia, 1856 ***9788.3*** *p4*
Blume, Theodore; New Orleans, 1848 ***1450.2*** *p15A*
Blume, Wilhelmine 15; America, 1881 ***4610.10*** *p159*
Blumenauer, Justus Henrich; Philadelphia, 1779 ***8137*** *p6*
Blumenauer, Melchior; Lancaster, PA, 1780 ***8137*** *p6*
Blumenberg, Joachim; Wisconsin, n.d. ***9675.4*** *p266*
Blumenberg, Julius; New York, 1868 ***1450.2*** *p16A*
Blumenfeld, Nathan; Arkansas, 1918 ***95.2*** *p20*
Blumenstoke, John; Baltimore, 1853 ***1450.2*** *p15A*
Blumentale, Eugene 26; New Orleans, 1838 ***778.5*** *p58*
Blumentale, Rose 24; New Orleans, 1838 ***778.5*** *p58*

Blumenthal, Joseph 30; Kansas, 1885 ***5240.1*** *p68*
Blumery, Florence 26; New Orleans, 1862 ***543.30*** *p108*
Blumes, Ann; Philadelphia, 1850 ***53.26*** *p4*
Blumes, Ann; Philadelphia, 1850 ***5704.8*** *p68*
Blumhart, . . .; Canada, 1776-1783 ***9786*** *p17*
Bluminell, . . .; Canada, 1776-1783 ***9786*** *p17*
Blumke, . . .; Canada, 1776-1783 ***9786*** *p18*
Blummell, . . .; Canada, 1776-1783 ***9786*** *p18*
Blumner, August 29; Baltimore, 1832 ***3702.7*** *p95*
*Brother:*Carl 27
*Wife:*Sophia Oesterley
Blumner, Carl 27 *SEE* Blumner, August
Blumner, Sophia Oesterley *SEE* Blumner, August
Blundell, Bryan 16; America, 1700 ***2212*** *p29*
Blundell, Charles 21; Maryland, 1774 ***1219.7*** *p211*
Blundell, Charles 29; Maryland, 1775 ***1219.7*** *p261*
*Wife:*Mary 29
Blundell, Jno 20; Virginia, 1704 ***2212*** *p41*
Blundell, Margery; Maryland or Virginia, 1697 ***2212*** *p3*
Blundell, Mary 29 *SEE* Blundell, Charles
Blundell, Wm; Virginia, 1698 ***2212*** *p16*
Blunden, Jas. 26; Canada, 1835 ***4535.10*** *p196*
Blunden, Thomas 17; West Indies, 1739 ***3690.1*** *p21*
Blunt, Charles 28; Jamaica, 1730 ***3690.1*** *p21*
Blunt, Harry C.; Arkansas, 1918 ***95.2*** *p20*
Blunt, Henry 35; Jamaica, 1736 ***3690.1*** *p21*
Blunt, James; America, 1737 ***4971*** *p36*
Blunt, Richard 18; Jamaica, 1734 ***3690.1*** *p21*
Blunter, John; Virginia, 1638 ***6219*** *p125*
Blurscvc, Blars; Iowa, 1866-1943 ***123.54*** *p9*
Bly, Elizabeth 21; Virginia, 1774 ***1219.7*** *p241*
Bly, Henry; Wisconsin, n.d. ***9675.4*** *p266*
Blystad, Ed; Colorado, 1904 ***9678.1*** *p154*
Blyth, Ann; America, 1698 ***2212*** *p6*
Blyth, John 32; Carolina, 1774 ***1219.7*** *p236*
Blyth, Joseph Henry; New York, NY, 1838 ***8208.4*** *p66*
Blyth, Sarah 30; Jamaica, 1774 ***1219.7*** *p180*
Blythe, Keziah; New York, NY, 1811 ***2859.11*** *p9*
Boadel, Jane 20; Wilmington, DE, 1831 ***6508.7*** *p161*
Boag, John 18; Jamaica, 1733 ***3690.1*** *p22*
Boag, Robert; Iowa, 1866-1943 ***123.54*** *p9*
Board, John 36; Virginia, 1774 ***1219.7*** *p226*
Boardman, Francis 21; Maryland or Virginia, 1699 ***2212*** *p21*
Boardman, James; Virginia, 1698 ***2212*** *p12*
Boardman, James 18; Maryland, 1729 ***3690.1*** *p22*
Boardman, Jerry 8; Massachusetts, 1848 ***5881.1*** *p8*
Boardman, Jerry 60; Massachusetts, 1848 ***5881.1*** *p8*
Boardman, John 17; Philadelphia, 1860 ***5704.8*** *p145*
Boardman, Mary; Maryland or Virginia, 1698 ***2212*** *p10*
Boardman, Osmond; Virginia, 1645 ***6219*** *p253*
Boarne, Joseph; Virginia, 1638 ***6219*** *p117*
Boas, Ann Maria 32; America, 1836 ***778.5*** *p58*
Boas, Christine 34; America, 1836 ***778.5*** *p58*
Boas, Elisabeth 23; America, 1836 ***778.5*** *p58*
Boasche, Joan; Illinois, 1857 ***7857*** *p2*
Boast, Francis 47; Nova Scotia, 1774 ***1219.7*** *p209*
With wife
With 5 children
Boast, John; Petersburg, VA, 1805 ***4778.1*** *p150*
Boate, Henry; Virginia, 1639 ***6219*** *p156*
Boates, Elizabeth Ward; Virginia, 1636 ***6219*** *p79*
Boaton, Thomas; Virginia, 1638 ***6219*** *p119*
Bob, Anna Felicitas Merckle *SEE* Bob, Hans Jerg
Bob, Bernhart; Pennsylvania, 1754 ***4525*** *p237*
*Relative:*Johan Georg
Bob, Hans Jerg; New York, 1717 ***3627*** *p9*
*Wife:*Anna Felicitas Merckle
Bob, Johan Georg *SEE* Bob, Bernhart
Bobacher, John M. 27; New Orleans, 1864 ***543.30*** *p249*
Bobainne, Madame 25; America, 1827 ***778.5*** *p58*
Bobainne, Joseph 26; America, 1827 ***778.5*** *p58*
Boban, Franke; Iowa, 1866-1943 ***123.54*** *p9*
Bobart, . . .; Canada, 1776-1783 ***9786*** *p41*
Bobe, . . .; Canada, 1776-1783 ***9786*** *p18*
Bober, August; Illinois, 1884 ***2896.5*** *p3*
Bober, Edward; Illinois, 1884 ***2896.5*** *p3*
Bobrov, Louis; Iowa, 1866-1943 ***123.54*** *p9*
Bobser, Jacob Frederick; New York, NY, 1838 ***8208.4*** *p64*
Boccheardo, James; Iowa, 1866-1943 ***123.54*** *p9*
Bochel, Mr. 39; New Orleans, 1831 ***778.5*** *p58*
Bocher, Catherine 30; New Orleans, 1835 ***778.5*** *p58*
Bocher, Ferdinand 6 mos; New Orleans, 1835 ***778.5*** *p58*
Bocher, Ferdinand 31; New Orleans, 1835 ***778.5*** *p58*
Bochius, Wilhelm; Charleston, SC, 1775-1781 ***8582.2*** *p52*
Bochmann, Gragor; Illinois, 1888 ***2896.5*** *p4*
Bochring, Ernest 35; New Orleans, 1862 ***543.30*** *p245*
Bochstader, Matthias; Ohio, 1851 ***1450.2*** *p16A*
Bocick, Peter; Wisconsin, n.d. ***9675.4*** *p266*
Bock, Andon; Philadelphia, 1756 ***4525*** *p261*
Bock, Anna Catharina Loze; Pennsylvania, 1743 ***4525*** *p239*
*Husband:*Thomas
Bock, Christian; America, 1850 ***1450.2*** *p16A*
Bock, F.W.; Missouri, 1833 ***3702.7*** *p97*
Bock, George; Wisconsin, n.d. ***9675.4*** *p266*
Bock, George 22; New Orleans, 1862 ***543.30*** *p483*
Bock, Oliver 21; Maryland, 1774 ***1219.7*** *p225*
Bock, Thomas *SEE* Bock, Anna Catharina Loze
Bockel, . . .; Ohio, 1881 ***3702.7*** *p430*
Bockel, Anna Catharina *SEE* Bockel, Georg Velten
Bockel, Anna Maria Rheinhard *SEE* Bockel, Georg Velten
Bockel, Georg Velten 32; Pennsylvania, 1732 ***1034.18*** *p5*
*Wife:*Anna Maria Rheinhard
*Child:*Maria Margaretha
*Child:*Anna Catharina
*Child:*Joh. Michael
Bockel, Joh. Michael *SEE* Bockel, Georg Velten
Bockel, Maria Margaretha *SEE* Bockel, Georg Velten
Bockels, Anna Elisabetha; Philadelphia, 1742 ***1034.18*** *p11*
Bocker, Franz Heinrich; America, 1856 ***4610.10*** *p121*
Bockham, William; Barbados, 1769 ***1219.7*** *p140*
Bockholder, Christian; Cincinnati, 1788-1848 ***8582.3*** *p89*
Bockhorn, George; New York, NY, 1835 ***8208.4*** *p41*
Bockius, Godfried; Philadelphia, 1760 ***9973.7*** *p34*
Bockman, Robt; South Carolina, 1788 ***7119*** *p202*
Bocwinska, Elzbieta 17; New York, 1912 ***9980.29*** *p52*
Boczkiewicz, . . .; New York, 1831 ***4606*** *p172*
Bodamer, Justina Catharina; Pennsylvania, 1751 ***2444*** *p216*
With parents
Bodamer, Margaretha Magdalena; Pennsylvania, 1752 ***2444*** *p139*
Bodd, James; New York, NY, 1811 ***2859.11*** *p9*
Boddicutt, Robert; Virginia, 1637 ***6219*** *p84*
Bode, Andreas; Wisconsin, n.d. ***9675.4*** *p266*
Bode, Anne Marie Engel; America, 1844 ***4610.10*** *p133*
Bode, Ernest 23; New Orleans, 1862 ***543.30*** *p243*
Bode, Gerhard Wilhelm; Ohio, 1815-1871 ***8582*** *p3*
Bode, Johann Andreas; Quebec, 1776 ***9786*** *p263*
Bode, Johann Friedrich; Quebec, 1776 ***9786*** *p260*
Bode, Joseph; Illinois, 1861 ***5012.38*** *p98*
Bode, Mathias; Wisconsin, n.d. ***9675.4*** *p266*
Bode, Nicholas S.; Wisconsin, n.d. ***9675.4*** *p266*
Bode, Wilhelm; Halifax, N.S., 1778 ***9786*** *p270*
Bode, Wilhelm; New York, 1776 ***9786*** *p270*
Bodecker, . . .; Canada, 1776-1783 ***9786*** *p18*
Bodely, Arthur; Virginia, 1642 ***6219*** *p194*
Bodemer, Justina Catharina; Pennsylvania, 1751 ***2444*** *p216*
With parents
Bodemer, Margaretha Magdalena; Pennsylvania, 1752 ***2444*** *p139*
Bodemeyer, George; Quebec, 1776 ***9786*** *p260*
Boden, Edward; Arizona, 1897 ***9228.30*** *p1*
Boden, Heinrich; Kentucky, 1798 ***8582.3*** *p94*
Boden, Hugh; New York, NY, 1815 ***2859.11*** *p25*
Boden, Hugh; Ohio, 1840 ***9892.11*** *p4*
Boden, John; Ohio, 1825-1830 ***9892.11*** *p4*
Boden, John; Ohio, 1840 ***9892.11*** *p4*
Boden, John; Quebec, 1824 ***9892.11*** *p4*
Boden, Thomas; America, 1739 ***4971*** *p24*
Bodenbinder, . . .; Canada, 1776-1783 ***9786*** *p18*
Bodenstein, Charles; Illinois, 1883 ***2896.5*** *p4*
Bodenstein, Christian; Illinois, 1879 ***2896.5*** *p4*
Boder, Alosia; Wisconsin, n.d. ***9675.4*** *p266*
Boder, Cecelia; Wisconsin, n.d. ***9675.4*** *p266*
Boder, Julia; Wisconsin, n.d. ***9675.4*** *p266*
Boderen, William; Wisconsin, n.d. ***9675.4*** *p266*
Bodevin, Michel; Wisconsin, n.d. ***9675.4*** *p266*
Bodhaine, Baynard; Colorado, 1904 ***9678.1*** *p155*
Bodhaine, Frank; Colorado, 1892 ***9678.1*** *p155*
Bodhaine, Frank; Colorado, 1904 ***9678.1*** *p155*
Bodhaine, Jules; Colorado, 1904 ***9678.1*** *p155*
Bodin, Adolph; Missouri, 1884 ***5240.1*** *p6*
Bodin, Frank; Wisconsin, n.d. ***9675.4*** *p266*
Bodin, John; Virginia, 1635 ***6219*** *p25*
Bodin, William; Wisconsin, n.d. ***9675.4*** *p266*
Bodis, Charles; Wisconsin, n.d. ***9675.4*** *p266*
Bodis, Edward; Wisconsin, n.d. ***9675.4*** *p266*
Bodis, Louis; Wisconsin, n.d. ***9675.4*** *p266*
Bodkin, Ann 7; Quebec, 1855 ***5704.8*** *p126*
Bodkin, Eliza; Quebec, 1852 ***5704.8*** *p94*
Bodkin, George 12; Quebec, 1855 ***5704.8*** *p125*
Bodkin, James; Quebec, 1851 ***5704.8*** *p75*
Bodkin, John 16; Quebec, 1853 ***5704.8*** *p104*
Bodkin, Margaret 11; Quebec, 1855 ***5704.8*** *p126*
Bodkin, Margaret 40; Quebec, 1855 ***5704.8*** *p125*
Bodkin, William; Philadelphia, 1867 ***5704.8*** *p219*
Bodkin, William 18; Quebec, 1853 ***5704.8*** *p104*
Bodkin, William 80; Quebec, 1855 ***5704.8*** *p125*
Bodley, James; West Virginia, 1803-1840 ***9788.3*** *p5*
Bodley, James; West Virginia, 1848 ***9788.3*** *p5*
Bodley, William 70; West Virginia, 1811 ***9788.3*** *p5*
Bodman, Andrew; Virginia, 1638 ***6219*** *p149*
Bodmann, Mr.; Cincinnati, 1831 ***8582.1*** *p51*
Bodmann, Ferdinand; America, 1822 ***8582.2*** *p61*
Bodmann, Ferdinand; Baltimore, 1822 ***8582.1*** *p3*
*Father:*Louis C.
With 2 brothers
Bodmann, Ferdinand; Cincinnati, 1869-1887 ***8582*** *p3*
Bodmann, Louis C. *SEE* Bodmann, Ferdinand
Bodmer, Carl; America, 1891 ***1450.2*** *p4B*
Bodney, Henry; Virginia, 1642 ***6219*** *p195*
Bodouin, Mr. 29; America, 1837 ***778.5*** *p59*
Body, Robert; Virginia, 1645 ***6219*** *p253*
Body, Thomas; Virginia, 1636 ***6219*** *p79*
Boe, Ellen 16; Massachusetts, 1849 ***5881.1*** *p7*
Boebinger, Jakob; Cincinnati, 1788-1876 ***8582.3*** *p81*
Boebinger, Margaretha; Cincinnati, 1833 ***8582.1*** *p41*
With father
Boeblinger, Abraham; Cincinnati, 1818 ***8582.1*** *p51*
Boeblinger, Johann; America, 1839 ***8582.2*** *p3*
Boecker, Anne Marie Engel *SEE* Boecker, Johann Heinrich
Boecker, Anne Marie Louise *SEE* Boecker, Johann Heinrich
Boecker, Johann Heinrich *SEE* Boecker, Johann Heinrich
Boecker, Johann Heinrich 44; America, 1850 ***4610.10*** *p142*
With wife
*Child:*Anne Marie Louise
*Child:*Anne Marie Engel
*Child:*Wilhelmine
*Child:*Johann Heinrich
Boecker, Wilhelmine *SEE* Boecker, Johann Heinrich
Boeckling, Anton; Cincinnati, 1788-1848 ***8582.3*** *p89*
Boegeholz, Carl Diedrich 39; America, 1850 ***4610.10*** *p142*
*Wife:*Christine Sander
*Child:*Carl Heinrich
*Child:*Wilhelm Carl Heinrich
*Child:*Friedrich Wilhelm
Boegeholz, Carl Heinrich *SEE* Boegeholz, Carl Diedrich
Boegeholz, Christine Sander *SEE* Boegeholz, Carl Diedrich
Boegeholz, Friedrich Wilhelm *SEE* Boegeholz, Carl Diedrich
Boegeholz, Wilhelm Carl Heinrich *SEE* Boegeholz, Carl Diedrich
Boeger, Johann Henrich; Trenton, NJ, 1776 ***8137*** *p6*
Boehler, Anna Catharine *SEE* Boehler, Francis
Boehler, Christian; America, 1830-1839 ***2896.5*** *p4*
Boehler, Elizabeth *SEE* Boehler, Peter
Boehler, Elizabeth *SEE* Boehler, Peter
Boehler, Francis; New York, 1752 ***3652*** *p76*
*Wife:*Anna Catharine
Boehler, Peter; New York, 1753 ***3652*** *p77*
*Wife:*Elizabeth
Boehler, Peter; New York, 1756 ***3652*** *p81*
Boehler, Peter; Philadelphia, 1742 ***3652*** *p55*
*Wife:*Elizabeth
Boehler, William; New York, 1756 ***3652*** *p81*
Boehm, . . .; Canada, 1776-1783 ***9786*** *p18*
Boehm, Mr.; America, 1715 ***8582.3*** *p75*
Boehm, Anton; America, 1700-1877 ***8582.3*** *p80*
Boehm, Baulus; Philadelphia, 1752 ***8125.6*** *p23*
Boehm, Frederick; New York, 1849 ***1450.2*** *p16A*
Boehme, . . .; Canada, 1776-1783 ***9786*** *p18*
Boehme, Adolph; Wisconsin, n.d. ***9675.4*** *p266*
Boehmer, Albert; Cincinnati, 1869-1887 ***8582*** *p3*
Boehmer, Margaret *SEE* Boehmer, Martin
Boehmer, Martin; New York, 1743 ***3652*** *p59*
*Wife:*Margaret
Boehmreuther, . . .; Canada, 1776-1783 ***9786*** *p18*
Boehne, Child; Illinois, 1822-1922 ***4610.10*** *p85*
With 3 siblings
Boehne, Christian Friedrich Ludwig; Illinois, 1822-1922 ***4610.10*** *p85*
Boehne, Christian Friedrich Wilhelm; Illinois, 1822-1922 ***4610.10*** *p85*
*Son:*Edward
Boehne, Christian Friedrich Wilhelm; Illinois, 1922 ***4610.10*** *p85*
Boehne, Edward *SEE* Boehne, Christian Friedrich Wilhelm
Boehner, Heinrich; Wisconsin, n.d. ***9675.4*** *p266*
Boehning, John; New York, NY, 1874 ***3455.2*** *p98*
Boehnisch, George; Pennsylvania, 1734 ***3652*** *p51*
Boehringer, Gertrude *SEE* Boehringer, John David
Boehringer, John David; New York, 1743 ***3652*** *p59*
*Wife:*Gertrude
Boeker, Karl Heinrich August; America, 1887 ***4610.10*** *p118*

Boeker, Wilhelmine Marie Christine; America, 1865 ***4610.10*** *p100*
Boekhoff, Tasso; Iroquois Co., IL, 1894 ***3455.1*** *p9*
Boeles, Krist; Arkansas, 1918 ***95.2*** *p20*
Boellner, Johann H.; Cincinnati, 1869-1887 ***8582*** *p4*
Boelzner, Ernst; America, 1854 ***8582.3*** *p7*
Boemeyer, A.M. Ilse Lubbing *SEE* Boemeyer, Ernst Heinrich
Boemeyer, Ernst Heinrich; America, 1840 ***4610.10*** *p111*
*Wife:*A.M. Ilse Lubbing
*Son:*Friedrich Wilhelm
Boemeyer, Friedrich Wilhelm *SEE* Boemeyer, Ernst Heinrich
Boening, Fred W.; Wisconsin, n.d. ***9675.4*** *p266*
Boenning, Herman; Wisconsin, n.d. ***9675.4*** *p266*
Boeres, Heinrich; America, 1849 ***8582.2*** *p4*
Boeres, Heinrich; New York, NY, 1849 ***8582.3*** *p7*
Boerger, Johannes Nicholas 33; Pennsylvania, 1753 ***4525*** *p202*
Boerjesson, Benjamin 20; Massachusetts, 1860 ***6410.32*** *p113*
Boers, Hendrieka 65; New York, NY, 1847 ***3377.6*** *p14*
Boers, Jane 20; New York, NY, 1847 ***3377.6*** *p14*
Boers, John 28; New York, NY, 1847 ***3377.6*** *p14*
Boers, Mannes 65; New York, NY, 1847 ***3377.6*** *p14*
Boesch, Christian; Illinois, 1869 ***5012.38*** *p99*
Boesel, Charles; Ohio, 1869-1887 ***8582*** *p4*
Boesmer, Hans Jerg; Pennsylvania, 1749 ***2444*** *p140*
Boesmer, Hans Jerg; Pennsylvania, 1749 ***2444*** *p163*
Boessler, Jacob; Wisconsin, n.d. ***9675.4*** *p266*
Boessmer, Anna Barbara *SEE* Boessmer, Hans Jerg
Boessmer, Christina *SEE* Boessmer, Hans Jerg
Boessmer, Cordula *SEE* Boessmer, Hans Jerg
Boessmer, Dorothea *SEE* Boessmer, Hans Jerg
Boessmer, Hans Jerg; Pennsylvania, 1750 ***2444*** *p140*
*Wife:*Anna Barbara
*Child:*Johann Caspar
*Child:*Maria Elisabetha
*Child:*Dorothea
*Child:*Christina
*Child:*Cordula
Boessmer, Johann Caspar *SEE* Boessmer, Hans Jerg
Boessmer, Maria Elisabetha *SEE* Boessmer, Hans Jerg
Boeswald, Karl; Kentucky, 1844 ***8582.3*** *p101*
Boetger, . . .; Canada, 1776-1783 ***9786*** *p18*
Boeth, Michael 50; New Orleans, 1839 ***9420.2*** *p70*
Boeth, Nikolaus; Philadelphia, 1779 ***8137*** *p6*
Boettcher, Charles; Wisconsin, n.d. ***9675.4*** *p266*
Boettcher, John; America, 1889 ***1450.2*** *p16A*
Boetticher, Julius; Philadelphia, 1832 ***8582.2*** *p4*
Boetz, Andreas; Pennsylvania, 1730-1779 ***2444*** *p140*
Boetz, Carl 27; New Orleans, 1862 ***543.30*** *p482*
Boetz, Herman 25; New Orleans, 1862 ***543.30*** *p482*
Boff, Geno; Iowa, 1866-1943 ***123.54*** *p9*
Bofield, Prere 29; New Orleans, 1862 ***543.30*** *p483*
Bogaard Family ; New York, NY, 1710 ***8582.3*** *p7*
Bogaart Family ; New York, NY, 1710 ***8582.3*** *p7*
Bogacki, Antoni; New York, 1835 ***4606*** *p179*
Bogagues, Pilar 68; Arizona, 1905 ***9228.40*** *p10*
Bogan, Alice 9; New Orleans, 1849 ***5704.8*** *p59*
Bogan, Ann 20; Massachusetts, 1849 ***5881.1*** *p6*
Bogan, Brien; New Orleans, 1849 ***5704.8*** *p59*
Bogan, Catherine; New Orleans, 1849 ***5704.8*** *p59*
Bogan, James 7; New Orleans, 1849 ***5704.8*** *p59*
Bogan, Laurince 3; New Orleans, 1849 ***5704.8*** *p59*
Bogan, Margaret; New York, NY, 1866 ***5704.8*** *p214*
Bogan, Mary; New York, NY, 1870 ***5704.8*** *p239*
Bogan, Michael; New York, NY, 1869 ***5704.8*** *p233*
Bogan, Patrick; New York, NY, 1870 ***5704.8*** *p239*
Bogan, Paul; Philadelphia, 1847 ***53.26*** *p4*
Bogan, Paul; Philadelphia, 1847 ***5704.8*** *p31*
Bogan, Sarah; New Orleans, 1849 ***5704.8*** *p59*
Bogan, Sarah 3; New Orleans, 1849 ***5704.8*** *p59*
Bogan, Sarah 20; Philadelphia, 1861 ***5704.8*** *p148*
Bogan, Susan; New York, NY, 1870 ***5704.8*** *p239*
Bogan, William; New York, NY, 1869 ***5704.8*** *p233*
Bogart Family ; New York, NY, 1710 ***8582.3*** *p7*
Bogart, John; Washington, 1859-1920 ***2872.1*** *p4*
Bogdonobicz, Mieczyelon; Arkansas, 1918 ***95.2*** *p20*
Boge, Archibald; North Carolina, 1739 ***1639.20*** *p14*
Bogehold, Anne M. L. C. Finke *SEE* Bogehold, Carl Heinrich
Bogehold, Carl Heinrich; America, 1841 ***4610.10*** *p138*
*Wife:*Anne M. L. C. Finke
*Son:*Johann Carl Diedrich
Bogehold, Johann Carl Diedrich *SEE* Bogehold, Carl Heinrich
Bogeholz, Miss; America, 1850 ***4610.10*** *p138*
Bogeholz, Carl Heinrich; America, 1850 ***4610.10*** *p139*
Bogeholz, Carl Heinrich; America, 1882 ***4610.10*** *p140*
Bogeholz, Hermann Heinrich; America, 1855 ***4610.10*** *p139*
Bogen, Georg *SEE* Bogen, Peter
Bogen, Georg; Cincinnati, 1869-1887 ***8582*** *p4*
Bogen, Peter; America, 1826 ***8582.2*** *p61*
*Brother:*Georg
Bogen, Peter; Cincinnati, 1869-1887 ***8582*** *p4*
Bogenschuetz, Karl; America, 1843 ***8582.3*** *p7*
Boger, Anna Maria *SEE* Boger, Joseph
Boger, Jacob Friedrich *SEE* Boger, Joseph
Boger, Joseph; Philadelphia, 1754 ***2444*** *p140*
*Wife:*Susanna
*Child:*Maria Margaretha
*Child:*Anna Maria
*Child:*Jacob Friedrich
Boger, Maria Margaretha *SEE* Boger, Joseph
Boger, Susanna *SEE* Boger, Joseph
Bogert, Peter; Pennsylvania, 1706 ***8582.3*** *p7*
Bogert, Peter; Philadelphia, 1744 ***8582.3*** *p8*
Boggs, Alexander; New York, NY, 1816 ***2859.11*** *p25*
Boggs, Isabella; St. John, N.B., 1847 ***5704.8*** *p5*
Boggs, James A.; America, 1861 ***2896.5*** *p4*
Bogle, Isabella; New York, NY, 1815 ***2859.11*** *p25*
Bogle, John; New York, NY, 1815 ***2859.11*** *p25*
Bogle, Robert; Wilmington, NC, 1751-1785 ***1639.20*** *p14*
Bogle, Robert 50; Grenada, 1774 ***1219.7*** *p184*
Bogle, Samuel; New York, NY, 1815 ***2859.11*** *p25*
Bogon, Franciszek 21; New York, 1912 ***9980.29*** *p61*
Bogue, Bernard 50; Massachusetts, 1850 ***5881.1*** *p6*
Bogue, Eliza 5; Massachusetts, 1850 ***5881.1*** *p7*
Bogue, Jane 9; Massachusetts, 1850 ***5881.1*** *p9*
Bogue, John 7; Massachusetts, 1850 ***5881.1*** *p9*
Bogue, Rose 45; Massachusetts, 1850 ***5881.1*** *p12*
Bogue, William 27; Philadelphia, 1774 ***1219.7*** *p216*
Boguslawski, Aleksander; New York, 1831 ***4606*** *p172*
Bohan, John R.; Wisconsin, n.d. ***9675.4*** *p266*
Bohan, Matthew; New York, NY, 1816 ***2859.11*** *p25*
Bohan, Thomas; Wisconsin, n.d. ***9675.4*** *p266*
Bohannan, John 30; Philadelphia, 1775 ***1219.7*** *p257*
Bohas, William 30; New Orleans, 1863 ***543.30*** *p362*
Bohckel, . . .; Ohio, 1881 ***3702.7*** *p436*
Bohde, Charles; New York, NY, 1840 ***8208.4*** *p109*
Bohde, Sebastian; Canada, 1783 ***9786*** *p38A*
Bohitz, August; Wisconsin, n.d. ***9675.4*** *p266*
Bohk, Christophe 33; America, 1838 ***778.5*** *p59*
Bohkel, . . .; New York, 1881 ***3702.7*** *p426*
Bohl, Peter; Cincinnati, 1869-1887 ***8582*** *p4*
Bohlaender, Conrad; America, 1839 ***8582.1*** *p4*
Bohlau, Ferdinand 35; New Orleans, 1839 ***9420.2*** *p483*
Bohle, . . .; Canada, 1776-1783 ***9786*** *p18*
Bohle, Christian; New York, 1756 ***3652*** *p81*
Bohlen, Barney; Illinois, 1905 ***5012.37*** *p63*
Bohlen, D. Augustus; America, 1849 ***1450.2*** *p16A*
Bohlen, Heinrich; America, 1861-1865 ***8582.3*** *p91*
Bohlender, Jost; Cincinnati, 1869-1887 ***8582*** *p4*
Bohler, Anna Barbara *SEE* Bohler, Hans Martin
Bohler, Catharina *SEE* Bohler, Hans Martin
Bohler, Catharina *SEE* Bohler, Hans Martin
Bohler, Catharina Elisabetha *SEE* Bohler, Hans Martin
Bohler, Catharina Elisabetha; Pennsylvania, 1738 ***1034.18*** *p15*
Bohler, Hans Martin *SEE* Bohler, Hans Martin
Bohler, Hans Martin; Pennsylvania, 1738 ***1034.18*** *p5*
*Wife:*Catharina
*Child:*Hans Martin
*Child:*Catharina Elisabetha
*Child:*Anna Barbara
*Child:*Maria Johannata
*Child:*Joh. Ludwig
*Child:*Catharina
Bohler, Jacob; New England, 1766 ***2854*** *p43*
With wife
With 5 children
Bohler, Joh. Ludwig *SEE* Bohler, Hans Martin
Bohler, Maria Johannata *SEE* Bohler, Hans Martin
Bohler, Peter; Philadelphia, 1742 ***3652*** *p54*
Bohling, . . .; Canada, 1776-1783 ***9786*** *p18*
Bohling, Heinrich; America, 1846 ***8582.1*** *p4*
Bohlman, Henry; Iroquois Co., IL, 1892 ***3455.1*** *p9*
Bohlmann, Henry; Iroquois Co., IL, 1894 ***3455.1*** *p9*
Bohls, Claus; New York, NY, 1840 ***8208.4*** *p113*
Bohm, August; Nebraska, 1874 ***2896.5*** *p4*
Bohm, Charles; Illinois, 1871 ***5012.39*** *p25*
Bohm, John; Illinois, 1871 ***5012.39*** *p25*
Bohman, C. P.; Minneapolis, 1868-1878 ***6410.35*** *p50*
Bohman, Fred; Minneapolis, 1874-1887 ***6410.35*** *p50*
Bohme, Amelia 17 *SEE* Bohme, Charles Gottl.
Bohme, Bertha 4 *SEE* Bohme, Wm. Aug.
Bohme, Carolina 24 *SEE* Bohme, Charles Gottl.
Bohme, Charles 5 *SEE* Bohme, Wm. Aug.
Bohme, Charles Gottl. 51; New Orleans, 1839 ***9420.2*** *p484*
*Wife:*Jane Christ Sophie 42
*Daughter:*Carolina 24
*Daughter:*Emma 19
*Daughter:*Amelia 17
*Daughter:*Mary 10
*Son:*Martin 9
Bohme, Emma 19 *SEE* Bohme, Charles Gottl.
Bohme, Jane Christ Sophie 42 *SEE* Bohme, Charles Gottl.
Bohme, Johanna 40 *SEE* Bohme, Wm. Aug.
Bohme, Louis 6 mos *SEE* Bohme, Wm. Aug.
Bohme, Martin 9 *SEE* Bohme, Charles Gottl.
Bohme, Mary 2 *SEE* Bohme, Wm. Aug.
Bohme, Mary 10 *SEE* Bohme, Charles Gottl.
Bohme, Wm. Aug. 28; New Orleans, 1839 ***9420.2*** *p359*
*Wife:*Johanna 40
*Son:*Charles 5
*Daughter:*Bertha 4
*Daughter:*Mary 2
*Son:*Louis 6 mos
Bohmeier, A.M. Ilse Lubbing *SEE* Bohmeier, Ernst Heinrich
Bohmeier, Ernst Heinrich; America, 1840 ***4610.10*** *p111*
*Wife:*A.M. Ilse Lubbing
*Son:*Friedrich Wilhelm
Bohmeier, Friedrich Wilhelm *SEE* Bohmeier, Ernst Heinrich
Bohment, Lucas 27; America, 1839 ***778.5*** *p59*
Bohmeyer, Carl Heinrich; America, 1868 ***4610.10*** *p140*
Bohn, Carl; Illinois, 1902 ***5012.40*** *p79*
Bohn, Frederick; Ohio, 1857-1861 ***9892.11*** *p4*
Bohn, Henry; Illinois, 1904 ***5012.39*** *p53*
Bohn, Louis; Illinois, 1904 ***5012.39*** *p53*
Bohnacker, Anna Durst *SEE* Bohnacker, David
Bohnacker, David; Nova Scotia, 1752 ***2444*** *p140*
*Wife:*Anna Durst
*Child:*Elisabetha
Bohnacker, Elisabetha *SEE* Bohnacker, David
Bohner, John; Savannah, GA, 1736 ***3652*** *p51*
Bohnert, Bernhard; Cincinnati, 1869-1887 ***8582*** *p4*
Bohning, George D.; Illinois, 1860 ***2896.5*** *p4*
Bohnisch, Matthias; Savannah, GA, 1736 ***3652*** *p51*
Bohnsack, . . .; Canada, 1776-1783 ***9786*** *p18*
Bohonett, Patrick; Virginia, 1641 ***6219*** *p184*
Bohrer, Georg A.; Cincinnati, 1869-1887 ***8582*** *p4*
Bohrer, Georges 18; America, 1836 ***778.5*** *p59*
Bohrer, Louise 29; America, 1836 ***778.5*** *p59*
Bohrtz, Charles; Wisconsin, n.d. ***9675.4*** *p266*
Bohuszewicz, Baltazar; New York, 1834 ***4606*** *p178*
Boid, John; Virginia, 1643 ***6219*** *p206*
Boijart, Mme. 56; America, 1839 ***778.5*** *p59*
Boilletot, Simon 26; New Orleans, 1838 ***778.5*** *p59*
Boimare, Mr. 23; New Orleans, 1821 ***778.5*** *p59*
Boimare, A. L. 34; New Orleans, 1820 ***778.5*** *p59*
Bois, Thomas 26; Massachusetts, 1847 ***5881.1*** *p12*
Boisibon, Pierre; Louisiana, 1789-1819 ***778.5*** *p555*
Boismare, A. 40; New Orleans, 1836 ***778.5*** *p59*
Boismare, A. L. 30; New Orleans, 1826 ***778.5*** *p59*
Boismare, R. L. 30; New Orleans, 1825 ***778.5*** *p59*
Boison, Francois 30; America, 1826 ***778.5*** *p59*
Boissau, Albert 42; America, 1839 ***778.5*** *p59*
Boisseau, Dominique 28; America, 1838 ***778.5*** *p60*
Boisseles, Eugene; New York, NY, 1838 ***8208.4*** *p73*
Boisson, Mr. 30; New Orleans, 1839 ***778.5*** *p60*
Boisson, Francois 35; New Orleans, 1837 ***778.5*** *p60*
Boisson, Guillaume; Port uncertain, 1839 ***778.5*** *p60*
Boisson, Jacques 30; New Orleans, 1837 ***778.5*** *p60*
Boiteux, Jean 28; New Orleans, 1838 ***778.5*** *p60*
Boiteux, Rosalie 24; New Orleans, 1838 ***778.5*** *p60*
Boiton, Philibert 28; America, 1835 ***778.5*** *p60*
Boizo, Abraham 17; Pennsylvania, 1719 ***3690.1*** *p22*
Bojack, . . .; Canada, 1776-1783 ***9786*** *p18*
Bok, Joseph; Illinois, 1873 ***5012.39*** *p26*
Bokalarza, John; Iowa, 1866-1943 ***123.54*** *p9*
Boke, Sohn; New York, NY, 1816 ***2859.11*** *p25*
Boker, Carl Heinrich Friedrich; America, 1891 ***4610.10*** *p103*
Boker, Franz Heinrich; America, 1856 ***4610.10*** *p121*
Boker, Jacob; Ohio, 1837 ***9892.11*** *p4*
Boker, Karl; America, 1892 ***4610.10*** *p52*
Boker, Marie Louise; America, 1891 ***4610.10*** *p103*
Bokseth, Peter; Washington, 1859-1920 ***2872.1*** *p4*
Bolan, John; America, 1736-1743 ***4971*** *p58*
Bolan, Maurice; America, 1736-1743 ***4971*** *p58*
Bolan, Patrick; Philadelphia, 1866 ***5704.8*** *p208*
Bolan, Unity; Philadelphia, 1866 ***5704.8*** *p208*
Bolan, William; America, 1736-1743 ***4971*** *p58*
Boland, . . .; Canada, 1776-1783 ***9786*** *p18*
Boland, Biddy 19; Philadelphia, 1854 ***5704.8*** *p122*
Boland, Bridget; New York, NY, 1868 ***5704.8*** *p229*
Boland, Conrad; Philadelphia, 1837 ***8582.3*** *p8*
With parents
Boland, John; Indiana, 1852 ***1450.2*** *p16A*
Boland, Penrigin; Virginia, 1642 ***6219*** *p199*
Bolander, C. A.; Iowa, 1866-1943 ***123.54*** *p9*
Bolans, John; Arkansas, 1918 ***95.2*** *p20*
Bolaus, David; Ohio, 1789 ***8582.2*** *p56*

Bolay, Anna Barbara Jetter *SEE* Bolay, Laurentius
Bolay, Anna Martha *SEE* Bolay, Laurentius
Bolay, Jean 30; America, 1839 ***778.5*** *p60*
Bolay, Laurentius; Pennsylvania, 1752 ***2444*** *p140*
*Wife:*Anna Barbara Jetter
*Child:*Anna Martha
Bolay, Peter 25; America, 1839 ***778.5*** *p60*
Bolcker, Friderick; Canada, 1783 ***9786*** *p38A*
Bold, Jacob; Wisconsin, n.d. ***9675.4*** *p266*
Boldason, Joseph; Arkansas, 1918 ***95.2*** *p20*
Bolden, John 15; Jamaica, 1730 ***3690.1*** *p22*
Bole, John; St. John, N.B., 1848 ***5704.8*** *p47*
Bole, John 18; Philadelphia, 1854 ***5704.8*** *p121*
Bole, Peter 20; New England, 1699 ***2212*** *p19*
Bolender, Jost; America, 1835 ***8582.2*** *p60*
Boles, Bennet 23; Philadelphia, 1803 ***53.26*** *p4*
Boles, Euge.; Virginia, 1637 ***6219*** *p83*
Boles, Jane 21; Massachusetts, 1849 ***5881.1*** *p8*
Bolf, Francois 23; America, 1838 ***778.5*** *p60*
Bolger, James; New Orleans, 1847 ***6013.19*** *p29*
Bolin, James; North Carolina, 1767-1794 ***1639.20*** *p14*
Bolin, Oscar; Minneapolis, 1880-1887 ***6410.35*** *p50*
Bolish, Christopher; America, 1852 ***6014.1*** *p1*
Bolks, Albert 7; New York, NY, 1847 ***3377.6*** *p11*
Bolks, Geertje 32; New York, NY, 1847 ***3377.6*** *p11*
Bolks, Gemaniel 6; New York, NY, 1847 ***3377.6*** *p11*
Bolks, Janet 15; New York, NY, 1847 ***3377.6*** *p11*
Bolks, Johanna 4; New York, NY, 1847 ***3377.6*** *p11*
Bolks, Seine 32; New York, NY, 1847 ***3377.6*** *p11*
Boll, Dominick; New York, NY, 1838 ***8208.4*** *p71*
Bollatti, John; Iowa, 1866-1943 ***123.54*** *p10*
Bolle, George; Illinois, 1885 ***2896.5*** *p4*
Bolle, Henry D.; America, 1818 ***1450.2*** *p16A*
Bollhorst, Wilhelm; Illinois, 1888 ***2896.5*** *p4*
Bollier, Paulus; America, 1854-1856 ***1450.2*** *p17A*
Bolliere, Alphonse 35; New Orleans, 1864 ***543.30*** *p249*
Bolling, Ernst Carl Friedrich; America, 1865 ***4610.10*** *p105*
Bolling, Louis 26; America, 1876 ***4610.10*** *p101*
*Wife:*Marie Louise 20
Bolling, Marie Louise 20 *SEE* Bolling, Louis
Bollinger, Peter; New Orleans, 1835 ***8582*** *p4*
Bollmann, . . .; Canada, 1776-1783 ***9786*** *p18*
Bollmann, A. M. Louise Wilhelmine; America, 1881 ***4610.10*** *p159*
Bollmann, Caroline W. Charlotte; America, 1884 ***4610.10*** *p160*
Bollmann, John 34; Kansas, 1885 ***5240.1*** *p67*
Bollnitz, v., Capit.; Quebec, 1776 ***9786*** *p105*
Bolm, N. F.; Minneapolis, 1881-1885 ***6410.35*** *p51*
Bolmer, Christian; Ohio, 1811 ***8582.1*** *p48*
Bolney, John 15; Maryland, 1775 ***1219.7*** *p272*
Bolnski, Jim; Arkansas, 1918 ***95.2*** *p20*
Boloe, Leon.; Virginia, 1636 ***6219*** *p23*
Bolous, David; Ohio, 1789 ***8582.2*** *p56*
Bolsee, Mrs. 26; New Orleans, 1827 ***778.5*** *p60*
Bolt, . . .; Canada, 1776-1783 ***9786*** *p41*
Bolte, Henry; Illinois, 1870 ***5240.1*** *p6*
Bolter, Nathan; Arkansas, 1918 ***95.2*** *p20*
Boltjes, John; Kansas, 1884 ***5240.1*** *p6*
Bolton, Daniel 22; Jamaica, 1736 ***3690.1*** *p23*
Bolton, Frank George; Arkansas, 1918 ***95.2*** *p20*
Bolton, James F. 41; California, 1871 ***2769.2*** *p5*
Bolton, Joane; Virginia, 1636 ***6219*** *p109*
Bolton, Jone; Virginia, 1635 ***6219*** *p72*
Bolton, Margaret; New York, NY, 1816 ***2859.11*** *p25*
Bolton, Richard 36; Maryland, 1773 ***1219.7*** *p173*
Bolton, Samuel 40; Massachusetts, 1848 ***5881.1*** *p12*
Bolton, Sarah 25; Canada, 1838 ***4535.12*** *p113*
Bolton, Thomas 9; Massachusetts, 1848 ***5881.1*** *p12*
Bolton, Thomas George 42; California, 1872 ***2769.2*** *p5*
Bolton, William 34; Maryland, 1775 ***1219.7*** *p272*
Bolts, Joseph 38; Maryland, 1774 ***1219.7*** *p191*
Boltz, Samuel, Jr.; Virginia, 1858 ***4626.16*** *p17*
Boltzius, Gertraud *SEE* Boltzius, Johann Martin
Boltzius, Gertraud Kroehr; Georgia, 1739 ***9332*** *p324*
Boltzius, Johann Martin; Georgia, 1739 ***9332*** *p325*
*Wife:*Gertraud
Bolz, Frederick; Shreveport, LA, 1876 ***7129*** *p44*
Bolze, Mr. 34; New Orleans, 1826 ***778.5*** *p60*
Bolzekeke, Steve; Arkansas, 1918 ***95.2*** *p21*
Bolzius, John Martin; Georgia, 1734 ***9332*** *p323A*
Bomant, Mr. 28; Port uncertain, 1838 ***778.5*** *p60*
Bombonnel, Charles 20; Port uncertain, 1836 ***778.5*** *p60*
Bomtz, George; Wisconsin, n.d. ***9675.4*** *p266*
Bomzutto, Carmelo; Arkansas, 1918 ***95.2*** *p21*
Bon, Gilles 25; New Orleans, 1821 ***778.5*** *p61*
Bon, Jesus 64; Arizona, 1906 ***9228.40*** *p10*
Bon, John 28; New Orleans, 1863 ***543.30*** *p247*
Bonacina, Lewis; Quebec, 1815 ***9229.18*** *p78*
Bonacker, Anna Durst *SEE* Bonacker, David
Bonacker, David; Nova Scotia, 1752 ***2444*** *p140*
*Wife:*Anna Durst
*Child:*Elisabetha
Bonacker, Elisabetha *SEE* Bonacker, David
Bonal, Jean 38; New Orleans, 1839 ***778.5*** *p61*
Bonamie, Pedro 40; New Orleans, 1831 ***778.5*** *p61*
Bonanno, Tony; Arkansas, 1918 ***95.2*** *p21*
Bonar, Eliza 24; St. John, N.B., 1861 ***5704.8*** *p149*
Bonar, Francis 23; St. John, N.B., 1862 ***5704.8*** *p150*
Bonar, Grace; St. John, N.B., 1850 ***5704.8*** *p67*
Bonar, Henry; America, 1853 ***1450.2*** *p17A*
Bonar, James; Philadelphia, 1850 ***53.26*** *p4*
Bonar, James; Philadelphia, 1850 ***5704.8*** *p59*
Bonath, Catharine; Milwaukee, 1875 ***4719.30*** *p257*
Bonato, Giuseppe; Iowa, 1866-1943 ***123.54*** *p57*
Bonato, Guiseppe; Iowa, 1866-1943 ***123.54*** *p57*
Bonchase, E. 24; New Orleans, 1825 ***778.5*** *p61*
Bonckell, . . .; Canada, 1776-1783 ***9786*** *p18*
Bond, Alexander; New York, NY, 1816 ***2859.11*** *p25*
Bond, Anne 27 *SEE* Bond, John
Bond, Barbara 2 *SEE* Bond, John
Bond, Conrad; Wisconsin, n.d. ***9675.4*** *p266*
Bond, Degery; Virginia, 1638 ***6219*** *p116*
Bond, Edw.; Virginia, 1636 ***6219*** *p108*
Bond, Elizabeth 20; Philadelphia, 1774 ***1219.7*** *p183*
Bond, Francis 23; Jamaica, 1725 ***3690.1*** *p22*
Bond, Henry; America, 1698 ***2212*** *p6*
Bond, James; St. John, N.B., 1851 ***5704.8*** *p72*
Bond, John; Philadelphia, 1852 ***5704.8*** *p92*
Bond, John; Virginia, 1638 ***6219*** *p146*
Bond, John 30; Jamaica, 1724 ***3690.1*** *p22*
Bond, John 32; Philadelphia, 1834 ***53.26*** *p5*
*Relative:*Anne 27
*Relative:*Mary 5
*Relative:*Margaret 2
*Relative:*Barbara 2
Bond, Jon.; Virginia, 1637 ***6219*** *p110*
Bond, Margaret 2 *SEE* Bond, John
Bond, Mary 5 *SEE* Bond, John
Bond, Mary Jane 20; Philadelphia, 1854 ***5704.8*** *p122*
Bond, Peggy; St. John, N.B., 1847 ***5704.8*** *p35*
Bond, Richard 17; Maryland, 1774 ***1219.7*** *p244*
Bond, Richard 21; Jamaica, 1736 ***3690.1*** *p22*
Bond, S. 27; Philadelphia, 1775 ***1219.7*** *p255*
Bond, Sarah; Virginia, 1642 ***6219*** *p199*
Bond, William 16; Maryland, 1775 ***1219.7*** *p254*
Bond, William 21; New York, 1775 ***1219.7*** *p268*
Bonda, Isadore 25; New Orleans, 1838 ***778.5*** *p61*
Bonda, Philipe 23; New Orleans, 1838 ***778.5*** *p61*
Bonde, . . .; Canada, 1776-1783 ***9786*** *p18*
Bondet, Josephe 40; New Orleans, 1838 ***778.5*** *p61*
Bonds, Nicholas; Virginia, 1642 ***6219*** *p198*
Bondscher, Johan Vetter; South Carolina, 1788 ***7119*** *p204*
Bone, Eliz. 2 *SEE* Bone, Wm.
Bone, Eliz. 20 *SEE* Bone, Richard
Bone, Eliz. 31 *SEE* Bone, Wm.
Bone, James 24; Port uncertain, 1849 ***4535.10*** *p198*
*Wife:*Mary Ann 20
Bone, Jose 20; Mexico, 1836 ***778.5*** *p61*
Bone, Mary Ann 6 *SEE* Bone, Wm.
Bone, Mary Ann 20 *SEE* Bone, James
Bone, Richard 21; Port uncertain, 1849 ***4535.10*** *p198*
*Wife:*Eliz. 20
Bone, Sarah 2 mos *SEE* Bone, Wm.
Bone, Thos. 4 *SEE* Bone, Wm.
Bone, Wm.; Virginia, 1643 ***6219*** *p199*
Bone, Wm. 33; Canada, 1852 ***4535.10*** *p197*
*Wife:*Eliz. 31
*Child:*Mary Ann 6
*Child:*Thos. 4
*Child:*Eliz. 2
*Child:*Sarah 2 mos
Boneau de St. Martin, Edward; New York, 1831 ***4606*** *p172*
Bonel, Martin; Iowa, 1866-1943 ***123.54*** *p10*
Bonelli, Louis; Colorado, 1904 ***9678.1*** *p155*
Bonelli, Paul F.; Colorado, 1904 ***9678.1*** *p155*
Bonenkamp, Ernst Carl Friedrich; America, 1867 ***4610.10*** *p117*
Boner, Adam; Indiana, 1848 ***9117*** *p16*
Boner, Ann Jane *SEE* Boner, Robert
Boner, Ann Jane; Philadelphia, 1847 ***5704.8*** *p14*
Boner, Biddy; St. John, N.B., 1853 ***5704.8*** *p99*
Boner, Catherine *SEE* Boner, Robert
Boner, Catherine; Philadelphia, 1847 ***5704.8*** *p14*
Boner, Catherine 17; Philadelphia, 1854 ***5704.8*** *p118*
Boner, Cicily 7; St. John, N.B., 1853 ***5704.8*** *p99*
Boner, Daniel 3; St. John, N.B., 1853 ***5704.8*** *p99*
Boner, Eliza; New York, NY, 1865 ***5704.8*** *p196*
Boner, Fanny 9 mos; St. John, N.B., 1853 ***5704.8*** *p99*
Boner, Harriett; Philadelphia, 1849 ***53.26*** *p5*
Boner, Harriett; Philadelphia, 1849 ***5704.8*** *p50*
Boner, James; New Orleans, 1849 ***5704.8*** *p59*
Boner, Margaret 14; Philadelphia, 1854 ***5704.8*** *p118*
Boner, Mary; St. John, N.B., 1853 ***5704.8*** *p99*
Boner, Mary 18; Quebec, 1866 ***5704.8*** *p167*
Boner, Neal; St. John, N.B., 1853 ***5704.8*** *p99*
Boner, Neal 10; St. John, N.B., 1853 ***5704.8*** *p99*
Boner, Owen 5; St. John, N.B., 1853 ***5704.8*** *p99*
Boner, Paddy 13; St. John, N.B., 1853 ***5704.8*** *p99*
Boner, Patrick 22; Philadelphia, 1856 ***5704.8*** *p128*
Boner, Rebecca; New York, NY, 1865 ***5704.8*** *p196*
Boner, Robert; Philadelphia, 1847 ***53.26*** *p5*
*Relative:*Ann Jane
*Relative:*Catherine
Boner, Robert; Philadelphia, 1847 ***5704.8*** *p14*
Boner, Robert 11; New Orleans, 1849 ***5704.8*** *p59*
Boner, Sarah; St. John, N.B., 1849 ***5704.8*** *p56*
Boner, Sarah; St. John, N.B., 1852 ***5704.8*** *p95*
Boner, Sarah; St. John, N.B., 1853 ***5704.8*** *p99*
Boner, Thomas; St. John, N.B., 1852 ***5704.8*** *p84*
Boness, Bernard 21; Kansas, 1880 ***5240.1*** *p62*
Bonetto, Charles; Arkansas, 1918 ***95.2*** *p21*
Bonfeather, Mr.; Quebec, 1815 ***9229.18*** *p74*
Bonfeer, Luis 26; New Orleans, 1830 ***778.5*** *p61*
Bonfig, George; Washington, 1859-1920 ***2872.1*** *p4*
Bong, Jorgen; Arkansas, 1918 ***95.2*** *p21*
Bonge, . . .; Canada, 1776-1783 ***9786*** *p41*
Bonge, Carl von; Cincinnati, 1788-1848 ***8582.3*** *p89*
Bonge, Carl von; Cincinnati, 1831 ***8582.1*** *p51*
Bongre, Alexander 35; Port uncertain, 1836 ***778.5*** *p61*
Boni, Frank; Arkansas, 1918 ***95.2*** *p21*
Boni, Giovanni Pietro; Arkansas, 1918 ***95.2*** *p21*
Bonicken, Robert; New York, NY, 1838 ***8208.4*** *p82*
Boniday, Wm.; Virginia, 1648 ***6219*** *p241*
Bonie, Thomas 18; St. John, N.B., 1864 ***5704.8*** *p157*
Boniface, Jacob A.; America, 1866 ***6014.1*** *p1*
Boniface, Richard 16; Maryland, 1775 ***1219.7*** *p264*
Bonifacio, Faglio; Arkansas, 1918 ***95.2*** *p21*
Bonin, Francois; Quebec, 1768 ***7603*** *p29*
Bonin, Joseph 20; New Orleans, 1830 ***778.5*** *p61*
Boning, . . .; Canada, 1776-1783 ***9786*** *p18*
Boninghausen, John Bartholomew; New York, 1756 ***3652*** *p81*
Bonis, Dominique 28; New Orleans, 1839 ***778.5*** *p61*
Bonis, P. F. 32; New Orleans, 1839 ***778.5*** *p61*
Bonivard, Joseph 7; America, 1836 ***778.5*** *p62*
Bonivard, Joseph 37; America, 1836 ***778.5*** *p61*
Bonland, David 28; Quebec, 1857 ***5704.8*** *p136*
Bonland, Mary Ann 27; Quebec, 1857 ***5704.8*** *p136*
Bonn, Henrich; Lancaster, PA, 1780 ***8137*** *p7*
Bonnabel, Mr. 26; New Orleans, 1825 ***778.5*** *p62*
Bonnabel, A. 26; New Orleans, 1826 ***778.5*** *p62*
Bonnaire, Mr. 24; America, 1838 ***778.5*** *p62*
Bonnanno, Tony; Arkansas, 1918 ***95.2*** *p21*
Bonnaud, P. 18; America, 1837 ***778.5*** *p62*
Bonne Molaise, Ms. 30; Louisiana, 1820 ***778.5*** *p62*
Bonnecase, Hypolite 18; New Orleans, 1838 ***778.5*** *p62*
Bonnefemme, Jean 21; New Orleans, 1839 ***778.5*** *p62*
Bonnefour, Mr. 27; America, 1835 ***778.5*** *p62*
Bonnefour, Mrs. 26; America, 1835 ***778.5*** *p62*
Bonnefour, Mrs. 50; America, 1835 ***778.5*** *p62*
Bonnefoux, Laurent; New York, NY, 1837 ***8208.4*** *p52*
Bonnel, John; New York, NY, 1811 ***2859.11*** *p9*
Bonnell, Loui; Iowa, 1866-1943 ***123.54*** *p10*
Bonnell, Louis; Iowa, 1866-1943 ***123.54*** *p10*
Bonnell, Lovin; Iowa, 1866-1943 ***123.54*** *p10*
Bonner, Francis 21; Maryland, 1724 ***3690.1*** *p22*
Bonner, John; New York, NY, 1864 ***5704.8*** *p171*
Bonner, John; Quebec, 1853 ***5704.8*** *p104*
Bonner, John; Virginia, 1638 ***6219*** *p124*
Bonner, John 14; Quebec, 1855 ***5704.8*** *p125*
Bonner, Joseph 26; Jamaica, 1731 ***3690.1*** *p22*
Bonner, Margaret 45; Quebec, 1855 ***5704.8*** *p125*
Bonner, Mary Jane 8; Quebec, 1855 ***5704.8*** *p125*
Bonner, Mathias 28; Maryland, 1774 ***1219.7*** *p235*
Bonner, Nancy; Philadelphia, 1866 ***5704.8*** *p203*
Bonner, Rich.; Virginia, 1643 ***6219*** *p202*
Bonner, Robert; Philadelphia, 1852 ***5704.8*** *p96*
Bonner, Robert 16; Quebec, 1855 ***5704.8*** *p125*
Bonner, Rudolph; Philadelphia, 1776 ***8582.3*** *p83*
Bonner, Rudolph; Philadelphia, 1776 ***8582.3*** *p84*
Bonner, Sarah 16; Philadelphia, 1864 ***5704.8*** *p161*
Bonner, Thomas; Virginia, 1638 ***6219*** *p145*
Bonner, Thomas; Virginia, 1647 ***6219*** *p247*
Bonner, William 15; Philadelphia, 1774 ***1219.7*** *p175*
Bonnet, Mr. 40; Port uncertain, 1820 ***778.5*** *p62*
Bonnet, Catherine *SEE* Bonnet, Jean, Jr.
Bonnet, Eugene 23; New Orleans, 1829 ***778.5*** *p62*
Bonnet, Jean *SEE* Bonnet, Jean, Jr.
Bonnet, Jean; America, 1753-1819 ***2444*** *p140*
Bonnet, Jean, Jr.; Pennsylvania, 1753 ***2444*** *p140*
*Wife:*Madeleine Germanet
*Child:*Marguerite
*Child:*Madeleine

Child:Jean
Child:Judith
Child:Catherine
Bonnet, Johann; America, 1830 8582.1 p4
Bonnet, Judith SEE Bonnet, Jean, Jr.
Bonnet, Leonard 27; Maryland, 1774 1219.7 p211
Bonnet, Madeleine SEE Bonnet, Jean, Jr.
Bonnet, Madeleine Germanet SEE Bonnet, Jean, Jr.
Bonnet, Marguerite SEE Bonnet, Jean, Jr.
Bonneth, John 15; Maryland, 1719 3690.1 p22
Bonnett, Thomas 23; Jamaica, 1724 3690.1 p22
Bonney, Henry; Virginia, 1636 6219 p77
Bonnicas, Mr. 28; New Orleans, 1837 778.5 p62
Bonnilli, Mr. 22; Port uncertain, 1825 778.5 p62
Bonnin, Charles; New York, NY, 1836 8208.4 p19
Bonnin, Louis 37; New Orleans, 1863 543.30 p248
Bonnor, Catarine; Philadelphia, 1864 5704.8 p188
Bonns, Jno; America, 1704 2212 p41
Bonnureau, Emily 22; Port uncertain, 1835 778.5 p63
Bonnureau, John A. 29; Port uncertain, 1835 778.5 p63
Bono, Thomas; Arkansas, 1918 95.2 p21
Bonovsky, George; America, 1889 7137 p168
Bonque, J. Julian 20; America, 1835 778.5 p63
Bonquetal, T. 26; Port uncertain, 1839 778.5 p63
Bonroe, Chas. G.; Wisconsin, n.d. 9675.4 p266
Bons, Louis 46; Port uncertain, 1823 778.5 p63
Bonsdall, Adaleide 7; New Orleans, 1838 778.5 p63
Bonsdall, Charles 24; New Orleans, 1838 778.5 p63
Bonsky, Thomas; Quebec, 1853 5704.8 p104
Bonsoivin, H. N. 24; New Orleans, 1837 778.5 p63
Bonson, Francis 32; New Orleans, 1838 778.5 p63
Bonstein, Jakob; Philadelphia, 1779 8137 p7
Bonstrom, Frank; Iowa, 1866-1943 123.54 p10
Bonte, . . .; Canada, 1776-1783 9786 p18
Bonthron, John; Charleston, SC, 1806 1639.20 p14
Bonvagnet, Francois 28; America, 1837 778.5 p63
Bonvagnet, Joseph 30; America, 1837 778.5 p63
Bonval, Mr. 26; Port uncertain, 1836 778.5 p63
Bonvillin, Mrs. 28; New Orleans, 1823 778.5 p63
Bonwicke, Benjamin 42; Jamaica, 1736 3690.1 p22
Bony, Henry; Virginia, 1642 6219 p199
Bony, Susanna; Virginia, 1637 6219 p82
Boo, George 20; Jamaica, 1736 3690.1 p23
Boob, Sebastian; Alberta, n.d. 5262 p58
Boodes, John; Virginia, 1637 6219 p83
Boods, John; Virginia, 1635 6219 p36
Boogaard, Albert; Washington, 1859-1920 2872.1 p4
Boogaard, Edna Gertrude; Washington, 1859-1920 2872.1 p4
Boogaard, Elizabeth; Washington, 1859-1920 2872.1 p4
Boogaard, Esther Isabel; Washington, 1859-1920 2872.1 p5
Boogaard, Hannes Uitden; Washington, 1859-1920 2872.1 p4
Boogaard, Jans; Washington, 1859-1920 2872.1 p4
Boogaard, Jennie; Washington, 1859-1920 2872.1 p4
Boogaard, Johannes; Washington, 1859-1920 2872.1 p4
Boogaard, Johannes Uitden; Washington, 1859-1920 2872.1 p4
Boogaard, Lundert; Washington, 1859-1920 2872.1 p4
Boogaard, Martha; Washington, 1859-1920 2872.1 p4
Boogard, Johannes Elsworth; Washington, 1859-1920 2872.1 p5
Boogard, Olive Maria; Washington, 1859-1920 2872.1 p5
Boogard, Sarah Martha; Washington, 1859-1920 2872.1 p5
Booker, Ann 19; Maryland, 1775 1219.7 p252
Booker, John; Ohio, 1837 9892.11 p4
Booker, John; Ohio, 1839 9892.11 p5
Booker, John 31; Maryland, 1738 3690.1 p23
Bookingham, William 19; Maryland, 1721 3690.1 p23
Bookm, John; South Carolina, 1788 7119 p201
Bookman, John; South Carolina, 1788 7119 p201
Bookter, Jacob; South Carolina, 1788 7119 p202
Booland, Susan; Philadelphia, 1865 5704.8 p191
Boomer, Michael; Illinois, 1854 7857 p2
Boomgaarden, Okke; Illinois, 1863 7857 p2
Boon, John 16; Pennsylvania, 1735 3690.1 p23
Boone, Adam; Philadelphia, 1760 9973.7 p34
Boone, Eliza.; Virginia, 1635 6219 p70
Boone, Wm.; Virginia, 1642 6219 p191
Booney, Harriett; New York, NY, 1811 2859.11 p9
Booney, Samuel; New York, NY, 1811 2859.11 p9
Booney, Sarah; New York, NY, 1811 2859.11 p9
Boopaci, Jno.; Iowa, 1866-1943 123.54 p10
Boora, John; Iowa, 1866-1943 123.54 p10
Boore, Richard; Virginia, 1643 6219 p229
Boorer, George 24; Virginia, 1774 1219.7 p186
Boorer, John 20; Jamaica, 1724 3690.1 p23
Boorman, John; New York, NY, 1830 8208.4 p30
Boorman, William; New York, NY, 1837 8208.4 p48
Boorn, John 15; Jamaica, 1733 3690.1 p23
Boorne, John; Virginia, 1636 6219 p16
Boortz, Mrs. E. A. 62; Washington, 1916-1919 1728.4 p251
Boortz, E. A. 63; Washington, 1916-1919 1728.4 p251
Boos, . . .; Canada, 1776-1783 9786 p18
Boos, Alexis 6 mos; America, 1839 778.5 p63
Boos, Elisabeth 27; America, 1839 778.5 p63
Boos, Joseph 20; America, 1839 778.5 p64
Boosy, Francoise Maria 21; America, 1838 778.5 p64
Boosy, Joseph 23; America, 1838 778.5 p64
Boot, Thomas 21; Maryland, 1774 1219.7 p206
Booth, Alex 9; Quebec, 1850 5704.8 p62
Booth, Ann 16; America, 1705 2212 p42
Booth, Archy 3; Quebec, 1850 5704.8 p62
Booth, Bessey; Quebec, 1850 5704.8 p62
Booth, Eliza.; Virginia, 1648 6219 p246
Booth, Elizabeth 20; Maryland, 1722 3690.1 p23
Booth, Emil 22; Kansas, 1892 5240.1 p77
Booth, Fred; Washington, 1859-1920 2872.1 p5
Booth, Fred E.; Washington, 1859-1920 2872.1 p5
Booth, George 31; Maryland, 1775 1219.7 p250
Booth, James 5; Quebec, 1850 5704.8 p62
Booth, John; Quebec, 1850 5704.8 p62
Booth, John; Washington, 1859-1920 2872.1 p5
Booth, John 7; Quebec, 1850 5704.8 p62
Booth, John C. 33; New Orleans, 1862 543.30 p108
Booth, Jon.; Virginia, 1642 6219 p191
Booth, Margaret; Quebec, 1850 5704.8 p63
Booth, Mary; Virginia, 1648 6219 p250
Booth, Mary 22; Virginia, 1700 2212 p32
Booth, Robert; Quebec, 1850 5704.8 p62
Booth, Samuel; New York, NY, 1836 8208.4 p22
Booth, Thomas; New York, NY, 1834 8208.4 p51
Booth, Wm.; Virginia, 1642 6219 p197
Boothes, Abra.; Virginia, 1646 6219 p242
Boothey, Joseph 19; New York, 1775 1219.7 p246
Bopp, Anna Felicitas Merckle SEE Bopp, Hans Jerg
Bopp, Hans Georg; Pennsylvania, 1769 4525 p237
Bopp, Hans Jerg; New York, 1717 3627 p8
Wife:Anna Felicitas Merckle
Boran, Jon.; Virginia, 1635 6219 p7
Boratto, Cesare; Iowa, 1866-1943 123.54 p57
Borchardt, August; Wisconsin, n.d. 9675.4 p266
Borchers, Nicalaus; Iroquois Co., IL, 1892 3455.1 p9
Borchert, Frederick; New York, NY, 1851 1450.2 p17A
Borck, von; Canada, 1780 9786 p181
Borck, Heinrich von; Halifax, N.S., 1780 9786 p268
Borck, Heinrich von; New York, 1776 9786 p268
Bord, Benjamin 28; Jamaica, 1736 3690.1 p23
Bordach, Stephan; Arkansas, 1918 95.2 p21
Bordal, Mr. 40; New Orleans, 1831 778.5 p64
Bordat, Lorenzo 42; Mexico, 1829 778.5 p64
Bordelais, Mr. 36; Port uncertain, 1836 778.5 p64
Bordelais, Mrs. 28; Port uncertain, 1836 778.5 p64
Bordelais, Ch. 29; New Orleans, 1827 778.5 p64
Bordelais, E. 11; Port uncertain, 1836 778.5 p64
Bordelais, Philibert 32; New Orleans, 1832 778.5 p64
Bordelle, Xavier 31; Louisville, KY, 1838 778.5 p64
Bordelois, Mrs. 30; New Orleans, 1839 778.5 p64
Bordelois, Emile 14; New Orleans, 1839 778.5 p64
Bordelois, Ernest 12; New Orleans, 1839 778.5 p64
Bordelois, P. 40; New Orleans, 1839 778.5 p64
Borden, Thomas 21; Virginia, 1773 1219.7 p169
Bordenave, Mr.; New Orleans, 1839 778.5 p65
Bordenave, Mr. 19; New Orleans, 1826 778.5 p65
Bordere, A. 21; New Orleans, 1823 778.5 p65
Bordere, B. 27; New Orleans, 1823 778.5 p65
Borderes, Mr. 28; New Orleans, 1820 778.5 p65
Bordes, H. N. E. 18; America, 1837 778.5 p65
Bordes, James; Arkansas, 1918 95.2 p21
Bordet, Lewis 60; New Orleans, 1829 778.5 p65
Bordier, Etienne 26; Port uncertain, 1820 778.5 p65
Bording, Ole Christian; Kansas, 1914 6013.40 p15
Bordman, Jake; Arkansas, 1918 95.2 p21
Bordman, John; Virginia, 1636 6219 p28
Bordman, John; Virginia, 1637 6219 p28
Borduzat, James 26; America, 1826 778.5 p65
Boreas, Frances 36; America, 1838 778.5 p65
Borechy, John 50; Kansas, 1878 5240.1 p59
Boredont, Miss 25; America, 1830 778.5 p65
Boree, Jean 50; New Orleans, 1823 778.5 p65
Borel, Miss 38; New Orleans, 1836 778.5 p66
Borel, A. 18; New Orleans, 1839 778.5 p65
Borel, A. 54; Port uncertain, 1836 778.5 p65
Borel, Albert Jules 30; Arkansas, 1918 95.2 p21
Borel, Anna Maria; Pennsylvania, 1750 2444 p140
Borel, Georg; Kentucky, 1839-1840 8582.3 p98
Borel, M. 45; New Orleans, 1836 778.5 p66
Borell, Anna Maria; Pennsylvania, 1750 2444 p140
Borell, M. 3; New Orleans, 1839 778.5 p66
Borelle, C. 26; New Orleans, 1829 778.5 p66
Boreman, Eliza.; Virginia, 1639 6219 p154
Boreman, John; Philadelphia, 1762 1219.7 p89
Borer, Georg; Virginia, 1637 6219 p82
Borg, Carl; Minneapolis, 1876-1881 6410.35 p51
Borg, Caroline Maria 42; Kansas, 1893 5240.1 p78
Borgart, Fred 24; Kansas, 1884 5240.1 p66
Borger, . . .; Pennsylvania, 1769 4525 p265
Borger, Frieda Elisabeth SEE Borger, Katharina Friederike
Borger, Friedrich; Cincinnati, 1844 8582.1 p4
Borger, Friedrich; Cincinnati, 1869-1887 8582 p4
Borger, Hans Michel; Pennsylvania, 1752 4525 p202
With wife
With 2 children
Borger, Helene Wilhelmine SEE Borger, Katharina Friederike
Borger, Johann Heinrich SEE Borger, Katharina Friederike
Borger, Johann Nicolaus 18; New England, 1753 4525 p202
Borger, Johann Nicolaus 18; Pennsylvania, 1753 4525 p202
Borger, Johann Nicolaus 33; Pennsylvania, 1753 4525 p202
With wife
With mother
With 3 children
Borger, Johanna Maria SEE Borger, Katharina Friederike
Borger, Katharina Friederike; America, 1883 4610.10 p124
Child:Helene Wilhelmine
Child:Johann Heinrich
Child:Frieda Elisabeth
Child:Johanna Maria
Borges, Wilhelmine; America, 1865 4610.10 p149
Borgeson, Carl August; Bangor, ME, 1890 6410.22 p126
Borgeson, John Aug.; Maine, 1882-1892 6410.22 p120
Borghardt, Johanne Sophie; America, 1867 4610.10 p117
Borgholthaus, G. W.; Illinois, 1838 8582.2 p50
Borgini, Norchie; Arkansas, 1918 95.2 p21
Borgioli, Amerigo; New York, NY, 1911 3455.3 p50
Borgman, Ferdinand; New York, 1882 1450.2 p4B
Borgmann, Frederich; America, 1857 1450.2 p17A
Borgmann, Hermann H.; Cincinnati, 1869-1887 8582 p4
Borgstram, John; Colorado, 1900 9678.1 p155
Borgstrom, Hjalmar; Arkansas, 1918 95.2 p21
Borhek, John Andrew; New York, 1750 3652 p74
Borhnholt, J. F.; Baltimore, 1838 8582 p4
Borilly, Mr.; Port uncertain, 1839 778.5 p66
Borion, Arsene 30; New Orleans, 1835 778.5 p66
Borjesson, Carl August; Bangor, ME, 1881-1892 6410.22 p121
Bork, Anna Maria SEE Bork, Michel
Bork, Elisabetha SEE Bork, Michel
Bork, Konrad SEE Bork, Michel
Bork, Michael 21; New Orleans, 1839 9420.2 p70
Bork, Michael 50; New Orleans, 1839 9420.2 p70
Bork, Michel; Connecticut, 1856 3702.7 p354
Wife:Anna Maria
Son:Konrad
Daughter:Elisabetha
Borke, Tobie; Virginia, 1635 6219 p16
Borkert, Joseph 34; West Virginia, 1900 9788.3 p5
Borko, Eenori; Washington, 1859-1920 2872.1 p32
Borko, John; Washington, 1859-1920 2872.1 p5
Borkowska, Bronislawa 7 SEE Borkowska, Wiktorya Piekarska
Borkowska, Stefania 4 SEE Borkowska, Wiktorya Piekarska
Borkowska, Wiktorya Piekarska 33; New York, 1912 9980.29 p53
Son:Wladyslaw 9
Daughter:Bronislawa 7
Daughter:Stefania 4
Borkowska, Wladyslaw 9 SEE Borkowska, Wiktorya Piekarska
Borkowski, . . .; New York, 1831 4606 p173
Borkowski, Jozef; New York, 1835 4606 p179
Borkowski, Mina 17; New York, 1912 9980.29 p55
Borland, Alex; Philadelphia, 1850 53.26 p5
Borland, Alex; Philadelphia, 1850 5704.8 p60
Borland, Peter; Philadelphia, 1852 5704.8 p92
Borleske, Anton; Wisconsin, n.d. 9675.4 p266
Borleske, Hildegard; Wisconsin, n.d. 9675.4 p266
Borleteau, Widow 44; New Orleans, 1837 778.5 p66
Borling, Hermann H.; Cincinnati, 1869-1887 8582 p4
Borlridge, Josiah; Philadelphia, 1816 2859.11 p25
Bormann, . . .; Canada, 1776-1783 9786 p18
Bormann, Andres, Jr.; Wisconsin, n.d. 9675.4 p266
Bormann, Carl Friedrich; America, 1869 4610.10 p152
Bormann, Friedrich; New York, NY, 1923 3455.4 p27
Bormann, Friedrick; America, 1923 3455.3 p83
Bormann, Gabriel 44; Kansas, 1888 5240.1 p6
Bormann, Gabriel 44; Kansas, 1888 5240.1 p71

Bormant, Mr. 28; Port uncertain, 1838 **778.5** *p60*
Born, Charles Christoph; Wisconsin, n.d. **9675.4** *p266*
Born, Wm. J.; Shreveport, LA, 1879 **7129** *p44*
Borne, Jean 40; America, 1838 **778.5** *p66*
Borne, Thomas; Virginia, 1648 **6219** *p252*
Bornemann, August Friedrich Heinrich; Quebec, 1776 **9786** *p253*
Bornemann, Bothmar; Quebec, 1776 **9786** *p104*
Borner, William; Wisconsin, n.d. **9675.4** *p266*
Bornet, Charles 32; New Orleans, 1862 **543.30** *p326*
Bornett, Dorothy; Virginia, 1637 **6219** *p115*
Bornhage, Herman; Illinois, 1880 **5240.1** *p6*
Bornholdt, John 28; Kansas, 1906 **5240.1** *p84*
Bornholdt, Peter; Kansas, 1899 **5240.1** *p6*
Bornholt, August 22; Kansas, 1890 **5240.1** *p74*
Bornholt, John 35; Kansas, 1890 **5240.1** *p6*
Bornholt, John 35; Kansas, 1890 **5240.1** *p74*
Bornholt, Peter; Kansas, 1899 **5240.1** *p6*
Bornholt, William; Iowa, 1887 **5240.1** *p6*
Bornmann, Jakob; Philadelphia, 1779 **8137** *p7*
Bornnman, Andrew; Wisconsin, n.d. **9675.4** *p266*
Bornstein, Heinrich; St. Louis, 1848-1853 **3702.7** *p326*
Borol, Mfarie 42; New Orleans, 1836 **778.5** *p66*
Boroni, Oresto; New York, 1898 **1450.2** *p4B*
Borowiec, Chester Arthur; Arkansas, 1918 **95.2** *p21*
Borowska, Dorotha 17; New York, 1912 **9980.29** *p73*
Borowska, Helena 27; New York, 1912 **9980.29** *p61*
Borowska, Irena 4; New York, 1912 **9980.29** *p61*
Borowski, Tadeusz 9 mos; New York, 1912 **9980.29** *p61*
Borr, James; New York, NY, 1816 **2859.11** *p25*
Borra, Loui; Iowa, 1866-1943 **123.54** *p10*
Borral, John 38; America, 1838 **778.5** *p66*
Borral, Josephine 5; America, 1838 **778.5** *p66*
Borral, Marie 50; America, 1838 **778.5** *p66*
Borral, Selestine 18 mos; America, 1838 **778.5** *p66*
Borral, Selestine 2; America, 1838 **778.5** *p66*
Borsch, Johann; Wisconsin, n.d. **9675.4** *p266*
Borse, Olympe 20; America, 1838 **778.5** *p66*
Borskin, George; New York, NY, 1816 **2859.11** *p25*
Borst, Thomas; Wisconsin, n.d. **9675.4** *p266*
Borsting, Andrew E.; Washington, 1859-1920 **2872.1** *p5*
Borstner, George 22; Kansas, 1884 **5240.1** *p65*
Borstner, Godfried 54; Kansas, 1884 **5240.1** *p6*
Borstner, Gottfrid 54; Kansas, 1884 **5240.1** *p66*
Bortoluzzi, Bortolo 41; West Virginia, 1904 **9788.3** *p5*
Bortsch, Joseph 44; New Orleans, 1862 **543.30** *p110*
Bortz, Charles; Wisconsin, n.d. **9675.4** *p266*
Borucki, Jan 25; New York, 1912 **9980.29** *p50*
Borzek, . . .; New York, 1831 **4606** *p173*
Bos, Hans; New Netherland, 1630-1646 **8582.2** *p51*
Bos, John; Arkansas, 1918 **95.2** *p21*
Bos, John 30; Arkansas, 1918 **95.2** *p21*
Bosaker, Edward; Virginia, 1636 **6219** *p12*
Bosch, Adam 47; Kansas, 1893 **5240.1** *p78*
Bosch, Catharina *SEE* Bosch, Johannes
Bosch, Catharina *SEE* Bosch, Johannes
Bosch, Conrad *SEE* Bosch, Johannes
Bosch, Conrad *SEE* Bosch, Johannes
Bosch, Ignatz; Alberta, n.d. **5262** *p58*
Bosch, Jacob *SEE* Bosch, Johannes
Bosch, Jacob *SEE* Bosch, Johannes
Bosch, Johann; Wisconsin, n.d. **9675.4** *p266*
Bosch, Johann Michael *SEE* Bosch, Johannes
Bosch, Johann Michael *SEE* Bosch, Johannes
Bosch, Johannes; New England, 1752 **2444** *p141*
*Wife:*Margaretha Gomeringer
*Child:*Catharina
*Child:*Johann Michael
*Child:*Conrad
*Child:*Jacob
Bosch, Johannes; Pennsylvania, 1752 **2444** *p141*
*Wife:*Margaretha Gomeringer
*Child:*Catharina
*Child:*Johann Michael
*Child:*Conrad
*Child:*Jacob
Bosch, Johannes 30; Kansas, 1893 **5240.1** *p78*
Bosch, Joseph 21; Kansas, 1893 **5240.1** *p78*
Bosch, Joseph 32; Kansas, 1893 **5240.1** *p78*
Bosch, Margaretha Gomeringer *SEE* Bosch, Johannes
Bosch, Margaretha Gomeringer *SEE* Bosch, Johannes
Bosch, Matthew 34; New Orleans, 1862 **543.30** *p326*
Bosch, Michael 23; Kansas, 1893 **5240.1** *p78*
Bosche, Miss; America, 1845 **4815.7** *p92*
Bosche, Heinrich Wilhelm; America, 1845 **4815.7** *p92*
*Wife:*Margarete D. Siegmann
With 5 children
Bosche, Johann; America, 1847 **8582.3** *p8*
Bosche, Margarete D. Siegmann *SEE* Bosche, Heinrich Wilhelm
Bosco, Antonio; Arkansas, 1918 **95.2** *p21*
Bose, Nicolas 30; New Orleans, 1838 **778.5** *p67*
Bose, Upland 23; New Orleans, 1838 **778.5** *p67*
Boseck, Oscar 31; Kansas, 1896 **5240.1** *p6*
Boseck, Oscar 31; Kansas, 1896 **5240.1** *p80*
Bosen, Philipp; Philadelphia, 1776 **8582.3** *p83*
Bosen, Philipp; Philadelphia, 1776 **8582.3** *p85*
Boset, William; America, 1869 **1450.2** *p17A*
Boshen, John Henry; Virginia, 1844 **4626.16** *p12*
Bosi, Lewis 21; Port uncertain, 1838 **778.5** *p67*
Bosinger, Conrad; Ohio, 1826 **8582.1** *p48*
Boskovich, Louis; Arkansas, 1918 **95.2** *p21*
Boslem, Alexander; Iowa, 1866-1943 **123.54** *p10*
Bosman, Henry; Arkansas, 1918 **95.2** *p21*
Bosquet, Mr. 22; Louisiana, 1826 **778.5** *p67*
Boss, . . .; Canada, 1776-1783 **9786** *p18*
Boss, Christian; Cincinnati, 1869-1887 **8582** *p4*
Boss, Georg A.; America, 1831 **8582.2** *p4*
Boss, Jacob; South Carolina, 1752-1753 **3689.17** *p21*
With wife
*Relative:*Johannes 8
Boss, Jesus 64; Arizona, 1906 **9228.40** *p10*
Boss, Johannes 8 *SEE* Boss, Jacob
Bossard, Samuel 31; Kansas, 1883 **5240.1** *p64*
Bosse, . . .; Canada, 1776-1783 **9786** *p18*
Bosse, Heinrich; Baltimore, 1839 **8582** *p4*
Bosse, Joseph 22; New Orleans, 1862 **543.30** *p326*
Bosseau, Zacharie 27; America, 1838 **778.5** *p67*
Bossert, John; America, 1854 **1450.2** *p17A*
Bossile, Peter 21; Grenada, 1774 **1219.7** *p231*
Bossinger, Benjamin; Cincinnati, 1788-1848 **8582.3** *p89*
Bossont, John; New York, NY, 1835 **8208.4** *p44*
Bostmann, Johannes George; Arkansas, 1918 **95.2** *p21*
Boston, Christina; Charleston, SC, 1750-1818 **1639.20** *p14*
Boston, Christina; Charleston, SC, 1750-1818 **1639.20** *p91*
Bostwick, Henry Adolphus; California, 1863 **2769.1** *p5*
Boswell, Benjamin 15; Philadelphia, 1775 **1219.7** *p258*
Boswell, Charles 23; Jamaica, 1738 **3690.1** *p23*
Boten, John; Illinois, 1892 **5012.37** *p62*
Botey, Victor 22; New Orleans, 1862 **543.30** *p325*
Botham, Isabella; New York, NY, 1816 **2859.11** *p25*
Botham, Robert; New York, NY, 1816 **2859.11** *p25*
Bothan, Ann; Quebec, 1863 **4537.30** *p13*
Bothe, Christian; Wisconsin, n.d. **9675.4** *p266*
Bothe, Johann C.; Ohio, 1869-1887 **8582** *p4*
Botheley, Joseph 22; Maryland, 1774 **1219.7** *p182*
Bother, Mathias; Wisconsin, n.d. **9675.4** *p266*
Bothin, Gustaf; Minneapolis, 1868-1880 **6410.35** *p51*
Bothmann, Wilhelmine 63; America, 1884 **4610.10** *p160*
Bothwell, Elizabeth 2; Quebec, 1847 **5704.8** *p17*
Bothwell, James; Quebec, 1847 **5704.8** *p17*
Bothwell, John; Charleston, SC, 1777 **1639.20** *p14*
Bothwell, Margaret; Quebec, 1847 **5704.8** *p17*
Botoini, D.; Wisconsin, n.d. **9675.4** *p266*
Bott, Adam; Philadelphia, 1761 **9973.7** *p36*
Bott, Henry; Philadelphia, 1761 **9973.7** *p35*
Bott, Herman; Philadelphia, 1750 **9973.7** *p31*
Bott, Jacob; Philadelphia, 1761 **9973.7** *p35*
Bottcher, . . .; Canada, 1776-1783 **9786** *p18*
Botteher, Wilhelm; Illinois, 1904 **5012.39** *p53*
Botterbusch, A. M. L. Caroline Kiel *SEE* Botterbusch, Carl Gottlieb W.
Botterbusch, A.M. Louise Caroline *SEE* Botterbusch, Carl Gottlieb W.
Botterbusch, Carl Gottlieb W.; America, 1881 **4610.10** *p152*
*Wife:*A. M. L. Caroline Kiel
*Child:*A.M. Louise Caroline
*Child:*Fr. W.
Botterbusch, Ernst Carl Wilhelm; America, 1870 **4610.10** *p159*
Botterbusch, Fr. W. *SEE* Botterbusch, Carl Gottlieb W.
Bottie, Georges 28; New Orleans, 1835 **778.5** *p67*
Bottie, Nicholas 28; New Orleans, 1835 **778.5** *p67*
Bottke, Eugene; America, 1896 **1450.2** *p4B*
Bottmann, . . .; Canada, 1776-1783 **9786** *p18*
Bottoher, Heinr. Wm. 28; New Orleans, 1839 **9420.2** *p168*
Botts, Rynhard; Philadelphia, 1761 **9973.7** *p35*
Botvidsson, N. F.; Minneapolis, 1880-1881 **6410.35** *p51*
Botz, Andreas; Pennsylvania, 1730-1779 **2444** *p140*
Bouanchaud, Pierre 16; Louisiana, 1820 **778.5** *p67*
Boube, Antoine 17; New Orleans, 1839 **778.5** *p67*
Bouby, Mr. 36; New Orleans, 1839 **778.5** *p67*
Bouce, Sarah 20; Philadelphia, 1857 **5704.8** *p134*
Bouch, Leonard; South Carolina, 1788 **7119** *p199*
Bouchard, Mr. 25; New Orleans, 1821 **778.5** *p67*
Bouchard, Adeline 18; New Orleans, 1837 **778.5** *p67*
Bouchard, Alexis 63; New Orleans, 1826 **778.5** *p67*
Bouchard, Karl; Philadelphia, 1779 **8137** *p7*
Bouchard, Pierre 31; Port uncertain, 1836 **778.5** *p67*
Bouchard, Victorine 19; New Orleans, 1837 **778.5** *p67*
Bouche, Mr. 19; New Orleans, 1838 **778.5** *p68*
Bouche, Barthely 32; New Orleans, 1838 **778.5** *p68*
Bouche, C. P.; America, 1830 **8582.1** *p41*
With wife
Bouche, Jean 38; New Orleans, 1838 **778.5** *p68*
Bouche, Jean 45; New Orleans, 1838 **778.5** *p68*
Boucher, Mr.; Quebec, 1815 **9229.18** *p80*
Boucher, Ann 20; Massachusetts, 1847 **5881.1** *p6*
Boucher, Felix 20; New Orleans, 1862 **543.30** *p112*
Boucher, Jaques 35; Port uncertain, 1832 **778.5** *p68*
Boucher, John 23; New Orleans, 1838 **778.5** *p68*
Boucher, Mary 2; Massachusetts, 1847 **5881.1** *p9*
Boucher, Thomas 34; Massachusetts, 1847 **5881.1** *p12*
Bouchere, Mr.; Quebec, 1815 **9229.18** *p82*
Bouchet, Antoine 21; Port uncertain, 1825 **778.5** *p68*
Boucker, Jeremiah 20; Virginia, 1700 **2212** *p30*
Boucker, Mary 22; Virginia, 1700 **2212** *p32*
Boudet, Mr. 25; Port uncertain, 1820 **778.5** *p68*
Boudin, Mr. 25; Louisiana, 1820 **778.5** *p68*
Boudler, James; America, 1698 **2212** *p6*
Boudreau, Eli; Iroquois Co., IL, 1892 **3455.1** *p9*
Boudrie, Alfred; Iowa, 1866-1943 **123.54** *p10*
Boufelle, Ms. 33; New Orleans, 1837 **778.5** *p68*
Boufelle, Sophie Laure 4; New Orleans, 1837 **778.5** *p68*
Boufett, William; Jamaica, 1757 **1219.7** *p58*
Boufett, William; Jamaica, 1757 **3690.1** *p23*
Bouffleur, W. A. 51; Washington, 1916-1919 **1728.4** *p251*
Bougee, T. 30; New Orleans, 1823 **778.5** *p68*
Bougere, Mr. 47; New Orleans, 1829 **778.5** *p68*
Bouget, Mr. 23; America, 1836 **778.5** *p68*
Bouget, Mr. 36; America, 1836 **778.5** *p68*
Boughton, . . .; Virginia, 1639 **6219** *p24*
Boughton, Tho.; Virginia, 1639 **6219** *p151*
Bougnin, Vincent 16; America, 1838 **778.5** *p69*
Bougon, Mr.; America, 1838 **778.5** *p69*
Bougon, Jean Louis 59; Port uncertain, 1836 **778.5** *p69*
Bougot, John 36; New Orleans, 1862 **543.30** *p481*
Bouillerot, Mr. 48; New Orleans, 1821 **778.5** *p69*
Bouillet, Jean 33; America, 1838 **778.5** *p69*
Bouillon, Mrs.; New York, 1882 **3702.7** *p476*
Bouillon, Adam 31; Halifax, N.S., 1752 **7074.6** *p208*
Bouillon, Pierre 40; America, 1838 **778.5** *p69*
Bouis, A. 15; America, 1827 **778.5** *p69*
Bouis, Joseph 37; America, 1826 **778.5** *p69*
Bouis, Pascal 20; New Orleans, 1838 **778.5** *p69*
Bouknecht, John; South Carolina, 1788 **7119** *p201*
Boukofsky, Gustave 36; California, 1872 **2769.2** *p3*
Boukofsky, Henry 24; California, 1872 **2769.2** *p3*
Boulanger, F. 35; New Orleans, 1825 **778.5** *p69*
Boulanger, Peter 49; Port uncertain, 1832 **778.5** *p69*
Boulard, Mr. 20; America, 1829 **778.5** *p69*
Boulard, Amand 19; Port uncertain, 1836 **778.5** *p69*
Boulard, Francois 23; Port uncertain, 1836 **778.5** *p70*
Boulard, H.; New Orleans, 1839 **778.5** *p70*
Boulard, Joseph 29; Port uncertain, 1836 **778.5** *p70*
Boulard, Josephine 29; Port uncertain, 1836 **778.5** *p70*
Boulard, Pierre 26; Port uncertain, 1832 **778.5** *p70*
Boulard, Pierre 30; Port uncertain, 1836 **778.5** *p70*
Boulard, Rose Josephine 7; Port uncertain, 1836 **778.5** *p70*
Boulau, John 23; Mexico, 1836 **778.5** *p70*
Bould, John; New York, NY, 1836 **8208.4** *p19*
Boulding, Thomas; Virginia, 1639 **6219** *p157*
Bouldler, James; Virginia, 1698 **2212** *p11*
Bouldridge, James; Savannah, GA, 1774 **1219.7** *p227*
Boulemet, Mr. 18; New Orleans, 1821 **778.5** *p70*
Boulenger, J. 15; Port uncertain, 1838 **778.5** *p70*
Boulet Desentier, Jules 17; America, 1836 **778.5** *p70*
Boulier, Aime 25; America, 1837 **778.5** *p70*
Bouliet, Agnes 55; America, 1831 **778.5** *p70*
Bouliet, Favien 18; America, 1831 **778.5** *p70*
Bouliet, Hypolite 8; America, 1831 **778.5** *p71*
Bouliet, Joseph 14; America, 1831 **778.5** *p71*
Bouliet, Stanislaus 50; America, 1831 **778.5** *p70*
Bouliet, Theodore 19; America, 1831 **778.5** *p71*
Bouliet, Virgenee 10; America, 1831 **778.5** *p71*
Boullier, Rene Jean 61; Kansas, 1875 **5240.1** *p56*
Boullion, Adam 31; Halifax, N.S., 1752 **7074.6** *p207*
Boulon, Pierre 38; New Orleans, 1839 **778.5** *p71*
Boulston, John; Philadelphia, 1847 **53.26** *p5*
Boulton, Ann; Virginia, 1634 **6219** *p32*
Boulton, Condery 16; Maryland, 1775 **1219.7** *p259*
Boulton, Daniel 22; Jamaica, 1736 **3690.1** *p23*
Boulton, Henry 15; Maryland, 1775 **1219.7** *p259*
Boulton, Jacob; America, 1697 **2212** *p9*
Boulton, Thomas; Virginia, 1628 **6219** *p31*
Bouluguet, Jean B.H.; New York, NY, 1836 **8208.4** *p9*
Bouma, Garrett Binnes; Arkansas, 1918 **95.2** *p21*
Boumonth, Peter; Ohio, 1867 **6014.2** *p7*
Bound, Ann 30; New York, 1855 **4535.10** *p197*
*Child:*Joseph 7
*Child:*Fred 6
*Child:*Selia 5
*Child:*Henry 3

*Child:*Chas. 2
With child 2 mos
Bound, Chas. 2 *SEE* Bound, Ann
Bound, Elianor; Virginia, 1637 ***6219*** *p107*
Bound, Fred 6 *SEE* Bound, Ann
Bound, George; New York, 1854-1855 ***4535.10*** *p197*
Bound, Henry 3 *SEE* Bound, Ann
Bound, Joseph 7 *SEE* Bound, Ann
Bound, Selia 5 *SEE* Bound, Ann
Bouneville, Joseph 29; America, 1835 ***778.5*** *p71*
Bouquet, Heinrich; America, 1775-1877 ***8582.3*** *p80*
Bouquet, Heinrich; Philadelphia, 1756 ***8582.3*** *p95*
Bouquet, Henry; North America, 1766 ***1219.7*** *p124*
Bouquet, Peter; Charleston, SC, 1775 ***8582.2*** *p51*
Bour, Charles; Wisconsin, n.d. ***9675.4*** *p266*
Bour, Nicolaus; New York, NY, 1829 ***8582*** *p4*
Bourand, Mr.; Quebec, 1815 ***9229.18*** *p77*
With wife
Bourboulas, Nichalas Michael; Arkansas, 1918 ***95.2*** *p22*
Bourcier, Master 4; America, 1838 ***778.5*** *p71*
Bourcier, Miss 2; America, 1838 ***778.5*** *p71*
Bourcier, Mr. 29; America, 1838 ***778.5*** *p71*
Bourcier, Mrs. 20; America, 1838 ***778.5*** *p71*
Bourdin, John 35; New Orleans, 1826 ***778.5*** *p71*
Bourdman, William; Arkansas, 1918 ***95.2*** *p22*
Bourejon, Mary C. 20; America, 1839 ***778.5*** *p71*
Bourgan, Dennis; New York, NY, 1865 ***5704.8*** *p194*
Bourgeois, . . .; New Orleans, 1829 ***778.5*** *p72*
Bourgeois, Madame 22; New Orleans, 1829 ***778.5*** *p72*
Bourgeois, Mme.; Port uncertain, 1839 ***778.5*** *p72*
Bourgeois, Mr. 18; New Orleans, 1822 ***778.5*** *p71*
Bourgeois, Mr. 23; New Orleans, 1829 ***778.5*** *p71*
Bourgeois, Adeaide 5; America, 1839 ***778.5*** *p72*
Bourgeois, Catherine *SEE* Bourgeois, Jacques
Bourgeois, Catherine 8; America, 1839 ***778.5*** *p72*
Bourgeois, David *SEE* Bourgeois, Jacques
Bourgeois, Elisabeth 32; America, 1839 ***778.5*** *p72*
Bourgeois, J. D. 20; New Orleans, 1826 ***778.5*** *p72*
Bourgeois, Jacques 40; Halifax, N.S., 1752 ***7074.6*** *p207*
With family of 4
Bourgeois, Jacques 40; Halifax, N.S., 1752 ***7074.6*** *p208*
*Wife:*Catherine
*Child:*Suzanne-Therese
*Child:*David
*Child:*Marguerite
Bourgeois, Jean 10; America, 1839 ***778.5*** *p72*
Bourgeois, Julie 28; Port uncertain, 1839 ***778.5*** *p72*
Bourgeois, Leop.; Port uncertain, 1839 ***778.5*** *p72*
Bourgeois, Marguerite *SEE* Bourgeois, Jacques
Bourgeois, Marie 3; America, 1839 ***778.5*** *p72*
Bourgeois, Marie 11; America, 1839 ***778.5*** *p72*
Bourgeois, Philippe 34; America, 1839 ***778.5*** *p72*
Bourgeois, Suzanne-Therese *SEE* Bourgeois, Jacques
Bourgerol, Mr. 34; New Orleans, 1825 ***778.5*** *p72*
Bourgier, Ezekiel 18; Maryland, 1727 ***3690.1*** *p23*
Bourgin, Barnaby 26; Jamaica, 1736 ***3690.1*** *p24*
Bourgogne, . . .; Halifax, N.S., 1752 ***7074.6*** *p230*
Bourgogne, Anne-Elisabeth *SEE* Bourgogne, Marc
Bourgogne, Catherine-Elisabeth *SEE* Bourgogne, Marc
Bourgogne, Jacques *SEE* Bourgogne, Marc
Bourgogne, Jean-David *SEE* Bourgogne, Marc
Bourgogne, Jean-George *SEE* Bourgogne, Marc
Bourgogne, Marc 33; Halifax, N.S., 1752 ***7074.6*** *p208*
*Wife:*Anne-Elisabeth
*Child:*Catherine-Elisabeth
*Child:*Jean-David
*Child:*Jean-George
*Child:*Jacques
Bouriny, Mr. 30; New Orleans, 1839 ***778.5*** *p72*
Bouris, James; Arkansas, 1918 ***95.2*** *p22*
Bourjon, J.les 29; New Orleans, 1839 ***778.5*** *p73*
Bourk, Colbert 46?; Arizona, 1890 ***2764.35*** *p7*
Bourk, Daniel; America, 1737 ***4971*** *p30*
Bourk, John; Philadelphia, 1741 ***4971*** *p92*
Bourk, Mary; America, 1742 ***4971*** *p27*
Bourk, Rowland; America, 1742 ***4971*** *p31*
Bourk, Susannah; Annapolis, MD, 1742 ***4971*** *p93*
Bourk, Theobald; America, 1742 ***4971*** *p27*
Bourk, Thomas; America, 1742 ***4971*** *p27*
Bourke, Barbara; America, 1737 ***4971*** *p45*
Bourke, Barbara; America, 1738 ***4971*** *p46*
Bourke, Barth.; America, 1742 ***4971*** *p50*
Bourke, Barthol.; America, 1742 ***4971*** *p49*
Bourke, Edmond; America, 1736-1743 ***4971*** *p57*
Bourke, Edmund; America, 1736-1743 ***4971*** *p58*
Bourke, James; America, 1741 ***4971*** *p29*
Bourke, James; America, 1741 ***4971*** *p56*
Bourke, John; America, 1740 ***4971*** *p15*
Bourke, John; America, 1741 ***4971*** *p42*
Bourke, John; America, 1741 ***4971*** *p60*
Bourke, John; Maryland, 1740 ***4971*** *p91*
Bourke, Joseph; Montreal, 1825 ***7603*** *p97*
Bourke, Margaret; America, 1741 ***4971*** *p49*
Bourke, Martin; America, 1735-1743 ***4971*** *p8*
Bourke, Mary 28; St. John, N.B., 1854 ***5704.8*** *p120*
Bourke, Michael; America, 1735-1743 ***4971*** *p79*
Bourke, Michael 30; Massachusetts, 1849 ***5881.1*** *p10*
Bourke, Patrick; America, 1735-1743 ***4971*** *p78*
Bourke, Patrick; America, 1741 ***4971*** *p35*
Bourke, Patrick; America, 1742 ***4971*** *p80*
Bourke, Susanna; America, 1741 ***4971*** *p16*
Bourke, William; America, 1735-1743 ***4971*** *p78*
Bourke, William; America, 1735-1743 ***4971*** *p79*
Bourke, William; America, 1738 ***4971*** *p80*
Bourke, William; America, 1742 ***4971*** *p81*
Bourlando, J. 24; America, 1838 ***778.5*** *p73*
Bourlard, Alphonse; Arkansas, 1918 ***95.2*** *p22*
Bourlier, Calixte; New York, NY, 1834 ***8208.4*** *p39*
Bourlier, Marguerite 48; America, 1835 ***778.5*** *p73*
Bourloton, Pierre 24; Quebec, 1689 ***4533*** *p130*
Bourman, James 21; Maryland, 1775 ***1219.7*** *p247*
Bourn, Mary 25; Philadelphia, 1774 ***1219.7*** *p195*
Bourn, Thomas 18; Maryland, 1774 ***1219.7*** *p185*
Bourne, Jon.; Virginia, 1637 ***6219*** *p109*
Bourne, Tho.; Virginia, 1648 ***6219*** *p252*
Bourne, Thomas; Virginia, 1638 ***6219*** *p146*
Bourner, James; New York, NY, 1836 ***2896.5*** *p4*
Bourner, William; Illinois, 1859 ***2896.5*** *p4*
Bournier, L. 42; New Orleans, 1830 ***778.5*** *p73*
Bouron, B.; Port uncertain, 1838 ***778.5*** *p73*
Bourquin, Mr. 33; America, 1839 ***778.5*** *p73*
Bourquin, Jean Jac; Boston, 1776 ***1219.7*** *p278*
Bourquin, Louise 20; America, 1839 ***778.5*** *p73*
Bourrell, Antonius; Port uncertain, 1752 ***2444*** *p141*
Bourrely, Sebastien 19; Port uncertain, 1839 ***778.5*** *p73*
Bourrey, Jenry 15; America, 1837 ***778.5*** *p73*
Bourrilhon, Mr. 30; America, 1823 ***778.5*** *p73*
Bourson, Francoise 28; America, 1836 ***778.5*** *p73*
Bourson, Joly 4; America, 1836 ***778.5*** *p73*
Bouschet, John; Illinois, 1881 ***2896.5*** *p4*
Bousignes, Marc 21; Port uncertain, 1832 ***778.5*** *p73*
Bousigues, Justin 23; America, 1837 ***778.5*** *p73*
Bousiguet, Marc 19; New Orleans, 1830 ***778.5*** *p73*
Bousquet, Mme. 20; New Orleans, 1839 ***778.5*** *p74*
Bousquet, Mme. 22; America, 1839 ***778.5*** *p74*
Bousquet, Mr. 23; Port uncertain, 1838 ***778.5*** *p74*
Bousquet, Mr. 24; Port uncertain, 1836 ***778.5*** *p74*
Bousquet, Mr. 25; New Orleans, 1839 ***778.5*** *p74*
Bousquet, Mr. 30; America, 1839 ***778.5*** *p74*
Bousquet, F...ich 48; New Orleans, 1839 ***778.5*** *p74*
Bousquet, Thomas 18; New Orleans, 1835 ***778.5*** *p74*
Bousson, Jean Augt. 22; America, 1838 ***778.5*** *p74*
Boute, Margaret 25; St. Louis, 1836 ***778.5*** *p74*
Bouteiller, . . .; Halifax, N.S., 1752 ***7074.6*** *p230*
Bouteiller, Francoise *SEE* Bouteiller, Jean
Bouteiller, Frederic *SEE* Bouteiller, Jean-George
Bouteiller, George 26; Halifax, N.S., 1752 ***7074.6*** *p209*
Bouteiller, Jacques 17 *SEE* Bouteiller, Jean-George
Bouteiller, Jacques 33; Halifax, N.S., 1752 ***7074.6*** *p209*
*Wife:*Marguerite
With 2 children
Bouteiller, Jean 29; Halifax, N.S., 1752 ***7074.6*** *p209*
*Wife:*Francoise
Bouteiller, Jean-George 26; Halifax, N.S., 1752 ***7074.6*** *p209*
Bouteiller, Jean-George 50; Halifax, N.S., 1752 ***7074.6*** *p209*
*Wife:*Sarah
*Child:*Frederic
*Son:*Jacques 17
*Child:*Jeanne
Bouteiller, Jean-Nicolas 21; Halifax, N.S., 1752 ***7074.6*** *p209*
Bouteiller, Jeanne *SEE* Bouteiller, Jean-George
Bouteiller, Marguerite *SEE* Bouteiller, Jacques
Bouteiller, Sarah *SEE* Bouteiller, Jean-George
Bouteillier, Jean George; North America, 1752 ***7074.6*** *p201*
With wife
With 4 children
Bouteloup, Mme. 29; New Orleans, 1820 ***778.5*** *p74*
Bouteloup, Mr. 28; New Orleans, 1820 ***778.5*** *p74*
Bouthillier, Guillaume; Quebec, 1777 ***7603*** *p47*
Boutilier, . . .; Halifax, N.S., 1752 ***7074.6*** *p230*
Boutilier, Frederic; Halifax, N.S., 1752 ***7074.6*** *p228*
Boutilier, Georges; Halifax, N.S., 1752 ***7074.6*** *p228*
Boutilier, Jacques; Halifax, N.S., 1752 ***7074.6*** *p228*
Boutilier, James; Halifax, N.S., 1752 ***7074.6*** *p228*
Boutilier, Jean; Halifax, N.S., 1752 ***7074.6*** *p228*
Boutilier, Jean-George; Halifax, N.S., 1752 ***7074.6*** *p228*
Boutillier, . . .; Halifax, N.S., 1752 ***7074.6*** *p230*
Boutillier, Frederic; Halifax, N.S., 1752 ***7074.6*** *p228*
Boutillier, George; Halifax, N.S., 1752 ***7074.6*** *p228*
Boutillier, Jacques; Halifax, N.S., 1752 ***7074.6*** *p228*
Boutillier, James; Halifax, N.S., 1752 ***7074.6*** *p228*
Boutillier, Jean; Halifax, N.S., 1752 ***7074.6*** *p228*
Boutlier, . . .; Halifax, N.S., 1752 ***7074.6*** *p230*
Boutonnier, Mr. 38; Port uncertain, 1838 ***778.5*** *p74*
Bouttelier, George 26; Halifax, N.S., 1752 ***7074.6*** *p207*
Boutton, . . .; Canada, 1776-1783 ***9786*** *p41*
Bouty, Theobald 26; New Orleans, 1831 ***778.5*** *p74*
Bouvais, Mr.; Port uncertain, 1839 ***778.5*** *p75*
Bouvard, Mr. 35; New Orleans, 1821 ***778.5*** *p75*
Bouvent, Miss 38; Port uncertain, 1838 ***778.5*** *p335*
Bouvet, Mlle. 30; New Orleans, 1839 ***778.5*** *p75*
Bouvet, Onesime 34; Port uncertain, 1838 ***778.5*** *p75*
Bouvier, Catherine 24; Port uncertain, 1839 ***778.5*** *p75*
Bouvier, Francois; Louisiana, 1789-1819 ***778.5*** *p555*
Bouvier, Jacob 32; America, 1836 ***778.5*** *p75*
Bouvier, Jean 20; New Orleans, 1862 ***543.30*** *p114*
Bouvier, Marie 2; America, 1836 ***778.5*** *p75*
Bouvier, Nanet 34; America, 1836 ***778.5*** *p75*
Bouwer, Jelle; Arkansas, 1918 ***95.2*** *p22*
Bouwer, Joela; Arkansas, 1918 ***95.2*** *p22*
Bouz, Ms. 40; New Orleans, 1839 ***778.5*** *p75*
Bouz, Catherine 22; America, 1835 ***778.5*** *p75*
Bouz, Philip 32; America, 1835 ***778.5*** *p75*
Bovaird, Alex; Quebec, 1850 ***5704.8*** *p63*
Bovaird, Jane; Quebec, 1848 ***5704.8*** *p42*
Bovaird, John; Quebec, 1848 ***5704.8*** *p41*
Bovaird, Letty; Quebec, 1848 ***5704.8*** *p42*
Bovaird, Margaret 30; Philadelphia, 1860 ***5704.8*** *p145*
Bovaird, Mary 18; Philadelphia, 1860 ***5704.8*** *p146*
Bovaird, Matilda; Quebec, 1852 ***5704.8*** *p87*
Bovard, Matilda; Quebec, 1852 ***5704.8*** *p91*
Bovas, Ludiz; Iowa, 1866-1943 ***123.54*** *p10*
Bovenkamp, Aaron; New York, NY, 1847 ***3377.6*** *p14*
Bovenkamp, Christian 56; New York, NY, 1847 ***3377.6*** *p14*
Bovenkamp, Gerrard 3; New York, NY, 1847 ***3377.6*** *p14*
Bovenkamp, Hendrick 6; New York, NY, 1847 ***3377.6*** *p14*
Bovenkamp, Jane 31; New York, NY, 1847 ***3377.6*** *p14*
Boveri, Joseph; Arkansas, 1918 ***95.2*** *p22*
Bovey, Thomas 27; Maryland, 1774 ***1219.7*** *p192*
Boving, William; Colorado, 1891 ***9678.1*** *p155*
Bovis, Eugenia 25; America, 1835 ***778.5*** *p75*
Bovyer, Stephen; San Francisco, 1850 ***4914.15*** *p10*
Bovyer, Stephen; San Francisco, 1850 ***4914.15*** *p14*
Bow, Jno 19; America, 1705 ***2212*** *p43*
Bow, Wm.; Virginia, 1634 ***6219*** *p84*
Bowden, Albert Augustus; Illinois, 1876 ***2896.5*** *p4*
Bowden, Phillip; Virginia, 1646 ***6219*** *p239*
Bowden, Robert; South Carolina, 1802 ***1639.20*** *p14*
Bowe, Charles; Wisconsin, n.d. ***9675.4*** *p266*
Bowe, Jeremiah; Wisconsin, n.d. ***9675.4*** *p266*
Bowe, Martin; Montreal, 1823 ***7603*** *p66*
Bowen, Captain; Quebec, 1815 ***9229.18*** *p78*
Bowen, Elizabeth; Philadelphia, 1852 ***5704.8*** *p84*
Bowen, G. W.; Washington, 1859-1920 ***2872.1*** *p5*
Bowen, George 5 *SEE* Bowen, Thomas
Bowen, J. N.; Washington, 1859-1920 ***2872.1*** *p5*
Bowen, James 21; Maryland, 1774 ***1219.7*** *p206*
*Wife:*Mary 21
Bowen, John 34; Virginia, 1774 ***1219.7*** *p239*
Bowen, John Thomas 32; Kansas, 1886 ***5240.1*** *p69*
Bowen, Mary 21 *SEE* Bowen, James
Bowen, Michael; New York, NY, 1838 ***8208.4*** *p65*
Bowen, Morris; Virginia, 1638 ***6219*** *p122*
Bowen, Patrick; New York, NY, 1832 ***8208.4*** *p30*
Bowen, Penelope 26 *SEE* Bowen, Thomas
Bowen, Peter; America, 1741 ***4971*** *p37*
Bowen, Phillip; Virginia, 1643 ***6219*** *p23*
Bowen, Samuel; Virginia, 1643 ***6219*** *p23*
Bowen, Susanna; New York, NY, 1811 ***2859.11*** *p9*
Bowen, Thomas 23; Maryland, 1774 ***1219.7*** *p181*
Bowen, Thomas 27; Philadelphia, 1774 ***1219.7*** *p189*
*Wife:*Penelope 26
*Son:*George 5
*Son:*William 1
Bowen, Thomas 35; New Orleans, 1862 ***543.30*** *p116*
Bowen, William 1 *SEE* Bowen, Thomas
Bowen, William 20; Virginia, 1773 ***1219.7*** *p171*
Bower, August; Washington, 1859-1920 ***2872.1*** *p5*
Bower, George 34; New Orleans, 1838 ***778.5*** *p75*
Bower, Henry; Virginia, 1637 ***6219*** *p114*
Bower, Jelle 26; Arkansas, 1918 ***95.2*** *p22*
Bower, John 34; Kansas, 1871 ***5240.1*** *p52*
Bower, Margerite 26; New Orleans, 1838 ***778.5*** *p75*
Bower, Martin; Philadelphia, 1751 ***9973.7*** *p31*
Bower, Martin 44; Pennsylvania, 1752-1753 ***2444*** *p136*
Bower, Michael; Philadelphia, 1761 ***9973.7*** *p36*
Bower, Robert; Virginia, 1698 ***2212*** *p11*
Bowers, Catharine 40; Massachusetts, 1849 ***5881.1*** *p7*
Bowers, Jacob 16; Virginia, 1729 ***3690.1*** *p24*
Bowers, Jonas; Virginia, 1637 ***6219*** *p113*
Bowers, Matthew 25; Jamaica, 1730 ***3690.1*** *p24*
Bowery, Peter 45; New Orleans, 1862 ***543.30*** *p109*

Bowes, John; Colorado, 1900 ***9678.1*** *p155*
Bowie, Alexander 47; Kansas, 1888 ***5240.1*** *p72*
Bowie, Alexander McLauchlan; Iowa, 1866-1943 ***123.54*** *p10*
Bowie, Allan C.; Iowa, 1866-1943 ***123.54*** *p10*
Bowie, Ann 36; Carolina, 1774 ***1219.7*** *p231*
Bowie, David; Iowa, 1866-1943 ***123.54*** *p10*
Bowie, Janet 1; Quebec, 1864 ***5704.8*** *p162*
Bowie, Janet 27; Quebec, 1864 ***5704.8*** *p162*
Bowie, John; Austin, TX, 1886 ***9777*** *p5*
Bowie, John C.; Iowa, 1866-1943 ***123.54*** *p10*
Bowie, John Stuart; Iowa, 1866-1943 ***123.54*** *p10*
Bowie, Margaret 5; Quebec, 1864 ***5704.8*** *p162*
Bowie, Robert 3; Quebec, 1864 ***5704.8*** *p162*
Bowie, Robert 30; Quebec, 1864 ***5704.8*** *p162*
Bowie, Robert Allan; Iowa, 1866-1943 ***123.54*** *p10*
Bowie, William; Iowa, 1866-1943 ***123.54*** *p10*
Bowigly, A. 23; Port uncertain, 1839 ***778.5*** *p76*
Bowker, Abraham 18; Virginia, 1700 ***2212*** *p32*
Bowker, John 24; Virginia, 1700 ***2212*** *p32*
Bowland, Ann 20; America, 1704 ***2212*** *p40*
Bowlar, Martin; America, 1852 ***1450.2*** *p17A*
Bowler, Aaron 21; Philadelphia, 1774 ***1219.7*** *p232*
Bowler, Dennis 7; Massachusetts, 1849 ***5881.1*** *p7*
Bowler, John 20; Massachusetts, 1849 ***5881.1*** *p9*
Bowler, Maria 9; Massachusetts, 1849 ***5881.1*** *p10*
Bowler, Mary 40; Newport, RI, 1851 ***6508.5*** *p20*
Bowler, William; Virginia, 1639 ***6219*** *p152*
Bowles, Edward; Virginia, 1639 ***6219*** *p162*
Bowles, Geo.; Virginia, 1636 ***6219*** *p21*
Bowles, Mrs. H.; New York, NY, 1811 ***2859.11*** *p9*
Bowles, Henry; America, 1742 ***4971*** *p32*
Bowles, Peter 21; Maryland, 1775 ***1219.7*** *p250*
Bowley, Isaac 16; Port uncertain, 1757 ***3690.1*** *p24*
Bowley, Jeremiah 23; Virginia, 1774 ***1219.7*** *p241*
Bowley, Samuell 21; Jamaica, 1734 ***3690.1*** *p24*
Bowling, Edward; South Carolina, 1767 ***1639.20*** *p14*
Bowling, John 18; Maryland, 1775 ***1219.7*** *p253*
Bowling, Timothy 38; Savannah, GA, 1733 ***4719.17*** *p310*
Bowlinger, Conrad; America, 1865 ***6014.1*** *p1*
Bowman, Catharine 7; Philadelphia, 1867 ***5704.8*** *p216*
Bowman, Edmund 20; Maryland, 1720 ***3690.1*** *p24*
Bowman, Ellen; Philadelphia, 1867 ***5704.8*** *p216*
Bowman, George; Iroquois Co., IL, 1892 ***3455.1*** *p9*
Bowman, Henry; Philadelphia, 1761 ***9973.7*** *p36*
Bowman, James 4; Philadelphia, 1867 ***5704.8*** *p216*
Bowman, John; Carolina, 1769 ***1639.20*** *p322*
Bowman, John; Charleston, SC, 1807 ***1639.20*** *p14*
Bowman, John 11; Philadelphia, 1867 ***5704.8*** *p216*
Bowman, John 19; New Orleans, 1862 ***543.30*** *p484*
Bowman, Mathew 9; Philadelphia, 1867 ***5704.8*** *p216*
Bowman, Patrick 1; Philadelphia, 1867 ***5704.8*** *p216*
Bowman, Peter; Illinois, 1870 ***5012.38*** *p99*
Bowman, Peter 69; Arizona, 1905 ***9228.40*** *p10*
Bowman, Thomas 18; Maryland, 1729 ***3690.1*** *p24*
Bowman, Walter; Virginia, 1643 ***6219*** *p200*
Bowmann, . . .; Canada, 1776-1783 ***9786*** *p18*
Bows, John 34; Kansas, 1879 ***5240.1*** *p60*
Bowser, Ann 20; Nova Scotia, 1774 ***1219.7*** *p195*
Bowser, Ann 60; Nova Scotia, 1774 ***1219.7*** *p195*
Bowser, Richard 29; Nova Scotia, 1774 ***1219.7*** *p195*
Bowser, William 20; Philadelphia, 1774 ***1219.7*** *p217*
Bowser, William 22; New England, 1774 ***1219.7*** *p191*
Bowtell, James 24; Virginia, 1775 ***1219.7*** *p261*
Bowyer, Anna *SEE* Bowyer, Johann Jakob
Bowyer, Elisabeth *SEE* Bowyer, Johann Jakob
Bowyer, Eva *SEE* Bowyer, Johann Jakob
Bowyer, Friederich *SEE* Bowyer, Johann Jakob
Bowyer, Jakob *SEE* Bowyer, Johann Jakob
Bowyer, Johann Jakob; Philadelphia, 1752 ***8582.2*** *p67*
  With wife & 12 children
  *Child:*Jakob
  *Child:*Katharina
  *Child:*Anna
  *Child:*Elisabeth
  *Child:*Eva
  *Child:*Friederich
  *Child:*Margaretha
Bowyer, Katharina *SEE* Bowyer, Johann Jakob
Bowyer, Margaretha *SEE* Bowyer, Johann Jakob
Box, Anth.; Virginia, 1629 ***6219*** *p8*
Box, Benj.; Virginia, 1637 ***6219*** *p13*
Box, John 18; Pennsylvania, 1728 ***3690.1*** *p24*
Box, John 26; Georgia, 1774 ***1219.7*** *p188*
Box, Mary; Virginia, 1636 ***6219*** *p75*
Box, Thomas, Jr.; Virginia, 1636 ***6219*** *p13*
Box, Thomas, Jr.; Virginia, 1636 ***6219*** *p146*
Boxberger, Antoine 33; New Orleans, 1862 ***543.30*** *p326*
Boxborough, James 16; Virginia, 1774 ***1219.7*** *p205*
Boxholts, Caroline Louise *SEE* Boxholts, Gottlieb
Boxholts, Chr. C. Friederike *SEE* Boxholts, Gottlieb
Boxholts, Christine Charlotte *SEE* Boxholts, Gottlieb
Boxholts, Gottlieb 68; America, 1872 ***4610.10*** *p109*
  *Wife:*Louise Meier
  *Child:*Chr. C. Friederike
  *Child:*Caroline Louise
  *Child:*Heinrich Wilhelm
  *Child:*Christine Charlotte
Boxholts, Heinrich Wilhelm *SEE* Boxholts, Gottlieb
Boxholts, Louise Meier *SEE* Boxholts, Gottlieb
Boxhorn, Charles; Wisconsin, n.d. ***9675.4*** *p266*
Boxhorn, William; Wisconsin, n.d. ***9675.4*** *p266*
Boy, John; America, 1736 ***4971*** *p77*
Boy, Tho.; Virginia, 1635 ***6219*** *p20*
Boy, William 22; Virginia, 1700 ***2212*** *p31*
Boyce, Ann 38 *SEE* Boyce, James
Boyce, Anne; New York, NY, 1816 ***2859.11*** *p25*
Boyce, Anne; Philadelphia, 1864 ***5704.8*** *p181*
Boyce, Bridget; New York, NY, 1865 ***5704.8*** *p191*
Boyce, Chr.; Virginia, 1645 ***6219*** *p232*
Boyce, Christ.; Virginia, 1642 ***6219*** *p198*
Boyce, David 13 *SEE* Boyce, James
Boyce, Dennis; St. John, N.B., 1847 ***5704.8*** *p5*
Boyce, George; Philadelphia, 1852 ***5704.8*** *p91*
Boyce, Hugh; St. John, N.B., 1847 ***5704.8*** *p21*
Boyce, James; Philadelphia, 1851 ***5704.8*** *p81*
Boyce, James 16 *SEE* Boyce, James
Boyce, James 40; Philadelphia, 1833-1834 ***53.26*** *p5*
  *Relative:*Ann 38
  *Relative:*John 18
  *Relative:*James 16
  *Relative:*David 13
  *Relative:*Leslie 10
Boyce, John; New York, NY, 1833 ***8208.4*** *p46*
Boyce, John; Philadelphia, 1867 ***5704.8*** *p224*
Boyce, John; St. John, N.B., 1847 ***5704.8*** *p34*
Boyce, John 18 *SEE* Boyce, James
Boyce, John 60; South Carolina, 1850 ***1639.20*** *p14*
Boyce, Leslie 10 *SEE* Boyce, James
Boyce, Margaret; New York, NY, 1866 ***5704.8*** *p212*
Boyce, Margaret 20; Philadelphia, 1854 ***5704.8*** *p116*
Boyce, Mary; America, 1866 ***5704.8*** *p215*
Boyce, Mary; Philadelphia, 1851 ***5704.8*** *p81*
Boyce, Mary Jane; Philadelphia, 1864 ***5704.8*** *p184*
Boyce, Samuel; New York, NY, 1851 ***6013.19*** *p89*
Boyce, Stephen; New York, NY, 1869 ***5704.8*** *p233*
Boyd, Mr.; Quebec, 1815 ***9229.18*** *p81*
Boyd, Alfred; Washington, 1859-1920 ***2872.1*** *p5*
Boyd, Andrew; Philadelphia, 1816 ***2859.11*** *p25*
Boyd, Ann Eliza 11 *SEE* Boyd, Robert
Boyd, Ann Eliza 11; Philadelphia, 1847 ***5704.8*** *p5*
Boyd, David; New York, NY, 1816 ***2859.11*** *p25*
Boyd, David 7; Philadelphia, 1865 ***5704.8*** *p165*
Boyd, Eliza; St. John, N.B., 1853 ***5704.8*** *p107*
Boyd, Eliza 15; Philadelphia, 1853 ***5704.8*** *p109*
Boyd, Eliza 20; Quebec, 1856 ***5704.8*** *p130*
Boyd, Elizabeth; St. John, N.B., 1851 ***5704.8*** *p79*
Boyd, Elizabeth 2; Philadelphia, 1865 ***5704.8*** *p165*
Boyd, Elizabeth 30; Philadelphia, 1865 ***5704.8*** *p165*
Boyd, Ellen *SEE* Boyd, Samuel
Boyd, Ellen; Philadelphia, 1811 ***2859.11*** *p9*
Boyd, Ellen 20; St. John, N.B., 1858 ***5704.8*** *p137*
Boyd, George; St. John, N.B., 1847 ***5704.8*** *p10*
Boyd, George 25; Maryland, 1775 ***1219.7*** *p254*
Boyd, Henry 40; Philadelphia, 1833-1834 ***53.26*** *p5*
Boyd, Isabella 11 *SEE* Boyd, Robert
Boyd, Isabella 11; Philadelphia, 1847 ***5704.8*** *p5*
Boyd, James; Iowa, 1882 ***2764.35*** *p6*
Boyd, James; Ohio, 1840 ***9892.11*** *p5*
Boyd, James; Philadelphia, 1852 ***5704.8*** *p92*
Boyd, James; Philadelphia, 1868 ***5704.8*** *p230*
Boyd, James; Quebec, 1847 ***5704.8*** *p27*
Boyd, James; Quebec, 1849 ***5704.8*** *p52*
Boyd, James; St. John, N.B., 1848 ***5704.8*** *p44*
Boyd, James 2; St. John, N.B., 1855 ***5704.8*** *p126*
Boyd, James 11; Philadelphia, 1865 ***5704.8*** *p165*
Boyd, James 26; Philadelphia, 1803 ***53.26*** *p5*
Boyd, James 26; Philadelphia, 1804 ***53.26*** *p5*
Boyd, James 28; St. John, N.B., 1855 ***5704.8*** *p126*
Boyd, Jane; America, 1865 ***5704.8*** *p203*
Boyd, Jane; St. John, N.B., 1852 ***5704.8*** *p95*
Boyd, Jane; St. John, N.B., 1853 ***5704.8*** *p107*
Boyd, Jane 7; Philadelphia, 1865 ***5704.8*** *p165*
Boyd, Jane 16; Philadelphia, 1854 ***5704.8*** *p123*
Boyd, John; America, 1743 ***4971*** *p69*
Boyd, John; New York, NY, 1811 ***2859.11*** *p9*
Boyd, John; Philadelphia, 1864 ***5704.8*** *p183*
Boyd, John; Virginia, 1638-1738 ***1639.20*** *p15*
Boyd, John 38; Quebec, 1864 ***5704.8*** *p159*
Boyd, John S.; Arizona, 1907 ***9228.40*** *p10*
Boyd, Letitia *SEE* Boyd, Robert
Boyd, Letitia; Philadelphia, 1847 ***5704.8*** *p5*
Boyd, Letitia 18; Philadelphia, 1859 ***5704.8*** *p142*
Boyd, Maitland Wilson; Charleston, SC, 1829 ***1639.20*** *p15*
Boyd, Margaret; America, 1864 ***5704.8*** *p190*
Boyd, Margaret; New York, NY, 1865 ***5704.8*** *p195*
Boyd, Margaret; New York, NY, 1870 ***5704.8*** *p239*
Boyd, Margaret; Philadelphia, 1865 ***5704.8*** *p191*
Boyd, Martha; Quebec, 1849 ***5704.8*** *p52*
Boyd, Mary; Philadelphia, 1850 ***5704.8*** *p64*
Boyd, Mary 28; Quebec, 1864 ***5704.8*** *p159*
Boyd, Mary Ann *SEE* Boyd, Samuel
Boyd, Mary-Ann; Philadelphia, 1811 ***2859.11*** *p9*
Boyd, Mary Jane 9; Quebec, 1849 ***5704.8*** *p52*
Boyd, Mary Jane 22; Philadelphia, 1854 ***5704.8*** *p118*
Boyd, Matilda; Philadelphia, 1847 ***53.26*** *p5*
Boyd, Matilda Ann; Philadelphia, 1847 ***5704.8*** *p32*
Boyd, Nancy 23; St. John, N.B., 1855 ***5704.8*** *p126*
Boyd, P.; New York, NY, 1816 ***2859.11*** *p25*
Boyd, Rachael; Philadelphia, 1864 ***5704.8*** *p183*
Boyd, Robert; Arkansas, 1918 ***95.2*** *p22*
Boyd, Robert; New York, NY, 1816 ***2859.11*** *p25*
Boyd, Robert; New York, NY, 1838 ***8208.4*** *p84*
Boyd, Robert; Philadelphia, 1847 ***53.26*** *p5*
  *Relative:*Sarah
  *Relative:*Letitia
  *Relative:*Ann Eliza 11
  *Relative:*Isabella 11
Boyd, Robert; Philadelphia, 1847 ***5704.8*** *p5*
Boyd, Robert 16; Philadelphia, 1865 ***5704.8*** *p165*
Boyd, Robert 29; New Orleans, 1862 ***543.30*** *p327*
Boyd, Samuel; New York, NY, 1816 ***2859.11*** *p25*
Boyd, Samuel; Philadelphia, 1811 ***53.26*** *p5*
  *Relative:*Mary Ann
  *Relative:*Ellen
Boyd, Samuel; Philadelphia, 1811 ***2859.11*** *p9*
Boyd, Samuel; Philadelphia, 1852 ***5704.8*** *p86*
Boyd, Sarah *SEE* Boyd, Robert
Boyd, Sarah; Philadelphia, 1847 ***5704.8*** *p5*
Boyd, Susan; Quebec, 1849 ***5704.8*** *p52*
Boyd, Thomas; Arkansas, 1918 ***95.2*** *p22*
Boyd, Thomas; New York, NY, 1816 ***2859.11*** *p25*
Boyd, Thomas; St. John, N.B., 1851 ***5704.8*** *p72*
Boyd, W.; New York, NY, 1816 ***2859.11*** *p25*
Boyd, William; Arkansas, 1918 ***95.2*** *p22*
Boyd, William; Charleston, SC, 1817 ***1639.20*** *p15*
Boyd, William; New York, NY, 1811 ***2859.11*** *p9*
  With family
Boyd, William; New York, NY, 1811 ***2859.11*** *p9*
Boyd, William; New York, NY, 1870 ***5704.8*** *p239*
Boyd, William; Philadelphia, 1851 ***5704.8*** *p79*
Boyd, William; Philadelphia, 1865 ***5704.8*** *p191*
Boyd, William; Quebec, 1849 ***5704.8*** *p52*
Boyd, William; Quebec, 1851 ***5704.8*** *p75*
Boyd, William; St. John, N.B., 1848 ***5704.8*** *p45*
Boyd, William 23; Jamaica, 1725 ***3690.1*** *p24*
Boyd, William 60; Philadelphia, 1865 ***5704.8*** *p164*
Boyd, William J. 9; Philadelphia, 1865 ***5704.8*** *p165*
Boyd, William John 4; Quebec, 1849 ***5704.8*** *p52*
Boyde, Leonora 27 *SEE* Boyde, William
Boyde, Robert 28; New York, 1775 ***1219.7*** *p269*
  With wife
  With child
Boyde, William 36; Maryland, 1775 ***1219.7*** *p251*
  *Wife:*Leonora 27
Boyden, John 17; Maryland, 1774 ***1219.7*** *p221*
Boydon, Charles F.; Iroquois Co., IL, 1894 ***3455.1*** *p9*
Boye, Johannes Temand; Arkansas, 1918 ***95.2*** *p22*
Boyer, Mme. 26; New Orleans, 1837 ***778.5*** *p76*
Boyer, Mr.; New Orleans, 1837 ***778.5*** *p76*
Boyer, Mr.; Port uncertain, 1839 ***778.5*** *p76*
Boyer, Andrew; Virginia, 1628 ***6219*** *p31*
Boyer, Anna *SEE* Boyer, Johann Jakob
Boyer, Dietrick; Iroquois Co., IL, 1893 ***3455.1*** *p9*
Boyer, Elisabeth *SEE* Boyer, Johann Jakob
Boyer, Eva *SEE* Boyer, Johann Jakob
Boyer, F. 50; Port uncertain, 1839 ***778.5*** *p76*
Boyer, Friederich *SEE* Boyer, Johann Jakob
Boyer, H. B.; Washington, 1859-1920 ***2872.1*** *p5*
Boyer, Jakob *SEE* Boyer, Johann Jakob
Boyer, Johann Jakob; Philadelphia, 1752 ***8582.2*** *p67*
  With wife & 12 children
  *Child:*Jakob
  *Child:*Katharina
  *Child:*Anna
  *Child:*Elisabeth
  *Child:*Eva
  *Child:*Friederich
  *Child:*Margaretha
Boyer, John 25; New Orleans, 1835 ***778.5*** *p76*
Boyer, John H. 42; New Orleans, 1837 ***778.5*** *p76*
Boyer, John P. 57; Washington, 1919 ***1728.4*** *p251*
Boyer, Katharina *SEE* Boyer, Johann Jakob
Boyer, L. 25; New Orleans, 1821 ***778.5*** *p76*
Boyer, Margaretha *SEE* Boyer, Johann Jakob
Boyer, Mary 20; Maryland or Virginia, 1719 ***3690.1*** *p24*
Boyer, Nicholas; Philadelphia, 1759 ***9973.7*** *p33*

Boyer, Tho.; Virginia, 1635 6219 p69
Boyer, Thomas; Virginia, 1628 6219 p31
Boyer, William; Virginia, 1636 6219 p27
Boyere, P. 55; New Orleans, 1836 778.5 p475
Boyers, Lewis; America, 1777-1778 8582.2 p69
Boyes, Elisabeth Campbell *SEE* Boyes, Thomas
Boyes, John; Canada, 1835 4535.10 p198
With wife
With 8 children
Boyes, John; New York, 1835 4535.10 p198
With wife
With 8 children
Boyes, Thomas; St. Johns, N.F., 1794 8894.2 p56
*Wife:*Elisabeth Campbell
Boyes, Wm 19; New Orleans, 1862 543.30 p242
Boyfield, Thomas 20; Maryland, 1774 1219.7 p225
Boylan, Patrick; Charles Town, SC, 1767 1219.7 p133
Boylan, Patrick 24; Philadelphia, 1774 1219.7 p233
Boyle, . . . 3 mos; New York, NY, 1865 5704.8 p197
Boyle, Miss; Quebec, 1815 9229.18 p75
Boyle, Mrs.; Philadelphia, 1848 5704.8 p40
Boyle, Agnes 5; Quebec, 1858 5704.8 p137
Boyle, Alexander; Philadelphia, 1851 5704.8 p76
Boyle, Alexander; Philadelphia, 1851 5704.8 p78
Boyle, Alice; New York, NY, 1868 5704.8 p225
Boyle, Alice; Philadelphia, 1864 5704.8 p176
Boyle, Andrew; New York, NY, 1870 5704.8 p238
Boyle, Ann; New York, NY, 1865 5704.8 p203
Boyle, Ann; Philadelphia, 1848 53.26 p5
*Relative:*Biddy
Boyle, Ann; Philadelphia, 1848 5704.8 p40
Boyle, Ann; Quebec, 1825 7603 p63
Boyle, Ann; St. John, N.B., 1847 5704.8 p26
Boyle, Ann; St. John, N.B., 1851 5704.8 p79
Boyle, Ann 3 *SEE* Boyle, Bridget
Boyle, Ann 3; Philadelphia, 1847 5704.8 p13
Boyle, Ann 6; St. John, N.B., 1851 5704.8 p79
Boyle, Ann 11; St. John, N.B., 1847 5704.8 p10
Boyle, Ann 12; St. John, N.B., 1854 5704.8 p120
Boyle, Ann 40; Philadelphia, 1860 5704.8 p145
Boyle, Anna 9; Quebec, 1858 5704.8 p137
Boyle, Anne; New York, NY, 1867 5704.8 p220
Boyle, Anne 18; Philadelphia, 1864 5704.8 p160
Boyle, Bernard; New Orleans, 1849 5704.8 p59
Boyle, Bernard; New York, NY, 1864 5704.8 p171
Boyle, Bernard; St. John, N.B., 1847 5704.8 p26
Boyle, Bernard 19; Quebec, 1858 5704.8 p138
Boyle, Biddy *SEE* Boyle, Ann
Boyle, Biddy *SEE* Boyle, Patrick
Boyle, Biddy; Philadelphia, 1848 53.26 p5
Boyle, Biddy; Philadelphia, 1848 5704.8 p40
Boyle, Biddy; Philadelphia, 1851 5704.8 p81
Boyle, Bridget *SEE* Boyle, John
Boyle, Bridget; New York, NY, 1865 5704.8 p202
Boyle, Bridget; Philadelphia, 1847 53.26 p5
*Relative:*Magy 5
*Relative:*Ann 3
*Relative:*Nora 3
*Relative:*Michael 2
*Relative:*Bridget 1 mo
*Relative:*Peggy
Boyle, Bridget; Philadelphia, 1847 5704.8 p13
Boyle, Bridget 1 mo *SEE* Boyle, Bridget
Boyle, Bridget 1 mo; Philadelphia, 1847 5704.8 p13
Boyle, Bridget 15; Quebec, 1858 5704.8 p137
Boyle, Bridget 20; Philadelphia, 1853 5704.8 p111
Boyle, Bridget 20; Philadelphia, 1860 5704.8 p146
Boyle, Catharine; New York, NY, 1865 5704.8 p202
Boyle, Catharine; Philadelphia, 1848 5704.8 p40
Boyle, Catharine; Philadelphia, 1864 5704.8 p182
Boyle, Catherine *SEE* Boyle, Patrick
Boyle, Catherine; Baltimore, 1811 2859.11 p9
Boyle, Catherine; Philadelphia, 1850 53.26 p5
Boyle, Catherine; Philadelphia, 1850 5704.8 p65
Boyle, Catherine; Philadelphia, 1851 5704.8 p79
Boyle, Catherine; Philadelphia, 1851 5704.8 p81
Boyle, Catherine; Philadelphia, 1854 5704.8 p116
Boyle, Catherine 20; Philadelphia, 1858 5704.8 p139
Boyle, Catherine 20; Philadelphia, 1861 5704.8 p148
Boyle, Cathr 40; Wilmington, DE, 1831 6508.7 p160
Boyle, Cecilia; Philadelphia, 1853 5704.8 p102
Boyle, Cecilia 20; Philadelphia, 1860 5704.8 p145
Boyle, Ceilia; New York, NY, 1868 5704.8 p225
Boyle, Charles *SEE* Boyle, John
Boyle, Charles; Philadelphia, 1847 5704.8 p13
Boyle, Charles; Philadelphia, 1864 5704.8 p179
Boyle, Charles; Philadelphia, 1864 5704.8 p182
Boyle, Charles 9 mos; Philadelphia, 1853 5704.8 p112
Boyle, Charles 11; Quebec, 1858 5704.8 p137
Boyle, Chr.; Philadelphia, 1816 2859.11 p25
Boyle, Cornelius; St. John, N.B., 1851 5704.8 p79
Boyle, Daniel *SEE* Boyle, John
Boyle, Daniel; Iowa, 1866-1943 123.54 p10
Boyle, Daniel; New York, NY, 1864 5704.8 p175
Boyle, Daniel; Philadelphia, 1847 5704.8 p13
Boyle, Daniel; Philadelphia, 1848 53.26 p6
Boyle, Daniel; Philadelphia, 1848 5704.8 p40
Boyle, Daniel; St. John, N.B., 1853 5704.8 p107
Boyle, Dennis; New York, NY, 1811 2859.11 p9
Boyle, Dennis; Philadelphia, 1867 5704.8 p221
Boyle, Edward; Quebec, 1847 5704.8 p38
Boyle, Edward; St. John, N.B., 1847 5704.8 p26
Boyle, Elenor 14; Philadelphia, 1861 5704.8 p147
Boyle, Eliza; New York, NY, 1868 5704.8 p225
Boyle, Eliza 20; Philadelphia, 1860 5704.8 p145
Boyle, Elizabeth 11; St. John, N.B., 1851 5704.8 p79
Boyle, Ellan; St. John, N.B., 1847 5704.8 p10
Boyle, Ellan 6; St. John, N.B., 1847 5704.8 p10
Boyle, Ellen; New York, NY, 1868 5704.8 p225
Boyle, Ellen; Philadelphia, 1864 5704.8 p185
Boyle, Ellen 20; Quebec, 1863 5704.8 p154
Boyle, Emanuel 24; Philadelphia, 1865 5704.8 p164
Boyle, Francis; America, 1795 4778.2 p141
Boyle, George B.; New York, NY, 1836 8208.4 p9
Boyle, Grace; New York, NY, 1864 5704.8 p175
Boyle, Grace; Philadelphia, 1864 5704.8 p185
Boyle, Grace 18; Philadelphia, 1853 5704.8 p112
Boyle, Hannah; St. John, N.B., 1851 5704.8 p79
Boyle, Henry; St. John, N.B., 1848 5704.8 p39
Boyle, Hugh; St. John, N.B., 1847 5704.8 p10
Boyle, Hugh; St. John, N.B., 1847 5704.8 p26
Boyle, Hugh 8; St. John, N.B., 1847 5704.8 p10
Boyle, Hugh 19; Wilmington, DE, 1831 6508.7 p160
Boyle, Hugh Stanford; New York, NY, 1838 8208.4 p86
Boyle, Isabella; St. John, N.B., 1848 5704.8 p44
Boyle, Isabella 4; St. John, N.B., 1851 5704.8 p79
Boyle, James *SEE* Boyle, Patrick
Boyle, James; America, 1869 5704.8 p232
Boyle, James; America, 1869 6014.1 p1
Boyle, James; New York, NY, 1836 8208.4 p20
Boyle, James; Pennsylvania, 1864 2764.35 p9
Boyle, James; Philadelphia, 1847 53.26 p6
Boyle, James; Philadelphia, 1847 5704.8 p14
Boyle, James; Philadelphia, 1848 5704.8 p40
Boyle, James; Philadelphia, 1851 5704.8 p78
Boyle, James; Philadelphia, 1865 5704.8 p200
Boyle, James; Quebec, 1848 5704.8 p42
Boyle, James; St. John, N.B., 1848 5704.8 p43
Boyle, James 3; St. John, N.B., 1847 5704.8 p10
Boyle, James 4; New York, NY, 1864 5704.8 p187
Boyle, James 20; St. John, N.B., 1863 5704.8 p152
Boyle, James 30; Philadelphia, 1864 5704.8 p161
Boyle, James 35; New Orleans, 1862 543.30 p484
Boyle, James 40; Philadelphia, 1804 53.26 p6
Boyle, Jane; Philadelphia, 1851 5704.8 p78
Boyle, Jane; Philadelphia, 1865 5704.8 p203
Boyle, Jane 10; St. John, N.B., 1847 5704.8 p10
Boyle, Jane 13; St. John, N.B., 1847 5704.8 p26
Boyle, Jane 14; Wilmington, DE, 1831 6508.7 p160
Boyle, Jane 18; Philadelphia, 1861 5704.8 p148
Boyle, Jane 40; St. John, N.B., 1861 5704.8 p147
Boyle, John *SEE* Boyle, Patrick
Boyle, John; America, 1739 4971 p47
Boyle, John; America, 1739 4971 p66
Boyle, John; Baltimore, 1811 2859.11 p9
Boyle, John; New York, NY, 1811 2859.11 p9
Boyle, John; New York, NY, 1835 8208.4 p6
Boyle, John; New York, NY, 1868 5704.8 p225
Boyle, John; Philadelphia, 1815 2859.11 p25
With wife & 3 children
Boyle, John; Philadelphia, 1847 53.26 p6
Boyle, John; Philadelphia, 1847 53.26 p6
*Relative:*Daniel
*Relative:*Charles
*Relative:*John 13
*Relative:*Bridget
*Relative:*Mary
Boyle, John; Philadelphia, 1847 5704.8 p13
Boyle, John; Philadelphia, 1847 5704.8 p23
Boyle, John; Philadelphia, 1848 5704.8 p40
Boyle, John; Philadelphia, 1851 5704.8 p78
Boyle, John; Philadelphia, 1866 5704.8 p200
Boyle, John; Philadelphia, 1866 5704.8 p205
Boyle, John 2; New York, NY, 1864 5704.8 p187
Boyle, John 13 *SEE* Boyle, John
Boyle, John 13; Philadelphia, 1847 5704.8 p13
Boyle, John 13; Quebec, 1858 5704.8 p137
Boyle, John 16; Philadelphia, 1861 5704.8 p148
Boyle, John 21; Massachusetts, 1849 5881.1 p9
Boyle, John 22; St. John, N.B., 1858 5704.8 p137
Boyle, John 40; Philadelphia, 1860 5704.8 p145
Boyle, John 42; Quebec, 1858 5704.8 p137
Boyle, Joseph 7; Quebec, 1858 5704.8 p137
Boyle, Joseph Jack; Philadelphia, 1851 5704.8 p78
Boyle, Judy 60; Massachusetts, 1849 5881.1 p9
Boyle, Maggie 11; New York, NY, 1868 5704.8 p225
Boyle, Magy 5 *SEE* Boyle, Bridget
Boyle, Magy 5; Philadelphia, 1847 5704.8 p13
Boyle, Manus; Philadelphia, 1849 53.26 p6
*Relative:*Mary
*Relative:*Mary 6
Boyle, Manus; Philadelphia, 1849 5704.8 p54
Boyle, Margaret *SEE* Boyle, Patrick
Boyle, Margaret; Philadelphia, 1848 5704.8 p40
Boyle, Margaret; Philadelphia, 1864 5704.8 p173
Boyle, Margaret; Philadelphia, 1865 5704.8 p199
Boyle, Margaret; Philadelphia, 1865 5704.8 p200
Boyle, Margaret; Quebec, 1847 5704.8 p38
Boyle, Margaret 20; Philadelphia, 1853 5704.8 p112
Boyle, Mary *SEE* Boyle, John
Boyle, Mary *SEE* Boyle, Manus
Boyle, Mary; New Orleans, 1849 5704.8 p59
Boyle, Mary; New York, NY, 1865 5704.8 p194
Boyle, Mary; Philadelphia, 1847 5704.8 p13
Boyle, Mary; Philadelphia, 1849 5704.8 p54
Boyle, Mary; Philadelphia, 1864 5704.8 p179
Boyle, Mary; Philadelphia, 1867 5704.8 p217
Boyle, Mary; St. John, N.B., 1847 5704.8 p10
Boyle, Mary; St. John, N.B., 1848 5704.8 p39
Boyle, Mary; St. John, N.B., 1850 5704.8 p67
Boyle, Mary 6 *SEE* Boyle, Manus
Boyle, Mary 6; Philadelphia, 1849 5704.8 p54
Boyle, Mary 9; St. John, N.B., 1851 5704.8 p79
Boyle, Mary 9; St. John, N.B., 1854 5704.8 p120
Boyle, Mary 40; Philadelphia, 1853 5704.8 p114
Boyle, Mary Ann; New York, NY, 1868 5704.8 p225
Boyle, Mary Ann; St. John, N.B., 1852 5704.8 p83
Boyle, Mary Ann; St. John, N.B., 1852 5704.8 p92
Boyle, Mary Ann 16; Philadelphia, 1860 5704.8 p145
Boyle, Mary Ann 24; St. John, N.B., 1858 5704.8 p140
Boyle, Matty 17; Philadelphia, 1854 5704.8 p118
Boyle, Michael; New York, NY, 1868 5704.8 p225
Boyle, Michael 2 *SEE* Boyle, Bridget
Boyle, Michael 2; Philadelphia, 1847 5704.8 p13
Boyle, Michael 24; Philadelphia, 1854 5704.8 p115
Boyle, Michael 25; Philadelphia, 1860 5704.8 p145
Boyle, Nancy; Philadelphia, 1851 5704.8 p78
Boyle, Nancy; St. John, N.B., 1847 5704.8 p26
Boyle, Nancy 13; Quebec, 1851 5704.8 p82
Boyle, Neil; Philadelphia, 1811 2859.11 p9
With family
Boyle, Nora 3 *SEE* Boyle, Bridget
Boyle, Nora 3; Philadelphia, 1847 5704.8 p13
Boyle, Owen; America, 1737 4971 p24
Boyle, Owen; Philadelphia, 1864 5704.8 p183
Boyle, Patrick; Illinois, 1860 5012.39 p89
Boyle, Patrick; New York, NY, 1839 8208.4 p101
Boyle, Patrick; New York, NY, 1864 5704.8 p176
Boyle, Patrick; Philadelphia, 1848 53.26 p6
With wife
*Relative:*Catherine
*Relative:*Margaret
*Relative:*Biddy
*Relative:*John
*Relative:*James
*Relative:*William 2
Boyle, Patrick; Philadelphia, 1848 5704.8 p40
Boyle, Patrick; Philadelphia, 1870 5704.8 p239
Boyle, Patrick; Quebec, 1851 5704.8 p82
Boyle, Patrick 22; Philadelphia, 1853 5704.8 p108
Boyle, Peggy *SEE* Boyle, Bridget
Boyle, Peggy; Philadelphia, 1847 5704.8 p13
Boyle, Peter 18; Philadelphia, 1856 5704.8 p128
Boyle, Phelix 24; Quebec, 1856 5704.8 p130
Boyle, Phil; St. John, N.B., 1847 5704.8 p10
Boyle, Richard 35; Massachusetts, 1849 5881.1 p11
Boyle, Robert; New York, NY, 1815 2859.11 p25
Boyle, Robert; St. John, N.B., 1847 5704.8 p10
Boyle, Robert; San Francisco, 1850 4914.15 p10
Boyle, Robert; San Francisco, 1850 4914.15 p12
Boyle, Robert 21; Maryland, 1774 1219.7 p204
Boyle, Robert 21; Maryland, 1775 1219.7 p267
Boyle, Rose; Philadelphia, 1847 53.26 p6
Boyle, Rose; Philadelphia, 1847 5704.8 p14
Boyle, Rose Ann; New York, NY, 1864 5704.8 p187
Boyle, Rossanna 38; Quebec, 1858 5704.8 p137
Boyle, Samuel; New York, NY, 1816 2859.11 p25
Boyle, Sarah; New York, NY, 1865 5704.8 p197
Boyle, Sarah; Philadelphia, 1864 5704.8 p180
Boyle, Sarah 20; St. John, N.B., 1855 5704.8 p126
Boyle, Sarah 22; Philadelphia, 1853 5704.8 p112
Boyle, Sophy; Philadelphia, 1864 5704.8 p185
Boyle, Stephen; Quebec, 1824 7603 p74
Boyle, Susan; Philadelphia, 1865 5704.8 p202
Boyle, Susan Maria 6 mos; Quebec, 1858 5704.8 p137
Boyle, Terance; Baltimore, 1811 2859.11 p9
Boyle, Thomas; Illinois, 1858 2896.5 p4
Boyle, Thomas; St. John, N.B., 1850 5704.8 p67
Boyle, Thomas 10; New York, NY, 1865 5704.8 p194

Boyle, Thomas 13; St. John, N.B., 1847 ***5704.8*** *p10*
Boyle, William; America, 1773-1774 ***2859.11*** *p7*
Boyle, William; Philadelphia, 1849 ***53.26*** *p6*
Boyle, William; Philadelphia, 1849 ***5704.8*** *p54*
Boyle, William; Philadelphia, 1851 ***5704.8*** *p78*
Boyle, William; St. John, N.B., 1851 ***5704.8*** *p79*
Boyle, William 2 *SEE* Boyle, Patrick
Boyle, William 2; Philadelphia, 1848 ***5704.8*** *p40*
Boyle, William 8?; Quebec, 1858 ***5704.8*** *p137*
Boyle, William 13; Quebec, 1847 ***5704.8*** *p38*
Boyle, William 16; Wilmington, DE, 1831 ***6508.7*** *p160*
Boyle, William 26; Virginia, 1773 ***1219.7*** *p169*
Boyles, Elmore 26; Arizona, 1890 ***2764.35*** *p4*
Boyles, Page 24; Arizona, 1890 ***2764.35*** *p4*
Boyne, Edmond; America, 1738 ***4971*** *p35*
Boyne, Thomas; Quebec, 1824 ***7603*** *p74*
Boyne, William 27; New Orleans, 1862 ***543.30*** *p117*
Boys, William 26; Kansas, 1884 ***5240.1*** *p65*
Boyse, Cheney; Virginia, 1636 ***6219*** *p74*
Boyse, Christopher; Virginia, 1639 ***6219*** *p157*
Boyse, Hannah; Virginia, 1635 ***6219*** *p74*
*Father:*Luke
Boyse, Luke *SEE* Boyse, Hannah
Boyse, Thomas 15; Grenada, 1774 ***1219.7*** *p240*
Boyter, Robert; Washington, 1859-1920 ***2872.1*** *p5*
Bozarth, A. L.; Washington, 1859-1920 ***2872.1*** *p5*
Bozen, Francis 24; America, 1832 ***778.5*** *p76*
Bozett, Charles; Illinois, 1882 ***2896.5*** *p4*
Bozett, Charles; Illinois, 1890 ***2896.5*** *p4*
Bozicevich, George; Iowa, 1866-1943 ***123.54*** *p10*
Bozich, Jacob; Wisconsin, n.d. ***9675.4*** *p266*
Bozora, John Anton; Wisconsin, n.d. ***9675.4*** *p266*
Bozwell, John 27; Maryland, 1774 ***1219.7*** *p211*
Braack, Otto; Washington, 1859-1920 ***2872.1*** *p5*
Braam, Arnold; Arkansas, 1918 ***95.2*** *p22*
Braasch, Caroline 23; New York, NY, 1857 ***9831.14*** *p153*
Braasch, Charlotte 29; New York, NY, 1857 ***9831.14*** *p153*
Braatz, . . .; Canada, 1776-1783 ***9786*** *p18*
Brabo, Durand 48; New Orleans, 1839 ***778.5*** *p76*
Brace, Walter; Virginia, 1642 ***6219*** *p198*
Brace, William 20; Jamaica, 1775 ***1219.7*** *p266*
Braceland, Mary A.; Philadelphia, 1868 ***5704.8*** *p228*
Braceland, Thomas; Philadelphia, 1867 ***5704.8*** *p218*
Bracele, William; Virginia, 1637 ***6219*** *p111*
Bracelin, John; St. John, N.B., 1851 ***5704.8*** *p72*
Brachmann, Mr.; Cincinnati, 1831 ***8582.1*** *p51*
Brachmann, Heinrich; America, 1829 ***8582.2*** *p61*
Brachmann, Heinrich; Cincinnati, 1788-1848 ***8582.3*** *p89*
Brachmann, Heinrich; Cincinnati, 1830 ***8582.1*** *p51*
Brachmann, Henry; America, 1829 ***8582.1*** *p5*
Brack, John; America, 1740 ***4971*** *p30*
Brack, Thomas; America, 1740 ***4971*** *p30*
Bracken, Garrett 46; Massachusetts, 1850 ***5881.1*** *p8*
Bracken, Marie 21; America, 1838 ***778.5*** *p76*
Bracken, Michael; Illinois, 1872 ***2896.5*** *p4*
Bracken, P. H.; Illinois, 1863 ***2764.35*** *p5*
Bracken, Robert; Illinois, 1862 ***7857*** *p2*
Brackenueck, Gottlieb; Illinois, 1846 ***8582.2*** *p51*
Brackett, William; Virginia, 1638 ***6219*** *p153*
Brackin, Hugh; St. John, N.B., 1849 ***5704.8*** *p48*
Brackman, Frederick; Illinois, 1876 ***2896.5*** *p4*
Brackmann Family ; America, 1885 ***4610.10*** *p76*
Brackmann, Anne Marie Engel; America, 1845 ***4610.10*** *p134*
Brackmann, Carl Friedrich Gottlieb; America, 1845 ***4610.10*** *p134*
Bradburd, Jno 22; America, 1705 ***2212*** *p43*
Bradbury, Mr.; Quebec, 1815 ***9229.18*** *p82*
Bradbury, John; Virginia, 1636 ***6219*** *p78*
Bradbury, John 19; Maryland, 1750 ***3690.1*** *p24*
Bradbury, John 19; Maryland, 1751 ***1219.7*** *p1*
Bradbury, Thomas 17; Jamaica, 1725 ***3690.1*** *p24*
Bradbury, Thomas 24; America, 1700 ***2212*** *p30*
Bradbury, Zachary 24; Jamaica, 1739 ***3690.1*** *p25*
Bradchater, Jacob; Virginia, 1637 ***6219*** *p82*
Braddagh, Shane; America, 1741 ***4971*** *p76*
Braddens, Robert 35; St. John, N.B., 1863 ***5704.8*** *p153*
Bradehoeft, Henry; Kansas, 1907 ***6013.40*** *p15*
Bradehoeft, Herny Klaus; Kansas, 1912 ***6013.40*** *p15*
Brademier, Christian; America, 1849 ***1450.2*** *p17A*
Braden, Hinrich; New York, NY, 1835 ***8208.4*** *p7*
Braden, John Joseph; Arkansas, 1918 ***95.2*** *p22*
Bradenbach, Michael; Ohio, 1817 ***8582.1*** *p48*
Brader, Franz; Illinois, 1866 ***2896.5*** *p5*
Bradermeir, Henry; America, 1844 ***1450.2*** *p18A*
Bradfeild, Cornelius; Virginia, 1639 ***6219*** *p156*
Bradfield, John 21; Massachusetts, 1849 ***5881.1*** *p9*
Bradford, Clement W.; Washington, 1859-1920 ***2872.1*** *p5*
Bradford, Elizabeth Soule *SEE* Bradford, William
Bradford, Graham; America, 1743 ***4971*** *p11*
Bradford, Jacob 18; Maryland, 1729 ***3690.1*** *p25*
Bradford, James; New York, NY, 1816 ***2859.11*** *p25*
Bradford, John 18; Maryland, 1774 ***1219.7*** *p181*
Bradford, John 30; Maryland, 1775 ***1219.7*** *p254*
Bradford, Nicho.; Virginia, 1647 ***6219*** *p248*
Bradford, Richard 19; Jamaica, 1736 ***3690.1*** *p25*
Bradford, Susan; Virginia, 1643 ***6219*** *p204*
Bradford, Thos.; Virginia, 1640 ***6219*** *p182*
Bradford, William; Pennsylvania, 1682 ***4962*** *p156*
Bradford, William; Pennsylvania, 1685 ***4962*** *p156*
*Wife:*Elizabeth Soule
Bradin, Eliz.; Virginia, 1638 ***6219*** *p145*
Bradley, . . . 3 mos; Philadelphia, 1869 ***5704.8*** *p234*
Bradley, Abraham; Philadelphia, 1852 ***5704.8*** *p89*
Bradley, Ann; St. John, N.B., 1848 ***5704.8*** *p39*
Bradley, Ann 21; Philadelphia, 1854 ***5704.8*** *p118*
Bradley, Ann 21; St. John, N.B., 1854 ***5704.8*** *p122*
Bradley, Annie; New York, NY, 1866 ***5704.8*** *p213*
Bradley, Annie; New York, NY, 1867 ***5704.8*** *p224*
Bradley, Archy 1; St. John, N.B., 1857 ***5704.8*** *p134*
Bradley, Barney 7; Philadelphia, 1865 ***5704.8*** *p197*
Bradley, Barney 11; New York, NY, 1866 ***5704.8*** *p206*
Bradley, Bernard; Philadelphia, 1864 ***5704.8*** *p176*
Bradley, Bessy; Philadelphia, 1850 ***5704.8*** *p64*
Bradley, Biddy; Philadelphia, 1847 ***53.26*** *p6*
Bradley, Biddy; Philadelphia, 1847 ***5704.8*** *p22*
Bradley, Biddy; Philadelphia, 1851 ***5704.8*** *p80*
Bradley, Biddy 5; St. John, N.B., 1852 ***5704.8*** *p95*
Bradley, Billey 11; Philadelphia, 1852 ***5704.8*** *p87*
Bradley, Bridget; Montreal, 1821 ***7603*** *p99*
Bradley, Bridget; Philadelphia, 1852 ***5704.8*** *p91*
Bradley, Bridget; Philadelphia, 1864 ***5704.8*** *p175*
Bradley, Bridget; St. John, N.B., 1852 ***5704.8*** *p95*
Bradley, Cath.; New York, NY, 1811 ***2859.11*** *p9*
Bradley, Catharine; New York, NY, 1866 ***5704.8*** *p213*
Bradley, Catharine 23; Massachusetts, 1849 ***5881.1*** *p7*
Bradley, Catherine; America, 1864 ***5704.8*** *p177*
Bradley, Catherine 5; St. John, N.B., 1859 ***5704.8*** *p143*
Bradley, Catherine 7; St. John, N.B., 1852 ***5704.8*** *p95*
Bradley, Catherine 18; Philadelphia, 1856 ***5704.8*** *p129*
Bradley, Catherine 18; Philadelphia, 1859 ***5704.8*** *p142*
Bradley, Catherine 19; St. John, N.B., 1855 ***5704.8*** *p127*
Bradley, Catherine 23; St. John, N.B., 1865 ***5704.8*** *p165*
Bradley, Charles 4; Philadelphia, 1869 ***5704.8*** *p234*
Bradley, Charles 22; Philadelphia, 1855 ***5704.8*** *p124*
Bradley, Cicily; New York, NY, 1865 ***5704.8*** *p194*
Bradley, Cicily 2; St. John, N.B., 1852 ***5704.8*** *p95*
Bradley, Daniel 6; Philadelphia, 1865 ***5704.8*** *p197*
Bradley, Daniel 9; St. John, N.B., 1852 ***5704.8*** *p95*
Bradley, Daniel 20; Philadelphia, 1854 ***5704.8*** *p116*
Bradley, Dennis 18; Philadelphia, 1860 ***5704.8*** *p145*
Bradley, Dorothy; Virginia, 1638 ***6219*** *p11*
*Wife:*Margt.
Bradley, Edward; St. John, N.B., 1847 ***5704.8*** *p2*
Bradley, Edward 18; Quebec, 1864 ***5704.8*** *p160*
Bradley, Eleanor; Philadelphia, 1850 ***53.26*** *p6*
Bradley, Eleanor; Philadelphia, 1850 ***5704.8*** *p69*
Bradley, Eleanor 17; Philadelphia, 1858 ***5704.8*** *p138*
Bradley, Eliza; Philadelphia, 1864 ***5704.8*** *p182*
Bradley, Eliza 22; Philadelphia, 1853 ***5704.8*** *p112*
Bradley, Elizabeth 7; St. John, N.B., 1857 ***5704.8*** *p134*
Bradley, Elizabeth 18; Philadelphia, 1854 ***5704.8*** *p122*
Bradley, Ellan 8; Philadelphia, 1852 ***5704.8*** *p87*
Bradley, Ellanor 41; Philadelphia, 1853 ***5704.8*** *p112*
Bradley, Ellen 17; Philadelphia, 1864 ***5704.8*** *p160*
Bradley, Emily; Philadelphia, 1852 ***5704.8*** *p89*
Bradley, Francis; New York, NY, 1811 ***2859.11*** *p9*
Bradley, Francis; Quebec, 1847 ***5704.8*** *p28*
Bradley, Francis 6; Philadelphia, 1851 ***5704.8*** *p78*
Bradley, Francis 27; Philadelphia, 1859 ***5704.8*** *p141*
Bradley, George 24; Maryland, 1774 ***1219.7*** *p225*
Bradley, Giley; Philadelphia, 1852 ***5704.8*** *p87*
Bradley, Hannah; New York, NY, 1866 ***5704.8*** *p213*
Bradley, Hannah; St. John, N.B., 1848 ***5704.8*** *p43*
Bradley, Henry; New York, NY, 1840 ***8208.4*** *p112*
Bradley, Henry; Virginia, 1640 ***6219*** *p160*
Bradley, Henry; Virginia, 1642 ***6219*** *p191*
Bradley, Hugh; New York, NY, 1865 ***5704.8*** *p195*
Bradley, Hugh; New York, NY, 1866 ***5704.8*** *p213*
Bradley, Hugh; New York, NY, 1867 ***5704.8*** *p222*
Bradley, Hugh; St. John, N.B., 1851 ***5704.8*** *p72*
Bradley, Hugh 19; Philadelphia, 1854 ***5704.8*** *p116*
Bradley, Hugh 26; St. John, N.B., 1853 ***5704.8*** *p109*
Bradley, Isabella; Philadelphia, 1867 ***5704.8*** *p217*
Bradley, Isabella 36; St. John, N.B., 1857 ***5704.8*** *p134*
Bradley, James; New York, NY, 1816 ***2859.11*** *p25*
Bradley, James; New York, NY, 1866 ***5704.8*** *p206*
Bradley, James; Quebec, 1853 ***5704.8*** *p103*
Bradley, James; St. John, N.B., 1847 ***5704.8*** *p18*
Bradley, James; St. John, N.B., 1848 ***5704.8*** *p39*
Bradley, James 2; Philadelphia, 1869 ***5704.8*** *p234*
Bradley, James 8; St. John, N.B., 1850 ***5704.8*** *p67*
Bradley, James 9; Philadelphia, 1852 ***5704.8*** *p87*
Bradley, James 14; Philadelphia, 1859 ***5704.8*** *p141*
Bradley, James 16; West Indies, 1722 ***3690.1*** *p25*
Bradley, James 20; Philadelphia, 1859 ***5704.8*** *p142*
Bradley, James 24; Quebec, 1864 ***5704.8*** *p159*
Bradley, James 50; Philadelphia, 1859 ***5704.8*** *p141*
Bradley, John; Iowa, 1866-1943 ***123.54*** *p10*
Bradley, John; New York, NY, 1811 ***2859.11*** *p9*
Bradley, John; New York, NY, 1816 ***2859.11*** *p25*
Bradley, John; New York, NY, 1865 ***5704.8*** *p195*
Bradley, John; Philadelphia, 1867 ***5704.8*** *p217*
Bradley, John; Philadelphia, 1869 ***5704.8*** *p234*
Bradley, John; St. John, N.B., 1847 ***5704.8*** *p33*
Bradley, John; St. John, N.B., 1848 ***5704.8*** *p39*
Bradley, John; St. John, N.B., 1848 ***5704.8*** *p43*
Bradley, John; South Carolina, 1785 ***1639.20*** *p15*
Bradley, John; Wisconsin, n.d. ***9675.4*** *p266*
Bradley, John 5; St. John, N.B., 1857 ***5704.8*** *p134*
Bradley, John 7; St. John, N.B., 1861 ***5704.8*** *p149*
Bradley, John 11; Philadelphia, 1865 ***5704.8*** *p197*
Bradley, John 21; St. John, N.B., 1854 ***5704.8*** *p121*
Bradley, John 23; St. John, N.B., 1864 ***5704.8*** *p158*
Bradley, Joseph 25; Maryland, 1733 ***3690.1*** *p25*
Bradley, Linn; New York, NY, 1866 ***5704.8*** *p206*
Bradley, Manus; St. John, N.B., 1847 ***5704.8*** *p20*
Bradley, Margaret; New York, NY, 1864 ***5704.8*** *p169*
Bradley, Margaret; St. John, N.B., 1851 ***5704.8*** *p79*
Bradley, Margaret 14; Massachusetts, 1849 ***5881.1*** *p10*
Bradley, Margaret 16; Philadelphia, 1857 ***5704.8*** *p134*
Bradley, Margaret 18; Philadelphia, 1853 ***5704.8*** *p112*
Bradley, Margaret 20; St. John, N.B., 1865 ***5704.8*** *p165*
Bradley, Margt. *SEE* Bradley, Dorothy
Bradley, Martha; Philadelphia, 1864 ***5704.8*** *p182*
Bradley, Mary; New York, NY, 1864 ***5704.8*** *p169*
Bradley, Mary; New York, NY, 1865 ***5704.8*** *p195*
Bradley, Mary; New York, NY, 1866 ***5704.8*** *p206*
Bradley, Mary; New York, NY, 1868 ***5704.8*** *p225*
Bradley, Mary; Philadelphia, 1847 ***53.26*** *p6*
Bradley, Mary; Philadelphia, 1847 ***5704.8*** *p32*
Bradley, Mary; Philadelphia, 1848 ***53.26*** *p6*
Bradley, Mary; Philadelphia, 1848 ***5704.8*** *p45*
Bradley, Mary; Philadelphia, 1851 ***5704.8*** *p80*
Bradley, Mary; Philadelphia, 1852 ***5704.8*** *p88*
Bradley, Mary; Philadelphia, 1852 ***5704.8*** *p91*
Bradley, Mary; Philadelphia, 1852 ***5704.8*** *p96*
Bradley, Mary; Philadelphia, 1864 ***5704.8*** *p176*
Bradley, Mary; Philadelphia, 1865 ***5704.8*** *p200*
Bradley, Mary; Philadelphia, 1866 ***5704.8*** *p206*
Bradley, Mary; Philadelphia, 1867 ***5704.8*** *p219*
Bradley, Mary; Philadelphia, 1868 ***5704.8*** *p225*
Bradley, Mary; St. John, N.B., 1848 ***5704.8*** *p43*
Bradley, Mary; St. John, N.B., 1849 ***5704.8*** *p48*
Bradley, Mary; St. John, N.B., 1850 ***5704.8*** *p66*
Bradley, Mary 11; St. John, N.B., 1852 ***5704.8*** *p95*
Bradley, Mary 18; Philadelphia, 1861 ***5704.8*** *p148*
Bradley, Mary 22; Quebec, 1864 ***5704.8*** *p159*
Bradley, Mary 43; Philadelphia, 1853 ***5704.8*** *p112*
Bradley, Mary 50; Quebec, 1855 ***5704.8*** *p126*
Bradley, Mary 83; North Carolina, 1850 ***1639.20*** *p15*
Bradley, Mary Ann; St. John, N.B., 1848 ***5704.8*** *p43*
Bradley, Mary Jane 18; Quebec, 1855 ***5704.8*** *p126*
Bradley, Matilda; Quebec, 1852 ***5704.8*** *p94*
Bradley, Michael; America, 1865 ***5704.8*** *p195*
Bradley, Michael; New York, NY, 1868 ***5704.8*** *p228*
Bradley, Michael; St. John, N.B., 1853 ***5704.8*** *p107*
Bradley, Michael 20; St. John, N.B., 1854 ***5704.8*** *p114*
Bradley, Nabla 18; Philadelphia, 1860 ***5704.8*** *p145*
Bradley, Oliver; Philadelphia, 1850 ***53.26*** *p6*
Bradley, Oliver; Philadelphia, 1850 ***5704.8*** *p68*
Bradley, Owen; Quebec, 1847 ***5704.8*** *p28*
Bradley, Owen; Wisconsin, n.d. ***9675.4*** *p266*
Bradley, Patrick *SEE* Bradley, William
Bradley, Patrick; Philadelphia, 1847 ***5704.8*** *p23*
Bradley, Patrick; Philadelphia, 1849 ***53.26*** *p6*
Bradley, Patrick; Philadelphia, 1849 ***5704.8*** *p58*
Bradley, Patrick; Philadelphia, 1864 ***5704.8*** *p181*
Bradley, Patrick; Philadelphia, 1866 ***5704.8*** *p209*
Bradley, Patrick; St. John, N.B., 1850 ***5704.8*** *p66*
Bradley, Patrick 4; St. John, N.B., 1859 ***5704.8*** *p143*
Bradley, Patrick 13; Philadelphia, 1853 ***5704.8*** *p112*
Bradley, Patrick 19; Philadelphia, 1860 ***5704.8*** *p145*
Bradley, Peggy; Quebec, 1847 ***5704.8*** *p28*
Bradley, Peggy; St. John, N.B., 1853 ***5704.8*** *p107*
Bradley, Peter; Charleston, SC, 1806 ***1639.20*** *p15*
Bradley, Peter; New York, NY, 1816 ***2859.11*** *p25*
Bradley, Peter 18; St. John, N.B., 1865 ***5704.8*** *p165*
Bradley, Philip; Philadelphia, 1816 ***2859.11*** *p25*
Bradley, Rebecca; Quebec, 1850 ***5704.8*** *p66*
Bradley, Richard; Virginia, 1643 ***6219*** *p203*
Bradley, Richard 21; Jamaica, 1736 ***3690.1*** *p25*
Bradley, Robert; Colorado, 1902 ***9678.1*** *p155*
Bradley, Robert 11; St. John, N.B., 1857 ***5704.8*** *p134*
Bradley, Rodger 18; St. John, N.B., 1853 ***5704.8*** *p110*
Bradley, Rose; St. John, N.B., 1847 ***5704.8*** *p20*

Bradley, Rose 8; Philadelphia, 1865 ***5704.8*** *p197*
Bradley, Rose 20; Philadelphia, 1861 ***5704.8*** *p148*
Bradley, Sally; Philadelphia, 1850 ***53.26*** *p6*
Bradley, Sally; Philadelphia, 1850 ***5704.8*** *p68*
Bradley, Samuel; Philadelphia, 1852 ***5704.8*** *p86*
Bradley, Samuel 8; St. John, N.B., 1857 ***5704.8*** *p134*
Bradley, Sarah; New York, NY, 1865 ***5704.8*** *p195*
Bradley, Sarah; Philadelphia, 1867 ***5704.8*** *p216*
Bradley, Sarah; St. John, N.B., 1849 ***5704.8*** *p55*
Bradley, Susan; America, 1865 ***5704.8*** *p195*
Bradley, Susan; New York, NY, 1867 ***5704.8*** *p224*
Bradley, Susan; New York, NY, 1868 ***5704.8*** *p231*
Bradley, Susan; Philadelphia, 1864 ***5704.8*** *p183*
Bradley, Susan; Philadelphia, 1869 ***5704.8*** *p234*
Bradley, Susan 21; St. John, N.B., 1861 ***5704.8*** *p147*
Bradley, Walter; Iowa, 1866-1943 ***123.54*** *p10*
Bradley, William; Jamaica, 1753 ***1219.7*** *p23*
Bradley, William; Jamaica, 1753 ***3690.1*** *p25*
Bradley, William; New York, NY, 1816 ***2859.11*** *p25*
Bradley, William; New York, NY, 1837 ***8208.4*** *p33*
Bradley, William; Philadelphia, 1847 ***53.26*** *p6*
*Relative:*Patrick
Bradley, William; Philadelphia, 1847 ***5704.8*** *p23*
Bradley, William; Philadelphia, 1864 ***5704.8*** *p181*
Bradley, William; St. John, N.B., 1848 ***5704.8*** *p39*
Bradley, William 34; Virginia, 1774 ***1219.7*** *p186*
Bradley, William Henry; Iowa, 1866-1943 ***123.54*** *p10*
Bradley, Wm.; New York, NY, 1816 ***2859.11*** *p25*
Bradly, Eliza.; Virginia, 1637 ***6219*** *p113*
Bradly, Frances *SEE* Bradly, Henry
Bradly, Francis *SEE* Bradly, Henry
Bradly, Henry; Virginia, 1636 ***6219*** *p74*
Bradly, Henry; Virginia, 1636 ***6219*** *p79*
*Wife:*Francis
Bradly, Henry; Virginia, 1637 ***6219*** *p116*
*Wife:*Frances
Bradly, Jon.; Virginia, 1642 ***6219*** *p198*
Bradner, William 17; Jamaica, 1736 ***3690.1*** *p25*
Bradon, Mary 27; St. John, N.B., 1864 ***5704.8*** *p159*
Bradon, William 40; St. John, N.B., 1864 ***5704.8*** *p159*
Bradshaw, Abigall 27; America, 1701 ***2212*** *p34*
Bradshaw, Ellen 14; America, 1705 ***2212*** *p44*
Bradshaw, George 39; Kansas, 1889 ***5240.1*** *p73*
Bradshaw, Hen.; Virginia, 1637 ***6219*** *p83*
Bradshaw, James 22; Maryland, 1775 ***1219.7*** *p262*
Bradshaw, John 31; New Orleans, 1862 ***543.30*** *p479*
Bradshaw, Peter 22; Maryland, 1775 ***1219.7*** *p259*
Bradshaw, Richard; Virginia, 1643 ***6219*** *p200*
Bradshaw, Robert; Virginia, 1640 ***6219*** *p182*
Bradshaw, Robert 26; Jamaica, 1730 ***3690.1*** *p25*
Bradshaw, Thomas 32; Virginia, 1774 ***1219.7*** *p240*
Bradshaw, Thomas 35; St. Kitts, 1774 ***1219.7*** *p239*
Bradshaw, William; Virginia, 1698 ***2212*** *p17*
Bradshaw, William; West Indies, 1766 ***1219.7*** *p118*
Bradshaw, Wm.; Virginia, 1648 ***6219*** *p246*
Bradshawe, John; Virginia, 1652 ***6251*** *p20*
Bradshawe, Robert; Virginia, 1652 ***6251*** *p20*
Bradston, Dorothy *SEE* Bradston, John
Bradston, John; Virginia, 1636 ***6219*** *p149*
*Wife:*Dorothy
Bradston, Jon.; Virginia, 1628 ***6219*** *p31*
Bradwell, George; Iowa, 1866-1943 ***123.54*** *p10*
Brady, Widow; Quebec, 1847 ***5704.8*** *p37*
Brady, Ann; Quebec, 1847 ***5704.8*** *p17*
Brady, Ann 7; Quebec, 1847 ***5704.8*** *p17*
Brady, Ann 8; Massachusetts, 1848 ***5881.1*** *p6*
Brady, Ann 55; Massachusetts, 1850 ***5881.1*** *p6*
Brady, Anne; New York, NY, 1816 ***2859.11*** *p25*
Brady, Anthony; Quebec, 1847 ***5704.8*** *p17*
Brady, Bridget 27; Massachusetts, 1848 ***5881.1*** *p6*
Brady, Catharine 10; Massachusetts, 1850 ***5881.1*** *p7*
Brady, Catharine 21; Massachusetts, 1847 ***5881.1*** *p6*
Brady, Catharine 30; Massachusetts, 1849 ***5881.1*** *p7*
Brady, Charles 23; Massachusetts, 1848 ***5881.1*** *p6*
Brady, Daniel; America, 1741 ***4971*** *p16*
Brady, Daniel 60; Massachusetts, 1849 ***5881.1*** *p7*
Brady, Edward; New York, NY, 1836 ***8208.4*** *p16*
Brady, Eliza 5; Massachusetts, 1850 ***5881.1*** *p7*
Brady, Eliza 35; Massachusetts, 1850 ***5881.1*** *p8*
Brady, Elizabeth; Quebec, 1847 ***5704.8*** *p37*
Brady, Elizabeth 11; Quebec, 1852 ***5704.8*** *p91*
Brady, Ellen 16; Massachusetts, 1850 ***5881.1*** *p7*
Brady, Ellen 30; Massachusetts, 1849 ***5881.1*** *p7*
Brady, Ellen 32; Massachusetts, 1850 ***5881.1*** *p7*
Brady, Honor; Quebec, 1825 ***7603*** *p74*
Brady, Hugh; America, 1738 ***4971*** *p13*
Brady, Hugh; New York, NY, 1816 ***2859.11*** *p25*
Brady, Hugh 12; St. John, N.B., 1847 ***5704.8*** *p25*
Brady, James; New York, NY, 1811 ***2859.11*** *p9*
With family
Brady, James; New York, NY, 1815 ***2859.11*** *p26*
Brady, James; Quebec, 1847 ***5704.8*** *p37*
Brady, James 4; Massachusetts, 1848 ***5881.1*** *p8*
Brady, James 11; Quebec, 1847 ***5704.8*** *p17*
Brady, James 24; Massachusetts, 1847 ***5881.1*** *p8*
Brady, James 27; New Orleans, 1862 ***543.30*** *p479*
Brady, James 40; California, 1872 ***2769.2*** *p4*
Brady, John; New York, NY, 1816 ***2859.11*** *p26*
Brady, John; New York, NY, 1835 ***8208.4*** *p42*
Brady, John; New York, NY, 1838 ***8208.4*** *p63*
Brady, John; Quebec, 1847 ***5704.8*** *p17*
Brady, John; Quebec, 1847 ***5704.8*** *p37*
Brady, John; Quebec, 1852 ***5704.8*** *p91*
Brady, John; St. John, N.B., 1847 ***5704.8*** *p25*
Brady, John; San Francisco, 1871 ***2764.35*** *p8*
Brady, John 2; Massachusetts, 1848 ***5881.1*** *p8*
Brady, John 8; Massachusetts, 1850 ***5881.1*** *p9*
Brady, John 22; New Orleans, 1862 ***543.30*** *p242*
Brady, John 24; New Orleans, 1862 ***543.30*** *p116*
Brady, Judith; America, 1742 ***4971*** *p17*
Brady, Judy 13; Quebec, 1847 ***5704.8*** *p17*
Brady, Luke 15; Massachusetts, 1850 ***5881.1*** *p9*
Brady, Luke 23; Virginia, 1774 ***1219.7*** *p240*
Brady, Margaret; America, 1737 ***4971*** *p71*
Brady, Margaret; Quebec, 1847 ***5704.8*** *p17*
Brady, Margaret; Quebec, 1847 ***5704.8*** *p36*
Brady, Margaret; St. John, N.B., 1847 ***5704.8*** *p25*
Brady, Maria 5; Massachusetts, 1849 ***5881.1*** *p10*
Brady, Mark 25; New York, 1774 ***1219.7*** *p188*
Brady, Mary 10; Massachusetts, 1848 ***5881.1*** *p9*
Brady, Mary 17; Massachusetts, 1847 ***5881.1*** *p9*
Brady, Mary 19; Massachusetts, 1847 ***5881.1*** *p9*
Brady, Mary 30; Newport, RI, 1851 ***6508.5*** *p20*
Brady, Maurice; New York, NY, 1815 ***2859.11*** *p26*
Brady, Michael 20; Jamaica, 1735 ***3690.1*** *p25*
Brady, Mick 35; Newport, RI, 1851 ***6508.5*** *p20*
Brady, Nicholas; New York, 1837 ***8208.4*** *p42*
Brady, Pat 6; Massachusetts, 1848 ***5881.1*** *p11*
Brady, Pat 21; Massachusetts, 1847 ***5881.1*** *p11*
Brady, Patrick; New York, NY, 1815 ***2859.11*** *p26*
Brady, Patrick; New York, NY, 1838 ***8208.4*** *p74*
Brady, Patrick; New York, NY, 1838 ***8208.4*** *p87*
Brady, Patrick; Philadelphia, 1815 ***2859.11*** *p26*
Brady, Patrick; Quebec, 1847 ***5704.8*** *p17*
Brady, Patrick 9; Quebec, 1847 ***5704.8*** *p17*
Brady, Peter 45; Kansas, 1880 ***5240.1*** *p62*
Brady, Phillip; New York, NY, 1838 ***8208.4*** *p87*
Brady, Phillip 64; Arizona, 1907 ***9228.40*** *p10*
Brady, Robert; America, 1743 ***4971*** *p11*
Brady, Robert 3; Newport, RI, 1851 ***6508.5*** *p20*
Brady, Rosey; Quebec, 1847 ***5704.8*** *p17*
Brady, Sarah; Philadelphia, 1865 ***5704.8*** *p197*
Brady, Sarah 12; Quebec, 1847 ***5704.8*** *p17*
Brady, Susan; New York, NY, 1816 ***2859.11*** *p26*
Brady, Terrence 35; California, 1873 ***2769.10*** *p3*
Brady, Thomas; New York, NY, 1816 ***2859.11*** *p26*
Brady, Thomas; Quebec, 1819 ***7603*** *p80*
Brady, Thomas 16; Massachusetts, 1850 ***5881.1*** *p12*
Brady, William; Quebec, 1847 ***5704.8*** *p17*
Brady, William 1; Newport, RI, 1851 ***6508.5*** *p20*
Brady, William 9; Massachusetts, 1850 ***5881.1*** *p12*
Brady, William 40; Massachusetts, 1848 ***5881.1*** *p12*
Braeher, Cathrina 22; America, 1838 ***778.5*** *p76*
Braeher, Cathrine 6; America, 1838 ***778.5*** *p77*
Bragg, Ann 20; Virginia, 1774 ***1219.7*** *p215*
Bragg, John; Kansas, 1870 ***5240.1*** *p51*
Bragg, Mary 50; Virginia, 1774 ***1219.7*** *p215*
Brahmer, John 44; New Orleans, 1862 ***543.30*** *p481*
Braid, Matthew; Charleston, SC, 1813 ***1639.20*** *p15*
Braidy, James; South Carolina, 1822 ***1639.20*** *p15*
Braihn, Albert; New Orleans, 1848 ***1450.2*** *p18A*
Brailsford, Rowland 51; Kansas, 1887 ***5240.1*** *p70*
Brain, John; Iowa, 1866-1943 ***123.54*** *p10*
Brain, Simeon; Iowa, 1866-1943 ***123.54*** *p10*
Brainard, Johann; Wisconsin, n.d. ***9675.4*** *p266*
Brainbridge, Samuel 24; Nova Scotia, 1774 ***1219.7*** *p209*
Braineid, Charles; New York, NY, 1816 ***2859.11*** *p26*
Braise, James 20; Jamaica, 1720 ***3690.1*** *p25*
Braith, William; New York, NY, 1815 ***2859.11*** *p26*
Braithwait, John 24; Maryland, 1774 ***1219.7*** *p230*
Braithwaite, Edward; Illinois, 1897 ***5012.40*** *p55*
Braithwaite, Henry Edward; Illinois, 1906 ***5012.39*** *p54*
Braithwaite, William 22; Maryland, 1775 ***1219.7*** *p247*
Braitsch, John 27; Kansas, 1872 ***5240.1*** *p6*
Braitsch, John 27; Kansas, 1872 ***5240.1*** *p52*
Braitsch, Konstantin 26; Kansas, 1882 ***5240.1*** *p6*
Braitsch, Konstantine 26; Kansas, 1882 ***5240.1*** *p6*
Braitsch, Konstantine 26; Kansas, 1882 ***5240.1*** *p63*
Brakbusch, Andreas; Illinois, 1874 ***2896.5*** *p5*
Brakenmann, Hermann; America, 1849 ***8582.3*** *p8*
Brakensiek, Anna; Illinois, 1815-1879 ***4610.10*** *p67*
Braker, Porcilette 32; New Orleans, 1823 ***778.5*** *p77*
Brakness, Oscar Olsen; Arkansas, 1918 ***95.2*** *p22*
Brakowska, Antoni 19 *SEE* Brakowska, Leokadia
Brakowska, Leokadia 17; New York, 1912 ***9980.29*** *p54*
*Brother:*Antoni 19
Brakowski, Antoni 19; New York, 1912 ***9980.29*** *p54*
*Sister:*Leokadia 17
Brakowski, Leokadia 17 *SEE* Brakowski, Antoni
Bral, Mell; Arkansas, 1918 ***95.2*** *p22*
Bram, Henry; America, 1740 ***4971*** *p81*
Bram, Leo 25; Kansas, 1890 ***5240.1*** *p75*
Brames, Blanch; Virginia, 1635 ***6219*** *p69*
Bramford, Ann Jane 9; Quebec, 1851 ***5704.8*** *p75*
Bramford, Charles 6; Quebec, 1851 ***5704.8*** *p75*
Bramford, Eliza 11; Quebec, 1851 ***5704.8*** *p75*
Bramford, Mary; Quebec, 1851 ***5704.8*** *p75*
Bramford, Rebecca 3; Quebec, 1851 ***5704.8*** *p75*
Bramford, William 7; Quebec, 1851 ***5704.8*** *p75*
Bramlage, Johann Gerhard Clemens; America, 1848 ***8582.3*** *p8*
Bramley, Charles; New York, NY, 1838 ***8208.4*** *p63*
Bramley, Hugh; Virginia, 1639 ***6219*** *p184*
Bramly, Francis; Virginia, 1633 ***6219*** *p31*
Brampton, Briar 31; Virginia, 1774 ***1219.7*** *p201*
Bramsche, Georg F.; Cincinnati, 1869-1887 ***8582*** *p4*
Bramston, Thomas; Virginia, 1638 ***6219*** *p11*
Bramwale, Jo; America, 1697-1707 ***2212*** *p9*
Brana, Mr. 21; Louisiana, 1820 ***778.5*** *p77*
Brana, Mr. 24; New Orleans, 1821 ***778.5*** *p77*
Branagan, Thomas; New York, NY, 1839 ***8208.4*** *p90*
Branagin, Peggy; Massachusetts, 1847 ***5881.1*** *p11*
Branan, Matthew 21; Maryland, 1774 ***1219.7*** *p229*
Branch, Antho.; Virginia, 1643 ***6219*** *p23*
Branch, Christopher; Virginia, 1638 ***6219*** *p145*
Branch, John; Virginia, 1639 ***6219*** *p162*
Branch, John; Virginia, 1646 ***6219*** *p235*
Branche, Christopher; Virginia, 1635 ***6219*** *p73*
Branches, Christ.; Virginia, 1638 ***6219*** *p122*
Brand, . . .; Canada, 1776-1783 ***9786*** *p18*
Brand, Mr.; Died enroute, 1752-1753 ***3689.17*** *p21*
Brand, Mr.; New York, 1771-1772 ***2444*** *p141*
Brand, Mrs. Dietrich Christian; America, 1845 ***4815.7*** *p92*
With 3 children
Brand, Elisabetha Christina *SEE* Brand, Johann Heinrich
Brand, Hermann Heinrich 27; Cincinnati, 1860 ***4815.7*** *p92*
Brand, James; Illinois, 1841 ***7857*** *p2*
Brand, James; Illinois, 1852 ***7857*** *p2*
Brand, Johann Heinrich *SEE* Brand, Johann Heinrich
Brand, Johann Heinrich; Mississippi, 1764 ***2444*** *p141*
*Wife:*Maria Magdalena Hoerz
*Child:*Johanna Catharina
*Child:*Johann Heinrich
*Child:*Elisabetha Christina
*Child:*Maria Barbara
Brand, Johanna Catharina *SEE* Brand, Johann Heinrich
Brand, Joseph; Kansas, 1893 ***5240.1*** *p6*
Brand, Maria Barbara *SEE* Brand, Johann Heinrich
Brand, Maria Magdalena Hoerz *SEE* Brand, Johann Heinrich
Brand, Robert W.; Wisconsin, n.d. ***9675.4*** *p266*
Brand, William; Illinois, 1863 ***7857*** *p2*
Brand, William; Iowa, 1866-1943 ***123.54*** *p10*
Brandan, . . .; Canada, 1776-1783 ***9786*** *p18*
Brande, John 23; Maryland, 1775 ***1219.7*** *p251*
Brandebas, Zephirin C.; Iowa, 1866-1943 ***123.54*** *p10*
Brandecker, Franz Xavier; Cincinnati, 1788-1848 ***8582.3*** *p89*
Brandelow, Gottfried; Illinois, 1868 ***2896.5*** *p5*
Branden, Ferdinand; Illinois, 1881 ***2896.5*** *p5*
Branden, Peter; New York, NY, 1836 ***8208.4*** *p22*
Brandenberger, Henri 32; America, 1837 ***778.5*** *p77*
Brander, Adam 25; Jamaica, 1774 ***1219.7*** *p196*
Brander, Ernst Christian Heinrich; Quebec, 1776 ***9786*** *p257*
Brandes, F.; Quebec, 1776 ***9786*** *p105*
Brandes, Henry 33; Virginia, 1773 ***1219.7*** *p170*
Brandhorst, . . .; Illinois, 1800-1900 ***4610.10*** *p67*
Brandhorst, August; Illinois, 1872-1930 ***4610.10*** *p67*
Brandin, Mr.; Died enroute, 1752-1753 ***3689.17*** *p21*
Brandin, Andrew; Quebec, 1852 ***5704.8*** *p94*
Brandin, Jean 33; New Orleans, 1839 ***778.5*** *p77*
Brandin, Maria Gottlieb; South Carolina, 1752-1753 ***3689.17*** *p21*
Brandin, Martha; Quebec, 1852 ***5704.8*** *p94*
Brandish, Thomas 22; Maryland, 1733 ***3690.1*** *p25*
Brandl, John; Wisconsin, n.d. ***9675.4*** *p266*
Brandmiller, John; New York, 1761 ***3652*** *p87*
Brandmiller, John; Philadelphia, 1742 ***3652*** *p55*
Brandner, Maria *SEE* Brandner, Matthias
Brandner, Maria; Pennsylvania, 1742 ***3652*** *p58*
Brandner, Maria Herlin *SEE* Brandner, Matthias
Brandner, Matthias; Georgia, 1738 ***9332*** *p321*
Brandner, Matthias; Georgia, 1739 ***9332*** *p323*
*Wife:*Maria Herlin
Brandner, Matthias; Georgia, 1739 ***9332*** *p326*
*Wife:*Maria

Brandon, Bessy; Quebec, 1852 ***5704.8*** *p94*
Brandon, Henry; Quebec, 1852 ***5704.8*** *p94*
Brandon, Hugh 11; Philadelphia, 1859 ***5704.8*** *p142*
Brandon, James 15; Philadelphia, 1859 ***5704.8*** *p142*
Brandon, John; Quebec, 1850 ***5704.8*** *p66*
Brandon, John 20; Quebec, 1853 ***5704.8*** *p105*
Brandon, John 24; Quebec, 1853 ***5704.8*** *p105*
Brandon, John 43; New Orleans, 1862 ***543.30*** *p110*
Brandon, Margaret; Quebec, 1850 ***5704.8*** *p66*
Brandon, Robert 19; Quebec, 1853 ***5704.8*** *p105*
Brandon, Robert 27; Philadelphia, 1860 ***5704.8*** *p145*
Brandon, Sidney; Quebec, 1851 ***5704.8*** *p73*
Brandon, William; Quebec, 1852 ***5704.8*** *p94*
Brandon, William 33; Kansas, 1874 ***5240.1*** *p55*
Brandsfield, Wm 23; New Orleans, 1862 ***543.30*** *p244*
Brandstatter, John; Arkansas, 1918 ***95.2*** *p22*
Brandstetter, Andreas; Georgia, 1738 ***9332*** *p319*
*Brother:*Jacob
*Sister:*Ursula
*Sister:*Anna
Brandstetter, Anna *SEE* Brandstetter, Andreas
Brandstetter, Georg; Georgia, 1738 ***9332*** *p319*
Brandstetter, Jacob *SEE* Brandstetter, Andreas
Brandstetter, Simon; Georgia, 1738 ***9332*** *p319*
Brandstetter, Ursula *SEE* Brandstetter, Andreas
Brandt, . . .; Canada, 1776-1783 ***9786*** *p18*
Brandt, Christophe; Canada, 1776-1783 ***9786*** *p243*
Brandt, Friedrich 25; Kansas, 1893 ***5240.1*** *p78*
Brandt, Friedrich Wilhelm; America, 1867 ***4610.10*** *p122*
Brandt, Gustaf Emanuel; Ohio, 1918 ***9892.11*** *p5*
Brandt, Gustave 28; Kansas, 1889 ***5240.1*** *p73*
Brandt, John; Dakota, 1887 ***3702.7*** *p265*
With brothers & sister
Brandt, Karl F.; Cincinnati, 1869-1887 ***8582*** *p4*
Brandt, Philipp; New Netherland, 1630-1646 ***8582.2*** *p51*
Brandt, William; America, 1893 ***1450.2*** *p4B*
Brandt, William, Jr.; Wisconsin, n.d. ***9675.4*** *p266*
Braney, Arthur 36; New Orleans, 1863 ***543.30*** *p247*
Brange, Bonaventure 28; New Orleans, 1839 ***778.5*** *p77*
Branick, Jane; New York, NY, 1816 ***2859.11*** *p26*
With child
Branigan, Catherine; Montreal, 1824 ***7603*** *p55*
Branigan, Thomas; New York, NY, 1811 ***2859.11*** *p9*
Brankin, Thomas; New York, NY, 1816 ***2859.11*** *p26*
Branley, Margaret; New York, NY, 1816 ***2859.11*** *p26*
Branley, Thomas Joseph; Arkansas, 1918 ***95.2*** *p22*
Brannan, Daniel 24; Massachusetts, 1849 ***5881.1*** *p7*
Brannan, James; New York, NY, 1864 ***5704.8*** *p172*
Brannan, Owen; New York, NY, 1834 ***8208.4*** *p37*
Brannan, Peggy 24; Massachusetts, 1849 ***5881.1*** *p11*
Brannegan, Mary 18; Massachusetts, 1849 ***5881.1*** *p10*
Brannen, Catherine; Philadelphia, 1847 ***53.26*** *p6*
Brannen, Catherine; Philadelphia, 1847 ***5704.8*** *p23*
Brannen, Francis; Ohio, 1842 ***8365.25*** *p12*
Brannen, Margaret; Quebec, 1849 ***5704.8*** *p52*
Brannen, Patrick 28; New Orleans, 1862 ***543.30*** *p109*
Brannen, William 13; Quebec, 1849 ***5704.8*** *p52*
Branner, Jacob 38; America, 1837 ***778.5*** *p77*
Brannilly, Pat 32; Massachusetts, 1849 ***5881.1*** *p11*
Brannin, Elizabeth; St. John, N.B., 1847 ***5704.8*** *p10*
Brannin, Mary 22; Philadelphia, 1858 ***5704.8*** *p138*
Brannin, Pat; St. John, N.B., 1847 ***5704.8*** *p10*
Brannin, Patrick 35; New Orleans, 1862 ***543.30*** *p113*
Brannon, Alexander 1; Quebec, 1854 ***5704.8*** *p119*
Brannon, Ann Jane 25; Philadelphia, 1854 ***5704.8*** *p120*
Brannon, Benjamin 42; Massachusetts, 1848 ***5881.1*** *p6*
Brannon, Catharine; New York, NY, 1865 ***5704.8*** *p196*
Brannon, Eleanor; Philadelphia, 1852 ***5704.8*** *p88*
Brannon, Elizabeth; Philadelphia, 1852 ***5704.8*** *p88*
Brannon, James; Philadelphia, 1850 ***53.26*** *p6*
Brannon, James; Philadelphia, 1850 ***5704.8*** *p69*
Brannon, James; St. John, N.B., 1848 ***5704.8*** *p47*
Brannon, Jane; New York, NY, 1865 ***5704.8*** *p196*
Brannon, John 12; Quebec, 1854 ***5704.8*** *p119*
Brannon, John 25; Quebec, 1854 ***5704.8*** *p119*
Brannon, Joseph 46; Massachusetts, 1848 ***5881.1*** *p8*
Brannon, Margaret 18; Massachusetts, 1847 ***5881.1*** *p9*
Brannon, Margaret 22; Massachusetts, 1847 ***5881.1*** *p9*
Brannon, Mary 18; Massachusetts, 1849 ***5881.1*** *p10*
Brannon, Mary Ann 3; Quebec, 1847 ***5704.8*** *p17*
Brannon, Mary Ann 24; Quebec, 1854 ***5704.8*** *p119*
Brannon, Michael 20; Massachusetts, 1847 ***5881.1*** *p9*
Brannon, Michael 24; St. John, N.B., 1854 ***5704.8*** *p119*
Brannon, Patrick; St. John, N.B., 1848 ***5704.8*** *p47*
Brannon, Patrick 25; Massachusetts, 1848 ***5881.1*** *p11*
Brannon, Robert; New York, NY, 1865 ***5704.8*** *p196*
Brannon, Sarah; Quebec, 1847 ***5704.8*** *p17*
Brannon, Sarah 7; Quebec, 1847 ***5704.8*** *p17*
Brannon, Thomas 11; Quebec, 1847 ***5704.8*** *p17*
Brannon, William; Philadelphia, 1852 ***5704.8*** *p87*
Brannon, William; Quebec, 1847 ***5704.8*** *p17*
Branson, Thomas 21; Maryland, 1775 ***1219.7*** *p260*
Branson, William 26; Philadelphia, 1774 ***1219.7*** *p196*
Branston, Thomas 42; Quebec, 1864 ***5704.8*** *p159*
Brant, Martha Wally; Wisconsin, n.d. ***9675.4*** *p266*
Brant, William 26; Maryland, 1775 ***1219.7*** *p273*
Brantly, Edward; Virginia, 1638 ***6219*** *p117*
Brantly, Edward; Virginia, 1638 ***6219*** *p150*
Branton, Edward; Virginia, 1637 ***6219*** *p83*
Branton, William 20; Maryland, 1729 ***3690.1*** *p26*
Braquet, John 29; America, 1839 ***778.5*** *p77*
Braquier, B. 25; New Orleans, 1837 ***778.5*** *p77*
Brarenton, Thomas 21; Maryland, 1774 ***1219.7*** *p221*
Brasch, Frank; America, 1869 ***1450.2*** *p18A*
Brascher, Heinrich; Kentucky, 1796 ***8582.3*** *p95*
Brascoup, John 18; Virginia, 1699 ***2212*** *p26*
Brase, William; Virginia, 1638 ***6219*** *p123*
Braseland, Catharine 10; New York, NY, 1870 ***5704.8*** *p240*
Braseland, George; New York, NY, 1870 ***5704.8*** *p240*
Braseland, Sarah; New York, NY, 1870 ***5704.8*** *p240*
Brasey, Foulke; Virginia, 1635 ***6219*** *p69*
Brasfeild, George; Virginia, 1698 ***2212*** *p11*
Brashridge, John; Virginia, 1643 ***6219*** *p201*
Brasington, Samuel 19; Maryland, 1775 ***1219.7*** *p252*
Brason, Jacob 17; Jamaica, 1731 ***3690.1*** *p26*
Brass, Thomas; Savannah, GA, 1774 ***1219.7*** *p227*
Brassard, Louis 53; America, 1835 ***778.5*** *p77*
Brassontra, Samson; New Orleans, 1839 ***778.5*** *p77*
Bratmuller, William; Wisconsin, n.d. ***9675.4*** *p266*
Bratt, John; West Virginia, 1844 ***9788.3*** *p5*
Brattan, Elizabeth 20; St. John, N.B., 1857 ***5704.8*** *p135*
Brattan, John 20; St. John, N.B., 1857 ***5704.8*** *p135*
Brattan, John 22; Philadelphia, 1860 ***5704.8*** *p145*
Brattan, Martha; Philadelphia, 1847 ***53.26*** *p6*
Brattan, Martha; Philadelphia, 1847 ***5704.8*** *p31*
Brattan, Mary; America, 1741 ***4971*** *p63*
Brattan, Rebecca; St. John, N.B., 1847 ***5704.8*** *p9*
Bratten, George; Philadelphia, 1847 ***53.26*** *p6*
Bratten, George; Philadelphia, 1847 ***5704.8*** *p5*
Bratten, James; St. John, N.B., 1847 ***5704.8*** *p25*
Bratten, Robert; New Orleans, 1849 ***5704.8*** *p59*
Bratton, Mary A.; Philadelphia, 1866 ***5704.8*** *p215*
Bratz, Johann; Ohio, 1825 ***8582.1*** *p46*
Bratzman, Andrew; America, 1836 ***1450.2*** *p18A*
Brauch, William; Kansas, 1860 ***2764.35*** *p5*
Braucheler, Theobald; Philadelphia, 1741 ***4349*** *p46*
Braucheller, Theobald; Philadelphia, 1741 ***4349*** *p46*
Brauchler, Theobald; Philadelphia, 1741 ***4349*** *p46*
Braue, Christoph 24; Louisiana, 1838 ***778.5*** *p77*
Brauer, Edmund; Ohio, 1884-1889 ***9892.11*** *p5*
Brauer, Edmund; Ohio, 1892 ***9892.11*** *p5*
Brauer, Michael; America, 1851 ***8582.3*** *p8*
Braugh, Edward; Virginia, 1642 ***6219*** *p195*
Braugh, Stephen 25; Massachusetts, 1847 ***5881.1*** *p12*
Braughal, Christopher 19; Jamaica, 1730 ***3690.1*** *p26*
Braughel, Christofer 19; Jamaica, 1730 ***3690.1*** *p26*
Brault, Jacques 21?; Montreal, 1676 ***4533*** *p131*
Braum, Frederick; New York, NY, 1838 ***8208.4*** *p64*
Braumberger, Matthias 31; Georgia, 1734 ***9332*** *p327*
Braumuller, Herman; Virginia, 1857 ***4626.16*** *p17*
Braun, . . .; Canada, 1776-1783 ***9786*** *p18*
Braun, . . .; Virginia, 1738-1739 ***9898*** *p39*
With 3 siblings
Braun, Adolph Rudolph; New York, 1883 ***1450.2*** *p4B*
Braun, August; Wisconsin, n.d. ***9675.4*** *p266*
Braun, Barbara; Pennsylvania, 1750 ***2444*** *p159*
Braun, Catharina von Wehrt; Virginia, 1738-1739 ***9898*** *p39*
With daughter
Braun, Christian; New York, 1895 ***1450.2*** *p4B*
Braun, Christian; Wisconsin, n.d. ***9675.4*** *p266*
Braun, Dietrich; Philadelphia, 1779 ***8137*** *p7*
Braun, Edward 81; Arizona, 1925 ***9228.40*** *p29*
Braun, Ferdinand; Cincinnati, 1869-1887 ***8582*** *p4*
Braun, Friederich; America, 1843 ***8582.3*** *p8*
Braun, Gabriel; Philadelphia, 1886 ***1450.2*** *p4B*
Braun, George 37; New Orleans, 1838 ***778.5*** *p77*
Braun, George 39; America, 1839 ***778.5*** *p77*
Braun, Gottlieb; New Orleans, 1840 ***8582.1*** *p5*
Braun, Hermann; Wisconsin, n.d. ***9675.4*** *p266*
Braun, Jean 22; New Orleans, 1838 ***778.5*** *p78*
Braun, Joh. 58; Washington, D.C., 1901 ***1763*** *p40C*
Braun, Johann; Ohio, 1800-1885 ***8582.2*** *p59*
Braun, Johann Jacob; America, 1754 ***2444*** *p141*
*Wife:*Maria E. Koerber
Braun, Johannes; Ohio, 1798-1818 ***8582.2*** *p53*
Braun, Johannes; Ohio, 1800-1885 ***8582.2*** *p59*
Braun, Joseph; New York, 1890 ***1450.2*** *p5B*
Braun, Joseph; Virginia, 1738-1739 ***9898*** *p39*
Braun, Maria; Quebec, 1876 ***9980.20*** *p49*
Braun, Maria E. Koerber *SEE* Braun, Johann Jacob
Braun, Stephen 37; Pennsylvania, 1738 ***2444*** *p143*
Braun, Theodore A.; America, 1847 ***1450.2*** *p18A*
Braunbronn, . . .; Canada, 1776-1783 ***9786*** *p18*
Braune, . . .; Canada, 1776-1783 ***9786*** *p18*
Brauner, Henry; Illinois, 1860 ***2896.5*** *p5*
Braunger, Fannie; New York, NY, 1922 ***3455.2*** *p80*
Braunn, Hans; Wisconsin, n.d. ***9675.4*** *p266*
Braunschweig, August; Wisconsin, n.d. ***9675.4*** *p266*
Braunschweig, John M.; Cincinnati, 1869-1887 ***8582*** *p4*
Braunsdorf, Chaplain; Quebec, 1778 ***9786*** *p267*
Braunsreiter, Adam 24; New Orleans, 1862 ***543.30*** *p110*
Braunstein, Franz X.; Cincinnati, 1869-1887 ***8582*** *p4*
Braunstein, Franz Xaver; New York, NY, 1832 ***8582.3*** *p8*
With father & family
Braunwarth, Jacob; New Orleans, 1849 ***2896.5*** *p5*
Braunworth, John L.; New York, NY, 1854 ***2896.5*** *p5*
Braunworth, Michael; New Orleans, 1849 ***2896.5*** *p5*
Braurodt, Helwig 45; New Orleans, 1862 ***543.30*** *p242*
Brautigam, John; New York, NY, 1839 ***8208.4*** *p94*
Brauwer, Hubert; Germantown, PA, 1684 ***2467.7*** *p5*
Bravin, George 29; Arizona, 1890 ***2764.35*** *p7*
Bravo, Andrew 23; New Orleans, 1863 ***543.30*** *p247*
Brawders, John; Montreal, 1821 ***7603*** *p81*
Brawley, Catherine; New York, NY, 1869 ***5704.8*** *p232*
Brawley, Elizabeth; New York, NY, 1867 ***5704.8*** *p222*
Brawley, Isabella; New York, NY, 1816 ***2859.11*** *p26*
Brawley, William, Jr.; New York, NY, 1816 ***2859.11*** *p26*
Brawley, William, Sr.; New York, NY, 1816 ***2859.11*** *p26*
Braxston, Thomas; Virginia, 1636 ***6219*** *p79*
Braxton, Robert; Virginia, 1639 ***6219*** *p155*
Bray, Ann; America, 1740 ***4971*** *p15*
Bray, Francis 27; New Orleans, 1820 ***778.5*** *p78*
Bray, John; America, 1742 ***4971*** *p25*
Bray, John 18; Virginia, 1720 ***3690.1*** *p26*
Bray, John 27; Arizona, 1890 ***2764.35*** *p7*
Bray, Patrick; America, 1743 ***4971*** *p23*
Bray, Peter 40; New Orleans, 1831 ***778.5*** *p78*
Bray, Robert 16; Maryland, 1775 ***1219.7*** *p264*
Braydon, Edward; Virginia, 1642 ***6219*** *p189*
Braz, Eliza 22; Port uncertain, 1835 ***778.5*** *p78*
Braz, Eugene 3; Port uncertain, 1835 ***778.5*** *p78*
Braz, Henry 1; Port uncertain, 1835 ***778.5*** *p78*
Braz, Paul 20; Port uncertain, 1835 ***778.5*** *p78*
Brazel, Helene Robins; Montreal, 1822 ***7603*** *p91*
Brazell, Margaret; Montreal, 1818 ***7603*** *p89*
Brazier, Alexander; America, 1871 ***5704.8*** *p240*
Brazier, Eliza; America, 1871 ***5704.8*** *p240*
Brazier, Isabella; America, 1871 ***5704.8*** *p240*
Brazier, William 19; Virginia, 1774 ***1219.7*** *p239*
Brazones, Martin; Arkansas, 1918 ***95.2*** *p22*
Brazzale, Guisippe; Iowa, 1866-1943 ***123.54*** *p57*
Brazzalle, Emma; Iowa, 1866-1943 ***123.54*** *p10*
Brazzole, Guiseppi; Iowa, 1866-1943 ***123.54*** *p10*
Bread, James 30; Virginia, 1774 ***1219.7*** *p227*
Breaden, Catherine 2; St. John, N.B., 1852 ***5704.8*** *p84*
Breaden, Elizabeth; St. John, N.B., 1852 ***5704.8*** *p84*
Breaden, George; St. John, N.B., 1852 ***5704.8*** *p84*
Breaden, George 3 mos; St. John, N.B., 1852 ***5704.8*** *p84*
Breaden, John 4; St. John, N.B., 1852 ***5704.8*** *p84*
Bready, Edward 30; Philadelphia, 1861 ***5704.8*** *p148*
Bready, Elizabeth; Quebec, 1852 ***5704.8*** *p87*
Bready, John; Quebec, 1852 ***5704.8*** *p87*
Bready, Mary-Ann; Quebec, 1821 ***7603*** *p74*
Bready, Nancy 23; Philadelphia, 1861 ***5704.8*** *p148*
Breager, John Georg; Illinois, 1888 ***2896.5*** *p5*
Breamer, Thomas; Virginia, 1638 ***6219*** *p120*
Brean, Eleonore; Quebec, 1763 ***7603*** *p94*
Brearly, Daniel 45; Philadelphia, 1774 ***1219.7*** *p232*
Breaton, D. J. 27; Kansas, 1876 ***5240.1*** *p57*
Brebner, Archibald; Charleston, SC, 1805 ***1639.20*** *p15*
Brebouef, . . .; America, n.d. ***8582.3*** *p75*
Brechard, John 23; New Orleans, 1836 ***778.5*** *p78*
Brechel, Andrew; Philadelphia, 1759 ***9973.7*** *p33*
Brecht, . . .; Canada, 1776-1783 ***9786*** *p18*
Brecht, August von; America, 1842 ***8582*** *p4*
Brecht, Christ Frederick; Illinois, 1877 ***2896.5*** *p5*
Brecian, Mary; St. John, N.B., 1848 ***5704.8*** *p39*
Breckwede, August; Illinois, 1835 ***8582.1*** *p56*
Bredemeier, Christian; America, 1838 ***1450.2*** *p18A*
Bredemeier, Christian; America, 1849 ***1450.2*** *p17A*
Breden, Nicholas; New York, NY, 1836 ***8208.4*** *p16*
Bredenhagen, Anne M. Louise Charlotte; America, 1869 ***4610.10*** *p95*
Bredenhagen, Anne Marie Louise C. *SEE* Bredenhagen, Carl Friedrich
Bredenhagen, Carl Friedrich; America, 1869 ***4610.10*** *p95*
*Wife:*Anne Marie Louise C.
*Son:*Heinrich Friedrich P.
Bredenhagen, Heinrich Friedrich P. *SEE* Bredenhagen, Carl Friedrich
Bredenkamp, Christian; Indiana, 1850 ***9117*** *p20*
Bredford, J. 25; New Orleans, 1835 ***778.5*** *p78*
Breeden, Richard 19; Windward Islands, 1722 ***3690.1*** *p26*

Breem, Henry; Arizona, 1898 9228.30 p7
Breen, Alice *SEE* Breen, Terrence
Breen, Alice; Philadelphia, 1847 5704.8 p32
Breen, Catharine 20; Massachusetts, 1850 5881.1 p7
Breen, Catherine *SEE* Breen, Terrence
Breen, Catherine; Philadelphia, 1847 5704.8 p32
Breen, Charles 32; New Orleans, 1862 543.30 p115
Breen, Ellen 17; Quebec, 1864 5704.8 p160
Breen, Henry; Philadelphia, 1867 5704.8 p218
Breen, James; America, 1868 5704.8 p228
Breen, James; New York, 1827-1841 7036 p122
Breen, James; Quebec, 1822 7603 p62
Breen, John; Quebec, 1849 5704.8 p51
Breen, John 7; New York, NY, 1864 5704.8 p174
Breen, Margaret 1; Massachusetts, 1850 5881.1 p11
Breen, Margaret 3; Massachusetts, 1850 5881.1 p11
Breen, Margaret 20; Massachusetts, 1850 5881.1 p11
Breen, Mary; New York, NY, 1864 5704.8 p174
Breen, Mary 20; Massachusetts, 1847 5881.1 p9
Breen, Mary 60; Massachusetts, 1849 5881.1 p10
Breen, Patrick *SEE* Breen, Terrence
Breen, Patrick; Philadelphia, 1847 5704.8 p32
Breen, Patrick 35; Massachusetts, 1850 5881.1 p11
Breen, Peter 28; New Orleans, 1862 543.30 p109
Breen, Rosanna *SEE* Breen, Terrence
Breen, Rosanna; Philadelphia, 1847 5704.8 p32
Breen, Sally 30; Massachusetts, 1850 5881.1 p12
Breen, Sally 35; Massachusetts, 1849 5881.1 p12
Breen, Terrence; Philadelphia, 1847 53.26 p6
*Relative:*Patrick
*Relative:*Alice
*Relative:*Catherine
*Relative:*Rosanna
Breen, Terrence; Philadelphia, 1847 5704.8 p32
Breen, Thomas; St. John, N.B., 1847 5704.8 p25
Breene, Daniel; America, 1742 4971 p56
Breer, Andrew 40; Massachusetts, 1860 6410.32 p115
Breer, Margaret 30; Massachusetts, 1860 6410.32 p115
Breerely, Samuell 15; Virginia, 1700 2212 p31
Breeslin, Mary; St. John, N.B., 1850 5704.8 p61
Breeson, Ann; St. John, N.B., 1847 5704.8 p10
Breeson, Hugh 40; Philadelphia, 1803 53.26 p7
Bregadow, Bracky; Arkansas, 1918 95.2 p22
Breganski, Ludwik; Arkansas, 1918 95.2 p22
Breger, Henry; Wisconsin, n.d. 9675.4 p266
Breh, Leopold; Pennsylvania, 1857 1450.2 p18A
Brehaut, Pierre; Quebec, 1792 7603 p48
Brehm, Andreas; Buffalo, NY, 1846 8582.3 p9
Brehm, Andreas; Cincinnati, 1869-1887 8582 p4
Brehm, Andreas; Quebec, 1846 8582.3 p9
Brehm, Bernhard 11; America, 1867 1450.2 p19A
Brehm, Georg; Ohio, 1824 8582.1 p46
Brehm, Gg. Ad. 25; America, 1853 9162.8 p36
Brehmer, Charle; Wisconsin, n.d. 9675.4 p266
Brehmer, Charles; Wisconsin, n.d. 9675.4 p266
Brehob, Frank; New York, 1898 1450.2 p5B
Brehob, Henry; America, 1887 1450.2 p18A
Breidenbach, Hannche 22; America, 1853 9162.7 p14
Breidenhart, Christof; Pennsylvania, 1753 4525 p202
Breigel, Jakob; Charleston, SC, 1766 8582.2 p65
Breimnas, Lars; Washington, 1859-1920 2872.1 p5
Breinl, Wenzel; America, 1849 8582.2 p5
Breisch, Jacob; Pennsylvania, 1764 2444 p143
Breisch, Joseph; Pennsylvania, 1764 2444 p143
Breiss, Georg; South Carolina, 1788 7119 p201
Breitenbach, . . .; Canada, 1776-1783 9786 p18
Breitenbucher, Abraham; America, 1765-1766 2444 p142
*Wife:*Catharina Friz
Breitenbucher, Catharina Friz *SEE* Breitenbucher, Abraham
Breitenbuecher, Abraham; America, 1765-1766 2444 p142
*Wife:*Catharina Friz
Breitenbuecher, Abraham; Pennsylvania, 1765 2444 p142
Breitenbuecher, Balthas; Pennsylvania, 1765 2444 p142
Breitenbuecher, Catharina Friz *SEE* Breitenbuecher, Abraham
Breitenducher, Abraham; Pennsylvania, 1765 2444 p142
Breitenheert, Christoph; Pennsylvania, 1753 4525 p202
Breitenherd, Dorothea Gross *SEE* Breitenherd, Johann Christoph
Breitenherd, Johann Christoph; Pennsylvania, 1753 4525 p202
*Wife:*Dorothea Gross
With 2 children
Breitenherdt, Johan Christoph; Pennsylvania, 1753 4525 p202
Breitfusz, Peter; Georgia, 1738 9332 p319
Breitmeyer, John G.; New York, NY, 1840 8208.4 p104
Breitschuh, . . .; Canada, 1776-1783 9786 p18
Breitschwert, Adam 43; New Orleans, 1862 543.30 p110
Breitung, William; Wisconsin, n.d. 9675.4 p266
Breitwieser, J. 14; America, 1854-1855 9162.6 p105
Brekke, Louis Knutson; Arkansas, 1918 95.2 p22
Brekky, Frank; Arkansas, 1918 95.2 p22
Breman, Patrick; New York, NY, 1816 2859.11 p26
Breman, Sarah; Virginia, 1637 6219 p84
Bremen, Ellen; New York, NY, 1816 2859.11 p26
With 2 children
Bremer, Ernst; America, 1847 8582.1 p5
Bremer, Ferdinand; America, 1839 8582.3 p9
Bremer, Joseph; Wisconsin, n.d. 9675.4 p266
Bremer, William; Wisconsin, n.d. 9675.4 p266
Bremmer, Leib 40; New York, NY, 1878 9253 p47
Bremnes, Lars; Washington, 1859-1920 2872.1 p5
Bremond, J. 20; Port uncertain, 1836 778.5 p78
Bremond, Jena 35; Port uncertain, 1838 778.5 p78
Brenan, James; New York, NY, 1816 2859.11 p26
Brenan, John; America, 1735-1743 4971 p51
Brench, Isaac; Illinois, 1860 2896.5 p5
Brendel, . . .; Canada, 1776-1783 9786 p18
Brendel, John; New York, NY, 1835 8208.4 p57
Brendel, Katharina 33; New York, NY, 1898-1899 7846 p39
Brendes, Charles 22; Massachusetts, 1850 5881.1 p7
Brendt, Henry; Washington, 1859-1920 2872.1 p3
Breneison, Rudolph; Philadelphia, 1760 9973.7 p34
Brener, John C. F.; Ohio, 1842 8365.25 p12
Brener, Julius; Wisconsin, n.d. 9675.4 p266
Brengelman, Henrick; New York, NY, 1837 8208.4 p34
Brengelmann, B. H.; Cincinnati, 1869-1887 8582 p4
Brening, Charles; Maryland, 1892 1450.2 p5B
Brening, John Malcour; Ohio, 1843 9892.11 p5
Brenker, Jan; Arkansas, 1918 95.2 p22
Brenker, William; Colorado, 1892 9678.1 p155
Brenkman, Charles; America, 1840 1450.2 p20A
Brenn, Henry; Wisconsin, n.d. 9675.4 p266
Brennan, Bridget; New York, NY, 1816 2859.11 p26
Brennan, Bridget; Philadelphia, 1853 5704.8 p102
Brennan, Catherine 8; Philadelphia, 1853 5704.8 p102
Brennan, Daniel 20; Massachusetts, 1848 5881.1 p7
Brennan, Daniel I.; Philadelphia, 1850 6013.19 p29
Brennan, Dennis; America, 1737 4971 p30
Brennan, James; Montreal, 1822 7603 p84
Brennan, John; New York, NY, 1839 8208.4 p97
Brennan, John 16; Massachusetts, 1849 5881.1 p9
Brennan, John 40; New Orleans, 1862 543.30 p242
Brennan, John, II 17; New Orleans, 1862 543.30 p244
Brennan, Kitty 21; Massachusetts, 1849 5881.1 p9
Brennan, Margaret 5; Philadelphia, 1853 5704.8 p102
Brennan, Mary 3; Philadelphia, 1853 5704.8 p102
Brennan, Mary 21; Massachusetts, 1850 5881.1 p11
Brennan, Michael; New York, NY, 1838 8208.4 p81
Brennan, Michael 19; Massachusetts, 1849 5881.1 p10
Brennan, Nicholas; Springfield, MA, 1841 7036 p119
Brennan, Patrick; Illinois, 1892 5012.40 p27
Brennan, Patrick; Montreal, 1825 7603 p81
Brennan, Patrick; New York, NY, 1816 2859.11 p26
Brennan, Richard; Indiana, 1866 1450.2 p19A
Brennan, Richard; New York, NY, 1849 6013.19 p29
Brennan, Thomas; Boston, 1840 7036 p123
Brennan, Unity; New York, NY, 1816 2859.11 p26
Brennand, David 22; Maryland, 1774 1219.7 p218
Brennecker, . . .; Canada, 1776-1783 9786 p18
Brennecki, . . .; Canada, 1776-1783 9786 p41
Brenneke, . . .; Canada, 1776-1783 9786 p18
Brenneker, . . .; Canada, 1776-1783 9786 p18
Brennen, James; Illinois, 1888 5012.39 p52
Brennen, John; New York, NY, 1839 8208.4 p102
Brennenstuhl, Christina *SEE* Brennenstuhl, Johann Michael
Brennenstuhl, Johann Michael *SEE* Brennenstuhl, Johann Michael
Brennenstuhl, Johann Michael; Port uncertain, 1754 2444 p142
*Wife:*Maria M. Schilling
*Child:*Johann Michael
*Child:*Christina
*Child:*Maria Magdalena
*Child:*Johann Ulrich
Brennenstuhl, Johann Ulrich *SEE* Brennenstuhl, Johann Michael
Brennenstuhl, Maria M. Schilling *SEE* Brennenstuhl, Johann Michael
Brennenstuhl, Maria Magdalena *SEE* Brennenstuhl, Johann Michael
Brenner, Adam; South Carolina, 1788 7119 p203
Brenner, August; Wisconsin, n.d. 9675.4 p266
Brenner, Leo Kasierer; Arkansas, 1918 95.2 p22
Brenner, Lui; Wisconsin, n.d. 9675.4 p266
Brennin, Dennis 12; Massachusetts, 1849 5881.1 p7
Brennin, Patrick 10; Massachusetts, 1849 5881.1 p11
Brennon, Biddy 19; Philadelphia, 1853 5704.8 p113
Brennon, Francis 4; Philadelphia, 1853 5704.8 p113
Brennon, Mary 20; Massachusetts, 1847 5881.1 p9
Brennon, Michael 30; Massachusetts, 1849 5881.1 p10
Brennon, P.S. 74; Arizona, 1920 9228.40 p23
Brenon, Henry; Illinois, 1858 2896.5 p5
Brent, Guillaume; Quebec, 1820 7603 p23
Brent, Hugh; Virginia, 1642 6219 p197
Brent, Thomas 29; New York, 1774 1219.7 p217
Brentano, Lorenz; Chicago, 1800-1877 8582.3 p92
Brentle, Michael; Kentucky, 1839-1840 8582.3 p98
Brentlinger, Daniel; Ohio, 1825 8582.1 p46
Brentt, Jacob; South Carolina, 1788 7119 p202
Brentzel, Daniel; Philadelphia, 1779 8137 p7
Brenza, John; Pennsylvania, 1900 7137 p168
Brenzighofer, Anna Maria Rieger *SEE* Brenzighofer, Hans Georg
Brenzighofer, Georg Christoph; Port uncertain, 1782-1800 2444 p142
Brenzighofer, Hans Georg; Port uncertain, 1752 2444 p201
*Wife:*Anna Maria Rieger
Brenzighofer, Jacob Friedrich; Philadelphia, 1776-1801 2444 p142
Brenzikofer, Frank; America, 1889 5240.1 p6
Brenzikofer, Fred; Kansas, 1891 5240.1 p6
Breplur, Daniel 19; Maryland, 1774 1219.7 p191
Bres, Mr. 19; America, 1839 778.5 p78
Breski, J.; Iowa, 1866-1943 123.54 p11
Breslan, Tracy; St. John, N.B., 1853 5704.8 p99
Bresland, Henry 36; Philadelphia, 1864 5704.8 p157
Breslin, Ellan; St. John, N.B., 1847 5704.8 p21
Breslin, Hanna 15; Philadelphia, 1853 5704.8 p111
Breslin, James; America, 1864 5704.8 p178
Breslin, John; Quebec, 1847 5704.8 p8
Breslin, Paddy; St. John, N.B., 1853 5704.8 p107
Breslinn, Daniel; Philadelphia, 1869 5704.8 p236
Bresna, Jeremiah 12; Massachusetts, 1849 5881.1 p9
Bresna, Margaret 9; Massachusetts, 1849 5881.1 p10
Bresna, Norry 31; Massachusetts, 1849 5881.1 p11
Bresnahan, Daniel 60; Massachusetts, 1849 5881.1 p7
Bresnahan, John 44; Massachusetts, 1849 5881.1 p8
Bresnan, Stephen 30; Massachusetts, 1849 5881.1 p12
Bresnehan, Catharine 30; Massachusetts, 1849 5881.1 p7
Breson, Bell; Quebec, 1851 5704.8 p74
Breson, Bridget; Philadelphia, 1850 53.26 p7
*Relative:*Michael
*Relative:*John 11
Breson, Bridget; Philadelphia, 1850 5704.8 p69
Breson, John 11 *SEE* Breson, Bridget
Breson, John 11; Philadelphia, 1850 5704.8 p69
Breson, Michael *SEE* Breson, Bridget
Breson, Michael; Philadelphia, 1850 5704.8 p69
Breson, Nancy; Philadelphia, 1851 5704.8 p81
Bressler, A. 36; Louisiana, 1820 778.5 p78
Bressler, Siegmond; Philadelphia, 1779 8137 p7
Bressnehan, John 23; Massachusetts, 1849 5881.1 p9
Bresson, Samuel 27; America, 1830 778.5 p78
Bressy, Mr. 28; America, 1839 778.5 p78
Bret, Mr. 37; America, 1838 778.5 p79
Brethauer, Anna M. I. Wickemeyer *SEE* Brethauer, Johann Friedrich Christian
Brethauer, Heinrich Wilhelm *SEE* Brethauer, Johann Friedrich Christian
Brethauer, Johann Friedrich Christian; America, 1854 4610.10 p156
*Wife:*Anna M. I. Wickemeyer
*Son:*Heinrich Wilhelm
Bretherston, Dennis; Virginia, 1637 6219 p114
Bretherton, John 20; Newfoundland, 1699-1700 2212 p18
Breton, Achille 37; America, 1837 778.5 p79
Breton, Charles 36; Port uncertain, 1826 778.5 p79
Brett, Alex.; Virginia, 1638 6219 p118
Brett, Anne 10; Quebec, 1863 5704.8 p154
Brett, Anne 36; Quebec, 1863 5704.8 p154
Brett, Eliza 4; Quebec, 1863 5704.8 p154
Brett, Elizabeth 25; Baltimore, 1775 1219.7 p271
Brett, Marie; Montreal, 1823 7603 p84
Brett, Richard; Virginia, 1637 6219 p109
Brett, Thomas; New York, 1858 3840.1 p16
Brett, William; Illinois, 1868 7857 p2
Brettemeye, Fredric; Wisconsin, n.d. 9675.4 p266
Bretthauer, Friedrich Wilhelm; America, 1858 4610.10 p158
Bretthauer, Heinrich; Cincinnati, 1869-1887 8582 p4
Bretthauer, Johann Friedrich; America, 1853 4610.10 p156
Bretthauer, William; Indiana, 1872 1450.2 p19A
Bretzmann, Louis; Iroquois Co., IL, 1892 3455.1 p9
Breuer, Albert; Wisconsin, n.d. 9675.4 p266
Breuer, Carl Heinrich Friedrich W.; America, 1882 4610.10 p96
Breuer, Ernst Heinrich Friedrich; America, 1840 4610.10 p95

Brindza, John; Pennsylvania, 1900 7137 p168
Brine, Henry; Ohio, 1870 9892.11 p5
Bringemann, Hermann; Ohio, 1836 8582.1 p47
Bringewatt, Mr.; America, 1832-1863 4610.10 p152
With wife
Bringewatt, Mr.; America, 1853 4610.10 p151
*Wife:*Anne C. C. Homburg 52
*Child:*Christian Friedrich
*Child:*Johann Heinrich
*Child:*Carl H. Friedrich
Bringewatt, Anne C. C. Homburg 52 *SEE* Bringewatt, Mr.
Bringewatt, Anne Marie; America, 1863 4610.10 p152
Bringewatt, Carl H. Friedrich *SEE* Bringewatt, Mr.
Bringewatt, Christian Friedrich *SEE* Bringewatt, Mr.
Bringewatt, Johann Heinrich *SEE* Bringewatt, Mr.
Brining, Adam; Ohio, 1844 9892.11 p5
Brining, Elizabeth 17; America, 1706 2212 p46
Brink, Christian A.D.; America, 1858 1450.2 p19A
Brink, Peter; New York, 1754 3652 p79
Brinker, Fritz; Illinois, 1892 5012.40 p26
Brinklow, Alfred 22; Kansas, 1888 5240.1 p72
Brinkman, Charles; America, 1840 1450.2 p20A
Brinkman, Heinrich; Iroquois Co., IL, 1892 3455.1 p9
Brinkman, John; Maine, 1875-1884 6410.22 p119
Brinkman, John Frederick; America, 1852 1450.2 p19A
Brinkman, John Henry Frederick Gotleib; New York, 1840 1450.2 p20A
Brinkman, Wilhelm A.; Wisconsin, n.d. 9675.4 p266
Brinkmann, Mr.; Cincinnati, 1848 3702.7 p89
Brinkmann, A M Louise J Stumeier *SEE* Brinkmann, Friedrich
Brinkmann, Anne M. C. Niedergerke *SEE* Brinkmann, Karl Heinrich August
Brinkmann, August; Illinois, 1888 5012.39 p122
Brinkmann, B.; New Orleans, 1846 3702.7 p84
Brinkmann, B.; New Orleans, 1846 3702.7 p89
Brinkmann, Carl Friedrich Gottlieb; America, 1860 4610.10 p136
Brinkmann, Caroline F. Louise *SEE* Brinkmann, Friedrich
Brinkmann, Christian Henry; America, 1850 1450.2 p20A
Brinkmann, Ernst Heinz Moritz; America, 1853 4610.10 p112
Brinkmann, Friederike Wilhelmine *SEE* Brinkmann, Friedrich
Brinkmann, Friedrich; America, 1887 4610.10 p110
*Wife:*A M Louise J Stumeier
*Child:*Friederike Wilhelmine
*Child:*Caroline F. Louise
*Child:*Minna Louise Charlotte
Brinkmann, Herm; Ohio, 1882 3702.7 p445
Brinkmann, Johann Heinrich *SEE* Brinkmann, Karl Heinrich August
Brinkmann, Karl Heinrich August; America, 1838 4610.10 p119
*Father:*Johann Heinrich
*Mother:*Anne M. C. Niedergerke
Brinkmann, Minna Louise Charlotte *SEE* Brinkmann, Friedrich
Brinkmann, Wilhelm; Illinois, 1869-1930 4610.10 p67
Brinkmans, Mr.; Cincinnati, 1848 3702.7 p89
Brinkmans, B.; New Orleans, 1846 3702.7 p89
Brinkwell, William 22; Maryland, 1774 1219.7 p221
Brinnain, Patrick; America, 1845 1450.2 p19A
Brinnan, James; New York, 1836 1450.2 p19A
Brinnan, James; Virginia, 1855 4626.16 p15
Brinnan, William; Montreal, 1824 7603 p84
Brintwell, Robert; Virginia, 1643 6219 p204
Brintzighofer, Caspar; Pennsylvania, 1752 2444 p201
Brinzey, John; Pennsylvania, 1900 7137 p168
Brisac, Felix; New York, NY, 1850 6013.19 p29
Brisat, Mr. 30; New Orleans, 1838 778.5 p80
Brisbane, Robert; South Carolina, 1733 1639.20 p16
Brisbane, William; South Carolina, 1732 1639.20 p16
Brisbe, Felix; New York, NY, 1850 6013.19 p29
Briscoe, Thomas 22; America, 1700 2212 p33
Brise, Andre 35; New Orleans, 1838 778.5 p80
Brisemeister, William; Wisconsin, n.d. 9675.4 p266
Briski, Frank; Arkansas, 1918 95.2 p23
Briskin, Jacob; Wisconsin, n.d. 9675.4 p266
Briskin, Molly; Wisconsin, n.d. 9675.4 p266
Brisland, Andrew 9; Massachusetts, 1849 5881.1 p6
Brisland, Henry 28; Philadelphia, 1857 5704.8 p133
Brisland, John 50; Massachusetts, 1849 5881.1 p8
Brisland, Kitty; Philadelphia, 1851 5704.8 p78
Brisland, Nancy; St. John, N.B., 1850 5704.8 p66
Brisland, Patrick 30; Wilmington, DE, 1831 6508.7 p161
Brislane, Morgan; America, 1735-1743 4971 p79
Brislawn, Eliza; Montreal, 1824 7603 p65
Brisley, John 28; Maryland, 1774 1219.7 p202
Brismanie, F. G. 40; New Orleans, 1823 778.5 p80
Brismetier, Elisabetha 24; Port uncertain, 1839 778.5 p80
Brison, Catherine; Quebec, 1852 5704.8 p87
Brison, Catherine; Quebec, 1852 5704.8 p91
Brison, Catherine 8 *SEE* Brison, Susan
Brison, Catherine 8; Philadelphia, 1847 5704.8 p1
Brison, Charlott 20; Philadelphia, 1854 5704.8 p123
Brison, John; Quebec, 1852 5704.8 p87
Brison, John; Quebec, 1852 5704.8 p91
Brison, Margaret; Quebec, 1852 5704.8 p87
Brison, Margaret; Quebec, 1852 5704.8 p91
Brison, Sarah; Quebec, 1852 5704.8 p87
Brison, Sarah; Quebec, 1852 5704.8 p91
Brison, Sarah 21; Philadelphia, 1854 5704.8 p123
Brison, Susan; Philadelphia, 1847 53.26 p7
*Relative:*Catherine 8
*Relative:*William 2
Brison, Susan; Philadelphia, 1847 5704.8 p1
Brison, William 2 *SEE* Brison, Susan
Brison, William 2; Philadelphia, 1847 5704.8 p1
Brison, William 9; Quebec, 1852 5704.8 p87
Brison, William 9; Quebec, 1852 5704.8 p91
Brissel, Biddy 26; Massachusetts, 1849 5881.1 p6
Brissel, Thomas 60; Massachusetts, 1849 5881.1 p12
Brisset, A. 27; New Orleans, 1832 778.5 p80
Brisset, Alexandre 38; New Orleans, 1838 778.5 p80
Brisset, Jean Jacque 38; New Orleans, 1838 778.5 p80
Brissil, James 30; Massachusetts, 1849 5881.1 p9
Briste, Mathew; Virginia, 1638 6219 p181
Bristoe, Fr.; Virginia, 1637 6219 p110
Bristoe, John; Virginia, 1637 6219 p112
Bristoe, Laurc.; Virginia, 1634 6219 p84
Bristol, Joseph; New York, 1764 1219.7 p99
Bristow, Thomas; Virginia, 1646 6219 p236
Brisven, Charles; Washington, 1859-1920 2872.1 p5
Brith, Mary 46; Massachusetts, 1849 5881.1 p10
Britmaier, Jakob 35; Port uncertain, 1839 778.5 p80
Britmann, Johann 13; Port uncertain, 1839 778.5 p80
Britsch, Philipp 24; New Orleans, 1862 543.30 p327
Brittain, Charles 19; Virginia, 1720 3690.1 p27
Brittain, James 18; Maryland, 1723 3690.1 p27
Brittaine, John; Virginia, 1638 6219 p145
Brittaine, Robt.; Virginia, 1635 6219 p26
Britten, Catharine; America, 1865 5704.8 p204
Britten, Francis J.; America, 1865 5704.8 p204
Brittin, John 22; America, 1700 2212 p34
Brittle, Joseph 28; Maryland, 1774 1219.7 p192
Brittlebank, Elizabeth 21; Baltimore, 1775 1219.7 p271
Brittner, Simon; Alberta, n.d. 5262 p58
Britton, Alexander; New York, NY, 1835 8208.4 p77
Britton, Elizabeth; Montreal, 1820 7603 p72
Britton, Hugh 45; Philadelphia, 1855 5704.8 p124
Britton, Peggy 25; Philadelphia, 1853 5704.8 p113
Britton, William; New York, NY, 1815 2859.11 p26
Britung, William; Wisconsin, n.d. 9675.4 p266
Britz, Mathias; Wisconsin, n.d. 9675.4 p266
Britzwein, Albert; America, 1853 8582.3 p9
Briva, Hermann 21; America, 1836 778.5 p80
Brix, Asmus; Washington, 1859-1920 2872.1 p5
Brix, Peter Frederick; Washington, 1859-1920 2872.1 p5
Broa, James 36; Massachusetts, 1847 5881.1 p8
Broad, Frank; Arizona, 1890 2764.35 p4
Broad, John; New York, NY, 1834 8208.4 p58
Broad, Tho.; Virginia, 1635 6219 p17
Broadbeck, Frederick; Pennsylvania, 1749 2444 p142
Broadbin, Micheal 30; St. John, N.B., 1855 5704.8 p126
Broade, Humphrey; Virginia, 1635 6219 p7
Broadfeild, Ann; Virginia, 1648 6219 p253
Broadfield, Richard 34; Port uncertain, 1774 1219.7 p176
Broadfoot, Andrew; North Carolina, 1810 1639.20 p16
Broadfoot, William; America, 1808 1639.20 p16
Broadfoot, William; Charleston, SC, 1798 1639.20 p16
Broadgate, Edward 21; Virginia, 1727 3690.1 p27
Broadue, George; Virginia, 1639 6219 p152
Broadway, John; Virginia, 1643 6219 p23
Broadway, Rowland 19; Jamaica, 1750 3690.1 p27
Broady, John 30; Massachusetts, 1847 5881.1 p8
Brobbin, Eliz.; America, 1697 2212 p9
Brobbin, Henry; America, 1697 2212 p9
Brobbin, Jno; America, 1697 2212 p9
Brobst, . . .; Pennsylvania, 1670-1730 8582.3 p9
Brobst, . . .; Philadelphia, 1733 8582.3 p10
Brobst Family ; New York, NY, 1694 8582.3 p10
Brocard, Francois 6 mos; America, 1835 778.5 p81
Brocard, Francois 20; America, 1835 778.5 p81
Brocard, Jean-Baptiste Albert 2; America, 1835 778.5 p81
Brocard, Julie 20; America, 1835 778.5 p81
Brocard, Madeleine 4; America, 1835 778.5 p81
Brocas, Georg; Virginia, 1642 6219 p193
Broces, Alexis 24; New Orleans, 1839 778.5 p81
Broche, Barbary *SEE* Broche, John
Broche, John; Virginia, 1637 6219 p112
*Wife:*Barbary
Brochheuser, Peter; Illinois, 1872 5012.39 p26
Brochowicz, Zofia 21; New York, 1912 9980.29 p55
Brock, B. F.; Washington, 1859-1920 2872.1 p5
Brock, Clarence T.; Washington, 1859-1920 2872.1 p5
Brock, Frederick Dese; New York, NY, 1849 6013.19 p29
Brock, John; Iowa, 1866-1943 123.54 p11
Brock, Patrick; New York, NY, 1836 8208.4 p20
Brock, Thomas; New York, 1887 2764.35 p7
Brock, William 17; Virginia, 1720 3690.1 p27
Brock, William 23; Virginia, 1774 1219.7 p239
Brock, Wm.; Virginia, 1635 6219 p23
Brockel, Adolphine Charlotte; America, 1836 4610.10 p141
Brockel, Louis; America, 1860 4610.10 p145
Brockelmeyer, William; Illinois, 1890 2896.5 p5
Brockelsby, John; Iroquois Co., IL, 1896 3455.1 p9
Brockmann, Bernhard; America, 1844 8582.3 p10
Brockmann, Bernhard; Ohio, 1869-1887 8582 p4
Brockmann, Frederick; Illinois, 1876 2896.5 p5
Brockmann, Johann Hermann; America, 1846 8582.1 p5
Brockmeyer, Anna Marie Elisabeth; America, 1846 4610.10 p95
Brocks, W. S.; Washington, 1859-1920 2872.1 p5
Brocksch, Andrew; New York, 1743 3652 p60
*Wife:*Anna Elizabeth
Brocksch, Andrew; New York, 1748 3652 p68
Brocksch, Anna Elizabeth *SEE* Brocksch, Andrew
Brocksmith, John Henry; Baltimore, 1846 1450.2 p20A
Brockwoldt, Henry; New Jersey, 1858 2896.5 p5
Brod, Katarzina 18; New York, 1912 9980.29 p67
Brodbeck, Anna *SEE* Brodbeck, Hans Jerg
Brodbeck, Anna Maria; Port uncertain, 1743-1800 2444 p188
Brodbeck, Conrad; America, 1847 8582.2 p5
Brodbeck, Georg Friedrich *SEE* Brodbeck, Hans Jerg
Brodbeck, Hans Jerg; Pennsylvania, 1749 2444 p142
*Wife:*Anna
*Child:*Georg Friedrich
Brodbeck, Jacob; Cincinnati, 1848 8582.1 p53
Brodbeck, Richard 38; New Orleans, 1862 543.30 p114
Brodda, William C.; Wisconsin, n.d. 9675.4 p266
Broder, Andrew Henderson; San Francisco, 1865 2769.1 p6
Broder, Michael; America, 1736-1743 4971 p57
Broder, Patrick; America, 1743 4971 p32
Broderhausen, Carl Heinrich; America, 1868 4610.10 p159
Broderhausen, Friedrich Wilhelm; America, 1857 4610.10 p157
Broderick, James 37; New Orleans, 1862 543.30 p113
Broderick, John; America, 1742 4971 p31
Broderick, Margaret 31; Massachusetts, 1847 5881.1 p9
Broderick, Michael; America, 1736-1743 4971 p57
Broderick, Patrick 26; New Orleans, 1862 543.30 p482
Broderick, William; Philadelphia, 1865 5704.8 p196
Broders, Fanny; Philadelphia, 1852 5704.8 p96
Brodhurst, Walter; Virginia, 1652 6251 p19
Brodie, Alexander; Charleston, SC, 1792 1639.20 p16
Brodie, George 21; Jamaica, 1734 3690.1 p27
Brodie, John C.; Colorado, 1903 9678.1 p155
Brodie, Thomas; Charleston, SC, 1798 1639.20 p16
Brodigan, Hugh 10; Massachusetts, 1849 5881.1 p8
Brodigan, Patrick 14; Massachusetts, 1849 5881.1 p11
Brodley, Alexander 28; Philadelphia, 1803 53.26 p7
Brodley, Patrick 19; Philadelphia, 1803 53.26 p7
Brodneer, Stephen; Ohio, 1840 9892.11 p5
Broe, Matthew; Illinois, 1872 5012.39 p25
Broeckelmann Family ; New York, 1765 8125.8 p436
Broeg, John; New York, NY, 1836 8208.4 p16
Broeke, Henry; Indiana, 1848 9117 p19
Broeker, Ernst Heinrich Ferdinand; America, 1840 4610.10 p95
Broemmelhaus, Heinrich; America, 1850 8582.3 p10
Broer, Mr.; Michigan, 1870 4610.10 p149
Broer, Heinrich Ludwig; America, 1881 4610.10 p149
Broer, Hermann Heinrich; America, 1865 4610.10 p149
Broersma, Thys 22; Arkansas, 1918 95.2 p23
Broetz, David; Ohio, 1883 5240.1 p7
Broffee, Edward 23; Port uncertain, 1774 1219.7 p176
Brogan, Anne; New York, NY, 1870 5704.8 p237
Brogan, Bridget 54; Philadelphia, 1856 5704.8 p128
Brogan, Catherine; Quebec, 1851 5704.8 p74
Brogan, Catherine 25; Philadelphia, 1861 5704.8 p148
Brogan, Charles; New York, NY, 1866 5704.8 p213
Brogan, Connell; St. John, N.B., 1852 5704.8 p83
Brogan, Dennis; New York, NY, 1870 5704.8 p237
Brogan, Dennis; New York, NY, 1870 5704.8 p238
Brogan, Dennis; Philadelphia, 1848 53.26 p7
Brogan, Dennis; Philadelphia, 1848 5704.8 p40
Brogan, Elizabeth; Philadelphia, 1864 5704.8 p177

Brogan, Hugh; New York, NY, 1870 5704.8 p237
Brogan, Isabella; Philadelphia, 1864 5704.8 p180
Brogan, James; Philadelphia, 1850 53.26 p7
Brogan, James; Philadelphia, 1850 5704.8 p60
Brogan, John; Baltimore, 1811 2859.11 p9
Brogan, John; Philadelphia, 1849 53.26 p7
Brogan, John; Philadelphia, 1849 5704.8 p53
Brogan, John; Philadelphia, 1867 5704.8 p217
Brogan, Maggie; New York, NY, 1870 5704.8 p238
Brogan, Margaret; Quebec, 1825 7603 p83
Brogan, Mary A.; Philadelphia, 1864 5704.8 p173
Brogan, Michael 52; Philadelphia, 1856 5704.8 p128
Brogan, Nancy; New York, NY, 1867 5704.8 p222
Brogan, Patrick; America, 1741 4971 p38
Brogan, Patrick; New York, NY, 1815 2859.11 p26
Brogan, Patrick; New York, NY, 1836 8208.4 p13
Brogan, Patrick; New York, NY, 1870 5704.8 p237
Brogan, Patrick 9; New York, NY, 1870 5704.8 p238
Brogan, Peggy; Quebec, 1848 5704.8 p42
Brogan, Unity; New York, NY, 1866 5704.8 p213
Brogden, Elsie May *SEE* Brogden, John
Brogden, John; Missouri, 1914 3455.2 p78
*Wife:*Elsie May
Brogden, Thomas 21; Maryland, 1775 1219.7 p262
Brogniez, Peter 39; West Virginia, 1898 9788.3 p5
Brohain, Pat 20; Massachusetts, 1848 5881.1 p11
Brohan, Thomas; Quebec, 1835 1450.2 p20A
Brohan, Thomas 25?; Indiana, 1838 1450.2 p20A
Brohkel, Heisterkamp; Ohio, 1881 3702.7 p434
Brohm, Theodore Julius 38; New Orleans, 1839 9420.2 p165
Broin, John 25; America, 1838 778.5 p81
Broisch, Anna Barbara *SEE* Broisch, Joseph
Broisch, Anna Barbara Kurz *SEE* Broisch, Joseph
Broisch, Jacob Friedrich *SEE* Broisch, Joseph
Broisch, Johann Michael *SEE* Broisch, Joseph
Broisch, Johannes *SEE* Broisch, Joseph
Broisch, Joseph *SEE* Broisch, Joseph
Broisch, Joseph; Philadelphia, 1764 2444 p142
*Wife:*Anna Barbara Kurz
*Child:*Johann Michael
*Child:*Johannes
*Child:*Joseph
*Child:*Maria Catharina
*Child:*Anna Barbara
*Child:*Jacob Friedrich
Broisch, Maria Catharina *SEE* Broisch, Joseph
Broise, John 25; America, 1838 778.5 p81
Broke, Robert; Charleston, SC, 1733 1639.20 p16
Brokey, Charles 25; Georgia, 1775 1219.7 p276
Brokmann, Anna Magdalene; America, 1837 4815.7 p92
Brokmann, Fritz 30; Kansas, 1884 5240.1 p66
Broksch, Elizabeth; New York, 1761 3652 p88
Brolig, Julius; Wisconsin, n.d. 9675.4 p266
Brolly, Catherine; St. John, N.B., 1851 5704.8 p78
Brolly, Catherine 18; Philadelphia, 1857 5704.8 p132
Brolly, Jane 18; St. John, N.B., 1855 5704.8 p126
Brolly, Nancy 19; Philadelphia, 1859 5704.8 p142
Brolly, Patrick 18; Philadelphia, 1854 5704.8 p116
Brolly, Sarah; St. John, N.B., 1847 5704.8 p9
Brolly, William; Philadelphia, 1852 5704.8 p96
Bromat, J. 40; New Orleans, 1827 778.5 p81
Brombach, William; Wisconsin, n.d. 9675.4 p266
Bromebane, John; America, 1739 4971 p56
Bromely, Daniel; Virginia, 1635 6219 p27
Bromfeild, Marke; Virginia, 1645 6219 p239
Bromley, Henry; America, 1756 1219.7 p49
Bromley, Joseph 22; Virginia, 1774 1219.7 p238
Bromley, Thomas; America, 1869 9892.11 p6
Bromly, Daniell; Virginia, 1638 6219 p145
Bromly, Luke; Virginia, 1639 6219 p151
Brondlin, John 49; Kansas, 1885 5240.1 p67
Bronislaw, Jarosz; Arkansas, 1918 95.2 p23
Bronleave, Thomas; Illinois, 1872 7857 p2
Bronner, Jean 22; New Orleans, 1837 778.5 p81
Bronner, Johann Michael; Port uncertain, 1753 2444 p143
Bronnj, Catharina; Port uncertain, 1748-1800 2444 p143
*Child:*Catharine
Bronnj, Catharine *SEE* Bronnj, Catharina
Brons, Dietrich; Kentucky, 1843 8582.3 p100
Bronsema, Thomas; Iroquois Co., IL, 1892 3455.1 p9
Bronston, Eshell; Kansas, 1900 5240.1 p7
Broo, John Alfred; Arkansas, 1918 95.2 p23
Brood, Hans Peter; Arkansas, 1918 95.2 p23
Brook, Ann 57; Jamaica, 1774 1219.7 p219
Brook, Catherine; St. John, N.B., 1847 5704.8 p35
Brook, Elizabeth 5; Quebec, 1850 5704.8 p70
Brook, Ellen 7; Quebec, 1850 5704.8 p70
Brook, James; Georgia, 1775 1219.7 p274
Brook, Jane 3; Quebec, 1850 5704.8 p70
Brook, John 36; America, 1838 778.5 p81
Brook, John Henry; Illinois, 1860 2896.5 p5
Brook, Lawrance 21; Maryland, 1774 1219.7 p187
Brook, Mary; Quebec, 1850 5704.8 p69
Brook, Mary 9; Quebec, 1850 5704.8 p69
Brookbanks, John 16; Maryland, 1729 3690.1 p27
Brooke, Mr.; Quebec, 1815 9229.18 p74
Brooke, Charles; Virginia, 1646 6219 p242
Brooke, Charles 19; Virginia, 1751 1219.7 p4
Brooke, Charles 19; Virginia, 1751 3690.1 p27
Brooke, Eliza.; Virginia, 1642 6219 p195
Brooke, Georg; Virginia, 1638 6219 p153
Brooke, Gilbert; Virginia, 1642 6219 p186
Brooke, Henry 15; Pennsylvania, 1720 3690.1 p27
Brooke, John; Virginia, 1640 6219 p187
Brooke, Mary; Quebec, 1847 5704.8 p17
Brooke, Nicholas 12; America, 1697-1707 2212 p25
Brooke, Sarah 21; Maryland, 1775 1219.7 p259
Brooke, Tho.; Virginia, 1645 6219 p233
Brooke, Thomas; Quebec, 1847 5704.8 p17
Brooke, Thomas; Virginia, 1635 6219 p72
Brooke, William; Virginia, 1628 6219 p9
Brooke, William; Virginia, 1643 6219 p229
With wife & 2 children
Brookes, Bestney; Virginia, 1643 6219 p202
Brookes, Culbert; Virginia, 1622 6219 p4
Brookes, Elizabeth 30?; Maryland or Virginia, 1705 2212 p44
Brookes, Georg; Virginia, 1638 6219 p145
Brookes, Georg; Virginia, 1639 6219 p162
Brookes, James 27; Maryland, 1773 1219.7 p173
Brookes, John; New York, NY, 1838 8208.4 p89
Brookes, John; Virginia, 1638 6219 p145
Brookes, John; Virginia, 1639 6219 p161
Brookes, John 17; Pennsylvania, Virginia or Maryland, 1719 3690.1 p27
Brookes, Peter; Virginia, 1638 6219 p121
Brookes, Walter; Virginia, 1638 6219 p118
Brookes, William 15; Philadelphia, 1774 1219.7 p216
Brookhart, Julius; Philadelphia, 1763 9973.7 p39
Brookins, John 26; Philadelphia, 1864 5704.8 p156
Brookmeir, Christian; Illinois, 1854 7857 p2
Brookmeir, Christopher; Illinois, 1854 7857 p2
Brookmeir, Frederich; Illinois, 1854 7857 p2
Brooks, Alfred 1; Massachusetts, 1848 5881.1 p6
Brooks, Ann 32; New York, 1774 1219.7 p217
Brooks, Charles 19; Virginia, 1751 3690.1 p27
Brooks, Dorothea; New York, NY, 1864 5704.8 p180
Brooks, Eliza 27; Massachusetts, 1848 5881.1 p7
Brooks, Francis 17; Philadelphia, 1774 1219.7 p217
Brooks, Geo.; Virginia, 1635 6219 p27
Brooks, George 15; Baltimore, 1775 1219.7 p271
Brooks, George 15; Virginia, 1720 3690.1 p27
Brooks, Henry 29; New Orleans, 1864 543.30 p248
Brooks, James; New York, NY, 1815 2859.11 p26
Brooks, James 22; Baltimore, 1775 1219.7 p269
Brook's, Jno.; Virginia, 1644 6219 p229
Brooks, John; Jamaica, 1754 1219.7 p29
Brooks, John; Jamaica, 1754 3690.1 p28
Brooks, John; St. John, N.B., 1847 5704.8 p20
Brooks, John; Virginia, 1647 6219 p247
Brooks, John 17; Pennsylvania, Virginia or Maryland, 1719 3690.1 p27
Brooks, John 29; Quebec, 1774 1219.7 p211
Brooks, John 30; New York, 1774 1219.7 p217
Brooks, Mary 21; Georgia, 1774 1219.7 p188
Brooks, Philip; Mobile, AL, 1766 1219.7 p118
Brooks, Philip 15; Philadelphia, 1774 1219.7 p215
Brooks, Richard 56; New York, 1774 1219.7 p217
Brooks, Samuel 23; Maryland, 1729 3690.1 p28
Brooks, Tho.; Virginia, 1643 6219 p208
Brooks, Thomas; Virginia, 1628 6219 p31
Brooks, Thomas 30; Maryland, 1775 1219.7 p266
Brooks, W. S.; Washington, 1859-1920 2872.1 p5
Brooks, William; New York, NY, 1864 5704.8 p180
Brookshank, Nathan; New York, NY, 1839 6013.19 p29
Brookson, James 18; Jamaica, 1774 1219.7 p234
Broom, Mary 19; Pennsylvania, 1731 3690.1 p28
Broome, Francis 42; Maryland, 1775 1219.7 p264
Broome, Robt.; Virginia, 1638 6219 p149
Broome, Sarah 27; Maryland, 1775 1219.7 p264
Broomfield, John 36; Virginia, 1774 1219.7 p185
Brooms, Peter; Washington, 1859-1920 2872.1 p5
Brooms, William; Quebec, 1814 7603 p21
Broon, Edward 25; St. John, N.B., 1854 5704.8 p115
Broon, James 40; St. John, N.B., 1853 5704.8 p110
Brophy, Anastasie; Montreal, 1823 7603 p85
Brophy, James; New York, NY, 1850 2896.5 p5
Brophy, Jeremiah; Philadelphia, 1816 2859.11 p26
Brophy, M. J.; San Diego, 1890 2764.35 p75
Brophy, Michael; New York, NY, 1816 2859.11 p26
Brophy, Michael; New York, NY, 1838 8208.4 p65
Brophy, Patrick; Wisconsin, n.d. 9675.4 p266
Brophy, W. H.; Arizona, 1888 2764.35 p5
Brophy, William; Montreal, 1823 7603 p85
Bropigan, Thomas; New York, NY, 1815 2859.11 p26
Brorstrom, Anders; Iowa, 1851 2090 p614
Bros, George 21; Pennsylvania, 1753 2444 p143
Brosalg, John; Kansas, 1887 5240.1 p7
Broscher, Henriette 24; New York, NY, 1857 9831.14 p154
Brosemer, Karl; Kentucky, 1820-1829 8582.3 p98
Brosents, Joseph; Virginia, 1698 2212 p15
Brosier, Joseph; America, 1697 2212 p7
Brosis, Abraham; Philadelphia, 1758 9973.7 p33
Brosmin, Francis 20; America, 1831 778.5 p81
Brosnahan, Con. 23; Newfoundland, 1789 4915.24 p56
Brosnehane, Hugh; America, 1742 4971 p56
Broson, John; Philadelphia, 1850 53.26 p7
*Relative:*Mary Ann
Broson, John; Philadelphia, 1850 5704.8 p60
Broson, Mary Ann *SEE* Broson, John
Broson, Mary Ann 12; Philadelphia, 1850 5704.8 p60
Bross, Hans Jerg 21; Pennsylvania, 1753 2444 p143
Brosse, Dominick 27; New Orleans, 1823 778.5 p81
Brossel, John; Wisconsin, n.d. 9675.4 p266
Brossier, Mr.; America, 1839 778.5 p81
Brossmer, Elisabeth; Cincinnati, 1834 8582.2 p39
With parents & siblings
Brost, Nicholas; Wisconsin, n.d. 9675.4 p266
Brosters, Jane 20 *SEE* Brosters, Thomas
Brosters, Mary 18 *SEE* Brosters, Thomas
Brosters, Thomas 20; Philadelphia, 1833 53.26 p7
*Relative:*Mary 18
*Relative:*Jane 20
Brostrom, Gunnar; Arkansas, 1918 95.2 p23
Brot, Josephine 20; Louisiana, 1837 778.5 p81
Brother, Mr.; Quebec, 1815 9229.18 p75
Brother, Mathew; Pennsylvania, 1752 2444 p143
Brothers, Mr.; Quebec, 1815 9229.18 p79
Brothers, Mr.; Quebec, 1815 9229.18 p80
Brothers, John 19; Massachusetts, 1849 5881.1 p8
Brotherson, James; Wilmington, NC, 1794-1831 1639.20 p16
Brotherston, Hester; Virginia, 1636 6219 p7
Brotherton, Dennis; Virginia, 1635 6219 p35
Brotherton, Hen.; Virginia, 1637 6219 p11
Brotherton, Hen.; Virginia, 1637 6219 p114
Brotherton, Thomas 21; Maryland, 1775 1219.7 p266
Brott, Charles 64; New Orleans, 1822 778.5 p81
Brou, Antoine 31; New Orleans, 1838 778.5 p82
Brouard, Mr. 24; New Orleans, 1822 778.5 p82
Brouard, Nicolas-Martin; Quebec, 1817 7603 p47
Brouet, M. 28; New Orleans, 1837 778.5 p82
Brouget, Louis Francis 24; America, 1831 778.5 p82
Brough, George; Savannah, GA, 1774 1219.7 p227
Brough, Hugh; Ohio, 1868 9892.11 p6
Brough, Margery; Virginia, 1647 6219 p243
Brough, Mary 20; Massachusetts, 1849 5881.1 p10
Brough, Tho.; Virginia, 1635 6219 p17
Brougham, George 23; Maryland, 1774 1219.7 p220
Broughton, Banks 25; Virginia, 1774 1219.7 p193
Broughton, Charles; Iowa, 1866-1943 123.54 p11
Broughton, Edward; Virginia, 1638 6219 p120
Broughton, F. 75; Washington, 1916-1919 1728.4 p251
Broughton, Henry; Virginia, 1618 6219 p200
Broughton, J. 40; Washington, 1916-1919 1728.4 p251
Broughton, Joseph 20; Jamaica, 1738 3690.1 p28
Broughton, Thomas; Virginia, 1652 6251 p20
Broughton, Thomas 16; Jamaica, 1739 3690.1 p28
Broughton, William; Virginia, 1643 6219 p207
Broughton, William 18; Maryland, 1775 1219.7 p250
Broughton, Wm.; Virginia, 1638 6219 p149
Brouil, Elisabeth Davis; Quebec, 1761 7603 p26
Brouillet, Michel; Quebec, 1665 4533 p129
Brouse, Robert; Virginia, 1639 6219 p156
Brousque, Jacques; Quebec, 1800 7603 p21
Broussac, Dr. 45; New Orleans, 1837 778.5 p82
Broussard, Mr. 38; New Orleans, 1831 778.5 p82
Broussard, Louis 42; New Orleans, 1829 778.5 p82
Brousset, . . .; America, 1837 778.5 p82
Brousset, Mme. 37; America, 1837 778.5 p82
Brouster, James; Philadelphia, 1847 53.26 p7
*Relative:*Samuel 13
*Relative:*James 11
Brouster, James; Philadelphia, 1847 5704.8 p31
Brouster, James 11 *SEE* Brouster, James
Brouster, James 11; Philadelphia, 1847 5704.8 p31
Brouster, Joseph 16; Philadelphia, 1859 5704.8 p141
Brouster, Samuel 13 *SEE* Brouster, James
Brouster, Samuel 13; Philadelphia, 1847 5704.8 p31
Brout, Henry; New York, NY, 1856 2764.35 p8
Brouwer, Gerrit 2; New York, NY, 1847 3377.6 p14
Brouwer, Henrick 65; New York, NY, 1847 3377.6 p14
Brouwer, John 36; New York, NY, 1847 3377.6 p14
Brouwer, Mary 26; New York, NY, 1847 3377.6 p14
Broverman, Benjamin; Arkansas, 1918 95.2 p23
Brow, Eleanor 24; Philadelphia, 1774 1219.7 p196

Brow, Weston; Virginia, 1645 ***6219*** *p233*
Broward, Robert; Virginia, 1642 ***6219*** *p195*
Brower, Frederick; Virginia, 1844 ***4626.16*** *p12*
Browinski, . . .; New York, 1831 ***4606*** *p173*
Browitt, John; Iowa, 1866-1943 ***123.54*** *p11*
Brown, . . .; Canada, 1776-1783 ***9786*** *p18*
Brown, . . .; Virginia, 1738-1739 ***9898*** *p39*
With 3 siblings
Brown, Colonel; Virginia, 1738-1739 ***9898*** *p39*
Brown, Mr.; Quebec, 1815 ***9229.18*** *p76*
Brown, Mr. 36; Dominica, 1774 ***1219.7*** *p223*
Brown, Mrs.; Colombia, SC, 1830 ***1639.20*** *p17*
Brown, Mrs. 30; Boston, 1774 ***1219.7*** *p203*
Brown, A.; Minneapolis, 1873-1878 ***6410.35*** *p51*
Brown, Abraham 78; North Carolina, 1850 ***1639.20*** *p16*
Brown, Adam; Charleston, SC, 1804 ***1639.20*** *p17*
Brown, Adam 16; Windward Islands, 1722 ***3690.1*** *p28*
Brown, Agnes; Quebec, 1849 ***5704.8*** *p52*
Brown, Alex; New York, NY, 1811 ***2859.11*** *p9*
With family
Brown, Alexander; New York, 1831 ***9892.11*** *p6*
Brown, Alexander; Ohio, 1812-1840 ***9892.11*** *p6*
Brown, Alexander; Ohio, 1840 ***9892.11*** *p6*
Brown, Alexander; Philadelphia, 1864 ***5704.8*** *p174*
Brown, Alexander; Quebec, 1849 ***5704.8*** *p52*
Brown, Alexander; St. John, N.B., 1847 ***5704.8*** *p10*
Brown, Alexander 13; St. John, N.B., 1847 ***5704.8*** *p10*
Brown, Alexander 47; North Carolina, 1850 ***1639.20*** *p17*
*Relative:*Grace 47
Brown, Alfred Alexander; California, 1867 ***2769.1*** *p6*
Brown, Alice *SEE* Brown, Nicho.
Brown, Ambrose 19; West Indies, 1722 ***3690.1*** *p28*
Brown, Andrew; New Orleans, 1849 ***5704.8*** *p59*
Brown, Andrew; New York, NY, 1815 ***2859.11*** *p26*
Brown, Andrew; New York, NY, 1831 ***8208.4*** *p38*
Brown, Andrew Peter; Shreveport, LA, 1878 ***7129*** *p44*
Brown, Angus; North Carolina, 1770 ***1639.20*** *p17*
Brown, Ann; Philadelphia, 1811 ***53.26*** *p7*
Brown, Ann; Philadelphia, 1811 ***2859.11*** *p9*
Brown, Ann; Philadelphia, 1816 ***2859.11*** *p26*
Brown, Ann 21; America, 1705 ***2212*** *p42*
Brown, Ann 25; St. John, N.B., 1854 ***5704.8*** *p120*
Brown, Ann 60; Philadelphia, 1854 ***5704.8*** *p116*
Brown, Anne; New York, NY, 1816 ***2859.11*** *p26*
Brown, Anne; Philadelphia, 1864 ***5704.8*** *p186*
Brown, August 21; New Orleans, 1862 ***543.30*** *p245*
Brown, B.; Washington, 1859-1920 ***2872.1*** *p5*
Brown, Benjamin 21; Pennsylvania, 1728 ***3690.1*** *p28*
Brown, Bernard; New York, NY, 1816 ***2859.11*** *p26*
Brown, Biddy; Philadelphia, 1851 ***5704.8*** *p71*
Brown, Biddy 38; Philadelphia, 1803 ***53.26*** *p7*
Brown, Bridget 32; Massachusetts, 1860 ***6410.32*** *p105*
Brown, Buie Archibald; America, 1775 ***1639.20*** *p17*
Brown, C. B.; Washington, 1859-1920 ***2872.1*** *p5*
Brown, Caroline 2; Quebec, 1849 ***5704.8*** *p52*
Brown, Casper; South Carolina, 1788 ***7119*** *p198*
Brown, Catharina von Wehrt; Virginia, 1738-1739 ***9898*** *p39*
With daughter
Brown, Catharine; St. John, N.B., 1850 ***5704.8*** *p61*
Brown, Catherine 18; Philadelphia, 1855 ***5704.8*** *p124*
Brown, Catherine 22; St. John, N.B., 1853 ***5704.8*** *p110*
Brown, Cecilia 6; Quebec, 1849 ***5704.8*** *p52*
Brown, Charles; Boston, 1848 ***6410.32*** *p122*
Brown, Charles; New York, NY, 1866 ***5704.8*** *p213*
Brown, Charles; Washington, 1859-1920 ***2872.1*** *p5*
Brown, Charles 22; Massachusetts, 1850 ***5881.1*** *p7*
Brown, Charles 23; New Orleans, 1862 ***543.30*** *p244*
Brown, Charles 34; Massachusetts, 1860 ***6410.32*** *p101*
Brown, Charles Erick; Illinois, 1874 ***5012.39*** *p26*
Brown, Charles-Francis; Quebec, 1825 ***7603*** *p26*
Brown, Charles J. 25; Massachusetts, 1860 ***6410.32*** *p105*
Brown, Christopher; America, 1841 ***7036*** *p126*
Brown, Colin 23; Massachusetts, 1849 ***5881.1*** *p7*
Brown, Conrad; Philadelphia, 1760 ***9973.7*** *p34*
Brown, Daniel; Montreal, 1820 ***7603*** *p53*
Brown, Daniel 20; Pennsylvania, 1728 ***3690.1*** *p28*
Brown, Daniel 35; New Orleans, 1862 ***543.30*** *p482*
Brown, Dav. S., Jr. 26; New York, NY, 1893 ***9026.4*** *p41*
Brown, David; America, 1737 ***4971*** *p64*
Brown, David; New York, NY, 1811 ***2859.11*** *p9*
With family
Brown, David; Quebec, 1818 ***7603*** *p36*
Brown, David; St. John, N.B., 1847 ***5704.8*** *p32*
Brown, David 35; Philadelphia, 1774 ***1219.7*** *p232*
Brown, Debora; Virginia, 1647 ***6219*** *p244*
Brown, Dennis 18; West Indies, 1722 ***3690.1*** *p28*
Brown, Duncan; North Carolina, 1804 ***1639.20*** *p17*
Brown, Duncan 23; St. John, N.B., 1866 ***5704.8*** *p166*
Brown, Duncan 24; St. John, N.B., 1866 ***5704.8*** *p166*
Brown, E. E.; Washington, 1859-1920 ***2872.1*** *p5*
Brown, E. L.; Washington, 1859-1920 ***2872.1*** *p5*
Brown, Edw.; Philadelphia, 1816 ***2859.11*** *p26*
Brown, Edward 5; Philadelphia, 1853 ***5704.8*** *p111*
Brown, Edward 35; Philadelphia, 1853 ***5704.8*** *p111*
Brown, Edward 45; Massachusetts, 1849 ***5881.1*** *p7*
Brown, Eliza. *SEE* Brown, Wm.
Brown, Eliza; Philadelphia, 1848 ***53.26*** *p7*
Brown, Eliza; Philadelphia, 1848 ***5704.8*** *p40*
Brown, Eliza; Philadelphia, 1853 ***5704.8*** *p103*
Brown, Eliza; Quebec, 1847 ***5704.8*** *p12*
Brown, Eliza Ann; Philadelphia, 1853 ***5704.8*** *p100*
Brown, Eliza Jane; St. John, N.B., 1847 ***5704.8*** *p10*
Brown, Elizabeth 3 mos; Quebec, 1853 ***5704.8*** *p104*
Brown, Elizabeth 8; New York, NY, 1867 ***5704.8*** *p224*
Brown, Elizabeth 19; Maryland, 1775 ***1219.7*** *p266*
Brown, Elizabeth 20; Pennsylvania, 1720 ***3690.1*** *p28*
Brown, Elizabeth 22; Maryland, 1775 ***1219.7*** *p262*
Brown, Elizabeth 30; Maryland, 1775 ***1219.7*** *p257*
Brown, Ellen; Philadelphia, 1850 ***53.26*** *p7*
Brown, Ellen; Philadelphia, 1850 ***5704.8*** *p65*
Brown, Ellen; Philadelphia, 1853 ***5704.8*** *p102*
Brown, Ellen; Philadelphia, 1864 ***5704.8*** *p180*
Brown, Ellen 39; Massachusetts, 1860 ***6410.32*** *p101*
Brown, Esther; Philadelphia, 1852 ***5704.8*** *p89*
Brown, Frances Edward 30; Kansas, 1891 ***5240.1*** *p76*
Brown, Francis; New York, NY, 1811 ***2859.11*** *p9*
Brown, Francis; Philadelphia, 1850 ***53.26*** *p7*
Brown, Francis; Philadelphia, 1850 ***5704.8*** *p68*
Brown, Francis 20; St. Kitts, 1775 ***1219.7*** *p275*
Brown, Frank J. 38; Arizona, 1890 ***2764.35*** *p4*
Brown, Frederich; Illinois, 1856 ***7857*** *p2*
Brown, G. B. 23; Kansas, 1904 ***5240.1*** *p83*
Brown, Geo.; New York, NY, 1811 ***2859.11*** *p9*
With wife & 7 children
Brown, George; St. John, N.B., 1847 ***5704.8*** *p15*
Brown, George 18; Maryland, 1719 ***3690.1*** *p28*
Brown, George 18; Maryland, 1774 ***1219.7*** *p207*
Brown, George 21; Jamaica, 1736 ***3690.1*** *p29*
Brown, George 21; Maryland, 1731 ***3690.1*** *p29*
Brown, George 45; Charleston, SC, 1850 ***1639.20*** *p17*
*Relative:*Margaret 32
Brown, George H.; Washington, 1859-1920 ***2872.1*** *p5*
Brown, Giley 40; Philadelphia, 1853 ***5704.8*** *p111*
Brown, Grace 18; Philadelphia, 1855 ***5704.8*** *p123*
Brown, Grace 47 *SEE* Brown, Alexander
Brown, Henry; New York, NY, 1811 ***2859.11*** *p9*
Brown, Henry; New York, NY, 1836 ***8208.4*** *p19*
Brown, Henry 35; Maryland, 1774 ***1219.7*** *p187*
Brown, Hishersay 18; Jamaica, 1731 ***3690.1*** *p29*
Brown, Hugh; Ohio, 1840 ***9892.11*** *p6*
Brown, Hugh 10; Philadelphia, 1855 ***5704.8*** *p124*
Brown, Iain; Philadelphia, 1852 ***5704.8*** *p85*
Brown, Isabell; South Carolina, 1767 ***1639.20*** *p17*
Brown, Isabella; Philadelphia, 1865 ***5704.8*** *p202*
Brown, Isabella 18; Philadelphia, 1853 ***5704.8*** *p113*
Brown, Ithama 8; Massachusetts, 1849 ***5881.1*** *p8*
Brown, J. Giles; Illinois, 1859 ***7857*** *p2*
Brown, Jacob; Boston, 1841 ***6410.32*** *p123*
Brown, Jacob; New York, NY, 1835 ***8208.4*** *p36*
Brown, Jacob 30?; New Orleans, 1862 ***543.30*** *p326*
Brown, Jacob 40; Massachusetts, 1860 ***6410.32*** *p105*
Brown, James *SEE* Brown, William
Brown, James; Austin, TX, 1886 ***9777*** *p5*
Brown, James; Colorado, 1889 ***9678.1*** *p155*
Brown, James; New Brunswick, 1808 ***9775.5*** *p205*
Brown, James; New Brunswick, 1824 ***7603*** *p60*
Brown, James; New York, NY, 1811 ***2859.11*** *p9*
Brown, James; New York, NY, 1815 ***2859.11*** *p26*
Brown, James; New York, NY, 1816 ***2859.11*** *p26*
Brown, James; New York, NY, 1832 ***8208.4*** *p41*
Brown, James; New York, NY, 1835 ***8208.4*** *p46*
Brown, James; New York, NY, 1839 ***8208.4*** *p92*
Brown, James; Philadelphia, 1816 ***2859.11*** *p26*
Brown, James; Philadelphia, 1850 ***5704.8*** *p65*
Brown, James; Philadelphia, 1851 ***5704.8*** *p71*
Brown, James; Quebec, 1847 ***5704.8*** *p7*
Brown, James; Quebec, 1847 ***5704.8*** *p16*
Brown, James; Quebec, 1853 ***5704.8*** *p104*
Brown, James 4; Massachusetts, 1849 ***5881.1*** *p8*
Brown, James 4; Quebec, 1849 ***5704.8*** *p52*
Brown, James 11; Quebec, 1848 ***5704.8*** *p41*
Brown, James 13; Quebec, 1847 ***5704.8*** *p7*
Brown, James 17; America, 1705 ***2212*** *p42*
Brown, James 17; Nova Scotia, 1774 ***1219.7*** *p194*
Brown, James 20; Jamaica, 1724 ***3690.1*** *p29*
Brown, James 21; America, 1702 ***2212*** *p38*
Brown, James 22; New York, 1774 ***1219.7*** *p203*
*Wife:*Mary 25
Brown, James 23; Maryland, 1774 ***1219.7*** *p208*
Brown, James 23; St. John, N.B., 1866 ***5704.8*** *p167*
Brown, James 24; Maryland, 1735 ***3690.1*** *p29*
Brown, James 30; Massachusetts, 1847 ***5881.1*** *p8*
Brown, James 30; New Orleans, 1862 ***543.30*** *p245*
Brown, James 50; Philadelphia, 1855 ***5704.8*** *p123*
Brown, James A.; Ohio, 1860 ***9892.11*** *p6*
Brown, James C.; New York, NY, 1835 ***8208.4*** *p5*
Brown, Jane; New York, NY, 1815 ***2859.11*** *p26*
Brown, Jane; Philadelphia, 1852 ***5704.8*** *p89*
Brown, Jane; Quebec, 1847 ***5704.8*** *p7*
Brown, Jane; Quebec, 1853 ***5704.8*** *p104*
Brown, Jane; St. John, N.B., 1850 ***5704.8*** *p61*
Brown, Jane 1 *SEE* Brown, William
Brown, Jane 6; Quebec, 1847 ***5704.8*** *p7*
Brown, Jane 7; St. John, N.B., 1847 ***5704.8*** *p10*
Brown, Jane 21 *SEE* Brown, William
Brown, Jane 24; St. John, N.B., 1857 ***5704.8*** *p134*
Brown, Jemima 13; Quebec, 1848 ***5704.8*** *p41*
Brown, Joanna; Montreal, 1823 ***7603*** *p100*
Brown, John; America, 1736-1743 ***4971*** *p58*
Brown, John; America, 1741 ***4971*** *p16*
Brown, John; Illinois, 1866 ***2896.5*** *p6*
Brown, John; New York, NY, 1811 ***2859.11*** *p9*
Brown, John; New York, NY, 1811 ***2859.11*** *p9*
With family
Brown, John; New York, NY, 1815 ***2859.11*** *p26*
Brown, John; New York, NY, 1816 ***2859.11*** *p26*
Brown, John; Quebec, 1847 ***5704.8*** *p7*
Brown, John; Quebec, 1851 ***5704.8*** *p73*
Brown, John; San Francisco, 1852 ***6013.19*** *p90*
Brown, John; Virginia, 1646 ***6219*** *p238*
*Wife:*Ursula
Brown, John; Virginia, 1698 ***2212*** *p14*
Brown, John 10; Philadelphia, 1865 ***5704.8*** *p191*
Brown, John 10; St. John, N.B., 1854 ***5704.8*** *p120*
Brown, John 11; St. John, N.B., 1847 ***5704.8*** *p10*
Brown, John 12; Philadelphia, 1855 ***5704.8*** *p123*
Brown, John 15; Maryland, 1718 ***3690.1*** *p29*
Brown, John 17; Maryland, 1719 ***3690.1*** *p29*
Brown, John 17; Philadelphia, 1774 ***1219.7*** *p232*
Brown, John 18; Charleston, SC, 1774 ***1639.20*** *p17*
Brown, John 18; Maryland, 1720 ***3690.1*** *p29*
Brown, John 20; Port uncertain, 1774 ***1219.7*** *p176*
Brown, John 21; Maryland, 1774 ***1219.7*** *p215*
Brown, John 21; Virginia, 1775 ***1219.7*** *p261*
Brown, John 22; Maryland, 1774 ***1219.7*** *p191*
Brown, John 22; Virginia, 1774 ***1219.7*** *p191*
Brown, John 23; Philadelphia, 1774 ***1219.7*** *p182*
Brown, John 23; Virginia, 1774 ***1219.7*** *p239*
Brown, John 24; Massachusetts, 1848 ***5881.1*** *p8*
Brown, John 25; Philadelphia, 1853 ***5704.8*** *p109*
Brown, John 25; St. John, N.B., 1866 ***5704.8*** *p167*
Brown, John 26; New Orleans, 1862 ***543.30*** *p117*
Brown, John 26; Norfolk, VA, 1774 ***1219.7*** *p222*
Brown, John 30; New York, 1775 ***1219.7*** *p268*
Brown, John 33; Maryland, 1774 ***1219.7*** *p208*
Brown, John C. 39; New Orleans, 1862 ***543.30*** *p244*
Brown, John George; America, 1848 ***1450.2*** *p20A*
Brown, John Henry; Illinois, 1898 ***2896.5*** *p6*
Brown, John Joseph; New York, NY, 1835 ***8208.4*** *p44*
Brown, John Jost; America, 1848 ***1450.2*** *p21A*
Brown, John L. 65; Arizona, 1904 ***9228.40*** *p5*
Brown, John P.; New York, NY, 1837 ***8208.4*** *p52*
Brown, John William; America, 1848 ***1450.2*** *p21A*
Brown, Jonathan 23; Maryland, 1727 ***3690.1*** *p29*
Brown, Jonathan 26; Jamaica, 1736 ***3690.1*** *p29*
Brown, Joseph Henry; Arkansas, 1918 ***95.2*** *p23*
Brown, Joseph Henry; Arkansas, 1918 ***95.2*** *p69*
Brown, Joshua; New York, NY, 1815 ***2859.11*** *p26*
Brown, Julia; New York, NY, 1815 ***2859.11*** *p26*
Brown, Katherine 26; Wilmington, NC, 1774 ***1639.20*** *p75*
Brown, L. P.; Washington, 1859-1920 ***2872.1*** *p5*
Brown, Lydia 18; Philadelphia, 1854 ***5704.8*** *p116*
Brown, Miss M. 20; New York, NY, 1893 ***9026.4*** *p41*
Brown, Mabel; Philadelphia, 1865 ***5704.8*** *p182*
Brown, Mabel; Philadelphia, 1865 ***5704.8*** *p190*
Brown, Malcolm; Charleston, SC, 1795 ***1639.20*** *p17*
Brown, Manis 11; Philadelphia, 1853 ***5704.8*** *p111*
Brown, Margaret *SEE* Brown, William
Brown, Margaret; New York, NY, 1815 ***2859.11*** *p26*
With child
Brown, Margaret; New York, NY, 1867 ***5704.8*** *p224*
Brown, Margaret; Philadelphia, 1847 ***53.26*** *p7*
Brown, Margaret; Philadelphia, 1847 ***5704.8*** *p23*
Brown, Margaret; Philadelphia, 1850 ***5704.8*** *p65*
Brown, Margaret; Quebec, 1847 ***5704.8*** *p17*
Brown, Margaret; Quebec, 1849 ***5704.8*** *p51*
Brown, Margaret; Quebec, 1851 ***5704.8*** *p75*
Brown, Margaret 6; Quebec, 1847 ***5704.8*** *p17*
Brown, Margaret 10; New York, NY, 1867 ***5704.8*** *p224*
Brown, Margaret 19; Georgia, 1775 ***1219.7*** *p277*
Brown, Margaret 22; St. John, N.B., 1866 ***5704.8*** *p167*
Brown, Margaret 24; Massachusetts, 1848 ***5881.1*** *p9*
Brown, Margaret 32 *SEE* Brown, George
Brown, Margaret 38; Massachusetts, 1860 ***6410.32*** *p105*
Brown, Margaret 40; St. John, N.B., 1859 ***5704.8*** *p140*
Brown, Margtte 18; America, 1699 ***2212*** *p29*
Brown, Maria; New York, NY, 1864 ***5704.8*** *p169*

Brown, Martha 5; Quebec, 1848 ***5704.8*** *p42*
Brown, Martha 8; Quebec, 1849 ***5704.8*** *p52*
Brown, Martin 26; New Orleans, 1862 ***543.30*** *p481*
Brown, Mary; Canada, 1841 ***7036*** *p124*
With brother
Brown, Mary; Massachusetts, 1841 ***7036*** *p124*
With brother
Brown, Mary; New York, NY, 1816 ***2859.11*** *p26*
Brown, Mary; New York, NY, 1867 ***5704.8*** *p224*
Brown, Mary; Philadelphia, 1849 ***53.26*** *p7*
Brown, Mary; Philadelphia, 1849 ***5704.8*** *p52*
Brown, Mary; Philadelphia, 1850 ***53.26*** *p7*
Brown, Mary; Philadelphia, 1850 ***5704.8*** *p61*
Brown, Mary; Philadelphia, 1853 ***5704.8*** *p103*
Brown, Mary; Quebec, 1849 ***5704.8*** *p51*
Brown, Mary; St. John, N.B., 1850 ***5704.8*** *p61*
Brown, Mary 13; St. John, N.B., 1859 ***5704.8*** *p140*
Brown, Mary 19; America, 1706 ***2212*** *p47*
Brown, Mary 20; Philadelphia, 1864 ***5704.8*** *p157*
Brown, Mary 21; Maryland, 1775 ***1219.7*** *p267*
Brown, Mary 25 *SEE* Brown, James
Brown, Mary 26; Nova Scotia, 1774 ***1219.7*** *p194*
Brown, Mathew; New York, NY, 1816 ***2859.11*** *p26*
Brown, Mathew 31; Kansas, 1887 ***5240.1*** *p70*
Brown, Matilda 10; St. John, N.B., 1847 ***5704.8*** *p32*
Brown, Matthew 18; Philadelphia, 1804 ***53.26*** *p7*
Brown, Michael; Philadelphia, 1865 ***5704.8*** *p176*
Brown, Michael 20; Philadelphia, 1859 ***5704.8*** *p142*
Brown, Michael 35; St. John, N.B., 1857 ***5704.8*** *p134*
Brown, Moses; Quebec, 1825 ***7603*** *p101*
Brown, Moses; Washington, 1859-1920 ***2872.1*** *p5*
Brown, Nancy 50; Philadelphia, 1853 ***5704.8*** *p112*
Brown, Nathaniel 21; Maryland, 1724 ***3690.1*** *p29*
Brown, Nicho.; Virginia, 1648 ***6219*** *p250*
*Wife:*Alice
Brown, Patience; Virginia, 1649 ***6219*** *p252*
Brown, Patrick; Philadelphia, 1816 ***2859.11*** *p26*
Brown, Patrick; Philadelphia, 1848 ***53.26*** *p8*
Brown, Patrick; Philadelphia, 1848 ***5704.8*** *p40*
Brown, Patrick; Philadelphia, 1849 ***53.26*** *p8*
Brown, Patrick; Philadelphia, 1849 ***5704.8*** *p50*
Brown, Patrick; St. John, N.B., 1853 ***5704.8*** *p107*
Brown, Patrick 20; Massachusetts, 1849 ***5881.1*** *p11*
Brown, Patrick 21; St. John, N.B., 1864 ***5704.8*** *p157*
Brown, Paul; Arkansas, 1918 ***95.2*** *p23*
Brown, Paul 24; Philadelphia, 1774 ***1219.7*** *p190*
Brown, Peter; Cape Fear, NC, 1752 ***1639.20*** *p17*
Brown, Peter; New York, NY, 1889 ***1450.2*** *p5B*
Brown, Peter 21; Massachusetts, 1848 ***5881.1*** *p11*
Brown, Peter 35; Massachusetts, 1860 ***6410.32*** *p119*
Brown, Philip; America, 1837 ***1450.2*** *p21A*
Brown, Philip; Philadelphia, 1756 ***9973.7*** *p32*
Brown, Pierre 22; Montreal, 1778 ***7603*** *p92*
Brown, Rachel; New York, NY, 1811 ***2859.11*** *p9*
Brown, Rebecca; Philadelphia, 1866 ***5704.8*** *p209*
Brown, Rebecca; St. John, N.B., 1847 ***5704.8*** *p10*
Brown, Rebecca; St. John, N.B., 1847 ***5704.8*** *p32*
Brown, Rebecca 12; St. John, N.B., 1847 ***5704.8*** *p32*
Brown, Richard; New England, 1840 ***7036*** *p119*
Brown, Richard; United States or West Indies, 1721 ***3690.1*** *p30*
Brown, Richard 15; Maryland, 1720 ***3690.1*** *p30*
Brown, Richard 15; West Indies, 1722 ***3690.1*** *p30*
Brown, Richard 27; Maryland, 1774 ***1219.7*** *p187*
Brown, Robert; Charleston, SC, 1796-1800 ***1639.20*** *p18*
Brown, Robert; Philadelphia, 1852 ***5704.8*** *p85*
Brown, Robert; Philadelphia, 1864 ***5704.8*** *p179*
Brown, Robert; St. John, N.B., 1853 ***5704.8*** *p109*
Brown, Robert 10; Quebec, 1849 ***5704.8*** *p52*
Brown, Robert 19; Maryland, 1731 ***3690.1*** *p30*
Brown, Robert 25; St. John, N.B., 1856 ***5704.8*** *p131*
Brown, Robert 28; Jamaica, 1734 ***3690.1*** *p30*
Brown, Robert 32; Grenada, 1773 ***1219.7*** *p173*
Brown, Rose; Philadelphia, 1868 ***5704.8*** *p230*
Brown, Rose; Quebec, 1851 ***5704.8*** *p75*
Brown, Rosetta; St. John, N.B., 1847 ***5704.8*** *p10*
Brown, Samuel *SEE* Brown, William
Brown, Samuel; New York, NY, 1816 ***2859.11*** *p26*
Brown, Samuel; Philadelphia, 1850 ***5704.8*** *p65*
Brown, Samuel 6 mos; St. John, N.B., 1847 ***5704.8*** *p10*
Brown, Samuel 18; Pennsylvania, Virginia or Maryland, 1719 ***3690.1*** *p30*
Brown, Samuel 19; Virginia, 1774 ***1219.7*** *p238*
Brown, Samuel 20; Philadelphia, 1859 ***5704.8*** *p141*
Brown, Samuel S.; Charleston, SC, 1798 ***1639.20*** *p18*
Brown, Sarah 7; Quebec, 1848 ***5704.8*** *p41*
Brown, Sarah 16; Quebec, 1853 ***5704.8*** *p104*
Brown, Sarah 25; St. John, N.B., 1856 ***5704.8*** *p131*
Brown, Sarah Jane; Philadelphia, 1852 ***5704.8*** *p85*
Brown, Seth; New York, NY, 1815 ***2859.11*** *p26*
Brown, Solomon; New York, NY, 1836 ***6410.32*** *p122*
Brown, Stephen 37; Pennsylvania, 1738 ***2444*** *p143*
Brown, Susan 8; Quebec, 1847 ***5704.8*** *p17*
Brown, Susanna 20; Philadelphia, 1774 ***1219.7*** *p190*
Brown, Thom 15; America, 1706 ***2212*** *p46*
Brown, Thomas; America, 1837 ***1450.2*** *p21A*
Brown, Thomas; America, 1865 ***5704.8*** *p199*
Brown, Thomas; Colorado, 1894 ***9678.1*** *p155*
Brown, Thomas; New Jersey, 1834 ***8208.4*** *p47*
Brown, Thomas; New York, NY, 1867 ***5704.8*** *p224*
Brown, Thomas; Philadelphia, 1815 ***2859.11*** *p26*
Brown, Thomas; Quebec, 1848 ***5704.8*** *p41*
Brown, Thomas; St. John, N.B., 1847 ***5704.8*** *p10*
Brown, Thomas 1; Massachusetts, 1849 ***5881.1*** *p12*
Brown, Thomas 2; Quebec, 1847 ***5704.8*** *p17*
Brown, Thomas 9; Quebec, 1847 ***5704.8*** *p7*
Brown, Thomas 16; Maryland, 1719 ***3690.1*** *p30*
Brown, Thomas 17; Virginia, 1749 ***3690.1*** *p30*
Brown, Thomas 19; Jamaica, 1733 ***3690.1*** *p30*
Brown, Thomas 20; Jamaica, 1730 ***3690.1*** *p30*
Brown, Thomas 20; Maryland, 1719 ***3690.1*** *p30*
Brown, Thomas 22; Maryland, 1774 ***1219.7*** *p230*
Brown, Thomas 22; Philadelphia, 1774 ***1219.7*** *p182*
Brown, Thomas 24; Maryland, 1730 ***3690.1*** *p30*
Brown, Thomas 29; Virginia, 1774 ***1219.7*** *p226*
Brown, Ursula *SEE* Brown, John
Brown, W. G.; Illinois, 1891 ***5012.39*** *p53*
Brown, W. S.; Iowa, 1866-1943 ***123.54*** *p11*
Brown, William; Antigua (Antego), 1758 ***1219.7*** *p63*
Brown, William; Colorado, 1890 ***9678.1*** *p155*
Brown, William; New York, NY, 1811 ***2859.11*** *p9*
Brown, William; New York, NY, 1816 ***2859.11*** *p26*
Brown, William; New York, NY, 1833 ***8208.4*** *p59*
Brown, William; New York, NY, 1837 ***8208.4*** *p29*
Brown, William; Ohio, 1822 ***9892.11*** *p6*
Brown, William; Ohio, 1838 ***9892.11*** *p6*
Brown, William; Philadelphia, 1847 ***53.26*** *p8*
Brown, William; Philadelphia, 1847 ***5704.8*** *p22*
Brown, William; Philadelphia, 1850 ***53.26*** *p8*
*Relative:*Margaret
*Relative:*James
*Relative:*Samuel
Brown, William; Philadelphia, 1850 ***5704.8*** *p65*
Brown, William; Philadelphia, 1865 ***5704.8*** *p190*
Brown, William; Philadelphia, 1867 ***5704.8*** *p221*
Brown, William; Quebec, 1764 ***9775.5*** *p203*
Brown, William; Quebec, 1814 ***7603*** *p21*
Brown, William; Quebec, 1847 ***5704.8*** *p8*
Brown, William; St. John, N.B., 1847 ***5704.8*** *p32*
Brown, William; St. John, N.B., 1847 ***5704.8*** *p34*
Brown, William; Toronto, n.d. ***9775.5*** *p216*
Brown, William; Virginia, 1642 ***6219*** *p187*
Brown, William; Wisconsin, n.d. ***9675.4*** *p266*
Brown, William 11; Quebec, 1847 ***5704.8*** *p7*
Brown, William 12; Quebec, 1849 ***5704.8*** *p52*
Brown, William 12; Quebec, 1853 ***5704.8*** *p104*
Brown, William 15; Philadelphia, 1775 ***1219.7*** *p259*
Brown, William 17; St. John, N.B., 1867 ***5704.8*** *p168*
Brown, William 18; Philadelphia, 1858 ***5704.8*** *p139*
Brown, William 18; Virginia, 1751 ***1219.7*** *p4*
Brown, William 18; Virginia, 1751 ***3690.1*** *p31*
Brown, William 20; Maryland, 1722 ***3690.1*** *p30*
Brown, William 21; Jamaica, 1735 ***3690.1*** *p31*
Brown, William 21; Jamaica, 1774 ***1219.7*** *p232*
Brown, William 21; Maryland, 1775 ***1219.7*** *p267*
Brown, William 21; Quebec, 1864 ***5704.8*** *p164*
Brown, William 22; Nova Scotia, 1774 ***1219.7*** *p194*
*Wife:*Jane 21
*Child:*Jane 1
Brown, William 22; Philadelphia, 1774 ***1219.7*** *p189*
Brown, William 25; Jamaica, 1776 ***1219.7*** *p281*
Brown, William 25; Maryland, 1736 ***3690.1*** *p31*
Brown, William 26; Kansas, 1888 ***5240.1*** *p71*
Brown, William 27; Massachusetts, 1849 ***5881.1*** *p12*
Brown, William 27; New Orleans, 1862 ***543.30*** *p484*
Brown, William 30; New Orleans, 1862 ***543.30*** *p109*
Brown, William 30; Philadelphia, 1833-1834 ***53.26*** *p8*
Brown, William 39; New Orleans, 1862 ***543.30*** *p116*
Brown, William 47; Tortola, 1776 ***1219.7*** *p282*
Brown, William 54; Kansas, 1881 ***5240.1*** *p63*
Brown, William Louie; Iowa, 1866-1943 ***123.54*** *p57*
Brown, Wm.; Austin, TX, 1886 ***9777*** *p5*
Brown, Wm.; Virginia, 1647 ***6219*** *p244*
*Wife:*Eliza.
Brown, Wm 28; New Orleans, 1864 ***543.30*** *p247*
Brown, Wm. H.; Iowa, 1866-1943 ***123.54*** *p11*
Browne, Ann; Virginia, 1634 ***6219*** *p84*
Browne, Anne; Philadelphia, 1866 ***5704.8*** *p210*
Browne, Antho.; Virginia, 1635 ***6219*** *p72*
Browne, Bridget *SEE* Browne, Patrick
Browne, Bridget; Philadelphia, 1811 ***2859.11*** *p9*
Browne, Catharine; Philadelphia, 1850 ***5704.8*** *p60*
Browne, Catherine; Philadelphia, 1850 ***53.26*** *p8*
Browne, Christopher; Virginia, 1642 ***6219*** *p189*
Browne, Cormick; New York, NY, 1864 ***5704.8*** *p185*
Browne, Daniel; Philadelphia, 1866 ***5704.8*** *p210*
Browne, Edward; Virginia, 1637 ***6219*** *p108*
Browne, Eliza.; Virginia, 1635 ***6219*** *p12*
Browne, Eliza; Virginia, 1638 ***6219*** *p11*
Browne, Elizabeth; America, 1741 ***4971*** *p16*
Browne, Ellen; Philadelphia, 1866 ***5704.8*** *p204*
Browne, Ellen; Virginia, 1642 ***6219*** *p189*
Browne, Ellin; Virginia, 1643 ***6219*** *p199*
Browne, Esther 25; Wilmington, DE, 1831 ***6508.7*** *p161*
Browne, George; Virginia, 1639 ***6219*** *p152*
Browne, Giles; Virginia, 1641 ***6219*** *p187*
Browne, Henry; Virginia, 1643 ***6219*** *p207*
Browne, Humph.; Virginia, 1636 ***6219*** *p21*
Browne, James; New York, NY, 1866 ***5704.8*** *p211*
Browne, Jno; Barbados, 1698 ***2212*** *p5*
Browne, Joan; America, 1737 ***4971*** *p45*
Browne, Joan; America, 1738 ***4971*** *p46*
Browne, John; New York, NY, 1816 ***2859.11*** *p26*
Browne, John; Virginia, 1636 ***6219*** *p7*
Browne, John; Virginia, 1636 ***6219*** *p80*
Browne, John; Virginia, 1642 ***6219*** *p187*
With wife
Browne, Jon.; Virginia, 1637 ***6219*** *p82*
Browne, Jos.; Virginia, 1635 ***6219*** *p22*
Browne, Joyce; Virginia, 1643 ***6219*** *p204*
Browne, Martha; Philadelphia, 1864 ***5704.8*** *p178*
Browne, Mary; Philadelphia, 1811 ***53.26*** *p8*
Browne, Mary; Philadelphia, 1811 ***2859.11*** *p9*
Browne, Mary J.; Philadelphia, 1864 ***5704.8*** *p178*
Browne, Nancy; America, 1867 ***5704.8*** *p219*
Browne, Nicholas; Virginia, 1636 ***6219*** *p78*
Browne, Nicholas; Virginia, 1642 ***6219*** *p198*
Browne, Patrick; Philadelphia, 1811 ***53.26*** *p8*
*Relative:*Bridget
Browne, Patrick; Philadelphia, 1811 ***2859.11*** *p9*
Browne, Randall; Virginia, 1637 ***6219*** *p82*
Browne, Randall; Virginia, 1637 ***6219*** *p109*
Browne, Rich.; Virginia, 1642 ***6219*** *p195*
Browne, Richard; Virginia, 1648 ***6219*** *p251*
Browne, Robert; Virginia, 1618 ***6219*** *p12*
Browne, Robert; Virginia, 1636 ***6219*** *p80*
Browne, Robert; Virginia, 1637 ***6219*** *p107*
Browne, Robert; Virginia, 1639 ***6219*** *p162*
Browne, Robert; Virginia, 1643 ***6219*** *p201*
Browne, Robert 21; Wilmington, DE, 1831 ***6508.7*** *p161*
Browne, Robt.; Virginia, 1635 ***6219*** *p12*
Browne, Samuell 16; Virginia, 1700 ***2212*** *p32*
Browne, Sarah; Virginia, 1639 ***6219*** *p154*
Browne, Stephen; Virginia, 1634 ***6219*** *p84*
Browne, Tho.; Virginia, 1637 ***6219*** *p13*
Browne, Tho.; Virginia, 1637 ***6219*** *p84*
Browne, Tho.; Virginia, 1638 ***6219*** *p18*
Browne, Tho.; Virginia, 1638 ***6219*** *p123*
Browne, Thomas; New York, NY, 1867 ***5704.8*** *p222*
Browne, Thomas; Philadelphia, 1853 ***5704.8*** *p103*
Browne, Thomas; Virginia, 1635 ***6219*** *p70*
Browne, Thomas; Virginia, 1636 ***6219*** *p180*
Browne, Thomas; Virginia, 1637 ***6219*** *p108*
Browne, Thomas; Virginia, 1639 ***6219*** *p162*
Browne, Thomas; Virginia, 1641 ***6219*** *p185*
Browne, Thomas 16; Philadelphia, 1860 ***5704.8*** *p145*
Browne, William; Virginia, 1642 ***6219*** *p187*
Browne, Wm.; Virginia, 1635 ***6219*** *p20*
Browne, Wm.; Virginia, 1642 ***6219*** *p191*
Browne, Wm.; Virginia, 1643 ***6219*** *p200*
Brownell, James Washington; Washington, 1859-1920 ***2872.1*** *p5*
Brownell, Mary; Washington, 1859-1920 ***2872.1*** *p5*
Brownelofe, John; Virginia, 1638 ***6219*** *p125*
Brownhead, Mr.; Quebec, 1815 ***9229.18*** *p79*
Browning, Elizabeth 18; America, 1728 ***3690.1*** *p31*
Browning, Elizabeth 20; Pennsylvania, 1731 ***3690.1*** *p31*
Browning, Geo.; Virginia, 1635 ***6219*** *p71*
Browning, Henry Bird; New York, NY, 1838 ***8208.4*** *p71*
Browning, Jon.; Virginia, 1635 ***6219*** *p26*
Browning, Joseph 36; Maryland, 1774 ***1219.7*** *p191*
Browning, Mary 18; Maryland or Virginia, 1720 ***3690.1*** *p31*
Browning, Richard 21; Maryland, 1774 ***1219.7*** *p187*
Browning, Thomas H.; Colorado, 1903 ***9678.1*** *p156*
Browning, William 16; Maryland, 1775 ***1219.7*** *p272*
Browning, William 21; Maryland, 1775 ***1219.7*** *p266*
Brownlee, Anne 19; Quebec, 1856 ***5704.8*** *p130*
Brownlee, Jane 11; Quebec, 1856 ***5704.8*** *p130*
Brownlee, Lavina 7; America, 1868 ***5704.8*** *p228*
Brownlee, Mary 18; Quebec, 1856 ***5704.8*** *p130*
Brownlee, Mary Ann 5; America, 1868 ***5704.8*** *p228*
Brownlee, Oliver; New York, NY, 1837 ***8208.4*** *p36*
Brownlee, Susan; America, 1868 ***5704.8*** *p228*
Brownlow, Eliza; Quebec, 1847 ***5704.8*** *p12*
Brownlow, Joseph 12; Quebec, 1847 ***5704.8*** *p12*
Brownlow, Mary Ann; Quebec, 1847 ***5704.8*** *p12*
Brownlow, Nancy; Philadelphia, 1853 ***5704.8*** *p108*
Brownlow, Sarah; Quebec, 1847 ***5704.8*** *p12*

Brownlow, Sarah 10; Quebec, 1847 ***5704.8*** *p12*
Brownlow, Thomas 22; Jamaica, 1730 ***3690.1*** *p31*
Brownlow, William; Quebec, 1847 ***5704.8*** *p12*
Brownridge, Math.; Virginia, 1637 ***6219*** *p11*
Brownrig, John 48; Ohio, 1840 ***9892.11*** *p6*
Brownser, Tho.; Virginia, 1635 ***6219*** *p69*
Brownworth, Valentin; America, 1840 ***1450.2*** *p21A*
Browson, Geo.; Virginia, 1643 ***6219*** *p200*
Broyer, Christian H.; Illinois, 1900 ***2896.5*** *p5*
Brozolis, John James; Arkansas, 1918 ***95.2*** *p23*
Brozovic, Nick; Iowa, 1866-1943 ***123.54*** *p11*
Brozzalle, Guiseppi; Iowa, 1866-1943 ***123.54*** *p11*
Brtisch, Philipp 24; New Orleans, 1862 ***543.30*** *p327*
Bru, Mr. 6; New Orleans, 1839 ***778.5*** *p82*
Bru, Mr. 36; New Orleans, 1839 ***778.5*** *p82*
Brubacher, Isaak; Charleston, SC, 1775-1781 ***8582.2*** *p52*
Bruce, Mrs. 30; Dominica, 1773 ***1219.7*** *p174*
Bruce, Anne; Quebec, 1852 ***5704.8*** *p87*
Bruce, David; Philadelphia, 1741 ***3652*** *p53*
Bruce, Eliza; Quebec, 1852 ***5704.8*** *p87*
Bruce, Eliza Jane 7; Quebec, 1852 ***5704.8*** *p87*
Bruce, George 35; Dominica, 1773 ***1219.7*** *p173*
Bruce, James; Quebec, 1847 ***5704.8*** *p29*
Bruce, James; Quebec, 1852 ***5704.8*** *p87*
Bruce, James 5; Quebec, 1852 ***5704.8*** *p87*
Bruce, John 15; Philadelphia, 1774 ***1219.7*** *p216*
Bruce, Robert 3; Quebec, 1852 ***5704.8*** *p87*
Bruce, Robert 34; New England, 1774 ***1219.7*** *p203*
Bruce, William; America, 1739 ***4971*** *p66*
Bruce, William; New York, NY, 1815 ***2859.11*** *p26*
Bruce, William; Philadelphia, 1847 ***53.26*** *p8*
Bruce, William; Philadelphia, 1847 ***5704.8*** *p31*
Bruce, William; Quebec, 1852 ***5704.8*** *p87*
Bruce, William 15; Virginia, 1774 ***1219.7*** *p225*
Bruce, William 42; New Orleans, 1862 ***543.30*** *p112*
Bruch, Peter; New York, NY, 1837 ***8208.4*** *p26*
Bruchhausen, . . .; Canada, 1776-1783 ***9786*** *p18*
Bruchler, Ann Sonette 60; America, 1831 ***778.5*** *p82*
Bruchler, Maria 18; America, 1831 ***778.5*** *p82*
Bruchler, Nicholas 63; America, 1831 ***778.5*** *p82*
Bruchmann, Albert; Illinois, 1900 ***5012.40*** *p79*
Bruck, Valentin; New York, NY, 1837 ***8582*** *p5*
Brucker, John; Ohio, 1838 ***9892.11*** *p6*
Brucker, John; Philadelphia, 1742 ***3652*** *p55*
*Wife:*Mary Barbara
Brucker, Mary Barbara *SEE* Brucker, John
Bruckhof, . . .; Canada, 1776-1783 ***9786*** *p18*
Bruckman, Edward *SEE* Bruckman, Thomas
Bruckman, Joan Bagham *SEE* Bruckman, Thomas
Bruckman, Mary *SEE* Bruckman, William
Bruckman, Ruth *SEE* Bruckman, William
Bruckman, Sarah *SEE* Bruckman, William
Bruckman, Sarah *SEE* Bruckman, William
Bruckman, Thomas *SEE* Bruckman, Thomas
Bruckman, Thomas; Died enroute, 1682 ***4960*** *p155*
*Grandmother:*Joan Bagham
*Uncle:*Edward
*Uncle:*Thomas
Bruckman, William; Pennsylvania, 1682 ***4960*** *p155*
*Wife:*Sarah
*Daughter:*Sarah
*Daughter:*Mary
*Sister:*Ruth
Bruckner, . . .; Canada, 1776-1783 ***9786*** *p18*
Bruckner, Aguste; Wisconsin, n.d. ***9675.4*** *p266*
Bruckner, Anna Margaretha Muller *SEE* Bruckner, Georg
Bruckner, Christopher; New York, NY, 1835 ***8208.4*** *p27*
Bruckner, Georg; Georgia, 1739 ***9332*** *p323*
*Wife:*Anna Margaretha Muller
Bruckner, Georg; Georgia, 1739 ***9332*** *p326*
Bruckner, George; Georgia, 1738 ***9332*** *p321*
Bruckshaw, Nathaniel; Iowa, 1866-1943 ***123.54*** *p11*
Bruder, . . .; Canada, 1776-1783 ***9786*** *p18*
Bruder, Ignace 31; America, 1836 ***778.5*** *p82*
Bruder, Marie *SEE* Bruder, Matthess
Bruder, Marie Sinquette *SEE* Bruder, Matthess
Bruder, Matthess; Pennsylvania, 1752 ***2444*** *p143*
*Wife:*Marie Sinquette
*Child:*Marie
With child
Brudis, Joe John; Arkansas, 1918 ***95.2*** *p23*
Brudschin, Andreas; Illinois, 1871 ***5012.39*** *p25*
Brue, Mr. 35; America, 1826 ***778.5*** *p83*
Bruebach, Peter; Halifax, N.S., 1778 ***9786*** *p270*
Bruebach, Peter; New York, 1776 ***9786*** *p270*
Bruecher, Edward; Wisconsin, n.d. ***9675.5*** *p49*
Bruecker, Julius; Wisconsin, n.d. ***9675.5*** *p49*
Brueckmann, John C.; Cincinnati, 1846 ***8582.1*** *p5*
Brueder, Stephen; Colorado, 1895 ***9678.1*** *p156*
Bruegge, Joseph; New York, 1889 ***1450.2*** *p5B*
Brueggemann, Adolph; America, 1848 ***8582.3*** *p10*
Brueggemann, August; America, 1849 ***8582.1*** *p5*
Bruegger, Charles; Illinois, 1885 ***2896.5*** *p6*
Bruegger, Christian; Illinois, 1885 ***2896.5*** *p6*
Bruehl, Dr.; America, 1834 ***8582.1*** *p53*
Bruehl, Gustav; Cincinnati, 1869-1887 ***8582*** *p5*
Bruell, Pecho 42; New Orleans, 1829 ***778.5*** *p83*
Bruemmer, Hermann 23; Kansas, 1888 ***5240.1*** *p72*
Bruen, Henry; America, 1735-1743 ***4971*** *p79*
Bruening, Edward; New York, 1852 ***1450.2*** *p21A*
Bruens, Hermann; Iroquois Co., IL, 1892 ***3455.1*** *p9*
Bruer, Adam; Indiana, 1848 ***9117*** *p19*
Brufas, Theodore; Arkansas, 1918 ***95.2*** *p23*
Bruff, Mary 19; Pennsylvania, 1725 ***3690.1*** *p31*
Bruff, William 33; Maryland, 1775 ***1219.7*** *p256*
Bruffin, John; Virginia, 1635 ***6219*** *p69*
Brugere, Mr.; Quebec, 1815 ***9229.18*** *p78*
Bruggemann, John; New York, NY, 1836 ***8208.4*** *p18*
Bruggemeier, Heinrich Carl; America, 1881 ***4610.10*** *p101*
Bruggemeyer, Friedrich Karl Heinrich; America, 1865 ***4610.10*** *p100*
Brugnot, Frs. 45; New Orleans, 1838 ***778.5*** *p83*
Bruhn, C. H.; Kansas, 1888 ***5240.1*** *p7*
Bruhn, Jacob; New York, NY, 1838 ***8208.4*** *p61*
Bruhn, Peter Christensen; Arkansas, 1918 ***95.2*** *p23*
Bruin, Jno; Virginia, 1698 ***2212*** *p13*
Bruin, John; Virginia, 1698 ***2212*** *p15*
Bruin, Richard; Virginia, 1637 ***6219*** *p114*
Bruing, Charles 23; Virginia, 1774 ***1219.7*** *p240*
Bruins, Henrick 14; New York, NY, 1847 ***3377.6*** *p14*
Bruins, Henry 13; New York, NY, 1847 ***3377.6*** *p14*
Bruins, Hourok 30; New York, NY, 1847 ***3377.6*** *p14*
Bruins, John 13; New York, NY, 1847 ***3377.6*** *p14*
Bruins, Mary 10; New York, NY, 1847 ***3377.6*** *p14*
Bruins, Thomas 5; New York, NY, 1847 ***3377.6*** *p14*
Bruins, Walter 39; New York, NY, 1847 ***3377.6*** *p14*
Bruins, William 12; New York, NY, 1847 ***3377.6*** *p14*
Brulard, Sebastien 15; Louisiana, 1820 ***778.5*** *p83*
Brulatour, Pierre 34; New Orleans, 1836 ***778.5*** *p83*
Bruley, Mme.; Port uncertain, 1839 ***778.5*** *p83*
Bruley, Mr.; Port uncertain, 1839 ***778.5*** *p83*
Brumard, William 41; America, 1831 ***778.5*** *p83*
Brumbacher, Caspar 33; New Orleans, 1862 ***543.30*** *p479*
Brumberg, David; Iowa, 1866-1943 ***123.54*** *p11*
Brumel, F. 40; New Orleans, 1831 ***778.5*** *p83*
Brumerly, William; America, 1855 ***6014.1*** *p1*
Brumgard, John; Arkansas, 1918 ***95.2*** *p23*
Brumm, Michael; Pennsylvania, 1752 ***2444*** *p143*
Brumme, August; Illinois, 1882 ***5240.1*** *p7*
Brumme, August, Sr.; Kansas, 1890 ***5240.1*** *p7*
Brumme, August, Sr. 64; Kansas, 1890 ***5240.1*** *p74*
Brumme, Maria 60; Kansas, 1893 ***5240.1*** *p78*
Brumme, Marie; Kansas, 1893 ***5240.1*** *p7*
Brumme, Otto; Illinois, 1886 ***5240.1*** *p7*
Brummer, J.B.; Cincinnati, 1838-1874 ***8582.1*** *p1*
Brummer, Johann B.; Cincinnati, 1869-1887 ***8582*** *p5*
Brummer, John; Illinois, 1887 ***5240.1*** *p7*
Brummit, Julian; Jamaica, 1764 ***1219.7*** *p104*
Brumohler, Charles; America, 1892 ***1450.2*** *p5B*
Brumshagen, Henrich; Iroquois Co., IL, 1896 ***3455.1*** *p9*
Brun, Mr. 22; New Orleans, 1821 ***778.5*** *p83*
Brun, Mr. 30; America, 1839 ***778.5*** *p83*
Brun, Elisee 18; New Orleans, 1832 ***778.5*** *p83*
Brun, Etienne; Port uncertain, 1753 ***2444*** *p143*
*Wife:*Marie Sinquette
With child
*Child:*Marie
Brun, Marie *SEE* Brun, Etienne
Brun, Marie Sinquette *SEE* Brun, Etienne
Brun, Marius 18; America, 1836 ***778.5*** *p83*
Brun, Steffe 37; Pennsylvania, 1738 ***2444*** *p143*
Brunce, John D.; Wisconsin, n.d. ***9675.5*** *p49*
Brunco, Gaetano 9 *SEE* Brunco, Mariangelo
Brunco, Maria 6 *SEE* Brunco, Mariangelo
Brunco, Mariangelo 34; New York, NY, 1893 ***9026.4*** *p41*
*Relative:*Gaetano 9
*Relative:*Santa 29
*Relative:*Rosana 9
*Relative:*Maria 6
Brunco, Rosana 9 *SEE* Brunco, Mariangelo
Brunco, Santa 29 *SEE* Brunco, Mariangelo
Brundage, John; Illinois, 1857 ***7857*** *p2*
Brundish, Thomas 22; Maryland, 1733 ***3690.1*** *p25*
Brundon, John 13; Philadelphia, 1853 ***5704.8*** *p113*
Brune, John C. 40; New Orleans, 1862 ***543.30*** *p117*
Brunean, Alphonse; Washington, 1859-1920 ***2872.1*** *p5*
Bruner, Catharina E. Thomas *SEE* Bruner, Josef
Bruner, Emmile 2; America, 1831 ***778.5*** *p83*
Bruner, Francis 41; America, 1831 ***778.5*** *p83*
Bruner, Heinrich Elias 6 *SEE* Bruner, Josef
Bruner, Johannes 18 *SEE* Bruner, Josef
Bruner, Josef; Philadelphia, 1729 ***2854*** *p43*
*Wife:*Catharina E. Thomas
*Child:*Maria Catharina 19
*Child:*Johannes 18
*Child:*Heinrich Elias 6
Bruner, Joseph A.; Kentucky, 1800-1877 ***8582.3*** *p101*
Bruner, Maria Catharina 19 *SEE* Bruner, Josef
Bruner, Napoleon 9; America, 1831 ***778.5*** *p84*
Bruner, Roman; America, 1850 ***1450.2*** *p21A*
Brunet, . . . 12; America, 1837 ***778.5*** *p84*
Brunet, . . . 15; America, 1837 ***778.5*** *p84*
Brunet, Mr.; Port uncertain, 1839 ***778.5*** *p84*
Brunet, Mr. 30; Louisiana, 1821 ***778.5*** *p84*
Brunet, Mr. 35; America, 1838 ***778.5*** *p84*
Brunet, Mr. 42; America, 1822 ***778.5*** *p84*
Brunet, Mr. 45; America, 1837 ***778.5*** *p84*
Brunet, Mrs. 40; America, 1837 ***778.5*** *p84*
Brunet, J. P. 17; New Orleans, 1831 ***778.5*** *p84*
Brunetude, Mr. 50; America, 1830 ***778.5*** *p84*
Bruning, Carl Heinrich *SEE* Bruning, Johann Carl Friedrich
Bruning, Friedrich Philipp; America, 1860 ***4610.10*** *p158*
Bruning, Hermann Wilhelm *SEE* Bruning, Johann Carl Friedrich
Bruning, Johann Carl Friedrich; America, 1850 ***4610.10*** *p142*
*Wife:*Louise C. Kroger
*Child:*Carl Heinrich
*Child:*Wilhelmine Engel
*Child:*Hermann Wilhelm
*Child:*Louise Wilhelmine
Bruning, Joseph; America, 1855 ***1450.2*** *p21A*
Bruning, Louise C. Kroger *SEE* Bruning, Johann Carl Friedrich
Bruning, Louise Wilhelmine *SEE* Bruning, Johann Carl Friedrich
Bruning, Wilhelmine Engel *SEE* Bruning, Johann Carl Friedrich
Brunner, Ann Barbara; Philadelphia, 1729 ***2854*** *p44*
Brunner, Catharina E. Thomas *SEE* Brunner, Josef
Brunner, Christian Frederick; Bangor, ME, 1874 ***6410.22*** *p124*
Brunner, Heinrich; Arkansas, 1918 ***95.2*** *p23*
Brunner, Heinrich 18; America, 1854-1855 ***9162.6*** *p104*
Brunner, Heinrich Elias 6 *SEE* Brunner, Josef
Brunner, Henry; Philadelphia, 1760 ***9973.7*** *p34*
Brunner, Henry; Wisconsin, n.d. ***9675.5*** *p49*
Brunner, J. J.; Milwaukee, 1875 ***4719.30*** *p257*
Brunner, Johannes 18 *SEE* Brunner, Josef
Brunner, John; South Carolina, 1788 ***7119*** *p199*
Brunner, John 43; New Orleans, 1862 ***543.30*** *p326*
Brunner, Josef; Philadelphia, 1729 ***2854*** *p43*
*Wife:*Catharina E. Thomas
*Child:*Maria Catharina 19
*Child:*Johannes 18
*Child:*Heinrich Elias 6
Brunner, Ludwig; New York, NY, 1926 ***3455.4*** *p81*
Brunner, Maria Catharina 19 *SEE* Brunner, Josef
Bruno, Salvatore; Washington, 1859-1920 ***2872.1*** *p5*
Brunotte, Henry 29; New Orleans, 1862 ***543.30*** *p111*
Bruns, . . .; Canada, 1776-1783 ***9786*** *p18*
Bruns, Anton; America, 1847 ***8582.3*** *p10*
Bruns, Dietrich; Kentucky, 1843 ***8582.3*** *p100*
Bruns, Heinrich; Cincinnati, 1869-1887 ***8582*** *p5*
Bruns, Heinrich Joseph; America, 1844 ***8582.2*** *p5*
Bruns, Herman Frederick; Arkansas, 1918 ***95.2*** *p23*
Bruns, Hermann Heinrich; America, 1841 ***4815.7*** *p92*
*Wife:*Sophie M. Abeling
Bruns, Hilmer; Iroquois Co., IL, 1892 ***3455.1*** *p9*
Bruns, Johann; Wisconsin, n.d. ***9675.5*** *p49*
Bruns, Sophie M. Abeling *SEE* Bruns, Hermann Heinrich
Brunse, A.; Minneapolis, 1882-1883 ***6410.35*** *p51*
Brunst, Peter; New York, NY, 1848 ***8582.3*** *p10*
Brunsteidell, . . .; Canada, 1776-1783 ***9786*** *p18*
Brunswick, Edward 27; Massachusetts, 1848 ***5881.1*** *p7*
Brunswick, John M.; Cincinnati, 1869-1887 ***8582*** *p5*
Brunswick, M.; Cincinnati, 1848 ***8582.1*** *p53*
Brunt, John W.; Iowa, 1866-1943 ***123.54*** *p11*
Brunt, Mary Ann; Quebec, 1850 ***5704.8*** *p63*
Bruntz, Mathin; Washington, 1859-1920 ***2872.1*** *p5*
Bruny, Ursule 42; America, 1837 ***778.5*** *p84*
Brurdin, Jean 32; New Orleans, 1822 ***778.5*** *p84*
Brus, Matth; Ohio, 1881 ***3702.7*** *p433*
Brusac, Ange 25; America, 1838 ***778.5*** *p84*
Bruse, James; Virginia, 1645 ***6219*** *p239*
Bruse, Rich.; Virginia, 1638 ***6219*** *p11*
Bruss, Mr.; Wisconsin, 1849-1850 ***3702.7*** *p314*
Bruss, Frank; Wisconsin, n.d. ***9675.5*** *p49*
Brussel, John; Wisconsin, n.d. ***9675.5*** *p49*
Brust, Mathias Joseph; Wisconsin, n.d. ***9675.5*** *p49*
Bruster, Anthony; Virginia, 1647 ***6219*** *p239*
Brustolin, Pietro; Iowa, 1866-1943 ***123.54*** *p11*
Brustolin, Vittore; Iowa, 1866-1943 ***123.54*** *p11*

Bruston, Sarah; Philadelphia, 1850 ***53.26*** *p8*
Bruston, Sarah; Philadelphia, 1850 ***5704.8*** *p59*
Brusven, Charles; Washington, 1859-1920 ***2872.1*** *p5*
Brute, Walter; Virginia, 1637 ***6219*** *p111*
Bruthee, Patrick 35; Massachusetts, 1850 ***5881.1*** *p11*
Brutier, L.; New Orleans, 1839 ***778.5*** *p85*
Bruton, Edward; Virginia, 1637 ***6219*** *p83*
Bruton, John; Virginia, 1643 ***6219*** *p206*
Bruton, Jon.; Virginia, 1635 ***6219*** *p68*
Brutschin, Andreas; Illinois, 1871 ***5012.39*** *p25*
Bruy, Alferiso 31; New York, NY, 1893 ***9026.4*** *p41*
Bruyn, Bernard De; America, 1848 ***8582.2*** *p5*
Bruz, L. 25; America, 1835 ***778.5*** *p85*
Bruzaud, Mr. 28; America, 1837 ***778.5*** *p85*
Bruzdzinski, Zygmunt; Arkansas, 1918 ***95.2*** *p23*
Brversma, Thys; Arkansas, 1918 ***95.2*** *p23*
Bry, Mr. 36; America, 1838 ***778.5*** *p85*
Bry, Jean 24; New Orleans, 1823 ***778.5*** *p85*
Bryan, Anne; New York, NY, 1811 ***2859.11*** *p9*
Bryan, Biddy; New York, NY, 1865 ***5704.8*** *p195*
Bryan, Bridget 25; Massachusetts, 1847 ***5881.1*** *p6*
Bryan, Brigitte; Quebec, 1823 ***7603*** *p59*
Bryan, Catharine 20; Massachusetts, 1849 ***5881.1*** *p7*
Bryan, Catharine 28; Massachusetts, 1850 ***5881.1*** *p7*
Bryan, Catharine 40; Massachusetts, 1849 ***5881.1*** *p7*
Bryan, Catherine; St. John, N.B., 1847 ***5704.8*** *p15*
Bryan, Daniel; America, 1743 ***4971*** *p42*
Bryan, Dennis 10; Massachusetts, 1850 ***5881.1*** *p7*
Bryan, Edmond; America, 1743 ***4971*** *p32*
Bryan, Edmund 30; Massachusetts, 1849 ***5881.1*** *p7*
Bryan, Edw.; Virginia, 1620 ***6219*** *p34*
Bryan, Edward; Virginia, 1638 ***6219*** *p147*
Bryan, Edward; Virginia, 1647 ***6219*** *p239*
Bryan, Ellen; Philadelphia, 1865 ***5704.8*** *p201*
Bryan, Garret; Virginia, 1643 ***6219*** *p207*
Bryan, Henry; Maryland, 1740 ***4971*** *p91*
Bryan, Henry; Philadelphia, 1741 ***4971*** *p92*
Bryan, Henry; Virginia, 1639 ***6219*** *p155*
Bryan, Humphrey 18; West Indies, 1722 ***3690.1*** *p31*
Bryan, James; America, 1742 ***4971*** *p49*
Bryan, James; America, 1743 ***4971*** *p50*
Bryan, James; New York, NY, 1811 ***2859.11*** *p9*
With wife
Bryan, James 25; Massachusetts, 1847 ***5881.1*** *p8*
Bryan, James 30; Massachusetts, 1849 ***5881.1*** *p8*
Bryan, Jane 10; Massachusetts, 1850 ***5881.1*** *p9*
Bryan, Jeremiah 2; Massachusetts, 1849 ***5881.1*** *p9*
Bryan, Johanna 7; Massachusetts, 1848 ***5881.1*** *p8*
Bryan, Johanna 40; Massachusetts, 1847 ***5881.1*** *p8*
Bryan, John; America, 1738 ***4971*** *p13*
Bryan, John; America, 1738 ***4971*** *p39*
Bryan, John; America, 1739 ***4971*** *p47*
Bryan, John; America, 1741 ***4971*** *p49*
Bryan, John; America, 1742 ***4971*** *p56*
Bryan, John 18; Massachusetts, 1849 ***5881.1*** *p9*
Bryan, John 19; Massachusetts, 1849 ***5881.1*** *p9*
Bryan, John 30; Maryland, 1774 ***1219.7*** *p224*
Bryan, Joseph 37; Massachusetts, 1848 ***5881.1*** *p8*
Bryan, Kennedy 11; Massachusetts, 1850 ***5881.1*** *p9*
Bryan, Lewis 19; Jamaica, 1734 ***3690.1*** *p26*
Bryan, Margaret; America, 1736-1743 ***4971*** *p57*
Bryan, Margaret; America, 1740 ***4971*** *p48*
Bryan, Margaret; America, 1741 ***4971*** *p49*
Bryan, Margaret 12; Massachusetts, 1849 ***5881.1*** *p10*
Bryan, Mary; America, 1736 ***4971*** *p12*
Bryan, Mary; America, 1739 ***4971*** *p40*
Bryan, Mary; America, 1741 ***4971*** *p41*
Bryan, Mary 10; Massachusetts, 1849 ***5881.1*** *p10*
Bryan, Mary 35; Massachusetts, 1849 ***5881.1*** *p11*
Bryan, Mary 45; Massachusetts, 1849 ***5881.1*** *p10*
Bryan, Mary A. 18; Massachusetts, 1849 ***5881.1*** *p10*
Bryan, Maurice; America, 1736 ***4971*** *p44*
Bryan, Maurice; America, 1737 ***4971*** *p45*
Bryan, Michael; Quebec, 1765 ***7603*** *p70*
Bryan, Michael 6; Massachusetts, 1849 ***5881.1*** *p10*
Bryan, Michael 10; Massachusetts, 1848 ***5881.1*** *p9*
Bryan, Michael 22; Massachusetts, 1848 ***5881.1*** *p9*
Bryan, Miles; America, 1739 ***4971*** *p14*
Bryan, Morgan; Virginia, 1642 ***6219*** *p192*
Bryan, Nancy; New York, NY, 1865 ***5704.8*** *p195*
Bryan, Pat 3 mos; Massachusetts, 1847 ***5881.1*** *p11*
Bryan, Patrick; America, 1735-1743 ***4971*** *p8*
Bryan, Richard; America, 1738 ***4971*** *p14*
Bryan, Robert; America, 1735-1743 ***4971*** *p8*
Bryan, Robert; Annapolis, MD, 1742 ***4971*** *p93*
Bryan, Robert; Virginia, 1637 ***6219*** *p17*
Bryan, Sally; Philadelphia, 1866 ***5704.8*** *p208*
Bryan, Sarah; America, 1741 ***4971*** *p10*
Bryan, Stumphy; America, 1738 ***4971*** *p68*
Bryan, Teigue; America, 1736-1743 ***4971*** *p57*
Bryan, Tho.; Virginia, 1648 ***6219*** *p250*
Bryan, Thomas; America, 1742 ***4971*** *p56*
Bryan, William; Iowa, 1866-1943 ***123.54*** *p11*
Bryan, William; New York, NY, 1865 ***5704.8*** *p195*
Bryan, William 8; Massachusetts, 1849 ***5881.1*** *p12*
Bryan, Xtopr.; Virginia, 1646 ***6219*** *p246*
Bryans, Ann; St. John, N.B., 1847 ***5704.8*** *p15*
Bryans, Mary; Quebec, 1847 ***5704.8*** *p36*
Bryans, Sarah; New York, NY, 1811 ***2859.11*** *p9*
Bryans, William; St. John, N.B., 1847 ***5704.8*** *p15*
Bryant, Abraham 22; Philadelphia, 1774 ***1219.7*** *p232*
Bryant, James 16; Philadelphia, 1774 ***1219.7*** *p183*
Bryant, Jeremiah 32; Port uncertain, 1774 ***1219.7*** *p176*
Bryant, John 21; Philadelphia, 1774 ***1219.7*** *p232*
Bryant, John 21; Virginia, 1774 ***1219.7*** *p201*
Bryant, Lewis 22; Virginia, 1773 ***1219.7*** *p168*
Bryant, Michaell; Virginia, 1636 ***6219*** *p77*
Bryant, Thomas 22; Maryland, 1774 ***1219.7*** *p184*
Bryce, Henry; Charleston, SC, 1806 ***1639.20*** *p18*
Bryce, Jane C. 49; South Carolina, 1850 ***1639.20*** *p18*
Bryce, Mary; Philadelphia, 1852 ***5704.8*** *p87*
Bryce, Nichol; Charleston, SC, 1805 ***1639.20*** *p18*
Bryce, Nichol 52; South Carolina, 1850 ***1639.20*** *p18*
Bryce, Peter 57; South Carolina, 1850 ***1639.20*** *p18*
Bryce, William; South Carolina, 1808 ***1639.20*** *p18*
Brydair, Jacob; South Carolina, 1788 ***7119*** *p203*
Bryden, Miss; Quebec, 1815 ***9229.18*** *p78*
Brydolf, Fabian; Cleveland, OH, 1841 ***2090*** *p608*
Bryen, Dennis; America, 1741 ***4971*** *p42*
Bryen, Teigue; America, 1741 ***4971*** *p40*
Bryham, Louise Mathilda; Wisconsin, n.d. ***9675.5*** *p49*
Bryham, Tobias; New York, NY, 1838 ***8208.4*** *p72*
Brynd, William; Illinois, 1888 ***5012.39*** *p121*
Bryne, Catharine; Philadelphia, 1865 ***5704.8*** *p202*
Bryne, John 22; Newfoundland, 1789 ***4915.24*** *p57*
Bryne, Peter; Philadelphia, 1851 ***5704.8*** *p76*
Bryner, William 18; Philadelphia, 1774 ***1219.7*** *p232*
Brynestad, Lars; Arkansas, 1918 ***95.2*** *p23*
Bryngelson, Carl August; Arkansas, 1918 ***95.2*** *p23*
Bryon, Thomas 22; Philadelphia, 1775 ***1219.7*** *p255*
Bryson, Mrs.; New York, NY, 1811 ***2859.11*** *p9*
Bryson, Ann; St. John, N.B., 1852 ***5704.8*** *p95*
Bryson, Ann 6 mos; St. John, N.B., 1852 ***5704.8*** *p95*
Bryson, Catherine; New Orleans, 1849 ***5704.8*** *p59*
Bryson, Jane; New York, NY, 1864 ***5704.8*** *p173*
Bryson, Mary; New Orleans, 1849 ***5704.8*** *p59*
Bryson, Mary; St. John, N.B., 1852 ***5704.8*** *p95*
Bryson, Mary 20; St. John, N.B., 1855 ***5704.8*** *p127*
Bryson, Samuel; New York, NY, 1868 ***5704.8*** *p228*
Bryson, Samuel; Philadelphia, 1852 ***5704.8*** *p89*
Bryzelius, Hannah; New York, 1754 ***3652*** *p79*
Bryzelius, Mary; New York, 1754 ***3652*** *p79*
Bryzelius, P. D.; New York, 1754 ***3652*** *p78*
Bryzelius, Paul Daniel; Philadelphia, 1742 ***3652*** *p55*
*Wife:*Regina
Bryzelius, Regina *SEE* Bryzelius, Paul Daniel
Bryzelius, Regina Dorothea; New York, 1754 ***3652*** *p78*
Bryzelius, Renatus; New York, 1754 ***3652*** *p79*
Brzezinski, Jozef; New York, 1831 ***4606*** *p172*
Bua, Mike; Iowa, 1866-1943 ***123.54*** *p11*
Buall, Don Pedro 24; Port uncertain, 1831 ***778.5*** *p85*
Buard, Henry 25; America, 1838 ***778.5*** *p85*
Bub, Nikolaus; America, 1848 ***8582.3*** *p11*
Bub, Sebastian; Alberta, n.d. ***5262*** *p58*
Buba, Frank; Arkansas, 1918 ***95.2*** *p23*
Buban, John; Iowa, 1866-1943 ***123.54*** *p11*
Buban, Jos.; Iowa, 1866-1943 ***123.54*** *p11*
Buban, Julia; Iowa, 1866-1943 ***123.54*** *p11*
Buban, Julijan; Iowa, 1866-1943 ***123.54*** *p11*
Buban, Tony; Iowa, 1866-1943 ***123.54*** *p11*
Bubang, Anton; Iowa, 1866-1943 ***123.54*** *p11*
Bubany, Frank; Iowa, 1866-1943 ***123.54*** *p11*
Bubany, Joseph; Iowa, 1866-1943 ***123.54*** *p11*
Bubban, Joc; Iowa, 1866-1943 ***123.54*** *p11*
Bubby, Michael 20; Massachusetts, 1849 ***5881.1*** *p10*
Bublitz, Albert; Wisconsin, n.d. ***9675.5*** *p49*
Bublitz, Charles; Wisconsin, n.d. ***9675.5*** *p49*
Bublitz, Ferdinand; Wisconsin, n.d. ***9675.5*** *p49*
Bubniak, Gabriela; Iowa, 1866-1943 ***123.54*** *p57*
Bubniak, Matej; Iowa, 1866-1943 ***123.54*** *p11*
Bubnick, Adam; Iowa, 1866-1943 ***123.54*** *p11*
Bubnjak, Adam; Iowa, 1866-1943 ***123.54*** *p11*
Bubony, John; Iowa, 1866-1943 ***123.54*** *p11*
Bubony, Phillipp; Iowa, 1866-1943 ***123.54*** *p11*
Bucannon, John; Virginia, 1775 ***1219.7*** *p275*
Buch, Barbara; Pennsylvania, 1751 ***4525*** *p203*
Buch, Charlotte; Wisconsin, n.d. ***9675.5*** *p49*
Buch, Frank 24; New Orleans, 1862 ***543.30*** *p479*
Buch, Georg Fridrich; South Carolina, 1788 ***7119*** *p199*
Buch, Johann Peter; Pennsylvania, 1854-1855 ***3702.7*** *p389*
Buch, Johann Phillipp; Pennsylvania, 1752 ***4525*** *p203*
Buch, John; Wisconsin, n.d. ***9675.5*** *p49*
Buch, Lehne; Ohio, 1861 ***3702.7*** *p402*
Buch, Peter; America, 1858 ***3702.7*** *p29*
Buch, Philipp; New England, 1752 ***4525*** *p203*
Buchan, George; New York, NY, 1816 ***2859.11*** *p26*
Buchanan, Mr.; Quebec, 1815 ***9229.18*** *p81*
Buchanan, Alexander; New York, NY, 1838 ***8208.4*** *p62*
Buchanan, Alice; Philadelphia, 1871 ***5704.8*** *p240*
Buchanan, Ann *SEE* Buchanan, John
Buchanan, Ann *SEE* Buchanan, Neil
Buchanan, Ann; Quebec, 1851 ***4537.30*** *p52*
Buchanan, Ann 18; Philadelphia, 1859 ***5704.8*** *p143*
Buchanan, Ann MacIver *SEE* Buchanan, Donald
Buchanan, Annabella *SEE* Buchanan, Neil
Buchanan, Archibald; Charleston, SC, 1797-1823 ***1639.20*** *p18*
Buchanan, Catherine *SEE* Buchanan, Kenneth
Buchanan, Catherine; Quebec, 1841 ***4537.30*** *p35*
Buchanan, Catherine 12; Philadelphia, 1852 ***5704.8*** *p95*
Buchanan, Charles; Philadelphia, 1871 ***5704.8*** *p240*
Buchanan, Donald *SEE* Buchanan, John
Buchanan, Donald; Quebec, 1852 ***4537.30*** *p3*
*Wife:*Ann MacIver
*Child:*Margaret
Buchanan, Duncan; America, 1792 ***1639.20*** *p18*
Buchanan, Effie *SEE* Buchanan, Neil
Buchanan, Elizabeth; Philadelphia, 1852 ***5704.8*** *p95*
Buchanan, Elizabeth; Philadelphia, 1865 ***5704.8*** *p201*
Buchanan, George; South Carolina, 1684 ***1639.20*** *p19*
Buchanan, Hannah; America, 1867 ***5704.8*** *p220*
Buchanan, Hugh; Charleston, SC, 1805 ***1639.20*** *p19*
Buchanan, James; Ohio, 1840 ***9892.11*** *p6*
Buchanan, James 21; Philadelphia, 1856 ***5704.8*** *p128*
Buchanan, Jean; Quebec, 1765 ***7603*** *p39*
Buchanan, John *SEE* Buchanan, John
Buchanan, John *SEE* Buchanan, Kenneth
Buchanan, John *SEE* Buchanan, Neil
Buchanan, John; America, 1792 ***1639.20*** *p19*
Buchanan, John; Philadelphia, 1871 ***5704.8*** *p240*
Buchanan, John; Quebec, 1855 ***4537.30*** *p4*
*Wife:*Mary MacLennan
*Child:*William
*Child:*Donald
*Child:*Mary
*Child:*Peter
*Child:*John
*Child:*Ann
Buchanan, John 79; North Carolina, 1850 ***1639.20*** *p19*
Buchanan, Kenneth; Quebec, 1855 ***4537.30*** *p4*
*Wife:*Margaret Nicolson
*Child:*Murdo
*Child:*Marion
*Child:*Mary Ann
*Child:*Norman
*Child:*John
*Child:*Catherine
Buchanan, Kirsty; Quebec, 1838 ***4537.30*** *p86*
Buchanan, Margaret *SEE* Buchanan, Donald
Buchanan, Margaret *SEE* Buchanan, Neil
Buchanan, Margaret 16; Philadelphia, 1859 ***5704.8*** *p143*
Buchanan, Margaret Nicolson *SEE* Buchanan, Kenneth
Buchanan, Marion *SEE* Buchanan, Kenneth
Buchanan, Martha; New York, NY, 1865 ***5704.8*** *p188*
Buchanan, Mary *SEE* Buchanan, John
Buchanan, Mary; Philadelphia, 1868 ***5704.8*** *p225*
Buchanan, Mary; Philadelphia, 1871 ***5704.8*** *p240*
Buchanan, Mary; Quebec, 1851 ***4537.30*** *p77*
Buchanan, Mary 20; Wilmington, DE, 1831 ***6508.7*** *p161*
Buchanan, Mary 50; North Carolina, 1850 ***1639.20*** *p19*
Buchanan, Mary Ann *SEE* Buchanan, Kenneth
Buchanan, Mary MacArthur *SEE* Buchanan, Neil
Buchanan, Mary MacLennan *SEE* Buchanan, John
Buchanan, Matilda 21; Wilmington, DE, 1831 ***6508.7*** *p161*
Buchanan, Murdo *SEE* Buchanan, Kenneth
Buchanan, Neil; Quebec, 1851 ***4537.30*** *p4*
*Wife:*Mary MacArthur
*Child:*John
*Child:*Ann
*Child:*Effie
*Child:*Annabella
*Child:*Margaret
Buchanan, Norman *SEE* Buchanan, Kenneth
Buchanan, Peter *SEE* Buchanan, John
Buchanan, Peter; South Carolina, 1818 ***1639.20*** *p19*
Buchanan, Samuel; New York, NY, 1815 ***2859.11*** *p26*
Buchanan, Samuel; New York, NY, 1865 ***5704.8*** *p188*
Buchanan, Sarah 17; Philadelphia, 1854 ***5704.8*** *p116*
Buchanan, Sarah Ann; Philadelphia, 1853 ***5704.8*** *p101*
Buchanan, Susan; Philadelphia, 1852 ***5704.8*** *p95*
Buchanan, Thomas; Philadelphia, 1850 ***5704.8*** *p64*
Buchanan, Thomas 25; Philadelphia, 1857 ***5704.8*** *p133*
Buchanan, William *SEE* Buchanan, John
Buchanan, William; South Carolina, 1737 ***1639.20*** *p19*
Buchanan, William 19; Philadelphia, 1854 ***5704.8*** *p116*
Buchanan, Wm.; New York, NY, 1811 ***2859.11*** *p9*
Buchannon, Mrs. 22; Quebec, 1864 ***5704.8*** *p160*

Buchannon, Alexander; Nova Scotia, 1830 ***7085.4*** *p44*
*Wife:*Jannet
*Child:*Duncan
*Child:*Malcolm
Buchannon, Ann; New York, NY, 1868 ***5704.8*** *p228*
Buchannon, Bridget; New York, NY, 1868 ***5704.8*** *p228*
Buchannon, Duncan *SEE* Buchannon, Alexander
Buchannon, George 30; Quebec, 1864 ***5704.8*** *p160*
Buchannon, Jane; Philadelphia, 1866 ***5704.8*** *p209*
Buchannon, Jannet *SEE* Buchannon, Alexander
Buchannon, Malcolm *SEE* Buchannon, Alexander
Buchannon, Margaret; Philadelphia, 1867 ***5704.8*** *p219*
Buchannon, Rebecca; Philadelphia, 1847 ***53.26*** *p8*
Buchannon, Rebecca 8; Philadelphia, 1847 ***5704.8*** *p23*
Buchannon, Robert 35; Philadelphia, 1861 ***5704.8*** *p147*
Buchannon, Robt 24; Philadelphia, 1845 ***6508.6*** *p115*
Buchanon, Alexander 9; Philadelphia, 1848 ***53.26*** *p8*
*Relative:*Edward 7
*Relative:*William 3
Buchanon, Alexander 9; Philadelphia, 1848 ***5704.8*** *p46*
Buchanon, David 4 *SEE* Buchanon, Watt
Buchanon, David 4; Philadelphia, 1847 ***5704.8*** *p5*
Buchanon, Edward 7 *SEE* Buchanon, Alexander
Buchanon, Edward 7; Philadelphia, 1848 ***5704.8*** *p46*
Buchanon, Eliza *SEE* Buchanon, Watt
Buchanon, Eliza; Philadelphia, 1847 ***5704.8*** *p5*
Buchanon, James 12 *SEE* Buchanon, Watt
Buchanon, James 12; Philadelphia, 1847 ***5704.8*** *p5*
Buchanon, James A.; Philadelphia, 1847 ***53.26*** *p8*
Buchanon, Jane *SEE* Buchanon, Watt
Buchanon, Jane; Philadelphia, 1847 ***5704.8*** *p5*
Buchanon, Jane; Philadelphia, 1848 ***53.26*** *p8*
*Relative:*Mary Jane 12
Buchanon, Jane; Philadelphia, 1848 ***5704.8*** *p46*
Buchanon, Jane 6 *SEE* Buchanon, Watt
Buchanon, Jane 6; Philadelphia, 1847 ***5704.8*** *p5*
Buchanon, John; New York, NY, 1811 ***2859.11*** *p9*
Buchanon, John Alexander; Philadelphia, 1847 ***5704.8*** *p14*
Buchanon, Margery *SEE* Buchanon, Watt
Buchanon, Margery; Philadelphia, 1847 ***5704.8*** *p5*
Buchanon, Martha *SEE* Buchanon, Uriah
Buchanon, Martha; Philadelphia, 1848 ***5704.8*** *p40*
Buchanon, Mary *SEE* Buchanon, Uriah
Buchanon, Mary; Philadelphia, 1848 ***5704.8*** *p40*
Buchanon, Mary Jane 12 *SEE* Buchanon, Jane
Buchanon, Mary Jane 12; Philadelphia, 1848 ***5704.8*** *p46*
Buchanon, Sarah; New York, NY, 1864 ***5704.8*** *p171*
Buchanon, Sarah; St. John, N.B., 1847 ***5704.8*** *p5*
Buchanon, Uriah; Philadelphia, 1848 ***53.26*** *p8*
*Relative:*Mary
*Relative:*Martha
Buchanon, Uriah; Philadelphia, 1848 ***5704.8*** *p40*
Buchanon, Watt; Philadelphia, 1847 ***53.26*** *p8*
*Relative:*Jane
*Relative:*Eliza
*Relative:*Margery
*Relative:*James 12
*Relative:*Watt 9
*Relative:*Jane 6
*Relative:*David 4
Buchanon, Watt; Philadelphia, 1847 ***5704.8*** *p5*
Buchanon, Watt 9 *SEE* Buchanon, Watt
Buchanon, Watt 9; Philadelphia, 1847 ***5704.8*** *p5*
Buchanon, William; St. John, N.B., 1866 ***5704.8*** *p167*
Buchanon, William 3 *SEE* Buchanon, Alexander
Buchanon, William 3; Philadelphia, 1848 ***5704.8*** *p46*
Buchard, John 23; New Orleans, 1836 ***778.5*** *p78*
Buchell, Peter; Indiana, 1844 ***9117*** *p18*
Bucher, Richard; Virginia, 1638 ***6219*** *p147*
Bucher, Wm.; Virginia, 1635 ***6219*** *p69*
Buchert, Henry; New York, NY, 1838 ***8208.4*** *p80*
Buchet, Edmond 30; America, 1836 ***778.5*** *p85*
Buchholtz, Henrick; Germantown, PA, 1684 ***2467.7*** *p5*
Buchholz, . . .; Illinois, 1800-1900 ***4610.10*** *p67*
Buchholz, Anne M. C. Schomburg *SEE* Buchholz, Johann Heinrich
Buchholz, Carl Christoph; America, 1850 ***4610.10*** *p147*
*Wife:*Louise E. Bultemeyer
*Child:*Carl H. Friedrich
*Child:*Carl Heinrich
*Child:*Christine Caroline
*Child:*Johann Heinrich
Buchholz, Carl H. Friedrich *SEE* Buchholz, Carl Christoph
Buchholz, Carl Heinrich *SEE* Buchholz, Carl Christoph
Buchholz, Caroline; America, 1872 ***4610.10*** *p109*
Buchholz, Caroline Louise *SEE* Buchholz, Gottlieb
Buchholz, Chr. C. Friederike *SEE* Buchholz, Gottlieb
Buchholz, Christian Heinrich *SEE* Buchholz, Johann Heinrich
Buchholz, Christine Caroline *SEE* Buchholz, Carl Christoph
Buchholz, Christine Charlotte *SEE* Buchholz, Gottlieb
Buchholz, Ferd. 22; New York, NY, 1857 ***9831.14*** *p153*
Buchholz, Gottlieb 68; America, 1872 ***4610.10*** *p109*
*Wife:*Louise Meier
*Child:*Chr. C. Friederike
*Child:*Caroline Louise
*Child:*Heinrich Wilhelm
*Child:*Christine Charlotte
Buchholz, Heinrich Wilhelm *SEE* Buchholz, Gottlieb
Buchholz, Johann Heinrich *SEE* Buchholz, Carl Christoph
Buchholz, Johann Heinrich; America, 1854 ***4610.10*** *p144*
*Wife:*Anne M. C. Schomburg
*Son:*Christian Heinrich
Buchholz, Louise E. Bultemeyer *SEE* Buchholz, Carl Christoph
Buchholz, Louise Meier *SEE* Buchholz, Gottlieb
Buchilly, Catherine; America, 1741 ***4971*** *p41*
Buchl, Joseph; Kansas, 1884 ***5240.1*** *p7*
Buchler, Elise 39; America, 1854-1855 ***9162.6*** *p105*
Buchler, Wilhelm 5; America, 1854-1855 ***9162.6*** *p105*
Buchman, Jacob; South Carolina, 1788 ***7119*** *p202*
Buchner, Werner; America, 1853 ***1450.2*** *p22A*
Buchs, . . .; Canada, 1776-1783 ***9786*** *p18*
Buchs, Jacob; Pennsylvania, 1751 ***2444*** *p143*
Buchter, Jacob; South Carolina, 1788 ***7119*** *p201*
Buchwalter, Anton *SEE* Buchwalter, Joseph
Buchwalter, Joseph; Ohio, 1798-1818 ***8582.2*** *p53*
*Brother:*Anton
*Brother:*Wilhelm
Buchwalter, Wilhelm *SEE* Buchwalter, Joseph
Bucido, Casimer; America, 1889 ***7137*** *p168*
Buck, Adolph; Illinois, 1883 ***2896.5*** *p6*
Buck, August; Illinois, 1873 ***5012.39*** *p26*
Buck, Christian *SEE* Buck, Jacob
Buck, Frederick; Illinois, 1886 ***2896.5*** *p6*
Buck, Henry 24; New Orleans, 1862 ***543.30*** *p482*
Buck, Jacob; Pennsylvania, 1751 ***2444*** *p143*
*Wife:*Magdalena Rautenb...
*Child:*Johann
*Child:*Sofia
*Child:*Christian
Buck, Johann *SEE* Buck, Jacob
Buck, John; Virginia, 1642 ***6219*** *p189*
Buck, John 7; Massachusetts, 1848 ***5881.1*** *p8*
Buck, Magdalena Rautenb... *SEE* Buck, Jacob
Buck, Peter; Virginia, 1635 ***6219*** *p16*
Buck, Richard 29; Virginia, 1775 ***1219.7*** *p246*
Buck, Robert 19; Jamaica, 1725 ***3690.1*** *p31*
Buck, Sofia *SEE* Buck, Jacob
Buck, Tho.; Virginia, 1640 ***6219*** *p182*
Buck, Thomas; Virginia, 1639 ***6219*** *p156*
Buckborough, Siegel A. 32; Kansas, 1904 ***5240.1*** *p83*
Buckell, . . .; Canada, 1776-1783 ***9786*** *p18*
Buckenberger, Frederick 29; New Orleans, 1862 ***543.30*** *p244*
Buckenham, Edward 28; Jamaica, 1736 ***3690.1*** *p31*
Buckenmeier, Effa 31; New Orleans, 1838 ***778.5*** *p85*
Buckenmeier, John 7; New Orleans, 1838 ***778.5*** *p85*
Buckenmeier, John 30; New Orleans, 1838 ***778.5*** *p85*
Buckenmeier, Magdalen 4; New Orleans, 1838 ***778.5*** *p85*
Buckerl, Michael 19; America, 1836 ***778.5*** *p85*
Buckholz, Nels; Arkansas, 1918 ***95.2*** *p23*
Buckhorn, Christian Frederick; New York, 1837 ***1450.2*** *p22A*
Buckhorn, John W.; New York, NY, 1839 ***8208.4*** *p98*
Buckingham, Chas; South Carolina, 1788 ***7119*** *p199*
Buckland, Charles; America, 1870 ***6014.1*** *p1*
Buckland, Jon.; Virginia, 1637 ***6219*** *p13*
Buckland, Richard; Virginia, 1645 ***6219*** *p239*
Buckle, Jacob; South Carolina, 1788 ***7119*** *p200*
Buckle, Thomas; South Carolina, 1788 ***7119*** *p200*
Buckler, Richard 18; Maryland, 1735 ***3690.1*** *p31*
Buckler, Wm. 12; Canada, 1838 ***4535.12*** *p113*
Buckley, Ann 22; America, 1700 ***2212*** *p30*
Buckley, Arth.; Virginia, 1647 ***6219*** *p241*
Buckley, Bessy 3; Massachusetts, 1849 ***5881.1*** *p6*
Buckley, Bessy 20; Massachusetts, 1849 ***5881.1*** *p6*
Buckley, Betty 16; Massachusetts, 1849 ***5881.1*** *p6*
Buckley, Catherine; New York, NY, 1811 ***2859.11*** *p9*
Buckley, Daniel; America, 1850 ***1450.2*** *p22A*
Buckley, Daniel 30; Massachusetts, 1849 ***5881.1*** *p7*
Buckley, Daniel 35; Massachusetts, 1850 ***5881.1*** *p7*
Buckley, Edwd; America, 1697 ***2212*** *p7*
Buckley, Ellen 1; Massachusetts, 1847 ***5881.1*** *p7*
Buckley, Ellen 23; Massachusetts, 1847 ***5881.1*** *p7*
Buckley, Ellen 24; Massachusetts, 1849 ***5881.1*** *p7*
Buckley, Ellen 24; Massachusetts, 1849 ***5881.1*** *p36*
Buckley, Fred 23; Kansas, 1884 ***5240.1*** *p7*
Buckley, Fred 23; Kansas, 1884 ***5240.1*** *p66*
Buckley, Humphry; Virginia, 1639 ***6219*** *p161*
Buckley, James; New York, NY, 1835 ***8208.4*** *p43*
Buckley, James B. 24; New Orleans, 1862 ***543.30*** *p116*
Buckley, Jane 19; America, 1700 ***2212*** *p30*
Buckley, Johanna 25; Massachusetts, 1849 ***5881.1*** *p8*
Buckley, John; New York, NY, 1835 ***8208.4*** *p6*
Buckley, John; Quebec, 1792 ***7603*** *p55*
Buckley, John 4; Massachusetts, 1849 ***5881.1*** *p8*
Buckley, Judith 20; Massachusetts, 1849 ***5881.1*** *p8*
Buckley, Margaret 70; Massachusetts, 1849 ***5881.1*** *p10*
Buckley, Mary 24; Massachusetts, 1847 ***5881.1*** *p9*
Buckley, Mathieu; Sorel, Que., 1785 ***7603*** *p102*
Buckley, Michael 20; Massachusetts, 1849 ***5881.1*** *p10*
Buckley, Monaghan 20; Massachusetts, 1850 ***5881.1*** *p11*
Buckley, Robert 18; Maryland, 1732 ***3690.1*** *p32*
Buckley, Robt 13; America, 1703 ***2212*** *p38*
Buckley, Robt 15; America, 1702 ***2212*** *p37*
Buckley, Thimothy; Quebec, 1795 ***7603*** *p55*
Buckley, Thomas Edmond; New York, NY, 1837 ***8208.4*** *p35*
Buckly, Rowland; Virginia, 1637 ***6219*** *p85*
Buckly, Rowld.; Virginia, 1636 ***6219*** *p79*
Buckman Family ; Pennsylvania, 1682 ***4963*** *p40*
Buckman, Edward *SEE* Buckman, Thomas
Buckman, Joan Bagham *SEE* Buckman, Thomas
Buckman, Mary *SEE* Buckman, William
Buckman, Ruth *SEE* Buckman, William
Buckman, Sarah *SEE* Buckman, William
Buckman, Sarah *SEE* Buckman, William
Buckman, Thomas *SEE* Buckman, Thomas
Buckman, Thomas; Died enroute, 1682 ***4960*** *p155*
*Grandmother:*Joan Bagham
*Uncle:*Edward
*Uncle:*Thomas
Buckman, William; Pennsylvania, 1682 ***4960*** *p154*
*Wife:*Sarah
*Daughter:*Sarah
*Daughter:*Mary
*Sister:*Ruth
Buckmaster, John; Virginia, 1623 ***6219*** *p24*
Buckminster, William 50; Massachusetts, 1850 ***5881.1*** *p12*
Bucknaw, Conrad; Virginia, 1855 ***4626.16*** *p15*
Buckner, Jacob; Illinois, 1860 ***5012.39*** *p90*
Buckow, Joseph 18; New Orleans, 1863 ***543.30*** *p248*
Buckram, O.P. 50; Massachusetts, 1860 ***6410.32*** *p115*
Buckrath, William; America, 1837 ***1450.2*** *p22A*
Buckridge, Isaac; New York, NY, 1837 ***8208.4*** *p33*
Buckridge, James; New York, NY, 1834 ***8208.4*** *p2*
Buckridge, James; New York, NY, 1837 ***8208.4*** *p33*
Bucksath, Henry; America, 1837 ***1450.2*** *p22A*
Bucksath, William; America, 1837 ***1450.2*** *p22A*
Bucktrell, Rich.; Virginia, 1636 ***6219*** *p26*
Buckworth, John; Virginia, 1638 ***6219*** *p11*
Bucs, Jacob; Pennsylvania, 1751 ***2444*** *p143*
Budd, Abigail 28; Massachusetts, 1849 ***5881.1*** *p6*
Budd, Giles; Virginia, 1639 ***6219*** *p162*
Budd, Rich.; Virginia, 1652 ***6251*** *p19*
Budde, Anne Marie Ahlersmeyer 28 *SEE* Budde, Cord Henrich Gottlieb
Budde, Anne Marie Engel 1 *SEE* Budde, Cord Henrich Gottlieb
Budde, Carl Christoph *SEE* Budde, Carl Heinrich
Budde, Carl Heinrich 55; America, 1850 ***4610.10*** *p142*
*Child:*Carl Christoph
*Child:*Louise 19
Budde, Cord Henrich Gottlieb; America, 1850 ***4610.10*** *p142*
*Wife:*Anne Marie Ahlersmeyer 28
*Daughter:*Anne Marie Engel 1
Budde, Friedrich Wilhelm; America, 1855 ***4610.10*** *p139*
Budde, H.; Ohio, 1843 ***8582.1*** *p51*
Budde, Heinrich Wilhelm; America, 1847 ***8582.2*** *p5*
Budde, Louise 19 *SEE* Budde, Carl Heinrich
Budde, Louise 21; America, 1886 ***4610.10*** *p160*
Budde, Louise Wilhelmine Friederike; America, 1886 ***4610.10*** *p102*
Budde, Marie; America, 1850 ***4610.10*** *p143*
Buddeberg, Christian; America, 1837 ***1450.2*** *p22A*
Budden, Nathaniel; Philadelphia, 1816 ***2859.11*** *p26*
Budden, Samuel 22; Baltimore, 1775 ***1219.7*** *p270*
Buddicker, Franz; America, 1893 ***1450.2*** *p22A*
Buden, James; New York, NY, 1811 ***2859.11*** *p9*
With family
Buderhill, Edward; Virginia, 1648 ***6219*** *p251*
Budesalic, John; Iowa, 1866-1943 ***123.54*** *p11*
Budge, John; Virginia, 1640 ***6219*** *p182*
Budge, John; Virginia, 1643 ***6219*** *p205*
Budge, William 22; Georgia, 1775 ***1219.7*** *p276*
Budgman, Jane 29; Virginia, 1774 ***1219.7*** *p240*
Budiselic, Slavo; Iowa, 1866-1943 ***123.54*** *p12*
Budiselich, George; Iowa, 1866-1943 ***123.54*** *p57*
Budiselich, Marija; Iowa, 1866-1943 ***123.54*** *p57*
Budiselich, Slavko; Iowa, 1866-1943 ***123.54*** *p57*
Budisilick, Stipan; Iowa, 1866-1943 ***123.54*** *p12*

Budler, B. 35; Port uncertain, 1838 ***778.5*** *p85*
Budles, Tom; Arkansas, 1918 ***95.2*** *p23*
Budnye, Richard; Virginia, 1639 ***6219*** *p155*
Budreckis, John; Wisconsin, n.d. ***9675.5*** *p49*
Budreckis, Stanislaus; Wisconsin, n.d. ***9675.5*** *p49*
Budzilo, Jozef; Arkansas, 1918 ***95.2*** *p24*
Buea, Archibald; Brunswick, NC, 1767 ***1639.20*** *p19*
With wife & son
Buea, Duncan; Brunswick, NC, 1767 ***1639.20*** *p20*
With wife & son
Buea, Duncan; Brunswick, NC, 1767 ***1639.20*** *p20*
Buea, Malcolm; Brunswick, NC, 1767 ***1639.20*** *p20*
Buea, Mary; Brunswick, NC, 1767 ***1639.20*** *p20*
Buea, Neill; Brunswick, NC, 1767 ***1639.20*** *p21*
Bueche, Fiedel; Cincinnati, 1869-1887 ***8582*** *p5*
Buechele, Ferdinand; Wisconsin, n.d. ***9675.5*** *p49*
Buecher, Vincenz; Wisconsin, n.d. ***9675.5*** *p49*
Buechner, Ludwig; Cincinnati, 1788-1848 ***8582.3*** *p90*
Buecker, Ernst; America, 1847 ***8582.3*** *p11*
Buecker, Henry; Illinois, 1860 ***2896.5*** *p6*
Bueenhart, Jacob; Illinois, 1886 ***2896.5*** *p6*
Buehle, Cretien 25; New Orleans, 1839 ***778.5*** *p85*
Buehler, Christian; Milwaukee, 1855 ***2896.5*** *p6*
Buehler, John 56; Indiana, 1906 ***1450.2*** *p5B*
Buehler, Joseph; America, 1835 ***1450.2*** *p22A*
Buehler, Ursula; America, 1746 ***2444*** *p165*
Buehmann, J. H.; America, 1837 ***8582.1*** *p5*
Buehner, Nicolaus; Pennsylvania, 1754 ***4525*** *p204*
With wife
Buehner, Thomas; Pennsylvania, 1754 ***4525*** *p204*
With wife
Buehrer, John; Illinois, 1895 ***2896.5*** *p6*
Buehrmann, John Heinrich; America, 1850 ***8582.3*** *p11*
Buelow, Freiherr von; Cincinnati, 1788-1848 ***8582.3*** *p89*
Buelow, Alexander von; Nicaragua, 1856 ***8582.3*** *p30*
Buenger, Otto Erich; Wisconsin, n.d. ***9675.5*** *p49*
Buening, Mr.; Cincinnati, 1866 ***8582.1*** *p15*
Buening, Johann Hermann; America, 1845 ***8582.3*** *p11*
Buente, Frederick; Indiana, 1848 ***9117*** *p19*
Buerckle, Johann Georg; Cincinnati, 1869-1887 ***8582*** *p5*
Buercklin, Christian *SEE* Buercklin, Eberhard
Buercklin, Eberhard *SEE* Buercklin, Eberhard
Buercklin, Eberhard; Pennsylvania, 1750-1776 ***2444*** *p144*
*Wife:*Margaretha Hoff
*Child:*Eberhard
*Child:*Johann Jacob
*Child:*Christian
*Child:*Joachim
*Child:*Johann Jacob
*Child:*Heinrich Adam
Buercklin, Heinrich Adam *SEE* Buercklin, Eberhard
Buercklin, Joachim *SEE* Buercklin, Eberhard
Buercklin, Johann Jacob *SEE* Buercklin, Eberhard
Buercklin, Johann Jacob *SEE* Buercklin, Eberhard
Buercklin, Margaretha Hoff *SEE* Buercklin, Eberhard
Buerger, Erich Herman; Wisconsin, n.d. ***9675.5*** *p49*
Buerger, George; Wisconsin, n.d. ***9675.5*** *p49*
Buerger, Johann Gottfried; Wisconsin, n.d. ***9675.5*** *p49*
Buerger, Johans Michel; Pennsylvania, 1752 ***4525*** *p202*
Buerger, Phillipp H.; Cincinnati, 1869-1887 ***8582*** *p5*
Buerger, Rudolph; Baltimore, 1834 ***1450.2*** *p23A*
Buergler, Havia; New York, 1890 ***1450.2*** *p5B*
Buerkel, Mathias; Kentucky, 1840-1845 ***8582.3*** *p100*
Buerkert, William 16; New York, NY, 1875 ***3702.7*** *p406*
Buerkle, . . .; Cincinnati, 1788-1848 ***8582.3*** *p90*
Buerkle, Franz Xavier; Cincinnati, 1869-1887 ***8582*** *p5*
Buerkle, Johann G. 24; Cincinnati, 1832 ***8582*** *p5*
Buet, Jean 26; New Orleans, 1829 ***778.5*** *p86*
Buettel, Andreas *SEE* Buettel, Hans Joerg
Buettel, Burkard; Pennsylvania, 1752 ***4525*** *p204*
With 2 children
Buettel, Christof; Pennsylvania, 1753 ***4525*** *p204*
With wife
Buettel, Hans Joerg; Pennsylvania, 1752 ***4525*** *p204*
With wife & 3 children
*Relative:*Andreas
Buetteman, Fr. Albert; Wisconsin, n.d. ***9675.5*** *p49*
Buettner, Johann Gotthilf; Cincinnati, 1788-1848 ***8582.3*** *p90*
Buff, Johann Jacob; Cincinnati, 1848 ***8582.1*** *p53*
Buff, Siro; Arkansas, 1918 ***95.2*** *p24*
Buffo, Carlo; Colorado, 1905 ***9678.1*** *p156*
Buffo, James; New York, NY, 1893 ***9678.1*** *p156*
Bufort, Rich.; Virginia, 1637 ***6219*** *p112*
Buga, Fred; Wisconsin, n.d. ***9675.5*** *p49*
Bugbye, Jon.; Virginia, 1635 ***6219*** *p20*
Buger, Peter; Philadelphia, 1760 ***9973.7*** *p35*
Buggy, Catharine 18; Massachusetts, 1847 ***5881.1*** *p6*
Bugliosi, Frank; Arkansas, 1918 ***95.2*** *p24*
Bugnara, Rafael 27; West Virginia, 1906 ***9788.3*** *p5*
Buher, John; New York, NY, 1816 ***2859.11*** *p26*
Buhlen, Peter; Wisconsin, n.d. ***9675.5*** *p49*
Buhler, . . .; Canada, 1776-1783 ***9786*** *p18*
Buhler, Elise 39; America, 1854-1855 ***9162.6*** *p105*
Buhler, Joseph 50; America, 1836 ***778.5*** *p86*
Buhler, Karolina 17; Port uncertain, 1839 ***778.5*** *p86*
Buhlmann, Joseph; Wisconsin, n.d. ***9675.5*** *p49*
Buhot, Louis; Louisiana, 1789-1819 ***778.5*** *p555*
Buhr, Herman; New York, 1884 ***1450.2*** *p5B*
Buhr, John; Illinois, 1892 ***5012.40*** *p27*
Buhr, Joseph; Cincinnati, 1869-1887 ***8582*** *p5*
Buhr, Peter; Ohio, 1847 ***8582.2*** *p58*
Buhs, Haye; Illinois, 1892 ***5012.40*** *p27*
Buia, Duncan; North Carolina, 1724-1819 ***1639.20*** *p20*
Buichel, Christian 44; New Orleans, 1862 ***543.30*** *p326*
Buictrich, Phillip; Iowa, 1866-1943 ***123.54*** *p12*
Buidler, Chat.; New Orleans, 1837 ***5647.5*** *p4*
Buie, Archibald; Brunswick, NC, 1739 ***1639.20*** *p19*
Buie, Archibald; North Carolina, 1764 ***1639.20*** *p19*
With family
Buie, Daniel; Brunswick, NC, 1739 ***1639.20*** *p20*
Buie, Duncan; Brunswick, NC, 1739 ***1639.20*** *p20*
Buie, Malcolm; North Carolina, 1764 ***1639.20*** *p20*
With family
Buie, William; North Carolina, 1770-1870 ***1639.20*** *p21*
Buirburk, John; Ohio, 1868 ***6014.2*** *p7*
Buison, Mr. 19; America, 1825 ***778.5*** *p86*
Buissard, Jean 26; New Orleans, 1837 ***778.5*** *p86*
Buist, Arthur; Charleston, SC, 1820 ***1639.20*** *p21*
Buist, George; Charleston, SC, 1793 ***1639.20*** *p21*
Buitkus, John; Wisconsin, n.d. ***9675.5*** *p49*
Buivid, Louis; Wisconsin, n.d. ***9675.5*** *p49*
Buivid, Victoria; Wisconsin, n.d. ***9675.5*** *p49*
Bujac, Mr. 21; America, 1838 ***778.5*** *p86*
Bujard, Victor 29; America, 1831 ***778.5*** *p86*
Bukingham, William 19; Maryland, 1721 ***3690.1*** *p23*
Bulach, Anton; America, 1866 ***1450.2*** *p23A*
Buland, G. L.; Washington, 1859-1920 ***2872.1*** *p5*
Bulcock, Tho 22; Virginia, 1699 ***2212*** *p27*
Bulcock, Will 17; Virginia, 1699 ***2212*** *p27*
Bulekens, Adolf Josef Francois; Arkansas, 1918 ***95.2*** *p24*
Bulger, Margaret 30; Massachusetts, 1850 ***5881.1*** *p11*
Bulger, Patrick; New York, NY, 1838 ***8208.4*** *p75*
Bulger, Winneford 3; Massachusetts, 1850 ***5881.1*** *p12*
Bulgin, Joseph 28; Maryland, 1774 ***1219.7*** *p193*
Bulit, P. 35; New Orleans, 1829 ***778.5*** *p86*
Bulitschek, Joseph; New York, 1754 ***3652*** *p79*
Bulkowski, Stanley; Arkansas, 1918 ***95.2*** *p24*
Bull, Mr. 40; Grenada, 1774 ***1219.7*** *p245*
Bull, Edward 18; West Indies, 1722 ***3690.1*** *p32*
Bull, Elz. 15; Canada, 1838 ***4535.12*** *p113*
Bull, Georg; Virginia, 1639 ***6219*** *p152*
Bull, Henry; Newport, RI, 1765 ***1219.7*** *p108*
Bull, James 15; Philadelphia, 1775 ***1219.7*** *p274*
Bull, John; New York, NY, 1811 ***2859.11*** *p9*
Bull, John 36; Kansas, 1879 ***5240.1*** *p60*
Bull, Mary; Philadelphia, 1811 ***53.26*** *p8*
Bull, Mary; Philadelphia, 1811 ***2859.11*** *p9*
Bull, Miles 20; Jamaica, 1722 ***3690.1*** *p32*
Bullan, Richard 19; Jamaica, 1725 ***3690.1*** *p32*
Bulland, Richard 19; Jamaica, 1725 ***3690.1*** *p32*
Bullard, J.; Washington, 1859-1920 ***2872.1*** *p5*
Bullard, Jon.; Virginia, 1642 ***6219*** *p190*
Bullard, Tho.; Virginia, 1637 ***6219*** *p114*
Bullen, Henry; New York, NY, 1811 ***2859.11*** *p9*
Bullen, John 18; Maryland, 1775 ***1219.7*** *p250*
Bullen, Joseph 16; Maryland, 1730 ***3690.1*** *p32*
Bullen, Mary; New York, NY, 1811 ***2859.11*** *p9*
Buller, Tho.; Virginia, 1642 ***6219*** *p196*
Buller, Tho.; Virginia, 1643 ***6219*** *p206*
Bullerstein, Fred; Wisconsin, n.d. ***9675.5*** *p49*
Bullet, Jules 27; America, 1837 ***778.5*** *p86*
Bulley, Mathew 20; Maryland, 1727 ***3690.1*** *p289*
Bulley, Thomas 24; Maryland, 1737 ***3690.1*** *p32*
Bulliard, Etienne; Louisiana, 1789-1819 ***778.5*** *p555*
Bullion, Biddy; Philadelphia, 1850 ***53.26*** *p8*
Bullion, Biddy; Philadelphia, 1850 ***5704.8*** *p59*
Bullman, Robert 25; Massachusetts, 1850 ***5881.1*** *p12*
Bullmann, Anne Marie Cath.; America, 1838-1846 ***4610.10*** *p155*
Bulloch, James; Charleston, SC, 1728 ***1639.20*** *p21*
Bullock, Geo.; Virginia, 1635 ***6219*** *p20*
Bullock, Geo.; Virginia, 1637 ***6219*** *p112*
Bullock, Joane; Virginia, 1636 ***6219*** *p78*
Bullock, Richard; Virginia, 1641 ***6219*** *p187*
Bullock, William; Virginia, 1638 ***6219*** *p147*
Bulman, Diana 4 *SEE* Bulman, George
Bulman, Elizabeth 36 *SEE* Bulman, George
Bulman, George 5 *SEE* Bulman, George
Bulman, George 46; Georgia, 1775 ***1219.7*** *p276*
*Wife:*Elizabeth 36
*Child:*George 5
*Child:*Diana 4
Bulmer, Benis; Virginia, 1635 ***6219*** *p71*
Bulmer, George 14 *SEE* Bulmer, John
Bulmer, Grace 46 *SEE* Bulmer, John
Bulmer, James 20 *SEE* Bulmer, John
Bulmer, John 45; Nova Scotia, 1774 ***1219.7*** *p194*
*Wife:*Grace 46
*Child:*James 20
*Child:*George 14
*Child:*Joseph 10
Bulmer, Joseph 10 *SEE* Bulmer, John
Bulmer, Thos.; Virginia, 1636 ***6219*** *p28*
Bulmur, Tho.; Virginia, 1637 ***6219*** *p28*
Bulotti, Abondi; Arizona, 1890 ***2764.35*** *p8*
Bulstermann, Anna; Iowa, 1848 ***8125.8*** *p436*
Bultemeier, Marie Caroline Friederike; America, 1845 ***4610.10*** *p120*
Bultemeyer, Louise Engel; America, 1850 ***4610.10*** *p147*
Bultmann, C. F.; Cincinnati, 1869-1887 ***8582*** *p5*
Bulz, Charles; Virginia, 1858 ***4626.16*** *p17*
Bumber, Edwd 14; Maryland or Virginia, 1699 ***2212*** *p23*
Bumbridge, Christopher; Virginia, 1639 ***6219*** *p152*
Bumiller, Theodor; America, 1850 ***8582.2*** *p5*
Bumont, Louis Nomen; Arkansas, 1918 ***95.2*** *p24*
Bumpas, Richard; Virginia, 1638-1700 ***6219*** *p150*
Bumpass, Richard; Virginia, 1636 ***6219*** *p23*
Bumruck, Charles 30; Massachusetts, 1860 ***6410.32*** *p99*
Bumster, John; New York, NY, 1838 ***8208.4*** *p64*
Bun, Allen 16; Maryland, 1729 ***3690.1*** *p32*
Bun, William 17; Pennsylvania, 1731 ***3690.1*** *p32*
Bunau, von; New York, 1776 ***9786*** *p279*
Bunce, Charles F.; New York, NY, 1840 ***8208.4*** *p106*
Bundt, August; Wisconsin, n.d. ***9675.5*** *p49*
Bunermann, A.M. Louise; America, 1843-1844 ***4610.10*** *p111*
Bunet, P. A. 30; America, 1839 ***778.5*** *p86*
Bunetin, Mr. 22; America, 1826 ***778.5*** *p86*
Bunetta, Vence; Iowa, 1866-1943 ***123.54*** *p12*
Bung, Joseph; Wisconsin, n.d. ***9675.5*** *p49*
Bunger, Clementine 15; New Orleans, 1839 ***9420.2*** *p166*
Bunger, Emilie 26; New Orleans, 1839 ***9420.1*** *p376*
Bunger, Ernst 21; New Orleans, 1839 ***9420.2*** *p166*
Bunger, Herrmann 14; New Orleans, 1839 ***9420.2*** *p166*
Bunger, Liddy 11; New Orleans, 1839 ***9420.2*** *p166*
Bunger, Theodor 17; New Orleans, 1839 ***9420.2*** *p166*
Bunham, Ann; New York, NY, 1811 ***2859.11*** *p9*
Bunk, Lukas; Arkansas, 1918 ***95.2*** *p24*
Bunkle, George; Georgia, 1734 ***1639.20*** *p21*
Bunn, John 24; Jamaica, 1738 ***3690.1*** *p32*
Bunnett, Thomas 23; Jamaica, 1724 ***3690.1*** *p22*
Bunta, Joseph 27; America, 1837 ***778.5*** *p86*
Bunte, Johann H.; Cincinnati, 1869-1887 ***8582*** *p5*
Bunte, John; New York, NY, 1868 ***1450.2*** *p6B*
Buntin, Bessy 17; Massachusetts, 1849 ***5881.1*** *p6*
Buntin, John 50; Massachusetts, 1849 ***5881.1*** *p8*
Bunting, Catharine 10; New York, NY, 1865 ***5704.8*** *p196*
Bunting, James; New York, NY, 1865 ***5704.8*** *p196*
Bunting, James; Philadelphia, 1865 ***5704.8*** *p201*
Bunting, Jane; New York, NY, 1865 ***5704.8*** *p196*
Bunton, John 28; Massachusetts, 1860 ***6410.32*** *p104*
Buntrey, Mrs.; Philadelphia, 1852 ***5704.8*** *p96*
Buntrey, David 7; Philadelphia, 1852 ***5704.8*** *p96*
Buntrey, Emly 9 mos; Philadelphia, 1852 ***5704.8*** *p96*
Buntrey, James 5; Philadelphia, 1852 ***5704.8*** *p96*
Buntrey, Jane 12; Philadelphia, 1852 ***5704.8*** *p96*
Buntrey, Sarah 3; Philadelphia, 1852 ***5704.8*** *p96*
Buntrey, Stewart; Philadelphia, 1852 ***5704.8*** *p96*
Buohilly, Daniel; America, 1742 ***4971*** *p56*
Buracivsky, Waldyslaw; Iowa, 1866-1943 ***123.54*** *p12*
Buras, Albert 7; New York, NY, 1862 ***9831.18*** *p16*
Buras, Carl 8; New York, NY, 1862 ***9831.18*** *p16*
Buras, Carl 41; New York, NY, 1862 ***9831.18*** *p16*
Buras, Charlotte 48; New York, NY, 1862 ***9831.18*** *p16*
Buras, Gustav 17; New York, NY, 1862 ***9831.18*** *p16*
Burbach, Caroline 24; New York, NY, 1857 ***9831.14*** *p153*
Burbach, Christian 14; New York, NY, 1857 ***9831.14*** *p153*
Burbach, Elisabeth 22; New York, NY, 1857 ***9831.14*** *p153*
Burbach, Friedrich 4; New York, NY, 1857 ***9831.14*** *p153*
Burbach, Joseph; Wisconsin, n.d. ***9675.5*** *p49*
Burbach, Louise 31; New York, NY, 1857 ***9831.14*** *p153*
Burbach, Louise 50; New York, NY, 1857 ***9831.14*** *p153*
Burbach, Ludwig 59; New York, NY, 1857 ***9831.14*** *p153*
Burbach, Wilhelmine 19; New York, NY, 1857 ***9831.14*** *p153*
Burbage, Tho.; Virginia, 1642 ***6219*** *p193*
Burbage, William; Virginia, 1638 ***6219*** *p153*
Burbidge, Thomas 19; Maryland, 1724 ***3690.1*** *p32*
Burbidge, Timothy 20; Maryland, 1725 ***3690.1*** *p32*
Burch, Anthony 19; Maryland, 1729 ***3690.1*** *p32*

Burch, Christian; America, 1854 ***1450.2*** *p23A*
Burch, John 30; Maryland, 1775 ***1219.7*** *p259*
Burch, Jon.; Virginia, 1637 ***6219*** *p85*
Burch, Michael 30?; New Orleans, 1862 ***543.30*** *p326*
Burch, Robert; Washington, 1859-1920 ***2872.1*** *p5*
Burch, Salmon 28; America, 1839 ***778.5*** *p86*
Burch, Thomas 16; Maryland, 1775 ***1219.7*** *p272*
Burch, Thomas 19; Maryland, 1720 ***3690.1*** *p33*
Burch, William; New York, NY, 1837 ***8208.4*** *p34*
Burchal, Edward 21; Maryland, 1774 ***1219.7*** *p235*
Burcham, A. J.; Washington, 1859-1920 ***2872.1*** *p5*
Burchard, . . .; Canada, 1776-1783 ***9786*** *p18*
Burchard, Christian H.; Illinois, 1869 ***5012.38*** *p99*
Burchard, Ferdinand; Wisconsin, n.d. ***9675.5*** *p49*
Burchard, G. W.; Washington, 1859-1920 ***2872.1*** *p5*
Burchard, William; Illinois, 1869 ***5012.38*** *p99*
Burchel, Joseph 24; New Orleans, 1862 ***543.30*** *p112*
Burchell, Hen.; Virginia, 1642 ***6219*** *p196*
Burcher, Abraham; Virginia, 1638 ***6219*** *p125*
Burcher, Edwd.; Virginia, 1643 ***6219*** *p200*
Burcher, Humphrey; Virginia, 1636 ***6219*** *p80*
Burcher, Humphrey; Virginia, 1639 ***6219*** *p161*
Burcher, Tho.; Virginia, 1638 ***6219*** *p116*
Burchett, Joseph; Antigua (Antego), 1765 ***1219.7*** *p113*
Burchett, Thomas 20; Jamaica, 1730 ***3690.1*** *p33*
Burchhard, . . .; Canada, 1776-1783 ***9786*** *p18*
Burchill, William; New York, NY, 1816 ***2859.11*** *p26*
Burchord, Deidrich; Kansas, 1888 ***5240.1*** *p7*
Burck, George; New York, NY, 1891 ***1450.2*** *p6B*
Burckard, . . .; Canada, 1776-1783 ***9786*** *p18*
Burckard, Joseph; America, 1850 ***8582.3*** *p11*
Burckart, F. X.; Cincinnati, 1869-1887 ***8582*** *p5*
Burckhard, Elisabetha Roth *SEE* Burckhard, Joachim
Burckhard, Jacob *SEE* Burckhard, Joachim
Burckhard, Joachim; America, 1755-1800 ***2444*** *p144*
*Wife:*Elisabetha Roth
*Child:*Jacob
Burckhardt, Dr. Louis; America, 1893 ***1450.2*** *p23A*
Burckhardt, Johannes; America, 1777-1778 ***8582.2*** *p67*
Burckmayer, Maria Catharina; Pennsylvania, 1749 ***2444*** *p138*
With 8 children
Burdeau, Francois 26; New Orleans, 1838 ***778.5*** *p87*
Burdek, Terkil; Arkansas, 1918 ***95.2*** *p24*
Burden, Edw.; Virginia, 1637 ***6219*** *p13*
Burden, John; Virginia, 1636 ***6219*** *p13*
Burden, John; Virginia, 1636 ***6219*** *p146*
Burden, John; Virginia, 1637 ***6219*** *p11*
Burden, Jon.; Virginia, 1637 ***6219*** *p10*
Burden, Jon.; Virginia, 1637 ***6219*** *p13*
Burdet, B. M. 20; New Orleans, 1820 ***778.5*** *p87*
Burdett, Chastene; Virginia, 1648 ***6219*** *p246*
Burdett, Elizabeth 18; Philadelphia, 1774 ***1219.7*** *p182*
Burdett, Fco. 30; New Orleans, 1831 ***778.5*** *p87*
Burdett, William; Virginia, 1639 ***6219*** *p162*
Burdin, Jean 32; New Orleans, 1822 ***778.5*** *p84*
Burditt, Thomas 20; West Indies, 1722 ***3690.1*** *p33*
Burdock, Benjamin 23; Maryland, 1775 ***1219.7*** *p262*
Burdock, George 34; Jamaica, 1731 ***3690.1*** *p33*
Burdon, Hannah 27; Virginia, 1774 ***1219.7*** *p240*
Burdon, Samuel 16; Jamaica, 1735 ***3690.1*** *p33*
Burdorf, Dietrich; Nebraska, 1894 ***5240.1*** *p7*
Burdus, Richard 20; Maryland, 1734 ***3690.1*** *p33*
Bureau, Louis Marcellin 34; Louisiana, 1820 ***778.5*** *p87*
Burelle, Angello 32; West Virginia, 1898 ***9788.3*** *p5*
Bureski, Mary; Iowa, 1866-1943 ***123.54*** *p57*
Burfe, James; Virginia, 1635 ***6219*** *p71*
Burfoote, Ann; Virginia, 1639 ***6219*** *p161*
Burfoote, Saml.; Virginia, 1634 ***6219*** *p84*
Burford, Edward 21; Maryland, 1775 ***1219.7*** *p247*
Burford, Geo., Jr.; Virginia, 1643 ***6219*** *p203*
Burford, Georg; Virginia, 1643 ***6219*** *p23*
Burford, Georg, Sr.; Virginia, 1643 ***6219*** *p203*
Burford, Wm.; Virginia, 1637 ***6219*** *p24*
Burfur, Wm.; Virginia, 1639 ***6219*** *p154*
Burg, Joseph; Arkansas, 1918 ***95.2*** *p24*
Burg, Joseph; Arkansas, 1918 ***95.2*** *p49*
Burgaila, Alexander; Wisconsin, n.d. ***9675.5*** *p49*
Burgaila, Mary; Wisconsin, n.d. ***9675.5*** *p49*
Burgand, Kaspar; Lancaster, PA, 1780 ***8137*** *p7*
Burgdorf, Henry; Indiana, 1850 ***9117*** *p20*
Burgdorff, Ludwig Traugott; Quebec, 1776 ***9786*** *p256*
Burgees, Catherine; Montreal, 1823 ***7603*** *p89*
Burgen, Evan; Virginia, 1643 ***6219*** *p230*
Burgender, Paul 29; America, 1838 ***778.5*** *p87*
Burgeois, Edem 36; Port uncertain, 1838 ***778.5*** *p87*
Burger, . . .; Pennsylvania, 1769 ***4525*** *p265*
Burger, Reverend; New Orleans, 1839 ***9420.1*** *p373*
Burger, Andw.; Newfoundland, 1834 ***8893*** *p263*
Burger, Catherine 2; America, 1837 ***778.5*** *p87*
Burger, Catherine 23; America, 1837 ***778.5*** *p87*
Burger, Elisa 21; America, 1837 ***778.5*** *p87*
Burger, Ernst Moritz; America, 1839 ***3702.7*** *p308*
Burger, Ernst Moritz 33; New Orleans, 1839 ***9420.1*** *p375*
Burger, Hans Michel; Pennsylvania, 1752 ***4525*** *p202*
Burger, Jacob 24; New Orleans, 1831 ***778.5*** *p87*
Burger, Jean 34; America, 1837 ***778.5*** *p87*
Burger, Johanna 26; New Orleans, 1839 ***9420.1*** *p375*
Burger, Johannes Nicholas 33; Pennsylvania, 1753 ***4525*** *p202*
Burger, John 50; New Orleans, 1831 ***778.5*** *p87*
Burger, Madeline 22; New Orleans, 1831 ***778.5*** *p87*
Burger, Margaret 20; New Orleans, 1831 ***778.5*** *p87*
Burger, Margaretha; Pennsylvania, 1750 ***2444*** *p146*
Burger, Martha 14; New Orleans, 1831 ***778.5*** *p87*
Burger, Martin 10 mos; New Orleans, 1839 ***9420.1*** *p375*
Burger, Mary 5; Massachusetts, 1849 ***5881.1*** *p10*
Burger, Mary 25; New Orleans, 1831 ***778.5*** *p88*
Burger, Mary 46; New Orleans, 1831 ***778.5*** *p88*
Burger, Paul 3; New Orleans, 1839 ***9420.1*** *p375*
Burgery, Peter; Philadelphia, 1850 ***53.26*** *p8*
Burgery, Peter; Philadelphia, 1850 ***5704.8*** *p60*
Burges, J. 21; Virginia, 1774 ***1219.7*** *p240*
Burges, James; Charleston, SC, 1788 ***1639.20*** *p21*
Burges, James; North Carolina, 1787 ***1639.20*** *p21*
Burges, James 25; Jamaica, 1733 ***3690.1*** *p33*
Burges, James 27; North Carolina, 1775 ***1639.20*** *p21*
*Wife:*Margaret Hogg
Burges, John; Virginia, 1635 ***6219*** *p73*
Burges, John; Virginia, 1639 ***6219*** *p153*
Burges, Jon.; Virginia, 1637 ***6219*** *p113*
Burges, Margaret Hogg *SEE* Burges, James
Burges, Mary; Virginia, 1643 ***6219*** *p208*
Burges, Richard; Virginia, 1637 ***6219*** *p117*
Burges, Wm.; Virginia, 1637 ***6219*** *p85*
Burgeson, Sven; Iowa, 1853 ***2090*** *p611*
Burgess, Mr. 26; Dominica, 1774 ***1219.7*** *p223*
Burgess, Alexander 43; Kansas, 1901 ***5240.1*** *p7*
Burgess, Alexander 43; Kansas, 1901 ***5240.1*** *p82*
Burgess, Arthur; Quebec, 1850 ***5704.8*** *p63*
Burgess, Francis 16; Jamaica, 1733 ***3690.1*** *p33*
Burgess, John; Quebec, 1850 ***5704.8*** *p63*
Burgess, Mary; Quebec, 1850 ***5704.8*** *p63*
Burgess, William 34; Virginia, 1773 ***1219.7*** *p170*
Burgesse, Georg 22; America, 1702 ***2212*** *p39*
Burget, Jakob; Cincinnati, 1824 ***8582.1*** *p51*
Burgets, William 40; Boston, 1774 ***1219.7*** *p188*
Burgey, Peter; Philadelphia, 1741 ***4349*** *p46*
Burgeyny, Rich.; Virginia, 1642 ***6219*** *p192*
Burgfeldt, Joseph 23; New Orleans, 1862 ***543.30*** *p480*
Burggrabe, Christian Heinrich; America, 1851 ***4610.10*** *p98*
Burggrabe, Johann Heinrich Friedrich; America, 1848 ***4610.10*** *p97*
Burgh, John 20; Philadelphia, 1774 ***1219.7*** *p197*
Burghardt, Jacob 26; New Orleans, 1863 ***543.30*** *p248*
Burghoff, . . .; Quebec, 1776 ***9786*** *p105*
Burghoff, Johann Friedrich Heinrich; Quebec, 1776 ***9786*** *p255*
Burgis, John; Virginia, 1639 ***6219*** *p161*
Burgis, John; Virginia, 1648 ***6219*** *p249*
Burgis, Joseph; Virginia, 1752 ***1219.7*** *p14*
Burgis, Richard; Virginia, 1640 ***6219*** *p182*
Burgogne, . . .; Halifax, N.S., 1752 ***7074.6*** *p230*
Burgoyne, . . .; Halifax, N.S., 1752 ***7074.6*** *p230*
Burgoyne, Alexander D.; Washington, 1859-1920 ***2872.1*** *p5*
Burgoyne, Catherine; Washington, 1859-1920 ***2872.1*** *p6*
Burgoyne, Florence; Washington, 1859-1920 ***2872.1*** *p6*
Burgoyne, John; Washington, 1859-1920 ***2872.1*** *p6*
Burgoyne, Joseph; Washington, 1859-1920 ***2872.1*** *p6*
Burgoyne, Lillian; Washington, 1859-1920 ***2872.1*** *p6*
Burgoyne, Teressa; Washington, 1859-1920 ***2872.1*** *p6*
Burgsdorf, v.; Quebec, 1776 ***9786*** *p105*
Burgsteiner, Agatha *SEE* Burgsteiner, Matthias
Burgsteiner, Agatha *SEE* Burgsteiner, Matthias
Burgsteiner, Matthias; Georgia, 1738 ***9332*** *p321*
Burgsteiner, Matthias; Georgia, 1739 ***9332*** *p324*
*Wife:*Agatha
Burgsteiner, Matthias; Georgia, 1739 ***9332*** *p326*
*Wife:*Agatha
Burgstrom, Charles W.; Illinois, 1888 ***5012.39*** *p121*
Burgueof, E. 26; Louisiana, 1831 ***778.5*** *p88*
Burguiere, Louis 25; New Orleans, 1822 ***778.5*** *p88*
Burgur, Robt.; Newfoundland, 1843 ***8893*** *p264*
Burgy, . . .; Canada, 1776-1783 ***9786*** *p18*
Burgy, John James; New York, NY, 1838 ***8208.4*** *p56*
Burhop, John Henry; Wisconsin, n.d. ***9675.5*** *p49*
Burin, Justina; Virginia, 1775 ***1219.7*** *p275*
Burk, Alice 1; Massachusetts, 1849 ***5881.1*** *p6*
Burk, Anna; Virginia, 1647 ***6219*** *p245*
Burk, Anna Maria *SEE* Burk, Michel
Burk, Bridget 3; Massachusetts, 1849 ***5881.1*** *p6*
Burk, Catherine 18; St. John, N.B., 1857 ***5704.8*** *p135*
Burk, Edward; St. John, N.B., 1856 ***5704.8*** *p131*
Burk, Edward 6; St. John, N.B., 1857 ***5704.8*** *p135*
Burk, Edward 27; Maryland, 1731 ***3690.1*** *p33*
Burk, Elisabetha *SEE* Burk, Michel
Burk, Elizabeth; South Carolina, 1767 ***1639.20*** *p22*
Burk, Elizabeth 8; St. John, N.B., 1857 ***5704.8*** *p135*
Burk, Elizabeth 18; Maryland, 1774 ***1219.7*** *p207*
Burk, James; Ohio, 1841 ***9892.11*** *p6*
Burk, James 11; Massachusetts, 1849 ***5881.1*** *p9*
Burk, John; New York, NY, 1836 ***8208.4*** *p25*
Burk, John 20; Philadelphia, 1864 ***5704.8*** *p161*
Burk, John 24; Maryland, 1774 ***1219.7*** *p192*
Burk, John 42; New Orleans, 1862 ***543.30*** *p327*
Burk, Konrad *SEE* Burk, Michel
Burk, Letitia 22; Philadelphia, 1868 ***5704.8*** *p225*
Burk, Margaret 8; St. John, N.B., 1857 ***5704.8*** *p135*
Burk, Mary 9; Massachusetts, 1849 ***5881.1*** *p10*
Burk, Mary 40; St. John, N.B., 1857 ***5704.8*** *p135*
Burk, Mary Jane 13; St. John, N.B., 1857 ***5704.8*** *p135*
Burk, Matty Ann 4; St. John, N.B., 1857 ***5704.8*** *p135*
Burk, Michael; Illinois, 1860 ***2896.5*** *p6*
Burk, Michael; New York, NY, 1816 ***2859.11*** *p26*
Burk, Michel; Connecticut, 1856 ***3702.7*** *p354*
*Wife:*Anna Maria
*Son:*Konrad
*Daughter:*Elisabetha
Burk, Nancy; Philadelphia, 1864 ***5704.8*** *p180*
Burk, Robert; New York, NY, 1811 ***2859.11*** *p9*
Burk, Robert 2; St. John, N.B., 1857 ***5704.8*** *p135*
Burk, Sarah 19; Philadelphia, 1856 ***5704.8*** *p128*
Burk, Sibby; New York, NY, 1816 ***2859.11*** *p26*
Burk, Thomas; America, 1742 ***4971*** *p17*
Burk, Tom; Arkansas, 1918 ***95.2*** *p24*
Burk, W. H.; Washington, 1859-1920 ***2872.1*** *p6*
Burk, William; New York, NY, 1816 ***2859.11*** *p26*
Burk, William 9; Massachusetts, 1849 ***5881.1*** *p12*
Burk, William 16; St. John, N.B., 1857 ***5704.8*** *p135*
Burkamp, Ernst; Wisconsin, n.d. ***9675.5*** *p49*
Burkamp, Frederick; Wisconsin, n.d. ***9675.5*** *p49*
Burkamp, Phillip; Wisconsin, n.d. ***9675.5*** *p49*
Burkard, F. Joseph; Cincinnati, 1869-1887 ***8582*** *p5*
Burkart, Peter; New York, 1831 ***9892.11*** *p6*
Burkart, Peter; Ohio, 1836 ***9892.11*** *p6*
Burke, Anne; New York, NY, 1816 ***2859.11*** *p26*
Burke, Bartle; Illinois, 1894 ***5012.40*** *p53*
Burke, Biddy 11; St. John, N.B., 1847 ***5704.8*** *p34*
Burke, Catherine; Philadelphia, 1848 ***53.26*** *p8*
Burke, Catherine; Philadelphia, 1848 ***5704.8*** *p46*
Burke, Catherine; St. John, N.B., 1847 ***5704.8*** *p34*
Burke, Charles 3 mos *SEE* Burke, John
Burke, Charles 3 mos; Philadelphia, 1847 ***5704.8*** *p5*
Burke, Charles 9; St. John, N.B., 1847 ***5704.8*** *p34*
Burke, Edmund 32; New Orleans, 1862 ***543.30*** *p482*
Burke, Edwd.; New York, NY, 1816 ***2859.11*** *p26*
Burke, Eliza 5; Massachusetts, 1850 ***5881.1*** *p7*
Burke, Ellan; Philadelphia, 1849 ***5704.8*** *p50*
Burke, Ellen; Philadelphia, 1849 ***53.26*** *p8*
Burke, Fanny; Quebec, 1851 ***5704.8*** *p73*
Burke, Francis; New York, NY, 1816 ***2859.11*** *p26*
Burke, Francis; Philadelphia, 1850 ***53.26*** *p8*
Burke, Francis; Philadelphia, 1850 ***5704.8*** *p68*
Burke, Francis 40; Philadelphia, 1833-1834 ***53.26*** *p8*
*Relative:*Mary 30
Burke, Frank E.; Colorado, 1906 ***9678.1*** *p156*
Burke, Honora 14; Massachusetts, 1849 ***5881.1*** *p8*
Burke, Honora 60; Massachusetts, 1848 ***5881.1*** *p8*
Burke, James; Quebec, 1795 ***7603*** *p74*
Burke, James; St. John, N.B., 1847 ***5704.8*** *p34*
Burke, James 9 mos; St. John, N.B., 1847 ***5704.8*** *p34*
Burke, James 2 *SEE* Burke, John
Burke, James 2; Philadelphia, 1847 ***5704.8*** *p5*
Burke, James 18; St. John, N.B., 1854 ***5704.8*** *p114*
Burke, James 28; New Orleans, 1862 ***543.30*** *p116*
Burke, James 50; Massachusetts, 1849 ***5881.1*** *p9*
Burke, Jane 5; St. John, N.B., 1847 ***5704.8*** *p34*
Burke, John; Illinois, 1895 ***5012.40*** *p54*
Burke, John; Montreal, 1814 ***7603*** *p56*
Burke, John; New York, NY, 1816 ***2859.11*** *p26*
Burke, John; Philadelphia, 1847 ***53.26*** *p9*
*Relative:*Rosey
*Relative:*Thomas 6
*Relative:*John 4
*Relative:*James 2
*Relative:*Charles 3 mos
Burke, John; Philadelphia, 1847 ***5704.8*** *p5*
Burke, John 4 *SEE* Burke, John
Burke, John 4; Philadelphia, 1847 ***5704.8*** *p5*
Burke, John 15; Massachusetts, 1849 ***5881.1*** *p8*
Burke, John 16; Tortola, 1774 ***1219.7*** *p237*
Burke, John 20; St. John, N.B., 1854 ***5704.8*** *p114*
Burke, John Martin; New York, NY, 1847 ***6013.19*** *p29*
Burke, John Michael 27; New Orleans, 1862 ***543.30*** *p116*
Burke, John R. 45; Arizona, 1890 ***2764.35*** *p5*

58 *FOR A COMPLETE EXPLANATION OF ENTRY, SEE "HOW TO READ A CITATION" SECTION*

Burke, Julie; Montreal, 1822 ***7603*** *p98*
Burke, Margaret 9; St. John, N.B., 1854 ***5704.8*** *p120*
Burke, Margaret 11; Massachusetts, 1849 ***5881.1*** *p11*
Burke, Margaret 56; Massachusetts, 1850 ***5881.1*** *p11*
Burke, Maria 15; Massachusetts, 1849 ***5881.1*** *p10*
Burke, Martin 22; Massachusetts, 1849 ***5881.1*** *p10*
Burke, Mary; Philadelphia, 1853 ***5704.8*** *p100*
Burke, Mary; Quebec, 1851 ***5704.8*** *p73*
Burke, Mary 3; St. John, N.B., 1847 ***5704.8*** *p34*
Burke, Mary 20; Massachusetts, 1849 ***5881.1*** *p10*
Burke, Mary 27; Massachusetts, 1850 ***5881.1*** *p11*
Burke, Mary 30 *SEE* Burke, Francis
Burke, Michael; Wisconsin, n.d. ***9675.5*** *p49*
Burke, Michael 5; Massachusetts, 1849 ***5881.1*** *p10*
Burke, Michael 20; America, 1853 ***2896.5*** *p6*
Burke, Michael 22; Massachusetts, 1849 ***5881.1*** *p10*
Burke, Michael 30; Massachusetts, 1847 ***5881.1*** *p9*
Burke, Michael 55; Massachusetts, 1849 ***5881.1*** *p10*
Burke, Michael Joseph; Arkansas, 1918 ***95.2*** *p24*
Burke, Ormsby; Quebec, 1825 ***7603*** *p83*
Burke, Pat 7; St. John, N.B., 1847 ***5704.8*** *p34*
Burke, Pat 23; Massachusetts, 1849 ***5881.1*** *p11*
Burke, Patrick; America, 1846 ***5240.1*** *p7*
Burke, Patrick; Wisconsin, n.d. ***9675.5*** *p49*
Burke, Patrick 11; Massachusetts, 1850 ***5881.1*** *p11*
Burke, Patrick 24; Quebec, 1863 ***5704.8*** *p154*
Burke, Patrick 40; Massachusetts, 1847 ***5881.1*** *p11*
Burke, Patrick J.; Illinois, 1896 ***5012.40*** *p54*
Burke, Richard; Quebec, 1825 ***7603*** *p74*
Burke, Rosey *SEE* Burke, John
Burke, Rosey; Philadelphia, 1847 ***5704.8*** *p5*
Burke, Sabina 23; Massachusetts, 1849 ***5881.1*** *p12*
Burke, Sally; Quebec, 1825 ***7603*** *p74*
Burke, Susanna; Maryland, 1742 ***4971*** *p107*
Burke, Thomas; Arkansas, 1918 ***95.2*** *p24*
Burke, Thomas; New York, 1881 ***1450.2*** *p6B*
Burke, Thomas; New York, NY, 1836 ***8208.4*** *p18*
Burke, Thomas; Philadelphia, 1848 ***53.26*** *p9*
Burke, Thomas; Philadelphia, 1848 ***5704.8*** *p40*
Burke, Thomas; St. John, N.B., 1848 ***5704.8*** *p44*
Burke, Thomas 5; Massachusetts, 1850 ***5881.1*** *p12*
Burke, Thomas 6 *SEE* Burke, John
Burke, Thomas 6; Philadelphia, 1847 ***5704.8*** *p5*
Burke, Thomas 24; Massachusetts, 1847 ***5881.1*** *p12*
Burke, Tobey 23; Massachusetts, 1850 ***5881.1*** *p12*
Burke, William; America, 1736 ***4971*** *p12*
Burke, William; Quebec, 1847 ***5704.8*** *p12*
Burke, William 25; Quebec, 1856 ***5704.8*** *p130*
Burke, William 26; Kansas, 1891 ***5240.1*** *p76*
Burke, Wm.; Virginia, 1856 ***4626.16*** *p16*
Burke, Wm.; Wisconsin, n.d. ***9675.5*** *p49*
Burkemeyer, Conrad; Charleston, SC, 1766 ***8582.2*** *p65*
Burkert, William 16; New York, NY, 1875 ***3702.7*** *p408*
Burkett, Ellins; Virginia, 1636 ***6219*** *p78*
Burkett, George 31; Jamaica, 1730 ***3690.1*** *p33*
Burkett, Thomas 19; Jamaica, 1719 ***3690.1*** *p33*
Burkey, Michael; Philadelphia, 1764 ***9973.7*** *p39*
Burkhalter, Christian; Cincinnati, 1788-1848 ***8582.3*** *p89*
Burkhard, George; Philadelphia, 1760 ***9973.7*** *p34*
Burkhard, John Michael; Wisconsin, n.d. ***9675.5*** *p49*
Burkhard, John Philip; Philadelphia, 1760 ***9973.7*** *p34*
Burkhardt, Andreas; Cincinnati, 1869-1887 ***8582*** *p5*
Burkhardt, Andreas; Philadelphia, 1764 ***8582.2*** *p65*
Burkhardt, Aug. German 1 *SEE* Burkhardt, Godfrey
Burkhardt, August; Wisconsin, n.d. ***9675.5*** *p49*
Burkhardt, Charles; Ohio, 1869-1887 ***8582*** *p5*
Burkhardt, Charlot Frederika 5 *SEE* Burkhardt, Christna. Gottl.
Burkhardt, Christna. Concor 27 *SEE* Burkhardt, Godfrey
Burkhardt, Christna. Gottl. 56; New Orleans, 1839 ***9420.2*** *p486*
*Wife:*Mary Rosine 50
*Son:*Gottlieb 16
*Child:*Jane Eleonor 9
*Child:*Charlot Frederika 5
Burkhardt, Godfrey 28; New Orleans, 1839 ***9420.2*** *p486*
*Wife:*Christna. Concor 27
*Child:*Aug. German 1
Burkhardt, Gottlieb 16 *SEE* Burkhardt, Christna. Gottl.
Burkhardt, Jane Eleonor 9 *SEE* Burkhardt, Christna. Gottl.
Burkhardt, John G. 42; Kansas, 1893 ***5240.1*** *p78*
Burkhardt, Mary Rosine 50 *SEE* Burkhardt, Christna. Gottl.
Burkhart, John; Illinois, 1872 ***7857*** *p2*
Burkholder, Martin; Philadelphia, 1760 ***9973.7*** *p34*
Burkholz, Peter; Wisconsin, n.d. ***9675.5*** *p49*
Burkley, Jacob; Illinois, 1860 ***5012.38*** *p97*
Burkman, August Lennard; Arkansas, 1918 ***95.2*** *p24*
Burkmeyer, John; Charleston, SC, 1775 ***8582.2*** *p52*
Burkmire, Daniel; Pennsylvania, 1749 ***2444*** *p138*
Burks, Patrick 18; Jamaica, 1739 ***3690.1*** *p33*
Burl, James 27; America, 1702 ***2212*** *p36*
Burland, Dorothy *SEE* Burland, John
Burland, John; Virginia, 1623-1639 ***6219*** *p156*
*Wife:*Dorothy
Burland, John; Virginia, 1634 ***6219*** *p29*
Burleigh, Alexander 16; Maryland, 1775 ***1219.7*** *p268*
Burleigh, John 19; Newfoundland, 1789 ***4915.24*** *p56*
Burleth, Adam 17; America, 1836 ***778.5*** *p88*
Burleth, Johanna 23; America, 1836 ***778.5*** *p88*
Burley, John 28; Baltimore, 1775 ***1219.7*** *p269*
Burlie, Alfred 37; New Orleans, 1864 ***543.30*** *p247*
Burling, Arthur John 24; Kansas, 1894 ***5240.1*** *p80*
Burlo, Henry 21; Massachusetts, 1847 ***5881.1*** *p8*
Burly, Francis; Virginia, 1637 ***6219*** *p117*
Burman, Rowland; Virginia, 1638 ***6219*** *p123*
Burmeister, Charles 27; New Orleans, 1862 ***543.30*** *p109*
Burmeister, Wilhelm; Missouri, 1859-1861 ***3702.7*** *p495*
Burmesch, Francis; Wisconsin, n.d. ***9675.5*** *p49*
Burmingham, Henry 21; Jamaica, 1734 ***3690.1*** *p34*
Burn, Ann Baron; South Carolina, 1788 ***1639.20*** *p322*
Burn, Arthur; Delaware, 1743 ***4971*** *p105*
Burn, Bryan 22; Philadelphia, 1775 ***1219.7*** *p273*
Burn, Catherine; Delaware, 1743 ***4971*** *p105*
Burn, Catherine; Maryland, 1742 ***4971*** *p107*
Burn, Dennis 17; Port uncertain, 1774 ***1219.7*** *p177*
Burn, Isaac; Delaware, 1743 ***4971*** *p105*
Burn, James; New York, NY, 1816 ***2859.11*** *p26*
Burn, John; Charleston, SC, 1773 ***1639.20*** *p22*
Burn, John 19; Jamaica, 1749 ***3690.1*** *p34*
Burn, Luke 40; Port uncertain, 1774 ***1219.7*** *p176*
Burn, Lydia 19; Maryland, 1774 ***1219.7*** *p207*
Burn, Mary; Annapolis, MD, 1742 ***4971*** *p92*
Burn, Michael; Ohio, 1868 ***6014.2*** *p7*
Burn, Michael 17; Port uncertain, 1774 ***1219.7*** *p176*
Burn, Oliver; Quebec, 1847 ***5704.8*** *p16*
Burn, Thomas 22; Maryland, 1774 ***1219.7*** *p229*
Burn, William; America, 1743 ***4971*** *p80*
Burnard, Richard 27; Jamaica, 1730 ***3690.1*** *p34*
Burnars, John; Colorado, 1903 ***9678.1*** *p156*
Burne, John 20; Philadelphia, 1775 ***1219.7*** *p256*
Burne, Mary; Maryland, 1742 ***4971*** *p106*
Burne, William; America, 1735-1743 ***4971*** *p78*
Burnell, Charles 20; Jamaica, 1725 ***3690.1*** *p34*
Burner, Samuel 22; Philadelphia, 1774 ***1219.7*** *p219*
Burnes, Charles D.; South Carolina, 1824 ***1639.20*** *p22*
Burnes, James; New York, NY, 1811 ***2859.11*** *p9*
Burnes, James 10; Massachusetts, 1850 ***5881.1*** *p9*
Burnes, Patrick; Iowa, 1866-1943 ***123.54*** *p12*
Burnes, Patrick; New York, NY, 1840 ***8208.4*** *p112*
Burnes, William; Illinois, 1860 ***5012.39*** *p90*
Burnet, Judge; Cincinnati, 1820 ***8582.3*** *p89*
Burnet, Andrew; South Carolina, 1752-1764 ***1639.20*** *p22*
Burnet, William 24; Maryland, 1739 ***3690.1*** *p34*
Burnett, Abigail; Virginia, 1698 ***2212*** *p14*
Burnett, Alexander 25; Virginia, 1774 ***1219.7*** *p186*
Burnett, James; Illinois, 1860 ***5012.38*** *p98*
Burnett, James; Virginia, 1639 ***6219*** *p152*
Burnett, James 17; Maryland, 1731 ***3690.1*** *p34*
Burnett, John; America, 1764 ***1219.7*** *p105*
Burnett, Nich.; Virginia, 1636 ***6219*** *p75*
Burnett, Robert; Virginia, 1641 ***6219*** *p184*
Burnett, Robert T.; Illinois, 1892 ***5012.37*** *p63*
Burnett, Samll.; Virginia, 1643 ***6219*** *p229*
Burnett, W.J.; Illinois, 1882 ***5012.39*** *p52*
Burnett, Walter; New York, NY, 1838 ***8208.4*** *p72*
Burney, Charles 22; St. John, N.B., 1864 ***5704.8*** *p159*
Burney, Jane; St. John, N.B., 1848 ***5704.8*** *p45*
Burney, Mary 18; St. John, N.B., 1864 ***5704.8*** *p157*
Burney, Samuel 22; St. John, N.B., 1856 ***5704.8*** *p131*
Burnham, John; Virginia, 1643 ***6219*** *p204*
Burnham, Rowland; Virginia, 1643 ***6219*** *p201*
Burningham, Henry 21; Jamaica, 1734 ***3690.1*** *p34*
Burns, Andrew B.; New York, NY, 1815 ***2859.11*** *p26*
Burns, Ann; Montreal, 1823 ***7603*** *p101*
Burns, Ann; Quebec, 1851 ***5704.8*** *p73*
Burns, Ann; St. John, N.B., 1847 ***5704.8*** *p3*
Burns, Ann 16; Massachusetts, 1847 ***5881.1*** *p6*
Burns, Ann Jane; Philadelphia, 1851 ***5704.8*** *p79*
Burns, Archibald; New York, NY, 1834 ***8208.4*** *p3*
Burns, Barnaby; America, 1737 ***4971*** *p83*
Burns, Bridget; America, 1869 ***5704.8*** *p236*
Burns, Bridget; St. John, N.B., 1847 ***5704.8*** *p11*
Burns, Bridget 6; Massachusetts, 1850 ***5881.1*** *p6*
Burns, Bridget 7; St. John, N.B., 1847 ***5704.8*** *p3*
Burns, Bridget 60; Massachusetts, 1849 ***5881.1*** *p6*
Burns, Catharine 23; Massachusetts, 1847 ***5881.1*** *p6*
Burns, Catharine 30; Massachusetts, 1850 ***5881.1*** *p7*
Burns, Catherine; America, 1740 ***4971*** *p73*
Burns, Catherine; New York, NY, 1811 ***2859.11*** *p9*
Burns, Daniel; Philadelphia, 1849 ***53.26*** *p9*
Burns, Daniel; Philadelphia, 1849 ***5704.8*** *p53*
Burns, Daniel; St. John, N.B., 1847 ***5704.8*** *p3*
Burns, Darby; New York, NY, 1811 ***2859.11*** *p9*
Burns, David 36; California, 1868 ***3840.1*** *p16*
Burns, Edward; Iowa, 1866-1943 ***123.54*** *p12*
Burns, Eliza; Philadelphia, 1865 ***5704.8*** *p186*
Burns, Elizabeth; New York, NY, 1811 ***2859.11*** *p9*
Burns, Elizabeth; Quebec, 1847 ***5704.8*** *p38*
Burns, Ellen 16; Massachusetts, 1850 ***5881.1*** *p7*
Burns, George; Illinois, 1722-1822 ***1639.20*** *p22*
Burns, Hannah; Philadelphia, 1865 ***5704.8*** *p198*
Burns, Henry; New York, NY, 1811 ***2859.11*** *p9*
Burns, Henry 12; Massachusetts, 1849 ***5881.1*** *p8*
Burns, Henry 22; Kansas, 1879 ***5240.1*** *p60*
Burns, Hugh; New York, NY, 1815 ***2859.11*** *p26*
Burns, Hugh 9; St. John, N.B., 1847 ***5704.8*** *p3*
Burns, James; New York, NY, 1811 ***2859.11*** *p9*
Burns, James; Philadelphia, 1866 ***5704.8*** *p211*
Burns, James; Quebec, 1823 ***7603*** *p97*
Burns, James; Quebec, 1851 ***5704.8*** *p73*
Burns, James 12; St. John, N.B., 1847 ***5704.8*** *p3*
Burns, James 20; Philadelphia, 1803 ***53.26*** *p9*
Burns, James 27; New Orleans, 1862 ***543.30*** *p484*
Burns, Jane 19; St. John, N.B., 1857 ***5704.8*** *p135*
Burns, John; Illinois, 1882 ***2896.5*** *p6*
Burns, John; New York, NY, 1811 ***2859.11*** *p9*
With family
Burns, John; New York, NY, 1816 ***2859.11*** *p26*
Burns, John; Philadelphia, 1851 ***5704.8*** *p81*
Burns, John; Quebec, 1851 ***5704.8*** *p73*
Burns, John; St. John, N.B., 1847 ***5704.8*** *p34*
Burns, John 8; Massachusetts, 1850 ***5881.1*** *p9*
Burns, John 22; New Orleans, 1862 ***543.30*** *p327*
Burns, John 23; Massachusetts, 1847 ***5881.1*** *p8*
Burns, John 23; St. John, N.B., 1864 ***5704.8*** *p159*
Burns, John 29; St. John, N.B., 1866 ***5704.8*** *p166*
Burns, Joseph; St. John, N.B., 1851 ***5704.8*** *p77*
Burns, Judy 3; Massachusetts, 1849 ***5881.1*** *p9*
Burns, Margaret; Quebec, 1851 ***5704.8*** *p73*
Burns, Margaret; St. John, N.B., 1847 ***5704.8*** *p3*
Burns, Maria 10; Massachusetts, 1849 ***5881.1*** *p10*
Burns, Martha; Philadelphia, 1851 ***5704.8*** *p76*
Burns, Mary; America, 1743 ***4971*** *p65*
Burns, Mary; Philadelphia, 1853 ***5704.8*** *p100*
Burns, Mary; Quebec, 1847 ***5704.8*** *p38*
Burns, Mary 3; Massachusetts, 1849 ***5881.1*** *p10*
Burns, Mary 14; Massachusetts, 1849 ***5881.1*** *p10*
Burns, Mary 14; Massachusetts, 1850 ***5881.1*** *p11*
Burns, Mary 20; Massachusetts, 1849 ***5881.1*** *p10*
Burns, Mary 21; Massachusetts, 1849 ***5881.1*** *p10*
Burns, Mary 22; Massachusetts, 1850 ***5881.1*** *p11*
Burns, Mary Ann 9; Philadelphia, 1864 ***5704.8*** *p161*
Burns, Mathew; St. John, N.B., 1847 ***5704.8*** *p3*
Burns, Matthew 35; New Orleans, 1862 ***543.30*** *p482*
Burns, Michael; America, 1738 ***4971*** *p68*
Burns, Michael; New York, NY, 1865 ***5704.8*** *p185*
Burns, Michael; Philadelphia, 1868 ***5704.8*** *p230*
Burns, Michael 27; New Orleans, 1862 ***543.30*** *p483*
Burns, Murphy; New York, NY, 1811 ***2859.11*** *p9*
Burns, Nancy 20; Philadelphia, 1854 ***5704.8*** *p118*
Burns, Owen; Iowa, 1866-1943 ***123.54*** *p12*
Burns, Patrick; Illinois, 1861 ***2896.5*** *p6*
Burns, Patrick; New York, NY, 1816 ***2859.11*** *p26*
Burns, Patrick; New York, NY, 1837 ***8208.4*** *p35*
Burns, Patrick; St. John, N.B., 1847 ***5704.8*** *p3*
Burns, Patrick; St. John, N.B., 1853 ***5704.8*** *p106*
Burns, Patrick 15; Massachusetts, 1849 ***5881.1*** *p11*
Burns, Richard; San Francisco, 1861 ***3840.1*** *p16*
Burns, Robert 57; Arizona, 1899 ***9228.40*** *p2*
Burns, Rose; Philadelphia, 1850 ***53.26*** *p9*
Burns, Rose; Philadelphia, 1850 ***5704.8*** *p69*
Burns, Rosey; St. John, N.B., 1847 ***5704.8*** *p11*
Burns, Samuel; New York, NY, 1811 ***2859.11*** *p9*
Burns, Samuel 3; Quebec, 1851 ***5704.8*** *p73*
Burns, Susan; Philadelphia, 1851 ***5704.8*** *p77*
Burns, Susan; St. John, N.B., 1847 ***5704.8*** *p3*
Burns, Thomas; America, 1820-1821 ***1450.2*** *p23A*
Burns, Thomas; New York, NY, 1811 ***2859.11*** *p9*
With family
Burns, Thomas 9; Massachusetts, 1849 ***5881.1*** *p12*
Burns, Thomas 18; St. John, N.B., 1853 ***5704.8*** *p110*
Burns, Thomas 48; Arizona, 1890 ***2764.35*** *p4*
Burns, Thomas H.; Kansas, 1901 ***5240.1*** *p7*
Burns, Timothy 27; Philadelphia, 1860 ***5704.8*** *p146*
Burns, William; New York, NY, 1811 ***2859.11*** *p9*
Burns, William; New York, NY, 1811 ***2859.11*** *p9*
With family
Burns, William; New York, NY, 1815 ***2859.11*** *p26*
Burns, William; Quebec, 1849 ***5704.8*** *p52*
Burns, William 13; Massachusetts, 1849 ***5881.1*** *p12*
Burns, William 35; California, 1867 ***3840.1*** *p16*
Burnside, Joseph; New York, NY, 1816 ***2859.11*** *p26*
With wife
Burnside, Mary; Philadelphia, 1869 ***5704.8*** *p236*
Burnside, Robert; New York, NY, 1821 ***8208.4*** *p60*
Burnside, Samuel; New York, NY, 1816 ***2859.11*** *p26*
Buron, Ferdinand; Illinois, 1872 ***5012.39*** *p26*

Buros, A. 27; New Orleans, 1837 ***778.5*** *p88*
Burot, Mr. 25; America, 1838 ***778.5*** *p88*
Burpott, Richard; Virginia, 1635 ***6219*** *p36*
Burr, Edward; Virginia, 1635 ***6219*** *p33*
Burr, Ernest Stanley; Washington, 1859-1920 ***2872.1*** *p6*
Burr, Jeremiah; Virginia, 1637 ***6219*** *p113*
Burr, John; New York, NY, 1816 ***2859.11*** *p26*
Burr, Lillian; Washington, 1859-1920 ***2872.1*** *p6*
Burran, J. 33; New Orleans, 1823 ***778.5*** *p88*
Burras, Jacob; New York, NY, 1838 ***8208.4*** *p80*
Burras, Mathew; Virginia, 1642 ***6219*** *p190*
Burras, Noah; New York, NY, 1839 ***8208.4*** *p101*
Burrell, Ann 19; Virginia, 1720 ***3690.1*** *p34*
Burrell, Bishop R.; Wisconsin, n.d. ***9675.5*** *p49*
Burrell, Elizabeth *SEE* Burrell, Wm.
Burrell, Ralph; Wisconsin, n.d. ***9675.5*** *p49*
Burrell, Thomas; Virginia, 1638 ***6219*** *p159*
Burrell, William; New York, NY, 1834 ***8208.4*** *p2*
Burrell, Wm.; Virginia, 1644 ***6219*** *p231*
*Wife:*Elizabeth
Burria, Guillaume 19; America, 1839 ***778.5*** *p88*
Burridg, Daniel 26; America, 1699 ***2212*** *p28*
Burridge, John 20; Maryland, 1775 ***1219.7*** *p256*
Burridge, Robert; Virginia, 1769 ***1219.7*** *p140*
Burrill, William 50; California, 1866 ***3840.1*** *p14*
Burris, Mr.; Quebec, 1815 ***9229.18*** *p78*
Burriss, Walter 38; New Orleans, 1862 ***543.30*** *p116*
Burritt, Richard 23; Jamaica, 1736 ***3690.1*** *p34*
Burrough, Roger; Virginia, 1647 ***6219*** *p245*
Burroughs, Ann *SEE* Burroughs, Christopher
Burroughs, Ann; Virginia, 1635 ***6219*** *p32*
Burroughs, Christopher; Virginia, 1636 ***6219*** *p73*
*Brother:*William
*Sister:*Ann
Burroughs, William *SEE* Burroughs, Christopher
Burroughs, Wm.; Virginia, 1635 ***6219*** *p32*
Burrow, Mathew; Virginia, 1639 ***6219*** *p154*
Burrows, Edward 21; Maryland, 1774 ***1219.7*** *p222*
Burrows, Eleanor; Annapolis, MD, 1742 ***4971*** *p93*
Burrows, Ellenor; Maryland, 1742 ***4971*** *p108*
Burrows, Jesse; West Virginia, 1839 ***9788.3*** *p5*
Burrows, Mathew; Virginia, 1635 ***6219*** *p69*
Bursan, Phillip 13; America, 1847 ***2896.5*** *p6*
Burston, Christo.; Virginia, 1636 ***6219*** *p12*
Burt, Edwd.; Virginia, 1635 ***6219*** *p69*
Burt, Elias 20; Virginia, 1720 ***3690.1*** *p34*
Burt, Moses 15; Philadelphia, 1774 ***1219.7*** *p234*
Burt, Patrick; South Carolina, 1675-1775 ***1639.20*** *p22*
Burt, Peter 18; Massachusetts, 1849 ***5881.1*** *p11*
Burt, William; South Carolina, 1765 ***1219.7*** *p108*
Burt, William 15; Philadelphia, 1774 ***1219.7*** *p234*
Burt, Wm.; Virginia, 1623 ***6219*** *p33*
Burtcher, Ann *SEE* Burtcher, George
Burtcher, Anne *SEE* Burtcher, George
Burtcher, George; Virginia, 1635 ***6219*** *p4*
*Wife:*Anne
*Daughter:*Ann
With stepchild
Burtenwood, Wm.; Virginia, 1648 ***6219*** *p246*
Burthen, Rich.; Virginia, 1635 ***6219*** *p26*
Burthoud, Mrs. 40; New Orleans, 1823 ***778.5*** *p88*
Burthoud, Ann 18; New Orleans, 1823 ***778.5*** *p88*
Burthoud, Charles 45; New Orleans, 1823 ***778.5*** *p88*
Burthoud, Julienne 16; New Orleans, 1823 ***778.5*** *p88*
Burtin, Antoine 21; New Orleans, 1838 ***778.5*** *p88*
Burtlett, Thomas; Virginia, 1637 ***6219*** *p8*
Burton, Mr.; Quebec, 1815 ***9229.18*** *p77*
Burton, Ally; New York, NY, 1811 ***2859.11*** *p9*
Burton, Bryan; Virginia, 1646 ***6219*** *p236*
Burton, Charlotte 13; St. John Island, 1775 ***1219.7*** *p273*
Burton, David 15; Maryland, 1718 ***3690.1*** *p34*
Burton, Francis 21; Maryland, 1775 ***1219.7*** *p255*
Burton, Henry; Iowa, 1866-1943 ***123.54*** *p12*
Burton, Henry George; Iowa, 1866-1943 ***123.54*** *p12*
Burton, James 40; Massachusetts, 1848 ***5881.1*** *p8*
Burton, Jean; Wisconsin, n.d. ***9675.5*** *p49*
Burton, John; Iowa, 1866-1943 ***123.54*** *p12*
Burton, John; Ohio, 1869-1888 ***9892.11*** *p6*
Burton, John; Ohio, 1891 ***9892.11*** *p7*
Burton, John; Wisconsin, n.d. ***9675.5*** *p49*
Burton, John 16; Virginia, 1720 ***3690.1*** *p34*
Burton, John 21; Maryland, 1774 ***1219.7*** *p181*
Burton, John 22; Virginia, 1774 ***1219.7*** *p186*
Burton, John 37; Jamaica, 1734 ***3690.1*** *p34*
Burton, Noah 46; California, 1872 ***2769.2*** *p4*
Burton, Richard; Charles Town, SC, 1763 ***1219.7*** *p96*
Burton, Thomas; Ohio, 1870-1888 ***9892.11*** *p7*
Burton, Thomas; West Indies, 1762 ***1219.7*** *p89*
Burton, William; Virginia, 1643 ***6219*** *p206*
Burton, William 22; Maryland, 1775 ***1219.7*** *p249*
Burton, William 50; Philadelphia, 1774 ***1219.7*** *p216*
Burton, William A. 63; Arizona, 1890 ***2764.35*** *p4*
Burtschi, Daniel; Illinois, 1869 ***2896.5*** *p6*
Burutti, Gagston 28; New Orleans, 1832 ***778.5*** *p89*
Burvent, E. 23; America, 1827 ***778.5*** *p89*
Burwash, Stephen; Illinois, 1869 ***5012.38*** *p99*
Burwell, Benjamin 23; Windward Islands, 1722 ***3690.1*** *p35*
Burwell, Elizabeth; Virginia, 1648 ***6219*** *p246*
Burwell, Fra. Harrison *SEE* Burwell, Wm.
Burwell, Geo.; Virginia, 1648 ***6219*** *p246*
Burwell, Lewis; Virginia, 1648 ***6219*** *p246*
Burwell, Wm.; Virginia, 1648 ***6219*** *p246*
*Wife:*Fra. Harrison
Burwell, Wm.; Virginia, 1648 ***6219*** *p246*
Burwick, James 32; Harris Co., TX, 1897 ***6254*** *p3*
Bury, Isaac 17; Maryland, 1774 ***1219.7*** *p229*
Bury, William 22; Maryland, 1775 ***1219.7*** *p267*
Busbaum, Rankin; Illinois, 1876 ***5012.39*** *p26*
Busboom, Rankin; Illinois, 1876 ***5012.39*** *p26*
Busby, John 22; Maryland, 1729 ***3690.1*** *p35*
Busby, John J.; Arizona, 1884 ***2764.35*** *p6*
Busby, Robert, Jr. 24; Philadelphia, 1833-1834 ***53.26*** *p9*
Busby, Thos.; Virginia, 1637 ***6219*** *p113*
Buscemi, Filippo; Iowa, 1866-1943 ***123.54*** *p12*
Buscemi, Gesualda; Iowa, 1866-1943 ***123.54*** *p12*
Buscemi, Gesualdo; Iowa, 1866-1943 ***123.54*** *p12*
Buscemi, Michele; Iowa, 1866-1943 ***123.54*** *p12*
Buscemi, Pietro; Iowa, 1866-1943 ***123.54*** *p12*
Busch, . . .; Canada, 1776-1783 ***9786*** *p18*
Busch, Eduard; Kentucky, 1840 ***8582.3*** *p99*
Busch, Elisabeth *SEE* Busch, Philipp
Busch, Ernst; Kentucky, 1840 ***8582.3*** *p99*
Busch, Friederike Meyer 58 *SEE* Busch, Johann Wilhelm
Busch, Heinrich W.; America, 1885 ***4610.10*** *p137*
Busch, Johann Wilhelm; America, 1856 ***4610.10*** *p157*
*Wife:*Friederike Meyer 58
Busch, Johannes; New England, 1752 ***2444*** *p141*
Busch, Johannes; Ohio, 1798-1818 ***8582.2*** *p54*
Busch, Johannes; Pennsylvania, 1752 ***2444*** *p141*
Busch, John; Illinois, 1892 ***5012.40*** *p26*
Busch, Mathias; Kansas, 1897 ***5240.1*** *p7*
Busch, Michael; Ohio, 1798-1818 ***8582.2*** *p54*
Busch, Philipp; Frankfort, KY, 1794 ***8582.3*** *p87*
*Wife:*Elisabeth
Busch, Philipp; Kentucky, 1810-1825 ***8582.3*** *p97*
Busch, William; Wisconsin, n.d. ***9675.5*** *p49*
Buschbeck, Colonel; Pennsylvania, 1861-1865 ***8582.3*** *p91*
Busche, Karl; Ohio, 1843 ***8582.1*** *p51*
Buschel, Colonel; New York, 1861-1865 ***8582.3*** *p91*
Buschenfeld, Carl Friedrich Wilhelm *SEE* Buschenfeld, Johann Christoph
Buschenfeld, Christine L. Kampmeyer *SEE* Buschenfeld, Johann Christoph
Buschenfeld, Christoph Carl Friedr. *SEE* Buschenfeld, Johann Christoph
Buschenfeld, Johann Christoph; America, 1844 ***4610.10*** *p119*
*Wife:*Christine L. Kampmeyer
*Child:*Carl Friedrich Wilhelm
*Child:*Christoph Carl Friedr.
Buschenfeld, Johann Hermann Heinrich; America, 1850 ***4610.10*** *p142*
Buscher, Ewald C.; Milwaukee, 1868 ***8125.8*** *p435*
Buscher, John 27; Kansas, 1890 ***5240.1*** *p75*
Buschjost, Friedrich Ludwig Anton; America, 1874 ***4610.10*** *p122*
Buschjost, Hermann Carl; America, 1881 ***4610.10*** *p122*
Buschle, Friedrich; America, 1848 ***8582.1*** *p6*
Buschmann, Miss; America, 1853 ***4610.10*** *p156*
Buschmann, Henriette; America, 1850 ***4610.10*** *p155*
Buschmeyer, Friedrich 30; America, 1881 ***4610.10*** *p146*
*Relative:*Wilhelmine 64
*Relative:*Wilhelmine 34
Buschmeyer, Wilhelmine 34 *SEE* Buschmeyer, Friedrich
Buschmeyer, Wilhelmine 64 *SEE* Buschmeyer, Friedrich
Buscitti, Gregonio; Wisconsin, n.d. ***9675.5*** *p49*
Buscker, Harm; New York, NY, 1924 ***3455.4*** *p53*
Busen, Bernard; Indiana, 1840 ***9117*** *p16*
Busenbark, Augusta 42; Kansas, 1885 ***5240.1*** *p68*
Busenhart, John; Illinois, 1882 ***2896.5*** *p6*
Busenhorst, John; Illinois, 1882 ***2896.5*** *p6*
Busenitz, Frank; America, 1893 ***5240.1*** *p7*
Busenitz, John A.; Kansas, 1894 ***5240.1*** *p8*
Busetto, Fortuneto; Iowa, 1866-1943 ***123.54*** *p57*
Busetto, George, Jr.; Iowa, 1866-1943 ***123.54*** *p57*
Busetto, Regina; Iowa, 1866-1943 ***123.54*** *p57*
Busfield, John 30; Nova Scotia, 1774 ***1219.7*** *p194*
Bush, Charles 18; Virginia, 1774 ***1219.7*** *p238*
Bush, Charles 31; Maryland, 1774 ***1219.7*** *p211*
*Wife:*Hepzibah 31
Bush, Charles J. 36?; Arizona, 1890 ***2764.35*** *p8*
Bush, Ed; Washington, 1859-1920 ***2872.1*** *p6*
Bush, Elizabeth *SEE* Bush, Elizabeth
Bush, Elizabeth; Virginia, 1619 ***6219*** *p2*
*Child:*Elizabeth
*Child:*Mary
Bush, Gaspar; South Carolina, 1788 ***7119*** *p202*
Bush, George; Philadelphia, 1760 ***9973.7*** *p34*
Bush, Hepzibah 31 *SEE* Bush, Charles
Bush, J. M.; Washington, 1859-1920 ***2872.1*** *p6*
Bush, Johannes; New England, 1752 ***2444*** *p141*
Bush, Johannes; Pennsylvania, 1752 ***2444*** *p141*
Bush, John; Virginia, 1618 ***6219*** *p2*
Bush, Margaret; America, 1740 ***4971*** *p48*
Bush, Mary *SEE* Bush, Elizabeth
Bush, Nich.; Virginia, 1639 ***6219*** *p155*
Bush, Tho.; Virginia, 1637 ***6219*** *p110*
Bush, Thomas; Virginia, 1638 ***6219*** *p121*
Bush, Thomas 40; West Indies, 1722 ***3690.1*** *p35*
Bush, W. E.; Washington, 1859-1920 ***2872.1*** *p6*
Bush, William; Jamaica, 1757 ***1219.7*** *p52*
Bush, William; Philadelphia, 1760 ***9973.7*** *p34*
Bushby, Elizabeth; Quebec, 1849 ***5704.8*** *p57*
Bushby, Jane 13; Quebec, 1849 ***5704.8*** *p57*
Bushell, Nich.; Virginia, 1635 ***6219*** *p33*
Bushell, Nich.; Virginia, 1642 ***6219*** *p191*
Busher, Henry; America, 1832 ***1450.2*** *p23A*
Busher, Mable; Virginia, 1635 ***6219*** *p73*
Bushey, Mrs. A. 36; Washington, 1916 ***1728.4*** *p251*
Bushey, Arthur 38; Washington, 1916 ***1728.4*** *p251*
Bushlin, John 20; Virginia, 1719 ***3690.1*** *p35*
Bushmann, John; Wisconsin, n.d. ***9675.5*** *p49*
Bushopp, Jon.; Virginia, 1635 ***6219*** *p12*
Bushy, Ann; Virginia, 1635 ***6219*** *p3*
Busilli, Tony; Arkansas, 1918 ***95.2*** *p24*
Busker, John; Indiana, 1848 ***9117*** *p16*
Busker, Peter; Illinois, 1878 ***5012.37*** *p60*
Busky, John 37; New Orleans, 1862 ***543.30*** *p111*
Busonworth, John 39; Maryland, 1774 ***1219.7*** *p191*
Buss, Johann Jacob; Cincinnati, 1848 ***8582.1*** *p53*
Buss, Mary 46; North Carolina, 1850 ***1639.20*** *p22*
Bussami, Emigho; Iowa, 1866-1943 ***123.54*** *p12*
Bussche, August Vanden; Arkansas, 1918 ***95.2*** *p24*
Busscher, Suppe 40; Kansas, 1884 ***5240.1*** *p8*
Busscher, Suppe 40; Kansas, 1884 ***5240.1*** *p66*
Busse, Anne Marie L. Engel *SEE* Busse, Carl Heinrich
Busse, Carl Friedrich Wilhelm *SEE* Busse, Friedr. Philipp
Busse, Carl Heinrich; America, 1854 ***4610.10*** *p156*
With wife
*Child:*Carl Heinrich Gustav
*Child:*Anne Marie L. Engel
*Child:*Heinrich Wilhelm
Busse, Carl Heinrich Gustav *SEE* Busse, Carl Heinrich
Busse, Charles 22?; New Orleans, 1862 ***543.30*** *p110*
Busse, Christian; Illinois, 1878 ***2896.5*** *p6*
Busse, Christian; Illinois, 1880 ***2896.5*** *p6*
Busse, Christian Friedrich; America, 1870 ***4610.10*** *p105*
Busse, Elizabeth *SEE* Busse, Joachim
Busse, Ernst Heinrich; America, 1868 ***4610.10*** *p159*
Busse, Ernst Heinrich August; America, 1852 ***4610.10*** *p156*
Busse, Ernst Heinrich Ludwig; America, 1852 ***4610.10*** *p104*
Busse, Ernst Wilhelm; America, 1865 ***4610.10*** *p100*
Busse, Ferdinand; Illinois, 1866 ***2896.5*** *p6*
Busse, Ferdinand Ludwig; America, 1846 ***4610.10*** *p95*
Busse, Friedr. Philipp; America, 1847 ***4610.10*** *p151*
*Wife:*Marg. E. Haubrock
*Son:*Carl Friedrich Wilhelm
Busse, Friedrich Philipp; America, 1857 ***4610.10*** *p157*
*Son:*Friedrich Wilhelm
Busse, Friedrich Wilhelm *SEE* Busse, Friedrich Philipp
Busse, Georg; Virginia, 1642 ***6219*** *p197*
*Wife:*Lydia
Busse, Heinrich Wilhelm *SEE* Busse, Carl Heinrich
Busse, Heinrich Wilhelm; America, 1844 ***4610.10*** *p154*
Busse, Joachim; New York, 1751 ***3652*** *p75*
*Wife:*Elizabeth
Busse, Joachim; New York, 1756 ***3652*** *p81*
Busse, Johann Joseph; America, 1846 ***8582.3*** *p11*
Busse, John; America, 1849 ***1450.2*** *p23A*
Busse, Joseph; Cincinnati, 1869-1887 ***8582*** *p5*
Busse, Lydia *SEE* Busse, Georg
Busse, Marg. E. Haubrock *SEE* Busse, Friedr. Philipp
Busse, Michael; America, 1853 ***2896.5*** *p6*
Bussert, William; America, 1869 ***1450.2*** *p17A*
Bussetti, Antonio 17; New York, NY, 1893 ***9026.4*** *p41*
Bussey, Ann; Virginia, 1637 ***6219*** *p86*
Bussey, James W. 27; Kansas, 1885 ***5240.1*** *p8*
Bussey, James W. 27; Kansas, 1885 ***5240.1*** *p68*
Bussey, Thomas 22; Philadelphia, 1774 ***1219.7*** *p182*
Bussing, Georg H. 16; Cincinnati, 1832 ***8582.3*** *p11*
Bussing, Henry; Indiana, 1848 ***9117*** *p15*
Busson, Georg; Virginia, 1635 ***6219*** *p3*
Bustad, Jake 23; Arkansas, 1918 ***95.2*** *p24*
Bustard, . . . 3 mos; St. John, N.B., 1847 ***5704.8*** *p26*

Bustard, Ann 8; Philadelphia, 1856 ***5704.8*** *p129*
Bustard, Ann 40; Philadelphia, 1856 ***5704.8*** *p129*
Bustard, Ann Jane 10; St. John, N.B., 1847 ***5704.8*** *p33*
Bustard, Arthur; Quebec, 1853 ***5704.8*** *p104*
Bustard, Catherine 40; Philadelphia, 1859 ***5704.8*** *p142*
Bustard, Charles; St. John, N.B., 1847 ***5704.8*** *p33*
Bustard, Eliza; St. John, N.B., 1847 ***5704.8*** *p26*
Bustard, Eliza 6; Philadelphia, 1856 ***5704.8*** *p129*
Bustard, George; St. John, N.B., 1852 ***5704.8*** *p84*
Bustard, Hannah 6 mos; St. John, N.B., 1847 ***5704.8*** *p33*
Bustard, Jane; St. John, N.B., 1847 ***5704.8*** *p26*
Bustard, Margaret; St. John, N.B., 1847 ***5704.8*** *p33*
Bustard, Margaret 8; St. John, N.B., 1847 ***5704.8*** *p33*
Bustard, Margaret 17; Philadelphia, 1858 ***5704.8*** *p139*
Bustard, Mariah 3; Philadelphia, 1856 ***5704.8*** *p129*
Bustard, Mary 21; St. John, N.B., 1854 ***5704.8*** *p115*
Bustard, Robert 22; Philadelphia, 1856 ***5704.8*** *p129*
Bustard, Robert 58; Philadelphia, 1856 ***5704.8*** *p129*
Bustard, Samuel 10; Philadelphia, 1859 ***5704.8*** *p142*
Bustard, Thomas; St. John, N.B., 1847 ***5704.8*** *p26*
Bustard, Thomas 12; Philadelphia, 1859 ***5704.8*** *p142*
Bustard, William 12; St. John, N.B., 1847 ***5704.8*** *p33*
Bustlet, Mr. 38; America, 1839 ***778.5*** *p89*
Butchart, Elizabeth 30; Maryland, 1774 ***1219.7*** *p211*
Butchcoe, John 21; Kansas, 1900 ***5240.1*** *p81*
Butcher, David D.; Colorado, 1895 ***9678.1*** *p156*
Butcher, Joseph; Colorado, 1894 ***9678.1*** *p156*
Butcher, Lavinor 3; New York, NY, 1847 ***3377.6*** *p12*
Butcher, Sophia 31; New York, NY, 1847 ***3377.6*** *p12*
Butcher, Tho.; Virginia, 1643 ***6219*** *p200*
Butcher, Thomas 15; Maryland, 1775 ***1219.7*** *p253*
Butcher, Thomas 21; Kansas, 1871 ***5240.1*** *p52*
Butcher, W. 31; New York, NY, 1847 ***3377.6*** *p12*
Butcher, Weymouth 6 mos; New York, NY, 1847 ***3377.6*** *p12*
Butcher, William; America, 1864 ***5704.8*** *p173*
Butcher, William; Virginia, 1642 ***6219*** *p197*
Butcher, William 6; New York, NY, 1847 ***3377.6*** *p12*
Butcher, William 29; Philadelphia, 1774 ***1219.7*** *p212*
Butcher, Wm.; Virginia, 1643 ***6219*** *p206*
Bute, James 58; Harris Co., TX, 1900 ***6254*** *p6*
Bute, Peter; California, 1874 ***2764.35*** *p5*
Buten, Herrmann Bernard; America, 1836 ***8582.2*** *p6*
Buth, William; Wisconsin, n.d. ***9675.5*** *p49*
Buthan, Edward 30; Massachusetts, 1848 ***5881.1*** *p7*
Butis, John 26; New Orleans, 1831 ***778.5*** *p89*
Butkovich, Ivan; Iowa, 1866-1943 ***123.54*** *p12*
Butkovich, Katrene; Iowa, 1866-1943 ***123.54*** *p57*
Butkovich, Valentine; Iowa, 1866-1943 ***123.54*** *p12*
Butkus, Stanislau; Wisconsin, n.d. ***9675.5*** *p49*
Butland, James 35; Philadelphia, 1774 ***1219.7*** *p205*
Butler, Andrew; New York, NY, 1816 ***2859.11*** *p26*
Butler, Ann; Quebec, 1849 ***5704.8*** *p57*
Butler, Ann 16; Maryland, 1775 ***1219.7*** *p256*
Butler, Ann 25 *SEE* Butler, John
Butler, Bridget 26; Massachusetts, 1849 ***5881.1*** *p6*
Butler, Catherine; America, 1738 ***4971*** *p14*
Butler, Charles; North Dakota, 1911 ***9892.11*** *p7*
Butler, Christophe; Quebec, 1823 ***7603*** *p99*
Butler, Edward; Virginia, 1637 ***6219*** *p117*
Butler, Edward B.; Chicago, 1856 ***2896.5*** *p6*
Butler, Eliza; New York, NY, 1816 ***2859.11*** *p26*
Butler, Eliza.; Virginia, 1643 ***6219*** *p202*
Butler, Elizabeth 8; America, 1704 ***2212*** *p40*
Butler, Ellan; Quebec, 1849 ***5704.8*** *p57*
Butler, Flora; Philadelphia, 1851 ***5704.8*** *p70*
Butler, Frederick 35; New Orleans, 1862 ***543.30*** *p483*
Butler, George; New York, NY, 1816 ***2859.11*** *p26*
Butler, George 17; Philadelphia, 1774 ***1219.7*** *p197*
Butler, Hannah 27; Maryland, 1774 ***1219.7*** *p235*
Butler, Hen.; Virginia, 1637 ***6219*** *p114*
Butler, Henry J.; New York, NY, 1835 ***8208.4*** *p5*
Butler, James; America, 1738 ***4971*** *p31*
Butler, James 20; Jamaica, 1729 ***3690.1*** *p35*
Butler, James 24; New York, 1775 ***1219.7*** *p246*
Butler, James 29; Maryland, 1774 ***1219.7*** *p236*
Butler, Joan; America, 1742 ***4971*** *p29*
Butler, Joan; Delaware, 1743 ***4971*** *p105*
Butler, Joane; Virginia, 1635 ***6219*** *p69*
Butler, Joane; Virginia, 1638 ***6219*** *p123*
Butler, John; Quebec, 1823 ***7603*** *p73*
Butler, John; Virginia, 1636 ***6219*** *p13*
Butler, John; Virginia, 1636 ***6219*** *p146*
Butler, John; Virginia, 1642 ***6219*** *p197*
Butler, John; Virginia, 1643 ***6219*** *p202*
Butler, John 23; Maryland, 1774 ***1219.7*** *p230*
Butler, John 25; Carolina, 1774 ***1219.7*** *p225*
*Wife:*Ann 25
Butler, John 25; Georgia, 1775 ***1219.7*** *p275*
Butler, John 46?; Arizona, 1890 ***2764.35*** *p8*
Butler, Jon.; Virginia, 1638 ***6219*** *p124*
Butler, Jon.; Virginia, 1643 ***6219*** *p202*
Butler, Joseph 17; Maryland, 1775 ***1219.7*** *p255*
Butler, Joseph 20; Jamaica, 1737 ***3690.1*** *p35*
Butler, Margaret; Philadelphia, 1851 ***5704.8*** *p70*
Butler, Margaret 13; Quebec, 1849 ***5704.8*** *p57*
Butler, Marguerite; Quebec, 1770 ***7603*** *p75*
Butler, Mark 33; Massachusetts, 1848 ***5881.1*** *p9*
Butler, Mary *SEE* Butler, Thomas
Butler, Mary; America, 1740 ***4971*** *p69*
Butler, Mary; Massachusetts, 1850 ***5881.1*** *p11*
Butler, Mary; New York, NY, 1811 ***2859.11*** *p9*
Butler, Mary; New York, NY, 1816 ***2859.11*** *p26*
Butler, Mary; Quebec, 1849 ***5704.8*** *p57*
Butler, Mary; St. John, N.B., 1847 ***5704.8*** *p3*
Butler, Mary; Virginia, 1643 ***6219*** *p202*
Butler, Mary 24; Massachusetts, 1850 ***5881.1*** *p11*
Butler, Mary 26; Massachusetts, 1849 ***5881.1*** *p10*
Butler, Michael; New York, NY, 1811 ***2859.11*** *p9*
Butler, Michael; New York, NY, 1834 ***8208.4*** *p38*
Butler, Michel; Quebec, 1819 ***7603*** *p93*
Butler, P. 23; Philadelphia, 1774 ***1219.7*** *p228*
Butler, Patrick; Illinois, 1860 ***5012.39*** *p89*
Butler, Pierce; America, 1740 ***4971*** *p31*
Butler, Pierce; America, 1741 ***4971*** *p41*
Butler, Richard; Illinois, 1863 ***5012.38*** *p98*
Butler, Robert; Virginia, 1635 ***6219*** *p72*
Butler, Robert 29; Maryland, 1775 ***1219.7*** *p255*
Butler, Sally 21; Philadelphia, 1853 ***5704.8*** *p113*
Butler, Samuel 15; Maryland, 1774 ***1219.7*** *p244*
Butler, Samuell; Virginia, 1641 ***6219*** *p185*
Butler, Stephen; Philadelphia, 1851 ***5704.8*** *p70*
Butler, Tho.; Virginia, 1638 ***6219*** *p119*
Butler, Tho.; Virginia, 1642 ***6219*** *p197*
Butler, Thomas; Virginia, 1623-1638 ***6219*** *p121*
*Wife:*Mary
Butler, Thomas 25; Massachusetts, 1850 ***5881.1*** *p12*
Butler, Tobias; America, 1742 ***4971*** *p17*
Butler, W. B.; Washington, 1859-1920 ***2872.1*** *p6*
Butler, Walter; America, 1738 ***4971*** *p31*
Butler, William; America, 1742 ***4971*** *p17*
Butler, William; Illinois, 1875 ***5012.39*** *p26*
Butler, William; Jamaica, 1753 ***1219.7*** *p20*
Butler, William; Jamaica, 1753 ***3690.1*** *p35*
Butler, William; Virginia, 1635 ***6219*** *p73*
Butler, William; Virginia, 1643 ***6219*** *p202*
Butler, William 20; Maryland, 1734 ***3690.1*** *p35*
Butler, William 20; Massachusetts, 1848 ***5881.1*** *p12*
Butler, William 27; Newfoundland, 1789 ***4915.24*** *p56*
Butlinge, Thos.; Virginia, 1636 ***6219*** *p74*
Butorac, Josip; Iowa, 1866-1943 ***123.54*** *p12*
Butress, Rich.; Virginia, 1637 ***6219*** *p114*
Butros, Antony 22; Kansas, 1893 ***5240.1*** *p77*
Butross, Rich.; Virginia, 1637 ***6219*** *p11*
Butsch, George; New York, 1840 ***1450.2*** *p23A*
Butsch, John; New York, 1840 ***1450.2*** *p24A*
Butsch, Joseph; New York, 1840 ***1450.2*** *p24A*
Butscher, Johannes; America, 1845 ***8582.3*** *p12*
Butt, William; Maryland, 1753 ***1219.7*** *p22*
Butt, William; Maryland, 1753 ***3690.1*** *p35*
Buttazzoni, Lino; Arkansas, 1918 ***95.2*** *p24*
Butteny, Jacob 23; Jamaica, 1736 ***3690.1*** *p35*
Butter, Robert; Virginia, 1640 ***6219*** *p160*
Butter, William 16; Jamaica, 1725 ***3690.1*** *p35*
Butterfeild, Henry 16; Virginia, 1699 ***2212*** *p26*
Butterfield, James 22; Pennsylvania, 1728 ***3690.1*** *p35*
Butterfield, John 16; Pennsylvania, 1728 ***3690.1*** *p36*
Butterfield, Mary; America, 1737 ***4971*** *p85*
Butterfield, Mary; America, 1737 ***4971*** *p95*
Butterfield, Mary; America, 1743 ***4971*** *p11*
Butternuth, John Frederick; California, 1867 ***2769.2*** *p3*
Buttersley, John; New York, NY, 1816 ***2859.11*** *p26*
Buttersley, Mary; New York, NY, 1816 ***2859.11*** *p26*
Butterton, Thomas; America, 1737 ***4971*** *p13*
Butterum, John; Virginia, 1637 ***6219*** *p29*
Butterweck, Friedrich; America, 1847 ***3702.7*** *p328*
With family
Butterweck, Karl; Port uncertain, 1853 ***3702.7*** *p327*
Butterworth, A.; New York, NY, 1815 ***2859.11*** *p26*
Butterworth, Edward; Virginia, 1639 ***6219*** *p156*
Butterworth, James; Virginia, 1698 ***2212*** *p12*
Butterworth, James; Virginia, 1844 ***4626.16*** *p13*
Butterworth, Joseph 37; Maryland, 1774 ***1219.7*** *p229*
Butterworth, Judith; Virginia, 1698 ***2212*** *p13*
Butterworth, Nicholas 19; Virginia, 1700 ***2212*** *p31*
Butterworth, Richard; Colorado, 1889 ***9678.1*** *p156*
Buttle, Ann *SEE* Buttle, Robert
Buttle, Ann *SEE* Buttle, Robert
Buttle, Margaret; New York, NY, 1816 ***2859.11*** *p26*
Buttle, Robert; Georgia, 1775 ***1219.7*** *p274*
*Wife:*Ann
With 5 children
Buttle, Robert 35; Savannah, GA, 1775 ***1219.7*** *p274*
*Wife:*Ann
With 5 children
Buttle, Samuel; New York, NY, 1816 ***2859.11*** *p26*
Buttler, Barbara 18; New Orleans, 1831 ***778.5*** *p89*
Buttler, Hans 50; New Orleans, 1831 ***778.5*** *p89*
Buttler, Joseph 12; New Orleans, 1831 ***778.5*** *p89*
Buttler, Maria 10; New Orleans, 1831 ***778.5*** *p89*
Buttler, Martha 16; New Orleans, 1831 ***778.5*** *p89*
Buttler, Mary 50; New Orleans, 1831 ***778.5*** *p89*
Buttler, Tho; America, 1701 ***2212*** *p34*
Buttler, William 20; Maryland, 1734 ***3690.1*** *p35*
Buttner, . . .; Canada, 1776-1783 ***9786*** *p18*
Buttner, Charlotte 8; New York, NY, 1878 ***9253*** *p46*
Buttner, Gottlob; Philadelphia, 1741 ***3652*** *p52*
Buttner, Nathan 6; New York, NY, 1878 ***9253*** *p46*
Button, Eliz.; Virginia, 1642 ***6219*** *p191*
Button, Georg; Philadelphia, 1776 ***8582.3*** *p84*
Button, John 21; Baltimore, 1775 ***1219.7*** *p269*
Butts, George; Washington, 1859-1920 ***2872.1*** *p6*
Butulia, John 31; Arizona, 1923 ***9228.40*** *p27*
Butz, Eduard; Kentucky, 1840 ***8582.3*** *p97*
Butz, Jean 28; Louisiana, 1820 ***778.5*** *p89*
Butz, Johann Friedrich; Pennsylvania, 1751 ***2444*** *p144*
Butz, Johannes; Pennsylvania, 1752 ***2444*** *p144*
Butz, Kaspar; Des Moines, IA, 1848-1885 ***8125.8*** *p435*
Butz, Louis 21; New Orleans, 1862 ***543.30*** *p114*
Butzen, August 28; New Orleans, 1862 ***543.30*** *p327*
Butzka, Ferdinand; Wisconsin, n.d. ***9675.5*** *p49*
Butzke, William; Colorado, 1897 ***9678.1*** *p156*
Buxton, Edward; San Francisco, 1850 ***4914.15*** *p10*
Buxton, Edward; San Francisco, 1850 ***4914.15*** *p14*
Buxton, John 57; Kansas, 1880 ***5240.1*** *p62*
Buxton, Jon.; Virginia, 1637 ***6219*** *p8*
Buxton, Robert; Virginia, 1646 ***6219*** *p236*
Buyan, Berto; Iowa, 1866-1943 ***123.54*** *p12*
Buyer, Mary; America, 1738 ***4971*** *p14*
Buyusel, Jose 34; Arizona, 1915 ***9228.40*** *p19*
Buzon, Charles 25; America, 1839 ***778.5*** *p89*
Buzzelli, Emillio; Arkansas, 1918 ***95.2*** *p24*
Buzzi, Antonio 39; Kansas, 1873 ***5240.1*** *p54*
Buzzi, James 39; California, 1868 ***3840.1*** *p16*
Buzzy, Eliz.; Virginia, 1635 ***6219*** *p3*
Byam, John 18; Maryland, 1774 ***1219.7*** *p229*
Byarly, Michael; Pennsylvania, 1730 ***4779.3*** *p13*
Byen, Christy; Quebec, 1847 ***5704.8*** *p17*
Byen, Christy 6; Quebec, 1847 ***5704.8*** *p17*
Byen, Elizabeth; Quebec, 1847 ***5704.8*** *p17*
Byen, Elizabeth 13; Quebec, 1847 ***5704.8*** *p17*
Byen, James; Quebec, 1847 ***5704.8*** *p17*
Byen, Mary Ann 12; Quebec, 1847 ***5704.8*** *p17*
Byen, Thomas 3; Quebec, 1847 ***5704.8*** *p17*
Byer, Jacob 17; New York, 1775 ***1219.7*** *p246*
Byerley, Samuel; New York, NY, 1838 ***8208.4*** *p57*
Byerly, John Michael; Pennsylvania, 1753 ***4779.3*** *p13*
Byerly, Oliver; Washington, 1859-1920 ***2872.1*** *p6*
Byers, Ann Jane 12; St. John, N.B., 1848 ***5704.8*** *p47*
Byers, Catherine; Philadelphia, 1853 ***5704.8*** *p100*
Byers, Catherine; St. John, N.B., 1847 ***5704.8*** *p3*
Byers, Catherine; St. John, N.B., 1853 ***5704.8*** *p106*
Byers, David; New York, NY, 1816 ***2859.11*** *p26*
Byers, Eliza 10; St. John, N.B., 1848 ***5704.8*** *p47*
Byers, James 8; St. John, N.B., 1854 ***5704.8*** *p119*
Byers, Joseph; St. John, N.B., 1849 ***5704.8*** *p55*
Byers, Joseph 12; St. John, N.B., 1853 ***5704.8*** *p106*
Byers, Margaret 13; St. John, N.B., 1853 ***5704.8*** *p106*
Byers, Mary 28; St. John, N.B., 1854 ***5704.8*** *p119*
Byers, Nixon 12; St. John, N.B., 1849 ***5704.8*** *p56*
Byers, Robert; Philadelphia, 1816 ***2859.11*** *p26*
Bynon, Henry; New York, NY, 1840 ***8208.4*** *p109*
Byram, Abraham; Virginia, 1652 ***6251*** *p19*
Byram, Nicholas; Virginia, 1637 ***6219*** *p9*
Byrd, Henry; New York, NY, 1835 ***8208.4*** *p7*
Byrd, Isaiah Francis 38; California, 1872 ***2769.1*** *p5*
Byrd, James; New York, NY, 1816 ***2859.11*** *p26*
Byrd, Jesse Albert 47; California, 1872 ***2769.1*** *p5*
Byrn, Catherine; America, 1742 ***4971*** *p95*
Byrn, Catherine 45; Philadelphia, 1861 ***5704.8*** *p148*
Byrn, Francis; America, 1742 ***4971*** *p64*
Byrn, John 25; Philadelphia, 1861 ***5704.8*** *p148*
Byrn, Judith; America, 1742 ***4971*** *p86*
Byrn, Judith; America, 1742 ***4971*** *p95*
Byrn, Martin; Montreal, 1821 ***7603*** *p68*
Byrn, Mary; America, 1742 ***4971*** *p26*
Byrn, Mary 24; Philadelphia, 1861 ***5704.8*** *p148*
Byrn, Patrick; America, 1736-1743 ***4971*** *p58*
Byrn, Patrick; America, 1738 ***4971*** *p46*
Byrn, Patrick; America, 1743 ***4971*** *p10*
Byrn, Thomas; America, 1737 ***4971*** *p26*
Byrn, William 20; Philadelphia, 1853 ***5704.8*** *p108*
Byrne, Ann 20; Massachusetts, 1849 ***5881.1*** *p6*
Byrne, Anne; New York, NY, 1867 ***5704.8*** *p220*
Byrne, Anthony 16; Maryland, 1775 ***1219.7*** *p253*
Byrne, Bartholomew; America, 1737 ***4971*** *p71*
Byrne, Bernard 16; Philadelphia, 1864 ***5704.8*** *p156*
Byrne, Bridget 14; Philadelphia, 1864 ***5704.8*** *p156*
Byrne, Catharine; Philadelphia, 1866 ***5704.8*** *p212*

Byrne, Catharine 22; Massachusetts, 1847 *5881.1 p6*
Byrne, Catherine; America, 1742 *4971 p22*
Byrne, Catherine; America, 1742 *4971 p86*
Byrne, Catherine; America, 1743 *4971 p18*
Byrne, Catherine 1; Philadelphia, 1864 *5704.8 p156*
Byrne, Charles; America, 1738 *4971 p35*
Byrne, Cornelius 26; St. John, N.B., 1862 *5704.8 p150*
Byrne, Cornelius 30; Philadelphia, 1854 *5704.8 p120*
Byrne, Daniel; Montreal, 1822 *7603 p58*
Byrne, Dominice 8; Massachusetts, 1850 *5881.1 p7*
Byrne, Dudley; America, 1743 *4971 p11*
Byrne, Edward; New York, NY, 1816 *2859.11 p26*
Byrne, Edward 11; Philadelphia, 1864 *5704.8 p156*
Byrne, Fammer 17; St. John, N.B., 1851 *5704.8 p77*
Byrne, Fanny 27; Massachusetts, 1850 *5881.1 p8*
Byrne, George; New York, NY, 1815 *2859.11 p26*
Byrne, Gerard 22; Pensacola, FL, 1774 *1219.7 p227*
Byrne, Hannah 40; Philadelphia, 1864 *5704.8 p156*
Byrne, Honora 10; Massachusetts, 1850 *5881.1 p8*
Byrne, Isaac; America, 1742 *4971 p70*
Byrne, James; America, 1743 *4971 p35*
Byrne, James; Illinois, 1886 *2896.5 p6*
Byrne, James; New York, NY, 1811 *2859.11 p9*
Byrne, James; New York, NY, 1815 *2859.11 p26*
Byrne, James 10; Philadelphia, 1864 *5704.8 p156*
Byrne, James 15; St. John, N.B., 1851 *5704.8 p77*
Byrne, James P.; Indiana, 1848 *9117 p16*
Byrne, Jane; Massachusetts, 1849 *5881.1 p9*
Byrne, John; New York, NY, 1815 *2859.11 p26*
Byrne, John; New York, NY, 1816 *2859.11 p26*
Byrne, John 12; St. John, N.B., 1851 *5704.8 p77*
Byrne, John 21; St. John, N.B., 1862 *5704.8 p150*

Byrne, John Williams; New York, NY, 1896 *9892.11 p7*
Byrne, Judith; America, 1742 *4971 p22*
Byrne, Margaret 3; Massachusetts, 1849 *5881.1 p10*
Byrne, Maria 6; Massachusetts, 1849 *5881.1 p10*
Byrne, Mary; America, 1735-1743 *4971 p8*
Byrne, Mary; America, 1739 *4971 p14*
Byrne, Mary; America, 1740 *4971 p22*
Byrne, Mary; America, 1741 *4971 p98*
Byrne, Mary; America, 1742 *4971 p30*
Byrne, Mary; America, 1743 *4971 p18*
Byrne, Mary; New York, NY, 1816 *2859.11 p26*
  With 3 children
Byrne, Mary 3; Philadelphia, 1864 *5704.8 p156*
Byrne, Mary 18; St. John, N.B., 1858 *5704.8 p137*
Byrne, Michael; New York, NY, 1816 *2859.11 p26*
Byrne, Miles; New York, NY, 1811 *2859.11 p9*
  With family
Byrne, Morgan; America, 1741 *4971 p35*
Byrne, Owen; America, 1740 *4971 p22*
Byrne, Owen; New York, NY, 1838 *8208.4 p74*
Byrne, Owen 50; Massachusetts, 1850 *5881.1 p11*
Byrne, Patk; New York, NY, 1816 *2859.11 p26*
Byrne, Patrick; America, 1737 *4971 p45*
Byrne, Patrick; America, 1743 *4971 p95*
Byrne, Patrick; New York, NY, 1835 *8208.4 p32*
Byrne, Patrick; New York, NY, 1838 *8208.4 p75*
Byrne, Patrick 22; St. John, N.B., 1860 *5704.8 p144*
Byrne, Patrick 50; Philadelphia, 1864 *5704.8 p156*
Byrne, Peter; Portland, ME, 1821-1838 *7036 p124*
Byrne, Peter; St. Johns, N.F., 1821 *7036 p124*
Byrne, Richard; Wisconsin, n.d. *9675.5 p49*
Byrne, Robert 22; Maryland, 1775 *1219.7 p264*

Byrne, Rose 6; Philadelphia, 1864 *5704.8 p156*
Byrne, Terence; America, 1737 *4971 p35*
Byrne, Thomas 22; Massachusetts, 1847 *5881.1 p12*
Byrne, Thomas 40; Massachusetts, 1850 *5881.1 p12*
Byrne, Timothy 30; Newfoundland, 1789 *4915.24 p57*
Byrnes, Bridget; New York, NY, 1811 *2859.11 p9*
Byrnes, C., Jr.; New York, NY, 1811 *2859.11 p9*
Byrnes, Hugh; New York, NY, 1816 *2859.11 p26*
Byrnes, John; New York, NY, 1811 *2859.11 p9*
Byrnes, Mary; New York, NY, 1816 *2859.11 p26*
Byrnes, Nicholas; New York, NY, 1811 *2859.11 p9*
Byrnes, Patrick; New York, NY, 1834 *8208.4 p4*
Byrnes, Patrick; New York, NY, 1836 *8208.4 p16*
Byrnes, Patrick 55; Massachusetts, 1850 *5881.1 p11*
Byrnes, Richard 42; New Orleans, 1862 *543.30 p483*
Byrnes, Thomas; New York, NY, 1834 *8208.4 p41*
Byrns, Bridget; New York, NY, 1867 *5704.8 p215*
Byrns, Michael; New York, NY, 1820-1841 *7036 p120*
Byrns, Michael; Prince Edward Island, 1820 *7036 p120*
Byron, James; New York, NY, 1836 *8208.4 p77*
Byron, Thomas 36; New Orleans, 1862 *543.30 p115*
Bysher, Matthias; Philadelphia, 1761 *9973.7 p36*
Byst, Nathaniel 30; Philadelphia, 1803 *53.26 p9*
Bystrom, A.; Washington, 1859-1920 *2872.1 p6*
Bystrom, Esther; Washington, 1859-1920 *2872.1 p6*
Bystrom, Lars John; Washington, 1859-1920 *2872.1 p6*
Bystrom, Marie; Washington, 1859-1920 *2872.1 p6*
Bystrom, O.; Washington, 1859-1920 *2872.1 p6*
Bystrom, Olaf; Washington, 1859-1920 *2872.1 p6*
Bystrzanowski, . . .; New York, 1831 *4606 p172*
Bywater, Joseph 35; California, 1867 *3840.1 p14*

C

Caas, Nicholas; Wisconsin, n.d. **9675.5** *p49*
Cabanne, Mr. 39; Louisiana, 1825 **778.5** *p89*
Cabares, J. 26; Port uncertain, 1839 **778.5** *p89*
Cabassart, Emile; Iowa, 1866-1943 **123.54** *p12*
Cabbannes, Joseph 27; New Orleans, 1862 **543.30** *p450*
Cabell, Ann 27; Baltimore, 1775 **1219.7** *p271*
Cabirac, Miss 2; New Orleans, 1827 **778.5** *p90*
Cabirac, Miss 7; New Orleans, 1826 **778.5** *p90*
Cabirac, Mr. 33; New Orleans, 1826 **778.5** *p90*
Cabirac, Mr. 33; New Orleans, 1827 **778.5** *p89*
Cabirac, Mrs. 20; New Orleans, 1827 **778.5** *p90*
Cabirac, Mrs. 28; New Orleans, 1826 **778.5** *p90*
Cabiro, Mr. 22; America, 1839 **778.5** *p90*
Cabiro, Jean 32; New Orleans, 1836 **778.5** *p90*
Cablanquer, Jean 32; New Orleans, 1837 **778.5** *p90*
Cabonne, Jean 21; America, 1838 **778.5** *p90*
Cabossart, Emile Joseph; Iowa, 1866-1943 **123.54** *p57*
Cabot, Philippe; Quebec, 1821 **7603** *p48*
Cabouret, Arthur 4; New Orleans, 1835 **778.5** *p90*
Cabouret, Clement 35; New Orleans, 1835 **778.5** *p90*
Cabouret, Gaspard 31; New Orleans, 1836 **778.5** *p90*
Cabouret, Hortence 8; New Orleans, 1835 **778.5** *p90*
Cabouret, Marie 33; New Orleans, 1835 **778.5** *p90*
Cabriao, A.; New Orleans, 1839 **778.5** *p90*
Cabrillac, B. 33; Port uncertain, 1836 **778.5** *p91*
Cabrot, J. 27; New Orleans, 1839 **778.5** *p91*
Cabrot, P. 24; New Orleans, 1839 **778.5** *p91*
Cachan, Mr. 24; New Orleans, 1837 **778.5** *p91*
Cachellin, J. L. 25; America, 1836 **778.5** *p91*
Cacherd, John B. 38; New Orleans, 1862 **543.30** *p455*
Cacirtad, Mr. 25; Port uncertain, 1836 **778.5** *p103*
Cacozza, Sylvester; Arkansas, 1918 **95.2** *p24*
Cadby, Thos.; Virginia, 1638 **6219** *p122*
Caddigan, John 57; Massachusetts, 1849 **5881.1** *p18*
Caddigan, Julia Ann 5; Massachusetts, 1849 **5881.1** *p18*
Caddigan, Julia Ann 58; Massachusetts, 1849 **5881.1** *p18*
Cade, Nicholas; New York, NY, 1838 **8208.4** *p66*
Cade, Simon; Illinois, 1873 **5012.39** *p26*
Cade, Walter; Virginia, 1648 **6219** *p249*
  With wife
Cade, William; Virginia, 1640 **6219** *p184*
Cadell, John A.; Minneapolis, 1882-1885 **6410.35** *p51*
Cadenhead, Wm.; Austin, TX, 1886 **9777** *p5*
Cadet, Mr. 21; America, 1826 **778.5** *p91*
Cadet, Mr. 35; New Orleans, 1823 **778.5** *p91*
Cadet, Mrs. 18; America, 1827 **778.5** *p91*
Cadet, Mrs. 30; New Orleans, 1822 **778.5** *p91*
Cadet, Francois 27; America, 1827 **778.5** *p91*
Cadete, Mars 40; America, 1820 **778.5** *p91*
Cadillan, Mr. 20; America, 1838 **778.5** *p91*
Cadillan, William 29; New Orleans, 1832 **778.5** *p91*
Cadir, Mr.; New Orleans, 1838 **778.5** *p91*
Cadres, Gabriel 26; New Orleans, 1838 **778.5** *p91*
Cadrue, Mrs. 33; America, 1823 **778.5** *p92*
Cadwallader, Humphry; Virginia, 1640 **6219** *p185*
Cadwell, W. A.; Washington, 1859-1920 **2872.7** *p6*
Cady, Ellen; Massachusetts, 1850 **5881.1** *p16*
Cady, Ellen 30; Massachusetts, 1850 **5881.1** *p16*
Caelle, Napoleon 22; America, 1835 **778.5** *p92*
Caen, Mme. 28; Louisiana, 1820 **778.5** *p92*
Caesar, Julius; Santa Clara Co., CA, 1871 **2764.35** *p14*
Caffaral, Paul 45; Pennsylvania, 1753 **2444** *p144*
Caffarel, Antoine *SEE* Caffarel, Paul
Caffarel, Catherine *SEE* Caffarel, Paul
Caffarel, Lucresse *SEE* Caffarel, Paul
Caffarel, Lucresse Chapelle *SEE* Caffarel, Paul

Caffarel, Marguerite *SEE* Caffarel, Paul
Caffarel, Paul; Pennsylvania, 1753 **2444** *p144*
  *Wife:*Lucresse Chapelle
  *Child:*Antoine
  *Child:*Suzanne
  *Child:*Catherine
  *Child:*Marguerite
  *Child:*Lucresse
Caffarel, Suzanne *SEE* Caffarel, Paul
Caffe, Michael; New York, NY, 1836 **8208.4** *p10*
Cafferty, Girzy; New York, NY, 1816 **2859.11** *p26*
Cafferty, Mary; New York, NY, 1816 **2859.11** *p26*
Caffoe, Connor; America, 1742 **4971** *p53*
Caffray, Edward; New York, NY, 1811 **2859.11** *p9*
Caffrey, John; New Jersey, 1841 **7036** *p122*
Caffry, Catherine; America, 1737 **4971** *p24*
Caffry, John; America, 1740 **4971** *p15*
Caffry, Nicholas; New York, NY, 1815 **2859.11** *p26*
Cafon, Jean-Francois 37; Louisiana, 1820 **778.5** *p92*
Caganski, Michael; Illinois, 1893 **5012.39** *p53*
Cagaux, Peter 26; Virginia, 1773 **1219.7** *p169*
Cage, John 17; United States or West Indies, 1718 **3690.1** *p36*
Cage, William 17; Jamaica, 1730 **3690.1** *p36*
Cager, Tho.; Virginia, 1643 **6219** *p199*
Caghy, Garret; America, 1735-1743 **4971** *p79*
Cagno, Vincent; Arkansas, 1918 **95.2** *p24*
Cahalan, Ellen 55; St. John, N.B., 1866 **5704.8** *p167*
Cahalan, James 20; St. John, N.B., 1866 **5704.8** *p167*
Cahalan, Jermiah 55; St. John, N.B., 1866 **5704.8** *p167*
Cahan, John; America, 1735-1743 **4971** *p78*
Cahan, John; America, 1742 **4971** *p80*
Cahane, Ellenor; America, 1743 **4971** *p43*
Cahane, Honor; America, 1736-1737 **4971** *p59*
Cahey, John; Arkansas, 1918 **95.2** *p24*
Caheyac, B. H. 18; New Orleans, 1839 **778.5** *p92*
Cahill, Ann 7; Massachusetts, 1849 **5881.1** *p13*
Cahill, Ann 36; Massachusetts, 1850 **5881.1** *p13*
Cahill, Ann 40; Massachusetts, 1849 **5881.1** *p13*
Cahill, Bridget 10; Massachusetts, 1850 **5881.1** *p14*
Cahill, Catharine 6; Massachusetts, 1850 **5881.1** *p14*
Cahill, Darby 26; Massachusetts, 1847 **5881.1** *p14*
Cahill, Edward 5; Massachusetts, 1850 **5881.1** *p16*
Cahill, Ellen 2; Massachusetts, 1850 **5881.1** *p16*
Cahill, James; Illinois, 1856 **7857** *p2*
Cahill, James; Massachusetts, 1847 **5881.1** *p17*
Cahill, James 11; Massachusetts, 1849 **5881.1** *p19*
Cahill, John; Ohio, 1841 **9892.11** *p7*
Cahill, John; Ohio, 1843 **9892.11** *p7*
Cahill, John 12; Massachusetts, 1850 **5881.1** *p17*
Cahill, John 17; Massachusetts, 1849 **5881.1** *p19*
Cahill, John 33; Maryland, 1774 **1219.7** *p192*
Cahill, Judith 70; Massachusetts, 1849 **5881.1** *p18*
Cahill, Julia 8; Massachusetts, 1850 **5881.1** *p19*
Cahill, Kate 17; Massachusetts, 1849 **5881.1** *p20*
Cahill, Maria 5; Massachusetts, 1849 **5881.1** *p22*
Cahill, Mary 10; Massachusetts, 1850 **5881.1** *p22*
Cahill, Mary 22; Massachusetts, 1849 **5881.1** *p22*
Cahill, Mathias 20; Massachusetts, 1847 **5881.1** *p20*
Cahill, Pat. 25; Massachusetts, 1848 **5881.1** *p24*
Cahill, Susan 9; Massachusetts, 1849 **5881.1** *p25*
Cahill, Thomas; America, 1737 **4971** *p85*
Cahill, Thomas; America, 1743 **4971** *p11*
Cahill, Timothy 9; Massachusetts, 1848 **5881.1** *p25*
Cahlin, Patrick 19; St. John, N.B., 1855 **5704.8** *p127*
Cahlman, Louis 45; New Orleans, 1862 **543.30** *p455*
Cahn, Jacques; America, 1839 **778.5** *p92*

Cahoon, Joseph; Quebec, 1848 **5704.8** *p42*
Cahoon, Martha 12; Quebec, 1848 **5704.8** *p42*
Cail, John 20; St. John, N.B., 1858 **5704.8** *p137*
Caillard, Mr. 27; New Orleans, 1839 **778.5** *p92*
Caillaux, Pierre 22; New Orleans, 1822 **778.5** *p92*
Caille, Jacques 38; New Orleans, 1837 **778.5** *p92*
Cailleres, John 19; New Orleans, 1832 **778.5** *p92*
Caillet, P. 30; New Orleans, 1830 **778.5** *p92*
Cailleteau, A. A. 28; New Orleans, 1829 **778.5** *p92*
Caimella, Joseph; Arkansas, 1918 **95.2** *p24*
Cain, Ann; Philadelphia, 1851 **5704.8** *p81*
Cain, Ann 4; St. John, N.B., 1850 **5704.8** *p66*
Cain, Bernard 17; Massachusetts, 1847 **5881.1** *p13*
Cain, Biddy 20; Philadelphia, 1857 **5704.8** *p132*
Cain, Bridget 40; Quebec, 1864 **5704.8** *p159*
Cain, Charles; New York, NY, 1816 **2859.11** *p26*
Cain, Cornelius; California, 1865 **3840.1** *p16*
Cain, Daniel 30; New Orleans, 1862-1865 **543.30** *p455*
Cain, Edward; Nevada, 1883 **2764.35** *p11*
Cain, Edward 27; Massachusetts, 1847 **5881.1** *p15*
Cain, Elizabeth 2; St. John, N.B., 1850 **5704.8** *p66*
Cain, Francis 8; St. John, N.B., 1850 **5704.8** *p66*
Cain, George; St. John, N.B., 1853 **5704.8** *p106*
Cain, Hannah; Quebec, 1848 **5704.8** *p42*
Cain, James; St. John, N.B., 1850 **5704.8** *p66*
Cain, John; New York, NY, 1838 **8208.4** *p69*
Cain, John 13; St. John, N.B., 1850 **5704.8** *p66*
Cain, John 18; Philadelphia, 1854 **5704.8** *p118*
Cain, Judy 40; Massachusetts, 1847 **5881.1** *p27*
Cain, Margaret; St. John, N.B., 1847 **5704.8** *p5*
Cain, Margaret 6; St. John, N.B., 1850 **5704.8** *p66*
Cain, Mary; Philadelphia, 1851 **5704.8** *p81*
Cain, Mary; St. John, N.B., 1847 **5704.8** *p11*
Cain, Mary 11; St. John, N.B., 1850 **5704.8** *p66*
Cain, Mary 14; Philadelphia, 1857 **5704.8** *p132*
Cain, Mary 25; St. John, N.B., 1854 **5704.8** *p119*
Cain, Mary Jane 3; Quebec, 1864 **5704.8** *p159*
Cain, Michael 1; Quebec, 1864 **5704.8** *p159*
Cain, Michael 19; Pennsylvania, 1722 **3690.1** *p36*
Cain, Michael 34; New Orleans, 1862 **543.30** *p459*
Cain, Nancy; St. John, N.B., 1850 **5704.8** *p66*
Cain, Patrick; New York, NY, 1816 **2859.11** *p26*
Cain, Peter; Illinois, 1867 **5012.39** *p98*
Cain, Peter 44; Massachusetts, 1847 **5881.1** *p23*
Cain, Sarah 21; Philadelphia, 1854 **5704.8** *p118*
Cain, Sissy; St. John, N.B., 1853 **5704.8** *p106*
Caine, Abraham; Virginia, 1638 **6219** *p150*
Caine, Abrahame; Virginia, 1638 **6219** *p2*
Caine, Elisabeth; Sorel, Que., 1818 **7603** *p41*
Caine, Francis 22; St. John, N.B., 1851 **5704.8** *p72*
Caird, Thomas 25; Massachusetts, 1849 **5881.1** *p25*
Caire, Antoine Ugene 17; America, 1838 **778.5** *p92*
Caire, Joseph Auguste 19; America, 1838 **778.5** *p92*
Cairnes, Mr.; Quebec, 1815 **9229.18** *p82*
Cairnes, Alexander; Virginia, 1761 **1219.7** *p80*
Cairney, Phelemy; America, 1741 **4971** *p74*
Cairns, Mr.; Quebec, 1815 **9229.18** *p77*
Cairns, Alexander; St. John, N.B., 1848 **5704.8** *p47*
Cairns, Ann; St. John, N.B., 1847 **5704.8** *p19*
Cairns, Archibald; New York, NY, 1866 **5704.8** *p206*
Cairns, Eliza; St. John, N.B., 1847 **5704.8** *p19*
Cairns, Frank; Iowa, 1866-1943 **123.54** *p12*
Cairns, James; St. John, N.B., 1847 **5704.8** *p19*
Cairns, James G. 50; North Carolina, 1850 **1639.20** *p22*
Cairns, Jane 25; Quebec, 1863 **5704.8** *p154*
Cairns, John; New York, NY, 1866 **5704.8** *p206*
Cairns, John; St. John, N.B., 1848 **5704.8** *p47*

Cairns, Mage 20; Philadelphia, 1860 ***5704.8*** *p144*
Cairns, Margaret; New York, NY, 1866 ***5704.8*** *p206*
Cairns, Martha 12; St. John, N.B., 1853 ***5704.8*** *p110*
Cairns, Mary; New York, NY, 1816 ***2859.11*** *p26*
Cairns, Robert; Philadelphia, 1853 ***5704.8*** *p108*
Cairns, Samuel; New York, NY, 1816 ***2859.11*** *p26*
Cairns, Sarah 25; St. John, N.B., 1854 ***5704.8*** *p115*
Cairns, Thomas; St. John, N.B., 1848 ***5704.8*** *p47*
Cairns, William; Philadelphia, 1849 ***53.26*** *p9*
Cairns, William; Philadelphia, 1849 ***5704.8*** *p54*
Cairns, William 22; St. John, N.B., 1866 ***5704.8*** *p167*
Cairns, William 30; Quebec, 1863 ***5704.8*** *p154*
Caissy, Roger; Acadia, 1668 ***7603*** *p75*
Caiters, James; Ohio, 1841 ***9892.11*** *p7*
Cajner, Joseph; Wisconsin, n.d. ***9675.5*** *p49*
Cakebread, Jon.; Virginia, 1643 ***6219*** *p206*
Cakebread, Tho.; Virginia, 1645 ***6219*** *p253*
Calabrese, Frank; Arkansas, 1918 ***95.2*** *p24*
Calaghan, Daniel 24; Maryland, 1774 ***1219.7*** *p192*
Calaghan, John 23; Virginia, 1774 ***1219.7*** *p240*
Calahan, Bryan; New York, NY, 1836 ***8208.4*** *p23*
Calahan, Hugh 57; Arizona, 1890 ***2764.35*** *p11*
Calahan, Thomas; Ohio, 1840 ***9892.11*** *p7*
Calam, Michael 27; Maryland, 1775 ***1219.7*** *p248*
Calame, Abraham 52; Halifax, N.S., 1752 ***7074.6*** *p209*
*Wife:*Suzanne
*Child:*Jeannette
*Child:*Marie
*Child:*Jacques
*Child:*Madeleine
*Child:*Catherine
Calame, Abram 52; Halifax, N.S., 1752 ***7074.6*** *p207*
With son
With family of 5
Calame, Catherine *SEE* Calame, Abraham
Calame, Jacques *SEE* Calame, Abraham
Calame, Jeannette *SEE* Calame, Abraham
Calame, Madeleine *SEE* Calame, Abraham
Calame, Marie *SEE* Calame, Abraham
Calame, Suzanne *SEE* Calame, Abraham
Calbe, Jean 50; America, 1836 ***778.5*** *p92*
Calcup, Bridget; Virginia, 1647 ***6219*** *p241*
Caldcleugh, Andrew; Lexington, NC, 1744-1821 ***1639.20*** *p23*
Calder, Alexander; Charleston, SC, 1803 ***1639.20*** *p22*
Calder, Alexander; Georgia, 1775 ***1219.7*** *p275*
Calder, Catherine; Georgia, 1775 ***1219.7*** *p275*
Calder, Christopher; Georgia, 1775 ***1219.7*** *p275*
Calder, Henrietta; Georgia, 1775 ***1219.7*** *p275*
Calder, Henry; South Carolina, 1820 ***1639.20*** *p22*
Calder, James; Charleston, SC, 1813 ***1639.20*** *p23*
Calder, James; Georgia, 1775 ***1219.7*** *p275*
Calder, James 60; Charleston, SC, 1850 ***1639.20*** *p23*
Calder, John; Georgia, 1775 ***1219.7*** *p275*
Calder, Margaret; Georgia, 1775 ***1219.7*** *p275*
Calder, Mary; South Carolina, 1823 ***1639.20*** *p23*
Calder, Richard 21; Maryland, 1775 ***1219.7*** *p254*
Calder, Robert; Georgia, 1775 ***1219.7*** *p275*
Calder, William; Charleston, SC, 1831 ***1639.20*** *p23*
Calder, William 50; Charleston, SC, 1850 ***1639.20*** *p23*
Calderono, Michelo; Arkansas, 1918 ***95.2*** *p24*
Caldrick, Martha 26; St. John, N.B., 1854 ***5704.8*** *p122*
Caldwell, Agnes 9 mos; St. John, N.B., 1866 ***5704.8*** *p167*
Caldwell, Andrew 3 mos; St. John, N.B., 1853 ***5704.8*** *p109*
Caldwell, Ann Jane 8; Quebec, 1847 ***5704.8*** *p12*
Caldwell, Donald 18; Wilmington, NC, 1774 ***1639.20*** *p23*
Caldwell, Eliza 14; St. John, N.B., 1857 ***5704.8*** *p136*
Caldwell, Eliza 50; Quebec, 1855 ***5704.8*** *p125*
Caldwell, Eliza Jane 20; Quebec, 1855 ***5704.8*** *p125*
Caldwell, Elizabeth 30; St. John, N.B., 1853 ***5704.8*** *p109*
Caldwell, Emily 7; St. John, N.B., 1858 ***5704.8*** *p137*
Caldwell, Ezekiel; New York, NY, 1815 ***2859.11*** *p26*
Caldwell, Francis 20; Quebec, 1858 ***5704.8*** *p138*
Caldwell, George 17; Quebec, 1855 ***5704.8*** *p125*
Caldwell, Henry; Quebec, 1852 ***5704.8*** *p86*
Caldwell, Henry; Quebec, 1852 ***5704.8*** *p91*
Caldwell, Hugh; New York, NY, 1864 ***5704.8*** *p172*
Caldwell, J. A. 31; Kansas, 1888 ***5240.1*** *p71*
Caldwell, James; Boston, 1774 ***1219.7*** *p231*
Caldwell, James; Philadelphia, 1848 ***5704.8*** *p45*
Caldwell, James 10; St. John, N.B., 1857 ***5704.8*** *p136*
Caldwell, James 21; St. John, N.B., 1861 ***5704.8*** *p149*
Caldwell, James 29 *SEE* Caldwell, John
Caldwell, James 34; Philadelphia, 1817 ***9892.11*** *p7*
Caldwell, Jane; St. John, N.B., 1847 ***5704.8*** *p11*
Caldwell, Jane 20; St. John, N.B., 1858 ***5704.8*** *p137*
Caldwell, Jane 56 *SEE* Caldwell, John
Caldwell, John; Iowa, 1866-1943 ***123.54*** *p12*
Caldwell, John; New York, NY, 1811 ***2859.11*** *p9*
With family
Caldwell, John; North Carolina, 1812 ***1639.20*** *p24*
Caldwell, John; Quebec, 1851 ***5704.8*** *p74*
Caldwell, John 21; Philadelphia, 1858 ***5704.8*** *p139*
Caldwell, John 24 *SEE* Caldwell, John
Caldwell, John 24; Wilmington, DE, 1831 ***6508.7*** *p161*
Caldwell, John 40; St. John, N.B., 1853 ***5704.8*** *p109*
Caldwell, John 51; North Carolina, 1850 ***1639.20*** *p24*
Caldwell, John 53; Charleston, SC, 1850 ***1639.20*** *p23*
*Relative:*Jane 56
*Relative:*James 29
*Relative:*John 24
*Relative:*Sarah 23
Caldwell, John W. 55; South Carolina, 1850 ***1639.20*** *p23*
Caldwell, Joseph; America, 1808 ***4778.2*** *p142*
Caldwell, Joseph; New Brunswick, 1820 ***9775.5*** *p204*
With son
Caldwell, Joseph; New York, NY, 1811 ***2859.11*** *p9*
Caldwell, Joseph; New York, NY, 1816 ***2859.11*** *p26*
Caldwell, Joseph; Quebec, 1847 ***5704.8*** *p17*
Caldwell, Margaret; Quebec, 1852 ***5704.8*** *p86*
Caldwell, Margaret; Quebec, 1852 ***5704.8*** *p91*
Caldwell, Margaret 20; St. John, N.B., 1866 ***5704.8*** *p167*
Caldwell, Margaret 22; St. John, N.B., 1856 ***5704.8*** *p131*
Caldwell, Martha 6; Quebec, 1847 ***5704.8*** *p12*
Caldwell, Mary; Philadelphia, 1847 ***53.26*** *p9*
Caldwell, Mary; Philadelphia, 1847 ***5704.8*** *p14*
Caldwell, Mary; Philadelphia, 1866 ***5704.8*** *p215*
Caldwell, Mary; Quebec, 1847 ***5704.8*** *p12*
Caldwell, Mary 6 mos; Quebec, 1847 ***5704.8*** *p12*
Caldwell, Mathew; St. John, N.B., 1848 ***5704.8*** *p47*
Caldwell, Matilda 15; Quebec, 1855 ***5704.8*** *p125*
Caldwell, Nancy 18; St. John, N.B., 1858 ***5704.8*** *p137*
Caldwell, Nancy 20; Wilmington, DE, 1831 ***6508.3*** *p101*
Caldwell, Nancy 50; St. John, N.B., 1858 ***5704.8*** *p137*
Caldwell, Peter 39; Philadelphia, 1817 ***9892.11*** *p7*
Caldwell, Rebecca 9; St. John, N.B., 1858 ***5704.8*** *p137*
Caldwell, Richard 40; Philadelphia, 1817 ***9892.11*** *p7*
Caldwell, Robert; America, 1802 ***4778.2*** *p141*
Caldwell, Robert; Virginia, 1646 ***6219*** *p239*
Caldwell, Robert 22; St. John, N.B., 1866 ***5704.8*** *p167*
Caldwell, Samuel; Philadelphia, 1867 ***5704.8*** *p217*
Caldwell, Samuel 22; St. John, N.B., 1856 ***5704.8*** *p131*
Caldwell, Samuel 45; St. John, N.B., 1857 ***5704.8*** *p136*
Caldwell, Sarah 23 *SEE* Caldwell, John
Caldwell, Sarah 42; St. John, N.B., 1853 ***5704.8*** *p109*
Caldwell, Thomas; Philadelphia, 1852 ***5704.8*** *p89*
Caldwell, Timothy; Philadelphia, 1848 ***5704.8*** *p45*
Caldwell, William; America, 1742 ***4971*** *p74*
Caldwell, William; America, 1793 ***1639.20*** *p24*
Caldwell, William; Quebec, 1847 ***5704.8*** *p12*
Caldwell, William 4; St. John, N.B., 1853 ***5704.8*** *p109*
Caldwell, William 10; Quebec, 1847 ***5704.8*** *p12*
Caldwell, William 21; Philadelphia, 1854 ***5704.8*** *p116*
Caldwell, William James 17; Quebec, 1853 ***5704.8*** *p105*
Caldwell, William John 21; St. John, N.B., 1856 ***5704.8*** *p131*
Cale, John 42; Maryland, 1774 ***1219.7*** *p230*
Caleaghan, Bryan; New York, NY, 1836 ***8208.4*** *p23*
Calenbach, Pierre 22; New Orleans, 1838 ***778.5*** *p93*
Calfe, Wm.; Virginia, 1637 ***6219*** *p113*
Calgan, Catherine; New York, NY, 1816 ***2859.11*** *p26*
Calgan, Mary; New York, NY, 1816 ***2859.11*** *p26*
Calgay, John 21; Quebec, 1854 ***5704.8*** *p119*
Calhoun, Catherine; America, 1790 ***1639.20*** *p24*
Calhoun, Catherine 60; North Carolina, 1850 ***1639.20*** *p24*
Calhoun, Duncan; America, 1790 ***1639.20*** *p24*
Calhoun, Duncan; America, 1791 ***1639.20*** *p24*
Calhoun, James; New York, NY, 1815 ***2859.11*** *p26*
Calhoun, James; South Carolina, 1684-1760 ***1639.20*** *p24*
Calhoun, John 20; Philadelphia, 1857 ***5704.8*** *p133*
Calhoun, Mary 21; Philadelphia, 1857 ***5704.8*** *p133*
Calhoun, Mary 55; North Carolina, 1850 ***1639.20*** *p24*
Calhoun, William; New York, NY, 1815 ***2859.11*** *p26*
Cali, Toni; Arkansas, 1918 ***95.2*** *p24*
Calighan, Charles; New York, NY, 1838 ***8208.4*** *p64*
Calimis, Vincent 29; America, 1836 ***778.5*** *p93*
Calisher, Henry I.; Virginia, 1848 ***4626.16*** *p13*
Call, Mary; New York, NY, 1868 ***5704.8*** *p226*
Call, Moses 18; Philadelphia, 1854 ***5704.8*** *p117*
Callagan, C. 35; Arizona, 1918 ***9228.40*** *p22*
Callagan, James; New York, NY, 1816 ***2859.11*** *p26*
Callaghan, Alice 5; Massachusetts, 1849 ***5881.1*** *p13*
Callaghan, Alice 65; Massachusetts, 1847 ***5881.1*** *p12*
Callaghan, Andrew; Philadelphia, 1848 ***5704.8*** *p41*
Callaghan, Ann; Philadelphia, 1847 ***53.26*** *p9*
Callaghan, Ann; Philadelphia, 1847 ***5704.8*** *p14*
Callaghan, Anne 9 mos; St. John, N.B., 1851 ***5704.8*** *p71*
Callaghan, Anne 2; Newport, RI, 1851 ***6508.5*** *p19*
Callaghan, Annie 9; Philadelphia, 1867 ***5704.8*** *p224*
Callaghan, Bate 1; Newport, RI, 1851 ***6508.5*** *p19*
Callaghan, Bernard; St. John, N.B., 1853 ***5704.8*** *p107*
Callaghan, Bessy 30; Massachusetts, 1849 ***5881.1*** *p13*
Callaghan, Betsey 32; Massachusetts, 1849 ***5881.1*** *p13*
Callaghan, Betty 35; Massachusetts, 1849 ***5881.1*** *p13*
Callaghan, Biddy; St. John, N.B., 1850 ***5704.8*** *p61*
Callaghan, Biddy; St. John, N.B., 1850 ***5704.8*** *p65*
Callaghan, Biddy 11; St. John, N.B., 1851 ***5704.8*** *p71*
Callaghan, Bridget 10; St. John, N.B., 1848 ***5704.8*** *p47*
Callaghan, Catharine 7; Massachusetts, 1849 ***5881.1*** *p14*
Callaghan, Catherine; Philadelphia, 1849 ***53.26*** *p9*
Callaghan, Catherine; Philadelphia, 1849 ***5704.8*** *p53*
Callaghan, Catherine; Philadelphia, 1852 ***5704.8*** *p88*
Callaghan, Catherine 8; St. John, N.B., 1848 ***5704.8*** *p47*
Callaghan, Catherine 11; St. John, N.B., 1853 ***5704.8*** *p107*
Callaghan, Catherine 20; Philadelphia, 1859 ***5704.8*** *p142*
Callaghan, Charles; New York, NY, 1869 ***5704.8*** *p233*
Callaghan, Charles 3; St. John, N.B., 1853 ***5704.8*** *p107*
Callaghan, Corm.; America, 1742 ***4971*** *p63*
Callaghan, Cornelius; America, 1741 ***4971*** *p53*
Callaghan, Daniel; America, 1738 ***4971*** *p52*
Callaghan, Daniel; America, 1739 ***4971*** *p56*
Callaghan, Daniel 21; Massachusetts, 1847 ***5881.1*** *p15*
Callaghan, Daniel 30; Massachusetts, 1848 ***5881.1*** *p15*
Callaghan, Denis; St. John, N.B., 1851 ***5704.8*** *p72*
Callaghan, Dennis 9; St. John, N.B., 1853 ***5704.8*** *p100*
Callaghan, Edward; New York, NY, 1816 ***2859.11*** *p26*
Callaghan, Edward 8; Massachusetts, 1849 ***5881.1*** *p16*
Callaghan, Edward 13; St. John, N.B., 1851 ***5704.8*** *p71*
Callaghan, Edward 25; Massachusetts, 1847 ***5881.1*** *p15*
Callaghan, Elisha 4; Massachusetts, 1847 ***5881.1*** *p15*
Callaghan, Elisha 9; Massachusetts, 1847 ***5881.1*** *p15*
Callaghan, Eliza 12; Massachusetts, 1849 ***5881.1*** *p16*
Callaghan, Eliza 40; Massachusetts, 1847 ***5881.1*** *p15*
Callaghan, Eliza 50; Massachusetts, 1849 ***5881.1*** *p16*
Callaghan, Eliza Jane; Philadelphia, 1850 ***53.26*** *p9*
Callaghan, Eliza Jane; Philadelphia, 1850 ***5704.8*** *p59*
Callaghan, Ellen; New York, NY, 1866 ***5704.8*** *p213*
Callaghan, Ellen 20; Massachusetts, 1849 ***5881.1*** *p16*
Callaghan, Ellen 23; Massachusetts, 1850 ***5881.1*** *p16*
Callaghan, Ellen 25; Massachusetts, 1847 ***5881.1*** *p15*
Callaghan, Ellen 26; Newport, RI, 1851 ***6508.5*** *p19*
Callaghan, Ellen 30; Massachusetts, 1850 ***5881.1*** *p16*
Callaghan, Francis 7; Massachusetts, 1847 ***5881.1*** *p16*
Callaghan, Francis 40; Massachusetts, 1847 ***5881.1*** *p16*
Callaghan, Frank 9; Massachusetts, 1849 ***5881.1*** *p16*
Callaghan, Hannah; St. John, N.B., 1847 ***5704.8*** *p34*
Callaghan, Honora 23; Massachusetts, 1849 ***5881.1*** *p17*
Callaghan, Honora 28; Massachusetts, 1850 ***5881.1*** *p17*
Callaghan, Hugh; Philadelphia, 1851 ***5704.8*** *p80*
Callaghan, James; Philadelphia, 1816 ***2859.11*** *p26*
Callaghan, James; Quebec, 1849 ***5704.8*** *p51*
Callaghan, James 13; Massachusetts, 1847 ***5881.1*** *p17*
Callaghan, James 24; St. John, N.B., 1854 ***5704.8*** *p114*
Callaghan, Jane 3; St. John, N.B., 1851 ***5704.8*** *p71*
Callaghan, Jane 3; St. John, N.B., 1853 ***5704.8*** *p100*
Callaghan, John; America, 1737 ***4971*** *p13*
Callaghan, John; America, 1741 ***4971*** *p16*
Callaghan, John; St. John, N.B., 1853 ***5704.8*** *p107*
Callaghan, John 21; Massachusetts, 1849 ***5881.1*** *p18*
Callaghan, John 22; Philadelphia, 1774 ***1219.7*** *p216*
Callaghan, John 24; Philadelphia, 1859 ***5704.8*** *p142*
Callaghan, Kerty; Philadelphia, 1850 ***53.26*** *p9*
Callaghan, Kerty; Philadelphia, 1850 ***5704.8*** *p60*
Callaghan, Margaret; New York, NY, 1816 ***2859.11*** *p26*
With 2 children
Callaghan, Margaret; St. John, N.B., 1853 ***5704.8*** *p107*
Callaghan, Margaret 5; St. John, N.B., 1853 ***5704.8*** *p100*
Callaghan, Margaret 13; St. John, N.B., 1853 ***5704.8*** *p107*
Callaghan, Margaret 25; Massachusetts, 1849 ***5881.1*** *p21*
Callaghan, Mary; Philadelphia, 1847 ***53.26*** *p9*
Callaghan, Mary; Philadelphia, 1847 ***5704.8*** *p24*
Callaghan, Mary; Philadelphia, 1848 ***5704.8*** *p40*
Callaghan, Mary; Philadelphia, 1851 ***5704.8*** *p79*
Callaghan, Mary; Philadelphia, 1853 ***5704.8*** *p108*
Callaghan, Mary; Quebec, 1825 ***7603*** *p83*
Callaghan, Mary; St. John, N.B., 1851 ***5704.8*** *p71*
Callaghan, Mary; St. John, N.B., 1853 ***5704.8*** *p100*
Callaghan, Mary 10; Massachusetts, 1849 ***5881.1*** *p21*
Callaghan, Mary 12; Massachusetts, 1847 ***5881.1*** *p20*
Callaghan, Mary 12; Massachusetts, 1849 ***5881.1*** *p22*
Callaghan, Mary 13; St. John, N.B., 1853 ***5704.8*** *p107*
Callaghan, Mary 23; Massachusetts, 1850 ***5881.1*** *p23*
Callaghan, Mary 30; Massachusetts, 1849 ***5881.1*** *p22*
Callaghan, Michael; Philadelphia, 1811 ***2859.11*** *p9*
Callaghan, Michael 7; St. John, N.B., 1853 ***5704.8*** *p100*
Callaghan, Michael 9; Massachusetts, 1847 ***5881.1*** *p20*
Callaghan, Nancy; Philadelphia, 1849 ***53.26*** *p9*
Callaghan, Nancy; Philadelphia, 1849 ***5704.8*** *p53*
Callaghan, Nancy; Philadelphia, 1849 ***5704.8*** *p54*
Callaghan, Nancy; St. John, N.B., 1851 ***5704.8*** *p71*
Callaghan, Nancy 13; Massachusetts, 1850 ***5881.1*** *p23*
Callaghan, Neal 19; Philadelphia, 1803 ***53.26*** *p9*
Callaghan, Nelly; Philadelphia, 1848 ***53.26*** *p9*

64 *FOR A COMPLETE EXPLANATION OF ENTRY, SEE "HOW TO READ A CITATION" SECTION*

Callaghan, Nelly; Philadelphia, 1848 ***5704.8*** *p40*
Callaghan, Owen; America, 1740 ***4971*** *p25*
Callaghan, Owen; America, 1740 ***4971*** *p47*
Callaghan, Owen; America, 1741 ***4971*** *p49*
Callaghan, Pat; Philadelphia, 1852 ***5704.8*** *p97*
Callaghan, Pat. 16; Massachusetts, 1847 ***5881.1*** *p23*
Callaghan, Pat. 29; Massachusetts, 1849 ***5881.1*** *p24*
Callaghan, Patrick; New York, NY, 1815 ***2859.11*** *p26*
Callaghan, Patrick; Philadelphia, 1851 ***5704.8*** *p79*
Callaghan, Patrick; St. John, N.B., 1851 ***5704.8*** *p71*
Callaghan, Patrick; St. John, N.B., 1853 ***5704.8*** *p100*
Callaghan, Patrick; St. John, N.B., 1853 ***5704.8*** *p106*
Callaghan, Patrick 11; Massachusetts, 1849 ***5881.1*** *p24*
Callaghan, Patrick 12; St. John, N.B., 1849 ***5704.8*** *p55*
Callaghan, Rachel 23; Philadelphia, 1859 ***5704.8*** *p141*
Callaghan, Richard; St. John, N.B., 1853 ***5704.8*** *p107*
Callaghan, Richard 7; St. John, N.B., 1853 ***5704.8*** *p107*
Callaghan, Rose 20; Massachusetts, 1849 ***5881.1*** *p25*
Callaghan, Rose 20; Philadelphia, 1857 ***5704.8*** *p133*
Callaghan, Rosy 5; St. John, N.B., 1853 ***5704.8*** *p107*
Callaghan, Sally; St. John, N.B., 1851 ***5704.8*** *p71*
Callaghan, Sophia 40; Massachusetts, 1848 ***5881.1*** *p25*
Callaghan, Ternce 39; Newport, RI, 1851 ***6508.5*** *p19*
Callaghan, Thomas; Philadelphia, 1867 ***5704.8*** *p224*
Callaghan, Thomas 11; Massachusetts, 1850 ***5881.1*** *p26*
Callaghan, Thomas 25; Massachusetts, 1849 ***5881.1*** *p25*
Callaghan, Tim. 30; Massachusetts, 1849 ***5881.1*** *p25*
Callaghan, Tim. 50; Massachusetts, 1847 ***5881.1*** *p25*
Callaghan, Unity; St. John, N.B., 1851 ***5704.8*** *p72*
Callaghan, William; Philadelphia, 1848 ***5704.8*** *p40*
Callaghan, William; St. John, N.B., 1853 ***5704.8*** *p107*
Callaghan, William 18; Massachusetts, 1849 ***5881.1*** *p26*
Callagher, Phillip 20; Massachusetts, 1847 ***5881.1*** *p23*
Callahan, Charles; America, 1866 ***5704.8*** *p211*
Callahan, Charles; Virginia, 1637 ***6219*** *p110*
Callahan, Constantine 37; California, 1866 ***3840.1*** *p16*
Callahan, Edward; America, 1866 ***5704.8*** *p211*
Callahan, James; Philadelphia, 1867 ***5704.8*** *p223*
Callahan, James; Philadelphia, 1869 ***5704.8*** *p236*
Callahan, John; New York, NY, 1839 ***8208.4*** *p97*
Callahan, Mary 28; Massachusetts, 1850 ***5881.1*** *p23*
Callahan, Michael 30; New Orleans, 1862 ***543.30*** *p453*
Callan, Alexander 22; Wilmington, NC, 1774 ***1639.20*** *p24*
Callan, Bryan; America, 1739 ***4971*** *p63*
Callan, Elleanor; St. John, N.B., 1849 ***5704.8*** *p55*
Callan, J. 24; New Orleans, 1835 ***778.5*** *p93*
Callan, Mary; New York, NY, 1864 ***5704.8*** *p170*
Callan, Patrick 3; St. John, N.B., 1849 ***5704.8*** *p55*
Callan, Sally; St. John, N.B., 1849 ***5704.8*** *p55*
Callan, Thomas; Illinois, 1858 ***5012.39*** *p54*
Callari, Pascal; Arkansas, 1918 ***95.2*** *p25*
Callaughan, Thomas 23; Philadelphia, 1803 ***53.26*** *p9*
Callaway, Edmund; Virginia, 1639 ***6219*** *p151*
Callegan, Biddy 16; Massachusetts, 1850 ***5881.1*** *p14*
Calleghan, John 21; Massachusetts, 1847 ***5881.1*** *p17*
Callen, Biddy; Quebec, 1849 ***5704.8*** *p57*
Callen, Catharine; Quebec, 1849 ***5704.8*** *p57*
Callen, Edward 25; Massachusetts, 1849 ***5881.1*** *p15*
Callen, James; Philadelphia, 1849 ***53.26*** *p9*
Callen, James; Philadelphia, 1849 ***5704.8*** *p54*
Callen, James 13; Quebec, 1849 ***5704.8*** *p57*
Callen, John; Philadelphia, 1850 ***53.26*** *p9*
Callen, John; Philadelphia, 1850 ***5704.8*** *p65*
Callen, Mary 17; Massachusetts, 1849 ***5881.1*** *p21*
Callen, Michael; Quebec, 1849 ***5704.8*** *p57*
Calleville, Mme. 26; New Orleans, 1838 ***778.5*** *p93*
Calleville, M. 29; New Orleans, 1838 ***778.5*** *p93*
Calligan, Thomas; New York, NY, 1837 ***8208.4*** *p35*
Callighan, Catharine 19; Massachusetts, 1847 ***5881.1*** *p14*
Callighan, Margery 7; Philadelphia, 1861 ***5704.8*** *p148*
Callighan, Pat; Philadelphia, 1847 ***53.26*** *p9*
Callighan, Pat; Philadelphia, 1847 ***5704.8*** *p13*
Callihan, Carl; Illinois, 1860 ***2896.5*** *p7*
Callihan, John; New York, NY, 1811 ***2859.11*** *p9*
Callihan, Timothy; New York, NY, 1836 ***8208.4*** *p11*
Callin, Robert; St. John, N.B., 1851 ***5704.8*** *p72*
Callin, Sarah; St. John, N.B., 1847 ***5704.8*** *p5*
Callister, Robert; New York, NY, 1840 ***8208.4*** *p103*
Calloghty, Owen; America, 1741 ***4971*** *p48*
Callon, Ann 22; Philadelphia, 1858 ***5704.8*** *p139*
Callony, Pat. 30; Massachusetts, 1849 ***5881.1*** *p24*
Callum, James; Carolina, 1666-1766 ***1639.20*** *p25*
Callum, Robert; Raleigh, NC, 1717-1817 ***1639.20*** *p25*
Callwell, William; New York, NY, 1838 ***8208.4*** *p90*
Calmus, Henry B.; Wisconsin, n.d. ***9675.5*** *p49*
Calnec, . . .; Canada, 1776-1783 ***9786*** *p18*
Calney, Mat; New York, NY, 1816 ***2859.11*** *p26*
Calonne, John B.; Colorado, 1906 ***9678.1*** *p156*
Caloon, Daniel 40; St. John, N.B., 1856 ***5704.8*** *p131*
Caloon, Mary 11; St. John, N.B., 1856 ***5704.8*** *p131*
Caloon, Mary Ann 54; St. John, N.B., 1856 ***5704.8*** *p131*
Caloon, Solomon 18; St. John, N.B., 1856 ***5704.8*** *p131*
Calot, Andre 28; America, 1831 ***778.5*** *p93*
Calot, Catherine 1; America, 1831 ***778.5*** *p93*
Calot, Catherine 26; America, 1831 ***778.5*** *p93*
Calpin, James; New York, 1841 ***7036*** *p123*
Calshan, Catherine; New York, NY, 1816 ***2859.11*** *p26*
Calte, Henry; Wisconsin, n.d. ***9675.5*** *p49*
Calteun, Peter; Wisconsin, n.d. ***9675.5*** *p49*
Calton, Thomas; Virginia, 1647 ***6219*** *p243*
Calve, Julia 20; America, 1837 ***778.5*** *p93*
Calvert, Anthony 30; Carolina, 1774 ***1219.7*** *p180*
Calvert, John; Virginia, 1643 ***6219*** *p202*
Calvert, Mary 42; Savannah, GA, 1733 ***4719.17*** *p310*
*Husband:*William 44
Calvert, Robert; Iowa, 1866-1943 ***123.54*** *p12*
Calvert, William 44 *SEE* Calvert, Mary
Calvey, John; Arkansas, 1918 ***95.2*** *p25*
Calvin, Daniel 4; St. John, N.B., 1847 ***5704.8*** *p20*
Calvin, Elizabeth; St. John, N.B., 1847 ***5704.8*** *p20*
Calvin, Jane 8; St. John, N.B., 1847 ***5704.8*** *p20*
Calvin, John; St. John, N.B., 1847 ***5704.8*** *p20*
Calvin, John 9; St. John, N.B., 1847 ***5704.8*** *p20*
Calvin, John 22; St. John, N.B., 1863 ***5704.8*** *p152*
Calvin, Martha 6; St. John, N.B., 1847 ***5704.8*** *p20*
Calvin, Mary; St. John, N.B., 1847 ***5704.8*** *p20*
Calvin, Mary Ann 4; St. John, N.B., 1847 ***5704.8*** *p20*
Calvin, Thomas; New York, NY, 1811 ***2859.11*** *p9*
Calvin, Thomas; New York, NY, 1840 ***8208.4*** *p108*
Calvo, Michel 24; America, 1838 ***778.5*** *p93*
Calwell, James; Boston, 1774 ***1219.7*** *p231*
Calwin, Margaret; Philadelphia, 1852 ***5704.8*** *p95*
Cam, Christopher; Philadelphia, 1816 ***2859.11*** *p26*
With wife & son
Cam, John 18; Jamaica, 1739 ***3690.1*** *p36*
Camajore, Eunima 30; New York, NY, 1893 ***9026.4*** *p41*
Camane, Pierre; Quebec, 1790 ***7603*** *p36*
Camara, Ludwick 21; Pennsylvania, 1736 ***4779.3*** *p13*
Camaran, Elizabeth; America, 1740 ***4971*** *p15*
Camas, E. 14; New Orleans, 1838 ***778.5*** *p93*
Cambell, Daniel 18; Maryland, 1720 ***3690.1*** *p36*
Cambell, John; Colorado, 1891 ***9678.1*** *p156*
Cambell, Patrick 18; St. Christopher, 1722 ***3690.1*** *p36*
Cambell, Robert; New York, NY, 1811 ***2859.11*** *p9*
Cambert, Jean-Baptiste 31; Alabama, 1837 ***778.5*** *p93*
Cambet, Anthony; New York, NY, 1839 ***8208.4*** *p90*
Camble, John; New York, NY, 1816 ***2859.11*** *p26*
Camble, Joseph; New York, NY, 1811 ***2859.11*** *p9*
Camblett, Robert; Virginia, 1646 ***6219*** *p246*
Cambon, Lewis 30; Port uncertain, 1837 ***778.5*** *p93*
Camden, Thomas; New York, NY, 1837 ***8208.4*** *p54*
Came, John 21; Maryland, 1774 ***1219.7*** *p184*
Camell, Edmund; Virginia, 1637 ***6219*** *p17*
Camell, Elizabeth 16; Virginia, 1700 ***2212*** *p32*
Camell, Jacob Coury; Arkansas, 1918 ***95.2*** *p25*
Camellim, Edmond; Virginia, 1638 ***6219*** *p118*
Cameo, Jus. 25; New Orleans, 1827 ***778.5*** *p93*
Camereno, Rosalina 32; California, 1867 ***3840.1*** *p16*
Camerlohr, Francis; Wisconsin, n.d. ***9675.5*** *p49*
Cameron, Agnes 20; St. John, N.B., 1866 ***5704.8*** *p167*
Cameron, Allan; Cape Fear, NC, 1790 ***1639.20*** *p25*
Cameron, Allan; New Jersey, 1765 ***1219.7*** *p111*
Cameron, Allan 28; Wilmington, NC, 1774 ***1639.20*** *p25*
Cameron, Allen; Wilmington, NC, 1700-1800 ***1639.20*** *p25*
Cameron, Amelia 45; New York, NY, 1828 ***6508.4*** *p143*
Cameron, Angus 18; Wilmington, NC, 1774 ***1639.20*** *p25*
*Wife:*Katrine 21
Cameron, Ann; Norfolk, VA, 1773 ***1639.20*** *p223*
Cameron, Anne *SEE* Cameron, Donald
Cameron, Anne *SEE* Cameron, Donald
Cameron, Betty; Philadelphia, 1851 ***5704.8*** *p80*
Cameron, Catherine 12; St. John, N.B., 1847 ***5704.8*** *p9*
Cameron, Charles *SEE* Cameron, Donald
Cameron, Donald; America, 1811 ***1639.20*** *p25*
Cameron, Donald; Kansas, 1890 ***5240.1*** *p8*
Cameron, Donald; Nova Scotia, 1830 ***7085.4*** *p45*
*Wife:*Anne
*Child:*Anne
*Child:*Charles
*Child:*Mary
Cameron, Donald; South Carolina, 1716 ***1639.20*** *p25*
Cameron, Dougald; North Carolina, 1850 ***1639.20*** *p25*
Cameron, E. 15; New York, NY, 1828 ***6508.4*** *p143*
Cameron, Eliza; Philadelphia, 1853 ***5704.8*** *p101*
Cameron, Elizabeth 8; St. John, N.B., 1847 ***5704.8*** *p9*
Cameron, Isabella 6 mos; St. John, N.B., 1847 ***5704.8*** *p9*
Cameron, James; America, 1791 ***1639.20*** *p26*
Cameron, James; Philadelphia, 1867 ***5704.8*** *p215*
Cameron, James; St. John, N.B., 1847 ***5704.8*** *p9*
Cameron, James 20; St. John, N.B., 1853 ***5704.8*** *p109*
Cameron, Jane; Philadelphia, 1867 ***5704.8*** *p222*
Cameron, Janet; Quebec, 1843 ***4537.30*** *p1*
Cameron, Jean 16; New York, NY, 1828 ***6508.4*** *p143*
Cameron, Jeanette; Philadelphia, 1864 ***5704.8*** *p182*
Cameron, John; America, 1790 ***1639.20*** *p26*
Cameron, John; Brunswick, NC, 1739 ***1639.20*** *p26*
Cameron, John; North Carolina, 1830 ***1639.20*** *p26*
Cameron, John; Philadelphia, 1850 ***5704.8*** *p64*
Cameron, John; South Carolina, 1716 ***1639.20*** *p26*
Cameron, John; South Carolina, 1802 ***1639.20*** *p26*
Cameron, John 4; St. John, N.B., 1847 ***5704.8*** *p9*
Cameron, John 22; St. John, N.B., 1862 ***5704.8*** *p150*
Cameron, John 22; St. John, N.B., 1866 ***5704.8*** *p167*
Cameron, John 35; Savannah, GA, 1733 ***4719.17*** *p310*
Cameron, John G. 14; New York, NY, 1828 ***6508.4*** *p143*
Cameron, Katrine 21 *SEE* Cameron, Angus
Cameron, Lewis 28; Maryland, 1774 ***1219.7*** *p187*
Cameron, Lily; Quebec, 1852 ***4537.30*** *p22*
Cameron, Margaret 17; Massachusetts, 1849 ***5881.1*** *p21*
Cameron, Marie-Louise 24; Quebec, 1787 ***7603*** *p35*
Cameron, Martha; Philadelphia, 1852 ***5704.8*** *p97*
Cameron, Mary *SEE* Cameron, Donald
Cameron, Mary; Philadelphia, 1868 ***5704.8*** *p226*
Cameron, Mary Ann; Philadelphia, 1850 ***5704.8*** *p64*
Cameron, Nancy; New York, NY, 1868 ***5704.8*** *p228*
Cameron, Norman; North Carolina, 1816 ***1639.20*** *p26*
Cameron, R. 44; South Carolina, 1850 ***1639.20*** *p26*
Cameron, Robert; St. John, N.B., 1849 ***5704.8*** *p55*
Cameron, Robert 10; St. John, N.B., 1847 ***5704.8*** *p9*
Cameron, Sarah; Philadelphia, 1868 ***5704.8*** *p226*
Cameron, Thomas; Quebec, 1772 ***7603*** *p41*
Cameron, Uphinia; St. John, N.B., 1847 ***5704.8*** *p9*
Cameron, William; Washington, 1859-1920 ***2872.1*** *p6*
Camicart, Elizabeth 19; Jamaica, 1774 ***1219.7*** *p188*
Caminade, Eduard 21; Port uncertain, 1836 ***778.5*** *p93*
Cammay, Jean 34; New Orleans, 1838 ***778.5*** *p94*
Camme, P. 22; New Orleans, 1827 ***778.5*** *p94*
Cammerer, Johann Ludwig 21; Pennsylvania, 1736 ***4779.3*** *p13*
Cammerhoff, Anna *SEE* Cammerhoff, J. C. F.
Cammerhoff, J. C. F.; Delaware, 1746 ***3652*** *p67*
*Wife:*Anna
Camock, Mary; Virginia, 1642 ***6219*** *p194*
Camon, Juan 26; Mexico, 1826 ***778.5*** *p94*
Camont, Raymond 44; New Orleans, 1839 ***778.5*** *p94*
Camp, Robert; Washington, 1859-1920 ***2872.1*** *p6*
Camp, Thomas 17; Philadelphia, 1774 ***1219.7*** *p182*
Campagna, Sam; Arkansas, 1918 ***95.2*** *p25*
Campanar, Leandro 23; Kansas, 1881 ***5240.1*** *p63*
Campbel, Donald; America, 1784 ***8894.2*** *p56*
Campbell, . . . 16; Philadelphia, 1861 ***5704.8*** *p149*
Campbell, Lieut.; Quebec, 1815 ***9229.18*** *p80*
Campbell, Mr.; Quebec, 1815 ***9229.18*** *p77*
Campbell, Mrs.; America, 1762-1774 ***1639.20*** *p142*
Campbell, A.; Quebec, 1815 ***9229.18*** *p75*
Campbell, A. A.; Washington, 1859-1920 ***2872.1*** *p6*
Campbell, Abraham; St. John, N.B., 1849 ***5704.8*** *p55*
Campbell, Adam; Ohio, 1891 ***9892.11*** *p7*
Campbell, Alex *SEE* Campbell, Alex
Campbell, Alex *SEE* Campbell, Murdo
Campbell, Alex; Quebec, 1887 ***4537.30*** *p11*
*Wife:*Mary MacDonald
*Child:*Donald
*Child:*Alex
*Child:*Kirsty Ann
Campbell, Alexander; New York, NY, 1834 ***8208.4*** *p4*
Campbell, Alexander; New York, NY, 1838 ***8208.4*** *p89*
Campbell, Alexander; North Carolina, 1787-1812 ***1639.20*** *p27*
Campbell, Alexander; North Carolina, 1792-1840 ***1639.20*** *p27*
Campbell, Alexander; Nova Scotia, 1830 ***7085.4*** *p44*
*Wife:*Christy
*Child:*John
Campbell, Alexander; Quebec, 1853 ***5704.8*** *p103*
Campbell, Alexander; St. John, N.B., 1853 ***5704.8*** *p99*
Campbell, Alexander; South Carolina, 1767 ***1639.20*** *p26*
Campbell, Alexander 8; Quebec, 1854 ***5704.8*** *p121*
Campbell, Alexander 12 *SEE* Campbell, Hector
Campbell, Alexander 16; Philadelphia, 1864 ***5704.8*** *p155*
Campbell, Alexander 22; Philadelphia, 1859 ***5704.8*** *p142*
Campbell, Alexander 58; North Carolina, 1850 ***1639.20*** *p27*
*Relative:*Flora 56
Campbell, Alexander 90; South Carolina, 1850 ***1639.20*** *p26*
*Relative:*Isabella 85
Campbell, Allan; Quebec, 1851 ***4537.30*** *p5*
*Wife:*Catherine MacIver
*Child:*Angus
*Child:*Donald
*Child:*John
Campbell, Allan 25; St. John, N.B., 1856 ***5704.8*** *p131*
Campbell, Allan 83; North Carolina, 1850 ***1639.20*** *p27*

Campbell, Andrew; Philadelphia, 1850 *53.26 p9*
Campbell, Andrew; Philadelphia, 1850 *5704.8 p59*
Campbell, Andrew; Philadelphia, 1851 *5704.8 p75*
Campbell, Andrew; Philadelphia, 1868 *5704.8 p230*
Campbell, Andrew 7; Quebec, 1852 *5704.8 p86*
Campbell, Andrew 7; Quebec, 1852 *5704.8 p90*
Campbell, Angus *SEE* Campbell, Allan
Campbell, Angus *SEE* Campbell, Donald
Campbell, Angus *SEE* Campbell, Kenneth
Campbell, Angus *SEE* Campbell, Norman
Campbell, Angus *SEE* Campbell, William
Campbell, Angus; North Carolina, 1788-1812 *1639.20 p27*
Campbell, Angus; Nova Scotia, 1830 *7085.4 p44*
  *Wife:*Ket
  *Child:*Anne
  *Child:*Ket
  *Child:*Duncan
Campbell, Angus; Quebec, 1863 *4537.30 p5*
  *Wife:*Catherine MacFarlane
  *Child:*Gormelia
Campbell, Angus; Quebec, 1873 *4537.30 p10*
  *Wife:*Kirsty Murray
  *Child:*William
  *Child:*Effie
  *Child:*Catherine
  *Child:*Donald
  *Child:*Margaret
  *Child:*Mary
  *Child:*John
Campbell, Ann *SEE* Campbell, Donald
Campbell, Ann *SEE* Campbell, Donald
Campbell, Ann *SEE* Campbell, John
Campbell, Ann *SEE* Campbell, Kenneth
Campbell, Ann *SEE* Campbell, William
Campbell, Ann; America, 1742 *4971 p67*
Campbell, Ann; New York, NY, 1864 *5704.8 p170*
Campbell, Ann; New York, NY, 1869 *5704.8 p234*
Campbell, Ann; Philadelphia, 1847 *53.26 p9*
  *Relative:*Rebecca
  *Relative:*Jane Ann 12
  *Relative:*David 3
Campbell, Ann; Philadelphia, 1847 *5704.8 p1*
Campbell, Ann; Philadelphia, 1851 *5704.8 p76*
Campbell, Ann; Philadelphia, 1868 *5704.8 p227*
Campbell, Ann; Quebec, 1845 *4537.30 p109*
Campbell, Ann; Quebec, 1847 *5704.8 p15*
Campbell, Ann; Quebec, 1849 *5704.8 p52*
Campbell, Ann; Quebec, 1873 *4537.30 p118*
Campbell, Ann; St. John, N.B., 1850 *5704.8 p65*
Campbell, Ann 1; Quebec, 1864 *5704.8 p162*
Campbell, Ann 25; Quebec, 1855 *5704.8 p126*
Campbell, Ann 26; Wilmington, NC, 1774 *1639.20 p238*
Campbell, Ann 66; Quebec, 1862 *5704.8 p152*
Campbell, Ann Jane; Wilmington, DE, 1831 *6508.7 p160*
Campbell, Ann MacLeod *SEE* Campbell, Donald
Campbell, Ann Murray *SEE* Campbell, Norman
Campbell, Anne *SEE* Campbell, Angus
Campbell, Anne *SEE* Campbell, Malcolm
Campbell, Anne *SEE* Campbell, Murdo
Campbell, Anne 9; Philadelphia, 1851 *5704.8 p71*
Campbell, Antho.; Philadelphia, 1811 *2859.11 p9*
Campbell, Anthony; Philadelphia, 1811 *53.26 p9*
Campbell, Archibald; Boston, 1775 *1219.7 p280*
Campbell, Archibald; New Brunswick, 1831 *9775.5 p205*
Campbell, Archibald; New York, NY, 1816 *2859.11 p26*
Campbell, Archibald; North Carolina, 1740 *1639.20 p27*
Campbell, Archibald; North Carolina, 1750-1853 *1639.20 p27*
Campbell, Archibald; North Carolina, 1770 *1639.20 p27*
Campbell, Archibald; Philadelphia, 1851 *5704.8 p70*
Campbell, Archibald 21; St. John, N.B., 1854 *5704.8 p114*
Campbell, Archibald 26; Quebec, 1864 *5704.8 p162*
Campbell, Archibald 38; Wilmington, NC, 1774 *1639.20 p27*
  *Wife:*Jean McNeill 32
  *Child:*Mary 7
  *Child:*Lachlan 2
  *Child:*Girzie 6
Campbell, Archibald 87; North Carolina, 1850 *1639.20 p28*
Campbell, Archibald B.; Illinois, 1892 *5012.37 p62*
Campbell, Arthur; St. John, N.B., 1847 *5704.8 p35*
Campbell, Bell *SEE* Campbell, Collin
Campbell, Bernard; Philadelphia, 1847 *53.26 p9*
  *Relative:*Catherine
  *Relative:*John
  *Relative:*Biddy
  *Relative:*Bernard 10

  *Relative:*Daniel 7
  *Relative:*Cicily 5
Campbell, Bernard; Philadelphia, 1847 *5704.8 p30*
Campbell, Bernard 10 *SEE* Campbell, Bernard
Campbell, Bernard 10; Philadelphia, 1847 *5704.8 p30*
Campbell, Bertha Mildred; Washington, 1859-1920 *2872.1 p6*
Campbell, Bessie; Philadelphia, 1865 *5704.8 p191*
Campbell, Betsy 47; Quebec, 1862 *5704.8 p151*
Campbell, Betty; Philadelphia, 1851 *5704.8 p71*
Campbell, Betty; Quebec, 1851 *5704.8 p74*
Campbell, Betty; St. John, N.B., 1847 *5704.8 p35*
Campbell, Betty 22; St. John, N.B., 1854 *5704.8 p114*
Campbell, Biddy *SEE* Campbell, Bernard
Campbell, Biddy; Philadelphia, 1847 *5704.8 p30*
Campbell, Biddy 24; Wilmington, DE, 1831 *6508.7 p161*
Campbell, Catharine; New York, NY, 1868 *5704.8 p229*
Campbell, Catharine; Philadelphia, 1867 *5704.8 p222*
Campbell, Catharine 21; Massachusetts, 1849 *5881.1 p14*
Campbell, Catherine *SEE* Campbell, Angus
Campbell, Catherine *SEE* Campbell, Bernard
Campbell, Catherine *SEE* Campbell, John
Campbell, Catherine *SEE* Campbell, Kenneth
Campbell, Catherine *SEE* Campbell, William
Campbell, Catherine; North Carolina, 1805 *1639.20 p28*
Campbell, Catherine; Philadelphia, 1847 *5704.8 p30*
Campbell, Catherine; Quebec, 1863 *4537.30 p20*
Campbell, Catherine 10; St. John, N.B., 1853 *5704.8 p110*
Campbell, Catherine 14; Quebec, 1862 *5704.8 p151*
Campbell, Catherine 28; Montreal, 1775 *7603 p37*
Campbell, Catherine 46; Wilmington, NC, 1774 *1639.20 p98*
Campbell, Catherine 47 *SEE* Campbell, Sarah
Campbell, Catherine Ann; Quebec, 1847 *5704.8 p29*
Campbell, Catherine MacFarlane *SEE* Campbell, Angus
Campbell, Catherine MacIver *SEE* Campbell, Allan
Campbell, Catherine MacLeod *SEE* Campbell, Malcolm
Campbell, Catherine Murray *SEE* Campbell, Murdo
Campbell, Cecilia; New York, NY, 1869 *5704.8 p232*
Campbell, Charles *SEE* Campbell, Collin
Campbell, Charles; Quebec, 1847 *5704.8 p27*
Campbell, Charles Overington; Chicago, 1899 *3455.1 p49*
  *Wife:*Susie
Campbell, Christian 48; South Carolina, 1850 *1639.20 p28*
  *Relative:*Duncan M. 20
Campbell, Christian McCaskill; North Carolina, 1750-1850 *1639.20 p124*
Campbell, Christy *SEE* Campbell, Alexander
Campbell, Cicily 5 *SEE* Campbell, Bernard
Campbell, Cicily 5; Philadelphia, 1847 *5704.8 p30*
Campbell, Colin; America, 1791 *1639.20 p28*
Campbell, Colin; Carolina, 1774 *1639.20 p28*
Campbell, Colin; Charleston, SC, 1691-1791 *1639.20 p28*
Campbell, Colin; Charleston, SC, 1810 *1639.20 p28*
Campbell, Colin; Georgia, 1783 *1639.20 p28*
Campbell, Colin; North America, 1782 *8894.2 p57*
Campbell, Colin; Nova Scotia, 1833 *9775.5 p208*
Campbell, Colin; South Carolina, 1783 *1639.20 p28*
Campbell, Colin; South Carolina, 1784 *1639.20 p28*
Campbell, Colin 25; Quebec, 1862 *5704.8 p152*
Campbell, Colin 36; Carolina, 1714 *1219.7 p180*
Campbell, Colin 42; Virginia, 1774 *1219.7 p193*
Campbell, Collin; Prince Edward Island, 1829-1830 *7085.4 p45*
  *Brother:*Charles
  *Brother:*Lach
  *Mother:*Bell
  With stepfather & brother
Campbell, Conrad; America, 1837 *8582.1 p6*
Campbell, D. 40; North Carolina, 1850 *1639.20 p31*
Campbell, D. F., Jr.; Washington, 1859-1920 *2872.1 p6*
Campbell, Daniel; America, 1788 *1639.20 p29*
Campbell, Daniel; America, 1790 *1639.20 p28*
Campbell, Daniel; America, 1802 *1639.20 p29*
Campbell, Daniel; North Carolina, 1800 *1639.20 p29*
Campbell, Daniel; St. John, N.B., 1847 *5704.8 p21*
Campbell, Daniel 7 *SEE* Campbell, Bernard
Campbell, Daniel 7; Philadelphia, 1847 *5704.8 p30*
Campbell, Daniel 21; Philadelphia, 1854 *5704.8 p116*
Campbell, Daniel 25; Wilmington, NC, 1774 *1639.20 p29*
Campbell, Daniel 76; South Carolina, 1850 *1639.20 p29*
Campbell, David; New York, NY, 1816 *2859.11 p26*
Campbell, David; Philadelphia, 1852 *5704.8 p86*
Campbell, David; Philadelphia, 1865 *5704.8 p191*
Campbell, David; St. John, N.B., 1853 *5704.8 p106*
Campbell, David 3 *SEE* Campbell, Ann
Campbell, David 9; Philadelphia, 1847 *5704.8 p1*
Campbell, David 30; Charleston, SC, 1774 *1639.20 p29*

Campbell, Donald *SEE* Campbell, Alex
Campbell, Donald *SEE* Campbell, Allan
Campbell, Donald *SEE* Campbell, Angus
Campbell, Donald *SEE* Campbell, Kenneth
Campbell, Donald; North Carolina, 1774 *1639.20 p29*
Campbell, Donald; Quebec, 1851 *4537.30 p5*
  *Wife:*Ann MacLeod
  *Child:*Ann
  *Child:*Mary
  *Child:*Angus
  *Child:*Donald
Campbell, Donald; Quebec, 1851 *4537.30 p6*
  *Wife:*Isabella MacLeod
  *Child:*Effie
  *Child:*Margaret
  *Child:*Marion
  *Child:*Ann
  *Child:*Malcolm
Campbell, Donald; Quebec, 1866 *4537.30 p6*
Campbell, Donald; Raleigh, NC, 1808-1885 *1639.20 p29*
Campbell, Donald 25; Quebec, 1862 *5704.8 p151*
Campbell, Donald 50; Wilmington, NC, 1774 *1639.20 p29*
  With wife
  With son 12
Campbell, Donald 60; Quebec, 1862 *5704.8 p152*
Campbell, Donald M.; Quebec, 1800-1860 *9775.5 p203*
Campbell, Dugald; North Carolina, 1771 *1639.20 p29*
  With father & family
Campbell, Duncan *SEE* Campbell, Angus
Campbell, Duncan *SEE* Campbell, William
Campbell, Duncan; America, 1802 *1639.20 p31*
Campbell, Duncan; New York, NY, 1816 *2859.11 p26*
Campbell, Duncan; North Carolina, 1739 *1639.20 p30*
Campbell, Duncan; North Carolina, 1804 *1639.20 p31*
Campbell, Duncan 50; St. John, N.B., 1866 *5704.8 p167*
Campbell, Duncan 55 *SEE* Campbell, Sarah
Campbell, Duncan 55; North Carolina, 1850 *1639.20 p31*
Campbell, Duncan 60; South Carolina, 1850 *1639.20 p30*
Campbell, Duncan M. 20 *SEE* Campbell, Christian
Campbell, Edward; Ohio, 1838 *9892.11 p7*
Campbell, Edward; South Carolina, 1800 *1639.20 p31*
  *Wife:*Mary McLellan
  With family
Campbell, Edward Greenestin; Iowa, 1866-1943 *123.54 p12*
Campbell, Effie *SEE* Campbell, Angus
Campbell, Effie *SEE* Campbell, Donald
Campbell, Effie *SEE* Campbell, Kenneth
Campbell, Effie; Quebec, 1855 *4537.30 p77*
Campbell, Effie 50; North Carolina, 1850 *1639.20 p31*
Campbell, Elisabeth; St. Johns, N.F., 1794 *8894.2 p56*
Campbell, Eliza; Philadelphia, 1866 *5704.8 p204*
Campbell, Eliza; Quebec, 1847 *5704.8 p27*
Campbell, Eliza 9 mos; Quebec, 1847 *5704.8 p27*
Campbell, Eliza 5; Philadelphia, 1865 *5704.8 p202*
Campbell, Eliza 19; St. John, N.B., 1856 *5704.8 p132*
Campbell, Eliza Jane; Philadelphia, 1851 *5704.8 p70*
Campbell, Elizabeth; Philadelphia, 1865 *5704.8 p202*
Campbell, Elizabeth; Quebec, 1847 *5704.8 p29*
Campbell, Elizabeth; St. John, N.B., 1847 *5704.8 p35*
Campbell, Elizabeth; St. John, N.B., 1852 *5704.8 p93*
Campbell, Elizabeth 9 mos; Philadelphia, 1851 *5704.8 p76*
Campbell, Ellen 8; Philadelphia, 1866 *5704.8 p215*
Campbell, Ellen 20; Philadelphia, 1854 *5704.8 p116*
Campbell, Ellen 21; Massachusetts, 1849 *5881.1 p16*
Campbell, Ellen 21; St. John, N.B., 1862 *5704.8 p150*
Campbell, Fanny *SEE* Campbell, John
Campbell, Fanny; Philadelphia, 1847 *5704.8 p13*
Campbell, Farquhar; North Carolina, 1740 *1639.20 p31*
Campbell, Flora 22; Quebec, 1862 *5704.8 p151*
Campbell, Flora 54; North Carolina, 1850 *1639.20 p31*
Campbell, Flora 56 *SEE* Campbell, Alexander
Campbell, Francis; New York, NY, 1816 *2859.11 p26*
Campbell, George; New York, NY, 1816 *2859.11 p26*
Campbell, George; New York, NY, 1839 *8208.4 p94*
Campbell, George; North Carolina, 1771 *1639.20 p32*
Campbell, George; Philadelphia, 1852 *5704.8 p88*
Campbell, George; St. John, N.B., 1853 *5704.8 p98*
Campbell, George; Washington, 1859-1920 *2872.1 p6*
Campbell, George 19; Pennsylvania, 1728 *3690.1 p36*
Campbell, George 19; Quebec, 1854 *5704.8 p121*
Campbell, Girzie 6 *SEE* Campbell, Archibald
Campbell, Gormelia *SEE* Campbell, Angus
Campbell, Gormelia *SEE* Campbell, Murdo
Campbell, Gormelia *SEE* Campbell, Norman
Campbell, Grace 60; Philadelphia, 1864 *5704.8 p161*
Campbell, Guillaume; Quebec, 1772 *7603 p41*
Campbell, Gustave 50; Massachusetts, 1860 *6410.32 p106*

Campbell, Hanah 11; St. John, N.B., 1854 *5704.8* p114
Campbell, Hannah; Raleigh, NC, 1810-1840 *1639.20* p32
Campbell, Hector 16; Wilmington, NC, 1774 *1639.20* p142
 Relative: Alexander 12
  With grandfather
Campbell, Henrietta; Charleston, SC, 1832 *1639.20* p32
Campbell, Henry; Quebec, 1825 *7603* p55
Campbell, Honour; America, 1735-1743 *4971* p51
Campbell, Hugh; America, 1804 *1639.20* p32
Campbell, Hugh; Cape Fear, NC, 1733 *1639.20* p32
Campbell, Hugh; Cape Fear, NC, 1733 *4814* p92
Campbell, Hugh; Quebec, 1847 *5704.8* p17
Campbell, Hugh; Quebec, 1852 *5704.8* p86
Campbell, Hugh; Quebec, 1852 *5704.8* p90
Campbell, Hugh 5; Quebec, 1847 *5704.8* p15
Campbell, Hugh 63 *SEE* Campbell, John
Campbell, Isabel 65; North Carolina, 1850 *1639.20* p32
Campbell, Isabella; St. John, N.B., 1848 *5704.8* p44
Campbell, Isabella 9; Quebec, 1854 *5704.8* p121
Campbell, Isabella 18; Philadelphia, 1864 *5704.8* p155
Campbell, Isabella 18; Quebec, 1854 *5704.8* p121
Campbell, Isabella 19; St. John, N.B., 1866 *5704.8* p166
Campbell, Isabella 85 *SEE* Campbell, Alexander
Campbell, Isabella MacLeod *SEE* Campbell, Donald
Campbell, James; America, 1742 *4971* p99
Campbell, James; Mississippi, 1822 *1639.20* p32
Campbell, James; North Carolina, 1739 *1639.20* p32
Campbell, James; Philadelphia, 1730 *1639.20* p32
Campbell, James; Philadelphia, 1847 *53.26* p10
Campbell, James; Philadelphia, 1847 *53.26* p10
 Relative: Nancy
Campbell, James; Philadelphia, 1847 *5704.8* p1
Campbell, James; Philadelphia, 1847 *5704.8* p21
Campbell, James; Philadelphia, 1865 *5704.8* p196
Campbell, James; Philadelphia, 1865 *5704.8* p200
Campbell, James; Quebec, 1825 *7603* p96
Campbell, James; Quebec, 1847 *5704.8* p15
Campbell, James; St. John, N.B., 1847 *5704.8* p19
Campbell, James; St. John, N.B., 1847 *5704.8* p24
Campbell, James; St. John, N.B., 1847 *5704.8* p25
Campbell, James; St. John, N.B., 1852 *5704.8* p83
Campbell, James; South Carolina, 1810 *1639.20* p32
Campbell, James 8; St. John, N.B., 1853 *5704.8* p110
Campbell, James 11 *SEE* Campbell, William
Campbell, James 11; Philadelphia, 1847 *5704.8* p1
Campbell, James 21; New York, NY, 1828 *6508.4* p143
Campbell, James 21; Philadelphia, 1860 *5704.8* p145
Campbell, James 21; Quebec, 1855 *5704.8* p126
Campbell, James 22; Philadelphia, 1860 *5704.8* p145
Campbell, James 24; St. John, N.B., 1862 *5704.8* p150
Campbell, James 28; Philadelphia, 1803 *53.26* p10
 Relative: Mary 20
Campbell, James 30; Quebec, 1855 *5704.8* p126
Campbell, Jane; New York, NY, 1811 *2859.11* p9
Campbell, Jane; North Carolina, 1850 *1639.20* p144
Campbell, Jane; Philadelphia, 1851 *5704.8* p70
Campbell, Jane; Philadelphia, 1851 *5704.8* p71
Campbell, Jane; Philadelphia, 1852 *5704.8* p85
Campbell, Jane; Quebec, 1849 *5704.8* p57
Campbell, Jane; Quebec, 1853 *5704.8* p104
Campbell, Jane 1 *SEE* Campbell, William
Campbell, Jane 1; Philadelphia, 1847 *5704.8* p1
Campbell, Jane 6; St. John, N.B., 1853 *5704.8* p110
Campbell, Jane 19; Quebec, 1857 *5704.8* p136
Campbell, Jane 30; St. John, N.B., 1853 *5704.8* p110
Campbell, Jane Ann 12 *SEE* Campbell, Ann
Campbell, Jane Ann 12; Philadelphia, 1847 *5704.8* p1
Campbell, Jane Anne 13; St. John, N.B., 1854 *5704.8* p114
Campbell, Janet 26; Quebec, 1864 *5704.8* p162
Campbell, Jean 24; Wilmington, NC, 1774 *1639.20* p214
Campbell, Jean McNeill 32 *SEE* Campbell, Archibald
Campbell, Jemimah; New York, NY, 1811 *2859.11* p9
Campbell, Jennet 91; North Carolina, 1850 *1639.20* p33
Campbell, John *SEE* Campbell, Alexander
Campbell, John *SEE* Campbell, Allan
Campbell, John *SEE* Campbell, Angus
Campbell, John *SEE* Campbell, Bernard
Campbell, John *SEE* Campbell, John
Campbell, John *SEE* Campbell, Kenneth
Campbell, John; America, 1735-1743 *4971* p8
Campbell, John; America, 1738-1743 *4971* p91
Campbell, John; America, 1764 *1639.20* p33
Campbell, John; America, 1788 *1639.20* p33
Campbell, John; America, 1792 *1639.20* p34
 With parents wife & 5 children
Campbell, John; Brunswick, NC, 1767 *1639.20* p33
 With wife & son
Campbell, John; Charleston, SC, 1739 *1639.20* p33
Campbell, John; Charleston, SC, 1796 *1639.20* p34
Campbell, John; Charleston, SC, 1825 *1639.20* p34
Campbell, John; New York, NY, 1811 *2859.11* p9

Campbell, John; New York, NY, 1815 *2859.11* p26
Campbell, John; New York, NY, 1815 *2859.11* p26
Campbell, John; New York, NY, 1838 *8208.4* p68
Campbell, John; New York, NY, 1840 *8208.4* p106
Campbell, John; New York, NY, 1869 *5704.8* p234
Campbell, John; North Carolina, 1815 *1639.20* p33
Campbell, John; North Carolina, 1818 *1639.20* p34
Campbell, John; Philadelphia, 1847 *53.26* p10
 Relative: Fanny
Campbell, John; Philadelphia, 1847 *5704.8* p13
Campbell, John; Philadelphia, 1847 *5704.8* p30
Campbell, John; Philadelphia, 1851 *5704.8* p70
Campbell, John; Philadelphia, 1864 *5704.8* p179
Campbell, John; Quebec, 1849 *5704.8* p52
Campbell, John; Quebec, 1863 *4537.30* p7
 Wife: Margaret Graham
 Child: Norman
 Child: Mary
Campbell, John; Quebec, 1863 *4537.30* p7
 Wife: Mary Morrison
 Child: William
 Child: John
Campbell, John; Quebec, 1863 *4537.30* p7
 Wife: Mary Murray
 Child: Margaret
 Child: Ann
 Child: Mary
 Child: Catherine
Campbell, John; St. John, N.B., 1847 *5704.8* p35
Campbell, John; St. John, N.B., 1849 *5704.8* p56
Campbell, John; St. John, N.B., 1851 *5704.8* p77
Campbell, John; Santa Clara Co., CA, 1859 *2769.3* p3
Campbell, John; South Carolina, 1716 *1639.20* p33
Campbell, John; South Carolina, 1821 *1639.20* p34
Campbell, John 3; Quebec, 1847 *5704.8* p15
Campbell, John 4; Philadelphia, 1865 *5704.8* p191
Campbell, John 7; Philadelphia, 1861 *5704.8* p148
Campbell, John 9; Quebec, 1852 *5704.8* p86
Campbell, John 9; Quebec, 1852 *5704.8* p90
Campbell, John 9; St. John, N.B., 1854 *5704.8* p114
Campbell, John 10; Quebec, 1847 *5704.8* p29
Campbell, John 11; Quebec, 1862 *5704.8* p151
Campbell, John 18 *SEE* Campbell, Richard
Campbell, John 18; Windward Islands, 1722 *3690.1* p36
Campbell, John 21; Philadelphia, 1864 *5704.8* p155
Campbell, John 56; Philadelphia, 1864 *5704.8* p155
Campbell, John 65; North Carolina, 1850 *1639.20* p33
Campbell, John 65; North Carolina, 1850 *1639.20* p34
 Relative: Hugh 63
 Relative: Mary 52
Campbell, John 66; Quebec, 1854 *5704.8* p121
Campbell, John 75; North Carolina, 1850 *1639.20* p33
 Relative: Nancy 55
Campbell, John Joseph; Arkansas, 1918 *95.2* p25
Campbell, John W. *SEE* Campbell, William
Campbell, Joseph; Philadelphia, 1867 *5704.8* p221
Campbell, Joseph 14; Philadelphia, 1864 *5704.8* p155
Campbell, Joseph 16; Philadelphia, 1861 *5704.8* p148
Campbell, Katherine 32 *SEE* Campbell, William
Campbell, Katy 60; North Carolina, 1850 *1639.20* p34
Campbell, Kenneth; Quebec, 1863 *4537.30* p8
 Wife: Mary Smith
 Child: Effie
 Child: Norman
 Child: Ann
 Child: Mary
 Child: Murdo
 Child: John
 Child: Angus
 Child: Catherine
 With child
Campbell, Ket *SEE* Campbell, Angus
Campbell, Ket *SEE* Campbell, Angus
Campbell, Kirsty *SEE* Campbell, William
Campbell, Kirsty; Quebec, 1842 *4537.30* p100
Campbell, Kirsty; Quebec, 1855 *4537.30* p58
Campbell, Kirsty; Quebec, 1864 *4537.30* p67
Campbell, Kirsty Ann *SEE* Campbell, Alex
Campbell, Kirsty Murray *SEE* Campbell, Angus
Campbell, Lach *SEE* Campbell, Collin
Campbell, Lachlan; Quebec, 1790 *9775.5* p198A
 With family of 4
Campbell, Lachlan 2 *SEE* Campbell, Archibald
Campbell, Laurence; Charleston, SC, 1804 *1639.20* p34
Campbell, Lavinia 13; Quebec, 1854 *5704.8* p121
Campbell, Louis; Quebec, 1763 *7603* p42
Campbell, Louisa 20; Philadelphia, 1857 *5704.8* p132
Campbell, Lucinda 11; Quebec, 1854 *5704.8* p121
Campbell, Maggie; America, 1865 *5704.8* p203
Campbell, Maggie; New York, NY, 1869 *5704.8* p234
Campbell, Malcolm *SEE* Campbell, Donald
Campbell, Malcolm *SEE* Campbell, William

Campbell, Malcolm; Nova Scotia, 1830 *7085.4* p44
 Wife: Anne
Campbell, Malcolm; Quebec, 1860-1869 *4537.30* p8
 Wife: Catherine MacLeod
Campbell, Malcolm 7; Quebec, 1862 *5704.8* p151
Campbell, Malcolm 11; Quebec, 1862 *5704.8* p152
Campbell, Malcolm 53; North Carolina, 1850 *1639.20* p34
Campbell, Malcolm 70; South Carolina, 1850 *1639.20* p34
Campbell, Margaret *SEE* Campbell, Angus
Campbell, Margaret *SEE* Campbell, Donald
Campbell, Margaret *SEE* Campbell, John
Campbell, Margaret *SEE* Campbell, Nancy
Campbell, Margaret; Philadelphia, 1849 *5704.8* p58
Campbell, Margaret; Philadelphia, 1851 *5704.8* p70
Campbell, Margaret; Philadelphia, 1852 *5704.8* p88
Campbell, Margaret; Quebec, 1822 *7603* p53
Campbell, Margaret 20; Philadelphia, 1860 *5704.8* p145
Campbell, Margaret 30; Wilmington, DE, 1831 *6508.7* p160
Campbell, Margaret 60; North Carolina, 1850 *1639.20* p35
Campbell, Margaret 61; South Carolina, 1850 *1639.20* p35
Campbell, Margaret 84; North Carolina, 1850 *1639.20* p34
Campbell, Margaret A. 10; Philadelphia, 1866 *5704.8* p215
Campbell, Margaret E. 2; Philadelphia, 1865 *5704.8* p191
Campbell, Margaret Graham *SEE* Campbell, John
Campbell, Marguerite; Quebec, 1790 *7603* p37
Campbell, Marion *SEE* Campbell, Donald
Campbell, Marion; Quebec, 1855 *4537.30* p41
Campbell, Martha; Philadelphia, 1851 *5704.8* p70
Campbell, Martha; Philadelphia, 1866 *5704.8* p215
Campbell, Martha; Philadelphia, 1868 *5704.8* p230
Campbell, Martha 20; Philadelphia, 1854 *5704.8* p118
Campbell, Mary *SEE* Campbell, Angus
Campbell, Mary *SEE* Campbell, Donald
Campbell, Mary *SEE* Campbell, John
Campbell, Mary *SEE* Campbell, Kenneth
Campbell, Mary *SEE* Campbell, Nancy
Campbell, Mary; Montreal, 1821 *7603* p85
Campbell, Mary; New York, NY, 1811 *2859.11* p9
Campbell, Mary; New York, NY, 1869 *5704.8* p234
Campbell, Mary; New York, NY, 1871 *5704.8* p240
Campbell, Mary; North Carolina, 1725-1825 *1639.20* p127
Campbell, Mary; Philadelphia, 1849 *5704.8* p58
Campbell, Mary; Philadelphia, 1851 *5704.8* p70
Campbell, Mary; Philadelphia, 1852 *5704.8* p85
Campbell, Mary; Philadelphia, 1852 *5704.8* p88
Campbell, Mary; Philadelphia, 1868 *5704.8* p230
Campbell, Mary; Quebec, 1847 *5704.8* p17
Campbell, Mary; Quebec, 1849 *5704.8* p57
Campbell, Mary; Quebec, 1852 *5704.8* p86
Campbell, Mary; Quebec, 1852 *5704.8* p90
Campbell, Mary; Quebec, 1870-1879 *4537.30* p72
Campbell, Mary; Quebec, 1872 *4537.30* p26
Campbell, Mary; St. John, N.B., 1850 *5704.8* p65
Campbell, Mary 7 *SEE* Campbell, Archibald
Campbell, Mary 13; Quebec, 1847 *5704.8* p29
Campbell, Mary 17; Philadelphia, 1857 *5704.8* p132
Campbell, Mary 18; Quebec, 1855 *5704.8* p126
Campbell, Mary 20 *SEE* Campbell, James
Campbell, Mary 20; Philadelphia, 1853 *5704.8* p111
Campbell, Mary 24; Massachusetts, 1849 *5881.1* p21
Campbell, Mary 24; St. John, N.B., 1854 *5704.8* p114
Campbell, Mary 25; Quebec, 1857 *5704.8* p136
Campbell, Mary 45; North Carolina, 1850 *1639.20* p35
Campbell, Mary 48; St. John, N.B., 1854 *5704.8* p114
Campbell, Mary 50; Massachusetts, 1860 *6410.32* p106
Campbell, Mary 52 *SEE* Campbell, John
Campbell, Mary 86; North Carolina, 1850 *1639.20* p35
Campbell, Mary Ann 12; Philadelphia, 1854 *5704.8* p118
Campbell, Mary Ann 22; Quebec, 1857 *5704.8* p136
Campbell, Mary J.; New York, NY, 1867 *5704.8* p218
Campbell, Mary MacDonald *SEE* Campbell, Alex
Campbell, Mary MacLeod *SEE* Campbell, William
Campbell, Mary Martin *SEE* Campbell, Murdo
Campbell, Mary McLellan *SEE* Campbell, Edward
Campbell, Mary Morrison *SEE* Campbell, John
Campbell, Mary Murray *SEE* Campbell, John
Campbell, Mary Smith *SEE* Campbell, Kenneth
Campbell, Matilda; Philadelphia, 1851 *5704.8* p78
Campbell, Matilda; Philadelphia, 1865 *5704.8* p191
Campbell, Matilda 7 *SEE* Campbell, William
Campbell, Matilda 7; Philadelphia, 1847 *5704.8* p1
Campbell, Matthew; New York, NY, 1816 *2859.11* p26

Campbell, Matty 22; Wilmington, DE, 1831 6508.7 p161
Campbell, Michael; Illinois, 1858 2896.5 p7
Campbell, Michael; Philadelphia, 1850 5704.8 p64
Campbell, Michel; New Brunswick, 1825 7603 p69
Campbell, Moses; Ohio, 1851 9892.11 p8
Campbell, Murdo *SEE* Campbell, Kenneth
Campbell, Murdo *SEE* Campbell, Norman
Campbell, Murdo; Nova Scotia, 1830 7085.4 p44
*Wife:*Anne
Campbell, Murdo; Quebec, 1841 4537.30 p9
*Wife:*Catherine Murray
*Child:*Alex
Campbell, Murdo; Quebec, 1855 4537.30 p9
*Wife:*Mary Martin
*Child:*Gormelia
Campbell, Nancy *SEE* Campbell, James
Campbell, Nancy; North Carolina, 1794-1873 1639.20 p35
Campbell, Nancy; Philadelphia, 1847 5704.8 p1
Campbell, Nancy; Philadelphia, 1848 53.26 p10
Campbell, Nancy; Philadelphia, 1848 5704.8 p45
Campbell, Nancy; Philadelphia, 1849 53.26 p10
*Relative:*Margaret
*Relative:*Mary
Campbell, Nancy; Philadelphia, 1849 5704.8 p58
Campbell, Nancy; Philadelphia, 1865 5704.8 p202
Campbell, Nancy 4; Philadelphia, 1851 5704.8 p75
Campbell, Nancy 55 *SEE* Campbell, John
Campbell, Nancy 59; North Carolina, 1850 1639.20 p77
Campbell, Nancy 60; North Carolina, 1850 1639.20 p35
Campbell, Nancy 68; North Carolina, 1850 1639.20 p35
Campbell, Nancy 72; North Carolina, 1850 1639.20 p215
Campbell, Nancy 75; South Carolina, 1850 1639.20 p35
Campbell, Neil; America, 1789 1639.20 p35
Campbell, Neil 19; Quebec, 1862 5704.8 p151
Campbell, Neil 57; Quebec, 1862 5704.8 p151
Campbell, Neill 85; North Carolina, 1850 1639.20 p35
*Relative:*Sarah 65
Campbell, Norman *SEE* Campbell, John
Campbell, Norman *SEE* Campbell, Kenneth
Campbell, Norman; Quebec, 1855 4537.30 p10
*Wife:*Ann Murray
*Child:*Murdo
*Child:*Gormelia
*Child:*Angus
Campbell, Owen; New York, NY, 1836 8208.4 p21
Campbell, Owen 26; Massachusetts, 1847 5881.1 p23
Campbell, Pat.; America, 1742 4971 p65
Campbell, Pat. 6; Massachusetts, 1849 5881.1 p24
Campbell, Patrick; New York, NY, 1811 2859.11 p9
With family
Campbell, Patrick; New York, NY, 1840 8208.4 p111
Campbell, Patrick; North Carolina, 1775 1639.20 p36
Campbell, Patrick 16; Quebec, 1855 5704.8 p126
Campbell, Patrick 60; Philadelphia, 1864 5704.8 p161
Campbell, Peter; Charleston, SC, 1809 1639.20 p36
Campbell, Peter; New York, NY, 1864 5704.8 p173
Campbell, Peter; South Carolina, 1800 1639.20 p36
Campbell, Peter 59; North Carolina, 1850 1639.20 p36
Campbell, Prisilla; Philadelphia, 1867 5704.8 p216
Campbell, Rachel; Philadelphia, 1851 5704.8 p75
Campbell, Rachel; Philadelphia, 1851 5704.8 p78
Campbell, Rachel 56; Philadelphia, 1864 5704.8 p155
Campbell, Ralph; Philadelphia, 1864 5704.8 p183
Campbell, Rebecca *SEE* Campbell, Ann
Campbell, Rebecca; New York, NY, 1867 5704.8 p224
Campbell, Rebecca; Philadelphia, 1847 5704.8 p1
Campbell, Rebecca; Philadelphia, 1851 5704.8 p70
Campbell, Rebecca 3; Quebec, 1852 5704.8 p86
Campbell, Rebecca 3; Quebec, 1852 5704.8 p90
Campbell, Richard 44; New York, 1801 9892.11 p8
*Son:*John 18
*Son:*Robert 14
Campbell, Robert; America, 1864 5704.8 p187
Campbell, Robert; Iowa, 1866-1943 123.54 p12
Campbell, Robert; Northwest Terr., 1800-1899 9775.5 p219
Campbell, Robert; Quebec, 1847 5704.8 p29
Campbell, Robert; St. John, N.B., 1852 5704.8 p93
Campbell, Robert; St. John, N.B., 1853 5704.8 p107
Campbell, Robert; Virginia, 1858 4626.16 p17
Campbell, Robert 2 *SEE* Campbell, William
Campbell, Robert 2; Philadelphia, 1851 5704.8 p70
Campbell, Robert 14 *SEE* Campbell, Richard
Campbell, Robert 26; Wilmington, DE, 1831 6508.3 p101
Campbell, Rosanna; St. John, N.B., 1847 5704.8 p35
Campbell, Rosanna 6 mos; St. John, N.B., 1847 5704.8 p35
Campbell, Rose; St. John, N.B., 1852 5704.8 p83
Campbell, Sallie; New York, NY, 1868 5704.8 p228
Campbell, Samuel; Philadelphia, 1867 5704.8 p219
Campbell, Samuel; Quebec, 1847 5704.8 p29
Campbell, Samuel 4; Quebec, 1847 5704.8 p29
Campbell, Samuel 5; Philadelphia, 1851 5704.8 p70
Campbell, Samuel 11; Philadelphia, 1853 5704.8 p100
Campbell, Sarah; New York, NY, 1864 5704.8 p186
Campbell, Sarah; Philadelphia, 1847 5704.8 p31
Campbell, Sarah; Quebec, 1847 5704.8 p15
Campbell, Sarah; St. John, N.B., 1847 5704.8 p25
Campbell, Sarah; St. John, N.B., 1848 5704.8 p44
Campbell, Sarah 18; Philadelphia, 1856 5704.8 p128
Campbell, Sarah 18; Philadelphia, 1861 5704.8 p148
Campbell, Sarah 65 *SEE* Campbell, Neill
Campbell, Sarah 65; North Carolina, 1850 1639.20 p36
Campbell, Sarah 80; North Carolina, 1850 1639.20 p36
*Relative:*Catherine 47
*Relative:*Duncan 55
Campbell, Stuart; Philadelphia, 1852 5704.8 p85
Campbell, Susie *SEE* Campbell, Charles Overington
Campbell, T. C.; Washington, 1859-1920 2872.1 p6
Campbell, Thomas; Iowa, 1866-1943 123.54 p12
Campbell, Thomas; Philadelphia, 1816 2859.11 p26
Campbell, Thomas; Philadelphia, 1849 53.26 p10
Campbell, Thomas; Philadelphia, 1849 5704.8 p53
Campbell, Thomas; Philadelphia, 1851 5704.8 p70
Campbell, Thomas; Philadelphia, 1866 5704.8 p206
Campbell, Thomas; St. John, N.B., 1847 5704.8 p35
Campbell, Thomas; St. John, N.B., 1848 5704.8 p43
Campbell, Thomas 7; Quebec, 1847 5704.8 p29
Campbell, Thomas 30; St. Vincent, 1775 1219.7 p251
Campbell, Thomas 50; Massachusetts, 1849 5881.1 p25
Campbell, Thomas Chambers; Washington, 1859-1920 2872.1 p6
Campbell, Valentine; Philadelphia, 1864 5704.8 p185
Campbell, Mrs. W.; New York, NY, 1811 2859.11 p9
Campbell, William *SEE* Campbell, Angus
Campbell, William *SEE* Campbell, John
Campbell, William; Arizona, 1903 9228.40 p5
Campbell, William; Carolina, 1737 1639.20 p36
Campbell, William; Carolina, 1763-1863 1639.20 p36
Campbell, William; Charleston, SC, 1763 1639.20 p36
Campbell, William; New York, NY, 1865 5704.8 p194
Campbell, William; New York, NY, 1866 5704.8 p212
Campbell, William; New York, NY, 1869 5704.8 p234
Campbell, William; Nova Scotia, 1765 9775.5 p208
Campbell, William; Philadelphia, 1815 2859.11 p26
Campbell, William; Philadelphia, 1847 53.26 p10
*Wife:*Ann
*Relative:*James 11
*Relative:*Matilda 7
*Relative:*Jane 1
Campbell, William; Philadelphia, 1847 5704.8 p1
Campbell, William; Philadelphia, 1852 5704.8 p85
Campbell, William; Philadelphia, 1865 5704.8 p190
Campbell, William; Philadelphia, 1865 5704.8 p193
Campbell, William; Quebec, 1847 5704.8 p16
Campbell, William; Quebec, 1849 5704.8 p52
Campbell, William; Quebec, 1855 4537.30 p10
*Wife:*Mary MacLeod
*Child:*Catherine
*Child:*Kirsty
*Child:*Malcolm
*Child:*Angus
*Child:*John W.
Campbell, William; St. John, N.B., 1848 5704.8 p43
Campbell, William; St. John, N.B., 1853 5704.8 p98
Campbell, William; St. John, N.B., 1853 5704.8 p99
Campbell, William 1; St. John, N.B., 1866 5704.8 p166
Campbell, William 4; Quebec, 1849 5704.8 p52
Campbell, William 4; St. John, N.B., 1853 5704.8 p110
Campbell, William 6; Philadelphia, 1853 5704.8 p108
Campbell, William 11; Quebec, 1852 5704.8 p86
Campbell, William 11; Quebec, 1852 5704.8 p90
Campbell, William 17; Philadelphia, 1854 5704.8 p121
Campbell, William 20; Philadelphia, 1858 5704.8 p139
Campbell, William 27; St. John, N.B., 1866 5704.8 p166
Campbell, William 28; Wilmington, NC, 1775 1639.20 p36
*Wife:*Katherine 32
*Child:*Robert 2
*Child:*Duncan
Campbell, William J. 9; Philadelphia, 1865 5704.8 p202
Campbell, Wm.; New York, NY, 1811 2859.11 p9
With family
Campbell of Kilduskland, Duncan; Cape Fear, NC, 1739 1639.20 p30
Campbell of Lossett, Alexander; Kingston, Jamaica, 1679-1779 1639.20 p26
Campbell of Lossett, Alexander; North Carolina, 1679-1779 1639.20 p26
Campbelly, Ann 52 *SEE* Campbelly, H.
Campbelly, H. 51; South Carolina, 1850 1639.20 p37
*Relative:*Ann 52
Campble, Thomas 26; Jamaica, 1773 1219.7 p173
Campian, Ann 21; Massachusetts, 1850 5881.1 p13
Campion, Daniel 50; Kansas, 1887 5240.1 p71
Campion, German 29; Virginia, 1773 1219.7 p171
Campion, Humphrey; Virginia, 1637 6219 p81
Campion, Mary *SEE* Campion, Percivall
Campion, Percivall; Virginia, 1637 6219 p86
*Wife:*Mary
Campion, Sarafina 25; New Orleans, 1862 543.30 p459
Campioni, Sarafina 25; New Orleans, 1862 543.30 p459
Campley, Archibald; North Carolina, 1739 1639.20 p37
Campo, Fibarcio 29; America, 1829 778.5 p94
Campos, Mendez 22; New Orleans, 1838 778.5 p94
Camron, John 20; Jamaica, 1734 3690.1 p36
Camsie, Edward; New York, NY, 1867 5704.8 p221
Camus, H.; New Orleans, 1839 778.5 p94
Camut, Louis 21; America, 1839 778.5 p94
Camworth, George 15; Quebec, 1856 5704.8 p130
Cana, Felecie 24; Port uncertain, 1839 778.5 p94
Canakes, Stavros; Arkansas, 1918 95.2 p25
Canalle, Ferdinand 34; New Orleans, 1862 543.30 p450
Canan, Francis; New York, NY, 1839 8208.4 p94
Canan, James 20; Maryland, 1774 1219.7 p181
Cananna, Juan 20; America, 1838 778.5 p94
Canbeurnery, Antoine 23; America, 1829 778.5 p94
Canda, Juana Canda 65; New Orleans, 1839 778.5 p94
Candea, Ann Jane 9 *SEE* Candea, John
Candea, Ann Jane 9; Philadelphia, 1847 5704.8 p31
Candea, Catherine *SEE* Candea, John
Candea, Catherine; Philadelphia, 1847 5704.8 p31
Candea, Elizabeth 1 *SEE* Candea, John
Candea, Elizabeth 1; Philadelphia, 1847 5704.8 p31
Candea, James 13 *SEE* Candea, John
Candea, James 13; Philadelphia, 1847 5704.8 p31
Candea, John; Philadelphia, 1847 53.26 p10
*Relative:*Catherine
*Relative:*James 13
*Relative:*Margaret 11
*Relative:*Ann Jane 9
*Relative:*John 7
*Relative:*Matilda 4
*Relative:*Elizabeth 1
Candea, John; Philadelphia, 1847 5704.8 p31
Candea, John 7 *SEE* Candea, John
Candea, John 7; Philadelphia, 1847 5704.8 p31
Candea, Margaret 11 *SEE* Candea, John
Candea, Margaret 11; Philadelphia, 1847 5704.8 p31
Candea, Matilda 4 *SEE* Candea, John
Candea, Matilda 4; Philadelphia, 1847 5704.8 p31
Canders, Mary Ann; St. John, N.B., 1847 5704.8 p18
Canders, May 24; Quebec, 1855 5704.8 p126
Canders, Thomas; St. John, N.B., 1847 5704.8 p18
Candevielle, Mr. 31; America, 1838 778.5 p94
Candin, Ann Maria 12; Massachusetts, 1849 5881.1 p13
Candle, Anne; America, 1864 5704.8 p180
Candless, James M.; Philadelphia, 1868 5704.8 p230
Candless, Mary; Philadelphia, 1868 5704.8 p230
Candy, Jacob 19; Jamaica, 1731 3690.1 p36
Cane, Charles; New York, NY, 1811 2859.11 p9
With family
Cane, John; Virginia, 1638 6219 p121
Cane, Margarett; Virginia, 1643 6219 p202
Cane, Maximilian 19; West Indies, 1722 3690.1 p36
Cane, Patrick; Virginia, 1642 6219 p186
Cane, Robert; Virginia, 1635 6219 p73
Cane, William; America, 1741 4971 p94
Canes, Mandolin; Virginia, 1635 6219 p72
Canfield, Patrick 14; Massachusetts, 1850 5881.1 p24
Canfreau, Francois 27; New Orleans, 1839 778.5 p94
Canglino, Antonio 28; Arkansas, 1918 95.2 p25
Canier, R. 36; New Orleans, 1826 778.5 p94
Canigan, Michael; New York, NY, 1816 2859.11 p26
Canikis, Harablus; Arkansas, 1918 95.2 p25
Canlon, John; America, 1741 4971 p23
Cann, Barny; Boston, 1776 1219.7 p277
Cann, Catherine 22; Philadelphia, 1853 5704.8 p112
Cann, John 19; Philadelphia, 1853 5704.8 p112
Cann, Tho.; Virginia, 1643 6219 p204
Cannaday, Clement; Virginia, 1642 6219 p194
Cannaday, John; Virginia, 1642 6219 p198
Cannelan, John; New York, NY, 1816 2859.11 p26
Canner, Harry 23; Canada, 1835 4535.10 p196
Cannery, Catherine 11; Quebec, 1866 5704.8 p167
Cannery, Catherine 40; Quebec, 1866 5704.8 p167
Cannery, Patrick 6; Quebec, 1866 5704.8 p167
Canney, Charles 28; Philadelphia, 1803 53.26 p10
Canney, Martha; New York, NY, 1868 5704.8 p228
Canney, Nancy; New York, NY, 1864 5704.8 p174
Cannig, Ann 17; Philadelphia, 1853 5704.8 p111
Canning, Andrew 7; St. John, N.B., 1854 5704.8 p115
Canning, Ann; St. John, N.B., 1848 5704.8 p44
Canning, Annyan 11 *SEE* Canning, John
Canning, Biddy; St. John, N.B., 1848 5704.8 p39
Canning, Catharine 15; Massachusetts, 1849 5881.1 p14

68 FOR A COMPLETE EXPLANATION OF ENTRY, SEE "HOW TO READ A CITATION" SECTION

Canning, Catherine 3; St. John, N.B., 1850 5704.8 p67
Canning, Catherine 10; Philadelphia, 1852 5704.8 p88
Canning, Charlotte; Philadelphia, 1852 5704.8 p85
Canning, Cornelius; Philadelphia, 1849 5704.8 p50
Canning, Daniel; Philadelphia, 1850 53.26 p10
Canning, Daniel; Philadelphia, 1850 5704.8 p60
Canning, Daniel; St. John, N.B., 1848 5704.8 p44
Canning, Daniel 2; St. John, N.B., 1854 5704.8 p115
Canning, David 24; Philadelphia, 1833-1834 53.26 p10
Canning, Dennis; St. John, N.B., 1850 5704.8 p67
Canning, Eliza 9 mos; St. John, N.B., 1850 5704.8 p67
Canning, Eliza 16; St. John, N.B., 1854 5704.8 p115
Canning, Francis; New York, NY, 1834 8208.4 p32
Canning, Hannah 12; Philadelphia, 1852 5704.8 p88
Canning, James; Quebec, 1851 5704.8 p74
Canning, James; St. John, N.B., 1848 5704.8 p44
Canning, James 4; St. John, N.B., 1854 5704.8 p115
Canning, James 15; St. John, N.B., 1864 5704.8 p157
Canning, Jane; St. John, N.B., 1850 5704.8 p61
Canning, John; St. John, N.B., 1851 5704.8 p79
Canning, John; St. John, N.B., 1853 5704.8 p106
Canning, John 2; Massachusetts, 1850 5881.1 p19
Canning, John 5; St. John, N.B., 1850 5704.8 p67
Canning, John 18; Philadelphia, 1833-1834 53.26 p10
*Relative:*Marcus 18
*Relative:*Annyan 11
Canning, John 20; Philadelphia, 1865 5704.8 p164
Canning, Marcus 18 *SEE* Canning, John
Canning, Margaret; St. John, N.B., 1848 5704.8 p39
Canning, Maria 13; St. John, N.B., 1854 5704.8 p115
Canning, Martha; St. John, N.B., 1848 5704.8 p44
Canning, Mary; Quebec, 1851 5704.8 p74
Canning, Mary; St. John, N.B., 1848 5704.8 p39
Canning, Mary; St. John, N.B., 1850 5704.8 p67
Canning, Mary 29; St. John, N.B., 1854 5704.8 p115
Canning, Mary Ann 16; St. John, N.B., 1864 5704.8 p157
Canning, Mary Ann 20; Philadelphia, 1854 5704.8 p116
Canning, Nancy; St. John, N.B., 1848 5704.8 p39
Canning, Nancy 9; St. John, N.B., 1854 5704.8 p115
Canning, Neal 17; Philadelphia, 1853 5704.8 p111
Canning, Patrick; Philadelphia, 1867 5704.8 p224
Canning, Patrick 19; Philadelphia, 1855 5704.8 p123
Canning, Peggy Jane 13; St. John, N.B., 1848 5704.8 p44
Canning, Rebecca; New York, NY, 1866 5704.8 p214
Canning, Robert; New York, NY, 1867 5704.8 p220
Canning, Robert; Philadelphia, 1851 5704.8 p75
Canning, Sally; St. John, N.B., 1850 5704.8 p61
Canning, Samuel; St. John, N.B., 1850 5704.8 p62
Canning, Samuel; St. John, N.B., 1851 5704.8 p79
Canning, Susan; St. John, N.B., 1848 5704.8 p44
Canning, Thomas; Quebec, 1851 5704.8 p74
Canning, William 9; St. John, N.B., 1848 5704.8 p44
Canning, William 11; St. John, N.B., 1854 5704.8 p115
Cannivan, Letitia *SEE* Cannivan, Maria
Cannivan, Letitia; Philadelphia, 1847 5704.8 p24
Cannivan, Maria; Philadelphia, 1847 53.26 p10
*Relative:*Letitia
Cannivan, Maria; Philadelphia, 1847 5704.8 p24
Cannon, . . .; New York, NY, 1811 2859.11 p9
With family
Cannon, Mrs. 36; Massachusetts, 1848 5881.1 p20
Cannon, Andrew 8; Massachusetts, 1848 5881.1 p12
Cannon, Ann *SEE* Cannon, Edward
Cannon, Ann; Philadelphia, 1851 5704.8 p79
Cannon, Bernard; Philadelphia, 1864 5704.8 p182
Cannon, Biddy 5; Quebec, 1851 5704.8 p75
Cannon, Bridget; New York, NY, 1816 2859.11 p26
Cannon, Bridget; Philadelphia, 1867 5704.8 p218
Cannon, Catherine; Philadelphia, 1852 5704.8 p85
Cannon, Catherine 50; Philadelphia, 1859 5704.8 p143
Cannon, Clemetine 3 *SEE* Cannon, Richard
Cannon, Cornelius 20; Philadelphia, 1853 5704.8 p112
Cannon, Daniel 12; Philadelphia, 1851 5704.8 p77
Cannon, David; Philadelphia, 1865 5704.8 p204
Cannon, Dennis; Arizona, 1898 9228.30 p11
Cannon, Dorah; Philadelphia, 1867 5704.8 p218
Cannon, Edward; Virginia, 1646 6219 p244
*Wife:*Ann
Cannon, Edward 28; Maryland, 1733 3690.1 p37
Cannon, Elijah; New York, NY, 1838 8208.4 p70
Cannon, Elizabeth; Quebec, 1821 7603 p69
Cannon, Ellen 16; Philadelphia, 1859 5704.8 p143
Cannon, Ellen 20; Philadelphia, 1864 5704.8 p155
Cannon, Hugh; New York, NY, 1815 2859.11 p26
Cannon, James; New York, NY, 1837 8208.4 p32
Cannon, James 7 mos; Died enroute, 1733 4719.17 p310
Cannon, James 14; St. John, N.B., 1858 5704.8 p137
Cannon, Jean; Quebec, 1808 7603 p75
Cannon, John; New York, NY, 1811 2859.11 p9
Cannon, John; Philadelphia, 1867 5704.8 p221
Cannon, John 3; Philadelphia, 1852 5704.8 p85
Cannon, John 9; Philadelphia, 1851 5704.8 p77
Cannon, John 12; St. John, N.B., 1848 5704.8 p43
Cannon, John 18; Philadelphia, 1774 1219.7 p182
Cannon, Louis; Arizona, 1882 2764.35 p14
Cannon, Margaret; Philadelphia, 1847 53.26 p10
Cannon, Margaret; Philadelphia, 1847 5704.8 p2
Cannon, Margaret; Philadelphia, 1852 5704.8 p88
Cannon, Margaret; Philadelphia, 1864 5704.8 p182
Cannon, Margaret; Quebec, 1851 5704.8 p75
Cannon, Margaret 48; St. John, N.B., 1858 5704.8 p137
Cannon, Marmaduke 9 *SEE* Cannon, Richard
Cannon, Mary 33 *SEE* Cannon, Richard
Cannon, Mary Jane; New York, NY, 1868 5704.8 p228
Cannon, Michael; St. John, N.B., 1850 5704.8 p67
Cannon, Michael 8; Philadelphia, 1851 5704.8 p77
Cannon, Moses; New York, NY, 1816 2859.11 p26
Cannon, Nancy; New York, NY, 1868 5704.8 p228
Cannon, Nathaniel; New York, NY, 1838 8208.4 p63
Cannon, Neal; Philadelphia, 1852 5704.8 p85
Cannon, Pat; St. John, N.B., 1850 5704.8 p67
Cannon, Patrick; New York, NY, 1811 2859.11 p9
Cannon, Peter; America, 1735-1743 4971 p8
Cannon, Peter; America, 1738-1743 4971 p91
Cannon, Philip; New York, NY, 1867 5704.8 p219
Cannon, Richard 36; Savannah, GA, 1733 4719.17 p310
*Daughter:*Clemetine 3
*Son:*Marmaduke 9
*Wife:*Mary 33
Cannon, Robert; New York, NY, 1816 2859.11 p26
Cannon, Robert 6 mos; Philadelphia, 1852 5704.8 p85
Cannon, Samuel; New York, NY, 1868 5704.8 p228
Cannon, Susan; St. John, N.B., 1847 5704.8 p19
Cannon, Thomas; Antigua (Antego), 1754 1219.7 p27
Cannon, Thomas; Washington, 1859-1920 2872.1 p6
Cannon, William; Philadelphia, 1847 53.26 p10
Cannon, William; Philadelphia, 1847 5704.8 p32
Cannon, William 15; St. John, N.B., 1858 5704.8 p137
Cannonge, Mr. 24; New Orleans, 1835 778.5 p95
Cannoughton, Patrick; New York, NY, 1816 2859.11 p26
Cannum, Thomas 17; Philadelphia, 1774 1219.7 p175
Canny, Biddy; St. John, N.B., 1849 5704.8 p55
Canny, Charles; New York, NY, 1864 5704.8 p172
Canny, Dorby 22; St. John, N.B., 1854 5704.8 p114
Canny, Edward; St. John, N.B., 1853 5704.8 p99
Canny, Edward 20; St. John, N.B., 1853 5704.8 p109
Canny, James; New York, NY, 1864 5704.8 p172
Canny, Magy; St. John, N.B., 1849 5704.8 p55
Canny, Margaret; New York, NY, 1867 5704.8 p219
Canny, Margaret; St. John, N.B., 1847 5704.8 p26
Canny, Margaret; St. John, N.B., 1852 5704.8 p83
Canny, Mary; St. John, N.B., 1849 5704.8 p49
Canny, Mary; St. John, N.B., 1853 5704.8 p107
Canny, Peggy; St. John, N.B., 1852 5704.8 p84
Canny, Richard; Virginia, 1638 6219 p186
Canny, Rose 15; St. John, N.B., 1854 5704.8 p114
Canogre, Francis 34; America, 1829 778.5 p95
Cantello, Joseph; Colorado, 1904 9678.1 p156
Canter, Thomas 18; Maryland, 1774 1219.7 p220
Canterbury, Samuel 16; Philadelphia, 1774 1219.7 p212
Cantillon, Thomas; America, 1743 4971 p11
Cantlay, Thomas; Boston, 1906 9892.11 p8
Cantle, Alexander 42; Jamaica, 1730 3690.1 p37
Cantlie, Alexander 42; Jamaica, 1730 3690.1 p37
Cantrello, Antino 40; New York, NY, 1893 9026.4 p41
Cantwell, James; America, 1738 4971 p28
Cantwell, John; Washington, 1859-1920 2872.1 p6
Cantwell, John 30; Massachusetts, 1850 5881.1 p19
Cantwell, Pearce 19; Maryland, 1735 3690.1 p37
Canty, Thomas; Quebec, 1804 7603 p75
Canway, Catherine; New York, NY, 1816 2859.11 p27
Canway, Mary; New York, NY, 1816 2859.11 p27
Canway, Owen; New York, NY, 1816 2859.11 p27
Capan, George; Iowa, 1866-1943 123.54 p57
Capdevielle, Mr. 31; America, 1838 778.5 p94
Capdeville, A. 28; New Orleans, 1835 778.5 p95
Capdeville, John 19; New Orleans, 1864 543.30 p462
Capdeville, John 21; New Orleans, 1862 543.30 p462
Capdeville, John 25; New Orleans, 1862 543.30 p460
Cape, Robert; Virginia, 1638 6219 p120
Capel, Catharine 72; Kansas, 1873 5240.1 p54
Capepa, Tony; Arkansas, 1918 95.2 p25
Caper, William; Virginia, 1639 6219 p162
Capera, Pierre 34; Mexico, 1835 778.5 p95
Caperi, Jno. Francis Payne; Shreveport, LA, 1876 7129 p44
Capet, Jean J. 50; America, 1838 778.5 p95
Capie, Dominique 25; America, 1837 778.5 p95
Capie, Joseph 21; America, 1837 778.5 p95
Capira, P. 32; New Orleans, 1829 778.5 p95
Capitaine, Z.; New Orleans, 1839 778.5 p95
Capitier, Roze 30; Port uncertain, 1836 778.5 p95
Caplap, John; Arkansas, 1918 95.2 p25
Caples, Samuel 17; Virginia, 1721 3690.1 p37
Capo, Modesto; Arkansas, 1918 95.2 p25
Caporali, Vincinzo; Wisconsin, n.d. 9675.5 p49
Capouladge, Antone 29; America, 1836 778.5 p95
Cappel, George Lewis; Virginia, 1768 1219.7 p138
Cappell, Wm.; Virginia, 1642 6219 p192
Cappellano, Andrea; Arkansas, 1918 95.2 p25
Cappellin, Domick; Iowa, 1866-1943 123.54 p12
Cappellin, John; Iowa, 1866-1943 123.54 p12
Cappellin, Silvio; Iowa, 1866-1943 123.54 p12
Cappellin, Vittorio; Iowa, 1866-1943 123.54 p12
Cappello, Vincenzo 29; Arkansas, 1918 95.2 p25
Capper, Thomas 19; Pennsylvania, Virginia or Maryland, 1723 3690.1 p37
Cappes, Louis 34; New Orleans, 1862 543.30 p455
Cappes, Peter; Vermont, 1777 8137 p7
Capple, Frederic 19; New Orleans, 1862 543.30 p456
Cappo, Martin John; Arkansas, 1918 95.2 p25
Caprice, Nicholas; Colorado, 1904 9678.1 p156
Capron, Charles H.; Colorado, 1905 9678.1 p156
Caps, Robert; Virginia, 1645 6219 p239
Capseck, Mr. 21; New Orleans, 1837 778.5 p95
Caputo, Giovanni; Arkansas, 1918 95.2 p25
Caquelin, Henry Adolphe; New York, NY, 1886 3455.1 p45
Car, Wm.; Virginia, 1642 6219 p188
Cara, Louis; Shreveport, LA, 1879 7129 p44
Carabine, Catherine; New York, NY, 1816 2859.11 p27
Carabine, Thomas; New York, NY, 1816 2859.11 p27
Caraccio, Francisco; Iowa, 1866-1943 123.54 p13
Caraccio, Pasquale; Arkansas, 1918 95.2 p25
Caradine, Richard; New York, NY, 1833 8208.4 p43
Caraghen, Thomas 19; Philadelphia, 1774 1219.7 p183
Caramel, Mr. 30; New Orleans, 1835 778.5 p95
Caramelli, Silvio; Washington, 1859-1920 2872.1 p6
Carano, Vincenzo; Arkansas, 1918 95.2 p25
Caraubon, Jean 22; New Orleans, 1836 778.5 p95
Caraux, Jacques 24; New Orleans, 1835 778.5 p95
Caravella, Joe; Arkansas, 1918 95.2 p25
Carazos, Christ Aristidis; Arkansas, 1918 95.2 p25
Carbam, Timothy; New York, NY, 1838 8208.4 p73
Carbary, Patrick 25; St. John, N.B., 1864 5704.8 p159
Carberry, Barney; Philadelphia, 1867 5704.8 p216
Carberry, Charles; New York, NY, 1870 5704.8 p237
Carberry, Grace; Philadelphia, 1866 5704.8 p214
Carberry, Hannah 19; Philadelphia, 1854 5704.8 p117
Carberry, Susan; New York, NY, 1869 5704.8 p232
Carbery, Margaret 18; Philadelphia, 1854 5704.8 p117
Carbery, William 20; Philadelphia, 1854 5704.8 p117
Carbonel, M. 30; New Orleans, 1827 778.5 p96
Carbonell, Thomas; North America, 1759 1219.7 p68
Carbouel, Mr.; Port uncertain, 1839 778.5 p96
Carbry, Cormick 17; Philadelphia, 1853 5704.8 p108
Carconichuit, Madame 58; New Orleans, 1827 778.5 p96
Carcoran, Michael 20; Philadelphia, 1853 5704.8 p113
Cardana, John; New York, NY, 1838 8208.4 p81
Carde, Pierre 35; Port uncertain, 1837 778.5 p96
Carde, Robert; Virginia, 1600-1642 6219 p192
Cardel, Mr. 29; New Orleans, 1829 778.5 p96
Carden, N.; New York, NY, 1811 2859.11 p9
With family
Carden, Owen 12; Massachusetts, 1848 5881.1 p23
Carden, Rose 9; Massachusetts, 1848 5881.1 p24
Cardenzana, Joseph; Iowa, 1866-1943 123.54 p13
Cardenzana, Phillip; Iowa, 1866-1943 123.54 p13
Cardet, M. 28; America, 1837 778.5 p96
Cardiff, Edward; New York, NY, 1840 8208.4 p104
Cardiffe, John; Delaware Bay or River, 1743 4971 p104
Cardinal, Johann Christoph; America, 1853 4610.10 p148
Cardinall, Robert 21; Jamaica, 1730 3690.1 p37
Cardivale, Augustino; Arkansas, 1918 95.2 p25
Cardon, Mary 13; Massachusetts, 1848 5881.1 p20
Cardot, Xavier 28; New Orleans, 1864 543.30 p464
Cardova, Enasius 64; Arizona, 1919 9228.40 p23
Care, J. 27; New Orleans, 1837 778.5 p96
Care, John 26; Maryland, 1774 1219.7 p222
Careant, Jean 30; Port uncertain, 1839 778.5 p96
Careless, John; America, 1737 4971 p27
Carels, John; Wisconsin, n.d. 9675.5 p49
Carels, Peter; Wisconsin, n.d. 9675.5 p49
Caresse, J. 35; Mexico, 1826 778.5 p96
Caret, Miss 16; New Orleans, 1839 778.5 p96
Caretta, Mr. 23; New Orleans, 1822 778.5 p96
Carew, Martin; America, 1736-1743 4971 p58
Carew, Thomas; America, 1736-1743 4971 p58
Carew, William 19; Massachusetts, 1849 5881.1 p26
Carey, Ann *SEE* Carey, William
Carey, Ann *SEE* Carey, William
Carey, Ann; Philadelphia, 1847 5704.8 p13
Carey, Ann; Philadelphia, 1847 5704.8 p23
Carey, Archy; St. John, N.B., 1847 5704.8 p21

Carey, Cath'rine 20; Massachusetts, 1849 ***5881.1*** *p14*
Carey, Darby 54; Newfoundland, 1789 ***4915.24*** *p57*
Carey, Eliza; Philadelphia, 1865 ***5704.8*** *p200*
Carey, Ellan; St. John, N.B., 1847 ***5704.8*** *p25*
Carey, George; Illinois, 1854 ***7857*** *p2*
Carey, James; Massachusetts, 1850 ***5881.1*** *p19*
Carey, James 26; New Orleans, 1862 ***543.30*** *p459*
Carey, Jane *SEE* Carey, William
Carey, Jane; Philadelphia, 1847 ***5704.8*** *p23*
Carey, Jane; St. John, N.B., 1847 ***5704.8*** *p21*
Carey, Jane 7 *SEE* Carey, William
Carey, Jane 7; Philadelphia, 1847 ***5704.8*** *p13*
Carey, John; America, 1859 ***6014.1*** *p1*
Carey, John 18; Pennsylvania, 1725 ***3690.1*** *p37*
Carey, John 20; Massachusetts, 1849 ***5881.1*** *p18*
Carey, Margaret 30; Massachusetts, 1850 ***5881.1*** *p23*
Carey, Marg'et 21; Massachusetts, 1849 ***5881.1*** *p21*
Carey, Mary *SEE* Carey, William
Carey, Mary; Philadelphia, 1847 ***5704.8*** *p23*
Carey, Mary 18; Massachusetts, 1850 ***5881.1*** *p22*
Carey, Mary 25; Massachusetts, 1847 ***5881.1*** *p20*
Carey, Mary 25; Massachusetts, 1850 ***5881.1*** *p22*
Carey, Mary Ann; St. John, N.B., 1847 ***5704.8*** *p21*
Carey, Michael; Philadelphia, 1816 ***2859.11*** *p27*
Carey, Michael 3 mos; St. John, N.B., 1847 ***5704.8*** *p25*
Carey, Nelly; St. John, N.B., 1847 ***5704.8*** *p25*
Carey, Patrick; Illinois, 1857 ***2896.5*** *p7*
Carey, Patrick; Ohio, 1840 ***9892.11*** *p8*
Carey, Patrick 16; Massachusetts, 1849 ***5881.1*** *p24*
Carey, Richard; New York, NY, 1811 ***2859.11*** *p9*
Carey, Robert; Philadelphia, 1864 ***5704.8*** *p177*
Carey, Thomas; Illinois, 1856 ***7857*** *p2*
Carey, Timothy; St. John, N.B., 1847 ***5704.8*** *p25*
Carey, Unity 3 mos; St. John, N.B., 1847 ***5704.8*** *p25*
Carey, William *SEE* Carey, William
Carey, William; America, 1737 ***4971*** *p75*
Carey, William; Philadelphia, 1847 ***53.26*** *p10*
*Relative:*Ann
*Relative:*William
*Relative:*Jane 7
Carey, William; Philadelphia, 1847 ***53.26*** *p11*
*Relative:*Ann
*Relative:*Mary
*Relative:*Jane
Carey, William; Philadelphia, 1847 ***5704.8*** *p13*
Carey, William; Philadelphia, 1847 ***5704.8*** *p23*
Carey, William 43; Massachusetts, 1849 ***5881.1*** *p26*
Cargile, Adam; Savannah, GA, 1774 ***1219.7*** *p227*
Cargile, Jennet; Savannah, GA, 1774 ***1219.7*** *p227*
Cargill, David 55; North Carolina, 1850 ***1639.20*** *p37*
Cargill, Sally 26; Philadelphia, 1854 ***5704.8*** *p118*
Cargo, John; New York, NY, 1837 ***8208.4*** *p25*
Cariaux, Denis 34; New Orleans, 1838 ***778.5*** *p96*
Cariaux, Marie 28; New Orleans, 1838 ***778.5*** *p96*
Carier, J.B. 45; Maryland, 1775 ***1219.7*** *p250*
Cariere, N. 33; America, 1835 ***778.5*** *p96*
Carigan, Ellen; St. John, N.B., 1849 ***5704.8*** *p55*
Carion, M. 18; America, 1835 ***778.5*** *p96*
Caristo, Dominico; Arkansas, 1918 ***95.2*** *p25*
Carl, . . .; Canada, 1776-1783 ***9786*** *p18*
Carl, Mr. 6 mos; New Orleans, 1835 ***778.5*** *p97*
Carl, Christian Friedrich Wilhelm; America, 1865 ***4610.10*** *p158*
Carl, John; New York, 1852 ***2896.5*** *p7*
Carl, Joseph; New York, NY, 1838 ***8208.4*** *p65*
Carlain, Michael 26; Philadelphia, 1804 ***53.26*** *p11*
Carlan, Patrick; New York, NY, 1816 ***2859.11*** *p27*
Carlan, Sarah; New York, NY, 1816 ***2859.11*** *p27*
Carland, Anne 3; St. John, N.B., 1848 ***5704.8*** *p43*
Carland, Catherine 22; Philadelphia, 1860 ***5704.8*** *p144*
Carland, George; Philadelphia, 1852 ***5704.8*** *p91*
Carland, John; New York, NY, 1838 ***8208.4*** *p74*
Carland, John 20; Quebec, 1857 ***5704.8*** *p136*
Carland, Margaret; St. John, N.B., 1847 ***5704.8*** *p24*
Carland, Philip; New York, NY, 1838 ***8208.4*** *p63*
Carland, Rose 22; Philadelphia, 1860 ***5704.8*** *p144*
Carlberg, Anders W.; Maine, 1881-1896 ***6410.22*** *p122*
Carle, Conrad; Ohio, 1869-1887 ***8582*** *p5*
Carle, John W.; New York, NY, 1816 ***2859.11*** *p27*
Carle, Michael; New York, NY, 1816 ***2859.11*** *p27*
Carle, Michael; South Carolina, 1788 ***7119*** *p204*
Carlestadt, Frederick; Indiana, 1847 ***9117*** *p16*
Carlet, F. A. 27; New Orleans, 1838 ***778.5*** *p97*
Carleton, Guy; Quebec, 1759 ***9786*** *p108*
Carleton, Hen.; Virginia, 1642 ***6219*** *p196*
Carleton, J.; New York, NY, 1816 ***2859.11*** *p27*
Carleton, M.; New York, NY, 1816 ***2859.11*** *p27*
Carli, Joseph 37?; Arizona, 1890 ***2764.35*** *p13*
Carlier, Lugien 25; Port uncertain, 1832 ***778.5*** *p97*
Carlile, Charles 34; Maryland, 1734 ***3690.1*** *p37*
Carlin, Baby; Died enroute, 1752 ***7074.6*** *p208*
With sibling
Carlin, Ann; St. John, N.B., 1847 ***5704.8*** *p8*
Carlin, Ann 25; Philadelphia, 1860 ***5704.8*** *p145*
Carlin, Barbara; New York, NY, 1866 ***5704.8*** *p213*
Carlin, Bernard 3; St. John, N.B., 1847 ***5704.8*** *p8*
Carlin, Biddy; St. John, N.B., 1847 ***5704.8*** *p8*
Carlin, Biddy 35; Wilmington, DE, 1831 ***6508.7*** *p160*
Carlin, Biddy 35; Wilmington, DE, 1831 ***6508.7*** *p161*
Carlin, Brian; St. John, N.B., 1847 ***5704.8*** *p8*
Carlin, Catharine; America, 1868 ***5704.8*** *p226*
Carlin, Catharine; Philadelphia, 1865 ***5704.8*** *p189*
Carlin, Catharine; Philadelphia, 1866 ***5704.8*** *p204*
Carlin, Catharine; Philadelphia, 1867 ***5704.8*** *p217*
Carlin, Catharine; Philadelphia, 1868 ***5704.8*** *p229*
Carlin, Catharine; Philadelphia, 1869 ***5704.8*** *p235*
Carlin, Catharine 18 mos; Philadelphia, 1865 ***5704.8*** *p189*
Carlin, Catherine *SEE* Carlin, Jean
Carlin, Catherine; Philadelphia, 1851 ***5704.8*** *p76*
Carlin, Catherine; St. John, N.B., 1847 ***5704.8*** *p3*
Carlin, Catherine 11 *SEE* Carlin, John
Carlin, Catherine 11; Philadelphia, 1847 ***5704.8*** *p24*
Carlin, Connor 25; Massachusetts, 1849 ***5881.1*** *p14*
Carlin, Elisabeth *SEE* Carlin, Jean
Carlin, Eliza; New York, NY, 1869 ***5704.8*** *p230*
Carlin, Eliza J.; Philadelphia, 1870 ***5704.8*** *p239*
Carlin, Elizabeth; Philadelphia, 1847 ***53.26*** *p11*
Carlin, Elizabeth; Philadelphia, 1847 ***5704.8*** *p14*
Carlin, Elizabeth 10; St. John, N.B., 1847 ***5704.8*** *p3*
Carlin, Ellan; Quebec, 1851 ***5704.8*** *p74*
Carlin, Fredrick; New York, NY, 1866 ***5704.8*** *p202*
Carlin, George; Quebec, 1847 ***5704.8*** *p12*
Carlin, George 25; St. John, N.B., 1864 ***5704.8*** *p158*
Carlin, Hannah; Philadelphia, 1848 ***53.26*** *p11*
Carlin, Hannah; Philadelphia, 1848 ***5704.8*** *p40*
Carlin, Hugh; St. John, N.B., 1847 ***5704.8*** *p8*
Carlin, Hugh 7 *SEE* Carlin, John
Carlin, Hugh 7; Philadelphia, 1847 ***5704.8*** *p24*
Carlin, James *SEE* Carlin, Mary
Carlin, James; New Orleans, 1852 ***5704.8*** *p98*
Carlin, James; New York, NY, 1816 ***2859.11*** *p27*
Carlin, James 28; Wilmington, DE, 1831 ***6508.7*** *p160*
Carlin, Jane; Philadelphia, 1847 ***5704.8*** *p24*
Carlin, Jane 5 *SEE* Carlin, John
Carlin, Jane 5; Philadelphia, 1847 ***5704.8*** *p24*
Carlin, Jane 19; Philadelphia, 1864 ***5704.8*** *p157*
Carlin, Jane 22; Philadelphia, 1854 ***5704.8*** *p123*
Carlin, Jean 38; Halifax, N.S., 1752 ***7074.6*** *p207*
With family of 3
Carlin, Jean 38; Halifax, N.S., 1752 ***7074.6*** *p209*
*Wife:*Elisabeth
*Daughter:*Judith
*Daughter:*Jeanne
Carlin, Jean 38; Halifax, N.S., 1752 ***7074.6*** *p209*
*Wife:*Catherine
With 2 children
Carlin, Jeanne *SEE* Carlin, Jean
Carlin, John; New York, NY, 1816 ***2859.11*** *p27*
Carlin, John; New York, NY, 1869 ***5704.8*** *p234*
Carlin, John; Philadelphia, 1847 ***53.26*** *p11*
*Relative:*Sarah
*Relative:*Michael 13
*Relative:*Catherine 11
*Relative:*William 9
*Relative:*Hugh 7
*Relative:*Jane 5
*Relative:*John 1
Carlin, John; Philadelphia, 1847 ***5704.8*** *p24*
Carlin, John; Philadelphia, 1851 ***5704.8*** *p80*
Carlin, John; St. John, N.B., 1847 ***5704.8*** *p3*
Carlin, John; St. John, N.B., 1847 ***5704.8*** *p8*
Carlin, John; St. John, N.B., 1848 ***5704.8*** *p45*
Carlin, John 3 mos; St. John, N.B., 1847 ***5704.8*** *p8*
Carlin, John 1 *SEE* Carlin, John
Carlin, John 1; Philadelphia, 1847 ***5704.8*** *p24*
Carlin, John 3; Philadelphia, 1865 ***5704.8*** *p189*
Carlin, John 20; Philadelphia, 1857 ***5704.8*** *p132*
Carlin, John 25; Philadelphia, 1856 ***5704.8*** *p129*
Carlin, Judith *SEE* Carlin, Jean
Carlin, Larry 4 mos; Philadelphia, 1865 ***5704.8*** *p189*
Carlin, Mage; Philadelphia, 1865 ***5704.8*** *p202*
Carlin, Margaret; Philadelphia, 1847 ***53.26*** *p11*
Carlin, Margaret; Philadelphia, 1847 ***5704.8*** *p22*
Carlin, Margaret; Philadelphia, 1864 ***5704.8*** *p177*
Carlin, Martha; St. John, N.B., 1847 ***5704.8*** *p3*
Carlin, Mary; Philadelphia, 1847 ***53.26*** *p11*
*Relative:*Patrick
*Relative:*James
Carlin, Mary; Philadelphia, 1847 ***5704.8*** *p24*
Carlin, Mary; Philadelphia, 1864 ***5704.8*** *p185*
Carlin, Mary; St. John, N.B., 1847 ***5704.8*** *p3*
Carlin, Mary; St. John, N.B., 1853 ***5704.8*** *p107*
Carlin, Mary A.; Philadelphia, 1870 ***5704.8*** *p239*
Carlin, Mary Ann 2; St. John, N.B., 1847 ***5704.8*** *p8*
Carlin, Matilda 18; St. John, N.B., 1864 ***5704.8*** *p158*
Carlin, Michael; Philadelphia, 1850 ***53.26*** *p11*
Carlin, Michael; Philadelphia, 1850 ***5704.8*** *p60*
Carlin, Michael; Philadelphia, 1864 ***5704.8*** *p185*
Carlin, Michael 13 *SEE* Carlin, John
Carlin, Michael 13; Philadelphia, 1847 ***5704.8*** *p24*
Carlin, Michl 22; Wilmington, DE, 1831 ***6508.7*** *p160*
Carlin, Nelly; St. John, N.B., 1847 ***5704.8*** *p8*
Carlin, Patrick *SEE* Carlin, Mary
Carlin, Patrick; Philadelphia, 1847 ***5704.8*** *p24*
Carlin, Patrick; Philadelphia, 1864 ***5704.8*** *p177*
Carlin, Patrick 7; St. John, N.B., 1847 ***5704.8*** *p3*
Carlin, Rosanna; New York, NY, 1869 ***5704.8*** *p234*
Carlin, Rose; Philadelphia, 1851 ***5704.8*** *p80*
Carlin, Sarah *SEE* Carlin, John
Carlin, Sarah; Philadelphia, 1847 ***5704.8*** *p24*
Carlin, Susan; Philadelphia, 1865 ***5704.8*** *p204*
Carlin, Susan; Quebec, 1851 ***5704.8*** *p74*
Carlin, Susan 20; St. John, N.B., 1864 ***5704.8*** *p158*
Carlin, Thomas; New York, NY, 1815 ***2859.11*** *p27*
Carlin, William; Philadelphia, 1850 ***53.26*** *p11*
Carlin, William; Philadelphia, 1850 ***5704.8*** *p68*
Carlin, William; St. John, N.B., 1847 ***5704.8*** *p3*
Carlin, William 9 *SEE* Carlin, John
Carlin, William 9; Philadelphia, 1847 ***5704.8*** *p24*
Carlind, Isabella; Philadelphia, 1849 ***53.26*** *p11*
Carlind, Isabella; Philadelphia, 1849 ***5704.8*** *p53*
Carline, Elizabeth; St. John, N.B., 1853 ***5704.8*** *p107*
Carling, C. J.; Minneapolis, 1882-1887 ***6410.35*** *p51*
Carling, Jean 38; Halifax, N.S., 1752 ***7074.6*** *p207*
With family of 3
Carling, Philip; New York, NY, 1811 ***2859.11*** *p9*
Carlini, Germano; Arkansas, 1918 ***95.2*** *p25*
Carlisle, James; New York, NY, 1815 ***2859.11*** *p27*
Carlisle, John; New York, NY, 1815 ***2859.11*** *p27*
Carlisle, William; New York, NY, 1839 ***8208.4*** *p100*
Carlo, Stanish 39; New Orleans, 1862 ***543.30*** *p458*
Carlo, Tom; Wisconsin, n.d. ***9675.5*** *p49*
Carlo, Virizini; Arkansas, 1918 ***95.2*** *p25*
Carlo, Wino; Iowa, 1866-1943 ***123.54*** *p13*
Carlon, Jane 25; St. John, N.B., 1866 ***5704.8*** *p166*
Carlot, Pierre 23; Port uncertain, 1836 ***778.5*** *p97*
Carlotto, Antonio; Iowa, 1866-1943 ***123.54*** *p13*
Carlovand, Herman; Iowa, 1866-1943 ***123.54*** *p13*
Carlsen, A. E.; Minneapolis, 1879-1885 ***6410.35*** *p51*
Carlsen, Andrew Christian; Arkansas, 1918 ***95.2*** *p25*
Carlsen, Carl G. 22; Kansas, 1884 ***5240.1*** *p67*
Carlsen, Gust Adolph; Arkansas, 1918 ***95.2*** *p25*
Carlson, Adolph; Arkansas, 1918 ***95.2*** *p26*
Carlson, Adrian Carl; Arkansas, 1918 ***95.2*** *p26*
Carlson, Albin; Minneapolis, 1869-1877 ***6410.35*** *p51*
Carlson, Alex Henning Leonard; Iowa, 1866-1943 ***123.54*** *p13*
Carlson, Ance Alice; Washington, 1859-1920 ***2872.1*** *p6*
Carlson, Andrew; Washington, 1859-1920 ***2872.1*** *p6*
Carlson, Anna Samuelson; Washington, 1859-1920 ***2872.1*** *p6*
Carlson, Anton; Arkansas, 1918 ***95.2*** *p26*
Carlson, Anton Emanuel 23; Arkansas, 1918 ***95.2*** *p26*
Carlson, August; Iowa, 1866-1943 ***123.54*** *p13*
Carlson, August; Washington, 1859-1920 ***2872.1*** *p6*
Carlson, August Philip; Minneapolis, 1880-1887 ***6410.35*** *p51*
Carlson, Axel; Iowa, 1866-1943 ***123.54*** *p13*
Carlson, Axel William; Arkansas, 1918 ***95.2*** *p26*
Carlson, C.; Iowa, 1866-1943 ***123.54*** *p13*
Carlson, C. J.; Iowa, 1866-1943 ***123.54*** *p13*
Carlson, C. J. 37; Kansas, 1878 ***5240.1*** *p59*
Carlson, C.W.; Iowa, 1866-1943 ***123.54*** *p13*
Carlson, Carl; Arkansas, 1918 ***95.2*** *p26*
Carlson, Carl; Washington, 1859-1920 ***2872.1*** *p6*
Carlson, Carl Alrick; Arkansas, 1918 ***95.2*** *p26*
Carlson, Carl Anders; Washington, 1859-1920 ***2872.1*** *p6*
Carlson, Carl Aron; Canada, 1883-1909 ***9892.11*** *p8*
Carlson, Carl Aron; Duluth, MN, 1883-1913 ***9892.11*** *p8*
Carlson, Carl Linus; Arkansas, 1918 ***95.2*** *p26*
Carlson, Carl T.; Arkansas, 1918 ***95.2*** *p26*
Carlson, Carl Victor; Iroquois Co., IL, 1894 ***3455.1*** *p9*
Carlson, Charley; Iowa, 1866-1943 ***123.54*** *p13*
Carlson, David; Washington, 1859-1920 ***2872.1*** *p6*
Carlson, E.; Washington, 1859-1920 ***2872.1*** *p6*
Carlson, E. A. 34; Kansas, 1893 ***5240.1*** *p78*
Carlson, Elias; Washington, 1859-1920 ***2872.1*** *p6*
Carlson, Emil; Washington, 1859-1920 ***2872.1*** *p6*
Carlson, Ernest Severin; Arkansas, 1918 ***95.2*** *p26*
Carlson, Ernest Waldermerk; Arkansas, 1918 ***95.2*** *p26*
Carlson, Evald; Iowa, 1866-1943 ***123.54*** *p13*
Carlson, Francis Conrad; Maine, 1839-1845 ***6410.22*** *p115*
Carlson, Frank; Arkansas, 1918 ***95.2*** *p26*
Carlson, Frank; Iroquois Co., IL, 1895 ***3455.1*** *p9*
Carlson, Frank; Minneapolis, 1879-1885 ***6410.35*** *p51*
Carlson, Frank; Washington, 1859-1920 ***2872.1*** *p6*
Carlson, Frans Oskar; Iowa, 1866-1943 ***123.54*** *p13*

70 *FOR A COMPLETE EXPLANATION OF ENTRY, SEE "HOW TO READ A CITATION" SECTION*

Carr, Ellen 40; Philadelphia, 1859 ***5704.8*** *p142*
Carr, Francis; New York, NY, 1865 ***5704.8*** *p189*
Carr, Francis 8; New York, NY, 1865 ***5704.8*** *p189*
Carr, Giley; Philadelphia, 1867 ***5704.8*** *p222*
Carr, Henry 60; Philadelphia, 1864 ***5704.8*** *p156*
Carr, Hyndman 9 mos; Quebec, 1853 ***5704.8*** *p103*
Carr, Isaac; New York, NY, 1816 ***2859.11*** *p27*
Carr, James; America, 1865 ***5704.8*** *p191*
Carr, James; New York, NY, 1864 ***5704.8*** *p174*
Carr, James; New York, NY, 1865 ***5704.8*** *p195*
Carr, James; New York, NY, 1871 ***5704.8*** *p240*
Carr, James; Philadelphia, 1849 ***53.26*** *p11*
Carr, James; Philadelphia, 1849 ***5704.8*** *p54*
Carr, James; Philadelphia, 1868 ***5704.8*** *p230*
Carr, James; Quebec, 1852 ***5704.8*** *p94*
Carr, James; Quebec, 1853 ***5704.8*** *p103*
Carr, James; St. John, N.B., 1847 ***5704.8*** *p35*
Carr, James 3 mos; Philadelphia, 1865 ***5704.8*** *p164*
Carr, James 2; Philadelphia, 1865 ***5704.8*** *p164*
Carr, James 2; Quebec, 1853 ***5704.8*** *p103*
Carr, James 12; Philadelphia, 1853 ***5704.8*** *p113*
Carr, James 20; Philadelphia, 1860 ***5704.8*** *p145*
Carr, James Allen 31; California, 1867 ***3840.1*** *p16*
Carr, Jane; New York, NY, 1865 ***5704.8*** *p189*
Carr, Jane; Philadelphia, 1864 ***5704.8*** *p185*
Carr, Jean; Quebec, 1810 ***7603*** *p68*
Carr, John; Maryland, 1751 ***1219.7*** *p3*
Carr, John; Maryland, 1751 ***3690.1*** *p38*
Carr, John; New York, NY, 1811 ***2859.11*** *p9*
Carr, John; New York, NY, 1816 ***2859.11*** *p27*
Carr, John; New York, NY, 1864 ***5704.8*** *p174*
Carr, John; New York, NY, 1866 ***5704.8*** *p209*
Carr, John; Philadelphia, 1867 ***5704.8*** *p217*
Carr, John; St. John, N.B., 1850 ***5704.8*** *p67*
Carr, John 4 mos; Philadelphia, 1865 ***5704.8*** *p164*
Carr, John 2; Philadelphia, 1865 ***5704.8*** *p164*
Carr, John 11; St. John, N.B., 1850 ***5704.8*** *p67*
Carr, John C.; Illinois, 1882 ***5240.1*** *p8*
Carr, Joseph; Philadelphia, 1811 ***2859.11*** *p9*
Carr, Margaret; Quebec, 1847 ***5704.8*** *p17*
Carr, Margaret; Quebec, 1853 ***5704.8*** *p103*
Carr, Margaret 14; Massachusetts, 1849 ***5881.1*** *p22*
Carr, Margaret 20; Massachusetts, 1849 ***5881.1*** *p22*
Carr, Margaret 22; Philadelphia, 1865 ***5704.8*** *p164*
Carr, Margery; Philadelphia, 1864 ***5704.8*** *p179*
Carr, Mary; New York, NY, 1865 ***5704.8*** *p189*
Carr, Mary; New York, NY, 1865 ***5704.8*** *p196*
Carr, Mary; New York, NY, 1865 ***5704.8*** *p202*
Carr, Mary; New York, NY, 1867 ***5704.8*** *p223*
Carr, Mary; Philadelphia, 1864 ***5704.8*** *p174*
Carr, Mary; Philadelphia, 1864 ***5704.8*** *p179*
Carr, Mary; Philadelphia, 1867 ***5704.8*** *p217*
Carr, Mary; Philadelphia, 1867 ***5704.8*** *p221*
Carr, Mary; St. John, N.B., 1847 ***5704.8*** *p21*
Carr, Mary; St. John, N.B., 1853 ***5704.8*** *p99*
Carr, Mary 2; Massachusetts, 1850 ***5881.1*** *p22*
Carr, Mary 4; New York, NY, 1865 ***5704.8*** *p189*
Carr, Mary 13; St. John, N.B., 1850 ***5704.8*** *p67*
Carr, Mary 14; Philadelphia, 1853 ***5704.8*** *p113*
Carr, Mary 17; Philadelphia, 1864 ***5704.8*** *p157*
Carr, Mary 18; St. John, N.B., 1854 ***5704.8*** *p119*
Carr, Mary 23; Massachusetts, 1849 ***5881.1*** *p21*
Carr, Mary 27; Massachusetts, 1850 ***5881.1*** *p22*
Carr, Mary A.; Quebec, 1852 ***5704.8*** *p93*
Carr, Mary Jane; America, 1864 ***5704.8*** *p189*
Carr, Mary Jane 9; Philadelphia, 1859 ***5704.8*** *p141*
Carr, Michael; America, 1735-1743 ***4971*** *p78*
Carr, Michael; New York, NY, 1838 ***8208.4*** *p62*
Carr, Michael 3; Philadelphia, 1853 ***5704.8*** *p113*
Carr, Michael 3; St. John, N.B., 1850 ***5704.8*** *p67*
Carr, Michael 8; Massachusetts, 1850 ***5881.1*** *p22*
Carr, Michael 13; Massachusetts, 1849 ***5881.1*** *p21*
Carr, Nancy; Quebec, 1851 ***5704.8*** *p82*
Carr, Nathaniel; New York, NY, 1815 ***2859.11*** *p27*
Carr, Nelly; St. John, N.B., 1848 ***5704.8*** *p43*
Carr, Pat. 46; Massachusetts, 1849 ***5881.1*** *p24*
Carr, Patrick; America, 1890 ***1450.2*** *p25A*
Carr, Patrick; Arkansas, 1918 ***95.2*** *p26*
Carr, Patrick; Philadelphia, 1867 ***5704.8*** *p217*
Carr, Patrick 4; Philadelphia, 1865 ***5704.8*** *p164*
Carr, Peter; New York, NY, 1865 ***5704.8*** *p189*
Carr, Rachael 10; Massachusetts, 1849 ***5881.1*** *p25*
Carr, Richard 18; Maryland, 1722 ***3690.1*** *p38*
Carr, Robert; New York, NY, 1816 ***2859.11*** *p27*
Carr, Robert 12; Philadelphia, 1859 ***5704.8*** *p141*
Carr, Rosana; St. John, N.B., 1850 ***5704.8*** *p67*
Carr, Rose; Philadelphia, 1867 ***5704.8*** *p216*
Carr, Rose 25; Massachusetts, 1849 ***5881.1*** *p25*
Carr, Rose 50; Philadelphia, 1853 ***5704.8*** *p113*
Carr, Samuel; America, 1738 ***4971*** *p76*
Carr, Samuel 16; Maryland, 1724 ***3690.1*** *p38*
Carr, Sarah; New York, NY, 1864 ***5704.8*** *p174*
Carr, Sarah 14; Philadelphia, 1859 ***5704.8*** *p141*
Carr, Sarah 40; Philadelphia, 1859 ***5704.8*** *p141*
Carr, Sarah Ann 4; Quebec, 1853 ***5704.8*** *p103*
Carr, Sophia; St. John, N.B., 1850 ***5704.8*** *p67*
Carr, William; America, 1743 ***4971*** *p11*
Carr, William; New York, NY, 1868 ***5704.8*** *p227*
Carr, William; Ohio, 1852 ***9892.11*** *p8*
Carr, William; Quebec, 1853 ***5704.8*** *p103*
Carr, William; St. John, N.B., 1853 ***5704.8*** *p99*
Carr, William 3 mos; St. John, N.B., 1850 ***5704.8*** *p67*
Carr, William 4; St. John, N.B., 1848 ***5704.8*** *p43*
Carr, William 20; Philadelphia, 1803 ***53.26*** *p11*
Carr, William 20; Philadelphia, 1859 ***5704.8*** *p141*
Carraghan, Henry; Quebec, 1847 ***5704.8*** *p6*
Carraghan, Nancy; Quebec, 1847 ***5704.8*** *p6*
Carragher, Patrick; America, 1742 ***4971*** *p25*
Carragrancio, Mr. 50; New Orleans, 1839 ***778.5*** *p97*
Carrall, Dennis; New York, NY, 1811 ***2859.11*** *p9*
Carrall, John; New York, NY, 1811 ***2859.11*** *p9*
Carran, Thomas; America, 1739 ***4971*** *p68*
Carraway, Joane; Virginia, 1641 ***6219*** *p185*
Carraway, Jon.; Virginia, 1642 ***6219*** *p198*
Carre, Felix 28; New Orleans, 1822 ***778.5*** *p97*
Carre, John; Virginia, 1642 ***6219*** *p186*
Carre, John 18; Philadelphia, 1864 ***5704.8*** *p155*
Carrel, John 25; Philadelphia, 1774 ***1219.7*** *p228*
Carren, John; St. John, N.B., 1847 ***5704.8*** *p9*
Carrere, Mr. 27; America, 1837 ***778.5*** *p97*
Carrere, F. 21; Louisiana, 1822 ***778.5*** *p97*
Carrere, John 37; New Orleans, 1838 ***778.5*** *p97*
Carrere, Marie 28; New Orleans, 1839 ***778.5*** *p97*
Carrew, Mr.; Grenada, 1774 ***1219.7*** *p210*
Carrick, Mr.; Tobago, W. Indies, 1775 ***1219.7*** *p265*
Carrick, Bryan; America, 1736 ***4971*** *p44*
Carrick, Bryan; America, 1737 ***4971*** *p45*
Carrick, John 31; New York, 1775 ***1219.7*** *p269*
Carrick, William; Colorado, 1844 ***9678.1*** *p157*
Carrie, Gabriel 27; New Orleans, 1839 ***778.5*** *p97*
Carrier, Jean 30; America, 1837 ***778.5*** *p97*
Carrier, M. 23; New Orleans, 1835 ***778.5*** *p98*
Carrier, Thomas; Virginia, 1750 ***3690.1*** *p38*
Carrier, Thomas; Virginia, 1751 ***1219.7*** *p2*
Carrier, Thomas 24; New Orleans, 1835 ***778.5*** *p98*
Carrier, William; Illinois, 1884 ***5012.37*** *p60*
Carrier, William W.; Arkansas, 1918 ***95.2*** *p26*
Carriere, Mr. 36; New Orleans, 1838 ***778.5*** *p98*
Carriere, Mrs. 20; New Orleans, 1838 ***778.5*** *p98*
Carriere, C. 5; New Orleans, 1838 ***778.5*** *p98*
Carriere, Emile 2; New Orleans, 1838 ***778.5*** *p98*
Carriere, Emma 4 mos; New Orleans, 1838 ***778.5*** *p98*
Carriere, Jules 4; New Orleans, 1838 ***778.5*** *p98*
Carrigan, Andrew; New York, NY, 1816 ***2859.11*** *p27*
Carrigan, Andrew Lambert; Arkansas, 1918 ***95.2*** *p26*
Carrigan, Ann; St. John, N.B., 1848 ***5704.8*** *p47*
Carrigan, James; America, 1736-1743 ***4971*** *p57*
Carrigan, James; America, 1864 ***5704.8*** *p189*
Carrigan, James; New York, NY, 1811 ***2859.11*** *p9*
Carrigan, Jane 19; Quebec, 1855 ***5704.8*** *p126*
Carrigan, John; Philadelphia, 1864 ***5704.8*** *p179*
Carrigan, John; Wisconsin, n.d. ***9675.5*** *p49*
Carrigan, John Hoseph; Kansas, 1916 ***6013.40*** *p15*
Carrigan, Joseph; Philadelphia, 1864 ***5704.8*** *p179*
Carrigan, Lakey; New York, NY, 1864 ***5704.8*** *p174*
Carrigan, Martha; New York, NY, 1866 ***5704.8*** *p212*
Carrigan, Mary; Philadelphia, 1865 ***5704.8*** *p180*
Carrigan, Mary; Philadelphia, 1868 ***5704.8*** *p230*
Carrigan, Mary Jane 2; St. John, N.B., 1848 ***5704.8*** *p47*
Carrigan, Matty 6 mos; St. John, N.B., 1848 ***5704.8*** *p47*
Carrigan, Patk; New York, NY, 1816 ***2859.11*** *p27*
Carrigan, Rosanna 19; Philadelphia, 1858 ***5704.8*** *p138*
Carrigan, Theresa 20; Massachusetts, 1848 ***5881.1*** *p25*
Carrigan, Wm.; New York, NY, 1811 ***2859.11*** *p9*
Carrill, Benjamin; Virginia, 1638 ***6219*** *p118*
*Wife:*Elizabeth
Carrill, Elizabeth *SEE* Carrill, Benjamin
Carrill, Henry; Virginia, 1638 ***6219*** *p118*
Carrillo, . . . 26; New Orleans, 1862 ***543.30*** *p452*
Carrillo, Pedro; Nevada, 1872 ***2764.35*** *p10*
Carrin, Jos. C. 22; Louisiana, 1820 ***778.5*** *p98*
Carrogan, Ann 35; Massachusetts, 1847 ***5881.1*** *p12*
Carrogan, Mary 1; Massachusetts, 1847 ***5881.1*** *p20*
Carrogan, Pat. 10; Massachusetts, 1847 ***5881.1*** *p24*
Carrol, Brian; America, 1739 ***4971*** *p52*
Carrol, Dennis; New York, NY, 1839 ***8208.4*** *p95*
Carrol, Edward; Illinois, 1872 ***5012.39*** *p26*
Carrol, Thomas 18; Maryland, 1773 ***1219.7*** *p173*
Carrole, James; Quebec, 1850 ***5704.8*** *p67*
Carroll, Ann 27; Massachusetts, 1849 ***5881.1*** *p13*
Carroll, Bridget 25; Massachusetts, 1847 ***5881.1*** *p13*
Carroll, Bridget 30; Massachusetts, 1849 ***5881.1*** *p13*
Carroll, Catharine 11; Massachusetts, 1849 ***5881.1*** *p14*
Carroll, Catherine; America, 1743 ***4971*** *p18*
Carroll, Cornelius 25; Massachusetts, 1847 ***5881.1*** *p14*
Carroll, Edward 3; Massachusetts, 1849 ***5881.1*** *p16*
Carroll, Elizabeth; America, 1739 ***4971*** *p47*
Carroll, Elizabeth; America, 1741 ***4971*** *p49*
Carroll, Ellen 26; Massachusetts, 1849 ***5881.1*** *p16*
Carroll, James; America, 1741 ***4971*** *p23*
Carroll, James; Boston, 1833-1841 ***7036*** *p124*
Carroll, James 22; Massachusetts, 1847 ***5881.1*** *p17*
Carroll, James 30; Massachusetts, 1847 ***5881.1*** *p17*
Carroll, James 32; New Orleans, 1862 ***543.30*** *p375C*
Carroll, James 32; New Orleans, 1862 ***543.30*** *p453*
Carroll, Jane; America, 1736 ***4971*** *p44*
Carroll, John; America, 1741 ***4971*** *p10*
Carroll, John; America, 1741 ***4971*** *p94*
Carroll, John; America, 1867 ***5704.8*** *p222*
Carroll, John; Illinois, 1888 ***5012.39*** *p122*
Carroll, John; Kansas, 1874 ***5240.1*** *p8*
Carroll, John; New York, NY, 1838 ***8208.4*** *p73*
Carroll, John; St. John, N.B., 1847 ***5704.8*** *p21*
Carroll, John; United States or West Indies, 1736 ***3690.1*** *p38*
Carroll, John 5 mos; Massachusetts, 1849 ***5881.1*** *p19*
Carroll, John 22; Maryland, 1774 ***1219.7*** *p230*
Carroll, John 30; Massachusetts, 1849 ***5881.1*** *p18*
Carroll, John 35; Massachusetts, 1847 ***5881.1*** *p17*
Carroll, Joseph; New York, NY, 1834 ***8208.4*** *p1*
Carroll, Kate 18; Massachusetts, 1849 ***5881.1*** *p20*
Carroll, Margaret 22; Quebec, 1867 ***5704.8*** *p168*
Carroll, Mary; America, 1737 ***4971*** *p12*
Carroll, Mary; New York, NY, 1816 ***2859.11*** *p27*
Carroll, Mary; Philadelphia, 1864 ***5704.8*** *p177*
Carroll, Mary 5; Massachusetts, 1849 ***5881.1*** *p21*
Carroll, Mary 11; Massachusetts, 1850 ***5881.1*** *p23*
Carroll, Mary 22; Massachusetts, 1849 ***5881.1*** *p22*
Carroll, Mary 30; Massachusetts, 1849 ***5881.1*** *p20*
Carroll, Mathew 20; Massachusetts, 1847 ***5881.1*** *p20*
Carroll, Michael; Illinois, 1851 ***2896.5*** *p7*
Carroll, Michael; Illinois, 1888 ***5012.39*** *p122*
Carroll, Michael; New York, NY, 1815 ***2859.11*** *p27*
Carroll, Norah Dayton; Montreal, 1822 ***7603*** *p81*
Carroll, Pat 25; Massachusetts, 1847 ***5881.1*** *p23*
Carroll, Patrick; America, 1741 ***4971*** *p16*
Carroll, Patrick; America, 1743 ***4971*** *p11*
Carroll, Patrick; America, 1743 ***4971*** *p95*
Carroll, Patrick; America, 1841 ***7036*** *p121*
Carroll, Patrick; New York, NY, 1816 ***2859.11*** *p27*
Carroll, Patrick; New York, NY, 1840 ***8208.4*** *p107*
Carroll, Patrick; New York, NY, 1852 ***2896.5*** *p7*
Carroll, Patrick 18; Jamaica, 1738 ***3690.1*** *p38*
Carroll, Peter; Montreal, 1822 ***7603*** *p89*
Carroll, Reuben N.; Illinois, 1867 ***2896.5*** *p7*
Carroll, Richard; America, 1743 ***4971*** *p32*
Carroll, Rose 7; Massachusetts, 1850 ***5881.1*** *p25*
Carroll, Terence; New York, NY, 1816 ***2859.11*** *p27*
Carroll, Thomas; America, 1738 ***4971*** *p14*
Carroll, Thomas; America, 1741 ***4971*** *p23*
Carroll, Thomas; Arizona, 1897 ***9228.30*** *p2*
Carroll, Thomas; Illinois, 1882 ***2896.5*** *p7*
Carroll, Thomas; New York, NY, 1852 ***2896.5*** *p7*
Carroll, Thomas; Philadelphia, 1864 ***5704.8*** *p177*
Carroll, Thomas; Quebec, 1823 ***7603*** *p73*
Carroll, Thomas; Washington, 1859-1920 ***2872.1*** *p7*
Carroll, Thomas 33; Massachusetts, 1847 ***5881.1*** *p25*
Carroll, Timothy; America, 1742-1743 ***4971*** *p42*
Carroll, Timothy; Illinois, 1860 ***2896.5*** *p7*
Carroll, Walter; Illinois, 1870 ***2896.5*** *p7*
Carroll, William; New York, NY, 1852 ***2896.5*** *p7*
Carroll, William; Philadelphia, 1816 ***2859.11*** *p27*
Carroll, William 25; Massachusetts, 1849 ***5881.1*** *p26*
Carroll, William 29; Philadelphia, 1775 ***1219.7*** *p255*
Carroll, William-Henry; Quebec, 1825 ***7603*** *p93*
Carrolton, Catharine; Philadelphia, 1849 ***5704.8*** *p53*
Carrolton, Catherine; Philadelphia, 1849 ***53.26*** *p11*
Carron, Hugh; Virginia, 1639 ***6219*** *p152*
Carrow, Jon.; Virginia, 1643 ***6219*** *p200*
Carruthers, Jno; Ohio, 1841 ***9892.11*** *p8*
Carruthers, John; North Carolina, 1710-1751 ***1639.20*** *p40*
Carruthers, John; Ohio, 1844 ***9892.11*** *p8*
Carry, James; New York, NY, 1865 ***5704.8*** *p195*
Carry, James 23; St. John, N.B., 1858 ***5704.8*** *p140*
Carry, John 24; Virginia, 1773 ***1219.7*** *p168*
Carry, M. Margaret 22; Quebec, 1863 ***5704.8*** *p154*
Carry, Nancy 20; Quebec, 1863 ***5704.8*** *p153*
Carry, William M. 20; Quebec, 1863 ***5704.8*** *p153*
Carse, Moses; Virginia, 1643 ***6219*** *p33*
Carse, William; New York, NY, 1811 ***2859.11*** *p9*
Carsenelle, Alexander 39; New Orleans, 1863 ***543.30*** *p463*
Carsin, Charles 60; Philadelphia, 1854 ***5704.8*** *p117*
Carsin, Easter 20; Philadelphia, 1854 ***5704.8*** *p117*
Carsin, Jane 19; Philadelphia, 1854 ***5704.8*** *p117*
Carsin, Rachel 50; Philadelphia, 1854 ***5704.8*** *p117*
Carsley, Joseph 19; Maryland, 1774 ***1219.7*** *p208*
Carslile, Hugh; New York, NY, 1816 ***2859.11*** *p27*

Carsner, Arthur; Washington, 1859-1920 ***2872.1*** *p7*
Carsner, F. M.; Washington, 1859-1920 ***2872.1*** *p7*
Carson, Andrew; Philadelphia, 1867 ***5704.8*** *p205*
Carson, Ann 2; Quebec, 1850 ***5704.8*** *p70*
Carson, Ann Jane 9; Philadelphia, 1851 ***5704.8*** *p70*
Carson, Anne; Philadelphia, 1864 ***5704.8*** *p187*
Carson, Aurora; Washington, 1859-1920 ***2872.1*** *p7*
Carson, Caldwell; Quebec, 1851 ***5704.8*** *p75*
Carson, Charles; New York, NY, 1864 ***5704.8*** *p181*
Carson, Christophe; Montreal, 1770 ***7603*** *p75*
Carson, David 40; New York, 1775 ***1219.7*** *p268*
With wife
With 4 children
Carson, Ed William; Washington, 1859-1920 ***2872.1*** *p7*
Carson, Eino; Washington, 1859-1920 ***2872.1*** *p7*
Carson, Elizabeth 9; Massachusetts, 1850 ***5881.1*** *p16*
Carson, Francis 6 mos; Quebec, 1850 ***5704.8*** *p70*
Carson, George; New York, NY, 1811 ***2859.11*** *p9*
Carson, George; New York, NY, 1816 ***2859.11*** *p27*
Carson, George; Philadelphia, 1867 ***5704.8*** *p205*
Carson, Helen 4; Massachusetts, 1850 ***5881.1*** *p17*
Carson, Helen 38; Massachusetts, 1850 ***5881.1*** *p17*
Carson, James; New York, NY, 1811 ***2859.11*** *p9*
Carson, James; New York, NY, 1816 ***2859.11*** *p27*
Carson, James; Philadelphia, 1867 ***5704.8*** *p216*
Carson, James; St. John, N.B., 1847 ***5704.8*** *p25*
Carson, James 12; Charleston, SC, 1774 ***1639.20*** *p41*
Carson, James 20; Philadelphia, 1859 ***5704.8*** *p142*
Carson, Jane; New York, NY, 1864 ***5704.8*** *p169*
Carson, Jane; Philadelphia, 1851 ***5704.8*** *p76*
Carson, Jane; Philadelphia, 1852 ***5704.8*** *p89*
Carson, Jane; Philadelphia, 1867 ***5704.8*** *p205*
Carson, Jane; Quebec, 1850 ***5704.8*** *p70*
Carson, Janet 9 mos; Massachusetts, 1850 ***5881.1*** *p19*
Carson, John; New York, NY, 1811 ***2859.11*** *p9*
Carson, John 7; Massachusetts, 1850 ***5881.1*** *p19*
Carson, John 38; Massachusetts, 1850 ***5881.1*** *p19*
Carson, Julian 44; New Orleans, 1863 ***543.30*** *p464*
Carson, Margaret; New York, NY, 1869 ***5704.8*** *p232*
Carson, Maria; Philadelphia, 1864 ***5704.8*** *p187*
Carson, Mary; Philadelphia, 1852 ***5704.8*** *p89*
Carson, Mary; Quebec, 1851 ***5704.8*** *p75*
Carson, Nick; Washington, 1859-1920 ***2872.1*** *p7*
Carson, P.; Arkansas, 1918 ***95.2*** *p64*
Carson, Pete; Arkansas, 1918 ***95.2*** *p27*
Carson, Robert; Mobile, AL, 1766 ***1219.7*** *p118*
Carson, Robert; Philadelphia, 1864 ***5704.8*** *p174*
Carson, Robert 20; Grenada, 1774 ***1219.7*** *p238*
Carson, Robert 21; Quebec, 1856 ***5704.8*** *p129*
Carson, Samuel; Philadelphia, 1864 ***5704.8*** *p187*
Carson, Sarah; St. John, N.B., 1847 ***5704.8*** *p25*
Carson, Thomas; St. John, N.B., 1847 ***5704.8*** *p21*
Carson, William; Charleston, SC, 1824 ***1639.20*** *p41*
Carson, William; Philadelphia, 1864 ***5704.8*** *p183*
Carson, William 11; Massachusetts, 1849 ***5881.1*** *p26*
Carson, William 23; Philadelphia, 1858 ***5704.8*** *p139*
Carswel, Agnes 17; Baltimore, 1775 ***1219.7*** *p269*
Carswell, John 27; Kansas, 1871 ***5240.1*** *p51*
Carswell, John 44; Maryland, 1775 ***1219.7*** *p268*
Cart, Abraham 32; New Orleans, 1836 ***778.5*** *p98*
Carta, Giovanni; Iowa, 1866-1943 ***123.54*** *p13*
Cartan, Patrick; New York, NY, 1811 ***2859.11*** *p9*
With family
Cartar, Wm.; Virginia, 1646 ***6219*** *p242*
Cartella, Mr. 30; New Orleans, 1827 ***778.5*** *p98*
Carten, James; St. John, N.B., 1851 ***5704.8*** *p72*
Carteo, Lionoldo 65; Arizona, 1909 ***9228.40*** *p10*
Carter, Albert; Washington, 1859-1920 ***2872.1*** *p7*
Carter, Alicia 40; Massachusetts, 1849 ***5881.1*** *p13*
Carter, Anne; Quebec, 1847 ***5704.8*** *p37*
Carter, Armistead; Washington, 1859-1920 ***2872.1*** *p7*
Carter, Barb.; Virginia, 1649 ***6219*** *p253*
Carter, Biddy; Quebec, 1847 ***5704.8*** *p37*
Carter, Catherine; Quebec, 1847 ***5704.8*** *p37*
Carter, Charles; Quebec, 1847 ***5704.8*** *p37*
Carter, Charles; Virginia, 1643 ***6219*** *p202*
Carter, Dennis 22; Maryland, 1775 ***1219.7*** *p250*
Carter, Edward 18; Antigua (Antego), 1736 ***3690.1*** *p38*
Carter, Elizabeth Lavinia; Washington, 1859-1920 ***2872.1*** *p7*
Carter, Erasmus; Virginia, 1635 ***6219*** *p5*
*Wife:*Phillis
Carter, George; Illinois, 1893 ***2896.5*** *p7*
Carter, Henry; Virginia, 1624 ***6219*** *p7*
Carter, Henry; Virginia, 1639 ***6219*** *p155*
Carter, Hester; Virginia, 1641 ***6219*** *p184*
Carter, Hugh 4; Massachusetts, 1850 ***5881.1*** *p17*
Carter, J. A.; Washington, 1859-1920 ***2872.1*** *p7*
Carter, J. Andrew; Washington, 1859-1920 ***2872.1*** *p7*
Carter, Jacob 27; Philadelphia, 1774 ***1219.7*** *p182*
Carter, James; North Carolina, 1736 ***3690.1*** *p38*
Carter, James; Ohio, 1839 ***9892.11*** *p8*
Carter, James; Washington, 1859-1920 ***2872.1*** *p7*
Carter, James 17; Virginia, 1720 ***3690.1*** *p38*
Carter, John; Illinois, 1860 ***5012.38*** *p98*
Carter, John; Iroquois Co., IL, 1894 ***3455.1*** *p10*
Carter, John; St. John, N.B., 1851 ***5704.8*** *p78*
Carter, John; Virginia, 1636 ***6219*** *p26*
Carter, John; Virginia, 1644 ***6219*** *p231*
Carter, John 1; Massachusetts, 1850 ***5881.1*** *p19*
Carter, John 17; Virginia, 1721 ***3690.1*** *p39*
Carter, John 18; South Carolina, 1723 ***3690.1*** *p39*
Carter, John 30; New York, 1774 ***1219.7*** *p197*
Carter, John 46; Kansas, 1885 ***5240.1*** *p67*
Carter, John 46; Kansas, 1885 ***5240.1*** *p68*
Carter, Joseph 26; Maryland, 1775 ***1219.7*** *p247*
Carter, Katherine Lavinia; Washington, 1859-1920 ***2872.1*** *p7*
Carter, Laurance 21; Jamaica, 1725 ***3690.1*** *p39*
Carter, Margaret; Quebec, 1847 ***5704.8*** *p37*
Carter, Mary; Quebec, 1847 ***5704.8*** *p37*
Carter, Mary Jane 24; Massachusetts, 1850 ***5881.1*** *p23*
Carter, Michael; Iroquois Co., IL, 1892 ***3455.1*** *p10*
Carter, Mick; Quebec, 1847 ***5704.8*** *p37*
Carter, Nath.; Virginia, 1637 ***6219*** *p117*
Carter, Nora Crosland; Washington, 1859-1920 ***2872.1*** *p7*
Carter, Patt; Quebec, 1847 ***5704.8*** *p37*
Carter, Phillis *SEE* Carter, Erasmus
Carter, Rich.; Virginia, 1637 ***6219*** *p11*
Carter, Richard; Virginia, 1642 ***6219*** *p190*
Carter, Richard; Virginia, 1643 ***6219*** *p202*
Carter, Richard 27; North America, 1774 ***1219.7*** *p200*
Carter, Robert; Illinois, 1904 ***5012.39*** *p53*
Carter, Robert; Illinois, 1904 ***5012.40*** *p80*
Carter, Robert; New York, NY, 1815 ***2859.11*** *p27*
Carter, Robert 22; Jamaica, 1736 ***3690.1*** *p39*
Carter, Tho.; Virginia, 1637 ***6219*** *p115*
Carter, Tho.; Virginia, 1638 ***6219*** *p150*
Carter, Thomas; Quebec, 1847 ***5704.8*** *p37*
Carter, Thomas; Virginia, 1638 ***6219*** *p180*
Carter, Thomas 22; Maryland, 1775 ***1219.7*** *p267*
Carter, Thomas 26; Virginia, 1774 ***1219.7*** *p241*
Carter, Timothy 22; Jamaica, 1731 ***3690.1*** *p39*
Carter, William; Virginia, 1636 ***6219*** *p76*
Carter, William; Virginia, 1638 ***6219*** *p145*
Carter, William; Virginia, 1648 ***6219*** *p245*
Carter, William 16; Maryland, 1733 ***3690.1*** *p39*
Carter, William 18; Maryland, 1722 ***3690.1*** *p39*
Carter, William 25; Philadelphia, 1774 ***1219.7*** *p196*
Carter, William 30; Jamaica, 1730 ***3690.1*** *p39*
Carteres, J. 37; New Orleans, 1826 ***778.5*** *p98*
Carters, Randle 20; America, 1700 ***2212*** *p33*
Cartey, Thomas 23; Maryland, 1736 ***3690.1*** *p39*
Carthew, Edmund 18; Maryland, 1774 ***1219.7*** *p181*
Carthy, Ann; America, 1737 ***4971*** *p13*
Carthy, Charles; America, 1742 ***4971*** *p49*
Carthy, Charles; America, 1742 ***4971*** *p50*
Carthy, Daniel; America, 1736-1743 ***4971*** *p58*
Carthy, Ellen 9; Massachusetts, 1850 ***5881.1*** *p16*
Carthy, Florence; America, 1739 ***4971*** *p47*
Carthy, Florence; America, 1741 ***4971*** *p49*
Carthy, Honora 12; Massachusetts, 1849 ***5881.1*** *p17*
Carthy, Joan; America, 1737 ***4971*** *p55*
Carthy, Joanna; America, 1736 ***4971*** *p39*
Carthy, John; America, 1741 ***4971*** *p41*
Carthy, John 14; Massachusetts, 1849 ***5881.1*** *p18*
Carthy, Judy 20; Massachusetts, 1849 ***5881.1*** *p18*
Carthy, Mary; America, 1737 ***4971*** *p32*
Carthy, Mary 30; Massachusetts, 1850 ***5881.1*** *p23*
Carthy, Michael 7; Massachusetts, 1850 ***5881.1*** *p22*
Carthy, Pat. 60; Massachusetts, 1849 ***5881.1*** *p24*
Carthy, Patrick 7; Massachusetts, 1850 ***5881.1*** *p24*
Carthy, Tho.; America, 1737 ***4971*** *p32*
Carthy, Timothy; America, 1737-1738 ***4971*** *p39*
Carthy, Timothy; America, 1743 ***4971*** *p32*
Cartier, Jacques; Quebec, 1535 ***9775.5*** *p197*
Cartin, Ann 52; Philadelphia, 1860 ***5704.8*** *p144*
Cartin, Elizabeth 22; St. John, N.B., 1858 ***5704.8*** *p137*
Cartin, Hugh 20; Philadelphia, 1860 ***5704.8*** *p144*
Cartin, Hugh 54; Philadelphia, 1860 ***5704.8*** *p144*
Cartin, Jane 16; Philadelphia, 1860 ***5704.8*** *p144*
Cartin, Margaret 16; St. John, N.B., 1853 ***5704.8*** *p109*
Cartin, Mary *SEE* Cartin, Nancy
Cartin, Mary; Philadelphia, 1847 ***5704.8*** *p5*
Cartin, Mary 18; Philadelphia, 1860 ***5704.8*** *p144*
Cartin, Mary Ann 28 *SEE* Cartin, Michael
Cartin, Michael 28; Philadelphia, 1833-1834 ***53.26*** *p11*
*Relative:*Mary Ann 28
Cartin, Nancy; Philadelphia, 1847 ***53.26*** *p11*
*Relative:*Mary
Cartin, Nancy; Philadelphia, 1847 ***5704.8*** *p5*
Cartin, Rosey 20; St. John, N.B., 1853 ***5704.8*** *p109*
Cartin, Susan 30; Philadelphia, 1860 ***5704.8*** *p144*
Cartine, Betty; St. John, N.B., 1849 ***5704.8*** *p49*
Cartis, William 25; Virginia, 1773 ***1219.7*** *p171*
Cartlidge, Ann 22; Jamaica, 1730 ***3690.1*** *p289*
Cartly, Alexander *SEE* Cartly, Mary
Cartly, Alexander; Philadelphia, 1850 ***5704.8*** *p69*
Cartly, Catherine 6 *SEE* Cartly, Mary
Cartly, Catherine 6; Philadelphia, 1850 ***5704.8*** *p69*
Cartly, Margaret 8 *SEE* Cartly, Mary
Cartly, Margaret 8; Philadelphia, 1850 ***5704.8*** *p69*
Cartly, Mary *SEE* Cartly, Mary
Cartly, Mary; Philadelphia, 1850 ***53.26*** *p11*
*Relative:*Alexander
*Relative:*Samuel 10
*Relative:*Margaret 8
*Relative:*Catherine 6
*Relative:*Mary
Cartly, Mary; Philadelphia, 1850 ***5704.8*** *p69*
Cartly, Samuel 10 *SEE* Cartly, Mary
Cartly, Samuel 10; Philadelphia, 1850 ***5704.8*** *p69*
Cartney, Terrence 37; Massachusetts, 1847 ***5881.1*** *p25*
Carton, Catherine; St. John, N.B., 1847 ***5704.8*** *p25*
Carton, David 21; St. John, N.B., 1853 ***5704.8*** *p109*
Carton, Ellen; St. John, N.B., 1847 ***5704.8*** *p25*
Carton, James; St. John, N.B., 1851 ***5704.8*** *p77*
Carton, Jane 22; Philadelphia, 1854 ***5704.8*** *p120*
Carton, John; America, 1742 ***4971*** *p24*
Carton, John 35; Philadelphia, 1803 ***53.26*** *p11*
Carton, Mary; St. John, N.B., 1850 ***5704.8*** *p61*
Carton, Patrick; St. John, N.B., 1851 ***5704.8*** *p77*
Carton, Peter; America, 1738 ***4971*** *p36*
Cartright, Jon.; Virginia, 1642 ***6219*** *p192*
Cartwright, Henry; Virginia, 1652 ***6251*** *p20*
Cartwright, James 30; Virginia, 1700 ***2212*** *p32*
Cartwright, Jno 19; Maryland or Virginia, 1699 ***2212*** *p24*
Cartwright, Joseph; Cincinnati, 1827 ***8582.1*** *p6*
Cartwright, Tho.; Virginia, 1639 ***6219*** *p162*
Cartwright, Thomas 14; Pennsylvania, 1738 ***3690.1*** *p39*
Cartwright, Thomas 16; Philadelphia, 1774 ***1219.7*** *p197*
Cartwright, William 23; Jamaica, 1774 ***1219.7*** *p223*
Carty, Bridget 12; Massachusetts, 1849 ***5881.1*** *p13*
Carty, Catharine 3; Massachusetts, 1848 ***5881.1*** *p14*
Carty, Catherine; America, 1738 ***4971*** *p52*
Carty, Daniel; South Carolina, 1824 ***1639.20*** *p40*
Carty, Dennis; America, 1741 ***4971*** *p40*
Carty, Dennis 9; Massachusetts, 1848 ***5881.1*** *p15*
Carty, Dennis 28; Massachusetts, 1849 ***5881.1*** *p15*
Carty, Ellen 14; Massachusetts, 1848 ***5881.1*** *p15*
Carty, Ellen 20; Massachusetts, 1850 ***5881.1*** *p16*
Carty, Gilbert 21; Maryland, 1775 ***1219.7*** *p264*
Carty, John 9; Massachusetts, 1850 ***5881.1*** *p19*
Carty, John 10; Massachusetts, 1849 ***5881.1*** *p18*
Carty, Julia 40; Massachusetts, 1848 ***5881.1*** *p17*
Carty, Margaret 11; Massachusetts, 1848 ***5881.1*** *p20*
Carty, Mary 21; Massachusetts, 1849 ***5881.1*** *p21*
Carty, Pat. 30; Massachusetts, 1847 ***5881.1*** *p23*
Carty, Pat. 40; Massachusetts, 1847 ***5881.1*** *p23*
Carty, Rice 18; Jamaica, 1736 ***3690.1*** *p39*
Carty, Thomas 14; Massachusetts, 1850 ***5881.1*** *p26*
Carty, Tim. 7; Massachusetts, 1848 ***5881.1*** *p25*
Carty, Tim 18; Massachusetts, 1847 ***5881.1*** *p25*
Carty, William; America, 1741 ***4971*** *p16*
Caruth, John; Charleston, SC, 1805 ***1639.20*** *p40*
Caruth, Peter; Charleston, SC, 1797 ***1639.20*** *p40*
Caruthers, Archibald; New York, NY, 1816 ***2859.11*** *p27*
Caruthers, Jane; New York, NY, 1816 ***2859.11*** *p27*
Caruthers, John; New York, NY, 1816 ***2859.11*** *p27*
Caruthers, M.; New York, NY, 1816 ***2859.11*** *p27*
Carvalho, Antoni; Arkansas, 1918 ***95.2*** *p27*
Carvedo, Anton; Virginia, 1855 ***4626.16*** *p15*
Carvel, Robert; Antigua (Antego), 1754 ***1219.7*** *p29*
Carvel, William; Antigua (Antego), 1773 ***1219.7*** *p167*
Carver, Agnes; New York, NY, 1811 ***2859.11*** *p9*
Carver, Eliza. *SEE* Carver, Lawr.
Carver, John 26; Georgia, 1774 ***1219.7*** *p188*
Carver, Lawr.; Virginia, 1643 ***6219*** *p203*
*Wife:*Eliza.
Carver, Thomas 16; Pennsylvania, Virginia or Maryland, 1723 ***3690.1*** *p39*
Carvill, Benjamin 20; Virginia, 1720 ***3690.1*** *p39*
Carwele, Henry 15; Philadelphia, 1774 ***1219.7*** *p232*
Carwell, James 35; Savannah, GA, 1733 ***4719.17*** *p310*
*Wife:*Margaret 32
Carwell, Margaret 32 *SEE* Carwell, James
Cary, George Thomas; St. John, N.B., 1847 ***5704.8*** *p33*
Cary, Margaret; Annapolis, MD, 1742 ***4971*** *p93*
Cary, Margaret 21; Massachusetts, 1849 ***5881.1*** *p95*
Cary, Michael 23; Maryland, 1775 ***1219.7*** *p268*
Cary, Richard; Virginia, 1639 ***6219*** *p184*
Casagrande, Maria 64; New York, NY, 1893 ***9026.4*** *p41*
Casale, Francesco; Iowa, 1866-1943 ***123.54*** *p13*
Casalotto, Carmelo; Iowa, 1866-1943 ***123.54*** *p57*
Casamajor, Mr.; Port uncertain, 1839 ***778.5*** *p98*
Casan, Michael 23; Maryland, 1774 ***1219.7*** *p244*
Casana, G. Batta 26; New York, NY, 1893 ***9026.4*** *p41*

Casanova, Giac 23; New York, NY, 1893 ***9026.4*** *p41*
Casara, M. 50; Arizona, 1909 ***9228.40*** *p10*
Casassa, Jiuseppe; Iowa, 1866-1943 ***123.54*** *p57*
Casat, Anders Martiniano; America, 1836 ***6410.32*** *p124*
Casat, Bernhardina Aurora Fredrika; Boston, 1835 ***6410.32*** *p124*
*Sister:*Eufemia A. Almanzora
Casat, Eufemia A. Almanzora *SEE* Casat, Bernhardina Aurora Fredrika
Cascia, Esidore; Arkansas, 1918 ***95.2*** *p27*
Casciato, Antonio; Arkansas, 1918 ***95.2*** *p27*
Cascill, John; Virginia, 1642 ***6219*** *p198*
Cascioli, Gaetano; Arkansas, 1918 ***95.2*** *p27*
Casdorf, Lewis; Illinois, 1894 ***5012.39*** *p53*
Case, Allen; Arizona, 1897 ***9228.30*** *p2*
Case, Chadwell 21; Jamaica, 1733 ***3690.1*** *p40*
Case, Mary; Virginia, 1698 ***2212*** *p17*
Caseaine, Henri 55; America, 1838 ***778.5*** *p98*
Caseame, Henri 55; America, 1838 ***778.5*** *p98*
Casearano, Nick; Washington, 1859-1920 ***2872.1*** *p7*
Caselle, Mr. 19; America, 1838 ***778.5*** *p98*
Caselly, Patrick; New York, NY, 1816 ***2859.11*** *p27*
Casenave, J. 17; New Orleans, 1839 ***778.5*** *p99*
Caseris, Henry 46; America, 1837 ***778.5*** *p99*
Caseris, Louis 20; America, 1820-1839 ***778.5*** *p99*
Caserta, Charles Dominick; Arkansas, 1918 ***95.2*** *p27*
Caset, Ise. Che. Andre; America, 1836 ***6410.32*** *p124*
Caset, Ise. Che. Andre 38; Massachusetts, 1860 ***6410.32*** *p108*
Casey, Mr.; New York, NY, 1815 ***2859.11*** *p27*
Casey, Alexander; New York, NY, 1871 ***2764.35*** *p11*
Casey, Bridget 10; Massachusetts, 1849 ***5881.1*** *p13*
Casey, Bridget 18; Massachusetts, 1849 ***5881.1*** *p13*
Casey, Bridget 30; Massachusetts, 1850 ***5881.1*** *p14*
Casey, Catherine; America, 1735-1743 ***4971*** *p78*
Casey, Catherine; Philadelphia, 1849 ***5704.8*** *p54*
Casey, Cath'ine 25; Massachusetts, 1849 ***5881.1*** *p14*
Casey, Cath'rine 20; Massachusetts, 1849 ***5881.1*** *p14*
Casey, Daniel; New York, NY, 1852 ***2764.35*** *p15*
Casey, David; California, 1865 ***3840.1*** *p16*
Casey, Edmond; Quebec, 1789 ***7603*** *p80*
Casey, Edmund 3; Massachusetts, 1850 ***5881.1*** *p16*
Casey, Edward 8; Massachusetts, 1849 ***5881.1*** *p16*
Casey, Ellen 20; Massachusetts, 1850 ***5881.1*** *p16*
Casey, Henry; New York, NY, 1838 ***8208.4*** *p70*
Casey, Honora 16; Massachusetts, 1849 ***5881.1*** *p17*
Casey, Hugh; St. John, N.B., 1848 ***5704.8*** *p45*
Casey, James; New York, NY, 1838 ***8208.4*** *p66*
Casey, James 32; Massachusetts, 1849 ***5881.1*** *p18*
Casey, Jane 60; Massachusetts, 1849 ***5881.1*** *p18*
Casey, Johanna 55; Massachusetts, 1850 ***5881.1*** *p19*
Casey, John; Kansas, 1858 ***2764.35*** *p12*
Casey, John; New York, NY, 1811 ***2859.11*** *p9*
Casey, John 2; Massachusetts, 1850 ***5881.1*** *p19*
Casey, John 4; Massachusetts, 1849 ***5881.1*** *p18*
Casey, John 21; Maryland, 1774 ***1219.7*** *p192*
Casey, John 25; Massachusetts, 1850 ***5881.1*** *p19*
Casey, John 35; New Orleans, 1863 ***543.30*** *p451*
Casey, Judith 24; Massachusetts, 1849 ***5881.1*** *p18*
Casey, Margaret 25; Massachusetts, 1849 ***5881.1*** *p21*
Casey, Mary; Montreal, 1821 ***7603*** *p81*
Casey, Mary 11; Massachusetts, 1849 ***5881.1*** *p22*
Casey, Mary 22; Massachusetts, 1849 ***5881.1*** *p22*
Casey, Mary 24; Massachusetts, 1849 ***5881.1*** *p22*
Casey, Mary, II 22; Massachusetts, 1850 ***5881.1*** *p22*
Casey, Mary Jane; St. John, N.B., 1847 ***5704.8*** *p20*
Casey, Mathew 20; Massachusetts, 1849 ***5881.1*** *p22*
Casey, Michael 12; Massachusetts, 1849 ***5881.1*** *p22*
Casey, Nora 15; Massachusetts, 1849 ***5881.1*** *p23*
Casey, Pat. 20; Massachusetts, 1849 ***5881.1*** *p24*
Casey, Patrick 30; New Orleans, 1862 ***543.30*** *p459*
Casey, Peggy 22; Massachusetts, 1849 ***5881.1*** *p24*
Casey, Peggy 26; Massachusetts, 1849 ***5881.1*** *p31*
Casey, Peter; New York, NY, 1811 ***2859.11*** *p9*
Casey, Richard; Jamaica, 1757 ***1219.7*** *p58*
Casey, Richard; Jamaica, 1757 ***3690.1*** *p40*
Casey, Roger; Acadia, 1668 ***7603*** *p75*
Casey, Thomas; Maryland, 1833-1841 ***7036*** *p125*
Casey, Thomas; Massachusetts, 1850 ***5881.1*** *p26*
Casey, Thomas; Montreal, 1823 ***7603*** *p91*
Casey, Thomas 5; Massachusetts, 1850 ***5881.1*** *p26*
Casey, Thomas 32; California, 1872 ***2769.3*** *p3*
Casey, Timothy; New York, NY, 1835 ***8208.4*** *p7*
Casey, Timothy 12; Massachusetts, 1849 ***5881.1*** *p25*
Casey, Walter 19; Virginia, 1719 ***3690.1*** *p40*
Casey, William 20; Massachusetts, 1849 ***5881.1*** *p26*
Cash, B. C.; Washington, 1859-1920 ***2872.1*** *p7*
Cash, Denis; New York, NY, 1840 ***8208.4*** *p108*
Casheday, Catherine; St. John, N.B., 1849 ***5704.8*** *p55*
Casheen, Mary; America, 1741 ***4971*** *p16*
Cashell, James 23; Newfoundland, 1789 ***4915.24*** *p56*
Casher, Anne; Philadelphia, 1816 ***2859.11*** *p27*
Casher, Bartholomew; Philadelphia, 1816 ***2859.11*** *p27*
Casher, M.; Philadelphia, 1816 ***2859.11*** *p27*
Casher, Margaret; Philadelphia, 1816 ***2859.11*** *p27*
Cashine, William 33; Maryland, 1774 ***1219.7*** *p204*
Cashman, Mary 30; Massachusetts, 1849 ***5881.1*** *p21*
Cashman, William; New York, NY, 1838 ***8208.4*** *p69*
Casila, E. 30; America, 1837 ***778.5*** *p99*
Casina, George; Arkansas, 1918 ***95.2*** *p27*
Casini, Antonio; Arkansas, 1918 ***95.2*** *p27*
Caskey, Ann 20 *SEE* Caskey, Samuel
Caskey, Ann 47 *SEE* Caskey, Samuel
Caskey, Eliz. 22 *SEE* Caskey, Samuel
Caskey, Elizabeth 34; St. John, N.B., 1859 ***5704.8*** *p141*
Caskey, John 22 *SEE* Caskey, Samuel
Caskey, Martha Jane; Philadelphia, 1850 ***53.26*** *p11*
Caskey, Martha Jane; Philadelphia, 1850 ***5704.8*** *p59*
Caskey, Mary 24 *SEE* Caskey, Samuel
Caskey, Milly 18 *SEE* Caskey, Samuel
Caskey, Samuel 50; Philadelphia, 1833-1834 ***53.26*** *p12*
*Relative:*Ann 47
*Relative:*John 22
*Relative:*Mary 24
*Relative:*Eliz. 22
*Relative:*Ann 20
*Relative:*Milly 18
Caskore, Alexander 11; Quebec, 1856 ***5704.8*** *p130*
Caskore, Ann Jane 9; Quebec, 1856 ***5704.8*** *p130*
Caskore, Catherine 7; Quebec, 1856 ***5704.8*** *p130*
Caskore, Eliza 15; Quebec, 1856 ***5704.8*** *p130*
Caskore, Jane 48; Quebec, 1856 ***5704.8*** *p130*
Caskore, Robert 4; Quebec, 1856 ***5704.8*** *p130*
Caskore, Thomas 50; Quebec, 1856 ***5704.8*** *p130*
Caslar, Lewis; Philadelphia, 1757 ***9973.7*** *p33*
Casley, Henry; Virginia, 1637 ***6219*** *p13*
Caslife, Tho.; Virginia, 1642 ***6219*** *p198*
Casparis, Lorenz; Shreveport, LA, 1879 ***7129*** *p44*
Casper, Marie 27; America, 1837 ***778.5*** *p99*
Caspers, Lawrence; Wisconsin, n.d. ***9675.5*** *p49*
Casperson, Alice Patria; Washington, 1859-1920 ***2872.1*** *p7*
Casperson, John Angel; Arkansas, 1918 ***95.2*** *p27*
Casperson, Olga Christine; Washington, 1859-1920 ***2872.1*** *p7*
Casperson, Peter; Washington, 1859-1920 ***2872.1*** *p8*
Casperson, Tejner; Washington, 1859-1920 ***2872.1*** *p8*
Cass, George 19; Nova Scotia, 1774 ***1219.7*** *p209*
Cass, John 18; Philadelphia, 1774 ***1219.7*** *p228*
Cass, John 44; New Orleans, 1862 ***543.30*** *p457*
Cassady, Anthony; New York, NY, 1816 ***2859.11*** *p27*
Cassady, Bridget 18; Massachusetts, 1850 ***5881.1*** *p14*
Cassady, Catherine; Quebec, 1822 ***7603*** *p93*
Cassady, James; Massachusetts, 1847 ***5881.1*** *p17*
Cassady, James; New York, NY, 1815 ***2859.11*** *p27*
Cassady, Mary 18; Massachusetts, 1847 ***5881.1*** *p20*
Cassady, Mary 20; Massachusetts, 1847 ***5881.1*** *p20*
Cassady, Michael; New York, NY, 1835 ***8208.4*** *p56*
Cassady, Pat. 38; Massachusetts, 1849 ***5881.1*** *p24*
Cassady, Rose 50; Massachusetts, 1849 ***5881.1*** *p25*
Cassady, Thomas 30; Massachusetts, 1849 ***5881.1*** *p26*
Cassady, Wm. 25; New Orleans, 1862 ***543.30*** *p459*
Cassagne, . . .; America, 1837 ***778.5*** *p99*
Cassagne, . . .; Port uncertain, 1839 ***778.5*** *p99*
Cassagne, Mme.; Port uncertain, 1839 ***778.5*** *p100*
Cassagne, Mme. 28; America, 1837 ***778.5*** *p100*
Cassagne, Mr.; America, 1839 ***778.5*** *p99*
Cassagne, Mr.; Port uncertain, 1839 ***778.5*** *p99*
Cassagne, Augustin 18; New Orleans, 1837 ***778.5*** *p99*
Cassagne, Jean Marie 18; America, 1838 ***778.5*** *p99*
Cassagne, Joseph 31; New Orleans, 1839 ***778.5*** *p100*
Cassagne, Noel 23; New Orleans, 1839 ***778.5*** *p100*
Cassagne, Noel 27; New Orleans, 1839 ***778.5*** *p100*
Cassagnet, Jean 26; New Orleans, 1838 ***778.5*** *p100*
Cassaigne, T.C. 22; New Orleans, 1836 ***778.5*** *p100*
Cassal, John 48; New Orleans, 1827 ***778.5*** *p100*
Cassamayon, A. 16; New Orleans, 1839 ***778.5*** *p100*
Cassan, Anty 20; Massachusetts, 1849 ***5881.1*** *p13*
Cassan, Michael 30; Massachusetts, 1847 ***5881.1*** *p20*
Cassan, William; St. John, N.B., 1853 ***5704.8*** *p107*
Cassassanta, Santa 37; New York, NY, 1893 ***9026.4*** *p41*
Cassat, Mr.; Cincinnati, 1841 ***8582.1*** *p46*
Cassat, Anders Martiniano; America, 1836 ***6410.32*** *p124*
Cassat, Bernhardina Aurora Fredrika; Boston, 1835 ***6410.32*** *p124*
*Sister:*Eufemia A. Almanzora
Cassat, Eufemia A. Almanzora *SEE* Cassat, Bernhardina Aurora Fredrika
Cassaty, Thomas 29; New Orleans, 1862 ***543.30*** *p458*
Casse, J. 26; America, 1835 ***778.5*** *p100*
Casse, Jean 28; New Orleans, 1823 ***778.5*** *p100*
Casse, Jean 30; New Orleans, 1822 ***778.5*** *p100*
Casse, Louis 23; America, 1839 ***778.5*** *p100*
Cassedy, Francis; America, 1741 ***4971*** *p37*
Cassedy, John; America, 1738 ***4971*** *p68*
Cassedy, Simon; America, 1742 ***4971*** *p71*
Cassel, Mr.; Quebec, 1815 ***9229.18*** *p74*
Cassel, Carl J.; Iowa, 1846 ***2090*** *p610*
Cassel, Christian; Philadelphia, 1760 ***9973.7*** *p35*
Cassel, Peter; New York, NY, 1838 ***8208.4*** *p86*
Cassell, Humphrey; Virginia, 1636 ***6219*** *p75*
Cassell, Patrick; New York, NY, 1816 ***2859.11*** *p27*
Casselman, . . .; Canada, 1776-1783 ***9786*** *p41*
Casselmann, . . .; Canada, 1776-1783 ***9786*** *p41*
Cassels, George; St. John, N.B., 1866 ***5704.8*** *p166*
Cassels, Patrick; New York, NY, 1838 ***8208.4*** *p69*
Cassels, Robert; Died enroute, 1750 ***1639.20*** *p41*
Cassely, Patrick; Philadelphia, 1811 ***2859.11*** *p9*
Cassen, Thomas; Virginia, 1643 ***6219*** *p204*
Cassey, James 27; St. John, N.B., 1866 ***5704.8*** *p167*
Cassi, Casey; Arkansas, 1918 ***95.2*** *p27*
Cassiday, Jane 26; St. John, N.B., 1854 ***5704.8*** *p119*
Cassiday, Robert; St. John, N.B., 1854 ***5704.8*** *p119*
Cassiday, Rose; America, 1864 ***5704.8*** *p179*
Cassidy, Alice; St. John, N.B., 1847 ***5704.8*** *p9*
Cassidy, Amy; Philadelphia, 1867 ***5704.8*** *p220*
Cassidy, Ann; Philadelphia, 1849 ***53.26*** *p12*
*Relative:*Mary
*Relative:*Roddy
Cassidy, Ann; Philadelphia, 1849 ***5704.8*** *p50*
Cassidy, Barney; America, 1864 ***5704.8*** *p185*
Cassidy, Bernard; Philadelphia, 1866 ***5704.8*** *p205*
Cassidy, Bernard 28; Kansas, 1884 ***5240.1*** *p67*
Cassidy, Bessy 12; St. John, N.B., 1847 ***5704.8*** *p9*
Cassidy, Catherine; New Orleans, 1848 ***5704.8*** *p48*
Cassidy, Catherine; Philadelphia, 1850 ***5704.8*** *p64*
Cassidy, Catherine; St. John, N.B., 1847 ***5704.8*** *p21*
Cassidy, Catherine 9; Philadelphia, 1861 ***5704.8*** *p148*
Cassidy, Charles 13; Quebec, 1847 ***5704.8*** *p27*
Cassidy, Edward; St. John, N.B., 1847 ***5704.8*** *p21*
Cassidy, Edward 20; St. John, N.B., 1856 ***5704.8*** *p131*
Cassidy, Elizabeth 19; St. John, N.B., 1854 ***5704.8*** *p122*
Cassidy, Ellen; St. John, N.B., 1847 ***5704.8*** *p9*
Cassidy, Ellen; St. John, N.B., 1849 ***5704.8*** *p56*
Cassidy, Francis; Baltimore, 1811 ***2859.11*** *p9*
Cassidy, Henry; Philadelphia, 1853 ***5704.8*** *p102*
Cassidy, Hugh; Philadelphia, 1850 ***53.26*** *p12*
*Relative:*Sarah
Cassidy, Hugh; Philadelphia, 1850 ***5704.8*** *p60*
Cassidy, Hugh; Quebec, 1823 ***7603*** *p75*
Cassidy, Hugh; St. John, N.B., 1851 ***5704.8*** *p72*
Cassidy, James; Quebec, 1824 ***7603*** *p68*
Cassidy, James; St. John, N.B., 1847 ***5704.8*** *p9*
Cassidy, James; St. John, N.B., 1853 ***5704.8*** *p107*
Cassidy, Jane; Philadelphia, 1847 ***53.26*** *p12*
Cassidy, Jane; Philadelphia, 1847 ***5704.8*** *p5*
Cassidy, John; Quebec, 1847 ***5704.8*** *p29*
Cassidy, John 4; St. John, N.B., 1847 ***5704.8*** *p9*
Cassidy, John 4; St. John, N.B., 1854 ***5704.8*** *p120*
Cassidy, John 25; Philadelphia, 1853 ***5704.8*** *p109*
Cassidy, Margaret; St. John, N.B., 1847 ***5704.8*** *p33*
Cassidy, Margaret 6; St. John, N.B., 1854 ***5704.8*** *p120*
Cassidy, Margaret 8; St. John, N.B., 1847 ***5704.8*** *p9*
Cassidy, Margaret 21; St. John, N.B., 1854 ***5704.8*** *p119*
Cassidy, Mary *SEE* Cassidy, Ann
Cassidy, Mary; Philadelphia, 1849 ***5704.8*** *p50*
Cassidy, Mary; Philadelphia, 1851 ***5704.8*** *p76*
Cassidy, Mary; Philadelphia, 1853 ***5704.8*** *p103*
Cassidy, Mary; Philadelphia, 1867 ***5704.8*** *p220*
Cassidy, Mary; Philadelphia, 1868 ***5704.8*** *p230*
Cassidy, Mary; St. John, N.B., 1849 ***5704.8*** *p56*
Cassidy, Mary; St. John, N.B., 1852 ***5704.8*** *p93*
Cassidy, Mary A.; Philadelphia, 1865 ***5704.8*** *p196*
Cassidy, Mary Jane; Quebec, 1851 ***5704.8*** *p74*
Cassidy, Maurice; America, 1738 ***4971*** *p72*
Cassidy, Michael; St. John, N.B., 1848 ***5704.8*** *p45*
Cassidy, Nancy 20; Philadelphia, 1854 ***5704.8*** *p116*
Cassidy, Owen; Philadelphia, 1865 ***5704.8*** *p196*
Cassidy, Owen; Philadelphia, 1868 ***5704.8*** *p230*
Cassidy, Patrick; Philadelphia, 1851 ***5704.8*** *p77*
Cassidy, Roddy *SEE* Cassidy, Ann
Cassidy, Roddy; Philadelphia, 1849 ***5704.8*** *p50*
Cassidy, Rose 22; Philadelphia, 1855 ***5704.8*** *p124*
Cassidy, Samuel 2; St. John, N.B., 1854 ***5704.8*** *p120*
Cassidy, Sarah *SEE* Cassidy, Hugh
Cassidy, Sarah; Philadelphia, 1850 ***5704.8*** *p60*
Cassidy, Terry 9; St. John, N.B., 1847 ***5704.8*** *p9*
Cassidy, Thomas; St. John, N.B., 1852 ***5704.8*** *p95*
Cassimus, Victor Marcus; Arkansas, 1918 ***95.2*** *p27*
Cassin, Mr. 27; Port uncertain, 1836 ***778.5*** *p100*
Cassind, Mme.; America, 1838 ***778.5*** *p101*
Cassind, Mr.; America, 1838 ***778.5*** *p100*
Cassind, Pierre Francois 41; America, 1838 ***778.5*** *p101*
Cassoe, Philip; America, 1737 ***4971*** *p59*
Casson, Mr.; New Orleans, 1839 ***778.5*** *p101*
Casson, Ann; Virginia, 1643 ***6219*** *p203*
Casson, Ant. 18; New Orleans, 1837 ***778.5*** *p101*
Casson, Eliza J.; Philadelphia, 1865 ***5704.8*** *p196*
Casson, John 19; Jamaica, 1731 ***3690.1*** *p40*

74 *FOR A COMPLETE EXPLANATION OF ENTRY, SEE "HOW TO READ A CITATION" SECTION*

Casson, Margaret; Philadelphia, 1867 ***5704.8*** *p218*
Casson, P.; New Orleans, 1839 ***778.5*** *p101*
Casson, Thos.; Virginia, 1635 ***6219*** *p69*
Cassos, Chris; Arkansas, 1918 ***95.2*** *p27*
Cassou, Ant. 18; New Orleans, 1837 ***778.5*** *p101*
Cassou, Jean 26; New Orleans, 1836 ***778.5*** *p101*
Casstet, Dominique 20; America, 1837 ***778.5*** *p101*
Cast, A. 21; America, 1836 ***778.5*** *p101*
Castaffin, George; Halifax, N.S., 1774 ***1219.7*** *p188*
Castagne, Mr. 22; New Orleans, 1836 ***778.5*** *p101*
Castagne, Alexandre 21; New Orleans, 1835 ***778.5*** *p101*
Castaing, Mme. 50; New Orleans, 1839 ***778.5*** *p101*
Castaing, Mr. 60; New Orleans, 1839 ***778.5*** *p101*
Castaing, Ms. 16; New Orleans, 1839 ***778.5*** *p101*
Castaing, Ms. 22; New Orleans, 1839 ***778.5*** *p101*
Castaing, Jean 17; New Orleans, 1836 ***778.5*** *p101*
Castake, William 21; Virginia, 1774 ***1219.7*** *p226*
Castaldi, Michele; Arkansas, 1918 ***95.2*** *p27*
Castallo, Jordan 31; Maryland, 1775 ***1219.7*** *p272*
Castaquet, Jean 28; America, 1838 ***778.5*** *p102*
Casteele, Wm.; Virginia, 1643 ***6219*** *p206*
Casteels, Gustave Pierre; Iowa, 1866-1943 ***123.54*** *p13*
Casteels, Mary; Iowa, 1866-1943 ***123.54*** *p13*
Castel, A. 28; Port uncertain, 1839 ***778.5*** *p102*
Castel, Augustin 26; New Orleans, 1837 ***778.5*** *p102*
Castel, Pierre 24; New Orleans, 1837 ***778.5*** *p102*
Castell, George 40; Maryland, 1775 ***1219.7*** *p252*
Castell, Henry; Virginia, 1639 ***6219*** *p152*
Castelleleon, L.; New Orleans, 1839 ***778.5*** *p102*
Castelli, Patrick 36; New Orleans, 1862 ***543.30*** *p461*
Castello, John; New York, NY, 1816 ***2859.11*** *p27*
Castello, Lawrence; Shreveport, LA, 1874 ***7129*** *p44*
Castello, Michael; New York, NY, 1816 ***2859.11*** *p27*
Castello, Thomas; New York, NY, 1816 ***2859.11*** *p27*
Castelnan, D. de 27; New Orleans, 1825 ***778.5*** *p102*
Castenada, J. M.; Arizona, 1872 ***2764.35*** *p15*
Castenaro, John; Iowa, 1866-1943 ***123.54*** *p13*
Castendyck, Capt.; Canada, 1776-1783 ***9786*** *p185*
Castendyck, Carl Wilhelm; Canada, 1777 ***9786*** *p266*
Castens, Charles B.; Wisconsin, n.d. ***9675.5*** *p49*
Caster, William 24; Antigua (Antego), 1733 ***3690.1*** *p40*
Castera, Miss 6; America, 1838 ***778.5*** *p102*
Castera, Mme. 55; America, 1838 ***778.5*** *p102*
Castero, Nativo 65; Arizona, 1910 ***9228.40*** *p15*
Castet, Hypolite 28; America, 1829 ***778.5*** *p102*
Castet, Jacques 23; New Orleans, 1839 ***778.5*** *p102*
Castets, Jean 21; America, 1838 ***778.5*** *p102*
Castex, Mr. 21; America, 1839 ***778.5*** *p102*
Castian, Emil 49; West Virginia, 1903 ***9788.3*** *p5*
Castie, J. 33; Mexico, 1825 ***778.5*** *p102*
Castigan, Thomas; New York, NY, 1816 ***2859.11*** *p27*
Castilla, Gorgoria; Arizona, 1916 ***9228.40*** *p20*
Castille, Dr. 31; America, 1829 ***778.5*** *p102*
Castille, Henry 34; America, 1838 ***778.5*** *p102*
Castillon, J. B. 25; Port uncertain, 1838 ***778.5*** *p103*
Castillon, L. 22; New Orleans, 1839 ***778.5*** *p103*
Castle, Mr.; Quebec, 1815 ***9229.18*** *p79*
Castle, Dorothy; Virginia, 1639 ***6219*** *p157*
Castle, Frederick; Arizona, 1889 ***2764.35*** *p11*
Castle, Geo.; Virginia, 1637 ***6219*** *p111*
Castle, Georg; Virginia, 1638 ***6219*** *p122*
Castle, Humphry; Virginia, 1643 ***6219*** *p203*
Castle, Robert; Virginia, 1648 ***6219*** *p250*
Castlewood, Hugh; New York, NY, 1816 ***2859.11*** *p27*
Castons, Robert; Virginia, 1637 ***6219*** *p8*
Castora, Stephen 30; New Orleans, 1862 ***543.30*** *p460*
Castres, J. 50; Port uncertain, 1839 ***778.5*** *p103*
Caswell, Lawrance 15; Maryland, 1774 ***1219.7*** *p202*
Catalano, Charley; Illinois, 1906 ***5012.37*** *p63*
Catcher, . . .; America, 1869-1885 ***8582.2*** *p6*
Catchett, John 26; New York, 1774 ***1219.7*** *p217*
Catchhof, . . .; Canada, 1776-1783 ***9786*** *p18*
Catchman, Tho.; Virginia, 1635 ***6219*** *p35*
Catelyn, Henry; Virginia, 1638 ***6219*** *p146*
Catenzara, Cosimo 35; New York, NY, 1893 ***9026.4*** *p41*
Catenzaro, Ginseppe 42; New York, NY, 1893 ***9026.4*** *p41*
Cater, Georg; Virginia, 1642 ***6219*** *p196*
Caterer, Char.; Virginia, 1648 ***6219*** *p246*
Caterson, Eliza J.; Philadelphia, 1865 ***5704.8*** *p190*
Caterson, Francis 10; Philadelphia, 1865 ***5704.8*** *p190*
Caterson, Frank; Philadelphia, 1864 ***5704.8*** *p182*
Cates, Samuel; Sorel, Que., 1794 ***7603*** *p26*
Catesby, June; Virginia, 1632 ***6219*** *p180*
Cathcart, Alan; New York, NY, 1839 ***8208.4*** *p100*
Cathcart, Alexander; New York, NY, 1816 ***2859.11*** *p27*
Cathcart, Catherine; New York, NY, 1816 ***2859.11*** *p27*
Cathcart, David; Quebec, 1853 ***5704.8*** *p104*
Cathcart, George 18; Quebec, 1857 ***5704.8*** *p136*
Cathcart, John; New York, NY, 1864 ***5704.8*** *p172*
Cathcart, William; North Carolina, 1737 ***1639.20*** *p41*
Cather, Ann 18; Quebec, 1858 ***5704.8*** *p138*
Cather, Anne 3; Quebec, 1858 ***5704.8*** *p138*
Cather, Charles 7; Quebec, 1858 ***5704.8*** *p138*
Cather, Ellen 29; Quebec, 1858 ***5704.8*** *p138*
Cather, James 9; Quebec, 1858 ***5704.8*** *p138*
Cather, Mary 1; Quebec, 1858 ***5704.8*** *p138*
Cather, Thomas 8; Quebec, 1858 ***5704.8*** *p138*
Cather, Wm.; Virginia, 1798 ***4778.2*** *p141*
Catheral, John 38; Virginia, 1774 ***1219.7*** *p240*
Catherall, Thomas; Iowa, 1866-1943 ***123.54*** *p13*
Catherina, Anton 38; New Orleans, 1862 ***543.30*** *p460*
Cathers, Margaret; New York, NY, 1870 ***5704.8*** *p237*
Catherson, . . .; Philadelphia, 1865 ***5704.8*** *p195*
Catherson, Margaret; New York, NY, 1865 ***5704.8*** *p195*
Catherson, Margaret J.; Philadelphia, 1865 ***5704.8*** *p195*
Catherwood, Hugh; New York, NY, 1811 ***2859.11*** *p9*
Catherwood, Letitia 9 mos; St. John, N.B., 1848 ***5704.8*** *p42*
Catherwood, Mary; St. John, N.B., 1851 ***5704.8*** *p72*
Catherwood, Robert; St. John, N.B., 1848 ***5704.8*** *p42*
Catherwood, Robert 2; St. John, N.B., 1848 ***5704.8*** *p42*
Catherwood, Susan; St. John, N.B., 1848 ***5704.8*** *p42*
Catherwood, Thomas; New York, NY, 1816 ***2859.11*** *p27*
Cathlina, Frank; Iowa, 1866-1943 ***123.54*** *p13*
Cathlina, Teresa; Iowa, 1866-1943 ***123.54*** *p57*
Cathridge, Hannah 33; Massachusetts, 1848 ***5881.1*** *p16*
Catlin, J. R.; Washington, 1859-1920 ***2872.1*** *p8*
Cato, James 28; Maryland, 1775 ***1219.7*** *p257*
Catoln, Barnard; Illinois, 1858 ***5012.39*** *p54*
Caton, William 22; Maryland, 1775 ***1219.7*** *p250*
Catt, John 28; Maryland, 1775 ***1219.7*** *p252*
Catt, Richard 37; Philadelphia, 1774 ***1219.7*** *p217*
Cattan, Samll.; Virginia, 1648 ***6219*** *p251*
Cattarall, Francis; Virginia, 1698 ***2212*** *p12*
Cattenach, John 50; Wilmington, NC, 1774 ***1639.20*** *p41*
With wife & 2 children
With child 7
With child 19
Catter, William; Wisconsin, n.d. ***9675.5*** *p49*
Catterall, Alice; Virginia, 1698 ***2212*** *p12*
Catterall, William 22; Maryland, 1724 ***3690.1*** *p40*
Catterell, Edward; Virginia, 1636 ***6219*** *p109*
Cattero, Jiocomo; Arkansas, 1918 ***95.2*** *p27*
Catto, Adam; Austin, TX, 1886 ***9777*** *p5*
Catton, B.E.; Illinois, 1888 ***5012.37*** *p61*
Cau, Me. 30; Port uncertain, 1836 ***778.5*** *p103*
Caubere, Francois 27; New Orleans, 1839 ***778.5*** *p103*
Cauchin, Julien 29; Louisiana, 1820 ***778.5*** *p103*
Caudell, Phillipp; Virginia, 1637 ***6219*** *p17*
Cauder, Joseph; Illinois, 1858 ***2896.5*** *p7*
Caufferel, Paul 45; Pennsylvania, 1753 ***2444*** *p144*
Caufield, Julia; Quebec, 1825 ***7603*** *p75*
Cauger, Michael; Kentucky, 1796 ***8582.3*** *p94*
Caughey, Mary; Baltimore, 1816 ***2859.11*** *p27*
Caughlan, Daniel 8; Massachusetts, 1850 ***5881.1*** *p15*
Caughlan, Johanna 11; Massachusetts, 1850 ***5881.1*** *p19*
Caughlan, Kate 5; Massachusetts, 1850 ***5881.1*** *p20*
Caughlan, Patrick 16; Massachusetts, 1850 ***5881.1*** *p24*
Caughlan, Peggy 2; Massachusetts, 1850 ***5881.1*** *p24*
Caughlan, Sarah 30; Massachusetts, 1850 ***5881.1*** *p25*
Caughlin, Bridget 26; Massachusetts, 1850 ***5881.1*** *p14*
Caulan, Edward; America, 1742 ***4971*** *p94*
Caulan, James; America, 1742 ***4971*** *p23*
Caulan, Patrick; America, 1740 ***4971*** *p15*
Caully, Robert; Virginia, 1637 ***6219*** *p86*
Caulseun, Anton; Wisconsin, n.d. ***9675.5*** *p49*
Caune, Celestin 25; Port uncertain, 1839 ***778.5*** *p103*
Caurtad, Mr. 25; Port uncertain, 1836 ***778.5*** *p103*
Causau, Mr. 40; New Orleans, 1839 ***778.5*** *p525*
Causby, Thomas; Virginia, 1636 ***6219*** *p26*
Cause, Catharine 36; America, 1774 ***1219.7*** *p191*
Cause, John 36; America, 1774 ***1219.7*** *p191*
Causey, Jane *SEE* Causey, Tho.
Causey, Tho.; Virginia, 1640 ***6219*** *p182*
*Wife:*Jane
Causland, William; New York, NY, 1816 ***2859.11*** *p27*
Causon, Nehemiah; Virginia, 1643 ***6219*** *p201*
Causs, Joseph; Arkansas, 1918 ***95.2*** *p27*
Caussat, Francois 19; America, 1838 ***778.5*** *p103*
Causse, S. 18; America, 1825 ***778.5*** *p103*
Causton, Thomas 40; Savannah, GA, 1733 ***4719.17*** *p310*
Cautez, F.; Port uncertain, 1832 ***778.5*** *p103*
Caux, . . .; Canada, 1776-1783 ***9786*** *p18*
Cauzlovic, Jacob; Iowa, 1866-1943 ***123.54*** *p13*
Cavalaris, Thomas James 22; Arkansas, 1918 ***95.2*** *p27*
Cavalene, Charles; Arkansas, 1918 ***95.2*** *p27*
Cavalier, Alexandrin. 2; New Orleans, 1836 ***778.5*** *p103*
Cavalier, Anna 34; New Orleans, 1836 ***778.5*** *p103*
Cavalier, Sabine 30; America, 1823 ***778.5*** *p103*
Cavallier, Jos.; Port uncertain, 1838 ***778.5*** *p104*
Cavallier, P.; Port uncertain, 1838 ***778.5*** *p104*
Cavanagh, Bridget; New York, NY, 1866 ***5704.8*** *p208*
Cavanagh, Edmond; America, 1743 ***4971*** *p30*
Cavanagh, Edward; Philadelphia, 1847 ***53.26*** *p12*
Cavanagh, Edward; Philadelphia, 1847 ***5704.8*** *p5*
Cavanagh, Elizabeth; Quebec, 1825 ***7603*** *p69*
Cavanagh, Jacques; Montreal, 1760 ***7603*** *p75*
Cavanagh, James; America, 1741 ***4971*** *p37*
Cavanagh, John; America, 1740 ***4971*** *p26*
Cavanagh, John; New York, NY, 1815 ***2859.11*** *p27*
Cavanagh, John 24; St. John, N.B., 1854 ***5704.8*** *p119*
Cavanagh, John 30; Philadelphia, 1853 ***5704.8*** *p112*
Cavanagh, Margaret; America, 1742 ***4971*** *p32*
Cavanagh, Michael; New York, NY, 1811 ***2859.11*** *p9*
Cavanagh, Peter; New York, NY, 1839 ***8208.4*** *p94*
Cavanagh, Tobias; America, 1735-1743 ***4971*** *p8*
Cavanagh, William 20; Philadelphia, 1855 ***5704.8*** *p124*
Cavanaugh, Anna 21; Massachusetts, 1849 ***5881.1*** *p13*
Cavanaugh, James 9; Massachusetts, 1849 ***5881.1*** *p18*
Cavanaugh, Kitty 20; Massachusetts, 1849 ***5881.1*** *p54*
Cavanaugh, M. S.; Washington, 1859-1920 ***2872.1*** *p8*
Cavanaugh, Michael; Illinois, 1886 ***5012.39*** *p120*
Cavanaugh, Susan 30; Massachusetts, 1849 ***5881.1*** *p25*
Cavanaugh, Thomas 26; Massachusetts, 1849 ***5881.1*** *p25*
Cave, Elizabeth 27; Maryland or Virginia, 1699 ***2212*** *p24*
Cave, James 46; Maryland, 1775 ***1219.7*** *p259*
Cave, James J.; New York, NY, 1839 ***8208.4*** *p98*
Cave, Patrick; Virginia, 1642 ***6219*** *p186*
Cave, Robert Henry 45; Kansas, 1893 ***5240.1*** *p78*
Cavelier, J. 45; New Orleans, 1829 ***778.5*** *p104*
Cavell, Ellen 28; Canada, 1838 ***4535.12*** *p113*
Cavell, Jane 1; Canada, 1838 ***4535.12*** *p113*
Cavell, Thos. 36; Canada, 1838 ***4535.12*** *p113*
Cavellier, Julian; Port uncertain, 1839 ***778.5*** *p104*
Cavelry, Miss; Milwaukee, 1875 ***4719.30*** *p257*
Cavelry, Mrs.; Milwaukee, 1875 ***4719.30*** *p257*
Cavena, John; New York, NY, 1839 ***8208.4*** *p94*
Cavenagh, Anthony; Philadelphia, 1852 ***5704.8*** *p92*
Cavenagh, Edmond; Delaware Bay or River, 1743 ***4971*** *p104*
Cavenagh, Honor; America, 1740 ***4971*** *p48*
Cavenagh, Joseph; New York, NY, 1840 ***8208.4*** *p107*
Cavenagh, Michael; America, 1738 ***4971*** *p22*
Cavenagh, Peter 8; America, 1866 ***5704.8*** *p214*
Cavenaugh, Kitty 20; Massachusetts, 1849 ***5881.1*** *p20*
Cavenaugh, Michael 6; Massachusetts, 1849 ***5881.1*** *p21*
Cavendish, John; New York, NY, 1852 ***9788.3*** *p5*
Cavers, George W.; Washington, 1859-1920 ***2872.1*** *p8*
Caves, Bartholomew 40; America, 1837 ***778.5*** *p104*
Caves, Madolin; Virginia, 1638 ***6219*** *p180*
Cavicchia, Cabnie; Colorado, 1904 ***9678.1*** *p157*
Cavicchia, Louis; Colorado, 1904 ***9678.1*** *p157*
Caviglia, Angelina 29?; Arizona, 1890 ***2764.35*** *p13*
Cavinagh, James; Quebec, 1852 ***5704.8*** *p94*
Cavoy, Ms. 39; New Orleans, 1838 ***778.5*** *p104*
Cavriol, J. 28; New Orleans, 1829 ***778.5*** *p104*
Caw, Alexander; Charleston, SC, 1817 ***1639.20*** *p41*
Caw, Thomas; Charleston, SC, 1773 ***1639.20*** *p41*
Cawker, John; Virginia, 1635 ***6219*** *p72*
Cawlan, Edward; America, 1743 ***4971*** *p11*
Cawlan, Edward; America, 1743 ***4971*** *p86*
Cawlan, Thomas Roe; America, 1743 ***4971*** *p25*
Cawley, Ellen 21; Massachusetts, 1847 ***5881.1*** *p15*
Cawwood, Richard 19; Pennsylvania, 1731 ***3690.1*** *p40*
Cay, James; New York, NY, 1816 ***2859.11*** *p27*
Cay, Michael; New York, NY, 1816 ***2859.11*** *p27*
Caye, Wm. 35; New Orleans, 1862 ***543.30*** *p454*
Cayton, William 43; Kansas, 1880 ***5240.1*** *p62*
Cazaley, Lewis 28; Grenada, 1774 ***1219.7*** *p191*
Cazanc, James 25; New Orleans, 1863 ***543.30*** *p462*
Cazanski, Michael; Illinois, 1900 ***5012.40*** *p77*
Cazauran, Auguste 29; New Orleans, 1838 ***778.5*** *p104*
Cazauran, Thresy 26; New Orleans, 1838 ***778.5*** *p104*
Cazaux, John Marie 37; America, 1830 ***778.5*** *p104*
Caze, Charles 23; America, 1839 ***778.5*** *p104*
Caze, Etienne 25; America, 1839 ***778.5*** *p104*
Cazeau, H. 20; New Orleans, 1835 ***778.5*** *p104*
Cazeau, Jean 22; America, 1837 ***778.5*** *p104*
Cazeau, Jean 28; America, 1837 ***778.5*** *p104*
Cazeaud, Dom. 33; New Orleans, 1838 ***778.5*** *p105*
Cazeaud, Pierre 18; New Orleans, 1838 ***778.5*** *p105*
Cazeaux, Mr. 21; New Orleans, 1822 ***778.5*** *p105*
Cazeaux, Bernard 13; New Orleans, 1839 ***778.5*** *p105*
Cazeaux, H. 21; America, 1835 ***778.5*** *p105*
Cazeaux, H. 24; New Orleans, 1836 ***778.5*** *p105*
Cazeaux, H. 24; New Orleans, 1837 ***778.5*** *p105*
Cazeaux, Jane 22; New Orleans, 1839 ***778.5*** *p105*
Cazeaux, Jean 29; New Orleans, 1838 ***778.5*** *p105*
Cazeaux, M. 15; Port uncertain, 1839 ***778.5*** *p105*
Cazeaux, P. 23; New Orleans, 1837 ***778.5*** *p105*
Cazedevant, Philip 25; New Orleans, 1832 ***778.5*** *p105*
Cazenabe, Jean 25; New Orleans, 1836 ***778.5*** *p105*
Cazenare, Mr. 22; New Orleans, 1836 ***778.5*** *p105*
Cazenave, Mr. 28; New Orleans, 1839 ***778.5*** *p105*

Cazenave, Andre 35; Texas, 1837 ***778.5*** *p106*
Cazeres, Miss 1; America, 1838 ***778.5*** *p106*
Cazeres, Miss 5; America, 1838 ***778.5*** *p106*
Cazeres, Mme. 32; America, 1838 ***778.5*** *p106*
Cazeres, Mr. 35; America, 1838 ***778.5*** *p106*
Cazes, Cesar 18; America, 1838 ***778.5*** *p106*
Cazes, Gaudens 21; America, 1838 ***778.5*** *p106*
Cdargrun, John; Iowa, 1866-1943 ***123.54*** *p13*
Ceacy, Edmond; Quebec, 1789 ***7603*** *p80*
Ceahy, James 20; Philadelphia, 1833-1834 ***53.26*** *p12*
Ceanfas, Jonas Clean; Virginia, 1775 ***1219.7*** *p275*
Cearing, Ludwick; Pennsylvania, 1753 ***4779.3*** *p13*
Cearl, John 40; Charleston, SC, 1774 ***1639.20*** *p41*
With wife 50
Cearns, Thomas; New York, NY, 1836 ***8208.4*** *p14*
Cebuhar, Mary; Iowa, 1866-1943 ***123.54*** *p59*
Cecchetti, Gisleno; Wisconsin, n.d. ***9675.5*** *p49*
Ceccone, Attilio; Arkansas, 1918 ***95.2*** *p27*
Cech, Franz; New York, NY, 1840 ***8208.4*** *p110*
Cechin, Celests; Iowa, 1866-1943 ***123.54*** *p13*
Ceely, Fran.; Virginia, 1648 ***6219*** *p252*
Ceely, Margery; Virginia, 1640 ***6219*** *p184*
Cehardard, Lombard 30; America, 1831 ***778.5*** *p106*
Cekrer, Friederig; Virginia, 1775 ***1219.7*** *p275*
Celesta, Florenz 27; America, 1836 ***778.5*** *p106*
Celeste, Giovani; Arkansas, 1918 ***95.2*** *p27*
Celgte, Forfnato; Iowa, 1866-1943 ***123.54*** *p13*
Celich, Anna; Iowa, 1866-1943 ***123.54*** *p13*
Celliam, Sarah; Virginia, 1698 ***2212*** *p13*
Celoni, Vincenzo; Washington, 1859-1920 ***2872.1*** *p8*
Cemen, R. 29; Port uncertain, 1839 ***778.5*** *p106*
Cemens, Mme. 40; America, 1839 ***778.5*** *p106*
Cempsey, Patrick; America, 1743 ***4971*** *p11*
Cena, Francesco; Iowa, 1866-1943 ***123.54*** *p13*
Cenac, Henriette 28; Port uncertain, 1839 ***778.5*** *p106*
Ceneray, Nicolas 28; New Orleans, 1831 ***778.5*** *p106*
Cenetier, Francois; Louisiana, 1789-1819 ***778.5*** *p555*
Cenly, Michael; Pennsylvania, 1750 ***2444*** *p173*
Ceola, Augustus; Arkansas, 1918 ***95.2*** *p27*
Ceoughan, James; Philadelphia, 1864 ***5704.8*** *p185*
Ceplack, Joe; Wisconsin, n.d. ***9675.5*** *p49*
Cerato, David; Iowa, 1866-1943 ***123.54*** *p13*
Ceregioni, S.; Wisconsin, n.d. ***9675.5*** *p49*
Cerf, Henry 24; New Orleans, 1839 ***778.5*** *p106*
Cerfbene, Mme. 25; New Orleans, 1825 ***778.5*** *p107*
Cerfbene, Mr. 45; New Orleans, 1825 ***778.5*** *p106*
Cerieu, Mr. 28; Louisiana, 1820 ***778.5*** *p107*
Cerlevato, Ferdinand 44; Arizona, 1890 ***2764.35*** *p13*
Cerr, Peter 48; Kansas, 1889 ***5240.1*** *p74*
Certier, . . .; Halifax, N.S., 1752 ***7074.6*** *p232*
Certier, Christine *SEE* Certier, Jean-Urbain
Certier, Etienne 18; Halifax, N.S., 1752 ***7074.6*** *p207*
Certier, Etienne 18; Halifax, N.S., 1752 ***7074.6*** *p209*
Certier, Jacques *SEE* Certier, Jean-Urbain
Certier, Jean-Urbain 34; Halifax, N.S., 1752 ***7074.6*** *p212*
*Wife:*Christine
*Son:*Pierre
*Son:*Jacques
Certier, Pierre *SEE* Certier, Jean-Urbain
Ceruich, Frank; Iowa, 1866-1943 ***123.54*** *p13*
Cerutty, Mike; Iowa, 1866-1943 ***123.54*** *p14*
Cesar, F. 50; Port uncertain, 1836 ***778.5*** *p107*
Cesar, N. 65; America, 1835 ***778.5*** *p107*
Cesarini, Taliana; Arkansas, 1918 ***95.2*** *p27*
Cesca, Pietro; Iowa, 1866-1943 ***123.54*** *p59*
Cesta, Antonio Incani 28; West Virginia, 1904 ***9788.3*** *p6*
Cesta, David 24; West Virginia, 1904 ***9788.3*** *p6*
Cesta, Demenico 31; West Virginia, 1903 ***9788.3*** *p6*
Cesta, Giambatista 22; West Virginia, 1904 ***9788.3*** *p6*
Cestianovse, Giovanni; Wisconsin, n.d. ***9675.5*** *p49*
Cestrac, P. 18; New Orleans, 1837 ***778.5*** *p107*
Ceut, Jos.; Wisconsin, n.d. ***9675.5*** *p49*
Cevalo, Gerenis; Arkansas, 1918 ***95.2*** *p27*
Ceyler, Charles 20; New Orleans, 1835 ***778.5*** *p107*
Ceyrin, William; Philadelphia, 1811 ***53.26*** *p12*
Ceyrin, Wm.; Philadelphia, 1811 ***2859.11*** *p9*
Ceyssedre, B. 23; Port uncertain, 1839 ***778.5*** *p107*
Chabat, Francois 24; New Orleans, 1838 ***778.5*** *p107*
Chabert, Mr. 30; Mexico, 1837 ***778.5*** *p107*
Chabert, D. 44; Mexico, 1825 ***778.5*** *p107*
Chabert, E. M. G. 18; New Orleans, 1836 ***778.5*** *p107*
Chabert, H. 35; Cuba, 1820 ***778.5*** *p107*
Chabert, M. 20; Mexico, 1825 ***778.5*** *p107*
Chabloz, Alexis; Indiana, 1888 ***1450.2*** *p6B*
Chabriyan, Anna; Iowa, 1866-1943 ***123.54*** *p59*
Chabrol, Mr.; Port uncertain, 1839 ***778.5*** *p107*
Chace, Thomas Taylor; New York, NY, 1838 ***8208.4*** *p81*
Chacet, Aron Moses 22; New York, NY, 1878 ***9253*** *p47*
Chacet, Lea 23; New York, NY, 1878 ***9253*** *p47*
Chaddock, James 22; New England, 1699 ***2212*** *p19*
Chaddock, Thom 12; America, 1705 ***2212*** *p43*
Chaddworth, Tho.; Virginia, 1643 ***6219*** *p206*
Chadevell, August 35; America, 1831 ***778.5*** *p108*
Chadwell, August 35; America, 1831 ***778.5*** *p108*
Chadwick, Edward 30; Massachusetts, 1850 ***5881.1*** *p16*
Chadwick, Elias 19; Pennsylvania, 1735 ***3690.1*** *p40*
Chadwick, Jane 24; America, 1702 ***2212*** *p36*
Chadwick, William 24; Maryland, 1773 ***1219.7*** *p173*
Chadwyck, Alice 20; America, 1703 ***2212*** *p39*
Chaere, Claude 22; America, 1838 ***778.5*** *p108*
Chaffers, James 33; Jamaica, 1773 ***1219.7*** *p170*
Chaffers, William-Unsworth; Quebec, 1822 ***7603*** *p25*
Chagnion, Alex. 23; New Orleans, 1836 ***778.5*** *p108*
Chaiffer, Bernard 18; America, 1835 ***778.5*** *p108*
Chaigneau, M. 19; New Orleans, 1829 ***778.5*** *p108*
Chaileroux, Jacques 21; Louisiana, 1820 ***778.5*** *p108*
Chain, J. B. 22; Mexico, 1825 ***778.5*** *p108*
Chaine, J. 18; America, 1835 ***778.5*** *p108*
Chaire, Claude 19; America, 1837 ***778.5*** *p108*
Chairn, Eliza 24; New Orleans, 1839 ***778.5*** *p108*
Chaise, L. 27; America, 1827 ***778.5*** *p108*
Chaise, Roger 32; New Orleans, 1827 ***778.5*** *p108*
Chaix, B. 26; Port uncertain, 1838 ***778.5*** *p108*
Chaix, J.; New Orleans, 1839 ***778.5*** *p108*
Chakey, Frank; Ohio, 1905-1936 ***9892.11*** *p8*
Chalaron, J. 28; New Orleans, 1827 ***778.5*** *p109*
Chalaron, J. 29; New Orleans, 1829 ***778.5*** *p109*
Chalaron, J. 35; America, 1825 ***778.5*** *p109*
Chalaron, Jacques 36; New Orleans, 1838 ***778.5*** *p109*
Chalaughan, Nicholas; Quebec, 1823 ***7603*** *p80*
Chaleron, J. J. 38; America, 1827 ***778.5*** *p109*
Chaley, William; New York, NY, 1811 ***2859.11*** *p9*
Chalich, Joe Marko; Arkansas, 1918 ***95.2*** *p27*
Chalis, Rob; America, 1697-1707 ***2212*** *p9*
Chalk, Stephen 32; Virginia, 1774 ***1219.7*** *p193*
Challaron, Jacques 23; New Orleans, 1822 ***778.5*** *p109*
Challe, Peter 23; Virginia, 1773 ***1219.7*** *p170*
Challgren, Charles; Washington, 1859-1920 ***2872.1*** *p8*
Challinor, Alexander; Virginia, 1698 ***2212*** *p15*
Challiot, F. 26; New Orleans, 1823 ***778.5*** *p109*
Challis, Edward; Virginia, 1639 ***6219*** *p155*
Chalmers, James Johnson; Arkansas, 1918 ***95.2*** *p27*
Chalmers, John; New York, NY, 1838 ***8208.4*** *p65*
Chalmers, Lionel; South Carolina, 1737 ***1639.20*** *p41*
Chalock, Juan 38; Mexico, 1838 ***778.5*** *p109*
Chalon, Mr. 18; Port uncertain, 1825 ***778.5*** *p109*
Cham, Casper; New York, NY, 1856 ***2896.5*** *p7*
Chamael, Mr. 34; Port uncertain, 1836 ***778.5*** *p109*
Chamael, Berry 32; Port uncertain, 1836 ***778.5*** *p109*
Chamael, Charles 2; Port uncertain, 1836 ***778.5*** *p109*
Chamael, Louis 8; Port uncertain, 1836 ***778.5*** *p109*
Chamael, Louise 12; Port uncertain, 1836 ***778.5*** *p109*
Chamael, Victor 5; Port uncertain, 1836 ***778.5*** *p110*
Chambaud, Mme.; New Orleans, 1839 ***778.5*** *p110*
Chambaud, G. 28; New Orleans, 1839 ***778.5*** *p110*
Chambaud, T. 37; New Orleans, 1826 ***778.5*** *p110*
Chamber, John 20; Philadelphia, 1803 ***53.26*** *p12*
Chamberlain, John 22; Maryland, 1775 ***1219.7*** *p247*
Chamberlain, Jonas 22; Maryland, 1775 ***1219.7*** *p247*
Chamberlain, Leon.; Virginia, 1637 ***6219*** *p11*
Chamberlain, Philip 22; Maryland, 1775 ***1219.7*** *p247*
Chamberlaine, Thomas 20; Pennsylvania, 1733 ***3690.1*** *p40*
Chamberlane, Jon.; Virginia, 1643 ***6219*** *p200*
Chamberlin, Benjamin 26; Maryland, 1774 ***1219.7*** *p208*
Chamberlin, Christ.; Virginia, 1643 ***6219*** *p200*
Chamberlin, James 23; Virginia, 1774 ***1219.7*** *p225*
Chamberlin, William 28; Baltimore, 1775 ***1219.7*** *p269*
Chambers, Agnes; New York, NY, 1816 ***2859.11*** *p27*
Chambers, Alex; Quebec, 1850 ***5704.8*** *p69*
Chambers, Andrew; Philadelphia, 1848 ***53.26*** *p12*
*Relative:*Margaret
Chambers, Andrew; Philadelphia, 1848 ***5704.8*** *p40*
Chambers, Andrew; Quebec, 1851 ***5704.8*** *p82*
Chambers, Ann Jane 6; Quebec, 1850 ***5704.8*** *p69*
Chambers, Anne 3; Philadelphia, 1852 ***5704.8*** *p96*
Chambers, Barbara; Philadelphia, 1852 ***5704.8*** *p85*
Chambers, Benjamin; Pennsylvania, 1682 ***4961*** *p168*
Chambers, Betsey 40; Massachusetts, 1849 ***5881.1*** *p13*
Chambers, Bridget 5; Massachusetts, 1849 ***5881.1*** *p13*
Chambers, Catherine 3; Quebec, 1850 ***5704.8*** *p69*
Chambers, Charles; New York, NY, 1816 ***2859.11*** *p27*
Chambers, Clarence; Washington, 1859-1920 ***2872.1*** *p8*
Chambers, Easter; Philadelphia, 1852 ***5704.8*** *p96*
Chambers, Edward 18; Philadelphia, 1854 ***5704.8*** *p117*
Chambers, Eliza; New York, NY, 1816 ***2859.11*** *p27*
Chambers, Eliza; Philadelphia, 1852 ***5704.8*** *p96*
Chambers, Eliza 18; Philadelphia, 1864 ***5704.8*** *p155*
Chambers, Eliza Jane 5; Philadelphia, 1852 ***5704.8*** *p96*
Chambers, Elizabeth; Savannah, GA, 1770 ***1219.7*** *p145*
Chambers, Ernest Joseph; Arkansas, 1918 ***95.2*** *p27*
Chambers, Esther; Quebec, 1851 ***5704.8*** *p74*
Chambers, Francis; Virginia, 1637 ***6219*** *p115*
Chambers, Francis; Virginia, 1642 ***6219*** *p197*
Chambers, George 18; St. John, N.B., 1855 ***5704.8*** *p127*
Chambers, George 30; Maryland, 1775 ***1219.7*** *p255*
Chambers, Isabella 15; Philadelphia, 1864 ***5704.8*** *p155*
Chambers, James; Illinois, 1859 ***5012.39*** *p89*
Chambers, James; New York, NY, 1816 ***2859.11*** *p27*
Chambers, James; Philadelphia, 1851 ***5704.8*** *p71*
Chambers, James; Philadelphia, 1852 ***5704.8*** *p84*
Chambers, James 9 mos; Quebec, 1850 ***5704.8*** *p69*
Chambers, Jane; Philadelphia, 1851 ***5704.8*** *p80*
Chambers, Jane; Philadelphia, 1852 ***5704.8*** *p97*
Chambers, Jane 20; Wilmington, DE, 1831 ***6508.7*** *p161*
Chambers, John; Iowa, 1866-1943 ***123.54*** *p14*
Chambers, John; Philadelphia, 1847 ***53.26*** *p12*
Chambers, John; Philadelphia, 1847 ***5704.8*** *p22*
Chambers, John; Philadelphia, 1847 ***5704.8*** *p30*
Chambers, John; Philadelphia, 1849 ***53.26*** *p12*
Chambers, John; Philadelphia, 1849 ***5704.8*** *p52*
Chambers, John; Philadelphia, 1852 ***5704.8*** *p97*
Chambers, John; Virginia, 1639 ***6219*** *p157*
Chambers, John; Virginia, 1642 ***6219*** *p192*
Chambers, John 1; Massachusetts, 1849 ***5881.1*** *p18*
Chambers, John 22; Jamaica, 1774 ***1219.7*** *p178*
Chambers, John 22; Philadelphia, 1854 ***5704.8*** *p116*
Chambers, John 23; Philadelphia, 1854 ***5704.8*** *p116*
Chambers, Jon.; Virginia, 1637 ***6219*** *p84*
Chambers, Joseph; South Carolina, 1716 ***1639.20*** *p42*
Chambers, Joseph 16; Philadelphia, 1864 ***5704.8*** *p155*
Chambers, Laurence; America, 1741 ***4971*** *p16*
Chambers, Margaret *SEE* Chambers, Andrew
Chambers, Margaret *SEE* Chambers, Robert
Chambers, Margaret; New York, NY, 1816 ***2859.11*** *p27*
Chambers, Margaret; Philadelphia, 1847 ***5704.8*** *p23*
Chambers, Margaret; Philadelphia, 1848 ***5704.8*** *p40*
Chambers, Margaret; Philadelphia, 1850 ***5704.8*** *p68*
Chambers, Margaret; Philadelphia, 1865 ***5704.8*** *p199*
Chambers, Margaret 8; Quebec, 1850 ***5704.8*** *p69*
Chambers, Margaret 30; Massachusetts, 1849 ***5881.1*** *p21*
Chambers, Mary; New York, NY, 1816 ***2859.11*** *p27*
Chambers, Mary Ann; Philadelphia, 1847 ***53.26*** *p12*
Chambers, Mary Ann; Philadelphia, 1847 ***5704.8*** *p22*
Chambers, Mathew; New York, NY, 1816 ***2859.11*** *p27*
Chambers, Matty; Philadelphia, 1852 ***5704.8*** *p96*
Chambers, Pat. 7; Massachusetts, 1849 ***5881.1*** *p24*
Chambers, Robert; Iowa, 1866-1943 ***123.54*** *p14*
Chambers, Robert; New York, NY, 1816 ***2859.11*** *p27*
Chambers, Robert; Philadelphia, 1847 ***53.26*** *p12*
*Relative:*Margaret
Chambers, Robert; Philadelphia, 1847 ***5704.8*** *p23*
Chambers, Robert; Virginia, 1639 ***6219*** *p158*
Chambers, Sarah; New York, NY, 1816 ***2859.11*** *p27*
Chambers, Sarah; Quebec, 1850 ***5704.8*** *p69*
Chambers, Soloman; Philadelphia, 1853 ***5704.8*** *p101*
Chambers, Solomon; Philadelphia, 1852 ***5704.8*** *p84*
Chambers, Susan; Quebec, 1851 ***5704.8*** *p74*
Chambers, Tho.; Virginia, 1643 ***6219*** *p200*
Chambers, Thomas; Ohio, 1840 ***9892.11*** *p8*
Chambers, Thomas, II; New York, NY, 1815 ***2859.11*** *p27*
Chambers, William; Arkansas, 1918 ***95.2*** *p28*
Chambers, William; Iowa, 1866-1943 ***123.54*** *p14*
Chambers, William; New York, NY, 1816 ***2859.11*** *p27*
Chambers, William; New York, NY, 1834 ***8208.4*** *p50*
Chambers, William; Philadelphia, 1850 ***53.26*** *p12*
Chambers, William; Philadelphia, 1850 ***5704.8*** *p69*
Chambers, William; Philadelphia, 1865 ***5704.8*** *p198*
Chambers, William 9; Massachusetts, 1849 ***5881.1*** *p26*
Chambers, William 28; Maryland, 1775 ***1219.7*** *p267*
Chambers, William W.; New York, NY, 1836 ***8208.4*** *p16*
Chambige, F. 31; America, 1839 ***778.5*** *p110*
Chamblit, Samuel 19; Maryland, 1724 ***3690.1*** *p40*
Chambon, Mr.; New Orleans, 1838 ***778.5*** *p110*
Chambond, John 48; California, 1872 ***2769.3*** *p4*
Chamell, John; Virginia, 1637 ***6219*** *p24*
Chamerlik, Anton; Arkansas, 1918 ***95.2*** *p28*
Chamieux, von; Costa Rica, 1853 ***8582.3*** *p30*
Chamness, Anthony 15; Maryland, 1724 ***3690.1*** *p40*
Chamouffet, Claude 20; New Orleans, 1838 ***778.5*** *p110*
Champes, Eugene 25; New Orleans, 1838 ***778.5*** *p110*
Champier, . . .; Canada, 1776-1783 ***9786*** *p18*
Champins, Francis; Virginia, 1637 ***6219*** *p28*
Champion, Edw.; Virginia, 1635 ***6219*** *p71*
Champion, John; Virginia, 1635 ***6219*** *p5*
Champion, John; Virginia, 1643 ***6219*** *p203*
Champion, John 19; Virginia, 1720 ***3690.1*** *p40*
Champion, Mary; Virginia, 1637 ***6219*** *p115*
Champion, Thady; America, 1743 ***4971*** *p29*
Champmela, Mr. 40; New Orleans, 1823 ***778.5*** *p110*
Chamson, Elizabeth; South Carolina, 1767 ***1639.20*** *p42*
Chance, James 35; Grenada, 1774 ***1219.7*** *p203*
Chance, Thomas; St. Augustine, FL, 1771 ***1219.7*** *p150*
Chanceller, Wm; America, 1698 ***2212*** *p5*
Chancerre, Mr. 18; Port uncertain, 1836 ***778.5*** *p110*
Chancy, William Joseph; Arkansas, 1918 ***95.2*** *p28*

Chandasues, Joseph 24; America, 1838 *778.5* p110
Chandelier, Mme. 39; America, 1838 *778.5* p110
Chandelier, M. 25; New Orleans, 1836 *778.5* p110
Chandey, Francois 28; America, 1839 *778.5* p110
Chandey, Genevieve 26; America, 1839 *778.5* p111
Chandler, Ann; America, 1705 *2212* p45
Chandler, Elizabeth *SEE* Chandler, John
Chandler, Henry 15; Maryland, 1723 *3690.1* p40
Chandler, John; New York, 1834 *8208.4* p47
Chandler, John; Virginia, 1632 *6219* p180
  *Wife:*Elizabeth
Chandler, John 19; Maryland, 1774 *1219.7* p235
Chandler, John 22; Maryland, 1775 *1219.7* p263
Chandler, R. 25; Boston, 1775 *1219.7* p258
Chandler, Samuel 22; Maryland, 1775 *1219.7* p250
Chandler, Susan; Virginia, 1642 *6219* p186
Chandler, Tho.; Virginia, 1628 *6219* p31
Chandler, William; Virginia, 1638 *6219* p186
Chandler, Wm.; Virginia, 1638 *6219* p124
Chandliss, Charles; Boston, 1775 *1219.7* p280
Chandy, Pierre 25; St. Louis, 1835 *778.5* p111
Channel, Henri 37; America, 1838 *778.5* p111
Channet, Louise; Pennsylvania, 1752 *2444* p199
Channing, John; New York, NY, 1839 *8208.4* p93
Channon, Geo.; Virginia, 1638 *6219* p119
Chant, Andrew; Virginia, 1628 *6219* p31
Chant, Andrew; Virginia, 1636 *6219* p74
Chantley, James 21; Maryland, 1775 *1219.7* p249
Chanvetier, Mrie 23; America, 1835 *778.5* p111
Chapella, Achille 16; New Orleans, 1829 *778.5* p111
Chapelle, Catherine; Pennsylvania, 1751 *2444* p226
Chapelle, Catherine Don *SEE* Chapelle, Pierre
Chapelle, Eberhard; Pennsylvania, 1751 *2444* p144
Chapelle, Germain *SEE* Chapelle, Pierre
Chapelle, Jaques *SEE* Chapelle, Jeremie
Chapelle, Jean Pierre *SEE* Chapelle, Pierre
Chapelle, Jeremie *SEE* Chapelle, Jeremie
Chapelle, Jeremie 25; Pennsylvania, 1753 *2444* p144
  *Wife:*Madeleine Rouchon
  *Child:*Jaques
  *Child:*Matthieu
  *Child:*Jeremie
  *Child:*Madeleine
Chapelle, Lucresse; Pennsylvania, 1753 *2444* p144
Chapelle, Madeleine *SEE* Chapelle, Jeremie
Chapelle, Madeleine *SEE* Chapelle, Pierre
Chapelle, Madeleine Rouchon *SEE* Chapelle, Jeremie
Chapelle, Marguerite *SEE* Chapelle, Pierre
Chapelle, Matthieu *SEE* Chapelle, Jeremie
Chapelle, Pierre 27; America, 1838 *778.5* p111
Chapelle, Pierre 30; Pennsylvania, 1753 *2444* p144
  *Wife:*Catherine Don
  *Child:*Jean Pierre
  *Child:*Marguerite
  *Child:*Madeleine
  *Child:*Germain
Chapellon, Maria 25; St. Louis, 1836 *778.5* p111
Chaperon, L. 47; America, 1831 *778.5* p111
Chaplin, Sarah; Virginia, 1639 *6219* p156
Chaplock, John; Wisconsin, n.d. *9675.5* p49
Chaplyn, Robt.; Virginia, 1637 *6219* p113
Chapman, A.; Iowa, 1866-1943 *123.54* p14
Chapman, A. B.; Washington, 1859-1920 *2872.1* p8
Chapman, Alex.; Virginia, 1638 *6219* p115
Chapman, Ann 1 *SEE* Chapman, William
Chapman, Ann 8 *SEE* Chapman, Lancelot
Chapman, Barbara Rutherford; Wilmington, NC, 1763 *1639.20* p42
Chapman, Barbary; Virginia, 1636 *6219* p21
Chapman, Barbary; Virginia, 1642 *6219* p193
Chapman, Benjamin 21; Virginia, 1774 *1219.7* p178
Chapman, Daniel 15; Maryland, 1718 *3690.1* p41
Chapman, David; Illinois, 1853 *7857* p2
Chapman, Frances 12 *SEE* Chapman, Lancelot
Chapman, Frances 42 *SEE* Chapman, Lancelot
Chapman, George; Illinois, 1861 *7857* p2
Chapman, George N.; Washington, 1859-1920 *2872.1* p8
Chapman, H.; Iowa, 1866-1943 *123.54* p14
Chapman, Hannah 4 *SEE* Chapman, Lancelot
Chapman, Henry 7 *SEE* Chapman, William
Chapman, Henry 19; Carolina, 1774 *1219.7* p179
Chapman, Humphrey; Virginia, 1640 *6219* p160
Chapman, James; Pennsylvania, 1757 *1219.7* p51
Chapman, James; Pennsylvania, 1757 *3690.1* p41
Chapman, James 23; Baltimore, 1775 *1219.7* p270
Chapman, Jane 15 *SEE* Chapman, William
Chapman, Jane 27; New York, NY, 1847 *3377.6* p12
Chapman, John; Virginia, 1639 *6219* p161
Chapman, John 13 *SEE* Chapman, William
Chapman, John 21; Maryland, 1775 *1219.7* p257
Chapman, John 22; Maryland, 1775 *1219.7* p249
Chapman, John 22; Maryland, 1775 *1219.7* p252

Chapman, Jon.; Virginia, 1636 *6219* p80
Chapman, Jon.; Virginia, 1642 *6219* p192
Chapman, Jonathan 5 *SEE* Chapman, William
Chapman, Lancelot 6 *SEE* Chapman, Lancelot
Chapman, Lancelot 49; North America, 1774 *1219.7* p198
  *Wife:*Frances 42
  *Child:*Rachael 14
  *Child:*Martin 10
  *Child:*Ann 8
  *Child:*Lancelot 6
  *Child:*Hannah 4
  *Child:*Thomas 18
  *Child:*Frances 12
Chapman, Margaret; Montreal, 1819 *7603* p94
Chapman, Martin 10 *SEE* Chapman, Lancelot
Chapman, Mary 9 *SEE* Chapman, William
Chapman, Mary 42 *SEE* Chapman, William
Chapman, Mathew; Virginia, 1642 *6219* p190
Chapman, Nathan; Iowa, 1866-1943 *123.54* p14
Chapman, Pascoe; Virginia, 1645 *6219* p233
Chapman, Peter 35; Maryland, 1774 *1219.7* p181
Chapman, Phill.; Virginia, 1637 *6219* p13
Chapman, Rachael 14 *SEE* Chapman, Lancelot
Chapman, Richard; Virginia, 1645 *6219* p233
Chapman, Roger; Virginia, 1639 *6219* p161
Chapman, Samuel; Charleston, SC, 1779-1806 *1639.20* p42
Chapman, Sarah 3 *SEE* Chapman, William
Chapman, Sarah 8; New York, NY, 1847 *3377.6* p12
Chapman, Susanna; America, 1825 *6410.32* p125
Chapman, Thomas 17 *SEE* Chapman, William
Chapman, Thomas 18 *SEE* Chapman, Lancelot
Chapman, Thos.; Virginia, 1637 *6219* p37
Chapman, William; Kansas, 1879 *5240.1* p8
Chapman, William; New York, NY, 1816 *2859.11* p27
Chapman, William; Virginia, 1639 *6219* p154
Chapman, William 16; South Carolina, 1751 *1219.7* p4
Chapman, William 16; South Carolina, 1751 *3690.1* p41
Chapman, William 18; Philadelphia, 1774 *1219.7* p233
Chapman, William 19 *SEE* Chapman, William
Chapman, William 27; Virginia, 1775 *1219.7* p246
Chapman, William 44; North America, 1774 *1219.7* p199
  *Wife:*Mary 42
  *Child:*William 19
  *Child:*Thomas 17
  *Child:*Jane 15
  *Child:*John 13
  *Child:*Mary 9
  *Child:*Henry 7
  *Child:*Jonathan 5
  *Child:*Sarah 3
  *Child:*Ann 1
Chapman, Wm.; Virginia, 1637 *6219* p115
Chapp, Izidor; Iowa, 1866-1943 *123.54* p14
Chappel, Jeremias 25; Pennsylvania, 1753 *2444* p145
Chappell, John; Virginia, 1638 *6219* p124
Chappell, John 30; Pennsylvania, 1753 *2444* p144
Chappell, Jon.; Virginia, 1638 *6219* p124
Chappell, Robt.; Virginia, 1639 *6219* p23
Chappell, Robt.; Virginia, 1642 *6219* p191
Chappell, Theo.; San Francisco, 1850 *4914.15* p13
Chappell, Theophilus; San Francisco, 1850 *4914.15* p10
Chappell, William 32; Maryland, 1774 *1219.7* p204
Chappelle, Jean Pierre 30; Pennsylvania, 1753 *2444* p144
Chappelle, Jeremie 25; Pennsylvania, 1753 *2444* p145
Chapple, John 16; Philadelphia, 1774 *1219.7* p175
Chapsky, Stanislaw; Arkansas, 1918 *95.2* p28
Chaptes, Jean Francois 33; New Orleans, 1826 *778.5* p111
Chapuis, Mr. 22; New Orleans, 1837 *778.5* p111
Charbonnier, A. 24; America, 1835 *778.5* p111
Charbonnier, Powell 32; Philadelphia, 1774 *1219.7* p183
Charby, Guillaume; Quebec, 1722 *7603* p21
Chardon, Antoine Charles 29; New Orleans, 1821 *778.5* p111
Chardon, Jeanne M. 28; New Orleans, 1821 *778.5* p111
Chardon, Joseph 66; New Orleans, 1822 *778.5* p112
Charel, Mr. 24; New Orleans, 1822 *778.5* p112
Charenton, A. 18; Port uncertain, 1839 *778.5* p112
Charignry, Mme. 19; America, 1838 *778.5* p112
Charitie, Philip 25; Grenada, 1774 *1219.7* p219
Charlerette, H. 26; New Orleans, 1838 *778.5* p112
Charles, Mr. 22; New Orleans, 1821 *778.5* p112
Charles, Arthur; Iowa, 1866-1943 *123.54* p59
Charles, Elizabeth; New York, NY, 1868 *5704.8* p229
Charles, Fredrick; New York, NY, 1868 *5704.8* p229
Charles, Henry 29; New Orleans, 1862 *543.30* p450
Charles, James; Charleston, SC, 1793 *1639.20* p322
Charles, John Libertade; Iowa, 1866-1943 *123.54* p59
Charles, John Libertate; Iowa, 1866-1943 *123.54* p59

Charles, Jon.; Virginia, 1637 *6219* p110
Charles, Louise 20; Port uncertain, 1836 *778.5* p112
Charles, Nancy; Philadelphia, 1851 *5704.8* p76
Charles, William; Georgia, 1775 *1219.7* p275
Charles, William; Virginia, 1638 *6219* p124
Charles, William; Virginia, 1643 *6219* p203
Charles, William 24; Savannah, GA, 1775 *1219.7* p274
Charleton, Edward; America, 1735-1743 *4971* p51
Charlie, John 30; New Orleans, 1862 *543.30* p462
Charlok, Marie; Quebec, 1808 *7603* p75
Charlot, A. 49; Port uncertain, 1837 *778.5* p112
Charlotte, . . .; Charleston, SC, 1775-1779 *8582.2* p6
Charlsen, Charles 27; Kansas, 1872 *5240.1* p53
Charlson, Charles 27; Kansas, 1872 *5240.1* p8
Charlston, Olof; Illinois, 1888 *5012.39* p121
Charlton, Daniel; Maryland, 1757 *1219.7* p58
Charlton, Edward; America, 1735-1743 *4971* p51
Charlton, George; Kansas, 1879 *5240.1* p8
Charlton, Jonathan 20; Maryland, 1729 *3690.1* p41
Charlton, Robert 17; North America, 1774 *1219.7* p198
Charlton, William 21; Quebec, 1862 *5704.8* p151
Charmichael, Samuel 10; Jamaica, 1773 *1219.7* p172
Charnack, Thomas 22; Maryland, 1725 *3690.1* p41
Charnas, Jacob; Arkansas, 1918 *95.2* p28
Charney, Charles 26; Ohio, 1838 *778.5* p112
Charnick, Henry 31; North America, 1774 *1219.7* p200
Charnock, Thomas 26; Maryland, 1774 *1219.7* p230
Charnock, William 23; Jamaica, 1736 *3690.1* p41
Charnocke, John; Virginia, 1643 *6219* p203
Charoit, Cyprian 20; America, 1839 *778.5* p112
Charowell, James; New York, NY, 1811 *2859.11* p9
Charpentier, Adolphe 37; New Orleans, 1862 *543.30* p455
Charpin, Mr.; Port uncertain, 1839 *778.5* p112
Charret, S. 32; New Orleans, 1823 *778.5* p112
Charrier, Camille 19; America, 1839 *778.5* p112
Charrier, Louis 38; New Orleans, 1831 *778.5* p112
Charry, J. 30; New Orleans, 1837 *778.5* p113
Charry, Jean 30; New Orleans, 1836 *778.5* p113
Charsberg, Charles 38; America, 1838 *778.5* p113
Charsberg, Jeannet 30; America, 1838 *778.5* p113
Charter, Charles 36; Jamaica, 1725 *3690.1* p41
Charter, Henry 20; Maryland, 1722 *3690.1* p41
Charter, Jon.; Virginia, 1639 *6219* p150
Charters, Arthur; New York, NY, 1816 *2859.11* p27
Charters, Frances Mary *SEE* Charters, Thomas
Charters, Frances Mary *SEE* Charters, Thomas
Charters, Francis; Quebec, 1851 *5704.8* p73
Charters, Henry; New York, NY, 1834 *8208.4* p2
Charters, John; New York, NY, 1815 *2859.11* p27
Charters, John Norris; Detroit, 1916 *3455.2* p78
Charters, John Norris; St. John, N.B., 1901-1916 *3455.2* p78
Charters, Thomas; Port Huron, MI, 1915 *3455.3* p54
Charters, Thomas; Port Huron, MI, 1915 *3455.3* p114
  *Wife:*Frances Mary
Charters, Thomas; Quebec, 1915 *3455.3* p54
  *Wife:*Frances Mary
Chartier, Paul; Quebec, 1667 *4533* p129
Charvit, S. 31; New Orleans, 1822 *778.5* p113
Charywell, Samll.; Virginia, 1639 *6219* p150
Chase, Hans Edward; Arkansas, 1918 *95.2* p28
Chase, Salmon P.; Cincinnati, 1788-1848 *8582.3* p90
Chase, William 23; Philadelphia, 1775 *1219.7* p258
Chase, William Hasleham; Antigua (Antego), 1758 *1219.7* p61
Chase, William Hasleham; Antigua (Antego), 1758 *3690.1* p41
Chassignol, Pierre 18; America, 1839 *778.5* p113
Chassin, Philipp 15; America, 1838 *778.5* p113
Chate, Edw. 40; America, 1839 *778.5* p113
Chate, Edward 40; America, 1838 *778.5* p113
Chateaubriand, G. G. von 41; Cincinnati, 1871 *8582* p5
Chateauneuf, Jean 25; Quebec, 1694 *4533* p130
Chatel, Aime 48; Louisiana, 1820 *778.5* p113
Chatel, Julien 40; America, 1836 *778.5* p113
Chatelain, Chatisne 32; America, 1838 *778.5* p113
Chater, Henry 20; Maryland, 1722 *3690.1* p41
Chatfield, Thomas; Nova Scotia, 1750 *3690.1* p41
Chatt, Robert 37; Virginia, 1734 *3690.1* p41
Chatten, Richard 39; California, 1872 *2769.3* p3
Chattoni, . . .; Canada, 1776-1783 *9786* p41
Chauchon, Louis 27; America, 1836 *778.5* p113
Chaud, Adele 6; America, 1836 *778.5* p113
Chaud, John 36; America, 1836 *778.5* p113
Chaudrien, Charles 42; America, 1838 *778.5* p114
Chaul, Mr. 24; New Orleans, 1822 *778.5* p113
Chaumond, Mr. 32; New Orleans, 1830 *778.5* p114
Chaumont, Lucien M. 26; Louisiana, 1820 *778.5* p114
Chaumot, Mr. 30; New Orleans, 1821 *778.5* p114
Chauncey, Daniel; New York, NY, 1839 *8208.4* p98
Chauret, Mr. 35; America, 1830 *778.5* p114

Chauson, Jacques; Nova Scotia, 1638 ***4533*** *p125*
*Wife:*Jeanne Chesson
Chauson, Jeanne Chesson *SEE* Chauson, Jacques
Chaussin, Marie 30; New Orleans, 1838 ***778.5*** *p114*
Chautas, Antoine 40; New Orleans, 1826 ***778.5*** *p114*
Chauve, Bernard 36; Port uncertain, 1836 ***778.5*** *p114*
Chauvin, J. S. 41; Havana, 1822 ***778.5*** *p114*
Chavaroche, Mr. 48; America, 1835 ***778.5*** *p114*
Chaves, Mariano 46; Arizona, 1890 ***2764.35*** *p14*
Chaves, Victoriano 32; Arizona, 1921 ***9228.40*** *p25*
Chavey, Jean 32; America, 1838 ***778.5*** *p114*
Chavez, Rafael 39; California, 1872 ***2769.3*** *p3*
Chavillac, Mr. 28; Louisiana, 1827 ***778.5*** *p114*
Chavrignoe, Andre 40; America, 1839 ***778.5*** *p114*
Chawke, John; Virginia, 1635 ***6219*** *p73*
Chayot, Bartolome 28; Louisiana, 1820 ***778.5*** *p114*
Chearhouse, C. 45; New Orleans, 1839 ***778.5*** *p114*
Cheatly, Eleanor; New York, NY, 1869 ***5704.8*** *p231*
Cheatly, Elizabeth; New York, NY, 1869 ***5704.8*** *p231*
Cheauvant, Thomas 20; Virginia, 1773 ***1219.7*** *p169*
Chebuchar, Joseph; Iowa, 1866-1943 ***123.54*** *p14*
Chedeville, Mr. 32; New Orleans, 1826 ***778.5*** *p115*
Chedville, A. 35; America, 1837 ***778.5*** *p115*
Chedville, Auguste 30; Texas, 1827 ***778.5*** *p115*
Cheeseman, Clement 26; Maryland, 1774 ***1219.7*** *p213*
Cheesman, Edward; Virginia, 1637 ***6219*** *p109*
Cheesome, Richard; Virginia, 1643 ***6219*** *p202*
Cheetum, John; Virginia, 1698 ***2212*** *p15*
Cheffer, . . .; Canada, 1776-1783 ***9786*** *p18*
Cheine, Elizabeth 24; Montreal, 1775 ***1219.7*** *p261*
Cheley, William John; Colorado, 1905 ***9678.1*** *p157*
Chelmedge, Wm.; Virginia, 1628 ***6219*** *p9*
Chelps, Richard 20; Maryland, 1751 ***3690.1*** *p41*
Cheltum, Andrew 19; Jamaica, 1724 ***3690.1*** *p42*
Chemal, Antoine 40; America, 1837 ***778.5*** *p115*
Chemchuk, Reil; Arkansas, 1918 ***95.2*** *p28*
Chemchuk, Reil; Arkansas, 1918 ***95.2*** *p109*
Chemin, Julie 25; New Orleans, 1837 ***778.5*** *p115*
Chenaille, . . .; Canada, 1776-1783 ***9786*** *p18*
Chenal, Francois 29; America, 1838 ***778.5*** *p115*
Chenee, Jules 24; Port uncertain, 1836 ***778.5*** *p115*
Chenet, Mr. 25; Mexico, 1838 ***778.5*** *p115*
Chenet, Eugene 29; Louisiana, 1821 ***778.5*** *p115*
Cheney, John; New York, NY, 1837 ***8208.4*** *p29*
Cheney, Mary; Died enroute, 1682 ***4961*** *p167*
Chennells, Adam Thomas; Virginia, 1855 ***4626.16*** *p15*
Chenon, Louis Francois 48; New Orleans, 1826 ***778.5*** *p115*
Chenot, Nicholas; New York, NY, 1839 ***8208.4*** *p97*
Chenoweth, John 20; West Indies, 1722 ***3690.1*** *p42*
Chentkowska, Sofia 9; New York, 1912 ***9980.29*** *p58*
With uncle
Chentkowski, Felix 8 *SEE* Chentkowski, Josef
Chentkowski, Josef 21; New York, 1912 ***9980.29*** *p58*
With niece
*Nephew:*Felix 8
Cheralien, Mr. 30; America, 1838 ***778.5*** *p115*
Cherberg, Alexandera 16; America, 1829 ***778.5*** *p115*
Cherberg, Antoinette 12; America, 1829 ***778.5*** *p115*
Cherberg, Magdalene 50; America, 1829 ***778.5*** *p115*
Cherbonnier, Mr. 45; Port uncertain, 1838 ***778.5*** *p115*
Cheret, L. 38; America, 1825 ***778.5*** *p116*
Cheribelli, Giac 25; New York, NY, 1893 ***9026.4*** *p41*
Chernal, Antoine 40; America, 1837 ***778.5*** *p115*
Cheron, Christopher 26; Port uncertain, 1838 ***778.5*** *p117*
Cherrieu, Jean 27; America, 1838 ***778.5*** *p116*
Cherry, . . .; America, 1869-1885 ***8582.2*** *p6*
Cherry, Franc.; Virginia, 1643 ***6219*** *p205*
Cherry, John; Virginia, 1637 ***6219*** *p110*
Cherry, Patrick; America, 1740 ***4971*** *p76*
Cherry, Robert; Iowa, 1866-1943 ***123.54*** *p14*
Cherry, Sarah 22; Virginia, 1775 ***1219.7*** *p248*
Cherteau, A. P. 26; Port uncertain, 1839 ***778.5*** *p116*
Cherville, William 28; New Orleans, 1827 ***778.5*** *p116*
Chery, Mr. 26; New Orleans, 1825 ***778.5*** *p116*
Chesaillez, Alexander 21; Virginia, 1773 ***1219.7*** *p169*
Cheshire, John 20; Pennsylvania, 1736 ***3690.1*** *p42*
Chesman, John 16; Maryland, 1729 ***3690.1*** *p42*
Chesne, Mr. 28; America, 1837 ***778.5*** *p116*
Chesnee, Jules 26; New Orleans, 1838 ***778.5*** *p116*
Chesnut, Elizabeth 13; St. John, N.B., 1848 ***5704.8*** *p43*
Chesnut, Henry; New York, NY, 1836 ***8208.4*** *p79*
Chesnut, Jane 7; St. John, N.B., 1848 ***5704.8*** *p43*
Chesnut, John; St. John, N.B., 1848 ***5704.8*** *p43*
Chesnut, John 4; St. John, N.B., 1848 ***5704.8*** *p43*
Chesnut, Margaret; St. John, N.B., 1848 ***5704.8*** *p43*
Chesnut, Margaret 9; St. John, N.B., 1848 ***5704.8*** *p43*
Chesnut, Mary 10; St. John, N.B., 1848 ***5704.8*** *p43*
Chesnut, Nancy 9 mos; St. John, N.B., 1848 ***5704.8*** *p43*
Chesnut, Robert 12; St. John, N.B., 1848 ***5704.8*** *p43*
Chessheire, Robt.; Virginia, 1635 ***6219*** *p69*
Chessom, Thomas 20; Jamaica, 1739 ***3690.1*** *p42*
Chesson, Jeanne; Nova Scotia, 1638 ***4533*** *p125*
Chestain, Benedictus 18; America, 1700 ***2212*** *p30*
Chester, William 24; Philadelphia, 1774 ***1219.7*** *p232*
Chestmore, John 14; Philadelphia, 1775 ***1219.7*** *p248*
Chestnut, Andrew 16; Philadelphia, 1864 ***5704.8*** *p156*
Chestnut, Benjamin *SEE* Chestnut, Isabella
Chestnut, C.; New York, NY, 1816 ***2859.11*** *p27*
Chestnut, Eliza J.; New York, NY, 1869 ***5704.8*** *p232*
Chestnut, Elizabeth 2; Philadelphia, 1864 ***5704.8*** *p156*
Chestnut, Elizabeth 40; Philadelphia, 1864 ***5704.8*** *p156*
Chestnut, George 11 *SEE* Chestnut, Isabella
Chestnut, Isabella; Philadelphia, 1847 ***53.26*** *p12*
*Relative:*Samuel
*Relative:*Margaret
*Relative:*Benjamin
*Relative:*George 11
Chestnut, James; Quebec, 1853 ***5704.8*** *p103*
Chestnut, John 4; Philadelphia, 1864 ***5704.8*** *p156*
Chestnut, John 45; Philadelphia, 1864 ***5704.8*** *p156*
Chestnut, M.; New York, NY, 1816 ***2859.11*** *p27*
Chestnut, Margaret *SEE* Chestnut, Isabella
Chestnut, Matty 17; Philadelphia, 1864 ***5704.8*** *p156*
Chestnut, S.; New York, NY, 1816 ***2859.11*** *p27*
Chestnut, Samuel *SEE* Chestnut, Isabella
Chestnut, Samuel; Philadelphia, 1811 ***53.26*** *p12*
Chestnut, Samuel; Philadelphia, 1811 ***2859.11*** *p9*
Chestnut, Susan 6; Philadelphia, 1864 ***5704.8*** *p156*
Chestnut, William; New York, NY, 1815 ***2859.11*** *p27*
Chestnutt, Benjamin; Philadelphia, 1847 ***5704.8*** *p24*
Chestnutt, George 11; Philadelphia, 1847 ***5704.8*** *p24*
Chestnutt, Isabella; Philadelphia, 1847 ***5704.8*** *p24*
Chestnutt, Margaret; Philadelphia, 1847 ***5704.8*** *p24*
Chestnutt, Samuel; Philadelphia, 1847 ***5704.8*** *p24*
Cheton, Marke; Virginia, 1642 ***6219*** *p195*
Cheusburg, A.; Iowa, 1866-1943 ***123.54*** *p14*
Chevaillier, Antony 21; Virginia, 1773 ***1219.7*** *p170*
Chevalier, Anthony 24; Jamaica, 1736 ***3690.1*** *p42*
Chevalier, E. 5; New Orleans, 1831 ***778.5*** *p116*
Chevalier, Francies 22; America, 1837 ***778.5*** *p116*
Chevalier, John; New York, NY, 1834 ***8208.4*** *p80*
Chevalier, P. 28; New Orleans, 1831 ***778.5*** *p116*
Chevallier, Jacques 31; New Orleans, 1838 ***778.5*** *p116*
Chevelier, Barbara 24; America, 1837 ***778.5*** *p116*
Chevelier, Frederick 1; America, 1837 ***778.5*** *p116*
Chevelier, John 29; America, 1837 ***778.5*** *p117*
Chevelier, Joseph 19; America, 1837 ***778.5*** *p117*
Chevelier, Michael 17; America, 1837 ***778.5*** *p117*
Chevilar, John 30; Port uncertain, 1838 ***778.5*** *p117*
Chevlier, Mme. 54; America, 1832 ***778.5*** *p117*
Chevlier, Mr. 57; America, 1832 ***778.5*** *p118*
Chevon, Christopher 26; Port uncertain, 1838 ***778.5*** *p117*
Chevonedemann, Augustin 28; New Orleans, 1832 ***778.5*** *p117*
Chew, John; Virginia, 1636 ***6219*** *p76*
Chew, Jon.; Virginia, 1622 ***6219*** *p76*
Chew, Jon.; Virginia, 1623 ***6219*** *p76*
Cheyney, Robert; Virginia, 1639 ***6219*** *p161*
Cheyny, Robertt; Virginia, 1636 ***6219*** *p80*
Chiapella, Mme. 54; America, 1837 ***778.5*** *p117*
Chiappa, A.F.J. 66; Arizona, 1924 ***9228.40*** *p28*
Chichester, Arthur; New York, NY, 1834 ***8208.4*** *p3*
Chick, Hugh; Virginia, 1648 ***6219*** *p250*
Chico, Mr. 30; Louisiana, 1829 ***778.5*** *p117*
Chicot, P. 25; America, 1832 ***778.5*** *p117*
Chicoy, M. 25; America, 1827 ***778.5*** *p117*
Chicoy, M. 30; Havana, 1827 ***778.5*** *p117*
Chicton, Mary; Virginia, 1636 ***6219*** *p77*
Chid, Peter; Wisconsin, n.d. ***9675.5*** *p49*
Chieger, Joseph; Wisconsin, n.d. ***9675.5*** *p49*
Chielby, Onesiphorus 18; Pennsylvania, 1738 ***3690.1*** *p42*
Chige, Mr. 25; New Orleans, 1825 ***778.5*** *p117*
Chigian, William; Virginia, 1641 ***6219*** *p185*
Chilberg, C.; Iowa, 1847 ***2090*** *p611*
With wife & 5 children
Chilcot, Thomas 25; Maryland, 1774 ***1219.7*** *p196*
Chilcott, Tho.; Virginia, 1635 ***6219*** *p69*
Child, Alexander; New York, NY, 1811 ***2859.11*** *p9*
Child, Daniell; Virginia, 1698 ***2212*** *p14*
Child, Richard; Virginia, 1635 ***6219*** *p35*
Child, Robert 21; Maryland, 1775 ***1219.7*** *p272*
Child, Tho.; Virginia, 1638 ***6219*** *p18*
Child, Tho.; Virginia, 1642 ***6219*** *p195*
Child, William 21; Philadelphia, 1775 ***1219.7*** *p256*
Child, William 23; Maryland, 1774 ***1219.7*** *p187*
Childs, Emma R. 44; Kansas, 1872 ***5240.1*** *p53*
Childs, Joseph 45; Kansas, 1870 ***5240.1*** *p51*
Childs, Rich.; Virginia, 1637 ***6219*** *p113*
Childs, Richard; Virginia, 1638 ***6219*** *p2*
Chiles, Walter; Virginia, 1638 ***6219*** *p118*
Chillingworth, Ralph 35; Virginia, 1774 ***1219.7*** *p201*
Chillman, John Augustus; Maine, 1876 ***6410.22*** *p124*
Chilman, Nicholas; Virginia, 1646 ***6219*** *p240*
Chily, Nicholas 30; Maryland, 1775 ***1219.7*** *p249*
Chimann, Frederic; Milwaukee, 1875 ***4719.30*** *p257*
Chimbouris, George D.; Ohio, 1890 ***1450.2*** *p6B*
Ching, Richard; Colorado, 1904 ***9678.1*** *p157*
Chink, . . .; Canada, 1776-1783 ***9786*** *p18*
Chink, George 21; New Orleans, 1862 ***543.30*** *p458*
Chinley, John; Virginia, 1648 ***6219*** *p252*
Chinn, William; Iowa, 1866-1943 ***123.54*** *p14*
Chinnick, Henry 20; Maryland, 1719 ***3690.1*** *p42*
Chinon, Mr. 44; New Orleans, 1823 ***778.5*** *p117*
Chiodo, Concetia 6 *SEE* Chiodo, Ginsefpina
Chiodo, Ginsefpina 34; New York, NY, 1893 ***9026.4*** *p41*
*Relative:*Maria 10
*Relative:*Michele 8
*Relative:*Concetia 6
Chiodo, Maria 10 *SEE* Chiodo, Ginsefpina
Chiodo, Michele 8 *SEE* Chiodo, Ginsefpina
Chiolier, Mme. 54; America, 1832 ***778.5*** *p117*
Chiolier, Mr. 57; America, 1832 ***778.5*** *p118*
Chipchase, Ann 35 *SEE* Chipchase, Thomas
Chipchase, Thomas 40; Maryland, 1774 ***1219.7*** *p206*
*Wife:*Ann 35
Chiphart, Vince; Iowa, 1866-1943 ***123.54*** *p14*
Chipmell, John; Petersburg, VA, 1810 ***4778.2*** *p141*
Chippendale, James Pedder; Illinois, 1892 ***5012.39*** *p53*
Chippendale, James Pedder; Illinois, 1894 ***5012.40*** *p53*
Chirkowsky, A.M.L.C. Lufelsmeyer *SEE* Chirkowsky, Wilhelm
Chirkowsky, Dorette C. Bertha *SEE* Chirkowsky, Wilhelm
Chirkowsky, Heinrich F. August *SEE* Chirkowsky, Wilhelm
Chirkowsky, Minna Dorette *SEE* Chirkowsky, Wilhelm
Chirkowsky, Wilhelm; America, 1884 ***4610.10*** *p113*
*Wife:*A.M.L.C. Lufelsmeyer
*Child:*Minna Dorette
*Child:*Heinrich F. August
*Child:*Dorette C. Bertha
Chirstensen, Fritz; Illinois, 1878 ***5240.1*** *p8*
Chisen, Eliza *SEE* Chisen, George
Chisen, Eliza; Philadelphia, 1848 ***5704.8*** *p40*
Chisen, George; Philadelphia, 1848 ***53.26*** *p12*
*Relative:*Eliza
Chisen, George; Philadelphia, 1848 ***5704.8*** *p40*
Chisham, Thomas 15; Jamaica, 1774 ***1219.7*** *p233*
Chisham, William 19; Philadelphia, 1774 ***1219.7*** *p233*
Chisholm, Miss; North Carolina, 1774 ***1639.20*** *p224*
Chisholm, Alex *SEE* Chisholm, Donald
Chisholm, Alexander; America, 1803 ***1639.20*** *p42*
Chisholm, Alexander; Georgia, 1735 ***1639.20*** *p42*
Chisholm, Alexander; San Francisco, 1879 ***2764.35*** *p15*
Chisholm, Alexander; South Carolina, 1717 ***1639.20*** *p42*
Chisholm, Alexander; South Carolina, 1746 ***1639.20*** *p42*
Chisholm, Alexander 58 *SEE* Chisholm, Daniel
Chisholm, Ann; Pictou, N.S., 1801 ***9775.5*** *p207A*
Chisholm, Ann 58; South Carolina, 1850 ***1639.20*** *p42*
Chisholm, Ann Stewart *SEE* Chisholm, Donald
Chisholm, Archd; Pictou, N.S., 1801 ***9775.5*** *p207A*
Chisholm, Cath; Pictou, N.S., 1801 ***9775.5*** *p207A*
Chisholm, Cath 12; Pictou, N.S., 1801 ***9775.5*** *p207A*
Chisholm, Catherine; North Carolina, 1783-1859 ***1639.20*** *p43*
Chisholm, Catherine 66; North Carolina, 1850 ***1639.20*** *p43*
Chisholm, Daniel 70; North Carolina, 1850 ***1639.20*** *p43*
*Relative:*Murdoch 60
*Relative:*Alexander 58
Chisholm, Donald; Quebec, 1863 ***4537.30*** *p11*
*Wife:*Ann Stewart
*Child:*Alex
Chisholm, Duncan; Pictou, N.S., 1801 ***9775.5*** *p207A*
Chisholm, Findlay; North Carolina, 1813 ***1639.20*** *p43*
Chisholm, George; Charleston, SC, 1809 ***1639.20*** *p43*
Chisholm, Hugh 48; North Carolina, 1850 ***1639.20*** *p43*
Chisholm, Isob; Pictou, N.S., 1801 ***9775.5*** *p207A*
Chisholm, J. C.; San Francisco, 1885 ***2764.35*** *p12*
Chisholm, James; America, 1803 ***1639.20*** *p43*
Chisholm, James; Arkansas, 1918 ***95.2*** *p28*
Chisholm, John; Carolina, 1701-1801 ***1639.20*** *p43*
Chisholm, John; Pictou, N.S., 1801 ***9775.5*** *p207A*
Chisholm, John; Quebec, 1771 ***7603*** *p37*
Chisholm, John Archie; Arkansas, 1918 ***95.2*** *p28*
Chisholm, Mary 40; South Carolina, 1850 ***1639.20*** *p43*
Chisholm, Murdoch 60 *SEE* Chisholm, Daniel
Chisholm, Nancy 80; North Carolina, 1850 ***1639.20*** *p43*
*Relative:*Rachael 60
Chisholm, Rachael 60 *SEE* Chisholm, Nancy
Chisim, Margaret 6; Philadelphia, 1853 ***5704.8*** *p111*
Chisim, Mary Ann 8; Philadelphia, 1853 ***5704.8*** *p111*
Chisim, Robert 10; Philadelphia, 1853 ***5704.8*** *p111*
Chisin, Sarah 21; Philadelphia, 1854 ***5704.8*** *p120*
Chism, Anne; St. John, N.B., 1847 ***5704.8*** *p9*
Chismo, John; America, 1885 ***7137*** *p168*
Chittick, Catherine; St. John, N.B., 1852 ***5704.8*** *p83*
Chittick, Christopher 13; Quebec, 1847 ***5704.8*** *p8*

Chittick, Henry; St. John, N.B., 1852 ***5704.8*** *p83*
Chittick, Henry 13; St. John, N.B., 1852 ***5704.8*** *p83*
Chittick, John; Quebec, 1847 ***5704.8*** *p8*
Chittick, Mary 3 mos; St. John, N.B., 1852 ***5704.8*** *p83*
Chittick, William; Arkansas, 1918 ***95.2*** *p28*
Chittock, Thomas; Quebec, 1851 ***5704.8*** *p73*
Chitwood, Wm.; Virginia, 1636 ***6219*** *p32*
Chivers, John 23; Virginia, 1774 ***1219.7*** *p193*
Chiverton, Wm. 26; Canada, 1838 ***4535.12*** *p113*
Chlopicki, Ludwik; New York, 1831 ***4606*** *p173*
Choderker, Froem; Arkansas, 1918 ***95.2*** *p28*
Choenin, Joseph 22; America, 1839 ***778.5*** *p118*
Choisne, Mr. 25; America, 1829 ***778.5*** *p118*
Choisne, L. 28; America, 1830 ***778.5*** *p118*
Choisne, M. 22; America, 1830 ***778.5*** *p118*
Cholans, Pierre 31; America, 1839 ***778.5*** *p118*
Cholmley, Thomas 16; Pennsylvania, 1725 ***3690.1*** *p42*
Cholmondeley, Margtt 20; America, 1705-1706 ***2212*** *p44*
Chopers, George P. 26; Kansas, 1889 ***5240.1*** *p74*
Chopin, Alex.; Port uncertain, 1839 ***778.5*** *p118*
Chopin, Victor 19; America, 1836 ***778.5*** *p118*
Chorane, Mary 20; Philadelphia, 1853 ***5704.8*** *p111*
Chorne, John; Arkansas, 1918 ***95.2*** *p28*
Chorter, Tho; America, 1701 ***2212*** *p35*
Choru, B. 30; America, 1837 ***778.5*** *p118*
Chose, J. 30; America, 1838 ***778.5*** *p118*
Chouette, Louis; California, 1876 ***2764.35*** *p13*
Choulz, . . .; Canada, 1776-1783 ***9786*** *p18*
Chourro, Francois 20; New Orleans, 1839 ***778.5*** *p118*
Chouvet, Mr. 27; America, 1838 ***778.5*** *p118*
Chouvrier, Mr. 45; America, 1837 ***778.5*** *p118*
Chovelot, A. 12; New Orleans, 1839 ***778.5*** *p118*
Chovier, Pierre 21; New Orleans, 1836 ***778.5*** *p118*
Chowning, Georg; Virginia, 1632 ***6219*** *p180*
Chraniewicz, Tomasz; Boston, 1834 ***4606*** *p179*
With wife
With children
Chrestowska, Stanislawa 18; New York, 1912 ***9980.29*** *p69*
Chris, Miller; Ohio, 1869-1878 ***9892.11*** *p8*
Chrishal, Michel 40; America, 1836 ***778.5*** *p119*
Chrisippe, Jno.; Virginia, 1645 ***6219*** *p232*
Chrisley, James 24; Jamaica, 1736 ***3690.1*** *p42*
Chriss, Miller; Ohio, 1869-1880 ***9892.11*** *p8*
Chriss, Miller 22; Ohio, 1888 ***9892.11*** *p9*
Christ, . . .; Canada, 1776-1783 ***9786*** *p41*
Christ, Mr.; Virginia, 1764 ***8582.1*** *p6*
With wife
Christ, Anna Mary *SEE* Christ, George
Christ, George; New York, 1743 ***3652*** *p59*
*Wife:*Anna Mary
Christ, Gottlieb; Georgia, 1739 ***9332*** *p327*
Christ, James 36; New York, 1774 ***1219.7*** *p203*
Christ, Philip; Pennsylvania, 1768 ***9973.8*** *p32*
Christ, Rudolph; Pennsylvania, 1750 ***2444*** *p145*
Christa, . . .; Canada, 1776-1783 ***9786*** *p18*
Christa, Adam; New York, NY, 1815 ***2859.11*** *p27*
Christansen, Niels Soren 24; Arkansas, 1918 ***95.2*** *p28*
Christe, Anna Wolfer *SEE* Christe, Rudolph
Christe, Johann Jacob *SEE* Christe, Rudolph
Christe, Johann Peter *SEE* Christe, Rudolph
Christe, Margaretha *SEE* Christe, Rudolph
Christe, Maria *SEE* Christe, Rudolph
Christe, Rudolph; Pennsylvania, 1750 ***2444*** *p145*
*Wife:*Anna Wolfer
*Child:*Maria
*Child:*Johann Jacob
*Child:*Johann Peter
*Child:*Margaretha
Christensen, C.; Washington, 1859-1920 ***2872.1*** *p8*
Christensen, Carl Chris; Arkansas, 1918 ***95.2*** *p28*
Christensen, Carl Gebhard; Arkansas, 1918 ***95.2*** *p28*
Christensen, Christen Nielsen; Arkansas, 1918 ***95.2*** *p28*
Christensen, Christian; Arkansas, 1918 ***95.2*** *p28*
Christensen, Claus Hansen; Arkansas, 1918 ***95.2*** *p28*
Christensen, Hans; Bangor, ME, 1889 ***6410.22*** *p126*
Christensen, James; Washington, 1859-1920 ***2872.1*** *p8*
Christensen, James B.; Washington, 1859-1920 ***2872.1*** *p8*
Christensen, James S.; Washington, 1859-1920 ***2872.1*** *p8*
Christensen, Jens Walter; Arkansas, 1918 ***95.2*** *p28*
Christensen, John 23; Arkansas, 1918 ***95.2*** *p28*
Christensen, Kund; Arkansas, 1918 ***95.2*** *p28*
Christensen, Lars Djernes; Arkansas, 1918 ***95.2*** *p28*
Christensen, Laurist Marino F. Magnus; Arkansas, 1918 ***95.2*** *p28*
Christensen, Magnus Christian; Arkansas, 1918 ***95.2*** *p28*
Christensen, Niels Andrew; Arkansas, 1918 ***95.2*** *p28*
Christensen, Paul; Bangor, ME, 1891-1898 ***6410.22*** *p123*
Christensen, Paul; Bangor, ME, 1894 ***6410.22*** *p127*
Christensen, Peter 23; Arkansas, 1918 ***95.2*** *p29*
Christenson, Carl; Colorado, 1904 ***9678.1*** *p157*
Christenson, Christ; Minneapolis, 1879-1883 ***6410.35*** *p52*
Christenson, Christan; Wisconsin, n.d. ***9675.5*** *p49*
Christenson, Hans; Bangor, ME, 1894 ***6410.22*** *p121*
Christer, Jon.; Virginia, 1632 ***6219*** *p180*
Christhoph, Pallansch; Wisconsin, n.d. ***9675.5*** *p49*
Christi, Anna Wolfer *SEE* Christi, Rudolph
Christi, Johann Jacob *SEE* Christi, Rudolph
Christi, Johann Peter *SEE* Christi, Rudolph
Christi, Margaretha *SEE* Christi, Rudolph
Christi, Maria *SEE* Christi, Rudolph
Christi, Rudolph; Pennsylvania, 1750 ***2444*** *p145*
*Wife:*Anna Wolfer
*Child:*Maria
*Child:*Johann Jacob
*Child:*Johann Peter
*Child:*Margaretha
Christian, Aslanis; Arkansas, 1918 ***95.2*** *p29*
Christian, Fredrick; Wisconsin, n.d. ***9675.5*** *p49*
Christian, Hans; New York, NY, 1834 ***8208.4*** *p78*
Christian, John; New York, NY, 1816 ***2859.11*** *p27*
Christian, Mary; America, 1738 ***4971*** *p13*
Christian, Mary; America, 1738-1743 ***4971*** *p91*
Christian, Richard; Virginia, 1643 ***6219*** *p200*
Christian, Steph 30; America, 1703 ***2212*** *p39*
Christian, Thomas 19; Maryland, 1729 ***3690.1*** *p42*
Christian, William 39; Kansas, 1894 ***5240.1*** *p79*
Christiane, Joh. 21; New Orleans, 1839 ***9420.2*** *p166*
Christians, Hemmo H.; Illinois, 1888 ***5012.39*** *p121*
Christiansen, Bernard; Wisconsin, n.d. ***9675.5*** *p49*
Christiansen, Carl Peter 25; Kansas, 1891 ***5240.1*** *p75*
Christiansen, Charles; Wisconsin, n.d. ***9675.5*** *p49*
Christiansen, Christ 24; Arkansas, 1918 ***95.2*** *p29*
Christiansen, Christian; New York, 1761 ***3652*** *p87*
Christiansen, Hans M. 39; Arizona, 1890 ***2764.35*** *p14*
Christiansen, John Christian; New York, 1751 ***3652*** *p75*
Christiansen, Lars 81; Arizona, 1927 ***9228.40*** *p31*
Christiansen, Neils Erick; Arkansas, 1918 ***95.2*** *p29*
Christiansen, Niels Loren; Arkansas, 1918 ***95.2*** *p29*
Christiansen, Sakarias M.; Washington, 1859-1920 ***2872.1*** *p8*
Christianson, Beruld; Wisconsin, n.d. ***9675.5*** *p49*
Christie, Ann Elizabeth; Charleston, SC, 1827 ***1639.20*** *p44*
Christie, Edward; Charleston, SC, 1797 ***1639.20*** *p44*
Christie, Elizabeth 29 *SEE* Christie, John
Christie, James Johnson; New York, NY, 1913 ***9892.11*** *p9*
Christie, John; Nevada, 1864 ***2764.35*** *p12*
Christie, John 35; California, 1872 ***2769.3*** *p4*
Christie, John 56; South Carolina, 1850 ***1639.20*** *p44*
*Relative:*Elizabeth 29
Christie, Margaret; New York, NY, 1811 ***2859.11*** *p9*
With child
Christie, Margaret; Philadelphia, 1852 ***5704.8*** *p87*
Christie, Mary; Philadelphia, 1851 ***5704.8*** *p81*
Christie, Mary Anne; Philadelphia, 1852 ***5704.8*** *p87*
Christie, Michael; Illinois, 1896 ***5012.40*** *p54*
Christie, Robert; America, 1836 ***8893*** *p266*
Christie, Thomas 32; Savannah, GA, 1733 ***4719.17*** *p310*
Christiny, . . .; Canada, 1776-1783 ***9786*** *p41*
Christirsen, Emil Peter; Arkansas, 1918 ***95.2*** *p29*
Christman, Phillip; Ohio, 1851 ***9892.11*** *p9*
Christmann, Jacob; Virginia, 1732 ***8582.3*** *p96*
With father-in-law
Christmas, Dictoris; Virginia, 1635 ***6219*** *p72*
*Wife:*Isabell
Christmas, Dictoris; Virginia, 1639 ***6219*** *p159*
*Wife:*Isbell
Christmas, Dictoris; Virginia, 1642 ***6219*** *p193*
*Wife:*Izabell
Christmas, Isabell *SEE* Christmas, Dictoris
Christmas, Isbell *SEE* Christmas, Dictoris
Christmas, Izabell *SEE* Christmas, Dictoris
Christmas, Rich.; Virginia, 1634 ***6219*** *p84*
Christner, Ilse Emma; Iowa, 1866-1943 ***123.54*** *p59*
Christofanelli, Victor; Arkansas, 1918 ***95.2*** *p29*
Christofelles, Nicholas; Arkansas, 1918 ***95.2*** *p29*
Christoffersen, Martin; Arkansas, 1918 ***95.2*** *p29*
Christofferson, Tarleit; Arkansas, 1918 ***95.2*** *p29*
Christofferson, Valenten H.; Iroquois Co., IL, 1892 ***3455.1*** *p10*
Christopher, Charles 19; Pennsylvania, 1738 ***3690.1*** *p42*
Christopher, Chrales 21; New Orleans, 1862 ***543.30*** *p462*
Christopher, Edward 33; Jamaica, 1733 ***3690.1*** *p43*
Christopher, John 32; St. Christopher, 1730 ***3690.1*** *p43*
Christopherson, Christopher Eggert; Bangor, ME, 1879-1892 ***6410.22*** *p121*
Christopulous, John Apostolos; Arkansas, 1918 ***95.2*** *p29*
Christy, Adam; New York, NY, 1816 ***2859.11*** *p27*
Christy, Charlotte; Philadelphia, 1851 ***5704.8*** *p79*
Christy, David; New York, NY, 1816 ***2859.11*** *p27*
Christy, Elizabeth; New York, NY, 1816 ***2859.11*** *p27*
Christy, George 19; Quebec, 1859 ***5704.8*** *p143*
Christy, Ingeborg; Iowa, 1866-1943 ***123.54*** *p59*
Christy, James 30; New Orleans, 1831 ***778.5*** *p119*
Christy, Jane; New York, NY, 1816 ***2859.11*** *p27*
Christy, Jane 18; Philadelphia, 1856 ***5704.8*** *p129*
Christy, John; New York, NY, 1816 ***2859.11*** *p27*
Christy, John 26; Philadelphia, 1853 ***5704.8*** *p108*
Christy, John 33; New Orleans, 1831 ***778.5*** *p119*
Christy, John 36; Quebec, 1864 ***5704.8*** *p159*
Christy, Margaret 26; New Orleans, 1831 ***778.5*** *p119*
Christy, Martha 20; New Orleans, 1831 ***778.5*** *p119*
Christy, Mary 29; New Orleans, 1831 ***778.5*** *p119*
Christy, Pat. 31; Massachusetts, 1847 ***5881.1*** *p24*
Christy, Peter 28; New Orleans, 1831 ***778.5*** *p119*
Christy, Phillipp; Washington, 1859-1920 ***2872.1*** *p8*
Christy, Rita; Iowa, 1866-1943 ***123.54*** *p59*
Christy, Robert; New York, NY, 1816 ***2859.11*** *p27*
Christy, Rudolph; Pennsylvania, 1750 ***2444*** *p145*
Christy, Sarah 21; Quebec, 1859 ***5704.8*** *p143*
Christy, William 23; Quebec, 1864 ***5704.8*** *p163*
Chrostowski, Bolislaw 26; New York, 1912 ***9980.29*** *p68*
Chrystal, Thomas 26; St. John, N.B., 1859 ***5704.8*** *p140*
Chrzaszcz, Jozef; Iowa, 1866-1943 ***123.54*** *p59*
Chubbick, Robert John 26; Arkansas, 1918 ***95.2*** *p29*
Chudille, D. 35; New Orleans, 1829 ***778.5*** *p119*
Chudzinski, Franciszek 29; New York, 1912 ***9980.29*** *p69*
Chukus, James; Arkansas, 1918 ***95.2*** *p29*
Chulot, A. 35; New Orleans, 1835 ***778.5*** *p119*
Chung, Joe 62; Arizona, 1912 ***9228.40*** *p16*
Church, Agnes; Quebec, 1847 ***5704.8*** *p28*
Church, Agnes 8; Quebec, 1847 ***5704.8*** *p28*
Church, Archibald 25; Quebec, 1863 ***5704.8*** *p154*
Church, Charles 19; Virginia, 1721 ***3690.1*** *p43*
Church, Clinton D. 20; Kansas, 1872 ***5240.1*** *p52*
Church, Edward 23; Maryland, 1775 ***1219.7*** *p268*
Church, Elizabeth 5; Quebec, 1847 ***5704.8*** *p28*
Church, Ernest; Iowa, 1866-1943 ***123.54*** *p14*
Church, George 25; Jamaica, 1736 ***3690.1*** *p43*
Church, Isabella 24; Quebec, 1863 ***5704.8*** *p154*
Church, James 12; Quebec, 1847 ***5704.8*** *p28*
Church, James 16; Maryland, 1722 ***3690.1*** *p43*
Church, John; Philadelphia, 1850 ***5704.8*** *p63*
Church, John 20; Jamaica, 1730 ***3690.1*** *p43*
Church, John 22; Quebec, 1863 ***5704.8*** *p154*
Church, Maitland C.; Kansas, 1875 ***5240.1*** *p8*
Church, Maitland H. 27; Kansas, 1875 ***5240.1*** *p56*
Church, Martin; Virginia, 1639 ***6219*** *p155*
Church, Mary T. 72; Kansas, 1889 ***5240.1*** *p74*
Church, Samuell; Virginia, 1636 ***6219*** *p78*
Church, Thomas; Virginia, 1645 ***6219*** *p239*
Church, Thomas 10; Quebec, 1847 ***5704.8*** *p28*
Church, William 2; Quebec, 1847 ***5704.8*** *p28*
Church, William, Jr.; New York, NY, 1838 ***8208.4*** *p87*
Church, William H. 27; Kansas, 1875 ***5240.1*** *p56*
Churchill, Edward; Antigua (Antego), 1764 ***1219.7*** *p99*
Churchill, John Charles 40; California, 1867 ***3840.1*** *p16*
Churchill, Joseph; New York, NY, 1835 ***8208.4*** *p8*
Churchill, O. F.; Washington, 1859-1920 ***2872.1*** *p8*
Churchill, Thomas 21; Jamaica, 1733 ***3690.1*** *p43*
Churchill, Thos 27; Philadelphia, 1845 ***6508.6*** *p115*
Churchley, Arthur G.; Washington, 1859-1920 ***2872.1*** *p8*
Churchs, John 20; Maryland, 1730 ***3690.1*** *p43*
Churden, Caroline 25; America, 1831 ***778.5*** *p119*
Churden, Michael 27; America, 1831 ***778.5*** *p119*
Churoy, Michel 25; America, 1827 ***778.5*** *p119*
Chusburg, John; Iowa, 1866-1943 ***123.54*** *p14*
Chusman, Alfred; Illinois, 1841 ***7857*** *p2*
Chute, Tho.; Virginia, 1635 ***6219*** *p19*
Chutkowski, Ignacy; New York, 1835 ***4606*** *p179*
Ciacentini, Joseph; Shreveport, LA, 1876 ***7129*** *p44*
Ciacio, Luigi; Arkansas, 1918 ***95.2*** *p29*
Cialdini, Alfredo; Wisconsin, n.d. ***9675.5*** *p49*
Ciallella, Cosmo; Colorado, 1904 ***9678.1*** *p157*
Cianci, Umberto; Arkansas, 1918 ***95.2*** *p29*
Ciaplinski, Benadict; Wisconsin, n.d. ***9675.5*** *p49*
Ciarnla, Constantino; Arkansas, 1918 ***95.2*** *p29*
Ciavarella, Nazario; Washington, 1859-1920 ***2872.1*** *p8*
Cibery, T. 29; Port uncertain, 1838 ***778.5*** *p119*
Ciborosski, Julius 25; Arkansas, 1918 ***95.2*** *p29*
Cican, David; Iowa, 1866-1943 ***123.54*** *p14*
Cicco, Joe; Iowa, 1866-1943 ***123.54*** *p59*
Cicco, Nicola Orlando; Iowa, 1866-1943 ***123.54*** *p59*
Ciccone, Antonio 39; New York, NY, 1893 ***9026.4*** *p41*
Cicha, Antonia 20; New York, 1912 ***9980.29*** *p67*
Cicks, James; Virginia, 1643 ***6219*** *p229*
Ciechanowski, . . .; New York, 1831 ***4606*** *p173*
Ciegeske, Adolf; Minnesota, 1879 ***5240.1*** *p8*
Cieplinski, Julyon; Wisconsin, n.d. ***9675.5*** *p49*
Cieplinski, K.; Wisconsin, n.d. ***9675.5*** *p49*

Cieslet, Stephen; Arkansas, 1918 95.2 p29
Cieszewski, Stanislaw 21; New York, 1912 9980.29 p60
Cifaldi, Mariano Gisumino; Arkansas, 1918 95.2 p29
Cifarelli, Joseph; Arkansas, 1918 95.2 p29
Cigrand, Jacob; Wisconsin, n.d. 9675.5 p49
Cigrand, Nicholas; Wisconsin, n.d. 9675.5 p49
Cikada, Mike; Iowa, 1866-1943 123.54 p14
Ciliak, . . .; Canada, 1776-1783 9786 p41
Ciliakc, . . .; Canada, 1776-1783 9786 p41
Cimarusti, Vito Antonio; Arkansas, 1918 95.2 p29
Cimbler, Jacob; Pennsylvania, 1743 2444 p180
Cimerman, John; Iowa, 1866-1943 123.54 p14
Cimmel, Jacob; Philadelphia, 1765 4779.3 p13
Cinley, Michael; Pennsylvania, 1750 2444 p173
Cinner, James; Arkansas, 1918 95.2 p29
Ciocci, Giuseppe; Arkansas, 1918 95.2 p29
Cioldini, A.; Wisconsin, n.d. 9675.5 p49
Cioldini, R.; Wisconsin, n.d. 9675.5 p49
Cioli, Albert; Wisconsin, n.d. 9675.5 p49
Ciolino, Salvador; Arkansas, 1918 95.2 p29
Cioni, Virgilio; Arkansas, 1918 95.2 p29
Cioro, Akin J.; Arkansas, 1918 95.2 p30
Ciotto, Domenico; Arkansas, 1918 95.2 p30
Circle, Maria; Cincinnati, 1885-1886 9461 p47
Ciriaco, Garofoni; Wisconsin, n.d. 9675.5 p49
Cisne, P. 23; New Orleans, 1839 778.5 p119
Cisneres, Juan 30; Arizona, 1913 9228.40 p17
Cissan, Paul 27; New Orleans, 1838 778.5 p119
Cist, Carl; Philadelphia, 1776 8582.3 p84
Ciste, Andre 27; America, 1837 778.5 p120
Civiri, Juan 24; New Orleans, 1831 778.5 p120
Civiry, J. 26; New Orleans, 1831 778.5 p120
Civitenovich, Joseph; Iowa, 1866-1943 123.54 p14
Civoy, M. 35; Port uncertain, 1835 778.5 p120
Claasen, Claas; New Orleans, 1844 8582.3 p12
Claasen, Wolbert; Cincinnati, 1845-1877 8582.3 p12
Claassen, Claas; America, 1844 8582.1 p6
Claassen, Claas; New Orleans, 1844 8582.3 p12
Claassen, Edward; Kansas, 1881 5240.1 p8
Claassen, John; Indiana, 1892 5240.1 p8
Claassen, Wolbert; America, 1848 8582.1 p6
Claassen, Wolbert; Cincinnati, 1845-1877 8582.3 p12
Clack, Abraham 23; Maryland, 1774 1219.7 p204
Clackett, Leonard; Virginia, 1638 6219 p121
Claeys, Charles; Arkansas, 1918 95.2 p30
Claeys, Leraphiem; Arkansas, 1918 95.2 p30
Clafferty, Bridget; Philadelphia, 1852 5704.8 p85
Clafferty, Margaret; Philadelphia, 1851 5704.8 p71
Claffy, Lavinia 24; Massachusetts, 1847 5881.1 p20
Claffy, Mary 20; Massachusetts, 1850 5881.1 p22
Claffy, Mary 33; Massachusetts, 1850 5881.1 p22
Claffy, Peter 11; Massachusetts, 1850 5881.1 p24
Clagasce, Mrs. 37; Missouri, 1837 778.5 p120
Clagasce, Auguste 4; Missouri, 1837 778.5 p120
Clagasce, Catherine 2; Missouri, 1837 778.5 p120
Clagasce, Frederick 8; Missouri, 1837 778.5 p120
Clagasce, Margaret 6; Missouri, 1837 778.5 p120
Clagasce, Peter 14; Missouri, 1837 778.5 p120
Clagasce, Pierre 37; Missouri, 1837 778.5 p120
Clagasce, Pierre Jacques 6; Missouri, 1837 778.5 p120
Clagasce, Susan 12; Missouri, 1837 778.5 p120
Clagasce, Susette 2; Missouri, 1837 778.5 p120
Clagher, Jane; New York, NY, 1811 2859.11 p9
Claick, . . .; Canada, 1776-1783 9786 p18
Claire, Robert; Quebec, 1825 7603 p21
Claiton, Samuel 19; Jamaica, 1737 3690.1 p46
Clamageran, Jean G. 45; New Orleans, 1823 778.5 p120
Clampton, Philip 26; Philadelphia, 1774 1219.7 p219
Clampton, Thomas 21; Philadelphia, 1774 1219.7 p219
Clan, . . .; Canada, 1776-1783 9786 p18
Clana, Nancy; New Orleans, 1848 5704.8 p48
Clancey, Catharine 9; Massachusetts, 1850 5881.1 p14
Clancey, Elizabeth 7; Massachusetts, 1850 5881.1 p16
Clancey, James; New York, NY, 1816 2859.11 p27
Clancey, John; New York, NY, 1816 2859.11 p27
Clancey, Mary; America, 1739 4971 p71
Clancey, Mary 23; Massachusetts, 1849 5881.1 p21
Clancey, Mary 30; Massachusetts, 1849 5881.1 p21
Clancey, Thomas 21; Quebec, 1859 5704.8 p143
Clancey, Timothy; New York, NY, 1838 8208.4 p75
Clancy, Ann 13; Quebec, 1847 5704.8 p18
Clancy, Bridget 18; Massachusetts, 1849 5881.1 p13
Clancy, Dennis 22; Massachusetts, 1849 5881.1 p15
Clancy, Ellen 30; Massachusetts, 1847 5881.1 p15
With 2 children
Clancy, James; Quebec, 1825 7603 p100
Clancy, Mary; America, 1739 4971 p14
Clancy, Michael 23; Massachusetts, 1849 5881.1 p22
Clancy, Robert; New York, NY, 1816 2859.11 p27
Clancy, Terence; St. John, N.B., 1847 5704.8 p34
Clancy, Thomas; Illinois, 1868 5012.38 p99
Clancy, Thomas; Illinois, 1872 5012.39 p91
Clancy, Thomas 9; Massachusetts, 1850 5881.1 p26
Clansey, James; Virginia, 1638 6219 p150
Clapier, Louis 26; New Orleans, 1829 778.5 p121
Clappier, Louis 27; New Orleans, 1830 778.5 p121
Claprood, . . .; Canada, 1776-1783 9786 p18
Clara, Mrs. 20; America, 1837 778.5 p121
Clara, Ms. 20; America, 1837 778.5 p121
Clara, Dennis 24; Massachusetts, 1847 5881.1 p14
Clara, Judy 30; Massachusetts, 1847 5881.1 p17
Clara, Mary 20; Massachusetts, 1847 5881.1 p20
Clarck, Joseph 16; Jamaica, 1730 3690.1 p44
Clare, John 22; Philadelphia, 1774 1219.7 p232
Clare, Patrick; Illinois, 1872 2896.5 p8
Clare, Rich.; Virginia, 1652 6251 p20
Clare, William Henry 32; Kansas, 1886 5240.1 p69
Clarence, Mr. 24; New Orleans, 1825 778.5 p121
Clariot, Peter 24; New Orleans, 1862 543.30 p457
Clarissa, Ms. 21; Louisiana, 1822 778.5 p121
Clark, Mr.; Quebec, 1815 9229.18 p76
With wife
With son
Clark, Adam; Illinois, 1862 5012.38 p98
Clark, Alexander; Brunswick, NC, 1739 1639.20 p44
Clark, Alfred; Ohio, 1880 9892.11 p9
Clark, Andrew; America, 1798 1639.20 p44
Clark, Andrew; North Carolina, 1759-1796 1639.20 p44
Clark, Ann SEE Clark, William
Clark, Ann; Philadelphia, 1811 2859.11 p9
Clark, Anne McNaughtan SEE Clark, John
Clark, Archibald; Brunswick, NC, 1739 1639.20 p44
Clark, Benjamin 17; Pennsylvania, Virginia or Maryland, 1722 3690.1 p43
Clark, Bridget; America, 1741 4971 p16
Clark, Bridget; Annapolis, MD, 1742 4971 p92
Clark, Bridget; Maryland, 1742 4971 p107
Clark, Bridget 10; Massachusetts, 1850 5881.1 p14
Clark, Catharine 5; Massachusetts, 1850 5881.1 p14
Clark, Cath'ine 20; Massachusetts, 1849 5881.1 p14
Clark, Charles; New York, NY, 1815 2859.11 p27
Clark, Charles 11 SEE Clark, Robert
Clark, Charles 21; Jamaica, 1737 3690.1 p45
Clark, Charles L.; Washington, 1859-1920 2872.1 p8
Clark, Daniel; Jamaica, 1760 1219.7 p78
Clark, Daniel 73; North Carolina, 1850 1639.20 p44
Clark, David; Illinois, 1882 2896.5 p7
Clark, David; Philadelphia, 1811 53.26 p12
Clark, David; Philadelphia, 1811 2859.11 p9
Clark, Edward; New York, NY, 1811 2859.11 p9
Clark, Edward; Virginia, 1698 2212 p15
Clark, Eleanor 57; South Carolina, 1850 1639.20 p45
Clark, Eleanor 61; North Carolina, 1850 1639.20 p44
Clark, Eliza Jane 18; St. John, N.B., 1853 5704.8 p110
Clark, Elizabeth 28; Quebec, 1855 5704.8 p125
Clark, Francis 16; Virginia, 1720 3690.1 p43
Clark, Francis 20; Windward Islands, 1722 3690.1 p44
Clark, Francis 48; North Carolina, 1850 1639.20 p45
Clark, George; Colorado, 1895 9678.1 p157
Clark, George; Colorado, 1898 9678.1 p157
Clark, George; St. John, N.B., 1852 5704.8 p83
Clark, George 2; Quebec, 1855 5704.8 p125
Clark, George 18; Virginia, 1773 1219.7 p168
Clark, George 22; Jamaica, 1730 3690.1 p289
Clark, George H.; Kansas, 1876 2764.35 p12
Clark, Hugh; New York, NY, 1816 2859.11 p27
Clark, Hugh; South Carolina, 1716 1639.20 p45
Clark, I. M.; Wisconsin, n.d. 9675.5 p49
Clark, Isabella; St. John, N.B., 1852 5704.8 p83
Clark, Isabella 7; Philadelphia, 1854 5704.8 p118
Clark, Isabella 10; Quebec, 1855 5704.8 p125
Clark, Jacob 23; Maryland, 1774 1219.7 p215
Clark, James; America, 1798 1639.20 p45
Clark, James; California, 1869 2764.35 p12
Clark, James; New York, NY, 1837 8208.4 p53
Clark, James; South Carolina, 1716 1639.20 p45
Clark, James 9 mos; Died enroute, 1733 4719.17 p310
Clark, James 6; Massachusetts, 1850 5881.1 p19
Clark, James 9; Massachusetts, 1849 5881.1 p19
Clark, James 9; Philadelphia, 1854 5704.8 p118
Clark, James 19; Maryland, 1719 3690.1 p44
Clark, James 41; Philadelphia, 1854 5704.8 p118
Clark, James 42; South Carolina, 1774 1219.7 p205
Clark, James A.; Washington, 1859-1920 2872.1 p8
Clark, Jane; New York, NY, 1816 2859.11 p27
Clark, Jane 6; Quebec, 1855 5704.8 p125
Clark, Jessie 24; Philadelphia, 1853 5704.8 p113
Clark, John; America, 1735-1743 4971 p8
Clark, John; America, 1741 4971 p63
Clark, John; America, 1776 8894.1 p192
Wife:Anne McNaughtan
Clark, John; Annapolis, MD, 1742 4971 p93
Clark, John; Canada, 1835 4535.10 p198
With child
Clark, John; Jamaica, 1750 3690.1 p44
Clark, John; Jamaica, 1751 1219.7 p2
Clark, John; Maryland, 1742 4971 p107
Clark, John; New York, 1835 4535.10 p198
With child
Clark, John; New York, NY, 1811 2859.11 p10
Clark, John; New York, NY, 1815 2859.11 p27
Clark, John; New York, NY, 1836 8208.4 p15
Clark, John; North Carolina, 1739 1639.20 p45
Clark, John; Philadelphia, 1816 2859.11 p27
Clark, John 7 mos; Massachusetts, 1849 5881.1 p18
Clark, John 9 mos; St. John, N.B., 1852 5704.8 p83
Clark, John 4 SEE Clark, Robert
Clark, John 14; Maryland or Virginia, 1720 3690.1 p44
Clark, John 18; Philadelphia, 1774 1219.7 p232
Clark, John 19; Jamaica, 1730 3690.1 p44
Clark, John 19; Jamaica, 1731 3690.1 p44
Clark, John 20; Jamaica, 1730 3690.1 p43
Clark, John 21; Jamaica, 1733 3690.1 p44
Clark, John 23; Jamaica, 1739 3690.1 p44
Clark, John 23; Maryland, 1775 1219.7 p262
Clark, John 24; New Orleans, 1862 543.30 p461
Clark, John 28; Virginia, 1774 1219.7 p238
Clark, John 29; New Orleans, 1863 543.30 p463
Clark, John 55; Nova Scotia, 1774 1219.7 p209
Clark, Jonathan; Virginia, 1698 2212 p11
Clark, Joseph 16; Jamaica, 1730 3690.1 p44
Clark, Joseph 17; Philadelphia, 1854 5704.8 p117
Clark, Joseph 18; Philadelphia, 1774 1219.7 p175
Clark, Joseph 21; Virginia, 1774 1219.7 p186
Clark, Judith 24 SEE Clark, Robert
Clark, Judy 8; Massachusetts, 1850 5881.1 p19
Clark, Malcolm; Brunswick, NC, 1739 1639.20 p45
Clark, Margaret; New York, NY, 1816 2859.11 p27
Clark, Margaret 8; Quebec, 1855 5704.8 p125
Clark, Margaret 20; Philadelphia, 1856 5704.8 p128
Clark, Margaret 26; Baltimore, 1775 1219.7 p271
Clark, Margaret 40; Philadelphia, 1854 5704.8 p118
Clark, Martha 20; St. John, N.B., 1863 5704.8 p152
Clark, Mary; Massachusetts, 1850 5881.1 p23
Clark, Mary; New York, NY, 1811 2859.11 p10
Clark, Mary 13 SEE Clark, William
Clark, Mary 50; Massachusetts, 1850 5881.1 p23
Clark, Mary 60; North Carolina, 1850 1639.20 p46
Clark, Mary 72; North Carolina, 1850 1639.20 p45
Clark, Mary Mackenzie; South Carolina, 1750-1757 1639.20 p175
Clark, Mary Schaw; America, 1815 8894.2 p56
Clark, Matthew; New York, NY, 1816 2859.11 p27
Clark, Michael 19; Massachusetts, 1848 5881.1 p20
Clark, Nancy; New York, NY, 1811 2859.11 p10
Clark, Neil; New York, NY, 1816 2859.11 p27
Clark, Neil 57; North Carolina, 1850 1639.20 p46
Clark, Neill; Brunswick, NC, 1767 1639.20 p46
Clark, Neill 75; North Carolina, 1850 1639.20 p46
Clark, Patrick 30; California, 1872 2769.3 p4
Clark, Peter 3 SEE Clark, Robert
Clark, Rachael 3 SEE Clark, William
Clark, Ralph 25; Jamaica, 1731 3690.1 p44
Clark, Richard; Antigua (Antego), 1751 1219.7 p1
Clark, Richard; New York, NY, 1815 2859.11 p27
With wife
Clark, Richard; New York, NY, 1835 8208.4 p46
Clark, Richard 9 SEE Clark, William
Clark, Richard 15; Maryland, 1730 3690.1 p44
Clark, Richard 30; Jamaica, 1774 1219.7 p238
Clark, Richard 50; Nova Scotia, 1774 1219.7 p209
Clark, Robert; America, 1697 2212 p9
Clark, Robert 24; Massachusetts, 1847 5881.1 p24
Clark, Robert 25; Maryland, 1774 1219.7 p220
Clark, Robert 33; Quebec, 1855 5704.8 p125
Clark, Robert 37; Savannah, GA, 1733 4719.17 p310
Son:Charles 11
Son:John 4
Wife:Judith 24
Son:Peter 3
Clark, Samuel; Jamaica, 1763 1219.7 p93
Clark, Samuel 15; Maryland or Virginia, 1719 3690.1 p44
Clark, Samuel 18; Quebec, 1855 5704.8 p126
Clark, Samuel 18; Virginia, 1718-1719 3690.1 p44
Clark, Sarah 12; Philadelphia, 1854 5704.8 p118
Clark, Sarah 19; St. John, N.B., 1853 5704.8 p110
Clark, Sarah 21; Massachusetts, 1849 5881.1 p25
Clark, Susanna 17; Maryland, 1773 1219.7 p173
Clark, Thady; America, 1740 4971 p30
Clark, Thomas; Iowa, 1866-1943 123.54 p59
Clark, Thomas; New York, 1764 1639.20 p46
Clark, Thomas; New York, NY, 1837 8208.4 p34
Clark, Thomas 17; Jamaica, 1720 3690.1 p45
Clark, Thomas 17; Jamaica, 1729 3690.1 p45
Clark, Thomas 18; Virginia, 1774 1219.7 p225
Clark, Thomas 19; Jamaica, 1731 3690.1 p45
Clark, Thomas 21; Baltimore, 1775 1219.7 p270
Clark, Thomas 26; Jamaica, 1733 3690.1 p45

Clark, Thomas 33; Port uncertain, 1774 ***1219.7*** *p176*
Clark, Thomas 39; Maryland, 1774 ***1219.7*** *p225*
Clark, Thomas 40; Maryland, 1774 ***1219.7*** *p178*
Clark, William; Arkansas, 1918 ***95.2*** *p30*
Clark, William; Colorado, 1904 ***9678.1*** *p157*
Clark, William; Illinois, 1853 ***7857*** *p2*
Clark, William; Iowa, 1866-1943 ***123.54*** *p14*
Clark, William; New York, NY, 1811 ***2859.11*** *p10*
Clark, William; New York, NY, 1815 ***2859.11*** *p27*
Clark, William; New York, NY, 1816 ***2859.11*** *p27*
Clark, William; Ohio, 1818-1828 ***9892.11*** *p9*
Clark, William; Philadelphia, 1811 ***53.26*** *p12*
*Relative:*Ann
Clark, William; Philadelphia, 1811 ***2859.11*** *p10*
Clark, William 10 *SEE* Clark, William
Clark, William 17; Jamaica, 1733 ***3690.1*** *p45*
Clark, William 17; Philadelphia, 1853 ***5704.8*** *p111*
Clark, William 19; Maryland, 1774 ***1219.7*** *p214*
Clark, William 19; Philadelphia, 1855 ***5704.8*** *p123*
Clark, William 20; Maryland, 1725 ***3690.1*** *p45*
Clark, William 22; Jamaica, 1773 ***1219.7*** *p168*
Clark, William 29; Maryland, 1775 ***1219.7*** *p253*
Clark, William 30; Port uncertain, 1774 ***1219.7*** *p176*
Clark, William 42; Annapolis, N.S., 1775 ***1219.7*** *p262*
*Child:*Mary 13
*Child:*William 10
*Child:*Richard 9
*Child:*Rachael 3
Clarke, . . .; Philadelphia, 1864 ***5704.8*** *p186*
Clarke, Mr. 38; Dominica, 1774 ***1219.7*** *p223*
Clarke, Alex.; Virginia, 1638 ***6219*** *p159*
Clarke, Alexander; St. John, N.B., 1849 ***5704.8*** *p55*
Clarke, Alexander 2; St. John, N.B., 1864 ***5704.8*** *p159*
Clarke, Alfred; San Francisco, 1851 ***6013.19*** *p90*
Clarke, Ally; Quebec, 1847 ***5704.8*** *p37*
Clarke, Ann; Philadelphia, 1851 ***5704.8*** *p79*
Clarke, Ann; Virginia, 1648 ***6219*** *p251*
Clarke, Anthony; Philadelphia, 1865 ***5704.8*** *p192*
Clarke, Barnabas 21; Virginia, 1775 ***1219.7*** *p261*
Clarke, Bernard 52; Kansas, 1876 ***5240.1*** *p57*
Clarke, Bridget; America, 1742 ***4971*** *p49*
Clarke, Bridget; America, 1742 ***4971*** *p50*
Clarke, Caroline 17; St. John, N.B., 1855 ***5704.8*** *p127*
Clarke, Catharine; Philadelphia, 1864 ***5704.8*** *p182*
Clarke, Catherine; Quebec, 1847 ***5704.8*** *p37*
Clarke, Catherine 13; Philadelphia, 1853 ***5704.8*** *p102*
Clarke, Charles; Virginia, 1638 ***6219*** *p120*
Clarke, Charles 21; Jamaica, 1737 ***3690.1*** *p45*
Clarke, Daniel; Jamaica, 1736 ***3690.1*** *p45*
Clarke, David; Quebec, 1848 ***5704.8*** *p42*
Clarke, David; Virginia, 1638 ***6219*** *p33*
Clarke, David 15; Wilmington, DE, 1831 ***6508.7*** *p161*
Clarke, David 19; St. John, N.B., 1854 ***5704.8*** *p114*
Clarke, Douglas; Virginia, 1637 ***6219*** *p110*
Clarke, Edw.; Virginia, 1637 ***6219*** *p113*
Clarke, Edw.; Virginia, 1643 ***6219*** *p200*
Clarke, Edward; New York, NY, 1864 ***5704.8*** *p173*
Clarke, Edward; Philadelphia, 1847 ***53.26*** *p12*
Clarke, Edward; Philadelphia, 1847 ***5704.8*** *p13*
Clarke, Edward; St. John, N.B., 1847 ***5704.8*** *p34*
Clarke, Edward; Virginia, 1638 ***6219*** *p120*
Clarke, Edward; Virginia, 1638 ***6219*** *p122*
Clarke, Edward 40; Philadelphia, 1803 ***53.26*** *p12*
Clarke, Eliz.; Virginia, 1637 ***6219*** *p113*
Clarke, Eliza *SEE* Clarke, Samuel
Clarke, Eliza; Philadelphia, 1847 ***5704.8*** *p30*
Clarke, Elizabeth; Philadelphia, 1853 ***5704.8*** *p102*
Clarke, Elizabeth; Quebec, 1848 ***5704.8*** *p42*
Clarke, Elizabeth; Virginia, 1638 ***6219*** *p147*
Clarke, Elizabeth; Virginia, 1646 ***6219*** *p236*
Clarke, Francis 7; Philadelphia, 1864 ***5704.8*** *p182*
Clarke, Francis 11; Philadelphia, 1864 ***5704.8*** *p182*
Clarke, Francis 21; Jamaica, 1739 ***3690.1*** *p45*
Clarke, Geo.; Virginia, 1636 ***6219*** *p34*
Clarke, Georg; Virginia, 1635 ***6219*** *p25*
Clarke, George 13; Quebec, 1848 ***5704.8*** *p42*
Clarke, Hugh 10; St. John, N.B., 1849 ***5704.8*** *p55*
Clarke, Isabella; Philadelphia, 1864 ***5704.8*** *p182*
Clarke, James; New York, NY, 1815 ***2859.11*** *p27*
Clarke, James; New York, NY, 1835 ***8208.4*** *p6*
Clarke, James; Philadelphia, 1847 ***53.26*** *p12*
Clarke, James; Philadelphia, 1847 ***5704.8*** *p23*
Clarke, James; Quebec, 1847 ***5704.8*** *p38*
Clarke, James; St. John, N.B., 1847 ***5704.8*** *p34*
Clarke, James; St. John, N.B., 1848 ***5704.8*** *p38*
Clarke, James 2; Philadelphia, 1852 ***5704.8*** *p85*
Clarke, James 4; St. John, N.B., 1864 ***5704.8*** *p159*
Clarke, James 17; New England, 1699 ***2212*** *p19*
Clarke, James 21; Philadelphia, 1775 ***1219.7*** *p271*
Clarke, James 23; Philadelphia, 1774 ***1219.7*** *p200*
Clarke, Jane *SEE* Clarke, Samuel
Clarke, Jane; Philadelphia, 1847 ***5704.8*** *p30*
Clarke, Jane; Philadelphia, 1849 ***53.26*** *p12*
Clarke, Jane; Philadelphia, 1849 ***5704.8*** *p55*
Clarke, Jane; Quebec, 1847 ***5704.8*** *p37*
Clarke, Jane 28; St. John, N.B., 1864 ***5704.8*** *p159*
Clarke, John; New York, NY, 1833 ***8208.4*** *p40*
Clarke, John; Philadelphia, 1851 ***5704.8*** *p79*
Clarke, John; Quebec, 1847 ***5704.8*** *p7*
Clarke, John; Quebec, 1847 ***5704.8*** *p37*
Clarke, John; Virginia, 1635 ***6219*** *p69*
Clarke, John; Virginia, 1637 ***6219*** *p84*
Clarke, John; Virginia, 1638 ***6219*** *p117*
Clarke, John; Virginia, 1644 ***6219*** *p230*
Clarke, John; Virginia, 1646 ***6219*** *p244*
Clarke, John; Virginia, 1757 ***1219.7*** *p57*
Clarke, John 20; Philadelphia, 1833 ***53.26*** *p12*
Clarke, John 20; Philadelphia, 1860 ***5704.8*** *p144*
Clarke, John 31; West Indies, 1734 ***3690.1*** *p45*
Clarke, John F.; Virginia, 1855 ***4626.16*** *p15*
Clarke, Jonathan; America, 1698 ***2212*** *p10*
Clarke, Joseph; New York, NY, 1749-1850 ***1639.20*** *p45*
Clarke, Joseph 18; Quebec, 1856 ***5704.8*** *p130*
Clarke, Kitty; Montreal, 1821 ***7603*** *p66*
Clarke, Margaret; Philadelphia, 1852 ***5704.8*** *p85*
Clarke, Margaret; Philadelphia, 1864 ***5704.8*** *p186*
Clarke, Margaret; Quebec, 1848 ***5704.8*** *p42*
Clarke, Margaret; St. John, N.B., 1849 ***5704.8*** *p55*
Clarke, Margaret Jane 9 mos; St. John, N.B., 1848 ***5704.8*** *p38*
Clarke, Mary *SEE* Clarke, Phillipp
Clarke, Mary; Philadelphia, 1848 ***53.26*** *p13*
Clarke, Mary; Philadelphia, 1848 ***5704.8*** *p46*
Clarke, Mary; Philadelphia, 1849 ***53.26*** *p13*
Clarke, Mary; Philadelphia, 1849 ***5704.8*** *p53*
Clarke, Mary; Quebec, 1847 ***5704.8*** *p8*
Clarke, Mary; Quebec, 1847 ***5704.8*** *p37*
Clarke, Mary 8; Quebec, 1848 ***5704.8*** *p42*
Clarke, Mary 9; Quebec, 1847 ***5704.8*** *p38*
Clarke, Mary Ann; St. John, N.B., 1848 ***5704.8*** *p38*
Clarke, Mary J.; Philadelphia, 1847 ***53.26*** *p13*
Clarke, Mary J.; Philadelphia, 1847 ***5704.8*** *p13*
Clarke, Mary Jane 17; Philadelphia, 1856 ***5704.8*** *p129*
Clarke, Mary Jane 21; Philadelphia, 1853 ***5704.8*** *p112*
Clarke, Matilda *SEE* Clarke, Samuel
Clarke, Matilda; Philadelphia, 1847 ***5704.8*** *p30*
Clarke, Michael; Quebec, 1847 ***5704.8*** *p37*
Clarke, Michaell; Virginia, 1642 ***6219*** *p186*
Clarke, Nathaniel; Virginia, 1636 ***6219*** *p16*
Clarke, Nathaniell; Virginia, 1637 ***6219*** *p109*
Clarke, Nicho.; Virginia, 1635 ***6219*** *p12*
Clarke, Nicholas; Virginia, 1638 ***6219*** *p120*
Clarke, Noble 28; St. John, N.B., 1864 ***5704.8*** *p159*
Clarke, Oliver 14; Philadelphia, 1860 ***5704.8*** *p144*
Clarke, Pat; Quebec, 1847 ***5704.8*** *p37*
Clarke, Patrick; Quebec, 1847 ***5704.8*** *p38*
Clarke, Patrick 13; Philadelphia, 1864 ***5704.8*** *p182*
Clarke, Patrick 21; Philadelphia, 1774 ***1219.7*** *p237*
Clarke, Peggy; Quebec, 1847 ***5704.8*** *p38*
Clarke, Philip 21; Philadelphia, 1774 ***1219.7*** *p237*
Clarke, Phillipp; Virginia, 1638 ***6219*** *p147*
*Wife:*Mary
Clarke, Randall; Virginia, 1642 ***6219*** *p197*
Clarke, Rich.; Virginia, 1635 ***6219*** *p20*
Clarke, Rich.; Virginia, 1643 ***6219*** *p199*
Clarke, Robert; Philadelphia, 1850 ***5704.8*** *p64*
Clarke, Robert; Virginia, 1647 ***6219*** *p247*
Clarke, Robert 11; Quebec, 1848 ***5704.8*** *p42*
Clarke, Robt.; Virginia, 1636 ***6219*** *p108*
Clarke, Rose; St. John, N.B., 1849 ***5704.8*** *p55*
Clarke, Sally 12; Quebec, 1847 ***5704.8*** *p38*
Clarke, Sally 25; Philadelphia, 1853 ***5704.8*** *p112*
Clarke, Samuel; Philadelphia, 1847 ***53.26*** *p13*
*Relative:*Jane
*Relative:*Matilda
*Relative:*Eliza
Clarke, Samuel; Philadelphia, 1847 ***5704.8*** *p30*
Clarke, Samuel; Quebec, 1848 ***5704.8*** *p42*
Clarke, Sarah Ann 12; St. John, N.B., 1849 ***5704.8*** *p55*
Clarke, Susan 18; Philadelphia, 1865 ***5704.8*** *p165*
Clarke, Tho.; Virginia, 1639 ***6219*** *p18*
Clarke, Tho.; Virginia, 1639 ***6219*** *p157*
Clarke, Thomas; Philadelphia, 1865 ***5704.8*** *p195*
Clarke, Thomas; Quebec, 1847 ***5704.8*** *p37*
Clarke, Thomas; Virginia, 1637 ***6219*** *p112*
Clarke, Thomas; Virginia, 1643 ***6219*** *p200*
Clarke, Thomas 12; St. John, N.B., 1847 ***5704.8*** *p34*
Clarke, Thomas 18; Maryland, 1773 ***1219.7*** *p173*
Clarke, Thomas 21; Jamaica, 1738 ***3690.1*** *p45*
Clarke, Thomas 21; St. John, N.B., 1859 ***5704.8*** *p140*
Clarke, Thomas 25; Maryland, 1737 ***3690.1*** *p45*
Clarke, Thomas Ann; Charles Town, SC, 1768 ***1219.7*** *p137*
Clarke, Uriah; Virginia, 1636 ***6219*** *p75*
Clarke, Walter 19; Philadelphia, 1861 ***5704.8*** *p148*
Clarke, William; Philadelphia, 1864 ***5704.8*** *p186*
Clarke, William; Quebec, 1848 ***5704.8*** *p42*
Clarke, William; St. John, N.B., 1847 ***5704.8*** *p34*
Clarke, William; Virginia, 1635 ***6219*** *p5*
Clarke, William 6 mos; St. John, N.B., 1849 ***5704.8*** *p55*
Clarke, William 18; Maryland, 1775 ***1219.7*** *p254*
Clarke, William 21; Virginia, 1775 ***1219.7*** *p261*
Clarke, Wm.; Virginia, 1637 ***6219*** *p13*
Clarkson, Andrew; Colorado, 1894 ***9678.1*** *p157*
Clarkson, Ann; Virginia, 1638 ***6219*** *p119*
Clarkson, Catharine 21; Massachusetts, 1849 ***5881.1*** *p14*
Clarkson, Charles 19; North America, 1774 ***1219.7*** *p200*
Clarkson, James; Carolina, 1684 ***1639.20*** *p46*
Clarkson, Jane; Virginia, 1638 ***6219*** *p119*
Clarmont, Mme.; America, 1839 ***778.5*** *p121*
Clarmont, Ms.; America, 1839 ***778.5*** *p121*
Clarmont, C.; America, 1839 ***778.5*** *p121*
Clary, Bridget 22; Philadelphia, 1853 ***5704.8*** *p114*
Clary, Catherine 16; Quebec, 1855 ***5704.8*** *p124*
Clary, Francis 22; Philadelphia, 1853 ***5704.8*** *p114*
Clary, John; Philadelphia, 1811 ***53.26*** *p13*
Clary, John; Philadelphia, 1811 ***2859.11*** *p10*
Clary, Morris 27; Massachusetts, 1847 ***5881.1*** *p20*
Clary, Patrick; Illinois, 1858 ***2896.5*** *p8*
Clary, Patrick 29; New Orleans, 1862 ***543.30*** *p452*
Clary, Thomas; Illinois, 1860 ***2896.5*** *p8*
Clary, Thomas; Virginia, 1642 ***6219*** *p18*
Clary, Thomas; Virginia, 1642 ***6219*** *p197*
Clasen, Fred; Wisconsin, n.d. ***9675.5*** *p49*
Clasheide, Henry; Cincinnati, 1869-1887 ***8582*** *p5*
Clason, Jon.; Virginia, 1637 ***6219*** *p111*
Class, John; New York, NY, 1811 ***2859.11*** *p10*
With family
Classe, Ms. 16; America, 1839 ***778.5*** *p121*
Classe, Ms. 18; America, 1839 ***778.5*** *p121*
Classe, Ms. 20; America, 1839 ***778.5*** *p121*
Classe, Thresa 37; America, 1839 ***778.5*** *p121*
Classen, . . .; Canada, 1776-1783 ***9786*** *p41*
Classon, Nicholas 19; Maryland, 1725 ***3690.1*** *p46*
Classons, Nicholas 19; Maryland, 1725 ***3690.1*** *p46*
Clatworthy, James 45 *SEE* Clatworthy, Janette
Clatworthy, Janette 38; South Carolina, 1850 ***1639.20*** *p46*
*Relative:*James 45
Claude, . . .; Canada, 1776-1783 ***9786*** *p18*
Claude, Francis 36; Port uncertain, 1836 ***778.5*** *p121*
Claudel, Miss 22; America, 1830 ***778.5*** *p121*
Claudet, Constant 27; New Orleans, 1835 ***778.5*** *p122*
Claudius, . . .; Canada, 1776-1783 ***9786*** *p18*
Claughey, . . .; New York, NY, 1815 ***2859.11*** *p27*
Claughey, James; New York, NY, 1816 ***2859.11*** *p27*
Claughey, John; New York, NY, 1816 ***2859.11*** *p27*
Claughey, Mary; New York, NY, 1816 ***2859.11*** *p27*
Claughey, Sarah; New York, NY, 1816 ***2859.11*** *p27*
Claughlin, Bridget 24; Massachusetts, 1848 ***5881.1*** *p13*
Claughlin, Eunice 12; Massachusetts, 1848 ***5881.1*** *p15*
Claughton, James; Virginia, 1652 ***6251*** *p20*
Claus, . . .; Canada, 1776-1783 ***9786*** *p18*
Claus, George 23; New Orleans, 1835 ***778.5*** *p122*
Claus, Gustave Adolf; Wisconsin, n.d. ***9675.5*** *p49*
Claus, Henry; Canada, 1776-1783 ***9786*** *p207A*
Claus, Jacob; Iroquois Co., IL, 1892 ***3455.1*** *p10*
Claus, Jacob; New York, NY, 1838 ***8208.4*** *p59*
Claus, Karl; Philadelphia, 1777-1782 ***8137*** *p7*
Claus, Thomas; Virginia, 1648 ***6219*** *p250*
Clausen, Anders Tranholm; Arkansas, 1918 ***95.2*** *p30*
Clausen, Casten 34; Kansas, 1904 ***5240.1*** *p83*
Clausen, Claus Jorgen; Arkansas, 1918 ***95.2*** *p30*
Clausen, Henry; New York, NY, 1836 ***8208.4*** *p13*
Clausen, Henry; Wisconsin, n.d. ***9675.5*** *p49*
Clausen, Peter 44; America, 1838 ***778.5*** *p122*
Clausen, Walter; Arkansas, 1918 ***95.2*** *p30*
Clausheide, Anna M. Brokmann *SEE* Clausheide, Johann Heinrich
Clausheide, Anna Margarete Luise; America, 1837 ***4815.7*** *p92*
Clausheide, Friedrich Heinrich; America, 1830 ***4815.7*** *p92*
Clausheide, Johann Heinrich; America, 1837 ***4815.7*** *p92*
*Wife:*Anna M. Brokmann
Clausheide, Wilhelmine E. Kaiser; America, 1837 ***4815.7*** *p92*
Clausing, Frederick; Wisconsin, n.d. ***9675.5*** *p49*
Clauso, Giovanni; Arkansas, 1918 ***95.2*** *p30*
Clauson, Cath'ine 20; Massachusetts, 1849 ***5881.1*** *p14*
Clauss, Johann Jost; Trenton, NJ, 1776 ***8137*** *p7*
Claussen, Andrew; Arkansas, 1918 ***95.2*** *p30*
Claussen, Christen Nilsen; Arkansas, 1918 ***95.2*** *p30*
Claussen, Emil Johanest; Arkansas, 1918 ***95.2*** *p30*
Claussen, Jens Christian 23; Arkansas, 1918 ***95.2*** *p30*
Claussen, Johann Christian Heinrich; America, 1842 ***8582.3*** *p12*
Claussen, Oscar; Arkansas, 1918 ***95.2*** *p30*
Clauvet, Widow 68; America, 1836 ***778.5*** *p122*

Clavau, John 32; New Orleans, 1838 ***778.5*** *p122*
Clave, Francois 31; New Orleans, 1832 ***778.5*** *p122*
Clave, John 22; New Orleans, 1832 ***778.5*** *p122*
Clave, Phillip; Virginia, 1648 ***6219*** *p250*
Clavel, Antoine 30; New Orleans, 1825 ***778.5*** *p122*
Claverie, J. B. 29; New Orleans, 1825 ***778.5*** *p122*
Clavet, J. 40; Port uncertain, 1836 ***778.5*** *p122*
Clavin, Catharine 60; Massachusetts, 1848 ***5881.1*** *p14*
Clavin, Ellen 15; Massachusetts, 1848 ***5881.1*** *p15*
Clawley, John 45; Massachusetts, 1848 ***5881.1*** *p17*
Clawley, Nancy 20; Massachusetts, 1848 ***5881.1*** *p23*
Clay, Henry 31; North Carolina, 1736 ***3690.1*** *p46*
Clay, Jno.; Virginia, 1643 ***6219*** *p208*
Clay, John; Barbados, 1771 ***1219.7*** *p149*
Clay, Jon.; Virginia, 1642 ***6219*** *p197*
Clay, Thomas; Virginia, 1646 ***6219*** *p244*
Clay, William 17; Jamaica, 1736 ***3690.1*** *p46*
Clayborne, Edward; Virginia, 1636 ***6219*** *p15*
Clayden, Ellianor; Virginia, 1638 ***6219*** *p122*
Claydon, Charles D.; Washington, 1859-1920 ***2872.1*** *p8*
Claydon, Lillian Rhoda; Washington, 1859-1920 ***2872.1*** *p8*
Claydon, Lily Eugenie; Washington, 1859-1920 ***2872.1*** *p8*
Claydon, Robert Henry; Arkansas, 1918 ***95.2*** *p30*
Claypoole, Helena Mercer *SEE* Claypoole, James
Claypoole, James; Pennsylvania, 1682 ***4961*** *p12*
Claypoole, James; Pennsylvania, 1683 ***4961*** *p13*
*Wife:*Helena Mercer
With children
Claypoole, John; Pennsylvania, 1682 ***4961*** *p13*
Clayton, Daniel; America, 1740 ***4971*** *p15*
Clayton, Daniel; America, 1740 ***4971*** *p86*
Clayton, Dennis; Maryland, 1740 ***4971*** *p91*
Clayton, Dennis; Philadelphia, 1741 ***4971*** *p92*
Clayton, Francis; Wilmington, NC, 1790 ***1639.20*** *p47*
Clayton, Henry 36; Maryland, 1773 ***1219.7*** *p173*
Clayton, James 16 *SEE* Clayton, James
Clayton, James 50; Pennsylvania, 1682 ***4961*** *p10*
*Wife:*Jane 48
*Child:*James 16
*Child:*Sarah 14
*Child:*John 11
*Child:*Mary 8
*Child:*Josuah 5
*Child:*Lydia 5
Clayton, Jane 48 *SEE* Clayton, James
Clayton, John; North Carolina, 1739 ***1639.20*** *p47*
Clayton, John; Pennsylvania, 1609-1744 ***4961*** *p12*
*Brother:*Paul
Clayton, John 11 *SEE* Clayton, James
Clayton, Joshua; Pennsylvania, 1682 ***4961*** *p10*
Clayton, Josuah 5 *SEE* Clayton, James
Clayton, Lydia 5 *SEE* Clayton, James
Clayton, Mary 8 *SEE* Clayton, James
Clayton, Mary 24; Virginia, 1699 ***2212*** *p26*
Clayton, Paul *SEE* Clayton, John
Clayton, Richard; Virginia, 1636 ***6219*** *p32*
Clayton, Richard 21; Maryland, 1774 ***1219.7*** *p224*
Clayton, Samuel 19; Jamaica, 1737 ***3690.1*** *p46*
Clayton, Sarah 14 *SEE* Clayton, James
Clayton, Sarah 17; Maryland, 1774 ***1219.7*** *p207*
Clayton, Tho.; Virginia, 1635 ***6219*** *p70*
Clayton, Tho.; Virginia, 1637 ***6219*** *p180*
Clayton, Thomas; North Carolina, 1793 ***1639.20*** *p47*
Clayton, Thomas; Virginia, 1698 ***2212*** *p12*
Clayton, Towers 18; Jamaica, 1730 ***3690.1*** *p46*
Clean, Richard 34; Virginia, 1774 ***1219.7*** *p244*
Clear, Mary; New York, NY, 1816 ***2859.11*** *p27*
Clearla, . . .; Canada, 1776-1783 ***9786*** *p18*
Cleary, Andrew; America, 1735-1743 ***4971*** *p8*
Cleary, Andrew; Philadelphia, 1816 ***2859.11*** *p27*
Cleary, Ann; Quebec, 1847 ***5704.8*** *p12*
Cleary, Bridget 23; Massachusetts, 1850 ***5881.1*** *p14*
Cleary, Darby; America, 1736 ***4971*** *p44*
Cleary, Edward 13; Quebec, 1847 ***5704.8*** *p12*
Cleary, Edward 23; Massachusetts, 1849 ***5881.1*** *p15*
Cleary, James 6; Quebec, 1847 ***5704.8*** *p12*
Cleary, John; Illinois, 1898 ***2896.5*** *p8*
Cleary, John; New York, NY, 1835 ***8208.4*** *p4*
Cleary, John; New York, NY, 1838 ***8208.4*** *p64*
Cleary, John 13; Quebec, 1847 ***5704.8*** *p12*
Cleary, Joseph 31; Kansas, 1879 ***5240.1*** *p60*
Cleary, Margaret 6 mos; Quebec, 1847 ***5704.8*** *p12*
Cleary, Martin; America, 1736-1743 ***4971*** *p58*
Cleary, Mary; Philadelphia, 1865 ***5704.8*** *p198*
Cleary, Mary 34; Massachusetts, 1849 ***5881.1*** *p21*
Cleary, Mary Ann 10; Quebec, 1847 ***5704.8*** *p12*
Cleary, Maurice 24; Massachusetts, 1849 ***5881.1*** *p21*
Cleary, Owen; America, 1740 ***4971*** *p53*
Cleary, Owen; America, 1741 ***4971*** *p62*
Cleary, Owen; Quebec, 1847 ***5704.8*** *p12*
Cleary, Patrick; Colorado, 1904 ***9678.1*** *p157*
Cleary, Patrick 8; Quebec, 1847 ***5704.8*** *p12*
Cleary, Rose; Philadelphia, 1865 ***5704.8*** *p198*
Cleary, Thomas; America, 1736-1743 ***4971*** *p58*
Cleary, Thomas; Massachusetts, 1850 ***5881.1*** *p26*
Cleary, Thomas 29; Massachusetts, 1850 ***5881.1*** *p26*
Cleary, William 3; Quebec, 1847 ***5704.8*** *p12*
Cleary, William 21; St. John, N.B., 1856 ***5704.8*** *p131*
Cleaton, James 16 *SEE* Cleaton, James
Cleaton, James 50; Pennsylvania, 1682 ***4961*** *p10*
*Wife:*Jane 48
*Child:*James 16
*Child:*Sarah 14
*Child:*John 11
*Child:*Mary 8
*Child:*Josuah 5
*Child:*Lydia 5
Cleaton, Jane 48 *SEE* Cleaton, James
Cleaton, John 11 *SEE* Cleaton, James
Cleaton, Josuah 5 *SEE* Cleaton, James
Cleaton, Lydia 5 *SEE* Cleaton, James
Cleaton, Mary 8 *SEE* Cleaton, James
Cleaton, Robert John 20; Jamaica, 1773 ***1219.7*** *p172*
Cleaton, Sarah 14 *SEE* Cleaton, James
Cleator, Edward; Washington, 1859-1920 ***2872.1*** *p8*
Cleaveland, Ann 14; St. John Island, 1775 ***1219.7*** *p273*
Cleaver, Charles; New York, NY, 1838 ***8208.4*** *p60*
Cleaver, Phillip; Virginia, 1637 ***6219*** *p85*
Cleaver, Thomas 22; Maryland, 1775 ***1219.7*** *p264*
Cleavin, Ann 34; Massachusetts, 1850 ***5881.1*** *p13*
Cleavin, Margaret 3; Massachusetts, 1850 ***5881.1*** *p22*
Cleavin, Mary 8; Massachusetts, 1850 ***5881.1*** *p22*
Cleavin, Peter 6 mos; Massachusetts, 1850 ***5881.1*** *p24*
Cleavin, Richard 6; Massachusetts, 1850 ***5881.1*** *p25*
Cleavin, William 2; Massachusetts, 1849 ***5881.1*** *p26*
Clebborn, Samuel; New York, NY, 1815 ***2859.11*** *p27*
Cleborne, Marie Nouby; Quebec, 1770 ***7603*** *p29*
Cleer, James 21; New Orleans, 1862 ***543.30*** *p454*
Cleff, Robert von; New Jersey, 1867-1873 ***8125.8*** *p435*
Clefford, Michael 25; Massachusetts, 1849 ***5881.1*** *p22*
Clegg, Joseph; New York, NY, 1816 ***2859.11*** *p27*
Clegg, Samuel 16; Massachusetts, 1849 ***5881.1*** *p25*
Clegg, Wm.; Iowa, 1873 ***5240.1*** *p8*
Clein, Gabriel; Virginia, 1775 ***1219.7*** *p275*
Clein, George Adam; Virginia, 1775 ***1219.7*** *p275*
Cleing, . . .; Canada, 1776-1783 ***9786*** *p18*
Cleing, Albert; Canada, 1776-1783 ***9786*** *p242*
Cleland, Dr.; Charleston, SC, 1647-1747 ***1639.20*** *p47*
Cleland, James 23; Jamaica, 1735 ***3690.1*** *p46*
Cleland, John; New York, NY, 1811 ***2859.11*** *p10*
Cleland, John; South Carolina, 1740 ***1639.20*** *p322*
Cleland, Samuel; New York, NY, 1811 ***2859.11*** *p10*
Clemando, Pierre 30; New Orleans, 1838 ***778.5*** *p122*
Clemason, George; Jamaica, 1751 ***1219.7*** *p1*
Clembolt, Frederick 19; Massachusetts, 1860 ***6410.32*** *p107*
Clembolt, John 50; Massachusetts, 1860 ***6410.32*** *p107*
Clembolt, Salley 48; Massachusetts, 1860 ***6410.32*** *p107*
Clembolt, Sally 12; Massachusetts, 1860 ***6410.32*** *p107*
Clemen, Rudolph 18; America, 1865 ***4610.10*** *p123*
Clemenceau, Robertine 19; New Orleans, 1826 ***778.5*** *p122*
Clemencon, Daniel 36; Halifax, N.S., 1752 ***7074.6*** *p209*
*Son:*Jacques-Christophe
Clemencon, Frederic 18; Halifax, N.S., 1752 ***7074.6*** *p209*
Clemencon, Jacques-Christophe *SEE* Clemencon, Daniel
Clemens, Alfred; Iowa, 1866-1943 ***123.54*** *p14*
Clemens, David; Iowa, 1866-1943 ***123.54*** *p14*
Clemens, Florentine; New York, 1859 ***8125.8*** *p436*
Clemens, J. W.; Washington, 1859-1920 ***2872.1*** *p8*
Clemens, Joseph; Ohio, 1798-1818 ***8582.2*** *p54*
Clemens, Thomas; Iowa, 1866-1943 ***123.54*** *p14*
Clemenshaw, Walter 24; Maryland, 1775 ***1219.7*** *p249*
Clement, Mr. 25; America, 1829 ***778.5*** *p122*
Clement, Charles 40; New Orleans, 1837 ***778.5*** *p122*
Clement, Edey *SEE* Clement, Jeremiah
Clement, Edouard; Quebec, 1710 ***7603*** *p24*
Clement, Ezekiel; Virginia, 1643 ***6219*** *p229*
Clement, Francis; New York, NY, 1837 ***8208.4*** *p25*
Clement, Francois Abel 29; America, 1835 ***778.5*** *p122*
Clement, James 25; Massachusetts, 1847 ***5881.1*** *p17*
Clement, Jeremiah; Virginia, 1635 ***6219*** *p69*
*Wife:*Edey
Clement, John; Virginia, 1635 ***6219*** *p69*
Clement, John 17; Maryland, 1724 ***3690.1*** *p46*
Clement, John 19; Pennsylvania, 1728 ***3690.1*** *p46*
Clement, Joseph Francois 35; America, 1835 ***778.5*** *p123*
Clement, Margarett; Virginia, 1635 ***6219*** *p36*
Clement, Nicolas 31; New Orleans, 1836 ***778.5*** *p123*
Clement, Pat. 20; Massachusetts, 1847 ***5881.1*** *p23*
Clement, Rich.; Virginia, 1623-1700 ***6219*** *p182*
Clement, Robert; Virginia, 1638 ***6219*** *p124*
Clement, William; New York, NY, 1811 ***2859.11*** *p10*
Clements, Mrs. 35; Georgia, 1738 ***9332*** *p331*
Clements, Amey; Virginia, 1643 ***6219*** *p229*
Clements, Ann 1; Philadelphia, 1845 ***6508.6*** *p115*
Clements, Cornelius; Virginia, 1643 ***6219*** *p202*
Clements, Edey *SEE* Clements, Jeremiah
Clements, Eliz. *SEE* Clements, Elizabeth
Clements, Elizabeth; Philadelphia, 1864 ***5704.8*** *p177*
Clements, Elizabeth; Virginia, 1617 ***6219*** *p5*
*Son:*Jeremiah
*Son:*Nicholas
*Son:*Ezekiel
*Daughter:*Eliz.
Clements, Ezekiel *SEE* Clements, Elizabeth
Clements, Geo.; Austin, TX, 1886 ***9777*** *p5*
Clements, George; Iowa, 1866-1943 ***123.54*** *p14*
Clements, Isabella; Philadelphia, 1865 ***5704.8*** *p196*
Clements, James; New York, NY, 1816 ***2859.11*** *p27*
Clements, James; Ohio, 1822 ***9892.11*** *p9*
Clements, Jane 21; America, 1704 ***2212*** *p40*
Clements, Jane 23; Philadelphia, 1845 ***6508.6*** *p115*
Clements, Jeremiah *SEE* Clements, Elizabeth
Clements, Jeremiah; Virginia, 1635 ***6219*** *p69*
*Wife:*Edey
Clements, John 22; Maryland, 1737 ***3690.1*** *p46*
Clements, Margaret; New York, NY, 1816 ***2859.11*** *p27*
Clements, Mary Latitia 15; Philadelphia, 1857 ***5704.8*** *p133*
Clements, Nicholas *SEE* Clements, Elizabeth
Clements, Rich.; Virginia, 1636 ***6219*** *p1*
Clements, Robert; Quebec, 1847 ***5704.8*** *p28*
Clements, Robert; Virginia, 1639 ***6219*** *p157*
Clements, Sally; Quebec, 1847 ***5704.8*** *p13*
Clements, Sarah; Philadelphia, 1864 ***5704.8*** *p177*
Clements, Stanley Curtis; Arkansas, 1918 ***95.2*** *p30*
Clements, William 20; Maryland, 1775 ***1219.7*** *p262*
Clemer, Henerich; Philadelphia, 1730 ***1034.18*** *p11*
*Son:*Johannes
Clemer, Johannes *SEE* Clemer, Henerich
Clemments, John; Philadelphia, 1864 ***5704.8*** *p181*
Clemments, Susan; Philadelphia, 1864 ***5704.8*** *p181*
Clemments, Thomas; Philadelphia, 1864 ***5704.8*** *p181*
Clemo, Thomas; Illinois, 1850 ***7857*** *p2*
Clemow, Captain; Quebec, 1815 ***9229.18*** *p78*
With wife
With 3 children
Clendener, Francis A.; Illinois, 1855 ***7857*** *p2*
Clendining, James 18; Philadelphia, 1803 ***53.26*** *p13*
Cleon, J. E. 28; Louisiana, 1839 ***778.5*** *p123*
Cleppen, Frederick; Ohio, 1856 ***6014.2*** *p7*
Cler, Anthony; Illinois, 1896 ***5012.40*** *p54*
Cler, Frank; Illinois, 1896 ***5012.40*** *p54*
Cler, John; Illinois, 1876 ***5012.37*** *p60*
Cler, John; Illinois, 1896 ***5012.37*** *p63*
Cler, Philipp; Illinois, 1896 ***5012.37*** *p63*
Clere, Francis; New York, NY, 1836 ***8208.4*** *p23*
Clerico, John; Iowa, 1866-1943 ***123.54*** *p14*
Clerk, Mr.; Quebec, 1815 ***9229.18*** *p82*
Clerk, Alexander; North Carolina, 1764 ***1639.20*** *p44*
With family
Clerk, Stephen 26; Grenada, 1774 ***1219.7*** *p231*
Clerk, Thomas; South Carolina, 1716 ***1639.20*** *p46*
Clerke, Genevieve; Quebec, 1794 ***7603*** *p99*
Clerke, J. W. 24; Kansas, 1893 ***5240.1*** *p78*
Clerke, Richard; Virginia, 1646 ***6219*** *p235*
Clerkin, Edward Joseph; Arkansas, 1918 ***95.2*** *p30*
Clerkin, Flan.; America, 1738 ***4971*** *p63*
Clery, John; Illinois, 1898 ***2896.5*** *p8*
Cleve, Lieuts.; Quebec, 1776 ***9786*** *p104*
Cleve, Frederick Christian; Canada, 1776-1783 ***9786*** *p252*
Cleve, Heinrich Urban; Quebec, 1776 ***9786*** *p260*
Cleveden, Wm.; Virginia, 1642 ***6219*** *p191*
Clever, Charles; Wisconsin, n.d. ***9675.5*** *p50*
Clevere, Marke; Virginia, 1638 ***6219*** *p147*
Clevex, Alexis 31; New Orleans, 1838 ***778.5*** *p123*
Clew, Danll 21; New England, 1699 ***2212*** *p19*
Clew, John; Virginia, 1652 ***6251*** *p20*
Clewley, Eliz.; Virginia, 1643 ***6219*** *p206*
Cley, John; Virginia, 1639 ***6219*** *p155*
Clide, Elizabeth; Philadelphia, 1847 ***53.26*** *p13*
Clide, Elizabeth; Philadelphia, 1847 ***5704.8*** *p31*
Clide, Robert 9; Massachusetts, 1847 ***5881.1*** *p24*
Cliff, Edward 24; Jamaica, 1735 ***3690.1*** *p46*
Cliffe, Nich.; Virginia, 1638 ***6219*** *p14*
Clifferty, Ann 18; Philadelphia, 1859 ***5704.8*** *p141*
Clifferty, Mary; New York, NY, 1866 ***5704.8*** *p213*
Clifford, E. 38; Arizona, 1890 ***2764.35*** *p13*
Clifford, Ellen 20; Massachusetts, 1849 ***5881.1*** *p16*
Clifford, Henry 34; Arizona, 1890 ***2764.35*** *p11*
Clifford, John; Illinois, 1892 ***5012.40*** *p27*
Clifford, John; Philadelphia, 1864 ***5704.8*** *p178*
Clifford, John 19; Jamaica, 1731 ***3690.1*** *p46*

Clifford, Mary 20; Massachusetts, 1848 *5881.1 p20*
 With child
Clifford, Michael; Quebec, 1824 *7603 p71*
Clifford, Oliver; Virginia, 1639 *6219 p184*
Clifford, Patrick 28; Massachusetts, 1850 *5881.1 p24*
Clifford, Patrick 30; Massachusetts, 1848 *5881.1 p24*
Clifford, Ralph; Arkansas, 1918 *95.2 p30*
Clifford, Thomas 18; New Orleans, 1862 *543.30 p452*
Clifford, Timothy 21; Massachusetts, 1849 *5881.1 p25*
Clifford, William; Philadelphia, 1864 *5704.8 p178*
Clifford, William 22; Maryland, 1774 *1219.7 p229*
Clift, Thomas; Colorado, 1903 *9678.1 p158*
Clifton, Lady; Virginia, 1648 *6219 p246*
 With daughter
Clifton, James 50; St. Kitts, 1774 *1219.7 p245*
Clifton, Mary; Port uncertain, 1718 *3690.1 p46*
Clifton, Richard; Virginia, 1642 *6219 p196*
Clifton, Thomas; Virginia, 1638 *6219 p146*
Clime, Martin; Charleston, SC, 1775-1781 *8582.2 p52*
Climer, . . .; Pennsylvania, n.d. *1034.18 p12*
Climmer, . . .; Pennsylvania, n.d. *1034.18 p12*
Climo, Thomas; Illinois, 1853 *7857 p2*
Clinch, James; New York, NY, 1815 *2859.11 p27*
Cline, Mr.; North Carolina, 1683-1817 *3702.7 p2*
Cline, Jonathan Herick; Philadelphia, 1761 *9973.7 p35*
Cline, Michael 22; Massachusetts, 1849 *5881.1 p22*
Clingalsmith, Daniel; Pennsylvania, 1738 *4779.3 p13*
 Relative: Frantz Daniel
Clingalsmith, Frantz Daniel *SEE* Clingalsmith, Daniel
Clinglesmith, Daniel; Pennsylvania, 1738 *4779.3 p13*
 Relative: Frantz Daniel
Clinglesmith, Frantz Daniel *SEE* Clinglesmith, Daniel
Clinhence, Nicholas; Ohio, 1841 *8365.25 p12*
Clinton, Anne 2; New York, NY, 1866 *5704.8 p211*
Clinton, Barthelemy; Montreal, 1815 *7603 p75*
Clinton, Bartholomew; New York, NY, 1816 *2859.11 p27*
Clinton, Bridget; New York, NY, 1866 *5704.8 p211*
Clinton, Edward; America, 1742 *4971 p24*
Clinton, Elizabeth 17; Philadelphia, 1853 *5704.8 p113*
Clinton, Isabella; Quebec, 1850 *5704.8 p66*
Clinton, James 26; New Orleans, 1862 *543.30 p456*
Clinton, John; Quebec, 1850 *5704.8 p66*
Clinton, John 5 mos; New York, NY, 1866 *5704.8 p211*
Clinton, John Henry; San Francisco, 1850 *6013.19 p29*
Clinton, William 19; Philadelphia, 1853 *5704.8 p113*
Clion, Jacques 37; America, 1838 *778.5 p123*
Cllayer, Wm. G. 46; Harris Co., TX, 1899 *6254 p5*
Cloane, W.; New York, NY, 1816 *2859.11 p27*
Clock, Mathw.; New York, NY, 1816 *2859.11 p27*
 With wife
Clodal, M. 31; New Orleans, 1837 *778.5 p123*
Clode, Stephen 21; New Orleans, 1837 *778.5 p123*
Clohecy, Mark; New York, NY, 1836 *8208.4 p21*
Clohecy, Mark 32; Kansas, 1884 *5240.1 p66*
Cloirec, Jean-Joseph; Louisiana, 1789-1819 *778.5 p555*
Clomet, Mr. 27; America, 1838 *778.5 p123*
Cloninger, J. S.; Washington, 1859-1920 *2872.1 p8*
Clonninger, J. S.; Washington, 1859-1920 *2872.1 p8*
Clooke, Tho.; Virginia, 1636 *6219 p74*
Cloon, Michael; America, 1743 *4971 p84*
Cloos, Jean Baptist; Wisconsin, n.d. *9675.5 p49*
Cloos, Jean Baptiste; Wisconsin, n.d. *9675.5 p49*
Cloos, Nic.; Wisconsin, n.d. *9675.5 p49*
Clos, Margaretha Catharina; Pennsylvania, 1766 *4349 p48*
Close, Ann 2 *SEE* Close, Henry
Close, Fred; Washington, 1859-1920 *2872.1 p8*
Close, Hanna 32 *SEE* Close, Henry
Close, Henry 42; Savannah, GA, 1733 *4719.17 p310*
 Daughter: Ann 2
 Wife: Hanna 32
Closkey, Thomas 45; Massachusetts, 1849 *5881.1 p25*
Closse, Patrick; Virginia, 1641 *6219 p185*
Closterman, Mr. 17; New Orleans, 1839 *778.5 p123*
Closterman, Mr. 50; New Orleans, 1839 *778.5 p123*
Closterman, Ms. 16; New Orleans, 1839 *778.5 p123*
Closterman, Ms. 46; New Orleans, 1839 *778.5 p123*
Clostermann, Heinrich; America, 1839 *8582.3 p12*
Cloteau, Louis; Louisiana, 1789-1819 *778.5 p555*
Clothard, Anthony; New York, NY, 1811 *2859.11 p10*
Clotworthy, James; Colorado, 1904 *9678.1 p158*
Clouchel, Antoine 19; Louisiana, 1839 *778.5 p123*
Cloud, Mary; America, 1697 *2212 p9*
Cloud, Robert; Virginia, 1643 *6219 p204*
Clough, John 40; Virginia, 1775 *1219.7 p261*
Clough, Sarah 17; Virginia, 1700 *2212 p31*
Clouvel, Leon 18; America, 1838 *778.5 p123*
Clouzell, C. 18; Port uncertain, 1839 *778.5 p124*
Clovss, Gregorius; Wisconsin, n.d. *9675.5 p50*
Clow, John C.; Iowa, 1866-1943 *123.54 p14*
Clowd, Mary; Virginia, 1698 *2212 p14*
Clowney, Mary Jane 11; Philadelphia, 1852 *5704.8 p97*

Clows, Danill 23; New England, 1699 *2212 p18*
Cloyd, Henry; Virginia, 1623-1648 *6219 p252*
Cloyes, Jon.; Virginia, 1635 *6219 p20*
Clozier, . . . 21; Grenada, 1774 *1219.7 p231*
Club, Alexander; Charleston, SC, 1802 *1639.20 p47*
Cluer, Elizabeth 33; Georgia, 1738 *9332 p331*
Cluever, Heinrich; New York, NY, 1925 *3455.4 p92*
Cluff, Margaret; Quebec, 1847 *5704.8 p17*
Cluff, Mary; Quebec, 1849 *5704.8 p51*
Cluff, Mary 13; Quebec, 1849 *5704.8 p51*
Cluff, William; Philadelphia, 1853 *5704.8 p101*
Cluly, Nicho.; Virginia, 1647 *6219 p247*
Clumb, Jacob; Wisconsin, n.d. *9675.5 p50*
Clump, John 28; New Orleans, 1831 *778.5 p124*
Clune, Thomas; Jamaica, 1753 *1219.7 p20*
Clune, Thomas; Jamaica, 1753 *3690.1 p46*
Clunie, Alice; Wilmington, NC, 1791 *1639.20 p47*
Cluq, Charles 22; Port uncertain, 1836 *778.5 p124*
Clures, John Eustration; Arkansas, 1918 *95.2 p30*
Cluver, Annie *SEE* Cluver, Heinrich Diedrich
Cluver, Heinrich Diedrich; New York, NY, 1909 *3455.2 p103*
 Wife: Annie
Cluver, John; Iroquois Co., IL, 1892 *3455.1 p10*
Clyatt, John 18; Maryland or Virginia, 1732 *3690.1 p47*
Clyde, Ann 9; Philadelphia, 1864 *5704.8 p161*
Clyde, Elizabeth 11; Philadelphia, 1853 *5704.8 p112*
Clyde, Elizabeth 17; Philadelphia, 1864 *5704.8 p161*
Clyde, James 17; Philadelphia, 1864 *5704.8 p157*
Clyde, Jane 11; Philadelphia, 1864 *5704.8 p161*
Clyde, Richard 7 mos; Philadelphia, 1864 *5704.8 p161*
Clyde, Robert 5; Philadelphia, 1864 *5704.8 p161*
Clyde, Rose 7; Philadelphia, 1864 *5704.8 p161*
Clyde, Rose 32; Philadelphia, 1864 *5704.8 p161*
Clymer, Georg; Philadelphia, 1776 *8582.3 p80*
Clynch, James; America, 1738 *4971 p13*
Clyncke, August; Colorado, 1904 *9678.1 p158*
Clyncke, Hupoliet; Colorado, 1904 *9678.1 p158*
Clyne, John; New York, NY, 1849 *6013.19 p29*
Clyne, John 21; Philadelphia, 1833-1834 *53.26 p13*
Cnscione, Frank 40; Kansas, 1889 *5240.1 p74*
Coach, Isabella; New York, NY, 1816 *2859.11 p27*
Coach, John; New York, NY, 1816 *2859.11 p27*
Coach, William; New York, NY, 1816 *2859.11 p27*
Coach, William M.; Philadelphia, 1867 *5704.8 p218*
Coache, . . .; Canada, 1776-1783 *9786 p19*
Coady, Edmond; Illinois, 1857 *2896.5 p8*
Coady, Michael; Illinois, 1860 *7857 p2*
Coady, Patrick; Illinois, 1857 *2896.5 p8*
Coaedy, Patrick; Illinois, 1860 *5012.39 p89*
Coagrefourq, Mme. 28; Port uncertain, 1839 *778.5 p124*
Coagrefourq, Mr. 30; Port uncertain, 1839 *778.5 p124*
Coaker, Jonathan 21; Jamaica, 1724 *3690.1 p47*
Coakley, Catharine 14; Massachusetts, 1849 *5881.1 p14*
Coakley, Ellen 15; Massachusetts, 1849 *5881.1 p16*
Coakley, Honora 15; Massachusetts, 1849 *5881.1 p17*
Coakley, John; Illinois, 1858 *2896.5 p8*
Coal, Alley; New York, NY, 1811 *2859.11 p10*
Coal, Catherine; New York, NY, 1811 *2859.11 p10*
 With family
Coal, James; New York, NY, 1811 *2859.11 p10*
Coales, Margt 16; Virginia, 1699 *2212 p27*
Coals, William 20; Maryland, 1729 *3690.1 p47*
Coan, Honora; America, 1735-1743 *4971 p78*
Coane, Catherine 16; Philadelphia, 1861 *5704.8 p148*
Coarraze, M. 25; Port uncertain, 1839 *778.5 p124*
Coasire, Louis David 35; America, 1829 *778.5 p124*
Coate, Abraham; Virginia, 1642 *6219 p194*
Coates, Elizabeth 17; Maryland, 1719 *3690.1 p47*
Coates, Mark J. 68; Kansas, 1880 *5240.1 p62*
Coats, Elizabeth 17; Maryland, 1719 *3690.1 p47*
Coats, Henry 37; Virginia, 1773 *1219.7 p171*
Cobb, Benjamin *SEE* Cobb, Joseph
Cobb, Elizabeth *SEE* Cobb, Joseph
Cobb, George 54; Kansas, 1889 *5240.1 p73*
Cobb, John 30; Pennsylvania, 1728 *3690.1 p47*
Cobb, John 31; Georgia, 1775 *1219.7 p276*
Cobb, Joseph *SEE* Cobb, Joseph
Cobb, Joseph; Virginia, 1637 *6219 p112*
 Wife: Elizabeth
 Son: Joseph
 Son: Benjamin
Cobb, Michael 27; Maryland, 1738 *3690.1 p47*
Cobb, Thomas; Virginia, 1643 *6219 p241*
Cobb, Wm.; Canada, 1836 *4535.10 p196*
 With wife
 With family
Cobbett, John 3; Massachusetts, 1849 *5881.1 p18*
Cobbett, John 30; Massachusetts, 1849 *5881.1 p18*
Cobbett, John 34; Massachusetts, 1849 *5881.1 p18*
Cobbledick, John; Wisconsin, n.d. *9675.5 p50*

Cobbs, Ambrose; Virginia, 1639 *6219 p154*
 Wife: Ann
 Son: Robert
 Daughter: Margarett
Cobbs, Ann *SEE* Cobbs, Ambrose
Cobbs, Margarett *SEE* Cobbs, Ambrose
Cobbs, Robert *SEE* Cobbs, Ambrose
Cobelage, Martin; New York, NY, 1838 *8208.4 p81*
Cobelance, Anna Catharina *SEE* Cobelance, Niclaus
Cobelance, Anna Maria *SEE* Cobelance, Niclaus
Cobelance, Joh. Adam *SEE* Cobelance, Niclaus
Cobelance, Joh. Herman *SEE* Cobelance, Niclaus
Cobelance, Joh. Peter *SEE* Cobelance, Niclaus
Cobelance, Joh. Philip *SEE* Cobelance, Niclaus
Cobelance, Johanna Dorothea *SEE* Cobelance, Niclaus
Cobelance, Maria Margaretha *SEE* Cobelance, Niclaus
Cobelance, Niclaus 45; Pennsylvania, 1743 *1034.18 p7*
 Wife: Anna Catharina
 Child: Joh. Adam
 Child: Joh. Philip
 Child: Joh. Peter
 Child: Joh. Herman
 Child: Maria Margaretha
 Child: Anna Maria
 Child: Johanna Dorothea
Cobelentz, Anna Catharina *SEE* Cobelentz, Johann Niclaus
Cobelentz, Anna Maria *SEE* Cobelentz, Johann Niclaus
Cobelentz, Joh. Adam *SEE* Cobelentz, Johann Niclaus
Cobelentz, Joh. Herman *SEE* Cobelentz, Johann Niclaus
Cobelentz, Joh. Peter *SEE* Cobelentz, Johann Niclaus
Cobelentz, Joh. Philip *SEE* Cobelentz, Johann Niclaus
Cobelentz, Johann Niclaus 45; Pennsylvania, 1743 *1034.18 p6*
 Wife: Anna Catharina
 Child: Joh. Adam
 Child: Joh. Philip
 Child: Joh. Peter
 Child: Joh. Herman
 Child: Maria Margaretha
 Child: Anna Maria
 Child: Johanna Dorothea
Cobelentz, Johanna Dorothea *SEE* Cobelentz, Johann Niclaus
Cobelentz, Maria Margaretha *SEE* Cobelentz, Johann Niclaus
Cobere, Barthelemy 18; America, 1838 *778.5 p124*
Cobewell, Robert 21; Maryland, 1729 *3690.1 p47*
Cobham, George; West Indies, 1752 *1219.7 p11*
Cobham, Robert 39; Philadelphia, 1774 *1219.7 p233*
Cobia, Daniel; Charleston, SC, 1775-1781 *8582.2 p52*
Cobia, Franz; Charleston, SC, 1775-1781 *8582.2 p52*
Cobia, Michael; Charleston, SC, 1775-1781 *8582.2 p52*
Cobin, George 22; Jamaica, 1730 *3690.1 p47*
Cobine, Adelaide 32; America, 1837 *778.5 p124*
Cobine, George; New York, NY, 1811 *2859.11 p10*
Cobine, Robert; New York, NY, 1811 *2859.11 p10*
Coblentz, Anna Catharina *SEE* Coblentz, Niclaus
Coblentz, Anna Maria *SEE* Coblentz, Niclaus
Coblentz, Joh. Adam *SEE* Coblentz, Niclaus
Coblentz, Joh. Herman *SEE* Coblentz, Niclaus
Coblentz, Joh. Peter *SEE* Coblentz, Niclaus
Coblentz, Joh. Philip *SEE* Coblentz, Niclaus
Coblentz, Johanna Dorothea *SEE* Coblentz, Niclaus
Coblentz, Maria Margaretha *SEE* Coblentz, Niclaus
Coblentz, Niclaus 45; Pennsylvania, 1743 *1034.18 p6*
 Wife: Anna Catharina
 Child: Joh. Adam
 Child: Joh. Philip
 Child: Joh. Peter
 Child: Joh. Herman
 Child: Maria Margaretha
 Child: Anna Maria
 Child: Johanna Dorothea
Coblenz, Anna Catharina *SEE* Coblenz, Joh. Nicholas
Coblenz, Anna Maria *SEE* Coblenz, Joh. Nicholas
Coblenz, Joh. Adam *SEE* Coblenz, Joh. Nicholas
Coblenz, Joh. Herman *SEE* Coblenz, Joh. Nicholas
Coblenz, Joh. Nicholas 45; Pennsylvania, 1743 *1034.18 p6*
 Wife: Anna Catharina
 Child: Joh. Adam
 Child: Joh. Philip
 Child: Joh. Peter
 Child: Joh. Herman
 Child: Maria Margaretha
 Child: Anna Maria
 Child: Johanna Dorothea
Coblenz, Joh. Peter *SEE* Coblenz, Joh. Nicholas
Coblenz, Joh. Philip *SEE* Coblenz, Joh. Nicholas
Coblenz, Johanna Dorothea *SEE* Coblenz, Joh. Nicholas
Coblenz, Maria Margaretha *SEE* Coblenz, Joh. Nicholas
Coborn, Elizabeth; America, 1828 *7036 p118*

Coborn, Wm.; New York, NY, 1811 ***2859.11*** *p10*
With family
Cobudge, Joseph 22; Virginia, 1774 ***1219.7*** *p240*
Coburn, Albemarla 24; Kansas, 1878 ***5240.1*** *p59*
Cochet, Jeanne Susanne; New England, 1753 ***2444*** *p156*
Cochet, Rachel; Pennsylvania, 1751 ***2444*** *p199*
Cochey, Benjamin 38; Port uncertain, 1838 ***778.5*** *p124*
Cochina, V. 31; Port uncertain, 1823 ***778.5*** *p124*
Cochlan, Peter; Maryland, 1740 ***4971*** *p91*
Cochlan, Peter; Philadelphia, 1741 ***4971*** *p92*
Cochlin, James; New York, NY, 1811 ***2859.11*** *p10*
Cochon, Jean 28; America, 1837 ***778.5*** *p124*
Cochraine, Agnes 11; Quebec, 1864 ***5704.8*** *p162*
Cochraine, Alexander 9; Quebec, 1864 ***5704.8*** *p162*
Cochraine, Archibald 1; Quebec, 1864 ***5704.8*** *p162*
Cochraine, Elizabeth 66; Philadelphia, 1857 ***5704.8*** *p132*
Cochraine, Henrettia 7; Quebec, 1864 ***5704.8*** *p162*
Cochraine, Hugh 3; Quebec, 1864 ***5704.8*** *p162*
Cochraine, Hugh 36; Quebec, 1864 ***5704.8*** *p162*
Cochraine, Mary 5; Quebec, 1864 ***5704.8*** *p162*
Cochraine, Mary 33; Quebec, 1864 ***5704.8*** *p162*
Cochran, Mr.; New York, NY, 1811 ***2859.11*** *p10*
Cochran, Adessa 6 *SEE* Cochran, James
Cochran, Adessa 6; Philadelphia, 1847 ***5704.8*** *p13*
Cochran, Agnes; New York, NY, 1815 ***2859.11*** *p27*
Cochran, Alexander 8; Quebec, 1847 ***5704.8*** *p27*
Cochran, Andrew 13; Philadelphia, 1851 ***5704.8*** *p76*
Cochran, Ann; Philadelphia, 1849 ***53.26*** *p13*
*Relative:*Hugh
Cochran, Ann; Philadelphia, 1849 ***5704.8*** *p53*
Cochran, Anne Fitzgerald; Quebec, 1795 ***7603*** *p76*
Cochran, David; New York, NY, 1833 ***8208.4*** *p39*
Cochran, Dennis; New York, NY, 1836 ***8208.4*** *p21*
Cochran, Elizabeth; Quebec, 1847 ***5704.8*** *p27*
Cochran, Elizabeth; St. John, N.B., 1852 ***5704.8*** *p84*
Cochran, Elizabeth 2 *SEE* Cochran, James
Cochran, Elizabeth 2; Philadelphia, 1847 ***5704.8*** *p13*
Cochran, Elizabeth 58; Philadelphia, 1853 ***5704.8*** *p111*
Cochran, George 52; St. John, N.B., 1851 ***5704.8*** *p72*
Cochran, Hugh *SEE* Cochran, Ann
Cochran, Hugh 8; Philadelphia, 1849 ***5704.8*** *p53*
Cochran, Hugues; Quebec, 1685 ***7603*** *p35*
Cochran, Isaac; New York, NY, 1815 ***2859.11*** *p27*
Cochran, Isaac 27; Philadelphia, 1803 ***53.26*** *p13*
Cochran, Isabella; Philadelphia, 1867 ***5704.8*** *p220*
Cochran, Isabella 8 *SEE* Cochran, James
Cochran, Isabella 8; Philadelphia, 1847 ***5704.8*** *p13*
Cochran, James; North Carolina, 1798 ***1639.20*** *p47*
Cochran, James; Philadelphia, 1847 ***53.26*** *p13*
Cochran, James; Philadelphia, 1847 ***53.26*** *p13*
*Relative:*Matilda
*Relative:*William 11
*Relative:*Matilda 9
*Relative:*Isabella 8
*Relative:*Robert 7
*Relative:*Adessa 6
*Relative:*Mary 4
*Relative:*Elizabeth 2
Cochran, James; Philadelphia, 1847 ***5704.8*** *p13*
Cochran, James; Philadelphia, 1847 ***5704.8*** *p22*
Cochran, James; St. John, N.B., 1848 ***5704.8*** *p47*
Cochran, James Gould; South Carolina, 1830 ***1639.20*** *p47*
Cochran, Jane; New York, NY, 1815 ***2859.11*** *p27*
Cochran, John; Philadelphia, 1811 ***53.26*** *p13*
Cochran, John; Philadelphia, 1811 ***2859.11*** *p10*
Cochran, John; Philadelphia, 1847 ***53.26*** *p13*
Cochran, John; Philadelphia, 1847 ***5704.8*** *p14*
Cochran, John; St. John, N.B., 1848 ***5704.8*** *p47*
Cochran, Margaret; Quebec, 1853 ***5704.8*** *p105*
Cochran, Margaret 13; St. John, N.B., 1848 ***5704.8*** *p47*
Cochran, Martha; Philadelphia, 1851 ***5704.8*** *p77*
Cochran, Mary; Jamaica, 1751 ***1219.7*** *p8*
Cochran, Mary; Jamaica, 1751 ***3690.1*** *p47*
Cochran, Mary; St. John, N.B., 1848 ***5704.8*** *p47*
Cochran, Mary 4 *SEE* Cochran, James
Cochran, Mary Ann; New York, NY, 1815 ***2859.11*** *p27*
Cochran, Mary Ann 4; Philadelphia, 1847 ***5704.8*** *p13*
Cochran, Matilda *SEE* Cochran, James
Cochran, Matilda; Philadelphia, 1847 ***5704.8*** *p13*
Cochran, Matilda 9 *SEE* Cochran, James
Cochran, Matilda Jane 9; Philadelphia, 1847 ***5704.8*** *p13*
Cochran, Michael 22; Maryland, 1775 ***1219.7*** *p256*
Cochran, Peggy Jane 6 mos; Quebec, 1847 ***5704.8*** *p27*
Cochran, Richard; New York, NY, 1815 ***2859.11*** *p27*
Cochran, Robert; New York, NY, 1816 ***2859.11*** *p27*
Cochran, Robert; New York, NY, 1838 ***8208.4*** *p61*
Cochran, Robert 6; Quebec, 1847 ***5704.8*** *p27*
Cochran, Robert 7 *SEE* Cochran, James
Cochran, Robert Hay 7; Philadelphia, 1847 ***5704.8*** *p13*
Cochran, Samuel; New York, NY, 1816 ***2859.11*** *p27*
Cochran, William; Quebec, 1847 ***5704.8*** *p27*
Cochran, William; St. John, N.B., 1851 ***5704.8*** *p72*
Cochran, William 6 mos; Quebec, 1853 ***5704.8*** *p105*
Cochran, William 4; Quebec, 1847 ***5704.8*** *p27*
Cochran, William 11 *SEE* Cochran, James
Cochran, William 20; Philadelphia, 1860 ***5704.8*** *p146*
Cochran, William 21; Philadelphia, 1854 ***5704.8*** *p123*
Cochran, William James 11; Philadelphia, 1847 ***5704.8*** *p13*
Cochrane, Mme. 45; America, 1839 ***778.5*** *p124*
Cochrane, Andrew 24; Philadelphia, 1833-1834 ***53.26*** *p13*
Cochrane, Arthur; Quebec, 1822 ***7603*** *p56*
Cochrane, Elizabeth; Quebec, 1847 ***5704.8*** *p36*
Cochrane, Henry; New York, NY, 1811 ***2859.11*** *p10*
Cochrane, James 24; Quebec, 1864 ***5704.8*** *p159*
Cochrane, Mary; St. John, N.B., 1852 ***5704.8*** *p84*
Cochrane, Robert; New York, NY, 1811 ***2859.11*** *p10*
Cochrane, William; New York, NY, 1811 ***2859.11*** *p10*
Cock, Ann; Virginia, 1642 ***6219*** *p189*
Cock, Charles F. 36; Massachusetts, 1860 ***6410.32*** *p105*
Cock, Edward; Virginia, 1648 ***6219*** *p252*
Cock, Jacob 20; Philadelphia, 1774 ***1219.7*** *p185*
Cock, Lewis; Virginia, 1638 ***6219*** *p123*
Cock, Ralph 37; Savannah, GA, 1774 ***1219.7*** *p226*
With wife
Cock, Rich.; Virginia, 1642 ***6219*** *p194*
Cock, Richard; Virginia, 1637 ***6219*** *p83*
Cock, Robert 25; Georgia, 1774 ***1219.7*** *p188*
Cock, William 15; Maryland, 1774 ***1219.7*** *p208*
Cockburn, Mrs. 26; Grenada, 1774 ***1219.7*** *p177*
Cockburn, Alexander 30; Grenada, 1774 ***1219.7*** *p177*
Cockcroft, Georg; Virginia, 1641 ***6219*** *p186*
Cocke, Lewis; Virginia, 1635 ***6219*** *p69*
Cocke, William; Virginia, 1652 ***6251*** *p20*
Cocker, Edward 29; North Carolina, 1736 ***3690.1*** *p47*
Cockerton, Robert 22; Maryland, 1774 ***1219.7*** *p206*
Cockerum, William; Virginia, 1639 ***6219*** *p156*
Cockett, John; Virginia, 1643 ***6219*** *p206*
Cockett, Ralph 15; America, 1701 ***2212*** *p34*
Cockett, Robert; Virginia, 1636 ***6219*** *p109*
Cockett, Samll.; Virginia, 1639 ***6219*** *p152*
Cocklan, Catharine 20; Massachusetts, 1847 ***5881.1*** *p14*
Cocklan, Catharine 40; Massachusetts, 1847 ***5881.1*** *p14*
Cocklan, James; Massachusetts, 1847 ***5881.1*** *p17*
Cocklin, Mary 30; Massachusetts, 1850 ***5881.1*** *p23*
Cockshott, Edw.; Virginia, 1635 ***6219*** *p26*
Cockshutte, Lawrence 20; America, 1705 ***2212*** *p43*
Cocle, Oliver 38; Jamaica, 1730 ***3690.1*** *p47*
Cocqfontaine, Mr.; Maryland, 1768 ***8582.3*** *p96*
Cocu, Mr. 22; America, 1826 ***778.5*** *p124*
Coda, Bart; West Virginia, 1883 ***9788.3*** *p6*
Coda, Bart; West Virginia, 1890 ***9788.3*** *p6*
Coda, John B. 44; West Virginia, 1895 ***9788.3*** *p6*
Coday, Anne 28; Philadelphia, 1861 ***5704.8*** *p148*
Coday, Michael 35; Philadelphia, 1861 ***5704.8*** *p148*
Coday, William 4; Philadelphia, 1861 ***5704.8*** *p148*
Codd, Edward; New York, NY, 1815 ***2859.11*** *p27*
Codd, James; New York, NY, 1815 ***2859.11*** *p27*
Codd, Thomas; Virginia, 1637 ***6219*** *p82*
Codd, Walter; America, 1741 ***4971*** *p99*
Codden, Patrick; New York, NY, 1839 ***8208.4*** *p91*
Coddy, Patrick; Illinois, 1876 ***5012.39*** *p91*
Codey, John; New York, NY, 1836 ***8208.4*** *p12*
Codne, Mary; Virginia, 1642 ***6219*** *p195*
Codran, Mme. 24; America, 1838 ***778.5*** *p125*
Codran, Mr.; America, 1838 ***778.5*** *p124*
Codran, Mr.; America, 1838 ***778.5*** *p125*
Codrau, Mme. 24; America, 1838 ***778.5*** *p125*
Codrau, Mr.; America, 1838 ***778.5*** *p124*
Codrau, Mr.; America, 1838 ***778.5*** *p125*
Codry, George 18; Jamaica, 1754 ***1219.7*** *p27*
Codry, George 18; Jamaica, 1754 ***3690.1*** *p47*
Cody, John; Illinois, 1856 ***7857*** *p2*
Cody, William; America, 1743 ***4971*** *p33*
Coe, . . .; New York, NY, 1811 ***2859.11*** *p10*
With sister
Coe, Joseph; Colorado, 1887 ***9678.1*** *p158*
Coen, Patrick; New York, NY, 1838 ***8208.4*** *p63*
Coens, Johannes; America, n.d. ***8125.8*** *p435*
Coenzler, Joseph; America, 1801-1869 ***8582*** *p5*
Coffe, Michael; New York, NY, 1836 ***8208.4*** *p10*
Coffe, Patrick; America, 1850 ***6013.19*** *p30*
Coffee, Ann 6; Massachusetts, 1849 ***5881.1*** *p13*
Coffee, Bridget 11; Massachusetts, 1849 ***5881.1*** *p13*
Coffee, Bridget 14; Massachusetts, 1849 ***5881.1*** *p13*
Coffee, Bridget 22; Massachusetts, 1847 ***5881.1*** *p13*
Coffee, Catharine 7; Massachusetts, 1850 ***5881.1*** *p14*
Coffee, Hannah 30; Massachusetts, 1849 ***5881.1*** *p17*
Coffee, Henry; America, 1740 ***4971*** *p15*
Coffee, James 22; Massachusetts, 1849 ***5881.1*** *p18*
Coffee, John 5; Massachusetts, 1849 ***5881.1*** *p18*
Coffee, Julia 1; Massachusetts, 1849 ***5881.1*** *p18*
Coffee, Larry 10; Massachusetts, 1849 ***5881.1*** *p20*
Coffee, Margaret 8; Massachusetts, 1849 ***5881.1*** *p21*
Coffee, Maria 3; Massachusetts, 1849 ***5881.1*** *p21*
Coffee, Mary 40; Massachusetts, 1849 ***5881.1*** *p21*
Coffee, Michael 23; Massachusetts, 1850 ***5881.1*** *p23*
Coffee, Pat. 12; Massachusetts, 1849 ***5881.1*** *p24*
Coffee, Pat. 13; Massachusetts, 1849 ***5881.1*** *p24*
Coffee, Patrick 30; Maryland, 1774 ***1219.7*** *p182*
Coffee, Rose 19; Massachusetts, 1849 ***5881.1*** *p25*
Coffee, Thomas 15; Massachusetts, 1849 ***5881.1*** *p25*
Coffey, Andrews R.; Iowa, 1866-1943 ***123.54*** *p14*
Coffey, Christopher; Shreveport, LA, 1878 ***7129*** *p44*
Coffey, G. M.; Washington, 1859-1920 ***2872.1*** *p8*
Coffey, James 25; New Orleans, 1863 ***543.30*** *p463*
Coffey, John; Arizona, 1898 ***9228.30*** *p6*
Coffey, Patrick 38; New Orleans, 1850-1859 ***543.30*** *p459*
Coffey, Robert C.; Iowa, 1866-1943 ***123.54*** *p14*
Coffey, William; Washington, 1859-1920 ***2872.1*** *p8*
Coffignial, Leonard 28; New Orleans, 1836 ***778.5*** *p125*
Coffin, Francis; Virginia, 1635 ***6219*** *p70*
Coffin, John; Virginia, 1637 ***6219*** *p112*
Coffinbury, . . .; Ohio, 1819 ***8582.1*** *p47*
Coffits, William; Indiana, 1836 ***9117*** *p15*
Coffman, William; West Virginia, 1856 ***9788.3*** *p6*
Cogan, Daniel; New York, NY, 1835 ***8208.4*** *p6*
Cogan, Ira; Arkansas, 1918 ***95.2*** *p30*
Cogan, John; New York, NY, 1836 ***8208.4*** *p21*
Coggerill, Mary; America, 1740 ***4971*** *p80*
Coggin, Sarah; Virginia, 1637 ***6219*** *p145*
Coggin, Thomas; Virginia, 1642 ***6219*** *p197*
Coggin, Thomas; Virginia, 1652 ***6251*** *p20*
Coghan, James; Montreal, 1821 ***7603*** *p102*
Cogher, Daniel; America, 1735-1743 ***4971*** *p79*
Coghlan, Bridget; New York, NY, 1816 ***2859.11*** *p27*
Coghlan, Catharine; Philadelphia, 1865 ***5704.8*** *p198*
Coghlan, Catherine; New York, NY, 1816 ***2859.11*** *p27*
Coghlan, Catherine; New York, NY, 1816 ***2859.11*** *p28*
Coghlan, Eliza; New York, NY, 1816 ***2859.11*** *p28*
Coghlan, Francis 10; Philadelphia, 1865 ***5704.8*** *p198*
Coghlan, Henry; Philadelphia, 1865 ***5704.8*** *p198*
Coghlan, James; America, 1739 ***4971*** *p14*
Coghlan, John 8; Philadelphia, 1865 ***5704.8*** *p198*
Coghlan, Joseph; Philadelphia, 1865 ***5704.8*** *p198*
Coghlan, Mary; New York, NY, 1816 ***2859.11*** *p28*
Coghlan, Michel; Montreal, 1818 ***7603*** *p64*
Coghlan, Patrick; New York, NY, 1816 ***2859.11*** *p28*
Coghlan, Peter; America, 1740 ***4971*** *p15*
Coghlan, Tim 14; Newport, RI, 1851 ***6508.5*** *p20*
Coghran, George; America, 1735-1743 ***4971*** *p79*
Coghy, Garret; America, 1739 ***4971*** *p82*
Cogly, Martin; New York, NY, 1815 ***2859.11*** *p28*
Cognity, Jean 31; America, 1838 ***778.5*** *p125*
Cogwell, Robert 21; Maryland, 1729 ***3690.1*** *p47*
Cohan, Abram 23; Arkansas, 1918 ***95.2*** *p30*
Cohan, Abram 23; Arkansas, 1918 ***95.2*** *p58*
Cohan, Max; Milwaukee, 1875 ***4719.30*** *p257*
Cohano, Lennis; Wisconsin, n.d. ***9675.5*** *p50*
Cohen, Benedict; New York, NY, 1835 ***8208.4*** *p48*
Cohen, Elias 45; New Orleans, 1863 ***543.30*** *p451*
Cohen, Golda *SEE* Cohen, Karl
Cohen, Golde *SEE* Cohen, Karl
Cohen, Goldie; New York, NY, 1923 ***3455.5*** *p7*
Cohen, Iro; Arkansas, 1918 ***95.2*** *p30*
Cohen, Isaac; Arkansas, 1918 ***95.2*** *p30*
Cohen, Karl; Detroit, 1913 ***3455.2*** *p76*
*Wife:*Golde
Cohen, Karl; Detroit, 1913 ***3455.3*** *p53*
*Wife:*Golda
Cohen, Max; Milwaukee, 1875 ***4719.30*** *p258*
Cohen, Morris; Arkansas, 1918 ***95.2*** *p30*
Cohen, Philip; New York, NY, 1836 ***8208.4*** *p22*
Cohen, Sam; Arkansas, 1918 ***95.2*** *p30*
Cohen, Samuel D.; Arkansas, 1918 ***95.2*** *p31*
Cohern, Ellen 18; Massachusetts, 1847 ***5881.1*** *p15*
Cohern, Sarah 40; Massachusetts, 1847 ***5881.1*** *p25*
Cohlmeyer Family ; Illinois, 1800-1899 ***4610.10*** *p66*
Cohn, Abraham M.; Nevada, 1869 ***2764.35*** *p10*
Cohn, B.; Iowa, 1866-1943 ***123.54*** *p14*
Cohn, David; Arizona, 1888 ***2764.35*** *p14*
Cohn, Fanny 32; New York, NY, 1878 ***9253*** *p46*
Cohn, Hirsch 6; New York, NY, 1878 ***9253*** *p46*
Cohn, Joe; Arkansas, 1918 ***95.2*** *p31*
Cohn, Liche 26; New York, NY, 1878 ***9253*** *p46*
Cohn, Reisel 11 mos; New York, NY, 1878 ***9253*** *p46*
Cohon, E.M.; Iowa, 1866-1943 ***123.54*** *p14*
Cohrs, Dora; Milwaukee, 1875 ***4719.30*** *p257*
Coik, Christina; America, 1896 ***7137*** *p168*
Coik, Stanislaus; America, 1885 ***7137*** *p168*
Coil, Ann; Quebec, 1852 ***5704.8*** *p86*
Coil, Ann; Quebec, 1852 ***5704.8*** *p90*
Coil, Ann Jane; Quebec, 1852 ***5704.8*** *p86*
Coil, Catherine; Quebec, 1852 ***5704.8*** *p86*
Coil, Catherine; Quebec, 1852 ***5704.8*** *p90*
Coil, Henry; Quebec, 1821 ***7603*** *p67*
Coil, Henry; Quebec, 1852 ***5704.8*** *p86*

Coil, Henry; Quebec, 1852 ***5704.8*** *p90*
Coil, James; Quebec, 1852 ***5704.8*** *p86*
Coil, James; Quebec, 1852 ***5704.8*** *p90*
Coil, Jane 18; St. John, N.B., 1864 ***5704.8*** *p158*
Coil, Mage 20; St. John, N.B., 1864 ***5704.8*** *p158*
Coil, Peter; New York, NY, 1811 ***2859.11*** *p10*
Coil, Rosa; New York, NY, 1811 ***2859.11*** *p10*
Coil, Sarah; New York, NY, 1811 ***2859.11*** *p10*
Coil, William; New York, NY, 1811 ***2859.11*** *p10*
Coile, Patrick; New York, NY, 1836 ***8208.4*** *p11*
Coile, Peter; Ohio, 1833 ***9892.11*** *p9*
Coillar, John 39; Louisiana, 1827 ***778.5*** *p125*
Coin, Ann; New York, NY, 1811 ***2859.11*** *p10*
With children
Coin, Mary 20; Massachusetts, 1850 ***5881.1*** *p22*
Coinlick, Daniel; Philadelphia, 1864 ***5704.8*** *p183*
Coisy, Antoine 36; Port uncertain, 1836 ***778.5*** *p125*
Coit, Catharine 22; Massachusetts, 1850 ***5881.1*** *p14*
Coje, . . .; Canada, 1776-1783 ***9786*** *p41*
Cokely, John 35; New Orleans, 1862 ***543.30*** *p457*
Coker, John; Virginia, 1636 ***6219*** *p77*
Colabrese, Feliciantonio; Colorado, 1903 ***9678.1*** *p158*
Colaco, Joe; Arkansas, 1918 ***95.2*** *p31*
Colaert, Omer; Arkansas, 1918 ***95.2*** *p31*
Colane, J. 30; America, 1837 ***778.5*** *p125*
Colar, Frank 25; Kansas, 1879 ***5240.1*** *p61*
Colb, Frank; Colorado, 1898 ***9678.1*** *p158*
Colberg, Grist; Illinois, 1884 ***5240.1*** *p8*
Colbert, Garrett 15; Massachusetts, 1850 ***5881.1*** *p16*
Colbert, Mary 23; Massachusetts, 1849 ***5881.1*** *p21*
Colbert, Patrick; Virginia, 1858 ***4626.16*** *p17*
Colbrook, Robert 28; Philadelphia, 1774 ***1219.7*** *p232*
Colby, Patrick; New York, NY, 1839 ***8208.4*** *p101*
Colchester, Ann; Virginia, 1643 ***6219*** *p202*
Colchester, Jone; Virginia, 1637 ***6219*** *p110*
Colclough, Mr.; Quebec, 1815 ***9229.18*** *p81*
With wife
With 2 children
Colclough, Beauchamp; Kansas, 1889 ***5240.1*** *p8*
Colclough, George; Virginia, 1652 ***6251*** *p19*
Colden, Thomas; New York, NY, 1837 ***8208.4*** *p34*
Coldron, Symon; Virginia, 1641 ***6219*** *p187*
Coldwater, George; Wisconsin, n.d. ***9675.5*** *p50*
Cole, Ann; Virginia, 1642 ***6219*** *p188*
Cole, Antho.; Virginia, 1641 ***6219*** *p184*
Cole, Anthony; Virginia, 1638 ***6219*** *p115*
Cole, Austin 20; Maryland, 1774 ***1219.7*** *p192*
Cole, Dorothy; Virginia, 1638 ***6219*** *p117*
Cole, Dorothy; Virginia, 1648 ***6219*** *p237*
Cole, Edward; Virginia, 1642 ***6219*** *p186*
Cole, Edward 17; Philadelphia, 1775 ***1219.7*** *p255*
Cole, George 17; Maryland, 1729 ***3690.1*** *p48*
Cole, Guy 27; Maryland, 1774 ***1219.7*** *p202*
Cole, Henry 24; Maryland, 1774 ***1219.7*** *p204*
Cole, Herbert 18; Jamaica, 1774 ***1219.7*** *p219*
Cole, John; New York, NY, 1816 ***2859.11*** *p28*
Cole, John; Nova Scotia, 1774 ***1219.7*** *p210*
Cole, John; Virginia, 1637 ***6219*** *p37*
Cole, John; Virginia, 1638 ***6219*** *p119*
Cole, John; Virginia, 1639 ***6219*** *p18*
Cole, John; Virginia, 1639 ***6219*** *p157*
Cole, John; Virginia, 1646 ***6219*** *p236*
Cole, John 17; Virginia, 1719 ***3690.1*** *p48*
Cole, John 21; Virginia, 1773 ***1219.7*** *p171*
Cole, Jon; Virginia, 1635 ***6219*** *p16*
Cole, Jon.; Virginia, 1636 ***6219*** *p74*
Cole, Jon.; Virginia, 1637 ***6219*** *p108*
Cole, Jon.; Virginia, 1638 ***6219*** *p11*
Cole, Louis Bogart; Illinois, 1868 ***5012.38*** *p99*
Cole, Mary; Philadelphia, 1851 ***5704.8*** *p81*
Cole, Millecent; Virginia, 1640 ***6219*** *p208*
Cole, Rich.; Virginia, 1635 ***6219*** *p69*
Cole, Robt.; Virginia, 1635 ***6219*** *p72*
Cole, Sarah; Virginia, 1638 ***6219*** *p118*
Cole, Tho.; Virginia, 1635 ***6219*** *p69*
Cole, Tho.; Virginia, 1640 ***6219*** *p182*
Cole, Tho.; Virginia, 1644 ***6219*** *p231*
Cole, Thomas; Virginia, 1635 ***6219*** *p5*
Cole, Thomas 17; Massachusetts, 1850 ***5881.1*** *p26*
Cole, Willi.; Virginia, 1635 ***6219*** *p69*
Cole, William; Virginia, 1638 ***6219*** *p11*
Cole, William; Virginia, 1643 ***6219*** *p206*
Cole, William 16; Philadelphia, 1774 ***1219.7*** *p175*
Cole, William 18; Virginia, 1719 ***3690.1*** *p48*
Cole, William 21; Maryland, 1775 ***1219.7*** *p253*
Cole, William 22; Baltimore, 1775 ***1219.7*** *p269*
Cole, Wm.; Virginia, 1635 ***6219*** *p12*
Cole, Wm. Ullin; Wisconsin, n.d. ***9675.5*** *p50*
Colealough, James 24; Philadelphia, 1775 ***1219.7*** *p274*
Colebourne, Rudolph G.; New York, 1900 ***1450.2*** *p6B*
Colebrooke, Harriet 21; Maryland, 1775 ***1219.7*** *p267*
Coleby, John 21; Maryland, 1775 ***1219.7*** *p267*
Colella, Angelo; Arkansas, 1918 ***95.2*** *p31*
Coleman, Adam; Ohio, 1842 ***8365.25*** *p12*
Coleman, Andrew; Washington, 1859-1920 ***2872.1*** *p8*
Coleman, Ann; Philadelphia, 1850 ***53.26*** *p13*
Coleman, Ann; Philadelphia, 1850 ***5704.8*** *p60*
Coleman, Ch. C. 48; New York, NY, 1893 ***9026.4*** *p41*
Coleman, Denis 36; New Orleans, 1862 ***543.30*** *p460*
Coleman, Edward; America, 1874 ***6014.1*** *p1*
Coleman, Edward; Illinois, 1868 ***7857*** *p2*
Coleman, Edward; Virginia, 1637 ***6219*** *p109*
Coleman, Eliza 20; Massachusetts, 1849 ***5881.1*** *p15*
Coleman, Ellen Alan; New York, NY, 1871 ***3455.2*** *p74*
Coleman, Ellen Alan; New York, NY, 1871 ***3455.3*** *p24*
Coleman, Ellen Alan; New York, NY, 1871 ***3455.3*** *p114*
Coleman, Francis; Illinois, 1854 ***7857*** *p3*
Coleman, Henry; Virginia, 1635 ***6219*** *p75*
*Wife:*Katherine
Coleman, Joan; America, 1740 ***4971*** *p47*
Coleman, John; America, 1741 ***4971*** *p49*
Coleman, John; Illinois, 1888 ***5012.39*** *p122*
Coleman, John; New York, NY, 1835 ***8208.4*** *p55*
Coleman, John 20; Maryland, 1729 ***3690.1*** *p48*
Coleman, John 22; Virginia, 1774 ***1219.7*** *p193*
Coleman, Katherine *SEE* Coleman, Henry
Coleman, Lucy; America, 1740 ***4971*** *p15*
Coleman, Lucy; Maryland, 1740 ***4971*** *p91*
Coleman, Lucy; Philadelphia, 1741 ***4971*** *p92*
Coleman, Margaret; St. John, N.B., 1849 ***5704.8*** *p55*
Coleman, Margaret 3; St. John, N.B., 1849 ***5704.8*** *p55*
Coleman, Mary 35; Massachusetts, 1849 ***5881.1*** *p21*
Coleman, Mary 55; Kansas, 1872 ***5240.1*** *p52*
Coleman, Michael; Virginia, 1856 ***4626.16*** *p16*
Coleman, Morris; Virginia, 1638 ***6219*** *p125*
Coleman, Patrick 28; Massachusetts, 1848 ***5881.1*** *p24*
Coleman, Philip; Pennsylvania, 1749-1800 ***2444*** *p173*
Coleman, Robert; Philadelphia, 1815 ***2859.11*** *p28*
With wife & child
Coleman, Robert; Virginia, 1637 ***6219*** *p11*
Coleman, Robert; Virginia, 1638 ***6219*** *p148*
Coleman, Robert; Virginia, 1639 ***6219*** *p157*
Coleman, Thomas 25; Massachusetts, 1847 ***5881.1*** *p25*
Colepicker, Antone; Illinois, 1860 ***5012.38*** *p97*
Colert, Chri.; Virginia, 1636 ***6219*** *p76*
Coles, Anna 13 *SEE* Coles, Joseph
Coles, Anna 32 *SEE* Coles, Joseph
Coles, George 15; Virginia, 1774 ***1219.7*** *p240*
Coles, Joseph 28; Savannah, GA, 1733 ***4719.17*** *p310*
*Wife:*Anna 32
*Daughter:*Anna 13
Coles, Richard; Virginia, 1637 ***6219*** *p10*
Coles, Richard 17; Philadelphia, 1749 ***3690.1*** *p48*
Colewell, Elias; Virginia, 1647 ***6219*** *p241*
Colfari, John; Iowa, 1866-1943 ***123.54*** *p14*
Colgan, Bridget; New York, NY, 1869 ***5704.8*** *p233*
Colgan, James; Philadelphia, 1864 ***5704.8*** *p169*
Colgan, John; New York, NY, 1833 ***8208.4*** *p50*
Colgan, Mary A.; Philadelphia, 1864 ***5704.8*** *p169*
Colgan, Mary Winifred; New York, NY, 1913 ***3455.3*** *p80*
Colgan, Mary Winifred; New York, NY, 1913 ***3455.4*** *p27*
Colgan, Rose Ann 20; Quebec, 1857 ***5704.8*** *p135*
Colgan, Thomas; Ohio, 1880-1884 ***9892.11*** *p9*
Colgan, Thomas; Ohio, 1886 ***9892.11*** *p9*
Colgan, William; St. John, N.B., 1851 ***5704.8*** *p78*
Colgrove, John 23; Virginia, 1774 ***1219.7*** *p239*
Colhannon, Mary 11; Massachusetts, 1850 ***5881.1*** *p22*
Colhoun, Alexander 24; Quebec, 1854 ***5704.8*** *p119*
Colhoun, Andrew; Philadelphia, 1847 ***53.26*** *p13*
Colhoun, Andrew; Philadelphia, 1847 ***5704.8*** *p30*
Colhoun, Anne 18; Quebec, 1859 ***5704.8*** *p143*
Colhoun, Eliza Jane 21; Quebec, 1854 ***5704.8*** *p119*
Colhoun, James; Philadelphia, 1852 ***5704.8*** *p85*
Colhoun, James 20; Philadelphia, 1853 ***5704.8*** *p108*
Colhoun, John; New York, NY, 1816 ***2859.11*** *p28*
Colhoun, Joseph 3 mos; Quebec, 1854 ***5704.8*** *p119*
Colhoun, Margaret; Philadelphia, 1852 ***5704.8*** *p85*
Colhoun, Martha 35; Philadelphia, 1860 ***5704.8*** *p145*
Colhoun, Mary; Philadelphia, 1852 ***5704.8*** *p85*
Colhoun, Mary 18; Philadelphia, 1853 ***5704.8*** *p108*
Colhoun, Mary Jane 3; Philadelphia, 1860 ***5704.8*** *p145*
Colhoun, Robert 60; Philadelphia, 1860 ***5704.8*** *p145*
Colhoun, William; St. John, N.B., 1851 ***5704.8*** *p78*
Colhoun, William James 30; Philadelphia, 1860 ***5704.8*** *p145*
Coligan, Henry 21; Philadelphia, 1861 ***5704.8*** *p148*
Coligan, Mary 9 mos; Philadelphia, 1861 ***5704.8*** *p148*
Coligan, Sarah 22; Philadelphia, 1861 ***5704.8*** *p148*
Colin, Anna 26; Port uncertain, 1839 ***778.5*** *p125*
Colin, Henry; New York, NY, 1811 ***2859.11*** *p10*
Colin, Jacques 32; Port uncertain, 1839 ***778.5*** *p125*
Coling, Peter; New York, NY, 1816 ***2859.11*** *p28*
Colison, John; Ohio, 1820 ***9892.11*** *p9*
Colison, John; Ohio, 1824 ***9892.11*** *p9*
Colkan, Thomas 21; Massachusetts, 1849 ***5881.1*** *p25*
Colkbrand, Tho.; Virginia, 1643 ***6219*** *p206*
Colkier, Jens; New York, 1754 ***3652*** *p79*
Coll, . . .; Canada, 1776-1783 ***9786*** *p19*
Coll, Barney; Philadelphia, 1867 ***5704.8*** *p211*
Coll, Betty; Philadelphia, 1849 ***53.26*** *p13*
*Relative:*Biddy
Coll, Betty; Philadelphia, 1849 ***5704.8*** *p52*
Coll, Biddy *SEE* Coll, Betty
Coll, Biddy; Philadelphia, 1849 ***5704.8*** *p52*
Coll, Bridget; Philadelphia, 1867 ***5704.8*** *p216*
Coll, Catharine; New York, NY, 1865 ***5704.8*** *p194*
Coll, Catharine; Philadelphia, 1866 ***5704.8*** *p209*
Coll, Catherine; Philadelphia, 1852 ***5704.8*** *p89*
Coll, Catherine 50; Philadelphia, 1859 ***5704.8*** *p142*
Coll, Charles; Philadelphia, 1847 ***53.26*** *p13*
Coll, Charles; Philadelphia, 1847 ***5704.8*** *p22*
Coll, Daniel 28; Philadelphia, 1864 ***5704.8*** *p161*
Coll, Denis; Philadelphia, 1866 ***5704.8*** *p209*
Coll, Dennis; New York, NY, 1816 ***2859.11*** *p28*
Coll, Dennis; New York, NY, 1865 ***5704.8*** *p191*
Coll, Dennis; Philadelphia, 1848 ***53.26*** *p13*
Coll, Dennis; Philadelphia, 1848 ***5704.8*** *p40*
Coll, Edward 21; Maryland, 1774 ***1219.7*** *p215*
Coll, Ellen 22; Philadelphia, 1864 ***5704.8*** *p156*
Coll, Hugh 20; Philadelphia, 1864 ***5704.8*** *p156*
Coll, James 20; Philadelphia, 1858 ***5704.8*** *p138*
Coll, James 20; Philadelphia, 1859 ***5704.8*** *p141*
Coll, John; New York, NY, 1869 ***5704.8*** *p232*
Coll, John; Philadelphia, 1864 ***5704.8*** *p180*
Coll, John 23; Philadelphia, 1864 ***5704.8*** *p156*
Coll, Margery; Quebec, 1850 ***5704.8*** *p62*
Coll, Maria 18; St. John, N.B., 1853 ***5704.8*** *p110*
Coll, Mary; Philadelphia, 1847 ***53.26*** *p13*
Coll, Mary; Philadelphia, 1847 ***5704.8*** *p5*
Coll, Mary 19; Philadelphia, 1864 ***5704.8*** *p156*
Coll, Mary 26; Philadelphia, 1861 ***5704.8*** *p148*
Coll, Moses; Philadelphia, 1852 ***5704.8*** *p96*
Coll, Nancy; Quebec, 1850 ***5704.8*** *p62*
Coll, Owen; Philadelphia, 1849 ***53.26*** *p13*
Coll, Owen; Philadelphia, 1849 ***5704.8*** *p54*
Coll, Patrick; America, 1868 ***5704.8*** *p231*
Coll, Patrick 15; Philadelphia, 1859 ***5704.8*** *p142*
Coll, Paul; St. John, N.B., 1847 ***5704.8*** *p26*
Coll, Peggy; Philadelphia, 1852 ***5704.8*** *p96*
Coll, Peggy 18; Philadelphia, 1858 ***5704.8*** *p138*
Coll, Rose 40; Philadelphia, 1854 ***5704.8*** *p123*
Coll, Sally 18; Philadelphia, 1860 ***5704.8*** *p146*
Coll, Susan; Philadelphia, 1865 ***5704.8*** *p201*
Coll, Thomas; Philadelphia, 1865 ***5704.8*** *p200*
Coll, Unity; Philadelphia, 1866 ***5704.8*** *p209*
Coll, Unity; Quebec, 1850 ***5704.8*** *p62*
Colland, George; Washington, 1859-1920 ***2872.1*** *p8*
Collannek, John; New York, NY, 1839 ***8208.4*** *p92*
Collart, William; Norfolk, VA, 1776 ***1219.7*** *p284*
Colle, Francis 25; Barbados, 1774 ***1219.7*** *p241*
Collect, Geo.; Virginia, 1636 ***6219*** *p74*
Colledge, Geo.; Virginia, 1637 ***6219*** *p114*
Collegan, Thomas; New York, NY, 1834 ***8208.4*** *p2*
Collens, Daniel 18; Philadelphia, 1859 ***5704.8*** *p142*
Collens, John 22; Philadelphia, 1859 ***5704.8*** *p142*
Collerton, John 16; Massachusetts, 1849 ***5881.1*** *p18*
Colles, Richard; Virginia, 1644 ***6219*** *p231*
Collet, Henry Louis 32; New Orleans, 1835 ***778.5*** *p125*
Collet, J. 18; America, 1835 ***778.5*** *p125*
Collet, Johann; Ohio, 1798 ***8582.2*** *p54*
Collett, Elizabeth; Virginia, 1637 ***6219*** *p110*
Collett, John; Virginia, 1642 ***6219*** *p188*
Collett, John 28; Jamaica, 1736 ***3690.1*** *p48*
Collett, Margarett; Virginia, 1640 ***6219*** *p182*
Collett, Richard; Virginia, 1642 ***6219*** *p197*
Collett, Thomas; Virginia, 1754 ***1219.7*** *p29*
Collett, Thomas; Virginia, 1754 ***3690.1*** *p48*
Colletti, Louis; Arkansas, 1918 ***95.2*** *p31*
Colley, James 20; Maryland, 1729 ***3690.1*** *p48*
Colley, William; Illinois, 1893 ***5012.40*** *p53*
Collier, Daniel; New York, 1763 ***1219.7*** *p94*
Collier, Daniell; Virginia, 1636 ***6219*** *p74*
Collier, Daniell; Virginia, 1637 ***6219*** *p108*
Collier, Henry; Virginia, 1648 ***6219*** *p252*
Collier, John; Illinois, 1853 ***7857*** *p3*
Collier, John 33; Kansas, 1876 ***5240.1*** *p57*
Collier, Ralph 25; America, 1705-1706 ***2212*** *p45*
Collier, Thomas 20; Jamaica, 1730 ***3690.1*** *p49*
Collier, Thomas 21; Maryland, 1774 ***1219.7*** *p215*
Colligan, Mary; America, 1741 ***4971*** *p10*
Collignan, Francis; New York, NY, 1839 ***8208.4*** *p96*
Collin, Francois 33; America, 1839 ***778.5*** *p125*
Collin, George 30; Maryland, 1775 ***1219.7*** *p268*
Collin, James; New York, NY, 1836 ***8208.4*** *p11*
Collin, Jeremiah; New York, NY, 1837 ***8208.4*** *p35*
Collin, Mary 22; Philadelphia, 1774 ***1219.7*** *p234*
Colling, . . .; Canada, 1776-1783 ***9786*** *p19*

Colling, Aaron 25; Philadelphia, 1775 1219.7 p274
Colling, Anne; Philadelphia, 1867 5704.8 p217
Colling, Mary E.; Philadelphia, 1867 5704.8 p217
Collingham, Esther; Quebec, 1814 7603 p28
Collings, Henry; Minneapolis, 1875-1880 6410.35 p52
Collingwood, John 28; Jamaica, 1736 3690.1 p48
Collingwood, Thomas; West Virginia, 1856 9788.3 p6
Collini, Nicola; Wisconsin, n.d. 9675.5 p50
Collins, Aeneas; America, 1743 4971 p65
Collins, Alex; New York, NY, 1864 5704.8 p170
Collins, Alice; America, 1735-1743 4971 p8
Collins, Andrew; New York, NY, 1811 2859.11 p10
Collins, Anne; Quebec, 1850 5704.8 p63
Collins, Anne Macdermott; Quebec, 1791 7603 p77
Collins, Barney; America, 1865 5704.8 p203
Collins, Bernard; America, 1868 5704.8 p226
Collins, Bernard 7; Philadelphia, 1864 5704.8 p156
Collins, Betty 30; St. John, N.B., 1854 5704.8 p115
Collins, Biddy; St. John, N.B., 1847 5704.8 p20
Collins, Biddy 11; St. John, N.B., 1853 5704.8 p99
Collins, Bridget 5; Philadelphia, 1864 5704.8 p156
Collins, Bridget 20; St. John, N.B., 1853 5704.8 p110
Collins, Bryan 45; Massachusetts, 1848 5881.1 p13
Collins, Catharine 3; Massachusetts, 1849 5881.1 p14
Collins, Catherine; Philadelphia, 1850 53.26 p13
Collins, Catherine; Philadelphia, 1850 5704.8 p68
Collins, Catherine 11; Philadelphia, 1864 5704.8 p156
Collins, Catherine 18; Philadelphia, 1864 5704.8 p157
Collins, Cornelius; New York, NY, 1838 8208.4 p69
Collins, Cornelius 25; Massachusetts, 1849 5881.1 p14
Collins, Daniel; America, 1736-1743 4971 p57
Collins, Daniel; Quebec, 1825 7603 p98
Collins, Daniel 4; St. John, N.B., 1866 5704.8 p166
Collins, Daniel 24; Massachusetts, 1847 5881.1 p15
Collins, Daniel 40; Massachusetts, 1850 5881.1 p15
Collins, Darby; America, 1743 4971 p42
Collins, Dennis 30; Philadelphia, 1854 5704.8 p117
Collins, Dennis 40; Massachusetts, 1849 5881.1 p15
Collins, Elias; Virginia, 1638 6219 p122
Collins, Elizabeth; Virginia, 1636 6219 p78
Collins, Ellen 7 mos; Massachusetts, 1849 5881.1 p16
Collins, Ellen 10; Massachusetts, 1850 5881.1 p16
Collins, Ellen 15; Philadelphia, 1864 5704.8 p156
Collins, Ellen 16; Massachusetts, 1850 5881.1 p16
Collins, Giles; Virginia, 1635 6219 p35
Collins, Grace 9; St. John, N.B., 1853 5704.8 p99
Collins, Hen.; Virginia, 1635 6219 p71
Collins, Honora 8; Massachusetts, 1850 5881.1 p17
Collins, Hugh 20; Philadelphia, 1864 5704.8 p157
Collins, Isabella; Philadelphia, 1866 5704.8 p209
Collins, James; New York, NY, 1811 2859.11 p10
Collins, James 8; Quebec, 1847 5704.8 p16
Collins, James 12; Massachusetts, 1847 5881.1 p17
Collins, James 19; Maryland, 1774 1219.7 p181
Collins, James 20; Massachusetts, 1849 5881.1 p18
Collins, James 20; Philadelphia, 1854 5704.8 p117
Collins, James 45; Quebec, 1864 5704.8 p160
Collins, James N.; New York, NY, 1834 8208.4 p33
Collins, Jane; Quebec, 1847 5704.8 p16
Collins, Jane 40; Philadelphia, 1860 5704.8 p144
Collins, Jeremiah; New York, NY, 1837 8208.4 p35
Collins, Jerry 8; Massachusetts, 1849 5881.1 p19
Collins, Johanna 35; Massachusetts, 1849 5881.1 p19
Collins, John; America, 1736 4971 p44
Collins, John; America, 1736 4971 p45
Collins, John; America, 1736 4971 p83
Collins, John; New York, NY, 1838 8208.4 p59
Collins, John; Philadelphia, 1847 53.26 p13
Collins, John; Philadelphia, 1847 5704.8 p14
Collins, John; Philadelphia, 1865 5704.8 p186
Collins, John; Quebec, 1847 5704.8 p16
Collins, John; Quebec, 1847 5704.8 p27
Collins, John; St. John, N.B., 1847 5704.8 p18
Collins, John; St. John, N.B., 1847 5704.8 p20
Collins, John; St. John, N.B., 1853 5704.8 p100
Collins, John 6; Quebec, 1847 5704.8 p16
Collins, John 14; Massachusetts, 1850 5881.1 p20
Collins, John 16; Massachusetts, 1849 5881.1 p19
Collins, John 18; Philadelphia, 1864 5704.8 p157
Collins, John 19; West Indies, 1722 3690.1 p48
Collins, John 20; Philadelphia, 1861 5704.8 p149
Collins, John 24; St. John, N.B., 1853 5704.8 p110
Collins, John 25; Virginia, 1775 1219.7 p246
Collins, John 28; Massachusetts, 1849 5881.1 p18
Collins, John 28; New Orleans, 1862 543.30 p457
Collins, John 30; Massachusetts, 1849 5881.1 p18
Collins, John 39; Maryland, 1773 1219.7 p173
Collins, John 42; Philadelphia, 1775 1219.7 p274
Collins, John 45; Philadelphia, 1864 5704.8 p156
Collins, John 85; Massachusetts, 1849 5881.1 p18
Collins, Jon.; Virginia, 1635 6219 p12
Collins, Jon.; Virginia, 1638 6219 p115
Collins, Joseph; Kansas, 1912 6013.40 p15
Collins, Joseph 20; Maryland, 1774 1219.7 p220
Collins, Julia 25; Massachusetts, 1849 5881.1 p19
With child
Collins, Julienne; Quebec, 1810 7603 p75
Collins, Larry 42; Massachusetts, 1849 5881.1 p20
Collins, Margaret; St. John, N.B., 1847 5704.8 p18
Collins, Margaret; St. John, N.B., 1852 5704.8 p95
Collins, Margaret 36; Massachusetts, 1850 5881.1 p23
Collins, Mary; America, 1869 5704.8 p233
Collins, Mary; Philadelphia, 1853 5704.8 p101
Collins, Mary; St. John, N.B., 1850 5704.8 p61
Collins, Mary 10; Quebec, 1847 5704.8 p16
Collins, Mary 25; Quebec, 1864 5704.8 p160
Collins, Mary 40; Massachusetts, 1849 5881.1 p21
Collins, Mary 40; Philadelphia, 1864 5704.8 p156
Collins, Mary 50; St. John, N.B., 1853 5704.8 p109
Collins, Mary 60; Philadelphia, 1860 5704.8 p144
Collins, Mary Ann 11 mos; Massachusetts, 1849 5881.1 p21
Collins, Mary Ann 4; Philadelphia, 1864 5704.8 p156
Collins, Mary Ann 17; St. John, N.B., 1866 5704.8 p166
Collins, Mary Ann 20; Philadelphia, 1853 5704.8 p113
Collins, Maurice 28; Massachusetts, 1849 5881.1 p21
Collins, Michael; America, 1740 4971 p48
Collins, Michael; America, 1741 4971 p49
Collins, Michael; America, 1867 5704.8 p221
Collins, Michael; New York, NY, 1840 8208.4 p109
Collins, Michael; Quebec, 1795 7603 p97
Collins, Michael; Quebec, 1803 7603 p75
Collins, Michael; Wisconsin, n.d. 9675.5 p50
Collins, Michael 13; Philadelphia, 1864 5704.8 p156
Collins, Michael 20; Virginia, 1750 3690.1 p48
Collins, Michael 20; Virginia, 1751 1219.7 p3
Collins, Michael 30; Massachusetts, 1849 5881.1 p21
Collins, Patrick 25; Maryland, 1775 1219.7 p248
Collins, Peter; Colorado, 1904 9678.1 p158
Collins, Peter; New York, NY, 1839 8208.4 p102
Collins, Peter 40; Virginia, 1774 1219.7 p186
Collins, Philip; Philadelphia, 1852 5704.8 p92
Collins, Richard; Virginia, 1646 6219 p239
Collins, Richard 21; Jamaica, 1735 3690.1 p48
Collins, Richard 37; Virginia, 1775 1219.7 p252
Collins, Rose; St. John, N.B., 1848 5704.8 p43
Collins, Rose 25; Philadelphia, 1854 5704.8 p116
Collins, Rose Ann; Philadelphia, 1868 5704.8 p225
Collins, S. W.; Washington, 1859-1920 2872.1 p8
Collins, Sally 20; St. John, N.B., 1856 5704.8 p131
Collins, Samuel 22; Philadelphia, 1854 5704.8 p118
Collins, Samuel 25; Virginia, 1727 3690.1 p49
Collins, Samuel Henry; California, 1862 2769.3 p3
Collins, Sarah; Philadelphia, 1864 5704.8 p169
Collins, Sarah; Philadelphia, 1867 5704.8 p221
Collins, Sarah 22; Philadelphia, 1861 5704.8 p148
Collins, Sarah Ann 2; Philadelphia, 1864 5704.8 p156
Collins, Susan; St. John, N.B., 1851 5704.8 p80
Collins, Susan 18; Philadelphia, 1853 5704.8 p113
Collins, Tho.; Virginia, 1635 6219 p12
Collins, Thomas; Illinois, 1861 2896.5 p8
Collins, Thomas; Illinois, 1900 5012.40 p77
Collins, Thomas; Virginia, 1772 1219.7 p160
Collins, Thomas 22; New Orleans, 1862 543.30 p460
Collins, Thomas 28; Maryland, 1774 1219.7 p192
Collins, Thomas 32; Maryland, 1774 1219.7 p191
Collins, Tim. 28; Massachusetts, 1849 5881.1 p25
Collins, Walter; Virginia, 1635 6219 p71
Collins, William; Montreal, 1822 7603 p65
Collins, William; Montreal, 1824 7603 p65
Collins, William; New York, NY, 1815 2859.11 p28
Collins, William; New York, NY, 1839 8208.4 p98
Collins, William; Ohio, 1830-1868 9892.11 p9
Collins, William; Virginia, 1638 6219 p125
Collins, William; Virginia, 1639 6219 p161
Collins, William; Virginia, 1698 2212 p14
Collins, William 14; Philadelphia, 1775 1219.7 p248
Collins, William 24; Maryland, 1774 1219.7 p228
Collins, William 24; Maryland, 1775 1219.7 p255
Collins, William 25; Massachusetts, 1849 5881.1 p26
Collins, William 30; Quebec, 1855 5704.8 p125
Collins, William J.; Illinois, 1898 5012.40 p55
Collis, Thomas 19; Maryland, 1730 3690.1 p49
Collison, Miles; Virginia, 1639 6219 p152
Collison, William; Norfolk, VA, 1819 9892.11 p9
Colliton, John 40; Charles Town, SC, 1775 1219.7 p265
With wife
With 3 children
Collity, Dermot; America, 1741 4971 p56
Collity, Michael; America, 1741 4971 p56
Collius, . . .; Canada, 1776-1783 9786 p19
Collmann, William; Philadelphia, 1894 1450.2 p6B
Collner, John 24; Pennsylvania, 1738 3690.1 p49
Collomb, Louis Alphonse 24; New Orleans, 1836 778.5 p125
Collon, . . .; Canada, 1776-1783 9786 p19
Collon, Thomas; St. John, N.B., 1847 5704.8 p21
Collongues, Mr. 28; America, 1837 778.5 p125
Collopy, James; America, 1738 4971 p52
Collowes, Step.; Virginia, 1645 6219 p233
Collue, Abraham 19; Maryland, 1724 3690.1 p49
Collum, W.E. 70; Arizona, 1924 9228.40 p28
Collup, William 15; Philadelphia, 1774 1219.7 p175
Collura, Joseph; Kansas, 1912 6013.40 p15
Colly, Tho.; Virginia, 1636 6219 p11
Collybancke, Sarah; Virginia, 1638 6219 p145
Collybant, Sarah; Virginia, 1635 6219 p27
Collyer, J. W.; Washington, 1859-1920 2872.1 p8
Collyer, Joseph W.; Washington, 1859-1920 2872.1 p8
Collyer, Thomas 20; Jamaica, 1730 3690.1 p49
Colmer, George 44; Maryland, 1774 1219.7 p213
Colmer, Thomas; Virginia, 1600-1643 6219 p200
Colnin, Catherine 20; Quebec, 1864 5704.8 p159
Coloct, John 11; Virginia, 1700 2212 p30
Colodon, Jacques 28; Port uncertain, 1837 778.5 p126
Cologan, Heran; New York, NY, 1839 8208.4 p93
Cologan, Mary; America, 1741 4971 p94
Colom, Catherine 24; Quebec, 1856 5704.8 p129
Colomb, Mrs. 47; Port uncertain, 1838 778.5 p126
Colomb, Francisco 40; Port uncertain, 1837 778.5 p126
Colomb, Jean Jacques 18; Port uncertain, 1839 778.5 p126
Colomb, Malanda 22; Port uncertain, 1837 778.5 p126
Colombo, Frank; Arkansas, 1918 95.2 p31
Colombo, Girolamo; Arkansas, 1918 95.2 p31
Colombo, Louis; Arkansas, 1918 95.2 p31
Colombos, Constantine Demitre; Arkansas, 1918 95.2 p31
Colomtal, Augustin 25; America, 1838 778.5 p126
Colon, Christobal; Arkansas, 1918 95.2 p31
Colon, H. O. 16; America, 1838 778.5 p126
Colonelli, Epimmaco; Arkansas, 1918 95.2 p31
Colonelli, Epimmaco; Wisconsin, n.d. 9675.5 p50
Colosono, Antonis; Arkansas, 1918 95.2 p31
Colound, J. D. 50; New Orleans, 1823 778.5 p126
Colpits, Robert 28; Nova Scotia, 1775 1219.7 p263
Colquhoun, Angus; America, 1790 1639.20 p47
Colquhoun, Ann 20 SEE Colquhoun, Mary
Colquhoun, Archibald; America, 1791 1639.20 p48
Colquhoun, Archibald; America, 1802 1639.20 p47
Colquhoun, Archibald; North Carolina, 1786 1639.20 p47
Colquhoun, Archibald 22 SEE Colquhoun, Mary
Colquhoun, Catherine; North Carolina, 1762-1841 1639.20 p181
Colquhoun, Duncan; America, 1790 1639.20 p48
Colquhoun, Mary 55; Wilmington, NC, 1775 1639.20 p38
*Child:*Archibald 22
*Child:*Ann 20
Colquhoun, Wm.; Virginia, 1802 4778.2 p141
Colsey, George; New York, NY, 1837 8208.4 p51
Colsey, Thomas Rhoades; New York, NY, 1837 8208.4 p51
Colso, Angelo; Iowa, 1866-1943 123.54 p14
Colson, Charles 25; Port uncertain, 1836 778.5 p126
Colson, Charles A. 25; Massachusetts, 1860 6410.32 p108
Colson, Elizabeth; Charles Town, SC, 1751 1219.7 p7
Colson, Emma 3; Massachusetts, 1860 6410.32 p107
Colson, Susan; Virginia, 1628 6219 p31
Colson, Thomas 18; Maryland or Virginia, 1699 2212 p21
Colston, Thomas 29; Philadelphia, 1774 1219.7 p184
Colten, Ally; St. John, N.B., 1848 5704.8 p44
Colten, Mary; St. John, N.B., 1848 5704.8 p44
Colter, Catherine 30; Quebec, 1853 5704.8 p105
Colter, Eliza 9; Quebec, 1858 5704.8 p137
Colter, Fanny 1; Quebec, 1853 5704.8 p105
Colter, Isabella 57; Quebec, 1853 5704.8 p105
Colter, James 11; Quebec, 1858 5704.8 p137
Colter, John 12; New Orleans, 1852 5704.8 p98
Colter, Robert 10; New Orleans, 1852 5704.8 p98
Colter, Thomas 6; Quebec, 1853 5704.8 p105
Colter, William 4; Quebec, 1853 5704.8 p105
Colter, William 58; Quebec, 1853 5704.8 p105
Colteusc, Peter; Wisconsin, n.d. 9675.5 p50
Colton, Ellen; Philadelphia, 1851 5704.8 p80
Colton, James; Philadelphia, 1851 5704.8 p80
Colton, John; Ohio, 1844 9892.11 p10
Colton, John 56; Massachusetts, 1849 5881.1 p18
Colton, Nicho.; Virginia, 1643 6219 p204
Colton, William 22; Virginia, 1774 1219.7 p244
Colty, Bridget 12; Massachusetts, 1849 5881.1 p13
Columban, Antoine 11; America, 1831 778.5 p126
Columban, Denis 44; America, 1831 778.5 p126
Columban, Jacob 5; America, 1831 778.5 p126
Columban, Joseph 15; America, 1831 778.5 p126
Columban, Lawrence 7; America, 1831 778.5 p126

Columban, Maria 17; America, 1831 778.5 p126
Columban, Maria Elizabeth 46; America, 1831 778.5 p127
Columban, Nicholas 9; America, 1831 778.5 p127
Columbu, Michael; Iowa, 1866-1943 123.54 p59
Columbus, John; Arkansas, 1918 95.2 p31
Colvard, William 24; Virginia, 1725 3690.1 p49
Colvens, John 22; Jamaica, 1725 3690.1 p49
Colvile, Andrew; Northwest Terr., 1880 9775.5 p218
Colvin, A. 21; New Orleans, 1835 778.5 p127
Colvin, Alexander; Brunswick, NC, 1739 1639.20 p48
Colvin, B. F.; Washington, 1859-1920 2872.1 p8
Colvin, Eliza 18; Quebec, 1859 5704.8 p143
Colvin, James; Philadelphia, 1811 2859.11 p10
Colvin, Jane; Philadelphia, 1811 53.26 p13
Colvin, John; Philadelphia, 1811 53.26 p14
Colvin, John; Philadelphia, 1811 2859.11 p10
Colvin, John 20; Quebec, 1859 5704.8 p143
Colvin, Margaret 16; Quebec, 1859 5704.8 p143
Colvin, Maria 19; Quebec, 1859 5704.8 p143
Colvin, Mary 25; Quebec, 1859 5704.8 p143
Colwell, George 16; Quebec, 1854 5704.8 p118
Colwell, John M. 50; New Orleans, 1862 543.30 p454
Colwell, Mary Jane 15; Quebec, 1854 5704.8 p118
Colwell, Rebecca; Philadelphia, 1867 5704.8 p217
Colwell, William M.; Washington, 1859-1920 2872.1 p8
Colwin, Mrs. 30; Baltimore, 1871 6508.6 p115
Colwin, James 28; Baltimore, 1871 6508.6 p115
Colwin, Jane 8; Baltimore, 1871 6508.6 p115
Coman, Lancelot; Montreal, 1824 7603 p98
Comat, Jacques 50; America, 1831 778.5 p127
Comat, Marie 48; America, 1831 778.5 p127
Combe, Jule 8; America, 1831 778.5 p127
Combe, Michael 36; America, 1831 778.5 p127
Combelle, Alexander 36; America, 1836 778.5 p127
Comberlander, John; South Carolina, 1788 7119 p201
Combes, Rich.; Virginia, 1635 6219 p72
Combes, William 15; Baltimore, 1775 1219.7 p269
Combey, Ann; Virginia, 1635 6219 p6
Combier, C. 20; New Orleans, 1823 778.5 p127
Comburre, S.M. 22; Port uncertain, 1838 778.5 p127
Come, Francois 19; New Orleans, 1836 778.5 p127
Comeings, Nicholas; Virginia, 1639 6219 p159
Comely, Chas. E. 23; Kansas, 1888 5240.1 p72
Comer, G. G.; Washington, 1859-1920 2872.1 p8
Comer, James 18; Maryland or Virginia, 1719 3690.1 p49
Comer, John 28; America, 1724 3690.1 p49
Comerford, James; America, 1742 4971 p31
Comerford, John; America, 1742 4971 p31
Comfort, Andrew; Philadelphia, 1762 9973.7 p37
Comfort, Helena; Montreal, 1818 7603 p73
Comfort, John; Philadelphia, 1762 9973.7 p37
Comings, Nicholas; Virginia, 1639 6219 p159
Comins, William; New York, NY, 1839 8208.4 p101
Comisky, James; Colorado, 1892 9678.1 p158
Comitez, Phillipie 37; America, 1827 778.5 p127
Comitis, Victor 32; New Orleans, 1836 778.5 p127
Commane, Dennis; America, 1741 4971 p42
Commane, Maurice; America, 1742 4971 p53
Commeford, Laurent; New Brunswick, 1822 7603 p98
Commet, Adalade 18; New Orleans, 1837 778.5 p127
Commet, John 31; New Orleans, 1837 778.5 p128
Commettier, Hector 31; America, 1835 778.5 p128
Commis, Donunis; Arkansas, 1918 95.2 p31
Commusky, Bryan 16; Massachusetts, 1847 5881.1 p13
Compoore, Ralph; Virginia, 1635 6219 p3
Compston, Thomas 24; St. John, N.B., 1865 5704.8 p165
Compte, Jean 27; America, 1837 778.5 p128
Compton, Catharine 24; Massachusetts, 1847 5881.1 p14
Compton, John; Virginia, 1643 6219 p203
Compton, William 25; Maryland, 1775 1219.7 p251
Comran, Peter 44; Massachusetts, 1847 5881.1 p23
Comras, Charles N.; Arkansas, 1918 95.2 p31
Comtessa, Nicolas 33; America, 1839 778.5 p128
Conaghan, . . .; Philadelphia, 1865 5704.8 p192
Conaghan, Ann; New York, NY, 1868 5704.8 p229
Conaghan, Ann; Philadelphia, 1865 5704.8 p192
Conaghan, Ann 20; Philadelphia, 1854 5704.8 p122
Conaghan, Bell; Quebec, 1853 5704.8 p104
Conaghan, Catharine; Philadelphia, 1865 5704.8 p192
Conaghan, Catherine 20; St. John, N.B., 1858 5704.8 p137
Conaghan, Corneilus; New York, NY, 1864 5704.8 p173
Conaghan, Daniel; Quebec, 1851 5704.8 p82
Conaghan, Hannah; St. John, N.B., 1848 5704.8 p43
Conaghan, Hugh; Philadelphia, 1851 5704.8 p78
Conaghan, Isabella; Philadelphia, 1847 53.26 p14
Conaghan, Isabella; Philadelphia, 1847 5704.8 p23
Conaghan, Isabella 8; Quebec, 1853 5704.8 p104
Conaghan, James; New York, NY, 1869 5704.8 p235
Conaghan, James 6 *SEE* Conaghan, Mary
Conaghan, James 6; Philadelphia, 1847 5704.8 p31
Conaghan, James 18; Philadelphia, 1861 5704.8 p149
Conaghan, John; Philadelphia, 1865 5704.8 p198
Conaghan, John; Quebec, 1853 5704.8 p104
Conaghan, John 3; Quebec, 1853 5704.8 p104
Conaghan, Margaret; Quebec, 1853 5704.8 p104
Conaghan, Margaret 6; Quebec, 1853 5704.8 p104
Conaghan, Margaret 8 *SEE* Conaghan, Mary
Conaghan, Margaret 8; Philadelphia, 1847 5704.8 p31
Conaghan, Margaret 22; St. John, N.B., 1855 5704.8 p127
Conaghan, Margery; Philadelphia, 1865 5704.8 p192
Conaghan, Mary; Philadelphia, 1847 53.26 p14
*Relative:*Margaret 8
*Relative:*James 6
Conaghan, Mary; Philadelphia, 1847 5704.8 p31
Conaghan, Mary; Philadelphia, 1864 5704.8 p179
Conaghan, Mary; Philadelphia, 1865 5704.8 p192
Conaghan, Mary; Philadelphia, 1865 5704.8 p198
Conaghan, Mary; Quebec, 1850 5704.8 p63
Conaghan, Mary; Quebec, 1853 5704.8 p104
Conaghan, Sarah J.; New York, NY, 1866 5704.8 p212
Conaghan, William 1; Quebec, 1853 5704.8 p104
Conaghy, Barnard; New York, NY, 1811 2859.11 p10
Conaghy, Thomas; New York, NY, 1811 2859.11 p10
Conahan, Anne 11; Quebec, 1855 5704.8 p125
Conahan, Mary 2; Quebec, 1855 5704.8 p125
Conahan, Mary 30; Quebec, 1855 5704.8 p125
Conahan, Paddy 7; Quebec, 1855 5704.8 p125
Conahan, Patt 40; Quebec, 1855 5704.8 p125
Conaly, Andrew 23; Maryland, 1775 1219.7 p248
Conard, Thomas; Louisiana, 1789-1819 778.5 p555
Conboy, J. E.; Washington, 1859-1920 2872.1 p8
Concannon, James; Virginia, 1764 1219.7 p104
Concannon, James 8; Massachusetts, 1850 5881.1 p19
Concannon, John; New York, NY, 1816 2859.11 p28
Concannon, Patrick; New York, NY, 1811 2859.11 p10
Concannon, Thomas; Ohio, 1884 2764.35 p12
Concannon, Timothy 23; Massachusetts, 1849 5881.1 p25
Concannon, William; New York, NY, 1816 2859.11 p28
Concelli, Charles; Arkansas, 1918 95.2 p31
Conda, Michael; Colorado, 1904 9678.1 p158
Condamine, De La; South America, 1700-1799 8582.3 p79
Conday, J. 25; America, 1835 778.5 p128
Conde, Mrs. 45; New Orleans, 1830 778.5 p128
Conde, D. 26; New Orleans, 1830 778.5 p128
Conden, Ellen 23; Massachusetts, 1849 5881.1 p16
Conden, Hannah; New York, NY, 1811 2859.11 p10
With family
Conden, Margaret 20; Massachusetts, 1849 5881.1 p21
Conden, Mary 30; Massachusetts, 1850 5881.1 p23
Conden, Richard 25; Massachusetts, 1849 5881.1 p25
Condier, A. 32; America, 1838 778.5 p128
Condin, Ellen 14; Massachusetts, 1849 5881.1 p16
Condinotte, Cementi; Iowa, 1866-1943 123.54 p14
Condinotti, Clemente; Iowa, 1866-1943 123.54 p14
Condon, Bridget 20; Massachusetts, 1849 5881.1 p13
Condon, Catherine; Montreal, 1824 7603 p85
Condon, David; America, 1742-1743 4971 p42
Condon, John; America, 1738-1739 4971 p59
Condon, Michael 12; Massachusetts, 1850 5881.1 p23
Condon, Norry 60; Massachusetts, 1850 5881.1 p23
Condon, Patrick; Illinois, 1861 2896.5 p8
Condon, Peter; Montreal, 1820 7603 p98
Condron, Richard; America, 1742 4971 p17
Condrum, John; Annapolis, MD, 1742 4971 p93
Cone, David; Virginia, 1641 6219 p184
Cone, John; Illinois, 1867 2896.5 p8
Coneghan, Patrick; New York, NY, 1816 2859.11 p28
Conen, Hugh 23; Philadelphia, 1854 5704.8 p118
Conerry, John; New York, NY, 1816 2859.11 p28
Conery, David 3; Massachusetts, 1849 5881.1 p15
Conery, Hannah 4; Massachusetts, 1849 5881.1 p16
Conery, John; Canada, 1841 7036 p124
*Sister:*Mary
Conery, John; Massachusetts, 1841 7036 p124
*Sister:*Mary
Conery, Mary *SEE* Conery, John
Conery, Mary *SEE* Conery, John
Conery, Mary 6; Massachusetts, 1849 5881.1 p21
Conery, Mary 24; Massachusetts, 1849 5881.1 p21
Conet, F...ois 24; America, 1838 778.5 p128
Confiotti, Umberto 24; New York, NY, 1893 9026.4 p41
Conford, John; America, 1741 4971 p16
Congalinon, Justin 38; Port uncertain, 1837 778.5 p128
Congden, John; Virginia, 1638 6219 p125
Conger, J. K.; Washington, 1859-1920 2872.1 p8
Conghlin, M.J.; Illinois, 1892 5012.37 p62
Congrave, John 23; Virginia, 1774 1219.7 p201
Congrave, Mary; America, 1743 4971 p11
Conhooe, William; Virginia, 1639 6219 p156
Coniella, Filippo 17 *SEE* Coniella, Vincenzo
Coniella, Vincenzo 37; New York, NY, 1893 9026.4 p41
*Relative:*Filippo 17
Conigan, Elizabeth; Philadelphia, 1847 53.26 p14
Conigan, Elizabeth; Philadelphia, 1847 5704.8 p22
Conigan, Henry; Philadelphia, 1847 53.26 p14
*Relative:*Jane
*Relative:*Isabella 11
*Relative:*Jane 9 mos
Conigan, Henry; Philadelphia, 1847 5704.8 p22
Conigan, Isabella 4; Philadelphia, 1847 5704.8 p22
Conigan, Isabella 11 *SEE* Conigan, Henry
Conigan, Jane *SEE* Conigan, Henry
Conigan, Jane; Philadelphia, 1847 5704.8 p22
Conigan, Jane 9 mos *SEE* Conigan, Henry
Conigan, Jane 9 mos; Philadelphia, 1847 5704.8 p22
Conigan, Stephen 25; Massachusetts, 1849 5881.1 p25
Conigham, Thomas 18; Philadelphia, 1803 53.26 p14
Conighen, Biddy 1; Philadelphia, 1859 5704.8 p141
Conighen, Isabella 30; Philadelphia, 1859 5704.8 p141
Conighen, Mary 2; Philadelphia, 1859 5704.8 p141
Coniot, John B. 39; West Virginia, 1902 9788.3 p6
Conkley, Dennis 50; Massachusetts, 1850 5881.1 p15
Conkley, Mary 45; Massachusetts, 1850 5881.1 p23
Conlan, Mrs. 35; Massachusetts, 1847 5881.1 p20
Conlan, Andre; Quebec, 1822 7603 p91
Conlan, Anna 38; Massachusetts, 1849 5881.1 p13
Conlan, Anna 38; Massachusetts, 1849 5881.1 p22
Conlan, Bridget 6; Massachusetts, 1847 5881.1 p13
Conlan, Bridget 13; Massachusetts, 1849 5881.1 p13
Conlan, Bridget 28; Massachusetts, 1847 5881.1 p13
Conlan, Eliza 16; Massachusetts, 1848 5881.1 p15
Conlan, James; St. John, N.B., 1853 5704.8 p99
Conlan, James 15; Massachusetts, 1849 5881.1 p19
Conlan, Jeremiah 6; Massachusetts, 1849 5881.1 p19
Conlan, Johanna 35; Massachusetts, 1847 5881.1 p17
Conlan, John 10; Massachusetts, 1847 5881.1 p17
Conlan, Julia 18; Massachusetts, 1847 5881.1 p17
Conlan, Margaret 8; Massachusetts, 1849 5881.1 p22
Conlan, Margaret 18; Massachusetts, 1847 5881.1 p20
Conlan, Margaret 50; Massachusetts, 1847 5881.1 p20
Conlan, Mary 17; Massachusetts, 1849 5881.1 p22
Conlan, Michael 11; Massachusetts, 1849 5881.1 p22
Conlan, Pat 8; Massachusetts, 1847 5881.1 p23
Conlan, Peter; New York, NY, 1832 8208.4 p36
Conlan, Peter 13; Massachusetts, 1849 5881.1 p24
Conlan, Thomas 11; Massachusetts, 1849 5881.1 p26
Conlen, Margaret; Quebec, 1825 7603 p83
Conley, Catharine 24; Massachusetts, 1847 5881.1 p14
Conley, Isabel; Maryland or Virginia, 1697 2212 p3
Conley, Isabell; Maryland or Virginia, 1697 2212 p3
Conley, Isabella 4; Massachusetts, 1849 5881.1 p19
Conley, James; Illinois, 1861 2896.5 p8
Conley, James 14; Massachusetts, 1850 5881.1 p20
Conley, John 27; Massachusetts, 1848 5881.1 p17
Conley, John 34; Massachusetts, 1849 5881.1 p19
Conley, Mary 1; Massachusetts, 1847 5881.1 p20
Conley, Mary 1; Massachusetts, 1849 5881.1 p22
Conley, Mary 26; Massachusetts, 1849 5881.1 p22
Conley, Mary 30; Massachusetts, 1847 5881.1 p20
Conley, Mary Jane 23; St. John, N.B., 1863 5704.8 p154
Conley, Michael; Massachusetts, 1849 5881.1 p22
Conley, Michael 25; Massachusetts, 1847 5881.1 p20
Conley, Sarah 3; Massachusetts, 1849 5881.1 p25
Conley, Sarah 25; Massachusetts, 1849 5881.1 p25
Conley, William 7; Massachusetts, 1849 5881.1 p26
Conley, William 50; Massachusetts, 1849 5881.1 p26
Conlin, Matthew; Illinois, 1866 7857 p3
Conlon, Michael 24; Maryland, 1774 1219.7 p218
Conly, Bryan; Massachusetts, 1847 5881.1 p13
Conly, John 7; Massachusetts, 1847 5881.1 p17
Conly, John 20; Massachusetts, 1850 5881.1 p19
Conly, William 9; Maryland or Virginia, 1699 2212 p21
Conn, Alexander; Baltimore, 1820 9892.11 p10
Conn, James; Baltimore, 1826 9892.11 p10
Conn, Jane; Baltimore, 1811 2859.11 p10
Conn, John; Ohio, 1821 9892.11 p10
Conn, Robert; Baltimore, 1811 2859.11 p10
Conn, Samuel; Baltimore, 1811 2859.11 p10
Conn, Samuel; Philadelphia, 1853 5704.8 p103
Conn, Samuel 28; St. John, N.B., 1861 5704.8 p146
Conn, Sarah; Baltimore, 1811 2859.11 p10
Connaghan, James; Quebec, 1852 5704.8 p94
Connagrave, Thomas; Virginia, 1635 6219 p69
Connahan, Nancy 20; Massachusetts, 1847 5881.1 p23
Connarsa, Antonio; Arkansas, 1918 95.2 p31
Connaughty, Thomas; America, 1743 4971 p11
Connaway, Jarman; Virginia, 1642 6219 p198
Connaway, Jon.; Virginia, 1638 6219 p11
Connay, Margaret; St. John, N.B., 1850 5704.8 p61
Connel, Honora; America, 1742 4971 p53
Connel, Jane; Philadelphia, 1847 53.26 p14
Connel, Jane; Philadelphia, 1847 5704.8 p1

Connel, John; Quebec, 1852 5704.8 p86
Connel, John; Quebec, 1852 5704.8 p91
Connel, Stephen; Baltimore, 1811 2859.11 p10
Connelan, Patrice; Montreal, 1814 7603 p93
Connell, Abby 16; Massachusetts, 1850 5881.1 p13
Connell, Ann 37; Massachusetts, 1849 5881.1 p13
Connell, Bartholemew 22; Massachusetts, 1849 5881.1 p13
Connell, Bridget; Philadelphia, 1865 5704.8 p203
Connell, Catharine 6; Massachusetts, 1850 5881.1 p14
Connell, Catharine 15; Massachusetts, 1850 5881.1 p14
Connell, Dennis 30; Massachusetts, 1850 5881.1 p15
Connell, Elizabeth 20; Massachusetts, 1849 5881.1 p16
Connell, Ellen 24; Massachusetts, 1850 5881.1 p16
Connell, Hannah 20; Massachusetts, 1849 5881.1 p17
Connell, Honora 30; Massachusetts, 1847 5881.1 p16
Connell, James; America, 1741 4971 p41
Connell, James; New York, NY, 1834 8208.4 p45
Connell, James; San Francisco, 1850 4914.15 p10
Connell, Joanna 2; Massachusetts, 1850 5881.1 p19
Connell, Johanna 9; Massachusetts, 1849 5881.1 p18
Connell, Johanna 38; Massachusetts, 1849 5881.1 p19
Connell, John; America, 1741-1742 4971 p60
Connell, John; Kansas, 1870 5240.1 p51
Connell, John 3; Massachusetts, 1849 5881.1 p18
Connell, John 24; Massachusetts, 1849 5881.1 p19
Connell, John 29; Massachusetts, 1850 5881.1 p19
Connell, John 39; Maryland, 1774 1219.7 p222
Connell, John McJeffry; America, 1739 4971 p56
Connell, Julia 30; Massachusetts, 1849 5881.1 p18
Connell, Kate 18; Massachusetts, 1849 5881.1 p20
Connell, Limerick; Philadelphia, 1850 5704.8 p64
Connell, Mary; Philadelphia, 1850 5704.8 p64
Connell, Mary 26; Massachusetts, 1849 5881.1 p21
Connell, Mary Ann 1; Philadelphia, 1850 5704.8 p64
Connell, Matty 26; Massachusetts, 1847 5881.1 p20
Connell, Michael 18; Massachusetts, 1847 5881.1 p20
Connell, Michael 32; New Orleans, 1863 543.30 p464
Connell, Pat. 50; Massachusetts, 1849 5881.1 p24
Connell, Patrick; New York, NY, 1816 2859.11 p28
Connell, Patrick 7; Massachusetts, 1850 5881.1 p24
Connell, Robert 30; Massachusetts, 1847 5881.1 p24
Connell, Robert John 3 mos; Philadelphia, 1850 5704.8 p64
Connell, Samuel; Philadelphia, 1852 5704.8 p84
Connell, Timothy; America, 1738 4971 p40
Connell, Timothy; America, 1741 4971 p40
Connell, Timothy; Quebec, 1825 7603 p60
Connell, William; Philadelphia, 1850 5704.8 p64
Connelley, Mary Ann 9; Philadelphia, 1851 5704.8 p79
Connellin, James; New York, NY, 1816 2859.11 p28
Connelly, . . .; Massachusetts, 1850 5881.1 p19
With child
Connelly, Anne; New York, NY, 1869 5704.8 p232
Connelly, Barney; California, 1824-1872 2769.3 p4
Connelly, Bartholomew 35; Massachusetts, 1849 5881.1 p13
Connelly, Biddy 9; Quebec, 1847 5704.8 p7
Connelly, Bridget 21; Massachusetts, 1847 5881.1 p13
Connelly, Catharine; Philadelphia, 1866 5704.8 p205
Connelly, Catharine 40; Massachusetts, 1850 5881.1 p14
Connelly, Denis 39; Kansas, 1880 5240.1 p62
Connelly, Edward; Quebec, 1847 5704.8 p7
Connelly, Joanna 24; Massachusetts, 1850 5881.1 p19
Connelly, John 5; Quebec, 1847 5704.8 p7
Connelly, John 19; Massachusetts, 1847 5881.1 p17
Connelly, John 20; Jamaica, 1736 3690.1 p49
Connelly, John 20; Massachusetts, 1850 5881.1 p19
Connelly, John 24; New Orleans, 1862 543.30 p460
Connelly, Mary; New York, NY, 1816 2859.11 p28
Connelly, Mary; New York, NY, 1869 5704.8 p232
Connelly, Mary 3; Quebec, 1847 5704.8 p7
Connelly, Mary 18; Massachusetts, 1847 5881.1 p20
Connelly, Mary 35; Massachusetts, 1849 5881.1 p22
Connelly, Mary 60; Massachusetts, 1847 5881.1 p20
Connelly, Matthew; America, 1735-1743 4971 p8
Connelly, Michael; America, 1735-1743 4971 p79
Connelly, Nelly; Quebec, 1847 5704.8 p7
Connelly, Owen; Philadelphia, 1865 5704.8 p192
Connelly, Pat. 26; Massachusetts, 1847 5881.1 p23
Connelly, Pat. 26; Massachusetts, 1847 5881.1 p24
Connelly, Patrick; Philadelphia, 1811 53.26 p14
Connelly, Patrick; Philadelphia, 1811 2859.11 p10
Connelly, Patrick 7; Quebec, 1847 5704.8 p7
Connelly, Patrick 30; Massachusetts, 1847 5881.1 p23
Connelly, Patrick 33; Philadelphia, 1804 53.26 p14
Connelly, Peter; New York, NY, 1815 2859.11 p28
Connelly, Rose 31; Philadelphia, 1804 53.26 p14
Connelly, Thomas; New York, NY, 1849 6013.19 p30
Connelly, Thomas 26; Arkansas, 1918 95.2 p31
Connelly, Thompson 25; St. John, N.B., 1864 5704.8 p159
Connelly, Timothy 22; Philadelphia, 1774 1219.7 p228
Connelly, William 23; Massachusetts, 1847 5881.1 p26
Conner, Anthony 7; St. John, N.B., 1849 5704.8 p55
Conner, Arthur; St. John, N.B., 1849 5704.8 p55
Conner, Bridget; Philadelphia, 1849 53.26 p14
Conner, Bridget; Philadelphia, 1849 5704.8 p53
Conner, Catherine 20; St. John, N.B., 1865 5704.8 p165
Conner, Cornelius 16; Massachusetts, 1849 5881.1 p14
Conner, Edward; Philadelphia, 1815 2859.11 p28
Conner, Edward; St. John, N.B., 1853 5704.8 p99
Conner, Edward 28; Kansas, 1874 5240.1 p55
Conner, Grace 5; Philadelphia, 1856 5704.8 p128
Conner, Hugh 10; Philadelphia, 1856 5704.8 p128
Conner, James; Philadelphia, 1847 53.26 p14
Conner, James; Philadelphia, 1847 5704.8 p21
Conner, James 3; St. John, N.B., 1849 5704.8 p55
Conner, James 7; Philadelphia, 1856 5704.8 p128
Conner, Jeremiah; New York, NY, 1815 2859.11 p28
Conner, John; Philadelphia, 1815 2859.11 p28
Conner, John 35; New Orleans, 1862 543.30 p458
Conner, Mary 6; Massachusetts, 1849 5881.1 p21
Conner, Mary 18; Massachusetts, 1849 5881.1 p21
With child
Conner, Mary 20; Massachusetts, 1849 5881.1 p22
Conner, Mary 28; Philadelphia, 1856 5704.8 p128
Conner, Mary 30; Massachusetts, 1849 5881.1 p21
Conner, Matty; St. John, N.B., 1849 5704.8 p56
Conner, Michael 3; Philadelphia, 1856 5704.8 p128
Conner, Michael 35; Philadelphia, 1856 5704.8 p128
Conner, Nancy 20; Philadelphia, 1861 5704.8 p149
Conner, Pat 7; Philadelphia, 1856 5704.8 p128
Conner, Pat 12; Philadelphia, 1849 53.26 p14
Conner, Pat 12; Philadelphia, 1849 5704.8 p52
Conner, Pat. 16; Massachusetts, 1849 5881.1 p24
Conner, Patrick 20; Quebec, 1854 5704.8 p119
Conner, Phillip; Virginia, 1638 6219 p153
Conner, Robert 50; Massachusetts, 1850 5881.1 p25
Conner, Susanna; Philadelphia, 1856 5704.8 p128
Conner, Thomas; Illinois, 1870 2896.5 p8
Conner, William 21; Philadelphia, 1854 5704.8 p118
Conners, Dennis; Illinois, 1861 2896.5 p8
Conners, Edward 27; New Orleans, 1862 543.30 p453
Conners, James; America, 1860 6014.1 p1
Conners, John; Illinois, 1870 5012.38 p99
Conners, John 27; New Orleans, 1862 543.30 p453
Conners, Mary 19; Massachusetts, 1849 5881.1 p22
Conners, Patrick; America, 1738 4971 p52
Conners, Thomas; America, 1735-1743 4971 p51
Conners, Tim. 18; Massachusetts, 1849 5881.1 p26
Connerty, Mary 20; Massachusetts, 1850 5881.1 p23
Connery, John 40; Virginia, 1774 1219.7 p185
Connery, Tim 16; Newfoundland, 1789 4915.24 p57
Connick, Laurence; America, 1743 4971 p34
Connifry, John 24; New Orleans, 1862 543.30 p452
Connil, Mr. 25; New Orleans, 1838 778.5 p128
Connill, Alexander 24; New York, 1775 1219.7 p268
With wife
Connily, Thom 26; Maryland or Virginia, 1699 2212 p24
Connington, Thomas; Indiana, 1848 9117 p16
Connolan, Thomas; New York, NY, 1815 2859.11 p28
Connolley, Easter 30; St. John, N.B., 1856 5704.8 p131
Connolli, Michael 34; New Orleans, 1862 543.30 p462
Connolly, Ann; America, 1743 4971 p10
Connolly, Bell; Quebec, 1847 5704.8 p6
Connolly, Biddy 7; Quebec, 1847 5704.8 p7
Connolly, Brian; St. John, N.B., 1853 5704.8 p100
Connolly, Catharine; America, 1865 5704.8 p204
Connolly, Charles 21; Quebec, 1854 5704.8 p119
Connolly, Dan 30; Newport, RI, 1851 6508.5 p20
Connolly, Dennis 3; Newport, RI, 1851 6508.5 p20
Connolly, Edmond; America, 1736 4971 p80
Connolly, Edmond; Montreal, 1815 7603 p69
Connolly, Eliza 3; Quebec, 1847 5704.8 p6
Connolly, Henry; New York, NY, 1816 2859.11 p28
With wife
Connolly, Henry; Quebec, 1847 5704.8 p7
Connolly, Henry 5; Quebec, 1847 5704.8 p6
Connolly, Henry 5; Quebec, 1847 5704.8 p7
Connolly, James; Quebec, 1847 5704.8 p6
Connolly, James 9; Quebec, 1847 5704.8 p6
Connolly, James 19; St. John, N.B., 1864 5704.8 p158
Connolly, Jane 13; Quebec, 1847 5704.8 p7
Connolly, John; Cleveland, OH, 1873 2764.35 p13
Connolly, John; Quebec, 1784 7603 p88
Connolly, John 7; Quebec, 1847 5704.8 p6
Connolly, John 40; Massachusetts, 1849 5881.1 p18
Connolly, Kate 30; Newport, RI, 1851 6508.5 p20
Connolly, Kitty Ann 11; Quebec, 1847 5704.8 p6
Connolly, Margaret; Quebec, 1847 5704.8 p6
Connolly, Margaret 11; Quebec, 1847 5704.8 p7
Connolly, Martin; Arkansas, 1918 95.2 p31
Connolly, Mary; Quebec, 1847 5704.8 p6
Connolly, Mary; Quebec, 1847 5704.8 p7
Connolly, Mary; South Carolina, 1767 1639.20 p48
Connolly, Mary 1; Newport, RI, 1851 6508.5 p20
Connolly, Mary 9; Quebec, 1847 5704.8 p7
Connolly, Mary 22; Massachusetts, 1849 5881.1 p22
Connolly, Mary A.; New York, NY, 1868 5704.8 p225
Connolly, Michael; America, 1740 4971 p81
Connolly, Michael; New York, NY, 1839 8208.4 p91
Connolly, Michael Joseph; Arkansas, 1918 95.2 p31
Connolly, Mick 30; Newport, RI, 1851 6508.5 p20
Connolly, Owen; Washington, 1859-1920 2872.1 p8
Connolly, Patrick 6 mos; Quebec, 1847 5704.8 p6
Connolly, Patt 22; Newport, RI, 1851 6508.5 p20
Connolly, Richard; New York, NY, 1838 8208.4 p63
Connolly, Rosey 3; Quebec, 1847 5704.8 p7
Connolly, Sarah 13; Quebec, 1847 5704.8 p6
Connolly, Thomas; San Francisco, 1851 6013.19 p90
Connolly, Thomas 28; Kansas, 1892 5240.1 p77
Connolly, William; Philadelphia, 1849 53.26 p14
Connolly, William; Philadelphia, 1849 5704.8 p50
Connolly, William; Quebec, 1847 5704.8 p7
Connoly, Rev.; New York, NY, 1815 2859.11 p28
Connor, Anastatia 15; Massachusetts, 1849 5881.1 p13
Connor, Ann; New York, NY, 1864 5704.8 p184
Connor, Bridget; America, 1735-1743 4971 p7
Connor, Bridget 14; Massachusetts, 1849 5881.1 p13
Connor, Bryan; America, 1742 4971 p29
Connor, Catherine; America, 1739 4971 p28
Connor, Catherine; St. John, N.B., 1852 5704.8 p93
Connor, Catherine 18; Philadelphia, 1865 5704.8 p164
Connor, Cecil; Philadelphia, 1850 53.26 p14
*Relative:*Patrick 8
*Relative:*John 6
Connor, Cecil; Philadelphia, 1850 5704.8 p68
Connor, Charles 24; Dominica, 1775 1219.7 p260
Connor, Cornelius 19; Jamaica, 1730 3690.1 p49
Connor, Dan 30; Massachusetts, 1847 5881.1 p15
Connor, Daniel 14; Massachusetts, 1847 5881.1 p14
Connor, Darby; America, 1741 4971 p56
Connor, David; Philadelphia, 1865 5704.8 p196
Connor, Dennis; America, 1740 4971 p56
Connor, Dennis; New York, NY, 1866 5704.8 p208
Connor, Edmund; America, 1738-1739 4971 p59
Connor, Edmund 1; Massachusetts, 1850 5881.1 p16
Connor, Edward; Brunswick, NC, 1739 1639.20 p48
Connor, Eliza 7; Massachusetts, 1850 5881.1 p16
Connor, Elleanor; St. John, N.B., 1847 5704.8 p35
Connor, Ellen; America, 1737 4971 p45
Connor, Ellen; New York, NY, 1865 5704.8 p196
Connor, Ellen 6; Massachusetts, 1850 5881.1 p16
Connor, Ellen 20; Massachusetts, 1849 5881.1 p15
Connor, Ellen 22; Massachusetts, 1848 5881.1 p15
Connor, Ellen 22; Massachusetts, 1849 5881.1 p16
Connor, Ellen 24; Massachusetts, 1849 5881.1 p15
Connor, Ellenor; America, 1743 4971 p57
Connor, Eugene 20; Massachusetts, 1849 5881.1 p15
Connor, Francis S.; New York, NY, 1835 8208.4 p8
Connor, Garet; America, 1741 4971 p49
Connor, Garret; America, 1740 4971 p48
Connor, Giley; New York, NY, 1868 5704.8 p229
Connor, Giley; Philadelphia, 1866 5704.8 p200
Connor, Gubby 20; Massachusetts, 1849 5881.1 p16
Connor, Hamilton; St. John, N.B., 1848 5704.8 p39
Connor, Henry; St. John, N.B., 1847 5704.8 p9
Connor, Hugh; New York, NY, 1816 2859.11 p28
Connor, James; America, 1735-1743 4971 p8
Connor, James; America, 1741 4971 p16
Connor, James; New York, NY, 1811 2859.11 p10
Connor, James; New York, NY, 1870 5704.8 p238
Connor, James; Philadelphia, 1851 5704.8 p71
Connor, James; St. John, N.B., 1847 5704.8 p35
Connor, James 20; Massachusetts, 1849 5881.1 p18
Connor, James 24; Maryland, 1775 1219.7 p250
Connor, James 24; Massachusetts, 1850 5881.1 p19
Connor, James 35; Massachusetts, 1849 5881.1 p18
Connor, Jane; New York, NY, 1811 2859.11 p10
With family
Connor, Jeremiah; America, 1839 6013.19 p90
Connor, Jeremiah; New York, NY, 1811 2859.11 p10
Connor, Joanna 8; Massachusetts, 1850 5881.1 p19
Connor, Johanna 12; Massachusetts, 1850 5881.1 p19
Connor, Johanna 20; Massachusetts, 1849 5881.1 p18
Connor, Johanna 40; Massachusetts, 1849 5881.1 p19
Connor, Johanna 40; Massachusetts, 1850 5881.1 p19
Connor, John; America, 1736 4971 p39
Connor, John; America, 1736-1737 4971 p59
Connor, John; America, 1737 4971 p55
Connor, John; America, 1738 4971 p36
Connor, John; America, 1739 4971 p27
Connor, John; America, 1741 4971 p23
Connor, John; America, 1742-1743 4971 p42
Connor, John; America, 1743 4971 p42
Connor, John; Charles Town, SC, 1768 1219.7 p136
Connor, John; New York, NY, 1816 2859.11 p28
Connor, John; New York, NY, 1868 5704.8 p229

Connor, John; Philadelphia, 1804 ***53.26*** *p14*
Connor, John 4; Massachusetts, 1847 ***5881.1*** *p17*
Connor, John 6 *SEE* Connor, Cecil
Connor, John 6; Philadelphia, 1850 ***5704.8*** *p68*
Connor, John 18; Massachusetts, 1847 ***5881.1*** *p17*
Connor, John 19; Virginia, 1775 ***1219.7*** *p247*
Connor, John 21; Maryland, 1775 ***1219.7*** *p260*
Connor, John 22; Massachusetts, 1847 ***5881.1*** *p17*
Connor, John 23; Massachusetts, 1847 ***5881.1*** *p17*
Connor, John 28; Massachusetts, 1849 ***5881.1*** *p18*
Connor, John 68; Massachusetts, 1849 ***5881.1*** *p18*
Connor, John P.; New York, NY, 1839 ***8208.4*** *p91*
Connor, Joseph; New York, NY, 1816 ***2859.11*** *p28*
Connor, Joseph 21; St. John, N.B., 1863 ***5704.8*** *p155*
Connor, Julia 20; Massachusetts, 1849 ***5881.1*** *p19*
Connor, Lawrence; Virginia, 1752 ***1219.7*** *p11*
Connor, Lawrence; Virginia, 1752 ***3690.1*** *p49*
Connor, Lawrence 50; Massachusetts, 1847 ***5881.1*** *p20*
Connor, Lizzee; New York, NY, 1866 ***5704.8*** *p208*
Connor, Luke; West Virginia, 1848-1850 ***9788.3*** *p6*
Connor, Luke; West Virginia, 1854 ***9788.3*** *p6*
Connor, Margaret; New York, NY, 1869 ***5704.8*** *p232*
Connor, Margaret 2; Massachusetts, 1850 ***5881.1*** *p23*
Connor, Margery; New York, NY, 1868 ***5704.8*** *p229*
Connor, Mary; America, 1867 ***5704.8*** *p223*
Connor, Mary; New York, NY, 1811 ***2859.11*** *p10*
Connor, Mary; New York, NY, 1866 ***5704.8*** *p208*
Connor, Mary; Philadelphia, 1871 ***5704.8*** *p240*
Connor, Mary 18; Massachusetts, 1850 ***5881.1*** *p23*
Connor, Mary 19; Massachusetts, 1847 ***5881.1*** *p20*
Connor, Mary 26; St. John, N.B., 1855 ***5704.8*** *p127*
Connor, Mary Anne; Quebec, 1781 ***7603*** *p75*
Connor, Matilda; New York, NY, 1870 ***5704.8*** *p238*
Connor, Michael 25; Massachusetts, 1849 ***5881.1*** *p21*
Connor, Michl; New York, NY, 1816 ***2859.11*** *p28*
Connor, Pat. 13; Massachusetts, 1849 ***5881.1*** *p24*
Connor, Patrick; America, 1735-1743 ***4971*** *p8*
Connor, Patrick; America, 1738-1743 ***4971*** *p91*
Connor, Patrick; America, 1741 ***4971*** *p56*
Connor, Patrick 8 *SEE* Connor, Cecil
Connor, Patrick 8; Philadelphia, 1850 ***5704.8*** *p68*
Connor, Patrick 25; Massachusetts, 1848 ***5881.1*** *p24*
Connor, Patrick 35; St. Vincent, 1775 ***1219.7*** *p251*
Connor, Peter 20; Massachusetts, 1849 ***5881.1*** *p24*
Connor, Philip; New York, NY, 1816 ***2859.11*** *p28*
Connor, Richard; New York, NY, 1816 ***2859.11*** *p28*
Connor, Roger; America, 1740 ***4971*** *p48*
Connor, Roger; America, 1741 ***4971*** *p49*
Connor, Sally 28; Massachusetts, 1850 ***5881.1*** *p25*
Connor, Thomas; America, 1739 ***4971*** *p14*
Connor, Thomas 23; New Orleans, 1862 ***543.30*** *p459*
Connor, Thomas 27; Massachusetts, 1848 ***5881.1*** *p25*
Connor, Timothy; America, 1741 ***4971*** *p56*
Connor, Timothy 4; Massachusetts, 1850 ***5881.1*** *p26*
Connor, Timothy 40; Massachusetts, 1850 ***5881.1*** *p26*
Connor, William; America, 1736 ***4971*** *p39*
Connor, William 24; Massachusetts, 1847 ***5881.1*** *p26*
Connors, Biddy 17; Massachusetts, 1847 ***5881.1*** *p13*
Connors, Catharine 20; Massachusetts, 1849 ***5881.1*** *p14*
Connors, Daniel; Quebec, 1822 ***7603*** *p66*
Connors, Daniel 17; Massachusetts, 1849 ***5881.1*** *p15*
Connors, Daniel 40; Massachusetts, 1849 ***5881.1*** *p15*
Connors, Edward; Quebec, 1785 ***7603*** *p73*
Connors, James B.; Illinois, 1880 ***2896.5*** *p8*
Connors, Julia 10; Massachusetts, 1849 ***5881.1*** *p19*
Connors, Margaret 25; Massachusetts, 1848 ***5881.1*** *p20*
Connors, Michael; Quebec, 1775 ***7603*** *p70*
Connors, Patrick; Quebec, 1821 ***7603*** *p57*
Connors, Patrick; Washington, 1859-1920 ***2872.1*** *p8*
Connue, Serrestine 27; Port uncertain, 1838 ***778.5*** *p128*
Connydon, John; Virginia, 1642 ***6219*** *p189*
With wife
Connyngton, John; Indiana, 1820-1850 ***9117*** *p16*
Conolan, Charles; New York, NY, 1815 ***2859.11*** *p28*
Conolan, James; New York, NY, 1815 ***2859.11*** *p28*
Conolly, Ann; America, 1737 ***4971*** *p85*
Conolly, Bryan; America, 1741 ***4971*** *p76*
Conolly, Catherine; America, 1740 ***4971*** *p15*
Conolly, David 21; Maryland, 1775 ***1219.7*** *p249*
Conolly, Ellan; Quebec, 1847 ***5704.8*** *p29*
Conolly, James; America, 1735-1743 ***4971*** *p79*
Conolly, James; New York, NY, 1816 ***2859.11*** *p28*
Conolly, James 22; Maryland, 1774 ***1219.7*** *p196*
Conolly, John; New York, NY, 1816 ***2859.11*** *p28*
Conolly, John; Philadelphia, 1851 ***5704.8*** *p80*
Conolly, M.; New York, NY, 1816 ***2859.11*** *p28*
Conolly, Margaret; America, 1741 ***4971*** *p16*
Conolly, Margaret; Quebec, 1847 ***5704.8*** *p29*
Conolly, Margaret 8; St. John, N.B., 1853 ***5704.8*** *p109*
Conolly, Mary 11; St. John, N.B., 1853 ***5704.8*** *p109*
Conolly, Michael; America, 1742 ***4971*** *p74*
Conolly, Michael; America, 1867 ***6014.1*** *p1*
Conolly, Patrick; Quebec, 1847 ***5704.8*** *p29*
Conolly, Patrick; St. John, N.B., 1847 ***5704.8*** *p35*
Conolly, Polly; New York, NY, 1811 ***2859.11*** *p10*
With family
Conolly, Thomas; New York, NY, 1816 ***2859.11*** *p28*
Conolly, Thomas; Quebec, 1847 ***5704.8*** *p29*
Conolly, William; New York, NY, 1816 ***2859.11*** *p28*
Conolly, William J.; New York, NY, 1816 ***2859.11*** *p28*
Conoly, Ann *SEE* Conoly, Owen
Conoly, Ann; Philadelphia, 1848 ***5704.8*** *p45*
Conoly, Bridget; St. John, N.B., 1847 ***5704.8*** *p33*
Conoly, Charles *SEE* Conoly, Owen
Conoly, Charles; Philadelphia, 1848 ***5704.8*** *p45*
Conoly, Elizabeth 14; St. John, N.B., 1854 ***5704.8*** *p122*
Conoly, Francis; St. John, N.B., 1847 ***5704.8*** *p25*
Conoly, Francis; St. John, N.B., 1847 ***5704.8*** *p33*
Conoly, Henry; St. John, N.B., 1847 ***5704.8*** *p26*
Conoly, John; New Orleans, 1848 ***5704.8*** *p48*
Conoly, John; St. John, N.B., 1847 ***5704.8*** *p26*
Conoly, John; St. John, N.B., 1847 ***5704.8*** *p35*
Conoly, John 20; St. John, N.B., 1854 ***5704.8*** *p115*
Conoly, Luke; Quebec, 1847 ***5704.8*** *p17*
Conoly, Margaret; St. John, N.B., 1847 ***5704.8*** *p33*
Conoly, Mary; St. John, N.B., 1847 ***5704.8*** *p33*
Conoly, Mary Jane 8; New Orleans, 1848 ***5704.8*** *p48*
Conoly, Nancy 5; New Orleans, 1848 ***5704.8*** *p48*
Conoly, Owen; Philadelphia, 1848 ***53.26*** *p14*
*Relative:*Ann
*Relative:*Charles
*Relative:*Susanna
Conoly, Own; Philadelphia, 1848 ***5704.8*** *p45*
Conoly, Patrick; St. John, N.B., 1847 ***5704.8*** *p35*
Conoly, Roger 12; St. John, N.B., 1854 ***5704.8*** *p120*
Conoly, Sarah Jane; New Orleans, 1848 ***5704.8*** *p48*
Conoly, Sarah Jane 3; New Orleans, 1848 ***5704.8*** *p48*
Conoly, Susanna *SEE* Conoly, Owen
Conoly, Susanna; Philadelphia, 1848 ***5704.8*** *p45*
Conoly, Terence; St. John, N.B., 1847 ***5704.8*** *p33*
Conoly, Unity; St. John, N.B., 1847 ***5704.8*** *p26*
Conoly, William; St. John, N.B., 1847 ***5704.8*** *p26*
Conrad, . . .; Canada, 1776-1783 ***9786*** *p19*
Conrad, Carl; Wisconsin, n.d. ***9675.5*** *p50*
Conrad, Christian; Wisconsin, n.d. ***9675.5*** *p50*
Conrad, Christopher; Wisconsin, n.d. ***9675.5*** *p50*
Conrad, Cunread *SEE* Conrad, Dennis
Conrad, Dennis; Pennsylvania, 1683 ***2155*** *p1*
*Wife:*Lijntijen Teissen
*Child:*Cunread
*Child:*Matthias
*Child:*Jan
Conrad, Eug. 18; America, 1839 ***778.5*** *p128*
Conrad, Friedrich; Philadelphia, 1749 ***4349*** *p48*
Conrad, Friedrich; Virginia, 1767 ***4349*** *p48*
Conrad, Georg; Canada, 1776-1783 ***9786*** *p243*
Conrad, George; Philadelphia, 1764 ***9973.7*** *p39*
Conrad, I.; Washington, 1859-1920 ***2872.1*** *p8*
Conrad, Jan *SEE* Conrad, Dennis
Conrad, Johann; Virginia, 1844 ***4626.16*** *p12*
Conrad, Johann Friedrich; Philadelphia, 1751 ***4349*** *p48*
Conrad, John; Iowa, 1866-1943 ***123.54*** *p15*
Conrad, John; New York, NY, 1840 ***8208.4*** *p113*
Conrad, Joseph; Ohio, 1798-1818 ***8582.2*** *p54*
Conrad, Kurt; Lancaster, PA, 1780 ***8137*** *p7*
Conrad, Lijntijen Teissen *SEE* Conrad, Dennis
Conrad, Matthias *SEE* Conrad, Dennis
Conrad, Oscar H.; Kentucky, 1846 ***8582.3*** *p98*
Conrad, Peter; Wisconsin, n.d. ***9675.5*** *p50*
Conrad, William; Wisconsin, n.d. ***9675.5*** *p50*
Conradi, . . .; Canada, 1776-1783 ***9786*** *p19*
Conradi, Carl Friedrich; Quebec, 1776 ***9786*** *p260*
Conradi, Charles; Washington, 1859-1920 ***2872.1*** *p8*
Conradi, Henry; Washington, 1859-1920 ***2872.1*** *p8*
Conradia, Charles; Washington, 1859-1920 ***2872.1*** *p8*
Conrahy, Edmond; America, 1743 ***4971*** *p29*
Conran, Edward 20; Pennsylvania, 1728 ***3690.1*** *p49*
Conran, John; America, 1742 ***4971*** *p29*
Conray, Hannah 36; Massachusetts, 1849 ***5881.1*** *p17*
Conray, Sarah 16; Massachusetts, 1849 ***5881.1*** *p25*
Conroy, Edward; Quebec, 1825 ***7603*** *p58*
Conroy, J. E.; Washington, 1859-1920 ***2872.1*** *p8*
Conroy, John; Montreal, 1823 ***7603*** *p91*
Conroy, Michael 43; New Orleans, 1862 ***543.30*** *p456*
Conry, Catherine; New York, NY, 1816 ***2859.11*** *p28*
Conry, James; New York, NY, 1816 ***2859.11*** *p28*
Conry, Judith; New York, NY, 1816 ***2859.11*** *p28*
Conry, Mary; New York, NY, 1816 ***2859.11*** *p28*
Conry, Michael; New York, NY, 1816 ***2859.11*** *p28*
Consay, Martin 22; Massachusetts, 1847 ***5881.1*** *p20*
Conscanran, Catharine 28; Massachusetts, 1849 ***5881.1*** *p14*
Conselman, Gottlieb; New York, NY, 1834 ***8208.4*** *p26*
Considine, William; Ohio, 1852 ***6014.2*** *p7*
Constable, Charles 13; Philadelphia, 1774 ***1219.7*** *p201*
Constable, Charles 19; America, 1774 ***1219.7*** *p237*
Constable, John 24; Baltimore, 1775 ***1219.7*** *p269*
Constable, Oliver; Iowa, 1866-1943 ***123.54*** *p59*
Constable, Robert; New York, NY, 1838 ***8208.4*** *p85*
Constable, William M.; Illinois, 1869 ***2764.35*** *p15*
Constans, Philip 30; New Orleans, 1862 ***543.30*** *p455*
Constant, Mr. 35; America, 1829 ***778.5*** *p128*
Constant, Charles 30; America, 1835 ***778.5*** *p128*
Constant, D. 25; America, 1839 ***778.5*** *p129*
Constant, M. 29; America, 1836 ***778.5*** *p129*
Constant, Martial 45; Louisiana, 1820 ***778.5*** *p129*
Constant, Nancy 23; Massachusetts, 1860 ***6410.32*** *p112*
Constant, William 31; Massachusetts, 1860 ***6410.32*** *p112*
Constantin, Jean; Louisiana, 1789-1819 ***778.5*** *p555*
Constantine, Christo; Arkansas, 1918 ***95.2*** *p31*
Constantine, F.; Wisconsin, n.d. ***9675.5*** *p50*
Constantine, Jon.; Virginia, 1637 ***6219*** *p82*
Constantino, Joseph Louis; Arkansas, 1918 ***95.2*** *p31*
Contat, Madeleine 29; America, 1831 ***778.5*** *p129*
Conte, Angelo; Arkansas, 1918 ***95.2*** *p31*
Conte, J. J. 51; New Orleans, 1837 ***778.5*** *p129*
Conte, Jean 33; Port uncertain, 1836 ***778.5*** *p129*
Conte, Joseph; Iowa, 1866-1943 ***123.54*** *p15*
Conte, Marie; Pennsylvania, 1751 ***2444*** *p226*
Conte Pierre, Mr. 38; Port uncertain, 1838 ***778.5*** *p74*
Contello, Catharine 20; Massachusetts, 1860 ***6410.32*** *p100*
Contello, David 23; Massachusetts, 1860 ***6410.32*** *p100*
Conter, Nic.; Wisconsin, n.d. ***9675.5*** *p50*
Contorenes, Michael Strate; Arkansas, 1918 ***95.2*** *p31*
Contretti, Angelo 40; New York, NY, 1893 ***9026.4*** *p41*
Conversi, Joseph; Arkansas, 1918 ***95.2*** *p32*
Convery, Bridget; America, 1864 ***5704.8*** *p189*
Convery, Henry; New York, NY, 1864 ***5704.8*** *p173*
Convery, Henry 22; Philadelphia, 1857 ***5704.8*** *p133*
Convery, Margaret 33; Philadelphia, 1854 ***5704.8*** *p122*
Convery, Mary 32; Philadelphia, 1853 ***5704.8*** *p113*
Convery, Mary Ann 8; Philadelphia, 1854 ***5704.8*** *p122*
Convery, Patrick 5; Philadelphia, 1853 ***5704.8*** *p113*
Convery, Patrick 6; Philadelphia, 1854 ***5704.8*** *p122*
Convery, Thomas; New York, NY, 1869 ***5704.8*** *p235*
Convery, Thomas 3; Philadelphia, 1853 ***5704.8*** *p113*
Convery, Thomas 4; Philadelphia, 1854 ***5704.8*** *p122*
Conway, Alice; Philadelphia, 1853 ***5704.8*** *p103*
Conway, Alice 54; Philadelphia, 1861 ***5704.8*** *p148*
Conway, Ann *SEE* Conway, Michael
Conway, Ann; America, 1864 ***5704.8*** *p184*
Conway, Ann; Philadelphia, 1847 ***5704.8*** *p23*
Conway, Ann 19; Philadelphia, 1857 ***5704.8*** *p132*
Conway, Aron; Virginia, 1642 ***6219*** *p191*
Conway, Bernard; New Orleans, 1849 ***5704.8*** *p59*
Conway, Bernard; Philadelphia, 1851 ***5704.8*** *p70*
Conway, Bernard 13 *SEE* Conway, Peter
Conway, Bernard 13; Philadelphia, 1847 ***5704.8*** *p14*
Conway, Bernard 18; Philadelphia, 1861 ***5704.8*** *p148*
Conway, Bridget 11 *SEE* Conway, Charles
Conway, Bridget 11; Philadelphia, 1849 ***5704.8*** *p52*
Conway, Catharine 20; Massachusetts, 1849 ***5881.1*** *p14*
Conway, Charles; Philadelphia, 1849 ***53.26*** *p14*
*Relative:*Martha
*Relative:*James 13
*Relative:*Margaret 13
*Relative:*Bridget 11
*Relative:*Nancy 9
*Relative:*Mary 7
*Relative:*Rosey 5
*Relative:*Martha 3
Conway, Charles; Philadelphia, 1849 ***5704.8*** *p52*
Conway, Charles 9; New York, NY, 1867 ***5704.8*** *p218*
Conway, Daniel; New York, NY, 1866 ***5704.8*** *p211*
Conway, Dennis *SEE* Conway, Michael
Conway, Dennis; Philadelphia, 1847 ***5704.8*** *p23*
Conway, Edmund; Philadelphia, 1853 ***5704.8*** *p102*
Conway, Edward; Philadelphia, 1851 ***5704.8*** *p81*
Conway, Ellen; Philadelphia, 1851 ***5704.8*** *p81*
Conway, Ellen; Philadelphia, 1853 ***5704.8*** *p103*
Conway, Ellen; Philadelphia, 1864 ***5704.8*** *p176*
Conway, Hannah *SEE* Conway, Peter
Conway, Hannah; Philadelphia, 1847 ***5704.8*** *p14*
Conway, Hugh; New York, NY, 1815 ***2859.11*** *p28*
Conway, Hugh; New York, NY, 1866 ***5704.8*** *p211*
Conway, Hugh; Philadelphia, 1865 ***5704.8*** *p197*
Conway, James; Philadelphia, 1850 ***53.26*** *p15*
Conway, James; Philadelphia, 1850 ***5704.8*** *p65*
Conway, James 13 *SEE* Conway, Charles
Conway, James 13; Philadelphia, 1849 ***5704.8*** *p52*
Conway, James 14; Philadelphia, 1861 ***5704.8*** *p148*
Conway, James 54; Philadelphia, 1861 ***5704.8*** *p148*
Conway, James C.; Colorado, 1893 ***9678.1*** *p158*
Conway, Johanna 26; Massachusetts, 1849 ***5881.1*** *p18*
Conway, John; America, 1743 ***4971*** *p11*
Conway, John; New York, NY, 1868 ***5704.8*** *p229*
Conway, John; Philadelphia, 1849 ***5704.8*** *p53*

Conway, John; St. John, N.B., 1853 ***5704.8*** *p111*
Conway, John 30; Massachusetts, 1849 ***5881.1*** *p18*
Conway, Kitty; St. John, N.B., 1849 ***5704.8*** *p55*
Conway, Margaret; New York, NY, 1867 ***5704.8*** *p218*
Conway, Margaret; Philadelphia, 1867 ***5704.8*** *p223*
Conway, Margaret 13 *SEE* Conway, Charles
Conway, Margaret 13; Philadelphia, 1849 ***5704.8*** *p52*
Conway, Martha *SEE* Conway, Charles
Conway, Martha; Philadelphia, 1849 ***5704.8*** *p52*
Conway, Martha; Philadelphia, 1864 ***5704.8*** *p172*
Conway, Martha 3 *SEE* Conway, Charles
Conway, Martha 3; Philadelphia, 1849 ***5704.8*** *p52*
Conway, Mary; Philadelphia, 1853 ***5704.8*** *p103*
Conway, Mary; Philadelphia, 1870 ***5704.8*** *p238*
Conway, Mary 7 *SEE* Conway, Charles
Conway, Mary 7; Philadelphia, 1849 ***5704.8*** *p52*
Conway, Mary Ann; Philadelphia, 1847 ***53.26*** *p15*
Conway, Mary Ann; Philadelphia, 1847 ***5704.8*** *p2*
Conway, Michael; Philadelphia, 1847 ***53.26*** *p15*
*Relative:*Dennis
*Relative:*Ann
Conway, Michael; Philadelphia, 1847 ***5704.8*** *p22*
Conway, Michael 20; Philadelphia, 1854 ***5704.8*** *p116*
Conway, Nancy 9 *SEE* Conway, Charles
Conway, Nancy 9; Philadelphia, 1849 ***5704.8*** *p52*
Conway, Neill 9 mos; Philadelphia, 1849 ***53.26*** *p15*
Conway, Neill 9 mos; Philadelphia, 1849 ***5704.8*** *p52*
Conway, Owen; New York, NY, 1837 ***8208.4*** *p43*
Conway, Pat. 26; Massachusetts, 1849 ***5881.1*** *p24*
Conway, Patrick 18; Philadelphia, 1854 ***5704.8*** *p117*
Conway, Patrick 22; Philadelphia, 1854 ***5704.8*** *p116*
Conway, Patrick 33; New Orleans, 1862 ***543.30*** *p450*
Conway, Peter; Philadelphia, 1847 ***53.26*** *p15*
Conway, Peter; Philadelphia, 1847 ***53.26*** *p15*
*Relative:*Hannah
*Relative:*Bernard 13
*Relative:*Rose 7
Conway, Peter; Philadelphia, 1847 ***5704.8*** *p14*
Conway, Peter; Philadelphia, 1847 ***5704.8*** *p22*
Conway, Peter; Philadelphia, 1864 ***5704.8*** *p172*
Conway, Robert 10; New York, NY, 1867 ***5704.8*** *p218*
Conway, Rose; Philadelphia, 1847 ***53.26*** *p15*
Conway, Rose; Philadelphia, 1847 ***5704.8*** *p14*
Conway, Rose 7 *SEE* Conway, Peter
Conway, Rose 7; Philadelphia, 1847 ***5704.8*** *p14*
Conway, Rosey; St. John, N.B., 1849 ***5704.8*** *p49*
Conway, Rosey 5 *SEE* Conway, Charles
Conway, Rosey 5; Philadelphia, 1849 ***5704.8*** *p52*
Conway, Sally; St. John, N.B., 1847 ***5704.8*** *p35*
Conway, Sarah 15; Philadelphia, 1861 ***5704.8*** *p148*
Conway, Sarah 19; St. John, N.B., 1865 ***5704.8*** *p165*
Conway, Susan 15; St. John, N.B., 1865 ***5704.8*** *p165*
Conway, Thomas; St. John, N.B., 1848 ***5704.8*** *p44*
Conway, Thomas 40; Massachusetts, 1849 ***5881.1*** *p25*
Conway, Wm.; America, 1742 ***4971*** *p32*
Conwell, James; St. John, N.B., 1852 ***5704.8*** *p84*
Conwell, William; St. John, N.B., 1852 ***5704.8*** *p83*
Conyngham, Alexander 21 *SEE* Conyngham, George
Conyngham, Andrew 6 *SEE* Conyngham, Andrew
Conyngham, Andrew 34; Philadelphia, 1804 ***53.26*** *p15*
*Relative:*Elitia 34
*Relative:*John 12
*Relative:*Andrew 6
Conyngham, Catherine 12 *SEE* Conyngham, George
Conyngham, Elitia 34 *SEE* Conyngham, Andrew
Conyngham, George 49; Philadelphia, 1804 ***53.26*** *p15*
*Relative:*Alexander 21
*Relative:*James 18
*Relative:*John 15
*Relative:*Catherine 12
Conyngham, Isabella 23 *SEE* Conyngham, William
Conyngham, Isabella 49 *SEE* Conyngham, John
Conyngham, James 18 *SEE* Conyngham, George
Conyngham, John 12 *SEE* Conyngham, Andrew
Conyngham, John 15 *SEE* Conyngham, George
Conyngham, John 55; Philadelphia, 1804 ***53.26*** *p15*
*Relative:*Isabella 49
Conyngham, William 26; Philadelphia, 1804 ***53.26*** *p15*
*Relative:*Isabella 23
Conyus, Wm.; South Carolina, 1788 ***7119*** *p202*
Conzelmann, Catharina Barbara *SEE* Conzelmann, Hans Jerg
Conzelmann, Hans Jerg; Pennsylvania, 1749 ***2444*** *p145*
With son
*Child:*Catharina Barbara
*Child:*Johann Georg
*Wife:*M. Rausenberger
Conzelmann, Johann Georg *SEE* Conzelmann, Hans Jerg
Conzelmann, M. Rausenberger *SEE* Conzelmann, Hans Jerg
Conzillio, Guisepp; Colorado, 1904 ***9678.1*** *p158*
Cooey, Alexander 45; Philadelphia, 1854 ***5704.8*** *p120*
Cooey, Mathew; Ohio, 1845 ***9892.11*** *p10*
Cooey, Matthew; Ohio, 1847 ***9892.11*** *p10*
Coogan, Peter; New York, NY, 1838 ***8208.4*** *p75*
Cooglar, John; Pennsylvania, 1752 ***2444*** *p181*
Coogler, John; Pennsylvania, 1752 ***2444*** *p181*
Cook, Miss; Quebec, 1815 ***9229.18*** *p79*
Cook, Ann 20; Massachusetts, 1849 ***5881.1*** *p12*
Cook, Anne; St. John, N.B., 1850 ***5704.8*** *p65*
Cook, Anton; America, 1845 ***8582.1*** *p6*
Cook, Charles 21; Jamaica, 1731 ***3690.1*** *p50*
Cook, Charles 23; Maryland, 1774 ***1219.7*** *p230*
Cook, Charles W.; New York, NY, 1836 ***8208.4*** *p14*
Cook, Cyrus Milton 26; Kansas, 1887 ***5240.1*** *p70*
Cook, Daniel; Quebec, 1825 ***7603*** *p58*
Cook, Edward; St. John, N.B., 1850 ***5704.8*** *p65*
Cook, Edward 16; Pennsylvania, 1730 ***3690.1*** *p50*
Cook, Edward 19; New England, 1699 ***2212*** *p19*
Cook, Elin; America, 1698 ***2212*** *p5*
Cook, Ellen 16; Massachusetts, 1847 ***5881.1*** *p15*
Cook, Esther; Quebec, 1738 ***7603*** *p26*
Cook, Franz; New York, NY, 1840 ***8208.4*** *p110*
Cook, George; Arkansas, 1918 ***95.2*** *p32*
Cook, George; New York, NY, 1840 ***8208.4*** *p113*
Cook, George 19; Maryland, 1750 ***3690.1*** *p50*
Cook, George 19; Maryland, 1751 ***1219.7*** *p3*
Cook, George 21; New Orleans, 1862 ***543.30*** *p455*
Cook, George Adam; Pennsylvania, 1754 ***4525*** *p229*
Cook, Hamilton 21; St. John, N.B., 1866 ***5704.8*** *p166*
Cook, Henry; New York, NY, 1811 ***2859.11*** *p10*
Cook, Henry; Wisconsin, n.d. ***9675.5*** *p50*
Cook, Henry 17; Jamaica, 1774 ***1219.7*** *p181*
Cook, Henry 32; Virginia, 1775 ***1219.7*** *p261*
Cook, Henry G. E. 32; Arizona, 1890 ***2764.35*** *p10*
Cook, Isabella; Quebec, 1853 ***5704.8*** *p104*
Cook, James; St. John, N.B., 1850 ***5704.8*** *p61*
Cook, James 18; Pennsylvania, 1730 ***3690.1*** *p50*
Cook, James 47; Arizona, 1890 ***2764.35*** *p12*
Cook, Jens Lauther; Arkansas, 1918 ***95.2*** *p32*
Cook, John; New Brunswick, 1840-1900 ***9775.5*** *p204*
Cook, John; New York, NY, 1850 ***6013.19*** *p30*
Cook, John; Philadelphia, 1757 ***9973.7*** *p33*
Cook, John 15; Philadelphia, 1774 ***1219.7*** *p175*
Cook, John 21; Maryland, 1774 ***1219.7*** *p222*
Cook, John 21; Virginia, 1774 ***1219.7*** *p243*
Cook, John 27; Massachusetts, 1847 ***5881.1*** *p17*
Cook, John 29; Maryland, 1775 ***1219.7*** *p252*
Cook, Jos.; New York, NY, 1816 ***2859.11*** *p28*
Cook, Joseph 18; Maryland, 1730 ***3690.1*** *p50*
Cook, Joseph 24; Virginia, 1774 ***1219.7*** *p225*
Cook, Margaret 16; Philadelphia, 1857 ***5704.8*** *p132*
Cook, Maria 50; South Carolina, 1850 ***1639.20*** *p48*
Cook, Mary 22; Massachusetts, 1850 ***5881.1*** *p23*
Cook, Melvin; Iroquois Co., IL, 1896 ***3455.1*** *p10*
Cook, Owen; New York, NY, 1838 ***8208.4*** *p74*
Cook, Ralph; Savannah, GA, 1774 ***1219.7*** *p227*
With wife
Cook, Robert 52; South Carolina, 1850 ***1639.20*** *p48*
Cook, Seth; Washington, 1859-1920 ***2872.1*** *p9*
Cook, Thomas; America, 1697 ***2212*** *p4*
Cook, Thomas; New England, 1816 ***2859.11*** *p28*
Cook, Thomas; New York, NY, 1816 ***2859.11*** *p28*
Cook, Thomas; Quebec, 1790 ***7603*** *p87*
Cook, Thomas 16; Maryland, 1730 ***3690.1*** *p50*
Cook, Thomas 17; Maryland, 1733 ***3690.1*** *p50*
Cook, Thomas 23; Philadelphia, 1774 ***1219.7*** *p182*
Cook, William 19; Maryland, 1729 ***3690.1*** *p50*
Cook, William 21; Maryland, 1774 ***1219.7*** *p236*
Cook, William 21; Maryland, 1775 ***1219.7*** *p257*
Cook, William 24; Maryland, 1774 ***1219.7*** *p235*
Cooke, Alice; Virginia, 1642 ***6219*** *p18*
Cooke, Alice; Virginia, 1642 ***6219*** *p197*
Cooke, Amy; Virginia, 1638 ***6219*** *p125*
Cooke, Ann; St. John, N.B., 1852 ***5704.8*** *p83*
Cooke, Ann; Virginia, 1635 ***6219*** *p26*
Cooke, Ann; Virginia, 1637 ***6219*** *p83*
Cooke, Ann 18?; America, 1705 ***2212*** *p45*
Cooke, Barth.; Virginia, 1636 ***6219*** *p75*
Cooke, Christ.; Virginia, 1643 ***6219*** *p204*
Cooke, David; New York, NY, 1816 ***2859.11*** *p28*
Cooke, Edward; Virginia, 1642 ***6219*** *p195*
Cooke, Eliza 9; Quebec, 1847 ***5704.8*** *p12*
Cooke, Elizabeth; St. John, N.B., 1851 ***5704.8*** *p71*
Cooke, George; Virginia, 1617 ***6219*** *p6*
Cooke, George L. 21; Kansas, 1878 ***5240.1*** *p8*
Cooke, George L. 21; Kansas, 1878 ***5240.1*** *p59*
Cooke, Gerrard; Virginia, 1637 ***6219*** *p145*
Cooke, Henry; Virginia, 1638 ***6219*** *p145*
Cooke, Hugh; New York, NY, 1816 ***2859.11*** *p28*
Cooke, James; St. John, N.B., 1847 ***5704.8*** *p25*
Cooke, James; Virginia, 1637 ***6219*** *p85*
Cooke, James; Virginia, 1648 ***6219*** *p246*
Cooke, James 24; Quebec, 1855 ***5704.8*** *p125*
Cooke, Jane; Quebec, 1847 ***5704.8*** *p12*
Cooke, Jane; St. John, N.B., 1847 ***5704.8*** *p19*
Cooke, John; Virginia, 1638 ***6219*** *p122*
Cooke, John; Virginia, 1639 ***6219*** *p161*
Cooke, John; Virginia, 1643 ***6219*** *p204*
Cooke, John 16; Philadelphia, 1856 ***5704.8*** *p128*
Cooke, Jon.; Virginia, 1636 ***6219*** *p80*
Cooke, Jon.; Virginia, 1637 ***6219*** *p83*
Cooke, Jon.; Virginia, 1638 ***6219*** *p11*
Cooke, Leonard 17; Canada, 1838 ***4535.12*** *p113*
Cooke, Margaret; Quebec, 1853 ***5704.8*** *p104*
Cooke, Margaret 17; Philadelphia, 1857 ***5704.8*** *p133*
Cooke, Mark 18; Jamaica, 1774 ***1219.7*** *p183*
Cooke, Martha; Philadelphia, 1850 ***53.26*** *p15*
Cooke, Martha; Philadelphia, 1850 ***5704.8*** *p68*
Cooke, Mary; Quebec, 1847 ***5704.8*** *p12*
Cooke, Mary 18; Philadelphia, 1864 ***5704.8*** *p156*
Cooke, Mary 29; Canada, 1838 ***4535.12*** *p113*
Cooke, Mathew 7; Quebec, 1847 ***5704.8*** *p12*
Cooke, Miles; Virginia, 1638 ***6219*** *p2*
Cooke, Mordecay; Virginia, 1639 ***6219*** *p157*
Cooke, Mordecay; Virginia, 1642 ***6219*** *p198*
Cooke, Rich.; Virginia, 1636 ***6219*** *p75*
Cooke, Richard; Virginia, 1636 ***6219*** *p80*
Cooke, Richard; Virginia, 1638 ***6219*** *p181*
Cooke, Richard; Virginia, 1639 ***6219*** *p161*
Cooke, Richard; Virginia, 1643 ***6219*** *p205*
Cooke, Robert; Quebec, 1847 ***5704.8*** *p12*
Cooke, Robert; Virginia, 1638 ***6219*** *p22*
Cooke, Robert 19; Quebec, 1864 ***5704.8*** *p162*
Cooke, Samuel 7; St. John, N.B., 1847 ***5704.8*** *p19*
Cooke, Thomas; America, 1740 ***4971*** *p99*
Cooke, Thomas; Philadelphia, 1850 ***53.26*** *p15*
Cooke, Thomas; Philadelphia, 1850 ***5704.8*** *p68*
Cooke, Thomas; Virginia, 1638 ***6219*** *p17*
Cooke, Thomas 13; Quebec, 1847 ***5704.8*** *p12*
Cooke, Thomas 18; Philadelphia, 1857 ***5704.8*** *p133*
Cooke, William; Quebec, 1847 ***5704.8*** *p12*
Cooke, William; Virginia, 1637 ***6219*** *p86*
Cooke, William 30; Virginia, 1774 ***1219.7*** *p240*
Cooke, Wm.; Virginia, 1636 ***6219*** *p26*
Cooke, Wm.; Virginia, 1636 ***6219*** *p77*
Cooke, Wm.; Virginia, 1642 ***6219*** *p186*
Cooke, Wm.; Virginia, 1642 ***6219*** *p199*
Cookson, John 26; Virginia, 1774 ***1219.7*** *p241*
Coolan, . . .; Halifax, N.S., 1752 ***7074.6*** *p230*
Coole, John 4; Massachusetts, 1850 ***5881.1*** *p19*
Coole, Thomas 3; Massachusetts, 1850 ***5881.1*** *p26*
Coolen, . . .; Halifax, N.S., 1752 ***7074.6*** *p230*
Cooler, Jacob; South Carolina, 1752-1753 ***3689.17*** *p21*
With wife
Cooley, John; Illinois, 1841 ***7857*** *p3*
Cooley, John 16; Virginia, 1774 ***1219.7*** *p186*
Cooley, Joseph 12; Virginia, 1774 ***1219.7*** *p186*
Cooley, Michael 35; New Orleans, 1862 ***543.30*** *p454*
Cooley, Patrick; America, 1741 ***4971*** *p16*
Cooley, Peter 38; Virginia, 1774 ***1219.7*** *p186*
Cooley, Peter, Jr. 18; Virginia, 1774 ***1219.7*** *p186*
Cooley, William 21; Maryland, 1774 ***1219.7*** *p229*
Cooling, Ellen 4; Massachusetts, 1848 ***5881.1*** *p15*
Cooling, Johanna 7; Massachusetts, 1848 ***5881.1*** *p17*
Cooling, Kitty 20; Massachusetts, 1848 ***5881.1*** *p20*
Cooling, Mary 2; Massachusetts, 1848 ***5881.1*** *p20*
Cooling, Mary 30; Massachusetts, 1848 ***5881.1*** *p20*
Cooling, Norry 30; Massachusetts, 1848 ***5881.1*** *p23*
Cooling, William 22; Jamaica, 1736 ***3690.1*** *p50*
Coolling, William 22; Jamaica, 1736 ***3690.1*** *p50*
Coombs, Edward 21; Virginia, 1774 ***1219.7*** *p238*
Coon, Caspar; South Carolina, 1788 ***7119*** *p202*
Coon, Francis; Philadelphia, 1764 ***2444*** *p181*
Coona, Edward 16; Quebec, 1855 ***5704.8*** *p125*
Coones, Nicholas; Illinois, 1865 ***2896.5*** *p8*
Cooney, Bridget; Philadelphia, 1849 ***53.26*** *p15*
Cooney, Bridget; Philadelphia, 1849 ***5704.8*** *p54*
Cooney, Bryan; Philadelphia, 1811 ***53.26*** *p15*
Cooney, Bryan; Philadelphia, 1811 ***2859.11*** *p10*
Cooney, John; Wisconsin, n.d. ***9675.5*** *p50*
Cooney, John 17; St. John, N.B., 1865 ***5704.8*** *p165*
Coop, Charles; Virginia, 1698 ***2212*** *p12*
Coope, Johan; New York, NY, 1840 ***8208.4*** *p110*
Cooper, Mr.; Quebec, 1815 ***9229.18*** *p75*
Cooper, Mr.; Quebec, 1815 ***9229.18*** *p79*
Cooper, Mrs.; New York, NY, 1811 ***2859.11*** *p10*
Cooper, A.W.; Iowa, 1866-1943 ***123.54*** *p15*
Cooper, Ann *SEE* Cooper, Justinian
Cooper, Ann; Philadelphia, 1865 ***5704.8*** *p191*
Cooper, Ann 52 *SEE* Cooper, Jonas
Cooper, Arthur; St. John, N.B., 1851 ***5704.8*** *p80*
Cooper, Barbara; South Carolina, 1767 ***1639.20*** *p48*
Cooper, Charles; Washington, 1859-1920 ***2872.1*** *p9*
Cooper, Charles 19; Windward Islands, 1722 ***3690.1*** *p50*
Cooper, Charles Henry 15; St. John, N.B., 1853 ***5704.8*** *p110*
Cooper, Christian 35; South Carolina, 1850 ***1639.20*** *p48*
Cooper, David 3; Quebec, 1864 ***5704.8*** *p162*

Cooper, Edward; Virginia, 1638 ***6219*** *p150*
Cooper, Edward 19 *SEE* Cooper, Jonas
Cooper, Eliz 24; America, 1704 ***2212*** *p40*
Cooper, Eliz. 25 *SEE* Cooper, Jonas
Cooper, Eliza; Philadelphia, 1866 ***5704.8*** *p215*
Cooper, Elizabeth 16; Pennsylvania, 1723 ***3690.1*** *p50*
Cooper, Elizabeth 26; Quebec, 1864 ***5704.8*** *p162*
Cooper, Elspet; America, 1844 ***8893*** *p265*
Cooper, Harriet 8 *SEE* Cooper, Jonas
Cooper, Hen.; Virginia, 1635 ***6219*** *p32*
Cooper, Henry 15 *SEE* Cooper, Jonas
Cooper, Henry 22; Baltimore, 1775 ***1219.7*** *p270*
Cooper, Jacob; Ohio, 1840 ***9892.11*** *p10*
Cooper, Jacob; Ohio, 1848 ***9892.11*** *p10*
Cooper, James; Austin, TX, 1886 ***9777*** *p5*
Cooper, James; Philadelphia, 1865 ***5704.8*** *p189*
Cooper, James; Virginia, 1787-1802 ***1639.20*** *p49*
Cooper, James 20; Wilmington, DE, 1831 ***6508.3*** *p100*
Cooper, James 60; Virginia, 1850 ***1639.20*** *p49*
Cooper, John; America, 1741 ***4971*** *p69*
Cooper, John; Ohio, 1840 ***9892.11*** *p10*
Cooper, John; Quebec, 1852 ***5704.8*** *p94*
Cooper, John; Virginia, 1617 ***6219*** *p11*
Cooper, John; Virginia, 1637 ***6219*** *p37*
Cooper, John; Virginia, 1639 ***6219*** *p162*
Cooper, John; Virginia, 1640 ***6219*** *p181*
Cooper, John; Virginia, 1645 ***6219*** *p252*
Cooper, John 9; Philadelphia, 1866 ***5704.8*** *p215*
Cooper, John 15; Jamaica, 1731 ***3690.1*** *p50*
Cooper, John 16; Tortola, 1773 ***1219.7*** *p172*
Cooper, John 20; Jamaica, 1735 ***3690.1*** *p50*
Cooper, John 29; Maryland, 1774 ***1219.7*** *p235*
Cooper, Jon.; Virginia, 1635 ***6219*** *p71*
Cooper, Jon.; Virginia, 1636 ***6219*** *p20*
Cooper, Jon.; Virginia, 1638 ***6219*** *p11*
Cooper, Jonas 52; Montreal, 1843 ***4535.10*** *p196*
*Wife:*Ann 52
*Child:*Edward 19
*Child:*Henry 15
*Child:*Eliz. 25
*Child:*Harriet 8
Cooper, Joseph 26; Virginia, 1774 ***1219.7*** *p240*
Cooper, Joseph 37; Savannah, GA, 1733 ***4719.17*** *p310*
Cooper, Joyce; Virginia, 1698 ***2212*** *p11*
Cooper, Joyce; Virginia, 1698 ***2212*** *p17*
Cooper, Justinian; Virginia, 1636 ***6219*** *p77*
Cooper, Justinian; Virginia, 1642 ***6219*** *p199*
*Wife:*Ann
Cooper, Lewis; Virginia, 1643 ***6219*** *p202*
Cooper, Martha 2; Canada, 1838 ***4535.12*** *p113*
Cooper, Mary 17; America, 1705 ***2212*** *p42*
Cooper, Mary 29; Maryland, 1774 ***1219.7*** *p187*
Cooper, Mary 30; Maryland, 1775 ***1219.7*** *p257*
Cooper, Maurice; Arkansas, 1918 ***95.2*** *p32*
Cooper, Nathanial 16; Maryland, 1719 ***3690.1*** *p51*
Cooper, Nathaniel 16; Virginia, 1720 ***3690.1*** *p51*
Cooper, Peeter; Virginia, 1643 ***6219*** *p206*
Cooper, Peter; Charleston, SC, 1797 ***1639.20*** *p49*
Cooper, Peter 19; Georgia, 1735 ***3690.1*** *p51*
Cooper, Richard; New York, NY, 1834 ***8208.4*** *p4*
Cooper, Richard; Virginia, 1639 ***6219*** *p152*
Cooper, Richard; Virginia, 1641 ***6219*** *p184*
Cooper, Richard; Virginia, 1642 ***6219*** *p193*
Cooper, Richard; Virginia, 1648 ***6219*** *p252*
Cooper, Richard 27; Jamaica, 1734 ***3690.1*** *p51*
Cooper, Robert; Philadelphia, 1865 ***5704.8*** *p191*
Cooper, Robert; Philadelphia, 1866 ***5704.8*** *p215*
Cooper, Robert 30; North Carolina, 1730 ***3690.1*** *p51*
Cooper, Samuel 22; Maryland, 1774 ***1219.7*** *p187*
Cooper, Sindney; St. John, N.B., 1851 ***5704.8*** *p80*
Cooper, Stephen 31; Maryland, 1774 ***1219.7*** *p179*
Cooper, Tho.; Virginia, 1642 ***6219*** *p191*
Cooper, Tho.; Virginia, 1642 ***6219*** *p198*
Cooper, Thomas; Virginia, 1636 ***6219*** *p78*
Cooper, Thomas; Virginia, 1646 ***6219*** *p241*
Cooper, Thomas; Washington, 1859-1920 ***2872.1*** *p9*
Cooper, Thomas 6; Philadelphia, 1866 ***5704.8*** *p215*
Cooper, Thomas 15; Maryland, 1719 ***3690.1*** *p51*
Cooper, Thomas 21; Maryland, 1774 ***1219.7*** *p202*
Cooper, Thomas 22; Virginia, 1775 ***1219.7*** *p246*
Cooper, William; Charleston, SC, 1821 ***1639.20*** *p49*
Cooper, William; New York, NY, 1838 ***8208.4*** *p73*
Cooper, William; Ohio, 1840 ***9892.11*** *p10*
Cooper, William 27; Philadelphia, 1774 ***1219.7*** *p216*
Cooper, William 40; Maryland, 1775 ***1219.7*** *p256*
Cooper, Wm.; Virginia, 1637 ***6219*** *p113*
Coordes, Reinhard Henry; New York, NY, 1924 ***3455.4*** *p56*
Coote, Adam; Virginia, 1639 ***6219*** *p161*
Cootes, John; Virginia, 1648 ***6219*** *p250*
Coother, Eliza; Philadelphia, 1865 ***5704.8*** *p197*
Coother, John; Philadelphia, 1865 ***5704.8*** *p197*
Coots, Jon.; Virginia, 1643 ***6219*** *p203*
Cope, Henry; Colorado, 1891 ***9678.1*** *p158*
Cope, James; New York, NY, 1820 ***9892.11*** *p10*
Cope, James; Ohio, 1835 ***9892.11*** *p10*
Cope, William D.; New York, NY, 1839 ***8208.4*** *p96*
Copeland, . . .; Virginia, 1638 ***6219*** *p120*
Copeland, Christopher 16; Jamaica, 1734 ***3690.1*** *p51*
Copeland, Frederick 28; Massachusetts, 1860 ***6410.32*** *p117*
Copeland, Hen.; Virginia, 1637 ***6219*** *p11*
Copeland, Hen.; Virginia, 1637 ***6219*** *p114*
Copeland, James; New York, NY, 1811 ***2859.11*** *p10*
Copeland, Leonard 35; Jamaica, 1738 ***3690.1*** *p51*
Copeland, Thomas; New York, NY, 1811 ***2859.11*** *p10*
Copeland, William 17; Maryland, 1718 ***3690.1*** *p51*
Copeland, William 30; Kansas, 1874 ***5240.1*** *p55*
Copeland, Wm.; New York, NY, 1811 ***2859.11*** *p10*
With family
Cophne, Johanna; St. Charles, 1801 ***7603*** *p75*
Copinsher, Mrs. 30; Boston, 1774 ***1219.7*** *p203*
Copjak, Steve; Arkansas, 1918 ***95.2*** *p32*
Copke, Valentine 32; Kansas, 1883 ***5240.1*** *p64*
Copland, John 40; Maryland, 1774 ***1219.7*** *p211*
Copleston, Annias; Virginia, 1637 ***6219*** *p180*
Coplestone, Annanias; Virginia, 1635 ***6219*** *p70*
Copley, Abraham 22; New York, 1774 ***1219.7*** *p202*
Coplon, Bennie; Arkansas, 1918 ***95.2*** *p32*
Coppay, . . .; Canada, 1776-1783 ***9786*** *p19*
Coppel, Jane 45; New York, 1774 ***1219.7*** *p203*
Copper, Thomas 16; Virginia, 1774 ***1219.7*** *p240*
Coppinger, James E.; New York, NY, 1836 ***8208.4*** *p8*
Coppler, Catharine 30; America, 1836 ***778.5*** *p129*
Coppler, Mathias 36; America, 1836 ***778.5*** *p129*
Coppler, Ursula 34; America, 1836 ***778.5*** *p129*
Copsey, Roger 19; Barbados, 1718 ***3690.1*** *p51*
Coquekpah, Sierley; Arkansas, 1918 ***95.2*** *p32*
Coquet, Mr. 23; America, 1839 ***778.5*** *p129*
Cora, Domenik; Iowa, 1866-1943 ***123.54*** *p59*
Cora, Guiseppe; Iowa, 1866-1943 ***123.54*** *p15*
Cora, Guiseppi; Iowa, 1866-1943 ***123.54*** *p15*
Cora, Olindo; Iowa, 1866-1943 ***123.54*** *p59*
Cora, Orlindo; Iowa, 1866-1943 ***123.54*** *p59*
Coragan, Ellen; Philadelphia, 1850 ***53.26*** *p15*
Coragan, Ellen; Philadelphia, 1850 ***5704.8*** *p60*
Coram, Elizabeth; Virginia, 1646 ***6219*** *p241*
Corban, Thomas; America, 1736-1737 ***4971*** *p59*
Corbe, Jean 28; Louisiana, 1820 ***778.5*** *p129*
Corbere, Jean 25; America, 1838 ***778.5*** *p129*
Corbet, Luther; New York, NY, 1839 ***8208.4*** *p99*
Corbet, Matthew 18; Maryland, 1729 ***3690.1*** *p51*
Corbet, Philip; America, 1738 ***4971*** *p14*
Corbett, Edward 20; Charleston, SC, 1774 ***1639.20*** *p49*
Corbett, Henry; Charleston, SC, 1824 ***1639.20*** *p49*
Corbett, Isaac 24; Jamaica, 1730 ***3690.1*** *p51*
Corbett, Michael 25; Massachusetts, 1849 ***5881.1*** *p21*
Corbett, Oswald 27; Jamaica, 1737 ***3690.1*** *p51*
Corbett, Robert; Virginia, 1635 ***6219*** *p72*
Corbett, William 31?; Arizona, 1890 ***2764.35*** *p13*
Corbetta, Joseph 34; New Orleans, 1838 ***778.5*** *p130*
Corbetto, Joseph 34; New Orleans, 1838 ***778.5*** *p130*
Corbeve, Jean 25; America, 1838 ***778.5*** *p129*
Corbin, Hun.; Virginia, 1645 ***6219*** *p240*
Corbin, Matthew 18; Maryland, 1729 ***3690.1*** *p51*
Corbitt, Michael; New York, NY, 1838 ***8208.4*** *p67*
Corbitt, Tim. 25; Massachusetts, 1847 ***5881.1*** *p25*
Corby, Benjamin 15; Maryland, 1775 ***1219.7*** *p264*
Corby, Concetta; Iowa, 1866-1943 ***123.54*** *p59*
Corby, Pete; Iowa, 1866-1943 ***123.54*** *p59*
Corcoran, Dennis; New York, NY, 1838 ***8208.4*** *p86*
Corcoran, Elizabeth 21; Massachusetts, 1850 ***5881.1*** *p16*
Corcoran, Ellen 45; Massachusetts, 1850 ***5881.1*** *p16*
Corcoran, Jean; New Brunswick, 1825 ***7603*** *p97*
Corcoran, John 30; Massachusetts, 1850 ***5881.1*** *p19*
Corcoran, Margaret 60; Massachusetts, 1848 ***5881.1*** *p20*
Corcoran, Thomas; New York, NY, 1811 ***2859.11*** *p10*
Corcoran, Wm.; New York, NY, 1811 ***2859.11*** *p10*
Corde, John; Virginia, 1642 ***6219*** *p196*
Cordel, Mathias 37; Kansas, 1886 ***5240.1*** *p69*
Cordes, . . .; Canada, 1776-1783 ***9786*** *p41*
Cordesman, H. J.; Cincinnati, 1869-1887 ***8582*** *p5*
Cordesmann, . . .; Ohio, 1832 ***8582.2*** *p49*
Cordey, Nathaniell; Virginia, 1637 ***6219*** *p82*
Cordez, Jean 36; America, 1827 ***778.5*** *p130*
Cordon, Robert 32; New Orleans, 1863 ***543.30*** *p452*
Cordschaper, Amalie Caroline *SEE* Cordschaper, Heinrich Gottlieb
Cordschaper, Anna Marie J. Engel *SEE* Cordschaper, Heinrich Gottlieb
Cordschaper, Anna Marie Wilhelmine *SEE* Cordschaper, Heinrich Gottlieb
Cordschaper, Carl Friedrich Wilhelm *SEE* Cordschaper, Heinrich Gottlieb
Cordschaper, Catharine M. C. Stucke *SEE* Cordschaper, Heinrich Gottlieb
Cordschaper, Ernst H. Gottlieb *SEE* Cordschaper, Heinrich Gottlieb
Cordschaper, Heinrich Gottlieb; America, 1844 ***4610.10*** *p154*
*Wife:*Catharine M. C. Stucke
*Stepchild:*Amalie Caroline
*Stepchild:*Anna Marie Wilhelmine
*Child:*Heinrich W. Gottlieb
*Child:*Ernst H. Gottlieb
*Child:*Anna Marie J. Engel
*Child:*Carl Friedrich Wilhelm
Cordschaper, Heinrich W. Gottlieb *SEE* Cordschaper, Heinrich Gottlieb
Core, Alexander; New York, NY, 1838 ***8208.4*** *p90*
Core, Ralph 22; Maryland, 1775 ***1219.7*** *p273*
Coredan, Michael; Iowa, 1866-1943 ***123.54*** *p15*
Corell, Andreas; Reading, PA, 1780 ***8137*** *p7*
Corell, John; America, 1848 ***8582.1*** *p6*
Corell, Konrad; Philadelphia, 1779 ***8137*** *p7*
Corell, Konrad; Philadelphia, 1779-1783 ***8137*** *p4*
Corentre, Nicolas 41; New Orleans, 1838 ***778.5*** *p130*
Corepel, John; Indiana, 1845 ***9117*** *p16*
Coressel, John; Indiana, 1845 ***9117*** *p16*
Coret, Jean 23; New Orleans, 1839 ***778.5*** *p130*
Corfield, Charles 18; Maryland, 1722 ***3690.1*** *p52*
Corgan, Thomas; Ohio, 1840 ***9892.11*** *p10*
Corgeil, John; Georgia, 1775 ***1219.7*** *p274*
Corget, . . .; Port uncertain, 1839 ***778.5*** *p130*
Corget, Mme.; Port uncertain, 1839 ***778.5*** *p130*
Corhoon, Cor.; Virginia, 1645 ***6219*** *p233*
Coriatti, Edwarda; Arkansas, 1918 ***95.2*** *p32*
Corigot, Dominique 23; New Orleans, 1837 ***778.5*** *p130*
Corin, Annie 9; Quebec, 1851 ***5704.8*** *p82*
Corin, Margaret; Quebec, 1851 ***5704.8*** *p82*
Corin, Margaret 11; Quebec, 1851 ***5704.8*** *p82*
Corin, Mary; Quebec, 1851 ***5704.8*** *p82*
Corish, James; New York, NY, 1816 ***2859.11*** *p28*
Cork, John; Ohio, 1850-1867 ***9892.11*** *p10*
Cork, John; Ohio, 1870 ***9892.11*** *p10*
Cork, Martha 25; Canada, 1838 ***4535.12*** *p113*
Corke, Jane; Virginia, 1637 ***6219*** *p112*
Corke, Wm.; Virginia, 1623-1700 ***6219*** *p182*
Corkeran, Philip; America, 1743 ***4971*** *p50*
Corkery, Jeremiah 30; Massachusetts, 1850 ***5881.1*** *p19*
Corkoran, Michael; New York, NY, 1816 ***2859.11*** *p28*
Corkran, Margaret 18; Philadelphia, 1853 ***5704.8*** *p113*
Corkran, Patrick; America, 1738 ***4971*** *p31*
Corlere, Philip; Iroquois Co., IL, 1894 ***3455.1*** *p10*
Corlinovi, Gesuina 20; New York, NY, 1893 ***9026.4*** *p41*
Corlis, Margaret 23; Massachusetts, 1847 ***5881.1*** *p20*
Cormack, Alexander; Charleston, SC, 1773 ***1639.20*** *p49*
Cormack, Alexandre; Quebec, 1764 ***7603*** *p42*
Cormack, Barthol.; America, 1737 ***4971*** *p27*
Cormack, Daniell; Virginia, 1643 ***6219*** *p202*
Cormack, Thomas 50; Massachusetts, 1850 ***5881.1*** *p26*
Cormack, William 20; Nevis, 1723 ***3690.1*** *p52*
Corman, Andy; Arkansas, 1918 ***95.2*** *p32*
Cormelly, Dennis 23; Maryland, 1774 ***1219.7*** *p204*
Cormens, Sarah Ann 21; St. John, N.B., 1861 ***5704.8*** *p149*
Cormett, Moses 18; Philadelphia, 1853 ***5704.8*** *p108*
Cormick, Mary 24; Maryland, 1774 ***1219.7*** *p228*
Cormier, Mme. 40; America, 1826 ***778.5*** *p130*
Cormier, J.C. 40; America, 1826 ***778.5*** *p130*
Cormir, William; Illinois, 1855 ***7857*** *p3*
Cormock, Mary 11; Savannah, GA, 1733 ***4719.17*** *p310*
Cormonis, Angel D.; Arkansas, 1918 ***95.2*** *p32*
Cornard, Louise; Quebec, 1810 ***7603*** *p100*
Cornberger, Gertraud Einecker *SEE* Cornberger, Hans
Cornberger, Hans; Georgia, 1739 ***9332*** *p323*
*Wife:*Gertraud Einecker
Cornberger, John; Georgia, 1738 ***9332*** *p321*
Cornbergerin, Anne; Georgia, 1738 ***9332*** *p319*
Corne, John; Virginia, 1643 ***6219*** *p207*
Cornebois, Hectore 29; New Orleans, 1822 ***778.5*** *p130*
Corneen, Mary 24; St. John, N.B., 1858 ***5704.8*** *p137*
Corneli, . . .; Canada, 1776-1783 ***9786*** *p41*
Cornelius, John P.; Illinois, 1888 ***5012.37*** *p61*
Cornelius, Philipp 29; America, 1838 ***778.5*** *p130*
Cornelius, Theodor; New Netherland, 1630-1646 ***8582.2*** *p51*
Cornell, George; South Carolina, 1716 ***1639.20*** *p49*
Cornely, Edouard; Quebec, 1822 ***7603*** *p99*
Corneps, Bernhard; Charleston, SC, 1851 ***6013.19*** *p30*
Corner, Martin; New Orleans, 1821 ***778.5*** *p130*
Corner, Rebecca; Philadelphia, 1850 ***53.26*** *p15*
Corner, Rebecca; Philadelphia, 1850 ***5704.8*** *p60*
Corney, Richard; Philadelphia, 1811 ***2859.11*** *p10*
Corney, Wm.; Virginia, 1637 ***6219*** *p13*
Cornforth, Elizabeth 4 *SEE* Cornforth, William
Cornforth, Mary 1 *SEE* Cornforth, William
Cornforth, Mary 26 *SEE* Cornforth, William

Cornforth, Paul 70; North America, 1774 ***1219.7*** *p198*
*Wife:*Phillis 68
Cornforth, Phillis 68 *SEE* Cornforth, Paul
Cornforth, William 34; North America, 1774 ***1219.7*** *p198*
*Wife:*Mary 26
*Child:*Elizabeth 4
*Child:*Mary 1
Cornily, John F.; America, 1853 ***6014.1*** *p1*
Cornily, Nicholas; America, 1853 ***6014.1*** *p1*
Corning, Aziel 20; Massachusetts, 1849 ***5881.1*** *p13*
Cornish, Isaac 22; Jamaica, 1736 ***3690.1*** *p52*
Cornish, John 38; Maryland, 1775 ***1219.7*** *p250*
Cornish, Robert; Virginia, 1637 ***6219*** *p109*
Cornish, William; Virginia, 1652 ***6251*** *p20*
Cornu, Aime 16; Louisiana, 1838 ***778.5*** *p130*
Cornu, Maria 1; New Orleans, 1838 ***778.5*** *p131*
Cornwall, John 22; St. John, N.B., 1859 ***5704.8*** *p140*
Cornwall, Robert 20; Maryland, 1729 ***3690.1*** *p52*
Cornwall, Thomas 29; Jamaica, 1737 ***3690.1*** *p52*
Cornwall, Thomas H. 38; Kansas, 1888 ***5240.1*** *p8*
Cornwall, Thomas H. 38; Kansas, 1888 ***5240.1*** *p71*
Cornwell, John; New York, NY, 1816 ***2859.11*** *p28*
Cornwell, Mary 20; Philadelphia, 1859 ***5704.8*** *p142*
Cornwell, Robert 20; Maryland, 1729 ***3690.1*** *p52*
Cornwell, William 27; Maryland, 1774 ***1219.7*** *p215*
Corp, James; Antigua (Antego), 1769 ***1219.7*** *p141*
Corr, Charles; New York, NY, 1866 ***5704.8*** *p207*
Corr, Daniel 9; New York, NY, 1866 ***5704.8*** *p207*
Corr, Elizabeth 45; St. John, N.B., 1861 ***5704.8*** *p147*
Corr, Ellan 10; St. John, N.B., 1861 ***5704.8*** *p147*
Corr, Grace; New York, NY, 1866 ***5704.8*** *p207*
Corr, James; America, 1869 ***5704.8*** *p234*
Corr, Mary; St. John, N.B., 1852 ***5704.8*** *p93*
Corr, Mary 7; New York, NY, 1866 ***5704.8*** *p207*
Corr, Mary Ann 16; St. John, N.B., 1861 ***5704.8*** *p147*
Corr, Richard 45; St. John, N.B., 1861 ***5704.8*** *p147*
Corran, Domnick; Quebec, 1849 ***5704.8*** *p57*
Corran, Eliza; Quebec, 1849 ***5704.8*** *p57*
Corran, James; America, 1739 ***4971*** *p30*
Corran, John 10; Quebec, 1849 ***5704.8*** *p57*
Corran, Michael; America, 1739 ***4971*** *p30*
Corran, Nancy; Quebec, 1849 ***5704.8*** *p57*
Corran, Patrick; Quebec, 1849 ***5704.8*** *p57*
Corran, Patrick 3; Quebec, 1849 ***5704.8*** *p57*
Corran, Peggy 12; Quebec, 1849 ***5704.8*** *p57*
Corran, Rose; Quebec, 1849 ***5704.8*** *p57*
Corran, Thomas 9; Quebec, 1849 ***5704.8*** *p57*
Corraway, Joane; Virginia, 1644 ***6219*** *p230*
Correia, Antone; Arkansas, 1918 ***95.2*** *p32*
Correll, Tho.; Virginia, 1642 ***6219*** *p198*
Correy, Patrick 30; New Orleans, 1862 ***543.30*** *p459*
Corridon, Timothy; Iowa, 1866-1943 ***123.54*** *p15*
Corrie, Alexander; Charleston, SC, 1803 ***1639.20*** *p49*
Corrie, John; America, 1791 ***1639.20*** *p49*
Corrie, John; Charleston, SC, 1803 ***1639.20*** *p49*
Corrie, John; South Carolina, 1791 ***1639.20*** *p49*
Corrie, Little; Philadelphia, 1864 ***5704.8*** *p186*
Corrigal, James; Georgia, 1775 ***1219.7*** *p274*
Corrigal, John; Georgia, 1775 ***1219.7*** *p274*
Corrigan, Edward; Wisconsin, n.d. ***9675.5*** *p50*
Corrigan, James; Wisconsin, n.d. ***9675.5*** *p50*
Corrigan, John; St. John, N.B., 1853 ***5704.8*** *p106*
Corrigan, Margaret; Quebec, 1823 ***7603*** *p85*
Corrigan, William; America, 1866 ***5704.8*** *p207*
Corrigan, William; New York, NY, 1840 ***8208.4*** *p107*
Corrigel, Elizabeth; Georgia, 1775 ***1219.7*** *p274*
Corrin, Farrigle; Philadelphia, 1847 ***53.26*** *p15*
Corrin, Farrigle; Philadelphia, 1847 ***5704.8*** *p24*
Corrine, Agniazio; Arkansas, 1918 ***95.2*** *p32*
Corrins, James; New York, NY, 1811 ***2859.11*** *p10*
Corronan, Denis; Quebec, 1824 ***7603*** *p75*
Corroran, Margaret; Philadelphia, 1852 ***5704.8*** *p85*
Corroy, John 18; New Orleans, 1862 ***543.30*** *p453*
Corrwinn, Margt 20; Maryland or Virginia, 1699 ***2212*** *p24*
Corry, Arthur; New York, NY, 1834 ***8208.4*** *p45*
Corry, Hugh; New York, NY, 1815 ***2859.11*** *p28*
Corry, James; New York, NY, 1816 ***2859.11*** *p28*
Corry, James; Virginia, 1698 ***2212*** *p14*
Corry, Robert 18; Philadelphia, 1854 ***5704.8*** *p118*
Corry, Samuel 20; Philadelphia, 1854 ***5704.8*** *p118*
Corry, Thomas 44; New York, 1774 ***1219.7*** *p222*
Corry, William; New York, NY, 1838 ***8208.4*** *p90*
Corsaden, James; Philadelphia, 1848 ***53.26*** *p15*
Corsar, Mrs. 30; Grenada, 1774 ***1219.7*** *p177*
Corsar, Frederick 35; Grenada, 1774 ***1219.7*** *p177*
Corscaden, Ann 15; Philadelphia, 1855 ***5704.8*** *p124*
Corscaden, Catherine; Philadelphia, 1847 ***53.26*** *p15*
*Relative:*Margaret
Corscaden, Catherine; Philadelphia, 1847 ***5704.8*** *p30*
Corscaden, James; Philadelphia, 1848 ***5704.8*** *p46*
Corscaden, Margaret *SEE* Corscaden, Catherine
Corscaden, Margaret; Philadelphia, 1847 ***5704.8*** *p30*
Corscaden, Mary 17; Philadelphia, 1855 ***5704.8*** *p124*
Corscaden, Robert 18; Quebec, 1856 ***5704.8*** *p130*
Corscaden, Thomas 44; Quebec, 1856 ***5704.8*** *p130*
Corscaden, William; Philadelphia, 1864 ***5704.8*** *p177*
Corscadin, Arthur; Philadelphia, 1847 ***53.26*** *p15*
Corscadin, Arthur; Philadelphia, 1847 ***5704.8*** *p31*
Corsell, Frank; Indiana, 1844 ***9117*** *p19*
Corso, Angelo; Iowa, 1866-1943 ***123.54*** *p15*
Corso, Antonia; Iowa, 1866-1943 ***123.54*** *p15*
Corso, David; Iowa, 1866-1943 ***123.54*** *p15*
Corso, Louie; Iowa, 1866-1943 ***123.54*** *p15*
Corso, Luigi; Iowa, 1866-1943 ***123.54*** *p15*
Corso, Peter; Iowa, 1866-1943 ***123.54*** *p15*
Corso, Thomas; Arkansas, 1918 ***95.2*** *p32*
Corsso, Geusppie; Iowa, 1866-1943 ***123.54*** *p15*
Corstorphin, James; North Carolina, 1716-1816 ***1639.20*** *p50*
Corstorphin, Robert; North Carolina, 1680-1778 ***1639.20*** *p50*
Corta, Victor; Iowa, 1866-1943 ***123.54*** *p15*
Cortal, B. 28; Port uncertain, 1838 ***778.5*** *p131*
Cortes, Christopher; Wisconsin, 1870 ***5240.1*** *p9*
Cortes, G. S. 29; America, 1832 ***778.5*** *p131*
Cortes, John; Virginia, 1637 ***6219*** *p112*
Cortes, Manuel 35; Port uncertain, 1838 ***778.5*** *p131*
Cortese, Alfredo; Arkansas, 1918 ***95.2*** *p32*
Cortesia, Francesco; Iowa, 1866-1943 ***123.54*** *p15*
Cortesio, Maggie; Iowa, 1866-1943 ***123.54*** *p15*
Cortesio, Pasqualino; Iowa, 1866-1943 ***123.54*** *p59*
Cortesio, Paszualino; Iowa, 1866-1943 ***123.54*** *p15*
Cortiana, Joe; Arkansas, 1918 ***95.2*** *p32*
Cortin, Thomas; New York, NY, 1853 ***2896.5*** *p8*
Corunot, Mr. 24; America, 1838 ***778.5*** *p131*
Corvaia, Concetta; Iowa, 1866-1943 ***123.54*** *p59*
Corvaia, Pietro; Iowa, 1866-1943 ***123.54*** *p59*
Corvance, Daniel; Kansas, 1883 ***5240.1*** *p9*
Corwin, James 24; Massachusetts, 1848 ***5881.1*** *p17*
Cory, Lewin 21; Philadelphia, 1774 ***1219.7*** *p233*
Cory, Margaret; Quebec, 1850 ***5704.8*** *p63*
Cory, Robert 16; Philadelphia, 1774 ***1219.7*** *p228*
Corye, Jon.; Virginia, 1638 ***6219*** *p122*
Cosby, Henry; New York, 1754 ***1219.7*** *p30*
Cosdier, Mr. 32; New Orleans, 1839 ***778.5*** *p131*
Cosebuchar, Geo.; Iowa, 1866-1943 ***123.54*** *p15*
Cosentino, Filippo Salvatore; Arkansas, 1918 ***95.2*** *p32*
Cosentino, Francesco; Arkansas, 1918 ***95.2*** *p32*
Cosentino, Giuseppe; Arkansas, 1918 ***95.2*** *p32*
Coser, Daniel; America, 1735-1743 ***4971*** *p79*
Cosey, Rich.; Virginia, 1636 ***6219*** *p77*
Cosgrave, James; New York, NY, 1816 ***2859.11*** *p28*
Cosgriff, Esther 16; Massachusetts, 1849 ***5881.1*** *p15*
Cosgrove, Hugh; St. John, N.B., 1847 ***5704.8*** *p11*
Cosgrove, John 50; St. John, N.B., 1867 ***5704.8*** *p167*
Cosgrove, Mary 18; Massachusetts, 1849 ***5881.1*** *p22*
Cosgrove, Mary Ann 9; St. John, N.B., 1847 ***5704.8*** *p34*
Cosgrove, Michael; Illinois, 1870 ***7857*** *p3*
Cosgrove, Michael; St. John, N.B., 1847 ***5704.8*** *p11*
Cosgrove, Michael; Wisconsin, n.d. ***9675.5*** *p50*
Cosgrove, Patrick; New York, NY, 1836 ***8208.4*** *p19*
Cosgrove, Peter 37; New Orleans, 1862 ***543.30*** *p452*
Cosgrove, Rose; Quebec, 1853 ***5704.8*** *p104*
Cosgrove, Thomas; New York, NY, 1816 ***2859.11*** *p28*
Cosgrove, Wm. 35; New Orleans, 1862 ***543.30*** *p450*
Coskry, Michael; America, 1741 ***4971*** *p42*
Coskry, Timothy; America, 1741 ***4971*** *p42*
Coslarger, James; New York, NY, 1811 ***2859.11*** *p10*
Cosly, Patrick; America, 1735-1743 ***4971*** *p79*
Cosmas, James George; Arkansas, 1918 ***95.2*** *p32*
Cosmouet, Louise; Quebec, 1701 ***7603*** *p21*
Cosnell, Phillip 19; Jamaica, 1736 ***3690.1*** *p52*
Cosones, Nich.; Virginia, 1637 ***6219*** *p115*
Coss, John; Virginia, 1639 ***6219*** *p162*
Cosse, John; Ohio, 1846 ***8365.27*** *p12*
Cossee, Honora; America, 1736 ***4971*** *p12*
Cosselli, Filippo; Arkansas, 1918 ***95.2*** *p32*
Cossen, Henry; Virginia, 1643 ***6219*** *p200*
Cossett, John 16; West Indies, 1722 ***3690.1*** *p52*
Costa, Alexander; Arkansas, 1918 ***95.2*** *p32*
Costa, Filippo; Iowa, 1866-1943 ***123.54*** *p15*
Costa, Giuseppe; Arkansas, 1918 ***95.2*** *p32*
Costa, Mickel; Iowa, 1866-1943 ***123.54*** *p59*
Costa, Wm. 22; New Orleans, 1862 ***543.30*** *p458*
Costagan, James; New York, NY, 1811 ***2859.11*** *p10*
Costantino, Cesare; Arkansas, 1918 ***95.2*** *p32*
Costanza, Giovanni; Arkansas, 1918 ***95.2*** *p32*
Coste, Mr. 25; New Orleans, 1836 ***778.5*** *p131*
Coste, E. 55; America, 1836 ***778.5*** *p131*
Coste, Eugene 14; Louisiana, 1838 ***778.5*** *p131*
Coste, Francois; America, 1833 ***778.5*** *p131*
Costebel, Marie; Port uncertain, 1753 ***2444*** *p135*
Costell, Eliza 20; Massachusetts, 1849 ***5881.1*** *p16*
Costell, John 20; Massachusetts, 1849 ***5881.1*** *p19*
Costello, Barclay J.; New York, NY, 1840 ***8208.4*** *p107*
Costello, Bridget 2; Massachusetts, 1850 ***5881.1*** *p14*
Costello, Cornelius 19; Massachusetts, 1850 ***5881.1*** *p14*
Costello, Edmund; America, 1741 ***4971*** *p60*
Costello, Ellen 4; Massachusetts, 1850 ***5881.1*** *p16*
Costello, John 28; Massachusetts, 1847 ***5881.1*** *p17*
Costello, John 40; Massachusetts, 1850 ***5881.1*** *p19*
Costello, Judy 20; Massachusetts, 1850 ***5881.1*** *p19*
Costello, Martin 35; Arizona, 1890 ***2764.35*** *p11*
Costello, Mary 50; Massachusetts, 1849 ***5881.1*** *p22*
With child
Costello, Michael 2; Massachusetts, 1849 ***5881.1*** *p22*
Costello, Nancy 30; Massachusetts, 1850 ***5881.1*** *p23*
Costello, Pat. 27; Massachusetts, 1849 ***5881.1*** *p24*
Costello, Peter; Philadelphia, 1868 ***5704.8*** *p230*
Costello, Robert 24; Massachusetts, 1850 ***5881.1*** *p25*
Costello, Thomas; New York, NY, 1815 ***2859.11*** *p28*
Costelloe, Ann; America, 1735-1743 ***4971*** *p8*
Costelloe, Bridget; America, 1736 ***4971*** *p81*
Costelloe, Charles; America, 1735-1743 ***4971*** *p78*
Costen, Georg; Virginia, 1635 ***6219*** *p72*
Coster, Adele; Iowa, 1866-1943 ***123.54*** *p59*
Coster, Clemence; Iowa, 1866-1943 ***123.54*** *p15*
Coster, David 22; Maryland, 1733 ***3690.1*** *p52*
Coster, Elie Frank; Iowa, 1866-1943 ***123.54*** *p61*
Coster, Lisette Alice; Iowa, 1866-1943 ***123.54*** *p15*
Costerdine, Franc.; Virginia, 1635 ***6219*** *p5*
Costes, Baptiste 36; America, 1838 ***778.5*** *p131*
Costigan, James; New York, NY, 1816 ***2859.11*** *p28*
Costika, Alex; Arkansas, 1918 ***95.2*** *p33*
Coston, Georg; Virginia, 1636 ***6219*** *p109*
Cote, Juan 49; Port uncertain, 1838 ***778.5*** *p131*
Cotel, Samuel 27; Jamaica, 1733 ***3690.1*** *p52*
Cotele, Samuel 27; Jamaica, 1733 ***3690.1*** *p52*
Coterson, Andrew 2; Philadelphia, 1866 ***5704.8*** *p204*
Coterson, James; Philadelphia, 1866 ***5704.8*** *p204*
Coterson, Margaret; Philadelphia, 1866 ***5704.8*** *p204*
Coti, Elia; Arkansas, 1918 ***95.2*** *p33*
Cottar, Barnaby; Wisconsin, n.d. ***9675.5*** *p50*
Cotter, Arthur; New York, NY, 1816 ***2859.11*** *p28*
Cotter, John; Charleston, SC, 1841 ***7036*** *p126*
Cotter, John 4; Massachusetts, 1849 ***5881.1*** *p18*
Cotter, John F.; Wisconsin, n.d. ***9675.5*** *p50*
Cotter, Maurice 20; Massachusetts, 1849 ***5881.1*** *p21*
Cotter, Patrick 6; Massachusetts, 1849 ***5881.1*** *p24*
Cotteral, Catherine; South Carolina, 1767 ***1639.20*** *p50*
Cotterell, Christopher; Bermuda, 1751 ***1219.7*** *p7*
Cotterell, Edwd.; Virginia, 1635 ***6219*** *p72*
Cotterill, Rebecca 17; Maryland, 1731 ***3690.1*** *p52*
Cottes, Edward 24; New Orleans, 1825 ***778.5*** *p131*
Cottez, John Edward 30; New Orleans, 1832 ***778.5*** *p131*
Cottin, Elize 31; America, 1835 ***778.5*** *p131*
Cottington, George; Virginia, 1636 ***6219*** *p28*
Cottle, Charles 29; Jamaica, 1737 ***3690.1*** *p52*
Cottle, John 20; Maryland, 1733 ***3690.1*** *p53*
Cottle, Thomas; Virginia, 1635 ***6219*** *p25*
Cotton, Ann Graves *SEE* Cotton, William
Cotton, Cicely; Virginia, 1637 ***6219*** *p115*
Cotton, Eliz 18; America, 1699 ***2212*** *p29*
Cotton, George 22; Jamaica, 1735 ***3690.1*** *p53*
Cotton, George 30; Maryland, 1774 ***1219.7*** *p180*
Cotton, John; Ohio, 1844 ***9892.11*** *p10*
Cotton, John 20; Maryland, 1724 ***3690.1*** *p53*
Cotton, John 40; Maryland, 1775 ***1219.7*** *p251*
Cotton, Joshua 29; Maryland, 1730 ***3690.1*** *p53*
Cotton, Margt.; Virginia, 1638 ***6219*** *p160*
Cotton, Michael 30; Maryland, 1775 ***1219.7*** *p272*
Cotton, Michel; Quebec, 1775 ***7603*** *p62*
Cotton, Rowland; Virginia, 1637 ***6219*** *p110*
Cotton, William; Virginia, 1637 ***6219*** *p84*
*Wife:*Ann Graves
Cotton, William; Virginia, 1638 ***6219*** *p122*
Cotton, William; Virginia, 1638 ***6219*** *p146*
Cottrell, Margaret 30; Massachusetts, 1850 ***5881.1*** *p22*
Cotz, Christoph; Pennsylvania, 1751 ***2444*** *p144*
Cotz, Christoph; Pennsylvania, 1751 ***2444*** *p178*
Cou, L. 19; New Orleans, 1839 ***778.5*** *p132*
Couado, Antoine 26; America, 1838 ***778.5*** *p132*
Couat, Mr. 34; America, 1838 ***778.5*** *p132*
Couch, Arthur 45; Maryland, 1774 ***1219.7*** *p214*
Couch, Charles 22; Maryland, 1774 ***1219.7*** *p220*
Couchot, Claude 19; New Orleans, 1837 ***778.5*** *p132*
Couday, J. 25; America, 1835 ***778.5*** *p128*
Coude, Joseph; America, 1839 ***8582.1*** *p6*
Couden, Hannah; New York, NY, 1811 ***2859.11*** *p10*
With family
Couder, Pierre 25; America, 1836 ***778.5*** *p132*
Coudere, J. P. P.; New Orleans, 1839 ***778.5*** *p132*
Coudert, Charles; New York, NY, 1835 ***8208.4*** *p54*
Cough, John; America, 1742 ***4971*** *p54*
Coughlan, Cornelius; America, 1736 ***4971*** *p39*
Coughlan, Ellen 42; Massachusetts, 1849 ***5881.1*** *p15*
Coughlan, James; New York, NY, 1815 ***2859.11*** *p28*

Coughlan, James 7; Massachusetts, 1850 ***5881.1*** *p19*
Coughlan, Margaret 9; Massachusetts, 1850 ***5881.1*** *p23*
Coughlan, Pat. 4; Massachusetts, 1850 ***5881.1*** *p24*
Coughlan, William 20; Massachusetts, 1849 ***5881.1*** *p26*
Coughland, Wm 13; Philadelphia, 1845 ***6508.6*** *p115*
Coughlin, Ann; Quebec, 1796 ***7603*** *p75*
Coughlin, Ann 20; Massachusetts, 1847 ***5881.1*** *p12*
Coughlin, John; Colorado, 1887 ***9678.1*** *p158*
Coughlin, Joseph P.; Illinois, 1868 ***7857*** *p3*
Coughton, Anthony 50; Massachusetts, 1849 ***5881.1*** *p12*
Cougot, Claude Francois 35; America, 1835 ***778.5*** *p132*
Couilland, J. 23; New Orleans, 1839 ***778.5*** *p132*
Coukoulis, George; Arkansas, 1918 ***95.2*** *p33*
Coulburne, Ann; America, 1697 ***2212*** *p8*
Couley, Henry 21; Baltimore, 1775 ***1219.7*** *p269*
Couling, George 31; Maryland, 1775 ***1219.7*** *p273*
Couling, James 21; Maryland, 1775 ***1219.7*** *p273*
Coulon, . . .; Halifax, N.S., 1752 ***7074.6*** *p230*
Coulon, Mr. 19; New Orleans, 1837 ***778.5*** *p132*
Coulon, Mr. 35; New Orleans, 1839 ***778.5*** *p132*
Coulon, Catherine *SEE* Coulon, Pierre
Coulon, David 17 *SEE* Coulon, Pierre
Coulon, Jacques *SEE* Coulon, Pierre
Coulon, Jean-George *SEE* Coulon, Jean Nicolas
Coulon, Jean-George *SEE* Coulon, Pierre
Coulon, Jean-Jacques *SEE* Coulon, Jean Nicolas
Coulon, Jean Nicolas 66; Halifax, N.S., 1752 ***7074.6*** *p207*
With family of 3
Coulon, Jean Nicolas 66; Halifax, N.S., 1752 ***7074.6*** *p209*
*Wife:*Suzanne
*Son:*Jean-George
*Son:*Jean-Jacques
With son
Coulon, Jonas *SEE* Coulon, Pierre
Coulon, Marie-Madeleine *SEE* Coulon, Pierre
Coulon, Pierre 19 *SEE* Coulon, Pierre
Coulon, Pierre 46; Halifax, N.S., 1752 ***7074.6*** *p209*
*Wife:*Marie-Madeleine
*Child:*Jacques
*Child:*Jean-George
*Child:*Jonas
*Child:*Catherine
*Son:*Pierre 19
*Son:*David 17
Coulon, Suzanne *SEE* Coulon, Jean Nicolas
Coulon, Thomas R.; New York, NY, 1836 ***8208.4*** *p18*
Coulson, John 20; North America, 1774 ***1219.7*** *p197*
*Wife:*Mary 20
Coulson, Mary 20 *SEE* Coulson, John
Coulson, William; Quebec, 1815 ***9229.18*** *p81*
Coulston, John 20; Maryland, 1725 ***3690.1*** *p53*
Coulta, James; New York, NY, 1816 ***2859.11*** *p28*
Coulter, Alexander 6; New Orleans, 1852 ***5704.8*** *p98*
Coulter, Allan 11; St. John, N.B., 1866 ***5704.8*** *p166*
Coulter, Allan 42; St. John, N.B., 1866 ***5704.8*** *p166*
Coulter, Andrew 11; Philadelphia, 1853 ***5704.8*** *p111*
Coulter, Andrew 60; Quebec, 1862 ***5704.8*** *p151*
Coulter, Ann; New York, NY, 1811 ***2859.11*** *p10*
Coulter, Ann 7; Philadelphia, 1853 ***5704.8*** *p111*
Coulter, Anne 8; Quebec, 1855 ***5704.8*** *p125*
Coulter, Anne 11; Quebec, 1862 ***5704.8*** *p151*
Coulter, Beck; Quebec, 1848 ***5704.8*** *p42*
Coulter, Catherine 6; Quebec, 1855 ***5704.8*** *p125*
Coulter, Charles; Ohio, 1840 ***9892.11*** *p11*
Coulter, Charles 5; St. John, N.B., 1866 ***5704.8*** *p166*
Coulter, Charles 13; Quebec, 1855 ***5704.8*** *p125*
Coulter, Charles 38; Quebec, 1855 ***5704.8*** *p125*
Coulter, Christopher; Quebec, 1855 ***5704.8*** *p125*
Coulter, David 8; Quebec, 1862 ***5704.8*** *p151*
Coulter, Eliza; New Orleans, 1849 ***5704.8*** *p58*
Coulter, Eliza 7; Quebec, 1848 ***5704.8*** *p42*
Coulter, Eliza 8; New Orleans, 1852 ***5704.8*** *p98*
Coulter, Eliza 16; Quebec, 1862 ***5704.8*** *p151*
Coulter, Eliza 36; Quebec, 1855 ***5704.8*** *p125*
Coulter, Ellen 10; Quebec, 1855 ***5704.8*** *p125*
Coulter, Ellen Jane; Quebec, 1862 ***5704.8*** *p151*
Coulter, Fanny; Quebec, 1848 ***5704.8*** *p42*
Coulter, Frank 64; Arizona, 1909 ***9228.40*** *p10*
Coulter, Hannah 10; Quebec, 1862 ***5704.8*** *p151*
Coulter, Hugh; New York, NY, 1811 ***2859.11*** *p10*
Coulter, Isabella 5; Quebec, 1862 ***5704.8*** *p151*
Coulter, Isabella 40; Quebec, 1862 ***5704.8*** *p151*
Coulter, James; Quebec, 1848 ***5704.8*** *p42*
Coulter, James 5; Quebec, 1848 ***5704.8*** *p42*
Coulter, James 19; Quebec, 1853 ***5704.8*** *p105*
Coulter, Jane; St. John, N.B., 1847 ***5704.8*** *p26*
Coulter, Jane 37; St. John, N.B., 1866 ***5704.8*** *p166*
Coulter, Jane 40; St. John, N.B., 1859 ***5704.8*** *p143*
Coulter, Jean 3; St. John, N.B., 1866 ***5704.8*** *p166*
Coulter, John; New York, NY, 1816 ***2859.11*** *p28*
Coulter, John; Ohio, 1846 ***9892.11*** *p11*
Coulter, John; Philadelphia, 1850 ***53.26*** *p16*
Coulter, John; Philadelphia, 1850 ***5704.8*** *p68*
Coulter, John 1; St. John, N.B., 1866 ***5704.8*** *p166*
Coulter, John 2; Quebec, 1855 ***5704.8*** *p125*
Coulter, John 3; Quebec, 1848 ***5704.8*** *p42*
Coulter, John 3; Quebec, 1862 ***5704.8*** *p151*
Coulter, John 9; Philadelphia, 1853 ***5704.8*** *p111*
Coulter, John 10; St. John, N.B., 1859 ***5704.8*** *p143*
Coulter, Margaret 14; Quebec, 1862 ***5704.8*** *p151*
Coulter, Margaret 19; Philadelphia, 1854 ***5704.8*** *p121*
Coulter, Margaret 20; St. John, N.B., 1859 ***5704.8*** *p143*
Coulter, Mary; New Orleans, 1852 ***5704.8*** *p98*
Coulter, Mary; Philadelphia, 1867 ***5704.8*** *p223*
Coulter, Mary 18; Philadelphia, 1856 ***5704.8*** *p129*
Coulter, Mary Jane 9; Quebec, 1848 ***5704.8*** *p42*
Coulter, Richard 21; Quebec, 1853 ***5704.8*** *p105*
Coulter, Robert 9; St. John, N.B., 1866 ***5704.8*** *p166*
Coulter, Ruth 11; Quebec, 1855 ***5704.8*** *p125*
Coulter, Sarah; New York, NY, 1811 ***2859.11*** *p10*
Coulter, Sarah 15; St. John, N.B., 1859 ***5704.8*** *p143*
Coulter, Sarah 27; Quebec, 1864 ***5704.8*** *p159*
Coulter, William 4; Quebec, 1855 ***5704.8*** *p125*
Coulter, Wm. 69; Arizona, 1913 ***9228.40*** *p18*
Coulthred, Mathew 26; St. Christopher, 1730 ***3690.1*** *p289*
Coultman, Anthony 19; Jamaica, 1731 ***3690.1*** *p53*
Coulty, Ann 40; Massachusetts, 1850 ***5881.1*** *p13*
Coumad, Melchior; New York, 1754 ***3652*** *p79*
Counce, Bartle 29; Pennsylvania, 1741 ***4779.3*** *p13*
Count, Mme. 38; New Orleans, 1839 ***778.5*** *p132*
Count, Barbey 4; New Orleans, 1838 ***778.5*** *p132*
Count, Elize 2; New Orleans, 1838 ***778.5*** *p132*
Count, Margerite 60; New Orleans, 1838 ***778.5*** *p132*
Countis, Dimitre A.; Iowa, 1866-1943 ***123.54*** *p15*
County, Patrick 18; Massachusetts, 1850 ***5881.1*** *p24*
Couples, Elizabeth; New York, NY, 1811 ***2859.11*** *p10*
Couples, James; New York, NY, 1811 ***2859.11*** *p10*
Couran, John; Maryland, 1742 ***4971*** *p106*
Courbe, Mr. 24; America, 1838 ***778.5*** *p132*
Courbe, Clara 20; New Orleans, 1826 ***778.5*** *p133*
Courbet, Jacques 27; New Orleans, 1839 ***778.5*** *p133*
Courcey, James; America, 1739 ***4971*** *p52*
Courcey, Susan 18; Philadelphia, 1853 ***5704.8*** *p108*
Courel, Mr. 40; America, 1835 ***778.5*** *p133*
Couret, B.; New Orleans, 1838 ***778.5*** *p133*
Couret, Bartholomew 24; America, 1838 ***778.5*** *p133*
Couret, Daniel 29; America, 1838 ***778.5*** *p133*
Couret, Francois 24; New Orleans, 1839 ***778.5*** *p133*
Couret, Hubert 28; America, 1838 ***778.5*** *p133*
Couret, Jean 21; Port uncertain, 1838 ***778.5*** *p133*
Courette, Frederic 37; New Orleans, 1862 ***543.30*** *p457*
Courier, Rufus M.; New York, NY, 1840 ***8208.4*** *p111*
Courmon, Mr. 30; New Orleans, 1839 ***778.5*** *p133*
Courne, Jerome 58; New Orleans, 1839 ***778.5*** *p133*
Courret, Louis; America, 1853 ***2896.5*** *p8*
Courrey, Mary Anne; Quebec, 1849 ***5704.8*** *p51*
Course, George 38; New Orleans, 1822 ***778.5*** *p133*
Coursey, Edward 28; Maryland, 1773 ***1219.7*** *p172*
Coursie, Richard; Virginia, 1642 ***6219*** *p199*
Courssisuer, Mr. 26; Port uncertain, 1839 ***778.5*** *p133*
Court, Charles 18; Dominica, 1774 ***1219.7*** *p205*
Court, Richard; Virginia, 1637 ***6219*** *p81*
Court, Richard 19; St. Christopher, 1722 ***3690.1*** *p53*
Court, William 18; Maryland, 1775 ***1219.7*** *p254*
Courtade, F. 19; New Orleans, 1839 ***778.5*** *p133*
Courtaud, J. 30; America, 1829 ***778.5*** *p133*
Courtet, A. 32; Mexico, 1823 ***778.5*** *p134*
Courtier, Wm.; Virginia, 1637 ***6219*** *p113*
Courting, Mary 20; Massachusetts, 1850 ***5881.1*** *p22*
Courtman, Thomas 28; Baltimore, 1775 ***1219.7*** *p270*
Courtnay, Margaret 18; Massachusetts, 1850 ***5881.1*** *p23*
Courtney, James; Virginia, 1635 ***6219*** *p69*
Courtney, John; West Virginia, 1798-1811 ***9788.3*** *p6*
Courtney, John 37; Jamaica, 1724 ***3690.1*** *p53*
Courtney, Margaret 24 *SEE* Courtney, Richard
Courtney, Margaret 56; Massachusetts, 1850 ***5881.1*** *p23*
Courtney, Michael; Canada, 1727-1827 ***9788.3*** *p7*
Courtney, Michael; West Virginia, 1798-1811 ***9788.3*** *p6*
Courtney, Michael; West Virginia, 1832 ***9788.3*** *p7*
Courtney, Michael 26; Massachusetts, 1849 ***5881.1*** *p21*
Courtney, Michael 40; West Virginia, 1827 ***9788.3*** *p7*
Courtney, Nancy; Philadelphia, 1853 ***5704.8*** *p108*
Courtney, Paul 23; Philadelphia, 1775 ***1219.7*** *p258*
Courtney, Peter; New York, NY, 1811 ***2859.11*** *p10*
Courtney, Richard 25; Philadelphia, 1804 ***53.26*** *p16*
*Relative:*Margaret 24
Courtney, Robert 54; West Virginia, 1811 ***9788.3*** *p7*
Courtney, Victoria; St. John, N.B., 1851 ***5704.8*** *p72*
Courtney, William; West Virginia, 1800-1906 ***9788.3*** *p2*
Courtney, William; West Virginia, 1833 ***9788.3*** *p7*
Courtney, William 28; West Virginia, 1811 ***9788.3*** *p7*
Courtois, Alexis 2; New Orleans, 1838 ***778.5*** *p134*
Courtois, Charles 7; New Orleans, 1838 ***778.5*** *p134*
Courtois, Eloise 11; New Orleans, 1838 ***778.5*** *p134*
Courtois, Francois 52; New Orleans, 1838 ***778.5*** *p134*
Courtois, Maria 48; New Orleans, 1838 ***778.5*** *p134*
Courtright, Joseph; Cincinnati, 1827 ***8582.1*** *p6*
Courts, Cesar 16; America, 1823 ***778.5*** *p134*
Courts, William; New York, NY, 1835 ***8208.4*** *p76*
Couruet, Mme. 36; America, 1839 ***778.5*** *p134*
Couruet, Mr. 45; America, 1839 ***778.5*** *p134*
Courvois, Mr. 31; New Orleans, 1839 ***778.5*** *p134*
Cousens, James; Virginia, 1637 ***6219*** *p114*
Cousin, Cesair 24; New Orleans, 1838 ***778.5*** *p134*
Cousins, Edward 19; Maryland, 1774 ***1219.7*** *p204*
Cousins, Fred; Iowa, 1866-1943 ***123.54*** *p15*
Cousins, Henry; California, 1843-1872 ***2769.3*** *p4*
Cousins, James; St. John, N.B., 1849 ***5704.8*** *p55*
Cousins, John; South Carolina, 1716 ***1639.20*** *p50*
Cousins, Mary Jane 1; St. John, N.B., 1849 ***5704.8*** *p55*
Cousirat, J. 18; America, 1835 ***778.5*** *p134*
Coussan, Jean 26; America, 1831 ***778.5*** *p134*
Coutanceau, Jacob; Virginia, 1652 ***6251*** *p19*
Coutard, Alexandre 9; Louisiana, 1820 ***778.5*** *p134*
Coutaud, Mr. 20; America, 1838 ***778.5*** *p134*
Coutelier, Mr. 28; New Orleans, 1835 ***778.5*** *p135*
Coutie, James 47; California, 1869 ***3840.1*** *p16*
Coutreau, Jean 19; New Orleans, 1829 ***778.5*** *p135*
Couts, Christopher; Indiana, 1836 ***9117*** *p15*
Coutts, John M.; America, 1890 ***1450.2*** *p6B*
Couturier, Mr. 20; America, 1839 ***778.5*** *p135*
Couturier, Jean 25; America, 1839 ***778.5*** *p135*
Couty, John; Charleston, SC, 1821 ***1639.20*** *p50*
Coutz, C. 38; Port uncertain, 1839 ***778.5*** *p135*
Couve, J.; New Orleans, 1838 ***778.5*** *p135*
Couvertie, J. B. 30; America, 1839 ***778.5*** *p135*
Covell, John; Virginia, 1637 ***6219*** *p109*
Covell, John; Virginia, 1641 ***6219*** *p187*
Covenagh, Robert; New York, NY, 1816 ***2859.11*** *p28*
Coventon, Nehemiah; Virginia, 1647 ***6219*** *p244*
Coventry, William 27; Virginia, 1774 ***1219.7*** *p185*
Coverly, Wm 25; Virginia, 1699 ***2212*** *p27*
Covill, Humphry 25; Windward Islands, 1722 ***3690.1*** *p53*
Covington, Mr.; Maryland, 1768 ***8582.3*** *p96*
Cow, John; Jamaica, 1756 ***1219.7*** *p41*
Cow, John; Jamaica, 1756 ***3690.1*** *p53*
Cowan, Catharine; Philadelphia, 1865 ***5704.8*** *p193*
Cowan, Charles; New York, NY, 1815 ***2859.11*** *p28*
Cowan, James 13; Quebec, 1851 ***5704.8*** *p82*
Cowan, John T.; Charleston, SC, 1798-1827 ***1639.20*** *p50*
Cowan, Mary; Philadelphia, 1848 ***53.26*** *p16*
Cowan, Mary; Philadelphia, 1848 ***5704.8*** *p46*
Cowan, Mary; Quebec, 1851 ***5704.8*** *p82*
Cowan, Patrick 10; Quebec, 1851 ***5704.8*** *p82*
Cowan, Robert 10; Quebec, 1851 ***5704.8*** *p82*
Cowan, Samuel E. 35?; Arizona, 1890 ***2764.35*** *p14*
Cowan, Thomas; Arizona, 1890 ***2764.35*** *p15*
Cowan, William; Nevada, 1880 ***2764.35*** *p11*
Cowan, William 7; Quebec, 1851 ***5704.8*** *p82*
Cowans, Robert 58; Kansas, 1872 ***5240.1*** *p53*
Cowans, William 23; Kansas, 1872 ***5240.1*** *p9*
Cowans, William 23; Kansas, 1872 ***5240.1*** *p53*
Coward, James 21; Port uncertain, 1774 ***1219.7*** *p177*
Coward, John; Iroquois Co., IL, 1894 ***3455.1*** *p10*
Coway, John; Philadelphia, 1849 ***53.26*** *p16*
Cowdell, Robert 17; Virginia, 1774 ***1219.7*** *p186*
Cowell, Elizabeth; Virginia, 1645 ***6219*** *p233*
Cowell, John 19; Barbados or Antigua, 1735 ***3690.1*** *p53*
Cowell, Peter; Illinois, 1871 ***7857*** *p3*
Cowell, Thomas 15; Virginia, 1749 ***3690.1*** *p53*
Cowen, J. 38; New Orleans, 1826 ***778.5*** *p135*
Cowen, James 25; Massachusetts, 1849 ***5881.1*** *p18*
Cowen, Thomas 21; Maryland, 1774 ***1219.7*** *p225*
Cowes, John; Virginia, 1634 ***6219*** *p32*
Cowey, Alexander 14; Philadelphia, 1854 ***5704.8*** *p121*
Cowham, Joel Foster; New York, NY, 1835 ***8208.4*** *p76*
Cowham, John M.; Louisiana, 1832 ***8208.4*** *p26*
Cowie, Alexander; Virginia, 1852 ***4626.16*** *p14*
Cowie, James; Colorado, 1884 ***9678.1*** *p158*
Cowie, Mary H.; Colorado, 1893 ***9678.1*** *p159*
Cowlan, Patrick; Maryland, 1740 ***4971*** *p91*
Cowlan, Patrick; Philadelphia, 1741 ***4971*** *p92*
Cowles, Thomas 16; New England, 1724 ***3690.1*** *p53*
Cowley, Charles; America, 1737 ***4971*** *p55*
Cowley, Robert 27; Maryland, 1774 ***1219.7*** *p221*
Cowley, William; New York, NY, 1840 ***8208.4*** *p107*
Cowley, Wm.; Virginia, 1647 ***6219*** *p239*
Cowlund, Richd; America, 1698 ***2212*** *p5*
Cowly, Mary; America, 1698 ***2212*** *p9*
Cowper, James 24; Jamaica, 1730 ***3690.1*** *p54*
Cowser, Eliza; New York, NY, 1811 ***2859.11*** *p10*
Cowser, James; New York, NY, 1811 ***2859.11*** *p10*
Cowser, Sophia; New York, NY, 1811 ***2859.11*** *p10*
Cowson, William; South Carolina, 1716 ***1639.20*** *p51*
Cox, Andrew; Quebec, 1850 ***5704.8*** *p67*
Cox, Anne; Quebec, 1847 ***5704.8*** *p12*

Cox, Annie; Quebec, 1850 ***5704.8*** *p67*
Cox, Bernard 14; Massachusetts, 1850 ***5881.1*** *p14*
Cox, Charles 26; Port uncertain, 1774 ***1219.7*** *p176*
Cox, Cicely 25; St. John, N.B., 1864 ***5704.8*** *p158*
Cox, Edward; St. John, N.B., 1847 ***5704.8*** *p9*
Cox, Eliz. 19; Port uncertain, 1849 ***4535.10*** *p198*
Cox, Eliza; Quebec, 1847 ***5704.8*** *p16*
Cox, Eliza 10; Philadelphia, 1852 ***5704.8*** *p97*
Cox, Eunice 3 *SEE* Cox, William
Cox, Francis 35 *SEE* Cox, William
Cox, Francis 36; St. John, N.B., 1864 ***5704.8*** *p158*
Cox, George; New York, NY, 1836 ***8208.4*** *p58*
Cox, Hugh; St. John, N.B., 1853 ***5704.8*** *p109*
Cox, Isabella 3; Quebec, 1847 ***5704.8*** *p16*
Cox, James; Quebec, 1847 ***5704.8*** *p12*
Cox, James; Quebec, 1847 ***5704.8*** *p16*
Cox, John 19; Jamaica, 1733 ***3690.1*** *p54*
Cox, John 20; Jamaica, 1729 ***3690.1*** *p54*
Cox, John 28; New Orleans, 1862 ***543.30*** *p458*
Cox, Jon.; Virginia, 1637 ***6219*** *p11*
Cox, Jon.; Virginia, 1637 ***6219*** *p13*
Cox, Jon.; Virginia, 1642 ***6219*** *p194*
Cox, Joseph; Virginia, 1639 ***6219*** *p155*
Cox, Joseph 21; Jamaica, 1739 ***3690.1*** *p54*
Cox, Laughlin; America, 1738 ***4971*** *p9*
Cox, Margaret 13; Quebec, 1847 ***5704.8*** *p12*
Cox, Martha 18; Philadelphia, 1854 ***5704.8*** *p123*
Cox, Mary; America, 1865 ***5704.8*** *p201*
Cox, Mary; Quebec, 1847 ***5704.8*** *p12*
Cox, Mary; Quebec, 1847 ***5704.8*** *p16*
Cox, Mary; Virginia, 1643 ***6219*** *p203*
Cox, Michael; New York, NY, 1840 ***8208.4*** *p112*
Cox, Robert 5; Quebec, 1847 ***5704.8*** *p16*
Cox, Rose 22; Philadelphia, 1854 ***5704.8*** *p123*
Cox, Samuel 17; Barbados, 1732 ***3690.1*** *p54*
Cox, Symon; Virginia, 1648 ***6219*** *p246*
Cox, Tho.; Virginia, 1637 ***6219*** *p113*
Cox, Thomas; Quebec, 1847 ***5704.8*** *p12*
Cox, Thomas 19; West Indies, 1722 ***3690.1*** *p54*
Cox, William; Illinois, 1861 ***5012.38*** *p98*
Cox, William; Illinois, 1865 ***5012.38*** *p98*
Cox, William; Virginia, 1643 ***6219*** *p203*
Cox, William 6; Philadelphia, 1852 ***5704.8*** *p97*
Cox, William 12 *SEE* Cox, William
Cox, William 16; Port uncertain, 1757 ***3690.1*** *p54*
Cox, William 41; Savannah, GA, 1733 ***4719.17*** *p310*
*Daughter:*Eunice 3
*Wife:*Francis 35
*Son:*William 12
Cox, William J. 7; Quebec, 1847 ***5704.8*** *p16*
Cox, Wm.; Virginia, 1637 ***6219*** *p8*
Cox, Wm.; Virginia, 1637 ***6219*** *p11*
Coxson, Thomas; Virginia, 1637 ***6219*** *p115*
Coy, Charles 5; New York, NY, 1869 ***5704.8*** *p233*
Coy, Eliza; New York, NY, 1869 ***5704.8*** *p233*
Coy, Joseph 7; New York, NY, 1869 ***5704.8*** *p233*
Coyd, Thomas 30; Jamaica, 1730 ***3690.1*** *p54*
Coyen, Bridget 25; St. John, N.B., 1854 ***5704.8*** *p119*
Coyl, Henry; New York, NY, 1834 ***8208.4*** *p49*
Coyl, John; New York, NY, 1838 ***8208.4*** *p89*
Coyle, Anabella 5; Philadelphia, 1866 ***5704.8*** *p205*
Coyle, Andrew; St. John, N.B., 1847 ***5704.8*** *p34*
Coyle, Andrew; St. John, N.B., 1850 ***5704.8*** *p66*
Coyle, Andrew 8; Philadelphia, 1853 ***5704.8*** *p111*
Coyle, Ann; Philadelphia, 1851 ***5704.8*** *p71*
Coyle, Ann; Philadelphia, 1851 ***5704.8*** *p76*
Coyle, Ann 20; Philadelphia, 1855 ***5704.8*** *p123*
Coyle, Ann 22; Philadelphia, 1853 ***5704.8*** *p108*
Coyle, Anne; Philadelphia, 1850 ***53.26*** *p16*
Coyle, Anne; Philadelphia, 1850 ***5704.8*** *p65*
Coyle, Anne; Philadelphia, 1864 ***5704.8*** *p182*
Coyle, Anthony; New York, NY, 1868 ***5704.8*** *p227*
Coyle, Anton; Philadelphia, 1850 ***5704.8*** *p64*
Coyle, Barney; America, 1865 ***5704.8*** *p192*
Coyle, Bernard; New York, NY, 1864 ***5704.8*** *p169*
Coyle, Bernard; Philadelphia, 1864 ***5704.8*** *p170*
Coyle, Betty 9; America, 1868 ***5704.8*** *p230*
Coyle, Biddy; Quebec, 1851 ***5704.8*** *p74*
Coyle, Biddy 40; Philadelphia, 1853 ***5704.8*** *p111*
Coyle, Bridget; New York, NY, 1868 ***5704.8*** *p227*
Coyle, Catharine; America, 1867 ***5704.8*** *p221*
Coyle, Catharine; New York, NY, 1865 ***5704.8*** *p188*
Coyle, Catharine; Philadelphia, 1864 ***5704.8*** *p170*
Coyle, Catharine; Philadelphia, 1867 ***5704.8*** *p218*
Coyle, Catharine 22; Massachusetts, 1850 ***5881.1*** *p14*
Coyle, Catherine; St. John, N.B., 1849 ***5704.8*** *p56*
Coyle, Catherine; St. John, N.B., 1851 ***5704.8*** *p72*
Coyle, Catherine 6; Philadelphia, 1854 ***5704.8*** *p116*
Coyle, Catherine 14; Philadelphia, 1861 ***5704.8*** *p148*
Coyle, Catherine 18; Philadelphia, 1853 ***5704.8*** *p113*
Coyle, Cecelia; Philadelphia, 1864 ***5704.8*** *p182*
Coyle, Charles 8; New York, NY, 1868 ***5704.8*** *p228*
Coyle, Charlotte 6; Philadelphia, 1853 ***5704.8*** *p111*
Coyle, Daniel *SEE* Coyle, John
Coyle, Daniel; New York, NY, 1865 ***5704.8*** *p199*
Coyle, Daniel; Philadelphia, 1811 ***2859.11*** *p10*
Coyle, Daniel 21; St. John, N.B., 1855 ***5704.8*** *p127*
Coyle, Daniel 50; Philadelphia, 1861 ***5704.8*** *p147*
Coyle, Danny; St. John, N.B., 1847 ***5704.8*** *p24*
Coyle, Eliza; Quebec, 1852 ***5704.8*** *p94*
Coyle, Eliza 12; Quebec, 1851 ***5704.8*** *p74*
Coyle, Eliza Jane; Philadelphia, 1864 ***5704.8*** *p187*
Coyle, Elizabeth; New York, NY, 1866 ***5704.8*** *p212*
Coyle, Elizabeth; New York, NY, 1868 ***5704.8*** *p231*
Coyle, Elizabeth; Philadelphia, 1865 ***5704.8*** *p200*
Coyle, Ellen; New York, NY, 1870 ***5704.8*** *p238*
Coyle, Ellen 9 mos; Philadelphia, 1853 ***5704.8*** *p111*
Coyle, Ellen 5; America, 1868 ***5704.8*** *p230*
Coyle, Ellen 28; Massachusetts, 1850 ***5881.1*** *p16*
Coyle, Ellen A.; Philadelphia, 1865 ***5704.8*** *p198*
Coyle, Eneas; Philadelphia, 1864 ***5704.8*** *p183*
Coyle, Fanny; Philadelphia, 1866 ***5704.8*** *p204*
Coyle, Francis; New York, NY, 1816 ***2859.11*** *p28*
Coyle, Francis 22; St. John, N.B., 1866 ***5704.8*** *p167*
Coyle, Hanna; Philadelphia, 1847 ***53.26*** *p16*
Coyle, Hanna; Philadelphia, 1847 ***5704.8*** *p1*
Coyle, Hannah; Philadelphia, 1852 ***5704.8*** *p88*
Coyle, Henry; New York, NY, 1838 ***8208.4*** *p75*
Coyle, Hugh; New York, NY, 1836 ***8208.4*** *p20*
Coyle, Hugh; New York, NY, 1865 ***5704.8*** *p199*
Coyle, Hugh; New York, NY, 1868 ***5704.8*** *p227*
Coyle, Hugh; Philadelphia, 1851 ***5704.8*** *p81*
Coyle, Hugh; Philadelphia, 1865 ***5704.8*** *p198*
Coyle, Hugh 9 mos; Philadelphia, 1851 ***5704.8*** *p76*
Coyle, Hugh 7; America, 1868 ***5704.8*** *p230*
Coyle, Hugh 22; Philadelphia, 1861 ***5704.8*** *p147*
Coyle, Hugh 25; Philadelphia, 1861 ***5704.8*** *p149*
Coyle, Isabella 13; St. John, N.B., 1853 ***5704.8*** *p110*
Coyle, Isabella 45; St. John, N.B., 1853 ***5704.8*** *p110*
Coyle, James; St. John, N.B., 1848 ***5704.8*** *p44*
Coyle, James; Washington, 1859-1920 ***2872.1*** *p9*
Coyle, James 4; Philadelphia, 1853 ***5704.8*** *p111*
Coyle, James 10; New York, NY, 1868 ***5704.8*** *p227*
Coyle, James 14; Philadelphia, 1860 ***5704.8*** *p146*
Coyle, Jane; Philadelphia, 1864 ***5704.8*** *p175*
Coyle, Jane; Quebec, 1851 ***5704.8*** *p74*
Coyle, Jane 16; Philadelphia, 1864 ***5704.8*** *p156*
Coyle, Jane 22; St. John, N.B., 1853 ***5704.8*** *p110*
Coyle, John; New York, NY, 1838 ***8208.4*** *p65*
Coyle, John; New York, NY, 1865 ***5704.8*** *p199*
Coyle, John; Philadelphia, 1811 ***53.26*** *p16*
*Relative:*Daniel
Coyle, John; Philadelphia, 1811 ***2859.11*** *p10*
Coyle, John; St. John, N.B., 1847 ***5704.8*** *p33*
Coyle, John 7; Philadelphia, 1852 ***5704.8*** *p89*
Coyle, John 16; Philadelphia, 1854 ***5704.8*** *p116*
Coyle, John 18; Quebec, 1856 ***5704.8*** *p130*
Coyle, John 21; Newfoundland, 1789 ***4915.24*** *p55*
Coyle, Joseph; Philadelphia, 1864 ***5704.8*** *p178*
Coyle, Julia; Philadelphia, 1867 ***5704.8*** *p219*
Coyle, Kate 11 mos; Philadelphia, 1866 ***5704.8*** *p205*
Coyle, Madge 4; Philadelphia, 1854 ***5704.8*** *p116*
Coyle, Manus 4; Philadelphia, 1851 ***5704.8*** *p77*
Coyle, Margaret; New York, NY, 1865 ***5704.8*** *p196*
Coyle, Margaret; Philadelphia, 1870 ***5704.8*** *p239*
Coyle, Margaret; St. John, N.B., 1847 ***5704.8*** *p10*
Coyle, Margaret 8; Philadelphia, 1864 ***5704.8*** *p187*
Coyle, Margery; Philadelphia, 1866 ***5704.8*** *p205*
Coyle, Martin; New York, NY, 1834 ***8208.4*** *p2*
Coyle, Mary; New York, NY, 1865 ***5704.8*** *p199*
Coyle, Mary; New York, NY, 1869 ***5704.8*** *p234*
Coyle, Mary; Philadelphia, 1866 ***5704.8*** *p209*
Coyle, Mary 7; Philadelphia, 1866 ***5704.8*** *p205*
Coyle, Mary 10; Philadelphia, 1853 ***5704.8*** *p111*
Coyle, Mary 18; Philadelphia, 1864 ***5704.8*** *p155*
Coyle, Mary 30; Massachusetts, 1850 ***5881.1*** *p23*
Coyle, Mary 30; Philadelphia, 1851 ***5704.8*** *p76*
Coyle, Mary 36; Philadelphia, 1853 ***5704.8*** *p111*
Coyle, Mary Ann 15; St. John, N.B., 1853 ***5704.8*** *p110*
Coyle, Matthew; New York, NY, 1836 ***8208.4*** *p25*
Coyle, Michael; Philadelphia, 1865 ***5704.8*** *p185*
Coyle, Nancy; America, 1868 ***5704.8*** *p230*
Coyle, Nancy 4; Philadelphia, 1853 ***5704.8*** *p111*
Coyle, Neal; Philadelphia, 1848 ***5704.8*** *p46*
Coyle, Patrick; Philadelphia, 1866 ***5704.8*** *p205*
Coyle, Patrick; Philadelphia, 1868 ***5704.8*** *p229*
Coyle, Patrick 10; St. John, N.B., 1853 ***5704.8*** *p110*
Coyle, Patrick 25; Philadelphia, 1861 ***5704.8*** *p147*
Coyle, Patrick 45; St. John, N.B., 1853 ***5704.8*** *p110*
Coyle, Peggy; Philadelphia, 1851 ***5704.8*** *p76*
Coyle, Peter; New York, NY, 1828 ***9892.11*** *p11*
Coyle, Peter; Philadelphia, 1869 ***5704.8*** *p235*
Coyle, Robert; St. John, N.B., 1850 ***5704.8*** *p65*
Coyle, Rose; Philadelphia, 1853 ***5704.8*** *p103*
Coyle, Rose Ann 2; Philadelphia, 1864 ***5704.8*** *p181*
Coyle, Sarah; New Orleans, 1848 ***5704.8*** *p48*
Coyle, Sarah; New York, NY, 1864 ***5704.8*** *p169*
Coyle, Sarah 20; St. John, N.B., 1853 ***5704.8*** *p110*
Coyle, Sophia 3; Philadelphia, 1866 ***5704.8*** *p205*
Coyle, Susan 22; St. John, N.B., 1862 ***5704.8*** *p150*
Coyle, Thomas; Philadelphia, 1847 ***53.26*** *p16*
Coyle, Thomas; Philadelphia, 1847 ***5704.8*** *p22*
Coyle, Thomas; Philadelphia, 1865 ***5704.8*** *p198*
Coyle, Thomas 17; St. John, N.B., 1861 ***5704.8*** *p149*
Coyle, Unity 30; Philadelphia, 1854 ***5704.8*** *p116*
Coyle, William; New York, NY, 1865 ***5704.8*** *p199*
Coyle, William; Philadelphia, 1851 ***5704.8*** *p71*
Coyle, William 6; Philadelphia, 1851 ***5704.8*** *p76*
Coyle, William 20; Philadelphia, 1854 ***5704.8*** *p120*
Coyley, Michael; Montreal, 1823 ***7603*** *p75*
Coyne, Bryan; America, 1735-1743 ***4971*** *p79*
Coyne, Bryan; America, 1741 ***4971*** *p82*
Coyne, John 40; New Orleans, 1862 ***543.30*** *p453*
Coyne, Joss 32; Kansas, 1881 ***5240.1*** *p63*
Coysh, George; Wisconsin, n.d. ***9675.5*** *p50*
Coyt, William; Virginia, 1638 ***6219*** *p120*
Coyte, Willi.; Virginia, 1637 ***6219*** *p83*
Coz., Sarah Dera.; Virginia, 1648 ***6219*** *p246*
Cozier, William; Virginia, 1636 ***6219*** *p77*
Crab, John 22; Philadelphia, 1775 ***1219.7*** *p259*
Crabb, Jon.; Virginia, 1635 ***6219*** *p73*
Crabb, Jon.; Virginia, 1637 ***6219*** *p113*
Crabb, Robert; South Carolina, 1811 ***1639.20*** *p50*
Crabbe, James 25; Massachusetts, 1848 ***5881.1*** *p17*
Crabbe, Roger; Virginia, 1638 ***6219*** *p124*
Crabill, Albert; Washington, 1859-1920 ***2872.1*** *p9*
Crabill, Albert G.; Washington, 1859-1920 ***2872.1*** *p9*
Crabill, Daniel; Washington, 1859-1920 ***2872.1*** *p9*
Crabtree, John; New York, NY, 1833 ***8208.4*** *p50*
Cracker, Tho.; Virginia, 1645 ***6219*** *p240*
Craddock, Charles Alfred; Washington, 1859-1920 ***2872.1*** *p9*
Craddock, George 16; Maryland, 1724 ***3690.1*** *p54*
Craddock, Thomas 20; Maryland, 1720 ***3690.1*** *p54*
Cradick, Thomas 16; Virginia, 1774 ***1219.7*** *p244*
Cradock, Robert; Virginia, 1637 ***6219*** *p24*
Craemer, Friedrich Wilhelm *SEE* Craemer, Heinrich David
Craemer, Heinrich David; America, 1839 ***4610.10*** *p154*
With wife
*Child:*Marie
*Child:*Friedrich Wilhelm
Craemer, Johann Daniel *SEE* Craemer, Johann Daniel Friedrich
Craemer, Johann Daniel Friedrich; America, 1750 ***2444*** *p145*
*Child:*Philipp Bernhard
*Child:*Wilhelm Jacob
*Wife:*Sofia Pfeil
*Child:*Johann Daniel
Craemer, Johann Friedrich; America, 1839 ***4610.10*** *p154*
With wife
With 2 daughters
Craemer, Marie *SEE* Craemer, Heinrich David
Craemer, Philipp Bernhard *SEE* Craemer, Johann Daniel Friedrich
Craemer, Sofia Pfeil *SEE* Craemer, Johann Daniel Friedrich
Craemer, Wilhelm Jacob *SEE* Craemer, Johann Daniel Friedrich
Crafford, Dorothy; Virginia, 1642 ***6219*** *p191*
Crafford, Martin; Virginia, 1647 ***6219*** *p241*
Craft, Bridgett; Virginia, 1636 ***6219*** *p77*
Craft, Jon.; Virginia, 1637 ***6219*** *p84*
Craftin, Tho.; Virginia, 1635 ***6219*** *p36*
Craftin, Thomas; Virginia, 1637 ***6219*** *p83*
Craftt, Oliver; Virginia, 1643 ***6219*** *p207*
Cragg, Richard 19; United States or West Indies, 1739 ***3690.1*** *p54*
Cragg, Thomas; Virginia, 1637 ***6219*** *p83*
Cragg, Thomas 22; Jamaica, 1731 ***3690.1*** *p54*
Cragg, Wm; Virginia, 1698 ***2212*** *p17*
Craggs, George 25; Maryland, 1773 ***1219.7*** *p172*
Craghan, Bridget; Philadelphia, 1866 ***5704.8*** *p207*
Cragie, Balfour; New York, NY, 1832 ***8208.4*** *p28*
Crago, Francis 30; Maryland, 1775 ***1219.7*** *p272*
Crahin, Dennis; America, 1841 ***7036*** *p127*
*Sister:*Judy
Crahin, Judy *SEE* Crahin, Dennis
Craid, James; New York, NY, 1868 ***5704.8*** *p228*
Craid, Madge; New York, NY, 1868 ***5704.8*** *p228*
Craid, Susan; New York, NY, 1868 ***5704.8*** *p228*
Craid, William; New York, NY, 1868 ***5704.8*** *p228*
Craig, . . . 1 wk; Philadelphia, 1860 ***5704.8*** *p146*
Craig, Alex 4; Philadelphia, 1851 ***5704.8*** *p70*
Craig, Andre; Quebec, 1795 ***7603*** *p39*
Craig, Andreas; Ohio, 1819 ***8582.1*** *p47*
Craig, Andrew; New York, NY, 1816 ***2859.11*** *p28*
Craig, Anne; Philadelphia, 1864 ***5704.8*** *p175*

Craig, Anne; Quebec, 1847 ***5704.8*** *p8*
Craig, Archibald; Charleston, SC, 1821 ***1639.20*** *p50*
*Child:*Jane
*Child:*James
Craig, Charles; New York, NY, 1864 ***5704.8*** *p173*
Craig, Charles M.; New York, NY, 1838 ***8208.4*** *p88*
Craig, Chas.; New York, NY, 1811 ***2859.11*** *p10*
With family
Craig, David; North Carolina, 1732-1785 ***1639.20*** *p50*
Craig, Eliza; Philadelphia, 1851 ***5704.8*** *p75*
Craig, Eliza 2; Philadelphia, 1860 ***5704.8*** *p146*
Craig, Eliza Mary 13; Philadelphia, 1853 ***5704.8*** *p102*
Craig, Elizabeth; Philadelphia, 1849 ***5704.8*** *p50*
Craig, Elizabeth; Philadelphia, 1864 ***5704.8*** *p188*
Craig, Elizabeth; Philadelphia, 1865 ***5704.8*** *p196*
Craig, Elizabeth 20; Philadelphia, 1854 ***5704.8*** *p118*
Craig, Elizabeth 42; Philadelphia, 1859 ***5704.8*** *p141*
Craig, Ellizabeth *SEE* Craig, Ross
Craig, Fanny; Quebec, 1847 ***5704.8*** *p38*
Craig, Fanny 8; Quebec, 1847 ***5704.8*** *p38*
Craig, George; Barbados, 1776 ***1219.7*** *p281*
Craig, George 27; Virginia, 1773 ***1219.7*** *p171*
Craig, Henry 20; St. John, N.B., 1861 ***5704.8*** *p149*
Craig, Hugh; Philadelphia, 1852 ***5704.8*** *p85*
Craig, Hugh 4; Philadelphia, 1851 ***5704.8*** *p70*
Craig, James *SEE* Craig, Archibald
Craig, James; Philadelphia, 1865 ***5704.8*** *p196*
Craig, James; Philadelphia, 1867 ***5704.8*** *p222*
Craig, James 9; Philadelphia, 1864 ***5704.8*** *p175*
Craig, James 60; Massachusetts, 1850 ***5881.1*** *p19*
Craig, Jane *SEE* Craig, Archibald
Craig, Jane 10; Quebec, 1847 ***5704.8*** *p38*
Craig, John; New York, NY, 1811 ***2859.11*** *p10*
Craig, John; New York, NY, 1838 ***8208.4*** *p85*
Craig, John; Philadelphia, 1851 ***5704.8*** *p75*
Craig, John; Philadelphia, 1852 ***5704.8*** *p88*
Craig, John; Philadelphia, 1864 ***5704.8*** *p175*
Craig, John; St. John, N.B., 1849 ***5704.8*** *p49*
Craig, John; St. John, N.B., 1850 ***5704.8*** *p61*
Craig, John 20; Philadelphia, 1833-1834 ***53.26*** *p16*
Craig, John 20; Philadelphia, 1860 ***5704.8*** *p144*
Craig, John 24; Wilmington, DE, 1831 ***6508.7*** *p160*
Craig, Jos.; New York, NY, 1811 ***2859.11*** *p10*
With family
Craig, Joseph; New York, NY, 1833 ***8208.4*** *p27*
Craig, Joseph 20; St. John, N.B., 1862 ***5704.8*** *p150*
Craig, Margaret; Philadelphia, 1864 ***5704.8*** *p175*
Craig, Margaret; St. John, N.B., 1848 ***5704.8*** *p43*
Craig, Margaret; St. John, N.B., 1849 ***5704.8*** *p49*
Craig, Margaret; St. John, N.B., 1850 ***5704.8*** *p61*
Craig, Margaret; St. John, N.B., 1850 ***5704.8*** *p65*
Craig, Margaret; Savannah, GA, 1774 ***1219.7*** *p227*
Craig, Margaret 9; Philadelphia, 1864 ***5704.8*** *p188*
Craig, Margaret 23; Philadelphia, 1860 ***5704.8*** *p146*
Craig, Margaret 68; Kansas, 1881 ***5240.1*** *p63*
Craig, Mark; New York, NY, 1864 ***5704.8*** *p171*
Craig, Martha; Philadelphia, 1847 ***53.26*** *p16*
Craig, Martha; Philadelphia, 1847 ***5704.8*** *p23*
Craig, Martha; Philadelphia, 1867 ***5704.8*** *p223*
Craig, Mary; Philadelphia, 1847 ***53.26*** *p16*
Craig, Mary; Philadelphia, 1847 ***5704.8*** *p1*
Craig, Mary; Philadelphia, 1850 ***5704.8*** *p64*
Craig, Mary; Quebec, 1850 ***5704.8*** *p63*
Craig, Mary E.; Philadelphia, 1864 ***5704.8*** *p175*
Craig, Mary Jane 22; Philadelphia, 1854 ***5704.8*** *p122*
Craig, Matilda; New York, NY, 1864 ***5704.8*** *p176*
Craig, Nancy; Philadelphia, 1867 ***5704.8*** *p222*
Craig, Nancy 22; Philadelphia, 1861 ***5704.8*** *p148*
Craig, Patrick 20; Philadelphia, 1865 ***5704.8*** *p165*
Craig, Peter; New Orleans, 1849 ***5704.8*** *p59*
Craig, Robert; Charleston, SC, 1806 ***1639.20*** *p51*
Craig, Robert; Philadelphia, 1864 ***5704.8*** *p184*
Craig, Robert; St. John, N.B., 1847 ***5704.8*** *p4*
Craig, Robert; St. John, N.B., 1850 ***5704.8*** *p65*
Craig, Robert 21; Quebec, 1854 ***5704.8*** *p119*
Craig, Roseann; Philadelphia, 1849 ***53.26*** *p16*
Craig, Roseann; Philadelphia, 1849 ***5704.8*** *p52*
Craig, Ross; Philadelphia, 1849 ***53.26*** *p16*
*Relative:*Ellizabeth
*Relative:*Sarah
Craig, Ross; Philadelphia, 1849 ***5704.8*** *p50*
Craig, Samuel; New York, NY, 1816 ***2859.11*** *p28*
Craig, Sarah *SEE* Craig, Ross
Craig, Sarah; New York, NY, 1866 ***5704.8*** *p211*
Craig, Sarah; Philadelphia, 1849 ***5704.8*** *p50*
Craig, Sarah 1; Philadelphia, 1860 ***5704.8*** *p146*
Craig, Sarah 7; Philadelphia, 1864 ***5704.8*** *p175*
Craig, Sarah 9; Philadelphia, 1864 ***5704.8*** *p188*
Craig, Scott 18; Quebec, 1854 ***5704.8*** *p121*
Craig, Thomas; Charleston, SC, 1799 ***1639.20*** *p51*
Craig, Thomas; Philadelphia, 1847 ***53.26*** *p16*
*Relative:*William
Craig, Thomas; Philadelphia, 1847 ***5704.8*** *p23*
Craig, Thomas; Philadelphia, 1867 ***5704.8*** *p222*
Craig, Thomas 22; Jamaica, 1774 ***1219.7*** *p232*
Craig, William *SEE* Craig, Thomas
Craig, William; Philadelphia, 1811 ***53.26*** *p16*
Craig, William; Philadelphia, 1847 ***5704.8*** *p23*
Craig, William; Philadelphia, 1851 ***5704.8*** *p78*
Craig, William; Philadelphia, 1865 ***5704.8*** *p202*
Craig, William; Quebec, 1847 ***5704.8*** *p8*
Craig, William 20; Philadelphia, 1857 ***5704.8*** *p134*
Craig, William 25; Philadelphia, 1860 ***5704.8*** *p146*
Craig, William 46; Philadelphia, 1859 ***5704.8*** *p141*
Craig, Winifred 16; Philadelphia, 1853 ***5704.8*** *p113*
Craig, Wm.; Philadelphia, 1811 ***2859.11*** *p10*
Craigen, Dennis 37; Virginia, 1774 ***1219.7*** *p243*
Craighan, Austin 29; Massachusetts, 1849 ***5881.1*** *p13*
Craighead, Alexander *SEE* Craighead, George
Craighead, Anne *SEE* Craighead, George
Craighead, Christian *SEE* Craighead, George
Craighead, Elizabeth *SEE* Craighead, George
Craighead, Elspet Cooper *SEE* Craighead, George
Craighead, George; America, 1844 ***8893*** *p265*
*Wife:*Elspet Cooper
*Daughter:*Elizabeth
*Daughter:*Anne
*Son:*Alexander
*Daughter:*Christian
*Son:*William
*Son:*James
*Son:*Thomas
Craighead, James *SEE* Craighead, George
Craighead, Thomas *SEE* Craighead, George
Craighead, William *SEE* Craighead, George
Craike, George 28; Virginia, 1775 ***1219.7*** *p248*
Crake, William 31; Maryland, 1730 ***3690.1*** *p54*
Cram, Sally 13; Massachusetts, 1849 ***5881.1*** *p25*
Crameey, Eleanor; Philadelphia, 1851 ***5704.8*** *p81*
Cramer, . . .; Canada, 1776-1783 ***9786*** *p19*
Cramer, . . .; Pennsylvania, n.d. ***1034.18*** *p13*
Cramer, Mrs.; Milwaukee, 1875 ***4719.30*** *p257*
Cramer, A. M. Ilsabein Lunte *SEE* Cramer, August Heinrich W.
Cramer, A. M. W. Karoline *SEE* Cramer, August Heinrich W.
Cramer, Adam; New York, 1754 ***3652*** *p79*
Cramer, August Heinrich W.; America, 1881 ***4610.10*** *p159*
*Wife:*A. M. Ilsabein Lunte
*Child:*A. M. W. Karoline
*Child:*Carl Friedrich W.
*Child:*Caroline Wilhelmine
*Child:*Ernst H. Friedrich W.
*Child:*Heinrich Friedrich W.
Cramer, Carl Friedrich W. *SEE* Cramer, August Heinrich W.
Cramer, Caroline Wilhelmine *SEE* Cramer, August Heinrich W.
Cramer, Christan; South Carolina, 1788 ***7119*** *p197*
Cramer, Christopher; Georgia, 1775 ***8582.2*** *p64*
Cramer, Daniel; Pennsylvania, 1752 ***2444*** *p145*
Cramer, Ernst H. Friedrich W. *SEE* Cramer, August Heinrich W.
Cramer, Heinrich Friedrich W. *SEE* Cramer, August Heinrich W.
Cramer, Henri; Canada, 1776-1783 ***9786*** *p243*
Cramer, John William; New York, NY, 1831 ***8208.4*** *p58*
Cramer, Joseph; New York, NY, 1846 ***8582.1*** *p6*
Cramer, Joseph; South Carolina, 1788 ***7119*** *p199*
Cramer, Oscar; Milwaukee, 1875 ***4719.30*** *p257*
Cramfeild, Wm.; Virginia, 1639 ***6219*** *p150*
Cramm, v., Lieut.; Quebec, 1776 ***9786*** *p104*
Cramm, Heinrich Wilhelm Gottfried; Quebec, 1776 ***9786*** *p256*
Cramp, Walter; America, 1698 ***2212*** *p13*
Crampsey, Daniel; St. John, N.B., 1847 ***5704.8*** *p24*
Crampsey, Edward; St. John, N.B., 1849 ***5704.8*** *p55*
Crampsey, Hugh; Quebec, 1848 ***5704.8*** *p42*
Crampsey, Mary; St. John, N.B., 1847 ***5704.8*** *p24*
Crampsey, Shane; St. John, N.B., 1847 ***5704.8*** *p24*
Crampsier, John; New York, NY, 1811 ***2859.11*** *p10*
Crampton, Thomas 15; Maryland, 1775 ***1219.7*** *p264*
Crampton, Walter; Virginia, 1698 ***2212*** *p15*
Crampy, John; Massachusetts, 1847 ***5881.1*** *p17*
Cramsey, William; Philadelphia, 1864 ***5704.8*** *p183*
Cramsie, John 13; St. John, N.B., 1853 ***5704.8*** *p110*
Cramsie, Philip 21; St. John, N.B., 1853 ***5704.8*** *p110*
Cramsie, Sicily 19; Philadelphia, 1858 ***5704.8*** *p139*
Cranage, Edmund *SEE* Cranage, William
Cranage, Eliza. *SEE* Cranage, William
Cranage, Eliza.; Virginia, 1639 ***6219*** *p159*
Cranage, Elizabeth *SEE* Cranage, William
Cranage, Marg. *SEE* Cranage, William
Cranage, Margarett *SEE* Cranage, William
Cranage, Margarett; Virginia, 1639 ***6219*** *p159*
Cranage, William; Virginia, 1637 ***6219*** *p116*
*Wife:*Elizabeth
*Child:*Margarett
*Child:*Eliza.
*Child:*Marg.
*Child:*Edmund
Cranage, William; Virginia, 1640 ***6219*** *p183*
Cranahan, Mary Ann 43; St. John, N.B., 1863 ***5704.8*** *p153*
Cranally, Edmond; America, 1735-1743 ***4971*** *p78*
Crandell, Reuben D.; Illinois, 1848 ***7857*** *p3*
Crane, A. W.; Washington, 1859-1920 ***2872.1*** *p9*
Crane, Caroline M.; Milwaukee, 1875 ***4719.30*** *p257*
Crane, Henry 18; Maryland, 1774 ***1219.7*** *p208*
Crane, John; Arkansas, 1918 ***95.2*** *p33*
Crane, Lawrance 23; Maryland, 1775 ***1219.7*** *p260*
Crane, Moses H.; New York, NY, 1840 ***8208.4*** *p111*
Crane, T. N.; Washington, 1859-1920 ***2872.1*** *p9*
Crane, Thomas; Ohio, 1840 ***9892.11*** *p11*
Crane, William 26; Baltimore, 1775 ***1219.7*** *p269*
Craney, Owen; New York, NY, 1838 ***8208.4*** *p62*
Cranfeild, Peter; Virginia, 1638 ***6219*** *p147*
Cranfield, Henry 20; Virginia, 1720 ***3690.1*** *p55*
Cranfin, Mary; New York, NY, 1811 ***2859.11*** *p10*
With family
Cranfurd, John 20; Jamaica, 1750 ***3690.1*** *p55*
Crannage, Edmond; Virginia, 1639 ***6219*** *p159*
Crannage, Eliza.; Virginia, 1639 ***6219*** *p159*
Crannage, Mary; Virginia, 1639 ***6219*** *p159*
Crannage, William; Virginia, 1639 ***6219*** *p159*
Cranne, Ultrel 21; New Orleans, 1835 ***778.5*** *p135*
Cranow, Simon; Arkansas, 1918 ***95.2*** *p33*
Cranston, James 25; Maryland, 1775 ***1219.7*** *p260*
Cranstone, John 19; Jamaica, 1730 ***3690.1*** *p55*
Crantz, . . .; America, 1700-1877 ***8582.3*** *p80*
Crany, John; New York, NY, 1815 ***2859.11*** *p28*
Craortt, Edward; Virginia, 1638 ***6219*** *p153*
Crapisi, Guiseppe; Arkansas, 1918 ***95.2*** *p33*
Crapp, Laura *SEE* Crapp, Thomas John Marshall
Crapp, Thomas John Marshall; New York, NY, 1908 ***3455.2*** *p101*
*Wife:*Laura
Crary, Samuel; New York, NY, 1811 ***2859.11*** *p10*
Crashaw, Joseph; Virginia, 1638 ***6219*** *p119*
Crathew, Mr.; Quebec, 1815 ***9229.18*** *p82*
Crathy, Pat.; Massachusetts, 1848 ***5881.1*** *p24*
Crause, Barbara *SEE* Crause, Leonhard
Crause, Barbara Einecker *SEE* Crause, Leonhard
Crause, Johannes; Philadelphia, 1779 ***8137*** *p7*
Crause, Leonhard; Georgia, 1738 ***9332*** *p321*
Crause, Leonhard; Georgia, 1739 ***9332*** *p323*
*Wife:*Barbara Einecker
Crause, Leonhard; Georgia, 1739 ***9332*** *p326*
*Wife:*Barbara
Crauthers, Joseph 62; Arizona, 1913 ***9228.40*** *p18*
Craven, Francis; Virginia, 1855 ***4626.16*** *p15*
Craven, James; Virginia, 1639 ***6219*** *p157*
Craven, James 19; Jamaica, 1731 ***3690.1*** *p55*
Craven, Jno. 25; Philadelphia, 1803 ***53.26*** *p16*
Craven, John; New York, NY, 1816 ***2859.11*** *p28*
Craven, Tho.; Virginia, 1642 ***6219*** *p194*
Craven, Thomas 18; Pennsylvania, 1728 ***3690.1*** *p55*
Crawe, Roger; Virginia, 1638 ***6219*** *p117*
Crawes, Henry; Virginia, 1640 ***6219*** *p184*
Crawford, Mr.; Quebec, 1815 ***9229.18*** *p79*
Crawford, Mrs.; Philadelphia, 1865 ***5704.8*** *p198*
Crawford, Agnes 11; Quebec, 1864 ***5704.8*** *p163*
Crawford, Alexander; Washington, 1859-1920 ***2872.1*** *p9*
Crawford, Andrew; Ohio, 1863 ***9892.11*** *p11*
Crawford, Andrew; Philadelphia, 1853 ***5704.8*** *p100*
Crawford, Andrew 23; Nova Scotia, 1774 ***1219.7*** *p195*
Crawford, Andrew 25; Quebec, 1864 ***5704.8*** *p159*
Crawford, Ann; Quebec, 1851 ***5704.8*** *p73*
Crawford, Ann; Virginia, 1635 ***6219*** *p17*
Crawford, Ann 21; St. John, N.B., 1864 ***5704.8*** *p159*
Crawford, Anne; Philadelphia, 1816 ***2859.11*** *p28*
With 3 children
Crawford, Arthur 4 *SEE* Crawford, Charles
Crawford, Arthur 4; Philadelphia, 1849 ***5704.8*** *p49*
Crawford, Charles; Philadelphia, 1849 ***53.26*** *p16*
*Relative:*Rosanna
*Relative:*Mary Ann
*Relative:*John 12
*Relative:*Margaret 9
*Relative:*Eliza Jane 7
*Relative:*Arthur 4
*Relative:*Charles 2
*Relative:*Matilda 6 mos
*Relative:*Rebecca 6 mos
Crawford, Charles; Philadelphia, 1849 ***5704.8*** *p49*
Crawford, Charles 2 *SEE* Crawford, Charles
Crawford, Charles 2; Philadelphia, 1849 ***5704.8*** *p49*
Crawford, Charles 29; California, 1872 ***2769.3*** *p4*

Crawford, Daniel; South Carolina, 1737 *1639.20 p51*
Crawford, David; New York, NY, 1816 *2859.11 p28*
Crawford, David; South Carolina, 1737 *1639.20 p51*
Crawford, David J.; Quebec, 1849 *5704.8 p57*
Crawford, Eliz. *SEE* Crawford, Martin
Crawford, Eliza 20; St. John, N.B., 1858 *5704.8 p137*
Crawford, Eliza J.; Philadelphia, 1866 *5704.8 p211*
Crawford, Eliza Jane 7 *SEE* Crawford, Charles
Crawford, Eliza Jane 7; Philadelphia, 1849 *5704.8 p49*
Crawford, Elizabeth; Philadelphia, 1847 *5704.8 p13*
Crawford, Elizabeth; Quebec, 1851 *5704.8 p73*
Crawford, Elizabeth; St. John, N.B., 1848 *5704.8 p42*
Crawford, Elizabeth 48 *SEE* Crawford, Robert
Crawford, English; New York, NY, 1816 *2859.11 p28*
Crawford, Fanny 26; St. John, N.B., 1857 *5704.8 p134*
Crawford, Francis; Quebec, 1853 *5704.8 p105*
Crawford, George 24; Quebec, 1856 *5704.8 p130*
Crawford, George 24; St. John, N.B., 1857 *5704.8 p134*
Crawford, Gideon; Carolina, 1684 *1639.20 p51*
Crawford, Henry; Philadelphia, 1865 *5704.8 p198*
Crawford, Henry; St. John, N.B., 1847 *5704.8 p33*
Crawford, Isabella; Philadelphia, 1865 *5704.8 p198*
Crawford, Isabella 18; Philadelphia, 1860 *5704.8 p145*
Crawford, J.; New York, NY, 1816 *2859.11 p28*
Crawford, James; New York, NY, 1816 *2859.11 p28*
Crawford, James; New York, NY, 1839 *8208.4 p94*
Crawford, James; Philadelphia, 1816 *2859.11 p28*
Crawford, James; St. John, N.B., 1848 *5704.8 p44*
Crawford, Jameson 4; Quebec, 1864 *5704.8 p163*
Crawford, Jameson 30; Quebec, 1864 *5704.8 p163*
Crawford, Jane; Quebec, 1851 *5704.8 p73*
Crawford, John; Charleston, SC, 1809 *1639.20 p51*
Crawford, John; New York, NY, 1816 *2859.11 p28*
Crawford, John; Philadelphia, 1852 *5704.8 p84*
Crawford, John; Philadelphia, 1866 *5704.8 p211*
Crawford, John; Quebec, 1795 *7603 p39*
Crawford, John; Quebec, 1852 *5704.8 p90*
Crawford, John 12 *SEE* Crawford, Charles
Crawford, John 12; Philadelphia, 1849 *5704.8 p49*
Crawford, Joseph; Philadelphia, 1864 *5704.8 p179*
Crawford, Joseph; Philadelphia, 1865 *5704.8 p198*
Crawford, Joseph 26; Philadelphia, 1833-1834 *53.26 p16*
Crawford, King 18; Philadelphia, 1856 *5704.8 p128*
Crawford, M.; New York, NY, 1816 *2859.11 p28*
Crawford, M. D.; Washington, 1859-1920 *2872.1 p9*
Crawford, Margaret; Philadelphia, 1865 *5704.8 p198*
Crawford, Margaret; Quebec, 1853 *5704.8 p105*
Crawford, Margaret; St. John, N.B., 1850 *5704.8 p67*
Crawford, Margaret 9 *SEE* Crawford, Charles
Crawford, Margaret 9; Philadelphia, 1849 *5704.8 p49*
Crawford, Margaret 19; St. John, N.B., 1854 *5704.8 p119*
Crawford, Margaret 30; Quebec, 1864 *5704.8 p163*
Crawford, Maria 24; St. John, N.B., 1857 *5704.8 p134*
Crawford, Martha; Philadelphia, 1847 *53.26 p16*
Crawford, Martha; Philadelphia, 1847 *5704.8 p32*
Crawford, Martin; Philadelphia, 1847 *53.26 p16*
*Relative:*Eliz.
*Relative:*Peggy
*Relative:*Peggy Jane 8
*Relative:*Nancy 4
*Relative:*Robert 2
Crawford, Martin; Philadelphia, 1847 *5704.8 p13*
Crawford, Mary; Philadelphia, 1816 *2859.11 p28*
Crawford, Mary; Philadelphia, 1852 *5704.8 p84*
Crawford, Mary; Philadelphia, 1852 *5704.8 p85*
Crawford, Mary; St. John, N.B., 1848 *5704.8 p42*
Crawford, Mary 20; St. John, N.B., 1859 *5704.8 p140*
Crawford, Mary 26; Quebec, 1864 *5704.8 p159*
Crawford, Mary Ann *SEE* Crawford, Charles
Crawford, Mary Ann; Philadelphia, 1847 *53.26 p17*
Crawford, Mary Ann; Philadelphia, 1847 *5704.8 p30*
Crawford, Mary Ann; Philadelphia, 1849 *5704.8 p49*
Crawford, Mary Ann 22; Philadelphia, 1859 *5704.8 p142*
Crawford, Mary J.; Philadelphia, 1864 *5704.8 p181*
Crawford, Matilda 6 mos *SEE* Crawford, Charles
Crawford, Matilda 6 mos; Philadelphia, 1849 *5704.8 p49*
Crawford, Matty 20; Quebec, 1855 *5704.8 p126*
Crawford, Montgomery; New York, NY, 1833 *8208.4 p60*
Crawford, Nancy 4 *SEE* Crawford, Martin
Crawford, Nancy 4; Philadelphia, 1847 *5704.8 p13*
Crawford, Otto 60; Arizona, 1906 *9228.40 p10*
Crawford, Patrick; New York, NY, 1837 *8208.4 p54*
Crawford, Peggy *SEE* Crawford, Martin
Crawford, Peggy; Philadelphia, 1847 *5704.8 p13*
Crawford, Peggy Jane 8 *SEE* Crawford, Martin
Crawford, Peggy Jane 8; Philadelphia, 1847 *5704.8 p13*
Crawford, Rebecca; New York, NY, 1811 *2859.11 p10*
Crawford, Rebecca; New York, NY, 1869 *5704.8 p232*
Crawford, Rebecca 6 mos *SEE* Crawford, Charles
Crawford, Rebecca 6 mos; Philadelphia, 1849 *5704.8 p49*
Crawford, Rebecca 18; Philadelphia, 1859 *5704.8 p141*
Crawford, Robert; Philadelphia, 1865 *5704.8 p198*
Crawford, Robert 2 *SEE* Crawford, Martin
Crawford, Robert 2; Philadelphia, 1847 *5704.8 p13*
Crawford, Robert 13; Quebec, 1854 *5704.8 p119*
Crawford, Robert 16; Georgia, 1775 *1219.7 p276*
Crawford, Robert 20; St. John, N.B., 1860 *5704.8 p143*
Crawford, Robert 22; Maryland, 1774 *1219.7 p185*
Crawford, Robert 23; Quebec, 1815 *9229.18 p80*
Crawford, Robert 50; South Carolina, 1850 *1639.20 p51*
*Relative:*Elizabeth 48
Crawford, Rosanna *SEE* Crawford, Charles
Crawford, Rosanna; Philadelphia, 1849 *5704.8 p49*
Crawford, Sally Jane; St. John, N.B., 1850 *5704.8 p67*
Crawford, Samuel 29; Philadelphia, 1853 *5704.8 p111*
Crawford, Sarah; Philadelphia, 1850 *53.26 p17*
Crawford, Sarah; Philadelphia, 1850 *5704.8 p65*
Crawford, Sarah; Philadelphia, 1864 *5704.8 p176*
Crawford, Thomas; Illinois, 1872 *5012.39 p25*
Crawford, Thomas; Petersburg, VA, 1810 *4778.2 p142*
Crawford, Thomas; St. John, N.B., 1850 *5704.8 p67*
Crawford, Thomas 40; Quebec, 1864 *5704.8 p159*
Crawford, William; Montreal, 1816 *7603 p69*
Crawford, William; New York, NY, 1815 *2859.11 p28*
Crawford, William; Philadelphia, 1865 *5704.8 p198*
Crawford, William; Quebec, 1847 *5704.8 p29*
Crawford, William; Quebec, 1851 *5704.8 p74*
Crawford, William 23; St. John, N.B., 1854 *5704.8 p114*
Crawford, William Carroll; Texas, 1895 *9777 p4*
Crawford, Willis; Washington, 1859-1920 *2872.1 p9*
Crawford, Wm.; Virginia, 1623-1648 *6219 p252*
Crawley, Bridget 17; Massachusetts, 1850 *5881.1 p14*
Crawley, Daniel; America, 1736-1743 *4971 p57*
Crawley, Ellen 15; Massachusetts, 1849 *5881.1 p15*
Crawley, Jerry 15; Massachusetts, 1848 *5881.1 p17*
Crawley, Lewis; New York, NY, 1816 *2859.11 p28*
Crawley, Margaret 20; Massachusetts, 1849 *5881.1 p21*
Crawley, Mary 5; Massachusetts, 1849 *5881.1 p21*
Crawley, Michael; New York, NY, 1816 *2859.11 p28*
Crawley, Michael; New York, NY, 1835 *8208.4 p78*
Crawley, Michael 26; Massachusetts, 1850 *5881.1 p22*
Crawley, Patrick W.; America, 1865 *5240.1 p9*
Crawley, Timothy; New York, NY, 1838 *8208.4 p69*
Crawlon, Patrick; New York, NY, 1816 *2859.11 p28*
Crawly, John; America, 1736 *4971 p45*
Crawly, Michaell; Virginia, 1641 *6219 p187*
Crawshaw, Rawleigh; Virginia, 1621 *6219 p4*
With wife
Crawson, James; St. John, N.B., 1847 *5704.8 p26*
Creadell, Eady; Virginia, 1648 *6219 p253*
Creak, Joseph 17; Pennsylvania, Virginia or Maryland, 1719 *3690.1 p55*
Creame, Samll.; Virginia, 1642 *6219 p193*
Creamer, William 35; New York, 1775 *1219.7 p246*
Creaser, Eliza.; Virginia, 1635 *6219 p32*
Creaser, Tho.; Virginia, 1634 *6219 p32*
Creathern, Mary 10; Massachusetts, 1850 *5881.1 p22*
Creatsener, Hance Yarah; Pennsylvania, 1743 *2444 p159*
Credden, John; America, 1868 *5704.8 p229*
Credy, Peter 25; Maryland, 1774 *1219.7 p230*
Creed, James; Newport, RI, 1765 *1219.7 p108*
Creed, Robert; Barbados, 1767 *1219.7 p129*
Creed, Thomas 21; Maryland, 1722 *3690.1 p55*
Creeden, Jeremiah; Quebec, 1837 *7036 p119*
Creeden, William 25; Newport, RI, 1851 *6508.5 p19*
Creek, Thomas; Jamaica, 1757 *1219.7 p58*
Creek, Thomas; Jamaica, 1757 *3690.1 p55*
Creen, Bridget 20; Massachusetts, 1849 *5881.1 p13*
Creenan, Daniel 34; Massachusetts, 1849 *5881.1 p15*
Creenan, Eliza 32; Massachusetts, 1849 *5881.1 p16*
Creenin, Honora 27; Massachusetts, 1848 *5881.1 p16*
Creese, William 22; Jamaica, 1736 *3690.1 p55*
Creger, Henry; New York, NY, 1836 *8208.4 p10*
Creger, Joseph; Illinois, 1859 *5012.38 p97*
Creighpaum, George; Ohio, 1839 *9892.11 p11*
Creighpaum, Jacob; Ohio, 1839 *9892.11 p11*
Creighton, Alexander 19; Quebec, 1859 *5704.8 p143*
Creighton, Catherine; Quebec, 1851 *5704.8 p73*
Creighton, Elleanor 20; Philadelphia, 1855 *5704.8 p124*
Creighton, Hugh; Philadelphia, 1848 *53.26 p17*
Creighton, Hugh; Philadelphia, 1848 *5704.8 p46*
Creighton, Isabella; Quebec, 1847 *5704.8 p27*
Creighton, James; Austin, TX, 1886 *9777 p5*
Creighton, James; New York, NY, 1816 *2859.11 p28*
Creighton, James; South Carolina, 1716 *1639.20 p51*
Creighton, James 33; Maryland, 1774 *1219.7 p193*
Creighton, John; Quebec, 1851 *5704.8 p73*
Creighton, John Morgan 42; California, 1872 *2769.3 p4*
Creighton, Mary; America, 1735-1743 *4971 p7*
Creighton, Robert 48; New Orleans, 1862 *543.30 p452*
Creiton, Ann 22; Philadelphia, 1833-1834 *53.26 p17*
*Relative:*Fanny 24
Creiton, Fanny 24 *SEE* Creiton, Ann
Crellin, John; Washington, 1859-1920 *2872.1 p9*
Cremin, Dennis 14; Massachusetts, 1849 *5881.1 p15*
Cremin, Pat. 23; Massachusetts, 1849 *5881.1 p24*
Cremmer, . . .; Pennsylvania, n.d. *1034.18 p13*
Cremmer, Elizabeth 6; Quebec, 1850 *5704.8 p66*
Cremmer, William 12; Quebec, 1850 *5704.8 p66*
Crenin, Catharine 25; Massachusetts, 1849 *5881.1 p14*
Crenin, Daniel 20; Massachusetts, 1849 *5881.1 p15*
Creron, James; Philadelphia, 1853 *5704.8 p101*
Crescent, . . .; Canada, 1776-1783 *9786 p42*
Crescent, A. D. 40; New Orleans, 1826 *778.5 p135*
Creslak, Feliksa 18; New York, 1912 *9980.29 p73*
Creslak, Ignacy; Long Island, 1912 *9980.29 p73*
Cresse, Isaac 21; Jamaica, 1736 *3690.1 p55*
Cressent, . . .; Canada, 1776-1783 *9786 p42*
Crestani, Vettore; Iowa, 1866-1943 *123.54 p61*
Creswell, Benjamin Samuel; Washington, 1859-1920 *2872.1 p9*
Creswell, Elizabeth *SEE* Creswell, James
Creswell, Elizabeth; Philadelphia, 1847 *5704.8 p14*
Creswell, Elizabeth 1 *SEE* Creswell, James
Creswell, Elizabeth 1; Philadelphia, 1847 *5704.8 p14*
Creswell, James; Philadelphia, 1847 *53.26 p17*
*Relative:*Elizabeth
*Relative:*Mary 8
*Relative:*Samuel 6
*Relative:*John 4
*Relative:*Elizabeth 1
Creswell, James; Philadelphia, 1847 *5704.8 p14*
Creswell, John; Philadelphia, 1852 *5704.8 p84*
Creswell, John 4 *SEE* Creswell, James
Creswell, John 4; Philadelphia, 1847 *5704.8 p14*
Creswell, Mary 8 *SEE* Creswell, James
Creswell, Mary 8; Philadelphia, 1847 *5704.8 p14*
Creswell, Mary Jane; Quebec, 1853 *5704.8 p104*
Creswell, Matilda; Philadelphia, 1851 *5704.8 p76*
Creswell, Samuel 6 *SEE* Creswell, James
Creswell, Samuel 6; Philadelphia, 1847 *5704.8 p14*
Creswell, William; Quebec, 1853 *5704.8 p104*
Crete, Jacques 30; America, 1831 *778.5 p135*
Cretelli, Giovanni 27; Arkansas, 1918 *95.2 p33*
Cretmick, Anton; Wisconsin, n.d. *9675.5 p50*
Creton, Rebecca; Quebec, 1847 *5704.8 p7*
Cretschmann, Christian; Canada, 1776-1783 *9786 p242*
Creutz, Jacob; America, 1846 *8582.3 p13*
Creutznacher, . . .; Canada, 1776-1783 *9786 p19*
Crevon, J. F. 48; New Orleans, 1821 *778.5 p135*
Crew, Humphrey 21; Jamaica, 1730 *3690.1 p55*
Crew, John 22; Philadelphia, 1774 *1219.7 p205*
Crew, Jon.; Virginia, 1642 *6219 p191*
Crew, Martin 29; Maryland, 1774 *1219.7 p229*
*Wife:*Mary 28
Crew, Marwood 22; Kansas, 1881 *5240.1 p63*
Crew, Mary 28 *SEE* Crew, Martin
Crew, William; Massachusetts, 1847 *5881.1 p26*
Crewe, Rebecca; Virginia, 1635 *6219 p16*
Criaux, M.; Port uncertain, 1832 *778.5 p135*
Crich, Rich.; Virginia, 1636 *6219 p75*
Crichton, David; America, 1879 *5240.1 p9*
Crichton, David 29; Kansas, 1906 *5240.1 p84*
Crichton, James; New York, NY, 1839 *8208.4 p92*
Crichton, James 17; Virginia, 1721 *3690.1 p55*
Crichton, John; Ohio, 1860 *2769.3 p3*
Crichton, William; Charleston, SC, 1780 *1639.20 p52*
Crichtoun, John; Carolina, 1684 *1639.20 p52*
Cricket, John 20; Virginia, 1718 *3690.1 p55*
Cricklock, Jon.; Virginia, 1642 *6219 p192*
Crief, John; Jamaica, 1776 *1219.7 p281*
Crigh, John; New York, NY, 1839 *8208.4 p94*
Crilley, Elizabeth; Philadelphia, 1850 *5704.8 p64*
Crilley, Mary Ann 24; St. John, N.B., 1862 *5704.8 p150*
Crilly, Eliza; St. John, N.B., 1847 *5704.8 p10*
Crilly, Jane 21; Philadelphia, 1864 *5704.8 p160*
Crilly, John; St. John, N.B., 1852 *5704.8 p83*
Crilly, Mary; St. John, N.B., 1847 *5704.8 p10*
Crily, John; Philadelphia, 1867 *5704.8 p223*
Crimes, Jonath 21; America, 1700 *2212 p25*
Crimm, Lorenz; South Carolina, 1788 *7119 p199*
Crimm, Zacharias; South Carolina, 1788 *7119 p199*
Crimmeen, Cornelius; America, 1741 *4971 p41*
Crimmeen, Margaret; America, 1741 *4971 p40*
Crimmis, James J.; Colorado, 1891 *9678.1 p159*
Crioyes, Leon 31; New Orleans, 1863 *543.30 p463*
Crippin, Kath.; Virginia, 1635 *6219 p71*
Cripps, John Splatt; Charles Town, SC, 1768 *1219.7 p137*
Cripps, Kath.; Virginia, 1635 *6219 p71*
Cripps, Sarah 25; Port uncertain, 1774 *1219.7 p176*
Crips, Eliza 20; Massachusetts, 1849 *5881.1 p15*
Crips, Nancy 20; Massachusetts, 1849 *5881.1 p23*

Crisman, Jacob; Ohio, 1844 ***9892.11*** *p11*
Crisman, Jacob; Ohio, 1847 ***9892.11*** *p11*
Crisp, Francis 25; Maryland, 1774 ***1219.7*** *p206*
Crisp, James; Indiana, 1837 ***9117*** *p15*
Crisp, William; Indiana, 1836 ***9117*** *p15*
Crispe, James; Virginia, 1643 ***6219*** *p200*
Crispe, John; Virginia, 1639 ***6219*** *p157*
Crispe, Jon.; Virginia, 1642 ***6219*** *p198*
Cristiano, Domenico 22; New York, NY, 1893 ***9026.4*** *p41*
Cristman, Jacob; Ohio, 1846 ***9892.11*** *p11*
Cristoff, Ruei; Arkansas, 1918 ***95.2*** *p33*
Critchley, John; California, 1879 ***2764.35*** *p12*
Crnkovich, Stjepan; Iowa, 1866-1943 ***123.54*** *p15*
Crnokrak, Nove; Arkansas, 1918 ***95.2*** *p33*
Croan, Henry; America, 1740 ***4971*** *p63*
Croat, G. William; Wisconsin, n.d. ***9675.5*** *p50*
Croat, Nicholas; Wisconsin, n.d. ***9675.5*** *p50*
Croat, William; Wisconsin, n.d. ***9675.5*** *p50*
Crobare, P. 23; Port uncertain, 1839 ***778.5*** *p135*
Crobat, Joseph A.; New Orleans, 1863 ***543.30*** *p463*
Crocen, John; America, 1742 ***4971*** *p50*
Crocker, James; Arkansas, 1918 ***95.2*** *p33*
Crocker, John 18; Philadelphia, 1774 ***1219.7*** *p197*
Crocker, Pascall; Virginia, 1635 ***6219*** *p5*
Crocker, Samuel 28; Kansas, 1873 ***5240.1*** *p54*
Crocket, George; Philadelphia, 1811 ***53.26*** *p17*
*Relative:*Samuel
Crocket, George; Philadelphia, 1811 ***2859.11*** *p10*
Crocket, Henry 21; Maryland, 1775 ***1219.7*** *p266*
Crocket, James; New York, NY, 1815 ***2859.11*** *p28*
Crocket, John; New York, NY, 1815 ***2859.11*** *p28*
Crocket, Samuel *SEE* Crocket, George
Crocket, Samuel; Philadelphia, 1811 ***2859.11*** *p10*
Crocket, William 74; North Carolina, 1850 ***1639.20*** *p52*
Crockett, Eliza 11; Quebec, 1847 ***5704.8*** *p27*
Crockett, George; Philadelphia, 1811 ***53.26*** *p17*
*Relative:*John
*Relative:*Robert
Crockett, George; Philadelphia, 1811 ***2859.11*** *p10*
Crockett, George; Quebec, 1847 ***5704.8*** *p27*
Crockett, Isabella 4; Quebec, 1847 ***5704.8*** *p27*
Crockett, James; South Carolina, 1665-1765 ***1639.20*** *p52*
Crockett, Jane 9 mos; Quebec, 1847 ***5704.8*** *p27*
Crockett, John *SEE* Crockett, George
Crockett, John; Charleston, SC, 1759 ***1639.20*** *p52*
Crockett, John; Philadelphia, 1811 ***2859.11*** *p10*
Crockett, John; South Carolina, 1716 ***1639.20*** *p52*
Crockett, Margaret Jane; Quebec, 1847 ***5704.8*** *p27*
Crockett, Nancy 7; Quebec, 1847 ***5704.8*** *p27*
Crockett, Robert *SEE* Crockett, George
Crockett, Robert; Philadelphia, 1811 ***2859.11*** *p10*
Crockett, Thomas W.; Colorado, 1903 ***9678.1*** *p159*
Croffeild, Robert; Virginia, 1638 ***6219*** *p160*
Croft, David; South Carolina, 1716 ***1639.20*** *p52*
Croft, Edward; Port uncertain, 1757 ***3690.1*** *p56*
Croft, Hen.; Virginia, 1637 ***6219*** *p8*
Croft, James; Pennsylvania, 1680 ***4962*** *p150*
Croft, Jon.; Virginia, 1635 ***6219*** *p27*
Croft, Jon.; Virginia, 1638 ***6219*** *p145*
Croft, Mary; Pennsylvania, 1680 ***4962*** *p150*
Crofts, Thomas; Indiana, 1848 ***9117*** *p16*
Croger, Jr. 27; Jamaica, 1774 ***1219.7*** *p190*
Crogh, Charles; Quebec, 1848 ***5704.8*** *p41*
Crogh, Charles 10; Quebec, 1848 ***5704.8*** *p41*
Crogh, Elizabeth 12; Quebec, 1848 ***5704.8*** *p41*
Crogh, James 3; Quebec, 1848 ***5704.8*** *p41*
Crogh, John; Quebec, 1848 ***5704.8*** *p41*
Crogh, Mary; Quebec, 1848 ***5704.8*** *p41*
Crogh, Mary Ann; Quebec, 1848 ***5704.8*** *p41*
Crogh, Robert 8; Quebec, 1848 ***5704.8*** *p41*
Crohare, P. 23; Port uncertain, 1839 ***778.5*** *p135*
Crohegan, Michael 20; Massachusetts, 1849 ***5881.1*** *p22*
Croiney, Thomas; Virginia, 1638 ***6219*** *p119*
Croise, J.; New Orleans, 1839 ***778.5*** *p135*
Croissart, Rene 42; America, 1839 ***778.5*** *p136*
Croix, James 15; Philadelphia, 1774 ***1219.7*** *p183*
Crolly, James; Quebec, 1849 ***5704.8*** *p57*
Crolly, Jermiah; Quebec, 1849 ***5704.8*** *p57*
Crolly, Peter; Montreal, 1825 ***7603*** *p101*
Cromartie, William; North Carolina, 1758 ***1639.20*** *p52*
Cromb, Elijah; South Carolina, 1788 ***7119*** *p199*
Cromer, Andrew 15 mos *SEE* Cromer, George
Cromer, George; South Carolina, 1752-1753 ***3689.17*** *p21*
With wife
*Relative:*John Michael 10
*Relative:*George 6
*Relative:*Andrew 15 mos
Cromer, George 6 *SEE* Cromer, George
Cromer, Godfrey; South Carolina, 1788 ***7119*** *p202*
Cromer, Godfrig; South Carolina, 1788 ***7119*** *p202*
Cromer, Hubert 28; America, 1838 ***778.5*** *p136*
Cromer, John Michael 10 *SEE* Cromer, George
Cromie, Alexander; St. John, N.B., 1847 ***5704.8*** *p20*
Cromie, Henry; St. John, N.B., 1847 ***5704.8*** *p20*
Cromie, Isaac 9; St. John, N.B., 1847 ***5704.8*** *p20*
Cromie, Martha; St. John, N.B., 1847 ***5704.8*** *p20*
Cromlish, Agnes 6 mos; Philadelphia, 1853 ***5704.8*** *p113*
Cromlish, Mary 32; Philadelphia, 1853 ***5704.8*** *p113*
Cromlish, Mary Jane 3; Philadelphia, 1853 ***5704.8*** *p113*
Cromlish, Philip 4; Philadelphia, 1853 ***5704.8*** *p113*
Crompton, Alice 25; America, 1705 ***2212*** *p44*
Crompton, Eliz; Virginia, 1698 ***2212*** *p13*
Crompton, Elizabeth 25; Maryland, 1775 ***1219.7*** *p249*
Cromwell, Gershon; Virginia, 1652 ***6251*** *p20*
Crona, Erenest; Colorado, 1900 ***9678.1*** *p159*
Crona, Sextus E.S.; Colorado, 1890 ***9678.1*** *p159*
Cronage, Jeremiah 17; America, 1699 ***2212*** *p29*
Cronan, John 35; New Orleans, 1863 ***543.30*** *p454*
Cronan, William; Washington, 1859-1920 ***2872.1*** *p9*
Cronau, Rudolf; America, 1855-1930 ***8125.8*** *p436*
Cronberger, Gertraud *SEE* Cronberger, Johann
Cronberger, Johann; Georgia, 1739 ***9332*** *p326*
*Wife:*Gertraud
Crone, Maria; Ohio, 1834-1839 ***8582.2*** *p59*
With family
Crone, Edward; Iowa, 1866-1943 ***123.54*** *p15*
Crone, John; Philadelphia, 1763 ***9973.7*** *p38*
Crone, William; New York, NY, 1811 ***2859.11*** *p10*
Croneen, Ellenor; America, 1742 ***4971*** *p54*
Croneen, Joan; America, 1736 ***4971*** *p44*
Croneen, Julian; America, 1736 ***4971*** *p43*
Croneen, Julian; America, 1736 ***4971*** *p45*
Cronen, Phillip; Wisconsin, n.d. ***9675.5*** *p50*
Croney, John 25; Maryland, 1725 ***3690.1*** *p56*
Cronie, Archie 20; Philadelphia, 1861 ***5704.8*** *p148*
Croniel, Timothy; Illinois, 1860 ***2896.5*** *p8*
Cronimus, Georg; New Orleans, 1820-1825 ***8582.3*** *p86*
With family
Cronimus, Jacob; Cincinnati, 1800-1877 ***8582.3*** *p86*
Cronin, Daniel 25; Massachusetts, 1849 ***5881.1*** *p15*
Cronin, Ellen 20; Massachusetts, 1849 ***5881.1*** *p15*
Cronin, Ellen 56; Arizona, 1914 ***9228.40*** *p18*
Cronin, Honora 16; Massachusetts, 1849 ***5881.1*** *p17*
Cronin, Johanna 20; Massachusetts, 1849 ***5881.1*** *p18*
Cronin, John; California, 1856 ***3840.1*** *p16*
Cronin, John 10; Massachusetts, 1849 ***5881.1*** *p18*
Cronin, John 20; Massachusetts, 1847 ***5881.1*** *p17*
Cronin, Margaret 23; Massachusetts, 1849 ***5881.1*** *p21*
Cronin, Margaret 25; Massachusetts, 1849 ***5881.1*** *p21*
Cronin, Michael 22; Massachusetts, 1849 ***5881.1*** *p21*
Cronin, Patrick; California, 1865 ***3840.1*** *p16*
Cronin, Stephen; New York, NY, 1811 ***2859.11*** *p10*
Cronin, Tim. 28; Massachusetts, 1849 ***5881.1*** *p25*
Cronin, Timothy 21; New Orleans, 1861-1865 ***543.30*** *p455*
Cronin, William 24; Massachusetts, 1849 ***5881.1*** *p26*
Cronin, William 60; Massachusetts, 1849 ***5881.1*** *p26*
Cronine, Edward R.; Ohio, 1847 ***9892.11*** *p11*
Cronise, Henry; America, 1867 ***6014.1*** *p1*
Cronkshaw, William; New York, NY, 1838 ***8208.4*** *p86*
Cronland, John W.; New York, NY, 1834 ***8208.4*** *p2*
Cronmiller, Martin; Philadelphia, 1762 ***9973.7*** *p37*
Cronne, . . .; Canada, 1776-1783 ***9786*** *p19*
Crook, David; Antigua (Antego), 1760 ***1219.7*** *p79*
Crook, John 22; Pennsylvania, 1738 ***3690.1*** *p56*
Crook, John 33; Maryland, 1775 ***1219.7*** *p250*
Crook, John 34; Maryland, 1775 ***1219.7*** *p251*
Crooke, James 13; Massachusetts, 1850 ***5881.1*** *p19*
Crooke, John 22; Pennsylvania, 1738 ***3690.1*** *p56*
Crooke, Sarah 25; Nevis, 1773 ***1219.7*** *p170*
Crooke, William; Virginia, 1636 ***6219*** *p15*
Crookneck, Nico.; Virginia, 1646 ***6219*** *p246*
Crooks, Andrew; St. John, N.B., 1847 ***5704.8*** *p35*
Crooks, James; Philadelphia, 1816 ***2859.11*** *p28*
Crooks, Samuel; Philadelphia, 1852 ***5704.8*** *p85*
Crookshank, James 22; Philadelphia, 1774 ***1219.7*** *p216*
Crookshanks, William; Jamaica, 1755 ***1219.7*** *p38*
Crookshanks, William; Jamaica, 1755 ***3690.1*** *p56*
Cropley, John 6 *SEE* Cropley, William
Cropley, William 33; Philadelphia, 1774 ***1219.7*** *p189*
*Son:*John 6
Cropp, Tho.; Virginia, 1629 ***6219*** *p8*
Crosan, Catherine; Quebec, 1847 ***5704.8*** *p12*
Crosbie, John; America, 1741 ***4971*** *p56*
Crosbie, Joseph 24; Maryland or Virginia, 1699 ***2212*** *p23*
Crosbie, Mary; New York, NY, 1864 ***5704.8*** *p185*
Crosby, Hen.; Virginia, 1642 ***6219*** *p198*
Crosby, Peter; West Virginia, 1856 ***9788.3*** *p7*
Crosby, Robert; New York, NY, 1816 ***2859.11*** *p28*
Crosby, Tho.; Virginia, 1637 ***6219*** *p8*
Crosby, Thomas; New York, NY, 1816 ***2859.11*** *p28*
Crosby, Timothy 28; Maryland, 1774 ***1219.7*** *p221*
Crosbye, Hen.; Virginia, 1635 ***6219*** *p71*
Crosfield, Anna 18; America, 1702 ***2212*** *p36*
Croshaw, Richd.; Virginia, 1643 ***6219*** *p207*
Croshen, Wm.; Virginia, 1637 ***6219*** *p110*
Croshow, Hugh 29; Barbados, 1737 ***3690.1*** *p56*
Crosia, Joseph; Virginia, 1637 ***6219*** *p82*
Crosier, Eliza; Baltimore, 1811 ***2859.11*** *p10*
Croskerry, James 16; Massachusetts, 1849 ***5881.1*** *p18*
Croskerry, Jane 12; Massachusetts, 1849 ***5881.1*** *p18*
Croskerry, Mary 18; Massachusetts, 1849 ***5881.1*** *p21*
Croskerry, Nancy 21; Massachusetts, 1849 ***5881.1*** *p23*
Croskerry, Thomas 10; Massachusetts, 1849 ***5881.1*** *p25*
Croskery, David 18 mos; Massachusetts, 1849 ***5881.1*** *p15*
Crosley, Sarah 21; Maryland, 1774 ***1219.7*** *p187*
Cross, Elizabeth; Philadelphia, 1811 ***53.26*** *p17*
Cross, Elizabeth; Philadelphia, 1811 ***2859.11*** *p10*
Cross, George Robert; New York, NY, 1837 ***8208.4*** *p34*
Cross, Henry 18; Maryland, 1718 ***3690.1*** *p56*
Cross, John; Illinois, 1868 ***7857*** *p3*
Cross, John 19; Virginia, 1774 ***1219.7*** *p201*
Cross, Joseph 20; Maryland, 1720 ***3690.1*** *p56*
Cross, Katherine; Virginia, 1643 ***6219*** *p206*
Cross, Margaret; New York, NY, 1815 ***2859.11*** *p28*
Cross, Nich.; Virginia, 1643 ***6219*** *p203*
Cross, Richard 16; Maryland, 1719 ***3690.1*** *p56*
Cross, Richard 38; Jamaica, 1774 ***1219.7*** *p219*
Cross, Thomas 18; Maryland, 1739 ***3690.1*** *p56*
Crossan, . . . 6 mos; St. John, N.B., 1847 ***5704.8*** *p26*
Crossan, Ann; St. John, N.B., 1849 ***5704.8*** *p49*
Crossan, Anne; St. John, N.B., 1847 ***5704.8*** *p26*
Crossan, Anne 10; Philadelphia, 1864 ***5704.8*** *p156*
Crossan, Barny; St. John, N.B., 1848 ***5704.8*** *p44*
Crossan, Catherine; Philadelphia, 1851 ***5704.8*** *p70*
Crossan, Catherine 7; St. John, N.B., 1847 ***5704.8*** *p3*
Crossan, Charles *SEE* Crossan, Charles
Crossan, Charles; Philadelphia, 1850 ***53.26*** *p17*
*Relative:*Charles
Crossan, Charles; Philadelphia, 1850 ***5704.8*** *p59*
Crossan, Cormick 40; Philadelphia, 1864 ***5704.8*** *p160*
Crossan, Domnick; St. John, N.B., 1849 ***5704.8*** *p56*
Crossan, Elleanor; St. John, N.B., 1847 ***5704.8*** *p3*
Crossan, Eugine; St. John, N.B., 1847 ***5704.8*** *p26*
Crossan, Hannah 16; Philadelphia, 1864 ***5704.8*** *p156*
Crossan, Hugh 4; St. John, N.B., 1847 ***5704.8*** *p26*
Crossan, Hugh 5; St. John, N.B., 1847 ***5704.8*** *p3*
Crossan, James; Philadelphia, 1853 ***5704.8*** *p102*
Crossan, James 22; Philadelphia, 1864 ***5704.8*** *p156*
Crossan, John; St. John, N.B., 1847 ***5704.8*** *p3*
Crossan, John; St. John, N.B., 1849 ***5704.8*** *p49*
Crossan, John; St. John, N.B., 1850 ***5704.8*** *p61*
Crossan, John 14; Philadelphia, 1864 ***5704.8*** *p156*
Crossan, Kate 46; Philadelphia, 1864 ***5704.8*** *p156*
Crossan, Margaret; Philadelphia, 1851 ***5704.8*** *p70*
Crossan, Margaret 18; Philadelphia, 1854 ***5704.8*** *p118*
Crossan, Mary 11; St. John, N.B., 1847 ***5704.8*** *p3*
Crossan, Mary 20; Philadelphia, 1864 ***5704.8*** *p156*
Crossan, Michael; New York, NY, 1815 ***2859.11*** *p28*
Crossan, Patrick; St. John, N.B., 1850 ***5704.8*** *p61*
Crossan, Rosonah 20; Philadelphia, 1854 ***5704.8*** *p116*
Crossan, Shelah 20; Philadelphia, 1864 ***5704.8*** *p155*
Crossan, Thomas 3; St. John, N.B., 1847 ***5704.8*** *p3*
Crossan, William; New York, NY, 1864 ***5704.8*** *p170*
Crossan, William; Quebec, 1851 ***5704.8*** *p74*
Crossan, William 16; Philadelphia, 1864 ***5704.8*** *p161*
Crosse, Katherine; Virginia, 1642 ***6219*** *p197*
Crossen, Ann 18; Philadelphia, 1860 ***5704.8*** *p144*
Crossen, Bernard 13; Quebec, 1847 ***5704.8*** *p30*
Crossen, Cornelius; Philadelphia, 1811 ***53.26*** *p17*
Crossen, Cornelius; Philadelphia, 1811 ***2859.11*** *p10*
Crossen, Edward; Quebec, 1847 ***5704.8*** *p30*
Crossen, Grace; Quebec, 1847 ***5704.8*** *p29*
Crossen, John 9; Quebec, 1847 ***5704.8*** *p30*
Crossen, Mary; New York, NY, 1866 ***5704.8*** *p208*
Crossen, Mary 6; Quebec, 1847 ***5704.8*** *p30*
Crossen, Mathew 9 mos; Quebec, 1847 ***5704.8*** *p30*
Crossen, Nancy 11; Quebec, 1847 ***5704.8*** *p30*
Crossen, Patrick; Quebec, 1847 ***5704.8*** *p29*
Crossen, William 4; Quebec, 1847 ***5704.8*** *p30*
Crossett, Andy 40; Massachusetts, 1850 ***5881.1*** *p13*
Crossin, Charles; Philadelphia, 1864 ***5704.8*** *p170*
Crossin, Elizabeth; Philadelphia, 1866 ***5704.8*** *p210*
Crossin, Patrick 20; Philadelphia, 1856 ***5704.8*** *p128*
Crossingham, Thomas; New York, NY, 1837 ***8208.4*** *p54*
Crossland, Geo.; Virginia, 1638 ***6219*** *p11*
Crossley, David; New York, NY, 1839 ***8208.4*** *p95*
Crossley, Esther 30; Quebec, 1864 ***5704.8*** *p163*
Crossley, John 32; Quebec, 1864 ***5704.8*** *p163*
Crossley, Leonard; America, 1773 ***1219.7*** *p167*
Crossley, William 7; Quebec, 1864 ***5704.8*** *p163*
Crossman, Charles 26; New Orleans, 1862 ***543.30*** *p451*
Crossman, William; Virginia, 1636 ***6219*** *p77*
Crossnall, Andrew 20; Maryland, 1729 ***3690.1*** *p56*
Crosson, Barney; Philadelphia, 1864 ***5704.8*** *p176*

Crosson, Bernard; Philadelphia, 1867 ***5704.8*** *p220*
Crosson, Charles; Philadelphia, 1865 ***5704.8*** *p201*
Crosson, Corneilus; America, 1868 ***5704.8*** *p229*
Crosson, Grace; New York, NY, 1864 ***5704.8*** *p170*
Crosson, Patrick; America, 1868 ***5704.8*** *p229*
Crosson, Patrick; Philadelphia, 1811 ***53.26*** *p17*
Crosson, Patrick; Philadelphia, 1811 ***2859.11*** *p10*
Crosson, Richard; Montreal, 1824 ***7603*** *p67*
Crosson, Sarah; Philadelphia, 1867 ***5704.8*** *p220*
Crosson, Thomas; Philadelphia, 1864 ***5704.8*** *p176*
Crosson, William; New York, NY, 1828 ***8208.4*** *p41*
Crosswhart, Ephraim 23; Antigua (Antego), 1737 ***3690.1*** *p56*
Croston, Ellen 17; America, 1705 ***2212*** *p42*
Croswell, Hanna 22; America, 1704 ***2212*** *p40*
Crothers, Ann *SEE* Crothers, John
Crothers, Hugh; New York, NY, 1811 ***2859.11*** *p10*
Crothers, James *SEE* Crothers, John
Crothers, John; Philadelphia, 1847 ***53.26*** *p17*
*Relative:*Ann
*Relative:*James
*Relative:*Mary Ann 11
*Relative:*Robert 9
*Relative:*John 6
Crothers, John 6 *SEE* Crothers, John
Crothers, Mary Ann 11 *SEE* Crothers, John
Crothers, Robert 9 *SEE* Crothers, John
Crothy, Patrick 15; Massachusetts, 1850 ***5881.1*** *p24*
Crothy, William 25; Massachusetts, 1849 ***5881.1*** *p26*
Crotty, Ellen 50; Massachusetts, 1850 ***5881.1*** *p16*
Crotty, Honor; America, 1736 ***4971*** *p39*
Crotty, Mary; America, 1741-1742 ***4971*** *p60*
Crotty, Michael; Quebec, 1822 ***7603*** *p100*
Crouch, Charles; Antigua (Antego), 1751 ***1219.7*** *p6*
Crouch, Edward; Kingston, Jamaica, 1766 ***1219.7*** *p123*
Crouch, Isaac William; South Carolina, 1759 ***1219.7*** *p72*
Crouch, James; Illinois, 1858 ***2896.5*** *p8*
Crouch, Margaret 27; Baltimore, 1775 ***1219.7*** *p271*
Crouch, Nicholas; Virginia, 1637 ***6219*** *p37*
Crouch, Thomas 25; Maryland, 1774 ***1219.7*** *p187*
Crouch, William; Illinois, 1877 ***2896.5*** *p8*
Crouch, Wm.; Virginia, 1635 ***6219*** *p20*
Crouch, Wm.; Virginia, 1637 ***6219*** *p112*
Crouere, Mr. 18; America, 1837 ***778.5*** *p136*
Crough, . . .; Virginia, 1643 ***6219*** *p229*
Crough, James; New York, NY, 1839 ***8208.4*** *p100*
Croutch, Tho.; Virginia, 1639 ***6219*** *p151*
Crouzet, John; Quebec, 1826 ***7603*** *p23*
Crow, Cornelius 48; Virginia, 1774 ***1219.7*** *p244*
Crow, Elizabeth; Quebec, 1847 ***5704.8*** *p12*
Crow, Francis; Quebec, 1847 ***5704.8*** *p12*
Crow, George 9 mos; Quebec, 1847 ***5704.8*** *p12*
Crow, Henry; Virginia, 1636 ***6219*** *p78*
Crow, Jane; New York, NY, 1811 ***2859.11*** *p10*
Crow, John; America, 1816 ***1639.20*** *p52*
Crow, John 3; Quebec, 1847 ***5704.8*** *p12*
Crow, Margaret; New York, NY, 1811 ***2859.11*** *p10*
Crow, Martha Jane 6; Quebec, 1847 ***5704.8*** *p12*
Crow, Mary 3; Quebec, 1847 ***5704.8*** *p12*
Crow, Mary 20; Philadelphia, 1858 ***5704.8*** *p139*
Crow, Mary Ann 10; Quebec, 1847 ***5704.8*** *p12*
Crow, Owen; America, 1739 ***4971*** *p27*
Crow, Robert 13; Quebec, 1847 ***5704.8*** *p12*
Crow, Susan 20; St. John, N.B., 1859 ***5704.8*** *p140*
Crow, William; New York, NY, 1811 ***2859.11*** *p10*
Crowblehome, J. 48; Ohio, 1826 ***778.5*** *p136*
Crowden, Samuel 22; Jamaica, 1774 ***1219.7*** *p189*
Crowe, Eleonore; Montreal, 1824 ***7603*** *p98*
Crowe, Ellen 40; Massachusetts, 1849 ***5881.1*** *p15*
Crowe, Martin 10; Massachusetts, 1850 ***5881.1*** *p23*
Crowe, Mary 10; Massachusetts, 1850 ***5881.1*** *p23*
Crowe, Patrick; Montreal, 1823 ***7603*** *p98*
Crowe, William 26; Harris Co., TX, 1898 ***6254*** *p5*
Croweldon, John; Virginia, 1636 ***6219*** *p7*
Crowley, Alice 25; Massachusetts, 1847 ***5881.1*** *p12*
Crowley, Bridget 20; Massachusetts, 1849 ***5881.1*** *p13*
Crowley, Catharine 7; Massachusetts, 1849 ***5881.1*** *p14*
Crowley, Catharine 50; Massachusetts, 1849 ***5881.1*** *p14*
Crowley, Charles; America, 1736 ***4971*** *p39*
Crowley, Cornelius 25; Massachusetts, 1849 ***5881.1*** *p14*
Crowley, Dan 11; Massachusetts, 1847 ***5881.1*** *p14*
Crowley, Daniel; America, 1736 ***4971*** *p39*
Crowley, Daniel; New York, NY, 1838 ***8208.4*** *p68*
Crowley, Dennis; America, 1741 ***4971*** *p41*
Crowley, Eliza 5; Massachusetts, 1849 ***5881.1*** *p16*
Crowley, Ellen 30; Newport, RI, 1851 ***6508.5*** *p19*
Crowley, Harry 44; Massachusetts, 1849 ***5881.1*** *p17*
Crowley, James 7; Massachusetts, 1847 ***5881.1*** *p17*
Crowley, Jeremiah; New York, NY, 1838 ***8208.4*** *p81*
Crowley, Jerry 50; Massachusetts, 1849 ***5881.1*** *p18*
Crowley, Johanna 22; Massachusetts, 1849 ***5881.1*** *p19*
Crowley, John; New York, NY, 1836 ***8208.4*** *p79*
Crowley, John; New York, NY, 1838 ***8208.4*** *p64*
Crowley, Judith 20; Massachusetts, 1849 ***5881.1*** *p19*
Crowley, Margaret 24; Massachusetts, 1850 ***5881.1*** *p23*
Crowley, Mary 5; Massachusetts, 1849 ***5881.1*** *p22*
Crowley, Mary 6; Massachusetts, 1849 ***5881.1*** *p21*
Crowley, Mary 9; Massachusetts, 1847 ***5881.1*** *p20*
Crowley, Mary 10; Massachusetts, 1850 ***5881.1*** *p23*
Crowley, Mary 40; Massachusetts, 1849 ***5881.1*** *p22*
Crowley, Michael 10; Massachusetts, 1849 ***5881.1*** *p22*
Crowley, Michael 24; Massachusetts, 1847 ***5881.1*** *p20*
Crowley, Pat. 13; Massachusetts, 1847 ***5881.1*** *p23*
Crowley, Patrick 2; Massachusetts, 1849 ***5881.1*** *p24*
Crowley, Patrick 6; Massachusetts, 1850 ***5881.1*** *p24*
Crowley, Robert; New York, NY, 1840 ***8208.4*** *p104*
Crowley, Susan 45; Massachusetts, 1847 ***5881.1*** *p25*
Crowley, Susannah; America, 1736 ***4971*** *p45*
Crowley, Timothy; New York, NY, 1834 ***8208.4*** *p33*
Crowley, Timothy; New York, NY, 1840 ***8208.4*** *p104*
Crowley, Timothy 50; Massachusetts, 1848 ***5881.1*** *p25*
Crowley, William 34; Massachusetts, 1849 ***5881.1*** *p26*
Crowly, Susanna; America, 1736 ***4971*** *p44*
Crown, Henry 43; Maryland, 1774 ***1219.7*** *p192*
Crowther, John 47; West Virginia, 1844 ***9788.3*** *p7*
Croxen, Thomas; Illinois, 1869 ***5012.38*** *p99*
Croxford, Joseph 23; Virginia, 1774 ***1219.7*** *p241*
Croxon, Alice; Virginia, 1636 ***6219*** *p75*
Croxon, Alice; Virginia, 1638 ***6219*** *p181*
Crozarde, J. B. 27; Port uncertain, 1839 ***778.5*** *p136*
Crozecz, Ivan; Iowa, 1866-1943 ***123.54*** *p15*
Crozet, Eliza 18; Port uncertain, 1839 ***778.5*** *p136*
Crozier, Ann Jane; Quebec, 1852 ***5704.8*** *p89*
Crozier, Christopher 13; Quebec, 1852 ***5704.8*** *p89*
Crozier, Eliza; New York, NY, 1811 ***2859.11*** *p10*
Crozier, Eliza; Quebec, 1852 ***5704.8*** *p89*
Crozier, Elizabeth; Quebec, 1852 ***5704.8*** *p89*
Crozier, John; Quebec, 1852 ***5704.8*** *p91*
Crozier, John 4; Quebec, 1852 ***5704.8*** *p89*
Crozier, Mary; Quebec, 1852 ***5704.8*** *p89*
Crozier, Richard; New York, NY, 1811 ***2859.11*** *p10*
Crozier, William 10; Quebec, 1852 ***5704.8*** *p89*
Cruau, G. 55; New Orleans, 1823 ***778.5*** *p136*
Cruche, J. 34; America, 1839 ***778.5*** *p136*
Crue, Diederick; New York, NY, 1836 ***8208.4*** *p16*
Cruger, Dederick; New York, NY, 1840 ***8208.4*** *p110*
Cruger, Friedrich D.; Charleston, SC, 1775-1781 ***8582.2*** *p52*
Cruger, Joseph; Illinois, 1859 ***5012.38*** *p97*
Cruhin, Ferdinand; Wisconsin, n.d. ***9675.5*** *p50*
Cruickshanks, George; Quebec, 1817 ***1639.20*** *p53*
Cruickshanks, George; South Carolina, 1818 ***1639.20*** *p53*
Cruikshanks, James; South Carolina, 1823 ***1639.20*** *p53*
Cruikshanks, William; Charleston, SC, 1793 ***1639.20*** *p53*
Cruise, James W.; New York, NY, 1839 ***8208.4*** *p102*
Cruise, Martha; Quebec, 1850 ***5704.8*** *p63*
Crum, David; South Carolina, 1788 ***7119*** *p197*
Crumblish, Michael; New York, NY, 1866 ***5704.8*** *p207*
Crumblisk, Charles; Philadelphia, 1864 ***5704.8*** *p184*
Crumley, Eleanor; Philadelphia, 1816 ***2859.11*** *p28*
With sister
Crumley, Rebecca 20; Philadelphia, 1860 ***5704.8*** *p145*
Crumlish, Ann; St. John, N.B., 1853 ***5704.8*** *p108*
Crumlish, Catherine; Philadelphia, 1851 ***5704.8*** *p81*
Crumlish, Ellen 50; Philadelphia, 1854 ***5704.8*** *p120*
Crumlish, John; Philadelphia, 1864 ***5704.8*** *p187*
Crumlish, Margaret; Philadelphia, 1851 ***5704.8*** *p79*
Crumlish, Matilda 20; Philadelphia, 1854 ***5704.8*** *p120*
Crumlish, Patrick; Philadelphia, 1869 ***5704.8*** *p236*
Crumlish, Thomas 50; Philadelphia, 1854 ***5704.8*** *p120*
Crumlisk, Mary; Philadelphia, 1850 ***53.26*** *p17*
Crumlisk, Mary; Philadelphia, 1850 ***5704.8*** *p69*
Crummer, Ann; Baltimore, 1811 ***2859.11*** *p10*
Crummer, Cathar.; Baltimore, 1811 ***2859.11*** *p10*
Crummer, Letitia; Baltimore, 1811 ***2859.11*** *p10*
Crummer, Mary; Baltimore, 1811 ***2859.11*** *p10*
Crummer, Nathl.; Baltimore, 1811 ***2859.11*** *p10*
Crummer, Saml.; Baltimore, 1811 ***2859.11*** *p10*
Crummin, William; Quebec, 1850 ***5704.8*** *p67*
Crump, Elizabeth 37; Kansas, 1879 ***5240.1*** *p60*
Crump, Giles; Virginia, 1637 ***6219*** *p11*
Crump, John; New York, NY, 1838 ***8208.4*** *p74*
Crump, Thomas; Montreal, 1769 ***7603*** *p21*
Crumpe, Thomas; Virginia, 1635 ***6219*** *p71*
Crumpler, Daniel 26; Maryland, 1775 ***1219.7*** *p257*
Crunedge, Henry 18; Maryland, 1774 ***1219.7*** *p208*
Cruney, Pat. 20; Massachusetts, 1849 ***5881.1*** *p24*
Cruse, Henry *SEE* Cruse, James
Cruse, Henry; Philadelphia, 1848 ***5704.8*** *p40*
Cruse, James; Philadelphia, 1848 ***53.26*** *p17*
*Relative:*Henry
Cruse, James; Philadelphia, 1848 ***5704.8*** *p40*
Cruse, Philipp Sigesmund; Quebec, 1776 ***9786*** *p263*
Cruse, Robert 35; Maryland, 1774 ***1219.7*** *p221*
Crut, John 36; Maryland, 1775 ***1219.7*** *p250*
Crutchfield, John; Pensacola, FL, 1766 ***1219.7*** *p119*
Cruz, Jesus 92; Arizona, 1914 ***9228.40*** *p19*
Cruz, Jose 30; Arizona, 1925 ***9228.40*** *p29*
Cruz, Jose 50; Port uncertain, 1839 ***778.5*** *p136*
Cruzbauer, Ms. 40; New Orleans, 1839 ***778.5*** *p136*
Cruzbauer, Armantine 8; New Orleans, 1839 ***778.5*** *p136*
Cruzbauer, Arthur 18 mos; New Orleans, 1839 ***778.5*** *p136*
Cruzbauer, Clodine 10; New Orleans, 1839 ***778.5*** *p136*
Cruzbauer, Otelli 14; New Orleans, 1839 ***778.5*** *p136*
Cryan, Bridget; New York, NY, 1816 ***2859.11*** *p28*
Cryan, Catharine; New York, NY, 1816 ***2859.11*** *p28*
Cryan, James; New York, NY, 1816 ***2859.11*** *p28*
Cryan, Martin; New York, NY, 1816 ***2859.11*** *p28*
Cryan, Mary; New York, NY, 1816 ***2859.11*** *p28*
Cryan, Michael; New York, NY, 1816 ***2859.11*** *p28*
Cryan, Michael 10; Massachusetts, 1850 ***5881.1*** *p23*
Cryan, Patrick; New York, NY, 1816 ***2859.11*** *p28*
Cryan, Timothy; New York, NY, 1816 ***2859.11*** *p28*
Cryder, Johannes *SEE* Cryder, Michael
Cryder, Michael; Ohio, 1796 ***8582.2*** *p57*
*Brother:*Johannes
Csaki, Ferencz; Ohio, 1905-1936 ***9892.11*** *p8*
Cubbert, Isaac; New York, NY, 1811 ***2859.11*** *p10*
Cubler, Jacob; Virginia, 1775 ***1219.7*** *p275*
Cucchiara, Baldasare; Iowa, 1866-1943 ***123.54*** *p61*
Cuckerson, Thomas 17; Boston, 1774 ***1219.7*** *p188*
Cuckney, Henry; Virginia, 1639 ***6219*** *p161*
Cuculich, Martin; Iowa, 1866-1943 ***123.54*** *p15*
Cue, Patrick 22; Philadelphia, 1803 ***53.26*** *p17*
Cueni, Bonaventura 46; Kansas, 1892 ***5240.1*** *p9*
Cueni, Bonaventura 46; Kansas, 1892 ***5240.1*** *p76*
Cuenod, Adrian 22; Kansas, 1876 ***5240.1*** *p9*
Cuenoll, Advieu 22; Kansas, 1876 ***5240.1*** *p57*
Cuff, Anthony 27; Massachusetts, 1849 ***5881.1*** *p13*
Cuff, Lawrence 25; Massachusetts, 1849 ***5881.1*** *p20*
Cugley, John; Virginia, 1635 ***6219*** *p23*
Cugly, Loughlin; America, 1735-1743 ***4971*** *p79*
Cugly, Michael; Montreal, 1823 ***7603*** *p101*
Cugne, Guillaume 48; Halifax, N.S., 1752 ***7074.6*** *p207*
With family of 6
Cugot, Mr. 25; Port uncertain, 1836 ***778.5*** *p136*
Culane, Daniel; America, 1741 ***4971*** *p40*
Culberson, William 35; Jamaica, 1730 ***3690.1*** *p289*
Culbert, Catherine 10; St. John, N.B., 1850 ***5704.8*** *p65*
Culbert, Ellen 15; Philadelphia, 1855 ***5704.8*** *p123*
Culbert, Fanny 18; St. John, N.B., 1854 ***5704.8*** *p122*
Culbert, George; Philadelphia, 1811 ***53.26*** *p17*
Culbert, George; Philadelphia, 1811 ***2859.11*** *p10*
Culbert, Hannah; Philadelphia, 1851 ***5704.8*** *p71*
Culbert, James 20; Massachusetts, 1848 ***5881.1*** *p17*
Culbert, Jane; Philadelphia, 1850 ***5704.8*** *p64*
Culbert, John 20; Wilmington, DE, 1831 ***6508.3*** *p101*
Culbert, Margaret 20; Philadelphia, 1853 ***5704.8*** *p108*
Culbert, Martha 20; St. John, N.B., 1854 ***5704.8*** *p114*
Culbert, Matthew; St. John, N.B., 1850 ***5704.8*** *p65*
Culbert, Samuel; Philadelphia, 1852 ***5704.8*** *p85*
Culbert, William 18; Philadelphia, 1853 ***5704.8*** *p108*
Culbertson, James; Philadelphia, 1850 ***5704.8*** *p64*
Culborson, Lawrence 17; Jamaica, 1731 ***3690.1*** *p56*
Culbreth, Archibald; America, 1792 ***1639.20*** *p53*
Culham, Thomas; Montreal, 1815 ***7603*** *p86*
Culhane, James 28; Kansas, 1874 ***5240.1*** *p9*
Culhane, James 28; Kansas, 1874 ***5240.1*** *p55*
Culhane, Patrick 30; Kansas, 1880 ***5240.1*** *p62*
Culin, Madame 60; New Orleans, 1835 ***778.5*** *p137*
Culin, Mlle. 20; New Orleans, 1835 ***778.5*** *p137*
Cull, John 20; Massachusetts, 1849 ***5881.1*** *p19*
Cullacott, John J.F.; Colorado, 1880 ***9678.1*** *p159*
Cullan, Peter; Ohio, 1840 ***9892.11*** *p11*
Cullane, Maurice; America, 1742 ***4971*** *p56*
Cullen, Allen; New York, NY, 1816 ***2859.11*** *p28*
Cullen, Catherine 18; Philadelphia, 1859 ***5704.8*** *p141*
Cullen, Catherine 26; Philadelphia, 1864 ***5704.8*** *p157*
Cullen, Fennal; America, 1739 ***4971*** *p63*
Cullen, Francis 16; Philadelphia, 1804 ***53.26*** *p17*
Cullen, George; America, 1741 ***4971*** *p35*
Cullen, Hugh 23; St. John, N.B., 1858 ***5704.8*** *p140*
Cullen, James; America, 1738 ***4971*** *p9*
Cullen, James; Ohio, 1840 ***9892.11*** *p12*
Cullen, James; Philadelphia, 1811 ***53.26*** *p17*
Cullen, James; Wisconsin, n.d. ***9675.5*** *p50*
Cullen, John; America, 1736 ***4971*** *p81*
Cullen, John; New York, NY, 1864 ***5704.8*** *p186*
Cullen, John; New York, NY, 1866 ***5704.8*** *p208*
Cullen, Margaret 10; New York, NY, 1864 ***5704.8*** *p186*
Cullen, Maria 8; Massachusetts, 1849 ***5881.1*** *p22*
Cullen, Mary; New York, NY, 1815 ***2859.11*** *p28*
Cullen, Mary 18; Quebec, 1856 ***5704.8*** *p129*
Cullen, Michael; Illinois, 1858 ***2896.5*** *p8*
Cullen, Michael; Virginia, 1852 ***4626.16*** *p14*
Cullen, Neal 15; Philadelphia, 1856 ***5704.8*** *p128*

98 *FOR A COMPLETE EXPLANATION OF ENTRY, SEE "HOW TO READ A CITATION" SECTION*

Cullen, Pat. 25; Massachusetts, 1849 ***5881.1*** *p24*
Cullen, Patrick 20; Massachusetts, 1848 ***5881.1*** *p24*
Cullen, Peter; America, 1738 ***4971*** *p99*
Cullen, Richard; Illinois, 1858 ***2896.5*** *p9*
Cullen, Sarah; New York, NY, 1864 ***5704.8*** *p186*
Cullen, Teresa 20; Massachusetts, 1849 ***5881.1*** *p26*
Cullen, Thomas 22; Quebec, 1856 ***5704.8*** *p129*
Cullen, William 19; Maryland, 1723 ***3690.1*** *p57*
Cullenan, Catharine 26; Massachusetts, 1849 ***5881.1*** *p14*
Culley, James S. 48; Kansas, 1879 ***5240.1*** *p61*
Cullin, Fergal; America, 1740 ***4971*** *p75*
Cullin, James; Philadelphia, 1811 ***2859.11*** *p10*
Cullin, Joane; Virginia, 1642 ***6219*** *p196*
Cullin, John; New York, NY, 1811 ***2859.11*** *p10*
Cullin, Mary; Philadelphia, 1866 ***5704.8*** *p207*
Cullin, Naller 25; Philadelphia, 1858 ***5704.8*** *p138*
Cullinn, Margaret 19; Philadelphia, 1858 ***5704.8*** *p139*
Cullion, Biddy; Philadelphia, 1853 ***5704.8*** *p100*
Cullion, John; Philadelphia, 1853 ***5704.8*** *p103*
Cullion, Patrick; Philadelphia, 1853 ***5704.8*** *p100*
Cullion, William 10; St. John, N.B., 1854 ***5704.8*** *p121*
Cullitagh, Dennis; America, 1736 ***4971*** *p39*
Cullmann, George; New York, NY, 1836 ***8208.4*** *p15*
Cullnagh, Thomas; America, 1735-1743 ***4971*** *p78*
Culloghty, Owen; America, 1742 ***4971*** *p49*
Cullon, William 19; Maryland, 1724 ***3690.1*** *p57*
Cullue, Patrick; America, 1741-1742 ***4971*** *p60*
Cullum, D. G.; Washington, 1859-1920 ***2872.1*** *p9*
Cullumbine, Rich.; Virginia, 1635 ***6219*** *p3*
Cully, James; New York, NY, 1838 ***8208.4*** *p89*
Culmann, Daniel; New York, 1880 ***1450.2*** *p7B*
Culnane, Mary 20; Massachusetts, 1849 ***5881.1*** *p21*
Culp, Philip; Philadelphia Co., PA, 1765 ***4779.3*** *p13*
Culpeper, Jno.; Virginia, 1646 ***6219*** *p246*
Culpin, Mr.; Quebec, 1815 ***9229.18*** *p76*
With wife
Culter, Margaret 21; Philadelphia, 1857 ***5704.8*** *p132*
Culver, John 19; Jamaica, 1722 ***3690.1*** *p57*
Cuming, . . .; South Carolina, 1684 ***1639.20*** *p53*
Cuming, Alfred G. 25; Kansas, 1895 ***5240.1*** *p80*
Cummack, James 10 mos; Massachusetts, 1849 ***5881.1*** *p18*
Cummack, Margaret 34; Massachusetts, 1849 ***5881.1*** *p21*
Cummack, Walter 3; Massachusetts, 1849 ***5881.1*** *p26*
Cummin, Edmond; America, 1736-1743 ***4971*** *p57*
Cummin, Patrick; America, 1740 ***4971*** *p70*
Cumming, Alexander; Illinois, 1860-1869 ***5012.38*** *p98*
Cumming, Charles 26; Maryland, 1775 ***1219.7*** *p262*
Cumming, Elizabeth; Montreal, 1822 ***7603*** *p64*
Cumming, Hans; New York, NY, 1815 ***2859.11*** *p28*
Cumming, Isobella Nichol *SEE* Cumming, James
Cumming, James; America, 1832 ***8893*** *p265*
*Wife:*Isobella Nichol
Cumming, James, Jr.; Petersburg, VA, 1808-1812 ***4778.1*** *p150*
Cumming, Robert; South Carolina, 1749 ***1639.20*** *p53*
Cumming, Tho.; New York, NY, 1815 ***2859.11*** *p28*
Cumming, Thomas, Jr.; New York, NY, 1836 ***8208.4*** *p17*
Cumming, William 21; Kansas, 1883 ***5240.1*** *p64*
Cummings, Alexander; Illinois, 1860-1869 ***5012.38*** *p98*
Cummings, Catharine; New York, NY, 1865 ***5704.8*** *p195*
Cummings, Edw. 7; Massachusetts, 1849 ***5881.1*** *p15*
Cummings, Eliza 20; St. John, N.B., 1858 ***5704.8*** *p137*
Cummings, James 38; Massachusetts, 1850 ***5881.1*** *p19*
Cummings, John; New York, NY, 1811 ***2859.11*** *p10*
Cummings, John; New York, NY, 1834 ***8208.4*** *p49*
Cummings, John; Philadelphia, 1811 ***53.26*** *p17*
Cummings, John; Philadelphia, 1811 ***2859.11*** *p10*
Cummings, Mary 22; Massachusetts, 1850 ***5881.1*** *p23*
Cummings, Michael 5; Massachusetts, 1849 ***5881.1*** *p21*
Cummings, Michael 25; New Orleans, 1862 ***543.30*** *p451*
Cummings, Sophia; Philadelphia, 1852 ***5704.8*** *p92*
Cummings, Thomas 24; Massachusetts, 1849 ***5881.1*** *p25*
Cummins, Catherine; New York, NY, 1816 ***2859.11*** *p28*
Cummins, James J. 47; Kansas, 1892 ***5240.1*** *p77*
Cummins, Jeremiah; New York, NY, 1834 ***8208.4*** *p58*
Cummins, Mary 19; Newport, RI, 1851 ***6508.5*** *p19*
Cummins, Thomas; New York, NY, 1816 ***2859.11*** *p28*
Cummiskey, James; America, 1841 ***7036*** *p124*
Cummiskey, John; America, 1841 ***7036*** *p124*
Cummiskey, Owen; America, 1841 ***7036*** *p124*
Cumpston, Henry; Illinois, 1871 ***5012.39*** *p25*
Cunard, Mr.; Quebec, 1815 ***9229.18*** *p82*
Cunard, Mr. 30; New Orleans, 1835 ***778.5*** *p137*
Cunaugh, Mary 6; Massachusetts, 1849 ***5881.1*** *p21*
Cunco, Maria 18; New York, NY, 1893 ***9026.4*** *p41*
Cundall, Benjamin; New York, NY, 1836 ***8208.4*** *p80*
Cunder, Joseph; Illinois, 1858 ***2896.5*** *p9*
Cundez, Jacques 20; Port uncertain, 1836 ***778.5*** *p137*
Cuneo, Andrew; America, 1859 ***6014.1*** *p1*
Cuniff, Mary 9; Massachusetts, 1849 ***5881.1*** *p21*
Cuniff, Peter 7; Massachusetts, 1849 ***5881.1*** *p24*
Cuninghorm, Jon.; Virginia, 1637 ***6219*** *p113*
Cunliffe, Esther 28; Maryland, 1775 ***1219.7*** *p264*
Cunliffe, J.W. 22; Virginia, 1775 ***1219.7*** *p247*
Cunliffe, John 27; New York, 1774 ***1219.7*** *p203*
Cunn, Peggy; Quebec, 1847 ***5704.8*** *p28*
Cunnay, Thomas; New York, NY, 1816 ***2859.11*** *p28*
Cunney, Hannah; Philadelphia, 1867 ***5704.8*** *p220*
Cunney, Henry; Virginia, 1639 ***6219*** *p162*
Cunnick, Robert 21; Port uncertain, 1774 ***1219.7*** *p176*
Cunnie, Edward; Philadelphia, 1851 ***5704.8*** *p76*
Cunniff, John 22; St. John, N.B., 1866 ***5704.8*** *p166*
Cunniff, Patrick; Albany, NY, 1841 ***7036*** *p119*
Cunniff, Patrick 35; St. John, N.B., 1866 ***5704.8*** *p166*
Cunnigham, Roger 30; Newport, RI, 1851 ***6508.5*** *p19*
Cunning, Isabella; Philadelphia, 1864 ***5704.8*** *p179*
Cunning, Margaret 20; Philadelphia, 1853 ***5704.8*** *p108*
Cunning, Mary; Philadelphia, 1864 ***5704.8*** *p179*
Cunningham, Adam; Philadelphia, 1852 ***5704.8*** *p85*
Cunningham, Alexander; New York, NY, 1815 ***2859.11*** *p28*
Cunningham, Alexander; Quebec, 1852 ***5704.8*** *p94*
Cunningham, Alexander 9 mos; Quebec, 1847 ***5704.8*** *p16*
Cunningham, Andrew; Quebec, 1847 ***5704.8*** *p16*
Cunningham, Andrew 14; St. John, N.B., 1861 ***5704.8*** *p149*
Cunningham, Ann; Philadelphia, 1868 ***5704.8*** *p226*
Cunningham, Anne; New York, NY, 1871 ***5704.8*** *p240*
Cunningham, Anne 18; Quebec, 1863 ***5704.8*** *p153*
Cunningham, Betty 7; Quebec, 1847 ***5704.8*** *p16*
Cunningham, Bridget 30; Massachusetts, 1849 ***5881.1*** *p13*
Cunningham, C.; New York, NY, 1811 ***2859.11*** *p10*
Cunningham, Catharine; Quebec, 1849 ***5704.8*** *p51*
Cunningham, Catharine 5; Massachusetts, 1849 ***5881.1*** *p14*
Cunningham, Catherine; St. John, N.B., 1847 ***5704.8*** *p35*
Cunningham, Charles 11; Quebec, 1847 ***5704.8*** *p16*
Cunningham, Charles, Jr.; New York, NY, 1840 ***8208.4*** *p104*
Cunningham, Christopher 6; Quebec, 1852 ***5704.8*** *p94*
Cunningham, Coudy; New York, NY, 1811 ***2859.11*** *p10*
Cunningham, Dan; New York, NY, 1811 ***2859.11*** *p10*
Cunningham, David; New York, NY, 1835 ***8208.4*** *p40*
Cunningham, Edward; Quebec, 1852 ***5704.8*** *p94*
Cunningham, Eliza 7; St. John, N.B., 1861 ***5704.8*** *p149*
Cunningham, Eliza 13; Quebec, 1852 ***5704.8*** *p94*
Cunningham, Eliza A. 40; St. John, N.B., 1861 ***5704.8*** *p149*
Cunningham, Eliza Jane; Quebec, 1851 ***5704.8*** *p74*
Cunningham, Elizabeth; Quebec, 1847 ***5704.8*** *p16*
Cunningham, Elizabeth 18; Philadelphia, 1854 ***5704.8*** *p116*
Cunningham, Ellan 9; Quebec, 1847 ***5704.8*** *p16*
Cunningham, Ellen 21; Massachusetts, 1847 ***5881.1*** *p15*
Cunningham, Fanny Ann 17; St. John, N.B., 1861 ***5704.8*** *p149*
Cunningham, Frances; New York, NY, 1811 ***2859.11*** *p10*
Cunningham, Francis; Philadelphia, 1866 ***5704.8*** *p209*
Cunningham, Frank John; Arkansas, 1918 ***95.2*** *p33*
Cunningham, George; New York, NY, 1839 ***8208.4*** *p103*
Cunningham, George; South Carolina, 1716 ***1639.20*** *p53*
Cunningham, George 20; Philadelphia, 1854 ***5704.8*** *p116*
Cunningham, Henry 24; St. John, N.B., 1851 ***5704.8*** *p72*
Cunningham, Honora 11; Massachusetts, 1847 ***5881.1*** *p16*
Cunningham, Hugh; New York, NY, 1811 ***2859.11*** *p10*
Cunningham, Hugh; Philadelphia, 1851 ***5704.8*** *p70*
Cunningham, Hugh; Quebec, 1847 ***5704.8*** *p36*
Cunningham, Hugh 24; St. John, N.B., 1855 ***5704.8*** *p127*
Cunningham, J.; New York, NY, 1811 ***2859.11*** *p10*
Cunningham, James; New York, NY, 1816 ***2859.11*** *p28*
Cunningham, James; Ohio, 1819 ***8582.1*** *p47*
Cunningham, James; Ohio, 1840 ***9892.11*** *p12*
Cunningham, James 9; Quebec, 1852 ***5704.8*** *p94*
Cunningham, James 17; Philadelphia, 1854 ***5704.8*** *p116*
Cunningham, James 17; Philadelphia, 1856 ***5704.8*** *p128*
Cunningham, James 22; Quebec, 1864 ***5704.8*** *p160*
Cunningham, James 28; Massachusetts, 1847 ***5881.1*** *p17*
Cunningham, Jane; St. John, N.B., 1847 ***5704.8*** *p35*
Cunningham, Jane 12; Philadelphia, 1848 ***53.26*** *p17*
*Relative:*Robert 10
Cunningham, Jane 12; Philadelphia, 1848 ***5704.8*** *p46*
Cunningham, Jane 20; Quebec, 1863 ***5704.8*** *p153*
Cunningham, Jane 22; Philadelphia, 1864 ***5704.8*** *p155*
Cunningham, Jean-Adam; Quebec, 1819 ***7603*** *p41*
Cunningham, Johannah 5; Quebec, 1852 ***5704.8*** *p94*
Cunningham, John *SEE* Cunningham, John
Cunningham, John; New York, NY, 1811 ***2859.11*** *p10*
Cunningham, John; New York, NY, 1865 ***5704.8*** *p190*
Cunningham, John; Ohio, 1840 ***9892.11*** *p12*
Cunningham, John; Philadelphia, 1815 ***2859.11*** *p28*
Cunningham, John; Philadelphia, 1848 ***53.26*** *p17*
*Relative:*Mary
*Relative:*John
Cunningham, John; Philadelphia, 1848 ***5704.8*** *p45*
Cunningham, John; Philadelphia, 1853 ***5704.8*** *p100*
Cunningham, John; St. John, N.B., 1847 ***5704.8*** *p15*
Cunningham, John; St. John, N.B., 1848 ***5704.8*** *p39*
Cunningham, John 7; Quebec, 1852 ***5704.8*** *p94*
Cunningham, John 18; Massachusetts, 1849 ***5881.1*** *p18*
Cunningham, Joseph; Quebec, 1847 ***5704.8*** *p16*
Cunningham, Joseph 12; Philadelphia, 1854 ***5704.8*** *p116*
Cunningham, Joseph 18; Quebec, 1858 ***5704.8*** *p138*
Cunningham, Joseph 48; Massachusetts, 1849 ***5881.1*** *p18*
Cunningham, Joseph 50; Philadelphia, 1854 ***5704.8*** *p116*
Cunningham, Julia 6; Massachusetts, 1847 ***5881.1*** *p17*
Cunningham, Lavina; Philadelphia, 1849 ***53.26*** *p17*
Cunningham, Lavina; Philadelphia, 1849 ***5704.8*** *p52*
Cunningham, Margaret; Quebec, 1847 ***5704.8*** *p17*
Cunningham, Margaret; Quebec, 1853 ***5704.8*** *p104*
Cunningham, Margaret 6; Philadelphia, 1864 ***5704.8*** *p156*
Cunningham, Margaret 9; Massachusetts, 1847 ***5881.1*** *p20*
Cunningham, Margaret 60; Massachusetts, 1850 ***5881.1*** *p23*
Cunningham, Margery 20; Philadelphia, 1864 ***5704.8*** *p155*
Cunningham, Mary *SEE* Cunningham, John
Cunningham, Mary; Montreal, 1825 ***7603*** *p91*
Cunningham, Mary; Philadelphia, 1848 ***5704.8*** *p45*
Cunningham, Mary; Philadelphia, 1866 ***5704.8*** *p209*
Cunningham, Mary; Philadelphia, 1870 ***5704.8*** *p239*
Cunningham, Mary; Quebec, 1852 ***5704.8*** *p94*
Cunningham, Mary 9; Massachusetts, 1849 ***5881.1*** *p21*
Cunningham, Mary 44; Massachusetts, 1847 ***5881.1*** *p20*
Cunningham, Mary Ann; Quebec, 1847 ***5704.8*** *p16*
Cunningham, Mary Ann 13; Massachusetts, 1847 ***5881.1*** *p20*
Cunningham, Mary Jane 9 mos; St. John, N.B., 1861 ***5704.8*** *p149*
Cunningham, Mathew; Quebec, 1847 ***5704.8*** *p17*
Cunningham, Matilda; Philadelphia, 1850 ***53.26*** *p18*
Cunningham, Matilda; Philadelphia, 1850 ***5704.8*** *p69*
Cunningham, Matilda 22; St. John, N.B., 1855 ***5704.8*** *p127*
Cunningham, Matthew; Quebec, 1851 ***5704.8*** *p75*
Cunningham, Michael; America, 1742 ***4971*** *p23*
Cunningham, Michael; Arkansas, 1918 ***95.2*** *p33*
Cunningham, Nehemiah; Virginia, 1641 ***6219*** *p187*
Cunningham, Owen 7; Massachusetts, 1849 ***5881.1*** *p23*
Cunningham, Patrick; Illinois, 1882 ***2896.5*** *p9*
Cunningham, Patrick 40; St. John, N.B., 1851 ***5704.8*** *p72*
Cunningham, Patt 30; Philadelphia, 1804 ***53.26*** *p18*
Cunningham, Pierre; Quebec, 1824 ***7603*** *p68*
Cunningham, Rachael; Quebec, 1849 ***5704.8*** *p57*
Cunningham, Rebecca; Philadelphia, 1847 ***53.26*** *p18*
Cunningham, Rebecca; Philadelphia, 1847 ***5704.8*** *p31*
Cunningham, Rebecca; Quebec, 1847 ***5704.8*** *p16*
Cunningham, Robert; Carolina, 1703 ***1639.20*** *p53*
Cunningham, Robert; New York, NY, 1811 ***2859.11*** *p10*
With family
Cunningham, Robert; Quebec, 1847 ***5704.8*** *p16*
Cunningham, Robert 10 *SEE* Cunningham, Jane
Cunningham, Robert 10; Philadelphia, 1848 ***5704.8*** *p46*
Cunningham, Sally 13; Quebec, 1847 ***5704.8*** *p16*
Cunningham, Samuel; Quebec, 1852 ***5704.8*** *p94*
Cunningham, Sarah Jane; Philadelphia, 1852 ***5704.8*** *p88*
Cunningham, Susan 20; Quebec, 1864 ***5704.8*** *p160*
Cunningham, Thomas; South Carolina, 1767 ***1639.20*** *p53*
Cunningham, Thomas 19; St. John, N.B., 1859 ***5704.8*** *p140*
Cunningham, Thomas 39; Philadelphia, 1864 ***5704.8*** *p156*
Cunningham, Thomas 40; Massachusetts, 1847 ***5881.1*** *p25*
Cunningham, William; Philadelphia, 1868 ***5704.8*** *p226*
Cunningham, William; Quebec, 1852 ***5704.8*** *p94*
Cunningham, William 3; Massachusetts, 1847 ***5881.1*** *p26*
Cunningham, William 20; Philadelphia, 1854 ***5704.8*** *p116*
Cunningham, William 30; Jamaica, 1750 ***3690.1*** *p57*
Cunningham, Wm.; Virginia, 1636 ***6219*** *p8*

Cunninghan, Timothy 26; Massachusetts, 1849 ***5881.1*** *p25*
Cunnis, John 19; Maryland, 1721 ***3690.1*** *p57*
Cupal, Henry Thomas; Arkansas, 1918 ***95.2*** *p33*
Cupidon, . . .; Louisiana, 1829 ***778.5*** *p137*
Cupidon, . . . 36; Louisiana, 1829 ***778.5*** *p137*
Cupit, James; Charleston, SC, 1737 ***1639.20*** *p54*
Cupperwhaite, Tho.; Virginia, 1635 ***6219*** *p17*
Cuprian, Anthony; Arkansas, 1918 ***95.2*** *p33*
Cuquith, Ann 22; America, 1705 ***2212*** *p45*
Curby, Alice *SEE* Curby, Samuel
Curby, Samuel; Virginia, 1636 ***6219*** *p77*
*Wife:*Alice
Curd, John 20; Maryland, 1723 ***3690.1*** *p57*
Curdie, George; New York, NY, 1909 ***9892.11*** *p12*
Cure, Mary 19; Baltimore, 1775 ***1219.7*** *p271*
Curet, P. 21; New Orleans, 1839 ***778.5*** *p137*
Curgin, Mary; St. John, N.B., 1847 ***5704.8*** *p11*
Curgin, Peter; St. John, N.B., 1847 ***5704.8*** *p11*
Curie, Jacques 27; Halifax, N.S., 1752 ***7074.6*** *p207*
With family of 1
Curie, Jacques 27; Halifax, N.S., 1752 ***7074.6*** *p209*
*Wife:*Marguerite
Curie, Marguerite *SEE* Curie, Jacques
Curien, Mr. 24; America, 1837 ***778.5*** *p137*
Curley, Brigitte; Quebec, 1822 ***7603*** *p53*
Curley, Ellen 15; Massachusetts, 1847 ***5881.1*** *p15*
Curley, Ellen 21; Massachusetts, 1847 ***5881.1*** *p15*
Curley, Jane 20; Massachusetts, 1849 ***5881.1*** *p18*
Curley, Jean; Quebec, 1804 ***7603*** *p23*
Curley, Pat. 14; Massachusetts, 1849 ***5881.1*** *p24*
Curley, Patrick 20; Philadelphia, 1803 ***53.26*** *p18*
Curley, Thomas 30; Massachusetts, 1848 ***5881.1*** *p25*
Curnin, John; St. John, N.B., 1847 ***5704.8*** *p10*
Curragan, Sarah; Philadelphia, 1811 ***53.26*** *p18*
Curragan, Sarah; Philadelphia, 1811 ***2859.11*** *p10*
Curran, Alexander; Philadelphia, 1869 ***5704.8*** *p236*
Curran, Alice Ann; Philadelphia, 1853 ***5704.8*** *p100*
Curran, Ann; America, 1866 ***5704.8*** *p214*
Curran, Ann; New York, NY, 1867 ***5704.8*** *p221*
Curran, Anne; Quebec, 1851 ***5704.8*** *p75*
Curran, Bernard; New York, NY, 1864 ***5704.8*** *p172*
Curran, David 30; Maryland or Virginia, 1699 ***2212*** *p22*
Curran, Edward 20; Philadelphia, 1853 ***5704.8*** *p109*
Curran, George; Philadelphia, 1853 ***5704.8*** *p100*
Curran, Jacques; Quebec, 1812 ***7603*** *p72*
Curran, James; Montreal, 1818 ***7603*** *p92*
Curran, James 20; Massachusetts, 1847 ***5881.1*** *p17*
Curran, John *SEE* Curran, William
Curran, John; Baltimore, 1830 ***9892.11*** *p12*
Curran, John; New York, NY, 1864 ***5704.8*** *p182*
Curran, John; Philadelphia, 1849 ***5704.8*** *p50*
Curran, John 19; Philadelphia, 1861 ***5704.8*** *p148*
Curran, John 25; Massachusetts, 1847 ***5881.1*** *p17*
Curran, Mary; New York, NY, 1866 ***5704.8*** *p214*
Curran, Mary 9; Massachusetts, 1849 ***5881.1*** *p22*
Curran, Michael; Ohio, 1840 ***9892.11*** *p12*
Curran, Michael 3; Massachusetts, 1849 ***5881.1*** *p21*
Curran, Mich'l 38; Massachusetts, 1850 ***5881.1*** *p22*
Curran, Mich'l 38; Massachusetts, 1850 ***5881.1*** *p43*
Curran, Pat. 8; Massachusetts, 1849 ***5881.1*** *p24*
Curran, Peter; Baltimore, 1830 ***9892.11*** *p12*
Curran, Peter; New York, NY, 1816 ***2859.11*** *p28*
Curran, Robert; New York, NY, 1838 ***8208.4*** *p68*
Curran, Thomas 29; New Orleans, 1862 ***543.30*** *p461*
Curran, William; Philadelphia, 1849 ***53.26*** *p18*
*Relative:*John
Curran, William; Philadelphia, 1849 ***5704.8*** *p50*
Curran, William 20; Philadelphia, 1857 ***5704.8*** *p133*
Currane, John; America, 1742 ***4971*** *p54*
Currane, Morris 22; Massachusetts, 1849 ***5881.1*** *p21*
Currans, James; Quebec, 1851 ***5704.8*** *p75*
Currant, Patrick; New York, NY, 1816 ***2859.11*** *p28*
Currant, Robert; Virginia, 1636 ***6219*** *p78*
Curraway, John; Virginia, 1644 ***6219*** *p230*
Curred, Bartholomew; New York, NY, 1816 ***2859.11*** *p28*
Curred, Bryan; New York, NY, 1816 ***2859.11*** *p28*
Curred, Dominick; New York, NY, 1816 ***2859.11*** *p28*
Curregan, Mary 18; Massachusetts, 1847 ***5881.1*** *p20*
Currell, Elizah; New York, NY, 1816 ***2859.11*** *p28*
Currell, George 16; Jamaica, 1730 ***3690.1*** *p57*
Currell, Susannah; New York, NY, 1816 ***2859.11*** *p28*
Curren, Ann; Quebec, 1823 ***7603*** *p62*
Curren, Catharine; Philadelphia, 1852 ***5704.8*** *p87*
Curren, Daniel 23; Philadelphia, 1864 ***5704.8*** *p155*
Curren, Jane 25; St. John, N.B., 1862 ***5704.8*** *p151*
Curren, Michael; Philadelphia, 1850 ***53.26*** *p18*
Curren, Michael; Philadelphia, 1850 ***5704.8*** *p60*
Curren, Robert 24; St. John, N.B., 1862 ***5704.8*** *p151*
Curren, Thomas; Wisconsin, n.d. ***9675.5*** *p50*
Curren, Thos. W. 36; New Orleans, 1862 ***543.30*** *p461*
Curren, William; Philadelphia, 1848 ***53.26*** *p18*
Curren, William; Philadelphia, 1848 ***5704.8*** *p40*
Current, Lawrence; New York, NY, 1811 ***2859.11*** *p10*
Curret, Mich.; Virginia, 1645 ***6219*** *p240*
Currican, Elizabeth 34; St. John, N.B., 1864 ***5704.8*** *p159*
Currican, John 8; St. John, N.B., 1864 ***5704.8*** *p159*
Currican, John 38; St. John, N.B., 1864 ***5704.8*** *p159*
Currican, Margaret 3; St. John, N.B., 1864 ***5704.8*** *p159*
Currican, Thomas 6; St. John, N.B., 1864 ***5704.8*** *p159*
Currie, Angus; America, 1790 ***1639.20*** *p54*
Currie, Angus; America, 1791 ***1639.20*** *p54*
Currie, Archibald; America, 1791 ***1639.20*** *p54*
Currie, Catherine 62; Wilmington, NC, 1774 ***1639.20*** *p284*
Currie, Flora; America, 1775 ***1639.20*** *p54*
Currie, Florah 80; North Carolina, 1850 ***1639.20*** *p54*
*Relative:*Nancy 60
Currie, John; America, 1805 ***1639.20*** *p54*
Currie, John; New Brunswick, 1840-1900 ***9775.5*** *p204*
Currie, John 70; North Carolina, 1850 ***1639.20*** *p55*
Currie, John 80; North Carolina, 1850 ***1639.20*** *p54*
Currie, Josias; New York, NY, 1811 ***2859.11*** *p10*
Currie, Lauchlen; America, 1791 ***1639.20*** *p55*
Currie, Mabel; Buffalo, NY, 1901 ***3455.2*** *p97*
Currie, Malcolm; North Carolina, 1790-1866 ***1639.20*** *p55*
Currie, Mungo; New York, NY, 1833 ***8208.4*** *p76*
Currie, Murdoch; North Carolina, 1715-1775 ***1639.20*** *p55*
Currie, Nancy 60 *SEE* Currie, Florah
Currie, Robert; Virginia, 1852 ***4626.16*** *p14*
Currie, William 13; Philadelphia, 1854 ***5704.8*** *p123*
Currier, Felix; Kansas, 1896 ***5240.1*** *p9*
Currin, Bernard; Quebec, 1852 ***5704.8*** *p86*
Currin, Bernard; Quebec, 1852 ***5704.8*** *p91*
Currin, Catherine 22; Philadelphia, 1854 ***5704.8*** *p118*
Currin, Hannah 21; Philadelphia, 1854 ***5704.8*** *p118*
Currin, John 20; Philadelphia, 1858 ***5704.8*** *p139*
Currin, Margaret; St. John, N.B., 1847 ***5704.8*** *p26*
Currin, Thady; America, 1741 ***4971*** *p31*
Currogan, Owen 10; Massachusetts, 1847 ***5881.1*** *p23*
Curron, Edward; America, 1866 ***5704.8*** *p212*
Curry, Alexander; New York, NY, 1816 ***2859.11*** *p28*
Curry, Andrew; New York, NY, 1870 ***5704.8*** *p238*
Curry, Catharine; Philadelphia, 1864 ***5704.8*** *p181*
Curry, Catherine; St. John, N.B., 1851 ***5704.8*** *p80*
Curry, Catherine 59; North Carolina, 1850 ***1639.20*** *p54*
Curry, Charlotte; Quebec, 1850 ***5704.8*** *p66*
Curry, Conell; New York, NY, 1811 ***2859.11*** *p10*
Curry, Daniel 64; Kansas, 1894 ***5240.1*** *p9*
Curry, Daniel 64; Kansas, 1894 ***5240.1*** *p79*
Curry, David; St. John, N.B., 1847 ***5704.8*** *p2*
Curry, Eassy 8; Philadelphia, 1853 ***5704.8*** *p113*
Curry, Eassy 8; Philadelphia, 1854 ***5704.8*** *p117*
Curry, Eliza; Philadelphia, 1869 ***5704.8*** *p236*
Curry, Eliza Jane; Quebec, 1850 ***5704.8*** *p66*
Curry, Elizabeth; Philadelphia, 1849 ***53.26*** *p18*
Curry, Elizabeth; Philadelphia, 1849 ***5704.8*** *p52*
Curry, Elizabeth; Quebec, 1847 ***5704.8*** *p36*
Curry, Elizabeth 10; Quebec, 1847 ***5704.8*** *p36*
Curry, George; Quebec, 1850 ***5704.8*** *p66*
Curry, James; New York, NY, 1838 ***8208.4*** *p68*
Curry, James; Quebec, 1847 ***5704.8*** *p36*
Curry, James; St. John, N.B., 1848 ***5704.8*** *p48*
Curry, James 15; Maryland, 1774 ***1219.7*** *p211*
Curry, James 19; Philadelphia, 1854 ***5704.8*** *p118*
Curry, James W. 31?; Arizona, 1890 ***2764.35*** *p13*
Curry, Jane; Quebec, 1850 ***5704.8*** *p66*
Curry, John; Philadelphia, 1811 ***2859.11*** *p10*
Curry, John 19; Philadelphia, 1854 ***5704.8*** *p118*
Curry, John 20; Massachusetts, 1849 ***5881.1*** *p18*
Curry, John 50; St. John, N.B., 1859 ***5704.8*** *p140*
Curry, Judith; Quebec, 1825 ***7603*** *p83*
Curry, Laughlin; Annapolis, MD, 1742 ***4971*** *p93*
Curry, Margaret J. 16; Philadelphia, 1853 ***5704.8*** *p112*
Curry, Martha; Philadelphia, 1848 ***53.26*** *p18*
Curry, Martha; Philadelphia, 1848 ***5704.8*** *p45*
Curry, Mary; New York, NY, 1811 ***2859.11*** *p10*
Curry, Mary 8; Quebec, 1847 ***5704.8*** *p36*
Curry, Mary 11; Philadelphia, 1853 ***5704.8*** *p112*
Curry, Mary 23; Massachusetts, 1847 ***5881.1*** *p20*
Curry, Mary 50; Massachusetts, 1849 ***5881.1*** *p21*
Curry, Mary Ann; Philadelphia, 1851 ***5704.8*** *p77*
Curry, Matilda; Quebec, 1851 ***5704.8*** *p75*
Curry, Michael; New York, NY, 1816 ***2859.11*** *p28*
Curry, Nancy 14; Philadelphia, 1853 ***5704.8*** *p112*
Curry, Patrick; St. John, N.B., 1848 ***5704.8*** *p48*
Curry, Robert; St. John, N.B., 1847 ***5704.8*** *p35*
Curry, Robert; St. John, N.B., 1851 ***5704.8*** *p80*
Curry, Robert 19; Philadelphia, 1853 ***5704.8*** *p113*
Curry, Robert 20; Philadelphia, 1854 ***5704.8*** *p117*
Curry, Robert 55; Philadelphia, 1853 ***5704.8*** *p112*
Curry, Susanna; Philadelphia, 1864 ***5704.8*** *p170*
Curry, William; Indiana, 1848 ***9117*** *p16*
Curry, William; New York, NY, 1816 ***2859.11*** *p28*
Curry, William; Quebec, 1850 ***5704.8*** *p66*
Curtain, David 25; Massachusetts, 1849 ***5881.1*** *p15*
Curtain, Guillaume; Quebec, 1761 ***7603*** *p59*
Curtain, Johanna 26; Massachusetts, 1849 ***5881.1*** *p18*
Curtain, Mary 25; Massachusetts, 1849 ***5881.1*** *p22*
Curtain, Pat. 24; Massachusetts, 1849 ***5881.1*** *p24*
Curtane, William; America, 1742 ***4971*** *p83*
Curtarel, Eugene 22; America, 1831 ***778.5*** *p137*
Curth, Mrs. 45; Port uncertain, 1832 ***778.5*** *p137*
Curth, Henrich; Philadelphia, 1779 ***8137*** *p7*
Curth, Johann Jost; Lancaster, PA, 1780 ***8137*** *p7*
Curth, Yenten 60; Port uncertain, 1832 ***778.5*** *p137*
Curtice, Alice; Virginia, 1639 ***6219*** *p184*
Curtillet, Jean Louis; New York, NY, 1836 ***8208.4*** *p14*
Curtin, Matthew William; San Francisco, 1870 ***2769.3*** *p4*
Curtin, Timothy; America, 1863 ***6014.1*** *p1*
Curtis, Alice; Virginia, 1645 ***6219*** *p253*
Curtis, Catharine 35; Massachusetts, 1850 ***5881.1*** *p14*
Curtis, Eliz.; Virginia, 1636 ***6219*** *p78*
Curtis, Eliza.; Virginia, 1643 ***6219*** *p204*
Curtis, Henry; America, 1736 ***4971*** *p12*
Curtis, James 16; Massachusetts, 1849 ***5881.1*** *p18*
Curtis, Joane; Virginia, 1645 ***6219*** *p253*
Curtis, John; Virginia, 1636 ***6219*** *p77*
Curtis, John 16; Massachusetts, 1849 ***5881.1*** *p18*
Curtis, John 21; Jamaica, 1735 ***3690.1*** *p57*
Curtis, John 27; Virginia, 1774 ***1219.7*** *p239*
Curtis, Jon.; Virginia, 1636 ***6219*** *p21*
Curtis, Jon.; Virginia, 1637 ***6219*** *p13*
Curtis, Sarah; Quebec, 1847 ***5704.8*** *p11*
Curtis, Sarah; Quebec, 1849 ***5704.8*** *p57*
Curtis, Sarah 18; Quebec, 1855 ***5704.8*** *p126*
Curtis, Tho.; Virginia, 1637 ***6219*** *p13*
Curtis, Thomas; America, 1739 ***4971*** *p14*
Curtis, Thomas 24; Philadelphia, 1774 ***1219.7*** *p183*
Curtis, William L.; New York, NY, 1836 ***8208.4*** *p9*
Curtisse, Eliza; Virginia, 1635 ***6219*** *p32*
Cury, Barber 18; Port uncertain, 1838 ***778.5*** *p137*
Curzon, Joseph; New York, NY, 1836 ***8208.4*** *p21*
Cusack, Betsey 10; Massachusetts, 1849 ***5881.1*** *p13*
Cusack, John 16; St. John, N.B., 1853 ***5704.8*** *p109*
Cusack, Mary 50; St. John, N.B., 1853 ***5704.8*** *p109*
Cusack, Patrick; New York, NY, 1816 ***2859.11*** *p28*
Cusato, Antonio; Ohio, 1881-1888 ***9892.11*** *p12*
Cuse, Mary 25; Massachusetts, 1849 ***5881.1*** *p22*
Cushan, Patrick; America, 1737 ***4971*** *p28*
Cushman, Eliza 20; Massachusetts, 1849 ***5881.1*** *p16*
Cushman, Hannah 22; Massachusetts, 1849 ***5881.1*** *p17*
Cushman, John 10; Massachusetts, 1849 ***5881.1*** *p18*
Cushman, Julia 45; Massachusetts, 1849 ***5881.1*** *p18*
Cushman, Margaret 16; Massachusetts, 1849 ***5881.1*** *p21*
Cushoe, John 30; Maryland, 1725 ***3690.1*** *p57*
Cusick, Hugh; New York, NY, 1834 ***8208.4*** *p42*
Cusick, Sarah; St. John, N.B., 1852 ***5704.8*** *p95*
Cusin, M.; New Orleans, 1835 ***778.5*** *p137*
Cussack, Robert; America, 1735-1743 ***4971*** *p8*
Custabader, Catharina 50; Georgia, 1738 ***9332*** *p333*
Custel, Augustin 31; Mexico, 1825 ***778.5*** *p138*
Custer, Paulus; Germantown, PA, 1684 ***2467.7*** *p5*
Cusumano, Mike; Arkansas, 1918 ***95.2*** *p33*
Cutchey, Jane 17; Philadelphia, 1854 ***5704.8*** *p123*
Cutchey, John 24; Philadelphia, 1854 ***5704.8*** *p123*
Cutclift, William 28; Maryland, 1774 ***1219.7*** *p220*
Cuthbert, David 19; Maryland, 1774 ***1219.7*** *p181*
Cuthbert, George; South Carolina, 1754 ***1639.20*** *p55*
Cuthbert, James; South Carolina, 1716-1758 ***1639.20*** *p55*
Cuthbert, James 18; St. John, N.B., 1854 ***5704.8*** *p122*
Cuthbert, James G.; North Carolina, 1814 ***1639.20*** *p55*
Cuthbert, John; Georgia, 1642-1742 ***1639.20*** *p55*
Cuthbert, John; New York, NY, 1838 ***8208.4*** *p68*
Cuthbert, William; North Carolina, 1823 ***1639.20*** *p55*
Cuthbertson, Isabella; Philadelphia, 1847 ***53.26*** *p18*
Cuthbertson, Isabella; Philadelphia, 1847 ***5704.8*** *p14*
Cuthbertson, Moses; Philadelphia, 1847 ***53.26*** *p18*
*Relative:*Rebecca
Cuthbertson, Moses; Philadelphia, 1847 ***5704.8*** *p23*
Cuthbertson, Rebecca *SEE* Cuthbertson, Moses
Cuthbertson, Rebecca; Philadelphia, 1847 ***5704.8*** *p23*
Cuthbirt, Maria 8; Philadelphia, 1854 ***5704.8*** *p115*
Cuthbirt, Martha 5; Philadelphia, 1854 ***5704.8*** *p115*
Cuthbirt, Peggy 50; Philadelphia, 1854 ***5704.8*** *p115*
Cuthbirt, Samuel 11; Philadelphia, 1854 ***5704.8*** *p115*
Cuthbirt, William 60; Philadelphia, 1854 ***5704.8*** *p115*
Cuthill, John; North Carolina, 1811 ***1639.20*** *p55*
Cutlar, Elizabeth 74; Wilmington, NC, 1850 ***1639.20*** *p56*
Cutler, Chr.; Virginia, 1637 ***6219*** *p112*
Cutlow, Mrs. R.; Milwaukee, 1875 ***4719.30*** *p257*
Cuttam, Kerenhappuck 63; Kansas, 1879 ***5240.1*** *p61*

Cutton, Mrs. R.; Milwaukee, 1875 *4719.30* p257
Cutts, Catherine 55; North Carolina, 1850 *1639.20* p56
Cutts, Christopher 26; Jamaica, 1734 *3690.1* p57
Cutwaltz, Adam; Philadelphia, 1760 *9973.7* p35
Cuvellier, Sophie 30; Port uncertain, 1832 *778.5* p138
Cuwillen, Antoinenette 19; Port uncertain, 1839 *778.5* p138
Cvitanovic, Jaso; Iowa, 1866-1943 *123.54* p15
Cvitanovich, Franjo; Iowa, 1866-1943 *123.54* p15
Cwierdzinski, . . .; New York, 1831 *4606* p173
Cydalise, Ms. 30; New Orleans, 1827 *778.5* p138
Cygan, Boleslaw 17; New York, 1912 *9980.29* p51
  With cousin
Cynarski, Stanislaw 16; New York, 1912 *9980.29* p67

Czajka, Antonina 25; New York, 1912 *9980.29* p73
  *Daughter:*Jan 4
  *Daughter:*Kazimierz 2
Czajka, Jan 4 *SEE* Czajka, Antonina
Czajka, Kasper; Iowa, 1866-1943 *123.54* p15
Czajka, Kazimierz 2 *SEE* Czajka, Antonina
Czajka, Wojciech; Cleveland, OH, 1912 *9980.29* p73
Czarcenski, Joseph; Arkansas, 1918 *95.2* p33
Czarnecki, Michal; New York, 1834 *4606* p178
Czechowski, Ignacy; New York, 1831 *4606* p173
Czechowski, Tytus; New York, 1831 *4606* p173
Czernicki, Jozef; New York, 1831 *4606* p173
Czerwinska, Anastasya 31; New York, 1912 *9980.29* p71

Czerwinska, Clara 8; New York, 1912 *9980.29* p72
Czerwinska, Lucia 6; New York, 1912 *9980.29* p72
Czerwinska, Monika 4 mos; New York, 1912 *9980.29* p72
Czerwinska, Wanda 9; New York, 1912 *9980.29* p72
Czerwinski, . . .; New York, 1831 *4606* p173
Czerwinski, Franciszek 11; New York, 1912 *9980.29* p71
Czerwinski, Wladyslaw 35; New York, 1912 *9980.29* p71
Czerwnsk, Raymond Charles; Arkansas, 1918 *95.2* p33
Czerwonka, August; Illinois, 1894 *5012.40* p54
Czerwonka, Christ.; Illinois, 1888 *5012.39* p121
Czesna, Simon; Wisconsin, n.d. *9675.5* p50

D

Daavie, John 29; St. John, N.B., 1866 *5704.8 p166*
Dabauval, B. 34; New Orleans, 1829 *778.5 p138*
Dabkovich, George Simon; Arkansas, 1918 *95.2 p33*
Daboral, Alexis Solomon 19; Louisiana, 1820 *778.5 p138*
Daboval, Mr. 28; New Orleans, 1827 *778.5 p138*
Dabrall, Willson 25; Carolina, 1774 *1219.7 p234*
Dabrall, Wilson 25; Carolina, 1774 *1639.20 p56*
Dabreuil, Jean 35; America, 1839 *778.5 p138*
Dabrowski, Adolf; New York, 1831 *4606 p173*
Dabrowski, Antoni; New York, 1831 *4606 p173*
Dabski, . . .; New York, 1831 *4606 p173*
Dacey, Mary 25; Massachusetts, 1849 *5881.1 p32*
Dacier, Mr. 67; New Orleans, 1837 *778.5 p138*
Dacosses, Francis 50; America, 1831 *778.5 p138*
Dacy, William; New York, NY, 1834 *8208.4 p1*
Daddy, . . . 9 mos; Philadelphia, 1867 *5704.8 p218*
Daddy, James 3; Philadelphia, 1867 *5704.8 p218*
Daddy, Matilda; Philadelphia, 1867 *5704.8 p218*
Daddy, Sarah 3; Philadelphia, 1867 *5704.8 p218*
Dadson, Tho.; Virginia, 1643 *6219 p200*
Dady, David 30; Massachusetts, 1849 *5881.1 p28*
Daehne, Ludwig Christian; New York, 1753 *3652 p77*
Daeman, Jon.; Virginia, 1643 *6219 p205*
Daenschaerez, Anna Margaretha; Pennsylvania, 1779 *4525 p205*
Daerick, Anna Sophia 30; Massachusetts, 1849 *5881.1 p26*
Daerick, Edward 10; Massachusetts, 1849 *5881.1 p28*
Daerick, Hidda 15; Massachusetts, 1849 *5881.1 p29*
Daerick, John 3; Massachusetts, 1849 *5881.1 p30*
Daerick, Maria C. 17; Massachusetts, 1849 *5881.1 p32*
Daesch, Anna Maria Gleichner *SEE* Daesch, Baltas
Daesch, Baltas; Pennsylvania, 1750 *2444 p146*
  *Wife:*Anna Maria Gleichner
Daeschler, David; Philadelphia, 1775-1776 *8582.3 p83*
Daeseele, Alfons; Arkansas, 1918 *95.2 p33*
Daeuble, Georg; Ohio, 1869-1887 *8582 p5*
Daeuble, Johann Georg; Cincinnati, 1832 *8582.2 p60*
Daeuble, John G.; Ohio, 1872 *8582.1 p6*
Dafflitto, Edwardo; Iowa, 1866-1943 *123.54 p15*
Dagase, Jean 21; America, 1838 *778.5 p138*
Dagert, M. 28; New Orleans, 1832 *778.5 p138*
Dagesse, Francois; Quebec, 1791 *7603 p21*
Daget, Remi 13; New Orleans, 1839 *778.5 p138*
Daglis, Samuel 17; Pennsylvania, Virginia or Maryland, 1723 *3690.1 p57*
Dagman, Christopher 30; California, 1867 *3840.1 p18*
Dagnell, Samuel; Virginia, 1698 *2212 p17*
Dahl, Jens Christian; Illinois, 1888 *5012.39 p121*
Dahl, Nels; Arkansas, 1918 *95.2 p33*
Dahl, William; Washington, 1859-1920 *2872.1 p9*
Dahlberg, . . .; Iowa, 1841 *2090 p608*
Dahlberg, George; Massachusetts, 1869-1879 *6410.22 p117*
Dahlberg, Harken; Iowa, 1866-1943 *123.54 p16*
Dahlberg, Oscar; Arkansas, 1918 *95.2 p34*
Dahlbom, Wm.; Shreveport, LA., 1877 *7129 p44*
Dahle, . . .; Canada, 1776-1783 *9786 p42*
Dahlen, Andrew; Arkansas, 1918 *95.2 p34*
Dahlenburg, Marie; Washington, 1859-1920 *2872.1 p9*
Dahler, . . .; Canada, 1776-1783 *9786 p19*
Dahler, Carl G.; Arkansas, 1918 *95.2 p34*
Dahlgreen, Mary L. 23; Massachusetts, 1860 *6410.32 p109*
Dahlgren, A. G. 27; Kansas, 1886 *5240.1 p68*
Dahlgren, C.; Illinois, 1876 *5012.39 p91*

Dahlheim, Olof; Minneapolis, 1862-1877 *6410.35 p52*
Dahlholm, Carl John 25; Arkansas, 1918 *95.2 p34*
Dahlin, D.; Minneapolis, 1881-1883 *6410.35 p52*
Dahlin, F.; Minneapolis, 1869-1883 *6410.35 p52*
Dahlin, Swan J.; Colorado, 1902 *9678.2 p15*
Dahllke, Gustave; Washington, 1859-1920 *2872.1 p9*
Dahlquist, O. N.; Washington, 1859-1920 *2872.1 p9*
Dahlstirna, Bernhard Rich; Quebec, 1776 *9786 p258*
Dahlstrom, Gustaf Edward; Illinois, 1889 *5012.39 p52*
Dahlstrom, John F.; Minneapolis, 1881-1887 *6410.35 p52*
Dahmer, Karthringen; Connecticut, 1856 *3702.7 p354*
Dahna, Charles; America, 1854 *1450.2 p26A*
Dahony, Den.; America, 1738 *4971 p46*
Daig, John; Indiana, 1843 *9117 p16*
Dail, Edward; New York, NY, 1811 *2859.11 p10*
  With family
Daile, Robert 21; Maryland, 1775 *1219.7 p267*
Dailey, Ann 20; Massachusetts, 1848 *5881.1 p26*
Dailey, Ann 20; Philadelphia, 1859 *5704.8 p142*
Dailey, Anne 7; Philadelphia, 1868 *5704.8 p231*
Dailey, Anne 40; Philadelphia, 1868 *5704.8 p231*
Dailey, Bridget 6; Massachusetts, 1850 *5881.1 p27*
Dailey, Bridget 9; Philadelphia, 1865 *5704.8 p204*
Dailey, Bridget 20; Massachusetts, 1850 *5881.1 p27*
Dailey, Catharine 11; Philadelphia, 1865 *5704.8 p204*
Dailey, Catharine 15; Massachusetts, 1848 *5881.1 p28*
Dailey, Catharine 20; Massachusetts, 1850 *5881.1 p28*
Dailey, Catharine 22; Massachusetts, 1847 *5881.1 p27*
Dailey, Charles 14; Massachusetts, 1850 *5881.1 p28*
Dailey, Cornelius 11; Massachusetts, 1850 *5881.1 p28*
Dailey, Edward; Philadelphia, 1865 *5704.8 p203*
Dailey, Edward 5; Philadelphia, 1868 *5704.8 p231*
Dailey, Eliza 18; Massachusetts, 1847 *5881.1 p28*
Dailey, Elizabeth; Philadelphia, 1868 *5704.8 p179*
Dailey, Ellen; New York, NY, 1864 *5704.8 p173*
Dailey, Ellen 30; Massachusetts, 1850 *5881.1 p28*
Dailey, Francis 3; Philadelphia, 1868 *5704.8 p231*
Dailey, Henry; Philadelphia, 1864 *5704.8 p171*
Dailey, James; Quebec, 1848 *5704.8 p42*
Dailey, James 11; Philadelphia, 1868 *5704.8 p231*
Dailey, John 9; Philadelphia, 1868 *5704.8 p231*
Dailey, John 13; Massachusetts, 1850 *5881.1 p30*
Dailey, Lydia; St. John, N.B., 1847 *5704.8 p10*
Dailey, Margaret 8; Massachusetts, 1850 *5881.1 p32*
Dailey, Mary; Philadelphia, 1865 *5704.8 p203*
Dailey, Mary 22; Massachusetts, 1848 *5881.1 p31*
Dailey, Michael 24; Massachusetts, 1850 *5881.1 p32*
Dailey, Nancy; Philadelphia, 1868 *5704.8 p85*
Dailey, Parrissa Curtis 52; California, 1872 *2769.3 p5*
Dailey, Patrick 11; Massachusetts, 1850 *5881.1 p34*
Dailey, Patrick 33; Massachusetts, 1848 *5881.1 p33*
Dailey, Phillis 20; Massachusetts, 1849 *5881.1 p33*
Dailey, Sarah 12; Massachusetts, 1847 *5881.1 p34*
Dailey, Steve; Arkansas, 1918 *95.2 p34*
Dailey, Thomas; Philadelphia, 1850 *5704.8 p60*
Dailey, Thomas 20; Massachusetts, 1848 *5881.1 p34*
Dailey, Thomas 24; Philadelphia, 1774 *1219.7 p233*
Dailey, Thomas 27; Massachusetts, 1849 *5881.1 p34*
Dailey, William; Philadelphia, 1865 *5704.8 p203*
Dailey, William; Philadelphia, 1866 *5704.8 p208*
Dailey, William 17; Massachusetts, 1849 *5881.1 p35*
Daily, Bridget; Philadelphia, 1865 *5704.8 p196*
Daily, Bridget 13; Massachusetts, 1848 *5881.1 p27*
Daily, Catharine 20; Massachusetts, 1847 *5881.1 p27*
Daily, Catharine 50; Massachusetts, 1850 *5881.1 p28*
Daily, Daniel; Philadelphia, 1868 *5704.8 p227*

Daily, David 30; Massachusetts, 1849 *5881.1 p28*
Daily, Henry; New York, NY, 1816 *2859.11 p28*
Daily, James; Philadelphia, 1864 *5704.8 p181*
Daily, John; Quebec, 1821 *7603 p71*
Daily, John 30; Massachusetts, 1849 *5881.1 p30*
Daily, Mary 20; Massachusetts, 1847 *5881.1 p31*
Daily, Mary 25; Massachusetts, 1848 *5881.1 p31*
Daily, Patrick; New York, NY, 1864 *5704.8 p173*
Daily, Patrick; New York, NY, 1869 *5704.8 p233*
Daily, Patrick; Philadelphia, 1865 *5704.8 p197*
Daily, Rose Ann; New York, NY, 1864 *5704.8 p173*
Daily, William; Montreal, 1818 *7603 p56*
Daily, William; Philadelphia, 1864 *5704.8 p181*
Daineen, Julia 26; Massachusetts, 1848 *5881.1 p29*
Daines, John Mark; Arkansas, 1918 *95.2 p34*
D'Air, Jean-Francois; Quebec, 1760 *7603 p21*
Dairey, John B. 31; New Orleans, 1862 *543.30 p219*
Daisac, Jose 33; Mexico, 1826 *778.5 p138*
Daisley, Susan Jane; Philadelphia, 1865 *5704.8 p189*
Daiyure, Mr. 27; New Orleans, 1839 *778.5 p139*
Dakin, John; New York, NY, 1834 *8208.4 p45*
Dakins, Gilbert; Virginia, 1638 *6219 p117*
Daklin, Charles E.; Colorado, 1904 *9678.2 p15*
Dalander, Mrs.; Iowa, 1846 *2090 p610*
  *Son:*Emil
  *Son:*Lars P.
  *Son:*John
  *Son:*Swan
  *Daughter:*Anna
  *Daughter:*Ulrica
Dalander, Anna *SEE* Dalander, Mrs.
Dalander, Emil *SEE* Dalander, Mrs.
Dalander, John *SEE* Dalander, Mrs.
Dalander, Lars P. *SEE* Dalander, Mrs.
Dalander, Swan *SEE* Dalander, Mrs.
Dalander, Ulrica *SEE* Dalander, Mrs.
Dalandez, J. 20; America, 1837 *778.5 p139*
Dalbe, Jean 31; Port uncertain, 1836 *778.5 p139*
Dalborn, Charles J. 25; Kansas, 1888 *5240.1 p9*
Dalborn, Charles J. 25; Kansas, 1888 *5240.1 p72*
Dalby, Arthur; Chicago, 1891 *1450.2 p26A*
Dal Cortina, Jeck; Iowa, 1866-1943 *123.54 p16*
Dale, Daniel; New York, NY, 1816 *2859.11 p28*
Dale, E. E.; Washington, 1859-1920 *2872.1 p9*
Dale, Edward; Virginia, 1642 *6219 p194*
Dale, George; New York, NY, 1815 *2859.11 p28*
Dale, Humphry; Virginia, 1638 *6219 p124*
Dale, James 22; Maryland, 1775 *1219.7 p257*
Dale, John; New York, NY, 1816 *2859.11 p28*
Dale, Jon.; Virginia, 1638 *6219 p14*
Dale, Jonas Daniel; New York, NY, 1837 *8208.4 p34*
Dale, Nicholas; Virginia, 1638 *6219 p121*
  With wife
Dale, Nicholas; Virginia, 1638 *6219 p124*
Dale, Samuel; New York, NY, 1816 *2859.11 p28*
Dale, Walter; Virginia, 1648 *6219 p237*
Dale, William; New York, NY, 1816 *2859.11 p28*
Dale, William; New York, NY, 1830 *8208.4 p104*
Dale, William 15; America, 1706 *2212 p47*
D'Alessandro, Flaviano; Arkansas, 1918 *95.2 p33*
Daletzas, Michael; Arkansas, 1918 *95.2 p34*
Daley, Ann; Philadelphia, 1847 *53.26 p18*
Daley, Ann; Philadelphia, 1847 *5704.8 p32*
Daley, Anne; St. John, N.B., 1853 *5704.8 p99*
Daley, Biddy; New Orleans, 1849 *5704.8 p58*
Daley, Denas; Ohio, 1845 *9892.11 p12*
Daley, James; Virginia, 1646 *6219 p242*

Daley, James 13; Massachusetts, 1849 ***5881.1*** *p30*
Daley, Kearn 23; Massachusetts, 1849 ***5881.1*** *p30*
Daley, Michael 21; Massachusetts, 1850 ***5881.1*** *p32*
Daley, Patrick 13; Newport, RI, 1851 ***6508.5*** *p19*
Daley, Patrick 25; New Orleans, 1864 ***543.30*** *p372*
Daley, Timothy 26; Massachusetts, 1849 ***5881.1*** *p34*
Dalezal, Joseph; Iowa, 1866-1943 ***123.54*** *p16*
Dalgairne, Alexander; Wilmington, NC, 1808 ***1639.20*** *p56*
D'Algans, Leon 31; America, 1839 ***778.5*** *p139*
Dalgetty, Alexander; South Carolina, 1716 ***1639.20*** *p56*
Dalhousie, Earl of; Nova Scotia, 1815 ***9775.5*** *p208*
Dalieu, John 28; New Orleans, 1827 ***778.5*** *p139*
Dalina, Mrs. 26; New Orleans, 1826 ***778.5*** *p139*
Dalina, Henry 29; New Orleans, 1826 ***778.5*** *p139*
Dalingan, Leland; Iowa, 1866-1943 ***123.54*** *p16*
Dall, Peter 24; Kansas, 1885 ***5240.1*** *p67*
Dalla Dora, Frank; Iowa, 1866-1943 ***123.54*** *p16*
Dallaire, . . .; Canada, 1776-1783 ***9786*** *p19*
Dallas, Alexander; New York, NY, 1815 ***2859.11*** *p28*
Dallas, Alexander; Wilmington, NC, 1820 ***1639.20*** *p56*
Dallas, Elizabeth 50; Philadelphia, 1864 ***5704.8*** *p156*
Dallas, Ellen 19; Philadelphia, 1864 ***5704.8*** *p156*
Dallas, George 31; New Orleans, 1862 ***543.30*** *p215*
Dallas, John 14; Philadelphia, 1864 ***5704.8*** *p156*
Dallas, Louis; Arkansas, 1918 ***95.2*** *p34*
Dallas, Madeleine 22; Quebec, 1771 ***7603*** *p37*
Dallas, Mary 24; Philadelphia, 1864 ***5704.8*** *p156*
Dallas, Peter; America, 1791 ***1639.20*** *p56*
Dallas, William; Philadelphia, 1866 ***5704.8*** *p211*
Dallas, William 26; Philadelphia, 1864 ***5704.8*** *p156*
Dallasta, Joseph 26; New Orleans, 1862 ***543.30*** *p60*
Dalle, L. 65; Port uncertain, 1829 ***778.5*** *p139*
Daller, Johann; Cincinnati, 1869-1887 ***8582*** *p5*
D'Allesandro, Atilio; Arkansas, 1918 ***95.2*** *p33*
Dallion, John; Virginia, 1639 ***6219*** *p162*
Dallke, Peter, Jr.; Kansas, 1879 ***5240.1*** *p9*
Dallman, Luie; Iroquois Co., IL, 1896 ***3455.1*** *p10*
Dalloe, John William 21; Kansas, 1906 ***5240.1*** *p84*
Dally, Edward; New York, NY, 1816 ***2859.11*** *p28*
Dally, Margaret 9; Quebec, 1847 ***5704.8*** *p38*
Dally, Teresa 11; Quebec, 1847 ***5704.8*** *p38*
Dally, Thomas 13; Quebec, 1847 ***5704.8*** *p38*
Dally, William 22; Philadelphia, 1864 ***5704.8*** *p155*
Dallyner, John 17; Maryland, 1724 ***3690.1*** *p57*
Dalmer, Henry Julius; Arkansas, 1918 ***95.2*** *p34*
Dalponte, Antonio; Iowa, 1866-1943 ***123.54*** *p16*
Dalponte, Bartalo; Iowa, 1866-1943 ***123.54*** *p16*
Dalponte, Guiseppe; Iowa, 1866-1943 ***123.54*** *p16*
Dal Ponte, Libera; Iowa, 1866-1943 ***123.54*** *p16*
Dalpra, Silvio; Colorado, 1904 ***9678.2*** *p15*
Dalrymple, Ann; North Carolina, 1766-1866 ***1639.20*** *p56*
Dalrymple, Ann 9 *SEE* Dalrymple, John
Dalrymple, Archibald 15 *SEE* Dalrymple, John
Dalrymple, Elizabeth 81; North Carolina, 1850 ***1639.20*** *p56*
Dalrymple, James 11 *SEE* Dalrymple, John
Dalrymple, Janet 7 *SEE* Dalrymple, John
Dalrymple, Jean 5 *SEE* Dalrymple, John
Dalrymple, John; North Carolina, 1767 ***1639.20*** *p56*
Dalrymple, John 17 *SEE* Dalrymple, John
Dalrymple, John 49; North Carolina, 1775 ***1639.20*** *p57*
*Wife:*Margaret Gordon 39
*Child:*Mary 19
*Child:*John 17
*Child:*Archibald 15
*Child:*James 11
*Child:*Ann 9
*Child:*Janet 7
*Child:*Jean 5
*Child:*William 2
Dalrymple, Margaret Gordon 39 *SEE* Dalrymple, John
Dalrymple, Mary; North Carolina, 1824 ***1639.20*** *p296*
Dalrymple, Mary 19 *SEE* Dalrymple, John
Dalrymple, William 2 *SEE* Dalrymple, John
Dalrymple, William 77; North Carolina, 1850 ***1639.20*** *p57*
Dalsinger, Ambrosius; Venezuela, n.d. ***8582.3*** *p79*
Dal Soggio, Anton; Arkansas, 1918 ***95.2*** *p34*
Dalton, Alice 18; Massachusetts, 1850 ***5881.1*** *p26*
Dalton, Barbe; Quebec, 1818 ***7603*** *p101*
Dalton, Bridget 22; Massachusetts, 1849 ***5881.1*** *p27*
Dalton, Bridget 35; Massachusetts, 1849 ***5881.1*** *p27*
Dalton, Daniel; America, 1840 ***7036*** *p117*
*Wife:*Ellen McCabe
Dalton, Edward 28; New England, 1774 ***1219.7*** *p203*
Dalton, Edward 31; Virginia, 1774 ***1219.7*** *p201*
Dalton, Ellen 35; Massachusetts, 1850 ***5881.1*** *p28*
Dalton, Ellen McCabe *SEE* Dalton, Daniel
Dalton, Henry; America, 1739 ***4971*** *p37*
Dalton, Henry; America, 1741 ***4971*** *p37*
Dalton, Henry; New York, NY, 1815 ***2859.11*** *p28*
Dalton, James; America, 1735-1743 ***4971*** *p78*
Dalton, John A.; America, 1869 ***6014.1*** *p1*
Dalton, Mary; Montreal, 1823 ***7603*** *p91*
Dalton, Patrick; America, 1736-1743 ***4971*** *p58*
Dalton, Richard 26; Maryland or Virginia, 1699 ***2212*** *p22*
Dalwingh, . . .; Canada, 1776-1783 ***9786*** *p19*
Daly, Anthony; New York, NY, 1815 ***2859.11*** *p28*
Daly, Bridget; New Brunswick, 1824 ***7603*** *p75*
Daly, Bridget Carroll 60; Kansas, 1880 ***5240.1*** *p62*
Daly, Bryan; America, 1742 ***4971*** *p70*
Daly, Bryan; New York, NY, 1816 ***2859.11*** *p28*
Daly, Catharine 13; Quebec, 1849 ***5704.8*** *p51*
Daly, Charles; Montreal, 1820 ***7603*** *p90*
Daly, Charles; Quebec, 1784 ***7603*** *p75*
Daly, Daniel; America, 1737 ***4971*** *p36*
Daly, Darby; America, 1743 ***4971*** *p54*
Daly, Dennis; America, 1735-1743 ***4971*** *p78*
Daly, Dennis; New York, NY, 1836 ***8208.4*** *p18*
Daly, Ellen; New York, NY, 1816 ***2859.11*** *p28*
With 3 children
Daly, Ellen; New York, NY, 1816 ***2859.11*** *p28*
Daly, Ellenor; America, 1743 ***4971*** *p25*
Daly, Henry; Quebec, 1849 ***5704.8*** *p51*
Daly, James; America, 1741 ***4971*** *p23*
Daly, James; New York, NY, 1838 ***8208.4*** *p67*
Daly, John; America, 1735-1743 ***4971*** *p78*
Daly, John; America, 1742 ***4971*** *p80*
Daly, John; Charles Town, SC, 1768 ***1219.7*** *p136*
Daly, John; Illinois, 1876 ***5012.39*** *p91*
Daly, John; Montreal, 1823 ***7603*** *p60*
Daly, John; New York, NY, 1866 ***5704.8*** *p207*
Daly, John; Quebec, 1822 ***7603*** *p60*
Daly, John, Jr.; Illinois, 1876 ***5012.37*** *p60*
Daly, Martin; New York, NY, 1816 ***2859.11*** *p29*
Daly, Mary; New Brunswick, 1824 ***7603*** *p75*
Daly, Michael; America, 1836 ***7036*** *p117*
Daly, Michael; New York, NY, 1816 ***2859.11*** *p29*
Daly, Neal; America, 1741 ***4971*** *p26*
Daly, P.; New York, NY, 1816 ***2859.11*** *p29*
Daly, Patrick; Quebec, 1848 ***5704.8*** *p41*
Daly, Peter *SEE* Daly, Peter
Daly, Peter; America, 1886 ***5240.1*** *p9*
*Father:*Peter
Daly, Peter 60; Kansas, 1886 ***5240.1*** *p69*
Daly, Samuel; St. John, N.B., 1849 ***5704.8*** *p56*
Daly, Thomas H.; New York, NY, 1838 ***8208.4*** *p74*
Daly, William; New York, NY, 1816 ***2859.11*** *p29*
Daly, William; Quebec, 1849 ***5704.8*** *p51*
Daly, William; Washington, 1859-1920 ***2872.1*** *p9*
Daly, Wm. George; New York, NY, 1815 ***2859.11*** *p29*
Dalzell, William 25; Carolina, 1774 ***1639.20*** *p57*
Dalziel, John; Carolina or Virginia, 1716 ***1639.20*** *p57*
Dalziel, William; South Carolina, 1716 ***1639.20*** *p57*
Dam, Eliza.; Virginia, 1643 ***6219*** *p204*
Dam, John Pedersen; Arkansas, 1918 ***95.2*** *p34*
Dambacher, Max; America, 1892 ***1450.2*** *p26A*
Damberaut, E. 40; Port uncertain, 1839 ***778.5*** *p139*
D'Ambrosio, Angelo Michele; Arkansas, 1918 ***95.2*** *p33*
Dambrun, J. M. 16; New Orleans, 1839 ***778.5*** *p139*
Dame, George 33; Virginia, 1773 ***1219.7*** *p169*
Damead, William 21; Philadelphia, 1774 ***1219.7*** *p197*
D'Amel, Henry 37; America, 1830 ***778.5*** *p139*
D'Amelio, Luigi; Arkansas, 1918 ***95.2*** *p33*
Damer, . . .; America, 1881 ***3702.7*** *p438*
Damer, Henrich; Philadelphia, 1779 ***8137*** *p7*
Dames, George Demetres; Arkansas, 1918 ***95.2*** *p34*
Damiani, Antonio; Colorado, 1904 ***9678.2*** *p15*
Damico, Onofrio; Arkansas, 1918 ***95.2*** *p34*
Damien, Jacques; Quebec, 1729 ***4533*** *p131*
Damm, Emil Johannes Kofoed; Arkansas, 1918 ***95.2*** *p34*
Damm, Emil John Kofeld; Arkansas, 1918 ***95.2*** *p34*
Damm, Heinerick; Canada, 1783 ***9786*** *p38A*
Damm, Heinrich; Pennsylvania, 1754 ***4525*** *p204*
With wife
Damm, Ludvig F.; Minneapolis, 1868-1876 ***6410.35*** *p52*
Damm, Peter 26; Arkansas, 1918 ***95.2*** *p34*
Damman, A. Henry; Washington, 1859-1920 ***2872.1*** *p9*
Dammann, Frederich Christoph; New York, 1891 ***5240.1*** *p9*
Damme, Francis E.; America, 1848 ***1450.2*** *p26A*
Dammeier, Frederick; America, 1843 ***1450.2*** *p26A*
Dammel, Anna Maria *SEE* Dammel, Johannes
Dammel, Johannes *SEE* Dammel, Johannes
Dammel, Johannes; Pennsylvania, 1754 ***2444*** *p146*
*Wife:*Anna Maria
*Child:*Johannes
Dampeau, John 26; America, 1822 ***778.5*** *p143*
Dampert, Lancelott; Virginia, 1639 ***6219*** *p155*
Damson, Johann Gottlieb; America, 1734-1800 ***2444*** *p146*
Damson, Johann Samuel; America, 1733-1800 ***2444*** *p146*
Damson, Jon.; Virginia, 1642 ***6219*** *p192*
Damson, Sixt Jacob; America, 1744-1800 ***2444*** *p146*
Danaby, Jeremiah; Virginia, 1858 ***4626.16*** *p17*
Danagh, Margaret 18; Quebec, 1855 ***5704.8*** *p125*
Danaho, Patrick; New York, NY, 1815 ***2859.11*** *p29*
Danahy, Patrick; New York, NY, 1836 ***8208.4*** *p11*
Danaker, Christian; Philadelphia, 1783 ***2444*** *p146*
Danay, George; Iowa, 1866-1943 ***123.54*** *p16*
Dancauve, Germain 32; Port uncertain, 1837 ***778.5*** *p139*
Dancer, Brill 18; Maryland, 1775 ***1219.7*** *p267*
Dancer, John; South Carolina, 1788 ***7119*** *p202*
Dancer, Peter; South Carolina, 1788 ***7119*** *p203*
Dancer, William 21; Maryland, 1774 ***1219.7*** *p187*
Dander, Sarah; New York, NY, 1811 ***2859.11*** *p10*
Dandey, Edward 16; Pennsylvania, 1728 ***3690.1*** *p58*
Dandignac, Joseph Victor; New York, NY, 1837 ***8208.4*** *p35*
Dandoff, . . .; Canada, 1776-1783 ***9786*** *p19*
Dandorff, . . .; Canada, 1776-1783 ***9786*** *p19*
Dandoulakis, Gregorius Emanuel; Arkansas, 1918 ***95.2*** *p34*
Dandrea, Serafino; Colorado, 1904 ***9678.2*** *p15*
Dane, Yorath; Virginia, 1636 ***6219*** *p1*
Danecker, Jacob; Pennsylvania, 1750 ***2444*** *p146*
Daner, John; New York, NY, 1853 ***2896.5*** *p9*
Danerhauer, Marc 12; America, 1836 ***778.5*** *p139*
Danet, Christine 30; Port uncertain, 1839 ***778.5*** *p139*
Daney, Richard; Virginia, 1639 ***6219*** *p151*
Danford, James; New York, NY, 1816 ***2859.11*** *p29*
Danford, Matty; Philadelphia, 1850 ***53.26*** *p18*
Danford, Matty; Philadelphia, 1850 ***5704.8*** *p59*
Danford, Ralph; New York, NY, 1816 ***2859.11*** *p29*
Danger, Joseph 9 mos; New York, NY, 1878 ***9253*** *p46*
Danger, Leib H. 19; New York, NY, 1878 ***9253*** *p46*
Danger, Lore 25; New York, NY, 1878 ***9253*** *p46*
Dangerfield, Elizabeth 19; Pennsylvania, 1719 ***3690.1*** *p58*
Dangerfield, Samuel 33; Kansas, 1883 ***5240.1*** *p64*
Dangerro, . . .; Canada, 1776-1783 ***9786*** *p42*
Danglades, P. 32; New Orleans, 1832 ***778.5*** *p139*
Danguard, Anders Petersen; Illinois, 1876 ***2896.5*** *p9*
Daniel, . . .; America, n.d. ***8582.3*** *p75*
Daniel, Alexander 15; Port uncertain, 1774 ***1219.7*** *p176*
Daniel, Elizabeth *SEE* Daniel, Henry
Daniel, Francis 27; Maryland, 1774 ***1219.7*** *p214*
Daniel, Henry; Virginia, 1635 ***6219*** *p6*
*Wife:*Elizabeth
Daniel, James; New York, NY, 1816 ***2859.11*** *p29*
Daniel, John 18; Antigua (Antego), 1728 ***3690.1*** *p58*
Daniel, John 21; Maryland, 1774 ***1219.7*** *p224*
Daniel, Jonathan 19; Maryland, 1725 ***3690.1*** *p58*
Daniel, Joseph 29; Virginia, 1774 ***1219.7*** *p244*
Daniel, Thomas 16; Virginia, 1720 ***3690.1*** *p58*
Daniel, Thomas 21; Maryland, 1774 ***1219.7*** *p208*
Daniele, Jen 18; Antigua (Antego), 1728 ***3690.1*** *p58*
Daniell, Edw.; Virginia, 1636 ***6219*** *p21*
Daniell, Edward; Virginia, 1644 ***6219*** *p231*
Daniell, Edwd.; Virginia, 1638 ***6219*** *p115*
Daniell, Hen.; Virginia, 1638 ***6219*** *p18*
Daniell, John; Virginia, 1642 ***6219*** *p196*
Daniell, John; Virginia, 1648 ***6219*** *p252*
Daniell, John; Virginia, 1649 ***6219*** *p252*
Daniels, Alexander V.; America, 1852 ***8582.3*** *p13*
Daniels, Benjamin 2; Massachusetts, 1847 ***5881.1*** *p27*
Daniels, Benjamin 24; Massachusetts, 1847 ***5881.1*** *p27*
Daniels, Mary Ann 4; Massachusetts, 1847 ***5881.1*** *p31*
Daniels, Ruth 24; Massachusetts, 1847 ***5881.1*** *p34*
Danielsen, Peter; New York, 1761 ***3652*** *p87*
Danielson, Anders; Iowa, 1852 ***2090*** *p615*
Danielson, Andrew; Washington, 1859-1920 ***2872.1*** *p9*
Danielson, Anna 36; Massachusetts, 1860 ***6410.32*** *p111*
Danielson, Anna A. 8; Massachusetts, 1860 ***6410.32*** *p111*
Danielson, Augustus 36; Massachusetts, 1860 ***6410.32*** *p111*
Danielson, Earnest; Maine, 1888-1896 ***6410.22*** *p123*
Danielson, Gustaf; America, 1853 ***6410.32*** *p124*
With wife
With child
Danielson, J. O. 22; Kansas, 1894 ***5240.1*** *p79*
Danielson, Katrina; Washington, 1859-1920 ***2872.1*** *p9*
Danielson, Signe Irene; Washington, 1859-1920 ***2872.1*** *p9*
Danielson, Theodore; Washington, 1859-1920 ***2872.1*** *p9*
Danielsson, Daniel; Minneapolis, 1881-1883 ***6410.35*** *p52*
d'Anieres, Jr.; Quebec, 1776 ***9786*** *p104*
Danils, Stephen; Iowa, 1866-1943 ***123.54*** *p16*
Danish, Michael 30; Massachusetts, 1850 ***5881.1*** *p33*
Dann, A. 24; Port uncertain, 1838 ***778.5*** *p140*
Dann, Henrich; Pennsylvania, 1754 ***4525*** *p204*
Danna, Gerlando; Illinois, 1904 ***5012.39*** *p53*
Danna, Giovanni; Arkansas, 1918 ***95.2*** *p34*
Dannan, John; New York, NY, 1816 ***2859.11*** *p29*
Dannckher, Jacob; Pennsylvania, 1750 ***2444*** *p146*
Danne, Jean Benoist 28; New Orleans, 1838 ***778.5*** *p140*

Dannecker, Christian; America, 1724-1800 ***2444*** *p146*
Dannecker, Christian; Philadelphia, 1783 ***2444*** *p146*
Danneckher, Christian *SEE* Danneckher, Jacob
Danneckher, Elisabetha Margaretha *SEE* Danneckher, Jacob
Danneckher, Jacob; Pennsylvania, 1750 ***2444*** *p146*
*Wife:*Margaretha Burger
*Child:*Johann Georg
*Child:*Elisabetha Margaretha
*Child:*Christian
Danneckher, Johann Georg *SEE* Danneckher, Jacob
Danneckher, Margaretha Burger *SEE* Danneckher, Jacob
Dannehower, George; Pennsylvania, 1746 ***2444*** *p147*
Dannenhauer, Catharina *SEE* Dannenhauer, Hans Jerg
Dannenhauer, Hans Jerg; Pennsylvania, 1746 ***2444*** *p146*
*Wife:*Catharina
*Child:*Rosina Catharina
Dannenhauer, Rosina Catharina *SEE* Dannenhauer, Hans Jerg
Dannenhold, Balthasar; America, 1833 ***8582.1*** *p6*
Dannenhold, Balthasar; Cincinnati, 1874 ***8582.3*** *p87*
Danner, Martin; Philadelphia, 1760 ***9973.7*** *p34*
D'Anniers, Carl Franz, II; Quebec, 1776 ***9786*** *p262*
Dannot, William 17; Maryland, 1775 ***1219.7*** *p256*
Danny, Samuel 18; Philadelphia, 1774 ***1219.7*** *p219*
Danny, Sarah 15; Philadelphia, 1774 ***1219.7*** *p219*
Danny, Sarah 36; Philadelphia, 1774 ***1219.7*** *p219*
With child
Danny, Thomas 21; Philadelphia, 1774 ***1219.7*** *p219*
Danoies, Pierre Louis 31; New Orleans, 1838 ***778.5*** *p140*
Danowski, Wladislaw 20; New York, 1912 ***9980.29*** *p53*
Dansac, A. 25; Port uncertain, 1835 ***778.5*** *p140*
Dansac, B. 20; Port uncertain, 1832 ***778.5*** *p140*
Dansac, B. 24; Port uncertain, 1839 ***778.5*** *p140*
Dansac, Louis 27; New Orleans, 1826 ***778.5*** *p140*
Dansar, Harry; South Carolina, 1788 ***7119*** *p202*
Dansey, Alice *SEE* Dansey, John
Dansey, John; Virginia, 1636 ***6219*** *p7*
*Wife:*Alice
Danson, Henry; Washington, 1859-1920 ***2872.1*** *p9*
Danss, Tobias 40; Philadelphia, 1774 ***1219.7*** *p183*
Dansye, John, Jr.; Virginia, 1621 ***6219*** *p2*
Dantac, Joseph 25; New Orleans, 1823 ***778.5*** *p140*
Dantey, Michael 22; New Orleans, 1862 ***543.30*** *p218*
Danth, Charles; New York, NY, 1839 ***8208.4*** *p93*
Danton, Mr.; Quebec, 1815 ***9229.18*** *p75*
Danton, Peter 27; New Orleans, 1862 ***543.30*** *p60*
Dantz, . . .; Canada, 1776-1783 ***9786*** *p19*
Dantzer, Carl; Milwaukee, 1875 ***4719.30*** *p258*
Danwoody, John; New York, NY, 1811 ***2859.11*** *p10*
Danwoody, Wm.; New York, NY, 1811 ***2859.11*** *p10*
Danz, Ernest; Arkansas, 1918 ***95.2*** *p34*
Danzer, Jacobina; Pennsylvania, 1752 ***2444*** *p175*
Danzero, Andrea Anton; Arkansas, 1918 ***95.2*** *p34*
Danziger, George E.; America, 1887 ***1450.2*** *p26A*
Danziger, Herman Joseph; Arkansas, 1918 ***95.2*** *p34*
Danzler, Jno Henry, Sr.; South Carolina, 1788 ***7119*** *p198*
Danzler, John Henry; South Carolina, 1788 ***7119*** *p198*
Dappler, Andres 23; Port uncertain, 1839 ***778.5*** *p140*
Dappler, Anton 23; Port uncertain, 1839 ***778.5*** *p140*
Dappler, Christiana 22; Port uncertain, 1839 ***778.5*** *p140*
Dappler, Franz 2; Port uncertain, 1839 ***778.5*** *p140*
Dappler, Nickolaus 5; Port uncertain, 1839 ***778.5*** *p140*
Daracnnas, Karl; Arkansas, 1918 ***95.2*** *p34*
Darah, James 20; Quebec, 1857 ***5704.8*** *p136*
Darand, Mr. 21; New Orleans, 1837 ***778.5*** *p140*
Darasz, John; Arkansas, 1918 ***95.2*** *p34*
Daraugh, Bernard; Quebec, 1822 ***7603*** *p53*
Daraugh, Patrick; Montreal, 1822 ***7603*** *p53*
Darbez, G.; New Orleans, 1839 ***778.5*** *p140*
Darbier, Mr. 77; America, 1839 ***778.5*** *p141*
Darbon, Francois 20; New Orleans, 1839 ***778.5*** *p141*
Darby, Ann 10; Massachusetts, 1849 ***5881.1*** *p26*
Darby, Francis 24; Jamaica, 1736 ***3690.1*** *p58*
Darby, John 40; North Carolina, 1774 ***1219.7*** *p215*
Darby, Tho.; Virginia, 1635 ***6219*** *p35*
Darbye, Jon.; Virginia, 1637 ***6219*** *p114*
Darcey, Thos.; New York, NY, 1815 ***2859.11*** *p29*
Darche, Leonard 35; New Orleans, 1829 ***778.5*** *p141*
Darche Dagardenis, L. 30; New Orleans, 1823 ***778.5*** *p141*
Darche D'Agardens, L. 44; New Orleans, 1837 ***778.5*** *p141*
Darche Dargadin, Leonard 42; New Orleans, 1836 ***778.5*** *p141*
Darcus, William 28; Quebec, 1857 ***5704.8*** *p136*
Darcy, Dennis; New York, NY, 1839 ***8208.4*** *p91*
Darcy, James; America, 1740 ***4971*** *p73*
Darcy, Miles; America, 1738 ***4971*** *p33*
Darcy, Miles; America, 1740 ***4971*** *p34*
Dare, Catherine *SEE* Dare, Nicolas
Dare, Jacques *SEE* Dare, Nicolas
Dare, James; New York, NY, 1834 ***8208.4*** *p2*
Dare, Jeanne *SEE* Dare, Nicolas
Dare, Nicolas 42; Halifax, N.S., 1752 ***7074.6*** *p209*
*Wife:*Suzanne
*Child:*Jeanne
*Child:*Catherine
*Child:*Jacques
With child
Dare, Suzanne *SEE* Dare, Nicolas
Dareing, Richd.; Virginia, 1648 ***6219*** *p250*
Daren, Anne; New York, NY, 1816 ***2859.11*** *p29*
Dares, . . .; Halifax, N.S., 1752 ***7074.6*** *p232*
Darey, . . .; Halifax, N.S., 1752 ***7074.6*** *p230*
Darey, Robert 20; Maryland, 1750 ***3690.1*** *p58*
Dargadens, D. 41; America, 1835 ***778.5*** *p141*
Dargan, Andrew; America, 1738 ***4971*** *p31*
Darganell, Alex; Iowa, 1866-1943 ***123.54*** *p16*
D'Argardens, D. 34; New Orleans, 1827 ***778.5*** *p141*
Dargarel, Thomas; New York, NY, 1838 ***8208.4*** *p64*
Dargent, P. 30; Port uncertain, 1839 ***778.5*** *p141*
Dargueding, Sarah 45; New Orleans, 1839 ***778.5*** *p141*
Dargy, Baptiste 8; America, 1838 ***778.5*** *p141*
Darian, Ann 3; St. John, N.B., 1857 ***5704.8*** *p134*
Darian, Catherine 49; St. John, N.B., 1857 ***5704.8*** *p134*
Darian, Charlott 27; St. John, N.B., 1857 ***5704.8*** *p134*
Darian, James 18; Philadelphia, 1857 ***5704.8*** *p132*
Darian, John 6 mos; St. John, N.B., 1857 ***5704.8*** *p134*
Darian, Margaret 4; St. John, N.B., 1857 ***5704.8*** *p134*
Darian, Patrick 40; St. John, N.B., 1857 ***5704.8*** *p134*
Daricutt, Robert; Virginia, 1639 ***6219*** *p156*
Darimon, Arnaud Eugene 31; Port uncertain, 1838 ***778.5*** *p141*
Da Rin, Daniele; Iowa, 1866-1943 ***123.54*** *p16*
Daringer, John; Ohio, 1851 ***9892.11*** *p12*
Dark, Alice 63?; Pennsylvania, 1684 ***4962*** *p150*
*Son:*John 17
Dark, Ann Knight; Pennsylvania, 1682 ***4962*** *p149*
Dark, John 17 *SEE* Dark, Alice
Dark, Samuel; Pennsylvania, 1680 ***4962*** *p150*
Dark, William 58?; Pennsylvania, 1680 ***4962*** *p150*
Darles, Eliza 16; St. John, N.B., 1854 ***5704.8*** *p115*
Darles, William 18; St. John, N.B., 1854 ***5704.8*** *p115*
Darley, Michael 35; Massachusetts, 1849 ***5881.1*** *p31*
Darling, Dorothy; Virginia, 1647 ***6219*** *p241*
Darling, George 35; Virginia, 1774 ***1219.7*** *p239*
Darling, Patrick; America, 1739 ***4971*** *p14*
Darling, Richard; Virginia, 1641 ***6219*** *p184*
Darnell, C. B.; Washington, 1859-1920 ***2872.1*** *p9*
Darnell, J. C.; Washington, 1859-1920 ***2872.1*** *p9*
Darnell, J. S.; Washington, 1859-1920 ***2872.1*** *p9*
Darnell, Robert 21; Jamaica, 1733 ***3690.1*** *p58*
Darning, James; Quebec, 1822 ***7603*** *p89*
Darnoly, Wm.; Virginia, 1635 ***6219*** *p69*
Darnstadt, Johanne Georg 24; New Orleans, 1839 ***9420.2*** *p71*
Darose, Mr. 33; Louisiana, 1820 ***778.5*** *p141*
Darozak, George; America, 1890 ***7137*** *p168*
Darque, Mr. 33; America, 1835 ***778.5*** *p141*
Darr, Mr.; Cincinnati, 1831 ***8582.1*** *p51*
Darr, Joseph; America, 1820 ***8582.2*** *p60*
Darr, Joseph; Cincinnati, 1827 ***8582.1*** *p51*
Darr, Joseph; Cincinnati, 1869-1887 ***8582*** *p5*
Darr, Philip; West Virginia, 1853 ***9788.3*** *p7*
Darrach, Jenny; Brunswick, NC, 1767 ***1639.20*** *p57*
Darrag, John; America, 1742 ***4971*** *p50*
Darragh, Ann 10; Quebec, 1847 ***5704.8*** *p8*
Darragh, Christina; Quebec, 1847 ***5704.8*** *p8*
Darragh, Elizabeth 12; Quebec, 1847 ***5704.8*** *p8*
Darragh, Jane; New York, NY, 1867 ***5704.8*** *p223*
Darragh, Jane; Philadelphia, 1868 ***5704.8*** *p226*
Darragh, Margaret; Quebec, 1847 ***5704.8*** *p8*
Darragh, Patrick; Philadelphia, 1847 ***53.26*** *p18*
*Relative:*Peggy
Darragh, Patrick; Philadelphia, 1847 ***5704.8*** *p31*
Darragh, Peggy *SEE* Darragh, Patrick
Darragh, Peggy; Philadelphia, 1847 ***5704.8*** *p31*
Darragh, Robert; New York, NY, 1865 ***5704.8*** *p195*
Darragh, Robert; Philadelphia, 1852 ***5704.8*** *p96*
Darragh, Siddy; Quebec, 1847 ***5704.8*** *p8*
Darragh, William; New York, NY, 1869 ***5704.8*** *p233*
Darraghty, John; Philadelphia, 1847 ***53.26*** *p18*
Darraghty, John; Philadelphia, 1847 ***5704.8*** *p22*
Darrel, Richd; America, 1698 ***2212*** *p7*
Darrel, Stephen; Arkansas, 1918 ***95.2*** *p34*
Darrell, Stephen; Arkansas, 1918 ***95.2*** *p34*
Darricau, Henry 37; Port uncertain, 1838 ***778.5*** *p142*
Darriff, William; New York, NY, 1865 ***5704.8*** *p203*
Darrigh, Elizabeth; New York, NY, 1869 ***5704.8*** *p232*
Darrigrand, Jean 23; Port uncertain, 1836 ***778.5*** *p142*
Darrimon, Mr. 31; America, 1838 ***778.5*** *p142*
Darris, William; Washington, 1859-1920 ***2872.1*** *p9*
Darson, Jonathan; Virginia, 1638 ***6219*** *p118*
Dartache, Mateo 24; New Orleans, 1831 ***778.5*** *p142*
D'Artague, Jacques 50; New Orleans, 1827 ***778.5*** *p142*
D'Artague, Pierre 25; New Orleans, 1827 ***778.5*** *p142*
Darter, William; America, 1697 ***2212*** *p9*
Dartigaud, Mr. 35; America, 1839 ***778.5*** *p142*
Dartigues, Jacques 40; America, 1829 ***778.5*** *p142*
Dartigues, Simeon 18; America, 1829 ***778.5*** *p142*
Darty, Lee 25; Arizona, 1916 ***9228.40*** *p20*
Dary, John; Virginia, 1638 ***6219*** *p153*
Dasar, Paulus 45; Pennsylvania, 1753 ***2444*** *p147*
Daser, Anna Catharine *SEE* Daser, Paulus Achatius
Daser, Anna Dorothea *SEE* Daser, Paulus Achatius
Daser, Elisabetha Friederica *SEE* Daser, Paulus Achatius
Daser, Frederick; South Carolina, 1788 ***7119*** *p197*
Daser, George Achatius *SEE* Daser, Paulus Achatius
Daser, Heinricke Charlotte *SEE* Daser, Paulus Achatius
Daser, Johanna Margaretha *SEE* Daser, Paulus Achatius
Daser, Ludwig Heinrich *SEE* Daser, Paulus Achatius
Daser, Margaretha G. Raymond *SEE* Daser, Paulus Achatius
Daser, Maria Christina *SEE* Daser, Paulus Achatius
Daser, Paul Friedrich Wilhelm *SEE* Daser, Paulus Achatius
Daser, Paulus Achatius; Pennsylvania, 1753 ***2444*** *p147*
*Wife:*Margaretha G. Raymond
*Child:*Johanna Margaretha
*Child:*Elisabetha Friederica
*Child:*George Achatius
*Child:*Regina Catharina
*Child:*Maria Christina
*Child:*Anna Dorothea
*Child:*Paul Friedrich Wilhelm
*Child:*Regina Margaretha
*Child:*Anna Catharine
*Child:*Ludwig Heinrich
*Child:*Heinricke Charlotte
Daser, Regina Catharina *SEE* Daser, Paulus Achatius
Daser, Regina Margaretha *SEE* Daser, Paulus Achatius
Dash, John 36; Virginia, 1774 ***1219.7*** *p201*
Dashall, William 24; Virginia, 1775 ***1219.7*** *p252*
Dashwood, Charles 26; New Orleans, 1862 ***543.30*** *p59*
Dashwood, Charles 26; New Orleans, 1862 ***543.30*** *p214*
Dasilva, Francis Persiva; Virginia, 1844 ***4626.16*** *p12*
Dasodes, Charles 23; New Orleans, 1826 ***778.5*** *p142*
Dass, John; Illinois, 1871 ***5012.39*** *p25*
Dass, Thomas; Maryland, 1751 ***1219.7*** *p3*
Dass, Thomas; Maryland, 1751 ***3690.1*** *p58*
Dasser, Paulus 45; Pennsylvania, 1753 ***2444*** *p147*
Dassieux, V. 20; Port uncertain, 1838 ***778.5*** *p142*
Dassimon, Mr. 31; America, 1838 ***778.5*** *p142*
Dast, Barbara; America, 1749 ***2444*** *p192*
Dast, Jacob; America, 1724-1800 ***2444*** *p147*
Dast, Jacob; Pennsylvania, 1750 ***2444*** *p147*
Dastie, J. 30; Port uncertain, 1838 ***778.5*** *p142*
Dastugue, Etienne 29; New Orleans, 1835 ***778.5*** *p142*
Dasvie, John; Virginia, 1646 ***6219*** *p236*
Dataiker, Julius 34; New Orleans, 1862 ***543.30*** *p220*
Dater, Adam; America, 1829 ***8582.2*** *p61*
Dater, Adam; Cincinnati, 1869-1887 ***8582*** *p5*
Dater, Gebhard; America, 1830 ***8582.2*** *p61*
Dater, Gebhard; Ohio, 1869-1887 ***8582*** *p5*
Dater, Peter; America, 1829 ***8582.2*** *p61*
Dater, Peter; Cincinnati, 1869-1887 ***8582*** *p5*
Dathe, Gottlieb 34; New Orleans, 1839 ***9420.2*** *p71*
Daton, Marg.; Virginia, 1648 ***6219*** *p246*
Datrie, William; Quebec, 1819 ***7603*** *p75*
Datugues, Mr. 33; Port uncertain, 1839 ***778.5*** *p142*
Daub, Friedr. W. 51; New York, NY, 1912 ***1763*** *p40D*
Daub, Henry 78; Pittsburgh, 1908 ***1763*** *p40D*
Daub, Joseph; Wisconsin, n.d. ***9675.5*** *p50*
Daub, Michael; Indiana, 1836 ***9117*** *p15*
Daubars, John; Wisconsin, n.d. ***9675.5*** *p50*
Daube, Konrad; Lancaster, PA, 1780 ***8137*** *p7*
Daubenschmidt, Anna Catharina; Pennsylvania, 1752 ***4525*** *p230*
Dauber, Carl 25; America, 1838 ***778.5*** *p143*
Daubert, Ferdinand 32; New Orleans, 1862 ***543.30*** *p62*
Daubert, Frederick 45; New Orleans, 1862 ***543.30*** *p61*
Daubert, Jean-Baptiste 40; New Orleans, 1821 ***778.5*** *p143*
Daubin, B. J. 23; Port uncertain, 1839 ***778.5*** *p143*
Daucker, Nels; Arkansas, 1918 ***95.2*** *p35*
D'Aucour, Count; Quebec, 1815 ***9229.18*** *p79*
With wife
Daudorf, . . .; Canada, 1776-1783 ***9786*** *p19*
Dauenhauer, John 34; New Orleans, 1862 ***543.30*** *p55*
Dauert, Augustin 40; Port uncertain, 1839 ***778.5*** *p143*
Dauert, Marie 50; Port uncertain, 1839 ***778.5*** *p143*
Dauert, Nicolas 16; Port uncertain, 1839 ***778.5*** *p143*
Dauert, Pierre 13; Port uncertain, 1839 ***778.5*** *p143*
Daugherty, Ann 23; Philadelphia, 1857 ***5704.8*** *p133*
Daugherty, Charles; Quebec, 1823 ***7603*** *p84*
Daugherty, Mary 20; St. John, N.B., 1857 ***5704.8*** *p135*
Daugherty, Mary Ann 17; Philadelphia, 1858 ***5704.8*** *p139*

Dauis, Henry; America, 1698 2212 p5
Dauis, Jno; America, 1697 2212 p7
Dauis, Jno 13; Maryland or Virginia, 1699 2212 p23
Dauis, Jno 28; Maryland or Virginia, 1699 2212 p23
Dauis, Jonas; America, 1698 2212 p6
Dauis, Maudlin; Maryland or Virginia, 1697 2212 p4
Dauis, Peter 13; Maryland or Virginia, 1699 2212 p23
Dauis, William; America, 1698 2212 p8
Dauis, William 19; Maryland or Virginia, 1699 2212 p24
Daukes, Walter; Virginia, 1637 6219 p113
Dauksha, Joseph; Wisconsin, n.d. 9675.5 p50
Daule, Marie 26; New Orleans, 1837 778.5 p143
Daum, Lewis; Indiana, 1845 9117 p16
Daum, Phillip; Wisconsin, n.d. 9675.5 p50
Daume, J. 23; New Orleans, 1837 778.5 p143
Daumer, John Chas. 25; New Orleans, 1839 9420.2 p362
Daumichen, Gustave; Wisconsin, n.d. 9675.5 p50
Daunis, Charli; Wisconsin, n.d. 9675.5 p50
Daunt, Mary; America, 1736 4971 p44
Daunt, Mary; America, 1737 4971 p45
Daunt, Phil.; America, 1736 4971 p44
Daunt, Phil.; America, 1737 4971 p45
Daunt, Philip; America, 1736 4971 p44
Dauphin, B. 22; New Orleans, 1829 778.5 p143
Dauphin, J.P.V. 45; Louisiana, 1820 778.5 p143
Dauphine, David 25; Halifax, N.S., 1752 7074.6 p207
With family of 3
Dauphine, David 25; Halifax, N.S., 1752 7074.6 p209
With child
Dauphine, Jean 26; Halifax, N.S., 1752 7074.6 p207
Dauphine, Jean 26; Halifax, N.S., 1752 7074.6 p209
Dauphinee, . . .; Halifax, N.S., 1752 7074.6 p230
Dauphinee, Ms.; Died enroute, 1752 7074.6 p208
With baby
Dauphinee, Christophe; Halifax, N.S., 1752 7074.6 p230
Dauphinee, George; Halifax, N.S., 1752 7074.6 p230
Dauphinee, Jean; Halifax, N.S., 1752 7074.6 p230
Dauphiney, . . .; Halifax, N.S., 1752 7074.6 p230
Dauphinie, . . .; Halifax, N.S., 1752 7074.6 p230
Daurss, Herman; Germantown, PA, 1684 2467.7 p5
Daury, . . .; Halifax, N.S., 1752 7074.6 p230
Daush, Jos.; Wisconsin, n.d. 9675.5 p50
Dausseau, John 26; America, 1822 778.5 p143
Daussogne, Frank; New York, NY, 1901 3455.2 p96
Dauter, Eliz.; Virginia, 1637 6219 p113
Dauterry, Joseph 33; Port uncertain, 1829 778.5 p143
Dauth, . . .; Canada, 1776-1783 9786 p19
Dautonis, Mr. 36; America, 1838 778.5 p143
Dautremare, Louis 45; Port uncertain, 1839 778.5 p144
DaVanney, Elisa 30; America, 1838 778.5 p144
Davatz, John; New York, 1889 1450.2 p7B
D'Avbraccio, Cosirno 35; New York, NY, 1893 9026.4 p41
*Wife:*Vincenza 34
D'Avbraccio, Vincenza 34 *SEE* D'Avbraccio, Cosirno
Davenport, Ann; Virginia, 1637 6219 p82
Davenport, Augusta; St. John, N.B., 1851 5704.8 p79
Davenport, Catherine; New York, NY, 1816 2859.11 p29
Davenport, Edward; Virginia, 1643 6219 p204
Davenport, James; Montreal, 1825 7603 p67
Davenport, James; Philadelphia, 1816 2859.11 p29
Davenport, Martha 50; Massachusetts, 1847 5881.1 p31
Davenport, William; Jamaica, 1758 1219.7 p61
Davenport, William; Jamaica, 1758 3690.1 p58
Davenport, William 15; Philadelphia, 1774 1219.7 p232
Daver, Daniel; America, 1735-1743 4971 p79
Daveride, Mr. 23; New Orleans, 1839 778.5 p144
Daveride, P. 30; New Orleans, 1839 778.5 p144
Davers, Henry; America, 1759 1219.7 p71
Davers, Jermyn; Virginia, 1751 1219.7 p3
Davey, Cornelius; New York, NY, 1816 2859.11 p29
Davey, Nancy; Philadelphia, 1852 5704.8 p89
Davey, Patrick 22; Harris Co., TX, 1898 6254 p3
Davezan, Mr. 18; New Orleans, 1822 778.5 p144
David, . . .; Canada, 1776-1783 9786 p19
David, Mr.; America, 1839 778.5 p144
David, Charles 18; America, 1839 778.5 p144
David, Charles 26; Maryland, 1774 1219.7 p230
David, Christian; New York, 1749 3652 p69
David, Christian; New York, 1749 3652 p71
David, Christian 36; New Orleans, 1835 778.5 p144
David, Evan; Virginia, 1641 6219 p184
David, John; New York, NY, 1898 1450.2 p7B
David, Jon.; Virginia, 1635 6219 p35
David, Joseph; Illinois, 1898 2896.5 p9
David, Victor 46; New Orleans, 1838 778.5 p144
David, Wm.; Virginia, 1623-1648 6219 p252
Davidson, Alexander G.; New York, NY, 1840 8208.4 p104
Davidson, Archibald H. 24; West Virginia, 1903 9788.3 p7
Davidson, David 25; Massachusetts, 1848 5881.1 p28
Davidson, Donald; South Carolina, 1716 1639.20 p57
Davidson, Elizabeth 21; Maryland, 1775 1219.7 p256
Davidson, Ellen 25; St. John, N.B., 1858 5704.8 p137
Davidson, Geo.; Austin, TX, 1886 9777 p5
Davidson, George 29; New Orleans, 1862 543.30 p215
Davidson, George 38; Virginia, 1774 1219.7 p239
Davidson, Gilbert; South Carolina, 1760-1783 1639.20 p57
Davidson, Isidore; Arkansas, 1918 95.2 p35
Davidson, James; Kansas, 1892 5240.1 p9
Davidson, James; Nova Scotia, 1767-1770 9775.5 p206
Davidson, James 17; Maryland, 1729 3690.1 p58
Davidson, James 19; St. John, N.B., 1859 5704.8 p140
Davidson, James 33; Kansas, 1875 5240.1 p56
Davidson, James V.; Boston, 1844 2896.5 p9
Davidson, John; Kansas, 1876 5240.1 p9
Davidson, John; Maryland, 1755 1219.7 p33
Davidson, John; Maryland, 1755 3690.1 p58
Davidson, John; New York, NY, 1811 2859.11 p10
Davidson, John; New York, NY, 1811 2859.11 p10
With family
Davidson, John; New York, NY, 1816 2859.11 p29
Davidson, John; New York, NY, 1854 1450.2 p26A
Davidson, John; North Carolina, 1773 1639.20 p57
Davidson, John 22; Maryland, 1774 1219.7 p235
Davidson, John 36; Quebec, 1879 2557.1 p39
Davidson, Joseph 24; Kansas, 1884 5240.1 p65
Davidson, Marion M. 45; Washington, 1916-1919 1728.4 p253
Davidson, Mathew; Virginia, 1801 4778.1 p150
Davidson, Matilda 23; Massachusetts, 1849 5881.1 p32
Davidson, Robert 21; Philadelphia, 1774 1219.7 p183
Davidson, Salomon 19; New York, NY, 1878 9253 p45
Davidson, Samuel 15; Maryland, 1774 1219.7 p235
Davidson, Thomas; Quebec, 1765 7603 p36
Davidson, Thomas 18; Virginia, 1719 3690.1 p60
Davidson, Thomas 25; Jamaica, 1731 3690.1 p59
Davidson, William; New Brunswick, 1765 9775.5 p204
Davidson, William; New York, NY, 1815 2859.11 p29
Davidson, William 20; Virginia, 1727 3690.1 p59
Davidson, William 52; Charleston, SC, 1850 1639.20 p58
Davidson, Wm 29; Kansas, 1888 5240.1 p71
Davidsson, Jon 36; Quebec, 1879 2557.1 p39
Davie, Hugh; Virginia, 1638 6219 p122
Davie, John; Virginia, 1638 6219 p121
Davie, John; Virginia, 1639 6219 p158
Davies, Caspar Heinrich; Kentucky, 1848 8582.3 p101
Davies, Dorithy 20; America, 1705 2212 p45
Davies, Edgar William; New York, NY, 1835 8208.4 p78
Davies, Elizabeth 24; Virginia, 1700 2212 p32
Davies, Ellis 20; America, 1706 2212 p47
Davies, Henry 33; Jamaica, 1730 3690.1 p59
Davies, Ida Margaretta; Wisconsin, n.d. 9675.5 p50
Davies, J. 21; New Orleans, 1835 778.5 p144
Davies, James; Colorado, 1900 9678.2 p15
Davies, James; New York, 1773 1219.7 p167
Davies, Jno 17; America, 1706-1707 2212 p48
Davies, John; America, 1698 2212 p10
Davies, John; New York, NY, 1816 2859.11 p29
Davies, John; Virginia, 1698 2212 p11
Davies, Margaret *SEE* Davies, Robert
Davies, Margaret; Philadelphia, 1849 5704.8 p49
Davies, Margaret; Philadelphia, 1850 53.26 p18
Davies, Margaret; Philadelphia, 1850 5704.8 p60
Davies, Octavius; Virginia, 1856 4626.16 p16
Davies, Phebe M.; New York, NY, 1836 8208.4 p23
Davies, Richard; Antigua (Antego), 1767 1219.7 p129
Davies, Robert; Philadelphia, 1849 53.26 p18
*Relative:*Margaret
Davies, Robert; Philadelphia, 1849 5704.8 p49
Davies, Robt 21; America, 1699 2212 p20
Davies, Ruth; Virginia, 1698 2212 p15
Davies, Samuel W.; Cincinnati, 1800-1877 8582.3 p86
Davies, Tho; America, 1697 2212 p7
Davies, William 21; America, 1700 2212 p33
Davies, William 24; America, 1700 2212 p33
Davies, William 24; Montserrat, 1700 2212 p22
Davies, Wm; Virginia, 1698 2212 p17
Davies, Zachariah; New York, NY, 1833 8208.4 p26
Davignon, . . .; New Orleans, 1839 778.5 p144
Davignon, Mme. 28; New Orleans, 1839 778.5 p144
Davignon, Mr. 45; New Orleans, 1839 778.5 p144
Daviknes, Ludvig; Arkansas, 1918 95.2 p35
Daviner, William 16; New York, 1774 1219.7 p203
Davis, Mr.; Quebec, 1815 9229.18 p79
Davis, Abram; Philadelphia, 1851 5704.8 p80
Davis, Alexander 22; Philadelphia, 1855 5704.8 p124
Davis, Alfred; Washington, 1859-1920 2872.1 p9
Davis, Ally 3; St. John, N.B., 1857 5704.8 p134
Davis, Ann; Virginia, 1643 6219 p229
Davis, Anne 11; St. John, N.B., 1857 5704.8 p134
Davis, Arthur; America, 1869 1450.2 p26A
Davis, Barnard; Philadelphia, 1811 53.26 p18
Davis, Barnard; Philadelphia, 1811 2859.11 p10
Davis, Benjamin 20; Jamaica, 1730 3690.1 p59
Davis, C. W.; Washington, 1859-1920 2872.1 p9
Davis, Caleb; Washington, 1859-1920 2872.1 p9
Davis, Charles; America, 1873 1450.2 p26A
Davis, Charles; New York, NY, 1811 2859.11 p10
Davis, Charles; Quebec, 1713 7603 p27
Davis, Charles 25; Maryland, 1774 1219.7 p214
Davis, Charles D.; Illinois, 1899 5012.40 p56
Davis, Charles S. 40; Kansas, 1889 5240.1 p74
Davis, Daniel; Iowa, 1866-1943 123.54 p16
Davis, Daniel 28; Jamaica, 1731 3690.1 p59
Davis, David; America, 1876 1450.2 p27A
Davis, David; Virginia, 1638 6219 p18
Davis, David 19; Jamaica, 1730 3690.1 p59
Davis, David 20; Maryland, 1774 1219.7 p220
Davis, Dorothy; Virginia, 1636 6219 p28
Davis, Edward; Illinois, 1890 5012.39 p53
Davis, Edward; Illinois, 1891 5012.40 p26
Davis, Edward 17; Jamaica, 1774 1219.7 p208
Davis, Edward 25; Maryland, 1774 1219.7 p230
Davis, Edward 25; Maryland, 1775 1219.7 p272
Davis, Elisabeth; Quebec, 1761 7603 p26
Davis, Eliz.; Virginia, 1642 6219 p189
Davis, Eliza 17; St. John, N.B., 1857 5704.8 p134
Davis, Eliza Jane 20; Philadelphia, 1855 5704.8 p124
Davis, Eliza Jane 22; Philadelphia, 1856 5704.8 p129
Davis, Elizabeth; St. John, N.B., 1851 5704.8 p79
Davis, Elizabeth; Virginia, 1638 6219 p117
Davis, Elizabeth 21; Virginia, 1774 1219.7 p228
Davis, Ellen 25; Massachusetts, 1847 5881.1 p28
Davis, Evan; Virginia, 1643 6219 p201
Davis, Evan 24; Maryland, 1774 1219.7 p211
Davis, Fanny; Philadelphia, 1864 5704.8 p173
Davis, Fanny 10; St. John, N.B., 1857 5704.8 p134
Davis, Francis 15; Maryland or Virginia, 1728 3690.1 p59
Davis, George 30; St. John, N.B., 1866 5704.8 p167
Davis, George James; West Virginia, 1896 9788.3 p7
Davis, George James 36; West Virginia, 1894 9788.3 p7
Davis, Griffeth; Virginia, 1647 6219 p245
Davis, Harry; Cincinnati, 1800-1877 8582.3 p86
Davis, Harry 23; Kansas, 1892 5240.1 p77
Davis, Henry; New York, NY, 1816 2859.11 p29
Davis, Henry; Virginia, 1646 6219 p239
Davis, Henry; Virginia, 1851 4626.16 p14
Davis, Henry A.; New York, NY, 1838 8208.4 p89
Davis, Herscherel; Arkansas, 1918 95.2 p35
Davis, Isaac 40; Kansas, 1900 5240.1 p81
Davis, James; Arkansas, 1918 95.2 p35
Davis, James; Iroquois Co., IL, 1895 3455.1 p10
Davis, James; Philadelphia, 1849 53.26 p18
Davis, James; Philadelphia, 1849 5704.8 p53
Davis, James; Quebec, 1852 5704.8 p97
Davis, James; Virginia, 1638 6219 p33
Davis, James; Virginia, 1640 6219 p182
Davis, James 21; Maryland, 1774 1219.7 p187
Davis, Jane; Virginia, 1639 6219 p150
Davis, Jane 6; St. John, N.B., 1857 5704.8 p134
Davis, Jane 29; Maryland, 1774 1219.7 p207
Davis, Joane; Virginia, 1636 6219 p28
Davis, Joane; Virginia, 1637 6219 p28
Davis, John; America, 1736 4971 p12
Davis, John; America, 1852 1450.2 p27A
Davis, John; Arkansas, 1918 95.2 p35
Davis, John; New York, NY, 1834 8208.4 p34
Davis, John; Virginia, 1637 6219 p109
Davis, John; Virginia, 1638 6219 p121
Davis, John; Virginia, 1638 6219 p124
Davis, John; Virginia, 1639 6219 p150
Davis, John; Virginia, 1642 6219 p194
*Wife:*Mary
Davis, John; Virginia, 1643 6219 p200
Davis, John; Virginia, 1643 6219 p208
Davis, John; Virginia, 1648 6219 p246
Davis, John 17; Quebec, 1856 5704.8 p129
Davis, John 19; Jamaica, 1730 3690.1 p59
Davis, John 20; Jamaica, 1732 3690.1 p59
Davis, John 20; Maryland, 1719 3690.1 p59
Davis, John 20; Maryland, 1723 3690.1 p59
Davis, John 20; Massachusetts, 1848 5881.1 p29
Davis, John 21; Maryland, 1774 1219.7 p192
Davis, John 21; Maryland, 1774 1219.7 p214
Davis, John 26; Kansas, 1889 5240.1 p73
Davis, John 26; Virginia, 1775 1219.7 p247
Davis, John 45; St. John, N.B., 1857 5704.8 p134
Davis, Jon.; Virginia, 1636 6219 p77
Davis, Jon.; Virginia, 1642 6219 p194
Davis, Jon.; Virginia, 1642 6219 p199
Davis, Jonas; Washington, 1859-1920 2872.1 p9
Davis, Jonathan; America, 1698 2212 p5
Davis, Joseph; Illinois, 1882 5240.1 p9
Davis, Joseph; Iroquois Co., IL, 1895 3455.1 p10
Davis, Justin; Virginia, 1649 6219 p252

Deacon, William; New York, NY, 1835 8208.4 p6
Deacon, William 22; Maryland, 1774 1219.7 p182
Deacres, James 17; Virginia, 1750 3690.1 p61
Deacres, James 17; Virginia, 1751 1219.7 p3
Deacy, James 50; Massachusetts, 1850 5881.1 p30
Deacy, Johan 24; Massachusetts, 1850 5881.1 p30
Deady, Bridget 20; Massachusetts, 1849 5881.1 p27
Deady, John 13; Massachusetts, 1849 5881.1 p29
Deady, John 50; Massachusetts, 1849 5881.1 p29
Deady, Michael; New York, NY, 1839 8208.4 p100
Deakes, William; Virginia, 1638 6219 p124
Deakin, Easter 22; America, 1703 2212 p39
Deaks, John 20; Jamaica, 1737 3690.1 p61
Deal, Peter; Philadelphia, 1760 9973.7 p34
Deale, Francis; New York, NY, 1815 2859.11 p29
Dealey, Biddy; Philadelphia, 1852 5704.8 p87
Deall, Peter 22; Jamaica, 1730 3690.1 p289
Dealy, John; New York, NY, 1811 2859.11 p10
Dealy, John 31; Maryland, 1775 1219.7 p260
Dealy, Mary 22; Maryland, 1775 1219.7 p260
Deams, Elizabeth; America, 1865 5704.8 p204
Dean, Adam; America, 1741 4971 p67
Dean, Bryan 43; Kansas, 1887 5240.1 p70
Dean, Charles; Maryland, 1775 1219.7 p265
Dean, Ellen 38; St. John, N.B., 1862 5704.8 p149
Dean, George; Philadelphia, 1868 5704.8 p231
Dean, Giles; Philadelphia, 1868 5704.8 p231
Dean, Henry; Philadelphia, 1851 5704.8 p70
Dean, Jacob 17; Maryland or Virginia, 1735 3690.1 p62
Dean, James; Arizona, 1897 9228.30 p2
Dean, James; Arizona, 1898 9228.30 p8
Dean, James; Philadelphia, 1851 5704.8 p70
Dean, James 40; St. John, N.B., 1862 5704.8 p149
Dean, Jane 40; St. John, N.B., 1862 5704.8 p149
Dean, John; Boston, 1829 6410.32 p126
Dean, John 18; Philadelphia, 1774 1219.7 p197
Dean, John 19; Georgia, 1775 1219.7 p276
Dean, John 19; New York, NY, 1835 6410.32 p126
Dean, John 45; Massachusetts, 1860 6410.32 p120
Dean, Margaret; Philadelphia, 1867 5704.8 p223
Dean, Margaret; St. John, N.B., 1847 5704.8 p20
Dean, Mary; St. John, N.B., 1847 5704.8 p20
Dean, Mary 26; Massachusetts, 1849 5881.1 p31
Dean, Robert; St. John, N.B., 1847 5704.8 p20
Dean, Robert 28; Nova Scotia, 1774 1219.7 p210
Dean, Samuel 21; Massachusetts, 1849 5881.1 p34
Dean, Sarah Ann 9; St. John, N.B., 1862 5704.8 p149
Dean, Susan 22; Massachusetts, 1849 5881.1 p34
Dean, Thomas; America, 1866 1450.2 p27A
Dean, Thomas 20; Jamaica, 1738 3690.1 p62
Dean, William 19; Maryland, 1775 1219.7 p253
Dean, William 24; Philadelphia, 1853 5704.8 p108
Dean, William 35; Maryland, 1775 1219.7 p262
Deane, Charlotte 37; Massachusetts, 1860 6410.32 p112
Deane, Elianor; Virginia, 1639 6219 p157
Deane, Eliza; Quebec, 1850 5704.8 p66
Deane, Jane; Quebec, 1850 5704.8 p66
Deane, John; South Carolina, 1723 1639.20 p58
Deane, John; Virginia, 1636 6219 p7
Deane, Joseph; Virginia, 1622 6219 p29
Deane, Nath.; Virginia, 1635 6219 p27
Deane, Nath.; Virginia, 1638 6219 p145
Deane, Rich; Virginia, 1635 6219 p27
Deane, Richard; Virginia, 1637 6219 p117
Deane, Richard; Virginia, 1639 6219 p155
Deane, Thomas 27; Maryland, 1774 1219.7 p220
Deane, William; Virginia, 1642 6219 p198
Deane, William 36; Maryland, 1775 1219.7 p251
Deane, Wm.; Virginia, 1637 6219 p8
Deaney, Bridget; Philadelphia, 1865 5704.8 p198
Deaney, Catharine; Philadelphia, 1864 5704.8 p180
Deaney, James; America, 1866 5704.8 p215
Deaney, John; Philadelphia, 1864 5704.8 p179
Deaney, John; Philadelphia, 1864 5704.8 p180
Deaney, Margaret; Philadelphia, 1865 5704.8 p198
Deaney, Mary 10; Philadelphia, 1867 5704.8 p218
Deaney, Nancy; Philadelphia, 1867 5704.8 p218
Deangelis, Guiseppe; Arkansas, 1918 95.2 p36
Deans, Ellen 31; St. John, N.B., 1855 5704.8 p126
Deans, George; Austin, TX, 1886 9777 p5
Deans, Jane; St. John, N.B., 1848 5704.8 p43
Deans, Robert; South Carolina, 1750 1639.20 p58
Deare, Joseph; Virginia, 1637 6219 p180
Dearie, Eliza; Philadelphia, 1864 5704.8 p182
Dearie, Hugh; Philadelphia, 1864 5704.8 p182
Deary, Dennis 28; Massachusetts, 1849 5881.1 p28
Deary, James; New York, NY, 1816 2859.11 p29
Deary, John 29; St. John, N.B., 1864 5704.8 p159
Deary, Margaret; Philadelphia, 1868 5704.8 p228
Deary, Michael 30; Massachusetts, 1849 5881.1 p31
Deas, David; Carolina, 1738 1639.20 p58
Deas, John; Charleston, SC, 1790 1639.20 p58
Deas, John; South Carolina, 1749 1639.20 p58
Deas, William; South Carolina, 1680-1830 1639.20 p58
Deashiah, Timothy; America, 1739 4971 p47
Death, Eliz.; Virginia, 1641 6219 p184
Death, Peter; Virginia, 1637 6219 p110
Death, Rich.; Virginia, 1641 6219 p184
Deaves, John; Quebec, 1815 9229.18 p78
Deavlin, Danl.; New York, NY, 1816 2859.11 p29
Deavlin, Neil; New York, NY, 1816 2859.11 p29
De Baconais, E. 22; America, 1837 778.5 p145
DeBaillon, Jean Marie; Louisiana, 1789-1819 778.5 p555
Debar, Edmund 25; New Orleans, 1862 543.30 p57
Debar, Peteer; Virginia, 1646 6219 p242
Debarlier, . . .; Port uncertain, 1839 778.5 p145
Debarlier, Mme.; Port uncertain, 1839 778.5 p145
Debarlier, Mr.; Port uncertain, 1839 778.5 p145
Debas, Pierre Antoine 65; America, 1823 778.5 p145
Debats, Louis 26; New Orleans, 1862 543.30 p58
Debbel, John; America, 1834 1450.2 p30A
De Beauprion, Pierre A. 30; America, 1838 778.5 p145
Debenham, Charles; Illinois, 1854 7857 p3
Debenharn, Thomas; Illinois, 1855 7857 p3
Debenharn, William; Illinois, 1855 7857 p3
Debeno, Anton; New York, NY, 1845 8582 p5
DeBiasio, Biagio 33; West Virginia, 1905 9788.3 p8
DeBiasio, Valentino 35; West Virginia, 1905 9788.3 p8
Debicki, Fortunat; New York, 1831 4606 p173
Debicki, Jozef; New York, 1831 4606 p173
Debicki, Wladyslaw; New York, 1831 4606 p173
Debieux, Mr. 38; New Orleans, 1837 778.5 p145
Deboar, Peter 39; New Orleans, 1862 543.30 p55
DeBocker, Leopold; Colorado, 1898 9678.2 p15
DeBoer, Charlie; Arkansas, 1918 95.2 p35
DeBoer, Louis; Arkansas, 1918 95.2 p35
Debois, E. Th. 42; Port uncertain, 1839 778.5 p145
De Bold, . . .; Canada, 1776-1783 9786 p19
DeBondt, Gustave; Arkansas, 1918 95.2 p35
De Boo, George; Arkansas, 1918 95.2 p35
Deborox, Joseph 22; Maryland, 1774 1219.7 p206
Debos, Pierre 23; America, 1835 778.5 p145
De Boss, Daniel; Ohio, 1798-1802 8582.2 p55
De Boss, Daniel; Ohio, 1798-1818 8582.2 p7
De Bourges, Ch. 33; Port uncertain, 1836 778.5 p145
Deboyne, Clodine 21; St. Louis, 1836 778.5 p145
DeBrot, Earnest E. 25; Kansas, 1903 5240.1 p82
DeBruin, John; Arkansas, 1918 95.2 p35
De Bruyn, Bernard; America, 1848 8582.2 p7
DeBuhr, Tonjes; Wisconsin, n.d. 9675.5 p50
De Castelnaer, Justin 33; Port uncertain, 1838 778.5 p146
Decaudin, Raymond; New York, NY, 1839 8208.4 p97
de Chambre, Jean 23; Quebec, 1666 4533 p130
De Chancel, Mr.; New Orleans, 1839 778.5 p146
De Chancel, A. 63; New Orleans, 1838 778.5 p146
Dechaux, A. 30; New Orleans, 1830 778.5 p146
Dechaux, C. 24; New Orleans, 1830 778.5 p146
Dechene, Constant 6 mos; Missouri, 1837 778.5 p146
Dechene, Francois 18; Missouri, 1837 778.5 p146
Dechene, Isidah 28; Missouri, 1837 778.5 p146
Dechene, Julian 20; Missouri, 1837 778.5 p146
Dechene, Maria 15; Missouri, 1837 778.5 p146
Dechene, Maria 27; Missouri, 1837 778.5 p146
Dechene, Maria Anne 57; Missouri, 1837 778.5 p146
Dechene, Nicolas 52; Missouri, 1837 778.5 p146
Dechene, Philibert 24; Missouri, 1837 778.5 p146
Dechene, Virginia 22; Louisiana, 1837 778.5 p146
Decher, Anna Maria 76; America, 1897 1763 p40D
Dechow, Carl Friedrich von; Halifax, N.S., 1780 9786 p269
Dechow, Carl Friedrich von; New York, 1776 9786 p269
Decigilus, Vidalis 32; America, 1837 778.5 p147
Deck, Henry; Cincinnati, 1869-1887 8582 p6
Deck, Johannes; Cincinnati, 1869-1887 8582 p6
Deck, John; New Orleans, 1843 8582.1 p6
Deckaer, Christoph; New York, NY, 1836 8208.4 p15
Deckebach, Mr.; Cincinnati, 1849 8582.3 p12
Deckebach, Friederich Christian; Cincinnati, 1849 8582.3 p13
With father
Deckebach, Friedrich Christian; America, 1849 8582.1 p7
Deckebach, Georg; America, 1849 8582.1 p7
Deckebach, Johann Georg; New York, NY, 1849 8582.3 p13
With children
Deckenbrock, Henrich William; Baltimore, 1850 1450.2 p27A
Decker, . . .; Canada, 1776-1783 9786 p19
Decker, Benjamin; New York, NY, 1835 8208.4 p39
Decker, Chien 28; Port uncertain, 1839 778.5 p147
Decker, Christoph; New York, NY, 1836 8208.4 p15
Decker, Franz; Kentucky, 1840-1845 8582.3 p100
Decker, Franz; Kentucky, 1843 8582.3 p100
Decker, G. Peter; Wisconsin, n.d. 9675.5 p50
Decker, Heinrich; Wisconsin, n.d. 9675.5 p50
Decker, Henry; Wisconsin, n.d. 9675.5 p50
Decker, John; Illinois, 1893 5012.39 p53
Decker, Martin; Ohio, 1810 8582.1 p48
Decker, Peter; Wisconsin, n.d. 9675.5 p50
Decker, Peter Joseph; Wisconsin, n.d. 9675.5 p50
Decker, William Henry; Wisconsin, n.d. 9675.5 p50
Deckritz, Mrs. August; Milwaukee, 1875 4719.30 p257
Deckritz, Hermann; Milwaukee, 1875 4719.30 p257
Declass, Joseph S.; Illinois, 1872 5012.39 p26
Declercq, Hector; Arkansas, 1918 95.2 p36
DeClercq, Victor; Arkansas, 1918 95.2 p35
DeCloss, Lambert 34; Kansas, 1889 5240.1 p74
Decocest, M. 32; New Orleans, 1827 778.5 p147
Decoeur, Guillaume; Quebec, 1758 7603 p75
Decorb, Amelie 10; America, 1839 778.5 p147
Decorb, Eugenie 7; America, 1839 778.5 p147
DeCorte, Julien Adolph; Arkansas, 1918 95.2 p35
De Coudre, . . .; Canada, 1776-1783 9786 p19
Decoudril, C. 53; Port uncertain, 1838 778.5 p147
Decourb, Marie 37; America, 1839 778.5 p147
DeCoury, Dennis; Illinois, 1862 7857 p3
Decoux, Madame 22; America, 1835 778.5 p147
De Cresent, M. A. 45; Port uncertain, 1827 778.5 p147
de Cude, Allin; Virginia, 1639 6219 p162
Decwski, Walter; Arkansas, 1918 95.2 p36
Deddeder, Peter; Wisconsin, n.d. 9675.5 p50
Dedenbier, Christoph; Philadelphia, 1780 8137 p7
Dederer, Anna Barbara *SEE* Dederer, Joh. Ludwig
Dederer, Joh. Ludwig; Pennsylvania, 1727 3627 p18
*Wife:*Anna Barbara
Dedering, Anton; Wisconsin, n.d. 9675.5 p50
Dedert, Louise; America, 1850 4610.10 p139
Dedet, William; America, 1854 1450.2 p27A
Dedier, John; Philadelphia, 1757 9973.7 p33
De Doirde, G. 30; New Orleans, 1837 778.5 p147
Deduk, Alek; Arkansas, 1918 95.2 p36
Dee, Patrick; New York, NY, 1837 8208.4 p52
Dee, Patrick; Virginia, 1858 4626.16 p17
Dee, Robert 33; Carolina, 1774 1219.7 p231
Dee, Robert 33; Georgia, 1775 1219.7 p275
Dee, William; Arizona, 1883 2764.35 p16
Deecke, Carl Louis; Wisconsin, n.d. 9675.5 p50
Deegan, William; Quebec, 1825 7603 p63
Deehan, Ellen; New York, NY, 1867 5704.8 p216
Deehan, Mary A.; New York, NY, 1867 5704.8 p216
Deek, Agnes; New York, NY, 1811 2859.11 p10
Deek, James; New York, NY, 1811 2859.11 p10
Deel, Adam; Philadelphia, 1764 9973.7 p39
Deel, George; Philadelphia, 1764 9973.7 p39
Deem, . . .; Pennsylvania, n.d. 4525 p206
Deem, . . .; Pennsylvania, n.d. 4525 p208
Deem, Jacob; Pennsylvania, 1752 4525 p207
Deen, Sarah 20; Philadelphia, 1864 5704.8 p155
Deeney, Eleanor; Philadelphia, 1867 5704.8 p220
Deeney, Margaret; New York, NY, 1864 5704.8 p186
Deeney, Margaret; New York, NY, 1865 5704.8 p195
Deening, Margaret 13; Quebec, 1850 5704.8 p69
Deeny, Catherine 14; Philadelphia, 1858 5704.8 p139
Deeny, Catherine 21; Quebec, 1855 5704.8 p126
Deeny, Daniel; New York, NY, 1868 5704.8 p228
Deeny, Daniel 22; Philadelphia, 1855 5704.8 p124
Deeny, Hannah; Quebec, 1849 5704.8 p52
Deeny, Hugh 9; Philadelphia, 1853 5704.8 p101
Deeny, Hugh 14; St. John, N.B., 1857 5704.8 p134
Deeny, James; Quebec, 1853 5704.8 p104
Deeny, Jane 40; St. John, N.B., 1857 5704.8 p134
Deeny, John; Philadelphia, 1852 5704.8 p88
Deeny, John; Philadelphia, 1865 5704.8 p198
Deeny, John 1; St. John, N.B., 1857 5704.8 p134
Deeny, John 7; Philadelphia, 1853 5704.8 p101
Deeny, John 7; Philadelphia, 1864 5704.8 p160
Deeny, John 11; Philadelphia, 1853 5704.8 p111
Deeny, John 20; Philadelphia, 1857 5704.8 p132
Deeny, John 25; Philadelphia, 1858 5704.8 p139
Deeny, John 48; St. John, N.B., 1857 5704.8 p134
Deeny, Joseph 12; Philadelphia, 1853 5704.8 p101
Deeny, Margaret 11; St. John, N.B., 1857 5704.8 p134
Deeny, Mary *SEE* Deeny, Sarah
Deeny, Mary; Philadelphia, 1849 5704.8 p53
Deeny, Mary; Philadelphia, 1853 5704.8 p101
Deeny, Mary 16; St. John, N.B., 1857 5704.8 p134
Deeny, Mary 20; Philadelphia, 1859 5704.8 p142
Deeny, Mathew 7; St. John, N.B., 1857 5704.8 p134
Deeny, Nancy 40; Philadelphia, 1854 5704.8 p122
Deeny, Rosy 11; Philadelphia, 1859 5704.8 p142
Deeny, Sarah; Philadelphia, 1849 53.26 p18
*Relative:*Mary
Deeny, Sarah; Philadelphia, 1849 5704.8 p53
Deepup, John 18; Barbados, 1720 3690.1 p62
Deer, George; Philadelphia, 1760 9973.7 p34
Deer, Mathias; Pennsylvania, 1754 2444 p148
Deer, Michel; Quebec, 1821 7603 p58

108 FOR A COMPLETE EXPLANATION OF ENTRY, SEE "HOW TO READ A CITATION" SECTION

Deer, Stephan; Pennsylvania, 1751 2444 p226
Deerin, Thomas; America, 1739 4971 p31
Deering, . . . 6 mos; Philadelphia, 1861 5704.8 p148
Deering, Adolph; Wisconsin, n.d. 9675.5 p50
Deering, Francis 25; Philadelphia, 1861 5704.8 p147
Deering, Jane 28; Philadelphia, 1861 5704.8 p148
Deering, Mary; America, 1737 4971 p12
Deering, Mary A. 18; Philadelphia, 1857 5704.8 p133
Deering, Thomas; Virginia, 1638 6219 p121
Deery, Ann; New York, NY, 1866 5704.8 p212
Deery, Bridget; New York, NY, 1866 5704.8 p213
Deery, Catharine 5; Philadelphia, 1865 5704.8 p202
Deery, Edward; America, 1847 1450.2 p27A
Deery, Elizabeth; Philadelphia, 1867 5704.8 p219
Deery, Elizabeth; St. John, N.B., 1848 5704.8 p47
Deery, Elizabeth; St. John, N.B., 1849 5704.8 p55
Deery, Hugh; Philadelphia, 1851 5704.8 p71
Deery, James; New York, NY, 1864 5704.8 p170
Deery, James; Philadelphia, 1848 53.26 p18
Deery, James; Philadelphia, 1848 5704.8 p40
Deery, James; Philadelphia, 1852 5704.8 p85
Deery, James 14; Philadelphia, 1853 5704.8 p112
Deery, John; Philadelphia, 1850 53.26 p18
Deery, John; Philadelphia, 1850 5704.8 p60
Deery, Mary SEE Deery, Michael
Deery, Mary; New York, NY, 1866 5704.8 p213
Deery, Mary; Philadelphia, 1847 53.26 p18
Relative: Rose
Deery, Mary; Philadelphia, 1847 5704.8 p14
Deery, Mary; Philadelphia, 1865 5704.8 p202
Deery, Mary 5; Philadelphia, 1848 5704.8 p40
Deery, Michael; Philadelphia, 1848 53.26 p18
Relative: Mary
Deery, Michael 8; Philadelphia, 1848 5704.8 p40
Deery, Nancy; St. John, N.B., 1847 5704.8 p4
Deery, Patrick; New York, NY, 1864 5704.8 p170
Deery, Philip; New York, NY, 1865 5704.8 p197
Deery, Rose SEE Deery, Mary
Deery, Rose 6; Philadelphia, 1847 5704.8 p14
Deery, Sally; Quebec, 1853 5704.8 p103
Deery, Susan; Philadelphia, 1866 5704.8 p210
Deery, Thomas; St. John, N.B., 1853 5704.8 p107
Deery, Unity; Philadelphia, 1847 53.26 p18
Deery, Unity; Philadelphia, 1847 5704.8 p14
Deery, William 3; Philadelphia, 1865 5704.8 p202
Deetz, B. A.; Washington, 1859-1920 2872.1 p9
Defer, Mrs. 35; Louisiana, 1823 778.5 p147
Defer, Eugene 5; Louisiana, 1823 778.5 p147
Defer, Henry 1; Louisiana, 1823 778.5 p147
Defer, J. B. 45; Louisiana, 1823 778.5 p147
Deffaulx, Louis Victor; America, 1853 1450.2 p27A
Deffit, Mr. 27; Port uncertain, 1839 778.5 p147
Deffner, . . .; Canada, 1776-1783 9786 p19
Deffry, Chatrine 22; Port uncertain, 1839 778.5 p148
Deffry, Francois 8; Port uncertain, 1839 778.5 p148
Deffry, Francois 54; Port uncertain, 1839 778.5 p148
Deffry, Josephine 6; Port uncertain, 1839 778.5 p148
Deffry, Marguerite 16; Port uncertain, 1839 778.5 p148
Deffry, Martin 12; Port uncertain, 1839 778.5 p148
Deffry, Ursule 10; Port uncertain, 1839 778.5 p148
Deffry, Ursule 47; Port uncertain, 1839 778.5 p148
Defis, J. B. 55; America, 1829 778.5 p148
De Fontenelle, Mrs. 40; New Orleans, 1835 778.5 p148
DeFoort, Morise 31; Arkansas, 1918 95.2 p35
De Fortmanoir, Mme.; New Orleans, 1839 778.5 p148
De Fortmanoir, P. 42; New Orleans, 1839 778.5 p148
Defournand, Antoine 42; New Orleans, 1862 543.30 p217
DeGabain, Armand; Colorado, 1894 9678.2 p15
Degail, John 25; America, 1829 778.5 p148
Degard, Alphonse 22; America, 1835 778.5 p148
Degaris, Elias; Virginia, 1643 6219 p205
Degarne, Madam 27; Grenada, 1774 1219.7 p245
Degarne, Jean 30; Grenada, 1774 1219.7 p245
Degase, Louis J. 26; New Orleans, 1826 778.5 p148
Degaugue, Alice Marie; Iowa, 1866-1943 123.54 p61
Degaugue, Charles; Iowa, 1866-1943 123.54 p61
Degele, Johann David; Port uncertain, 1747-1800 2444 p147
Wife: Juliana
Child: Margaretha Barbara
Degele, Juliana SEE Degele, Johann David
Degele, Margaretha Barbara SEE Degele, Johann David
Degen, . . .; Canada, 1776-1783 9786 p19
Degenhard, . . .; Canada, 1776-1783 9786 p19
Degenhardt, August; America, 1849 8582.1 p7
Degenhart, Christian; Virginia, 1847 4626.16 p13
Degenstein, Peter; Alberta, n.d. 5262 p58
Degerstrom, John; Maine, 1871-1881 6410.22 p121
Deglapion, . . . 23; Grenada, 1774 1219.7 p231
Deglow, Herman Rudolph; America, 1851 8582.3 p13
Degn, Hans Nelson; Arkansas, 1918 95.2 p36
Degnan, Barnard 30; Massachusetts, 1850 5881.1 p27
Degnan, Margaret 50; Massachusetts, 1850 5881.1 p33
Degnan, Peter; Quebec, 1847 5704.8 p37
Degnitz, Herman; Wisconsin, n.d. 9675.5 p50
De Goer, Hte. 28; America, 1835 778.5 p149
De Graillay, Mr. 28; New Orleans, 1835 778.5 p149
De Greif, Jakob; America, 1851 8582.3 p13
De Groot, Catharinus 25; Kansas, 1905 5240.1 p83
DeGroot, Tys; Arkansas, 1918 95.2 p35
de Grote, Antonia; Virginia, 1639 6219 p154
De Haas, Philipp; Philadelphia, 1756 8582.3 p95
Dehall, Vincent; Virginia, 1636 6219 p79
De Hart, Edward; New York, NY, 1811 2859.11 p10
Dehaven, A.; Ohio, 1811 8582.1 p48
Dehaven, Abraham; Ohio, 1811 8582.1 p48
Dehaven, Jakob; Ohio, 1811 8582.1 p48
Dehayes, Mrs. 46; America, 1837 778.5 p149
Dehayes, Etienne 19; America, 1837 778.5 p149
Dehayes, Etienne 46; America, 1837 778.5 p149
Deheyden, Joseph; New York, NY, 1823 8208.4 p57
Dehl, Charles; Philadelphia, 1763 9973.7 p38
Dehl, Daniel; Philadelphia, 1761 9973.7 p35
Dehlern, Ludwig 38; New Orleans, 1862 543.30 p55
Dehmer, Joseph; Wisconsin, n.d. 9675.5 p50
Dehne, . . .; Canada, 1776-1783 9786 p19
Dehner, Anton; America, 1838 1450.2 p28A
Dehner, Daniel; Ohio, 1869-1887 8582 p6
Dehner, Georg; Savannah, GA, 1779 8582.2 p52
Dehner, Hilarius; America, 1846 8582.1 p7
Dehner, Hilarius 27; New Orleans, 1846 8582.2 p7
With wife & 2 children
Dehner, Peter; Charleston, SC, 1775-1781 8582.2 p7
Dehnert, . . .; Canada, 1776-1783 9786 p19
Dehnhardt, . . .; Canada, 1776-1783 9786 p19
Deho, Wilhelm; Cincinnati, 1869-1887 8582 p6
Deho, Wilhelm; New York, NY, 1836 8582.3 p14
Dehony, Thomas; America, 1736-1743 4971 p57
DeHoog, Gerret; Arkansas, 1918 95.2 p35
DeHoog, Gerrett 28; Arkansas, 1918 95.2 p35
Dehue, . . .; Canada, 1776-1783 9786 p42
Dehueres, Samuel; Halifax, N.S., 1752 7074.6 p216
Dehull, Cornelius; Virginia, 1636 6219 p79
Deibel, Marg. 52; Pennsylvania, 1906 1763 p40C
Deibel, Maria 68; America, 1895 1763 p40C
Deickmann, August Gerhard 20; Jamaica, 1753 1219.7 p22
Deickmann, August Gerhard 20; Jamaica, 1753 3690.1 p62
Deie, John; Cincinnati, 1869-1887 8582 p6
Deierlein, Friedrich; America, 1845 8582.1 p7
Deierling, Jacob; Cincinnati, 1820-1869 8582 p6
Deighan, Bridget; Philadelphia, 1870 5704.8 p239
Deighan, Joseph; New York, NY, 1816 2859.11 p29
Deighan, Kate; Philadelphia, 1870 5704.8 p239
Deighan, Patrick; Philadelphia, 1870 5704.8 p239
Deighan, Sarah; Philadelphia, 1870 5704.8 p239
Deighton, Thomas 20; New York, 1774 1219.7 p202
Deikert, Jacob; America, 1852 1450.2 p30A
Deikus, John; Wisconsin, n.d. 9675.5 p50
Deil, August 31; New Orleans, 1862 543.30 p60
Deischmer, John; Illinois, 1869 5012.38 p99
Deisler, Conrad; America, 1849 8582.3 p14
Deisler, John; America, 1853 1450.2 p28A
Deissinger, . . .; Canada, 1776-1783 9786 p19
Deist, Elisabeth SEE Deist, Elisabeth
Deist, Elisabeth; America, 1857 3702.7 p206
Father: Hermann
Mother: Elisabeth
With brothers & sisters
Deist, Hermann SEE Deist, Elisabeth
Deiter, August 21; Kansas, 1880 5240.1 p9
Deitrick, Jacob; Philadelphia, 1760 9973.7 p34
Deitsch, Nicholas; Wisconsin, n.d. 9675.5 p50
Deitz, Mr. 24; New Orleans, 1821 778.5 p149
Deitz, Carmann; America, 1853 1450.2 p28A
Deitz, Elisabeth SEE Deitz, Elisabeth
Deitz, Elisabeth; America, 1857 3702.7 p206
Father: Hermann
Mother: Elisabeth
With brothers
With sisters
Deitz, Frederick; America, 1848 1450.2 p28A
Deitz, George 28; Louisiana, 1863 543.30 p374
Deitz, Hermann SEE Deitz, Elisabeth
Deitz, John; America, 1844 1450.2 p31A
Dejamme, V.; America, 1839 778.5 p149
Dejardin, Albert; Wisconsin, n.d. 9675.5 p50
Dejardin, Leopold; Wisconsin, n.d. 9675.5 p50
Dejax, Mr. 48; New Orleans, 1836 778.5 p149
Dejean, Bartholomew; Louisiana, 1789-1819 778.5 p555
Dejon, Mr.; Port uncertain, 1839 778.5 p149
Dejon, F.; New Orleans, 1839 778.5 p149
De Jos, M. 28; America, 1829 778.5 p149
Dekert, Joseph; Kansas, 1879 5240.1 p10
De Kovadchy, . . .; Canada, 1776-1783 9786 p19
Dela Rey, Jaques; Virginia, 1635 6219 p75
Delabar, Anton; Illinois, 1836 8582.1 p55
Delabeere, Richard; Virginia, 1638 6219 p117
Delabien, F. 18; New Orleans, 1832 778.5 p149
Delabraise, Alex; America, 1839 778.5 p149
Delabroye, Charles 19; New Orleans, 1838 778.5 p149
Delabroye, Pierre 30; New Orleans, 1838 778.5 p150
Delabroye, Theodore 28; New Orleans, 1838 778.5 p150
Delabroye, Theophile 22; New Orleans, 1838 778.5 p150
de Lacetiere, Florent; Quebec, 1687 4533 p129
De la Chaise, Leonard 21; New Orleans, 1821 778.5 p150
Delachaux, L. 20; Louisiana, 1820 778.5 p150
Delacomb, A. 30; New Orleans, 1836 778.5 p150
Delacroix, Francois 20; New Orleans, 1832 778.5 p150
Delaforgue, Frederick; Colorado, 1889 9678.2 p15
Delage, Mlle. 25; Port uncertain, 1832 778.5 p150
Delahanty, Maurice Edgar; Arkansas, 1918 95.2 p36
Delahunt, John; New York, NY, 1836 8208.4 p19
Delahunt, Thomas; New York, NY, 1815 2859.11 p29
Delahunty, Simon; America, 1739 4971 p26
Delail, Miss; New Orleans, 1839 778.5 p150
Delalande, J. 35; New Orleans, 1830 778.5 p150
Delamar, Peter Alexander 20; Pennsylvania, 1731 3690.1 p62
Delamare, Gustave 22; Louisiana, 1822 778.5 p150
Delamarre, . . .; Canada, 1776-1783 9786 p42
Delamarre, Jean; New Brunswick, 1798 7603 p49
Delamnundayes, Mareene; Virginia, 1638 6219 p158
Delamotte, Charles; Savannah, GA, 1736 3652 p51
Delancan, John 24; Louisiana, 1820 778.5 p150
Delandy, William; Arkansas, 1918 95.2 p36
Delaney, Alexander; Virginia, 1851 4626.16 p14
Delaney, Cornelius 48?; Arizona, 1890 2764.35 p18
Delaney, Dennis; New York, NY, 1867 2764.35 p19
Delaney, Edmund 20; Newport, RI, 1851 6508.5 p20
Delaney, Eliza 16; Newport, RI, 1851 6508.5 p20
Delaney, Forrest 11; Newport, RI, 1851 6508.5 p20
Delaney, George; New York, NY, 1866 5704.8 p212
Delaney, James; St. John, N.B., 1850 5704.8 p62
Delaney, Kate 20; Newport, RI, 1851 6508.5 p20
Delaney, Martin 21; Newport, RI, 1851 6508.5 p20
Delaney, Michael 18; Maryland, 1774 1219.7 p220
Delaney, Michael 21; Carolina, 1774 1219.7 p227
Delaney, Michael 22; Newfoundland, 1789 4915.24 p57
Delaney, Patrick; New York, NY, 1866 5704.8 p212
Delaney, Wm 28; Newport, RI, 1851 6508.5 p20
Delange, Escobant 42; America, 1837 778.5 p150
Delanie, Peter 25; America, 1829 778.5 p150
Delanne, Mme. 30; America, 1838 778.5 p151
Delanoe, Aristides 34; America, 1832 778.5 p151
Delanul, Alexandre 22; New Orleans, 1835 778.5 p151
Delany, Mr.; Quebec, 1815 9229.18 p78
Delany, Ann 9; St. John, N.B., 1852 5704.8 p83
Delany, Bridget; St. John, N.B., 1852 5704.8 p83
Delany, Catherine; America, 1741 4971 p10
Delany, Catherine; America, 1741 4971 p94
Delany, Cavan 22; Maryland, 1730 3690.1 p290
Delany, Charles; America, 1740 4971 p28
Delany, Edmund 36; New Orleans, 1862 543.30 p54
Delany, Edward; St. John, N.B., 1847 5704.8 p11
Delany, Edward; St. John, N.B., 1852 5704.8 p83
Delany, Elizabeth; St. John, N.B., 1852 5704.8 p83
Delany, Ellen; America, 1863-1871 5704.8 p224
Delany, Fanny 1; Massachusetts, 1850 5881.1 p29
Delany, Francis 11; St. John, N.B., 1852 5704.8 p83
Delany, Grizel; America, 1739 4971 p28
Delany, James; America, 1743 4971 p10
Delany, James; America, 1743 4971 p95
Delany, John; America, 1738 4971 p31
Delany, John 50; Massachusetts, 1849 5881.1 p29
Delany, Kitty 35; Massachusetts, 1850 5881.1 p31
Delany, Margaret 1; Massachusetts, 1849 5881.1 p31
Delany, Margaret 30; Massachusetts, 1849 5881.1 p31
Delany, Mary; Quebec, 1821 7603 p74
Delany, Mary 10; St. John, N.B., 1847 5704.8 p11
Delany, Mary 40; Massachusetts, 1849 5881.1 p31
Delany, Mary 46; Massachusetts, 1850 5881.1 p33
Delany, Michael; New York, NY, 1838 8208.4 p57
Delany, Michael 7; Massachusetts, 1849 5881.1 p31
Delany, Nicholas; New York, NY, 1816 2859.11 p29
Delany, Peggy 30; Massachusetts, 1849 5881.1 p33
Delany, Thomas; New York, NY, 1811 2859.11 p10
Delany, Thomas; New York, NY, 1838 8208.4 p85
Delany, William; America, 1742 4971 p29
Delany, William; Maryland, 1742 4971 p106
Delany, William 13; St. John, N.B., 1847 5704.8 p11
Delany, William 35; Massachusetts, 1849 5881.1 p34
Delanzac, George 19; New Orleans, 1862 543.30 p58
Delap, Alexander 5; St. John, N.B., 1848 5704.8 p43
Delap, Andrew 42; St. John, N.B., 1856 5704.8 p131
Delap, James 20; Philadelphia, 1854 5704.8 p118

Delap, Jane 3; St. John, N.B., 1848 ***5704.8*** *p43*
Delap, John 18; Philadelphia, 1859 ***5704.8*** *p141*
Delap, Margaret 35; St. John, N.B., 1856 ***5704.8*** *p131*
Delap, Rebecca; St. John, N.B., 1848 ***5704.8*** *p43*
Delap, Samuel; Philadelphia, 1850 ***53.26*** *p18*
Delap, Samuel; Philadelphia, 1850 ***5704.8*** *p69*
Delap, William 9 mos; St. John, N.B., 1848 ***5704.8*** *p43*
Delaport, Mr. 36; America, 1831 ***778.5*** *p151*
Delaporte, Mr. 26; America, 1839 ***778.5*** *p151*
De la Porte, Rose 16; Port uncertain, 1836 ***778.5*** *p151*
Delarive, A. 32; America, 1839 ***778.5*** *p151*
Delarive, Avril 24; America, 1839 ***778.5*** *p151*
Delaroche, A. 28; New Orleans, 1839 ***778.5*** *p151*
Delassele, Emma 23; America, 1838 ***778.5*** *p151*
Delaunay, Alexandre; New York, NY, 1834 ***8208.4*** *p45*
Delaunay, Elisa 26; America, 1835 ***778.5*** *p151*
Delaunay, Eliza 27; America, 1837 ***778.5*** *p151*
De Launnay de la Blarduse, Mr. 63; New Orleans, 1830 ***778.5*** *p151*
Delaunre, Mr. 29; America, 1838 ***778.5*** *p151*
Delaure, Mlle. 21; America, 1838 ***778.5*** *p151*
Delaure, Mme. 25; America, 1838 ***778.5*** *p152*
Delaure, Mr. 29; America, 1838 ***778.5*** *p151*
DeLaux, Francois 32; America, 1838 ***778.5*** *p152*
Delavalette, St. George 37; New Orleans, 1821 ***778.5*** *p152*
De la Vega, J. 22; New Orleans, 1862 ***543.30*** *p217*
Delavigne, F. 38; New Orleans, 1832 ***778.5*** *p152*
DelaVille, Mr. 26; Port uncertain, 1838 ***778.5*** *p152*
Delaville, V. 55; New Orleans, 1836 ***778.5*** *p152*
Delaware, Esau; Virginia, 1637 ***6219*** *p13*
Delayhaye, Gringall; Virginia, 1641 ***6219*** *p187*
Delbocci, Guizappi; Wisconsin, n.d. ***9675.5*** *p50*
DelBoccio, Venanzio; Wisconsin, n.d. ***9675.5*** *p50*
DelBociio, Panfilo; Wisconsin, n.d. ***9675.5*** *p50*
DelBocio, Donato; Wisconsin, n.d. ***9675.5*** *p50*
Delbocio, Salvatoro; Wisconsin, n.d. ***9675.5*** *p50*
Delbosio, Giovarneo; Wisconsin, n.d. ***9675.5*** *p50*
Delbridge, Edward; Virginia, 1750 ***3690.1*** *p62*
Delbridge, Robert 21; Baltimore, 1775 ***1219.7*** *p270*
Delbruge, Mr.; Baltimore, 1833 ***3702.7*** *p68*
Delcker, Adam; Pennsylvania, 1751 ***2444*** *p149*
Delcourneau, Mr. 30; New Orleans, 1839 ***778.5*** *p152*
Delega, Joseph; Wisconsin, n.d. ***9675.5*** *p50*
Delehante, P.J.; Arizona, 1890 ***2764.35*** *p19*
Delehanty, Patrick; New York, NY, 1838 ***8208.4*** *p81*
Delehaunty, William; New York, 1841 ***7036*** *p120*
Delenable, Louis P. 24; America, 1838 ***778.5*** *p152*
Deleo, Guiseppe; Arkansas, 1918 ***95.2*** *p36*
Deletra, Miss 28; New Orleans, 1836 ***778.5*** *p152*
DeLetra, Lewis 21; New Orleans, 1829 ***778.5*** *p152*
DeLetrass, L. 40; New Orleans, 1826 ***778.5*** *p152*
DeLetre, Luis 49; New Orleans, 1826 ***778.5*** *p152*
Delevran, Charles 36; New Orleans, 1838 ***778.5*** *p152*
Delevrau, Charles 36; New Orleans, 1838 ***778.5*** *p152*
Delfeld, Mathias; Wisconsin, n.d. ***9675.5*** *p50*
Delfini, Ermenegildo; Arkansas, 1918 ***95.2*** *p36*
Delfoget, Piere 30; America, 1839 ***778.5*** *p153*
Delfs, Detlof; New York, 1754 ***3652*** *p79*
Delgado, Bacilio 64; Arizona, 1915 ***9228.40*** *p19*
DelGallo, Liberato; Wisconsin, n.d. ***9675.5*** *p50*
Delgallo, Venanzi; Wisconsin, n.d. ***9675.5*** *p50*
Delger, Adam; Pennsylvania, 1751 ***2444*** *p149*
*Wife:*Eva Stortz
*Child:*Sara
Delger, Eva Stortz *SEE* Delger, Adam
Delger, Sara *SEE* Delger, Adam
Delhome, J. M.; Shreveport, LA, 1879 ***7129*** *p44*
De L'Hoste, Mme.; America, 1835 ***778.5*** *p153*
De L'Hoste, J. 25; America, 1835 ***778.5*** *p153*
Delitombe, Francois 36; Ohio, 1820 ***778.5*** *p153*
Delivronel, C. 37; Port uncertain, 1838 ***778.5*** *p153*
Delka, Joh, Sr.; Charleston, SC, 1775-1781 ***8582.2*** *p52*
Delker, Adam; Pennsylvania, 1751 ***2444*** *p149*
Dell, . . .; Canada, 1776-1783 ***9786*** *p19*
Dell, John; America, 1834 ***1450.2*** *p28A*
Dell, John; New York, 1833 ***1450.2*** *p28A*
Dell, William; America, 1834 ***1450.2*** *p28A*
Dellair, Mr.; Quebec, 1815 ***9229.18*** *p77*
Dellebere, Henry 14; Jamaica, 1733 ***3690.1*** *p62*
Dellemore, Robert 22; Virginia, 1773 ***1219.7*** *p168*
Deller, Thomas 18; Jamaica, 1738 ***3690.1*** *p62*
Dellert, Charles; America, 1847 ***1450.2*** *p29A*
Delles, John; Wisconsin, n.d. ***9675.5*** *p50*
Delles, Martin; Wisconsin, n.d. ***9675.5*** *p50*
Delles, Peter; Wisconsin, n.d. ***9675.5*** *p50*
Delles, Peter K.; Wisconsin, n.d. ***9675.5*** *p50*
Dellgren, August; Minneapolis, 1883-1886 ***6410.35*** *p52*
Dellit, Andreas Francis 30; New Orleans, 1839 ***9420.2*** *p167*
Delmas, Antoine 26; Port uncertain, 1837 ***778.5*** *p153*
Delmenhorst, Friedrich; Philadelphia, 1779 ***8137*** *p7*
Delmenhorst, Henrich; Lancaster, PA, 1780 ***8137*** *p7*
Delmore, Richard 40; New Orleans, 1862 ***543.30*** *p220*
Delnow, Jonath 11; America, 1706 ***2212*** *p46*
Deloanna, Mme. 30; America, 1838 ***778.5*** *p151*
Deloche, Mr. 35; Port uncertain, 1832 ***778.5*** *p153*
Delope, P.A. 21; New York, NY, 1893 ***9026.4*** *p41*
Deloroches, Joseph 18; Port uncertain, 1839 ***778.5*** *p153*
De Lorodriges, Estmath 48; Arizona, 1911 ***9228.40*** *p15*
Delouvre, Jules 25; New Orleans, 1836 ***778.5*** *p153*
Delpench, Mr. 25; New Orleans, 1825 ***778.5*** *p153*
Delpeuche, Ant. 40; New Orleans, 1838 ***778.5*** *p153*
Delphin, Joseph 27; New Orleans, 1836 ***778.5*** *p153*
Delpit, Mr. 14; New Orleans, 1826 ***778.5*** *p153*
Delpit, Mr. 25; New Orleans, 1839 ***778.5*** *p153*
Delpit, Mr. 28; New Orleans, 1838 ***778.5*** *p153*
Delpit, Mrs. 35; New Orleans, 1826 ***778.5*** *p154*
Delpit, Adrien 16; New Orleans, 1821 ***778.5*** *p154*
Delpit, Jean 40; New Orleans, 1826 ***778.5*** *p154*
Delpuget, Annais 17; New Orleans, 1837 ***778.5*** *p154*
Delpuget, Celina 11; New Orleans, 1837 ***778.5*** *p154*
Delpuget, M. 42; New Orleans, 1837 ***778.5*** *p154*
Delpujet, David 23; New Orleans, 1838 ***778.5*** *p154*
Deltombe, Anatolie 36; Ohio, 1820 ***778.5*** *p154*
DeLuca, Nickolas; Arkansas, 1918 ***95.2*** *p35*
DeLuca, Raphael 38; Kansas, 1891 ***5240.1*** *p76*
de Lucke, Major; Quebec, 1776 ***9786*** *p264*
Delusin, Mr. 24; New Orleans, 1830 ***778.5*** *p154*
Delussan, Mrs. 20; America, 1835 ***778.5*** *p154*
Delussan, P. 35; America, 1835 ***778.5*** *p154*
Deluvian, Louis 22; America, 1829 ***778.5*** *p154*
Deluzan, Henri; New Orleans, 1831 ***778.5*** *p154*
Delvaille, Louis 48; New Orleans, 1827 ***778.5*** *p154*
Delvaille, M. 41; Port uncertain, 1820 ***778.5*** *p154*
Del Vallate, Mr. 27; Mexico, 1835 ***778.5*** *p155*
Delvalle, A. 26; America, 1835 ***778.5*** *p155*
Delves, John; Kingston, Jamaica, 1752 ***1219.7*** *p13*
Delvis, Alice; Virginia, 1641 ***6219*** *p187*
Delz, Gaspard 22; New Orleans, 1863 ***543.30*** *p222*
Demache, Charles 16; Louisiana, 1820 ***778.5*** *p155*
Demacheto, Christian; Virginia, 1643 ***6219*** *p203*
DeMaeght, Jeron; Arkansas, 1918 ***95.2*** *p35*
DeMagnus, J. 50; America, 1837 ***778.5*** *p155*
Demaio, Anthony; Arkansas, 1918 ***95.2*** *p36*
DeMaio, James; Arkansas, 1918 ***95.2*** *p35*
Demann, Van; America, 1869-1885 ***8582.2*** *p7*
De Marchi, Pietro; Iowa, 1866-1943 ***123.54*** *p61*
DeMarco, Mattia; Arkansas, 1918 ***95.2*** *p35*
DeMarco, Mattia; Arkansas, 1918 ***95.2*** *p36*
DeMarco, Mattio; Arkansas, 1918 ***95.2*** *p36*
Demarco, Paul; Arkansas, 1918 ***95.2*** *p36*
DeMarens, Mme. 50; America, 1835 ***778.5*** *p155*
DeMarens, Ch. D. 64; America, 1835 ***778.5*** *p155*
DeMarens, Charles 17; America, 1835 ***778.5*** *p155*
DeMargne, John 24; America, 1838 ***778.5*** *p155*
Demario, Angelo; Colorado, 1904 ***9678.2*** *p15*
Demarteni, Lorenzo; Iowa, 1866-1943 ***123.54*** *p16*
Demartini, Paul A.; Nevada, 1875 ***2764.35*** *p17*
Demarun, Jules 20; Port uncertain, 1838 ***778.5*** *p155*
Demas, Peter 35; America, 1835 ***778.5*** *p155*
Demasse, J. 28; New Orleans, 1837 ***778.5*** *p155*
Demattei, Antonio; Arkansas, 1918 ***95.2*** *p36*
DeMaught, Alphonse; Arkansas, 1918 ***95.2*** *p36*
Demberg, Caspar Heinrich Gottlieb; America, 1858 ***4610.10*** *p140*
Dembergsmeyer, Anne Marie Wilhelmine; America, 1845 ***4610.10*** *p120*
Dembicki, . . .; New York, 1831 ***4606*** *p173*
Dembowski, Wladyslaw; Arkansas, 1918 ***95.2*** *p36*
Demedina, Miss 28; America, 1839 ***778.5*** *p155*
Demedina, Mme. 25; America, 1839 ***778.5*** *p155*
Demedina, Mr. 30; America, 1839 ***778.5*** *p155*
Demerch, John Adam; Wisconsin, n.d. ***9675.5*** *p50*
Demere, Paul; South Carolina, 1765 ***1219.7*** *p115*
Demers, Baptiste; New Hampshire, 1889 ***3455.3*** *p107*
Demers, Joseph; Illinois, 1906 ***3455.3*** *p23*
Demesh, Tony; Arkansas, 1918 ***95.2*** *p36*
Demet, Marie *SEE* Demet, Pierre
Demet, Pierre 26; Halifax, N.S., 1752 ***7074.6*** *p209*
*Wife:*Marie
Demetrakoupoulos, Vasilous John; Arkansas, 1918 ***95.2*** *p37*
Demeyne, John; Washington, 1859-1920 ***2872.1*** *p9*
Demicolo, Ella; Washington, 1859-1920 ***2872.1*** *p10*
Demicolo, Joe; Washington, 1859-1920 ***2872.1*** *p10*
Demien, John Chr. Theo.; Illinois, 1888 ***5012.39*** *p122*
Demien, John Christian Theodore; Illinois, 1883 ***5012.39*** *p52*
Demier, John Christian Theodore; Illinois, 1883 ***5012.39*** *p52*
Demisich, Philip; Wisconsin, n.d. ***9675.5*** *p50*
Demjan, John; Pennsylvania, 1900 ***7137*** *p168*
Demkowicz, Marianna 9 *SEE* Demkowicz, Stefania
Demkowicz, Michal 3 *SEE* Demkowicz, Stefania
Demkowicz, Michalina 7 *SEE* Demkowicz, Stefania
Demkowicz, Silvester; Massachusetts, 1912 ***9980.29*** *p65*
Demkowicz, Stefania 16; New York, 1912 ***9980.29*** *p65*
*Sister:*Marianna 9
*Sister:*Michalina 7
*Brother:*Michal 3
Demming, Bryan 4; Massachusetts, 1849 ***5881.1*** *p27*
Demming, Hugh 11; Massachusetts, 1849 ***5881.1*** *p29*
Demming, John 5; Massachusetts, 1849 ***5881.1*** *p30*
Demming, Patrick 7; Massachusetts, 1849 ***5881.1*** *p33*
Demmler, Elisabetha Margaretha; Pennsylvania, 1753 ***2444*** *p237*
Demmler, Regina Cath.; Philadelphia, 1754 ***2444*** *p224*
Demolliers, Victor Amedee 25; Port uncertain, 1839 ***778.5*** *p155*
Demond, John; Washington, 1859-1920 ***2872.1*** *p10*
Demond, Martin; Virginia, 1638 ***6219*** *p147*
Demonjie, Louis 40; New Orleans, 1863 ***543.30*** *p221*
Demornay, Fanny 30; New Orleans, 1823 ***778.5*** *p156*
Demos, Wm. John; Arkansas, 1918 ***95.2*** *p37*
Demose, Joseph; Arkansas, 1918 ***95.2*** *p37*
Dempewolfe, Theodore 30; Kansas, 1880 ***5240.1*** *p61*
Dempsey, Ann 3; Massachusetts, 1847 ***5881.1*** *p26*
Dempsey, Catherine; New York, NY, 1816 ***2859.11*** *p29*
Dempsey, Catherine 28; St. John, N.B., 1864 ***5704.8*** *p157*
Dempsey, Cornelius 3; St. John, N.B., 1864 ***5704.8*** *p157*
Dempsey, Daniel 29; St. John, N.B., 1864 ***5704.8*** *p157*
Dempsey, Edward 10; Massachusetts, 1849 ***5881.1*** *p28*
Dempsey, Eliza 25; Massachusetts, 1847 ***5881.1*** *p28*
Dempsey, Ellen 15; Massachusetts, 1849 ***5881.1*** *p28*
Dempsey, James 8; Massachusetts, 1850 ***5881.1*** *p30*
Dempsey, James 22; Massachusetts, 1849 ***5881.1*** *p30*
Dempsey, Jane 4; Massachusetts, 1847 ***5881.1*** *p29*
Dempsey, Jane 26; Massachusetts, 1850 ***5881.1*** *p30*
Dempsey, John; New England, 1816 ***2859.11*** *p29*
Dempsey, John; New York, NY, 1815 ***2859.11*** *p29*
Dempsey, John 22; Philadelphia, 1864 ***5704.8*** *p156*
Dempsey, Margaret 1; Massachusetts, 1847 ***5881.1*** *p31*
Dempsey, Margaret 19; Massachusetts, 1849 ***5881.1*** *p31*
Dempsey, Mary 5; St. John, N.B., 1864 ***5704.8*** *p157*
Dempsey, Mary 15; Massachusetts, 1849 ***5881.1*** *p32*
Dempsey, Mary 22; Massachusetts, 1849 ***5881.1*** *p32*
Dempsey, Matt. 21; Newfoundland, 1789 ***4915.24*** *p55*
Dempsey, Michael; Wisconsin, n.d. ***9675.5*** *p50*
Dempsey, Patrick; America, 1738 ***4971*** *p85*
Dempsey, Patrick; America, 1738 ***4971*** *p95*
Dempsey, Timothy 16; Massachusetts, 1849 ***5881.1*** *p34*
Dempsey, Timothy 20; Massachusetts, 1850 ***5881.1*** *p34*
Dempsey, William; America, 1741 ***4971*** *p16*
Dempsey, William; Illinois, 1892 ***5012.40*** *p27*
Dempsey, William 9 mos; St. John, N.B., 1864 ***5704.8*** *p157*
Dempsey, William 45; Massachusetts, 1849 ***5881.1*** *p34*
Dempster, George; Charleston, SC, 1734 ***1639.20*** *p59*
Dempster, Isabella; Charleston, SC, 1815 ***8894.2*** *p56*
Dempster, John; Philadelphia, 1850 ***5704.8*** *p64*
Dempsy, Murtey; New York, NY, 1836 ***8208.4*** *p22*
Dempwolf, August; New Orleans, 1862 ***543.30*** *p55*
Demsay, James; America, 1773-1774 ***2859.11*** *p7*
Demsay, James 21; Virginia, 1773 ***1219.7*** *p168*
Demson, Rowland; Virginia, 1640 ***6219*** *p160*
Demuth, . . .; Canada, 1776-1783 ***9786*** *p19*
Demuth, Anna Mary *SEE* Demuth, Christopher
Demuth, Christopher; New York, 1743 ***3652*** *p60*
*Wife:*Anna Mary
Demuth, Gotthard; Savannah, GA, 1735 ***3652*** *p51*
Demuth, Gottlieb; Savannah, GA, 1736 ***3652*** *p51*
*Relative:*Regina
Demuth, Regina *SEE* Demuth, Gottlieb
De Muylder, John B. 37; Kansas, 1883 ***5240.1*** *p65*
De Nanteuil, Augustus; New York, NY, 1835 ***8208.4*** *p76*
Denashiah, Timothy; America, 1739 ***4971*** *p47*
Dencausse, Henri 23; New Orleans, 1839 ***778.5*** *p156*
D'Encausse, Jean 20; America, 1838 ***778.5*** *p156*
D'Encausse, Pierre 19; America, 1838 ***778.5*** *p156*
Denchfeild, Jeffery; Virginia, 1643 ***6219*** *p204*
Dencke, Jeremiah; New York, 1761 ***3652*** *p87*
Dene, Eliz 27; America, 1705 ***2212*** *p43*
Dene, Jno 14; Maryland or Virginia, 1699 ***2212*** *p23*
Deneau, Edmund 45; Virginia, 1773 ***1219.7*** *p168*
Deneby, Michael; Montreal, 1813 ***7603*** *p75*
Denechaud, Antoine 35; New Orleans, 1838 ***778.5*** *p156*
Denecke, Friedrich Ludwig; Quebec, 1776 ***9786*** *p257*
Denefre, Francis 22; New Orleans, 1862 ***543.30*** *p218*
Denehy, Patrick; New York, NY, 1836 ***8208.4*** *p11*
Dener, Peter; Charleston, SC, 1775-1781 ***8582.2*** *p52*
Deneston, Fanny A.; New York, NY, 1869 ***5704.8*** *p233*
Deneston, Isabella 9; New York, NY, 1869 ***5704.8*** *p233*
Deneston, James 11; New York, NY, 1869 ***5704.8*** *p233*
Deneston, Jane; New York, NY, 1869 ***5704.8*** *p233*
Deneston, John; New York, NY, 1869 ***5704.8*** *p233*
Deng, Carl; Illinois, 1875 ***2896.5*** *p9*

Dengel, Jacob; Wisconsin, n.d. 9675.5 p50
Dengen, . . .; Canada, 1776-1783 9786 p19
Dengen, Caspard; Canada, 1776-1783 9786 p207A
Dengle, Jacob 31; Louisiana, 1863 543.30 p374
Dengler, F. X.; Cincinnati, 1869-1887 8582 p6
Dengler, John; Pennsylvania, 1753 2444 p148
Denham, Thomas; Virginia, 1643 6219 p229
Denichaud, A. 38; New Orleans, 1839 778.5 p156
Denicon, Michael; America, 1735-1743 4971 p79
Denigusse, P. 40; Port uncertain, 1839 778.5 p156
Denis, Fortune Rene Marie; New York, NY, 1836 8208.4 p19
Denis, Phillip 24; America, 1821 778.5 p156
Denishaud, A. 34; New Orleans, 1837 778.5 p156
Denison, James 23; Maryland, 1774 1219.7 p215
Denison, Margaret 35; Maryland, 1775 1219.7 p259
Denison, Myers; Shreveport, LA, 1878 7129 p44
Denison, Patrick 17; Maryland, 1774 1219.7 p215
Denison, William; Quebec, 1847 5704.8 p12
Denker, August; New Jersey, 1882-1887 3702.7 p603
Denker, Henrich; Trenton, NJ, 1776 8137 p7
Denman, Campbell C.; Arkansas, 1918 95.2 p37
Denman, Henry; Colorado, 1896 9678.2 p15
Denman, John; New York, NY, 1839 8208.4 p98
Denman, Mathias; Ohio, 1801 8582.2 p55
Denmann, Mathias; Ohio, 1801 8582.2 p55
Denmarke, Fr.; Virginia, 1636 6219 p34
Denmmer, Robert; Illinois, 1889 5012.39 p122
Denn, Basil 18; Maryland, 1774 1219.7 p214
Denn, Christ.; Virginia, 1637 6219 p11
Denne, Dennis; Illinois, 1860 7857 p3
Denneen, John; America, 1742 4971 p56
Dennehy, Jerry 16; Massachusetts, 1850 5881.1 p30
Dennes, Humphrey; Virginia, 1639 6219 p161
Dennes, John; Virginia, 1639 6219 p153
Dennet, John; Arkansas, 1888 5240.1 p10
Dennett, John; Virginia, 1635 6219 p69
Dennevall, Robert 19; Jamaica, 1730 3690.1 p62
Denney, Daniel 6 mos; St. John, N.B., 1854 5704.8 p115
Denney, Daniel 35; St. John, N.B., 1854 5704.8 p115
Denney, Hugh 4; St. John, N.B., 1854 5704.8 p115
Denney, John 2; St. John, N.B., 1854 5704.8 p115
Denney, Mary Ann; St. John, N.B., 1847 5704.8 p11
Dennhof, John G.; Wisconsin, n.d. 9675.5 p50
Denning, Hugh; Iowa, 1866-1943 123.54 p16
Denning, Patrick; New York, NY, 1834 8208.4 p31
Dennington, Oliver; Virginia, 1636 6219 p78
Dennis, Edward 21; Maryland, 1775 1219.7 p266
Dennis, Francois; Quebec, 1815 7603 p21
Dennis, James; America, 1743 4971 p64
Dennis, Joan; America, 1741 4971 p63
Dennis, John; Virginia, 1635 6219 p5
Dennis, John; Virginia, 1652 6251 p19
Dennis, Jon.; Virginia, 1636 6219 p79
Dennis, Jonas 43; New Orleans, 1862 543.30 p56
Dennis, Joseph 21; Maryland, 1775 1219.7 p259
Dennis, Philip; Ohio, 1844 9892.11 p12
Dennis, Richard 24; Virginia, 1773 1219.7 p171
Dennis, Richard James; Colorado, 1902 9678.2 p15
Dennis, Samuel 21; Baltimore, 1775 1219.7 p269
Dennison, James; Charleston, SC, 1796 1639.20 p59
Dennison, Margaret 3; Massachusetts, 1850 5881.1 p32
Dennison, Thomas 30; Maryland, 1775 1219.7 p257
Dennison, William 16; Maryland, 1775 1219.7 p264
Dennison, William 20; Philadelphia, 1857 5704.8 p133
Dennisson, Richard; New York, NY, 1816 2859.11 p29
Denniston, William; Philadelphia, 1850 53.26 p18
Denniston, William; Philadelphia, 1850 5704.8 p69
Denniswoods, Edward 16; Maryland or Virginia, 1720 3690.1 p62
Dennon, Charles; New York, NY, 1839 8208.4 p95
Dennscherz, Lorenz Joseph; Pennsylvania, 1752 4525 p204
Dennscherz, Lorenz Joseph; Pennsylvania, 1752 4525 p277
Denny, Elizabeth; St. John, N.B., 1853 5704.8 p107
Denny, James 20; Massachusetts, 1849 5881.1 p30
Denny, Margaret 20; Quebec, 1856 5704.8 p130
Denny, Mary; St. John, N.B., 1847 5704.8 p35
Denny, Neal; St. John, N.B., 1847 5704.8 p15
Denois, Mr. 32; Port uncertain, 1839 778.5 p156
Denson, William; Virginia, 1637 6219 p117
Dent, Eliza.; Virginia, 1643 6219 p204
Dent, George 32; Maryland, 1774 1219.7 p214
Dent, James 22; Maryland, 1735 3690.1 p62
Dent, William 19; Jamaica, 1729 3690.1 p62
Denton, Preston; Boston, 1776 1219.7 p278
Denton, William 23; Maryland, 1775 1219.7 p251
Denvant, Michael; New York, NY, 1811 2859.11 p10
Denvelden, Wilhelm von; Canada, 1777 9786 p266
Denzler, John; Virginia, 1855 4626.16 p14
Deoghoe, John; America, 1738 4971 p35
Deolin, Arthur; New York, NY, 1811 2859.11 p10
Deolin, Daniel; New York, NY, 1811 2859.11 p10
DePanfilis, William; Arkansas, 1918 95.2 p36
DePaolo, Dome 32; West Virginia, 1904 9788.3 p8
DePaolo, Stefono 34; West Virginia, 1906 9788.3 p9
Depas, P. 38; New Orleans, 1838 778.5 p156
DePasalon, Mr. 22; America, 1838 778.5 p156
DePaulo, Antonio 30; West Virginia, 1906 9788.3 p8
Depean, G. 30; Port uncertain, 1839 778.5 p156
DePelletier, Juliette 18; New Orleans, 1826 778.5 p156
De Pencier, . . .; Canada, 1776-1783 9786 p19
DePhillip, Jack; Colorado, 1900 9678.2 p15
Depiesse, Jacob; Wisconsin, n.d. 9675.5 p50
Depiesse, Jean B.; Wisconsin, n.d. 9675.5 p50
Deplaigne, Jacques 26; America, 1836 778.5 p157
Deplaine, B. 26; Port uncertain, 1838 778.5 p157
Depleigne, Jacques 28; America, 1838 778.5 p157
Depleigne, Jean 27; New Orleans, 1837 778.5 p157
Depleigne, Polien 25; America, 1838 778.5 p157
Deplich, Benjamin 19; Jamaica, 1731 3690.1 p63
Depoma, Lewis; Virginia, 1635 6219 p71
DePontalba, Mr. 22; America, 1837 778.5 p157
Deponthe, Mr.; Tobago, W. Indies, 1775 1219.7 p265
Deporte, Miss 18; America, 1839 778.5 p157
Deporte, Elenor. 40; America, 1839 778.5 p157
Depouilly, Miss 7; America, 1839 778.5 p157
Depouilly, Miss 8; America, 1839 778.5 p157
Depouilly, Mme. 30; America, 1839 778.5 p157
Depouviller, C. A. S. 24; New Orleans, 1823 778.5 p157
Deppe, Hartwig; New York, 1857 1450.2 p29A
Deppermann, Edmund; America, 1848 8582.3 p14
Depping, Caspar Heinrich *SEE* Depping, Johann Diederich
Depping, Johann Diederich; America, 1854 4610.10 p144
With wife
*Son:*Caspar Heinrich
Deppisch, John; Wisconsin, n.d. 9675.5 p50
Deppisch, Ludwig; Wisconsin, n.d. 9675.5 p50
Deprau, Saml. 35; New Orleans, 1839 778.5 p157
Depre, James L. 18; America, 1823 778.5 p157
Deprez, John A.; New York, NY, 1839 8208.4 p99
Deprot, Mr. 28; New Orleans, 1823 778.5 p157
DePrun, Mme. 24; New Orleans, 1839 778.5 p158
Depuy, Mr. 45; America, 1825 778.5 p158
D'Equilles, Lewis 25; America, 1839 778.5 p158
DeRamefert, Widow 31; New Orleans, 1829 778.5 p158
DeRancourt, Mr. 33; America, 1839 778.5 p158
Deratt, Charles; Virginia, 1642 6219 p197
Derbacher, Franz; Kentucky, 1839-1840 8582.3 p98
Derbas, Mr. 15; New Orleans, 1827 778.5 p158
Derbyshire, Elizabeth 21; Maryland, 1774 1219.7 p229
Derbyshire, Peter; Virginia, 1858 4626.16 p17
Derder, Antony; Philadelphia, 1758 9973.7 p33
Deregowska, Helena 20; New York, 1912 9980.29 p49
Derenbacher, Jacob; New York, NY, 1840 8208.4 p104
Derengowski, Helena 20; New York, 1912 9980.29 p49
Derenom, Jean; Quebec, 1713 7603 p64
Derenthal, Anton; New York, NY, 1838 8208.4 p75
Derepas, Etienne 31; New Orleans, 1829 778.5 p158
Derepas, Vincent 33; New Orleans, 1837 778.5 p158
Deresches, Abram; Iowa, 1866-1943 123.54 p16
Deretich, Sam; Washington, 1859-1920 2872.1 p10
Dereve, Victor 21; New Orleans, 1838 778.5 p158
Derhas, Xaareus; New York, NY, 1835 8208.4 p56
Derick, Mrs. 26; Georgia, 1738 9332 p331
*Daughter:*Elizabeth 8
*Son:*Malchier 7
*Son:*Jacob 5
*Daughter:*Margeretta 1
Derick, Elizabeth 8 *SEE* Derick, Mrs.
Derick, Jacob 5 *SEE* Derick, Mrs.
Derick, Malchier 7 *SEE* Derick, Mrs.
Derick, Margeretta 1 *SEE* Derick, Mrs.
Derin, Peter 56; Philadelphia, 1803 53.26 p18
Deringer, Christopher; Pennsylvania, 1752 2444 p226
Deringer, Stophel; Pennsylvania, 1752 2444 p226
Derivaux, Laurent 24; New Orleans, 1838 778.5 p158
Derlin, Anne; New York, NY, 1816 2859.11 p29
Dermitt, Margaret; New York, NY, 1866 5704.8 p211
Dermody, Murtagh; America, 1742 4971 p80
Dermody, Murtogh; America, 1735-1743 4971 p78
Dermody, Patrick; America, 1742 4971 p80
Dermody, Peter; Montreal, 1824 7603 p87
Dermot, Thomas 25; Maryland, 1774 1219.7 p192
Dermott, Betty; St. John, N.B., 1847 5704.8 p35
Dermott, Betty; St. John, N.B., 1850 5704.8 p65
Dermott, Eleanor 18; St. John, N.B., 1854 5704.8 p114
Dermott, Peggy; St. John, N.B., 1847 5704.8 p35
Dermott, Rose; America, 1866 5704.8 p205
Dernier, Francois 25; New Orleans, 1838 778.5 p158
De Rocco, Antonio; Iowa, 1866-1943 123.54 p61
De Rocco, Maria; Iowa, 1866-1943 123.54 p61
Deroche, Joseph 41; New Orleans, 1862 543.30 p58
Derollers, Mr. 21; America, 1838 778.5 p158
DeRouault, M. 20; Port uncertain, 1839 778.5 p158
Deroy, Edward; New York, NY, 1815 2859.11 p29
Deroy, Eugene 13; New Orleans, 1836 778.5 p158
Deroy, James; New York, NY, 1815 2859.11 p29
DeRozat, Mr. 23; New Orleans, 1836 778.5 p158
Derr, George; America, 1847 1450.2 p29A
Derr, Mathias; Pennsylvania, 1754 2444 p148
Derr, Michael; Pennsylvania, 1754 2444 p148
Derragh, Eliza; New York, NY, 1811 2859.11 p10
Derragh, Ellen; New York, NY, 1811 2859.11 p10
Derragh, John; New York, NY, 1811 2859.11 p10
Derrenger, George; New York, NY, 1837 8208.4 p34
Derrey, Mme. 32; Ohio, 1837 778.5 p159
Derrey, John B. 32; America, 1837 778.5 p159
Derrick, Francis; Virginia, 1639 6219 p154
Derrick, G. M.; Washington, 1859-1920 2872.1 p10
Derry, George 25; Philadelphia, 1774 1219.7 p216
Derry, Jean Baptiste 32; America, 1838 778.5 p159
Derry, John 45; Georgia, 1775 1219.7 p277
Derry, Robt.; Virginia, 1635 6219 p17
Dersch, K. Marg. 58; America, 1853 9162.8 p36
Derubski, Jan 19; New York, 1912 9980.29 p52
Dery, John; America, 1848 1450.2 p29A
Deryke, John; Arkansas, 1918 95.2 p37
Desache, Mr.; Port uncertain, 1839 778.5 p159
Desachy, E.; New Orleans, 1839 778.5 p159
Desachy, N.; New Orleans, 1839 778.5 p159
DeSaint Mart, George M. Francis; New York, NY, 1851 9788.3 p8
DeSaint Mart, George M. Francis; West Virginia, 1858 9788.3 p8
De Saint Vital, Mr.; Port uncertain, 1839 778.5 p159
DeSanto, Cosino; Colorado, 1904 9678.2 p16
DeSanto, Salvatore; Arkansas, 1918 95.2 p36
Desare, M. 28; America, 1838 778.5 p159
Desbat, Mr. 30; America, 1837 778.5 p159
Desbats, P. 25; New Orleans, 1837 778.5 p159
Desbes, Mr. 21; Port uncertain, 1838 778.5 p159
Desbiens, Etienne; Montreal, 1691 4533 p129
Des Biens, Marie 18; America, 1827 778.5 p159
Desbois, Phillippe Severin; Vermont, 1904 3455.2 p50
Desbois, Phillippe Severin; Vermont, 1904 3455.3 p113
Desbrit, William; Annapolis, MD, 1742 4971 p93
Descannet, Mr. 33; New Orleans, 1839 778.5 p160
Descartes, Miss 5; Louisiana, 1820 778.5 p159
Descartes, A. 45; Louisiana, 1820 778.5 p159
Descaudin, Jean 60; America, 1839 778.5 p160
Descaunet, Mr. 33; New Orleans, 1839 778.5 p160
Desceux, Notaire J. 40; New Orleans, 1826 778.5 p160
Deschamp, Mr. 48; Port uncertain, 1838 778.5 p160
Deschamp, Mr. 51; America, 1838 778.5 p160
Deschamp, Bernard 34; New Orleans, 1862 543.30 p58
Deschamp, Louis 28; America, 1825 778.5 p160
Deschamps, Mr. 25; New Orleans, 1822 778.5 p160
Deschamps, Mr. 32; America, 1837 778.5 p160
Deschamps, Mr. 40; Grenada, 1774 1219.7 p245
Deschamps, Mrs. 22; New Orleans, 1822 778.5 p160
Deschamps, Louis 20; America, 1820 778.5 p160
Deschler, David; Philadelphia, 1765 8582.3 p84
Deschler, Louis 24; America, 1839 778.5 p160
Deschmer, . . .; Canada, 1776-1783 9786 p19
Deschong, Friedrich; Philadelphia, 1776 8582.3 p85
Des Coudres, . . .; Canada, 1776-1783 9786 p19
Descury, Simon; Ohio, 1763 1219.7 p94
Desedes, A. 35; America, 1836 778.5 p160
Deseindre, . . .; Canada, 1776-1783 9786 p19
Desel, Karl; Charleston, SC, 1775-1781 8582.2 p52
Desenne, Mr. 35; America, 1839 778.5 p160
Desera, A. 38; America, 1826 778.5 p160
Desertembo, John 25; Maryland, 1775 1219.7 p263
Des Franssai, Lewis 32; America, 1825 778.5 p161
De Shane, Paul 33; Kansas, 1874 5240.1 p55
Desider, . . .; Canada, 1776-1783 9786 p19
Desini, Anne 40; Louisiana, 1837 778.5 p161
Desire, P. F. 45; New Orleans, 1822 778.5 p161
Desjardias, Aime 22; America, 1838 778.5 p161
Desjardins, Mrs. 23; Port uncertain, 1838 778.5 p161
Desjardins, A. 37; Port uncertain, 1838 778.5 p161
Desjardins, Theophile 31?; Arizona, 1890 2764.35 p17
Deslick, Geo.; Iowa, 1866-1943 123.54 p16
Desloges, Joseph; Montreal, 1709 4533 p128
Desmond, Miss; Newport, RI, 1851 6508.5 p20
Desmond, Catharine 6; Massachusetts, 1847 5881.1 p27
Desmond, Catharine 40; Massachusetts, 1847 5881.1 p27
Desmond, Con 25; Newport, RI, 1851 6508.5 p20
Desmond, Cornelius 24; Massachusetts, 1847 5881.1 p27
Desmond, Dudy 10; Massachusetts, 1849 5881.1 p28
Desmond, Ellen 10; Massachusetts, 1847 5881.1 p28
Desmond, Ellen 17; Massachusetts, 1850 5881.1 p28
Desmond, Ellen 40; Massachusetts, 1850 5881.1 p28
Desmond, Humphrey 40; Massachusetts, 1849 5881.1 p29
Desmond, Jerry 3; Massachusetts, 1848 5881.1 p29

Desmond, Mary 4; Massachusetts, 1849 ***5881.1*** *p31*
Desmond, Mary 6; Massachusetts, 1849 ***5881.1*** *p31*
Desmond, Mary 25; Newport, RI, 1851 ***6508.5*** *p20*
Desmond, Merry 9; Massachusetts, 1849 ***5881.1*** *p31*
Desmond, Patrick 15; Massachusetts, 1849 ***5881.1*** *p33*
Desmortiers, Mrs.; New Orleans, 1823 ***778.5*** *p161*
Desmortiers, Ms.; New Orleans, 1823 ***778.5*** *p161*
Desmortiers, N. J. 37; New Orleans, 1823 ***778.5*** *p161*
Desmoulins, Silvestre 30; America, 1838 ***778.5*** *p161*
Desormeaux, Jean; Louisiana, 1789-1819 ***778.5*** *p555*
Despais, Charles 23; Port uncertain, 1838 ***778.5*** *p161*
Despard, William; Maryland, 1742 ***4971*** *p106*
Despaux, Vincent 25; New Orleans, 1838 ***778.5*** *p161*
Desper, Ernest; New York, 1848 ***1450.2*** *p29A*
Desperous, Mme. 22; America, 1838 ***778.5*** *p161*
Desperous, M. 34; America, 1838 ***778.5*** *p161*
Despinoze, . . .; New Orleans, 1839 ***778.5*** *p162*
Despinoze, Mr. 32; New Orleans, 1839 ***778.5*** *p162*
Despinoze, Mrs. 25; New Orleans, 1839 ***778.5*** *p162*
Despit, Pierre 25; Port uncertain, 1837 ***778.5*** *p162*
Desploux, Pierre 29; New Orleans, 1838 ***778.5*** *p162*
Despluces, Pierre 25; New Orleans, 1838 ***778.5*** *p162*
Despourey, Batiste 23; New Orleans, 1839 ***778.5*** *p162*
Despres, Alexis A. 50; New Orleans, 1825 ***778.5*** *p162*
Desranleau, Jean 25; Quebec, 1694 ***4533*** *p130*
Desrochers, Pierre; Quebec, 1694 ***4533*** *p130*
Desrue, Jacob 38; New Orleans, 1862 ***543.30*** *p58*
Dessales, Pierre 29; America, 1838 ***778.5*** *p162*
Dessar, Leo C.; America, 1851 ***1450.2*** *p29A*
Dessar, Lewis; America, 1852 ***1450.2*** *p29A*
Dessauze, Mr. 28; New Orleans, 1837 ***778.5*** *p162*
Dessecker, Johann Jacob *SEE* Dessecker, Peter
Dessecker, Michael *SEE* Dessecker, Peter
Dessecker, Peter *SEE* Dessecker, Peter
Dessecker, Peter; America, 1748-1800 ***2444*** *p147*
*Child:*Johann Jacob
*Child:*Michael
*Child:*Peter
Dessepent, Miss 3; America, 1827 ***778.5*** *p162*
Dessepent, Annette 31; America, 1827 ***778.5*** *p162*
Dessinger, . . .; Canada, 1776-1783 ***9786*** *p19*
Dessome, Eugene; America, 1838 ***778.5*** *p163*
Destaing, Peter 32; New Orleans, 1827 ***778.5*** *p163*
Dester, Thomas 21; Jamaica, 1739 ***3690.1*** *p63*
Desterberg, Henry 16; Maryland, 1774 ***1219.7*** *p229*
Destino, Jeneroso; Arkansas, 1918 ***95.2*** *p37*
Desty, Eugene 65; Arizona, 1902 ***9228.40*** *p5*
Desvoge, Firmin 19; New Orleans, 1823 ***778.5*** *p163*
Dete, Joseph 32; Port uncertain, 1839 ***778.5*** *p163*
Detering, Anne Marie Louise; America, 1857 ***4610.10*** *p158*
Determann, Heinrich; Cincinnati, 1829 ***8582*** *p6*
Deters, Franz Heinrich; America, 1850 ***8582.3*** *p14*
Deters, Henry Clemens; America, 1849 ***8582.3*** *p14*
Detlaf, John 30; Carolina, 1774 ***1219.7*** *p221*
*Wife:*Sarah 25
Detlaf, Sarah 25 *SEE* Detlaf, John
Detloff, Christian; Wisconsin, n.d. ***9675.5*** *p50*
Detloff, John; New York, NY, 1878 ***2764.35*** *p17*
Detmer, George; New York, NY, 1839 ***8208.4*** *p101*
Detmering, Charles; Wisconsin, n.d. ***9675.5*** *p50*
Detraber, Mlle.; Port uncertain, 1839 ***778.5*** *p163*
Detrie, . . .; Canada, 1776-1783 ***9786*** *p19*
Detrui, . . .; Canada, 1776-1783 ***9786*** *p19*
Dettelshausen, Michael V.; New York, 1870 ***1450.2*** *p29A*
Detter, Mathias; Pennsylvania, 1770 ***9973.8*** *p32*
Detterer, Ludwig; Pennsylvania, 1727 ***3627*** *p18*
Detterey, Ludwig; Pennsylvania, 1727 ***3627*** *p18*
Dettgen, . . .; Cincinnati, 1826 ***8582.1*** *p51*
Dettmer, . . .; Canada, 1776-1783 ***9786*** *p19*
Dettmer, Bernhard; Cincinnati, 1869-1887 ***8582*** *p6*
Dettmer, Dietrich; Cincinnati, 1869-1887 ***8582*** *p6*
Dettmers, Ferdinand Jacob; New York, 1761 ***3652*** *p87*
Deubner, Christopher; America, 1848 ***8582.2*** *p7*
Deuceux, Victor 30; America, 1838 ***778.5*** *p163*
Deuceux, Victor, Mme. 30?; America, 1838 ***778.5*** *p163*
Deuffel, Michel; New England, 1754 ***4525*** *p252*
Deugler, George; Wisconsin, n.d. ***9675.5*** *p50*
Deulher, . . .; Canada, 1776-1783 ***9786*** *p19*
Deulin, Wm.; New York, NY, 1816 ***2859.11*** *p29*
Deuschle, Christian Willhelm; Colorado, 1894 ***9678.2*** *p16*
Deussing, Berthold 27; Kansas, 1888 ***5240.1*** *p72*
Deuster, P. V.; Wisconsin, n.d. ***9675.5*** *p50*
Deutch, Levi 15; Philadelphia, 1774 ***1219.7*** *p185*
Deutcher, Ernest William; Illinois, 1900 ***5012.40*** *p77*
Deutcher, Franz Henry; Illinois, 1900 ***5012.40*** *p77*
Deuter, Philip; Canada, 1783 ***9786*** *p38A*
Deuther, . . .; Canada, 1776-1783 ***9786*** *p19*
Deutscher, Ernest William; Illinois, 1897 ***5012.39*** *p53*
Deutscher, Franz Henry; Illinois, 1897 ***5012.39*** *p53*
Deutscher, Henry W.; Illinois, 1897 ***5012.40*** *p55*
Deutscher, Henry William; Illinois, 1894 ***5012.39*** *p53*
Deutschman, Antoine 3 mos; New Orleans, 1838 ***778.5*** *p163*
Deutschman, Antoine 34; New Orleans, 1838 ***778.5*** *p163*
Deutschman, Chatrine 7; New Orleans, 1838 ***778.5*** *p163*
Deutschman, Chatrine 27; New Orleans, 1838 ***778.5*** *p163*
Deutschman, Jacob 31; New Orleans, 1862 ***543.30*** *p61*
Deutschman, Julianne 4; New Orleans, 1838 ***778.5*** *p163*
Deutschmann, Caroline 5; New York, NY, 1878 ***9253*** *p46*
Deutschmann, Elisabeth 20; New York, NY, 1878 ***9253*** *p46*
Deutschmann, Friedrich 8; New York, NY, 1878 ***9253*** *p46*
Deutschmann, Georg 22; New York, NY, 1878 ***9253*** *p46*
Deutschmann, Georg 44; New York, NY, 1878 ***9253*** *p46*
Deutschmann, Helene 11 mos; New York, NY, 1878 ***9253*** *p46*
Deutschmann, Jacob 1 mo; New York, NY, 1878 ***9253*** *p46*
Deutschmann, Johann 17; New York, NY, 1878 ***9253*** *p46*
Deutschmann, Martin 20; New York, NY, 1878 ***9253*** *p46*
Deutschmann, Peter 13; New York, NY, 1878 ***9253*** *p46*
Deutschmann, Regina 40; New York, NY, 1878 ***9253*** *p46*
Devall, John; Virginia, 1642 ***6219*** *p195*
Devall, Jon.; Virginia, 1642 ***6219*** *p194*
Devalle, Alfred 18; America, 1838 ***778.5*** *p163*
Devan, Francis; New York, NY, 1811 ***2859.11*** *p10*
Devan, Francis; New York, NY, 1811 ***2859.11*** *p11*
Devaney, Owin; Illinois, 1852 ***7857*** *p3*
DeVanney, Elisa 30; America, 1838 ***778.5*** *p144*
Devanny, Pat 25; Kansas, 1900 ***5240.1*** *p81*
Devans, Mary 8; Massachusetts, 1850 ***5881.1*** *p32*
Devaux, Mr.; Port uncertain, 1839 ***778.5*** *p163*
Devaux, A. 21; New Orleans, 1831 ***778.5*** *p164*
Devaux, Josephine 15; America, 1838 ***778.5*** *p164*
Deveau, Mrs. 30; New Orleans, 1835 ***778.5*** *p164*
Devehy, Michel; Isle aux Noix, Que., 1813 ***7603*** *p62*
Develin, Jane 32 *SEE* Develin, Roger
Develin, Roger 35; Philadelphia, 1803 ***53.26*** *p18*
*Relative:*Jane 32
Deven, Mary 7; Massachusetts, 1849 ***5881.1*** *p32*
Deven, Susan 4; Massachusetts, 1849 ***5881.1*** *p34*
Devenne, Alexander; St. John, N.B., 1849 ***5704.8*** *p49*
Devenny, Ann; Philadelphia, 1852 ***5704.8*** *p96*
Devenny, Catherine 26; Philadelphia, 1854 ***5704.8*** *p122*
Devenny, Cornelus; Philadelphia, 1864 ***5704.8*** *p179*
Devenny, David 24; Quebec, 1856 ***5704.8*** *p129*
Devenny, Eleanor 50; Philadelphia, 1854 ***5704.8*** *p116*
Devenny, Elinor 27; Philadelphia, 1804 ***53.26*** *p19*
Devenny, Elizabeth; Philadelphia, 1851 ***5704.8*** *p76*
Devenny, Elizabeth 20; Philadelphia, 1854 ***5704.8*** *p116*
Devenny, Hannah; America, 1867 ***5704.8*** *p216*
Devenny, Hannah; St. John, N.B., 1848 ***5704.8*** *p43*
Devenny, Hugh; St. John, N.B., 1847 ***5704.8*** *p21*
Devenny, Hugh 15; Philadelphia, 1854 ***5704.8*** *p116*
Devenny, James; St. John, N.B., 1847 ***5704.8*** *p19*
Devenny, James; St. John, N.B., 1848 ***5704.8*** *p43*
Devenny, John 25; Philadelphia, 1854 ***5704.8*** *p116*
Devenny, Margaret 18; Philadelphia, 1854 ***5704.8*** *p116*
Devenny, Mary; St. John, N.B., 1847 ***5704.8*** *p19*
Devenny, Mary 25; Philadelphia, 1861 ***5704.8*** *p148*
Devenny, Mary Ann; Philadelphia, 1849 ***53.26*** *p19*
Devenny, Mary Ann; Philadelphia, 1849 ***5704.8*** *p53*
Devenny, Neal 22; Philadelphia, 1854 ***5704.8*** *p123*
Devenny, Patrick 22; Philadelphia, 1865 ***5704.8*** *p165*
Devenny, Sarah; Philadelphia, 1851 ***5704.8*** *p76*
Devenny, Stephen 22; Philadelphia, 1857 ***5704.8*** *p132*
Devenny, Thomas; America, 1868 ***5704.8*** *p231*
Devenny, Thomas; New Orleans, 1848 ***5704.8*** *p48*
Devens, Patrick; Chicago, 1880 ***2764.35*** *p20*
Deveny, Thomas; New York, NY, 1889 ***1450.2*** *p7B*
Dever, Ann; Philadelphia, 1867 ***5704.8*** *p214*
Dever, Brigidt 55; Philadelphia, 1803 ***53.26*** *p19*
Dever, Edward; New York, NY, 1811 ***2859.11*** *p11*
With family
Dever, Fanny; Philadelphia, 1848 ***53.26*** *p19*
*Relative:*Mary 10
Dever, Fanny; Philadelphia, 1848 ***5704.8*** *p46*
Dever, Frank; Missouri, 1890 ***2764.35*** *p17*
Dever, Hugh; New York, NY, 1866 ***5704.8*** *p212*
Dever, James; St. John, N.B., 1847 ***5704.8*** *p26*
Dever, Mary 10 *SEE* Dever, Fanny
Dever, Mary 10; Philadelphia, 1848 ***5704.8*** *p46*
Dever, Mary 20; Philadelphia, 1861 ***5704.8*** *p149*
Dever, Mary A.; New York, NY, 1866 ***5704.8*** *p213*
Dever, Michael; St. John, N.B., 1847 ***5704.8*** *p20*
Dever, Patrick; St. John, N.B., 1847 ***5704.8*** *p26*
Dever, Sarah; St. John, N.B., 1847 ***5704.8*** *p20*
Dever, Sarah 12; St. John, N.B., 1847 ***5704.8*** *p20*
Deverall, Daniel; Jamaica, 1752 ***1219.7*** *p15*
Deverall, Daniel; Jamaica, 1752 ***3690.1*** *p63*
Deverall, Jonathan 16; Jamaica, 1730 ***3690.1*** *p63*
Deveray, Hugh 22; Kansas, 1873 ***5240.1*** *p54*
Devereaux, James; Philadelphia, 1816 ***2859.11*** *p29*
Deverell, Georg; Virginia, 1628 ***6219*** *p9*
Deverell, Jonathan 16; Jamaica, 1730 ***3690.1*** *p63*
Devereux, Marguerite; Quebec, 1823 ***7603*** *p91*
Devereux, Patrice; Quebec, 1818 ***7603*** *p81*
Devereux, Thomas; America, 1741 ***4971*** *p34*
Devet, Margaret 19; Philadelphia, 1864 ***5704.8*** *p156*
Devig, Erling; Arkansas, 1918 ***95.2*** *p37*
Devigner, Pierre Joseph 40; America, 1838 ***778.5*** *p164*
Deville, Adolphe 14; America, 1839 ***778.5*** *p164*
Deville, Clemence 16; America, 1839 ***778.5*** *p164*
Deville, Julius 45; America, 1839 ***778.5*** *p164*
Deville, Narcisse 19; America, 1839 ***778.5*** *p164*
Deville, Prudence 18; New Orleans, 1829 ***778.5*** *p164*
Deville, Victor 22; New Orleans, 1829 ***778.5*** *p164*
Devilleray, Mr.; Quebec, 1815 ***9229.18*** *p74*
Devillez, Nicolas 27; America, 1838 ***778.5*** *p164*
Devilt, James; Philadelphia, 1811 ***2859.11*** *p11*
Devilt, John; Philadelphia, 1811 ***53.26*** *p19*
Devilt, Thomas; Philadelphia, 1811 ***53.26*** *p19*
Devilt, Thomas; Philadelphia, 1811 ***2859.11*** *p11*
Devin, Ann; New York, NY, 1869 ***5704.8*** *p233*
Devin, Bryan; America, 1735-1743 ***4971*** *p8*
Devin, Catharine; New York, NY, 1869 ***5704.8*** *p233*
Devin, Edward; New York, NY, 1869 ***5704.8*** *p233*
Devin, James 8; Massachusetts, 1849 ***5881.1*** *p29*
Devin, John; New York, NY, 1869 ***5704.8*** *p233*
Devin, Patrick; America, 1739 ***4971*** *p14*
Devin, William 25; Massachusetts, 1849 ***5881.1*** *p34*
Devine, Ann; Philadelphia, 1847 ***53.26*** *p19*
Devine, Ann; Philadelphia, 1847 ***5704.8*** *p23*
Devine, Ann; Philadelphia, 1867 ***5704.8*** *p217*
Devine, Ann; Philadelphia, 1867 ***5704.8*** *p220*
Devine, Ann 13; St. John, N.B., 1853 ***5704.8*** *p100*
Devine, Ann 40; Massachusetts, 1849 ***5881.1*** *p26*
Devine, Arthur; Philadelphia, 1851 ***5704.8*** *p76*
Devine, Barney 17; Philadelphia, 1857 ***5704.8*** *p134*
Devine, Bernard 35; St. John, N.B., 1864 ***5704.8*** *p158*
Devine, Bridget 24; Philadelphia, 1854 ***5704.8*** *p120*
Devine, Catharine; New York, NY, 1870 ***5704.8*** *p237*
Devine, Catharine; Philadelphia, 1864 ***5704.8*** *p177*
Devine, Catharine; Philadelphia, 1867 ***5704.8*** *p220*
Devine, Catharine 6; Massachusetts, 1847 ***5881.1*** *p27*
Devine, Catherine; Philadelphia, 1847 ***53.26*** *p19*
Devine, Catherine; Philadelphia, 1847 ***5704.8*** *p22*
Devine, Catherine; Quebec, 1821 ***7603*** *p60*
Devine, Catherine 11; Philadelphia, 1864 ***5704.8*** *p177*
Devine, Catherine 13; St. John, N.B., 1847 ***5704.8*** *p19*
Devine, Catherine 17; Philadelphia, 1860 ***5704.8*** *p146*
Devine, Catherine 23; Philadelphia, 1858 ***5704.8*** *p139*
Devine, Charles; Philadelphia, 1852 ***5704.8*** *p88*
Devine, Charles 6 mos; Philadelphia, 1851 ***5704.8*** *p76*
Devine, Charles 20; Philadelphia, 1751 ***1219.7*** *p6*
Devine, Charles 20; Philadelphia, 1751 ***3690.1*** *p63*
Devine, Daniel 11 *SEE* Devine, Mary
Devine, Daniel 11; Philadelphia, 1849 ***5704.8*** *p52*
Devine, Elizabeth; Philadelphia, 1851 ***5704.8*** *p76*
Devine, Elizabeth; Philadelphia, 1852 ***5704.8*** *p91*
Devine, Elizabeth; St. John, N.B., 1849 ***5704.8*** *p49*
Devine, Francis 21; Philadelphia, 1854 ***5704.8*** *p117*
Devine, Hannah; America, 1868 ***5704.8*** *p230*
Devine, Henry; New York, NY, 1865 ***5704.8*** *p201*
Devine, James; Ohio, 1840 ***9892.11*** *p13*
Devine, James; Philadelphia, 1864 ***5704.8*** *p177*
Devine, James; Philadelphia, 1867 ***5704.8*** *p222*
Devine, James; St. John, N.B., 1847 ***5704.8*** *p33*
Devine, James 10; St. John, N.B., 1853 ***5704.8*** *p109*
Devine, James 18; Philadelphia, 1853 ***5704.8*** *p113*
Devine, John; Illinois, 1868 ***7857*** *p3*
Devine, John; New York, NY, 1866 ***5704.8*** *p209*
Devine, John; Philadelphia, 1848 ***53.26*** *p19*
*Relative:*Sarah
Devine, John; Philadelphia, 1848 ***5704.8*** *p46*
Devine, John; Philadelphia, 1851 ***5704.8*** *p79*
Devine, John; Philadelphia, 1865 ***5704.8*** *p200*
Devine, John; Philadelphia, 1867 ***5704.8*** *p220*
Devine, John; Philadelphia, 1868 ***5704.8*** *p227*
Devine, John; Quebec, 1492-1825 ***7603*** *p21*
Devine, John; St. John, N.B., 1851 ***5704.8*** *p72*
Devine, John; St. John, N.B., 1853 ***5704.8*** *p100*
Devine, John; St. John, N.B., 1853 ***5704.8*** *p109*
Devine, John 19; St. John, N.B., 1864 ***5704.8*** *p159*
Devine, John 25; Wilmington, DE, 1831 ***6508.3*** *p101*
Devine, John 26; Wilmington, DE, 1831 ***6508.7*** *p161*
Devine, John 28; Massachusetts, 1849 ***5881.1*** *p29*
Devine, John 29; Montreal, 1752 ***7603*** *p72*

Devine, John 30; Philadelphia, 1833-1834 ***53.26*** *p19*
Devine, John 65; St. John, N.B., 1853 ***5704.8*** *p109*
Devine, Joseph 9 mos; Philadelphia, 1853 ***5704.8*** *p113*
Devine, Joseph 8; Massachusetts, 1849 ***5881.1*** *p30*
Devine, Margaret *SEE* Devine, Michael
Devine, Margaret; Philadelphia, 1847 ***5704.8*** *p5*
Devine, Margaret 19; Philadelphia, 1854 ***5704.8*** *p116*
Devine, Margaret 38; St. John, N.B., 1864 ***5704.8*** *p158*
Devine, Martha 46; Philadelphia, 1853 ***5704.8*** *p113*
Devine, Mary; New York, NY, 1867 ***5704.8*** *p218*
Devine, Mary; Philadelphia, 1849 ***53.26*** *p19*
*Relative:*Daniel 11
*Relative:*Mary 9
*Relative:*Michael 7
*Relative:*Thomas 4
*Relative:*Robert 3 mos
Devine, Mary; Philadelphia, 1849 ***5704.8*** *p52*
Devine, Mary; Philadelphia, 1851 ***5704.8*** *p76*
Devine, Mary; Philadelphia, 1871 ***5704.8*** *p241*
Devine, Mary; St. John, N.B., 1847 ***5704.8*** *p5*
Devine, Mary; St. John, N.B., 1849 ***5704.8*** *p49*
Devine, Mary 9 *SEE* Devine, Mary
Devine, Mary 9; Philadelphia, 1849 ***5704.8*** *p52*
Devine, Mary 9; Philadelphia, 1864 ***5704.8*** *p177*
Devine, Mary 19; Philadelphia, 1854 ***5704.8*** *p116*
Devine, Mary A.; New York, NY, 1866 ***5704.8*** *p205*
Devine, Mary E.; Philadelphia, 1864 ***5704.8*** *p178*
Devine, Michael; New York, NY, 1811 ***2859.11*** *p11*
Devine, Michael; Philadelphia, 1847 ***53.26*** *p19*
*Relative:*Margaret
Devine, Michael; Philadelphia, 1847 ***5704.8*** *p5*
Devine, Michael 7 *SEE* Devine, Mary
Devine, Michael 7; Philadelphia, 1849 ***5704.8*** *p52*
Devine, Michael 30; New Orleans, 1862 ***543.30*** *p221*
Devine, Neil; Philadelphia, 1848 ***53.26*** *p19*
Devine, Neil; Philadelphia, 1848 ***5704.8*** *p40*
Devine, Neil 20; Philadelphia, 1854 ***5704.8*** *p117*
Devine, Nicholas 5; Massachusetts, 1849 ***5881.1*** *p33*
Devine, Patrick; New York, NY, 1866 ***5704.8*** *p209*
Devine, Patrick; New York, NY, 1869 ***5704.8*** *p232*
Devine, Patrick 10; Massachusetts, 1849 ***5881.1*** *p33*
Devine, Patrick 18; Philadelphia, 1854 ***5704.8*** *p115*
Devine, Patrick 20; St. John, N.B., 1854 ***5704.8*** *p114*
Devine, Patrick 21; New Orleans, 1862 ***543.30*** *p220*
Devine, Patrick 22; Philadelphia, 1854 ***5704.8*** *p116*
Devine, Patrick 40; Massachusetts, 1848 ***5881.1*** *p33*
Devine, Phillip 22; Massachusetts, 1849 ***5881.1*** *p33*
Devine, Robert 3 mos *SEE* Devine, Mary
Devine, Robert 3 mos; Philadelphia, 1849 ***5704.8*** *p52*
Devine, Robert 18; St. John, N.B., 1864 ***5704.8*** *p158*
Devine, Rose 69; St. John, N.B., 1853 ***5704.8*** *p109*
Devine, Sarah *SEE* Devine, John
Devine, Sarah; Philadelphia, 1848 ***5704.8*** *p46*
Devine, Susanna; New York, NY, 1866 ***5704.8*** *p205*
Devine, Thomas; Philadelphia, 1848 ***53.26*** *p19*
Devine, Thomas 9 mos; Philadelphia, 1848 ***5704.8*** *p46*
Devine, Thomas 4 *SEE* Devine, Mary
Devine, Thomas 4; Philadelphia, 1849 ***5704.8*** *p52*
Devine, Thomas 18; Massachusetts, 1849 ***5881.1*** *p34*
Devine, Thomas 24; Massachusetts, 1847 ***5881.1*** *p34*
Devine, William; Philadelphia, 1851 ***5704.8*** *p76*
Devineenzi, G. B.; California, 1880 ***2764.35*** *p19*
Devingt, Laurence 24; Louisiana, 1838 ***778.5*** *p164*
Devinny, Catharine; Philadelphia, 1867 ***5704.8*** *p218*
Devir, Anne; New York, NY, 1870 ***5704.8*** *p239*
Devir, Elizabeth; New York, NY, 1870 ***5704.8*** *p238*
Devir, James; New York, NY, 1870 ***5704.8*** *p238*
Devir, John; New York, NY, 1870 ***5704.8*** *p238*
Devir, Matty; Philadelphia, 1853 ***5704.8*** *p102*
Devir, Michael; New York, NY, 1867 ***5704.8*** *p213*
Devir, Sarah; New York, NY, 1870 ***5704.8*** *p239*
Deviss, Charles; Quebec, 1713 ***7603*** *p27*
Devit, Margaret 11; Quebec, 1851 ***5704.8*** *p82*
Devit, Sarah 13; Quebec, 1851 ***5704.8*** *p82*
Devitt, Ann 35; St. John, N.B., 1861 ***5704.8*** *p147*
Devitt, Anne 8; Quebec, 1853 ***5704.8*** *p105*
Devitt, Catherine 6; Quebec, 1853 ***5704.8*** *p105*
Devitt, Catherine 30; Quebec, 1853 ***5704.8*** *p105*
Devitt, John; St. John, N.B., 1853 ***5704.8*** *p99*
Devitt, John 2; Quebec, 1853 ***5704.8*** *p105*
Devitt, John 11; St. John, N.B., 1861 ***5704.8*** *p147*
Devitt, Winne 8; Massachusetts, 1849 ***5881.1*** *p34*
Devlin, Alice 16; Philadelphia, 1854 ***5704.8*** *p121*
Devlin, Ann; Quebec, 1850 ***5704.8*** *p67*
Devlin, Ann 9 mos; St. John, N.B., 1848 ***5704.8*** *p38*
Devlin, Ann 22; Quebec, 1855 ***5704.8*** *p125*
Devlin, Bernard; St. John, N.B., 1853 ***5704.8*** *p99*
Devlin, Bernard 28; Philadelphia, 1857 ***5704.8*** *p133*
Devlin, Biddy; Quebec, 1852 ***5704.8*** *p86*
Devlin, Biddy; Quebec, 1852 ***5704.8*** *p90*
Devlin, Biddy 7; St. John, N.B., 1848 ***5704.8*** *p38*
Devlin, Biddy 12; St. John, N.B., 1849 ***5704.8*** *p56*
Devlin, Bridget; New York, NY, 1864 ***5704.8*** *p182*
Devlin, Catharine; Philadelphia, 1865 ***5704.8*** *p189*
Devlin, Catharine 10; St. John, N.B., 1849 ***5704.8*** *p56*
Devlin, Catherine; St. John, N.B., 1852 ***5704.8*** *p95*
Devlin, Catherine; St. John, N.B., 1853 ***5704.8*** *p99*
Devlin, Catherine 19; Quebec, 1855 ***5704.8*** *p126*
Devlin, Charles; St. John, N.B., 1849 ***5704.8*** *p55*
Devlin, Charles 3 mos; St. John, N.B., 1850 ***5704.8*** *p61*
Devlin, Chas. 11; Wilmington, DE, 1831 ***6508.7*** *p161*
Devlin, Cormick; St. John, N.B., 1847 ***5704.8*** *p11*
Devlin, Daniel; Philadelphia, 1852 ***5704.8*** *p84*
Devlin, Daniel; Philadelphia, 1864 ***5704.8*** *p181*
Devlin, Daniel 5; St. John, N.B., 1847 ***5704.8*** *p11*
Devlin, Edward 13; St. John, N.B., 1848 ***5704.8*** *p44*
Devlin, Eleanor 23; St. John, N.B., 1851 ***5704.8*** *p77*
Devlin, Eliza 11; St. John, N.B., 1848 ***5704.8*** *p44*
Devlin, Elizabeth; St. John, N.B., 1851 ***5704.8*** *p72*
Devlin, Ellen; Philadelphia, 1869 ***5704.8*** *p236*
Devlin, Fanny; St. John, N.B., 1850 ***5704.8*** *p65*
Devlin, Fanny; St. John, N.B., 1853 ***5704.8*** *p106*
Devlin, Francis 48; Quebec, 1857 ***5704.8*** *p136*
Devlin, Hannah; St. John, N.B., 1848 ***5704.8*** *p44*
Devlin, Hannah 3; St. John, N.B., 1848 ***5704.8*** *p44*
Devlin, Henry; St. John, N.B., 1848 ***5704.8*** *p38*
Devlin, Henry 22; Philadelphia, 1861 ***5704.8*** *p148*
Devlin, Isabelle; Montreal, 1823 ***7603*** *p86*
Devlin, James; New York, NY, 1865 ***5704.8*** *p189*
Devlin, James; Quebec, 1824 ***7603*** *p60*
Devlin, James; St. John, N.B., 1848 ***5704.8*** *p44*
Devlin, James 3 mos; St. John, N.B., 1848 ***5704.8*** *p44*
Devlin, James 20; Quebec, 1863 ***5704.8*** *p154*
Devlin, James 21; St. John, N.B., 1851 ***5704.8*** *p77*
Devlin, Jane; America, 1864 ***5704.8*** *p188*
Devlin, Jane 7; St. John, N.B., 1847 ***5704.8*** *p11*
Devlin, Jane 16; Philadelphia, 1859 ***5704.8*** *p142*
Devlin, John; New York, NY, 1816 ***2859.11*** *p29*
Devlin, John 6 mos; Quebec, 1850 ***5704.8*** *p67*
Devlin, John 4; St. John, N.B., 1848 ***5704.8*** *p38*
Devlin, John 13; Philadelphia, 1854 ***5704.8*** *p123*
Devlin, John 21; Quebec, 1853 ***5704.8*** *p105*
Devlin, Lawrence 29; New Orleans, 1864 ***543.30*** *p222*
Devlin, Mary; Philadelphia, 1849 ***5704.8*** *p50*
Devlin, Mary; Philadelphia, 1852 ***5704.8*** *p96*
Devlin, Mary; St. John, N.B., 1847 ***5704.8*** *p11*
Devlin, Mary; St. John, N.B., 1849 ***5704.8*** *p49*
Devlin, Mary 5; St. John, N.B., 1848 ***5704.8*** *p44*
Devlin, Mary 22; Quebec, 1859 ***5704.8*** *p143*
Devlin, Mary 30; St. John, N.B., 1853 ***5704.8*** *p110*
Devlin, Mary A.; Philadelphia, 1867 ***5704.8*** *p216*
Devlin, Mary Ann; America, 1864 ***5704.8*** *p188*
Devlin, Mary Ann; St. John, N.B., 1849 ***5704.8*** *p56*
Devlin, Michael; America, 1864 ***5704.8*** *p188*
Devlin, Michael; New York, NY, 1865 ***5704.8*** *p190*
Devlin, Michael; St. John, N.B., 1853 ***5704.8*** *p99*
Devlin, Michael 1; St. John, N.B., 1848 ***5704.8*** *p44*
Devlin, Michl; New York, NY, 1816 ***2859.11*** *p29*
Devlin, Nancy 9; Philadelphia, 1854 ***5704.8*** *p121*
Devlin, Neal; Philadelphia, 1852 ***5704.8*** *p96*
Devlin, Pat 9; St. John, N.B., 1848 ***5704.8*** *p44*
Devlin, Patrick; Philadelphia, 1865 ***5704.8*** *p190*
Devlin, Patrick; St. John, N.B., 1848 ***5704.8*** *p38*
Devlin, Patrick 2; St. John, N.B., 1847 ***5704.8*** *p11*
Devlin, Patrick 3; St. John, N.B., 1848 ***5704.8*** *p38*
Devlin, Patrick 5; St. John, N.B., 1850 ***5704.8*** *p61*
Devlin, Patrick 7; Philadelphia, 1854 ***5704.8*** *p121*
Devlin, Peggy; St. John, N.B., 1849 ***5704.8*** *p49*
Devlin, Peggy; St. John, N.B., 1850 ***5704.8*** *p61*
Devlin, Peggy 3; St. John, N.B., 1850 ***5704.8*** *p61*
Devlin, Rose 21; Philadelphia, 1860 ***5704.8*** *p145*
Devlin, Rose 46; Massachusetts, 1847 ***5881.1*** *p34*
Devlin, Rosey; St. John, N.B., 1851 ***5704.8*** *p72*
Devlin, Sally; New York, NY, 1811 ***2859.11*** *p11*
Devlin, Sarah; St. John, N.B., 1851 ***5704.8*** *p72*
Devlin, Sarah 22; Philadelphia, 1861 ***5704.8*** *p148*
Devlin, Susanna; Philadelphia, 1847 ***53.26*** *p19*
Devlin, Susanna; Philadelphia, 1847 ***5704.8*** *p31*
Devlin, Unity; Philadelphia, 1865 ***5704.8*** *p195*
Devlin, William; Philadelphia, 1864 ***5704.8*** *p170*
Devlin, William 26; Philadelphia, 1860 ***5704.8*** *p145*
Devoss, Daniel; Ohio, 1798-1818 ***8582.2*** *p54*
Devotto, Jean-Baptiste 20; America, 1820 ***778.5*** *p164*
DeVries, Joe; Arkansas, 1918 ***95.2*** *p36*
DeVries, Walter; Arkansas, 1918 ***95.2*** *p36*
Devrincy, Eugene; New York, NY, 1851 ***6013.19*** *p90*
Devut, R. 27; America, 1826 ***778.5*** *p164*
Dew, John; Virginia, 1652 ***6251*** *p20*
Dew, Thomas; New York, NY, 1816 ***2859.11*** *p29*
Dew, Thomas; Virginia, 1643 ***6219*** *p207*
Dewald, Daniel; Philadelphia, 1761 ***9973.7*** *p35*
Dewalz, Napoleon 26; New Orleans, 1830 ***778.5*** *p164*
Dewar, Duncan 36; New Orleans, 1862 ***543.30*** *p216*
Dewar, James; New York, NY, 1837 ***8208.4*** *p36*
Dewar, Michael; Montreal, 1821 ***7603*** *p92*
Deward, John; St. John, N.B., 1849 ***5704.8*** *p56*
Dewars, Alexander; South Carolina, 1730 ***1639.20*** *p59*
Dewe, Tho.; Virginia, 1638 ***6219*** *p159*
Deweex, David; Virginia, 1640 ***6219*** *p187*
Dewer, Mary 11; Massachusetts, 1848 ***5881.1*** *p31*
Dewess, Stophel; Pennsylvania, 1740 ***4779.3*** *p13*
Dewey, Margaret 18; Philadelphia, 1858 ***5704.8*** *p139*
Dewey, Nancy 16; Philadelphia, 1858 ***5704.8*** *p139*
Dewhurst, Arthur 10; America, 1699 ***2212*** *p28*
DeWilde, Albert Nicholas; Arkansas, 1918 ***95.2*** *p36*
Dewis, Samuel; Boston, 1776 ***1219.7*** *p277*
Dewitt, Jacob; Virginia, 1637 ***6219*** *p86*
DeWitte, Zackarias; Wisconsin, n.d. ***9675.5*** *p50*
De Wolf, Joseph; Ohio, 1812 ***8582.1*** *p49*
DeWorle, Edmund 29; Arkansas, 1918 ***95.2*** *p36*
Dewthwaite, James 34; Nova Scotia, 1774 ***1219.7*** *p209*
Dewyer, Anthony 20; Maryland, 1775 ***1219.7*** *p271*
Dexon, John 22; Philadelphia, 1856 ***5704.8*** *p128*
Dexter, Ann 17; Pennsylvania, 1731 ***3690.1*** *p63*
Dexter, Dan; Arkansas, 1918 ***95.2*** *p37*
Dexter, John; New York, NY, 1892 ***3455.2*** *p94*
Deyarmatt, Fanny 20; Philadelphia, 1857 ***5704.8*** *p133*
Deymour, William; New York, NY, 1815 ***2859.11*** *p29*
Deynes, Phillis *SEE* Deynes, William
Deynes, William; Virginia, 1646 ***6219*** *p235*
*Wife:*Phillis
DeYoung, Lieuwe Foekert; Arkansas, 1918 ***95.2*** *p36*
Deyr, John; New York, NY, 1815 ***2859.11*** *p29*
Dezadre, Charles 19; Maryland, 1724 ***3690.1*** *p63*
Dezen, August; Wisconsin, n.d. ***9675.5*** *p50*
De Zorzi, Antonio; Iowa, 1866-1943 ***123.54*** *p16*
Dezzani, John; Arkansas, 1918 ***95.2*** *p37*
Dhoren, . . .; Canada, 1776-1783 ***9786*** *p19*
Dhoullieu, P. 28; America, 1838 ***778.5*** *p165*
Dia, Antonio 28; New Orleans, 1863 ***543.30*** *p372*
Diailey, Mary Ann 36; Philadelphia, 1864 ***5704.8*** *p160*
Diamere, J.; New York, NY, 1816 ***2859.11*** *p29*
Diamond, James 20; Philadelphia, 1864 ***5704.8*** *p156*
Diamond, John; New York, NY, 1816 ***2859.11*** *p29*
Diamond, John; St. John, N.B., 1852 ***5704.8*** *p95*
Diamond, John 4 *SEE* Diamond, Mary
Diamond, John 18; Philadelphia, 1864 ***5704.8*** *p156*
Diamond, Mary 6; Philadelphia, 1833-1834 ***53.26*** *p19*
*Relative:*John 4
Diamond, Patrick; New York, NY, 1865 ***5704.8*** *p193*
Diamond, Richard 25; New Orleans, 1862 ***543.30*** *p56*
Diamond, Wm. D. 32; New Orleans, 1863 ***543.30*** *p372*
DiAndrea, Domenico 31; West Virginia, 1903 ***9788.3*** *p8*
Dianto, Leon J.; Arkansas, 1918 ***95.2*** *p37*
DiBartolo, Benifacio Di; Wisconsin, n.d. ***9675.5*** *p50*
Dibbel, John; America, 1834 ***1450.2*** *p30A*
Dibbell, John; America, 1834 ***1450.2*** *p30A*
Dibbens, Arthur 27; Kansas, 1874 ***5240.1*** *p10*
Dibbens, Arthur 27; Kansas, 1874 ***5240.1*** *p55*
DiBella, Gioseppe; Arkansas, 1918 ***95.2*** *p37*
DiBerardino, Nicola Antonio; Arkansas, 1918 ***95.2*** *p37*
DiBiase, Clementi; Wisconsin, n.d. ***9675.5*** *p50*
DiBiase, Luigi; Wisconsin, n.d. ***9675.5*** *p50*
DiBiase, Vinanzio; Wisconsin, n.d. ***9675.5*** *p50*
Dibon, William; Jamaica, 1762 ***1219.7*** *p85*
Dichot, H.; America, 1838 ***778.5*** *p165*
Dichtel, Johann Georg; Pennsylvania, 1752 ***2444*** *p147*
*Wife:*Magdalen Blaich
Dichtel, Magdalen Blaich *SEE* Dichtel, Johann Georg
Dick, Adam; Ohio, 1843 ***8582.1*** *p51*
Dick, Adam; Pennsylvania, 1768 ***9973.8*** *p32*
Dick, Alexander; South Carolina, 1642-1742 ***1639.20*** *p59*
Dick, Anton; Wisconsin, n.d. ***9675.5*** *p50*
Dick, David; St. John, N.B., 1848 ***5704.8*** *p45*
Dick, George *SEE* Dick, Mary
Dick, Grizel 4 *SEE* Dick, John
Dick, J. F. 33; Kansas, 1902 ***5240.1*** *p82*
Dick, James 50; South Carolina, 1850 ***1639.20*** *p59*
Dick, Jane 13 *SEE* Dick, John
Dick, Jervis; Virginia, 1637 ***6219*** *p111*
Dick, John; New York, NY, 1811 ***2859.11*** *p11*
Dick, John; Petersburg, VA, 1806 ***4778.2*** *p141*
Dick, John; South Carolina, 1753 ***1639.20*** *p59*
Dick, John 14; Georgia, 1775 ***1219.7*** *p276*
Dick, John 46; Georgia, 1775 ***1219.7*** *p276*
*Wife:*Mary 33
*Child:*Jane 13
*Child:*Grizel 4
Dick, Mary; Carolina, 1796 ***1639.20*** *p59*
*Father:*George
Dick, Mary 33 *SEE* Dick, John
Dick, Peter; Philadelphia, 1760 ***9973.7*** *p34*
Dick, Philip; Philadelphia, 1760 ***9973.7*** *p34*
Dick, Robert 64; West Virginia, 1800 ***9788.3*** *p8*
Dick, Susan; Detroit, 1790 ***8894.1*** *p191*
Dick, Thomas 32; Philadelphia, 1803 ***53.26*** *p19*
Dick, William; Arkansas, 1918 ***95.2*** *p37*
Dickel, Colonel; New York, 1861-1865 ***8582.3*** *p92*
Dickel, Gg. Adam 76; America, 1897 ***1763*** *p40C*

Dicken, Emil; Baltimore, 1910 *3455.3 p55*
Dicken, Emil; Illinois, 1915-1922 *3455.3 p55*
Dickens, William; Virginia, 1643 *6219 p206*
Dickenson, Wm.; Virginia, 1635 *6219 p68*
Dicker, Edward; Virginia, 1638 *6219 p123*
Dickerhof, Peter; Ohio, 1811 *8582.1 p48*
Dickerhoff, Peter; Ohio, 1811 *8582.1 p48*
Dickerson, William 25; Philadelphia, 1775 *1219.7 p258*
Dickes, Eliza.; Virginia, 1637 *6219 p114*
Dickes, Wm.; Virginia, 1633 *6219 p111*
Dickescheid, Wendel; America, 1847 *8582.1 p7*
Dickeson, Peter; Virginia, 1622 *6219 p4*
Dickey, Isaac 20; Philadelphia, 1804 *53.26 p19*
Dickey, James; Philadelphia, 1811 *53.26 p19*
Dickey, James; Philadelphia, 1811 *2859.11 p11*
Dickey, Nathaniel; Philadelphia, 1811 *53.26 p19*
Dickey, Nathaniel; Philadelphia, 1811 *2859.11 p11*
Dickey, Samuel; New York, NY, 1816 *2859.11 p29*
Dickey, Samuel; Philadelphia, 1811 *53.26 p19*
Dickey, Samuel; Philadelphia, 1811 *2859.11 p11*
Dickhaut, . . .; Canada, 1776-1783 *9786 p19*
Dickhoff, Heinrich; America, 1842 *8582.3 p14*
Dickhut, Friederich Wilhelm; Illinois, 1842 *8582.2 p50*
Dickie, John; New Brunswick, 1822 *9775.5 p204*
  With family
Dickie, William; Austin, TX, 1886 *9777 p5*
Dickin, Elizabeth; Virginia, 1698 *2212 p17*
Dickinson, Andrew; Virginia, 1648 *6219 p237*
Dickinson, Anthony; Virginia, 1640 *6219 p184*
Dickinson, Joseph; Cincinnati, 1800-1877 *8582.3 p86*
Dickinson, Margtte 22; America, 1703 *2212 p40*
Dickinson, Peter 27; Maryland, 1735 *3690.1 p63*
Dickinson, Robert 26; New York, 1774 *1219.7 p217*
Dickinson, Thom 15; America, 1704 *2212 p41*
Dickinson, Timothy 35; America, 1702 *2212 p37*
Dickinson, William; America, 1697 *2212 p7*
Dickinson, William 14; Maryland or Virginia, 1699 *2212 p21*
Dickinson, Wm.; Virginia, 1645 *6219 p232*
Dickman, Bernhard Frederick; America, 1838 *1450.2 p30A*
Dickman, Francis; America, 1819 *1450.2 p30A*
Dickmann, Gerhard; Cincinnati, 1841 *8582.3 p16*
Dickmann, Wilhelm; Ohio, 1869-1887 *8582 p6*
Dickmans, Heinriette; Baltimore, 1846 *3702.7 p86*
Dickner, . . .; Canada, 1776-1783 *9786 p19*
Dicks, Edward; Virginia, 1623-1648 *6219 p252*
Dicks, William 29; Allegany Co., MD, 1840 *1450.2 p30A*
Dickson, Christian; Virginia, 1647 *6219 p239*
Dickson, David; New York, NY, 1815 *2859.11 p29*
Dickson, Eacy; St. John, N.B., 1850 *5704.8 p66*
Dickson, Eliza; New York, NY, 1816 *2859.11 p29*
Dickson, Hugh; New York, NY, 1816 *2859.11 p29*
Dickson, J.; New York, NY, 1811 *2859.11 p11*
  With family
Dickson, James 23; Philadelphia, 1864 *5704.8 p156*
Dickson, Jane; New York, NY, 1816 *2859.11 p29*
Dickson, Jane; St. John, N.B., 1852 *5704.8 p93*
Dickson, John; New York, NY, 1816 *2859.11 p29*
Dickson, John; New York, NY, 1865 *5704.8 p195*
Dickson, John; North Carolina, 1809 *1639.20 p59*
Dickson, John; Philadelphia, 1811 *2859.11 p11*
Dickson, John 27; Virginia, 1727 *3690.1 p64*
Dickson, Lundy; Philadelphia, 1850 *5704.8 p64*
Dickson, Mary Ann; New York, NY, 1816 *2859.11 p29*
Dickson, Matilda; Quebec, 1847 *5704.8 p36*
Dickson, Richard; Virginia, 1647 *6219 p239*
Dickson, Sally; New York, NY, 1816 *2859.11 p29*
Dickson, Samuel; New York, NY, 1816 *2859.11 p29*
Dickson, Tho.; Virginia, 1638 *6219 p148*
Dickson, Thomas; North Carolina, 1809 *1639.20 p59*
Dickson, William; Ontario, 1815 *9775.5 p214*
Dicky, Jane; St. John, N.B., 1852 *5704.8 p95*
Dicky, R.J. 75; Arizona, 1914 *9228.40 p18*
DiDiana, Dominico; Arkansas, 1918 *95.2 p37*
Didier, August; Iroquois Co., IL, 1896 *3455.1 p10*
Didier, Francis; New York, NY, 1840 *8208.4 p105*
Didier, Scipion 30; America, 1827 *778.5 p165*
DiDominico, Sabatino; Colorado, 1904 *9678.2 p16*
Dieber, Johan; Pennsylvania, 1753 *2444 p226*
Diebitz, Walter; Wisconsin, n.d. *9675.5 p50*
Diebo, Charles; New York, NY, 1837 *8208.4 p24*
Diebold, George 30; New Orleans, 1862 *543.30 p62*
Diebold, Michael; New York, NY, 1836 *8582.1 p7*
Diebolt, Joseph; Cincinnati, 1820-1871 *8582 p6*
Diechtel, Johann Georg; Pennsylvania, 1752 *2444 p147*
  *Wife:*Magdalen Blaich
Diechtel, Magdalen Blaich *SEE* Diechtel, Johann Georg
Dieck, Abraham; Kansas, 1885 *5240.1 p10*
Dieckman, Engel; Canada, 1783 *9786 p38A*
Dieckmann, Carl; Illinois, 1877 *2896.5 p9*
Dieckmann, Eberhard; America, 1846 *3702.7 p87*
Dieckmann, Ernest; Illinois, 1895 *2896.5 p9*

Dieckmann, Heinrich August; New Orleans, 1841 *2896.5 p9*
Dieckmann, Heinriette; Baltimore, 1846 *3702.7 p87*
Dieckmann, Henrich Conrad; New Orleans, 1839 *2896.5 p9*
Diederichs, Johann Fr.; New York, 1847 *8125.8 p436*
Diedering, Henry; Wisconsin, n.d. *9675.5 p50*
Diederk, Nicholas; Wisconsin, n.d. *9675.5 p50*
Diedrich, Frederick; Illinois, 1871 *5012.39 p25*
Diedrichs, . . .; Canada, 1776-1783 *9786 p19*
Diefel, Michael; Pennsylvania, 1754 *4525 p253*
Diefenbach, Georg; Ohio, 1869-1887 *8582 p6*
Diefenbach, Jacob; Illinois, 1874 *5240.1 p10*
Diefenbach, Joseph 31; Kansas, 1876 *5240.1 p10*
Diefenbach, Joseph 31; Kansas, 1876 *5240.1 p57*
Diefenbach, Paul; Minnesota, 1875 *5240.1 p10*
Diefenbach, Peter William 41; Kansas, 1877 *5240.1 p58*
Dieffenderfer, Heinrich; Pennsylvania, 1735 *4480 p312*
Dieffenderfer, Jacob; Pennsylvania, 1735 *4480 p312*
Dieffenderfer, Kilian; Pennsylvania, 1735 *4480 p312*
Diehl, . . .; Canada, 1776-1783 *9786 p19*
Diehl, Gabriel; New York, NY, 1840 *8208.4 p106*
Diehl, Henry; Ohio, 1850 *9892.11 p13*
Diehl, Jacob; Baltimore, 1840 *8582.1 p7*
Diehl, Jacob; Cincinnati, 1869-1887 *8582 p6*
Diehl, Jacob; Illinois, 1853 *7857 p3*
Diehl, Jacob; Ohio, 1844 *9892.11 p13*
Diehl, Jacob; Ohio, 1846 *9892.11 p13*
Diehl, Jacob; Ohio, 1848 *9892.11 p13*
Diehl, Johann; Illinois, 1842 *8582.2 p51*
Diehl, John; Illinois, 1869 *7857 p3*
Diehl, John; Illinois, 1871 *7857 p3*
Diehl, John Justus; Canada, 1776-1783 *9786 p241*
Diehl, Louise 21; Illinois, 1836 *778.5 p165*
Diehl, Theobald; Ohio, 1843 *9892.11 p13*
Diehm, Adam; New England, 1753 *4525 p205*
Diehm, Adam; Pennsylvania, 1749 *4525 p206*
Diehm, Adam; Pennsylvania, 1751 *4525 p206*
Diehm, Adam; Pennsylvania, 1753 *4525 p206*
Diehm, Adam; Pennsylvania, 1754 *4525 p206*
  *Relative:*Hans Adam
Diehm, Andreas; Pennsylvania, 1753 *4525 p206*
  With wife
Diehm, Andreas; Pennsylvania, 1773 *4525 p206*
Diehm, Franz; America, 1847 *8582.2 p7*
Diehm, Hans Adam *SEE* Diehm, Adam
Diehm, Hans Adam; Pennsylvania, 1753 *4525 p207*
Diehm, Hans Adam; Pennsylvania, 1754 *4525 p206*
  With wife
  With children
Diehm, Hans Thomas; Pennsylvania, 1753 *4525 p208*
  With wife
  With children
Diehm, Jacob; Pennsylvania, 1752 *4525 p206*
Diehm, Johann Adam; New England, 1753 *4525 p207*
Diehm, Peter; New England, 1773 *4525 p207*
Diehm, Peter; Pennsylvania, 1752 *4525 p207*
  With wife
  With 4 children
Diehm, Peter; Pennsylvania, 1773 *4525 p207*
  With wife
Diehm, Thomas; Pennsylvania, 1752 *4525 p207*
  With wife
  With 3 children
Dieken, Emil; Baltimore, 1908-1910 *3455.2 p53*
Dieken, Emma; Baltimore, 1910 *3455.4 p56*
Dieken, Herman Remmers; Baltimore, 1910 *3455.2 p71*
Dieker, Anton; America, 1836 *8582 p6*
Diekman, Martin; Kentucky, 1869-1887 *8582 p6*
Diekmann, Mr.; America, 1840-1858 *4610.10 p158*
  With daughters
  With sons
  With wife
Diekmann, Anna Margarete Elisabeth; America, 1831 *4815.7 p92*
Diekmann, Bernhard Heinrich; America, 1858 *4610.10 p158*
Diekmann, C. F.; America, 1853 *4610.10 p148*
Diekmann, Carl August; America, 1853 *4610.10 p156*
Diekmann, Carl Fr. W.; America, 1892 *4610.10 p161*
Diekmann, Christian Friedrich August; America, 1868 *4610.10 p117*
Diekmann, Friedrich; America, 1831 *4815.7 p92*
  *Wife:*Sophie Leonore Barking
  With 3 children
Diekmann, Gerhard; Cincinnati, 1837 *8582 p6*
Diekmann, Heinrich Adolf Louis; America, 1853 *4610.10 p116*
Diekmann, Johann Christoph Ludwig; America, 1848 *4610.10 p115*
Diekmann, Sophie Leonore Barking *SEE* Diekmann, Friedrich
Diel, Konrad 77; Pennsylvania, 1904 *1763 p40C*
Dieler, . . .; Canada, 1776-1783 *9786 p19*

Dieler, Jean; Canada, 1776-1783 *9786 p207A*
Dielzel, . . .; Canada, 1776-1783 *9786 p35*
Diem, . . .; Pennsylvania, n.d. *4525 p206*
Diem, . . .; Pennsylvania, n.d. *4525 p207*
Diem, . . .; Pennsylvania, n.d. *4525 p208*
Diem, Andrew; Pennsylvania, 1753 *4525 p206*
Diemard, Augustin de; Quebec, 1790 *7603 p29*
Dieme, . . .; Pennsylvania, n.d. *4525 p208*
Diemer, Franz Christopher; New York, 1754 *3652 p79*
Diemert, Louis 18; New Orleans, 1862 *543.30 p57*
Diener, Amelia; Wisconsin, n.d. *9675.5 p50*
Diener, Henry; Wisconsin, n.d. *9675.5 p50*
Dienie, Theresa 21; America, 1838 *778.5 p165*
Dieraiks, Cameil; Arkansas, 1918 *95.2 p37*
Dieringer, Coelestin; America, 1849 *8582.1 p7*
Dieringer, Josephine; Wisconsin, n.d. *9675.5 p50*
Dierkes, Charles 34; New Orleans, 1863 *543.30 p221*
Dierks, Henry; Washington, 1859-1920 *2872.1 p10*
Dierksen, . . .; New Netherland, 1630-1646 *8582.2 p51*
Diers, Joseph; New Orleans, 1849 *3840.1 p16*
Dierstein, Martin; Illinois, 1841 *8582.2 p50*
Diessner, Elsie; Wisconsin, n.d. *9675.5 p50*
Diessner, Max; Wisconsin, n.d. *9675.5 p50*
Dietel, John 30; New Orleans, 1862 *543.30 p62*
Dieter, August 21; Kansas, 1880 *5240.1 p62*
Dieter, Ernst; America, 1853 *1450.2 p30A*
Dieter, J. P. 21; Kansas, 1872 *5240.1 p53*
Dieterich, Christian P. 75; Washington, D.C., 1908 *1763 p40C*
Dieterich, Gustav 66; New York, NY, 1909 *1763 p40C*
Dieterle, Andreas; America, 1852 *8582.3 p14*
Dieterlin, Anna Barbara; Port uncertain, 1728-1800 *2444 p148*
Diether, Bastian; Died enroute, 1738 *9898 p42*
  With wife & children
Diether, George; Virginia, 1700-1738 *9898 p42*
Diether, Margareta; Philadelphia, 1737 *9898 p42*
Dietker, Anton; America, 1834 *8582.2 p60*
Dietrich, . . .; Canada, 1776-1783 *9786 p19*
Dietrich, Adolph Lorenz; Quebec, 1776 *9786 p254*
Dietrich, Christian Gotthelf; America, 1850 *1450.2 p30A*
Dietrich, Clemens; Cincinnati, 1834 *8582.1 p52*
Dietrich, Conrad; Wisconsin, n.d. *9675.5 p50*
Dietrich, Jacob; Philadelphia, 1776 *8582.3 p83*
Dietrich, John; Illinois, 1892 *5012.40 p27*
Dietrich, John; Wisconsin, n.d. *9675.5 p50*
Dietrich, Joseph 22; America, 1835 *778.5 p165*
Dietrich, Lisette 20; America, 1854-1855 *9162.6 p105*
Dietrich, Louis 72; Washington, D.C., 1904 *1763 p40C*
Dietrich, Marian 22; America, 1835 *778.5 p165*
Dietrich, Michael; America, 1835 *8582.1 p7*
Dietrich, Michel; Canada, 1776-1783 *9786 p207A*
Dietrich, Phillip; Wisconsin, n.d. *9675.5 p50*
Dietrichs, Willial; Baltimore, 1852 *1450.2 p30A*
Diets, Ferdinand; America, 1853 *1450.2 p31A*
Dietsch, Walter; Wisconsin, n.d. *9675.5 p50*
Dietz, Christophe 29; America, 1838 *778.5 p165*
Dietz, Conrad; Philadelphia, 1838 *8137 p4*
Dietz, Eva 45; America, 1837 *778.5 p165*
Dietz, George; New York, NY, 1838 *8208.4 p68*
Dietz, George; Pennsylvania, 1737-1782 *2444 p148*
Dietz, Johann Michael; America, 1851 *8582.3 p14*
Dietz, Johannes; America, 1844 *1450.2 p31A*
Dietz, John; America, 1844 *1450.2 p31A*
Dietz, John George; Indiana, 1861 *1450.2 p7B*
Dietz, Konrad; Philadelphia, 1779 *8137 p7*
Dietz, Maria Catherine; New York, 1752 *3652 p76*
Dietz, Rosina; New York, 1749 *3652 p72*
Dietz, Theodore; America, 1844 *1450.2 p28A*
Dietze, Ernst Herman; Wisconsin, n.d. *9675.5 p121*
Dietzel, . . .; Canada, 1776-1783 *9786 p19*
Diewes, Johan Christ.; Pennsylvania, 1740 *4779.3 p13*
Diewos, Johanrich; Pennsylvania, 1740 *4779.3 p13*
Diez, Anna Maria *SEE* Diez, Hans Jerg
Diez, Hans Jerg; Pennsylvania, 1737-1782 *2444 p148*
  *Wife:*Anna Maria
  *Child:*Johann Caspar
Diez, Johann Caspar *SEE* Diez, Hans Jerg
Diezen, Peter; Wisconsin, n.d. *9675.5 p121*
Diezmann Family ; Costa Rica, 1853 *8582.3 p30*
Diffiderfer, Michael; Philadelphia, 1759 *9973.7 p34*
Digel, Anna Barbara *SEE* Digel, Hans Jacob
Digel, Hans Jacob; Pennsylvania, 1752 *2444 p148*
  *Wife:*Ursula
  *Child:*Johann Jacob
  *Child:*Anna Barbara
Digel, Johann Jacob *SEE* Digel, Hans Jacob
Digel, Ursula *SEE* Digel, Hans Jacob
Digeon, David; New York, 1743 *3652 p60*
  *Wife:*Mary
Digeon, Mary *SEE* Digeon, David
Di Georgio, Thomas; Arkansas, 1918 *95.2 p37*
Digesu, Sam; Arkansas, 1918 *95.2 p37*

Diggins, David; Iowa, 1866-1943 ***123.54*** *p16*
Diggins, James 6; Massachusetts, 1850 ***5881.1*** *p30*
Diggins, Margaret 10; Massachusetts, 1850 ***5881.1*** *p32*
Diggles, Alice 27; Maryland or Virginia, 1699 ***2212*** *p23*
Diggs, Richard; Virginia, 1645 ***6219*** *p232*
Dighton, Benjamin 16; Maryland, 1723 ***3690.1*** *p63*
DiGiacomo, Mariano; Colorado, 1904 ***9678.2*** *p16*
DiGiacomo, Nichola; Colorado, 1904 ***9678.2*** *p16*
DiGioio, Salvoutore; Wisconsin, n.d. ***9675.5*** *p121*
Digle, Jacob; Pennsylvania, 1752 ***2444*** *p148*
Dignac, J. 17; Louisiana, 1820 ***778.5*** *p165*
Dignam, Teresa; America, 1741 ***4971*** *p94*
Dignam, Terress; America, 1741 ***4971*** *p10*
Dignan, Bernard 22; Massachusetts, 1849 ***5881.1*** *p27*
Dignan, Honora 26; Massachusetts, 1849 ***5881.1*** *p29*
Dignan, Michael 10; Massachusetts, 1849 ***5881.1*** *p32*
Dignan, Phillip 14; Massachusetts, 1850 ***5881.1*** *p33*
D'Ignoti, Ginseppe 7; New York, NY, 1893 ***9026.4*** *p41*
Digris, John; Wisconsin, n.d. ***9675.5*** *p121*
Digwell, Nich.; Virginia, 1642 ***6219*** *p191*
Dihm, Adam; Pennsylvania, 1754 ***4525*** *p206*
Dihm, Andreas; Pennsylvania, 1753 ***4525*** *p206*
Dihm, Hans Adam; Pennsylvania, 1754 ***4525*** *p206*
Dihm, Hans Adam; Pennsylvania, 1754 ***4525*** *p208*
Dihm, Hans Thomas; Pennsylvania, 1752 ***4525*** *p208*
Dihm, Johan Lorentz; Pennsylvania, 1773 ***4525*** *p233*
Dihm, Johann Peter; Pennsylvania, 1753 ***4525*** *p207*
Dihm, Thomas; Pennsylvania, 1754 ***4525*** *p206*
Dilg, Mr.; Cincinnati, 1847 ***8582.2*** *p8*
Dilg, Adam; America, 1847 ***8582.1*** *p7*
Dilg, Adam; New York, NY, 1847 ***8582.2*** *p8*
*Wife:*Catharina Spiess
With child
Dilg, Catharina Spiess *SEE* Dilg, Adam
Dilg, Christian; America, 1840 ***8582.1*** *p7*
Dilg, Georg; America, 1847 ***8582.1*** *p7*
Dilg, Heinrich; America, 1836 ***8582.1*** *p7*
Dilg, Peter; Cincinnati, 1869-1887 ***8582*** *p6*
Dilgen, John; Wisconsin, n.d. ***9675.5*** *p121*
Dilger, Captain; America, 1861-1865 ***8582.3*** *p92*
Dilger, Alois; St. Louis, 1931 ***3702.7*** *p515*
Dilger, Emma; Brazil, 1894 ***3702.7*** *p498*
Dilger, Ludwig; St. Louis, 1881-1882 ***3702.7*** *p486*
Dilke, Clement; Virginia, 1622 ***6219*** *p6*
*Wife:*Elizabeth
Dilke, Elizabeth *SEE* Dilke, Clement
Dill, Johann Caspar; Pennsylvania, 1791 ***4525*** *p208*
Dill, Johann Michael; Pennsylvania, 1754 ***4525*** *p208*
Dill, Michael; Pennsylvania, 1754 ***4525*** *p208*
Dillan, David; New York, NY, 1816 ***2859.11*** *p29*
Dillane, David; America, 1741 ***4971*** *p41*
Dillane, John; America, 1742 ***4971*** *p56*
Dillemann, . . .; Canada, 1776-1783 ***9786*** *p19*
Dillen, Edmund 50; Massachusetts, 1847 ***5881.1*** *p28*
Dillen, Ellen 20; Philadelphia, 1860 ***5704.8*** *p144*
Diller, . . .; Canada, 1776-1783 ***9786*** *p19*
Diller, Mr.; Canada, 1776-1783 ***9786*** *p232*
Dilles, Omer 28; Port uncertain, 1838 ***778.5*** *p165*
Dilley, Page; Washington, 1859-1920 ***2872.1*** *p10*
Dillhoff, Clemens; West Virginia, 1905 ***9788.3*** *p9*
Dilli, Stephen; America, 1889 ***1450.2*** *p31A*
Dillin, Catherine 20; Philadelphia, 1857 ***5704.8*** *p134*
Dilling, Andreas; America, 1846 ***8582.3*** *p14*
Dilling, Johann Leonhard; America, 1846 ***8582.3*** *p14*
Dillion, W. F.; Washington, 1859-1920 ***2872.1*** *p10*
Dillman, . . .; Canada, 1776-1783 ***9786*** *p19*
Dillman, Jacob; Ohio, 1856 ***6014.2*** *p7*
Dillman, Jacob 30; New Orleans, 1862 ***543.30*** *p220*
Dillmann, . . .; Canada, 1776-1783 ***9786*** *p19*
Dillmann, Johanne Henrietta; New York, NY, 1925 ***3455.4*** *p56*
*Husband:*Otto
Dillmann, Otto *SEE* Dillmann, Johanne Henrietta
Dilloe, Tho.; Virginia, 1637 ***6219*** *p85*
Dillon, Christopher; New York, NY, 1836 ***8208.4*** *p22*
Dillon, Edward; New York, NY, 1834 ***8208.4*** *p48*
Dillon, Edward 22; Maryland, 1775 ***1219.7*** *p251*
Dillon, Ellen; New York, NY, 1816 ***2859.11*** *p29*
Dillon, Francis 6; Massachusetts, 1850 ***5881.1*** *p29*
Dillon, Hannah 8; Massachusetts, 1849 ***5881.1*** *p29*
Dillon, James; New York, NY, 1816 ***2859.11*** *p29*
Dillon, Jane; New York, NY, 1869 ***5704.8*** *p234*
Dillon, John; New York, NY, 1815 ***2859.11*** *p29*
Dillon, John 20; Massachusetts, 1847 ***5881.1*** *p29*
Dillon, Julia 23; Massachusetts, 1849 ***5881.1*** *p30*
Dillon, Margaret; America, 1743 ***4971*** *p18*
Dillon, Margaret; Delaware Bay or River, 1743 ***4971*** *p104*
Dillon, Mary; America, 1735-1743 ***4971*** *p7*
Dillon, Mary; Philadelphia, 1847 ***53.26*** *p19*
Dillon, Mary; Philadelphia, 1847 ***5704.8*** *p22*
Dillon, Mary Ann 4; Philadelphia, 1854 ***5704.8*** *p118*
Dillon, Mary Ann 9; Massachusetts, 1850 ***5881.1*** *p32*
Dillon, Michael 11; Massachusetts, 1849 ***5881.1*** *p32*
Dillon, Michael 28; Massachusetts, 1847 ***5881.1*** *p31*
Dillon, Patrick; New York, NY, 1838 ***8208.4*** *p63*
Dillon, Patrick; Philadelphia, 1816 ***2859.11*** *p29*
Dillon, Patrick; Quebec, 1825 ***7603*** *p86*
Dillon, Patrick 40; Louisiana, 1863 ***543.30*** *p373*
Dillon, Peter; Illinois, 1872 ***5012.39*** *p91*
Dillon, Richard; New York, NY, 1816 ***2859.11*** *p29*
Dillon, Robert; New York, NY, 1838 ***8208.4*** *p73*
Dillon, Rosana 4; Massachusetts, 1850 ***5881.1*** *p34*
Dillon, Susan 2; Massachusetts, 1850 ***5881.1*** *p34*
Dilmore, Bridget 6; Massachusetts, 1850 ***5881.1*** *p27*
Dilon, Charles 25; Port uncertain, 1825 ***778.5*** *p165*
Dils, Jacob; Philadelphia, 1752 ***8125.6*** *p23*
Dils, Moritz Wilhelm; Philadelphia, 1752 ***8125.6*** *p23*
Dils, Peder; Philadelphia, 1752 ***8125.6*** *p23*
Dilss, Peter; America, 1750-1752 ***8125.6*** *p23*
Dilworth, Patrick; New York, NY, 1837 ***8208.4*** *p33*
Dimarzo, Guiseppe; Arkansas, 1918 ***95.2*** *p37*
Dimiaco, Gast; Arkansas, 1918 ***95.2*** *p37*
Dimine, Sophia 26; America, 1831 ***778.5*** *p165*
Dimitri, Konstantin; Arkansas, 1918 ***95.2*** *p37*
Dimitroff, Kosta; Arkansas, 1918 ***95.2*** *p38*
Dimm, Christana 22; Port uncertain, 1839 ***778.5*** *p165*
Dimmer, Charles; Wisconsin, n.d. ***9675.5*** *p121*
Dimmery, Daniel 17; Jamaica, 1731 ***3690.1*** *p63*
Dimock, M.D.; Milwaukee, 1875 ***4719.30*** *p257*
Dimock, Martin; Virginia, 1637 ***6219*** *p11*
Dimock, Miss S.; Milwaukee, 1875 ***4719.30*** *p257*
Dimond, Alice 24; North America, 1774 ***1219.7*** *p200*
Dimond, Raymond 33; New Orleans, 1862 ***543.30*** *p216*
Dimore, Daniel 20; Windward Islands, 1722 ***3690.1*** *p63*
Dimpsey, James 23; Baltimore, 1775 ***1219.7*** *p269*
Dinaghy, Daniel; America, 1741 ***4971*** *p56*
Dinaghy, Teigue; America, 1741 ***4971*** *p56*
Dinaghy, William 21; Philadelphia, 1854 ***5704.8*** *p117*
Dinan, Mary; Quebec, 1805 ***7603*** *p64*
Dinar, Harry; Arizona, 1898 ***9228.30*** *p7*
DiNardis, Tommasso; Arkansas, 1918 ***95.2*** *p37*
Dinckel, Anna Elisabetha; Pennsylvania, 1753 ***4525*** *p254*
Dinckel, Michael; Pennsylvania, 1752 ***4525*** *p209*
Dinckel, Michael; Pennsylvania, 1752 ***4525*** *p226*
Dinckle, Daniel; Philadelphia, 1764 ***9973.7*** *p39*
Dineen, Michael 40; Massachusetts, 1850 ***5881.1*** *p32*
Dinehart, Conrod; Ohio, 1842 ***8365.25*** *p12*
Dineley, Samuel 37; California, 1872 ***2769.3*** *p5*
Ding, Yee 63; Arizona, 1922 ***9228.40*** *p26*
Dingeldine, Leonh. 17; America, 1853 ***9162.8*** *p36*
Dinger, August; America, 1845 ***8582.3*** *p14*
Dinger, John 18; Massachusetts, 1847 ***5881.1*** *p29*
Dingerson, Charles 34; Kansas, 1889 ***5240.1*** *p73*
Dingledein, Gg. Ph. 48; America, 1853 ***9162.8*** *p36*
Dingler, Johannes *SEE* Dingler, Johannes
Dingler, Johannes; America, 1750-1800 ***2444*** *p148*
*Wife:*Maria M. Gaertner
*Child:*Johannes
Dingler, John; Pennsylvania, 1753 ***2444*** *p148*
Dingler, Maria M. Gaertner *SEE* Dingler, Johannes
Dinglor, Frederick 27; New Orleans, 1864 ***543.30*** *p221*
Dinholm, Grace; Quebec, 1822 ***8894.2*** *p57*
Dinigan, Michael; Montreal, 1824 ***7603*** *p87*
Diniger, Barbara 7; Port uncertain, 1839 ***778.5*** *p165*
Diniger, Casper 53; Port uncertain, 1839 ***778.5*** *p166*
Diniger, Christiana 14; Port uncertain, 1839 ***778.5*** *p166*
Diniger, Elisabeth 50; Port uncertain, 1839 ***778.5*** *p166*
Diniger, Katherina 3; Port uncertain, 1839 ***778.5*** *p166*
Diniger, Marian 25; Port uncertain, 1839 ***778.5*** *p166*
Diniger, Michael 24; Port uncertain, 1839 ***778.5*** *p166*
Dining, David; Iowa, 1866-1943 ***123.54*** *p16*
Dinkel, Michael; New England, 1752 ***4525*** *p209*
With wife & children
Dinkel, Michael; Pennsylvania, 1752 ***4525*** *p226*
Dinkel, Nicolaus; Pennsylvania, 1785 ***4525*** *p209*
With wife
With 4 children
Dinkelmeyer, Kaspar; New Jersey, 1780 ***8137*** *p7*
Dinneen, Patrick; Illinois, 1888 ***5012.37*** *p60*
Dinneford, William; Washington, D.C., 1825 ***8208.4*** *p37*
Dinning, Mathew; Iowa, 1866-1943 ***123.54*** *p16*
Dinning, Robert; Iowa, 1866-1943 ***123.54*** *p16*
Dinninger, Heinrich; America, 1847 ***8582.3*** *p14*
Dinnis, Mr.; Cincinnati, 1843-1877 ***8582.3*** *p26*
Dinnison, John 9; Philadelphia, 1854 ***5704.8*** *p117*
Dinohugh, Andrew 17; St. John, N.B., 1856 ***5704.8*** *p132*
Dinohugh, James 15; St. John, N.B., 1856 ***5704.8*** *p132*
Dinsdale, Thomas; Virginia, 1638 ***6219*** *p159*
Dinsdall, Richd 32; America, 1701 ***2212*** *p34*
Dinsmore, Andrew; New York, NY, 1867 ***5704.8*** *p222*
Dinsmore, Elizabeth; New York, NY, 1867 ***5704.8*** *p222*
Dinsmore, Isabella; New York, NY, 1867 ***5704.8*** *p222*
Dinsmore, Isabella; Philadelphia, 1850 ***53.26*** *p19*
Dinsmore, Isabella; Philadelphia, 1850 ***5704.8*** *p68*
Dinsmore, James 20; Philadelphia, 1856 ***5704.8*** *p128*
Dinwiddie, William 40; Philadelphia, 1804 ***53.26*** *p19*
Dion, Emma *SEE* Dion, Louis
Dion, Louis; Chicago, 1901 ***3455.2*** *p47*
Dion, Louis; Chicago, 1901 ***3455.3*** *p108*
*Wife:*Emma
Dion, Nazaire; Chicago, 1900 ***3455.2*** *p47*
Diontona, Carmine 25; West Virginia, 1892 ***9788.3*** *p9*
Dioz, Joseph 19; America, 1831 ***778.5*** *p166*
Dipatarain, N. 19; New Orleans, 1837 ***778.5*** *p166*
DiPietro, Joseph; Arkansas, 1918 ***95.2*** *p37*
DiPilla, James; Colorado, 1904 ***9678.2*** *p16*
DiPitro, Gio; Arkansas, 1918 ***95.2*** *p37*
DiPonzio, Domenico 40; West Virginia, 1904 ***9788.3*** *p9*
Dipp, Henrich; Lancaster, PA, 1780 ***8137*** *p7*
Dippietro, Donato; Wisconsin, n.d. ***9675.5*** *p121*
Dipple, Jon.; Virginia, 1636 ***6219*** *p80*
Dippold, George; Missouri, 1869 ***2896.5*** *p9*
Dir, Hans Michel; Pennsylvania, 1754 ***2444*** *p148*
Dir, Matthaeus; Pennsylvania, 1754 ***2444*** *p148*
DiRaimo, Nicola; Arkansas, 1918 ***95.2*** *p37*
Direjeka, Joseph; Arkansas, 1918 ***95.2*** *p38*
Dirkie, Mary; South Carolina, 1767 ***1639.20*** *p59*
Dirksen, Catharina; Ohio, 1811 ***8582.1*** *p48*
Dirlam, Wigand; Philadelphia, 1779 ***8137*** *p7*
Dirlam, Wigand; Philadelphia, 1779-1783 ***8137*** *p4*
Dirr, Matthaeus; Port uncertain, 1743-1800 ***2444*** *p148*
Dirr, Michael; Port uncertain, 1743-1800 ***2444*** *p148*
Disache, A. M. 32; New Orleans, 1839 ***778.5*** *p166*
Disbonne, Charles 30; Virginia, 1773 ***1219.7*** *p170*
Disch, Dominick; New York, NY, 1839 ***8208.4*** *p101*
Discher, . . .; Canada, 1776-1783 ***9786*** *p19*
Discher, Caspar; Canada, 1776-1783 ***9786*** *p242*
Dischinger, Raymund; Lexington, MO, 1869-1887 ***8582*** *p6*
Discord, J.; New York, NY, 1816 ***2859.11*** *p29*
Disemer, John; Illinois, 1869 ***5012.38*** *p99*
Diserenz, Friedrich; Cincinnati, 1829 ***8582.1*** *p51*
Dish, Christopher; New York, NY, 1840 ***8208.4*** *p111*
DiShenna, Alfredo 21; West Virginia, 1904 ***9788.3*** *p9*
Disier, Mr. 23; New Orleans, 1839 ***778.5*** *p166*
Dismore, Henry 21; Maryland, 1775 ***1219.7*** *p250*
Disney, John 28; Maryland, 1723 ***3690.1*** *p63*
Disperati, Eva; Washington, 1859-1920 ***2872.1*** *p10*
Disperati, Ferruccio; Washington, 1859-1920 ***2872.1*** *p10*
Disperati, Filippo; Washington, 1859-1920 ***2872.1*** *p10*
Disperati, Frank; Washington, 1859-1920 ***2872.1*** *p10*
Disperati, Ida; Washington, 1859-1920 ***2872.1*** *p10*
Disperati, Jim; Washington, 1859-1920 ***2872.1*** *p10*
Disperati, Mary; Washington, 1859-1920 ***2872.1*** *p10*
Diss, F. G.; Ohio, 1869-1887 ***8582*** *p6*
Dissauze, Mr.; Port uncertain, 1839 ***778.5*** *p166*
Disser, Catharine 3; America, 1836 ***778.5*** *p166*
Disser, Catharine 28; America, 1836 ***778.5*** *p166*
Disser, Louise 1; America, 1836 ***778.5*** *p166*
Disser, Marianne 9; America, 1836 ***778.5*** *p166*
Disser, Michal 6; America, 1836 ***778.5*** *p167*
Disser, Michal 38; America, 1836 ***778.5*** *p167*
Distelli, Jacob 43; New Orleans, 1862 ***543.30*** *p216*
Distler, Johann Adam; America, 1847 ***8582.1*** *p7*
Ditch, Andrew; Virginia, 1645 ***6219*** *p233*
Diterichs, Capt.; Quebec, 1776 ***9786*** *p105*
DiTrapano, Albert; Arkansas, 1918 ***95.2*** *p37*
Ditrich, Frederick; Wisconsin, n.d. ***9675.5*** *p121*
Dittlie, . . .; Canada, 1776-1783 ***9786*** *p19*
Dittmar, Adam; Philadelphia, 1779 ***8137*** *p7*
Dittmer, Fredrick Jurgend; Kansas, 1907 ***6013.40*** *p15*
Dittmer, John Henry; Kansas, 1907 ***6013.40*** *p15*
Dittmeyer, Charles 35; Kansas, 1874 ***5240.1*** *p10*
Dittmeyer, Charles 35; Kansas, 1874 ***5240.1*** *p56*
Dittus, Tobias; America, 1738-1775 ***2444*** *p148*
With child
Ditz, Alexandrin. 22; New Orleans, 1838 ***778.5*** *p167*
Ditz, Henry 32; New Orleans, 1838 ***778.5*** *p167*
Ditzel, . . .; Canada, 1776-1783 ***9786*** *p19*
Ditzel, John; Canada, 1776-1783 ***9786*** *p207A*
Divan, Catherine *SEE* Divan, John
Divan, Catherine; Philadelphia, 1847 ***5704.8*** *p23*
Divan, Eliza 50; Massachusetts, 1849 ***5881.1*** *p28*
Divan, James 30; Massachusetts, 1849 ***5881.1*** *p30*
Divan, John; Philadelphia, 1847 ***53.26*** *p19*
*Relative:*Catherine
Divan, John; Philadelphia, 1847 ***5704.8*** *p23*
Divan, Michael 9; Massachusetts, 1849 ***5881.1*** *p32*
Divan, Nancy 24; St. John, N.B., 1859 ***5704.8*** *p141*
Divan, Patrick 2; Massachusetts, 1849 ***5881.1*** *p33*
Diven, Henry; Philadelphia, 1851 ***5704.8*** *p75*
Diven, John 25; Quebec, 1864 ***5704.8*** *p159*
Diven, Owen; St. John, N.B., 1851 ***5704.8*** *p78*
Diven, Pat 28; Philadelphia, 1803 ***53.26*** *p19*
Diven, Patrick; Philadelphia, 1851 ***5704.8*** *p75*
Diver, Alicia 19; Philadelphia, 1865 ***5704.8*** *p165*
Diver, Ann; St. John, N.B., 1851 ***5704.8*** *p77*
Diver, Ann 24; Quebec, 1857 ***5704.8*** *p136*

Diver, Ann 25; Philadelphia, 1859 ***5704.8*** *p142*
Diver, Biddy; St. John, N.B., 1848 ***5704.8*** *p43*
Diver, Biddy; St. John, N.B., 1849 ***5704.8*** *p55*
Diver, Biddy 20; Philadelphia, 1854 ***5704.8*** *p123*
Diver, Bridget; St. John, N.B., 1847 ***5704.8*** *p15*
Diver, Bridget 8; New York, NY, 1869 ***5704.8*** *p235*
Diver, Catherine; St. John, N.B., 1848 ***5704.8*** *p43*
Diver, Charles; New York, NY, 1852 ***1450.2*** *p31A*
Diver, Charles; St. John, N.B., 1847 ***5704.8*** *p15*
Diver, Charles 10; St. John, N.B., 1847 ***5704.8*** *p15*
Diver, Cornelius; New York, NY, 1869 ***5704.8*** *p235*
Diver, Denis; Philadelphia, 1867 ***5704.8*** *p222*
Diver, Edward; New York, NY, 1865 ***5704.8*** *p203*
Diver, Edward; Philadelphia, 1816 ***2859.11*** *p29*
Diver, Edward; St. John, N.B., 1847 ***5704.8*** *p18*
Diver, Edward; St. John, N.B., 1849 ***5704.8*** *p55*
Diver, Eliza; Philadelphia, 1850 ***5704.8*** *p64*
Diver, Eliza; St. John, N.B., 1851 ***5704.8*** *p77*
Diver, Eliza 3; Quebec, 1862 ***5704.8*** *p151*
Diver, Elizabeth; New York, NY, 1867 ***5704.8*** *p222*
Diver, Elizabeth; St. John, N.B., 1848 ***5704.8*** *p38*
Diver, Elizabeth; St. John, N.B., 1849 ***5704.8*** *p55*
Diver, Ellin; New York, NY, 1869 ***5704.8*** *p235*
Diver, George; New York, NY, 1816 ***2859.11*** *p29*
Diver, Grace; New York, NY, 1864 ***5704.8*** *p169*
Diver, Hannah; Quebec, 1848 ***5704.8*** *p42*
Diver, Hugh; Philadelphia, 1864 ***5704.8*** *p179*
Diver, Hugh; Quebec, 1848 ***5704.8*** *p42*
Diver, Hugh; St. John, N.B., 1851 ***5704.8*** *p77*
Diver, Hugh 6 *SEE* Diver, Sarah
Diver, Hugh 6; Philadelphia, 1849 ***5704.8*** *p58*
Diver, James; New York, 1849 ***1450.2*** *p31A*
Diver, James; New York, NY, 1864 ***5704.8*** *p169*
Diver, James; St. John, N.B., 1848 ***5704.8*** *p43*
Diver, James; St. John, N.B., 1848 ***5704.8*** *p47*
Diver, James 11; St. John, N.B., 1849 ***5704.8*** *p55*
Diver, James 35; Quebec, 1862 ***5704.8*** *p151*
Diver, Jane; Philadelphia, 1864 ***5704.8*** *p177*
Diver, John; New York, NY, 1867 ***5704.8*** *p220*
Diver, John; Philadelphia, 1865 ***5704.8*** *p190*
Diver, John; Philadelphia, 1867 ***5704.8*** *p222*
Diver, John; St. John, N.B., 1847 ***5704.8*** *p15*
Diver, John 12; Quebec, 1848 ***5704.8*** *p42*
Diver, John 45; Quebec, 1858 ***5704.8*** *p137*
Diver, Madge 11; New York, NY, 1869 ***5704.8*** *p235*
Diver, Margaret; Philadelphia, 1850 ***5704.8*** *p64*
Diver, Margery; St. John, N.B., 1847 ***5704.8*** *p15*
Diver, Mary; New York, NY, 1816 ***2859.11*** *p29*
Diver, Mary; Philadelphia, 1865 ***5704.8*** *p197*
Diver, Mary; St. John, N.B., 1852 ***5704.8*** *p95*
Diver, Mary 9; St. John, N.B., 1849 ***5704.8*** *p55*
Diver, Mary 39; Quebec, 1858 ***5704.8*** *p137*
Diver, Mary A.; Philadelphia, 1865 ***5704.8*** *p198*
Diver, Mary Ann 19; Philadelphia, 1859 ***5704.8*** *p142*
Diver, Mary Jane 10; Quebec, 1850 ***5704.8*** *p62*
Diver, Matilda; Quebec, 1850 ***5704.8*** *p62*
Diver, Matty; Philadelphia, 1848 ***53.26*** *p19*
Diver, Matty; Philadelphia, 1848 ***5704.8*** *p45*
Diver, Michael 2; St. John, N.B., 1848 ***5704.8*** *p43*
Diver, Neill 10 *SEE* Diver, Sarah
Diver, Neill 10; Philadelphia, 1849 ***5704.8*** *p58*
Diver, Paddy; Philadelphia, 1853 ***5704.8*** *p102*
Diver, Patrick; New York, NY, 1816 ***2859.11*** *p29*
Diver, Patrick; Philadelphia, 1848 ***53.26*** *p19*
Diver, Patrick; Philadelphia, 1848 ***5704.8*** *p45*
Diver, Patrick; St. John, N.B., 1848 ***5704.8*** *p43*
Diver, Patrick 13; St. John, N.B., 1847 ***5704.8*** *p3*
Diver, Patrick 13; St. John, N.B., 1848 ***5704.8*** *p43*
Diver, Peggy 11; St. John, N.B., 1847 ***5704.8*** *p3*
Diver, Peter; New York, NY, 1867 ***5704.8*** *p220*
Diver, Phillip; St. John, N.B., 1847 ***5704.8*** *p3*
Diver, Rebecca 18; Philadelphia, 1854 ***5704.8*** *p115*
Diver, Sally; St. John, N.B., 1848 ***5704.8*** *p47*
Diver, Samuel; New York, NY, 1867 ***5704.8*** *p224*
Diver, Samuel 2; Quebec, 1862 ***5704.8*** *p151*
Diver, Sarah; Philadelphia, 1849 ***53.26*** *p20*
  *Relative:*Neill 10
  *Relative:*Hugh 6
Diver, Sarah; Philadelphia, 1849 ***5704.8*** *p58*
Diver, Sarah 21; Philadelphia, 1865 ***5704.8*** *p164*
Diver, Sarah 22; Quebec, 1862 ***5704.8*** *p151*
Diver, Sicily; St. John, N.B., 1847 ***5704.8*** *p15*
Diver, Sicily 8; St. John, N.B., 1847 ***5704.8*** *p15*
Diver, Sidney; New York, NY, 1816 ***2859.11*** *p29*
Diver, Susan; New York, NY, 1816 ***2859.11*** *p29*
Diver, Susan; Quebec, 1851 ***5704.8*** *p74*
Diver, Susan; St. John, N.B., 1847 ***5704.8*** *p3*
Diver, Susan 7; St. John, N.B., 1849 ***5704.8*** *p55*
Diver, Susanna; Philadelphia, 1853 ***5704.8*** *p102*
Diver, Thomas; Quebec, 1852 ***5704.8*** *p90*
Diver, Thomas 25; Philadelphia, 1804 ***53.26*** *p20*
Diver, William; New York, NY, 1816 ***2859.11*** *p29*
Diver, William; Quebec, 1852 ***5704.8*** *p90*
Diver, William 13; Quebec, 1850 ***5704.8*** *p62*
Diver, William 20; Philadelphia, 1853 ***5704.8*** *p113*
Diver, William 45; Quebec, 1857 ***5704.8*** *p136*
Divin, Henry; Philadelphia, 1852 ***5704.8*** *p85*
Divin, Nancy; Philadelphia, 1849 ***53.26*** *p20*
Divin, Nancy; Philadelphia, 1849 ***5704.8*** *p53*
Divin, Patrick; New York, NY, 1811 ***2859.11*** *p11*
Divin, Sally 21; Wilmington, DE, 1831 ***6508.7*** *p161*
Divine, Bernard 21; Philadelphia, 1860 ***5704.8*** *p145*
Divine, Catherine; St. John, N.B., 1853 ***5704.8*** *p99*
Divine, James; New York, NY, 1838 ***8208.4*** *p69*
Divine, James 23; Philadelphia, 1859 ***5704.8*** *p141*
Divine, John; New York, NY, 1835 ***8208.4*** *p7*
Divine, Mary 35; Massachusetts, 1849 ***5881.1*** *p32*
Divine, Michael 18; Quebec, 1856 ***5704.8*** *p129*
Divine, Peter; New York, NY, 1838 ***8208.4*** *p68*
Divine, Robert; New York, NY, 1838 ***8208.4*** *p71*
Divine, William; New York, NY, 1811 ***2859.11*** *p11*
Divininy, Rose; America, 1735-1743 ***4971*** *p7*
Divir, William; Quebec, 1852 ***5704.8*** *p87*
Diwane, Michael; America, 1736-1743 ***4971*** *p57*
Dix, Hen.; Virginia, 1637 ***6219*** *p113*
Dix, Henry; Wisconsin, n.d. ***9675.5*** *p121*
Dix, John 20; Jamaica, 1730 ***3690.1*** *p64*
Dix, Jon.; Virginia, 1642 ***6219*** *p192*
Dix, Wellborn 34; Pennsylvania, 1728 ***3690.1*** *p64*
Dixon, Adam; Virginia, 1622 ***6219*** *p6*
  *Wife:*Ann
  *Daughter:*Elizabeth
Dixon, Adam William 23; Arkansas, 1918 ***95.2*** *p38*
Dixon, Alexander 8; Quebec, 1849 ***5704.8*** *p51*
Dixon, Ann *SEE* Dixon, Adam
Dixon, Anne 25; Philadelphia, 1860 ***5704.8*** *p144*
Dixon, B.; New Orleans, 1839 ***778.5*** *p167*
Dixon, Catherine; New York, NY, 1816 ***2859.11*** *p29*
Dixon, Charles; Colorado, 1888 ***9678.2*** *p16*
Dixon, Charles; Jamaica, 1762 ***1219.7*** *p89*
Dixon, Charlotte *SEE* Dixon, James
Dixon, Charlotte; Philadelphia, 1848 ***5704.8*** *p40*
Dixon, Christopher; Virginia, 1636 ***6219*** *p10*
Dixon, Christopher; Virginia, 1638 ***6219*** *p146*
Dixon, Eliz 20; America, 1702 ***2212*** *p38*
Dixon, Eliza 5; Quebec, 1849 ***5704.8*** *p51*
Dixon, Elizabeth *SEE* Dixon, Adam
Dixon, Elizabeth 20; St. John, N.B., 1864 ***5704.8*** *p157*
Dixon, Ellen; St. John, N.B., 1850 ***5704.8*** *p65*
Dixon, Ellen 6 mos; Quebec, 1849 ***5704.8*** *p51*
Dixon, Geo.; Virginia, 1643 ***6219*** *p202*
Dixon, George 12; Maryland, 1719 ***3690.1*** *p64*
Dixon, Henry 48; Jamaica, 1730 ***3690.1*** *p290*
Dixon, Isabella 7; Quebec, 1849 ***5704.8*** *p51*
Dixon, Iszabella; Virginia, 1639 ***6219*** *p154*
Dixon, James; Philadelphia, 1848 ***53.26*** *p20*
  *Relative:*Charlotte
Dixon, James; Philadelphia, 1848 ***5704.8*** *p40*
Dixon, James 25; Port uncertain, 1774 ***1219.7*** *p176*
Dixon, Jane; St. John, N.B., 1850 ***5704.8*** *p66*
Dixon, Joanna; New York, NY, 1811 ***2859.11*** *p11*
Dixon, Joanna 54; Massachusetts, 1860 ***6410.32*** *p103*
Dixon, John; Philadelphia, 1816 ***2859.11*** *p29*
Dixon, John; Quebec, 1849 ***5704.8*** *p50*
Dixon, John; St. John, N.B., 1851 ***5704.8*** *p79*
Dixon, John; Virginia, 1638 ***6219*** *p147*
Dixon, John 21; Philadelphia, 1860 ***5704.8*** *p146*
Dixon, John 21; Virginia, 1737 ***3690.1*** *p64*
Dixon, John 27; Virginia, 1727 ***3690.1*** *p64*
Dixon, John 50; Massachusetts, 1860 ***6410.32*** *p103*
Dixon, Joseph; Philadelphia, 1850 ***5704.8*** *p64*
Dixon, Joseph; St. John, N.B., 1850 ***5704.8*** *p65*
Dixon, Joseph 9; Quebec, 1849 ***5704.8*** *p51*
Dixon, Lonna; Philadelphia, 1850 ***5704.8*** *p64*
Dixon, Margaret 21; Philadelphia, 1864 ***5704.8*** *p160*
Dixon, Martin; New York, NY, 1838 ***8208.4*** *p83*
Dixon, Mary 1; St. John, N.B., 1850 ***5704.8*** *p66*
Dixon, Mary Ann; New York, NY, 1811 ***2859.11*** *p11*
Dixon, Mary Ann; Philadelphia, 1847 ***53.26*** *p20*
Dixon, Mary Ann; Philadelphia, 1847 ***5704.8*** *p5*
Dixon, Math.; Virginia, 1638 ***6219*** *p124*
Dixon, P.T.; San Francisco, 1884 ***2764.35*** *p16*
Dixon, Patrick; Illinois, 1878 ***5012.37*** *p60*
Dixon, Rebecca; Quebec, 1849 ***5704.8*** *p50*
Dixon, Rebecca 2; Quebec, 1849 ***5704.8*** *p51*
Dixon, Rich.; Virginia, 1636 ***6219*** *p75*
Dixon, Richard 17; St. Christopher, 1722 ***3690.1*** *p64*
Dixon, Richard 24; Maryland, 1774 ***1219.7*** *p181*
Dixon, Robert; Philadelphia, 1847 ***53.26*** *p20*
Dixon, Robert; Philadelphia, 1847 ***5704.8*** *p5*
Dixon, Robt 16; America, 1706 ***2212*** *p47*
Dixon, Rose 2; St. John, N.B., 1850 ***5704.8*** *p66*
Dixon, Thomas; New York, NY, 1811 ***2859.11*** *p11*
Dixon, Thomas 27; New Orleans, 1862 ***543.30*** *p62*
Dixon, William; America, 1738 ***4971*** *p66*
Dixon, William; Jamaica, 1754 ***1219.7*** *p31*
Dixon, William; Jamaica, 1754 ***3690.1*** *p64*
Dixon, William; New York, NY, 1834 ***8208.4*** *p2*
Dixon, William; Pennsylvania, 1749 ***3652*** *p73*
Dixon, William 15; Maryland, 1719 ***3690.1*** *p64*
Dixon, Wm.; Virginia, 1642 ***6219*** *p194*
Dixson, Nicholas; Virginia, 1646 ***6219*** *p240*
Dluski, Aleksander; New York, 1831 ***4606*** *p173*
Dmuchowski, Kazimierz; Boston, 1834 ***4606*** *p179*
Doak, Andrew; Philadelphia, 1852 ***5704.8*** *p87*
Doak, Andrew 11; St. John, N.B., 1847 ***5704.8*** *p9*
Doak, David; New York, NY, 1811 ***2859.11*** *p11*
Doak, George; St. John, N.B., 1847 ***5704.8*** *p9*
Doak, James 74; Arizona, 1912 ***9228.40*** *p16*
Doak, Margaret; New York, NY, 1815 ***2859.11*** *p29*
Doak, Margaret; Philadelphia, 1853 ***5704.8*** *p101*
Doak, Michael; New York, NY, 1815 ***2859.11*** *p29*
Doak, Robert 8; St. John, N.B., 1847 ***5704.8*** *p9*
Doake, David; Philadelphia, 1847 ***53.26*** *p20*
Doake, David; Philadelphia, 1847 ***5704.8*** *p22*
Doake, Francis 20; Wilmington, DE, 1831 ***6508.7*** *p161*
Doakey, Martha; New York, NY, 1867 ***5704.8*** *p219*
Doane, Alexandre 25; Texas, 1839 ***778.5*** *p167*
Doane, Pierce; America, 1844 ***1450.2*** *p31A*
Doas, Peter 22; Port uncertain, 1839 ***778.5*** *p167*
Dobberhow, William 23; Maryland, 1775 ***1219.7*** *p266*
Dobberphul, Herman; Wisconsin, n.d. ***9675.5*** *p121*
Dobbin, Mrs.; New York, NY, 1811 ***2859.11*** *p11*
Dobbin, John; St. John, N.B., 1853 ***5704.8*** *p98*
Dobbin, Leonard; New York, NY, 1811 ***2859.11*** *p11*
Dobbins, Brigitte; Quebec, 1823 ***7603*** *p90*
Dobbins, Henry 23; Antigua (Antego), 1734 ***3690.1*** *p64*
Dobbins, Patrick 39; New Orleans, 1862 ***543.30*** *p56*
Dobbis, Edward 21; Maryland, 1775 ***1219.7*** *p264*
Dobbis, Mary 29; Maryland, 1775 ***1219.7*** *p264*
Dobbling, Friedrich; Cincinnati, 1869-1887 ***8582*** *p6*
Dobbs, Samuel 21; Maryland, 1774 ***1219.7*** *p220*
Dobbyn, Richard; Savannah, GA, 1770 ***1219.7*** *p144*
Dobeneck, Hans Philipp Heinrich; Quebec, 1776 ***9786*** *p260*
Dober, Andrew; Savannah, GA, 1736 ***3652*** *p51*
  *Relative:*Anna
Dober, Anna *SEE* Dober, Andrew
Doberval, Dr. 37; New Orleans, 1837 ***778.5*** *p167*
Dobler, Jacob Christian; America, 1776-1800 ***2444*** *p148*
  With 2 children
Dobritzberger, Fritz; Wisconsin, n.d. ***9675.5*** *p121*
Dobrovnik, Tony; Wisconsin, n.d. ***9675.5*** *p121*
Dobrowolska, Janina 9; New York, 1912 ***9980.29*** *p51*
  With mother
  With grandmother
Dobrowolski, Apolonan 23; New York, 1912 ***9980.29*** *p69*
Dobrowolski, Kazemer; Wisconsin, n.d. ***9675.5*** *p121*
Dobson, Barbara 12; St. John, N.B., 1848 ***5704.8*** *p43*
Dobson, Edward; Virginia, 1638 ***6219*** *p124*
Dobson, Eliza 10; St. John, N.B., 1848 ***5704.8*** *p43*
Dobson, Fanny; New York, NY, 1815 ***2859.11*** *p29*
Dobson, James; New York, NY, 1815 ***2859.11*** *p29*
Dobson, James 19; Pennsylvania, 1731 ***3690.1*** *p64*
Dobson, Jno; America, 1698 ***2212*** *p6*
Dobson, John; New York, NY, 1815 ***2859.11*** *p29*
Dobson, John; Virginia, 1698 ***2212*** *p11*
Dobson, John 6; St. John, N.B., 1848 ***5704.8*** *p43*
Dobson, Margaret 8; St. John, N.B., 1848 ***5704.8*** *p43*
Dobson, Mary; New York, NY, 1815 ***2859.11*** *p29*
Dobson, Richard; Virginia, 1643 ***6219*** *p203*
Dobson, Richard 72; North America, 1774 ***1219.7*** *p199*
Dobson, Sarah 17; Baltimore, 1775 ***1219.7*** *p271*
Dobson, Susan; New York, NY, 1815 ***2859.11*** *p29*
Dobson, Thomas 23; Jamaica, 1739 ***3690.1*** *p64*
Dobson, William; New York, NY, 1815 ***2859.11*** *p29*
Dobson, William 20; Windward Islands, 1722 ***3690.1*** *p64*
Dochester, William 28; Jamaica, 1731 ***3690.1*** *p64*
Dockar, John; Washington, 1859-1920 ***2872.1*** *p10*
Dockenwadel, Agnes; Pennsylvania, 1754 ***2444*** *p149*
  With son
Dockenwadel, Anna Maria Majer *SEE* Dockenwadel, Georg Friedrich
Dockenwadel, Elisabetha Dorothea *SEE* Dockenwadel, Georg Friedrich
Dockenwadel, Georg Friedrich; Pennsylvania, 1754 ***2444*** *p149*
  *Mother:*Maria Agnes Schneider
  *Wife:*Anna Maria Majer
  *Child:*Matthaus
  *Child:*Philipp Friedrich
  *Child:*Johann Georg
  *Child:*Elisabetha Dorothea
  *Child:*Ludwig
Dockenwadel, Johann Georg *SEE* Dockenwadel, Georg Friedrich
Dockenwadel, Ludwig *SEE* Dockenwadel, Georg Friedrich

Doherty, Con; St. John, N.B., 1847 ***5704.8*** *p24*
Doherty, Daniel; America, 1867 ***5704.8*** *p221*
Doherty, Daniel; New York, NY, 1815 ***2859.11*** *p29*
Doherty, Daniel; New York, NY, 1816 ***2859.11*** *p29*
Doherty, Daniel; New York, NY, 1866 ***5704.8*** *p213*
Doherty, Daniel; Philadelphia, 1851 ***5704.8*** *p81*
Doherty, Daniel; St. John, N.B., 1847 ***5704.8*** *p4*
Doherty, Daniel; St. John, N.B., 1847 ***5704.8*** *p25*
Doherty, Daniel; St. John, N.B., 1848 ***5704.8*** *p39*
Doherty, Daniel; St. John, N.B., 1848 ***5704.8*** *p42*
Doherty, Daniel; St. John, N.B., 1849 ***5704.8*** *p55*
Doherty, Daniel; St. John, N.B., 1849 ***5704.8*** *p56*
Doherty, Daniel; St. John, N.B., 1851 ***5704.8*** *p72*
Doherty, Daniel; St. John, N.B., 1851 ***5704.8*** *p78*
Doherty, Daniel 6; Philadelphia, 1857 ***5704.8*** *p134*
Doherty, Daniel 6; St. John, N.B., 1847 ***5704.8*** *p2*
Doherty, Daniel 6; St. John, N.B., 1851 ***5704.8*** *p79*
Doherty, Daniel 20; St. John, N.B., 1854 ***5704.8*** *p114*
Doherty, Daniel 22; Philadelphia, 1858 ***5704.8*** *p138*
Doherty, Daniel 24; St. John, N.B., 1854 ***5704.8*** *p115*
Doherty, Daniel 24; St. John, N.B., 1865 ***5704.8*** *p165*
Doherty, Daniel 27; St. John, N.B., 1856 ***5704.8*** *p131*
Doherty, Daniel 40; Philadelphia, 1860 ***5704.8*** *p146*
Doherty, Danny; Philadelphia, 1852 ***5704.8*** *p84*
Doherty, David; New York, NY, 1816 ***2859.11*** *p29*
Doherty, David 21; Philadelphia, 1857 ***5704.8*** *p133*
Doherty, David 38; St. John, N.B., 1854 ***5704.8*** *p122*
Doherty, Denis; Philadelphia, 1853 ***5704.8*** *p102*
Doherty, Denis; St. John, N.B., 1848 ***5704.8*** *p39*
Doherty, Dennis; St. John, N.B., 1847 ***5704.8*** *p9*
Doherty, Dennis; St. John, N.B., 1853 ***5704.8*** *p100*
Doherty, Dolly 18; St. John, N.B., 1855 ***5704.8*** *p126*
Doherty, Dominick; St. John, N.B., 1851 ***5704.8*** *p72*
Doherty, Edward; New York, NY, 1865 ***5704.8*** *p197*
Doherty, Edward; Philadelphia, 1852 ***5704.8*** *p84*
Doherty, Edward; Philadelphia, 1853 ***5704.8*** *p100*
Doherty, Edward; Philadelphia, 1866 ***5704.8*** *p206*
Doherty, Edward; St. John, N.B., 1847 ***5704.8*** *p3*
Doherty, Edward; St. John, N.B., 1847 ***5704.8*** *p4*
Doherty, Edward; St. John, N.B., 1847 ***5704.8*** *p15*
Doherty, Edward; St. John, N.B., 1847 ***5704.8*** *p21*
Doherty, Edward; St. John, N.B., 1847 ***5704.8*** *p24*
Doherty, Edward; St. John, N.B., 1851 ***5704.8*** *p72*
Doherty, Edward; St. John, N.B., 1852 ***5704.8*** *p92*
Doherty, Edward; St. John, N.B., 1853 ***5704.8*** *p107*
Doherty, Edward 9 mos; St. John, N.B., 1847 ***5704.8*** *p25*
Doherty, Edward 1; St. John, N.B., 1849 ***5704.8*** *p56*
Doherty, Edward 9; St. John, N.B., 1847 ***5704.8*** *p33*
Doherty, Edward 13; Philadelphia, 1848 ***53.26*** *p20*
*Relative:*Catherine 11
*Relative:*Eleanor 9
*Relative:*Ann 7
Doherty, Edward 13; Philadelphia, 1848 ***5704.8*** *p45*
Doherty, Edward 25 *SEE* Doherty, William
Doherty, Edward 25; Philadelphia, 1833-1834 ***53.26*** *p20*
Doherty, Edward 30; St. John, N.B., 1862 ***5704.8*** *p150*
Doherty, Eleanor; Philadelphia, 1851 ***5704.8*** *p70*
Doherty, Eleanor; St. John, N.B., 1847 ***5704.8*** *p25*
Doherty, Eleanor 9 *SEE* Doherty, Edward
Doherty, Elen; St. John, N.B., 1852 ***5704.8*** *p92*
Doherty, Eliza; Philadelphia, 1852 ***5704.8*** *p97*
Doherty, Eliza; Philadelphia, 1866 ***5704.8*** *p206*
Doherty, Eliza; St. John, N.B., 1847 ***5704.8*** *p15*
Doherty, Eliza; St. John, N.B., 1848 ***5704.8*** *p39*
Doherty, Eliza; St. John, N.B., 1851 ***5704.8*** *p78*
Doherty, Eliza; St. John, N.B., 1851 ***5704.8*** *p79*
Doherty, Eliza 5; Quebec, 1863 ***5704.8*** *p153*
Doherty, Eliza 8; St. John, N.B., 1854 ***5704.8*** *p122*
Doherty, Eliza 9 *SEE* Doherty, Robert
Doherty, Eliza 9; Philadelphia, 1847 ***5704.8*** *p24*
Doherty, Eliza 10; Quebec, 1849 ***5704.8*** *p57*
Doherty, Eliza 12 *SEE* Doherty, George
Doherty, Eliza 12; Philadelphia, 1848 ***5704.8*** *p46*
Doherty, Elizabeth; Philadelphia, 1851 ***5704.8*** *p77*
Doherty, Elizabeth; Philadelphia, 1853 ***5704.8*** *p102*
Doherty, Elizabeth; St. John, N.B., 1847 ***5704.8*** *p32*
Doherty, Elizabeth; St. John, N.B., 1853 ***5704.8*** *p107*
Doherty, Elizabeth 26; St. John, N.B., 1863 ***5704.8*** *p153*
Doherty, Ellan; St. John, N.B., 1847 ***5704.8*** *p24*
Doherty, Ellan; St. John, N.B., 1847 ***5704.8*** *p34*
Doherty, Ellan; St. John, N.B., 1848 ***5704.8*** *p39*
Doherty, Elleanor *SEE* Doherty, William
Doherty, Elleanor; Philadelphia, 1849 ***5704.8*** *p52*
Doherty, Elleanor; Quebec, 1850 ***5704.8*** *p63*
Doherty, Elleanor; St. John, N.B., 1848 ***5704.8*** *p38*
Doherty, Elleanor; St. John, N.B., 1848 ***5704.8*** *p43*
Doherty, Elleanor 9; Philadelphia, 1848 ***5704.8*** *p45*
Doherty, Ellen; Philadelphia, 1852 ***5704.8*** *p89*
Doherty, Ellen; Philadelphia, 1852 ***5704.8*** *p96*
Doherty, Ellen; St. John, N.B., 1847 ***5704.8*** *p24*
Doherty, Ellen; St. John, N.B., 1848 ***5704.8*** *p45*
Doherty, Ellen; St. John, N.B., 1853 ***5704.8*** *p107*
Doherty, Ellen; St. John, N.B., 1853 ***5704.8*** *p108*
Doherty, Ellen 3; Philadelphia, 1860 ***5704.8*** *p146*
Doherty, Ellen 4; Philadelphia, 1857 ***5704.8*** *p134*
Doherty, Ellen 6; St. John, N.B., 1850 ***5704.8*** *p61*
Doherty, Ellen 11; Philadelphia, 1866 ***5704.8*** *p206*
Doherty, Ellinah; Philadelphia, 1850 ***53.26*** *p20*
Doherty, Ellinah; Philadelphia, 1850 ***5704.8*** *p60*
Doherty, Eugene 9; St. John, N.B., 1849 ***5704.8*** *p55*
Doherty, Fanny; Philadelphia, 1849 ***53.26*** *p20*
*Relative:*Roger 7
*Relative:*Rose 5
Doherty, Fanny; Philadelphia, 1849 ***5704.8*** *p54*
Doherty, Fanny; Philadelphia, 1850 ***5704.8*** *p64*
Doherty, Fanny; St. John, N.B., 1853 ***5704.8*** *p107*
Doherty, Fanny 2; St. John, N.B., 1847 ***5704.8*** *p2*
Doherty, Fanny 12; St. John, N.B., 1849 ***5704.8*** *p55*
Doherty, Fanny 21; Philadelphia, 1860 ***5704.8*** *p145*
Doherty, Fanny 25; St. John, N.B., 1864 ***5704.8*** *p158*
Doherty, Francis; Philadelphia, 1851 ***5704.8*** *p70*
Doherty, Geily; St. John, N.B., 1851 ***5704.8*** *p77*
Doherty, George; Philadelphia, 1847 ***53.26*** *p20*
*Relative:*Rebecca
Doherty, George; Philadelphia, 1847 ***5704.8*** *p32*
Doherty, George; Philadelphia, 1848 ***53.26*** *p20*
Doherty, George; Philadelphia, 1848 ***53.26*** *p20*
*Relative:*Eliza 12
Doherty, George; Philadelphia, 1848 ***5704.8*** *p46*
Doherty, George; St. John, N.B., 1847 ***5704.8*** *p19*
Doherty, George; St. John, N.B., 1850 ***5704.8*** *p65*
Doherty, George 10; St. John, N.B., 1847 ***5704.8*** *p34*
Doherty, George 24; Philadelphia, 1859 ***5704.8*** *p141*
Doherty, Giley; St. John, N.B., 1848 ***5704.8*** *p43*
Doherty, Gilley; New York, NY, 1864 ***5704.8*** *p170*
Doherty, Ginney; St. John, N.B., 1847 ***5704.8*** *p18*
Doherty, Grace; New York, NY, 1864 ***5704.8*** *p170*
Doherty, Grace; St. John, N.B., 1847 ***5704.8*** *p3*
Doherty, Grace; St. John, N.B., 1847 ***5704.8*** *p33*
Doherty, Grace; St. John, N.B., 1850 ***5704.8*** *p68*
Doherty, Grace; St. John, N.B., 1853 ***5704.8*** *p107*
Doherty, Gracey; New Orleans, 1852 ***5704.8*** *p98*
Doherty, Gracey; St. John, N.B., 1847 ***5704.8*** *p2*
Doherty, Gracey 8; St. John, N.B., 1852 ***5704.8*** *p95*
Doherty, Gracy 7; St. John, N.B., 1851 ***5704.8*** *p79*
Doherty, Hannah; Philadelphia, 1851 ***5704.8*** *p71*
Doherty, Hannah; St. John, N.B., 1849 ***5704.8*** *p56*
Doherty, Hannah; St. John, N.B., 1853 ***5704.8*** *p108*
Doherty, Helen; Quebec, 1820 ***7603*** *p56*
Doherty, Henry; Philadelphia, 1849 ***53.26*** *p20*
Doherty, Henry; Philadelphia, 1849 ***5704.8*** *p54*
Doherty, Honora 18; Massachusetts, 1849 ***5881.1*** *p29*
Doherty, Hugh *SEE* Doherty, Patrick
Doherty, Hugh; New York, NY, 1816 ***2859.11*** *p29*
Doherty, Hugh; New York, NY, 1864 ***5704.8*** *p170*
Doherty, Hugh; Philadelphia, 1847 ***5704.8*** *p22*
Doherty, Hugh; Philadelphia, 1852 ***5704.8*** *p91*
Doherty, Hugh; Philadelphia, 1867 ***5704.8*** *p216*
Doherty, Hugh; Philadelphia, 1868 ***5704.8*** *p225*
Doherty, Hugh; St. John, N.B., 1847 ***5704.8*** *p2*
Doherty, Hugh; St. John, N.B., 1847 ***5704.8*** *p4*
Doherty, Hugh; St. John, N.B., 1847 ***5704.8*** *p32*
Doherty, Hugh; St. John, N.B., 1848 ***5704.8*** *p43*
Doherty, Hugh; St. John, N.B., 1850 ***5704.8*** *p61*
Doherty, Hugh; St. John, N.B., 1852 ***5704.8*** *p93*
Doherty, Hugh 1 *SEE* Doherty, Sarah
Doherty, Hugh 1; Philadelphia, 1847 ***5704.8*** *p2*
Doherty, Hugh 8 *SEE* Doherty, William
Doherty, Hugh 8; Philadelphia, 1849 ***5704.8*** *p52*
Doherty, Hugh 19; Philadelphia, 1864 ***5704.8*** *p156*
Doherty, Hugh 20; St. John, N.B., 1854 ***5704.8*** *p114*
Doherty, Hugh 29; Philadelphia, 1857 ***5704.8*** *p132*
Doherty, Isabella; Philadelphia, 1852 ***5704.8*** *p92*
Doherty, Isabella; St. John, N.B., 1849 ***5704.8*** *p48*
Doherty, Jackey; St. John, N.B., 1851 ***5704.8*** *p79*
Doherty, James *SEE* Doherty, Robert
Doherty, James; America, 1867 ***5704.8*** *p221*
Doherty, James; Philadelphia, 1847 ***5704.8*** *p24*
Doherty, James; Philadelphia, 1850 ***53.26*** *p20*
Doherty, James; Philadelphia, 1850 ***5704.8*** *p69*
Doherty, James; Philadelphia, 1851 ***5704.8*** *p81*
Doherty, James; Philadelphia, 1853 ***5704.8*** *p102*
Doherty, James; St. John, N.B., 1847 ***5704.8*** *p3*
Doherty, James; St. John, N.B., 1847 ***5704.8*** *p9*
Doherty, James; St. John, N.B., 1847 ***5704.8*** *p19*
Doherty, James; St. John, N.B., 1847 ***5704.8*** *p33*
Doherty, James; St. John, N.B., 1848 ***5704.8*** *p39*
Doherty, James; St. John, N.B., 1848 ***5704.8*** *p43*
Doherty, James; St. John, N.B., 1848 ***5704.8*** *p44*
Doherty, James; St. John, N.B., 1849 ***5704.8*** *p48*
Doherty, James; St. John, N.B., 1849 ***5704.8*** *p49*
Doherty, James; St. John, N.B., 1851 ***5704.8*** *p78*
Doherty, James; St. John, N.B., 1852 ***5704.8*** *p95*
Doherty, James 3 mos *SEE* Doherty, John
Doherty, James 3 mos; Philadelphia, 1847 ***5704.8*** *p22*
Doherty, James 1 *SEE* Doherty, John
Doherty, James 1; Philadelphia, 1847 ***5704.8*** *p1*
Doherty, James 5; St. John, N.B., 1853 ***5704.8*** *p109*
Doherty, James 6 *SEE* Doherty, Jane
Doherty, James 6; Philadelphia, 1849 ***5704.8*** *p58*
Doherty, James 7; St. John, N.B., 1849 ***5704.8*** *p55*
Doherty, James 7; St. John, N.B., 1851 ***5704.8*** *p78*
Doherty, James 8; St. John, N.B., 1849 ***5704.8*** *p48*
Doherty, James 10 *SEE* Doherty, Sarah
Doherty, James 10; Philadelphia, 1847 ***5704.8*** *p2*
Doherty, James 12; St. John, N.B., 1852 ***5704.8*** *p92*
Doherty, James 12; St. John, N.B., 1853 ***5704.8*** *p110*
Doherty, James 14; Philadelphia, 1860 ***5704.8*** *p144*
Doherty, James 17; St. John, N.B., 1862 ***5704.8*** *p150*
Doherty, James 18; Philadelphia, 1854 ***5704.8*** *p117*
Doherty, James 18; St. John, N.B., 1855 ***5704.8*** *p127*
Doherty, James 20; St. John, N.B., 1854 ***5704.8*** *p115*
Doherty, James 21; St. John, N.B., 1857 ***5704.8*** *p134*
Doherty, James 21; St. John, N.B., 1860 ***5704.8*** *p144*
Doherty, James 22; St. John, N.B., 1859 ***5704.8*** *p143*
Doherty, James 22; Wilmington, DE, 1831 ***6508.7*** *p161*
Doherty, James 28; Philadelphia, 1804 ***53.26*** *p20*
Doherty, James 40; St. John, N.B., 1858 ***5704.8*** *p137*
Doherty, Jane; Philadelphia, 1849 ***53.26*** *p20*
*Relative:*James 6
*Relative:*John 9 mos
Doherty, Jane; Philadelphia, 1849 ***5704.8*** *p58*
Doherty, Jane; St. John, N.B., 1847 ***5704.8*** *p9*
Doherty, Jane 8; St. John, N.B., 1847 ***5704.8*** *p2*
Doherty, Jane 12; St. John, N.B., 1850 ***5704.8*** *p67*
Doherty, Jane 16; Philadelphia, 1853 ***5704.8*** *p108*
Doherty, Jane 30; St. John, N.B., 1858 ***5704.8*** *p140*
Doherty, Johanna; Philadelphia, 1850 ***5704.8*** *p64*
Doherty, John *SEE* Doherty, John
Doherty, John *SEE* Doherty, Michael
Doherty, John *SEE* Doherty, Patrick
Doherty, John; New York, NY, 1816 ***2859.11*** *p29*
Doherty, John; New York, NY, 1835 ***8208.4*** *p6*
Doherty, John; Philadelphia, 1847 ***53.26*** *p21*
*Relative:*Bridgit
*Relative:*John
*Relative:*Catherine
*Relative:*Mary 7
*Relative:*Patrick 5
*Relative:*Biddy 3
*Relative:*James 1
Doherty, John; Philadelphia, 1847 ***53.26*** *p21*
*Relative:*Rosey
*Relative:*William 3
*Relative:*James 3 mos
*Relative:*Marg. Ann 4
Doherty, John; Philadelphia, 1847 ***5704.8*** *p1*
Doherty, John; Philadelphia, 1847 ***5704.8*** *p22*
Doherty, John; Philadelphia, 1849 ***53.26*** *p21*
Doherty, John; Philadelphia, 1849 ***5704.8*** *p50*
Doherty, John; Philadelphia, 1849 ***5704.8*** *p53*
Doherty, John; Philadelphia, 1850 ***5704.8*** *p59*
Doherty, John; Philadelphia, 1850 ***5704.8*** *p60*
Doherty, John; Philadelphia, 1852 ***5704.8*** *p87*
Doherty, John; Philadelphia, 1852 ***5704.8*** *p89*
Doherty, John; Philadelphia, 1852 ***5704.8*** *p97*
Doherty, John; Philadelphia, 1865 ***5704.8*** *p196*
Doherty, John; Philadelphia, 1866 ***5704.8*** *p206*
Doherty, John; Quebec, 1849 ***5704.8*** *p57*
Doherty, John; Quebec, 1852 ***5704.8*** *p91*
Doherty, John; St. John, N.B., 1847 ***5704.8*** *p2*
Doherty, John; St. John, N.B., 1847 ***5704.8*** *p4*
Doherty, John; St. John, N.B., 1847 ***5704.8*** *p9*
Doherty, John; St. John, N.B., 1847 ***5704.8*** *p15*
Doherty, John; St. John, N.B., 1847 ***5704.8*** *p26*
Doherty, John; St. John, N.B., 1847 ***5704.8*** *p33*
Doherty, John; St. John, N.B., 1848 ***5704.8*** *p47*
Doherty, John; St. John, N.B., 1849 ***5704.8*** *p48*
Doherty, John; St. John, N.B., 1849 ***5704.8*** *p56*
Doherty, John; St. John, N.B., 1850 ***5704.8*** *p61*
Doherty, John; St. John, N.B., 1851 ***5704.8*** *p78*
Doherty, John; St. John, N.B., 1852 ***5704.8*** *p84*
Doherty, John; St. John, N.B., 1853 ***5704.8*** *p99*
Doherty, John; St. John, N.B., 1853 ***5704.8*** *p107*
Doherty, John; St. John, N.B., 1853 ***5704.8*** *p108*
Doherty, John 9 mos *SEE* Doherty, Jane
Doherty, John 9 mos; Philadelphia, 1849 ***5704.8*** *p58*
Doherty, John 3 *SEE* Doherty, Sarah
Doherty, John 3; Philadelphia, 1847 ***5704.8*** *p2*
Doherty, John 4; St. John, N.B., 1850 ***5704.8*** *p61*
Doherty, John 6; Philadelphia, 1852 ***5704.8*** *p97*
Doherty, John 6; St. John, N.B., 1849 ***5704.8*** *p56*
Doherty, John 7; Quebec, 1863 ***5704.8*** *p153*
Doherty, John 7; St. John, N.B., 1847 ***5704.8*** *p33*
Doherty, John 9; Quebec, 1852 ***5704.8*** *p87*
Doherty, John 10; St. John, N.B., 1847 ***5704.8*** *p9*
Doherty, John 11; St. John, N.B., 1858 ***5704.8*** *p137*
Doherty, John 12; Philadelphia, 1859 ***5704.8*** *p142*
Doherty, John 16; Philadelphia, 1859 ***5704.8*** *p142*

Doherty, John 17; St. John, N.B., 1854 ***5704.8*** *p114*
Doherty, John 19; Massachusetts, 1849 ***5881.1*** *p30*
Doherty, John 21; Philadelphia, 1857 ***5704.8*** *p133*
Doherty, John 21; Philadelphia, 1858 ***5704.8*** *p139*
Doherty, John 21; St. John, N.B., 1860 ***5704.8*** *p143*
Doherty, John 22; Quebec, 1854 ***5704.8*** *p121*
Doherty, John 22; St. John, N.B., 1863 ***5704.8*** *p155*
Doherty, John 23; St. John, N.B., 1860 ***5704.8*** *p144*
Doherty, John 25; Philadelphia, 1858 ***5704.8*** *p139*
Doherty, John 26; Philadelphia, 1859 ***5704.8*** *p142*
Doherty, John 30; Philadelphia, 1804 ***53.26*** *p21*
*Relative:*Mary 26
Doherty, John 30; St. John, N.B., 1864 ***5704.8*** *p158*
Doherty, John 35; Philadelphia, 1854 ***5704.8*** *p118*
Doherty, John 42; Quebec, 1863 ***5704.8*** *p153*
Doherty, John 54; Quebec, 1864 ***5704.8*** *p162*
Doherty, John-Patrice 30; Montreal, 1796 ***7603*** *p88*
Doherty, Joseph; New Orleans, 1848 ***5704.8*** *p48*
Doherty, Joseph; Washington, 1859-1920 ***2872.1*** *p10*
Doherty, Joseph 26; Kansas, 1890 ***5240.1*** *p75*
Doherty, Julia 19; Philadelphia, 1857 ***5704.8*** *p133*
Doherty, Keatty; St. John, N.B., 1848 ***5704.8*** *p43*
Doherty, Kitty; St. John, N.B., 1851 ***5704.8*** *p72*
Doherty, Magy; St. John, N.B., 1847 ***5704.8*** *p19*
Doherty, Magy; St. John, N.B., 1851 ***5704.8*** *p72*
Doherty, Magy 2; St. John, N.B., 1849 ***5704.8*** *p48*
Doherty, Magy 3; St. John, N.B., 1851 ***5704.8*** *p78*
Doherty, Mandy; Philadelphia, 1847 ***53.26*** *p21*
Doherty, Mandy; Philadelphia, 1847 ***5704.8*** *p14*
Doherty, Marg. Ann 4 *SEE* Doherty, John
Doherty, Margaret *SEE* Doherty, William
Doherty, Margaret; Philadelphia, 1849 ***5704.8*** *p52*
Doherty, Margaret; Philadelphia, 1850 ***5704.8*** *p64*
Doherty, Margaret; Philadelphia, 1866 ***5704.8*** *p206*
Doherty, Margaret; St. John, N.B., 1847 ***5704.8*** *p3*
Doherty, Margaret; St. John, N.B., 1847 ***5704.8*** *p15*
Doherty, Margaret; St. John, N.B., 1848 ***5704.8*** *p39*
Doherty, Margaret; St. John, N.B., 1850 ***5704.8*** *p65*
Doherty, Margaret; St. John, N.B., 1853 ***5704.8*** *p106*
Doherty, Margaret 9 mos; Quebec, 1863 ***5704.8*** *p153*
Doherty, Margaret 1; Quebec, 1849 ***5704.8*** *p57*
Doherty, Margaret 12; Philadelphia, 1857 ***5704.8*** *p134*
Doherty, Margaret 12; St. John, N.B., 1849 ***5704.8*** *p56*
Doherty, Margaret 15; Massachusetts, 1847 ***5881.1*** *p31*
Doherty, Margaret 15; Philadelphia, 1860 ***5704.8*** *p146*
Doherty, Margaret 17; Philadelphia, 1859 ***5704.8*** *p141*
Doherty, Margaret 18; St. John, N.B., 1853 ***5704.8*** *p110*
Doherty, Margaret 23; Quebec, 1864 ***5704.8*** *p163*
Doherty, Margaret 40; Philadelphia, 1853 ***5704.8*** *p111*
Doherty, Margaret Ann 4; Philadelphia, 1847 ***5704.8*** *p22*
Doherty, Margery 19; St. John, N.B., 1857 ***5704.8*** *p134*
Doherty, Maria; New York, NY, 1816 ***2859.11*** *p29*
Doherty, Maria; Philadelphia, 1853 ***5704.8*** *p108*
Doherty, Maria 13; St. John, N.B., 1854 ***5704.8*** *p122*
Doherty, Martha; Philadelphia, 1849 ***53.26*** *p21*
Doherty, Martha; Philadelphia, 1849 ***5704.8*** *p53*
Doherty, Mary *SEE* Doherty, Neal
Doherty, Mary; America, 1869 ***5704.8*** *p232*
Doherty, Mary; New Orleans, 1852 ***5704.8*** *p98*
Doherty, Mary; New York, NY, 1815 ***2859.11*** *p29*
Doherty, Mary; New York, NY, 1865 ***5704.8*** *p196*
Doherty, Mary; New York, NY, 1866 ***5704.8*** *p214*
Doherty, Mary; New York, NY, 1867 ***5704.8*** *p216*
Doherty, Mary; Philadelphia, 1847 ***53.26*** *p21*
Doherty, Mary; Philadelphia, 1847 ***5704.8*** *p14*
Doherty, Mary; Philadelphia, 1848 ***5704.8*** *p46*
Doherty, Mary; Philadelphia, 1849 ***53.26*** *p21*
Doherty, Mary; Philadelphia, 1849 ***5704.8*** *p54*
Doherty, Mary; Philadelphia, 1851 ***5704.8*** *p70*
Doherty, Mary; Philadelphia, 1853 ***5704.8*** *p100*
Doherty, Mary; Philadelphia, 1865 ***5704.8*** *p204*
Doherty, Mary; Quebec, 1851 ***5704.8*** *p74*
Doherty, Mary; St. John, N.B., 1847 ***5704.8*** *p2*
Doherty, Mary; St. John, N.B., 1847 ***5704.8*** *p4*
Doherty, Mary; St. John, N.B., 1847 ***5704.8*** *p8*
Doherty, Mary; St. John, N.B., 1847 ***5704.8*** *p9*
Doherty, Mary; St. John, N.B., 1847 ***5704.8*** *p18*
Doherty, Mary; St. John, N.B., 1847 ***5704.8*** *p24*
Doherty, Mary; St. John, N.B., 1847 ***5704.8*** *p33*
Doherty, Mary; St. John, N.B., 1848 ***5704.8*** *p38*
Doherty, Mary; St. John, N.B., 1848 ***5704.8*** *p43*
Doherty, Mary; St. John, N.B., 1849 ***5704.8*** *p49*
Doherty, Mary; St. John, N.B., 1849 ***5704.8*** *p55*
Doherty, Mary; St. John, N.B., 1849 ***5704.8*** *p56*
Doherty, Mary; St. John, N.B., 1850 ***5704.8*** *p61*
Doherty, Mary; St. John, N.B., 1850 ***5704.8*** *p66*
Doherty, Mary; St. John, N.B., 1850 ***5704.8*** *p67*
Doherty, Mary; St. John, N.B., 1851 ***5704.8*** *p72*
Doherty, Mary; St. John, N.B., 1851 ***5704.8*** *p77*
Doherty, Mary; St. John, N.B., 1851 ***5704.8*** *p78*
Doherty, Mary; St. John, N.B., 1853 ***5704.8*** *p99*
Doherty, Mary; St. John, N.B., 1853 ***5704.8*** *p107*
Doherty, Mary 1; St. John, N.B., 1850 ***5704.8*** *p61*
Doherty, Mary 2; St. John, N.B., 1849 ***5704.8*** *p56*
Doherty, Mary 3; Massachusetts, 1850 ***5881.1*** *p32*
Doherty, Mary 4 *SEE* Doherty, William
Doherty, Mary 4; Philadelphia, 1849 ***5704.8*** *p52*
Doherty, Mary 6; St. John, N.B., 1852 ***5704.8*** *p95*
Doherty, Mary 6; St. John, N.B., 1865 ***5704.8*** *p165*
Doherty, Mary 7 *SEE* Doherty, John
Doherty, Mary 7; Philadelphia, 1847 ***5704.8*** *p1*
Doherty, Mary 10; St. John, N.B., 1847 ***5704.8*** *p2*
Doherty, Mary 10; St. John, N.B., 1849 ***5704.8*** *p48*
Doherty, Mary 12; St. John, N.B., 1847 ***5704.8*** *p2*
Doherty, Mary 13; Philadelphia, 1860 ***5704.8*** *p146*
Doherty, Mary 13; St. John, N.B., 1849 ***5704.8*** *p48*
Doherty, Mary 13; St. John, N.B., 1854 ***5704.8*** *p114*
Doherty, Mary 17; St. John, N.B., 1854 ***5704.8*** *p119*
Doherty, Mary 18; St. John, N.B., 1862 ***5704.8*** *p150*
Doherty, Mary 19; Philadelphia, 1859 ***5704.8*** *p141*
Doherty, Mary 20; Philadelphia, 1853 ***5704.8*** *p111*
Doherty, Mary 20; Philadelphia, 1857 ***5704.8*** *p134*
Doherty, Mary 20; Philadelphia, 1860 ***5704.8*** *p144*
Doherty, Mary 20; St. John, N.B., 1858 ***5704.8*** *p137*
Doherty, Mary 20; St. John, N.B., 1862 ***5704.8*** *p150*
Doherty, Mary 22; St. John, N.B., 1856 ***5704.8*** *p131*
Doherty, Mary 25; Philadelphia, 1857 ***5704.8*** *p132*
Doherty, Mary 26 *SEE* Doherty, John
Doherty, Mary 35; Philadelphia, 1860 ***5704.8*** *p146*
Doherty, Mary 54; Quebec, 1864 ***5704.8*** *p162*
Doherty, Mary A.; Philadelphia, 1867 ***5704.8*** *p217*
Doherty, Mary A. 27; Philadelphia, 1857 ***5704.8*** *p134*
Doherty, Mary Ann; Philadelphia, 1851 ***5704.8*** *p76*
Doherty, Mary Ann; Philadelphia, 1852 ***5704.8*** *p97*
Doherty, Mary Ann 6 mos; Philadelphia, 1857 ***5704.8*** *p132*
Doherty, Mary Ann 8; Quebec, 1863 ***5704.8*** *p153*
Doherty, Mary Ann 9; St. John, N.B., 1851 ***5704.8*** *p78*
Doherty, Mary Anne 30; Philadelphia, 1859 ***5704.8*** *p142*
Doherty, Matilda; Philadelphia, 1866 ***5704.8*** *p206*
Doherty, Matty; Philadelphia, 1850 ***5704.8*** *p64*
Doherty, Michael *SEE* Doherty, Charles
Doherty, Michael; New York, NY, 1816 ***2859.11*** *p29*
Doherty, Michael; New York, NY, 1865 ***5704.8*** *p196*
Doherty, Michael; Philadelphia, 1847 ***5704.8*** *p1*
Doherty, Michael; Philadelphia, 1849 ***53.26*** *p21*
Doherty, Michael; Philadelphia, 1849 ***5704.8*** *p52*
Doherty, Michael; Philadelphia, 1850 ***53.26*** *p21*
*Relative:*John
Doherty, Michael; Philadelphia, 1850 ***5704.8*** *p59*
Doherty, Michael; Philadelphia, 1852 ***5704.8*** *p84*
Doherty, Michael; Philadelphia, 1853 ***5704.8*** *p102*
Doherty, Michael; Philadelphia, 1865 ***5704.8*** *p197*
Doherty, Michael; Quebec, 1850 ***5704.8*** *p66*
Doherty, Michael; St. John, N.B., 1847 ***5704.8*** *p3*
Doherty, Michael; St. John, N.B., 1847 ***5704.8*** *p4*
Doherty, Michael; St. John, N.B., 1848 ***5704.8*** *p39*
Doherty, Michael; St. John, N.B., 1850 ***5704.8*** *p66*
Doherty, Michael; St. John, N.B., 1851 ***5704.8*** *p72*
Doherty, Michael; St. John, N.B., 1852 ***5704.8*** *p84*
Doherty, Michael 2; St. John, N.B., 1848 ***5704.8*** *p43*
Doherty, Michael 5; St. John, N.B., 1847 ***5704.8*** *p2*
Doherty, Michael 14; Philadelphia, 1859 ***5704.8*** *p142*
Doherty, Michael 20; Philadelphia, 1859 ***5704.8*** *p142*
Doherty, Michael 21; Philadelphia, 1865 ***5704.8*** *p164*
Doherty, Michael 24; Philadelphia, 1833-1834 ***53.26*** *p21*
Doherty, Michael 25; St. John, N.B., 1854 ***5704.8*** *p115*
Doherty, Micky; Philadelphia, 1852 ***5704.8*** *p86*
Doherty, Nancy; Philadelphia, 1868 ***5704.8*** *p226*
Doherty, Nancy; St. John, N.B., 1847 ***5704.8*** *p3*
Doherty, Nancy; St. John, N.B., 1847 ***5704.8*** *p9*
Doherty, Nancy; St. John, N.B., 1847 ***5704.8*** *p24*
Doherty, Nancy; St. John, N.B., 1849 ***5704.8*** *p56*
Doherty, Nancy 11; St. John, N.B., 1851 ***5704.8*** *p72*
Doherty, Nancy 12 *SEE* Doherty, Sarah
Doherty, Nancy 12; Philadelphia, 1847 ***5704.8*** *p2*
Doherty, Nancy 22; Philadelphia, 1833-1834 ***53.26*** *p21*
Doherty, Nancy 50; Massachusetts, 1849 ***5881.1*** *p33*
Doherty, Neal; Philadelphia, 1848 ***53.26*** *p21*
*Relative:*Peggy
*Relative:*Mary
*Relative:*Sally
Doherty, Neal; Philadelphia, 1848 ***5704.8*** *p46*
Doherty, Neal; Quebec, 1849 ***5704.8*** *p51*
Doherty, Neal; St. John, N.B., 1847 ***5704.8*** *p4*
Doherty, Neal; St. John, N.B., 1851 ***5704.8*** *p77*
Doherty, Nelly; St. John, N.B., 1847 ***5704.8*** *p9*
Doherty, Nelly; St. John, N.B., 1850 ***5704.8*** *p62*
Doherty, Nelly; St. John, N.B., 1851 ***5704.8*** *p72*
Doherty, Nelly 11; St. John, N.B., 1850 ***5704.8*** *p61*
Doherty, Nola 23; Philadelphia, 1853 ***5704.8*** *p112*
Doherty, Owen *SEE* Doherty, Charles
Doherty, Owen; Philadelphia, 1847 ***5704.8*** *p1*
Doherty, Owen; Philadelphia, 1852 ***5704.8*** *p88*
Doherty, Owen; St. John, N.B., 1847 ***5704.8*** *p5*
Doherty, Owen; St. John, N.B., 1847 ***5704.8*** *p33*
Doherty, Owen; St. John, N.B., 1850 ***5704.8*** *p65*
Doherty, Owen 12; St. John, N.B., 1847 ***5704.8*** *p33*
Doherty, Owen 23; Philadelphia, 1853 ***5704.8*** *p112*
Doherty, Own; St. John, N.B., 1847 ***5704.8*** *p24*
Doherty, Pady; St. John, N.B., 1847 ***5704.8*** *p25*
Doherty, Pat *SEE* Doherty, William
Doherty, Pat; Philadelphia, 1849 ***5704.8*** *p52*
Doherty, Pat; Philadelphia, 1851 ***5704.8*** *p71*
Doherty, Pat 50; St. John, N.B., 1855 ***5704.8*** *p126*
Doherty, Patrick *SEE* Doherty, Phillip
Doherty, Patrick; America, 1866 ***5704.8*** *p205*
Doherty, Patrick; New York, NY, 1864 ***5704.8*** *p169*
Doherty, Patrick; Philadelphia, 1847 ***53.26*** *p21*
*Relative:*Hugh
Doherty, Patrick; Philadelphia, 1847 ***5704.8*** *p22*
Doherty, Patrick; Philadelphia, 1849 ***53.26*** *p21*
Doherty, Patrick; Philadelphia, 1849 ***5704.8*** *p50*
Doherty, Patrick; Philadelphia, 1849 ***5704.8*** *p55*
Doherty, Patrick; Philadelphia, 1850 ***53.26*** *p21*
*Relative:*John
*Relative:*Catherine
Doherty, Patrick; Philadelphia, 1850 ***5704.8*** *p60*
Doherty, Patrick; Philadelphia, 1851 ***5704.8*** *p76*
Doherty, Patrick; Philadelphia, 1851 ***5704.8*** *p80*
Doherty, Patrick; Philadelphia, 1852 ***5704.8*** *p84*
Doherty, Patrick; Philadelphia, 1866 ***5704.8*** *p206*
Doherty, Patrick; Quebec, 1852 ***5704.8*** *p98*
Doherty, Patrick; St. John, N.B., 1847 ***5704.8*** *p3*
Doherty, Patrick; St. John, N.B., 1847 ***5704.8*** *p21*
Doherty, Patrick; St. John, N.B., 1848 ***5704.8*** *p43*
Doherty, Patrick; St. John, N.B., 1850 ***5704.8*** *p61*
Doherty, Patrick; St. John, N.B., 1850 ***5704.8*** *p65*
Doherty, Patrick; St. John, N.B., 1850 ***5704.8*** *p66*
Doherty, Patrick; St. John, N.B., 1851 ***5704.8*** *p72*
Doherty, Patrick; St. John, N.B., 1851 ***5704.8*** *p77*
Doherty, Patrick; St. John, N.B., 1852 ***5704.8*** *p92*
Doherty, Patrick; St. John, N.B., 1853 ***5704.8*** *p107*
Doherty, Patrick; Wisconsin, n.d. ***9675.5*** *p121*
Doherty, Patrick 4; St. John, N.B., 1850 ***5704.8*** *p61*
Doherty, Patrick 5 *SEE* Doherty, John
Doherty, Patrick 5; Philadelphia, 1847 ***5704.8*** *p1*
Doherty, Patrick 6 *SEE* Doherty, Sarah
Doherty, Patrick 6; Philadelphia, 1847 ***5704.8*** *p2*
Doherty, Patrick 8; St. John, N.B., 1847 ***5704.8*** *p25*
Doherty, Patrick 10; Massachusetts, 1849 ***5881.1*** *p33*
Doherty, Patrick 11; Quebec, 1864 ***5704.8*** *p162*
Doherty, Patrick 12; Massachusetts, 1849 ***5881.1*** *p33*
Doherty, Patrick 12; St. John, N.B., 1849 ***5704.8*** *p55*
Doherty, Patrick 13; Quebec, 1863 ***5704.8*** *p153*
Doherty, Patrick 18; St. John, N.B., 1864 ***5704.8*** *p158*
Doherty, Patrick 20; St. John, N.B., 1859 ***5704.8*** *p140*
Doherty, Patrick 22; St. John, N.B., 1854 ***5704.8*** *p115*
Doherty, Patrick 28; Quebec, 1856 ***5704.8*** *p130*
Doherty, Patrick 30; St. John, N.B., 1862 ***5704.8*** *p150*
Doherty, Patrick 62; St. John, N.B., 1854 ***5704.8*** *p121*
Doherty, Patrick 65; Philadelphia, 1858 ***5704.8*** *p138*
Doherty, Peggy *SEE* Doherty, Charles
Doherty, Peggy *SEE* Doherty, Neal
Doherty, Peggy; Philadelphia, 1847 ***5704.8*** *p1*
Doherty, Peggy; Philadelphia, 1848 ***5704.8*** *p46*
Doherty, Peggy; Philadelphia, 1853 ***5704.8*** *p103*
Doherty, Peggy; St. John, N.B., 1847 ***5704.8*** *p9*
Doherty, Peggy; St. John, N.B., 1850 ***5704.8*** *p61*
Doherty, Peggy; St. John, N.B., 1851 ***5704.8*** *p72*
Doherty, Peggy; St. John, N.B., 1851 ***5704.8*** *p78*
Doherty, Peggy 10; St. John, N.B., 1847 ***5704.8*** *p3*
Doherty, Peter; Philadelphia, 1850 ***5704.8*** *p64*
Doherty, Peter 3; St. John, N.B., 1851 ***5704.8*** *p78*
Doherty, Peter 50; St. John, N.B., 1853 ***5704.8*** *p110*
Doherty, Phelix 3; Quebec, 1863 ***5704.8*** *p153*
Doherty, Philip; New York, NY, 1816 ***2859.11*** *p29*
Doherty, Philip; New York, NY, 1838 ***8208.4*** *p63*
Doherty, Philip; Philadelphia, 1852 ***5704.8*** *p92*
Doherty, Philip; St. John, N.B., 1848 ***5704.8*** *p43*
Doherty, Philip; St. John, N.B., 1851 ***5704.8*** *p72*
Doherty, Phillip; Philadelphia, 1849 ***53.26*** *p21*
*Relative:*Patrick
Doherty, Phillip; Philadelphia, 1849 ***5704.8*** *p55*
Doherty, Phillip 3; St. John, N.B., 1850 ***5704.8*** *p61*
Doherty, Phillip 4; St. John, N.B., 1847 ***5704.8*** *p33*
Doherty, Rachel; St. John, N.B., 1847 ***5704.8*** *p2*
Doherty, Rebecca *SEE* Doherty, George
Doherty, Rebecca; Philadelphia, 1847 ***5704.8*** *p32*
Doherty, Robert; Philadelphia, 1847 ***53.26*** *p21*
*Relative:*Betty
Doherty, Robert; Philadelphia, 1847 ***53.26*** *p21*
*Relative:*Catherine 11
*Relative:*Eliza 9
*Relative:*James
Doherty, Robert; Philadelphia, 1847 ***5704.8*** *p24*
Doherty, Robert; Philadelphia, 1847 ***5704.8*** *p30*
Doherty, Robert; St. John, N.B., 1848 ***5704.8*** *p43*
Doherty, Robert 24; Philadelphia, 1860 ***5704.8*** *p144*

Doherty, Robert 40; Philadelphia, 1854 ***5704.8*** *p123*
Doherty, Roddy; St. John, N.B., 1850 ***5704.8*** *p61*
Doherty, Rodey; St. John, N.B., 1847 ***5704.8*** *p24*
Doherty, Roger 7 *SEE* Doherty, Fanny
Doherty, Roger 7; Philadelphia, 1849 ***5704.8*** *p54*
Doherty, Roger A. 22; St. John, N.B., 1860 ***5704.8*** *p144*
Doherty, Rosanna 8; St. John, N.B., 1847 ***5704.8*** *p33*
Doherty, Rose; Philadelphia, 1866 ***5704.8*** *p205*
Doherty, Rose; Philadelphia, 1866 ***5704.8*** *p207*
Doherty, Rose; Philadelphia, 1867 ***5704.8*** *p215*
Doherty, Rose; St. John, N.B., 1847 ***5704.8*** *p18*
Doherty, Rose; St. John, N.B., 1847 ***5704.8*** *p20*
Doherty, Rose; St. John, N.B., 1848 ***5704.8*** *p39*
Doherty, Rose 5 *SEE* Doherty, Fanny
Doherty, Rose 5; Philadelphia, 1849 ***5704.8*** *p54*
Doherty, Rose 16; Philadelphia, 1858 ***5704.8*** *p138*
Doherty, Rose 17; Philadelphia, 1856 ***5704.8*** *p129*
Doherty, Rose 20; Philadelphia, 1855 ***5704.8*** *p124*
Doherty, Rose 24; St. John, N.B., 1853 ***5704.8*** *p110*
Doherty, Rose 30; Philadelphia, 1865 ***5704.8*** *p165*
Doherty, Rose 37; Massachusetts, 1847 ***5881.1*** *p34*
Doherty, Rose 59; Philadelphia, 1858 ***5704.8*** *p138*
Doherty, Rose Ann; Philadelphia, 1852 ***5704.8*** *p96*
Doherty, Rose Ann 6 mos; Philadelphia, 1857 ***5704.8*** *p134*
Doherty, Rosey *SEE* Doherty, John
Doherty, Rosey; Philadelphia, 1847 ***5704.8*** *p22*
Doherty, Rosey; Philadelphia, 1851 ***5704.8*** *p78*
Doherty, Rosey; St. John, N.B., 1847 ***5704.8*** *p8*
Doherty, Rosey; St. John, N.B., 1852 ***5704.8*** *p93*
Doherty, Rosy 24; St. John, N.B., 1855 ***5704.8*** *p126*
Doherty, Sally *SEE* Doherty, Neal
Doherty, Sally; Philadelphia, 1848 ***5704.8*** *p46*
Doherty, Sally; St. John, N.B., 1848 ***5704.8*** *p40*
Doherty, Sally; St. John, N.B., 1848 ***5704.8*** *p43*
Doherty, Sally 10; St. John, N.B., 1847 ***5704.8*** *p2*
Doherty, Sally 13; St. John, N.B., 1847 ***5704.8*** *p3*
Doherty, Sally 50; St. John, N.B., 1854 ***5704.8*** *p115*
Doherty, Samuel 8 *SEE* Doherty, Sarah
Doherty, Samuel 8; Philadelphia, 1847 ***5704.8*** *p2*
Doherty, Sarah; New York, NY, 1867 ***5704.8*** *p219*
Doherty, Sarah; Philadelphia, 1847 ***53.26*** *p22*
Doherty, Sarah; Philadelphia, 1847 ***53.26*** *p22*
*Relative:*Nancy 12
*Relative:*James 10
*Relative:*Samuel 8
*Relative:*Patrick 6
*Relative:*John 3
*Relative:*Hugh 1
Doherty, Sarah; Philadelphia, 1847 ***5704.8*** *p2*
Doherty, Sarah; Philadelphia, 1847 ***5704.8*** *p31*
Doherty, Sarah; Philadelphia, 1852 ***5704.8*** *p85*
Doherty, Sarah; Philadelphia, 1867 ***5704.8*** *p220*
Doherty, Sarah; St. John, N.B., 1847 ***5704.8*** *p3*
Doherty, Sarah; St. John, N.B., 1847 ***5704.8*** *p26*
Doherty, Sarah; St. John, N.B., 1852 ***5704.8*** *p95*
Doherty, Sarah 3 mos; St. John, N.B., 1849 ***5704.8*** *p56*
Doherty, Sarah 15; Massachusetts, 1847 ***5881.1*** *p34*
Doherty, Sarah 19; Philadelphia, 1857 ***5704.8*** *p133*
Doherty, Sarah 45; St. John, N.B., 1854 ***5704.8*** *p122*
Doherty, Shan; Philadelphia, 1851 ***5704.8*** *p79*
Doherty, Shane; Philadelphia, 1852 ***5704.8*** *p84*
Doherty, Sisley; St. John, N.B., 1850 ***5704.8*** *p67*
Doherty, Susan; Philadelphia, 1852 ***5704.8*** *p91*
Doherty, Susan; Philadelphia, 1853 ***5704.8*** *p100*
Doherty, Susan; Philadelphia, 1866 ***5704.8*** *p206*
Doherty, Susan; Quebec, 1847 ***5704.8*** *p27*
Doherty, Susan; St. John, N.B., 1847 ***5704.8*** *p9*
Doherty, Susan; St. John, N.B., 1852 ***5704.8*** *p93*
Doherty, Susanna; St. John, N.B., 1849 ***5704.8*** *p55*
Doherty, Teresa 13; St. John, N.B., 1849 ***5704.8*** *p55*
Doherty, Thomas; St. John, N.B., 1847 ***5704.8*** *p33*
Doherty, Thomas 10; Quebec, 1863 ***5704.8*** *p153*
Doherty, Thomas 15; Philadelphia, 1854 ***5704.8*** *p120*
Doherty, Timothy; New York, NY, 1864 ***5704.8*** *p172*
Doherty, Unity; America, 1863 ***5704.8*** *p169*
Doherty, Unity; St. John, N.B., 1850 ***5704.8*** *p61*
Doherty, Walter Peter 8; Philadelphia, 1859 ***5704.8*** *p142*
Doherty, William; New York, NY, 1816 ***2859.11*** *p29*
Doherty, William; New York, NY, 1865 ***5704.8*** *p197*
Doherty, William; Philadelphia, 1847 ***53.26*** *p22*
Doherty, William; Philadelphia, 1847 ***5704.8*** *p2*
Doherty, William; Philadelphia, 1849 ***53.26*** *p22*
Doherty, William; Philadelphia, 1849 ***53.26*** *p22*
*Relative:*Margaret
*Relative:*Pat
*Relative:*Elleanor
*Relative:*Hugh 8
*Relative:*Mary 4
Doherty, William; Philadelphia, 1849 ***5704.8*** *p52*
Doherty, William; Philadelphia, 1849 ***5704.8*** *p54*
Doherty, William; Philadelphia, 1850 ***53.26*** *p22*
Doherty, William; Philadelphia, 1850 ***5704.8*** *p69*
Doherty, William; Philadelphia, 1852 ***5704.8*** *p86*
Doherty, William; Philadelphia, 1852 ***5704.8*** *p97*
Doherty, William; Philadelphia, 1866 ***5704.8*** *p210*
Doherty, William; Quebec, 1851 ***5704.8*** *p74*
Doherty, William; St. John, N.B., 1847 ***5704.8*** *p3*
Doherty, William; St. John, N.B., 1847 ***5704.8*** *p4*
Doherty, William; St. John, N.B., 1849 ***5704.8*** *p56*
Doherty, William; St. John, N.B., 1850 ***5704.8*** *p61*
Doherty, William; St. John, N.B., 1851 ***5704.8*** *p78*
Doherty, William; St. John, N.B., 1853 ***5704.8*** *p106*
Doherty, William 9 mos; St. John, N.B., 1848 ***5704.8*** *p39*
Doherty, William 3 *SEE* Doherty, John
Doherty, William 3; Philadelphia, 1847 ***5704.8*** *p22*
Doherty, William 12; St. John, N.B., 1859 ***5704.8*** *p141*
Doherty, William 15; Massachusetts, 1849 ***5881.1*** *p34*
Doherty, William 18; St. John, N.B., 1862 ***5704.8*** *p150*
Doherty, William 22; Philadelphia, 1833-1834 ***53.26*** *p22*
Doherty, William 22; Philadelphia, 1833-1834 ***53.26*** *p22*
*Relative:*Edward 25
Doherty, William 22; Quebec, 1853 ***5704.8*** *p105*
Doherty, William 23; Philadelphia, 1804 ***53.26*** *p22*
Doherty, William 23; Philadelphia, 1853 ***5704.8*** *p112*
Doherty, William 24; Philadelphia, 1833-1834 ***53.26*** *p22*
Doherty, William 30; Massachusetts, 1847 ***5881.1*** *p34*
Dohimann, Otto; New York, NY, 1839 ***8208.4*** *p100*
Dohirty, Michael; Providence, RI, 1853 ***6013.19*** *p90*
Dohla, Johann Conrad; Maryland, 1783 ***9786*** *p201*
Dohlen, Harm; Illinois, 1865 ***7857*** *p3*
Dohm, John 18; New Orleans, 1862 ***543.30*** *p220*
Dohmprobst, . . .; Canada, 1776-1783 ***9786*** *p19*
Doholy, Edward; New York, NY, 1811 ***2859.11*** *p11*
Dohren, . . .; Canada, 1776-1783 ***9786*** *p19*
Dohrn, Henry William; Arkansas, 1918 ***95.2*** *p38*
Doig, Jacques; Quebec, 1777 ***7603*** *p38*
Doig, John 22; Quebec, 1862 ***5704.8*** *p152*
Doin, . . .; Port uncertain, 1839 ***778.5*** *p167*
Doin, Mme.; Port uncertain, 1839 ***778.5*** *p167*
Doin, Mr.; Port uncertain, 1839 ***778.5*** *p167*
Doini, Bordolo; Arkansas, 1918 ***95.2*** *p38*
Dolan, Ann; Quebec, 1852 ***5704.8*** *p93*
Dolan, Ann 5; America, 1866 ***5704.8*** *p205*
Dolan, Ann 15; Massachusetts, 1848 ***5881.1*** *p26*
Dolan, Anne; America, 1866 ***5704.8*** *p209*
Dolan, Biddy 11; Quebec, 1847 ***5704.8*** *p17*
Dolan, Bridget; America, 1743 ***4971*** *p11*
Dolan, Bridget; New York, NY, 1869 ***5704.8*** *p232*
Dolan, Bridget 7; Quebec, 1852 ***5704.8*** *p93*
Dolan, Bridget 9; Philadelphia, 1865 ***5704.8*** *p190*
Dolan, Bridget 28; Massachusetts, 1849 ***5881.1*** *p27*
Dolan, Catharine 9; Massachusetts, 1847 ***5881.1*** *p27*
Dolan, Catherine *SEE* Dolan, John
Dolan, Catherine; Philadelphia, 1847 ***5704.8*** *p14*
Dolan, Daniel; America, 1743 ***4971*** *p10*
Dolan, Daniel; America, 1743 ***4971*** *p95*
Dolan, George; Philadelphia, 1864 ***5704.8*** *p173*
Dolan, Henry; New York, NY, 1836 ***8208.4*** *p25*
Dolan, Isabella 20; Philadelphia, 1854 ***5704.8*** *p122*
Dolan, James 7; St. John, N.B., 1849 ***5704.8*** *p56*
Dolan, James 35; New Orleans, 1863 ***543.30*** *p374*
Dolan, Jane 22; Massachusetts, 1848 ***5881.1*** *p29*
Dolan, John; Philadelphia, 1847 ***53.26*** *p22*
*Relative:*Catherine
Dolan, John; Philadelphia, 1847 ***5704.8*** *p14*
Dolan, John; Philadelphia, 1866 ***5704.8*** *p211*
Dolan, John; St. John, N.B., 1849 ***5704.8*** *p56*
Dolan, John; St. John, N.B., 1853 ***5704.8*** *p99*
Dolan, John 13; Quebec, 1852 ***5704.8*** *p93*
Dolan, John 13; Quebec, 1852 ***5704.8*** *p94*
Dolan, John 30; Massachusetts, 1847 ***5881.1*** *p29*
Dolan, John 38; Massachusetts, 1849 ***5881.1*** *p29*
Dolan, John 41; Harris Co., TX, 1898 ***6254*** *p5*
Dolan, John 54; Kansas, 1894 ***5240.1*** *p79*
Dolan, Lawrence; New York, NY, 1834 ***8208.4*** *p3*
Dolan, Margaret; Philadelphia, 1865 ***5704.8*** *p190*
Dolan, Margaret; St. John, N.B., 1849 ***5704.8*** *p56*
Dolan, Margaret 50; Massachusetts, 1849 ***5881.1*** *p32*
Dolan, Margaret A.; Philadelphia, 1865 ***5704.8*** *p190*
Dolan, Margaret J.; Philadelphia, 1865 ***5704.8*** *p190*
Dolan, Maria 23; Massachusetts, 1849 ***5881.1*** *p32*
Dolan, Mary; Massachusetts, 1849 ***5881.1*** *p32*
Dolan, Mary; Philadelphia, 1864 ***5704.8*** *p184*
Dolan, Mary; St. John, N.B., 1849 ***5704.8*** *p56*
Dolan, Mary 13; Quebec, 1847 ***5704.8*** *p17*
Dolan, Mary 48; Massachusetts, 1849 ***5881.1*** *p32*
Dolan, Michael 17; Massachusetts, 1849 ***5881.1*** *p31*
Dolan, Mike 36; Massachusetts, 1849 ***5881.1*** *p32*
Dolan, Patrick; America, 1866 ***5704.8*** *p205*
Dolan, Patrick 21; Massachusetts, 1848 ***5881.1*** *p33*
Dolan, Patrick H. 21; New Orleans, 1862 ***543.30*** *p218*
Dolan, Peter 50; Massachusetts, 1849 ***5881.1*** *p33*
Dolan, Richard 34; Massachusetts, 1847 ***5881.1*** *p34*
Dolan, Susan; St. John, N.B., 1849 ***5704.8*** *p56*
Dolan, Susan 13; St. John, N.B., 1849 ***5704.8*** *p56*
Dolan, Thomas; Quebec, 1852 ***5704.8*** *p93*
Dolan, William 38; Massachusetts, 1849 ***5881.1*** *p34*
Doland, James; New York, NY, 1834 ***8208.4*** *p3*
Doland, Lawrence; New York, NY, 1834 ***8208.4*** *p3*
Dolanowski, Edward; New York, 1834 ***4606*** *p178*
Dolbin, John; Virginia, 1640 ***6219*** *p18*
Dolby, Edward 21; Jamaica, 1733 ***3690.1*** *p65*
Dolby, John 19; Jamaica, 1722 ***3690.1*** *p65*
Dolby, Jon.; Virginia, 1642 ***6219*** *p191*
Dolcher, George 24; America, 1838 ***778.5*** *p167*
Dolen, Ann 13; St. John, N.B., 1847 ***5704.8*** *p25*
Dolen, James 7; St. John, N.B., 1847 ***5704.8*** *p25*
Dolen, Margaret; St. John, N.B., 1847 ***5704.8*** *p25*
Dolen, Margaret 9; St. John, N.B., 1847 ***5704.8*** *p25*
Dolen, Mary 11; St. John, N.B., 1847 ***5704.8*** *p25*
Dolezal, Joseph; Iowa, 1866-1943 ***123.54*** *p61*
Dolezal, Josip; Iowa, 1866-1943 ***123.54*** *p61*
Dolezol, Mary; Iowa, 1866-1943 ***123.54*** *p61*
Dolfapa, Fiorentina 24; New York, NY, 1893 ***9026.4*** *p41*
Doligherty, Margaret; New York, NY, 1864 ***5704.8*** *p174*
Dolinar, John; Wisconsin, n.d. ***9675.5*** *p121*
Doliner, Brandul *SEE* Doliner, Max
Doliner, Max; New York, NY, 1914 ***3455.2*** *p76*
*Wife:*Brandul
Doll, John; Virginia, 1844 ***4626.16*** *p12*
Doll, Lorenz; Wisconsin, n.d. ***9675.5*** *p121*
Dollan, John; America, 1739 ***4971*** *p63*
Dollert, E. Wilhelm; Wisconsin, n.d. ***9675.5*** *p121*
Dollin, Wm.; Virginia, 1643 ***6219*** *p200*
Dollinger, Barbara; South Dakota, 1889 ***1641*** *p41*
Dollinger, Barbara, Jr.; South Dakota, 1889 ***1641*** *p41*
Dollinger, Barbara Rott *SEE* Dollinger, Phillip
Dollinger, Christian; South Dakota, 1889 ***1641*** *p41*
Dollinger, Christiana; Dakota, 1881-1980 ***1641*** *p43*
Dollinger, Christina; Dakota, 1806-1900 ***1641*** *p43*
Dollinger, Christina; Dakota, 1878-1978 ***1641*** *p43*
Dollinger, Elizabeth; Dakota, 1806-1900 ***1641*** *p43*
Dollinger, Elizabeth; Dakota, 1877-1977 ***1641*** *p43*
Dollinger, Frederick; Dakota, 1806-1900 ***1641*** *p43*
Dollinger, Frederick; Dakota, 1889 ***1641*** *p43*
*Wife:*Rosina
Dollinger, Fredericka; Dakota, 1867-1967 ***1641*** *p43*
Dollinger, Gottlieb; Dakota, 1806-1900 ***1641*** *p43*
Dollinger, Gottlieb; Dakota, 1884 ***1641*** *p43*
Dollinger, Gottlieb; South Dakota, 1889 ***1641*** *p41*
Dollinger, Jacob; Dakota, 1875-1975 ***1641*** *p43*
Dollinger, Jakob; South Dakota, 1889 ***1641*** *p41*
Dollinger, Johann; South Dakota, 1889 ***1641*** *p41*
Dollinger, John; Dakota, 1806-1900 ***1641*** *p43*
Dollinger, John; Dakota, 1871-1971 ***1641*** *p43*
Dollinger, Katherina; South Dakota, 1889 ***1641*** *p41*
Dollinger, Kathrina; Dakota, 1806-1900 ***1641*** *p43*
Dollinger, Kathrina; Dakota, 1869-1969 ***1641*** *p43*
Dollinger, Magdalena; Dakota, 1883-1980 ***1641*** *p43*
Dollinger, Phillip; South Dakota, 1889 ***1641*** *p41*
Dollinger, Phillip; South Dakota, 1889 ***1641*** *p43*
*Wife:*Barbara Rott
Dollinger, Rosina *SEE* Dollinger, Frederick
Dollinger, Rosina; Dakota, 1868-1968 ***1641*** *p43*
Dollton, Obediah 24; Jamaica, 1735 ***3690.1*** *p65*
Dolly, Jeanne 21; New Orleans, 1836 ***778.5*** *p168*
Dolmetsch, Eugene C.; America, 1869 ***1450.2*** *p31A*
Dolonson, Hugh; New York, NY, 1811 ***2859.11*** *p11*
With family
Dolph, Chester V.; Washington, 1859-1920 ***2872.1*** *p10*
Dolson, Andrew; Virginia, 1649 ***6219*** *p253*
Dolson, Edward; New York, NY, 1834 ***8208.4*** *p26*
Dolten, Edward; Quebec, 1776 ***7603*** *p72*
Dolten, Thomas; New York, NY, 1837 ***8208.4*** *p53*
Doltie, Owen; Virginia, 1638 ***6219*** *p153*
Doly, Altha; Philadelphia, 1816 ***2859.11*** *p29*
Doly, Arthur; Philadelphia, 1816 ***2859.11*** *p29*
Doly, Henrietta; Philadelphia, 1816 ***2859.11*** *p29*
Doly, Jane; Philadelphia, 1816 ***2859.11*** *p29*
Doly, Maria; Philadelphia, 1816 ***2859.11*** *p29*
Dom, Jacob; Pennsylvania, 1754 ***2444*** *p226*
Domange, J. 34; New Orleans, 1830 ***778.5*** *p168*
Domanh, Peter; Iowa, 1866-1943 ***123.54*** *p16*
Domanski, Ludwik; Boston, 1834 ***4606*** *p179*
With wife
Domb, Louis; New Jersey, 1898 ***1450.2*** *p7B*
Dombrowski, Anton; Wisconsin, n.d. ***9675.5*** *p121*
Dombrowski, Dominik; Wisconsin, n.d. ***9675.5*** *p121*
Domenico, Dona; Colorado, 1888 ***9678.2*** *p16*
Domeniko, Castijo; Wisconsin, n.d. ***9675.5*** *p121*
Domerby, Mr. 22; New Orleans, 1832 ***778.5*** *p168*
Domester, John 16; Port uncertain, 1838 ***778.5*** *p168*
Domijancic, Stefen; Iowa, 1866-1943 ***123.54*** *p16*
Domijancich, Matt; Iowa, 1866-1943 ***123.54*** *p16*
Domijancie, Anton; Iowa, 1866-1943 ***123.54*** *p16*
Domingo, Vito; Philadelphia, 1851 ***6013.19*** *p30*
Domingues, Jose 58; Arizona, 1925 ***9228.40*** *p29*

Dominic, Mana; Wisconsin, n.d. ***9675.5*** *p121*
Dominica, Peter 17; Philadelphia, 1774 ***1219.7*** *p175*
Dominick, Andreas; America, 1752 ***2444*** *p149*
*Wife:*Barbara Reyler
*Child:*Walpurga
Dominick, Angelo 22; West Virginia, 1896 ***9788.3*** *p9*
Dominick, Barbara Reyler *SEE* Dominick, Andreas
Dominick, Maria; New York, 1749 ***3652*** *p72*
Dominick, Walpurga *SEE* Dominick, Andreas
Dominico, Anastasio 31; America, 1836 ***778.5*** *p168*
Dominiq, J. 22; New Orleans, 1821 ***778.5*** *p168*
Dominique, Mr. 23; New Orleans, 1822 ***778.5*** *p168*
Dominique, Mr. 25; New Orleans, 1838 ***778.5*** *p168*
Dominique, Mr. 45; Louisiana, 1821 ***778.5*** *p168*
Dominique, Jerome 37; New Orleans, 1862 ***543.30*** *p216*
Dominique, Olmia 27; New Orleans, 1862 ***543.30*** *p56*
Dominique, Philippe 30; New Orleans, 1839 ***778.5*** *p168*
Dominish, Ribon 30; New York, NY, 1893 ***9026.4*** *p41*
Dominy, Andrew; South Carolina, 1788 ***7119*** *p203*
Domitz, John; Arkansas, 1918 ***95.2*** *p38*
Dommes, August Friedrich; Quebec, 1776 ***9786*** *p262*
Domri, Catharina 9; America, 1839 ***778.5*** *p168*
Domri, George 1; America, 1839 ***778.5*** *p168*
Domri, Henry 7; America, 1839 ***778.5*** *p168*
Domri, Jacques 2; America, 1839 ***778.5*** *p168*
Domri, Michel 14; America, 1839 ***778.5*** *p168*
Domri, Michel 39; America, 1839 ***778.5*** *p169*
Domri, Salomea 11; America, 1839 ***778.5*** *p169*
Domri, Salomea 38; America, 1839 ***778.5*** *p169*
Domyancich, George; Iowa, 1866-1943 ***123.54*** *p16*
Domyansich, Matt; Iowa, 1866-1943 ***123.54*** *p16*
Don, Alexander; Charleston, SC, 1814 ***1639.20*** *p60*
Don, Catherine; Pennsylvania, 1753 ***2444*** *p144*
Don, Henry 18; New Orleans, 1862 ***543.30*** *p57*
Don, James 29; Jamaica, 1739 ***3690.1*** *p68*
Don Luis, Mr. 39; New Orleans, 1820 ***778.5*** *p169*
With nephew 12
Dona..., Vincenzo 26; New York, NY, 1893 ***9026.4*** *p41*
Donagan, Thomas; St. John, N.B., 1850 ***5704.8*** *p67*
Donagh, Catherine 15; Philadelphia, 1857 ***5704.8*** *p132*
Donagh, Hugh 21; St. John, N.B., 1864 ***5704.8*** *p158*
Donagh, Rose 18; Philadelphia, 1857 ***5704.8*** *p132*
Donaghe, Henry; New York, NY, 1816 ***2859.11*** *p29*
Donagher, Ann; Quebec, 1825 ***7603*** *p94*
Donaghey, Ann; New York, NY, 1811 ***2859.11*** *p11*
Donaghey, Barney; Baltimore, 1811 ***2859.11*** *p11*
Donaghey, Bridget; Philadelphia, 1865 ***5704.8*** *p201*
Donaghey, Edward 6; Philadelphia, 1856 ***5704.8*** *p129*
Donaghey, James; New York, NY, 1867 ***5704.8*** *p220*
Donaghey, Jane; Philadelphia, 1864 ***5704.8*** *p180*
Donaghey, Jane; Philadelphia, 1864 ***5704.8*** *p182*
Donaghey, John; Philadelphia, 1864 ***5704.8*** *p180*
Donaghey, John 5; Philadelphia, 1856 ***5704.8*** *p129*
Donaghey, Margaret 1; Philadelphia, 1856 ***5704.8*** *p129*
Donaghey, Michael 41; Philadelphia, 1856 ***5704.8*** *p129*
Donaghey, Pat; Baltimore, 1811 ***2859.11*** *p11*
Donaghey, Rosey 39; Philadelphia, 1856 ***5704.8*** *p129*
Donaghey, Thomas 1 mo; Philadelphia, 1856 ***5704.8*** *p129*
Donaghoe, Cornelius; America, 1741 ***4971*** *p49*
Donaghoe, Thomas; America, 1735-1743 ***4971*** *p78*
Donaghue, Catharine; Philadelphia, 1864 ***5704.8*** *p177*
Donaghue, Ellen; Philadelphia, 1864 ***5704.8*** *p177*
Donaghue, Rose Ann; Philadelphia, 1864 ***5704.8*** *p177*
Donaghue, William; Quebec, 1797 ***7603*** *p75*
Donaghy, Ann; Philadelphia, 1865 ***5704.8*** *p200*
Donaghy, Ann 6; Philadelphia, 1852 ***5704.8*** *p84*
Donaghy, Anne; New York, NY, 1815 ***2859.11*** *p29*
Donaghy, Ar.; New York, NY, 1811 ***2859.11*** *p11*
Donaghy, Archibald 8; St. John, N.B., 1848 ***5704.8*** *p43*
Donaghy, Arthur; New York, NY, 1868 ***5704.8*** *p227*
Donaghy, Biddy; St. John, N.B., 1847 ***5704.8*** *p34*
Donaghy, Biddy 12 *SEE* Donaghy, Patrick
Donaghy, Biddy 12; Philadelphia, 1847 ***5704.8*** *p1*
Donaghy, Bridget *SEE* Donaghy, Peter
Donaghy, Bridget; Philadelphia, 1847 ***5704.8*** *p32*
Donaghy, Bridget 24; Quebec, 1853 ***5704.8*** *p105*
Donaghy, Catherine *SEE* Donaghy, Patrick
Donaghy, Catherine; Philadelphia, 1847 ***5704.8*** *p1*
Donaghy, Catherine; St. John, N.B., 1853 ***5704.8*** *p100*
Donaghy, Catherine 40; Philadelphia, 1856 ***5704.8*** *p128*
Donaghy, Charles 14; Philadelphia, 1856 ***5704.8*** *p128*
Donaghy, Cicily; St. John, N.B., 1848 ***5704.8*** *p47*
Donaghy, Eliza; New York, NY, 1866 ***5704.8*** *p213*
Donaghy, Elizabeth; Philadelphia, 1851 ***5704.8*** *p70*
Donaghy, Elizabeth 12; St. John, N.B., 1847 ***5704.8*** *p34*
Donaghy, Ellen 2 *SEE* Donaghy, Patrick
Donaghy, Ellen 2; Philadelphia, 1847 ***5704.8*** *p1*
Donaghy, Fanny; New York, NY, 1868 ***5704.8*** *p228*
Donaghy, Fanny; Philadelphia, 1867 ***5704.8*** *p223*
Donaghy, George; St. John, N.B., 1847 ***5704.8*** *p11*
Donaghy, Ginny; St. John, N.B., 1847 ***5704.8*** *p11*
Donaghy, Henry; St. John, N.B., 1853 ***5704.8*** *p100*
Donaghy, Henry 9 *SEE* Donaghy, Peter
Donaghy, Henry 9; Philadelphia, 1847 ***5704.8*** *p32*
Donaghy, Henry 20; Philadelphia, 1861 ***5704.8*** *p148*
Donaghy, Hugh; Philadelphia, 1852 ***5704.8*** *p85*
Donaghy, James; New York, NY, 1866 ***5704.8*** *p213*
Donaghy, James; Philadelphia, 1847 ***53.26*** *p22*
*Relative:*Mary
Donaghy, James; Philadelphia, 1847 ***5704.8*** *p5*
Donaghy, James; St. John, N.B., 1848 ***5704.8*** *p47*
Donaghy, James 4 *SEE* Donaghy, Patrick
Donaghy, James 4; Philadelphia, 1847 ***5704.8*** *p1*
Donaghy, James 10; St. John, N.B., 1848 ***5704.8*** *p43*
Donaghy, James 11; Philadelphia, 1847 ***53.26*** *p22*
*Relative:*Mary Ann 9
Donaghy, James 11; Philadelphia, 1847 ***5704.8*** *p30*
Donaghy, James 18; Philadelphia, 1857 ***5704.8*** *p132*
Donaghy, James 24; Philadelphia, 1857 ***5704.8*** *p132*
Donaghy, James 30; Philadelphia, 1857 ***5704.8*** *p132*
Donaghy, Jane; New York, NY, 1866 ***5704.8*** *p213*
Donaghy, Jane; Philadelphia, 1868 ***5704.8*** *p225*
Donaghy, Jane 9; Philadelphia, 1852 ***5704.8*** *p84*
Donaghy, Jane 13; Quebec, 1850 ***5704.8*** *p67*
Donaghy, John; New York, NY, 1811 ***2859.11*** *p11*
Donaghy, John; New York, NY, 1815 ***2859.11*** *p29*
Donaghy, John; Philadelphia, 1850 ***53.26*** *p22*
*Relative:*Mary Ann
Donaghy, John; Philadelphia, 1850 ***5704.8*** *p68*
Donaghy, John; Philadelphia, 1851 ***5704.8*** *p70*
Donaghy, John; Philadelphia, 1852 ***5704.8*** *p84*
Donaghy, John; Quebec, 1849 ***5704.8*** *p51*
Donaghy, John; St. John, N.B., 1848 ***5704.8*** *p43*
Donaghy, John 3 *SEE* Donaghy, Patrick
Donaghy, John 3; Philadelphia, 1847 ***5704.8*** *p1*
Donaghy, John 4; Philadelphia, 1852 ***5704.8*** *p84*
Donaghy, John 12; St. John, N.B., 1848 ***5704.8*** *p43*
Donaghy, John 22; Philadelphia, 1859 ***5704.8*** *p142*
Donaghy, Joseph; Philadelphia, 1852 ***5704.8*** *p84*
Donaghy, Joseph 9 mos; St. John, N.B., 1848 ***5704.8*** *p43*
Donaghy, Joseph 20; Philadelphia, 1861 ***5704.8*** *p147*
Donaghy, Margaret *SEE* Donaghy, Peter
Donaghy, Margaret; New York, NY, 1868 ***5704.8*** *p228*
Donaghy, Margaret; Philadelphia, 1847 ***5704.8*** *p32*
Donaghy, Margaret; Philadelphia, 1851 ***5704.8*** *p81*
Donaghy, Margaret; St. John, N.B., 1848 ***5704.8*** *p43*
Donaghy, Margaret 18; Quebec, 1863 ***5704.8*** *p154*
Donaghy, Maria 5; St. John, N.B., 1848 ***5704.8*** *p43*
Donaghy, Mary *SEE* Donaghy, James
Donaghy, Mary; New York, NY, 1866 ***5704.8*** *p213*
Donaghy, Mary; Philadelphia, 1847 ***5704.8*** *p5*
Donaghy, Mary; St. John, N.B., 1848 ***5704.8*** *p38*
Donaghy, Mary; St. John, N.B., 1848 ***5704.8*** *p47*
Donaghy, Mary; St. John, N.B., 1849 ***5704.8*** *p56*
Donaghy, Mary 6; Philadelphia, 1852 ***5704.8*** *p84*
Donaghy, Mary 20; Philadelphia, 1853 ***5704.8*** *p114*
Donaghy, Mary Ann *SEE* Donaghy, John
Donaghy, Mary Ann 9 *SEE* Donaghy, James
Donaghy, Mary Ann 9; Philadelphia, 1847 ***5704.8*** *p30*
Donaghy, Mary Anne; Philadelphia, 1850 ***5704.8*** *p68*
Donaghy, Matilda; New York, NY, 1864 ***5704.8*** *p185*
Donaghy, Matilda; Philadelphia, 1851 ***5704.8*** *p76*
Donaghy, Michael 6 mos; St. John, N.B., 1847 ***5704.8*** *p11*
Donaghy, Patrick; Philadelphia, 1847 ***53.26*** *p22*
*Relative:*Catherine
*Relative:*Biddy 12
*Relative:*John 3
*Relative:*James 4
*Relative:*Ellen 2
Donaghy, Patrick; Philadelphia, 1847 ***5704.8*** *p1*
Donaghy, Patrick; St. John, N.B., 1848 ***5704.8*** *p47*
Donaghy, Peter; New Orleans, 1849 ***5704.8*** *p58*
Donaghy, Peter; Philadelphia, 1847 ***53.26*** *p22*
*Relative:*Margaret
*Relative:*Peter 11
*Relative:*Henry 9
*Relative:*Bridget
Donaghy, Peter; Philadelphia, 1847 ***5704.8*** *p32*
Donaghy, Peter 11 *SEE* Donaghy, Peter
Donaghy, Peter 11; Philadelphia, 1847 ***5704.8*** *p32*
Donaghy, Rachel; Philadelphia, 1852 ***5704.8*** *p84*
Donaghy, Robert; St. John, N.B., 1847 ***5704.8*** *p5*
Donaghy, Rose; Philadelphia, 1847 ***53.26*** *p23*
Donaghy, Rose; Philadelphia, 1847 ***5704.8*** *p22*
Donaghy, Rosey; St. John, N.B., 1848 ***5704.8*** *p47*
Donaghy, Sally 20; Philadelphia, 1853 ***5704.8*** *p114*
Donaghy, Samuel 9; St. John, N.B., 1848 ***5704.8*** *p43*
Donaghy, Sarah; New York, NY, 1868 ***5704.8*** *p228*
Donaghy, Sarah 6; Quebec, 1850 ***5704.8*** *p67*
Donaghy, Sarah 10; New York, NY, 1866 ***5704.8*** *p213*
Donaghy, Sarah 22; Philadelphia, 1864 ***5704.8*** *p161*
Donaghy, Sarah A.; Philadelphia, 1867 ***5704.8*** *p223*
Donaghy, Thomas; Philadelphia, 1864 ***5704.8*** *p177*
Donaghy, Unity 6; St. John, N.B., 1848 ***5704.8*** *p47*
Donaghy, William; New Orleans, 1849 ***5704.8*** *p58*
Donaghy, William; New York, NY, 1864 ***5704.8*** *p183*
Donaghy, William; St. John, N.B., 1852 ***5704.8*** *p93*
Donaghy, William 13; St. John, N.B., 1848 ***5704.8*** *p43*
Donaghy, William 55; Philadelphia, 1858 ***5704.8*** *p139*
Donaher, Martin 24; New Orleans, 1862 ***543.30*** *p214*
Donahew, Bryan; Ohio, 1840 ***9892.11*** *p13*
Donahoe, Ann 15; Massachusetts, 1850 ***5881.1*** *p26*
Donahoe, Cornelius; America, 1742-1743 ***4971*** *p42*
Donahoe, James; Wisconsin, n.d. ***9675.5*** *p121*
Donahoe, John; Wisconsin, n.d. ***9675.5*** *p121*
Donahoe, John 18; Massachusetts, 1849 ***5881.1*** *p30*
Donahoe, Michael; New York, NY, 1833 ***8208.4*** *p58*
Donahoo, Bryan; Ohio, 1847 ***9892.11*** *p13*
Donahoo, John; Ohio, 1840 ***9892.11*** *p13*
Donahoo, John; Ohio, 1843 ***9892.11*** *p13*
Donahoo, Morris; Ohio, 1843 ***9892.11*** *p13*
Donahowr, George; Pennsylvania, 1746 ***2444*** *p147*
Donahue, Betty 16; Massachusetts, 1849 ***5881.1*** *p27*
Donahue, Bridget; Philadelphia, 1864 ***5704.8*** *p183*
Donahue, Bridget 22; Massachusetts, 1849 ***5881.1*** *p27*
Donahue, Catharine 4; Massachusetts, 1850 ***5881.1*** *p28*
Donahue, Catharine 8; Massachusetts, 1850 ***5881.1*** *p28*
Donahue, Catharine 10; Massachusetts, 1850 ***5881.1*** *p28*
Donahue, Catharine 12; Massachusetts, 1847 ***5881.1*** *p27*
Donahue, Catharine 50; Massachusetts, 1847 ***5881.1*** *p27*
Donahue, Charles 16; Massachusetts, 1847 ***5881.1*** *p27*
Donahue, Daniel; New York, NY, 1838 ***8208.4*** *p87*
Donahue, Dennis 24; Massachusetts, 1847 ***5881.1*** *p28*
Donahue, Dennis 31; Massachusetts, 1850 ***5881.1*** *p28*
Donahue, Ellen; Massachusetts, 1850 ***5881.1*** *p28*
Donahue, Ellen 12; Massachusetts, 1850 ***5881.1*** *p28*
Donahue, Ellen 30; Massachusetts, 1849 ***5881.1*** *p28*
Donahue, Honora 29; Massachusetts, 1850 ***5881.1*** *p29*
Donahue, James; Philadelphia, 1851 ***5704.8*** *p77*
Donahue, Jeremiah 15; Massachusetts, 1849 ***5881.1*** *p29*
Donahue, Johanna 7; Massachusetts, 1849 ***5881.1*** *p30*
Donahue, Johanna 12; Massachusetts, 1849 ***5881.1*** *p30*
Donahue, John; Philadelphia, 1866 ***5704.8*** *p215*
Donahue, John 5; Massachusetts, 1849 ***5881.1*** *p30*
Donahue, John 22; Massachusetts, 1849 ***5881.1*** *p30*
Donahue, John 50; Massachusetts, 1849 ***5881.1*** *p30*
Donahue, Margaret; Philadelphia, 1850 ***5704.8*** *p64*
Donahue, Margery; America, 1866 ***5704.8*** *p213*
Donahue, Martin 26; Massachusetts, 1849 ***5881.1*** *p31*
Donahue, Mary; Philadelphia, 1865 ***5704.8*** *p196*
Donahue, Mary 2; Massachusetts, 1850 ***5881.1*** *p33*
Donahue, Mary 2; Philadelphia, 1864 ***5704.8*** *p183*
Donahue, Mary 4; Massachusetts, 1850 ***5881.1*** *p33*
Donahue, Mary 10; Massachusetts, 1849 ***5881.1*** *p31*
Donahue, Mary 12; Massachusetts, 1849 ***5881.1*** *p31*
Donahue, Mary 18; Massachusetts, 1848 ***5881.1*** *p31*
Donahue, Mary 19; Massachusetts, 1847 ***5881.1*** *p31*
Donahue, Michael 9; Massachusetts, 1847 ***5881.1*** *p31*
Donahue, Michael 20; Massachusetts, 1850 ***5881.1*** *p32*
Donahue, Michael 40; Massachusetts, 1849 ***5881.1*** *p31*
Donahue, Patrick 8; Massachusetts, 1849 ***5881.1*** *p33*
Donahue, Patrick 10; Philadelphia, 1864 ***5704.8*** *p183*
Donahue, Patrick 21; Massachusetts, 1849 ***5881.1*** *p33*
Donahue, Patrick 25; Massachusetts, 1850 ***5881.1*** *p33*
Donahue, Patrick 26; Massachusetts, 1849 ***5881.1*** *p33*
Donahue, Peter; Philadelphia, 1864 ***5704.8*** *p182*
Donahue, Phillip 8; Massachusetts, 1849 ***5881.1*** *p33*
Donahue, Phillip 30; Massachusetts, 1848 ***5881.1*** *p33*
Donahue, Sally; Philadelphia, 1850 ***5704.8*** *p64*
Donahue, Sarah 11; Philadelphia, 1851 ***5704.8*** *p77*
Donahue, Thomas 22; Massachusetts, 1849 ***5881.1*** *p34*
Donahue, William 40; Massachusetts, 1849 ***5881.1*** *p35*
Donald, Barney; New York, NY, 1811 ***2859.11*** *p11*
Donald, Bryan; America, 1737 ***4971*** *p30*
Donald, Christian; St. John, N.B., 1852 ***5704.8*** *p93*
Donald, Edward; Colorado, 1904 ***9678.2*** *p16*
Donald, Eleanor; New York, NY, 1811 ***2859.11*** *p11*
Donald, George; Virginia, 1801 ***4778.1*** *p150*
Donald, John; Maryland, 1742 ***4971*** *p106*
Donald, John; Philadelphia, 1852 ***5704.8*** *p84*
Donald, Michael; New York, NY, 1811 ***2859.11*** *p11*
Donald, Nelson; Colorado, 1904 ***9678.2*** *p16*
Donald, Patrick; Philadelphia, 1852 ***5704.8*** *p84*
Donald, Patrick 50; Philadelphia, 1803 ***53.26*** *p23*
Donald, Toal; Philadelphia, 1852 ***5704.8*** *p84*
Donald, William; Maryland, 1742 ***4971*** *p106*
Donaldsen, James 37; California, 1869 ***3840.1*** *p18*
Donaldson, Bell 36 *SEE* Donaldson, Robert
Donaldson, Ellen 9 mos; St. John, N.B., 1847 ***5704.8*** *p4*
Donaldson, James; New York, NY, 1837 ***8208.4*** *p36*
Donaldson, Jane 5 *SEE* Donaldson, Robert
Donaldson, John; New York, NY, 1838 ***8208.4*** *p63*
Donaldson, John; Quebec, 1847 ***5704.8*** *p12*
Donaldson, John 6; St. John, N.B., 1847 ***5704.8*** *p4*
Donaldson, John 18; Maryland, 1718 ***3690.1*** *p65*
Donaldson, Margaret 6; St. John, N.B., 1847 ***5704.8*** *p4*
Donaldson, Mary 20; Philadelphia, 1803 ***53.26*** *p23*

Donaldson, Mary 24 *SEE* Donaldson, Robert
Donaldson, Mathew; St. John, N.B., 1847 ***5704.8*** *p4*
Donaldson, Peter 33; Dominica, 1773 ***1219.7*** *p170*
Donaldson, Robert 46; Philadelphia, 1803 ***53.26*** *p23*
*Relative:*Bell 36
*Relative:*Mary 24
*Relative:*Jane 5
Donaldson, Sarah 3; St. John, N.B., 1847 ***5704.8*** *p4*
Donaldson, Thomas; New York, NY, 1811 ***2859.11*** *p11*
Donaldson, Walter; Illinois, 1841 ***7857*** *p3*
Donaldson, William; Illinois, 1841 ***7857*** *p3*
Donaldson, William; New York, NY, 1834 ***8208.4*** *p49*
Donally, Bridget; Quebec, 1847 ***5704.8*** *p38*
Donally, Edward; Philadelphia, 1849 ***53.26*** *p23*
Donally, Edward; Philadelphia, 1849 ***5704.8*** *p58*
Donally, John; Philadelphia, 1847 ***53.26*** *p23*
*Relative:*Mary
Donally, John; Philadelphia, 1847 ***5704.8*** *p31*
Donally, Mary *SEE* Donally, John
Donally, Mary; Philadelphia, 1847 ***5704.8*** *p31*
Donally, Michael; St. Louis, 1845 ***6013.19*** *p30*
Donally, Rose 18; Massachusetts, 1849 ***5881.1*** *p34*
Donally, Timothy 28; Massachusetts, 1849 ***5881.1*** *p34*
Donan, Thomas 23; Philadelphia, 1803 ***53.26*** *p23*
Donaty, Pete; Arkansas, 1918 ***95.2*** *p38*
Donaugey, Archibald; Quebec, 1825 ***7603*** *p62*
Donaugho, Elizabeth 22; Dominica, 1774 ***1219.7*** *p207*
Donaugho, John 34; Dominica, 1774 ***1219.7*** *p207*
Donaughy, Pierre; Quebec, 1824 ***7603*** *p55*
Donavan, Ann 20; Massachusetts, 1850 ***5881.1*** *p26*
Donavan, Bart 14; Massachusetts, 1849 ***5881.1*** *p27*
Donavan, Bridget 22; Massachusetts, 1849 ***5881.1*** *p27*
Donavan, Catharine 18; Massachusetts, 1850 ***5881.1*** *p28*
Donavan, Catharine 20; Massachusetts, 1847 ***5881.1*** *p27*
Donavan, Catharine 50; Massachusetts, 1847 ***5881.1*** *p27*
Donavan, Daniel 15; Massachusetts, 1849 ***5881.1*** *p28*
Donavan, Daniel 40; Massachusetts, 1849 ***5881.1*** *p28*
Donavan, Dennis 23; Massachusetts, 1849 ***5881.1*** *p28*
Donavan, Ellen 50; Massachusetts, 1849 ***5881.1*** *p28*
Donavan, Frederic 22; Massachusetts, 1847 ***5881.1*** *p29*
Donavan, James; America, 1847 ***1450.2*** *p32A*
Donavan, John 30; Massachusetts, 1850 ***5881.1*** *p30*
Donavan, John 43; Massachusetts, 1850 ***5881.1*** *p30*
Donavan, John 50; California, 1867 ***3840.1*** *p18*
Donavan, Julia 20; Massachusetts, 1849 ***5881.1*** *p33*
Donavan, Margaret 18; Massachusetts, 1848 ***5881.1*** *p31*
Donavan, Martin 26; Massachusetts, 1847 ***5881.1*** *p31*
Donavan, Mary 30; Massachusetts, 1850 ***5881.1*** *p32*
Donavan, Mary Ann 30; Massachusetts, 1849 ***5881.1*** *p31*
Donavan, Mathew 17; Massachusetts, 1847 ***5881.1*** *p31*
Donavan, Michael 36; Massachusetts, 1848 ***5881.1*** *p31*
Donavan, Thomas 20; Massachusetts, 1850 ***5881.1*** *p34*
Donavan, Timothy 28; Massachusetts, 1849 ***5881.1*** *p34*
Donavan, William; New York, NY, 1834 ***8208.4*** *p4*
Donavan, William 26; Massachusetts, 1849 ***5881.1*** *p34*
Donaven, Ernest A.; Kansas, 1890 ***5240.1*** *p10*
Donavich, Ivan; Iowa, 1866-1943 ***123.54*** *p16*
Donblesky, Walter; Arkansas, 1918 ***95.2*** *p38*
Dondagon, Anne; Philadelphia, 1864 ***5704.8*** *p181*
Dondekin, Patrick; New York, NY, 1839 ***8208.4*** *p95*
Dondekin, Thomas; New York, NY, 1839 ***8208.4*** *p95*
Dondelinger, Charles; Wisconsin, n.d. ***9675.5*** *p121*
Dondle, Jacob; Philadelphia, 1757 ***9973.7*** *p32*
Done, William; Virginia, 1618 ***6219*** *p200*
Donegan, Francis 46; California, 1868 ***3840.1*** *p18*
Doneghy, Mary Ann; St. John, N.B., 1848 ***5704.8*** *p44*
Donehoe, James E. 21; West Virginia, 1887 ***9788.3*** *p9*
Donehy, Michael 18; Massachusetts, 1849 ***5881.1*** *p32*
Donell, Jane; New York, NY, 1811 ***2859.11*** *p11*
Donelly, Charles; America, 1737 ***4971*** *p73*
Donelly, Francis; Illinois, 1858 ***5012.39*** *p54*
Donelly, Michael; St. John, N.B., 1850 ***5704.8*** *p62*
Donelly, Michael 30; Massachusetts, 1849 ***5881.1*** *p32*
Donelly, Sarah; America, 1742 ***4971*** *p35*
Donelly, Sarah; Annapolis, MD, 1742 ***4971*** *p93*
Donelly, Sarah; Maryland, 1742 ***4971*** *p106*
Donevan, Daniel 36; New Orleans, 1862 ***543.30*** *p217*
Donevan, Florence 20; Massachusetts, 1849 ***5881.1*** *p29*
Dongus, Gustav; America, 1884 ***1450.2*** *p7B*
Dongworth, John; West Indies, 1764 ***1219.7*** *p101*
Doniche, Hermann; Wisconsin, n.d. ***9675.5*** *p121*
Donildson, Daniel; New York, NY, 1868 ***5704.8*** *p229*
Donildson, Jane; New York, NY, 1868 ***5704.8*** *p229*
Donlan, Catharine 18; Massachusetts, 1847 ***5881.1*** *p27*
Donlan, John 22; Massachusetts, 1849 ***5881.1*** *p30*
Donlan, Katie O'Neil 66; Arizona, 1909 ***9228.40*** *p11*
Donlan, Martin 21; Massachusetts, 1849 ***5881.1*** *p32*
Donlea, Cornelius; Montreal, 1825 ***7603*** *p98*
Donley, Catherine; Philadelphia, 1852 ***5704.8*** *p88*
Donley, Jane 18; Philadelphia, 1864 ***5704.8*** *p156*
Donley, Patrick 18; Massachusetts, 1847 ***5881.1*** *p33*
Donly, Michael 18; St. John, N.B., 1853 ***5704.8*** *p110*
Donn, Arthur; Virginia, 1643 ***6219*** *p205*
Donn, Clemt.; Virginia, 1639 ***6219*** *p162*
Donn, Mary; Philadelphia, 1851 ***5704.8*** *p76*
Donnac, Bon. 40; New Orleans, 1836 ***778.5*** *p169*
Donnan, David; America, 1816 ***1450.2*** *p31A*
Donnat, Mr. 26; New Orleans, 1839 ***778.5*** *p169*
Donne, . . .; Canada, 1776-1783 ***9786*** *p42*
Donne, Richard; Virginia, 1639 ***6219*** *p157*
Donnebauer, Michael; Wisconsin, n.d. ***9675.5*** *p121*
Donned, . . .; Virginia, 1648 ***6219*** *p246*
Donnehover, George; Pennsylvania, 1746 ***2444*** *p146*
Donnel, Barney 10; Philadelphia, 1852 ***5704.8*** *p91*
Donnel, Charles; Quebec, 1850 ***5704.8*** *p67*
Donnel, Ellen 8; Philadelphia, 1852 ***5704.8*** *p91*
Donnel, John; Philadelphia, 1852 ***5704.8*** *p91*
Donnel, Margaret; Philadelphia, 1847 ***53.26*** *p23*
Donnel, Margaret; Philadelphia, 1847 ***5704.8*** *p31*
Donnel, Sarah; Philadelphia, 1852 ***5704.8*** *p91*
Donnel, Susan; Philadelphia, 1852 ***5704.8*** *p91*
Donnel, William 20; Wilmington, DE, 1831 ***6508.7*** *p160*
Donnell, . . . 8 mos; New York, NY, 1866 ***5704.8*** *p214*
Donnell, Brine 3; St. John, N.B., 1847 ***5704.8*** *p26*
Donnell, Catherine; Philadelphia, 1852 ***5704.8*** *p88*
Donnell, Catherine; St. John, N.B., 1847 ***5704.8*** *p26*
Donnell, Catherine 9; Philadelphia, 1857 ***5704.8*** *p133*
Donnell, Catherine 24; Philadelphia, 1854 ***5704.8*** *p122*
Donnell, Charles 23; Philadelphia, 1854 ***5704.8*** *p118*
Donnell, Daniel; New York, NY, 1816 ***2859.11*** *p29*
Donnell, Daniel; Quebec, 1849 ***5704.8*** *p57*
Donnell, Daniel 2; Quebec, 1849 ***5704.8*** *p57*
Donnell, Dennis 15; Philadelphia, 1861 ***5704.8*** *p148*
Donnell, Edward 22; Philadelphia, 1864 ***5704.8*** *p155*
Donnell, Edward 28; Philadelphia, 1859 ***5704.8*** *p141*
Donnell, Elizabeth; Philadelphia, 1811 ***2859.11*** *p11*
Donnell, Ellen; Quebec, 1853 ***5704.8*** *p104*
Donnell, Ellen 2; New York, NY, 1866 ***5704.8*** *p214*
Donnell, Francis; Philadelphia, 1851 ***5704.8*** *p79*
Donnell, Giles 18; Philadelphia, 1856 ***5704.8*** *p128*
Donnell, Isabella 20; Philadelphia, 1854 ***5704.8*** *p116*
Donnell, Isabella 22; Philadelphia, 1854 ***5704.8*** *p121*
Donnell, James; New York, NY, 1816 ***2859.11*** *p29*
Donnell, James; Philadelphia, 1853 ***5704.8*** *p102*
Donnell, James; Quebec, 1853 ***5704.8*** *p104*
Donnell, Jane; Philadelphia, 1868 ***5704.8*** *p226*
Donnell, Jane; St. John, N.B., 1847 ***5704.8*** *p5*
Donnell, Jane 8; Quebec, 1853 ***5704.8*** *p104*
Donnell, John; Philadelphia, 1851 ***5704.8*** *p70*
Donnell, John; Philadelphia, 1854 ***5704.8*** *p116*
Donnell, John; Quebec, 1850 ***5704.8*** *p67*
Donnell, John; Quebec, 1853 ***5704.8*** *p104*
Donnell, John; St. John, N.B., 1853 ***5704.8*** *p98*
Donnell, John 1; St. John, N.B., 1847 ***5704.8*** *p26*
Donnell, John 4; Quebec, 1849 ***5704.8*** *p57*
Donnell, John 19; Philadelphia, 1853 ***5704.8*** *p108*
Donnell, Maggie; Philadelphia, 1868 ***5704.8*** *p226*
Donnell, Manus; New York, NY, 1864 ***5704.8*** *p170*
Donnell, Margaret; Philadelphia, 1852 ***5704.8*** *p91*
Donnell, Margaret; Philadelphia, 1853 ***5704.8*** *p101*
Donnell, Mary; New York, NY, 1865 ***5704.8*** *p191*
Donnell, Mary 17; Philadelphia, 1854 ***5704.8*** *p118*
Donnell, Mary 20; Philadelphia, 1864 ***5704.8*** *p155*
Donnell, Mary A.; New York, NY, 1866 ***5704.8*** *p214*
Donnell, Michael; Philadelphia, 1847 ***53.26*** *p23*
Donnell, Michael; Philadelphia, 1847 ***5704.8*** *p14*
Donnell, Nancy; Philadelphia, 1850 ***53.26*** *p23*
Donnell, Nancy; Philadelphia, 1850 ***5704.8*** *p59*
Donnell, Nancy 40; Philadelphia, 1861 ***5704.8*** *p148*
Donnell, Neal 18; Philadelphia, 1853 ***5704.8*** *p113*
Donnell, Patrick; America, 1736 ***4971*** *p80*
Donnell, Rebecca; St. John, N.B., 1851 ***5704.8*** *p72*
Donnell, Robert; Philadelphia, 1850 ***5704.8*** *p63*
Donnell, Robert 15; St. John, N.B., 1865 ***5704.8*** *p165*
Donnell, Samuel 9; Quebec, 1849 ***5704.8*** *p57*
Donnell, Susan A.; New York, NY, 1865 ***5704.8*** *p191*
Donnell, Teresa; America, 1865 ***5704.8*** *p204*
Donnell, Teressa 3 mos; Quebec, 1851 ***5704.8*** *p74*
Donnell, Thomas 4; Quebec, 1853 ***5704.8*** *p104*
Donnell, William; Philadelphia, 1852 ***5704.8*** *p91*
Donnell, William; Quebec, 1849 ***5704.8*** *p57*
Donnell, William 17; St. John, N.B., 1858 ***5704.8*** *p137*
Donnelley, John; Philadelphia, 1849 ***53.26*** *p23*
Donnelley, John; Philadelphia, 1849 ***5704.8*** *p54*
Donnelly, Miss; Philadelphia, 1864 ***5704.8*** *p178*
Donnelly, Alice; Philadelphia, 1850 ***5704.8*** *p64*
Donnelly, Alice; Philadelphia, 1864 ***5704.8*** *p174*
Donnelly, Ann; Philadelphia, 1851 ***5704.8*** *p80*
Donnelly, Ann 2; Massachusetts, 1849 ***5881.1*** *p26*
Donnelly, Ann 6 *SEE* Donnelly, Ellen
Donnelly, Ann 6; Philadelphia, 1848 ***5704.8*** *p46*
Donnelly, Ann 20; Philadelphia, 1860 ***5704.8*** *p145*
Donnelly, Anthony 20; Massachusetts, 1847 ***5881.1*** *p26*
Donnelly, Beranrd 10 *SEE* Donnelly, Ellen
Donnelly, Bernard; New York, NY, 1868 ***5704.8*** *p227*
Donnelly, Bernard 10; Philadelphia, 1848 ***5704.8*** *p46*
Donnelly, Bridget 10; Massachusetts, 1849 ***5881.1*** *p27*
Donnelly, Catharine 20; Massachusetts, 1847 ***5881.1*** *p28*
Donnelly, Catharine 25; Massachusetts, 1847 ***5881.1*** *p27*
Donnelly, Catherine; Canada, 1840 ***7036*** *p122*
*Sister:*Mary
Donnelly, Catherine 4 *SEE* Donnelly, Ellen
Donnelly, Catherine 4; Philadelphia, 1848 ***5704.8*** *p46*
Donnelly, Catherine 17; Philadelphia, 1861 ***5704.8*** *p149*
Donnelly, Charles 28; New Orleans, 1862 ***543.30*** *p216*
Donnelly, Edmond; America, 1742 ***4971*** *p70*
Donnelly, Edward 27; Philadelphia, 1803 ***53.26*** *p23*
Donnelly, Ellen; Philadelphia, 1848 ***53.26*** *p23*
*Relative:*William
*Relative:*Beranrd 10
*Relative:*Margaret 8
*Relative:*Ann 6
*Relative:*Catherine 4
*Relative:*Hugh 2
Donnelly, Ellen; Philadelphia, 1848 ***5704.8*** *p46*
Donnelly, Ellen; Quebec, 1851 ***5704.8*** *p75*
Donnelly, Ellen 5; Philadelphia, 1861 ***5704.8*** *p149*
Donnelly, Ellen 8; Philadelphia, 1851 ***5704.8*** *p79*
Donnelly, Ellen 50; Philadelphia, 1861 ***5704.8*** *p149*
Donnelly, Francis; New York, NY, 1838 ***8208.4*** *p64*
Donnelly, Henry; St. John, N.B., 1852 ***5704.8*** *p93*
Donnelly, Henry 40; Massachusetts, 1847 ***5881.1*** *p29*
Donnelly, Honora 4; Massachusetts, 1849 ***5881.1*** *p29*
Donnelly, Honora 35; Massachusetts, 1849 ***5881.1*** *p29*
Donnelly, Hugh 2 *SEE* Donnelly, Ellen
Donnelly, Hugh 2; Philadelphia, 1848 ***5704.8*** *p46*
Donnelly, Isabella; Quebec, 1852 ***5704.8*** *p98*
Donnelly, James; America, 1866 ***5704.8*** *p209*
Donnelly, James; New York, NY, 1816 ***2859.11*** *p29*
Donnelly, James; New York, NY, 1866 ***5704.8*** *p212*
Donnelly, James; Philadelphia, 1850 ***53.26*** *p23*
Donnelly, James; Philadelphia, 1850 ***5704.8*** *p68*
Donnelly, James; Philadelphia, 1864 ***5704.8*** *p172*
Donnelly, James; Philadelphia, 1864 ***5704.8*** *p178*
Donnelly, James; Quebec, 1851 ***5704.8*** *p75*
Donnelly, James; St. John, N.B., 1850 ***5704.8*** *p66*
Donnelly, James 6; Philadelphia, 1861 ***5704.8*** *p149*
Donnelly, James 7; Philadelphia, 1864 ***5704.8*** *p176*
Donnelly, James 18; Massachusetts, 1847 ***5881.1*** *p29*
Donnelly, James 24; St. John, N.B., 1853 ***5704.8*** *p110*
Donnelly, James 31; California, 1867 ***3840.1*** *p18*
Donnelly, Jane; America, 1866 ***5704.8*** *p206*
Donnelly, Jane; St. John, N.B., 1850 ***5704.8*** *p67*
Donnelly, Jane 7; Philadelphia, 1861 ***5704.8*** *p149*
Donnelly, Jane 24; Philadelphia, 1854 ***5704.8*** *p120*
Donnelly, John; New York, NY, 1816 ***2859.11*** *p29*
Donnelly, John; Philadelphia, 1847 ***53.26*** *p23*
Donnelly, John; Philadelphia, 1847 ***5704.8*** *p31*
Donnelly, John; Quebec, 1849 ***5704.8*** *p52*
Donnelly, John 3 mos; Philadelphia, 1851 ***5704.8*** *p80*
Donnelly, John 3; St. John, N.B., 1852 ***5704.8*** *p93*
Donnelly, John 5; Philadelphia, 1864 ***5704.8*** *p176*
Donnelly, John 6; Philadelphia, 1851 ***5704.8*** *p79*
Donnelly, John 18; Philadelphia, 1864 ***5704.8*** *p157*
Donnelly, John 25; Massachusetts, 1850 ***5881.1*** *p30*
Donnelly, John 50; Philadelphia, 1861 ***5704.8*** *p149*
Donnelly, Margaret; New York, NY, 1866 ***5704.8*** *p206*
Donnelly, Margaret 8 *SEE* Donnelly, Ellen
Donnelly, Margaret 8; Philadelphia, 1848 ***5704.8*** *p46*
Donnelly, Margaret 12; Massachusetts, 1849 ***5881.1*** *p32*
Donnelly, Margaret 18; Quebec, 1858 ***5704.8*** *p138*
Donnelly, Martha; America, 1736 ***4971*** *p12*
Donnelly, Mary *SEE* Donnelly, Catherine
Donnelly, Mary; Philadelphia, 1864 ***5704.8*** *p178*
Donnelly, Mary; St. John, N.B., 1847 ***5704.8*** *p19*
Donnelly, Mary 11; Philadelphia, 1851 ***5704.8*** *p79*
Donnelly, Mary 12; Philadelphia, 1861 ***5704.8*** *p149*
Donnelly, Mary 20; Philadelphia, 1857 ***5704.8*** *p132*
Donnelly, Mason; America, 1741 ***4971*** *p16*
Donnelly, Matilda; Philadelphia, 1848 ***53.26*** *p23*
Donnelly, Matilda; Philadelphia, 1848 ***5704.8*** *p45*
Donnelly, Michael; New York, NY, 1834 ***8208.4*** *p1*
Donnelly, Mick; Philadelphia, 1847 ***53.26*** *p23*
Donnelly, Mick; Philadelphia, 1847 ***5704.8*** *p22*
Donnelly, Patrick; America, 1866 ***5704.8*** *p214*
Donnelly, Patrick; New York, NY, 1816 ***2859.11*** *p29*
Donnelly, Patrick; New York, NY, 1836 ***8208.4*** *p14*
Donnelly, Patrick 4; Philadelphia, 1851 ***5704.8*** *p79*
Donnelly, Patrick 10; St. John, N.B., 1850 ***5704.8*** *p67*
Donnelly, Patrick 15; Philadelphia, 1861 ***5704.8*** *p149*
Donnelly, Patrick 40; Massachusetts, 1848 ***5881.1*** *p33*
Donnelly, Peter; New York, NY, 1837 ***8208.4*** *p52*
Donnelly, Peter 13; Massachusetts, 1849 ***5881.1*** *p33*
Donnelly, Robert; New York, NY, 1816 ***2859.11*** *p29*
Donnelly, Robert Joseph 21; Kansas, 1888 ***5240.1*** *p72*
Donnelly, Rosa; St. John, N.B., 1852 ***5704.8*** *p93*
Donnelly, Rose; America, 1866 ***5704.8*** *p209*
Donnelly, Rose; Philadelphia, 1847 ***53.26*** *p23*
Donnelly, Rose; Philadelphia, 1847 ***5704.8*** *p2*

122 *FOR A COMPLETE EXPLANATION OF ENTRY, SEE "HOW TO READ A CITATION" SECTION*

Donnelly, Rose; Philadelphia, 1864 ***5704.8*** *p177*
Donnelly, Sarah; Quebec, 1847 ***5704.8*** *p36*
Donnelly, Sarah 18; Philadelphia, 1853 ***5704.8*** *p108*
Donnelly, Stephen 20; Philadelphia, 1857 ***5704.8*** *p133*
Donnelly, Susan; Philadelphia, 1867 ***5704.8*** *p217*
Donnelly, Thomas; Quebec, 1822 ***7603*** *p62*
Donnelly, Thomas 8; Massachusetts, 1849 ***5881.1*** *p34*
Donnelly, William *SEE* Donnelly, Ellen
Donnelly, William; New York, NY, 1811 ***2859.11*** *p11*
Donnelly, William; New York, NY, 1838 ***8208.4*** *p82*
Donnelly, William; Philadelphia, 1848 ***5704.8*** *p46*
Donnely, Catherine; Philadelphia, 1850 ***5704.8*** *p69*
Donnely, Chas. M. 38; New York, NY, 1893 ***9026.4*** *p41*
Donnely, Ellen; Philadelphia, 1850 ***5704.8*** *p69*
Donnely, James; Philadelphia, 1850 ***5704.8*** *p69*
Donnely, Michael; Philadelphia, 1850 ***5704.8*** *p69*
Donner, Barbara Baumann *SEE* Donner, Heinrich
Donner, Berhnard 24; Port uncertain, 1839 ***778.5*** *p169*
Donner, Franzrois 23; Port uncertain, 1839 ***778.5*** *p169*
Donner, Fred; Ohio, 1860 ***5647.5*** *p63*
Donner, George 22; America, 1838 ***778.5*** *p169*
Donner, H. 27; New York, NY, 1839 ***5647.5*** *p45*
Donner, Heinrich 27; New York, NY, 1839 ***5647.5*** *p45*
*Wife:*Barbara Baumann
Donner, Sophia M.; Ohio, 1837-1839 ***5647.5*** *p59*
Donner, Sophia M.; Ohio, 1839 ***5647.5*** *p4*
Donnersberger, Anton; Cincinnati, 1830 ***8582.1*** *p51*
Donnersberger, Anton; Cincinnati, 1860 ***8582.2*** *p66*
Donnersberger, Anton; New Orleans, 1819 ***8582*** *p7*
Donneville, Charlotte 18; Quebec, 1853 ***5704.8*** *p104*
Donniger, Daniel 22; Maryland, 1722 ***3690.1*** *p65*
Donninger, Michael; Indiana, 1848 ***9117*** *p16*
Donnings, Georg; Virginia, 1642 ***6219*** *p196*
Donny, . . .; Canada, 1776-1783 ***9786*** *p19*
Donny, Eliza; Quebec, 1847 ***5704.8*** *p36*
Donny, Eliza 11; Quebec, 1847 ***5704.8*** *p37*
Donny, Mary 13; Quebec, 1847 ***5704.8*** *p36*
Donoghoe, Cornelius; America, 1739 ***4971*** *p46*
Donoghoe, Cornelius; America, 1739 ***4971*** *p47*
Donoghoe, Cornelius; America, 1741 ***4971*** *p56*
Donoghoe, James; America, 1737 ***4971*** *p36*
Donoghoe, John; America, 1743 ***4971*** *p43*
Donoghoe, Michael; America, 1738 ***4971*** *p9*
Donoghoe, Thomas; America, 1742 ***4971*** *p80*
Donoghue, Oliver R.; Indiana, 1837 ***9117*** *p15*
Donoghue, Timothy; Arkansas, 1918 ***95.2*** *p38*
Donoher, Simon; New England, 1816 ***2859.11*** *p29*
Donohin, James; New York, NY, 1864 ***5704.8*** *p176*
Donoho, William; New York, NY, 1836 ***8208.4*** *p22*
Donohoe, James; Philadelphia, 1848 ***53.26*** *p23*
*Relative:*Margaret
Donohoe, James; Philadelphia, 1848 ***5704.8*** *p46*
Donohoe, Margaret *SEE* Donohoe, James
Donohoe, Margaret; America, 1736 ***4971*** *p44*
Donohoe, Margaret; Philadelphia, 1848 ***5704.8*** *p46*
Donohoe, Mary Ann; Philadelphia, 1848 ***53.26*** *p23*
Donohoe, Mary Ann 3 mos; Philadelphia, 1848 ***5704.8*** *p46*
Donohoe, Michael; America, 1741 ***4971*** *p29*
Donohoe, Thomas; New York, NY, 1838 ***8208.4*** *p73*
Donohoe, Timothy; America, 1742-1743 ***4971*** *p42*
Donohoe, Wm.; America, 1738 ***4971*** *p31*
Donohoo, James; New York, NY, 1815 ***2859.11*** *p29*
Donohue, Ann; Quebec, 1823 ***7603*** *p80*
Donohue, Anne; Philadelphia, 1870 ***5704.8*** *p239*
Donohue, Biddy 20; Philadelphia, 1855 ***5704.8*** *p124*
Donohue, James; New York, NY, 1869 ***5704.8*** *p233*
Donohue, Jean-Baptiste; Quebec, 1769 ***7603*** *p89*
Donohue, Martin Patrick; Arkansas, 1918 ***95.2*** *p38*
Donohue, Owen; Nevada, 1865 ***2764.35*** *p17*
Donohue, Thomas; Montreal, 1767 ***7603*** *p64*
Donoly, Hannah; Philadelphia, 1850 ***5704.8*** *p64*
Donoly, Patrick; Philadelphia, 1850 ***5704.8*** *p64*
Donoly, Rosanna 3 mos; Philadelphia, 1850 ***5704.8*** *p64*
Donovan, Ann 20; Massachusetts, 1849 ***5881.1*** *p26*
Donovan, Bartholimew; New York, NY, 1838 ***8208.4*** *p81*
Donovan, Daniel; America, 1736 ***4971*** *p44*
Donovan, Daniel; America, 1741 ***4971*** *p42*
Donovan, Daniel; Quebec, 1823 ***7603*** *p65*
Donovan, Daniel 16; Philadelphia, 1774 ***1219.7*** *p175*
Donovan, James; America, 1740 ***4971*** *p15*
Donovan, James; Maryland, 1740 ***4971*** *p91*
Donovan, James; Philadelphia, 1741 ***4971*** *p92*
Donovan, James 22; New Orleans, 1862 ***543.30*** *p58*
Donovan, James 27; Philadelphia, 1774 ***1219.7*** *p175*
Donovan, James J.; Washington, 1859-1920 ***2872.1*** *p10*
Donovan, Jeremiah; New York, NY, 1840 ***8208.4*** *p109*
Donovan, Johanna 18; Massachusetts, 1850 ***5881.1*** *p30*
Donovan, John; Illinois, 1860 ***5012.39*** *p90*
Donovan, Julia 20; Massachusetts, 1849 ***5881.1*** *p30*
Donovan, Margaret; America, 1740 ***4971*** *p15*
Donovan, Martin; Sorel, Que., 1803 ***7603*** *p75*
Donovan, Michael; Wisconsin, n.d. ***9675.5*** *p121*
Donovan, Rickard; America, 1736 ***4971*** *p44*
Donovan, Rickard; America, 1736 ***4971*** *p45*
Donovan, Thomas 30; Harris Co., TX, 1898 ***6254*** *p4*
Donovan, Timothy 23; Maryland, 1775 ***1219.7*** *p247*
Donragh, William; Quebec, 1851 ***5704.8*** *p75*
Donshea, Isaac; New York, NY, 1833 ***8208.4*** *p79*
Donthart, Isabella; Philadelphia, 1853 ***5704.8*** *p102*
Donthart, Jane 3; Philadelphia, 1853 ***5704.8*** *p102*
Donveau, Mr. 49; New Orleans, 1829 ***778.5*** *p169*
Donzell, Anne-Barbe *SEE* Donzell, George
Donzell, George 40; Halifax, N.S., 1752 ***7074.6*** *p207*
With family of 1
Donzell, George 40; Halifax, N.S., 1752 ***7074.6*** *p209*
*Wife:*Anne-Barbe
Doobees, Jon.; Virginia, 1638 ***6219*** *p14*
Doodle, Mary; Quebec, 1809 ***7603*** *p98*
Doody, John 15; Massachusetts, 1849 ***5881.1*** *p30*
Doody, Nicholas; New York, NY, 1836 ***8208.4*** *p13*
Doody, Richard; Massachusetts, 1847 ***5881.1*** *p34*
Doogan, Edward 21; St. John, N.B., 1861 ***5704.8*** *p147*
Doogan, John; New York, NY, 1816 ***2859.11*** *p29*
Doogan, Sophia 19; St. John, N.B., 1862 ***5704.8*** *p150*
Doogan, Sophia 19; St. John, N.B., 1862 ***5704.8*** *p151*
Doogan, William; America, 1742 ***4971*** *p29*
Doohan, Catherine 25; Philadelphia, 1854 ***5704.8*** *p117*
Doohan, Edward 12; St. John, N.B., 1852 ***5704.8*** *p95*
Doohan, Margaret 22; Philadelphia, 1857 ***5704.8*** *p134*
Doohan, Mary; Philadelphia, 1852 ***5704.8*** *p96*
Doohan, Mary; Philadelphia, 1866 ***5704.8*** *p215*
Doohan, Mary 7; St. John, N.B., 1852 ***5704.8*** *p95*
Doohan, Michael; St. John, N.B., 1852 ***5704.8*** *p95*
Doohan, Thomas; St. John, N.B., 1852 ***5704.8*** *p84*
Dooher, James; St. John, N.B., 1847 ***5704.8*** *p34*
Doolan, Margaret 40; Massachusetts, 1850 ***5881.1*** *p32*
Doolan, Patrick; Illinois, 1855 ***7857*** *p3*
Dooley, Ann 10; Massachusetts, 1850 ***5881.1*** *p26*
Dooley, Bridget 40; Massachusetts, 1849 ***5881.1*** *p27*
Dooley, Cornelius; New York, NY, 1836 ***8208.4*** *p13*
Dooley, Frank 45; Massachusetts, 1849 ***5881.1*** *p29*
Dooley, Jeremiah 29; Massachusetts, 1849 ***5881.1*** *p30*
Dooley, John; Virginia, 1844 ***4626.16*** *p12*
Dooley, John 38; Massachusetts, 1848 ***5881.1*** *p29*
Dooley, Martin 22; Massachusetts, 1848 ***5881.1*** *p31*
Dooley, Martin 22; Massachusetts, 1850 ***5881.1*** *p33*
Dooley, Mary 13; Massachusetts, 1850 ***5881.1*** *p32*
Dooley, Michael 11; Massachusetts, 1849 ***5881.1*** *p32*
Dooley, Patrick 13; Massachusetts, 1849 ***5881.1*** *p33*
Dooley, Patrick 29; New Orleans, 1862 ***543.30*** *p221*
Dooley, Patrick 29; New Orleans, 1863 ***543.30*** *p374*
Dooley, Thomas; Massachusetts, 1841 ***7036*** *p125*
Doolin, Maurice; America, 1740 ***4971*** *p56*
Doolin, Thomas; America, 1740 ***4971*** *p56*
Dooling, Darby; America, 1741 ***4971*** *p60*
Dooling, Michael; New York, NY, 1815 ***2859.11*** *p29*
Doona, Julia 30; Massachusetts, 1850 ***5881.1*** *p30*
Doonan, Bryan 20; Massachusetts, 1848 ***5881.1*** *p27*
Doonan, Frank 10; Massachusetts, 1850 ***5881.1*** *p29*
Doonan, John; Quebec, 1852 ***5704.8*** *p86*
Doonan, John; Quebec, 1852 ***5704.8*** *p90*
Doonan, Patrick 12; Massachusetts, 1850 ***5881.1*** *p33*
Dooney, John; New York, NY, 1816 ***2859.11*** *p29*
Dooney, Timothy 24; Massachusetts, 1849 ***5881.1*** *p34*
Dooris, Bernard; Philadelphia, 1852 ***5704.8*** *p92*
Dooris, Bridget 18; Philadelphia, 1864 ***5704.8*** *p157*
Dooris, Felix 11; Philadelphia, 1864 ***5704.8*** *p157*
Dooris, John 50; St. John, N.B., 1853 ***5704.8*** *p110*
Dooris, Patrick 15; Philadelphia, 1864 ***5704.8*** *p157*
Dooris, William 20; Philadelphia, 1864 ***5704.8*** *p157*
Doorish, Bernard; New York, NY, 1811 ***2859.11*** *p11*
Doowe, Herman; Washington, 1859-1920 ***2872.1*** *p11*
Dopkus, John; Wisconsin, n.d. ***9675.5*** *p121*
Dopler, Francois 35; New Orleans, 1836 ***778.5*** *p169*
Doppel, Andrew; Wisconsin, n.d. ***9675.5*** *p121*
Doppes, Johann Bernard; America, 1847 ***8582.2*** *p8*
Doppler, Andreas; Cincinnati, 1869-1887 ***8582*** *p7*
Doppler, Andreas; New Orleans, 1834 ***8582.1*** *p7*
Doppler, Elisa 30; Port uncertain, 1839 ***778.5*** *p169*
Doppler, Schosephina 24; Port uncertain, 1839 ***778.5*** *p169*
Dopson, John; Quebec, 1492-1825 ***7603*** *p75*
Dor, Simon 44; New Orleans, 1862 ***543.30*** *p214*
Doran, Mrs. 20; Massachusetts, 1848 ***5881.1*** *p31*
Doran, Bridget; St. John, N.B., 1850 ***5704.8*** *p65*
Doran, Bridget 3; St. John, N.B., 1850 ***5704.8*** *p65*
Doran, Bridget 24; Massachusetts, 1849 ***5881.1*** *p27*
Doran, Bridget 40; Massachusetts, 1849 ***5881.1*** *p27*
Doran, Bryan; America, 1742 ***4971*** *p30*
Doran, Bryan; Annapolis, MD, 1742 ***4971*** *p93*
Doran, Bryan; Maryland, 1742 ***4971*** *p106*
Doran, Catherine *SEE* Doran, Thomas
Doran, Catherine; Philadelphia, 1847 ***5704.8*** *p14*
Doran, Catherine 35; Quebec, 1858 ***5704.8*** *p137*
Doran, Daniel; New York, NY, 1864 ***5704.8*** *p171*
Doran, Ellen 4; Quebec, 1858 ***5704.8*** *p137*
Doran, Francis 32; Massachusetts, 1848 ***5881.1*** *p29*
Doran, Henry; New York, NY, 1864 ***5704.8*** *p173*
Doran, Hugh 23; Massachusetts, 1849 ***5881.1*** *p29*
Doran, James; America, 1738 ***4971*** *p31*
Doran, James; America, 1741 ***4971*** *p16*
Doran, James; Philadelphia, 1850 ***53.26*** *p23*
Doran, James; Philadelphia, 1850 ***5704.8*** *p61*
Doran, James 9 mos; Quebec, 1858 ***5704.8*** *p137*
Doran, James 11; Philadelphia, 1865 ***5704.8*** *p192*
Doran, Lawrence 22; Massachusetts, 1848 ***5881.1*** *p31*
Doran, Margaret 2 *SEE* Doran, Thomas
Doran, Margaret 2; Philadelphia, 1847 ***5704.8*** *p14*
Doran, Mary *SEE* Doran, Thomas
Doran, Mary; New York, NY, 1867 ***5704.8*** *p218*
Doran, Mary; Philadelphia, 1847 ***5704.8*** *p14*
Doran, Mary 7 *SEE* Doran, Thomas
Doran, Mary 7; Philadelphia, 1847 ***5704.8*** *p14*
Doran, Mary 25; Massachusetts, 1849 ***5881.1*** *p32*
Doran, Michael; New York, NY, 1840 ***8208.4*** *p112*
Doran, Patrick; America, 1740 ***4971*** *p69*
Doran, Patrick; St. John, N.B., 1852 ***5704.8*** *p95*
Doran, Paul; New York, NY, 1816 ***2859.11*** *p29*
Doran, Phelemy; America, 1742 ***4971*** *p69*
Doran, Richard; California, 1863 ***3840.1*** *p16*
Doran, Robert 49; California, 1873 ***2769.10*** *p3*
Doran, Sarah; Philadelphia, 1866 ***5704.8*** *p210*
Doran, Sarah 4 *SEE* Doran, Thomas
Doran, Sarah 4; Philadelphia, 1847 ***5704.8*** *p14*
Doran, Thomas; Philadelphia, 1847 ***53.26*** *p23*
*Relative:*Catherine
*Relative:*Mary
*Relative:*Mary 7
*Relative:*Sarah 4
*Relative:*Margaret 2
Doran, Thomas; Philadelphia, 1847 ***5704.8*** *p14*
Doran, William; St. John, N.B., 1851 ***5704.8*** *p77*
Doran, William 6; Quebec, 1858 ***5704.8*** *p137*
Dorare, Rosetta; Philadelphia, 1864 ***5704.8*** *p185*
Doraty, Daniel 15; Massachusetts, 1847 ***5881.1*** *p28*
Dorcey, Patrick 21; Massachusetts, 1849 ***5881.1*** *p33*
Dorder, . . .; Canada, 1776-1783 ***9786*** *p19*
Dore, James 21; Canada, 1838 ***4535.12*** *p113*
Dore, John; New York, NY, 1836 ***8208.4*** *p13*
Dore, Thomas 23; Virginia, 1774 ***1219.7*** *p238*
Doren, . . .; Canada, 1776-1783 ***9786*** *p19*
Doren, John; Quebec, 1823 ***7603*** *p90*
Doren, Susy; St. John, N.B., 1847 ***5704.8*** *p25*
Dorey, . . .; Halifax, N.S., 1752 ***7074.6*** *p230*
Dorfel, . . .; Ohio, 1881 ***3702.7*** *p439*
Dorfeuille, Joseph; Cincinnati, 1823 ***8582.3*** *p88*
Dorffer, . . .; Canada, 1776-1783 ***9786*** *p19*
Dorffler, . . .; Canada, 1776-1783 ***9786*** *p20*
Dorgain, P. 23; New Orleans, 1829 ***778.5*** *p169*
Dorgan, Mr. 32; Port uncertain, 1839 ***778.5*** *p170*
Dorgan, Catharine 4; Massachusetts, 1847 ***5881.1*** *p27*
Dorgan, Jeremiah 22; New Orleans, 1862 ***543.30*** *p219*
Dorgan, Patrick; New York, NY, 1839 ***8208.4*** *p94*
Dorgaten, Matth; New York, 1881 ***3702.7*** *p445*
Dorgathen, Matth; Halifax, N.S., 1881 ***3702.7*** *p462*
Dorgathen, Matth; New York, 1881 ***3702.7*** *p462*
Dorgau, Mr. 32; Port uncertain, 1839 ***778.5*** *p170*
Dorge, . . .; Canada, 1776-1783 ***9786*** *p20*
Dorian, Charles; Shreveport, LA, 1878 ***7129*** *p44*
Dorian, Susan 21; Philadelphia, 1865 ***5704.8*** *p164*
Dorich, Anton; Iowa, 1866-1943 ***123.54*** *p16*
Dorie, Mrs. 22; New Orleans, 1827 ***778.5*** *p170*
Dorien, John; New York, NY, 1839 ***8208.4*** *p102*
Dorin, Edward 20; Philadelphia, 1865 ***5704.8*** *p164*
Doring, . . .; Canada, 1776-1783 ***9786*** *p20*
Doring, Andreas 84; America, 1897 ***1763*** *p40D*
Doring, Elisabetha Schmidt 65; Indiana, 1901 ***1763*** *p40C*
Doring, Franz; Saratoga, NY, 1777 ***8137*** *p7*
Doring, Henrich; Philadelphia, 1779 ***8137*** *p7*
Doring, Otto; Washington, 1859-1920 ***2872.1*** *p10*
Doring, Patrick; Ohio, 1850 ***9892.11*** *p13*
Dorion, A. 30; America, 1836 ***778.5*** *p170*
Dorion, Neal 29; New Orleans, 1864 ***543.30*** *p374*
Dority, J.B. 98; Arizona, 1908 ***9228.40*** *p11*
Dorman, John; America, 1741 ***4971*** *p9*
Dorman, John; America, 1741 ***4971*** *p94*
Dorman, John; Virginia, 1648 ***6219*** *p246*
Dorman, Wm.; Virginia, 1638 ***6219*** *p121*
Dormant, William 25; Philadelphia, 1775 ***1219.7*** *p248*
Dormay, Jeremiah 27; Massachusetts, 1850 ***5881.1*** *p30*
Dormay, Johanna 27; Massachusetts, 1850 ***5881.1*** *p30*
Dormay, Mary 2; Massachusetts, 1850 ***5881.1*** *p32*
Dormet, Francis 20; Philadelphia, 1803 ***53.26*** *p24*
Dormeyer, . . .; Canada, 1776-1783 ***9786*** *p20*
Dormillion, Nelly 35; Massachusetts, 1849 ***5881.1*** *p33*
Dormillion, Thomas 35; Massachusetts, 1849 ***5881.1*** *p34*
Dorn, Nicolas 25; New Orleans, 1862 ***543.30*** *p58*

Dorn, Peter; South Carolina, 1788 ***7119*** *p203*
Dornan, Eliza 22; Philadelphia, 1860 ***5704.8*** *p145*
Dornau, Eugene 6; Port uncertain, 1838 ***778.5*** *p170*
Dornau, Lesin 8; Port uncertain, 1838 ***778.5*** *p170*
Dornau, Maria 33; Port uncertain, 1838 ***778.5*** *p170*
Dornau, Nicholas 10; Port uncertain, 1838 ***778.5*** *p170*
Dornau, Nicholas 34; Port uncertain, 1838 ***778.5*** *p170*
Dornau, Vera 4; Port uncertain, 1838 ***778.5*** *p170*
Dorne, Christian; Cincinnati, 1869-1887 ***8582*** *p7*
Dornis, H. 30; New Orleans, 1827 ***778.5*** *p170*
Dorochowicz, Jacob; Arkansas, 1918 ***95.2*** *p38*
Doroney, John 35; Massachusetts, 1849 ***5881.1*** *p30*
Dorr, Ludwig Peter; Pennsylvania, 1855 ***3702.7*** *p389*
Dorr, Marg. 22; America, 1853 ***9162.8*** *p36*
Dorr, Peter 57; Ontario, 1908 ***1763*** *p40C*
Dorrean, Bridget; New York, NY, 1865 ***5704.8*** *p190*
Dorrell, Wm.; Virginia, 1643 ***6219*** *p200*
Dorren, Edward; New York, NY, 1870 ***5704.8*** *p239*
Dorrian, Patrick; New York, NY, 1865 ***5704.8*** *p194*
Dorrington, Edwin 31; Kansas, 1880 ***5240.1*** *p62*
Dorrmann, Friedrich; America, 1848 ***8582.1*** *p7*
Dorrmann, Friedrich; Cincinnati, 1869-1887 ***8582*** *p7*
Dorrsam, Anna Barb. 18; America, 1853 ***9162.8*** *p36*
Dorrsam, Kath. 17; America, 1853 ***9162.8*** *p36*
Dorrsam, Kath. 24; America, 1853 ***9162.8*** *p36*
Dorrsam, Leonh. 3 mos; America, 1853 ***9162.8*** *p36*
Dorrsam, Marg.; America, 1853 ***9162.8*** *p36*
Dorrsam, Marg. 9 mos; America, 1853 ***9162.8*** *p36*
Dorrsam, Ph. 21; America, 1853 ***9162.7*** *p14*
Dorrsam, Rosene 56; America, 1853 ***9162.8*** *p36*
Dorry, . . .; Halifax, N.S., 1752 ***7074.6*** *p230*
Dors, Herman; Germantown, PA, 1684 ***2467.7*** *p5*
Dorsch, . . .; Canada, 1776-1783 ***9786*** *p20*
Dorsch, Adam; Pennsylvania, 1786 ***4525*** *p209*
With wife
*Child:*Maria Sallemie
*Child:*Margarieta
Dorsch, Margarieta *SEE* Dorsch, Adam
Dorsch, Maria Sallemie *SEE* Dorsch, Adam
Dorsel, Johann Christian; America, 1854 ***8582.3*** *p15*
Dorsett, Jon.; Virginia, 1643 ***6219*** *p203*
Dorsey, Edward; Virginia, 1646 ***6219*** *p245*
Dorsey, Michael; Ohio, 1840 ***9892.11*** *p13*
Dorvall, Jane 30; New Orleans, 1829 ***778.5*** *p170*
Dorwaite, James 20; Maryland, 1721 ***3690.1*** *p65*
Dorwin, Tho.; Virginia, 1647 ***6219*** *p245*
Doryan, Lily; St. John, N.B., 1847 ***5704.8*** *p25*
Doryan, Mary 9 mos; St. John, N.B., 1847 ***5704.8*** *p25*
Doryan, Michael; St. John, N.B., 1847 ***5704.8*** *p25*
Dosalek, John; Wisconsin, n.d. ***9675.5*** *p121*
Dosch, Mr.; Pennsylvania, 1769 ***4525*** *p265*
With brother
Dosch, Adam; Pennsylvania, 1786 ***4525*** *p209*
With wife
With child
Dosch, Anna Margaret *SEE* Dosch, John Michael
Dosch, Anna Margaretha; New England, 1773 ***4525*** *p209*
Dosch, Anna Margaretha; Pennsylvania, 1773 ***4525*** *p209*
Dosch, Christoph; Pennsylvania, 1752 ***4525*** *p209*
*Wife:*Maria Elisabeth
Dosch, Friedrich; New England, 1773 ***4525*** *p210*
With wife
With 2 children
Dosch, Hans Georg; Pennsylvania, 1752 ***4525*** *p210*
With wife
With 4 children
Dosch, Joh Mich; Philadelphia, 1756 ***4525*** *p262*
Dosch, Johann Christoph; Pennsylvania, 1752 ***4525*** *p210*
With wife
With 2 children
Dosch, Johann Michael; Pennsylvania, 1753 ***4525*** *p210*
Dosch, Johann Michael; Pennsylvania, 1754 ***4525*** *p210*
Dosch, John Michael; Lancaster, PA, 1754 ***4525*** *p210*
*Wife:*Anna Margaret
Dosch, Maria Elisabeth *SEE* Dosch, Christoph
Dosch, Michael; Pennsylvania, 1769 ***4525*** *p210*
Dosch, Peter; Pennsylvania, 1773 ***4525*** *p210*
With wife
With 4 children
Doscher, John 41; California, 1869 ***3840.1*** *p18*
Dosda, Franz 38; Kansas, 1890 ***5240.1*** *p75*
Dose, John; Wisconsin, n.d. ***9675.5*** *p121*
Doser, Johann; America, 1843 ***8582.2*** *p9*
Dosh, Barbara; Pennsylvania, 1786 ***4525*** *p209*
Dosh, Christopher; Pennsylvania, 1752 ***4525*** *p210*
Dosh, Hans George; Pennsylvania, 1752 ***4525*** *p210*
Dosik, David; Arkansas, 1918 ***95.2*** *p38*
Doss, John; Illinois, 1871 ***5012.39*** *p25*
Dosselberger, . . .; Canada, 1776-1783 ***9786*** *p20*
Dossmann, F. A.; Cincinnati, 1869-1887 ***8582*** *p7*
Dostman, Johan Martin; Pennsylvania, 1752 ***4525*** *p211*
Dostmann, Mr.; Pennsylvania, 1752 ***4525*** *p211*
With sister
Dotaro, Michael 43; West Virginia, 1904 ***9788.3*** *p9*
Dotona, Martin 23; New Orleans, 1838 ***778.5*** *p170*
Dotson, E. P.; Washington, 1859-1920 ***2872.1*** *p10*
Dotter, Nicolaus; Pennsylvania, 1749 ***4525*** *p205*
Dotterer, Anna Barbara *SEE* Dotterer, Ludwig
Dotterer, Ludwig; Pennsylvania, 1727 ***3627*** *p18*
*Wife:*Anna Barbara
Dotterweich, Andr; New York, 1876-1877 ***8582.3*** *p61*
Dotton, Thomas; Quebec, 1821 ***7603*** *p55*
Doty, C. A.; Washington, 1859-1920 ***2872.1*** *p10*
Douaron, Franc. 25; New Orleans, 1826 ***778.5*** *p170*
Douas, Victor 22; New Orleans, 1838 ***778.5*** *p170*
Douat, Jacques 18; New Orleans, 1839 ***778.5*** *p171*
Doubert, George 25; Louisiana, 1820 ***778.5*** *p171*
Doubly, Mary; Virginia, 1637 ***6219*** *p113*
Doubte, Sampson; Virginia, 1636 ***6219*** *p77*
Douce, Mlle. 8; Mexico, 1829 ***778.5*** *p171*
Douce, A., Mme. 30; Mexico, 1829 ***778.5*** *p171*
Doucez, Mr. 18; New Orleans, 1838 ***778.5*** *p171*
Doucot, Felicia 26; America, 1835 ***778.5*** *p171*
Doud, Ellen 20; Massachusetts, 1849 ***5881.1*** *p66*
Doud, John 13; Quebec, 1851 ***5704.8*** *p82*
Doud, William 50; Massachusetts, 1849 ***5881.1*** *p34*
Doudes, Bernard; New York, NY, 1838 ***8208.4*** *p72*
Douds, Elleanor *SEE* Douds, Mary
Douds, Elleanor; Philadelphia, 1848 ***5704.8*** *p40*
Douds, Isabella 24; Philadelphia, 1856 ***5704.8*** *p129*
Douds, John *SEE* Douds, Mary
Douds, John; Philadelphia, 1848 ***5704.8*** *p40*
Douds, Margaret; Philadelphia, 1851 ***5704.8*** *p76*
Douds, Mary; Philadelphia, 1848 ***53.26*** *p24*
*Relative:*Elleanor
*Relative:*John
Douds, Mary; Philadelphia, 1848 ***5704.8*** *p40*
Douet, Mr. 53; New Orleans, 1839 ***778.5*** *p171*
Doufinee, George; Halifax, N.S., 1752 ***7074.6*** *p228*
Doufinee, Jean; Halifax, N.S., 1752 ***7074.6*** *p228*
Douflin, Martin; Virginia, 1637 ***6219*** *p112*
Doufour, Germain 38; America, 1837 ***778.5*** *p171*
Dougal, Margaret; South Carolina, 1767 ***1639.20*** *p60*
Dougal, Nathaniel; New York, NY, 1865 ***5704.8*** *p194*
Dougall, William; Wilmington, NC, 1796-1837 ***1639.20*** *p60*
Dougan, Catherine 7; Philadelphia, 1864 ***5704.8*** *p155*
Dougan, Ellan; Quebec, 1847 ***5704.8*** *p38*
Dougan, Ellen 26; Philadelphia, 1864 ***5704.8*** *p156*
Dougan, Farrigle; Philadelphia, 1847 ***5704.8*** *p24*
Dougan, Hannah 3; Philadelphia, 1864 ***5704.8*** *p155*
Dougan, Henry; Quebec, 1847 ***5704.8*** *p38*
Dougan, James 35; Philadelphia, 1864 ***5704.8*** *p155*
Dougan, James 62; Arizona, 1901 ***9228.40*** *p5*
Dougan, John; Philadelphia, 1847 ***5704.8*** *p32*
Dougan, John 5; Philadelphia, 1864 ***5704.8*** *p155*
Dougan, Manus; Philadelphia, 1852 ***5704.8*** *p89*
Dougan, Mary 30; Philadelphia, 1864 ***5704.8*** *p155*
Dougan, Neil 6 mos; Philadelphia, 1864 ***5704.8*** *p155*
Dougan, Sarah; New York, NY, 1867 ***5704.8*** *p217*
Dougan, Thomas; Philadelphia, 1853 ***5704.8*** *p101*
Dougan, William; New York, NY, 1867 ***5704.8*** *p217*
Dough, Mary 26; Philadelphia, 1859 ***5704.8*** *p142*
Doughan, Mary 19; Philadelphia, 1860 ***5704.8*** *p144*
Doughan, William 16; Philadelphia, 1854 ***5704.8*** *p118*
Dougharty, Edward 20; Virginia, 1774 ***1219.7*** *p186*
Dougher, James; New York, NY, 1836 ***8208.4*** *p24*
Dougher, Patrick; St. John, N.B., 1847 ***5704.8*** *p32*
Dougherty, . . . 5 mos; New York, NY, 1866 ***5704.8*** *p210*
Dougherty, Mrs.; Philadelphia, 1864 ***5704.8*** *p186*
Dougherty, Abigail; Philadelphia, 1811 ***2859.11*** *p11*
Dougherty, Abigale *SEE* Dougherty, Thomas
Dougherty, Alexander; Philadelphia, 1864 ***5704.8*** *p180*
Dougherty, Anabella; Philadelphia, 1865 ***5704.8*** *p202*
Dougherty, Andrew; Philadelphia, 1864 ***5704.8*** *p174*
Dougherty, Andrew; St. John, N.B., 1848 ***5704.8*** *p39*
Dougherty, Ann; Philadelphia, 1847 ***53.26*** *p24*
Dougherty, Ann; Philadelphia, 1847 ***5704.8*** *p22*
Dougherty, Ann; Philadelphia, 1865 ***5704.8*** *p192*
Dougherty, Ann; St. John, N.B., 1848 ***5704.8*** *p39*
Dougherty, Ann 9; St. John, N.B., 1848 ***5704.8*** *p39*
Dougherty, Ann 12; Philadelphia, 1858 ***5704.8*** *p139*
Dougherty, Ann 45; Philadelphia, 1858 ***5704.8*** *p139*
Dougherty, Anne; New York, NY, 1864 ***5704.8*** *p171*
Dougherty, Annie 9; New York, NY, 1864 ***5704.8*** *p172*
Dougherty, Anthony *SEE* Dougherty, Henry
Dougherty, Anthony; Philadelphia, 1864 ***5704.8*** *p171*
Dougherty, Anthony 23; Philadelphia, 1854 ***5704.8*** *p117*
Dougherty, Anthy.; Philadelphia, 1811 ***2859.11*** *p11*
Dougherty, Archibald 4; Quebec, 1852 ***5704.8*** *p86*
Dougherty, Archy 5; Quebec, 1852 ***5704.8*** *p90*
Dougherty, Bell; New York, NY, 1869 ***5704.8*** *p234*
Dougherty, Bernard; New York, 1847 ***1450.2*** *p32A*
Dougherty, Bernard; New York, NY, 1868 ***5704.8*** *p228*
Dougherty, Bernard; New York, NY, 1869 ***5704.8*** *p232*
Dougherty, Bernard; New York, NY, 1869 ***5704.8*** *p236*
Dougherty, Bridget; America, 1864 ***5704.8*** *p186*
Dougherty, Bridget; America, 1866 ***5704.8*** *p208*
Dougherty, Bridget; New York, NY, 1815 ***2859.11*** *p29*
Dougherty, Bridget; New York, NY, 1864 ***5704.8*** *p178*
Dougherty, Bridget; New York, NY, 1869 ***5704.8*** *p232*
Dougherty, Bridget; New York, NY, 1869 ***5704.8*** *p233*
Dougherty, Bridget; New York, NY, 1869 ***5704.8*** *p234*
Dougherty, Bridget; Philadelphia, 1847 ***53.26*** *p24*
*Relative:*Margaret
Dougherty, Bridget; Philadelphia, 1847 ***5704.8*** *p2*
Dougherty, Bridget; Philadelphia, 1865 ***5704.8*** *p193*
Dougherty, Bridget; Philadelphia, 1868 ***5704.8*** *p226*
Dougherty, Bridget 7; Philadelphia, 1853 ***5704.8*** *p101*
Dougherty, Cath.; Philadelphia, 1811 ***2859.11*** *p11*
Dougherty, Catharine; America, 1868 ***5704.8*** *p231*
Dougherty, Catharine; New York, NY, 1869 ***5704.8*** *p232*
Dougherty, Catharine; New York, NY, 1869 ***5704.8*** *p236*
Dougherty, Catharine; New York, NY, 1870 ***5704.8*** *p236*
Dougherty, Catharine; Philadelphia, 1864 ***5704.8*** *p177*
Dougherty, Catharine; Philadelphia, 1864 ***5704.8*** *p180*
Dougherty, Catharine; Philadelphia, 1865 ***5704.8*** *p198*
Dougherty, Catharine; Philadelphia, 1868 ***5704.8*** *p226*
Dougherty, Catherine *SEE* Dougherty, Henry
Dougherty, Catherine; Philadelphia, 1851 ***5704.8*** *p70*
Dougherty, Catherine 10; Philadelphia, 1854 ***5704.8*** *p117*
Dougherty, Catherine 13; Philadelphia, 1864 ***5704.8*** *p177*
Dougherty, Cecilia; Philadelphia, 1853 ***5704.8*** *p101*
Dougherty, Charles; Philadelphia, 1853 ***5704.8*** *p103*
Dougherty, Charles; Quebec, 1847 ***5704.8*** *p29*
Dougherty, Charles 18; Philadelphia, 1855 ***5704.8*** *p124*
Dougherty, Charles 23; Philadelphia, 1860 ***5704.8*** *p146*
Dougherty, Dan 63; Arizona, 1903 ***9228.40*** *p5*
Dougherty, Daniel; America, 1868 ***5704.8*** *p229*
Dougherty, Daniel; New York, NY, 1868 ***5704.8*** *p228*
Dougherty, Daniel; Philadelphia, 1864 ***5704.8*** *p179*
Dougherty, Daniel; Philadelphia, 1866 ***5704.8*** *p208*
Dougherty, Daniel 32; Kansas, 1893 ***5240.1*** *p78*
Dougherty, Darby 25; Philadelphia, 1803 ***53.26*** *p24*
Dougherty, Dennis; New York, NY, 1869 ***5704.8*** *p233*
Dougherty, Dennis; Philadelphia, 1865 ***5704.8*** *p198*
Dougherty, Dudly.; New York, NY, 1811 ***2859.11*** *p11*
Dougherty, Edward; America, 1867 ***5704.8*** *p224*
Dougherty, Edward; Philadelphia, 1849 ***53.26*** *p24*
Dougherty, Edward; Philadelphia, 1849 ***5704.8*** *p50*
Dougherty, Edward 11; New York, NY, 1864 ***5704.8*** *p172*
Dougherty, Elenor; Philadelphia, 1865 ***5704.8*** *p195*
Dougherty, Eliza; Quebec, 1848 ***5704.8*** *p41*
Dougherty, Eliza 9 mos; St. John, N.B., 1848 ***5704.8*** *p39*
Dougherty, Eliza J.; New York, NY, 1870 ***5704.8*** *p237*
Dougherty, Elizabeth; New York, NY, 1868 ***5704.8*** *p226*
Dougherty, Elizabeth; New York, NY, 1868 ***5704.8*** *p231*
Dougherty, Elizabeth; Philadelphia, 1867 ***5704.8*** *p218*
Dougherty, Elizabeth; Quebec, 1851 ***5704.8*** *p74*
Dougherty, Elizabeth 6 mos; Quebec, 1852 ***5704.8*** *p86*
Dougherty, Elizabeth 9 mos; Quebec, 1852 ***5704.8*** *p90*
Dougherty, Ellan; Philadelphia, 1849 ***5704.8*** *p49*
Dougherty, Ellen *SEE* Dougherty, Ellen
Dougherty, Ellen; New York, NY, 1864 ***5704.8*** *p170*
Dougherty, Ellen; New York, NY, 1868 ***5704.8*** *p228*
Dougherty, Ellen; New York, NY, 1869 ***5704.8*** *p232*
Dougherty, Ellen; New York, NY, 1869 ***5704.8*** *p233*
Dougherty, Ellen; Philadelphia, 1849 ***53.26*** *p24*
*Relative:*Ellen
Dougherty, Ellen; Philadelphia, 1869 ***5704.8*** *p235*
Dougherty, Ellen; St. John, N.B., 1851 ***5704.8*** *p72*
Dougherty, Ellen 6; Philadelphia, 1864 ***5704.8*** *p177*
Dougherty, Ellen 10; Philadelphia, 1858 ***5704.8*** *p139*
Dougherty, Ellen 26; Philadelphia, 1864 ***5704.8*** *p161*
Dougherty, Fanny; America, 1864 ***5704.8*** *p181*
Dougherty, Fanny 3; New York, NY, 1866 ***5704.8*** *p210*
Dougherty, Francis; New York, NY, 1866 ***5704.8*** *p210*
Dougherty, Francis; St. John, N.B., 1848 ***5704.8*** *p39*
Dougherty, Francis 7; St. John, N.B., 1848 ***5704.8*** *p39*
Dougherty, George; Philadelphia, 1864 ***5704.8*** *p178*
Dougherty, George; Quebec, 1847 ***5704.8*** *p12*
Dougherty, George; Quebec, 1848 ***5704.8*** *p41*
Dougherty, George 12; Philadelphia, 1854 ***5704.8*** *p117*
Dougherty, Giley; St. John, N.B., 1853 ***5704.8*** *p107*
Dougherty, Grace; New York, NY, 1868 ***5704.8*** *p227*
Dougherty, Hannah 4; Philadelphia, 1864 ***5704.8*** *p177*
Dougherty, Henry; New York, NY, 1865 ***5704.8*** *p193*
Dougherty, Henry; Philadelphia, 1811 ***53.26*** *p24*
*Relative:*Catherine
*Relative:*Anthony
Dougherty, Henry; Philadelphia, 1811 ***2859.11*** *p11*
Dougherty, Henry; Quebec, 1848 ***5704.8*** *p42*
Dougherty, Henry 7; New York, NY, 1869 ***5704.8*** *p233*
Dougherty, Hugh; Philadelphia, 1865 ***5704.8*** *p198*
Dougherty, Hugh 5; New York, NY, 1869 ***5704.8*** *p233*

Dougherty, Hugh 8; Philadelphia, 1854 *5704.8 p117*
Dougherty, Hugh 36; Massachusetts, 1849 *5881.1 p29*
Dougherty, Jack; New York, NY, 1869 *5704.8 p232*
Dougherty, James; New York, NY, 1811 *2859.11 p11*
Dougherty, James; New York, NY, 1815 *2859.11 p29*
Dougherty, James; New York, NY, 1870 *5704.8 p237*
Dougherty, James; Philadelphia, 1850 *53.26 p24*
Dougherty, James; Philadelphia, 1850 *5704.8 p60*
Dougherty, James; Philadelphia, 1865 *5704.8 p195*
Dougherty, James; Quebec, 1851 *5704.8 p74*
Dougherty, James; St. John, N.B., 1853 *5704.8 p106*
Dougherty, James 2 *SEE* Dougherty, Mary
Dougherty, James 2; Philadelphia, 1850 *5704.8 p69*
Dougherty, James 13; St. John, N.B., 1848 *5704.8 p39*
Dougherty, James 26; Massachusetts, 1849 *5881.1 p30*
Dougherty, James 32; Quebec, 1863 *5704.8 p154*
Dougherty, James 33; Philadelphia, 1804 *53.26 p24*
Dougherty, James 45; Philadelphia, 1854 *5704.8 p117*
Dougherty, James, Jr.; New York, NY, 1840 *8208.4 p107*
Dougherty, Jane; New York, NY, 1869 *5704.8 p234*
Dougherty, Jane; Philadelphia, 1864 *5704.8 p180*
Dougherty, Jane; Philadelphia, 1864 *5704.8 p182*
Dougherty, Jane; Quebec, 1847 *5704.8 p29*
Dougherty, Jane; Quebec, 1852 *5704.8 p86*
Dougherty, Jane; Quebec, 1852 *5704.8 p90*
Dougherty, Jane 4; St. John, N.B., 1848 *5704.8 p39*
Dougherty, Jeffery; New York, NY, 1869 *5704.8 p234*
Dougherty, Johanna 23; Philadelphia, 1855 *5704.8 p124*
Dougherty, John; Baltimore, 1811 *2859.11 p11*
Dougherty, John; California, 1875 *2764.35 p18*
Dougherty, John; New York, NY, 1811 *2859.11 p11*
Dougherty, John; New York, NY, 1835 *8208.4 p6*
Dougherty, John; New York, NY, 1864 *5704.8 p170*
Dougherty, John; New York, NY, 1865 *5704.8 p196*
Dougherty, John; New York, NY, 1867 *5704.8 p219*
Dougherty, John; New York, NY, 1869 *5704.8 p234*
Dougherty, John; New York, NY, 1870 *5704.8 p236*
Dougherty, John; Philadelphia, 1816 *2859.11 p29*
Dougherty, John; Philadelphia, 1850 *53.26 p24*
*Relative:*Michael
Dougherty, John; Philadelphia, 1850 *5704.8 p69*
Dougherty, John; Philadelphia, 1853 *5704.8 p101*
Dougherty, John; Philadelphia, 1864 *5704.8 p180*
Dougherty, John; Philadelphia, 1864 *5704.8 p186*
Dougherty, John; Philadelphia, 1865 *5704.8 p188*
Dougherty, John; Philadelphia, 1866 *5704.8 p210*
Dougherty, John; Philadelphia, 1869 *5704.8 p236*
Dougherty, John; St. John, N.B., 1853 *5704.8 p107*
Dougherty, John 9; Quebec, 1852 *5704.8 p86*
Dougherty, John 9; Quebec, 1852 *5704.8 p90*
Dougherty, John 10; Philadelphia, 1864 *5704.8 p177*
Dougherty, John 12; Philadelphia, 1857 *5704.8 p133*
Dougherty, John 13; Quebec, 1848 *5704.8 p41*
Dougherty, John 18; Philadelphia, 1857 *5704.8 p133*
Dougherty, Joseph; St. John, N.B., 1848 *5704.8 p39*
Dougherty, Manuel 4; New York, NY, 1866 *5704.8 p210*
Dougherty, Margaret *SEE* Dougherty, Bridget
Dougherty, Margaret; America, 1864 *5704.8 p181*
Dougherty, Margaret; New York, NY, 1864 *5704.8 p172*
Dougherty, Margaret; New York, NY, 1864 *5704.8 p174*
Dougherty, Margaret; New York, NY, 1866 *5704.8 p210*
Dougherty, Margaret; New York, NY, 1866 *5704.8 p212*
Dougherty, Margaret; New York, NY, 1868 *5704.8 p227*
Dougherty, Margaret; Philadelphia, 1847 *5704.8 p2*
Dougherty, Margaret; Philadelphia, 1848 *53.26 p24*
*Relative:*Patrick 5
*Relative:*Michael 3
Dougherty, Margaret; Philadelphia, 1848 *5704.8 p41*
Dougherty, Margaret; Philadelphia, 1850 *53.26 p24*
Dougherty, Margaret; Philadelphia, 1850 *5704.8 p68*
Dougherty, Margaret; Philadelphia, 1851 *5704.8 p71*
Dougherty, Margaret; Philadelphia, 1863-1871 *5704.8 p199*
Dougherty, Margaret; Philadelphia, 1865 *5704.8 p198*
Dougherty, Margaret; Philadelphia, 1866 *5704.8 p203*
Dougherty, Margaret; Philadelphia, 1867 *5704.8 p223*
Dougherty, Margaret 3; Philadelphia, 1864 *5704.8 p177*
Dougherty, Margaret 8; St. John, N.B., 1853 *5704.8 p106*
Dougherty, Margaret 11; St. John, N.B., 1851 *5704.8 p72*
Dougherty, Margaret 17; Philadelphia, 1859 *5704.8 p142*
Dougherty, Martha 8; St. John, N.B., 1853 *5704.8 p106*
Dougherty, Mary; New York, NY, 1864 *5704.8 p174*
Dougherty, Mary; New York, NY, 1866 *5704.8 p211*
Dougherty, Mary; New York, NY, 1867 *5704.8 p224*
Dougherty, Mary; New York, NY, 1868 *5704.8 p228*
Dougherty, Mary; Philadelphia, 1850 *53.26 p24*
*Relative:*James 2
*Relative:*Nancy 6 mos
Dougherty, Mary; Philadelphia, 1850 *5704.8 p69*
Dougherty, Mary; Philadelphia, 1851 *5704.8 p77*
Dougherty, Mary; Philadelphia, 1853 *5704.8 p102*
Dougherty, Mary; Philadelphia, 1866 *5704.8 p208*
Dougherty, Mary; Philadelphia, 1869 *5704.8 p236*
Dougherty, Mary; Philadelphia, 1871 *5704.8 p241*
Dougherty, Mary; Quebec, 1848 *5704.8 p41*
Dougherty, Mary 3; Philadelphia, 1864 *5704.8 p180*
Dougherty, Mary 11; St. John, N.B., 1848 *5704.8 p39*
Dougherty, Mary 30; Philadelphia, 1864 *5704.8 p161*
Dougherty, Mary 60; Philadelphia, 1855 *5704.8 p124*
Dougherty, Mary A.; New York, NY, 1865 *5704.8 p201*
Dougherty, Mary A.; Philadelphia, 1869 *5704.8 p235*
Dougherty, Mary A.; Philadelphia, 1869 *5704.8 p236*
Dougherty, Mary Ann; St. John, N.B., 1853 *5704.8 p106*
Dougherty, Mary Ann 6; Quebec, 1852 *5704.8 p86*
Dougherty, Mary Ann 7; Quebec, 1852 *5704.8 p90*
Dougherty, Matilda; St. John, N.B., 1853 *5704.8 p106*
Dougherty, Michael *SEE* Dougherty, John
Dougherty, Michael; America, 1849 *1450.2 p32A*
Dougherty, Michael; America, 1865 *5704.8 p193*
Dougherty, Michael; America, 1866 *5704.8 p209*
Dougherty, Michael; New York, NY, 1864 *5704.8 p173*
Dougherty, Michael; Philadelphia, 1850 *5704.8 p69*
Dougherty, Michael; Philadelphia, 1851 *5704.8 p77*
Dougherty, Michael 3 *SEE* Dougherty, Margaret
Dougherty, Michael 3; Philadelphia, 1848 *5704.8 p41*
Dougherty, Michael 24; Philadelphia, 1854 *5704.8 p117*
Dougherty, Mike 58; Massachusetts, 1850 *5881.1 p33*
Dougherty, Nancy; New York, NY, 1864 *5704.8 p185*
Dougherty, Nancy; Philadelphia, 1865 *5704.8 p198*
Dougherty, Nancy 6 mos *SEE* Dougherty, Mary
Dougherty, Nancy 6 mos; Philadelphia, 1850 *5704.8 p69*
Dougherty, Nancy 22; St. John, N.B., 1854 *5704.8 p122*
Dougherty, Neal; New York, NY, 1811 *2859.11 p11*
Dougherty, Neal 20; Philadelphia, 1803 *53.26 p24*
Dougherty, Neal 25; Philadelphia, 1864 *5704.8 p156*
Dougherty, Owen; New York, NY, 1864 *5704.8 p174*
Dougherty, Owen; New York, NY, 1865 *5704.8 p201*
Dougherty, Owen; New York, NY, 1866 *5704.8 p209*
Dougherty, Owen; Philadelphia, 1867 *5704.8 p218*
Dougherty, Patrick; Illinois, 1860 *2896.5 p9*
Dougherty, Patrick; Philadelphia, 1848 *5704.8 p40*
Dougherty, Patrick; Philadelphia, 1865 *5704.8 p198*
Dougherty, Patrick 5 *SEE* Dougherty, Margaret
Dougherty, Patrick 5; Philadelphia, 1848 *5704.8 p41*
Dougherty, Patrick 8; Philadelphia, 1864 *5704.8 p177*
Dougherty, Patrick 10; New York, NY, 1869 *5704.8 p233*
Dougherty, Patrick 11; Philadelphia, 1864 *5704.8 p156*
Dougherty, Patrick 14; Philadelphia, 1858 *5704.8 p139*
Dougherty, Patrick 21; Massachusetts, 1849 *5881.1 p33*
Dougherty, Peter; New York, NY, 1838 *8208.4 p72*
Dougherty, Peter; New York, NY, 1865 *5704.8 p194*
Dougherty, Philip; New York, NY, 1811 *2859.11 p11*
Dougherty, Philip; New York, NY, 1865 *5704.8 p203*
Dougherty, Rebecca; Philadelphia, 1864 *5704.8 p180*
Dougherty, Rebecca 2; Philadelphia, 1864 *5704.8 p180*
Dougherty, Richard 36; Philadelphia, 1803 *53.26 p24*
Dougherty, Robert 18; Philadelphia, 1854 *5704.8 p120*
Dougherty, Roger; America, 1735-1743 *4971 p8*
Dougherty, Rose; New York, NY, 1865 *5704.8 p194*
Dougherty, Rose; Philadelphia, 1865 *5704.8 p173*
Dougherty, Rose; Philadelphia, 1866 *5704.8 p209*
Dougherty, Rose; St. John, N.B., 1853 *5704.8 p107*
Dougherty, Rose 18; Philadelphia, 1864 *5704.8 p161*
Dougherty, Sarah; New York, NY, 1866 *5704.8 p212*
Dougherty, Sarah; New York, NY, 1869 *5704.8 p233*
Dougherty, Sarah; Philadelphia, 1864 *5704.8 p176*
Dougherty, Sarah; Philadelphia, 1864 *5704.8 p185*
Dougherty, Sarah; St. John, N.B., 1851 *5704.8 p72*
Dougherty, Silena 11; St. John, N.B., 1853 *5704.8 p106*
Dougherty, Susan; Philadelphia, 1853 *5704.8 p101*
Dougherty, Thomas; Arizona, 1890 *2764.35 p16*
Dougherty, Thomas; Philadelphia, 1811 *53.26 p24*
*Relative:*Abigale
Dougherty, Thomas; Philadelphia, 1864 *5704.8 p176*
Dougherty, Thomas; St. John, N.B., 1853 *5704.8 p106*
Dougherty, Thomas 13; St. John, N.B., 1853 *5704.8 p106*
Dougherty, Thomas 18; Philadelphia, 1854 *5704.8 p117*
Dougherty, Thos.; Philadelphia, 1811 *2859.11 p11*
Dougherty, Unity; Philadelphia, 1865 *5704.8 p202*
Dougherty, William; America, 1849 *1450.2 p32A*
Dougherty, William; New York, NY, 1811 *2859.11 p11*
Dougherty, William; Philadelphia, 1816 *2859.11 p29*
Dougherty, William; Philadelphia, 1851 *5704.8 p70*
Dougherty, William; Philadelphia, 1864 *5704.8 p175*
Dougherty, William; Philadelphia, 1864 *5704.8 p178*
Dougherty, William; Philadelphia, 1864 *5704.8 p181*
Dougherty, William; Philadelphia, 1865 *5704.8 p186*
Dougherty, William; Quebec, 1852 *5704.8 p86*
Dougherty, William; Quebec, 1852 *5704.8 p90*
Dougherty, William; St. John, N.B., 1853 *5704.8 p106*
Dougherty, William; St. John, N.B., 1853 *5704.8 p107*
Dougherty, William 2; Quebec, 1852 *5704.8 p86*
Dougherty, William 20; Philadelphia, 1854 *5704.8 p120*
Dougherty, Wm.; Virginia, 1856 *4626.16 p16*
Doughrey, Margaret; St. John, N.B., 1853 *5704.8 p107*
Doughten, Stephen 18; Pennsylvania, 1730 *3690.1 p65*
Doughty, Charles; St. Christopher, 1760 *1219.7 p76*
Douglas, Mr.; Quebec, 1815 *9229.18 p75*
With wife
Douglas, Alexander 22; Carolina, 1774 *1219.7 p242*
Douglas, Alexander 22; Carolina, 1774 *1639.20 p60*
Douglas, Alexander 46; South Carolina, 1850 *1639.20 p60*
Douglas, Angus; North Carolina, 1759-1819 *1639.20 p60*
Douglas, Anthony 42; South Carolina, 1850 *1639.20 p60*
Douglas, Archibald; North Carolina, 1740 *1639.20 p60*
Douglas, Benjamin W.; New Orleans, 1846 *1450.2 p32A*
Douglas, Campbell; Charleston, SC, 1813 *1639.20 p60*
Douglas, Campbell 69; Charleston, SC, 1850 *1639.20 p60*
Douglas, Catherine Read; South Carolina, 1789 *1639.20 p269*
Douglas, Charles 17; Jamaica, 1731 *3690.1 p65*
Douglas, Charles Joseph; Quebec, 1745 *9775.5 p197*
Douglas, Daniel; North Carolina, 1735-1816 *1639.20 p60*
Douglas, d'Hortore; Quebec, 1745 *9775.5 p197*
Douglas, George; Quebec, 1847 *5704.8 p12*
Douglas, George 18; Virginia, 1721 *3690.1 p65*
Douglas, James; British Columbia, 1858 *9775.5 p222*
Douglas, James; Charleston, SC, 1804 *1639.20 p61*
Douglas, James; Charleston, SC, 1805 *1639.20 p61*
Douglas, James Kennedy; Charleston, SC, 1804 *1639.20 p61*
Douglas, Jane; St. John, N.B., 1853 *5704.8 p106*
Douglas, John; America, 1788 *1639.20 p61*
Douglas, John; Charleston, SC, 1802 *1639.20 p61*
Douglas, John; South Carolina, 1799 *1639.20 p61*
Douglas, John 9 mos; Quebec, 1847 *5704.8 p12*
Douglas, John 17; Port uncertain, 1757 *3690.1 p65*
Douglas, John 18; Windward Islands, 1722 *3690.1 p65*
Douglas, John 20; Georgia, 1775 *1219.7 p276*
Douglas, John 50; South Carolina, 1850 *1639.20 p61*
Douglas, John 60; South Carolina, 1850 *1639.20 p61*
Douglas, Joseph; St. John, N.B., 1847 *5704.8 p4*
Douglas, Mary; Quebec, 1847 *5704.8 p12*
Douglas, Sholto; North America, 1759 *1219.7 p69*
Douglass, Andrew; New York, NY, 1815 *2859.11 p29*
Douglass, Catharine; Philadelphia, 1868 *5704.8 p227*
Douglass, Charles 17; Jamaica, 1731 *3690.1 p65*
Douglass, Edward 22; California, 1872 *2769.3 p5*
Douglass, Elizabeth 20; Wilmington, DE, 1831 *6508.3 p100*
Douglass, James; New York, NY, 1815 *2859.11 p29*
Douglass, James; Virginia, 1698 *2212 p14*
Douglass, John 38; Philadelphia, 1804 *53.26 p24*
*Relative:*Mary 38
Douglass, John Stephen 21; California, 1873 *2769.10 p3*
Douglass, Joseph; New York, NY, 1811 *2859.11 p11*
Douglass, Joseph; Philadelphia, 1811 *53.26 p24*
Douglass, Joseph; Philadelphia, 1811 *2859.11 p11*
Douglass, Joseph; Philadelphia, 1851 *5704.8 p79*
Douglass, Mary 10; Philadelphia, 1867 *5704.8 p220*
Douglass, Mary 38 *SEE* Douglass, John
Douglass, Matthew 21; Philadelphia, 1833-1834 *53.26 p24*
Douglass, Robert; New York, NY, 1811 *2859.11 p11*
Douglass, Robert 15; Jamaica, 1721 *3690.1 p68*
Douglass, Sarah; Philadelphia, 1868 *5704.8 p230*
Douglass, Thomas; New York, NY, 1852 *2896.5 p9*
Doujos, Mme.; America, 1839 *778.5 p171*
Doujos, Mr. 52; America, 1839 *778.5 p171*
Doulan, William 24; Virginia, 1774 *1219.7 p244*
Doulet, Louis; Arkansas, 1918 *95.2 p38*
Doulin, Michael; New York, NY, 1838 *8208.4 p89*
Doulle, Alexandre 29; America, 1829 *778.5 p171*
Doumecq, Mr.; Port uncertain, 1839 *778.5 p171*
Doumeiny, Emile 28; America, 1825 *778.5 p171*
Doumerq, Mr.; Port uncertain, 1839 *778.5 p171*
Doune, Clement; Virginia, 1639 *6219 p153*
Dounes, Laurence; America, 1698 *2212 p5*
Doupan, Mr. 36; New Orleans, 1821 *778.5 p171*
Dourage, John 22; Quebec, 1857 *5704.8 p136*
Dours, Mr. 22; Port uncertain, 1836 *778.5 p172*
Douse, Barbara; Virginia, 1645 *6219 p253*
Doussan, A. 22; America, 1832 *778.5 p172*
Doussan, A. G. 37; America, 1832 *778.5 p172*
Doutherd, Hannah; Philadelphia, 1848 *53.26 p24*
Doutherd, Hannah; Philadelphia, 1848 *5704.8 p46*
Douthit, Elizabeth; St. John, N.B., 1847 *5704.8 p21*
Douthwit, Jane *SEE* Douthwit, Thomas
Douthwit, Thomas; Philadelphia, 1849 *53.26 p24*
*Relative:*Jane
Douthwitt, Stephen; Philadelphia, 1847 *53.26 p24*

Douthwitt, Stephen; Philadelphia, 1847 ***5704.8*** *p5*
Dove, Andrew 15; Maryland, 1775 ***1219.7*** *p266*
Dove, Catherine 74; South Carolina, 1850 ***1639.20*** *p61*
Dove, Edward; New York, NY, 1811 ***2859.11*** *p11*
Dove, Heinrich Anton David; Quebec, 1776 ***9786*** *p258*
Dove, John; Virginia, 1638 ***6219*** *p145*
Dove, William; Virginia, 1618 ***6219*** *p200*
Dove, William 24; Philadelphia, 1774 ***1219.7*** *p216*
Dover, Mary 17; Virginia, 1719 ***3690.1*** *p66*
Doves, James 28; Virginia, 1774 ***1219.7*** *p244*
Doving, Otto; Washington, 1859-1920 ***2872.1*** *p10*
Dow, G.; Charleston, SC, 1755 ***1639.20*** *p61*
Dow, M. A. 41; Kansas, 1889 ***5240.1*** *p73*
Dowd, Ann 17; Massachusetts, 1850 ***5881.1*** *p26*
Dowd, Bridget; St. John, N.B., 1850 ***5704.8*** *p61*
Dowd, Bridget 28; Massachusetts, 1847 ***5881.1*** *p27*
Dowd, Christopher; America, 1740 ***4971*** *p22*
Dowd, Hugh 11; Massachusetts, 1850 ***5881.1*** *p29*
Dowd, Mathew; New York, NY, 1853 ***2764.35*** *p16*
Dowdall, Edward; America, 1742 ***4971*** *p26*
Dowdd, Steve; Iowa, 1866-1943 ***123.54*** *p16*
Dowden, George; Virginia, 1856 ***4626.16*** *p16*
Dowding, Edward 19; Maryland, 1724 ***3690.1*** *p66*
Dowdle, Michael; Philadelphia, 1764 ***9973.7*** *p39*
Dowds, Catherine; Philadelphia, 1848 ***53.26*** *p24*
Dowds, Catherine; Philadelphia, 1848 ***5704.8*** *p41*
Dowds, Charles; California, 1860 ***3840.1*** *p16*
Dowdy, John 16; Maryland, 1720 ***3690.1*** *p66*
Dowe, John 27; Massachusetts, 1849 ***5881.1*** *p29*
Dowe, Thomas; New York, NY, 1815 ***2859.11*** *p29*
Dowen, Robert; Virginia, 1648 ***6219*** *p246*
Dower, Henry 45; New Orleans, 1863 ***543.30*** *p373*
Dowlan, William 40; Massachusetts, 1849 ***5881.1*** *p34*
Dowler, William 20; Antigua (Antego), 1728 ***3690.1*** *p66*
Dowley, John 19; Massachusetts, 1849 ***5881.1*** *p30*
Dowlin, Dennis 27; Virginia, 1774 ***1219.7*** *p241*
Dowling, Charles 30; Maryland, 1775 ***1219.7*** *p250*
Dowling, Fr.; Virginia, 1643 ***6219*** *p200*
Dowling, James; America, 1740 ***4971*** *p32*
Dowling, Jerry 4; Massachusetts, 1849 ***5881.1*** *p29*
Dowling, John; America, 1741 ***4971*** *p16*
Dowling, John 16; Pennsylvania, 1731 ***3690.1*** *p66*
Dowling, Mary; America, 1737 ***4971*** *p85*
Dowling, Mary; America, 1737 ***4971*** *p95*
Dowling, Mary; America, 1743 ***4971*** *p11*
Dowling, Michael; New York, NY, 1816 ***2859.11*** *p29*
Dowling, Patrick; America, 1739 ***4971*** *p9*
Dowling, Patrick; America, 1739 ***4971*** *p85*
Dowling, Patrick; America, 1739 ***4971*** *p103*
Dowling, Patrick; New York, NY, 1839 ***8208.4*** *p99*
Dowling, Robert 30; Kansas, 1871 ***5240.1*** *p52*
Dowling, Sarah 3; Massachusetts, 1849 ***5881.1*** *p34*
Dowling, Thomas; America, 1741 ***4971*** *p16*
Dowling, William; America, 1735-1743 ***4971*** *p8*
Dowling, William 17; Jamaica, 1729 ***3690.1*** *p66*
Dowlman, John William 21; Kansas, 1882 ***5240.1*** *p63*
Down, Joanna 21; Massachusetts, 1849 ***5881.1*** *p30*
Down, William 18; Pennsylvania, 1735 ***3690.1*** *p66*
Downe, John; Illinois, 1861 ***2896.5*** *p9*
Downes, Agnes 24; St. John, N.B., 1856 ***5704.8*** *p131*
Downes, Eustace; Virginia, 1637 ***6219*** *p11*
Downes, Fr.; Virginia, 1638 ***6219*** *p14*
Downes, James 29; Virginia, 1774 ***1219.7*** *p186*
Downes, Jeremiah; Charleston, SC, 1796 ***1639.20*** *p61*
Downes, Robert 21; St. John, N.B., 1856 ***5704.8*** *p131*
Downes, Walter; Virginia, 1637 ***6219*** *p85*
Downes, Walter; Virginia, 1642 ***6219*** *p189*
Downes, Watkin; Virginia, 1643 ***6219*** *p208*
Downes, William; Quebec, 1822 ***7603*** *p92*
Downes, William; Virginia, 1637 ***6219*** *p108*
Downes, William 22; New York, 1774 ***1219.7*** *p217*
Downey, Bryan; America, 1738 ***4971*** *p25*
Downey, Darby; America, 1738 ***4971*** *p55*
Downey, Dennis; America, 1739 ***4971*** *p56*
Downey, Eliza; Philadelphia, 1848 ***5704.8*** *p46*
Downey, John; America, 1846 ***1450.2*** *p32A*
Downey, John 28; Kansas, 1880 ***5240.1*** *p62*
Downey, John 35; Massachusetts, 1849 ***5881.1*** *p32*
Downey, Julia 5; Massachusetts, 1849 ***5881.1*** *p30*
Downey, Margaret 18; Massachusetts, 1849 ***5881.1*** *p32*
Downey, Mary; St. John, N.B., 1851 ***5704.8*** *p80*
Downey, Mary 6; Massachusetts, 1849 ***5881.1*** *p32*
Downey, Matilda; New York, NY, 1867 ***5704.8*** *p223*
Downey, Michael; America, 1847 ***1450.2*** *p32A*
Downey, Michael; New York, NY, 1815 ***2859.11*** *p29*
Downey, Patrick 2; Massachusetts, 1849 ***5881.1*** *p33*
Downey, Patrick 26; Massachusetts, 1849 ***5881.1*** *p33*
Downey, Philip; America, 1740 ***4971*** *p15*
Downey, Robert; Kansas, 1873 ***2764.35*** *p16*
Downey, Sarah; Quebec, 1824 ***7603*** *p97*
Downham, John; Virginia, 1620 ***6219*** *p18*
Downham, Thomas 20; Pennsylvania, 1735 ***3690.1*** *p66*
Downie, Christian 30; Wilmington, NC, 1774 ***1639.20*** *p218*
Downie, Joseph *SEE* Downie, Mary
Downie, Mary 4; Wilmington, NC, 1775 ***1639.20*** *p227*
*Brother:*Joseph
With mother
Downie, Mary 35; Wilmington, NC, 1774 ***1639.20*** *p166*
Downie, Robert 20; Jamaica, 1724 ***3690.1*** *p66*
Downie, Robert 60; Charleston, SC, 1850 ***1639.20*** *p62*
Downing, Ann; Quebec, 1847 ***5704.8*** *p29*
Downing, Arthur 16; Jamaica, 1736 ***3690.1*** *p66*
Downing, Charles; Washington, 1859-1920 ***2872.1*** *p10*
Downing, Hugh; Philadelphia, 1849 ***53.26*** *p24*
Downing, Hugh; Philadelphia, 1849 ***5704.8*** *p58*
Downing, James; Quebec, 1847 ***5704.8*** *p29*
Downing, James; Washington, 1859-1920 ***2872.1*** *p10*
Downing, James 20; Tortola, 1774 ***1219.7*** *p237*
Downing, James L.; Washington, 1859-1920 ***2872.1*** *p10*
Downing, John; Quebec, 1847 ***5704.8*** *p29*
Downing, John 30; Massachusetts, 1847 ***5881.1*** *p29*
Downing, John 40; Massachusetts, 1847 ***5881.1*** *p29*
Downing, Mary; Quebec, 1847 ***5704.8*** *p29*
Downing, Sally; Quebec, 1847 ***5704.8*** *p29*
Downing, Timothy 24; Massachusetts, 1847 ***5881.1*** *p34*
Downing, Wm.; Virginia, 1647 ***6219*** *p241*
Downs, Hugh; New York, NY, 1837 ***8208.4*** *p52*
Downs, John; Iowa, 1866-1943 ***123.54*** *p17*
Downs, John 14; Massachusetts, 1847 ***5881.1*** *p29*
Downy, Brigitte; Quebec, 1822 ***7603*** *p68*
Downy, Christian 25; Wilmington, NC, 1775 ***1639.20*** *p62*
Dowry, Duncan; St. John, N.B., 1847 ***5704.8*** *p15*
Dowry, John 12; St. John, N.B., 1847 ***5704.8*** *p15*
Dowse, Charles; Virginia, 1643 ***6219*** *p199*
Dowse, Katherine; Virginia, 1637 ***6219*** *p115*
Dowsing, Jeremiah 30; Philadelphia, 1775 ***1219.7*** *p274*
Dowson, Geor.; Virginia, 1643 ***6219*** *p200*
Dowson, George 16; Philadelphia, 1774 ***1219.7*** *p232*
Dowson, Gilbert; Virginia, 1636 ***6219*** *p74*
Dowthwit, Jane; Philadelphia, 1849 ***5704.8*** *p49*
Dowthwit, Thomas; Philadelphia, 1849 ***5704.8*** *p49*
Doyl, Michael; America, 1743 ***4971*** *p35*
Doyle, Mrs. 26; Massachusetts, 1847 ***5881.1*** *p31*
With child
Doyle, Alexander; St. John, N.B., 1847 ***5704.8*** *p33*
Doyle, Alexander 12; St. John, N.B., 1847 ***5704.8*** *p33*
Doyle, Andrew; America, 1742 ***4971*** *p31*
Doyle, Bartholomew; New York, 1840 ***7036*** *p123*
Doyle, Bernard 6; Massachusetts, 1849 ***5881.1*** *p27*
Doyle, Biddy 10; St. John, N.B., 1847 ***5704.8*** *p33*
Doyle, Catharine 40; Massachusetts, 1847 ***5881.1*** *p27*
Doyle, Catherine; America, 1741 ***4971*** *p16*
Doyle, Catherine; Annapolis, MD, 1742 ***4971*** *p93*
Doyle, Catherine; Maryland, 1742 ***4971*** *p107*
Doyle, Catherine; Montreal, 1824 ***7603*** *p65*
Doyle, Catherine; Philadelphia, 1811 ***53.26*** *p24*
Doyle, Catherine; Philadelphia, 1811 ***2859.11*** *p11*
Doyle, Catherine; St. John, N.B., 1848 ***5704.8*** *p43*
Doyle, Cornelius; Quebec, 1820 ***7603*** *p64*
Doyle, David; America, 1742 ***4971*** *p83*
Doyle, David; New York, NY, 1811 ***2859.11*** *p11*
Doyle, David 11; Philadelphia, 1864 ***5704.8*** *p155*
Doyle, Denis; Quebec, 1809 ***7603*** *p58*
Doyle, Dennis; America, 1742 ***4971*** *p30*
Doyle, Dennis; Annapolis, MD, 1742 ***4971*** *p93*
Doyle, Dennis; Maryland, 1742 ***4971*** *p106*
Doyle, Dennis; New York, NY, 1811 ***2859.11*** *p11*
Doyle, Dennis 22; Massachusetts, 1849 ***5881.1*** *p28*
Doyle, Dennis Thomas; Arkansas, 1918 ***95.2*** *p38*
Doyle, Edmond; America, 1743 ***4971*** *p54*
Doyle, Edmund 10; Massachusetts, 1849 ***5881.1*** *p28*
Doyle, Edward; Illinois, 1852 ***7857*** *p3*
Doyle, Edward; Quebec, 1808 ***7603*** *p81*
Doyle, Eliza; New York, NY, 1816 ***2859.11*** *p29*
With child
Doyle, Feelix; Annapolis, MD, 1742 ***4971*** *p93*
Doyle, Feelix; Maryland, 1742 ***4971*** *p107*
Doyle, Felix; America, 1742 ***4971*** *p86*
Doyle, Foelix; America, 1742 ***4971*** *p95*
Doyle, Francis; Quebec, 1822 ***7603*** *p57*
Doyle, George; New York, NY, 1835 ***8208.4*** *p43*
Doyle, George 24; Massachusetts, 1848 ***5881.1*** *p29*
Doyle, Helen 5; Philadelphia, 1864 ***5704.8*** *p155*
Doyle, Honora; Quebec, 1823 ***7603*** *p58*
Doyle, Jackey; St. John, N.B., 1847 ***5704.8*** *p33*
Doyle, James; America, 1740 ***4971*** *p30*
Doyle, James; America, 1741 ***4971*** *p34*
Doyle, James; California, 1879 ***2764.35*** *p19*
Doyle, James; New York, NY, 1838 ***8208.4*** *p81*
Doyle, James; New York, NY, 1850 ***6013.19*** *p90*
Doyle, James 8; Massachusetts, 1849 ***5881.1*** *p30*
Doyle, James 28; Virginia, 1774 ***1219.7*** *p243*
Doyle, James L.; Illinois, 1890 ***2896.5*** *p9*
Doyle, Jane; Quebec, 1847 ***5704.8*** *p17*
Doyle, John; America, 1739 ***4971*** *p26*
Doyle, John; America, 1742 ***4971*** *p35*
Doyle, John; Annapolis, MD, 1742 ***4971*** *p93*
Doyle, John; Boston, 1839-1840 ***7036*** *p117*
Doyle, John; Illinois, 1871 ***5012.38*** *p99*
Doyle, John; Maryland, 1742 ***4971*** *p106*
Doyle, John; New York, NY, 1811 ***2859.11*** *p11*
Doyle, John; New York, NY, 1816 ***2859.11*** *p29*
Doyle, John; New York, NY, 1837 ***8208.4*** *p55*
Doyle, John; Quebec, 1825 ***7603*** *p69*
Doyle, John; St. John, N.B., 1839 ***7036*** *p117*
Doyle, John; St. John, N.B., 1847 ***5704.8*** *p33*
Doyle, John; Virginia, 1856 ***4626.16*** *p16*
Doyle, John 6 mos; Massachusetts, 1849 ***5881.1*** *p30*
Doyle, John 19; Massachusetts, 1849 ***5881.1*** *p30*
Doyle, John 27; New Orleans, 1862 ***543.30*** *p59*
Doyle, John P.; Illinois, 1871 ***5012.39*** *p25*
Doyle, Joseph 20; St. John, N.B., 1866 ***5704.8*** *p167*
Doyle, Joseph 24; Philadelphia, 1774 ***1219.7*** *p232*
Doyle, Kate 18; Massachusetts, 1849 ***5881.1*** *p30*
Doyle, Kitty 5; St. John, N.B., 1847 ***5704.8*** *p33*
Doyle, Lawrence; Quebec, 1824 ***7603*** *p71*
Doyle, Lawrence 26; New Orleans, 1862 ***543.30*** *p59*
Doyle, Margaret; New York, NY, 1816 ***2859.11*** *p29*
Doyle, Margaret; St. John, N.B., 1848 ***5704.8*** *p43*
Doyle, Martin; New York, NY, 1816 ***2859.11*** *p29*
Doyle, Martin 22; Virginia, 1774 ***1219.7*** *p243*
Doyle, Martin 23; St. John, N.B., 1864 ***5704.8*** *p157*
Doyle, Martin Madden; New York, NY, 1836 ***8208.4*** *p12*
Doyle, Mary; Montreal, 1824 ***7603*** *p101*
Doyle, Mary; Quebec, 1825 ***7603*** *p93*
Doyle, Mary; St. John, N.B., 1847 ***5704.8*** *p33*
Doyle, Mary; St. John, N.B., 1852 ***5704.8*** *p95*
Doyle, Mary 6; Massachusetts, 1849 ***5881.1*** *p31*
Doyle, Mary 8; St. John, N.B., 1847 ***5704.8*** *p33*
Doyle, Mary 10; Massachusetts, 1850 ***5881.1*** *p32*
Doyle, Mary 24; Massachusetts, 1849 ***5881.1*** *p32*
Doyle, Mary 41; Philadelphia, 1864 ***5704.8*** *p155*
Doyle, Michael; America, 1742 ***4971*** *p17*
Doyle, Michael; Delaware, 1743 ***4971*** *p105*
Doyle, Michael; New York, NY, 1811 ***2859.11*** *p11*
Doyle, Michael 40; Philadelphia, 1864 ***5704.8*** *p155*
Doyle, Morgan; Quebec, 1787 ***7603*** *p75*
Doyle, Moses; New York, NY, 1816 ***2859.11*** *p29*
Doyle, Murtagh; America, 1743 ***4971*** *p34*
Doyle, Nancy; St. John, N.B., 1847 ***5704.8*** *p33*
Doyle, Ned 3; St. John, N.B., 1847 ***5704.8*** *p33*
Doyle, Nicholas 27; St. John, N.B., 1865 ***5704.8*** *p165*
Doyle, Nilly 8; St. John, N.B., 1847 ***5704.8*** *p33*
Doyle, Patrick; New Brunswick, 1824 ***7603*** *p76*
Doyle, Patrick; New Orleans, 1850 ***2896.5*** *p9*
Doyle, Patrick; New York, NY, 1816 ***2859.11*** *p29*
Doyle, Patrick 8; Massachusetts, 1849 ***5881.1*** *p33*
Doyle, Patrick 22; Massachusetts, 1848 ***5881.1*** *p33*
Doyle, Patrick 22; St. John, N.B., 1865 ***5704.8*** *p165*
Doyle, Patt 17; Newport, RI, 1851 ***6508.5*** *p20*
Doyle, Paul; New York, NY, 1837 ***8208.4*** *p53*
Doyle, Peter; Virginia, 1856 ***4626.16*** *p16*
Doyle, Richard 30; Massachusetts, 1849 ***5881.1*** *p34*
Doyle, Thomas; New York, NY, 1838 ***8208.4*** *p65*
Doyle, Thomas; St. John, N.B., 1847 ***5704.8*** *p33*
Doyle, Thomas 5; Massachusetts, 1850 ***5881.1*** *p34*
Doyle, Thomas 22; Virginia, 1774 ***1219.7*** *p239*
Doyle, Timothy 17; Massachusetts, 1849 ***5881.1*** *p34*
Doyle, William; New Brunswick, 1824 ***7603*** *p57*
Doyley, James 26; Maryland, 1775 ***1219.7*** *p249*
Doyne, Charles; New York, NY, 1815 ***2859.11*** *p29*
Dpyle, James 31; Arizona, 1890 ***2764.35*** *p17*
Drabble, Samuel; West Virginia, 1818 ***9788.3*** *p9*
Drabble, Samuel; West Virginia, 1820 ***9788.3*** *p9*
Drabwell, Charles 29; Maryland, 1775 ***1219.7*** *p261*
Drach, Andres; Pennsylvania, 1752 ***4525*** *p211*
Drach, Mrs. George; New England, 1752 ***4525*** *p211*
With 6 children
Drach, Petter; Pennsylvania, 1752 ***4525*** *p211*
Drach, Rudolf; Pennsylvania, 1754 ***4525*** *p211*
Drach, Wilhelm von; Halifax, N.S., 1780 ***9786*** *p269*
Drach, Wilhelm von; New York, 1776 ***9786*** *p269*
Dracott, Wm.; Virginia, 1642 ***6219*** *p194*
Dradge, John 24; Philadelphia, 1774 ***1219.7*** *p175*
Drady, Catharine 30; Massachusetts, 1847 ***5881.1*** *p27*
Dragash, Acim J.; Washington, 1859-1920 ***2872.1*** *p10*
Drago, Louis Vincent; Arkansas, 1918 ***95.2*** *p38*
Draheim, Elisabeth 26; New York, NY, 1862 ***9831.18*** *p16*
Draher, John, Jr.; New York, NY, 1840 ***8208.4*** *p109*
Drahmann, Johann Bernhard; America, 1848 ***8582.3*** *p15*
Drahmann, Johann Heinrich; America, 1848 ***8582.3*** *p15*
Drain, Henry; New York, NY, 1811 ***2859.11*** *p11*
Drain, John; New York, NY, 1811 ***2859.11*** *p11*
Drain, John; New York, NY, 1816 ***2859.11*** *p29*
Drain, Richard; New York, NY, 1816 ***2859.11*** *p29*

Drake, Ann; Virginia, 1638 6219 p120
Drake, Elizabeth *SEE* Drake, Robert
Drake, Francis; New York, NY, 1838 8208.4 p69
Drake, Henry; New York, NY, 1811 2859.11 p11
Drake, James; Virginia, 1639 6219 p156
Drake, Joane *SEE* Drake, Robert
Drake, John; Ohio, 1851 9892.11 p14
Drake, John; Virginia, 1637 6219 p82
Drake, Peter 24; Jamaica, 1736 3690.1 p66
Drake, Robert; Virginia, 1636 6219 p7
*Wife:*Joane
*Daughter:*Elizabeth
With son
Drake, Thomas 20; Antigua (Antego), 1728 3690.1 p66
Dralle, Henry 31; West Virginia, 1844 9788.3 p9
Dralle, John; Baltimore, 1904 3455.1 p48
Drandakis, John Andro; Arkansas, 1918 95.2 p38
Drangenstein, Johannes; Reading, PA, 1780 8137 p7
Draper, Elizabeth 26; Baltimore, 1775 1219.7 p271
Draper, George 25; Jamaica, 1730 3690.1 p66
Draper, James 18; Jamaica, 1733 3690.1 p67
Draper, John; Virginia, 1635 6219 p35
Draper, John 29; New Orleans, 1862 543.30 p57
Draper, Robt.; Virginia, 1624 6219 p2
Draper, Thomas 17; Maryland, 1718 3690.1 p67
Draper, Thomas 22; Virginia, 1773 1219.7 p168
Draper, William 18; Maryland, 1718 3690.1 p67
Draper, William 24; Kansas, 1878 5240.1 p10
Draper, William 24; Kansas, 1878 5240.1 p59
Draper, William Henry; Kansas, 1902 5240.1 p10
Dratt, Anth.; Virginia, 1643 6219 p200
Dravautz, Frank L. 21; Illinois, 1890 2896.5 p10
Drawater, Ann; Virginia, 1637 6219 p83
Drawter, Ann; Virginia, 1635 6219 p26
Draysey, Thomas 15; Philadelphia, 1775 1219.7 p248
Draywood, Thos.; Virginia, 1637 6219 p24
Draz, Francis; New York, NY, 1834 8208.4 p51
Dreaner, Mary 21; St. John, N.B., 1854 5704.8 p115
Dreaton, Jon.; Virginia, 1642 6219 p194
Drebot, Stephen; Arkansas, 1918 95.2 p38
Drechsler, . . .; Canada, 1776-1783 9786 p20
Dreckmeyer, Anne Marie Wilhelmine; America, 1854 4610.10 p156
Dreckmeyer, Christian Friedr. Conrad; America, 1881 4610.10 p109
Drees, Miss; America, 1845 3702.7 p85
Drees, John; Wisconsin, n.d. 9675.5 p121
Dreesmann, Bernard; America, 1839 8582.3 p15
Dreesmann, Heinrich; America, 1840 8582.3 p15
Dregis, Victor 20; New York, NY, 1878 9253 p47
Dreher, . . .; Canada, 1776-1783 9786 p20
Dreher, Andreas; Cayenne, 1764 2854 p44
*Wife:*Maria Anna
*Child:*Appolonia
*Child:*Maria Eva
*Child:*Catharina
*Child:*Johann Peter
Dreher, Andreas; Philadelphia, 1767 2854 p44
Dreher, Appolonia *SEE* Dreher, Andreas
Dreher, Appolonia; America, 1764 2854 p43
With 4 daughters
Dreher, Catharina *SEE* Dreher, Andreas
Dreher, Johann Peter *SEE* Dreher, Andreas
Dreher, Margaretha; New England, 1752 2444 p213
Dreher, Maria Anna *SEE* Dreher, Andreas
Dreher, Maria Eva *SEE* Dreher, Andreas
Dreher, Paul L.; Illinois, 1871 5012.39 p25
Dreher, Paul L.; Illinois, 1873 5012.39 p91
Drehr, Christian; South Carolina, 1788 7119 p199
Drehr, Georg Johannes; South Carolina, 1788 7119 p200
Drehr, Godfrey, Jr.; South Carolina, 1788 7119 p199
Drehr, Gottfrid; South Carolina, 1788 7119 p199
Drehr, John; South Carolina, 1788 7119 p199
Drehr, John; South Carolina, 1788 7119 p201
Drehr, Michl; South Carolina, 1788 7119 p197
Dreier, August 2 *SEE* Dreier, Gottfried
Dreier, Gottfried 37; America, 1839 3702.7 p307
*Wife:*Wilhelmine Wussow 28
*Son:*August 2
Dreier, Wilhelmine Wussow 28 *SEE* Dreier, Gottfried
Dreis, Michael; Wisconsin, n.d. 9675.5 p121
Dreisbach, Johannes 82; Ohio, 1871 8582 p7
Dreison, Anah.; New York, NY, 1811 2859.11 p11
Drenkhahn, Heinrich 23; New Orleans, 1839 9420.2 p71
Drennan, Catharine 5; Massachusetts, 1847 5881.1 p27
Drennan, Michael 7; Massachusetts, 1847 5881.1 p31
Drenner, John; West Virginia, 1855 9788.3 p9
Dres, Conrad; Pennsylvania, 1746 2444 p149
Dresback, Martin; Philadelphia, 1760 9973.7 p34
Dreschen, John 29; Kansas, 1882 5240.1 p63
Drescher, Adam; Philadelphia, 1779 8137 p7
Drescher, Anna Maria *SEE* Drescher, Hans Jerg
Drescher, Anna Maria *SEE* Drescher, Hans Jerg
Drescher, Georg Adam *SEE* Drescher, Hans Jerg
Drescher, Hans Jerg; Pennsylvania, 1746 2444 p150
*Wife:*Anna Maria
*Child:*Johann Georg
*Child:*Georg Adam
*Child:*Anna Maria
*Child:*Ursula
Drescher, Johann Georg *SEE* Drescher, Hans Jerg
Drescher, Ursula *SEE* Drescher, Hans Jerg
Dreschmeier, Franziska E. D. Dorette 37; America, 1882 4610.10 p118
Dresel, Otto; America, 1849 8582.3 p15
Dreseler, August; Missouri, 1854 4610.10 p17
Dreseler, August; New Orleans, 1853 4610.10 p41
Dreseler, L.; Died enroute, 1853 4610.10 p41
Dreseler, Wischen; Died enroute, 1853 4610.10 p40
Dreseman, Harmon H.; Ohio, 1843 8365.26 p12
Dresher, George; Pennsylvania, 1746 2444 p150
Dresler, Johann Andreas; Pennsylvania, 1749 4525 p211
Dresmann, Gerhard; Kentucky, 1843 8582.3 p100
Dress, Conrad; Pennsylvania, 1746 2444 p149
Dressler, Mr.; Pennsylvania, 1750-1761 4525 p211
Dressler, Andreas; Pennsylvania, 1752 4525 p211
Dressler, Sophia Margaret; New York, 1749 3652 p72
Dressmann, Arnold Heinrich; Kentucky, 1848 8582.3 p101
Dressmann, Bernard; Kentucky, 1839 8582.3 p99
Dressmann, Bernard; Kentucky, 1874-1875 8582.3 p99
Dressmann, Franz; Kentucky, 1848 8582.3 p101
Dressmann, Heinrich; Kentucky, 1839 8582.3 p99
Dressmann, Heinrich; Kentucky, 1848 8582.3 p101
Dreux, Mr. 16; New Orleans, 1826 778.5 p172
Dreves, Ernest 53; Kansas, 1884 5240.1 p10
Dreves, Ernst 53; Kansas, 1884 5240.1 p66
Drew, Edmund 14; Massachusetts, 1850 5881.1 p29
Drew, Edward; Virginia, 1647 6219 p244
Drew, Francis Abraham; New York, NY, 1835 8208.4 p56
Drew, Fred; Iowa, 1866-1943 123.54 p17
Drew, George; Philadelphia, 1847 53.26 p24
*Relative:*Nancy
*Relative:*Jane
Drew, George; Philadelphia, 1847 5704.8 p23
Drew, Hen.; Virginia, 1635 6219 p71
Drew, Jane *SEE* Drew, George
Drew, Jane; Philadelphia, 1847 5704.8 p23
Drew, Jerry 4; Massachusetts, 1849 5881.1 p30
Drew, John; Kansas, 1888 2764.35 p18
Drew, John 15; Virginia, 1727 3690.1 p67
Drew, Jon.; Virginia, 1642 6219 p195
Drew, Mary 2; Massachusetts, 1849 5881.1 p32
Drew, Nancy *SEE* Drew, George
Drew, Nancy; Philadelphia, 1847 5704.8 p23
Drew, Nancy 40; Massachusetts, 1849 5881.1 p33
Drew, Symon; Virginia, 1638 6219 p147
Drew, Timothy; Massachusetts, 1849 5881.1 p34
Drew, William; Iowa, 1866-1943 123.54 p17
Drew, Wm.; Virginia, 1636 6219 p32
Drewer, Joseph; Virginia, 1639 6219 p150
Drewett, John; Virginia, 1643 6219 p200
Drewlo, Gustav; Arkansas, 1918 95.2 p38
Drewrey, George; New York, NY, 1838 8208.4 p82
Drewry, Abigail; Virginia, 1639 6219 p154
Drewry, Robert; Virginia, 1638 6219 p124
Drews, Margaret; New York, 1749 3652 p72
Drews, Peter; New York, 1749 3652 p71
Drewyre, Alice; Virginia, 1637 6219 p111
Drey, Louis L. 20; New Orleans, 1862 543.30 p219
Dreyer, . . .; Canada, 1776-1783 9786 p20
Dreyer, Anne M. C. Wilhelmine *SEE* Dreyer, Ernst Carl Wilhelm
Dreyer, Anne Marie C. Muller *SEE* Dreyer, Friedrich Wilhelm
Dreyer, August 2 *SEE* Dreyer, Gottfried
Dreyer, Carl Heinrich *SEE* Dreyer, Friedrich Wilhelm
Dreyer, Ernst Carl Wilhelm; America, 1844 4610.10 p150
*Sister:*Anne M. C. Wilhelmine
Dreyer, Friedrich Wilhelm; America, 1839 4610.10 p119
*Father:*Carl Heinrich
*Mother:*Anne Marie C. Muller
Dreyer, Gottfried 37; America, 1839 3702.7 p307
*Wife:*Wilhelmine Wussow 28
*Son:*August 2
Dreyer, Wilhelmine Wussow 28 *SEE* Dreyer, Gottfried
Dreyfous, Abel; New York, NY, 1839 8208.4 p97
Dreyfus, Simon; Illinois, 1901 5012.40 p77
Dreyfuss, Abraham; America, 1840 8582.1 p8
Dreyfuss, Gerard; Shreveport, LA, 1877 7129 p44
Dreyspring, Carl J.; New York, 1754 3652 p79
Drezey, Thomas 21; Jamaica, 1733 3690.1 p67
Drezle, Joseph 31; New Orleans, 1862 543.30 p220
Dries, Gertrude; New Netherland, 1630-1646 8582.2 p51
*Relative:*Heinrich
Dries, Heinrich *SEE* Dries, Gertrude
Dries, John; Wisconsin, n.d. 9675.5 p121
Drieschmann, Henrich; Philadelphia, 1779 8137 p7
Drill, . . .; Canada, 1776-1783 9786 p20
Dring, Francis 19; Maryland, 1733 3690.1 p67
Drinkot, William; America, 1845 1450.2 p32A
Drinkwater, John; Jamaica, 1754 1219.7 p31
Drinkwater, Jon.; Virginia, 1637 6219 p113
Drinkwater, William; Boston, 1776 1219.7 p278
Drinkwater, William; Colorado, 1894 9678.2 p16
Drinnan, Thomas; Maine, 1835 1450.2 p33A
Drinner, Charles; West Virginia, 1855 9788.3 p9
Dripps, James; New York, NY, 1815 2859.11 p29
Driscol, Daniel; New York, NY, 1832 8208.4 p39
Driscol, Florence 40; New Orleans, 1862 543.30 p217
Driscoll, Mrs. 30; Massachusetts, 1849 5881.1 p31
Driscoll, Anne; Quebec, 1819 7603 p84
Driscoll, Catharine 8; Massachusetts, 1847 5881.1 p27
Driscoll, Catharine 20; Massachusetts, 1850 5881.1 p28
Driscoll, Cornelius; New York, NY, 1834 8208.4 p28
Driscoll, Cornelius; New York, NY, 1834 8208.4 p33
Driscoll, Darby; America, 1741 4971 p41
Driscoll, Dennis; America, 1742-1743 4971 p42
Driscoll, Eliza 9; Massachusetts, 1849 5881.1 p28
Driscoll, Ellen 16; Massachusetts, 1850 5881.1 p28
Driscoll, Florence 40; New Orleans, 1862 543.30 p217
Driscoll, Jeremiah; New York, NY, 1838 8208.4 p83
Driscoll, Jeremiah 17; Massachusetts, 1849 5881.1 p30
Driscoll, John; Arizona, 1897 9228.30 p2
Driscoll, John 14; Massachusetts, 1850 5881.1 p30
Driscoll, Margaret 1; Massachusetts, 1850 5881.1 p32
Driscoll, Margaret 10; Massachusetts, 1850 5881.1 p32
Driscoll, Mary 22; Massachusetts, 1850 5881.1 p32
Driscoll, Patrice; Quebec, 1819 7603 p53
Driscoll, Patrick 15; Massachusetts, 1849 5881.1 p33
Drisdale, Alexander 19; Philadelphia, 1774 1219.7 p183
Drissler, Jacob; Washington, 1859-1920 2872.1 p10
Dritscher, Peter; Georgia, 1738 9332 p319
Driver, Edward 19; Maryland, 1774 1219.7 p222
Driver, John 38; Port uncertain, 1730 3690.1 p290
Driver, Thomas 26; Georgia, 1774 1219.7 p188
Droculot, Nickenlas 39; Louisiana, 1835 778.5 p172
Droege, Ignatius; America, 1849 8582.3 p15
Droege, Lorenz; America, 1853 8582.3 p15
Droenan, Bridget; Quebec, 1847 5704.8 p37
Droenan, Edward; Quebec, 1847 5704.8 p37
Droenan, James; Quebec, 1847 5704.8 p37
Droenan, Margaret; Quebec, 1847 5704.8 p37
Droenan, Mary; Quebec, 1847 5704.8 p37
Droenan, Pat; Quebec, 1847 5704.8 p37
Droenan, Terrence; Quebec, 1847 5704.8 p37
Drolez, G. W. 30; Mexico, 1829 778.5 p172
Dromgoole, Christian 20; Massachusetts, 1847 5881.1 p27
Drone, P. S. 22; Port uncertain, 1825 778.5 p172
Dronet, Antoine; Louisiana, 1789-1819 778.5 p555
Drongoal, John; Montreal, 1822 7603 p76
Drop, Mike Steve; Arkansas, 1918 95.2 p38
Droppelmann, Johann Heinrich; America, 1844 8582.2 p9
Dros, Louisa 36; New Orleans, 1829 778.5 p172
Drose, John 19; Leeward Islands, 1729 3690.1 p67
Droste, Anne Marie Louise Caroline; America, 1871 4610.10 p100
Droste, Caroline 15; America, 1883 4610.10 p102
Droste, Herman Heinrich; America, 1839 8582.3 p15
Droste, Hermina 51; New York, NY, 1847 3377.6 p15
Droste, John; Philadelphia, 1754 1219.7 p29
Droste, John Hendrick 56; New York, NY, 1847 3377.6 p15
Drott, Johann; America, 1849 8582.2 p9
Drouet, Auguste 27; Port uncertain, 1821 778.5 p172
Drouillett, John; America, 1827 778.5 p172
Drouin, A.; Shreveport, LA, 1877 7129 p44
Droves, Lorenz 33; New Orleans, 1862 543.30 p62
Droyer, Timothy 26; New Orleans, 1862 543.30 p55
Drozke, Andrew 30; Arkansas, 1918 95.2 p38
Drozki, Andrew; Arkansas, 1918 95.2 p38
Druce, John 17; Maryland, 1739 3690.1 p67
Drue, Mary-Ann; Quebec, 1732 7603 p23
Drue, Richard; Virginia, 1639 6219 p157
Druecker, Joseph; Wisconsin, n.d. 9675.5 p121
Druhe, John Harvey; Baltimore, 1850 6013.19 p30
Druid, Charles 28; New Orleans, 1862 543.30 p61
Druit, Wm.; Virginia, 1648 6219 p252
Drum, Ann; Quebec, 1847 5704.8 p13
Drum, Johann Simon; Pennsylvania, 1742 4779.3 p13
Drum, Mary 16 *SEE* Drum, William
Drum, Nathaniel 34 *SEE* Drum, Thomas
Drum, Roger; Quebec, 1847 5704.8 p17

Drum, Thomas 36; Philadelphia, 1803 ***53.26*** *p24*
*Relative:*Nathaniel 34
Drum, William 20; Philadelphia, 1803 ***53.26*** *p24*
*Relative:*Mary 16
Drumgold, John; New York, NY, 1838 ***8208.4*** *p90*
Drumm, Louise; Iroquois Co., IL, 1894 ***3455.1*** *p10*
Drummer, Robert 15; Maryland or Virginia, 1718 ***3690.1*** *p67*
Drummond, Mr.; Quebec, 1815 ***9229.18*** *p79*
With wife
Drummond, David; Ohio, 1842 ***9892.11*** *p14*
Drummond, Emanuel Rudolph; Arkansas, 1918 ***95.2*** *p38*
Drummond, Frederick 27; Kansas, 1891 ***5240.1*** *p76*
Drummond, Hugh; St. John, N.B., 1847 ***5704.8*** *p34*
Drummond, John; Brunswick, NC, 1775 ***1639.20*** *p62*
Drummond, John; Charleston, SC, 1825 ***1639.20*** *p62*
Drummond, William; North Carolina, 1664 ***1639.20*** *p62*
Drummond, William; Prince Edward Island, 1770 ***9775.5*** *p210*
Drummond, William; Virginia, 1637 ***6219*** *p83*
Drummond, William; Virginia, 1639 ***6219*** *p182*
Drumond, John 18; Antigua (Antego), 1728 ***3690.1*** *p67*
Drumond, Michael; Philadelphia, 1851 ***5704.8*** *p70*
Drung, Ally; Quebec, 1847 ***5704.8*** *p37*
Drung, Edward; Quebec, 1847 ***5704.8*** *p37*
Drung, Ellen; Quebec, 1847 ***5704.8*** *p37*
Drung, Frank; Quebec, 1847 ***5704.8*** *p37*
Drung, James; Quebec, 1847 ***5704.8*** *p37*
Drung, John; Quebec, 1847 ***5704.8*** *p37*
Drung, Mary; Quebec, 1847 ***5704.8*** *p37*
Drung, Sarah; Quebec, 1847 ***5704.8*** *p37*
Druon, H. 27; New Orleans, 1835 ***778.5*** *p172*
Drury, Eleanor 23; Maryland or Virginia, 1699 ***2212*** *p24*
Drury, Henry 20; Massachusetts, 1849 ***5881.1*** *p29*
Drury, Mary; America, 1743 ***4971*** *p18*
Drury, Mary; Delaware Bay or River, 1743 ***4971*** *p104*
Dry, George 42; New Orleans, 1862 ***543.30*** *p219*
Dry, Thomas H.; Wisconsin, n.d. ***9675.5*** *p121*
Dryden, Adam; Savannah, GA, 1774 ***1219.7*** *p227*
Dryden, Adam 28; Savannah, GA, 1774 ***1219.7*** *p226*
With wife
With 3 children
Dryfus, Joshua; Shreveport, LA, 1878 ***7129*** *p44*
Drygyer, John; New York, NY, 1834 ***8208.4*** *p3*
Dryhurst, Thomas; Virginia, 1618 ***6219*** *p4*
Dryniewicz, . . .; New York, 1831 ***4606*** *p173*
Dsyat, Catherine 6 mos; Quebec, 1863 ***5704.8*** *p153*
Dsyat, Mary 21; Quebec, 1863 ***5704.8*** *p153*
Dsyat, Patrick 22; Quebec, 1863 ***5704.8*** *p153*
Duane, Timothy; America, 1736 ***4971*** *p39*
Duat, Germain 27; New Orleans, 1835 ***778.5*** *p172*
Dubac, Dominique 25; New Orleans, 1862 ***543.30*** *p215*
Dubache, Mr. 23; New Orleans, 1837 ***778.5*** *p172*
Dubacher, Frank; Arizona, 1888 ***2764.35*** *p18*
Dubacher, Henry; Salt Lake City, 1877 ***2764.35*** *p16*
Dubail, Theophile 25; America, 1836 ***778.5*** *p172*
Dubains, Francois 45; America, 1825 ***778.5*** *p172*
Dubal, Benjamin 30; New Orleans, 1826 ***778.5*** *p173*
Dubarry, Mr. 22; America, 1835 ***778.5*** *p173*
Dubas, Luc 24; New Orleans, 1839 ***778.5*** *p176*
Dubat, Pierre 24; New Orleans, 1838 ***778.5*** *p173*
Dubberley, William 19; Maryland, 1724 ***3690.1*** *p67*
Dubeau, Simon 26; Louisiana, 1820 ***778.5*** *p173*
Dubinski, Alex; Arkansas, 1918 ***95.2*** *p38*
Duboc, Chs. 24; New Orleans, 1839 ***778.5*** *p173*
Dubois, Mr.; New York, NY, 1834 ***8582.2*** *p23*
Dubois, Mr. 20; New Orleans, 1823 ***778.5*** *p173*
Dubois, Mr. 40; America, 1838 ***778.5*** *p173*
Dubois, Mr. 40; New Orleans, 1825 ***778.5*** *p173*
Dubois, A. 37; America, 1838 ***778.5*** *p173*
Dubois, Ch. Jos. 3; America, 1836 ***778.5*** *p173*
DuBois, Edward; America, 1893 ***1450.2*** *p33A*
Dubois, Guillaume Germain; Louisiana, 1789-1819 ***778.5*** *p555*
Dubois, J. F. 33; New Orleans, 1823 ***778.5*** *p174*
Dubois, Jean 25; America, 1838 ***778.5*** *p173*
Dubois, Jean Bapte. 19; New Orleans, 1838 ***778.5*** *p173*
Dubois, John 33; New Orleans, 1862 ***543.30*** *p56*
Dubois, Jules 41; West Virginia, 1904 ***9788.3*** *p9*
DuBois, Louis 46; Kansas, 1879 ***5240.1*** *p61*
Dubois, M. 21; America, 1836 ***778.5*** *p173*
Dubois, Octave 17; Port uncertain, 1839 ***778.5*** *p173*
Dubois, Pierre; Louisiana, 1789-1819 ***778.5*** *p555*
Dubois, Prisque; Quebec, 1714 ***7603*** *p21*
Dubois, Sophie 30; New Orleans, 1829 ***778.5*** *p173*
Duboist, James 36; Port uncertain, 1829 ***778.5*** *p174*
Dubold, Eliza 14; America, 1835 ***778.5*** *p174*
Dubons, A. 22; New Orleans, 1826 ***778.5*** *p174*
Dubord, Dr.; Quebec, 1815 ***9229.18*** *p79*
Dubosq, Mr. 40; America, 1837 ***778.5*** *p174*
Dubourdieu, Charles 17; Jamaica, 1731 ***3690.1*** *p67*
Dubourg, Adolphe 7; America, 1835 ***778.5*** *p174*
Dubourg, Celine 1; America, 1835 ***778.5*** *p174*
Dubourg, Charles 34; New Orleans, 1836 ***778.5*** *p174*
Dubourg, Francois 27; America, 1837 ***778.5*** *p174*
Dubourg, Martin 45; Louisiana, 1820 ***778.5*** *p174*
Dubourg, Nicholas 30; New Orleans, 1839 ***778.5*** *p174*
Dubourg, Sophie 28; America, 1835 ***778.5*** *p174*
Dubourg, Victor 5; America, 1835 ***778.5*** *p174*
Dubourjas, Francois. 22; New Orleans, 1838 ***778.5*** *p174*
Dubrege, Louis 35; New Orleans, 1838 ***778.5*** *p174*
Dubret, Estelle 13; America, 1839 ***778.5*** *p175*
Dubret, P. A. 45; America, 1839 ***778.5*** *p175*
Dubreuil, Mme. 22; America, 1839 ***778.5*** *p175*
Dubreuil, Mr. 34; America, 1839 ***778.5*** *p175*
Dubreuil, Mr. 36; America, 1839 ***778.5*** *p175*
Dubreuil, Francois 30; New Orleans, 1827 ***778.5*** *p175*
Dubreuil, J. 30; Mexico, 1831 ***778.5*** *p175*
Dubreuill, Victor 31; America, 1838 ***778.5*** *p175*
Dubreye, Louis 35; New Orleans, 1838 ***778.5*** *p174*
Dubriel, Andrien; Colorado, 1904 ***9678.2*** *p16*
Dubroca, Mr. 22; New Orleans, 1839 ***778.5*** *p175*
Dubuck, Andre 24; New Orleans, 1839 ***778.5*** *p175*
Dubunois, Barth. 69; Port uncertain, 1839 ***778.5*** *p175*
Duburg, E. B. 33; Port uncertain, 1835 ***778.5*** *p175*
Dubus, Mme.; America, 1838 ***778.5*** *p175*
Dubus, Mr. 45; America, 1838 ***778.5*** *p175*
Ducall, Victor; Washington, 1859-1920 ***2872.1*** *p10*
Ducarre, Charles Marie; Port uncertain, 1839 ***778.5*** *p175*
Ducas, George 20; America, 1836 ***778.5*** *p176*
Ducas, J. B. 50; Port uncertain, 1823 ***778.5*** *p176*
Ducas, Jean-Baptiste; Quebec, 1715 ***7603*** *p21*
Ducas, Luc 24; New Orleans, 1839 ***778.5*** *p176*
Ducas, V. 25; Port uncertain, 1836 ***778.5*** *p176*
Ducasse, Mr.; America, 1839 ***778.5*** *p176*
Ducastaing, Jean 23; New Orleans, 1838 ***778.5*** *p176*
Ducat, Charles M. 26; New Orleans, 1838 ***778.5*** *p176*
Ducaurneau, Mr. 44; New Orleans, 1829 ***778.5*** *p176*
Duch, Charlotte 43; America, 1854-1855 ***9162.6*** *p105*
Duch, Frz. Jos. 13; America, 1854-1855 ***9162.6*** *p105*
Duch, Jon.; Virginia, 1637 ***6219*** *p113*
Duchanfour, Mr. 18; New Orleans, 1822 ***778.5*** *p176*
Duchemin, Francois; Quebec, 1793 ***7603*** *p47*
Ducherer, Anton 35; New Orleans, 1835 ***778.5*** *p176*
Duchesnay, Major; Quebec, 1815 ***9229.18*** *p82*
With wife
Duchesne, Amedee 26; New Orleans, 1836 ***778.5*** *p176*
Duchesne, J. B. 44; New Orleans, 1822 ***778.5*** *p176*
Duchey, David 21; New Orleans, 1862 ***543.30*** *p220*
Duchien, Mr. 31; New Orleans, 1839 ***778.5*** *p15*
Duchow, Christian; Illinois, 1862 ***2896.5*** *p10*
Duck, John; Wisconsin, n.d. ***9675.5*** *p121*
Ducke, William; Virginia, 1639 ***6219*** *p158*
Duckener, David; Philadelphia, 1760 ***9973.7*** *p35*
Ducker, Jno; America, 1698 ***2212*** *p6*
Ducker, Thomas 18; New Orleans, 1862 ***543.30*** *p215*
Duckes, Thomas; America, 1698 ***2212*** *p9*
Ducket, John; Virginia, 1646 ***6219*** *p246*
Duckett, Guillaume; Quebec, 1824 ***7603*** *p76*
Duckett, Thomas 18; New Orleans, 1862 ***543.30*** *p215*
Duckfield, Susannah; Died enroute, 1875 ***4719.30*** *p258*
Duckley, Luce; Virginia, 1639 ***6219*** *p161*
Duckus, Fredk.; Wisconsin, n.d. ***9675.5*** *p121*
Duckworth, Edmund; New York, NY, 1838 ***8208.4*** *p81*
Duclos, Mr. 23; New Orleans, 1822 ***778.5*** *p176*
Ducluzeau, C. 28; America, 1839 ***778.5*** *p176*
Ducluzeau, Henry; New York, NY, 1839 ***8208.4*** *p97*
Ducoin, F. 42; New Orleans, 1823 ***778.5*** *p177*
Ducommun, Henriette 27; New Orleans, 1822 ***778.5*** *p177*
Ducos, Mr. 40; America, 1837 ***778.5*** *p177*
Ducournau, Mr. 20; New Orleans, 1825 ***778.5*** *p177*
Ducournau, Mr. 26; New Orleans, 1836 ***778.5*** *p177*
Ducournau, L. 23; New Orleans, 1836 ***778.5*** *p177*
Ducret, Alphonse 26; Kansas, 1879 ***5240.1*** *p59*
Ducret, Jean 26; Kansas, 1880 ***5240.1*** *p61*
Ducret, Paul 26; Kansas, 1876 ***5240.1*** *p57*
Ducros, Mr. 24; New Orleans, 1837 ***778.5*** *p177*
Ducrow, Stephen 25; Jamaica, 1735 ***3690.1*** *p67*
Dudar, Anielina 19; New York, 1912 ***9980.29*** *p59*
Duddy, Biddy 6; Philadelphia, 1865 ***5704.8*** *p165*
Duddy, George; Philadelphia, 1864 ***5704.8*** *p173*
Duddy, Hannah 8; Philadelphia, 1865 ***5704.8*** *p165*
Duddy, Henry; Baltimore, 1811 ***2859.11*** *p11*
Duddy, Hugh 10; Philadelphia, 1865 ***5704.8*** *p165*
Duddy, Hugh 48; Philadelphia, 1864 ***5704.8*** *p161*
Duddy, Jane 55; Philadelphia, 1865 ***5704.8*** *p165*
Duddy, Margaret; Philadelphia, 1868 ***5704.8*** *p225*
Duddy, Mary J.; Philadelphia, 1864 ***5704.8*** *p173*
Duddy, Mary Jane 1; Philadelphia, 1864 ***5704.8*** *p161*
Duddy, Mary Jane 20; Philadelphia, 1865 ***5704.8*** *p165*
Duddy, Richard; St. John, N.B., 1850 ***5704.8*** *p65*
Duddy, William; Baltimore, 1811 ***2859.11*** *p11*
Dudek, Jan 10 mos *SEE* Dudek, Wiktoria
Dudek, Wiktoria 23; New York, 1912 ***9980.29*** *p66*
*Son:*Jan 10 mos
Duden, August; New York, 1891 ***1450.2*** *p8B*
Duden, George E.; Illinois, 1893 ***5012.40*** *p53*
Duden, Gottfried; Baltimore, 1824 ***8582.1*** *p54*
Duden, Hans; America, 1891 ***1450.2*** *p8B*
Dudenheiffer, Jacob 26; New Orleans, 1862 ***543.30*** *p61*
Dudenhofer, Elisabeth; America, 1913 ***1763*** *p40D*
Dudenhoffer, Joseph 22; New Orleans, 1862 ***543.30*** *p57*
Dudgeon, Catharine 18; Massachusetts, 1850 ***5881.1*** *p28*
Dudgeon, Robert; Philadelphia, 1849 ***53.26*** *p25*
Dudgeon, Robert John; Philadelphia, 1849 ***5704.8*** *p53*
Dudis, Anton; Arkansas, 1918 ***95.2*** *p39*
Dudley, Christian Lester; Washington, 1859-1920 ***2872.1*** *p10*
Dudley, George 18; Maryland or Virginia, 1733 ***3690.1*** *p68*
Dudley, James 16; Maryland, 1730 ***3690.1*** *p68*
Dudley, James Stephen; Washington, 1859-1920 ***2872.1*** *p10*
Dudley, Jewel Kethleen; Washington, 1859-1920 ***2872.1*** *p10*
Dudley, Lillei May; Washington, 1859-1920 ***2872.1*** *p10*
Dudley, Margaret; New York, NY, 1815 ***2859.11*** *p30*
Dudley, Matthew; America, 1741 ***4971*** *p23*
Dudley, Robert; Montreal, 1824 ***7603*** *p100*
Dudley, Sherman; Dakota, 1882 ***5240.1*** *p10*
Dudloff, . . .; Canada, 1776-1783 ***9786*** *p20*
Dudly, Edward; Virginia, 1637 ***6219*** *p82*
Dudo, Gus; Arkansas, 1918 ***95.2*** *p39*
Dudouyt, Mr. 37; Port uncertain, 1837 ***778.5*** *p177*
Duduit, Jacq. 23; Port uncertain, 1839 ***778.5*** *p177*
Duduit, Mathilde 24; Port uncertain, 1839 ***778.5*** *p177*
Dudun, Mrs. P. 40?; New Orleans, 1826 ***778.5*** *p177*
Duebel, Andreas; America, 1836 ***8582.1*** *p8*
Dueck, Abraham; Quebec, 1876 ***9980.20*** *p49*
Dueck, Anna; Quebec, 1875 ***9980.20*** *p48*
Dueck, Anna; Quebec, 1876 ***9980.20*** *p49*
Dueck, Anna Friesen; Quebec, 1876 ***9980.20*** *p49*
Dueck, Elisabeth; Quebec, 1875 ***9980.20*** *p48*
Dueck, Elizabeth; Quebec, 1875 ***9980.20*** *p48*
Dueck, Helena; Quebec, 1875 ***9980.20*** *p48*
Dueck, Helena Fehr; Quebec, 1875 ***9980.20*** *p48*
Dueck, Herrmann; Quebec, 1875 ***9980.20*** *p48*
Dueck, Isaak 18; Quebec, 1875 ***9980.20*** *p48*
Dueck, Isak; Quebec, 1875 ***9980.20*** *p48*
Dueck, Jacob; Quebec, 1877 ***9980.20*** *p49*
Dueck, Jacob 15; Quebec, 1875 ***9980.20*** *p48*
Dueck, Johann; Quebec, 1875 ***9980.20*** *p48*
Dueck, Margaretha; Quebec, 1875 ***9980.20*** *p48*
Dueck, Peter; Quebec, 1875 ***9980.20*** *p48*
Dueck, Peter; Quebec, 1876 ***9980.20*** *p49*
Dueck, Susana Vehr; Quebec, 1875 ***9980.20*** *p48*
Dueck, Susanna; Quebec, 1875 ***9980.20*** *p48*
Dueckel, Nikolaus; Philadelphia, 1779 ***8137*** *p8*
Duee, John; Colorado, 1904 ***9678.2*** *p16*
Duemmler, Georg Peter; Pennsylvania, 1724-1765 ***2444*** *p150*
Duenckel, Anna Elisabeth *SEE* Duenckel, Johann Michael
Duenckel, Johann Michael; Pennsylvania, 1752 ***4525*** *p209*
*Wife:*Anna Elisabeth
Duerrbaum, J. Philip; New York, 1749 ***3652*** *p71*
Duett, Joh.; Pennsylvania, 1753 ***2444*** *p169*
Duette, David; Pennsylvania, 1751 ***2444*** *p150*
Dufain, . . . 6 wks; New Orleans, 1827 ***778.5*** *p177*
Dufain, Mme. 17; New Orleans, 1827 ***778.5*** *p177*
Dufain, Jos. 21; New Orleans, 1827 ***778.5*** *p177*
Dufais, . . .; Canada, 1776-1783 ***9786*** *p42*
Dufar, J. 32; America, 1838 ***778.5*** *p177*
Dufard, S. 33; New Orleans, 1830 ***778.5*** *p178*
Dufart, John 24; New Orleans, 1831 ***778.5*** *p178*
Dufau, John B.; New York, NY, 1836 ***8208.4*** *p20*
Dufaut, Louis 38; America, 1838 ***778.5*** *p178*
Dufaux, Mr. 40; New Orleans, 1839 ***778.5*** *p178*
Dufendorffer, Heinrich; Pennsylvania, 1735 ***4480*** *p312*
Dufendorffer, Jacob; Pennsylvania, 1735 ***4480*** *p312*
Dufendorffer, Kilian; Pennsylvania, 1735 ***4480*** *p312*
Dufetel, L. A. 23; New Orleans, 1832 ***778.5*** *p178*
Duff, . . .; Canada, 1776-1783 ***9786*** *p20*
Duff, Ann 10; Jamaica, 1773 ***1219.7*** *p172*
Duff, Dan.; America, 1736 ***4971*** *p44*
Duff, Donald; South Carolina, 1716 ***1639.20*** *p62*
Duff, Eliza; New York, NY, 1815 ***2859.11*** *p30*
Duff, James N. 27; Kansas, 1890 ***5240.1*** *p10*
Duff, James N. 27; Kansas, 1890 ***5240.1*** *p74*
Duff, Jane; New York, NY, 1816 ***2859.11*** *p30*
Duff, John; New York, NY, 1816 ***2859.11*** *p30*
Duff, John; New York, NY, 1836 ***8208.4*** *p12*
Duff, John 20; North Carolina, 1775 ***1639.20*** *p62*
Duff, Margaret; New York, NY, 1816 ***2859.11*** *p30*
Duff, Paul; Wisconsin, n.d. ***9675.5*** *p121*
Duff, Samuel; New York, NY, 1815 ***2859.11*** *p30*
Duff, Thomas; New York, NY, 1816 ***2859.11*** *p30*

Duff, Thomas; South Carolina, 1716 ***1639.20*** *p62*
Duff, William M. 37; Kansas, 1880 ***5240.1*** *p62*
Duffas, Jean 36; Port uncertain, 1837 ***778.5*** *p178*
Duffee, Margaret 1; Massachusetts, 1849 ***5881.1*** *p32*
Duffey, Anne 21; Philadelphia, 1860 ***5704.8*** *p145*
Duffey, John; New York, NY, 1811 ***2859.11*** *p11*
Duffey, Phillip 20; St. John, N.B., 1866 ***5704.8*** *p167*
Duffey, Thomas 21; Ohio, 1842 ***9892.11*** *p14*
Duffie, Ellen; Philadelphia, 1865 ***5704.8*** *p195*
Duffield, George; Iroquois Co., IL, 1892 ***3455.1*** *p10*
Duffin, Anne; Philadelphia, 1816 ***2859.11*** *p30*
Duffin, Catherine *SEE* Duffin, John
Duffin, Catherine; Philadelphia, 1848 ***5704.8*** *p40*
Duffin, Charles 7 *SEE* Duffin, John
Duffin, Charles 7; Philadelphia, 1848 ***5704.8*** *p40*
Duffin, Daniel; Ohio, 1841 ***8365.25*** *p12*
Duffin, Edward 23; Windward Islands, 1722 ***3690.1*** *p68*
Duffin, Felix; Ohio, 1842 ***8365.25*** *p12*
Duffin, James 6 *SEE* Duffin, John
Duffin, James 6; Philadelphia, 1848 ***5704.8*** *p40*
Duffin, Jane 9 *SEE* Duffin, John
Duffin, Jane 9; Philadelphia, 1848 ***5704.8*** *p40*
Duffin, John; Philadelphia, 1848 ***53.26*** *p25*
*Relative:*Catherine
*Relative:*Jane 9
*Relative:*Charles 7
*Relative:*James 6
*Relative:*Sarah 4
Duffin, John; Philadelphia, 1848 ***5704.8*** *p40*
Duffin, Sarah 4 *SEE* Duffin, John
Duffin, Sarah 4; Philadelphia, 1848 ***5704.8*** *p40*
Duffiney, . . .; Halifax, N.S., 1752 ***7074.6*** *p230*
Dufft, . . .; Canada, 1776-1783 ***9786*** *p20*
Duffus, Alexander; Charleston, SC, 1806 ***1639.20*** *p62*
Duffy, Ann; Philadelphia, 1851 ***5704.8*** *p80*
Duffy, Anne; Philadelphia, 1864 ***5704.8*** *p175*
Duffy, Anne; St. John, N.B., 1853 ***5704.8*** *p106*
Duffy, Annie; New York, NY, 1867 ***5704.8*** *p224*
Duffy, Anthoney; Philadelphia, 1868 ***5704.8*** *p225*
Duffy, Barny; St. John, N.B., 1847 ***5704.8*** *p15*
Duffy, Bell; St. John, N.B., 1847 ***5704.8*** *p15*
Duffy, Bernard; Philadelphia, 1865 ***5704.8*** *p190*
Duffy, Bernard 28; St. John, N.B., 1853 ***5704.8*** *p110*
Duffy, Biddy; St. John, N.B., 1847 ***5704.8*** *p10*
Duffy, Biddy; St. John, N.B., 1847 ***5704.8*** *p24*
Duffy, Biddy 22; St. John, N.B., 1865 ***5704.8*** *p165*
Duffy, Bridget; Montreal, 1825 ***7603*** *p99*
Duffy, Bridget; Philadelphia, 1847 ***53.26*** *p25*
*Relative:*Mary 11
Duffy, Bridget; Philadelphia, 1847 ***5704.8*** *p14*
Duffy, Catharine; New York, NY, 1869 ***5704.8*** *p232*
Duffy, Catharine; Philadelphia, 1849 ***5704.8*** *p54*
Duffy, Catharine 40; Massachusetts, 1847 ***5881.1*** *p27*
Duffy, Catherine; Philadelphia, 1849 ***53.26*** *p25*
Duffy, Catherine; St. John, N.B., 1847 ***5704.8*** *p11*
Duffy, Catherine; St. John, N.B., 1851 ***5704.8*** *p77*
Duffy, Catherine 6 mos; St. John, N.B., 1847 ***5704.8*** *p15*
Duffy, Catherine 20; St. John, N.B., 1856 ***5704.8*** *p132*
Duffy, Charles; New York, NY, 1816 ***2859.11*** *p30*
Duffy, Charles; Philadelphia, 1853 ***5704.8*** *p100*
Duffy, Charles; St. John, N.B., 1847 ***5704.8*** *p20*
Duffy, Charles; St. John, N.B., 1850 ***5704.8*** *p67*
Duffy, Charles 22; Philadelphia, 1856 ***5704.8*** *p129*
Duffy, Daniel; Philadelphia, 1851 ***5704.8*** *p81*
Duffy, Daniel; St. John, N.B., 1853 ***5704.8*** *p106*
Duffy, Daniel 21; Philadelphia, 1857 ***5704.8*** *p132*
Duffy, Dennis; New York, NY, 1864 ***5704.8*** *p171*
Duffy, Edward; Philadelphia, 1851 ***5704.8*** *p75*
Duffy, Eliza; New York, NY, 1868 ***5704.8*** *p227*
Duffy, Eliza Jane 19; Philadelphia, 1864 ***5704.8*** *p157*
Duffy, Elizabeth; Philadelphia, 1865 ***5704.8*** *p190*
Duffy, Elizabeth; Philadelphia, 1866 ***5704.8*** *p208*
Duffy, Ellen; America, 1867 ***5704.8*** *p223*
Duffy, Ellen; New York, NY, 1868 ***5704.8*** *p227*
Duffy, Ellen; St. John, N.B., 1847 ***5704.8*** *p15*
Duffy, Ellen 1; St. John, N.B., 1853 ***5704.8*** *p107*
Duffy, Fanny; New York, NY, 1816 ***2859.11*** *p30*
Duffy, Fanny; St. John, N.B., 1853 ***5704.8*** *p106*
Duffy, Fanny 17; Philadelphia, 1864 ***5704.8*** *p156*
Duffy, Fargus; New York, NY, 1811 ***2859.11*** *p11*
Duffy, Francis; New York, NY, 1811 ***2859.11*** *p11*
Duffy, Francis; New York, NY, 1833 ***8208.4*** *p40*
Duffy, Francis 3; St. John, N.B., 1853 ***5704.8*** *p106*
Duffy, George; America, 1864 ***5704.8*** *p188*
Duffy, Hannah 26; New Orleans, 1858 ***5704.8*** *p140*
Duffy, Hyacinth; St. Louis, 1850 ***6013.19*** *p30*
Duffy, Isabella; Philadelphia, 1865 ***5704.8*** *p197*
Duffy, James; New York, NY, 1811 ***2859.11*** *p11*
Duffy, James; New York, NY, 1949 ***6013.19*** *p30*
Duffy, James; Ohio, 1844 ***9892.11*** *p14*
Duffy, James; Ohio, 1847 ***9892.11*** *p14*
Duffy, James; St. John, N.B., 1847 ***5704.8*** *p15*
Duffy, James 15; Philadelphia, 1854 ***5704.8*** *p118*
Duffy, John; America, 1740 ***4971*** *p70*
Duffy, John; America, 1864 ***5704.8*** *p190*
Duffy, John; New York, NY, 1816 ***2859.11*** *p30*
Duffy, John; New York, NY, 1865 ***5704.8*** *p195*
Duffy, John; New York, NY, 1868 ***5704.8*** *p227*
Duffy, John; Philadelphia, 1853 ***5704.8*** *p101*
Duffy, John; Philadelphia, 1866 ***5704.8*** *p208*
Duffy, John; St. John, N.B., 1847 ***5704.8*** *p10*
Duffy, John; Washington, 1859-1920 ***2872.1*** *p10*
Duffy, John 30; Philadelphia, 1853 ***5704.8*** *p111*
Duffy, John 30; Philadelphia, 1854 ***5704.8*** *p123*
Duffy, John 38; New Orleans, 1862 ***543.30*** *p61*
Duffy, John 39; Nevada, 1890 ***2764.35*** *p18*
Duffy, Julia 18; Massachusetts, 1850 ***5881.1*** *p30*
Duffy, Margaret; New York, NY, 1868 ***5704.8*** *p227*
Duffy, Margaret; Philadelphia, 1864 ***5704.8*** *p169*
Duffy, Margaret; Philadelphia, 1865 ***5704.8*** *p190*
Duffy, Margaret; Quebec, 1847 ***5704.8*** *p29*
Duffy, Margaret; St. John, N.B., 1849 ***5704.8*** *p49*
Duffy, Margaret 30; Philadelphia, 1854 ***5704.8*** *p118*
Duffy, Margaret McLaughlin *SEE* Duffy, Patrick
Duffy, Martin; New York, 1847 ***1450.2*** *p33A*
Duffy, Mary; New York, NY, 1816 ***2859.11*** *p30*
With child
Duffy, Mary; New York, NY, 1864 ***5704.8*** *p170*
Duffy, Mary; Philadelphia, 1847 ***53.26*** *p25*
*Relative:*Sally
Duffy, Mary; Philadelphia, 1847 ***5704.8*** *p5*
Duffy, Mary; Philadelphia, 1866 ***5704.8*** *p208*
Duffy, Mary; Philadelphia, 1868 ***5704.8*** *p225*
Duffy, Mary 4; St. John, N.B., 1853 ***5704.8*** *p107*
Duffy, Mary 5; St. John, N.B., 1853 ***5704.8*** *p106*
Duffy, Mary 11 *SEE* Duffy, Bridget
Duffy, Mary 11; Philadelphia, 1847 ***5704.8*** *p14*
Duffy, Mary 18; Philadelphia, 1853 ***5704.8*** *p109*
Duffy, Mary 18; St. John, N.B., 1856 ***5704.8*** *p131*
Duffy, Mary 19; St. John, N.B., 1865 ***5704.8*** *p165*
Duffy, Mary 34; Massachusetts, 1849 ***5881.1*** *p32*
Duffy, Mary Ann 2; New York, NY, 1868 ***5704.8*** *p227*
Duffy, Michael; Philadelphia, 1847 ***53.26*** *p25*
*Relative:*Nancy
Duffy, Michael; Philadelphia, 1847 ***5704.8*** *p1*
Duffy, Michael; St. John, N.B., 1847 ***5704.8*** *p15*
Duffy, Michael 9; St. John, N.B., 1853 ***5704.8*** *p107*
Duffy, Nancy *SEE* Duffy, Michael
Duffy, Nancy; Philadelphia, 1847 ***5704.8*** *p1*
Duffy, Nancy; St. John, N.B., 1853 ***5704.8*** *p106*
Duffy, Natty; St. John, N.B., 1847 ***5704.8*** *p20*
Duffy, Ned 40; Massachusetts, 1847 ***5881.1*** *p33*
Duffy, Owen; New York, NY, 1811 ***2859.11*** *p11*
Duffy, Patrick; America, 1740 ***4971*** *p15*
Duffy, Patrick; America, 1864 ***5704.8*** *p176*
Duffy, Patrick; New York, NY, 1816 ***2859.11*** *p30*
Duffy, Patrick; New York, NY, 1867 ***5704.8*** *p223*
Duffy, Patrick; Philadelphia, 1836 ***7036*** *p116*
*Wife:*Margaret McLaughlin
Duffy, Patrick 12; Philadelphia, 1854 ***5704.8*** *p118*
Duffy, Patrick 19; St. John, N.B., 1854 ***5704.8*** *p122*
Duffy, Patrick 19; St. John, N.B., 1864 ***5704.8*** *p158*
Duffy, Patrick 20; Massachusetts, 1849 ***5881.1*** *p33*
Duffy, Peggy 21; St. John, N.B., 1858 ***5704.8*** *p137*
Duffy, Peter; New York, NY, 1816 ***2859.11*** *p30*
Duffy, Peter 25; Massachusetts, 1850 ***5881.1*** *p33*
Duffy, Phillip 20; St. John, N.B., 1867 ***5704.8*** *p168*
Duffy, Sally *SEE* Duffy, Mary
Duffy, Sally; Philadelphia, 1847 ***5704.8*** *p5*
Duffy, Sally; St. John, N.B., 1850 ***5704.8*** *p65*
Duffy, Sally 20; Philadelphia, 1853 ***5704.8*** *p111*
Duffy, Sarah; Quebec, 1847 ***5704.8*** *p29*
Duffy, Sarah 53; St. John, N.B., 1854 ***5704.8*** *p122*
Duffy, Susan; St. John, N.B., 1847 ***5704.8*** *p15*
Duffy, Susan 9 mos; St. John, N.B., 1853 ***5704.8*** *p106*
Duffy, Timothy; New York, NY, 1840 ***8208.4*** *p105*
Duffy, William; Philadelphia, 1849 ***53.26*** *p25*
Duffy, William; Philadelphia, 1849 ***5704.8*** *p54*
Duffy, William; Philadelphia, 1853 ***5704.8*** *p101*
Duffy, William; Philadelphia, 1866 ***5704.8*** *p208*
Duffy, William; St. John, N.B., 1847 ***5704.8*** *p25*
Duffy, William 13; St. John, N.B., 1854 ***5704.8*** *p122*
Duffy, William 18; Philadelphia, 1854 ***5704.8*** *p117*
Duffy, William 29; Philadelphia, 1854 ***5704.8*** *p116*
Dufiard, Mme. 50; New Orleans, 1826 ***778.5*** *p178*
Dufilho, Lady 32; New Orleans, 1820 ***778.5*** *p178*
Dufilho, Mr. 5; New Orleans, 1820 ***778.5*** *p178*
Dufilho, Eugene 34; New Orleans, 1820 ***778.5*** *p178*
Dufiney, . . .; Halifax, N.S., 1752 ***7074.6*** *p230*
Dufner, Karl; Illinois, 1904 ***5012.40*** *p80*
Dufon, M. 33; New Orleans, 1832 ***778.5*** *p178*
Dufort, Mme.; America, 1836 ***778.5*** *p178*
Dufour, Mr. 27; New Orleans, 1829 ***778.5*** *p178*
Dufour, Widow 57; New Orleans, 1827 ***778.5*** *p179*
Dufour, Alexis 14; New Orleans, 1839 ***778.5*** *p178*
Dufour, Charles 35; New Orleans, 1837 ***778.5*** *p179*
Dufour, Francois 30; New Orleans, 1826 ***778.5*** *p179*
Dufour, Franz; Cincinnati, 1788-1848 ***8582.3*** *p89*
Dufour, Hippolite 35; Port uncertain, 1832 ***778.5*** *p179*
Dufour, Johann Jakob; Cincinnati, 1788-1848 ***8582.3*** *p89*
Dufrasne, Adelson Florent; Iowa, 1866-1943 ***123.54*** *p61*
Dufrasne, Josephine Marie; Iowa, 1866-1943 ***123.54*** *p61*
Dufrayer, A. 29; America, 1832 ***778.5*** *p179*
Dufrene, Mr. 18; America, 1839 ***778.5*** *p179*
DuFresne, Albert; Iowa, 1866-1943 ***123.54*** *p61*
Dufresne, Elia; Iowa, 1866-1943 ***123.54*** *p61*
Dufresne, Isidore 32; New Orleans, 1839 ***778.5*** *p179*
Dufton, John 27; Baltimore, 1775 ***1219.7*** *p270*
Dufur, George G.; Washington, 1859-1920 ***2872.1*** *p10*
Dufus, George G.; Washington, 1859-1920 ***2872.1*** *p10*
Dugall, Margaret 12; Philadelphia, 1858 ***5704.8*** *p139*
Dugan, Andrew; New Jersey, 1806 ***9892.11*** *p14*
Dugan, Andrew; Ohio, 1822 ***9892.11*** *p14*
Dugan, Ann; Philadelphia, 1867 ***5704.8*** *p218*
Dugan, Anne; Philadelphia, 1864 ***5704.8*** *p187*
Dugan, Barney; New York, NY, 1838 ***8208.4*** *p75*
Dugan, Bernard; Philadelphia, 1867 ***5704.8*** *p222*
Dugan, Bill; St. John, N.B., 1852 ***5704.8*** *p94*
Dugan, Catherine; Philadelphia, 1852 ***5704.8*** *p96*
Dugan, Catherine 5; St. John, N.B., 1852 ***5704.8*** *p94*
Dugan, Charles; Philadelphia, 1866 ***5704.8*** *p206*
Dugan, Cormick; New York, NY, 1869 ***5704.8*** *p233*
Dugan, Cormick; Philadelphia, 1868 ***5704.8*** *p226*
Dugan, Daniel 24; Philadelphia, 1854 ***5704.8*** *p121*
Dugan, Dennis; Philadelphia, 1854 ***5704.8*** *p116*
Dugan, Farrigle; Philadelphia, 1847 ***53.26*** *p25*
Dugan, George; New York, NY, 1863 ***1450.2*** *p33A*
Dugan, Grace; St. John, N.B., 1852 ***5704.8*** *p94*
Dugan, Grace 28; Philadelphia, 1854 ***5704.8*** *p120*
Dugan, Hannah; St. John, N.B., 1852 ***5704.8*** *p94*
Dugan, Hugh; New York, NY, 1869 ***5704.8*** *p232*
Dugan, James; America, 1890 ***1450.2*** *p33A*
Dugan, James; Arizona, 1898 ***9228.30*** *p5*
Dugan, James; Ohio, 1841 ***9892.11*** *p14*
Dugan, James 8; Philadelphia, 1865 ***5704.8*** *p202*
Dugan, Jane; Philadelphia, 1852 ***5704.8*** *p86*
Dugan, John; New York, NY, 1868 ***5704.8*** *p228*
Dugan, John; Philadelphia, 1847 ***53.26*** *p25*
Dugan, John; Philadelphia, 1865 ***5704.8*** *p194*
Dugan, John 3; St. John, N.B., 1852 ***5704.8*** *p94*
Dugan, John 20; Philadelphia, 1860 ***5704.8*** *p146*
Dugan, Margaret; New York, NY, 1864 ***5704.8*** *p181*
Dugan, Margaret; Philadelphia, 1864 ***5704.8*** *p179*
Dugan, Margaret; Philadelphia, 1865 ***5704.8*** *p201*
Dugan, Margaret J. 6; Philadelphia, 1865 ***5704.8*** *p202*
Dugan, Maria; Philadelphia, 1865 ***5704.8*** *p202*
Dugan, Martha; Philadelphia, 1865 ***5704.8*** *p202*
Dugan, Mary; New York, NY, 1864 ***5704.8*** *p181*
Dugan, Mary 24; Philadelphia, 1864 ***5704.8*** *p160*
Dugan, Mathew; St. John, N.B., 1852 ***5704.8*** *p94*
Dugan, Mathew 6 mos; St. John, N.B., 1852 ***5704.8*** *p94*
Dugan, Michael 12; St. John, N.B., 1852 ***5704.8*** *p94*
Dugan, Neal; New York, NY, 1853 ***1450.2*** *p33A*
Dugan, Patrick; New York, NY, 1838 ***8208.4*** *p66*
Dugan, Patrick; Philadelphia, 1854 ***5704.8*** *p116*
Dugan, Peter; Wisconsin, n.d. ***9675.5*** *p121*
Dugan, Rasan 16; Philadelphia, 1857 ***5704.8*** *p133*
Dugan, Rose; Philadelphia, 1865 ***5704.8*** *p194*
Dugan, Sarah; Philadelphia, 1866 ***5704.8*** *p206*
Dugan, Susan 21; Philadelphia, 1864 ***5704.8*** *p156*
Dugan, T. D.; Washington, 1859-1920 ***2872.1*** *p10*
Dugan, Thomas; Philadelphia Co., PA, 1851 ***1450.2*** *p33A*
Dugan, William; Philadelphia, 1865 ***5704.8*** *p202*
Dugan, William 2; Philadelphia, 1865 ***5704.8*** *p202*
Dugdale, Benj.; Virginia, 1638 ***6219*** *p160*
Dugg, Robt.; Virginia, 1635 ***6219*** *p69*
Duggan, Ann 8; Philadelphia, 1864 ***5704.8*** *p160*
Duggan, Catharine 8; Massachusetts, 1850 ***5881.1*** *p28*
Duggan, Cornelius 4; Philadelphia, 1860 ***5704.8*** *p144*
Duggan, Daniel 18; Philadelphia, 1864 ***5704.8*** *p156*
Duggan, Daniel 23; Massachusetts, 1847 ***5881.1*** *p28*
Duggan, Daniel 36; Massachusetts, 1849 ***5881.1*** *p28*
Duggan, Eliza 2; Massachusetts, 1850 ***5881.1*** *p28*
Duggan, Ellen 44; Philadelphia, 1864 ***5704.8*** *p160*
Duggan, Hannah 22; Massachusetts, 1847 ***5881.1*** *p29*
Duggan, Jeanna; Montreal, 1825 ***7603*** *p65*
Duggan, Jeremie; Quebec, 1760 ***7603*** *p88*
Duggan, Johanna 6; Massachusetts, 1850 ***5881.1*** *p30*
Duggan, John 19; Philadelphia, 1864 ***5704.8*** *p156*
Duggan, John 20; Massachusetts, 1849 ***5881.1*** *p30*
Duggan, Margaret 18; Massachusetts, 1849 ***5881.1*** *p31*
Duggan, Mary 22; Massachusetts, 1847 ***5881.1*** *p31*
Duggan, Mary 32; Massachusetts, 1849 ***5881.1*** *p32*
Duggan, Mary Ann 4; Massachusetts, 1849 ***5881.1*** *p32*
Duggan, Peggy 4; Massachusetts, 1850 ***5881.1*** *p33*
Duggan, Susan 30; Philadelphia, 1860 ***5704.8*** *p144*
Duggan, William 40; Philadelphia, 1864 ***5704.8*** *p160*
Duggin, William 20; Newport, RI, 1851 ***6508.5*** *p20*

Duglas, Robert 15; Jamaica, 1721 *3690.1 p68*
Duglas, Thomas 29; Virginia, 1700 *2212 p31*
Dugom, John 6; St. John, N.B., 1847 *5704.8 p34*
Dugom, Margaret; St. John, N.B., 1847 *5704.8 p34*
Dugom, Margaret 9 mos; St. John, N.B., 1847 *5704.8 p34*
Dugom, Rosanna 4; St. John, N.B., 1847 *5704.8 p34*
Dugom, Susan 9; St. John, N.B., 1847 *5704.8 p34*
Dugren, Daniel; America, 1852 *6014.1 p1*
Dugue, Adolph 19; New Orleans, 1839 *778.5 p179*
Duhart, Peter 21; America, 1831 *778.5 p179*
Duhigg, O., Mme.; Port uncertain, 1839 *778.5 p179*
Duhme, Dietrich *SEE* Duhme, Herman Heinrich, Jr.
Duhme, H. H.; Cincinnati, 1869-1887 *8582 p7*
Duhme, Herman *SEE* Duhme, Herman Heinrich, Jr.
Duhme, Herman Heinrich, Jr.; Ohio, 1834 *8582.1 p8*
  *Father:*Hermann Heinrich, Sr.
  With mother & 4 sisters
  *Brother:*Johann
  *Brother:*Herman
  *Brother:*Dietrich
Duhme, Hermann; Cincinnati, 1869-1887 *8582 p7*
Duhme, Hermann Heinrich, Sr. *SEE* Duhme, Herman Heinrich, Jr.
Duhme, Johann *SEE* Duhme, Herman Heinrich, Jr.
Duhring, Adolph; Illinois, 1881 *2896.5 p10*
Duigan, Anne; New York, NY, 1816 *2859.11 p30*
Duigan, Bridget; New York, NY, 1816 *2859.11 p30*
Duigan, Eliza; New York, NY, 1816 *2859.11 p30*
Duigan, Michael; Montreal, 1822 *7603 p85*
Duigan, Wm; New York, NY, 1816 *2859.11 p30*
Duigenan, Hugh; Montreal, 1825 *7603 p86*
Duitsmann, Frederick J.; Illinois, 1888 *5012.37 p61*
Duitsmann, Henry J.; Illinois, 1888 *5012.37 p61*
Duitsmann, John W.; Illinois, 1876 *5012.39 p120*
Duivenkate, Gerritdina 23; New York, NY, 1847 *3377.6 p14*
Dujardin, Mr. 28; America, 1839 *778.5 p179*
Duke, Geo.; Virginia, 1648 *6219 p246*
Duke, John 25; Nova Scotia, 1774 *1219.7 p209*
Duke, Peter; New York, NY, 1838 *8208.4 p64*
Dukro, Alfred; Arizona, 1897 *9228.30 p1*
Dulagh, Sarah; America, 1739 *4971 p53*
Dulan, Jean 28; New Orleans, 1821 *778.5 p179*
Dulanivert, Mr. 18; New Orleans, 1839 *778.5 p180*
Dulanse, Edw. 35; Port uncertain, 1836 *778.5 p180*
Dulany, William; Annapolis, MD, 1742 *4971 p93*
Dulass, M. 21; New Orleans, 1827 *778.5 p180*
Dulau, Gabriella; Wisconsin, n.d. *9675.5 p121*
Dulberly, William 19; Maryland, 1724 *3690.1 p67*
Dulby Nielsen, Annie Marie *SEE* Dulby Nielsen, Niels Peter
Dulby Nielsen, Niels Peter; New York, NY, 1911 *3455.2 p102*
  *Wife:*Annie Marie
Duleplange, Signe 29; Port uncertain, 1836 *778.5 p180*
Duleplange Signe, Miss 29; Port uncertain, 1836 *778.5 p180*
Duley, Joseph; Iowa, 1866-1943 *123.54 p17*
Dulfert, Hartmann; Philadelphia, 1779 *8137 p8*
Dull, Sebastian; Illinois, 1874 *5012.39 p26*
Dullnick, Catharina *SEE* Dullnick, Matthaeus
Dullnick, Justina Catharina *SEE* Dullnick, Matthaeus
Dullnick, Margaretha *SEE* Dullnick, Matthaeus
Dullnick, Matthaeus; Pennsylvania, 1751 *2444 p150*
  *Wife:*Justina Catharina
  *Child:*Margaretha
  *Child:*Catharina
  With child
Dulock, August; Illinois, 1874 *2896.5 p10*
Dulondet, Adolphe 33; New Orleans, 1838 *778.5 p180*
Dulong, Jean; Port uncertain, 1839 *778.5 p180*
Duls, Mike George; Arkansas, 1918 *95.2 p39*
Dulson, Edward; New York, NY, 1834 *8208.4 p26*
Duluc, Miss 11; New Orleans, 1822 *778.5 p180*
Duluc, Mrs. 36; New Orleans, 1822 *778.5 p180*
Duluzeau, J. B. 29; New Orleans, 1838 *778.5 p180*
Duluzeau, Marie 29; New Orleans, 1838 *778.5 p180*
Duluzeau, Rene 26; New Orleans, 1838 *778.5 p180*
Dum, Jacob; Pennsylvania, 1754 *2444 p226*
Dumahan, Michael 22; Massachusetts, 1849 *5881.1 p32*
Dumaine, Mme. 22; New Orleans, 1839 *778.5 p180*
Dumaine, Mr. 35; New Orleans, 1839 *778.5 p180*
Dumaresq, John; New York, NY, 1836 *8208.4 p15*
Dumarselay, L. 28; Mexico, 1827 *778.5 p180*
Dumarshell, E. 22; Port uncertain, 1827 *778.5 p180*
Dumas, Aime 19; Port uncertain, 1839 *778.5 p181*
Dumas, Pierre 30; America, 1838 *778.5 p181*
Dumbile, Ann; Virginia, 1698 *2212 p15*
Dumblanski, Joseph; Arkansas, 1918 *95.2 p39*
Dumbruske, Henry; Arkansas, 1918 *95.2 p39*
Dumerneilt, Caper; Philadelphia, 1757 *9973.7 p33*
Dumerneilt, David; Philadelphia, 1757 *9973.7 p33*

Dumey, Jean B. 26; New Orleans, 1836 *778.5 p181*
Dummar, Henry; Wisconsin, n.d. *9675.5 p121*
Dummler, . . .; Canada, 1776-1783 *9786 p20*
Dumond, George; Kansas, 1890 *5240.1 p10*
Dumont, Alexander 45; Kentucky, 1820 *778.5 p181*
Dumont, Francois 25; New Orleans, 1826 *778.5 p181*
Dumont, M. 37; America, 1836 *778.5 p181*
Dumont, P. 32; New Orleans, 1837 *778.5 p181*
Dumont, Pascal 23; America, 1838 *778.5 p181*
Dumontet, Jean; Quebec, 1712 *7603 p21*
Dumouchel, Mlle. 30; New Orleans, 1825 *778.5 p181*
Dun, James 29; Jamaica, 1739 *3690.1 p68*
Dunache, O. S. 34; Texas, 1827 *778.5 p181*
Dunbalin, Thomas; America, 1698 *2212 p6*
Dunbar, Annie McPherson *SEE* Dunbar, William
Dunbar, David 19; St. John, N.B., 1856 *5704.8 p131*
Dunbar, Fanny; St. John, N.B., 1847 *5704.8 p34*
Dunbar, John; Philadelphia, 1851 *5704.8 p70*
Dunbar, William; Pictou, N.S., 1846 *8893 p265*
  *Wife:*Annie McPherson
Dunbarr, James; America, 1737 *4971 p75*
Dunberbeach, Elianor; Virginia, 1635 *6219 p69*
Dunberg, Daniel; New York, NY, 1870 *5704.8 p237*
Duncan, . . . 23; St. John, N.B., 1857 *5704.8 p135*
Duncan, Alexander; Wilmington, NC, 1767 *1639.20 p63*
Duncan, Andrew 19; St. John, N.B., 1857 *5704.8 p134*
Duncan, Ann 18; Philadelphia, 1861 *5704.8 p148*
Duncan, Becky; St. John, N.B., 1853 *5704.8 p106*
Duncan, Bridget 8; Massachusetts, 1848 *5881.1 p27*
Duncan, Brougham Gowan; Arkansas, 1918 *95.2 p39*
Duncan, David; South Carolina, 1767 *1639.20 p63*
Duncan, Eleanor; St. John, N.B., 1853 *5704.8 p106*
Duncan, Elizabeth; Quebec, 1853 *5704.8 p104*
Duncan, Elizabeth; St. John, N.B., 1853 *5704.8 p106*
Duncan, Fanny 22; Philadelphia, 1853 *5704.8 p113*
Duncan, George; Charleston, SC, 1799 *1639.20 p63*
Duncan, George; Quebec, 1849 *5704.8 p51*
Duncan, George 22; St. John, N.B., 1866 *5704.8 p166*
Duncan, James; Philadelphia, 1847 *53.26 p25*
Duncan, James; Philadelphia, 1847 *5704.8 p30*
Duncan, James; Quebec, 1853 *5704.8 p104*
Duncan, James 18; St. John, N.B., 1858 *5704.8 p137*
Duncan, James 27; Wilmington, NC, 1774 *1639.20 p63*
  With wife & 2 children
Duncan, Jane 9 mos; St. John, N.B., 1857 *5704.8 p134*
Duncan, Jane 23; St. John, N.B., 1857 *5704.8 p134*
Duncan, John; Charleston, SC, 1747-1830 *1639.20 p63*
Duncan, John; St. John, N.B., 1853 *5704.8 p106*
Duncan, John; South Carolina, 1752 *1639.20 p63*
Duncan, John 33; New Orleans, 1862 *543.30 p55*
Duncan, Margaret; Philadelphia, 1811 *53.26 p25*
Duncan, Margaret; Philadelphia, 1811 *2859.11 p11*
Duncan, Margaret 5; Massachusetts, 1848 *5881.1 p31*
Duncan, Margaret 24; Quebec, 1864 *5704.8 p162*
Duncan, Maria 14; Philadelphia, 1865 *5704.8 p200*
Duncan, Mary 2; St. John, N.B., 1857 *5704.8 p134*
Duncan, Peter; New York, NY, 1840 *8208.4 p104*
Duncan, Richard; New York, NY, 1816 *2859.11 p30*
Duncan, Robert; St. John, N.B., 1853 *5704.8 p106*
Duncan, Robert 16; St. John, N.B., 1863 *5704.8 p153*
Duncan, Robert 20; Philadelphia, 1856 *5704.8 p128*
Duncan, Samuel; New York, NY, 1865 *5704.8 p194*
Duncan, Stephan; St. John, N.B., 1853 *5704.8 p106*
Duncan, Thomas; America, 1868 *5704.8 p229*
Duncan, Thomas; Illinois, 1880 *5012.39 p52*
Duncan, Thomas 13; Newfoundland, 1789 *4915.24 p58*
Duncan, William; New York, NY, 1815 *2859.11 p30*
Duncan, William; North Carolina, 1744-1779 *1639.20 p63*
Duncan, William 11; Massachusetts, 1847 *5881.1 p34*
Duncan, William 21; Virginia, 1774 *1219.7 p243*
Duncanson, William 22; St. John, N.B., 1864 *5704.8 p158*
Duncason, Hugh 18; St. Vincent, 1774 *1219.7 p184*
Duncker, Henry; California, 1882 *2764.35 p16*
Dunckley, Edwd.; Virginia, 1638 *6219 p124*
Duncombe, John; Virginia, 1637 *6219 p85*
Duncome, Jon.; Virginia, 1636 *6219 p79*
Dundas, Anne; Quebec, 1851 *5704.8 p74*
Dundas, Eleanora E. Home *SEE* Dundas, Thomas
Dundas, Elizabeth 20; St. John, N.B., 1857 *5704.8 p135*
Dundas, Ellen 24; St. John, N.B., 1853 *5704.8 p110*
Dundas, George; Prince Edward Island, 1864 *9775.5 p211*
Dundas, James 9 mos; St. John, N.B., 1853 *5704.8 p110*
Dundas, John 7; Massachusetts, 1850 *5881.1 p30*
Dundas, Mary; Quebec, 1850 *5704.8 p67*
Dundas, Richard 4; Massachusetts, 1850 *5881.1 p34*
Dundas, Thomas; Quebec, 1787 *8894.2 p57*
  *Wife:*Eleanora E. Home
Dundas, Thomas 24; St. John, N.B., 1857 *5704.8 p135*
Dundass, Barbara; St. John, N.B., 1848 *5704.8 p45*
Dundass, Margaret; St. John, N.B., 1848 *5704.8 p45*

Dundee, David; South Carolina, 1744 *1639.20 p63*
Dunder, Jacob; Philadelphia, 1760 *9973.7 p34*
Dundon, Marguerite; Montreal, 1822 *7603 p86*
Dundzik, Stanislawa 27; New York, 1912 *9980.29 p74*
Duneen, Daniel; New York, NY, 1816 *2859.11 p30*
Dunehou, Hugh; Ohio, 1843 *8365.26 p12*
Dunell, Francis; Virginia, 1638 *6219 p119*
Dunery, John; Virginia, 1648 *6219 p252*
Dunet, Francois 25; New Orleans, 1838 *778.5 p181*
Duney, Robert; New England, 1816 *2859.11 p30*
Dungan, James; America, 1741 *4971 p37*
Dungan, John 24; Jamaica, 1724 *3690.1 p68*
Dungan, Saragh; America, 1738-1743 *4971 p91*
Dungan, Sarah; America, 1738 *4971 p13*
Dunham, C. E.; Washington, 1859-1920 *2872.1 p10*
Dunham, H. C.; Washington, 1859-1920 *2872.1 p10*
Dunham, Harry; Washington, 1859-1920 *2872.1 p10*
Dunham, Harry C.; Washington, 1859-1920 *2872.1 p10*
Duniess, . . .; Canada, 1776-1783 *9786 p20*
Duniho, Cornelius; America, 1831 *1450.2 p33A*
Dunilton, John 21; Philadelphia, 1774 *1219.7 p232*
Duning, Rich.; Virginia, 1635 *6219 p72*
Duning, Richard; Virginia, 1636 *6219 p109*
Duningham, Rich.; Virginia, 1635 *6219 p69*
Dunk, . . .; Milwaukee, 1875 *4719.30 p258*
Dunk, John 15; Maryland, 1733 *3690.1 p68*
Dunkarn, Thomas 20; Philadelphia, 1774 *1219.7 p185*
Dunkel, Margarite 35; New Orleans, 1836 *778.5 p181*
Dunker, Paul; Colorado, 1880-1894 *9678.2 p16*
Dunkers, Brunke; Iroquois Co., IL, 1892 *3455.1 p10*
Dunkie, James; New York, NY, 1837 *8208.4 p51*
Dunkin, Andrew; St. John, N.B., 1847 *5704.8 p3*
Dunkin, Andrew 23; St. John, N.B., 1860 *5704.8 p143*
Dunkin, Mary Ann 20; St. John, N.B., 1860 *5704.8 p143*
Dunkin, Nancy; St. John, N.B., 1847 *5704.8 p3*
Dunkin, Patk 35; Maryland or Virginia, 1699 *2212 p24*
Dunkley, William 18; Maryland, 1775 *1219.7 p247*
Dunlap, Mr. 22; Louisiana, 1820 *778.5 p181*
Dunlap, David 5; St. John, N.B., 1847 *5704.8 p20*
Dunlap, Elizabeth; Philadelphia, 1866 *5704.8 p208*
Dunlap, James; Illinois, 1860 *5012.39 p89*
Dunlap, James; Philadelphia, 1866 *5704.8 p210*
Dunlap, James; St. John, N.B., 1847 *5704.8 p20*
Dunlap, James 7; St. John, N.B., 1847 *5704.8 p20*
Dunlap, James 20; St. John, N.B., 1864 *5704.8 p159*
Dunlap, William; Philadelphia, 1866 *5704.8 p208*
Dunlea, Edward 32; Massachusetts, 1849 *5881.1 p28*
Dunleary, Ann 10; Philadelphia, 1851 *5704.8 p81*
Dunleary, Bridget; Philadelphia, 1851 *5704.8 p81*
Dunleary, Catharine 18; Massachusetts, 1848 *5881.1 p28*
Dunleary, Catherine; Philadelphia, 1851 *5704.8 p81*
Dunleary, Daniel 2; Philadelphia, 1851 *5704.8 p81*
Dunleary, Honora 8; Massachusetts, 1849 *5881.1 p29*
Dunleary, James 8; Philadelphia, 1851 *5704.8 p81*
Dunleary, Jane 22; Philadelphia, 1859 *5704.8 p142*
Dunleary, Margaret 4; Philadelphia, 1851 *5704.8 p81*
Dunleary, Mary 2; Massachusetts, 1849 *5881.1 p31*
Dunleary, Mary 12; Massachusetts, 1849 *5881.1 p31*
Dunleary, Patrick 6; Philadelphia, 1851 *5704.8 p81*
Dunleary, William 12; Philadelphia, 1851 *5704.8 p81*
Dunleavy, Peter 6; Massachusetts, 1849 *5881.1 p33*
Dunleory, Mary 20; Philadelphia, 1854 *5704.8 p120*
Dunlevy, Patrick; New York, NY, 1839 *8208.4 p94*
Dunlop, Alexander; Carolina, 1684 *1639.20 p63*
Dunlop, Ann 40; St. John, N.B., 1861 *5704.8 p149*
Dunlop, Daniel 48; Quebec, 1857 *5704.8 p135*
Dunlop, Douglas *SEE* Dunlop, Jesse, Sr.
Dunlop, Eliza 48; Quebec, 1857 *5704.8 p135*
Dunlop, Isabella; New York, NY, 1868 *5704.8 p227*
Dunlop, James *SEE* Dunlop, Jesse, Sr.
Dunlop, James; South Carolina, 1716 *1639.20 p64*
Dunlop, James 20; Quebec, 1856 *5704.8 p130*
Dunlop, James 20; St. John, N.B., 1866 *5704.8 p166*
Dunlop, James 27; St. John, N.B., 1866 *5704.8 p166*
Dunlop, Jane; Philadelphia, 1847 *53.26 p25*
  *Relative:*Thomas 10
  *Relative:*Sarah 6
  *Relative:*John 2
Dunlop, Jane; Philadelphia, 1847 *5704.8 p23*
Dunlop, Jane 21; St. John, N.B., 1861 *5704.8 p149*
Dunlop, Jesse, Sr.; America, 1805 *1639.20 p64*
  *Son:*James
  *Son:*Douglas
Dunlop, John; New York, NY, 1836 *1450.2 p33A*
Dunlop, John 2 *SEE* Dunlop, Jane
Dunlop, John 2; Philadelphia, 1847 *5704.8 p23*
Dunlop, Joseph 11; Quebec, 1857 *5704.8 p135*
Dunlop, Margaret; Philadelphia, 1852 *5704.8 p96*
Dunlop, Mary *SEE* Dunlop, Samuel
Dunlop, Mary; Philadelphia, 1847 *5704.8 p13*
Dunlop, Mary 9 mos *SEE* Dunlop, Samuel
Dunlop, Mary 9 mos; Philadelphia, 1847 *5704.8 p13*
Dunlop, Mary 30; St. John, N.B., 1866 *5704.8 p167*

Dunlop, Patrick; Charleston, SC, 1767 ***1639.20*** *p64*
Dunlop, Robert 20; Quebec, 1855 ***5704.8*** *p125*
Dunlop, Samuel; Philadelphia, 1847 ***53.26*** *p25*
*Relative:*Mary
*Relative:*Mary 9 mos
Dunlop, Samuel; Philadelphia, 1847 ***5704.8*** *p13*
Dunlop, Sarah 6 *SEE* Dunlop, Jane
Dunlop, Sarah 6; Philadelphia, 1847 ***5704.8*** *p23*
Dunlop, Thomas 10 *SEE* Dunlop, Jane
Dunlop, Thomas 10; Philadelphia, 1847 ***5704.8*** *p23*
Dunlop, Thomas 18; St. John, N.B., 1861 ***5704.8*** *p149*
Dunlop, William; Ontario, 1827 ***9775.5*** *p214*
Dunlop, William 5; St. John, N.B., 1866 ***5704.8*** *p167*
Dunlop, William 30; St. John, N.B., 1866 ***5704.8*** *p166*
Dunn, Miss 20; Barbados, 1774 ***1219.7*** *p212*
Dunn, Mr.; Quebec, 1815 ***9229.18*** *p82*
Dunn, A. C.; Washington, 1859-1920 ***2872.1*** *p10*
Dunn, Adam; America, 1832 ***1450.2*** *p34A*
Dunn, Adm. 30; Philadelphia, 1803 ***53.26*** *p25*
Dunn, Anastatia 30; Massachusetts, 1849 ***5881.1*** *p26*
Dunn, Andrew 20; Pennsylvania, 1728 ***3690.1*** *p68*
Dunn, Angus C.; Washington, 1859-1920 ***2872.1*** *p10*
Dunn, Catharine 8; Massachusetts, 1847 ***5881.1*** *p27*
Dunn, Catharine 50; Massachusetts, 1847 ***5881.1*** *p27*
Dunn, Catherine; Quebec, 1825 ***7603*** *p57*
Dunn, Charles; Philadelphia, 1850 ***53.26*** *p25*
*Relative:*Patrick 12
Dunn, Charles; Philadelphia, 1850 ***5704.8*** *p60*
Dunn, Darby; America, 1739-1740 ***4971*** *p59*
Dunn, Dennis; America, 1735-1743 ***4971*** *p8*
Dunn, Dennis; Maryland, 1740 ***4971*** *p91*
Dunn, Dennis; Philadelphia, 1741 ***4971*** *p92*
Dunn, Edmund 20; Massachusetts, 1847 ***5881.1*** *p28*
Dunn, Edward; New York, 1849 ***2896.5*** *p10*
Dunn, Edward 21; Maryland, 1774 ***1219.7*** *p229*
Dunn, Elizabeth; America, 1743 ***4971*** *p35*
Dunn, Elizabeth; Delaware, 1743 ***4971*** *p105*
Dunn, Elizabeth; Philadelphia, 1816 ***2859.11*** *p30*
Dunn, Ellen; Montreal, 1825 ***7603*** *p85*
Dunn, Ellen 19; Massachusetts, 1850 ***5881.1*** *p28*
Dunn, Ellen 35; Massachusetts, 1847 ***5881.1*** *p28*
Dunn, Hugh; America, 1735-1743 ***4971*** *p78*
Dunn, Hugh; America, 1742 ***4971*** *p80*
Dunn, James; Wisconsin, n.d. ***9675.5*** *p121*
Dunn, James 24; Philadelphia, 1804 ***53.26*** *p25*
*Relative:*Mary 19
Dunn, Jane 20; Georgia, 1775 ***1219.7*** *p277*
Dunn, Jane 21; Quebec, 1856 ***5704.8*** *p130*
Dunn, John; America, 1833 ***1450.2*** *p34A*
Dunn, John; New Orleans, 1864 ***543.30*** *p372*
Dunn, John; New York, NY, 1811 ***2859.11*** *p11*
Dunn, John; New York, NY, 1864 ***5704.8*** *p182*
Dunn, John; Washington, 1859-1920 ***2872.1*** *p10*
Dunn, John; Wisconsin, n.d. ***9675.5*** *p121*
Dunn, John 17; Maryland, 1732 ***3690.1*** *p68*
Dunn, John 19; Newport, RI, 1851 ***6508.5*** *p20*
Dunn, John 20; St. John, N.B., 1857 ***5704.8*** *p135*
Dunn, John 25; St. John, N.B., 1863 ***5704.8*** *p153*
Dunn, John 27; New Orleans, 1862 ***543.30*** *p219*
Dunn, John 28; Massachusetts, 1847 ***5881.1*** *p29*
Dunn, John 30; Virginia, 1774 ***1219.7*** *p200*
Dunn, John 35; St. John, N.B., 1858 ***5704.8*** *p137*
Dunn, John 74; South Carolina, 1850 ***1639.20*** *p64*
Dunn, Joseph 19; New Orleans, 1863 ***543.30*** *p222*
Dunn, Keatty; St. John, N.B., 1847 ***5704.8*** *p35*
Dunn, Margaret 13; St. John, N.B., 1850 ***5704.8*** *p65*
Dunn, Margaret 17; Massachusetts, 1847 ***5881.1*** *p31*
Dunn, Margaret 30; Philadelphia, 1853 ***5704.8*** *p113*
Dunn, Maria 13; Massachusetts, 1847 ***5881.1*** *p31*
Dunn, Mary; Philadelphia, 1816 ***2859.11*** *p30*
Dunn, Mary; South Carolina, 1767 ***1639.20*** *p64*
Dunn, Mary 7; Massachusetts, 1849 ***5881.1*** *p32*
Dunn, Mary 19 *SEE* Dunn, James
Dunn, Mary Jane; St. John, N.B., 1847 ***5704.8*** *p20*
Dunn, Mathew *SEE* Dunn, Thomas
Dunn, Mathew; Philadelphia, 1816 ***2859.11*** *p30*
Dunn, Maurice 40; Massachusetts, 1849 ***5881.1*** *p31*
Dunn, Michael 23; New Orleans, 1862 ***543.30*** *p58*
Dunn, Michael 25; Philadelphia, 1858 ***5704.8*** *p139*
Dunn, Nicholas 35; Massachusetts, 1847 ***5881.1*** *p33*
Dunn, Owen; America, 1737 ***4971*** *p26*
Dunn, Owen 32; Maryland, 1774 ***1219.7*** *p214*
Dunn, Patrick; New York, 1849 ***2896.5*** *p10*
Dunn, Patrick 12 *SEE* Dunn, Charles
Dunn, Patrick 12; Philadelphia, 1850 ***5704.8*** *p60*
Dunn, Patrick 28; New Orleans, 1862 ***543.30*** *p60*
Dunn, Paul; America, 1741 ***4971*** *p29*
Dunn, Peter; America, 1741 ***4971*** *p34*
Dunn, Peter; Montreal, 1823 ***7603*** *p58*
Dunn, Peter; Philadelphia, 1816 ***2859.11*** *p30*
Dunn, Peter; St. John, N.B., 1850 ***5704.8*** *p65*
Dunn, Richard; America, 1740 ***4971*** *p35*
Dunn, Theresa 13; St. John, N.B., 1850 ***5704.8*** *p65*
Dunn, Thomas; New Orleans, 1840 ***7036*** *p117*
*Brother:*Mathew
Dunn, Thomas; Petersburg, VA, 1811 ***4778.2*** *p142*
Dunn, Thomas 45; New Orleans, 1863 ***543.30*** *p222*
Dunn, Timothy 35; Massachusetts, 1849 ***5881.1*** *p34*
Dunn, Walter; Petersburg, VA, 1810 ***4778.2*** *p142*
Dunn, William; America, 1736-1743 ***4971*** *p58*
Dunn, William; North Carolina, 1794-1818 ***1639.20*** *p64*
Dunn, William; Philadelphia, 1816 ***2859.11*** *p30*
Dunn, William 20; Maryland, 1729 ***3690.1*** *p68*
Dunn, William 30; Massachusetts, 1847 ***5881.1*** *p34*
Dunn, William 36; Virginia, 1774 ***1219.7*** *p186*
Dunn, William A.; America, 1845 ***1450.2*** *p34A*
Dunnahough, Thomas; New York, NY, 1811 ***2859.11*** *p11*
Dunnanbark, Christian; America, 1838 ***1450.2*** *p34A*
Dunnary, Ellen 18; Massachusetts, 1847 ***5881.1*** *p28*
Dunne, James; Wisconsin, n.d. ***9675.5*** *p121*
Dunne, Michael 27; New Orleans, 1861-1865 ***543.30*** *p61*
Dunner, Barbara Baumann *SEE* Dunner, Heinrich
Dunner, Heinrich 27; New York, NY, 1839 ***5647.5*** *p45*
*Wife:*Barbara Baumann
Dunnet, Anna 24; America, 1836 ***778.5*** *p181*
Dunniff, Michael 25; St. John, N.B., 1866 ***5704.8*** *p167*
Dunnigan, Jane 4; Massachusetts, 1848 ***5881.1*** *p29*
Dunnigan, John 7; Massachusetts, 1848 ***5881.1*** *p29*
Dunnigan, Phillip 9; Massachusetts, 1848 ***5881.1*** *p33*
Dunnigan, Stephen 3; Massachusetts, 1848 ***5881.1*** *p34*
Dunning, John 24; North America, 1774 ***1219.7*** *p199*
Dunning, Theophilus 15; Philadelphia, 1775 ***1219.7*** *p259*
Dunning, Thomas; New York, NY, 1839 ***8208.4*** *p99*
Dunnings, Georg; Virginia, 1642 ***6219*** *p198*
Dunnion, Nancy 22; Philadelphia, 1864 ***5704.8*** *p161*
Dunphy, James; America, 1741 ***4971*** *p34*
Dunreith, Ann 16; Philadelphia, 1857 ***5704.8*** *p133*
Dunreith, James 20; Philadelphia, 1857 ***5704.8*** *p133*
Dunreith, James 48; Philadelphia, 1857 ***5704.8*** *p133*
Dunreith, Mary 48; Philadelphia, 1857 ***5704.8*** *p133*
Dunsleman, John Frederick; California, 1868 ***2769.3*** *p5*
Dunsmore, Jane 20; Wilmington, DE, 1831 ***6508.3*** *p100*
Dunsmore, Samuel 26; Wilmington, DE, 1831 ***6508.3*** *p100*
Dunsmuir, Robert; British Columbia, n.d. ***9775.5*** *p222*
Dunst, Herman; Wisconsin, n.d. ***9675.5*** *p121*
Dunster, Elizabeth 21 *SEE* Dunster, William
Dunster, William 22; Baltimore, 1775 ***1219.7*** *p270*
Dunster, William 40; Maryland, 1774 ***1219.7*** *p235*
*Wife:*Elizabeth 21
Dunston, Cicely *SEE* Dunston, John
Dunston, George 21; Maryland, 1729 ***3690.1*** *p68*
Dunston, John; Virginia, 1636 ***6219*** *p7*
*Wife:*Cicely
Dunstone, George 21; Maryland, 1729 ***3690.1*** *p68*
Dunton, Thomas; Virginia, 1647 ***6219*** *p243*
Duoret, Edward Nicholas Radenheimer; Philadelphia, 1834 ***8208.4*** *p58*
Duos, Mr. 23; America, 1839 ***778.5*** *p181*
DuPard, Julien 24; Louisiana, 1820 ***778.5*** *p182*
Dupart, Julien 26; New Orleans, 1823 ***778.5*** *p182*
Dupart, Julien 30; Mexico, 1829 ***778.5*** *p182*
Dupart, Julien 30; New Orleans, 1826 ***778.5*** *p182*
Dupas, Mr. 35; Port uncertain, 1838 ***778.5*** *p182*
Dupas, S. 35; America, 1839 ***778.5*** *p182*
Dupass, James 21; America, 1831 ***778.5*** *p182*
Dupat, S. 35; America, 1839 ***778.5*** *p182*
Dupathorn, Mr.; Quebec, 1815 ***9229.18*** *p77*
Dupay, Pierre 19; New Orleans, 1838 ***778.5*** *p182*
Dupen, James; Virginia, 1642 ***6219*** *p194*
Dupenack, . . .; Canada, 1776-1783 ***9786*** *p20*
Duperin, Catherine; Halifax, N.S., 1752 ***7074.6*** *p216*
Duperrin, Anne-Marie *SEE* Duperrin, Pierre
Duperrin, Catherine *SEE* Duperrin, Pierre
Duperrin, Catherine *SEE* Duperrin, Pierre
Duperrin, Marguerite *SEE* Duperrin, Pierre
Duperrin, Pierre 46; Halifax, N.S., 1752 ***7074.6*** *p207*
With family of 5
Duperrin, Pierre 46; Halifax, N.S., 1752 ***7074.6*** *p209*
*Wife:*Catherine
*Child:*Catherine
*Child:*Anne-Marie
*Child:*Marguerite
*Child:*Pierre-Nicolas
Duperrin, Pierre-Nicolas *SEE* Duperrin, Pierre
Dupetel, L. A. 23; New Orleans, 1832 ***778.5*** *p178*
DuPiereau, Antoine 35; Louisiana, 1827 ***778.5*** *p182*
Dupieris, J.; New Orleans, 1839 ***778.5*** *p182*
Duplantier, D. 45; New Orleans, 1831 ***778.5*** *p182*
Duplantier, John B. 31; New Orleans, 1822 ***778.5*** *p182*
Duplessis, Mr. 25; New Orleans, 1822 ***778.5*** *p182*
Duplessis, A. 45; Port uncertain, 1820 ***778.5*** *p183*
Dupont, . . .; Port uncertain, 1838 ***778.5*** *p183*
Dupont, Mr.; Port uncertain, 1839 ***778.5*** *p183*
Dupont, Mr. 36; New Orleans, 1821 ***778.5*** *p171*
Dupont, Mrs. 22; Port uncertain, 1838 ***778.5*** *p183*
Dupont, Auguste 36; New Orleans, 1839 ***778.5*** *p183*
Dupont, Fanny 35; America, 1837 ***778.5*** *p183*
Dupont, Francis 20; South Carolina, 1725 ***3690.1*** *p68*
Dupont, J. L. 21; New Orleans, 1839 ***778.5*** *p183*
DuPont, Jack Maria 35; New Orleans, 1838 ***778.5*** *p183*
Dupont, M. 30; America, 1837 ***778.5*** *p183*
Duport, Robert; Halifax, N.S., 1755 ***1219.7*** *p33*
Duport, St. Clair 31; Port uncertain, 1836 ***778.5*** *p183*
Dupossou, Augustine 33; America, 1831 ***778.5*** *p183*
Dupot, Pedra 29; Port uncertain, 1825 ***778.5*** *p183*
Dupouy, Dominique 26; New Orleans, 1836 ***778.5*** *p183*
Dupoy, Theodore 19; New Orleans, 1835 ***778.5*** *p183*
Duprat, Mr. 25; New Orleans, 1839 ***778.5*** *p184*
Dupre, Mr.; Port uncertain, 1839 ***778.5*** *p184*
Dupre, Andre 58; New Orleans, 1836 ***778.5*** *p184*
Dupre, Gustavus C.H.; New York, NY, 1835 ***8208.4*** *p77*
Dupre, Julien 30; New Orleans, 1830 ***778.5*** *p184*
Dupres, Jean Marie 30; New Orleans, 1838 ***778.5*** *p184*
Duprevois, C. 3; New Orleans, 1838 ***778.5*** *p184*
Duprevois, G. 22; New Orleans, 1838 ***778.5*** *p184*
Duprevois, J. 35; New Orleans, 1838 ***778.5*** *p184*
Duprey, Clemence 18; America, 1837 ***778.5*** *p184*
Dupuis, . . . 36; America, 1839 ***778.5*** *p184*
Dupuis, Mr. 25; Port uncertain, 1836 ***778.5*** *p184*
Dupuis, Adolphe 15; New Orleans, 1831 ***778.5*** *p184*
Dupuis, Auguste 1; America, 1838 ***778.5*** *p184*
Dupuis, Catherine *SEE* Dupuis, Jean Nicolas
Dupuis, Edward 2; America, 1838 ***778.5*** *p184*
Dupuis, Jean Bapt. 29; America, 1838 ***778.5*** *p184*
Dupuis, Jean Bapt. 29; New Orleans, 1838 ***778.5*** *p185*
Dupuis, Jean Nicolas 27; Halifax, N.S., 1752 ***7074.6*** *p207*
With family of 2
Dupuis, Jean Nicolas 27; Halifax, N.S., 1752 ***7074.6*** *p209*
*Wife:*Catherine
*Son:*Pierre
Dupuis, Jeannete 27; America, 1838 ***778.5*** *p185*
Dupuis, Pierre *SEE* Dupuis, Jean Nicolas
Dupusse, Nicolas 28; New Orleans, 1827 ***778.5*** *p185*
Dupuy, Mr. 25; New Orleans, 1827 ***778.5*** *p185*
Dupuy, Mr. 28; America, 1835 ***778.5*** *p185*
Dupuy, Mr. 28; America, 1838 ***778.5*** *p185*
Dupuy, Dorotee 28; New Orleans, 1822 ***778.5*** *p185*
Dupuy, George; America, 1836 ***778.5*** *p185*
Dupuy, Mrs. George; America, 1836 ***778.5*** *p185*
Dupuy, J. 23; America, 1835 ***778.5*** *p185*
Dupuy, J. 32; Port uncertain, 1839 ***778.5*** *p185*
Dupuy, John; Colorado, 1888 ***9678.2*** *p16*
Dupuy, Jules 20; New Orleans, 1838 ***778.5*** *p185*
Dupuy, Minus 30; Port uncertain, 1836 ***778.5*** *p185*
Dupuy, P. 25; New Orleans, 1839 ***778.5*** *p185*
Dupuy, Theodore 19; New Orleans, 1835 ***778.5*** *p183*
Duquaine, Joseph; Quebec, 1492-1825 ***7603*** *p21*
Duquid, Thomas; New York, NY, 1838 ***8208.4*** *p56*
Duquillon, Victor 37; Port uncertain, 1838 ***778.5*** *p185*
Durain, Christophe 32; New Orleans, 1837 ***778.5*** *p186*
Dural, Corneil; Quebec, 1783 ***7603*** *p76*
Duran, Andres 62; Arizona, 1912 ***9228.40*** *p17*
Durand, Mr. 15; Port uncertain, 1836 ***778.5*** *p186*
Durand, A. F. 25; Port uncertain, 1827 ***778.5*** *p186*
Durand, Auguste 30; New Orleans, 1838 ***778.5*** *p186*
Durand, C. 25; America, 1825 ***778.5*** *p186*
Durand, Charles 26; New Orleans, 1862 ***543.30*** *p55*
Durand, Delphine 30; New Orleans, 1838 ***778.5*** *p186*
Durand, Etienne 20; New Orleans, 1821 ***778.5*** *p186*
Durand, Eugene 28; New Orleans, 1864 ***543.30*** *p372*
Durand, Jacques; New York, 1773 ***7074.6*** *p214*
Durand, Jacques 38; Port uncertain, 1839 ***778.5*** *p186*
Durand, Jean 24; Halifax, N.S., 1752 ***7074.6*** *p207*
Durand, Jean 24; Halifax, N.S., 1752 ***7074.6*** *p209*
Durand, Julien 16; New Orleans, 1826 ***778.5*** *p186*
Durand, P. 35; America, 1825 ***778.5*** *p186*
Durand, Peter; America, 1752 ***7074.6*** *p214*
Durand, Sylvain 20; America, 1838 ***778.5*** *p186*
Durand, William; Virginia, 1639 ***6219*** *p156*
Durand, Wm.; Virginia, 1635 ***6219*** *p3*
Durano, Luigi; Arkansas, 1918 ***95.2*** *p39*
Durant, Thomas 20; Maryland, 1774 ***1219.7*** *p229*
Duranti, Aless 30; New York, NY, 1893 ***9026.4*** *p41*
Duranti, Dco. 42; New York, NY, 1893 ***9026.4*** *p41*
Duranton, Mr.; Port uncertain, 1839 ***778.5*** *p186*
Duras, Marie; Wisconsin, n.d. ***9675.5*** *p121*
Durasier, Jacob 27; America, 1838 ***778.5*** *p186*
Durass, Biddy; St. John, N.B., 1847 ***5704.8*** *p9*
Durass, Ellen; St. John, N.B., 1847 ***5704.8*** *p9*
Durass, James 10; St. John, N.B., 1847 ***5704.8*** *p9*
Durass, John; St. John, N.B., 1847 ***5704.8*** *p9*
Durass, Mary; St. John, N.B., 1847 ***5704.8*** *p9*
Durass, Patrick; America, 1741 ***4971*** *p35*
Durass, Terry; St. John, N.B., 1847 ***5704.8*** *p9*
Durass, Terry 12; St. John, N.B., 1847 ***5704.8*** *p9*

Durastain, Jean 22; New Orleans, 1839 778.5 p187
Durbin, Charles L.; Ohio, 1842 9892.11 p14
Durdy, . . .; Canada, 1776-1783 9786 p20
Dure, Samuel 24; Halifax, N.S., 1752 7074.6 p209
Durel, F. 25; New Orleans, 1829 778.5 p187
Durel, N. 40; New Orleans, 1829 778.5 p187
Durenoyer, Antoine 48; America, 1831 778.5 p187
Durenoyer, Christine 49; America, 1831 778.5 p187
Durenoyer, Jane 17; America, 1831 778.5 p187
Durey, Miss 7; New Orleans, 1839 778.5 p187
Durey, Ms. 40; New Orleans, 1839 778.5 p187
Durgin, Edgar E. 27; New Orleans, 1864 543.30 p374
Durham, James; New York, NY, 1811 2859.11 p11
Durham, James; New York, NY, 1837 8208.4 p35
Durham, Margaret; New York, NY, 1811 2859.11 p11
Durham, Mary 21; Baltimore, 1775 1219.7 p269
Durham, Michael 40; New Orleans, 1863 543.30 p222
Durham, Richard; America, 1738 4971 p99
Durholt, Mr.; Illinois, 1875 8582.2 p51
Duriau, Bertrand 18; New Orleans, 1830 778.5 p187
Duriau, Francois 34; New Orleans, 1830 778.5 p187
Durieux, Jean Paul 28; New Orleans, 1839 778.5 p187
Durin, Jeremiah; America, 1848 6014.1 p1
Durish, Francis; Virginia, 1638 6219 p145
Durk, Edmond; America, 1735-1743 4971 p78
Durka, Stanislas; Arkansas, 1918 95.2 p39
Durken, Luke; New York, NY, 1836 8208.4 p25
Durkin, John 30; New Orleans, 1863 543.30 p222
Durkin, Mary; Iowa, 1866-1943 123.54 p61
Durmon, Patrick; Philadelphia, 1851 5704.8 p81
Durmond, Patrick; Quebec, 1825 7603 p83
Durnay, Daniel 24; Pennsylvania, 1740 4779.3 p14A
Durnin, Catherine; New York, NY, 1864 5704.8 p171
Durnin, Charles 6 SEE Durnin, Margaret
Durnin, Charles 6; Philadelphia, 1847 5704.8 p1
Durnin, Grace; Philadelphia, 1867 5704.8 p219
Durnin, James 20; Philadelphia, 1865 5704.8 p164
Durnin, Julia; Philadelphia, 1867 5704.8 p219
Durnin, Margaret; New York, NY, 1864 5704.8 p171
Durnin, Margaret; Philadelphia, 1847 53.26 p25
  Relative:Mary 9
  Relative:Charles 6
Durnin, Margaret; Philadelphia, 1847 5704.8 p1
Durnin, Margaret; Philadelphia, 1866 5704.8 p207
Durnin, Margery; Philadelphia, 1864 5704.8 p184
Durnin, Mary 9 SEE Durnin, Margaret
Durnin, Mary 9; Philadelphia, 1847 5704.8 p1
Durning, James 26; Philadelphia, 1858 5704.8 p139
Durnion, Alex 4; Quebec, 1849 5704.8 p56
Durnion, Catharine 13; Quebec, 1849 5704.8 p56
Durnion, Darl; Quebec, 1849 5704.8 p56
Durnion, Grace; Quebec, 1849 5704.8 p56
Durnion, John; Quebec, 1849 5704.8 p56
Durnion, John 18; Philadelphia, 1859 5704.8 p142
Durnion, Margaret 6; Quebec, 1849 5704.8 p56
Durnion, Margaret 19; St. John, N.B., 1854 5704.8 p114
Durno, Andrew; Austin, TX, 1886 9777 p5
Durnon, Dennis; New York, NY, 1870 5704.8 p239
DuRocher, Mr. 27; New Orleans, 1829 778.5 p187
du Roi, . . .; Quebec, 1776 9786 p105
du Roi, August Wilhelm; Quebec, 1776 9786 p255
Duron, Martin; Ohio, 1840 9892.11 p14
Duross, John 21; Philadelphia, 1804 53.26 p25
Duroux, Mr. 29; America, 1837 778.5 p187
Durr, . . .; Canada, 1776-1783 9786 p42
Durrant, Richard; Virginia, 1635 6219 p6
  With wife
Durred, William 15; Virginia, 1773 1219.7 p171
Durrington, Richard; Virginia, 1643 6219 p201
Durrsee, John 38; New Orleans, 1862 543.30 p60
Dursee, John 38; New Orleans, 1862 543.30 p55
Durst, Mr.; America, 1855 3702.7 p156
Durst, Anna; Nova Scotia, 1752 2444 p140
Durumis, George; Arkansas, 1918 95.2 p39
Durward, Alexander; Colorado, 1888 9678.2 p17
Durward, Alexander 36?; Arizona, 1890 2764.35 p17
Dury, John; Baltimore, 1811 2859.11 p11
Dus, Christian; Charleston, SC, 1766 8582.2 p65
Dusalle, J. P.; America, 1838 778.5 p187
Dusan, Mr. 24; New Orleans, 1839 778.5 p188
Dusard, Dr. 30; Baton Rouge, LA, 1822 778.5 p188
Dusautoy, Alfred 52; America, 1837 778.5 p188
Duseigneur, C. 35; New Orleans, 1835 778.5 p188
Dush, . . .; Pennsylvania, n.d. 4525 p210
Dush, Francis; Virginia, 1844 4626.16 p12
Dusiard, Mme. 50; New Orleans, 1826 778.5 p178
Duspiva, Frank; Illinois, 1885 2896.5 p10
Duss, Anna Maria SEE Duss, Christian Jacob
Duss, Anna Maria Roller SEE Duss, Christian Jacob
Duss, Christian Jacob; America, 1751-1800 2444 p150
  Child:Magdalena
  Child:Anna Maria
  Wife:Anna Maria Roller
Duss, Magdalena SEE Duss, Christian Jacob
Dussart, Julien 38; New Orleans, 1827 778.5 p188
Dussass, James 21; America, 1831 778.5 p182
Dussaux, Mr. 30; Port uncertain, 1836 778.5 p188
Dusseaus, Alfred 35; America, 1838 778.5 p188
Dusseaux, Joseph; Philadelphia, 1756 8582.3 p95
Dust, Christoph; Illinois, 1868 5012.38 p98
Dust, Gottfried; New York, 1754 3652 p79
Dust, Henry; Illinois, 1862 5012.38 p98
Dustman, . . .; Pennsylvania, n.d. 4525 p211
Dusumier, Mr. 20; Louisiana, 1820 778.5 p188
Dut, George; Pennsylvania, 1751 2444 p150
Dutarb, C. J. 30; Port uncertain, 1835 778.5 p188
D'Utassy, Colonel; New York, 1861-1865 8582.3 p91
Dutch, Cornelius 27; Maryland, 1775 1219.7 p250
Dutch, James 16; Maryland, 1775 1219.7 p250
Dutch, John 23; Maryland, 1775 1219.7 p250
  Wife:Mary 23
Dutch, Mary 23 SEE Dutch, John
Dutch, Peter 29; New Orleans, 1862 543.30 p219
Dutch, Robert; Virginia, 1645 6219 p232
Dutch, Thomas 21; Maryland, 1775 1219.7 p250
Dutch, Walter; Wisconsin, n.d. 9675.5 p121
Dute, Hans George; Pennsylvania, 1751 2444 p150
Dutertre, Mr. 25; Louisiana, 1820 778.5 p188
Duth, Hannes; Pennsylvania, 1751 2444 p150
Duthel, Mr. 37; Port uncertain, 1838 778.5 p188
Duthil, Jacques 50; Louisiana, 1838 778.5 p188
Duthilois, Jules 27?; Port uncertain, 1839 778.5 p188
Dutihl, P. 14; New Orleans, 1821 778.5 p188
Dutkoski, Frank; America, 1884 7137 p168
  Wife:Josephine
Dutkoski, Josephine SEE Dutkoski, Frank
Dutone, Dominique 31; New Orleans, 1862 543.30 p57
Dutruissan, P. B. 48; New Orleans, 1827 778.5 p189
Dutt, David; Pennsylvania, 1751 2444 p150
Dutt, Johann Georg; Pennsylvania, 1751 2444 p150
Dutt, Johann Michael; Port uncertain, 1751 2444 p151
Dutt, Johannes; Pennsylvania, 1751 2444 p150
Dutten, Samuel; New Orleans, 1849 5704.8 p58
Dutton, James 71; Arizona, 1917 9228.40 p21
Dutton, John 15; Grenada, 1773 1219.7 p173
Dutton, Thomas 23; Maryland, 1775 1219.7 p247
Duty, Thomas; Antigua (Antego), 1758 1219.7 p61
Duty, Thomas; Antigua (Antego), 1758 3690.1 p68
Duval, . . . 16; Grenada, 1774 1219.7 p231
Duval, Mme.; New Orleans, 1839 778.5 p189
Duval, Mme. 20; America, 1829 778.5 p190
Duval, Mr.; New Orleans, 1839 778.5 p189
Duval, Mr. 25; America, 1822 778.5 p189
Duval, Mr. 27; America, 1829 778.5 p190
Duval, Mr. 30; America, 1822 778.5 p189
Duval, A.; New Orleans, 1839 778.5 p189
Duval, Benjamin 23; Louisiana, 1826 778.5 p189
Duval, David 24; Kansas, 1880 5240.1 p62
Duval, H. 30; New Orleans, 1825 778.5 p189
Duval, J. 24; New Orleans, 1827 778.5 p189
Duval, J. J. H. 26; Louisiana, 1821 778.5 p189
Duval, L. 4; America, 1829 778.5 p189
Duval, Marie Rene 23; New Orleans, 1827 778.5 p189
Duvas, Terance; Baltimore, 1811 2859.11 p11
Duveneck, Joseph; America, 1847 8582.3 p16
Duverge, Pierre 30; New Orleans, 1829 778.5 p190
Duverger, J. 13; New Orleans, 1839 778.5 p190
Duverger, Jean En. 20; New Orleans, 1836 778.5 p190
Duverger, Suzanne; Montreal, 1660 7603 p26
Duvert, Armand 14; New Orleans, 1838 778.5 p190
Duvert, Claudine 37; New Orleans, 1838 778.5 p190
Duvert, Theodore 36; New Orleans, 1838 778.5 p190
Duvie, Antoine 19; America, 1838 778.5 p190
Duvie, Joseph 45; New Orleans, 1839 778.5 p190
Duvinet, . . .; Canada, 1776-1783 9786 p20
Duvinett, . . .; Canada, 1776-1783 9786 p20
Duvoisin, Charles 24; New Orleans, 1838 778.5 p190
Duvoisin, Daniel SEE Duvoisin, Jean-Henri
Duvoisin, Daniel; Philadelphia, 1750-1768 7074.6 p214
Duvoisin, Jean-Henri; Halifax, N.S., 1750 7074.6 p210
  Wife:Marguerite
  Son:Daniel
  With 2 children
Duvoisin, Marguerite SEE Duvoisin, Jean-Henri
Duwe, William; Wisconsin, n.d. 9675.5 p121
Dux, Jacob; Baltimore, 1867 1450.2 p8B
Dux, Paul; America, 1892 1450.2 p8B
Duynes, . . .; Canada, 1776-1783 9786 p20
Dvorak, Joseph Frank; Arkansas, 1918 95.2 p39
Dvorink, John; Wisconsin, n.d. 9675.5 p121
Dwason, Iver; Iowa, 1866-1943 123.54 p17
Dwire, William 25; New Orleans, 1862 543.30 p216
Dwyer, Anthony; America, 1736-1743 4971 p57
Dwyer, Biddy 12; Massachusetts, 1850 5881.1 p27
Dwyer, Catharine 13; Massachusetts, 1850 5881.1 p28
Dwyer, Honora 48; Massachusetts, 1849 5881.1 p29
Dwyer, James; New York, NY, 1834 8208.4 p3
Dwyer, James 2; Massachusetts, 1849 5881.1 p30
Dwyer, Jean; Quebec, 1752 7603 p92
Dwyer, John; America, 1742 4971 p50
Dwyer, John; America, 1742 4971 p53
Dwyer, John; America, 1743 4971 p50
Dwyer, John; New York, NY, 1816 2859.11 p30
Dwyer, John; New York, NY, 1839 8208.4 p97
Dwyer, John 22; Massachusetts, 1847 5881.1 p29
Dwyer, John 35; New Orleans, 1862 543.30 p218
Dwyer, Kate 16; Massachusetts, 1849 5881.1 p31
Dwyer, Mary 55; Massachusetts, 1849 5881.1 p32
Dwyer, Michael 22; New Orleans, 1862 543.30 p57
Dwyer, Patrick; America, 1742 4971 p31
Dwyer, Patrick; New York, NY, 1833 8208.4 p29
Dwyer, Patrick 16; Massachusetts, 1849 5881.1 p33
Dwyer, Patrick 64; California, 1866 3840.1 p16
Dwyer, Patrick, Jr. 21; Kansas, 1873 5240.1 p54
Dwyer, Richard 18; Massachusetts, 1847 5881.1 p34
Dwyer, T.J. 47; Arizona, 1899 9228.40 p2
Dwyer, Thomas 18; Massachusetts, 1849 5881.1 p34
Dwyer, Timothy 20; Massachusetts, 1847 5881.1 p34
Dwyer, William; America, 1736-1743 4971 p57
Dwyer, William 25; New Orleans, 1862 543.30 p216
Dwyer, William 26; Massachusetts, 1847 5881.1 p34
Dyal, Mary 23; Jamaica, 1775 1219.7 p265
Dyas, John; Virginia, 1642 6219 p188
Dyatt, . . . 9 mos; New York, NY, 1865 5704.8 p194
Dyatt, Daniel; New York, NY, 1865 5704.8 p194
Dyatt, Elizabeth; New York, NY, 1865 5704.8 p194
Dyck, Abraham; Quebec, 1876 9980.20 p49
Dyck, Anna; Quebec, 1875 9980.20 p48
Dyck, Anna; Quebec, 1876 9980.20 p49
Dyck, Anna Friesen; Quebec, 1876 9980.20 p49
Dyck, Dietrich; Washington, 1859-1920 2872.1 p10
Dyck, Elizabeth; Quebec, 1875 9980.20 p48
Dyck, Helena; Kansas, 1882 5240.1 p10
Dyck, Helena; Quebec, 1875 9980.20 p48
Dyck, Helena Fehr; Quebec, 1875 9980.20 p48
Dyck, Hermann; Kansas, 1882 5240.1 p10
Dyck, Herrmann; Quebec, 1875 9980.20 p48
Dyck, Isaak 18; Quebec, 1875 9980.20 p48
Dyck, Jacob 15; Quebec, 1875 9980.20 p48
Dyck, Johann; Quebec, 1875 9980.20 p48
Dyck, Peter; Quebec, 1875 9980.20 p48
Dyck, Peter; Quebec, 1876 9980.20 p49
Dycle, John; New York, NY, 1815 2859.11 p30
Dycle, Robert; New York, NY, 1815 2859.11 p30
Dye, Henry 21; Maryland, 1729 3690.1 p69
Dye, Robt.; Virginia, 1637 6219 p110
Dyer, Ann; Virginia, 1643 6219 p23
Dyer, Jno.; Virginia, 1647 6219 p239
Dyer, John; Virginia, 1629 6219 p31
Dyer, Joseph 17; New York, 1775 1219.7 p246
Dyer, Joseph 21; Maryland, 1774 1219.7 p224
Dyer, Joseph 21; South Carolina, 1774 1219.7 p234
Dyer, Mary 11; Massachusetts, 1850 5881.1 p32
Dyer, Mary 18; Massachusetts, 1850 5881.1 p32
Dyer, Mary 20; Massachusetts, 1847 5881.1 p31
Dyer, Patrick 15; Massachusetts, 1850 5881.1 p33
Dyer, Peter 12; Massachusetts, 1850 5881.1 p33
Dyer, Robert 18; Maryland, 1729 3690.1 p69
Dyer, Tho.; Virginia, 1638 6219 p159
Dyer, Thomas; America, 1736 4971 p44
Dyet, Catherine; New York, NY, 1864 5704.8 p175
Dyet, Robert; New York, NY, 1864 5704.8 p175
Dykeman, Peter Simon; Washington, 1859-1920 2872.1 p10
Dyken, Marcus Ludwig; Arkansas, 1918 95.2 p39
Dykes, John 35; St. John, N.B., 1858 5704.8 p140
Dykoski, Frank; America, 1884 7137 p168
  Wife:Josephine
Dykoski, Josephine SEE Dykoski, Frank
Dykstra, Everdina Hermina; Washington, 1859-1920 2872.1 p11
Dykstra, Gerrit Hendrick; Washington, 1859-1920 2872.1 p11
Dykstra, Hendrika Reindina; Washington, 1859-1920 2872.1 p11
Dykstra, Herman; Washington, 1859-1920 2872.1 p11
Dykstra, Jelle; Iroquois Co., IL, 1896 3455.1 p10
Dykstra, Nick 29; Arkansas, 1918 95.2 p39
Dykstra, Ruth; Washington, 1859-1920 2872.1 p11
Dykstra, Theodorus Bernhardus; Washington, 1859-1920 2872.1 p11
Dymer, Charles 20; Virginia, 1721 3690.1 p69
Dymoer, Daniel 20; Windward Islands, 1722 3690.1 p63
Dyne, Luke; Virginia, 1652 6251 p20
Dyner, Thos.; Virginia, 1635 6219 p5
Dynes, Margaret; New York, NY, 1867 5704.8 p218
Dynowski, . . .; New York, 1831 4606 p173
Dyos, Thomas; Virginia, 1642 6219 p15
Dyos, Thomas; Virginia, 1642 6219 p190

Dysart, Anne 12; St. John, N.B., 1849 *5704.8 p56*
Dysart, George; South Carolina, 1716 *1639.20 p64*
Dysart, Jane 10; St. John, N.B., 1849 *5704.8 p56*
Dysart, Sarah; St. John, N.B., 1849 *5704.8 p56*
Dyson, William 18; West Indies, 1722 *3690.1 p69*
Dyson, William 21; Maryland, 1724 *3690.1 p69*
Dystler, Henry L.; Virginia, 1844 *4626.16 p13*

Dysz, Franciszek 25; New York, 1912 *9980.29 p53*
Dyt, Cornelius 36; Kansas, 1872 *5240.1 p52*
Dytche, William 20; Virginia, 1774 *1219.7 p241*
Dzallakowki, Michael; Illinois, 1890 *5012.40 p25*
Dziadulewicz, Sigmund; Arkansas, 1918 *95.2 p39*
Dziarmann, Onufry 27; New York, 1912 *9980.29 p64*
Dziewanowski, . . .; New York, 1831 *4606 p173*

Dziklinski, Stanislaw; Arkansas, 1918 *95.2 p39*
Dzuirda, Daniel; Arkansas, 1918 *95.2 p39*
Dzunda, John; America, 1896 *7137 p168*
Dzunda, Michael; America, 1896 *7137 p168*
Dzwierzynski, Josef 30; New York, 1912 *9980.29 p71*
Dzwik, Wikton; Arkansas, 1918 *95.2 p39*

E

Eade, Henry John; Illinois, 1884 *2896.5 p10*
Eades, Laurance 19; Pennsylvania, 1728 *3690.1 p69*
Eadie, William G.; New York, NY, 1831 *8208.4 p30*
Eadly, Ambrose; Virginia, 1637 *6219 p108*
Eagan, Patrick; New York, NY, 1816 *2859.11 p30*
Eagan, Richard; New York, NY, 1834 *8208.4 p2*
Eager, Robert; New York, NY, 1816 *2859.11 p30*
Eager, Tho.; Virginia, 1643 *6219 p199*
Eagle, Geo.; Virginia, 1635 *6219 p26*
Eagleston, Moses; Ohio, 1840 *9892.11 p14*
Eakens, Sarah; New York, NY, 1811 *2859.11 p11*
Eakin, Alex. 26; Philadelphia, 1833-1834 *53.26 p25*
Eakin, Alexander 28; Philadelphia, 1803 *53.26 p25*
Eakin, Ann Jane 11; St. John, N.B., 1847 *5704.8 p19*
Eakin, Isabella 6 mos; St. John, N.B., 1848 *5704.8 p44*
Eakin, John; Quebec, 1851 *5704.8 p73*
Eakin, Margaret; St. John, N.B., 1848 *5704.8 p44*
Eakin, Margaret 6; St. John, N.B., 1847 *5704.8 p19*
Eakin, Mary; St. John, N.B., 1847 *5704.8 p19*
Eakin, Robert; St. John, N.B., 1847 *5704.8 p19*
Eakin, Robert 4; St. John, N.B., 1847 *5704.8 p19*
Eakin, Robert 4; St. John, N.B., 1848 *5704.8 p44*
Eakin, William; St. John, N.B., 1848 *5704.8 p44*
Eakins, Margaret; New York, NY, 1811 *2859.11 p11*
Eakins, Margaret, Jr.; New York, NY, 1811 *2859.11 p11*
Eakins, Rosannah; New York, NY, 1811 *2859.11 p11*
Ealerye, Emerie; Virginia, 1637 *6219 p112*
Eales, Francis 21; Maryland, 1775 *1219.7 p267*
Eall, Christian; Wisconsin, n.d. *9675.5 p121*
Eally, John; Philadelphia, 1868 *5704.8 p230*
Eardly, Catharine 24; Massachusetts, 1849 *5881.1 p35*
Earl, Charles 19; St. John, N.B., 1866 *5704.8 p166*
Earl, Isaac; Illinois, 1856 *7857 p3*
Earl, Isaac T.; Colorado, 1897 *9678.2 p17*
Earl, John; Jamaica, 1752 *1219.7 p15*
Earl, John 36; New Orleans, 1862 *543.30 p482A*
Earl, Joseph; Illinois, 1854 *7857 p3*
Earl, Joseph; Illinois, 1856 *7857 p3*
Earl, Thomas 19; Pennsylvania, 1731 *3690.1 p69*
Earle, James 24; St. John, N.B., 1856 *5704.8 p131*
Earle, John; Virginia, 1652 *6251 p20*
Earle, John 25; Philadelphia, 1774 *1219.7 p214*
Earle, Joseph 19; Pennsylvania, 1735 *3690.1 p69*
Earles, James; St. John, N.B., 1853 *5704.8 p99*
Earley, Ann; Philadelphia, 1850 *53.26 p25*
Earley, Ann; Philadelphia, 1850 *5704.8 p60*
Earley, Daniel; New York, NY, 1865 *5704.8 p183*
Earley, Daniel; St. John, N.B., 1851 *5704.8 p78*
Earley, Daniel 7; St. John, N.B., 1851 *5704.8 p78*
Earley, Edward; St. John, N.B., 1851 *5704.8 p78*
Earley, Francis; Quebec, 1847 *5704.8 p37*
Earley, Francis 7; St. John, N.B., 1847 *5704.8 p35*
Earley, Hannah; St. John, N.B., 1851 *5704.8 p78*
Earley, James; Quebec, 1848 *5704.8 p42*
Earley, Jane; Quebec, 1848 *5704.8 p42*
Earley, Patrick 5; St. John, N.B., 1851 *5704.8 p78*
Earley, Rebecca; Quebec, 1848 *5704.8 p42*
Earley, William 5; St. John, N.B., 1847 *5704.8 p35*
Earlsman, Edward 30; Jamaica, 1774 *1219.7 p223*
Early, Alice; Philadelphia, 1866 *5704.8 p215*
Early, Bernard 9; St. John, N.B., 1847 *5704.8 p14*
Early, Bessy; St. John, N.B., 1847 *5704.8 p14*
Early, Biddy; St. John, N.B., 1847 *5704.8 p34*
Early, Catherine; St. John, N.B., 1847 *5704.8 p15*
Early, Ceclia; Philadelphia, 1866 *5704.8 p215*
Early, Charles 35; Massachusetts, 1849 *5881.1 p35*
Early, Donald; Quebec, 1825 *7603 p82*

Early, Edward; St. John, N.B., 1847 *5704.8 p14*
Early, Edward 9 mos; St. John, N.B., 1847 *5704.8 p15*
Early, Henry; Philadelphia, 1852 *5704.8 p97*
Early, Henry; St. John, N.B., 1847 *5704.8 p14*
Early, Jacob; Pennsylvania, 1750 *2444 p198*
Early, James 10; St. John, N.B., 1847 *5704.8 p15*
Early, James 22; Philadelphia, 1854 *5704.8 p117*
Early, Jane 10; St. John, N.B., 1847 *5704.8 p14*
Early, John 9 mos; St. John, N.B., 1847 *5704.8 p34*
Early, John 35; New Orleans, 1862 *543.30 p480A*
Early, Kate 20; Philadelphia, 1861 *5704.8 p148*
Early, Manus 40; Quebec, 1858 *5704.8 p137*
Early, Mary; Philadelphia, 1852 *5704.8 p97*
Early, Mary; Philadelphia, 1866 *5704.8 p215*
Early, Mary 9 mos; St. John, N.B., 1847 *5704.8 p14*
Early, Mary 10; St. John, N.B., 1847 *5704.8 p34*
Early, Thomas; St. John, N.B., 1847 *5704.8 p34*
Early, Thomas 3; St. John, N.B., 1847 *5704.8 p34*
Early, Thomas 6; St. John, N.B., 1847 *5704.8 p14*
Early, William 4; St. John, N.B., 1847 *5704.8 p14*
Earnst, Michael; Pennsylvania, 1741-1783 *2444 p152*
Earrie, Edward; New York, NY, 1816 *2859.11 p30*
Eartes, Joane; Virginia, 1642 *6219 p189*
Earthead, John 18; America, 1702 *2212 p36*
Easdale, James 20; Quebec, 1858 *5704.8 p138*
Easill, Christ.; Virginia, 1637 *6219 p108*
Easmes, Louis; Illinois, 1871 *5012.39 p25*
Eason, Edward; Virginia, 1637 *6219 p108*
Eason, Robert; Charleston, SC, 1804 *1639.20 p64*
East, John 18; Maryland, 1737 *3690.1 p69*
East, William; Virginia, 1643 *6219 p201*
East, Wm.; Virginia, 1638 *6219 p11*
Eastcote, Jon.; Virginia, 1635 *6219 p69*
Easter, William A.; Washington, 1859-1920 *2872.1 p11*
Easterley, Jane 48; South Carolina, 1850 *1639.20 p64*
Eastet, Jean 38; America, 1837 *778.5 p190*
Eastman, Joseph; Maryland, 1775 *1219.7 p265*
Easton, Alexander; New York, NY, 1836 *8208.4 p25*
Easton, Edward; New York, NY, 1840 *8208.4 p112*
Easton, Edward Warren; Washington, 1859-1920 *2872.1 p11*
Easton, Thomas 19; Maryland, 1719 *3690.1 p69*
Eastvold, John M.; Arkansas, 1918 *95.2 p39*
Eastwood, Edw.; Virginia, 1621 *6219 p67*
Eastwood, Richard; Virginia, 1642 *6219 p186*
Eastwood, Sarah 16; South Carolina, 1774 *1219.7 p234*
Easun, William 37; Maryland, 1774 *1219.7 p191*
Easware, Battis 30; New Orleans, 1838 *778.5 p190*
Easware, Virginia 37; New Orleans, 1838 *778.5 p190*
Eatock, Ada; Iowa, 1866-1943 *123.54 p61*
Eatock, Edmond; Iowa, 1866-1943 *123.54 p17*
Eatock, Samuel; Iowa, 1866-1943 *123.54 p17*
Eatock, Samuel; Iowa, 1866-1943 *123.54 p61*
Eaton, David 19; Philadelphia, 1864 *5704.8 p155*
Eaton, George; Quebec, 1852 *5704.8 p87*
Eaton, George; Quebec, 1852 *5704.8 p90*
Eaton, Henry; Virginia, 1638 *6219 p115*
Eaton, J. P.; Washington, 1859-1920 *2872.1 p11*
Eaton, James 32; Maryland, 1775 *1219.7 p247*
Eaton, James P.; Washington, 1859-1920 *2872.1 p11*
Eaton, John; Virginia, 1643 *6219 p201*
Eaton, John 16; New York, 1774 *1219.7 p203*
Eaton, John 29; Jamaica, 1733 *3690.1 p69*
Eaton, Nathaniell; Virginia, 1635 *6219 p69*
Eaton, Peter; Virginia, 1637 *6219 p28*
Eaton, Robert; Philadelphia, 1849 *53.26 p25*
Eaton, Robert; Philadelphia, 1849 *5704.8 p50*

Eaton, Sam.; Virginia, 1635 *6219 p71*
Eaton, Sarah 20; America, 1699 *2212 p29*
Eatros, James; Arkansas, 1918 *95.2 p39*
Eaworth, Mary; Virginia, 1635 *6219 p69*
Ebacher, . . .; Canada, 1776-1783 *9786 p20*
Ebbage, James; Iowa, 1866-1943 *123.54 p17*
Ebbell, Eliz.; Virginia, 1648 *6219 p251*
Ebbernathy, William 18; Maryland, 1723 *3690.1 p69*
Ebbers, Heinrich; America, 1851 *8582.3 p16*
Ebberts, Martha 40; Massachusetts, 1848 *5881.1 p35*
Ebbly, Martin; Pennsylvania, 1751 *2444 p152*
Ebbly, Martin; Pennsylvania, 1751 *2444 p171*
Ebbot, Ann 15; Massachusetts, 1848 *5881.1 p35*
Ebbot, Mary 50; Massachusetts, 1848 *5881.1 p35*
Ebbs, Barbara 13 SEE Ebbs, Daniel
Ebbs, Daniel; South Carolina, 1752-1753 *3689.17 p21*
  With wife
  Relative: Daniel 18
  Relative: Barbara 13
  Relative: Magdalene 8
Ebbs, Daniel 18 SEE Ebbs, Daniel
Ebbs, Magdalene 8 SEE Ebbs, Daniel
Ebel, Joseph; Wisconsin, n.d. *9675.5 p121*
Ebel, M. 45; America, 1836 *778.5 p190*
Ebel, Philipp 47; America, 1836 *778.5 p191*
Ebel, Philippe 21; America, 1836 *778.5 p191*
Ebel, Pierre 12; America, 1836 *778.5 p191*
Ebel, Rosina 18; America, 1836 *778.5 p191*
Ebeling, Andrew; Canada, 1783 *9786 p38A*
Ebeling, John; Pennsylvania, 1749 *2444 p151*
Ebell, John; New Jersey, 1780 *8137 p8*
Ebenhardt, . . .; Canada, 1776-1783 *9786 p20*
Eberal, William 35; New Orleans, 1863 *543.30 p484A*
Eberard, . . .; Canada, 1776-1783 *9786 p20*
Eberhard, Franz; Cincinnati, 1830 *8582.1 p51*
Eberhard, Henry; Philadelphia, 1763 *9973.7 p38*
Eberhard, Magdalena 25; Port uncertain, 1839 *778.5 p191*
Eberhard, Magdelena 18; Port uncertain, 1839 *778.5 p191*
Eberhard, Marie 28; Port uncertain, 1839 *778.5 p191*
Eberhard, Michael 29; Port uncertain, 1839 *778.5 p191*
Eberhard, Nikolaus; Philadelphia, 1779 *8137 p8*
Eberharda, Sister M.; Wisconsin, n.d. *9675.6 p268*
Eberhardi, Anna Gwinner SEE Eberhardi, Ludwig David
Eberhardi, Catharina Susanna SEE Eberhardi, Ludwig David
Eberhardi, Ludwig David; America, 1709 *2444 p151*
  Wife: Anna Gwinner
  Child: Salome Gertraute
  Child: Wilhelm Benedict
  Child: Regina Barbara
  Child: Catharina Susanna
Eberhardi, Regina Barbara SEE Eberhardi, Ludwig David
Eberhardi, Salome Gertraute SEE Eberhardi, Ludwig David
Eberhardi, Wilhelm Benedict SEE Eberhardi, Ludwig David
Eberhardt, John; New York, 1846 *1450.2 p35A*
Eberhardt, Katharine; New York, 1873 *1450.2 p8B*
Eberhardt, Nicholas Henry; New York, 1752 *3652 p76*
Eberharter, Louis; Colorado, 1898 *9678.2 p17*
Eberharter, Louis; Colorado, 1898 *9678.2 p17*
Eberharter, Ludwig; Colorado, 1898 *9678.2 p17*
Eberl, Frank; Colorado, 1904 *9678.2 p17*
Eberl, Joseph; Colorado, 1891 *9678.2 p17*

Eberle, Adam 7; America, 1838 ***778.5*** *p191*
Eberle, Anna Barb. 26; America, 1853 ***9162.7*** *p14*
Eberle, Anna Maria 30; America, 1853 ***9162.7*** *p14*
Eberle, Apollonia 14; America, 1838 ***778.5*** *p191*
Eberle, Carl 22; America, 1838 ***778.5*** *p191*
Eberle, Catharine 20; America, 1838 ***778.5*** *p191*
Eberle, Catharine 46; America, 1838 ***778.5*** *p191*
Eberle, Earnest; Illinois, 1888 ***5012.37*** *p61*
Eberle, Franz 20; America, 1853 ***9162.7*** *p14*
Eberle, George 16; America, 1838 ***778.5*** *p191*
Eberle, Gustav 3; America, 1853 ***9162.7*** *p14*
Eberle, Jacob 28; America, 1853 ***9162.7*** *p14*
Eberle, Johann 6 mos; America, 1853 ***9162.7*** *p14*
Eberle, Johannes; Pennsylvania, 1749 ***2444*** *p151*
Eberle, Magdalena; Baltimore, 1829 ***8582.1*** *p47*
Eberle, Valentin 18; America, 1838 ***778.5*** *p192*
Eberle, Valentin 50; America, 1838 ***778.5*** *p191*
Eberlen, Anna Barbara *SEE* Eberlen, Johannes
Eberlen, Johann Conrad *SEE* Eberlen, Johannes
Eberlen, Johannes; Pennsylvania, 1749 ***2444*** *p151*
*Wife:*Anna Barbara
*Child:*Johann Conrad
Eberli, Anna Maria; Port uncertain, 1727 ***3627*** *p19*
Eberly, John; Pennsylvania, 1749 ***2444*** *p151*
Ebermeyer, Margaret; New York, 1752 ***3652*** *p76*
Eberomy, Gartwragh; Virginia, 1648 ***6219*** *p250*
Ebersolt, Ernst; Illinois, 1900 ***2896.5*** *p10*
Ebert, . . .; Canada, 1776-1783 ***9786*** *p20*
Ebert, Ad. 39; America, 1853 ***9162.7*** *p14*
Ebert, Adam; America, 1849 ***8582.3*** *p16*
Ebert, Adolph 32; New Orleans, 1862 ***543.30*** *p480A*
Ebert, Anna Cath. 4; America, 1853 ***9162.7*** *p14*
Ebert, Christian; Wisconsin, n.d. ***9675.5*** *p121*
Ebert, Elis. 7; America, 1853 ***9162.7*** *p14*
Ebert, Elisabetha 48; America, 1853 ***9162.7*** *p14*
Ebert, Ernest; Washington, 1859-1920 ***2872.1*** *p11*
Ebert, Fred 41; Arizona, 1910 ***9228.40*** *p15*
Ebert, Heinrich; America, 1853 ***8582.3*** *p16*
Ebert, John 42; Arizona, 1910 ***9228.40*** *p11*
Ebert, Maria 10; America, 1853 ***9162.7*** *p14*
Ebert, Martin; Philadelphia, 1751 ***9973.7*** *p31*
Ebert, Michael; Philadelphia, 1751 ***9973.7*** *p31*
Ebert, Otto Hugo; Washington, 1859-1920 ***2872.1*** *p11*
Ebert, Susan; Washington, 1859-1920 ***2872.1*** *p11*
Eberths, . . .; Canada, 1776-1783 ***9786*** *p20*
Eberwein, Anna; Pennsylvania, 1748 ***2444*** *p199*
Eberwein, Anna; Pennsylvania, 1749 ***2444*** *p199*
Ebi, Barbara; Pennsylvania, 1717 ***3627*** *p13*
Ebin, Barbara; Pennsylvania, 1717 ***3627*** *p13*
Ebinger, Johann Caspar; Pennsylvania, 1752 ***2444*** *p151*
Ebinnger, Gottlieb; South Carolina, 1788 ***7119*** *p198*
Ebisoh, Christian 23; New Orleans, 1836 ***778.5*** *p192*
Ebison, Thomas 22; Jamaica, 1733 ***3690.1*** *p70*
Eble, Christian Benedict; New York, NY, 1835 ***8208.4*** *p7*
Eble, Martin; Pennsylvania, 1751 ***2444*** *p152*
Ebner, Balthasar; Georgia, 1738 ***9332*** *p319*
Ebner, Hans; Georgia, 1738 ***9332*** *p319*
Eby, Barbara; Pennsylvania, 1717 ***3627*** *p13*
Eccles, Ann; Virginia, 1698 ***2212*** *p12*
Eccles, Griffin 24; North Carolina, 1736 ***3690.1*** *p70*
Eccles, James; America, 1697 ***2212*** *p4*
Eccles, John 12 *SEE* Eccles, William
Eccles, Martha McKenzie 45 *SEE* Eccles, William
Eccles, Robert; St. John, N.B., 1852 ***5704.8*** *p95*
Eccles, William 40; North Carolina, 1775 ***1639.20*** *p64*
*Wife:*Martha McKenzie 45
*Son:*John 12
Eccleston, Eliz 20; America, 1706 ***2212*** *p47*
Echair, A. 25; Mexico, 1829 ***778.5*** *p192*
Echard, George; New York, NY, 1811 ***2859.11*** *p11*
Echarte, Francis; New York, NY, 1835 ***8208.4*** *p5*
Echtzel, Gottfried; New Jersey, 1780 ***8137*** *p8*
Eck, Kath. 20; America, 1853 ***9162.7*** *p14*
Eck, Michael; New Orleans, 1847 ***1450.2*** *p35A*
Eckardt, Charles G. 36; Kansas, 1873 ***5240.1*** *p10*
Eckardt, Hermann August; Illinois, 1888 ***5012.39*** *p121*
Eckardt, Jeremias; Pennsylvania, 1754 ***2444*** *p151*
Eckart, August; Illinois, 1875 ***2896.5*** *p10*
Eckart, Charles G. 36; Kansas, 1873 ***5240.1*** *p54*
Eckart, William; New York, NY, 1840 ***8208.4*** *p105*
Eckaus, Julius; Arkansas, 1918 ***95.2*** *p39*
Eckehardt, . . .; Ohio, 1825-1829 ***8582.1*** *p46*
Eckel, . . .; Canada, 1776-1783 ***9786*** *p42*
Eckel, Elize 18; Port uncertain, 1838 ***778.5*** *p192*
Eckel, F. 20; Port uncertain, 1838 ***778.5*** *p192*
Eckel, J. 18; Port uncertain, 1838 ***778.5*** *p192*
Eckel, P. H. 51; Port uncertain, 1838 ***778.5*** *p192*
Eckell, Adam Carl 25; Kansas, 1900 ***5240.1*** *p81*
Eckelmann, Heinrich Bernard; America, 1844 ***8582.2*** *p9*
Eckeman, Hartman; Indiana, 1844 ***9117*** *p18*
Ecker, Frank 24; West Virginia, 1898 ***9788.3*** *p9*
Ecker, Frantz; Georgia, 1738 ***9332*** *p320*
Ecker, Joseph 57; West Virginia, 1899 ***9788.3*** *p9*
Eckerly, John 28; New Orleans, 1862 ***543.30*** *p481A*
Eckerstrom, Fredrik Tolf; Minneapolis, 1880-1884 ***6410.35*** *p52*
Eckerstrom, John; Iroquois Co., IL, 1894 ***3455.1*** *p10*
Eckert, Mr.; Philadelphia, 1835 ***8582.3*** *p16*
Eckert, Jeremiah; Pennsylvania, 1754 ***2444*** *p151*
Eckert, Jerimias; Pennsylvania, 1754 ***2444*** *p151*
Eckert, Joseph 20; Harris Co., TX, 1898 ***6254*** *p3*
Eckert, Michael; Cincinnati, 1800-1877 ***8582.3*** *p86*
Eckert, Michael; Cincinnati, 1861 ***8582.3*** *p87*
Eckert, Michael; Cincinnati, 1869-1887 ***8582*** *p7*
Eckert, Michael; New York, NY, 1835 ***8582.3*** *p16*
Eckert, Valentin; Ohio, 1869-1887 ***8582*** *p7*
Eckesparre, Adolph; New York, 1756 ***3652*** *p81*
Eckhard, . . .; Canada, 1776-1783 ***9786*** *p20*
Eckhard, Emile 22; New Orleans, 1862 ***543.30*** *p480A*
Eckhard, Georg Christoph; Philadelphia, 1777-1779 ***8137*** *p8*
Eckhard, Johann Georg; New Jersey, 1777 ***8137*** *p8*
Eckhard, Justus; Philadelphia, 1779 ***8137*** *p8*
Eckhard, Zacharias; New York, 1750 ***3652*** *p74*
Eckhardt, . . .; Canada, 1776-1783 ***9786*** *p20*
Eckhart, Elis. Marg. 11; America, 1853 ***9162.8*** *p36*
Eckhoff, George J.; Illinois, 1881 ***2896.5*** *p10*
Eckhoff, John Henry; Illinois, 1879 ***2896.5*** *p10*
Eckstein, Friederich; Cincinnati, 1826 ***8582.3*** *p87*
Ecrot, Francois 24; America, 1838 ***778.5*** *p192*
Ecrot, Marguerite 25; America, 1838 ***778.5*** *p192*
Ed, John Magnus; Minneapolis, 1881-1886 ***6410.35*** *p52*
Edberg, Maria; Boston, 1833 ***6410.32*** *p124*
Edden, John; Virginia, 1642 ***6219*** *p193*
Edelman, Louis; Arkansas, 1918 ***95.2*** *p39*
Edelman, Samuel; Arkansas, 1918 ***95.2*** *p39*
Edelman, Tom; Wisconsin, n.d. ***9675.5*** *p121*
Edelsahn, Debora 22; New York, NY, 1878 ***9253*** *p45*
Eden, Edo; New York, NY, 1923 ***3455.3*** *p85*
Eden, Hilma M.; Washington, 1859-1920 ***2872.1*** *p11*
Eden, Johan E.; Washington, 1859-1920 ***2872.1*** *p11*
Eden, Jonas Wilhelm; Washington, 1859-1920 ***2872.1*** *p11*
Eden, Karl W.; Washington, 1859-1920 ***2872.1*** *p11*
Eden, Marta Olivia; Washington, 1859-1920 ***2872.1*** *p11*
Eden, Ruth M.; Washington, 1859-1920 ***2872.1*** *p11*
Eden, Stina E.; Washington, 1859-1920 ***2872.1*** *p11*
Edens, Claus; Illinois, 1871 ***5012.39*** *p25*
Edens, John; Illinois, 1890 ***5012.40*** *p25*
Edens, William 42; Kansas, 1887 ***5240.1*** *p69*
Eder, Frank; Colorado, 1887 ***9678.2*** *p17*
Edes, Alice; Virginia, 1635 ***6219*** *p71*
Edes, Eliza.; Virginia, 1638 ***6219*** *p123*
Edgar, Charles; Virginia, 1642 ***6219*** *p195*
Edgar, David; Kansas, 1877 ***5240.1*** *p10*
Edgar, Isabella; America, 1869 ***5704.8*** *p235*
Edgar, James; Charleston, SC, 1805 ***1639.20*** *p65*
Edgar, James; Kansas, 1881 ***5240.1*** *p10*
Edgar, John 18; Maryland, 1720 ***3690.1*** *p70*
Edgar, William F.; Kansas, 1887 ***5240.1*** *p11*
Edgcomb, John; Virginia, 1648 ***6219*** *p237*
Edge, Bessy 15; Massachusetts, 1850 ***5881.1*** *p35*
Edge, Henry 38; Montreal, 1777 ***7603*** *p29*
Edge, Joseph; Montreal, 1775 ***7603*** *p22*
Edge, Tho 16; America, 1706 ***2212*** *p46*
Edge, Thos.; Virginia, 1637 ***6219*** *p13*
Edge, Wm 17; America, 1702 ***2212*** *p36*
Edgen, Henry 19; Virginia, 1720 ***3690.1*** *p70*
Edger, David 40; New York, 1775 ***1219.7*** *p269*
With wife
With 2 children
Edgerler, John 24; Maryland, 1774 ***1219.7*** *p191*
Edgerton, George 19; Maryland, 1728 ***3690.1*** *p70*
Edghill, Thomas; Virginia, 1637 ***6219*** *p9*
Edie, George 28; Virginia, 1775 ***1219.7*** *p261*
Ediford, Wm.; Virginia, 1643 ***6219*** *p203*
Edin, Thomas 23; Jamaica, 1731 ***3690.1*** *p70*
Edison, Hans; Arkansas, 1918 ***95.2*** *p39*
Edison, Swan; Colorado, 1896 ***9678.2*** *p17*
Edkins, Edward 31; Kansas, 1886 ***5240.1*** *p69*
Edler, Caroline Henriette; America, 1883 ***4610.10*** *p118*
Edler, Fritz; Illinois, 1840-1890 ***4610.10*** *p59*
Edler, Heinrich; Kentucky, 1842 ***8582.3*** *p99*
Edler, Henry; New York, NY, 1840 ***8208.4*** *p109*
Edler, John; New York, NY, 1840 ***8208.4*** *p109*
Edlin, John; Virginia, 1638 ***6219*** *p121*
Edloe, Alice; Virginia, 1635 ***6219*** *p8*
Edloe, Alice; Virginia, 1635 ***6219*** *p74*
Edloe, Mathew; Virginia, 1637 ***6219*** *p8*
Edlund, P. 24; Kansas, 1874 ***5240.1*** *p11*
Edlund, P. 24; Kansas, 1874 ***5240.1*** *p55*
Edmenston, Agnes; New York, NY, 1865 ***5704.8*** *p203*
Edmenston, Mary Ann 1; New York, NY, 1865 ***5704.8*** *p203*
Edminson, Letitia 32; St. John, N.B., 1855 ***5704.8*** *p127*
Edminson, Samuel John 6; St. John, N.B., 1855 ***5704.8*** *p127*
Edminson, Wright 11; St. John, N.B., 1855 ***5704.8*** *p127*
Edminston, Margaret; New York, NY, 1864 ***5704.8*** *p169*
Edmond, Eric Valentine; Arkansas, 1918 ***95.2*** *p39*
Edmond, William 41; Philadelphia, 1804 ***53.26*** *p25*
Edmondon, James; Philadelphia, 1811 ***53.26*** *p25*
Edmonds, Ann; Virginia, 1638 ***6219*** *p24*
Edmonds, Ann; Virginia, 1638 ***6219*** *p119*
Edmonds, Ann; Virginia, 1639 ***6219*** *p151*
Edmonds, Evan 46; Maryland, 1775 ***1219.7*** *p257*
Edmonds, Howell; Virginia, 1637 ***6219*** *p11*
Edmonds, John; Virginia, 1622 ***6219*** *p30*
Edmonds, John 12; Dominica, 1774 ***1219.7*** *p223*
Edmonds, Thomas 19; St. John Island, 1775 ***1219.7*** *p273*
Edmonds, William; New York, 1754 ***3652*** *p79*
Edmondson, James; Philadelphia, 1811 ***2859.11*** *p11*
Edmonston, Eliza; Quebec, 1851 ***5704.8*** *p75*
Edmonston, Samuel 11; Quebec, 1851 ***5704.8*** *p75*
Edmund, Grace 20; America, 1699 ***2212*** *p28*
Edmund, James; South Carolina, 1817 ***1639.20*** *p65*
Edmund, Jean; Quebec, 1693 ***7603*** *p76*
Edmunds, Jno; America, 1698 ***2212*** *p8*
Edmunds, Wm 12; Maryland or Virginia, 1699 ***2212*** *p24*
Edmunston, Charles; Charleston, SC, 1799 ***1639.20*** *p65*
Edmunston, Charles 68; Charleston, SC, 1850 ***1639.20*** *p65*
Ednall, Edwd.; Virginia, 1638 ***6219*** *p115*
Edone, Mr. 35; New Orleans, 1837 ***778.5*** *p192*
Edorado, Miniggio E.; Iowa, 1866-1943 ***123.54*** *p17*
Edouard, P. 30; Port uncertain, 1836 ***778.5*** *p192*
Edoue, Mr. 35; New Orleans, 1837 ***778.5*** *p192*
Edsonne, Francis; Virginia, 1637 ***6219*** *p83*
Edsten, A. H.; Minneapolis, 1864-1884 ***6410.35*** *p52*
Edward, Anne 25; Virginia, 1700 ***2212*** *p32*
Edward, Elizabeth; South Carolina, 1658-1721 ***1639.20*** *p252*
Edward, James; Carolina, 1684 ***1639.20*** *p65*
Edward, Jane 27 *SEE* Edward, John
Edward, John 18; America, 1699 ***2212*** *p20*
Edward, John 26; South Carolina, 1774 ***1219.7*** *p205*
*Wife:*Jane 27
Edward, Richd; America, 1697 ***2212*** *p7*
Edward, Walter; Virginia, 1648 ***6219*** *p252*
Edwards, Mr.; Quebec, 1815 ***9229.18*** *p81*
Edwards, Alice; Virginia, 1648 ***6219*** *p246*
Edwards, Andrew; Virginia, 1639 ***6219*** *p22*
Edwards, Ann 18; Philadelphia, 1774 ***1219.7*** *p183*
Edwards, Benjamin 22; Virginia, 1773 ***1219.7*** *p169*
Edwards, Charles; New York, NY, 1834 ***8208.4*** *p4*
Edwards, Charles 12; America, 1700 ***2212*** *p31*
Edwards, Charles 15; Philadelphia, 1774 ***1219.7*** *p215*
Edwards, Christina Lillian; Washington, 1859-1920 ***2872.1*** *p11*
Edwards, Christopher; Virginia, 1638 ***6219*** *p24*
Edwards, Christopher; Virginia, 1639 ***6219*** *p24*
Edwards, Christopher R.; New York, NY, 1839 ***8208.4*** *p92*
Edwards, Dorothy; America, 1698 ***2212*** *p8*
Edwards, Dorothy *SEE* Edwards, William
Edwards, Dorothy Maud; Washington, 1859-1920 ***2872.1*** *p11*
Edwards, Edmond; Virginia, 1638 ***6219*** *p119*
Edwards, Edward 20; Jamaica, 1736 ***3690.1*** *p70*
Edwards, Edward 22; Maryland, 1775 ***1219.7*** *p252*
Edwards, Elizabeth; Virginia, 1640 ***6219*** *p182*
Edwards, Elizabeth 18; Maryland or Virginia, 1699 ***2212*** *p21*
Edwards, Elizabeth 21; Quebec, 1853 ***5704.8*** *p105*
Edwards, Ellen; Virginia, 1638 ***6219*** *p121*
Edwards, Ernest Albert; Washington, 1859-1920 ***2872.1*** *p11*
Edwards, Evan 26; America, 1699 ***2212*** *p25*
Edwards, Francis 18; Maryland, 1729 ***3690.1*** *p70*
Edwards, G.; New York, NY, 1811 ***2859.11*** *p11*
With family
Edwards, George; Austin, TX, 1886 ***9777*** *p5*
Edwards, Henry 17; Virginia, 1774 ***1219.7*** *p227*
Edwards, Henry T.; Colorado, 1901 ***9678.2*** *p17*
Edwards, Humphrye; Virginia, 1635 ***6219*** *p36*
Edwards, Isaac 17; Jamaica, 1734 ***3690.1*** *p70*
Edwards, Isabella; Philadelphia, 1849 ***53.26*** *p25*
Edwards, Isabella; Philadelphia, 1849 ***5704.8*** *p49*
Edwards, James; Austin, TX, 1886 ***9777*** *p5*
Edwards, James; New York, NY, 1835 ***8208.4*** *p77*
Edwards, Jane; St. John, N.B., 1851 ***5704.8*** *p72*
Edwards, Jane 35; Massachusetts, 1849 ***5881.1*** *p35*
Edwards, John; Maryland, 1755 ***1219.7*** *p39*
Edwards, John; Maryland, 1755 ***3690.1*** *p71*
Edwards, John; Virginia, 1638 ***6219*** *p147*
Edwards, John 16; Maryland, 1774 ***1219.7*** *p180*
Edwards, John 17; Pennsylvania, 1722 ***3690.1*** *p70*
Edwards, John 18; Jamaica, 1729 ***3690.1*** *p70*

Edwards, John 18; Maryland, 1720 *3690.1 p70*
Edwards, John 20; Jamaica, 1729 *3690.1 p71*
Edwards, John 20; Philadelphia, 1774 *1219.7 p185*
Edwards, John 25; New York, NY, 1851 *9555.10 p26*
Edwards, John J.; Illinois, 1860 *5012.39 p89*
Edwards, Jon.; Virginia, 1618 *6219 p72*
Edwards, Jon.; Virginia, 1634 *6219 p105*
Edwards, Luke; Illinois, 1886 *2896.5 p10*
Edwards, Margaret 18; St. John, N.B., 1854 *5704.8 p119*
Edwards, Mary; New York, NY, 1851 *9555.10 p26*
Edwards, Mary; Virginia, 1646 *6219 p242*
Edwards, Mary 20; Pennsylvania, 1728 *3690.1 p71*
Edwards, Mary 24; New York, NY, 1851 *9555.10 p26*
Edwards, Rebecca; Virginia, 1638 *6219 p159*
Edwards, Reginald Edgar; Washington, 1859-1920
  2872.1 p11
Edwards, Rich.; Virginia, 1634 *6219 p84*
Edwards, Rich.; Virginia, 1637 *6219 p83*
Edwards, Richard; Edenton, NC, 1757 *1219.7 p58*
Edwards, Richard; New York, NY, 1816 *2859.11 p30*
Edwards, Richard 14; America, 1699 *2212 p20*
Edwards, Richard 19; Maryland or Virginia, 1699 *2212
  p23*
Edwards, Richard 23; Philadelphia, 1775 *1219.7 p255*
Edwards, Richd; America, 1698 *2212 p9*
Edwards, Robert; Virginia, 1638 *6219 p160*
Edwards, Robert; Virginia, 1643 *6219 p204*
Edwards, Robert 22; Maryland or Virginia, 1699 *2212
  p23*
Edwards, Robert 22; Virginia, 1774 *1219.7 p243*
Edwards, Rose; Washington, 1859-1920 *2872.1 p11*
Edwards, Samll.; Virginia, 1642 *6219 p191*
Edwards, Samuel 15; Maryland, 1775 *1219.7 p256*
Edwards, Sidney 18; St. John, N.B., 1854 *5704.8 p119*
Edwards, Sidney 48; St. John, N.B., 1854 *5704.8 p119*
Edwards, Simon 9; Quebec, 1850 *5704.8 p63*
Edwards, Tho.; Virginia, 1639 *6219 p152*
Edwards, Thomas; Virginia, 1637 *6219 p110*
Edwards, Thomas; Virginia, 1638 *6219 p24*
Edwards, Thomas; Virginia, 1638 *6219 p119*
Edwards, Thomas; Virginia, 1639 *6219 p151*
Edwards, Thomas 19; Maryland, 1774 *1219.7 p230*
Edwards, Thomas 21; Baltimore, 1775 *1219.7 p270*
Edwards, William; Quebec, 1850 *5704.8 p63*
Edwards, William; Virginia, 1648 *6219 p250*
  *Wife:*Dorothy
Edwards, William 13; Quebec, 1850 *5704.8 p63*
Edwards, William 25; Quebec, 1853 *5704.8 p105*
Edwards, William 36; Philadelphia, 1775 *1219.7 p258*
Edwards, William 40; Philadelphia, 1774 *1219.7 p217*
Edwards, William James; Washington, 1859-1920 *2872.1
  p11*
Edwards, Wm.; Virginia, 1628 *6219 p31*
Edwards, Wm.; Virginia, 1635 *6219 p26*
Edwards, Wm.; Virginia, 1636 *6219 p77*
Edwards, Wm.; Virginia, 1642 *6219 p191*
Edwards, Wm.; Virginia, 1643 *6219 p199*
Edwards, Wm 10; America, 1700 *2212 p31*
Edwds, Charles 12; America, 1700 *2212 p31*
Edwin, James; Virginia, 1642 *6219 p186*
Edwin, Thomas; Virginia, 1642 *6219 p186*
Eeck, John; Illinois, 1882 *2896.5 p10*
Eells, Robert 25; Jamaica, 1733 *3690.1 p71*
Eerala, Matti; Washington, 1859-1920 *2872.1 p11*
Effinger, Henry; Pennsylvania, 1745-1799 *2444 p198*
Effinger, Johannes Ignatius; America, 1777-1778 *8582.2
  p67*
Effinger, John Ignatius; Philadelphia, 1783 *8582.2 p66*
Efinger, Georg Heinrich; Pennsylvania, 1745-1779 *2444
  p198*
Efstathew, John; Arkansas, 1918 *95.2 p39*
Egan, Edmond; New York, NY, 1834 *8208.4 p2*
Egan, Eliza *SEE* Egan, Peter
Egan, Eliza; Philadelphia, 1850 *5704.8 p59*
Egan, Eliza 15; Massachusetts, 1850 *5881.1 p35*
Egan, James 60; Massachusetts, 1849 *5881.1 p35*
Egan, John; America, 1741 *4971 p60*
Egan, John; New York, NY, 1836 *8208.4 p11*
Egan, John 7; Massachusetts, 1848 *5881.1 p35*
Egan, Judy 40; Massachusetts, 1850 *5881.1 p35*
Egan, Margaret *SEE* Egan, Peter
Egan, Margaret; Philadelphia, 1850 *5704.8 p59*
Egan, Margaret 5; Massachusetts, 1848 *5881.1 p35*
Egan, Margaret 40; Massachusetts, 1848 *5881.1 p35*
Egan, Martin 9; Massachusetts, 1848 *5881.1 p35*
Egan, Mary 50; Massachusetts, 1850 *5881.1 p35*
Egan, Peter; Philadelphia, 1850 *53.26 p26*
  *Relative:*Margaret
  *Relative:*Eliza
Egan, Peter; Philadelphia, 1850 *5704.8 p59*
Egan, Rachael; Philadelphia, 1864 *5704.8 p180*
Egan, Thomas; New York, NY, 1815 *2859.11 p30*
Egan, Thomas; New York, NY, 1838 *8208.4 p72*

Egan, Thomas 18; Massachusetts, 1847 *5881.1 p35*
Egan, Timothy; New York, NY, 1838 *8208.4 p89*
Egar, Jane; Philadelphia, 1811 *2859.11 p11*
Egart, Josep; Wisconsin, n.d. *9675.5 p121*
Egart, Say; Wisconsin, n.d. *9675.5 p121*
Egberow, William; Virginia, 1647 *6219 p245*
Egbert, Archibald; New York, NY, 1840 *8208.4 p111*
Egell, . . .; Canada, 1776-1783 *9786 p20*
Egellton, Richard 19; Jamaica, 1732 *3690.1 p71*
Egemo, Tores; Arkansas, 1918 *95.2 p39*
Eggen, James; Bangor, ME, 1898 *6410.22 p128*
Eggener, Miss; America, 1843 *3702.7 p242*
Eggert, August 46; Harris Co., TX, 1898 *6254 p5*
Eggert, Louis 28; Kansas, 1879 *5240.1 p60*
Eggleston, Arthur; Virginia, 1634 *6219 p32*
Eggleston, Christopher; America, 1858 *5240.1 p11*
Eggoe, John; South Carolina, 1716 *1639.20 p65*
Eggoe, William; South Carolina, 1716 *1639.20 p65*
Egland, Gustav; Arkansas, 1918 *95.2 p40*
Egle, John; Philadelphia, 1759 *9973.7 p33*
Egler, Margaretha Barbara; America, 1753 *2444 p151*
Egleston, Richard; Virginia, 1637 *6219 p82*
Egleton, Francis 17; Jamaica, 1739 *3690.1 p71*
Eglin, Stephen 25; Carolina, 1714 *1219.7 p234*
Eglin, Thomas; New York, NY, 1837 *8208.4 p48*
Eglington, Florinda 17; Philadelphia, 1853 *5704.8 p109*
Eglington, Peter 24; Maryland, 1773 *1219.7 p172*
Eglington, Stewart; St. John, N.B., 1848 *5704.8 p43*
Eglinton, Samuel; Philadelphia, 1850 *53.26 p26*
Eglinton, Samuel; Philadelphia, 1850 *5704.8 p69*
Egly, Jean 43; America, 1838 *778.5 p192*
Egly, Joseph; Cincinnati, 1869-1887 *8582 p7*
Egly, Joseph E.; America, 1840-1849 *8582.1 p8*
Egly, Pauline 72; America, 1838 *778.5 p192*
Egly, Veronique 30; America, 1838 *778.5 p192*
Egly, Victor 9; America, 1838 *778.5 p192*
Egly, Virginie 11; America, 1838 *778.5 p193*
Egly, Weitmine 6; America, 1838 *778.5 p193*
Egnbersen, Heinrich; New Orleans, 1847 *8582.3 p17*
  *Father:*Johann Heinrich
  *Son:*Wilhelm
Egnbersen, Johann Heinrich *SEE* Egnbersen, Heinrich
Egnbersen, Wilhelm *SEE* Egnbersen, Heinrich
Egner, . . .; Canada, 1776-1783 *9786 p20*
Egner, Christian; Colorado, 1904 *9678.2 p17*
Egnoetc, Martin; Arkansas, 1918 *95.2 p40*
Egolf, William; Illinois, 1920 *3455.4 p94*
Egolf, William; New York, NY, 1913 *3455.3 p25*
Egolf, William; New York, NY, 1913 *3455.4 p81*
Egry, W.; Dayton, OH, 1869-1887 *8582 p7*
Ehalt, Michael; Wisconsin, n.d. *9675.5 p121*
Ehinger, Georg; Venezuela, n.d. *8582.3 p79*
Ehle, Henrich; Trenton, NJ, 1776 *8137 p8*
Ehle, John F.; Wisconsin, n.d. *9675.5 p121*
Ehlenbast, Bartholomaeus; America, 1852 *8582.3 p16*
Ehler, Ferdinand 23; Kansas, 1870 *5240.1 p51*
Ehler, Gerd; Illinois, 1888 *5012.37 p61*
Ehler, John W.; Illinois, 1888 *5012.37 p61*
Ehler, Wattie W.; Illinois, 1888 *5012.37 p61*
Ehler, Wattie W.; Illinois, 1888 *5012.39 p122*
Ehlers, . . .; Canada, 1776-1783 *9786 p20*
Ehlers, John Heinrich; Wisconsin, n.d. *9675.5 p121*
Ehlers, John William Emmanuel 31; Arkansas, 1918 *95.2
  p40*
Ehlin, Erik Jansson; Boston, 1854-1858 *6410.32 p125*
Ehlin, Leonard; Arkansas, 1918 *95.2 p40*
Ehlin, Lottie 12; Massachusetts, 1860 *6410.32 p115*
Ehlinger, Charles 12; America, 1838 *778.5 p193*
Ehlinger, Joseph 46; America, 1838 *778.5 p193*
Ehlinger, Marie 6; America, 1838 *778.5 p193*
Ehlinger, Marie 38; America, 1838 *778.5 p193*
Ehlinger, Martin 10; America, 1838 *778.5 p193*
Ehmen, Dick; Illinois, 1905 *5012.39 p54*
Ehmen, Emil Hinrich; America, 1911 *3455.3 p54*
  *Wife:*Laura
Ehmen, Emil Hinrich; New York, NY, 1911 *3455.3 p17*
Ehmen, Ernest; New York, NY, 1911 *3455.3 p18*
Ehmen, Hinrich Edward; New York, NY, 1914 *3455.3
  p105*
Ehmen, Laura *SEE* Ehmen, Emil Hinrich
Ehmer, Joseph; America, 1845 *8582.2 p9*
Ehmke, Charles; Wisconsin, n.d. *9675.5 p121*
Ehmrnn, George; Baltimore, 1849 *1450.2 p35A*
Ehmrun, George; Baltimore, 1849 *1450.2 p35A*
Ehnes, Franz; Alberta, n.d. *5262 p58*
Ehney, Eberhard; Charleston, SC, 1766 *8582.2 p65*
Ehrat, George J.; Illinois, 1884 *2896.5 p10*
Ehrat, Gottfried; Illinois, 1880 *2896.5 p10*
Ehrat, Jacob; Illinois, 1876 *2896.5 p10*
Ehrecke, . . .; Canada, 1776-1783 *9786 p20*
Ehrenkrock, Carl Friedrich; Quebec, 1776 *9786 p257*
Ehrenkrock, Johann Gustavus; Quebec, 1776 *9786 p259*
Ehrenkrook, von; Canada, 1777 *9786 p140*

Ehrenkrook, J.G. von; Canada, 1776 *9786 p109*
Ehrenmann, Johann; Cincinnati, 1869-1887 *8582 p7*
Ehrenmann, Johannes; Cincinnati, 1835 *8582.2 p60*
Ehrensperger, . . .; Canada, 1776-1783 *9786 p20*
Ehrenstein, . . .; Canada, 1776-1783 *9786 p20*
Ehrenstrom, Karl Wilhelm; Wisconsin, 1845-1847
  3702.7 p312
Ehrenzeller, Jacob; Philadelphia, 1757 *9973.7 p32*
Ehrenzeller, Jacob; Philadelphia, 1776 *8582.3 p84*
Ehret, Julius; Illinois, 1870 *5012.38 p99*
Ehrhardt, Andreas 34; Kansas, 1887 *5240.1 p70*
Ehrhardt, Gottfried; South Carolina, 1788 *7119 p200*
Ehrhart, Caspar; Charleston, SC, 1775-1781 *8582.2 p52*
Ehrhart, Jacob 24; America, 1836 *778.5 p193*
Ehrhartt, Valentine 27; Kansas, 1887 *5240.1 p70*
Ehrmann, Albrecht 96; Louisville, KY, 1869 *8582 p7*
Ehrnsperger, John; Wisconsin, n.d. *9675.5 p121*
Eibet, Jean 32; Port uncertain, 1838 *778.5 p193*
Eichelberger, Anna; Wisconsin, n.d. *9675.5 p121*
Eichelberger, Elsa; Wisconsin, n.d. *9675.5 p121*
Eichelmann, . . .; Canada, 1776-1783 *9786 p20*
Eichely, Jacob 28; Pennsylvania, 1754 *2444 p132*
Eichenberg, . . .; Canada, 1776-1783 *9786 p20*
Eichenlaub, Franz; Ohio, 1843 *8582.1 p51*
Eichenlaub, Georg Franz; New York, NY, 1832 *8582 p7*
Eichenlaub, Johann Jakob; Ohio, 1800-1885 *8582.2 p59*
Eichenlaub, Valentin; New Orleans, 1837 *8582 p8*
Eichhorn, John; New York, 1831 *1450.2 p35A*
Eichler, Frederick; Arkansas, 1918 *95.2 p40*
Eichler, Julius; New York, 1867 *1450.2 p35A*
Eichmann, Peter; Vermont, 1777 *8137 p8*
Eichstedt, Fred; Wisconsin, n.d. *9675.5 p121*
Eichwald, Frank Otto; Wisconsin, n.d. *9675.5 p121*
Eicke, Christian; Canada, 1783 *9786 p38A*
Eickel, Agnes Wolf 32 *SEE* Eickel, Jean
Eickel, Jean 30; New York, 1865 *3702.7 p210*
  *Wife:*Agnes Wolf 32
Eickhart, Fredrick; Illinois, 1860 *5012.38 p98*
Eickhoff, Anna W. Dorothee *SEE* Eickhoff, Johann
  Heinrich
Eickhoff, Anne Marie Lunte; Illinois, 1800-1900 *4610.10
  p67*
Eickhoff, Anton; New York, NY, 1800-1877 *8582.3 p92*
Eickhoff, August; America, 1877 *4610.10 p113*
  *Wife:*Louise Lubbing
Eickhoff, Carl Friedrich August *SEE* Eickhoff, Johann
  Heinrich
Eickhoff, Christine L.C. Lubbing *SEE* Eickhoff, Johann
  Heinrich
Eickhoff, Johann Heinrich; America, 1883 *4610.10 p113*
  *Wife:*Christine L.C. Lubbing
  *Child:*Carl Friedrich August
  *Child:*Anna W. Dorothee
Eickhoff, Louise Lubbing *SEE* Eickhoff, August
Eickhoff, Mathilde; America, 1883 *4610.10 p114*
Eickmeier, Christine Petersmeier *SEE* Eickmeier,
  Friedrich Wilhelm August
Eickmeier, Friedrich Wilhelm *SEE* Eickmeier, Friedrich
  Wilhelm August
Eickmeier, Friedrich Wilhelm August; America, 1893
  4610.10 p107
  *Child:*Friedrich Wilhelm
  *Child:*Heinrich Carl
  *Child:*Heinrich F. Wilhelm
  *Wife:*Christine Petersmeier
Eickmeier, Heinrich Carl *SEE* Eickmeier, Friedrich
  Wilhelm August
Eickmeier, Heinrich F. Wilhelm *SEE* Eickmeier,
  Friedrich Wilhelm August
Eickmeier, Johann Berthold; America, 1864 *4610.10
  p122*
Eickmeyer, Anna Marie Cath. Engel; America, 1844
  4610.10 p134
Eickmeyer, Carl Friedrich Wilhelm; America, 1843
  4610.10 p133
Eickmeyer, Friedrich Wilhelm; America, 1857 *4610.10
  p149*
Eickmeyer, Heinrich Friedrich *SEE* Eickmeyer, Heinrich
  Friedrich
Eickmeyer, Heinrich Friedrich 34; America, 1854
  4610.10 p156
  With wife
  *Son:*Heinrich Friedrich
  With 3 daughters
Eidam, . . .; Canada, 1776-1783 *9786 p20*
Eide, Hadle Jacob; Arkansas, 1918 *95.2 p40*
Eidenberger, Crescens Mary; Wisconsin, n.d. *9675.5
  p121*
Eidenberger, Frank; Wisconsin, n.d. *9675.5 p121*
Eidenberger, John; Wisconsin, n.d. *9675.5 p121*
Eidenberger, Joseph; Wisconsin, n.d. *9675.5 p121*
Eidenberger, Leopold; Wisconsin, n.d. *9675.5 p121*
Eidenberger, Louis; Wisconsin, n.d. *9675.5 p121*

Eidenberger, Mathias; Wisconsin, n.d. ***9675.5*** *p121*
Eidenmuller, Peter 18; America, 1854-1855 ***9162.6*** *p105*
Eidennkas, Konstantin; Wisconsin, n.d. ***9675.5*** *p121*
Eidler, Maurice 28; West Virginia, 1889 ***9788.3*** *p9*
Eidman, . . .; Canada, 1776-1783 ***9786*** *p20*
Eif, Jacob; New York, NY, 1836 ***8208.4*** *p77*
Eifert, Wilhelm; America, 1849 ***8582.3*** *p17*
Eigell, . . .; Canada, 1776-1783 ***9786*** *p20*
Eigemann, Friedrich; Wisconsin, n.d. ***9675.5*** *p121*
Eigenbrod, Wilhelm; Philadelphia, 1779 ***8137*** *p8*
Eigenmann, Fritz; Wisconsin, n.d. ***9675.5*** *p121*
Eigenmann, Karl; Wisconsin, n.d. ***9675.5*** *p121*
Eihuser, Herman; Illinois, 1880 ***2896.5*** *p10*
Eikel, Schan; New York, 1865 ***3702.7*** *p209*
With wife
Eilering, Louis; America, 1858 ***1450.2*** *p35A*
Eilers, Bernard; America, 1847 ***8582.3*** *p17*
Eilers, Johann; America, 1843 ***8582.1*** *p8*
Eilers, Johann F.; New York, NY, 1923 ***3455.4*** *p25*
Eimecke, . . .; Canada, 1776-1783 ***9786*** *p20*
Eimer, Barbara Schlegel; America, 1897 ***1763*** *p40C*
Eimmermann, George Philipp; Wisconsin, n.d. ***9675.5*** *p121*
Einarsdottir, Gudjon 25; Quebec, 1879 ***2557.1*** *p38*
Einarsdottir, Gudrun 21; Quebec, 1879 ***2557.1*** *p39*
Einarsdottir, Hallgrimur 26; Quebec, 1879 ***2557.1*** *p38*
Einarsdottir, Jacobina 2; Quebec, 1879 ***2557.1*** *p39*
Einarsdottir, Jon 11; Quebec, 1879 ***2557.2*** *p36*
Einarsdottir, Jonina 6 mos; Quebec, 1879 ***2557.1*** *p20*
Einarsdottir, Jonina 25; Quebec, 1879 ***2557.2*** *p36*
Einarsdottir, Rosdamundur 13?; Quebec, 1879 ***2557.2*** *p36*
Einarsdottir, Stefania 19?; Quebec, 1879 ***2557.2*** *p36*
Einarsson, Asmundur 4 *SEE* Einarsson, Kristjan
Einarsson, Benedikt 13; Quebec, 1879 ***2557.1*** *p39*
Einarsson, Einar 6 mos *SEE* Einarsson, Kristjan
Einarsson, Einar 44; Quebec, 1879 ***2557.1*** *p39*
Einarsson, Fridfinnur 10 *SEE* Einarsson, Kristjan
Einarsson, Gudjon 25; Quebec, 1879 ***2557.1*** *p38*
Einarsson, Hallgrimur 26; Quebec, 1879 ***2557.1*** *p38*
Einarsson, Kristjan 13; Quebec, 1879 ***2557.1*** *p39*
*Relative:*Fridfinnur 10
*Relative:*Sigurdur 7
*Relative:*Asmundur 4
*Relative:*Einar 6 mos
Einarsson, Sigurdur 7 *SEE* Einarsson, Kristjan
Einatz, Anthony; America, 1850 ***1450.2*** *p35A*
Einecker, Barbara; Georgia, 1739 ***9332*** *p323*
Einecker, Gertraud; Georgia, 1739 ***9332*** *p323*
Einer, Adam 22; Kansas, 1887 ***5240.1*** *p71*
Einfalt, Frank; Illinois, 1885 ***2896.5*** *p10*
Einfalt, John; Illinois, 1887 ***2896.5*** *p10*
Einfalt, Paul; Illinois, 1888 ***2896.5*** *p10*
Einstein, . . .; Pennsylvania, 1861-1865 ***8582.3*** *p91*
Eirch, Johan Michel; Pennsylvania, 1786 ***4525*** *p219*
With mother & stepfather
Eirich, Andreas; New England, 1752 ***4525*** *p211*
With wife
With 6 children
Eirich, Anna Barbara *SEE* Eirich, Johann Adam
Eirich, Johann Adam; Pennsylvania, 1753-1754 ***4525*** *p211*
*Sister:*Anna Barbara
Eirich, Maria Barbara; Pennsylvania, 1752 ***4525*** *p212*
Eirich, Michael; Pennsylvania, 1786 ***4525*** *p212*
Eirich, Philipp; America, 1752 ***4525*** *p212*
Eirichs, . . .; Pennsylvania, n.d. ***4525*** *p211*
Eis, Charlotte; New York, 1749 ***3652*** *p72*
Eischbacher, Philip; Georgia, 1738 ***9332*** *p319*
Eischberger, Maria *SEE* Eischberger, Ruprecht
Eischberger, Maria Riedelsberger *SEE* Eischberger, Ruprecht
Eischberger, Rupr.; Georgia, 1738 ***9332*** *p321*
Eischberger, Ruprecht; Georgia, 1739 ***9332*** *p323*
*Wife:*Maria Riedelsberger
Eischberger, Ruprecht; Georgia, 1739 ***9332*** *p326*
*Wife:*Maria
Eischenthal, Zacharias; Canada, 1783 ***9786*** *p38A*
Eischer, Leonhard; Wisconsin, n.d. ***9675.5*** *p121*
Eischstadt, Charles; Wisconsin, n.d. ***9675.5*** *p121*
Eisebraun, Matthaeus; Carolina, 1745-1800 ***2444*** *p151*
Eisel, M. F.; Ohio, 1869-1887 ***8582*** *p8*
Eisele, Johann; America, 1856 ***8582.3*** *p17*
Eiselen, Mr.; Cincinnati, 1848 ***8582.2*** *p63*
Eiselen, J. A.; Cincinnati, 1848 ***8582.2*** *p63*
Eisemann, Adam; South Dakota, 1889 ***1641*** *p41*
Eisemann, Magdalena; South Dakota, 1889 ***1641*** *p41*
Eisemnam, John Jacob; Philadelphia, 1880 ***3455.2*** *p43*
Eisen, Anton; Cincinnati, 1847 ***8582.1*** *p8*
Eisenach, Henrich; Philadelphia, 1779 ***8137*** *p8*
Eisenach, Kaspar; Philadelphia, 1779 ***8137*** *p8*
Eisenbach, M.; Wisconsin, n.d. ***9675.5*** *p121*
Eisenburg, William; Arkansas, 1918 ***95.2*** *p40*
Eisener, Anna; Milwaukee, 1875 ***4719.30*** *p257*
Eisenhard, Andrew; Pennsylvania, 1751 ***2444*** *p151*
Eisenhard, George; Philadelphia, 1764 ***9973.7*** *p39*
Eisenhardt, Andreas; Pennsylvania, 1751 ***2444*** *p151*
*Wife:*Anna Margaretha Herter
*Child:*Johann Andreas
*Child:*Joseph
*Child:*Johann Jacob
*Child:*Catharina Barbara
*Child:*Lorenz Simon
Eisenhardt, Anna Margaretha Herter *SEE* Eisenhardt, Andreas
Eisenhardt, Catharina Barbara *SEE* Eisenhardt, Andreas
Eisenhardt, Johann Andreas *SEE* Eisenhardt, Andreas
Eisenhardt, Johann Jacob *SEE* Eisenhardt, Andreas
Eisenhardt, Joseph *SEE* Eisenhardt, Andreas
Eisenhardt, Lorenz Simon *SEE* Eisenhardt, Andreas
Eisenhart, Andrew; Pennsylvania, 1751 ***2444*** *p151*
Eisenhauer, Eva Kath. 36; America, 1853 ***9162.8*** *p36*
Eisenhauer, Katharine 4; America, 1853 ***9162.8*** *p36*
Eisenhauer, Maria Elis. 7; America, 1853 ***9162.8*** *p36*
Eisenhauer, Maria Eva 9; America, 1853 ***9162.8*** *p36*
Eisenhoffer, Hans; Georgia, 1738 ***9332*** *p319*
Eisenhouse, Frank; Ohio, 1841 ***9892.11*** *p14*
Eisenkolben, . . .; Canada, 1776-1783 ***9786*** *p20*
Eisenmann, Anna *SEE* Eisenmann, John Jacob
Eisenmann, Hans Philipp; Port uncertain, 1717-1800 ***2444*** *p152*
Eisenmann, John Jacob; Philadelphia, 1880 ***3455.3*** *p106*
*Wife:*Anna
Eisenschmidt, Fredk. Berh. 23; New Orleans, 1839 ***9420.2*** *p362*
Eisfelder, Anna Maria Volsing 86; Illinois, 1897 ***1763*** *p40D*
Eisinbry, Peter 27; Pennsylvania, 1753 ***2444*** *p132*
Eisinger, Julius 32; New Orleans, 1864 ***543.30*** *p484A*
Eisner, Anna; Milwaukee, 1875 ***4719.30*** *p257*
Eison, Thomas 25; Nova Scotia, 1774 ***1219.7*** *p210*
Eissenhard, Andrew; Pennsylvania, 1751 ***2444*** *p151*
Eitel, Baby 6 mos; America, 1854-1855 ***9162.6*** *p104*
Eitel, Adam; America, 1772 ***2444*** *p152*
Eitel, Adam 10; America, 1854-1855 ***9162.6*** *p104*
Eitel, Agnes *SEE* Eitel, Matthias Johannes
Eitel, Agnes *SEE* Eitel, Matthias Johannes
Eitel, Catharina *SEE* Eitel, Matthias Johannes
Eitel, Catharina *SEE* Eitel, Matthias Johannes
Eitel, Christina 27; America, 1854-1855 ***9162.6*** *p104*
Eitel, Georg 4; America, 1854-1855 ***9162.6*** *p104*
Eitel, George F.; America, 1869 ***1450.2*** *p35A*
Eitel, Hans H. von; New York, 1776 ***9786*** *p278*
Eitel, Jacob; America, 1772 ***2444*** *p152*
Eitel, Johann Bernhard *SEE* Eitel, Matthias Johannes
Eitel, Johann Bernhard *SEE* Eitel, Matthias Johannes
Eitel, Kathr. 8; America, 1854-1855 ***9162.6*** *p104*
Eitel, Margaretha *SEE* Eitel, Matthias Johannes
Eitel, Margaretha *SEE* Eitel, Matthias Johannes
Eitel, Margaretha; Pennsylvania, 1754 ***4525*** *p212*
Eitel, Mathias Frederick; Virginia, 1858 ***4626.16*** *p17*
Eitel, Matthias Johannes; America, 1749-1800 ***2444*** *p152*
*Wife:*Agnes
*Child:*Margaretha
*Child:*Johann Bernhard
*Child:*Catharina
Eitel, Matthias Johannes; Pennsylvania, 1749-1800 ***2444*** *p152*
*Wife:*Agnes
*Child:*Margaretha
*Child:*Johann Bernhard
*Child:*Catharina
Eitel, Peter, III 33; America, 1854-1855 ***9162.6*** *p104*
Eitelbuss, Anna; America, 1754 ***2444*** *p203*
Eiteljoerg, August; Cincinnati, 1829 ***8582.1*** *p51*
Eitelmien, Chris; Shreveport, LA, 1878 ***7129*** *p44*
Eitrhein, Nels Olsen; Arkansas, 1918 ***95.2*** *p40*
Eives, Elizabeth 24 *SEE* Eives, John
Eives, John 31; Georgia, 1775 ***1219.7*** *p277*
*Wife:*Elizabeth 24
*Child:*William 7
Eives, William 7 *SEE* Eives, John
Eivimas, Caspar; Wisconsin, n.d. ***9675.5*** *p121*
Eivinas, Stanislaus; Wisconsin, n.d. ***9675.5*** *p121*
Ekart, Elisabeth 33; New Orleans, 1838 ***778.5*** *p193*
Ekart, Francois 12; New Orleans, 1838 ***778.5*** *p193*
Ekart, George 35; New Orleans, 1838 ***778.5*** *p193*
Ekdahl, Henry 30; Kansas, 1877 ***5240.1*** *p58*
Ekerstrom, Fredrik; Minneapolis, 1880-1884 ***6410.35*** *p52*
Ekerstrom, J. A.; Minneapolis, 1869-1877 ***6410.35*** *p52*
Ekerstrom, John F.; Minneapolis, 1853-1879 ***6410.35*** *p52*
Eklaf, John; Iowa, 1866-1943 ***123.54*** *p17*
Eklof, Johan Fabian; Iowa, 1866-1943 ***123.54*** *p17*
Eklund, Thomas; Boston, 1846 ***6410.32*** *p125*
Ekonom, George; Arkansas, 1918 ***95.2*** *p40*
Ekstam, Claes A. 26; Kansas, 1884 ***5240.1*** *p67*
Ekstegner, Catherine; South Carolina, 1752-1753 ***3689.17*** *p21*
*Relative:*Marie Elizabeth 2
*Relative:*Letitie Margarita 7
Ekstegner, Letitie Margarita 7 *SEE* Ekstegner, Catherine
Ekstegner, Marie Elizabeth 2 *SEE* Ekstegner, Catherine
Ekstein, Martin 6; America, 1839 ***778.5*** *p193*
Elam, Joseph 50; Norfolk, VA, 1774 ***1219.7*** *p222*
Elam, Robert; Virginia, 1638-1700 ***6219*** *p150*
Elam, Thomas 17; Jamaica, 1739 ***3690.1*** *p71*
Elay, Lancelott; Virginia, 1638 ***6219*** *p146*
Elb, Anna Margaretha; New England, 1753 ***2444*** *p231*
Elberry, Wm.; Virginia, 1622 ***6219*** *p31*
Elbone, Henry 16; Maryland, 1718 ***3690.1*** *p71*
Elcock, Robert 22; Baltimore, 1775 ***1219.7*** *p269*
Eldam, . . .; Canada, 1776-1783 ***9786*** *p20*
Elden, William John 19; Philadelphia, 1853 ***5704.8*** *p111*
Elder, Alexander 4; St. John, N.B., 1847 ***5704.8*** *p19*
Elder, Daniel 21; Barbados, 1774 ***1219.7*** *p178*
Elder, Eliza Jane; St. John, N.B., 1847 ***5704.8*** *p19*
Elder, Elizabeth 8; Philadelphia, 1854 ***5704.8*** *p118*
Elder, James; Charleston, SC, 1830 ***1639.20*** *p65*
Elder, James; New York, NY, 1816 ***2859.11*** *p30*
Elder, James 46; Philadelphia, 1854 ***5704.8*** *p118*
Elder, Jane; Quebec, 1850 ***5704.8*** *p69*
Elder, Jane; Quebec, 1852 ***5704.8*** *p91*
Elder, Jane Matilda; Quebec, 1852 ***5704.8*** *p87*
Elder, John; New York, NY, 1816 ***2859.11*** *p30*
Elder, Joseph 3 mos; St. John, N.B., 1847 ***5704.8*** *p19*
Elder, Mary Jane; Philadelphia, 1852 ***5704.8*** *p88*
Elder, Richard; St. John, N.B., 1847 ***5704.8*** *p19*
Elder, Samuel; St. John, N.B., 1847 ***5704.8*** *p19*
Elder, Samuel 2; St. John, N.B., 1847 ***5704.8*** *p19*
Elder, Samuel 6; Philadelphia, 1854 ***5704.8*** *p118*
Elder, William; Philadelphia, 1849 ***53.26*** *p26*
Elder, William; Philadelphia, 1849 ***5704.8*** *p50*
Elder, William 3; Philadelphia, 1854 ***5704.8*** *p118*
Elder, William 21; Barbados, 1774 ***1219.7*** *p179*
Eldrege, Samll.; Virginia, 1642 ***6219*** *p199*
Eldridge, Samll.; Virginia, 1636 ***6219*** *p77*
Eldridge, Thomas 26; Baltimore, 1775 ***1219.7*** *p271*
Eleazer, Semeon; South Carolina, 1788 ***7119*** *p202*
Eles, Jon.; Virginia, 1637 ***6219*** *p83*
Eley, Adam; Wisconsin, n.d. ***9675.5*** *p121*
Eley, Robert; Virginia, 1639 ***6219*** *p156*
Elfers, Christian 22; New Orleans, 1862 ***543.30*** *p483A*
Elgian, James 23; Virginia, 1774 ***1219.7*** *p240*
Elgin, James 10; Philadelphia, 1803 ***53.26*** *p26*
Elgin, Mathew; Quebec, 1851 ***5704.8*** *p75*
Elias, Henry; New York, NY, 1834 ***8208.4*** *p2*
Eliason, August; America, 1882 ***1450.2*** *p36A*
Eliason, Edward Elias 26; Arkansas, 1918 ***95.2*** *p40*
Elie, Adolphe 23; New Orleans, 1826 ***778.5*** *p193*
Elie, J. B. Victor 19; New Orleans, 1836 ***778.5*** *p193*
Eligmear, Frederick 24; Dominica, 1774 ***1219.7*** *p207*
Elimen, Emil Hinrich; New York, NY, 1911 ***3455.2*** *p79*
Elisson, Arvid; Arkansas, 1918 ***95.2*** *p40*
Eliza, Mrs. 26; New Orleans, 1835 ***778.5*** *p194*
Elke, Chas.; Wisconsin, n.d. ***9675.5*** *p121*
Elken, Annie; New York, NY, 1867 ***5704.8*** *p219*
Elken, Mary J.; New York, NY, 1867 ***5704.8*** *p219*
Elkin, Elizabeth; Virginia, 1752 ***1219.7*** *p14*
Elkin, Jane; Quebec, 1847 ***5704.8*** *p12*
Elkin, John; St. John, N.B., 1847 ***5704.8*** *p24*
Elkin, Mary 20; Philadelphia, 1859 ***5704.8*** *p142*
Elkin, Robert; Quebec, 1847 ***5704.8*** *p12*
Elkin, William; Philadelphia, 1850 ***53.26*** *p26*
Elkin, William; Philadelphia, 1850 ***5704.8*** *p69*
Elkins, William 25; Maryland, 1774 ***1219.7*** *p230*
Elkouri, Eid 23; Kansas, 1901 ***5240.1*** *p82*
Elkouri, Salim 27; Kansas, 1901 ***5240.1*** *p82*
Elkton, Wm.; Virginia, 1637 ***6219*** *p10*
Ell, Valentin; New York, NY, 1839 ***8208.4*** *p93*
Ellam, Robert; Virginia, 1636 ***6219*** *p23*
Elleman, Mme. 26; America, 1838 ***778.5*** *p194*
Ellems, Robert 25; Maryland, 1774 ***1219.7*** *p185*
Ellenbecker, Nicholas; Wisconsin, n.d. ***9675.5*** *p121*
Ellenbecker, Nicholaus G.; Wisconsin, n.d. ***9675.5*** *p121*
Ellerick, Herman; Pike Co., IN, 1855 ***2896.5*** *p11*
Ellermann, Anne Marie Elisabeth; America, 1844 ***4610.10*** *p146*
Ellermann, Anne Marie Louise Charlotte; America, 1840 ***4610.10*** *p119*
Ellermann, Caroline Justine 39; America, 1844 ***4610.10*** *p141*
Ellermann, Heinrich; Cincinnati, 1842 ***8582.1*** *p8*
Ellermannmeier, Anne M. L. Charlotte; America, 1840 ***4610.10*** *p119*
Ellershausen, George; Canada, 1783 ***9786*** *p38A*
Ellert, John; New York, NY, 1836 ***8208.4*** *p21*
Ellerye, Charity; Virginia, 1638 ***6219*** *p120*

138 *FOR A COMPLETE EXPLANATION OF ENTRY, SEE "HOW TO READ A CITATION" SECTION*

Ellesar, Jacob; South Carolina, 1788 ***7119*** *p202*
Elleser, Anna E. Landvatter *SEE* Elleser, Joh. Conrad
Elleser, Elisabetha *SEE* Elleser, Joh. Conrad
Elleser, Joh. Conrad; Port uncertain, 1717 ***3627*** *p16*
*Wife:*Anna E. Landvatter
*Child:*Johann Bartholomaus
*Child:*Johann Jacob
*Child:*Elisabetha
*Child:*Maria Barbara
Elleser, Johann Bartholomaus *SEE* Elleser, Joh. Conrad
Elleser, Johann Jacob *SEE* Elleser, Joh. Conrad
Elleser, Maria Barbara *SEE* Elleser, Joh. Conrad
Elleson, Thom 12; America, 1702 ***2212*** *p38*
Ellice, Elianor; Virginia, 1639 ***6219*** *p181*
Ellickson, John; California, 1879 ***2764.35*** *p21*
Ellig, Jacob 21; Louisiana, 1820 ***778.5*** *p194*
Ellin, William; Virginia, 1638 ***6219*** *p160*
Ellingson, Emil Bernhab; Arkansas, 1918 ***95.2*** *p40*
Ellingworth, Daniel 30; Arkansas, 1918 ***95.2*** *p40*
Ellins, Bridgett; Virginia, 1645 ***6219*** *p252*
Elliot, Alexander; Philadelphia, 1866 ***5704.8*** *p207*
Elliot, Andrew 6 *SEE* Elliot, Hamilton
Elliot, Charles; North Carolina, 1756 ***1639.20*** *p65*
Elliot, Eliza; America, 1866 ***5704.8*** *p208*
Elliot, George; America, 1767 ***1639.20*** *p66*
Elliot, George R.; Colorado, 1895 ***9678.2*** *p17*
Elliot, Hamilton; Philadelphia, 1847 ***53.26*** *p26*
*Relative:*Nancy
*Relative:*Margaret
*Relative:*William 10
*Relative:*Thomas 8
*Relative:*Andrew 6
*Relative:*Hamilton 4
Elliot, Hamilton 4 *SEE* Elliot, Hamilton
Elliot, J.; New York, NY, 1815 ***2859.11*** *p30*
Elliot, James; Antigua (Antego), 1763 ***1219.7*** *p96*
Elliot, James; Savannah, GA, 1774 ***1219.7*** *p227*
Elliot, James 35; Savannah, GA, 1774 ***1219.7*** *p226*
With wife
Elliot, John; America, 1866 ***5704.8*** *p206*
Elliot, Lewis; Virginia, 1648 ***6219*** *p250*
Elliot, Lucy; Philadelphia, 1866 ***5704.8*** *p207*
Elliot, Margaret *SEE* Elliot, Hamilton
Elliot, Nancy *SEE* Elliot, Hamilton
Elliot, Robert; America, 1738 ***4971*** *p66*
Elliot, Robert; Baltimore, 1816 ***2859.11*** *p30*
Elliot, Robert; Quebec, 1820 ***7603*** *p73*
Elliot, Thomas; New York, NY, 1866 ***5704.8*** *p208*
Elliot, Thomas 8 *SEE* Elliot, Hamilton
Elliot, Thomas 25; Jamaica, 1728 ***3690.1*** *p71*
Elliot, William; New York, NY, 1811 ***2859.11*** *p11*
Elliot, William; Philadelphia, 1866 ***5704.8*** *p207*
Elliot, William 10 *SEE* Elliot, Hamilton
Elliott, Alexander; Philadelphia, 1864 ***5704.8*** *p177*
Elliott, Andrew; Quebec, 1850 ***5704.8*** *p62*
Elliott, Andrew; Savannah, GA, 1775 ***1219.7*** *p252*
Elliott, Andrew 6; Philadelphia, 1847 ***5704.8*** *p23*
Elliott, Archibald; New York, NY, 1811 ***2859.11*** *p11*
With family
Elliott, Archy; Illinois, 1870 ***7857*** *p3*
Elliott, Arthur; America, 1865 ***5704.8*** *p202*
Elliott, Arthur; St. John, N.B., 1847 ***5704.8*** *p26*
Elliott, C. L.; Washington, 1859-1920 ***2872.1*** *p11*
Elliott, Charles; Philadelphia, 1852 ***5704.8*** *p86*
Elliott, Charles; Quebec, 1847 ***5704.8*** *p17*
Elliott, Elizabeth; America, 1868 ***5704.8*** *p231*
Elliott, Elizabeth 11; Quebec, 1850 ***5704.8*** *p62*
Elliott, Elizabeth 26; St. John, N.B., 1863 ***5704.8*** *p152*
Elliott, Elizabeth 30; Quebec, 1856 ***5704.8*** *p130*
Elliott, Elizabeth 50; Philadelphia, 1861 ***5704.8*** *p147*
Elliott, Fanny 17; Philadelphia, 1854 ***5704.8*** *p118*
Elliott, Francis 20; Philadelphia, 1854 ***5704.8*** *p123*
Elliott, George; New York, NY, 1838 ***8208.4*** *p73*
Elliott, George 13; Quebec, 1851 ***5704.8*** *p82*
Elliott, George 21; Philadelphia, 1857 ***5704.8*** *p132*
Elliott, George 21; Quebec, 1856 ***5704.8*** *p130*
Elliott, Hamilton; Philadelphia, 1847 ***5704.8*** *p23*
Elliott, Hamilton 4; Philadelphia, 1847 ***5704.8*** *p23*
Elliott, Humphrey; Philadelphia, 1865 ***5704.8*** *p200*
Elliott, J. 22; Philadelphia, 1845 ***6508.6*** *p115*
Elliott, James 9; Quebec, 1863 ***5704.8*** *p154*
Elliott, James 19; Quebec, 1857 ***5704.8*** *p136*
Elliott, James 32; Philadelphia, 1774 ***1219.7*** *p233*
Elliott, Jane; New York, NY, 1865 ***5704.8*** *p204*
Elliott, Jane; Philadelphia, 1851 ***5704.8*** *p70*
Elliott, Jane; Quebec, 1847 ***5704.8*** *p8*
Elliott, Jane; St. John, N.B., 1852 ***5704.8*** *p95*
Elliott, Jane 32 *SEE* Elliott, William
Elliott, John; Quebec, 1847 ***5704.8*** *p12*
Elliott, John 9; Quebec, 1850 ***5704.8*** *p62*
Elliott, John 20; Philadelphia, 1854 ***5704.8*** *p116*
Elliott, Joseph; New York, NY, 1839 ***8208.4*** *p93*
Elliott, Louisa 43; Massachusetts, 1860 ***6410.32*** *p107*
Elliott, Margaret; Philadelphia, 1847 ***5704.8*** *p23*
Elliott, Margaret; Quebec, 1852 ***5704.8*** *p97*
Elliott, Margaret 18; Quebec, 1853 ***5704.8*** *p104*
Elliott, Margaret 39; Quebec, 1863 ***5704.8*** *p154*
Elliott, Mary 20; Philadelphia, 1854 ***5704.8*** *p118*
Elliott, Mary A.; Philadelphia, 1867 ***5704.8*** *p221*
Elliott, Mary Ann 11; Quebec, 1863 ***5704.8*** *p154*
Elliott, Mary Ann 12; Quebec, 1852 ***5704.8*** *p97*
Elliott, Mathew 20; Philadelphia, 1864 ***5704.8*** *p157*
Elliott, Nancy; Philadelphia, 1847 ***5704.8*** *p23*
Elliott, Nancy 24; Philadelphia, 1864 ***5704.8*** *p157*
Elliott, Patrick; Quebec, 1851 ***5704.8*** *p74*
Elliott, Patrick; Quebec, 1852 ***5704.8*** *p94*
Elliott, Rebecca; Quebec, 1852 ***5704.8*** *p90*
Elliott, Rebecca 15; Quebec, 1863 ***5704.8*** *p154*
Elliott, Robert; Philadelphia, 1852 ***5704.8*** *p85*
Elliott, Robert 49; Quebec, 1863 ***5704.8*** *p154*
Elliott, Samuel; Quebec, 1847 ***5704.8*** *p8*
Elliott, Samuel 36; Massachusetts, 1860 ***6410.32*** *p107*
Elliott, Sarah; Quebec, 1850 ***5704.8*** *p62*
Elliott, Sarah 20; Philadelphia, 1857 ***5704.8*** *p132*
Elliott, Sarah J.; Philadelphia, 1866 ***5704.8*** *p210*
Elliott, Sarah Jane 13; Quebec, 1850 ***5704.8*** *p62*
Elliott, Simon 6; Quebec, 1852 ***5704.8*** *p97*
Elliott, Susanna 2; St. John, N.B., 1852 ***5704.8*** *p95*
Elliott, Thomas 8; Philadelphia, 1847 ***5704.8*** *p23*
Elliott, Thomas 21; Quebec, 1857 ***5704.8*** *p136*
Elliott, Thomas 25; Jamaica, 1728 ***3690.1*** *p71*
Elliott, William; Iowa, 1866-1943 ***123.54*** *p17*
Elliott, William; Philadelphia, 1852 ***5704.8*** *p85*
Elliott, William; Philadelphia, 1864 ***5704.8*** *p177*
Elliott, William; Quebec, 1847 ***5704.8*** *p8*
Elliott, William; Quebec, 1850 ***5704.8*** *p67*
Elliott, William; St. John, N.B., 1849 ***5704.8*** *p56*
Elliott, William 8; Quebec, 1852 ***5704.8*** *p97*
Elliott, William 10; Philadelphia, 1847 ***5704.8*** *p23*
Elliott, William 20; St. John, N.B., 1855 ***5704.8*** *p126*
Elliott, William 27; Quebec, 1856 ***5704.8*** *p130*
Elliott, William 33; New York, 1774 ***1219.7*** *p207*
*Wife:*Jane 32
Elliott, William 38; Philadelphia, 1774 ***1219.7*** *p216*
Elliott, Wm.; Virginia, 1643 ***6219*** *p202*
Ellis, Andrew; New Orleans, 1852 ***5704.8*** *p98*
Ellis, Andrew; Philadelphia, 1851 ***5704.8*** *p78*
Ellis, Ann 23; America, 1699 ***2212*** *p28*
Ellis, Bartholomew; New York, NY, 1816 ***2859.11*** *p30*
Ellis, Charles; America, 1698 ***2212*** *p10*
Ellis, Charles; Virginia, 1698 ***2212*** *p11*
Ellis, David; New York, NY, 1837 ***8208.4*** *p35*
Ellis, David; Virginia, 1642 ***6219*** *p194*
Ellis, Edward; America, 1741 ***4971*** *p67*
Ellis, Edward 27; Virginia, 1774 ***1219.7*** *p241*
Ellis, Edwd.; Virginia, 1638 ***6219*** *p118*
Ellis, Eliz. 20; America, 1699 ***2212*** *p28*
Ellis, Eliza 2; Quebec, 1857 ***5704.8*** *p135*
Ellis, Elizabeth; Philadelphia, 1850 ***5704.8*** *p64*
Ellis, Fanny 9; Quebec, 1858 ***5704.8*** *p138*
Ellis, Fanny 36; Quebec, 1858 ***5704.8*** *p138*
Ellis, Henry; Iowa, 1866-1943 ***123.54*** *p17*
Ellis, Isaac; Virginia, 1640 ***6219*** *p185*
Ellis, James; New York, NY, 1836 ***8208.4*** *p20*
Ellis, James; Philadelphia, 1850 ***5704.8*** *p64*
Ellis, James; Washington, 1859-1920 ***2872.1*** *p11*
Ellis, James N. 33; Kansas, 1891 ***5240.1*** *p76*
Ellis, Jane 9; Quebec, 1857 ***5704.8*** *p135*
Ellis, John; New York, NY, 1838 ***8208.4*** *p88*
Ellis, John; Virginia, 1642 ***6219*** *p188*
Ellis, John 5; Quebec, 1857 ***5704.8*** *p135*
Ellis, John 17; St. Christopher, 1722 ***3690.1*** *p71*
Ellis, John 18; West Indies, 1722 ***3690.1*** *p71*
Ellis, John 37; California, 1867 ***3840.1*** *p18*
Ellis, Jon; Virginia, 1635 ***6219*** *p20*
Ellis, Joseph; New York, NY, 1816 ***2859.11*** *p30*
Ellis, Margt 28; Pennsylvania, Virginia or Maryland, 1699 ***2212*** *p20*
Ellis, Mark 26; Jamaica, 1730 ***3690.1*** *p71*
Ellis, Mary Ann; Philadelphia, 1851 ***5704.8*** *p79*
Ellis, Matilda; Philadelphia, 1851 ***5704.8*** *p79*
Ellis, Maxwell; Quebec, 1857 ***5704.8*** *p135*
Ellis, Michaell; Virginia, 1642 ***6219*** *p188*
Ellis, Phebe 34; Quebec, 1857 ***5704.8*** *p135*
Ellis, Ralph; New York, NY, 1839 ***8208.4*** *p92*
Ellis, Rebecca; Philadelphia, 1850 ***5704.8*** *p64*
Ellis, Richard 37; Quebec, 1857 ***5704.8*** *p135*
Ellis, Robert 29; Georgia, 1774 ***1219.7*** *p188*
Ellis, Samuel 18; Newfoundland, 1789 ***4915.24*** *p55*
Ellis, Samuel 27; Jamaica, 1733 ***3690.1*** *p72*
Ellis, Samuell; Virginia, 1635 ***6219*** *p73*
Ellis, Samuell; Virginia, 1636 ***6219*** *p79*
Ellis, Sarah; America, 1866 ***5704.8*** *p214*
Ellis, Sarah; Virginia, 1643 ***6219*** *p199*
Ellis, Stephen 21; Maryland, 1774 ***1219.7*** *p221*
Ellis, Thomas; America, 1698 ***2212*** *p6*
Ellis, Thomas 16; Maryland, 1722 ***3690.1*** *p72*
Ellis, Thomas 17; Savannah, GA, 1733 ***4719.17*** *p310*
Ellis, Thomas Graham; Washington, 1859-1920 ***2872.1*** *p11*
Ellis, Willi.; Virginia, 1641 ***6219*** *p184*
Ellis, William; Arkansas, 1918 ***95.2*** *p40*
Ellis, William 20; Maryland, 1729 ***3690.1*** *p72*
Ellis, William 24; Nova Scotia, 1774 ***1219.7*** *p208*
With wife & child
Ellis, William 40; Quebec, 1858 ***5704.8*** *p138*
Ellis, Wm; America, 1698 ***2212*** *p8*
Ellis, Wm.; Virginia, 1637 ***6219*** *p13*
Ellis, Wm 26; Pennsylvania, Virginia or Maryland, 1699 ***2212*** *p20*
Ellison, Andrew; Philadelphia, 1853 ***5704.8*** *p102*
Ellison, Elizabeth 10; Philadelphia, 1853 ***5704.8*** *p109*
Ellison, Fred; New York, 1857 ***1450.2*** *p36A*
Ellison, Hannah; St. John, N.B., 1849 ***5704.8*** *p49*
Ellison, Jane 17; America, 1705 ***2212*** *p43*
Ellison, John; New York, NY, 1815 ***2859.11*** *p30*
Ellison, John 19; Maryland, 1774 ***1219.7*** *p181*
Ellison, Jonath.; Virginia, 1629 ***6219*** *p8*
Ellison, Oliver; Quebec, 1851 ***5704.8*** *p73*
Ellison, Robert; Albany, NY, 1756 ***1219.7*** *p45*
Ellison, Robert 13; St. John, N.B., 1849 ***5704.8*** *p49*
Ellison, Seth; Iroquois Co., IL, 1892 ***3455.1*** *p10*
Ellison, Thomas; Ohio, 1846 ***9892.11*** *p14*
Ellison, William 16; Philadelphia, 1853 ***5704.8*** *p109*
Ellisson, Fr. Will 25; New Orleans, 1862 ***543.30*** *p482A*
Elliston, Mrs. 50; Jamaica, 1776 ***1219.7*** *p281*
Elliston, Robert; Philadelphia, 1816 ***2859.11*** *p30*
Ellistone, Ambrose 23; Jamaica, 1736 ***3690.1*** *p72*
Ellit, Richard; Virginia, 1643 ***6219*** *p230*
Ellmann, Clemens; America, 1851 ***8582.3*** *p17*
Ellord, William; America, 1739 ***4971*** *p28*
Ellors, Roger 14; America, 1706 ***2212*** *p47*
Ellott, James; St. John, N.B., 1847 ***5704.8*** *p26*
Ellsworth, Racheal 26; Massachusetts, 1849 ***5881.1*** *p35*
Ellwanger, Mr.; Cincinnati, 1831 ***8582.1*** *p51*
Ellward, Patrick; Quebec, 1814 ***7603*** *p98*
Ellyott, Anthony; Virginia, 1643 ***6219*** *p233*
Elmes, James 18; Georgia, 1774 ***1219.7*** *p188*
Elmes, Thomas; America, 1740 ***4971*** *p15*
Elmes, William 30; Baltimore, 1775 ***1219.7*** *p270*
Elmitt, John T. 29; Kansas, 1892 ***5240.1*** *p77*
Elmore, Patrick A.; Ohio, 1880-1890 ***9892.11*** *p14*
Elms, James; New England, 1816 ***2859.11*** *p30*
Elmund, John 26; Kansas, 1877 ***5240.1*** *p58*
Elphinstone, Alexander; Austin, TX, 1886 ***9777*** *p5*
Elsasser, William C.; America, 1891 ***1450.2*** *p36A*
Else, Stephen 33; Kansas, 1878 ***5240.1*** *p59*
Elsen, Mike 37; Kansas, 1888 ***5240.1*** *p72*
Elsen, Nick 28; Kansas, 1895 ***5240.1*** *p11*
Elsen, Nick 28; Kansas, 1895 ***5240.1*** *p80*
Elsenheimer, J. G.; Louisville, KY, 1869-1887 ***8582*** *p8*
Elsigood, Edmund 24; St. Kitts, 1773 ***1219.7*** *p170*
Elsinga, Fred; Arkansas, 1918 ***95.2*** *p40*
Elsinore, Alexander; Charleston, SC, 1768 ***1219.7*** *p137*
Elsner, . . .; Canada, 1776-1783 ***9786*** *p20*
Elsner, Anna; Milwaukee, 1875 ***4719.30*** *p257*
Elsner, Ewald Alfred Bruno; Wisconsin, n.d. ***9675.5*** *p121*
Elstermeier, Anne Marie Louise; America, 1857 ***4610.10*** *p136*
Elstermeyer Family ; America, 1884 ***4610.10*** *p137*
Elstermeyer, Mr.; America, 1856 ***4610.10*** *p135*
With wife
*Child:*Anne Marie C. Louise 20
*Child:*Anne M. C. Luise Engel 17
*Child:*Louise Friederike 13
*Child:*Johann F. Wilhelm
Elstermeyer, Anne M. C. Luise Engel 17 *SEE* Elstermeyer, Mr.
Elstermeyer, Anne Marie C. Louise 20 *SEE* Elstermeyer, Mr.
Elstermeyer, Caspar Fr. W.; America, 1884 ***4610.10*** *p137*
Elstermeyer, Johann F. Wilhelm *SEE* Elstermeyer, Mr.
Elstermeyer, Louise Friederike 13 *SEE* Elstermeyer, Mr.
Elstob, Thomas 40; Halifax, N.S., 1774 ***1219.7*** *p213*
Elstrod, Henry; America, 1854 ***1450.2*** *p36A*
Elsworth, Ann; Virginia, 1637 ***6219*** *p13*
Elsworth, Anth.; Virginia, 1637 ***6219*** *p13*
Elting, August; America, 1846 ***8582.1*** *p8*
Elton, Frank John; Arkansas, 1918 ***95.2*** *p40*
Elton, Olaf; Wisconsin, n.d. ***9675.5*** *p121*
Elton, William 46; North Carolina, 1850 ***1639.20*** *p66*
Eltzer, . . .; Canada, 1776-1783 ***9786*** *p20*
Eluson, John; Iowa, 1866-1943 ***123.54*** *p17*
Elvert, Max Henry; Arkansas, 1918 ***95.2*** *p40*
Elvin, Ann Jane; Philadelphia, 1852 ***5704.8*** *p84*
Elvin, John; Philadelphia, 1852 ***5704.8*** *p84*
Elwick, Frank; Wisconsin, n.d. ***9675.5*** *p121*

Elwood, Jno.; Virginia, 1645 ***6219*** *p232*
Elwood, Joseph 19; America, 1699 ***2212*** *p20*
Elwood, Joseph 19; America, 1699 ***2212*** *p29*
Elworthy, Thomas 21; Maryland, 1775 ***1219.7*** *p254*
Ely, Mr. 18; America, 1838 ***778.5*** *p194*
Ely, Armand 28; New Orleans, 1863 ***543.30*** *p483A*
Ely, George; Illinois, 1859 ***5012.39*** *p89*
Ely, Joane; Virginia, 1636 ***6219*** *p80*
Elye, Joane; Virginia, 1639 ***6219*** *p161*
Elys, P. Eugene 34; America, 1839 ***778.5*** *p194*
Emanuella, Pietro; Arkansas, 1918 ***95.2*** *p40*
Emberg, John 16; South Carolina, 1737 ***3690.1*** *p72*
Embery, John 16; South Carolina, 1737 ***3690.1*** *p72*
Emde, William 29; Kansas, 1888 ***5240.1*** *p72*
Emden, Michael; America, 1864 ***1450.2*** *p36A*
Emelian, Mr. 3; Louisiana, 1822 ***778.5*** *p194*
Emeric, Vidal F.; Wisconsin, n.d. ***9675.5*** *p121*
Emerich, Henry; America, 1854 ***1450.2*** *p36A*
Emeroy, Lydia; Virginia, 1647 ***6219*** *p245*
Emersley, John D.; Nevada, 1874 ***2764.35*** *p20*
Emerson, Mrs.; New York, NY, 1811 ***2859.11*** *p11*
With family
Emerson, Arthur; Virginia, 1640 ***6219*** *p208*
Emerson, Nicholas; Virginia, 1642 ***6219*** *p188*
Emerson, William; Kingston, Jamaica, 1755 ***1219.7*** *p33*
Emerson, William M.; Bangor, ME, 1880-1894 ***6410.22*** *p121*
Emerton, Henry 21; Maryland, 1775 ***1219.7*** *p264*
Emerton, Joseph 21; Maryland, 1775 ***1219.7*** *p264*
Emerton, William 28; Maryland, 1774 ***1219.7*** *p181*
Emery, Andrew; St. John, N.B., 1853 ***5704.8*** *p98*
Emery, Andrew; Virginia, 1638 ***6219*** *p145*
Emery, Andrew 8; St. John, N.B., 1853 ***5704.8*** *p98*
Emery, Edward 6; St. John, N.B., 1853 ***5704.8*** *p98*
Emery, Eliza 25; Quebec, 1863 ***5704.8*** *p153*
Emery, Isabella 12; St. John, N.B., 1853 ***5704.8*** *p98*
Emery, James 10; St. John, N.B., 1853 ***5704.8*** *p98*
Emery, Margaret; St. John, N.B., 1853 ***5704.8*** *p98*
Emery, Margaret 10; Quebec, 1863 ***5704.8*** *p153*
Emery, Oliver 12; St. John, N.B., 1853 ***5704.8*** *p98*
Emery, Rebecca 1 mo; Quebec, 1863 ***5704.8*** *p153*
Emery, Thomas 29; Quebec, 1863 ***5704.8*** *p153*
Emery, William 4; St. John, N.B., 1853 ***5704.8*** *p98*
Emes, John Phillip; America, 1834 ***1450.2*** *p36A*
Emett, Robert 18; Virginia, 1699 ***2212*** *p27*
Emig, John; Philadelphia, 1762 ***9973.7*** *p38*
Emkes, Wilke; Illinois, 1888 ***5012.39*** *p122*
Emmasdottir, Jonina 6 mos; Quebec, 1879 ***2557.1*** *p20*
Emmel, Frederick; Illinois, 1870 ***2896.5*** *p11*
Emmelmann, Henry; America, 1870 ***1450.2*** *p36A*
Emmenegger, Peter 36; West Virginia, 1902 ***9788.3*** *p10*
Emmerich, . . .; Canada, 1776-1783 ***9786*** *p20*
Emmerson, Edward; Quebec, 1847 ***5704.8*** *p16*
Emmerson, Isabella; Quebec, 1847 ***5704.8*** *p16*
Emmerson, James 13; Quebec, 1847 ***5704.8*** *p17*
Emmerson, John; Quebec, 1847 ***5704.8*** *p16*
Emmerson, Robert; Quebec, 1847 ***5704.8*** *p16*
Emmerson, Thomas; Quebec, 1847 ***5704.8*** *p16*
Emmert, Dorothea; Philadelphia, 1717 ***3627*** *p9*
Emmert, F. L.; Cincinnati, 1788-1848 ***8582.3*** *p90*
Emmert, F. L.; Cincinnati, 1869-1887 ***8582*** *p8*
Emmert, Leopold; Saratoga, NY, 1777 ***8137*** *p8*
Emmerton, Alice; Virginia, 1636 ***6219*** *p74*
Emmerton, Ann; Virginia, 1636 ***6219*** *p20*
Emmett, Catherine 20; Virginia, 1749 ***3690.1*** *p72*
Emmett, Henry 32; Philadelphia, 1775 ***1219.7*** *p256*
Emmett, Mary 25; Massachusetts, 1850 ***5881.1*** *p35*
Emmins, William 27; Virginia, 1773 ***1219.7*** *p168*
Emmis, Edward; New York, NY, 1835 ***8208.4*** *p40*
Emmonds, Peter 27; New Orleans, 1862 ***543.30*** *p481A*
Emonaud, Frederic 24; Halifax, N.S., 1752 ***7074.6*** *p207*
With family of 1
Emonaud, Samuel 50; Halifax, N.S., 1752 ***7074.6*** *p207*
With family of 3
Emond, Thomas; Petersburg, VA, 1802 ***1639.20*** *p66*
Emoneau, . . .; Halifax, N.S., 1752 ***7074.6*** *p232*
Emoneau, Anne-Elisabeth *SEE* Emoneau, Samuel
Emoneau, Elisabeth *SEE* Emoneau, Frederic
Emoneau, Elisabeth *SEE* Emoneau, Samuel
Emoneau, Frederic 24; Halifax, N.S., 1752 ***7074.6*** *p210*
*Wife:*Elisabeth
Emoneau, Judith *SEE* Emoneau, Samuel
Emoneau, Samuel 50; Halifax, N.S., 1752 ***7074.6*** *p210*
*Wife:*Elisabeth
*Daughter:*Judith
*Daughter:*Anne-Elisabeth
Emong, . . .; Canada, 1776-1783 ***9786*** *p20*
Emorson, Joseph 24; Quebec, 1863 ***5704.8*** *p154*
Emory, Catharine; New York, NY, 1864 ***5704.8*** *p187*
Emory, William; New York, NY, 1865 ***5704.8*** *p188*
Empaytag, Franklin F.; Washington, 1859-1920 ***2872.1*** *p11*
Empaytaz, Franklin F.; Washington, 1859-1920 ***2872.1*** *p11*
Emperor, Charles 20; Jamaica, 1729 ***3690.1*** *p72*
Emperor, John 31; New Orleans, 1862 ***543.30*** *p481A*
Empersfield, John 21; Jamaica, 1736 ***3690.1*** *p72*
Empey, Thaddeus M.; Nevada, 1872 ***2764.35*** *p20*
Empson, William; Virginia, 1635 ***6219*** *p7*
Enax, Johann Gottfried; Philadelphia, 1776 ***8582.3*** *p83*
Ende, Johann Christoph von; Halifax, N.S., 1778 ***9786*** *p270*
Ende, Johann Christoph von; New York, 1776 ***9786*** *p270*
Endel, Moses; Virginia, 1856 ***4626.16*** *p16*
Ender, Jacob 45; Kansas, 1888 ***5240.1*** *p71*
Ender, Johannes, Jr.; Pennsylvania, 1749 ***4525*** *p212*
Enderlan, Christian; America, 1851 ***1450.2*** *p37A*
Enders, Conrad 48; New Orleans, 1862 ***543.30*** *p482A*
Enders, Wilhelm; Indiana, 1860-1870 ***3702.7*** *p567*
Enderson, John; America, 1740 ***4971*** *p15*
Endres, Andreas Philipp; Kentucky, 1790 ***4525*** *p281*
Endres, Anna Eulalia; America, 1748-1749 ***8125.6*** *p23*
Endres, Johann; Pennsylvania, 1752 ***4525*** *p212*
Endres, Johann Michael; Pennsylvania, 1753 ***4525*** *p212*
Endres, Johann Zacharias 40; Philadelphia, 1766 ***4525*** *p280*
Endres, Johannes; Pennsylvania, 1749 ***4525*** *p212*
Endres, Johannes; Pennsylvania, 1752 ***4525*** *p212*
Endres, Michel; Pennsylvania, 1767 ***4525*** *p212*
Endres, Thomas; Pennsylvania, 1754 ***4525*** *p213*
With wife
With child 11
With child 13
With child 16
Endres, Zacharias; Pennsylvania, 1766 ***4525*** *p213*
Endress, Paul; Kentucky, 1839-1840 ***8582.3*** *p98*
Endress, Zacharias; Pennsylvania, 1766 ***4525*** *p213*
Endress, Zacharias 40; Philadelphia, 1766 ***4525*** *p282*
Endter, John George; Philadelphia, 1742 ***3652*** *p55*
Enegren, Andrew 63; Kansas, 1892 ***5240.1*** *p77*
Enegren, John 27; Kansas, 1890 ***5240.1*** *p11*
Enegren, John 27; Kansas, 1890 ***5240.1*** *p75*
Energico, Dominico; Arkansas, 1918 ***95.2*** *p40*
Enersen, Enert; New York, 1749 ***3652*** *p71*
Enesmark, John; Illinois, 1891 ***5012.40*** *p25*
Eng, Heinrich; Ohio, 1884 ***3702.7*** *p461*
Engard, Charles; Virginia, 1646 ***6219*** *p242*
Engbersen, Heinrich *SEE* Engbersen, Johann Heinrich
Engbersen, Johann Heinrich; New Orleans, 1847 ***8582.3*** *p17*
*Son:*Heinrich
*Son:*Wilhelm
Engbersen, John; America, 1846 ***8582.2*** *p9*
Engbersen, Wilhelm *SEE* Engbersen, Johann Heinrich
Engdahl, Robert; Minneapolis, 1879-1886 ***6410.35*** *p52*
Engeilfeld, John 15; South Carolina, 1736 ***3690.1*** *p72*
Engel, . . .; Canada, 1776-1783 ***9786*** *p20*
Engel, Adam; Cincinnati, 1869-1887 ***8582*** *p8*
Engel, Adam; New York, NY, 1836 ***8582.2*** *p9*
Engel, Anne Marie Cath.; America, 1846 ***4610.10*** *p134*
Engel, Audones; Philadelphia, 1758 ***9973.7*** *p33*
Engel, Barbara 16; America, 1836 ***778.5*** *p194*
Engel, Barbara 40; America, 1836 ***778.5*** *p194*
Engel, Carl Louis; America, 1846 ***8582.1*** *p8*
Engel, Catherina 14; America, 1836 ***778.5*** *p194*
Engel, Charles; Illinois, 1884 ***2896.5*** *p11*
Engel, Christian 5; America, 1836 ***778.5*** *p194*
Engel, Conrad 54; New York, NY, 1902 ***1763*** *p40C*
Engel, David; Cincinnati, 1837 ***8582.1*** *p8*
Engel, Franz; America, 1812 ***8582.2*** *p58*
Engel, Frederick; Illinois, 1880 ***2896.5*** *p11*
Engel, Gustav; Illinois, 1884 ***2896.5*** *p44*
Engel, Henrich; Philadelphia, 1779 ***8137*** *p8*
Engel, J. Godfrey; New York, 1749 ***3652*** *p71*
Engel, Joseph 19; America, 1836 ***778.5*** *p194*
Engel, Joseph 44; America, 1836 ***778.5*** *p194*
Engel, Magdeline 8; America, 1836 ***778.5*** *p194*
Engel, Maria 8; America, 1836 ***778.5*** *p194*
Engel, Morris 23; Kansas, 1888 ***5240.1*** *p72*
Engel, Paul; Philadelphia, 1774 ***8582.3*** *p85*
Engel, Peter; Wisconsin, n.d. ***9675.5*** *p121*
Engeland, Johannes, Jr.; Philadelphia, 1779 ***8137*** *p8*
Engeland, Johannes, Sr.; Philadelphia, 1779 ***8137*** *p8*
Engelbert, John; Wisconsin, n.d. ***9675.5*** *p121*
Engelbrecht, Georg Martin; Pennsylvania, 1751 ***2444*** *p152*
Engelbrecht, Maria Gottliebin; Port uncertain, 1680-1780 ***2444*** *p152*
Engelbrecht, Martin; Pennsylvania, 1751 ***2444*** *p152*
Engeler, . . .; Pennsylvania, n.d. ***4525*** *p214*
Engelhard, . . .; Canada, 1776-1783 ***9786*** *p20*
Engelhardt, Henry; New York, NY, 1839 ***8208.4*** *p90*
Engelhardt, John; America, 1849 ***8582.1*** *p8*
Engelhardt, Klara; Wisconsin, n.d. ***9675.5*** *p121*
Engelke, Frederick; America, 1848 ***1450.2*** *p37A*
Engelke, John; Illinois, 1861 ***2896.5*** *p1*
Engelkenjohn, Wilhelm; Illinois, 1874 ***2896.5*** *p11*
Engelmann, John Andrew William; America, 1847 ***1450.2*** *p37A*
Engelmann, Louis 21; New Orleans, 1838 ***778.5*** *p194*
Engels, Charles; Wisconsin, n.d. ***9675.5*** *p121*
Engert, Adam; Kentucky, 1839-1840 ***8582.3*** *p98*
*Brother:*Gustav
Engert, Gustav *SEE* Engert, Adam
Engert, Victor Caspar; America, 1834 ***8582.3*** *p17*
Engert, Victor Kaspar; Kentucky, 1834 ***8582.3*** *p99*
Engeser, Joseph; New York, 1890 ***1450.2*** *p37A*
Enghauser, Seraphine 40; New Orleans, 1862 ***543.30*** *p481A*
Englader, John 28; New Orleans, 1823 ***778.5*** *p195*
England, C. T.; Washington, 1859-1920 ***2872.1*** *p11*
England, Humphrey *SEE* England, Humphrey
England, Humphrey; Virginia, 1636 ***6219*** *p8*
*Wife:*Mary
*Brother:*John
*Son:*Humphrey
England, Humphrey; Virginia, 1637 ***6219*** *p107*
England, John *SEE* England, Humphrey
England, John; Virginia, 1637 ***6219*** *p107*
England, Jon.; Virginia, 1638 ***6219*** *p115*
England, Jurgen 21; Kansas, 1872 ***5240.1*** *p53*
England, Mary *SEE* England, Humphrey
England, Maurits Enar; Arkansas, 1918 ***95.2*** *p40*
England, Sarah; Virginia, 1642 ***6219*** *p197*
Englefield, John 15; South Carolina, 1736 ***3690.1*** *p72*
Englekenk, Henry; America, 1837 ***1450.2*** *p37A*
Engleman, Joseph; Washington, 1859-1920 ***2872.1*** *p11*
Engler, Casper; New Orleans, 1845 ***2896.5*** *p11*
Engler, Christopher; Pennsylvania, 1750 ***2444*** *p152*
Engler, George; Pennsylvania, 1751-1752 ***2444*** *p152*
Engler, Joseph; America, 1837 ***8582.1*** *p9*
Engler, Maria Elizabeth; New York, 1749 ***3652*** *p72*
Englert, Caspar; Philadelphia, 1756 ***4525*** *p261*
Englert, Georg 18; New England, 1752 ***4525*** *p214*
Englert, Hans Juerg; Pennsylvania, 1752 ***2444*** *p152*
Englert, Hans Juerg; Pennsylvania, 1752 ***4525*** *p214*
Englert, J. K.; Washington, 1859-1920 ***2872.1*** *p11*
Englert, Johann Christoph; Pennsylvania, 1750 ***2444*** *p152*
Englert, Johann Geoerg; Pennsylvania, 1751 ***2444*** *p152*
Englert, Johann Georg; Pennsylvania, 1751 ***4525*** *p214*
Englert, Johann Georg; Pennsylvania, 1752 ***2444*** *p152*
Englert, Johann Georg; Pennsylvania, 1752 ***4525*** *p214*
Englerth, Hans Christoph; Pennsylvania, 1750 ***2444*** *p152*
Engleson, Olaf; Washington, 1859-1920 ***2872.1*** *p11*
Englibright, Martin; Philadelphia, 1762 ***9973.7*** *p37*
English, Abraham; Virginia, 1638 ***6219*** *p9*
English, Abraham; Virginia, 1638 ***6219*** *p120*
English, Abraham; Virginia, 1642 ***6219*** *p189*
With wife
English, Alexander 20; Jamaica, 1773 ***1219.7*** *p172*
English, August; Wisconsin, n.d. ***9675.5*** *p121*
English, Charles; New York, NY, 1864 ***5704.8*** *p183*
English, Edward; New York, 1832 ***1450.2*** *p37A*
English, James; America, 1736 ***4971*** *p39*
English, James; Jamaica, 1736 ***3690.1*** *p72*
English, James; Philadelphia, 1811 ***2859.11*** *p11*
English, Jane 20; Maryland, 1738 ***3690.1*** *p72*
English, Joane; Virginia, 1623-1642 ***6219*** *p192*
English, John; America, 1736-1743 ***4971*** *p58*
English, Jon.; Virginia, 1637 ***6219*** *p107*
English, Joseph; Pennsylvania, 1682 ***4962*** *p150*
English, King 35; Maryland, 1775 ***1219.7*** *p267*
English, Laurence; America, 1739 ***4971*** *p52*
English, Mary; America, 1739 ***4971*** *p52*
English, Mary; Pennsylvania, 1682 ***4962*** *p149*
English, Mary; St. John, N.B., 1848 ***5704.8*** *p47*
English, Patrick; America, 1742 ***4971*** *p25*
English, Richard; America, 1741 ***4971*** *p16*
English, Robert; Iowa, 1866-1943 ***123.54*** *p17*
English, Robert; New York, NY, 1811 ***2859.11*** *p11*
English, Robert; New York, NY, 1864 ***5704.8*** *p174*
English, Samuel 23; Maryland, 1775 ***1219.7*** *p264*
English, Tho 14; United States or West Indies, 1706 ***2212*** *p47*
English, Thomas; New York, NY, 1811 ***2859.11*** *p11*
With family
English, William; New York, NY, 1839 ***8208.4*** *p102*
English, William; Virginia, 1638 ***6219*** *p125*
English, William; Virginia, 1638 ***6219*** *p147*
English, Wm; Barbados, 1698 ***2212*** *p4*
Englist, George; Illinois, 1863 ***2896.5*** *p11*
Englund, L.P.; Iowa, 1866-1943 ***123.54*** *p17*
Engstrom, Andrew Ole; Washington, 1859-1920 ***2872.1*** *p11*
Engstrom, John; Maine, 1871-1878 ***6410.22*** *p116*
Engstrom, John L.; Maine, 1890-1896 ***6410.22*** *p122*
Engstrom, P. N.; Minneapolis, 1870-1886 ***6410.35*** *p52*

Evans, Tho., Jr.; Virginia, 1643 *6219 p200*
Evans, Tho., Sr.; Virginia, 1642 *6219 p191*
Evans, Thomas; Pennsylvania, 1698 *2212 p4*
Evans, Thomas; Virginia, 1638 *6219 p125*
Evans, Thomas; Virginia, 1639 *6219 p155*
Evans, Thomas 26; Barbados, 1774 *1219.7 p234*
Evans, Thomas 29; Maryland, 1774 *1219.7 p204*
Evans, Thomas 36; Virginia, 1774 *1219.7 p201*
Evans, William; Arkansas, 1918 *95.2 p41*
Evans, William; Iowa, 1866-1943 *123.54 p17*
Evans, William; Massachusetts, 1849 *5881.1 p35*
Evans, William 9 mos; St. John, N.B., 1862 *5704.8 p150*
Evans, William 19; Virginia, 1775 *1219.7 p247*
Evans, William 35; Maryland, 1774 *1219.7 p179*
Evans, William 40; Philadelphia, 1774 *1219.7 p183*
Evans, William 70; Massachusetts, 1850 *5881.1 p35*
Evans, Wm; New York, NY, 1816 *2859.11 p30*
Evans, Wm 23; Maryland or Virginia, 1699 *2212 p22*
Evans, Wm. Henry; Wisconsin, n.d. *9675.5 p122*
Evaresto, Ravanelle; Iowa, 1866-1943 *123.54 p17*
Evart, David; New York, NY, 1811 *2859.11 p11*
Eve, William 18; Jamaica, 1737 *3690.1 p74*
Evelapon, Mr. 28; America, 1838 *778.5 p199*
Evelin, Mary; Virginia, 1648 *6219 p246*
Even, Adam; Wisconsin, n.d. *9675.5 p122*
Even, John; Wisconsin, n.d. *9675.5 p122*
Evenden, Richard; St. Christopher, 1754 *1219.7 p27*
Evenden, Richard; St. Christopher, 1754 *3690.1 p74*
Evenett, Elizabeth 21; Virginia, 1774 *1219.7 p240*
Evens, John 20; Jamaica, 1730 *3690.1 p74*
Evens, Robert; Iowa, 1866-1943 *123.54 p17*
Evensen, John; Washington, 1859-1920 *2872.1 p12*
Everard, James, Jr.; New York, NY, 1836 *8208.4 p12*
Everard, Thomas; Virginia, 1648 *6219 p241*
Everched, Mr.; Quebec, 1815 *9229.18 p81*
Evere, John; Virginia, 1645 *6219 p233*
Everedge, William; Virginia, 1636 *6219 p78*
Everell, Thomas; Montreal, 1812 *7603 p24*
Everett, Christo.; Virginia, 1635 *6219 p72*
Everett, Richard A.; America, 1853 *1450.2 p38A*
Everett, Robert 15; Pennsylvania, Virginia or Maryland, 1723 *3690.1 p74*
Everett, Robert 21; Virginia, 1774 *1219.7 p193*
Everhard, . . .; Canada, 1776-1783 *9786 p20*
Everhard, Francois; Canada, 1776-1783 *9786 p243*
Everhart, Henry; Indiana, 1848 *9117 p16*
Everitt, William; New York, NY, 1815 *2859.11 p30*
Everly, Jacob; Philadelphia, 1757 *9973.7 p32*
Everly, Peter; Philadelphia, 1757 *9973.7 p32*
Evers, Patrick; New York, NY, 1832 *8208.4 p38*
Eversden, Elizabeth 27; Maryland, 1731 *3690.1 p74*
Eversmann, Hermann H.; Cincinnati, 1869-1887 *8582 p8*
Eversmann, Peter; America, 1836 *8582.2 p10*
Eversmeyer, Fritz; Died enroute, 1853 *4610.10 p41*
Everston, Rachel; America, 1741 *4971 p94*
Everton, Julia 18; Massachusetts, 1850 *5881.1 p35*
Eves, John; Virginia, 1637 *6219 p85*
Eves, Jon.; Virginia, 1636 *6219 p79*
Eveslage, B. G.; America, 1841 *8582.2 p10*

Eveslage, Joseph; Baltimore, 1838 *8582.1 p9*
  With parents
Eveslage, Joseph; Cincinnati, 1869-1887 *8582 p8*
Evil, Fred'k; Pennsylvania, 1753 *2444 p226*
Evins, Samuel; New York, NY, 1816 *2859.11 p30*
Evisston, Rachel; America, 1741 *4971 p10*
Evolga, Sergie D.; Arkansas, 1918 *95.2 p41*
Evory, Edmond; Maryland, 1742 *4971 p106*
Evos, John 15; Pennsylvania, 1725 *3690.1 p74*
Ewald, Capt.; New York, 1776 *9786 p279*
Ewan, James; Austin, TX, 1886 *9777 p5*
Ewang, George 19; Dominica, 1773 *1219.7 p170*
Ewart, Jean; Charleston, SC, 1821 *1639.20 p66*
Ewart, John; New York, NY, 1811 *2859.11 p11*
Ewart, Thomas; Charleston, SC, 1831 *1639.20 p66*
Ewbank, James; New York, NY, 1834 *8208.4 p79*
Ewen, Job; Carson City, NV, 1874 *2764.35 p21*
Ewen, Nicholas; Virginia, 1638 *6219 p9*
Ewen, Richard; Virginia, 1638 *6219 p9*
Ewen, William; Virginia, 1648 *6219 p250*
Ewens, Ann *SEE* Ewens, John
Ewens, John; Virginia, 1642 *6219 p196*
  *Wife:*Ann
Ewenson, Jean; Newfoundland, 1842 *8893 p264*
Ewert, Frank; Arkansas, 1918 *95.2 p41*
Ewert, Frank; Kansas, 1894 *5240.1 p11*
Ewert, Gerhard; Kansas, 1879 *5240.1 p11*
Ewert, Henry; Kansas, 1880 *5240.1 p11*
Ewert, Herman; Kansas, 1894 *5240.1 p12*
Ewert, J. G.; America, 1874 *5240.1 p12*
Ewertz, Adam 22; Kansas, 1884 *5240.1 p12*
Ewertz, Adam 22; Kansas, 1884 *5240.1 p66*
Ewertz, Peter 33; Kansas, 1884 *5240.1 p12*
Ewertz, Peter 33; Kansas, 1884 *5240.1 p67*
Ewes, Thomas 20; America, 1699 *2212 p28*
Ewin, Joseph 20; Jamaica, 1731 *3690.1 p74*
Ewin, Wm.; Virginia, 1636 *6219 p80*
Ewing, Alex *SEE* Ewing, Joseph
Ewing, Alex; Philadelphia, 1850 *5704.8 p59*
Ewing, Alexander 21; Philadelphia, 1854 *5704.8 p116*
Ewing, Alexander D.; New York, NY, 1815 *2859.11 p30*
Ewing, Ann; Philadelphia, 1849 *53.26 p26*
Ewing, Ann; Philadelphia, 1849 *5704.8 p54*
Ewing, Charles; New York, NY, 1834 *8208.4 p46*
Ewing, Daniel; Charleston, SC, 1807 *1639.20 p66*
Ewing, Elizabeth 21; Philadelphia, 1857 *5704.8 p132*
Ewing, Gabriel; New York, NY, 1826 *8208.4 p39*
Ewing, Henry 21; Philadelphia, 1853 *5704.8 p113*
Ewing, Jane *SEE* Ewing, Joseph
Ewing, Jane; New York, NY, 1866 *5704.8 p214*
Ewing, Jane; Philadelphia, 1850 *5704.8 p59*
Ewing, John; Charleston, SC, 1753 *1639.20 p66*
Ewing, John 18; Philadelphia, 1854 *5704.8 p116*
Ewing, John 20; Philadelphia, 1803 *53.26 p26*
Ewing, Joseph; Philadelphia, 1850 *53.26 p26*
  *Relative:*Jane
  *Relative:*Alex
Ewing, Joseph; Philadelphia, 1850 *5704.8 p59*
Ewing, Mary 18; Philadelphia, 1856 *5704.8 p128*

Ewing, Mathew 12; Philadelphia, 1854 *5704.8 p116*
Ewing, Nancy 15; Philadelphia, 1856 *5704.8 p128*
Ewing, Rebecca; Philadelphia, 1850 *53.26 p26*
Ewing, Rebecca; Philadelphia, 1850 *5704.8 p60*
Ewing, William; New York, NY, 1834 *8208.4 p41*
Ewing, William; Philadelphia, 1847 *53.26 p26*
Ewing, William; Philadelphia, 1847 *5704.8 p5*
Ewins, Clement; Virginia, 1642 *6219 p199*
Ewrin, Margaret 50; Philadelphia, 1861 *5704.8 p147*
Excoffier, Ambrose 26; America, 1838 *778.5 p199*
Excoffier, Jean Claude 33; America, 1838 *778.5 p199*
Excoffier, Joseph 28; America, 1838 *778.5 p199*
Exley, George 20; Jamaica, 1722 *3690.1 p74*
Exley, Nathaniel; Barbados, 1751 *1219.7 p7*
Exnowski, Aline; Wisconsin, n.d. *9675.5 p122*
Expert, Pierre 37; New Orleans, 1836 *778.5 p199*
Extine, Frederick; New York, 1829 *9892.11 p15*
Extine, Frederick; Ohio, 1840 *9892.11 p15*
Exton, Geo.; Virginia, 1643 *6219 p207*
Exton, William; Virginia, 1635 *6219 p27*
Exx, James; Virginia, 1698 *2212 p12*
Eyberts, . . .; Canada, 1776-1783 *9786 p20*
Eycott, William 30; Jamaica, 1774 *1219.7 p197*
  With wife
Eydam, . . .; Canada, 1776-1783 *9786 p20*
Eyer, Andrew; Illinois, 1900 *5012.40 p77*
Eyer, Jacob; Iroquois Co., IL, 1896 *3455.1 p10*
Eyerle, Jacob; New York, 1753 *3652 p77*
Eyers, Michael; America, 1736 *4971 p45*
Eyestone, Martin; New York, NY, 1832 *2896.5 p11*
Eygle, Jacob 28; Pennsylvania, 1754 *2444 p132*
Eykel, . . .; Canada, 1776-1783 *9786 p42*
Eyl, Nikolaus; Philadelphia, 1779 *8137 p8*
Eyler, Anna Christina *SEE* Eyler, Philipp
Eyler, Johann Michael *SEE* Eyler, Philipp
Eyler, Philipp; Pennsylvania, 1752 *2444 p153*
  *Wife:*Rosina
  *Child:*Johann Michael
  *Child:*Anna Christina
Eyler, Rosina *SEE* Eyler, Philipp
Eyles, Elizabeth; Quebec, 1850 *5704.8 p66*
Eyles, Samuel 22; Barbados, 1730 *3690.1 p74*
Eyma, Mr.; New Orleans, 1838 *778.5 p199*
Eymann, Carl; America, 1845 *8582.1 p9*
Eymann, Louis; America, 1850 *8582.3 p18*
Eyre, John 22; Maryland, 1775 *1219.7 p257*
Eyres, Jon.; Virginia, 1600-1642 *6219 p192*
Eyres, Robert; Virginia, 1642 *6219 p187*
Eyres, William; Virginia, 1636 *6219 p7*
Eyrich, Anderas; Pennsylvania, 1770 *4525 p211*
Eyrich, Johann Philip; Pennsylvania, 1753 *4525 p212*
Eyrich, Matheas; Pennsylvania, 1750 *4525 p212*
Eyrich, Michael; Pennsylvania, 1750 *4525 p212*
Eyselie, Albert; Santa Clara Co., CA, 1871 *2764.35 p21*
Eysenbreit, Peter; Pennsylvania, 1753 *2444 p207*
Eysmont, . . .; New York, 1831 *4606 p173*
Ezel, Andrew; Pennsylvania, 1750 *4525 p235*

F

Faab, August 32; New Orleans, 1862 *543.30 p223B*
Fabaroni, Gabr. 22; America, 1838 *778.5 p199*
Fabens, . . .; Nicaragua, 1856 *8582.3 p31*
Faber, . . .; Canada, 1776-1783 *9786 p42*
Faber, Miss; America, 1838-1858 *8582 p30*
Faber, Andrien 73; New Orleans, 1830 *778.5 p199*
Faber, Catharina 3; New Orleans, 1836 *778.5 p199*
Faber, Frederick 23; Grenada, 1773 *1219.7 p170*
Faber, George 1; New Orleans, 1836 *778.5 p199*
Faber, John 38; New Orleans, 1862 *543.30 p31*
Faber, John 42; Kansas, 1882 *5240.1 p63*
Faber, Joseph; Kentucky, 1840-1845 *8582.3 p100*
Faber, Nicolas 24; New Orleans, 1836 *778.5 p200*
Faber, Susana 22; New Orleans, 1836 *778.5 p200*
Faber, Thevin 29; America, 1831 *778.5 p200*
Fabet, . . .; Canada, 1776-1783 *9786 p42*
Fabhri, Guiseppe; Arkansas, 1918 *95.2 p41*
Fabian, Baby 1; America, 1853 *9162.7 p14*
Fabian, Mr. 31; New Orleans, 1823 *778.5 p200*
Fabian, Ad. 9; America, 1853 *9162.7 p14*
Fabian, Christoph 30; New York, NY, 1862 *9831.18 p16*
Fabian, Eduard 11 mos; New York, NY, 1862 *9831.18 p16*
Fabian, Elis. 33; America, 1853 *9162.7 p14*
Fabian, Friederike 4; New York, NY, 1862 *9831.18 p16*
Fabian, George 32; New Orleans, 1862 *543.30 p224B*
Fabian, Gilbert; Virginia, 1648 *6219 p237*
Fabian, Margarethe 30; New York, NY, 1862 *9831.18 p16*
Fabian, Nickl. 31; America, 1853 *9162.7 p14*
Fabian, Richard 17; New York, NY, 1862 *9831.18 p16*
Fabiani, Salvatore; Arkansas, 1918 *95.2 p41*
Fabore, Mr. 37; New Orleans, 1837 *778.5 p200*
Fabre, Mr. 48; New Orleans, 1823 *778.5 p200*
Fabre, Mrs. 49; New Orleans, 1823 *778.5 p200*
Fabre, A. C., Mme. 45; America, 1823 *778.5 p200*
Fabre, Charles 10; New Orleans, 1823 *778.5 p200*
Fabre, Francis 35; America, 1829 *778.5 p200*
Fabre, Helena 14; New Orleans, 1823 *778.5 p200*
Fabre, Hermana 17; New Orleans, 1823 *778.5 p200*
Fabre, John 35; America, 1829 *778.5 p200*
Fabre, Louis 17; Louisiana, 1827 *778.5 p200*
Fabre, Pierre 27; New Orleans, 1838 *778.5 p200*
Fabricius, . . .; Canada, 1776-1783 *9786 p20*
Fabricius, George Christian; New York, 1753 *3652 p77*
Fabrier, P. 29; Mexico, 1829 *778.5 p201*
Fabrizio, Antonio; Colorado, 1903 *9678.2 p18*
Fabueres, Barbara 17; America, 1837 *778.5 p201*
Facest, Nicolas 19; America, 1836 *778.5 p201*
Facest, Nicolas 20; America, 1836 *778.5 p201*
Fachter, George; Wisconsin, n.d. *9675.5 p122*
Fackh, Anna Margaretha Loser *SEE* Fackh, Philipp Jacob
Fackh, Philipp Jacob; Port uncertain, 1754 *2444 p153*
  With 2 daughters
  *Wife:*Anna Margaretha Loser
Fackler, Jacob; Philadelphia, 1750 *9973.7 p31*
Facobjohn, Isak 26; New York, NY, 1878 *9253 p47*
Facquet, Augustine 45; New York, NY, 1893 *9026.4 p41*
Fadesco, Luigi; Iowa, 1866-1943 *123.54 p17*
Fadiga, Andro; Iowa, 1866-1943 *123.54 p17*
Fadiga, Barbara; Iowa, 1866-1943 *123.54 p61*
Faehr, Jacob; Quebec, 1875 *9980.20 p48*
Faehr, Jacob; Quebec, 1876 *9980.20 p49*
Faehr, Maria; Quebec, 1876 *9980.20 p49*
Faehr, Maria Braun; Quebec, 1876 *9980.20 p49*
Faehr, Stephan; Ohio, 1843 *8582.1 p51*
Faessler, Joseph 32; New Orleans, 1862 *543.30 p31*

Fagan, James 25; Massachusetts, 1847 *5881.1 p37*
Fagan, John; New York, NY, 1835 *8208.4 p40*
Fagan, John; New York, NY, 1840 *8208.4 p106*
Fagan, Michael; New York, NY, 1815 *2859.11 p30*
Fagan, Thomas; America, 1840 *7036 p124*
Fagan, Thomas; St. John, N.B., 1840 *7036 p124*
Fagan, Wm. 40; New Orleans, 1862 *543.30 p223B*
Fage, William 20; Jamaica, 1754 *1219.7 p27*
Fagel, Jake; Arkansas, 1918 *95.2 p41*
Fagerstadt, Frank; Colorado, 1894 *9678.2 p18*
Fagerston, Charlotta Svensson *SEE* Fagerston, Magnus
Fagerston, Jenny *SEE* Fagerston, Magnus
Fagerston, Magnus; Boston, 1851 *6410.32 p124*
  *Wife:*Charlotta Svensson
  *Daughter:*Jenny
Fagerstrom, Carl; Washington, 1859-1920 *2872.1 p12*
Fagerstrom, Charlotta Svensson *SEE* Fagerstrom,
  Magnus
Fagerstrom, Edd; Iowa, 1847 *2090 p611*
Fagerstrom, J. R.; Minneapolis, 1872-1884 *6410.35 p53*
Fagerstrom, Jenny *SEE* Fagerstrom, Magnus
Fagerstrom, Magnus; Boston, 1851 *6410.32 p124*
  *Wife:*Charlotta Svensson
  *Daughter:*Jenny
Faget, Mr. 40; Port uncertain, 1839 *778.5 p201*
Faggart, Margaret 28 *SEE* Faggart, Samuel
Faggart, Samuel 30; Philadelphia, 1803 *53.26 p26*
  *Relative:*Margaret 28
Fagin, Henry 28; Massachusetts, 1848 *5881.1 p37*
Fagin, William 26; Massachusetts, 1849 *5881.1 p41*
Fagnano, Franciso; Colorado, 1887 *9678.2 p18*
Fagot, L. 39; Port uncertain, 1836 *778.5 p201*
Fagundes, Francis M.; Virginia, 1844 *4626.16 p12*
Fagundes, Joseph Machado; Virginia, 1847 *4626.16 p13*
Fahay, John; California, 1871 *2769.4 p3*
Fahey, Ann 17; Massachusetts, 1850 *5881.1 p35*
Fahey, Garrit; New York, NY, 1816 *2859.11 p30*
Fahey, Honora 26; Massachusetts, 1848 *5881.1 p37*
Fahey, John; California, 1860 *2769.4 p3*
Fahey, John 25; Massachusetts, 1847 *5881.1 p37*
Fahey, Martin 18; Massachusetts, 1850 *5881.1 p39*
Fahey, Mary; New York, NY, 1816 *2859.11 p30*
Fahey, Mary 17; Massachusetts, 1847 *5881.1 p38*
Fahey, Michael 25; Massachusetts, 1850 *5881.1 p39*
Fahey, Michael 60; Massachusetts, 1849 *5881.1 p39*
Fahey, Peter 40; Massachusetts, 1849 *5881.1 p40*
Fahey, Thomas; America, 1841 *7036 p122*
Fahey, Mrs. Thomas; America, 1841 *7036 p122*
  With child
  With sister-in-law
Fahey, Tim T.; New York, NY, 1816 *2859.11 p30*
Fahr, John; Wisconsin, n.d. *9675.5 p122*
Fahrbach, Gottfried; America, 1849 *8582.1 p9*
Fahrback, Christian; Ohio, 1850 *6013.19 p30*
Fahrbeck, Godfrey; America, 1840 *1450.2 p39A*
Fahrenbruch, Ella; Wisconsin, n.d. *9675.5 p122*
Fahrenbruch, Richard; Wisconsin, n.d. *9675.5 p122*
Fahrenbruch, Wilhelm; Wisconsin, n.d. *9675.5 p122*
Fahrenkrog, Henry; Illinois, 1878 *2896.5 p11*
Fahrenkrog, William; Illinois, 1878 *2896.5 p11*
Fahrion, Christian; Pennsylvania, 1856 *1450.2 p39A*
Fahrner, Henry; America, 1881 *1450.2 p39A*
Fahrni, Ulrich; Pennsylvania, 1709-1710 *4480 p311*
Fahs, Regina; Pennsylvania, 1753 *2444 p153*
Fahy, Andrew; New York, NY, 1816 *2859.11 p30*
Fahy, John; America, 1742-1743 *4971 p60*
Fahy, John 26; New Orleans, 1862 *543.30 p30*

Fahy, Michael; America, 1735-1743 *4971 p78*
Fahy, Michael; America, 1742 *4971 p83*
Faichney, Ann; South Carolina, 1797 *1639.20 p66*
Fail, . . .; Canada, 1776-1783 *9786 p20*
Faille, . . .; Canada, 1776-1783 *9786 p20*
Faillot, Celine 3; America, 1839 *778.5 p201*
Fainot, George-Frederic 24; Halifax, N.S., 1752 *7074.6 p210*
Fair, Alexander; New York, NY, 1816 *2859.11 p30*
Fair, Andrew 20; Philadelphia, 1854 *5704.8 p120*
Fair, Ann; New York, NY, 1811 *2859.11 p11*
Fair, Bridget; Quebec, 1850 *5704.8 p66*
Fair, James; New York, NY, 1811 *2859.11 p11*
Fair, Jane 10; Quebec, 1850 *5704.8 p66*
Fair, Jane 17; Quebec, 1853 *5704.8 p105*
Fair, Margaret; Quebec, 1847 *5704.8 p29*
Fair, Mary Ann; Quebec, 1850 *5704.8 p66*
Fair, Maxwell; Quebec, 1850 *5704.8 p66*
Fair, Michael 6; Quebec, 1850 *5704.8 p66*
Fair, Thomas; New York, NY, 1811 *2859.11 p11*
Fair, Thomas 8; Quebec, 1850 *5704.8 p66*
Fair, William 22; Philadelphia, 1775 *1219.7 p248*
Fairar, John 16; Nevis, 1773 *1219.7 p170*
Fairbos, J. 20; New Orleans, 1839 *778.5 p201*
Fairbrother, Henry; Iowa, 1866-1943 *123.54 p17*
Fairbrother, Nath.; Virginia, 1638 *6219 p33*
Fairclough, Margery 14; Virginia, 1699 *2212 p27*
Fairclough, Margt 16; Virginia, 1699 *2212 p27*
Faire, Mathew; Virginia, 1643 *6219 p200*
Faire, Richard; Virginia, 1643 *6219 p200*
Fairefax, Margery *SEE* Fairefax, William
Fairefax, William; Virginia, 1611 *6219 p152*
  *Wife:*Margery
Fairface, James 20; Georgia, 1775 *1219.7 p276*
Fairfax, William; Antigua (Antego), 1755 *1219.7 p36*
Fairfax, William; Antigua (Antego), 1755 *3690.1 p74*
Fairlclough, Ann 37; Virginia, 1699 *2212 p27*
Fairlie, James; New York, NY, 1839 *8208.4 p103*
Fairly, Alexander; North Carolina, 1753-1827 *1639.20 p67*
Fairly, Flora 49; North Carolina, 1850 *1639.20 p67*
Fairman, Jane; St. John, N.B., 1850 *5704.8 p62*
Fairman, Robert; Philadelphia, 1849 *53.26 p26*
Fairman, Robert; Philadelphia, 1849 *5704.8 p50*
Fairman, Robert; St. John, N.B., 1847 *5704.8 p10*
Fairman, Samuel; St. John, N.B., 1850 *5704.8 p62*
Fairmstrum, Augustus 22; New Orleans, 1862 *543.30 p227B*
Fairry, Edward; St. John, N.B., 1853 *5704.8 p99*
Fairstein, Nicholas; Wisconsin, n.d. *9675.5 p122*
Fairweather, Edwin; Iowa, 1866-1943 *123.54 p17*
Fairweather, Robert; Charleston, SC, 1763 *1639.20 p67*
Fairweather, William H.; New York, NY, 1835 *8208.4 p80*
Fais, Peter; America, 1836 *8582.2 p60*
Fais, Peter; Cincinnati, 1869-1887 *8582 p8*
Faisant, Victor 19; New Orleans, 1835 *778.5 p201*
Faith, Elizabeth; Philadelphia, 1851 *5704.8 p76*
Faith, Nancy; Philadelphia, 1847 *53.26 p26*
Faith, Nancy; Philadelphia, 1847 *5704.8 p14*
Faivre, James; New York, NY, 1836 *8208.4 p23*
Faivre, John C.; America, 1828 *1450.2 p39A*
Faivre, Joseph; Colorado, 1870 *9678.2 p18*
Faivre, Peter; New York, NY, 1836 *8208.4 p23*
Falahee, Mathew; New York, NY, 1838 *8208.4 p65*
Falare, Mrs. 42; New Orleans, 1839 *778.5 p201*
Falatck, Andrew; America, 1888 *7137 p168*

Falatck, Anna; America, 1896 ***7137*** *p168*
Falatck, John; America, 1886 ***7137*** *p168*
Falatck, Mary; America, 1889 ***7137*** *p168*
Falatck, Michael; America, 1886 ***7137*** *p168*
Falatic, Andrew; America, 1888 ***7137*** *p168*
Falatic, Anna; America, 1896 ***7137*** *p168*
Falatic, John; America, 1886 ***7137*** *p168*
Falatic, Mary; America, 1889 ***7137*** *p168*
Falcinelli, August; Wisconsin, n.d. ***9675.5*** *p122*
Falconer, Alexander; North Carolina, 1818 ***1639.20*** *p67*
Falconer, George 13; St. John, N.B., 1866 ***5704.8*** *p167*
Falconer, Mary A.; New York, NY, 1869 ***5704.8*** *p232*
Falconer, Richard; Virginia, 1638 ***6219*** *p14*
Falconer, William 37; St. John, N.B., 1866 ***5704.8*** *p167*
Falconi, George A. 38; New Orleans, 1862 ***543.30*** *p32*
Faldo, Robert 18; Antigua (Antego), 1728 ***3690.1*** *p75*
Faleide, Arnold Bernt; Arkansas, 1918 ***95.2*** *p41*
Falender, Louis; New York, 1890 ***1450.2*** *p8B*
Faley, F. 35; Arizona, 1906 ***9228.40*** *p11*
Faley, Thomas; New York, NY, 1815 ***2859.11*** *p30*
Faley, William; New York, NY, 1816 ***2859.11*** *p30*
Falin, Mary; New York, NY, 1816 ***2859.11*** *p30*
Falk, Emil; Kansas, 1890 ***5240.1*** *p12*
Falk, George Oscar; Arkansas, 1918 ***95.2*** *p41*
Falk, Gust; Washington, 1859-1920 ***2872.1*** *p12*
Falk, Max C.; Kansas, 1890 ***5240.1*** *p12*
Falk, Swen; Iowa, 1866-1943 ***123.54*** *p17*
Falke, Simon; America, 1857 ***4610.10*** *p149*
Falkenbach, Joseph; America, 1848 ***8582.3*** *p18*
Falkener, John 19; Maryland, 1736 ***3690.1*** *p75*
Falkener, Mary 6; St. John, N.B., 1849 ***5704.8*** *p55*
Falkener, Pat; St. John, N.B., 1849 ***5704.8*** *p55*
Falkener, Pat 4; St. John, N.B., 1849 ***5704.8*** *p55*
Falkener, Rosey; St. John, N.B., 1849 ***5704.8*** *p55*
Falkener, William 8; St. John, N.B., 1849 ***5704.8*** *p55*
Falker, Adam; Philadelphia, 1757 ***9973.7*** *p32*
Falkingham, Frederick R.; Indiana, 1894 ***2896.5*** *p11*
Falkner, Ann; St. John, N.B., 1847 ***5704.8*** *p3*
Falkner, Arnold; Kentucky, 1844 ***8582.3*** *p99*
Falkner, David; St. John, N.B., 1847 ***5704.8*** *p3*
Falkner, Dorothy 45 *SEE* Falkner, Ralph
Falkner, Eliza; St. John, N.B., 1847 ***5704.8*** *p3*
Falkner, Jane; St. John, N.B., 1847 ***5704.8*** *p3*
Falkner, John; Wisconsin, n.d. ***9675.5*** *p122*
Falkner, Mary; St. John, N.B., 1847 ***5704.8*** *p3*
Falkner, Mary 30 *SEE* Falkner, Ralph
Falkner, Obadiah 21; Pennsylvania, 1728 ***3690.1*** *p75*
Falkner, Ralph 30; Philadelphia, 1774 ***1219.7*** *p225*
*Wife:*Mary 30
Falkner, Ralph 50; Philadelphia, 1774 ***1219.7*** *p225*
*Wife:*Dorothy 45
Falkner, William 5; St. John, N.B., 1847 ***5704.8*** *p3*
Falkner, William 21; Maryland, 1774 ***1219.7*** *p180*
Falko, Josef 28; New York, NY, 1878 ***9253*** *p47*
Falkouski, John; Arkansas, 1918 ***95.2*** *p41*
Falkovic, Ellen; America, 1900 ***7137*** *p168*
Falkovic, John; America, 1884 ***7137*** *p168*
Falkovic, Mary; America, 1900 ***7137*** *p168*
Falkovic, Susan; America, 1896 ***7137*** *p168*
Fallan, William; New York, NY, 1816 ***2859.11*** *p30*
Fallar, Wm 17; America, 1705-1706 ***2212*** *p45*
Falldorf, Erna Margaretha Grete; New York, NY, 1928 ***3455.4*** *p93*
Falle, Florian; Wisconsin, n.d. ***9675.5*** *p122*
Falle, Frank; Wisconsin, n.d. ***9675.5*** *p122*
Fallen, Esther 40; Massachusetts, 1849 ***5881.1*** *p37*
Fallen, Lars; Iowa, 1850-1855 ***2090*** *p613*
Fallenach, Joseph; Ohio, 1795 ***8582.2*** *p53*
Fallert, Antone; Washington, 1859-1920 ***2872.1*** *p12*
Fallert, Antonia; Washington, 1859-1920 ***2872.1*** *p12*
Falles, Ann 21; Maryland, 1775 ***1219.7*** *p256*
Falless, William 23; New England, 1774 ***1219.7*** *p196*
Fallevolte, Benedetto 40; Maryland, 1775 ***1219.7*** *p266*
Falliant, August 20; New Orleans, 1862 ***543.30*** *p27*
Fallick, Josef; Arkansas, 1918 ***95.2*** *p42*
Falline, Lontena; Iowa, 1866-1943 ***123.54*** *p18*
Fallis, Edward 11; Quebec, 1847 ***5704.8*** *p29*
Fallis, Elizabeth; Quebec, 1850 ***5704.8*** *p63*
Fallis, Jane; Quebec, 1847 ***5704.8*** *p29*
Fallis, Thomas 13; Quebec, 1847 ***5704.8*** *p29*
Fallmenn, Joe; Illinois, 1874 ***5012.39*** *p26*
Fallon, Bridget 30; Massachusetts, 1849 ***5881.1*** *p36*
Fallon, Catharine 8; Massachusetts, 1849 ***5881.1*** *p36*
Fallon, Daniel; Massachusetts, 1847 ***5881.1*** *p36*
Fallon, Jane 12; Massachusetts, 1849 ***5881.1*** *p37*
Fallon, John; Iroquois Co., IL, 1892 ***3455.1*** *p10*
Fallon, John 4; Massachusetts, 1849 ***5881.1*** *p37*
Fallon, John 16; Massachusetts, 1849 ***5881.1*** *p37*
Fallon, Maria 10; Massachusetts, 1850 ***5881.1*** *p39*
Fallon, Michael; Massachusetts, 1849 ***5881.1*** *p39*
Fallon, Patrick 18; Massachusetts, 1848 ***5881.1*** *p40*
Fallon, Peter 5; Massachusetts, 1849 ***5881.1*** *p40*
Fallon, Thomas 10; Massachusetts, 1849 ***5881.1*** *p40*
Fallon, Thomas 20; Massachusetts, 1849 ***5881.1*** *p40*
Fallon, Thomas 21; Massachusetts, 1848 ***5881.1*** *p40*
Fallon, Thomas 21; Massachusetts, 1850 ***5881.1*** *p40*
Fallone, Biddy 21; Massachusetts, 1849 ***5881.1*** *p36*
Fallow, Bridget 26; Massachusetts, 1850 ***5881.1*** *p36*
Fallowfield, Wharton; Virginia, 1698 ***2212*** *p15*
Falls, Adam 34; New Orleans, 1862 ***543.30*** *p226B*
Falls, Archibald 10; Quebec, 1852 ***5704.8*** *p97*
Falls, Ellen 7; Quebec, 1852 ***5704.8*** *p97*
Falls, John; Quebec, 1852 ***5704.8*** *p97*
Falls, John 19; Philadelphia, 1854 ***5704.8*** *p116*
Falls, Margaret; Quebec, 1852 ***5704.8*** *p97*
Falls, Mary; St. John, N.B., 1847 ***5704.8*** *p24*
Falls, Robert 12; Quebec, 1852 ***5704.8*** *p97*
Falls, Stewart; Quebec, 1852 ***5704.8*** *p97*
Fallydown, Patience 22; Halifax, N.S., 1775 ***1219.7*** *p262*
Falmann, Octave 28; New Orleans, 1836 ***778.5*** *p201*
Falston, Eliz.; Virginia, 1642 ***6219*** *p191*
Falter, Adam 15; America, 1853 ***9162.7*** *p14*
Falter, Elis. 53; America, 1853 ***9162.8*** *p36*
Falter, Elisabetha 16; America, 1853 ***9162.8*** *p36*
Falter, Johs. 18; America, 1853 ***9162.8*** *p36*
Falter, Niklaus 10; America, 1853 ***9162.8*** *p36*
Falutck, Andrew; America, 1888 ***7137*** *p168*
Falutck, Anna; America, 1896 ***7137*** *p168*
Falvel, Luke A.; New York, NY, 1835 ***8208.4*** *p5*
Falvey, Richard 29; New Orleans, 1862 ***543.30*** *p224B*
Falvy, Johanna 22; Massachusetts, 1849 ***5881.1*** *p38*
Famester, Berry; New York, NY, 1838 ***8208.4*** *p87*
Fanan, John; New York, NY, 1811 ***2859.11*** *p11*
Fanara, Guiseppe; Arkansas, 1918 ***95.2*** *p42*
Fanara, Joseph; Arkansas, 1918 ***95.2*** *p42*
Fanbridge, Charles; Arkansas, 1918 ***95.2*** *p42*
Fancke, Carl; Wisconsin, n.d. ***9675.5*** *p122*
Fanclik, John; America, 1890 ***7137*** *p168*
Fanco, Francis 25; America, 1700 ***2212*** *p30*
Faneett, Ann; Quebec, 1851 ***5704.8*** *p73*
Fanell, Willi.; Virginia, 1640 ***6219*** *p160*
Fanen, John; New York, NY, 1811 ***2859.11*** *p11*
Fangher, Charles Frederick; America, 1839 ***1450.2*** *p39A*
Fangmeyer, Luise Dorothee; Died enroute, 1853 ***4815.7*** *p92*
Fangney, Daniel J. 49; Kansas, 1884 ***5240.1*** *p65*
Fangohr, Charles Frederick; America, 1839 ***1450.2*** *p39A*
Fanherd, Karl 21; Port uncertain, 1839 ***778.5*** *p201*
Fani, Paul; Indiana, 1848 ***9117*** *p19*
Faniter, James; New York, 1832 ***1450.2*** *p39A*
Fankhanel, Fredrick 29; Kansas, 1873 ***5240.1*** *p55*
Fanlon, Ann 12; Massachusetts, 1847 ***5881.1*** *p35*
Fanly, John; America, 1735-1743 ***4971*** *p79*
Fann, Wm.; Virginia, 1635 ***6219*** *p69*
Fannell, Catharine 40; Massachusetts, 1849 ***5881.1*** *p36*
Fannen, Ann; Quebec, 1824 ***7603*** *p89*
Fanning, Frank 55; Arizona, 1902 ***9228.40*** *p6*
Fanning, Patrick 10; Massachusetts, 1849 ***5881.1*** *p40*
Fanning, Peter 20; Pennsylvania, 1730 ***3690.1*** *p75*
Fannon, Bridget 18; Massachusetts, 1850 ***5881.1*** *p36*
Fannon, Bridget 20; Massachusetts, 1850 ***5881.1*** *p36*
Fannon, Honora 20; Massachusetts, 1848 ***5881.1*** *p37*
Fannon, Honora 20; Massachusetts, 1850 ***5881.1*** *p35*
Fannon, Honora 20; Massachusetts, 1850 ***5881.1*** *p37*
Fanshawe, John; New York, NY, 1837 ***8208.4*** *p52*
Fant, Jacob Teris; Arkansas, 1918 ***95.2*** *p42*
Fantleroy, George; Virginia, 1643 ***6219*** *p230*
Fantleroy, Moore; Virginia, 1643 ***6219*** *p230*
Fanton, Franc; Iowa, 1866-1943 ***123.54*** *p18*
Fanton, John 21; Jamaica, 1737 ***3690.1*** *p75*
Faoro, Arnaldo; Iowa, 1866-1943 ***123.54*** *p18*
Faoro, Emma; Iowa, 1866-1943 ***123.54*** *p61*
Faoro, Frank; Iowa, 1866-1943 ***123.54*** *p18*
Faoro, Giovanni; Iowa, 1866-1943 ***123.54*** *p18*
Faoro, Joseph; Iowa, 1866-1943 ***123.54*** *p61*
Faoro, Regena Italia; Iowa, 1866-1943 ***123.54*** *p18*
Farb, Harry Edward; Arkansas, 1918 ***95.2*** *p42*
Farbach, Gottfried; America, 1849 ***8582.1*** *p9*
Farbarne, Lawrence; Virginia, 1636 ***6219*** *p78*
Farber, Johannes; Dakota, 1880 ***5240.1*** *p12*
Farburne, Lawrance; Virginia, 1637 ***6219*** *p84*
Fardig, Anders Christian; Minneapolis, 1868-1881 ***6410.35*** *p54*
Faree, Dominck; Arkansas, 1918 ***95.2*** *p42*
Faren, Owen; Philadelphia, 1864 ***5704.8*** *p178*
Faren, Thomas; New York, NY, 1811 ***2859.11*** *p11*
Farer, Marie 34; America, 1835 ***778.5*** *p201*
Farer, Xavier 38; America, 1835 ***778.5*** *p201*
Faresdahl, Andrew 28; Arkansas, 1918 ***95.2*** *p42*
Farese, Salvatore; Arkansas, 1918 ***95.2*** *p42*
Farey, John 25; Pennsylvania, 1733 ***3690.1*** *p75*
Fargason, Thomas; Virginia, 1639 ***6219*** *p151*
Fargrieve, George 2; Massachusetts, 1849 ***5881.1*** *p37*
Fargrieve, Margaret 23; Massachusetts, 1849 ***5881.1*** *p39*
Fargue, L. 29; New Orleans, 1839 ***778.5*** *p202*
Fargue, Louis 26; Port uncertain, 1835 ***778.5*** *p202*
Fargue, Louis 28; New Orleans, 1837 ***778.5*** *p202*
Fargue, Louis 30; New Orleans, 1839 ***778.5*** *p202*
Fargy, Elizabeth; Quebec, 1852 ***5704.8*** *p87*
Fargy, Elizabeth 2; Quebec, 1852 ***5704.8*** *p91*
Farha, Albert 21; Kansas, 1901 ***5240.1*** *p82*
Farhat, Nagib; Arkansas, 1918 ***95.2*** *p42*
Fario, Antonio 30; Arkansas, 1918 ***95.2*** *p42*
Fark, Peter; Virginia, 1847 ***4626.16*** *p13*
Farkas, John; Washington, 1859-1920 ***2872.1*** *p12*
Farland, Margaret; New York, NY, 1811 ***2859.11*** *p11*
Farley, Ann 19; Massachusetts, 1848 ***5881.1*** *p35*
Farley, James 20; Massachusetts, 1847 ***5881.1*** *p37*
Farley, John 16; Maryland, 1727 ***3690.1*** *p75*
Farley, Martin 14; Massachusetts, 1850 ***5881.1*** *p40*
Farley, Owen; New York, NY, 1816 ***2859.11*** *p30*
Farley, Patrick 18; Massachusetts, 1849 ***5881.1*** *p40*
Farley, Patrick 19; New Orleans, 1863 ***543.30*** *p229B*
Farley, Sarah 20; Virginia, 1775 ***1219.7*** *p246*
Farley, Terrence; New York, NY, 1811 ***2859.11*** *p11*
Farlo, Joice; Virginia, 1648 ***6219*** *p250*
Farlow, William; Philadelphia, 1850 ***5704.8*** *p64*
Farly, Ann; Virginia, 1643 ***6219*** *p203*
Farly, Antoine; Quebec, 1710 ***7603*** *p72*
Farly, John; Montreal, 1823 ***7603*** *p87*
Farm, Anton; Arkansas, 1918 ***95.2*** *p42*
Farm, Anton 29; Arkansas, 1918 ***95.2*** *p42*
Farmakis, Pantalas; Arkansas, 1918 ***95.2*** *p42*
Farmer, Alfred A.; Wisconsin, n.d. ***9675.5*** *p122*
Farmer, Ferdinand; Pennsylvania, 1869-1885 ***8582.2*** *p65*
Farmer, Francis 22; Kansas, 1887 ***5240.1*** *p71*
Farmer, John; New York, NY, 1816 ***2859.11*** *p30*
Farmer, John; Virginia, 1639 ***6219*** *p157*
Farmer, John 22; Maryland, 1775 ***1219.7*** *p251*
Farmer, John 25; Massachusetts, 1849 ***5881.1*** *p37*
Farmer, Joseph; Ohio, 1800-1885 ***8582.2*** *p58*
Farmer, Ludwig; Philadelphia, 1764 ***8582.2*** *p65*
Farmer, Ludwig; Philadelphia, 1776 ***8582.3*** *p84*
Farmer, Thomas 17; Virginia, 1721 ***3690.1*** *p75*
Farming, Frank 55; Arizona, 1902 ***9228.40*** *p6*
Farms, Ellen; New York, NY, 1815 ***2859.11*** *p30*
Farms, Mary; New York, NY, 1815 ***2859.11*** *p30*
Farms, Robert; New York, NY, 1815 ***2859.11*** *p30*
Farnacht, John; Canada, 1776-1783 ***9786*** *p207A*
Farnan, Nanny; St. John, N.B., 1851 ***5704.8*** *p72*
Farnborow, Alexander 19; Pennsylvania, Virginia or Maryland, 1728 ***3690.1*** *p75*
Farnborow, Jacob 21; Pennsylvania, 1728 ***3690.1*** *p75*
Farne, Mme. 30; New Orleans, 1835 ***778.5*** *p202*
Farnell, John 33; New Orleans, 1862 ***543.30*** *p32*
Farnell, Jonathan 23; Maryland, 1735 ***3690.1*** *p75*
Farnen, Patrick; Philadelphia, 1852 ***5704.8*** *p88*
Farner, Gotthold 33; Kansas, 1876 ***5240.1*** *p57*
Farney, Bessy 18; Massachusetts, 1850 ***5881.1*** *p36*
Farnish, Peter; Wisconsin, n.d. ***9675.5*** *p122*
Farnon, Anthony; Philadelphia, 1865 ***5704.8*** *p187*
Farnon, Bridget; Philadelphia, 1865 ***5704.8*** *p187*
Farnon, Henry; Philadelphia, 1865 ***5704.8*** *p187*
Farnon, Nancy; Philadelphia, 1865 ***5704.8*** *p187*
Farnsworth, . . .; Cincinnati, 1810 ***8582.3*** *p88*
Farques, Louis 30; New Orleans, 1838 ***778.5*** *p202*
Farquhar, George; Canada, 1827 ***8893*** *p266*
Farquhar, Robert; Charleston, SC, 1783 ***1639.20*** *p67*
Farquhar, Robert; Charleston, SC, 1795 ***1639.20*** *p67*
Farquharson, Alexander; Halifax, N.S., 1795 ***8894.1*** *p191*
*Wife:*Elisabeth Gullet
Farquharson, Elisabeth Gullet *SEE* Farquharson, Alexander
Farquharson, James; South Carolina, 1780 ***1639.20*** *p67*
Farquher, Alexander 15; Pennsylvania, 1728 ***3690.1*** *p75*
Farr, Edward 18; Virginia, 1774 ***1219.7*** *p243*
Farr, Henry; Philadelphia, 1866 ***5704.8*** *p214*
Farr, Henry 22; Jamaica, 1732 ***3690.1*** *p76*
Farr, John; Virginia, 1635 ***6219*** *p72*
Farr, Thomas; Antigua (Antego), 1756 ***1219.7*** *p49*
Farr, Thomas; Antigua (Antego), 1756 ***3690.1*** *p76*
Farr, William; Antigua (Antego), 1756 ***1219.7*** *p49*
Farr, William; Antigua (Antego), 1756 ***3690.1*** *p76*
Farrall, Michael; Illinois, 1861 ***2896.5*** *p11*
Farran, Augustine 28; Jamaica, 1736 ***3690.1*** *p76*
Farran, Biddy; St. John, N.B., 1847 ***5704.8*** *p35*
Farran, Eleanor; St. John, N.B., 1852 ***5704.8*** *p83*
Farran, Elleanonr; Philadelphia, 1848 ***53.26*** *p26*
Farran, Elleanor; St. John, N.B., 1847 ***5704.8*** *p25*
Farran, Elleanor 10; Philadelphia, 1848 ***5704.8*** *p45*
Farran, Jane; St. John, N.B., 1851 ***5704.8*** *p80*
Farran, John; St. John, N.B., 1847 ***5704.8*** *p4*
Farran, John 26; America, 1838 ***778.5*** *p202*
Farran, Peggy; Philadelphia, 1848 ***53.26*** *p26*
Farran, Peggy; Philadelphia, 1848 ***5704.8*** *p45*
Farran, Sally; St. John, N.B., 1853 ***5704.8*** *p106*
Farran, Sarah; St. John, N.B., 1850 ***5704.8*** *p66*
Farran, Sarah 17; St. John, N.B., 1862 ***5704.8*** *p150*

146 *FOR A COMPLETE EXPLANATION OF ENTRY, SEE "HOW TO READ A CITATION" SECTION*

Farran, William; St. John, N.B., 1849 ***5704.8*** *p56*
Farrant, Henry; New York, 1768 ***1219.7*** *p137*
Farrar, Ann.; Virginia, 1647 ***6219*** *p245*
Farrarello, Caromelo; Arkansas, 1918 ***95.2*** *p42*
Farrarhoe, . . .; Virginia, 1645 ***6219*** *p233*
Farras, Nauf 28; Arkansas, 1918 ***95.2*** *p42*
Farrel, Anne; New York, NY, 1816 ***2859.11*** *p30*
Farrel, Edward; New York, NY, 1816 ***2859.11*** *p30*
Farrel, John 20; Pennsylvania, 1738 ***3690.1*** *p76*
Farrel, Matthew; America, 1740 ***4971*** *p66*
Farrel, Patrick 38; Maryland, 1774 ***1219.7*** *p192*
Farrel, Thomas; America, 1697 ***2212*** *p7*
Farrel, Thos 21; Wilmington, DE, 1831 ***6508.7*** *p161*
Farrell, Miss; New York, NY, 1815 ***2859.11*** *p30*
Farrell, Ann 20; St. John, N.B., 1855 ***5704.8*** *p127*
Farrell, Anna; Montreal, 1822 ***7603*** *p87*
Farrell, Biddy 16; St. John, N.B., 1855 ***5704.8*** *p127*
Farrell, Biddy 21; Massachusetts, 1849 ***5881.1*** *p36*
Farrell, Bridget 17; Massachusetts, 1850 ***5881.1*** *p36*
Farrell, Bridget 30; Massachusetts, 1849 ***5881.1*** *p36*
Farrell, Bryan; America, 1735-1743 ***4971*** *p8*
Farrell, Bryan; New York, NY, 1832 ***8208.4*** *p30*
Farrell, Catharine 26; Massachusetts, 1848 ***5881.1*** *p36*
Farrell, Christopher; New York, NY, 1838 ***8208.4*** *p64*
Farrell, Darby; America, 1735-1743 ***4971*** *p78*
Farrell, Edward 24; Massachusetts, 1847 ***5881.1*** *p36*
Farrell, Ellen; New York, NY, 1816 ***2859.11*** *p30*
Farrell, Faughney; America, 1739 ***4971*** *p85*
Farrell, Faughny; America, 1743 ***4971*** *p11*
Farrell, Francis; New York, NY, 1836 ***8208.4*** *p25*
Farrell, Garrett; Virginia, 1637 ***6219*** *p113*
Farrell, Garrett; Virginia, 1638 ***6219*** *p159*
Farrell, George 24; Massachusetts, 1850 ***5881.1*** *p37*
Farrell, James; America, 1735-1743 ***4971*** *p79*
Farrell, James; West Virginia, 1847-1852 ***9788.3*** *p10*
Farrell, James 21; Maryland, 1774 ***1219.7*** *p181*
Farrell, James 32; New Orleans, 1862 ***543.30*** *p375C*
Farrell, James 50; Massachusetts, 1850 ***5881.1*** *p38*
Farrell, Jean; Quebec, 1779 ***7603*** *p85*
Farrell, John; America, 1735-1743 ***4971*** *p78*
Farrell, John; America, 1735-1743 ***4971*** *p79*
Farrell, John; America, 1740 ***4971*** *p81*
Farrell, John; America, 1741 ***4971*** *p94*
Farrell, John; America, 1742 ***4971*** *p53*
Farrell, John; America, 1743 ***4971*** *p11*
Farrell, John; New York, NY, 1835 ***8208.4*** *p6*
Farrell, John; New York, NY, 1836 ***8208.4*** *p22*
Farrell, John; New York, NY, 1839 ***8208.4*** *p96*
Farrell, John 14; Newfoundland, 1789 ***4915.24*** *p55*
Farrell, John 20; Massachusetts, 1850 ***5881.1*** *p38*
Farrell, John 22; New Orleans, 1862 ***543.30*** *p225B*
Farrell, John 25; Maryland, 1773 ***1219.7*** *p173*
Farrell, John H.; Colorado, 1904 ***9678.2*** *p18*
Farrell, Margaret 16; Philadelphia, 1853 ***5704.8*** *p108*
Farrell, Mary; America, 1742 ***4971*** *p17*
Farrell, Mary; Philadelphia, 1865 ***5704.8*** *p197*
Farrell, Mary 18; St. John, N.B., 1855 ***5704.8*** *p127*
Farrell, Mary 28; Massachusetts, 1847 ***5881.1*** *p38*
Farrell, Matthew; New Brunswick, 1820 ***7603*** *p58*
Farrell, Michael 26; New Orleans, 1862 ***543.30*** *p225B*
Farrell, Michel; New Brunswick, 1820 ***7603*** *p61*
Farrell, Patrick; America, 1740 ***4971*** *p31*
Farrell, Patrick; America, 1869 ***5704.8*** *p234*
Farrell, Patrick; Quebec, 1821 ***7603*** *p57*
Farrell, Patrick; Virginia, 1638 ***6219*** *p147*
Farrell, Patrick 12; Massachusetts, 1847 ***5881.1*** *p40*
Farrell, Patrick 20; Massachusetts, 1847 ***5881.1*** *p40*
Farrell, Peter; New York, NY, 1816 ***2859.11*** *p30*
Farrell, Philip; New York, NY, 1838 ***8208.4*** *p81*
Farrell, Richard; New York, NY, 1815 ***2859.11*** *p30*
Farrell, Roger; America, 1740 ***4971*** *p30*
Farrell, Roger; America, 1742 ***4971*** *p37*
Farrell, Sarah 50; St. John, N.B., 1855 ***5704.8*** *p127*
Farrell, Thomas; America, 1736 ***4971*** *p12*
Farrell, Thomas; New York, 1836 ***8208.4*** *p60*
Farrell, Thomas 32; St. John, N.B., 1866 ***5704.8*** *p166*
Farrell, Walter; America, 1736 ***4971*** *p12*
Farrell, William; Montreal, 1811 ***7603*** *p93*
Farrell, William; New York, NY, 1838 ***8208.4*** *p88*
Farrell, William James; New York, NY, 1816 ***2859.11*** *p30*
Farrell, Winnefred 70; Massachusetts, 1850 ***5881.1*** *p41*
Farrelly, Patrick; New York, NY, 1838 ***8208.4*** *p67*
Farren, Bernard 19; Philadelphia, 1856 ***5704.8*** *p128*
Farren, Bernard P. 20; Philadelphia, 1864 ***5704.8*** *p157*
Farren, Bridget 20; Philadelphia, 1864 ***5704.8*** *p156*
Farren, Catherine 17; Philadelphia, 1864 ***5704.8*** *p157*
Farren, Charles 22; St. John, N.B., 1862 ***5704.8*** *p150*
Farren, Cicily 20; St. John, N.B., 1854 ***5704.8*** *p114*
Farren, Edward; St. John, N.B., 1847 ***5704.8*** *p20*
Farren, Ellen 21; Massachusetts, 1849 ***5881.1*** *p36*
Farren, Fanny 19; St. John, N.B., 1857 ***5704.8*** *p134*
Farren, Felix; New York, NY, 1811 ***2859.11*** *p11*
Farren, George 2; St. John, N.B., 1847 ***5704.8*** *p20*
Farren, Hugh; St. John, N.B., 1852 ***5704.8*** *p83*
Farren, James; New York, NY, 1811 ***2859.11*** *p11*
Farren, John; Nevada, 1874 ***2764.35*** *p23*
Farren, John; Philadelphia, 1852 ***5704.8*** *p85*
Farren, John 20; St. John, N.B., 1854 ***5704.8*** *p122*
Farren, Martha; St. John, N.B., 1847 ***5704.8*** *p20*
Farren, Mary; St. John, N.B., 1852 ***5704.8*** *p84*
Farren, Michael 23; Philadelphia, 1857 ***5704.8*** *p133*
Farren, Neal 30; Philadelphia, 1860 ***5704.8*** *p145*
Farren, Owen 25; Massachusetts, 1849 ***5881.1*** *p40*
Farren, Rose 17; Philadelphia, 1855 ***5704.8*** *p124*
Farren, Sally; New York, NY, 1811 ***2859.11*** *p11*
Farren, Samuel 6; St. John, N.B., 1847 ***5704.8*** *p20*
Farren, Sarah 16; Philadelphia, 1855 ***5704.8*** *p124*
Farren, Sarah 52; Quebec, 1854 ***5704.8*** *p121*
Farren, William 21; St. John, N.B., 1854 ***5704.8*** *p114*
Farren, William 53; Quebec, 1854 ***5704.8*** *p121*
Farrer, William; United States or West Indies, 1736 ***3690.1*** *p76*
Farrer, William Ward; West Indies, 1775 ***1219.7*** *p252*
Farrett, Ann 25; Quebec, 1855 ***5704.8*** *p125*
Farrett, Bessy 23; Quebec, 1855 ***5704.8*** *p125*
Farrett, Edward 18; Quebec, 1855 ***5704.8*** *p125*
Farrett, John 13; Quebec, 1855 ***5704.8*** *p125*
Farrett, John 60; Quebec, 1855 ***5704.8*** *p125*
Farrett, Mary 27; Quebec, 1855 ***5704.8*** *p125*
Farrett, Mary 50; Quebec, 1855 ***5704.8*** *p125*
Farrett, Robert 17; Quebec, 1855 ***5704.8*** *p125*
Farrington, Cha.; Virginia, 1635 ***6219*** *p69*
Farrington, Edwd 20; Maryland or Virginia, 1699 ***2212*** *p24*
Farrington, John 27; Jamaica, 1730 ***3690.1*** *p76*
Farrington, Richard; New York, NY, 1837 ***8208.4*** *p48*
Farris, Mary-Ann Walton; Quebec, 1786 ***7603*** *p86*
Farrolly, Edward 18; Massachusetts, 1850 ***5881.1*** *p37*
Farrolly, John 40; Massachusetts, 1848 ***5881.1*** *p37*
Farrolly, Mary 50; Massachusetts, 1848 ***5881.1*** *p38*
Farron, Ann; St. John, N.B., 1850 ***5704.8*** *p67*
Farron, Annie 20; Massachusetts, 1849 ***5881.1*** *p35*
Farron, Biddy; St. John, N.B., 1847 ***5704.8*** *p9*
Farron, Bridget; Quebec, 1850 ***5704.8*** *p67*
Farron, Bridget; St. John, N.B., 1853 ***5704.8*** *p108*
Farron, Daniel; St. John, N.B., 1851 ***5704.8*** *p72*
Farron, Eleanor; America, 1867 ***5704.8*** *p222*
Farron, James; St. John, N.B., 1851 ***5704.8*** *p72*
Farron, Margaret; St. John, N.B., 1852 ***5704.8*** *p83*
Farron, Mary; St. John, N.B., 1851 ***5704.8*** *p72*
Farron, Mary; St. John, N.B., 1852 ***5704.8*** *p84*
Farron, Michael; St. John, N.B., 1850 ***5704.8*** *p66*
Farron, Patrick 21; St. John, N.B., 1862 ***5704.8*** *p149*
Farron, Rose 18; St. John, N.B., 1862 ***5704.8*** *p150*
Farron, Sally 18; Philadelphia, 1859 ***5704.8*** *p142*
Farror, John; Virginia, 1623-1648 ***6219*** *p252*
Farrow, Henry 17; Jamaica, 1729 ***3690.1*** *p76*
Farrow, John 19; Jamaica, 1719 ***3690.1*** *p76*
Farrow, Jon; Virginia, 1635 ***6219*** *p35*
Farrow, Sarah; Philadelphia, 1853 ***5704.8*** *p103*
Farsmann, Carl; Washington, 1859-1920 ***2872.1*** *p12*
Farson, James 5; St. John, N.B., 1863 ***5704.8*** *p152*
Farson, Jane 40; St. John, N.B., 1863 ***5704.8*** *p152*
Farson, John 17; St. John, N.B., 1863 ***5704.8*** *p152*
Farson, Paul 11; St. John, N.B., 1863 ***5704.8*** *p152*
Farson, Thomas 9 mos; St. John, N.B., 1863 ***5704.8*** *p152*
Farson, William 8; St. John, N.B., 1863 ***5704.8*** *p152*
Farth, Jon.; Virginia, 1637 ***6219*** *p114*
Farthin, Robt.; Virginia, 1636 ***6219*** *p76*
Farthing, Barr.; Virginia, 1636 ***6219*** *p78*
Farthing, John 15; Virginia, 1720 ***3690.1*** *p76*
Fartley, Wm; America, 1698 ***2212*** *p13*
Farwick, Bernard; Kentucky, 1844 ***8582.3*** *p101*
Farye, Ann *SEE* Farye, Joseph
Farye, Joseph; Virginia, 1638 ***6219*** *p119*
*Wife:*Ann
Fasc, Henry; Wisconsin, n.d. ***9675.5*** *p122*
Fasking, George; Iroquois Co., IL, 1892 ***3455.1*** *p10*
Fasnacht, . . .; Canada, 1776-1783 ***9786*** *p20*
Fasnacht, John; Canada, 1776-1783 ***9786*** *p207A*
Fasold, August; Wisconsin, n.d. ***9675.5*** *p122*
Fassan, Margaret; Philadelphia, 1865 ***5704.8*** *p200*
Fassario, John; Arkansas, 1918 ***95.2*** *p42*
Fassbender, Ferdinand 24; Kansas, 1878 ***5240.1*** *p59*
Fassbender, Peter 22; Kansas, 1878 ***5240.1*** *p59*
Fasser, Joseph 41; New Orleans, 1864 ***543.30*** *p230B*
Fast, August 21; Kansas, 1887 ***5240.1*** *p70*
Fastnacht, Michael; America, 1847 ***1450.2*** *p39A*
Fatchell, . . .; Canada, 1776-1783 ***9786*** *p20*
Fatino, Domenico; Iowa, 1866-1943 ***123.54*** *p18*
Fatino, Francesco; Iowa, 1866-1943 ***123.54*** *p18*
Fattiger, Martha Elise; America, 1840 ***4610.10*** *p119*
Fattner, B. 27; New Orleans, 1837 ***778.5*** *p202*
Fau, Michel 23; New Orleans, 1835 ***778.5*** *p202*
Fauche, H. 20; New Orleans, 1831 ***778.5*** *p202*
Faucher, Mr. 58; New Orleans, 1825 ***778.5*** *p202*
Faucitt, Supply Officer; Canada, 1776 ***9786*** *p137*
Fauconnier, J. P. 28; Port uncertain, 1827 ***778.5*** *p202*
Fauille, Jean 28; New Orleans, 1835 ***778.5*** *p202*
Faulkender, Jane Ann; St. John, N.B., 1847 ***5704.8*** *p21*
Faulkender, Patk; New York, NY, 1816 ***2859.11*** *p30*
Faulkner, Ann 20; Massachusetts, 1849 ***5881.1*** *p35*
Faulkner, Bridget 16; Philadelphia, 1857 ***5704.8*** *p134*
Faulkner, Carey; St. John, N.B., 1847 ***5704.8*** *p2*
Faulkner, Catherine; St. John, N.B., 1847 ***5704.8*** *p19*
Faulkner, Catherine 6 mos; St. John, N.B., 1847 ***5704.8*** *p19*
Faulkner, Catherine 2; St. John, N.B., 1847 ***5704.8*** *p2*
Faulkner, E. R.; America, 1852 ***6014.1*** *p2*
Faulkner, Fanny; St. John, N.B., 1847 ***5704.8*** *p2*
Faulkner, George 7; St. John, N.B., 1847 ***5704.8*** *p2*
Faulkner, James 20; Philadelphia, 1774 ***1219.7*** *p228*
Faulkner, John 9 mos; St. John, N.B., 1847 ***5704.8*** *p8*
Faulkner, Margaret 13; Philadelphia, 1864 ***5704.8*** *p161*
Faulkner, Margarett *SEE* Faulkner, Thomas
Faulkner, Mary; Virginia, 1698 ***2212*** *p17*
Faulkner, Neal; St. John, N.B., 1847 ***5704.8*** *p8*
Faulkner, Neal; St. John, N.B., 1847 ***5704.8*** *p19*
Faulkner, Richd 15; Maryland or Virginia, 1699 ***2212*** *p23*
Faulkner, Rose; St. John, N.B., 1847 ***5704.8*** *p8*
Faulkner, Sarah; St. John, N.B., 1850 ***5704.8*** *p62*
Faulkner, Thomas; Virginia, 1639 ***6219*** *p153*
*Wife:*Margarett
Faulkner, William 3; St. John, N.B., 1847 ***5704.8*** *p2*
Faulstich, Phillip 28; New Orleans, 1862 ***543.30*** *p223B*
Faulstroth, . . .; Canada, 1776-1783 ***9786*** *p20*
Faunat, Francoise 7; America, 1839 ***778.5*** *p202*
Faunat, Francoise 32; America, 1839 ***778.5*** *p202*
Faunat, Joseph 2; America, 1839 ***778.5*** *p203*
Faunat, Nicolas 39; America, 1839 ***778.5*** *p203*
Faundelakis, Nick; Arkansas, 1918 ***95.2*** *p42*
Fauquet, Mr. 30; Port uncertain, 1836 ***778.5*** *p203*
Faure, F. 23; New Orleans, 1832 ***778.5*** *p203*
Faure, Ferdinand 26; New Orleans, 1829 ***778.5*** *p203*
Faure, M. 24; New Orleans, 1837 ***778.5*** *p203*
Faure, Pierre 25; America, 1838 ***778.5*** *p203*
Fausel, . . .; Canada, 1776-1783 ***9786*** *p20*
Fauser, Anna; America, 1766 ***2444*** *p153*
*Child:*Catharina
Fauser, Catharina *SEE* Fauser, Anna
Fauser, Hans Jerg *SEE* Fauser, Margaretha
Fauser, Margaretha; Carolina, 1737-1800 ***2444*** *p153*
*Brother:*Hans Jerg
Fausse, . . .; Canada, 1776-1783 ***9786*** *p20*
Fausser, Johannes; Philadelphia, 1790 ***2444*** *p153*
Fausset, Auguste 25; New Orleans, 1832 ***778.5*** *p203*
Faussett, Isabella; Quebec, 1850 ***5704.8*** *p63*
Faust, . . .; Canada, 1776-1783 ***9786*** *p20*
Faust, Anna Maria; America, 1853 ***9162.7*** *p14*
Faust, Casper, Jr.; South Carolina, 1788 ***7119*** *p203*
Faust, Daniel; South Carolina, 1788 ***7119*** *p203*
Faust, Frederik Ferdinand 28; Kansas, 1886 ***5240.1*** *p69*
Faust, Jacob; South Carolina, 1788 ***7119*** *p202*
Faust, Johann 26; America, 1853 ***9162.7*** *p14*
Faust, John; South Carolina, 1788 ***7119*** *p202*
Fauster, Elizabeth 21; America, 1705 ***2212*** *p44*
Fauth, Anton; Alberta, n.d. ***5262*** *p58*
Faux, Edward 19; New England, 1699 ***2212*** *p19*
Faux, Robt; America, 1698 ***2212*** *p9*
Favani, R. 25; Port uncertain, 1839 ***778.5*** *p203*
Favarone, Luigi 25; New York, NY, 1893 ***9026.4*** *p41*
*Relative:*Theresa 21
Favarone, Theresa 21 *SEE* Favarone, Luigi
Favell, James 26; Maryland, 1775 ***1219.7*** *p267*
Favereau, Mrs. 42; America, 1836 ***778.5*** *p203*
Favereau, Victor 7; America, 1836 ***778.5*** *p203*
Faviraux, Denis 33; New Orleans, 1837 ***778.5*** *p203*
Fawceit, Jane 28 *SEE* Fawceit, John
Fawceit, John 29; Nova Scotia, 1774 ***1219.7*** *p195*
*Wife:*Jane 28
*Child:*Mary 4
Fawceit, Mary 4 *SEE* Fawceit, John
Fawcet, Arthur 19; Philadelphia, 1804 ***53.26*** *p26*
Fawcett, Catherine 21; Philadelphia, 1804 ***53.26*** *p26*
Fawcett, Frederick; New York, NY, 1837 ***8208.4*** *p38*
Fawcett, George; Quebec, 1823 ***7603*** *p60*
Fawcett, Michael 22; Quebec, 1858 ***5704.8*** *p137*
Fawcett, Susan 19; Quebec, 1858 ***5704.8*** *p137*
Fawent, Robert 30; Nova Scotia, 1774 ***1219.7*** *p193*
Fawne, Wm.; Virginia, 1633 ***6219*** *p32*
Fawsett, Bryan 15; Maryland, 1730 ***3690.1*** *p76*
Fax, Peter; New York, NY, 1815 ***2859.11*** *p30*
Fay, James; New York, NY, 1816 ***2859.11*** *p30*
Fay, Luke; New York, NY, 1815 ***2859.11*** *p30*
Fay, Patrick; New York, NY, 1816 ***2859.11*** *p30*
Fay, Thomas 21; Massachusetts, 1847 ***5881.1*** *p40*

Fayden, Jonathan; Virginia, 1637 ***6219*** *p115*
Faye, Michael; Illinois, 1870 ***5012.38*** *p99*
Faye, Pierre; Quebec, 1688 ***4533*** *p127*
Faye, William 20; Jamaica, 1754 ***3690.1*** *p76*
Fayet, Mr. 30; America, 1837 ***778.5*** *p203*
Faymero, P. 40; New Orleans, 1826 ***778.5*** *p203*
Fayne, John 21; Maryland, 1774 ***1219.7*** *p221*
Fayolle, Edmond 26; New Orleans, 1835 ***778.5*** *p203*
Fayret, P. 20; Louisiana, 1820 ***778.5*** *p204*
Fays, Jean Pierre 30; Port uncertain, 1839 ***778.5*** *p204*
Faysau, L. 24; America, 1831 ***778.5*** *p204*
Fayt, J.; Quebec, 1815 ***9229.18*** *p80*
Fazan, J.B. 35; America, 1838 ***778.5*** *p204*
Fazzini, Francesco; Arkansas, 1918 ***95.2*** *p42*
Fazzolari, Rocco; Arkansas, 1918 ***95.2*** *p42*
Fea, William 13; St. John, N.B., 1850 ***5704.8*** *p65*
Feach, Nicholas 23; America, 1831 ***778.5*** *p204*
Feagan, John 21; Kansas, 1870 ***5240.1*** *p12*
Feagan, John 21; Kansas, 1870 ***5240.1*** *p51*
Feagean, Peter 22; Kansas, 1873 ***5240.1*** *p55*
Feakin, Albert; Washington, 1859-1920 ***2872.1*** *p12*
Feakin, Edward; Washington, 1859-1920 ***2872.1*** *p12*
Feakin, John; Washington, 1859-1920 ***2872.1*** *p12*
Feakin, Maggie; Washington, 1859-1920 ***2872.1*** *p12*
Feakin, Mathew; Washington, 1859-1920 ***2872.1*** *p12*
Fearby, George 19; Jamaica, 1734 ***3690.1*** *p77*
Feard, Ulrich; South Carolina, 1788 ***7119*** *p202*
Fearebrace, Roger; Virginia, 1635 ***6219*** *p12*
Fearey, John 25; Pennsylvania, 1733 ***3690.1*** *p75*
Fearis, Catherine; New York, NY, 1816 ***2859.11*** *p30*
Fearis, John; New York, NY, 1816 ***2859.11*** *p30*
Fearis, Margaret; New York, NY, 1816 ***2859.11*** *p30*
Fearis, Mary; New York, NY, 1816 ***2859.11*** *p30*
Fearn, William; Washington, 1859-1920 ***2872.1*** *p12*
Fearnley, John 29; New York, NY, 1821 ***1450.2*** *p39A*
*Wife:*Martha 23
*Child:*Mary Ann 6
*Child:*Prissilla 4
Fearnley, Martha 23 *SEE* Fearnley, John
Fearnley, Mary Ann 6 *SEE* Fearnley, John
Fearnley, Prissilla 4 *SEE* Fearnley, John
Feasly, Robert; Virginia, 1642 ***6219*** *p199*
Feather, Peter; Philadelphia, 1759 ***9973.7*** *p33*
Feathergill, Chris.; Virginia, 1623-1648 ***6219*** *p252*
Featherman, Sebastian; Illinois, 1862 ***2896.5*** *p11*
Featherston, John 20; Jamaica, 1724 ***3690.1*** *p77*
Featherston, John 25; Massachusetts, 1847 ***5881.1*** *p37*
Featson, Henry 22; Virginia, 1774 ***1219.7*** *p186*
Feber, George; Illinois, 1860 ***2896.5*** *p11*
Febiarn, Angelo; Wisconsin, n.d. ***9675.5*** *p122*
February, John; Virginia, 1638 ***6219*** *p124*
Febures, Lewis 19; South Carolina, 1725 ***3690.1*** *p77*
Fechheimer, Marcus; America, 1837 ***8582.3*** *p18*
Fechter, Wolfgang; Wisconsin, n.d. ***9675.5*** *p122*
Fedder, Richard; Wisconsin, n.d. ***9675.5*** *p122*
Fedder, Snade 18; Maryland, 1730 ***3690.1*** *p77*
Fedele, Deida 25; Harris Co., TX, 1898 ***6254*** *p4*
Feder, John 38; New Orleans, 1862 ***543.30*** *p228B*
Federer, Joseph A.; West Virginia, 1857 ***9788.3*** *p10*
Federico, Felippo; Arkansas, 1918 ***95.2*** *p42*
Federmann, Hans; Venezuela, n.d. ***8582.3*** *p79*
Federole, Nicols; South Carolina, 1788 ***7119*** *p200*
Federowicz, Franciszek; Buffalo, NY, 1912 ***9980.29*** *p56*
Federowicz, Stanislawa Gisowska 23; New York, 1912 ***9980.29*** *p56*
Federspiel, August; America, 1840 ***8582.2*** *p10*
Federspiel, John; Illinois, 1852 ***7857*** *p3*
Fedigan, Patrick; America, 1739 ***4971*** *p25*
Fedora, Phillip; America, 1899 ***7137*** *p168*
Fedorowis, Ignatz; Arkansas, 1918 ***95.2*** *p42*
Fedorowitch, Kazmery; Arkansas, 1918 ***95.2*** *p42*
Fedorski, Julian 20; New York, 1912 ***9980.29*** *p53*
Fedran, Frank; Wisconsin, n.d. ***9675.5*** *p122*
Fedran, John; Wisconsin, n.d. ***9675.5*** *p122*
Fedroin, John; Wisconsin, n.d. ***9675.5*** *p122*
Feduji, Biagio; Wisconsin, n.d. ***9675.5*** *p122*
Fee, Ann 12 *SEE* Fee, Mary
Fee, Ann 12; Philadelphia, 1847 ***5704.8*** *p23*
Fee, Biddy; St. John, N.B., 1847 ***5704.8*** *p35*
Fee, Catherine; Philadelphia, 1851 ***5704.8*** *p79*
Fee, Henri; Quebec, 1819 ***7603*** *p99*
Fee, Hugh; Philadelphia, 1816 ***2859.11*** *p30*
Fee, James; Philadelphia, 1811 ***53.26*** *p26*
Fee, James; Philadelphia, 1811 ***2859.11*** *p11*
Fee, Mary; Philadelphia, 1847 ***53.26*** *p26*
*Relative:*Ann 12
*Relative:*Sarah 10
Fee, Mary; Philadelphia, 1847 ***5704.8*** *p23*
Fee, Neale; Virginia, 1642 ***6219*** *p192*
Fee, Patrick; Philadelphia, 1811 ***53.26*** *p26*
Fee, Patrick; Philadelphia, 1811 ***2859.11*** *p11*
Fee, Rosy; St. John, N.B., 1847 ***5704.8*** *p35*
Fee, Sarah 10 *SEE* Fee, Mary
Fee, Sarah 10; Philadelphia, 1847 ***5704.8*** *p23*
Fee, Thomas; Philadelphia, 1864 ***5704.8*** *p169*
Fee, Thomas; Philadelphia, 1868 ***5704.8*** *p226*
Fee, Thomas 20; Massachusetts, 1850 ***5881.1*** *p40*
Feederee, Richard; Milwaukee, 1875 ***4719.30*** *p257*
Feederle, Richard; Milwaukee, 1875 ***4719.30*** *p257*
Feegan, Mary 25; Massachusetts, 1849 ***5881.1*** *p39*
Feegan, Thomas 21; Massachusetts, 1849 ***5881.1*** *p40*
Feeharay, Lawrence 29; Montreal, 1796 ***7603*** *p98*
Feeley, John 23; Philadelphia, 1865 ***5704.8*** *p164*
Feely, Martin; St. John, N.B., 1852 ***5704.8*** *p83*
Feely, Thomas; America, 1862 ***6014.1*** *p2*
Feeney, Charles; Philadelphia, 1865 ***5704.8*** *p184*
Feeney, Luke; Quebec, 1840 ***7036*** *p125*
Feeney, Martin; New York, NY, 1816 ***2859.11*** *p30*
Feeney, Patrick; Philadelphia, 1865 ***5704.8*** *p184*
Feeney, William; Philadelphia, 1864 ***5704.8*** *p181*
Feeny, Andrew 50; St. John, N.B., 1865 ***5704.8*** *p165*
Feeny, Ann 22; Philadelphia, 1856 ***5704.8*** *p128*
Feeny, Bernard 27; St. John, N.B., 1866 ***5704.8*** *p167*
Feeny, Biddy; St. John, N.B., 1852 ***5704.8*** *p93*
Feeny, Catherine 21; St. John, N.B., 1861 ***5704.8*** *p147*
Feeny, John; Philadelphia, 1847 ***53.26*** *p26*
*Relative:*Mary
Feeny, John; Philadelphia, 1847 ***5704.8*** *p21*
Feeny, John 20; Philadelphia, 1861 ***5704.8*** *p147*
Feeny, John 22; St. John, N.B., 1865 ***5704.8*** *p165*
Feeny, Mary *SEE* Feeny, John
Feeny, Mary; Philadelphia, 1847 ***5704.8*** *p21*
Feeny, Michael; New York, NY, 1816 ***2859.11*** *p30*
Feeny, Patrick; Philadelphia, 1851 ***5704.8*** *p77*
Feeny, Patt 21; St. John, N.B., 1854 ***5704.8*** *p115*
Feeny, Rose Ann 26; Philadelphia, 1854 ***5704.8*** *p123*
Feeny, William; Montreal, 1824 ***7603*** *p96*
Feepound, Joseph 18; Jamaica, 1737 ***3690.1*** *p77*
Feer, Anna Dorothea *SEE* Feer, Johannes
Feer, Catharina Dorothea *SEE* Feer, Johannes
Feer, Jacob Cunrad *SEE* Feer, Johannes
Feer, Johannes; Pennsylvania, 1751 ***2444*** *p155*
*Wife:*Anna Dorothea
*Child:*Jacob Cunrad
*Child:*Catharina Dorothea
Feeterer, Carl; Illinois, 1888 ***5012.39*** *p121*
Feeton, Nicho.; Virginia, 1648 ***6219*** *p250*
Fegan, Arthur; New York, NY, 1836 ***8208.4*** *p22*
Fegan, Francis; America, 1742 ***4971*** *p65*
Fegan, Francis; New York, NY, 1836 ***8208.4*** *p24*
Fegan, Hugh; Colorado, 1904 ***9678.2*** *p18*
Fegan, Manus; America, 1741 ***4971*** *p65*
Fegan, Marcus N.; Colorado, 1887 ***9678.2*** *p18*
Fegan, Nich.; New York, NY, 1815 ***2859.11*** *p30*
With wife
Fegan, Richd; New York, NY, 1816 ***2859.11*** *p30*
Fegan, Terence; America, 1741 ***4971*** *p65*
Feghorn, Friederich; Cincinnati, 1788-1876 ***8582.3*** *p81*
Fehan, Margaret; Quebec, 1852 ***5704.8*** *p97*
Fehan, Robert; Quebec, 1852 ***5704.8*** *p97*
Fehl, Andreas; America, 1749 ***2444*** *p154*
Fehl, Andreas; Pennsylvania, 1749 ***2444*** *p154*
Fehlandt, Carl; Wisconsin, n.d. ***9675.5*** *p122*
Fehlhaber, Emilia Carolina Margaretha; America, 1881 ***4610.10*** *p110*
Fehling, Cord 23; Kansas, 1894 ***5240.1*** *p12*
Fehling, Cord 23; Kansas, 1894 ***5240.1*** *p79*
Fehling, Frederick William; America, 1845 ***1450.2*** *p40A*
Fehr, . . .; Milwaukee, 1875 ***4719.30*** *p258*
Fehr, Anna; Quebec, 1875 ***9980.20*** *p49*
Fehr, Anna; Quebec, 1876 ***9980.20*** *p49*
Fehr, Frank 35; Kansas, 1890 ***5240.1*** *p74*
Fehr, Helena; Quebec, 1875 ***9980.20*** *p48*
Fehr, Johannes; Pennsylvania, 1753 ***2444*** *p155*
Fehrabarker, Heironamous; Indiana, 1848 ***9117*** *p19*
Fehre, Anna Niessen; Quebec, 1876 ***9980.20*** *p48*
Fehre, Cathariena; Quebec, 1876 ***9980.20*** *p48*
Fehre, Johann; Quebec, 1876 ***9980.20*** *p48*
Fehre, Maria; Quebec, 1876 ***9980.20*** *p48*
Fehren, Ferdinand L. 13; New Orleans, 1850 ***2896.5*** *p12*
Fehrenback, Flavian 40; Kansas, 1883 ***5240.1*** *p64*
Fehring, Christoph Hermann Heinrich; America, 1880 ***4610.10*** *p140*
Fehse, Frederick; America, 1848 ***1450.2*** *p40A*
Feichel, Friedrich Wilhelm; Quebec, 1776 ***9786*** *p260*
Feichtel, Charles; America, 1853 ***1450.2*** *p40A*
Feichtt, Peter; Colorado, 1904 ***9678.2*** *p18*
Feick, Valentin; Cincinnati, 1869-1887 ***8582*** *p8*
Feidler, George; Wisconsin, n.d. ***9675.5*** *p122*
Feie, Gerhard B.; America, 1841 ***8582.1*** *p9*
Feiertag, Georg; America, 1848 ***8582.1*** *p9*
Feiertag, Georg; New York, NY, 1848 ***8582.2*** *p10*
Feight, George; Philadelphia, 1762-1776 ***2444*** *p227*
Feil, Peter H.; New York, 1828 ***8208.4*** *p28*
Feild, Ann; Virginia, 1643 ***6219*** *p202*
Feild, Charles; Virginia, 1642 ***6219*** *p199*
Feild, Christopher; Virginia, 1638 ***6219*** *p147*
Feild, Daniel; Virginia, 1637 ***6219*** *p84*
Feild, Danll.; Virginia, 1648 ***6219*** *p251*
Feild, James; Virginia, 1642 ***6219*** *p196*
Feild, Jon.; Virginia, 1635 ***6219*** *p72*
Feild, Richard; Virginia, 1638 ***6219*** *p147*
Feild, Tho.; Virginia, 1637 ***6219*** *p13*
Feild, Tho.; Virginia, 1643 ***6219*** *p202*
Feiler, Gottfried; Pennsylvania, 1753 ***2444*** *p153*
*Wife:*Regina Fahs
With 5 children
Feiler, Regina Fahs *SEE* Feiler, Gottfried
Feilt, Antone 14; America, 1836 ***778.5*** *p204*
Feilt, Cherese 10; America, 1836 ***778.5*** *p204*
Feilt, George 38; America, 1836 ***778.5*** *p204*
Feilt, Guertrult 40; America, 1836 ***778.5*** *p204*
Feilt, Joseph 16; America, 1836 ***778.5*** *p204*
Feilt, Michael 12; America, 1836 ***778.5*** *p204*
Fein, Louis; Ohio, 1869-1887 ***8582*** *p8*
Feine, Andreas Wilhelm Carl; America, 1850 ***8582.2*** *p10*
Feinere, Jacques; Halifax, N.S., 1752 ***7074.6*** *p217*
Feino, Henry 25; New Orleans, 1862 ***543.30*** *p28*
Feinon, Jacques; Halifax, N.S., 1752 ***7074.6*** *p217*
Feinstein, Frank Louis; Arkansas, 1918 ***95.2*** *p42*
Feinthal, Friederich Jakob; America, 1849 ***8582.3*** *p18*
Feiny, Neal; Philadelphia, 1852 ***5704.8*** *p89*
Feireizen, Jacob; Wisconsin, n.d. ***9675.5*** *p122*
Feisser, Jonathan; Philadelphia, 1761 ***9973.7*** *p36*
Feissler, Martha; Pennsylvania, 1749 ***2444*** *p175*
Feissler, Martha; Port uncertain, 1749 ***2444*** *p175*
Feist, Carl Frederick; Washington, 1859-1920 ***2872.1*** *p12*
Feist, Henry; Washington, 1859-1920 ***2872.1*** *p12*
Feist, Leonhard; Alberta, n.d. ***5262*** *p58*
Feist, William; America, 1887 ***1450.2*** *p8B*
Feistel, August; Wisconsin, n.d. ***9675.5*** *p122*
Feit, John; Wisconsin, n.d. ***9675.5*** *p122*
Feit, Mich'l; Pennsylvania, 1751 ***2444*** *p227*
Feitel, Kalman; New York, 1891 ***1450.2*** *p40A*
Feith, . . .; Canada, 1776-1783 ***9786*** *p20*
Feith, Andreas; Pennsylvania, 1753 ***4525*** *p253*
Feketik, Andro; Iowa, 1866-1943 ***123.54*** *p18*
Feketik, Guro; Iowa, 1866-1943 ***123.54*** *p18*
Felber, Catharina; Pennsylvania, 1751-1800 ***2444*** *p153*
*Child:*Johann Jacob
Felber, Johann Jacob *SEE* Felber, Catharina
Felberg, August; Washington, 1859-1920 ***2872.1*** *p12*
Felberg, Gustaf; Washington, 1859-1920 ***2872.1*** *p12*
Felberg, Wilhelm; Washington, 1859-1920 ***2872.1*** *p12*
Feldberg, August; Washington, 1859-1920 ***2872.1*** *p12*
Feldberg, Gustaf; Washington, 1859-1920 ***2872.1*** *p12*
Feldberg, Wilhelm; Washington, 1859-1920 ***2872.1*** *p12*
Feldbinder, John; Illinois, 1890 ***5012.40*** *p25*
Felder, Fred; South Carolina, 1788 ***7119*** *p198*
Felder, Friederick; Wisconsin, n.d. ***9675.5*** *p122*
Felder, H.; South Carolina, 1788 ***7119*** *p197*
Feldhaus, Hermann; Kentucky, 1840 ***8582.3*** *p100*
Feldhausen, Christopher; New York, 1750 ***3652*** *p75*
Feldhausen, Henry; New York, 1750 ***3652*** *p74*
Feldhausen, J. Christopher; New York, 1750 ***3652*** *p74*
Feldkamp, Franz; America, 1845 ***8582.3*** *p18*
Feldkamp, J. B. H.; Cincinnati, 1869-1887 ***8582*** *p8*
Feldkamp, Joseph; America, 1854 ***8582.3*** *p18*
Feldman, Frank; Arkansas, 1918 ***95.2*** *p42*
Feldmann, . . .; Ohio, 1832 ***8582.2*** *p49*
With family
Feldmann, Breinrel 6; New York, NY, 1878 ***9253*** *p47*
Feldmann, Hermann; America, 1849 ***1450.2*** *p40A*
Feldmann, Isaack 38; New York, NY, 1878 ***9253*** *p47*
Feldmann, Israel 28; New York, NY, 1878 ***9253*** *p45*
Feldmann, John W.; America, 1846 ***8582.1*** *p9*
Feldmann, William; Wisconsin, n.d. ***9675.5*** *p122*
Feldpush, John; America, 1854 ***1450.2*** *p40A*
Feldsch, . . .; Quebec, 1776 ***9786*** *p105*
Feldscher, Ernst Friedrich Wilhelm; America, 1839 ***4610.10*** *p154*
With wife
*Son:*Friedrich August
Feldscher, Friedrich August *SEE* Feldscher, Ernst Friedrich Wilhelm
Feldstein, Jacob 23; New York, NY, 1878 ***9253*** *p47*
Feldz, Carl; America, 1881 ***1450.2*** *p40A*
Felezak, Stanley; Arkansas, 1918 ***95.2*** *p43*
Felgate, Erasmus *SEE* Felgate, Robert
Felgate, Erasmus; Virginia, 1637 ***6219*** *p9*
Felgate, Judith *SEE* Felgate, Robert
Felgate, Margarett *SEE* Felgate, Robert
Felgate, Robert; Virginia, 1628 ***6219*** *p9*
With son
Felgate, Robert; Virginia, 1639 ***6219*** *p181*
*Wife:*Margarett
*Son:*Erasmus
*Daughter:*Judith
Felgate, Toby; Virginia, 1632 ***6219*** *p9*

Felgher, August; Wisconsin, n.d. ***9675.5*** *p122*
Felico, Mathew; Arkansas, 1918 ***95.2*** *p43*
Felieux, Remon 43; Mexico, 1822 ***778.5*** *p204*
Felinski, . . .; New York, 1831 ***4606*** *p173*
Felis, Narvarre; California, 1867 ***2769.4*** *p4*
Felix, Franz; Cincinnati, 1869-1887 ***8582*** *p8*
Felix, Paul 19; New Orleans, 1822 ***778.5*** *p204*
Felix, Peter; America, 1846 ***8582.3*** *p18*
Felke, Christian; Wisconsin, n.d. ***9675.5*** *p122*
Fell, James 34; Philadelphia, 1774 ***1219.7*** *p200*
Fell, James 45; Ohio, 1897 ***1450.2*** *p40A*
Fell, John; Arkansas, 1918 ***95.2*** *p43*
Fell, John D.; Illinois, 1869 ***5012.38*** *p99*
Fell, Phillip; Barbados, 1752 ***1219.7*** *p15*
Fell, William 32; New Orleans, 1862 ***543.30*** *p28*
Fellberg, Rachel 9; New York, NY, 1878 ***9253*** *p46*
Fellberg, Sara 8; New York, NY, 1878 ***9253*** *p46*
Fellenger, Joseph; America, 1833 ***1450.2*** *p41A*
Fellenger, Peter; America, 1833 ***1450.2*** *p41A*
Fellenzer, Jacob; America, 1839 ***1450.2*** *p41A*
Fellenzer, Joseph; America, 1839 ***1450.2*** *p41A*
Feller, Herman; Illinois, 1871 ***2896.5*** *p12*
Fellerson, Carl; Iowa, 1849-1860 ***2090*** *p613*
Fellery, John 26; America, 1836 ***778.5*** *p204*
Fellett, Thomas 22; Philadelphia, 1774 ***1219.7*** *p197*
Felley, John 17; Maryland, 1774 ***1219.7*** *p236*
Fellgate, James 24; Philadelphia, 1774 ***1219.7*** *p183*
Fellman, Wolf; Arkansas, 1918 ***95.2*** *p43*
Fellnagel, Julius; Ohio, 1832 ***8582.1*** *p46*
Fellows, Jonathan 31; Jamaica, 1736 ***3690.1*** *p77*
Fellows, Joseph 39; Maryland, 1775 ***1219.7*** *p265*
Fells, John; Virginia, 1638 ***6219*** *p121*
Fells, John; Virginia, 1645 ***6219*** *p232*
Fells, Jon.; Virginia, 1642 ***6219*** *p198*
Fellwock, Ernst; Illinois, 1868 ***2896.5*** *p12*
Fellwock, John F.; Illinois, 1866 ***2896.5*** *p12*
Fellwock, William E.; Illinois, 1867 ***2896.5*** *p12*
Felon, J. B. J. M. 28; Port uncertain, 1839 ***778.5*** *p204*
Felrery, Thomas 30; St. John, N.B., 1854 ***5704.8*** *p114*
Fels, Medard; Ohio, 1869-1887 ***8582*** *p8*
Felser, Georg; Georgia, 1734 ***9332*** *p328*
Felstead, Richard 26; Jamaica, 1731 ***3690.1*** *p77*
Felstead, William; Indiana, 1848 ***9117*** *p16*
Feltham, John; New York, NY, 1837 ***8208.4*** *p55*
Felthaus, Heinrich; Kentucky, 1840-1845 ***8582.3*** *p100*
Felthaus, Hermann Heinrich; Kentucky, 1843 ***8582.3*** *p100*
Feltmann, Hermann; America, 1849 ***1450.2*** *p40A*
Felton, John; Illinois, 1858 ***2896.5*** *p12*
Felton, John; Virginia, 1639 ***6219*** *p162*
Felton, John; Virginia, 1640 ***6219*** *p160*
Felton, John; Virginia, 1642 ***6219*** *p191*
Felton, Jon.; Virginia, 1637 ***6219*** *p116*
Felton, Thomas 21; Virginia, 1774 ***1219.7*** *p240*
Felz, . . .; Canada, 1776-1783 ***9786*** *p20*
Femlleras, John 21; New Orleans, 1862 ***543.30*** *p223B*
Femmeling, . . .; Canada, 1776-1783 ***9786*** *p20*
Fenay, John 20; St. John, N.B., 1854 ***5704.8*** *p115*
Fenby, Robert 26; Nova Scotia, 1774 ***1219.7*** *p195*
Fenchter, Christ; New York, 1882 ***1450.2*** *p8B*
Fender, Anton; Cincinnati, 1872-1874 ***8582.1*** *p9*
Fendlay, Napshall; New York, NY, 1811 ***2859.11*** *p11*
Fenel, Johann; Ohio, 1798 ***8582.2*** *p54*
Fenelly, Daniel 40; Massachusetts, 1849 ***5881.1*** *p36*
Fenelon, Mr.; New Orleans, 1839 ***778.5*** *p205*
Fenger, G. Heinrich; America, 1844 ***8582.3*** *p18*
Fenili, Agostino; Arkansas, 1918 ***95.2*** *p43*
Fenili, Domenico 41; New York, NY, 1893 ***9026.4*** *p41*
Fenley, Charles; Quebec, 1822 ***7603*** *p95*
Fenlison, Peter 20; Jamaica, 1723 ***3690.1*** *p77*
Fenlon, Bridget 22; Massachusetts, 1849 ***5881.1*** *p36*
Fenman, Nich.; Virginia, 1643 ***6219*** *p205*
Fenn, Henry 11; Massachusetts, 1848 ***5881.1*** *p37*
Fenn, Julia 7; Massachusetts, 1849 ***5881.1*** *p38*
Fenn, Mary *SEE* Fenn, Tymothy
Fenn, Mary 9; Massachusetts, 1849 ***5881.1*** *p39*
Fenn, Robert 19; Virginia, 1751 ***1219.7*** *p3*
Fenn, Robert 19; Virginia, 1751 ***3690.1*** *p77*
Fenn, Saml.; Virginia, 1637 ***6219*** *p109*
Fenn, Stephen 22; Georgia, 1774 ***1219.7*** *p188*
Fenn, Tymothy; Virginia, 1642 ***6219*** *p194*
*Daughter:*Mary
Fenn, William; Virginia, 1642 ***6219*** *p186*
Fennan, Nicho.; Virginia, 1648 ***6219*** *p246*
Fenne, Thomas 24; Virginia, 1700 ***2212*** *p32*
Fennelens, Elizabeth-Marie; Quebec, 1747 ***7603*** *p21*
Fennell, Nathaniel R. 51; Kansas, 1888 ***5240.1*** *p73*
Fennelly, Bridget 21; Massachusetts, 1850 ***5881.1*** *p36*
Fennely, Patrick; New York, NY, 1816 ***2859.11*** *p30*
Fenner, Ferdinand 25; America, 1838 ***778.5*** *p205*
Fenner, Georg Heinrich; Halifax, N.S., 1778 ***9786*** *p270*
Fenner, Georg Heinrich; New York, 1776 ***9786*** *p270*
Fenner, Hans Henrich; Philadelphia, 1779 ***8137*** *p8*
Fenner, Henrich; Philadelphia, 1779 ***8137*** *p8*
Fenner, Henry; New York, NY, 1836 ***8208.4*** *p23*
Fenner, Johannes; Lancaster, PA, 1780 ***8137*** *p8*
Fenner, Johannes; Philadelphia, 1779 ***8137*** *p8*
Fenner, Nikolaus; Reading, PA, 1780 ***8137*** *p8*
Fennimore, William 20; Maryland, 1725 ***3690.1*** *p77*
Fenning, James 21; Port uncertain, 1774 ***1219.7*** *p176*
Fenning, John; New York, NY, 1833 ***8208.4*** *p52*
Fenning, John 28; Maryland, 1774 ***1219.7*** *p196*
Fenny, Bridget; New York, NY, 1868 ***5704.8*** *p229*
Fenny, Catherine 22; Philadelphia, 1857 ***5704.8*** *p133*
Fenny, Sarah 21; Philadelphia, 1857 ***5704.8*** *p133*
Fenny, Thomas 24; Massachusetts, 1850 ***5881.1*** *p40*
Fenray, Peter 20; Massachusetts, 1849 ***5881.1*** *p40*
Fenton, Alexander 19; Antigua (Antego), 1738 ***3690.1*** *p77*
Fenton, Geo.; New York, NY, 1816 ***2859.11*** *p30*
Fenton, Henry; Virginia, 1638 ***6219*** *p17*
Fenton, John 21; New York, 1774 ***1219.7*** *p217*
Fenton, John 22; Massachusetts, 1847 ***5881.1*** *p37*
Fenton, Mary 9; Halifax, N.S., 1775 ***1219.7*** *p263*
Fenton, Richard; Savannah, GA, 1774 ***1219.7*** *p227*
With wife
With 2 children
Fenton, Richard 26; Savannah, GA, 1774 ***1219.7*** *p226*
With wife
With children
Fenton, Sarah 15; Halifax, N.S., 1775 ***1219.7*** *p263*
Fenton, Thomas 15; Philadelphia, 1774 ***1219.7*** *p233*
Fenton, William 23; Maryland, 1775 ***1219.7*** *p251*
Fentrice, Ro.; Virginia, 1645 ***6219*** *p232*
Fentrice, Robert; Virginia, 1642 ***6219*** *p198*
Fenwick, Edward 28; North America, 1774 ***1219.7*** *p199*
Fenwick, George; New York, NY, 1839 ***8208.4*** *p95*
Fenwick, Mary 18; Maryland, 1723 ***3690.1*** *p78*
Fenwick, Mathew 16; North America, 1774 ***1219.7*** *p200*
Feola, Givanni 16 *SEE* Feola, Michele
Feola, Michele 42; New York, NY, 1893 ***9026.4*** *p41*
*Relative:*Givanni 16
Feran, James 10; St. John, N.B., 1866 ***5704.8*** *p167*
Feran, John 1; St. John, N.B., 1866 ***5704.8*** *p167*
Ferand, Pierre 31; New Orleans, 1839 ***778.5*** *p205*
Ferary, Mr. 45; New Orleans, 1820 ***778.5*** *p205*
Feraud, Ms. 54; America, 1836 ***778.5*** *p205*
Feraud, Louis Franc. Aug. H. 32; America, 1822 ***778.5*** *p205*
Feraud, Pierre 31; New Orleans, 1839 ***778.5*** *p205*
Ferber, Peter; Wisconsin, n.d. ***9675.5*** *p122*
Ferbitz, . . .; Canada, 1776-1783 ***9786*** *p20*
Ferchere, Mr. 21; New Orleans, 1839 ***778.5*** *p205*
Fercy, Peter 25; Maryland, 1774 ***1219.7*** *p207*
Ferdig, Johan Christoffel; Pennsylvania, 1769 ***4525*** *p215*
Ferdig, Johan Christoffel; Pennsylvania, 1769 ***4525*** *p237*
Ferdinand, . . .; Canada, 1776-1783 ***9786*** *p20*
Ferdinand, Massillon Trosseven; America, 1869 ***2896.5*** *p12*
Ferdinandeg, Cerldo; Arkansas, 1918 ***95.2*** *p43*
Ferdinandsen, Charles C.; Illinois, 1899 ***5012.40*** *p76*
Ferdinandsen, Viggo; Illinois, 1905 ***5012.39*** *p53*
Ferdinandson, Charles C.; Illinois, 1896 ***5012.39*** *p53*
Ferepoint, Jon.; Virginia, 1637 ***6219*** *p83*
Fergue, Eliza; Philadelphia, 1816 ***2859.11*** *p30*
Fergue, James; Philadelphia, 1816 ***2859.11*** *p30*
Fergus, James; North Carolina, 1740 ***1639.20*** *p67*
Fergus, John; North Carolina, 1758-1802 ***1639.20*** *p67*
Ferguson, . . .; Philadelphia, 1811 ***2859.11*** *p11*
Ferguson, Agnes Maitland *SEE* Ferguson, Alexander
Ferguson, Alexander; Chicago, 1851 ***8893*** *p266*
*Wife:*Agnes Maitland
Ferguson, Ann 8; Quebec, 1854 ***5704.8*** *p121*
Ferguson, Bridget 22; St. John, N.B., 1864 ***5704.8*** *p158*
Ferguson, Catherine 5; Quebec, 1854 ***5704.8*** *p121*
Ferguson, Catherine 49 *SEE* Ferguson, Neill
Ferguson, Charles; New York, NY, 1815 ***2859.11*** *p30*
Ferguson, Charles 49; South Carolina, 1850 ***1639.20*** *p67*
Ferguson, Charlotta Svensson *SEE* Ferguson, Magnus
Ferguson, Charlotte 43; Massachusetts, 1860 ***6410.32*** *p110*
Ferguson, Daniel; South Carolina, 1826 ***1639.20*** *p67*
Ferguson, Daniel 55; North Carolina, 1850 ***1639.20*** *p67*
Ferguson, David; Philadelphia, 1850 ***53.26*** *p27*
Ferguson, David; Philadelphia, 1850 ***5704.8*** *p60*
Ferguson, Duncan; Carolina, 1684 ***1639.20*** *p68*
Ferguson, Duncan; North Carolina, 1793 ***1639.20*** *p68*
Ferguson, Edward; New York, NY, 1816 ***2859.11*** *p30*
Ferguson, Effie; Quebec, 1855 ***4537.30*** *p102*
Ferguson, Eleanor; New York, NY, 1816 ***2859.11*** *p30*
Ferguson, Eliza.; New York, NY, 1816 ***2859.11*** *p30*
Ferguson, Elizabeth 17; Jamaica, 1774 ***1219.7*** *p188*
Ferguson, Ellen 16; Philadelphia, 1845 ***6508.6*** *p115*
Ferguson, Ellen 21; Philadelphia, 1856 ***5704.8*** *p128*
Ferguson, Euphemier 16; Jamaica, 1774 ***1219.7*** *p188*
Ferguson, Finlay; South Carolina, 1716 ***1639.20*** *p68*
Ferguson, George 1; Philadelphia, 1854 ***5704.8*** *p121*
Ferguson, George 10; Quebec, 1854 ***5704.8*** *p121*
Ferguson, H. 20; Jamaica, 1773 ***1219.7*** *p168*
Ferguson, Hugh; New York, NY, 1811 ***2859.11*** *p11*
Ferguson, Hugh W.; South Carolina, 1822 ***1639.20*** *p68*
Ferguson, James; New York, NY, 1816 ***2859.11*** *p30*
Ferguson, James; New York, NY, 1867 ***5704.8*** *p224*
Ferguson, James; South Carolina, 1700 ***1639.20*** *p68*
Ferguson, James 11; Philadelphia, 1864 ***5704.8*** *p161*
Ferguson, James 11; Quebec, 1854 ***5704.8*** *p121*
Ferguson, James 16; St. John, N.B., 1863 ***5704.8*** *p153*
Ferguson, James 23; Philadelphia, 1856 ***5704.8*** *p128*
Ferguson, James C.; Washington, 1859-1920 ***2872.1*** *p12*
Ferguson, Jane Eliza 14; Philadelphia, 1864 ***5704.8*** *p161*
Ferguson, Jennie 10; Massachusetts, 1860 ***6410.32*** *p110*
Ferguson, Jenny *SEE* Ferguson, Magnus
Ferguson, John; Charleston, SC, 1813 ***1639.20*** *p68*
Ferguson, John; Illinois, 1872 ***7857*** *p3*
Ferguson, John; New York, NY, 1815 ***2859.11*** *p30*
Ferguson, John; New York, NY, 1816 ***2859.11*** *p30*
Ferguson, John; New York, NY, 1839 ***8208.4*** *p92*
Ferguson, John; North Carolina, 1793-1865 ***1639.20*** *p68*
Ferguson, John; North Carolina, 1821 ***1639.20*** *p68*
Ferguson, John; Philadelphia, 1850 ***5704.8*** *p64*
Ferguson, John; Plymouth, NC, 1826 ***1639.20*** *p68*
Ferguson, John 19; Wilmington, NC, 1774 ***1639.20*** *p68*
Ferguson, John 20; Philadelphia, 1856 ***5704.8*** *p128*
Ferguson, Magnus; Boston, 1851 ***6410.32*** *p124*
*Wife:*Charlotta Svensson
*Daughter:*Jenny
Ferguson, Margaret; Philadelphia, 1850 ***5704.8*** *p64*
Ferguson, Margaret 20; St. John, N.B., 1864 ***5704.8*** *p158*
Ferguson, Martha Jane 30; Philadelphia, 1861 ***5704.8*** *p147*
Ferguson, Mary; New York, NY, 1869 ***5704.8*** *p235*
Ferguson, Mary 18; Quebec, 1854 ***5704.8*** *p121*
Ferguson, Mary 22; Maryland, 1733 ***3690.1*** *p78*
Ferguson, Mary 46; Quebec, 1854 ***5704.8*** *p121*
Ferguson, Mary Ann; New York, NY, 1816 ***2859.11*** *p30*
Ferguson, Mary Jane 26; Quebec, 1856 ***5704.8*** *p129*
Ferguson, Mathew; New York, NY, 1815 ***2859.11*** *p30*
Ferguson, Mongus 41; Massachusetts, 1860 ***6410.32*** *p110*
Ferguson, Murdo; America, 1803 ***1639.20*** *p69*
Ferguson, Neill 49; North Carolina, 1850 ***1639.20*** *p69*
*Relative:*Catherine 49
Ferguson, Rebecca 36; Philadelphia, 1861 ***5704.8*** *p148*
Ferguson, Robert; Illinois, 1875 ***7857*** *p3*
Ferguson, Robert; North Carolina, 1700-1794 ***1639.20*** *p69*
Ferguson, Sally; New York, NY, 1816 ***2859.11*** *p30*
Ferguson, Sarah 13; Quebec, 1854 ***5704.8*** *p121*
Ferguson, Susannah; New York, NY, 1816 ***2859.11*** *p30*
Ferguson, Thomas 7; Quebec, 1854 ***5704.8*** *p121*
Ferguson, W. 24; Philadelphia, 1857 ***5704.8*** *p134*
Ferguson, Walter; North Carolina, 1763-1789 ***1639.20*** *p69*
Ferguson, William; New York, NY, 1816 ***2859.11*** *p30*
With wife
Ferguson, William; Philadelphia, 1847 ***53.26*** *p27*
Ferguson, William; Philadelphia, 1847 ***5704.8*** *p22*
Ferguson, William; Philadelphia, 1853 ***5704.8*** *p101*
Ferguson, William 14; Philadelphia, 1854 ***5704.8*** *p121*
Ferguson, William 24; St. John, N.B., 1866 ***5704.8*** *p166*
Fergusson, John; America, 1736 ***4971*** *p12*
Ferhs, Mr. 22; New Orleans, 1837 ***778.5*** *p205*
Fermer, Rich.; Virginia, 1637 ***6219*** *p84*
Fernais, Mrs. 28; New Orleans, 1829 ***778.5*** *p205*
Fernan, John 22; St. John, N.B., 1857 ***5704.8*** *p134*
Fernandez, Mr. 24; New Orleans, 1839 ***778.5*** *p205*
Fernandez, Manuel; New York, NY, 1836 ***8208.4*** *p13*
Fernandos, Guadalupe 29; Arizona, 1917 ***9228.40*** *p21*
Fernauer, Johann; Ohio, 1798-1818 ***8582.2*** *p54*
Fernder, Christine 60; New York, NY, 1857 ***9831.14*** *p153*
Fernder, Fried. 23; New York, NY, 1857 ***9831.14*** *p153*
Fernder, Gottlieb 68; New York, NY, 1857 ***9831.14*** *p153*
Ferndon, John 22; Maryland, 1775 ***1219.7*** *p250*
Ferne, Auguste 19; New Orleans, 1835 ***778.5*** *p205*
Ferneding Family ; America, 1830-1849 ***8582.1*** *p22*
Ferneding, Joseph; America, 1830-1849 ***8582.1*** *p9*
Ferneding, Joseph; Baltimore, 1832 ***8582*** *p8*
Ferney, Ann; Philadelphia, 1852 ***5704.8*** *p91*
Ferney, Elizabeth; Philadelphia, 1852 ***5704.8*** *p91*
Ferney, James 6; Philadelphia, 1852 ***5704.8*** *p91*
Ferney, John 8; Philadelphia, 1852 ***5704.8*** *p91*
Ferney, Nancy 10; Philadelphia, 1852 ***5704.8*** *p91*
Ferney, Sarah; Philadelphia, 1852 ***5704.8*** *p91*
Ferney, Thomas 12; Philadelphia, 1852 ***5704.8*** *p91*
Fernhaber, Jacob Nicolaus; Pennsylvania, 1773 ***4525*** *p216*

Fernhaber, Johan Christoph; Pennsylvania, 1753 ***4525*** *p216*
Fernhaber, Johann; Pennsylvania, 1773 ***4525*** *p216*
Fernier, Mr. 25; America, 1829 ***778.5*** *p205*
Ferns, Henry; Montreal, 1821 ***7603*** *p101*
Fernsly, James; America, 1739 ***4971*** *p14*
Fernstermaker, Christian; Philadelphia, 1759 ***9973.7*** *p33*
Ferran, Alice 18; Massachusetts, 1850 ***5881.1*** *p35*
Ferran, Daniel 20; Massachusetts, 1850 ***5881.1*** *p36*
Ferran, Mary 22; Massachusetts, 1850 ***5881.1*** *p39*
Ferrand, Mr. 45; Port uncertain, 1825 ***778.5*** *p205*
Ferrand, F. 30; New Orleans, 1823 ***778.5*** *p205*
Ferrand, Jean Dominique 18; Port uncertain, 1838 ***778.5*** *p206*
Ferrand, Marie 18; New Orleans, 1836 ***778.5*** *p206*
Ferrand, Pierre 32; Port uncertain, 1838 ***778.5*** *p206*
Ferrant, Dominique 31; America, 1837 ***778.5*** *p206*
Ferrante, Aldina 16 *SEE* Ferrante, Cesare
Ferrante, Cesare 23; New York, NY, 1893 ***9026.4*** *p41*
*Relative:*Pia 18
*Relative:*Aldina 16
Ferrante, Pia 18 *SEE* Ferrante, Cesare
Ferrante, Thomas Antonio; Arkansas, 1918 ***95.2*** *p43*
Ferrario, Tony; Arkansas, 1918 ***95.2*** *p43*
Ferrau, Mr. 31; America, 1838 ***778.5*** *p206*
Ferraud, F. 30; New Orleans, 1823 ***778.5*** *p205*
Ferreby, Tho.; Virginia, 1635 ***6219*** *p17*
Ferrell, Bryan; America, 1737 ***4971*** *p13*
Ferrell, Frank; Illinois, 1861 ***2896.5*** *p12*
Ferrell, John; America, 1741 ***4971*** *p10*
Ferrer, George 19; Maryland, 1774 ***1219.7*** *p181*
Ferres, William 24; Massachusetts, 1849 ***5881.1*** *p41*
Ferret, Mrs. 24; New Orleans, 1837 ***778.5*** *p206*
Ferret, Francois 24; New Orleans, 1837 ***778.5*** *p206*
Ferri, Frank; Washington, 1859-1920 ***2872.1*** *p12*
Ferrier, Mr.; Port uncertain, 1839 ***778.5*** *p206*
Ferrier, James 24; Philadelphia, 1803 ***53.26*** *p27*
Ferries, . . .; Canada, 1776-1783 ***9786*** *p20*
Ferriman, William; Salem, MA, 1766 ***1219.7*** *p117*
Ferriot, Mr. 22; New Orleans, 1829 ***778.5*** *p206*
Ferris, Ann; Quebec, 1847 ***5704.8*** *p27*
Ferris, Ann 32 *SEE* Ferris, William
Ferris, Ann Jane 22; Philadelphia, 1860 ***5704.8*** *p146*
Ferris, Anne; Quebec, 1847 ***5704.8*** *p17*
Ferris, Bernard 26; St. John, N.B., 1861 ***5704.8*** *p146*
Ferris, Bridget 20; Massachusetts, 1849 ***5881.1*** *p36*
Ferris, Catherine 20; St. John, N.B., 1859 ***5704.8*** *p140*
Ferris, Charles; New York, NY, 1811 ***2859.11*** *p11*
Ferris, Daniel; Philadelphia, 1849 ***53.26*** *p27*
Ferris, Daniel; Philadelphia, 1849 ***5704.8*** *p53*
Ferris, David; New York, NY, 1816 ***2859.11*** *p30*
Ferris, Eliza 17; Philadelphia, 1864 ***5704.8*** *p160*
Ferris, Henry 13; Quebec, 1847 ***5704.8*** *p27*
Ferris, Isabella 17; Philadelphia, 1854 ***5704.8*** *p117*
Ferris, James; New York, NY, 1811 ***2859.11*** *p11*
Ferris, James; New York, NY, 1816 ***2859.11*** *p30*
Ferris, James 9; Quebec, 1847 ***5704.8*** *p17*
Ferris, James 25; Quebec, 1864 ***5704.8*** *p160*
Ferris, Jane 4; Quebec, 1847 ***5704.8*** *p17*
Ferris, John; Quebec, 1847 ***5704.8*** *p17*
Ferris, John 16; St. John, N.B., 1858 ***5704.8*** *p137*
Ferris, John 20; St. John, N.B., 1863 ***5704.8*** *p154*
Ferris, Joseph; Quebec, 1847 ***5704.8*** *p27*
Ferris, Margaret; New York, NY, 1811 ***2859.11*** *p11*
With family
Ferris, Margaret; Quebec, 1847 ***5704.8*** *p27*
Ferris, Margaret 6 mos; Quebec, 1847 ***5704.8*** *p17*
Ferris, Margaret Ann 26; St. John, N.B., 1864 ***5704.8*** *p159*
Ferris, Martha 8; Quebec, 1847 ***5704.8*** *p27*
Ferris, Mary 22; St. John, N.B., 1858 ***5704.8*** *p137*
Ferris, Nancy 18; St. John, N.B., 1859 ***5704.8*** *p140*
Ferris, Owen; America, 1741 ***4971*** *p56*
Ferris, Owen; Philadelphia, 1850 ***5704.8*** *p64*
Ferris, Patrick; Philadelphia, 1852 ***5704.8*** *p88*
Ferris, Rich.; Virginia, 1636 ***6219*** *p75*
Ferris, Robert 23; Philadelphia, 1854 ***5704.8*** *p117*
Ferris, Sarah 6; Quebec, 1847 ***5704.8*** *p27*
Ferris, Unity 22; Philadelphia, 1860 ***5704.8*** *p146*
Ferris, William 7; Quebec, 1847 ***5704.8*** *p17*
Ferris, William 25; Philadelphia, 1804 ***53.26*** *p27*
*Relative:*Ann 32
Ferris, William John 20; St. John, N.B., 1857 ***5704.8*** *p135*
Ferriter, Thomas; America, 1848 ***1450.2*** *p41A*
Ferry, Alexandre C. 26; Port uncertain, 1838 ***778.5*** *p206*
Ferry, Ann 9 mos; St. John, N.B., 1847 ***5704.8*** *p34*
Ferry, Biddy 18; Philadelphia, 1861 ***5704.8*** *p148*
Ferry, Bridget; Philadelphia, 1868 ***5704.8*** *p231*
Ferry, Bridget 4; New York, NY, 1870 ***5704.8*** *p237*
Ferry, Catharine; New York, NY, 1866 ***5704.8*** *p214*
Ferry, Catharine; Philadelphia, 1850 ***5704.8*** *p60*
Ferry, Catherine *SEE* Ferry, John
Ferry, Catherine; Philadelphia, 1847 ***53.26*** *p27*
Ferry, Catherine; Philadelphia, 1847 ***5704.8*** *p32*
Ferry, Catherine; St. John, N.B., 1847 ***5704.8*** *p34*
Ferry, Catherine 4; St. John, N.B., 1847 ***5704.8*** *p34*
Ferry, Catherine 18; Philadelphia, 1857 ***5704.8*** *p133*
Ferry, Charles 20; Philadelphia, 1864 ***5704.8*** *p155*
Ferry, Domnick; Philadelphia, 1868 ***5704.8*** *p231*
Ferry, Edward; New York, NY, 1866 ***5704.8*** *p210*
Ferry, Edward; Philadelphia, 1864 ***5704.8*** *p182*
Ferry, Eliza 12; St. John, N.B., 1847 ***5704.8*** *p34*
Ferry, Ellen; Philadelphia, 1864 ***5704.8*** *p182*
Ferry, Ellen; Philadelphia, 1864 ***5704.8*** *p188*
Ferry, Ellen 34; Philadelphia, 1853 ***5704.8*** *p111*
Ferry, Hannah; New York, NY, 1866 ***5704.8*** *p210*
Ferry, Hannah 11; Philadelphia, 1864 ***5704.8*** *p182*
Ferry, Hannah 18; Philadelphia, 1855 ***5704.8*** *p123*
Ferry, Hannah 20; St. John, N.B., 1866 ***5704.8*** *p166*
Ferry, Hugh 11; New York, NY, 1870 ***5704.8*** *p237*
Ferry, James; America, 1865 ***5704.8*** *p196*
Ferry, James 19; Virginia, 1774 ***1219.7*** *p227*
Ferry, James 20; Philadelphia, 1854 ***5704.8*** *p118*
Ferry, James 20; Philadelphia, 1859 ***5704.8*** *p142*
Ferry, Jean 32; America, 1836 ***778.5*** *p206*
Ferry, John; Philadelphia, 1847 ***53.26*** *p27*
Ferry, John; Philadelphia, 1847 ***5704.8*** *p22*
Ferry, John; Philadelphia, 1850 ***53.26*** *p27*
*Relative:*Catherine
Ferry, John; Philadelphia, 1850 ***5704.8*** *p60*
Ferry, John; Quebec, 1847 ***5704.8*** *p29*
Ferry, John 10; St. John, N.B., 1847 ***5704.8*** *p34*
Ferry, Joseph 17; Virginia, 1774 ***1219.7*** *p227*
Ferry, Joseph D. 20; Louisiana, 1820 ***778.5*** *p206*
Ferry, Magy; Quebec, 1847 ***5704.8*** *p29*
Ferry, Margaret; New York, NY, 1867 ***5704.8*** *p224*
Ferry, Margaret S.; St. John, N.B., 1847 ***5704.8*** *p24*
Ferry, Mary; Philadelphia, 1866 ***5704.8*** *p214*
Ferry, Mary 5; Philadelphia, 1866 ***5704.8*** *p214*
Ferry, Mary 8; St. John, N.B., 1847 ***5704.8*** *p34*
Ferry, Maurice; New York, NY, 1811 ***2859.11*** *p11*
Ferry, Michael; Philadelphia, 1867 ***5704.8*** *p221*
Ferry, Michael 2; New York, NY, 1870 ***5704.8*** *p237*
Ferry, Nancy; New York, NY, 1870 ***5704.8*** *p237*
Ferry, Owen 25; Philadelphia, 1864 ***5704.8*** *p155*
Ferry, Paddy; Philadelphia, 1852 ***5704.8*** *p85*
Ferry, Patrick; New York, NY, 1865 ***5704.8*** *p193*
Ferry, Patrick; Philadelphia, 1853 ***5704.8*** *p103*
Ferry, Patrick 6; New York, NY, 1870 ***5704.8*** *p237*
Ferry, Peter; Philadelphia, 1864 ***5704.8*** *p188*
Ferry, Phillip 8; New York, NY, 1870 ***5704.8*** *p237*
Ferry, Robert 44; Virginia, 1774 ***1219.7*** *p227*
Ferry, Rose; Philadelphia, 1867 ***5704.8*** *p219*
Ferry, Rose 9; Philadelphia, 1866 ***5704.8*** *p214*
Ferry, Rose 20; Philadelphia, 1864 ***5704.8*** *p161*
Ferry, Sally 20; Philadelphia, 1856 ***5704.8*** *p128*
Ferry, Susan 20; Philadelphia, 1853 ***5704.8*** *p109*
Ferry, Unity; Philadelphia, 1853 ***5704.8*** *p112*
Ferry, Wener von; Halifax, N.S., 1780 ***9786*** *p269*
Ferry, Wener von; New York, 1776 ***9786*** *p269*
Ferry, William; Philadelphia, 1847 ***53.26*** *p27*
Ferry, William; Philadelphia, 1847 ***5704.8*** *p5*
Ferson, Paul 40; St. John, N.B., 1862 ***5704.8*** *p150*
Ferson, Susanna 15; St. John, N.B., 1862 ***5704.8*** *p150*
Ferson, William 24; Philadelphia, 1833-1834 ***53.26*** *p27*
Fertal, Mr. 25; America, 1838 ***778.5*** *p206*
Ferthyn, Anton 4; America, 1839 ***778.5*** *p206*
Ferthyn, Dorathea 25; America, 1839 ***778.5*** *p207*
Ferthyn, Valentine 32; America, 1839 ***778.5*** *p207*
Fertig, Andreas; America, 1749 ***4525*** *p214*
Fertig, Andreas; Pennsylvania, 1754 ***4525*** *p214*
Fertig, Andreas; Pennsylvania, 1762 ***4525*** *p274*
Fertig, Conrad; America, 1833 ***1450.2*** *p41A*
Fertig, Francis; America, 1849 ***1450.2*** *p41A*
Fertig, Hans; America, 1754 ***4525*** *p215*
Fertig, Hans; New England, 1752 ***4525*** *p215*
With wife
Fertig, Hans; Pennsylvania, 1752 ***4525*** *p215*
Fertig, Johann Adam; Pennsylvania, 1754 ***4525*** *p215*
Fertig, Johann Christoph; Pennsylvania, 1769 ***4525*** *p215*
Fertig, Johannas; Pennsylvania, 1782 ***4525*** *p273*
Fertig, Matthaeus; Pennsylvania, 1754 ***4525*** *p215*
Fertig, Michael; Pennsylvania, 1764 ***4525*** *p215*
Fertig, Michel; Philadelphia Co., PA, 1782 ***4525*** *p273*
Fertig, Regina; Pennsylvania, 1755-1784 ***4525*** *p216*
Fervent, Peter; San Francisco, 1870 ***2764.35*** *p24*
Fervie, Widow 50; New Orleans, 1831 ***778.5*** *p207*
Ferynes, Wm.; Virginia, 1643 ***6219*** *p204*
Fesenbeck, . . .; America, 1836 ***8582.1*** *p39*
Feshel, James 30; America, 1701 ***2212*** *p35*
Fesler, Jacob; Pennsylvania, 1752 ***2444*** *p154*
Fesnacht, John; Canada, 1776-1783 ***9786*** *p207A*
Fessel, Dr. 40; New Orleans, 1823 ***778.5*** *p207*
Fessner, . . .; Canada, 1776-1783 ***9786*** *p21*
Feste, John Gerhard 40; New Orleans, 1862 ***543.30*** *p228B*
Fester, A. 28; Port uncertain, 1839 ***778.5*** *p207*
Fester, Frank; Iowa, 1866-1943 ***123.54*** *p18*
Fetherston, Ellen; Virginia, 1642 ***6219*** *p189*
Fetherston, Thomas 26; Jamaica, 1733 ***3690.1*** *p78*
Fetis, Mr. 26; Port uncertain, 1820 ***778.5*** *p207*
Fette, George; America, 1853 ***1450.2*** *p41A*
Fetter, . . .; Canada, 1776-1783 ***9786*** *p21*
Fetter, Ellis 29; New York, 1774 ***1219.7*** *p218*
Fetter, Jean; Canada, 1776-1783 ***9786*** *p207A*
Fetter, John 31; New York, 1774 ***1219.7*** *p217*
Fetter, Louis 30; America, 1838 ***778.5*** *p207*
Fetter, Marie Marguerite 21; America, 1838 ***778.5*** *p207*
Fettig, Franz; Alberta, n.d. ***5262*** *p58*
Fettke, Charles 21; Kansas, 1879 ***5240.1*** *p60*
Fettweis, C.L.; Cincinnati, 1848 ***8582.2*** *p63*
Fettweis, C.L.; Cincinnati, 1869-1885 ***8582.2*** *p52*
Fettweiss, Carl Leopold; America, 1847 ***8582.1*** *p9*
Feuer, George; Wisconsin, n.d. ***9675.5*** *p122*
Feulade, Mr. 34; America, 1837 ***778.5*** *p207*
Feull, James 24; Philadelphia, 1774 ***1219.7*** *p232*
Feumelan, Edmond 13; New Orleans, 1838 ***778.5*** *p207*
Feumelan, V..ve 30; New Orleans, 1838 ***778.5*** *p207*
Feury, William; Illinois, 1857 ***7857*** *p3*
Feusier, Henry; New York, NY, 1836 ***8208.4*** *p22*
Feuss, Wilhelm David; America, 1848 ***8582.3*** *p18*
Fever, James; America, 1742 ***4971*** *p34*
Fevete, J.P. 22; Maryland, 1775 ***1219.7*** *p250*
Fevre, Catherine *SEE* Fevre, Pierre
Fevre, Jacques *SEE* Fevre, Pierre
Fevre, Jacques *SEE* Fevre, Pierre
Fevre, Jean-Pierre 17; Halifax, N.S., 1752 ***7074.6*** *p210*
Fevre, Pierre 26; Halifax, N.S., 1752 ***7074.6*** *p210*
*Wife:*Catherine
*Son:*Jacques
*Brother:*Jacques
Fevry, Hugh; New York, NY, 1815 ***2859.11*** *p30*
Fewkes, Joseph; New York, NY, 1832 ***8208.4*** *p37*
Fewson, Edw.; Virginia, 1637 ***6219*** *p11*
Fey, Conrad 65; America, 1895 ***1763*** *p40D*
Fey, Jane 22; St. John, N.B., 1855 ***5704.8*** *p126*
Fey, Susanne Philippina; New York, 1858 ***3702.7*** *p352*
Feyen, Joseph 26; Kansas, 1888 ***5240.1*** *p72*
Feyer, Lewis; Ohio, 1840 ***9892.11*** *p15*
Feyet, Francois 28; New Orleans, 1836 ***778.5*** *p207*
Fezde, Jaleor 35; Harris Co., TX, 1899 ***6254*** *p6*
Ffitzwater, George *SEE* Ffitzwater, Thomas
Ffitzwater, Josiah *SEE* Ffitzwater, Mary Cheney
Ffitzwater, Mary *SEE* Ffitzwater, Mary Cheney
Ffitzwater, Mary Cheney; Died enroute, 1682 ***4961*** *p167*
*Child:*Josiah
*Child:*Mary
Ffitzwater, Thomas *SEE* Ffitzwater, Thomas
Ffitzwater, Thomas; Pennsylvania, 1682 ***4961*** *p167*
*Child:*Thomas
*Child:*George
Fflurgel, Melchoir; South Carolina, 1788 ***7119*** *p198*
Ffunk, Hans; Pennsylvania, 1709 ***3627*** *p17*
Fiala, Vaclav; Arkansas, 1918 ***95.2*** *p43*
Fiber, Heinrich; Kentucky, 1843 ***8582.3*** *p100*
Fibolet, Albrecht; Ohio, 1868 ***6014.2*** *p7*
Fichte, Catherine; New York, 1749 ***3652*** *p72*
Fichte, Jacob 18; New Orleans, 1862 ***543.30*** *p28*
Fichtel, Charles; America, 1853 ***1450.2*** *p40A*
Fichter, Jacob; Died enroute, 1738 ***9898*** *p44*
*Relative:*Maria
Fichter, Jacob 18; New Orleans, 1862 ***543.30*** *p28*
Fichter, Margaretha; Pennsylvania, 1754 ***2444*** *p175*
Fichter, Maria *SEE* Fichter, Jacob
Fick, Friedrich; Cincinnati, 1869-1887 ***8582*** *p9*
Fick, Friedrick; Wisconsin, n.d. ***9675.5*** *p122*
Fickbohm, Johann William; New York, NY, 1923 ***3455.4*** *p80*
Ficke, Hermann; Cincinnati, 1869-1887 ***8582*** *p9*
Ficken, Jakob; Kentucky, 1844 ***8582.3*** *p100*
Ficklen, Ernestine 3; New Orleans, 1839 ***9420.2*** *p70*
Ficklen, Gottlob 30; New Orleans, 1839 ***9420.2*** *p70*
Ficklen, Justine 28; New Orleans, 1839 ***9420.2*** *p70*
Ficks, . . .; Ohio, 1881 ***3702.7*** *p429*
Ficollier, Peter 30; New Orleans, 1836 ***778.5*** *p518*
Fiddelke, John Henry 68; Kansas, 1903 ***5240.1*** *p12*
Fiddelke, John Henry 68; Kansas, 1903 ***5240.1*** *p82*
Fidderling, Voith; Pennsylvania, 1752 ***4525*** *p217*
Fiddis, Jane; Quebec, 1850 ***5704.8*** *p63*
Fiddis, Sarah; Quebec, 1850 ***5704.8*** *p63*
Fiddis, William; Quebec, 1850 ***5704.8*** *p63*
Fiddler, Melchior; Pennsylvania, 1752-1779 ***2444*** *p153*
Fideldey, J. C.; America, 1839 ***8582.1*** *p9*
Fidelis, Fritz 33; New Orleans, 1862 ***543.30*** *p228B*
Fidians, Randle 22; America, 1700 ***2212*** *p33*
Fidler, Anna *SEE* Fidler, Melchior
Fidler, Charles; Arkansas, 1918 ***95.2*** *p43*

Fidler, Johann Jacob *SEE* Fidler, Melchior
Fidler, Johann Martin *SEE* Fidler, Melchior
Fidler, Melchior; Pennsylvania, 1752-1779 2444 p153
*Wife:*Anna
*Child:*Johann Jacob
*Child:*Johann Martin
Fidon, Pierre Ignare 46; America, 1838 778.5 p207
Fidura, Phillip; America, 1899 7137 p168
Fieber, Johann; America, 1825 8582.2 p61
Fieber, Johann; Cincinnati, 1869-1887 8582 p9
Fieber, Johann 14; Philadelphia, 1825 8582.2 p11
With parents
Fieber, Simon; Cincinnati, 1869-1887 8582 p9
Fieber, Simon; Ohio, 1800-1885 8582.2 p61
Fiebrand, Ludwig Carl 38; Kansas, 1880 5240.1 p62
Fiederling, Voith; Pennsylvania, 1752 4525 p216
Fiedler, . . .; Canada, 1776-1783 9786 p21
Fiedler, Gus 31; Kansas, 1890 5240.1 p12
Fiedler, Gust 31; Kansas, 1890 5240.1 p75
Fiedler, Sam; Kansas, 1900 5240.1 p12
Fiegenbaum, Ernst; Cincinnati, 1847 3702.7 p84
Fiegs, John; Wisconsin, n.d. 9675.5 p122
Fiel, Jean-Baptiste 30; America, 1838 778.5 p207
Field, Charles 21; Maryland, 1774 1219.7 p223
Field, Charles 21; Maryland, 1774 1219.7 p236
Field, Eliel; Washington, 1859-1920 2872.1 p12
Field, George 23; Maryland, 1774 1219.7 p181
Field, George 29; Maryland, 1775 1219.7 p272
Field, Henry 14; New England, 1724 3690.1 p78
Field, James; America, 1738 4971 p14
Field, James; New York, NY, 1840 8208.4 p111
Field, Joan; America, 1741 4971 p49
Field, John; New York, NY, 1811 2859.11 p11
Field, John; New York, NY, 1815 2859.11 p30
Field, John 24; Maryland, 1722 3690.1 p78
Field, John 28; Maryland, 1775 1219.7 p249
Field, Luke 22; Virginia, 1775 1219.7 p261
Field, Margaret 1; Massachusetts, 1850 5881.1 p39
Field, Michael 20; Massachusetts, 1849 5881.1 p39
Field, Samuel 21; Jamaica, 1737 3690.1 p78
Field, Thomas 30; Maryland, 1774 1219.7 p222
Field, William; Washington, 1859-1920 2872.1 p12
Field, William 21; Jamaica, 1736 3690.1 p78
Field, Wm.; Arizona, 1897 9228.30 p2
Fielder, William 18; Jamaica, 1723 3690.1 p78
Fielding, Arnistead 42; Nova Scotia, 1774 1219.7 p194
*Wife:*Elizabeth 40
*Child:*John 15
*Child:*William 14
*Child:*Nicholas 12
*Child:*Hannah 8
*Child:*Esther 5
*Child:*Joseph 2
Fielding, Elizabeth 40 *SEE* Fielding, Arnistead
Fielding, Esther 5 *SEE* Fielding, Arnistead
Fielding, Hannah 8 *SEE* Fielding, Arnistead
Fielding, John 15 *SEE* Fielding, Arnistead
Fielding, Joseph 2 *SEE* Fielding, Arnistead
Fielding, Mary 25; Massachusetts, 1849 5881.1 p39
Fielding, Nicholas 12 *SEE* Fielding, Arnistead
Fielding, William 14 *SEE* Fielding, Arnistead
Fields, Aida; Washington, 1859-1920 2872.1 p12
Fields, Armas; Washington, 1859-1920 2872.1 p12
Fields, Charles; Washington, 1859-1920 2872.1 p12
Fields, Eino; Washington, 1859-1920 2872.1 p12
Fields, Eliel; Washington, 1859-1920 2872.1 p12
Fields, Else; Washington, 1859-1920 2872.1 p12
Fields, Erho; Washington, 1859-1920 2872.1 p12
Fields, George; Illinois, 1856 7857 p3
Fields, Hilla; Washington, 1859-1920 2872.1 p12
Fields, Hilmi; Washington, 1859-1920 2872.1 p12
Fields, James; Philadelphia, 1865 5704.8 p202
Fields, Jenne; Washington, 1859-1920 2872.1 p12
Fields, Johanna; Washington, 1859-1920 2872.1 p12
Fields, Kestti; Washington, 1859-1920 2872.1 p12
Fields, Tyyne; Washington, 1859-1920 2872.1 p12
Fields, Weikko; Washington, 1859-1920 2872.1 p12
Fields, William; Washington, 1859-1920 2872.1 p12
Fielitz, John; Wisconsin, n.d. 9675.5 p122
Fieser, Friedrich; Cincinnati, 1841 8582.3 p90
Fievre, Peter 32; Port uncertain, 1835 778.5 p208
Fife, Alexander 24; Jamaica, 1774 1219.7 p189
Fife, Ann 14; Quebec, 1847 5704.8 p12
Fife, James; Charleston, SC, 1804 1639.20 p69
Fife, James; Philadelphia, 1811 53.26 p27
Fife, James; Philadelphia, 1811 2859.11 p11
Fife, James 12; Quebec, 1847 5704.8 p12
Fife, James 35; Charleston, SC, 1774 1639.20 p69
Fife, John; New York, NY, 1816 2859.11 p30
Fife, Margaret; Quebec, 1847 5704.8 p12
Fife, Margaret 6; Quebec, 1847 5704.8 p12
Fife, Mary; New York, NY, 1816 2859.11 p30
Fife, Mary 8; Quebec, 1847 5704.8 p12
Fife, Matty 10; Quebec, 1847 5704.8 p12
Fife, Robert; Quebec, 1847 5704.8 p12
Fife, William Nicol; Utah, 1868 2764.35 p76
Fiffer, John 31; New Orleans, 1862 543.30 p227B
Fiffre, . . .; Canada, 1776-1783 9786 p21
Figdon, Julius; Baltimore, 1865 1450.2 p41A
Figel, Andrew; America, 1890 7137 p168
Figg, John; Virginia, 1636 6219 p78
Figg, Jon.; Virginia, 1643 6219 p200
Figg, William 19; Virginia, 1775 1219.7 p260
Figueroa, Jesus Lopes; Arkansas, 1918 95.2 p43
Figux, Francois; New York, NY, 1839 8208.4 p93
Fihe, John H.; Indiana, 1869-1887 8582 p9
Fik, John; Virginia, 1851 4626.16 p14
Fike, Clinton Earl; Arkansas, 1918 95.2 p43
Fiken, Henry 30; New Orleans, 1862 543.30 p28
Filadelfo, Mogono; Arkansas, 1918 95.2 p43
Filadelfo, Nugano; Arkansas, 1918 95.2 p43
Filb, Johann; Pennsylvania, 1747 2444 p165
Filby, Joane; Virginia, 1640 6219 p160
Filce, Thomas 23; Maryland, 1774 1219.7 p193
Filer, Henry; Colorado, 1894 9678.2 p18
Filete, . . .; America, 1839 778.5 p208
Filete, J. 25; America, 1839 778.5 p208
Filhe, Mr. 28; New Orleans, 1838 778.5 p208
Fili, Angelo; Arkansas, 1918 95.2 p43
Filiguier, Lucien B.; Shreveport, LA, 1878 7129 p44
Filip, Samuel; Wisconsin, n.d. 9675.5 p122
Filipowski, . . .; New York, 1831 4606 p173
Filleul, John 22; America, 1838 778.5 p208
Fillhouer, Charles H.; America, 1862 6014.1 p1
Filliance, Jean 49; Port uncertain, 1839 778.5 p208
Filliance, Marguerite 13; Port uncertain, 1839 778.5 p208
Filliance, Marie 21; Port uncertain, 1839 778.5 p208
Filpon, Augustin 22; New Orleans, 1826 778.5 p208
Fils, Jasmin 22; New Orleans, 1830 778.5 p208
Filsoffer, . . .; Canada, 1776-1783 9786 p21
Filson, Jean; Kentucky, 1781 8582.3 p93
Filtz, Thomas; Vermont, 1777 8137 p8
Fimmen, Fimme Eilts 54; Kansas, 1896 5240.1 p80
Fimpel, Agnes *SEE* Fimpel, Johannes
Fimpel, Jerg *SEE* Fimpel, Johannes
Fimpel, Johann Michael *SEE* Fimpel, Johannes
Fimpel, Johannes; Pennsylvania, 1752 2444 p153
*Wife:*Agnes
*Child:*Jerg
*Child:*Johann Michael
*Child:*Maria Agnes
Fimpel, Maria Agnes *SEE* Fimpel, Johannes
Fimple, John; Pennsylvania, 1752 2444 p153
Fin, Henry; New York, NY, 1836 8208.4 p23
Fin, Richd; Virginia, 1698 2212 p17
Finally, John; America, 1739 4971 p47
Finana, Daniel 36; Virginia, 1775 1219.7 p246
Finarty, Frank 35; New Orleans, 1862 543.30 p223B
Finch, Frances; Virginia, 1638 6219 p11
Finch, Henry; New York, NY, 1838 8208.4 p69
Finch, Isabella; Charleston, SC, 1761 1639.20 p69
Finch, John; Virginia, 1637 6219 p24
Finch, John; Virginia, 1652 6251 p20
Finch, John 15; Philadelphia, 1774 1219.7 p175
Finch, Robert; Virginia, 1698 2212 p14
Finch, Roger 45; America, 1704 2212 p41
Finch, William 11; Jamaica, 1774 1219.7 p231
Finch, Wm 16; America, 1704 2212 p41
Fincher, Charles 30; Maryland, 1774 1219.7 p207
Fincher, Henry 25; Pennsylvania, 1728 3690.1 p78
Finck, Jacob; New York, NY, 1837 8208.4 p31
Finck, Karl; Philadelphia, 1777-1779 8137 p8
Fincke, Johannes Christoph; America, 1852 8582.3 p19
Findel, Bernhard; Wisconsin, n.d. 9675.5 p122
Finder, Mr.; Quebec, 1815 9229.18 p80
With wife
With 3 children
Finder, August; Illinois, 1890 5012.40 p25
Finder, Friedrich Wilhelm; Illinois, 1873 5012.39 p26
Findlater, William; Charleston, SC, 1796 1639.20 p69
Findlay, Alexander; South Carolina, 1784 1639.20 p69
Findlay, Jane *SEE* Findlay, Rachel
Findlay, Jane; Philadelphia, 1847 5704.8 p32
Findlay, Rachel; Philadelphia, 1847 53.26 p27
*Relative:*Jane
Findlay, Rachel; Philadelphia, 1847 5704.8 p32
Findlayson, Angus 60; North Carolina, 1850 1639.20 p69
*Relative:*Catherine 58
Findlayson, Catherine 58 *SEE* Findlayson, Angus
Findon, John; New Jersey, 1835 8208.4 p47
Fineash, Francis; Virginia, 1639 6219 p155
Fineau, Etienne 40; New Orleans, 1838 778.5 p208
Finegan, Robert; New York, NY, 1840 8208.4 p110
Finegan, Thomas; New York, NY, 1815 2859.11 p30
Fineghy, Wm. 30; Massachusetts, 1849 5881.1 p41
Finer, John 17; Jamaica, 1725 3690.1 p78
Fines, Sarah 22; Georgia, 1774 1219.7 p188
Finey, Kate 25; Kansas, 1880 5240.1 p61
Finger, Theodore; New Orleans, 1837 6013.19 p30
Finges, Frederick 30; Ohio, 1844 1450.2 p42A
Fingusin, Michael; New York, NY, 1815 2859.11 p30
Finhold, Melchior 22; Pennsylvania, 1753 2444 p191
Finigan, Hugh; Philadelphia, 1816 2859.11 p30
Finigan, James; New York, NY, 1816 2859.11 p30
Finigan, Matthew; New York, NY, 1816 2859.11 p30
Fink, . . .; Canada, 1776-1783 9786 p21
Fink, Albert; America, 1700-1877 8582.3 p80
Fink, Christopf 62; Pittsburgh, 1901 1763 p40C
Fink, Henry; America, 1834 1450.2 p42A
Fink, Henry; Indiana, 1844 9117 p16
Fink, Jacob 45; New Orleans, 1862 543.30 p31
Fink, Johann Peter; America, 1847 8582.3 p19
Fink, Joseph; Shreveport, LA, 1877 7129 p44
Fink, Wilhelm; Philadelphia, 1850-1860 3702.7 p163
Finke, Anne Christine Louise; America, 1838-1844 4610.10 p138
Finke, Anne Marie Louise Christine; America, 1841 4610.10 p138
Finke, Caspar Heinrich Wilhelm; America, 1844 4610.10 p138
Finke, Heinrich; Cincinnati, 1869-1887 8582 p9
Finke, Johann Friedrich 51; America, 1857 4610.10 p105
*Wife:*Karoline 60
Finke, Joseph; America, 1848 8582.1 p10
Finke, Karoline 60 *SEE* Finke, Johann Friedrich
Finkelstein, Chaie 53; New York, NY, 1878 9253 p46
Finkelstein, Hirsch 20; New York, NY, 1878 9253 p45
Finkelstein, Jacob 61; New York, NY, 1878 9253 p46
Finkelstein, Josef 15; New York, NY, 1878 9253 p46
Finkelstein, Leon; Arkansas, 1918 95.2 p43
Finkelstein, Mariam 9; New York, NY, 1878 9253 p46
Finkelstein, Rachel 20; New York, NY, 1878 9253 p46
Finkelstein, Riefkl 17; New York, NY, 1878 9253 p46
Finkie, Charlie; Arkansas, 1918 95.2 p43
Finkman, Charles; America, 1891 1450.2 p42A
Finlan, Bridget; New York, NY, 1816 2859.11 p30
Finlan, James; New York, NY, 1816 2859.11 p30
Finlan, John; New York, NY, 1816 2859.11 p30
Finlan, Mary; New York, NY, 1816 2859.11 p30
Finlan, Owen; New York, NY, 1816 2859.11 p30
Finlan, Patrick; New York, NY, 1816 2859.11 p30
Finlay, Mr.; Quebec, 1815 9229.18 p81
Finlay, Andrew; Philadelphia, 1847 53.26 p27
Finlay, Andrew; Philadelphia, 1847 5704.8 p22
Finlay, Charles; New York, NY, 1816 2859.11 p30
Finlay, Elizabeth; Philadelphia, 1852 5704.8 p97
Finlay, Isabella; Philadelphia, 1851 5704.8 p70
Finlay, James; America, 1741 4971 p37
Finlay, James; Canada, 1761-1784 9775.5 p199
Finlay, James, Jr.; Canada, 1784-1789 9775.5 p199
Finlay, John; New York, NY, 1811 2859.11 p11
Finlay, Joseph 19; St. John, N.B., 1856 5704.8 p131
Finlay, Pidgeon; America, 1741 4971 p16
Finlay, William John; Philadelphia, 1852 5704.8 p97
Finlayson, Alex.; Nova Scotia, 1830 7085.4 p45
*Wife:*Christy
*Child:*Angus
*Child:*Christy
*Child:*Anne
Finlayson, Angus *SEE* Finlayson, Alex.
Finlayson, Ann; Quebec, 1845 4537.30 p81
Finlayson, Anne *SEE* Finlayson, Alex.
Finlayson, Christy *SEE* Finlayson, Alex.
Finlayson, Christy *SEE* Finlayson, Alex.
Finlayson, Ella J. 25; Kansas, 1893 5240.1 p79
Finlayson, George 21; Maryland, 1774 1219.7 p235
Finlayson, Jane; Quebec, 1873 4537.30 p36
Finlayson, John; Quebec, 1875 4537.30 p11
Finlayson, Mary; North Carolina, 1769-1817 1639.20 p70
Finlayson, Rachel; Quebec, 1842 4537.30 p111
Finley, Mrs.; Grenada, 1775 1219.7 p280
Finley, James 8; Massachusetts, 1848 5881.1 p37
Finley, John 27; Massachusetts, 1849 5881.1 p38
Finley, Joseph L. 24; New Orleans, 1862 543.30 p227B
Finley, Mary 42; Massachusetts, 1848 5881.1 p38
Finley, Richard 5; Massachusetts, 1848 5881.1 p40
Finley, William; New York, NY, 1838 8208.4 p84
Finmore, Francis 50; Georgia, 1775 1219.7 p275
Finn, Ann 30; Massachusetts, 1849 5881.1 p35
Finn, Ellen 22; Massachusetts, 1849 5881.1 p36
Finn, James; Philadelphia, 1816 2859.11 p30
Finn, James 19; Newfoundland, 1789 4915.24 p56
Finn, Johann; America, 1846 8582.3 p19
Finn, John; America, 1847 1450.2 p42A
Finn, John; Virginia, 1698 2212 p17
Finn, John 13; Massachusetts, 1850 5881.1 p38
Finn, John 18; Massachusetts, 1850 5881.1 p38

Finn, John 23; Massachusetts, 1860 ***6410.32*** *p117*
Finn, Kath. 25; America, 1853 ***9162.7*** *p14*
Finn, Mary 26; Massachusetts, 1860 ***6410.32*** *p117*
Finn, Michael 30; New Orleans, 1862 ***543.30*** *p30*
Finn, Michel; Quebec, 1805 ***7603*** *p76*
Finn, Patrick; America, 1739 ***4971*** *p14*
Finn, Patrick; New York, 1837 ***1450.2*** *p42A*
Finn, Patrick 40; New Orleans, 1862 ***543.30*** *p224B*
Finn, Philip; Virginia, 1698 ***2212*** *p17*
Finn, Thomas; America, 1740 ***4971*** *p15*
Finn, Thomas; Maryland, 1740 ***4971*** *p91*
Finn, Thomas; Philadelphia, 1741 ***4971*** *p92*
Finn, William 21; Maryland, 1733 ***3690.1*** *p78*
Finnan, James; New York, NY, 1834 ***8208.4*** *p38*
Finnegan, Ann; Baltimore, 1811 ***2859.11*** *p11*
Finnegan, Henry; America, 1743 ***4971*** *p23*
Finnegan, James 32; Massachusetts, 1849 ***5881.1*** *p37*
Finnegan, John; America, 1738 ***4971*** *p26*
Finnegan, John 20; Massachusetts, 1850 ***5881.1*** *p38*
Finnegan, Mary 8; Massachusetts, 1849 ***5881.1*** *p38*
Finnegan, Patrick 7; Massachusetts, 1849 ***5881.1*** *p40*
Finnell, Jacob; America, 1867 ***6014.1*** *p2*
Finnelly, Wm. 30; Massachusetts, 1849 ***5881.1*** *p41*
Finneran, Catharine 9; Massachusetts, 1850 ***5881.1*** *p36*
Finneran, Mary 11; Massachusetts, 1850 ***5881.1*** *p39*
Finnerty, Ann 20; Massachusetts, 1849 ***5881.1*** *p35*
Finnerty, Martin; California, 1876 ***2764.35*** *p22*
Finnerty, Michael 22; Massachusetts, 1849 ***5881.1*** *p39*
Finnerty, Patrick 25; Massachusetts, 1848 ***5881.1*** *p40*
Finnerty, Thomas 20; Massachusetts, 1848 ***5881.1*** *p40*
Finnestan, Reinert Emil 25; Arkansas, 1918 ***95.2*** *p43*
Finney, Catharine; Philadelphia, 1865 ***5704.8*** *p189*
Finney, Dennis; America, 1867 ***5704.8*** *p217*
Finney, Ellen 10; Massachusetts, 1849 ***5881.1*** *p36*
Finney, George 15; Pennsylvania, 1728 ***3690.1*** *p78*
Finney, Isaac; Iowa, 1866-1943 ***123.54*** *p18*
Finney, James 5; Philadelphia, 1865 ***5704.8*** *p189*
Finney, James W.; Illinois, 1903 ***5012.40*** *p79*
Finney, Jane 3 mos; Philadelphia, 1865 ***5704.8*** *p189*
Finney, John 32; Maryland, 1774 ***1219.7*** *p220*
Finney, Margaret 16; Massachusetts, 1849 ***5881.1*** *p39*
Finney, Matthew; New York, NY, 1811 ***2859.11*** *p11*
Finney, Patrick; New York, NY, 1811 ***2859.11*** *p11*
Finney, Robert; Philadelphia, 1865 ***5704.8*** *p189*
Finnie, William; Boston, 1775 ***1219.7*** *p279*
Finnigan, Henry; Delaware Bay or River, 1743 ***4971*** *p104*
Finnigan, Thomas; New York, NY, 1835 ***8208.4*** *p50*
Finnin, Bridget 2; Massachusetts, 1849 ***5881.1*** *p36*
Finnin, John 40; Massachusetts, 1849 ***5881.1*** *p37*
Finnin, Patrick; New York, NY, 1837 ***8208.4*** *p41*
Finnin, Patrick 1; Massachusetts, 1849 ***5881.1*** *p40*
Finnon, Ann; Massachusetts, 1850 ***5881.1*** *p35*
Finnon, Charles 9; Massachusetts, 1850 ***5881.1*** *p36*
Finnon, Mary 7; Massachusetts, 1850 ***5881.1*** *p39*
Finny, Richard; Virginia, 1639 ***6219*** *p158*
Finos, Mike; Arkansas, 1918 ***95.2*** *p43*
Finselbach, Friedrich Ludwig; America, 1853 ***4610.10*** *p148*
Finsterer, . . .; Canada, 1776-1783 ***9786*** *p21*
Finsterwald, . . .; Canada, 1776-1783 ***9786*** *p21*
Finsterwalt, . . .; Canada, 1776-1783 ***9786*** *p21*
Finton, John 25; St. John, N.B., 1863 ***5704.8*** *p152*
Finton, Patrick; America, 1849 ***1450.2*** *p42A*
Fintzen, John; Wisconsin, n.d. ***9675.5*** *p122*
Finzel, Georg; Ohio, 1869-1887 ***8582*** *p9*
Fiogere, Claude 32; America, 1837 ***778.5*** *p208*
Fiohamer, Luis 27; Port uncertain, 1836 ***778.5*** *p522*
Fiorelli, Anestasio; Wisconsin, n.d. ***9675.5*** *p122*
Fiorletta, Goetano; Arkansas, 1918 ***95.2*** *p43*
Firainaud, Amedee 26; America, 1839 ***778.5*** *p208*
Firestone, Nicholas; Philadelphia, 1763 ***9973.7*** *p38*
Firmant, Samuell; Virginia, 1638 ***6219*** *p123*
Firmins, William 23; Maryland, 1774 ***1219.7*** *p223*
Firnhaber, Jacob Nicolaus; Pennsylvania, 1773 ***4525*** *p216*
Firnhaber, Johann Nicolaus; Pennsylvania, 1773 ***4525*** *p216*
Firnhaber, Margaret Catharine; America, 1753 ***4525*** *p216*
Firnkaes, Margaretha; New York, NY, 1846 ***8582.3*** *p29*
Firnkaes, Mathias; Cincinnati, 1846 ***8582.3*** *p29*
Firth, George 30; Nova Scotia, 1774 ***1219.7*** *p194*
Firth, Isaac; America, 1698 ***2212*** *p13*
Fisch, George; Wisconsin, n.d. ***9675.5*** *p122*
Fischbach, Peter 21; Kansas, 1884 ***5240.1*** *p66*
Fischback, William 29; New Orleans, 1862 ***543.30*** *p225B*
Fischel Family ; Pennsylvania, n.d. ***1034.18*** *p12*
Fischen, . . .; Ohio, 1881 ***3702.7*** *p429*
Fischer, . . .; Canada, 1776-1783 ***9786*** *p21*
Fischer, Miss; America, 1852 ***4610.10*** *p147*
Fischer, Adam 7; New York, NY, 1889 ***7846*** *p39*
Fischer, Agnes *SEE* Fischer, Thomas
Fischer, Albert; America, 1846 ***8582.3*** *p19*
Fischer, Albert; Wisconsin, n.d. ***9675.5*** *p122*
Fischer, Alwina Fredca. 6 mos *SEE* Fischer, John Fredk.
Fischer, Andrew; America, 1884 ***7137*** *p168*
*Wife:*Anna
Fischer, Anna *SEE* Fischer, Andrew
Fischer, Anne M. C. Stratmeier *SEE* Fischer, Johann Wilhelm
Fischer, Anne Marie Louise *SEE* Fischer, Johann Wilhelm
Fischer, Anne Marie Wippermann *SEE* Fischer, Daniel
Fischer, Arthur; Ohio, 1895 ***1450.2*** *p42A*
Fischer, Aug. Adolph 26; New Orleans, 1839 ***9420.2*** *p361*
*Wife:*Sophia 29
Fischer, Bernhardt; Illinois, 1900 ***5012.40*** *p77*
Fischer, Carl August; Wisconsin, n.d. ***9675.5*** *p122*
Fischer, Carl Friedrich *SEE* Fischer, Daniel
Fischer, Carl Heinrich *SEE* Fischer, Daniel
Fischer, Carl Johan; Wisconsin, n.d. ***9675.5*** *p122*
Fischer, Caroline Sophia 8 *SEE* Fischer, Jane Sophia
Fischer, Casper; New York, 1754 ***3652*** *p79*
Fischer, Cath. 76; America, 1895 ***1763*** *p40D*
Fischer, Catharina 17; New York, NY, 1889 ***7846*** *p39*
Fischer, Catherine; New York, 1749 ***3652*** *p72*
Fischer, Charles; America, 1876 ***1450.2*** *p43A*
Fischer, Christ Friedrich Wilhelm; America, 1850 ***4610.10*** *p147*
Fischer, Christa Mary 11 *SEE* Fischer, John Fredk.
Fischer, Conrad; Wisconsin, n.d. ***9675.5*** *p122*
Fischer, Daniel 39; America, 1850 ***4610.10*** *p142*
*Wife:*Anne Marie Wippermann
*Child:*Carl Heinrich
*Child:*Carl Friedrich
*Child:*Heinrich Carl
*Child:*Heinrich Daniel
Fischer, Daniel Heinrich; America, 1851 ***4610.10*** *p147*
Fischer, Elisabeth 54; New York, NY, 1889 ***7846*** *p39*
Fischer, Ernst; Wisconsin, n.d. ***9675.5*** *p122*
Fischer, Ernst Heinrich Wilhelm *SEE* Fischer, Johann Wilhelm
Fischer, F. B.; Cincinnati, 1830-1849 ***8582*** *p9*
Fischer, Frank; Wisconsin, n.d. ***9675.5*** *p122*
Fischer, Fredk. Albert 12 *SEE* Fischer, John Fredk.
Fischer, Fredk. Ferdind. 6 *SEE* Fischer, John Fredk.
Fischer, G.; America, 1876-1877 ***8582.3*** *p19*
Fischer, George; Wisconsin, n.d. ***9675.5*** *p122*
Fischer, Gottfried; New York, NY, 1921 ***3455.2*** *p79*
Fischer, Hans Jerg; Pennsylvania, 1749 ***2444*** *p154*
Fischer, Heinrich Carl *SEE* Fischer, Daniel
Fischer, Heinrich Daniel *SEE* Fischer, Daniel
Fischer, Herman; Wisconsin, n.d. ***9675.5*** *p122*
Fischer, Jacob 44; Harris Co., TX, 1900 ***6254*** *p6*
Fischer, Jane Sophia 49; New Orleans, 1839 ***9420.2*** *p487*
*Child:*Caroline Sophia 8
*Child:*John Ehregod 3 mos
Fischer, Johan Carl Gottlieb; Wisconsin, n.d. ***9675.5*** *p122*
Fischer, Johann 13; New York, NY, 1889 ***7846*** *p39*
Fischer, Johann 59; New York, NY, 1889 ***7846*** *p39*
Fischer, Johann Wilhelm; America, 1857 ***4610.10*** *p152*
*Wife:*Anne M. C. Stratmeier
*Child:*Anne Marie Louise
*Child:*Ernst Heinrich Wilhelm
Fischer, John 40; Kansas, 1893 ***5240.1*** *p78*
Fischer, John Ehregod 3 mos *SEE* Fischer, Jane Sophia
Fischer, John Fredk. 38; New Orleans, 1839 ***9420.2*** *p361*
*Wife:*Marie Doroth. 38
*Son:*Fredk. Albert 12
*Daughter:*Christa Mary 11
*Son:*Fredk. Ferdind. 6
*Daughter:*Alwina Fredca. 6 mos
Fischer, Josef 27; New York, NY, 1889 ***7846*** *p39*
Fischer, Julius 16; New Orleans, 1839 ***9420.2*** *p166*
Fischer, Leo Degar.; Cincinnati, 1869-1887 ***8582*** *p9*
Fischer, Maria Agnes; Pennsylvania, 1752 ***2444*** *p154*
Fischer, Marie 9; New York, NY, 1889 ***7846*** *p39*
Fischer, Marie Doroth. 38 *SEE* Fischer, John Fredk.
Fischer, Michael; Ohio, 1801-1802 ***8582.2*** *p55*
Fischer, Michael; Ohio, 1841 ***8582.1*** *p48*
Fischer, Michael; Ohio, 1869-1887 ***8582*** *p9*
Fischer, Michael 8 mos; New York, NY, 1889 ***7846*** *p39*
Fischer, Paul; America, 1873 ***1450.2*** *p42A*
Fischer, R.; Wheeling, WV, 1852 ***8582.3*** *p78*
Fischer, Rosalie 18; New York, NY, 1889 ***7846*** *p39*
Fischer, Sebestian 11; New York, NY, 1889 ***7846*** *p39*
Fischer, Sophia 29 *SEE* Fischer, Aug. Adolph
Fischer, Theresia 26; New York, NY, 1889 ***7846*** *p39*
Fischer, Thomas; New York, 1743 ***3652*** *p59*
*Wife:*Agnes
Fischer, Wilhelm; America, 1848 ***8582.3*** *p19*
Fischer, William; Wisconsin, n.d. ***9675.5*** *p122*
Fischkorn, Bernhard; Virginia, 1847 ***4626.16*** *p13*
Fischmeier, Antlon Frederick; Baltimore, 1839 ***1450.2*** *p43A*
Fiseher, Margurite 26; America, 1838 ***778.5*** *p208*
Fiseher, Marie 23; America, 1838 ***778.5*** *p208*
Fish, Charles 37; Kansas, 1887 ***5240.1*** *p71*
Fish, Joshua 19; Virginia, 1773 ***1219.7*** *p171*
Fish, Mary 29; America, 1702 ***2212*** *p37*
Fish, Mary 29; Maryland or Virginia, 1702 ***2212*** *p36*
Fishbach, Peter 21; Kansas, 1884 ***5240.1*** *p12*
Fishborn, Philip; Pennsylvania, 1772 ***9973.8*** *p33*
Fishburn, George; America, 1742 ***4971*** *p27*
Fishell, Frederick; Philadelphia, 1763 ***9973.7*** *p38*
Fishell, John; Philadelphia, 1761 ***9973.7*** *p36*
Fisher, Mr.; Quebec, 1815 ***9229.18*** *p77*
Fisher, Abigail; Philadelphia, 1850 ***5704.8*** *p69*
Fisher, Abigale; Philadelphia, 1850 ***53.26*** *p27*
Fisher, Albert; Wisconsin, n.d. ***9675.5*** *p122*
Fisher, Alexander; New York, NY, 1834 ***8208.4*** *p4*
Fisher, Andrew; America, 1884 ***7137*** *p168*
*Wife:*Anna
Fisher, Andrew; Philadelphia, 1851 ***5704.8*** *p80*
Fisher, Anna *SEE* Fisher, Andrew
Fisher, Archibald; North Carolina, 1820 ***1639.20*** *p70*
Fisher, Ballaras; Virginia, 1858 ***4626.16*** *p17*
Fisher, Benjamin 25; Dominica, 1774 ***1219.7*** *p205*
Fisher, Bridgett; Virginia, 1636 ***6219*** *p22*
Fisher, Catharine 34; Philadelphia, 1774 ***1219.7*** *p214*
Fisher, Charles; America, 1876 ***1450.2*** *p43A*
Fisher, Charles Godfred; America, 1850 ***1450.2*** *p43A*
Fisher, Christian; Virginia, 1640 ***6219*** *p160*
Fisher, Conrad; Illinois, 1852 ***3840.1*** *p18*
Fisher, Daniel; South Carolina, 1791 ***1639.20*** *p70*
Fisher, Daniel 18; Philadelphia, 1865 ***5704.8*** *p164*
Fisher, Ebenezer; New Bern, NC, 1739-1767 ***1639.20*** *p70*
Fisher, Edward; Virginia, 1642 ***6219*** *p192*
Fisher, Edward 28; New York, 1775 ***1219.7*** *p268*
With wife
With 2 children
Fisher, Eliz.; Virginia, 1640 ***6219*** *p184*
Fisher, Ellen 18; America, 1706 ***2212*** *p46*
Fisher, Frederick 28; New Orleans, 1839 ***778.5*** *p209*
Fisher, George; Illinois, 1860 ***2896.5*** *p12*
Fisher, George; Philadelphia, 1847 ***53.26*** *p27*
Fisher, George; Philadelphia, 1847 ***5704.8*** *p5*
Fisher, George 21; Kansas, 1874 ***5240.1*** *p55*
Fisher, George 27; America, 1831 ***778.5*** *p209*
Fisher, George 36; Philadelphia, 1774 ***1219.7*** *p183*
Fisher, George 43; Kansas, 1874 ***5240.1*** *p56*
Fisher, Gustave; Arizona, 1890 ***2764.35*** *p24*
Fisher, H.; Quebec, 1815 ***9229.18*** *p75*
Fisher, H.T. 48; New Orleans, 1839 ***9420.2*** *p165*
*Wife:*Julie
Fisher, Henry 26; Virginia, 1774 ***1219.7*** *p227*
Fisher, Henry 30; Maryland, 1775 ***1219.7*** *p257*
Fisher, Henry 32; New Orleans, 1862 ***543.30*** *p227B*
Fisher, Hugh; New York, NY, 1816 ***2859.11*** *p30*
Fisher, James; New York, NY, 1816 ***2859.11*** *p30*
With wife & 5 children
Fisher, James; Philadelphia, 1848 ***5704.8*** *p46*
Fisher, James 10 *SEE* Fisher, Martha
Fisher, Jane; New York, NY, 1870 ***5704.8*** *p239*
Fisher, John *SEE* Fisher, Martha
Fisher, John; America, 1874 ***1450.2*** *p43A*
Fisher, John; Indiana, 1848 ***9117*** *p16*
Fisher, John; New York, 1830 ***1450.2*** *p42A*
Fisher, John; New York, NY, 1839 ***8208.4*** *p93*
Fisher, John; Virginia, 1643 ***6219*** *p204*
Fisher, John; Virginia, 1698 ***2212*** *p14*
Fisher, John; Wisconsin, n.d. ***9675.5*** *p122*
Fisher, John; Wisconsin, 1898 ***1450.2*** *p9B*
Fisher, John 6; Philadelphia, 1848 ***5704.8*** *p46*
Fisher, John George; Wisconsin, n.d. ***9675.5*** *p122*
Fisher, Jon.; Virginia, 1632 ***6219*** *p180*
Fisher, Joseph; New York, NY, 1835 ***8208.4*** *p40*
Fisher, Joseph; Wisconsin, n.d. ***9675.5*** *p122*
Fisher, Joseph 25; Jamaica, 1731 ***3690.1*** *p78*
Fisher, Joseph P.; Indiana, 1836 ***9117*** *p15*
Fisher, Julie *SEE* Fisher, H.T.
Fisher, Julius; Kansas, 1884 ***5240.1*** *p12*
Fisher, Leonard; New York, NY, 1839 ***8208.4*** *p94*
Fisher, Margaret; New York, NY, 1816 ***2859.11*** *p30*
Fisher, Margaret; Philadelphia, 1849 ***53.26*** *p27*
*Relative:*Ruth
Fisher, Margaret; Philadelphia, 1849 ***5704.8*** *p53*
Fisher, Margaret 8 *SEE* Fisher, Martha
Fisher, Margaret 10; Philadelphia, 1848 ***5704.8*** *p46*
Fisher, Martha *SEE* Fisher, Martha
Fisher, Martha; Philadelphia, 1848 ***53.26*** *p27*
*Relative:*Martha
*Relative:*James 10
*Relative:*Margaret 8

152 *FOR A COMPLETE EXPLANATION OF ENTRY, SEE "HOW TO READ A CITATION" SECTION*

*Relative:*Samuel 6
*Relative:*John
Fisher, Martha; Philadelphia, 1848 ***5704.8*** *p46*
Fisher, Martin; Philadelphia, 1760 ***9973.7*** *p34*
Fisher, Mary; St. John, N.B., 1847 ***5704.8*** *p34*
Fisher, Masld; Virginia, 1645 ***6219*** *p253*
Fisher, Matilda 26; Philadelphia, 1853 ***5704.8*** *p111*
Fisher, Michael; New York, NY, 1816 ***2859.11*** *p30*
Fisher, Moritz; Wisconsin, n.d. ***9675.5*** *p122*
Fisher, Peter; South Carolina, 1798 ***1639.20*** *p70*
Fisher, Robert 18; Philadelphia, 1860 ***5704.8*** *p145*
Fisher, Robert 25; Newfoundland, 1789 ***4915.24*** *p55*
Fisher, Ruth *SEE* Fisher, Margaret
Fisher, Ruth; Philadelphia, 1849 ***5704.8*** *p53*
Fisher, Samuel; Philadelphia, 1847 ***53.26*** *p27*
Fisher, Samuel; Philadelphia, 1847 ***5704.8*** *p1*
Fisher, Samuel 6 *SEE* Fisher, Martha
Fisher, Samuel 8; Philadelphia, 1848 ***5704.8*** *p46*
Fisher, Samuel 19; Maryland, 1738 ***3690.1*** *p79*
Fisher, Sarah; Quebec, 1819 ***7603*** *p26*
Fisher, Sarah; Virginia, 1636 ***6219*** *p22*
Fisher, Sarah; Virginia, 1645 ***6219*** *p233*
Fisher, Stephen 30; New York, 1774 ***1219.7*** *p227*
Fisher, Theodore; Wisconsin, n.d. ***9675.5*** *p122*
Fisher, Tho.; Virginia, 1638 ***6219*** *p123*
Fisher, Thomas; New York, NY, 1834 ***8208.4*** *p41*
Fisher, Thomas 19; Maryland, 1774 ***1219.7*** *p220*
Fisher, Thomas 27; Virginia, 1774 ***1219.7*** *p227*
Fisher, W.; Quebec, 1815 ***9229.18*** *p75*
Fisher, William; Virginia, 1639 ***6219*** *p156*
Fisher, William 24; Jamaica, 1730 ***3690.1*** *p79*
Fishpen, Conrad 30; America, 1837 ***778.5*** *p209*
Fiske, Louis; Colorado, 1904 ***9678.2*** *p18*
Fisler, Durst; Philadelphia, 1759 ***9973.7*** *p33*
Fissler, Dorothea *SEE* Fissler, Jacob
Fissler, Eva *SEE* Fissler, Jacob
Fissler, Jacob; Pennsylvania, 1752 ***2444*** *p154*
*Wife:*Eva
*Child:*Dorothea
*Child:*Johannes
Fissler, Johann Georg; Pennsylvania, 1752 ***2444*** *p154*
Fissler, Johann Michael; Pennsylvania, 1752 ***2444*** *p154*
Fissler, Johannes *SEE* Fissler, Jacob
Fister, Bastien 19; New Orleans, 1863 ***543.30*** *p230B*
Fister, Florko; Iowa, 1866-1943 ***123.54*** *p63*
Fister, Frink; Iowa, 1866-1943 ***123.54*** *p18*
Fister, George; Iowa, 1866-1943 ***123.54*** *p18*
Fister, Gos; Iowa, 1866-1943 ***123.54*** *p18*
Fister, Gov.; Iowa, 1866-1943 ***123.54*** *p18*
Fister, Ignas; Iowa, 1866-1943 ***123.54*** *p18*
Fister, Jean P. 22; America, 1831 ***778.5*** *p209*
Fistic, Jean 31; America, 1838 ***778.5*** *p209*
Fistie, Jean 31; America, 1838 ***778.5*** *p209*
Fitch, John 30; Massachusetts, 1849 ***5881.1*** *p38*
Fitch, Mary; Virginia, 1646 ***6219*** *p239*
Fitch, Samuell; Virginia, 1638-1700 ***6219*** *p150*
Fitchett, John; Virginia, 1635 ***6219*** *p33*
Fitchgerrard, Edwd 30; Virginia, 1700 ***2212*** *p32*
Fitgibbons, Thomas; Quebec, 1792 ***7603*** *p86*
Fithail, George; Arkansas, 1918 ***95.2*** *p43*
Fitheal, George; Arkansas, 1918 ***95.2*** *p43*
Fitiar, Herman; Philadelphia, 1764 ***9973.7*** *p39*
Fitman, Robert 20; Massachusetts, 1847 ***5881.1*** *p40*
Fitspatrick, James 37; Philadelphia, 1803 ***53.26*** *p27*
Fitspatrick, Mary 32; Philadelphia, 1803 ***53.26*** *p27*
Fitsummons, Ellen; Quebec, 1849 ***5704.8*** *p51*
Fitt, Frank 39; New Orleans, 1862 ***543.30*** *p225B*
Fitterer, Peter; Alberta, n.d. ***5262*** *p58*
Fitterling, Voith; Pennsylvania, 1752 ***4525*** *p216*
With wife
With 8 children
Fitting, Carl; Wisconsin, n.d. ***9675.5*** *p122*
Fitton, John J.; Illinois, 1868 ***5012.38*** *p99*
Fitts, Carry; Virginia, 1648 ***6219*** *p252*
Fitture, Jean 40; New Orleans, 1839 ***778.5*** *p209*
Fitz, Anna Barbara *SEE* Fitz, Michael
Fitz, Jacob *SEE* Fitz, Michael
Fitz, Margaretha *SEE* Fitz, Michael
Fitz, Michael *SEE* Fitz, Michael
Fitz, Michael; Pennsylvania, 1754 ***2444*** *p200*
*Wife:*Anna Barbara
*Child:*Margaretha
*Child:*Michael
*Child:*Jacob
Fitzer, Jacob F.; Ohio, 1840 ***9892.11*** *p15*
Fitzgarret, Redmond; Virginia, 1635 ***6219*** *p4*
Fitzgerald, Mrs. 40; Massachusetts, 1849 ***5881.1*** *p39*
Fitzgerald, Ann; Quebec, 1824 ***7603*** *p63*
Fitzgerald, Ann 5; Massachusetts, 1849 ***5881.1*** *p35*
Fitzgerald, Ann 13; Massachusetts, 1849 ***5881.1*** *p35*
Fitzgerald, Anne; Quebec, 1795 ***7603*** *p76*
Fitzgerald, Anthony 3; Massachusetts, 1849 ***5881.1*** *p35*
Fitzgerald, Badeline 11; Massachusetts, 1849 ***5881.1*** *p36*
Fitzgerald, C.D. 30; Maryland, 1775 ***1219.7*** *p260*
Fitzgerald, Catherine; America, 1743 ***4971*** *p57*
Fitzgerald, Catherine; New Brunswick, 1824 ***7603*** *p65*
Fitzgerald, Charles 8; Massachusetts, 1849 ***5881.1*** *p36*
Fitzgerald, Darby 7; Massachusetts, 1849 ***5881.1*** *p36*
Fitzgerald, David 1; Massachusetts, 1850 ***5881.1*** *p36*
Fitzgerald, Edmund; America, 1741 ***4971*** *p16*
Fitzgerald, Edmund 10; Massachusetts, 1849 ***5881.1*** *p36*
Fitzgerald, Edmund 30; Massachusetts, 1847 ***5881.1*** *p36*
Fitzgerald, Edward; Indiana, 1850 ***9117*** *p20*
Fitzgerald, Edward 3; St. John, N.B., 1854 ***5704.8*** *p114*
Fitzgerald, Edward 20; Massachusetts, 1849 ***5881.1*** *p37*
Fitzgerald, Edward 43; New Orleans, 1864 ***543.30*** *p230B*
Fitzgerald, Edward 45; St. John, N.B., 1854 ***5704.8*** *p114*
Fitzgerald, Eliza 20; Massachusetts, 1849 ***5881.1*** *p37*
Fitzgerald, Elizabeth 16; Maryland, 1775 ***1219.7*** *p256*
Fitzgerald, Elleanor 35; St. John, N.B., 1854 ***5704.8*** *p114*
Fitzgerald, Francis; America, 1738 ***4971*** *p33*
Fitzgerald, Gerald; New York, NY, 1834 ***8208.4*** *p56*
Fitzgerald, Honora 10; Massachusetts, 1848 ***5881.1*** *p37*
Fitzgerald, James; America, 1738 ***4971*** *p52*
Fitzgerald, James; Arkansas, 1918 ***95.2*** *p43*
Fitzgerald, James; Montreal, 1805 ***7603*** *p80*
Fitzgerald, James 9; Massachusetts, 1849 ***5881.1*** *p38*
Fitzgerald, James 10; Massachusetts, 1849 ***5881.1*** *p37*
Fitzgerald, James 14; Massachusetts, 1849 ***5881.1*** *p38*
Fitzgerald, James 30; Massachusetts, 1849 ***5881.1*** *p38*
Fitzgerald, James 32; Massachusetts, 1848 ***5881.1*** *p37*
Fitzgerald, James 40; Massachusetts, 1849 ***5881.1*** *p38*
Fitzgerald, Johanna 24; Massachusetts, 1850 ***5881.1*** *p38*
Fitzgerald, John; America, 1735-1743 ***4971*** *p79*
Fitzgerald, John; America, 1736 ***4971*** *p44*
Fitzgerald, John; America, 1736-1743 ***4971*** *p57*
Fitzgerald, John; America, 1738 ***4971*** *p28*
Fitzgerald, John; America, 1740 ***4971*** *p81*
Fitzgerald, John; New York, NY, 1811 ***2859.11*** *p11*
Fitzgerald, John; New York, NY, 1815 ***2859.11*** *p30*
Fitzgerald, John; Wisconsin, n.d. ***9675.5*** *p122*
Fitzgerald, John 1; Massachusetts, 1849 ***5881.1*** *p38*
Fitzgerald, John 9; Massachusetts, 1849 ***5881.1*** *p38*
Fitzgerald, John 20; Massachusetts, 1849 ***5881.1*** *p37*
Fitzgerald, John 20; Massachusetts, 1850 ***5881.1*** *p38*
Fitzgerald, John 45; Massachusetts, 1849 ***5881.1*** *p38*
Fitzgerald, Lucy 30; Massachusetts, 1850 ***5881.1*** *p38*
Fitzgerald, Margaret; America, 1739 ***4971*** *p47*
Fitzgerald, Margaret 20; Massachusetts, 1849 ***5881.1*** *p39*
Fitzgerald, Maria 4; Massachusetts, 1849 ***5881.1*** *p39*
Fitzgerald, Martin; Quebec, 1811 ***7603*** *p101*
Fitzgerald, Mary; America, 1738 ***4971*** *p13*
Fitzgerald, Mary; America, 1738 ***4971*** *p40*
Fitzgerald, Mary; America, 1741 ***4971*** *p40*
Fitzgerald, Mary; America, 1742 ***4971*** *p17*
Fitzgerald, Mary; New York, NY, 1815 ***2859.11*** *p30*
Fitzgerald, Mary 5; Massachusetts, 1849 ***5881.1*** *p39*
Fitzgerald, Mary 7; St. John, N.B., 1854 ***5704.8*** *p114*
Fitzgerald, Mary 8; Massachusetts, 1850 ***5881.1*** *p40*
Fitzgerald, Mary 9; Massachusetts, 1849 ***5881.1*** *p39*
Fitzgerald, Mary 12; Massachusetts, 1849 ***5881.1*** *p39*
Fitzgerald, Mary 40; Massachusetts, 1849 ***5881.1*** *p39*
Fitzgerald, Mary 50; Massachusetts, 1849 ***5881.1*** *p39*
Fitzgerald, Matthew; New York, NY, 1815 ***2859.11*** *p30*
Fitzgerald, Maurice; America, 1741 ***4971*** *p48*
Fitzgerald, Maurice; America, 1742 ***4971*** *p49*
Fitzgerald, Maurice; New York, NY, 1834 ***8208.4*** *p1*
Fitzgerald, Michael 7; Massachusetts, 1849 ***5881.1*** *p39*
Fitzgerald, Michael 11; Massachusetts, 1849 ***5881.1*** *p39*
Fitzgerald, Michael 33; New Orleans, 1862 ***543.30*** *p229B*
Fitzgerald, Michael 40; Massachusetts, 1849 ***5881.1*** *p39*
Fitzgerald, Michael 40; Massachusetts, 1850 ***5881.1*** *p39*
Fitzgerald, Morris; New York, NY, 1811 ***2859.11*** *p11*
Fitzgerald, Nancy; Quebec, 1786 ***7603*** *p76*
Fitzgerald, Patrick; New York, NY, 1834 ***8208.4*** *p2*
Fitzgerald, Patrick; Quebec, 1820 ***7603*** *p76*
Fitzgerald, Patrick 1; Massachusetts, 1849 ***5881.1*** *p40*
Fitzgerald, Patrick 25; New Orleans, 1862 ***543.30*** *p29*
Fitzgerald, Patrick 30; Massachusetts, 1847 ***5881.1*** *p40*
Fitzgerald, Patrick 60; Massachusetts, 1850 ***5881.1*** *p40*
Fitzgerald, Philip; America, 1740 ***4971*** *p28*
Fitzgerald, Richard 8; St. John, N.B., 1854 ***5704.8*** *p114*
Fitzgerald, Robert 21; Massachusetts, 1847 ***5881.1*** *p40*
Fitzgerald, Thomas; America, 1742-1743 ***4971*** *p42*
Fitzgerald, Thomas; New York, 1828 ***1450.2*** *p43A*
Fitzgerald, Thomas; New York, NY, 1816 ***2859.11*** *p30*
Fitzgerald, Thomas; Philadelphia, 1815 ***2859.11*** *p30*
Fitzgerald, Thomas 19; Maryland, 1723 ***3690.1*** *p79*
Fitzgerald, William; America, 1736 ***4971*** *p44*
Fitzgerald, William; America, 1736 ***4971*** *p45*
Fitzgerald, William; America, 1739 ***4971*** *p27*
Fitzgerald, William; America, 1739 ***4971*** *p46*
Fitzgerald, William; America, 1739 ***4971*** *p47*
Fitzgerald, William 3 mos; St. John, N.B., 1854 ***5704.8*** *p114*
Fitzgerald, William 13; Massachusetts, 1849 ***5881.1*** *p41*
Fitzgerald, William 24; Massachusetts, 1847 ***5881.1*** *p40*
Fitzgerald, William 25; Massachusetts, 1847 ***5881.1*** *p40*
Fitzgerild, Thomas 19; Maryland, 1723 ***3690.1*** *p79*
Fitz Gibbon, David; America, 1735-1743 ***4971*** *p78*
Fitzgibbon, Louise Cornard; Quebec, 1810 ***7603*** *p100*
Fitzgibbons, James 28; Harris Co., TX, 1897 ***6254*** *p3*
Fitzharris, Michael; America, 1740 ***4971*** *p35*
Fitzhenry, John 32; New Orleans, 1864 ***543.30*** *p228B*
Fitz Henry, Joseph; Iowa, 1866-1943 ***123.54*** *p18*
Fitzhofen, . . .; Canada, 1776-1783 ***9786*** *p21*
Fitzimmons, Andrew; Philadelphia, 1811 ***2859.11*** *p11*
Fitzmorris, James; America, 1736 ***4971*** *p81*
Fitzpatrick, Widow; Philadelphia, 1864 ***5704.8*** *p182*
Fitzpatrick, Acheson 28; Quebec, 1864 ***5704.8*** *p162*
Fitzpatrick, Bernard; New York, NY, 1838 ***8208.4*** *p82*
Fitzpatrick, Bernd; New York, NY, 1816 ***2859.11*** *p30*
Fitzpatrick, Bessy 16; Massachusetts, 1850 ***5881.1*** *p36*
Fitzpatrick, Bridget; Quebec, 1820 ***7603*** *p60*
Fitzpatrick, Bridget 24; Massachusetts, 1847 ***5881.1*** *p35*
Fitzpatrick, Daniel; New York, NY, 1816 ***2859.11*** *p30*
Fitzpatrick, Daniel; Philadelphia, 1834 ***8208.4*** *p49*
Fitzpatrick, Dennis; New York, NY, 1816 ***2859.11*** *p30*
Fitzpatrick, Edmund; New York, NY, 1816 ***2859.11*** *p30*
Fitzpatrick, Edward 31; Virginia, 1774 ***1219.7*** *p185*
Fitzpatrick, Elizabeth 60; Quebec, 1864 ***5704.8*** *p164*
Fitzpatrick, James; America, 1738 ***4971*** *p85*
Fitzpatrick, James; America, 1738 ***4971*** *p95*
Fitzpatrick, James; America, 1743 ***4971*** *p11*
Fitzpatrick, James; New York, NY, 1816 ***2859.11*** *p30*
Fitzpatrick, James; New York, NY, 1838 ***8208.4*** *p71*
Fitzpatrick, Jane 27; Quebec, 1864 ***5704.8*** *p162*
Fitzpatrick, Johanna; Philadelphia, 1864 ***5704.8*** *p182*
Fitzpatrick, John; America, 1737 ***4971*** *p71*
Fitzpatrick, John; America, 1739 ***4971*** *p31*
Fitzpatrick, John; Quebec, 1781 ***7603*** *p93*
Fitzpatrick, John 24; Philadelphia, 1774 ***1219.7*** *p183*
Fitzpatrick, John 27?; New Orleans, 1862 ***543.30*** *p30*
Fitzpatrick, John M.; Wisconsin, n.d. ***9675.5*** *p122*
Fitzpatrick, Judith; Montreal, 1824 ***7603*** *p87*
Fitzpatrick, Mary; Quebec, 1823 ***7603*** *p80*
Fitzpatrick, Mary 4 mos; Massachusetts, 1847 ***5881.1*** *p38*
Fitzpatrick, Mary 22; Massachusetts, 1849 ***5881.1*** *p39*
Fitzpatrick, Mary Ann; New York, NY, 1816 ***2859.11*** *p30*
Fitzpatrick, Michael; Montreal, 1820 ***7603*** *p92*
Fitzpatrick, Peter; America, 1742 ***4971*** *p30*
Fitzpatrick, Peter; Annapolis, MD, 1742 ***4971*** *p93*
Fitzpatrick, Peter; Maryland, 1742 ***4971*** *p106*
Fitzpatrick, Sally; New York, NY, 1816 ***2859.11*** *p31*
Fitzpatrick, Samuel 3; Quebec, 1864 ***5704.8*** *p162*
Fitzpatrick, T.; New York, NY, 1811 ***2859.11*** *p11*
With family
Fitzpatrick, Terence; America, 1737 ***4971*** *p71*
Fitzpatrick, Terence; New York, NY, 1816 ***2859.11*** *p31*
Fitzpatrick, Thomas; New York, NY, 1816 ***2859.11*** *p31*
Fitzpatrick, Thomas; Philadelphia, 1852 ***5704.8*** *p89*
Fitzpatrick, Thomas; Quebec, 1822 ***7603*** *p82*
Fitzpatrick, Thomas 5; Quebec, 1864 ***5704.8*** *p162*
Fitzpatrick, Timothy 20; Massachusetts, 1849 ***5881.1*** *p40*
Fitzpatrick, William; America, 1740 ***4971*** *p64*
Fitzpatrick, William 7 mos; Quebec, 1864 ***5704.8*** *p162*
Fitzpatrick, Wm.; New York, NY, 1811 ***2859.11*** *p11*
FitzRoy, G. D. Seymour; Kansas, 1890 ***5240.1*** *p12*
Fitzsimmon, James 40; Arizona, 1897 ***9228.40*** *p2*
Fitzsimmons, Alfred; Iowa, 1866-1943 ***123.54*** *p18*
Fitzsimmons, Christopher 42; New Orleans, 1862 ***543.30*** *p30*
Fitzsimmons, Eliza 5; Massachusetts, 1850 ***5881.1*** *p37*
Fitzsimmons, Eliza 33; Massachusetts, 1850 ***5881.1*** *p37*
Fitzsimmons, Henry; America, 1741 ***4971*** *p16*
Fitzsimmons, James; Arizona, 1897 ***9228.30*** *p1*
Fitzsimmons, James; Philadelphia, 1852 ***5704.8*** *p92*
Fitzsimmons, John; New York, NY, 1840 ***8208.4*** *p111*
Fitzsimmons, John 3; Massachusetts, 1850 ***5881.1*** *p38*
Fitzsimmons, Mary; America, 1742 ***4971*** *p17*
Fitzsimmons, Michael 7; Massachusetts, 1850 ***5881.1*** *p39*
Fitzsimons, Bryan; America, 1738 ***4971*** *p14*
Fitzsimons, Henry 16; Quebec, 1864 ***5704.8*** *p163*
Fitzsimons, James 4; Quebec, 1864 ***5704.8*** *p163*
Fitzsimons, John; Philadelphia, 1811 ***2859.11*** *p11*
Fitzsimons, Margaret 38; Quebec, 1864 ***5704.8*** *p163*
Fitzsimons, Philip; America, 1735-1743 ***4971*** *p8*
Fitzsimons, Sarah 11; Quebec, 1864 ***5704.8*** *p163*
Fitzsimons, William 9; Quebec, 1864 ***5704.8*** *p163*
Fitzsimons, William 39; Quebec, 1864 ***5704.8*** *p163*
Fitz-Symons, James; America, 1743 ***4971*** *p24*
Fitzwalter, George *SEE* Fitzwalter, Thomas

Fitzwalter, Joseph 31; Savannah, GA, 1733 *4719.17* p310
Fitzwalter, Josiah SEE Fitzwalter, Mary Cheney
Fitzwalter, Mary SEE Fitzwalter, Mary Cheney
Fitzwalter, Mary Cheney; Died enroute, 1682 *4961* p167
  Child:Josiah
  Child:Mary
Fitzwalter, Thomas SEE Fitzwalter, Thomas
Fitzwalter, Thomas; Pennsylvania, 1682 *4961* p167
  Child:Thomas
  Child:George
Fitzwater, George SEE Fitzwater, Thomas
Fitzwater, Josiah SEE Fitzwater, Mary Cheney
Fitzwater, Mary SEE Fitzwater, Mary Cheney
Fitzwater, Mary Cheney; Died enroute, 1682 *4961* p167
  Child:Josiah
  Child:Mary
Fitzwater, Thomas SEE Fitzwater, Thomas
Fitzwater, Thomas; Pennsylvania, 1682 *4960* p158
Fitzwater, Thomas; Pennsylvania, 1682 *4961* p167
  Child:Thomas
  Child:George
Fitzwilliams, Henry; Annapolis, MD, 1742 *4971* p93
Fitzwilliams, Henry; Maryland, 1742 *4971* p106
Fix, . . .; Canada, 1776-1783 *9786* p42
Fixari, Mr. 24; America, 1839 *778.5* p209
Fixmus, Richard; Virginia, 1644 *6219* p231
Fizgerald, William; America, 1741 *4971* p49
Fjallman, Charles; Minneapolis, 1879-1885 *6410.35* p53
Flach, Dorothea SEE Flach, Ludwig
Flach, Johann Georg SEE Flach, Ludwig
Flach, Karl; Cincinnati, 1869-1887 *8582* p9
Flach, Ludwig; America, 1746-1800 *2444* p154
  Wife:Dorothea
  Child:Johann Georg
  Child:Maria Catharina
Flach, Maria Catharina SEE Flach, Ludwig
Flaches, Ella; Milwaukee, 1875 *4719.30* p257
Flachmeier, Anna Marie Engel SEE Flachmeier, Johann Heinrich
Flachmeier, Carl Heinrich F. SEE Flachmeier, Johann Heinrich
Flachmeier, Johann Heinrich; America, 1844 *4610.10* p141
  Wife:Anna Marie Engel
  Child:Carl Heinrich F.
  Child:Peter Friedrich W.
Flachmeier, Peter Friedrich W. SEE Flachmeier, Johann Heinrich
Flachmeyer, Anna M. Louise Stucke 34 SEE Flachmeyer, Johann Barthold
Flachmeyer, Anna Marie Louise SEE Flachmeyer, Johann Barthold
Flachmeyer, Anna Marie Louise SEE Flachmeyer, Johann Barthold
Flachmeyer, Caspar Heinrich SEE Flachmeyer, Johann Barthold
Flachmeyer, Friedrich W.A. Leopold SEE Flachmeyer, Johann Barthold
Flachmeyer, Hermann H. Friedrich SEE Flachmeyer, Johann Barthold
Flachmeyer, Johann Barthold 51; America, 1843 *4610.10* p133
  Wife:Anna M. Louise Stucke 34
  Child:Anna Marie Louise
  Child:Caspar Heinrich
  Child:Friedrich W.A. Leopold
  Child:Hermann H. Friedrich
  Child:Anna Marie Louise
Flachs, Elisabetha 11; America, 1853 *9162.7* p14
Flachs, Johannes 9; America, 1853 *9162.7* p14
Flachs, Katharina 2; America, 1853 *9162.7* p14
Flachs, Margaretha 6; America, 1853 *9162.7* p14
Flachs, Marie Elis. 26; America, 1853 *9162.7* p14
Flack, A. 40; New Orleans, 1830 *778.5* p209
Flack, A. 50; New Orleans, 1830 *778.5* p209
Flack, Adam; Arkansas, 1918 *95.2* p43
Flack, B. 12; New Orleans, 1830 *778.5* p209
Flack, Joseph 21; Maryland, 1774 *1219.7* p207
Flack, Ludwig; Pennsylvania, 1749 *2444* p154
Flack, S. 15; New Orleans, 1830 *778.5* p209
Flack, W. 9; New Orleans, 1830 *778.5* p209
Flacks, Ella; Milwaukee, 1875 *4719.30* p257
Flaczenski, Adam; Arkansas, 1918 *95.2* p43
Flaeming, Julius; Arkansas, 1918 *95.2* p44
Flafferty, Anne; New York, NY, 1864 *5704.8* p186
Flagdin, Henry 19; Jamaica, 1730 *3690.1* p290
Flaharty, John 25; Ohio, 1852 *1450.2* p43A
Flaherty, Daniel Michael; Arkansas, 1918 *95.2* p44
Flaherty, Edward 38; California, 1867 *3840.1* p18
Flaherty, Margaret; Philadelphia, 1816 *2859.11* p31
Flaherty, Martin 20; Massachusetts, 1849 *5881.1* p39
Flaherty, Martin 30; Massachusetts, 1849 *5881.1* p39

Flaherty, Michael; New York, NY, 1870 *5704.8* p238
Flaherty, Michael 47; Massachusetts, 1849 *5881.1* p39
Flaherty, Patrick; Illinois, 1892 *5012.40* p26
Flaherty, Patrick; New York, NY, 1815 *2859.11* p31
Flaherty, Thomas; America, 1735-1743 *4971* p78
Flaherty, Thomas; America, 1742 *4971* p80
Flaherty, William; New Brunswick, 1806 *7603* p76
Flaherty, William 21; Philadelphia, 1857 *5704.8* p133
Flake, Robert; Virginia, 1640 *6219* p182
Flaker, Sarah 16; Maryland, 1774 *1219.7* p229
Flameng, John; West Indies, 1764 *1219.7* p101
Flamon, Patrice 24; Montreal, 1782 *7603* p90
Flanagan, Ann; St. John, N.B., 1847 *5704.8* p26
Flanagan, Bridget; America, 1743 *4971* p74
Flanagan, Bridget 22; Philadelphia, 1853 *5704.8* p108
Flanagan, Catherine 22; Quebec, 1856 *5704.8* p130
Flanagan, Charles 36; New Orleans, 1863 *543.30* p230B
Flanagan, Dominick; New York, NY, 1816 *2859.11* p31
Flanagan, Ellen 20; Philadelphia, 1853 *5704.8* p108
Flanagan, Henry; New York, NY, 1838 *8208.4* p90
Flanagan, James; America, 1743 *4971* p74
Flanagan, James 21; Jamaica, 1774 *1219.7* p232
Flanagan, John; America, 1738 *4971* p46
Flanagan, John; Philadelphia, 1847 *53.26* p27
  Relative:Mary
Flanagan, John; Philadelphia, 1847 *5704.8* p32
Flanagan, John; Philadelphia, 1865 *5704.8* p201
Flanagan, John; Quebec, 1852 *5704.8* p97
Flanagan, Mary SEE Flanagan, John
Flanagan, Mary; New York, NY, 1868 *5704.8* p227
Flanagan, Mary; Philadelphia, 1847 *5704.8* p32
Flanagan, Michel; Quebec, 1774 *7603* p60
Flanagan, Patrick; America, 1738 *4971* p36
Flanagan, Patrick; New York, NY, 1816 *2859.11* p31
Flanagan, Patrick; Philadelphia, 1811 *53.26* p27
Flanagan, Patrick; Philadelphia, 1811 *2859.11* p11
Flanagan, Rose 17; Quebec, 1856 *5704.8* p130
Flanagan, Samuel; New York, NY, 1816 *2859.11* p31
Flanagan, Sarah 30; Philadelphia, 1853 *5704.8* p113
Flanagan, Thady; America, 1738-1743 *4971* p91
Flanagan, Thomas 40; New Orleans, 1862 *543.30* p223B
Flanagan, Timothy; Vermont, 1819-1841 *7036* p126
Flanaghan, John; Philadelphia, 1851 *5704.8* p81
Flanaghan, Peter; Philadelphia, 1849 *53.26* p27
Flanaghan, Peter; Philadelphia, 1849 *5704.8* p53
Flandin, John Francis Elie; New York, NY, 1838 *8208.4* p67
Flanegan, Patrick; America, 1735-1743 *4971* p79
Flanery, M.; New York, NY, 1811 *2859.11* p11
  With family
Flanger, Martin; Kansas, 1868 *5240.1* p12
Flanigan, Charles 34; Philadelphia, 1804 *53.26* p27
  Relative:Mary 28
  Relative:Jno. 6
Flanigan, Jane; Philadelphia, 1851 *5704.8* p71
Flanigan, Jno. 6 SEE Flanigan, Charles
Flanigan, John; New York, NY, 1811 *2859.11* p11
Flanigan, John; Philadelphia, 1851 *5704.8* p71
Flanigan, Mary 28 SEE Flanigan, Charles
Flanigan, Patrick; New York, NY, 1811 *2859.11* p11
Flanigan, Timothy; America, 1735-1743 *4971* p8
Flannagan, Patrick 12; Massachusetts, 1849 *5881.1* p40
Flannagan, Bridget 35; Massachusetts, 1849 *5881.1* p36
Flannegan, Ivory 10; Massachusetts, 1849 *5881.1* p37
Flannegan, James 8; Massachusetts, 1849 *5881.1* p38
Flannegan, Mary 20; Massachusetts, 1847 *5881.1* p38
Flannegan, Mary 45; Massachusetts, 1849 *5881.1* p39
Flannegan, Patrick; America, 1741 *4971* p82
Flannegan, Sylvester 55; Massachusetts, 1850 *5881.1* p40
Flannegan, Thomas 5; Massachusetts, 1849 *5881.1* p40
Flannelly, James; New York, NY, 1838 *8208.4* p89
Flannelly, Timothy; New York, NY, 1837 *8208.4* p11
Flannery, John 25; Kansas, 1885 *5240.1* p68
Flannigan, Brigitte; Quebec, 1823 *7603* p64
Flannigan, Charles 39; New Orleans, 1862 *543.30* p30
Flannigan, James; America, 1736-1743 *4971* p58
Flannigan, Lawrence H.; New York, NY, 1839 *8208.4* p96
Flannigan, Pierce; America, 1736-1743 *4971* p58
Flarity, Patrick 27; New Orleans, 1862 *543.30* p29
Flath, Peter; Pennsylvania, 1764 *4525* p216
  With family
Flath, Peter; South America, 1764 *4525* p216
  With family
Flatman, John 35; Maryland, 1774 *1219.7* p196
Flatman, Thomas 23; Jamaica, 1725 *3690.1* p79
Flatt, James 25; Carolina, 1774 *1219.7* p237
Flatt, James H.; Illinois, 1871 *5012.39* p25
Flatt, Peter; Pennsylvania, 1764 *4525* p216
Flatt, Peter; South America, 1764 *4525* p216
Flatter, Alphonse 26; America, 1835 *778.5* p209
Flavel, Job; Illinois, 1886 *2896.5* p12

Flaxman, Thomas 44; Maryland, 1775 *1219.7* p272
Flaxton, Jno.; Virginia, 1648 *6219* p250
Flecheur, Edouard; Quebec, 1710 *7603* p28
Fleck, J. C.; Ohio, 1843 *8582* p9
Fleck, Johanna Her 65; New York, NY, 1911 *1763* p40C
Fleckenstein, Elise 3; America, 1854-1855 *9162.6* p105
Fleckenstein, Elise 17; America, 1854-1855 *9162.6* p105
Fleckenstein, Eva Elis. 58; America, 1854-1855 *9162.6* p105
Fleckenstein, Heinrich 18; America, 1854-1855 *9162.6* p105
Flecker, Adam; America, 1785 *4525* p217
Flecker, Adam; Pennsylvania, 1785 *4525* p217
Fleckstein, . . .; Canada, 1776-1783 *9786* p21
Flecksteiner, Alexander; America, 1845 *8582.3* p19
Fleese, Michael; Philadelphia, 1759 *9973.7* p33
Fleet, Abraham 21; Jamaica, 1724 *3690.1* p79
Fleet, Benjamin 21; Virginia, 1774 *1219.7* p201
Fleet, Jno.; Virginia, 1646 *6219* p239
Fleetcroft, Thomas 19; United States or West Indies, 1718 *3690.1* p79
Fleete, Robt.; Virginia, 1643 *6219* p207
Fleett, Abraham 21; Jamaica, 1724 *3690.1* p79
Flegeler, Andrew; Pennsylvania, 1773 *4525* p217
Flegger, Christoph; Wisconsin, n.d. *9675.5* p122
Flegler Family ; Pennsylvania, 1785 *4525* p225
Flegler, Miss; Pennsylvania, 1752 *4525* p219
Flegler, Andreas; Pennsylvania, 1773 *4525* p217
Flegler, Dorothy SEE Flegler, Valentine
Flegler, Eva SEE Flegler, Valentine
Flegler, Johann Leonhard; Pennsylvania, 1752 *4525* p217
  With wife
  With child
Flegler, Maria; New England, 1752 *4525* p217
Flegler, Maria; Pennsylvania, 1752 *4525* p217
Flegler, Nich's SEE Flegler, Valentine
Flegler, Valentin, Jr.; America, 1785 *4525* p217
  With wife
  With 2 children
Flegler, Valentine; Pennsylvania, 1785 *4525* p217
  Relative:Eva
  Relative:Dorothy
  Relative:Nich's
Flegler, Zacharias; America, 1709 *4525* p217
Flegler, Zacharias; Pennsylvania, 1709 *4525* p217
Fleischer, . . .; Canada, 1776-1783 *9786* p21
Fleischer, Andrew; Canada, 1783 *9786* p38A
Fleischer, Gustav W. T. F. 39; Kansas, 1889 *5240.1* p74
Fleischhaner, Franz; Kansas, 1887 *5240.1* p12
Fleischman, Andrew; Wisconsin, n.d. *9675.5* p122
Fleischman, Edward 25; New Orleans, 1862 *543.30* p225B
Fleischman, Moses; California, 1872 *2769.4* p4
Fleischmann, . . .; Canada, 1776-1783 *9786* p42
Fleischmann, Mr.; Cincinnati, 1831 *8582* p51
Fleischmann, Christina 22; America, 1853 *9162.8* p36
Fleischmann, Johann Christoph; Pennsylvania, 1753 *2444* p154
  Wife:Maria Clara Mehlhaefin
Fleischmann, Maria Clara Mehlhaefin SEE Fleischmann, Johann Christoph
Fleischmann, Mathias; Wisconsin, n.d. *9675.5* p122
Fleischmann, Willibald; Kansas, 1889 *5240.1* p12
Fleisner, Gregor; Wisconsin, n.d. *9675.5* p122
Fleiss, Balthasar 27; Georgia, 1734 *9332* p327
Fleissner, Joseph; Wisconsin, n.d. *9675.5* p122
Fleith, Francois 50; America, 1837 *778.5* p209
Fleman, Betsy; New York, NY, 1811 *2859.11* p11
Fleman, Joseph; New York, NY, 1811 *2859.11* p11
Fleming, Alexander 23; St. John, N.B., 1864 *5704.8* p158
Fleming, Andrew; Philadelphia, 1866 *5704.8* p215
Fleming, Andrew 19; Quebec, 1858 *5704.8* p138
Fleming, Ann 27; St. John, N.B., 1864 *5704.8* p158
Fleming, Ann 50; Philadelphia, 1854 *5704.8* p116
Fleming, Annie; Philadelphia, 1865 *5704.8* p195
Fleming, Belle; Philadelphia, 1866 *5704.8* p215
Fleming, Betty; Quebec, 1853 *5704.8* p103
Fleming, Catherine 18; Philadelphia, 1861 *5704.8* p147
Fleming, Christina 10; St. John, N.B., 1864 *5704.8* p158
Fleming, David; Charleston, SC, 1809 *1639.20* p70
Fleming, Edward Z. 38; Kansas, 1904 *5240.1* p83
Fleming, Eliz 28; Wilmington, DE, 1831 *6508.7* p160
Fleming, Eliza Anne 11; Philadelphia, 1854 *5704.8* p116
Fleming, Isabella 13; Philadelphia, 1854 *5704.8* p116
Fleming, James; Philadelphia, 1865 *5704.8* p195
Fleming, James; Quebec, 1847 *5704.8* p8
Fleming, James 1; St. John, N.B., 1864 *5704.8* p158
Fleming, James 18; Philadelphia, 1854 *5704.8* p116
Fleming, James 60; Philadelphia, 1861 *5704.8* p147
Fleming, Jane 18; Philadelphia, 1858 *5704.8* p139
Fleming, Jane 18; St. John, N.B., 1864 *5704.8* p158
Fleming, John; Carolina, 1684 *1639.20* p70

Fleming, John; South Carolina, 1810 ***1639.20*** *p70*
Fleming, John 20; St. John, N.B., 1864 ***5704.8*** *p158*
Fleming, John 21; Philadelphia, 1774 ***1219.7*** *p228*
Fleming, John 24; Philadelphia, 1803 ***53.26*** *p27*
Fleming, John 30; Wilmington, DE, 1831 ***6508.7*** *p160*
Fleming, John 56; St. John, N.B., 1864 ***5704.8*** *p158*
Fleming, John C. W.; Kansas, 1901 ***5240.1*** *p12*
Fleming, Joseph 50; Philadelphia, 1854 ***5704.8*** *p116*
Fleming, Margaret 14; St. John, N.B., 1864 ***5704.8*** *p158*
Fleming, Margaret 18; Philadelphia, 1854 ***5704.8*** *p116*
Fleming, Margaret 42; St. John, N.B., 1864 ***5704.8*** *p158*
Fleming, Martha 7; Wilmington, DE, 1831 ***6508.7*** *p160*
Fleming, Martin; Illinois, 1862 ***7857*** *p3*
Fleming, Mary; America, 1868 ***5704.8*** *p230*
Fleming, Mary; New York, NY, 1871 ***5704.8*** *p240*
Fleming, Mary; Philadelphia, 1865 ***5704.8*** *p195*
Fleming, Mary 6; St. John, N.B., 1864 ***5704.8*** *p158*
Fleming, Mary 17; Philadelphia, 1858 ***5704.8*** *p139*
Fleming, Mary Ann 3; Wilmington, DE, 1831 ***6508.7*** *p160*
Fleming, Matilda 6; Philadelphia, 1854 ***5704.8*** *p116*
Fleming, Matilda 30; Philadelphia, 1861 ***5704.8*** *p147*
Fleming, Morris; New York, NY, 1834 ***8208.4*** *p77*
Fleming, Nancy; Philadelphia, 1852 ***5704.8*** *p88*
Fleming, Nancy 20; Philadelphia, 1861 ***5704.8*** *p147*
Fleming, Nicholas; Wisconsin, n.d. ***9675.5*** *p122*
Fleming, Richard; Virginia, 1643 ***6219*** *p203*
Fleming, Richard 25; Quebec, 1864 ***5704.8*** *p161*
Fleming, Robert; New York, NY, 1864 ***5704.8*** *p172*
Fleming, Robert; Virginia, 1643 ***6219*** *p207*
Fleming, Robert 11; St. John, N.B., 1864 ***5704.8*** *p158*
Fleming, Roger; Illinois, 1862 ***7857*** *p3*
Fleming, Samuel 23; Philadelphia, 1854 ***5704.8*** *p116*
Fleming, Sandford; Canada, 1864 ***9775.5*** *p211*
Fleming, Sandford; Ontario, 1800-1880 ***9775.5*** *p216*
Fleming, Sarah 24; Philadelphia, 1854 ***5704.8*** *p118*
Fleming, Tho.; America, 1742 ***4971*** *p30*
Fleming, Thomas; Annapolis, MD, 1742 ***4971*** *p93*
Fleming, Thomas; Maryland, 1742 ***4971*** *p106*
Fleming, William; New Brunswick, 1765-1828 ***9775.5*** *p204*
Fleming, William; South Carolina, 1788 ***7119*** *p201*
Fleming, William 5; Wilmington, DE, 1831 ***6508.7*** *p160*
Fleming, William 15; Philadelphia, 1861 ***5704.8*** *p147*
Flemme, . . .; Canada, 1776-1783 ***9786*** *p21*
Flemming, David 12; Massachusetts, 1850 ***5881.1*** *p36*
Flemming, Elizabeth 5; Massachusetts, 1849 ***5881.1*** *p36*
Flemming, Fanny; New Orleans, 1852 ***5704.8*** *p98*
Flemming, Franci *SEE* Flemming, Mary Ann
Flemming, Francis; Philadelphia, 1847 ***5704.8*** *p14*
Flemming, Henry; Philadelphia, 1847 ***53.26*** *p27*
Flemming, Henry; Philadelphia, 1847 ***5704.8*** *p22*
Flemming, Isabella 2; Quebec, 1847 ***5704.8*** *p16*
Flemming, James; Philadelphia, 1847 ***53.26*** *p27*
Flemming, James; Philadelphia, 1847 ***5704.8*** *p23*
Flemming, James; St. John, N.B., 1847 ***5704.8*** *p20*
Flemming, James 26; Virginia, 1773 ***1219.7*** *p170*
Flemming, Jane; Quebec, 1847 ***5704.8*** *p16*
Flemming, Jane 9 mos; Quebec, 1847 ***5704.8*** *p16*
Flemming, Joan 28; Massachusetts, 1849 ***5881.1*** *p37*
Flemming, Johanna 11; Massachusetts, 1850 ***5881.1*** *p38*
Flemming, John 16; Massachusetts, 1847 ***5881.1*** *p37*
Flemming, John 20; Massachusetts, 1849 ***5881.1*** *p37*
Flemming, John 20; Quebec, 1863 ***5704.8*** *p154*
Flemming, John 27; Virginia, 1775 ***1219.7*** *p261*
Flemming, Joseph 4; Quebec, 1847 ***5704.8*** *p16*
Flemming, Mary 23; Massachusetts, 1849 ***5881.1*** *p39*
Flemming, Mary Ann; Philadelphia, 1847 ***53.26*** *p27*
*Relative:*Franci
Flemming, Mary Ann; Philadelphia, 1847 ***5704.8*** *p14*
Flemming, Mary Jane 3 mos; St. John, N.B., 1847 ***5704.8*** *p20*
Flemming, Michael; Quebec, 1803 ***7603*** *p76*
Flemming, Michael 30; Massachusetts, 1849 ***5881.1*** *p39*
Flemming, Patrick 13; Massachusetts, 1850 ***5881.1*** *p40*
Flemming, Rebecca 2; Quebec, 1847 ***5704.8*** *p16*
Flemming, Richard; America, 1742 ***4971*** *p49*
Flemming, Richard; America, 1742 ***4971*** *p50*
Flemming, Robert; New York, NY, 1836 ***8208.4*** *p10*
Flemming, Samuel; Philadelphia, 1848 ***53.26*** *p27*
Flemming, Samuel; Philadelphia, 1848 ***5704.8*** *p46*
Flemming, Thomas; Indiana, 1837 ***7036*** *p123*
Flemming, Thomas; Philadelphia, 1848 ***53.26*** *p28*
*Relative:*William
Flemming, Thomas; Philadelphia, 1848 ***5704.8*** *p46*
Flemming, Thomas 19; Philadelphia, 1803 ***53.26*** *p28*
Flemming, William *SEE* Flemming, Thomas
Flemming, William; New York, NY, 1816 ***2859.11*** *p31*
Flemming, William; Philadelphia, 1848 ***5704.8*** *p46*
Flemming, William; Quebec, 1847 ***5704.8*** *p16*
Flemming, Wm.; New York, NY, 1811 ***2859.11*** *p11*
Flennig, Frank; Wisconsin, n.d. ***9675.5*** *p122*
Flensbach, Christoph Ludwig *SEE* Flensbach, Melchior Leonhard
Flensbach, Georg Martin *SEE* Flensbach, Melchior Leonhard
Flensbach, Johann Adam *SEE* Flensbach, Melchior Leonhard
Flensbach, Melchior Leonhard; Pennsylvania, 1753 ***2444*** *p154*
*Wife:*Sophia C. Rembold
*Child:*Johann Adam
*Child:*Georg Martin
*Child:*Christoph Ludwig
*Child:*Sophia Catharina
*Child:*Rosmaria
*Child:*Regina Margaretha
Flensbach, Regina Margaretha *SEE* Flensbach, Melchior Leonhard
Flensbach, Rosmaria *SEE* Flensbach, Melchior Leonhard
Flensbach, Sophia C. Rembold *SEE* Flensbach, Melchior Leonhard
Flensbach, Sophia Catharina *SEE* Flensbach, Melchior Leonhard
Flesner, Andrew; Illinois, 1888 ***5012.37*** *p61*
Flesner, Ekke E., Jr.; Illinois, 1888 ***5012.37*** *p61*
Flesner, Minke; Illinois, 1895 ***5012.40*** *p54*
Fletcher, Angus 46; Wilmington, NC, 1774 ***1639.20*** *p70*
*Wife:*Katherine McIntyre
*Child:*Euphane 10
*Child:*Mary 6
*Child:*Nancy 3
Fletcher, Anthony; Virginia, 1643 ***6219*** *p187*
Fletcher, C. John 17; Philadelphia, 1853 ***5704.8*** *p113*
Fletcher, Charles 18; Windward Islands, 1722 ***3690.1*** *p79*
Fletcher, Edwd 24; Wilmington, DE, 1831 ***6508.7*** *p161*
Fletcher, Eleazer 25; Maryland or Virginia, 1699 ***2212*** *p24*
Fletcher, Elizabeth *SEE* Fletcher, Hannibal
Fletcher, Ellen; St. John, N.B., 1853 ***5704.8*** *p99*
Fletcher, Ernest; Arkansas, 1918 ***95.2*** *p44*
Fletcher, Euphane 10 *SEE* Fletcher, Angus
Fletcher, George; Virginia, 1652 ***6251*** *p20*
Fletcher, Hannibal; Virginia, 1634 ***6219*** *p10*
*Wife:*Elizabeth
Fletcher, James; Virginia, 1635 ***6219*** *p69*
Fletcher, James 33; Quebec, 1857 ***5704.8*** *p136*
Fletcher, Jno.; Virginia, 1646 ***6219*** *p241*
Fletcher, John; New York, NY, 1811 ***2859.11*** *p11*
Fletcher, John; Virginia, 1639 ***6219*** *p154*
Fletcher, John; Port uncertain, 1757 ***3690.1*** *p79*
Fletcher, Jon.; Virginia, 1643 ***6219*** *p204*
Fletcher, Jonie 22; Virginia, 1700 ***2212*** *p31*
Fletcher, Katherine McIntyre *SEE* Fletcher, Angus
Fletcher, Mary 6 *SEE* Fletcher, Angus
Fletcher, Mary 16; America, 1702 ***2212*** *p38*
Fletcher, Mary 21; America, 1703 ***2212*** *p40*
Fletcher, Mary Ann 6 mos; Quebec, 1857 ***5704.8*** *p136*
Fletcher, Michaell; Virginia, 1642 ***6219*** *p194*
Fletcher, Nancy 3 *SEE* Fletcher, Angus
Fletcher, Peter; Virginia, 1643 ***6219*** *p200*
Fletcher, Samuel 16; Virginia, 1774 ***1219.7*** *p241*
Fletcher, Stephen 21; Pennsylvania, Virginia or Maryland, 1699 ***2212*** *p19*
Fletcher, Tho.; Virginia, 1643 ***6219*** *p204*
Fletcher, Thomas 26; Philadelphia, 1774 ***1219.7*** *p228*
Fletcher, Thomas 29; Maryland, 1774 ***1219.7*** *p187*
Fletcher, Valent.; Virginia, 1636 ***6219*** *p80*
Fletcher, Vallentine; Virginia, 1639 ***6219*** *p161*
Fletcher, William 20; Virginia, 1730 ***3690.1*** *p79*
Fletcher, William 22; Maryland, 1724 ***3690.1*** *p79*
Fletcher, Wm.; Virginia, 1634 ***6219*** *p32*
Fletef, Joseph; Iowa, 1866-1943 ***123.54*** *p18*
Fleti, Michael 22; New Orleans, 1862 ***543.30*** *p224B*
Flett, Henry 24; Kansas, 1871 ***5240.1*** *p52*
Flett, John; Canada, 1830 ***8893*** *p266*
Fleurant, . . .; Canada, 1776-1783 ***9786*** *p42*
Fleuri, Jean 23; New Orleans, 1839 ***778.5*** *p209*
Fleuriau de Belleman, Mr. 30; Louisiana, 1821 ***778.5*** *p210*
Fleury, Mrs. A. 20; New Orleans, 1837 ***778.5*** *p210*
Fleury, E. 2; New Orleans, 1837 ***778.5*** *p210*
Fleury, F. 18; New Orleans, 1831 ***778.5*** *p210*
Fleury, L. D. 35; New Orleans, 1837 ***778.5*** *p210*
Fleury, Louis 26; Louisiana, 1820 ***778.5*** *p210*
Fleury, Marg.; Port uncertain, 1839 ***778.5*** *p210*
Flewellin, Ann; Virginia, 1643 ***6219*** *p23*
Flewellin, Tho.; Virginia, 1643 ***6219*** *p23*
Flewelling, Charles H.; Illinois, 1888 ***5012.39*** *p122*
Flex, Elias; New York, 1749 ***3652*** *p71*
Fleyneye, Thos.; Virginia, 1637 ***6219*** *p10*
Flicker, Michael; Pennsylvania, 1786 ***4525*** *p209*
Flickert, Adam; America, 1785 ***4525*** *p217*
With wife
With 6 children
Flickert, Adam; Pennsylvania, 1785 ***4525*** *p217*
With wife
With 6 children
Flickert, Joh Mich; Pennsylvania, 1786 ***4525*** *p209*
With wife & 4 children
Flickert, Johann Michael; Pennsylvania, 1786 ***4525*** *p217*
Fliegenschmidt, Carl; America, 1895 ***1450.2*** *p9B*
Flierl, George; Wisconsin, n.d. ***9675.5*** *p122*
Flierl, Johann; Illinois, 1892 ***2896.5*** *p12*
Fligny, Francois 17; Port uncertain, 1839 ***778.5*** *p210*
Fligny, Francois 24; Port uncertain, 1839 ***778.5*** *p210*
Fligny, Francois 63; Port uncertain, 1839 ***778.5*** *p210*
Fligny, Marguerite 29; Port uncertain, 1839 ***778.5*** *p210*
Fliker, Anna Elizabeth *SEE* Fliker, Michael
Fliker, Johan Christoph *SEE* Fliker, Michael
Fliker, Johan Michel *SEE* Fliker, Michael
Fliker, Maria Dorothea *SEE* Fliker, Michael
Fliker, Michael; Pennsylvania, 1786 ***4525*** *p218*
With wife
*Child:*Maria Dorothea
*Child:*Johan Christoph
*Child:*Johan Michel
*Child:*Anna Elizabeth
Flikker, Anna Elizabeth *SEE* Flikker, Michael
Flikker, Johan Christoph *SEE* Flikker, Michael
Flikker, Johan Michel *SEE* Flikker, Michael
Flikker, Maria Dorothea *SEE* Flikker, Michael
Flikker, Michael; Pennsylvania, 1786 ***4525*** *p218*
With wife
*Child:*Maria Dorothea
*Child:*Johan Christoph
*Child:*Johan Michel
*Child:*Anna Elizabeth
Flimaning, John 31; Maryland, 1775 ***1219.7*** *p251*
Flin, William; America, 1742 ***4971*** *p22*
Flinchbach, Heinrich; Ohio, 1820-1829 ***8582*** *p9*
Flinchbough, . . .; Pennsylvania, n.d. ***2444*** *p154*
Fling, John; Virginia, 1639 ***6219*** *p150*
Flink, Gust Carl; Arkansas, 1918 ***95.2*** *p44*
Flinn, Catherine; Philadelphia, 1847 ***5704.8*** *p22*
Flinn, Catherine 2; Philadelphia, 1847 ***5704.8*** *p22*
Flinn, Hugh; Philadelphia, 1847 ***5704.8*** *p22*
Flinn, Isabella 11; Philadelphia, 1847 ***5704.8*** *p22*
Flinn, James; Philadelphia, 1816 ***2859.11*** *p31*
Flinn, James; Philadelphia, 1849 ***53.26*** *p28*
Flinn, James; Philadelphia, 1849 ***5704.8*** *p54*
Flinn, Jane 6; Philadelphia, 1847 ***5704.8*** *p22*
Flinn, John; America, 1736-1743 ***4971*** *p57*
Flinn, John; Maryland, 1828-1838 ***1450.2*** *p43A*
Flinn, John; Pennsylvania, 1828-1838 ***1450.2*** *p43A*
Flinn, John 9; Philadelphia, 1847 ***5704.8*** *p22*
Flinn, Patrick; America, 1739 ***4971*** *p98*
Flinn, Rebecca 18; Philadelphia, 1853 ***5704.8*** *p112*
Flinn, Thomas; New York, NY, 1837 ***8208.4*** *p48*
Flinn, Thomas; Wisconsin, n.d. ***9675.5*** *p122*
Flinn, William; America, 1742 ***4971*** *p95*
Flinn, William; Philadelphia, 1816 ***2859.11*** *p31*
Flinsback, Hans Philip 22; Pennsylvania, 1753 ***2444*** *p154*
Flinshbach, . . .; Pennsylvania, n.d. ***2444*** *p154*
Flinspach, Johann Philipp 22; Pennsylvania, 1753 ***2444*** *p154*
Flinspach, Melchior 24; Pennsylvania, 1753 ***2444*** *p154*
Flint, Abigail 42; Massachusetts, 1848 ***5881.1*** *p35*
Flint, James; South Carolina, 1716 ***1639.20*** *p70*
Flint, James 15; Maryland, 1774 ***1219.7*** *p208*
Flint, Richard; Virginia, 1645 ***6219*** *p239*
Flint, William 26; Maryland, 1775 ***1219.7*** *p264*
Flinton, Eliza.; Virginia, 1638 ***6219*** *p117*
Flinton, Pharoah; Virginia, 1623 ***6219*** *p9*
Flintshback, Melchior 24; Pennsylvania, 1753 ***2444*** *p154*
Floerch., Carl; Georgia, 1738 ***9332*** *p321*
Floerch., Hans; Georgia, 1738 ***9332*** *p321*
Floerl, Johann; Georgia, 1775 ***8582.2*** *p64*
Flogden, Andrew 16; Philadelphia, 1774 ***1219.7*** *p233*
Flohr, Friedrich; Cincinnati, 1869-1887 ***8582*** *p9*
Flohr, H.; Cincinnati, 1869-1887 ***8582*** *p9*
Flonius, . . .; Canada, 1776-1783 ***9786*** *p21*
Flood, Ann; Quebec, 1824 ***7603*** *p82*
Flood, Bryan 45; Philadelphia, 1853 ***5704.8*** *p111*
Flood, Daniel; New York, NY, 1815 ***2859.11*** *p31*
Flood, David; Virginia, 1637 ***6219*** *p113*
Flood, Edward; New York, NY, 1838 ***8208.4*** *p70*
Flood, Elizabeth; Philadelphia, 1865 ***5704.8*** *p191*
Flood, Francis; America, 1735-1743 ***4971*** *p8*
Flood, James; America, 1737 ***4971*** *p12*
Flood, James; New York, NY, 1834 ***8208.4*** *p43*
Flood, James; Philadelphia, 1865 ***5704.8*** *p191*
Flood, John 28; Philadelphia, 1864 ***5704.8*** *p161*
Flood, John Joseph; New York, 1899 ***1450.2*** *p9B*

Flood, Jon.; Virginia, 1635 ***6219*** *p71*
Flood, Margaret; Philadelphia, 1867 ***5704.8*** *p220*
Flood, Mary; Philadelphia, 1865 ***5704.8*** *p191*
Flood, Patrick; New York, NY, 1835 ***8208.4*** *p56*
Flood, Patrick; New York, NY, 1840 ***8208.4*** *p105*
Flood, Patrick 26; St. John, N.B., 1864 ***5704.8*** *p157*
Flood, Rich.; Virginia, 1635 ***6219*** *p71*
Flood, Richard; Virginia, 1642 ***6219*** *p186*
Flood, Robert; Virginia, 1637 ***6219*** *p10*
Flood, Samll.; Virginia, 1634 ***6219*** *p84*
Flood, Samuel; New York, NY, 1815 ***2859.11*** *p31*
Flood, Thomas; New York, NY, 1868 ***5704.8*** *p229*
Flood, Thomas; Philadelphia, 1865 ***5704.8*** *p191*
Flood, Thomas; West Virginia, 1856 ***9788.3*** *p10*
Flopkins, Suzanne; Montreal, 1818 ***7603*** *p67*
Flora, Thomas 17; Maryland, 1719 ***3690.1*** *p79*
Florance, Michel 19; Port uncertain, 1836 ***778.5*** *p210*
Floranne, Michel 19; Port uncertain, 1836 ***778.5*** *p210*
Florat, J. 10; America, 1830 ***778.5*** *p210*
Florcak, Stanislaw 23; New York, 1912 ***9980.29*** *p67*
Floreday, Morgan; Virginia, 1600-1642 ***6219*** *p193*
Florel, Anna Maria *SEE* Florel, Hans
Florel, Anna Maria Hopflinger *SEE* Florel, Hans
Florel, Carl; Georgia, 1739 ***9332*** *p323*
Florel, Hans; Georgia, 1739 ***9332*** *p323*
*Wife:*Anna Maria Hopflinger
Florel, Hans; Georgia, 1739 ***9332*** *p326*
*Wife:*Anna Maria
Florel, Karl; Georgia, 1739 ***9332*** *p327*
Florence, Miles; St. John, N.B., 1866 ***5704.8*** *p167*
Florentier, Jean 25; New Orleans, 1826 ***778.5*** *p210*
Florer, . . .; Canada, 1776-1783 ***9786*** *p21*
Florer, John; Canada, 1776-1783 ***9786*** *p207A*
Flores, Juan; Arizona, 1907 ***9228.40*** *p11*
Flores, Meliton 70; Arizona, 1926 ***9228.40*** *p30*
Floreth, Peter William; Illinois, 1868 ***2896.5*** *p12*
Florez, E. 48; Arizona, 1911 ***9228.40*** *p16*
Florez, Inez 45; Arizona, 1918 ***9228.40*** *p22*
Florian, Mr.; New Orleans, 1838 ***778.5*** *p210*
Florian, Frank; Arkansas, 1918 ***95.2*** *p44*
Floriau, Mr.; New Orleans, 1838 ***778.5*** *p210*
Floridor, Hugues; Quebec, 1685 ***7603*** *p35*
Florig, Ph. 22; America, 1853 ***9162.8*** *p36*
Florjancic, Frank; Wisconsin, n.d. ***9675.5*** *p122*
Florjancic, Jacob; Wisconsin, n.d. ***9675.5*** *p122*
Floro, Joseph; Ohio, 1816 ***8582.1*** *p47*
Florsheim, Simon; Shreveport, LA, 1879 ***7129*** *p44*
Floter, Christian 32; California, 1872 ***2769.4*** *p3*
Floto, Ernest; Illinois, 1861 ***7857*** *p3*
Floto, Luis; Illinois, 1854 ***7857*** *p3*
Floughsby, Wm.; New York, NY, 1811 ***2859.11*** *p11*
Flous, Adolphe 22; New Orleans, 1823 ***778.5*** *p211*
Flousty, Raimond 23; New Orleans, 1836 ***778.5*** *p211*
Flower, Etherel; Boston, 1776 ***1219.7*** *p277*
Flower, John 21; Virginia, 1774 ***1219.7*** *p238*
Flower, Joseph 22; Virginia, 1727 ***3690.1*** *p79*
Flower, Thomas 28; Virginia, 1775 ***1219.7*** *p246*
Flower, William 21; Virginia, 1774 ***1219.7*** *p201*
Flowerday, Eliza.; Virginia, 1644 ***6219*** *p231*
Flowerdew, Eliza.; Virginia, 1642 ***6219*** *p198*
Flowers, Mr.; Grenada, 1775 ***1219.7*** *p280*
Flowers, James; Colorado, 1895 ***9678.2*** *p18*
Floyd, Ann; Philadelphia, 1867 ***5704.8*** *p222*
Floyd, Arth.; Virginia, 1647 ***6219*** *p241*
Floyd, Cecilia; Philadelphia, 1852 ***5704.8*** *p85*
Floyd, Ellen; Philadelphia, 1867 ***5704.8*** *p217*
Floyd, Flug; Virginia, 1637 ***6219*** *p11*
Floyd, John; Baltimore, 1811 ***2859.11*** *p11*
Floyd, John; Philadelphia, 1867 ***5704.8*** *p217*
Floyd, John 18; Barbados, 1718 ***3690.1*** *p79*
Floyd, Joseph 16; Maryland, 1775 ***1219.7*** *p267*
Floyd, Mary; America, 1698 ***2212*** *p10*
Floyd, Mary 24; Quebec, 1855 ***5704.8*** *p126*
Floyd, Melchesedick; Virginia, 1638 ***6219*** *p122*
Floyd, Nowell; Virginia, 1637 ***6219*** *p114*
Floyd, Rice; Virginia, 1639 ***6219*** *p152*
Floyd, Robert; Virginia, 1637 ***6219*** *p111*
Floyd, Samuel; Philadelphia, 1853 ***5704.8*** *p102*
Floyd, Tho.; Virginia, 1639 ***6219*** *p154*
Floyd, Thomas; Philadelphia, 1867 ***5704.8*** *p217*
Floyd, William 18; Jamaica, 1731 ***3690.1*** *p80*
Floyne, Joane *SEE* Floyne, John
Floyne, John; Virginia, 1640 ***6219*** *p185*
*Wife:*Joane
Fluck, Ludwig; Pennsylvania, 1749 ***2444*** *p154*
Flucks, Henry; Ohio, 1861 ***6014.2*** *p7*
Flud, John 20; Pennsylvania, 1730 ***3690.1*** *p80*
Fludd, John; Virginia, 1638 ***6219*** *p11*
Fludd, John; Virginia, 1648 ***6219*** *p251*
Fludd, John, Jr.; Virginia, 1638 ***6219*** *p11*
Fludd, Martha; Virginia, 1638 ***6219*** *p14*
Fludd, William 25; Virginia, 1737 ***3690.1*** *p80*
Fludernik, Franz; Wisconsin, n.d. ***9675.5*** *p122*
Fludernik, Joseph; Wisconsin, n.d. ***9675.5*** *p122*
Fluhrer, . . .; Canada, 1776-1783 ***9786*** *p21*
Flurent, Marguerite 35; America, 1838 ***778.5*** *p211*
Flurn, Pack; New York, NY, 1816 ***2859.11*** *p31*
Flushing, Eleanor; New York, NY, 1816 ***2859.11*** *p31*
Flushing, George; New York, NY, 1816 ***2859.11*** *p31*
Flushing, John; New York, NY, 1816 ***2859.11*** *p31*
Flute, Robt.; Virginia, 1638 ***6219*** *p14*
Flux, John 22; Canada, 1838 ***4535.12*** *p113*
Flux, Richard 28; Jamaica, 1738 ***3690.1*** *p80*
Flye, John; Virginia, 1637 ***6219*** *p107*
Flyn, James; New York, NY, 1816 ***2859.11*** *p31*
Flyn, Luke; New York, NY, 1811 ***2859.11*** *p11*
Flyn, William; America, 1742 ***4971*** *p86*
Flynn, Biddy 24; Massachusetts, 1849 ***5881.1*** *p36*
Flynn, Bridget; Quebec, 1820 ***7603*** *p56*
Flynn, Bridget 70; Massachusetts, 1850 ***5881.1*** *p36*
Flynn, Catharine 6; Massachusetts, 1849 ***5881.1*** *p36*
Flynn, Catharine 12; Massachusetts, 1849 ***5881.1*** *p36*
Flynn, Catherine *SEE* Flynn, Hugh
Flynn, Catherine 2 *SEE* Flynn, Hugh
Flynn, Charles 24; Maryland, 1775 ***1219.7*** *p266*
Flynn, Cornelius; Quebec, 1823 ***7603*** *p64*
Flynn, Cornelius 4; Massachusetts, 1849 ***5881.1*** *p36*
Flynn, Daniel 38; Massachusetts, 1850 ***5881.1*** *p36*
Flynn, David; Quebec, 1784 ***7603*** *p88*
Flynn, David 35; New Orleans, 1862 ***543.30*** *p226B*
Flynn, David 37; Massachusetts, 1849 ***5881.1*** *p36*
Flynn, Dennis 4; Massachusetts, 1850 ***5881.1*** *p36*
Flynn, Dennis 4; Massachusetts, 1850 ***5881.1*** *p58*
Flynn, Dennis 6; Massachusetts, 1849 ***5881.1*** *p36*
Flynn, Dennis 16; Massachusetts, 1849 ***5881.1*** *p36*
Flynn, Dennis 45; Massachusetts, 1849 ***5881.1*** *p36*
Flynn, Dominick; America, 1738 ***4971*** *p24*
Flynn, Edmond; America, 1736-1743 ***4971*** *p57*
Flynn, Edward; New York, NY, 1834 ***8208.4*** *p2*
Flynn, Edward; Pennsylvania, 1826-1840 ***7036*** *p119*
Flynn, Edward; Quebec, 1825 ***7036*** *p119*
Flynn, Ellen; Massachusetts, 1849 ***5881.1*** *p37*
Flynn, Ellen 13; Massachusetts, 1849 ***5881.1*** *p37*
Flynn, Ellen 35; Massachusetts, 1849 ***5881.1*** *p36*
Flynn, Ellen 50; Massachusetts, 1849 ***5881.1*** *p36*
Flynn, Hannah; St. John, N.B., 1852 ***5704.8*** *p93*
Flynn, Honora 28; Massachusetts, 1848 ***5881.1*** *p37*
Flynn, Hugh; New York, NY, 1816 ***2859.11*** *p31*
Flynn, Hugh; Philadelphia, 1847 ***53.26*** *p28*
*Relative:*Catherine
*Relative:*Isabella 11
*Relative:*John 9
*Relative:*Jane 6
*Relative:*Catherine 2
Flynn, Isabella 11 *SEE* Flynn, Hugh
Flynn, James; New York, NY, 1837 ***8208.4*** *p56*
Flynn, James 12; Massachusetts, 1849 ***5881.1*** *p38*
Flynn, James 16; Massachusetts, 1849 ***5881.1*** *p38*
Flynn, Jane 6 *SEE* Flynn, Hugh
Flynn, Jerry 33; New Orleans, 1864 ***543.30*** *p230B*
Flynn, Joanna 10; Massachusetts, 1849 ***5881.1*** *p38*
Flynn, Joanna 16; Massachusetts, 1849 ***5881.1*** *p38*
Flynn, Johanna 9; Massachusetts, 1849 ***5881.1*** *p38*
Flynn, Johanna 11; Massachusetts, 1849 ***5881.1*** *p38*
Flynn, John; Philadelphia, 1816 ***2859.11*** *p31*
Flynn, John; Quebec, 1799 ***7603*** *p71*
Flynn, John; Quebec, 1812 ***7603*** *p76*
Flynn, John 9 *SEE* Flynn, Hugh
Flynn, John 11; Massachusetts, 1850 ***5881.1*** *p38*
Flynn, John 20; Massachusetts, 1849 ***5881.1*** *p37*
Flynn, John 28; Massachusetts, 1847 ***5881.1*** *p37*
Flynn, John 40; Massachusetts, 1850 ***5881.1*** *p38*
Flynn, John, Jr.; Philadelphia, 1816 ***2859.11*** *p31*
Flynn, John P.; Arkansas, 1918 ***95.2*** *p44*
Flynn, Joseph; New York, NY, 1816 ***2859.11*** *p31*
Flynn, Julia; Massachusetts, 1841 ***7036*** *p121*
Flynn, Julia 12; Massachusetts, 1849 ***5881.1*** *p38*
Flynn, Luke; Illinois, 1874 ***5012.37*** *p59*
Flynn, Margaret 8; Massachusetts, 1849 ***5881.1*** *p39*
Flynn, Margaret 15; Massachusetts, 1849 ***5881.1*** *p39*
Flynn, Margaret 18; Massachusetts, 1849 ***5881.1*** *p39*
Flynn, Margaret 40; Massachusetts, 1849 ***5881.1*** *p39*
Flynn, Mary; Philadelphia, 1816 ***2859.11*** *p31*
Flynn, Mary 7; Massachusetts, 1849 ***5881.1*** *p39*
Flynn, Mary 17; Massachusetts, 1849 ***5881.1*** *p39*
Flynn, Mary 18; Massachusetts, 1847 ***5881.1*** *p38*
Flynn, Mary 20; Massachusetts, 1849 ***5881.1*** *p39*
Flynn, Mary 40; Massachusetts, 1849 ***5881.1*** *p39*
Flynn, Michael 7; Massachusetts, 1850 ***5881.1*** *p40*
Flynn, Michael 7; Massachusetts, 1850 ***5881.1*** *p61*
Flynn, Michael 21; Newfoundland, 1789 ***4915.24*** *p56*
Flynn, Patrick; America, 1738 ***4971*** *p9*
Flynn, Patrick; New York, NY, 1837 ***8208.4*** *p56*
Flynn, Patrick 10; Massachusetts, 1847 ***5881.1*** *p40*
Flynn, Patrick 13; Massachusetts, 1849 ***5881.1*** *p40*
Flynn, Patrick 14; Massachusetts, 1849 ***5881.1*** *p40*
Flynn, Patrick 18; Massachusetts, 1847 ***5881.1*** *p40*
Flynn, Patrick 40; New Orleans, 1863 ***543.30*** *p228B*
Flynn, Patrick 45; Massachusetts, 1849 ***5881.1*** *p40*
Flynn, Patrick M.; Sacramento, CA, 1861 ***2764.35*** *p24*
Flynn, Peter 43; Louisiana, 1863 ***543.30*** *p230B*
Flynn, Phillip 24; Massachusetts, 1849 ***5881.1*** *p40*
Flynn, Robert; New York, NY, 1839 ***8208.4*** *p94*
Flynn, Thady; America, 1735-1743 ***4971*** *p79*
Flynn, Thomas; Quebec, 1778 ***7603*** *p64*
Flynn, Timothy; Massachusetts, 1849 ***5881.1*** *p40*
Flynn, William; St. John, N.B., 1852 ***5704.8*** *p93*
Flynn, William 20; Massachusetts, 1849 ***5881.1*** *p41*
Flynt, Ri.; Virginia, 1652 ***6251*** *p19*
Foaley, Patrick; New York, NY, 1811 ***2859.11*** *p11*
Foanes, Thomas; Virginia, 1629 ***6219*** *p8*
Foard, John; Virginia, 1643 ***6219*** *p204*
Foard, Jon.; Virginia, 1636 ***6219*** *p80*
Fobee, John 42; Kansas, 1882 ***5240.1*** *p13*
Focht, Catharina C. Winner *SEE* Focht, Simon
Focht, Simon; New York, 1709 ***3627*** *p6*
*Wife:*Catharina C. Winner
Fock, Fred; Wisconsin, n.d. ***9675.5*** *p122*
Fock, Friedrich; Wisconsin, n.d. ***9675.5*** *p122*
Fockel, Godfrey; New York, 1750 ***3652*** *p74*
Fockel, John Godfrey; New York, 1750 ***3652*** *p74*
Fockel, Samuel; New York, 1750 ***3652*** *p74*
Fockler, John; Philadelphia, 1762 ***9973.7*** *p36*
Fodder, Isaac 15; Pennsylvania, 1735 ***3690.1*** *p80*
Foeger, Joseph; Wisconsin, n.d. ***9675.5*** *p122*
Foeger, Rosa Lener; Wisconsin, n.d. ***9675.5*** *p122*
Foehl, Andreas; America, 1749 ***2444*** *p154*
Foehl, Andreas; Pennsylvania, 1749 ***2444*** *p154*
Foehl, Andreas; Pennsylvania, 1749 ***2444*** *p182*
Foehr, Anna Dorothea *SEE* Foehr, Johannes
Foehr, Catharina Dorothea *SEE* Foehr, Johannes
Foehr, Jacob Cunrad *SEE* Foehr, Johannes
Foehr, Johannes; Pennsylvania, 1751 ***2444*** *p155*
*Wife:*Anna Dorothea
*Child:*Jacob Cunrad
*Child:*Catharina Dorothea
Foersh, Henry R.; New York, NY, 1837 ***8208.4*** *p51*
Foerster, Charles; Indiana, 1872 ***1450.2*** *p43A*
Foerster, Daniel; Cincinnati, 1869-1887 ***8582*** *p9*
Foerster, Daniel; New York, NY, 1831 ***8582.3*** *p19*
With parents
Foetchenhauer, Carl; Washington, 1859-1920 ***2872.1*** *p13*
Foeth, Ludwig 30; New York, NY, 1889 ***7846*** *p40*
Foeth, Magdalen 6 mos; New York, NY, 1889 ***7846*** *p40*
Foeth, Regina 26; New York, NY, 1889 ***7846*** *p40*
Foeth, Therese 4; New York, NY, 1889 ***7846*** *p40*
Foeth, Wendelin 2; New York, NY, 1889 ***7846*** *p40*
Fogarty, Anna M.; Washington, 1859-1920 ***2872.1*** *p13*
Fogarty, James; Philadelphia, 1839 ***7036*** *p122*
Fogarty, James 23; Massachusetts, 1849 ***5881.1*** *p38*
Fogarty, James A.; Washington, 1859-1920 ***2872.1*** *p13*
Fogarty, John; Illinois, 1840 ***7036*** *p118*
Fogarty, Joseph 26; Arkansas, 1918 ***95.2*** *p44*
Fogarty, Margaret 6 mos; Massachusetts, 1849 ***5881.1*** *p39*
Fogarty, Martin; America, 1741 ***4971*** *p60*
Fogarty, Terence; America, 1739 ***4971*** *p52*
Fogarty, William; America, 1851 ***1450.2*** *p43A*
Fogelin, Olof P.; Maine, 1871-1882 ***6410.22*** *p116*
Fogelman, Melcher; Pennsylvania, 1749 ***2444*** *p228*
Fogelstrone, Frank; Iowa, 1882 ***5240.1*** *p13*
Fogerty, Cornelius 30; Virginia, 1774 ***1219.7*** *p241*
Fogerty, James; New York, NY, 1811 ***2859.11*** *p12*
Fogerty, James 27; Virginia, 1774 ***1219.7*** *p241*
Fogerty, Patrick 44; New Orleans, 1862 ***543.30*** *p227B*
Fogerty, Timothy 25; Massachusetts, 1849 ***5881.1*** *p40*
Fogg, Benjamin 19; Maryland, 1774 ***1219.7*** *p192*
Fogg, Nath; America, 1698 ***2212*** *p13*
Fogg, William 23; Virginia, 1773 ***1219.7*** *p169*
Foggett, Charles 17; Philadelphia, 1774 ***1219.7*** *p232*
Fogherty, Ellenora; Montreal, 1825 ***7603*** *p98*
Fogherty, Mathew 19; Massachusetts, 1849 ***5881.1*** *p39*
Foglio, Secondina 37; New York, NY, 1893 ***9026.4*** *p41*
Fohr, . . .; Canada, 1776-1783 ***9786*** *p21*
Foidl, Alois; Colorado, 1886 ***9678.2*** *p19*
Fokes, Chas. 10; Canada, 1838 ***4535.12*** *p113*
Fokes, Emma 13; Canada, 1838 ***4535.12*** *p113*
Fokes, James 39; Canada, 1838 ***4535.12*** *p113*
Folder, Katherine; Virginia, 1637 ***6219*** *p11*
Folen, Joseph 25; Massachusetts, 1849 ***5881.1*** *p38*
Foleveilor, Andreas 32; America, 1839 ***778.5*** *p211*
Foley, Anne; New York, NY, 1816 ***2859.11*** *p31*
Foley, Anthony 29; New Orleans, 1862 ***543.30*** *p29*
Foley, Bridget; St. John, N.B., 1849 ***5704.8*** *p56*
Foley, Catharine 18; Massachusetts, 1850 ***5881.1*** *p36*
Foley, Darby; America, 1742 ***4971*** *p30*
Foley, David; New York, NY, 1839 ***8208.4*** *p99*
Foley, Ellen 24; Massachusetts, 1849 ***5881.1*** *p7*

Foley, Ellen 24; Massachusetts, 1849 ***5881.1*** *p36*
Foley, James; America, 1840 ***1450.2*** *p44A*
Foley, James; Illinois, 1900 ***5012.40*** *p77*
Foley, Jeremiah 29; Massachusetts, 1849 ***5881.1*** *p37*
Foley, Johanna 60; Massachusetts, 1848 ***5881.1*** *p37*
Foley, John; New York, NY, 1836 ***8208.4*** *p13*
Foley, John 19; Newfoundland, 1789 ***4915.24*** *p56*
Foley, John 20; Massachusetts, 1849 ***5881.1*** *p37*
Foley, John 22; Massachusetts, 1849 ***5881.1*** *p38*
Foley, John 25; Massachusetts, 1849 ***5881.1*** *p37*
Foley, Margaret; Quebec, 1840 ***7036*** *p122*
Foley, Margaret 18; Massachusetts, 1847 ***5881.1*** *p38*
Foley, Margaret 23; Massachusetts, 1850 ***5881.1*** *p39*
Foley, Maria 25; Massachusetts, 1850 ***5881.1*** *p39*
Foley, Mary 16; Massachusetts, 1847 ***5881.1*** *p38*
Foley, Mary 25; Massachusetts, 1849 ***5881.1*** *p38*
Foley, Mary 28; Massachusetts, 1849 ***5881.1*** *p39*
Foley, Maurice; Sacramento Co., CA, 1876 ***2764.35*** *p22*
Foley, Michael; America, 1840 ***1450.2*** *p44A*
Foley, Michael; New York, NY, 1834 ***8208.4*** *p44*
Foley, Patrick 13; St. John, N.B., 1849 ***5704.8*** *p56*
Foley, Patrick 14; Massachusetts, 1849 ***5881.1*** *p40*
Foley, Thomas 20; St. John, N.B., 1853 ***5704.8*** *p110*
Foley, Thomas J. 20; Harris Co., TX, 1897 ***6254*** *p3*
Foley, Tim. 40; Massachusetts, 1849 ***5881.1*** *p40*
Foley, William; New York, NY, 1816 ***2859.11*** *p31*
Foley, William 50; Massachusetts, 1849 ***5881.1*** *p40*
Folhall, Laurin; Philadelphia, 1811 ***53.26*** *p28*
Folhall, Laurin; Philadelphia, 1811 ***2859.11*** *p12*
Folik, Catharina 40; New York, NY, 1889 ***7846*** *p40*
Folik, Cyril 46; New York, NY, 1889 ***7846*** *p40*
Folik, Eva 2; New York, NY, 1889 ***7846*** *p40*
Folik, Jacob 13; New York, NY, 1889 ***7846*** *p40*
Folik, Josef 9; New York, NY, 1889 ***7846*** *p40*
Folik, Peter 5; New York, NY, 1889 ***7846*** *p40*
Foliles, H. C. 24; New Orleans, 1837 ***778.5*** *p211*
Folin, Bryan; New York, NY, 1816 ***2859.11*** *p31*
Folkard, P. 28; St. Kitts, 1774 ***1219.7*** *p184*
Folkard, Philip 29; Virginia, 1775 ***1219.7*** *p247*
Folkening, Charles D.L.; America, 1843 ***1450.2*** *p44A*
Folkers, Folket; Illinois, 1891 ***5012.40*** *p25*
Folkert, Evert Jan 50; New York, NY, 1847 ***3377.6*** *p13*
Folkert, Hermanus 6; New York, NY, 1847 ***3377.6*** *p13*
Folkert, Janna 43; New York, NY, 1847 ***3377.6*** *p13*
Follard, John 20; Virginia, 1774 ***1219.7*** *p244*
Folle, Carl Diedrich 39; America, 1850 ***4610.10*** *p142*
*Wife:*Christine Sander
*Child:*Carl Heinrich
*Child:*Wilhelm Carl Heinrich
*Child:*Friedrich Wilhelm
Folle, Carl Heinrich *SEE* Folle, Carl Diedrich
Folle, Carl Heinrich Wilhelm *SEE* Folle, Ernst Heinrich
Folle, Christine Caroline *SEE* Folle, Ernst Heinrich
Folle, Christine L.C. Kroeger *SEE* Folle, Samuel Heinrich
Folle, Christine Louise Engel *SEE* Folle, Samuel Heinrich
Folle, Christine Sander *SEE* Folle, Carl Diedrich
Folle, Daniel Heinrich Samuel *SEE* Folle, Ernst Heinrich
Folle, Ernst Friedrich Samuel; America, 1848 ***4610.10*** *p142*
Folle, Ernst Heinrich; America, 1850 ***4610.10*** *p142*
*Wife:*Louise Kramer
*Child:*Carl Heinrich Wilhelm
*Child:*Daniel Heinrich Samuel
*Child:*Johanne C. Louise
*Child:*Christine Caroline
Folle, Friederike L. Engel *SEE* Folle, Samuel Heinrich
Folle, Friedrich Wilhelm *SEE* Folle, Carl Diedrich
Folle, Johanne C. Louise *SEE* Folle, Ernst Heinrich
Folle, Louise Kramer *SEE* Folle, Ernst Heinrich
Folle, Samuel Heinrich 26; America, 1850 ***4610.10*** *p142*
*Wife:*Christine L.C. Kroeger
*Child:*Friederike L. Engel
*Child:*Christine Louise Engel
Folle, Wilhelm Carl Heinrich *SEE* Folle, Carl Diedrich
Follenius, . . .; New Orleans, 1834 ***8582.1*** *p53*
Follenius, Paul; Missouri, 1830-1834 ***3702.7*** *p8*
Follett, Francis 20; Maryland, 1731 ***3690.1*** *p80*
Folley, Thomas; Washington, 1831 ***1450.2*** *p44A*
Follope, M. W. 40; America, 1827 ***778.5*** *p211*
Folly, Peter; New York, NY, 1811 ***2859.11*** *p12*
Folmar, Henry; Baltimore, 1845 ***1450.2*** *p44A*
Folp, Christian; New York, 1883 ***1450.2*** *p9B*
Folrey, Daniel; America, 1860 ***6014.1*** *p1*
Foltynski, Maryian; Arkansas, 1918 ***95.2*** *p44*
Folz, Carl; America, 1829 ***8582.2*** *p61*
Folz, Charles; Cincinnati, 1869-1887 ***8582*** *p9*
Folz, Michael; Wisconsin, n.d. ***9675.5*** *p122*
Fon, J. L. 35; Port uncertain, 1820 ***778.5*** *p211*
Fonclaire, Mlle. 6; Mexico, 1829 ***778.5*** *p211*
Fonclaire, Mme. 28; Mexico, 1829 ***778.5*** *p211*
Fonclaire, Mr. 30; Mexico, 1829 ***778.5*** *p211*
Fondahn, Peter; Colorado, 1896 ***9678.2*** *p19*
Fondary, Mr. 22; America, 1839 ***778.5*** *p211*
Fondary, P. 28; America, 1839 ***778.5*** *p211*
Fondelarue, Michael 20; Port uncertain, 1836 ***778.5*** *p211*
Fondevielle, Michel 30; Port uncertain, 1837 ***778.5*** *p211*
Fonsica, Pablo 36; New Orleans, 1862 ***543.30*** *p32*
Fontain, Pierre 32; New Orleans, 1835 ***778.5*** *p211*
Fontaine, Eug. 20; Port uncertain, 1839 ***778.5*** *p212*
Fontaine, Francois; Louisiana, 1789-1819 ***778.5*** *p555*
Fontaine, Louis 40; New Orleans, 1862 ***543.30*** *p32*
Fontaine, Nicholaus; Wisconsin, n.d. ***9675.5*** *p189*
Fontan, Guillaume 32; Port uncertain, 1838 ***778.5*** *p212*
Fontana, Girolamo 23; Arkansas, 1918 ***95.2*** *p44*
Fontanes, Franz; Boston, 1923 ***3455.4*** *p51*
Fontbonne, Antoinette 30; St. Louis, 1836 ***778.5*** *p212*
Fontbonne, M. A. 23; St. Louis, 1836 ***778.5*** *p212*
Fonte, Achilles; Wisconsin, n.d. ***9675.5*** *p189*
Fonte, Cesidio; Wisconsin, n.d. ***9675.5*** *p189*
Fonte, Venanzio; Wisconsin, n.d. ***9675.5*** *p189*
Fontelieu, John 16; New Orleans, 1830 ***778.5*** *p212*
Fontont, John 25; New Orleans, 1862 ***543.30*** *p27*
Foo, Adam 22; New Orleans, 1862 ***543.30*** *p228B*
Foogood, Arthur 25; Newport, RI, 1851 ***6508.5*** *p20*
Foogood, Mary 18; Newport, RI, 1851 ***6508.5*** *p20*
Fookes, Ann; Virginia, 1638 ***6219*** *p147*
Fooles, Jno 25; America, 1702 ***2212*** *p37*
Foon, C.; New Orleans, 1839 ***778.5*** *p212*
Foord, Adrian; Virginia, 1643 ***6219*** *p204*
Foote, Samuel E.; Cincinnati, 1800-1877 ***8582.3*** *p86*
Foppiano, John; New York, 1855 ***1450.2*** *p9B*
Foquet, John 35; New Orleans, 1862 ***543.30*** *p27*
Foran, John 20; Massachusetts, 1847 ***5881.1*** *p37*
Foran, Mary; America, 1739 ***4971*** *p28*
Forande, Mr. 17; Port uncertain, 1838 ***778.5*** *p212*
Forave, Honora; America, 1742 ***4971*** *p83*
Foray, Martin; Illinois, 1890 ***5012.40*** *p25*
Forber, Richard 17; America, 1702 ***2212*** *p37*
Forbes, Alexander; Charleston, SC, 1807 ***1639.20*** *p71*
Forbes, Alexander; Quebec, 1820 ***7603*** *p25*
Forbes, Alexander 19; Jamaica, 1731 ***3690.1*** *p80*
Forbes, Alexander Malpes; California, 1865 ***3840.1*** *p18*
Forbes, Ann; Philadelphia, 1864 ***5704.8*** *p174*
Forbes, C. A. 22; Kansas, 1887 ***5240.1*** *p70*
Forbes, Daniel; Quebec, 1772 ***7603*** *p37*
Forbes, Fanny; New York, NY, 1816 ***2859.11*** *p31*
Forbes, Francis A.; Wisconsin, n.d. ***9675.5*** *p189*
Forbes, George; Charleston, SC, 1781 ***1639.20*** *p71*
Forbes, George; Jamaica, 1681-1781 ***1639.20*** *p71*
Forbes, George; South Carolina, 1716 ***1639.20*** *p71*
Forbes, Grant 22; Kansas, 1889 ***5240.1*** *p73*
Forbes, Hugh; Charleston, SC, 1734 ***1639.20*** *p71*
Forbes, J.; Quebec, 1815 ***9229.18*** *p75*
Forbes, Jacques; Quebec, 1770 ***7603*** *p37*
Forbes, James; Philadelphia, 1851 ***5704.8*** *p71*
Forbes, Jane; New York, NY, 1816 ***2859.11*** *p31*
Forbes, Jean; Charleston, SC, 1781 ***1639.20*** *p71*
Forbes, Jean; Sorel, Que., 1781 ***7603*** *p40*
Forbes, John; New York, NY, 1816 ***2859.11*** *p31*
Forbes, John; Quebec, 1819 ***7603*** *p35*
Forbes, John 22; Massachusetts, 1849 ***5881.1*** *p37*
Forbes, John 25; Jamaica, 1774 ***1219.7*** *p231*
Forbes, John 30; Philadelphia, 1774 ***1219.7*** *p217*
Forbes, Luc; Quebec, 1764 ***7603*** *p67*
Forbes, Susan; Philadelphia, 1851 ***5704.8*** *p70*
Forbes, Thomas; St. John, N.B., 1847 ***5704.8*** *p15*
Forbes, Thomas 22; Jamaica, 1731 ***3690.1*** *p80*
Forbes, William; Cape Fear, NC, 1733 ***4814*** *p92*
Forbes, William; North Carolina, 1733 ***1639.20*** *p71*
Forbes, William; Quebec, 1852 ***5704.8*** *p86*
Forbes, William; Quebec, 1852 ***5704.8*** *p90*
Forbes, William 30; Tobago, W. Indies, 1775 ***1219.7*** *p251*
Forbes, William 53; Kansas, 1889 ***5240.1*** *p73*
Forbes, William, Jr.; New York, NY, 1816 ***2859.11*** *p31*
Forbes, William, Sr.; New York, NY, 1816 ***2859.11*** *p31*
Forbey, William 15; Baltimore, 1775 ***1219.7*** *p269*
Forbush, Jon.; Virginia, 1638 ***6219*** *p122*
Forcade, . . .; Canada, 1776-1783 ***9786*** *p42*
Forcade, J.B. 52; New Orleans, 1822 ***778.5*** *p212*
Forcade, William; New York, NY, 1811 ***2859.11*** *p12*
With family
Forcetini, Lingi 22; Arkansas, 1918 ***95.2*** *p44*
Ford, Alexander 26; Virginia, 1774 ***1219.7*** *p240*
Ford, Ambrose; New York, NY, 1835 ***8208.4*** *p39*
Ford, Ann 25; Massachusetts, 1848 ***5881.1*** *p35*
Ford, Ann 45; Massachusetts, 1847 ***5881.1*** *p35*
Ford, Bridget 10; Massachusetts, 1847 ***5881.1*** *p35*
Ford, Daniel 23; Massachusetts, 1850 ***5881.1*** *p36*
Ford, Elizabeth 19; Virginia, 1720 ***3690.1*** *p80*
Ford, George; Iowa, 1866-1943 ***123.54*** *p18*
Ford, Henry; Maryland, 1756 ***1219.7*** *p43*
Ford, Henry; Maryland, 1756 ***3690.1*** *p80*
Ford, Hester; Virginia, 1698 ***2212*** *p12*
Ford, James 40; Massachusetts, 1847 ***5881.1*** *p37*
Ford, James, Jr. 16; Massachusetts, 1847 ***5881.1*** *p37*
Ford, Jane 22; Quebec, 1855 ***5704.8*** *p126*
Ford, John; Virginia, 1637 ***6219*** *p86*
Ford, John; Virginia, 1637 ***6219*** *p112*
Ford, John 17; Philadelphia, 1774 ***1219.7*** *p233*
Ford, John 20; Maryland, 1729 ***3690.1*** *p80*
Ford, John 50; Massachusetts, 1850 ***5881.1*** *p38*
Ford, Jon.; Virginia, 1635 ***6219*** *p3*
Ford, Margaret 22; Massachusetts, 1849 ***5881.1*** *p39*
Ford, Mary 30; Massachusetts, 1849 ***5881.1*** *p39*
Ford, Michael 24; Massachusetts, 1847 ***5881.1*** *p38*
Ford, Patrick 14; Massachusetts, 1847 ***5881.1*** *p40*
Ford, Peter 22; New Orleans, 1862 ***543.30*** *p229B*
Ford, Ralph 22; Maryland, 1775 ***1219.7*** *p257*
Ford, Richard; Virginia, 1638 ***6219*** *p160*
Ford, Robert; Boston, 1837 ***7036*** *p126*
Ford, Robert 40; Carolina, 1775 ***1219.7*** *p278*
Ford, Samuel L.; Illinois, 1904 ***2896.5*** *p12*
Ford, Thomas; Virginia, 1856 ***4626.16*** *p16*
Ford, Thomas 32; Virginia, 1774 ***1219.7*** *p186*
Ford, Thomas 34; New Orleans, 1862 ***543.30*** *p224B*
Ford, Wm.; Virginia, 1636 ***6219*** *p76*
Forden, Mathew; Virginia, 1637 ***6219*** *p11*
Forden, William; Illinois, 1887 ***5012.39*** *p121*
Fordham, Thomas; New York, NY, 1836 ***8208.4*** *p21*
Fordice, William; Ohio, 1829 ***9892.11*** *p15*
Fordred, William 25; Maryland, 1730 ***3690.1*** *p80*
Fordyce, William Dingwall; Charleston, SC, 1798-1839 ***1639.20*** *p71*
Fore, Owen 33; Massachusetts, 1849 ***5881.1*** *p40*
Forein, James; New Brunswick, 1824 ***7603*** *p76*
Foreman, Eleanor 20; Georgia, 1775 ***1219.7*** *p277*
Foreman, George; Iroquois Co., IL, 1894 ***3455.1*** *p10*
Foreman, Thomas 19; Jamaica, 1725 ***3690.1*** *p80*
Fores, Jmre; Arkansas, 1918 ***95.2*** *p44*
Foresight, David 18; Jamaica, 1722 ***3690.1*** *p81*
Forest, . . .; Canada, 1776-1783 ***9786*** *p42*
Forest, Mr. 39; Port uncertain, 1837 ***778.5*** *p212*
Forest, John; New York, NY, 1816 ***2859.11*** *p31*
Forest, Thomas 24; Virginia, 1774 ***1219.7*** *p201*
Forestier, Mr. 24; America, 1826 ***778.5*** *p212*
Forestier, Ami; New York, NY, 1920 ***3455.3*** *p79*
Forestier, Ami; New York, NY, 1920 ***3455.4*** *p24*
Forestier, Jean.e 24; New Orleans, 1839 ***778.5*** *p212*
Forestier, Jules; Iroquois Co., IL, 1894 ***3455.1*** *p10*
Forestreet, Thomas 24; Jamaica, 1774 ***1219.7*** *p241*
Forfar, Alexander 20; Tortola, 1773 ***1219.7*** *p172*
Forgerot, J. C. 22; America, 1825 ***778.5*** *p212*
Forget, Auguste; Port uncertain, 1839 ***778.5*** *p212*
Forgue, Mr. 30; America, 1839 ***778.5*** *p212*
Forhan, Patrick; America, 1898 ***1450.2*** *p9B*
Foristall, Tobias; Quebec, 1820 ***7603*** *p76*
Forke, Tho.; Virginia, 1643 ***6219*** *p204*
Forley, Felix; New York, NY, 1838 ***8208.4*** *p74*
Forley, Patrick; New York, NY, 1811 ***2859.11*** *p12*
Formax, Coonrod; Illinois, 1862 ***2896.5*** *p12*
Formborow, Alexander 19; Pennsylvania, Virginia or Maryland, 1728 ***3690.1*** *p75*
Formichetti, Valerio; Arkansas, 1918 ***95.2*** *p44*
Fornelli, Spirit; Iowa, 1866-1943 ***123.54*** *p18*
Fornery, M. 24; New Orleans, 1827 ***778.5*** *p213*
Forney, Marcus; Philadelphia, 1753 ***9973.7*** *p32*
Forney, Nicholas; Pennsylvania, 1772 ***9973.8*** *p33*
Forragher, Patrick; America, 1736 ***4971*** *p81*
Forragher, Thomas; America, 1736 ***4971*** *p81*
Forres, Charles 40; New Orleans, 1832 ***778.5*** *p213*
Forrest, . . .; Canada, 1776-1783 ***9786*** *p42*
Forrest, Aly 6 *SEE* Forrest, Esther
Forrest, Aly 6; Philadelphia, 1847 ***5704.8*** *p31*
Forrest, Ann; Quebec, 1849 ***5704.8*** *p52*
Forrest, Anthony; Philadelphia, 1758 ***9973.7*** *p33*
Forrest, Bessie; Philadelphia, 1865 ***5704.8*** *p202*
Forrest, Daniel; Philadelphia, 1849 ***53.26*** *p28*
Forrest, Daniel; Philadelphia, 1849 ***5704.8*** *p54*
Forrest, Eliza 12 *SEE* Forrest, Esther
Forrest, Eliza 14; Philadelphia, 1847 ***5704.8*** *p31*
Forrest, Elizabeth 26; Baltimore, 1775 ***1219.7*** *p271*
Forrest, Esther; Philadelphia, 1847 ***53.26*** *p28*
*Relative:*Eliza 12
*Relative:*Mary Jane 11
*Relative:*Rachel 7
*Relative:*Aly 6
Forrest, Esther; Philadelphia, 1847 ***5704.8*** *p31*
Forrest, Fanny; New York, NY, 1864 ***5704.8*** *p171*
Forrest, Henry 33; Nevis, 1774 ***1219.7*** *p197*
Forrest, James; New York, NY, 1864 ***5704.8*** *p186*
Forrest, James 35; Jamaica, 1736 ***3690.1*** *p81*
Forrest, John 57; Charleston, SC, 1850 ***1639.20*** *p71*
Forrest, Lesley; Philadelphia, 1865 ***5704.8*** *p202*
Forrest, Margaret; New York, NY, 1864 ***5704.8*** *p173*
Forrest, Mary Jane 11 *SEE* Forrest, Esther
Forrest, Mary Jane 11; Philadelphia, 1847 ***5704.8*** *p31*
Forrest, Michael; America, 1741 ***4971*** *p41*
Forrest, Michael; New York, NY, 1838 ***8208.4*** *p63*

Forrest, Rachel 7 *SEE* Forrest, Esther
Forrest, Rachel 7; Philadelphia, 1847 ***5704.8*** *p31*
Forrest, Richard; West Virginia, 1840 ***9788.3*** *p10*
Forrest, William; America, 1738 ***4971*** *p66*
Forrest, William 18; Philadelphia, 1854 ***5704.8*** *p116*
Forrester, Elizabeth 50; Philadelphia, 1854 ***5704.8*** *p118*
Forrester, George; America, 1741 ***4971*** *p10*
Forrester, Henry 24; Philadelphia, 1803 ***53.26*** *p28*
Forrester, James 20; Philadelphia, 1774 ***1219.7*** *p228*
Forrester, Mary; Philadelphia, 1864 ***5704.8*** *p180*
Forsary, . . . 28; America, 1838 ***778.5*** *p213*
Forscue, Martin; Virginia, 1639 ***6219*** *p157*
Forshew, Hugh; Virginia, 1642 ***6219*** *p186*
Forson, Trygos; Arkansas, 1918 ***95.2*** *p44*
Forsons, John 27; New Orleans, 1862 ***543.30*** *p27*
Forssen, Alex; Iowa, 1866-1943 ***123.54*** *p18*
Forssman, Grest A.; Iowa, 1866-1943 ***123.54*** *p18*
Forstenson, Arvid Julious; Arkansas, 1918 ***95.2*** *p44*
Forster, Carl William; Wisconsin, n.d. ***9675.5*** *p189*
Forster, Mrs. E.; Milwaukee, 1875 ***4719.30*** *p257*
With 2 children
Forster, George; America, 1741 ***4971*** *p94*
Forster, George 11; Jamaica, 1774 ***1219.7*** *p237*
Forster, George 15; Jamaica, 1730 ***3690.1*** *p81*
Forster, Henry 12; Jamaica, 1774 ***1219.7*** *p238*
Forster, Henry 30; Kansas, 1888 ***5240.1*** *p71*
Forster, Herman 24; New Orleans, 1862 ***543.30*** *p222B*
Forster, John 17; Philadelphia, 1774 ***1219.7*** *p233*
Forster, John 24; North Carolina, 1774 ***1219.7*** *p215*
Forster, John 30; Philadelphia, 1775 ***1219.7*** *p258*
Forster, Jonathan 20; Virginia, 1774 ***1219.7*** *p240*
Forster, Mary 55; North Carolina, 1850 ***1639.20*** *p71*
Forster, Thomas; West Virginia, 1854 ***9788.3*** *p10*
Forster, Thomas 18; Maryland, 1774 ***1219.7*** *p244*
Forstner, Heinrich Friedrich; Quebec, 1776 ***9786*** *p257*
Forsyth, Ann; Quebec, 1827 ***8893*** *p263*
Forsyth, Berobeer 22; Carolina, 1774 ***1219.7*** *p234*
Forsyth, Bezabeer 22; Carolina, 1774 ***1639.20*** *p71*
Forsyth, George; New York, NY, 1815 ***2859.11*** *p31*
Forsyth, George 16; Quebec, 1864 ***5704.8*** *p163*
Forsyth, George 50; Quebec, 1864 ***5704.8*** *p163*
Forsyth, James; New York, NY, 1815 ***2859.11*** *p31*
Forsyth, James; Ohio, 1832-1838 ***9892.11*** *p15*
Forsyth, James; Ohio, 1840 ***9892.11*** *p15*
Forsyth, James R.; Colorado, 1880 ***9678.2*** *p19*
Forsyth, John; New York, NY, 1811 ***2859.11*** *p12*
Forsyth, John; Quebec, 1798 ***7603*** *p35*
Forsyth, John; Quebec, 1815 ***9229.18*** *p75*
With wife
With daughter
Forsyth, John 14; Quebec, 1864 ***5704.8*** *p163*
Forsyth, John A.; North Carolina, 1818 ***1639.20*** *p72*
Forsyth, Mary; New York, NY, 1811 ***2859.11*** *p12*
Forsyth, Mary 25; St. John, N.B., 1860 ***5704.8*** *p144*
Forsyth, Nancy 3; St. John, N.B., 1860 ***5704.8*** *p144*
Forsyth, Robert; New York, NY, 1811 ***2859.11*** *p12*
Forsyth, Sarah; New York, NY, 1811 ***2859.11*** *p12*
Forsyth, Thomas 6; St. John, N.B., 1860 ***5704.8*** *p144*
Forsyth, Thomas 14; Quebec, 1855 ***5704.8*** *p125*
Forsyth, Thomas 47; Maryland, 1775 ***1219.7*** *p261*
Forsyth, Valentine; New York, NY, 1811 ***2859.11*** *p12*
Forsyth, William 17; Jamaica, 1774 ***1219.7*** *p189*
Forsythe, Alexander 18; Quebec, 1857 ***5704.8*** *p136*
Forsythe, Ann; Philadelphia, 1853 ***5704.8*** *p101*
Forsythe, Anne Jane 10; Quebec, 1855 ***5704.8*** *p125*
Forsythe, Elizabeth 14; Quebec, 1855 ***5704.8*** *p125*
Forsythe, James; Quebec, 1853 ***5704.8*** *p104*
Forsythe, Jemima 7; Quebec, 1855 ***5704.8*** *p125*
Forsythe, Jemima 48; Quebec, 1855 ***5704.8*** *p125*
Forsythe, John 13; St. John, N.B., 1853 ***5704.8*** *p107*
Forsythe, John 19; Philadelphia, 1853 ***5704.8*** *p112*
Forsythe, John 27; St. John, N.B., 1858 ***5704.8*** *p137*
Forsythe, John 44; Quebec, 1855 ***5704.8*** *p125*
Forsythe, Martha; Philadelphia, 1853 ***5704.8*** *p101*
Forsythe, William; Ohio, 1840 ***9892.11*** *p15*
Fortclough, Wm 12; Virginia, 1699 ***2212*** *p27*
Fortescue, Nich.; Virginia, 1635 ***6219*** *p35*
Forth, John; Georgia, 1775 ***1219.7*** *p274*
Forth, Jon.; Virginia, 1637 ***6219*** *p11*
Fortier, Clemence 11; America, 1837 ***778.5*** *p213*
Fortier, Hardy 4; Louisiana, 1833 ***778.5*** *p213*
Fortier, Jean 40; America, 1835 ***778.5*** *p213*
Fortier, Jean Marie 40; Louisiana, 1833 ***778.5*** *p213*
Fortier, L. B. 2; New Orleans, 1839 ***778.5*** *p213*
Fortier, Rosalie 17; Louisiana, 1833 ***778.5*** *p213*
Fortier, Rosalie 40; Louisiana, 1833 ***778.5*** *p213*
Fortier, Sophie 7; Louisiana, 1833 ***778.5*** *p213*
Fortier, Victorine 11; Louisiana, 1833 ***778.5*** *p213*
Fortin, Pierre Benoit; Wisconsin, n.d. ***9675.5*** *p189*
Fortino, Giacomo; Arkansas, 1918 ***95.2*** *p44*
Fortmann, Franz; Cincinnati, 1835-1875 ***8582.3*** *p47*
Fortmann, Heinrich Anton; America, 1852 ***8582.3*** *p19*
Fortnam, John 34; Kansas, 1892 ***5240.1*** *p13*
Fortnam, John 34; Kansas, 1892 ***5240.1*** *p77*
Fortt, Lewis; Illinois, 1866 ***2896.5*** *p12*
Fortune, Andrew; America, 1743 ***4971*** *p34*
Fortune, Andrew 38; New Orleans, 1862 ***543.30*** *p226B*
Fortune, Catherine; Quebec, 1811 ***7603*** *p101*
Fortune, John; Quebec, 1812 ***7603*** *p101*
Fortune, Michael; New York, NY, 1838 ***8208.4*** *p67*
Fortune, Moses; Quebec, 1825 ***7603*** *p101*
Fortune, Patrick; New York, NY, 1816 ***2859.11*** *p31*
Fortwengler, Benjamin; Illinois, 1880 ***2896.5*** *p12*
Forward, William; Washington, 1859-1920 ***2872.1*** *p13*
Fos, Bernard 32; America, 1838 ***778.5*** *p213*
Fos, Eutrope 22; America, 1838 ***778.5*** *p213*
Fos, Guillaume 31; Port uncertain, 1838 ***778.5*** *p213*
Foscett, Symon; Virginia, 1642 ***6219*** *p188*
Foser, . . .; Canada, 1776-1783 ***9786*** *p21*
Foss, Henry; Cincinnati, 1869-1887 ***8582*** *p9*
Foss, Nestor; Colorado, 1900 ***9678.2*** *p19*
Foss, Peter J.; New York, NY, 1853 ***2896.5*** *p12*
Fosse, Christian 18; America, 1837 ***778.5*** *p214*
Fossel, Nels; Arkansas, 1918 ***95.2*** *p44*
Fossen, Arnold van; Germantown, PA, 1684 ***2467.7*** *p5*
Fossett, Robert; Virginia, 1637 ***6219*** *p85*
Fossett, Robert; Virginia, 1642 ***6219*** *p189*
Fossett, Robt.; Virginia, 1629 ***6219*** *p8*
Fossey, John 23; Jamaica, 1736 ***3690.1*** *p81*
Fost, . . .; Canada, 1776-1783 ***9786*** *p20*
Foster, . . .; New York, NY, 1815 ***2859.11*** *p31*
Foster, Mrs. 39; New York, NY, 1893 ***9026.4*** *p41*
*Relative:*Newton 6
*Relative:*Anna 4
Foster, Andrew; Philadelphia, 1851 ***5704.8*** *p70*
Foster, Anna 4 *SEE* Foster, Mrs.
Foster, Armstrong; Virginia, 1635 ***6219*** *p69*
Foster, Bridgett *SEE* Foster, John
Foster, Eliza; Virginia, 1637 ***6219*** *p11*
Foster, Elizabeth 19; Maryland, 1722 ***3690.1*** *p81*
Foster, Ellen 27; Virginia, 1700 ***2212*** *p31*
Foster, Francis; New York, NY, 1838 ***8208.4*** *p83*
Foster, George; New York, NY, 1840 ***8208.4*** *p112*
Foster, Giles; Virginia, 1643 ***6219*** *p203*
Foster, Henry; St. John, N.B., 1853 ***5704.8*** *p106*
Foster, Henry; Virginia, 1638 ***6219*** *p124*
Foster, Henry; Virginia, 1646 ***6219*** *p243*
Foster, Isaac; America, 1741 ***4971*** *p34*
Foster, James; New York, NY, 1811 ***2859.11*** *p12*
Foster, James; Virginia, 1642 ***6219*** *p195*
Foster, James; Virginia, 1643 ***6219*** *p241*
Foster, James; Virginia, 1646 ***6219*** *p238*
Foster, Jane; America, 1698 ***2212*** *p5*
Foster, Jane; Virginia, 1639 ***6219*** *p159*
Foster, John; America, 1698 ***2212*** *p6*
Foster, John; America, 1864 ***5704.8*** *p190*
Foster, John; New York, NY, 1811 ***2859.11*** *p12*
Foster, John; New York, NY, 1815 ***2859.11*** *p31*
Foster, John; New York, NY, 1838 ***8208.4*** *p85*
Foster, John; Virginia, 1636 ***6219*** *p21*
Foster, John; Virginia, 1641 ***6219*** *p184*
Foster, John; Virginia, 1643 ***6219*** *p207*
*Wife:*Bridgett
Foster, John; Wisconsin, 1866 ***5240.1*** *p13*
Foster, John 19; Jamaica, 1722 ***3690.1*** *p81*
Foster, John 26; Maryland, 1774 ***1219.7*** *p236*
Foster, John 33; Jamaica, 1738 ***3690.1*** *p81*
Foster, John 40; New England, 1774 ***1219.7*** *p191*
Foster, Joseph 16; Maryland, 1722 ***3690.1*** *p81*
Foster, Margaret; New York, NY, 1811 ***2859.11*** *p12*
Foster, Margarett; Virginia, 1638 ***6219*** *p11*
Foster, Margery; America, 1864 ***5704.8*** *p189*
Foster, Mark; Virginia, 1635 ***6219*** *p36*
Foster, Mary; New York, NY, 1811 ***2859.11*** *p12*
Foster, Mary; Virginia, 1642 ***6219*** *p199*
Foster, Mary 18; Georgia, 1775 ***1219.7*** *p277*
Foster, Newton 6 *SEE* Foster, Mrs.
Foster, Nicholas; Virginia, 1635 ***6219*** *p71*
Foster, Pauline; Milwaukee, 1875 ***4719.30*** *p257*
With child
Foster, Pemett; Virginia, 1645 ***6219*** *p252*
Foster, Phillip; Virginia, 1636 ***6219*** *p80*
Foster, Richard; Quebec, 1850 ***5704.8*** *p70*
Foster, Richard; Virginia, 1638 ***6219*** *p122*
Foster, Robert; New York, NY, 1838 ***8208.4*** *p89*
Foster, Robert; Philadelphia, 1852 ***5704.8*** *p84*
Foster, Robert; Philadelphia, 1868 ***5704.8*** *p230*
Foster, Thomas; Iowa, 1866-1943 ***123.54*** *p18*
Foster, Thomas 29; Port uncertain, 1774 ***1219.7*** *p176*
Foster, William; America, 1864 ***5704.8*** *p189*
Foster, William; New York, NY, 1837 ***8208.4*** *p25*
Foster, William; Virginia, 1642 ***6219*** *p187*
Foster, William 17; Philadelphia, 1774 ***1219.7*** *p175*
Foster, Wm.; Virginia, 1637 ***6219*** *p83*
Foster, Zachariah; Virginia, 1635 ***6219*** *p72*
Fosti, John 28; New Orleans, 1838 ***778.5*** *p214*
Fostonski, Stanley; Arkansas, 1918 ***95.2*** *p44*
Fotcher, Silvester; Virginia, 1638 ***6219*** *p148*
Foth, Fred; Indiana, 1848 ***9117*** *p16*
Foth, Henry; Kansas, 1884 ***5240.1*** *p13*
Foth, Jacob H.; Kansas, 1882 ***5240.1*** *p13*
Fotheringham, Alexander; America, 1841 ***8893*** *p266*
Fotheringham, John; South Carolina, 1716 ***1639.20*** *p72*
Fothn, Peter; America, 1697 ***2212*** *p8*
Foti, Louis 23; New Orleans, 1838 ***778.5*** *p214*
Foti, Stefano; Arkansas, 1918 ***95.2*** *p44*
Fotts, Hannah 22; Maryland, 1775 ***1219.7*** *p253*
Foucaud, Pierre 69; America, 1839 ***778.5*** *p214*
Fouche, Mr. 46; New Orleans, 1821 ***778.5*** *p214*
Fouche, Nelson 38; America, 1839 ***778.5*** *p214*
Fouga, John 33; Mexico, 1826 ***778.5*** *p214*
Fouga, Pierre 26; New Orleans, 1820 ***778.5*** *p214*
Fougard, Joseph 40; America, 1839 ***778.5*** *p214*
Foughler, Harry 39; New Orleans, 1862 ***543.30*** *p32*
Fougue, Jos. 20; New Orleans, 1830 ***778.5*** *p214*
Fouilliol, Marie J. 49; America, 1836 ***778.5*** *p214*
Foukett, Mr. 30; Grenada, 1774 ***1219.7*** *p185*
Foul, Julius; Washington, 1859-1920 ***2872.1*** *p13*
Foulger, Benjamin 14 *SEE* Foulger, Thomas
Foulger, Mary 40 *SEE* Foulger, Thomas
Foulger, Rebecca 18 *SEE* Foulger, Thomas
Foulger, Thomas 16 *SEE* Foulger, Thomas
Foulger, Thomas 42; Philadelphia, 1774 ***1219.7*** *p239*
*Wife:*Mary 40
*Child:*Rebecca 18
*Child:*Thomas 16
*Child:*Benjamin 14
Foulks, Ellen 38; Massachusetts, 1849 ***5881.1*** *p37*
Foulon, Mr. 26; New Orleans, 1829 ***778.5*** *p214*
Foulon, Francis 22; New Orleans, 1862 ***543.30*** *p227B*
Founier, Isaac 24; Baltimore, 1775 ***1219.7*** *p270*
Fountain, Colbert; California, 1879 ***2764.35*** *p22*
Fountain, Lewis 28; Maryland, 1775 ***1219.7*** *p249*
Fountaine, Francis 17; Jamaica, 1725 ***3690.1*** *p81*
Fountaine, John 17; Jamaica, 1727 ***3690.1*** *p81*
Founten, John 17; Jamaica, 1727 ***3690.1*** *p81*
Fouquet, Jean; Port uncertain, 1839 ***778.5*** *p214*
Fourcade, Mme. 25; Port uncertain, 1837 ***778.5*** *p215*
Fourcade, Mr.; Port uncertain, 1839 ***778.5*** *p214*
Fourcade, Mr. 30; Port uncertain, 1837 ***778.5*** *p214*
Fourcade, Jacob 14; New Orleans, 1822 ***778.5*** *p215*
Fourcar, Mr. 50; Louisiana, 1820 ***778.5*** *p215*
Fourchy, Alexandre 37; Port uncertain, 1824 ***778.5*** *p215*
Fourcomichalopoulos, Constantine Elion; Arkansas, 1918 ***95.2*** *p44*
Fourdran, Antoni 26; America, 1839 ***778.5*** *p215*
Fourment, Jean 38; New Orleans, 1839 ***778.5*** *p215*
Fournier, John; Washington, 1859-1920 ***2872.1*** *p13*
Fouroux, Joseph 22; New Orleans, 1831 ***778.5*** *p215*
Fourrault, J. Bapt. 24; Died enroute, 1835 ***778.5*** *p215*
Fouskey, Catharine 23; New York, NY, 1868 ***5704.8*** *p225*
Fout, Charley; Iowa, 1866-1943 ***123.54*** *p18*
Fout, Fredrick W.; New York, 1855 ***1450.2*** *p44A*
Fouta, Mr. 30; America, 1839 ***778.5*** *p215*
Fouteaux, J. M. 30; New Orleans, 1839 ***778.5*** *p215*
Fouyd, B. 30; Port uncertain, 1839 ***778.5*** *p215*
Fowell, Edmund 25; Jamaica, 1736 ***3690.1*** *p81*
Fowell, James 18; Windward Islands, 1722 ***3690.1*** *p81*
Fowen, Francis 15; Philadelphia, 1774 ***1219.7*** *p212*
Fowey, Thomas; New York, NY, 1811 ***2859.11*** *p12*
Fowin, Robert; New York, NY, 1868 ***5704.8*** *p229*
Fowke, John; Virginia, 1635 ***6219*** *p36*
Fowke, Wm.; Virginia, 1646 ***6219*** *p236*
Fowks, William 21; Jamaica, 1724 ***3690.1*** *p82*
Fowler, A. J.; Washington, 1859-1920 ***2872.1*** *p13*
Fowler, Charles; St. Kitts, 1776 ***1219.7*** *p284*
Fowler, James; New York, NY, 1833 ***8208.4*** *p77*
Fowler, James; Virginia, 1635 ***6219*** *p71*
Fowler, James C.; Illinois, 1872 ***5012.39*** *p25*
Fowler, John; Charleston, SC, 1799 ***1639.20*** *p72*
Fowler, John 22; Kansas, 1886 ***5240.1*** *p68*
Fowler, John 36; Maryland, 1775 ***1219.7*** *p253*
Fowler, Mary; Virginia, 1643 ***6219*** *p205*
Fowler, Mary 22; Maryland, 1775 ***1219.7*** *p257*
Fowler, Mary 22; Philadelphia, 1774 ***1219.7*** *p212*
Fowler, Mrs. Richard 23; Jamaica, 1774 ***1219.7*** *p190*
Fowler, Richard 26; Jamaica, 1724 ***3690.1*** *p82*
Fowler, Tho.; Virginia, 1638 ***6219*** *p124*
Fowler, Thomas; California, 1869 ***2769.4*** *p3*
Fowler, Wm.; Virginia, 1635 ***6219*** *p3*
Fowley, Dennis; Montreal, 1824 ***7603*** *p65*
Fowley, John; America, 1736-1743 ***4971*** *p57*
Fowley, Michel; Quebec, 1822 ***7603*** *p82*
Fowley, Robert; Quebec, 1810 ***7603*** *p100*
Fowley, William; Montreal, 1824 ***7603*** *p101*
Fox, Mr.; Cincinnati, 1838 ***8582.1*** *p15*
Fox, Aaron; Iowa, 1866-1943 ***123.54*** *p18*
Fox, Abraham 31; Maryland, 1735 ***3690.1*** *p82*

Fox, Alexander; St. John, N.B., 1847 ***5704.8*** *p19*
Fox, Ann; St. John, N.B., 1847 ***5704.8*** *p11*
Fox, Christopher; Ohio, 1851 ***9892.11*** *p15*
Fox, Daniel; America, 1738 ***4971*** *p85*
Fox, Daniel; America, 1738 ***4971*** *p95*
Fox, Daniel; America, 1743 ***4971*** *p11*
Fox, Daniel; Illinois, 1902 ***5012.40*** *p77*
Fox, David; America, 1777-1778 ***8582.2*** *p68*
Fox, Edward; Virginia, 1639 ***6219*** *p159*
Fox, Edward 21; Maryland, 1774 ***1219.7*** *p210*
Fox, Eliza 11; St. John, N.B., 1847 ***5704.8*** *p19*
Fox, Elizabeth 19; Maryland, 1720 ***3690.1*** *p82*
Fox, Ellen 9; Massachusetts, 1849 ***5881.1*** *p36*
Fox, Ellen 25; Massachusetts, 1850 ***5881.1*** *p37*
Fox, Francis; Virginia, 1639 ***6219*** *p155*
Fox, George; Maryland, 1753 ***1219.7*** *p22*
Fox, George; Maryland, 1753 ***3690.1*** *p82*
Fox, George 2; Massachusetts, 1850 ***5881.1*** *p37*
Fox, Grace 23; Maryland, 1773 ***1219.7*** *p173*
Fox, H.; Iowa, 1866-1943 ***123.54*** *p18*
Fox, Henry; Colorado, 1891 ***9678.2*** *p19*
Fox, Hugh; Virginia, 1637 ***6219*** *p113*
Fox, Jacob; America, 1844 ***8582.3*** *p19*
Fox, Jacob; Iowa, 1866-1943 ***123.54*** *p18*
Fox, Jacob; Philadelphia, 1783 ***8582.2*** *p67*
Fox, James; Iowa, 1866-1943 ***123.54*** *p18*
Fox, James 2; St. John, N.B., 1847 ***5704.8*** *p11*
Fox, James 8; Massachusetts, 1850 ***5881.1*** *p38*
Fox, James 11; Massachusetts, 1849 ***5881.1*** *p37*
Fox, James 40; Philadelphia, 1803 ***53.26*** *p28*
Fox, Jane; St. John, N.B., 1847 ***5704.8*** *p11*
Fox, Jane; St. John, N.B., 1847 ***5704.8*** *p19*
Fox, John; New York, NY, 1838 ***8208.4*** *p73*
Fox, John; St. John, N.B., 1847 ***5704.8*** *p19*
Fox, John 6; Massachusetts, 1850 ***5881.1*** *p38*
Fox, John 16; Maryland, 1774 ***1219.7*** *p220*
Fox, John 21; Port uncertain, 1774 ***1219.7*** *p176*
Fox, John 26; Maryland, 1773 ***1219.7*** *p173*
Fox, John 70; Arizona, 1909 ***9228.40*** *p11*
Fox, Joseph; Illinois, 1860 ***2896.5*** *p12*
Fox, L.; Iowa, 1866-1943 ***123.54*** *p18*
Fox, Maria 25; Massachusetts, 1850 ***5881.1*** *p40*
Fox, Mary; St. John, N.B., 1847 ***5704.8*** *p19*
Fox, Mary 6; Massachusetts, 1850 ***5881.1*** *p39*
Fox, Mary 13; St. John, N.B., 1847 ***5704.8*** *p19*
Fox, Matthew 21; Maryland, 1774 ***1219.7*** *p206*
Fox, Michael; Illinois, 1903 ***5012.39*** *p53*
Fox, Michael 4; St. John, N.B., 1847 ***5704.8*** *p11*
Fox, Michael 7; Massachusetts, 1849 ***5881.1*** *p39*
Fox, Morris 38; New Orleans, 1862 ***543.30*** *p29*
Fox, Robert; St. John, N.B., 1847 ***5704.8*** *p19*
Fox, Sam; Iowa, 1866-1943 ***123.54*** *p18*
Fox, Samuel 9; St. John, N.B., 1847 ***5704.8*** *p19*
Fox, Samuel 22; Virginia, 1774 ***1219.7*** *p240*
Fox, Thomas; St. John, N.B., 1847 ***5704.8*** *p11*
Fox, Thomas; St. John, N.B., 1852 ***5704.8*** *p83*
Fox, Walter 35; Savannah, GA, 1733 ***4719.17*** *p311*
Fox, William; Virginia, 1698 ***2212*** *p12*
Fox, William 5; Massachusetts, 1849 ***5881.1*** *p41*
Fox, William 26; Virginia, 1775 ***1219.7*** *p261*
Foxcraft, Hugh 18; Maryland, 1720 ***3690.1*** *p82*
Foxly, Mary; Virginia, 1646 ***6219*** *p246*
Foxmond, Edm.; Virginia, 1648 ***6219*** *p250*
Foxwell, Joseph 20; Maryland, 1739 ***3690.1*** *p82*
Foy, Capt.; Quebec, 1776 ***9786*** *p104*
Foy, Jacob; Ohio, 1838 ***9892.11*** *p15*
Foy, Jacob; Ohio, 1840 ***9892.11*** *p15*
Foy, Jacques 47; New Orleans, 1838 ***778.5*** *p215*
Foy, Mary 20; St. John, N.B., 1854 ***5704.8*** *p114*
Foy, Patrick; Quebec, 1823 ***7603*** *p66*
Fozzolare, Natale; Arkansas, 1918 ***95.2*** *p44*
Fraber, Charles; Wisconsin, n.d. ***9675.5*** *p189*
Fraber, Gottlieb; Wisconsin, n.d. ***9675.5*** *p189*
Frabotta, Mario; Arkansas, 1918 ***95.2*** *p44*
Fraccica, Angelo; Arkansas, 1918 ***95.2*** *p44*
Fracco, Pete; Arkansas, 1918 ***95.2*** *p44*
Fraedrich, August; Wisconsin, n.d. ***9675.5*** *p189*
Fraford, Victo; Virginia, 1633 ***6219*** *p31*
Fraham, Charles; Milwaukee, 1875 ***4719.30*** *p258*
Frahm, Carl; Milwaukee, 1875 ***4719.30*** *p257*
Frahm, Charles; Milwaukee, 1875 ***4719.30*** *p258*
Frahm, John 26; Kansas, 1883 ***5240.1*** *p64*
Frahm, William; Milwaukee, 1875 ***4719.30*** *p257*
Fraidevoir, Louis 29; America, 1837 ***778.5*** *p215*
Frain, John; America, 1737 ***4971*** *p27*
Frain, Thomas Joseph; Arkansas, 1918 ***95.2*** *p44*
Frais, Louis; Wisconsin, n.d. ***9675.5*** *p189*
Fraiser, John 28; Baltimore, 1775 ***1219.7*** *p270*
Fraisse, Paul 16; New Orleans, 1863 ***543.30*** *p230B*
Fraisse, Pierre 43; New Orleans, 1863 ***543.30*** *p229B*
Fraki, Ivari; Washington, 1859-1920 ***2872.1*** *p13*
Fraly, Thomas; America, 1742 ***4971*** *p53*
Frame, Alexander; Port Huron, MI, 1881 ***9678.2*** *p19*
Frame, James; Philadelphia, 1852 ***5704.8*** *p89*
Frame, John; New York, NY, 1815 ***2859.11*** *p31*
Frame, Jon.; Virginia, 1637 ***6219*** *p11*
Frame, Margaret *SEE* Frame, Thomas
Frame, Margaret; Philadelphia, 1847 ***5704.8*** *p24*
Frame, Thomas; Philadelphia, 1847 ***53.26*** *p28*
*Relative:*Margaret
Frame, Thomas; Philadelphia, 1847 ***5704.8*** *p24*
Framerville, Widow 42; America, 1839 ***778.5*** *p215*
Framm, Peter; Wisconsin, n.d. ***9675.5*** *p189*
Franc, Henry 36; America, 1838 ***778.5*** *p215*
Franc, Jean 18; America, 1838 ***778.5*** *p216*
Francaise, Marie 31; America, 1836 ***778.5*** *p216*
France, Adam; Virginia, 1856 ***4626.16*** *p16*
France, Jno; Virginia, 1698 ***2212*** *p17*
France, John 23; Kansas, 1891 ***5240.1*** *p76*
France, Mareny; Wisconsin, n.d. ***9675.5*** *p189*
Francee, John 28; New Orleans, 1862 ***543.30*** *p228B*
Frances, Mr. 16; New Orleans, 1826 ***778.5*** *p216*
Frances, George; Arkansas, 1918 ***95.2*** *p45*
Frances, Samuel; Jamaica, 1771 ***1219.7*** *p151*
Franceschini, Giulio; Wisconsin, n.d. ***9675.5*** *p189*
Franceskini, B.; Wisconsin, n.d. ***9675.5*** *p189*
Franceskini, Guielio; Wisconsin, n.d. ***9675.5*** *p189*
Franceskini, R.; Wisconsin, n.d. ***9675.5*** *p189*
Franceway, Norwood 17; Maryland, 1719 ***3690.1*** *p82*
Francey, Mary 25; St. John, N.B., 1855 ***5704.8*** *p127*
Francey, William 30; Virginia, 1774 ***1219.7*** *p238*
Franche, Frederick; America, 1843 ***1450.2*** *p44A*
Franche, Jean-Baptiste; Quebec, 1730 ***7603*** *p21*
Franchick, Frank; Wisconsin, n.d. ***9675.5*** *p189*
Franchis, Louis; Arkansas, 1918 ***95.2*** *p45*
Franchiss, Thomas; Virginia, 1648 ***6219*** *p241*
Franciosci, Agostino; Arkansas, 1918 ***95.2*** *p45*
Francis, August; Iowa, 1866-1943 ***123.54*** *p18*
Francis, Bedford; Virginia, 1642 ***6219*** *p199*
Francis, Charles 25; New Orleans, 1826 ***778.5*** *p216*
Francis, Charles 35; New Orleans, 1862 ***543.30*** *p223B*
Francis, Miss Day; New York, NY, 1816 ***2859.11*** *p31*
Francis, Francis 27; Port uncertain, 1774 ***1219.7*** *p176*
Francis, James; Virginia, 1639 ***6219*** *p184*
Francis, James 30; Massachusetts, 1849 ***5881.1*** *p37*
Francis, James A.; Colorado, 1898 ***9678.2*** *p19*
Francis, John; New York, NY, 1840 ***8208.4*** *p113*
Francis, John; Virginia, 1623-1700 ***6219*** *p189*
Francis, John; Virginia, 1635 ***6219*** *p3*
Francis, John 42; Port uncertain, 1837 ***778.5*** *p216*
Francis, John H.; New York, NY, 1839 ***8208.4*** *p99*
Francis, John L. 39; New Orleans, 1838 ***778.5*** *p216*
Francis, Joseph Day; New York, NY, 1816 ***2859.11*** *p31*
Francis, Martha; New York, NY, 1811 ***2859.11*** *p12*
Francis, Mary; Virginia, 1648 ***6219*** *p253*
Francis, Michael 48; North Carolina, 1850 ***1639.20*** *p72*
Francis, Nicholas; Philadelphia, 1759 ***9973.7*** *p33*
Francis, Palos; Virginia, 1846 ***4626.16*** *p13*
Francis, Peter 19; St. Christopher, 1722 ***3690.1*** *p82*
Francis, Rebecca; Virginia, 1642 ***6219*** *p191*
Francis, Redmond Day; New York, NY, 1816 ***2859.11*** *p31*
Francis, Richard 26; Philadelphia, 1774 ***1219.7*** *p232*
Francis, Tho 24; Maryland or Virginia, 1699 ***2212*** *p24*
Francis, Thomas; Virginia, 1638 ***6219*** *p149*
Francis, William 15; Virginia, 1775 ***1219.7*** *p261*
Francis, William 33; Maryland, 1774 ***1219.7*** *p215*
Francis, Wm.; New York, NY, 1811 ***2859.11*** *p12*
Francisca, . . .; Canada, 1776-1783 ***9786*** *p21*
Francisco, Assolin; Iowa, 1866-1943 ***123.54*** *p18*
Francise, Maheen; Arkansas, 1918 ***95.2*** *p45*
Franciskovic, Augustin; Iowa, 1866-1943 ***123.54*** *p19*
Franck, . . .; Canada, 1776-1783 ***9786*** *p21*
Franck, Adam 10; America, 1853 ***9162.7*** *p14*
Franck, Anna Elis. 6; America, 1853 ***9162.7*** *p14*
Franck, Daniel; Virginia, 1622 ***6219*** *p25*
Franck, John; California, 1860 ***3840.1*** *p18*
Franck, Kath. 8; America, 1853 ***9162.7*** *p14*
Franck, Marg. 17; America, 1853 ***9162.7*** *p14*
Franck, Peter 15; America, 1853 ***9162.7*** *p14*
Franck, Robert; Wisconsin, n.d. ***9675.5*** *p189*
Francke, . . .; Canada, 1776-1783 ***9786*** *p21*
Francke, August Henry; New York, 1754 ***3652*** *p79*
Francke, George; Canada, 1783 ***9786*** *p38A*
Francke, Philipp; Reading, PA, 1780 ***8137*** *p8*
Francken, von; Canada, 1776-1783 ***9786*** *p185*
Francken, Hermann Albrecht von; Canada, 1777 ***9786*** *p266*
Franckh, Michael; Mississippi, 1723 ***2854*** *p44*
Franckiewicz, Marianna 17; New York, 1912 ***9980.29*** *p56*
Franckleberger, John; Philadelphia, 1753 ***9973.7*** *p32*
Francklin, Francis; Virginia, 1634 ***6219*** *p10*
Francklin, John; Virginia, 1637 ***6219*** *p108*
Francklyn, Robert 19; Maryland, 1725 ***3690.1*** *p82*
Franco, Morris; Arkansas, 1918 ***95.2*** *p45*
Francois, Mr. 23; America, 1839 ***778.5*** *p216*
Francois, Andre 19; Port uncertain, 1832 ***778.5*** *p216*
Francois, C. 31; New Orleans, 1839 ***778.5*** *p216*
Francois, C. C. 26; New Orleans, 1839 ***778.5*** *p216*
Francois, Charles 4; America, 1837 ***778.5*** *p216*
Francois, Claude 24; New Orleans, 1838 ***778.5*** *p216*
Francois, Eugene 1; America, 1837 ***778.5*** *p216*
Francois, F. B. 24; Port uncertain, 1839 ***778.5*** *p216*
Francois, Francoise 32; America, 1837 ***778.5*** *p216*
Francois, J. 19; New Orleans, 1836 ***778.5*** *p217*
Francois, J. 30; New Orleans, 1839 ***778.5*** *p217*
Francois, Jean 28; Maryland, 1774 ***1219.7*** *p211*
Francois, Jeanne 34; America, 1837 ***778.5*** *p217*
Francois, Joseph Jean 32; America, 1837 ***778.5*** *p217*
Francois, Jules 3; America, 1837 ***778.5*** *p217*
Francois, Oges Pierre Marie 31; America, 1837 ***778.5*** *p217*
Francois, Passanieux 32; New Orleans, 1835 ***778.5*** *p217*
Francois, Poulard 37; America, 1837 ***778.5*** *p217*
Francois, Sourdille 25; America, 1837 ***778.5*** *p217*
Francois, Sylvie 30; America, 1837 ***778.5*** *p217*
Francois, Thereze 21; New Orleans, 1836 ***778.5*** *p217*
Francois, Ursule 16; America, 1837 ***778.5*** *p217*
Francoise, Ms. 22; New Orleans, 1829 ***778.5*** *p217*
Francques, Etienne 24; New Orleans, 1839 ***778.5*** *p217*
Francus, Wladyslaw 20; New York, 1912 ***9980.29*** *p59*
Frand, Isodar; New York, 1900 ***1450.2*** *p9B*
Frandorf, Philipp; Ohio, 1869-1887 ***8582*** *p9*
Franich, Dujo; Arkansas, 1918 ***95.2*** *p45*
Franisco, . . .; Canada, 1776-1783 ***9786*** *p21*
Frank, Mr. 24; America, 1838 ***778.5*** *p217*
Frank, Abraham; America, 1851 ***8582.3*** *p19*
Frank, Alex Konstantine; Arkansas, 1918 ***95.2*** *p45*
Frank, Bernard; Wisconsin, n.d. ***9675.5*** *p189*
Frank, Charles; Colorado, 1904 ***9678.2*** *p19*
Frank, Charles 45; Kansas, 1873 ***5240.1*** *p54*
Frank, Christian; Illinois, 1873 ***5012.39*** *p26*
Frank, Christoph; Illinois, 1855 ***7857*** *p3*
Frank, Frank 21; New Orleans, 1862 ***543.30*** *p224B*
Frank, Frederich; New Orleans, 1862 ***543.30*** *p28*
Frank, Frederick G.; Illinois, 1886 ***5012.39*** *p120*
Frank, G. A.; Cincinnati, 1869-1887 ***8582*** *p9*
Frank, Georg; America, 1895 ***1763*** *p40D*
Frank, Giovanna Petralia; Iowa, 1866-1943 ***123.54*** *p63*
Frank, Guiseppe; Iowa, 1866-1943 ***123.54*** *p63*
Frank, Hans Gorg; Philadelphia, 1756 ***4525*** *p261*
Frank, Herman; Kansas, 1881 ***5240.1*** *p13*
Frank, Jacob; Savannah, GA, 1736 ***3652*** *p51*
Frank, Jakob; Kentucky, 1839-1840 ***8582.3*** *p98*
Frank, Joe; Iowa, 1866-1943 ***123.54*** *p63*
Frank, Joseph; Arkansas, 1918 ***95.2*** *p45*
Frank, Joseph; Kentucky, 1844 ***8582.3*** *p101*
Frank, Max; America, 1850 ***8582.3*** *p20*
Frank, Nicolas J.; Colorado, 1892 ***9678.2*** *p19*
Frank, Peter; America, 1862 ***6014.1*** *p1*
Frank, Peter; Wisconsin, n.d. ***9675.5*** *p189*
Frank, Samuel H.; Cincinnati, 1869-1887 ***8582*** *p9*
Frank, William; Colorado, 1904 ***9678.2*** *p19*
Frank, Wm.; Ohio, 1857 ***6014.2*** *p7*
Franke, Anthony; America, 1841 ***1450.2*** *p44A*
Franke, Christina *SEE* Franke, Christopher
Franke, Christopher; Pennsylvania, 1742 ***3652*** *p58*
*Wife:*Christina
Franke, Emil; Wisconsin, n.d. ***9675.5*** *p189*
Franke, Joseph; New York, NY, 1834 ***8208.4*** *p42*
Franke, Otto; Wisconsin, n.d. ***9675.5*** *p189*
Franke, Robert; Virginia, 1642 ***6219*** *p192*
Franke, William; Missouri, 1863 ***2896.5*** *p12*
Frankel, Mack; Arkansas, 1918 ***95.2*** *p45*
Frankenstein Family ; America, 1826 ***8582.3*** *p88*
Frankenstein, Franz *SEE* Frankenstein, Johann P.
Frankenstein, Georg *SEE* Frankenstein, Johann P.
Frankenstein, Gottfried *SEE* Frankenstein, Johann P.
Frankenstein, Johann P.; Cincinnati, 1826-1831 ***8582.3*** *p88*
*Brother:*Gottfried
*Brother:*Franz
*Brother:*Georg
With sister
Frankill, Sally M. 70; North Carolina, 1850 ***1639.20*** *p72*
Frankitt, Thomas 16; Pennsylvania, Virginia or Maryland, 1723 ***3690.1*** *p82*
Franklaine, Ann; Virginia, 1643 ***6219*** *p229*
Frankland, Mr. 58; Philadelphia, 1775 ***1219.7*** *p260*
Frankland, John 21; Virginia, 1700 ***2212*** *p32*
Franklin, George 30; Quebec, 1858 ***5704.8*** *p138*
Franklin, Henry; Virginia, 1634 ***6219*** *p32*
Franklin, John; Illinois, 1859 ***2896.5*** *p12*
Franklin, John 22; Jamaica, 1735 ***3690.1*** *p82*
Franklin, Martin; Illinois, 1861 ***2896.5*** *p13*
Franklin, Mary 26; Quebec, 1858 ***5704.8*** *p138*
Franklin, William 14; Massachusetts, 1848 ***5881.1*** *p40*
Franklin, William 23; Newfoundland, 1789 ***4915.24*** *p55*

Franklind, Ann; Virginia, 1643 6219 p229
Franklyn, John 22; Jamaica, 1735 3690.1 p82
Franklyn, Peter 24; Philadelphia, 1775 1219.7 p255
Franko, Mateos; America, 1893 1450.2 p45A
Frankport, Frank; Wisconsin, n.d. 9675.5 p189
Franks, . . .; America, 1836 8582.1 p39
Franks, . . .; Cincinnati, 1837-1838 8582.1 p45
Franks, Friederich; Cincinnati, 1828 8582.3 p88
Franks, H.B.; Philadelphia, 1755 9973.7 p32
Franks, Henry 14; Pennsylvania, Virginia or Maryland, 1719 3690.1 p83
Franks, Jakob; Illinois, 1828 8582.1 p54
Franks, James; Wisconsin, n.d. 9675.5 p189
Franks, Robert 17; Maryland, 1734 3690.1 p17A
Franks, Robert 17; Maryland, 1734 3690.1 p83
Franler, John 38; Maryland, 1774 1219.7 p214
Franlini, Angelo; Arkansas, 1918 95.2 p45
Franoy, Dennis 39; New Orleans, 1863 543.30 p27
Franquez, Bernard 24; America, 1838 778.5 p218
Frans, Achillos 26; Arkansas, 1918 95.2 p45
Fransiole, Charles 18; America, 1837 778.5 p218
Fransioli, Charles 28; America, 1837 778.5 p218
Franson, Martin; Arkansas, 1918 95.2 p45
Frantz, . . .; Canada, 1776-1783 9786 p21
Frantz, Friederich 26; New Orleans, 1862 543.30 p224B
Frantzen, Gerhard; Wisconsin, n.d. 9675.5 p189
Franz, . . .; Canada, 1776-1783 9786 p21
Franz, Friedrich; Illinois, 1888 5012.37 p60
Franz, Margarethe 27; America, 1838 778.5 p218
Franz, Nicolas 27; America, 1838 778.5 p218
Franz, Peter; America, 1852 1450.2 p45A
Franzel, Herman 25; New Orleans, 1862 543.30 p29
Franzen, Bernhard; Wisconsin, n.d. 9675.5 p189
Franzen, Harm; Illinois, 1876 5012.39 p91
Franzen, Philip; Wisconsin, n.d. 9675.5 p189
Franzes, George; Wisconsin, n.d. 9675.5 p189
Franziole, Casper 37; America, 1837 778.5 p218
Fraomaer, Casper; America, 1848 1450.2 p45A
Frarey, James; Illinois, 1864 5012.38 p98
Frarichs, Henry; Illinois, 1860 7857 p3
Fraser, Miss; Quebec, 1815 9229.18 p75
Fraser, Mr.; Quebec, 1815 9229.18 p76
Fraser, Alexander; Charleston, SC, 1792 1639.20 p72
Fraser, Alexander; Illinois, 1875 7857 p3
Fraser, Alexander; South Carolina, 1680-1830 1639.20 p72
Fraser, Andrew; Colorado, 1903 9678.2 p19
Fraser, Augustin; Quebec, 1763 7603 p36
Fraser, Charles-George; Quebec, 1796 7603 p37
Fraser, Daniel 35 SEE Fraser, Malcolm
Fraser, Donald; Quebec, 1790 9775.5 p198A
With family of 3
Fraser, George; America, 1835 8893 p264
Fraser, Guillaume; Quebec, 1768 7603 p37
Fraser, Hugh; Charleston, SC, 1817 1639.20 p73
Fraser, Hugh; New York, 1764 9775.5 p199
Fraser, Hugh; South Carolina, 1763-1838 1639.20 p73
Fraser, Hugh Cameron; California, 1879 2764.35 p22
Fraser, Isabel 64 SEE Fraser, Malcolm
Fraser, Isabell Grant SEE Fraser, Simon
Fraser, James A.; New York, NY, 1838 8208.4 p84
Fraser, Jean; Quebec, 1765 7603 p40
Fraser, Jean; Quebec, 1775 7603 p36
Fraser, Jean; Quebec, 1777 7603 p40
Fraser, Joel; Quebec, 1782 7603 p21
Fraser, John; Carolina, 1700 1639.20 p73
Fraser, John; Charleston, SC, 1807 1639.20 p73
Fraser, John; Charleston, SC, 1810 1639.20 p73
Fraser, John; Quebec, 1765 7603 p40
Fraser, John; South Carolina, 1716 1639.20 p73
Fraser, John 70; Charleston, SC, 1850 1639.20 p73
Fraser, John A.; Colorado, 1889 9678.2 p19
Fraser, Joseph; North Carolina, 1838 1639.20 p73
Fraser, Malcolm 66; North Carolina, 1850 1639.20 p73
*Relative:*Isabel 64
*Relative:*Daniel 35
Fraser, Mary 30; Philadelphia, 1774 1219.7 p226
Fraser, Simon; Canada, 1769-1792 9775.5 p199
Fraser, Simon; New York, 1769 9775.5 p199
*Wife:*Isabell Grant
Fraser, Simon 17; St. Kitts, 1774 1219.7 p205
Fraser, William; Quebec, 1784 7603 p39
Fraser, William 21; Jamaica, 1731 3690.1 p83
Fraser, William 40; Philadelphia, 1774 1219.7 p226
With 3 children
Frash, Frederick; Baltimore, 1834 9892.11 p50
Frash, Frederick; Ohio, 1840 9892.11 p50
Frashier, Angus 42 SEE Frashier, Catherine
Frashier, Catherine 75; North Carolina, 1850 1639.20 p74
*Relative:*William 44
*Relative:*Angus 42
Frashier, William 44 SEE Frashier, Catherine
Frasier, James; New York, NY, 1811 2859.11 p12
Frasier, John; New York, NY, 1839 8208.4 p101
Frasier, Robert; New York, NY, 1811 2859.11 p12
Frasse, Louis; Wisconsin, n.d. 9675.5 p189
Fratnik, Joe; Wisconsin, n.d. 9675.5 p189
Fratschell, . . .; Canada, 1776-1783 9786 p21
Frauciskovic, Andrew; Iowa, 1866-1943 123.54 p19
Fraudsen, Andreas 29; Kansas, 1873 5240.1 p54
Frauer, Herman E.; Indiana, 1894 1450.2 p45A
Frawley, James; Illinois, 1864 5012.38 p98
Frayer, Mr. 20; St. Kitts, 1773 1219.7 p174
Frayle, Tego; Virginia, 1642 6219 p195
Frayne, James; New York, NY, 1815 2859.11 p31
Frayne, William; New York, NY, 1815 2859.11 p31
Frazer, . . .; Canada, 1776-1783 9786 p21
Frazer, Duncan; South Carolina, 1716 1639.20 p72
Frazer, Eliza; America, 1863-1871 5704.8 p240
Frazer, Eliza; New York, NY, 1815 2859.11 p31
Frazer, Francis 15; Maryland, 1775 1219.7 p251
Frazer, Hugh; South Carolina, 1716 1639.20 p72
Frazer, Isabella; America, 1863-1871 5704.8 p240
Frazer, Jane; New York, NY, 1815 2859.11 p31
Frazer, John; New York, NY, 1815 2859.11 p31
Frazer, John; New York, NY, 1836 2896.5 p13
Frazer, Joseph; New York, NY, 1815 2859.11 p31
Frazer, Margaret; New York, NY, 1815 2859.11 p31
Frazer, Mary; New York, NY, 1864 5704.8 p171
Frazer, Robert John 47; California, 1873 2769.10 p3
Frazer, Sarah; New York, NY, 1815 2859.11 p31
Frazer, Thomas; St. Christopher, 1757 1219.7 p56
Frazer, William; South Carolina, 1716 1639.20 p73
Frazier, Anne; Quebec, 1847 5704.8 p8
Frazier, John; Quebec, 1847 5704.8 p8
Frazier, John 21; Kansas, 1870 5240.1 p51
Frazior, Elizabeth 19; Barbados, 1718 3690.1 p83
Frea, Peter; Harris Co., TX, 1898 6254 p4
Freah, Peter; Wisconsin, n.d. 9675.5 p189
Freal, Honor; New York, NY, 1816 2859.11 p31
Freal, Owen; New York, NY, 1816 2859.11 p31
Frear, Joseph, Jr.; New York, NY, 1836 8208.4 p11
Frebel, Carl Alfred; Arkansas, 1918 95.2 p45
Frech, Anna Catharina; West Indies, 1752 2444 p172
Frech, Pauline 25; Kansas, 1900 5240.1 p81
Freche, Bernard 4; New Orleans, 1837 778.5 p218
Frede, Anton 35; New Orleans, 1863 543.30 p229B
Fredeaux, J. 35; America, 1835 778.5 p218
Fredelissy, Mr. 48; Port uncertain, 1837 778.5 p218
Fredell, Carl Johan; Minneapolis, 1882-1887 6410.35 p51
Fredell, J.; Minneapolis, 1869-1878 6410.35 p53
Fredere, Michael; Quebec, 1772 7603 p76
Frederic, . . .; Canada, 1776-1783 9786 p21
Frederichs Family ; New York, 1765 8125.8 p436
Frederichs, Albert 8; New York, NY, 1878 9253 p46
Frederichs, Jacob 43; New York, NY, 1878 9253 p46
Frederichs, Jean 3; New York, NY, 1878 9253 p46
Frederichs, Lucy 6; New York, NY, 1878 9253 p46
Frederichs, Marie 19; New York, NY, 1878 9253 p46
Frederichs, Marie 38; New York, NY, 1878 9253 p46
Frederick, Andrew; Philadelphia, 1763 9973.7 p38
Frederick, Anna Maria; America, 1832 8582.3 p20
With husband & 7 children
Frederick, Anthony 32; New Orleans, 1862 543.30 p29
Frederick, Antoine 36; New Orleans, 1829 778.5 p218
Frederick, August F.; Wisconsin, n.d. 9675.5 p189
Frederick, Charles; New York, 1754 3652 p79
Frederick, Charles 35; New Orleans, 1821 778.5 p218
Frederick, George; Philadelphia, 1760 9973.7 p35
Frederick, Jacob 29; America, 1831 778.5 p218
Frederick, John; Virginia, 1638 6219 p122
Frederick, Peter; South Carolina, 1788 7119 p197
Fredericks, Gisela; Akron, OH, 1922 9892.11 p16
Frederickson, Oscar; Wisconsin, n.d. 9675.5 p189
Fredersdorff, Wilhelm Ludwig; Quebec, 1776 9786 p260
Fredewest, Joseph; America, 1857 8582.2 p66
Fredewest, Joseph; Cincinnati, 1788-1848 8582.3 p90
Fredrick, Emil; America, 1846 6014.1 p2
Fredrick, Henry 24; Jamaica, 1730 3690.1 p83
Fredricksen, Martin Wilhelm; Washington, 1859-1920 2872.1 p13
Fredrickson, C. F.; Minneapolis, 1880-1886 6410.35 p53
Fredrickson, Mathias; Washington, 1859-1920 2872.1 p13
Fredrickson, P. J.; Minneapolis, 1881-1886 6410.35 p53
Fredriksson, Carl Fredrik; Minneapolis, 1880-1886 6410.35 p53
Fredriksson, Peter Johan; Minneapolis, 1881-1886 6410.35 p53
Freeberg, Gustav Oscar; Arkansas, 1918 95.2 p45
Freeborn, John; Ohio, 1844 9892.11 p15
Freeborn, John; Ohio, 1848 9892.11 p15
Freeborn, John, Jr.; Ohio, 1848 9892.11 p15
Freeborn, Sarah 24; Philadelphia, 1775 1219.7 p257
Freeborn, Thomas; New York, NY, 1811 2859.11 p12
With family
Freeborn, William; New York, NY, 1834 8208.4 p2
Freeburn, George 21; Quebec, 1864 5704.8 p159
Freeburn, Margaret; Philadelphia, 1852 5704.8 p85
Freeburn, Robert; West Virginia, 1824-1840 9788.3 p10
Freed, Peter; Philadelphia, 1765 9973.7 p40
Freedline, John; Indiana, 1848 9117 p16
Freedman, Isidore 23; Arkansas, 1918 95.2 p45
Freedman, Morris S.; Illinois, 1901 5012.40 p77
Freeds, Margaretha; Pennsylvania, 1752 2444 p155
Freegard, Elizabeth Mary 33; Kansas, 1891 5240.1 p76
Freegard, H. J.; Kansas, 1881 5240.1 p13
Freeh, George; Wisconsin, n.d. 9675.5 p189
Freehorne, Jno.; Virginia, 1640 6219 p208
Freeje, H. H.; Cincinnati, 1869-1887 8582 p9
Freel, . . .; Canada, 1776-1783 9786 p21
Freel, Ann; St. John, N.B., 1847 5704.8 p35
Freel, Anne 15; Philadelphia, 1859 5704.8 p142
Freel, Bernard; St. John, N.B., 1847 5704.8 p35
Freel, Biddy; St. John, N.B., 1847 5704.8 p35
Freel, Catherine; St. John, N.B., 1847 5704.8 p35
Freel, Catherine 17; Philadelphia, 1859 5704.8 p142
Freel, Catherine 20; Philadelphia, 1853 5704.8 p112
Freel, Charles 8; Philadelphia, 1859 5704.8 p142
Freel, Dennis; Philadelphia, 1852 5704.8 p88
Freel, Ellan; St. John, N.B., 1847 5704.8 p35
Freel, Francis 22; Philadelphia, 1853 5704.8 p113
Freel, Grace; St. John, N.B., 1847 5704.8 p3
Freel, Hannah; St. John, N.B., 1847 5704.8 p35
Freel, Hugh 20; Philadelphia, 1853 5704.8 p113
Freel, Isabella; St. John, N.B., 1847 5704.8 p35
Freel, James; St. John, N.B., 1847 5704.8 p35
Freel, Mary; Philadelphia, 1847 53.26 p28
Freel, Mary; Philadelphia, 1847 5704.8 p31
Freel, Mary; Philadelphia, 1852 5704.8 p85
Freel, Mary; Philadelphia, 1867 5704.8 p220
Freel, Michael 51; Philadelphia, 1859 5704.8 p142
Freel, Nancy 50; Philadelphia, 1859 5704.8 p142
Freel, Patrick; Philadelphia, 1853 5704.8 p100
Freel, Patrick; Philadelphia, 1867 5704.8 p220
Freel, Rose; Philadelphia, 1864 5704.8 p178
Freel, Sally; St. John, N.B., 1847 5704.8 p35
Freel, Susan; Philadelphia, 1851 5704.8 p80
Freel, Thomas; St. John, N.B., 1847 5704.8 p3
Freeland, Elizabeth; Washington, 1859-1920 2872.1 p13
Freeland, Jakob; Washington, 1859-1920 2872.1 p13
Freeland, Johny; Washington, 1859-1920 2872.1 p13
Freeland, Richard; Virginia, 1636 6219 p10
With wife
With 2 children
Freeland, Sophia; Washington, 1859-1920 2872.1 p13
Freeland, Wm.; New York, NY, 1811 2859.11 p12
Freeland, Wm.; Virginia, 1643 6219 p230
Freelum, Richard 23; Philadelphia, 1854 5704.8 p122
Freeman, Alexander 28; Quebec, 1857 5704.8 p136
Freeman, Ann; Virginia, 1642 6219 p193
Freeman, Ann 9; Massachusetts, 1849 5881.1 p35
Freeman, Benjamin 61; Kansas, 1880 5240.1 p62
Freeman, Bennett SEE Freeman, Bridges
Freeman, Bridges; Virginia, 1635 6219 p10
*Wife:*Bridgett
*Brother:*Bennett
Freeman, Bridgett SEE Freeman, Bridges
Freeman, Catharine 11; Massachusetts, 1849 5881.1 p36
Freeman, George William; Antigua (Antego), 1757 1219.7 p56
Freeman, Gust; Minneapolis, 1880-1887 6410.35 p53
Freeman, James 16; Maryland, 1729 3690.1 p83
Freeman, James 20; Virginia, 1774 1219.7 p186
Freeman, John; Virginia, 1637 6219 p111
Freeman, John 12; Massachusetts, 1849 5881.1 p38
Freeman, John 23; Maryland, 1774 1219.7 p235
Freeman, John 34; Jamaica, 1736 3690.1 p83
Freeman, Jone; Virginia, 1637 6219 p113
Freeman, Judith; America, 1742 4971 p22
Freeman, Judith; America, 1742 4971 p86
Freeman, Judith; America, 1742 4971 p95
Freeman, Judith; Annapolis, MD, 1742 4971 p92
Freeman, Judith; Maryland, 1742 4971 p107
Freeman, Margaret 13; Massachusetts, 1849 5881.1 p39
Freeman, Richard; Virginia, 1636 6219 p26
Freeman, Robert; Quebec, 1761 7603 p86
Freeman, Samuel; New York, NY, 1811 2859.11 p12
Freeman, Samuel 19; Maryland, 1719 3690.1 p83
Freeman, Samuel 27; Maryland, 1774 1219.7 p236
Freeman, Sarah 17; South Carolina, 1722 3690.1 p83
Freeman, William; Virginia, 1637 6219 p86
Freeman, William; Virginia, 1647 6219 p244
Freeman, William 20; Maryland, 1774 1219.7 p192
Freemann, Henry; Wisconsin, n.d. 9675.5 p189
Freeme, Anne SEE Freeme, John

Freeme, John; Virginia, 1643 ***6219*** *p202*
*Wife:*Anne
Freemen, Mill.; Virginia, 1635 ***6219*** *p70*
Freemount, Robert 23; Maryland, 1774 ***1219.7*** *p215*
Freerksen, Henry; Illinois, 1875 ***7857*** *p3*
Frees, . . .; Canada, 1776-1783 ***9786*** *p21*
Frees, Kate 26; Kansas, 1872 ***5240.1*** *p53*
Frees, Mary 24; Kansas, 1872 ***5240.1*** *p53*
Freesen, Charles 22; Jamaica, 1731 ***3690.1*** *p83*
Freethorne, John; Virginia, 1636 ***6219*** *p26*
Freez, Arnall; Virginia, 1622 ***6219*** *p76*
Freeze, Rachel; Virginia, 1636 ***6219*** *p15*
Frei, Mr.; Cincinnati, 1844-1855 ***8582.2*** *p45*
Frei, Friedrich; Ohio, 1798-1818 ***8582.2*** *p54*
Freibaum, Lee; Arkansas, 1918 ***95.2*** *p45*
Freiberg, Joseph; America, 1870 ***1450.2*** *p45A*
Freiboth, Carl; Iroquois Co., IL, 1893 ***3455.1*** *p10*
Freiburg, Johan; Wisconsin, n.d. ***9675.5*** *p189*
Freiemmuth, Otto; Wisconsin, n.d. ***9675.5*** *p189*
Freier, Lydia; Wisconsin, n.d. ***9675.5*** *p189*
Freige, Chas.; America, 1892 ***1450.2*** *p45A*
Freigee, David; America, 1889 ***1450.2*** *p45A*
Freihaber, Johan Christoph; Pennsylvania, 1753 ***4525*** *p216*
Freije, Fred; New York, 1899 ***1450.2*** *p10B*
Freije, George; America, 1897 ***1450.2*** *p10B*
Freil, Adam; Philadelphia, 1851 ***5704.8*** *p78*
Freil, Bridget; New York, NY, 1866 ***5704.8*** *p212*
Freil, Bridget; Philadelphia, 1864 ***5704.8*** *p184*
Freil, Catharine; New York, NY, 1864 ***5704.8*** *p176*
Freil, Catharine; Philadelphia, 1864 ***5704.8*** *p176*
Freil, Dennis; Philadelphia, 1852 ***5704.8*** *p85*
Freil, Edward; Philadelphia, 1864 ***5704.8*** *p178*
Freil, Edward; Philadelphia, 1868 ***5704.8*** *p222*
Freil, James; Philadelphia, 1864 ***5704.8*** *p177*
Freil, John; New York, NY, 1866 ***5704.8*** *p212*
Freil, John; Philadelphia, 1864 ***5704.8*** *p178*
Freil, Mary; America, 1864 ***5704.8*** *p185*
Freil, Michael; New York, NY, 1864 ***5704.8*** *p169*
Freil, Nancy; New York, NY, 1864 ***5704.8*** *p169*
Freil, Patrick; America, 1864 ***5704.8*** *p185*
Freil, Rose; New York, NY, 1867 ***5704.8*** *p222*
Freil, Susan 20; Philadelphia, 1853 ***5704.8*** *p113*
Freimuth, A.M. Charl. Kracht *SEE* Freimuth, Ernst Ludwig
Freimuth, Anna Marie Engel; America, 1840-1842 ***4610.10*** *p111*
Freimuth, Carl Heinrich August *SEE* Freimuth, Ernst Ludwig
Freimuth, Ernst Ludwig; America, 1857 ***4610.10*** *p112*
*Wife:*A.M. Charl. Kracht
*Son:*Carl Heinrich August
Freind, Peter; Virginia, 1643 ***6219*** *p207*
Freis, Joseph; Ohio, 1843 ***8582.1*** *p51*
Freiston, Robert; Virginia, 1639 ***6219*** *p150*
Freitach, Joseph; New York, NY, 1838 ***8208.4*** *p86*
Freitag, Friedrich; Illinois, 1880 ***2896.5*** *p13*
Freitag, Friedrich Wilhelm A.; Wisconsin, n.d. ***9675.5*** *p189*
Freitzsch, Johan; Pennsylvania, 1754 ***2444*** *p155*
Frej, Johann; Illinois, 1860 ***5012.38*** *p98*
Frelick, Joseph 21; America, 1835 ***778.5*** *p218*
Fremau, Mme. 30; America, 1830 ***778.5*** *p218*
Fremaux, Mr. 53; America, 1839 ***778.5*** *p218*
Frement, Mathew N. 31; New Orleans, 1827 ***778.5*** *p219*
Fremhaber, Johan Christoph; Pennsylvania, 1753 ***4525*** *p216*
Frencerip, Frederich 21; New Orleans, 1862 ***543.30*** *p28*
French, Edward 5; Massachusetts, 1849 ***5881.1*** *p36*
French, Eliza; St. John, N.B., 1852 ***5704.8*** *p93*
French, Elizabeth; St. John, N.B., 1852 ***5704.8*** *p93*
French, George 33; West Virginia, 1844 ***9788.3*** *p10*
French, Honora 8; Massachusetts, 1848 ***5881.1*** *p37*
French, Isabella; St. John, N.B., 1851 ***5704.8*** *p77*
French, James; St. John, N.B., 1852 ***5704.8*** *p93*
French, James 18; St. John, N.B., 1864 ***5704.8*** *p157*
French, James 25; Maryland, 1775 ***1219.7*** *p264*
French, Jane; St. John, N.B., 1852 ***5704.8*** *p93*
French, Jane 21; Maryland or Virginia, 1699 ***2212*** *p23*
French, John; Quebec, 1822 ***7603*** *p55*
French, John; St. John, N.B., 1851 ***5704.8*** *p77*
French, John 23; Pennsylvania, 1728 ***3690.1*** *p83*
French, Joseph 9; Massachusetts, 1849 ***5881.1*** *p38*
French, Joseph 16; Jamaica, 1730 ***3690.1*** *p83*
French, Lawrence 26; Montserrat, 1699-1700 ***2212*** *p22*
French, Margaret 3; Massachusetts, 1849 ***5881.1*** *p39*
French, Matilda; St. John, N.B., 1852 ***5704.8*** *p93*
French, Richard 25; Jamaica, 1725 ***3690.1*** *p83*
French, Robert; St. John, N.B., 1851 ***5704.8*** *p77*
French, William 25; Virginia, 1774 ***1219.7*** *p193*
French, William 46; Port uncertain, 1774 ***1219.7*** *p176*
Frendenberg, J. 42; Kansas, 1890 ***5240.1*** *p74*
Frenighty, Daniel; America, 1740 ***4971*** *p56*
Frenk, George; Illinois, 1889 ***5012.39*** *p52*
Frenk, John George; Illinois, 1892 ***5012.40*** *p26*
Frenkel, Benedict; Cincinnati, 1869-1887 ***8582*** *p9*
Frenken, Hubert 22; Kansas, 1884 ***5240.1*** *p66*
Frenly, Bryan 14; Massachusetts, 1847 ***5881.1*** *p35*
Frensch, Mathias; America, 1851 ***8582.3*** *p20*
Frensemeyer, Mr.; America, 1856 ***4610.10*** *p135*
With wife
*Child:*Anne Marie C. Louise 20
*Child:*Anne M.C. Luise Engel 17
*Child:*Louise Friederike 13
*Child:*Johann F. Wilhelm
Frensemeyer, Anne M.C. Luise Engel 17 *SEE* Frensemeyer, Mr.
Frensemeyer, Anne Marie C. Louise 20 *SEE* Frensemeyer, Mr.
Frensemeyer, Johann F. Wilhelm *SEE* Frensemeyer, Mr.
Frensemeyer, Louise Friederike 13 *SEE* Frensemeyer, Mr.
Frenz, Friedrich; Illinois, 1888 ***5012.37*** *p60*
Frere, Alexandre; Louisiana, 1789-1819 ***778.5*** *p555*
Frere, Edward 55; Port uncertain, 1836 ***778.5*** *p219*
Frere, Robert; Virginia, 1641 ***6219*** *p185*
Frerichs, Frank Mennen; New York, NY, 1926 ***3455.4*** *p79*
Frescazes, Bertrand 19; America, 1838 ***778.5*** *p219*
Fresdenberger, Ernst Louis; New York, NY, 1838 ***8208.4*** *p80*
Frese, Charles; America, 1852 ***1450.2*** *p45A*
Frese, Jean 32; America, 1838 ***778.5*** *p219*
Frese, Joseph; Cincinnati, 1869-1887 ***8582*** *p9*
Frese, Mary 20; America, 1838 ***778.5*** *p219*
Fresh, Frederick; Ohio, 1840 ***9892.11*** *p15*
Freshmuth, Daniel; Pennsylvania, 1766 ***4525*** *p218*
Frett, Ann 22; Tortola, 1773 ***1219.7*** *p172*
With husband
Frett, Florence 21; Tortola, 1773 ***1219.7*** *p172*
Frett, Peter; Philadelphia, 1763 ***9973.7*** *p38*
Frette, J. 20; New Orleans, 1821 ***778.5*** *p219*
Fretto, Vingenzo; Arkansas, 1918 ***95.2*** *p45*
Fretwell, William 21; Jamaica, 1731 ***3690.1*** *p84*
Freudenberger, Heinrich; America, 1851 ***8582.3*** *p20*
Freund, . . .; Canada, 1776-1783 ***9786*** *p21*
Freund, Charles; New York, 1868 ***1450.2*** *p9B*
Freund, Christian Friedrich Wilhelm; America, 1868 ***4610.10*** *p159*
With family
Freund, Ernst Friedrich Christian; America, 1867 ***4610.10*** *p158*
Freund, Jacob H.; Cincinnati, 1869-1887 ***8582*** *p9*
Freund, John; Illinois, 1875 ***2896.5*** *p13*
Freund, Math; Wisconsin, 1881 ***5240.1*** *p13*
Freundt, Gottlieb Ferdinand August; America, 1853 ***4610.10*** *p156*
Frew, William; Iowa, 1866-1943 ***123.54*** *p19*
Frewin, Thomas 21; Philadelphia, 1774 ***1219.7*** *p212*
Frey, . . .; Canada, 1776-1783 ***9786*** *p21*
Frey, Mr.; America, 1840-1860 ***4610.10*** *p52*
Frey, Mr.; Cincinnati, 1831 ***8582.1*** *p51*
Frey, Catharine *SEE* Frey, Michael
Frey, Conrad 45; Arizona, 1890 ***2764.35*** *p23*
Frey, Doris; Kentucky, 1840-1845 ***8582.3*** *p100*
Frey, Elisabetha *SEE* Frey, Michael
Frey, Heinrich; Pennsylvania, 1675 ***8125.8*** *p436*
Frey, Humphrey; Virginia, 1639 ***6219*** *p151*
Frey, Johann; Ohio, 1869-1887 ***8582*** *p9*
Frey, Johann Jacob; Cincinnati, 1833 ***8582.2*** *p60*
Frey, Johann Jacob; Cincinnati, 1869-1887 ***8582*** *p10*
Frey, Johann Martin; Pennsylvania, 1771 ***2444*** *p155*
Frey, John; Kansas, 1888 ***5240.1*** *p13*
Frey, John 42; New Orleans, 1862 ***543.30*** *p31*
Frey, Ludwig; Cincinnati, 1828 ***8582.1*** *p51*
Frey, Marg. Elis. 22; America, 1853 ***9162.8*** *p36*
Frey, Mathias; Wisconsin, n.d. ***9675.5*** *p189*
Frey, Michael; Pennsylvania, 1771 ***2444*** *p155*
*Wife:*Catharine
*Child:*Elisabetha
Frey, Nicolaus; Wisconsin, n.d. ***9675.5*** *p189*
Frey, Philipp; America, 1778 ***4349*** *p47*
Frey, Philipp; Philadelphia, 1754 ***4349*** *p47*
Frey, Valentine 41; New Orleans, 1862 ***543.30*** *p228B*
Frey, William; New York, NY, 1839 ***8208.4*** *p95*
Freyden, Engelbrecht von; Halifax, N.S., 1778 ***9786*** *p270*
Freyden, Engelbrecht von; New York, 1776 ***9786*** *p270*
Freye, Charles; New York, 1898 ***1450.2*** *p10B*
Freyenhagen, . . .; Canada, 1776-1783 ***9786*** *p21*
Freyenhagen, Lieut.; Quebec, 1776 ***9786*** *p105*
Freyenhagen, Heinrich Julius; Quebec, 1776 ***9786*** *p256*
Freyenmuth, Otto; Wisconsin, n.d. ***9675.5*** *p189*
Freyensoner, . . .; Canada, 1776-1783 ***9786*** *p21*
Freyfogel, Jacob; Virginia, 1844 ***4626.16*** *p13*
Freyhube, Andrew; New York, 1750 ***3652*** *p74*
Freyling, John Peter; Wisconsin, n.d. ***9675.5*** *p189*
Freyman, George; Ohio, 1842 ***9892.11*** *p15*
Freyman, George; Ohio, 1845 ***9892.11*** *p16*
Freymuth, . . .; Canada, 1776-1783 ***9786*** *p21*
Freytaeger, Walter; Wisconsin, n.d. ***9675.5*** *p189*
Freytag, Anna Elisabetha *SEE* Freytag, Nicholas
Freytag, Catharina Elisabetha *SEE* Freytag, Nicholas
Freytag, Johann Martin *SEE* Freytag, Nicholas
Freytag, Nicholas; Pennsylvania, 1738 ***1034.18*** *p7*
*Wife:*Anna Elisabetha
*Child:*Catharina Elisabetha
*Child:*Johann Martin
Friberg, Albin Natanael; Arkansas, 1918 ***95.2*** *p45*
Friberg, Soren Nelson; Washington, 1859-1920 ***2872.1*** *p13*
Friccio, Loizi; Iowa, 1866-1943 ***123.54*** *p19*
Frich, Bernhard; Quebec, 1776 ***9786*** *p260*
Frichman, Adam; Pennsylvania, 1765 ***4779.3*** *p13*
Frick, J. H.; Washington, 1859-1920 ***2872.1*** *p13*
Frick, John; Illinois, 1861 ***5012.38*** *p98*
Fricke, . . .; Canada, 1776-1783 ***9786*** *p21*
Fricke, Capt.; Quebec, 1776 ***9786*** *p104*
Fricke, George Friedrich Gebhard; Quebec, 1776 ***9786*** *p263*
Fricke, Heinrich Christian; Quebec, 1776 ***9786*** *p252*
Fricke, Heinrich Ernst; America, 1883 ***4610.10*** *p124*
Fricke, Louis 42; Kansas, 1893 ***5240.1*** *p79*
Fricke, Theodore; Wisconsin, n.d. ***9675.5*** *p189*
Fricker, Jacob; Cincinnati, 1869-1887 ***8582*** *p10*
Fricker, John; Virginia, 1638 ***6219*** *p124*
Frico, John 39; America, 1836 ***778.5*** *p219*
Friday, John; South Carolina, 1788 ***7119*** *p199*
Friday, Saml; South Carolina, 1788 ***7119*** *p199*
Friday, Steve; Wisconsin, n.d. ***9675.5*** *p189*
Fride, . . .; Canada, 1776-1783 ***9786*** *p21*
Fridel, . . .; Canada, 1776-1783 ***9786*** *p21*
Friderici, . . .; Canada, 1776-1783 ***9786*** *p21*
Fridle, Hans Jerg; Pennsylvania, 1751 ***2444*** *p155*
Fridley, George; Pennsylvania, 1751 ***2444*** *p155*
Fridlin, Hans Jerg; Pennsylvania, 1751 ***2444*** *p155*
Fridly, George; Pennsylvania, 1751 ***2444*** *p155*
Fridrich, Andreas; South Carolina, 1788 ***7119*** *p197*
Fridriksdottir, Agusta 10; Quebec, 1879 ***2557.1*** *p21*
Fridriksdottir, Fridrig 55; Quebec, 1879 ***2557.2*** *p36*
*Relative:*Sigvaldi 14
Fridriksdottir, Kristin 21; Quebec, 1879 ***2557.1*** *p38*
Fridriksdottir, Sigvaldi 14 *SEE* Fridriksdottir, Fridrig
Fridriksson, Fredjburn 18; Quebec, 1879 ***2557.1*** *p21*
Fridriksson, Fridrik 13; Quebec, 1879 ***2557.1*** *p21*
*Brother:*Valgerdur 12
Fridriksson, Olgeir 16; Quebec, 1879 ***2557.1*** *p22*
Fridriksson, Thorgrimur 22; Quebec, 1879 ***2557.1*** *p38*
Fridriksson, Valgerdur 12 *SEE* Fridriksson, Fridrik
Fridsteinsson, Sigurdur 3; Quebec, 1879 ***2557.2*** *p36*
Frieble, Christian; New York, 1754 ***3652*** *p79*
Fried, Anna *SEE* Fried, Margaretha Loeffler
Fried, Dennis 35; New Orleans, 1862 ***543.30*** *p225B*
Fried, Frederich 40; New Orleans, 1862 ***543.30*** *p222B*
Fried, Frederick 40; New Orleans, 1864 ***543.30*** *p229B*
Fried, Johann Georg *SEE* Fried, Margaretha Loeffler
Fried, Margaretha *SEE* Fried, Margaretha Loeffler
Fried, Margaretha Loeffler; Pennsylvania, 1752 ***2444*** *p155*
*Child:*Maria Catharina
*Child:*Anna
*Child:*Johann Georg
*Child:*Margaretha
Fried, Maria Catharina *SEE* Fried, Margaretha Loeffler
Friedaner, Christian; Kansas, 1896 ***5240.1*** *p13*
Friedemann, . . .; Canada, 1776-1783 ***9786*** *p21*
Frieden, Henry; Illinois, 1896 ***5012.40*** *p55*
Friederich, Anna Maria; America, 1832 ***8582.3*** *p20*
With husband & 7 children
Friederick, Robert Henry; Wisconsin, n.d. ***9675.5*** *p189*
Friedering, George Neinrich; Virginia, 1775 ***1219.7*** *p275*
Friedert, Hans Gorg; Philadelphia, 1756 ***4525*** *p262*
Friedgen, Michael; Wisconsin, n.d. ***9675.5*** *p189*
Friedl, Andrew Joe; Arkansas, 1918 ***95.2*** *p45*
Friedler, Johannes; Ohio, 1799 ***8582.2*** *p54*
Friedman, Jacob B. 25?; Arizona, 1890 ***2764.35*** *p23*
Friedman, Michael; New York, NY, 1882 ***1450.2*** *p10B*
Friedmann, Levi; America, 1836 ***8582.3*** *p20*
Friedrich, . . .; Canada, 1776-1783 ***9786*** *p21*
Friedrich, Balthas. 17; America, 1854-1855 ***9162.6*** *p105*
Friedrich, Leonhard; Wisconsin, n.d. ***9675.5*** *p189*
Friedrich, Robert H.; Wisconsin, n.d. ***9675.5*** *p189*
Friedrichsmeyer, Anna Ilsabein; America, 1853 ***4610.10*** *p148*
Friedrichsmeyer, Mathilde Louise 33; America, 1850 ***4610.10*** *p142*
Friedrichsmeyer, O. H.; Illinois, 1901-1960 ***4610.10*** *p67*
Friehaut, Philip; Indiana, 1847 ***9117*** *p19*
Friel, Alex 9 mos; St. John, N.B., 1847 ***5704.8*** *p10*

Friel, Ann 3; St. John, N.B., 1847 5704.8 p15
Friel, Ann 20; Philadelphia, 1859 5704.8 p142
Friel, Anthony; Philadelphia, 1866 5704.8 p207
Friel, Anthony; Quebec, 1848 5704.8 p41
Friel, Bernard; America, 1868 5704.8 p225
Friel, Bessey 8; Philadelphia, 1853 5704.8 p108
Friel, Biddy; Quebec, 1848 5704.8 p41
Friel, Biddy; St. John, N.B., 1847 5704.8 p9
Friel, Bridget SEE Friel, Manus
Friel, Bridget; Philadelphia, 1849 5704.8 p49
Friel, Bridget; Philadelphia, 1853 5704.8 p101
Friel, Bridget; Philadelphia, 1866 5704.8 p207
Friel, Bridget; Philadelphia, 1868 5704.8 p230
Friel, Bridget 15; Philadelphia, 1868 5704.8 p225
Friel, Bridget 20; Philadelphia, 1865 5704.8 p164
Friel, Bryan 20; Philadelphia, 1856 5704.8 p128
Friel, Catharine; New York, NY, 1864 5704.8 p169
Friel, Catharine; New York, NY, 1867 5704.8 p222
Friel, Catharine; Quebec, 1848 5704.8 p41
Friel, Catherine; Philadelphia, 1853 5704.8 p108
Friel, Catherine; St. John, N.B., 1847 5704.8 p15
Friel, Catherine; St. John, N.B., 1849 5704.8 p56
Friel, Charles; Philadelphia, 1847 53.26 p28
Relative:Isabella
Relative:Ellen 11
Friel, Charles; Philadelphia, 1847 5704.8 p14
Friel, Daniel; St. John, N.B., 1847 5704.8 p10
Friel, Dougal; Philadelphia, 1851 5704.8 p71
Friel, Edward 5; St. John, N.B., 1847 5704.8 p10
Friel, Elleanor 3; St. John, N.B., 1847 5704.8 p10
Friel, Ellen; Quebec, 1852 5704.8 p94
Friel, Ellen 4 mos; Quebec, 1852 5704.8 p94
Friel, Ellen 7; Philadelphia, 1853 5704.8 p112
Friel, Ellen 11 SEE Friel, Charles
Friel, Ellen 11; Philadelphia, 1847 5704.8 p14
Friel, Fanny; Philadelphia, 1870 5704.8 p238
Friel, Francis 6; Philadelphia, 1853 5704.8 p108
Friel, Grace; Philadelphia, 1853 5704.8 p102
Friel, Hannah 9; Philadelphia, 1853 5704.8 p112
Friel, Hannah 10; Philadelphia, 1853 5704.8 p108
Friel, Hugh 9 mos; St. John, N.B., 1847 5704.8 p15
Friel, Hugh 5; Philadelphia, 1853 5704.8 p112
Friel, Isabella SEE Friel, Charles
Friel, Isabella; Philadelphia, 1847 5704.8 p14
Friel, James; New York, NY, 1864 5704.8 p169
Friel, James; Quebec, 1848 5704.8 p41
Friel, James; St. John, N.B., 1847 5704.8 p4
Friel, James 9 mos; Philadelphia, 1853 5704.8 p108
Friel, James 10; St. John, N.B., 1847 5704.8 p10
Friel, James 11; Philadelphia, 1853 5704.8 p112
Friel, James 11; Quebec, 1848 5704.8 p41
Friel, James 20; Philadelphia, 1855 5704.8 p124
Friel, Jane; Philadelphia, 1869 5704.8 p235
Friel, John; New York, NY, 1836 8208.4 p11
Friel, John; New York, NY, 1838 8208.4 p71
Friel, John; Philadelphia, 1847 53.26 p28
Friel, John; Philadelphia, 1847 5704.8 p31
Friel, John; St. John, N.B., 1847 5704.8 p2
Friel, John; St. John, N.B., 1847 5704.8 p4
Friel, John 10; Philadelphia, 1853 5704.8 p108
Friel, John 13; St. John, N.B., 1847 5704.8 p10
Friel, John 19; St. John, N.B., 1858 5704.8 p140
Friel, John 22; Philadelphia, 1859 5704.8 p142
Friel, John 22; Quebec, 1857 5704.8 p136
Friel, John 24; Philadelphia, 1864 5704.8 p155
Friel, Manus; Philadelphia, 1849 53.26 p28
Relative:Bridget
Friel, Manus; Philadelphia, 1849 5704.8 p49
Friel, Margaret; New York, NY, 1866 5704.8 p206
Friel, Margaret; Philadelphia, 1853 5704.8 p101
Friel, Margery 21; Philadelphia, 1864 5704.8 p156
Friel, Mary; New York, NY, 1864 5704.8 p169
Friel, Mary; St. John, N.B., 1847 5704.8 p2
Friel, Mary 9 mos; Philadelphia, 1864 5704.8 p156
Friel, Mary 2; Quebec, 1852 5704.8 p94
Friel, Mary 9; St. John, N.B., 1849 5704.8 p56
Friel, Mary 12; Philadelphia, 1853 5704.8 p101
Friel, Mary 40; Philadelphia, 1865 5704.8 p164
Friel, Mary Ann 4; Quebec, 1848 5704.8 p41
Friel, Michael; Philadelphia, 1847 53.26 p28
Friel, Michael; Philadelphia, 1847 5704.8 p24
Friel, Michael; Philadelphia, 1851 5704.8 p70
Friel, Michael; Philadelphia, 1866 5704.8 p207
Friel, Nancy; Philadelphia, 1865 5704.8 p196
Friel, Nancy; Philadelphia, 1866 5704.8 p207
Friel, Nancy 1; St. John, N.B., 1847 5704.8 p15
Friel, Neal; St. John, N.B., 1847 5704.8 p15
Friel, Nelly 22; Philadelphia, 1858 5704.8 p139
Friel, Patrick; America, 1869 5704.8 p235
Friel, Patrick; New York, NY, 1864 5704.8 p169
Friel, Patrick; Philadelphia, 1849 5704.8 p50
Friel, Patrick 18; Philadelphia, 1865 5704.8 p164
Friel, Peter 12; Quebec, 1848 5704.8 p41
Friel, Rose 18; Philadelphia, 1861 5704.8 p149
Friel, Rose 30; Philadelphia, 1853 5704.8 p112
Friel, Rose Ann; Philadelphia, 1853 5704.8 p102
Friel, Sally; St. John, N.B., 1847 5704.8 p10
Friel, Sally 52; Philadelphia, 1864 5704.8 p156
Friel, Susan; Philadelphia, 1866 5704.8 p207
Friel, William 4; Quebec, 1852 5704.8 p94
Friel, William 20; Philadelphia, 1854 5704.8 p118
Frieman, Peter; Wisconsin, n.d. 9675.5 p189
Friend, Henrey; Milwaukee, 1875 4719.30 p257
Friend, Mrs. Henrey; Milwaukee, 1875 4719.30 p257
Friend, John 21; Kansas, 1887 5240.1 p70
Frierke, Franz; Cincinnati, 1869-1887 8582 p10
Friery, James 11; Massachusetts, 1848 5881.1 p37
Friery, Mary 9; Massachusetts, 1848 5881.1 p38
Friery, Mary 38; Massachusetts, 1848 5881.1 p38
Fries, Mr. 23; America, 1839 778.5 p219
Fries, Carl Christian 22; Kansas, 1900 5240.1 p81
Fries, Hannah 22; Kansas, 1872 5240.1 p53
Friese, Hiram; Illinois, 1888 5012.39 p122
Friesen, Abram; Quebec, 1877 9980.20 p49
Friesen, Anna; Quebec, 1875 9980.20 p48
Friesen, Anna; Quebec, 1876 9980.20 p49
Friesen, Elisb.; Quebec, 1876 9980.20 p48
Friesen, Maria; Quebec, 1875 9980.20 p48
Friesen, Marie 71; Quebec, 1875 9980.20 p48
Friesen, Peter; Quebec, 1875 9980.20 p48
Friesing, Wilhelm; New Jersey, 1780 8137 p8
Frieson, Balthar 50; New York, NY, 1889 7846 p40
Frieson, Balthasar 4; New York, NY, 1889 7846 p40
Frieson, Catharina 15; New York, NY, 1889 7846 p40
Frieson, Eva 29; New York, NY, 1889 7846 p40
Frieson, Franciska 6 mos; New York, NY, 1889 7846 p40
Frieson, Genefefa 6; New York, NY, 1889 7846 p40
Frieson, Helena 16; New York, NY, 1889 7846 p40
Frieson, Joseph 28; New York, NY, 1889 7846 p40
Frieson, Luckartta 44; New York, NY, 1889 7846 p40
Frieson, Ludwig 3; New York, NY, 1889 7846 p40
Frieson, Philipp 18; New York, NY, 1889 7846 p40
Frigaroa, Joseph 34; Kansas, 1876 5240.1 p58
Fright, Mathew 33; Virginia, 1774 1219.7 p186
Frigout, Edwin C. 34; Kansas, 1883 5240.1 p64
Frigout, Eugenie 21; New Orleans, 1838 778.5 p219
Frigout, Jean Louis 20; New Orleans, 1838 778.5 p219
Frigout, Jean Pierre 50; New Orleans, 1838 778.5 p219
Friis, Jacob; New York, 1753 3652 p77
Friis, Peter; Kansas, 1890 5240.1 p13
Friis, Peter 27; Kansas, 1890 5240.1 p75
Frileogh, William; America, 1850 1450.2 p46A
Frillmann, Conrad; New York, NY, 1836 8208.4 p20
Friment, Francis; New York, NY, 1839 8208.4 p99
Frinbrecht, . . .; Canada, 1776-1783 9786 p21
Frintz, Juliana; Cincinnati, 1834 8582.2 p11
Friquet, Mrs. F. 32; America, 1838 778.5 p219
Frisby, Ann; Virginia, 1637 6219 p113
Frisby, Frederick; New York, NY, 1853 2896.5 p13
Frisch, Charles; Illinois, 1877 2896.5 p13
Frisch, Julius; Kansas, 1881 5240.1 p13
Frischkorn, Johannes; Vermont, 1777 8137 p8
Frischmuth, Daniel; Pennsylvania, 1766 4525 p218
Frischmuth, M.; Pennsylvania, 1780 4525 p283
Frisell, Victor; Washington, 1859-1920 2872.1 p13
Friser, . . .; Canada, 1776-1783 9786 p21
Frissonier, C. 30; Mexico, 1825 778.5 p219
Frissonier, Henriette 30; Mexico, 1825 778.5 p219
Frissonier, Jules 7; Mexico, 1825 778.5 p219
Frissonier, P. 35; Mexico, 1825 778.5 p220
Frissonier, Sarah Ann 9; Mexico, 1825 778.5 p220
Fristedt, John A.; Minneapolis, 1852-1879 6410.35 p53
Fritch, Carl N.; Illinois, 1887 2896.5 p13
Fritche, Charles; America, 1867 1450.2 p46A
Fritchman, Adam; Pennsylvania, 1765 4779.3 p13
Frith, Henry; Virginia, 1647 6219 p244
Frith, James 19; Jamaica, 1721 3690.1 p84
Frith, Thomas 20; Grenada, 1774 1219.7 p185
Fritsch, Martin; America, 1867 1450.2 p46A
Fritsche, Anna Margaret SEE Fritsche, John C.
Fritsche, Henry; New York, 1749 3652 p71
Fritsche, John; Wisconsin, n.d. 9675.5 p189
Fritsche, John C.; New York, 1743 3652 p59
Wife:Anna Margaret
Fritsche, Paul; New York, 1749 3652 p71
Fritsohe, Regine 35; New Orleans, 1839 9420.2 p166
Fritz, Mr.; New York, 1882 3702.7 p476
Fritz, Alexander; Alberta, 1909-1950 5262 p58
Fritz, Anna Catharina SEE Fritz, Caspar
Fritz, August 33; Kansas, 1884 5240.1 p66
Fritz, Carl 43; America, 1839 778.5 p220
Fritz, Caspar; Pennsylvania, 1744 2444 p155
Wife:Anna Catharina
Child:Jacob
Fritz, David; Alberta, 1909-1950 5262 p58
Fritz, George 27; New Orleans, 1862 543.30 p225B
Fritz, J.; Arizona, 1898 9228.30 p12
Fritz, Jacob SEE Fritz, Caspar
Fritz, Jacob; America, 1870 1450.2 p46A
Fritz, Jacob; Ohio, 1840 9892.11 p16
Fritz, Johannes; Pennsylvania, 1749 2444 p155
Fritz, Johannes; Pennsylvania, 1749-1754 2444 p155
Fritz, Johannes; Pennsylvania, 1754 2444 p155
Fritz, Johannes; Philadelphia, 1764 8582.2 p65
Fritz, John Gerald 43; Jamaica, 1737 3690.1 p84
Fritz, Kath. Etling 53; America, 1895 1763 p40D
Fritz, Mich.; Wisconsin, n.d. 9675.5 p189
Fritz, Samuel; America, 1700-1877 8582.3 p80
Fritz, Samuel; South America, n.d. 8582.3 p79
Fritzgerald, John; America, 1862 6014.1 p1
Fritzsche, Augustus 6 SEE Fritzsche, John Praisegod
Fritzsche, Eva Rose 30 SEE Fritzsche, John Praisegod
Fritzsche, John Praisegod 36; New Orleans, 1839 9420.2 p487
Wife:Eva Rose 30
Child:William 7
Child:Augustus 6
Fritzsche, William 7 SEE Fritzsche, John Praisegod
Friz, Catharina; America, 1765-1766 2444 p142
Friz, Felix; America, 1845 8582.3 p20
Friz, Henry; New York, 1750 3652 p74
Frizzle, Letitia; St. John, N.B., 1850 5704.8 p65
Frizzle, Margaret; St. John, N.B., 1848 5704.8 p43
Froberg, Emil Leonard; Arkansas, 1918 95.2 p45
Froberg, Robert; New York, NY, 1903 3455.1 p49
Frobisher, Joseph; Montreal, 1792 9775.5 p202
Frobisher, Joseph; Quebec, 1779 7603 p24
Froche, Agnes 24; New Orleans, 1839 9420.2 p483
Frocheke, William; Illinois, 1872 5012.39 p25
Frochiher, Joseph 3; America, 1831 778.5 p220
Frochiher, Joseph 35; America, 1831 778.5 p220
Frochiher, Louis 1; America, 1831 778.5 p220
Frochiher, Marie 26; America, 1831 778.5 p220
Frochisser, Joseph 3; America, 1831 778.5 p220
Frochisser, Joseph 35; America, 1831 778.5 p220
Frochisser, Louis 1; America, 1831 778.5 p220
Frochisser, Marie 26; America, 1831 778.5 p220
Frochlke, William; Illinois, 1872 5012.39 p25
Froddermann, Christoph Heinrich; America, 1837 4610.10 p119
Frodermann, Anne Marie C. Muller SEE Frodermann, Friedrich Wilhelm
Frodermann, Carl Heinrich SEE Frodermann, Friedrich Wilhelm
Frodermann, Friedrich Wilhelm; America, 1839 4610.10 p119
Father:Carl Heinrich
Mother:Anne Marie C. Muller
Froebe, . . .; Canada, 1776-1783 9786 p21
Froeber, Catharina; New England, 1753 4525 p218
Froeber, Catharina; Pennsylvania, 1753 4525 p218
Froehlech, John; America, 1848 1450.2 p46A
Froehlich, Anton 31; New Orleans, 1862 543.30 p224B
Froehlich, August 36; New Orleans, 1862 543.30 p222B
Froehlich, Carl Friderich; South Carolina, 1788 7119 p203
Froehlich, Christian; Philadelphia, 1740 3652 p52
Froehlich, Victor Wilhelm; Cincinnati, 1788-1848 8582.3 p90
Froelich, Christian; New York, 1744 3652 p63
Froelich, Esther; Delaware, 1746 3652 p67
Froelich, Henry; Indiana, 1848 9117 p16
Froelich, Johannes; Philadelphia, 1779 8137 p8
Froelick, Lewis; New York, NY, 1834 8208.4 p30
Froeling, John; Iroquois Co., IL, 1892 3455.1 p10
Froelking, Aug; America, 1848 8582.1 p10
Froemming, Gottlieb; Wisconsin, n.d. 9675.5 p189
Froese, Elisabeth; Quebec, 1876 9980.20 p48
Froese, Elisb. Friesen; Quebec, 1876 9980.20 p48
Froese, Franz; Quebec, 1876 9980.20 p48
Froese, Johann; Quebec, 1876 9980.20 p48
Froese, Maria; Quebec, 1876 9980.20 p48
Froese, Peter; Quebec, 1876 9980.20 p48
Froger, Jean-Baptiste 37; Mexico, 1837 778.5 p220
Froget, Mr. 25; New Orleans, 1823 778.5 p221
Froheley, Daniel; New York, NY, 1816 2859.11 p31
Frohlich, Jane Christa. 40; New Orleans, 1839 9420.2 p485
Frohlioh, Aug. Ernst 28; New Orleans, 1839 9420.2 p166
Frohmann, Ludwig; America, 1842 8582.3 p20
Froibel, Jakob 24; Port uncertain, 1839 778.5 p220
Froid, Jean 22; America, 1838 778.5 p220
Froidcoeur, August Joseph; New York, NY, 1903 3455.2 p71
Froidcoeur, August Joseph; New York, NY, 1903 3455.3 p54
Wife:Flora

162 FOR A COMPLETE EXPLANATION OF ENTRY, SEE "HOW TO READ A CITATION" SECTION

Fulton, Nancy 1 *SEE* Fulton, Margaret
Fulton, Nancy 1; Philadelphia, 1848 *5704.8 p41*
Fulton, Nancy 31; Philadelphia, 1804 *53.26 p29*
Fulton, Nealy 20; Philadelphia, 1860 *5704.8 p145*
Fulton, Richard T.; Colorado, 1904 *9678.2 p19*
Fulton, Robert; Philadelphia, 1852 *5704.8 p87*
Fulton, Robert 13; Quebec, 1847 *5704.8 p29*
Fulton, Robert 43; Philadelphia, 1804 *53.26 p29*
Fulton, Rosanna 3 *SEE* Fulton, Margaret
Fulton, Rosanna 3; Philadelphia, 1848 *5704.8 p41*
Fulton, Rose; Quebec, 1847 *5704.8 p29*
Fulton, Rose Ann; Quebec, 1847 *5704.8 p29*
Fulton, Sally; Quebec, 1850 *5704.8 p66*
Fulton, Samuel; Iowa, 1866-1943 *123.54 p19*
Fulton, Samuel 2; Philadelphia, 1851 *5704.8 p76*
Fulton, Samuel 14 *SEE* Fulton, Margaret
Fulton, Samuel Thomas 1; Quebec, 1852 *5704.8 p86*
Fulton, Samuel Thomas 1; Quebec, 1852 *5704.8 p90*
Fulton, Sandy 7; Philadelphia, 1851 *5704.8 p76*
Fulton, Thomas; Baltimore, 1811 *2859.11 p12*
Fulton, Thomas; Philadelphia, 1851 *5704.8 p76*
Fulton, Thomas; Philadelphia, 1865 *5704.8 p189*
Fulton, Thomas 8 *SEE* Fulton, Margaret
Fulton, Walter; Philadelphia, 1864 *5704.8 p184*
Fulton, William; Quebec, 1850 *5704.8 p66*
Fulton, William 5 *SEE* Fulton, Margaret
Fulton, William 5; Philadelphia, 1848 *5704.8 p41*
Fulton, William 11; Quebec, 1847 *5704.8 p29*
Fulton, William H.; Illinois, 1848 *7857 p3*
Fulwell, George; America, 1880 *1450.2 p46A*
Fuman, Michael; New York, NY, 1816 *2859.11 p31*
Fumella, Ardiuno; Wisconsin, n.d. *9675.5 p189*
Fummerton, W. J. 21; Kansas, 1887 *5240.1 p70*
Fums, Giacento; Arkansas, 1918 *95.2 p46*
Funaro, Antonio Ross 22; Arkansas, 1918 *95.2 p46*
Funck, Benedict; Pennsylvania, 1751 *2444 p156*
   *Wife:*Johanna Dorothea
Funck, Hans; Pennsylvania, 1709 *3627 p17*
Funck, Heinrich; Pennsylvania, 1729 *3627 p17*
Funck, Heinrich; Port uncertain, 1717 *3627 p17*
   With wife
   With children
Funck, Johanna Dorothea *SEE* Funck, Benedict
Funck, Martin; Port uncertain, 1717 *3627 p17*
   With wife
   With children
Fungins, Ferdinand; New York, NY, 1840 *8208.4 p110*
Funk, Benedick; Pennsylvania, 1751 *2444 p156*
Funk, Georg; Ohio, 1812-1814 *8582.2 p59*
Funk, Hans; Pennsylvania, 1709 *3627 p17*
Funk, Hans Nicholas; New York, 1754 *3652 p79*

Funk, Heinrich; Philadelphia, 1776 *8582.3 p84*
Funk, John; Wisconsin, n.d. *9675.5 p189*
Funke, Carl Friedrich August; Louisville, KY, 1810-1871
   8582 p10
Funke, Charlotte; Wisconsin, n.d. *9675.5 p189*
Funke, Wilhelm; Ohio, 1869-1887 *8582 p10*
Funston, Andrew; New York, NY, 1811 *2859.11 p12*
Funston, Anne; New York, NY, 1815 *2859.11 p31*
Funston, Francis; New York, NY, 1815 *2859.11 p31*
Funston, John; New York, NY, 1815 *2859.11 p31*
Funston, John 18; Quebec, 1857 *5704.8 p135*
Funston, Joseph; New York, NY, 1815 *2859.11 p31*
Funston, Nancy 53; Quebec, 1857 *5704.8 p135*
Funston, Robert; New York, NY, 1815 *2859.11 p31*
Funston, Thomas 22; Quebec, 1857 *5704.8 p135*
Funston, Thomas 60; Quebec, 1857 *5704.8 p135*
Funte, August Gottlieb; America, 1854 *4610.10 p148*
Funte, Caroline 18; America, 1853 *4610.10 p148*
Funte, Friederike 20; America, 1853 *4610.10 p148*
Funte, Friedrich Wilhelm; America, 1853 *4610.10 p121*
Funte, Otto; America, 1870 *4610.10 p123*
Fupin, Mr. 25; New Orleans, 1836 *778.5 p279*
Furbringer, Ottonar 28; New Orleans, 1839 *9420.2 p357*
Furbush, Fr.; Virginia, 1636 *6219 p7*
Furchtenicht, Ernst; New Orleans, 1849 *1450.2 p46A*
Furgens, . . .; Canada, 1776-1783 *9786 p42*
Furger, John 19; Maryland, 1774 *1219.7 p235*
Furgerson, Anna 60; Massachusetts, 1849 *5881.1 p35*
Furgerson, Ellen 7; Massachusetts, 1847 *5881.1 p36*
Furgerson, Susan 50; Massachusetts, 1849 *5881.1 p40*
Furguson, Abel 19; Jamaica, 1734 *3690.1 p84*
Furiou, J. 17; America, 1835 *778.5 p221*
Furlin, Angelo; Iowa, 1866-1943 *123.54 p63*
Furlin, Anna; Iowa, 1866-1943 *123.54 p63*
Furlin, Antonio; Iowa, 1866-1943 *123.54 p63*
Furlin, Donato; Iowa, 1866-1943 *123.54 p19*
Furlin, Giovanna; Iowa, 1866-1943 *123.54 p63*
Furlin, John; Iowa, 1866-1943 *123.54 p19*
Furlin, John 33; Dominican Republic, 1822 *778.5 p221*
Furlin, Peter; Iowa, 1866-1943 *123.54 p19*
Furlin, Semplico; Iowa, 1866-1943 *123.54 p19*
Furlin, Simplicio; Iowa, 1866-1943 *123.54 p19*
Furlon, Nicholas; Annapolis, MD, 1742 *4971 p93*
Furlong, Daniel 22; Philadelphia, 1774 *1219.7 p212*
Furlong, Edward; New York, NY, 1811 *2859.11 p12*
Furlong, John; New York, NY, 1816 *2859.11 p31*
Furlong, Lawrance 40; Philadelphia, 1774 *1219.7 p201*
Furlong, Mathew; Philadelphia, 1816 *2859.11 p31*
Furlong, Matthew; Montreal, 1824 *7603 p101*
Furlong, Michael; Montreal, 1820 *7603 p101*
Furlong, Michael 22; Massachusetts, 1847 *5881.1 p38*

Furlong, Nicholas; America, 1742 *4971 p17*
Furlong, Nicholas; Maryland, 1742 *4971 p107*
Furlong, Thomas 26; Maryland, 1775 *1219.7 p247*
Furlong, William; New York, NY, 1838 *8208.4 p64*
Furnaux, Louis 25; America, 1823 *778.5 p222*
Furness, Edward 20; Massachusetts, 1849 *5881.1 p37*
Furprud, Margaret 14; America, 1838 *778.5 p222*
Furrance, John 21; Maryland, 1775 *1219.7 p259*
Furrer, Johan; Iroquois Co., IL, 1896 *3455.1 p10*
Furst, Joseph; New Orleans, 1847 *1450.2 p46A*
Furstenberg, John C. 48; Kansas, 1878 *5240.1 p59*
Furtado, Solomon; Missouri, 1881 *5240.1 p13*
Fury, Bernard; Philadelphia, 1850 *5704.8 p64*
Furze, Henry; New York, NY, 1837 *8208.4 p32*
Fush, Frederick; Baltimore, 1834 *9892.11 p16*
Fush, Frederick; Ohio, 1840 *9892.11 p16*
Fushir, Ignatz; Wisconsin, n.d. *9675.5 p189*
Fusinato, Celeste; Iowa, 1866-1943 *123.54 p63*
Fusir, Ignaz; Wisconsin, n.d. *9675.5 p189*
Fuss, Frederick; California, 1867 *2764.35 p23*
Fuss, Lucas; New York, 1750 *3652 p74*
Fusseder, Francis; Wisconsin, n.d. *9675.5 p189*
Fussner, Johann A.; America, 1848 *8582.1 p10*
Futajest, M. 20; New Orleans, 1835 *778.5 p222*
Futhren, David 29; America, 1831 *778.5 p222*
Futoransky, Max; Iowa, 1866-1943 *123.54 p19*
Futterer, . . .; Canada, 1776-1783 *9786 p21*
Futur, M.; Quebec, 1815 *9229.18 p82*
Fuyes, P. J. 37; Port uncertain, 1827 *778.5 p222*
Fuzir, Anton; Wisconsin, n.d. *9675.5 p189*
Fyalka, John; Washington, 1859-1920 *2872.1 p13*
Fyann, Richard; America, 1742 *4971 p32*
Fybill, Jacob; Virginia, 1643 *6219 p206*
Fyder, Chas; Wisconsin, n.d. *9675.5 p189*
Fyffe, Alexander; South Carolina, 1750-1759 *1639.20
   p74*
Fyffe, David; South Carolina, 1750-1759 *1639.20 p74*
Fyffe, William; South Carolina, 1750-1759 *1639.20 p74*
Fynewever, Berendina 31; New York, NY, 1847 *3377.6
   p16*
Fynewever, Dine 6; New York, NY, 1847 *3377.6 p16*
Fynewever, Gerrit Jan 30; New York, NY, 1847 *3377.6
   p16*
Fynewever, Gerrit Jan 56; New York, NY, 1847 *3377.6
   p16*
Fynewever, Harm Jan 24; New York, NY, 1847 *3377.6
   p16*
Fynewever, Jennie 62; New York, NY, 1847 *3377.6 p16*
Fysol, George; New York, 1897 *1450.2 p10B*

G

Gabard, Mrs. 30; New Orleans, 1839 *778.5 p222*
Gabard, A. 33; New Orleans, 1839 *778.5 p222*
Gabard, Amelie 6; New Orleans, 1839 *778.5 p222*
Gabarrau, Th. 15; New Orleans, 1837 *778.5 p222*
Gabathuler, Fred; Arkansas, 1918 *95.2 p46*
Gabel, Anna Maria 10 SEE Gabel, Hans Georg
Gabel, Antoni 12 SEE Gabel, Hans Georg
Gabel, Barbara 38 SEE Gabel, Hans Georg
Gabel, Frank; Colorado, 1888 *9678.2 p20*
Gabel, Hans Georg 40; Philadelphia, 1733 *2854 p44*
  Wife: Barbara 38
  Child: Antoni 12
  Child: Anna Maria 10
  Child: Magdalena 8
  Child: Jerg Adam 5
  Child: Hans Jerg 3
Gabel, Hans Jerg 3 SEE Gabel, Hans Georg
Gabel, Jerg Adam 5 SEE Gabel, Hans Georg
Gabel, Magdalena 8 SEE Gabel, Hans Georg
Gabel, William; Ohio, 1879 *9892.11 p16*
Gabilson, Ida 24; Kansas, 1872 *5240.1 p52*
Gabinq, Pierre 23; Port uncertain, 1839 *778.5 p222*
Gabler, Joh. Gottlob 40; New Orleans, 1839 *9420.2 p169*
Gably, Hugh 18; Philadelphia, 1803 *53.26 p29*
Gabriel, . . .; Canada, 1776-1783 *9786 p21*
Gabriel, Mr. 38; America, 1835 *778.5 p222*
Gabriel, Andreas; Alberta, n.d. *5262 p58*
Gabriel, August; Illinois, 1886 *2896.5 p13*
Gabriel, Frank J.; Illinois, 1889 *5012.40 p25*
Gabriel, Hermann; America, 1828 *8582 p10*
Gabrielson, August 21; Kansas, 1884 *5240.1 p13*
Gabrielson, August 21; Kansas, 1884 *5240.1 p65*
Gabrielson, Axel 23; Kansas, 1890 *5240.1 p75*
Gabrielson, Charles; Washington, 1859-1920 *2872.1 p13*
Gabrielson, Charles 22; Kansas, 1886 *5240.1 p69*
Gabrielson, Emil 22; Kansas, 1888 *5240.1 p13*
Gabrielson, Emil 22; Kansas, 1888 *5240.1 p73*
Gachapin, Mr. 35; Port uncertain, 1839 *778.5 p222*
Gachis, Demetrois George; Arkansas, 1918 *95.2 p46*
Gacki, Apolonary 21; New York, 1912 *9980.29 p70*
Gackstatter, Gertrude; Washington, 1859-1920 *2872.1 p13*
Gadd, Charles N.; Washington, 1859-1920 *2872.1 p13*
Gadd, Charley; Washington, 1859-1920 *2872.1 p13*
Gadd, Nicholas; Washington, 1859-1920 *2872.1 p13*
Gadd, Nick; Washington, 1859-1920 *2872.1 p13*
Gaddis, John 36; Maryland, 1774 *1219.7 p192*
Gadecki, Philip; Iowa, 1866-1943 *123.54 p63*
Gadefrey, C. 40; New Orleans, 1839 *778.5 p222*
Gadeke, Henry 23; Kansas, 1888 *5240.1 p73*
Gader, Frank 24; Kansas, 1876 *5240.1 p58*
Gader, John N.; Kansas, 1880 *5240.1 p61*
Gades, Harman 25; Jamaica, 1774 *1219.7 p189*
Gadesis, Ligor Thomas Spiro; Arkansas, 1918 *95.2 p46*
Gadirin, Minasa; Arkansas, 1918 *95.2 p46*
Gadisin, Morris; Arkansas, 1918 *95.2 p46*
Gadle, Nathan; Virginia, 1637 *6219 p112*
Gadowska, Agnieska 14 SEE Gadowska, Katarina
Gadowska, Bronislawa 7 SEE Gadowska, Katarina
Gadowska, Katarina 35; New York, 1912 *9980.29 p66*
  Child: Agnieska 14
  Child: Katarzyna 11
  Child: Bronislawa 7
Gadowska, Katarzyna 11 SEE Gadowska, Katarina
Gadowska, Teodor; Cleveland, OH, 1912 *9980.29 p66*
Gadowski, Agnieska 14 SEE Gadowski, Katarina
Gadowski, Bronislawa 7 SEE Gadowski, Katarina

Gadowski, Katarina 35; New York, 1912 *9980.29 p66*
  Child: Agnieska 14
  Child: Katarzyna 11
  Child: Bronislawa 7
Gadowski, Katarzyna 11 SEE Gadowski, Katarina
Gadowski, Teodor; Cleveland, OH, 1912 *9980.29 p66*
Gadsby, Henry 19; Pennsylvania, 1724 *3690.1 p85*
Gadsby, John 19; Maryland, 1774 *1219.7 p191*
Gadsby, Ralph 21; Maryland, 1775 *1219.7 p250*
Gady, Pierre 19; Port uncertain, 1839 *778.5 p222*
Gaeling, John 33; Maryland, 1774 *1219.7 p180*
Gaertner, A.; Ohio, 1819 *8582.1 p47*
Gaertner, Elsa; Wisconsin, n.d. *9675.5 p189*
Gaertner, Maria Magdalena; America, 1750-1800 *2444 p148*
Gaertner, Mathias; Wisconsin, n.d. *9675.5 p189*
Gaetano, Shiantar 24; America, 1838 *778.5 p222*
Gaetz, Ignatz; Alberta, 1909-1950 *5262 p58*
Gaffee, Thomas 20; Massachusetts, 1849 *5881.1 p44*
Gafferny, Michael 15; Massachusetts, 1849 *5881.1 p43*
Gaffin, James; New York, NY, 1811 *2859.11 p12*
Gaffney, Bridget 14; Massachusetts, 1849 *5881.1 p41*
Gaffney, Elleanor; St. John, N.B., 1848 *5704.8 p43*
Gaffney, Francis 18; Massachusetts, 1849 *5881.1 p42*
Gaffney, James; New York, NY, 1838 *8208.4 p81*
Gaffney, James 10; Massachusetts, 1850 *5881.1 p43*
Gaffney, James 18; Massachusetts, 1847 *5881.1 p42*
Gaffney, Jane; America, 1736 *4971 p94*
Gaffney, John; America, 1742 *4971 p53*
Gaffney, John; Philadelphia, 1833 *8208.4 p50*
Gaffney, William; New York, NY, 1838 *8208.4 p89*
Gafney, James; New York, NY, 1815 *2859.11 p31*
Gafney, James; New York, NY, 1840 *8208.4 p107*
Gagan, William 58; Kansas, 1880 *5240.1 p62*
Gagarty, John; America, 1741 *4971 p94*
Gage, John 22; Virginia, 1700 *2212 p31*
Gage, Wm.; Virginia, 1638 *6219 p11*
Gage, Wm.; Virginia, 1638 *6219 p117*
Gaghey, John; Quebec, 1852 *5704.8 p94*
Gagne, . . .; Canada, 1776-1783 *9786 p21*
Gagne, . . .; Canada, 1776-1783 *9786 p215*
Gagnon, M.; Quebec, 1815 *9229.18 p74*
Gahagan, Mary 11; Massachusetts, 1849 *5881.1 p43*
Gahagan, Peter; New York, NY, 1839 *8208.4 p93*
Gahaghan, James 10; Massachusetts, 1849 *5881.1 p42*
Gahbert, . . .; Canada, 1776-1783 *9786 p42*
Gahl, John Henry; California, 1856 *2764.35 p25*
Gahn, Charles; Illinois, 1873 *5012.39 p91*
Gahn, John; America, 1851 *1450.2 p47A*
Gahnet, Lewis; America, 1872 *6014.1 p2*
Gaiar, Adam; America, 1838 *1450.2 p47A*
Gaige, Francis; Wisconsin, n.d. *9675.5 p189*
Gaigl, Francis; Wisconsin, n.d. *9675.5 p189*
Gaigle, Franz; Wisconsin, n.d. *9675.5 p189*
Gailey, Charles; Philadelphia, 1847 *53.26 p29*
  Relative: Margaret
Gailey, Charles; Philadelphia, 1847 *5704.8 p13*
Gailey, Margaret SEE Gailey, Charles
Gailey, Margaret; Philadelphia, 1847 *5704.8 p13*
Gaileys, . . .; Philadelphia, 1848 *53.26 p29*
Gaileys, . . .; Philadelphia, 1848 *5704.8 p46*
Gaillard, Mr. 17; Port uncertain, 1832 *778.5 p223*
Gaillard, Mrs. 18; Port uncertain, 1836 *778.5 p223*
Gaillard, John Francis 31; America, 1836 *778.5 p223*
Gaillard, Joseph; America, 1839 *778.5 p223*
Gaillard, Mad. 23; New Orleans, 1837 *778.5 p223*
Gaillard, P. 21; Port uncertain, 1836 *778.5 p223*

Gaillardet, Frederick 30; New Orleans, 1838 *778.5 p223*
Gailot, Mr. 35; America, 1835 *778.5 p223*
Gaily, Joseph; Philadelphia, 1864 *5704.8 p183*
Gaily, Martha; Philadelphia, 1864 *5704.8 p183*
Gaily, Sarah; Philadelphia, 1864 *5704.8 p183*
Gaine, Abdul; Arkansas, 1918 *95.2 p46*
Gaines, Thomas 37; California, 1873 *2769.10 p4*
Gainnie, Robt.; Virginia, 1634 *6219 p32*
Gainpord, John 18; Newfoundland, 1789 *4915.24 p56*
Gainsford, Mathias 28; Maryland, 1774 *1219.7 p214*
Gainton, Thomas; Shreveport, LA, 1878 *7129 p44*
Gainye, Wm.; Virginia, 1617 *6219 p11*
Gair, Katherine Ross; Louisiana, 1849 *8893 p263*
Gairber, Pierre 21; America, 1836 *778.5 p223*
Gairdner, John; Carolina, 1684 *1639.20 p74*
Gairns, John; Cape Fear, NC, 1752 *1639.20 p74*
Gaiser, Benjamin; America, 1848 *8582.3 p21*
Gaiser, John; Illinois, 1901 *5012.40 p79*
Gaites, Edwin; New York, NY, 1834 *8208.4 p55*
Gaither, E. W.; Washington, 1859-1920 *2872.1 p13*
Gaither, Eli; Washington, 1859-1920 *2872.1 p13*
Gaitly, Thomas 26; New Orleans, 1862 *543.30 p376C*
Gaivreault, Francois; Louisiana, 1789-1819 *778.5 p555*
Gajer, Anna Magdalena SEE Gajer, Johann Caspar
Gajer, Anna Maria; Port uncertain, 1748-1800 *2444 p231*
Gajer, Anna Maria Walther SEE Gajer, Johann Caspar
Gajer, Christina Catharina SEE Gajer, Johann Caspar
Gajer, Johann Caspar; Pennsylvania, 1753 *2444 p156*
  Wife: Anna Maria Walther
  Child: Regina Barbara
  Child: Christina Catharina
  Child: Anna Magdalena
Gajer, Johann Caspar; Pennsylvania, 1754 *2444 p157*
Gajer, Regina Barbara SEE Gajer, Johann Caspar
Gajewska, Bronislawa 32; New York, 1912 *9980.29 p65*
Gajewska, Helena 8; New York, 1912 *9980.29 p65*
Gajewska, Stanislawa 3?; New York, 1912 *9980.29 p65*
Gak, Golda SEE Gak, Koftse
Gak, Koftse; Detroit, 1913 *3455.3 p53*
  Wife: Golda
Gakstetter, Charles; New York, 1881 *1450.2 p10B*
Gakstetter, Philip; New York, 1873 *1450.2 p10B*
Galaf, J.; New Orleans, 1839 *778.5 p223*
Galaher, John; America, 1864 *6014.1 p2*
Galangher, James; New York, NY, 1816 *2859.11 p31*
Galanis, George Peter; Arkansas, 1918 *95.2 p46*
Galant, Abram; Rochester, NY, 1896 *1450.2 p47A*
Galant, H. 22; America, 1826 *778.5 p223*
Galat, Miss 3; New Orleans, 1839 *778.5 p223*
Galavan, Patrick; America, 1739-1740 *4971 p59*
Galbraith, Ann 55; Quebec, 1862 *5704.8 p152*
Galbraith, Anne; New York, NY, 1815 *2859.11 p31*
Galbraith, Catherine 14; Quebec, 1863 *5704.8 p154*
Galbraith, Charles; New York, NY, 1815 *2859.11 p31*
Galbraith, Donald 72; Quebec, 1862 *5704.8 p152*
Galbraith, Eliza; New York, NY, 1815 *2859.11 p31*
Galbraith, Eliza 18; Quebec, 1863 *5704.8 p154*
Galbraith, Ellen 16; Quebec, 1863 *5704.8 p154*
Galbraith, Flora 2; Quebec, 1862 *5704.8 p152*
Galbraith, Florenola 60; Wilmington, DE, 1831 *6508.3 p101*
Galbraith, James; Quebec, 1851 *5704.8 p74*
Galbraith, Jane; Quebec, 1851 *5704.8 p82*
Galbraith, Jane; St. John, N.B., 1847 *5704.8 p9*
Galbraith, Jane 23; Quebec, 1863 *5704.8 p154*
Galbraith, Jane 40; Quebec, 1863 *5704.8 p154*
Galbraith, John; Philadelphia, 1851 *5704.8 p77*

Galbraith, John 20; Quebec, 1863 ***5704.8*** *p154*
Galbraith, Laughlan 27; Quebec, 1862 ***5704.8*** *p152*
Galbraith, Margaret; Philadelphia, 1865 ***5704.8*** *p204*
Galbraith, Margaret 24; Quebec, 1863 ***5704.8*** *p154*
Galbraith, Marion 23; Quebec, 1862 ***5704.8*** *p152*
Galbraith, Martha; Philadelphia, 1851 ***5704.8*** *p77*
Galbraith, Mary Ann 21; Quebec, 1863 ***5704.8*** *p154*
Galbraith, Samuel 30; Quebec, 1856 ***5704.8*** *p130*
Galbraith, Susan 24; Quebec, 1855 ***5704.8*** *p125*
Galbraith, Thomas; St. John, N.B., 1847 ***5704.8*** *p10*
Galbraith, William; New York, NY, 1815 ***2859.11*** *p31*
Galbraith, William 50; Quebec, 1863 ***5704.8*** *p154*
Galbreath, Alexander 50; North Carolina, 1850 ***1639.20*** *p75*
Galbreath, Angus 30; Wilmington, NC, 1774 ***1639.20*** *p75*
*Wife:*Katherine Brown 26
Galbreath, James; New York, NY, 1815 ***2859.11*** *p31*
Galbreath, Katherine Brown 26 *SEE* Galbreath, Angus
Galbreath, Mathew; St. John, N.B., 1848 ***5704.8*** *p43*
Galbreath, Rachael; New York, NY, 1815 ***2859.11*** *p31*
Galbroner, Louis; America, 1866 ***6014.1*** *p2*
Galdanagh, Owen; America, 1740 ***4971*** *p75*
Gale, Mr.; Quebec, 1815 ***9229.18*** *p82*
Gale, John 25; Maryland, 1774 ***1219.7*** *p204*
Galeota, Demetrangelo 36; West Virginia, 1905 ***9788.3*** *p10*
Galeota, Demetro 30; West Virginia, 1905 ***9788.3*** *p10*
Galere, Jacques 30; New Orleans, 1826 ***778.5*** *p223*
Galey, Anne; New York, NY, 1816 ***2859.11*** *p31*
Galey, Eliza; New York, NY, 1816 ***2859.11*** *p31*
Galey, Thomas; Florida, 1766 ***1219.7*** *p119*
Galey, William; Philadelphia, 1816 ***2859.11*** *p31*
Galey, Wister; Philadelphia, 1816 ***2859.11*** *p31*
Galgenmeyer, Sabina Catharina *SEE* Galgenmeyer, Simon
Galgenmeyer, Simon; America, 1752 ***2444*** *p156*
*Wife:*Sabina Catharina
Galin, Jean Louis 21; America, 1838 ***778.5*** *p223*
Gall, Alois Dominie; New York, 1842 ***1450.2*** *p47A*
Gall, Alois Dominie; Pittsburgh, 1843 ***1450.2*** *p47A*
Gall, Charles F.; Wisconsin, n.d. ***9675.5*** *p189*
Gall, John Michael; Wisconsin, n.d. ***9675.5*** *p189*
Gall, Luke; Quebec, 1803 ***7603*** *p81*
Gall, Margaretha E.; Wisconsin, n.d. ***9675.5*** *p189*
Gall, W.R. von; Quebec, 1776 ***9786*** *p102*
Gallagan, Andrew; New York, NY, 1837 ***8208.4*** *p32*
Gallagan, Thomas 18; Massachusetts, 1849 ***5881.1*** *p44*
Gallager, Bridget; New York, NY, 1816 ***2859.11*** *p31*
Gallager, James; Illinois, 1860 ***5012.39*** *p90*
Gallager, Peter; New York, NY, 1816 ***2859.11*** *p31*
Gallaghan, Ann 24; Massachusetts, 1849 ***5881.1*** *p41*
Gallaghan, James 26; Massachusetts, 1849 ***5881.1*** *p43*
Gallaghan, John 25; Massachusetts, 1849 ***5881.1*** *p43*
Gallaghan, Joseph 11; Massachusetts, 1850 ***5881.1*** *p43*
Gallaghan, Malachi 17; Massachusetts, 1849 ***5881.1*** *p43*
Gallaghan, Patrick; New York, NY, 1838 ***8208.4*** *p85*
Gallaghan, Peter 44; Massachusetts, 1850 ***5881.1*** *p44*
Gallaghan, Sally Anne; Philadelphia, 1851 ***5704.8*** *p70*
Gallagher, . . . 4; America, 1864 ***5704.8*** *p177*
Gallagher, . . . 8; America, 1864 ***5704.8*** *p177*
Gallagher, . . . 10; America, 1864 ***5704.8*** *p177*
Gallagher, Alice 18; Massachusetts, 1847 ***5881.1*** *p41*
Gallagher, Andrew 3 mos; St. John, N.B., 1847 ***5704.8*** *p26*
Gallagher, Ann *SEE* Gallagher, James
Gallagher, Ann; New York, NY, 1864 ***5704.8*** *p174*
Gallagher, Ann; New York, NY, 1866 ***5704.8*** *p213*
Gallagher, Ann; Philadelphia, 1849 ***5704.8*** *p53*
Gallagher, Ann; Philadelphia, 1865 ***5704.8*** *p196*
Gallagher, Ann 4; St. John, N.B., 1863 ***5704.8*** *p153*
Gallagher, Ann 11; St. John, N.B., 1862 ***5704.8*** *p151*
Gallagher, Ann 16; St. John, N.B., 1862 ***5704.8*** *p151*
Gallagher, Ann 19; St. John, N.B., 1862 ***5704.8*** *p150*
Gallagher, Ann 20; St. John, N.B., 1857 ***5704.8*** *p134*
Gallagher, Ann 48; St. John, N.B., 1862 ***5704.8*** *p151*
Gallagher, Ann 55; St. John, N.B., 1854 ***5704.8*** *p122*
Gallagher, Anne; America, 1864 ***5704.8*** *p171*
Gallagher, Anne; New York, NY, 1865 ***5704.8*** *p189*
Gallagher, Anne; New York, NY, 1869 ***5704.8*** *p232*
Gallagher, Anne; Philadelphia, 1867 ***5704.8*** *p217*
Gallagher, Anne 12; Philadelphia, 1864 ***5704.8*** *p160*
Gallagher, Anne 22; St. John, N.B., 1854 ***5704.8*** *p114*
Gallagher, Anne 24; Philadelphia, 1853 ***5704.8*** *p109*
Gallagher, Anne 36; Quebec, 1866 ***5704.8*** *p167*
Gallagher, Anne Jane 19; Philadelphia, 1858 ***5704.8*** *p139*
Gallagher, Annie; Philadelphia, 1864 ***5704.8*** *p174*
Gallagher, Bart. 8; Massachusetts, 1849 ***5881.1*** *p41*
Gallagher, Bernard; New York, NY, 1864 ***5704.8*** *p174*
Gallagher, Bernard 6 mos; Philadelphia, 1860 ***5704.8*** *p145*
Gallagher, Betsey; New York, NY, 1816 ***2859.11*** *p31*
Gallagher, Betty; Philadelphia, 1868 ***5704.8*** *p225*
Gallagher, Betty; St. John, N.B., 1848 ***5704.8*** *p47*
Gallagher, Betty; St. John, N.B., 1850 ***5704.8*** *p61*
Gallagher, Biddy; New York, NY, 1864 ***5704.8*** *p174*
Gallagher, Biddy; St. John, N.B., 1851 ***5704.8*** *p78*
Gallagher, Biddy 4 *SEE* Gallagher, James
Gallagher, Biddy 4; Philadelphia, 1848 ***5704.8*** *p45*
Gallagher, Biddy 4; Philadelphia, 1864 ***5704.8*** *p160*
Gallagher, Biddy 19; St. John, N.B., 1854 ***5704.8*** *p115*
Gallagher, Bridget; New York, NY, 1865 ***5704.8*** *p201*
Gallagher, Bridget; Philadelphia, 1847 ***53.26*** *p29*
*Relative:*John 7
*Relative:*Bridget 5
Gallagher, Bridget; Philadelphia, 1847 ***5704.8*** *p22*
Gallagher, Bridget; Philadelphia, 1865 ***5704.8*** *p193*
Gallagher, Bridget; St. John, N.B., 1850 ***5704.8*** *p61*
Gallagher, Bridget; St. John, N.B., 1853 ***5704.8*** *p98*
Gallagher, Bridget 5 *SEE* Gallagher, Bridget
Gallagher, Bridget 5; Philadelphia, 1847 ***5704.8*** *p22*
Gallagher, Bridget 19; Massachusetts, 1850 ***5881.1*** *p41*
Gallagher, Bridget 20; Massachusetts, 1849 ***5881.1*** *p41*
Gallagher, Bridget 20; Philadelphia, 1864 ***5704.8*** *p155*
Gallagher, Bridget 21; Philadelphia, 1864 ***5704.8*** *p155*
Gallagher, Bridget 24; Philadelphia, 1860 ***5704.8*** *p146*
Gallagher, Bridget 31; Massachusetts, 1849 ***5881.1*** *p41*
Gallagher, Bridget 50; St. John, N.B., 1855 ***5704.8*** *p127*
Gallagher, Catharine; America, 1867 ***5704.8*** *p217*
Gallagher, Catharine; New York, NY, 1864 ***5704.8*** *p170*
Gallagher, Catharine; New York, NY, 1864 ***5704.8*** *p174*
Gallagher, Catharine; New York, NY, 1867 ***5704.8*** *p217*
Gallagher, Catharine; Philadelphia, 1864 ***5704.8*** *p183*
Gallagher, Catharine; Philadelphia, 1866 ***5704.8*** *p215*
Gallagher, Catharine; Philadelphia, 1868 ***5704.8*** *p226*
Gallagher, Catharine 5; New York, NY, 1867 ***5704.8*** *p217*
Gallagher, Catharine 20; Massachusetts, 1847 ***5881.1*** *p41*
Gallagher, Catharine 21; Massachusetts, 1847 ***5881.1*** *p41*
Gallagher, Catherine *SEE* Gallagher, James
Gallagher, Catherine *SEE* Gallagher, Mary
Gallagher, Catherine; Philadelphia, 1847 ***53.26*** *p29*
Gallagher, Catherine; Philadelphia, 1847 ***5704.8*** *p22*
Gallagher, Catherine; Philadelphia, 1848 ***5704.8*** *p45*
Gallagher, Catherine; Philadelphia, 1851 ***5704.8*** *p71*
Gallagher, Catherine; Philadelphia, 1852 ***5704.8*** *p89*
Gallagher, Catherine; Philadelphia, 1853 ***5704.8*** *p102*
Gallagher, Catherine; Quebec, 1849 ***5704.8*** *p56*
Gallagher, Catherine; Quebec, 1850 ***5704.8*** *p66*
Gallagher, Catherine; Quebec, 1851 ***5704.8*** *p74*
Gallagher, Catherine; St. John, N.B., 1847 ***5704.8*** *p11*
Gallagher, Catherine; St. John, N.B., 1847 ***5704.8*** *p19*
Gallagher, Catherine; St. John, N.B., 1847 ***5704.8*** *p20*
Gallagher, Catherine; St. John, N.B., 1853 ***5704.8*** *p107*
Gallagher, Catherine 17; St. John, N.B., 1855 ***5704.8*** *p126*
Gallagher, Catherine 18; Philadelphia, 1861 ***5704.8*** *p148*
Gallagher, Catherine 21; Quebec, 1857 ***5704.8*** *p136*
Gallagher, Catherine 27; Quebec, 1858 ***5704.8*** *p137*
Gallagher, Catherine 30; Philadelphia, 1860 ***5704.8*** *p145*
Gallagher, Caty; Philadelphia, 1852 ***5704.8*** *p96*
Gallagher, Celia 1; Massachusetts, 1849 ***5881.1*** *p41*
Gallagher, Charles *SEE* Gallagher, Robert
Gallagher, Charles; Philadelphia, 1811 ***53.26*** *p29*
Gallagher, Charles; Philadelphia, 1850 ***5704.8*** *p61*
Gallagher, Charles; Philadelphia, 1864 ***5704.8*** *p176*
Gallagher, Charles; Philadelphia, 1865 ***5704.8*** *p198*
Gallagher, Charles; St. John, N.B., 1848 ***5704.8*** *p47*
Gallagher, Charles 6; Philadelphia, 1860 ***5704.8*** *p145*
Gallagher, Con; New York, NY, 1864 ***5704.8*** *p169*
Gallagher, Con; St. John, N.B., 1852 ***5704.8*** *p95*
Gallagher, Con; St. John, N.B., 1853 ***5704.8*** *p98*
Gallagher, Condy; Philadelphia, 1864 ***5704.8*** *p179*
Gallagher, Curty 21; St. John, N.B., 1854 ***5704.8*** *p115*
Gallagher, Daniel; Philadelphia, 1847 ***53.26*** *p29*
Gallagher, Daniel; Philadelphia, 1847 ***5704.8*** *p5*
Gallagher, Daniel; Philadelphia, 1847 ***5704.8*** *p22*
Gallagher, Daniel; Philadelphia, 1847 ***5704.8*** *p24*
Gallagher, Daniel 2; Philadelphia, 1864 ***5704.8*** *p160*
Gallagher, Daniel 9; New York, NY, 1864 ***5704.8*** *p174*
Gallagher, Daniel 12; Massachusetts, 1847 ***5881.1*** *p41*
Gallagher, Daniel 18; Philadelphia, 1853 ***5704.8*** *p112*
Gallagher, Daniel 20; Philadelphia, 1864 ***5704.8*** *p156*
Gallagher, Daniel 23; Philadelphia, 1860 ***5704.8*** *p145*
Gallagher, Daniel 40; Philadelphia, 1864 ***5704.8*** *p160*
Gallagher, Dennis; Philadelphia, 1849 ***53.26*** *p29*
Gallagher, Dennis; Philadelphia, 1849 ***5704.8*** *p55*
Gallagher, Dennis; Philadelphia, 1864 ***5704.8*** *p179*
Gallagher, Dennis; St. John, N.B., 1847 ***5704.8*** *p20*
Gallagher, Dennis 9; St. John, N.B., 1862 ***5704.8*** *p151*
Gallagher, Dennis 18; Philadelphia, 1856 ***5704.8*** *p128*
Gallagher, Dennis 25; St. John, N.B., 1862 ***5704.8*** *p151*
Gallagher, Dominick; St. John, N.B., 1848 ***5704.8*** *p39*
Gallagher, Dudley; America, 1739 ***4971*** *p75*
Gallagher, Edmond; America, 1741 ***4971*** *p76*
Gallagher, Edmund 5; Massachusetts, 1850 ***5881.1*** *p42*
Gallagher, Edward; St. John, N.B., 1852 ***5704.8*** *p84*
Gallagher, Edward; St. John, N.B., 1853 ***5704.8*** *p98*
Gallagher, Edward 15; Philadelphia, 1864 ***5704.8*** *p155*
Gallagher, Edward 20; Philadelphia, 1857 ***5704.8*** *p132*
Gallagher, Edward 22; St. John, N.B., 1861 ***5704.8*** *p147*
Gallagher, Elenor 16; Philadelphia, 1861 ***5704.8*** *p148*
Gallagher, Eliza 8; Quebec, 1866 ***5704.8*** *p167*
Gallagher, Eliza 13; St. John, N.B., 1853 ***5704.8*** *p106*
Gallagher, Eliza 18; Philadelphia, 1854 ***5704.8*** *p116*
Gallagher, Elizabeth; New York, NY, 1864 ***5704.8*** *p171*
Gallagher, Elizabeth; Philadelphia, 1850 ***53.26*** *p29*
*Relative:*Fanny
Gallagher, Elizabeth; Philadelphia, 1850 ***5704.8*** *p69*
Gallagher, Elizabeth; Philadelphia, 1853 ***5704.8*** *p102*
Gallagher, Elizabeth 6 *SEE* Gallagher, James
Gallagher, Elizabeth 6; New York, NY, 1864 ***5704.8*** *p174*
Gallagher, Elizabeth 6; Philadelphia, 1850 ***5704.8*** *p68*
Gallagher, Elizabeth 10; St. John, N.B., 1861 ***5704.8*** *p146*
Gallagher, Elizabeth 45; St. John, N.B., 1861 ***5704.8*** *p146*
Gallagher, Elleanor 12; St. John, N.B., 1847 ***5704.8*** *p3*
Gallagher, Elleanor 20; St. John, N.B., 1856 ***5704.8*** *p131*
Gallagher, Ellen; New York, NY, 1868 ***5704.8*** *p231*
Gallagher, Ellen 18; Philadelphia, 1856 ***5704.8*** *p128*
Gallagher, Ellen 21; Philadelphia, 1864 ***5704.8*** *p155*
Gallagher, Ellen 24; St. John, N.B., 1854 ***5704.8*** *p121*
Gallagher, Ellen 40; Philadelphia, 1853 ***5704.8*** *p111*
Gallagher, Elly 3 mos; St. John, N.B., 1863 ***5704.8*** *p153*
Gallagher, Eugine 10; St. John, N.B., 1856 ***5704.8*** *p131*
Gallagher, Fanny *SEE* Gallagher, Elizabeth
Gallagher, Fanny; Philadelphia, 1847 ***53.26*** *p29*
*Relative:*Mary
Gallagher, Fanny; Philadelphia, 1847 ***5704.8*** *p24*
Gallagher, Fanny; Philadelphia, 1850 ***5704.8*** *p69*
Gallagher, Fanny; Philadelphia, 1865 ***5704.8*** *p192*
Gallagher, Fanny; Quebec, 1851 ***5704.8*** *p82*
Gallagher, Fanny 2 *SEE* Gallagher, James
Gallagher, Fanny 2; Philadelphia, 1847 ***5704.8*** *p5*
Gallagher, Fergal; America, 1741 ***4971*** *p76*
Gallagher, Francis; America, 1849 ***1450.2*** *p47A*
Gallagher, Francis; America, 1864 ***5704.8*** *p177*
Gallagher, Francis; Philadelphia, 1853 ***5704.8*** *p102*
Gallagher, Francis; St. John, N.B., 1847 ***5704.8*** *p33*
Gallagher, Francis; St. John, N.B., 1852 ***5704.8*** *p84*
Gallagher, Francis 7; Massachusetts, 1850 ***5881.1*** *p42*
Gallagher, Francis 11; Philadelphia, 1853 ***5704.8*** *p102*
Gallagher, Francis 11; St. John, N.B., 1850 ***5704.8*** *p62*
Gallagher, Francis 22; Quebec, 1854 ***5704.8*** *p119*
Gallagher, Frank 18; Philadelphia, 1855 ***5704.8*** *p124*
Gallagher, George; Philadelphia, 1847 ***53.26*** *p29*
Gallagher, George; Philadelphia, 1847 ***5704.8*** *p1*
Gallagher, George; Philadelphia, 1848 ***53.26*** *p29*
Gallagher, George; Philadelphia, 1848 ***5704.8*** *p40*
Gallagher, George; West Virginia, 1818-1852 ***9788.3*** *p10*
Gallagher, George 14; Philadelphia, 1853 ***5704.8*** *p112*
Gallagher, George 16; St. John, N.B., 1863 ***5704.8*** *p153*
Gallagher, Giles; Philadelphia, 1847 ***53.26*** *p29*
*Relative:*Mary 12
*Relative:*John 4
*Relative:*Nancy 1
Gallagher, Giles; Philadelphia, 1847 ***5704.8*** *p31*
Gallagher, Giley; St. John, N.B., 1847 ***5704.8*** *p20*
Gallagher, Giley 18; Philadelphia, 1853 ***5704.8*** *p111*
Gallagher, Gilly; Philadelphia, 1852 ***5704.8*** *p96*
Gallagher, Grace; America, 1865 ***5704.8*** *p200*
Gallagher, Grace; New York, NY, 1865 ***5704.8*** *p201*
Gallagher, Grace; Philadelphia, 1867 ***5704.8*** *p223*
Gallagher, Grace 9 mos; Philadelphia, 1864 ***5704.8*** *p160*
Gallagher, Grace 13; Philadelphia, 1861 ***5704.8*** *p148*
Gallagher, Grace 19; Philadelphia, 1854 ***5704.8*** *p121*
Gallagher, Grace 30; Philadelphia, 1854 ***5704.8*** *p120*
Gallagher, Grace 35; Philadelphia, 1864 ***5704.8*** *p160*
Gallagher, Hannah; New York, NY, 1865 ***5704.8*** *p199*
Gallagher, Hannah; New York, NY, 1866 ***5704.8*** *p211*
Gallagher, Hannah; Philadelphia, 1851 ***5704.8*** *p76*
Gallagher, Hannah; Philadelphia, 1865 ***5704.8*** *p197*
Gallagher, Hannah 50; Massachusetts, 1849 ***5881.1*** *p42*
Gallagher, Hannah J.; Philadelphia, 1865 ***5704.8*** *p199*
Gallagher, Hugh *SEE* Gallagher, Mary
Gallagher, Hugh; America, 1738 ***4971*** *p75*
Gallagher, Hugh; New York, NY, 1815 ***2859.11*** *p31*
Gallagher, Hugh; New York, NY, 1816 ***2859.11*** *p31*
Gallagher, Hugh; New York, NY, 1836 ***8208.4*** *p21*
Gallagher, Hugh; Philadelphia, 1864 ***5704.8*** *p174*
Gallagher, Hugh; Philadelphia, 1871 ***5704.8*** *p241*
Gallagher, Hugh; Quebec, 1851 ***5704.8*** *p75*

Gallagher, Rosey; St. John, N.B., 1847 ***5704.8*** *p15*
Gallagher, Rosey 15; Philadelphia, 1853 ***5704.8*** *p111*
Gallagher, Rosy; Quebec, 1847 ***5704.8*** *p27*
Gallagher, Sally; America, 1841 ***7036*** *p125*
Gallagher, Sally; Philadelphia, 1852 ***5704.8*** *p92*
Gallagher, Sally; St. John, N.B., 1850 ***5704.8*** *p65*
Gallagher, Sally 26; Philadelphia, 1853 ***5704.8*** *p111*
Gallagher, Sarah; America, 1866 ***5704.8*** *p213*
Gallagher, Sarah; America, 1871 ***5704.8*** *p240*
Gallagher, Sarah; Philadelphia, 1865 ***5704.8*** *p192*
Gallagher, Sarah; St. John, N.B., 1848 ***5704.8*** *p42*
Gallagher, Sarah; St. John, N.B., 1853 ***5704.8*** *p106*
Gallagher, Sarah 8; Philadelphia, 1864 ***5704.8*** *p160*
Gallagher, Sarah 12; America, 1864 ***5704.8*** *p177*
Gallagher, Sarah 16; St. John, N.B., 1859 ***5704.8*** *p143*
Gallagher, Sarah 40; St. John, N.B., 1863 ***5704.8*** *p153*
Gallagher, Sarah Jane 13; Philadelphia, 1864 ***5704.8*** *p155*
Gallagher, Shan 11; St. John, N.B., 1863 ***5704.8*** *p153*
Gallagher, Shane; St. John, N.B., 1850 ***5704.8*** *p65*
Gallagher, Susan; Boston, 1832-1841 ***7036*** *p125*
Gallagher, Susan; Philadelphia, 1853 ***5704.8*** *p102*
Gallagher, Susan; Quebec, 1832 ***7036*** *p125*
Gallagher, Susan; St. John, N.B., 1847 ***5704.8*** *p26*
Gallagher, Susan 4; Philadelphia, 1860 ***5704.8*** *p145*
Gallagher, Susan 18; Philadelphia, 1859 ***5704.8*** *p141*
Gallagher, Susan 19; St. John, N.B., 1857 ***5704.8*** *p134*
Gallagher, Susan 20; Philadelphia, 1859 ***5704.8*** *p142*
Gallagher, Suzanna; Quebec, 1825 ***7603*** *p84*
Gallagher, Thomas; New York, NY, 1816 ***2859.11*** *p31*
Gallagher, Thomas; New York, NY, 1866 ***5704.8*** *p211*
Gallagher, Thomas; New York, NY, 1867 ***5704.8*** *p217*
Gallagher, Thomas; St. John, N.B., 1847 ***5704.8*** *p35*
Gallagher, Thomas 26; St. John, N.B., 1856 ***5704.8*** *p131*
Gallagher, Thomas 40; St. John, N.B., 1863 ***5704.8*** *p153*
Gallagher, Unity; New York, NY, 1868 ***5704.8*** *p231*
Gallagher, Unity 16; Philadelphia, 1864 ***5704.8*** *p155*
Gallagher, William *SEE* Gallagher, James
Gallagher, William; New York, NY, 1815 ***2859.11*** *p31*
Gallagher, William; New York, NY, 1866 ***5704.8*** *p211*
Gallagher, William; Philadelphia, 1847 ***5704.8*** *p5*
Gallagher, William; Philadelphia, 1850 ***53.26*** *p30*
Gallagher, William; Philadelphia, 1850 ***5704.8*** *p69*
Gallagher, William; Philadelphia, 1853 ***5704.8*** *p100*
Gallagher, William; Philadelphia, 1854 ***5704.8*** *p116*
Gallagher, William; Philadelphia, 1864 ***5704.8*** *p171*
Gallagher, William; St. John, N.B., 1847 ***5704.8*** *p9*
Gallagher, William; St. John, N.B., 1847 ***5704.8*** *p32*
Gallagher, William 9; Philadelphia, 1864 ***5704.8*** *p155*
Gallagher, William 10 *SEE* Gallagher, James
Gallagher, William 10; Philadelphia, 1850 ***5704.8*** *p68*
Gallagher, William 13; St. John, N.B., 1847 ***5704.8*** *p25*
Gallagher, William 16; Philadelphia, 1864 ***5704.8*** *p160*
Gallagher, William 29; Philadelphia, 1859 ***5704.8*** *p142*
Gallagher, William John 27; Quebec, 1858 ***5704.8*** *p138*
Gallaher, . . . 9 mos; America, 1864 ***5704.8*** *p175*
Gallaher, Ansley; Philadelphia, 1870 ***5704.8*** *p238*
Gallaher, Anthony; America, 1864 ***5704.8*** *p175*
Gallaher, Anthony; New York, NY, 1865 ***5704.8*** *p190*
Gallaher, Bell; Philadelphia, 1867 ***5704.8*** *p218*
Gallaher, Catharine; Philadelphia, 1867 ***5704.8*** *p217*
Gallaher, Catharine; Philadelphia, 1867 ***5704.8*** *p222*
Gallaher, Ellen; America, 1864 ***5704.8*** *p175*
Gallaher, Ellen; America, 1870 ***5704.8*** *p239*
Gallaher, Fanny; Philadelphia, 1867 ***5704.8*** *p223*
Gallaher, Giley; Philadelphia, 1867 ***5704.8*** *p223*
Gallaher, Grace 3; America, 1864 ***5704.8*** *p175*
Gallaher, Hugh; New York, NY, 1867 ***5704.8*** *p220*
Gallaher, Hugh; New York, NY, 1870 ***5704.8*** *p238*
Gallaher, Hugh; Philadelphia, 1867 ***5704.8*** *p217*
Gallaher, James; Philadelphia, 1867 ***5704.8*** *p215*
Gallaher, John; America, 1870 ***5704.8*** *p239*
Gallaher, John; Virginia, 1856 ***4626.16*** *p16*
Gallaher, Margaret; New York, NY, 1867 ***5704.8*** *p222*
Gallaher, Mary; New York, NY, 1869 ***5704.8*** *p232*
Gallaher, Mary; Philadelphia, 1870 ***5704.8*** *p238*
Gallaher, Mary 5; America, 1864 ***5704.8*** *p175*
Gallaher, Mary Ann 11; Philadelphia, 1864 ***5704.8*** *p187*
Gallaher, Patrick; Philadelphia, 1867 ***5704.8*** *p218*
Gallaher, Samuel 3; Philadelphia, 1870 ***5704.8*** *p238*
Gallaher, Susan; New York, NY, 1870 ***5704.8*** *p239*
Gallaher, William 9; Philadelphia, 1864 ***5704.8*** *p187*
Gallalore, Denis; America, 1869 ***5704.8*** *p236*
Gallanagh, James 22; Philadelphia, 1859 ***5704.8*** *p142*
Gallanan, Hugh 48; Massachusetts, 1847 ***5881.1*** *p42*
Galland, . . .; Canada, 1776-1783 ***9786*** *p21*
Galland, Mr. 27; Port uncertain, 1836 ***778.5*** *p223*
Galland, Caspar; Cincinnati, 1869-1887 ***8582*** *p10*
Galland, Charles-Belletisse; Quebec, 1778 ***7603*** *p23*
Galland, Fs. 21; Port uncertain, 1836 ***778.5*** *p224*
Galland, Samuel 39; Maryland, 1775 ***1219.7*** *p249*
Gallandt, . . .; Canada, 1776-1783 ***9786*** *p21*
Gallanes, Anthony; Arkansas, 1918 ***95.2*** *p46*
Gallard, Wm.; Virginia, 1643 ***6219*** *p200*
Gallatin, Abraham Albert Alphons von; Boston, 1780 ***8582.1*** *p10*
Gallatin, Albert; America, 1776-1877 ***8582.3*** *p80*
Gallatin, Albert; America, 1800-1877 ***8582.3*** *p92*
Gallaugher, Cath.; Philadelphia, 1811 ***2859.11*** *p12*
Gallaugher, Catherine 25; Philadelphia, 1857 ***5704.8*** *p132*
Gallaugher, Chas.; Philadelphia, 1811 ***2859.11*** *p12*
Gallaugher, Hugh; Philadelphia, 1811 ***2859.11*** *p12*
Gallaugher, Hugh 25; Philadelphia, 1857 ***5704.8*** *p132*
Gallaugher, James; Philadelphia, 1852 ***5704.8*** *p84*
Gallaugher, James; Quebec, 1851 ***5704.8*** *p74*
Gallaugher, Mary; Philadelphia, 1811 ***2859.11*** *p12*
Gallaugher, Mary 2; Philadelphia, 1857 ***5704.8*** *p132*
Gallaugher, Mich.; Philadelphia, 1811 ***2859.11*** *p12*
Gallaugher, Patk.; Philadelphia, 1811 ***2859.11*** *p12*
Gallaugher, William 4; Philadelphia, 1857 ***5704.8*** *p132*
Gallavan, Matthias; America, 1741 ***4971*** *p56*
Gallaway, David; New York, NY, 1838 ***8208.4*** *p81*
Gallaway, Mary; Virginia, 1646 ***6219*** *p241*
Gallaway, Wm.; Virginia, 1623 ***6219*** *p7*
Gallay, Tera 51; America, 1835 ***778.5*** *p224*
Galle, Rosina; New York, 1749 ***3652*** *p72*
Gallee, Auguste 27; America, 1836 ***778.5*** *p224*
Gallen, Biddy *SEE* Gallen, Hugh
Gallen, Biddy; Philadelphia, 1811 ***2859.11*** *p12*
Gallen, Catherine *SEE* Gallen, Hugh
Gallen, Catherine; Philadelphia, 1811 ***2859.11*** *p12*
Gallen, Charles 23; Philadelphia, 1864 ***5704.8*** *p161*
Gallen, Fanny Ester; Washington, 1859-1920 ***2872.1*** *p13*
Gallen, Grace; St. John, N.B., 1847 ***5704.8*** *p25*
Gallen, Heidi Linca; Washington, 1859-1920 ***2872.1*** *p13*
Gallen, Hilma; Washington, 1859-1920 ***2872.1*** *p13*
Gallen, Hugh; Philadelphia, 1811 ***53.26*** *p30*
*Relative:*Mary
*Relative:*Margaret
*Relative:*Owen
*Relative:*Sally
*Relative:*Biddy
*Relative:*Mary
*Relative:*James
*Relative:*Catherine
Gallen, Hugh; Philadelphia, 1811 ***2859.11*** *p12*
Gallen, James *SEE* Gallen, Hugh
Gallen, James; Philadelphia, 1811 ***2859.11*** *p12*
Gallen, Margaret *SEE* Gallen, Hugh
Gallen, Margaret; Philadelphia, 1811 ***2859.11*** *p12*
Gallen, Margaret; St. John, N.B., 1847 ***5704.8*** *p25*
Gallen, Mary *SEE* Gallen, Hugh
Gallen, Mary *SEE* Gallen, Hugh
Gallen, Mary; Philadelphia, 1811 ***2859.11*** *p12*
Gallen, Owen *SEE* Gallen, Hugh
Gallen, Owen; Philadelphia, 1811 ***2859.11*** *p12*
Gallen, Paul; Washington, 1859-1920 ***2872.1*** *p13*
Gallen, Sally *SEE* Gallen, Hugh
Gallen, Sally; Philadelphia, 1811 ***2859.11*** *p12*
Galler, Hans Conrad; Port uncertain, 1715-1800 ***2444*** *p156*
Gallery, Eliza; New York, NY, 1811 ***2859.11*** *p12*
Gallery, James; New York, NY, 1811 ***2859.11*** *p12*
Gallery, Morgan; America, 1740 ***4971*** *p48*
Gallery, Morgan; America, 1741 ***4971*** *p49*
Gallet, . . .; America, 1838 ***778.5*** *p224*
Gallet, Mrs. 35; America, 1838 ***778.5*** *p224*
Gallet, F.P. 36; America, 1838 ***778.5*** *p224*
Galli, Vincent; Arkansas, 1918 ***95.2*** *p46*
Galliburn, Eliza 18; Maryland or Virginia, 1699 ***2212*** *p22*
Galligan, Andrew; Quebec, 1825 ***7603*** *p83*
Galligan, Daniel 20; Massachusetts, 1849 ***5881.1*** *p41*
Galligan, John; New York, NY, 1837 ***8208.4*** *p32*
Galligan, Robert 17; Massachusetts, 1850 ***5881.1*** *p44*
Galliger, Cornelius 27; New Orleans, 1862 ***543.30*** *p375C*
Gallighan, Mathew 22; Massachusetts, 1849 ***5881.1*** *p43*
Galligher, M. A. 35; Kansas, 1887 ***5240.1*** *p14*
Galligher, Mathew 12; Massachusetts, 1849 ***5881.1*** *p43*
Galligher, Patrick 31; Massachusetts, 1849 ***5881.1*** *p44*
Galligher, Thaddeus 10; Massachusetts, 1849 ***5881.1*** *p44*
Gallinagh, Patrick; Philadelphia, 1852 ***5704.8*** *p92*
Gallinah, Catherine 9 mos; St. John, N.B., 1864 ***5704.8*** *p158*
Gallinah, Daniel 6; St. John, N.B., 1864 ***5704.8*** *p158*
Gallinah, Edward 32; St. John, N.B., 1864 ***5704.8*** *p158*
Gallinah, Mary Ann 4; St. John, N.B., 1864 ***5704.8*** *p158*
Gallinah, Mary Ann 26; St. John, N.B., 1864 ***5704.8*** *p158*
Gallinah, Rebecca 2; St. John, N.B., 1864 ***5704.8*** *p158*
Gallinger, Jacob; Cincinnati, 1869-1887 ***8582*** *p10*
Gallion, Bell 46; Massachusetts, 1850 ***5881.1*** *p41*
Galliott, John; Virginia, 1639 ***6219*** *p162*
Gallivan, Bridget; New York, NY, 1811 ***2859.11*** *p12*
Gallivan, Patrick 42; Kansas, 1889 ***5240.1*** *p74*
Galliway, David; New York, NY, 1838 ***8208.4*** *p81*
Gallmagh, Ann *SEE* Gallmagh, Nancy
Gallmagh, Ann; Philadelphia, 1848 ***5704.8*** *p46*
Gallmagh, Nancy; Philadelphia, 1848 ***53.26*** *p30*
*Relative:*Ann
Gallmagh, Nancy; Philadelphia, 1848 ***5704.8*** *p46*
Gallmeister, Robert; Illinois, 1880 ***2896.5*** *p13*
Gallo, Antonia; Iowa, 1866-1943 ***123.54*** *p63*
Gallo, Giovanni Battista; Iowa, 1866-1943 ***123.54*** *p63*
Gallo, Teresa; Iowa, 1866-1943 ***123.54*** *p63*
Gallon, Ann; Quebec, 1847 ***5704.8*** *p29*
Gallon, Edward; Philadelphia, 1852 ***5704.8*** *p88*
Gallon, Edward 50; Massachusetts, 1850 ***5881.1*** *p42*
Gallon, Else; Philadelphia, 1852 ***5704.8*** *p88*
Gallon, Grace 30; St. John, N.B., 1866 ***5704.8*** *p167*
Gallon, Lettece; Philadelphia, 1852 ***5704.8*** *p88*
Gallon, Margaret 5 *SEE* Gallon, Patrick
Gallon, Margaret 5; Philadelphia, 1847 ***5704.8*** *p30*
Gallon, Mary *SEE* Gallon, Patrick
Gallon, Mary; Philadelphia, 1847 ***5704.8*** *p30*
Gallon, Mary 9 mos *SEE* Gallon, Patrick
Gallon, Mary 9 mos; Philadelphia, 1847 ***5704.8*** *p30*
Gallon, Michael; Philadelphia, 1847 ***53.26*** *p30*
Gallon, Michael; Philadelphia, 1847 ***5704.8*** *p1*
Gallon, Patrick; Philadelphia, 1847 ***53.26*** *p31*
*Relative:*Mary
*Relative:*Margaret 5
*Relative:*Mary 9 mos
Gallon, Patrick; Philadelphia, 1847 ***5704.8*** *p30*
Gallon, Sally; Quebec, 1847 ***5704.8*** *p29*
Gallopin, Wm.; Virginia, 1635 ***6219*** *p69*
Gallossi, Albert 62; Arizona, 1923 ***9228.40*** *p27*
Gallotti, Frank 30; Kansas, 1873 ***5240.1*** *p54*
Galloway, Charles; Virginia, 1728-1770 ***1639.20*** *p75*
Galloway, Daniel; Quebec, 1765 ***7603*** *p80*
Galloway, Gallia 21 *SEE* Galloway, John
Galloway, James; North Carolina, 1742-1799 ***1639.20*** *p75*
Galloway, John 22; Philadelphia, 1774 ***1219.7*** *p182*
*Wife:*Gallia 21
Galloway, Richard; Virginia, 1646 ***6219*** *p240*
Galloway, Robert; America, 1783 ***1639.20*** *p75*
Galloway, T. C.; Washington, 1859-1920 ***2872.1*** *p13*
Galloway, Thomas 20; Maryland, 1719 ***3690.1*** *p85*
Gallway, John; America, 1735-1743 ***4971*** *p79*
Gally, Miss 22; America, 1837 ***778.5*** *p224*
Gally, Mme. 45; America, 1837 ***778.5*** *p224*
Gally, Mr. 10; America, 1837 ***778.5*** *p224*
Gally, Mr. 16; New Orleans, 1825 ***778.5*** *p224*
Gally, Mr. 50; America, 1837 ***778.5*** *p224*
Gally, Mrs. 35; New Orleans, 1826 ***778.5*** *p224*
Gally, Charles 15; America, 1835 ***778.5*** *p224*
Gally, Joane; Virginia, 1639 ***6219*** *p155*
Gally, Julius; America, 1890 ***1450.2*** *p10B*
Gally, Louis 40; New Orleans, 1826 ***778.5*** *p224*
Gally, Richard; Virginia, 1637 ***6219*** *p24*
Gally, Sopie 12; Louisiana, 1829 ***778.5*** *p225*
Galmen, Joseph; Wisconsin, n.d. ***9675.5*** *p189*
Galmiche, Felicite 36; America, 1831 ***778.5*** *p225*
Galmiche, Hortense 29; America, 1831 ***778.5*** *p225*
Galny, August; New Orleans, 1850 ***2896.5*** *p13*
Galop, Jean 19; New Orleans, 1839 ***778.5*** *p225*
Galos, C. 25; Port uncertain, 1839 ***778.5*** *p225*
Galt, Hamilton; Quebec, 1851 ***5704.8*** *p82*
Galt, John; Ontario, 1827 ***9775.5*** *p214*
Galt, William; Virginia, 1742 ***8894.2*** *p55*
Galteland, Niels F.; Wisconsin, n.d. ***9675.5*** *p189*
Galuscak, Ella; America, 1893 ***7137*** *p168*
Galuscak, Nicholas; America, 1891 ***7137*** *p168*
Galuschick, Ella; America, 1893 ***7137*** *p168*
Galuschick, Nicholas; America, 1891 ***7137*** *p168*
Galvan, Jeremiah; New York, NY, 1837 ***8208.4*** *p32*
Galvin, John; New York, NY, 1838 ***8208.4*** *p71*
Galvin, Michael; Ohio, 1840 ***9892.11*** *p16*
Galvin, Patrick; Quebec, 1825 ***7603*** *p83*
Galway, Hugh 25; St. John, N.B., 1864 ***5704.8*** *p158*
Galway, John; America, 1741 ***4971*** *p81*
Galway, Moore; Philadelphia, 1819 ***1450.2*** *p47A*
Gam, George; America, 1852 ***1450.2*** *p48A*
Gaman, Richard 16; South Carolina, 1751 ***1219.7*** *p4*
Gaman, Richard 16; South Carolina, 1751 ***3690.1*** *p85*
Gamareklian, Ezekiel G. 42; Indiana, 1904 ***1450.2*** *p10B*
Gambell, Adam; North Carolina, 1709 ***1639.20*** *p75*
Gambell, James; Virginia, 1698 ***2212*** *p12*
Gambier, Cendre S. 55; America, 1820 ***778.5*** *p225*
Gamble, Ann 20; Quebec, 1857 ***5704.8*** *p135*
Gamble, Bell; New York, NY, 1811 ***2859.11*** *p12*
Gamble, Catharine Amelia; Georgia, 1811 ***8894.2*** *p55*
Gamble, Catherine; Quebec, 1848 ***5704.8*** *p42*
Gamble, Catherine; Quebec, 1851 ***5704.8*** *p82*
Gamble, David 40; Quebec, 1863 ***5704.8*** *p153*
Gamble, Eliza; New York, NY, 1811 ***2859.11*** *p12*
Gamble, Eliza 21; Philadelphia, 1774 ***1219.7*** *p212*

Gamble, Elizabeth *SEE* Gamble, Jane
Gamble, Elizabeth; Philadelphia, 1848 *5704.8 p46*
Gamble, Elizabeth; Philadelphia, 1849 *53.26 p31*
*Relative:*Joseph 8
Gamble, Elizabeth; Philadelphia, 1849 *5704.8 p53*
Gamble, Ellen; St. John, N.B., 1847 *5704.8 p24*
Gamble, Fanny 3; St. John, N.B., 1847 *5704.8 p20*
Gamble, George; New York, NY, 1811 *2859.11 p12*
Gamble, George; St. John, N.B., 1848 *5704.8 p42*
Gamble, Isabella; Philadelphia, 1852 *5704.8 p92*
Gamble, Isabella 36; Quebec, 1864 *5704.8 p164*
Gamble, James; New York, NY, 1811 *2859.11 p12*
Gamble, James; New York, NY, 1816 *2859.11 p31*
Gamble, James 17; Philadelphia, 1854 *5704.8 p116*
Gamble, Jane; Philadelphia, 1848 *53.26 p31*
*Relative:*Elizabeth
*Relative:*William 5
*Relative:*Sarah 2
Gamble, Jane; Philadelphia, 1848 *5704.8 p46*
Gamble, Jane; St. John, N.B., 1848 *5704.8 p42*
Gamble, John; New York, NY, 1811 *2859.11 p12*
Gamble, John; St. John, N.B., 1847 *5704.8 p20*
Gamble, John 2; St. John, N.B., 1855 *5704.8 p127*
Gamble, Joseph; New York, NY, 1811 *2859.11 p12*
Gamble, Joseph 8 *SEE* Gamble, Elizabeth
Gamble, Joseph 8; Philadelphia, 1849 *5704.8 p53*
Gamble, Margaret 25; Philadelphia, 1859 *5704.8 p142*
Gamble, Mary; Philadelphia, 1850 *53.26 p31*
Gamble, Mary; Philadelphia, 1850 *5704.8 p65*
Gamble, Mary 1; St. John, N.B., 1847 *5704.8 p20*
Gamble, Mary 30; St. John, N.B., 1855 *5704.8 p126*
Gamble, Mary Ann 26; Quebec, 1863 *5704.8 p153*
Gamble, Matilda 2; St. John, N.B., 1847 *5704.8 p20*
Gamble, Nancy 14; St. John, N.B., 1856 *5704.8 p131*
Gamble, Prudence; Philadelphia, 1864 *5704.8 p180*
Gamble, Rachel; Philadelphia, 1852 *5704.8 p91*
Gamble, Robert; Philadelphia, 1847 *53.26 p31*
Gamble, Robert; Philadelphia, 1847 *5704.8 p30*
Gamble, Robert; Philadelphia, 1864 *5704.8 p179*
Gamble, Robert 1; St. John, N.B., 1848 *5704.8 p42*
Gamble, Robert 21; St. John, N.B., 1856 *5704.8 p131*
Gamble, Robert 24; Quebec, 1864 *5704.8 p164*
Gamble, Robert John 3 mos; Quebec, 1864 *5704.8 p164*
Gamble, Rosanna; Quebec, 1847 *5704.8 p17*
Gamble, Samuel; New York, NY, 1811 *2859.11 p12*
Gamble, Samuel 18; St. John, N.B., 1856 *5704.8 p131*
Gamble, Samuel 36; Philadelphia, 1855 *5704.8 p123*
Gamble, Sarah; Philadelphia, 1847 *53.26 p31*
Gamble, Sarah; Philadelphia, 1847 *5704.8 p30*
Gamble, Sarah; Quebec, 1851 *5704.8 p82*
Gamble, Sarah 2 *SEE* Gamble, Jane
Gamble, Sarah 2; Philadelphia, 1848 *5704.8 p46*
Gamble, Susan; Quebec, 1851 *5704.8 p82*
Gamble, William; New York, NY, 1811 *2859.11 p12*
Gamble, William; Quebec, 1851 *5704.8 p82*
Gamble, William 2; St. John, N.B., 1848 *5704.8 p42*
Gamble, William 5 *SEE* Gamble, Jane
Gamble, William 5; Philadelphia, 1848 *5704.8 p46*
Gamble, William 20; Massachusetts, 1849 *5881.1 p44*
Gambling, Josias; Virginia, 1636 *6219 p12*
Gambling, Josias; Virginia, 1636 *6219 p77*
Gambold, Hector; Philadelphia, 1742 *3652 p55*
Gamboni, Domenick; Iowa, 1866-1943 *123.54 p63*
Gamel, Andrew; New York, NY, 1815 *2859.11 p31*
Gamelin, Mr.; Pennsylvania, 1776 *8582.2 p56*
With wife
Gamerdinger, Gottlieb; Pennsylvania, 1753-1800 *2444 p156*
With wife
*Child:*Maria Magdalena
Gamerdinger, Maria Magdalena *SEE* Gamerdinger, Gottlieb
Gamerelinger, Jacob; New York, 1852 *1450.2 p48A*
Gamlin, Israel; California, 1847-1872 *2769.4 p5*
Gamm, Julius; Baltimore, 1904 *3455.1 p46*
Gammerdinger, . . .; Canada, 1776-1783 *9786 p21*
Gammern, Juliana Benedicta von; New York, 1761 *3652 p88*
Gammock, Robert; Virginia, 1639 *6219 p152*
Gammon, Dennis 25; California, 1873 *2769.10 p4*
Gamond, Fel.. 16; New Orleans, 1836 *778.5 p225*
Gamsby, Ann 8 *SEE* Gamsby, John
Gamsby, Dorothy 10 *SEE* Gamsby, John
Gamsby, George 6 *SEE* Gamsby, John
Gamsby, John 7 *SEE* Gamsby, John
Gamsby, John 33; Boston, 1774 *1219.7 p210*
*Wife:*Margaret 30
*Child:*Dorothy 10
*Child:*Ann 8
*Child:*John 7
*Child:*George 6
*Child:*Peter 1
Gamsby, Margaret 30 *SEE* Gamsby, John
Gamsby, Peter 1 *SEE* Gamsby, John
Gamsford, Frederick; New Jersey, 1832 *8208.4 p47*
Gamutie, L. 30; Port uncertain, 1835 *778.5 p225*
Gamy, Joseph; America, 1892 *7137 p168*
Ganangino, Joe; Arkansas, 1918 *95.2 p46*
Gance, C. M.; Illinois, 1861 *2896.5 p13*
Gander, Carl F.; Illinois, 1893 *2896.5 p13*
Gander, Charles; Jamaica, 1772 *1219.7 p158*
Gandy, . . . 73; South Carolina, 1850 *1639.20 p75*
Ganel, Eugene 23; Port uncertain, 1839 *778.5 p225*
Ganel, Prosper 17; Port uncertain, 1836 *778.5 p225*
Ganes, Richard; Virginia, 1636 *6219 p77*
Ganeske, August; Illinois, 1878 *2896.5 p13*
Ganet, James 30; Philadelphia, 1803 *53.26 p31*
Ganey, Richard; Virginia, 1639 *6219 p157*
Gang, John; Illinois, 1900 *5012.40 p77*
Gangloff, Joseph; New York, NY, 1839 *8208.4 p101*
Gangloff, Philip; America, 1872 *6014.1 p2*
Gangwer, Georg; America, 1777-1778 *8582.2 p69*
Gangwer, George; Philadelphia, 1783 *8582.2 p66*
Gangwyer, Jacob; Pennsylvania, 1727 *4779.3 p13*
Ganley, Michael; New York, NY, 1838 *8208.4 p68*
Ganly, John; New York, NY, 1816 *2859.11 p31*
Ganly, Thomas; New York, NY, 1816 *2859.11 p31*
Gann, Anna Catharina *SEE* Gann, Hans Jerg
Gann, Anna Maria *SEE* Gann, Hans Jerg
Gann, Hans Jerg; New England, 1728-1800 *2444 p156*
*Wife:*Anna Catharina
*Child:*Anna Maria
Gannan, Hugh; New York, NY, 1816 *2859.11 p31*
Gannare, Joseph 28; America, 1829 *778.5 p225*
Gannel, Joseph 30; America, 1838 *778.5 p225*
Gannel, Josephine 20; America, 1838 *778.5 p225*
Ganner, Dennis; New York, NY, 1816 *2859.11 p31*
Gannings, Hugh 25; Massachusetts, 1847 *5881.1 p42*
Gannings, John 30; Massachusetts, 1847 *5881.1 p42*
Gannon, Catharine 27; Massachusetts, 1847 *5881.1 p41*
Gannon, Edward 25; New Orleans, 1862 *543.30 p375C*
Gannon, James 25; Massachusetts, 1847 *5881.1 p42*
Gannon, John; New York, NY, 1840 *8208.4 p109*
Gannon, John 60; Massachusetts, 1849 *5881.1 p42*
Gannon, Richard; Arkansas, 1918 *95.2 p46*
Gannon, Robert; New York, NY, 1838 *8208.4 p70*
Gannon, Timothy; New York, NY, 1840 *8208.4 p108*
Gannon, William; New York, NY, 1816 *2859.11 p31*
Ganon, Anna 38; New Orleans, 1838 *778.5 p228*
Ganon, Francis 2; New Orleans, 1838 *778.5 p228*
Ganon, Francis 33; New Orleans, 1838 *778.5 p228*
Ganon, John N. 14; New Orleans, 1838 *778.5 p228*
Ganon, Maria 14; New Orleans, 1838 *778.5 p228*
Ganon, Peter 5; New Orleans, 1838 *778.5 p228*
Ganquene, Dominic; Wisconsin, n.d. *9675.5 p189*
Gans, . . .; Canada, 1776-1783 *9786 p21*
Gans, Franz; Wisconsin, n.d. *9675.5 p189*
Ganseman, Bartel 25; America, 1838 *778.5 p225*
Ganss, Johann Justus; Ohio, 1869-1887 *8582 p10*
Gant, Thomas; Quebec, 1776 *1219.7 p282*
Ganta, John; America, 1861 *6014.1 p2*
Gantenberg, Bernard; America, 1848 *8582.3 p21*
Ganter, John; New York, NY, 1837 *8208.4 p54*
Ganter, Martin; Cincinnati, 1869-1887 *8582 p10*
Ganter, Peter; America, 1854 *8582.3 p21*
Gantillon, P. 26; New Orleans, 1839 *778.5 p225*
Gantner, Philip; Wisconsin, n.d. *9675.5 p189*
Gantum, James 22; Maryland, 1735 *3690.1 p85*
Gantum, James 24; Jamaica, 1735 *3690.1 p85*
Gantz, Frederick; America, 1848 *1450.2 p48A*
Gantz, Henry; Indiana, 1820-1850 *9117 p19*
Gantzarow, Harry; Wisconsin, n.d. *9675.5 p189*
Ganway, Bernard; New York, NY, 1816 *2859.11 p31*
Gany, Alice; Virginia, 1642 *6219 p191*
Gany, Ann *SEE* Gany, William
Gany, Ann *SEE* Gany, William
Gany, Henry *SEE* Gany, William
Gany, William *SEE* Gany, William
Gany, William; Virginia, 1635 *6219 p12*
*Wife:*Ann
*Son:*William
*Daughter:*Ann
*Brother:*Henry
Ganz, Ferdinand 25; New Orleans, 1862 *543.30 p382C*
Ganz, John; Wisconsin, n.d. *9675.5 p189*
Ganz, Julius; Wisconsin, n.d. *9675.5 p189*
Garahis, Adam; Ohio, 1867 *6014.2 p7*
Garalaght, Bartholomew; America, 1738 *4971 p39*
Garay, Echevaria 31; America, 1839 *778.5 p226*
Garbaczuk, Alexandra 18; New York, 1912 *9980.29 p65*
Garbarczyk, . . .; New York, 1831 *4606 p173*
Garbe, Paul; Wisconsin, n.d. *9675.5 p189*
Garbel, Ephrahim Benedikt; New England, 1753 *4525 p218*
With wife
With child
Garbel, Ephraim Bendedigt; Pennsylvania, 1753 *4525 p219*
Garbella, Bartolomeo; Colorado, 1902 *9678.2 p19*
Garbella, Frank; Colorado, 1902 *9678.2 p20*
Garbella, John; Colorado, 1888 *9678.2 p20*
Garber, George; Iroquois Co., IL, 1894 *3455.1 p10*
Garbo, Sam, Jr.; Arkansas, 1918 *95.2 p46*
Garbrecht, Henry L.; New York, NY, 1834 *8208.4 p48*
Garbutt, Richard 34; Nova Scotia, 1774 *1219.7 p209*
With wife
With 6 children
Garce, Martin; Colorado, 1896 *9678.2 p20*
Garce, Steven; Colorado, 1896 *9678.2 p20*
Garcia, Charles 38; Arizona, 1890 *2764.35 p28*
Garcia, Domiano A Delmo 45 days; Arizona, 1914 *9228.40 p19*
Garcia, Felipia 24; Arizona, 1922 *9228.40 p26*
Garcia, Frank 70; Arizona, 1921 *9228.40 p25*
Garcia, Gardo 22; New Orleans, 1863 *543.30 p378C*
Garcia, Jesus; Arizona, 1898 *9228.30 p8*
Garcia, Joseph; Kansas, 1913 *6013.40 p15*
Garcia, Joseph F. 40; New Orleans, 1862 *543.30 p375C*
Garcia, Louis 36?; New Orleans, 1862 *543.30 p374C*
Garcia, Manuel 38; New Orleans, 1863 *543.30 p379C*
Garcia, Marcelino; Arkansas, 1918 *95.2 p46*
Garcia, Raphael 27; New Orleans, 1863 *543.30 p378C*
Garcia, S.; Arizona, 1912 *9228.40 p16*
Garcia, Santiago 20; New Orleans, 1863 *543.30 p378C*
Garcia, Thomas 56; Arizona, 1918 *9228.40 p22*
Garcin, Anne 26; Port uncertain, 1838 *778.5 p226*
Garcis, Eugene 15; New Orleans, 1839 *778.5 p226*
Gardais, Jean 28; America, 1820 *778.5 p226*
Gardame, Madame 35; America, 1829 *778.5 p226*
Gardame, Mr. 40; America, 1829 *778.5 p226*
Gardame, Cossimer 16; America, 1829 *778.5 p226*
Gardame, Julie 15; America, 1829 *778.5 p226*
Gardame, Laurence; America, 1829 *778.5 p226*
Garden, Alexander; Charleston, SC, 1719 *1639.20 p75*
Garden, Alexander; Charleston, SC, 1753-1830 *1639.20 p75*
Garden, Francis; Charleston, SC, 1768-1770 *1639.20 p76*
Garden, G.; Quebec, 1815 *9229.18 p75*
With wife
Garden, J. 39; Kansas, 1895 *5240.1 p14*
Garden, J. 39; Kansas, 1895 *5240.1 p80*
Gardener, Edward 18; Maryland, 1775 *1219.7 p272*
Gardener, James; Philadelphia, 1847 *53.26 p31*
Gardener, James; Philadelphia, 1847 *5704.8 p24*
Gardener, Jane; Quebec, 1823 *7603 p93*
Gardenir, James 22; St. John, N.B., 1866 *5704.8 p167*
Gardenir, William 24; St. John, N.B., 1866 *5704.8 p167*
Gardery, P. 39; America, 1838 *778.5 p226*
Gardes, Alphonse 27; America, 1837 *778.5 p226*
Gardey, B. 22; Port uncertain, 1839 *778.5 p226*
Gardey, Joseph 29; New Orleans, 1862 *543.30 p382C*
Gardie, Antony 14; America, 1838 *778.5 p227*
Gardie, N. Phillip 50; America, 1838 *778.5 p227*
Gardiner, A.; Ohio, 1819 *8582.1 p47*
Gardiner, Bryan; Virginia, 1639 *6219 p157*
Gardiner, Isaac; New York, NY, 1835 *8208.4 p5*
Gardiner, James; San Francisco, 1850 *4914.15 p10*
Gardiner, John; Colorado, 1892 *9678.2 p20*
Gardiner, Margaret; Philadelphia, 1852 *5704.8 p89*
Gardiner, Marie; Quebec, 1814 *7603 p76*
Gardiner, Richard; Virginia, 1638 *6219 p149*
Gardiner, Richard; Virginia, 1753 *1219.7 p20*
Gardiner, Richard; Virginia, 1753 *3690.1 p85*
Gardiner, Rosa; America, 1816 *8894.2 p56*
Gardiner, Thomas; Boston, 1776 *1219.7 p284*
Gardiner, Thomas; Virginia, 1642 *6219 p196*
Gardit, Oswald; Wisconsin, n.d. *9675.5 p189*
Gardneer, Jacob 44; Harris Co., TX, 1900 *6254 p6*
Gardner, Mrs.; Charleston, SC, 1806 *1639.20 p76*
Gardner, Arthur; New York, NY, 1815 *2859.11 p31*
Gardner, Arthur, Jr.; New York, NY, 1815 *2859.11 p31*
Gardner, Charles 45; New Orleans, 1862 *543.30 p379C*
Gardner, Debarah; New York, NY, 1815 *2859.11 p31*
Gardner, Edward 18; Maryland, 1774 *1219.7 p208*
Gardner, Eleanor; New York, NY, 1815 *2859.11 p31*
Gardner, Eliza 9; Massachusetts, 1850 *5881.1 p42*
Gardner, Elizabeth; New York, NY, 1815 *2859.11 p31*
Gardner, Elizabeth 12; Philadelphia, 1851 *5704.8 p76*
Gardner, Francis 7; Massachusetts, 1849 *5881.1 p42*
Gardner, George 19; Maryland, 1774 *1219.7 p222*
Gardner, Godtholdt 18; New Orleans, 1864 *543.30 p379C*
Gardner, Henry 21; Maryland, 1775 *1219.7 p255*
Gardner, Isabel 50 *SEE* Gardner, William
Gardner, Jacob; America, 1848 *8582.1 p10*
Gardner, James; New York, NY, 1816 *2859.11 p31*
Gardner, Jane 7; Massachusetts, 1850 *5881.1 p43*
Gardner, Jane 11; Massachusetts, 1849 *5881.1 p42*
Gardner, John; Illinois, 1852 *7857 p3*

Gardner, John; New York, NY, 1837 8208.4 p53
Gardner, John 4; Massachusetts, 1850 5881.1 p43
Gardner, John 6; Philadelphia, 1851 5704.8 p76
Gardner, John 19; Maryland, 1731 3690.1 p85
Gardner, John 30; Virginia, 1774 1219.7 p193
Gardner, John 35; New Orleans, 1862 543.30 p375C
Gardner, Margaret 43 *SEE* Gardner, Thomas
Gardner, Marie Gardiner; Quebec, 1814 7603 p76
Gardner, Mary; Philadelphia, 1850 53.26 p31
Gardner, Mary; Philadelphia, 1850 5704.8 p60
Gardner, Mary 10; Philadelphia, 1851 5704.8 p76
Gardner, N. B.; Washington, 1859-1920 2872.1 p13
Gardner, Patrick; South Carolina, 1716 1639.20 p76
Gardner, Rebecca 7 *SEE* Gardner, Thomas
Gardner, Richard 18; Pennsylvania, 1735 3690.1 p85
Gardner, Richard 21; Maryland, 1774 1219.7 p224
Gardner, Sarah 14; Massachusetts, 1849 5881.1 p44
Gardner, Simon 16 *SEE* Gardner, Thomas
Gardner, Theodore 21; Kansas, 1890 5240.1 p75
Gardner, Thomas 20 *SEE* Gardner, Thomas
Gardner, Thomas 44; Boston, 1774 1219.7 p205
*Wife:*Margaret 43
*Child:*Simon 16
*Child:*Rebecca 7
*Child:*Thomas 20
Gardner, William 57; South Carolina, 1850 1639.20 p76
*Relative:*Isabel 50
Gardnier, Joseph; Illinois, 1892 5012.40 p26
Gardy, Mr. 28; Mexico, 1830 778.5 p227
Gardyne, Samuel; Charleston, SC, 1680-1830 1639.20 p76
Gare, Robert; Virginia, 1649 6219 p252
Gareckas, Wicent; Wisconsin, n.d. 9675.5 p189
Gareille, Michel; Louisiana, 1789-1819 778.5 p555
Garek, Sylvester 27; New Orleans, 1831 778.5 p227
Garelan, William; New York, NY, 1816 2859.11 p31
Gares, Jean Casimir 28; New Orleans, 1837 778.5 p227
Gareuil, Michel; Louisiana, 1789-1819 778.5 p555
Garfoot, Jonathan 15; Windward Islands, 1722 3690.1 p85
Gargame, Ellis; Virginia, 1639 6219 p161
Gargan, Bryan; America, 1737 4971 p71
Gargrave, Isam; Virginia, 1635 6219 p17
Garice, Juan 22; America, 1838 778.5 p227
Garin, Pier.e 29; America, 1839 778.5 p227
Garland, Bernard; New York, NY, 1837 8208.4 p33
Garland, Frank; Arizona, 1890 2764.35 p28
Garland, Mary; America, 1866 5704.8 p214
Garland, Richard; Kingston, Jamaica, 1752 1219.7 p11
Garland, William; New York, NY, 1838 8208.4 p68
Garlepied, V..ve 34; New Orleans, 1838 778.5 p227
Garlick, John 27; Massachusetts, 1847 5881.1 p42
Garlin, Domenic; Iowa, 1866-1943 123.54 p19
Garling, Frederick; Illinois, 1896 5012.40 p55
Garlipad, Jean Edouard 10; Port uncertain, 1838 778.5 p227
Garman, James; New Brunswick, 1789-1793 7603 p76
Garmer, Kude; Wisconsin, n.d. 9675.5 p189
Garnar, James 16; Pennsylvania, Virginia or Maryland, 1735 3690.1 p85
Garner, . . . 8 mos; New York, NY, 1869 5704.8 p232
Garner, Mr.; Quebec, 1815 9229.18 p75
Garner, Alex.; Virginia, 1635 6219 p3
Garner, Ann; Virginia, 1648 6219 p250
Garner, Caroline 2; New York, NY, 1869 5704.8 p232
Garner, Charles; New York, 1835 1450.2 p48A
Garner, Daniell; Virginia, 1638 6219 p122
Garner, Elizabeth 6; New York, NY, 1869 5704.8 p232
Garner, Ellen; Virginia, 1640 6219 p185
Garner, James; New York, NY, 1869 5704.8 p232
Garner, Jane; New York, NY, 1869 5704.8 p232
Garner, John; Virginia, 1637 6219 p11
Garner, Jon.; Virginia, 1637 6219 p13
Garner, Joseph; Washington, 1859-1920 2872.1 p13
Garner, Mary; Virginia, 1639 6219 p150
Garner, Michaell; Virginia, 1637 6219 p114
Garner, Rich.; Virginia, 1637 6219 p11
Garner, Richard; Virginia, 1637 6219 p116
Garner, Sarah 9; New York, NY, 1869 5704.8 p232
Garner, Violet; Philadelphia, 1851 5704.8 p79
Garner, William; Virginia, 1635 6219 p186
Garnett, Mr.; Died enroute, 1741 8582.2 p12
With wife
Garnett, Mr.; Norfolk, VA, 1741 8582.2 p12
Garnett, J. 27; Port uncertain, 1825 778.5 p227
Garnett, Thomas 19; Maryland, 1724 3690.1 p85
Garnett, Wm.; Virginia, 1648 6219 p250
Garnette, James 22; Newfoundland, 1699 2212 p22
Garney, Michel; New York, NY, 1816 2859.11 p31
Garnie, S. 25; Port uncertain, 1837 778.5 p227
Garnier, August; New York, 1858 1450.2 p48A
Garnier, Cladomir 28; New Orleans, 1862 543.30 p382C
Garnier, Etienne Prosper 21; America, 1835 778.5 p227
Garnier, John B.; Indiana, 1869-1887 8582 p10
Garnier, Laurent 52; New Orleans, 1822 778.5 p227
Garnier, Nicolas Felix 13; Port uncertain, 1825 778.5 p227
Garnier, P. 28; Port uncertain, 1839 778.5 p228
Garnier, Sophie 43; Port uncertain, 1825 778.5 p228
Garnison, John; Maine, 1874 6410.22 p124
Garnitz, Henry; Indiana, 1844 9117 p16
Garnor, John 18; Philadelphia, 1856 5704.8 p128
Garnor, Margaret 40; Philadelphia, 1856 5704.8 p128
Garnum, Richard; Virginia, 1640 6219 p183
Garnwath, Charles; St. John, N.B., 1852 5704.8 p83
Garoufalis, Nick Christ; Arkansas, 1918 95.2 p46
Garr, Lewis Franklin; Kansas, 1916 6013.40 p15
Garrad, John 27; Jamaica, 1730 3690.1 p85
Garrad, Thomas 18; Maryland or Virginia, 1719 3690.1 p85
Garraed, William 19; Jamaica, 1730 3690.1 p86
Garragh, Patrick 23; Philadelphia, 1861 5704.8 p148
Garrahee, John 23; Kansas, 1872 5240.1 p52
Garral, James 32; New Orleans, 1862 543.30 p375C
Garraty, Patrick 19; Massachusetts, 1849 5881.1 p44
Garraway, Evans; Virginia, 1637 6219 p113
Garreau, Pierre 35; New Orleans, 1821 778.5 p228
Garrecht, . . .; Pennsylvania, 1752 4525 p219
Garrecht, Catharina *SEE* Garrecht, Christoph
Garrecht, Christoph; Pennsylvania, 1786 4525 p212
With family
Garrecht, Christoph; Pennsylvania, 1786 4525 p219
With wife
With stepchild
*Child:*Pieter Willem Andries
*Child:*Catharina
*Child:*Orchille
Garrecht, Orchille *SEE* Garrecht, Christoph
Garrecht, Pieter Willem Andries *SEE* Garrecht, Christoph
Garrecht, Veit; Philadelphia, 1752 4525 p219
With wife
With 2 children
Garrechts, Veit; Philadelphia, 1752 4525 p219
Garreffa, Rocco 24; Arkansas, 1918 95.2 p46
Garrel, Prosper 17; Port uncertain, 1836 778.5 p225
Garrell, George 11; Quebec, 1847 5704.8 p8
Garrell, Jane; Quebec, 1847 5704.8 p8
Garrell, John Fitz; Virginia, 1636 6219 p76
Garrell, Robert 13; Quebec, 1847 5704.8 p8
Garrell, William; Quebec, 1847 5704.8 p8
Garret, Edward; Quebec, 1816 7603 p76
Garret, Eliza.; Virginia, 1647 6219 p248
Garret, John; Virginia, 1647 6219 p247
Garret, Tho.; Virginia, 1647 6219 p247
Garrett, Adam 22; Maryland, 1775 1219.7 p250
Garrett, Adrey; Virginia, 1637 6219 p83
Garrett, Andrew 40?; Arizona, 1890 2764.35 p27
Garrett, Eliz.; Virginia, 1632 6219 p180
Garrett, Eliz.; Virginia, 1642 6219 p199
Garrett, Francis; Virginia, 1639 6219 p161
Garrett, Geo. 22; Canada, 1835 4535.10 p196
Garrett, George; Charles Town, SC, 1771 1219.7 p150
Garrett, Hugh; Illinois, 1854 7857 p3
Garrett, Hugh; New York, NY, 1815 2859.11 p31
Garrett, James; Illinois, 1870 2896.5 p13
Garrett, James; Sacramento, CA, 1864 2764.35 p25
Garrett, John; Halifax, N.S., 1771 1219.7 p150
Garrett, John; Virginia, 1636 6219 p7
Garrett, John; Virginia, 1637 6219 p85
Garrett, John; Virginia, 1642 6219 p186
Garrett, John 15; Philadelphia, 1774 1219.7 p175
Garrett, Rowland; Virginia, 1637 6219 p37
Garrett, Thomas; Illinois, 1854 7857 p3
Garrett, Thomas; Virginia, 1640 6219 p181
Garrett, William; Virginia, 1640 6219 p188
Garrett, William 16; Maryland, 1720 3690.1 p86
Garrety, Pascal 35; Massachusetts, 1849 5881.1 p44
Garrey, Bridget 30; Massachusetts, 1849 5881.1 p41
Garrigue Flaujeac, Paul Joseph Louis; Louisiana, 1789-1819 778.5 p555
Garrigue Flaujeau, Pierre Jean-Antoine; Louisiana, 1789-1819 778.5 p555
Garrince, John; Virginia, 1638 6219 p160
Garriott, James 24; Maryland, 1774 1219.7 p214
Garrison, Benjamin; New York, 1754 3652 p79
Garrison, Mary Ann; New York, 1754 3652 p78
Garrison, Nicholas; New York, 1763 3652 p89
With wife
Garrison, Nicholas, Jr.; New York, 1754 3652 p79
Garrity, Dan; Arkansas, 1918 95.2 p46
Garrity, Edward; St. John, N.B., 1851 5704.8 p79
Garrity, Mary 50; Massachusetts, 1849 5881.1 p43
Garro, Estien 24; America, 1838 778.5 p228
Garron, John 9; Massachusetts, 1848 5881.1 p42
Garrot, Robert 18; Jamaica, 1733 3690.1 p86
Garrott, Robert 18; Jamaica, 1733 3690.1 p86
Garry, William 27; Philadelphia, 1864 5704.8 p155
Garsford, John 22; Maryland, 1774 1219.7 p184
Garson, Anna 38; New Orleans, 1838 778.5 p228
Garson, Francis 2; New Orleans, 1838 778.5 p228
Garson, Francis 33; New Orleans, 1838 778.5 p228
Garson, John N. 14; New Orleans, 1838 778.5 p228
Garson, Maria 14; New Orleans, 1838 778.5 p228
Garson, Peter 5; New Orleans, 1838 778.5 p228
Garson, Robert; Georgia, 1775 1219.7 p274
Gart, John 41; Port uncertain, 1820 778.5 p228
Garth, Charles 45; New Orleans, 1862 543.30 p376C
Garth, George 24; Philadelphia, 1774 1219.7 p216
Garth, John 39; Virginia, 1773 1219.7 p169
Garthan, Thomas 19; Maryland, 1774 1219.7 p192
Garthley, James 14; Philadelphia, 1853 5704.8 p111
Garthwaitt, Jane 22; Georgia, 1775 1219.7 p277
Gartley, John; Philadelphia, 1865 5704.8 p200
Gartman, Bartholome; South Carolina, 1788 7119 p200
Gartman, Danl; South Carolina, 1788 7119 p200
Gartman, George; South Carolina, 1788 7119 p200
Gartman, Johan P.; South Carolina, 1788 7119 p200
Gartman, Philip; South Carolina, 1788 7119 p200
Gartner, . . .; Canada, 1776-1783 9786 p42
Gartner, Anna Barb. 11 mos; America, 1853 9162.7 p14
Gartner, Elis. 21; America, 1853 9162.8 p36
Gartner, Georg 9; America, 1853 9162.7 p14
Gartner, Kath. 28; America, 1853 9162.7 p14
Gartner, Ludwig 6; America, 1853 9162.7 p14
Gartner, Marg. 10; America, 1853 9162.7 p14
Garton, James 16; Maryland, 1774 1219.7 p192
Gartzich, Andrew; New York, NY, 1836 8208.4 p19
Garvan, Bridget 60; Philadelphia, 1864 5704.8 p161
Garvan, Edward 23; St. John, N.B., 1862 5704.8 p150
Garvan, John 20; St. John, N.B., 1856 5704.8 p131
Garvan, Neal 18; St. John, N.B., 1856 5704.8 p131
Garvay, Michael; America, 1849 1450.2 p48A
Garven, Ellen 24; Massachusetts, 1849 5881.1 p42
Garven, William; New York, NY, 1816 2859.11 p31
Garverick, . . .; Pennsylvania, n.d. 4525 p220
Garvey, Ellen 16; Massachusetts, 1849 5881.1 p42
Garvey, John; New York, NY, 1834 8208.4 p4
Garvey, Patrick; America, 1738 4971 p13
Garvey, Patrick; New York, NY, 1840 8208.4 p108
Garvey, Susan; New York, NY, 1868 5704.8 p221
Garvey, Thomas; Boston, 1840 1450.2 p48A
Garvey, William; America, 1735-1743 4971 p79
Garvey, William; New York, NY, 1869 5704.8 p233
Garvin, Daniel; America, 1742 4971 p23
Garvin, Michael; Philadelphia, 1866 5704.8 p207
Garvin, Patrick; New York, NY, 1811 2859.11 p12
Garwood, Abraham 19; Virginia, 1723 3690.1 p86
Gary, Mr. 18; New Orleans, 1821 778.5 p228
Gary, Walter; Virginia, 1639 6219 p161
Garye, John; Virginia, 1637 6219 p17
Gascha, Peter; Philadelphia, 1765 9973.7 p40
Gasche, Gott; Baltimore, 1833 8582.1 p10
Gaschler, Aloes 34; West Virginia, 1900 9788.3 p11
Gascioli, Alderico; Arkansas, 1918 95.2 p46
Gascon, Raimond; New York, NY, 1827 8208.4 p39
Gascoyne, Thomas 19; Jamaica, 1733 3690.1 p86
Gascoyne, Thomas 22; Maryland, 1774 1219.7 p206
Gash, Mathew 21; New York, 1774 1219.7 p218
Gashjian, Armenag; Arkansas, 1918 95.2 p46
Gasik, Stanley; Arkansas, 1918 95.2 p46
Gasiorowski, . . .; New York, 1831 4606 p173
Gaskell, Lawrence 24; Maryland, 1774 1219.7 p180
Gaskell, Thomas; Iowa, 1866-1943 123.54 p19
Gaskin, Covell; Virginia, 1638 6219 p120
Gaskines, Thomas; Virginia, 1652 6251 p19
Gaskins, Alice; Virginia, 1636 6219 p12
Gaskins, Alice; Virginia, 1636 6219 p77
Gaskins, Eliz.; Virginia, 1636 6219 p12
Gaskins, Eliz.; Virginia, 1636 6219 p77
Gaskins, Josias; Virginia, 1636 6219 p12
Gaskins, Josias; Virginia, 1636 6219 p77
Gaskins, Mary; Virginia, 1636 6219 p12
Gaskins, Mary; Virginia, 1636 6219 p77
Gaskins, Thomas; Virginia, 1636 6219 p12
Gaskins, Thomas; Virginia, 1636 6219 p77
Gaskins, Thomas; Virginia, 1652 6251 p19
Gasparac, George; Iowa, 1866-1943 123.54 p19
Gaspard, Mr. 3; New Orleans, 1839 778.5 p228
Gaspard, Ms. 50; New Orleans, 1839 778.5 p228
Gaspard, Charles 29; America, 1839 778.5 p228
Gaspard, Marguerite 23; America, 1839 778.5 p229
Gaspare, Fca. 30; New York, NY, 1893 9026.4 p41
*Relative:*Val 27
Gaspare, Val 27 *SEE* Gaspare, Fca.
Gasparini, Joe; Wisconsin, n.d. 9675.5 p189
Gasparovic, Blaz; Iowa, 1866-1943 123.54 p19
Gasparpvic, Ivan; Iowa, 1866-1943 123.54 p19
Gasper, John; Wisconsin, n.d. 9675.5 p189

170 *FOR A COMPLETE EXPLANATION OF ENTRY, SEE "HOW TO READ A CITATION" SECTION*

Gasporovic, Ivan; Iowa, 1866-1943 ***123.54*** *p19*
Gasporovic, Sliv; Iowa, 1866-1943 ***123.54*** *p19*
Gass, . . .; Ohio, 1819 ***8582.1*** *p47*
Gass, John Heinrich 54; Indiana, 1849 ***1450.2*** *p48A*
Gass, Jon.; Virginia, 1635 ***6219*** *p70*
Gassees, Jean 60; New Orleans, 1827 ***778.5*** *p229*
Gassenberger, Henry 26; California, 1872 ***2769.4*** *p4*
Gasser, John; Wisconsin, n.d. ***9675.5*** *p189*
Gasser, Magdaline; Wisconsin, n.d. ***9675.5*** *p189*
Gasser, Mary; Wisconsin, n.d. ***9675.5*** *p189*
Gassies, Mr. 26; New Orleans, 1823 ***778.5*** *p229*
Gassin, Mr. 33; New Orleans, 1835 ***778.5*** *p229*
Gassin, Floriau 24; America, 1838 ***778.5*** *p229*
Gassing, . . .; Port uncertain, 1839 ***778.5*** *p229*
Gassing, Mme.; Port uncertain, 1839 ***778.5*** *p229*
Gassius, Victor 23; New Orleans, 1862 ***543.30*** *p383C*
Gassner, Johann; Cincinnati, 1869-1887 ***8582*** *p10*
Gastens, . . .; Canada, 1776-1783 ***9786*** *p21*
Gastino, Charles 44; America, 1838 ***778.5*** *p229*
Gastino, M. 29; America, 1838 ***778.5*** *p229*
Gaston, Anna; Philadelphia, 1847 ***53.26*** *p31*
Gaston, Anna; Philadelphia, 1847 ***5704.8*** *p30*
Gaston, E. 25; Texas, 1838 ***778.5*** *p229*
Gastons, Mary; Philadelphia, 1867 ***5704.8*** *p221*
Gastrey, Thomas; Virginia, 1648 ***6219*** *p241*
Gastrock, Wm.; Virginia, 1633 ***6219*** *p32*
Gasway, John; Virginia, 1698 ***2212*** *p12*
Gately, John; Virginia, 1636 ***6219*** *p26*
Gately, Martin; New York, NY, 1835 ***8208.4*** *p38*
Gatens, Guillaume; Quebec, 1820 ***7603*** *p47*
Gatens, Patrick; Washington, 1859-1920 ***2872.1*** *p14*
Gater, Joane *SEE* Gater, John
Gater, John; Virginia, 1636 ***6219*** *p12*
*Wife:*Joane
Gaterson, James; Virginia, 1637 ***6219*** *p24*
Gates, Charles 24; Kansas, 1888 ***5240.1*** *p71*
Gates, Duncan; Illinois, 1859 ***7857*** *p3*
Gates, George; Illinois, 1855 ***7857*** *p3*
Gates, John 17; Maryland, 1774 ***1219.7*** *p229*
Gates, John H.; San Francisco, 1850 ***4914.15*** *p11*
Gates, John H., Jr.; San Francisco, 1850 ***4914.15*** *p10*
Gates, Jon.; Virginia, 1643 ***6219*** *p204*
Gates, Louis 31; Kansas, 1897 ***5240.1*** *p81*
Gates, Mathew; Virginia, 1639 ***6219*** *p157*
Gates, Thomas; Virginia, 1751 ***1219.7*** *p1*
Gates, William 36; Virginia, 1734 ***3690.1*** *p86*
Gath, Jno 20; Virginia, 1700 ***2212*** *p33*
Gatham, Gustar Christopher; Baltimore, 1894 ***3455.1*** *p47*
Gathburg, Charles; Iroquois Co., IL, 1896 ***3455.1*** *p10*
Gatley, Thomas 17; Baltimore, 1775 ***1219.7*** *p269*
Gaton, Georg; Virginia, 1638 ***6219*** *p120*
Gatt, James; Baltimore, 1811 ***2859.11*** *p12*
Gatt, William; New York, NY, 1811 ***2859.11*** *p12*
Gatten, Hugh 18; Jamaica, 1730 ***3690.1*** *p86*
Gattens, William 26; Maryland, 1774 ***1219.7*** *p191*
Gattermeyer, J. Leonard; New York, 1749 ***3652*** *p71*
Gattoni, Jacob 62; Arizona, 1901 ***9228.40*** *p6*
Gatus, Alexander 19; Maryland, 1733 ***3690.1*** *p86*
Gatzen, Herman; Kansas, 1908 ***6013.40*** *p15*
Gauarrella, Jeoczhino; Arkansas, 1918 ***95.2*** *p46*
Gaub, Joe; Arkansas, 1918 ***95.2*** *p46*
Gauber, Pierre 21; America, 1836 ***778.5*** *p223*
Gaubert, Mrs. 18; New Orleans, 1822 ***778.5*** *p230*
Gaubert, A. 25; New Orleans, 1822 ***778.5*** *p229*
Gaubert, Jean-Marie 37; Louisiana, 1820 ***778.5*** *p229*
Gaubert, John Theodore 31; America, 1823 ***778.5*** *p229*
Gaubert, Peter; Kentucky, 1839-1840 ***8582.3*** *p98*
Gauch, Jean 18; America, 1836 ***778.5*** *p230*
Gauche, Jean 21; America, 1839 ***778.5*** *p230*
Gauche, Jean 28; America, 1838 ***778.5*** *p230*
Gauche, Peter; Wisconsin, n.d. ***9675.5*** *p189*
Gaud, J. 40; Port uncertain, 1823 ***778.5*** *p230*
Gaudault, Mr. 15; New Orleans, 1825 ***778.5*** *p230*
Gaudens, Mr. 32; America, 1839 ***778.5*** *p230*
Gaudiere, Mr. 35; Port uncertain, 1839 ***778.5*** *p230*
Gaudinot, J. 50; New Orleans, 1820 ***778.5*** *p230*
Gaudry, . . .; Halifax, N.S., 1752 ***7074.6*** *p230*
Gaudy, B. 50; New Orleans, 1837 ***778.5*** *p230*
Gauers, . . .; Canada, 1776-1783 ***9786*** *p21*
Gauers, Andrew; Canada, 1783 ***9786*** *p38A*
Gauffres, A.; New York, NY, 1853 ***4610.10*** *p34*
Gauffres, A.; New York, NY, 1853 ***4610.10*** *p38*
Gaug, Anna Maria Eberli *SEE* Gaug, Heinrich
Gaug, Heinrich; Port uncertain, 1727 ***3627*** *p19*
*Wife:*Anna Maria Eberli
*Child:*Joh. Ludwig
*Child:*Johann Friedrich
*Child:*Johann Michael
Gaug, Joh. Ludwig *SEE* Gaug, Heinrich
Gaug, Johann Friedrich *SEE* Gaug, Heinrich
Gaug, Johann Michael *SEE* Gaug, Heinrich
Gauger, Anna Maria Eberli *SEE* Gauger, Heinrich
Gauger, Heinrich; Port uncertain, 1727 ***3627*** *p19*
*Wife:*Anna Maria Eberli
*Child:*Joh. Ludwig
*Child:*Johann Friedrich
*Child:*Johann Michael
Gauger, Joh. Ludwig *SEE* Gauger, Heinrich
Gauger, Johann Friedrich *SEE* Gauger, Heinrich
Gauger, Johann Michael *SEE* Gauger, Heinrich
Gauger, Vital 26; New Orleans, 1822 ***778.5*** *p230*
Gaughan, Michael; Illinois, 1852 ***7857*** *p3*
Gaul, Guillaume; Quebec, 1802 ***7603*** *p76*
Gaule, John Joseph; Iowa, 1866-1943 ***123.54*** *p19*
Gaulhoac, Mr. 26; New Orleans, 1825 ***778.5*** *p230*
Gaullter, Scarlett 22; Pennsylvania, 1738 ***3690.1*** *p86*
Gault, Catherine; St. John, N.B., 1852 ***5704.8*** *p84*
Gault, G.; New York, NY, 1815 ***2859.11*** *p31*
Gault, George; New York, NY, 1816 ***2859.11*** *p31*
Gault, Jakob; Ohio, 1854 ***8582.2*** *p58*
Gault, Mary; Philadelphia, 1848 ***53.26*** *p31*
Gault, Mary; Philadelphia, 1848 ***5704.8*** *p46*
Gault, Robert; New York, NY, 1815 ***2859.11*** *p31*
Gault, Sarah Jane 22; Philadelphia, 1853 ***5704.8*** *p109*
Gault, Thompson; New York, NY, 1815 ***2859.11*** *p31*
Gault, William; New York, NY, 1839 ***8208.4*** *p100*
Gaultier, Vincent 19; Ohio, 1837 ***778.5*** *p230*
Gaume, J. B. 18; America, 1832 ***778.5*** *p230*
Gaumon, Mr. 17; America, 1837 ***778.5*** *p231*
Gaumont, Miss 6; Cayenne, 1820 ***778.5*** *p231*
Gaumont, Mr. 1; Cayenne, 1820 ***778.5*** *p231*
Gaumont, Gertrude 20; Cayenne, 1820 ***778.5*** *p231*
Gaumont, Jean Louis Etienne 30; Cayenne, 1820 ***778.5*** *p231*
Gaunt, Jeffery; Virginia, 1642 ***6219*** *p188*
Gaunt, Rich.; Virginia, 1637 ***6219*** *p117*
Gaunt, Robt.; Virginia, 1637 ***6219*** *p83*
Gaupp, Dorothea; New York, 1752 ***3652*** *p76*
Gaurdan, Katharina 18; America, 1853 ***9162.7*** *p14*
Gaurdotte, Isaac 26; America, 1838 ***778.5*** *p231*
Gaurrato, Mike; Arkansas, 1918 ***95.2*** *p47*
Gausepohl, Bernard; Kentucky, 1843 ***8582.3*** *p100*
Gausley, Jno.; Philadelphia, 1816 ***2859.11*** *p31*
Gauss, Eugene; America, 1868 ***1450.2*** *p49A*
Gauss, Johann Justus; Ohio, 1869-1887 ***8582*** *p10*
Gaussenois, Antoine 28; Port uncertain, 1839 ***778.5*** *p231*
Gaussenois, Marguerite 27; Port uncertain, 1839 ***778.5*** *p231*
Gauter, Martin; Cincinnati, 1869-1887 ***8582*** *p10*
Gauthier, Francois; Louisiana, 1789-1819 ***778.5*** *p555*
Gauthier, Jacques; Quebec, 1729 ***4533*** *p127*
Gauthier, Jeane 26; New Orleans, 1838 ***778.5*** *p231*
Gauthier, Johann; Pennsylvania, 1855 ***3702.7*** *p389*
*Brother:*Wilhelm
Gauthier, M. 25; America, 1836 ***778.5*** *p231*
Gauthier, Wilhelm *SEE* Gauthier, Johann
Gautie, Mr. 27; Port uncertain, 1839 ***778.5*** *p231*
Gautier, Mr. 2; New Orleans, 1839 ***778.5*** *p232*
Gautier, Mr. 3; New Orleans, 1839 ***778.5*** *p232*
Gautier, Mr. 28; Port uncertain, 1838 ***778.5*** *p231*
Gautier, Mr. 30; Port uncertain, 1827 ***778.5*** *p231*
Gautier, Mr. 47; New Orleans, 1836 ***778.5*** *p231*
Gautier, Mrs. 25; New Orleans, 1839 ***778.5*** *p232*
Gautier, Aimable; Port uncertain, 1839 ***778.5*** *p231*
Gautier, Catherine Rachel *SEE* Gautier, Jaques
Gautier, Isaac *SEE* Gautier, Jaques
Gautier, Jaques; New England, 1753 ***2444*** *p156*
*Wife:*Jeanne Susanne Cochet
*Child:*Marie Susanne
*Child:*Marguerite
*Child:*Catherine Rachel
*Child:*Isaac
Gautier, Jeanne Susanne Cochet *SEE* Gautier, Jaques
Gautier, John; New Orleans, 1830 ***778.5*** *p232*
Gautier, Louis 8; America, 1839 ***778.5*** *p232*
Gautier, M. 31; America, 1825 ***778.5*** *p232*
Gautier, Marguerite *SEE* Gautier, Jaques
Gautier, Marie Susanne *SEE* Gautier, Jaques
Gautier, Maurice 38; New Orleans, 1839 ***778.5*** *p232*
Gautier, Melie 3; America, 1839 ***778.5*** *p232*
Gautier, Melie 30; America, 1839 ***778.5*** *p232*
Gautier, Michel 24; New Orleans, 1838 ***778.5*** *p232*
Gautier, Pierre 31; Pennsylvania, 1753 ***2444*** *p156*
Gautner, Jean 42; America, 1836 ***778.5*** *p232*
Gautner, Madelena 11; America, 1836 ***778.5*** *p232*
Gautner, Madelena 44; America, 1836 ***778.5*** *p232*
Gautner, Marguerite 2; America, 1836 ***778.5*** *p232*
Gautner, Marie 9; America, 1836 ***778.5*** *p232*
Gautner, Marie Anne 13; America, 1836 ***778.5*** *p233*
Gautner, Ursulle 8; America, 1836 ***778.5*** *p233*
Gautraud, Frederick 22; New Orleans, 1835 ***778.5*** *p233*
Gautuil, E. 30; Port uncertain, 1838 ***778.5*** *p233*
Gautz, John; Wisconsin, n.d. ***9675.5*** *p189*
Gavagan, Thomas 30; Massachusetts, 1849 ***5881.1*** *p44*
Gavaler, George; America, 1900 ***7137*** *p169*
Gavan, Charles; St. John, N.B., 1851 ***5704.8*** *p80*
Gavan, Felix; Montreal, 1822 ***7603*** *p60*
Gavan, John; Quebec, 1851 ***5704.8*** *p73*
Gave, Alfred 24; New Orleans, 1830 ***778.5*** *p233*
Gaveault, D. 38; New Orleans, 1838 ***778.5*** *p233*
Gaven, Bernard; Quebec, 1853 ***5704.8*** *p105*
Gaven, William; Quebec, 1853 ***5704.8*** *p105*
Gavin, James 20; Massachusetts, 1847 ***5881.1*** *p42*
Gavin, Thomas 24; Maryland, 1774 ***1219.7*** *p192*
Gawny, Joan; America, 1740 ***4971*** *p81*
Gawny, John; America, 1735-1743 ***4971*** *p79*
Gawron, Jan; Illinois, 1912 ***9980.29*** *p62*
Gawron, Jozef 17; New York, 1912 ***9980.29*** *p62*
*Sister:*Salomea 9
*Brother:*Stanislaw 7
Gawron, Salomea 9 *SEE* Gawron, Jozef
Gawron, Stanislaw 7 *SEE* Gawron, Jozef
Gawronski, Leon; New York, 1835 ***4606*** *p179*
Gay, Andre 35; New Orleans, 1838 ***778.5*** *p233*
Gay, F. 34; New Orleans, 1830 ***778.5*** *p233*
Gay, John 32; Mexico, 1825 ***778.5*** *p233*
Gay, Mathew; Delaware, 1801 ***9788.3*** *p11*
Gayer, Joh. Casper; Pennsylvania, 1753 ***2444*** *p156*
Gaygakian, Elisha S. 26; West Virginia, 1904 ***9788.3*** *p11*
Gaying, Bernard; Virginia, 1643 ***6219*** *p200*
Gaykowski, . . .; New York, 1831 ***4606*** *p173*
Gaylen, Margtt 36; America, 1703 ***2212*** *p38*
Gaynor, Edward; Illinois, 1858 ***2896.5*** *p13*
Gaynor, James; America, 1736 ***4971*** *p81*
Gayton, Roger 26; Maryland, 1774 ***1219.7*** *p184*
Gazeley, Nathaniel 15; Maryland, 1720 ***3690.1*** *p86*
Gazelle, Joseph; America, 1833 ***778.5*** *p233*
Gazes, James; Arkansas, 1918 ***95.2*** *p47*
Gazet, Peter; Illinois, 1860 ***5012.39*** *p89*
Gazette, John 35; Massachusetts, 1860 ***6410.32*** *p108*
Gazoti, Tom; Arkansas, 1918 ***95.2*** *p47*
Gazzell, Mitchell; Arkansas, 1918 ***95.2*** *p47*
Geabe, John; Virginia, 1640 ***6219*** *p185*
Geagan, Catharine 16; Massachusetts, 1849 ***5881.1*** *p41*
Geagin, John; America, 1736-1743 ***4971*** *p57*
Geaks, Charles 28; New Orleans, 1862 ***543.30*** *p376C*
Geamaugh, Ellen 7; Massachusetts, 1850 ***5881.1*** *p42*
Geamaugh, John 9; Massachusetts, 1850 ***5881.1*** *p43*
Geamaugh, Lawrence 15; Massachusetts, 1850 ***5881.1*** *p43*
Geamaugh, Rose 14; Massachusetts, 1850 ***5881.1*** *p44*
Gear, John 17; Virginia, 1774 ***1219.7*** *p227*
Geard, Louis 30; New Orleans, 1822 ***778.5*** *p233*
Gearhart, George; America, 1883 ***7137*** *p168*
Geary, John; New York, NY, 1837 ***8208.4*** *p53*
Geary, John 25; Philadelphia, 1856 ***5704.8*** *p128*
Geary, Patrick; New York, NY, 1816 ***2859.11*** *p31*
Geat, Wm.; Virginia, 1637 ***6219*** *p113*
Geatanganas, Tom; Arkansas, 1918 ***95.2*** *p47*
Geattus, Alexander 19; Maryland, 1733 ***3690.1*** *p86*
Geaux, Jean; Montreal, 1723 ***7603*** *p86*
Gebaner, Emil 40; Kansas, 1905 ***5240.1*** *p83*
Gebbie, Thomas; Iowa, 1866-1943 ***123.54*** *p19*
Gebert, Jerg; Died enroute, 1738 ***9898*** *p42*
Gebert, Mrs. Jerg; Philadelphia, 1738 ***9898*** *p42*
Gebhard, . . .; Quebec, 1776 ***9786*** *p104*
Gebhard, Henry 73; America, 1895 ***1763*** *p40C*
Gebhard, Ignace 27; Kansas, 1872 ***5240.1*** *p52*
Gebhard, Johanna; America, 1854-1855 ***9162.6*** *p105*
Gebhard, Theodore Friedrich; Quebec, 1776 ***9786*** *p261*
Gebhardt, George; Wisconsin, n.d. ***9675.5*** *p189*
Gebhart, John Henry; Arkansas, 1918 ***95.2*** *p47*
Gebhart, Peter; Wisconsin, n.d. ***9675.5*** *p189*
Gebran, Mike Oscar; Arkansas, 1918 ***95.2*** *p47*
Gebsheimer, Lorenz 22; Kansas, 1887 ***5240.1*** *p70*
Gecks, Charles; New Orleans, 1862 ***543.30*** *p373C*
Geddes, James E.; New York, NY, 1838 ***8208.4*** *p66*
Geddie, James Donald; Cape Fear, NC, 1772 ***1639.20*** *p76*
Gederowicz, Wincentas 21; New York, 1912 ***9980.29*** *p67*
Gedlin, William 18; Virginia, 1701 ***2212*** *p35*
Gedlundn, Peter; Wisconsin, n.d. ***9675.5*** *p189*
Gedon, Anne; Virginia, 1636 ***6219*** *p76*
Gee, Edward; Virginia, 1643 ***6219*** *p230*
Gee, Jon.; Virginia, 1637 ***6219*** *p117*
Gee, Richard 21; Maryland, 1774 ***1219.7*** *p225*
Gee, Wilfred W.; Arkansas, 1918 ***95.2*** *p47*
Gee, William; Virginia, 1639 ***6219*** *p153*
Gee, William 27; Jamaica, 1733 ***3690.1*** *p86*
Geelhaus, Johann Friedrich; America, 1852 ***4610.10*** *p98*
Geer, John; Philadelphia, 1760 ***9973.7*** *p35*
Geeran, Edward; New York, NY, 1869 ***5704.8*** *p234*
Geers, Herrmann H.; Indiana, 1830-1849 ***8582*** *p10*
Geerts, Bernard Herman; Arkansas, 1918 ***95.2*** *p47*
Geetle, Louis 35; West Virginia, 1900 ***9788.3*** *p11*
Geezy, Jacob; Philadelphia, 1749-1773 ***9973.7*** *p40*

Geffrard, Josue; Quebec, 1786 7603 p49
Geffre, . . .; Canada, 1776-1783 9786 p21
Geffrey, Armel 26; America, 1832 778.5 p233
Gegere, Louis 31; New Orleans, 1830 778.5 p233
Gegoue, J. 25; New Orleans, 1839 778.5 p233
Gegout, Charles 22; America, 1838 778.5 p233
Gegrand, Nicholas 21; Port uncertain, 1839 778.5 p234
Gegraud, Nicholas 21; Port uncertain, 1839 778.5 p234
Gehart, Mr. 28; New Orleans, 1836 778.5 p234
Gehaut, Mr. 28; New Orleans, 1836 778.5 p234
Gehl, Philipp; Philadelphia, 1779 8137 p8
Gehler, George 32; Kansas, 1891 5240.1 p76
Gehring, Albert; Wisconsin, n.d. 9675.5 p189
Gehringer, John 32; New Orleans, 1862 543.30 p382C
Gehrke, Charlotte 48; New York, NY, 1862 9831.18 p16
Gehrke, Christian 50; New York, NY, 1862 9831.18 p16
Gehrke, Fred; Wisconsin, n.d. 9675.5 p189
Gehrke, Friedrich; Iroquois Co., IL, 1896 3455.1 p10
Gehrke, Laurette 19; New York, NY, 1862 9831.18 p16
Gehrke, Reinhold 8; New York, NY, 1862 9831.18 p16
Gehrke, Wilhelm 14; New York, NY, 1862 9831.18 p16
Gehrung, Margaretha; America, 1753-1800 2444 p196
Geidel, Charles; Wisconsin, n.d. 9675.5 p189
Geider, Heinrich; Cincinnati, 1788-1848 8582.3 p91
Geidt, Claudie; Virginia, 1851 4626.16 p14
Geier, Franz; America, 1849 8582.2 p12
Geier, Henry; Wisconsin, n.d. 9675.5 p190
Geiger, . . .; Canada, 1776-1783 9786 p21
Geiger, Mrs. Caspar 43; Philadelphia, 1752 4525 p219
Geiger, Christian; Wisconsin, n.d. 9675.5 p190
Geiger, Fred. G. 22; Kansas, 1886 5240.1 p68
Geiger, Henry C.; New York, NY, 1887 1450.2 p11B
Geiger, Jacob; Pennsylvania, 1744 2444 p157
Geiger, Jacob; Pennsylvania, 1751 2444 p157
Geiger, Johann Michael; Pennsylvania, 1744 2444 p157
Geiger, Johann Michael; Pennsylvania, 1752 2444 p157
Geiger, John; South Carolina, 1788 7119 p203
Geikie, Catharine A. Gamble *SEE* Geikie, James Henry
Geikie, James Henry; Georgia, 1811 8894.2 p55
*Wife:*Catharine A. Gamble
Geil, Georg L.; Charleston, SC, 1775-1781 8582.2 p52
Geiler, Bernhard; New York, NY, 1834 8208.4 p4
Geilfuss, Ludwig; Cincinnati, 1869-1887 8582 p10
Geilker, Anna Wilhelmine *SEE* Geilker, Caspar Heinrich
Geilker, August F. Wilhelm *SEE* Geilker, Caspar Heinrich
Geilker, August H. Wilhelm *SEE* Geilker, Caspar Heinrich
Geilker, Carl Heinrich *SEE* Geilker, Caspar Heinrich
Geilker, Caspar Heinrich *SEE* Geilker, Caspar Heinrich
Geilker, Caspar Heinrich 42; America, 1850 4610.10 p142
*Wife:*M. L. Friedrichsmeyer 33
*Child:*Louise 22
*Child:*August H. Wilhelm
*Child:*Zacharias Heinrich
*Child:*Caspar Heinrich
*Child:*Carl Heinrich
*Child:*August F. Wilhelm
*Child:*Anna Wilhelmine
Geilker, Friedrich Wilhelm; America, 1850 4610.10 p138
Geilker, Louise 22 *SEE* Geilker, Caspar Heinrich
Geilker, M. L. Friedrichsmeyer 33 *SEE* Geilker, Caspar Heinrich
Geilker, Zacharias Heinrich *SEE* Geilker, Caspar Heinrich
Geimer, Dominic; Wisconsin, n.d. 9675.5 p190
Geimer, Peter; Wisconsin, n.d. 9675.5 p190
Geiphart, John; Illinois, 1870 7857 p3
Geir, Johann; Wisconsin, n.d. 9675.5 p190
Geis, Adam; Cincinnati, 1869-1887 8582 p10
Geis, Adam 36; Kansas, 1873 5240.1 p54
Geis, Christoph; Cincinnati, 1869-1887 8582 p10
Geis, Christopher; New York, NY, 1845 8582.3 p21
Geis, George; Wisconsin, n.d. 9675.5 p190
Geis, Joseph; Cincinnati, 1800-1877 8582.3 p87
Geis, Martin 45; New Orleans, 1862 543.30 p384C
Geisbauer, Carl; America, 1830 8582.2 p61
Geisbauer, Charles; Kentucky, 1869-1887 8582 p10
Geisbauer, Karl; Ohio, 1830 8582.3 p98
Geise, William; America, 1837 1450.2 p49A
Geisel, Henrich; Lancaster, PA, 1780 8137 p8
Geisel, Henry; America, 1848 1450.2 p49A
Geisendorf, Louis 28; Kansas, 1876 5240.1 p57
Geisenheimer, George; New Orleans, 1862 543.30 p376C
Geisenhoffer, Otto; Arizona, 1878 2764.35 p26
Geiserdorf, Louis 28; Kansas, 1876 5240.1 p14
Geisert, August 24; America, 1854-1855 9162.6 p104
Geisler, George; Philadelphia, 1759 9973.7 p34
Geisler, Jacob; Indiana, 1836 9117 p14
Geismar, Friedrich von; Quebec, 1776 9786 p265
Geismeyer, August Ernst Friedrich *SEE* Geismeyer, Marie Wilhelmine
Geismeyer, Marie Wilhelmine; America, 1851 4610.10 p155
*Son:*August Ernst Friedrich
Geispert, Marie 27; America, 1854-1855 9162.6 p105
Geissler, Arthur Herman; Kansas, 1897 5240.1 p14
Geissler, Michael; Ohio, 1869-1887 8582 p10
Geissler, S. August; Wisconsin, n.d. 9675.5 p190
Geist, Caspar; Cincinnati, 1869-1887 8582 p10
Geist, Heinrich; Cincinnati, 1872-1874 8582.1 p10
Geist, Matthew 30; New Orleans, 1862 543.30 p374C
Geist, Wilh. 17; America, 1854-1855 9162.6 p105
Geitner, Anton; Wisconsin, n.d. 9675.5 p190
Geitner, John G.; New York, 1748 3652 p68
Geittler, Joseph; Wisconsin, n.d. 9675.5 p190
Geitzen, John Joseph; Wisconsin, n.d. 9675.5 p190
Gejdos, Adam; Iowa, 1866-1943 123.54 p63
Gejdos, Ondraj; Iowa, 1866-1943 123.54 p63
Gejer, Andreas *SEE* Gejer, Johann Caspar
Gejer, Anna B. Kienzlein *SEE* Gejer, Johann Caspar
Gejer, Anna Barbara *SEE* Gejer, Johann Caspar
Gejer, Anna Maria *SEE* Gejer, Johann Caspar
Gejer, Christina *SEE* Gejer, Johann Caspar
Gejer, Johann Caspar *SEE* Gejer, Johann Caspar
Gejer, Johann Caspar; Pennsylvania, 1754 2444 p156
*Wife:*Anna B. Kienzlein
*Child:*Anna Barbara
*Child:*Johann Caspar
*Child:*Anna Maria
*Child:*Christina
*Child:*Andreas
*Child:*Johannes
Gejer, Johannes *SEE* Gejer, Johann Caspar
Gel, Benj. 22; New Orleans, 1832 778.5 p234
Gelding, Elizabeth; Virginia, 1648 6219 p253
Geldmeier, Louise 18; New York, NY, 1867 3702.7 p571
Gelencir, Frank Joseph; Arkansas, 1918 95.2 p47
Gelhaus, Mr.; America, 1839-1859 4610.10 p99
Gelhaus, Bernhard Friedrich Ludwig; America, 1859 4610.10 p99
Gelinet, Pierre 33; Ohio, 1820 778.5 p234
Gelison, Samuel; New York, NY, 1811 2859.11 p12
With family
Gellback, Caroline 19; America, 1838 778.5 p234
Gellback, Guillaume 14; America, 1838 778.5 p234
Gellback, Jean 17; America, 1838 778.5 p234
Gellert, Paul; America, 1889 1450.2 p11B
Gellez, Joseph 27; New Orleans, 1838 778.5 p234
Gellie, George; New York, 1763 1219.7 p92
Gelman, Adolph H.; New York, 1879 1450.2 p11B
Gelman, Elias; New York, 1880 1450.2 p11B
Gelman, Samuel; New York, 1883 1450.2 p11B
Gelmo, Louis; Arkansas, 1918 95.2 p47
Gelpke, . . .; Canada, 1776-1783 9786 p21
Gels, Bernhardt 57; Kansas, 1890 5240.1 p75
Gelston, James; New York, NY, 1811 2859.11 p12
Gembrini, Frank; Colorado, 1895 9678.2 p20
Gemer, John; Iowa, 1866-1943 123.54 p19
Gemind, Chatin 22; America, 1837 778.5 p234
Gemler, Gg. 39; America, 1853 9162.8 p36
Gemmel, Mr.; America, 1884 3702.7 p484
With son-in-law
Gemmell, Captain; Quebec, 1815 9229.18 p81
Gemmen, Antone; Wisconsin, n.d. 9675.5 p190
Gemmer, Conrad; America, 1847 1450.2 p49A
Gemmer, Peter 41; Kansas, 1880 5240.1 p61
Gemmingen, Philipp, Freiherr von; Cincinnati, 1788-1848 8582.3 p89
Gemmingen, Philipp, Freiherr von; Cincinnati, 1788-1848 8582.3 p90
Gemuender, Mr.; America, 1847 8582.3 p21
Gemuender, Georg; America, 1847 8582.3 p21
Gen, Mr.; Port uncertain, 1839 778.5 p237
Genagal, Mary; Philadelphia, 1811 53.26 p31
Genagal, Mary; Philadelphia, 1811 2859.11 p12
Genais, Mr. 34; New Orleans, 1836 778.5 p234
Genarty, James; America, 1738 4971 p35
Genazzi, Emilio; Arkansas, 1918 95.2 p47
Gender, Gottliebin; Port uncertain, 1712-1800 2444 p157
Gendrian, Joseph 37; New Orleans, 1838 778.5 p234
Geneau de Fort Manoir, Paul 40; Port uncertain, 1838 778.5 p234
Geney, Jean J. 21; America, 1836 778.5 p234
Genger, . . .; Canada, 1776-1783 9786 p21
Gengerich, John; Illinois, 1904 5012.39 p53
Gengler, Peter; Wisconsin, n.d. 9675.5 p190
Genies, Henry; Washington, 1859-1920 2872.1 p14
Genis, Constentine; Arkansas, 1918 95.2 p47
Genner, Theodore; Wisconsin, n.d. 9675.5 p190
Gennevine, Leonard; Philadelphia, 1764 9973.7 p39
Gennine, D. Zenon; Louisiana, 1826 778.5 p235
Genova, Pete; New Orleans, 1899 3455.2 p49
Gens, Jean-Baptiste; Quebec, 1730 7603 p21
Gensvittle, Bernard; Kentucky, 1839-1840 8582.3 p98
Genthaler, . . .; Canada, 1776-1783 9786 p21
Gentil, Francis 46; New Orleans, 1863 543.30 p373C
Gentil, Jacque Pernet; New York, NY, 1836 8208.4 p9
Gentile, Nick; Arkansas, 1918 95.2 p47
Gentin, Mrs. 55; New Orleans, 1822 778.5 p235
Gentin, Louis 62; New Orleans, 1822 778.5 p235
Gentle, James; America, 1837 1450.2 p49A
Gentle, Robert; Jamaica, 1750 3690.1 p86
Gentner, Augustinus; Pennsylvania, 1749 2444 p157
With wife
Gentner, George; Pennsylvania, 1781 2444 p186
Gentner, Johannes *SEE* Gentner, Johannes
Gentner, Johannes; Pennsylvania, 1748-1749 2444 p157
*Wife:*Maria Agnes
*Child:*Johannes
Gentner, Maria Agnes *SEE* Gentner, Johannes
Gentsch, Carol 30; New Orleans, 1839 9420.2 p169
Genty, Jean Louis 53; America, 1829 778.5 p235
Gentzler, Conrad; Philadelphia, 1761 9973.7 p35
Gentzler, Philip; Philadelphia, 1763 9973.7 p38
Genz, Herman; Wisconsin, n.d. 9675.5 p190
Genz, Richard William; San Francisco, 1850 6013.19 p30
Genzel, Fred; Iroquois Co., IL, 1892 3455.1 p10
Geoculine, Ghilardi; Iowa, 1866-1943 123.54 p19
Geoffois, Robert; Quebec, 1764 7603 p39
Geogarty, John; America, 1741 4971 p94
Geoghegan, Henry; Philadelphia, 1815 2859.11 p31
Geoghegan, Murtoch; Philadelphia, 1815 2859.11 p31
Geohegan, Christopher; New England, 1816 2859.11 p31
Geoman, Albert; America, 1880 5240.1 p14
Geoman, Frank; America, 1880 5240.1 p14
Geono, Peter; Iowa, 1866-1943 123.54 p19
Georg, Griffith; Virginia, 1643 6219 p203
Georg, Jacobine 16; New York, NY, 1857 9831.14 p153
Georg, Jane *SEE* Georg, John
Georg, John; Virginia, 1638 6219 p122
*Wife:*Jane
Georg, Thomas; Virginia, 1638 6219 p123
George, . . .; Canada, 1776-1783 9786 p21
George, . . .; Canada, 1776-1783 9786 p42
George, Mr.; Quebec, 1815 9229.18 p78
George, Adam; Philadelphia, 1811 53.26 p31
George, Adam; Philadelphia, 1811 2859.11 p12
George, Alex. 21; Philadelphia, 1833-1834 53.26 p31
George, Alexander; New York, NY, 1811 2859.11 p12
George, Andrew; Baltimore, 1847 1450.2 p49A
George, Andrew; New York, NY, 1811 2859.11 p12
George, Caroline 22; Massachusetts, 1848 5881.1 p41
George, Catharine 36; Port uncertain, 1838 778.5 p235
George, Charlie; Arkansas, 1918 95.2 p47
George, David 29; Arkansas, 1918 95.2 p47
George, E. 25; New Orleans, 1827 778.5 p235
George, Eliza; New York, NY, 1811 2859.11 p12
George, Griffeth; Virginia, 1648 6219 p250
George, Gus; Arkansas, 1918 95.2 p47
George, Gust; Arkansas, 1918 95.2 p47
George, Isaac 19; Virginia, 1730 3690.1 p86
George, James 22; Maryland, 1774 1219.7 p220
George, James 29; Maryland, 1774 1219.7 p202
George, Jane *SEE* George, John
George, Jena; Wisconsin, n.d. 9675.5 p190
George, John; Arkansas, 1918 95.2 p47
George, John; New York, NY, 1811 2859.11 p12
With family
George, John; New York, NY, 1816 2859.11 p31
George, John; New York, NY, 1836 8208.4 p17
George, John; Philadelphia, 1811 53.26 p31
George, John; Philadelphia, 1811 2859.11 p12
George, John; Virginia, 1635 6219 p12
George, John; Virginia, 1638 6219 p33
George, John; Virginia, 1638 6219 p122
*Wife:*Jane
George, John; Virginia, 1640 6219 p185
George, John; Wisconsin, n.d. 9675.5 p190
George, John 16; Philadelphia, 1774 1219.7 p183
George, John 18; West Indies, 1722 3690.1 p87
George, John 37; Maryland, 1774 1219.7 p230
George, Louis 1; Port uncertain, 1838 778.5 p235
George, Lucy 11; Port uncertain, 1838 778.5 p235
George, M.; New York, NY, 1811 2859.11 p12
George, Martha; New York, NY, 1811 2859.11 p12
George, Mary Ann; New Orleans, 1852 5704.8 p98
George, Matthew 32; New Orleans, 1862 543.30 p375C
George, Mike; Arkansas, 1918 95.2 p47
George, Nicholas 8; Port uncertain, 1838 778.5 p235
George, Nicolas 21; New Orleans, 1837 778.5 p235
George, Pierre 42; Port uncertain, 1838 778.5 p235
George, R.D.; Colorado, 1904 9678.2 p20
George, Rady; Arkansas, 1918 95.2 p47
George, Robert; Virginia, 1642 6219 p193

George, Tony 47; Kansas, 1890 *5240.1* p75
George, William; New York, NY, 1811 *2859.11* p12
George, William; New York, NY, 1811 *2859.11* p12
  With family
George, William 20; Maryland, 1723 *3690.1* p87
George, William 24; Maryland, 1774 *1219.7* p229
George, William 29; Philadelphia, 1775 *1219.7* p255
Georgenberger, Benedict; Colorado, 1900 *9678.2* p20
Georges, Andrew; Arkansas, 1918 *95.2* p47
Georges, Ferdinand 49; New Orleans, 1839 *778.5* p235
Georget, Francois 14; New Orleans, 1838 *778.5* p235
Georget, Francoise 39; New Orleans, 1838 *778.5* p235
Georget, Michael; Indiana, 1848 *9117* p19
Georgii, Eduard C.; Wisconsin, n.d. *9675.5* p190
Gephart, Elizabeth 14; Georgia, 1738 *9332* p330
Gephart, Eva 10; Georgia, 1738 *9332* p330
Gephart, Hans George *SEE* Gephart, Philip
Gephart, Magdalen 19; Georgia, 1738 *9332* p330
Gephart, Maria Catherina 17 *SEE* Gephart, Philip
Gephart, Martha 43 *SEE* Gephart, Philip
Gephart, Philip 6 *SEE* Gephart, Philip
Gephart, Philip 45; Georgia, 1738 *9332* p331
  *Wife:*Martha 43
  *Daughter:*Maria Catherina 17
  *Son:*Philip 6
  *Son:*Hans George
Geran, Ellen 20; Massachusetts, 1849 *5881.1* p42
Gerando, John; Iowa, 1866-1943 *123.54* p19
Geranson, Gust Alfred; Colorado, 1903 *9678.2* p20
Gerard, Mme. 54; America, 1839 *778.5* p236
Gerard, Mr.; Quebec, 1815 *9229.18* p75
Gerard, Ms. 18; America, 1839 *778.5* p236
Gerard, A. 28; America, 1838 *778.5* p236
Gerard, Celestin; Iowa, 1866-1943 *123.54* p19
Gerard, Celestine; Iowa, 1866-1943 *123.54* p19
Gerard, E. 28; New Orleans, 1821 *778.5* p236
Gerard, Elise 24; America, 1838 *778.5* p236
Gerard, Emile; Iowa, 1866-1943 *123.54* p19
Gerard, George 25; America, 1838 *778.5* p236
Gerard, Huchet 33; America, 1831 *778.5* p236
Gerard, Leon 7; America, 1831 *778.5* p236
Gerard, Paul 5; America, 1831 *778.5* p236
Gerard, Rosette 33; America, 1831 *778.5* p236
Gerardet, Mr. 26; America, 1836 *778.5* p236
Gerassin, Paul 21; New Orleans, 1838 *778.5* p236
Gerati, Giovani; Arkansas, 1918 *95.2* p47
Geraud, Mme. 25; America, 1839 *778.5* p236
Geraud, Mme. 60; America, 1839 *778.5* p236
Geraud, Mr. 30; America, 1839 *778.5* p236
Gerbatowicz, Marianna 20; New York, 1912 *9980.29* p54
Gerber, Barbara 9; Philadelphia, 1738 *9898* p43
  With brother 6
Gerber, Christmann; Pennsylvania, 1738 *9898* p27
Gerber, David; Kansas, 1891 *5240.1* p14
Gerber, Georg 74; America, 1895 *1763* p40D
Gerber, Heinrich; Died enroute, 1738 *9898* p44
Gerber, Johann Jacob; Died enroute, 1738 *9898* p43
  With wife
  With father
  With 3 children
Gerber, John 35; New Orleans, 1862 *543.30* p374C
Gerber, Louis; America, 1850 *8582.3* p22
Gerber, Peter; Pennsylvania, 1709-1710 *4480* p311
  *Wife:*Verena Aeschlimann
Gerber, Verena Aeschlimann *SEE* Gerber, Peter
Gerber'ch, Peter; Pennsylvania, 1765 *4525* p220
Gerberich, Andrew; Pennsylvania, 1754 *4525* p220
Gerberich, Anna Barbara *SEE* Gerberich, Hans
Gerberich, Apollonia *SEE* Gerberich, Hans
Gerberich, Christine *SEE* Gerberich, Hans
Gerberich, Hans; Pennsylvania, 1751 *4525* p220
  *Wife:*Christine
  *Child:*Apollonia
  *Child:*Margaretha
  *Child:*Maria Margareta
  *Child:*Johannes
  *Child:*Anna Barbara
  *Child:*Johann Michael
Gerberich, Hans; Pennsylvania, 1752 *4525* p220
Gerberich, Hans Michael; Pennsylvania, 1751 *4525* p220
Gerberich, Johann Michael *SEE* Gerberich, Hans
Gerberich, Johannes *SEE* Gerberich, Hans
Gerberich, Johannes; Pennsylvania, 1751 *4525* p220
Gerberich, Margaretha *SEE* Gerberich, Hans
Gerberich, Maria Margareta *SEE* Gerberich, Hans
Gerberich, Peter; Pennsylvania, 1765 *4525* p220
Gerberick, John; Pennsylvania, 1751-1752 *4525* p220
Gerbers, Menke H.; Illinois, 1888 *5012.39* p122
Gerbig, . . .; Canada, 1776-1783 *9786* p21
Gercken, John; Iroquois Co., IL, 1895 *3455.1* p10
Gerd-To-Berns, Heinrich; New York, NY, 1923 *3455.4* p94

Gerdes, Bernard J. K.; Allegany Co., MD, 1850 *2896.5* p13
Gerdes, Carl Fred George; New York, NY, 1913 *3455.3* p26
Gerdes, Frederick; Baltimore, 1849 *2896.5* p13
Gerdes, George; Iroquois Co., IL, 1892 *3455.1* p10
Gerdes, George; New York, 1924 *3455.4* p79
Gerdes, Henry; Iroquois Co., IL, 1894 *3455.1* p10
Gerdes, Max Julius; America, 1892 *4610.10* p125
Gerdes, Renke; Illinois, 1858 *2896.5* p13
Gerdes, Ubbe; Illinois, 1888 *5012.39* p122
Gerdes, Wm. H.; Illinois, 1888 *5012.39* p52
Gerding, Mr.; New York, 1837 *8582.2* p23
Gerdts, John; America, 1859 *1450.2* p49A
Gerecke, . . .; Canada, 1776-1783 *9786* p21
Gereghy, Paul; New York, NY, 1816 *2859.11* p31
Gereke, William; America, 1853 *2896.5* p13
Gereschach, Julius; Shreveport, LA, 1874 *7129* p44
Geretz, Patrick; Illinois, 1872 *5012.39* p91
Gerey, . . .; Virginia, 1642 *6219* p194
Gerford, John; Virginia, 1646 *6219* p239
Gerger, . . .; Canada, 1776-1783 *9786* p21
Gergerich, Hans; Pennsylvania, 1752 *4525* p220
Gergman, Charles Ivar; Washington, 1859-1920 *2872.1* p3
Gerhard, . . .; Canada, 1776-1783 *9786* p21
Gerhard Brothers ; Illinois, 1842 *8582.2* p51
Gerhard, George; America, 1883 *7137* p168
Gerhard, Gottlieb; Wisconsin, n.d. *9675.5* p190
Gerhard, Ingle; Illinois, 1867 *2896.5* p14
Gerhard, John 80; America, 1895 *1763* p40C
Gerhard, Theodore; Illinois, 1876 *2896.5* p14
Gerhardt, Catherine; New York, 1752 *3652* p76
Gerhart, Edurt; Illinois, 1869 *2896.5* p14
Gerichs, William; America, 1853 *2896.5* p13
Gerighaty, Owen; New York, NY, 1811 *2859.11* p12
Geriks, Christian; New Orleans, 1843 *2896.5* p14
Gering, Jacob P.; America, 1874 *5240.1* p14
Gering, Peter 47; Kansas, 1879 *5240.1* p14
Gering, Peter 47; Kansas, 1881 *5240.1* p61
Gerke, Anne Marie L. W. C. *SEE* Gerke, Johann Friedrich Wilhelm
Gerke, Carl Friedrich Wilhelm *SEE* Gerke, Johann Friedrich Wilhelm
Gerke, Friedrich; America, 1844 *4610.10* p150
  *Daughter:*Marie Catharine F.C.
Gerke, Friedrich W. Gottlieb *SEE* Gerke, Johann Friedrich Wilhelm
Gerke, Heinrich E. Wilhelm *SEE* Gerke, Johann Friedrich Wilhelm
Gerke, Johann; New York, NY, 1843 *8582.3* p22
  *Wife:*Margaretha Konnen
Gerke, Johann Friedrich Wilhelm; America, 1844 *4610.10* p150
  *Wife:*Marie C. F. Charlotte
  *Child:*Anne Marie L. W. C.
  *Child:*Friedrich W. Gottlieb
  *Child:*Carl Friedrich Wilhelm
  *Child:*Heinrich E. Wilhelm
  With father-in-law
Gerke, Johannes; Ohio, 1869-1887 *8582* p10
Gerke, Margaretha Konnen *SEE* Gerke, Johann Friedrich Wilhelm
Gerke, Marie C. F. Charlotte *SEE* Gerke, Johann Friedrich Wilhelm
Gerke, Marie Catharine F.C. *SEE* Gerke, Friedrich
Gerke, Marie Catharine Friederike C.; America, 1844 *4610.10* p150
Gerken, Haman; New York, NY, 1840 *8208.4* p105
Gerken, Lizzie *SEE* Gerken, Wilhelm
Gerken, Wilhelm; New York, NY, 1911 *3455.3* p19
  *Wife:*Lizzie
Gerkensmeier, Carl Friedrich Wilhelm; America, 1872 *4610.10* p106
Gerkensmeier, Friederike; America, 1893 *4610.10* p118
Gerkensmeyer, Ernst Heinrich Dietrich; America, 1885 *4610.10* p102
Gerky, Friedrick 36; Kansas, 1875 *5240.1* p56
Gerlach, . . .; Canada, 1776-1783 *9786* p21
Gerlach, Capt.; Quebec, 1776 *9786* p104
Gerlach, Charles; Wisconsin, n.d. *9675.5* p190
Gerlach, Christian; Wisconsin, n.d. *9675.5* p190
Gerlach, Heinrich Jan.; Canada, 1776-1783 *9786* p252
Gerlach, Wilhelm; Wisconsin, n.d. *9675.5* p190
Gerleich, Gust; Wisconsin, n.d. *9675.5* p190
Gerletz, Christian Frederick; Illinois, 1860 *5012.38* p98
Gerlier, Mme. 30; New Orleans, 1839 *778.5* p237
Gerlier, Mr. 48; New Orleans, 1839 *778.5* p237
Gerlier, M. 13; New Orleans, 1839 *778.5* p237
Gerlig, . . .; Canada, 1776-1783 *9786* p21
Gerling, Ernst Heinrich Carl; America, 1881 *4610.10* p96
Gerling, Joseph 25; Kansas, 1885 *5240.1* p68
Germain, Albro 16; Ohio, 1838 *778.5* p237
Germain, Bertholet 32; America, 1837 *778.5* p237

Germain, Jean 25; New Orleans, 1839 *778.5* p237
Germain, Louis; California, 1869 *2769.4* p5
Germain, Louis 26; New Orleans, 1862 *543.30* p384C
German, . . .; Canada, 1776-1783 *9786* p42
German, Frederick; New York, NY, 1839 *8208.4* p90
German, J. B.; Cincinnati, 1834 *8582.1* p52
German, James H.; Iroquois Co., IL, 1894 *3455.1* p10
German, Patrick; New York, NY, 1816 *2859.11* p31
German, Phillip; Ohio, 1865 *9892.11* p16
German, Robert H.; Iroquois Co., IL, 1894 *3455.1* p10
German, Thomas 26; Virginia, 1773 *1219.7* p168
German, Thomas H.; Iroquois Co., IL, 1894 *3455.1* p10
Germanet, Madeleine; Pennsylvania, 1753 *2444* p140
Germann, August Friedrich von; Quebec, 1776 *9786* p265
Germann, Rudolf; New York, NY, 1906 *3455.2* p97
Germans, Jacques 25; New Orleans, 1835 *778.5* p237
Germanson, Ferdinand; Wisconsin, n.d. *9675.5* p190
Germanson, Germund; Wisconsin, n.d. *9675.5* p190
Germershausen, Johanna 18; New York, 1865 *3702.7* p210
Germershausen, Marie 20; New York, 1865 *3702.7* p210
Gern, Leonh. 15; America, 1853 *9162.7* p14
Gern, M. L. 46; America, 1837 *778.5* p237
Gerner, . . .; Canada, 1776-1783 *9786* p21
Gerner, John; Wisconsin, n.d. *9675.5* p190
Gernerzervic, Porter; Arkansas, 1918 *95.2* p47
Gerngross, Christiane Dorothea *SEE* Gerngross, Johann
Gerngross, Georg Heinrich *SEE* Gerngross, Johann
Gerngross, Johann; America, 1742-1800 *2444* p157
  *Wife:*Maria B. Neuberth
  *Child:*Georg Heinrich
  *Child:*Sophia Catharina
  *Child:*Christiane Dorothea
  *Child:*Johann Ludwig
Gerngross, Johann Ludwig *SEE* Gerngross, Johann
Gerngross, Maria B. Neuberth *SEE* Gerngross, Johann
Gerngross, Sophia Catharina *SEE* Gerngross, Johann
Gernhoff, Henry Ludwig; Wisconsin, n.d. *9675.5* p190
Geroffi, P. 50; Port uncertain, 1839 *778.5* p237
Geroin, A. 18; New Orleans, 1837 *778.5* p237
Gerold, Jean 23; America, 1839 *778.5* p237
Geromi, Joseph; Arkansas, 1918 *95.2* p48
Geromini, Cerillo; Arkansas, 1918 *95.2* p48
Gerraghty, Garrit; New York, NY, 1835 *8208.4* p4
Gerrard, Ann 33 *SEE* Gerrard, Thomas
Gerrard, Gilbert; Virginia, 1643 *6219* p200
Gerrard, Jon.; Virginia, 1635 *6219* p17
Gerrard, Thomas 28; Philadelphia, 1774 *1219.7* p217
  *Wife:*Ann 33
Gerrecht, Catharina *SEE* Gerrecht, Christoph
Gerrecht, Christoph; Pennsylvania, 1786 *4525* p209
Gerrecht, Christoph; Pennsylvania, 1786 *4525* p219
  With wife & stepchild
  *Child:*Pieter Willem Andries
  *Child:*Catharina
  *Child:*Orchille
Gerrecht, Orchille *SEE* Gerrecht, Christoph
Gerrecht, Pieter Willem Andries *SEE* Gerrecht, Christoph
Gerrich, Veit; Philadelphia, 1752 *4525* p219
Gerrichs, Andreas; New Orleans, 1853 *2896.5* p14
Gerrick, Albert; Arkansas, 1918 *95.2* p48
Gerrih, William John; America, 1867 *5704.8* p224
Gerring, William B.; New York, NY, 1840 *8208.4* p103
Gerris, Stephen; Virginia, 1642 *6219* p197
Gerrish, John; Virginia, 1641 *6219* p185
Gerry, Ann 9; Massachusetts, 1850 *5881.1* p41
Gerry, Ellen 11; Massachusetts, 1850 *5881.1* p42
Gerry, John 27; Massachusetts, 1847 *5881.1* p42
Gerry, Jon.; Virginia, 1638 *6219* p118
Gerry, Patrick 8; Massachusetts, 1850 *5881.1* p44
Gerschau, Jozefa 21; New York, 1912 *9980.29* p56
Gerschke, Frank; Wisconsin, n.d. *9675.5* p190
Gerschke, John; Wisconsin, n.d. *9675.5* p190
Gersdorf, Susan von; New York, 1763 *3652* p89
Gershak, Gilbert 24; Arkansas, 1918 *95.2* p48
Gerske, Tony; Arkansas, 1918 *95.2* p48
Gersmeyer, A.M. Louise W Bollmann *SEE* Gersmeyer, Johann Carl Fr.
Gersmeyer, Anna Marie Elisabeth *SEE* Gersmeyer, Conrad Friedrich
Gersmeyer, Carl E. Heinrich *SEE* Gersmeyer, Johann Carl Fr.
Gersmeyer, Conrad Friedrich; America, 1844 *4610.10* p154
  *Wife:*Anna Marie Elisabeth
  *Son:*Ernst Heinrich
Gersmeyer, Ernst Heinrich *SEE* Gersmeyer, Conrad Friedrich
Gersmeyer, Ernst Heinrich *SEE* Gersmeyer, Johann Carl Fr.

Gersmeyer, Heinrich Fr. W. *SEE* Gersmeyer, Johann Carl Fr.
Gersmeyer, Johann Carl Fr.; America, 1881 ***4610.10*** *p159*
*Wife:*A.M. Louise W Bollmann
*Child:*Carl E. Heinrich
*Child:*Heinrich Fr. W.
*Child:*Ernst Heinrich
Gerstaecker, Friederich; New York, NY, 1837 ***8582.1*** *p45*
Gerstberger, Henry; New York, 1750 ***3652*** *p75*
Gerstenmeyer, Mr. 13; New Orleans, 1839 ***778.5*** *p237*
Gerstewitz, Gotfried; Wisconsin, n.d. ***9675.5*** *p190*
Gerstkamper, Anna Marie C. Schnacke *SEE* Gerstkamper, Christian Moritz
Gerstkamper, Christian Moritz; America, 1852 ***4610.10*** *p98*
*Wife:*Anna Marie C. Schnacke
*Son:*Heinrich F. Wilhelm
Gerstkamper, Ernst Heinrich Friedrich; America, 1851 ***4610.10*** *p98*
Gerstkamper, Heinrich F. Wilhelm *SEE* Gerstkamper, Christian Moritz
Gerstle, Friedrich Wilhelm; Cincinnati, 1869-1887 ***8582*** *p10*
Gerstner, Christian J.; America, 1882 ***1450.2*** *p49A*
Gerteis, Joseph 28; Kansas, 1871 ***5240.1*** *p14*
Gerteis, Joseph 28; Kansas, 1871 ***5240.1*** *p51*
Gertel, Leopold 32; New Orleans, 1862 ***543.30*** *p383C*
Gerth, Peter; Indiana, 1848 ***9117*** *p16*
Gertheis, Fredalene; Wisconsin, 1867 ***5240.1*** *p14*
Gerthilda, Augusta 35; Massachusetts, 1860 ***6410.32*** *p98*
Gerthmann, . . .; Canada, 1776-1783 ***9786*** *p21*
Gertman, . . .; Canada, 1776-1783 ***9786*** *p21*
Geruand, Phillip 36; Kansas, 1876 ***5240.1*** *p57*
Gervais, . . .; Canada, 1776-1783 ***9786*** *p21*
Gervan, Richard 18; Maryland, 1773 ***1219.7*** *p173*
Gervasi, Sam; Arkansas, 1918 ***95.2*** *p48*
Gervers, Caspar Henry; Cincinnati, 1869-1887 ***8582*** *p10*
Gervers, John; Cincinnati, 1869-1887 ***8582*** *p10*
Gervis, Sarah 18; Philadelphia, 1859 ***5704.8*** *p142*
Gerwe, F. A. J.; Cincinnati, 1869-1887 ***8582*** *p10*
Gerwers, Friedrich; Ohio, 1832 ***8582.2*** *p49*
With family
Gerwien, Herman; San Francisco, 1872 ***2764.35*** *p26*
Gerwig, A.; Wheeling, WV, 1852 ***8582.3*** *p78*
Gerwin, Carl; Illinois, 1888 ***5012.39*** *p121*
Gescheidle, . . .; Canada, 1776-1783 ***9786*** *p21*
Gescheidt, Anton; New York, NY, 1835 ***8582.2*** *p23*
Geschke, . . .; Canada, 1776-1783 ***9786*** *p22*
Geschunn, Joseph 19; America, 1835 ***778.5*** *p237*
Geschwandel, Thomas; Georgia, 1738 ***9332*** *p321*
Gesell, Adam; Illinois, 1888 ***2896.5*** *p14*
Gesell, Andrew; Illinois, 1886 ***2896.5*** *p14*
Gesell, William; Wisconsin, n.d. ***9675.5*** *p190*
Gesler, William; Ohio, 1841 ***8365.25*** *p12*
Gessert, Heinrich; Cincinnati, 1869-1887 ***8582*** *p10*
Gessert, Jacob; Cincinnati, 1835 ***8582.1*** *p10*
Gessler, . . .; Canada, 1776-1783 ***9786*** *p22*
Gessner, Johann A.; Cincinnati, 1813 ***8582.1*** *p51*
Gest, Thomas 25; Philadelphia, 1774 ***1219.7*** *p216*
Gestman, Michael; South Carolina, 1752-1753 ***3689.17*** *p21*
With wife
Gestner, John; Wisconsin, n.d. ***9675.5*** *p190*
Geth, John; New York, NY, 1840 ***8208.4*** *p105*
Getke, Edward; Wisconsin, n.d. ***9675.5*** *p190*
Getrost, Leonh. 33; America, 1853 ***9162.7*** *p14*
Getting, John 23; Philadelphia, 1774 ***1219.7*** *p232*
Gettires, William; Quebec, 1852 ***5704.8*** *p97*
Getto, Peter 26; Kansas, 1872 ***5240.1*** *p14*
Getto, Peter 26; Kansas, 1872 ***5240.1*** *p53*
Getty, Arthur; Philadelphia, 1848 ***53.26*** *p31*
Getty, Arthur; Philadelphia, 1848 ***5704.8*** *p46*
Getty, Henry; New York, NY, 1867 ***5704.8*** *p219*
Getty, James; New York, NY, 1811 ***2859.11*** *p12*
Getty, Jane; Philadelphia, 1865 ***5704.8*** *p202*
Getty, Joseph 20; Philadelphia, 1833-1834 ***53.26*** *p31*
*Relative:*Martha
Getty, Martha *SEE* Getty, Joseph
Getty, Moore; New York, NY, 1866 ***5704.8*** *p213*
Getty, Robert; New York, NY, 1867 ***5704.8*** *p219*
Getty, Sarah; New York, NY, 1867 ***5704.8*** *p218*
Getty, Sarah; Philadelphia, 1852 ***5704.8*** *p88*
Getzelman, . . .; Pennsylvania, n.d. ***4525*** *p221*
Getzelmann, . . .; Pennsylvania, n.d. ***4525*** *p221*
Getzunger, Banerman; South Carolina, 1788 ***7119*** *p204*
Geu, Mr.; Port uncertain, 1839 ***778.5*** *p237*
Geurly, Jane; Philadelphia, 1849 ***53.26*** *p31*
Geurly, Jane; Philadelphia, 1849 ***5704.8*** *p49*
Geuzendam, John Theunis; Arkansas, 1918 ***95.2*** *p48*
Geveshomme, Stanislas 45; America, 1839 ***778.5*** *p238*
Gevry, Josephine 34; Port uncertain, 1839 ***778.5*** *p238*
Geyer, Casper; Pennsylvania, 1754 ***2444*** *p156*
Geyer, Jacob; Pennsylvania, 1744 ***2444*** *p157*
Geyer, Joh. Casper; Pennsylvania, 1753 ***2444*** *p156*
Geyer, Joh Jacob; Pennsylvania, 1753 ***2444*** *p156*
Geyer, Johannes; America, 1829 ***8582.2*** *p61*
Geyer, Johannes; Cincinnati, 1869-1887 ***8582*** *p10*
Geyger, Jacob; Pennsylvania, 1744 ***2444*** *p157*
Geyger, Johann Michael; Pennsylvania, 1744 ***2444*** *p157*
Geyso, Carl; Quebec, 1776 ***9786*** *p262*
Geysow, Ludwig Ferdinand von; Halifax, N.S., 1780 ***9786*** *p269*
Geysow, Ludwig Ferdinand von; New York, 1776 ***9786*** *p269*
Ghenet, Frederik 22; America, 1837 ***778.5*** *p238*
Ghezzi, Primo; Arkansas, 1918 ***95.2*** *p48*
Giaciomorro, Vincenzo; Arkansas, 1918 ***95.2*** *p48*
Giamarchi, M. 37; America, 1838 ***778.5*** *p238*
Gianello, Joseph 21; America, 1837 ***778.5*** *p238*
Gianetta, Dominico 20; Harris Co., TX, 1898 ***6254*** *p5*
Gianini, Peter; New York, NY, 1837 ***8208.4*** *p25*
Giantoiriaso, Donato 38; New York, NY, 1893 ***9026.4*** *p41*
*Relative:*Libera 32
*Relative:*Vincenzo 8
Giantoiriaso, Libera 32 *SEE* Giantoiriaso, Donato
Giantoiriaso, Vincenzo 8 *SEE* Giantoiriaso, Donato
Giardulli, Gioranni 34; West Virginia, 1904 ***9788.3*** *p11*
Giardullo, Nicola 21; West Virginia, 1903 ***9788.3*** *p11*
Giaretta, Giovanni 25; Kansas, 1893 ***5240.1*** *p79*
Giaretta, John; Kansas, 1893 ***5240.1*** *p14*
Giaretta, Peter 25; Kansas, 1899 ***5240.1*** *p14*
Giaretta, Peter 25; Kansas, 1899 ***5240.1*** *p81*
Giauas, Dave; Iowa, 1866-1943 ***123.54*** *p20*
Gibb, Mr.; Quebec, 1815 ***9229.18*** *p77*
With wife
Gibb, Alec; Austin, TX, 1886 ***9777*** *p5*
Gibb, Alexander 31; Maryland, 1730 ***3690.1*** *p87*
Gibb, Bernard; Kentucky, 1843 ***8582.3*** *p100*
Gibb, Robert; South Carolina, 1754 ***1639.20*** *p322*
Gibb, Robert 24; St. John, N.B., 1865 ***5704.8*** *p165*
Gibbard, Henry 35; Virginia, 1774 ***1219.7*** *p244*
Gibbert, John; Illinois, 1892 ***5012.40*** *p27*
Gibbin, Thomas 31; Nova Scotia, 1774 ***1219.7*** *p210*
Gibbins, Biddy 13; St. John, N.B., 1848 ***5704.8*** *p43*
Gibbins, Brian; St. John, N.B., 1851 ***5704.8*** *p78*
Gibbins, Catharine; New York, NY, 1866 ***5704.8*** *p210*
Gibbins, Thomas 21; Maryland, 1774 ***1219.7*** *p204*
Gibbon, Maurice; America, 1742 ***4971*** *p53*
Gibbons, Mr.; Charleston, SC, 1724 ***1639.20*** *p76*
Gibbons, Mr.; Quebec, 1815 ***9229.18*** *p77*
Gibbons, Biddy 26; Philadelphia, 1853 ***5704.8*** *p112*
Gibbons, Charles; Philadelphia, 1849 ***53.26*** *p31*
Gibbons, Charles; Philadelphia, 1849 ***5704.8*** *p50*
Gibbons, Ellan 6; Philadelphia, 1847 ***5704.8*** *p30*
Gibbons, Ellen 6 *SEE* Gibbons, William
Gibbons, Fanny 13; Philadelphia, 1853 ***5704.8*** *p112*
Gibbons, H.; New York, NY, 1816 ***2859.11*** *p31*
Gibbons, Hannah 7; St. John, N.B., 1853 ***5704.8*** *p99*
Gibbons, J.; New York, NY, 1816 ***2859.11*** *p31*
Gibbons, James 12 *SEE* Gibbons, William
Gibbons, James 12; Philadelphia, 1847 ***5704.8*** *p30*
Gibbons, James 12; St. John, N.B., 1853 ***5704.8*** *p99*
Gibbons, John; St. John, N.B., 1847 ***5704.8*** *p4*
Gibbons, John; Virginia, 1641 ***6219*** *p187*
Gibbons, John 20; Philadelphia, 1859 ***5704.8*** *p141*
Gibbons, John 32; Kansas, 1870 ***5240.1*** *p14*
Gibbons, John 32; Kansas, 1870 ***5240.1*** *p51*
Gibbons, Julia 4 *SEE* Gibbons, William
Gibbons, Julia 4; Philadelphia, 1847 ***5704.8*** *p30*
Gibbons, M.; New York, NY, 1816 ***2859.11*** *p31*
Gibbons, Margey 10; St. John, N.B., 1853 ***5704.8*** *p99*
Gibbons, Mary; Philadelphia, 1867 ***5704.8*** *p218*
Gibbons, Mary 15; Philadelphia, 1853 ***5704.8*** *p112*
Gibbons, Nancy 9 mos; Philadelphia, 1853 ***5704.8*** *p112*
Gibbons, Neil 2 *SEE* Gibbons, William
Gibbons, Neil 2; Philadelphia, 1847 ***5704.8*** *p30*
Gibbons, Oliver; Virginia, 1642 ***6219*** *p189*
Gibbons, Rose *SEE* Gibbons, William
Gibbons, Rose; Philadelphia, 1847 ***5704.8*** *p30*
Gibbons, Sally 14; St. John, N.B., 1853 ***5704.8*** *p99*
Gibbons, Sarah; St. John, N.B., 1849 ***5704.8*** *p55*
Gibbons, Sarah; Virginia, 1698 ***2212*** *p17*
Gibbons, Thomas; Bermuda, 1764 ***1219.7*** *p100*
Gibbons, William; America, 1742 ***4971*** *p37*
Gibbons, William; Jamaica, 1752 ***1219.7*** *p16*
Gibbons, William; Jamaica, 1752 ***3690.1*** *p87*
Gibbons, William; Philadelphia, 1847 ***53.26*** *p31*
*Relative:*Rose
*Relative:*James 12
*Relative:*Ellen 6
*Relative:*Julia 4
*Relative:*Neil 2
Gibbons, William; Philadelphia, 1847 ***5704.8*** *p30*
Gibbons, William 22; Newfoundland, 1789 ***4915.24*** *p55*
Gibbs, Edward; Virginia, 1638 ***6219*** *p123*
Gibbs, Ellen 20; Massachusetts, 1848 ***5881.1*** *p41*
Gibbs, George 21; Virginia, 1774 ***1219.7*** *p238*
Gibbs, Humphry; Virginia, 1639 ***6219*** *p156*
Gibbs, John; New York, NY, 1816 ***2859.11*** *p31*
Gibbs, John; New York, NY, 1836 ***8208.4*** *p23*
Gibbs, John 20; Virginia, 1721 ***3690.1*** *p87*
Gibbs, John 27; Virginia, 1775 ***1219.7*** *p261*
Gibbs, Joseph 25; Baltimore, 1775 ***1219.7*** *p269*
Gibbs, Joseph 26; Maryland, 1774 ***1219.7*** *p234*
Gibbs, Mary; New York, NY, 1816 ***2859.11*** *p31*
Gibbs, Mary; Virginia, 1698 ***2212*** *p12*
Gibbs, Max; America, 1863 ***1450.2*** *p49A*
Gibbs, Robert 19; Tortola, 1773 ***1219.7*** *p172*
Gibbs, Ruth; New York, NY, 1816 ***2859.11*** *p31*
Gibbs, Thomas 18; Maryland, 1719 ***3690.1*** *p87*
Gibbs, William Henry; New York, NY, 1834 ***8208.4*** *p43*
Gibeausset, Mr. 50; America, 1823 ***778.5*** *p238*
Gibetta, Ange 27; America, 1838 ***778.5*** *p238*
Giblin, John; Virginia, 1857 ***4626.16*** *p17*
Gibson, . . .; Virginia, 1637 ***6219*** *p82*
Gibson, Alexander; America, 1805 ***1639.20*** *p76*
Gibson, Alexander 68; South Carolina, 1850 ***1639.20*** *p76*
Gibson, Andrew; Philadelphia, 1811 ***53.26*** *p31*
Gibson, Andrew; Philadelphia, 1811 ***2859.11*** *p12*
Gibson, Andrew 21; St. John, N.B., 1864 ***5704.8*** *p157*
Gibson, Ann; Philadelphia, 1816 ***2859.11*** *p31*
Gibson, Ann; Philadelphia, 1848 ***5704.8*** *p40*
Gibson, Biddy; Philadelphia, 1848 ***5704.8*** *p40*
Gibson, Catherine 26; St. John, N.B., 1864 ***5704.8*** *p157*
Gibson, Christian 50; St. John, N.B., 1864 ***5704.8*** *p157*
Gibson, David; New York, NY, 1840 ***8208.4*** *p104*
Gibson, David; Philadelphia, 1811 ***2859.11*** *p12*
Gibson, David 57; South Carolina, 1850 ***1639.20*** *p76*
Gibson, Eassy Ann; St. John, N.B., 1853 ***5704.8*** *p107*
Gibson, Edward; Virginia, 1637 ***6219*** *p114*
Gibson, Edward 11; St. John, N.B., 1864 ***5704.8*** *p157*
Gibson, Eliza; Philadelphia, 1852 ***5704.8*** *p86*
Gibson, Elizabeth 17; Philadelphia, 1864 ***5704.8*** *p161*
Gibson, Elizabeth 19; Maryland, 1775 ***1219.7*** *p249*
Gibson, George; Illinois, 1866 ***5012.38*** *p98*
Gibson, George; New York, NY, 1834 ***8208.4*** *p33*
Gibson, George 36; North America, 1774 ***1219.7*** *p200*
Gibson, George 50; St. John, N.B., 1864 ***5704.8*** *p157*
Gibson, Hannah *SEE* Gibson, Jane
Gibson, Hannah; Philadelphia, 1847 ***5704.8*** *p31*
Gibson, Hugh; America, 1737 ***4971*** *p66*
Gibson, Hugh; New York, NY, 1816 ***2859.11*** *p31*
Gibson, James; New York, NY, 1816 ***2859.11*** *p31*
Gibson, James; Philadelphia, 1848 ***5704.8*** *p40*
Gibson, James 21; Quebec, 1853 ***5704.8*** *p105*
Gibson, James 34; St. Louis, 1889 ***1450.2*** *p50A*
Gibson, James G.; New York, NY, 1840 ***8208.4*** *p112*
Gibson, Jane; Montreal, 1823 ***7603*** *p68*
Gibson, Jane; Philadelphia, 1847 ***53.26*** *p31*
*Relative:*Hannah
Gibson, Jane; Philadelphia, 1847 ***5704.8*** *p31*
Gibson, Jane 10; Philadelphia, 1852 ***5704.8*** *p86*
Gibson, Jane Ann 2; Philadelphia, 1852 ***5704.8*** *p86*
Gibson, John; New York, NY, 1816 ***2859.11*** *p31*
Gibson, John; Philadelphia, 1847 ***53.26*** *p31*
*Relative:*Mary
Gibson, John; Philadelphia, 1847 ***5704.8*** *p14*
Gibson, John; Philadelphia, 1848 ***5704.8*** *p40*
Gibson, John; Virginia, 1635 ***6219*** *p73*
Gibson, John 8; Philadelphia, 1852 ***5704.8*** *p86*
Gibson, John 22; Maryland, 1775 ***1219.7*** *p249*
Gibson, John 22; Philadelphia, 1856 ***5704.8*** *p128*
Gibson, John 50; Philadelphia, 1803 ***53.26*** *p31*
Gibson, Jon.; Virginia, 1637 ***6219*** *p11*
Gibson, Jon.; Virginia, 1643 ***6219*** *p202*
Gibson, Joseph; Illinois, 1854 ***7857*** *p3*
Gibson, Joseph 16; America, 1700 ***2212*** *p33*
Gibson, Margaret; New York, NY, 1816 ***2859.11*** *p31*
Gibson, Margaret; Philadelphia, 1852 ***5704.8*** *p86*
Gibson, Martha 20; Philadelphia, 1857 ***5704.8*** *p132*
Gibson, Mary *SEE* Gibson, John
Gibson, Mary; Philadelphia, 1847 ***5704.8*** *p14*
Gibson, Mary 20; Philadelphia, 1861 ***5704.8*** *p147*
Gibson, Mary Ann 18; St. John, N.B., 1864 ***5704.8*** *p157*
Gibson, Nich.; Virginia, 1642 ***6219*** *p198*
Gibson, Nicholas; Virginia, 1638 ***6219*** *p123*
Gibson, Oliver 15; St. John, N.B., 1864 ***5704.8*** *p157*
Gibson, Robert; New York, NY, 1815 ***2859.11*** *p31*
Gibson, Robert; Philadelphia, 1811 ***2859.11*** *p12*
Gibson, Robert 30; Maryland or Virginia, 1736 ***3690.1*** *p87*
Gibson, Robert 37; Jamaica, 1730 ***3690.1*** *p87*
Gibson, Tho.; Virginia, 1639 ***6219*** *p154*
Gibson, Thomas; Iowa, 1866-1943 ***123.54*** *p19*
Gibson, Thomas; Virginia, 1647 ***6219*** *p248*
Gibson, Thomas 42; New Orleans, 1862 ***543.30*** *p384C*

174

FOR A COMPLETE EXPLANATION OF ENTRY, SEE "HOW TO READ A CITATION" SECTION

Gibson, Walter; Virginia, 1639 ***6219*** *p24*
Gibson, William; Charleston, SC, 1798 ***1639.20*** *p76*
Gibson, William; Philadelphia, 1811 ***2859.11*** *p12*
With family
Gibson, William 5; Philadelphia, 1852 ***5704.8*** *p86*
Gibson, William 19; Quebec, 1864 ***5704.8*** *p161*
Gibson, William B.; Arizona, 1882 ***2764.35*** *p28*
Gibson, Wm; Maryland or Virginia, 1697 ***2212*** *p3*
Giceppe, Pongetti; Wisconsin, n.d. ***9675.5*** *p190*
Gickey, Anne 6; New York, NY, 1867 ***5704.8*** *p218*
Gickey, Susan; New York, NY, 1867 ***5704.8*** *p218*
Gickey, William; New York, NY, 1867 ***5704.8*** *p218*
Gicquel, Madame 40; America, 1829 ***778.5*** *p238*
Gicquel, Miss 18; America, 1829 ***778.5*** *p238*
Giddes, Joseph; Iowa, 1866-1943 ***123.54*** *p19*
Giddings, Charles 32; Virginia, 1774 ***1219.7*** *p201*
Giddons, James 25; Jamaica, 1774 ***1219.7*** *p238*
Gide, Pierre 38; America, 1829 ***778.5*** *p238*
Gidio, Cialdini; Wisconsin, n.d. ***9675.5*** *p190*
Gidle, Lewis 39; West Virginia, 1902 ***9788.3*** *p11*
Gidney, John; Virginia, 1639 ***6219*** *p154*
Giecewicz, Walter; Arkansas, 1918 ***95.2*** *p48*
Giedricz, Marianna 18; New York, 1912 ***9980.29*** *p56*
Giefer, Mat. Joe; America, 1871 ***5240.1*** *p14*
Giekert, Henry; Philadelphia, 1760 ***9973.7*** *p34*
Giekie, James; North Carolina, 1774-1793 ***1639.20*** *p77*
Gielow, Carl; Wisconsin, n.d. ***9675.5*** *p190*
Gienger, Mr.; America, 1849 ***3702.7*** *p534*
Gienger, Christian; America, 1849-1900 ***3702.7*** *p534*
Giequal, Jane Marie 45; America, 1830 ***778.5*** *p238*
Gierke, William F.A.; America, 1894 ***1450.2*** *p50A*
Giers, Joseph; New York, 1754 ***3652*** *p80*
Giersch, Christian; New York, 1750 ***3652*** *p74*
Giershal, Friedrich 10; Port uncertain, 1839 ***778.5*** *p238*
Giershal, Georg 12; Port uncertain, 1839 ***778.5*** *p238*
Giershal, Georg 34; Port uncertain, 1839 ***778.5*** *p238*
Giershal, Henry 5; Port uncertain, 1839 ***778.5*** *p238*
Giershal, Henry 5; Port uncertain, 1839 ***778.5*** *p239*
Giershal, Julie 7; Port uncertain, 1839 ***778.5*** *p239*
Giershal, Louise 1; Port uncertain, 1839 ***778.5*** *p239*
Giershal, Marguerite 38; Port uncertain, 1839 ***778.5*** *p239*
Giershal, Philipp; Port uncertain, 1839 ***778.5*** *p239*
Gies, Geo. 35; New Orleans, 1862 ***543.30*** *p382C*
Gies, Konrad; Philadelphia, 1779 ***8137*** *p8*
Giesbrecht, Anna; Quebec, 1875 ***9980.20*** *p49*
Giesbrecht, Anna Fehr; Quebec, 1875 ***9980.20*** *p49*
Giesbrecht, Cornelius; Quebec, 1875 ***9980.20*** *p49*
Giesbrecht, Elisabeth; Quebec, 1875 ***9980.20*** *p49*
Giesbrecht, Isak; Quebec, 1875 ***9980.20*** *p49*
Giesbrecht, Jacob; Quebec, 1875 ***9980.20*** *p49*
Giesbrecht, Johann; Quebec, 1875 ***9980.20*** *p49*
Giesbrecht, Magaretha; Quebec, 1875 ***9980.20*** *p49*
Gieschen, Henry; San Francisco, 1865 ***3840.1*** *p18*
Giese, Mr.; Cincinnati, 1831 ***8582.1*** *p51*
Giese, Ella; Wisconsin, n.d. ***9675.5*** *p190*
Giese, Henrich; Philadelphia, 1779 ***8137*** *p8*
Giese, Irene M.; Wisconsin, n.d. ***9675.5*** *p190*
Giese, Johann Jost; Philadelphia, 1779 ***8137*** *p9*
Giese, Max; Wisconsin, n.d. ***9675.5*** *p190*
Giese, Siegfried; New York, NY, 1923 ***3455.4*** *p25*
Giese, William; Illinois, 1876 ***5012.39*** *p91*
Gieselmann, Ernst Friedrich Dietrich; America, 1892 ***4610.10*** *p110*
Giesen, . . .; Ohio, 1881 ***3702.7*** *p436*
Giesler, . . .; Canada, 1776-1783 ***9786*** *p22*
Giesselmann, Ernst Heinrich Wilhelm; America, 1857 ***4610.10*** *p105*
Giesselmann, Friedrich Wilhelm; America, 1852 ***4610.10*** *p116*
Giessleman, Michael; Philadelphia, 1761 ***9973.7*** *p35*
Giessler, Carl Gotth. 33; New Orleans, 1839 ***9420.2*** *p167*
*Wife:*Juliane 21
Giessler, Juliane 21 *SEE* Giessler, Carl Gotth.
Gieswein, Johann Adam; America, 1847 ***8582.3*** *p23*
Gietzen, Antony; Wisconsin, n.d. ***9675.5*** *p190*
Giezendanner, Anna Barbara Brunner *SEE* Giezendanner, Christian
Giezendanner, Christian; Philadelphia, 1729 ***2854*** *p44*
*Wife:*Anna Barbara Brunner
With son 6
With daughter 5
Giezendanner, John; America, 1856 ***1450.2*** *p50A*
Giffard, John 29; New Orleans, 1830 ***778.5*** *p239*
Giger, Jacob; Pennsylvania, 1744 ***2444*** *p157*
Giger, Jacob; Pennsylvania, 1751 ***2444*** *p157*
Giger, John; Ohio, 1830 ***9892.11*** *p16*
Giger, Philip; New York, NY, 1838 ***8208.4*** *p88*
Giger, Tobias; South Carolina, 1788 ***7119*** *p202*
Giglio, Salvador; Arkansas, 1918 ***95.2*** *p48*
Gigliotto, Paul 23; Arkansas, 1918 ***95.2*** *p48*
Gigliotto, Paul 23; Arkansas, 1918 ***95.2*** *p75*
Gihl, Claudius; Pittsburgh, 1854 ***1450.2*** *p50A*
Gil, Aniela Kaminska 25; New York, 1912 ***9980.29*** *p59*
*Daughter:*Franciszek 2
Gil, Franciszek 2 *SEE* Gil, Aniela Kaminska
Gil, Josef; Scranton, PA, 1912 ***9980.29*** *p59*
Gil, Julia 18; New York, 1912 ***9980.29*** *p61*
Gilber, Lewis; New York, NY, 1834 ***8208.4*** *p3*
Gilberd, William 18; Maryland, 1719 ***3690.1*** *p87*
Gilbert, . . .; Virginia, 1637 ***6219*** *p13*
Gilbert, Mr. 15; New Orleans, 1835 ***778.5*** *p239*
Gilbert, Adam H.; Wisconsin, n.d. ***9675.5*** *p190*
Gilbert, Ann; New York, NY, 1811 ***2859.11*** *p12*
Gilbert, Ann; South Carolina, 1767 ***1639.20*** *p77*
Gilbert, Armand 23; New Orleans, 1822 ***778.5*** *p239*
Gilbert, B. F.; Washington, 1859-1920 ***2872.1*** *p14*
Gilbert, Eliz.; Virginia, 1635 ***6219*** *p3*
Gilbert, Elizabeth; Virginia, 1637 ***6219*** *p86*
Gilbert, F. E.; Washington, 1859-1920 ***2872.1*** *p14*
Gilbert, George; Virginia, 1635 ***6219*** *p16*
Gilbert, George 33; Maryland, 1775 ***1219.7*** *p250*
Gilbert, James; America, 1871 ***1450.2*** *p50A*
Gilbert, James; San Francisco, 1850 ***6013.19*** *p30*
Gilbert, James; Wisconsin, n.d. ***9675.5*** *p190*
Gilbert, Jane; Virginia, 1643 ***6219*** *p204*
Gilbert, John; Canada, 1842 ***8893*** *p266*
*Wife:*Margaret Hosack
Gilbert, John; New York, NY, 1811 ***2859.11*** *p12*
Gilbert, John; Pennsylvania, 1682 ***4961*** *p13*
Gilbert, John 16; Virginia, 1774 ***1219.7*** *p243*
Gilbert, John 20; Maryland, 1774 ***1219.7*** *p214*
Gilbert, Joseph; Illinois, 1860 ***7857*** *p3*
Gilbert, Joseph; New York, NY, 1811 ***2859.11*** *p12*
Gilbert, Junian; South Carolina, 1767 ***1639.20*** *p77*
Gilbert, Margaret Hosack *SEE* Gilbert, John
Gilbert, Mary Ann; New York, NY, 1811 ***2859.11*** *p12*
Gilbert, Rich.; Virginia, 1637 ***6219*** *p107*
Gilbert, Robt.; Virginia, 1643 ***6219*** *p203*
Gilbert, Roger, Jr.; Virginia, 1645 ***6219*** *p253*
Gilbert, Roger, Sr.; Virginia, 1645 ***6219*** *p253*
Gilbert, Sam.; Virginia, 1645 ***6219*** *p240*
Gilbert, Thomas; Virginia, 1645 ***6219*** *p233*
Gilbert, Thomas 26; Maryland, 1775 ***1219.7*** *p255*
Gilbert, William 17; Maryland, 1774 ***1219.7*** *p204*
Gilbert, William 18; Maryland, 1719 ***3690.1*** *p87*
Gilbert, William 25; Jamaica, 1775 ***1219.7*** *p253*
Gilbise, Mary; Philadelphia, 1864 ***5704.8*** *p180*
Gilboa, Mr. 53; Port uncertain, 1835 ***778.5*** *p239*
Gilborson, Charles 22; Kansas, 1886 ***5240.1*** *p68*
Gilbraith, John 16; St. John, N.B., 1854 ***5704.8*** *p114*
Gilbraith, Rebecca 48; St. John, N.B., 1854 ***5704.8*** *p114*
Gilbraith, William 18; St. John, N.B., 1854 ***5704.8*** *p114*
Gilburt, John; Virginia, 1698 ***2212*** *p14*
Gilchrest, Isabella; Quebec, 1804 ***7603*** *p37*
Gilchrist, Angus 25; Wilmington, NC, 1774 ***1639.20*** *p77*
Gilchrist, Catherine 30 *SEE* Gilchrist, James
Gilchrist, Eliza; Philadelphia, 1864 ***5704.8*** *p172*
Gilchrist, George 32 *SEE* Gilchrist, James
Gilchrist, Isabella 60; North Carolina, 1850 ***1639.20*** *p77*
*Relative:*Mary 50
Gilchrist, James; Philadelphia, 1864 ***5704.8*** *p173*
Gilchrist, James 60; North Carolina, 1850 ***1639.20*** *p77*
*Relative:*George 32
*Relative:*Catherine 30
Gilchrist, John; North Carolina, 1770 ***1639.20*** *p77*
Gilchrist, John 25; Wilmington, NC, 1774 ***1639.20*** *p77*
*Wife:*Marion Taylor 21
Gilchrist, Margaret; Died enroute, 1680-1736 ***1639.20*** *p291*
Gilchrist, Margaret; Quebec, 1852 ***5704.8*** *p94*
Gilchrist, Margaret 55; North Carolina, 1850 ***1639.20*** *p77*
Gilchrist, Marion Taylor 21 *SEE* Gilchrist, John
Gilchrist, Mary 50 *SEE* Gilchrist, Isabella
Gilchrist, Susan; Philadelphia, 1864 ***5704.8*** *p172*
Gilchrist, Thomas 27; Maryland, 1774 ***1219.7*** *p235*
Gilchrist, William; Charleston, SC, 1821 ***1639.20*** *p77*
Gilchrist, William 60; Kansas, 1871 ***5240.1*** *p52*
Gildart, John 19; North America, 1774 ***1219.7*** *p200*
Gildart, Joshua 48; North America, 1774 ***1219.7*** *p200*
Gildart, Richard 30; New York, 1774 ***1219.7*** *p218*
Gilday, John 22; Massachusetts, 1848 ***5881.1*** *p42*
Gilday, Michael 40; New Orleans, 1862 ***543.30*** *p382C*
Gildea, Alice; Philadelphia, 1867 ***5704.8*** *p215*
Gilder, Henry; South Carolina, 1788 ***7119*** *p199*
Gildner, . . .; Canada, 1776-1783 ***9786*** *p22*
Gildner, Marg. Mog 76; America, 1895 ***1763*** *p40D*
Gildner, Simon; Canada, 1776-1783 ***9786*** *p207A*
Gileault, Nicolas 39; New Orleans, 1837 ***778.5*** *p239*
Giles, Agnes; New York, NY, 1864 ***5704.8*** *p169*
Giles, Ed.; America, 1740 ***4971*** *p66*
Giles, Georg; Virginia, 1639 ***6219*** *p154*
Giles, Henry; Virginia, 1635 ***6219*** *p16*
Giles, Henry 44; Kansas, 1876 ***5240.1*** *p57*
Giles, James; New York, NY, 1839 ***8208.4*** *p102*
Giles, James; Virginia, 1639 ***6219*** *p181*
Giles, John; New York, NY, 1811 ***2859.11*** *p12*
Giles, John; Virginia, 1635 ***6219*** *p69*
Giles, John; Virginia, 1639 ***6219*** *p154*
Giles, John; Virginia, 1642 ***6219*** *p189*
Giles, John 32; Tortola, 1773 ***1219.7*** *p172*
Giles, Robert; New York, NY, 1839 ***8208.4*** *p92*
Giles, Robert 19; Maryland, 1723 ***3690.1*** *p87*
Gilespie, Mr.; Quebec, 1815 ***9229.18*** *p74*
Gilet, Mme. 30; Port uncertain, 1836 ***778.5*** *p239*
Gilet, Francois 24; America, 1838 ***778.5*** *p239*
Gilfeather, Arthur; Washington, 1859-1920 ***2872.1*** *p14*
Gilfeather, James; New York, NY, 1836 ***8208.4*** *p22*
Gilfelland, Ann; Philadelphia, 1851 ***5704.8*** *p76*
Gilfillan, Anne; Philadelphia, 1864 ***5704.8*** *p182*
Gilfillan, James; Philadelphia, 1866 ***5704.8*** *p214*
Gilfillan, Jane 16; Philadelphia, 1853 ***5704.8*** *p109*
Gilfillan, Margaret; Philadelphia, 1850 ***53.26*** *p32*
Gilfillan, Margaret; Philadelphia, 1850 ***5704.8*** *p68*
Gilfillan, Margaret; Philadelphia, 1866 ***5704.8*** *p214*
Gilfillan, Matilda; Philadelphia, 1852 ***5704.8*** *p85*
Gilfillin, John; New York, NY, 1816 ***2859.11*** *p31*
Gilfoile, William; Montreal, 1818 ***7603*** *p93*
Gilfoyle, Micahel; Illinois, 1866 ***2896.5*** *p14*
Gilgodan, Mary 16; Massachusetts, 1849 ***5881.1*** *p43*
Gilgulin, Catherine 18; St. John, N.B., 1864 ***5704.8*** *p159*
Gilgulin, Daniel 16; St. John, N.B., 1864 ***5704.8*** *p159*
Gilhaus, Gerhard W.; America, 1851 ***8582.3*** *p23*
Giligan, Andrew; New Orleans, 1848 ***1450.2*** *p50A*
Gilks, Edward 22; North Carolina, 1774 ***1219.7*** *p215*
Gill, Mrs.; Philadelphia, 1774 ***1219.7*** *p224*
With children
Gill, Ann *SEE* Gill, Stephen
Gill, Ann 10 *SEE* Gill, Richard
Gill, Ann 46 *SEE* Gill, Richard
Gill, Annie 6; New York, NY, 1865 ***5704.8*** *p197*
Gill, Biddy; St. John, N.B., 1847 ***5704.8*** *p24*
Gill, Catherine 17; Wilmington, DE, 1831 ***6508.7*** *p160*
Gill, Dennis; America, 1739 ***4971*** *p14*
Gill, Edw.; Virginia, 1636 ***6219*** *p21*
Gill, Elizabeth; Philadelphia, 1852 ***5704.8*** *p84*
Gill, Elizabeth 20; Philadelphia, 1774 ***1219.7*** *p196*
Gill, Henry; South Carolina, 1716 ***1639.20*** *p78*
Gill, James; Quebec, 1847 ***5704.8*** *p29*
Gill, James 17; Virginia, 1699 ***2212*** *p27*
Gill, Jane 7; New York, NY, 1865 ***5704.8*** *p197*
Gill, John; New York, NY, 1837 ***8208.4*** *p35*
Gill, John; Philadelphia, 1850 ***5704.8*** *p60*
Gill, John; Philadelphia, 1851 ***5704.8*** *p70*
Gill, Jon.; Virginia, 1636 ***6219*** *p32*
Gill, Jon.; Virginia, 1637 ***6219*** *p113*
Gill, Joseph; Iowa, 1866-1943 ***123.54*** *p19*
Gill, Mary; America, 1738 ***4971*** *p33*
Gill, Mary; New York, NY, 1865 ***5704.8*** *p197*
Gill, Mary; Philadelphia, 1851 ***5704.8*** *p71*
Gill, Mary; Philadelphia, 1851 ***5704.8*** *p79*
Gill, Mary 1; St. John, N.B., 1847 ***5704.8*** *p35*
Gill, Mary 11; New York, NY, 1865 ***5704.8*** *p197*
Gill, Michael; Philadelphia, 1853 ***5704.8*** *p101*
Gill, Owen; Philadelphia, 1851 ***5704.8*** *p71*
Gill, Patrick; New York, NY, 1865 ***5704.8*** *p197*
Gill, Patrick; Philadelphia, 1849 ***53.26*** *p32*
Gill, Patrick; Philadelphia, 1849 ***5704.8*** *p54*
Gill, Peggy; St. John, N.B., 1847 ***5704.8*** *p24*
Gill, Peter 38?; Arizona, 1890 ***2764.35*** *p27*
Gill, Pier.. 20; America, 1839 ***778.5*** *p239*
Gill, Richard; Virginia, 1643 ***6219*** *p204*
Gill, Richard 6 *SEE* Gill, Richard
Gill, Richard 40; New York, 1774 ***1219.7*** *p202*
*Wife:*Sarah 41
*Child:*Ann 10
*Child:*Richard 6
*Sister:*Ann 46
Gill, Roger; St. John, N.B., 1853 ***5704.8*** *p98*
Gill, Rosy 24; St. John, N.B., 1854 ***5704.8*** *p115*
Gill, Sarah; New York, NY, 1870 ***5704.8*** *p238*
Gill, Sarah; Philadelphia, 1851 ***5704.8*** *p70*
Gill, Sarah; St. John, N.B., 1847 ***5704.8*** *p35*
Gill, Sarah 41 *SEE* Gill, Richard
Gill, Stephen; Virginia, 1636 ***6219*** *p13*
*Wife:*Ann
Gill, Stephen; Virginia, 1642 ***6219*** *p199*
Gill, Thomas; New York, NY, 1864 ***5704.8*** *p171*
Gill, Unity; St. John, N.B., 1853 ***5704.8*** *p98*
Gill, William; Virginia, 1635 ***6219*** *p71*
Gill, William 30; Virginia, 1774 ***1219.7*** *p244*
Gill, Winne 21; Massachusetts, 1849 ***5881.1*** *p44*
Gillan, Darby; New York, NY, 1815 ***2859.11*** *p31*
Gillan, Sally; New York, NY, 1815 ***2859.11*** *p31*
Gilland, Richard 22; Philadelphia, 1861 ***5704.8*** *p148*
Gillane, John 8; Massachusetts, 1849 ***5881.1*** *p43*
Gillane, Kate 10; Massachusetts, 1849 ***5881.1*** *p43*
Gillane, Mary 6; Massachusetts, 1849 ***5881.1*** *p43*

Gillane, Mary 46; Massachusetts, 1849 ***5881.1*** *p43*
Gillane, Maurice; America, 1736 ***4971*** *p44*
Gillane, Maurice; America, 1737 ***4971*** *p45*
Gillard, Pierre 42; New Orleans, 1838 ***778.5*** *p239*
Gillard, Thomas 21; Maryland, 1774 ***1219.7*** *p184*
Gillaspie, James; Philadelphia, 1811 ***2859.11*** *p12*
Gillberg, Andrew; Iowa, 1866-1943 ***123.54*** *p19*
Gillberg, Ernst; Wisconsin, n.d. ***9675.5*** *p190*
Gille, . . .; Canada, 1776-1783 ***9786*** *p22*
Gilleece, Judy; St. John, N.B., 1847 ***5704.8*** *p25*
Gilleise, Patrick 24; Philadelphia, 1861 ***5704.8*** *p149*
Gillen, . . . 7; America, 1864 ***5704.8*** *p179*
Gillen, Ann 20; Philadelphia, 1859 ***5704.8*** *p141*
Gillen, Anthony 18; Quebec, 1853 ***5704.8*** *p105*
Gillen, Biddy; St. John, N.B., 1851 ***5704.8*** *p72*
Gillen, Bridget; Quebec, 1852 ***5704.8*** *p89*
Gillen, Catherine 52; Quebec, 1853 ***5704.8*** *p105*
Gillen, Daniel; St. John, N.B., 1851 ***5704.8*** *p72*
Gillen, Dennis 29; West Virginia, 1855 ***9788.3*** *p11*
Gillen, Elizabeth; Philadelphia, 1852 ***5704.8*** *p86*
Gillen, Elizabeth; St. John, N.B., 1847 ***5704.8*** *p18*
Gillen, Ellen 18; St. John, N.B., 1858 ***5704.8*** *p137*
Gillen, Francis; America, 1864 ***5704.8*** *p179*
Gillen, George 13; St. John, N.B., 1847 ***5704.8*** *p18*
Gillen, George 20; Philadelphia, 1854 ***5704.8*** *p118*
Gillen, Henry; New York, NY, 1815 ***2859.11*** *p31*
Gillen, Henry; Philadelphia, 1865 ***5704.8*** *p201*
Gillen, Isabella 6; St. John, N.B., 1847 ***5704.8*** *p15*
Gillen, James; St. John, N.B., 1847 ***5704.8*** *p18*
Gillen, James 6; St. John, N.B., 1847 ***5704.8*** *p18*
Gillen, James 11; St. John, N.B., 1852 ***5704.8*** *p92*
Gillen, John; New York, NY, 1816 ***2859.11*** *p31*
Gillen, John; Philadelphia, 1864 ***5704.8*** *p181*
Gillen, John; St. John, N.B., 1847 ***5704.8*** *p15*
Gillen, John; St. John, N.B., 1847 ***5704.8*** *p18*
Gillen, John 8; St. John, N.B., 1847 ***5704.8*** *p15*
Gillen, John 13; St. John, N.B., 1852 ***5704.8*** *p92*
Gillen, Martin; New York, NY, 1836 ***8208.4*** *p21*
Gillen, Mary; Philadelphia, 1864 ***5704.8*** *p184*
Gillen, Mary; St. John, N.B., 1847 ***5704.8*** *p18*
Gillen, Mary 20; St. John, N.B., 1856 ***5704.8*** *p131*
Gillen, Mary 25; Quebec, 1853 ***5704.8*** *p105*
Gillen, Nancy; St. John, N.B., 1847 ***5704.8*** *p15*
Gillen, Patrick; New York, NY, 1816 ***2859.11*** *p31*
Gillen, Patrick; St. John, N.B., 1851 ***5704.8*** *p72*
Gillen, Patrick 5; St. John, N.B., 1847 ***5704.8*** *p15*
Gillen, Rosy; St. John, N.B., 1851 ***5704.8*** *p72*
Gillen, Thomas 17; Maryland, 1774 ***1219.7*** *p221*
Gillen, William; Philadelphia, 1865 ***5704.8*** *p189*
Gillen, William; St. John, N.B., 1847 ***5704.8*** *p18*
Gillen, William 20; Quebec, 1853 ***5704.8*** *p105*
Gillen, William 50; Quebec, 1853 ***5704.8*** *p105*
Giller, Jacob; New York, NY, 1811 ***2859.11*** *p12*
Gilles, Angus *SEE* Gilles, Archibald
Gilles, Angus *SEE* Gilles, Murdo
Gilles, Angus; Nova Scotia, 1830 ***7085.4*** *p44*
*Wife:*Flora
Gilles, Archibald *SEE* Gilles, John
Gilles, Archibald; Nova Scotia, 1830 ***7085.4*** *p44*
*Wife:*Ket
*Child:*Murdo
*Child:*Margaret
*Child:*Angus
Gilles, Christy *SEE* Gilles, John
Gilles, Christy *SEE* Gilles, Murdo
Gilles, Donald *SEE* Gilles, Murdo
Gilles, Duncan *SEE* Gilles, John
Gilles, Flora *SEE* Gilles, Angus
Gilles, Flora *SEE* Gilles, John
Gilles, James *SEE* Gilles, Murdo
Gilles, Jannet *SEE* Gilles, John
Gilles, John *SEE* Gilles, John
Gilles, John; Nova Scotia, 1830 ***7085.4*** *p44*
*Wife:*Flora
*Child:*Sarah
*Child:*Duncan
*Child:*Mary
*Child:*Archibald
*Child:*Christy
Gilles, John; Nova Scotia, 1830 ***7085.4*** *p44*
*Wife:*Jannet
*Child:*John
Gilles, K. 61; North Carolina, 1850 ***1639.20*** *p79*
Gilles, Ket *SEE* Gilles, Archibald
Gilles, Malcolm *SEE* Gilles, Murdo
Gilles, Margaret *SEE* Gilles, Archibald
Gilles, Margaret *SEE* Gilles, Murdo
Gilles, Mary *SEE* Gilles, John
Gilles, Murdo *SEE* Gilles, Archibald
Gilles, Murdo; Nova Scotia, 1830 ***7085.4*** *p44*
*Wife:*Margaret
*Child:*Christy
*Child:*Angus
*Child:*Malcolm
*Child:*James
*Child:*Donald
*Child:*Susan
Gilles, Sarah *SEE* Gilles, John
Gilles, Susan *SEE* Gilles, Murdo
Gillespie, Alice; Quebec, 1852 ***5704.8*** *p86*
Gillespie, Alice; Quebec, 1852 ***5704.8*** *p91*
Gillespie, Ann; St. John, N.B., 1851 ***5704.8*** *p79*
Gillespie, Archibald 38; Quebec, 1855 ***5704.8*** *p126*
Gillespie, Biddy; St. John, N.B., 1848 ***5704.8*** *p39*
Gillespie, Bridget; St. John, N.B., 1851 ***5704.8*** *p77*
Gillespie, Catherine; St. John, N.B., 1851 ***5704.8*** *p72*
Gillespie, Catherine 25; Philadelphia, 1860 ***5704.8*** *p146*
Gillespie, Charles; Philadelphia, 1852 ***5704.8*** *p87*
Gillespie, Clements; St. John, N.B., 1847 ***5704.8*** *p35*
Gillespie, Cornelius; Philadelphia, 1866 ***5704.8*** *p211*
Gillespie, Daniel; St. John, N.B., 1847 ***5704.8*** *p3*
Gillespie, Dennis 24; Massachusetts, 1847 ***5881.1*** *p41*
Gillespie, Eliza; New York, NY, 1816 ***2859.11*** *p31*
Gillespie, Ellan; St. John, N.B., 1847 ***5704.8*** *p33*
Gillespie, Ellen 16; St. John, N.B., 1855 ***5704.8*** *p127*
Gillespie, Fanny; New York, NY, 1811 ***2859.11*** *p12*
Gillespie, Francis; New York, NY, 1811 ***2859.11*** *p12*
Gillespie, Frank; America, 1864 ***5704.8*** *p184*
Gillespie, George; America, 1700 ***1639.20*** *p80*
Gillespie, Hannah; Philadelphia, 1864 ***5704.8*** *p175*
Gillespie, Harriet; Philadelphia, 1867 ***5704.8*** *p213*
Gillespie, Henry; St. John, N.B., 1847 ***5704.8*** *p25*
Gillespie, Isabella; New York, NY, 1815 ***2859.11*** *p31*
Gillespie, James; New York, NY, 1816 ***2859.11*** *p31*
Gillespie, James; Philadelphia, 1811 ***53.26*** *p32*
Gillespie, James; Philadelphia, 1847 ***53.26*** *p32*
Gillespie, James; Philadelphia, 1847 ***5704.8*** *p14*
Gillespie, James; Philadelphia, 1849 ***53.26*** *p32*
*Relative:*John
Gillespie, James; Philadelphia, 1849 ***5704.8*** *p53*
Gillespie, James; Quebec, 1851 ***5704.8*** *p75*
Gillespie, James 9 mos; Quebec, 1852 ***5704.8*** *p86*
Gillespie, James 9 mos; Quebec, 1852 ***5704.8*** *p91*
Gillespie, James 10; St. John, N.B., 1855 ***5704.8*** *p127*
Gillespie, Jane; New York, NY, 1868 ***5704.8*** *p229*
Gillespie, Jane 20; Philadelphia, 1860 ***5704.8*** *p145*
Gillespie, John *SEE* Gillespie, James
Gillespie, John; America, 1849 ***1450.2*** *p50A*
Gillespie, John; Philadelphia, 1849 ***5704.8*** *p53*
Gillespie, John; Philadelphia, 1852 ***5704.8*** *p97*
Gillespie, John 17; St. John, N.B., 1854 ***5704.8*** *p120*
Gillespie, Lecke; Philadelphia, 1864 ***5704.8*** *p178*
Gillespie, Margaret; America, 1864 ***5704.8*** *p180*
Gillespie, Margaret; Philadelphia, 1865 ***5704.8*** *p197*
Gillespie, Margaret; Quebec, 1852 ***5704.8*** *p87*
Gillespie, Margaret 16; Philadelphia, 1860 ***5704.8*** *p145*
Gillespie, Maria 12; Philadelphia, 1860 ***5704.8*** *p144*
Gillespie, Maria 28; Massachusetts, 1848 ***5881.1*** *p43*
Gillespie, Mary; New York, NY, 1816 ***2859.11*** *p31*
Gillespie, Mary; Philadelphia, 1864 ***5704.8*** *p172*
Gillespie, Mary; St. John, N.B., 1850 ***5704.8*** *p66*
Gillespie, Mary 22; Philadelphia, 1864 ***5704.8*** *p161*
Gillespie, Mary Ann; Philadelphia, 1850 ***5704.8*** *p64*
Gillespie, Mary Anne; New York, NY, 1816 ***2859.11*** *p31*
Gillespie, Mathew; Ohio, 1812-1840 ***9892.11*** *p16*
Gillespie, Michael; New York, NY, 1811 ***2859.11*** *p12*
Gillespie, Michael; Philadelphia, 1852 ***5704.8*** *p87*
Gillespie, Michael; Quebec, 1852 ***5704.8*** *p86*
Gillespie, Michael; Quebec, 1852 ***5704.8*** *p91*
Gillespie, Michael 19; Philadelphia, 1854 ***5704.8*** *p123*
Gillespie, Nancy; Philadelphia, 1866 ***5704.8*** *p211*
Gillespie, Neal; St. John, N.B., 1852 ***5704.8*** *p83*
Gillespie, Owen; Ohio, 1855 ***3840.1*** *p18*
Gillespie, Owen 9; Quebec, 1852 ***5704.8*** *p86*
Gillespie, Peter; New York, NY, 1864 ***5704.8*** *p185*
Gillespie, Rose; Philadelphia, 1864 ***5704.8*** *p172*
Gillespie, Sally; St. John, N.B., 1847 ***5704.8*** *p3*
Gillespie, Sally; St. John, N.B., 1851 ***5704.8*** *p72*
Gillespie, Sally 16; Philadelphia, 1860 ***5704.8*** *p144*
Gillespie, Sarah; St. John, N.B., 1851 ***5704.8*** *p77*
Gillespie, Susan; Philadelphia, 1851 ***5704.8*** *p80*
Gillespie, Thomas; America, 1817 ***1639.20*** *p80*
Gillespie, Thomas D.; New York, NY, 1835 ***8208.4*** *p37*
Gillespie, Unity; St. John, N.B., 1851 ***5704.8*** *p72*
Gillespie, Unity 2; Quebec, 1852 ***5704.8*** *p86*
Gillespie, Unity 2; Quebec, 1852 ***5704.8*** *p91*
Gillespie, William; Philadelphia, 1849 ***53.26*** *p32*
Gillespie, William; Philadelphia, 1849 ***5704.8*** *p54*
Gillespie, William; Philadelphia, 1851 ***5704.8*** *p78*
Gillespie, William; Philadelphia, 1852 ***5704.8*** *p84*
Gillespie, William 21; Massachusetts, 1850 ***5881.1*** *p44*
Gillespie, William 26; Quebec, 1853 ***5704.8*** *p105*
Gillespy, Patt 35; Philadelphia, 1804 ***53.26*** *p32*
*Relative:*Peggy 24
Gillespy, Peggy 24 *SEE* Gillespy, Patt
Gillett, John; Washington, 1859-1920 ***2872.1*** *p14*
Gillett, Jon.; Virginia, 1637 ***6219*** *p11*
Gillett, Thomas; Pennsylvania, 1682 ***4962*** *p152*
Gillfilland, Alison 8; Philadelphia, 1851 ***5704.8*** *p71*
Gillfilland, Eliza 11; Philadelphia, 1851 ***5704.8*** *p71*
Gillfilland, John 6; Philadelphia, 1851 ***5704.8*** *p71*
Gillfilland, Joseph; Philadelphia, 1851 ***5704.8*** *p71*
Gillfilland, Joseph 10; Philadelphia, 1851 ***5704.8*** *p71*
Gillfilland, Martha; Philadelphia, 1851 ***5704.8*** *p71*
Gillfilland, Nancy; Philadelphia, 1851 ***5704.8*** *p71*
Gillfilland, Robert; Philadelphia, 1851 ***5704.8*** *p71*
Gillgate, John; Virginia, 1638 ***6219*** *p33*
Gillgrass, Johie; Iowa, 1866-1943 ***123.54*** *p20*
Gillgrist, Law; Maryland or Virginia, 1697 ***2212*** *p3*
Gillhuber, John; Wisconsin, n.d. ***9675.5*** *p190*
Gilliat, Elizabeth 4 *SEE* Gilliat, William
Gilliat, Mary 1 *SEE* Gilliat, William
Gilliat, Rebecca 30 *SEE* Gilliat, William
Gilliat, William 3 *SEE* Gilliat, William
Gilliat, William 34; Nova Scotia, 1774 ***1219.7*** *p209*
*Wife:*Rebecca 30
*Child:*William 3
*Child:*Elizabeth 4
*Child:*Mary 1
Gilliaume, Celestin 32; New Orleans, 1862 ***543.30*** *p377C*
Gillie, James 21; Philadelphia, 1774 ***1219.7*** *p183*
Gillies, Alex *SEE* Gillies, Angus
Gillies, Angus *SEE* Gillies, Peter
Gillies, Angus; Quebec, 1855 ***4537.30*** *p12*
*Wife:*Catherine MacIver
*Child:*John
*Child:*Kirsty
*Child:*Mary Ann
*Child:*Alex
Gillies, Catherine MacIver *SEE* Gillies, Angus
Gillies, Christian 85; North Carolina, 1850 ***1639.20*** *p78*
Gillies, Donald; America, 1810 ***1639.20*** *p78*
Gillies, Duncan; America, 1810 ***1639.20*** *p78*
Gillies, Duncan; Quebec, 1790 ***9775.5*** *p198A*
With family of 6
Gillies, John *SEE* Gillies, Angus
Gillies, John; Quebec, 1790 ***9775.5*** *p198A*
With family of 3
Gillies, Kirsty *SEE* Gillies, Angus
Gillies, Margaret MacLean *SEE* Gillies, Peter
Gillies, Marion *SEE* Gillies, Peter
Gillies, Mary Ann *SEE* Gillies, Angus
Gillies, Norman; Quebec, 1838 ***4537.30*** *p12*
Gillies, Peter; Quebec, 1843 ***4537.30*** *p12*
*Wife:*Margaret MacLean
*Child:*Angus
*Child:*Marion
Gillies, Robert; North Carolina, 1776 ***1639.20*** *p80*
Gilligan, Daniel; New York, NY, 1839 ***8208.4*** *p94*
Gilligan, Hugh; California, 1871 ***2769.4*** *p5*
Gilligan, John; New York, NY, 1834 ***8208.4*** *p50*
Gilligan, John 25; New Orleans, 1862 ***543.30*** *p376C*
Gillilan, William; New York, NY, 1815 ***2859.11*** *p31*
Gilliland, William; New York, NY, 1837 ***8208.4*** *p53*
Gillin, Barbie 28; New Orleans, 1838 ***778.5*** *p240*
Gillin, Daniel 44; New Orleans, 1838 ***778.5*** *p240*
Gillin, Francis; New York, NY, 1815 ***2859.11*** *p31*
Gillin, Georg; Virginia, 1638 ***6219*** *p33*
Gillin, James; New York, NY, 1815 ***2859.11*** *p31*
Gillin, Margaret; New York, NY, 1815 ***2859.11*** *p32*
Gillinger, Etienne 22; America, 1831 ***778.5*** *p240*
Gillingham, Henry; Virginia, 1642 ***6219*** *p193*
Gillingham, Thomas 22; Pennsylvania, 1728 ***3690.1*** *p87*
Gillings, Edward 3; Massachusetts, 1848 ***5881.1*** *p41*
Gillings, Patrick 7; Massachusetts, 1848 ***5881.1*** *p44*
Gillings, Winnefred 30; Massachusetts, 1848 ***5881.1*** *p44*
With child
Gillis, Alexander; America, 1802 ***1639.20*** *p78*
Gillis, Alexander; Massachusetts, 1847 ***5881.1*** *p41*
Gillis, Archibald; America, 1788 ***1639.20*** *p78*
Gillis, Daniel 40 *SEE* Gillis, Nancy
Gillis, David W.; Arkansas, 1918 ***95.2*** *p48*
Gillis, Hector; America, 1811 ***1639.20*** *p78*
Gillis, John; America, 1788 ***1639.20*** *p78*
Gillis, John 45; North Carolina, 1850 ***1639.20*** *p79*
Gillis, Kenneth Edward; America, 1810 ***1639.20*** *p79*
Gillis, Malcolm; America, 1789 ***1639.20*** *p79*
Gillis, Malcolm; America, 1802 ***1639.20*** *p79*
Gillis, Malcolm; North Carolina, 1776-1862 ***1639.20*** *p79*
Gillis, Malcolm 85; North Carolina, 1850 ***1639.20*** *p79*
*Relative:*Mary 65
Gillis, Mary 60; North Carolina, 1850 ***1639.20*** *p79*
Gillis, Mary 65 *SEE* Gillis, Malcolm
Gillis, Nancy 67; North Carolina, 1850 ***1639.20*** *p79*
*Relative:*Daniel 40
Gillis, Neill; America, 1811 ***1639.20*** *p80*
Gillis, Norman; America, 1788 ***1639.20*** *p80*
Gillis, Roderick; America, 1789 ***1639.20*** *p80*

Gillis, Swain; America, 1788 ***1639.20*** *p80*
Gillispie, Andrew; Iowa, 1866-1943 ***123.54*** *p20*
Gillispie, Ann 35; St. John, N.B., 1854 ***5704.8*** *p122*
Gillispie, Bernard 34; St. John, N.B., 1853 ***5704.8*** *p110*
Gillispie, Connell 13; St. John, N.B., 1854 ***5704.8*** *p122*
Gillispie, Mary; America, 1741 ***4971*** *p74*
Gillispie, Mary 15; St. John, N.B., 1854 ***5704.8*** *p122*
Gillmer, Hugh 24; New Orleans, 1862 ***543.30*** *p374C*
Gilloby, Bridget 23; Massachusetts, 1849 ***5881.1*** *p41*
Gilloe, Alexander; Philadelphia, 1811 ***2859.11*** *p12*
Gillogley, Bell; St. John, N.B., 1847 ***5704.8*** *p33*
Gillogley, Christopher 6; St. John, N.B., 1847 ***5704.8*** *p33*
Gillogley, Ellan; St. John, N.B., 1847 ***5704.8*** *p33*
Gillogley, Hugh; St. John, N.B., 1847 ***5704.8*** *p33*
Gillogley, James; St. John, N.B., 1847 ***5704.8*** *p33*
Gillogley, Mary 9 mos; St. John, N.B., 1847 ***5704.8*** *p33*
Gillogley, Matilda 9; St. John, N.B., 1847 ***5704.8*** *p33*
Gillogley, Sally 3; St. John, N.B., 1847 ***5704.8*** *p33*
Gillogley, Susan 12; St. John, N.B., 1847 ***5704.8*** *p33*
Gillon, Alexander; Charleston, SC, 1775 ***8582.2*** *p51*
Gillon, Alexandre-Edouard; Quebec, 1822 ***7603*** *p38*
Gillon, Andrew 22; Philadelphia, 1859 ***5704.8*** *p141*
Gillooly, Patrick; America, 1864 ***6014.1*** *p2*
Gillott, Thomas; Pennsylvania, 1682 ***4962*** *p152*
Gillown, Anne; New York, NY, 1816 ***2859.11*** *p32*
Gillown, Owen; New York, NY, 1816 ***2859.11*** *p32*
Gills, Adam; Philadelphia, 1779 ***8137*** *p9*
Gills, Joseph; Philadelphia, 1848 ***53.26*** *p32*
Gills, Joseph; Philadelphia, 1848 ***5704.8*** *p45*
Gills, Owen; St. John, N.B., 1848 ***5704.8*** *p43*
Gillsepie, John 32; Quebec, 1862 ***5704.8*** *p152*
Gillson, James 18; Jamaica, 1729 ***3690.1*** *p87*
Gilly, Mr. 18; New Orleans, 1827 ***778.5*** *p240*
Gilly, William; America, 1840 ***7036*** *p118*
Gilman, Leonora 30; Philadelphia, 1774 ***1219.7*** *p228*
With 3 children
Gilman, Lewes; Virginia, 1652 ***6251*** *p20*
Gilman, Saul; Arkansas, 1918 ***95.2*** *p48*
Gilmartin, Dennis; America, 1735-1743 ***4971*** *p79*
Gilmartin, Patrick; New York, NY, 1838 ***8208.4*** *p85*
Gilmer, Samuel; New York, NY, 1811 ***2859.11*** *p12*
Gilmer, William; New York, NY, 1837 ***8208.4*** *p39*
Gilmor, Hugh; Quebec, 1830 ***4719.7*** *p21*
Gilmore, Christopher; New York, NY, 1816 ***2859.11*** *p32*
Gilmore, James; Philadelphia, 1816 ***2859.11*** *p32*
Gilmore, James; Philadelphia, 1852 ***5704.8*** *p91*
Gilmore, James; Philadelphia, 1853 ***5704.8*** *p113*
Gilmore, Jane; Philadelphia, 1853 ***5704.8*** *p113*
Gilmore, Jane 21; Quebec, 1864 ***5704.8*** *p159*
Gilmore, John; New York, NY, 1815 ***2859.11*** *p32*
Gilmore, John; New York, NY, 1816 ***2859.11*** *p32*
Gilmore, John; Philadelphia, 1851 ***5704.8*** *p76*
Gilmore, Margaret; New York, NY, 1816 ***2859.11*** *p32*
Gilmore, Mary; New York, NY, 1816 ***2859.11*** *p32*
Gilmore, Matthew; New York, NY, 1816 ***2859.11*** *p32*
Gilmore, Robert B.; America, 1892 ***1450.2*** *p50A*
Gilmore, Thomas; America, 1848 ***1450.2*** *p50A*
Gilmore, William; New York, NY, 1816 ***2859.11*** *p32*
Gilmore, William 30; Quebec, 1864 ***5704.8*** *p159*
Gilmore, William, Jr.; New York, NY, 1816 ***2859.11*** *p32*
Gilmour, Andy 9; Quebec, 1847 ***5704.8*** *p27*
Gilmour, Ann; Quebec, 1847 ***5704.8*** *p27*
Gilmour, Ann 15 *SEE* Gilmour, James
Gilmour, Felix; New York, NY, 1815 ***2859.11*** *p32*
Gilmour, Isabella; Quebec, 1847 ***5704.8*** *p27*
Gilmour, James; New York, NY, 1838 ***8208.4*** *p66*
Gilmour, James; Philadelphia, 1847 ***53.26*** *p32*
*Relative:*Ann 15
Gilmour, James; Philadelphia, 1847 ***5704.8*** *p1*
Gilmour, John; Philadelphia, 1811 ***53.26*** *p32*
Gilmour, John; Philadelphia, 1811 ***2859.11*** *p12*
Gilmour, John; Quebec, 1847 ***5704.8*** *p27*
Gilmour, John Alexander; New York, NY, 1838 ***8208.4*** *p66*
Gilmour, Joseph; New York, NY, 1816 ***2859.11*** *p32*
Gilmour, Mary; Quebec, 1847 ***5704.8*** *p27*
Gilmour, Mary Jane 20; Philadelphia, 1856 ***5704.8*** *p129*
Gilmour, Michael; New York, NY, 1815 ***2859.11*** *p32*
Gilmour, Robert; Philadelphia, 1851 ***5704.8*** *p80*
Gilmour, Robert; Quebec, 1847 ***5704.8*** *p27*
Gilmour, Samuel 20; Philadelphia, 1803 ***53.26*** *p32*
Gilmour, Thomas; Quebec, 1764 ***9775.5*** *p203*
Gilmour, Thomas 11; Quebec, 1847 ***5704.8*** *p27*
Gilois, Mr. 23; America, 1836 ***778.5*** *p240*
Gilroy, Alice; Quebec, 1847 ***5704.8*** *p8*
Gilroy, Daniel; Quebec, 1847 ***5704.8*** *p8*
Gilroy, Francis; St. John, N.B., 1847 ***5704.8*** *p15*
Gilroy, Mary; St. John, N.B., 1847 ***5704.8*** *p15*
Gilroy, Nancy; St. John, N.B., 1847 ***5704.8*** *p15*
Gilroy, Owen; Quebec, 1821 ***7603*** *p91*
Gilroy, P.; Quebec, 1847 ***5704.8*** *p8*
Gilroy, Patrick; New York, NY, 1839 ***8208.4*** *p99*
Gilroy, Patrick; St. John, N.B., 1847 ***5704.8*** *p15*
Gilsa, Colonel; New York, 1861-1865 ***8582.3*** *p91*
Gilson, John; New York, NY, 1816 ***2859.11*** *p32*
Gilson, John N.; Wisconsin, n.d. ***9675.5*** *p190*
Gilson, John Peter; Wisconsin, n.d. ***9675.5*** *p190*
Gilson, Margaret; Wisconsin, n.d. ***9675.5*** *p190*
Gilson, Michael; Wisconsin, n.d. ***9675.5*** *p190*
Gilson, Nicolas; Wisconsin, n.d. ***9675.5*** *p190*
Gilson, Philip; Wisconsin, n.d. ***9675.5*** *p190*
Gilson, Theodor; Wisconsin, n.d. ***9675.5*** *p190*
Gilston, Eliza Jane 4; Quebec, 1864 ***5704.8*** *p163*
Gilston, James 38; Quebec, 1864 ***5704.8*** *p163*
Gilston, Martha 9 mos; Quebec, 1864 ***5704.8*** *p163*
Gilston, Mary 29; Quebec, 1864 ***5704.8*** *p163*
Gilston, William 7; Quebec, 1864 ***5704.8*** *p163*
Gilstrap, John; America, 1739 ***4971*** *p14*
Gilwicks, Frederick; Philadelphia, 1760 ***9973.7*** *p34*
Gimaz, Carlos; Colorado, 1904 ***9678.2*** *p20*
Gimbel, Hans Henrich; Trenton, NJ, 1776 ***8137*** *p9*
Gimbel, Henrich; Philadelphia, 1779-1783 ***8137*** *p4*
Gimbel, Michael; New York, 1846 ***1450.2*** *p51A*
Gimbell, Henrich; Lancaster, PA, 1780 ***8137*** *p9*
Gimber, Nicholas; America, 1848 ***1450.2*** *p51A*
Gimble, . . .; Canada, 1776-1783 ***9786*** *p22*
Gimmele, Matthias; New York, 1754 ***3652*** *p80*
Gina, Marke; Virginia, 1643 ***6219*** *p206*
Ginalia, Michael 31; New Orleans, 1863 ***543.30*** *p378C*
Ginau, Mr. 22; New Orleans, 1839 ***778.5*** *p240*
Gincotite, J. 22; America, 1829 ***778.5*** *p240*
Gindele, Stephan; Chicago, 1700-1877 ***8582.3*** *p80*
Gingell, James 32; New York, 1775 ***1219.7*** *p246*
Gingley, George 28; Maryland, 1774 ***1219.7*** *p178*
Gingrass, Oliver V.; America, 1874 ***5240.1*** *p15*
Ginn, Elizabeth 14; Philadelphia, 1854 ***5704.8*** *p120*
Ginn, Ellen 33; Philadelphia, 1854 ***5704.8*** *p120*
Ginn, Mary Ann 2; Philadelphia, 1854 ***5704.8*** *p120*
Ginn, Matilda 5; Philadelphia, 1854 ***5704.8*** *p120*
Ginn, Robert 20; Antigua (Antego), 1728 ***3690.1*** *p88*
Ginn, Thomas 16; Maryland, 1730 ***3690.1*** *p88*
Ginnanane, Ellenor; America, 1743 ***4971*** *p43*
Ginnerty, Patrick 24; Massachusetts, 1850 ***5881.1*** *p44*
Ginness, Robert; Philadelphia, 1851 ***5704.8*** *p81*
Ginnings, Mr. 25; Carolina, 1774 ***1219.7*** *p215*
Ginocchio, Henry; Arkansas, 1918 ***95.2*** *p48*
Ginsberg, Harry; Iowa, 1866-1943 ***123.54*** *p20*
Ginsberg, Sol; Iowa, 1866-1943 ***123.54*** *p20*
Ginsel, Fred'k 28; Philadelphia, 1753 ***2444*** *p171*
Gintner, Augustinus; Pennsylvania, 1749 ***2444*** *p157*
Gintner, Johannes; Pennsylvania, 1748 ***2444*** *p194*
Gintner, Johannes 30; Pennsylvania, 1748 ***2444*** *p157*
Giocomoni, Csore; Wisconsin, n.d. ***9675.5*** *p190*
Giordano, Giacomo; Arkansas, 1918 ***95.2*** *p48*
Giorvzia, Ferdinando; Arkansas, 1918 ***95.2*** *p48*
Giorzelli, Peter; Colorado, 1904 ***9678.2*** *p20*
Giovani, Genesio; Colorado, 1898 ***9678.2*** *p20*
Giovanni, Bolzan 31; West Virginia, 1903 ***9788.3*** *p11*
Giovanni, Zucco; Iowa, 1866-1943 ***123.54*** *p20*
Giovinco, Tony; Arkansas, 1918 ***95.2*** *p48*
Gir-Fray, Mr. 30; America, 1827 ***778.5*** *p240*
Giraghty, Daniel; America, 1738 ***4971*** *p85*
Girard, Mme. 21; New Orleans, 1829 ***778.5*** *p241*
Girard, Mr. 24; America, 1839 ***778.5*** *p240*
Girard, Mr. 35; New Orleans, 1827 ***778.5*** *p240*
Girard, Mr. 35; New Orleans, 1829 ***778.5*** *p241*
Girard, Ant.; New Orleans, 1839 ***778.5*** *p240*
Girard, Eloi 14 mos; New Orleans, 1829 ***778.5*** *p240*
Girard, Guillaume; Quebec, 1791 ***7603*** *p48*
Girard, Guillaume Francois; Port uncertain, 1839 ***778.5*** *p240*
Girard, Jacques 34; New Orleans, 1832 ***778.5*** *p240*
Girard, Mrs. T. 34; New Orleans, 1836 ***778.5*** *p241*
Girard, Thomas 31; New Orleans, 1836 ***778.5*** *p241*
Girardeau, J. 33; America, 1826 ***778.5*** *p241*
Girardin, A. 30; Port uncertain, 1836 ***778.5*** *p241*
Girardo, Tony; Colorado, 1904 ***9678.2*** *p20*
Girardot, Mlle. 25; New Orleans, 1829 ***778.5*** *p241*
Girau, Mr. 22; New Orleans, 1839 ***778.5*** *p240*
Giraud, Mme. 25; New Orleans, 1838 ***778.5*** *p241*
Giraud, Mr. 25; New Orleans, 1838 ***778.5*** *p241*
Giraudeau, Mr. 32; New Orleans, 1826 ***778.5*** *p241*
Girault, Mrs. 40; America, 1835 ***778.5*** *p241*
Girault, A. 50; America, 1839 ***778.5*** *p241*
Girault, Aug. 50; America, 1835 ***778.5*** *p241*
Girbeau Adelle, Mr. 45; America, 1827 ***778.5*** *p241*
Girczis, John; Wisconsin, n.d. ***9675.5*** *p190*
Girczis, Julius; Wisconsin, n.d. ***9675.5*** *p190*
Girdler, Charles 17; Maryland, 1775 ***1219.7*** *p267*
Gireaudeau, Mr. 24; Port uncertain, 1836 ***778.5*** *p241*
Girilli, Albans; Arkansas, 1918 ***95.2*** *p48*
Girod, Mr. 22; America, 1832 ***778.5*** *p242*
Girod, Mr. 28; Port uncertain, 1836 ***778.5*** *p242*
Girod, Michel 23; New Orleans, 1822 ***778.5*** *p242*
Girolamo, Giuseppe; Arkansas, 1918 ***95.2*** *p48*
Girondeau, Francois 40; Port uncertain, 1838 ***778.5*** *p242*
Giroux, Theodore F.; Colorado, 1895 ***9678.2*** *p21*
Girraghty, Daniel; America, 1738 ***4971*** *p95*
Girrens, John Joseph 21; Kansas, 1881 ***5240.1*** *p15*
Girrens, John Joseph 21; Kansas, 1881 ***5240.1*** *p63*
Girsewald, v., Cap.; Quebec, 1776 ***9786*** *p105*
Girsewald, Ernst Heinrich Wilhelm; Quebec, 1776 ***9786*** *p256*
Girvan, John; St. John, N.B., 1853 ***5704.8*** *p99*
Girvin, Ann 8; St. John, N.B., 1852 ***5704.8*** *p93*
Girvin, John; St. John, N.B., 1852 ***5704.8*** *p93*
Gisch, Mattes; Philadelphia, 1733 ***4349*** *p48*
Gisch, Matthes; America, 1733 ***4349*** *p48*
Gisel, John 18; St. John, N.B., 1855 ***5704.8*** *p126*
Gisel, Margaret 19; St. John, N.B., 1855 ***5704.8*** *p126*
Gisfry, Richard; Virginia, 1642 ***6219*** *p197*
Gisgen, Margarethe; America, 1853 ***3702.7*** *p340*
Gisladottir, Gisli 4; Quebec, 1879 ***2557.1*** *p38*
Gisladottir, Helga 37; Quebec, 1879 ***2557.1*** *p39A*
Gisladottir, Rosa 34; Quebec, 1879 ***2557.1*** *p38*
Gislason, Adalbjorg 43 *SEE* Gislason, Bjorn
Gislason, Arni *SEE* Gislason, Bjorn
Gislason, Bjorn 5 *SEE* Gislason, Bjorn
Gislason, Bjorn 52; Quebec, 1879 ***2557.1*** *p22*
*Wife:*Adalbjorg 43
*Relative:*Olof 12
*Relative:*Thorvaldur 9
*Relative:*Jon 7
*Relative:*Bjorn 5
*Relative:*Ingibjorg 6
*Relative:*Halldor 3
*Relative:*Arni
Gislason, Grimur 48; Quebec, 1879 ***2557.1*** *p22*
Gislason, Gudmundur 60; Quebec, 1879 ***2557.1*** *p38A*
Gislason, Halldor 3 *SEE* Gislason, Bjorn
Gislason, Ingibjorg 6 *SEE* Gislason, Bjorn
Gislason, Jon 7 *SEE* Gislason, Bjorn
Gislason, Olof 12 *SEE* Gislason, Bjorn
Gislason, Sigvaldi 50; Quebec, 1879 ***2557.1*** *p22*
Gislason, Thorvaldur 9 *SEE* Gislason, Bjorn
Gislasson, Bjorn 52; Quebec, 1879 ***2557.1*** *p22*
Gislayson, Grimur 48; Quebec, 1879 ***2557.1*** *p22*
Gisler, Conrad; America, 1880 ***1450.2*** *p51A*
Gislow, . . .; Canada, 1776-1783 ***9786*** *p22*
Gisowska, Stanislawa 23; New York, 1912 ***9980.29*** *p56*
Giss, Jane 17; Baltimore, 1775 ***1219.7*** *p269*
Gissen, . . .; Ohio, 1881 ***3702.7*** *p430*
Gissler, George; South Carolina, 1788 ***7119*** *p200*
Gissomi, Joseph; Arkansas, 1918 ***95.2*** *p48*
Giszkiwiz, Steve; Arkansas, 1918 ***95.2*** *p48*
Gite, Jozefa 28; New York, 1912 ***9980.29*** *p55*
Gitins, Thomas 18; Pennsylvania, 1730 ***3690.1*** *p88*
Gitrin, Nicolas Charles 36; Ohio, 1820 ***778.5*** *p242*
Gittally, John 20; Massachusetts, 1847 ***5881.1*** *p42*
Gittally, Mary 30; Massachusetts, 1847 ***5881.1*** *p43*
Gittens, Bridget 20; Quebec, 1853 ***5704.8*** *p105*
Gittens, Owen 23; Quebec, 1853 ***5704.8*** *p105*
Gittinger, John; Philadelphia, 1760 ***9973.7*** *p34*
Gittrich, Albert; Kansas, 1884 ***5240.1*** *p15*
Gitty, James; New York, NY, 1816 ***2859.11*** *p32*
Gitty, John; New York, NY, 1816 ***2859.11*** *p32*
Giuffre, Joseph; America, 1896 ***1450.2*** *p51A*
Giuliano, Jos.; Kentucky, 1886 ***1450.2*** *p51A*
Givachin, Donetta 23; America, 1837 ***778.5*** *p242*
Givancericz, Dzan; Iowa, 1866-1943 ***123.54*** *p20*
Givas, Conrad 22; America, 1831 ***778.5*** *p242*
Givaudau, Joseph 29; Port uncertain, 1835 ***778.5*** *p242*
Givaudau, Justine 25; Port uncertain, 1835 ***778.5*** *p242*
Given, Alexander 25; St. John, N.B., 1865 ***5704.8*** *p165*
Given, Andrew 22; Wilmington, DE, 1831 ***6508.3*** *p100*
Given, Charles 27; St. John, N.B., 1854 ***5704.8*** *p115*
Given, Ellen 20; Massachusetts, 1849 ***5881.1*** *p42*
Given, James; New York, NY, 1811 ***2859.11*** *p12*
Given, James; Philadelphia, 1852 ***5704.8*** *p89*
Given, James; Philadelphia, 1864 ***5704.8*** *p179*
Given, John; New York, NY, 1811 ***2859.11*** *p12*
Given, John; New York, NY, 1815 ***2859.11*** *p32*
Given, John; Philadelphia, 1852 ***5704.8*** *p96*
Given, Joseph; New York, NY, 1816 ***2859.11*** *p32*
Given, Margaret; New York, NY, 1811 ***2859.11*** *p12*
Given, Mary 11; Philadelphia, 1852 ***5704.8*** *p96*
Given, Moses; New York, NY, 1864 ***5704.8*** *p178*
Given, Sally 25; St. John, N.B., 1860 ***5704.8*** *p144*
Given, Samuel; New York, NY, 1816 ***2859.11*** *p32*
Given, Thomas; Philadelphia, 1849 ***53.26*** *p32*
Given, Thomas; Philadelphia, 1849 ***5704.8*** *p53*
Given, William 25; St. John, N.B., 1865 ***5704.8*** *p165*
Givens, Eliza; New York, NY, 1867 ***5704.8*** *p224*
Givens, William; New York, NY, 1867 ***5704.8*** *p216*
Givianni, Peter 24; America, 1837 ***778.5*** *p242*
Givry, Alphonse 44; New Orleans, 1836 ***778.5*** *p242*
Givry, Joanty Laima 30; New Orleans, 1836 ***778.5*** *p242*
Givun, John; New York, NY, 1811 ***2859.11*** *p12*
Giwonesky, Solomon; New York, NY, 1884 ***5240.1*** *p15*

Glachin, Betty 20; Philadelphia, 1853 ***5704.8*** *p108*
Glackemeyer, . . .; Canada, 1776-1783 ***9786*** *p22*
Glackemeyer, Friedrich Heinrich; Canada, 1776-1783 ***9786*** *p237*
Glacken, Margaret; New York, NY, 1864 ***5704.8*** *p175*
Glacken, Nancy; New York, NY, 1866 ***5704.8*** *p211*
Glackin, Daniel; Philadelphia, 1865 ***5704.8*** *p200*
Glackin, Edward; New York, NY, 1866 ***5704.8*** *p213*
Glackin, Patrick; New York, NY, 1864 ***5704.8*** *p184*
Glackin, William; Philadelphia, 1849 ***53.26*** *p32*
Glackin, William; Philadelphia, 1849 ***5704.8*** *p54*
Glade, Francis; New York, NY, 1865 ***5704.8*** *p202*
Glade, Mary 11; New York, NY, 1865 ***5704.8*** *p202*
Glade, Nancy; New York, NY, 1865 ***5704.8*** *p202*
Gladen, Johann Gottlieb; Quebec, 1776 ***9786*** *p263*
Gladfeld, Carl; America, 1880 ***4610.10*** *p124*
Gladin, Richard 19; Antigua (Antego), 1728 ***3690.1*** *p88*
Glading, Mary 25; Pennsylvania, 1735 ***3690.1*** *p88*
Gladston, Jno.; Virginia, 1643 ***6219*** *p207*
Gladwin, Richard 19; Jamaica, 1724 ***3690.1*** *p88*
Glaeser, Carl F. W.; Wisconsin, n.d. ***9675.5*** *p190*
Glaeser, J. C.; Illinois, 1846 ***8582.2*** *p51*
Glaess, Herman; Wisconsin, n.d. ***9675.5*** *p190*
Glaessener, Jacob; Wisconsin, n.d. ***9675.5*** *p190*
Glaidy, John; Philadelphia, 1761 ***9973.7*** *p35*
Glaise, J. 50; America, 1835 ***778.5*** *p242*
Glance, David 19; Jamaica, 1725 ***3690.1*** *p88*
Glancy, Ann; Quebec, 1847 ***5704.8*** *p36*
Glancy, Bernard; Quebec, 1847 ***5704.8*** *p36*
Glancy, David 1; Quebec, 1847 ***5704.8*** *p36*
Glancy, Eliza 11; Quebec, 1847 ***5704.8*** *p36*
Glancy, James; Quebec, 1850 ***5704.8*** *p62*
Glancy, James 2; Quebec, 1847 ***5704.8*** *p36*
Glancy, Robert 4; Quebec, 1847 ***5704.8*** *p36*
Glancy, William 7; Quebec, 1847 ***5704.8*** *p36*
Glanfeild, Joane; Virginia, 1642 ***6219*** *p193*
Glanford, Fran; Virginia, 1698 ***2212*** *p17*
Glanney, Catherine; Philadelphia, 1867 ***5704.8*** *p224*
Glanz, Sebastian; Georgia, 1734 ***9332*** *p327*
Glasbrenner, George; New York, 1854 ***1450.2*** *p51A*
Glasco, Margaret; America, 1741 ***4971*** *p16*
Glascock, Rich.; Virginia, 1635 ***6219*** *p3*
Glascocke, Jane *SEE* Glascocke, Thomas
Glascocke, Thomas; Virginia, 1643 ***6219*** *p203*
*Wife:*Jane
Glascoe, Hugh; America, 1739 ***4971*** *p9*
Glascoe, Hugh; America, 1739 ***4971*** *p103*
Glaser, . . .; Canada, 1776-1783 ***9786*** *p22*
Glaser, Fred 57; Arizona, 1910 ***9228.40*** *p15*
Glaser, Frida; Wisconsin, n.d. ***9675.5*** *p190*
Glaser, Jacob; Cincinnati, 1869-1887 ***8582*** *p10*
Glaser, Jacob Friedrich 62; Cincinnati, 1872 ***8582.1*** *p11*
Glaser, Julius; Ohio, 1853 ***1450.2*** *p51A*
Glaser, Samuel; America, 1844 ***8582.3*** *p23*
Glasgau, John; Philadelphia, 1811 ***2859.11*** *p12*
Glasken, Jane; Quebec, 1849 ***5704.8*** *p57*
Glason, John 15; Massachusetts, 1849 ***5881.1*** *p42*
Glaspey, Catharine 17; Massachusetts, 1849 ***5881.1*** *p41*
Glass, . . .; Canada, 1776-1783 ***9786*** *p42*
Glass, Alex; New York, NY, 1811 ***2859.11*** *p12*
Glass, Alexander 11 *SEE* Glass, Andrew
Glass, Alexander 11; Philadelphia, 1847 ***5704.8*** *p2*
Glass, Alicia 2; Wilmington, DE, 1831 ***6508.3*** *p100*
Glass, Alicia 28; Wilmington, DE, 1831 ***6508.3*** *p100*
Glass, Andrew; Philadelphia, 1847 ***53.26*** *p32*
*Relative:*Martha
*Relative:*Alexander 11
*Relative:*Edward 10
*Relative:*Samuel 7
*Relative:*Margaret 5
*Relative:*Andrew 2
Glass, Andrew; Philadelphia, 1847 ***5704.8*** *p2*
Glass, Andrew 2 *SEE* Glass, Andrew
Glass, Andrew 2; Philadelphia, 1847 ***5704.8*** *p2*
Glass, Edward 10 *SEE* Glass, Andrew
Glass, Edward 10; Philadelphia, 1847 ***5704.8*** *p2*
Glass, Eliza 9; Quebec, 1847 ***5704.8*** *p6*
Glass, Ellen 22; Philadelphia, 1859 ***5704.8*** *p142*
Glass, Henry; St. John, N.B., 1847 ***5704.8*** *p34*
Glass, Hugh 25; St. John, N.B., 1864 ***5704.8*** *p157*
Glass, Isabella; New York, NY, 1811 ***2859.11*** *p12*
Glass, Isabella; Quebec, 1847 ***5704.8*** *p6*
Glass, Isabella 5; Quebec, 1847 ***5704.8*** *p6*
Glass, James; New York, NY, 1811 ***2859.11*** *p12*
Glass, James; Quebec, 1847 ***5704.8*** *p6*
Glass, John; New York, NY, 1811 ***2859.11*** *p12*
Glass, John; Philadelphia, 1867 ***5704.8*** *p220*
Glass, John James 2; Quebec, 1847 ***5704.8*** *p6*
Glass, Lorenz; Cincinnati, 1869-1887 ***8582*** *p10*
Glass, Margaret 5 *SEE* Glass, Andrew
Glass, Margaret 5; Philadelphia, 1847 ***5704.8*** *p2*
Glass, Martha *SEE* Glass, Andrew
Glass, Martha; Philadelphia, 1847 ***5704.8*** *p2*
Glass, Martha 13; Quebec, 1847 ***5704.8*** *p6*
Glass, Mary 5; Wilmington, DE, 1831 ***6508.3*** *p100*
Glass, Mary 12; Quebec, 1847 ***5704.8*** *p6*
Glass, Robert; Philadelphia, 1816 ***2859.11*** *p32*
Glass, Samuel 7 *SEE* Glass, Andrew
Glass, Samuel 7; Philadelphia, 1847 ***5704.8*** *p2*
Glassan, David; America, 1735-1743 ***4971*** *p51*
Glassey, Matthew; New York, NY, 1816 ***2859.11*** *p32*
Glassey, Robert; New York, NY, 1816 ***2859.11*** *p32*
Glassman, John J.; Arkansas, 1918 ***95.2*** *p48*
Glassmann, Pierre 25; America, 1839 ***778.5*** *p242*
Glassup, Jonathan 15; Maryland, 1723 ***3690.1*** *p88*
Glasul, Martin 13; Port uncertain, 1838 ***778.5*** *p242*
Glatt, Julius; Pennsylvania, 1877 ***3702.7*** *p415*
With wife
Glattsfelder, Casper; Philadelphia, 1763 ***9973.7*** *p38*
Glaub, Helena; Iowa, 1866-1943 ***123.54*** *p63*
Glaub, Helena Puda; Iowa, 1866-1943 ***123.54*** *p63*
Glaub, Stanley; Iowa, 1866-1943 ***123.54*** *p63*
Glaubenskindt, Auguste-France; Canada, 1776-1783 ***9786*** *p229*
Glauville, John; Illinois, 1854 ***7857*** *p4*
Glave, Jno 19; America, 1699 ***2212*** *p28*
Glavel, A.; New Orleans, 1839 ***778.5*** *p243*
Glavin, Barthol.; America, 1741 ***4971*** *p16*
Glavin, Bridget 5; Massachusetts, 1850 ***5881.1*** *p41*
Glavin, Edward 7; Massachusetts, 1850 ***5881.1*** *p42*
Glavin, Margaret 3; Massachusetts, 1850 ***5881.1*** *p43*
Gleare, Peter; Virginia, 1637 ***6219*** *p112*
Gleason, Mr.; Quebec, 1815 ***9229.18*** *p78*
Gleason, Catharine 40; Massachusetts, 1849 ***5881.1*** *p41*
Gleason, Daniel 16; Massachusetts, 1849 ***5881.1*** *p41*
Gleason, John 10; Massachusetts, 1849 ***5881.1*** *p42*
Gleason, Martin; Illinois, 1892 ***2896.5*** *p14*
Gleason, Mary; Montreal, 1821 ***7603*** *p90*
Gleason, Mary 40; Massachusetts, 1849 ***5881.1*** *p43*
Gleason, Mary 70; Massachusetts, 1848 ***5881.1*** *p43*
Gleason, Michael 20; Massachusetts, 1849 ***5881.1*** *p43*
Gleason, Morris 34; Kansas, 1872 ***5240.1*** *p52*
Gleason, Patrick 24; Massachusetts, 1849 ***5881.1*** *p44*
Gleason, William 13; Massachusetts, 1849 ***5881.1*** *p44*
Gleason, Winne 21; Massachusetts, 1849 ***5881.1*** *p44*
Gleddale, Mary 20; New England, 1699 ***2212*** *p18*
Gleed, Tho.; Virginia, 1638 ***6219*** *p33*
Gleesen, Daniel 28; New Orleans, 1862 ***543.30*** *p375C*
Gleeson, John; America, 1834 ***1450.2*** *p51A*
Gleeson, John; Montreal, 1823 ***7603*** *p98*
Gleeson, Thomas; New York, NY, 1846 ***1450.2*** *p51A*
Gleger, Cornelius; Ohio, 1843 ***9892.11*** *p16*
Glegly, John, Jr.; South Carolina, 1788 ***7119*** *p199*
Gleich, Balthasar; America, 1850 ***8582.2*** *p13*
Gleich, Johann Friedrich; Cincinnati, 1869-1887 ***8582*** *p10*
Gleichner, Anna Maria; Pennsylvania, 1750 ***2444*** *p146*
Gleiger, Cornelius; Ohio, 1847 ***9892.11*** *p16*
Gleighman, John; Indiana, 1836 ***9117*** *p14*
Gleik, Leopold; America, 1846 ***8582.3*** *p23*
Gleissenberg, . . .; Canada, 1776-1783 ***9786*** *p22*
Gleissenberg, Gottlief Joachim; Quebec, 1776 ***9786*** *p262*
Gleit, Leopold; America, 1846 ***8582.3*** *p23*
Gleitzinter, Adam; Wisconsin, n.d. ***9675.5*** *p190*
Glen, Alexander 7; St. John, N.B., 1853 ***5704.8*** *p99*
Glen, Eliza 11; Quebec, 1852 ***5704.8*** *p94*
Glen, Ellen 4; St. John, N.B., 1853 ***5704.8*** *p99*
Glen, James; South Carolina, 1743 ***1639.20*** *p80*
Glen, Jane; Philadelphia, 1849 ***53.26*** *p32*
Glen, Jane; Quebec, 1852 ***5704.8*** *p94*
Glen, John 13; Quebec, 1852 ***5704.8*** *p94*
Glen, Joseph 9; Quebec, 1852 ***5704.8*** *p94*
Glen, Margaret; Philadelphia, 1852 ***5704.8*** *p96*
Glen, Margaret 9; Quebec, 1852 ***5704.8*** *p94*
Glen, Mary; St. John, N.B., 1853 ***5704.8*** *p99*
Glen, Patrick 21; Kansas, 1876 ***5240.1*** *p57*
Glen, Robert; Philadelphia, 1849 ***53.26*** *p32*
Glen, Robert; Philadelphia, 1849 ***5704.8*** *p50*
Glen, Robert 9; St. John, N.B., 1853 ***5704.8*** *p99*
Glen, Samuel; Philadelphia, 1811 ***53.26*** *p32*
Glen, Samuel; Philadelphia, 1811 ***2859.11*** *p12*
Glen, Sarah 1; St. John, N.B., 1853 ***5704.8*** *p99*
Glen, William; St. John, N.B., 1853 ***5704.8*** *p99*
Glency, Hannah; Philadelphia, 1851 ***5704.8*** *p78*
Glendenen, Robert 25; St. John, N.B., 1866 ***5704.8*** *p167*
Glendenery, Mr.; Quebec, 1815 ***9229.18*** *p77*
With wife
With child
Glendinning, Mary 18; Philadelphia, 1857 ***5704.8*** *p133*
Glendinning, William; New York, NY, 1866 ***5704.8*** *p206*
Glendinning, William; North Carolina, 1816 ***1639.20*** *p80*
Glendt, John; Illinois, 1869 ***5012.38*** *p99*
Glenfuld, Edward; New York, NY, 1811 ***2859.11*** *p12*
Glenie, James; New Brunswick, 1791 ***9775.5*** *p205*
Glenister, Robt.; Virginia, 1636 ***6219*** *p1*
Glenn, Andrew; Ohio, 1812-1840 ***9892.11*** *p16*
Glenn, David; America, 1867 ***5704.8*** *p224*
Glenn, Hamilton 22; St. John, N.B., 1859 ***5704.8*** *p140*
Glenn, Henry 20; Philadelphia, 1857 ***5704.8*** *p132*
Glenn, Hugh; America, 1850 ***1450.2*** *p52A*
Glenn, Hugh 60; Kansas, 1873 ***5240.1*** *p54*
Glenn, James; Philadelphia, 1849 ***53.26*** *p32*
Glenn, James; Philadelphia, 1849 ***5704.8*** *p53*
Glenn, James 22; St. John, N.B., 1858 ***5704.8*** *p137*
Glenn, Jane; Philadelphia, 1849 ***5704.8*** *p53*
Glenn, John 22; Philadelphia, 1855 ***5704.8*** *p124*
Glenn, Margaret; America, 1867 ***5704.8*** *p224*
Glenn, Mary; America, 1867 ***5704.8*** *p224*
Glenn, Nancy 20; St. John, N.B., 1859 ***5704.8*** *p140*
Glenn, Patrick; Wisconsin, n.d. ***9675.5*** *p190*
Glenn, William; America, 1849 ***1450.2*** *p52A*
Glenn, William; America, 1864 ***5704.8*** *p178*
Glenn, William; Ohio, 1862-1880 ***9892.11*** *p17*
Glenn, William 30; Jamaica, 1730 ***3690.1*** *p88*
Glenn, William 30; Kansas, 1873 ***5240.1*** *p54*
Glenn, William A.; Ohio, 1862-1880 ***9892.11*** *p17*
Glenn, William A.; Ohio, 1880 ***9892.11*** *p17*
Glennie, George; Austin, TX, 1886 ***9777*** *p5*
Glenning, Bridget 60; Massachusetts, 1850 ***5881.1*** *p41*
Glennon, Christopher 51; Arizona, 1890 ***2764.35*** *p25*
Glesner, Jean 28; New Orleans, 1838 ***778.5*** *p243*
Gleubert, Justus Henrich; Lancaster, PA, 1780 ***8137*** *p9*
Gleyman, Gottlieb; Illinois, 1868 ***2896.5*** *p14*
Glickman, Walter Selig; Arkansas, 1918 ***95.2*** *p48*
Glieber, John; Wisconsin, n.d. ***9675.5*** *p190*
Glight, Thomas; Virginia, 1642 ***6219*** *p196*
Glimm, Christian; New York, NY, 1840 ***8208.4*** *p112*
Glin, William 25; Philadelphia, 1803 ***53.26*** *p32*
Glinchy, John; Baltimore, 1811 ***2859.11*** *p12*
Glinn, John; Ohio, 1843 ***8365.26*** *p12*
Glinski, . . .; New York, 1831 ***4606*** *p173*
Glisan, Catherine; America, 1736-1743 ***4971*** *p57*
Glissan, James; America, 1736-1743 ***4971*** *p57*
Glissing, George Frederick; New York, NY, 1838 ***8208.4*** *p71*
Gliszcynski, Vincent; Arkansas, 1918 ***95.2*** *p48*
Glitzenstein, Carl; New York, 1885 ***1450.2*** *p11B*
Gloak, Amey 26; Port uncertain, 1838 ***778.5*** *p243*
Gloak, Andres 15; Port uncertain, 1838 ***778.5*** *p243*
Gloak, Catherine 18; Port uncertain, 1838 ***778.5*** *p243*
Gloak, Henry 61; Port uncertain, 1838 ***778.5*** *p243*
Gloak, Henry, Jr. 22; Port uncertain, 1838 ***778.5*** *p243*
Gloak, John 18; Port uncertain, 1838 ***778.5*** *p243*
Gloak, William 28; Port uncertain, 1838 ***778.5*** *p243*
Globenskindt, . . .; Canada, 1776-1783 ***9786*** *p22*
Globensky, . . .; Canada, 1776-1783 ***9786*** *p22*
Globensky, Auguste-France; Canada, 1776-1783 ***9786*** *p229*
Globes, Rapol; Wisconsin, n.d. ***9675.5*** *p190*
Globoenick, Johan; Wisconsin, n.d. ***9675.5*** *p190*
Glock, Peter; Connecticut, 1856 ***3702.7*** *p357*
Glock, Mrs. Peter; Connecticut, 1857 ***3702.7*** *p359*
Glockh, Hans Caspar; Pennsylvania, 1744 ***2444*** *p157*
Glod, Peter 24; Maryland, 1735 ***3690.1*** *p88*
Glodek, Franciszek 28; New York, 1912 ***9980.29*** *p62*
Gloede, Andrew; Illinois, 1875 ***2896.5*** *p14*
Gloger, Otto; Baltimore, 1895 ***1450.2*** *p11B*
Glojeck, Frannz; Wisconsin, n.d. ***9675.5*** *p190*
Gloor, Gottfreid; Washington, 1859-1920 ***2872.1*** *p14*
Glorias, Irian; Iowa, 1866-1943 ***123.54*** *p20*
Glorie, Thos.; Virginia, 1635 ***6219*** *p35*
Glory, Eliza 23; Massachusetts, 1847 ***5881.1*** *p41*
Glory, Henry 48; New Orleans, 1864 ***543.30*** *p380C*
Gloser, Andreas; Georgia, 1754 ***7829*** *p8*
Gloss, David; Boston, 1776 ***1219.7*** *p278*
Glossner, Charles, Sr.; Cincinnati, 1869-1887 ***8582*** *p11*
Glotz, Anna Barbara; Port uncertain, 1717 ***3627*** *p13*
Glouer, Richd 22; America, 1706 ***2212*** *p46*
Glovas, Daniel; Iowa, 1866-1943 ***123.54*** *p20*
Glovas, Daniel; Iowa, 1866-1943 ***123.54*** *p63*
Glove, Gottfreid; Washington, 1859-1920 ***2872.1*** *p14*
Gloven, Thomas; Illinois, 1863 ***7857*** *p4*
Glover, Christiana 60; North Carolina, 1850 ***1639.20*** *p80*
Glover, Dorothy; Virginia, 1637 ***6219*** *p112*
Glover, Edward; Virginia, 1638 ***6219*** *p33*
Glover, Edward 20; New England, 1699 ***2212*** *p19*
Glover, Henry; Antigua (Antego), 1765 ***1219.7*** *p114*
Glover, John; New York, NY, 1838 ***8208.4*** *p61*
Glover, John 16; Maryland, 1723 ***3690.1*** *p88*
Glover, John 28; New York, 1774 ***1219.7*** *p189*
Glover, Lattimor 19; Maryland, 1724 ***3690.1*** *p27A*
Glover, Morgan; Virginia, 1639 ***6219*** *p151*
Glover, Morgan; Virginia, 1643 ***6219*** *p203*
Glover, Sarah; Virginia, 1637 ***6219*** *p8*
Glover, Thomas 24; Maryland, 1775 ***1219.7*** *p272*
Glover, William 16; Maryland, 1775 ***1219.7*** *p272*
Glover, Wm.; Virginia, 1638 ***6219*** *p150*

178 *FOR A COMPLETE EXPLANATION OF ENTRY, SEE "HOW TO READ A CITATION" SECTION*

Glowacka, Barbara Pietrowska 40; New York, 1912 ***9980.29** p55*
*Son:*Marcin 20
Glowacka, Jan; New Bedford, MA, 1912 ***9980.29** p56*
Glowacka, Marcin 20 *SEE* Glowacka, Barbara Pietrowska
Glowacka, Martha 28; New York, 1912 ***9980.29** p56*
Glowacka, Stanislawa 20; New York, 1912 ***9980.29** p57*
With sister-in-law
Glowacki, Barbara Pietrowska 40; New York, 1912 ***9980.29** p55*
*Son:*Marcin 20
Glowacki, Ignacy; New York, 1831 ***4606** p173*
Glowacki, Jan; New Bedford, MA, 1912 ***9980.29** p56*
Glowacki, Marcin 20 *SEE* Glowacki, Barbara Pietrowska
Glowacki, Maria 30; New York, 1912 ***9980.29** p67*
Glowacki, Martha 28; New York, 1912 ***9980.29** p56*
Glowata, Maryanna 19; New York, 1912 ***9980.29** p66*
Glowney, Bessy 20; Massachusetts, 1847 ***5881.1** p41*
Gloystim, C.F. Dietrich; Wisconsin, n.d. ***9675.5** p190*
Glubiak, John; Arkansas, 1918 ***95.2** p49*
Gluckman, Samuel; Arkansas, 1918 ***95.2** p49*
Glueck, Jacob; America, 1846 ***8582.3** p23*
Gluer, Ludwig von; Canada, 1780 ***9786** p268*
Gluer, Ludwig von; New York, 1776 ***9786** p268*
Gluirfmann, Johann Nicol; Indiana, 1836 ***9117** p14*
Gluke, Frank; Wisconsin, n.d. ***9675.5** p190*
Glumaz, John; California, 1868 ***2764.35** p29*
Gluszewski, . . .; New York, 1831 ***4606** p173*
Glyndcamp, Christopher 32; New Orleans, 1862 ***543.30** p383C*
Glynn, John 30; Massachusetts, 1847 ***5881.1** p42*
Glynn, Joseph; New York, NY, 1816 ***2859.11** p32*
Glynn, Michael 19; Massachusetts, 1849 ***5881.1** p43*
Glynn, Patrick 5; Massachusetts, 1849 ***5881.1** p44*
Glyster, David; Antigua (Antego), 1756 ***1219.7** p41*
Gmibando, Andrea; Iowa, 1866-1943 ***123.54** p19*
Gmiter, Joseph H.; America, 1870 ***7137** p168*
Gmiter, Margaret A.; America, 1864 ***7137** p168*
Gmter, Joseph H.; America, 1870 ***7137** p168*
Gmter, Margaret A.; America, 1864 ***7137** p168*
Gnall, Mihall; Arkansas, 1918 ***95.2** p49*
Gnehm, Paul Werner; Arkansas, 1918 ***95.2** p49*
Gniewkowski, Seweryn; New York, 1835 ***4606** p179*
Gnoedler, Hans Jerg; Pennsylvania, 1750 ***2444** p166*
Gnoedler, Hans Jerg; Pennsylvania, 1750 ***2444** p176*
Gnudschmit, Francis; Canada, 1776-1783 ***9786** p207A*
Goa, Mr. 40; New Orleans, 1822 ***778.5** p243*
Goa, Mrs. 22; New Orleans, 1822 ***778.5** p243*
Goaden, Peter; Wisconsin, n.d. ***9675.5** p190*
Goadley, Thomas; New York, NY, 1836 ***8208.4** p18*
Goardlad, Tho.; Virginia, 1643 ***6219** p204*
Goare, Mary 22; Virginia, 1699 ***2212** p27*
Goba, Solomon; Iowa, 1866-1943 ***123.54** p20*
Gobble, Coonrod; Ohio, 1844 ***9892.11** p17*
Gobble, Coonrod; Ohio, 1848 ***9892.11** p17*
Gobble, David; Ohio, 1840 ***9892.11** p17*
Gobble, Peter; Ohio, 1855-1861 ***9892.11** p17*
Gobble, Peter; Ohio, 1855-1868 ***9892.11** p17*
Gobby, Ann; Virginia, 1647 ***6219** p247*
Gobe, Charles 28; New Orleans, 1838 ***778.5** p243*
Gobel, Andrew; Ohio, 1838 ***9892.11** p17*
Gobel, Anna Maria 10 *SEE* Gobel, Hans Georg
Gobel, Antoni 12 *SEE* Gobel, Hans Georg
Gobel, Barbara 38 *SEE* Gobel, Hans Georg
Gobel, Hans Georg 40; Philadelphia, 1733 ***2854** p44*
*Wife:*Barbara 38
*Child:*Antoni 12
*Child:*Anna Maria 10
*Child:*Magdalena 8
*Child:*Jerg Adam 5
*Child:*Hans Jerg 3
Gobel, Hans Jerg 3 *SEE* Gobel, Hans Georg
Gobel, Jerg Adam 5 *SEE* Gobel, Hans Georg
Gobel, Magdalena 8 *SEE* Gobel, Hans Georg
Gobell, Vallentin; South Carolina, 1788 ***7119** p200*
Gobels, Nicholas; Illinois, 1890 ***2896.5** p14*
Gobet, Henry 27; New Orleans, 1829 ***778.5** p243*
Gobet, John 23; New Orleans, 1829 ***778.5** p243*
Gobl, Anna Maria 10 *SEE* Gobl, Hans Georg
Gobl, Antoni 12 *SEE* Gobl, Hans Georg
Gobl, Barbara 38 *SEE* Gobl, Hans Georg
Gobl, Hans Georg 40; Philadelphia, 1733 ***2854** p44*
*Wife:*Barbara 38
*Child:*Antoni 12
*Child:*Anna Maria 10
*Child:*Magdalena 8
*Child:*Jerg Adam 5
*Child:*Hans Jerg 3
Gobl, Hans Jerg 3 *SEE* Gobl, Hans Georg
Gobl, Jerg Adam 5 *SEE* Gobl, Hans Georg
Gobl, Magdalena 8 *SEE* Gobl, Hans Georg
Goble, Andrew 15 *SEE* Goble, Andrew
Goble, Andrew 37?; New York, NY, 1833 ***9892.11** p17*
*Relative:*Peter 18
*Relative:*Andrew 15
*Relative:*Joseph 8
Goble, Joseph 8 *SEE* Goble, Andrew
Goble, Peter 18 *SEE* Goble, Andrew
Gock, Dieterich; New York, NY, 1836 ***8208.4** p15*
Gockel, William; Cincinnati, 1869-1887 ***8582** p11*
Gocken, Siebelt; Iroquois Co., IL, 1892 ***3455.1** p10*
Gocken, Siebelt; Iroquois Co., IL, 1894 ***3455.1** p10*
Gockstatter, Fred; Washington, 1859-1920 ***2872.1** p13*
Gockstatter, Gertrude; Washington, 1859-1920 ***2872.1** p13*
Godaifroy, D. 32; New Orleans, 1829 ***778.5** p244*
Godard, Alexis 23; New Orleans, 1823 ***778.5** p244*
Godard, Athanase; Quebec, 1764 ***7603** p94*
Godbeare, Hector; Virginia, 1635 ***6219** p70*
Godbeare, Hester; Virginia, 1637 ***6219** p180*
Godbere, Hestor; Virginia, 1639 ***6219** p151*
Godberson, Jes; Illinois, 1888 ***2896.5** p14*
Godbery, Joane; Virginia, 1636 ***6219** p8*
Godby, Thomas; Virginia, 1647 ***6219** p247*
Godbye, Tho.; Virginia, 1637 ***6219** p115*
Goddard, . . .; America, 1839 ***778.5** p244*
Goddard, Arthur 20; Antigua (Antego), 1728 ***3690.1** p88*
Goddard, Napolean 40; America, 1839 ***778.5** p244*
Goddard, Napolean, Mme.; America, 1839 ***778.5** p244*
Godeck, Johann Conrad; Canada, 1776-1782 ***9786** p252*
Godecke, . . .; Canada, 1776-1783 ***9786** p22*
Godecke, Johann Heinrich; Quebec, 1776 ***9786** p260*
Godeffroy, Alfred; San Francisco, 1849 ***6013.19** p30*
Godeffroy, Alfred; San Francisco, 1851 ***6013.19** p90*
Godefroy, Mr. 8; New Orleans, 1821 ***778.5** p244*
Godereski, Peter; Wisconsin, n.d. ***9675.5** p190*
Godersky, John; Wisconsin, n.d. ***9675.5** p190*
Godfretson, P.R.; Illinois, 1876 ***5012.39** p120*
Godfrey, George; Philadelphia, 1847 ***53.26** p32*
Godfrey, John; America, 1736 ***4971** p44*
Godfrey, John; America, 1736 ***4971** p45*
Godfrey, John; New York, NY, 1838 ***8208.4** p81*
Godfrey, John 22; Virginia, 1774 ***1219.7** p243*
Godfrey, John 40; New Orleans, 1862 ***543.30** p383C*
Godfrey, Joseph 21; Maryland, 1774 ***1219.7** p224*
Godfrey, Margaret 45; Montreal, 1777 ***7603** p58*
Godfrey, Mary A.; Philadelphia, 1867 ***5704.8** p222*
Godfrey, Michael; Ohio, 1842 ***8365.25** p12*
Godfrey, Robert; New York, NY, 1868 ***5704.8** p227*
Godfrey, Thomas; New York, NY, 1815 ***2859.11** p32*
Godfrey, Thomas 21; Jamaica, 1738 ***3690.1** p89*
Godfrey, Timothy 30; Massachusetts, 1849 ***5881.1** p44*
Godfrey, William; Virginia, 1640 ***6219** p183*
Godfry, David; New York, NY, 1869 ***5704.8** p233*
Godfry, Eleanor; Quebec, 1847 ***5704.8** p36*
Godfry, George; Philadelphia, 1847 ***5704.8** p22*
Godfry, Margaret; Quebec, 1847 ***5704.8** p36*
Godfry, Wm.; Virginia, 1637 ***6219** p85*
Godfrye, John; Virginia, 1638 ***6219** p147*
Godfrye, Jon.; Virginia, 1618 ***6219** p72*
Godfrye, Jon; Virginia, 1634 ***6219** p105*
Godiche, . . .; Canada, 1776-1783 ***9786** p22*
Godkin, Henry; New York, NY, 1815 ***2859.11** p32*
Godles, Joseph; Arkansas, 1918 ***95.2** p49*
Godlewski, Jan 20; New York, 1912 ***9980.29** p49*
Godlewski, Kazimierz; Arkansas, 1918 ***95.2** p49*
Godley, Richard; Virginia, 1637 ***6219** p37*
Godona, Peter 17; Maryland, 1775 ***1219.7** p249*
Godoni, Antonia 16; New York, NY, 1893 ***9026.4** p41*
Godowia, Aldoph; Arkansas, 1918 ***95.2** p49*
Godschal, . . .; Canada, 1776-1783 ***9786** p22*
Godschalk, Louis 36; Kansas, 1880 ***5240.1** p15*
Godschalk, Louis 36; Kansas, 1880 ***5240.1** p61*
Godsland, Tom; Illinois, 1886 ***5012.39** p52*
Godson, John 19; Jamaica, 1733 ***3690.1** p89*
Godwin, Daniel; Virginia, 1635 ***6219** p27*
Godwin, Henry 19; Jamaica, 1736 ***3690.1** p89*
Godwin, Jno.; Virginia, 1647 ***6219** p241*
Godwin, Michl; Virginia, 1698 ***2212** p15*
Godwin, Step.; Virginia, 1638 ***6219** p145*
Godzwan, Alexander 25; New York, 1912 ***9980.29** p70*
Godzwon, Louis; Arkansas, 1918 ***95.2** p49*
Goebel, Christopher; Indiana, 1849 ***9117** p16*
Goebel, George; Indiana, 1849 ***9117** p16*
Goebel, Henrich; Lancaster, PA, 1780 ***8137** p9*
Goebel, Henrich; Philadelphia, 1779 ***8137** p9*
Goebel, Henry; Indiana, 1845 ***9117** p16*
Goebel, Jacob 37; New Orleans, 1862 ***543.30** p376C*
Goebel, Jean 30; America, 1838 ***778.5** p244*
Goebel, John; Ohio, 1869-1887 ***8582** p11*
Goebel, John Christopher; Washington, 1859-1920 ***2872.1** p14*
Goebel, Philip; Indiana, 1849 ***9117** p16*
Goebel, Wiegand; Philadelphia, 1779 ***8137** p9*
Goebel, Wilhelm; America, 1854 ***8582.3** p23*
Goebel, Wilhelm 24; New York, NY, 1854 ***8582.3** p23*
Goebel, William; Washington, 1859-1920 ***2872.1** p14*
Goebell, . . .; Canada, 1776-1783 ***9786** p22*
Goebils, Nicholas; Illinois, 1888 ***2896.5** p14*
Goeble, John; Washington, 1859-1920 ***2872.1** p14*
Goebman, Leopold 24; America, 1836 ***778.5** p244*
Goeckell, . . .; Canada, 1776-1783 ***9786** p22*
Goedecke, O.F.C.; Quebec, 1776 ***9786** p104*
Goeden, Peter; Wisconsin, n.d. ***9675.5** p190*
Goedert, Nic; Wisconsin, n.d. ***9675.5** p190*
Goedick, . . .; Canada, 1776-1783 ***9786** p22*
Goedick, Fred. Louis; Canada, 1776-1783 ***9786** p207A*
Goedicke, . . .; Canada, 1776-1783 ***9786** p22*
Goehring, . . .; Alberta, 1909-1950 ***5262** p58*
Goehring, Gottlieb Friedrich *SEE* Goehring, Johann Jacob
Goehring, Johann Jacob *SEE* Goehring, Johann Jacob
Goehring, Johann Jacob; Port uncertain, 1753-1800 ***2444** p157*
*Wife:*Magdalena
*Child:*Johann Jacob
*Child:*Gottlieb Friedrich
Goehring, Magdalena *SEE* Goehring, Johann Jacob
Goeiner, Martin; New York, NY, 1834 ***8208.4** p1*
Goekaler, Christian; America, 1853 ***1450.2** p52A*
Goekel, . . .; Canada, 1776-1783 ***9786** p22*
Goekel, Anthy; Canada, 1776-1783 ***9786** p207A*
Goeller, Katherine; Wisconsin, n.d. ***9675.5** p190*
Goellner, Gerhard; Wisconsin, n.d. ***9675.5** p190*
Goenne, William; Arkansas, 1918 ***95.2** p49*
Goepp, August; Illinois, 1888 ***5012.39** p121*
Goepp, E.; Wheeling, WV, 1852 ***8582.3** p78*
Goepper, Frederick 23?; Philadelphia Co., PA, 1849 ***1450.2** p52A*
Goepper, Karl; America, 1849 ***8582.2** p13*
Goepper, Michael; Cincinnati, 1869-1887 ***8582** p11*
Goepper, Wilhelm; America, 1848 ***8582.3** p23*
Goercke, Jakob; Philadelphia, 1779 ***8137** p9*
Goerdes, Friederich; America, 1849 ***8582.3** p23*
Goerent, Henry; Wisconsin, n.d. ***9675.5** p190*
Goerent, John; Wisconsin, n.d. ***9675.5** p190*
Goerig, John; Washington, 1859-1920 ***2872.1** p14*
Goerke, Heinrich; Illinois, 1845 ***8582.2** p51*
Goertz, August; New Jersey, 1867 ***8125.8** p436*
Goeser, August; America, 1848 ***8582.2** p13*
Goessler, Johannes; America, 1853 ***8582.3** p23*
Goethals, Camiel; Arkansas, 1918 ***95.2** p49*
Goethel, Heins; Washington, 1859-1920 ***2872.1** p14*
Goethel, Johanna Milta; Washington, 1859-1920 ***2872.1** p14*
Goethel, Paul Walter; Washington, 1859-1920 ***2872.1** p14*
Goethel, Walter Cl...de; Washington, 1859-1920 ***2872.1** p14*
Goethmann, Friederic 36; Port uncertain, 1839 ***778.5** p244*
Goetje, Anna Barbara *SEE* Goetje, Peter
Goetje, Peter; New York, 1743 ***3652** p59*
*Wife:*Anna Barbara
Goetjen, Herman; Kansas, 1908 ***6013.40** p15*
Goetjens, Charles A.; Chicago, 1873 ***2764.35** p26*
Goettheim, F.B.; America, 1872-1874 ***8582.1** p11*
Goettler, George; Wisconsin, n.d. ***9675.5** p190*
Goettscha, F. C. H.; New York, 1886 ***1450.2** p11B*
Goetz, . . .; Canada, 1776-1783 ***9786** p22*
Goetz, Anna *SEE* Goetz, Hans Mich.el
Goetz, Anna; Pennsylvania, 1744 ***2444** p158*
With sons
Goetz, Anna Barbara *SEE* Goetz, Hans Mich.el
Goetz, Francois 29; America, 1837 ***778.5** p244*
Goetz, Friederich; Kentucky, 1833 ***8582.3** p99*
Goetz, Friedrich; Kentucky, 1869-1887 ***8582** p11*
Goetz, Gottlieb Friedrich; Baltimore, 1833 ***8582** p11*
Goetz, Hans Mich.el; Pennsylvania, 1744 ***2444** p158*
*Wife:*Anna
*Child:*Johann Georg
*Child:*Johann Heinrich
*Child:*Anna Barbara
*Child:*Johannes
*Child:*Johann Michael
Goetz, Jacob; Illinois, 1854 ***7857** p4*
Goetz, Jacob; Illinois, 1858 ***7857** p4*
Goetz, Johann Georg *SEE* Goetz, Hans Mich.el
Goetz, Johann Heinrich *SEE* Goetz, Hans Mich.el
Goetz, Johann Michael *SEE* Goetz, Hans Mich.el
Goetz, Johann Michael; Pennsylvania, 1767 ***2444** p158*
Goetz, Johannes *SEE* Goetz, Hans Mich.el
Goetz, Philip; Illinois, 1854 ***7857** p4*
Goetz, Philip; Illinois, 1858 ***7857** p4*
Goetz, William; Illinois, 1854 ***7857** p4*
Goetze, . . .; Canada, 1776-1783 ***9786** p22*
Goetze, Henry 32; New Orleans, 1862 ***543.30** p374C*
Goetzelman, J. Jacob; Pennsylvania, 1752 ***4525** p221*

Goodburn, George; Antigua (Antego), 1757 3690.1 p90
Goodcross, James; Virginia, 1646 6219 p240
Goodgaine, Henry; Virginia, 1642 6219 p189
Goodgame, William 27; Jamaica, 1737 3690.1 p90
Goodier, Jacob 27; Pennsylvania, 1753 2444 p156
Goodier, Peter 31; Pennsylvania, 1753 2444 p156
Goodin, Georg; Virginia, 1622 6219 p76
Goodlatt, Alexander; North Carolina, 1713-1813 1639.20 p81
Goodleaf, Abraham *SEE* Goodleaf, Jacob
Goodleaf, Henry *SEE* Goodleaf, Jacob
Goodleaf, Jacob *SEE* Goodleaf, Jacob
Goodleaf, Jacob; Ohio, 1823 9892.11 p49
Goodleaf, Jacob; Philadelphia, 1818 9892.11 p17
*Wife:*Maria Rye
*Child:*Abraham
*Child:*Henry
*Child:*Jacob
Goodleaf, Maria Rye *SEE* Goodleaf, Jacob
Goodleive, Abraham *SEE* Goodleive, Jacob
Goodleive, Henry *SEE* Goodleive, Jacob
Goodleive, Jacob *SEE* Goodleive, Jacob
Goodleive, Jacob; Philadelphia, 1818 9892.11 p17
*Wife:*Maria Rye
*Child:*Abraham
*Child:*Henry
*Child:*Jacob
Goodleive, Maria Rye *SEE* Goodleive, Jacob
Goodley, John 23; Virginia, 1773 1219.7 p171
Goodling, John Peter; Philadelphia, 1762 9973.7 p36
Goodlive, Jacob; Ohio, 1840 9892.11 p17
Goodlive, Jacob, Sr.; Ohio, 1841 9892.11 p18
Goodman, Mr.; Indiana, 1856 3702.7 p225
Goodman, Abram; New York, 1889 1450.2 p53A
Goodman, Catherine; New York, NY, 1815 2859.11 p32
Goodman, Francis; Virginia, 1637 6219 p111
Goodman, Francis; Virginia, 1638 6219 p122
Goodman, Johann Christian; Kentucky, 1860-1866 9460 p647
Goodman, Johann Christian; Kentucky, 1885-1886 9461 p47
Goodman, John; Virginia, 1638 6219 p153
Goodman, Joseph C.; Arkansas, 1918 95.2 p50
Goodman, Richard; America, 1741 4971 p99
Goodman, Richard; New York, NY, 1815 2859.11 p32
Goodman, Richard; Virginia, 1638 6219 p121
Goodman, Thomas; Annapolis, MD, 1742 4971 p93
Goodnought, Luke; Virginia, 1642 6219 p186
Goodpaller, Peter; America, 1851 1450.2 p53A
Goodridge, Ann; Virginia, 1637 6219 p10
Goodriffe, Grace; Virginia, 1649 6219 p252
Goods, Wm.; Virginia, 1643 6219 p199
Goodshalk, Daniel 22; Maryland, 1774 1219.7 p181
Goodson, Jon.; Virginia, 1635 6219 p71
Goodson, Margaret 18; Baltimore, 1775 1219.7 p271
Goodson, Margaret 18; Maryland, 1775 1219.7 p260
Goodwell, Thomas 28; Massachusetts, 1849 5881.1 p44
Goodwill, Louis 26; New Orleans, 1862 543.30 p374C
Goodwin, Ann 22; America, 1701 2212 p34
Goodwin, Daniell; Virginia, 1638 6219 p145
Goodwin, Henry; Montreal, 1821 7603 p99
Goodwin, Henry 30; Maryland, 1775 1219.7 p255
Goodwin, Jabez W.; New York, NY, 1836 8208.4 p11
Goodwin, James 12; Jamaica, 1749 3690.1 p90
Goodwin, John; New York, NY, 1834 8208.4 p1
Goodwin, John; Virginia, 1637 6219 p83
Goodwin, Jon.; Virginia, 1635 6219 p36
Goodwin, Lawrence; New York, NY, 1838 8208.4 p67
Goodwin, Patrick; Wisconsin, n.d. 9675.5 p190
Goodwin, Robt 22; Virginia, 1700 2212 p33
Goodwin, Sarah; America, 1742 4971 p17
Goodwin, Sarah; Virginia, 1643 6219 p204
Goodwin, Step.; Virginia, 1635 6219 p27
Goodwin, Thomas; America, 1742 4971 p29
Goodwin, Thomas; Maryland, 1742 4971 p106
Goodwin, Thomas 20; St. John, N.B., 1866 5704.8 p166
Goodwin, William 17; Virginia, 1720 3690.1 p90
Goodyer, Thomas 20; Maryland or Virginia, 1719 3690.1 p90
Gookin, Daniell; Virginia, 1642 6219 p195
Gookins, Daniell; Virginia, 1642 6219 p195
Gookins, Mary; Virginia, 1642 6219 p195
Gookins, Samll.; Virginia, 1642 6219 p195
Goole, Mary; Philadelphia, 1851 5704.8 p76
Goore, Fr.; Virginia, 1638 6219 p122
Goorley, David 6; St. John, N.B., 1852 5704.8 p95
Goorley, Eliza 8; St. John, N.B., 1852 5704.8 p95
Goorley, John 2; St. John, N.B., 1852 5704.8 p95
Goorley, Margaret; St. John, N.B., 1852 5704.8 p95
Goorley, Mary Ann 4; St. John, N.B., 1852 5704.8 p95
Goorley, Robert; St. John, N.B., 1852 5704.8 p95
Goorley, Robert 3 mos; St. John, N.B., 1852 5704.8 p95
Goorly, Catherine; Philadelphia, 1851 5704.8 p79
Goorly, Jane; Philadelphia, 1851 5704.8 p79
Goorly, Mary Ann; Philadelphia, 1851 5704.8 p79
Goos, Adam; Philadelphia, 1759 9973.7 p34
Goper, Charles 19; America, 1838 778.5 p245
Gopfert, Hans; Carolina, 1738 9898 p35
Gora, John; Iowa, 1866-1943 123.54 p20
Gorad, Henry 17; Jamaica, 1734 3690.1 p90
Gorad, John 19; Jamaica, 1734 3690.1 p90
Gorchow, Joe; Arkansas, 1918 95.2 p50
Gordan, Bridget; America, 1865 5704.8 p204
Gordan, Edward; America, 1865 5704.8 p204
Gordan, Elleanor *SEE* Gordan, Mary Ann
Gordan, Elleanor; Philadelphia, 1848 5704.8 p40
Gordan, Mary Ann; Philadelphia, 1848 53.26 p32
*Relative:*Elleanor
Gordan, Mary Ann; Philadelphia, 1848 5704.8 p40
Gordan, Robert 23; Kansas, 1879 5240.1 p60
Gorden, Henry 29; Maryland, 1733 3690.1 p90
Gorden, Mark 28; New York, 1774 1219.7 p242
Gorden, Mary 12; Quebec, 1850 5704.8 p67
Gorden, Sarah 8; Quebec, 1850 5704.8 p67
Gording, Carl; Illinois, 1886 2896.5 p14
Gordon, . . .; South Carolina, 1734 1639.20 p82
Gordon, Mr.; Quebec, 1815 9229.18 p81
Gordon, Mr. 45; Mexico, 1826 778.5 p245
Gordon, Alexander; Charleston, SC, 1824 1639.20 p81
Gordon, Alexander; South Carolina, 1708-1754 1639.20 p81
Gordon, Alexander 50; South Carolina, 1850 1639.20 p81
Gordon, Andrew; Philadelphia, 1870 5704.8 p239
Gordon, Anne; New York, NY, 1865 5704.8 p203
Gordon, Charles; South Carolina, 1759 1639.20 p81
Gordon, Easter; New York, NY, 1811 2859.11 p12
Gordon, Edward 46; Barbados, 1774 1219.7 p190
Gordon, Eliza 22; Philadelphia, 1860 5704.8 p144
Gordon, Elizabeth; New York, NY, 1816 2859.11 p32
Gordon, Elizabeth; Philadelphia, 1853 5704.8 p101
Gordon, Ellen; New York, NY, 1869 5704.8 p235
Gordon, Fanny 16; Quebec, 1855 5704.8 p126
Gordon, George; Antigua (Antego), 1757 3690.1 p90
Gordon, George; Philadelphia, 1828 1639.20 p81
Gordon, George 39; Virginia, 1774 1219.7 p244
Gordon, Hugh 22; Georgia, 1775 1219.7 p276
Gordon, James; America, 1742 4971 p37
Gordon, James; Charleston, SC, 1817 1639.20 p81
Gordon, James; Delaware Bay or River, 1743 4971 p104
Gordon, James; New York, NY, 1811 2859.11 p12
With family
Gordon, James 15; Philadelphia, 1861 5704.8 p149
Gordon, Jane; Philadelphia, 1849 53.26 p32
Gordon, Jane; Philadelphia, 1849 5704.8 p54
Gordon, John; New York, NY, 1816 2859.11 p32
Gordon, John; Petersburg, VA, 1809 4778.2 p141
Gordon, John; Philadelphia, 1811 53.26 p32
Gordon, John; Philadelphia, 1811 2859.11 p12
Gordon, John; Philadelphia, 1865 5704.8 p203
Gordon, John 16; Philadelphia, 1854 5704.8 p116
Gordon, John 17; Jamaica, 1737 3690.1 p90
Gordon, John 19; Antigua (Antego), 1736 3690.1 p90
Gordon, John 24; Jamaica, 1730 3690.1 p90
Gordon, John 27; Maryland, 1775 1219.7 p253
Gordon, John 28; Maryland, 1774 1219.7 p230
Gordon, John 36; Philadelphia, 1804 53.26 p32
Gordon, Joseph George; Arkansas, 1918 95.2 p50
Gordon, Katherine 28 *SEE* Gordon, Peter
Gordon, Letitia; St. John, N.B., 1847 5704.8 p11
Gordon, Magey; St. John, N.B., 1853 5704.8 p107
Gordon, Margaret; St. John, N.B., 1853 5704.8 p107
Gordon, Margaret 39; North Carolina, 1775 1639.20 p57
Gordon, Mary 24; Quebec, 1863 5704.8 p153
Gordon, Nich.; Virginia, 1635 6219 p12
Gordon, Peter 34; Savannah, GA, 1733 4719.17 p311
*Wife:*Katherine 28
Gordon, Robert; Carolina, 1684 1639.20 p81
Gordon, Robert 12; Quebec, 1855 5704.8 p126
Gordon, Robert 23; Philadelphia, 1854 5704.8 p117
Gordon, Thomas; New York, NY, 1816 2859.11 p32
Gordon, Thomas 17; Jamaica, 1773 1219.7 p170
Gordon, Thomas 18; Quebec, 1855 5704.8 p126
Gordon, Thomas 23; Maryland, 1774 1219.7 p192
Gordon, Thomas 25; Maryland, 1774 1219.7 p204
Gordon, William; Charleston, SC, 1765-1817 1639.20 p82
Gordon, William; New York, NY, 1811 2859.11 p12
Gordon, William; New York, NY, 1816 2859.11 p32
Gordon, William; Philadelphia, 1847 53.26 p32
Gordon, William; Philadelphia, 1847 5704.8 p23
Gordon, William; Quebec, 1798 7603 p37
Gordon, William; St. John, N.B., 1852 5704.8 p93
Gordon, William 36?; Arizona, 1890 2764.35 p27
Gordon, William 39; California, 1872 2769.4 p5
Gordon, William 60; Wilmington, NC, 1774 1639.20 p81
With 6 children daughters-in-law & grandchildren
Gore, Mr.; Quebec, 1815 9229.18 p81
Gore, Luke; New York, NY, 1816 2859.11 p32
Goreby, Joseph 19; Pennsylvania, 1738 3690.1 p90
Gorecki, Jan; New York, 1834 4606 p178
Gorfinkel, Nathan Isidore; Arkansas, 1918 95.2 p50
Gorgaine, Eliz.; Virginia, 1636 6219 p80
Gorham, Eugene 11; Massachusetts, 1847 5881.1 p41
Gorham, Jeremiah 26; Massachusetts, 1847 5881.1 p42
Gorham, Johanna 17; Massachusetts, 1847 5881.1 p42
Gorham, John 14; Massachusetts, 1847 5881.1 p42
Gorham, Samuell 23; Jamaica, 1734 3690.1 p91
Gorham, Thomas 50; Massachusetts, 1847 5881.1 p44
Gorie, John; North Carolina, 1813 1639.20 p82
Goring, Gottfried 12; New Orleans, 1839 9420.2 p70
Goring, Gottlieb 18; New Orleans, 1839 9420.2 p70
Goring, John M.; New York, NY, 1836 8208.4 p79
Goring, Justine 11; New Orleans, 1839 9420.2 p70
Goring, Rosine 45; New Orleans, 1839 9420.2 p70
Gorm, Mary; New York, NY, 1866 5704.8 p207
Gormally, Catharine 17; Massachusetts, 1849 5881.1 p41
Gorman, Ann; America, 1866 5704.8 p213
Gorman, Ann; St. John, N.B., 1851 5704.8 p77
Gorman, Bernard; Philadelphia, 1854 5704.8 p117
Gorman, Biddy 3; Quebec, 1855 5704.8 p125
Gorman, Bridget; Philadelphia, 1847 53.26 p32
Gorman, Bridget; Philadelphia, 1847 5704.8 p22
Gorman, Bridget 7; Massachusetts, 1849 5881.1 p41
Gorman, Catharine; Philadelphia, 1864 5704.8 p179
Gorman, Catherine 11; St. John, N.B., 1849 5704.8 p49
Gorman, Catherine 12; Quebec, 1855 5704.8 p125
Gorman, Edward 15; Quebec, 1855 5704.8 p125
Gorman, Eliza 60; Massachusetts, 1850 5881.1 p42
Gorman, Ellen; St. John, N.B., 1850 5704.8 p66
Gorman, Francis; St. John, N.B., 1850 5704.8 p67
Gorman, Hannah; America, 1866 5704.8 p209
Gorman, Honora; America, 1736 4971 p12
Gorman, Hugh; New York, NY, 1816 2859.11 p32
Gorman, Hugh; New York, NY, 1865 5704.8 p196
Gorman, Hugh 13; Quebec, 1855 5704.8 p125
Gorman, Hugh 19; St. John, N.B., 1854 5704.8 p114
Gorman, James; New York, 1880 1450.2 p12B
Gorman, James; New York, NY, 1834 8208.4 p3
Gorman, James; Philadelphia, 1853 5704.8 p100
Gorman, James 5; Quebec, 1855 5704.8 p125
Gorman, James 50; Quebec, 1855 5704.8 p125
Gorman, Jane 8; Massachusetts, 1850 5881.1 p43
Gorman, John 3; Massachusetts, 1849 5881.1 p42
Gorman, John 9; St. John, N.B., 1849 5704.8 p49
Gorman, John 16; Philadelphia, 1864 5704.8 p156
Gorman, John 17; Quebec, 1855 5704.8 p125
Gorman, John 29; Kansas, 1872 5240.1 p15
Gorman, John 29; Kansas, 1872 5240.1 p52
Gorman, Judith; America, 1737 4971 p12
Gorman, Lawrance 23; Philadelphia, 1774 1219.7 p183
Gorman, Margaret; Philadelphia, 1865 5704.8 p197
Gorman, Mary; America, 1743 4971 p11
Gorman, Mary; America, 1743 4971 p95
Gorman, Mary; New York, NY, 1816 2859.11 p32
Gorman, Mary; St. John, N.B., 1850 5704.8 p67
Gorman, Mary 5; Massachusetts, 1849 5881.1 p43
Gorman, Mary 10; Massachusetts, 1849 5881.1 p43
Gorman, Mary 10; Quebec, 1855 5704.8 p125
Gorman, Mary 25; Quebec, 1856 5704.8 p130
Gorman, Mary 45; Quebec, 1855 5704.8 p125
Gorman, Michael; New York, NY, 1816 2859.11 p32
Gorman, Michael; New York, NY, 1837 8208.4 p51
Gorman, Michael; New York, NY, 1837 8208.4 p52
Gorman, Michael; Philadelphia, 1864 5704.8 p180
Gorman, Michael 7; Massachusetts, 1850 5881.1 p43
Gorman, Michael 12; Massachusetts, 1849 5881.1 p43
Gorman, Michael 20; Massachusetts, 1849 5881.1 p43
Gorman, Michael 21; Philadelphia, 1859 5704.8 p142
Gorman, Nancy 15; St. John, N.B., 1854 5704.8 p119
Gorman, Neil; St. John, N.B., 1847 5704.8 p19
Gorman, Patrick; Philadelphia, 1865 5704.8 p197
Gorman, Patrick 18; Massachusetts, 1849 5881.1 p44
Gorman, Patt 20; Quebec, 1855 5704.8 p125
Gorman, Penelope; America, 1741 4971 p16
Gorman, Sarah; Philadelphia, 1866 5704.8 p209
Gorman, Sarah; St. John, N.B., 1847 5704.8 p19
Gorman, Susan 22; St. John, N.B., 1856 5704.8 p131
Gorman, Thomas; America, 1773-1774 2859.11 p7
Gorman, Thomas; Illinois, 1870 5012.38 p99
Gorman, Thomas; Philadelphia, 1811 2859.11 p12
With family
Gorman, Thomas; Philadelphia, 1864 5704.8 p180
Gorman, Thomas; Quebec, 1822 7603 p81
Gorman, Thomas; St. John, N.B., 1849 5704.8 p49
Gorman, Thomas; Wisconsin, n.d. 9675.5 p190
Gorman, Thomas 26; Philadelphia, 1859 5704.8 p141
Gorman, William; New Orleans, 1849 5704.8 p59

Gorman, William; New York, NY, 1816 2859.11 p32
Gorman, William; West Virginia, 1847-1852 9788.3 p11
Gorment, James; New Brunswick, 1789-1793 7603 p76
Gormill, Roger; America, 1742 4971 p29
Gormill, Roger; Delaware, 1743 4971 p105
Gormily, Margaret 19; Philadelphia, 1857 5704.8 p132
Gormin, Catherine; Quebec, 1847 5704.8 p12
Gormley, Bernard; America, 1868 5704.8 p229
Gormley, Bernard; New York, NY, 1816 2859.11 p32
Gormley, Bernard; New York, NY, 1840 8208.4 p105
Gormley, Bridget; Philadelphia, 1864 5704.8 p181
Gormley, Cath.; Philadelphia, 1864 5704.8 p184
Gormley, Catherine 4; St. John, N.B., 1847 5704.8 p15
Gormley, Edward; Ohio, 1844 9892.11 p18
Gormley, Edward; Ohio, 1846 9892.11 p18
Gormley, Edward; Philadelphia, 1864 5704.8 p178
Gormley, Eliza; St. John, N.B., 1847 5704.8 p15
Gormley, Henry; Philadelphia, 1847 53.26 p33
Gormley, Henry; Philadelphia, 1847 5704.8 p23
Gormley, Hugh; New York, NY, 1840 8208.4 p109
Gormley, James; Ohio, 1849 9892.11 p18
Gormley, James; Philadelphia, 1864 5704.8 p183
Gormley, John; New York, NY, 1867 5704.8 p219
Gormley, Martin; New York, NY, 1816 2859.11 p32
Gormley, Mary; Philadelphia, 1864 5704.8 p186
Gormley, Matthew; New York, NY, 1838 8208.4 p61
Gormley, Michael; Philadelphia, 1864 5704.8 p181
Gormley, Michael; St. John, N.B., 1847 5704.8 p15
Gormley, Patrick; Ohio, 1848 9892.11 p18
Gormley, Patrick; Ohio, 1850 9892.11 p18
Gormley, Peter; Philadelphia, 1867 5704.8 p221
Gormley, Rose 25; Philadelphia, 1865 5704.8 p164
Gormley, Sarah; New York, NY, 1868 5704.8 p230
Gormley, Sarah; Philadelphia, 1868 5704.8 p226
Gormly, Alice; Philadelphia, 1847 5704.8 p31
Gormly, Andrew 9 mos; St. John, N.B., 1847 5704.8 p15
Gormly, Ann; Quebec, 1847 5704.8 p17
Gormly, Arthur; St. John, N.B., 1850 5704.8 p67
Gormly, Arthur 7; Quebec, 1847 5704.8 p38
Gormly, Bernard; St. John, N.B., 1852 5704.8 p84
Gormly, Biddy; St. John, N.B., 1852 5704.8 p84
Gormly, Biddy 18; Philadelphia, 1854 5704.8 p116
Gormly, Bridget; St. John, N.B., 1847 5704.8 p11
Gormly, Catherine; Quebec, 1847 5704.8 p17
Gormly, Catherine; Quebec, 1851 5704.8 p74
Gormly, Catherine 3; St. John, N.B., 1847 5704.8 p15
Gormly, Charles; Philadelphia, 1853 5704.8 p103
Gormly, Charles; Quebec, 1847 5704.8 p17
Gormly, Charles; Quebec, 1851 5704.8 p74
Gormly, Charles 3 mos; Quebec, 1847 5704.8 p17
Gormly, Cornelius; America, 1740 4971 p73
Gormly, David; Quebec, 1851 5704.8 p74
Gormly, Elizabeth 6; Philadelphia, 1857 5704.8 p133
Gormly, Ellan 1; Quebec, 1847 5704.8 p17
Gormly, Ellen; St. John, N.B., 1852 5704.8 p95
Gormly, Ellen 20; Philadelphia, 1854 5704.8 p121
Gormly, Fergus; Quebec, 1847 5704.8 p38
Gormly, Francis; Philadelphia, 1848 53.26 p33
Gormly, Francis; Philadelphia, 1848 5704.8 p41
Gormly, George; Philadelphia, 1853 5704.8 p101
Gormly, Henry; Quebec, 1847 5704.8 p17
Gormly, Henry 8; Massachusetts, 1850 5881.1 p42
Gormly, James; Ohio, 1842 9892.11 p18
Gormly, James; St. John, N.B., 1847 5704.8 p11
Gormly, James; St. John, N.B., 1848 5704.8 p45
Gormly, James 6 mos; St. John, N.B., 1847 5704.8 p21
Gormly, Jane; Quebec, 1847 5704.8 p17
Gormly, Jane; Quebec, 1851 5704.8 p74
Gormly, John; New York, NY, 1836 8208.4 p79
Gormly, John; Quebec, 1847 5704.8 p17
Gormly, John; St. John, N.B., 1848 5704.8 p47
Gormly, John 2; St. John, N.B., 1847 5704.8 p11
Gormly, Joseph 2; Quebec, 1847 5704.8 p38
Gormly, Margaret *SEE* Gormly, Sarah
Gormly, Margaret; Philadelphia, 1849 5704.8 p58
Gormly, Margaret; Quebec, 1847 5704.8 p38
Gormly, Margaret; St. John, N.B., 1847 5704.8 p15
Gormly, Margaret; St. John, N.B., 1850 5704.8 p67
Gormly, Mary; Quebec, 1847 5704.8 p17
Gormly, Mary; Quebec, 1847 5704.8 p38
Gormly, Mary; Quebec, 1851 5704.8 p74
Gormly, Mary; St. John, N.B., 1847 5704.8 p21
Gormly, Mary; St. John, N.B., 1849 5704.8 p56
Gormly, Mary 4; St. John, N.B., 1847 5704.8 p11
Gormly, Mary 5; Quebec, 1847 5704.8 p38
Gormly, Michael 18; Philadelphia, 1854 5704.8 p117
Gormly, Mick *SEE* Gormly, Patrick
Gormly, Mick; Philadelphia, 1848 5704.8 p40
Gormly, Neal; St. John, N.B., 1847 5704.8 p19
Gormly, Pat; Philadelphia, 1852 5704.8 p92
Gormly, Patrick; Philadelphia, 1848 53.26 p33
*Relative:*Mick
Gormly, Patrick; Philadelphia, 1848 5704.8 p40
Gormly, Patrick; St. John, N.B., 1847 5704.8 p20
Gormly, Patrick; St. John, N.B., 1847 5704.8 p26
Gormly, Patrick 23; Philadelphia, 1854 5704.8 p116
Gormly, Patt; St. John, N.B., 1847 5704.8 p15
Gormly, Rose 11; Quebec, 1847 5704.8 p38
Gormly, Rose 16; Philadelphia, 1854 5704.8 p116
Gormly, Roseanna; Philadelphia, 1850 53.26 p33
Gormly, Roseanna; Philadelphia, 1850 5704.8 p69
Gormly, Sally 40; Massachusetts, 1850 5881.1 p44
Gormly, Sarah; Philadelphia, 1849 53.26 p33
*Relative:*Margaret
Gormly, Sarah; Philadelphia, 1849 5704.8 p58
Gormly, Sarah 8; Quebec, 1851 5704.8 p74
Gormly, Susan; Philadelphia, 1852 5704.8 p96
Gormly, Thomas; New Orleans, 1852 5704.8 p98
Gormly, Thomas; New York, NY, 1835 8208.4 p41
Gormly, Thomas 9; Quebec, 1847 5704.8 p38
Gormly, Thomas 18; Philadelphia, 1854 5704.8 p121
Gormly, William; Philadelphia, 1849 53.26 p33
Gormly, William; Philadelphia, 1849 5704.8 p53
Gormly, William; Quebec, 1851 5704.8 p74
Gormly, William; St. John, N.B., 1847 5704.8 p21
Gorney, John; Arkansas, 1918 95.2 p50
Gorrad, Henry 17; Jamaica, 1734 3690.1 p90
Gorrcoup, Robert 50; Port uncertain, 1836 778.5 p245
Gorrel, Ellen 13; St. John, N.B., 1859 5704.8 p143
Gorrel, James 12; St. John, N.B., 1859 5704.8 p143
Gorrell, Anne 18; Philadelphia, 1864 5704.8 p161
Gorrie, Daniel 29; Maryland, 1775 1219.7 p253
Gorrie, David; South Carolina, 1821 1639.20 p82
Gorrie, John; America, 1807 1639.20 p82
Gorrie, Joseph; Wilmington, NC, 1830 1639.20 p82
Gors, Carl; Kansas, 1887 5240.1 p15
Gorse, John; New York, NY, 1837 8208.4 p37
Gorska, Julia 22; New York, 1912 9980.29 p55
Gorski, Boleslaw; Wisconsin, n.d. 9675.5 p190
Gorvorn, Michael; New York, NY, 1816 2859.11 p32
Gorwell, Sackvild 21; Maryland, 1735 3690.1 p91
Gosall, Jon.; Virginia, 1638 6219 p118
Gosar, Luis 28; America, 1829 778.5 p245
Goschka, Heinrich 29; Kansas, 1882 5240.1 p63
Gosden, Richard 16; Maryland, 1720 3690.1 p91
Gosdzewski, Gotfrid; Illinois, 1896 5012.40 p54
Gosen, D. von; New York, 1776 9786 p277
Gosenflo, Gusta; America, 1860 6014.1 p2
Gosewehr, Carl Henry; Wisconsin, n.d. 9675.5 p190
Gosewehr, William; Wisconsin, n.d. 9675.5 p190
Goslar, Joachim; Illinois, 1856 2896.5 p14
Goslicki, Wincenty 20; New York, 1912 9980.29 p58
With niece
Goslin, Ellen 21; Massachusetts, 1849 5881.1 p42
Gosling, James 34; Maryland, 1774 1219.7 p235
Gosling, Jon.; Virginia, 1643 6219 p201
Gosman, Agnes 3 *SEE* Gosman, Andrew
Gosman, Andrew; Ohio, 1825 9892.11 p18
Gosman, Andrew; Philadelphia, 1817 9892.11 p18
*Relative:*Agnes 3
*Relative:*Frederic 4
Gosman, Frederic 4 *SEE* Gosman, Andrew
Gosman, Michael; New York, NY, 1838 8208.4 p69
Gosmore, Eliz.; Virginia, 1633 6219 p31
Gospole, Bernard; Kentucky, 1843 8582.3 p100
Gospole, Karl; Kentucky, 1843 8582.3 p100
Goss, Johann; Ohio, 1808 8582.1 p49
Goss, John 15; Maryland, 1724 3690.1 p91
Goss, Stanley; Arkansas, 1918 95.2 p50
Gossain Buch, Pierre 30; New Orleans, 1826 778.5 p245
Gossan, Jebron; Nebraska, 1900 5240.1 p15
Gossard, Jakob *SEE* Gossard, Johann
Gossard, Johann; Ohio, 1808 8582.2 p56
*Brother:*Philipp
*Brother:*Jakob
Gossard, Philipp *SEE* Gossard, Johann
Gossart, . . .; Canada, 1776-1783 9786 p22
Gosse, Christopher; Virginia, 1637 6219 p8
Gosselin, Francois 38; New Orleans, 1862 543.30 p373C
Gosser, Christian; Indiana, 1848 9117 p16
Gossert, John Lewis, Jr.; New York, NY, 1840 8208.4 p107
Gossling, . . .; Illinois, 1800-1900 4610.10 p67
Gossling, Marie; America, 1909 4610.10 p55
Gostas, Tony; Arkansas, 1918 95.2 p50
Gotchaud, Mayer; Port uncertain, 1839 778.5 p245
Gotear, Benjamin 18; Jamaica, 1729 3690.1 p91
Goter, Benjamin 18; Jamaica, 1729 3690.1 p91
Gothberg, Andrew; Iroquois Co., IL, 1892 3455.1 p11
Gothberg, Charles; New York, NY, 1921 3455.4 p29
*Wife:*Huldah
Gothberg, Huldah *SEE* Gothberg, Charles
Gothburg, John; Iroquois Co., IL, 1894 3455.1 p11
Gother, James; Jamaica, 1751 1219.7 p7
Gother, James; Jamaica, 1751 3690.1 p91
Gothie, Johann; Pennsylvania, 1855 3702.7 p389
*Brother:*Wilhelm
Gothie, Wilhelm *SEE* Gothie, Johann
Gothier, John James 37; New Orleans, 1838 778.5 p245
Gothier, Jules 4; New Orleans, 1838 778.5 p245
Gothier, Julian 8; New Orleans, 1838 778.5 p246
Gothier, Mary Pouland 32; New Orleans, 1838 778.5 p246
Gothman, William 24; New Orleans, 1864 543.30 p379C
Gott, Henry A.; Cincinnati, 1869-1887 8582 p11
Gott, John; New Jersey, 1853 1450.2 p53A
Gottdank, Samuel; America, 1900 1450.2 p53A
Gotteland, Niels T.; Wisconsin, n.d. 9675.5 p190
Gotterey, William 15; Jamaica, 1725 3690.1 p91
Gottermann, William; Wisconsin, n.d. 9675.5 p190
Gottfrieda, Sister M.; Wisconsin, n.d. 9675.7 p129
Gottker, John Harman; New York, NY, 1833 8208.4 p44
Gottlob, Carl 17; New Orleans, 1839 9420.2 p169
Gottman, Andrew; Indiana, 1847 9117 p18
Gottman, George Philippe 26; Kansas, 1882 5240.1 p63
Gottner, Ben; Arkansas, 1918 95.2 p50
Gottschalk, Charles; Kansas, 1872 5240.1 p15
Gottschalk, Georg; Philadelphia, 1779 8137 p9
Gottschalk, Jacob; America, 1854 4610.10 p99
Gottschalksson, Jon 12; Quebec, 1879 2557.1 p39
Gottschall, Agatha; America, 1750 2444 p158
*Brother:*Heinrich
With brother-in-law
Gottschall, Anna; Pennsylvania, 1751 2444 p195
Gottschall, Dorothea; America, 1750 2444 p137
Gottschall, Heinrich *SEE* Gottschall, Agatha
Gottshalk, Matthias Gottlieb; Delaware, 1746 3652 p68
Gottskuldsson, Jon 12; Quebec, 1879 2557.1 p39
Gottsschalck, . . .; Canada, 1776-1783 9786 p42
Gottsshall, . . .; Canada, 1776-1783 9786 p42
Gottzejer, Joseph; Illinois, 1868 2896.5 p15
Gotz, Mr. 25; New Orleans, 1823 778.5 p246
Gotz, Anna Barbara Brunner *SEE* Gotz, Christian
Gotz, Catherine 58; Kansas, 1879 5240.1 p61
Gotz, Christian; Philadelphia, 1729 2854 p43
Gotz, Christian; Philadelphia, 1729 2854 p44
*Wife:*Anna Barbara Brunner
With son 6
With daughter 5
Gotze, . . .; Canada, 1776-1783 9786 p22
Gotze, Gustave; Wisconsin, n.d. 9675.5 p190
Gotzelmann, Christoffel; Philadelphia, 1769 4525 p265
Gotzendanner, Anna Barbara Brunner *SEE* Gotzendanner, Christian
Gotzendanner, Christian; Philadelphia, 1729 2854 p43
Gotzendanner, Christian; Philadelphia, 1729 2854 p44
*Wife:*Anna Barbara Brunner
With son 6
With daughter 5
Gotzger, Anna Barbara *SEE* Gotzger, Christian
Gotzger, Anna Barbara *SEE* Gotzger, Christian
Gotzger, Anna Maria *SEE* Gotzger, Christian
Gotzger, Christian; Pennsylvania, 1754 2444 p158
*Wife:*Anna Barbara
*Child:*Anna Barbara
*Child:*Anna Maria
Gouan, Bd. 32; Havana, 1839 778.5 p246
Gouardette, Jean 25; New Orleans, 1838 778.5 p246
Gouardette, Marie 26; New Orleans, 1838 778.5 p246
Goubaux, Hubert 31; Port uncertain, 1839 778.5 p246
Goubaux, Julie 6 mos; Port uncertain, 1839 778.5 p246
Goubaux, Marie 26; Port uncertain, 1839 778.5 p246
Gouch, Mathew; Virginia, 1636 6219 p79
Goudeau, Desiree Marguerite 3; New Orleans, 1821 778.5 p246
Goudecheaur, Henry 24; America, 1831 778.5 p246
Goudecheaur, Levy 26; America, 1831 778.5 p246
Goudie, John; Quebec, 1822 7603 p39
Goudon, Mr. 19; America, 1836 778.5 p246
Gouffard, Mr.; New Orleans, 1839 778.5 p246
Gouffie, T. 22; New Orleans, 1827 778.5 p246
Gouffier, Mr. 26; New Orleans, 1823 778.5 p247
Gouffier, Mr. 30; Port uncertain, 1820 778.5 p247
Gouffroy, Leon 15; America, 1838 778.5 p247
Gough, John 33; Maryland, 1775 1219.7 p266
Gough, Mathew; Virginia, 1639 6219 p154
Gough, Richard 15; Philadelphia, 1775 1219.7 p248
Gough, Thomas; Wisconsin, n.d. 9675.5 p263
Gouhil de la Piqueliere, Mr. 20; New Orleans, 1825 778.5 p247
Gouhot, C. 31; America, 1832 778.5 p247
Gouin, Jeremiah 18; Pennsylvania, 1722 3690.1 p91
Goujon, Jeremiah 18; Pennsylvania, 1722 3690.1 p91
Goujon, Louis 26; America, 1837 778.5 p247
Goul, Bess 15; St. John, N.B., 1856 5704.8 p131
Goul, William 11; St. John, N.B., 1856 5704.8 p131
Goulby, John 24; Maryland, 1774 1219.7 p207
Gould, Edward 31; Jamaica, 1723 3690.1 p91

182 FOR A COMPLETE EXPLANATION OF ENTRY, SEE "HOW TO READ A CITATION" SECTION

Gould, Patrick; America, 1738 *4971 p39*
Gould, Thomas 21; Maryland, 1775 *1219.7 p273*
Goulding, Wm.; Virginia, 1635 *6219 p35*
Gouldmann, Jacob; New York, NY, 1854 *1450.2 p53A*
Gouldsmith, John 20; Jamaica, 1729 *3690.1 p91*
Gouldy, David; New York, NY, 1840 *8208.4 p103*
Goule, Mr. 20; America, 1837 *778.5 p247*
Goulson, Danll.; Virginia, 1648 *6219 p241*
Goumard, Mlle. 36; New Orleans, 1838 *778.5 p247*
Goumard, Charles 31; New Orleans, 1836 *778.5 p247*
Goumard, Rose 20; New Orleans, 1836 *778.5 p247*
Goumas, Mike; Arkansas, 1918 *95.2 p50*
Gouray, Jules 18; America, 1836 *778.5 p247*
Gourdon, Jules G. 22; New Orleans, 1836 *778.5 p247*
Gourdy, Victor 21; New Orleans, 1836 *778.5 p247*
Goure, Mr. 10; New Orleans, 1825 *778.5 p247*
Goure, Mr. 36; New Orleans, 1825 *778.5 p247*
Goure, Jacob 17; Maryland or Virginia, 1720 *3690.1 p91*
Gourlay, James; South Carolina, 1774 *1639.20 p82*
Gourley, Ann 10; St. John, N.B., 1853 *5704.8 p109*
Gourley, Eliza; St. John, N.B., 1847 *5704.8 p20*
Gourley, Eliza 11; St. John, N.B., 1847 *5704.8 p20*
Gourley, John 13; St. John, N.B., 1853 *5704.8 p109*
Gourley, Linnia; St. John, N.B., 1847 *5704.8 p20*
Gourley, Margaret; St. John, N.B., 1847 *5704.8 p20*
Gourley, Mary Jane; St. John, N.B., 1847 *5704.8 p20*
Gourley, Nancy 40; Wilmington, DE, 1831 *6508.7 p160*
Gourley, Robert; St. John, N.B., 1847 *5704.8 p20*
Gourley, Robert 19; Philadelphia, 1857 *5704.8 p132*
Gourley, Sarah; St. John, N.B., 1847 *5704.8 p20*
Gourley, Sarah 6; St. John, N.B., 1853 *5704.8 p109*
Gourley, William 13; St. John, N.B., 1847 *5704.8 p20*
Gourley, William 15; St. John, N.B., 1853 *5704.8 p109*
Gourley, William 40; Wilmington, DE, 1831 *6508.7 p160*
Gourmoin, H. 35; New Orleans, 1827 *778.5 p248*
Goursac, Mr. 32; Port uncertain, 1820 *778.5 p248*
Goursac, Mr. 35; New Orleans, 1821 *778.5 p248*
Goursac, Francois 55; New Orleans, 1838 *778.5 p248*
Gourtin, Laurent 18; New Orleans, 1838 *778.5 p248*
Goussaud, Antoine 35; Port uncertain, 1825 *778.5 p248*
Goutasgnier, Peter; New York, NY, 1837 *8208.4 p45*
Goutier, Jaque 27; Pennsylvania, 1753 *2444 p156*
Gouy, Mr. 33; New Orleans, 1839 *778.5 p248*
Gouye, Mr. 32; America, 1838 *778.5 p248*
Gouz, Louis 23; America, 1836 *778.5 p248*
Gouze, Arnold; New York, NY, 1850 *2896.5 p15*
Govan, Helen; Charleston, SC, 1782 *1639.20 p266*
Gove, Edward 21; New Orleans, 1863 *543.30 p378C*
Gover, Aaron 16; Philadelphia, 1775 *1219.7 p248*
Gover, John; Maryland, 1750 *3690.1 p92*
Gover, John; Maryland, 1751 *1219.7 p2*
Gover, John 15; Maryland, 1775 *1219.7 p272*
Gover, William 22; Maryland, 1774 *1219.7 p204*
Goveran, Peter; New York, NY, 1816 *2859.11 p32*
Goverman, Simon; Arkansas, 1918 *95.2 p50*
Goviella, Eugene 4; New Orleans, 1838 *778.5 p248*
Goviella, Louisa Marie 21; New Orleans, 1838 *778.5 p248*
Goviella, Matilda 2; New Orleans, 1838 *778.5 p248*
Gow, Andrew; Charleston, SC, 1798 *1639.20 p82*
Gow, Anstace; America, 1742 *4971 p50*
Gow, David; America, 1832 *8893 p263*
Gow, James 15; Quebec, 1864 *5704.8 p163*
Gow, James 40; Quebec, 1864 *5704.8 p163*
Gow, Janet 3; Quebec, 1864 *5704.8 p164*
Gow, John 5; Quebec, 1864 *5704.8 p164*
Gow, Mary 8; Quebec, 1864 *5704.8 p163*
Gow, Rose 18; St. John, N.B., 1856 *5704.8 p131*
Gowan, Henry; New York, NY, 1815 *2859.11 p32*
Gowan, James; Philadelphia, 1816 *2859.11 p32*
Gowan, Peter; Charleston, SC, 1848 *1639.20 p82*
Gowan, Peter 58; South Carolina, 1850 *1639.20 p82*
Gowdie, Ellen; Quebec, 1852 *5704.8 p90*
Gowen, Mr.; Quebec, 1815 *9229.18 p76*
Gowen, Francis 13; St. John, N.B., 1847 *5704.8 p4*
Gowen, Matilda 11; St. John, N.B., 1847 *5704.8 p4*
Gowen, Peter 20; Virginia, 1700 *2212 p32*
Gower, Henry 23; Philadelphia, 1775 *1219.7 p255*
Gower, John 17; Jamaica, 1729 *3690.1 p92*
Gower, Nich.; Virginia, 1637 *6219 p86*
Gower, Nich.; Virginia, 1638 *6219 p115*
Gower, William; New York, NY, 1835 *8208.4 p46*
Gowie, Alexander 23; Jamaica, 1774 *1219.7 p207*
Gowing, Richard; Quebec, 1783 *7603 p63*
Gowley, Cath'ine 25; Massachusetts, 1849 *5881.1 p41*
 With child
Gowley, Patrick 30; Massachusetts, 1849 *5881.1 p44*
Gowning, Jon.; Virginia, 1635 *6219 p71*
Gowran, John; New York, NY, 1815 *2859.11 p32*
Gowring, Richard; Quebec, 1783 *7603 p76*
Goyer, Mr.; New Orleans, 1839 *778.5 p248*

Goyer, Charles Lewis 26; New Orleans, 1839 *9420.2 p483*
Goyer, Natalie 23; New Orleans, 1839 *9420.2 p483*
Goyett, David 33; Kansas, 1887 *5240.1 p70*
Graaf, Nicholas; Illinois, 1892 *5012.40 p27*
Grab, George; Colorado, 1896 *9678.2 p21*
Grab, John; Indiana, 1848 *9117 p19*
Graban, Max; Kansas, 1885 *5240.1 p15*
Grabau, Johann; New York, 1839 *3702.7 p300*
Grabbe, Carl Anton Heinrich; America, 1886 *4610.10 p114*
Grabbe, Frederick; Indiana, 1850 *9117 p20*
Grabben, Thomas; New York, NY, 1865 *5704.8 p193*
Grabbin, Peter; New York, NY, 1811 *2859.11 p12*
Grabe, Anne Marie Heermeier SEE Grabe, Carl Heinrich
Grabe, Carl Heinrich; America, 1841 *4610.10 p111*
 Wife:Anne Marie Heermeier
 Son:Karl H. Ferdinand
Grabe, Karl H. Ferdinand SEE Grabe, Carl Heinrich
Graber, William; Illinois, 1898 *2896.5 p15*
Grabher, August; Illinois, 1884 *2896.5 p15*
Grabhorn, Anthony; America, 1849 *1450.2 p55A*
Grabhorn, J. H.; Indiana, 1850 *9117 p16*
Grabner, Anton; Wisconsin, n.d. *9675.5 p263*
Grabner, Johann; Wisconsin, n.d. *9675.5 p263*
Grabner, John; Wisconsin, n.d. *9675.5 p263*
Grabow, Pastor; New York, 1839 *3702.7 p304*
Grabowska, Irena 2; New York, 1912 *9980.29 p53*
Grabowska, Janina 8; New York, 1912 *9980.29 p53*
Grabowska, Maryanna Jelinska 29; New York, 1912 *9980.29 p53*
Grabowski, Anton 22; New York, 1912 *9980.29 p64*
Grabowski, Jan 7; New York, 1912 *9980.29 p53*
Grabowski, Maryanna Jelinska 29; New York, 1912 *9980.29 p53*
Grabowski, Sylvester; New York, 1831 *4606 p173*
Grabowski, Trofil; Arkansas, 1918 *95.2 p50*
Grabs, Anna Mary SEE Grabs, John Godfrey
Grabs, John Godfrey; New York, 1743 *3652 p59*
 Wife:Anna Mary
Grace, Francis; New York, NY, 1815 *2859.11 p32*
Grace, Georg; Virginia, 1639 *6219 p152*
Grace, Henri; Quebec, 1758 *7603 p27*
Grace, James 19; Maryland, 1774 *1219.7 p236*
Grace, John; Quebec, 1825 *7603 p76*
Grace, Patrick; America, 1742 *4971 p29*
Grace, Patrick; America, 1743 *4971 p32*
Grace, Patrick; Annapolis, MD, 1742 *4971 p93*
Grace, Patrick; Maryland, 1742 *4971 p106*
Grace, Richard; Quebec, 1765 *7603 p69*
Grace, Robt.; Virginia, 1635 *6219 p10*
Grace, Roger; Virginia, 1637 *6219 p10*
Gracey, William; New York, NY, 1816 *2859.11 p32*
Grachan, Frank; Iowa, 1866-1943 *123.54 p20*
Gradel, Johann; America, 1850 *8582.3 p24*
Gradel, Julian; Colorado, 1894 *9678.2 p21*
Gradick, Jacob, Jr.; South Carolina, 1788 *7119 p203*
Gradiezsky, Francis; Pennsylvania, 1900 *7137 p168*
Gradin, Edwd.; Virginia, 1637 *6219 p114*
Grados, . . .; Port uncertain, 1839 *778.5 p248*
Grados, . . .; Port uncertain, 1839 *778.5 p249*
Grados, Alex.; Port uncertain, 1839 *778.5 p249*
Grady, Ann 16; Massachusetts, 1847 *5881.1 p41*
Grady, Catharine 19; Massachusetts, 1849 *5881.1 p41*
Grady, Daniel O.; West Virginia, 1876 *9788.3 p11*
Grady, George; New York, NY, 1811 *2859.11 p12*
 With niece
Grady, Honora 20; Massachusetts, 1850 *5881.1 p42*
Grady, Honora 21; Massachusetts, 1850 *5881.1 p42*
Grady, James; New York, NY, 1838 *8208.4 p76*
Grady, James; Philadelphia, 1850 *6013.19 p20*
Grady, Johanna 20; Massachusetts, 1850 *5881.1 p43*
Grady, John 33; New Orleans, 1862 *543.30 p383C*
Grady, Mary 16; Massachusetts, 1849 *5881.1 p43*
Grady, Patrick; America, 1736-1737 *4971 p61*
Grady, Patrick; America, 1736-1743 *4971 p57*
Grady, Patrick 26; Massachusetts, 1848 *5881.1 p44*
Grady, Thomas; America, 1840 *7036 p118*
Grady, Thomas; St. Johns, N.F., 1840 *7036 p118*
Grady, Timothy 25; Massachusetts, 1849 *5881.1 p44*
Grady, Wm; New York, NY, 1816 *2859.11 p32*
Graeber, Anna Barbara SEE Graeber, Hieronymus
Graeber, Anna Maria SEE Graeber, Hieronymus
Graeber, August 44; New Orleans, 1839 *9420.2 p167*
Graeber, Hieronymus; New England, 1747 *2444 p158*
 Wife:Anna Maria
 Child:Anna Barbara
Graefe, Cornet; Quebec, 1776 *9786 p104*
Graeff, . . .; Canada, 1776-1783 *9786 p22*
Graeff, Abraham op den; Pennsylvania, 1683 *2155 p1*
 Wife:Catharina
 Child:Isaac
 Child:Jacob

 Child:Anne
 Child:Margaret
Graeff, Anne SEE Graeff, Abraham op den
Graeff, Catharina SEE Graeff, Abraham op den
Graeff, Dirck op den; Pennsylvania, 1683 *2155 p1*
 Wife:Nolken Vojten
Graeff, Gerhard; Lancaster, PA, 1773 *9973.8 p33*
Graeff, Greitjen Peiters op den; Philadelphia, 1683-1700 *2155 p2*
Graeff, Herman op den; Pennsylvania, 1683 *2155 p1*
 Wife:Lisbet I. van Bebber
Graeff, Isaac SEE Graeff, Abraham op den
Graeff, Jacob SEE Graeff, Abraham op den
Graeff, Lisbet I. van Bebber SEE Graeff, Herman op den
Graeff, Margaret SEE Graeff, Abraham op den
Graeff, Margaret op den; Pennsylvania, 1683-1700 *2155 p2*
Graeff, Nolken Vojten SEE Graeff, Dirck op den
Graehling, Henry; Illinois, 1861 *7857 p4*
Graeme, David; South Carolina, 1753 *1639.20 p84*
Graemiger, Otto B.; Arkansas, 1918 *95.2 p50*
Graeser, Louis; America, 1848 *8582.3 p24*
Graeter, . . .; Canada, 1776-1783 *9786 p22*
Graetsch, . . .; Canada, 1776-1783 *9786 p22*
Graetz, Mr.; Pennsylvania, 1754 *4525 p221*
Graetz, Andreas; Pennsylvania, 1751 *4525 p221*
Graez, Christian; Pennsylvania, 1752 *4525 p221*
Graf, Adolph; Wisconsin, n.d. *9675.5 p263*
Graf, Anne 7 SEE Graf, Augustus
Graf, August; America, 1871 *1450.2 p53A*
Graf, Augustus 30; New Orleans, 1839 *9420.2 p486*
 Wife:Wilhelmina 26
 Child:Gilian 12
 Child:Rosamond 9
 Child:Anne 7
Graf, Carl August; Wisconsin, n.d. *9675.5 p263*
Graf, Catharina; Pennsylvania, 1744 *2444 p158*
Graf, David; America, 1849 *8582.2 p13*
Graf, Gilian 12 SEE Graf, Augustus
Graf, Joseph; Maryland, 1820-1829 *8582.1 p46*
Graf, Jost 82; America, 1897 *1763 p40C*
Graf, Leopold; Arizona, 1890 *2764.35 p28*
Graf, Leopold 45; Arizona, 1890 *2764.35 p27*
Graf, Mathias; Wisconsin, n.d. *9675.5 p263*
Graf, Otto; New York, NY, 1896 *1450.2 p12B*
Graf, Rosamond 9 SEE Graf, Augustus
Graf, Wilhelmina 26 SEE Graf, Augustus
Grafe, August; Wisconsin, n.d. *9675.5 p263*
Grafe, August Ludwig Lucas; Quebec, 1776 *9786 p253*
Grafe, Gottlieb; Wisconsin, n.d. *9675.5 p263*
Grafenstein, William; America, 1858 *1450.2 p53A*
Graff, Carl Wilhelm; Halifax, N.S., 1778 *9786 p270*
Graff, Carl Wilhelm; New York, 1776 *9786 p270*
Graff, David; New York, NY, 1838 *8208.4 p60*
Graff, Fred; Illinois, 1896 *5012.40 p54*
Graff, Gertrude SEE Graff, John Michael
Graff, Herman 42; New Orleans, 1862 *543.30 p383C*
Graff, John Michael; New York, 1751 *3652 p75*
 Wife:Gertrude
Graff, L. 30; New Orleans, 1830 *778.5 p249*
Graff, Michael; Wisconsin, n.d. *9675.5 p263*
Graff, Michel 46; New Orleans, 1862 *543.30 p373C*
Graff, Peter; Wisconsin, n.d. *9675.5 p263*
Graff, Teopkiel 48; Kansas, 1883 *5240.1 p64*
Graff, Thomas 35; New Orleans, 1862 *543.30 p382C*
Graff, William 31; New Orleans, 1863 *543.30 p379C*
Graffe, Christopher; Philadelphia, 1760 *9973.7 p34*
Graffe, John Casper; Philadelphia, 1760 *9973.7 p34*
Graffenstein, Frederick; America, 1867 *1450.2 p53A*
Grafft, George; Philadelphia, 1761 *9973.7 p35*
Graftmuller, Max; America, 1876 *6014.1 p2*
Grafton, John 25; Carolina, 1774 *1219.7 p213*
Gragg, Michael 19; Jamaica, 1729 *3690.1 p92*
Graghan, Mich'l 38; Massachusetts, 1850 *5881.1 p22*
Graghty, Michael 50; Massachusetts, 1850 *5881.1 p43*
Graghty, Peter 12; Massachusetts, 1850 *5881.1 p44*
Graham, Alex SEE Graham, John
Graham, Alex; Quebec, 1863 *4537.30 p14*
 Wife:Sibla MacIver
 Child:Margaret
 Child:Catherine
 Child:Margaret
Graham, Alexander; Baltimore, 1816 *2859.11 p32*
 With wife
Graham, Alexander; North Carolina, 1771 *1639.20 p82*
Graham, Alexander 17; Philadelphia, 1854 *5704.8 p118*
Graham, Alexander 24; Quebec, 1859 *5704.8 p143*
Graham, Alexander 50; Charlotte, NC, 1850 *1639.20 p83*
 Relative:Catherine 74
Graham, Alexander 62; North Carolina, 1850 *1639.20 p83*

Graham, Alexander 69; North Carolina, 1850 ***1639.20*** *p83*
Graham, Andrew; America, 1735-1743 ***4971*** *p8*
Graham, Andrew; Ohio, 1840 ***9892.11*** *p18*
Graham, Andrew 11; St. John, N.B., 1855 ***5704.8*** *p127*
Graham, Andrew 63; St. John, N.B., 1855 ***5704.8*** *p127*
Graham, Angus *SEE* Graham, John
Graham, Angus *SEE* Graham, John
Graham, Angus; Quebec, 1851 ***4537.30*** *p13*
*Wife:*Margaret Maclean
*Child:*Margaret
*Child:*John
*Child:*Donald
*Child:*Murdo
Graham, Ann *SEE* Graham, John
Graham, Ann *SEE* Graham, Murdo
Graham, Ann *SEE* Graham, Norman
Graham, Ann; Quebec, 1873 ***4537.30*** *p33*
Graham, Ann 12; Philadelphia, 1864 ***5704.8*** *p176*
Graham, Ann 17; Quebec, 1854 ***5704.8*** *p119*
Graham, Ann 89; North Carolina, 1850 ***1639.20*** *p83*
Graham, Ann Jane; Philadelphia, 1868 ***5704.8*** *p230*
Graham, Annabella MacIver *SEE* Graham, John
Graham, Anne; Quebec, 1847 ***5704.8*** *p38*
Graham, Anne 4; Quebec, 1847 ***5704.8*** *p38*
Graham, Anthony 53; California, 1872 ***2769.4*** *p5*
Graham, Archibald; America, 1804 ***1639.20*** *p83*
Graham, Archibald 45; North Carolina, 1850 ***1639.20*** *p83*
Graham, Archibald 60; North Carolina, 1850 ***1639.20*** *p83*
Graham, Archibald 65; North Carolina, 1850 ***1639.20*** *p83*
Graham, Cath.; New York, NY, 1811 ***2859.11*** *p12*
With family
Graham, Catherine *SEE* Graham, Alex
Graham, Catherine *SEE* Graham, Murdo
Graham, Catherine *SEE* Graham, Norman
Graham, Catherine; Philadelphia, 1852 ***5704.8*** *p89*
Graham, Catherine; Quebec, 1875 ***4537.30*** *p71*
Graham, Catherine 12; Quebec, 1855 ***5704.8*** *p126*
Graham, Catherine 44; Quebec, 1855 ***5704.8*** *p126*
Graham, Catherine 74 *SEE* Graham, Alexander
Graham, Catherine MacDonald *SEE* Graham, John
Graham, Catherine MacRitchie *SEE* Graham, Murdo
Graham, Christopher 20; Quebec, 1854 ***5704.8*** *p119*
Graham, Daniel; America, 1788 ***1639.20*** *p83*
Graham, Daniel; America, 1803 ***1639.20*** *p84*
Graham, Daniel; St. John, N.B., 1848 ***5704.8*** *p45*
Graham, Daniel 25; Virginia, 1774 ***1219.7*** *p228*
Graham, Daniel 65; North Carolina, 1850 ***1639.20*** *p84*
Graham, Daniel 90; North Carolina, 1850 ***1639.20*** *p84*
Graham, David 18; Quebec, 1861 ***5704.8*** *p149*
Graham, David 76; North Carolina, 1850 ***1639.20*** *p84*
Graham, Donald *SEE* Graham, Angus
Graham, Donald *SEE* Graham, John
Graham, Donald *SEE* Graham, John
Graham, Donald *SEE* Graham, Norman
Graham, Dora; Philadelphia, 1868 ***5704.8*** *p230*
Graham, Dorah 55; Philadelphia, 1859 ***5704.8*** *p141*
Graham, Dugald; America, 1803 ***1639.20*** *p84*
Graham, Duncan 55; North Carolina, 1850 ***1639.20*** *p84*
Graham, Edmund; America, 1741 ***4971*** *p9*
Graham, Edward; America, 1741 ***4971*** *p94*
Graham, Effie *SEE* Graham, John
Graham, Eliza 10; Philadelphia, 1864 ***5704.8*** *p176*
Graham, Eliza 19; Quebec, 1855 ***5704.8*** *p126*
Graham, Eliza 33; Massachusetts, 1847 ***5881.1*** *p41*
Graham, Elizabeth; New York, NY, 1864 ***5704.8*** *p184*
Graham, Elizabeth; Philadelphia, 1850 ***53.26*** *p33*
*Relative:*Rebecca
Graham, Elizabeth; Philadelphia, 1850 ***5704.8*** *p68*
Graham, Elizabeth; St. John, N.B., 1850 ***5704.8*** *p65*
Graham, Elizabeth 13; St. John, N.B., 1853 ***5704.8*** *p99*
Graham, Elizabeth 16; St. John, N.B., 1855 ***5704.8*** *p127*
Graham, Elizabeth 48; St. John, N.B., 1855 ***5704.8*** *p127*
Graham, Ellen 20; Quebec, 1859 ***5704.8*** *p143*
Graham, Emily 6; Massachusetts, 1847 ***5881.1*** *p41*
Graham, George; America, 1804 ***1639.20*** *p84*
Graham, George 17; Maryland, 1774 ***1219.7*** *p235*
Graham, George 40; Quebec, 1864 ***5704.8*** *p163*
Graham, George, Jr.; Cincinnati, 1800-1877 ***8582.3*** *p86*
Graham, Henrettia 40; Quebec, 1864 ***5704.8*** *p162*
Graham, Henry 26; Georgia, 1775 ***1219.7*** *p277*
Graham, Hugh; Colorado, 1894 ***9678.2*** *p21*
Graham, Hugh; St. John, N.B., 1850 ***5704.8*** *p65*
Graham, Hugh 21; Quebec, 1861 ***5704.8*** *p149*
Graham, Humphry 50; Philadelphia, 1804 ***53.26*** *p33*
Graham, Isabella; New York, NY, 1867 ***5704.8*** *p223*
Graham, Isabella 1 *SEE* Graham, Margaret
Graham, Isabella 1; Philadelphia, 1847 ***5704.8*** *p24*
Graham, J. Keaney; America, 1874 ***1450.2*** *p54A*
Graham, James; America, 1803 ***1639.20*** *p84*
Graham, James; Charleston, SC, 1802 ***1639.20*** *p84*
Graham, James; Illinois, 1872 ***5012.39*** *p26*
Graham, James; Montreal, 1823 ***7603*** *p53*
Graham, James; New York, NY, 1811 ***2859.11*** *p12*
Graham, James; New York, NY, 1816 ***2859.11*** *p32*
Graham, James; New York, NY, 1838 ***8208.4*** *p83*
Graham, James; New York, NY, 1867 ***5704.8*** *p222*
Graham, James; Philadelphia, 1853 ***5704.8*** *p101*
Graham, James; Quebec, 1853 ***5704.8*** *p104*
Graham, James; St. John, N.B., 1848 ***5704.8*** *p38*
Graham, James 8; Quebec, 1864 ***5704.8*** *p162*
Graham, James 9; Quebec, 1864 ***5704.8*** *p163*
Graham, Jane; Charleston, SC, 1817 ***1639.20*** *p84*
Graham, Jane; Philadelphia, 1864 ***5704.8*** *p181*
Graham, Jane 9; Quebec, 1847 ***5704.8*** *p38*
Graham, Jane 18; Quebec, 1864 ***5704.8*** *p162*
Graham, Jane 24; Philadelphia, 1855 ***5704.8*** *p124*
Graham, John *SEE* Graham, Angus
Graham, John *SEE* Graham, Norman
Graham, John; America, 1803 ***1639.20*** *p85*
Graham, John; America, 1868 ***5704.8*** *p227*
Graham, John; Charleston, SC, 1797 ***1639.20*** *p85*
Graham, John; Charleston, SC, 1817 ***1639.20*** *p85*
Graham, John; Georgia, 1733 ***1639.20*** *p85*
Graham, John; New Orleans, 1848 ***2896.5*** *p15*
Graham, John; New Orleans, 1849 ***5704.8*** *p59*
Graham, John; New York, NY, 1811 ***2859.11*** *p12*
Graham, John; New York, NY, 1815 ***2859.11*** *p32*
Graham, John; North Carolina, 1769 ***1639.20*** *p85*
Graham, John; Philadelphia, 1866 ***5704.8*** *p208*
Graham, John; Quebec, 1851 ***4537.30*** *p13*
*Wife:*Catherine MacDonald
Graham, John; Quebec, 1863 ***4537.30*** *p13*
*Wife:*Mary Paterson
*Child:*Angus
*Child:*Effie
*Child:*Donald
*Child:*Alex
*Sister:*Ann
Graham, John; Quebec, 1874 ***4537.30*** *p15*
*Wife:*Annabella MacIver
*Child:*Angus
*Child:*Donald
Graham, John; St. John, N.B., 1847 ***5704.8*** *p21*
Graham, John; St. John, N.B., 1850 ***5704.8*** *p65*
Graham, John 5 *SEE* Graham, Margaret
Graham, John 5; Philadelphia, 1847 ***5704.8*** *p24*
Graham, John 6; Quebec, 1847 ***5704.8*** *p38*
Graham, John 11; Quebec, 1864 ***5704.8*** *p162*
Graham, John 11; St. John, N.B., 1853 ***5704.8*** *p99*
Graham, John 40; Quebec, 1864 ***5704.8*** *p162*
Graham, John 77; South Carolina, 1850 ***1639.20*** *p85*
Graham, John K.; Colorado, 1894 ***9678.2*** *p21*
Graham, John Robert 8; Quebec, 1851 ***5704.8*** *p82*
Graham, Joseph; Philadelphia, 1848 ***5704.8*** *p40*
Graham, Joseph 3 *SEE* Graham, Margaret
Graham, Joseph 3; Philadelphia, 1847 ***5704.8*** *p24*
Graham, Joseph 14; Quebec, 1864 ***5704.8*** *p162*
Graham, Kirsty *SEE* Graham, Murdo
Graham, Kirsty MacLeod; Quebec, 1875 ***4537.30*** *p15*
*Son:*Norman
*Son:*Murdo
Graham, Letitia 8; Quebec, 1861 ***5704.8*** *p149*
Graham, Louisa; St. John, N.B., 1847 ***5704.8*** *p24*
Graham, Margaret *SEE* Graham, Alex
Graham, Margaret *SEE* Graham, Alex
Graham, Margaret *SEE* Graham, Angus
Graham, Margaret; New Orleans, 1849 ***5704.8*** *p59*
Graham, Margaret; New York, NY, 1867 ***5704.8*** *p222*
Graham, Margaret; Philadelphia, 1847 ***53.26*** *p33*
*Relative:*Mary 7
*Relative:*John 5
*Relative:*Joseph 3
*Relative:*Isabella 1
Graham, Margaret; Philadelphia, 1847 ***5704.8*** *p24*
Graham, Margaret; Philadelphia, 1864 ***5704.8*** *p177*
Graham, Margaret; Philadelphia, 1866 ***5704.8*** *p208*
Graham, Margaret; Philadelphia, 1868 ***5704.8*** *p230*
Graham, Margaret; Quebec, 1863 ***4537.30*** *p7*
Graham, Margaret 10; Quebec, 1855 ***5704.8*** *p126*
Graham, Margaret 15; Philadelphia, 1859 ***5704.8*** *p141*
Graham, Margaret Jane; St. John, N.B., 1848 ***5704.8*** *p45*
Graham, Margaret Maclean *SEE* Graham, Angus
Graham, Marion *SEE* Graham, Murdo
Graham, Martha 17; Quebec, 1861 ***5704.8*** *p149*
Graham, Martin; New York, NY, 1816 ***2859.11*** *p32*
Graham, Mary *SEE* Graham, Murdo
Graham, Mary *SEE* Graham, Norman
Graham, Mary *SEE* Graham, Thomas
Graham, Mary; New York, NY, 1816 ***2859.11*** *p32*
Graham, Mary; New York, NY, 1865 ***5704.8*** *p196*
Graham, Mary; Philadelphia, 1847 ***53.26*** *p33*
Graham, Mary; Philadelphia, 1847 ***5704.8*** *p22*
Graham, Mary; Philadelphia, 1847 ***5704.8*** *p30*
Graham, Mary; Philadelphia, 1852 ***5704.8*** *p89*
Graham, Mary; Philadelphia, 1868 ***5704.8*** *p230*
Graham, Mary 7 *SEE* Graham, Margaret
Graham, Mary 7; Philadelphia, 1847 ***5704.8*** *p24*
Graham, Mary 11; Quebec, 1847 ***5704.8*** *p38*
Graham, Mary 15; Quebec, 1861 ***5704.8*** *p149*
Graham, Mary 34; Virginia, 1775 ***1219.7*** *p248*
Graham, Mary A.; Philadelphia, 1867 ***5704.8*** *p221*
Graham, Mary Jane 11; Quebec, 1851 ***5704.8*** *p82*
Graham, Mary MacDonald *SEE* Graham, Norman
Graham, Mary Paterson *SEE* Graham, John
Graham, Murdo *SEE* Graham, Angus
Graham, Murdo *SEE* Graham, Kirsty MacLeod
Graham, Murdo; Quebec, 1841 ***4537.30*** *p14*
*Wife:*Catherine MacRitchie
*Child:*Norman
*Child:*Mary
*Child:*Marion
*Child:*Catherine
*Child:*Kirsty
*Child:*Ann
Graham, Nancy; New Orleans, 1849 ***5704.8*** *p59*
Graham, Nappy; St. John, N.B., 1850 ***5704.8*** *p67*
Graham, Neil 66; North Carolina, 1850 ***1639.20*** *p85*
Graham, Neill; America, 1804 ***1639.20*** *p85*
Graham, Norman *SEE* Graham, Kirsty MacLeod
Graham, Norman *SEE* Graham, Murdo
Graham, Norman; Quebec, 1863 ***4537.30*** *p14*
*Wife:*Mary MacDonald
*Child:*John
*Child:*Donald
*Child:*Catherine
*Child:*Ann
*Child:*Mary
Graham, Patrick; Montreal, 1823 ***7603*** *p85*
Graham, Patrick; New York, NY, 1815 ***2859.11*** *p32*
Graham, Patrick; St. John, N.B., 1850 ***5704.8*** *p67*
Graham, Peter 10; Massachusetts, 1847 ***5881.1*** *p43*
Graham, Peter 18; Maryland, 1774 ***1219.7*** *p202*
Graham, Rebecca *SEE* Graham, Elizabeth
Graham, Rebecca; Philadelphia, 1850 ***5704.8*** *p68*
Graham, Rebecca 17; Philadelphia, 1857 ***5704.8*** *p133*
Graham, Robert; America, 1742 ***4971*** *p71*
Graham, Robert 11; Philadelphia, 1859 ***5704.8*** *p141*
Graham, Robert 20; Maryland, 1750 ***3690.1*** *p92*
Graham, Robert 20; Philadelphia, 1803 ***53.26*** *p33*
Graham, Robert W.; Illinois, 1892 ***5012.39*** *p53*
Graham, Robert W.; Illinois, 1895 ***5012.40*** *p54*
Graham, Samuel; Philadelphia, 1866 ***5704.8*** *p208*
Graham, Sarah; New York, NY, 1866 ***5704.8*** *p214*
Graham, Sarah; Philadelphia, 1866 ***5704.8*** *p210*
Graham, Sarah 4; Quebec, 1864 ***5704.8*** *p163*
Graham, Sarah 38; Quebec, 1864 ***5704.8*** *p163*
Graham, Sarah Ann 20; Philadelphia, 1857 ***5704.8*** *p133*
Graham, Sibla MacIver *SEE* Graham, Alex
Graham, Sidney 55; Quebec, 1861 ***5704.8*** *p149*
Graham, Thomas; New York, NY, 1816 ***2859.11*** *p32*
Graham, Thomas; New York, NY, 1833 ***8208.4*** *p46*
Graham, Thomas; New York, NY, 1864 ***5704.8*** *p184*
Graham, Thomas; Philadelphia, 1847 ***53.26*** *p33*
*Relative:*Mary
*Relative:*William
Graham, Thomas; Philadelphia, 1847 ***5704.8*** *p30*
Graham, Thomas; St. John, N.B., 1850 ***5704.8*** *p66*
Graham, Thomas; St. John, N.B., 1850 ***5704.8*** *p67*
Graham, Thomas 6; St. John, N.B., 1855 ***5704.8*** *p127*
Graham, Thomas 18; St. John, N.B., 1855 ***5704.8*** *p127*
Graham, Thomas 19; Jamaica, 1736 ***3690.1*** *p92*
Graham, Thomas 36; Philadelphia, 1804 ***53.26*** *p33*
Graham, Thomas J.; New York, NY, 1866 ***5704.8*** *p214*
Graham, Thomas William 13; Quebec, 1851 ***5704.8*** *p82*
Graham, William *SEE* Graham, Thomas
Graham, William; Philadelphia, 1847 ***5704.8*** *p30*
Graham, William; Philadelphia, 1867 ***5704.8*** *p224*
Graham, William; Quebec, 1830 ***4719.7*** *p21*
Graham, William; Quebec, 1847 ***5704.8*** *p7*
Graham, William; Quebec, 1847 ***5704.8*** *p38*
Graham, William 9 mos; Quebec, 1847 ***5704.8*** *p38*
Graham, William 14; St. John Island, 1775 ***1219.7*** *p273*
Graham, William 15; St. John, N.B., 1855 ***5704.8*** *p127*
Graham, William 19; Quebec, 1863 ***5704.8*** *p154*
Graham, William 30; Massachusetts, 1849 ***5881.1*** *p44*
Graham, William 45; Quebec, 1855 ***5704.8*** *p126*
Grahame, Archibald; South Carolina, 1809 ***1639.20*** *p83*
Grahber, Joseph; Illinois, 1867 ***2896.5*** *p15*
Grahser, John; Wisconsin, n.d. ***9675.5*** *p263*
Graies, Thomas; Virginia, 1628 ***6219*** *p67*
Graig, Thomas 20; St. John, N.B., 1862 ***5704.8*** *p150*
Grail, Mr. 20; America, 1839 ***778.5*** *p249*
Grainger, Mr.; Quebec, 1815 ***9229.18*** *p80*
Grainger, Hen.; Virginia, 1639 ***6219*** *p153*
Graird, Dominique 47; New Orleans, 1823 ***778.5*** *p249*

Grakes, Gust; Arkansas, 1918 95.2 p50
Gralewitz, Anna 18; New York, 1912 9980.29 p63
Gralewitz, Jozef 28; New York, 1912 9980.29 p63
Gramens, Herman; Iowa, 1866-1943 123.54 p20
Grames, Wm.; Virginia, 1639 6219 p151
Gramhausen, Bernhard; Cincinnati, 1869-1887 8582 p11
Gramlein, Anton; Kentucky, 1848 8582.3 p101
Gramlein, Johann Adam; Kentucky, 1848 8582.3 p101
Gramlich, Maria Barbara; Pennsylvania, 1749 2444 p228
Gramling, Joseph; Illinois, 1894 1450.2 p12B
Grammer, Johannes; America, 1852 8582.3 p24
Gramoll, Frederick; Wisconsin, n.d. 9675.5 p263
Gramshey, Danny; Philadelphia, 1852 5704.8 p84
Gramshey, Unity; Philadelphia, 1852 5704.8 p84
Grana, Alberto; Arkansas, 1918 95.2 p50
Grana, Antonino; Arkansas, 1918 95.2 p50
Granaghan, Jane; Philadelphia, 1865 5704.8 p199
Granahan, Margery 20; Philadelphia, 1864 5704.8 p157
Granato, Antonio; Arkansas, 1918 95.2 p50
Grand, Augustus 24; Port uncertain, 1835 778.5 p249
Grand, Bertrand 29; New Orleans, 1862 543.30 p373C
Grand, Dennis 23; Philadelphia, 1860 5704.8 p145
Grand, Francois 36; America, 1839 778.5 p249
Grand, Mary; Virginia, 1639 6219 p155
Grand, Mary 18; Philadelphia, 1860 5704.8 p145
Grandfield, Ernest A. 24; Kansas, 1885 5240.1 p15
Grandfield, Ernest A. 24; Kansas, 1885 5240.1 p67
Grandfield, Joseph 57; Kansas, 1885 5240.1 p67
Grandies, Antoine 38; America, 1839 778.5 p249
Grandjean, Jacques-Frederic 21; Halifax, N.S., 1752 7074.6 p210
Grando, Giuseppe; Iowa, 1866-1943 123.54 p65
Grando, Guiseppe; Iowa, 1866-1943 123.54 p65
Grandolphe, Pierre 27; America, 1838 778.5 p249
Grandt, Emil; Illinois, 1887 2896.5 p15
Grandy, John; Virginia, 1635 6219 p69
Grandy, Patrick; America, 1740 4971 p28
Grane, John; Virginia, 1639 6219 p159
Granell, C. A.; Minneapolis, 1869-1879 6410.35 p54
Graner, Christopher C.; Arizona, 1888 2764.35 p28
Grange, Edouard 26; America, 1836 778.5 p249
Grange, John; Virginia, 1637 6219 p85
Grange, Stephen 38; Virginia, 1775 1219.7 p247
Granger, Jean Marc Louis; New York, NY, 1834 8208.4 p77
Granger, John; New York, NY, 1836 8208.4 p11
Granger, Leger; Quebec, 1642 4533 p126
Granger, Rose 22; Philadelphia, 1854 5704.8 p123
Granger, William; Virginia, 1641 6219 p187
Granger, Wm.; Virginia, 1637 6219 p13
Granghan, Mich'l 38; Massachusetts, 1850 5881.1 p43
Granier, Joseph A. 40; America, 1838 778.5 p249
Granley, Jone; Virginia, 1638 6219 p11
Granny, Biddy; St. John, N.B., 1850 5704.8 p61
Granny, Charles; Philadelphia, 1851 5704.8 p76
Granny, Ellen; St. John, N.B., 1849 5704.8 p55
Granny, John; St. John, N.B., 1847 5704.8 p3
Granny, Keatty 25; Philadelphia, 1853 5704.8 p113
Granny, Margaret; St. John, N.B., 1848 5704.8 p43
Granny, Rodger 19; Philadelphia, 1854 5704.8 p118
Granny, Rosey; Philadelphia, 1852 5704.8 p84
Granny, Sally; Philadelphia, 1852 5704.8 p87
Granoti, Guiseppe; Arkansas, 1918 95.2 p50
Granstrom, Carl J. 33; Arizona, 1890 2764.35 p27
Grant, Mr.; Quebec, 1815 9229.18 p79
Grant, Mr. 40; Grenada, 1774 1219.7 p245
Grant, Mrs. 36; Grenada, 1774 1219.7 p245
Grant, A. F.; Minneapolis, 1880-1883 6410.35 p54
Grant, Alexander; Charleston, SC, 1807 1639.20 p86
Grant, Alexander; Georgia, 1775 1219.7 p275
Grant, Alexander; Havana, 1766 1219.7 p117
Grant, Alexander; New York, NY, 1836 8208.4 p14
Grant, Alexander; Ontario, 1749 9775.5 p213
Grant, Alexander; South Carolina, 1827 1639.20 p86
Grant, Alfred 21; Kansas, 1904 5240.1 p83
Grant, Alice; Philadelphia, 1865 5704.8 p202
Grant, C. A.; Minneapolis, 1882-1883 6410.35 p54
Grant, Catherine; Quebec, 1823 7603 p54
Grant, Charles W. 21; Kansas, 1889 5240.1 p73
Grant, Cuthbert; Montreal, 1792 9775.5 p202
Grant, Daniel 19; Massachusetts, 1847 5881.1 p41
Grant, Donald; Colorado, 1894 9678.2 p21
Grant, Edward; New York, NY, 1836 8208.4 p15
Grant, Edward 32; Maryland, 1774 1219.7 p204
Grant, Frank 45; Kansas, 1897 5240.1 p80
Grant, George 20; Wilmington, NC, 1774 1639.20 p86
Grant, George 22; Virginia, 1774 1219.7 p226
Grant, Harry; Charleston, SC, 1680-1830 1639.20 p322
Grant, Harry; Charleston, SC, 1792 1639.20 p86
Grant, Henry; Philadelphia, 1865 5704.8 p202
Grant, Isabell; New York, 1769 9775.5 p199
Grant, Isabella 38; Massachusetts, 1860 6410.32 p98
Grant, James; America, 1746 1639.20 p86
Grant, James; New York, NY, 1836 8208.4 p21
Grant, James; New York, NY, 1838 8208.4 p85
Grant, James; North Carolina, 1783-1828 1639.20 p86
Grant, James 19; Newfoundland, 1789 4915.24 p56
Grant, James 22; Virginia, 1774 1219.7 p201
Grant, James 30; West Virginia, 1896 9788.3 p11
Grant, James M.; New York, NY, 1840 8208.4 p107
Grant, Jean; New Brunswick, 1790 7603 p37
Grant, Jean; Quebec, 1768 7603 p42
Grant, Jean Forbes; Charleston, SC, 1781 1639.20 p71
Grant, John; America, 1802 1639.20 p86
Grant, John; Austin, TX, 1886 9777 p5
Grant, John; Boston, 1844 6410.32 p122
Grant, John; Canada, 1832 8893 p263
Grant, John; Montreal, 1823 7603 p102
Grant, John; Virginia, 1638 6219 p145
Grant, John 19; Maryland, 1739 3690.1 p92
Grant, John 36; Kansas, 1889 5240.1 p73
Grant, John 37; Georgia, 1774 1219.7 p188
Grant, John 45; Massachusetts, 1860 6410.32 p98
Grant, John Allan 26; Kansas, 1889 5240.1 p73
Grant, Ludovick; South Carolina, 1716 1639.20 p86
Grant, Mungo; Jamaica, 1753 1219.7 p21
Grant, Mungo; Jamaica, 1753 3690.1 p92
Grant, Nancy; Philadelphia, 1865 5704.8 p202
Grant, Norman; Arkansas, 1918 95.2 p50
Grant, Patrick; New York, NY, 1840 8208.4 p112
Grant, Patrick 17; Jamaica, 1750 3690.1 p92
Grant, Peter 32; Kansas, 1900 5240.1 p81
Grant, Robert M.; New York, NY, 1840 8208.4 p106
Grant, Thomas; Washington, 1859-1920 2872.1 p14
Grant, Thomas 25; Maryland, 1774 1219.7 p244
Grant, William; Quebec, 1788 7603 p35
Grant, William 20; Philadelphia, 1859 5704.8 p142
Grant, William 24; Virginia, 1774 1219.7 p201
Grant, William 28; Grenada, 1776 1219.7 p282
Grant, William R.; Illinois, 1896 5012.40 p55
Granth, Jane 23; America, 1702 2212 p37
Granthorn, Henry I.; New York, NY, 1816 2859.11 p32
Granval, J. 23; New Orleans, 1832 778.5 p249
Granwels, Victor; Arkansas, 1918 95.2 p50
Grany, Cornelius; America, 1743 4971 p42
Granzo, Bruno; Arkansas, 1918 95.2 p50
Grapes, Wilhelm; America, 1848 8582.3 p24
Grappini, Andrew; Virginia, 1856 4626.16 p16
Grasel, Michael; New Orleans, 1848 1450.2 p54A
Grasheare, John; Virginia, 1643 6219 p203
Grasmuck, Mrs. Franz 30; America, 1854-1855 9162.6 p105
Grasmuck, Helena 9; America, 1854-1855 9162.6 p105
Grasmuck, Wilh. 4; America, 1854-1855 9162.6 p105
Grass, C. 25; New Orleans, 1830 778.5 p249
Grass, E. 20; New Orleans, 1830 778.5 p249
Grasse, Charles Fred; Wisconsin, n.d. 9675.5 p263
Grasser, John; Wisconsin, n.d. 9675.5 p263
Grasser, Nicholas; Wisconsin, n.d. 9675.5 p263
Grassman, Fred William; Wisconsin, n.d. 9675.5 p263
Grasso, Andrea; Iowa, 1866-1943 123.54 p65
Grasz, Michel 32; America, 1835 778.5 p249
Grasz, Salome 25; America, 1835 778.5 p250
Gratelanel, Philippe 22; Port uncertain, 1836 778.5 p250
Grattan, Patrick Hugh 21; Kansas, 1875 5240.1 p56
Grattan, Peter 22; Kansas, 1872 5240.1 p52
Gratteau, George; Halifax, N.S., 1752 7074.6 p226
Gratto, . . .; Halifax, N.S., 1752 7074.6 p232
Gratton, Mary 35; Massachusetts, 1848 5881.1 p43
Gratz, Anna Maria SEE Gratz, Johann Jacob
Gratz, Jacob; Philadelphia, 1760 9973.7 p34
Gratz, Johann David SEE Gratz, Johann Jacob
Gratz, Johann Georg SEE Gratz, Johann Jacob
Gratz, Johann Jacob; Pennsylvania, 1749 2444 p158
Wife:Anna Maria
Child:Johann David
Child:Maria Catharina
Child:Johann Georg
Child:Rosina Dorothea
Gratz, Maria Catharina SEE Gratz, Johann Jacob
Gratz, Rosina Dorothea SEE Gratz, Johann Jacob
Gratze, Jacob; Pennsylvania, 1749 2444 p158
Grau, . . .; Canada, 1776-1783 9786 p22
Grau, Alexander; New York, 1888 1450.2 p12B
Grau, Julius; New York, 1888 1450.2 p12B
Graubner, Christian Ludwig; America, 1845-1847 3702.7 p320
Wife:Johannette Berthold
Child:Heinrich Carl L. F.
Child:Georg Friedrich H. L.
Graubner, Georg Friedrich H. L. SEE Graubner, Christian Ludwig
Graubner, Heinrich Carl L. F. SEE Graubner, Christian Ludwig
Graubner, Johannette Berthold SEE Graubner, Christian Ludwig
Grauel, Gottlieb; Cincinnati, 1869-1887 8582 p11
Grauer, Anna Maria SEE Grauer, Johannes
Grauer, Christian SEE Grauer, Johannes
Grauer, Hans Jerg SEE Grauer, Johannes
Grauer, Johannes SEE Grauer, Johannes
Grauer, Johannes; Pennsylvania, 1749 2444 p158
Wife:Anna Maria
Child:Johannes
Child:Christian
Child:Joseph David
Child:Hans Jerg
Child:Margaretha
Grauer, Joseph David SEE Grauer, Johannes
Grauer, Margaretha SEE Grauer, Johannes
Graugnard, Adolphe 30; America, 1839 778.5 p250
Graul, Gottlieb; America, 1837 8582.3 p24
Graulich, Balsar; New York, NY, 1838 8208.4 p82
Grauling, . . .; Canada, 1776-1783 9786 p22
Grauling, Henry; Canada, 1776-1783 9786 p207A
Graumenz, Fred; Illinois, 1896 2896.5 p15
Graunt, Christo.; Virginia, 1637 6219 p114
Graunt, Joane; Virginia, 1639 6219 p151
Grauss, Christine 25; Port uncertain, 1839 778.5 p250
Grauss, Jacob 40; Port uncertain, 1839 778.5 p250
Grauss, Magdaline 4; Port uncertain, 1839 778.5 p250
Grauss, Minick 6; Port uncertain, 1839 778.5 p250
Grauss, Pierre 3; Port uncertain, 1839 778.5 p250
Grautmann, C. F.; Cincinnati, 1869-1887 8582 p11
Grave, John; Annapolis, MD, 1757 1219.7 p54
Graveldinger, Christopher; Wisconsin, n.d. 9675.5 p263
Graven, John 40; St. Kitts, 1774 1219.7 p239
Gravenstein, Friederich; Charleston, SC, 1775-1781 8582.2 p52
Graves, Ann; Virginia, 1637 6219 p84
Graves, Chr.; Virginia, 1647 6219 p244
Graves, Edm.; Virginia, 1647 6219 p241
Graves, Gerry; Virginia, 1642 6219 p187
Graves, Isaac 34; Maryland, 1730 3690.1 p92
Graves, John; Virginia, 1637 6219 p13
With wife & 2 sons
Graves, John; Virginia, 1637 6219 p13
Graves, John 25; Philadelphia, 1774 1219.7 p234
Graves, John 36; Philadelphia, 1775 1219.7 p259
Graves, Katherine; Virginia, 1637 6219 p13
Graves, Rich.; Virginia, 1637 6219 p117
Graves, Richard; Virginia, 1636 6219 p21
Graves, Robert; Virginia, 1643 6219 p200
Graves, Robert 35; Arizona, 1907 9228.40 p11
Graves, Thomas; Virginia, 1637 6219 p13
Graves, Wm.; Virginia, 1639 6219 p24
Gravier, John 25; America, 1836 778.5 p250
Gravis, Tho.; Virginia, 1637 6219 p115
Gray, . . .; Prince Edward Island, 1764-1864 9775.5 p211
Gray, Alexander 11; Philadelphia, 1854 5704.8 p122
Gray, Alexander 36; Philadelphia, 1774 1219.7 p232
Gray, Andrew 16; St. John, N.B., 1867 5704.8 p167
Gray, Ann; Philadelphia, 1816 2859.11 p32
Gray, Ann 18; Quebec, 1855 5704.8 p125
Gray, Ann 19; South Carolina, 1736 3690.1 p92
Gray, Avis; Virginia, 1623-1638 6219 p149
Gray, Avis; Virginia, 1635 6219 p12
Gray, Benjamin 24; Maryland, 1775 1219.7 p266
Gray, Charles 25; Port uncertain, 1774 1219.7 p176
Gray, David; Illinois, 1860 2896.5 p15
Gray, Eliza 5; Quebec, 1855 5704.8 p125
Gray, Eliza 7; Quebec, 1849 5704.8 p51
Gray, Eliza Jane SEE Gray, John
Gray, Eliza Jane; Philadelphia, 1847 5704.8 p1
Gray, Elizabeth; New York, NY, 1811 2859.11 p12
Gray, Fran.; Virginia, 1635 6219 p16
Gray, Francis 21; Maryland, 1775 1219.7 p266
Gray, George; New York, NY, 1811 2859.11 p12
Gray, Henry; New York, NY, 1815 2859.11 p32
Gray, Isaac; Austin, TX, 1886 9777 p5
Gray, Isabella 35; Philadelphia, 1854 5704.8 p122
Gray, James SEE Gray, John
Gray, James; Carolina, 1684 1639.20 p86
Gray, James; Jamaica, 1685 1639.20 p86
Gray, James; New York, NY, 1811 2859.11 p12
Gray, James; New York, NY, 1864 5704.8 p174
Gray, James; Philadelphia, 1771 1219.7 p151
Gray, James; Philadelphia, 1847 5704.8 p1
Gray, James 9; Quebec, 1849 5704.8 p51
Gray, James 16; Quebec, 1855 5704.8 p125
Gray, Jane; New York, NY, 1811 2859.11 p12
Gray, Jane; Quebec, 1849 5704.8 p51
Gray, Jane; St. John, N.B., 1848 5704.8 p44
Gray, John; Boston, 1776 1219.7 p278
Gray, John; Illinois, 1871 5240.1 p15
Gray, John; New York, NY, 1811 2859.11 p12
Gray, John; North Carolina, 1690-1717 1639.20 p87

Gray, John; Philadelphia, 1847 ***53.26*** *p33*
*Relative:*James
*Relative:*Eliza Jane
*Relative:*John 3
*Relative:*William 3 mos
Gray, John; Philadelphia, 1847 ***5704.8*** *p1*
Gray, John; Quebec, 1849 ***5704.8*** *p51*
Gray, John; St. John, N.B., 1853 ***5704.8*** *p107*
Gray, John 3 *SEE* Gray, John
Gray, John 3; Philadelphia, 1847 ***5704.8*** *p1*
Gray, John 3; Quebec, 1849 ***5704.8*** *p51*
Gray, John 6; Philadelphia, 1854 ***5704.8*** *p123*
Gray, John 10; Quebec, 1855 ***5704.8*** *p125*
Gray, John 18; St. John, N.B., 1864 ***5704.8*** *p157*
Gray, John 21; Virginia, 1774 ***1219.7*** *p243*
Gray, John 25; Jamaica, 1773 ***1219.7*** *p172*
*Wife:*Sarah 25
Gray, John 27; Antigua (Antego), 1728 ***3690.1*** *p92*
Gray, John 28; Maryland, 1775 ***1219.7*** *p267*
Gray, Joseph; Philadelphia, 1849 ***53.26*** *p33*
*Relative:*Susan
Gray, Joseph; Philadelphia, 1849 ***5704.8*** *p53*
Gray, Joseph; Quebec, 1847 ***5704.8*** *p7*
Gray, Joseph 16; Maryland, 1729 ***3690.1*** *p92*
Gray, Joseph 19; Maryland, 1775 ***1219.7*** *p272*
Gray, Margaret; New York, NY, 1866 ***5704.8*** *p212*
Gray, Margaret 15; Philadelphia, 1854 ***5704.8*** *p122*
Gray, Mary; Philadelphia, 1847 ***53.26*** *p33*
Gray, Mary; Philadelphia, 1847 ***5704.8*** *p32*
Gray, Mary 10; Massachusetts, 1849 ***5881.1*** *p43*
Gray, Mary 12; Quebec, 1855 ***5704.8*** *p125*
Gray, Mary Ann; St. John, N.B., 1853 ***5704.8*** *p107*
Gray, Michael; America, 1737 ***4971*** *p36*
Gray, Michael 25; Maryland, 1775 ***1219.7*** *p251*
Gray, Oliver; St. John, N.B., 1849 ***5704.8*** *p49*
Gray, Patrick; New York, NY, 1838 ***8208.4*** *p61*
Gray, Patrick 11; Massachusetts, 1849 ***5881.1*** *p44*
Gray, Rebecca *SEE* Gray, Thomas
Gray, Rebecca; Virginia, 1635 ***6219*** *p12*
Gray, Rebecca 9 mos; Quebec, 1855 ***5704.8*** *p125*
Gray, Rebecca 34; Quebec, 1855 ***5704.8*** *p125*
Gray, Robert 6 mos; Quebec, 1849 ***5704.8*** *p51*
Gray, Robert 14; Antigua (Antego), 1749 ***3690.1*** *p92*
Gray, Robert 15; Maryland, 1775 ***1219.7*** *p250*
Gray, Samuel; New York, NY, 1811 ***2859.11*** *p12*
Gray, Samuel; New York, NY, 1816 ***2859.11*** *p32*
Gray, Samuel 16; Baltimore, 1775 ***1219.7*** *p271*
Gray, Sarah 25 *SEE* Gray, John
Gray, Susan *SEE* Gray, Joseph
Gray, Susan; Philadelphia, 1849 ***5704.8*** *p53*
Gray, Thady; America, 1738 ***4971*** *p85*
Gray, Thady; America, 1738-1743 ***4971*** *p91*
Gray, Tho.; Virginia, 1638 ***6219*** *p149*
Gray, Thomas *SEE* Gray, Thomas
Gray, Thomas; Virginia, 1635 ***6219*** *p12*
*Son:*Wm.
*Son:*Thomas
Gray, Thomas; Virginia, 1638 ***6219*** *p149*
*Wife:*Rebecca
Gray, Thomas 19; Maryland or Virginia, 1733 ***3690.1*** *p93*
Gray, Thomas 23; Philadelphia, 1774 ***1219.7*** *p182*
Gray, Thomas 31; Nova Scotia, 1774 ***1219.7*** *p209*
Gray, Thos. 65; Washington, 1916-1919 ***1728.4*** *p253*
Gray, Tom; St. John, N.B., 1849 ***5704.8*** *p56*
Gray, Walter; New York, NY, 1811 ***2859.11*** *p12*
Gray, William; America, 1868 ***6014.1*** *p2*
Gray, William; Boston, 1776 ***1219.7*** *p277*
Gray, William; Charleston, SC, 1813 ***1639.20*** *p87*
Gray, William; New York, NY, 1811 ***2859.11*** *p12*
Gray, William; New York, NY, 1815 ***2859.11*** *p32*
Gray, William 3 mos *SEE* Gray, John
Gray, William 3 mos; Philadelphia, 1847 ***5704.8*** *p1*
Gray, William 3; Philadelphia, 1854 ***5704.8*** *p123*
Gray, William 17; Virginia, 1774 ***1219.7*** *p238*
Gray, William 21; Maryland, 1724 ***3690.1*** *p93*
Gray, William 21; Philadelphia, 1775 ***1219.7*** *p259*
Gray, William 24; Philadelphia, 1803 ***53.26*** *p33*
Gray, William 30; Quebec, 1854 ***5704.8*** *p119*
Gray, Wm. *SEE* Gray, Thomas
Gray, Wm.; Virginia, 1638 ***6219*** *p149*
Grayes, Thomas; Virginia, 1638 ***6219*** *p123*
Grayne, James; Virginia, 1638 ***6219*** *p14*
Grayne, Jonathan; Virginia, 1638 ***6219*** *p180*
Grayne, Rowland; Virginia, 1638 ***6219*** *p14*
Graystock, Lucy 21; Maryland, 1775 ***1219.7*** *p253*
Grazina, Peter; Iowa, 1866-1943 ***123.54*** *p20*
Gready, John 22; Savannah, GA, 1733 ***4719.17*** *p311*
Gready, Patrick 19; Massachusetts, 1850 ***5881.1*** *p44*
Grealis, Patrick; Arkansas, 1918 ***95.2*** *p50*
Greally, Bridget 19; Massachusetts, 1849 ***5881.1*** *p41*
Greally, Honora 30; Massachusetts, 1849 ***5881.1*** *p42*
Greaues, Mary 27; America, 1706 ***2212*** *p46*
Greaves, George F. 53; Kansas, 1880 ***5240.1*** *p62*
Greb, Peter; Virginia, 1847 ***4626.16*** *p13*
Grebbell, John 21; Jamaica, 1731 ***3690.1*** *p93*
Grebe, Franz Friedrich; Canada, 1780 ***9786*** *p268*
Grebe, Franz Friedrich; New York, 1776 ***9786*** *p268*
Grebe, Nikolaus; Trenton, NJ, 1776 ***8137*** *p9*
Greben, . . .; Canada, 1776-1783 ***9786*** *p22*
Greber, Hieronimus; Pennsylvania, 1747 ***2444*** *p158*
Greco, Jastano; Arkansas, 1918 ***95.2*** *p50*
Greedy, William 28; Maryland, 1775 ***1219.7*** *p257*
Greegan, Sarah; New York, NY, 1867 ***5704.8*** *p222*
Greeke, Rich.; Virginia, 1637 ***6219*** *p11*
Greeley, Catharine 7; Massachusetts, 1849 ***5881.1*** *p41*
Green, . . .; America, 1697-1707 ***2212*** *p3*
Green, A.; Iowa, 1866-1943 ***123.54*** *p20*
Green, Abraham 19; Maryland, 1729 ***3690.1*** *p93*
Green, Amos; Boston, 1776 ***1219.7*** *p278*
Green, Ann; America, 1698 ***2212*** *p5*
Green, Bartholomew; Pennsylvania, 1682 ***4962*** *p152*
Green, Biddy 11; St. John, N.B., 1857 ***5704.8*** *p135*
Green, Bridget; Philadelphia, 1867 ***5704.8*** *p217*
Green, Bridget 6; Philadelphia, 1865 ***5704.8*** *p197*
Green, Candy 42; St. John, N.B., 1857 ***5704.8*** *p135*
Green, Catharine; America, 1866 ***5704.8*** *p213*
Green, Catharine; Philadelphia, 1865 ***5704.8*** *p196*
Green, Catherine *SEE* Green, Dennis
Green, Catherine; Philadelphia, 1847 ***5704.8*** *p30*
Green, Catherine 20; Philadelphia, 1857 ***5704.8*** *p133*
Green, Charles 24; Philadelphia, 1857 ***5704.8*** *p133*
Green, Daniel; Philadelphia, 1852 ***5704.8*** *p96*
Green, David; Quebec, 1847 ***5704.8*** *p7*
Green, Dennis; Philadelphia, 1847 ***53.26*** *p33*
*Relative:*Catherine
*Relative:*Sarah 6
*Relative:*Michael 4
*Relative:*Hugh 2
Green, Dennis; Philadelphia, 1847 ***5704.8*** *p30*
Green, Edmond; Virginia, 1647 ***6219*** *p241*
Green, Edmund 27; Jamaica, 1731 ***3690.1*** *p93*
Green, Edward 17; Philadelphia, 1856 ***5704.8*** *p129*
Green, Edward 42; Baltimore, 1775 ***1219.7*** *p270*
Green, Eliza; Philadelphia, 1847 ***53.26*** *p33*
Green, Eliza; Philadelphia, 1847 ***5704.8*** *p30*
Green, Ellan; Quebec, 1847 ***5704.8*** *p29*
Green, Francis 6; St. John, N.B., 1857 ***5704.8*** *p135*
Green, George; Austin, TX, 1886 ***9777*** *p5*
Green, George; Virginia, 1852 ***4626.16*** *p14*
Green, George 15; Maryland, 1775 ***1219.7*** *p253*
Green, Giles 17; Maryland or Virginia, 1719 ***3690.1*** *p93*
Green, Hannah 9 mos; Philadelphia, 1852 ***5704.8*** *p96*
Green, Harry J. 36; Kansas, 1880 ***5240.1*** *p62*
Green, Henry; New York, NY, 1816 ***2859.11*** *p32*
Green, Henry 22; Jamaica, 1730 ***3690.1*** *p93*
Green, Horace; California, 1856 ***2769.4*** *p5*
Green, Hugh 2 *SEE* Green, Dennis
Green, Hugh 2; Philadelphia, 1847 ***5704.8*** *p30*
Green, J. W. 32; Kansas, 1892 ***5240.1*** *p77*
Green, James; New York, NY, 1816 ***2859.11*** *p32*
Green, James; New York, NY, 1836 ***8208.4*** *p10*
Green, James; Quebec, 1848 ***5704.8*** *p41*
Green, James 9 mos; Quebec, 1847 ***5704.8*** *p7*
Green, James, Children; New York, NY, 1816 ***2859.11*** *p32*
Green, Jane; America, 1869 ***5704.8*** *p232*
Green, Jane; Philadelphia, 1867 ***5704.8*** *p214*
Green, Jane; St. John, N.B., 1849 ***5704.8*** *p49*
Green, Jesse; New York, NY, 1834 ***8208.4*** *p59*
Green, John; America, 1863 ***5240.1*** *p15*
Green, John; New York, NY, 1870 ***5704.8*** *p237*
Green, John; Philadelphia, 1847 ***53.26*** *p33*
Green, John; Philadelphia, 1847 ***5704.8*** *p1*
Green, John; Quebec, 1850 ***5704.8*** *p67*
Green, John; Virginia, 1647 ***6219*** *p249*
Green, John 4; Quebec, 1847 ***5704.8*** *p7*
Green, John 8; St. John, N.B., 1857 ***5704.8*** *p135*
Green, John 19; Philadelphia, 1856 ***5704.8*** *p128*
Green, John 20; Virginia, 1721 ***3690.1*** *p93*
Green, John 25; Virginia, 1774 ***1219.7*** *p243*
Green, John 30; Kansas, 1889 ***5240.1*** *p74*
Green, Jonathan 15; Jamaica, 1733 ***3690.1*** *p93*
Green, Jonathan 15; Maryland, 1733 ***3690.1*** *p93*
Green, Joseph 21; Barbados or Jamaica, 1733 ***3690.1*** *p93*
Green, Juda Harry; Arkansas, 1918 ***95.2*** *p50*
Green, Leonard; Arkansas, 1918 ***95.2*** *p50*
Green, Margaret; New York, NY, 1867 ***5704.8*** *p224*
Green, Margaret; Quebec, 1847 ***5704.8*** *p7*
Green, Margery; America, 1866 ***5704.8*** *p206*
Green, Martha 26; Maryland, 1724 ***3690.1*** *p93*
Green, Mary; New York, NY, 1867 ***5704.8*** *p224*
Green, Mary; Quebec, 1848 ***5704.8*** *p41*
Green, Mary; Virginia, 1643 ***6219*** *p207*
Green, Mary 3 mos; Quebec, 1848 ***5704.8*** *p41*
Green, Mary 40; St. John, N.B., 1857 ***5704.8*** *p135*
Green, Mary 48; Massachusetts, 1850 ***5881.1*** *p43*
Green, Mary Jane 2; Quebec, 1847 ***5704.8*** *p7*
Green, Michael 4 *SEE* Green, Dennis
Green, Michael 4; Philadelphia, 1847 ***5704.8*** *p30*
Green, Mick 3; St. John, N.B., 1857 ***5704.8*** *p135*
Green, Patrick; New York, NY, 1865 ***5704.8*** *p192*
Green, Patrick 11; Philadelphia, 1865 ***5704.8*** *p196*
Green, Patrick 16; Massachusetts, 1849 ***5881.1*** *p44*
Green, Peder; Washington, 1859-1920 ***2872.1*** *p14*
Green, Peter 25; Baltimore, 1775 ***1219.7*** *p269*
Green, Richard 18; Virginia, 1774 ***1219.7*** *p238*
Green, Richard 35; Maryland, 1774 ***1219.7*** *p182*
Green, Richard 35; Virginia, 1774 ***1219.7*** *p186*
Green, Robert; New York, NY, 1838 ***8208.4*** *p75*
Green, Rose; New York, NY, 1867 ***5704.8*** *p224*
Green, S. H.; Washington, 1859-1920 ***2872.1*** *p14*
Green, Sally; New York, NY, 1811 ***2859.11*** *p12*
Green, Samuel 26; Maryland, 1774 ***1219.7*** *p191*
Green, Sarah 6 *SEE* Green, Dennis
Green, Sarah 6; Philadelphia, 1847 ***5704.8*** *p30*
Green, Sarah 8; Philadelphia, 1865 ***5704.8*** *p196*
Green, Stephen; New York, NY, 1864 ***5704.8*** *p169*
Green, Thomas; America, 1736-1743 ***4971*** *p57*
Green, Thomas; Virginia, 1648 ***6219*** *p250*
Green, Thomas 15; Baltimore, 1775 ***1219.7*** *p271*
Green, Thomas 19; Jamaica, 1733 ***3690.1*** *p93*
Green, Thomas 24; Pennsylvania, 1735 ***3690.1*** *p94*
Green, William; Ohio, 1840 ***9892.11*** *p18*
Green, William; Port uncertain, 1757 ***3690.1*** *p94*
Green, William 13; Quebec, 1847 ***5704.8*** *p29*
Green, William 15; Port uncertain, 1774 ***1219.7*** *p176*
Green, William 17; New England, 1721 ***3690.1*** *p94*
Green, William 20; Maryland, 1722 ***3690.1*** *p94*
Green, William 22; Maryland or Virginia, 1734 ***3690.1*** *p94*
Green, Wm.; Quebec, 1830 ***4719.7*** *p21*
Greenall, Joseph; Iowa, 1866-1943 ***123.54*** *p20*
Greenan, Mary 20; Quebec, 1858 ***5704.8*** *p138*
Greenan, Michael 22; Quebec, 1858 ***5704.8*** *p138*
Greenaway, Robert; Pennsylvania, 1682 ***4962*** *p152*
Greenberg, Albert 24; Arkansas, 1918 ***95.2*** *p51*
Greenberg, Harry W.; Arkansas, 1918 ***95.2*** *p51*
Greenberg, William; Arkansas, 1918 ***95.2*** *p51*
Greenbu, Fabian; Iowa, 1866-1943 ***123.54*** *p20*
Greene, Charles; Virginia, 1637 ***6219*** *p113*
Greene, Dorothy; Virginia, 1617 ***6219*** *p5*
Greene, Miss E.; Milwaukee, 1875 ***4719.30*** *p257*
Greene, Eliz.; Virginia, 1636 ***6219*** *p74*
Greene, Eliz.; Virginia, 1637 ***6219*** *p108*
Greene, George; Virginia, 1639 ***6219*** *p152*
Greene, Hugh; New York, NY, 1816 ***2859.11*** *p32*
Greene, James; Virginia, 1642 ***6219*** *p192*
Greene, John; America, 1736-1737 ***4971*** *p59*
Greene, John; Virginia, 1639 ***6219*** *p153*
Greene, John; Virginia, 1643 ***6219*** *p33*
Greene, John; Virginia, 1648 ***6219*** *p250*
Greene, Jon.; Virginia, 1635 ***6219*** *p69*
Greene, Judith; Virginia, 1635 ***6219*** *p71*
Greene, Judith; Virginia, 1648 ***6219*** *p250*
Greene, Peter; Virginia, 1642 ***6219*** *p192*
Greene, Richard; Virginia, 1642 ***6219*** *p196*
Greene, Robert; Virginia, 1637 ***6219*** *p17*
Greene, Thomas; Virginia, 1639 ***6219*** *p161*
Greene, Thomas 27?; America, 1701 ***2212*** *p35*
Greene, William; Cincinnati, 1800-1877 ***8582.3*** *p86*
Greene, William; Virginia, 1638 ***6219*** *p124*
Greene, Wm.; Virginia, 1637 ***6219*** *p113*
Greenfeild, John; Virginia, 1638 ***6219*** *p124*
Greenfeild, John; Virginia, 1638 ***6219*** *p150*
Greenfield, Charles 16; Savannah, GA, 1733 ***4719.17*** *p311*
Greenfield, Robert; Virginia, 1635 ***6219*** *p25*
Greenfield, Sarah 16; Savannah, GA, 1733 ***4719.17*** *p311*
Greenfield, William 19; Savannah, GA, 1733 ***4719.17*** *p311*
Greenhalgh, Ann 20; America, 1705 ***2212*** *p44*
Greenhalgh, Mary 15; America, 1705 ***2212*** *p44*
Greenham, Mary; New York, NY, 1816 ***2859.11*** *p32*
Greenham, Wm.; Port uncertain, 1849 ***4535.10*** *p198*
Greenhill, Joseph 33; Montreal, 1711 ***7603*** *p30*
Greenhill, Martha; Virginia, 1636 ***6219*** *p32*
Greening, Elizabeth *SEE* Greening, James
Greening, James; New York, 1743 ***3652*** *p60*
*Wife:*Elizabeth
Greening, John 30; Jamaica, 1730 ***3690.1*** *p94*
Greenland, Herrmann M.; Cincinnati, 1869-1887 ***8582*** *p11*
Greenland, Richard 14; Jamaica, 1733 ***3690.1*** *p94*
Greenleafe, Robt.; Virginia, 1636 ***6219*** *p21*
Greenleafe, Susan; Virginia, 1636 ***6219*** *p21*
Greenlee, John 35; St. John, N.B., 1864 ***5704.8*** *p159*
Greenlees, John 25; Wilmington, NC, 1774 ***1639.20*** *p87*
*Wife:*Mary Howie 25

Greenlees, Mary Howie 25 *SEE* Greenlees, John
Greenluse, Ann; Quebec, 1847 5704.8 p7
Greenluse, John 13; Quebec, 1847 5704.8 p7
Greenluse, Margaret; Quebec, 1847 5704.8 p7
Greenluse, Moses; Quebec, 1847 5704.8 p7
Greenluse, Sonah 9; Quebec, 1847 5704.8 p7
Greenluse, Thomas; Quebec, 1847 5704.8 p7
Greenluse, Thomas 11; Quebec, 1847 5704.8 p7
Greenman, Robert; Pennsylvania, 1682 4962 p152
Greenough, James 30; Virginia, 1774 1219.7 p200
Greenwald, Reinhold; Washington, 1859-1920 2872.1 p14
Greenwalt, Philip; Philadelphia, 1759 9973.7 p34
Greenway, Robert; Pennsylvania, 1682 4962 p152
Greenwill, Jas.; Virginia, 1642 6219 p198
Greenwood, Elizabeth 36 *SEE* Greenwood, John
Greenwood, Emily 2; Massachusetts, 1850 5881.1 p42
Greenwood, Jane 5; Massachusetts, 1850 5881.1 p43
Greenwood, John 40; Halifax, N.S., 1774 1219.7 p213
  *Wife:*Elizabeth 36
  With child 10
  With child 8
  With child 6
  With child 4
Greenwood, Joseph 18; Virginia, 1721 3690.1 p94
Greenwood, Mary Ann 7; Massachusetts, 1850 5881.1 p43
Greenwood, Miles 20; Maryland, 1720 3690.1 p94
Greenwood, Miles 29; Jamaica, 1730 3690.1 p94
Greenwood, Raphael; Iroquois Co., IL, 1865 3455.1 p11
Greenwood, Richard; Virginia, 1637 6219 p24
Greenwoods, Eliza.; Virginia, 1637 6219 p82
Greep, John; America, 1884 5240.1 p15
Greep, Robert 23; Kansas, 1901 5240.1 p82
Greep, Thomas P.; Kansas, 1900 5240.1 p15
Greep, W. J.; Kansas, 1900 5240.1 p15
Greer, Adam *SEE* Greer, Marcus
Greer, Adam; Philadelphia, 1850 5704.8 p60
Greer, Alexander; Quebec, 1852 5704.8 p91
Greer, Andrew; Quebec, 1851 5704.8 p73
Greer, Anne; Quebec, 1851 5704.8 p74
Greer, Anne 21; Philadelphia, 1864 5704.8 p155
Greer, Catherine 6 mos; Philadelphia, 1864 5704.8 p155
Greer, Charles 25; Philadelphia, 1864 5704.8 p155
Greer, David 17; Wilmington, DE, 1831 6508.3 p100
Greer, Elias; Ohio, 1840 9892.11 p18
Greer, Elizabeth; Philadelphia, 1849 53.26 p33
Greer, Elizabeth; Philadelphia, 1849 5704.8 p54
Greer, Elizabeth; Quebec, 1852 5704.8 p97
Greer, Elizabeth 60; Philadelphia, 1864 5704.8 p155
Greer, Francis; Ohio, 1840 9892.11 p18
Greer, Francis; St. John, N.B., 1852 5704.8 p84
Greer, George; Ohio, 1840 9892.11 p18
Greer, Henry 5; Quebec, 1852 5704.8 p97
Greer, James; Philadelphia, 1850 53.26 p33
Greer, James; Philadelphia, 1850 5704.8 p65
Greer, James; Philadelphia, 1853 5704.8 p101
Greer, James; Quebec, 1851 5704.8 p74
Greer, James 2; Philadelphia, 1864 5704.8 p155
Greer, James 8; Quebec, 1852 5704.8 p97
Greer, James H.; Colorado, 1902 9678.2 p21
Greer, Jane 1; Philadelphia, 1864 5704.8 p156
Greer, Jane 20; Philadelphia, 1864 5704.8 p156
Greer, Jane Mary *SEE* Greer, Robert
Greer, Jane Mary; Philadelphia, 1850 5704.8 p60
Greer, John; St. John, N.B., 1847 5704.8 p14
Greer, John 1 mo; Quebec, 1852 5704.8 p97
Greer, John 18; St. John, N.B., 1856 5704.8 p131
Greer, John 25; Philadelphia, 1864 5704.8 p155
Greer, John 26; Philadelphia, 1864 5704.8 p156
Greer, Joseph; Ohio, 1812-1840 9892.11 p18
Greer, Joseph 5; Quebec, 1858 5704.8 p138
Greer, Keatty *SEE* Greer, Marcus
Greer, Keatty; Philadelphia, 1850 5704.8 p60
Greer, Letitia 44; Quebec, 1858 5704.8 p138
Greer, Marcus; Philadelphia, 1850 53.26 p34
  *Relative:*Keatty
  *Relative:*Adam
Greer, Marcus; Philadelphia, 1850 5704.8 p60
Greer, Margaret; Philadelphia, 1850 53.26 p34
Greer, Margaret; Philadelphia, 1850 5704.8 p65
Greer, Maria 14; Quebec, 1858 5704.8 p138
Greer, Mary; Quebec, 1851 5704.8 p73
Greer, Mary; St. John, N.B., 1850 5704.8 p62
Greer, Matty; Philadelphia, 1847 53.26 p34
Greer, Matty; Philadelphia, 1847 5704.8 p13
Greer, Rebecca; Quebec, 1852 5704.8 p97
Greer, Robert; Philadelphia, 1850 53.26 p34
  *Relative:*Jane Mary
Greer, Robert; Philadelphia, 1850 5704.8 p60
Greer, Susan 13; Philadelphia, 1853 5704.8 p101
Greer, Susanna 11; Quebec, 1852 5704.8 p97
Greer, William 3; Philadelphia, 1864 5704.8 p156
Greer, William 44; Quebec, 1858 5704.8 p138
Greere, David; Virginia, 1648 6219 p250
Greet, John 18; South Carolina, 1720 3690.1 p94
Greete, Richard; Virginia, 1636 6219 p79
Greete, Richard; Virginia, 1637 6219 p13
Greeve, Peter; America, 1735-1743 4971 p79
Greg, James 46; Philadelphia, 1803 53.26 p34
  *Relative:*Thomas 18
  *Relative:*John 19
Greg, John 19 *SEE* Greg, James
Greg, Thomas 18 *SEE* Greg, James
Greganti, Livis; Wisconsin, n.d. 9675.5 p263
Gregen, Frederic; Wisconsin, 1856 5240.1 p16
Greger, Frederic; Wisconsin, 1856 5240.1 p16
Gregerick, Benjamin; Maryland, 1750 3690.1 p94
Gregersen, George Jensen; Arkansas, 1918 95.2 p51
Gregerson, Eskild Christianson; Arkansas, 1918 95.2 p51
Gregg, Alexander; America, 1820 1639.20 p87
Gregg, Hannah; St. John, N.B., 1850 5704.8 p66
Gregg, John; New York, NY, 1837 8208.4 p34
Gregg, Joseph 22; America, 1701 2212 p35
Gregg, Margaret; Philadelphia, 1850 53.26 p34
Gregg, Margaret; Philadelphia, 1850 5704.8 p65
Gregg, Margaret 20; Philadelphia, 1861 5704.8 p149
Gregg, Mary A.; America, 1867 5704.8 p221
Greggory, George; Ohio, 1839 9892.11 p18
Gregoire, Mr. 38; New Orleans, 1839 778.5 p250
Gregoire, Stanislase 28; America, 1835 778.5 p250
Gregorie, Daniel; New York, NY, 1840 8208.4 p113
Gregorie, James; Charleston, SC, 1803 1639.20 p87
Gregory, Mr.; Quebec, 1815 9229.18 p82
Gregory, Alexander; North Carolina, 1793 1639.20 p87
Gregory, Benjamine; Virginia, 1637 6219 p84
Gregory, Bridget; New York, NY, 1816 2859.11 p32
  With 2 children
Gregory, Mrs. C.; Milwaukee, 1875 4719.30 p257
Gregory, Edward 38; Maryland, 1774 1219.7 p224
Gregory, Frank; Milwaukee, 1875 4719.30 p257
Gregory, Georg; Virginia, 1635 6219 p27
Gregory, Georg; Virginia, 1638 6219 p145
Gregory, John; New York, NY, 1811 2859.11 p12
Gregory, M.; New York, NY, 1811 2859.11 p12
  With family
Gregory, Margaret 20; Philadelphia, 1859 5704.8 p142
Gregory, Mary; New Jersey, 1791-1880 8894.2 p57
Gregory, Peter Mallard; Alexandria, VA, 1797-1817 8894.2 p57
Gregory, Richard; Virginia, 1628 6219 p9
Gregory, Richard 32; Jamaica, 1736 3690.1 p95
Gregory, Samuel; America, 1866 5704.8 p206
Gregory, Sarah; New York, NY, 1869 5704.8 p234
Gregory, Tho.; Virginia, 1637 6219 p113
Gregory, Tho.; Virginia, 1638 6219 p121
Gregory, William; Alexandria, VA, 1789-1875 8894.2 p57
Greider, Caspar 39; New Orleans, 1863 543.30 p373C
Greif, Charles; Wisconsin, n.d. 9675.5 p263
Greig, Alec; Austin, TX, 1886 9777 p5
Greighton, Margaret; Philadelphia, 1851 5704.8 p81
Greignaud, Mr.; Died enroute, 1752 7074.6 p208
Greignaud, Jean Abraham 46; Halifax, N.S., 1752 7074.6 p207
  With family of 2
Greignaud, Jean-Abraham 46; Halifax, N.S., 1752 7074.6 p210
  *Wife:*Marie
  With child
Greignaud, Marie *SEE* Greignaud, Jean-Abraham
Greiko, John; Iowa, 1866-1943 123.54 p20
Greilich, Joseph 42; New Orleans, 1862 543.30 p382C
Greimann, Wilhelm; Illinois, 1842-1915 4610.10 p66
Grein, Christian; Illinois, 1860 5012.39 p90
Grein, John; Illinois, 1860 5012.39 p90
Grein, Ludw. 75; Ontario, 1909 1763 p40D
Greindl, Joseph; Wisconsin, n.d. 9675.5 p263
Greindl, Ludwig; Wisconsin, n.d. 9675.5 p263
Greiner, Anna Catharina; Port uncertain, 1749 2444 p190
Greiner, Catharina *SEE* Greiner, Johann Dieterich
Greiner, David; New York, NY, 1837 8208.4 p52
Greiner, Dorothea Emmert *SEE* Greiner, Joh. Dieterich
Greiner, Joh. Dieterich; Philadelphia Co., PA, 1717 3627 p9
  *Wife:*Dorothea Emmert
  *Daughter:*Maria Catharina
  With sister
Greiner, Johann Dieterich; Pennsylvania, 1717 3627 p3
  With wife
  *Daughter:*Catharina
Greiner, Maria Catharina *SEE* Greiner, Joh. Dieterich
Greiner, Mathias 18; New Orleans, 1836 778.5 p250
Greiner, Nicolas 26; New Orleans, 1836 778.5 p250
Greisch, J. P.; Wisconsin, n.d. 9675.5 p263
Greisch, Joseph; Wisconsin, n.d. 9675.5 p263
Greisheimer, Marcus; Illinois, 1882 2896.5 p15
Greismann, Jean 29; New Orleans, 1835 778.5 p250
Greison, . . .; Quebec, 1852 5704.8 p87
Greison, John; Quebec, 1852 5704.8 p87
Greitter, Gottfried; Colorado, 1894 9678.2 p21
Greiveldinger, John; Wisconsin, n.d. 9675.5 p263
Greiving, G. H.; America, 1848 8582.1 p11
Greme, D. 26; Boston, 1773 1219.7 p172
Greme, J. 30; Boston, 1773 1219.7 p172
Gremiliure, Jacob 30; Port uncertain, 1821 778.5 p251
Gremillion, Jacob 30; Port uncertain, 1821 778.5 p251
Gren, Johan August; Minneapolis, 1881-1883 6410.35 p60
Grendle, Robert; New York, NY, 1811 2859.11 p12
Grendle, Sarah; New York, NY, 1811 2859.11 p12
Grene, Giles 17; Maryland or Virginia, 1719 3690.1 p93
Grene, John 14; America, 1706 2212 p47
Grenet, Delphine 27; America, 1838 778.5 p251
Grenholm, John; Illinois, 1868 7857 p4
Grenhow, William 37; Kansas, 1880 5240.1 p62
Grenier, C. 30; America, 1829 778.5 p251
Grenier, F. 43; Port uncertain, 1838 778.5 p251
Grenier, Francois; Quebec, 1750 7603 p48
Grenkigram, Vincent; Iowa, 1866-1943 123.54 p20
Grenko, Anton; Iowa, 1866-1943 123.54 p21
Grenko, Antonia; Iowa, 1866-1943 123.54 p65
Grenko, Antonija; Iowa, 1866-1943 123.54 p65
Grenko, Antony; Iowa, 1866-1943 123.54 p21
Grenko, Josip; Iowa, 1866-1943 123.54 p21
Grenko, Juraj; Iowa, 1866-1943 123.54 p21
Grenko, Maty; Iowa, 1866-1943 123.54 p21
Grenko, Mike; Iowa, 1866-1943 123.54 p21
Grenko, Romo; Iowa, 1866-1943 123.54 p21
Grenko, Wensel; Iowa, 1866-1943 123.54 p21
Grennwats, . . .; Canada, 1776-1783 9786 p22
Grenoz, M. 29; Mexico, 1829 778.5 p251
Grenville, Edward 29; Georgia, 1774 1219.7 p188
Grenz, Georg A. 30; America, 1854-1855 9162.6 p105
Gres, Eucher; Arizona, 1888 2764.35 p27
Gresail, Ludwig; Wisconsin, n.d. 9675.5 p263
Greser, John 19; New Orleans, 1862 543.30 p375C
Gresett, Ole; Washington, 1859-1920 2872.1 p14
Gresham, John; Virginia, 1652 6251 p19
Gresmeyer, Heinrich Friedrich Wilhelm; America, 1853 4610.10 p156
Gress, . . .; Canada, 1776-1783 9786 p22
Gresse, . . .; Canada, 1776-1783 9786 p22
Gressmeier, Heinrich Friedrich Wilhelm; America, 1848 4610.10 p155
Grete, Frantz; New York, NY, 1851 6013.19 p90
Greter, Joseph; Wisconsin, n.d. 9675.5 p263
Gretteau, . . .; Halifax, N.S., 1752 7074.6 p232
Gretteau, Anne-Catherine *SEE* Gretteau, Jean-George
Gretteau, Elisabeth-Marguerite *SEE* Gretteau, Jean-George
Gretteau, Jean-George 35; Halifax, N.S., 1752 7074.6 p210
  *Child:*Louis-Nicolas
  *Child:*Anne-Catherine
  *Child:*Elisabeth-Marguerite
  With wife
  With child
Gretteau, Louis-Nicolas *SEE* Gretteau, Jean-George
Gretton, George 19; Virginia, 1774 1219.7 p240
Gretzing, Agnes; Pennsylvania, 1752 2444 p192
Gretzing, Anna Maria *SEE* Gretzing, Hans Jerg
Gretzing, Hans Jerg; Carolina, 1743 2444 p158
  *Child:*Anna Maria
Gretzinger, Hans Jerg; Pennsylvania, 1743 2444 p159
Greu, P. 20; Louisiana, 1820 778.5 p251
Greubuehl, John; Cincinnati, 1869-1887 8582 p11
Greuling, Christian 52; America, 1838 778.5 p251
Greveldinger, John; Wisconsin, n.d. 9675.5 p263
Greven, Johann H.; Cincinnati, 1829 8582.1 p51
Grever, Franz A.; Cincinnati, 1830-1849 8582 p11
Grewe, Anne Marie Heermeier *SEE* Grewe, Carl Heinrich
Grewe, Carl Heinrich; America, 1841 4610.10 p111
  *Wife:*Anne Marie Heermeier
  *Son:*Karl H. Ferdinand
Grewe, Eduard; Cincinnati, 1869-1887 8582 p11
Grewe, Herman; America, 1854 8582.3 p24
Grewe, Karl H. Ferdinand *SEE* Grewe, Carl Heinrich
Grey, . . .; Canada, 1776-1783 9786 p42
Grey, . . . 12 wks; New York, NY, 1865 5704.8 p193
Grey, . . . 14 mos; New York, NY, 1865 5704.8 p193
Grey, Fred 21; Kansas, 1893 5240.1 p79
Grey, Isaac; New York, NY, 1816 2859.11 p32
Grey, James; New York, NY, 1811 2859.11 p12
Grey, Margaret; Philadelphia, 1848 53.26 p34
Grey, Margaret; Philadelphia, 1848 5704.8 p46
Grey, Robert; New York, NY, 1865 5704.8 p193
Grey, Sophia; New York, NY, 1865 5704.8 p193

Grey, Strickly Wray 26; St. John, N.B., 1865 ***5704.8*** *p165*
Grey, Thady; America, 1743 ***4971*** *p11*
Greyson, James; Arizona, 1898 ***9228.30*** *p5*
Gribben, John; Philadelphia, 1851 ***5704.8*** *p70*
Gribbin, Hugh; Illinois, 1900 ***5012.40*** *p77*
Gribbin, Hugh; St. John, N.B., 1848 ***5704.8*** *p39*
Gribe, Gottlieb 26; Kansas, 1870 ***5240.1*** *p51*
Gribi, Gottlieb 26; Kansas, 1870 ***5240.1*** *p16*
Grichel, . . .; Canada, 1776-1783 ***9786*** *p22*
Gridwell, Henry; Virginia, 1643 ***6219*** *p205*
Griebel, Charles; Illinois, 1860 ***5012.39*** *p90*
Griem, Fritz 22; Kansas, 1881 ***5240.1*** *p63*
Griem, John Henry; Wisconsin, n.d. ***9675.5*** *p263*
Grieme, Theodor; Cincinnati, 1869-1887 ***8582*** *p11*
Griemert, Marie Margarethe Ilsabein; America, 1850 ***4610.10*** *p143*
Grier, Alexander; New York, NY, 1815 ***2859.11*** *p32*
Grier, James; Philadelphia, 1851 ***5704.8*** *p81*
Grier, Jane 23 *SEE* Grier, Thomas
Grier, John; Ohio, 1839 ***9892.11*** *p19*
Grier, Mary Ann 9 mos; Philadelphia, 1850 ***5704.8*** *p64*
Grier, Sarah; Philadelphia, 1850 ***5704.8*** *p64*
Grier, Thomas 30; Philadelphia, 1804 ***53.26*** *p34*
*Relative:*Jane 23
Gries, Johann; New York, NY, 1852 ***8582.3*** *p24*
Gries, Michael; America, 1847 ***8582.1*** *p11*
Griesbach, Herman; Wisconsin, n.d. ***9675.5*** *p263*
Griesbaum, Johann; America, 1846 ***8582.1*** *p11*
Griese, Caspar Christian Heinrich; America, 1848 ***4610.10*** *p155*
Griese, Christian Friedrich; America, 1853 ***4610.10*** *p156*
Griese, Franz; America, 1854 ***1450.2*** *p54A*
Griese, Joh. 76; Illinois, 1907 ***1763*** *p40D*
Grieser, Anna Kath. 1; America, 1853 ***9162.7*** *p14*
Grieser, Barth. 3; America, 1853 ***9162.7*** *p14*
Grieser, Elis. 30; America, 1853 ***9162.7*** *p14*
Grieser, Peter 37; America, 1853 ***9162.7*** *p14*
Grieser, Ph. 7; America, 1853 ***9162.7*** *p14*
Griesinger, . . .; Canada, 1776-1783 ***9786*** *p22*
Griesman, . . .; Canada, 1776-1783 ***9786*** *p22*
Griesmann, . . .; Canada, 1776-1783 ***9786*** *p22*
Griesser, . . .; Canada, 1776-1783 ***9786*** *p22*
Griete, Joseph 32; New Orleans, 1836 ***778.5*** *p251*
Grieve, William; Carolina, 1684 ***1639.20*** *p87*
Grievely, Richard 47; Jamaica, 1774 ***1219.7*** *p180*
Griffen, Andrew; St. John, N.B., 1852 ***5704.8*** *p93*
Griffen, Ann; Virginia, 1645 ***6219*** *p252*
Griffen, Anthony; St. John, N.B., 1852 ***5704.8*** *p93*
Griffen, Bridget; Philadelphia, 1866 ***5704.8*** *p215*
Griffen, Bridget 22; St. John, N.B., 1860 ***5704.8*** *p144*
Griffen, Evans 20; Philadelphia, 1856 ***5704.8*** *p128*
Griffen, George; St. John, N.B., 1852 ***5704.8*** *p93*
Griffen, James; Philadelphia, 1853 ***5704.8*** *p100*
Griffen, Patrick; New York, NY, 1865 ***5704.8*** *p193*
Griffeth, Biddy *SEE* Griffeth, Rose
Griffeth, Biddy; Philadelphia, 1811 ***2859.11*** *p12*
Griffeth, George; Philadelphia, 1852 ***5704.8*** *p88*
Griffeth, Mary Jane; Philadelphia, 1852 ***5704.8*** *p88*
Griffeth, Rose; Philadelphia, 1811 ***53.26*** *p34*
*Relative:*Biddy
Griffeth, Rose; Philadelphia, 1811 ***2859.11*** *p12*
Griffeth, Samuel 9 mos; Philadelphia, 1852 ***5704.8*** *p88*
Griffeth, Tho.; Virginia, 1647 ***6219*** *p244*
Griffett, Herbert; Virginia, 1639 ***6219*** *p159*
Griffey, Martin William; New York, NY, 1895 ***3455.3*** *p49*
Griffin, Mrs. 36; Massachusetts, 1848 ***5881.1*** *p43*
Griffin, Abraham 11; Massachusetts, 1850 ***5881.1*** *p41*
Griffin, Ann; Virginia, 1637 ***6219*** *p82*
Griffin, Ann; Virginia, 1638 ***6219*** *p123*
Griffin, Anne; Quebec, 1849 ***5704.8*** *p51*
Griffin, Biddy 12; St. John, N.B., 1847 ***5704.8*** *p35*
Griffin, Catharine; America, 1867 ***5704.8*** *p223*
Griffin, Catharine; Philadelphia, 1865 ***5704.8*** *p200*
Griffin, Catharine 19; Massachusetts, 1849 ***5881.1*** *p41*
Griffin, Charles; America, 1833 ***1450.2*** *p54A*
Griffin, Daw; Philadelphia, 1811 ***2859.11*** *p12*
Griffin, Edward; Virginia, 1637 ***6219*** *p113*
Griffin, Edward; Virginia, 1638 ***6219*** *p116*
Griffin, Elias; Virginia, 1637 ***6219*** *p13*
Griffin, Elizabeth; Philadelphia, 1865 ***5704.8*** *p200*
Griffin, Ellen; Philadelphia, 1864 ***5704.8*** *p172*
Griffin, Ellen 20; Philadelphia, 1861 ***5704.8*** *p148*
Griffin, Georg; Virginia, 1638 ***6219*** *p120*
Griffin, Georg; Virginia, 1638 ***6219*** *p122*
Griffin, George; Philadelphia, 1865 ***5704.8*** *p200*
Griffin, Henry 20; America, 1700 ***2212*** *p30*
Griffin, Honora 28; Massachusetts, 1849 ***5881.1*** *p42*
Griffin, Hopkin; Virginia, 1643 ***6219*** *p200*
Griffin, James; Massachusetts, 1773 ***1219.7*** *p166*
Griffin, James; Philadelphia, 1864 ***5704.8*** *p175*
Griffin, James 25; Massachusetts, 1847 ***5881.1*** *p42*
Griffin, Jane 16; Philadelphia, 1864 ***5704.8*** *p161*
Griffin, Johanna 6; Massachusetts, 1849 ***5881.1*** *p43*
Griffin, Johanna 19; Massachusetts, 1848 ***5881.1*** *p42*
Griffin, John; Philadelphia, 1865 ***5704.8*** *p200*
Griffin, John; St. John, N.B., 1847 ***5704.8*** *p35*
Griffin, John; Virginia, 1641 ***6219*** *p187*
Griffin, John 20; Maryland, 1775 ***1219.7*** *p253*
Griffin, John 21; Leeward Islands, 1724 ***3690.1*** *p95*
Griffin, John 48; Massachusetts, 1849 ***5881.1*** *p42*
Griffin, John 60; Massachusetts, 1849 ***5881.1*** *p42*
Griffin, Julia 12; Massachusetts, 1848 ***5881.1*** *p42*
Griffin, Kate 20; Massachusetts, 1849 ***5881.1*** *p43*
Griffin, Margaret; Philadelphia, 1865 ***5704.8*** *p200*
Griffin, Mary; America, 1740 ***4971*** *p56*
Griffin, Mary; Quebec, 1849 ***5704.8*** *p51*
Griffin, Mary; Virginia, 1643 ***6219*** *p229*
Griffin, Mary 24; Quebec, 1864 ***5704.8*** *p160*
Griffin, Mathew; Virginia, 1643 ***6219*** *p204*
Griffin, Michael 21; Indianapolis, 1870 ***1450.2*** *p54A*
Griffin, Michael 21; Maryland, 1775 ***1219.7*** *p260*
Griffin, Michael 34; Philadelphia, 1865 ***5704.8*** *p164*
Griffin, Michael 40; Massachusetts, 1848 ***5881.1*** *p43*
Griffin, Michael 50; Massachusetts, 1849 ***5881.1*** *p43*
Griffin, Patrick; America, 1833 ***1450.2*** *p54A*
Griffin, Patrick; America, 1850 ***1450.2*** *p54A*
Griffin, Patrick; Philadelphia, 1864 ***5704.8*** *p175*
Griffin, Patrick; Philadelphia, 1865 ***5704.8*** *p200*
Griffin, Patrick 21; Massachusetts, 1849 ***5881.1*** *p44*
Griffin, Patrick 28; Kansas, 1877 ***5240.1*** *p58*
Griffin, Peggy 20; Massachusetts, 1849 ***5881.1*** *p44*
Griffin, Reginald; Virginia, 1621 ***6219*** *p30*
Griffin, Richard 6; Massachusetts, 1850 ***5881.1*** *p44*
Griffin, Richard 15; Philadelphia, 1774 ***1219.7*** *p175*
Griffin, Sally; Philadelphia, 1864 ***5704.8*** *p172*
Griffin, Samuel 15; Quebec, 1854 ***5704.8*** *p119*
Griffin, Sarah; Philadelphia, 1865 ***5704.8*** *p200*
Griffin, Sarah Jane 18; Philadelphia, 1857 ***5704.8*** *p133*
Griffin, Symon; Virginia, 1638 ***6219*** *p123*
Griffin, Tho.; Virginia, 1642 ***6219*** *p187*
Griffin, Tho.; Virginia, 1642 ***6219*** *p193*
Griffin, Thomas; Virginia, 1642 ***6219*** *p194*
Griffin, Thomas 9; Massachusetts, 1848 ***5881.1*** *p44*
Griffin, Thomas 28; Massachusetts, 1849 ***5881.1*** *p44*
Griffin, Willi.; Virginia, 1637 ***6219*** *p83*
Griffin, William; America, 1735-1743 ***4971*** *p79*
Griffin, William; Philadelphia, 1865 ***5704.8*** *p200*
Griffin, William; Virginia, 1638 ***6219*** *p159*
Griffin, William 24; Baltimore, 1775 ***1219.7*** *p269*
Griffin, Winnefred 58; Massachusetts, 1850 ***5881.1*** *p44*
Griffin, Wm.; Virginia, 1635 ***6219*** *p27*
Griffin, Wm.; Virginia, 1636 ***6219*** *p108*
Griffin, Wm.; Virginia, 1638 ***6219*** *p145*
Griffis, Edward 25; Philadelphia, 1774 ***1219.7*** *p182*
Griffis, John 15; Jamaica, 1730 ***3690.1*** *p95*
Griffis, John 19; Maryland, 1751 ***1219.7*** *p3*
Griffis, John 19; Maryland, 1751 ***3690.1*** *p95*
Griffis, Robert 20; Maryland, 1729 ***3690.1*** *p95*
Griffis, William 21; Jamaica, 1735 ***3690.1*** *p95*
Griffis, William 34; Philadelphia, 1803 ***53.26*** *p34*
Griffiss, Griffith 25; Jamaica, 1738 ***3690.1*** *p95*
Griffith, Ann 24; St. John, N.B., 1854 ***5704.8*** *p121*
Griffith, Anne 17; Philadelphia, 1857 ***5704.8*** *p133*
Griffith, Archibald; Philadelphia, 1849 ***53.26*** *p34*
*Relative:*Hannah
Griffith, Archibald; Philadelphia, 1849 ***5704.8*** *p52*
Griffith, Catherine 32; New York, NY, 1851 ***9555.10*** *p26*
Griffith, Daniel; St. John, N.B., 1853 ***5704.8*** *p100*
Griffith, Daniel 8; St. John, N.B., 1853 ***5704.8*** *p110*
Griffith, Esther 2; Wilmington, DE, 1831 ***6508.7*** *p160*
Griffith, Evan 3; New York, NY, 1851 ***9555.10*** *p26*
Griffith, Evan 20; Virginia, 1751 ***1219.7*** *p4*
Griffith, Evan 20; Virginia, 1751 ***3690.1*** *p95*
Griffith, George 23; Pennsylvania, Virginia or Maryland, 1699 ***2212*** *p20*
Griffith, Hannah *SEE* Griffith, Archibald
Griffith, Hannah; Philadelphia, 1849 ***5704.8*** *p52*
Griffith, Howell 32; New York, NY, 1851 ***9555.10*** *p26*
Griffith, Jane; Baltimore, 1811 ***2859.11*** *p12*
Griffith, John; Philadelphia, 1850 ***53.26*** *p34*
Griffith, John; Philadelphia, 1850 ***5704.8*** *p69*
Griffith, John 12; Virginia, 1700 ***2212*** *p30*
Griffith, Joseh 17; America, 1700 ***2212*** *p31*
Griffith, Joseph 33; New Orleans, 1838 ***778.5*** *p251*
Griffith, Josiah; New York, NY, 1840 ***8208.4*** *p104*
Griffith, Louis 11 mos; New York, NY, 1851 ***9555.10*** *p26*
Griffith, Margaret 11?; America, 1705 ***2212*** *p45*
Griffith, Margt. 5; New York, NY, 1851 ***9555.10*** *p26*
Griffith, Mary; Baltimore, 1811 ***2859.11*** *p12*
Griffith, Mary 38; St. John, N.B., 1853 ***5704.8*** *p110*
Griffith, Mary Jane 10; St. John, N.B., 1853 ***5704.8*** *p110*
Griffith, Maurice; America, 1699 ***2212*** *p25*
Griffith, Michael; America, 1742 ***4971*** *p54*
Griffith, Nancy 26; Wilmington, DE, 1831 ***6508.7*** *p160*
Griffith, Patrick 16; St. John, N.B., 1853 ***5704.8*** *p110*
Griffith, R. B.; Washington, 1859-1920 ***2872.1*** *p14*
Griffith, Ralph; Virginia, 1641 ***6219*** *p184*
Griffith, Rebecca; New York, NY, 1864 ***5704.8*** *p173*
Griffith, Robert; Baltimore, 1811 ***2859.11*** *p12*
Griffith, Robert 58; Arizona, 1924 ***9228.40*** *p28*
Griffith, Tho.; Virginia, 1643 ***6219*** *p199*
Griffith, Tho.; Virginia, 1646 ***6219*** *p236*
Griffith, Thomas; Shreveport, LA, 1881 ***7129*** *p44*
Griffith, Thomas 25; Virginia, 1727 ***3690.1*** *p95*
Griffith, Timothy 40; Arizona, 1890 ***2764.35*** *p26*
Griffith, William; Quebec, 1822 ***7603*** *p96*
Griffith, William P. 41; California, 1872 ***2769.4*** *p5*
Griffiths, Benjamin 19; Maryland, 1750 ***3690.1*** *p95*
Griffiths, Benjamin 19; Maryland, 1751 ***1219.7*** *p2*
Griffiths, Henry; New York, NY, 1816 ***2859.11*** *p32*
Griffiths, James 16; Maryland, 1775 ***1219.7*** *p256*
Griffiths, James C.; Colorado, 1885 ***9678.2*** *p21*
Griffiths, Jane 17; St. John, N.B., 1854 ***5704.8*** *p119*
Griffiths, Jane 23; Maryland, 1774 ***1219.7*** *p179*
Griffiths, John 15; Jamaica, 1730 ***3690.1*** *p95*
Griffiths, John 19; Maryland, 1775 ***1219.7*** *p256*
Griffiths, John 22; Maryland, 1774 ***1219.7*** *p185*
Griffiths, John 26; Maryland, 1774 ***1219.7*** *p236*
Griffiths, John 27; Jamaica, 1775 ***1219.7*** *p248*
Griffiths, Joseph 30; Philadelphia, 1774 ***1219.7*** *p183*
Griffiths, Samuel 19; Maryland, 1774 ***1219.7*** *p230*
Griffiths, Samuel 22; Maryland, 1775 ***1219.7*** *p263*
Griffiths, Thomas; Colorado, 1904 ***9678.2*** *p21*
Griffiths, William 19; St. John, N.B., 1854 ***5704.8*** *p119*
Griffitt, John; Virginia, 1637 ***6219*** *p81*
Griffon, Henry 35; Port uncertain, 1838 ***778.5*** *p251*
Griffy, Martin William; New York, NY, 1895 ***3455.2*** *p53*
Grigere, Andrew 22; America, 1839 ***778.5*** *p251*
Grigg, Thomas; Nevis, 1757 ***1219.7*** *p55*
Grigge, Mrs. 28; Port uncertain, 1839 ***778.5*** *p251*
Griggs, George; Shreveport, LA, 1878 ***7129*** *p44*
Griggs, Mrs. Luciene 27; Port uncertain, 1832 ***778.5*** *p251*
Griggs, Tho.; Virginia, 1649 ***6219*** *p252*
Griggs, Thos.; Virginia, 1637 ***6219*** *p13*
Grigs, John; Virginia, 1639 ***6219*** *p157*
Grigson, Jone; Virginia, 1637 ***6219*** *p81*
Grigson, Richard; Virginia, 1637 ***6219*** *p81*
Grikas, Felex; Wisconsin, n.d. ***9675.5*** *p263*
Griksas, Felix; Wisconsin, n.d. ***9675.5*** *p263*
Grikszas, Joseph; Wisconsin, n.d. ***9675.5*** *p263*
Grilli, Amilia; Wisconsin, n.d. ***9675.5*** *p263*
Grilli, Endry; Wisconsin, n.d. ***9675.5*** *p263*
Grillis, Catharine 21; Port uncertain, 1838 ***778.5*** *p251*
Grillis, Charles 3; Port uncertain, 1838 ***778.5*** *p251*
Grillis, Frances 9; Port uncertain, 1838 ***778.5*** *p252*
Grillis, Harriet 16; Port uncertain, 1838 ***778.5*** *p252*
Grillis, Henry 18; Port uncertain, 1838 ***778.5*** *p252*
Grillis, Joseph 23; Port uncertain, 1838 ***778.5*** *p252*
Grillis, Louis 51; Port uncertain, 1838 ***778.5*** *p252*
Grillis, Maria 48; Port uncertain, 1838 ***778.5*** *p252*
Grillis, Nicola. 13; Port uncertain, 1838 ***778.5*** *p252*
Grillot, George 26; Port uncertain, 1839 ***778.5*** *p252*
Grillot, Henry 36; Port uncertain, 1839 ***778.5*** *p252*
Grillot, Marguerite 17; Port uncertain, 1839 ***778.5*** *p252*
Grillozet, Joseph 21; Port uncertain, 1839 ***778.5*** *p252*
Grim, Ettmann; Pittsburgh, 1882 ***3702.7*** *p475*
Grim, J. P.; Washington, 1859-1920 ***2872.1*** *p14*
Grim, Jacob; Indiana, 1844 ***9117*** *p16*
Grim, James P.; Washington, 1859-1920 ***2872.1*** *p14*
Grimard, Jean 26; Port uncertain, 1838 ***778.5*** *p252*
Grimbaum, Koppel 19; New York, NY, 1878 ***9253*** *p46*
Grimer, John B. 40; Kansas, 1890 ***5240.1*** *p75*
Grimert, Franz Heinrich Wilhelm *SEE* Grimert, Johann Henrich
Grimert, Hermann Heinrich *SEE* Grimert, Johann Henrich
Grimert, Johann Henrich; America, 1850 ***4610.10*** *p138*
With wife
*Child:*Hermann Heinrich
*Child:*Franz Heinrich Wilhelm
Grimes, Ann; Virginia, 1642 ***6219*** *p189*
Grimes, Arthur; Virginia, 1638 ***6219*** *p123*
Grimes, Catharine 8; Massachusetts, 1850 ***5881.1*** *p41*
Grimes, Charles; Philadelphia, 1864 ***5704.8*** *p179*
Grimes, Edward; Virginia, 1643 ***6219*** *p203*
Grimes, Francis 5; Massachusetts, 1850 ***5881.1*** *p42*
Grimes, James; Philadelphia, 1811 ***53.26*** *p34*
Grimes, James; Philadelphia, 1811 ***2859.11*** *p12*
Grimes, Jeremiah 18; Antigua (Antego), 1728 ***3690.1*** *p95*
Grimes, John 25; Virginia, 1773 ***1219.7*** *p171*
Grimes, Jon.; Virginia, 1635 ***6219*** *p20*
Grimes, Patrick; New York, NY, 1839 ***8208.4*** *p101*

Grimes, Peter O. 22; Kansas, 1877 *5240.1 p58*
Grimes, Walter; Virginia, 1635 *6219 p6*
Griminsk, Henry; America, 1859 *6014.1 p2*
Griminsk, Peter; America, 1860 *6014.1 p2*
Grimm, . . .; Canada, 1776-1783 *9786 p22*
Grimm, Claus Hinrich; Illinois, 1874 *5012.39 p26*
Grimm, F. W. 67; Washington, 1916-1919 *1728.4 p253*
Grimm, Franz; America, 1844 *8582.1 p11*
Grimm, Jacob; America, 1850 *1450.2 p54A*
Grimm, M.; Cincinnati, 1843 *8582.1 p11*
Grimm, Wendelin; America, 1858 *1450.2 p55A*
Grimm, William; Kansas, 1902 *5240.1 p16*
Grimmenger, Andreas; Georgia, 1739 *9332 p324*
Grimmer, Andreas; Illinois, 1842 *8582.2 p51*
Grimmer, Jean 18; America, 1836 *778.5 p252*
Grimmert, Anne Marie Luise; America, 1858 *4610.10 p149*
Grimmiger, Andreas; Georgia, 1739 *9332 p327*
Grimmiger, Sabina; Georgia, 1734 *9332 p327*
Grimming, . . .; Canada, 1776-1783 *9786 p22*
Grimpe, . . .; Canada, 1776-1783 *9786 p22*
Grimpe, Ensign; Quebec, 1776 *9786 p259*
Grimsdottir, Fumefa 51; Quebec, 1879 *2557.1 p39*
Grimshaw, John; Iowa, 1866-1943 *123.54 p21*
Grimshaw, Miles; Maryland or Virginia, 1698 *2212 p10*
Grimsmann, August 25; Kansas, 1884 *5240.1 p65*
Grimsmann, August 45; Kansas, 1884 *5240.1 p16*
Grimston, Anthony; Virginia, 1637 *6219 p85*
Grinaker, Johannes; Arkansas, 1918 *95.2 p51*
Grindal, Elizabeth 32; Baltimore, 1775 *1219.7 p269*
Grindall, Thomas; Virginia, 1638 *6219 p119*
Grindall, Thomas; Virginia, 1639 *6219 p151*
Grindan, Samuell 17; Antigua (Antego), 1720 *3690.1 p96*
Grindell, Thomas; Virginia, 1638 *6219 p23*
Grinden, Jacob Rangvald; Arkansas, 1918 *95.2 p51*
Grinden, Samuell 17; Antigua (Antego), 1720 *3690.1 p96*
Grindlay, James; Charleston, SC, 1765 *1639.20 p87*
Grindle, Ragnvald Larsen 25; Arkansas, 1918 *95.2 p51*
Grindler, Philipp Jacob 50; Pennsylvania, 1754 *2444 p159*
Grindley, Joseph; Illinois, 1892 *5012.40 p27*
Grindley, Joseph S.; Illinois, 1876 *5012.39 p91*
Grindon, Tho.; Virginia, 1637 *6219 p83*
Griner, Dorothea Emmert *SEE* Griner, John Theodore
Griner, John Theodore; Philadelphia Co., PA, 1717 *3627 p9*
  *Wife:*Dorothea Emmert
  *Daughter:*Maria Catharina
  With sister
Griner, Maria Catharina *SEE* Griner, John Theodore
Grinett, Alice; Virginia, 1635 *6219 p12*
Grinett, Elizabeth; Virginia, 1635 *6219 p12*
Grinett, John; Virginia, 1635 *6219 p12*
Grinfeild, Robert; Virginia, 1639 *6219 p159*
Gringer, Robert; Virginia, 1643 *6219 p202*
Grinler, Philip Jacob 50; Pennsylvania, 1754 *2444 p159*
Grinslade, John 20; Jamaica, 1731 *3690.1 p96*
Grinspan, A.; Iowa, 1866-1943 *123.54 p21*
Grinwall, Jacob 29; New Orleans, 1838 *778.5 p252*
Grinwood, Dorothy; Virginia, 1641 *6219 p184*
Grinwood, Mary *SEE* Grinwood, Thomas
Grinwood, Thomas; Virginia, 1641 *6219 p184*
  *Wife:*Mary
Grisaffi, Salvatore; Wisconsin, n.d. *9675.5 p263*
Grisburg, Henry; New York, NY, 1838 *8208.4 p63*
Grischy, Heinrich; America, 1852 *8582.3 p24*
Grisdell, Joseph 19; Jamaica, 1736 *3690.1 p96*
Griselt, George 23; New Orleans, 1862 *543.30 p376C*
Grisier, Ms. 32; New Orleans, 1839 *778.5 p252*
Griskin, Dederick 30; Philadelphia, 1774 *1219.7 p233*
Grisman, John 18; Port uncertain, 1838 *778.5 p253*
Grison, Gustav 28; Kansas, 1892 *5240.1 p77*
Grispan, Benjamini; Iowa, 1866-1943 *123.54 p21*
Grispan, Marcus; Iowa, 1866-1943 *123.54 p21*
Grissim, Jasper; Philadelphia, 1848 *5704.8 p41*
Grissim, Sarah; Philadelphia, 1848 *5704.8 p41*
Grissum, Jasper; Philadelphia, 1848 *53.26 p34*
  *Relative:*Sarah
Grissum, Sarah *SEE* Grissum, Jasper
Grist, Adam 24; New Orleans, 1862 *543.30 p375C*
Griswell, John; New York, NY, 1816 *2859.11 p32*
Griswell, Mary; New York, NY, 1816 *2859.11 p32*
Griswell, Robert; New York, NY, 1816 *2859.11 p32*
Griswell, William; New York, NY, 1816 *2859.11 p32*
Grivas, Peter G.; Arkansas, 1918 *95.2 p51*
Griver, Peter; America, 1742 *4971 p37*
Grivey, John; Delaware Bay or River, 1743 *4971 p104*
Grizell, Humphrey; Virginia, 1636 *6219 p75*
Groat, Randle 32; Kansas, 1878 *5240.1 p59*
Grob, Karl 65; Baltimore, 1903 *1763 p40D*
Grob, Walter; Arkansas, 1918 *95.2 p51*

Grobin, Rosine Marie 28; New Orleans, 1839 *9420.2 p166*
Grochow, John; Wisconsin, n.d. *9675.5 p263*
Grodhaus, G. P.; Ohio, 1831 *8582 p11*
Grodos, Alexandre 39; America, 1838 *778.5 p253*
Grodotski, Emma; Wisconsin, n.d. *9675.5 p263*
Grodotski, Otto; Wisconsin, n.d. *9675.5 p263*
Grodson, Jon.; Virginia, 1637 *6219 p110*
Groefar, Valentine; Wisconsin, n.d. *9675.5 p263*
Groen, John George; New York, 1750 *3652 p74*
Groene, J. H. F.; America, 1849 *8582.2 p13*
Groene, P. H. F.; Cincinnati, 1869-1887 *8582 p11*
Groenland, Herrmann M.; Cincinnati, 1869-1887 *8582 p11*
Groenwalt, Henry; America, 1852 *1450.2 p55A*
Groenweld, Heiko; Illinois, 1853 *7857 p4*
Groeschel, Gottwerth; Wisconsin, n.d. *9675.5 p263*
Groetsch, Andreas; Wisconsin, n.d. *9675.5 p263*
Groezinger, Catharina; Pennsylvania, 1751 *2444 p229*
Grof, Joseph; Maryland, 1820-1829 *8582.1 p46*
Grogham, Ann; Montreal, 1823 *7603 p91*
Groh, George A.; Iowa, 1866-1943 *123.54 p21*
Groh, Jost; Philadelphia, 1779 *8137 p9*
Groisard, Joseph 32; America, 1836 *778.5 p253*
Grole, Benoit 40; Louisiana, 1823 *778.5 p253*
Grolinger, Peter; Wisconsin, n.d. *9675.5 p263*
Groliverse, . . . 2; America, 1838 *778.5 p253*
Groliverse, Madame 27; America, 1838 *778.5 p253*
Gromoll, Frederick; Wisconsin, n.d. *9675.5 p263*
Gromwell, Gersion; Virginia, 1638 *6219 p150*
Gromwell, Gerson; Virginia, 1638 *6219 p117*
Gronan, John; Kansas, 1884 *5240.1 p16*
Gronau, Catharina *SEE* Gronau, Israel Christian
Gronau, Catharina Kroehr; Georgia, 1739 *9332 p324*
Gronau, Israel Christian; Georgia, 1739 *9332 p325*
  *Wife:*Catharina
Gronauer, Frank; New York, 1886 *1450.2 p12B*
Gronemeyer, Dietrich; Wisconsin, n.d. *9675.5 p263*
Gronemeyer, Heinrich; Wisconsin, n.d. *9675.5 p263*
Groneweg, Friederich; America, 1849 *8582.2 p13*
Groning, Johann; Charleston, SC, 1775-1781 *8582.2 p52*
Gronnert, Henry; New York, 1882 *1450.2 p12B*
Grono, . . .; Halifax, N.S., 1752 *7074.6 p230*
Grono, Carmono 25; West Virginia, 1898 *9788.3 p11*
Gronros, Isak Hjalmar; Washington, 1859-1920 *2872.1 p14*
Gronwoldt, John; America, 1848 *1450.2 p55A*
Groom, George; Illinois, 1857 *7857 p4*
Grope, . . .; Canada, 1776-1783 *9786 p22*
Gropmann, Gustavus; America, 1847 *1450.2 p55A*
Gropp, August; Kansas, 1871 *5240.1 p16*
Groree, James 15; Maryland, 1774 *1219.7 p244*
Gros, . . .; America, 1837 *778.5 p253*
Gros, Mme.; America, 1837 *778.5 p254*
Gros, Mr. 30; America, 1837 *778.5 p253*
Gros, George 26; New Orleans, 1838 *778.5 p253*
Gros, J. F. 19; America, 1836 *778.5 p253*
Gros, John Christhoff; Washington, 1859-1920 *2872.1 p14*
Gros, Philipp; Cincinnati, 1869-1887 *8582 p11*
Grosbois, Anne 37; New Orleans, 1838 *778.5 p254*
Grosbois, Claude 37; New Orleans, 1838 *778.5 p254*
Grosch, John; America, 1847 *1450.2 p55A*
Grose, Mr. 30?; New Orleans, 1837 *778.5 p254*
Groshel, William; Illinois, 1871 *2896.5 p15*
Grosklaus, Frank; Wisconsin, n.d. *9675.5 p263*
Grosman, Lewis; South Carolina, 1788 *7119 p198*
Grosmann, George 16; America, 1836 *778.5 p254*
Grosregnault, . . .; Halifax, N.S., 1752 *7074.6 p230*
Grosrenauld, Francoise *SEE* Grosrenauld, Jean-Jacques
Grosrenauld, Jean-Christophe *SEE* Grosrenauld, Jean-Jacques
Grosrenauld, Jean-Jacques 36; Halifax, N.S., 1752 *7074.6 p210*
  *Wife:*Marguerite
  *Child:*Pierre
  *Child:*Jean-Christophe
  *Child:*Francoise
Grosrenauld, Marguerite *SEE* Grosrenauld, Jean-Jacques
Grosrenauld, Pierre *SEE* Grosrenauld, Jean-Jacques
Grosrenault, Hedwige; Halifax, N.S., 1752 *7074.6 p213*
Gross, . . .; Canada, 1776-1783 *9786 p22*
Gross, Andreas; Cincinnati, 1834 *8582.1 p52*
Gross, Andrew; Arkansas, 1918 *95.2 p51*
Gross, Andrew; New York, 1750 *3652 p75*
Gross, Anna *SEE* Gross, Heinrich, Jr.
Gross, Apollonia *SEE* Gross, Heinrich, Jr.
Gross, August; New York, NY, 1836 *8208.4 p20*
Gross, Christoph; America, 1801 *8582 p11*
Gross, Daniel; Pennsylvania, 1884 *2691.4 p167*
Gross, Dorothea; Pennsylvania, 1753 *4525 p202*
Gross, Francois; New York, NY, 1834 *8208.4 p28*
Gross, Frederick; Illinois, 1888 *5012.39 p52*

Gross, Heinrich, Jr.; Pennsylvania, 1752 *2444 p159*
  *Wife:*Apollonia
  *Child:*Anna
  *Child:*Johann Jacob
Gross, Henriette 19; New York, NY, 1878 *9253 p47*
Gross, Johann Jacob *SEE* Gross, Heinrich, Jr.
Gross, John Christhoff; Washington, 1859-1920 *2872.1 p14*
Gross, Mattes; Philadelphia, 1756 *4525 p261*
Gross, Philipp; Minnesota, 1856 *8582.3 p82*
Gross, S. J.; Washington, 1859-1920 *2872.1 p14*
Gross, Sampson; Virginia, 1637 *6219 p115*
Gross, Theodore; Illinois, 1877 *2896.5 p15*
Gross, Valentine; Arkansas, 1918 *95.2 p51*
Grosse, Christiane 52; New Orleans, 1839 *9420.2 p485*
  *Son:*Ferdinand 31
  *Son:*Maurice 25
  *Son:*Frederick 22
Grosse, Ferdinand 31 *SEE* Grosse, Christiane
Grosse, Frederick 22 *SEE* Grosse, Christiane
Grosse, Maurice 25 *SEE* Grosse, Christiane
Grosse-Knefelkamp, A. M. Luise; America, 1893 *4610.10 p153*
Grosse-Knefelkamp, Fr.; America, 1893 *4610.10 p153*
Grossens, Frank Haveer; Arkansas, 1918 *95.2 p51*
Grossius, Johann; America, 1850 *8582.3 p24*
Grossman, . . .; Canada, 1776-1783 *9786 p22*
Grossman, Edward; Arkansas, 1918 *95.2 p51*
Grossman, Nicolaus 32; New Orleans, 1862 *543.30 p374C*
Grossmann, Dorothee Louise; America, 1851 *4610.10 p98*
Grosso-Nicolio, Antonia 23; New York, NY, 1893 *9026.4 p41*
Grostephan, Michael; Illinois, 1876 *5012.37 p60*
Groszer, Margaret; New York, 1749 *3652 p72*
Grot, Tebbe; Illinois, 1888 *5012.37 p61*
Grote, . . .; Illinois, 1800-1900 *4610.10 p67*
Grote, Charles; Illinois, 1880 *2896.5 p15*
Grote, Christian; Illinois, 1880 *2896.5 p15*
Grote, J. G. F.; America, 1849 *8582.3 p24*
Groteluschen, Fred; Wisconsin, n.d. *9675.5 p263*
Groteluschen, Henry; Wisconsin, n.d. *9675.5 p263*
Groteluschen, John; Wisconsin, n.d. *9675.5 p263*
Groth, Carl; Wisconsin, n.d. *9675.5 p263*
Groth, Ferdinand; Wisconsin, n.d. *9675.5 p263*
Groth, Frank L.; Wisconsin, n.d. *9675.5 p263*
Groth, Joachim F.; Wisconsin, n.d. *9675.5 p263*
Groth, Johan; Wisconsin, n.d. *9675.5 p263*
Groth, Jouchnin; Wisconsin, n.d. *9675.5 p263*
Groth, Martin Friedrich; Wisconsin, n.d. *9675.5 p263*
Grothe, . . .; Canada, 1776-1783 *9786 p22*
Grothe, Edward 45; New Orleans, 1862 *543.30 p376C*
Grotvik, Alang; Washington, 1859-1920 *2872.1 p14*
Grotvik, Anna Beatrice; Washington, 1859-1920 *2872.1 p14*
Grotvik, Einar; Washington, 1859-1920 *2872.1 p14*
Grotvik, Halvor; Washington, 1859-1920 *2872.1 p14*
Grotz, Jacob; Pennsylvania, 1749 *2444 p158*
Grotz, John; Wisconsin, n.d. *9675.5 p263*
Groudmann, Elard; New York, NY, 1839 *8208.4 p92*
Grove, Benjamin 24; North Carolina, 1736 *3690.1 p96*
Grove, Charles 33; Virginia, 1730 *3690.1 p96*
Grove, Francis; Philadelphia, 1761 *9973.7 p36*
Grove, Gazeley 29; Jamaica, 1730 *3690.1 p96*
Grove, Jacob; Philadelphia, 1760 *9973.7 p35*
Grove, Joane; Virginia, 1639 *6219 p156*
Grove, John; Philadelphia, 1761 *9973.7 p36*
Grove, John 23; Baltimore, 1775 *1219.7 p270*
Grove, John Matthew; St. Christopher, 1753 *1219.7 p26*
Grover, John; Georgia, 1774 *1219.7 p242*
Grover, Jonathan 17; Philadelphia, 1774 *1219.7 p234*
Grover, William; Florida, 1768 *1219.7 p135*
Groves, Catherine 6 *SEE* Groves, George
Groves, Catherine Ann 6; Philadelphia, 1848 *5704.8 p46*
Groves, Edward 11 *SEE* Groves, George
Groves, Edward 11; Philadelphia, 1848 *5704.8 p46*
Groves, George; Philadelphia, 1847 *53.26 p34*
  *Relative:*Thomas
Groves, George; Philadelphia, 1847 *5704.8 p31*
Groves, George; Philadelphia, 1848 *53.26 p34*
  *Relative:*Nancy
  *Relative:*Edward 11
  *Relative:*Catherine 6
  *Relative:*Mary 4
Groves, George; Philadelphia, 1848 *5704.8 p46*
Groves, John 44; Maryland, 1775 *1219.7 p255*
Groves, Mary 4 *SEE* Groves, George
Groves, Mary 4; Philadelphia, 1848 *5704.8 p46*
Groves, Nancy *SEE* Groves, George
Groves, Nancy; Philadelphia, 1848 *5704.8 p46*
Groves, Thomas *SEE* Groves, George
Groves, Thomas; Nevada, 1864 *2764.35 p28*

Groves, Thomas; Philadelphia, 1847 ***5704.8*** *p31*
Groyman, Cosmero 33; Arizona, 1918 ***9228.40*** *p22*
Groz, Anna Maria; Pennsylvania, 1740-1800 ***2444*** *p182*
Groz, Anna Maria Keppler *SEE* Groz, Johann Martin
Groz, Johann Georg *SEE* Groz, Johann Martin
Groz, Johann Martin; Pennsylvania, 1737-1800 ***2444*** *p159*
*Wife:*Anna Maria Keppler
*Child:*Johann Georg
Grubb, . . .; Ohio, 1812-1814 ***8582.2*** *p59*
Grubbe, Daniel; Illinois, 1860 ***5012.38*** *p97*
Grubbel, Ernst Wilhelm August; America, 1886 ***4610.10*** *p114*
Grubber, Christian; Philadelphia, 1760 ***9973.7*** *p34*
Grube, Bernhard Adam; New York, 1748 ***3652*** *p68*
Grubenheim, Soph. Kathr. 19; America, 1854-1855 ***9162.6*** *p105*
Grubenstein, . . .; Canada, 1776-1783 ***9786*** *p22*
Gruber, . . .; Canada, 1776-1783 ***9786*** *p22*
Gruber, Balth; Georgia, 1738 ***9332*** *p320*
Gruber, Carl; Charleston, SC, 1766 ***8582.2*** *p65*
Gruber, Catharina Christian *SEE* Gruber, Friedrich
Gruber, Christian; Charleston, SC, 1775-1781 ***8582.2*** *p52*
Gruber, Ernst; America, 1845 ***1450.2*** *p55A*
Gruber, Frank 37; New Orleans, 1862 ***543.30*** *p374C*
Gruber, Friedrich; Pennsylvania, 1753 ***2444*** *p159*
*Child:*Johanna Gottliebin
*Wife:*Margaretha D. Staud
*Child:*Johanna Friederica
*Child:*Margaretha Dorothea
*Child:*Catharina Christian
*Child:*Rosina
Gruber, Hans 45; Georgia, 1734 ***9332*** *p327*
Gruber, Joh; Charleston, SC, 1775-1781 ***8582.2*** *p52*
Gruber, Johanna Friederica *SEE* Gruber, Friedrich
Gruber, Johanna Gottliebin *SEE* Gruber, Friedrich
Gruber, Joseph John; Arkansas, 1918 ***95.2*** *p51*
Gruber, Karl; Charleston, SC, 1775-1781 ***8582.2*** *p52*
Gruber, Margaretha D. Staud *SEE* Gruber, Friedrich
Gruber, Margaretha Dorothea *SEE* Gruber, Friedrich
Gruber, Maria Kroehr *SEE* Gruber, Peter
Gruber, Maria Mosshammer *SEE* Gruber, Peter
Gruber, Peter; Georgia, 1738 ***9332*** *p321*
Gruber, Peter; Georgia, 1739 ***9332*** *p323*
*Wife:*Maria Kroehr
Gruber, Peter; Georgia, 1739 ***9332*** *p325*
*Wife:*Maria Mosshammer
Gruber, Rosina *SEE* Gruber, Friedrich
Gruber, Wilhelm; Georgia, 1738 ***9332*** *p320*
Gruberic, Simon; Iowa, 1866-1943 ***123.54*** *p21*
Grubesse, Armant 27; Port uncertain, 1836 ***778.5*** *p254*
Grubio, Marija; Iowa, 1866-1943 ***123.54*** *p65*
Grubio, Matt; Iowa, 1866-1943 ***123.54*** *p65*
Grubisic, Anton; Iowa, 1866-1943 ***123.54*** *p21*
Grubisich, Loura; Iowa, 1866-1943 ***123.54*** *p21*
Gruchy, Brigitte 20; New Orleans, 1836 ***778.5*** *p254*
Gruddy, Catherine; St. John, N.B., 1852 ***5704.8*** *p93*
Gruden, Frank; Wisconsin, n.d. ***9675.5*** *p263*
Grueau, Francois 14; New Orleans, 1836 ***778.5*** *p254*
Gruen, Mr. 49; Port uncertain, 1836 ***778.5*** *p254*
Gruen, Pierre 35; New Orleans, 1823 ***778.5*** *p254*
Gruendelmayer, Jacob; Port uncertain, 1766 ***2444*** *p159*
Gruendler, . . .; Canada, 1776-1783 ***9786*** *p22*
Gruendler, Anna Magdalena *SEE* Gruendler, Philipp Jacob
Gruendler, Christina Catharina *SEE* Gruendler, Philipp Jacob
Gruendler, Dorothea *SEE* Gruendler, Philipp Jacob
Gruendler, Maria Agnes *SEE* Gruendler, Philipp Jacob
Gruendler, Maria Elisabetha *SEE* Gruendler, Philipp Jacob
Gruendler, Philipp Jacob; New England, 1747-1800 ***2444*** *p159*
*Wife:*Maria Elisabetha
*Child:*Anna Magdalena
*Child:*Maria Agnes
*Child:*Dorothea
*Child:*Christina Catharina
Gruenenwald, Christian; Wisconsin, n.d. ***9675.5*** *p263*
Gruener, Peter; America, 1871 ***1450.2*** *p56A*
Gruenzweig, Eva Catharina; Pennsylvania, 1749 ***2444*** *p202*
Gruesser, Wendel; America, 1848 ***8582.1*** *p11*
Grueter, Johann Heinrich; Cincinnati, 1800-1877 ***8582.3*** *p87*
Gruetter, Frederick John; Arkansas, 1918 ***95.2*** *p51*
Grughan, Patrick; Buffalo, NY, 1844 ***2896.5*** *p15*
Grugnet, Catherine 40; New Orleans, 1836 ***778.5*** *p254*
Gruir, John; New York, NY, 1811 ***2859.11*** *p12*
With family
Grumble, David 21; Maryland, 1775 ***1219.7*** *p256*
Grumey, Antoine 18; America, 1838 ***778.5*** *p254*
Grumitt, John 22; Jamaica, 1730 ***3690.1*** *p96*
Grummer, Paul 21; America, 1838 ***778.5*** *p254*
Grumpold, Hans; Georgia, 1738 ***9332*** *p320*
Grun, Joh. 85; Ontario, 1901 ***1763*** *p40D*
Grund, John George 32; Philadelphia, 1852 ***1450.2*** *p55A*
Grundberg, Helena; New York, 1749 ***3652*** *p72*
Grundin, Charles F.; Boston, 1853 ***6410.32*** *p123*
Grundin, Charles F. 36; Massachusetts, 1860 ***6410.32*** *p105*
Grundin, Mary 32; Massachusetts, 1860 ***6410.32*** *p105*
Grundler, . . .; Canada, 1776-1783 ***9786*** *p22*
Grundler, Friedrich; Canada, 1776-1783 ***9786*** *p243*
Grundner, Martin; Georgia, 1738 ***9332*** *p320*
Grundrum, Henry; America, 1832 ***1450.2*** *p55A*
Grundtish, Frank; Ohio, 1867 ***6014.2*** *p7*
Grundy, Adam; Iowa, 1866-1943 ***123.54*** *p21*
Grune, . . .; Canada, 1776-1783 ***9786*** *p22*
Gruner, Karl 30; Kansas, 1878 ***5240.1*** *p59*
Grunewald, . . .; Canada, 1776-1783 ***9786*** *p22*
Grunewald, Gustav; Illinois, 1922 ***3455.4*** *p26*
Grunewald, John Henry; New York, 1754 ***3652*** *p80*
Grunewald, Ludwig Christian; New York, 1761 ***3652*** *p87*
Grunewald, Peter 16; America, 1854-1855 ***9162.6*** *p105*
Grunewald, Valentin; America, 1853 ***2853.7*** *p109*
Grunhagen, Mr.; Milwaukee, 1843 ***3702.7*** *p310*
Gruning, Friedrich 26; New York, NY, 1862 ***9831.18*** *p16*
Grunko, John; Iowa, 1866-1943 ***123.54*** *p21*
Grunsdish, Jon.; Virginia, 1642 ***6219*** *p192*
Grunwald, Jacob 30; Kansas, 1876 ***5240.1*** *p58*
Grunwald, Zelde 25; New York, 1912 ***9980.29*** *p49*
Grunwalt, Henry; America, 1852 ***1450.2*** *p55A*
Grunz, Florent 32; America, 1838 ***778.5*** *p254*
Grupe, Karl; Wisconsin, n.d. ***9675.5*** *p263*
Grusemper, Villello; Iowa, 1866-1943 ***123.54*** *p21*
Grussen, Joseph 42; America, 1831 ***778.5*** *p254*
Grussen, Percete 36; America, 1831 ***778.5*** *p255*
Grutschmit, . . .; Canada, 1776-1783 ***9786*** *p22*
Grutze, Carl Gustav; Colorado, 1894 ***9678.2*** *p21*
Gruver, J. G.; Washington, 1859-1920 ***2872.1*** *p14*
Gryffeth, Eliz; America, 1698 ***2212*** *p8*
Gryffeth, Hugh; America, 1697 ***2212*** *p4*
Gryffeth, Wm; America, 1697 ***2212*** *p4*
Gryffin, Edw 25; America, 1699 ***2212*** *p29*
Gryffin, Jn; America, 1697 ***2212*** *p4*
Gryffith, Jno 17; Maryland or Virginia, 1699 ***2212*** *p23*
Gryffith, Mary; America, 1697 ***2212*** *p7*
Gryffith, Wm; Barbados, 1698 ***2212*** *p5*
Gryffith, Wm 13; Maryland or Virginia, 1699 ***2212*** *p23*
Grylski, . . .; New York, 1831 ***4606*** *p173*
Grymes, William; Virginia, 1638 ***6219*** *p145*
Grymsditch, John; Virginia, 1638 ***6219*** *p149*
With wife
Grysingher, . . .; Canada, 1776-1783 ***9786*** *p22*
Grzegorzewska, Anna 23; New York, 1912 ***9980.29*** *p69*
Grzeskiewicz, Roman 29; Arkansas, 1918 ***95.2*** *p51*
Grzeszkiewicz, Roman 29; Arkansas, 1918 ***95.2*** *p51*
Gschwandel, Margaretha; Georgia, 1734 ***9332*** *p327*
Gschwandel, Margaretha 7 *SEE* Gschwandel, Thomas
Gschwandel, Sibylla Resch *SEE* Gschwandel, Thomas
Gschwandel, Sibylla Schwab *SEE* Gschwandel, Thomas
Gschwandel, Thomas; Georgia, 1739 ***9332*** *p323*
*Wife:*Sibylla Schwab
Gschwandel, Thomas; Georgia, 1739 ***9332*** *p325*
*Wife:*Sibylla Resch
*Daughter:*Margaretha 7
Gschwind, . . .; Canada, 1776-1783 ***9786*** *p22*
Gsell, Anna Dorothea Hoffmann *SEE* Gsell, Ludwig
Gsell, Ludwig; Pennsylvania, 1727 ***3627*** *p18*
*Wife:*Anna Dorothea Hoffmann
Gstach, Andreas; Wisconsin, n.d. ***9675.5*** *p263*
Gualadi, Louigi; Iowa, 1866-1943 ***123.54*** *p21*
Gualodi, Lovigi; Iowa, 1866-1943 ***123.54*** *p21*
Guanella, Thomas; New York, NY, 1837 ***8208.4*** *p41*
Guarder, Antone 67; Arizona, 1920 ***9228.40*** *p23*
Guarino, Antonio; Arkansas, 1918 ***95.2*** *p51*
Guarino, Pellegrino; New Orleans, 1901 ***3455.2*** *p74*
Guarrella, Jeoczhino; Arkansas, 1918 ***95.2*** *p83*
Gubbin, Neal; St. John, N.B., 1853 ***5704.8*** *p106*
Gubbin, Tessa; St. John, N.B., 1851 ***5704.8*** *p72*
Gubbins, Ann; New York, 1837-1841 ***7036*** *p121*
*Sister:*Jane
*Sister:*Ellen
Gubbins, Ellen *SEE* Gubbins, Ann
Gubbins, Jane *SEE* Gubbins, Ann
Gubbins, William; Quebec, 1816 ***7603*** *p76*
Gube, George 51; New Orleans, 1839 ***9420.2*** *p166*
Gubitz, Frank; St. Louis, 1876 ***5240.1*** *p16*
Gubs, Peter; Wisconsin, n.d. ***9675.5*** *p263*
Gubsar, Frank 28; New Orleans, 1862 ***543.30*** *p384C*
Guchan, Louis 23; New Orleans, 1837 ***778.5*** *p255*
Guchereau, Mr. 22; America, 1839 ***778.5*** *p255*
Guchereau, Mr. 32; America, 1839 ***778.5*** *p255*
Guchereau, Bertrand 24; New Orleans, 1839 ***778.5*** *p255*
Gucherl, Joseph 25; Port uncertain, 1839 ***778.5*** *p255*
Gudelke, Nora; Wisconsin, n.d. ***9675.5*** *p263*
Gudge, Mrs.; America, 1839 ***778.5*** *p255*
Gudge, C.; America, 1839 ***778.5*** *p255*
Gudger, William; Maryland, 1752-1775 ***1639.20*** *p87*
Gudjonsson, Arni 6 mos; Quebec, 1879 ***2557.1*** *p38*
Gudjonsson, Sigtryggur 4; Quebec, 1879 ***2557.1*** *p38*
Gudle, Nathan; Virginia, 1636 ***6219*** *p80*
Gudlikis, John; Wisconsin, n.d. ***9675.5*** *p263*
Gudmundsdottir, Anna 7; Quebec, 1879 ***2557.2*** *p36*
Gudmundsdottir, Anna 23; Quebec, 1879 ***2557.2*** *p36*
Gudmundsdottir, Gislina 13; Quebec, 1879 ***2557.1*** *p38A*
Gudmundsdottir, Gudbjorg 40; Quebec, 1879 ***2557.1*** *p39*
*Relative:*Kristjan 13
Gudmundsdottir, Jonina 6 mos; Quebec, 1879 ***2557.2*** *p36*
Gudmundsdottir, Kristjan 13 *SEE* Gudmundsdottir, Gudbjorg
Gudmundsdottir, Siguros 6 mos; Quebec, 1879 ***2557.2*** *p36*
Gudmundsdottir, Thordys 28; Quebec, 1879 ***2557.1*** *p22*
Gudmundsson, Adaljon 28; Quebec, 1879 ***2557.2*** *p36*
Gudmundsson, Gisli 13; Quebec, 1879 ***2557.1*** *p38A*
Gudmundsson, Gudmundur 60; Quebec, 1879 ***2557.2*** *p36*
Gudmundsson, Gunnlogr 44; Quebec, 1879 ***2557.1*** *p21*
Gudmundsson, Kristjan; Quebec, 1879 ***2557.1*** *p22*
Gudmundsson, Magnus 21; Quebec, 1879 ***2557.2*** *p37*
Gudmundsson, Sigurbjorn 25; Quebec, 1879 ***2557.2*** *p36*
Gudmundsson, Sigurbjorn 50; Quebec, 1879 ***2557.2*** *p37*
Gue, . . .; Canada, 1776-1783 ***9786*** *p22*
Guedon, Mme. 23; New Orleans, 1838 ***778.5*** *p255*
Guedon, Theodore 30; New Orleans, 1838 ***778.5*** *p255*
Guegnon, Nicholas; Baltimore, 1832 ***1450.2*** *p56A*
Guehlich, Jakob; America, 1807 ***8582.2*** *p60*
Guekert, Chatrine 22; Port uncertain, 1839 ***778.5*** *p255*
Guekert, Elizabeth 48; Port uncertain, 1839 ***778.5*** *p255*
Guekert, Jean 17; Port uncertain, 1839 ***778.5*** *p255*
Guekert, Martin 26; America, 1838 ***778.5*** *p256*
Guekert, Valentin 60; Port uncertain, 1839 ***778.5*** *p256*
Guelain, George Christopher; South Carolina, 1752-1753 ***3689.17*** *p21*
With wife
*Relative:*John Mathias 20
*Relative:*John George 8
Guelain, John George 8 *SEE* Guelain, George Christopher
Guelain, John Mathias 20 *SEE* Guelain, George Christopher
Guelich, Jacob; Baltimore, 1807 ***8582*** *p11*
Guelich, Jacob; West Indies, 1808 ***8582*** *p11*
Guelich, Jakob; Cincinnati, 1788-1876 ***8582.3*** *p81*
Guelich, Jakob; Cincinnati, 1817 ***8582.3*** *p90*
Guenden, Catherine 20; America, 1836 ***778.5*** *p256*
Guenet, Melchior 22; America, 1822 ***778.5*** *p256*
Guenoz, G.; New Orleans, 1839 ***778.5*** *p256*
Guenther, Frederick; Wisconsin, n.d. ***9675.5*** *p263*
Guenther, Joseph; America, 1851 ***8582.3*** *p25*
Guenthon, Herman; Philadelphia Co., PA, 1884 ***5240.1*** *p16*
Guerard, . . .; Canada, 1776-1783 ***9786*** *p22*
Guerard, Mr. 20; Port uncertain, 1838 ***778.5*** *p256*
Guerard, J. A. 28; America, 1832 ***778.5*** *p256*
Guereon, Mr. 24; America, 1838 ***778.5*** *p256*
Guerguin, Mr. 40; America, 1837 ***778.5*** *p256*
Guerin, Mr. 28; America, 1837 ***778.5*** *p256*
Guerin, John 29; New Orleans, 1822 ***778.5*** *p255*
Guerin, Louis; Quebec, 1712 ***4533*** *p128*
Guerin, P. 27; Havana, 1825 ***778.5*** *p256*
Gueritt, Edward; Quebec, 1816 ***7603*** *p76*
Guero, Selso 40; Arizona, 1914 ***9228.40*** *p19*
Guerousse, Leon Leonard 14; New Orleans, 1832 ***778.5*** *p255*
Guerra, Francisco 23; Mexico, 1830 ***778.5*** *p256*
Guerre, Jules; Shreveport, LA, 1877 ***7129*** *p44*
Guerry, Mr. 23; St. Louis, 1821 ***778.5*** *p256*
Guerther, Peter; Wisconsin, n.d. ***9675.5*** *p263*
Guesching, Conrad 29; America, 1838 ***778.5*** *p256*
Guesme, Francois 30; America, 1839 ***778.5*** *p257*
Guesnon, Mathieu 37; New Orleans, 1820 ***778.5*** *p257*
Guess, James; New York, NY, 1811 ***2859.11*** *p12*
Guest, Abraham 18; Maryland, 1723 ***3690.1*** *p96*
Guest, Geo.; Virginia, 1647 ***6219*** *p247*
Guest, Job 16; Jamaica, 1730 ***3690.1*** *p96*
Guet, Louis 25; New Orleans, 1837 ***778.5*** *p257*
Guetschow, William; Kansas, 1889 ***5240.1*** *p16*
Guettler, George; Wisconsin, n.d. ***9675.5*** *p263*
Guetzlaff, Karl A. 59; Arizona, 1913 ***9228.40*** *p17*
Guevorlst, Mr. 62; New Orleans, 1823 ***778.5*** *p257*
Gugg, John; Wisconsin, n.d. ***9675.5*** *p263*

Gurry, John; New York, NY, 1811 *2859.11 p13*
  With wife
Gurski, Antoni; New York, 1831 *4606 p173*
Gurski, Michal; New York, 1831 *4606 p173*
Gurtler, . . .; Canada, 1776-1783 *9786 p42*
Gurtner, Leby 29; Kansas, 1880 *5240.1 p61*
Gurton, G. 28; America, 1839 *778.5 p261*
Gurttler, . . .; Canada, 1776-1783 *9786 p42*
Gurvan, Elizabeth; Philadelphia, 1851 *5704.8 p79*
Gurvan, Fanny; Philadelphia, 1851 *5704.8 p79*
Gurvan, James; Philadelphia, 1851 *5704.8 p79*
Gusanzat, Lewis 25; Port uncertain, 1836 *778.5 p261*
Gusecratty, Jean 35; Port uncertain, 1837 *778.5 p261*
Guskrick, William 17; Philadelphia, 1774 *1219.7 p231*
Gusman, Mr. 22; New Orleans, 1829 *778.5 p261*
Gusman, Vallentin; South Carolina, 1788 *7119 p202*
Gussman, John 28; New Orleans, 1862 *543.30 p376C*
Gust, William; Illinois, 1866 *5012.38 p98*
Gustafsen, Oscar; New York, NY, 1911 *3455.3 p111*
Gustafson, Axel; Illinois, 1896 *5012.40 p54*
Gustafson, Axel; Minneapolis, 1881-1886 *6410.35 p54*
Gustafson, C. W.; Minneapolis, 1871-1882 *6410.35 p54*
Gustafson, Charles 23; Kansas, 1872 *5240.1 p53*
Gustafson, E.; Minneapolis, 1882-1883 *6410.35 p54*
Gustafson, Emil; Minneapolis, 1879-1880 *6410.35 p54*
Gustafson, Erick Gustaf 25; Arkansas, 1918 *95.2 p52*
Gustafson, Joseph T.; Arkansas, 1918 *95.2 p52*
Gustafson, William; Colorado, 1904 *9678.2 p21*
Gustafsson, Alexander; Minneapolis, 1880-1884 *6410.35 p49*
Gustafsson, Axel; Minneapolis, 1881-1886 *6410.35 p54*
Gustafsson, Carl Victor; Minneapolis, 1871-1882 *6410.35 p54*
Gustafsson, Erik; Minneapolis, 1882-1883 *6410.35 p54*
Gustafsson, Hilmer; Arkansas, 1918 *95.2 p52*
Gustafsson, Jordan; Minneapolis, 1882-1887 *6410.35 p50*
Gustafsson, Nils Fabian; Minneapolis, 1881-1885 *6410.35 p51*
Gustaphenson, Oscar; New York, NY, 1911 *3455.2 p47*
Gustas, Antanas; Arkansas, 1918 *95.2 p52*
Gustave, Mrs. 30; New Orleans, 1827 *778.5 p262*
Gustave, J. S. 30; New Orleans, 1827 *778.5 p261*
Gusten, Alfred; Minneapolis, 1880-1886 *6410.35 p54*
Gustipson, Daniel; Iowa, 1866-1943 *123.54 p21*
Gustofson, Alex; Iowa, 1866-1943 *123.54 p21*
Gustofson, Andrew 30; Washington, 1916 *1728.4 p255*
Gustofson, Axel; Iowa, 1866-1943 *123.54 p21*
Gustofson, Carolina 29; Washington, 1916 *1728.4 p255*
Gustofson, David; Iowa, 1866-1943 *123.54 p21*
Gustofson, David Herbert; Iowa, 1866-1943 *123.54 p21*
Guston, Phillip 26; Kansas, 1876 *5240.1 p58*
Gusuegher, Mr. 23; America, 1838 *778.5 p262*
Gutbrod, Dorothea; America, 1772 *2444 p188*
Gutbrod, Ludwig; Pennsylvania, 1731 *2444 p160*
Gutcke, . . .; Canada, 1776-1783 *9786 p22*
Gutekunst, Barbara *SEE* Gutekunst, Hans Jerg
Gutekunst, Barbara Braun *SEE* Gutekunst, Hans Jerg
Gutekunst, Hans Jerg; Pennsylvania, 1750 *2444 p159*
  Wife: Barbara Braun
  Child: Philipp Jacob
  Child: Barbara
  Child: Paul
Gutekunst, Paul *SEE* Gutekunst, Hans Jerg
Gutekunst, Philipp Jacob *SEE* Gutekunst, Hans Jerg
Gutfelder, Alois; Colorado, 1899 *9678.2 p21*
Guth, Adam *SEE* Guth, Johann Jacob
Guth, Clarisa 23; New Orleans, 1835 *778.5 p262*
Guth, Edward; America, 1853 *1450.2 p56A*
Guth, Elisabetha *SEE* Guth, Johann Jacob
Guth, Frank; Arkansas, 1918 *95.2 p52*
Guth, Henri 26; America, 1838 *778.5 p262*
Guth, Jacob; Pennsylvania, 1751 *2444 p159*
Guth, Jacob; Pennsylvania, 1752 *2444 p159*
Guth, Johan Georg; Pennsylvania, 1752 *2444 p159*
Guth, Johan Michael; Pennsylvania, 1752 *2444 p159*

Guth, Johann Jacob; Pennsylvania, 1750 *2444 p159*
  Wife: Elisabetha
  Child: Adam
Guth, Mathias; Cincinnati, 1869-1887 *8582 p12*
Guth, Peter; Indiana, 1848 *9117 p16*
Guthardt, Elias; America, 1852 *8582.3 p25*
Gutheil, Johannes; Philadelphia, 1779 *8137 p9*
Guthier, Georg 18; America, 1853 *9162.7 p14*
Guthier, Georg 27; America, 1853 *9162.8 p36*
Guthier, Johannes 25; America, 1853 *9162.8 p36*
Guthire, Adam; Savannah, GA, 1774 *1219.7 p227*
Guthire, Helen; Savannah, GA, 1774 *1219.7 p227*
Guthire, Jane; Savannah, GA, 1774 *1219.7 p227*
Guthire, John; Savannah, GA, 1774 *1219.7 p227*
Guthire, Margaret; Savannah, GA, 1774 *1219.7 p227*
Guthire, Thomas; Savannah, GA, 1774 *1219.7 p227*
Guthire, Thomas, Jr.; Savannah, GA, 1774 *1219.7 p227*
Guthmann, Peter; Ohio, 1798-1818 *8582.2 p53*
Guthrey, John; New York, NY, 1816 *2859.11 p32*
Guthrie, Eaves 13; St. John, N.B., 1847 *5704.8 p9*
Guthrie, Eliza 14; St. John, N.B., 1856 *5704.8 p131*
Guthrie, Fanny 17; Philadelphia, 1861 *5704.8 p147*
Guthrie, George; St. John, N.B., 1847 *5704.8 p9*
Guthrie, James 16; St. John, N.B., 1856 *5704.8 p131*
Guthrie, John; New York, NY, 1837 *8208.4 p35*
Guthrie, John; South Carolina, 1716 *1639.20 p88*
Guthrie, Robert; South Carolina, 1716 *1639.20 p88*
Guthrie, William; St. John, N.B., 1847 *5704.8 p99*
Guthwirt, Bernard; Arkansas, 1918 *95.2 p52*
Gutier, H. 30; Port uncertain, 1837 *778.5 p262*
Gutling, Benjamin 32; Maryland, 1774 *1219.7 p185*
Gutman, Max; Harris Co., TX, 1884 *2764.35 p26*
Gutmann, Mr.; Indiana, 1856 *3702.7 p225*
Gutmann, Anna Sabina; Cincinnati, 1886-1888 *9460 p647*
Gutmann, Johann Christian; Kentucky, 1860-1866 *9460 p647*
Gutmann, Johann Christian; Kentucky, 1885-1886 *9461 p47*
Gutmann, Margaretha Barbara; Wisconsin, 1872 *9460 p646*
Gutmann, Mathilde 20; New York, NY, 1878 *9253 p45*
Gutowski, . . .; New York, 1831 *4606 p173*
Gutt, Henry; Virginia, 1645 *6219 p233*
Gutt, William 21; Maryland, 1775 *1219.7 p264*
Guttbrod, Joerg Peter; Port uncertain, 1724-1800 *2444 p160*
Guttbrod, Johann Ludwig; Pennsylvania, 1731 *2444 p160*
Guttbrod, Johannes; Port uncertain, 1701-1800 *2444 p160*
Guttbrod, Philippus; Port uncertain, 1726-1800 *2444 p160*
Guttekunts, George; Pennsylvania, 1750 *2444 p159*
Guttermann, Wm; America, 1844 *8582.1 p11*
Gutthaeter, Sebastian; Arkansas, 1885 *3688 p7*
Guttler, Joseph; Wisconsin, n.d. *9675.5 p263*
Guttridge, Albert Edward 21; Kansas, 1887 *5240.1 p70*
Guttrige, Peter; Virginia, 1648 *6219 p246*
Guttschmitt, . . .; Canada, 1776-1783 *9786 p22*
Guttshall, John; New York, 1836 *1450.2 p56A*
Guttwasser, Charles; Wisconsin, n.d. *9675.5 p263*
Guvenneton, Joseph 32; New Orleans, 1838 *778.5 p262*
Guvier, Victorina 45; Havana, 1831 *778.5 p262*
Guy, Allen 35; America, 1838 *778.5 p262*
Guy, Edwd 34; Maryland or Virginia, 1699 *2212 p23*
Guy, Gilbert; Virginia, 1636 *6219 p1*
Guy, Henry; Virginia, 1637 *6219 p112*
Guy, Isaac 16; Maryland, 1719 *3690.1 p97*
Guy, Isaac 16; Maryland, 1720 *3690.1 p97*
Guy, J. M. F. 33; Mexico, 1825 *778.5 p262*
Guy, John; St. John, N.B., 1847 *5704.8 p34*
Guy, John; Virginia, 1647 *6219 p248*
Guy, Robert; Illinois, 1856 *7857 p4*
Guy, Roger 18; Maryland, 1729 *3690.1 p97*
Guy, William; Quebec, 1852 *5704.8 p94*

Guy, Wm; Virginia, 1698 *2212 p14*
Guyard, Nicolas; Port uncertain, 1839 *778.5 p262*
Guyerick, Benjamin; Maryland, 1750 *3690.1 p94*
Guyerick, Benjamin; Maryland, 1751 *1219.7 p2*
Guyler, Michael; Illinois, 1859 *2896.5 p15*
Guynan, Pierre; Quebec, 1822 *7603 p89*
Guyol de Gueran, Miss 35; New Orleans, 1823 *778.5 p262*
Guyon, Mr.; Port uncertain, 1839 *778.5 p262*
Guyot, Eugenie 60; Kansas, 1873 *5240.1 p54*
Guyot, Eugenie 61; Kansas, 1873 *5240.1 p16*
Guyot, Henry; America, 1874 *5240.1 p16*
Guyot, Henry 28; Kansas, 1877 *5240.1 p58*
Guyot, J. B. 40; America, 1838 *778.5 p262*
Guyschalk, John 21; America, 1839 *778.5 p262*
Guyse, Carl Friedrich; Philadelphia, 1816 *8582.1 p39*
Guysi, Carl Friedrich; Philadelphia, 1816 *8582.1 p39*
Guyton, Benjamin 17; United States or West Indies, 1719 *3690.1 p97*
Guzowski, John; Arkansas, 1918 *95.2 p52*
Gwin, A.; Jamaica, 1775 *1219.7 p258*
Gwin, David 3 mos; Quebec, 1851 *5704.8 p75*
Gwin, Ellen; Quebec, 1851 *5704.8 p75*
Gwin, James 27; Massachusetts, 1847 *5881.1 p42*
Gwin, William; Quebec, 1851 *5704.8 p75*
Gwinczewski, Felix; New York, 1831 *4606 p173*
Gwinner, Anna; America, 1709 *2444 p151*
Gwinner, Ernst; Cincinnati, 1869-1887 *8582 p12*
Gwinner, Ernst; New York, NY, 1842 *8582.3 p15*
Gwinner, Maximilian Ferdinand; New York, NY, 1836 *8208.4 p76*
Gwisadeins, Dilladora; Iowa, 1866-1943 *123.54 p21*
Gwyn, Alexander; St. John, N.B., 1847 *5704.8 p2*
Gwyn, Ann; Virginia, 1642 *6219 p197*
Gwyn, Anne 12; St. John, N.B., 1847 *5704.8 p2*
Gwyn, David; Philadelphia, 1849 *53.26 p34*
  Relative: Margaret
  Relative: Thomas
  Relative: Margaret
  Relative: Mary Jane 13
  Relative: Isabella 8
  Relative: David 3
Gwyn, David; Philadelphia, 1849 *5704.8 p50*
Gwyn, David 3 *SEE* Gwyn, David
Gwyn, David 3; Philadelphia, 1849 *5704.8 p50*
Gwyn, Elizabeth; St. John, N.B., 1849 *5704.8 p48*
Gwyn, Hugh; Virginia, 1642 *6219 p198*
Gwyn, Isabella 8 *SEE* Gwyn, David
Gwyn, Isabella 8; Philadelphia, 1849 *5704.8 p50*
Gwyn, Isabella 9; St. John, N.B., 1849 *5704.8 p48*
Gwyn, James; St. John, N.B., 1849 *5704.8 p48*
Gwyn, James; St. John, N.B., 1853 *5704.8 p100*
Gwyn, James 11; St. John, N.B., 1849 *5704.8 p48*
Gwyn, Jane 13; St. John, N.B., 1849 *5704.8 p48*
Gwyn, Margaret *SEE* Gwyn, David
Gwyn, Margaret *SEE* Gwyn, David
Gwyn, Margaret; Philadelphia, 1849 *5704.8 p50*
Gwyn, Mary Jane 13 *SEE* Gwyn, David
Gwyn, Mary Jane 13; Philadelphia, 1849 *5704.8 p50*
Gwyn, Rachael 7; St. John, N.B., 1849 *5704.8 p48*
Gwyn, Thomas *SEE* Gwyn, David
Gwyn, Thomas; Philadelphia, 1849 *5704.8 p50*
Gwynn, Elizabeth 18; St. John, N.B., 1854 *5704.8 p115*
Gwynn, James 26; Maryland, 1774 *1219.7 p204*
Gwynn, James 26; St. John, N.B., 1854 *5704.8 p115*
Gwynn, Josiah 19; Jamaica, 1739 *3690.1 p97*
Gwynne, Evan 22; Maryland, 1773 *1219.7 p173*
Gye, Gilbert; Virginia, 1633 *6219 p32*
Gyer, John G.; Philadelphia, 1832 *9892.11 p19*
Gyer, Paul; Philadelphia, 1762 *9973.7 p37*
Gyles, William 22; Philadelphia, 1774 *1219.7 p175*
Gyllom, Hen.; Virginia, 1637 *6219 p11*
Gylyard, Richard; Virginia, 1637 *6219 p82*
Gzowski, Kazimierz; New York, 1831 *4606 p173*
Gztanfil, George; Iowa, 1866-1943 *123.54 p21*

H

Haack, Christian G.; Iowa, 1856 *8125.8 p436*
Haacke, Heinrich; America, 1851 *8582.3 p25*
Haaff, James; New York, NY, 1816 *2859.11 p32*
Haag, George; New York, NY, 1836 *8208.4 p19*
Haag, Marx; Port uncertain, 1738 *3627 p19*
　With wife
　With 3 children
Haaga, Anna Maria *SEE* Haaga, Hans Martin
Haaga, Catharina *SEE* Haaga, Hans Martin
Haaga, Dorothea *SEE* Haaga, Hans Martin
Haaga, Hans Martin; Pennsylvania, 1752-1800 *2444 p160*
　*Wife:*Catharina
　*Child:*Dorothea
　*Child:*Magdalena
　*Child:*Anna Maria
Haaga, Magdalena *SEE* Haaga, Hans Martin
Haak, Helmuth G.; Wisconsin, n.d. *9675.5 p263*
Haak, Marianna; Wisconsin, n.d. *9675.5 p263*
Haake, A. M. Louise; America, 1890 *4610.10 p137*
Haake, Anton; America, 1845 *8582.3 p25*
Haake, Marie 17; America, 1883 *4610.10 p102*
Haaland, Karl 22; Arkansas, 1918 *95.2 p52*
Haan, Jacob; Philadelphia, 1775-1776 *8582.3 p83*
Haan, Peter; Wisconsin, n.d. *9675.5 p263*
Haardt, William; Colorado, 1884 *9678.2 p22*
Haarmeyer, Heinrich August; America, 1850 *8582.3 p25*
Haas, . . .; Ohio, 1884 *3702.7 p461*
Haas, Mr.; Virginia, 1821 *8582.3 p89*
Haas, Carl; America, 1847 *8582.1 p11*
Haas, Charles; America, 1889 *1450.2 p57A*
Haas, Dr. de; America, 1847 *8125.8 p436*
Haas, Gattefried; Arkansas, 1918 *95.2 p52*
Haas, Georg; America, 1725-1800 *2444 p160*
Haas, Georg; Pennsylvania, 1749 *2444 p160*
Haas, Georg; Pennsylvania, 1752 *2444 p160*
Haas, Georg; Pennsylvania, 1753 *2444 p160*
Haas, Georg; Pennsylvania, 1764 *2444 p160*
Haas, George; New York, NY, 1857 *1450.2 p57A*
Haas, Joseph; Colorado, 1887 *9678.2 p22*
Haas, Karl; New Haven, CT, 1880 *8125.8 p436*
Haas, Karl; New York, NY, 1847 *8582.3 p25*
Haas, Michael; America, 1845 *1450.2 p57A*
Haas, Peter; Philadelphia, 1759 *9973.7 p34*
Haase, Mrs. C. F.; Milwaukee, 1875 *4719.30 p257*
Haase, Charles F.; Milwaukee, 1875 *4719.30 p257*
Haase, Lewis; New York, 1869 *1450.2 p57A*
Haase, Rudolph; Wisconsin, n.d. *9675.5 p263*
Haass, Hans Jerg; America, 1725-1800 *2444 p160*
Haass, Hans Jerg; Pennsylvania, 1749 *2444 p160*
Haass, Hans Jerg; Pennsylvania, 1752 *2444 p160*
Haass, Hans Jerg; Pennsylvania, 1753 *2444 p160*
Haass, Hans Jerg; Pennsylvania, 1764 *2444 p160*
Haass, Heinrich 27; Kansas, 1882 *5240.1 p64*
Haataja, Josephine; Washington, 1859-1920 *2872.1 p14*
Haataja, Matt; Washington, 1859-1920 *2872.1 p14*
Haataja, Matt Enori Howard; Washington, 1859-1920 *2872.1 p14*
Haataja, Salmi Hilda Ellen; Washington, 1859-1920 *2872.1 p14*
Haataja, Selma Ethel; Washington, 1859-1920 *2872.1 p14*
Habacker, . . .; Pennsylvania, n.d. *2444 p169*
Habat, Marie 2; Port uncertain, 1839 *778.5 p262*
Habbe, Christine Louise; America, 1839 *4610.10 p97*
Habbel, Heinrich; America, 1836 *8582.3 p25*
Habecker, . . .; Pennsylvania, n.d. *2444 p169*

Habekotte, Johann G. F.; Cincinnati, 1869-1887 *8582 p12*
Habenmeier, John 34; Indiana, 1838 *1450.2 p57A*
Haber, Henry; New York, NY, 1838 *8208.4 p67*
Haber, Jacob; Nevada, 1878 *2764.35 p32*
Haberdinck, Levin; Germantown, PA, 1684 *2467.7 p5*
Haberecht, Gottfried; Savannah, GA, 1735 *3652 p51*
Haberecht, Rosina; Savannah, GA, 1736 *3652 p51*
Haberer, Anna Barbara *SEE* Haberer, Jacob Friedrich
Haberer, Jacob Friedrich; America, 1736-1800 *2444 p160*
　*Wife:*Anna Barbara
　*Child:*Philipp
Haberer, Philipp *SEE* Haberer, Jacob Friedrich
Haberern, Michael; America, 1881 *1450.2 p13B*
Haberfehner, Frantz; Georgia, 1734 *9332 p328*
Haberfehner, Magdalena 15; Georgia, 1739 *9332 p327*
Haberfehner, Maria; Georgia, 1734 *9332 p328*
Haberfehner, Susanna 17; Georgia, 1739 *9332 p327*
Haberland, Anna Helena *SEE* Haberland, Michael
Haberland, George *SEE* Haberland, Michael
Haberland, Joseph; New York, 1753 *3652 p77*
Haberland, Juliana; New York, 1749 *3652 p72*
Haberland, Michael; New York, 1749 *3652 p71*
　*Wife:*Anna Helena
Haberland, Michael; Savannah, GA, 1735 *3652 p51*
　*Relative:*George
Haberlin, Raimund Gottlieb; Quebec, 1776 *9786 p257*
Habermann, . . .; Canada, 1776-1783 *9786 p22*
Habermann, Gustav; New Hampshire, 1882 *1450.2 p57A*
Habermehl, Karl 65; Ontario, 1897 *1763 p40D*
Habershett, Mr.; Quebec, 1815 *9229.18 p82*
　With wife
Haberttich, Mr. 31; New Orleans, 1839 *778.5 p263*
Habetill, Geo.; Virginia, 1637 *6219 p112*
Habich, . . .; Canada, 1776-1783 *9786 p42*
Habicht, Carl Edward *SEE* Habicht, Susanna Chapman
Habicht, Susanna Chapman; America, 1825 *6410.32 p125*
　*Son:*Carl Edward
Habig, Peter; Kentucky, 1840 *8582.3 p99*
Habishaw, William 18; Nova Scotia, 1774 *1219.7 p209*
Hablitzel, Jacob D.; Ohio, 1875 *6014.1 p2*
Haborn, Hannah 20; Pennsylvania, Virginia or Maryland, 1719 *3690.1 p97*
Hachard, Mme.; New Orleans, 1839 *778.5 p263*
Hachard, Mr.; New Orleans, 1839 *778.5 p263*
Hache, Theodosius 15; New Orleans, 1839 *9420.2 p168*
Hachenberg, F. von; New York, 1776 *9786 p277*
Hachenberger, . . .; Canada, 1776-1783 *9786 p22*
Hachler, Fritz; Wisconsin, n.d. *9675.5 p263*
Hachorne, John; Virginia, 1638 *6219 p122*
Hack, Isaac; Virginia, 1643 *6219 p200*
Hackbarth, Herman; Wisconsin, n.d. *9675.5 p263*
Hackbarth, Julius; Wisconsin, n.d. *9675.5 p263*
Hackcarth, Christian; Wisconsin, n.d. *9675.5 p263*
Hacke, John; Canada, 1783 *9786 p38A*
Hackenmiller, John Alright; Philadelphia, 1759 *9973.7 p34*
Hackens, Henry 20; Jamaica, 1758 *1219.7 p59*
Hackens, Henry 20; Jamaica, 1758 *3690.1 p98*
Hacker, Alice *SEE* Hacker, Walter
Hacker, John; New York, NY, 1835 *8208.4 p26*
Hacker, John; Virginia, 1636 *6219 p73*
Hacker, John; Virginia, 1645 *6219 p234*
Hacker, Margery; Virginia, 1637 *6219 p111*

Hacker, Walter; Virginia, 1636 *6219 p78*
　*Wife:*Alice
Hackes, Elell; Virginia, 1639 *6219 p149*
Hacket, Edmond; America, 1735-1743 *4971 p8*
Hacket, James; Wisconsin, n.d. *9675.5 p263*
Hackett, Dr.; Quebec, 1815 *9229.18 p75*
Hackett, Ann; Quebec, 1849 *5704.8 p52*
Hackett, Ann 11; Quebec, 1847 *5704.8 p27*
Hackett, Bridget; Quebec, 1849 *5704.8 p52*
Hackett, Bridget 25; Massachusetts, 1849 *5881.1 p45*
Hackett, Catharine 30; Massachusetts, 1849 *5881.1 p45*
Hackett, Charles 22; Maryland, 1774 *1219.7 p220*
Hackett, Elizabeth; Quebec, 1847 *5704.8 p27*
Hackett, Elleanor; Quebec, 1847 *5704.8 p27*
Hackett, Henry 60; California, 1872 *2769.5 p4*
Hackett, John; America, 1736-1743 *4971 p58*
Hackett, John; Quebec, 1847 *5704.8 p27*
Hackett, John; Wisconsin, n.d. *9675.5 p263*
Hackett, John 6 mos; Quebec, 1847 *5704.8 p27*
Hackett, John 17; Pennsylvania, 1734 *3690.1 p98*
Hackett, John 41; Maryland, 1774 *1219.7 p187*
Hackett, Joseph 8; Quebec, 1847 *5704.8 p27*
Hackett, Lawrance 32; Maryland, 1774 *1219.7 p229*
Hackett, Margaret 13; Quebec, 1847 *5704.8 p27*
Hackett, Michael; America, 1736-1743 *4971 p57*
Hackett, Michael; Philadelphia, 1848 *53.26 p34*
Hackett, Michael; Philadelphia, 1848 *5704.8 p40*
Hackett, Thomas; Philadelphia, 1851 *5704.8 p71*
Hackett, Thomas; Virginia, 1623-1700 *6219 p189*
Hackley, Jno.; Virginia, 1638 *6219 p120*
Hackley, Thomas 29; Virginia, 1774 *1219.7 p201*
Hackman, Henry; America, 1833 *1450.2 p25*
Hackmann, Heinrich Jos; America, 1847 *8582.3 p25*
Hackmann, Nicolaus Heinrich; Cincinnati, 1869-1887 *8582 p12*
Hackney, Wm.; Virginia, 1638 *6219 p119*
Hackvar, Vili; Wisconsin, n.d. *9675.5 p263*
Hackwell, Katherine; Virginia, 1637 *6219 p83*
Hacther, Aug. Fr. 56; New Orleans, 1839 *9420.2 p166*
　*Wife:*Christiane Lybille 55
　*Son:*Friedrich 20
Hacther, Christiane Lybille 55 *SEE* Hacther, Aug. Fr.
Hacther, Friedrich 20 *SEE* Hacther, Aug. Fr.
Haddad, William; Arkansas, 1918 *95.2 p52*
Haddam, . . .; America, 1697-1707 *2212 p3*
Hadden, William J.; Illinois, 1876 *5012.39 p120*
Haddock, Joseph 27; Philadelphia, 1803 *53.26 p34*
Haddock, Richd 14; Maryland or Virginia, 1699 *2212 p24*
Haddy, John; Virginia, 1600-1642 *6219 p193*
Haddy, John; Virginia, 1639 *6219 p156*
Hadeskey, J.; Philadelphia, 1865 *5704.8 p184*
Hadfield, John; New York, NY, 1833 *8208.4 p32*
Hadfield, Samuel; Illinois, 1876 *5012.37 p59*
Hadjinicholas, Gust; Arkansas, 1918 *95.2 p52*
Hadler, Charles; Wisconsin, n.d. *9675.5 p263*
Hadler, Frederick; Wisconsin, n.d. *9675.5 p263*
Hadler, Heinrich; Wisconsin, n.d. *9675.5 p263*
Hadley, John 25; Virginia, 1774 *1219.7 p240*
Hadnell, Mr.; Quebec, 1815 *9229.18 p75*
Hadock, Thomas 21; Quebec, 1859 *5704.8 p143*
Hadon, William 19; Maryland, 1876 *3690.1 p98*
Hadwell, Wm.; Virginia, 1643 *6219 p206*
Hadwig, Gan; Indianapolis, 1870 *3702.7 p586*
Haeberle, Mr.; Port uncertain, 1752 *2444 p160*
Haeberlein, . . .; Canada, 1776-1783 *9786 p23*
Haeberlin, Joachim Lorenz; Virginia, 1738 *9898 p24*

Haeberlin, Joachim Lorenz; Virginia, 1738-1739 ***9898*** *p39*
Haecker, Karl; Iroquois Co., IL, 1896 ***3455.1*** *p11*
Haedman, Christina 28; Massachusetts, 1860 ***6410.32*** *p104*
Haedman, Peter; America, 1847 ***6410.32*** *p123*
Haedman, Peter 38; Massachusetts, 1860 ***6410.32*** *p104*
Haegin, Anna; New England, 1750 ***2444*** *p229*
Haehl, Jacob; Ohio, 1869-1887 ***8582*** *p12*
Haemel, . . .; Canada, 1776-1783 ***9786*** *p23*
Haemmerlin, Elisabetha; Pennsylvania, 1751 ***2444*** *p162*
Haens, Heinrich; Philadelphia, 1770 ***8582.3*** *p84*
Haensel, John Christian; New York, 1750 ***3652*** *p75*
Haeper, Anne Marie Louise *SEE* Haeper, Hermann Heinrich
Haeper, Emilie Wilhelmine *SEE* Haeper, Hermann Heinrich
Haeper, Ernst H. Gottlieb *SEE* Haeper, Hermann Heinrich
Haeper, Hermann Heinrich 55; America, 1852 ***4610.10*** *p143*
With wife
*Child:*Ernst H. Gottlieb
*Child:*Peter F. Wilhelm
*Child:*Anne Marie Louise
*Child:*Emilie Wilhelmine
Haeper, Peter F. Wilhelm *SEE* Haeper, Hermann Heinrich
Haerder, Anna Margaretha; Pennsylvania, 1751 ***2444*** *p151*
Haerle, William; America, 1857 ***1450.2*** *p57A*
Haerlin, Johannes; Port uncertain, 1751 ***2444*** *p167*
Haerness, Joseph; Ohio, 1798 ***8582.2*** *p55*
Haerr, Haenry; Iroquois Co., IL, 1896 ***3455.1*** *p11*
Haerter, Anna Margaretha; Pennsylvania, 1751 ***2444*** *p151*
Haerter, Dorothea; Pennsylvania, 1746 ***2444*** *p138*
Haerting, Herman Gustav; New York, 1854 ***1450.2*** *p57A*
Haferd, Frank; America, 1853 ***6014.1*** *p2*
Haferd, Rudolph; America, 1853 ***6014.1*** *p2*
Haffner, John Christian 28; Maryland, 1774 ***1219.7*** *p230*
Hafforty, Daniel 6; St. John, N.B., 1847 ***5704.8*** *p32*
Hafforty, Jane; St. John, N.B., 1847 ***5704.8*** *p32*
Hafforty, John 7; St. John, N.B., 1847 ***5704.8*** *p32*
Hafforty, Michael; St. John, N.B., 1847 ***5704.8*** *p32*
Hafforty, Rebecca 2; St. John, N.B., 1847 ***5704.8*** *p32*
Hafforty, Sarah 12; St. John, N.B., 1847 ***5704.8*** *p32*
Hafforty, Susan; St. John, N.B., 1847 ***5704.8*** *p32*
Hafforty, Thomas 1; St. John, N.B., 1847 ***5704.8*** *p32*
Haffy, Condy; Illinois, 1861 ***2896.5*** *p15*
Haffy, Thomas; New York, NY, 1837 ***8208.4*** *p34*
Hafner, Johann Adam; Cincinnati, 1869-1887 ***8582*** *p12*
Hafstrom, Axel Ferdinand; Boston, 1906 ***3455.3*** *p23*
Hafy, Mary; Quebec, 1823 ***7603*** *p60*
Hag, Anna Elisabetha; Pennsylvania, 1750-1796 ***4525*** *p221*
Haga, William; Illinois, 1860 ***2896.5*** *p15*
Hagais, Peter; Arkansas, 1918 ***95.2*** *p52*
Hagall, Michael; Annapolis, MD, 1742 ***4971*** *p93*
Hagan, Alexander 19; Philadelphia, 1864 ***5704.8*** *p177*
Hagan, Ann; America, 1865 ***5704.8*** *p196*
Hagan, Anne; Philadelphia, 1867 ***5704.8*** *p220*
Hagan, Bernard 17; St. John, N.B., 1858 ***5704.8*** *p140*
Hagan, Catharine; New York, NY, 1870 ***5704.8*** *p238*
Hagan, Charles; Philadelphia, 1865 ***5704.8*** *p199*
Hagan, Charles 20; Quebec, 1857 ***5704.8*** *p135*
Hagan, Charles 30; Quebec, 1855 ***5704.8*** *p126*
Hagan, Daniel; Quebec, 1852 ***5704.8*** *p90*
Hagan, Daniel 5; Quebec, 1852 ***5704.8*** *p86*
Hagan, Darby 22; Maryland, 1774 ***1219.7*** *p220*
Hagan, Edward; New York, NY, 1816 ***2859.11*** *p32*
Hagan, Edward; Quebec, 1852 ***5704.8*** *p86*
Hagan, Edward; Quebec, 1852 ***5704.8*** *p90*
Hagan, Eliza 11; Philadelphia, 1864 ***5704.8*** *p181*
Hagan, Elizabeth; America, 1866 ***5704.8*** *p214*
Hagan, Elizabeth; St. John, N.B., 1847 ***5704.8*** *p18*
Hagan, George 4; Philadelphia, 1864 ***5704.8*** *p181*
Hagan, Henry; America, 1867 ***5704.8*** *p224*
Hagan, Henry; America, 1867 ***5704.8*** *p225*
Hagan, James; New York, NY, 1834 ***8208.4*** *p46*
Hagan, James; Philadelphia, 1816 ***2859.11*** *p32*
Hagan, James; Philadelphia, 1864 ***5704.8*** *p177*
Hagan, James; Philadelphia, 1867 ***5704.8*** *p220*
Hagan, James 19; Massachusetts, 1850 ***5881.1*** *p48*
Hagan, John; New York, NY, 1815 ***2859.11*** *p32*
Hagan, John 19; St. John, N.B., 1862 ***5704.8*** *p150*
Hagan, Joseph; Arizona, 1890 ***2764.35*** *p32*
Hagan, Margaret; America, 1743 ***4971*** *p65*
Hagan, Margaret; Philadelphia, 1851 ***5704.8*** *p79*
Hagan, Margaret; St. John, N.B., 1851 ***5704.8*** *p72*
Hagan, Mary; Philadelphia, 1852 ***5704.8*** *p85*
Hagan, Mary; Quebec, 1852 ***5704.8*** *p90*
Hagan, Mary 3; Quebec, 1852 ***5704.8*** *p86*
Hagan, Mary 9; Philadelphia, 1864 ***5704.8*** *p181*
Hagan, Mary 20; Philadelphia, 1861 ***5704.8*** *p148*
Hagan, Mary A.; Philadelphia, 1864 ***5704.8*** *p181*
Hagan, Michael 27; Philadelphia, 1865 ***5704.8*** *p165*
Hagan, Pat; Philadelphia, 1850 ***53.26*** *p34*
Hagan, Pat; Philadelphia, 1850 ***5704.8*** *p68*
Hagan, Patrick; New York, NY, 1836 ***8208.4*** *p21*
Hagan, Peter; Philadelphia, 1864 ***5704.8*** *p177*
Hagan, Peter; Quebec, 1822 ***7603*** *p85*
Hagan, Peter 6; Philadelphia, 1864 ***5704.8*** *p177*
Hagan, Rose; Quebec, 1852 ***5704.8*** *p86*
Hagan, Rose; Quebec, 1852 ***5704.8*** *p90*
Hagan, Rose 22; Quebec, 1857 ***5704.8*** *p135*
Hagan, Sally; Philadelphia, 1867 ***5704.8*** *p221*
Hagan, Sally; Quebec, 1852 ***5704.8*** *p90*
Hagan, Sally 9 mos; Quebec, 1852 ***5704.8*** *p86*
Hagan, Sarah; Philadelphia, 1864 ***5704.8*** *p177*
Hagan, Susan 7; Philadelphia, 1864 ***5704.8*** *p181*
Hagan, Unity; America, 1870 ***5704.8*** *p239*
Hagan, Unity; Philadelphia, 1867 ***5704.8*** *p220*
Hagan, William John 2; Philadelphia, 1864 ***5704.8*** *p181*
Hagar, John; Washington, 1859-1920 ***2872.1*** *p15*
Hagarty, Cornelius 19; Baltimore, 1775 ***1219.7*** *p269*
Hagarty, Daniel; America, 1741 ***4971*** *p41*
Hagarty, Richard; America, 1736 ***4971*** *p39*
Hagate, James; Virginia, 1639 ***6219*** *p155*
Hage, Anna Elisabetha; Pennsylvania, 1750-1796 ***4525*** *p221*
Hage, John 22; Philadelphia, 1774 ***1219.7*** *p214*
Hagedorn, Conrad; America, 1844 ***8582.1*** *p11*
Hagedorn, Hermann; America, 1834 ***8582*** *p12*
Hagedorn, John; New York, NY, 1836 ***8208.4*** *p8*
Hagedorn, Lewis; West Virginia, 1855 ***9788.3*** *p12*
Hagelberg, H. Zacharias; Pennsylvania, 1752 ***4779.3*** *p14*
Hagele, Adam; South Dakota, 1889 ***1641*** *p41*
Hagele, Adam, Jr.; South Dakota, 1889 ***1641*** *p41*
Hagele, Katharina; South Dakota, 1889 ***1641*** *p41*
Hagele, Rosina; South Dakota, 1889 ***1641*** *p41*
Hagemann, . . .; Canada, 1776-1783 ***9786*** *p23*
Hagemann, Mrs.; Died enroute, 1853 ***4610.10*** *p40*
With son
Hagemann, Mrs.; Died enroute, 1853 ***4610.10*** *p41*
With 2 children
Hagemann, Carl Friedrich Christoph; America, 1839 ***4610.10*** *p97*
Hagemann, George Leopold; Quebec, 1776 ***9786*** *p263*
Hagemanolakes, Nicholas Hage; Arkansas, 1918 ***95.2*** *p52*
Hagemeier, Marie Wilhelmine; America, 1851 ***4610.10*** *p98*
Hagemeir, Frank; Virginia, 1851 ***4626.16*** *p14*
Hagemeyer, Carl Heinrich Wilhelm; America, 1845 ***4610.10*** *p155*
Hagemeyer, Christoph Heinrich; America, 1850 ***4610.10*** *p147*
Hagemeyer, Friedrich Wilhelm; America, 1850 ***4610.10*** *p143*
Hagemeyer, Friedrich Wilhelm; America, 1856 ***4610.10*** *p149*
Hagemeyer, Heinrich 22; America, 1886 ***4610.10*** *p161*
Hagen, . . .; Canada, 1776-1783 ***9786*** *p23*
Hagen, Adolph K.; Arkansas, 1918 ***95.2*** *p53*
Hagen, August; Illinois, 1884 ***2896.5*** *p15*
Hagen, Georg; Cincinnati, 1832-1836 ***8582.1*** *p15*
Hagen, James T.; Arkansas, 1918 ***95.2*** *p53*
Hagen, Johann Georg; New Orleans, 1837 ***8582*** *p12*
Hagen, Johann Georg; New York, NY, 1831 ***8582*** *p12*
Hagen, Julius; Illinois, 1874 ***2896.5*** *p16*
Hagen, Mary; St. John, N.B., 1847 ***5704.8*** *p9*
Hagen, Ole; Arkansas, 1918 ***95.2*** *p53*
Hagen, Robert; New York, NY, 1850 ***6013.19*** *p30*
Hagen, Valentin; Kentucky, 1843 ***8582.3*** *p100*
Hagenlocher, Ann Maria *SEE* Hagenlocher, Joseph Bernhard
Hagenlocher, Johann Georg *SEE* Hagenlocher, Joseph Bernhard
Hagenlocher, Johann Stephen *SEE* Hagenlocher, Joseph Bernhard
Hagenlocher, Joseph Bernhard; Port uncertain, 1754 ***2444*** *p160*
*Wife:*Maria C. Rotenbach
*Child:*Johann Georg
*Child:*Sibylla
*Child:*Margaretha
*Child:*Johann Stephen
*Child:*Ann Maria
Hagenlocher, Margaretha *SEE* Hagenlocher, Joseph Bernhard
Hagenlocher, Maria C. Rotenbach *SEE* Hagenlocher, Joseph Bernhard
Hagenlocher, Sibylla *SEE* Hagenlocher, Joseph Bernhard
Hagenmacher, Casper 21; America, 1837 ***778.5*** *p263*
Hagenmaur, George; Indiana, 1893 ***1450.2*** *p13B*
Hager, . . .; America, 1836 ***778.5*** *p263*
Hager, Pierre 67; America, 1836 ***778.5*** *p263*
Hager, Samuel; Maryland, 1751 ***3690.1*** *p98*
Hagerhorst, Charles; America, 1840 ***1450.2*** *p58A*
Hagerhorst, Charles Frederick; America, 1838 ***1450.2*** *p58A*
Hagermann, Johann; Ohio, 1816 ***8582.1*** *p47*
Hagerty, Andrew; Wisconsin, n.d. ***9675.5*** *p263*
Hagerty, Daniel; New York, NY, 1811 ***2859.11*** *p13*
Hagerty, Eliza; Philadelphia, 1853 ***5704.8*** *p109*
Hagerty, Ellen 18; Philadelphia, 1853 ***5704.8*** *p112*
Hagerty, James; Illinois, 1886 ***2896.5*** *p16*
Hagerty, James D.; America, 1888 ***1450.2*** *p58A*
Hagerty, Maggy; St. John, N.B., 1849 ***5704.8*** *p55*
Hagerty, Michael; Boston, 1847 ***1450.2*** *p58A*
Hagerty, Michael; New York, NY, 1811 ***2859.11*** *p13*
Hagerty, Rose; Philadelphia, 1864 ***5704.8*** *p184*
Hagerty, Sarah; Philadelphia, 1864 ***5704.8*** *p184*
Hagerty, Susan; Philadelphia, 1853 ***5704.8*** *p109*
Hagerty, Thomas; Philadelphia, 1849 ***53.26*** *p34*
Hagerty, Thomas; Philadelphia, 1849 ***5704.8*** *p54*
Hagg, Arvid; Maine, 1890-1896 ***6410.22*** *p123*
Haggart, James, Jr.; New York, NY, 1838 ***8208.4*** *p82*
Haggarty, John; Virginia, 1698 ***2212*** *p16*
Hagger, Robert; Carolina, 1752 ***1219.7*** *p15*
Hagger, Samuel; Maryland, 1751 ***1219.7*** *p3*
Hagger, Samuel; Maryland, 1751 ***3690.1*** *p98*
Haggerty, Gubby 8; Massachusetts, 1849 ***5881.1*** *p46*
Haggerty, Jeremiah; Illinois, 1874 ***7857*** *p4*
Haggerty, Julia 6; Massachusetts, 1849 ***5881.1*** *p47*
Haggerty, Mary; New York, NY, 1811 ***2859.11*** *p13*
Haggerty, Michael 18; Massachusetts, 1847 ***5881.1*** *p48*
Haggerty, Rose; New York, NY, 1865 ***5704.8*** *p196*
Haggin, Bernard 18; St. John, N.B., 1854 ***5704.8*** *p122*
Haggman, William; Washington, 1859-1920 ***2872.1*** *p15*
Haghey, Robert 17; Philadelphia, 1860 ***5704.8*** *p145*
Haghy, John; St. John, N.B., 1852 ***5704.8*** *p83*
Haghy, Michael; St. John, N.B., 1852 ***5704.8*** *p83*
Haghy, Peter; St. John, N.B., 1852 ***5704.8*** *p83*
Haghy, Rose; St. John, N.B., 1852 ***5704.8*** *p83*
Hagler, Adam; Ohio, 1812-1814 ***8582.2*** *p59*
Hagman, John; Illinois, 1867 ***5240.1*** *p16*
Hagman, Leander; Washington, 1859-1920 ***2872.1*** *p15*
Hagmann, Alexander; Wisconsin, n.d. ***9675.5*** *p263*
Hagner, John; Pennsylvania, 1769 ***9973.8*** *p32*
Hagney, Lawrence 32; Massachusetts, 1847 ***5881.1*** *p48*
Hague, John 21; Jamaica, 1725 ***3690.1*** *p98*
Hague, Ralph 24; Maryland, 1774 ***1219.7*** *p235*
Haher, George H.; Indiana, 1848 ***9117*** *p19*
Hahlen, John; Colorado, 1894 ***9678.2*** *p22*
Hahn, . . .; Canada, 1776-1783 ***9786*** *p23*
Hahn, Abel; Philadelphia, 1779 ***8137*** *p9*
Hahn, Anna Katharina; America, 1712-1715 ***9982*** *p24*
Hahn, Charles Frederick; Cincinnati, 1854-1855 ***1450.2*** *p58A*
Hahn, Christ. Auguste. Wme. 27; New Orleans, 1839 ***9420.2*** *p168*
Hahn, Georg; Philadelphia, 1779 ***8137*** *p9*
Hahn, Georg Philipp; Philadelphia Co., PA, 1723-1779 ***2444*** *p160*
Hahn, Gottlieb Herm.; Wisconsin, n.d. ***9675.5*** *p263*
Hahn, Henry; Illinois, 1868 ***2896.5*** *p16*
Hahn, Isaac *SEE* Hahn, Sabina
Hahn, Jacob; New York, NY, 1883 ***1450.2*** *p13B*
Hahn, Joh. Heinr. 74; Ontario, 1902 ***1763*** *p40D*
Hahn, John; Indiana, 1848 ***9117*** *p19*
Hahn, John; Wisconsin, n.d. ***9675.5*** *p263*
Hahn, John 19; America, 1835 ***778.5*** *p263*
Hahn, Ludwig; Philadelphia, 1779 ***8137*** *p9*
Hahn, M.; Milwaukee, 1875 ***4719.30*** *p257*
Hahn, Maria Keth. 75; Illinois, 1911 ***1763*** *p40D*
Hahn, Mathias; Wisconsin, n.d. ***9675.5*** *p263*
Hahn, Peter; Wisconsin, n.d. ***9675.5*** *p263*
Hahn, Sabina *SEE* Hahn, Sabina
Hahn, Sabina; Nova Scotia, 1751 ***2444*** *p161*
*Father:*Isaac
*Mother:*Sabina
Hahn, Steffen 27; Kansas, 1885 ***5240.1*** *p16*
Hahn, Stephen 27; Kansas, 1885 ***5240.1*** *p68*
Hahn, Wilh H. 61; America, 1914 ***1763*** *p40D*
Hahn, Wilhelm; Wisconsin, n.d. ***9675.5*** *p263*
Hahne, . . .; Canada, 1776-1783 ***9786*** *p23*
Hahne, Carl Franz Heinrich; America, 1852 ***4610.10*** *p147*
Hahne, Carl Heinrich Dietrich; America, 1853 ***4610.10*** *p148*
Hahne, Johann Friedrich; America, 1853 ***4610.10*** *p148*
Hahniohen, Benj. Ferd. 35; New Orleans, 1839 ***9420.2*** *p168*
Haider, Solomon; New York, 1894 ***1450.2*** *p13B*
Haidik, Joe 27; Arkansas, 1918 ***95.2*** *p53*
Haidt, Catherine; New York, 1754 ***3652*** *p78*
Haidt, J. Valentine; New York, 1754 ***3652*** *p78*

194 *FOR A COMPLETE EXPLANATION OF ENTRY, SEE "HOW TO READ A CITATION" SECTION*

Haies, Alex.; Virginia, 1643 ***6219*** *p203*
Haies, Ann *SEE* Haies, Robert
Haies, Isabell; Virginia, 1643 ***6219*** *p203*
Haies, Nath.; Virginia, 1643 ***6219*** *p203*
Haies, Richard; Virginia, 1637 ***6219*** *p86*
Haies, Robert; Virginia, 1643 ***6219*** *p203*
*Wife:*Ann
Haig, Agnes Ritchie; Charleston, SC, 1817 ***1639.20*** *p88*
Haig, Mrs. David; Charleston, SC, 1805 ***1639.20*** *p88*
Haig, Lillia; South Carolina, 1742 ***1639.20*** *p88*
Haigess, Anna Luippold *SEE* Haigess, Valentin
Haigess, Anna Maria *SEE* Haigess, Valentin
Haigess, Jerg; America, 1727-1800 ***2444*** *p161*
Haigess, Johann Georg *SEE* Haigess, Valentin
Haigess, Johannes *SEE* Haigess, Valentin
Haigess, Valentin; America, 1750 ***2444*** *p161*
*Wife:*Anna Luippold
*Child:*Johann Georg
*Child:*Anna Maria
*Child:*Johannes
Haight, Gilbert; Illinois, 1864 ***7857*** *p4*
Hail, Anna Maria; Pennsylvania, 1752 ***2444*** *p186*
Hail, Hubert J.; Iowa, 1866-1943 ***123.54*** *p22*
Hail, William Charles; Iowa, 1866-1943 ***123.54*** *p22*
Haile, Thomas; Virginia, 1652 ***6251*** *p20*
Haile, William 22; Philadelphia, 1774 ***1219.7*** *p197*
Hailer, Georg Friedrich; Philadelphia, 1735-1809 ***2444*** *p161*
Hailmann, Johannes; Pennsylvania, 1733 ***2444*** *p161*
Hailmann, Maria Barbara Plieninger; Pennsylvania, 1753 ***2444*** *p161*
Haim, Martin; Wisconsin, n.d. ***9675.5*** *p263*
Haimsell, Stophel; Philadelphia, 1759 ***9973.7*** *p33*
Hain, Frank; Illinois, 1892 ***5012.40*** *p27*
Hain, Job 32; Maryland, 1775 ***1219.7*** *p262*
Haine, George 21; Philadelphia, 1854 ***5704.8*** *p116*
Haine, William 24; Antigua (Antego), 1739 ***3690.1*** *p98*
Haines, Andrew 16; Virginia, 1774 ***1219.7*** *p240*
Haines, Henry; Virginia, 1638 ***6219*** *p160*
Haines, Henry 15; Maryland, 1735 ***3690.1*** *p98*
Haines, John 26; Jamaica, 1733 ***3690.1*** *p98*
Haines, Katherine *SEE* Haines, Richard
Haines, Marcus; Philadelphia, 1762 ***9973.7*** *p38*
Haines, Perry E. 21; Kansas, 1872 ***5240.1*** *p52*
Haines, Richard; Virginia, 1643 ***6219*** *p203*
*Wife:*Katherine
Haines, Richd.; Virginia, 1645 ***6219*** *p232*
Haines, Robert; Virginia, 1646 ***6219*** *p236*
Hains, Joseph; Quebec, 1710 ***7603*** *p21*
Hains, William; Philadelphia, 1760 ***9973.7*** *p34*
Hainson, Mathilda 19; Massachusetts, 1860 ***6410.32*** *p118*
Haintel, Emil 30; Kansas, 1901 ***5240.1*** *p16*
Haintol, Emil 30; Kansas, 1901 ***5240.1*** *p82*
Hair, James 21; St. John, N.B., 1866 ***5704.8*** *p166*
Hair, John; Philadelphia, 1816 ***2859.11*** *p32*
Hairclipe, Hannah 27; America, 1703 ***2212*** *p40*
Haire, James; Virginia, 1642 ***6219*** *p198*
Hairison, William 20; Maryland, 1722 ***3690.1*** *p105*
Hairs, Jane 37; St. John, N.B., 1851 ***5704.8*** *p73*
Haisch, Catharine Hanselmann *SEE* Haisch, Hans Jerg
Haisch, Hans Jerch; Pennsylvania, 1749 ***2444*** *p192*
Haisch, Hans Jerch; Pennsylvania, 1749 ***2444*** *p235*
Haisch, Hans Jerg; America, 1749 ***2444*** *p162*
*Wife:*Catharine Hanselmann
Haist, Elisabetha *SEE* Haist, Johanna
Haist, Johanna; America, 1743-1800 ***2444*** *p162*
*Child:*Elisabetha
Haiste, James 34; Virginia, 1774 ***1219.7*** *p241*
Haitsma, Jerry; Iroquois Co., IL, 1896 ***3455.1*** *p11*
Haitsma, Johannes; Iroquois Co., IL, 1896 ***3455.1*** *p11*
Hajgli, Antol; Baltimore, 1902 ***9892.11*** *p19*
Hak, John; Virginia, 1858 ***4626.16*** *p17*
Hakanen, David; Washington, 1859-1920 ***2872.1*** *p15*
Hakanson, M. F.; Iowa, 1847 ***2090*** *p609*
Hakansson, Andrew Christen; Minneapolis, 1868-1881 ***6410.35*** *p54*
Hake, Heinrich; New York, NY, 1836-1875 ***4610.10*** *p66*
Hake, Karl Friedrich; America, 1850 ***8582.3*** *p26*
Hakemann, Friedrich Ludwig 23; America, 1858 ***4815.7*** *p92*
Hakensen, Andrew; Colorado, 1903 ***9678.2*** *p22*
Hakkinen, Albin; Washington, 1859-1920 ***2872.1*** *p15*
Hakkinen, David; Washington, 1859-1920 ***2872.1*** *p15*
Hakkinen, Oscar; Washington, 1859-1920 ***2872.1*** *p15*
Hakmann, Anna Wilhelmine; America, 1831 ***4815.7*** *p92*
Halabuda, Anton; Wisconsin, n.d. ***9675.5*** *p263*
Halabuda, Mary; Wisconsin, n.d. ***9675.5*** *p263*
Halanke, Joseph; Wisconsin, n.d. ***9675.5*** *p264*
Halay, Nicholas; Pennsylvania, 1900 ***7137*** *p168*
Halbach Family ; New York, 1765 ***8125.8*** *p436*
Halbenthaler, Maria; Georgia, 1739 ***9332*** *p323*
Halberstadt, William; Wisconsin, n.d. ***9675.5*** *p264*
Halbert, Caroline Charlotte; America, 1882 ***4610.10*** *p110*
Halbert, Ernst Friedr. Ferdinand; America, 1887 ***4610.10*** *p107*
Halbert, Johann Diedrich Carl; America, 1845 ***4610.10*** *p141*
Halbleib, Rudolph; Virginia, 1858 ***4626.16*** *p17*
Halchy, Judy 20; Massachusetts, 1850 ***5881.1*** *p47*
Halder, Baldauf 30; Port uncertain, 1839 ***778.5*** *p263*
Halder, Francois 30; Port uncertain, 1839 ***778.5*** *p263*
Haldersdottir, Kristin 36; Quebec, 1879 ***2557.1*** *p39*
Haldi, Alfred; Colorado, 1895 ***9678.2*** *p22*
Haldi, Peter, Sr.; Colorado, 1890 ***9678.2*** *p22*
Haldiman, Benedicht; Illinois, 1876 ***2896.5*** *p16*
Haldimand, Frederick; Canada, 1778 ***9786*** *p166*
Haldimann, Katherine; Pennsylvania, 1709-1710 ***4480*** *p311*
Haldy, Friederich Philipp; America, 1849 ***8582.3*** *p26*
Hale, Ann; Virginia, 1641 ***6219*** *p184*
Hale, Anthony 17; Maryland, 1775 ***1219.7*** *p273*
Hale, Barbery; Virginia, 1638 ***6219*** *p122*
Hale, J.; Quebec, 1815 ***9229.18*** *p77*
With family
Hale, Jacob; Ohio, 1869-1887 ***8582*** *p12*
Hale, John 23; North Carolina, 1736 ***3690.1*** *p98*
Hale, Leslie J.; Arkansas, 1918 ***95.2*** *p53*
Hale, Robert; New York, NY, 1815 ***2859.11*** *p32*
Hale, Tho.; Virginia, 1636 ***6219*** *p12*
Halenkamp, F. W.; Cincinnati, 1869-1887 ***8582*** *p12*
Halero, Joseph; Arizona, 1880 ***2764.35*** *p32*
Hales, John; Virginia, 1600-1642 ***6219*** *p193*
Hales, Sarah 18; Pennsylvania, 1728 ***3690.1*** *p98*
Hales, Thomas; New York, NY, 1811 ***2859.11*** *p13*
Hales, Thomas; Virginia, 1652 ***6251*** *p19*
Hales, William 25; Jamaica, 1750 ***3690.1*** *p98*
Halewood, Henry 25; West Indies, 1698-1699 ***2212*** *p18*
Haley, Abby 20; Massachusetts, 1847 ***5881.1*** *p44*
Haley, Anna 20; Massachusetts, 1849 ***5881.1*** *p45*
Haley, Catharine 30; Massachusetts, 1849 ***5881.1*** *p45*
Haley, Charles 20; Massachusetts, 1849 ***5881.1*** *p45*
Haley, Christine 1; Massachusetts, 1849 ***5881.1*** *p45*
Haley, James; Quebec, 1847 ***5704.8*** *p8*
Haley, Johanna 19; Massachusetts, 1849 ***5881.1*** *p47*
Haley, John; New York, NY, 1864 ***5704.8*** *p169*
Haley, Joseph; Pennsylvania, 1749 ***3652*** *p73*
Haley, Margaret; St. John, N.B., 1853 ***5704.8*** *p99*
Haley, Margaret 40; Massachusetts, 1849 ***5881.1*** *p48*
Haley, Michael 20; Massachusetts, 1849 ***5881.1*** *p48*
Haley, Owen 20; Massachusetts, 1847 ***5881.1*** *p49*
Haley, Peter; Quebec, 1847 ***5704.8*** *p8*
Haley, Peter 20; Quebec, 1857 ***5704.8*** *p136*
Haley, Thomas; New York, NY, 1835 ***8208.4*** *p50*
Haley, Timothy 37; California, 1867 ***3840.2*** *p14*
Haley, William; Illinois, 1858 ***2896.5*** *p16*
Halfdansdottir, Ingiridur 24; Quebec, 1879 ***2557.1*** *p37A*
Halfdermeir, Ana 25; America, 1838 ***778.5*** *p263*
Halfmann, Martin 39; Kansas, 1890 ***5240.1*** *p16*
Halfmann, Martin 39; Kansas, 1890 ***5240.1*** *p75*
Halford, Richard 21; Maryland, 1775 ***1219.7*** *p267*
Halfpenny, James 23; Newfoundland, 1789 ***4915.24*** *p55*
Halfpenny, Louisa 16; Canada, 1838 ***4535.12*** *p113*
Halfpenny, Mary; America, 1740 ***4971*** *p15*
Halfpenny, Mary; Maryland, 1740 ***4971*** *p91*
Halfpenny, Mary; Philadelphia, 1741 ***4971*** *p92*
Halfpin, John; America, 1738 ***4971*** *p77*
Halfsdottir, Ingridur 24; Quebec, 1879 ***2557.1*** *p37A*
Haliwale, Ralph; Virginia, 1698 ***2212*** *p16*
Halker, Ferdinand; America, 1869-1887 ***8582*** *p12*
Halket, William R.; Illinois, 1902 ***2896.5*** *p16*
Hall, . . .; Canada, 1776-1783 ***9786*** *p42*
Hall, Alex 11; Quebec, 1853 ***5704.8*** *p105*
Hall, Alexander; New York, NY, 1811 ***2859.11*** *p13*
Hall, Andrew; Arkansas, 1918 ***95.2*** *p53*
Hall, Ann 28; Massachusetts, 1847 ***5881.1*** *p44*
Hall, Ann Smith 20; Philadelphia, 1860 ***5704.8*** *p145*
Hall, August; Iowa, 1866-1943 ***123.54*** *p22*
Hall, Catherine 56; Philadelphia, 1854 ***5704.8*** *p122*
Hall, Charles 16; Virginia, 1775 ***1219.7*** *p261*
Hall, Daniel 19; Jamaica, 1733 ***3690.1*** *p98*
Hall, David *SEE* Hall, George
Hall, Edm. *SEE* Hall, George
Hall, Edw.; Virginia, 1635 ***6219*** *p69*
Hall, Edward 20; Jamaica, 1724 ***3690.1*** *p99*
Hall, Eliza *SEE* Hall, George
Hall, Elizabeth *SEE* Hall, Robert
Hall, Elizabeth White *SEE* Hall, Robert
Hall, Fra.; Virginia, 1648 ***6219*** *p250*
Hall, G. F.; Washington, 1859-1920 ***2872.1*** *p15*
Hall, Georg; Virginia, 1636 ***6219*** *p76*
Hall, George *SEE* Hall, Robert
Hall, George; Charleston, SC, 1812 ***1639.20*** *p88*
Hall, George; Illinois, 1869 ***5012.38*** *p99*
Hall, George; New York, NY, 1836 ***8208.4*** *p77*
Hall, George; Virginia, 1648 ***6219*** *p246*
*Wife:*Eliza
*Son:*Edm.
*Son:*David
Hall, George; Virginia, 1648 ***6219*** *p253*
Hall, George 65; Massachusetts, 1849 ***5881.1*** *p46*
Hall, Harvey; Cincinnati, 1825 ***8582.3*** *p88*
Hall, Henry 26; Maryland, 1774 ***1219.7*** *p225*
Hall, Hobert; New York, NY, 1811 ***2859.11*** *p13*
With family
Hall, Hugh; Virginia, 1623 ***6219*** *p9*
Hall, Hum.; Virginia, 1646 ***6219*** *p244*
Hall, James; New York, 1756 ***3652*** *p81*
Hall, James 11; Maryland or Virginia, 1699 ***2212*** *p21*
Hall, James 26; Virginia, 1700 ***2212*** *p32*
Hall, James 27; Massachusetts, 1847 ***5881.1*** *p47*
Hall, Johann Friederich; America, 1832 ***8582.3*** *p26*
Hall, John; America, 1742 ***4971*** *p37*
Hall, John; Arkansas, 1918 ***95.2*** *p53*
Hall, John; New York, NY, 1811 ***2859.11*** *p13*
Hall, John; New York, NY, 1839 ***8208.4*** *p91*
Hall, John; Philadelphia, 1851 ***5704.8*** *p77*
Hall, John; South Carolina, 1824 ***1639.20*** *p88*
Hall, John; Virginia, 1637 ***6219*** *p110*
Hall, John 8; Quebec, 1853 ***5704.8*** *p105*
Hall, John 15; Philadelphia, 1774 ***1219.7*** *p182*
Hall, John 20; Jamaica, 1720 ***3690.1*** *p99*
Hall, John 20; St. John, N.B., 1858 ***5704.8*** *p140*
Hall, John 21; Maryland, 1738 ***3690.1*** *p99*
Hall, John 21; Maryland, 1774 ***1219.7*** *p224*
Hall, John 22; Maryland, 1775 ***1219.7*** *p254*
Hall, John 22; Philadelphia, 1774 ***1219.7*** *p182*
Hall, John 25; Maryland, 1774 ***1219.7*** *p221*
Hall, John A.; North Carolina, 1803-1828 ***1639.20*** *p89*
Hall, Jon.; Virginia, 1643 ***6219*** *p200*
Hall, Jonathan; New York, 1768 ***1219.7*** *p135*
Hall, Joseph; New York, NY, 1837 ***8208.4*** *p34*
Hall, Joseph 23; Maryland, 1774 ***1219.7*** *p192*
Hall, Joseph, Jr.; America, 1806 ***6410.32*** *p125*
Hall, Josiah 45; New Orleans, 1837 ***778.5*** *p263*
Hall, Marshall 22; Philadelphia, 1775 ***1219.7*** *p273*
Hall, Mary; Philadelphia, 1851 ***5704.8*** *p77*
Hall, Mary 22; Maryland, 1733 ***3690.1*** *p99*
Hall, Mary 26; Maryland, 1775 ***1219.7*** *p252*
Hall, Mary 30; Philadelphia, 1854 ***5704.8*** *p117*
Hall, Mary 66; South Carolina, 1850 ***1639.20*** *p88*
Hall, Miles; Montreal, 1823 ***7603*** *p101*
Hall, Rebecca 17; Philadelphia, 1860 ***5704.8*** *p146*
Hall, Richard 16; Virginia, 1774 ***1219.7*** *p241*
Hall, Richard 18; Maryland or Virginia, 1719 ***3690.1*** *p99*
Hall, Richard 19; Maryland, 1774 ***1219.7*** *p221*
Hall, Robert; New York, NY, 1811 ***2859.11*** *p13*
Hall, Robert; Pennsylvania, 1682 ***4961*** *p13*
*Wife:*Elizabeth White
*Daughter:*Elizabeth
*Son:*George
Hall, Robert; Quebec, 1815 ***9229.18*** *p80*
Hall, Robert; Virginia, 1642 ***6219*** *p191*
Hall, Robert 4; Philadelphia, 1851 ***5704.8*** *p77*
Hall, Samuel; New York, NY, 1811 ***2859.11*** *p13*
Hall, Samuel; New York, NY, 1834 ***8208.4*** *p34*
Hall, Samuel; Virginia, 1643 ***6219*** *p23*
Hall, Sarah 20; Quebec, 1853 ***5704.8*** *p105*
Hall, Sophia 26; Massachusetts, 1860 ***6410.32*** *p104*
Hall, Susan; Virginia, 1646 ***6219*** *p241*
Hall, Susanna; America, 1825 ***6410.32*** *p125*
Hall, Susannah 51; Massachusetts, 1860 ***6410.32*** *p116*
Hall, Thomas; New York, NY, 1838 ***8208.4*** *p84*
Hall, Thomas; New York, NY, 1838 ***8208.4*** *p88*
Hall, Thomas; Quebec, 1815 ***9229.18*** *p81*
Hall, Thomas; San Francisco, 1869 ***2764.35*** *p36*
Hall, Thomas 6; Quebec, 1853 ***5704.8*** *p105*
Hall, Thomas 14; Maryland or Virginia, 1719 ***3690.1*** *p99*
Hall, Thomas 25; Jamaica, 1730 ***3690.1*** *p99*
Hall, Thomas 28; Maryland, 1775 ***1219.7*** *p254*
Hall, William; Charleston, SC, 1804 ***1639.20*** *p89*
Hall, William; New Orleans, 1849 ***1450.2*** *p58A*
Hall, William; New York, NY, 1816 ***2859.11*** *p32*
Hall, William; New York, NY, 1836 ***8208.4*** *p20*
Hall, William 2; Philadelphia, 1851 ***5704.8*** *p77*
Hall, William 16; Jamaica, 1774 ***1219.7*** *p233*
Hall, William 17; Antigua (Antego), 1728 ***3690.1*** *p99*
Hall, William 17; Philadelphia, 1775 ***1219.7*** *p248*
Hall, William 20; Maryland, 1719 ***3690.1*** *p99*
Hall, William 21; Maryland, 1774 ***1219.7*** *p184*
Hall, William 30; Massachusetts, 1849 ***5881.1*** *p51*
Hall, William 40; Halifax, N.S., 1774 ***1219.7*** *p213*
Hall, William 45; Massachusetts, 1860 ***6410.32*** *p104*
Hall, William F.; New York, NY, 1838 ***8208.4*** *p82*
Hall, Wm 21; Maryland or Virginia, 1699 ***2212*** *p24*
Hallack, Andrew; Virginia, 1643 ***6219*** *p200*
Hallaghan, Johanna 28; Massachusetts, 1849 ***5881.1*** *p47*
Halland, Mr.; Quebec, 1815 ***9229.18*** *p75*

Hallar, David; New York, 1890 ***1450.2*** *p13B*
Halldorsdottir, Kristin 36; Quebec, 1879 ***2557.1*** *p39*
Halle, H. 24; America, 1839 ***778.5*** *p263*
Halle, Louis F. 36; New Orleans, 1831 ***778.5*** *p263*
Halle, Martin 23; New Orleans, 1823 ***778.5*** *p263*
Halle, Thomas; New York, NY, 1816 ***2859.11*** *p32*
Halleck, George V.; Washington, 1859-1920 ***2872.1*** *p15*
Hallen, Ivar Elmer; Arkansas, 1918 ***95.2*** *p53*
Hallenkann, Peter Joseph; Wisconsin, n.d. ***9675.5*** *p264*
Haller, . . .; Canada, 1776-1783 ***9786*** *p23*
Haller, J.F. 19; Philadelphia, 1774 ***1219.7*** *p215*
Hallersy, Timothy 5; Massachusetts, 1849 ***5881.1*** *p50*
Hallett, Charles 21; Philadelphia, 1774 ***1219.7*** *p232*
Halley, Mercifull; Virginia, 1633 ***6219*** *p31*
Hallgrimsd, Thorsteinn 11; Quebec, 1879 ***2557.1*** *p39*
Hallgrimsdottir, Jon 12; Quebec, 1879 ***2557.1*** *p39*
Hallgrimsdottir, Jona 48; Quebec, 1879 ***2557.1*** *p39*
Hallgrimsdottir, Julianna 24; Quebec, 1879 ***2557.2*** *p37*
Halliburton, David; America, 1746 ***1639.20*** *p89*
Halliburton, Lawden 25; Philadelphia, 1774 ***1219.7*** *p237*
Halliday, Adam; Illinois, 1876 ***5012.39*** *p26*
Halliday, Alex 28; St. John, N.B., 1864 ***5704.8*** *p157*
Halliday, Hugh; St. John, N.B., 1849 ***5704.8*** *p56*
Halliday, John 26; Maryland, 1775 ***1219.7*** *p259*
Halliday, Robert; Iowa, 1866-1943 ***123.54*** *p22*
Hallifax, Thomas 40; Georgia, 1735 ***3690.1*** *p99*
Halligan, Ellen 10; Massachusetts, 1849 ***5881.1*** *p46*
Hallihan, John; New York, NY, 1839 ***8208.4*** *p93*
Hallinan, Michael; America, 1741 ***4971*** *p60*
Hallinan, Thomas; America, 1741 ***4971*** *p61*
Halling, C. A.; Minneapolis, 1872-1883 ***6410.35*** *p54*
Halling, Lorentz; Minneapolis, 1867-1878 ***6410.35*** *p54*
Hallingdottir, Julianna 24; Quebec, 1879 ***2557.2*** *p37*
Hallingsdottir, Sigurdur 6 mos; Quebec, 1879 ***2557.2*** *p37*
Halliwell, Richard 25; New York, 1774 ***1219.7*** *p202*
Hallome, Francis; Virginia, 1642 ***6219*** *p195*
Hallome, Robert; Virginia, 1642 ***6219*** *p195*
Halloran, Johan 22; Massachusetts, 1849 ***5881.1*** *p47*
Halloran, Patrick; Washington, 1859-1920 ***2872.1*** *p15*
Halloran, Thomas 35; Massachusetts, 1849 ***5881.1*** *p50*
Halloran, Timothy; New York, NY, 1836 ***8208.4*** *p22*
Hallott, William 17; Virginia, 1720 ***3690.1*** *p99*
Halloway, John; Virginia, 1636 ***6219*** *p21*
Hallowes, John; Virginia, 1652 ***6251*** *p20*
Hallquist, Anders Johan; Washington, 1859-1920 ***2872.1*** *p15*
Hallugan, Richard; New York, NY, 1811 ***2859.11*** *p13*
Hallum, Robert; Virginia, 1635 ***6219*** *p74*
Hally, Jos.; Virginia, 1636 ***6219*** *p76*
Hally, Joseph; Virginia, 1637 ***6219*** *p108*
Hallyach, Ann Jane; Philadelphia, 1853 ***5704.8*** *p101*
Halm, . . .; Canada, 1776-1783 ***9786*** *p23*
Halma, Charles 36; New Orleans, 1835 ***778.5*** *p264*
Halmer, Morris; Virginia, 1643 ***6219*** *p204*
Halojohn, Jacob; Wisconsin, n.d. ***9675.5*** *p264*
Halow, Elizabeth; Savannah, GA, 1774 ***1219.7*** *p227*
Halow, Magnus; Savannah, GA, 1774 ***1219.7*** *p227*
Halpen, James; Philadelphia, 1816 ***2859.11*** *p32*
Halpen, William; Indiana, 1844 ***9117*** *p16*
Halpin, Bernard; Philadelphia, 1816 ***2859.11*** *p32*
Halpin, Mary 40; Massachusetts, 1849 ***5881.1*** *p48*
Halpin, Patrick; Wisconsin, n.d. ***9675.5*** *p264*
Halpin, Thomas; New Orleans, 1848 ***5704.8*** *p48*
Halprin, Patric 46; Arizona, 1921 ***9228.40*** *p25*
Halsey, John 22; Jamaica, 1736 ***3690.1*** *p99*
Halsey, Jon.; Virginia, 1623-1700 ***6219*** *p182*
Halsey, Robert; Virginia, 1639 ***6219*** *p155*
Halstenberg, . . .; Illinois, 1800-1900 ***4610.10*** *p67*
Halstenberg, Ernst Carl Friedrich; America, 1872 ***4610.10*** *p100*
Halstenberg, Ernst Heinrich Friedrich; America, 1885 ***4610.10*** *p110*
Halstenberg, Friedrich Wilhelm; America, 1857 ***4610.10*** *p109*
Haltenwerth, Jakob; Cincinnati, 1829 ***8582.1*** *p51*
Halter, Casper; Philadelphia, 1738 ***9898*** *p43*
Halter, Johann Martin; Philadelphia, 1738 ***9898*** *p43*
Halter, John Reinhold 21; Illinois, 1884 ***2896.5*** *p16*
Halterman, George; New York, NY, 1834 ***8208.4*** *p26*
Haltion, George 18; Windward Islands, 1722 ***3690.1*** *p100*
Haltiwanger, Angelica 8 *SEE* Haltiwanger, Jacob
Haltiwanger, Christopher 10 *SEE* Haltiwanger, Jacob
Haltiwanger, Jacob; South Carolina, 1752-1753 ***3689.17*** *p21*
With wife
*Relative:*Christopher 10
*Relative:*Angelica 8
Halton, George 18; Windward Islands, 1722 ***3690.1*** *p100*
Halton, James 16; Maryland, 1775 ***1219.7*** *p268*
Halverson, Astack; California, 1863 ***3840.2*** *p14*
Halvorsen, Halvor E.; Arkansas, 1918 ***95.2*** *p53*
Halwax, Joseph; Arkansas, 1918 ***95.2*** *p53*
Halworth, Henry 23; Maryland, 1774 ***1219.7*** *p230*
Haly, David; America, 1736-1743 ***4971*** *p58*
Haly, Edward; Quebec, 1825 ***7603*** *p74*
Haly, Honor; America, 1738 ***4971*** *p52*
Halyer, Thomas 36; Maryland, 1774 ***1219.7*** *p179*
Ham, James 21; Maryland, 1775 ***1219.7*** *p267*
Ham, Jeremiah 16; Maryland or Virginia, 1733 ***3690.1*** *p100*
Ham, Martin; Canada, 1776-1783 ***9786*** *p207A*
Ham, Richard; Nevada, 1874 ***2764.35*** *p35*
Ham, Richard 16; Philadelphia, 1774 ***1219.7*** *p175*
Hamad, Ollie; Iowa, 1866-1943 ***123.54*** *p22*
Hamageorgakis, Pauteles; Arkansas, 1918 ***95.2*** *p53*
Haman, Herman Ernst; Wisconsin, n.d. ***9675.5*** *p264*
Haman, John; Virginia, 1637 ***6219*** *p86*
Haman, Mark; Virginia, 1638 ***6219*** *p160*
Hamann, . . .; Canada, 1776-1783 ***9786*** *p23*
Hamann, Hermann; Wisconsin, n.d. ***9675.5*** *p264*
Hamant, Eugene 26; Kansas, 1883 ***5240.1*** *p16*
Hamant, Eugene 26; Kansas, 1883 ***5240.1*** *p64*
Hamant, Hubert 36; Kansas, 1879 ***5240.1*** *p60*
Hamard, Michael; New York, NY, 1811 ***2859.11*** *p13*
Hambach, Captain; Canada, 1776-1783 ***9786*** *p170*
Hambach, v., Cap.; Quebec, 1776 ***9786*** *p104*
Hambach, August Wilhelm; Quebec, 1776 ***9786*** *p261*
Hamberry, James 21; Jamaica, 1730 ***3690.1*** *p100*
Hambleton, Edouard; Quebec, 1738 ***7603*** *p69*
Hamblin, James 18; Maryland, 1734 ***3690.1*** *p100*
Hamblyn, Stephen; Virginia, 1638 ***6219*** *p147*
Hambour, Bern. 44; Port uncertain, 1839 ***778.5*** *p264*
Hambright, Adam; Philadelphia, 1760 ***9973.7*** *p34*
Hamburger, . . .; Canada, 1776-1783 ***9786*** *p42*
Hamburger, Jacob; America, 1851 ***8582.3*** *p26*
Hamburger, Johannes; New York, NY, 1839 ***8208.4*** *p91*
Hamburger, Joseph; New York, NY, 1839 ***8208.4*** *p91*
Hambury, Benjamin 15; Virginia, 1774 ***1219.7*** *p244*
Hamel, . . .; Canada, 1776-1783 ***9786*** *p23*
Hamel, Carl Friedrich Wilhelm; America, 1869 ***4610.10*** *p152*
Hamel, John; Canada, 1783 ***9786*** *p38A*
Hamel, Marg.; Detroit, 1904 ***1763*** *p40D*
Hamelmann Family ; America, 1885 ***4610.10*** *p76*
Hamelmann, Caspar Fr. W.; America, 1885 ***4610.10*** *p137*
Hamelton, Isabella 20; Philadelphia, 1854 ***5704.8*** *p118*
Hamelton, James 14; Philadelphia, 1854 ***5704.8*** *p116*
Hamelton, Jane 45; Philadelphia, 1854 ***5704.8*** *p116*
Hamelton, Joseph; Antigua (Antego), 1757 ***3690.1*** *p100*
Hamelton, Rebecca 27; St. John, N.B., 1854 ***5704.8*** *p122*
Hamelton, Rebecca 70; St. John, N.B., 1854 ***5704.8*** *p122*
Hamelton, Robert 11; Philadelphia, 1854 ***5704.8*** *p116*
Hamelton, Robert 21; St. John, N.B., 1854 ***5704.8*** *p122*
Hamelton, Robert 30; St. John, N.B., 1854 ***5704.8*** *p122*
Hamelton, Sarah 16; Philadelphia, 1854 ***5704.8*** *p116*
Hamemann, William; Wisconsin, n.d. ***9675.5*** *p264*
Hamer, Edw.; Virginia, 1635 ***6219*** *p26*
Hamer, Jane 28; Massachusetts, 1848 ***5881.1*** *p47*
Hamerla, . . .; Canada, 1776-1783 ***9786*** *p23*
Hamerman, Luis; Colorado, 1893 ***1450.2*** *p58A*
Hamersky, Anton; America, 1866 ***5240.1*** *p16*
Hamerston, Thomas 22; Virginia, 1774 ***1219.7*** *p238*
Hamerton, William; America, 1736-1743 ***4971*** *p57*
Hamill, John; New York, NY, 1811 ***2859.11*** *p13*
Hamill, John; Philadelphia, 1811 ***53.26*** *p35*
Hamill, John; Philadelphia, 1811 ***2859.11*** *p13*
Hamill, Nicholas; America, 1743 ***4971*** *p23*
Hamilton, Miss; Quebec, 1815 ***9229.18*** *p75*
Hamilton, Mr.; Quebec, 1815 ***9229.18*** *p75*
Hamilton, Alexander; North Carolina, 1787-1803 ***1639.20*** *p89*
Hamilton, Alexander 4; St. John, N.B., 1861 ***5704.8*** *p147*
Hamilton, Alexander 11; Quebec, 1849 ***5704.8*** *p51*
Hamilton, Alexander 22; Kansas, 1876 ***5240.1*** *p57*
Hamilton, And; Virginia, 1698 ***2212*** *p17*
Hamilton, Andrew; Quebec, 1849 ***5704.8*** *p51*
Hamilton, Andrew 13; Quebec, 1849 ***5704.8*** *p51*
Hamilton, Ann; Quebec, 1852 ***5704.8*** *p97*
Hamilton, Ann 9; St. John, N.B., 1861 ***5704.8*** *p147*
Hamilton, Ann 15; Philadelphia, 1858 ***5704.8*** *p139*
Hamilton, Ann 40; Philadelphia, 1854 ***5704.8*** *p123*
Hamilton, Annie 8; New York, NY, 1865 ***5704.8*** *p192*
Hamilton, Archibald; North Carolina, 1776 ***1639.20*** *p89*
Hamilton, Bridget; New York, NY, 1868 ***5704.8*** *p226*
Hamilton, Catharine; St. John, N.B., 1847 ***5704.8*** *p35*
Hamilton, Catherine; America, 1741 ***4971*** *p40*
Hamilton, Catherine 8; St. John, N.B., 1861 ***5704.8*** *p147*
Hamilton, Charles; Ohio, 1826 ***2769.4*** *p6*
Hamilton, Charles; Philadelphia, 1811 ***53.26*** *p35*
*Relative:*Daniel
Hamilton, Charles; Philadelphia, 1811 ***2859.11*** *p13*
Hamilton, Charles 16; Antigua (Antego), 1773 ***1219.7*** *p171*
Hamilton, Charles 22; Quebec, 1855 ***5704.8*** *p124*
Hamilton, Conway; New York, NY, 1811 ***2859.11*** *p13*
Hamilton, Daniel *SEE* Hamilton, Charles
Hamilton, Daniel; Philadelphia, 1811 ***2859.11*** *p13*
Hamilton, David; Philadelphia, 1852 ***5704.8*** *p88*
Hamilton, E. R.; Washington, 1859-1920 ***2872.1*** *p15*
Hamilton, Edw.; New York, NY, 1811 ***2859.11*** *p13*
Hamilton, Eliza; Philadelphia, 1816 ***2859.11*** *p32*
Hamilton, Eliza; Philadelphia, 1864 ***5704.8*** *p181*
Hamilton, Eliza; Philadelphia, 1866 ***5704.8*** *p205*
Hamilton, Eliza; Quebec, 1851 ***5704.8*** *p73*
Hamilton, Eliza; Quebec, 1852 ***5704.8*** *p89*
Hamilton, Eliza 7; Quebec, 1847 ***5704.8*** *p7*
Hamilton, Eliza 16; St. John, N.B., 1860 ***5704.8*** *p143*
Hamilton, Elizabeth; New York, NY, 1811 ***2859.11*** *p13*
Hamilton, Elizabeth; New York, NY, 1867 ***5704.8*** *p223*
Hamilton, Elizabeth 7; Massachusetts, 1847 ***5881.1*** *p46*
Hamilton, Ellen 5; New York, NY, 1868 ***5704.8*** *p226*
Hamilton, Ellen 11; St. John, N.B., 1861 ***5704.8*** *p147*
Hamilton, Ellen 30; Philadelphia, 1854 ***5704.8*** *p121*
Hamilton, Ellen 40; St. John, N.B., 1861 ***5704.8*** *p147*
Hamilton, Frank; Arkansas, 1886 ***3688*** *p7*
Hamilton, George 19; Maryland, 1774 ***1219.7*** *p230*
Hamilton, George 23; Virginia, 1774 ***1219.7*** *p213*
Hamilton, George W.; New York, NY, 1840 ***8208.4*** *p111*
Hamilton, Hannah 6; Massachusetts, 1850 ***5881.1*** *p46*
Hamilton, Hariet; Philadelphia, 1852 ***5704.8*** *p89*
Hamilton, Hariet 12; Philadelphia, 1852 ***5704.8*** *p89*
Hamilton, Henry; St. John, N.B., 1851 ***5704.8*** *p80*
Hamilton, Hugh; Philadelphia, 1864 ***5704.8*** *p180*
Hamilton, Hugh 6; St. John, N.B., 1848 ***5704.8*** *p44*
Hamilton, Isaac 6; Quebec, 1849 ***5704.8*** *p51*
Hamilton, Isabella; New York, NY, 1867 ***5704.8*** *p223*
Hamilton, James; Antigua (Antego), 1757 ***1219.7*** *p50*
Hamilton, James; Antigua (Antego), 1757 ***3690.1*** *p100*
Hamilton, James; Carolina, 1684 ***1639.20*** *p89*
Hamilton, James; Charleston, SC, 1797 ***1639.20*** *p89*
Hamilton, James; Kansas, 1871 ***5240.1*** *p17*
Hamilton, James; New York, NY, 1839 ***8208.4*** *p97*
Hamilton, James; Philadelphia, 1850 ***53.26*** *p35*
Hamilton, James; Philadelphia, 1850 ***5704.8*** *p59*
Hamilton, James; Philadelphia, 1854 ***5704.8*** *p123*
Hamilton, James; Quebec, 1849 ***5704.8*** *p51*
Hamilton, James; Quebec, 1851 ***5704.8*** *p73*
Hamilton, James; St. John, N.B., 1852 ***5704.8*** *p92*
Hamilton, James; St. John, N.B., 1858 ***5704.8*** *p140*
Hamilton, James 11; Quebec, 1847 ***5704.8*** *p7*
Hamilton, James 20; Philadelphia, 1864 ***5704.8*** *p161*
Hamilton, James 23; Philadelphia, 1803 ***53.26*** *p35*
Hamilton, James 30; Quebec, 1862 ***5704.8*** *p152*
Hamilton, James 40; Massachusetts, 1847 ***5881.1*** *p47*
Hamilton, James 40; Philadelphia, 1854 ***5704.8*** *p123*
Hamilton, James A.; St. John, N.B., 1847 ***5704.8*** *p35*
Hamilton, James Martin; Iowa, 1866-1943 ***123.54*** *p22*
Hamilton, Jane; New York, NY, 1864 ***5704.8*** *p173*
Hamilton, Jane; New York, NY, 1869 ***5704.8*** *p235*
Hamilton, Jane; Quebec, 1847 ***5704.8*** *p7*
Hamilton, Jane; St. John, N.B., 1848 ***5704.8*** *p39*
Hamilton, Jane 10; Quebec, 1847 ***5704.8*** *p16*
Hamilton, Jane Ann 20; St. John, N.B., 1860 ***5704.8*** *p143*
Hamilton, John; America, 1741 ***4971*** *p76*
Hamilton, John; Antigua (Antego), 1757 ***1219.7*** *p51*
Hamilton, John; Antigua (Antego), 1757 ***3690.1*** *p100*
Hamilton, John; New York, NY, 1811 ***2859.11*** *p13*
Hamilton, John; Quebec, 1847 ***5704.8*** *p7*
Hamilton, John; Quebec, 1849 ***5704.8*** *p52*
Hamilton, John 4; Philadelphia, 1854 ***5704.8*** *p123*
Hamilton, John 9; Quebec, 1847 ***5704.8*** *p7*
Hamilton, John 14; St. John, N.B., 1855 ***5704.8*** *p127*
Hamilton, John 21; Maryland, 1774 ***1219.7*** *p192*
Hamilton, John 21; Quebec, 1855 ***5704.8*** *p125*
Hamilton, John 22; Maryland, 1775 ***1219.7*** *p247*
Hamilton, John 22; Philadelphia, 1864 ***5704.8*** *p160*
Hamilton, John 32; Virginia, 1774 ***1219.7*** *p244*
Hamilton, John 59; St. John, N.B., 1855 ***5704.8*** *p127*
Hamilton, Joseph; Antigua (Antego), 1757 ***1219.7*** *p50*
Hamilton, Joseph; New York, NY, 1838 ***8208.4*** *p85*
Hamilton, Joseph; Philadelphia, 1867 ***5704.8*** *p217*
Hamilton, Joseph 13; Quebec, 1849 ***5704.8*** *p52*
Hamilton, Joseph 45; St. John, N.B., 1861 ***5704.8*** *p147*
Hamilton, Joseph C.; America, 1873 ***1450.2*** *p58A*
Hamilton, Margaret; America, 1864 ***5704.8*** *p182*
Hamilton, Margaret; New York, NY, 1811 ***2859.11*** *p13*
Hamilton, Margaret; Philadelphia, 1865 ***5704.8*** *p197*
Hamilton, Margaret; Quebec, 1850 ***5704.8*** *p62*
Hamilton, Margaret; St. John, N.B., 1848 ***5704.8*** *p47*
Hamilton, Margaret 2; Quebec, 1847 ***5704.8*** *p7*
Hamilton, Margaret 9; Philadelphia, 1854 ***5704.8*** *p123*
Hamilton, Margaret 25; Massachusetts, 1847 ***5881.1*** *p48*

Hamilton, Margaret 60; St. John, N.B., 1854 ***5704.8*** *p120*
Hamilton, Margaret I. 4; Massachusetts, 1850 ***5881.1*** *p49*
Hamilton, Mary *SEE* Hamilton, Robert
Hamilton, Mary; New York, NY, 1811 ***2859.11*** *p13*
Hamilton, Mary; Philadelphia, 1847 ***5704.8*** *p24*
Hamilton, Mary; Philadelphia, 1851 ***5704.8*** *p77*
Hamilton, Mary; Philadelphia, 1853 ***5704.8*** *p103*
Hamilton, Mary; St. John, N.B., 1848 ***5704.8*** *p43*
Hamilton, Mary 7; New York, NY, 1868 ***5704.8*** *p226*
Hamilton, Mary 10; Philadelphia, 1854 ***5704.8*** *p123*
Hamilton, Mary 18; St. John, N.B., 1861 ***5704.8*** *p147*
Hamilton, Mary 24; Wilmington, DE, 1831 ***6508.7*** *p160*
Hamilton, Mary Ann; Quebec, 1852 ***5704.8*** *p86*
Hamilton, Mary Ann; Quebec, 1852 ***5704.8*** *p90*
Hamilton, Mary Ann 14; Massachusetts, 1850 ***5881.1*** *p49*
Hamilton, Mary J.; Philadelphia, 1864 ***5704.8*** *p180*
Hamilton, Matilda; Philadelphia, 1851 ***5704.8*** *p77*
Hamilton, Nancy; Quebec, 1849 ***5704.8*** *p52*
Hamilton, Nancy 22; St. John, N.B., 1853 ***5704.8*** *p110*
Hamilton, P. 61; North Carolina, 1850 ***1639.20*** *p89*
Hamilton, Patrick; America, 1807 ***1639.20*** *p89*
Hamilton, Paul; South Carolina, 1680-1830 ***1639.20*** *p90*
Hamilton, Peter 21; Philadelphia, 1861 ***5704.8*** *p148*
Hamilton, Rebecca; Quebec, 1849 ***5704.8*** *p51*
Hamilton, Rebecca; Quebec, 1850 ***5704.8*** *p62*
Hamilton, Rebecca; Quebec, 1850 ***5704.8*** *p63*
Hamilton, Robert; America, 1798 ***1639.20*** *p90*
Hamilton, Robert; New York, NY, 1811 ***2859.11*** *p13*
Hamilton, Robert; New York, NY, 1839 ***8208.4*** *p98*
Hamilton, Robert; North Carolina, 1799 ***1639.20*** *p90*
Hamilton, Robert; Philadelphia, 1811 ***53.26*** *p35*
Hamilton, Robert; Philadelphia, 1811 ***2859.11*** *p13*
Hamilton, Robert; Philadelphia, 1847 ***53.26*** *p35*
*Relative:*Mary
Hamilton, Robert; Philadelphia, 1847 ***5704.8*** *p24*
Hamilton, Robert; Quebec, 1849 ***5704.8*** *p51*
Hamilton, Robert; Quebec, 1850 ***5704.8*** *p63*
Hamilton, Robert 4; Quebec, 1849 ***5704.8*** *p51*
Hamilton, Robert 10; Quebec, 1849 ***5704.8*** *p52*
Hamilton, Robert 18; St. John, N.B., 1864 ***5704.8*** *p159*
Hamilton, Robert 24; Maryland, 1775 ***1219.7*** *p272*
Hamilton, Robert 42; New York, 1775 ***1219.7*** *p268*
With wife
With 3 children
Hamilton, Rosey; Philadelphia, 1851 ***5704.8*** *p81*
Hamilton, Ruth; Quebec, 1847 ***5704.8*** *p16*
Hamilton, Samuel; New York, NY, 1835 ***8208.4*** *p43*
Hamilton, Sarah; Philadelphia, 1852 ***5704.8*** *p89*
Hamilton, Sarah; Quebec, 1851 ***5704.8*** *p74*
Hamilton, Sarah 20; Philadelphia, 1860 ***5704.8*** *p145*
Hamilton, Thomas; New York, NY, 1811 ***2859.11*** *p13*
Hamilton, Thomas; Quebec, 1847 ***5704.8*** *p12*
Hamilton, Thomas; Quebec, 1852 ***5704.8*** *p94*
Hamilton, Thomas; St. John, N.B., 1847 ***5704.8*** *p15*
Hamilton, Thomas 9 mos; Quebec, 1852 ***5704.8*** *p97*
Hamilton, Thomas 5; Quebec, 1847 ***5704.8*** *p7*
Hamilton, Thomas 20; Maryland, 1738 ***3690.1*** *p100*
Hamilton, Thomas 21; Quebec, 1855 ***5704.8*** *p126*
Hamilton, Thomas J.; America, 1856 ***1450.2*** *p59A*
Hamilton, W.; New York, NY, 1816 ***2859.11*** *p32*
Hamilton, William; New York, NY, 1837 ***8208.4*** *p52*
Hamilton, William; New York, NY, 1864 ***5704.8*** *p173*
Hamilton, William; North Carolina, 1799 ***1639.20*** *p90*
Hamilton, William; Philadelphia, 1811 ***53.26*** *p35*
Hamilton, William; Philadelphia, 1816 ***2859.11*** *p32*
Hamilton, William 6 mos; Quebec, 1847 ***5704.8*** *p7*
Hamilton, William 5; Philadelphia, 1854 ***5704.8*** *p123*
Hamilton, William 8; Quebec, 1852 ***5704.8*** *p97*
Hamilton, William 9; Quebec, 1849 ***5704.8*** *p51*
Hamilton, William 19; Jamaica, 1736 ***3690.1*** *p100*
Hamilton, William 26; Grenada, 1774 ***1219.7*** *p242*
Hamilton, Wm.; Philadelphia, 1811 ***2859.11*** *p13*
Hamilton, Wm; Philadelphia, 1816 ***2859.11*** *p32*
Haming, Wm.; Virginia, 1642 ***6219*** *p187*
Hamkens, Louis; Wisconsin, n.d. ***9675.5*** *p264*
Hamlet, Christopher 42; New York, 1774 ***1219.7*** *p217*
Hamlet, Wm 10; America, 1702 ***2212*** *p38*
Hamlin, Robert 20; Jamaica, 1722 ***3690.1*** *p100*
Hamm, . . .; Canada, 1776-1783 ***9786*** *p23*
Hamm, Andrew M.; California, 1880 ***2764.35*** *p30*
Hamm, Deitriech 27; America, 1831 ***778.5*** *p269*
Hammanburg, Anna 35; Massachusetts, 1860 ***6410.32*** *p116*
Hammanburg, James; Boston, 1838 ***6410.32*** *p125*
Hammanburg, James 42; Massachusetts, 1860 ***6410.32*** *p116*
Hammann, Friederich; Kentucky, 1840-1845 ***8582.3*** *p100*
Hammann, H.; Ohio, 1843 ***8582.1*** *p51*
Hammar, Samuel; Maine, 1869-1882 ***6410.22*** *p118*
Hammarberg, Johan August; Boston, 1838 ***6410.32*** *p125*
Hamme, Valentine; Philadelphia, 1763 ***9973.7*** *p38*
Hammel, Frederic; Wisconsin, n.d. ***9675.5*** *p264*
Hammel, George; California, 1860 ***3840.2*** *p14*
Hammel, Godfrey; New York, NY, 1838 ***8208.4*** *p71*
Hammel, Johann; Kentucky, 1844 ***8582.3*** *p101*
Hammel, John M.; Pittsburgh, 1881 ***3702.7*** *p466*
Hammel, Kath. Zogner 71; Cleveland, OH, 1902 ***1763*** *p40D*
Hammel, Maria 62; America, 1895 ***1763*** *p40D*
Hammel, Philipp; America, 1846 ***8582.3*** *p26*
Hammel, Samuel; Kentucky, 1840 ***8582.3*** *p99*
Hammell, . . .; Canada, 1776-1783 ***9786*** *p23*
Hammelmann, A. M. Louise; America, 1852 ***4610.10*** *p112*
Hammelmann, Amalie Caroline *SEE* Hammelmann, Heinrich Gottlieb
Hammelmann, Anna Marie J. Engel *SEE* Hammelmann, Heinrich Gottlieb
Hammelmann, Anna Marie Wilhelmine *SEE* Hammelmann, Heinrich Gottlieb
Hammelmann, Anne Cath Louise Engel *SEE* Hammelmann, Heinrich Wilhelm Conrad
Hammelmann, Anne M. L. Cath. Engel *SEE* Hammelmann, Heinrich Wilhelm Conrad
Hammelmann, Anne M. Louise Engel *SEE* Hammelmann, Heinrich Wilhelm Conrad
Hammelmann, Anne Marie Cath. Wilh. *SEE* Hammelmann, Heinrich Wilhelm Conrad
Hammelmann, Anne Marie Engel Bode *SEE* Hammelmann, Heinrich Wilhelm Conrad
Hammelmann, Carl Friedrich Gottlieb; America, 1844 ***4610.10*** *p133*
Hammelmann, Carl Friedrich Wilhelm *SEE* Hammelmann, Heinrich Gottlieb
Hammelmann, Catharine M. C. Stucke *SEE* Hammelmann, Heinrich Gottlieb
Hammelmann, Ernst H. Gottlieb *SEE* Hammelmann, Heinrich Gottlieb
Hammelmann, Heinrich Gottlieb; America, 1844 ***4610.10*** *p154*
*Wife:*Catharine M. C. Stucke
*Stepchild:*Amalie Caroline
*Stepchild:*Anna Marie Wilhelmine
*Child:*Heinrich W. Gottlieb
*Child:*Ernst H. Gottlieb
*Child:*Anna Marie J. Engel
*Child:*Carl Friedrich Wilhelm
Hammelmann, Heinrich W. Gottlieb *SEE* Hammelmann, Heinrich Gottlieb
Hammelmann, Heinrich Wilhelm Conrad; America, 1844 ***4610.10*** *p133*
*Wife:*Anne Marie Engel Bode
*Child:*Anne Cath Louise Engel
*Child:*Anne M. L. Cath. Engel
*Child:*Anne Marie Cath. Wilh.
*Child:*Anne M. Louise Engel
With child
Hammer, Anna Maria; New York, 1749 ***3652*** *p72*
Hammer, Balthass *SEE* Hammer, Johann Melchior, Jr.
Hammer, Bruno Richard; Minnesota, 1888 ***5012.40*** *p80*
Hammer, Dorothea; New York, 1761 ***3652*** *p88*
Hammer, Elisabetha Haemmerlin *SEE* Hammer, Johann Melchior, Jr.
Hammer, Hans Michael *SEE* Hammer, Johann Melchior, Jr.
Hammer, Johann Caspar *SEE* Hammer, Johann Melchior, Jr.
Hammer, Johann Melchior *SEE* Hammer, Johann Melchior, Jr.
Hammer, Johann Melchior, Jr.; Pennsylvania, 1751 ***2444*** *p162*
*Wife:*Elisabetha Haemmerlin
*Child:*Johann Melchior
*Child:*Balthass
*Child:*Hans Michael
*Child:*Maria Elisabetha
*Child:*Johann Caspar
*Child:*Maria Agnes
Hammer, John; Colorado, 1887 ***9678.2*** *p22*
Hammer, Maria Agatha; Port uncertain, 1751 ***2444*** *p177*
Hammer, Maria Agnes *SEE* Hammer, Johann Melchior, Jr.
Hammer, Maria Elisabetha *SEE* Hammer, Johann Melchior, Jr.
Hammer, Melcher; Pennsylvania, 1751 ***2444*** *p177*
Hammerin, Erik; Washington, 1859-1920 ***2872.1*** *p15*
Hammerl, Marie; Wisconsin, n.d. ***9675.5*** *p264*
Hammerole, Peter; New York, NY, 1882 ***1450.2*** *p13B*
Hammerstied, Casper; New York, NY, 1835 ***8208.4*** *p28*
Hammes Family ; New York, 1765 ***8125.8*** *p436*
Hammeter, Johann Sebastian; Pennsylvania, 1753 ***4525*** *p221*
Hammeter, Johann Sebastian; Pennsylvania, 1753 ***4525*** *p278*
Hammill, Patrick; Philadelphia, 1816 ***2859.11*** *p32*
Hammilton, John 28; Virginia, 1731 ***3690.1*** *p100*
Hammiter, Adam; South Carolina, 1788 ***7119*** *p203*
Hammon, Edward; America, 1735-1743 ***4971*** *p51*
Hammon, Martin; Virginia, 1636 ***6219*** *p7*
Hammon, Paul; Wisconsin, n.d. ***9675.5*** *p264*
Hammon, Saul; Wisconsin, n.d. ***9675.5*** *p264*
Hammond, Catherine; St. John, N.B., 1850 ***5704.8*** *p68*
Hammond, Corker 15; Maryland, 1724 ***3690.1*** *p100*
Hammond, George; South Carolina, 1716 ***1639.20*** *p90*
Hammond, Henry 5 *SEE* Hammond, Henry
Hammond, Henry 21; Massachusetts, 1849 ***5881.1*** *p46*
Hammond, Henry 31; North America, 1774 ***1219.7*** *p199*
*Wife:*Margaret 27
*Child:*Henry 5
*Child:*Jane 3
*Child:*Margaret 1
Hammond, Hugh; New York, NY, 1816 ***2859.11*** *p32*
Hammond, Jane 3 *SEE* Hammond, Henry
Hammond, John; Virginia, 1638 ***6219*** *p124*
Hammond, John 15; Jamaica, 1749 ***3690.1*** *p101*
Hammond, John 20; Maryland, 1738 ***3690.1*** *p101*
Hammond, John 20; Massachusetts, 1847 ***5881.1*** *p47*
Hammond, John 37; Virginia, 1774 ***1219.7*** *p244*
Hammond, Joseph 19; America, 1728 ***3690.1*** *p101*
Hammond, Joseph 21; Maryland, 1774 ***1219.7*** *p212*
Hammond, Joseph 22; Jamaica, 1730 ***3690.1*** *p101*
Hammond, Margaret 1 *SEE* Hammond, Henry
Hammond, Margaret 27 *SEE* Hammond, Henry
Hammond, Mary Ann 27; Philadelphia, 1804 ***53.26*** *p35*
Hammond, Samuel; New York, NY, 1868 ***5704.8*** *p229*
Hamon, Christo.; Virginia, 1637 ***6219*** *p82*
Hamond, Christopher; Virginia, 1638 ***6219*** *p116*
Hamond, Hugh; St. John, N.B., 1853 ***5704.8*** *p99*
Hamond, James; Philadelphia, 1852 ***5704.8*** *p84*
Hamond, Joseph; Jamaica, 1736 ***3690.1*** *p101*
Hamond, Mary Jane; Philadelphia, 1852 ***5704.8*** *p84*
Hamond, Ollie; Iowa, 1866-1943 ***123.54*** *p22*
Hampsey, John; New York, NY, 1869 ***5704.8*** *p234*
Hampsey, Mary 18; Philadelphia, 1865 ***5704.8*** *p165*
Hampsey, Nancy; New York, NY, 1869 ***5704.8*** *p234*
Hampsey, Sarah 16; Philadelphia, 1865 ***5704.8*** *p165*
Hampshire, Mary 40; Massachusetts, 1860 ***6410.32*** *p105*
Hampshire, William 35; Massachusetts, 1860 ***6410.32*** *p105*
Hampsie, Esther; Philadelphia, 1867 ***5704.8*** *p220*
Hampson, John; New York, NY, 1864 ***5704.8*** *p172*
Hampson, Mary; Philadelphia, 1865 ***5704.8*** *p200*
Hampston, Quinlan; Nevada, 1876 ***2764.35*** *p30*
Hampton, Eliza.; Virginia, 1639 ***6219*** *p184*
Hampton, Grace; Virginia, 1639 ***6219*** *p184*
Hampton, Joane *SEE* Hampton, William
Hampton, John; Virginia, 1637 ***6219*** *p114*
Hampton, John; Virginia, 1638 ***6219*** *p125*
Hampton, Richard 16; Maryland, 1725 ***3690.1*** *p101*
Hampton, Thomas; Virginia, 1637 ***6219*** *p82*
Hampton, Willi.; Virginia, 1639 ***6219*** *p184*
Hampton, William; Virginia, 1639 ***6219*** *p184*
*Wife:*Joane
Hampton, William 33; Maryland, 1774 ***1219.7*** *p222*
Hams, Herman 22; Kansas, 1885 ***5240.1*** *p68*
Hamson, Samuel 32; Jamaica, 1730 ***3690.1*** *p101*
Hamson, Thomas; Antigua (Antego), 1762 ***1219.7*** *p90*
Hamson, Thomas 22; America, 1700 ***2212*** *p27*
Hamssen, Charles J.; Washington, 1859-1920 ***2872.1*** *p15*
Hanabry, John; New York, NY, 1836 ***8208.4*** *p17*
Hanagan, Denis; New York, NY, 1811 ***2859.11*** *p13*
Hanagan, James; Quebec, 1823 ***7603*** *p98*
Hanagan, John 22; St. John, N.B., 1864 ***5704.8*** *p159*
Hanagan, Thomas; Illinois, 1870 ***5240.1*** *p17*
Hanah, Mary 10; New York, NY, 1864 ***5704.8*** *p185*
Hanah, Samuel 24; Quebec, 1856 ***5704.8*** *p130*
Hanamny, John; Montreal, 1819 ***7603*** *p91*
Hanan, Isabella; Philadelphia, 1853 ***5704.8*** *p102*
Hananage, James; America, 1739 ***4971*** *p98*
Hanbury, Peter; Virginia, 1639 ***6219*** *p156*
Hanby, John; Charleston, SC, 1804 ***1639.20*** *p90*
Hanby, Rich.; Virginia, 1642 ***6219*** *p199*
Hanby, Sarah; Virginia, 1642 ***6219*** *p199*
Hance, William; Virginia, 1642 ***6219*** *p186*
Hancke, Elizabeth *SEE* Hancke, Matthew
Hancke, Matthew; New York, 1743 ***3652*** *p59*
*Wife:*Elizabeth
Hancock, Arnold 20; Pennsylvania, 1721 ***3690.1*** *p101*
Hancock, Charles; Nevada, 1878 ***2764.35*** *p33*
Hancock, Henry 24; Jamaica, 1737 ***3690.1*** *p101*
Hancock, James; San Francisco, 1850 ***4914.15*** *p10*
Hancock, Richard 21; Port uncertain, 1774 ***1219.7*** *p177*
Hancock, Robert 15; Philadelphia, 1774 ***1219.7*** *p212*
Hancock, Stephen 16; Maryland, 1775 ***1219.7*** *p273*
Hancock, Thomas 29; Maryland, 1775 ***1219.7*** *p266*

Hancocke, John; Virginia, 1639 ***6219*** *p155*
Hancorne, Thos. Walter 33; California, 1869 ***3840.2*** *p14*
Hand, James 41; Harris Co., TX, 1897 ***6254*** *p3*
Hand, Laurence; Delaware, 1743 ***4971*** *p105*
Hand, Lawrence; America, 1743 ***4971*** *p28*
Hand, Margaret; America, 1742 ***4971*** *p17*
Hand, Margaret; Maryland, 1742 ***4971*** *p107*
Hand, Mary Matheson; America, 1812 ***8893*** *p266*
Hand, Michael; New York, NY, 1837 ***8208.4*** *p52*
Hand, Owen; Iowa, 1866-1943 ***123.54*** *p22*
Hand, Robert; Virginia, 1646 ***6219*** *p242*
Hand, Robert 43; Harris Co., TX, 1897 ***6254*** *p3*
Hand, Thomas; Virginia, 1621 ***6219*** *p2*
Handell, . . .; Canada, 1776-1783 ***9786*** *p23*
Handiside, Mr.; Quebec, 1815 ***9229.18*** *p81*
Handke, Christ; Iowa, 1866-1943 ***123.54*** *p22*
Handle, Michael; Illinois, 1860 ***2896.5*** *p16*
Handley, James 21; Maryland, 1775 ***1219.7*** *p259*
Handley, Wm.; Virginia, 1648 ***6219*** *p250*
Handlon, Bridget; Quebec, 1784 ***7603*** *p90*
Handmann, Friedrich; America, 1869-1887 ***8582*** *p12*
Handock, Frank 36; Kansas, 1889 ***5240.1*** *p73*
Handonno, J.; New Orleans, 1839 ***778.5*** *p264*
Handrihan, Michael 35; Massachusetts, 1849 ***5881.1*** *p48*
Handrup, Mary *SEE* Handrup, Vitus
Handrup, Vitus; Delaware, 1746 ***3652*** *p68*
*Wife:*Mary
Handwick, Elizabeth 24 *SEE* Handwick, James
Handwick, James 34; North America, 1774 ***1219.7*** *p199*
*Wife:*Elizabeth 24
Handy, Elias; Iowa, 1866-1943 ***123.54*** *p22*
Handy, Robert; America, 1739 ***4971*** *p14*
Hanegan, Mary; St. John, N.B., 1852 ***5704.8*** *p84*
Hanekratt, . . .; Canada, 1776-1783 ***9786*** *p23*
Haner, . . .; Canada, 1776-1783 ***9786*** *p23*
Haner, John 24; Port uncertain, 1774 ***1219.7*** *p176*
Hanes, Joseph; Wisconsin, n.d. ***9675.5*** *p264*
Haney, Ann; Philadelphia, 1847 ***53.26*** *p35*
*Relative:*Ellen
Haney, Ann; Philadelphia, 1847 ***5704.8*** *p22*
Haney, Catherine 10; St. John, N.B., 1848 ***5704.8*** *p43*
Haney, Ellen *SEE* Haney, Ann
Haney, Ellen; Philadelphia, 1847 ***5704.8*** *p22*
Haney, James; Philadelphia, 1847 ***53.26*** *p35*
Haney, James; St. John, N.B., 1848 ***5704.8*** *p43*
Haney, John 13; St. John, N.B., 1848 ***5704.8*** *p43*
Haney, Margaret; St. John, N.B., 1848 ***5704.8*** *p43*
Haney, Susan; Philadelphia, 1847 ***53.26*** *p35*
Haney, Susan; Philadelphia, 1865 ***5704.8*** *p201*
Haney, Susan; St. John, N.B., 1848 ***5704.8*** *p43*
Hanf, Kristina 20; America, 1853 ***9162.8*** *p36*
Hanfbauer, Michael; Wisconsin, n.d. ***9675.5*** *p264*
Hang, Biddy 2; St. John, N.B., 1854 ***5704.8*** *p119*
Hang, Henry 13; St. John, N.B., 1854 ***5704.8*** *p119*
Hang, James 6; St. John, N.B., 1854 ***5704.8*** *p119*
Hang, John 40; St. John, N.B., 1854 ***5704.8*** *p119*
Hang, Mary 9; St. John, N.B., 1854 ***5704.8*** *p119*
Hang, Mary 32; St. John, N.B., 1854 ***5704.8*** *p119*
Hang, Patrick 16; St. John, N.B., 1854 ***5704.8*** *p119*
Hang, Rose 45; St. John, N.B., 1854 ***5704.8*** *p119*
Hang, Rudolf; America, 1887 ***1450.2*** *p59A*
Hangmeyer, Deaphilas 26; Boston, 1774 ***1219.7*** *p188*
Hanham, Thomas 21; Virginia, 1773 ***1219.7*** *p168*
Hanhart, J. 24; New Orleans, 1835 ***778.5*** *p264*
Hanhauser, Bernhard; America, 1869-1887 ***8582*** *p12*
Hanhauser, Bernhard; New Orleans, 1842 ***8582.3*** *p26*
Hanhauser, J. G.; Kentucky, 1839-1840 ***8582.3*** *p98*
Hanhauser, Jakob; America, 1835-1837 ***8582.3*** *p26*
With brother
Hanhauser, Jakob; Cincinnati, 1869 ***8582*** *p12*
Hanhauser, Jakob; Kentucky, 1839-1840 ***8582.3*** *p98*
Hanhauser, Johann; Cincinnati, 1869-1887 ***8582*** *p12*
Haniett, Mr. 35; America, 1839 ***778.5*** *p264*
Hanig, Werner; New York, NY, 1922 ***3455.3*** *p81*
Hanigan, . . .; New York, NY, 1867 ***5704.8*** *p224*
Hanigan, Con; New York, NY, 1867 ***5704.8*** *p224*
Hanigan, Jane; New York, NY, 1867 ***5704.8*** *p224*
Hanigan, William; New York, NY, 1867 ***5704.8*** *p224*
Hanisch, John; Illinois, 1892 ***5012.40*** *p26*
Hanitsch, Werner 88; America, 1895 ***1763*** *p40D*
Hanity, Dennis; Philadelphia, 1853 ***5704.8*** *p109*
Hank, Jim Leon; Arkansas, 1918 ***95.2*** *p53*
Hanke Family ; Costa Rica, 1853 ***8582.3*** *p30*
Hanke, Carl Friedrich *SEE* Hanke, Caroline Friederike Wiele
Hanke, Caroline Friederike Henriette; America, 1881 ***4610.10*** *p117*
Hanke, Caroline Friederike Wiele; America, 1881 ***4610.10*** *p117*
*Son:*Carl Friedrich
Hanke, Heinrich Friedrich; America, 1867 ***4610.10*** *p105*
Hanke, Johann Friedrich Christian; America, 1837 ***4610.10*** *p119*
Hanke, Joseph; Wisconsin, n.d. ***9675.5*** *p264*
Hanker, Fritz 35; California, 1872 ***2769.5*** *p4*
Hankin, Geor; Virginia, 1639 ***6219*** *p184*
Hanks, Edward 16; Maryland, 1775 ***1219.7*** *p268*
Hanks, Isaac 25; Philadelphia, 1775 ***1219.7*** *p274*
Hanks, Thomas 20; Maryland, 1723 ***3690.1*** *p101*
Hanlan, Darby; America, 1742 ***4971*** *p94*
Hanlan, Darby; America, 1743 ***4971*** *p86*
Hanlan, Edward; America, 1736-1743 ***4971*** *p58*
Hanlan, James 29; Maryland, 1775 ***1219.7*** *p261*
Hanlan, John; Philadelphia, 1811 ***53.26*** *p35*
Hanlan, John; Philadelphia, 1811 ***2859.11*** *p13*
Hanlan, Letty 27; St. John, N.B., 1863 ***5704.8*** *p152*
Hanlan, Margaret; New York, NY, 1811 ***2859.11*** *p13*
With family
Hanlan, Moses 22; St. John, N.B., 1863 ***5704.8*** *p152*
Hanlan, Thomas; Philadelphia, 1847 ***53.26*** *p35*
Hanlan, Thomas; Philadelphia, 1847 ***5704.8*** *p22*
Hanlay, Ardsal 22; Philadelphia, 1803 ***53.26*** *p35*
Hanlen, Patrick; Philadelphia, 1850 ***53.26*** *p35*
Hanlen, Patrick; Philadelphia, 1850 ***5704.8*** *p59*
Hanley, Daniel; Philadelphia, 1849 ***53.26*** *p35*
Hanley, Daniel; Philadelphia, 1849 ***5704.8*** *p50*
Hanley, James; New York, NY, 1816 ***2859.11*** *p32*
Hanley, John 48; Arizona, 1890 ***2764.35*** *p30*
Hanley, John Lynch; Arkansas, 1918 ***95.2*** *p53*
Hanley, Mary; New York, NY, 1816 ***2859.11*** *p32*
Hanley, Sarah; New York, NY, 1865 ***5704.8*** *p196*
Hanley, Stophel; Philadelphia, 1759 ***9973.7*** *p33*
Hanlin, Ann 11; St. John, N.B., 1861 ***5704.8*** *p147*
Hanlin, Anne 10; St. John, N.B., 1857 ***5704.8*** *p135*
Hanlin, Benjamin 5; St. John, N.B., 1861 ***5704.8*** *p147*
Hanlin, Christopher 5; St. John, N.B., 1857 ***5704.8*** *p135*
Hanlin, Ellen 9; St. John, N.B., 1861 ***5704.8*** *p147*
Hanlin, Henry 2; St. John, N.B., 1857 ***5704.8*** *p135*
Hanlin, Isabella 7; St. John, N.B., 1857 ***5704.8*** *p135*
Hanlin, Isabella 30; St. John, N.B., 1857 ***5704.8*** *p135*
Hanlin, James 3 mos; St. John, N.B., 1857 ***5704.8*** *p135*
Hanlin, Jane 18; St. John, N.B., 1857 ***5704.8*** *p135*
Hanlin, Joana 7; St. John, N.B., 1861 ***5704.8*** *p147*
Hanlin, John 45; St. John, N.B., 1861 ***5704.8*** *p147*
Hanlin, Margaret; New York, NY, 1866 ***5704.8*** *p212*
Hanlin, Moses 42; St. John, N.B., 1857 ***5704.8*** *p135*
Hanlin, Sally 40; St. John, N.B., 1861 ***5704.8*** *p147*
Hanlin, Susan 4; Massachusetts, 1850 ***5881.1*** *p50*
Hanlin, Susan 32; Massachusetts, 1850 ***5881.1*** *p50*
Hanlin, William 20; St. John, N.B., 1857 ***5704.8*** *p135*
Hanlon, Ann 20; St. John, N.B., 1867 ***5704.8*** *p168*
Hanlon, Catharine 40; Massachusetts, 1848 ***5881.1*** *p45*
Hanlon, Daniel 4; Massachusetts, 1848 ***5881.1*** *p46*
Hanlon, Daniel 9; Massachusetts, 1848 ***5881.1*** *p46*
Hanlon, Edmond; America, 1741 ***4971*** *p70*
Hanlon, Eliza Jane 8; St. John, N.B., 1867 ***5704.8*** *p168*
Hanlon, Isabella 3; St. John, N.B., 1861 ***5704.8*** *p149*
Hanlon, John; Illinois, 1860 ***2896.5*** *p16*
Hanlon, John 11; Massachusetts, 1848 ***5881.1*** *p47*
Hanlon, John O.; New York, NY, 1816 ***2859.11*** *p32*
Hanlon, Mary 25; St. John, N.B., 1861 ***5704.8*** *p149*
Hanlon, Milton; Arkansas, 1918 ***95.2*** *p53*
Hanlon, Thaddy 6; Massachusetts, 1848 ***5881.1*** *p50*
Hanlon, William 50; St. John, N.B., 1867 ***5704.8*** *p168*
Hanly, Ann; America, 1740 ***4971*** *p15*
Hanly, Dan 26; Newport, RI, 1851 ***6508.5*** *p20*
Hanly, Dennis; New York, NY, 1838 ***8208.4*** *p73*
Hanly, Dennis 20; Newport, RI, 1851 ***6508.5*** *p20*
Hanly, Julia 60; Newport, RI, 1851 ***6508.5*** *p20*
Hanly, Margt 20; Newport, RI, 1851 ***6508.5*** *p20*
Hanly, Mary 16; Newport, RI, 1851 ***6508.5*** *p20*
Hanly, Patt 15; Newport, RI, 1851 ***6508.5*** *p20*
Hanly, Thady; America, 1741 ***4971*** *p38*
Hanna, Agnes; St. John, N.B., 1847 ***5704.8*** *p4*
Hanna, Capp; Virginia, 1600-1642 ***6219*** *p193*
Hanna, Elizabeth 40; Wilmington, DE, 1831 ***6508.7*** *p161*
Hanna, Isabella 11; St. John, N.B., 1847 ***5704.8*** *p4*
Hanna, Isabella 20; Wilmington, DE, 1831 ***6508.7*** *p161*
Hanna, John; St. John, N.B., 1847 ***5704.8*** *p4*
Hanna, John 18; Philadelphia, 1860 ***5704.8*** *p144*
Hanna, John 20; Philadelphia, 1853 ***5704.8*** *p112*
Hanna, John 25; Philadelphia, 1864 ***5704.8*** *p157*
Hanna, Joseph; St. John, N.B., 1847 ***5704.8*** *p4*
Hanna, Letty; St. John, N.B., 1847 ***5704.8*** *p4*
Hanna, Mary; New York, NY, 1866 ***5704.8*** *p214*
Hanna, Mary Ann 13; St. John, N.B., 1847 ***5704.8*** *p4*
Hanna, Mary Ann 16; Philadelphia, 1860 ***5704.8*** *p144*
Hanna, Nancy; Philadelphia, 1865 ***5704.8*** *p195*
Hanna, Robert; New York, NY, 1816 ***2859.11*** *p32*
Hanna, Samuel 27; Quebec, 1864 ***5704.8*** *p159*
Hannabran, Dennis 26; Massachusetts, 1849 ***5881.1*** *p46*
Hannafan, Mary 30; Massachusetts, 1850 ***5881.1*** *p49*
Hannah, Alex Kelley; Arkansas, 1918 ***95.2*** *p53*
Hannah, Andrew; Charleston, SC, 1807 ***1639.20*** *p90*
Hannah, David 9; Wilmington, DE, 1831 ***6508.7*** *p160*
Hannah, Ellen 1; Quebec, 1864 ***5704.8*** *p164*
Hannah, James; New York, NY, 1811 ***2859.11*** *p13*
With family
Hannah, James 11; Quebec, 1864 ***5704.8*** *p164*
Hannah, James 30; Wilmington, DE, 1831 ***6508.7*** *p161*
Hannah, Jane 7; Quebec, 1864 ***5704.8*** *p164*
Hannah, John 20; Massachusetts, 1849 ***5881.1*** *p47*
Hannah, John 24; Philadelphia, 1860 ***5704.8*** *p145*
Hannah, John 35; Quebec, 1864 ***5704.8*** *p164*
Hannah, Margaret 33; Quebec, 1864 ***5704.8*** *p164*
Hannah, William 5; Quebec, 1864 ***5704.8*** *p164*
Hannahan, James 27; Massachusetts, 1849 ***5881.1*** *p47*
Hannahan, Patrick 40; Massachusetts, 1849 ***5881.1*** *p50*
Hannam, James 45; New York, 1774 ***1219.7*** *p203*
Hannam, John 30; New York, 1774 ***1219.7*** *p203*
Hannan, Elisabeth; Quebec, 1824 ***7603*** *p101*
Hannan, John; New York, NY, 1834 ***8208.4*** *p77*
Hannan, John; New York, NY, 1838 ***8208.4*** *p61*
Hannan, Michael 28; Massachusetts, 1847 ***5881.1*** *p48*
Hannan, Patrick; New York, NY, 1837 ***8208.4*** *p33*
Hannaven, Patrick; Montreal, 1824 ***7603*** *p89*
Hannawalt, Johann; Ohio, 1820 ***8582.2*** *p56*
Hannegan, Bridget 16; Massachusetts, 1849 ***5881.1*** *p45*
Hannegan, Mary 25; Massachusetts, 1849 ***5881.1*** *p48*
Hannehan, Patrick 26; Massachusetts, 1849 ***5881.1*** *p50*
Hannellen, Michael; Illinois, 1858 ***2896.5*** *p16*
Hannemann, Johann Caspar; Quebec, 1776 ***9786*** *p263*
Hannen, Peter; Wisconsin, n.d. ***9675.5*** *p264*
Hannifin, Michael 16; Massachusetts, 1849 ***5881.1*** *p48*
Hannigan, Catharine; America, 1865 ***5704.8*** *p204*
Hannigan, Daniel; Virginia, 1856 ***4626.16*** *p16*
Hannigan, James; St. John, N.B., 1852 ***5704.8*** *p83*
Hannock, Ann 40; Massachusetts, 1847 ***5881.1*** *p44*
Hannock, Barbara 13; Massachusetts, 1847 ***5881.1*** *p45*
Hannock, Bridget 8; Massachusetts, 1847 ***5881.1*** *p45*
Hannon, Bridget 22; Massachusetts, 1849 ***5881.1*** *p45*
Hannon, Darby; America, 1742 ***4971*** *p53*
Hannon, John 15; Massachusetts, 1849 ***5881.1*** *p47*
Hannon, Margaret 57; Massachusetts, 1849 ***5881.1*** *p48*
Hannon, Michael 60; Massachusetts, 1849 ***5881.1*** *p48*
Hannon, Patrick; America, 1889 ***1450.2*** *p13B*
Hannon, Patrick 30; Kansas, 1879 ***5240.1*** *p61*
Hannowin, Bridget 18; Massachusetts, 1850 ***5881.1*** *p45*
Hannowin, Bridget 40; Massachusetts, 1850 ***5881.1*** *p45*
Hanowin, Hugh 2; Massachusetts, 1850 ***5881.1*** *p46*
Hanpmann, Henry; New York, NY, 1850 ***6013.19*** *p73*
Hanrahan, John; California, 1860 ***3840.2*** *p14*
Hanrahan, Mary 11; Massachusetts, 1850 ***5881.1*** *p49*
Hanrahan, Michael 37; California, 1869 ***3840.2*** *p14*
Hans, Frederick; Illinois, 1860 ***2896.5*** *p16*
Hans, Jacques 37; America, 1838 ***778.5*** *p264*
Hans, Johann; Cincinnati, 1869-1887 ***8582*** *p12*
Hans, The. 27; New Orleans, 1831 ***778.5*** *p264*
Hansberger, Ulrick; Philadelphia, 1759 ***9973.7*** *p33*
Hanschen, Fred W. 30; Kansas, 1883 ***5240.1*** *p64*
Hanschen, Frederica Wme. 38 *SEE* Hanschen, John Davy
Hanschen, Gilmer Wme. 14 *SEE* Hanschen, John Davy
Hanschen, Gustav Fraugott 2 *SEE* Hanschen, John Davy
Hanschen, Jane Henriette 15 *SEE* Hanschen, John Davy
Hanschen, John Davy 36; New Orleans, 1839 ***9420.2*** *p483*
*Wife:*Frederica Wme. 38
*Child:*Jane Henriette 15
*Child:*Sophia Charlot 6
*Child:*Mary Louise 4
*Child:*Gustav Fraugott 2
*Child:*Gilmer Wme. 14
Hanschen, Mary Louise 4 *SEE* Hanschen, John Davy
Hanschen, Sophia Charlot 6 *SEE* Hanschen, John Davy
Hanscom, Alicia 26; Massachusetts, 1860 ***6410.32*** *p117*
Hanscom, Frederick; Boston, 1876 ***6410.32*** *p125*
Hanscom, Frederick 27; Massachusetts, 1860 ***6410.32*** *p117*
Hanscome, Tho.; Virginia, 1643 ***6219*** *p204*
Hanse, Joseph; Wisconsin, n.d. ***9675.5*** *p264*
Hanselman, George; Pennsylvania, 1749 ***2444*** *p163*
Hanselman, Philip; Germantown, PA, 1684 ***2467.7*** *p5*
Hanselmann, Mr.; Cincinnati, 1831 ***8582.1*** *p51*
Hanselmann, Anna Barbara; America, 1754-1756 ***2444*** *p162*
Hanselmann, C. F.; Cincinnati, 1824 ***8582.1*** *p51*
Hanselmann, Catharina; America, 1754-1756 ***2444*** *p162*
Hanselmann, Catharine; America, 1749 ***2444*** *p162*
Hanselmann, Christina; America, 1754-1756 ***2444*** *p162*
Hanselmann, Christine; Cincinnati, 1822 ***8582.1*** *p12*
With parents
Hanselmann, Christoph Friederich; America, 1817 ***8582.2*** *p60*
Hanselmann, Christopher Friedrich; Philadelphia, 1817 ***8582.1*** *p11*
Hanselmann, Friedrich C.; Cincinnati, 1869-1887 ***8582*** *p12*
Hanselmann, Hans Jerg; Pennsylvania, 1749 ***2444*** *p163*

Hanselmann, Hans Jerg; Pennsylvania, 1749 ***2444*** *p192*
Hanselmann, Hans Jerg; Pennsylvania, 1749 ***2444*** *p235*
Hanselmann, Mich. 26; America, 1853 ***9162.8*** *p36*
Hansen, A. 23; Arizona, 1905 ***9228.40*** *p12*
Hansen, A. N.; Washington, 1859-1920 ***2872.1*** *p15*
Hansen, Adam; Wisconsin, n.d. ***9675.5*** *p264*
Hansen, Alfred Otto; Arkansas, 1918 ***95.2*** *p53*
Hansen, Alfred Schneider; Arkansas, 1918 ***95.2*** *p53*
Hansen, Andrew; Arkansas, 1918 ***95.2*** *p53*
Hansen, Andrew J.; Colorado, 1891 ***9678.2*** *p22*
Hansen, Bernhard 23; Arkansas, 1918 ***95.2*** *p53*
Hansen, Carl; Arkansas, 1918 ***95.2*** *p53*
Hansen, Carle Frederick; Arkansas, 1918 ***95.2*** *p53*
Hansen, Charles; California, 1863 ***3840.2*** *p14*
Hansen, Charles H.F.; New York, NY, 1855 ***1450.2*** *p59A*
Hansen, Christian; New York, NY, 1834 ***8208.4*** *p44*
Hansen, Christian 38; Arizona, 1890 ***2764.35*** *p33*
Hansen, Claus; Illinois, 1886 ***5012.39*** *p120*
Hansen, Claus Barger; Arkansas, 1918 ***95.2*** *p53*
Hansen, Einar Ferdinand; Arkansas, 1918 ***95.2*** *p53*
Hansen, Elias; Charleston, SC, 1775-1779 ***8582.2*** *p14*
Hansen, Emma; Milwaukee, 1875 ***4719.30*** *p257*
With child
Hansen, Eugene 26; Kansas, 1885 ***5240.1*** *p17*
Hansen, Eugene 28; Kansas, 1885 ***5240.1*** *p68*
Hansen, Franz; Wisconsin, n.d. ***9675.5*** *p264*
Hansen, Hans; Arkansas, 1918 ***95.2*** *p53*
Hansen, Hans Andrew; Arkansas, 1918 ***95.2*** *p54*
Hansen, Hans Christian; Arkansas, 1918 ***95.2*** *p54*
Hansen, Hans Jasper; Kansas, 1885 ***5240.1*** *p17*
Hansen, Hans Laurence; Arkansas, 1918 ***95.2*** *p54*
Hansen, Hans Martin; Arkansas, 1918 ***95.2*** *p54*
Hansen, Hans Peter; Bangor, ME, 1893 ***6410.22*** *p126*
Hansen, Henry; Illinois, 1886 ***5012.39*** *p120*
Hansen, J.P.; Wisconsin, n.d. ***9675.5*** *p264*
Hansen, James P.; New York, 1891 ***1450.2*** *p59A*
Hansen, James P.; Washington, 1859-1920 ***2872.1*** *p15*
Hansen, John; Washington, 1859-1920 ***2872.1*** *p15*
Hansen, John; Wisconsin, n.d. ***9675.5*** *p264*
Hansen, John 30; Kansas, 1873 ***5240.1*** *p17*
Hansen, John 30; Kansas, 1873 ***5240.1*** *p55*
Hansen, Laurits Frederick; Washington, 1859-1920 ***2872.1*** *p15*
Hansen, Laurits John; Arkansas, 1918 ***95.2*** *p54*
Hansen, Louis Andres; Wisconsin, n.d. ***9675.5*** *p264*
Hansen, Matthias; Colorado, 1892 ***9678.2*** *p22*
Hansen, Michael; Wisconsin, n.d. ***9675.5*** *p264*
Hansen, Nels; Colorado, 1904 ***9678.2*** *p22*
Hansen, Nels Peter 23; Arkansas, 1918 ***95.2*** *p54*
Hansen, Niels Julius; New York, NY, 1913 ***95.2*** *p6*
Hansen, Niels Julius 22; Arkansas, 1918 ***95.2*** *p54*
Hansen, Ole; Wisconsin, n.d. ***9675.5*** *p264*
Hansen, Olof; Colorado, 1888 ***9678.2*** *p22*
Hansen, Ottinus; Arkansas, 1918 ***95.2*** *p54*
Hansen, Peter; Bangor, ME, 1882 ***6410.22*** *p125*
Hansen, Peter; Illinois, 1873 ***5012.39*** *p26*
Hansen, Peter; Maine, 1893 ***6410.22*** *p126*
Hansen, Peter Charles; Arkansas, 1918 ***95.2*** *p54*
Hansen, Philip; New York, NY, 1835 ***8208.4*** *p44*
Hansen, Rasmus; New York, 1888 ***1450.2*** *p14B*
Hansen, Severin; Wisconsin, n.d. ***9675.5*** *p264*
Hansen, Simon; California, 1885 ***2764.35*** *p34*
Hansen, Soren; New York, 1867 ***1450.2*** *p13B*
Hansen, Thom A.; Colorado, 1896 ***9678.2*** *p22*
Hansen, Thomas T.; New York, 1888 ***1450.2*** *p14B*
Hansen, Walter Emil; Arkansas, 1918 ***95.2*** *p54*
Hanser, Andrew; South Carolina, 1752-1753 ***3689.17*** *p21*
With wife
*Relative:*Elizabeth Catherine 12
*Relative:*John Christian 11
*Relative:*Barbara 5
Hanser, Barbara 5 *SEE* Hanser, Andrew
Hanser, Elias; Charleston, SC, 1775-1781 ***8582.2*** *p52*
Hanser, Elizabeth Catherine 12 *SEE* Hanser, Andrew
Hanser, John Christian 11 *SEE* Hanser, Andrew
Hanshaw, David; New York, NY, 1811 ***2859.11*** *p13*
Hansholder, Madelin 19; New Orleans, 1838 ***778.5*** *p264*
Hansholder, Martin 62; New Orleans, 1838 ***778.5*** *p264*
Hansholder, Mary 26; New Orleans, 1838 ***778.5*** *p264*
Hanshorne, Henry; Virginia, 1647 ***6219*** *p244*
Hansing, Christian; America, 1844 ***1450.2*** *p59A*
Hansler, Renhart; New York, NY, 1835 ***8208.4*** *p48*
Hansmeyer, August Carl Friedrich; America, 1872 ***4610.10*** *p122*
*Relative:*Friedrich 14
*Relative:*Henriette 10
Hansmeyer, Friedrich 14 *SEE* Hansmeyer, August Carl Friedrich
Hansmeyer, Hanna Justine Henriette; America, 1865 ***4610.10*** *p122*
Hansmeyer, Henriette 10 *SEE* Hansmeyer, August Carl Friedrich
Hanson, Adolf; Iowa, 1849-1860 ***2090*** *p613*
Hanson, Adolph; Iowa, 1850-1855 ***2090*** *p613*
Hanson, Adolph 43; Washington, 1916-1919 ***1728.4*** *p255*
Hanson, Alexander W.; Washington, 1859-1920 ***2872.1*** *p15*
Hanson, Alice Sophia; Washington, 1859-1920 ***2872.1*** *p15*
Hanson, Anna *SEE* Hanson, Hans Peter
Hanson, August; Maine, 1872-1884 ***6410.22*** *p119*
Hanson, Bert 61; Washington, 1916-1919 ***1728.4*** *p255*
Hanson, Betsy 25; Massachusetts, 1860 ***6410.32*** *p115*
Hanson, Carl; New York, NY, 1907 ***3455.2*** *p104*
Hanson, Carl; Wisconsin, n.d. ***9675.5*** *p264*
Hanson, Carl J.; Maine, 1872-1881 ***6410.22*** *p116*
Hanson, Charles; Washington, 1859-1920 ***2872.1*** *p15*
Hanson, Christian; Washington, 1859-1920 ***2872.1*** *p15*
Hanson, Emma 48; Washington, 1916-1919 ***1728.4*** *p255*
Hanson, Emma 50; Washington, 1916-1919 ***1728.4*** *p255*
Hanson, Fred Robert; Washington, 1859-1920 ***2872.1*** *p15*
Hanson, Frederick; Bangor, ME, 1872-1876 ***6410.22*** *p116*
Hanson, Frederick; Boston, 1876 ***6410.32*** *p125*
Hanson, Frederick; Maine, 1876 ***6410.22*** *p124*
Hanson, Fredrick Oscar; Arkansas, 1918 ***95.2*** *p54*
Hanson, Frnak Walter; Washington, 1859-1920 ***2872.1*** *p15*
Hanson, George; Washington, 1859-1920 ***2872.1*** *p15*
Hanson, Hans; Iowa, 1849-1860 ***2090*** *p613*
Hanson, Hans A.; Washington, 1859-1920 ***2872.1*** *p15*
Hanson, Hans Henrich; Kansas, 1875 ***5240.1*** *p17*
Hanson, Hans Jacob; Washington, 1859-1920 ***2872.1*** *p15*
Hanson, Hans Peter; New York, NY, 1906 ***3455.3*** *p22*
*Wife:*Anna
Hanson, Harold; Arkansas, 1918 ***95.2*** *p54*
Hanson, Harry Edward; Washington, 1859-1920 ***2872.1*** *p15*
Hanson, Harry Johnson; Baltimore, 1897 ***3455.2*** *p46*
Hanson, Harry Johnson; Baltimore, 1897 ***3455.3*** *p104*
Hanson, Ida; Washington, 1859-1920 ***2872.1*** *p15*
Hanson, Ida Helen; Washington, 1859-1920 ***2872.1*** *p15*
Hanson, Jacob; Arkansas, 1918 ***95.2*** *p54*
Hanson, James P.; Washington, 1859-1920 ***2872.1*** *p15*
Hanson, John; Maine, 1854 ***6410.22*** *p124*
Hanson, John A.; Minneapolis, 1870-1882 ***6410.35*** *p55*
Hanson, Nels; Iowa, 1866-1943 ***123.54*** *p22*
Hanson, Nels; New York, NY, 1904 ***3455.2*** *p52*
Hanson, Nels; New York, NY, 1904 ***3455.3*** *p20*
Hanson, Nels; New York, NY, 1904 ***3455.4*** *p55*
Hanson, Nick; Washington, 1859-1920 ***2872.1*** *p15*
Hanson, Niels; Washington, 1859-1920 ***2872.1*** *p15*
Hanson, O. H.; Washington, 1859-1920 ***2872.1*** *p15*
Hanson, Olaf Siverin; Arkansas, 1918 ***95.2*** *p54*
Hanson, Oscar 40; Washington, 1916-1919 ***1728.4*** *p255*
Hanson, Peder 27; Kansas, 1872 ***5240.1*** *p53*
Hanson, Peter; Bangor, ME, 1851-1882 ***6410.22*** *p120*
Hanson, Peter; Bangor, ME, 1883-1895 ***6410.22*** *p121*
Hanson, Peter; Iowa, 1866-1943 ***123.54*** *p22*
Hanson, Peter; Maine, 1890-1896 ***6410.22*** *p122*
Hanson, Peter P.; Minneapolis, 1874-1877 ***6410.35*** *p55*
Hanson, Samuel 15; Maryland, 1775 ***1219.7*** *p267*
Hanson, Samuel 32; Jamaica, 1730 ***3690.1*** *p101*
Hanson, Selma 25; Washington, 1916-1919 ***1728.4*** *p255*
Hanson, Sigoart 50; Washington, 1916-1919 ***1728.4*** *p255*
Hanson, William; Iowa, 1866-1943 ***123.54*** *p22*
Hanssmann, Henry; New York, NY, 1850 ***6013.19*** *p73*
Hansson, Johannes; Minneapolis, 1870-1882 ***6410.35*** *p55*
Hanstein, Ludwig August von; Canada, 1780 ***9786*** *p268*
Hanstein, Ludwig August von; New York, 1776 ***9786*** *p268*
Hanstey, James 19; Barbados, 1775 ***1219.7*** *p279*
Hanton, Darby; America, 1743 ***4971*** *p11*
Hanton, Peter; America, 1741 ***4971*** *p34*
Hantsch, Anna Regina; New York, 1743 ***3652*** *p60*
Hantsch, John George, Jr.; New York, 1743 ***3652*** *p60*
Hantsch, John George, Sr.; New York, 1743 ***3652*** *p60*
*Wife:*Regina
Hantsch, Regina *SEE* Hantsch, John George, Sr.
Hanus, John; Wisconsin, 1872 ***5240.1*** *p17*
Hanvy, Patrick; America, 1742 ***4971*** *p69*
Hany, Catharine 33; Maryland, 1775 ***1219.7*** *p265*
Hany, James; Philadelphia, 1847 ***5704.8*** *p21*
Hany, Susan; Philadelphia, 1847 ***5704.8*** *p22*
Hape, Richard; Maryland, 1753 ***3690.1*** *p101*
Hapicker, . . .; Pennsylvania, n.d. ***2444*** *p169*
Happa, John; Washington, 1859-1920 ***2872.1*** *p14*
Happel, Henrich; Philadelphia, 1779 ***8137*** *p9*
Happel, Henrich; Philadelphia, 1780 ***8137*** *p9*
Happel, Johannes; Philadelphia, 1779 ***8137*** *p9*
Happel, Konrad, Jr.; Philadelphia, 1779 ***8137*** *p9*
Happel, Konrad, Sr.; Philadelphia, 1779 ***8137*** *p9*
Happer, John; Quebec, 1847 ***5704.8*** *p28*
Happer, Margaret; Quebec, 1852 ***5704.8*** *p87*
Happer, Margaret; Quebec, 1852 ***5704.8*** *p90*
Happer, William; Quebec, 1852 ***5704.8*** *p87*
Happer, William; Quebec, 1852 ***5704.8*** *p90*
Har, Daniel 30; Maryland, 1775 ***1219.7*** *p247*
Hara, Ellen; St. John, N.B., 1851 ***5704.8*** *p77*
Hara, Sarah; St. John, N.B., 1851 ***5704.8*** *p77*
Haraghton, William; America, 1736-1743 ***4971*** *p58*
Haraghy, Edward 28; Kansas, 1873 ***5240.1*** *p54*
Haraingser, A. 50; America, 1827 ***778.5*** *p264*
Haran, Ellen 20; St. John, N.B., 1859 ***5704.8*** *p140*
Haran, Mary; New York, NY, 1816 ***2859.11*** *p32*
Haran, Sally 18; St. John, N.B., 1859 ***5704.8*** *p140*
Haranghan, Peter; New York, NY, 1837 ***8208.4*** *p32*
Harback, Hen.; Virginia, 1639 ***6219*** *p151*
Harbard, Ann; Virginia, 1642 ***6219*** *p188*
Harbec, . . .; Canada, 1776-1783 ***9786*** *p23*
Harber, Fra.; Virginia, 1647 ***6219*** *p244*
Harbique, . . .; Canada, 1776-1783 ***9786*** *p23*
Harbison, Alexander; America, 1834 ***1450.2*** *p59A*
Harbison, Henry; Philadelphia, 1816 ***2859.11*** *p32*
Harbison, Robert; New York, 1834 ***1450.2*** *p59A*
Harbord, . . .; Canada, 1776-1783 ***9786*** *p23*
Harbord, Capit.; Quebec, 1776 ***9786*** *p105*
Harbord, Gottlieb Benjamin; Quebec, 1776 ***9786*** *p256*
Harborth, . . .; Canada, 1776-1783 ***9786*** *p23*
Harborth, Ernst; Canada, 1776-1783 ***9786*** *p241*
Harbott, Richard; Virginia, 1643 ***6219*** *p200*
Harcan, Bridget; America, 1735-1743 ***4971*** *p79*
Harcan, Bridget; America, 1740 ***4971*** *p81*
Harcan, Rosanne; America, 1735-1743 ***4971*** *p79*
Harcevich, Blar; Iowa, 1866-1943 ***123.54*** *p22*
Harch, August; Illinois, 1877 ***2896.5*** *p16*
Harch, Julius; Illinois, 1885 ***2896.5*** *p16*
Harcocke, Jon.; Virginia, 1636 ***6219*** *p7*
Harcott, Benjamin 15; South Carolina, 1723 ***3690.1*** *p101*
Harcourt, Anne; New York, NY, 1815 ***2859.11*** *p32*
Harcourt, Richard; New York, NY, 1815 ***2859.11*** *p32*
Hard, Carl August; Minneapolis, 1873-1878 ***6410.35*** *p55*
Hard, Catherine; Quebec, 1794 ***7603*** *p37*
Hard, Sven Magnus; Minneapolis, 1865-1881 ***6410.35*** *p55*
Hardcastle, Elizabeth 27 *SEE* Hardcastle, Samuel
Hardcastle, Samuel 28; Maryland, 1775 ***1219.7*** *p272*
*Wife:*Elizabeth 27
Hardcastle, William 19; Jamaica, 1720 ***3690.1*** *p102*
Hardel, Barb 30; Port uncertain, 1839 ***778.5*** *p264*
Hardel, Barb. 30; Port uncertain, 1839 ***778.5*** *p264*
Hardel, Catherine 2; America, 1839 ***778.5*** *p264*
Hardel, Catherine 33; America, 1839 ***778.5*** *p264*
Hardel, Jacob 30; America, 1839 ***778.5*** *p265*
Hardel, Valentin 6; America, 1839 ***778.5*** *p265*
Hardeman, Pete; Arkansas, 1918 ***95.2*** *p54*
Harden, Ja.; Virginia, 1646 ***6219*** *p246*
Hardenbroeck, Abel; New York, 1662 ***8125.8*** *p436*
*Wife:*Annetje Meynards
With child
Hardenbroeck, Adolf; New York, 1661 ***8125.8*** *p436*
With wife
With son
Hardenbroeck, Annetje Meynards *SEE* Hardenbroeck, Abel
Hardenbroeck, Catharine; New York, 1684 ***8125.8*** *p436*
Hardenbroeck, Johannes; New York, 1664 ***8125.8*** *p436*
Hardenbroeck, Johannes; New York, 1686 ***8125.8*** *p436*
Hardenbroeck, Margariet; New York, 1649 ***8125.8*** *p436*
Hardenbroeck, Peter; New York, 1700 ***8125.8*** *p436*
Harder, Adolph; America, 1870 ***1450.2*** *p59A*
Harder, Bernhard H.; Kansas, 1896 ***5240.1*** *p17*
Harder, Ernst 30; Kansas, 1884 ***5240.1*** *p65*
Harder, Gustav; Kansas, 1879 ***5240.1*** *p17*
Harder, Helena; Kansas, 1887 ***5240.1*** *p17*
Harder, Jack; Kansas, 1885 ***5240.1*** *p17*
Harder, John; Kansas, 1884 ***5240.1*** *p17*
Harder, John F.; Kansas, 1884 ***5240.1*** *p17*
Hardey, George; Virginia, 1648 ***6219*** *p250*
With wife
Hardgrace, Ann 22; America, 1701 ***2212*** *p35*
Hardgrave, William 36; Maryland, 1774 ***1219.7*** *p212*
Hardie, Marian 56; North Carolina, 1850 ***1639.20*** *p90*
Hardie, Thomas 21; Philadelphia, 1774 ***1219.7*** *p183*
Hardie, Thomas 22; St. John, N.B., 1866 ***5704.8*** *p167*
Hardigan, Ellen 20; St. John, N.B., 1857 ***5704.8*** *p135*
Hardiman, Mary 35; Massachusetts, 1850 ***5881.1*** *p49*
Hardiman, Thomas 15; Massachusetts, 1847 ***5881.1*** *p50*
Hardiman, Valentine 20; Maryland, 1722 ***3690.1*** *p102*
Hardiment, Henry; Illinois, 1892 ***5012.39*** *p53*
Hardin, David; America, 1740 ***4971*** *p26*
Hardinent, Henry; Illinois, 1895 ***5012.40*** *p54*
Harding, Charles; Philadelphia, 1811 ***2859.11*** *p13*
Harding, Charles 21; Maryland, 1775 ***1219.7*** *p260*

Harding, Conrad; New York, 1743 3652 p60
Harding, Francis 39; Maryland, 1735 3690.1 p102
Harding, Georg; Virginia, 1642 6219 p197
Harding, George 21; Maryland, 1775 1219.7 p267
Harding, Harry 21; Kansas, 1884 5240.1 p66
Harding, Jakob; Kentucky, 1840-1845 8582.3 p100
Harding, James 17; Maryland, 1729 3690.1 p102
Harding, Joane; Virginia, 1642 6219 p186
Harding, John; New York, NY, 1816 2859.11 p32
Harding, John 22; Maryland, 1775 1219.7 p249
Harding, John 22; Maryland, 1775 1219.7 p252
Harding, John 23; Maryland, 1774 1219.7 p179
Harding, Mary; Virginia, 1635 6219 p3
Harding, Matthew 38?; California, 1867 3840.2 p14
Harding, Peter 17; Maryland, 1723 3690.1 p102
Harding, Richard 19; New England, 1721 3690.1 p102
Harding, Robert; America, 1737 4971 p13
Harding, Robert; Pennsylvania, 1869-1885 8582.2 p65
Harding, Robert 24; Jamaica, 1730 3690.1 p102
Harding, Sarah; Virginia, 1643 6219 p208
Harding, Thomas; Virginia, 1639 6219 p154
Harding, Thomas 31; Kansas, 1879 5240.1 p60
Harding, William; New York, NY, 1811 2859.11 p13
With wife
Hardke, Charles August; Arkansas, 1918 95.2 p54
Hardke, Herman Albert; Arkansas, 1918 95.2 p54
Hardld, Christopher; Pennsylvania, 1743 2444 p168
Hardman, Darby; New York, NY, 1816 2859.11 p32
Hardman, Edward; Pennsylvania, 1698 2212 p10
Hardman, John 20; Massachusetts, 1848 5881.1 p47
Hardman, L. B.; Washington, 1859-1920 2872.1 p15
Hardman, Rebecca 22; Massachusetts, 1850 5881.1 p50
Hardman, Thomas 30; Virginia, 1700 2212 p33
Hardouin, Mrs. 41; America, 1837 778.5 p265
Hardouin, Francois 5; America, 1837 778.5 p265
Hardouin, Louis 11; America, 1837 778.5 p265
Hardouin, Louis 40; America, 1837 778.5 p265
Hardouin, Ludovic 4; America, 1837 778.5 p265
Hardouin, Marie Victoire 29; America, 1837 778.5 p265
Hardouin, Prospert 8; America, 1837 778.5 p265
Hardouin, Victorine 2; America, 1837 778.5 p265
Hards, Ann 25; Maryland, 1724 3690.1 p102
Hardt, Henry L.; Wisconsin, n.d. 9675.5 p264
Hardwick, John 21; America, 1724 3690.1 p102
Hardwin, Grace; Virginia, 1643 6219 p206
Hardy, Ann; America, 1841 8893 p266
Hardy, Ann 19; Canada, 1838 4535.12 p113
Hardy, George 20; Jamaica, 1722 3690.1 p102
Hardy, Henry; Grenada, 1771 1219.7 p150
Hardy, Henry 32; Jamaica, 1736 3690.1 p102
Hardy, John; Iowa, 1866-1943 123.54 p65
Hardy, John; Virginia, 1647 6219 p241
Hardy, Robert; Philadelphia, 1851 5704.8 p81
Hardy, Thomas; Virginia, 1642 6219 p197
Hardy, Thomas 18; Maryland, 1719 3690.1 p102
Hardy, William; Iowa, 1866-1943 123.54 p22
Hardy, William; New York, NY, 1875 1450.2 p59A
Hardy, William 25; Nova Scotia, 1774 1219.7 p209
Hardyman, James 22; Jamaica, 1734 3690.1 p102
Hare, Charles; Baltimore, 1850 6013.19 p30
Hare, Charles 22; Maryland, 1775 1219.7 p250
Hare, Eberhardt; Ohio, 1798 8582.2 p54
Hare, Eberhardt; Ohio, 1798-1818 8582.2 p14
Hare, Henry 19; Pennsylvania, 1730 3690.1 p103
Hare, Richard; New York, NY, 1838 8208.4 p63
Hare, Susan; Virginia, 1638 6219 p121
Hare, Thomas; Boston, 1841 7036 p120
Hare, Thomas 21; Maryland, 1774 1219.7 p179
Hare, William 18; Maryland, 1722 3690.1 p103
Harefoote, Mary 19; America, 1701 2212 p34
Harel, Mr. 28; New Orleans, 1823 778.5 p265
Harelis, Stefanos John; Arkansas, 1918 95.2 p54
Hares, George 17; Pennsylvania, Virginia or Maryland, 1718 3690.1 p105
Harford, Elizabeth 18; Jamaica, 1730 3690.1 p103
Harford, Margt.; Virginia, 1637 6219 p107
Harford, Mary; Virginia, 1636 6219 p26
Hargaden, Patrick; New York, NY, 1816 2859.11 p32
Hargan, Henry 20; Philadelphia, 1857 5704.8 p132
Hargan, John; Quebec, 1853 5704.8 p104
Hargas, Geo.; Virginia, 1642 6219 p194
Hargen, Sjur Hallover; Arkansas, 1918 95.2 p54
Hargesefstiaem, Fred George; Arkansas, 1918 95.2 p54
Harginson, Alexander 5; Virginia, 1700 2212 p31
Hargitt, Samuel Leonard; Arkansas, 1918 95.2 p54
Hargon, Bessy; Quebec, 1849 5704.8 p52
Hargon, John; Quebec, 1849 5704.8 p52
Hargon, William; New York, NY, 1816 2859.11 p32
Hargrave, Christopher; Virginia, 1637 6219 p81
Hargrave, Christopher; Virginia, 1639 6219 p151
Hargrave, Joseph 20; Pennsylvania, 1723 3690.1 p103
Hargraves, Abra.; Virginia, 1646 6219 p246
Hargreaves, Bridget *SEE* Hargreaves, Edward
Hargreaves, Edward; New York, NY, 1857 3455.1 p45
*Wife:*Bridget
Hari, Gilgian; Iroquois Co., IL, 1893 3455.1 p11
Hari, Paul; New York, NY, 1893 3455.1 p55
Harigon, David; West Virginia, 1859 9788.3 p12
Harisky, Paddy; Philadelphia, 1852 5704.8 p85
Harison, Biddy; Philadelphia, 1853 5704.8 p109
Harison, Fra.; Virginia, 1644 6219 p231
Harju, Peter; Washington, 1859-1920 2872.1 p15
Harke, Theodore; Wisconsin, n.d. 9675.5 p264
Harken, Ann 20; St. John, N.B., 1854 5704.8 p114
Harken, Edward; Philadelphia, 1867 5704.8 p220
Harken, Patrick; Philadelphia, 1867 5704.8 p220
Harken, Peter 19; St. John, N.B., 1854 5704.8 p114
Harken, Sarah; Philadelphia, 1867 5704.8 p218
Harkens, Anne; America, 1868 5704.8 p228
Harkens, John; Philadelphia, 1868 5704.8 p226
Harker, John; New York, NY, 1837 8208.4 p48
Harket, Michael; Quebec, 1852 5704.8 p86
Harket, Michael; Quebec, 1852 5704.8 p90
Harkett, John 32; Georgia, 1774 1219.7 p188
Harkin, Ann; Philadelphia, 1852 5704.8 p84
Harkin, Anne; Philadelphia, 1866 5704.8 p210
Harkin, Anne; Philadelphia, 1867 5704.8 p215
Harkin, Anne; Philadelphia, 1869 5704.8 p236
Harkin, Barney; Philadelphia, 1847 53.26 p35
Harkin, Barney; Philadelphia, 1847 5704.8 p14
Harkin, Bernard; St. John, N.B., 1848 5704.8 p39
Harkin, Biddy; Philadelphia, 1853 5704.8 p100
Harkin, Biddy; St. John, N.B., 1848 5704.8 p38
Harkin, Biddy; St. John, N.B., 1848 5704.8 p39
Harkin, Biddy 11; St. John, N.B., 1849 5704.8 p55
Harkin, Biddy 22; Philadelphia, 1864 5704.8 p155
Harkin, Bridget; New York, NY, 1866 5704.8 p212
Harkin, Bridget; St. John, N.B., 1847 5704.8 p9
Harkin, Bridget 17; Philadelphia, 1858 5704.8 p139
Harkin, Bridget 17; St. John, N.B., 1854 5704.8 p119
Harkin, Catharine; New York, NY, 1868 5704.8 p229
Harkin, Catharine; Philadelphia, 1849 5704.8 p54
Harkin, Catharine; Philadelphia, 1864 5704.8 p177
Harkin, Catharine 25; Massachusetts, 1850 5881.1 p45
Harkin, Catherine; Philadelphia, 1849 53.26 p35
Harkin, Catherine; Philadelphia, 1852 5704.8 p84
Harkin, Catherine; Philadelphia, 1852 5704.8 p89
Harkin, Catherine; St. John, N.B., 1847 5704.8 p3
Harkin, Catherine 10; St. John, N.B., 1847 5704.8 p35
Harkin, Catherine 40; St. John, N.B., 1853 5704.8 p110
Harkin, Charles; New York, NY, 1871 5704.8 p240
Harkin, Charles; Philadelphia, 1847 53.26 p35
Harkin, Charles; Philadelphia, 1847 5704.8 p5
Harkin, Charles; Philadelphia, 1850 5704.8 p64
Harkin, Charles 4; St. John, N.B., 1847 5704.8 p35
Harkin, Daniel; St. John, N.B., 1848 5704.8 p38
Harkin, Daniel; St. John, N.B., 1849 5704.8 p56
Harkin, Daniel 12; St. John, N.B., 1853 5704.8 p110
Harkin, Daniel 20; St. John, N.B., 1860 5704.8 p143
Harkin, Dennis; St. John, N.B., 1851 5704.8 p72
Harkin, Edward; Philadelphia, 1852 5704.8 p96
Harkin, Edward 6; St. John, N.B., 1853 5704.8 p110
Harkin, Eleanor; St. John, N.B., 1851 5704.8 p77
Harkin, Eliza; New York, NY, 1864 5704.8 p170
Harkin, Elleanor 10; Philadelphia, 1853 5704.8 p100
Harkin, Ellen 16; Philadelphia, 1860 5704.8 p145
Harkin, Fanny; St. John, N.B., 1847 5704.8 p11
Harkin, Fanny; St. John, N.B., 1851 5704.8 p72
Harkin, Fanny 13; St. John, N.B., 1849 5704.8 p55
Harkin, Grace 3; St. John, N.B., 1853 5704.8 p110
Harkin, Hannah 11; St. John, N.B., 1851 5704.8 p72
Harkin, Hugh; New York, NY, 1811 2859.11 p13
Harkin, Hugh 15; St. John, N.B., 1853 5704.8 p110
Harkin, Isabella; New York, NY, 1868 5704.8 p228
Harkin, James; America, 1868 5704.8 p226
Harkin, James; Philadelphia, 1852 5704.8 p96
Harkin, James; Philadelphia, 1866 5704.8 p207
Harkin, James; St. John, N.B., 1847 5704.8 p3
Harkin, James; St. John, N.B., 1850 5704.8 p62
Harkin, James 25; Philadelphia, 1864 5704.8 p155
Harkin, Jane; Philadelphia, 1871 5704.8 p240
Harkin, John; New York, NY, 1816 2859.11 p32
Harkin, John; New York, NY, 1870 5704.8 p238
Harkin, John; Philadelphia, 1852 5704.8 p84
Harkin, John; Philadelphia, 1852 5704.8 p89
Harkin, John; Philadelphia, 1864 5704.8 p170
Harkin, John; Philadelphia, 1869 5704.8 p236
Harkin, John; St. John, N.B., 1848 5704.8 p47
Harkin, John; St. John, N.B., 1850 5704.8 p61
Harkin, John; St. John, N.B., 1851 5704.8 p72
Harkin, John 16; St. John, N.B., 1856 5704.8 p131
Harkin, John 18; Philadelphia, 1855 5704.8 p124
Harkin, John 28; St. John, N.B., 1854 5704.8 p115
Harkin, Keatty; Philadelphia, 1849 53.26 p35
Harkin, Keatty; Philadelphia, 1849 5704.8 p55
Harkin, Laurence; New York, NY, 1816 2859.11 p32
Harkin, Letty; St. John, N.B., 1848 5704.8 p47
Harkin, Margaret; New York, NY, 1866 5704.8 p212
Harkin, Margaret; Philadelphia, 1851 5704.8 p81
Harkin, Margaret 10; St. John, N.B., 1853 5704.8 p110
Harkin, Mary; New York, NY, 1816 2859.11 p32
With 3 children
Harkin, Mary; New York, NY, 1870 5704.8 p237
Harkin, Mary; Philadelphia, 1851 5704.8 p81
Harkin, Mary; Philadelphia, 1869 5704.8 p236
Harkin, Mary; St. John, N.B., 1847 5704.8 p20
Harkin, Mary; St. John, N.B., 1848 5704.8 p38
Harkin, Mary; St. John, N.B., 1849 5704.8 p48
Harkin, Mary; St. John, N.B., 1850 5704.8 p61
Harkin, Mary; St. John, N.B., 1851 5704.8 p79
Harkin, Mary; St. John, N.B., 1852 5704.8 p92
Harkin, Mary 6; St. John, N.B., 1851 5704.8 p72
Harkin, Mary 12; St. John, N.B., 1848 5704.8 p47
Harkin, Mary 18; Philadelphia, 1854 5704.8 p122
Harkin, Mary 20; St. John, N.B., 1864 5704.8 p158
Harkin, Mary 24; Philadelphia, 1854 5704.8 p122
Harkin, Michael; Philadelphia, 1864 5704.8 p181
Harkin, Michael 6; St. John, N.B., 1847 5704.8 p35
Harkin, Michael 10; St. John, N.B., 1856 5704.8 p131
Harkin, Nancy; Philadelphia, 1865 5704.8 p195
Harkin, Nancy 18; Philadelphia, 1853 5704.8 p111
Harkin, Nancy 30; Philadelphia, 1803 53.26 p35
*Relative:*William 6
*Relative:*Nelly 4
Harkin, Neil; St. John, N.B., 1848 5704.8 p47
Harkin, Nelly 4 *SEE* Harkin, Nancy
Harkin, Owen; Philadelphia, 1850 53.26 p35
Harkin, Owen; Philadelphia, 1850 5704.8 p65
Harkin, Pat; Philadelphia, 1847 53.26 p35
Harkin, Pat; Philadelphia, 1847 5704.8 p1
Harkin, Pat 21; Philadelphia, 1855 5704.8 p124
Harkin, Patrick; New York, NY, 1816 2859.11 p32
Harkin, Patrick; New York, NY, 1864 5704.8 p180
Harkin, Patrick; Philadelphia, 1852 5704.8 p84
Harkin, Patrick; Philadelphia, 1853 5704.8 p100
Harkin, Patrick; Philadelphia, 1853 5704.8 p101
Harkin, Patrick; Philadelphia, 1868 5704.8 p230
Harkin, Patrick; St. John, N.B., 1848 5704.8 p38
Harkin, Patrick 4; Philadelphia, 1853 5704.8 p111
Harkin, Patrick 21; St. John, N.B., 1864 5704.8 p158
Harkin, Patrick 30; Philadelphia, 1859 5704.8 p142
Harkin, Peter; New York, NY, 1864 5704.8 p170
Harkin, Rose; St. John, N.B., 1848 5704.8 p47
Harkin, Rose; St. John, N.B., 1851 5704.8 p78
Harkin, Rose 8; St. John, N.B., 1853 5704.8 p110
Harkin, Rose 8; St. John, N.B., 1856 5704.8 p131
Harkin, Rosey; St. John, N.B., 1847 5704.8 p26
Harkin, Sally; Philadelphia, 1853 5704.8 p102
Harkin, Sarah; St. John, N.B., 1847 5704.8 p3
Harkin, Susan; Philadelphia, 1865 5704.8 p184
Harkin, Susan 3; St. John, N.B., 1851 5704.8 p72
Harkin, Thomas; New York, NY, 1871 5704.8 p240
Harkin, Thomas; Philadelphia, 1866 5704.8 p210
Harkin, William; Philadelphia, 1853 5704.8 p101
Harkin, William; St. John, N.B., 1848 5704.8 p47
Harkin, William 6 *SEE* Harkin, Nancy
Harkin, William 25; Philadelphia, 1804 53.26 p35
Harkins, Bernard; Philadelphia, 1866 5704.8 p210
Harkins, Daniel; Philadelphia, 1866 5704.8 p210
Harkins, Hugh; Philadelphia, 1866 5704.8 p210
Harkins, John; New York, NY, 1840 8208.4 p112
Harkins, Mary; Philadelphia, 1866 5704.8 p210
Harkins, Mary; Philadelphia, 1868 5704.8 p231
Harkins, Mary; Philadelphia, 1870 5704.8 p238
Harkins, Philip; Ohio, 1840 9892.11 p19
Harkins, Phillip; Philadelphia, 1821 9892.11 p19
Harkins, William; America, 1864 5704.8 p186
Harkness, . . .; Cincinnati, 1800-1877 8582.3 p86
Harkwood, Benj.; Virginia, 1643 6219 p199
Harland, Georg; Virginia, 1642 6219 p198
Harland, John 30; Halifax, N.S., 1774 1219.7 p213
Harland, William; San Francisco, 1854 2769.4 p6
Harland, William 23; North America, 1774 1219.7 p197
Harlay, Cornelius; Quebec, 1810 7603 p64
Harle, Martin 19; Louisiana, 1820 778.5 p265
Harleston, Georg; Virginia, 1643 6219 p200
Harley, Ann 7; Massachusetts, 1850 5881.1 p45
Harley, Anne; New York, NY, 1866 5704.8 p209
Harley, Catherine; Philadelphia, 1847 53.26 p35
Harley, Catherine; Philadelphia, 1847 5704.8 p5
Harley, Eleanor 60; Philadelphia, 1864 5704.8 p161
Harley, Elleanor 28; Philadelphia, 1864 5704.8 p161
Harley, Hannah; St. John, N.B., 1848 5704.8 p44
Harley, Jane 22; Maryland, 1775 1219.7 p262
Harley, John; New York, NY, 1866 5704.8 p209
Harley, John; New York, NY, 1867 5704.8 p222
Harley, John 23; Philadelphia, 1857 5704.8 p132
Harley, Margaret 34; Philadelphia, 1864 5704.8 p161
Harley, Mary; Philadelphia, 1852 5704.8 p88

Harley, Mary 20; Philadelphia, 1857 *5704.8 p132*
Harley, Michael 10; Massachusetts, 1850 *5881.1 p49*
Harley, Nancy 32; Philadelphia, 1864 *5704.8 p161*
Harley, Patrick 30; Philadelphia, 1864 *5704.8 p161*
Harley, Phillip; Quebec, 1853 *5704.8 p103*
Harley, William; Philadelphia, 1851 *5704.8 p79*
Harley, William; St. John, N.B., 1848 *5704.8 p44*
Harley, William 9 mos; Philadelphia, 1857 *5704.8 p132*
Harlfinger, August; America, 1850 *8582.3 p26*
Harlin, Jno. 30; Pennsylvania, 1753 *2444 p167*
Harlin, Margaret 20; St. John, N.B., 1862 *5704.8 p150*
Harling, James 17; Philadelphia, 1774 *1219.7 p216*
Harlow, Agnis *SEE* Harlow, John
Harlow, Alice; America, 1698 *2212 p9*
Harlow, Ann *SEE* Harlow, John
Harlow, Ann; Virginia, 1642 *6219 p188*
Harlow, Henry Joseph; Arkansas, 1918 *95.2 p54*
Harlow, John; Virginia, 1636 *6219 p77*
   *Wife:*Ann
   *Sister:*Agnis
   *Son:*Step.
Harlow, John 30; Dominica, 1773 *1219.7 p168*
Harlow, Step. *SEE* Harlow, John
Harlow, Stephen; Virginia, 1642 *6219 p188*
Harlowe, . . .; Canada, 1776-1783 *9786 p23*
Harly, Eleanor 18; Philadelphia, 1853 *5704.8 p108*
Harman, . . .; Canada, 1776-1783 *9786 p23*
Harman, Bridget; New York, NY, 1811 *2859.11 p13*
Harman, Elias; Virginia, 1636 *6219 p21*
Harman, George 17; Maryland, 1719 *3690.1 p103*
Harman, Jacob; South Carolina, 1788 *7119 p200*
Harman, James 20; Maryland, 1774 *1219.7 p180*
Harman, Joane; Virginia, 1636 *6219 p77*
Harman, John; Ohio, 1840 *9892.11 p19*
Harman, Mary 5; Massachusetts, 1850 *5881.1 p49*
Harman, Peter 26; Maryland, 1736 *3690.1 p103*
Harman, William; Ohio, 1823 *9892.11 p19*
Harman, William; Philadelphia, 1818 *9892.11 p19*
Harmaning, Christian; America, 1845 *1450.2 p60A*
Harmata, Abraham; Virginia, 1642 *6219 p193*
Harmel, Matthias; Georgia, 1738 *9332 p319*
Harmening, William; America, 1840 *1450.2 p60A*
Harmer, Ann *SEE* Harmer, Charles
Harmer, Charles; Virginia, 1635 *6219 p69*
   *Wife:*Ann
Harmer, Stuart 28; Arkansas, 1918 *95.2 p54*
Harmon, Charles; Austin, TX, 1886 *9777 p5*
Harmon, Elizabeth; Boston, 1835 *7036 p118*
Harmon, John; Virginia, 1639 *6219 p18*
Harmon, John; Virginia, 1639 *6219 p157*
Harmon, John 17; St. Christopher, 1723 *3690.1 p103*
Harmon, Wm.; Virginia, 1648 *6219 p246*
Harms, A. G.; Kansas, 1882 *5240.1 p17*
Harms, Anna 1; Quebec, 1875 *9980.20 p48*
Harms, Benjamin J.; Kansas, 1892 *5240.1 p17*
Harms, Cath. 22; Quebec, 1875 *9980.20 p48*
Harms, Christian; Wisconsin, n.d. *9675.5 p264*
Harms, Cornelius; Kansas, 1882 *5240.1 p17*
Harms, Dirk; Illinois, 1896 *5012.40 p54*
Harms, Eliz. 2; Quebec, 1875 *9980.20 p48*
Harms, Elizabeth; Quebec, 1875 *9980.20 p48*
Harms, Frederick; Wisconsin, n.d. *9675.5 p264*
Harms, G. N.; Kansas, 1890 *5240.1 p17*
Harms, H. F.; Kansas, 1890 *5240.1 p17*
Harms, H. H.; Kansas, 1884 *5240.1 p18*
Harms, Herman; Iroquois Co., IL, 1892 *3455.1 p11*
Harms, J. C.; America, 1874 *5240.1 p18*
Harms, Jacob; Quebec, 1875 *9980.20 p48*
Harms, Jacob J.; Kansas, 1893 *5240.1 p18*
Harms, Johann R.; Kansas, 1879 *5240.1 p18*
Harms, Johannes; Illinois, 1863 *7857 p4*
Harms, John M.; Kansas, 1894 *5240.1 p18*
Harms, John Z.; Kansas, 1894 *5240.1 p18*
Harms, P. J.; America, 1874 *5240.1 p18*
Harms, Peter; Kansas, 1877 *5240.1 p18*
Harms, Peter; Kansas, 1879 *5240.1 p18*
Harms, Peter; Quebec, 1875 *9980.20 p48*
Harms, Peter 24; Quebec, 1875 *9980.20 p48*
Harms, Sebo Johanes; Baltimore, 1905 *3455.1 p48*
Harms, Wesley; Illinois, 1869 *7857 p4*
Harmsen, Heinrich; Wisconsin, n.d. *9675.5 p264*
Harmum, William 25; Philadelphia, 1775 *1219.7 p248*
Harnack, Frederick; Illinois, 1870 *5012.38 p99*
Harnack, Frederick; Illinois, 1872 *5012.39 p91*
Harnault, Mr. 15; America, 1836 *778.5 p265*
Harncour, Jean-Baptiste; Quebec, 1825 *7603 p76*
Harnekratt, . . .; Canada, 1776-1783 *9786 p23*
Harner, George; Pennsylvania, 1752 *4525 p224*
Harner, John; Baltimore, 1833 *1450.2 p60A*
Harner, Michael; New England, 1753 *4525 p225*
Harner, Michael; Pennsylvania, 1753 *4525 p225*
Harnett, Helene; New Brunswick, 1824 *7603 p61*
Harney, Joseph; Colorado, 1904 *9678.2 p22*

Harney, Michael 40; Massachusetts, 1850 *5881.1 p49*
Harnish, Samuel; Philadelphia, 1749-1773 *9973.7 p40*
Harnisoh, Anna Dorothea 6 *SEE* Harnisoh, Gottfr. Dan.
Harnisoh, Gottfr. Dan. 47; New Orleans, 1839 *9420.2 p168*
   *Wife:*Joh. Friedke. 46
   *Child:*Joh. Adolph 12
   *Child:*Anna Dorothea 6
Harnisoh, Joh. Adolph 12 *SEE* Harnisoh, Gottfr. Dan.
Harnisoh, Joh. Friedke. 46 *SEE* Harnisoh, Gottfr. Dan.
Harnold, Jacob; Cincinnati, 1869-1887 *8582 p12*
Harold, Christopher; Pennsylvania, 1743 *2444 p168*
Haron, William; Quebec, 1847 *5704.8 p12*
Harp, Madge 17; Philadelphia, 1857 *5704.8 p133*
Harp, Peter 14; Philadelphia, 1857 *5704.8 p133*
Harper, Alexander; Philadelphia, 1816 *2859.11 p32*
Harper, Andw.; Newfoundland, 1834 *8893 p263*
Harper, Catharine 7 *SEE* Harper, Christopher
Harper, Catherine; New York, NY, 1811 *2859.11 p13*
Harper, Charlotte 6 *SEE* Harper, Christopher
Harper, Christopher 40; Nova Scotia, 1774 *1219.7 p195*
Harper, Christopher 45; Nova Scotia, 1775 *1219.7 p263*
   *Wife:*Elizabeth 40
   *Child:*Hannah 15
   *Child:*Elizabeth 14
   *Child:*John 13
   *Child:*Thomas 12
   *Child:*Catharine 7
   *Child:*Charlotte 6
   *Child:*William 4
Harper, David; St. John, N.B., 1847 *5704.8 p21*
Harper, Elizabeth 14 *SEE* Harper, Christopher
Harper, Elizabeth 40 *SEE* Harper, Christopher
Harper, Francis; Virginia, 1635 *6219 p71*
Harper, Hannah 15 *SEE* Harper, Christopher
Harper, Henry 23; Jamaica, 1730 *3690.1 p290*
Harper, James; America, 1738 *4971 p68*
Harper, James 15; Philadelphia, 1774 *1219.7 p183*
Harper, Jane; New York, NY, 1811 *2859.11 p13*
Harper, John; Jamaica, 1765 *1219.7 p115*
Harper, John; Philadelphia, 1864 *5704.8 p173*
Harper, John; Virginia, 1642 *6219 p190*
Harper, John 13 *SEE* Harper, Christopher
Harper, Joseph; Maryland, 1753 *1219.7 p22*
Harper, Joseph; Maryland, 1753 *3690.1 p103*
Harper, Joseph; New York, NY, 1811 *2859.11 p13*
Harper, Louis; Quebec, 1791 *7603 p35*
Harper, Margaret; Philadelphia, 1864 *5704.8 p173*
Harper, Mary; St. John, N.B., 1847 *5704.8 p21*
Harper, Nancy; New Orleans, 1849 *5704.8 p59*
Harper, Richard; New York, NY, 1811 *2859.11 p13*
Harper, Robert; America, 1743 *4971 p100*
Harper, Robert 6; Quebec, 1849 *5704.8 p51*
Harper, Samuel 8; Quebec, 1849 *5704.8 p51*
Harper, Sarah; Quebec, 1849 *5704.8 p51*
Harper, Sarah 21; Maryland, 1775 *1219.7 p264*
Harper, Thomas 12 *SEE* Harper, Christopher
Harper, William; New York, NY, 1816 *2859.11 p32*
Harper, William 4 *SEE* Harper, Christopher
Harper, William 10; Quebec, 1849 *5704.8 p51*
Harper, Wm.; Virginia, 1642 *6219 p192*
Harpham, Robert 31; Maryland, 1775 *1219.7 p273*
Harpman, Thomas 21; Maryland, 1774 *1219.7 p181*
Harpowitz, Joseph; Arkansas, 1918 *95.2 p55*
Harps, Charles; Ohio, 1842 *8365.25 p12*
Harpur, James; New York, NY, 1811 *2859.11 p13*
Harpur, William; New York, NY, 1816 *2859.11 p32*
Harra, John; Massachusetts, 1847 *5881.1 p47*
Harrambourd, Dominique 36; New Orleans, 1839 *778.5 p265*
Harran, Alexander 7 *SEE* Harran, William
Harran, Ann 13 *SEE* Harran, William
Harran, Barbara 11 *SEE* Harran, William
Harran, Elizabeth 37 *SEE* Harran, William
Harran, Jane 8 *SEE* Harran, William
Harran, Jane 13 *SEE* Harran, William
Harran, Jane 32 *SEE* Harran, William
Harran, John 10 *SEE* Harran, William
Harran, L. B. 27; America, 1836 *778.5 p266*
Harran, Susan; Philadelphia, 1849 *53.26 p35*
Harran, Susan; Philadelphia, 1849 *5704.8 p58*
Harran, William 37; Philadelphia, 1804 *53.26 p35*
   *Relative:*Elizabeth 37
   *Relative:*Ann 13
   *Relative:*Jane 13
   *Relative:*John 10
   *Relative:*Alexander 7
Harran, William 37; Philadelphia, 1804 *53.26 p36*
   *Relative:*Jane 32
   *Relative:*Barbara 11
   *Relative:*Jane 8
Harratt, Jon.; Virginia, 1637 *6219 p11*
Harratt, Jon.; Virginia, 1637 *6219 p114*

Harre, A. M. W. Caroline *SEE* Harre, Ernst Carl Fr.
Harre, Anne Marie; America, 1855 *4610.10 p151*
Harre, Caroline W.C. Bollmann *SEE* Harre, Ernst Carl Fr.
Harre, Ernst Carl Fr.; America, 1884 *4610.10 p160*
   *Wife:*Caroline W.C. Bollmann
   *Child:*A. M. W. Caroline
   *Child:*Louise W. Sophie
Harre, Ernst Friedrich Conrad; America, 1872 *4610.10 p109*
Harre, Louise W. Sophie *SEE* Harre, Ernst Carl Fr.
Harrel, Mr. 28; New Orleans, 1823 *778.5 p265*
Harrel, Victor 28; New Orleans, 1822 *778.5 p266*
Harrias, Mr. 19; New Orleans, 1837 *778.5 p266*
Harrick, John; America, 1739 *4971 p37*
Harries, . . .; Canada, 1776-1783 *9786 p23*
Harriet, Susanna; Philadelphia, 1851 *5704.8 p76*
Harrigan, Catherine; Philadelphia, 1852 *5704.8 p92*
Harrigan, David; Illinois, 1888 *5012.39 p122*
Harrigan, Edmund 25; Massachusetts, 1850 *5881.1 p46*
Harrigan, Edward 30; Massachusetts, 1849 *5881.1 p46*
Harrigan, Joseph D. 30; Kansas, 1886 *5240.1 p68*
Harrigan, Winnefred 50; Massachusetts, 1849 *5881.1 p51*
Harriland, Ann 10; St. John, N.B., 1848 *5704.8 p43*
Harrin, John 40; Maryland, 1775 *1219.7 p251*
Harringham, Phillipp; Virginia, 1638 *6219 p122*
Harrington, Bridget 20; Massachusetts, 1850 *5881.1 p45*
Harrington, Catherine; America, 1743 *4971 p43*
Harrington, Daniel; Massachusetts, 1840 *7036 p118*
Harrington, Dennis 73; Arizona, 1898 *9228.40 p2*
Harrington, Edward; Virginia, 1643 *6219 p200*
Harrington, George W.; New York, NY, 1836 *8208.4 p22*
Harrington, Honora; Quebec, 1825 *7603 p60*
Harrington, John; America, 1741 *4971 p40*
Harrington, John 3; Massachusetts, 1849 *5881.1 p47*
Harrington, John 20; Massachusetts, 1847 *5881.1 p47*
Harrington, Mary; America, 1739 *4971 p46*
Harrington, Mary; America, 1739 *4971 p47*
Harrington, Mary 21; Massachusetts, 1847 *5881.1 p48*
Harrington, Patrick; St. John, N.B., 1841 *7036 p125*
Harrington, Ralph; Virginia, 1642 *6219 p186*
Harrington, Timothy 8; Massachusetts, 1847 *5881.1 p50*
Harrington, Timothy 50; Massachusetts, 1850 *5881.1 p51*
Harris, Adry *SEE* Harris, Thomas
Harris, Anthony; Virginia, 1640 *6219 p187*
Harris, Archibald; Philadelphia, 1851 *5704.8 p71*
Harris, Catharine; New York, NY, 1868 *5704.8 p229*
Harris, Catherine *SEE* Harris, Margaret
Harris, Catherine; Philadelphia, 1847 *5704.8 p13*
Harris, Charles; America, 1865 *5704.8 p194*
Harris, Charles; California, 1879 *2764.35 p30*
Harris, Charles; Wilmington, NC, 1817 *1639.20 p90*
Harris, Charles 62; North Carolina, 1850 *1639.20 p90*
   *Relative:*Rosa 47
Harris, Christina Boston; Charleston, SC, 1750-1818 *1639.20 p14*
Harris, Christina Boston; Charleston, SC, 1750-1818 *1639.20 p91*
Harris, Edward 37; Maryland, 1775 *1219.7 p265*
Harris, Elias; Virginia, 1642 *6219 p191*
Harris, Eliz.; Virginia, 1638 *6219 p146*
Harris, Eliza; Virginia, 1637 *6219 p82*
Harris, Eliza.; Virginia, 1642 *6219 p196*
Harris, Elizabeth 19; Maryland, 1775 *1219.7 p265*
Harris, George E.; America, 1865 *5240.1 p18*
Harris, Harm W.; Illinois, 1869 *7857 p4*
Harris, Hen.; Virginia, 1635 *6219 p35*
Harris, Hen.; Virginia, 1635 *6219 p69*
Harris, Henry; Virginia, 1637 *6219 p114*
Harris, Israell; Virginia, 1643 *6219 p206*
Harris, Israell; Virginia, 1647 *6219 p241*
Harris, James; St. John, N.B., 1849 *5704.8 p56*
Harris, James; Washington, 1859-1920 *2872.1 p15*
Harris, James 15; Philadelphia, 1774 *1219.7 p216*
Harris, James 20; St. Kitts, 1775 *1219.7 p275*
Harris, James A.; Colorado, 1904 *9678.2 p22*
Harris, Jane; America, 1868 *5704.8 p226*
Harris, Jane; Virginia, 1639 *6219 p152*
Harris, Jane; Virginia, 1642 *6219 p193*
Harris, Jane 23; Maryland, 1775 *1219.7 p253*
Harris, Jno; America, 1698 *2212 p9*
Harris, John; America, 1868 *5704.8 p226*
Harris, John; Arkansas, 1918 *95.2 p55*
Harris, John; Virginia, 1628 *6219 p31*
Harris, John; Virginia, 1636 *6219 p78*
Harris, John; Virginia, 1639 *6219 p153*
Harris, John; Virginia, 1639 *6219 p157*
Harris, John 15; Maryland, 1730 *3690.1 p103*
Harris, John 15; Virginia, 1718 *3690.1 p103*
Harris, John 20; Windward Islands, 1722 *3690.1 p103*

Harris, John 21; Jamaica, 1736 3690.1 p104
Harris, John 29; Jamaica, 1736 3690.1 p104
Harris, John 29; Maryland, 1775 1219.7 p264
Harris, John 32; United States or West Indies, 1734 3690.1 p103
Harris, John L.; Washington, 1859-1920 2872.1 p15
Harris, Jon.; Virginia, 1637 6219 p113
Harris, Jon.; Virginia, 1642 6219 p191
Harris, Joseph; Philadelphia, 1856 1450.2 p60A
Harris, Joseph 15; Philadelphia, 1774 1219.7 p234
Harris, Margaret; Philadelphia, 1847 53.26 p36
Relative:Catherine
Harris, Margaret; Philadelphia, 1847 5704.8 p13
Harris, Margaret 11 mos; Massachusetts, 1849 5881.1 p48
Harris, Mary; New York, NY, 1811 2859.11 p13
Harris, Mary; New York, NY, 1815 2859.11 p32
Harris, Mary 25; Philadelphia, 1774 1219.7 p225
Harris, Mary 26; Maryland, 1775 1219.7 p257
Harris, Mary A.; New York, NY, 1868 5704.8 p229
Harris, Michael; New Brunswick, 1821 7603 p63
Harris, Owen; Virginia, 1639 6219 p153
Harris, Owen; Virginia, 1639 6219 p162
Harris, Paul-David; Quebec, 1823 7603 p47
Harris, Richard; Virginia, 1636 6219 p21
Harris, Richard; Virginia, 1637 6219 p82
Harris, Richard; Virginia, 1642 6219 p186
Harris, Richard; Virginia, 1642 6219 p189
Harris, Richard 16; Maryland, 1775 1219.7 p272
Harris, Richard 26; Virginia, 1699 2212 p26
Harris, Richard 29; Virginia, 1774 1219.7 p186
Harris, Richard 35; Virginia, 1773 1219.7 p169
Harris, Robert; North Carolina, 1714-1798 1639.20 p91
Harris, Roger; Virginia, 1643 6219 p202
Harris, Rosa 47 SEE Harris, Charles
Harris, Samuel; New York, NY, 1811 2859.11 p13
Harris, Samuel 20; Maryland, 1734 3690.1 p104
Harris, Samuel 20; Pennsylvania, 1723 3690.1 p104
Harris, Samuell 24; Virginia, 1734 3690.1 p19A
Harris, Samuell 24; Virginia, 1734 3690.1 p104
Harris, Sarah 21; Virginia, 1773 1219.7 p170
Harris, Tho.; Virginia, 1636 6219 p74
Harris, Tho.; Virginia, 1637 6219 p108
Harris, Tho.; Virginia, 1644 6219 p208
Harris, Thomas; Colorado, 1904 9678.2 p22
Harris, Thomas; New York, NY, 1811 2859.11 p13
Harris, Thomas; New York, NY, 1840 8208.4 p106
Harris, Thomas; Virginia, 1634 6219 p105
Harris, Thomas; Virginia, 1638 6219 p146
Wife:Adry
Harris, Thomas; Virginia, 1643 6219 p241
Harris, Thomas; Virginia, 1648 6219 p251
Harris, Thomas 19; Philadelphia, 1751 1219.7 p6
Harris, Thomas 19; Philadelphia, 1751 3690.1 p104
Harris, Thomas 19; Philadelphia, 1774 1219.7 p182
Harris, Thomas 20; Jamaica, 1750 3690.1 p104
Harris, Thomas 38; Arizona, 1890 2764.35 p33
Harris, Thos.; Virginia, 1628 6219 p9
Harris, Waldo; Washington, 1859-1920 2872.1 p15
Harris, William; Arizona, 1890 2764.35 p34
Harris, William; Virginia, 1636 6219 p11
Harris, William; Virginia, 1639 6219 p161
Harris, William; Virginia, 1643 6219 p206
Harris, William 18; Jamaica, 1739 3690.1 p104
Harris, William Riley 37; California, 1873 2769.10 p4
Harris, Wm.; Virginia, 1621 6219 p4
Harris, Wm.; Virginia, 1636 6219 p80
Harris, Wm.; Virginia, 1637 6219 p112
Harris, Wm.; Virginia, 1648 6219 p246
Harrison, Alfred 47; Kansas, 1891 5240.1 p18
Harrison, Alfred 47; Kansas, 1891 5240.1 p76
Harrison, Ann 18; America, 1706 2212 p46
Harrison, Ann 19; Maryland or Virginia, 1699 2212 p24
Harrison, Benjamin 19; Jamaica, 1722 3690.1 p104
Harrison, Eleanor 48; North America, 1774 1219.7 p200
Harrison, Elizabeth 32 SEE Harrison, Samuel
Harrison, Eras.; Virginia, 1636 6219 p80
Harrison, Erasmus; Virginia, 1639 6219 p161
Harrison, Fra.; Virginia, 1643 6219 p229
Harrison, Fra.; Virginia, 1648 6219 p246
Harrison, Francis; Barbados, 1758 1219.7 p60
Harrison, Francis; New York, NY, 1840 8208.4 p110
Harrison, Francis 47; Kansas, 1898 5240.1 p81
Harrison, Frederick William; Arkansas, 1918 95.2 p55
Harrison, Georg; Virginia, 1636 6219 p80
Harrison, Georg; Virginia, 1639 6219 p161
Harrison, George; Virginia, 1638 6219 p17
Harrison, Harry; Washington, 1859-1920 2872.1 p15
Harrison, Hen.; Virginia, 1635 6219 p26
Harrison, James; New York, NY, 1816 2859.11 p32
Harrison, James; St. John, N.B., 1850 5704.8 p66
Harrison, James; Virginia, 1635 6219 p26
Harrison, James; Virginia, 1638 6219 p122
Harrison, James 19; Maryland, 1774 1219.7 p221
Harrison, James Lashly 21; Georgia, 1735 3690.1 p104
Harrison, Jane; New York, NY, 1811 2859.11 p13
Harrison, Jane 10; Massachusetts, 1850 5881.1 p48
Harrison, Jane 20; Nova Scotia, 1774 1219.7 p194
Harrison, Jno; Virginia, 1698 2212 p5
Harrison, Jno 24; America, 1702 2212 p37
Harrison, John; America, 1698 2212 p10
Harrison, John; New York, NY, 1811 2859.11 p13
Harrison, John; Virginia, 1638 6219 p186
Harrison, John; Virginia, 1639 6219 p158
Harrison, John; Virginia, 1698 2212 p11
Harrison, John 21; Virginia, 1700 2212 p33
Harrison, John 23; Maryland, 1774 1219.7 p207
Harrison, John 24; Maryland, 1774 1219.7 p213
Harrison, John 54; Nova Scotia, 1774 1219.7 p210
With wife
With 9 children
Harrison, Jon.; Virginia, 1635 6219 p16
Harrison, Jon.; Virginia, 1642 6219 p196
Harrison, Jon.; Virginia, 1642 6219 p198
Harrison, Katherine; Virginia, 1638 6219 p122
Harrison, M.; Milwaukee, 1875 4719.30 p257
Harrison, Maria 16; Maryland, 1775 1219.7 p256
Harrison, Mary; New York, NY, 1811 2859.11 p13
Harrison, Mary 17; North America, 1774 1219.7 p198
Harrison, Michael 22; Massachusetts, 1849 5881.1 p48
Harrison, Nathan 20; Jamaica, 1732 3690.1 p104
Harrison, Nathaniel; Pennsylvania, 1682 4962 p152
Harrison, Peter 24; Virginia, 1700 2212 p33
Harrison, Richard 16; Barbados, 1718 3690.1 p105
Harrison, Richard 17; Jamaica, 1731 3690.1 p105
Harrison, Richard 71; Kansas, 1891 5240.1 p18
Harrison, Richard 71; Kansas, 1891 5240.1 p76
Harrison, Robert; Virginia, 1646 6219 p244
Harrison, Robert 20; Maryland, 1723 3690.1 p105
Harrison, Robert 38; Savannah, GA, 1774 1219.7 p226
Harrison, Robt 15; America, 1705 2212 p44
Harrison, Samuel; Albany, NY, 1759 1219.7 p71
Harrison, Samuel 21; Kansas, 1881 5240.1 p63
Harrison, Samuel 41; Philadelphia, 1774 1219.7 p219
Wife:Elizabeth 32
With 4 children
Harrison, Sarah 11; Massachusetts, 1850 5881.1 p50
Harrison, Thomas; New York, NY, 1811 2859.11 p13
Harrison, Thomas; New York, NY, 1816 2859.11 p32
Harrison, Thomas; Virginia, 1636 6219 p7
Harrison, Thomas 15; Maryland, 1718 3690.1 p105
Harrison, Thomas 21; Maryland, 1773 1219.7 p173
Harrison, Thomas 21; Maryland, 1775 1219.7 p256
Harrison, Thomas 24; North America, 1774 1219.7 p198
Harrison, Thomas 28; Nova Scotia, 1774 1219.7 p195
Harrison, William; Virginia, 1638 6219 p148
Harrison, William; Virginia, 1638 6219 p159
Harrison, William 18; Maryland, 1774 1219.7 p179
Harrison, William 20; Maryland, 1722 3690.1 p105
Harrison, William 21; Maryland, 1775 1219.7 p256
Harrison, William 23; Philadelphia, 1775 1219.7 p258
Harrison, William 25; Jamaica, 1736 3690.1 p105
Harrison, William 39; Maryland, 1774 1219.7 p221
Harrison, William 49; Kansas, 1882 5240.1 p63
Harriss, John 17; Jamaica, 1739 3690.1 p104
Harriss, Thomas 19; Jamaica, 1739 3690.1 p104
Harrisson, Isaac 13; America, 1699 2212 p29
Harrisson, John 21; Maryland or Virginia, 1699 2212 p25
Harrity, Catherine 18; Philadelphia, 1864 5704.8 p157
Harrity, Flow; Quebec, 1851 5704.8 p82
Harrity, Hugh 26; Philadelphia, 1854 5704.8 p118
Harrity, James; Philadelphia, 1852 5704.8 p89
Harrity, John; Philadelphia, 1849 53.26 p36
Harrity, John; Philadelphia, 1849 5704.8 p54
Harrity, John; Philadelphia, 1852 5704.8 p96
Harrity, Madge 23; Philadelphia, 1854 5704.8 p118
Harrity, Margery; Philadelphia, 1852 5704.8 p96
Harrity, Mary; Philadelphia, 1847 53.26 p36
Harrity, Mary; Philadelphia, 1847 5704.8 p5
Harrity, Mary; Philadelphia, 1852 5704.8 p96
Harrity, Mary 25; Philadelphia, 1854 5704.8 p118
Harrity, Michael 32; Philadelphia, 1859 5704.8 p142
Harrity, Neal 20; Philadelphia, 1864 5704.8 p157
Harrity, Patrick 13; Philadelphia, 1854 5704.8 p123
Harrity, William; Philadelphia, 1852 5704.8 p96
Harrod, Henry 30; Maryland, 1774 1219.7 p179
Harrod, Jacob; Kentucky, 1774 8582.3 p96
Harrod, John 18; Maryland, 1718 3690.1 p105
Harrold, James; New York, NY, 1811 2859.11 p13
Harrold, John; Wisconsin, n.d. 9675.5 p264
Harrold, Thomas 18; Pennsylvania, 1730 3690.1 p105
Harrop, Samuel; Colorado, 1904 9678.2 p23
Harrowdin, Margaret 1 SEE Harrowdin, William
Harrowdin, Margaret 1; Philadelphia, 1847 5704.8 p32
Harrowdin, Sarah SEE Harrowdin, William
Harrowdin, Sarah; Philadelphia, 1847 5704.8 p32
Harrowdin, Sarah 5 SEE Harrowdin, William
Harrowdin, Sarah 5; Philadelphia, 1847 5704.8 p32
Harrowdin, Susan 7 SEE Harrowdin, William
Harrowdin, Susan 7; Philadelphia, 1847 5704.8 p32
Harrowdin, William; Philadelphia, 1847 53.26 p36
Relative:Sarah
Relative:Susan 7
Relative:Sarah 5
Relative:Margaret 1
Harrowdin, William; Philadelphia, 1847 5704.8 p32
Harrower, John 40; Virginia, 1774 1219.7 p186
Harrower, William; America, 1741 4971 p76
Harry, Frederick; Colorado, 1900 9678.2 p23
Harry, Martin; Philadelphia, 1763 9973.7 p38
Hars, George 17; Pennsylvania, Virginia or Maryland, 1718 3690.1 p105
Harsch, Christian Gottlieb; America, 1848 1450.2 p60A
Harsch, Jakob; Ohio, 1811 8582.1 p48
Harsch, Simeon; Ohio, 1811 8582.1 p48
Harsdorf, Frederick Gottl. 6 SEE Harsdorf, Jane Christa.
Harsdorf, Jane Christa. 27; New Orleans, 1839 9420.2 p486
Child:Frederick Gottl. 6
Child:Mary Theresa 4
Harsdorf, Mary Theresa 4 SEE Harsdorf, Jane Christa.
Harsh, Goodlive; Ohio, 1840 9892.11 p19
Harsh, Jacob; Ohio, 1838 9892.11 p19
Harsh, John; Ohio, 1838 9892.11 p19
Harsh, John; Philadelphia, 1832 9892.11 p19
Harsh, Martin; New England, 1749 2444 p167
Harsh, Martin; Pennsylvania, 1749 2444 p167
Harshaw, John; Baltimore, 1811 2859.11 p13
Harshaw, John; New York, NY, 1811 2859.11 p13
With family
Harshaw, Margaret; Baltimore, 1811 2859.11 p13
Harshaw, William; Baltimore, 1811 2859.11 p13
Harshaw, William; New York, NY, 1811 2859.11 p13
Harsinger, Samuel; Ohio, 1800-1885 8582.2 p58
Harsnett, John; Virginia, 1643 6219 p203
Harson, Walter; Virginia, 1648 6219 p241
Harssen, Catherine 22; America, 1831 778.5 p266
Harssen, Charles 29; America, 1831 778.5 p266
Hart, Andrew; North Carolina, 1830 1639.20 p91
Hart, Bridget; New York, NY, 1816 2859.11 p32
Hart, Catherine 21; Philadelphia, 1774 1219.7 p182
Hart, Daniell; Virginia, 1640 6219 p184
Hart, Danl 11; Newport, RI, 1851 6508.5 p19
Hart, David; America, 1861 6014.1 p2
Hart, David 26; Kansas, 1877 5240.1 p58
Hart, Edward 1; St. John, N.B., 1863 5704.8 p153
Hart, Eliza; Virginia, 1635 6219 p10
Hart, Elizabeth SEE Hart, Henry
Hart, Frank; Arizona, 1879 2764.35 p35
Hart, George; New York, NY, 1868 5704.8 p224
Hart, Henry; Virginia, 1634 6219 p84
Hart, Henry; Virginia, 1637 6219 p85
Wife:Elizabeth
Hart, Hugh; New York, NY, 1816 2859.11 p32
Hart, Isaac 23; Maryland, 1774 1219.7 p220
Hart, Isabella 20; Philadelphia, 1855 5704.8 p124
Hart, James 3; St. John, N.B., 1863 5704.8 p153
Hart, James 50; Massachusetts, 1849 5881.1 p47
Hart, John; New York, NY, 1815 2859.11 p32
Hart, John; New York, NY, 1816 2859.11 p32
Hart, John; New York, NY, 1837 8208.4 p35
Hart, John; Virginia, 1855 4626.16 p15
Hart, John 20; New England, 1724 3690.1 p110
Hart, Joseph; Hartford, CT, 1789 8582.1 p48
Hart, Joseph 16; Maryland or Virginia, 1699 2212 p23
Hart, Joseph 21; Maryland, 1774 1219.7 p193
Hart, Margaret; New York, NY, 1816 2859.11 p32
Hart, Mark; New York, NY, 1816 2859.11 p32
Hart, Mark; New York, NY, 1840 8208.4 p111
Hart, Martha 5; St. John, N.B., 1863 5704.8 p153
Hart, Mary 16; Massachusetts, 1847 5881.1 p48
Hart, Mary 20; Philadelphia, 1855 5704.8 p124
Hart, Mary 30; Newport, RI, 1851 6508.5 p19
Hart, Mary 36; St. John, N.B., 1863 5704.8 p153
Hart, Mary 40; Philadelphia, 1855 5704.8 p124
Hart, Mathew 24; Maryland, 1775 1219.7 p250
Hart, Matthew 9; Newport, RI, 1851 6508.5 p19
Hart, Michael 16; Massachusetts, 1850 5881.1 p49
Hart, Patrick 14; Newfoundland, 1789 4915.24 p56
Hart, Robert; America, 1738 4971 p9
Hart, Roger; America, 1737 4971 p32
Hart, Roger; New York, NY, 1840 8208.4 p103
Hart, Sarah SEE Hart, Sarah
Hart, Sarah; Philadelphia, 1850 53.26 p36
Relative:Sarah
Hart, Sarah; Philadelphia, 1850 5704.8 p68
Hart, Stephen 20; Philadelphia, 1751 1219.7 p6
Hart, Stephen 20; Philadelphia, 1751 3690.1 p105

Hart, Tho.; Virginia, 1638 *6219 p119*
Hart, Thom 17; America, 1702 *2212 p36*
Hart, Thomas; Virginia, 1638 *6219 p160*
Hart, William 3; Newport, RI, 1851 *6508.5 p19*
Hart, William 11; St. John, N.B., 1863 *5704.8 p153*
Hart, William 22; Jamaica, 1774 *1219.7 p178*
Hart, William 23; Massachusetts, 1849 *5881.1 p51*
Hart, William 27; Maryland, 1774 *1219.7 p207*
Hart, Winifred; Montreal, 1824 *7603 p91*
Hartau, Anna Margarete Elisabeth; Texas, 1845 *4815.7 p92*
Hartcliff, Edward B. 16; Massachusetts, 1848 *5881.1 p46*
Harte, Henry; Virginia, 1635 *6219 p71*
  *Wife:*Robena
Harte, Robena *SEE* Harte, Henry
Harte, Thomas; Virginia, 1600-1642 *6219 p192*
Hartel, Friedr. 30; New York, NY, 1857 *9831.14 p154*
Harten, Elizabeth *SEE* Harten, George
Harten, George; Philadelphia, 1742 *3652 p55*
  *Wife:*Elizabeth
Harten, Patrick; Philadelphia, 1851 *5704.8 p70*
Harten, Thomas; Philadelphia, 1851 *5704.8 p70*
Harter, E. 24; New Orleans, 1831 *778.5 p266*
Harter, Elisabeth; Ohio, 1811 *8582.1 p48*
Harter, John; Philadelphia, 1852 *5704.8 p87*
Hartery, John 30; Arizona, 1890 *2764.35 p33*
Hartgerink, Engelbert 23; New York, NY, 1847 *3377.6 p14*
Harth, M.; America, 1845 *8582.1 p12*
Harth, Seligmann; New York, NY, 1849 *8582.3 p26*
  With family
Hartigan, Edmond; Quebec, 1821 *7603 p59*
Hartin, Edward; Philadelphia, 1850 *53.26 p36*
Hartin, Edward; Philadelphia, 1850 *5704.8 p60*
Hartin, Edward; St. John, N.B., 1849 *5704.8 p49*
Hartin, Hugh; Philadelphia, 1853 *5704.8 p102*
Hartin, John; Philadelphia, 1853 *5704.8 p102*
Hartin, Margaret; Philadelphia, 1853 *5704.8 p102*
Hartin, Mary 20; Philadelphia, 1857 *5704.8 p133*
Hartin, Phillip; Philadelphia, 1853 *5704.8 p102*
Harting, Christian; America, 1845 *1450.2 p60A*
Harting, Henry; America, 1845 *1450.2 p60A*
Hartke, Auguste 6 mos; New York, NY, 1857 *9831.14 p153*
Hartke, Christian 42; New York, NY, 1857 *9831.14 p153*
Hartke, Johann Gerhard; America, 1840 *8582.1 p12*
Hartke, Maria 7; New York, NY, 1857 *9831.14 p153*
Hartke, Maria 36; New York, NY, 1857 *9831.14 p153*
Hartke, Wilhelmine 4; New York, NY, 1857 *9831.14 p153*
Hartlaub, Christoph; Philadelphia, 1756 *4525 p261*
Hartleb, Karl; New Orleans, 1847 *8582.3 p26*
  With family
Hartless, Saml; America, 1703 *2212 p40*
Hartley, John 18; Maryland, 1719 *3690.1 p105*
Hartley, Letitia 12; Massachusetts, 1849 *5881.1 p48*
Hartley, Richard 50; Massachusetts, 1848 *5881.1 p50*
Hartley, Tho.; Virginia, 1642 *6219 p198*
Hartley, Thomas 20; South Carolina, 1720 *3690.1 p105*
Hartley, William; Wisconsin, n.d. *9675.5 p264*
Hartley, William 25; Massachusetts, 1849 *5881.1 p51*
Hartley, Wm.; New York, NY, 1811 *2859.11 p13*
Hartlieb, Carl; America, 1847 *8582.1 p13*
Hartline, . . .; Canada, 1776-1783 *9786 p23*
Hartline, Adam; Canada, 1776-1783 *9786 p207A*
Hartly, John U.; Washington, 1859-1920 *2872.1 p15*
Hartly, Jonath 18; New England, 1699 *2212 p19*
Hartman, . . .; Canada, 1776-1783 *9786 p23*
Hartman, Charles; America, 1838 *1450.2 p60A*
Hartman, Charles; America, 1844 *1450.2 p61A*
Hartman, Charles; America, 1861 *1450.2 p61A*
Hartman, Charles 50?; America, 1839 *1450.2 p60A*
Hartman, Christophe; Canada, 1776-1783 *9786 p242*
Hartman, Frederich; Illinois, 1858 *7857 p4*
Hartman, Frederick C.; America, 1850 *1450.2 p61A*
Hartman, George; Philadelphia, 1760 *9973.7 p35*
Hartman, Justus; Ohio, 1840 *9892.11 p20*
Hartman, Matthias; Pennsylvania, 1769 *9973.8 p32*
Hartman, Michael; Wisconsin, n.d. *9675.5 p264*
Hartman, Samuel B.; Iowa, 1866-1943 *123.54 p22*
Hartman, William; Wisconsin, n.d. *9675.5 p264*
Hartmann, . . .; Canada, 1776-1783 *9786 p23*
Hartmann, . . .; Cincinnati, 1832-1836 *8582.1 p15*
Hartmann, Anne Cath. Wilhelmine *SEE* Hartmann, Carl Heinrich
Hartmann, Anne Marie Catherine; America, 1844 *4610.10 p134*
Hartmann, Anton 29; Kansas, 1887 *5240.1 p71*
Hartmann, Auguste C. Charlotte *SEE* Hartmann, Carl Friedrich Wilhelm
Hartmann, Carl Friedrich Wilhelm *SEE* Hartmann, Carl Heinrich

Hartmann, Carl Friedrich Wilhelm; America, 1891 *4610.10 p107*
  *Wife:*Caroline L C Schuster
  *Child:*Auguste C. Charlotte
  *Child:*Marie Karoline Louise
  *Child:*Karl Heinrich Wilhelm
  *Child:*Heinrich F. Wilhelm
  *Child:*Marie F. Johanne
  *Child:*Louise Johanne Marie
Hartmann, Carl Heinrich; America, 1845 *4610.10 p134*
  *Wife:*Anne Cath. Wilhelmine
  *Son:*Carl Friedrich Wilhelm
  With family
Hartmann, Carl Heinrich; America, 1857 *4610.10 p121*
Hartmann, Caroline L C Schuster *SEE* Hartmann, Carl Friedrich Wilhelm
Hartmann, Catharina; Pennsylvania, 1750 *2444 p218*
Hartmann, Christine 17; America, 1853 *9162.7 p14*
Hartmann, Elisabeth; America, 1840 *4610.10 p138*
Hartmann, Fred; Ohio, 1882-1889 *9892.11 p19*
Hartmann, Fred; Ohio, 1892 *9892.11 p20*
Hartmann, Friedrich Wilhelm; Cincinnati, 1872-1874 *8582.1 p13*
Hartmann, Georg 7; America, 1853 *9162.8 p36*
Hartmann, Heinrich F. Wilhelm *SEE* Hartmann, Carl Friedrich Wilhelm
Hartmann, Johann 17; America, 1854-1855 *9162.6 p104*
Hartmann, Johann 20; New York, NY, 1898-1899 *7846 p39*
Hartmann, Johann Carl C. Dietrich; America, 1855 *4610.10 p121*
Hartmann, Karl Heinrich Wilhelm *SEE* Hartmann, Carl Friedrich Wilhelm
Hartmann, Louise Johanne Marie *SEE* Hartmann, Carl Friedrich Wilhelm
Hartmann, Marg. 24; America, 1853 *9162.8 p36*
Hartmann, Marg. Elis. 4; America, 1853 *9162.8 p36*
Hartmann, Marie F. Johanne *SEE* Hartmann, Carl Friedrich Wilhelm
Hartmann, Marie Karoline Louise *SEE* Hartmann, Carl Friedrich Wilhelm
Hartmann, Vincent; Illinois, 1870 *5240.1 p18*
Hartnatt, Richard; New York, NY, 1834 *8208.4 p1*
Hartness, George; New York, NY, 1816 *2859.11 p32*
Hartnett, Bridget 24; Massachusetts, 1849 *5881.1 p45*
Hartnett, Cornelius 14; Massachusetts, 1849 *5881.1 p45*
Hartnett, Dennis 30; Massachusetts, 1849 *5881.1 p46*
Hartnett, Ellen 21; Massachusetts, 1849 *5881.1 p46*
Hartnett, John 20; Massachusetts, 1849 *5881.1 p47*
Hartnett, John 30; Massachusetts, 1849 *5881.1 p47*
Hartnett, Lawrence 26; Massachusetts, 1849 *5881.1 p48*
Hartnett, Mary 20; Massachusetts, 1849 *5881.1 p48*
Hartnett, Mary 28; Massachusetts, 1849 *5881.1 p48*
Hartnett, Patrick 40; Massachusetts, 1849 *5881.1 p50*
Hartnett, William 28; Massachusetts, 1849 *5881.1 p51*
Hartog, . . .; Canada, 1776-1783 *9786 p23*
Harton, . . .; Canada, 1776-1783 *9786 p23*
Harton, James; St. John, N.B., 1849 *5704.8 p55*
Harton, Rebecca; St. John, N.B., 1849 *5704.8 p55*
Harton, William; St. John, N.B., 1849 *5704.8 p55*
Hartop, Edward; Virginia, 1637 *6219 p114*
Hartopp, John; Virginia, 1698 *2212 p16*
Hartstein, Gottfried; New York, NY, 1838 *8208.4 p80*
Hartt, John Lebedie; New York, NY, 1835 *8208.4 p8*
Hartung, . . .; Canada, 1776-1783 *9786 p23*
Hartung, William; New York, NY, 1840 *8208.4 p108*
Hartwell, Edwd.; Virginia, 1637 *6219 p117*
Hartwell, Hen.; Virginia, 1636 *6219 p69*
Hartwell, John 21; Jamaica, 1732 *3690.1 p106*
Hartwig, Adam; America, 1867 *1450.2 p61A*
Hartwig, Anne M. Ellermannmeier *SEE* Hartwig, Christian Heinrich
Hartwig, Anton Heinrich *SEE* Hartwig, Friedrich Wilhelm August
Hartwig, Caroline 57; America, 1899 *4610.10 p118*
Hartwig, Charles; Wisconsin, n.d. *9675.5 p264*
Hartwig, Christian Heinrich; America, 1840 *4610.10 p119*
  *Father:*Johann Christian
  *Mother:*Anne M. Ellermannmeier
Hartwig, Friederike C. Henke *SEE* Hartwig, Friedrich Wilhelm August
Hartwig, Friedrich Wilhelm August; America, 1841 *4610.10 p119*
  *Father:*Anton Heinrich
  *Mother:*Friederike C. Henke
Hartwig, Johann Christian *SEE* Hartwig, Christian Heinrich
Hartwig, Johann Friedrich Christoph; America, 1840 *4610.10 p119*
Hartwig, John Henry 22; Philadelphia, 1774 *1219.7 p182*
Hartwig, Maria Magdaline; Wisconsin, n.d. *9675.5 p264*

Hartwig, William; Wisconsin, n.d. *9675.5 p264*
Harty, David 45; Massachusetts, 1849 *5881.1 p46*
Harty, Nikolaus; Alberta, n.d. *5262 p58*
Hartz, Lieut.; Quebec, 1776 *9786 p105*
Hartzmann, Frantz 20; America, 1838 *778.5 p266*
Hartzog, Tobias; South Carolina, 1788 *7119 p197*
Harvanek, Andreas; Wisconsin, n.d. *9675.5 p264*
Harvath, Ferencz; Iowa, 1866-1943 *123.54 p22*
Harvay, Michael; New York, NY, 1835 *8208.4 p79*
Harver, Edward; New York, NY, 1811 *2859.11 p13*
Harvey, Mrs.; New York, NY, 1811 *2859.11 p13*
Harvey, Alexander; New York, NY, 1869 *5704.8 p235*
Harvey, Alice 18; Maryland, 1775 *1219.7 p260*
Harvey, Andrew; Quebec, 1850 *5704.8 p62*
Harvey, Ann; Quebec, 1851 *5704.8 p75*
Harvey, Anne; New York, NY, 1816 *2859.11 p32*
Harvey, Anne; Philadelphia, 1864 *5704.8 p183*
Harvey, Annie; Philadelphia, 1867 *5704.8 p224*
Harvey, Anthony 14; Massachusetts, 1850 *5881.1 p45*
Harvey, Barney 10; Quebec, 1851 *5704.8 p75*
Harvey, Bessy 5; Quebec, 1851 *5704.8 p75*
Harvey, Betty; Quebec, 1850 *5704.8 p62*
Harvey, Bridget; Philadelphia, 1865 *5704.8 p200*
Harvey, Bridget 50; Massachusetts, 1850 *5881.1 p45*
Harvey, Catharine; St. John, N.B., 1847 *5704.8 p33*
Harvey, Catherine; New York, NY, 1816 *2859.11 p32*
Harvey, Charles; New York, NY, 1838 *8208.4 p88*
Harvey, Charles 13; Quebec, 1851 *5704.8 p75*
Harvey, Christopher; Colorado, 1904 *9678.2 p23*
Harvey, Daniel; Philadelphia, 1853 *5704.8 p103*
Harvey, Daniel; St. John, N.B., 1847 *5704.8 p19*
Harvey, Daniel 30; Philadelphia, 1774 *1219.7 p214*
  *Wife:*Mary 26
  With child 2
Harvey, David; Philadelphia, 1811 *53.26 p36*
Harvey, David; Philadelphia, 1811 *2859.11 p13*
Harvey, Edward; America, 1737 *4971 p63*
Harvey, Edward 32; Maryland, 1774 *1219.7 p187*
Harvey, Eliza; Quebec, 1850 *5704.8 p62*
Harvey, Elizabeth 23 *SEE* Harvey, Mary
Harvey, Ellen 9 mos; Quebec, 1851 *5704.8 p75*
Harvey, Francis; Boston, 1840 *7036 p119*
Harvey, H. H.; Washington, 1859-1920 *2872.1 p15*
Harvey, Henry; Virginia, 1640 *6219 p184*
Harvey, Jacob; New York, NY, 1816 *2859.11 p32*
Harvey, John *SEE* Harvey, Thomas
Harvey, John; New York, NY, 1869 *5704.8 p232*
Harvey, John; St. John, N.B., 1847 *5704.8 p84*
Harvey, John; St. John, N.B., 1853 *5704.8 p107*
Harvey, John 12; Quebec, 1847 *5704.8 p36*
Harvey, John 35; Maryland, 1775 *1219.7 p247*
Harvey, John 60; Massachusetts, 1850 *5881.1 p47*
Harvey, Jonas S.; America, 1867 *6014.1 p2*
Harvey, Joseph 18; Philadelphia, 1774 *1219.7 p175*
Harvey, Margaret; Quebec, 1851 *5704.8 p75*
Harvey, Mary *SEE* Harvey, Thomas
Harvey, Mary; New York, NY, 1866 *5704.8 p210*
Harvey, Mary 26 *SEE* Harvey, Daniel
Harvey, Mary 45; Philadelphia, 1803 *53.26 p36*
  *Relative:*Elizabeth 23
Harvey, Mary Ann 7; Quebec, 1851 *5704.8 p75*
Harvey, Matilda; Quebec, 1850 *5704.8 p62*
Harvey, Michael; Quebec, 1535 *9775.5 p197*
Harvey, Michael; Quebec, 1850 *5704.8 p62*
Harvey, Michael; Quebec, 1850 *5704.8 p75*
Harvey, Patrick; Quebec, 1850 *5704.8 p62*
Harvey, Patrick; Quebec, 1852 *5704.8 p86*
Harvey, Patrick; Quebec, 1852 *5704.8 p90*
Harvey, Robert; New York, NY, 1811 *2859.11 p13*
Harvey, Robert 19; Philadelphia, 1861 *5704.8 p148*
Harvey, Robert 48; Philadelphia, 1803 *53.26 p36*
Harvey, Rodger; Quebec, 1850 *5704.8 p62*
Harvey, Rose; Philadelphia, 1865 *5704.8 p192*
Harvey, Rose; Quebec, 1850 *5704.8 p62*
Harvey, Sarah; St. John, N.B., 1852 *5704.8 p92*
Harvey, Thomas; St. John, N.B., 1851 *5704.8 p78*
Harvey, Thomas; Virginia, 1640 *6219 p182*
  *Wife:*Mary
  *Son:*John
Harvey, Thomas 23; Maryland, 1775 *1219.7 p266*
Harvey, Wiloughby 38; Maryland, 1775 *1219.7 p262*
Harvick, Nicholas; Philadelphia, 1749-1773 *9973.7 p40*
Harvie Family ; Nova Scotia, 1744 *8894.2 p56*
Harvie, Alexander; Wilmington, NC, 1763 *1639.20 p91*
Harvie, Robert; New Brunswick, 1840-1900 *9775.5 p204*
Harvie, William; Nova Scotia, 1744 *8894.2 p56*
  With family
Harvy, James 12; Massachusetts, 1850 *5881.1 p48*
Harvy, Rice; Virginia, 1638 *6219 p186*
Harward, Humphrey; Virginia, 1638 *6219 p123*
Harwell, John; Virginia, 1635 *6219 p72*
Harwell, John; Virginia, 1636 *6219 p109*
Harwood, Georg; Virginia, 1643 *6219 p205*

Harwood, Giles; Virginia, 1637 6219 p107
Harwood, Humphry; Virginia, 1642 6219 p195
Harwood, John; Virginia, 1638 6219 p22
Harwood, John 21; Virginia, 1774 1219.7 p243
Harwood, Peter; Virginia, 1641 6219 p184
Harwood, Ralph; Virginia, 1635 6219 p33
Harwood, Robert; Virginia, 1645 6219 p253
Harwood, Tho.; Virginia, 1643 6219 p206
Harwood, Thomas; Virginia, 1638 6219 p146
Harwood, Thomas 34; Nova Scotia, 1774 1219.7 p194
Hary, Nicholas; Wisconsin, n.d. 9675.5 p264
Haryu, Arvid; Washington, 1859-1920 2872.1 p15
Haryu, Peter; Washington, 1859-1920 2872.1 p15
Harz, Johann Friedrich; Quebec, 1776 9786 p254
Hasbruck, Francis; New York, NY, 1838 8208.4 p65
Hasby, Robert; New York, NY, 1811 2859.11 p13
Hascao, Harry; Arkansas, 1918 95.2 p55
Hasebrock, Heinrich; America, 1848 8582.3 p27
Haselbarth, Barney; Wisconsin, n.d. 9675.5 p264
Hasemeyer, Johann; America, 1842 8582.3 p27
Hasen, Franz; Wisconsin, n.d. 9675.5 p264
Hasenclever, Franz; Philadelphia, 1775 8582.3 p85
Hasenclever, Peter; New York, 1765 8125.8 p436
Hasenjager, Anne M. C. C. Begemann *SEE* Hasenjager, Johann Christoph
Hasenjager, Anne M. C. Stuhmeyer *SEE* Hasenjager, Johann Christoph
Hasenjager, Carl August *SEE* Hasenjager, Friederike
Hasenjager, Carl Ludwig *SEE* Hasenjager, Friedrich Wilhelm
Hasenjager, Christine L. Wehmeyer *SEE* Hasenjager, Friedrich Wilhelm
Hasenjager, Christine Nolting *SEE* Hasenjager, Friedrich Wilhelm
Hasenjager, Ernst Heinrich *SEE* Hasenjager, Friedrich Wilhelm
Hasenjager, Friederike; America, 1839 4610.10 p104
*Son:*Carl August
Hasenjager, Friedrich Wilhelm *SEE* Hasenjager, Friedrich Wilhelm
Hasenjager, Friedrich Wilhelm *SEE* Hasenjager, Johann Christoph
Hasenjager, Friedrich Wilhelm; America, 1843 4610.10 p141
*Wife:*Christine Nolting
*Son:*Johann F. Wilhelm
Hasenjager, Friedrich Wilhelm; America, 1844 4610.10 p111
*Wife:*Christine L. Wehmeyer
*Child:*Friedrich Wilhelm
*Child:*Carl Ludwig
*Child:*Ernst Heinrich
Hasenjager, Friedrich Wilhelm; America, 1847 4610.10 p120
Hasenjager, Friedrich Wilhelm; America, 1853 4610.10 p108
Hasenjager, Friedrich Wilhelm Heinrich; America, 1880 4610.10 p106
Hasenjager, Johann Christoph; America, 1846 4610.10 p111
*Wife:*Anne M. C. Stuhmeyer
*Son:*Johann Friedrich
Hasenjager, Johann Christoph; America, 1850 4610.10 p147
*Wife:*Anne M. C. C. Begemann
*Son:*Friedrich Wilhelm
Hasenjager, Johann F. Wilhelm *SEE* Hasenjager, Friedrich Wilhelm
Hasenjager, Johann Friedrich *SEE* Hasenjager, Johann Christoph
Hasenohr, George; Virginia, 1856 4626.16 p16
Hasenstab, Alois; New York, 1886 1450.2 p14B
Hasert, Gottleib; America, 1880 1450.2 p14B
Hasher, Henry 16; Maryland, 1718 3690.1 p106
Haskett, Massy; New York, NY, 1811 2859.11 p13
Haskett, Richard; New York, NY, 1811 2859.11 p13
Haskins, James 13; Philadelphia, 1774 1219.7 p231
Haskins, John 28; Pennsylvania, 1738 3690.1 p106
Haslam, Margaret; Baltimore, 1811 2859.11 p13
Haslam, William; Baltimore, 1811 2859.11 p13
Hasle, James 26; Maryland, 1774 1219.7 p207
Hasle, Martin 22; New Orleans, 1822 778.5 p266
Hasle, Martin 22; New Orleans, 1823 778.5 p266
Haslem, Alexander 50; St. John, N.B., 1861 5704.8 p147
Haslem, Andrew 15; St. John, N.B., 1861 5704.8 p146
Haslem, Andrew K. 3; St. John, N.B., 1861 5704.8 p146
Haslem, Ann 4; St. John, N.B., 1861 5704.8 p147
Haslem, Bella Jane; St. John, N.B., 1861 5704.8 p146
Haslem, Ben 7; St. John, N.B., 1861 5704.8 p147
Haslem, Catherine 17; St. John, N.B., 1861 5704.8 p147
Haslem, Eliza 18; St. John, N.B., 1861 5704.8 p147
Haslem, Eliza 35; St. John, N.B., 1861 5704.8 p146
Haslem, Eliza Anne 9; St. John, N.B., 1861 5704.8 p146
Haslem, Elizabeth 75; St. John, N.B., 1861 5704.8 p147
Haslem, Jane 9; St. John, N.B., 1861 5704.8 p147
Haslem, Jane 48; St. John, N.B., 1861 5704.8 p147
Haslem, John 11; St. John, N.B., 1861 5704.8 p147
Haslem, John 45; St. John, N.B., 1861 5704.8 p146
Haslem, John 76; St. John, N.B., 1861 5704.8 p146
Haslem, John James 7; St. John, N.B., 1861 5704.8 p146
Haslem, Ruth 11; St. John, N.B., 1861 5704.8 p146
Haslem, Samuel C.P. 5; St. John, N.B., 1861 5704.8 p146
Haslem, William 15; St. John, N.B., 1861 5704.8 p147
Hasler, Jacob; Cincinnati, 1848 8582.1 p53
Hasleton, Priscilla; Virginia, 1643 6219 p202
Hasleton, Symon; Virginia, 1643 6219 p204
Haslett, Ann; Philadelphia, 1865 5704.8 p195
Haslett, Ann; St. John, N.B., 1847 5704.8 p9
Haslett, Dorethea 3; St. John, N.B., 1854 5704.8 p120
Haslett, Fortescue; New York, NY, 1815 2859.11 p32
Haslett, James 30; Quebec, 1855 5704.8 p126
Haslett, John; Philadelphia, 1847 53.26 p36
Haslett, John; Philadelphia, 1847 5704.8 p2
Haslett, John 26; St. John, N.B., 1854 5704.8 p120
Haslett, Letitia 54; Quebec, 1855 5704.8 p126
Haslett, Margaret; New York, NY, 1868 5704.8 p226
Haslett, Margaret Jane 20; St. John, N.B., 1854 5704.8 p120
Haslett, Martha 20; Quebec, 1855 5704.8 p125
Haslett, Mary; America, 1868 5704.8 p227
Haslett, Mary A.; America, 1868 5704.8 p230
Haslett, Samuel; St. John, N.B., 1854 5704.8 p120
Haslett, Sarah 24; Quebec, 1855 5704.8 p126
Haslett, William; New Orleans, 1852 5704.8 p98
Haslett, William; Quebec, 1850 5704.8 p67
Haslett, William 30; Quebec, 1855 5704.8 p125
Haslewood, Edward; Virginia, 1639 6219 p155
Haslewood, Rich.; Virginia, 1640 6219 p160
Haslewood, Walter; Virginia, 1622 6219 p76
Haslewood, William; North America, 1759 1219.7 p69
Haslington, Arthur; Virginia, 1636 6219 p80
Haslop, Isabella 21; Maryland, 1774 1219.7 p187
Haslop, William 22; Philadelphia, 1774 1219.7 p183
Hasly, John 3; Massachusetts, 1849 5881.1 p54
Hasman, James 21; Jamaica, 1738 3690.1 p106
Hason, Bridget 14; Philadelphia, 1860 5704.8 p144
Hason, Bridget 46; Philadelphia, 1860 5704.8 p144
Hason, Catherine 7; Philadelphia, 1860 5704.8 p144
Hason, John 17; Philadelphia, 1860 5704.8 p144
Hason, Margaret 19; Philadelphia, 1860 5704.8 p144
Hass, Abraham; New York, NY, 1887 1450.2 p61A
Hass, Anna F. Mercklin *SEE* Hass, Joh. Georg
Hass, David 24; Port uncertain, 1835 778.5 p266
Hass, Joh. Georg; Germantown, PA, 1717 3627 p12
*Wife:*Anna F. Mercklin
Hass, Joseph; Kansas, 1876 5240.1 p18
Hassan, Alexander; New York, NY, 1816 2859.11 p32
Hassan, Ann 16; Philadelphia, 1860 5704.8 p145
Hassan, Bridget; Philadelphia, 1864 5704.8 p182
Hassan, Francis; America, 1864 5704.8 p179
Hassan, John; New York, NY, 1816 2859.11 p32
Hassan, Mary; New York, NY, 1864 5704.8 p175
Hassan, Mary; Philadelphia, 1864 5704.8 p182
Hassan, Patrick 6 mos; Philadelphia, 1864 5704.8 p182
Hassan, Roseann; Philadelphia, 1850 53.26 p36
Hassan, Roseann; Philadelphia, 1850 5704.8 p60
Hassan, Thomas 18; Philadelphia, 1860 5704.8 p145
Hassan, Thomas J.; Philadelphia, 1864 5704.8 p182
Hassard, Edward; Philadelphia, 1853 5704.8 p101
Hassaurek, Friederich; America, 1849 8582.2 p14
Hassaurek, Friederich; Cincinnati, 1788-1848 8582.3 p90
Hasse, August; Illinois, 1867 2896.5 p16
Hasse, Wilhelm; Memphis, TN, 1869-1887 8582 p12
Hassebrock, Henry; Illinois, 1880 2896.5 p16
Hassebrock, Henry F. W.; Illinois, 1888 2896.5 p16
Hassebrock, William; Illinois, 1890 2896.5 p16
Hasselbacker, John; Colorado, 1887 9678.2 p23
Hasselberg, Abraham; New York, 1750 3652 p74
Hasselberg, Jens; Washington, 1859-1920 2872.1 p15
Hasselmann, . . .; Canada, 1776-1783 9786 p23
Hasselmann, . . .; New York, 1748 3652 p68
Hassen, Bryan; New York, NY, 1816 2859.11 p32
Hassen, Nave; Arkansas, 1918 95.2 p55
Hassen, Ollie; Arkansas, 1918 95.2 p55
Hassett, Thomas; New York, NY, 1838 8208.4 p81
Hassett, William; Arizona, 1890 2764.35 p32
Hassett, William 25; Massachusetts, 1849 5881.1 p51
Hassfeldt, John Adam; New York, 1754 3652 p80
Hasslinger, . . .; Canada, 1776-1783 9786 p23
Hasson, Andrew; St. John, N.B., 1847 5704.8 p3
Hasson, Anne; St. John, N.B., 1847 5704.8 p3
Hasson, Catherine 49; Philadelphia, 1860 5704.8 p145
Hasson, Elizabeth 8; St. John, N.B., 1847 5704.8 p3
Hasson, Fayis Mahmond 22; Kansas, 1904 5240.1 p83
Hasson, Grace; Philadelphia, 1865 5704.8 p204
Hasson, Henry; St. John, N.B., 1847 5704.8 p3
Hasson, Jane; St. John, N.B., 1847 5704.8 p3
Hasson, John; America, 1741 4971 p76
Hasson, John; Quebec, 1847 5704.8 p36
Hasson, John 9; Quebec, 1847 5704.8 p36
Hasson, John 24; Philadelphia, 1803 53.26 p36
Hasson, Letitia 10; St. John, N.B., 1847 5704.8 p3
Hasson, Margaret; Philadelphia, 1851 5704.8 p76
Hasson, Margaret; Quebec, 1847 5704.8 p36
Hasson, Margaret 6; Quebec, 1847 5704.8 p36
Hasson, Margaret 7; St. John, N.B., 1853 5704.8 p109
Hasson, Margaret 30; St. John, N.B., 1853 5704.8 p109
Hasson, Mary 11; Quebec, 1847 5704.8 p36
Hasson, Robert George 3; Quebec, 1847 5704.8 p36
Hasson, Sarah; New York, NY, 1868 5704.8 p228
Hasson, Sarah Ann 9 mos; Quebec, 1847 5704.8 p36
Hasson, William 13; Quebec, 1847 5704.8 p36
Hasstinger, . . .; Canada, 1776-1783 9786 p23
Hasswander, John 33; Kansas, 1887 5240.1 p71
Hast, George; Wisconsin, n.d. 9675.5 p264
Hast, William 21; Maryland, 1725 3690.1 p106
Haste, Richard 30; New York, 1774 1219.7 p203
Hastie, Alexander 8; Quebec, 1864 5704.8 p163
Hastie, Eliza 36; Quebec, 1864 5704.8 p163
Hastie, Hugh 11; Quebec, 1864 5704.8 p163
Hastie, James 38; Quebec, 1864 5704.8 p163
Hastie, Nancy Jane 6; Quebec, 1864 5704.8 p163
Hastie, Sarah 2; Quebec, 1864 5704.8 p163
Hastin, Jno.; Virginia, 1648 6219 p246
Hasting, Elizabeth; New York, NY, 1811 2859.11 p13
Hastings, Constant 45; America, 1836 778.5 p266
Hastings, George 18; Philadelphia, 1774 1219.7 p217
Hastings, Jane 18; Quebec, 1856 5704.8 p129
Hastings, John; Philadelphia, 1847 53.26 p36
Hastings, John; Philadelphia, 1847 5704.8 p14
Hastings, John 21; Philadelphia, 1803 53.26 p36
Hastings, John Joseph; Arkansas, 1918 95.2 p55
Hastings, Robert; Philadelphia, 1850 53.26 p36
Hastings, Robert; Philadelphia, 1850 5704.8 p65
Hastings, Sarah 16; Quebec, 1856 5704.8 p129
Hastings, William; Virginia, 1639 6219 p161
Hastings, Wm.; Virginia, 1636 6219 p80
Hastreiter, Dominic 40; Tennessee, 1850 1450.2 p61A
Hastwell, Arthur 17; New York, 1774 1219.7 p218
Hastwell, Betty 15; New York, 1774 1219.7 p218
Hastwell, Edward 1; New York, 1774 1219.7 p218
Hastwell, Isabella 4; New York, 1774 1219.7 p218
Hastwell, John 23; New York, 1774 1219.7 p218
Hastwell, John 46; New York, 1774 1219.7 p218
Hastwell, Joseph 21; New York, 1774 1219.7 p218
Hastwell, Margaret 5; New York, 1774 1219.7 p218
Hastwell, Mary 12; New York, 1774 1219.7 p218
Hastwell, Mary 34; New York, 1774 1219.7 p218
Hastwell, Richard 7; New York, 1774 1219.7 p218
Hastwell, Robert 19; New York, 1774 1219.7 p218
Hastwell, Thomas 9; New York, 1774 1219.7 p218
Hasty, John 3; Massachusetts, 1849 5881.1 p47
Hasty, John 9; Massachusetts, 1849 5881.1 p47
Hasty, Mary 6; Massachusetts, 1849 5881.1 p49
Hasty, Mary 40; Massachusetts, 1849 5881.1 p49
Hasty, Selia 11; Massachusetts, 1849 5881.1 p50
Hatch, Matthew; Georgia, 1765 1219.7 p109
Hatch, Thomas; New York, NY, 1816 2859.11 p32
Hatcher, Mr.; Quebec, 1815 9229.18 p75
Hatcher, Sarah; Virginia, 1632 6219 p180
Hatcher, Tho.; Virginia, 1645 6219 p232
Hatcher, William; Virginia, 1636 6219 p74
Hatcher, William; Virginia, 1637 6219 p84
Hatchett, Elizabeth; Virginia, 1642 6219 p195
Hatchway, Thomas; Virginia, 1643 6219 p207
Hatchwell, James 18; Philadelphia, 1774 1219.7 p197
Hatcock, Tho.; Virginia, 1635 6219 p69
Hate, Susan; Virginia, 1637 6219 p113
Hatfield, Edward 31; Maryland, 1774 1219.7 p179
Hatfield, Henry; Iowa, 1866-1943 123.54 p22
Hatfield, Thomas 24; Maryland, 1734 3690.1 p106
Hathaway, Matthias; Boston, 1761 1219.7 p80
Hathaway, Thomas; Virginia, 1638 6219 p146
Hathazi, John; Arkansas, 1918 95.2 p55
Hatherell, William 22; St. Christopher, 1736 3690.1 p106
Hatine, Henry 39; New Orleans, 1838 778.5 p266
Hatred, Mary; Virginia, 1637 6219 p113
Hatrick, Anne 30; St. John, N.B., 1854 5704.8 p114
Hatrick, Catherine 4; St. John, N.B., 1854 5704.8 p115
Hatrick, Eliza Ann 12; St. John, N.B., 1854 5704.8 p114
Hatrick, Ellen; Philadelphia, 1850 53.26 p36
Hatrick, Ellen; Philadelphia, 1850 5704.8 p68
Hatrick, Isabella 8; St. John, N.B., 1854 5704.8 p115
Hatrick, James 58; St. John, N.B., 1854 5704.8 p114
Hatrick, John 2 mos; St. John, N.B., 1854 5704.8 p115
Hatrick, John 40; St. John, N.B., 1853 5704.8 p110
Hatrick, Margaret 6; St. John, N.B., 1854 5704.8 p115

Hatrick, Matilda Jane 10; St. John, N.B., 1854 ***5704.8*** *p114*
Hatrick, William James 2; St. John, N.B., 1854 ***5704.8*** *p115*
Hatschenberger, . . .; Canada, 1776-1783 ***9786*** *p23*
Hattendorf, Eckhard; Philadelphia, 1779 ***8137*** *p9*
Hattendorf, Henry; America, 1853 ***1450.2*** *p61A*
Hatter, George 18; Kansas, 1896 ***5240.1*** *p18*
Hatter, George 18; Kansas, 1896 ***5240.1*** *p80*
Hatter, Leonard 21; Kansas, 1893 ***5240.1*** *p18*
Hatter, Leonhardt 21; Kansas, 1893 ***5240.1*** *p78*
Hattersley, Josiah 21; Maryland, 1775 ***1219.7*** *p247*
Hatteson, Christian; Arizona, 1883 ***2764.35*** *p30*
Hattfield, Thomas; Virginia, 1637 ***6219*** *p16*
Hattich, Bartholomew; California, 1877 ***2764.35*** *p30*
Hatton, James; Nevada, 1876 ***2764.35*** *p36*
Hatton, James 14; America, 1702 ***2212*** *p37*
Hatton, Jeffery; Virginia, 1635 ***6219*** *p20*
Hatton, John; New York, NY, 1836 ***8208.4*** *p16*
Hatton, John; Virginia, 1638 ***6219*** *p117*
Hatton, John; Virginia, 1643 ***6219*** *p206*
Hatton, Richard 29; America, 1702 ***2212*** *p36*
Hatton, Sarah; New York, NY, 1869 ***5704.8*** *p235*
Hatton, Tho.; Virginia, 1638 ***6219*** *p160*
Hatton, William 21; Maryland, 1775 ***1219.7*** *p266*
Hattridge, Alexander; America, 1804 ***1639.20*** *p91*
Hattridge, William; North Carolina, 1781-1809 ***1639.20*** *p91*
Hatty, Samuel; Philadelphia, 1867 ***5704.8*** *p217*
Hatzfeld, Col.; Halifax, N.S., 1781-1783 ***9786*** *p270*
Hatzinger, Anton; Wisconsin, n.d. ***9675.5*** *p264*
Haubald, Ernst F.; Wisconsin, n.d. ***9675.5*** *p264*
Haubensacker, Catharina; Pennsylvania, 1753 ***2444*** *p222*
Hauber, Jacob; South Carolina, 1788 ***7119*** *p204*
Hauberlin, F.; Quebec, 1776 ***9786*** *p105*
Haubrich, Adam; America, 1867 ***1450.2*** *p61A*
Haubrock, Marg. Elisabeth; America, 1847 ***4610.10*** *p151*
Hauck, Barbara *SEE* Hauck, Johann Peter
Hauck, Bartholomaeus; America, 1828 ***8582.1*** *p13*
Hauck, Bartholomaeus; Illinois, 1845 ***8582.2*** *p50*
Hauck, Caspar Anton *SEE* Hauck, Johann Peter
Hauck, Georg Peter *SEE* Hauck, Johann Peter
Hauck, George; Wisconsin, n.d. ***9675.5*** *p264*
Hauck, Hans Jerg; Port uncertain, 1738 ***3627*** *p19*
With wife & 6 children
Hauck, Johan Petter; Philadelphia, 1763 ***2854*** *p45*
Hauck, Johann Peter; America, 1764 ***2854*** *p45*
*Wife:*Barbara
*Child:*Georg Peter
*Child:*Wilhelm
*Child:*Caspar Anton
*Child:*Maria Susanna
*Child:*Nicolaus
Hauck, Johann Valatin; Philadelphia, 1763 ***2854*** *p45*
Hauck, John; Cincinnati, 1869-1887 ***8582*** *p12*
Hauck, John Peter; America, 1857 ***1450.2*** *p61A*
Hauck, Maria Susanna *SEE* Hauck, Johann Peter
Hauck, Michael; New York, 1852 ***2853.7*** *p107*
Hauck, N.; Ohio, 1839 ***8582.1*** *p13*
Hauck, Nicolaus *SEE* Hauck, Johann Peter
Hauck, Wilhelm *SEE* Hauck, Johann Peter
Haucke, Johann Michael; Wisconsin, n.d. ***9675.5*** *p264*
Haue, . . .; Canada, 1776-1783 ***9786*** *p23*
Haueisen, Robert 26; Indiana, 1877 ***1450.2*** *p61A*
Haueisen, William; America, 1854 ***1450.2*** *p61A*
Hauenberg, Zamach 24; New York, NY, 1878 ***9253*** *p46*
Hauer, . . .; New York, 1854 ***3702.7*** *p371*
Hauer, Michael; New York, NY, 1839 ***8582.1*** *p13*
Hauf, . . .; Canada, 1776-1783 ***9786*** *p23*
Hauf, Michael; Arkansas, 1918 ***95.2*** *p55*
Haufler, John; America, 1853 ***1450.2*** *p62A*
Haug, Anna Sara Negle *SEE* Haug, Georg Friedrich
Haug, August; Indianapolis, 1883 ***1450.2*** *p14B*
Haug, Catharina Magdalena *SEE* Haug, Georg Friedrich
Haug, Christina; Pennsylvania, 1751 ***2444*** *p165*
Haug, Georg Friedrich; Pennsylvania, 1750 ***2444*** *p163*
*Wife:*Anna Sara Negle
*Child:*Catharina Magdalena
*Child:*Johann Friedrich
*Child:*Johann Georg
Haug, Hans Jerg; Port uncertain, 1738 ***3627*** *p19*
With wife & 6 children
Haug, Jacob; Cincinnati, 1869-1887 ***8582*** *p13*
Haug, Johann Friedrich *SEE* Haug, Georg Friedrich
Haug, Johann Georg *SEE* Haug, Georg Friedrich
Haughey, Benjamin; New York, NY, 1811 ***2859.11*** *p13*
Haughey, Catharine; Philadelphia, 1866 ***5704.8*** *p209*
Haughey, John; Philadelphia, 1850 ***5704.8*** *p64*
Haughey, John; Philadelphia, 1865 ***5704.8*** *p200*
Haughey, John; Philadelphia, 1866 ***5704.8*** *p209*
Haughey, Margaret 22; Philadelphia, 1857 ***5704.8*** *p132*
Haughey, Mary; Philadelphia, 1865 ***5704.8*** *p189*
Haughey, Peter; New York, NY, 1811 ***2859.11*** *p13*
Haughey, Thomas; New York, NY, 1864 ***5704.8*** *p172*
Haughey, William; New York, NY, 1838 ***8208.4*** *p68*
Hauk, John Peter; America, 1857 ***1450.2*** *p61A*
Haukenhaupt, John; Wisconsin, n.d. ***9675.5*** *p264*
Haulon, P. J. Siver 25; New Orleans, 1838 ***778.5*** *p266*
Haulun, Mr.; Port uncertain, 1839 ***778.5*** *p267*
Haumann, . . .; Canada, 1776-1783 ***9786*** *p23*
Haun, Henry; Philadelphia, 1758 ***9973.7*** *p33*
Haunss, Ziriack; Indiana, 1890 ***1450.2*** *p14B*
Haupson, Ralph; Iowa, 1866-1943 ***123.54*** *p22*
Haupt, Charles; America, 1881 ***1450.2*** *p62A*
Haupt, Johannes; Trenton, NJ, 1776 ***8137*** *p9*
Haupt, Peter; Wisconsin, n.d. ***9675.5*** *p264*
Hauptmeier, Mr.; America, 1876-1893 ***4610.10*** *p103*
Hauptmeier, Anna M Caroline Wilhelmine; America, 1887 ***4610.10*** *p102*
Hauptmeier, Ernst Heinrich; America, 1893 ***4610.10*** *p103*
Hauptmeier, Ernst Heinrich Friedrich; America, 1887 ***4610.10*** *p102*
Hauraham, Philip; America, 1739 ***4971*** *p40*
Haurat, Alfred 14; Louisiana, 1839 ***778.5*** *p267*
Hauri, Hans; Pennsylvania, 1709-1710 ***4480*** *p311*
Haus, Frons 30; America, 1836 ***778.5*** *p267*
Haus, Peter; Philadelphia, 1760 ***9973.7*** *p35*
Haus, Rosina; New York, 1749 ***3652*** *p73*
Hausch, Catharina *SEE* Hausch, Johannes
Hausch, Hans Adam *SEE* Hausch, Johannes
Hausch, Johannes; Pennsylvania, 1750 ***2444*** *p163*
*Child:*Hans Adam
*Child:*Maria Barbara
*Child:*Catharina
Hausch, Maria Barbara *SEE* Hausch, Johannes
Hauschild, Carle; America, 1866 ***1450.2*** *p62A*
Hausdorf, Eduard; Illinois, 1883 ***2896.5*** *p16*
Hausee, Henrich; Philadelphia, 1779 ***8137*** *p9*
Hauser, Casper 38?; Arizona, 1890 ***2764.35*** *p32*
Hauser, Eberhard 24; Kansas, 1883 ***5240.1*** *p64*
Hauser, Elias; Charleston, SC, 1775-1779 ***8582.2*** *p14*
Hauser, Friedrich 31; Philadelphia, 1805 ***2444*** *p187*
Hauser, Klemenz 23; Kansas, 1883 ***5240.1*** *p64*
Hauser, Philipp; Cincinnati, 1788-1848 ***8582.3*** *p90*
Hausman, Johannes; Pennsylvania, 1749 ***2444*** *p163*
Hausman, John; Pennsylvania, 1750 ***2444*** *p163*
Hausman, Joseph; Pennsylvania, 1749 ***2444*** *p163*
Hausman, Paulus; Pennsylvania, 1749 ***2444*** *p163*
Hausmann, David; Pennsylvania, 1752 ***2444*** *p163*
Hausmann, Frederick Ludwig; Baltimore, 1842 ***2896.5*** *p16*
Haussarek, Friederich; America, 1849 ***8582.2*** *p14*
Hausserek, Friederich; America, 1849 ***8582.2*** *p14*
Haussler, Joh. Gg. 17; America, 1854-1855 ***9162.6*** *p105*
Haussmann, David; Pennsylvania, 1751 ***2444*** *p163*
*Wife:*Elisabetha
*Child:*Johann Michael
*Child:*Margaretha
Haussmann, Elisabetha *SEE* Haussmann, David
Haussmann, Jacob; Port uncertain, 1743-1800 ***2444*** *p163*
Haussmann, Johann Georg *SEE* Haussmann, Johannes
Haussmann, Johann Michael *SEE* Haussmann, David
Haussmann, Johannes; Pennsylvania, 1750 ***2444*** *p163*
*Wife:*Margaretha
*Child:*Johann Georg
Haussmann, Margaretha *SEE* Haussmann, David
Haussmann, Margaretha *SEE* Haussmann, Johannes
Haussmann, Walburga; Pennsylvania, 1752 ***2444*** *p218*
Haust, Henrich; Philadelphia, 1779 ***8137*** *p9*
Haust, Paulus; Lancaster, PA, 1780 ***8137*** *p9*
Haut, Cretien 16; America, 1836 ***778.5*** *p267*
Hauteloup, Mathurin 34; America, 1836 ***778.5*** *p267*
Hauton, Mathew; Virginia, 1637 ***6219*** *p81*
Havegan, Owen 40; Massachusetts, 1849 ***5881.1*** *p49*
Havekotte, . . .; Cincinnati, 1826 ***8582.1*** *p51*
Havelin, Daniel 22; St. John, N.B., 1862 ***5704.8*** *p150*
Havelin, John; St. John, N.B., 1847 ***5704.8*** *p4*
Havelin, Nelis; St. John, N.B., 1847 ***5704.8*** *p18*
Havelin, William; St. John, N.B., 1847 ***5704.8*** *p4*
Haveline, . . .; Canada, 1776-1783 ***9786*** *p23*
Havell, Henry 25; Philadelphia, 1774 ***1219.7*** *p228*
Haver, Edward H. 37; Harris Co., TX, 1898 ***6254*** *p4*
Haverell, Georg; Virginia, 1636 ***6219*** *p78*
Haverly, Bridget 6; Massachusetts, 1849 ***5881.1*** *p45*
Haverly, John 10; Massachusetts, 1849 ***5881.1*** *p47*
Haverstock, Thomas 42?; Arizona, 1890 ***2764.35*** *p33*
Haverstraw, Christian; Wisconsin, n.d. ***9675.5*** *p264*
Havert, William; Virginia, 1639 ***6219*** *p18*
Havert, William; Virginia, 1639 ***6219*** *p157*
Havert, Wm.; Virginia, 1637 ***6219*** *p113*
Haverty, Elizabeth; America, 1743 ***4971*** *p18*
Havey, Patrick; America, 1841 ***7036*** *p125*
Havich, George; Wisconsin, n.d. ***9675.5*** *p263*
Havland, John; Arkansas, 1918 ***95.2*** *p55*
Havlin, Biddy; St. John, N.B., 1847 ***5704.8*** *p21*
Havlin, James; St. John, N.B., 1849 ***5704.8*** *p48*
Havord, Alice; Virginia, 1641 ***6219*** *p185*
Haw, Francis 24; Virginia, 1774 ***1219.7*** *p201*
Haw, Hamlett; Virginia, 1642 ***6219*** *p191*
Haw, John; Philadelphia, 1849 ***5704.8*** *p54*
Haw, Peter; Illinois, 1860 ***5012.39*** *p89*
Haward, Ben.; Virginia, 1646 ***6219*** *p242*
Haward, John; Virginia, 1642 ***6219*** *p195*
Haward, Jon.; Virginia, 1636 ***6219*** *p34*
Hawbridge, Jane 39 *SEE* Hawbridge, Samuel
Hawbridge, Samuel 40; New York, 1774 ***1219.7*** *p202*
*Wife:*Jane 39
Hawerkost, Henry; Wisconsin, n.d. ***9675.5*** *p264*
Hawes, Michael 18; Antigua (Antego), 1728 ***3690.1*** *p106*
Hawes, Richard; Virginia, 1639 ***6219*** *p158*
Hawiar, Walter; Arkansas, 1918 ***95.2*** *p55*
Hawke, John S.; Pennsylvania, 1890 ***1450.2*** *p14B*
Hawker, Richard 16; Maryland, 1733 ***3690.1*** *p106*
Hawkes, Ellin; Virginia, 1643 ***6219*** *p23*
Hawkes, Mary; Virginia, 1635 ***6219*** *p71*
Hawkes, Mary; Virginia, 1643 ***6219*** *p23*
Hawkes, William; Illinois, 1870 ***5012.38*** *p99*
Hawkin, Robert; Virginia, 1639 ***6219*** *p151*
Hawkins, Edward; Iowa, 1866-1943 ***123.54*** *p22*
Hawkins, Hen.; Virginia, 1644 ***6219*** *p208*
Hawkins, Henry; Virginia, 1648 ***6219*** *p251*
Hawkins, Henry 18; West Indies, 1722 ***3690.1*** *p106*
Hawkins, J. A.; Iowa, 1866-1943 ***123.54*** *p22*
Hawkins, James; Virginia, 1639 ***6219*** *p161*
Hawkins, John; Jamaica, 1751 ***1219.7*** *p8*
Hawkins, John; New York, 1767 ***1219.7*** *p129*
Hawkins, John; San Francisco, 1850 ***4914.15*** *p10*
Hawkins, John 15; St. John Island, 1775 ***1219.7*** *p273*
Hawkins, John Lacy; New York, 1761 ***1219.7*** *p80*
Hawkins, Phillipp; Virginia, 1643 ***6219*** *p201*
Hawkins, Sampson; Jamaica, 1753 ***1219.7*** *p25*
Hawkins, Sampson; Jamaica, 1753 ***3690.1*** *p106*
Hawkins, Thomas; New York, NY, 1816 ***2859.11*** *p32*
Hawkins, William 19; Jamaica, 1750 ***3690.1*** *p106*
Hawkins, William 19; Jamaica, 1751 ***1219.7*** *p1*
Hawkins, William 21; Philadelphia, 1775 ***1219.7*** *p274*
Hawkins, Wm.; Virginia, 1637 ***6219*** *p83*
Hawkinson, Carl Berger; Arkansas, 1918 ***95.2*** *p55*
Hawkinson, Wm.; Virginia, 1635 ***6219*** *p69*
Hawks, Eliza *SEE* Hawks, George
Hawks, Eliza; Philadelphia, 1847 ***5704.8*** *p1*
Hawks, George; Philadelphia, 1847 ***53.26*** *p36*
*Relative:*Isabella
*Relative:*Eliza
*Relative:*Mary Ann 11
*Relative:*George 10
*Relative:*John 4
*Relative:*William 2
*Relative:*Martha 3 mos
*Relative:*Isabella 6
Hawks, George; Philadelphia, 1847 ***5704.8*** *p1*
Hawks, George 10 *SEE* Hawks, George
Hawks, George 10; Philadelphia, 1847 ***5704.8*** *p1*
Hawks, Isabella *SEE* Hawks, George
Hawks, Isabella; Philadelphia, 1847 ***5704.8*** *p1*
Hawks, Isabella 6 *SEE* Hawks, George
Hawks, Isabella 6; Philadelphia, 1847 ***5704.8*** *p1*
Hawks, John 4 *SEE* Hawks, George
Hawks, John 4; Philadelphia, 1847 ***5704.8*** *p1*
Hawks, Martha 3 mos *SEE* Hawks, George
Hawks, Martha 6 mos; Philadelphia, 1847 ***5704.8*** *p1*
Hawks, Mary Ann 11 *SEE* Hawks, George
Hawks, Mary Ann 11; Philadelphia, 1847 ***5704.8*** *p1*
Hawks, Sarah; New York, NY, 1867 ***5704.8*** *p218*
Hawks, William 2 *SEE* Hawks, George
Hawks, William 2; Philadelphia, 1847 ***5704.8*** *p1*
Hawksford, William 21; Maryland, 1775 ***1219.7*** *p267*
Hawkshaw, Tho; America, 1698 ***2212*** *p13*
Hawkshaw, Thos; Virginia, 1698 ***2212*** *p15*
Hawksworth, William 25; Jamaica, 1734 ***3690.1*** *p107*
Hawkworth, Adam 34; Nova Scotia, 1774 ***1219.7*** *p209*
With wife
With 4 children
Hawley, Alice *SEE* Hawley, James
Hawley, Ann *SEE* Hawley, James
Hawley, Francis Ann *SEE* Hawley, James
Hawley, James; Virginia, 1641 ***6219*** *p184*
*Wife:*Ann
*Child:*Francis Ann
*Child:*Alice
Hawly, Leonard; Virginia, 1643 ***6219*** *p200*
Hawstead, Jane 17; Jamaica, 1730 ***3690.1*** *p107*
Hawten, Richard; Virginia, 1643 ***6219*** *p204*
Hawthorn, Agnes; New York, NY, 1811 ***2859.11*** *p13*
Hawthorn, Bill; New York, NY, 1816 ***2859.11*** *p32*
Hawthorn, Charles 17; Maryland, 1721 ***3690.1*** *p107*
Hawthorn, Charles E.; New York, 1844 ***1450.2*** *p62A*

Hawthorn, David; New York, NY, 1811 ***2859.11*** *p13*
With family
Hawthorn, Eliza 17; Quebec, 1854 ***5704.8*** *p119*
Hawthorn, Eliza 21; St. John, N.B., 1856 ***5704.8*** *p131*
Hawthorn, Ellen; New York, NY, 1816 ***2859.11*** *p33*
Hawthorn, Esther; New York, NY, 1816 ***2859.11*** *p33*
Hawthorn, James 9; Quebec, 1854 ***5704.8*** *p119*
Hawthorn, John; New York, NY, 1811 ***2859.11*** *p13*
Hawthorn, John; New York, NY, 1816 ***2859.11*** *p33*
Hawthorn, Letitia 26; Quebec, 1854 ***5704.8*** *p119*
Hawthorn, Mary 20; Quebec, 1854 ***5704.8*** *p119*
Hawthorn, Mary 45; Quebec, 1854 ***5704.8*** *p119*
Hawthorn, Robert 20; Philadelphia, 1858 ***5704.8*** *p139*
Hawthorn, Thomas; New York, NY, 1816 ***2859.11*** *p33*
Hawthorn, Thomas 56; Quebec, 1854 ***5704.8*** *p119*
Hawthorn, William 15; St. John, N.B., 1863 ***5704.8*** *p153*
Hawthorne, John 14; St. John, N.B., 1865 ***5704.8*** *p165*
Hawthorne, Margaret 40; St. John, N.B., 1865 ***5704.8*** *p165*
Hawthorne, Sarah 17; St. John, N.B., 1865 ***5704.8*** *p165*
Hawton, William 19; Virginia, 1720 ***3690.1*** *p107*
Hax, Henry; Illinois, 1892 ***5012.40*** *p27*
Haxaire, Nicolas 37; America, 1838 ***778.5*** *p267*
Haxford, John 18; Jamaica, 1723 ***3690.1*** *p107*
Hay, Aaron; Ohio, 1850 ***6014.2*** *p7*
Hay, Alexander; America, 1798 ***1639.20*** *p91*
Hay, Alexander; America, 1828 ***1639.20*** *p91*
Hay, Ann 22; Massachusetts, 1848 ***5881.1*** *p44*
Hay, Charles; Boston, 1773 ***1219.7*** *p164*
Hay, Elizabeth 63; Massachusetts, 1849 ***5881.1*** *p46*
Hay, Ernst 42; Kansas, 1887 ***5240.1*** *p70*
Hay, George; New York, NY, 1864 ***5704.8*** *p174*
Hay, Hamilton; St. John, N.B., 1852 ***5704.8*** *p94*
Hay, Heinrich 72; Kansas, 1887 ***5240.1*** *p70*
Hay, Hugh; Philadelphia, 1849 ***53.26*** *p36*
Hay, Hugh; Philadelphia, 1849 ***5704.8*** *p58*
Hay, James; Wilmington, NC, 1775 ***1639.20*** *p91*
Hay, James 29; Philadelphia, 1774 ***1219.7*** *p232*
Hay, Jane 18; Philadelphia, 1861 ***5704.8*** *p148*
Hay, John; Arkansas, 1918 ***95.2*** *p55*
Hay, John; New York, NY, 1816 ***2859.11*** *p33*
Hay, John; New York, NY, 1838 ***8208.4*** *p90*
Hay, John; North Carolina, 1700-1735 ***1639.20*** *p92*
Hay, John; Philadelphia, 1851 ***5704.8*** *p76*
Hay, John; South Carolina, 1733 ***1639.20*** *p91*
Hay, John 3; Massachusetts, 1848 ***5881.1*** *p47*
Hay, John 23; Virginia, 1774 ***1219.7*** *p193*
Hay, Robert; New York, NY, 1816 ***2859.11*** *p33*
Hay, Robert; North Carolina, 1814 ***1639.20*** *p92*
Hay, Robert; Philadelphia, 1816 ***2859.11*** *p33*
Hay, Robert, Sr. 96; North Carolina, 1850 ***1639.20*** *p92*
Hay, Thomas; Massachusetts, 1848 ***5881.1*** *p50*
Hay, Thomas; New York, NY, 1834 ***8208.4*** *p37*
Hay, Thomas 1; Massachusetts, 1848 ***5881.1*** *p50*
Hay, William; Jamaica, 1754 ***1219.7*** *p27*
Hay, William; Maryland, 1754 ***3690.1*** *p107*
Hay, William; New York, NY, 1816 ***2859.11*** *p33*
Hay, William Henry; Montreal, 1848 ***8893*** *p267*
Hay, William J.; America, 1896 ***1450.2*** *p62A*
Hayborn, Hannah; Philadelphia, 1850 ***53.26*** *p36*
Hayborn, Hannah; Philadelphia, 1850 ***5704.8*** *p60*
Hayd, Anna Barbara *SEE* Hayd, Johannes
Hayd, Anna Eva Catharina *SEE* Hayd, Johannes
Hayd, Anna Maria *SEE* Hayd, Johannes
Hayd, Anna Maria Schultze *SEE* Hayd, Johannes
Hayd, Joh. Martinus *SEE* Hayd, Johannes
Hayd, Johannes; New York, 1709 ***3627*** *p4*
*Wife:*Anna Maria Schultze
*Daughter:*Anna Eva Catharina
*Daughter:*Anna Maria
*Daughter:*Anna Barbara
*Son:*Joh. Martinus
Hayd, Regina; Port uncertain, 1743-1800 ***2444*** *p163*
Hayden, Bridget; New York, NY, 1815 ***2859.11*** *p33*
Hayden, Bridget, Jr.; New York, NY, 1815 ***2859.11*** *p33*
Hayden, Elizabeth; Virginia, 1620 ***6219*** *p18*
Hayden, Patrick; New York, NY, 1816 ***2859.11*** *p33*
Haydock, Thomas; Illinois, 1876 ***5012.37*** *p60*
Haydon, Edward 30; Maryland, 1775 ***1219.7*** *p257*
Haydon, Joseph 18; Baltimore, 1775 ***1219.7*** *p270*
Haydon, Mary; Maryland, 1742 ***4971*** *p107*
Haydon, William; New York, NY, 1832 ***8208.4*** *p40*
Hayer, Herman; Wisconsin, n.d. ***9675.5*** *p264*
Hayer, Johan Friderich 23; Pennsylvania, 1743 ***1034.18*** *p7*
*Brother:*Vallandien 18
Hayer, Philip 31; Pennsylvania, 1743 ***1034.18*** *p7*
Hayer, Vallandien 18 *SEE* Hayer, Johan Friderich
Hayes, A. E.; Washington, 1859-1920 ***2872.1*** *p15*
Hayes, Andrew 25; Massachusetts, 1849 ***5881.1*** *p45*
Hayes, Ann *SEE* Hayes, Robert
Hayes, Anna 13; Quebec, 1851 ***5704.8*** *p74*
Hayes, Anthony; Virginia, 1639 ***6219*** *p157*
Hayes, Betty; Quebec, 1851 ***5704.8*** *p74*
Hayes, Bridget 20; Massachusetts, 1850 ***5881.1*** *p45*
Hayes, Caleb 25; Port uncertain, 1774 ***1219.7*** *p176*
Hayes, Daniel 30; Massachusetts, 1850 ***5881.1*** *p46*
Hayes, David; Virginia, 1638 ***6219*** *p11*
Hayes, Debora 30; Massachusetts, 1850 ***5881.1*** *p46*
Hayes, Dennis 22; Massachusetts, 1849 ***5881.1*** *p46*
Hayes, Eliza.; Virginia, 1638 ***6219*** *p117*
Hayes, Ellen 11; Massachusetts, 1850 ***5881.1*** *p46*
Hayes, Ellen 20; Massachusetts, 1849 ***5881.1*** *p46*
Hayes, Fanny J.; Philadelphia, 1850 ***5704.8*** *p64*
Hayes, George; Philadelphia, 1850 ***5704.8*** *p63*
Hayes, Grissy; Philadelphia, 1850 ***5704.8*** *p63*
Hayes, Henry; Virginia, 1638 ***6219*** *p117*
Hayes, Hugh; Virginia, 1635 ***6219*** *p69*
Hayes, James; Virginia, 1638 ***6219*** *p117*
Hayes, Johanna 25; Massachusetts, 1849 ***5881.1*** *p47*
Hayes, John; Montreal, 1823 ***7603*** *p86*
Hayes, John; New Jersey, 1811 ***9892.11*** *p20*
Hayes, John; Virginia, 1617 ***6219*** *p18*
Hayes, John; Virginia, 1856 ***4626.16*** *p16*
Hayes, John 15; Maryland, 1724 ***3690.1*** *p107*
Hayes, John 20; Maryland or Virginia, 1733 ***3690.1*** *p107*
Hayes, John 26; Philadelphia, 1774 ***1219.7*** *p175*
Hayes, John 34; Massachusetts, 1849 ***5881.1*** *p47*
Hayes, Malachi 40; Massachusetts, 1849 ***5881.1*** *p49*
Hayes, Margaret; Quebec, 1851 ***5704.8*** *p74*
Hayes, Margaret 40; Massachusetts, 1850 ***5881.1*** *p49*
Hayes, Mary; Philadelphia, 1850 ***5704.8*** *p63*
Hayes, Mary; Virginia, 1637 ***6219*** *p29*
Hayes, Mary 7; Massachusetts, 1850 ***5881.1*** *p49*
Hayes, Mary 25; Massachusetts, 1849 ***5881.1*** *p48*
Hayes, Michael 20; Massachusetts, 1849 ***5881.1*** *p48*
Hayes, Moses; Quebec, 1824 ***7603*** *p91*
Hayes, Patrick 3; Massachusetts, 1850 ***5881.1*** *p50*
Hayes, Patrick 30; Massachusetts, 1847 ***5881.1*** *p49*
Hayes, Patrick 45; Massachusetts, 1849 ***5881.1*** *p50*
Hayes, Peggy 25; Massachusetts, 1850 ***5881.1*** *p50*
Hayes, Rich.; Virginia, 1635 ***6219*** *p3*
Hayes, Richard 25; Massachusetts, 1850 ***5881.1*** *p50*
Hayes, Robert; Philadelphia, 1850 ***5704.8*** *p64*
Hayes, Robert; Virginia, 1637 ***6219*** *p113*
With wife
Hayes, Robert; Virginia, 1642 ***6219*** *p194*
Hayes, Robert; Virginia, 1643 ***6219*** *p203*
*Wife:*Ann
Hayes, Samuel; Antigua (Antego), 1755 ***1219.7*** *p36*
Hayes, Samuel; Antigua (Antego), 1755 ***3690.1*** *p107*
Hayes, Thom 30; Maryland, 1705 ***2212*** *p43*
Hayes, Thomas; New York, NY, 1835 ***8208.4*** *p5*
Hayes, Thomas; Philadelphia, 1865 ***5704.8*** *p202*
Hayes, Thomas; Virginia, 1637 ***6219*** *p17*
Hayes, Thomas 24; Massachusetts, 1849 ***5881.1*** *p50*
Hayes, Thomas 40; Massachusetts, 1849 ***5881.1*** *p50*
Hayes, Timothy 12; Massachusetts, 1849 ***5881.1*** *p50*
Hayes, William; Illinois, 1862 ***5012.38*** *p98*
Hayes, William; Philadelphia, 1850 ***5704.8*** *p64*
Hayes, William; Virginia, 1638 ***6219*** *p121*
Hayes, William 15; Philadelphia, 1775 ***1219.7*** *p259*
Hayes, William 17; America, 1728 ***3690.1*** *p107*
Hayes, William 21; Maryland, 1774 ***1219.7*** *p224*
Hayes, William 21; Quebec, 1854 ***5704.8*** *p121*
Hayes, William 48; Kansas, 1873 ***5240.1*** *p54*
Hayfield, Mary 20; Philadelphia, 1774 ***1219.7*** *p212*
Hayhes, Allen; Virginia, 1642 ***6219*** *p186*
Hayle, David 20; St. John, N.B., 1866 ***5704.8*** *p167*
Hayle, Dougal 26; St. John, N.B., 1866 ***5704.8*** *p167*
Hayle, Nicho.; Virginia, 1645 ***6219*** *p233*
Hayler, Thomas 35; Philadelphia, 1774 ***1219.7*** *p237*
Hayles, Jer.; Virginia, 1638 ***6219*** *p180*
Hayly, Georg; Virginia, 1638 ***6219*** *p147*
Hayman, William 22; Philadelphia, 1774 ***1219.7*** *p232*
Hayn, . . .; Canada, 1776-1783 ***9786*** *p23*
Hayn, Elisabetha; Pennsylvania, 1754 ***2444*** *p192*
Hayner, Thomas; Illinois, 1896 ***2896.5*** *p16*
Haynes, Edward 14; Jamaica, 1736 ***3690.1*** *p107*
Haynes, Eliza 14; Massachusetts, 1849 ***5881.1*** *p46*
Haynes, Elizabeth 22; Maryland, 1774 ***1219.7*** *p228*
Haynes, Elizabeth 30; Massachusetts, 1848 ***5881.1*** *p46*
Haynes, Ernest; Illinois, 1896 ***2896.5*** *p16*
Haynes, George; Virginia, 1645 ***6219*** *p232*
Haynes, George 28; Jamaica, 1734 ***3690.1*** *p107*
Haynes, James; Illinois, 1894 ***2896.5*** *p17*
Haynes, John 22; Philadelphia, 1775 ***1219.7*** *p258*
Haynes, Peggy 15; Massachusetts, 1847 ***5881.1*** *p49*
Haynes, Richard; Virginia, 1642 ***6219*** *p198*
Haynes, Thomas; Illinois, 1894 ***2896.5*** *p17*
Haynie, John; Virginia, 1652 ***6251*** *p19*
Hays, David; Kansas, 1887 ***5240.1*** *p18*
Hays, David; New York, NY, 1839 ***8208.4*** *p98*
Hays, Ellen 11; Philadelphia, 1868 ***5704.8*** *p225*
Hays, James; New York, NY, 1838 ***8208.4*** *p63*
Hays, Jane 20; Wilmington, DE, 1831 ***6508.3*** *p100*
Hays, John; New York, NY, 1838 ***8208.4*** *p88*
Hays, John; Philadelphia, 1867 ***5704.8*** *p224*
Hays, Leopold; Kansas, 1887 ***5240.1*** *p18*
Hays, Martha 19; Wilmington, DE, 1831 ***6508.3*** *p100*
Hays, Mary; Philadelphia, 1864 ***5704.8*** *p188*
Hays, Michael; Ohio, 1840 ***9892.11*** *p20*
Hays, Patrick; New York, NY, 1834 ***8208.4*** *p1*
Hays, Richard; Illinois, 1865 ***5012.38*** *p98*
Hays, Robert; Philadelphia, 1864 ***5704.8*** *p188*
Hays, Thomas; Montreal, 1823 ***7603*** *p101*
Hays, Thomas; New York, NY, 1816 ***2859.11*** *p33*
Hays, William; Illinois, 1862 ***5012.38*** *p98*
Hays, William 17; America, 1728 ***3690.1*** *p107*
Hays, William 40; Wilmington, DE, 1831 ***6508.3*** *p100*
Hayson, Susanna; New York, NY, 1811 ***2859.11*** *p13*
Hayssen, Gerhard; Wisconsin, n.d. ***9675.5*** *p264*
Haystrom, John; Washington, 1859-1920 ***2872.1*** *p15*
Haystrom, Y. E.; Washington, 1859-1920 ***2872.1*** *p15*
Hayton, George 32; Nova Scotia, 1774 ***1219.7*** *p194*
Hayton, John 27; Jamaica, 1731 ***3690.1*** *p108*
Hayts, Jeremiah; Virginia, 1636 ***6219*** *p76*
Hayward, Ann *SEE* Hayward, Mathew
Hayward, Ellen *SEE* Hayward, William
Hayward, Ellin *SEE* Hayward, William
Hayward, Francis; Virginia, 1639 ***6219*** *p156*
Hayward, Howell; Virginia, 1635 ***6219*** *p35*
Hayward, Hugh; Virginia, 1638 ***6219*** *p147*
Hayward, John; Virginia, 1652 ***6251*** *p19*
Hayward, Mathew; Virginia, 1638 ***6219*** *p119*
*Wife:*Ann
Hayward, Robert 22; Philadelphia, 1775 ***1219.7*** *p258*
Hayward, Samuel; Iowa, 1866-1943 ***123.54*** *p22*
Hayward, Susan; Virginia, 1638 ***6219*** *p147*
Hayward, Tom; Washington, 1859-1920 ***2872.1*** *p16*
Hayward, William; Virginia, 1638 ***6219*** *p118*
*Wife:*Ellen
Hayward, William; Virginia, 1642 ***6219*** *p193*
*Wife:*Ellin
Hayward, William 20; Maryland, 1725 ***3690.1*** *p108*
Haywood, Alfred; New York, NY, 1839 ***8208.4*** *p98*
Haywood, Colquit 16; Virginia, 1774 ***1219.7*** *p190*
Haywood, Ebenezer; New York, NY, 1838 ***8208.4*** *p72*
Haywood, Elizabeth 25; Maryland, 1775 ***1219.7*** *p249*
Haywood, Francis 24; Virginia, 1774 ***1219.7*** *p193*
Haywood, John 27; New York, 1774 ***1219.7*** *p218*
Haywood, Robert; Virginia, 1638 ***6219*** *p124*
Haywood, William 29; New York, 1774 ***1219.7*** *p218*
Haywood, Wm.; Virginia, 1643 ***6219*** *p204*
Hayworth, John; Virginia, 1638 ***6219*** *p146*
Hazar, Jacques 21; New Orleans, 1839 ***778.5*** *p267*
Hazel, W.; South Carolina, 1717-1737 ***1639.20*** *p92*
Hazelbarth, Morris; Wisconsin, n.d. ***9675.5*** *p264*
Hazelton, Samuel; New York, NY, 1836 ***8208.4*** *p19*
Hazle, Isabella 1; St. John, N.B., 1865 ***5704.8*** *p165*
Hazle, John 24; St. John, N.B., 1865 ***5704.8*** *p165*
Hazle, Mary 24; St. John, N.B., 1865 ***5704.8*** *p165*
Hazletine, Charles 16; Philadelphia, 1774 ***1219.7*** *p183*
Hazleton, Edward; New York, NY, 1811 ***2859.11*** *p13*
Hazleton, John; New York, NY, 1811 ***2859.11*** *p13*
Hazlett, Alexander 46; Philadelphia, 1859 ***5704.8*** *p141*
Hazlett, Ann 19; Philadelphia, 1859 ***5704.8*** *p141*
Hazlett, Charles 35; Philadelphia, 1833 ***53.26*** *p36*
Hazlett, Elizabeth 22; Philadelphia, 1859 ***5704.8*** *p141*
Hazlett, Francis 11; Philadelphia, 1859 ***5704.8*** *p141*
Hazlett, George 14; Philadelphia, 1859 ***5704.8*** *p141*
Hazlett, James 18; Philadelphia, 1859 ***5704.8*** *p141*
Hazlett, Martha 16; Philadelphia, 1859 ***5704.8*** *p141*
Hazlett, Martha 40; Philadelphia, 1859 ***5704.8*** *p141*
Hazlewood, Robert 25; Maryland, 1774 ***1219.7*** *p187*
Hazlewood, Thomas 16; Philadelphia, 1774 ***1219.7*** *p175*
Heaber, John; New York, NY, 1838 ***8208.4*** *p68*
Head, James; Virginia, 1636 ***6219*** *p21*
Head, James; Virginia, 1639 ***6219*** *p162*
Head, John 17; Virginia, 1774 ***1219.7*** *p239*
Head, Jonathan 20; Antigua (Antego), 1723 ***3690.1*** *p108*
Head, Tho.; Virginia, 1638 ***6219*** *p122*
Head, William 23; Maryland, 1774 ***1219.7*** *p179*
Header, Richard; Virginia, 1638 ***6219*** *p125*
Headstrum, Lester O.; Arkansas, 1918 ***95.2*** *p55*
Heakley, Henry; Virginia, 1646 ***6219*** *p246*
*Wife:*Mary
Heakley, Mary *SEE* Heakley, Henry
Heal, Jn 21; Virginia, 1700 ***2212*** *p33*
Heale, Richard; Virginia, 1622 ***6219*** *p31*
Healey, Bridget 40; Massachusetts, 1849 ***5881.1*** *p45*
Healey, Catherine 18; St. John, N.B., 1863 ***5704.8*** *p152*
Healey, Ellen 28; Massachusetts, 1849 ***5881.1*** *p46*
Healey, Henry 20; St. John, N.B., 1863 ***5704.8*** *p152*
Healey, James 28; Massachusetts, 1850 ***5881.1*** *p48*
Healey, Joseph 22; Maryland, 1730 ***3690.1*** *p290*
Healey, Margt 20; Newport, RI, 1851 ***6508.5*** *p20*
Healey, Mary 20; Massachusetts, 1850 ***5881.1*** *p49*

Healey, Patrick 19; Newfoundland, 1789 *4915.24* p56
Healey, Simon; New York, NY, 1838 *8208.4* p66
Heally, Owen 12; St. John, N.B., 1851 *5704.8* p80
Heally, Patrick; St. John, N.B., 1851 *5704.8* p80
Healy, Ann 14; Philadelphia, 1858 *5704.8* p139
Healy, Annie; Philadelphia, 1865 *5704.8* p200
Healy, Bryan; New York, NY, 1816 *2859.11* p33
Healy, Catherine 12; Philadelphia, 1858 *5704.8* p139
Healy, Denis J. 24; Kansas, 1906 *5240.1* p84
Healy, Edmund; Iowa, 1869 *1450.2* p62A
Healy, Ellen 55; Massachusetts, 1850 *5881.1* p46
Healy, James; Iroquois Co., IL, 1868 *3455.1* p11
Healy, James; New York, NY, 1807 *8208.4* p58
Healy, James; Philadelphia, 1867 *5704.8* p216
Healy, John; New York, NY, 1816 *2859.11* p33
Healy, John 24; Massachusetts, 1850 *5881.1* p48
Healy, John James 3; Philadelphia, 1865 *5704.8* p200
Healy, Joseph; Arizona, 1898 *9228.30* p7
Healy, Joseph 37; Arizona, 1898 *9228.40* p2
Healy, Leary; America, 1855 *1450.2* p62A
Healy, Luke 50; Massachusetts, 1850 *5881.1* p48
Healy, Maggie 7; Philadelphia, 1865 *5704.8* p200
Healy, Margaret; America, 1740 *4971* p48
Healy, Margaret; New York, NY, 1816 *2859.11* p33
Healy, Mary; New York, NY, 1816 *2859.11* p33
Healy, Mary 9; Massachusetts, 1849 *5881.1* p48
Healy, Michael; New York, NY, 1816 *2859.11* p33
Healy, Nancy; Massachusetts, 1847 *5881.1* p49
Healy, Patrick; New York, NY, 1816 *2859.11* p33
Healy, Patrick Oliver; New York, NY, 1839 *8208.4* p101
Healy, Thomas; America, 1740 *4971* p47
Healy, Thomas; America, 1742 *4971* p17
Healy, Thomas 20; Massachusetts, 1849 *5881.1* p50
Healy, Willie 5; Philadelphia, 1865 *5704.8* p200
Healy, Wm.; Virginia, 1856 *4626.16* p15
Heanes, Henry 15; Maryland, 1735 *3690.1* p98
Heanes, Phillipp; Virginia, 1642 *6219* p190
Heanes, Sarah 21; America, 1701 *2212* p35
Heaney, Charles 9 mos; St. John, N.B., 1847 *5704.8* p18
Heaney, Dennis; St. John, N.B., 1847 *5704.8* p18
Heaney, Elizabeth 3; St. John, N.B., 1847 *5704.8* p18
Heaney, Elizabeth 28; St. John, N.B., 1863 *5704.8* p155
Heaney, Hugh 12; St. John, N.B., 1847 *5704.8* p18
Heaney, James; St. John, N.B., 1847 *5704.8* p18
Heaney, James 6; St. John, N.B., 1847 *5704.8* p18
Heaney, John; St. John, N.B., 1847 *5704.8* p18
Heaney, Mary; St. John, N.B., 1847 *5704.8* p18
Heaney, Patrick 30; St. John, N.B., 1863 *5704.8* p155
Heaney, Sarah; St. John, N.B., 1852 *5704.8* p95
Heaney, William 14; St. John, N.B., 1847 *5704.8* p18
Heany, Ann; Philadelphia, 1865 *5704.8* p196
Heany, Darby; America, 1737 *4971* p12
Heany, Francis; New York, NY, 1816 *2859.11* p33
Heany, Hugh 11; Philadelphia, 1850 *5704.8* p64
Heany, James; America, 1735-1743 *4971* p79
Heany, Mary; America, 1740 *4971* p15
Heany, Mary; America, 1742 *4971* p17
Heap, John 15; Philadelphia, 1774 *1219.7* p233
Heap, Mary 21; America, 1705 *2212* p42
Heape, Richard; Maryland, 1753 *1219.7* p22
Heape, Richard; Maryland, 1753 *3690.1* p101
Heard, Anthony; North Carolina, 1817 *1639.20* p92
Heard, John 21; Maryland, 1774 *1219.7* p229
Hearn, James; New York, NY, 1836 *8208.4* p12
Hearnden, William 22; Maryland, 1774 *1219.7* p206
Hearne, John; Virginia, 1639 *6219* p161
Hearne, Jon.; Virginia, 1636 *6219* p80
Hearne, Thomas; Virginia, 1639 *6219* p161
Hearney, Ann 23; Philadelphia, 1804 *53.26* p37
   *Relative:*Patrick 12
   *Relative:*John 9
   *Relative:*Biddy 7
   *Relative:*Nanny 4
Hearney, Biddy 7 SEE Hearney, Ann
Hearney, John 9 SEE Hearney, Ann
Hearney, Nanny 4 SEE Hearney, Ann
Hearney, Patrick 12 SEE Hearney, Ann
Hearton, George 27; St. Vincent, 1774 *1219.7* p238
Heary, Mary 23; Massachusetts, 1849 *5881.1* p49
Heary, Michael 12; Massachusetts, 1849 *5881.1* p49
Heas, Darby; America, 1736-1743 *4971* p58
Heas, Dennis 25; Newport, RI, 1851 *6508.5* p19
Heas, John; America, 1736-1743 *4971* p58
Heas, Maurice; America, 1739 *4971* p47
Hease, John; America, 1742 *4971* p56
Heasell, Robert; Virginia, 1628 *6219* p31
Heastie, John 30; Charleston, SC, 1774 *1639.20* p92
Heates, Thomas 16; Maryland, 1773 *1219.7* p173
Heath, Mr.; Quebec, 1815 *9229.18* p80
Heath, Ferdinand; Virginia, 1642 *6219* p195
Heath, George 20; Virginia, 1750 *3690.1* p108
Heath, Jane; Virginia, 1643 *6219* p33
Heath, John 16; Pennsylvania, 1730 *3690.1* p108

Heath, John 17; West Indies, 1722 *3690.1* p108
Heath, John 19; Virginia, 1751 *1219.7* p4
Heath, John 19; Virginia, 1751 *3690.1* p108
Heath, John 19; Virginia, 1751 *3690.1* p108
Heath, John 21; Jamaica, 1725 *3690.1* p108
Heath, Jon.; Virginia, 1635 *6219* p26
Heath, Mary; Virginia, 1647 *6219* p244
Heath, Robert 19; Jamaica, 1723 *3690.1* p108
Heath, Tho.; Virginia, 1637 *6219* p85
Heath, Thomas; Virginia, 1636 *6219* p79
Heath, Thomas 20; Maryland, 1739 *3690.1* p108
Heath, William 16; Jamaica, 1730 *3690.1* p108
Heather, Richd.; Virginia, 1647 *6219* p248
Heaton, Alice; Virginia, 1698 *2212* p12
Heaton, Edward; Virginia, 1698 *2212* p12
Heaton, Eliz; Virginia, 1698 *2212* p12
Heaton, Margaret 28; Philadelphia, 1803 *53.26* p37
Heaton, Mary; Savannah, GA, 1774 *1219.7* p227
Heaton, Richd; Virginia, 1698 *2212* p12
Heaton, Wm; Virginia, 1698 *2212* p15
Heauke, Jacob; Philadelphia, 1757 *9973.7* p32
Heavey, Patrick 22; Massachusetts, 1850 *5881.1* p50
Heayes, Catherine; Quebec, 1835 *7036* p125
Hebberd, John 26; Jamaica, 1724 *3690.1* p109
Hebbett, Margrett 21; Virginia, 1700 *2212* p31
Hebdin, Thomas 17; Jamaica, 1736 *3690.1* p109
Hebenstrat, Franz; Wisconsin, n.d. *9675.5* p264
Hebenstreuil, Moris 22; New Orleans, 1836 *778.5* p267
Hebert, . . .; Canada, 1776-1783 *9786* p23
Hebert, Louis; Michigan, 1864 *5240.1* p19
Hebrock, Ernst Heinrich W.; America, 1893 *4610.10* p153
Hebting, Hans Jacob; Pennsylvania, 1752 *2444* p164
Hecher, John; Virginia, 1636 *6219* p76
Hechinger, Joseph; America, 1817 *8582.2* p60
Hechinger, Joseph; Cincinnati, 1833 *8582.1* p52
Hechinger, Joseph; Ohio, 1869-1887 *8582* p13
Hecht, Jacob; Cincinnati, 1869-1887 *8582* p13
Heck, Mr.; Boston, 1837 *8582.3* p59
Heck, Angela Spoo 28 SEE Heck, Nikolaus
Heck, Georg; Maryland, 1820-1829 *8582.1* p46
Heck, Gerhard; Ohio, 1824 *8582.1* p46
Heck, John; Philadelphia, 1762 *9973.7* p37
Heck, Nikolaus 29; New York, 1854 *3702.7* p367
   *Wife:*Angela Spoo 28
Heckenroth, . . .; Canada, 1776-1783 *9786* p23
Hecker, Mr.; Cincinnati, 1848 *8582.2* p63
Hecker, Johann Egidius; Pennsylvania, 1751 *2444* p186
Heckerott, . . .; Canada, 1776-1783 *9786* p23
Heckert, Henry F.; America, 1848 *8582.1* p13
Heckewelder, . . .; America, 1700-1877 *8582.3* p80
Heckewelder, Christian; New York, 1754 *3652* p79
Heckewelder, David; New York, 1754 *3652* p78
Heckewelder, David; New York, 1754 *3652* p79
Heckewelder, John; New York, 1754 *3652* p79
Heckewelder, Mary; New York, 1754 *3652* p79
Heckewelder, Regina; New York, 1754 *3652* p78
Heckler, Andrew; New York, 1866 *1450.2* p62A
Heckler, Henry; Virginia, 1847 *4626.16* p13
Heckler, Peter; Virginia, 1852 *4626.16* p14
Heckman, Anton; America, 1870 *1450.2* p62A
Heckmann, Friederich Wilhelm; America, 1849 *8582.3* p27
Heckmann, Peter; Cincinnati, 1846 *8582.1* p13
Heckrodt, M. A.; Illinois, 1844 *8582.2* p51
Heckstall, Abraham 19; Antigua (Antego), 1736 *3690.1* p109
Heclerc, Charles 20; America, 1838 *778.5* p267
Heclim, James 20; Philadelphia, 1856 *5704.8* p129
Hecourtine, J.; New Orleans, 1839 *778.5* p267
Hector, Adolph A.; Colorado, 1903 *9678.2* p23
Hector, John 26; New Orleans, 1831 *778.5* p267
Hector, Robert; Philadelphia, 1811 *53.26* p37
Hector, Robert; Philadelphia, 1811 *2859.11* p13
Hed, Henry; Virginia, 1623-1648 *6219* p252
Hedborg, Olie; Iowa, 1866-1943 *123.54* p22
Heddeman, Catharine 22; Massachusetts, 1849 *5881.1* p45
Heddinton, George; New York, NY, 1839 *8208.4* p101
Heddle, Alexander; Savannah, GA, 1774 *1219.7* p227
Hedge, John 30; Jamaica, 1730 *3690.1* p109
Hedger, Francis; Canada, 1776-1783 *9786* p207A
Hedges, Farclife; Pennsylvania, 1682 *4961* p6
Hedlen, Jon.; Virginia, 1635 *6219* p12
Hedley, John; Iowa, 1866-1943 *123.54* p22
Hedley, Thomas A.; Iowa, 1866-1943 *123.54* p22
Hedman, August; Iowa, 1866-1943 *123.54* p22
Hedman, Carl Peter; America, 1847 *6410.32* p123
Hedman, John Frederick; Colorado, 1890 *9678.2* p23
Hedstrom, E. J.; Minneapolis, 1833-1888 *6410.35* p55
Hedstrom, John 41; Harris Co., TX, 1899 *6254* p6
Hedwall, C. O.; Minneapolis, 1881-1886 *6410.35* p55
Heeds, Mary 21; Maryland, 1775 *1219.7* p253
Heeken, Andrew 5; St. John, N.B., 1863 *5704.8* p153

Heeken, Peggy 20; St. John, N.B., 1863 *5704.8* p153
Heekendorn, Jonathan; Philadelphia, 1761 *9973.7* p36
Heekendorn, Martin; Philadelphia, 1759 *9973.7* p34
Heele, George; Virginia, 1635 *6219* p25
Heeling, William 17; Maryland, 1737 *3690.1* p109
Heely, Mary; Philadelphia, 1816 *2859.11* p33
Heemann, Friederich; New Orleans, 1849 *8582.3* p27
Heemann, Friedrich; America, 1849 *8582.1* p13
Heemeier, Heinr. Fr.; America, 1881 *4610.10* p152
   *Wife:*Sophie L. C. Schaper
Heemeier, Sophie L. C. Schaper SEE Heemeier, Heinr. Fr.
Heenan, David 32; Kansas, 1900 *5240.1* p19
Heenan, David 32; Kansas, 1900 *5240.1* p81
Heendrey, Jonathan 14; America, 1705 *2212* p43
Heeper, Mrs.; America, 1849 *4610.10* p135
   *Child:*Carl Friedrich
   *Child:*Caspar H. Friedrich
Heeper, Anna Marie Scheidt SEE Heeper, Friedrich Wilhelm
Heeper, Anne Marie Engel 30; America, 1850 *4610.10* p135
Heeper, Anne Marie Louise SEE Heeper, Hermann Heinrich
Heeper, Carl Friedrich SEE Heeper, Mrs.
Heeper, Caspar H. Friedrich SEE Heeper, Mrs.
Heeper, Emilie Wilhelmine SEE Heeper, Hermann Heinrich
Heeper, Ernst H. Gottlieb SEE Heeper, Hermann Heinrich
Heeper, Franz Heinrich; America, 1854 *4610.10* p144
Heeper, Friedrich Wilhelm; America, 1850 *4610.10* p143
   *Wife:*Anna Marie Scheidt
   *Daughter:*Louise Johanne
Heeper, Hermann; America, 1850 *4610.10* p143
Heeper, Hermann Heinrich 55; America, 1852 *4610.10* p143
   With wife
   *Child:*Ernst H. Gottlieb
   *Child:*Peter F. Wilhelm
   *Child:*Anne Marie Louise
   *Child:*Emilie Wilhelmine
Heeper, Louise Johanne SEE Heeper, Friedrich Wilhelm
Heeper, Peter F. Wilhelm SEE Heeper, Hermann Heinrich
Heer, . . .; Canada, 1776-1783 *9786* p23
Heer, Anna; Port uncertain, 1713-1800 *2444* p163
Heer, Johann Henrich; Lancaster, PA, 1780 *8137* p9
Heer, Louis Chretien; Canada, 1776-1783 *9786* p239
Heermeier, Anne Marie; America, 1841 *4610.10* p111
Heermeier, Karl Diedrich; America, 1844 *4610.10* p97
Heerskowitz, Moses; America, 1873 *6014.1* p2
Heerskowitz, Sam; America, 1873 *6014.1* p2
Heery, Thomas; New York, NY, 1834 *8208.4* p39
Heesemann, Carl Friedrich; America, 1860 *4610.10* p99
Heesemann, Caroline Louise SEE Heesemann, Gottlieb
Heesemann, Caroline Louise Friederike; America, 1860 *4610.10* p99
Heesemann, Chr. C. Friederike SEE Heesemann, Gottlieb
Heesemann, Christian Friedrich; America, 1860 *4610.10* p99
Heesemann, Christine Charlotte SEE Heesemann, Gottlieb
Heesemann, Ernst Heinrich Wilhelm; America, 1851 *4610.10* p98
Heesemann, Friedrich 22; America, 1876 *4610.10* p101
   *Wife:*Wilhelmine F. Caroline
Heesemann, Friedrich Wilhelm; America, 1852 *4610.10* p98
Heesemann, Gottlieb 68; America, 1872 *4610.10* p109
   *Wife:*Louise Meier
   *Child:*Chr. C. Friederike
   *Child:*Caroline Louise
   *Child:*Heinrich Wilhelm
   *Child:*Christine Charlotte
Heesemann, Heinrich Wilhelm SEE Heesemann, Gottlieb
Heesemann, Johann Friedrich Wilhelm; America, 1851 *4610.10* p98
Heesemann, Louise Meier SEE Heesemann, Gottlieb
Heesemann, Wilhelmine F. Caroline SEE Heesemann, Friedrich
Hefelbauer, Philip 30; Pennsylvania, 1748 *2444* p167
Hefelbower, Philip 30; Pennsylvania, 1748 *2444* p167
Heferlen, Martin 27; America, 1836 *778.5* p267
Heffernan, Bridget 6; Massachusetts, 1849 *5881.1* p45
Heffernan, Catharine 11; Massachusetts, 1849 *5881.1* p45
Heffernan, Catharine 20; Massachusetts, 1849 *5881.1* p45
Heffernan, Dennis 2; Massachusetts, 1850 *5881.1* p46
Heffernan, Johanna 16; Massachusetts, 1849 *5881.1* p47
Heffernan, Johanna 19; Massachusetts, 1849 *5881.1* p47
Heffernan, Margaret 50; Massachusetts, 1850 *5881.1* p49

Heffernan, Mary 10; Massachusetts, 1849 5881.1 p49
Heffernan, Mary 20; Massachusetts, 1847 5881.1 p48
Heffernan, Michael 30; Massachusetts, 1850 5881.1 p49
Heffernan, Patrick 8; Massachusetts, 1849 5881.1 p50
Heffernan, Patrick 50; Massachusetts, 1850 5881.1 p50
Heffernan, Thomas 16; Massachusetts, 1849 5881.1 p50
Hefflinger, Emil; Illinois, 1897 5012.39 p53
Hefflinger, Emil; Illinois, 1900 5012.40 p77
Heffner, Auguste; America, 1852 1450.2 p58A
Hefke, W. H. 29; Kansas, 1896 5240.1 p80
Hefti, Ernest; Arkansas, 1918 95.2 p55
Heftin, Hans Jacob; Pennsylvania, 1752 2444 p164
Hegaghty, Hannah 50; Philadelphia, 1856 5704.8 p129
Hegaghty, Mandy 13; Philadelphia, 1856 5704.8 p129
Hegaghty, Mary 8; Philadelphia, 1856 5704.8 p129
Hegaghty, Michael 11; Philadelphia, 1856 5704.8 p129
Hegan, Edward; New York, NY, 1838 8208.4 p62
Hegan, John; Quebec, 1847 5704.8 p29
Hegarty, Andrew; Philadelphia, 1866 5704.8 p209
Hegarty, Anne 18; St. John, N.B., 1862 5704.8 p150
Hegarty, Anne 20; St. John, N.B., 1863 5704.8 p152
Hegarty, Biddy *SEE* Hegarty, James
Hegarty, Biddy; Philadelphia, 1849 5704.8 p54
Hegarty, Biddy 20; Philadelphia, 1853 5704.8 p113
Hegarty, Bridget; Philadelphia, 1864 5704.8 p183
Hegarty, Catharine; Philadelphia, 1866 5704.8 p215
Hegarty, Con 18; Philadelphia, 1865 5704.8 p165
Hegarty, Edward; St. John, N.B., 1849 5704.8 p56
Hegarty, Eleanor 25; St. John, N.B., 1854 5704.8 p115
Hegarty, Eliza Jane; Philadelphia, 1865 5704.8 p206
Hegarty, Ellen; St. John, N.B., 1847 5704.8 p15
Hegarty, Fanny; Philadelphia, 1864 5704.8 p175
Hegarty, Hannah; Philadelphia, 1852 5704.8 p89
Hegarty, Hugh 20; Philadelphia, 1857 5704.8 p133
Hegarty, James; America, 1884 1450.2 p63A
Hegarty, James; New York, NY, 1866 5704.8 p210
Hegarty, James; Philadelphia, 1849 53.26 p37
*Relative:*Biddy
Hegarty, James; Philadelphia, 1849 5704.8 p54
Hegarty, James; Philadelphia, 1864 5704.8 p183
Hegarty, Jane; Philadelphia, 1852 5704.8 p92
Hegarty, John; Philadelphia, 1847 53.26 p37
Hegarty, John; Philadelphia, 1847 5704.8 p21
Hegarty, John; Philadelphia, 1867 5704.8 p218
Hegarty, John 12; Philadelphia, 1853 5704.8 p113
Hegarty, John 20; St. John, N.B., 1854 5704.8 p115
Hegarty, John 35; Philadelphia, 1861 5704.8 p148
Hegarty, Margaret; Philadelphia, 1852 5704.8 p89
Hegarty, Margaret; St. John, N.B., 1853 5704.8 p107
Hegarty, Margaret 21; St. John, N.B., 1851 5704.8 p77
Hegarty, Margaret 24; Philadelphia, 1860 5704.8 p145
Hegarty, Margaret 28; Philadelphia, 1857 5704.8 p133
Hegarty, Margery 30; Philadelphia, 1854 5704.8 p117
Hegarty, Mary; America, 1864 5704.8 p178
Hegarty, Mary; St. John, N.B., 1848 5704.8 p39
Hegarty, Mary 17; Philadelphia, 1859 5704.8 p142
Hegarty, Mary 22; St. John, N.B., 1863 5704.8 p152
Hegarty, Nancy 21; Wilmington, DE, 1831 6508.7 p160
Hegarty, Thomas 23; Philadelphia, 1857 5704.8 p132
Hegarty, William; St. John, N.B., 1847 5704.8 p24
Hegdale, O. F.; Washington, 1859-1920 2872.1 p16
Hege, Balthaser; New York, 1750 3652 p74
Hegeman, Mrs. A. M. 27; New York, NY, 1893 9026.4 p41
Hegenberg, . . .; Canada, 1776-1783 9786 p23
Heggarty, James; Philadelphia, 1865 5704.8 p196
Heggarty, Nancy; New York, NY, 1866 5704.8 p212
Heggarty, Susan; Philadelphia, 1865 5704.8 p194
Hegge, Bernard Hermann; America, 1848 8582.3 p27
Heggerty, Catharine; Philadelphia, 1866 5704.8 p208
Hegner, Gottfried; America, 1845 8582.3 p27
Hegole, Ms.; America, 1838 778.5 p267
Hegole, Marie 44; America, 1838 778.5 p267
Heh, . . .; Canada, 1776-1783 9786 p23
Hehemann, Wm; America, 1836 8582.1 p13
Hehir, Charles; America, 1741 4971 p83
Hehl, Anna Maria *SEE* Hehl, Matthew
Hehl, Matthew; New York, 1752 3652 p76
*Wife:*Anna Maria
Hehr, Georg; Cincinnati, 1834 8582.1 p52
Hehr, Philipp; Ohio, 1801-1802 8582.2 p55
Heibert, Isaak; Cincinnati, 1869-1887 8582 p13
Heichd, Michael; South Carolina, 1788 7119 p200
Heid, Jacob; Ohio, 1869-1887 8582 p13
Heid, Sebastian 30; America, 1853 9162.7 p14
Heidacker, Eberhardt H.; Ohio, 1869-1887 8582 p13
Heidel, Charles; America, 1840 1450.2 p63A
Heidemann, Johannes; Philadelphia, 1781 8137 p9
Heiden, Frederick; Illinois, 1866 2896.5 p17
Heidkamp, Adolph; Wisconsin, n.d. 9675.5 p264
Heidkamp, Joseph; America, 1845 8582.3 p27
Heidke, Friedrich; Milwaukee, 1847 3702.7 p312
Heidmeier, Heinrich Carl; America, 1889 4610.10 p107
Heidt, Georg; America, 1849 8582.2 p15
Heidtke, Martin Friedrich 23; America, 1843 3702.7 p309
With parents
With uncle
Heienbrock, Anne Marie L. Nagel *SEE* Heienbrock, Heinrich Wilhelm
Heienbrock, Carl Heinrich *SEE* Heienbrock, Heinrich Wilhelm
Heienbrock, Heinrich Wilhelm; America, 1839 4610.10 p154
*Wife:*Anne Marie L. Nagel
*Son:*Carl Heinrich
Heifdel, Joseph 6; America, 1838 778.5 p268
Heifdel, Marie 22; America, 1838 778.5 p268
Heifdel, Michel 2; America, 1838 778.5 p268
Heifdel, Nicolas 35; America, 1838 778.5 p268
Heifelbower, Yerick Baltus 24; Pennsylvania, 1748 2444 p167
Heigis, Jerg; Pennsylvania, 1750 2444 p161
Heijer, Conrad; Canada, 1783 9786 p38A
Heikka, Hillie; Washington, 1859-1920 2872.1 p16
Heikkela, Thomas Eli; Washington, 1859-1920 2872.1 p16
Heikkila, Kalle; Washington, 1859-1920 2872.1 p16
Heikkila, Thomas Eli; Washington, 1859-1920 2872.1 p16
Heikkinen, Konstu; Washington, 1859-1920 2872.1 p16
Heil, . . .; Canada, 1776-1783 9786 p23
Heil, Andrew; Ohio, 1870-1875 9892.11 p20
Heil, Andrew; Ohio, 1877 9892.11 p20
Heil, Daniel; Ohio, 1884-1887 9892.11 p20
Heil, Mathias; Canada, 1776-1783 9786 p207A
Heil, Philipp; America, 1849 8582.1 p13
Heile, Bernhard Johann; America, 1850 8582.3 p27
Heile, Johann Franz; America, 1849 8582.3 p27
Heile, Johann Heinrich; America, 1850 8582.3 p27
Heiler, Frederick; Philadelphia, 1735-1809 2444 p161
Heill, . . .; Canada, 1776-1783 9786 p23
Heillmann, . . .; Canada, 1776-1783 9786 p23
Heillmann, Johannes; Pennsylvania, 1749 2444 p166
Heilman, Eva; Evansville, IN, 1836-1857 5647.5 p125
With father
Heilman, William; Indiana, 1849 9117 p16
Heilmann, Adam; New York, 1882 1450.2 p14B
Heilmann, Jakob 34; America, 1853 9162.7 p14
Heilmann, Johannes 16; Pennsylvania, 1732 2444 p162
Heilmann, Marg. 31; America, 1853 9162.7 p14
Heilmann, Marthin; Pennsylvania, 1732 2444 p162
Heilmann, Michael; Illinois, 1871 8582 p14
Heilmann, Ph. 11 mos; America, 1853 9162.7 p14
Heily, Ewin; Virginia, 1643 6219 p202
Heim, Conrad 5; America, 1853 9162.8 p36
Heim, Francois 38; Louisiana, 1820 778.5 p268
Heim, John Ruland; Philadelphia, 1830 1450.2 p63A
Heim, Joseph; Colorado, 1884 9678.2 p23
Heim, Magdalena 26; America, 1853 9162.8 p36
Heim, Wilhelm; America, 1839 8582.2 p15
Heiman, Julius Robert; Arkansas, 1918 95.2 p55
Heimann, Gerhard; Illinois, 1838 8582.2 p50
Heimbach, Johann Adam; Cincinnati, 1869-1887 8582 p13
Heimbach, John; New York, NY, 1845 8582.1 p13
Heimbrink, Anna Marie Elisabeth *SEE* Heimbrink, Conrad Friedrich
Heimbrink, Conrad Friedrich; America, 1844 4610.10 p154
*Wife:*Anna Marie Elisabeth
*Son:*Ernst Heinrich
Heimbrink, Ernst Heinrich *SEE* Heimbrink, Conrad Friedrich
Heimbrock, Friedrich Wilhelm August; America, 1854 4610.10 p156
Heimbruch, Anne Marie L. Nagel *SEE* Heimbruch, Heinrich Wilhelm
Heimbruch, Carl Heinrich *SEE* Heimbruch, Heinrich Wilhelm
Heimbruch, Heinrich Wilhelm; America, 1839 4610.10 p154
*Wife:*Anne Marie L. Nagel
*Son:*Carl Heinrich
Heimbuch, Caspar; Cincinnati, 1869-1887 8582 p13
Heimburger, John; Illinois, 1889 5012.39 p52
Heimburger, John; Illinois, 1891 5012.40 p25
Heimlicher, Frederick; Illinois, 1895 5012.37 p63
Heimsoth, Henry; Illinois, 1905 5012.39 p54
Hein, . . .; Canada, 1776-1783 9786 p23
Hein, Adolph; Wisconsin, n.d. 9675.5 p264
Hein, Barthel 22; Louisiana, 1820 778.5 p268
Hein, Johanna 46; New York, NY, 1878 9253 p46
Hein, Mathias; Wisconsin, n.d. 9675.5 p264
Hein, Peter; Wisconsin, n.d. 9675.5 p264
Heinbaugh, Joseph; Baltimore, 1843 1450.2 p63A
Heinberger, Andreas; Illinois, 1871 5012.39 p25
Heindel, Margaret; New York, 1749 3652 p73
Heindrick, Adam 16; New York, 1775 1219.7 p246
Heine, . . .; Canada, 1776-1783 9786 p23
Heine, A. 20; Havana, 1831 778.5 p268
Heine, Anthony Diederich; America, 1842 1450.2 p63A
Heine, Chas. 43; New Orleans, 1839 9420.2 p362
*Wife:*John Regina 45
Heine, Christine Caroline Charlotte; America, 1849-1850 4610.10 p112
Heine, David; Pennsylvania, 1806 8582.1 p48
Heine, Dr. Joseph; New York, NY, 1840 8208.4 p105
Heine, Gustavus; Arizona, 1884 2764.35 p31
Heine, Heinerich; Canada, 1783 9786 p38A
Heine, Hermann Wilhelm Heinrich; America, 1883 4610.10 p113
Heine, Hubert E.; America, 1885 1450.2 p14B
Heine, John Regina 45 *SEE* Heine, Chas.
Heine, John S.; Colorado, 1903 9678.2 p23
Heineburger, John; Illinois, 1891 5012.40 p25
Heinecke, . . .; Canada, 1776-1783 9786 p23
Heinecke, Carl; Illinois, 1843 8582.2 p51
Heinecker, . . .; Canada, 1776-1783 9786 p23
Heinecker, Friederich J.; Illinois, 1843 8582.2 p51
Heineken, G.A.; Baltimore, 1826 8582 p29
Heineman, . . .; Canada, 1776-1783 9786 p23
Heinemann, . . .; Canada, 1776-1783 9786 p24
Heinemann, Christian Friedrich; Canada, 1776-1783 9786 p241
Heinemann, Henrich; Philadelphia, 1779 8137 p9
Heinen, John; Wisconsin, n.d. 9675.5 p264
Heines, Andreas *SEE* Heines, Friedrich
Heines, Friedrich; Ohio, 1800-1885 8582.2 p58
*Relative:*Andreas
Heinhaus, August; Wisconsin, n.d. 9675.5 p264
Heinig, Eleonor 10 *SEE* Heinig, John Godfrey
Heinig, Frederick 4 *SEE* Heinig, John Godfrey
Heinig, Jane Christine 37 *SEE* Heinig, John Godfrey
Heinig, John Godfrey 47; New Orleans, 1839 9420.2 p486
*Wife:*Jane Christine 37
*Child:*Eleonor 10
*Child:*Frederick 4
Heiniger, . . .; Canada, 1776-1783 9786 p23
Heininger, Jacob; Pennsylvania, 1749 2444 p164
Heininger, Johannes; Pennsylvania, 1749 2444 p164
Heink, Max; Washington, 1859-1920 2872.1 p16
Heinkliman, Charles; America, 1848 6014.1 p2
Heinlein, John; Virginia, 1856 4626.16 p16
Heinlin, Charles; Virginia, 1856 4626.16 p16
Heinllein, . . .; Canada, 1776-1783 9786 p23
Heinllen, Andre; Canada, 1776-1783 9786 p243
Heinman, . . .; Canada, 1776-1783 9786 p23
Heinmen, Hannes Sulo; Arkansas, 1918 95.2 p55
Heinmueller, Henrich; Philadelphia, 1779 8137 p9
Heinmueller, Johann Henrich; Philadelphia, 1779 8137 p9
Heinmueller, Johannes; Philadelphia, 1779 8137 p9
Heinnemann, . . .; Canada, 1776-1783 9786 p23
Heinold, George; Philadelphia, 1851 6013.19 p73
Heinrich, . . .; Canada, 1776-1783 9786 p23
Heinrich, Anna Magdalena *SEE* Heinrich, Peter
Heinrich, Hermann 24; New Orleans, 1839 9420.1 p378
Heinrich, Juliana *SEE* Heinrich, Peter
Heinrich, Peter; Savannah, GA, 1738 9898 p43
*Wife:*Juliana
With 3 children
*Daughter:*Anna Magdalena
Heinrich, Wilhelmina 23; New Orleans, 1839 9420.1 p378
Heinrichs, Albert C. 21; Kansas, 1901 5240.1 p82
Heinrichs, Herman 28; Kansas, 1876 5240.1 p57
Heinrichs, Michael 28; Kansas, 1876 5240.1 p19
Heinrichshoven, Wilhelm; America, 1842 8582.1 p13
Heinrichsmeier, Carl Ernst Ludwig; America, 1875 4610.10 p101
Heinrichsmeyer, Anton Friedrich; America, 1839 4610.10 p97
*Wife:*Christine L. Habbe
*Son:*Friedrich Wilhelm G.
Heinrichsmeyer, Christine L. Habbe *SEE* Heinrichsmeyer, Anton Friedrich
Heinrichsmeyer, Friedrich Wilhelm G. *SEE* Heinrichsmeyer, Anton Friedrich
Heinricks, Michel 28; Kansas, 1876 5240.1 p57
Heinsheimer, J. H.; America, 1836 8582.1 p13
Heintz, Charles; Iroquois Co., IL, 1892 3455.1 p11
Heintz, Chatrine 6; New Orleans, 1838 778.5 p268
Heintz, Elizabeth 4; New Orleans, 1838 778.5 p268
Heintz, Elizabeth 32; New Orleans, 1838 778.5 p268
Heintz, Frederic 25; America, 1838 778.5 p268
Heintz, George 3 mos; New Orleans, 1838 778.5 p268
Heintz, Jacob 8; New Orleans, 1838 778.5 p268

Heintz, Jacob 28; New Orleans, 1838 *778.5 p268*
Heintz, Michael; Shreveport, LA, 1879 *7129 p44*
Heintz, Nikolaus; Ohio, 1847 *8582.1 p48*
Heintzelman, George; Pennsylvania, 1749 *2444 p163*
Heintzelmann, Anna Maria *SEE* Heintzelmann, Simon
Heintzelmann, Anna Maria *SEE* Heintzelmann, Simon
Heintzelmann, Catharina *SEE* Heintzelmann, Simon
Heintzelmann, Lucia *SEE* Heintzelmann, Simon
Heintzelmann, Margaretha; Pennsylvania, 1753 *2444 p180*
Heintzelmann, Simon; Pennsylvania, 1749-1800 *2444 p164*
   Wife: Anna Maria
   Child: Catharina
   Child: Anna Maria
   Child: Lucia
Heintzmann, Anna Maria; Pennsylvania, 1750-1800 *2444 p181*
Heinz, Joseph; Kansas, 1880 *5240.1 p19*
Heinze, . . .; Canada, 1776-1783 *9786 p23*
Heinzen, Karl; Louisville, KY, 1855 *3702.7 p125*
Heir, Eliza 20; Massachusetts, 1850 *5881.1 p46*
Heiron, William 20; Antigua (Antego), 1728 *3690.1 p109*
Heischman, . . .; Canada, 1776-1783 *9786 p23*
Heise, . . .; Canada, 1776-1783 *9786 p23*
Heise, August; America, 1862 *2896.5 p17*
Heise, Edward; New York, NY, 1927 *3455.4 p83*
Heiselmann, Franz; America, 1853 *9162.8 p36*
Heisenbuttel, Christian; New York, NY, 1836 *8208.4 p11*
Heiser, Charles; Wisconsin, n.d. *9675.5 p264*
Heiser, Georg; New York, NY, 1840 *8208.4 p110*
Heiser, John; America, 1855 *1450.2 p63A*
Heisflug, Herman; Ohio, 1882 *9892.11 p20*
Heish, George; America, 1749 *2444 p162*
Heisinger, Herman; Wisconsin, n.d. *9675.5 p264*
Heisler, Christian; Pennsylvania, 1750 *2444 p166*
Heisler, Jacob; Illinois, 1880 *2896.5 p17*
Heiss, . . .; Canada, 1776-1783 *9786 p23*
Heiss, John P.; Nicaragua, 1856 *8582.3 p31*
Heiss, Michael; Kentucky, 1843 *8582.3 p101*
Heissler, Peter; Charleston, SC, 1775-1781 *8582.2 p52*
Heist, Bo; New York, 1881 *3702.7 p426*
Heist, John Nicholas; Philadelphia, 1757 *9973.7 p32*
Heist, John Philip; Philadelphia, 1756 *9973.7 p32*
Heister, Philip von; New York, 1776 *9786 p277*
Heisterkamp, . . .; New York, 1881 *3702.7 p426*
Heiszler, Christoph; Pennsylvania, 1750 *2444 p166*
Heit, Jost; Virginia, 1732 *8582.3 p96*
   With sons & son-in-law
Heitbring, Adam H.; America, 1848 *8582.1 p13*
Heitland, Henry 20; Maryland, 1774 *1219.7 p204*
Heitmann, Franz H.; Cincinnati, 1844 *8582.1 p13*
Heitmann, H.; Columbus, OH, 1875 *8582.2 p52*
Heitmann, Johann Friederich; New York, NY, 1836 *8208.4 p10*
Heitmeier, Heinrich Carl; America, 1889 *4610.10 p107*
Heitsman, Martin; New York, 1854 *1450.2 p63A*
Heittman, John; America, 1854 *1450.2 p63A*
Heitto, Jalmar; Washington, 1859-1920 *2872.1 p16*
Heitz, Frank 27; Kansas, 1880 *5240.1 p61*
Heitz, Lewis; America, 1847 *1450.2 p63A*
Heitzler, Wilwar 21; Louisiana, 1838 *778.5 p268*
Heitzman, Anthony; Indiana, 1844 *9117 p16*
Heiz, Andrew; New Orleans, 1850 *2896.5 p17*
Helan Potet, Mathieu 38; New Orleans, 1838 *778.5 p269*
Helart, Joseph; Colorado, 1904 *9678.2 p23*
Helay, James; America, 1742 *4971 p53*
Helberg, Charles; Colorado, 1904 *9678.2 p23*
Helbig, Jane 37 *SEE* Helbig, Loveged
Helbig, Loveged 40; New Orleans, 1839 *9420.2 p483*
   Wife: Jane 37
Helbock, John; Illinois, 1878 *2896.5 p17*
Helbock, Stephen; Illinois, 1866 *2896.5 p17*
Helburn, William 19; Jamaica, 1722 *3690.1 p109*
Held, . . .; Canada, 1776-1783 *9786 p23*
Held, Anna I Friedrichsmeyer *SEE* Held, Carl Friedrich
Held, Anna Maria 22; America, 1853 *9162.8 p36*
Held, Anna Marie C Friedrike *SEE* Held, Christoph Heinrich
Held, Anne M. E. Ellermann *SEE* Held, Christoph Heinrich
Held, August; Wisconsin, n.d. *9675.5 p264*
Held, Carl Friedrich; America, 1838-1854 *4610.10 p148*
   Wife: Cath. I. F. Meyer
Held, Carl Friedrich; America, 1853 *4610.10 p148*
   Son: Anna I Friedrichsmeyer
Held, Carl Heinrich; America, 1850 *4610.10 p147*
Held, Carl Heinrich Hermann; America, 1854 *4610.10 p148*
Held, Caroline Louise *SEE* Held, Christoph Heinrich

Held, Caspar Heinrich; America, 1832 *4610.10 p47*
Held, Caspar Heinrich; America, 1850 *4610.10 p138*
Held, Cath. I. F. Meyer *SEE* Held, Carl Friedrich
Held, Christian; America, 1854 *4610.10 p116*
Held, Christian Heinrich *SEE* Held, Christoph Heinrich
Held, Christian Heinrich; America, 1853 *4610.10 p148*
   With wife 27
   Son: Peter Heinrich
Held, Christoph Heinrich *SEE* Held, Christoph Heinrich
Held, Christoph Heinrich; America, 1844 *4610.10 p146*
   Wife: Anne M. E. Ellermann
   Child: Christoph Heinrich
   Child: Hermann Heinrich
   Child: Anna Marie C Friedrike
   Child: Caroline Louise
   Child: Justine W. Henriette
   Child: Christian Heinrich
   Child: Joh. F. Christian
Held, Georg; Ohio, 1832 *8582 p13*
Held, Hermann Heinrich *SEE* Held, Christoph Heinrich
Held, Joh. F. Christian *SEE* Held, Christoph Heinrich
Held, Johann Carl Wilhelm *SEE* Held, Carl Friedrich
Held, Johann Karl Ludwig; America, 1852 *4610.10 p116*
Held, Justine W. Henriette *SEE* Held, Christoph Heinrich
Held, Peter Heinrich *SEE* Held, Christian Heinrich
Heldmayer, Eva Margaretha; Pennsylvania, 1754 *2444 p221*
Heldt, August Heinrich; America, 1890 *4610.10 p114*
Heldt, Condrit 52; Georgia, 1738 *9332 p333*
   Wife: Elizabeth 53
   Son: Hans Michael 23
   Daughter: Elizabeth 17
Heldt, Elizabeth 17 *SEE* Heldt, Condrit
Heldt, Elizabeth 53 *SEE* Heldt, Condrit
Heldt, Ernst Heinrich August; America, 1857 *4610.10 p117*
Heldt, Hans Michael 23 *SEE* Heldt, Condrit
Heldt, Johann Friedrich Christoph; America, 1856 *4610.10 p117*
Hele, George; Virginia, 1652 *6251 p19*
Helen Potet, Mathieu 38; New Orleans, 1838 *778.5 p269*
Helenberg, Frank 26; Harris Co., TX, 1899 *6254 p6*
Helerin, Johannes 30; Pennsylvania, 1753 *2444 p167*
Heley, Jane 9; Quebec, 1857 *5704.8 p135*
Heley, Sarah 15; Quebec, 1857 *5704.8 p135*
Helfenstein, Dorothea; Georgia, 1739 *9332 p326*
   Daughter: Maria Friederica 18
   Son: Johann Friedrich 16
   Daughter: Maria Christina 14
   Son: Johann Jacob 12
   Son: Jeremias 10
   Son: Johannes 6
Helfenstein, Jeremias 10 *SEE* Helfenstein, Dorothea
Helfenstein, Joh. Jac.; Georgia, 1739 *9332 p328*
Helfenstein, Johann Conrad Albert; Lancaster, PA, 1776 *8582.3 p85*
Helfenstein, Johann Friedrich 16 *SEE* Helfenstein, Dorothea
Helfenstein, Johann Jacob 12 *SEE* Helfenstein, Dorothea
Helfenstein, Johannes 6 *SEE* Helfenstein, Dorothea
Helfenstein, Maria Christina 14 *SEE* Helfenstein, Dorothea
Helfenstein, Maria Friederica 18 *SEE* Helfenstein, Dorothea
Helfer, Jean 69; America, 1837 *778.5 p269*
Helferich, Martin 20; America, 1838 *778.5 p269*
Helferick, Charles; New York, NY, 1833 *8208.4 p30*
Helfert, Barbara 34; America, 1853 *9162.8 p36*
Helfert, Elisabetha 15; America, 1853 *9162.8 p36*
Helfert, Gg. 43; America, 1853 *9162.8 p36*
Helfert, Margaretha 11; America, 1853 *9162.8 p36*
Helfert, Maria 8; America, 1853 *9162.8 p36*
Helfert, Maria Eva 24; America, 1853 *9162.8 p36*
Helfert, Valentin 9 mos; America, 1853 *9162.8 p36*
Helferty, Catharine; New York, NY, 1864 *5704.8 p178*
Helferty, Charles 32; Philadelphia, 1857 *5704.8 p134*
Helferty, John; St. John, N.B., 1853 *5704.8 p110*
Helferty, Mary; New York, NY, 1866 *5704.8 p214*
Helferty, Mary; St. John, N.B., 1849 *5704.8 p48*
Helferty, Mary Ann 10; St. John, N.B., 1853 *5704.8 p110*
Helferty, Thomas 5; St. John, N.B., 1853 *5704.8 p110*
Helferty, Thomas 42; St. John, N.B., 1853 *5704.8 p110*
Helferty, William; Philadelphia, 1851 *5704.8 p70*
Helferty, William 20; Philadelphia, 1854 *5704.8 p117*
Helfferich, Francis; Cincinnati, 1869-1887 *8582 p13*
Helfferich, Franz; Cincinnati, 1848 *8582.2 p63*
Helfrick, John Phillip; New York, NY, 1836 *8208.4 p16*
Helgeland, Osmond; Arkansas, 1918 *95.2 p55*
Helger, Francis; Canada, 1776-1783 *9786 p207A*
Helish, George; Wisconsin, n.d. *9675.5 p264*
Helker, Frederick; Illinois, 1868 *2896.5 p17*
Hell, August; Wisconsin, n.d. *9675.5 p264*

Hellberg, . . .; Canada, 1776-1783 *9786 p23*
Helle, Louis; America, 1859 *1450.2 p63A*
Hellebusch, B. H. F.; America, 1834 *8582.1 p13*
Hellebusch, Clemens; America, 1848 *8582.2 p15*
Hellemayer, Anne Marie 48; New Orleans, 1838 *778.5 p269*
Hellemayer, Bernard 16; New Orleans, 1838 *778.5 p269*
Hellemayer, George 60; New Orleans, 1838 *778.5 p269*
Hellemayer, Josephe 20; New Orleans, 1838 *778.5 p269*
Hellems, Fred B.R.; Colorado, 1904 *9678.2 p23*
Heller, . . .; Canada, 1776-1783 *9786 p23*
Heller, Adolph I. C. 25; Kansas, 1888 *5240.1 p72*
Heller, Georg Vincent; Ohio, 1795 *8582.2 p53*
   Brother: Jakob
Heller, Gottfried; Wisconsin, n.d. *9675.5 p264*
Heller, H. O. 22; Kansas, 1888 *5240.1 p19*
Heller, H. O. 22; Kansas, 1888 *5240.1 p71*
Heller, Jakob *SEE* Heller, Georg Vincent
Heller, Joseph; Wisconsin, n.d. *9675.5 p264*
Heller, William; Kansas, 1868 *5240.1 p19*
Hellerich, John Gottfried; New York, NY, 1836 *8208.4 p19*
Hellerman, Casper George; New York, 1756 *3652 p81*
Hellet, Albert; Arkansas, 1918 *95.2 p55*
Helley, David 21; Maryland, 1774 *1219.7 p180*
Hellier, Jon.; Virginia, 1637 *6219 p13*
Helling, Frederick William; Colorado, 1899 *9678.2 p23*
Helling, Ole 29; Arkansas, 1918 *95.2 p55*
Hellis, William John; America, 1851 *1450.2 p64A*
Hellman, Lambertine P.; Maryland, 1882 *1450.2 p15B*
Hellman, William; America, 1850 *1450.2 p64A*
Hellmann, Louis; Indianapolis, 1870 *1450.2 p15B*
Hellminger, Charles; Wisconsin, n.d. *9675.5 p264*
Hellmuth, . . .; Canada, 1776-1783 *9786 p23*
Hellmuth, Anton Julius; Wisconsin, n.d. *9675.5 p264*
Hellmuth, Henry 25; Kansas, 1906 *5240.1 p84*
Hellsten, Eric J.; Arkansas, 1918 *95.2 p55*
Hellsten, Erick Albert; Arkansas, 1918 *95.2 p55*
Hellwig, Gottl. 48; New Orleans, 1839 *9420.2 p166*
Hellwriggle, David; New York, 1834 *9892.11 p20*
Helm, Charles; Wisconsin, n.d. *9675.5 p264*
Helm, Johannes; Indianapolis, 1869-1887 *8582 p13*
Helm, Louis; Arkansas, 1874 *3688 p7*
Helm, Peter; Saratoga, NY, 1777 *8137 p9*
Helmann, Bernhard H.; Kentucky, 1845 *8582.3 p101*
Helmcke, Lieut.; Quebec, 1776 *9786 p104*
Helme, Samuel; Iowa, 1866-1943 *123.54 p22*
Helmecke, August Wilhelm; Quebec, 1776 *9786 p261*
Helmer, Jean 45; America, 1836 *778.5 p269*
Helmer, Matheus 50; America, 1836 *778.5 p269*
Helmer, Victor Frank; Kansas, 1910 *6013.40 p15*
Helmich, Wm; America, 1848 *8582.1 p13*
Helmig, Frederick; Illinois, 1870 *2896.5 p17*
Helming, Frederick; Illinois, 1868 *2896.5 p17*
Helmkamp, Christopher H.; America, 1840 *8582.1 p14*
Helmreich, Chr.; Iroquois Co., IL, 1892 *3455.1 p11*
Helms, Johannes; New Netherland, 1630-1646 *8582.2 p51*
Helmsmeier, Carl; America, 1896 *1450.2 p15B*
Helmstatter, Adam 17; America, 1854-1855 *9162.6 p104*
Helmstatter, Georg 20; America, 1854-1855 *9162.6 p104*
Helmstetter, Karl; Wisconsin, n.d. *9675.5 p264*
Helmwig, Frederick; Illinois, 1879 *2896.5 p17*
Helpenstall, Ludwig C.; Washington, 1859-1920 *2872.1 p16*
Helpenstell, Ludwig C.; Washington, 1859-1920 *2872.1 p16*
Helpfferer, Ruprecht; Georgia, 1738 *9332 p319*
Helpin, Dennis M.; Ohio, 1838 *9892.11 p20*
Helps, Christina; Colorado, 1906 *9678.2 p23*
Helps, Ernest Albert; Arkansas, 1918 *95.2 p55*
Helreigle, David; New York, 1834 *9892.11 p20*
Helrigle, Charles; Ohio, 1840 *9892.11 p20*
Helsby, Richard 19; Jamaica, 1731 *3690.1 p109*
Helsel, Tobias; Philadelphia, 1761 *9973.7 p36*
Helten, John; America, 1890 *5240.1 p19*
Helten, Leonard 43; Kansas, 1890 *5240.1 p19*
Helten, Leonard 43; Kansas, 1890 *5240.1 p75*
Helten, Peter; America, 1890 *5240.1 p19*
Heltermann, Hermann Gerhard; New York, NY, 1836 *8208.4 p19*
Helwin, Jane 7; Massachusetts, 1850 *5881.1 p48*
Helwin, William 9; Massachusetts, 1850 *5881.1 p51*
Hely, John; Virginia, 1637 *6219 p11*
Hely, John; Virginia, 1643 *6219 p208*
Hely, Willi.; Virginia, 1637 *6219 p112*
Hem, Thomas 26; Kansas, 1871 *5240.1 p51*
Heman, Thomas 35; St. John, N.B., 1866 *5704.8 p166*
Hemann, . . .; Canada, 1776-1783 *9786 p23*
Hemann, Henry; Illinois, 1880 *2896.5 p17*
Hemann, Henry; Illinois, 1882 *2896.5 p17*
Hemann, Joseph A.; Cincinnati, 1841 *8582.1 p46*
Hemann, Joseph A.; Cincinnati, 1869-1887 *8582 p13*

Hemann, Joseph Anton; Cincinnati, 1788-1848 ***8582.3*** *p89*
Hemann, Joseph Anton; Cincinnati, 1840-1841 ***8582.2*** *p52*
Hemann, William; Illinois, 1880 ***2896.5*** *p17*
Hemberger, Joseph 23; Kansas, 1877 ***5240.1*** *p58*
Hembrock, Clemens; Kentucky, 1840 ***8582.3*** *p100*
Hemer, Auguste 23; Louisiana, 1827 ***778.5*** *p269*
Hemes, John; Wisconsin, n.d. ***9675.5*** *p264*
Hemeyer, Carl Heinrich; America, 1868 ***4610.10*** *p152*
Hemicker, Michael; Pennsylvania, 1771 ***9973.8*** *p32*
Hemig, Gottleib; New Jersey, 1870 ***5240.1*** *p19*
Hemingway, Mary 27; Maryland, 1775 ***1219.7*** *p256*
Hemlock, Patrick; Wisconsin, n.d. ***9675.5*** *p264*
Hemlock, William; Wisconsin, n.d. ***9675.5*** *p264*
Hemlock, William 28; Massachusetts, 1849 ***5881.1*** *p51*
Hemmelgarn, Mr.; Cincinnati, 1866 ***8582.1*** *p15*
Hemmelgarn, Heinrich; America, 1869-1887 ***8582*** *p13*
Hemmerle, . . .; Canada, 1776-1783 ***9786*** *p23*
Hemmerle, Jakob; Ohio, 1798-1818 ***8582.2*** *p54*
Hemming, Samuell; America, 1698 ***2212*** *p10*
Hemminger, Agatha *SEE* Hemminger, Georg Friedrich
Hemminger, Andreas *SEE* Hemminger, Johannes, Jr.
Hemminger, Anna M Schlotterbecker *SEE* Hemminger, Georg Friedrich
Hemminger, Barbara; Pennsylvania, 1753 ***2444*** *p237*
Hemminger, Georg Friedrich *SEE* Hemminger, Johannes, Jr.
Hemminger, Georg Friedrich; Pennsylvania, 1753 ***2444*** *p164*
*Wife:*Anna M Schlotterbecker
*Child:*Agatha
Hemminger, Johannes *SEE* Hemminger, Johannes, Jr.
Hemminger, Johannes, Jr.; Pennsylvania, 1749 ***2444*** *p164*
*Wife:*Margaretha
*Child:*Johannes
*Child:*Georg Friedrich
*Child:*Sophia
*Child:*Andreas
Hemminger, Margaretha *SEE* Hemminger, Johannes, Jr.
Hemminger, Sophia *SEE* Hemminger, Johannes, Jr.
Hemminghaus, Hermann; Illinois, 1861-1940 ***4610.10*** *p67*
Hemmingsson, Johan August; Minneapolis, 1881-1884 ***6410.35*** *p60*
Hempel, John William; New York, NY, 1838 ***8208.4*** *p72*
Hempfield, William; New York, NY, 1818 ***9892.11*** *p20*
Hempfield, William; Ohio, 1835 ***9892.11*** *p20*
Hemphill, . . . 6 mos; Quebec, 1848 ***5704.8*** *p42*
Hemphill, David; New York, NY, 1864 ***5704.8*** *p174*
Hemphill, Hugh 27; Philadelphia, 1833-1834 ***53.26*** *p37*
Hemphill, James; Philadelphia, 1851 ***5704.8*** *p70*
Hemphill, John; New York, NY, 1811 ***2859.11*** *p13*
With family
Hemphill, John; New York, NY, 1864 ***5704.8*** *p180*
Hemphill, John; Quebec, 1848 ***5704.8*** *p42*
Hemphill, Margaret; Quebec, 1848 ***5704.8*** *p42*
Hemphill, Mary 20; Philadelphia, 1857 ***5704.8*** *p133*
Hemphill, Mary 25; Quebec, 1851 ***5704.8*** *p73*
Hemphill, Mary J.; New York, NY, 1867 ***5704.8*** *p218*
Hemphill, Mary Jane; Philadelphia, 1847 ***53.26*** *p37*
Hemphill, Mary Jane; Philadelphia, 1847 ***5704.8*** *p31*
Hemphill, Sarah; Philadelphia, 1849 ***53.26*** *p37*
Hemphill, Sarah; Philadelphia, 1849 ***5704.8*** *p53*
Hemphill, Wallace 15; Philadelphia, 1857 ***5704.8*** *p133*
Hemphry, William; Indiana, 1837 ***9117*** *p15*
Hempsey, Susan; Philadelphia, 1852 ***5704.8*** *p86*
Hempson, Margaret; Philadelphia, 1866 ***5704.8*** *p204*
Hempton, Eliza; Philadelphia, 1852 ***5704.8*** *p85*
Hempton, William; Philadelphia, 1852 ***5704.8*** *p85*
Hemsel, William 31; Nova Scotia, 1774 ***1219.7*** *p210*
With wife
With 3 children
Henaghan, Catherine; America, 1742 ***4971*** *p80*
Henan, William 11; Philadelphia, 1851 ***5704.8*** *p76*
Henar, G.; Cincinnati, 1869-1887 ***8582*** *p13*
Henard, F. 30; New Orleans, 1827 ***778.5*** *p269*
Henborne, Kath.; Virginia, 1637 ***6219*** *p111*
Henchley, Sarah; Virginia, 1638 ***6219*** *p117*
Hencing, Jon.; Virginia, 1636 ***6219*** *p79*
Hencke, Christopher; New York, 1743 ***3652*** *p60*
*Wife:*Elizabeth
Hencke, Elizabeth *SEE* Hencke, Christopher
Henckel, . . .; Canada, 1776-1783 ***9786*** *p23*
Henckel, Mr.; Canada, 1776-1783 ***9786*** *p232*
Henckel, Jacob; Canada, 1776-1783 ***9786*** *p242*
Henckelmann, Johann Heinrich; Halifax, N.S., 1778 ***9786*** *p270*
Henckelmann, Johann Heinrich; New York, 1776 ***9786*** *p270*
Hend, Winifred; Quebec, 1823 ***7603*** *p64*
Hendel, Heinrich; Wisconsin, n.d. ***9675.5*** *p264*
Hendel, Maria Barbara; New York, 1749 ***3652*** *p73*
Hendershot, Henry Herbert 26; Kansas, 1882 ***5240.1*** *p19*
Hendershot, Henry Herbert 26; Kansas, 1882 ***5240.1*** *p63*
Henderson, . . . 3; Philadelphia, 1865 ***5704.8*** *p192*
Henderson, Major; Quebec, 1815 ***9229.18*** *p80*
With wife
Henderson, Mr.; Quebec, 1815 ***9229.18*** *p79*
Henderson, Mr. 25; Tobago, W. Indies, 1774 ***1219.7*** *p224*
Henderson, Agnes 9; St. John, N.B., 1847 ***5704.8*** *p3*
Henderson, Agnes 18; St. John, N.B., 1866 ***5704.8*** *p167*
Henderson, Alexander; St. John, N.B., 1853 ***5704.8*** *p106*
Henderson, Alexander 4; Quebec, 1864 ***5704.8*** *p162*
Henderson, Alexander 6 *SEE* Henderson, Robert
Henderson, Alexander 18; Philadelphia, 1859 ***5704.8*** *p141*
Henderson, Andrew; New York, NY, 1838 ***8208.4*** *p81*
Henderson, Andrew; Pennsylvania, 1841 ***7036*** *p123*
*Brother:*John
Henderson, Andrew; Quebec, 1847 ***5704.8*** *p11*
Henderson, Ann 1 *SEE* Henderson, Robert
Henderson, Ann 6; Quebec, 1864 ***5704.8*** *p162*
Henderson, Ann 8 *SEE* Henderson, Robert
Henderson, Ann 35; Quebec, 1864 ***5704.8*** *p162*
Henderson, Anne; New York, NY, 1815 ***2859.11*** *p33*
Henderson, Carolin; Philadelphia, 1866 ***5704.8*** *p207*
Henderson, Catherine; New York, NY, 1815 ***2859.11*** *p33*
Henderson, Catherine; Quebec, 1852 ***5704.8*** *p87*
Henderson, Catherine; Quebec, 1852 ***5704.8*** *p90*
Henderson, Catherine; St. John, N.B., 1847 ***5704.8*** *p3*
Henderson, Catherine; St. John, N.B., 1853 ***5704.8*** *p106*
Henderson, Charles James 7; St. John, N.B., 1847 ***5704.8*** *p3*
Henderson, Christopher; New York, NY, 1815 ***2859.11*** *p33*
Henderson, Mrs. David; America, 1836 ***8893*** *p264*
With family
Henderson, David; North Carolina, 1735 ***1639.20*** *p92*
Henderson, David; Philadelphia, 1847 ***53.26*** *p37*
Henderson, David; Philadelphia, 1847 ***5704.8*** *p31*
Henderson, David 9 *SEE* Henderson, Robert
Henderson, David 21; Maryland, 1774 ***1219.7*** *p187*
Henderson, Donald; Quebec, 1790 ***9775.5*** *p198A*
Henderson, Eleanor; New York, NY, 1816 ***2859.11*** *p33*
Henderson, Elenor 18 *SEE* Henderson, Robert
Henderson, Elenor 44 *SEE* Henderson, Robert
Henderson, Eliza 13; Massachusetts, 1849 ***5881.1*** *p46*
Henderson, Elizabeth 40; Kansas, 1886 ***5240.1*** *p69*
Henderson, Francis; New York, NY, 1815 ***2859.11*** *p33*
Henderson, G.; Quebec, 1815 ***9229.18*** *p74*
Henderson, George; New York, NY, 1815 ***2859.11*** *p33*
Henderson, George; New York, NY, 1816 ***2859.11*** *p33*
Henderson, George 11 *SEE* Henderson, Robert
Henderson, George 23; St. John, N.B., 1863 ***5704.8*** *p153*
Henderson, Henry; Iowa, 1866-1943 ***123.54*** *p22*
Henderson, Henry; San Francisco, 1870 ***2764.35*** *p31*
Henderson, Isabella; St. John, N.B., 1851 ***5704.8*** *p79*
Henderson, James; America, 1803 ***1639.20*** *p92*
Henderson, James; New York, 1770 ***1219.7*** *p147*
Henderson, James; New York, NY, 1811 ***2859.11*** *p13*
With family
Henderson, James; New York, NY, 1815 ***2859.11*** *p33*
Henderson, James; New York, NY, 1816 ***2859.11*** *p33*
Henderson, James; Quebec, 1852 ***5704.8*** *p87*
Henderson, James; Quebec, 1852 ***5704.8*** *p90*
Henderson, James 15; Quebec, 1864 ***5704.8*** *p162*
Henderson, James 20; Maryland, 1751 ***1219.7*** *p3*
Henderson, James 20; Maryland, 1751 ***3690.1*** *p109*
Henderson, Jane; New York, NY, 1815 ***2859.11*** *p33*
Henderson, Jane 15 *SEE* Henderson, Robert
Henderson, Jane 22; St. John, N.B., 1858 ***5704.8*** *p140*
Henderson, Jane 26; St. John, N.B., 1863 ***5704.8*** *p153*
Henderson, Jane 26; Wilmington, DE, 1831 ***6508.7*** *p161*
Henderson, Janet 11; Quebec, 1864 ***5704.8*** *p162*
Henderson, John *SEE* Henderson, Andrew
Henderson, John; Iowa, 1866-1943 ***123.54*** *p22*
Henderson, John; New York, NY, 1811 ***2859.11*** *p13*
Henderson, John; New York, NY, 1815 ***2859.11*** *p33*
Henderson, John; North Carolina, 1825 ***1639.20*** *p92*
Henderson, John; Petersburg, VA, 1811 ***4778.2*** *p142*
Henderson, John; Philadelphia, 1816 ***2859.11*** *p33*
Henderson, John; Philadelphia, 1864 ***5704.8*** *p169*
Henderson, John; Quebec, 1847 ***5704.8*** *p11*
Henderson, John; St. John, N.B., 1853 ***5704.8*** *p106*
Henderson, John 9; Quebec, 1864 ***5704.8*** *p162*
Henderson, John 25; Jamaica, 1774 ***1219.7*** *p189*
Henderson, John 37; Quebec, 1864 ***5704.8*** *p162*
Henderson, John 42; St. John, N.B., 1866 ***5704.8*** *p166*
Henderson, Joseph; New York, NY, 1815 ***2859.11*** *p33*
Henderson, Joseph; St. John, N.B., 1847 ***5704.8*** *p5*
Henderson, Marg.; Baltimore, 1811 ***2859.11*** *p13*
Henderson, Margaret; Quebec, 1847 ***5704.8*** *p11*
Henderson, Margaret; Quebec, 1852 ***5704.8*** *p87*
Henderson, Margaret; Quebec, 1852 ***5704.8*** *p90*
Henderson, Margaret; St. John, N.B., 1853 ***5704.8*** *p106*
Henderson, Margaret 22; Kansas, 1886 ***5240.1*** *p69*
Henderson, Martha; Philadelphia, 1865 ***5704.8*** *p192*
Henderson, Mary; Quebec, 1847 ***5704.8*** *p11*
Henderson, Mary; St. John, N.B., 1847 ***5704.8*** *p3*
Henderson, Mary 18; Philadelphia, 1864 ***5704.8*** *p161*
Henderson, Mary J.; Philadelphia, 1864 ***5704.8*** *p169*
Henderson, Nancy; Philadelphia, 1864 ***5704.8*** *p169*
Henderson, Peter 29; Kansas, 1884 ***5240.1*** *p66*
Henderson, Prudence 13 *SEE* Henderson, Robert
Henderson, Robert; Baltimore, 1811 ***2859.11*** *p13*
Henderson, Robert; New York, NY, 1815 ***2859.11*** *p33*
Henderson, Robert; New York, NY, 1816 ***2859.11*** *p33*
Henderson, Robert; St. John, N.B., 1847 ***5704.8*** *p3*
Henderson, Robert 1; Quebec, 1864 ***5704.8*** *p162*
Henderson, Robert 6 *SEE* Henderson, Robert
Henderson, Robert 22; Barbados, 1735 ***3690.1*** *p109*
Henderson, Robert 34; New York, 1774 ***1219.7*** *p223*
*Wife:*Susanna 30
*Child:*David 9
*Child:*Robert 6
*Child:*Susanna 4
*Child:*Ann 1
Henderson, Robert 45; Philadelphia, 1804 ***53.26*** *p37*
*Relative:*Elenor 44
*Relative:*Elenor 18
*Relative:*Jane 15
*Relative:*Prudence 13
*Relative:*George 11
*Relative:*Ann 8
*Relative:*Alexander 6
Henderson, Robt.; Petersburg, VA, 1810 ***4778.2*** *p142*
Henderson, Roseanna; St. John, N.B., 1847 ***5704.8*** *p3*
Henderson, S.; New York, NY, 1811 ***2859.11*** *p13*
Henderson, Sarah; Philadelphia, 1849 ***53.26*** *p37*
Henderson, Sarah; Philadelphia, 1849 ***5704.8*** *p54*
Henderson, Sarah 20; Wilmington, DE, 1831 ***6508.7*** *p161*
Henderson, Stuart; Philadelphia, 1865 ***5704.8*** *p192*
Henderson, Susanna 4 *SEE* Henderson, Robert
Henderson, Susanna 30 *SEE* Henderson, Robert
Henderson, Thomas; New York, NY, 1816 ***2859.11*** *p33*
Henderson, Thomas; New York, NY, 1865 ***5704.8*** *p203*
Henderson, Thomas; Philadelphia, 1849 ***53.26*** *p37*
Henderson, Thomas; Philadelphia, 1849 ***5704.8*** *p50*
Henderson, Thomas; St. John, N.B., 1852 ***5704.8*** *p93*
Henderson, Thomas; South Carolina, 1775 ***1639.20*** *p92*
Henderson, Thos.; Newfoundland, 1835 ***8893*** *p264*
Henderson, William; America, 1738 ***4971*** *p72*
Henderson, William; Baltimore, 1811 ***2859.11*** *p13*
Henderson, William; New York, NY, 1815 ***2859.11*** *p33*
Henderson, William; New York, NY, 1816 ***2859.11*** *p33*
Henderson, William; Quebec, 1847 ***5704.8*** *p11*
Henderson, William; Quebec, 1849 ***5704.8*** *p51*
Henderson, William; Quebec, 1852 ***5704.8*** *p87*
Henderson, William; Quebec, 1852 ***5704.8*** *p90*
Henderson, William; St. John, N.B., 1853 ***5704.8*** *p106*
Henderson, William; South Carolina, 1716 ***1639.20*** *p93*
Henderson, William 10; St. John, N.B., 1847 ***5704.8*** *p3*
Henderson, William 20; St. John, N.B., 1866 ***5704.8*** *p166*
Henderson, William 28; Maryland, 1774 ***1219.7*** *p202*
Henderson, Williams; New York, NY, 1815 ***2859.11*** *p33*
Hendey, Charles; Illinois, 1896 ***5012.40*** *p55*
Hendorf, . . .; Canada, 1776-1783 ***9786*** *p23*
Hendorff, Friedrich Christoph; Canada, 1780 ***9786*** *p268*
Hendorff, Friedrich Christoph; New York, 1776 ***9786*** *p268*
Hendrick, Alexander; South Carolina, 1767 ***1639.20*** *p93*
Hendrick, David; America, 1740 ***4971*** *p86*
Hendrick, Eliza; New York, NY, 1816 ***2859.11*** *p33*
Hendrick, John; New York, NY, 1816 ***2859.11*** *p33*
Hendrick, Patrick; New York, NY, 1835 ***8208.4*** *p6*
Hendricks, Gerhard; Germantown, PA, 1684 ***2467.7*** *p5*
Hendricksen, Hendrich; Washington, 1859-1920 ***2872.1*** *p16*
Hendrickson, Andrew; Washington, 1859-1920 ***2872.1*** *p16*
Hendrickson, Emil; Washington, 1859-1920 ***2872.1*** *p16*
Hendrie, Andrew; South Carolina, 1766 ***1639.20*** *p93*
Hendry, Catherine 35; Wilmington, NC, 1774 ***1639.20*** *p205*
Hendry, James 40; New York, 1775 ***1219.7*** *p268*
With wife
With 3 children
Hendry, Neil 27; Wilmington, NC, 1774 ***1639.20*** *p93*
Hendrye, John; Virginia, 1636 ***6219*** *p21*
Hendschel, Franz; Wisconsin, n.d. ***9675.5*** *p264*
Hene, Moritz; Philadelphia, 1752 ***8125.6*** *p23*
Henebry, Michael; Illinois, 1901 ***5012.39*** *p53*
Henegan, James; New York, NY, 1816 ***2859.11*** *p33*

Heneguocy, Mr. 15; America, 1837 ***778.5*** *p269*
Henery, Robert 22; Philadelphia, 1833-1834 ***53.26*** *p37*
Henes, William; Virginia, 1642 ***6219*** *p197*
With wife
Henessy, John; America, 1742 ***4971*** *p49*
Henesy, John; New York, 1852 ***1450.2*** *p64A*
Henesy, Timothy; America, 1861 ***6014.1*** *p2*
Henet, Corline 30; America, 1838 ***778.5*** *p269*
Heney, Matilda; Philadelphia, 1850 ***53.26*** *p37*
Heney, Matilda; Philadelphia, 1850 ***5704.8*** *p68*
Hengehold, Bernhold; Cincinnati, 1811-1848 ***8582.3*** *p89*
Hengel, Franz; Wisconsin, n.d. ***9675.5*** *p264*
Hengel, John; Wisconsin, n.d. ***9675.5*** *p264*
Hengelbrock, David; America, 1846 ***8582.3*** *p28*
Henicke, Frederick Augustus; New York, NY, 1835 ***8208.4*** *p29*
Henin, Jean 32; New Orleans, 1825 ***778.5*** *p269*
Hening, William 25; Maryland, 1775 ***1219.7*** *p272*
Heninger, George; America, 1836 ***1450.2*** *p64A*
Henis, Anna 2 *SEE* Henis, John
Henis, John; South Carolina, 1752-1753 ***3689.17*** *p21*
With wife
*Relative:*Anna 2
Henk, Julius; Illinois, 1860 ***5012.38*** *p97*
Henke, Agnes Catharine Louise; America, 1857 ***4610.10*** *p157*
Henke, Anna 14 *SEE* Henke, Heinrich August Carl
Henke, Bernard 45; Kansas, 1890 ***5240.1*** *p75*
Henke, Friederike Charlotte; America, 1841 ***4610.10*** *p119*
Henke, Heinrich August Carl; America, 1881 ***4610.10*** *p124*
*Sister:*Anna 14
Henke, Heinrich August Hubert Florenz; America, 1893 ***4610.10*** *p125*
Henkel, . . .; Canada, 1776-1783 ***9786*** *p23*
Henkel, Chaplain; Quebec, 1776 ***9786*** *p262*
Henkel, Reg-Feldsch; Quebec, 1776 ***9786*** *p104*
Henkel, Jacob; Canada, 1776-1783 ***9786*** *p207A*
Henken, John; Arkansas, 1918 ***95.2*** *p55*
Henkes, Joseph; Wisconsin, n.d. ***9675.5*** *p264*
Henley, John 19; Jamaica, 1734 ***3690.1*** *p109*
Henly, Edward; Virginia, 1652 ***6251*** *p20*
Henly, Marcia 7; Massachusetts, 1849 ***5881.1*** *p48*
Henman, Jno.; Virginia, 1648 ***6219*** *p246*
Henn, Anna Eulalia; America, 1750-1752 ***8125.6*** *p23*
Henn, Falleck; Wisconsin, n.d. ***9675.5*** *p264*
Henn, Frank; Wisconsin, n.d. ***9675.5*** *p264*
Henn, Heinrich; America, 1850 ***8582.3*** *p28*
Henn, Johann Jacob; Philadelphia, 1744 ***8125.6*** *p22*
Henn, Johann Peder; Philadelphia, 1744 ***8125.6*** *p22*
Henn, Matheis; Philadelphia, 1744 ***8125.6*** *p22*
Hennassy, Thomas; Illinois, 1861 ***2896.5*** *p17*
Hennecke, Anne M Christine Tugel *SEE* Hennecke, Johann Diedrich
Hennecke, Ernst Heinrich *SEE* Hennecke, Johann Diedrich
Hennecke, Johann Diedrich; America, 1837 ***4610.10*** *p138*
*Father:*Ernst Heinrich
*Mother:*Anne M Christine Tugel
Hennecus, Michael 15; Jamaica, 1731 ***3690.1*** *p109*
Hennelly, Dan.; America, 1736 ***4971*** *p44*
Hennelly, Teddy 24; Massachusetts, 1849 ***5881.1*** *p50*
Henneman, . . .; Canada, 1776-1783 ***9786*** *p23*
Hennepin, Ludwig; America, 1700-1877 ***8582.3*** *p80*
Henner, Deitriech 27; America, 1831 ***778.5*** *p269*
Henner, Jacob; Cincinnati, 1869-1887 ***8582*** *p13*
Hennesey, Anne 6 mos; St. John, N.B., 1860 ***5704.8*** *p144*
Hennesey, Anne 34; St. John, N.B., 1860 ***5704.8*** *p144*
Hennesey, James 40; St. John, N.B., 1860 ***5704.8*** *p144*
Hennesey, Joseph 34; Kansas, 1873 ***5240.1*** *p53*
Hennesey, Mary 16; St. John, N.B., 1860 ***5704.8*** *p144*
Hennesey, Sarah 4; St. John, N.B., 1860 ***5704.8*** *p144*
Henness, Wilhelm; Ohio, 1812-1814 ***8582.2*** *p59*
Hennessee, Patrick; New York, 1836 ***1450.2*** *p64A*
Hennessey, Patrick; Illinois, 1872 ***5012.39*** *p25*
Hennessy, Anastasia; Quebec, 1824 ***7603*** *p73*
Hennessy, Dennis 55; Massachusetts, 1850 ***5881.1*** *p46*
Hennessy, Edmund; Quebec, 1801 ***7603*** *p76*
Hennessy, Ellen 30; Massachusetts, 1850 ***5881.1*** *p46*
Hennessy, George; New York, NY, 1835 ***8208.4*** *p26*
Hennessy, James 25; Massachusetts, 1849 ***5881.1*** *p47*
Hennessy, John; America, 1735-1743 ***4971*** *p51*
Hennessy, John; America, 1742 ***4971*** *p50*
Hennessy, John; Quebec, 1805 ***7603*** *p81*
Hennessy, Martin 27; Massachusetts, 1849 ***5881.1*** *p49*
Hennessy, Mary 20; Massachusetts, 1849 ***5881.1*** *p48*
Hennessy, Michael 40; Massachusetts, 1850 ***5881.1*** *p49*
Hennessy, Nathaniel 19; Massachusetts, 1849 ***5881.1*** *p49*
Hennessy, Patrick 30; Massachusetts, 1849 ***5881.1*** *p50*
Hennessy, William 20; Massachusetts, 1850 ***5881.1*** *p51*
Hennessy, William 28; Massachusetts, 1849 ***5881.1*** *p51*
Hennesy, Eleonore; Quebec, 1811 ***7603*** *p82*
Hennesy, Morris; Washington, 1859-1920 ***2872.1*** *p16*
Hennesy, Richard; America, 1741 ***4971*** *p41*
Henney, Peter; New York, NY, 1815 ***2859.11*** *p33*
Henney, Thomas 18; Antigua (Antego), 1754 ***3690.1*** *p110*
Henni, Johann Martin; Cincinnati, 1788-1848 ***8582.3*** *p89*
Hennig, Christfield; Wisconsin, n.d. ***9675.5*** *p264*
Hennig, Frederick 47; New Orleans, 1839 ***9420.2*** *p359*
Hennig, Paul; New York, 1750 ***3652*** *p75*
Henning, . . .; Canada, 1776-1783 ***9786*** *p23*
Henning, Christ; Wisconsin, n.d. ***9675.5*** *p264*
Henning, Frederich; America, 1849 ***1450.2*** *p64A*
Henning, Herman; Wisconsin, n.d. ***9675.5*** *p264*
Henning, Hieronimus; Philadelphia, 1759 ***9973.7*** *p34*
Henning, John A.; Illinois, 1892 ***5012.40*** *p26*
Henning, Joseph; New York, NY, 1839 ***8208.4*** *p100*
Henning, Julius; Wisconsin, n.d. ***9675.5*** *p264*
Henning, Leonhard; New York, NY, 1838 ***8208.4*** *p62*
Henning, Matth Wilhelm; Pennsylvania, 1752 ***4525*** *p221*
Henning, Ranke; Illinois, 1888 ***5012.37*** *p61*
Henning, Veter; South Carolina, 1788 ***7119*** *p201*
Henning, William; Wisconsin, n.d. ***9675.5*** *p264*
Henninger, Johannes; America, 1808 ***8582.3*** *p76*
Henninger, Karl; America, 1850 ***8582.3*** *p28*
Henninger, Richard; New York, 1850 ***1450.2*** *p64A*
Henninghausen, Konrad; Philadelphia, 1779 ***8137*** *p9*
Hennings, Henry 34; Kansas, 1890 ***5240.1*** *p19*
Hennings, Henry 34; Kansas, 1890 ***5240.1*** *p74*
Hennings, William; Wisconsin, n.d. ***9675.5*** *p264*
Henningsen, Carl Friederich; America, 1849-1856 ***8582.3*** *p30*
Henningsen, Carl Friederich; Nicaragua, 1856 ***8582.3*** *p31*
Henningsmeyer, Ernst Friedrich; America, 1854 ***4610.10*** *p156*
With wife
With 4 daughters
Hennissy, William; New York, NY, 1839 ***8208.4*** *p91*
Hennonin, Mr.; New Orleans, 1839 ***778.5*** *p270*
Henny, Thomas 18; Antigua (Antego), 1754 ***1219.7*** *p28*
Henny, Thomas 18; Antigua (Antego), 1754 ***3690.1*** *p110*
Heno, Vincent; Washington, 1859-1920 ***2872.1*** *p16*
Henochsberg, Moses; America, 1840 ***8582.1*** *p14*
Henochsberg, Moses 25; New York, NY, 1840 ***8582.3*** *p28*
Henonin, Mr.; New Orleans, 1839 ***778.5*** *p270*
Henonin, J.; New Orleans, 1839 ***778.5*** *p270*
Henraid, Numa 18; Port uncertain, 1838 ***778.5*** *p270*
Henrard, Jacques 28; America, 1822 ***778.5*** *p270*
Henri, Anne 30; Port uncertain, 1839 ***778.5*** *p270*
Henri, Ariz 48; Port uncertain, 1839 ***778.5*** *p270*
Henri, Barbe 8; Port uncertain, 1839 ***778.5*** *p270*
Henri, Elizabeth 33; America, 1837 ***778.5*** *p270*
Henri, Elizabeth 38; Port uncertain, 1839 ***778.5*** *p270*
Henri, Jacques 17; America, 1838 ***778.5*** *p270*
Henri, Louisa 7; America, 1837 ***778.5*** *p270*
Henri, Marie 6 mos; Port uncertain, 1839 ***778.5*** *p270*
Henri, Pierre Paul 29; Port uncertain, 1839 ***778.5*** *p270*
Henrich, George; Kansas, 1876 ***5240.1*** *p19*
Henrich, Johan Friederich; Pennsylvania, n.d. ***4779.3*** *p14*
Henrich, Johann; America, 1773 ***2444*** *p199*
Henrichs, Eibe; Illinois, 1876 ***5012.39*** *p26*
Henrichsmeyer, Ernst; Illinois, 1882 ***2896.5*** *p17*
Henrici, Mr.; Illinois, 1874 ***8582.2*** *p50*
Henrici, Anna Maria; Philadelphia, 1738-1768 ***4525*** *p281*
Henrici, Daniel Frederick; America, 1829 ***1450.2*** *p64A*
Henrick, Catherina 20; Georgia, 1738 ***9332*** *p330*
Henrick, Eve Barbara 22 *SEE* Henrick, Peter
Henrick, Jacob; Philadelphia, 1762 ***9973.7*** *p38*
Henrick, Juliana 54 *SEE* Henrick, Peter
Henrick, Margarett 15; Georgia, 1738 ***9332*** *p330*
Henrick, Peter 48; Georgia, 1738 ***9332*** *p330*
*Wife:*Juliana 54
*Daughter:*Eve Barbara 22
Henricks, Charles; New York, 1847 ***1450.2*** *p64A*
Henricks, Joachim; Wisconsin, n.d. ***9675.5*** *p264*
Henricksen, Albert 29; Arkansas, 1918 ***95.2*** *p55*
Henricksen, Frederick; Arkansas, 1918 ***95.2*** *p56*
Henrickson, Charles P.; Washington, 1859-1920 ***2872.1*** *p16*
Henrietta, Frances; New York, NY, 1811 ***2859.11*** *p13*
Henrietta, Francis; New York, NY, 1811 ***2859.11*** *p13*
Henriette, Ch. 29; America, 1836 ***778.5*** *p270*
Henrik, Sven; Minneapolis, 1883-1884 ***6410.35*** *p65*
Henriksen, Viggo Valdemar; Arkansas, 1918 ***95.2*** *p56*
Henriksson, Carl Henrik; America, 1843 ***6410.32*** *p124*
Henriksson, Mathias; America, 1830 ***6410.32*** *p124*
Henris, Clemence 8; America, 1837 ***778.5*** *p271*
Henry, . . .; New England, 1816 ***2859.11*** *p33*
With daughter
Henry, Mr. 35; New Orleans, 1837 ***778.5*** *p271*
Henry, Mr. 38; America, 1839 ***778.5*** *p271*
Henry, Alexander; Canada, 1761 ***9775.5*** *p197*
Henry, Alexander; Michigan, 1761 ***9775.5*** *p197*
Henry, Alexander 9; Massachusetts, 1848 ***5881.1*** *p44*
Henry, Andrew 5; Philadelphia, 1851 ***5704.8*** *p81*
Henry, Ann 9; Quebec, 1847 ***5704.8*** *p28*
Henry, Ann 28; Massachusetts, 1848 ***5881.1*** *p44*
Henry, Ann Jane *SEE* Henry, Catherine
Henry, Ann Jane; Philadelphia, 1849 ***5704.8*** *p58*
Henry, Anne; New York, NY, 1816 ***2859.11*** *p33*
Henry, Arthur 9 *SEE* Henry, Catherine
Henry, Arthur 9; Philadelphia, 1849 ***5704.8*** *p58*
Henry, Augustus; New York, NY, 1811 ***2859.11*** *p13*
Henry, Betty; Philadelphia, 1850 ***53.26*** *p37*
*Relative:*Mathew
Henry, Betty; Philadelphia, 1850 ***5704.8*** *p68*
Henry, Bridget; America, 1865 ***5704.8*** *p201*
Henry, Catharine; Philadelphia, 1849 ***5704.8*** *p58*
Henry, Catharine 22; Philadelphia, 1868 ***5704.8*** *p225*
Henry, Catherine *SEE* Henry, William
Henry, Catherine; North Carolina, 1735-1811 ***1639.20*** *p93*
Henry, Catherine; Philadelphia, 1849 ***53.26*** *p37*
*Relative:*Ann Jane
*Relative:*John 13
*Relative:*Mick 11
*Relative:*Arthur 9
*Relative:*David 7
Henry, Catherine; Philadelphia, 1849 ***5704.8*** *p58*
Henry, Charlotte *SEE* Henry, William
Henry, Charlotte; Philadelphia, 1848 ***5704.8*** *p45*
Henry, Daniel; Illinois, 1871 ***5012.39*** *p25*
Henry, Daniel; Philadelphia, 1851 ***5704.8*** *p81*
Henry, David; New York, NY, 1816 ***2859.11*** *p33*
Henry, David 7 *SEE* Henry, Catherine
Henry, David 7; Philadelphia, 1849 ***5704.8*** *p58*
Henry, David 13; Quebec, 1847 ***5704.8*** *p28*
Henry, Eliza; Quebec, 1847 ***5704.8*** *p28*
Henry, Eliza 5 *SEE* Henry, William
Henry, Eliza 5; Philadelphia, 1849 ***5704.8*** *p58*
Henry, Fanny; Quebec, 1847 ***5704.8*** *p28*
Henry, Francis 16; Philadelphia, 1860 ***5704.8*** *p145*
Henry, Francis 25; Philadelphia, 1861 ***5704.8*** *p149*
Henry, Francois 31; New Orleans, 1837 ***778.5*** *p271*
Henry, Fredk; Pennsylvania, n.d. ***4779.3*** *p14*
Henry, George; New York, NY, 1816 ***2859.11*** *p33*
Henry, George; Quebec, 1765 ***9775.5*** *p202*
Henry, Hugh; Philadelphia, 1853 ***5704.8*** *p100*
Henry, Hugh; Quebec, 1847 ***5704.8*** *p28*
Henry, James; Montreal, 1825 ***7603*** *p25*
Henry, James; New Orleans, 1849 ***5704.8*** *p58*
Henry, James 1; Massachusetts, 1848 ***5881.1*** *p47*
Henry, James W.; New York, NY, 1816 ***2859.11*** *p33*
Henry, Jane; America, 1865 ***5704.8*** *p201*
Henry, Jane 22; Philadelphia, 1864 ***5704.8*** *p160*
Henry, Jean Marie 43; America, 1838 ***778.5*** *p271*
Henry, Joe Fitz; Iowa, 1866-1943 ***123.54*** *p22*
Henry, John; New York, NY, 1811 ***2859.11*** *p13*
Henry, John; New York, NY, 1816 ***2859.11*** *p33*
Henry, John; New York, NY, 1835 ***8208.4*** *p29*
Henry, John; New York, NY, 1838 ***8208.4*** *p75*
Henry, John; Ohio, 1840 ***9892.11*** *p20*
Henry, John; Philadelphia, 1852 ***5704.8*** *p88*
Henry, John; St. John, N.B., 1853 ***5704.8*** *p110*
Henry, John 8; Quebec, 1847 ***5704.8*** *p28*
Henry, John 13 *SEE* Henry, Catherine
Henry, John 13; Philadelphia, 1849 ***5704.8*** *p58*
Henry, John 16; Massachusetts, 1850 ***5881.1*** *p48*
Henry, John 30; Grenada, 1774 ***1219.7*** *p231*
Henry, John G.; New York, NY, 1838 ***8208.4*** *p62*
Henry, Joseph; Quebec, 1847 ***5704.8*** *p28*
Henry, Margaret; Philadelphia, 1853 ***5704.8*** *p100*
Henry, Margaret 6 *SEE* Henry, William
Henry, Margaret 6; Philadelphia, 1849 ***5704.8*** *p58*
Henry, Margaret 13; Philadelphia, 1851 ***5704.8*** *p81*
Henry, Margaret 13; Quebec, 1847 ***5704.8*** *p28*
Henry, Margaret 18; New Orleans, 1860 ***5704.8*** *p144*
Henry, Margaret 24; Philadelphia, 1864 ***5704.8*** *p156*
Henry, Margaret Jane; Philadelphia, 1852 ***5704.8*** *p88*
Henry, Martha; Philadelphia, 1851 ***5704.8*** *p81*
Henry, Martice; Ohio, 1841 ***8365.25*** *p12*
Henry, Mary; Philadelphia, 1864 ***5704.8*** *p181*
Henry, Mary 11; Philadelphia, 1851 ***5704.8*** *p81*
Henry, Mathew *SEE* Henry, Betty
Henry, Mathew; Philadelphia, 1850 ***5704.8*** *p68*
Henry, Matilda; New York, NY, 1864 ***5704.8*** *p171*
Henry, Michael; Philadelphia, 1811 ***2859.11*** *p13*
With family
Henry, Mick 11 *SEE* Henry, Catherine
Henry, Mick 11; Philadelphia, 1849 ***5704.8*** *p58*
Henry, Molly 40; Philadelphia, 1833-1834 ***53.26*** *p37*
Henry, Patrick *SEE* Henry, William
Henry, Patrick; America, 1865 ***5704.8*** *p201*

Henry, Patrick; Philadelphia, 1849 ***5704.8*** *p58*
Henry, Patrick; Philadelphia, 1865 ***5704.8*** *p190*
Henry, Patrick 19; Philadelphia, 1860 ***5704.8*** *p145*
Henry, Peter; Quebec, 1851 ***5704.8*** *p73*
Henry, Robert; New York, NY, 1811 ***2859.11*** *p13*
Henry, Robert 8; Philadelphia, 1851 ***5704.8*** *p81*
Henry, Robert 36; Maryland, 1774 ***1219.7*** *p236*
Henry, Rose; Philadelphia, 1865 ***5704.8*** *p190*
Henry, Samuel; New York, NY, 1816 ***2859.11*** *p33*
Henry, Thomas; Philadelphia, 1864 ***5704.8*** *p176*
Henry, Thomas 3; Massachusetts, 1848 ***5881.1*** *p50*
Henry, William; New York, NY, 1811 ***2859.11*** *p13*
Henry, William; New York, NY, 1815 ***2859.11*** *p33*
Henry, William; North Carolina, 1783 ***1639.20*** *p93*
Henry, William; Philadelphia, 1848 ***53.26*** *p38*
*Relative:*Charlotte
Henry, William; Philadelphia, 1849 ***53.26*** *p37*
*Relative:*Catherine
*Relative:*Patrick
*Relative:*Margaret 6
*Relative:*Eliza 5
Henry, William; Philadelphia, 1849 ***5704.8*** *p58*
Henry, William; Quebec, 1847 ***5704.8*** *p28*
Henry, William 20; New Orleans, 1860 ***5704.8*** *p144*
Henry, William J.; Philadelphia, 1848 ***5704.8*** *p45*
Henrykowski, . . .; New York, 1831 ***4606*** *p173*
Hens, John; Wisconsin, n.d. ***9675.5*** *p264*
Henschell, . . .; Canada, 1776-1783 ***9786*** *p23*
Henschen, F.; New Orleans, 1846 ***3702.7*** *p84*
Henschen, John F.; Indiana, 1856 ***1450.2*** *p15B*
Henschen, Wilhelm; New Orleans, 1846 ***3702.7*** *p84*
Henschen, Wilhelmiene; New Orleans, 1846 ***3702.7*** *p84*
Henschuber, Morris; Arkansas, 1918 ***95.2*** *p56*
Hense, John; Wisconsin, n.d. ***9675.5*** *p264*
Hensel, Barbara; Wisconsin, n.d. ***9675.5*** *p264*
Hensel, Carl; Wisconsin, n.d. ***9675.5*** *p264*
Hensel, Elizabeth Miller; Wisconsin, n.d. ***9675.5*** *p264*
Hensen, Bernard; America, 1837 ***8582.1*** *p14*
Hensinger, Andreas *SEE* Hensinger, Hans
Hensinger, Barbara *SEE* Hensinger, Hans
Hensinger, Dorothea *SEE* Hensinger, Hans
Hensinger, Hans 26; Pennsylvania, 1753 ***2444*** *p164*
*Wife:*Barbara
*Child:*Dorothea
*Child:*Andreas
Hensinkveld, Berend; Illinois, 1863 ***2896.5*** *p17*
Henson, Joseph 35; Maryland, 1775 ***1219.7*** *p253*
Henson, Peter; America, 1866 ***1450.2*** *p65A*
Henss, . . .; Canada, 1776-1783 ***9786*** *p23*
Hensse, . . .; Canada, 1776-1783 ***9786*** *p23*
Henssell, . . .; Canada, 1776-1783 ***9786*** *p23*
Hentlands, Jon.; Virginia, 1637 ***6219*** *p11*
Hentlands, Jon.; Virginia, 1637 ***6219*** *p114*
Hentrich, Gotfried; Washington, 1859-1920 ***2872.1*** *p16*
Hentz, Anna Barbara Oertler *SEE* Hentz, Michael
Hentz, Michael; America, 1753 ***2444*** *p164*
*Wife:*Anna Barbara Oertler
Hentz, Nikolaus Martin; Cincinnati, 1788-1848 ***8582.3*** *p89*
Hentzen, Carl Hermann Gustav Julius; America, 1884 ***4610.10*** *p118*
*Brother:*Julius Carl Theodor
Hentzen, Carl Wilhelm Hermann; America, 1885 ***4610.10*** *p118*
Hentzen, Julius Carl Theodor *SEE* Hentzen, Carl Hermann Gustav Julius
Hentzinger, Andreas *SEE* Hentzinger, Hans
Hentzinger, Barbara *SEE* Hentzinger, Hans
Hentzinger, Dorothea *SEE* Hentzinger, Hans
Hentzinger, Hans 26; Pennsylvania, 1753 ***2444*** *p164*
*Wife:*Barbara
*Child:*Dorothea
*Child:*Andreas
Henwright, Patrick 26; Massachusetts, 1849 ***5881.1*** *p50*
Henzel, Ph. 25; America, 1839 ***778.5*** *p271*
Henzell, . . .; Canada, 1776-1783 ***9786*** *p23*
Henzey, Anthony; New York, NY, 1840 ***8208.4*** *p105*
Henzler, David 26; Kansas, 1890 ***5240.1*** *p74*
Henzler, Johann N.; America, 1847 ***8582.2*** *p15*
Hepburn, Charles; Cape Fear, NC, 1741 ***1639.20*** *p93*
Hepding, Catharina *SEE* Hepding, Johann Adam
Hepding, Christian *SEE* Hepding, Hans Jacob
Hepding, Christina B. Osiander *SEE* Hepding, Johann Adam
Hepding, Hans Jacob; Pennsylvania, 1752 ***2444*** *p164*
*Wife:*Johanna Benz
*Child:*Christian
Hepding, Johann Adam; Pennsylvania, 1749 ***2444*** *p164*
*Wife:*Christina B. Osiander
*Child:*Catharina
*Child:*Johann Jacob
*Child:*Matthias
Hepding, Johann Adam; Port uncertain, 1743-1800 ***2444*** *p165*
Hepding, Johann Jacob *SEE* Hepding, Johann Adam
Hepding, Johanna Benz *SEE* Hepding, Hans Jacob
Hepding, Matthias *SEE* Hepding, Johann Adam
Heper, Caspar Karl Heinrich Friedrich; America, 1844 ***4610.10*** *p133*
Heper, Ernestine Wilhelmine Henriette; America, 1881 ***4610.10*** *p137*
Hepp, Christian; America, 1842 ***1450.2*** *p65A*
Hepp, George; America, 1847 ***1450.2*** *p65A*
Hepp, John K.; America, 1852 ***1450.2*** *p65A*
Hepp, Otto; America, 1851 ***8582.3*** *p28*
Hepting, Hans Jacob; Pennsylvania, 1752 ***2444*** *p164*
Hequily, Francois 32; New Orleans, 1836 ***778.5*** *p271*
Her, Johanna 65; New York, NY, 1911 ***1763*** *p40C*
Heraghty, Catharine; New York, NY, 1870 ***5704.8*** *p239*
Heraghty, James; Philadelphia, 1868 ***5704.8*** *p220*
Heraghty, Michael; New York, NY, 1865 ***5704.8*** *p192*
Herald, Ann 16; Philadelphia, 1854 ***5704.8*** *p117*
Herald, Barbara 18; Philadelphia, 1854 ***5704.8*** *p117*
Herald, Georg Christoph; Pennsylvania, 1743 ***2444*** *p235*
Herald, Johan Earah; Pennsylvania, 1743 ***2444*** *p168*
Heralde, Christaf; Pennsylvania, 1743 ***2444*** *p168*
Heran, Martha; New York, NY, 1811 ***2859.11*** *p13*
Herancourt, G. M.; America, 1829 ***8582.2*** *p61*
Herancourt, Georg M.; Cincinnati, 1869-1887 ***8582*** *p13*
Herard, Virgil; Kansas, 1911 ***6013.40*** *p15*
Heraty, Margaret; Philadelphia, 1866 ***5704.8*** *p208*
Heraughty, Magy 10; Philadelphia, 1853 ***5704.8*** *p112*
Heraughty, Mary 8; Philadelphia, 1853 ***5704.8*** *p112*
Heraughty, Susan; Philadelphia, 1849 ***53.26*** *p38*
Heraughty, Susan; Philadelphia, 1849 ***5704.8*** *p53*
Herbault, Chs. 36; New Orleans, 1839 ***778.5*** *p271*
Herbault, E. 36; New Orleans, 1839 ***778.5*** *p271*
Herbault, Edward 27; New Orleans, 1821 ***778.5*** *p271*
Herbault, Fanny 24; Port uncertain, 1836 ***778.5*** *p271*
Herbeck, . . .; Canada, 1776-1783 ***9786*** *p24*
Herbeck, Joseph; Illinois, 1863 ***5012.39*** *p90*
Herbecke, . . .; Canada, 1776-1783 ***9786*** *p23*
Herbecke, . . .; Canada, 1776-1783 ***9786*** *p24*
Herber, George; Arkansas, 1918 ***95.2*** *p56*
Herberig, Melchior; New Jersey, 1780 ***8137*** *p9*
Herbers, Gerrard; New York, 1891 ***1450.2*** *p15B*
Herbers, Mathew Anthony; New York, 1901 ***1450.2*** *p15B*
Herbert, Lieutenant; Quebec, 1815 ***9229.18*** *p81*
Herbert, Allecia 9; Massachusetts, 1849 ***5881.1*** *p45*
Herbert, Catherine; Quebec, 1852 ***5704.8*** *p98*
Herbert, Ellen 11; Massachusetts, 1849 ***5881.1*** *p46*
Herbert, Isaac 23; Savannah, GA, 1775 ***1219.7*** *p274*
Herbert, John; Virginia, 1639 ***6219*** *p155*
Herbert, John 16; Jamaica, 1729 ***3690.1*** *p110*
Herbert, John, Jr.; New York, NY, 1834 ***8208.4*** *p3*
Herbert, Kelean; Iowa, 1866-1943 ***123.54*** *p22*
Herbert, L. F. 24; New Orleans, 1820 ***778.5*** *p271*
Herbert, Lawrence; Virginia, 1856 ***4626.16*** *p16*
Herbert, Margaret 13; Massachusetts, 1849 ***5881.1*** *p49*
Herbertz, Florentine Clemens *SEE* Herbertz, Karl
Herbertz, Karl; New York, 1859 ***8125.8*** *p436*
*Wife:*Florentine Clemens
With 6 children
Herbin, P. J. 31; Port uncertain, 1838 ***778.5*** *p271*
Herbnett, Richard 25; Massachusetts, 1849 ***5881.1*** *p50*
Herbst, Felix; Ohio, 1809-1871 ***8582*** *p13*
Herbst, John Henry; New York, 1750 ***3652*** *p74*
Herbst, John William; New York, NY, 1833 ***8208.4*** *p28*
Herbst, Laetitia; Kentucky, 1840-1845 ***8582.3*** *p100*
Herbst, Peter; Alberta, n.d. ***5262*** *p58*
Herbstreit, Mathias; New York, NY, 1831 ***8582.3*** *p28*
With parents
Herbstreit, Matthias; Cincinnati, 1869-1887 ***8582*** *p13*
Herby, Thomas; Virginia, 1750 ***3690.1*** *p110*
Herby, Thomas; Virginia, 1751 ***1219.7*** *p1*
Herchberg, Herman; Iowa, 1866-1943 ***123.54*** *p22*
Herchberg, M.; Iowa, 1866-1943 ***123.54*** *p22*
Herchberg, Samuel; Iowa, 1866-1943 ***123.54*** *p22*
Herchfield, . . .; Canada, 1776-1783 ***9786*** *p24*
Herchner, . . .; Canada, 1776-1783 ***9786*** *p24*
Herd, John; America, 1857 ***1450.2*** *p65A*
Herd, John; South Carolina, 1716 ***1639.20*** *p93*
Herde, William 25; Quebec, 1864 ***5704.8*** *p162*
Herder, Gustav; Baltimore, 1832 ***8125.8*** *p436*
Herdermann, Christine 36; America, 1836 ***778.5*** *p271*
Herdie, James 30; Baltimore, 1775 ***1219.7*** *p270*
Herdt, . . .; Canada, 1776-1783 ***9786*** *p24*
Here, Johannes; America, 1817 ***8582.2*** *p61*
Here, Johannes; America, 1872-1874 ***8582.1*** *p14*
Herfert, Josef; Washington, 1859-1920 ***2872.1*** *p16*
Herfurth, Wilhelm; Wisconsin, n.d. ***9675.5*** *p264*
Hergen, Louis; New York, NY, 1839 ***8208.4*** *p102*
Hergenroether, Franz; Kentucky, 1869-1887 ***8582*** *p13*
Herick, Ann *SEE* Herick, Henry
Herick, Henry; Virginia, 1644 ***6219*** *p230*
*Wife:*Ann
Herick Cline, Jonathan; Philadelphia, 1761 ***9973.7*** *p35*
Heril, Unity; Philadelphia, 1866 ***5704.8*** *p207*
Hering, Catherine; Milwaukee, 1875 ***4719.30*** *p257*
Hering, Constantin; Philadelphia, 1832 ***8582.3*** *p28*
Hering, Constantin; Surinam, 1800-1832 ***8582.3*** *p28*
Heringhty, Daniel 2; Philadelphia, 1853 ***5704.8*** *p100*
Heringhty, Hugh 4; Philadelphia, 1853 ***5704.8*** *p100*
Heringhty, Mary; Philadelphia, 1853 ***5704.8*** *p100*
Heringhty, Mary 8; Philadelphia, 1853 ***5704.8*** *p100*
Heringlacke, Henry; America, 1836 ***1450.2*** *p65A*
Heriot, Alexander; Carolina, 1684 ***1639.20*** *p93*
Heriott, Ann; Philadelphia, 1694-1695 ***4961*** *p164*
Heriott, Mary; Pennsylvania, 1682 ***4961*** *p164*
Heriott, Thomas; Pennsylvania, 1682 ***4960*** *p159*
Heriott, Thomas; Pennsylvania, 1682 ***4961*** *p164*
Herivel, Nicholas R.; Colorado, 1888 ***9678.2*** *p23*
Herkens, Elizabeth *SEE* Herkens, Peter
Herkens, Peter; New York, NY, 1883 ***3455.3*** *p47*
*Wife:*Elizabeth
Herker, James; New York, NY, 1811 ***2859.11*** *p13*
Herkins, Lovisa 18; Massachusetts, 1860 ***6410.32*** *p115*
Herkins, Peter; New York, NY, 1883 ***3455.2*** *p45*
Herlein, Johannes 30; Pennsylvania, 1753 ***2444*** *p167*
Herlemann, Nikolaus; Illinois, 1834 ***8582.1*** *p55*
Herlin, Maria; Georgia, 1739 ***9332*** *p323*
Herling, Carl; Charleston, SC, 1845 ***8582*** *p13*
Herling, Lewis; Illinois, 1858 ***2896.5*** *p17*
Herman, August; Illinois, 1880 ***2896.5*** *p17*
Herman, August; Wisconsin, n.d. ***9675.5*** *p264*
Herman, Benjamin; Arkansas, 1918 ***95.2*** *p56*
Herman, Gerg; Pennsylvania, 1747 ***2444*** *p165*
Herman, Henry; Arkansas, 1918 ***95.2*** *p56*
Herman, Henry; Pennsylvania, 1750 ***2444*** *p165*
Herman, Jacob; Indiana, 1848 ***9117*** *p19*
Herman, Johan Mich'l; Pennsylvania, 1754 ***2444*** *p165*
Herman, Johann Georg; Pennsylvania, 1750 ***2444*** *p165*
Herman, John; America, 1855 ***1450.2*** *p65A*
Herman, Louis; New York, NY, 1888 ***5240.1*** *p19*
Herman, Michael; Illinois, 1854 ***7857*** *p4*
Herman, Valentine; America, 1837 ***1450.2*** *p65A*
Hermandes, Juan 46; California, 1873 ***2769.10*** *p4*
Hermann, . . .; Canada, 1776-1783 ***9786*** *p24*
Hermann, . . .; Cincinnati, 1826 ***8582.1*** *p51*
Hermann, Agnes Barbara *SEE* Hermann, Johannes
Hermann, Anna Maria *SEE* Hermann, Johannes
Hermann, Babette 25; America, 1854-1855 ***9162.6*** *p105*
Hermann, Barbara *SEE* Hermann, Johannes
Hermann, Barbara; Pennsylvania, 1753 ***2444*** *p201*
Hermann, Eva Christine Walz *SEE* Hermann, Michael, Jr.
Hermann, Friederich; Kentucky, 1844 ***8582.3*** *p100*
Hermann, Gerg; Pennsylvania, 1747 ***2444*** *p165*
Hermann, Gottlieb; Iroquois Co., IL, 1896 ***3455.1*** *p11*
Hermann, Hans Jacob *SEE* Hermann, Michael, Jr.
Hermann, Hans Jerg *SEE* Hermann, Johannes
Hermann, Jacob; Pennsylvania, 1748 ***2444*** *p165*
Hermann, Jacob; Port uncertain, 1743-1800 ***2444*** *p165*
Hermann, Johannes; Pennsylvania, 1747 ***2444*** *p165*
*Child:*Anna Maria
*Child:*Agnes Barbara
With wife
Hermann, Johannes; Philadelphia, 1741-1800 ***2444*** *p165*
*Wife:*Barbara
*Child:*Hans Jerg
Hermann, Margaretha 81; Ontario, 1908 ***1763*** *p48D*
Hermann, Michael *SEE* Hermann, Michael
Hermann, Michael *SEE* Hermann, Michael, Jr.
Hermann, Michael; America, 1746 ***2444*** *p165*
*Wife:*Ursula Buehler
*Child:*Michael
Hermann, Michael, Jr.; America, 1753 ***2444*** *p165*
*Wife:*Eva Christine Walz
*Child:*Michael
With parents
*Child:*Hans Jacob
Hermann, Ursula Buehler *SEE* Hermann, Michael
Hermans, Albuns; Washington, 1859-1920 ***2872.1*** *p16*
Hermans, Erik Albinus; Washington, 1859-1920 ***2872.1*** *p16*
Hermans, John; Washington, 1859-1920 ***2872.1*** *p16*
Hermant, A. 23; New Orleans, 1823 ***778.5*** *p272*
Hermemesm, Gustav; Wisconsin, n.d. ***9675.5*** *p264*
Hermen, Bartholemew; Ohio, 1836 ***9892.11*** *p21*
Hermes, Joseph; America, 1853 ***8582.3*** *p29*
Hermes, Joseph; Kentucky, 1876-1877 ***8582.3*** *p99*
Hermicke, John Nicholas; Philadelphia, 1759 ***9973.7*** *p34*
Hermiger, Jane; Savannah, GA, 1774 ***1219.7*** *p227*
Hermiger, John; Savannah, GA, 1774 ***1219.7*** *p227*
Hermit of Sorel ; Canada, 1776-1783 ***9786*** *p233*
Hermitage, Jean 42; Montreal, 1798 ***7603*** *p30*
Hermling, John; New York, NY, 1853 ***1450.2*** *p65A*

Hermmeyer, Anne M. E. Korfmacher *SEE* Hermmeyer, Carl Friedrich
Hermmeyer, Carl Friedrich; America, 1852 ***4610.10*** *p98*
*Wife:*Anne M. E. Korfmacher
*Son:*Christian C. Friedrich
Hermmeyer, Christian C. Friedrich *SEE* Hermmeyer, Carl Friedrich
Hermo, Richard; Washington, 1859-1920 ***2872.1*** *p16*
Hermsdorf, Christian Adolph von; Savannah, GA, 1736 ***3652*** *p51*
Hermsdorff, . . .; Canada, 1776-1783 ***9786*** *p24*
Hermsen, John; Wisconsin, n.d. ***9675.5*** *p264*
Hermsmeyer, Ernst Christian Friedrich; America, 1881 ***4610.10*** *p101*
Hermstadt, Johann Gottfried 40; Halifax, N.S., 1752 ***7074.6*** *p207*
With family of 4
Hern, Georg; Pennsylvania, 1753 ***2444*** *p170*
Hern, Thomas; America, 1743 ***4971*** *p24*
Hernadez, Serido; Arkansas, 1918 ***95.2*** *p56*
Hernandez, Bridigo 30; Arizona, 1918 ***9228.40*** *p22*
Hernandez, Conception 42; Arizona, 1922 ***9228.40*** *p26*
Hernandez, Efren 25; Kansas, 1904 ***5240.1*** *p83*
Hernandez, Rafales 23; Arizona, 1926 ***9228.40*** *p30*
Hernberger, Anna Justina Unselt *SEE* Hernberger, Frantz
Hernberger, Frantz; Georgia, 1739 ***9332*** *p324*
*Wife:*Anna Justina Unselt
Hernberger, Frantz; Georgia, 1739 ***9332*** *p327*
*Wife:*Justina
Hernberger, Justina *SEE* Hernberger, Frantz
Herne, Christian; Milwaukee, 1875 ***4719.30*** *p257*
Herne, Mary; Philadelphia, 1866 ***5704.8*** *p209*
Herner, . . .; Canada, 1776-1783 ***9786*** *p24*
Herner, George; Pennsylvania, 1752 ***4525*** *p224*
Herner, Nicholas; Philadelphia, 1760 ***9973.7*** *p34*
Hernir, Auguste 23; Louisiana, 1827 ***778.5*** *p269*
Herns, John; America, 1736-1743 ***4971*** *p57*
Herntschier, Anton; New York, 1882 ***1450.2*** *p65A*
Herold, Adam; America, 1837 ***1763*** *p40D*
Herold, Andreas; Cincinnati, 1846 ***8582.1*** *p14*
Herold, Andreas; New York, NY, 1846 ***8582.3*** *p29*
Herold, Anna Maria; New York, 1717 ***3627*** *p12*
Herold, Christopher; Pennsylvania, 1743 ***2444*** *p168*
Herold, Emil 23; Kansas, 1906 ***5240.1*** *p83*
Herold, Fredrick; California, 1879 ***2764.35*** *p34*
Herold, Friedrich 28; St. Louis, 1871 ***8582*** *p13*
Herold, Henry 22; Kansas, 1879 ***5240.1*** *p60*
Herold, Henry 24; Kansas, 1897 ***5240.1*** *p19*
Herold, Henry Karl 24; Kansas, 1897 ***5240.1*** *p81*
Herold, Johann; Kentucky, 1869-1887 ***8582*** *p13*
Heroldt, Georg Christoph; Pennsylvania, 1743 ***2444*** *p168*
Heron, James; Philadelphia, 1848 ***53.26*** *p38*
Heron, James; Philadelphia, 1848 ***5704.8*** *p40*
Heron, James; Philadelphia, 1852 ***5704.8*** *p97*
Heron, James 38; St. John, N.B., 1866 ***5704.8*** *p166*
Heron, Jane; Philadelphia, 1868 ***5704.8*** *p231*
Heron, Margaret 16; Philadelphia, 1865 ***5704.8*** *p164*
Heron, Matilda; Philadelphia, 1867 ***5704.8*** *p218*
Heron, Michael; America, 1869 ***5704.8*** *p234*
Heron, P.; New Orleans, 1839 ***778.5*** *p272*
Heron, Samuel; Charleston, SC, 1803 ***1639.20*** *p93*
Herpel, John 82; Washington, D.C., 1911 ***1763*** *p40D*
Herpin, Mr. 20; New Orleans, 1823 ***778.5*** *p272*
Herpin, Mr. 60; America, 1835 ***778.5*** *p272*
Herport, . . .; Canada, 1776-1783 ***9786*** *p42*
Herr, Mrs. Daniel; Ohio, 1797 ***8582.2*** *p54*
With children
Herr, Daniel; Ohio, 1796 ***8582.2*** *p54*
Herr, Eberhard; Ohio, 1798-1818 ***8582.2*** *p54*
Herr, Eberhardt; Ohio, 1798 ***8582.2*** *p54*
Herr, Godfried; New York, 1860 ***2896.5*** *p17*
Herr, Jacob; America, 1753 ***2444*** *p163*
Herr, Jacob; New York, 1753 ***3652*** *p77*
Herr, John; Pennsylvania, 1709-1710 ***4480*** *p311*
Herr, Samuel; New York, 1750 ***3652*** *p74*
Herr, Valentine; America, 1854 ***2896.5*** *p18*
Herran, George; New York, NY, 1816 ***2859.11*** *p33*
Herreraz, Manuel; Arizona, 1900 ***9228.40*** *p6*
Herrick, Ann *SEE* Herrick, Henry
Herrick, Henry; Virginia, 1644 ***6219*** *p230*
*Wife:*Ann
Herrick, Jakob; New Netherland, 1630-1646 ***8582.2*** *p51*
Herrick, Tho., Jr.; Virginia, 1632 ***6219*** *p180*
Herrick, Tho., Sr.; Virginia, 1632 ***6219*** *p180*
Herricke, . . .; Canada, 1776-1783 ***9786*** *p24*
Herriford, John; Washington, 1859-1920 ***2872.1*** *p16*
Herrig, John; America, 1883 ***5240.1*** *p19*
Herrigan, Sarah; New York, NY, 1868 ***5704.8*** *p227*
Herriges, Gerhard; Wisconsin, n.d. ***9675.5*** *p264*
Herril, Neal 20; St. John, N.B., 1864 ***5704.8*** *p158*
Herril, Patrick 20; St. John, N.B., 1860 ***5704.8*** *p143*
Herrin, Thomas; New York, NY, 1815 ***2859.11*** *p33*
Herring, Christ.; Illinois, 1864 ***5012.38*** *p98*
Herring, John; Virginia, 1642 ***6219*** *p187*
Herring, Jon.; Virginia, 1642 ***6219*** *p192*
Herring, Michael 37; Georgia, 1774 ***1219.7*** *p187*
Herring, William 27; Virginia, 1775 ***1219.7*** *p246*
Herrit, Margaret; Philadelphia, 1853 ***5704.8*** *p100*
Herrit, Matilda; Philadelphia, 1852 ***5704.8*** *p89*
Herrit, Thomas; Philadelphia, 1853 ***5704.8*** *p101*
Herrity, Patrick 18; Massachusetts, 1849 ***5881.1*** *p50*
Herrman, Frederick Emmanuel; New York, 1750 ***3652*** *p75*
Herrman, Henry; New York, NY, 1836 ***8208.4*** *p15*
Herrman, Jacob; New York, 1750 ***3652*** *p74*
Herrman, John; America, 1837 ***1450.2*** *p66A*
Herrman, Susan Maria; New York, 1750 ***3652*** *p75*
Herrmann, Adolph 19 *SEE* Herrmann, Mary
Herrmann, Christina Haug *SEE* Herrmann, Johann Georg
Herrmann, Eleonore 30 *SEE* Herrmann, Mary
Herrmann, Elisabetha *SEE* Herrmann, Johann Georg
Herrmann, Feist 27; America, 1854-1855 ***9162.6*** *p105*
Herrmann, Friedrich; America, 1845 ***8582.1*** *p14*
Herrmann, Henry; New York, NY, 1873 ***1450.2*** *p66A*
Herrmann, Johann Georg; Pennsylvania, 1751 ***2444*** *p165*
*Wife:*Christina Haug
*Child:*Elisabetha
*Child:*Philipp Jacob
Herrmann, Maria Magdalena; Died enroute, 1744 ***2444*** *p165*
Herrmann, Mary 57; New Orleans, 1839 ***9420.2*** *p360*
*Daughter:*Roselle 31
*Daughter:*Eleonore 30
*Son:*Adolph 19
Herrmann, Philipp Jacob *SEE* Herrmann, Johann Georg
Herrmann, Philipp Jacob; Pennsylvania, 1744 ***2444*** *p165*
*Wife:*Sybilla C. Kullin
Herrmann, Rosalie 21; New Orleans, 1839 ***9420.2*** *p168*
Herrmann, Roselle 31 *SEE* Herrmann, Mary
Herrmann, Seligmann 21; America, 1854-1855 ***9162.6*** *p105*
Herrmann, Sybilla C. Kullin *SEE* Herrmann, Philipp Jacob
Herrmann, Zerle 16; America, 1854-1855 ***9162.6*** *p105*
Herrol, Georg; Charleston, SC, 1775-1781 ***8582.2*** *p52*
Herrold, George; Pennsylvania, 1743 ***2444*** *p168*
Herroll, Eleanor 4; St. John, N.B., 1852 ***5704.8*** *p83*
Herroll, James 5; St. John, N.B., 1852 ***5704.8*** *p83*
Herroll, John 6; St. John, N.B., 1852 ***5704.8*** *p83*
Herroll, Joseph 1; St. John, N.B., 1852 ***5704.8*** *p83*
Herroll, Mary 3; St. John, N.B., 1852 ***5704.8*** *p83*
Herroll, Michael; St. John, N.B., 1852 ***5704.8*** *p83*
Herroll, Owen 8; St. John, N.B., 1852 ***5704.8*** *p83*
Herron, Mr. 50; Port uncertain, 1839 ***778.5*** *p272*
Herron, Arthur 9 mos; Quebec, 1854 ***5704.8*** *p121*
Herron, George; Ohio, 1851 ***9892.11*** *p21*
Herron, Mary; New York, NY, 1865 ***5704.8*** *p195*
Herron, Mary; New York, NY, 1865 ***5704.8*** *p203*
Herron, Mary 5; Philadelphia, 1864 ***5704.8*** *p181*
Herron, Sarah 25; Quebec, 1854 ***5704.8*** *p121*
Herron, William 27; Quebec, 1854 ***5704.8*** *p121*
Herry, Lawrence; Virginia, 1643 ***6219*** *p200*
Herrzing, Philipp; Ohio, 1869-1887 ***8582*** *p13*
Hersche, . . .; America, 1800-1813 ***8582.3*** *p76*
Hersckowitz, Isadore M.; Arkansas, 1918 ***95.2*** *p56*
Hersey, Peter 16; Massachusetts, 1849 ***5881.1*** *p50*
Hersher, Lawrence; Philadelphia, 1762 ***9973.7*** *p37*
Hershkourtz, Moses; Iowa, 1866-1943 ***123.54*** *p22*
Herskovitz, Benjamin; America, 1889 ***1450.2*** *p66A*
Herst, John; Virginia, 1639 ***6219*** *p161*
Hert, G. 41; New Orleans, 1831 ***778.5*** *p272*
Herteen, John; Iowa, 1866-1943 ***123.54*** *p22*
Hertel, Daniel Arnold; Quebec, 1776 ***9786*** *p258*
Hertel, Morritz; Wisconsin, n.d. ***9675.5*** *p264*
Herter, Anna Margaretha; Pennsylvania, 1751 ***2444*** *p151*
Herterich, . . .; Canada, 1776-1783 ***9786*** *p24*
Herth, . . .; Canada, 1776-1783 ***9786*** *p24*
Herth, Peter; Wisconsin, n.d. ***9675.5*** *p264*
Hertland, Will 11; Virginia, 1699 ***2212*** *p27*
Hertlein, . . .; Canada, 1776-1783 ***9786*** *p24*
Hertny, Patrick; Wisconsin, n.d. ***9675.5*** *p264*
Hertsteiner, Otto F.W.; America, 1892 ***1450.2*** *p66A*
Hertz, . . .; Canada, 1776-1783 ***9786*** *p24*
Hertz, Francis 26; America, 1831 ***778.5*** *p272*
Hertz, Henry 23; California, 1872 ***2769.5*** *p4*
Hertz, Michel 17; America, 1838 ***778.5*** *p272*
Hertzer, Barbara E. *SEE* Hertzer, John Henry
Hertzer, John Henry; New York, 1743 ***3652*** *p60*
*Wife:*Barbara E.
Hertzog, Martin; Georgia, 1739 ***9332*** *p325*
Herve, Mme.; New Orleans, 1839 ***778.5*** *p272*
Herve, G.; New Orleans, 1839 ***778.5*** *p272*
Hervela, Andrew; Washington, 1859-1920 ***2872.1*** *p16*
Hervey, Barkie; Savannah, GA, 1774 ***1219.7*** *p227*
Hervey, George 12; Philadelphia, 1854 ***5704.8*** *p117*
Hervey, George 30; Philadelphia, 1854 ***5704.8*** *p117*
Hervey, James 10; Philadelphia, 1854 ***5704.8*** *p117*
Hervey, John 20; Philadelphia, 1854 ***5704.8*** *p117*
Hervey, Mary Ann 13; Philadelphia, 1854 ***5704.8*** *p117*
Hervey, Patrick 8; Philadelphia, 1854 ***5704.8*** *p117*
Herwick, Jacob, Jr.; Pennsylvania, 1750 ***2444*** *p166*
With 3 stepchildren
Herwig, Henry; West Virginia, 1855 ***9788.3*** *p12*
Herwood, Robert 17; Virginia, 1734 ***3690.1*** *p110*
Herz, Adolph 34; Kansas, 1902 ***5240.1*** *p19*
Herz, Adolph 34; Kansas, 1902 ***5240.1*** *p82*
Herz, Andreas; Wisconsin, n.d. ***9675.5*** *p264*
Herz, Charles 31; New Orleans, 1829 ***778.5*** *p272*
Herzberger, Johann; America, 1846 ***8582.3*** *p29*
Herzen, Jacob 38; Kansas, 1879 ***5240.1*** *p59*
Herziger, Carl Ferdinand; Wisconsin, n.d. ***9675.5*** *p264*
Herzmark, Mendell 21; Kansas, 1893 ***5240.1*** *p78*
Herzog, Friedrich; Cincinnati, 1824 ***8582.1*** *p51*
Herzog, H.; Iowa, 1866-1943 ***123.54*** *p22*
Herzog, Leonard 30; Kansas, 1887 ***5240.1*** *p71*
Herzog, Martin; Georgia, 1739 ***9332*** *p323*
Herzog, Martin; New York, NY, 1839 ***8208.4*** *p99*
Herzog, Otto W. H. 26; Harris Co., TX, 1900 ***6254*** *p6*
Herzog, Theobald; America, 1852 ***8582.3*** *p29*
Hesanti, Mr.; New Orleans, 1839 ***778.5*** *p272*
Heselton, William 32; Maryland, 1724 ***3690.1*** *p110*
Hesemann, Mr.; America, 1840-1863 ***4610.10*** *p99*
With brother
Hesemann, Christian Friedrich Wilhelm; America, 1863 ***4610.10*** *p99*
Hesemann, Friedrich Wilhelm; America, 1861 ***4610.10*** *p99*
Heshie, George 29; America, 1838 ***778.5*** *p272*
Hesing, Anton C.; America, 1840 ***8582.2*** *p16*
Hesjedal, Anders; Arkansas, 1918 ***95.2*** *p56*
Hesletine, William 32; Maryland, 1724 ***3690.1*** *p110*
Heslinga, Andrew Auke; Arkansas, 1918 ***95.2*** *p56*
Heson, William; New York, NY, 1811 ***2859.11*** *p13*
Hespeden, . . .; Canada, 1776-1783 ***9786*** *p24*
Hesper, . . .; Canada, 1776-1783 ***9786*** *p24*
Hespy, J. B. 26; America, 1823 ***778.5*** *p272*
Hess, . . .; Baltimore, 1872-1874 ***8582.1*** *p40*
Hess, Anna Maria; Port uncertain, 1735-1800 ***2444*** *p185*
Hess, Barbara *SEE* Hess, Johann Michael
Hess, Charles; America, 1875 ***1450.2*** *p66A*
Hess, Charles L.; America, 1836 ***1450.2*** *p66A*
Hess, Christian; Baltimore, 1836 ***1450.2*** *p66A*
Hess, Johann Martin; Pennsylvania, 1764 ***2444*** *p168*
Hess, Johann Michael; Philadelphia, 1741-1800 ***2444*** *p166*
*Wife:*Barbara
*Child:*Michael
Hess, Michael *SEE* Hess, Johann Michael
Hess, Peter; Wisconsin, n.d. ***9675.5*** *p264*
Hess, Ulrick; Philadelphia, 1764 ***9973.7*** *p39*
Hess, William; Wisconsin, n.d. ***9675.5*** *p264*
Hesse, . . .; Canada, 1776-1783 ***9786*** *p24*
Hesse, Captain; Nicaragua, 1856 ***8582.3*** *p31*
Hesse, Anna Charlotta; America, 1850 ***6410.32*** *p123*
Hesse, Charles Frederick; America, 1836 ***1450.2*** *p66A*
Hesse, Frank; Wisconsin, n.d. ***9675.5*** *p264*
Hesse, Henrich; Philadelphia, 1779 ***8137*** *p9*
Hesse, John 40; Kansas, 1878 ***5240.1*** *p20*
Hesse, John 40; Kansas, 1878 ***5240.1*** *p59*
Hesse, Marie; Milwaukee, 1875 ***4719.30*** *p257*
With child
Hesse, Stephan 24; Kansas, 1882 ***5240.1*** *p64*
Hesse, Stephen 24; Kansas, 1882 ***5240.1*** *p20*
Hessel, Christina 9 mos; America, 1853 ***9162.8*** *p36*
Hessel, Edward 27; Jamaica, 1738 ***3690.1*** *p110*
Hessel, Franz 10; America, 1853 ***9162.8*** *p36*
Hessel, Johs. 14; America, 1853 ***9162.8*** *p36*
Hessel, Julius Albin; Wisconsin, n.d. ***9675.5*** *p264*
Hessel, Kath. 3; America, 1853 ***9162.8*** *p36*
Hessel, Maria Kath. 38; America, 1853 ***9162.8*** *p36*
Hessel, Niklaus 40; America, 1853 ***9162.8*** *p36*
Hessell, G. Edward; Illinois, 1859 ***5012.39*** *p90*
Hessell, Thomas; New York, NY, 1838 ***8208.4*** *p82*
Hesser, Frederich; Germantown, PA, 1717 ***3627*** *p13*
Hesseran, Thady; America, 1741 ***4971*** *p33*
Hessernan, James; America, 1742 ***4971*** *p53*
Hessing, . . .; Canada, 1776-1783 ***9786*** *p24*
Hessler, . . .; Canada, 1776-1783 ***9786*** *p24*
Hessler, Abraham; New York, 1743 ***3652*** *p59*
*Wife:*Anna Mary
Hessler, Anna Mary *SEE* Hessler, Abraham
Hessler, Christian; Georgia, 1739 ***9332*** *p324*
Hessler, Christian; Georgia, 1739 ***9332*** *p326*
Hessler, Curt; Quebec, 1776 ***9786*** *p260*
Hessling, Bernard; America, 1858 ***1450.2*** *p66A*
Hessmann, Michel 23; America, 1839 ***778.5*** *p272*
Hester, Christian; Georgia, 1738 ***9332*** *p321*

Hester, Franz; Ohio, 1798-1818 ***8582.2*** *p54*
*Wife:*Maria
Hester, Franz; Ohio, 1869-1885 ***8582.2*** *p56*
Hester, Harman 44; Virginia, 1774 ***1219.7*** *p187*
Hester, Heinrich; Ohio, 1812-1814 ***8582.2*** *p59*
Hester, Maria *SEE* Hester, Franz
Hester, William 17; Maryland, 1722 ***3690.1*** *p110*
Hestin, Eliza.; Virginia, 1639 ***6219*** *p156*
Hetchcock, Mary 15; Maryland, 1775 ***1219.7*** *p249*
Hetebreug, Paul; Wisconsin, n.d. ***9675.5*** *p264*
Heterich, Nikolaus, Family; America, 1804-1923 ***2691.4*** *p172*
Hether, John; Virginia, 1635 ***6219*** *p12*
Hetherington, Benjamin F.; America, 1842 ***1450.2*** *p66A*
Hetherington, Christopher 45; New York, 1775 ***1219.7*** *p268*
With wife
With 7 children
Hetherington, George; Quebec, 1852 ***5704.8*** *p90*
Hetherington, Grace; Quebec, 1852 ***5704.8*** *p87*
Hetherington, John; New York, NY, 1816 ***2859.11*** *p33*
Hetherington, John; Philadelphia, 1851 ***5704.8*** *p80*
Hetherington, Joseph H. 45; Kansas, 1880 ***5240.1*** *p62*
Hetherington, Mary; Philadelphia, 1852 ***5704.8*** *p95*
Hetherington, Rebecca; New York, NY, 1864 ***5704.8*** *p179*
Hetherington, Sarah; New York, NY, 1816 ***2859.11*** *p33*
With 5 children
Hetherington, William; New York, NY, 1864 ***5704.8*** *p179*
Hetherton, Betsy; New York, NY, 1811 ***2859.11*** *p13*
Hethrington, Charles 40; Philadelphia, 1803 ***53.26*** *p38*
*Relative:*Susan 40
*Relative:*Josh 14
*Relative:*Elizabeth 16
*Relative:*George 10
Hethrington, Christy 36; Philadelphia, 1803 ***53.26*** *p38*
Hethrington, Elizabeth 16 *SEE* Hethrington, Charles
Hethrington, George 10 *SEE* Hethrington, Charles
Hethrington, Josh 14 *SEE* Hethrington, Charles
Hethrington, Susan 40 *SEE* Hethrington, Charles
Hetlich, C. F.; America, 1847 ***8582.1*** *p14*
Hetten, Joseph 47; Kansas, 1876 ***5240.1*** *p57*
Hettig, . . .; Canada, 1776-1783 ***9786*** *p24*
Hettler, . . .; Canada, 1776-1783 ***9786*** *p24*
Hettmann, Adam; Ohio, 1836 ***8582.1*** *p47*
Hettmeusperger, John 29; Kansas, 1890 ***5240.1*** *p75*
Hettrick, Peter 37; Ohio, 1855 ***1450.2*** *p67A*
Hettum, E.; Washington, 1859-1920 ***2872.1*** *p16*
Hetzel, Agnes *SEE* Hetzel, Christian
Hetzel, Agnes *SEE* Hetzel, Christian
Hetzel, Anna B. Schlotterer *SEE* Hetzel, Christian
Hetzel, Anna B. Schlotterer *SEE* Hetzel, Christian
Hetzel, Anna Barbara *SEE* Hetzel, Christian
Hetzel, Anna Barbara *SEE* Hetzel, Christian
Hetzel, Christian; America, 1766 ***2444*** *p166*
*Child:*Johann Bernhard
*Child:*Agnes
*Wife:*Anna B. Schlotterer
*Child:*Anna Barbara
Hetzel, Christian; Philadelphia Co., PA, 1766-1779 ***2444*** *p166*
*Wife:*Anna B. Schlotterer
*Child:*Johann Bernhard
*Child:*Agnes
*Child:*Anna Barbara
Hetzel, Gottlieb; Indiana, 1855 ***3702.7*** *p549*
*Brother:*Jacob
Hetzel, Jacob *SEE* Hetzel, Gottlieb
Hetzel, Johann Bernhard *SEE* Hetzel, Christian
Hetzel, Johann Bernhard *SEE* Hetzel, Christian
Hetzer, . . .; Canada, 1776-1783 ***9786*** *p24*
Hetzler, . . .; Canada, 1776-1783 ***9786*** *p24*
Hetzler, Henry; Iowa, 1866-1943 ***123.54*** *p23*
Hetzler, Henry C.; New York, 1874 ***1450.2*** *p67A*
Heubner, William 29; Arkansas, 1918 ***95.2*** *p56*
Heuburger, Mathias; Wisconsin, n.d. ***9675.6*** *p51*
Heuchert, Karl; Washington, 1859-1920 ***2872.1*** *p16*
Heucke, Hermann Friedrich; America, 1852 ***4610.10*** *p144*
Heucke, Johann Friedrich; America, 1856 ***4610.10*** *p145*
Heuer, . . .; Canada, 1776-1783 ***9786*** *p24*
Heuer, Frederick; Wisconsin, n.d. ***9675.6*** *p51*
Heuer, Paul; South Carolina, 1788 ***7119*** *p198*
Heuer, William; Illinois, 1872 ***5012.37*** *p59*
Heugel, William; Arkansas, 1918 ***95.2*** *p56*
Heuke, Anna Marie Hauptmeier *SEE* Heuke, Ernst Friedrich Wilhelm
Heuke, Carl Hermann Ludwig *SEE* Heuke, Ernst Friedrich Wilhelm
Heuke, Christian H. Wilhelm *SEE* Heuke, Ernst Friedrich Wilhelm
Heuke, Ernst Friedrich Wilhelm; America, 1887 ***4610.10*** *p102*
*Wife:*Anna Marie Hauptmeier
*Child:*Friederike W. Caroline
*Child:*Wilhelmine Charlotte
*Child:*Christian H. Wilhelm
*Child:*Carl Hermann Ludwig
*Child:*Marie K. Friederike
Heuke, Friederike W. Caroline *SEE* Heuke, Ernst Friedrich Wilhelm
Heuke, Friedrich; America, 1885 ***4610.10*** *p102*
Heuke, Heinrich Friedrich Wilhelm; America, 1885 ***4610.10*** *p102*
Heuke, Marie K. Friederike *SEE* Heuke, Ernst Friedrich Wilhelm
Heuke, Wilhelmine Charlotte *SEE* Heuke, Ernst Friedrich Wilhelm
Heuker, Mrs. 22; New Orleans, 1835 ***778.5*** *p273*
Heuker, J. 25; New Orleans, 1835 ***778.5*** *p273*
Heurtin, Mr. 35; Louisiana, 1823 ***778.5*** *p273*
Heurtin, Mrs. 25; Louisiana, 1823 ***778.5*** *p273*
Heurtin, Baptiste 2; Louisiana, 1823 ***778.5*** *p273*
Heus, Fritz; New Orleans, 1852 ***2896.5*** *p18*
Heuselstein, John 28; Port uncertain, 1839 ***778.5*** *p273*
Heusen, Bernard; America, 1837 ***8582.1*** *p14*
Heuser, L.F.; Wisconsin, n.d. ***9675.6*** *p51*
Heusler, Christian; Pennsylvania, 1750 ***2444*** *p166*
Heusler, Christian; Pennsylvania, 1750 ***2444*** *p176*
Heuss, Frederick A.; America, 1881 ***1450.2*** *p15B*
Heusse, . . .; Canada, 1776-1783 ***9786*** *p24*
Heussler, Christian *SEE* Heussler, Christian
Heussler, Christian; America, 1750 ***2444*** *p166*
*Wife:*Eva Elisabetha
*Child:*Maria Elisabetha
*Child:*Margaretha
*Child:*Eberhardina
*Child:*Christian
*Child:*Christina
Heussler, Christina *SEE* Heussler, Christian
Heussler, Eberhardina *SEE* Heussler, Christian
Heussler, Eva Elisabetha *SEE* Heussler, Christian
Heussler, Margaretha *SEE* Heussler, Christian
Heussler, Maria Elisabetha *SEE* Heussler, Christian
Heussler, Maria Elisabetha; America, 1750 ***2444*** *p176*
Heussner, Sophie 23; America, 1854-1855 ***9162.6*** *p104*
Heust, Anna Elisabetha Hag; Pennsylvania, 1750-1796 ***4525*** *p221*
*Husband:*Georg
Heust, Georg *SEE* Heust, Anna Elisabetha Hag
Heusted, Patrick; New York, NY, 1835 ***8208.4*** *p5*
Heuvard, G. 26; America, 1835 ***778.5*** *p273*
Hevarid, A. 21; New Orleans, 1837 ***778.5*** *p273*
Heverd, William 20; Philadelphia, 1774 ***1219.7*** *p205*
Heveron, Biddy 48; Massachusetts, 1850 ***5881.1*** *p45*
Heveron, Honora 13; Massachusetts, 1850 ***5881.1*** *p46*
Heveron, Mary Ann 16; Philadelphia, 1860 ***5704.8*** *p146*
Heveron, Michael 11; Massachusetts, 1850 ***5881.1*** *p49*
Hevy, Daniel 30; New Orleans, 1839 ***778.5*** *p273*
Hew, John 24; Philadelphia, 1774 ***1219.7*** *p184*
Heward, Ann 20; America, 1702 ***2212*** *p36*
Hewe, Willm.; Virginia, 1645 ***6219*** *p232*
Hewes, Francis; Virginia, 1637 ***6219*** *p84*
Hewes, Garrett; Virginia, 1636 ***6219*** *p7*
Hewes, James; Virginia, 1638 ***6219*** *p118*
Hewes, John; Virginia, 1618 ***6219*** *p25*
Hewes, Ralph; Virginia, 1635 ***6219*** *p3*
Hewes, Rich.; Virginia, 1638 ***6219*** *p11*
Hewes, Richard; Virginia, 1636 ***6219*** *p79*
Hewes, Richard; Virginia, 1642 ***6219*** *p194*
Hewes, Robert 31; Maryland, 1773 ***1219.7*** *p173*
Hewes, Tho.; Virginia, 1638 ***6219*** *p122*
Hewes, Wm.; Virginia, 1646 ***6219*** *p243*
Heweson, Hugen 26; Jamaica, 1722 ***3690.1*** *p110*
Hewet, Anne; Quebec, 1805 ***7603*** *p37*
Hewet, Gyles; Virginia, 1643 ***6219*** *p207*
Hewett, Antho.; Virginia, 1636 ***6219*** *p15*
Hewett, Elizabeth 35; Massachusetts, 1849 ***5881.1*** *p46*
Hewett, James; New York, NY, 1815 ***2859.11*** *p33*
Hewett, John; Virginia, 1636 ***6219*** *p80*
Hewett, William; Charles Town, SC, 1766 ***1219.7*** *p125*
Hewing, Bernard; America, 1833 ***8582.3*** *p29*
Hewing, Bernard; Kentucky, 1833 ***8582.3*** *p99*
Hewison, William 20; Georgia, 1775 ***1219.7*** *p277*
Hewit, David; New York, NY, 1816 ***2859.11*** *p33*
Hewit, John 8; Massachusetts, 1849 ***5881.1*** *p47*
Hewitson, Thomas 24; Jamaica, 1724 ***3690.1*** *p110*
Hewitt, Charles 14; Virginia, 1733 ***3690.1*** *p110*
Hewitt, Floyd; Washington, 1859-1920 ***2872.1*** *p16*
Hewitt, George 22; Maryland, 1774 ***1219.7*** *p181*
Hewitt, John; Philadelphia, 1849 ***53.26*** *p38*
Hewitt, John; Philadelphia, 1849 ***5704.8*** *p50*
Hewitt, John 29; Philadelphia, 1774 ***1219.7*** *p213*
*Wife:*Martha 24
With 2 children
Hewitt, Joseph 18; Maryland, 1727 ***3690.1*** *p110*
Hewitt, Joshua 25; Maryland, 1724 ***3690.1*** *p111*
Hewitt, Lousia 50; St. John, N.B., 1861 ***5704.8*** *p146*
Hewitt, Martha 24 *SEE* Hewitt, John
Hewitt, Mary 10; Massachusetts, 1849 ***5881.1*** *p49*
Hewitt, Rich.; Virginia, 1648 ***6219*** *p246*
Hewitt, Richard; New York, NY, 1839 ***8208.4*** *p98*
Hewitt, Richard; Virginia, 1637 ***6219*** *p110*
Hewitt, Richard 19; Maryland, 1725 ***3690.1*** *p111*
Hewitt, Robert; New York, NY, 1834 ***8208.4*** *p3*
Hewitte, Hannah 21; America, 1705 ***2212*** *p42*
Hewkes, Edward 36; Virginia, 1774 ***1219.7*** *p240*
Hewlett, Elizabeth 26; Maryland, 1775 ***1219.7*** *p253*
Hewlett, John 21; Maryland, 1774 ***1219.7*** *p181*
Hewlett, William; Colorado, 1894 ***9678.2*** *p23*
Hewreisen, Bernhard; Philadelphia, 1761 ***9973.7*** *p36*
Hews, Ann 19; Massachusetts, 1847 ***5881.1*** *p44*
Hews, James 19; Maryland, 1718 ***3690.1*** *p111*
Hews, John 37; Massachusetts, 1850 ***5881.1*** *p48*
Hews, Lancelot 18; Maryland, 1719 ***3690.1*** *p111*
Hewson, David; South Carolina, 1767 ***1639.20*** *p94*
Hewster, James 17; Virginia, 1719 ***3690.1*** *p111*
Hewston, Ann 50; Quebec, 1867 ***5704.8*** *p168*
Hewston, John 15; Quebec, 1867 ***5704.8*** *p168*
Hewston, Thomas 55; Quebec, 1867 ***5704.8*** *p168*
Hexler, John; New York, NY, 1833 ***8208.4*** *p42*
Hexon, Ralph; Virginia, 1642 ***6219*** *p188*
Hexter, Silas; Milwaukee, 1875 ***4719.30*** *p257*
Hexter, Silas; Milwaukee, 1875 ***4719.30*** *p258*
Hey, John; Pennsylvania, 1682 ***4960*** *p157*
Hey, John 21; Maryland, 1724 ***3690.1*** *p111*
Heyd, Anna Barbara *SEE* Heyd, Johannes
Heyd, Anna Eva Catharina *SEE* Heyd, Johannes
Heyd, Anna Maria *SEE* Heyd, Johannes
Heyd, Anna Maria Mercklin *SEE* Heyd, Justus
Heyd, Anna Maria Schultze *SEE* Heyd, Johannes
Heyd, Inger; New York, 1752 ***3652*** *p76*
Heyd, Joh. Martinus *SEE* Heyd, Johannes
Heyd, Johannes; New York, 1709 ***3627*** *p4*
*Wife:*Anna Maria Schultze
*Daughter:*Anna Eva Catharina
*Daughter:*Anna Maria
*Daughter:*Anna Barbara
*Son:*Joh. Martinus
Heyd, Justus; New York, 1709 ***3627*** *p4*
*Wife:*Anna Maria Mercklin
Heydecker, Jacob; New York, 1750 ***3652*** *p74*
Heydecker, John C.; Philadelphia, 1742 ***3652*** *p55*
Heydefuss, . . .; Canada, 1776-1783 ***9786*** *p24*
Heyden, Charles; Indiana, 1850 ***9117*** *p20*
Heyden, John; New York, 1884 ***1450.2*** *p15B*
Heydon, Mary; America, 1741 ***4971*** *p16*
Heydt, Anna Maria Mercklin *SEE* Heydt, Hans Justus
Heydt, Eduard von der; New York, 1862 ***8125.8*** *p437*
Heydt, George 24; America, 1839 ***778.5*** *p273*
Heydt, Hans Justus; New York, 1709 ***3627*** *p4*
*Wife:*Anna Maria Mercklin
Heyer, C. F.; Philadelphia, 1820-1825 ***8582.1*** *p14*
Heyer, Frederick Augustus; Virginia, 1856 ***4626.16*** *p16*
Heyer, Johan Friderich 23; Pennsylvania, 1743 ***1034.18*** *p7*
*Brother:*Vallandien 18
Heyer, John Gottlieb; Virginia, 1856 ***4626.16*** *p16*
Heyer, Vallandien 18 *SEE* Heyer, Johan Friderich
Heyes, John 15; America, 1706 ***2212*** *p47*
Heyes, Martin; Maryland or Virginia, 1697 ***2212*** *p3*
Heyes, Peter; Virginia, 1635 ***6219*** *p33*
Heyes, Sarah; Virginia, 1698 ***2212*** *p12*
Heyes, Wm 16; America, 1702 ***2212*** *p38*
Heygis, Valentin; Pennsylvania, 1750 ***2444*** *p161*
Heygis, Vallentin; Pennsylvania, 1750 ***2444*** *p161*
Heyl, Christian; Baltimore, 1800 ***8582*** *p13*
With father & family
Heyl, Jacob; America, 1845 ***8582.1*** *p14*
Heyl, Jacob; Cincinnati, 1845 ***8582.2*** *p60*
Heyl, Jacob; New York, NY, 1845 ***8582.3*** *p29*
Heyl, Val; America, 1845 ***8582.1*** *p14*
Heyl, Valentin; Cincinnati, 1869-1887 ***8582*** *p13*
Heyland, Dennis; America, 1741 ***4971*** *p37*
Heyland, Patrick; America, 1742 ***4971*** *p23*
Heyley, Elianor *SEE* Heyley, Willis
Heyley, Robert *SEE* Heyley, Willis
Heyley, Willis; Virginia, 1635 ***6219*** *p73*
*Wife:*Elianor
*Brother:*Robert
Heylman, Johannes 16; Pennsylvania, 1732 ***2444*** *p162*
Heylman, Martien; Pennsylvania, 1732 ***2444*** *p162*
Heylmann, Hans Michael; Port uncertain, 1716-1800 ***2444*** *p166*
Heylmann, Johannes; Pennsylvania, 1749 ***2444*** *p166*

Heyly, Wm.; Virginia, 1635 ***6219*** *p20*
Heymel, Ernst Philipp Wilhelm; Halifax, N.S., 1780 ***9786*** *p269*
Heymel, Ernst Philipp Wilhelm; New York, 1776 ***9786*** *p269*
Heymel, Karl Philipp; Philadelphia, 1779 ***8137*** *p9*
Heymets, Michel 29; New Orleans, 1835 ***778.5*** *p273*
Heyn, Alexander; Wisconsin, n.d. ***9675.6*** *p51*
Heyn, William; San Francisco, 1872 ***2764.35*** *p35*
Heyne, . . .; Canada, 1776-1783 ***9786*** *p24*
Heyne, Frederica 41 *SEE* Heyne, Samuel
Heyne, Frederick W. 56; Arizona, 1890 ***2764.35*** *p32*
Heyne, Herman W.; America, 1848 ***8582.2*** *p16*
Heyne, Justus Henrich; Trenton, NJ, 1776 ***8137*** *p9*
Heyne, Samuel 39; New Orleans, 1839 ***9420.2*** *p361*
*Wife:*Frederica 41
Heynemand, . . .; Canada, 1776-1783 ***9786*** *p24*
Heynemand, Christian Friedrich; Canada, 1776-1783 ***9786*** *p241*
Heynert, . . .; Canada, 1776-1783 ***9786*** *p24*
Heynes, Mary; Virginia, 1637 ***6219*** *p11*
Heynes, William, Jr.; Virginia, 1621 ***6219*** *p29*
Heyns, James; Charleston, SC, 1813 ***1639.20*** *p94*
Heyob, Charles 15; New Orleans, 1836 ***778.5*** *p273*
Heyob, Josephine 19; New Orleans, 1836 ***778.5*** *p273*
Heyot, Charles 15; New Orleans, 1836 ***778.5*** *p273*
Heyot, Josephine 19; New Orleans, 1836 ***778.5*** *p273*
Heyt, Anna Maria Mercklin *SEE* Heyt, Joost
Heyt, Joost; New York, 1709 ***3627*** *p5*
*Wife:*Anna Maria Mercklin
Heyward, Ann *SEE* Heyward, Mathew
Heyward, Ann; Virginia, 1639 ***6219*** *p152*
Heyward, Humphrey; Virginia, 1634 ***6219*** *p32*
Heyward, Jon.; Virginia, 1635 ***6219*** *p69*
Heyward, Mathew; Virginia, 1638 ***6219*** *p119*
*Wife:*Ann
Heyward, Rand; Virginia, 1637 ***6219*** *p8*
Heyward, Wm.; Virginia, 1643 ***6219*** *p201*
Heywood, Herbert John 23; Kansas, 1886 ***5240.1*** *p69*
Heywood, Mary 18; America, 1705 ***2212*** *p42*
Hiams, Moses 24; Philadelphia, 1775 ***1219.7*** *p258*
Hibbrown, Mr.; Quebec, 1815 ***9229.18*** *p82*
Hibernois, Jean; Quebec, 1697 ***7603*** *p99*
Hibert, Nicholas 9 *SEE* Hibert, Nicholas
Hibert, Nicholas 34; Georgia, 1774 ***1219.7*** *p241*
*Child:*Nicholas 9
Hibo, . . .; Canada, 1776-1783 ***9786*** *p42*
Hibos, Mr. 24; Port uncertain, 1836 ***778.5*** *p273*
Hibran, J. 30; Philadelphia, 1804 ***53.26*** *p38*
*Relative:*Joseph 23
Hibran, Joseph 23 *SEE* Hibran, J.
Hibschan, Mathias; Wisconsin, n.d. ***9675.6*** *p51*
Hibsham, Gerrahrt; Philadelphia, 1760 ***9973.7*** *p34*
Hice, Eleanor; New York, NY, 1815 ***2859.11*** *p33*
Hichel, Justus; Philadelphia, 1779 ***8137*** *p9*
Hichman, George 23; Maryland, 1774 ***1219.7*** *p224*
Hick, Mr.; Quebec, 1815 ***9229.18*** *p81*
With wife
With 2 children
Hick, Mathew 25; Norfolk, VA, 1774 ***1219.7*** *p222*
Hicke, T. Michael; South Carolina, 1788 ***7119*** *p202*
Hickel, George; America, 1868 ***6014.1*** *p2*
Hickel, Judith; Delaware, 1746 ***3652*** *p68*
Hickenbottom, John 17; Philadelphia, 1774 ***1219.7*** *p215*
Hickes, George; Pennsylvania, 1750 ***2444*** *p161*
Hickes, John; Virginia, 1642 ***6219*** *p187*
Hickes, Samuel; Virginia, 1637 ***6219*** *p16*
Hickey, Ann; Maine, 1840 ***7036*** *p119*
With 3 children
Hickey, Christopher; America, 1740 ***4971*** *p15*
Hickey, Daniel 11; Massachusetts, 1849 ***5881.1*** *p46*
Hickey, Johanna 5; Massachusetts, 1849 ***5881.1*** *p47*
Hickey, John; Arkansas, 1918 ***95.2*** *p56*
Hickey, John; New York, NY, 1835 ***8208.4*** *p5*
Hickey, John 24; Massachusetts, 1849 ***5881.1*** *p47*
Hickey, Margaret 30; Massachusetts, 1850 ***5881.1*** *p49*
Hickey, Mary; America, 1740 ***4971*** *p48*
Hickey, Mary 5; Massachusetts, 1850 ***5881.1*** *p49*
Hickey, Mary 18; Massachusetts, 1849 ***5881.1*** *p48*
Hickey, Michael 2; Massachusetts, 1849 ***5881.1*** *p48*
Hickey, Michael 6; Massachusetts, 1849 ***5881.1*** *p48*
Hickey, Owen; America, 1741 ***4971*** *p41*
Hickey, Patrick; Illinois, 1854 ***7857*** *p4*
Hickey, Patrick 20; Massachusetts, 1849 ***5881.1*** *p50*
Hickey, Patrick 26; Massachusetts, 1849 ***5881.1*** *p50*
Hickey, Pierre; Quebec, 1820 ***7603*** *p73*
Hickey, Thomas; America, 1776 ***8582.2*** *p67*
Hickey, Thomas; California, 1863 ***3840.2*** *p14*
Hickey, Thomas; Ohio, 1843 ***8365.26*** *p12*
Hickey, Timothy 6; Massachusetts, 1849 ***5881.1*** *p50*
Hickey, William; Arkansas, 1918 ***95.2*** *p56*
Hickie, Daniel; America, 1742 ***4971*** *p53*
Hickie, John Henry; Iowa, 1866-1943 ***123.54*** *p23*
Hickings, Patrick; New York, NY, 1811 ***2859.11*** *p13*
Hickings, William; New York, NY, 1811 ***2859.11*** *p13*
Hickins, Francis; Virginia, 1642 ***6219*** *p189*
Hickison, William 26; Maryland, 1774 ***1219.7*** *p224*
Hickling, Thomas 30; Kansas, 1877 ***5240.1*** *p58*
Hickman, Hen.; Virginia, 1635 ***6219*** *p70*
Hickman, Henry; Virginia, 1637 ***6219*** *p86*
Hickman, James; Barbados, 1765 ***1219.7*** *p110*
Hickman, Nath.; Virginia, 1652 ***6251*** *p20*
Hickman, Sarah; Virginia, 1641 ***6219*** *p187*
Hickmore, Sarah; Virginia, 1629 ***6219*** *p8*
Hicks, James; Virginia, 1637 ***6219*** *p110*
Hicks, Jane; America, 1740 ***4971*** *p48*
Hicks, Mary; Savannah, GA, 1733 ***4719.17*** *p311*
Hicks, Maurice; Philadelphia, 1816 ***2859.11*** *p33*
Hicks, Samuell; Virginia, 1637 ***6219*** *p29*
Hicks, Timothy 16; Virginia, 1700 ***2212*** *p31*
Hicks, William 15; Pennsylvania, 1728 ***3690.1*** *p111*
Hicks, Wm 22; Virginia, 1700 ***2212*** *p31*
Hickson, Catharine 18; Massachusetts, 1849 ***5881.1*** *p45*
Hickson, Johanna 20; Massachusetts, 1849 ***5881.1*** *p47*
Hickson, Joseph 21; Maryland, 1724 ***3690.1*** *p111*
Hicky, Christopher; Maryland, 1740 ***4971*** *p91*
Hicky, Christopher; Philadelphia, 1741 ***4971*** *p92*
Hidden, Johann W.; New York, NY, 1924 ***3455.4*** *p52*
Hidder, Edward Nicholas 29; Arkansas, 1918 ***95.2*** *p56*
Hide, Jane; America, 1698 ***2212*** *p10*
Hide, Patrick; New York, 1826 ***9892.11*** *p21*
Hide, Patrick; Ohio, 1840 ***9892.11*** *p21*
Hide, Richard; Virginia, 1636 ***6219*** *p20*
Hide, Samll.; Virginia, 1643 ***6219*** *p202*
Hide, Thomas 17; Maryland, 1722 ***3690.1*** *p111*
Hieatt, Joseph 18; Philadelphia, 1774 ***1219.7*** *p183*
Hieber, George Michael; America, 1769 ***2444*** *p166*
Hieber, Michael; Pennsylvania, 1768 ***2444*** *p166*
Hieber, Michael; Pennsylvania, 1768 ***2444*** *p210*
Hiebher, George; Pennsylvania, 1768 ***2444*** *p166*
Hien, Jacob; New York, NY, 1838 ***8208.4*** *p85*
Hienn, Jean 24; America, 1831 ***778.5*** *p273*
Hienn, Joseph 30; America, 1831 ***778.5*** *p274*
Hiep, . . .; Canada, 1776-1783 ***9786*** *p24*
Hietzmann, Jakob 22; Port uncertain, 1839 ***778.5*** *p274*
Higbie, Edmd.; Virginia, 1646 ***6219*** *p236*
Higgans, Eliza J.; Philadelphia, 1865 ***5704.8*** *p201*
Higgans, Mary; Philadelphia, 1865 ***5704.8*** *p201*
Higgans, Patrick; America, 1867 ***5704.8*** *p224*
Higgans, Rachael; Philadelphia, 1865 ***5704.8*** *p201*
Higgans, Richard; Philadelphia, 1865 ***5704.8*** *p201*
Higgans, Thomas; Philadelphia, 1865 ***5704.8*** *p201*
Higgens, John 11; America, 1865 ***5704.8*** *p191*
Higgens, Margaret; America, 1865 ***5704.8*** *p191*
Higgens, Sarah; Philadelphia, 1865 ***5704.8*** *p191*
Higgenson, Wm.; Virginia, 1638 ***6219*** *p181*
Higgeson, Joane; Virginia, 1637 ***6219*** *p32*
Higgin, William 20; Wilmington, DE, 1831 ***6508.7*** *p160*
Higginbottom, Mr.; Quebec, 1815 ***9229.18*** *p78*
Higgins, Agnes 31; Quebec, 1864 ***5704.8*** *p163*
Higgins, Andrew; Santa Clara Co., CA, 1867 ***3840.2*** *p14*
Higgins, Barnaby; America, 1736 ***4971*** *p12*
Higgins, Betty 30; Massachusetts, 1849 ***5881.1*** *p45*
Higgins, Catherine; St. John, N.B., 1853 ***5704.8*** *p107*
Higgins, Catherine 6 mos; St. John, N.B., 1847 ***5704.8*** *p4*
Higgins, Catherine 11; St. John, N.B., 1847 ***5704.8*** *p4*
Higgins, Catherine 21; St. John, N.B., 1854 ***5704.8*** *p114*
Higgins, Catherine 26; St. John, N.B., 1864 ***5704.8*** *p159*
Higgins, Daniel; St. John, N.B., 1847 ***5704.8*** *p4*
Higgins, David 2; St. John, N.B., 1864 ***5704.8*** *p159*
Higgins, David 20; St. John, N.B., 1861 ***5704.8*** *p147*
Higgins, Dennis; America, 1735-1743 ***4971*** *p79*
Higgins, Dennis; America, 1740 ***4971*** *p81*
Higgins, Eliza; St. John, N.B., 1847 ***5704.8*** *p4*
Higgins, Eliza 10; St. John, N.B., 1853 ***5704.8*** *p107*
Higgins, Ellen 35; Massachusetts, 1850 ***5881.1*** *p46*
Higgins, Eneas Dillon; New York, NY, 1835 ***8208.4*** *p4*
Higgins, Fanny 19; Philadelphia, 1857 ***5704.8*** *p133*
Higgins, Georg; Virginia, 1639 ***6219*** *p151*
Higgins, George; Carolina, 1684 ***1639.20*** *p94*
Higgins, Henry 1 mo; Quebec, 1864 ***5704.8*** *p163*
Higgins, James; St. John, N.B., 1853 ***5704.8*** *p107*
Higgins, James 4; St. John, N.B., 1864 ***5704.8*** *p159*
Higgins, James 22; Philadelphia, 1865 ***5704.8*** *p164*
Higgins, James 22; St. John, N.B., 1857 ***5704.8*** *p134*
Higgins, James 26; Arizona, 1890 ***2764.35*** *p36*
Higgins, James 28; St. John, N.B., 1862 ***5704.8*** *p150*
Higgins, James 30; Massachusetts, 1847 ***5881.1*** *p47*
Higgins, Jane 3; St. John, N.B., 1853 ***5704.8*** *p107*
Higgins, John; America, 1864 ***5704.8*** *p187*
Higgins, John; New York, NY, 1816 ***2859.11*** *p33*
Higgins, John; New York, NY, 1840 ***8208.4*** *p103*
Higgins, John; St. John, N.B., 1853 ***5704.8*** *p107*
Higgins, John; Virginia, 1639 ***6219*** *p151*
Higgins, John; Virginia, 1639 ***6219*** *p159*
Higgins, John 3 mos; St. John, N.B., 1864 ***5704.8*** *p159*
Higgins, John 8; St. John, N.B., 1853 ***5704.8*** *p107*
Higgins, John 11; Philadelphia, 1865 ***5704.8*** *p164*
Higgins, John 37; St. John, N.B., 1863 ***5704.8*** *p153*
Higgins, Jone; Virginia, 1638 ***6219*** *p119*
Higgins, Margaret 18; Philadelphia, 1865 ***5704.8*** *p164*
Higgins, Margaret 36; Massachusetts, 1850 ***5881.1*** *p49*
Higgins, Margaret 50; St. John, N.B., 1862 ***5704.8*** *p150*
Higgins, Martin; New York, NY, 1816 ***2859.11*** *p33*
Higgins, Mary 13; Massachusetts, 1850 ***5881.1*** *p49*
Higgins, Mary 17; Philadelphia, 1857 ***5704.8*** *p133*
Higgins, Mary 26; Massachusetts, 1849 ***5881.1*** *p49*
Higgins, Maurice 22; Maryland, 1774 ***1219.7*** *p180*
Higgins, Patrick; America, 1735-1743 ***4971*** *p51*
Higgins, Patrick; New York, NY, 1840 ***8208.4*** *p111*
Higgins, Patrick; Philadelphia, 1849 ***53.26*** *p38*
Higgins, Patrick; Philadelphia, 1849 ***5704.8*** *p53*
Higgins, Patrick 20; St. John, N.B., 1854 ***5704.8*** *p114*
Higgins, Peggy; Quebec, 1851 ***5704.8*** *p73*
Higgins, Robert; St. John, N.B., 1853 ***5704.8*** *p107*
Higgins, Robert 6; St. John, N.B., 1853 ***5704.8*** *p107*
Higgins, Robert 19; Antigua (Antego), 1728 ***3690.1*** *p111*
Higgins, Robert Harpur; Boston, 1776 ***1219.7*** *p282*
Higgins, Sarah; St. John, N.B., 1847 ***5704.8*** *p33*
Higgins, Susan; St. John, N.B., 1847 ***5704.8*** *p4*
Higgins, Teigue; America, 1736-1743 ***4971*** *p58*
Higgins, Thomas; New York, 1867 ***2764.35*** *p33*
Higgins, Thomas; Quebec, 1851 ***5704.8*** *p74*
Higgins, Thomas; St. John, N.B., 1853 ***5704.8*** *p107*
Higgins, Thomas 20; Jamaica, 1731 ***3690.1*** *p111*
Higgins, Thomas 32; Arizona, 1902 ***9228.40*** *p6*
Higgins, William; St. John, N.B., 1850 ***5704.8*** *p66*
Higgins, William 8; Quebec, 1864 ***5704.8*** *p163*
Higgins, William 17; Jamaica, 1739 ***3690.1*** *p111*
Higgins, William 22; Maryland, 1775 ***1219.7*** *p264*
Higgins, William 23; St. John, N.B., 1853 ***5704.8*** *p110*
Higgins, William 31; Quebec, 1864 ***5704.8*** *p163*
Higgins, Wm.; Shreveport, LA, 1874 ***7129*** *p44*
Higginson, Christo.; Virginia, 1642 ***6219*** *p197*
Higginson, Edward; New York, NY, 1850 ***5240.1*** *p20*
Higginson, Eliza.; Virginia, 1642 ***6219*** *p198*
Higginson, Peter; Virginia, 1642 ***6219*** *p188*
Higginson, Peter; Virginia, 1648 ***6219*** *p245*
Higgison, Peter; Virginia, 1636 ***6219*** *p76*
Higham, Tho; America, 1698 ***2212*** *p11*
Highbargin, John 18; Jamaica, 1718 ***3690.1*** *p111*
Highet, James; America, 1840 ***1450.2*** *p67A*
Highland, Even; Arkansas, 1918 ***95.2*** *p56*
Highland, Patrick; Ohio, 1865 ***9892.11*** *p21*
Highland, Severen Nels; Arkansas, 1918 ***95.2*** *p56*
Highlands, Mary; St. John, N.B., 1848 ***5704.8*** *p43*
Highlands, William; New York, NY, 1866 ***5704.8*** *p213*
Highmoore, Joseph 29; Sacramento Co., CA, 1850 ***6013.19*** *p73*
Higman, Edward 18; Maryland, 1774 ***1219.7*** *p221*
Higney, Hannah; Philadelphia, 1854 ***5704.8*** *p117*
Higson, George 23; New York, 1774 ***1219.7*** *p217*
Higson, John 43; New York, 1774 ***1219.7*** *p217*
Higson, Relph; Virginia, 1638 ***6219*** *p149*
Hiland, Patrick; Ohio, 1837-1863 ***9892.11*** *p21*
Hilbrand, Helena; Quebec, 1878 ***9980.20*** *p49*
Hild, Augustus; America, 1858 ***1450.2*** *p67A*
Hild, Karl; Cincinnati, 1875 ***8582.3*** *p87*
Hildebrand, Edwin 55; Arizona, 1924 ***9228.40*** *p28*
Hildebrand, Friederike; America, 1850 ***4610.10*** *p143*
Hildebrand, Georg; New York, NY, 1838 ***8208.4*** *p88*
Hildebrand, Jakob; Philadelphia, 1779 ***8137*** *p9*
Hildebrand, Philipp Jacques; Canada, 1776-1777 ***9786*** *p266*
Hildebrandt, Lt.; Canada, 1776-1783 ***9786*** *p150*
Hildebrandt, Anne Marie Charlotte; America, 1844 ***4610.10*** *p138*
Hildebrandt, John; America, 1889 ***1450.2*** *p16B*
Hildebrandt, William H.; Arizona, 1890 ***2764.35*** *p35*
Hildebrant, . . .; Canada, 1776-1783 ***9786*** *p24*
Hildehand, . . .; Canada, 1776-1783 ***9786*** *p24*
Hildemann, Mr.; Wisconsin, 1842 ***3702.7*** *p309*
Hildenbrand, Andreas; Pennsylvania, 1751 ***2444*** *p167*
*Wife:*Anna Magdalena Wagner
*Child:*Catharina
Hildenbrand, Anna Magdalena Wagner *SEE* Hildenbrand, Andreas
Hildenbrand, Catharina *SEE* Hildenbrand, Andreas
Hildenbrandt, Andreas; Pennsylvania, 1751 ***2444*** *p167*
Hilditch, Rebecca 27; Maryland, 1775 ***1219.7*** *p265*
Hildner, . . .; Canada, 1776-1783 ***9786*** *p24*
Hileman, George 39; California, 1872 ***2769.5*** *p4*
Hileman, Michael; Illinois, 1871 ***8582*** *p14*
Hilemann, George; New York, NY, 1839 ***8208.4*** *p92*
Hiler, Francois 24; America, 1835 ***778.5*** *p274*
Hiler, Jacob; Illinois, 1856 ***7857*** *p4*
Hilfer, Gottfried; New York, NY, 1838 ***8208.4*** *p76*
Hilferty, Mary; New York, NY, 1870 ***5704.8*** *p237*

Hilferty, Mary 16; Philadelphia, 1853 ***5704.8*** *p111*
Hilgard, Heinrich; New York, 1900 ***2691.4*** *p167*
Hilgard, Theo 63; Illinois, 1871 ***8582*** *p14*
Hilgart, Joseph; Wisconsin, n.d. ***9675.6*** *p51*
Hilgemeier, Henry Ludwig; Wisconsin, n.d. ***9675.6*** *p51*
Hilgen, Ernst; Wisconsin, n.d. ***9675.6*** *p51*
Hilgen, Gerhard; Wisconsin, n.d. ***9675.6*** *p51*
Hilgen, Peter; Wisconsin, n.d. ***9675.6*** *p51*
Hilgenberg, Christopher; America, 1848 ***1450.2*** *p67A*
Hilgendorf, Emil; Wisconsin, n.d. ***9675.6*** *p51*
Hilger, Frederick; Illinois, 1861 ***7857*** *p4*
Hilger, Joseph; Kansas, 1887 ***5240.1*** *p20*
Hilger, Joseph 22; Kansas, 1885 ***5240.1*** *p68*
Hilger, Mathias 21; Kansas, 1892 ***5240.1*** *p77*
Hilgmeier, Christian; America, 1856 ***1450.2*** *p67A*
Hilint, Elizabeth 21; Maryland, 1774 ***1219.7*** *p236*
Hilker, Frederick; Illinois, 1841 ***2896.5*** *p18*
Hill, Abraham; Virginia, 1636 ***6219*** *p73*
Hill, Adam; New York, NY, 1816 ***2859.11*** *p33*
Hill, Alexander; Philadelphia, 1853 ***5704.8*** *p102*
Hill, Alexander 56?; Arizona, 1890 ***2764.35*** *p33*
Hill, Ann; Virginia, 1648 ***6219*** *p250*
Hill, Ann 21; Philadelphia, 1774 ***1219.7*** *p212*
Hill, Ann 24; Carolina, 1775 ***1219.7*** *p278*
Hill, Anne; New York, NY, 1816 ***2859.11*** *p33*
Hill, Anne; St. John, N.B., 1853 ***5704.8*** *p98*
Hill, Anthony; Virginia, 1637 ***6219*** *p109*
Hill, Anthony 57; Nova Scotia, 1774 ***1219.7*** *p194*
Hill, Barbery; Virginia, 1648 ***6219*** *p250*
Hill, Biddy 48; St. John, N.B., 1855 ***5704.8*** *p126*
Hill, Calvin; Ohio, 1819 ***8582.1*** *p47*
Hill, Casper; Wisconsin, n.d. ***9675.6*** *p51*
Hill, Charles; Virginia, 1645 ***6219*** *p232*
Hill, Charles 16; Maryland, 1773 ***1219.7*** *p173*
Hill, Charles 25; St. John, N.B., 1855 ***5704.8*** *p126*
Hill, Chas. 7 *SEE* Hill, Timothy
Hill, Duncan; Charleston, SC, 1799 ***1639.20*** *p94*
Hill, Edward; Virginia, 1638 ***6219*** *p122*
Hill, Elianor; Virginia, 1637 ***6219*** *p84*
Hill, Eliza Jane; Philadelphia, 1852 ***5704.8*** *p91*
Hill, Elizabeth 2 *SEE* Hill, John
Hill, Ellen 6 *SEE* Hill, Timothy
Hill, Ellen 28 *SEE* Hill, Timothy
Hill, G. W.; Washington, 1859-1920 ***2872.1*** *p16*
Hill, George; Illinois, 1861 ***7857*** *p4*
Hill, George; New York, NY, 1816 ***2859.11*** *p33*
Hill, George; Virginia, 1648 ***6219*** *p245*
Hill, George 9 mos; Philadelphia, 1853 ***5704.8*** *p102*
Hill, George W.; Washington, 1859-1920 ***2872.1*** *p16*
Hill, Harman; New York, NY, 1839 ***8208.4*** *p101*
Hill, Henry; Arizona, 1897 ***9228.30*** *p3*
Hill, Henry; Virginia, 1634 ***6219*** *p32*
Hill, Henry; Virginia, 1648 ***6219*** *p250*
Hill, Henry 38; Maryland, 1774 ***1219.7*** *p192*
Hill, Hugh; Philadelphia, 1853 ***5704.8*** *p102*
Hill, James; Ohio, 1848 ***9892.11*** *p21*
Hill, James; Quebec, 1849 ***5704.8*** *p57*
Hill, James 16; Jamaica, 1725 ***3690.1*** *p112*
Hill, James 21; Jamaica, 1734 ***3690.1*** *p112*
Hill, James 21; St. John, N.B., 1854 ***5704.8*** *p114*
Hill, James 38; Massachusetts, 1848 ***5881.1*** *p47*
Hill, James A.; California, 1864 ***2769.5*** *p3*
Hill, Jane; Philadelphia, 1853 ***5704.8*** *p102*
Hill, Jane; Quebec, 1847 ***5704.8*** *p28*
Hill, Jane; Quebec, 1852 ***5704.8*** *p86*
Hill, Jane; Quebec, 1852 ***5704.8*** *p90*
Hill, Jane 28 *SEE* Hill, John
Hill, Jane 39; Massachusetts, 1848 ***5881.1*** *p47*
Hill, Jesse 4 *SEE* Hill, Timothy
Hill, John; America, 1741 ***4971*** *p9*
Hill, John; America, 1741 ***4971*** *p94*
Hill, John; Maryland, 1740 ***4971*** *p91*
Hill, John; New York, NY, 1816 ***2859.11*** *p33*
Hill, John; New York, NY, 1837 ***8208.4*** *p47*
Hill, John; Philadelphia, 1741 ***4971*** *p92*
Hill, John; Quebec, 1847 ***5704.8*** *p28*
Hill, John; St. John, N.B., 1852 ***5704.8*** *p95*
Hill, John; St. John, N.B., 1853 ***5704.8*** *p98*
Hill, John; Virginia, 1635 ***6219*** *p16*
Hill, John; Virginia, 1639 ***6219*** *p155*
Hill, John; Virginia, 1639 ***6219*** *p156*
Hill, John; Virginia, 1644 ***6219*** *p229*
Hill, John; Virginia, 1647 ***6219*** *p247*
Hill, John 18; Antigua (Antego), 1736 ***3690.1*** *p112*
Hill, John 20; Virginia, 1721 ***3690.1*** *p112*
Hill, John 21; Maryland, 1724 ***3690.1*** *p112*
Hill, John 24; Virginia, 1773 ***1219.7*** *p168*
Hill, John 25; North America, 1774 ***1219.7*** *p199*
*Wife:*Jane 28
*Child:*Thomas 2
*Child:*Elizabeth 2
*Child:*Mary 1
Hill, John 29; Jamaica, 1735 ***3690.1*** *p112*
Hill, John W.; New York, NY, 1840 ***8208.4*** *p112*
Hill, Jon.; Virginia, 1634 ***6219*** *p32*
Hill, Joseph; Philadelphia, 1853 ***5704.8*** *p102*
Hill, Joseph 16; St. John, N.B., 1860 ***5704.8*** *p144*
Hill, Joseph 21; Maryland, 1775 ***1219.7*** *p272*
Hill, Julia 15; Massachusetts, 1849 ***5881.1*** *p47*
Hill, Katherine *SEE* Hill, Richard
Hill, Littleton; South Carolina, 1752 ***1219.7*** *p12*
Hill, Margaret; Quebec, 1847 ***5704.8*** *p28*
Hill, Margaret 12; Philadelphia, 1853 ***5704.8*** *p102*
Hill, Margaret 22; Massachusetts, 1849 ***5881.1*** *p48*
Hill, Margaret 28; Philadelphia, 1854 ***5704.8*** *p122*
Hill, Margrett 20; South Carolina, 1749 ***3690.1*** *p112*
Hill, Maria 6; Philadelphia, 1853 ***5704.8*** *p102*
Hill, Marianne 1 *SEE* Hill, Timothy
Hill, Martin; New York, NY, 1816 ***2859.11*** *p33*
Hill, Mary *SEE* Hill, Robert
Hill, Mary; Philadelphia, 1853 ***5704.8*** *p102*
Hill, Mary; Quebec, 1849 ***5704.8*** *p57*
Hill, Mary; Virginia, 1634 ***6219*** *p32*
Hill, Mary 1 *SEE* Hill, John
Hill, Mary 3; Quebec, 1849 ***5704.8*** *p57*
Hill, Mary 22; St. John, N.B., 1855 ***5704.8*** *p126*
Hill, Mary 30; Philadelphia, 1854 ***5704.8*** *p122*
Hill, Mary, Jr.; Virginia, 1635 ***6219*** *p32*
Hill, Mary Ann 14; St. John, N.B., 1853 ***5704.8*** *p109*
Hill, Mathew 50; Philadelphia, 1855 ***5704.8*** *p124*
Hill, Matilda; New York, NY, 1816 ***2859.11*** *p33*
Hill, Michel; Montreal, 1823 ***7603*** *p85*
Hill, Nathaniel; North Carolina, 1769-1842 ***1639.20*** *p94*
Hill, Nicholas; Arizona, 1898 ***9228.30*** *p12*
Hill, Nicholas; Virginia, 1637 ***6219*** *p112*
Hill, Nicholas 64; Arizona, 1905 ***9228.40*** *p12*
Hill, Peter; Virginia, 1637 ***6219*** *p114*
Hill, Peter; Virginia, 1637 ***6219*** *p115*
Hill, Peter; Virginia, 1639 ***6219*** *p151*
Hill, Peter 29; Jamaica, 1724 ***3690.1*** *p112*
Hill, Rebecca; St. John, N.B., 1852 ***5704.8*** *p95*
Hill, Rebecca 50; St. John, N.B., 1853 ***5704.8*** *p109*
Hill, Rich.; Virginia, 1636 ***6219*** *p80*
Hill, Rich.; Virginia, 1637 ***6219*** *p108*
Hill, Richard; Virginia, 1637 ***6219*** *p84*
Hill, Richard; Virginia, 1638 ***6219*** *p121*
*Wife:*Katherine
Hill, Richard; Virginia, 1638 ***6219*** *p121*
Hill, Richard; Virginia, 1638 ***6219*** *p122*
Hill, Richard; Virginia, 1639 ***6219*** *p161*
Hill, Richard 24; Philadelphia, 1774 ***1219.7*** *p216*
Hill, Richard 25; Pennsylvania, 1738 ***3690.1*** *p112*
Hill, Richard 37; Maryland, 1774 ***1219.7*** *p204*
Hill, Richard 53; Massachusetts, 1849 ***5881.1*** *p50*
Hill, Robert; Pennsylvania, 1832 ***8208.4*** *p36*
Hill, Robert; Philadelphia, 1853 ***5704.8*** *p102*
Hill, Robert; Virginia, 1642 ***6219*** *p196*
*Wife:*Mary
Hill, Robert 19; St. John, N.B., 1854 ***5704.8*** *p114*
Hill, Robert 20; Jamaica, 1725 ***3690.1*** *p112*
Hill, Rose; Virginia, 1636 ***6219*** *p7*
Hill, Rose; Virginia, 1638 ***6219*** *p181*
Hill, Rosey; New Orleans, 1849 ***5704.8*** *p59*
Hill, Samuel; New York, NY, 1815 ***2859.11*** *p33*
Hill, Samuel; New York, NY, 1816 ***2859.11*** *p33*
Hill, Samuel 9 mos; Quebec, 1849 ***5704.8*** *p57*
Hill, Sarah; Quebec, 1849 ***5704.8*** *p57*
Hill, Sarah 4; Philadelphia, 1853 ***5704.8*** *p102*
Hill, Tho.; Virginia, 1639 ***6219*** *p151*
Hill, Tho.; Virginia, 1639 ***6219*** *p156*
Hill, Thom 16; America, 1705-1706 ***2212*** *p45*
Hill, Thomas; New York, NY, 1839 ***8208.4*** *p93*
Hill, Thomas; St. John, N.B., 1852 ***5704.8*** *p95*
Hill, Thomas; South Carolina, 1775 ***1639.20*** *p94*
Hill, Thomas; Virginia, 1639 ***6219*** *p151*
Hill, Thomas; Washington, 1859-1920 ***2872.1*** *p16*
Hill, Thomas 2 *SEE* Hill, John
Hill, Thomas 11; St. John, N.B., 1855 ***5704.8*** *p126*
Hill, Thomas 19; Maryland, 1730 ***3690.1*** *p112*
Hill, Thomas 22; Maryland, 1774 ***1219.7*** *p206*
Hill, Thomas 23; Jamaica, 1731 ***3690.1*** *p112*
Hill, Thomas 35; Virginia, 1773 ***1219.7*** *p170*
Hill, Thos; New York, NY, 1816 ***2859.11*** *p33*
Hill, Timothy 30; Port uncertain, 1849 ***4535.10*** *p198*
*Wife:*Ellen 28
*Child:*Chas. 7
*Child:*Ellen 6
*Child:*Jesse 4
*Child:*Marianne 1
Hill, Victor; Washington, 1859-1920 ***2872.1*** *p16*
Hill, William; America, 1741 ***4971*** *p25*
Hill, William; Quebec, 1847 ***5704.8*** *p28*
Hill, William; St. John, N.B., 1853 ***5704.8*** *p98*
Hill, William; Virginia, 1639 ***6219*** *p161*
Hill, William 8; Philadelphia, 1853 ***5704.8*** *p102*
Hill, William 11; Massachusetts, 1849 ***5881.1*** *p51*
Hill, William 16; Jamaica, 1725 ***3690.1*** *p113*
Hill, William 50; St. John, N.B., 1855 ***5704.8*** *p126*
Hill, Wm.; Virginia, 1636 ***6219*** *p15*
Hill, Wm.; Virginia, 1644 ***6219*** *p229*
Hill, Yajo; Washington, 1859-1920 ***2872.1*** *p16*
Hillam, William J.; New York, NY, 1838 ***8208.4*** *p88*
Hilland, Mary; Massachusetts, 1847 ***5881.1*** *p48*
Hilland, Michael; Massachusetts, 1847 ***5881.1*** *p48*
Hillard, Ellan; Philadelphia, 1853 ***5704.8*** *p101*
Hillard, James; Philadelphia, 1849 ***53.26*** *p38*
Hillard, James; Philadelphia, 1849 ***5704.8*** *p55*
Hillard, John; Philadelphia, 1867 ***5704.8*** *p222*
Hillard, Thomas; Quebec, 1851 ***5704.8*** *p73*
Hillars, John 26; Massachusetts, 1848 ***5881.1*** *p47*
Hillars, William 18; Massachusetts, 1848 ***5881.1*** *p51*
Hille, . . .; Canada, 1776-1783 ***9786*** *p24*
Hille, v., Major; Quebec, 1776 ***9786*** *p105*
Hille, von; Canada, 1776-1783 ***9786*** *p184*
Hille, Freidrich Wilhelm; Quebec, 1776 ***9786*** *p254*
Hille, Georg Wilhelm; Canada, 1780 ***9786*** *p268*
Hille, Georg Wilhelm; New York, 1776 ***9786*** *p268*
Hille, Henrich Reinhard; Canada, 1780 ***9786*** *p268*
Hille, Henrich Reinhard; New York, 1776 ***9786*** *p268*
Hillebrandt, Johann Henry; New York, NY, 1836 ***8208.4*** *p10*
Hilleck, Ann 36; Quebec, 1856 ***5704.8*** *p129*
Hilleck, Eliza Jane 17; Quebec, 1856 ***5704.8*** *p129*
Hilleck, James 7; Quebec, 1856 ***5704.8*** *p129*
Hilleck, Margaret 10; Quebec, 1856 ***5704.8*** *p129*
Hilleck, Robert 11; Quebec, 1856 ***5704.8*** *p129*
Hilleck, Thomas 35; Quebec, 1856 ***5704.8*** *p129*
Hillegas, Michael; Philadelphia, 1774 ***8582.3*** *p85*
Hillegas, William; Philadelphia, 1776 ***8582.3*** *p83*
Hillegass, Michael; Philadelphia, 1775-1781 ***8582.3*** *p81*
Hillen, Ann 20; St. John, N.B., 1855 ***5704.8*** *p127*
Hillen, John 20; St. John, N.B., 1854 ***5704.8*** *p114*
Hillenhagen, William; Illinois, 1857 ***2769.5*** *p3*
Hiller, . . .; Canada, 1776-1783 ***9786*** *p24*
Hiller, Johann Georg; America, 1777-1778 ***8582.2*** *p68*
Hiller, Joseph; Wisconsin, n.d. ***9675.6*** *p51*
Hiller, Konrad; New York, NY, 1893 ***1450.2*** *p16B*
Hiller, Richard 21; Virginia, 1773 ***1219.7*** *p169*
Hillerecht, Alexander; Illinois, 1830 ***8582.1*** *p55*
Hilley, Ellan *SEE* Hilley, James
Hilley, Ellan; Philadelphia, 1847 ***5704.8*** *p14*
Hilley, Hugh *SEE* Hilley, James
Hilley, Hugh; Philadelphia, 1847 ***5704.8*** *p14*
Hilley, James; Philadelphia, 1847 ***53.26*** *p38*
*Relative:*Hugh
*Relative:*Ellan
*Relative:*Mary
Hilley, James; Philadelphia, 1847 ***5704.8*** *p14*
Hilley, Mary *SEE* Hilley, James
Hilley, Mary; Philadelphia, 1847 ***5704.8*** *p14*
Hilliar, Frederick 27; Virginia, 1774 ***1219.7*** *p178*
Hilliard, Ann; Quebec, 1847 ***5704.8*** *p13*
Hilliard, Charlotte 9; Massachusetts, 1849 ***5881.1*** *p45*
Hilliard, Charlotte 36; Massachusetts, 1849 ***5881.1*** *p45*
Hilliard, Emma 6; Massachusetts, 1849 ***5881.1*** *p46*
Hilliard, Geo.; Virginia, 1638 ***6219*** *p11*
Hilliard, James 18; Port uncertain, 1757 ***3690.1*** *p113*
Hilliard, Jane 6 mos; Quebec, 1847 ***5704.8*** *p13*
Hilliard, John; Quebec, 1847 ***5704.8*** *p13*
Hilliard, Robert 3; Quebec, 1847 ***5704.8*** *p13*
Hilliard, Thomas 6; Quebec, 1847 ***5704.8*** *p13*
Hillicher, Anna Elisabeth Roth *SEE* Hillicher, Nicolaus
Hillicher, Christina Maria *SEE* Hillicher, Nicolaus
Hillicher, Gustavus *SEE* Hillicher, Nicolaus
Hillicher, Johan Henrich *SEE* Hillicher, Nicolaus
Hillicher, Johannes Martinus *SEE* Hillicher, Nicolaus
Hillicher, Nicolaus; New York, 1717 ***3627*** *p9*
*Wife:*Anna Elisabeth Roth
*Child:*Johan Henrich
*Child:*Christina Maria
*Child:*Johannes Martinus
*Child:*Gustavus
Hillicker, Anna Elisabeth Roth *SEE* Hillicker, Jacob Nicolaus
Hillicker, Christina Maria *SEE* Hillicker, Jacob Nicolaus
Hillicker, Gustavus *SEE* Hillicker, Jacob Nicolaus
Hillicker, Jacob Nicolaus; New York, 1717 ***3627*** *p9*
*Wife:*Anna Elisabeth Roth
*Child:*Johan Henrich
*Child:*Christina Maria
*Child:*Johannes Martinus
*Child:*Gustavus
Hillicker, Johan Henrich *SEE* Hillicker, Jacob Nicolaus
Hillicker, Johannes Martinus *SEE* Hillicker, Jacob Nicolaus
Hillier, David 30; Philadelphia, 1774 ***1219.7*** *p216*
Hillier, James 26; Maryland, 1774 ***1219.7*** *p221*
Hillier, William; Colorado, 1894 ***9678.2*** *p24*
Hillis, James; New Orleans, 1849 ***5704.8*** *p59*

Hillis, John; New Orleans, 1849 ***5704.8*** *p59*
Hillison, John; Illinois, 1892 ***5012.37*** *p62*
Hillman, Deiderich 78; Kansas, 1888 ***5240.1*** *p73*
Hillman, Deidrich 21; Kansas, 1879 ***5240.1*** *p20*
Hillman, Diedrich 21; Kansas, 1879 ***5240.1*** *p60*
Hillman, John 36; Kansas, 1879 ***5240.1*** *p61*
Hillmann, Fredericka Dorothea 72; Kansas, 1891 ***5240.1*** *p76*
Hillmann, Rebecca 32; Kansas, 1877 ***5240.1*** *p58*
Hillner, Bruno; Wisconsin, n.d. ***9675.6*** *p51*
Hillner, Dorothea; Wisconsin, n.d. ***9675.6*** *p51*
Hillner, Katie; Wisconsin, n.d. ***9675.6*** *p51*
Hillner, Paul; Wisconsin, n.d. ***9675.6*** *p51*
Hills, Wm.; Virginia, 1638 ***6219*** *p118*
Hillyard, Simon 15; Barbados, 1718 ***3690.1*** *p113*
Hillyer, William 21; Virginia, 1774 ***1219.7*** *p238*
Hilo, Pierre 22; America, 1836 ***778.5*** *p274*
Hilscher, Georg; Philadelphia, 1779 ***8137*** *p9*
Hilsdorf, Henry; America, 1834 ***8582.2*** *p16*
Hilstrom, Charles 29; Massachusetts, 1860 ***6410.32*** *p108*
Hilstrom, Christene 21; Massachusetts, 1860 ***6410.32*** *p108*
Hiltchen, Mathias; Wisconsin, n.d. ***9675.6*** *p51*
Hilton, Charlotte 18; Quebec, 1791 ***7603*** *p26*
Hilton, Hannah 4; Massachusetts, 1849 ***5881.1*** *p46*
Hilton, John; New York, NY, 1811 ***2859.11*** *p13*
Hilton, John; Virginia, 1647 ***6219*** *p247*
Hilton, Mary 16; Massachusetts, 1849 ***5881.1*** *p48*
Hilton, Richard; Maryland or Virginia, 1697 ***2212*** *p3*
Hilton, Sarah 25; Virginia, 1699 ***2212*** *p26*
Hilts, Jeremiah; Illinois, 1868 ***2896.5*** *p18*
Hiltunen, Matti; Washington, 1859-1920 ***2872.1*** *p16*
Hiltz, Martin; Wisconsin, n.d. ***9675.6*** *p51*
Himde, Kristian; Ohio, 1881 ***3702.7*** *p442*
Himler, Heinrich; South Carolina, 1788 ***7119*** *p197*
Himler, Thomas 34; Virginia, 1774 ***1219.7*** *p239*
Himton, Jane 35; Philadelphia, 1804 ***53.26*** *p38*
Hinagan, Catherine; America, 1735-1743 ***4971*** *p78*
Hinan, John 22; Philadelphia, 1774 ***1219.7*** *p216*
Hinch, Sarah 21; Philadelphia, 1774 ***1219.7*** *p212*
Hinchy, Bridget 21; Massachusetts, 1849 ***5881.1*** *p45*
Hinck, Arend; New York, NY, 1840 ***8208.4*** *p103*
Hinck, Lorens; New York, NY, 1836 ***8208.4*** *p10*
Hincke, Augusta 34; Massachusetts, 1860 ***6410.32*** *p113*
Hincke, Gustavus 34; Massachusetts, 1860 ***6410.32*** *p113*
Hincke, Julius 6; Massachusetts, 1860 ***6410.32*** *p113*
Hincke, Julius 37; Massachusetts, 1860 ***6410.32*** *p113*
Hincke, Theressa 8; Massachusetts, 1860 ***6410.32*** *p113*
Hinckel, George; South Carolina, 1788 ***7119*** *p197*
Hinckley, Tho.; Virginia, 1635 ***6219*** *p69*
Hind, . . .; Canada, 1776-1783 ***9786*** *p24*
Hind, Isaac 32; Maryland, 1774 ***1219.7*** *p208*
Hind, John; Philadelphia, 1775 ***1219.7*** *p265*
Hind, John 21; Maryland, 1774 ***1219.7*** *p221*
Hind, John 40; Philadelphia, 1774 ***1219.7*** *p182*
Hinde, . . .; Ohio, 1881 ***3702.7*** *p430*
Hinde, Crist; Ohio, 1881 ***3702.7*** *p444*
Hinde, Heinrich; Ohio, 1881 ***3702.7*** *p433*
Hinde, John 23; Jamaica, 1733 ***3690.1*** *p113*
Hinde, Rich.; Virginia, 1638 ***6219*** *p11*
Hinde, William; Virginia, 1642 ***6219*** *p188*
Hinde, Wm.; Virginia, 1647 ***6219*** *p249*
With wife
With 3 children
Hindelach, Christian; Canada, 1783 ***9786*** *p38A*
Hinden, John; New Orleans, 1854 ***2896.5*** *p18*
Hinderkarker, . . .; Canada, 1776-1783 ***9786*** *p24*
Hinderkirchen, . . .; Canada, 1776-1783 ***9786*** *p24*
Hindermann, Anna Catharina *SEE* Hindermann, Martin
Hindermann, Anna Catharina; Pennsylvania, 1753 ***2444*** *p167*
Hindermann, Anna Catharina; Pennsylvania, 1753 ***2444*** *p207*
Hindermann, Christina *SEE* Hindermann, Martin
Hindermann, Martin; Died enroute, 1753 ***2444*** *p167*
Hindermann, Martin; Pennsylvania, 1753 ***2444*** *p167*
*Wife:*Christina
*Child:*Anna Catharina
Hindley, James; Iowa, 1866-1943 ***123.54*** *p23*
Hindley, Major Llewellyn; Iowa, 1866-1943 ***123.54*** *p23*
Hinds, John; New York, NY, 1811 ***2859.11*** *p13*
Hinds, Richard; New York, NY, 1811 ***2859.11*** *p13*
With family
Hindson, Joseph 22; Jamaica, 1733 ***3690.1*** *p113*
Hines, Mrs. 31; Massachusetts, 1849 ***5881.1*** *p49*
Hines, William; Virginia, 1629 ***6219*** *p31*
Hinet, Mr.; New Orleans, 1839 ***778.5*** *p274*
Hing, Gon 80; Arizona, 1920 ***9228.40*** *p24*
Hinger, Nicholas; New York, NY, 1838 ***8208.4*** *p87*
Hingst, John Zum; New York, NY, 1907 ***3455.2*** *p102*
Hinkling, C. R.; Washington, 1859-1920 ***2872.1*** *p16*
Hinkner, Johannes 30; Pennsylvania, 1748 ***2444*** *p157*
Hinoiossa, George 20; Jamaica, 1720 ***3690.1*** *p113*
Hinrich, Ulfert; Illinois, 1892 ***5012.37*** *p62*
Hinrichs, Christoph; Illinois, 1893 ***2896.5*** *p18*
Hinrichs, Curt Wilken; New York, NY, 1903 ***3455.2*** *p98*
*Wife:*Eda
Hinrichs, Dirk; Iroquois Co., IL, 1892 ***3455.1*** *p11*
Hinrichs, Eda *SEE* Hinrichs, Curt Wilken
Hinrichs, Jacob; Iroquois Co., IL, 1894 ***3455.1*** *p11*
Hinrichs, Johann; Iroquois Co., IL, 1892 ***3455.1*** *p11*
Hinrichs, Thomas; Iroquois Co., IL, 1896 ***3455.1*** *p11*
Hinricks, Curt Wilken; New York, NY, 1903 ***3455.2*** *p98*
*Wife:*Eda
Hinricks, Eda *SEE* Hinricks, Curt Wilken
Hinricks, Ernest; Arkansas, 1918 ***95.2*** *p56*
Hins, Mme. 50; America, 1837 ***778.5*** *p274*
Hins, Ms.; America, 1837 ***778.5*** *p274*
Hinse, . . .; Canada, 1776-1783 ***9786*** *p24*
Hinshaw, Tho.; Virginia, 1646 ***6219*** *p241*
Hinsom, Colby 18; Jamaica, 1727 ***3690.1*** *p113*
Hinson, Heinrich; Ohio, 1800-1885 ***8582.2*** *p58*
Hinson, Henry 18; Jamaica, 1722 ***3690.1*** *p113*
Hinte, . . .; Ohio, 1881 ***3702.7*** *p428*
Hinte, Christian; Ohio, 1881 ***3702.7*** *p433*
Hinten, Crist; Ohio, 1881 ***3702.7*** *p438*
Hinton, James 23; Maryland, 1774 ***1219.7*** *p213*
Hinton, John; Virginia, 1642 ***6219*** *p196*
Hinton, Tho.; Virginia, 1634 ***6219*** *p84*
Hinton, Wm.; Virginia, 1636 ***6219*** *p80*
Hintz, Adolph; Wisconsin, n.d. ***9675.6*** *p51*
Hintz, Carl; Wisconsin, n.d. ***9675.6*** *p51*
Hintz, Ferdinand; Wisconsin, n.d. ***9675.6*** *p51*
Hintz, Julius; Wisconsin, n.d. ***9675.6*** *p51*
Hintze, . . .; Canada, 1776-1783 ***9786*** *p24*
Hintze, William; Wisconsin, n.d. ***9675.6*** *p51*
Hintzer, Henry J.; Indiana, 1848 ***9117*** *p16*
Hintzer, J. N.; Indiana, 1845 ***9117*** *p16*
Hintzer, John H.; Indiana, 1848 ***9117*** *p16*
Hinze, Richard; New York, NY, 1887 ***1450.2*** *p16B*
Hiolig, Bartholemy 40; America, 1831 ***778.5*** *p274*
Hiolig, Elisabeth 20; America, 1831 ***778.5*** *p274*
Hiorne, William 26; Maryland, 1774 ***1219.7*** *p196*
Hipolite, J. 28; America, 1835 ***778.5*** *p274*
Hipp, Baby Boy; Died enroute, 1857 ***8582.3*** *p31*
Hipp, Anna Maria; America, 1770-1809 ***2444*** *p139*
Hipp, Franziska Bibend; New York, NY, 1857 ***8582.3*** *p31*
With daughter
Hipp, Wilhelm Christian; Nicaragua, 1853 ***8582.3*** *p30*
Hipp, Wilhelm Christian; Virginia, 1844 ***8582.3*** *p30*
With father & family
Hipp, Wilhelm Christian; West Virginia, 1844 ***8582.3*** *p30*
With father & family
Hippesley, Joseph 16; Maryland, 1774 ***1219.7*** *p208*
Hippolite, Mr. 44; America, 1827 ***778.5*** *p274*
Hipson, Mary; New York, NY, 1864 ***5704.8*** *p186*
Hirchert, John; Wisconsin, n.d. ***9675.6*** *p51*
Hirl, Anne; St. John, N.B., 1848 ***5704.8*** *p38*
Hirl, Biddy; St. John, N.B., 1847 ***5704.8*** *p3*
Hirl, Brien; St. John, N.B., 1847 ***5704.8*** *p3*
Hirl, Magy; St. John, N.B., 1848 ***5704.8*** *p38*
Hirl, Mary; New York, NY, 1867 ***5704.8*** *p224*
Hirl, Mary; St. John, N.B., 1847 ***5704.8*** *p3*
Hirl, Mary 12; St. John, N.B., 1847 ***5704.8*** *p3*
Hirlean, Charles; St. John, N.B., 1849 ***5704.8*** *p48*
Hirm, Mr. 14; New Orleans, 1839 ***778.5*** *p274*
Hirm, Mr. 16; New Orleans, 1839 ***778.5*** *p274*
Hirm, Joseph; America, 1817 ***8582.2*** *p56*
Hirn, Johannes *SEE* Hirn, Joseph
Hirn, John; Wisconsin, n.d. ***9675.6*** *p51*
Hirn, Joseph; America, 1817 ***8582.2*** *p56*
Hirn, Joseph; Ohio, 1798-1818 ***8582.2*** *p54*
*Brother:*Johannes
Hirnei, Christian; Milwaukee, 1875 ***4719.30*** *p257*
Hirnschal, Catharina von Buhl; Virginia, 1737 ***9898*** *p27*
*Son:*Georg
Hirnschal, Georg *SEE* Hirnschal, Catharina von Buhl
Hirnschal, Tillmanus 55; Virginia, 1736 ***9898*** *p27*
Hirrel, Michael; St. John, N.B., 1851 ***5704.8*** *p71*
Hirrtz, Adolph 25; Harris Co., TX, 1899 ***6254*** *p6*
Hirsch, Anton; Cincinnati, 1869-1887 ***8582*** *p14*
Hirsch, Leohnhard; Canada, 1783 ***9786*** *p38A*
Hirsch, Louis E. A.; New York, NY, 1891 ***1450.2*** *p16B*
Hirsch, Martin; New England, 1749 ***2444*** *p167*
Hirsch, Martin; Pennsylvania, 1749 ***2444*** *p167*
Hirsch, Nathan 25; New York, NY, 1878 ***9253*** *p47*
Hirschau, Samuel; Ohio, 1800-1812 ***8582.2*** *p57*
Hirschauer, Philipp; Cincinnati, 1869-1887 ***8582*** *p14*
Hirschbach, . . .; Canada, 1776-1783 ***9786*** *p24*
Hirschbeck, John; Wisconsin, n.d. ***9675.6*** *p51*
Hirschberg, Isaac; Iowa, 1866-1943 ***123.54*** *p23*
Hirschmann, . . .; Canada, 1776-1783 ***9786*** *p24*
Hirschmann, Johann Leonhard; Wisconsin, 1872 ***9460*** *p646*
*Wife:*Margaretha B. Gutmann
Hirschmann, Margaretha B. Gutmann *SEE* Hirschmann, Johann Leonhard
Hirsh, Seligmann; America, 1849 ***8582.2*** *p16*
Hirst, John; Pennsylvania, 1749 ***3652*** *p73*
Hirt, Jacob; Wisconsin, n.d. ***9675.6*** *p51*
Hirt, Katherine; Wisconsin, n.d. ***9675.6*** *p51*
Hirt, Thomas; Wisconsin, n.d. ***9675.6*** *p51*
Hirte, John Tobias; New York, 1743 ***3652*** *p59*
*Wife:*Mary
Hirte, Mary *SEE* Hirte, John Tobias
Hirtz, Jacob; Ohio, 1842 ***9892.11*** *p21*
Hirvela, Andrew; Washington, 1859-1920 ***2872.1*** *p16*
His, Georges 24; America, 1838 ***778.5*** *p274*
His, Valentin 37; America, 1838 ***778.5*** *p274*
Hisme, Andrew 30; Jamaica, 1774 ***1219.7*** *p223*
Hiss, Samuel 19; Virginia, 1718 ***3690.1*** *p113*
Hiss, Sebastian; America, 1852 ***1450.2*** *p67A*
Hissey, Charles 17; Maryland, 1719 ***3690.1*** *p113*
Hister, Joseph; Philadelphia, 1758 ***9973.7*** *p33*
Hitchcock, Joseph; New York, NY, 1836 ***8208.4*** *p22*
Hitchcox, Hen.; Virginia, 1642 ***6219*** *p195*
Hitchcox, John; Virginia, 1639 ***6219*** *p157*
Hitchcox, Richard; Virginia, 1635 ***6219*** *p72*
Hitchcox, Richard; Virginia, 1636 ***6219*** *p23*
Hitchcox, Richard; Virginia, 1637 ***6219*** *p24*
Hitchfield, George 19; Pennsylvania, Virginia or Maryland, 1719 ***3690.1*** *p113*
Hitchin, John 21; Maryland, 1774 ***1219.7*** *p220*
Hitchins, John; Iowa, 1866-1943 ***123.54*** *p23*
Hite, Anna Maria Mercklin *SEE* Hite, Jost
Hite, Jost; New York, 1709 ***3627*** *p4*
*Wife:*Anna Maria Mercklin
Hite, Jost; Virginia, 1732 ***8582.3*** *p96*
With sons & son-in-law
Hites, Louis; Ohio, 1838 ***9892.11*** *p21*
Hiton, Richard 22; New York, 1774 ***1219.7*** *p202*
Hittel, . . .; Canada, 1776-1783 ***9786*** *p24*
Hitton, Henry; Virginia, 1643 ***6219*** *p205*
Hitzelberger, Christopher; New York, NY, 1838 ***8208.4*** *p89*
Hitzfeld, Anna Margarete Hartau *SEE* Hitzfeld, Friedrich Heinrich
Hitzfeld, Friedrich Heinrich; Texas, 1845 ***4815.7*** *p92*
*Wife:*Anna Margarete Hartau
Hix, Samuel 16; Philadelphia, 1774 ***1219.7*** *p182*
Hix, William; Virginia, 1638 ***6219*** *p124*
Hixams, Robert; Virginia, 1648 ***6219*** *p246*
Hixenbaugh, Johann Adam *SEE* Hixenbaugh, Johannes Wilhelm
Hixenbaugh, Johannes Wilhelm; Philadelphia, 1744 ***8125.6*** *p22*
With family
*Son:*Johann Adam
Hjellum, Olaf; Arkansas, 1918 ***95.2*** *p56*
Hjelm, Josef Emil; Arkansas, 1918 ***95.2*** *p56*
Hjertquist, Charles; Colorado, 1904 ***9678.2*** *p24*
Hladky, Emil; Arkansas, 1918 ***95.2*** *p56*
Hlemm, Joh. Fr. 39; New Orleans, 1839 ***9420.2*** *p166*
Hndlicha, Joseph; Arkansas, 1918 ***95.2*** *p56*
Hoa, Mr. 10; America, 1837 ***778.5*** *p275*
Hoa, Mrs. 40; America, 1837 ***778.5*** *p275*
Hoaf, Catharina Muller *SEE* Hoaf, John
Hoaf, Elisabetha Barbara *SEE* Hoaf, John
Hoaf, John 27; Pennsylvania, 1730 ***1034.18*** *p9*
*Wife:*Catharina Muller
*Child:*Elisabetha Barbara
Hoag, Jacob 57; Kansas, 1888 ***5240.1*** *p73*
Hoag, William E. 28; Kansas, 1886 ***5240.1*** *p68*
Hoague, Jno; Virginia, 1698 ***2212*** *p15*
Hoak, George; Pennsylvania, 1754-1773 ***2444*** *p167*
Hoalas, Leo Thomas; Arkansas, 1918 ***95.2*** *p56*
Hoan, Hugh; Philadelphia, 1847 ***53.26*** *p38*
Hoan, Hugh; Philadelphia, 1847 ***5704.8*** *p23*
Hoan, Patrick; New York, NY, 1833 ***8208.4*** *p27*
Hoar, Ellen 11; Massachusetts, 1849 ***5881.1*** *p46*
Hoar, James; Illinois, 1856 ***7857*** *p4*
Hoar, Margaret 24; Massachusetts, 1850 ***5881.1*** *p49*
Hoar, William; Nevada, 1878 ***2764.35*** *p30*
Hoare, Christopher 18; Pennsylvania, 1737 ***3690.1*** *p113*
Hoare, John 22; Maryland, 1775 ***1219.7*** *p254*
Hoare, Thomas T.; Arkansas, 1918 ***95.2*** *p56*
Hoatson, Margaret; Michigan, 1855 ***5240.1*** *p20*
Hobach, Adam; Pennsylvania, 1753 ***2444*** *p169*
Hobacker, . . .; Pennsylvania, n.d. ***2444*** *p169*
Hoban, Edmond; America, 1742 ***4971*** *p33*
Hobba, William 35; Arizona, 1890 ***2764.35*** *p33*
Hobbacher, Adam; Pennsylvania, 1753 ***2444*** *p169*
Hobbart, Edward; New York, NY, 1816 ***2859.11*** *p33*
Hobbin, Mary 17; Massachusetts, 1849 ***5881.1*** *p48*
Hobbs, Ann *SEE* Hobbs, Richard

Hobbs, John; Virginia, 1638 *6219 p2*
Hobbs, Jone; Virginia, 1643 *6219 p205*
Hobbs, Joseph 19; Leeward Islands, 1729 *3690.1 p113*
Hobbs, Mary; America, 1737 *4971 p85*
Hobbs, Mary; America, 1737 *4971 p95*
Hobbs, Mary; America, 1743 *4971 p11*
Hobbs, Richard 33; St. Christopher, 1773 *1219.7 p171*
  Sister: Ann
Hobbs, Thomas; Virginia, 1642 *6219 p190*
Hobec, Thomas 20; Maryland, 1775 *1219.7 p268*
Hoben, Christian August von; Canada, 1780 *9786 p268*
Hoben, Christian August von; New York, 1776 *9786 p268*
Hober, . . .; Canada, 1776-1783 *9786 p24*
Hoberg, Carl Friedrich; America, 1864 *4610.10 p122*
Hoberg, Carl Heinrich August; America, 1855 *4610.10 p121*
Hoberg, Herrmann Chr; America, 1845 *8582.1 p14*
Hoberg, Johann Heinrich; America, 1850 *8582.3 p31*
Hobert, Bertram; Virginia, 1600-1642 *6219 p192*
  Wife: Sarah
Hobert, Sarah *SEE* Hobert, Bertram
Hobsch, Joseph; New York, 1748 *3652 p68*
Hobson, John; Virginia, 1648 *6219 p241*
Hobson, Robert; Virginia, 1647 *6219 p239*
Hoburs, J. J. 41; Washington, 1916-1919 *1728.4 p255*
Hoch, Andrew; Virginia, 1856 *4626.16 p16*
Hoch, Christina *SEE* Hoch, Hans Jerg
Hoch, Christina Loeffler *SEE* Hoch, Hans Jerg
Hoch, Georg Fridrich; South Carolina, 1788 *7119 p202*
Hoch, Hans Jerg; Pennsylvania, 1754-1773 *2444 p167*
  Wife: Christina Loeffler
  Child: Johann Martin
  Child: Maria Magdalena
  Child: Johannes
  Child: Christina
Hoch, Hennig; Canada, 1783 *9786 p38A*
Hoch, Jacob; New York, NY, 1837 *8208.4 p35*
Hoch, Jenrich; South Carolina, 1788 *7119 p203*
Hoch, Johann 28; America, 1854-1855 *9162.6 p104*
Hoch, Johann Martin *SEE* Hoch, Hans Jerg
Hoch, Johannes *SEE* Hoch, Hans Jerg
Hoch, Louis; Shreveport, LA, 1877 *7129 p44*
Hoch, Maria Magdalena *SEE* Hoch, Hans Jerg
Hoch, Nikl. 19; America, 1854-1855 *9162.6 p104*
Hochwegger, Anna; New York, NY, 1831-1833 *8582.3 p46*
Hock, . . .; Canada, 1776-1783 *9786 p24*
Hock, Konrad; Vermont, 1777 *8137 p9*
Hockaday, William; Virginia, 1642 *6219 p190*
Hockelberger, H. Zacharias; Pennsylvania, 1752 *4779.3 p14*
Hockett, Philip; North Carolina, 1687-1783 *1639.20 p94*
Hockett, Philip; North Carolina, 1687-1783 *1639.20 p95*
Hocking, Joseph; Colorado, 1904 *9678.2 p24*
Hockins, Georg; Virginia, 1637 *6219 p82*
Hockinson, Gust; Colorado, 1904 *9678.2 p24*
Hockinson, Helma; Colorado, 1904 *9678.2 p24*
Hockinson, Martina; Colorado, 1904 *9678.2 p24*
Hocquart, Mr. 24; Port uncertain, 1836 *778.5 p275*
Hoct, Catharine; Philadelphia, 1850 *5704.8 p61*
Hodann, Henry; Wisconsin, n.d. *9675.6 p51*
Hoddin, Christian *SEE* Hoddin, John
Hoddin, John; Virginia, 1643 *6219 p204*
  Wife: Christian
Hodge, Adassa 13; St. John, N.B., 1847 *5704.8 p4*
Hodge, Ann; St. John, N.B., 1847 *5704.8 p4*
Hodge, Joseph 37; Carolina, 1775 *1219.7 p278*
Hodge, Margaret 9; St. John, N.B., 1847 *5704.8 p4*
Hodge, Rachel 5; St. John, N.B., 1847 *5704.8 p4*
Hodge, Robert; St. John, N.B., 1847 *5704.8 p4*
Hodge, Sarah 11; St. John, N.B., 1847 *5704.8 p4*
Hodge, William; Iowa, 1866-1943 *123.54 p23*
Hodge, Wm.; Virginia, 1636 *6219 p7*
Hodgen, John; Virginia, 1638 *6219 p146*
Hodges, Eliza.; Virginia, 1637 *6219 p10*
Hodges, Elizabeth 16 *SEE* Hodges, Richard
Hodges, Giles 28; Port uncertain, 1774 *1219.7 p176*
Hodges, Harriet; Pennsylvania, 1682 *4961 p6*
Hodges, Joane; Virginia, 1641 *6219 p184*
Hodges, John; Virginia, 1638 *6219 p22*
Hodges, John; Virginia, 1643 *6219 p206*
Hodges, Jon.; Virginia, 1637 *6219 p84*
Hodges, Mary 18 *SEE* Hodges, Richard
Hodges, Mary 42 *SEE* Hodges, Richard
Hodges, Richard 22; Virginia, 1774 *1219.7 p241*
Hodges, Richard 50; Savannah, GA, 1733 *4719.17 p311*
  Daughter: Elizabeth 16
  Wife: Mary 42
  Daughter: Sarah 5
  Daughter: Mary 18
Hodges, Robert; Virginia, 1636 *6219 p146*
Hodges, Robt.; Virginia, 1636 *6219 p13*

Hodges, Samuel 35; Philadelphia, 1774 *1219.7 p219*
Hodges, Sarah 5 *SEE* Hodges, Richard
Hodges, Thomas 24; Virginia, 1775 *1219.7 p246*
Hodges, Thomas 25; Jamaica, 1775 *1219.7 p247*
Hodgkins, Mary; Virginia, 1638 *6219 p122*
Hodgkins, William; Virginia, 1698 *2212 p15*
Hodgkinson, Cecil 34; America, 1700 *5240.1 p81*
Hodgkinson, John 9; America, 1700 *2212 p33*
Hodgkinson, Tho 19; Maryland or Virginia, 1699 *2212 p22*
Hodgsdon, John; New York, NY, 1811 *2859.11 p13*
Hodgskins, Jasper; Virginia, 1638 *6219 p146*
Hodgson, Barnabas S.; San Francisco, 1850 *4914.15 p10*
Hodgson, Catherine 40 *SEE* Hodgson, Thomas
Hodgson, Ellen; America, 1703 *2212 p39*
Hodgson, John 22; Kansas, 1874 *5240.1 p20*
Hodgson, John 22; Kansas, 1874 *5240.1 p56*
Hodgson, John 26; Maryland, 1775 *1219.7 p273*
Hodgson, John 30; Philadelphia, 1774 *1219.7 p219*
Hodgson, John Hyatt; New York, NY, 1832 *8208.4 p39*
Hodgson, Joshua; New York, NY, 1836 *8208.4 p9*
Hodgson, Thomas; Colorado, 1886 *9678.2 p24*
Hodgson, Thomas; Philadelphia, 1811 *2859.11 p13*
Hodgson, Thomas 38; Nova Scotia, 1774 *1219.7 p209*
Hodgson, Thomas 39; Philadelphia, 1774 *1219.7 p219*
  Wife: Catherine 40
  With child
Hodgson, William 22; Nova Scotia, 1774 *1219.7 p194*
Hodgson, William P.; Virginia, 1806 *4778.2 p142*
Hodor, George; America, 1900 *7137 p168*
Hodson, Jon.; Virginia, 1637 *6219 p85*
Hodson, Thomas 16; Maryland, 1729 *3690.1 p114*
Hodson, William 15; Philadelphia, 1774 *1219.7 p233*
Hoe, George; Pennsylvania, 1754-1773 *2444 p167*
Hoe, Rice; Virginia, 1638 *6219 p180*
  With wife
Hoechstenbach, Anna Elisabetha Klein *SEE* Hoechstenbach, Johannes Wilhelm
Hoechstenbach, Johann Adam *SEE* Hoechstenbach, Johannes Wilhelm
Hoechstenbach, Johann Adam *SEE* Hoechstenbach, Johannes Wilhelm
Hoechstenbach, Johannes Wilhelm; America, 1744 *8125.6 p22*
  Wife: Anna Elisabetha Klein
  Child: Maria Elisabetha
  Child: Johann Adam
Hoechstenbach, Johannes Wilhelm; Philadelphia, 1744 *8125.6 p22*
  With family
  Son: Johann Adam
Hoechstenbach, Maria Elisabetha *SEE* Hoechstenbach, Johannes Wilhelm
Hoechster, Emil; New York, 1855 *8125.8 p437*
Hoecker, Franz; America, 1848 *8582.3 p31*
Hoefelbauer, Joerg Balthas 24; Pennsylvania, 1748 *2444 p167*
Hoefelbauer, Philipp Jacob 30; Pennsylvania, 1748 *2444 p167*
  With wife
Hoefer, . . .; Canada, 1776-1783 *9786 p24*
Hoefer, William; Wisconsin, n.d. *9675.6 p51*
Hoeffelbauer, Georg Balthas 24; Pennsylvania, 1748 *2444 p167*
Hoeffelbauer, Philipp 30; Pennsylvania, 1748 *2444 p167*
Hoeffer, Mr.; Baltimore, 1800-1876 *8582.3 p81*
  With wife
Hoeffer, Franz *SEE* Hoeffer, Nikolaus
Hoeffer, Franz; Cincinnati, 1869-1887 *8582 p14*
Hoeffer, Georg Franz *SEE* Hoeffer, Nikolaus
Hoeffer, Heinrich; Cincinnati, 1800-1810 *8582.3 p81*
Hoeffer, Nicolaus; Cincinnati, 1869-1887 *8582 p14*
Hoeffer, Nikolaus; Cincinnati, 1833 *8582.1 p52*
Hoeffer, Nikolaus; New York, NY, 1832 *8582.1 p14*
  Father: Georg Franz
  With mother
  With sister 4
  With brother 11
  Brother: Franz
Hoeffer, Nikolaus; Ohio, 1843 *8582.1 p51*
Hoeffner, Auguste; America, 1852 *1450.2 p58A*
Hoefler, Joseph; Arizona, 1888 *2764.35 p322*
Hoefs, Johann; Wisconsin, n.d. *9675.6 p51*
Hoeger, Andrew; New York, 1754 *3652 p79*
Hoeger, Philip Jacob; New York, 1761 *3652 p87*
Hoehn, . . .; Canada, 1776-1783 *9786 p24*
Hoehn, Heinrich; Ohio, 1869-1887 *8582 p14*
Hoehn, Jacob; Ohio, 1844 *9892.11 p21*
Hoek, Hennig; Canada, 1783 *9786 p38A*
Hoekstra, Ulbe; Arkansas, 1918 *95.2 p56*
Hoeland, Johannes; Philadelphia, 1779 *8137 p9*
Hoellebold, Wilhelm; New York, NY, 1840 *8208.4 p111*
Hoeller, Joseph; Wisconsin, n.d. *9675.6 p51*

Hoeller, Peter 31; Kansas, 1898 *5240.1 p81*
Hoelscher, Herman 46; Kansas, 1893 *5240.1 p79*
Hoelterhoff, Robert; America, 1850 *8125.8 p437*
Hoen, . . .; Canada, 1776-1783 *9786 p24*
Hoene, Franz; America, 1845 *8582.3 p32*
Hoenner, Sebastian; Pennsylvania, 1753 *4525 p224*
Hoenningen, Erns Christian von; Canada, 1780 *9786 p268*
Hoenningen, Erns Christian von; New York, 1776 *9786 p268*
Hoepfner, Christian Henry; New York, 1750 *3652 p74*
Hoepfner, John C.; New York, 1743 *3652 p59*
  Wife: Mary M.
Hoepfner, Mary M. *SEE* Hoepfner, John C.
Hoer, Andrew; Virginia, 1637 *6219 p83*
Hoerer, Andrew; Indiana, 1806-1850 *5647.5 p41*
Hoerer, Andrew; Ohio, 1835 *5647.5 p4*
Hoerer, Henry; Philadelphia, 1759 *9973.7 p34*
Hoerer, Magdalena 22; New Orleans, 1837 *5647.5 p3*
Hoereth, Conrad; America, 1891 *1450.2 p16B*
Hoering, Edward Joseph 29; Kansas, 1906 *5240.1 p84*
Hoerlin, Johannes; Port uncertain, 1751 *2444 p167*
Hoermann, Anna Maria; Pennsylvania, 1751 *2444 p206*
Hoerner, Adam; New England, 1753 *4525 p224*
Hoerner, Adam; Pennsylvania, 1753 *4525 p224*
Hoerner, Anna Eva Koehler *SEE* Hoerner, Hans Albert
Hoerner, Anna Kunigunda *SEE* Hoerner, Valentin
Hoerner, Barbara *SEE* Hoerner, Valentin
Hoerner, Barbara; New England, 1753 *4525 p224*
  Child: Margaretha
  Child: Maria
  Child: Sebastian
Hoerner, Georg *SEE* Hoerner, Johans
Hoerner, Georg; Pennsylvania, 1752 *4525 p224*
Hoerner, Hans; New England, 1752 *4525 p221*
Hoerner, Hans; New England, 1752 *4525 p224*
  With wife
  With 2 children
Hoerner, Hans Albert; Pennsylvania, 1753 *4525 p224*
  Wife: Anna Eva Koehler
  With 2 children
Hoerner, Joerg; New England, 1752 *4525 p221*
Hoerner, Joerg; New England, 1752 *4525 p225*
  With wife
  With child
Hoerner, Joerg; Pennsylvania, 1752 *4525 p225*
  With wife & child
Hoerner, Johann Georg; New England, 1752 *4525 p224*
Hoerner, Johann Heinerich; Pennsylvania, 1786 *4525 p225*
Hoerner, Johann Jacob; Pennsylvania, 1752 *4525 p224*
Hoerner, Johann Jacob; Pennsylvania, 1752 *4525 p224*
  Relative: Johans
Hoerner, Johann Joerg; Pennsylvania, 1785 *4525 p224*
Hoerner, Johans *SEE* Hoerner, Johann Jacob
Hoerner, Johans; Pennsylvania, 1752 *4525 p224*
  Relative: Georg
Hoerner, Margaretha *SEE* Hoerner, Barbara
Hoerner, Margaretha; Pennsylvania, 1754 *4525 p225*
Hoerner, Maria *SEE* Hoerner, Barbara
Hoerner, Maria; New England, 1752 *4525 p221*
Hoerner, Maria Barbara *SEE* Hoerner, Michael
Hoerner, Maria Barbara *SEE* Hoerner, Michael
Hoerner, Marie; New England, 1752-1753 *4525 p225*
Hoerner, Marie; Pennsylvania, 1752-1753 *4525 p225*
Hoerner, Michael; New England, 1753 *4525 p225*
  Wife: Maria Barbara
  With 2 children
Hoerner, Michael; Pennsylvania, 1753 *4525 p225*
  Wife: Maria Barbara
  With 2 children
Hoerner, Philipp; Pennsylvania, 1786 *4525 p209*
  With wife & 3 children
Hoerner, Philipp; Pennsylvania, 1786 *4525 p225*
  With wife
  With 3 children
Hoerner, Sebastian *SEE* Hoerner, Barbara
Hoerner, Valentin; Pennsylvania, 1754 *4525 p225*
  Wife: Anna Kunigunda
  Daughter: Barbara
Hoerold, Anna Maria *SEE* Hoerold, Georg Christoph
Hoerold, Georg Christoff *SEE* Hoerold, Georg Christoph
Hoerold, Georg Christoph; America, 1734-1800 *2444 p168*
  Wife: Maria Christina
  Child: Maria Margaretha
  Child: Georg Christoff
  Child: Anna Maria
  Child: Johann Georg
  Child: Regina Catharina
Hoerold, Johann Georg *SEE* Hoerold, Georg Christoph
Hoerold, Maria Christina *SEE* Hoerold, Georg Christoph

FOR A COMPLETE EXPLANATION OF ENTRY, SEE "HOW TO READ A CITATION" SECTION

Hoerold, Maria Margaretha *SEE* Hoerold, Georg Christoph
Hoerold, Regina Catharina *SEE* Hoerold, Georg Christoph
Hoerr, Abraham; Iroquois Co., IL, 1895 *3455.1 p11*
Hoerr, Louis; Iroquois Co., IL, 1895 *3455.1 p11*
Hoerr, Regina 27; America, 1854-1855 *9162.6 p104*
Hoerz, Agnes *SEE* Hoerz, Hans Georg
Hoerz, Anna *SEE* Hoerz, Hans Georg
Hoerz, Hans Georg; Port uncertain, 1752-1800 *2444 p168*
   Wife:Anna
   Child:Agnes
Hoerz, Maria Magdalena; Mississippi, 1764 *2444 p141*
Hoess, Anna Barbara *SEE* Hoess, Johann Martin
Hoess, Anna Catharina *SEE* Hoess, Johann Martin
Hoess, Johann Georg *SEE* Hoess, Johann Martin
Hoess, Johann Martin; Pennsylvania, 1754 *2444 p168*
   Wife:Anna Barbara
   Child:Johann Georg
   Child:Anna Catharina
Hoetscher, Heinr.; America, 1895 *1763 p40D*
Hoey, Anne; America, 1742 *4971 p30*
Hoey, Thomas; America, 1741 *4971 p94*
Hof, Gus 21; Harris Co., TX, 1898 *6254 p4*
Hofe, Fra.; Virginia, 1646 *6219 p241*
Hofecker, . . .; Pennsylvania, n.d. *2444 p169*
Hofeld, Carl; Arkansas, 1918 *95.2 p57*
Hofelen, Johann Jacob; Pennsylvania, 1765 *2444 p168*
Hofelin, Anna C. Staudenmayer *SEE* Hofelin, Johann Peter
Hofelin, Johann Jacob *SEE* Hofelin, Johann Peter
Hofelin, Johann Peter; America, 1739-1800 *2444 p168*
   Wife:Anna C. Staudenmayer
   Child:Johann Jacob
Hofer, Christian; Kansas, 1886 *5240.1 p20*
Hofer, John; Kansas, 1886 *5240.1 p20*
Hoferbert, Regina 33; America, 1854-1855 *9162.6 p104*
Hoff, Adam; Pennsylvania, 1762 *1034.18 p9*
Hoff, Adam; Philadelphia, 1762 *9973.7 p38*
Hoff, Catharina Muller *SEE* Hoff, Johan Adam
Hoff, Elisabetha Barbara *SEE* Hoff, Johan Adam
Hoff, Emil 28; Kansas, 1892 *5240.1 p76*
Hoff, Friederich; Charleston, SC, 1766 *8582.2 p65*
Hoff, Jacob L.; Illinois, 1898 *2896.5 p18*
Hoff, Johan Adam 27; Pennsylvania, 1730 *1034.18 p9*
   Wife:Catharina Muller
   Child:Elisabetha Barbara
Hoff, Lars 23; Kansas, 1893 *5240.1 p79*
Hoff, Margaretha; Pennsylvania, 1750-1776 *2444 p144*
Hoff, Nick; Wisconsin, n.d. *9675.6 p51*
Hoffacher, . . .; Pennsylvania, n.d. *2444 p169*
Hoffacre, . . .; Pennsylvania, n.d. *2444 p169*
Hoffe, Evert in den; Germantown, PA, 1684 *2467.7 p5*
Hoffenrath, . . .; Canada, 1776-1783 *9786 p24*
Hoffer, Henry; Ohio, 1840 *9892.11 p21*
Hofferbert, Heinrich 29; America, 1854-1855 *9162.6 p104*
Hoffheimer, Max; America, 1848 *8582.3 p32*
Hoffinger, John; New York, 1893 *1450.2 p16B*
Hoffman, . . .; Canada, 1776-1783 *9786 p24*
Hoffman, Abe A.; Arkansas, 1918 *95.2 p57*
Hoffman, Adam; Canada, 1776-1783 *9786 p242*
Hoffman, August; New York, 1854 *2896.5 p18*
Hoffman, Charles; Washington, 1859-1920 *2872.1 p16*
Hoffman, Fred Aug.; Wisconsin, n.d. *9675.6 p51*
Hoffman, Fredk.; Canada, 1776-1783 *9786 p207A*
Hoffman, Gottfried; New York, 1748 *3652 p68*
Hoffman, Heinrich; Philadelphia, 1769 *4525 p265*
Hoffman, Heinrich Neitzert; America, 1748-1749 *8125.6 p23*
Hoffman, John; Illinois, 1862 *2896.5 p18*
Hoffman, John; Wisconsin, n.d. *9675.6 p51*
Hoffman, John Gottlob; New York, 1750 *3652 p74*
Hoffman, John William; Philadelphia, 1760 *9973.7 p34*
Hoffman, Lena; Kansas, 1899 *5240.1 p20*
Hoffman, Michael; America, 1849 *1450.2 p68A*
Hoffman, Michael; Philadelphia, 1757 *9973.7 p33*
Hoffman, Nicholas; Philadelphia, 1764 *9973.7 p39*
Hoffman, Peter; Illinois, 1862 *2896.5 p18*
Hoffman, Peter; Kansas, 1874 *5240.1 p20*
Hoffman, Peter H. J.; Kansas, 1892 *5240.1 p20*
Hoffman, Reinhold; Arkansas, 1918 *95.2 p57*
Hoffman, Sebastian; South Carolina, 1788 *7119 p202*
Hoffman, Thomas; New York, 1750 *3652 p74*
Hoffman, Valentine; New York, NY, 1884 *1450.2 p16B*
Hoffman, Wilhelm; America, 1884 *1450.2 p68A*
Hoffman, William 21; Kansas, 1886 *5240.1 p68*
Hoffmann, . . .; Canada, 1776-1783 *9786 p24*
Hoffmann, Mr. 19; America, 1836 *778.5 p275*
Hoffmann, Abraham; America, 1849 *8582.1 p16*
Hoffmann, Adam 15; America, 1853 *9162.7 p14*
Hoffmann, Agnes 18 *SEE* Hoffmann, Frederick

Hoffmann, Amely 9 *SEE* Hoffmann, Frederick
Hoffmann, Anna Dorothea; Pennsylvania, 1727 *3627 p18*
Hoffmann, August; Wisconsin, n.d. *9675.6 p51*
Hoffmann, Augusta 5 *SEE* Hoffmann, Frederick
Hoffmann, Benjamin 30; New Orleans, 1839 *9420.2 p484*
Hoffmann, C.; Wheeling, WV, 1852 *8582.3 p78*
Hoffmann, Charles Aug. 34; New Orleans, 1839 *9420.2 p484*
Hoffmann, Christian 32; New York, NY, 1857 *9831.14 p86*
Hoffmann, Christiana 30; New Orleans, 1839 *9420.2 p484*
Hoffmann, Eleanor 36 *SEE* Hoffmann, Frederick
Hoffmann, Elias; Kentucky, 1840 *8582.3 p100*
Hoffmann, Emily 24 *SEE* Hoffmann, Frederick
Hoffmann, Fred August; Wisconsin, n.d. *9675.6 p51*
Hoffmann, Frederich; Wisconsin, n.d. *9675.6 p51*
Hoffmann, Frederick 11 *SEE* Hoffmann, Frederick
Hoffmann, Frederick 42; New Orleans, 1839 *9420.2 p484*
   Wife:Eleanor 36
   Daughter:Agnes 18
   Daughter:Gilian 11
   Daughter:Amely 9
   Daughter:Augusta 5
   Daughter:Emily 24
   Son:Frederick 11
Hoffmann, Gilian 11 *SEE* Hoffmann, Frederick
Hoffmann, Gilian Christa. 27; New Orleans, 1839 *9420.2 p484*
Hoffmann, Gottlieb; Wisconsin, n.d. *9675.6 p51*
Hoffmann, H. 75; Illinois, 1901 *1763 p40D*
Hoffmann, Henry; Wisconsin, n.d. *9675.6 p51*
Hoffmann, Henry 25; New Orleans, 1839 *9420.2 p484*
Hoffmann, Jakob; Kentucky, 1840 *8582.3 p100*
Hoffmann, Jakob; Ohio, 1798-1818 *8582.2 p54*
Hoffmann, Jane Ros. 68; New Orleans, 1839 *9420.2 p484*
Hoffmann, Johan Theis; Philadelphia, 1752 *8125.6 p23*
Hoffmann, Johann; Cincinnati, 1827 *8582.1 p51*
Hoffmann, Johann; Cincinnati, 1869-1887 *8582 p14*
Hoffmann, Johann Wilhelm; Philadelphia, 1776 *8582.3 p83*
Hoffmann, Johannes; Kentucky, 1842 *8582.3 p98*
Hoffmann, John; Wisconsin, n.d. *9675.6 p51*
Hoffmann, Julius; America, 1849 *8582.1 p16*
Hoffmann, Julius; Cincinnati, 1869-1885 *8582.2 p69*
Hoffmann, Lovegod 30; New Orleans, 1839 *9420.2 p484*
Hoffmann, Marg. 17; America, 1853 *9162.7 p14*
Hoffmann, Michael; Cincinnati, 1848 *8582.1 p16*
Hoffmann, Peter; Wisconsin, n.d. *9675.6 p51*
Hoffmann, Philipp; America, 1849 *8582.1 p16*
Hoffmeister, . . .; Canada, 1776-1783 *9786 p24*
Hoffmeister, Charles W.; California, 1884 *2764.35 p34*
Hoffmeister, Ferdinand; New York, NY, 1836 *8208.4 p24*
Hoffnagel, Johannes; Ohio, 1798-1818 *8582.2 p54*
Hoffner, Jakob; Cincinnati, 1800-1876 *8582.3 p81*
Hoffregen, John; Canada, 1783 *9786 p38A*
Hoffsaess, Anna Maria; Pennsylvania, 1748 *2444 p168*
Hoffsaess, Margaretha; Pennsylvania, 1748 *2444 p168*
Hoffsaess, Maria; Pennsylvania, 1750 *2444 p168*
Hoffsess, George; Pennsylvania, 1749 *2444 p169*
Hoffsess, Margaretha; Pennsylvania, 1748 *2444 p168*
Hoffsess, Maria; Pennsylvania, 1750 *2444 p168*
Hofman, Constantine; Washington, 1859-1920 *2872.1 p16*
Hofman, Friederich; Wisconsin, n.d. *9675.6 p51*
Hofman, Joha. Rosine 31; New Orleans, 1839 *9420.2 p361*
   Daughter:Jul. Bernhd. 13
Hofman, John; Canada, 1776-1783 *9786 p207A*
Hofman, Jul. Bernhd. 13 *SEE* Hofman, Joha. Rosine
Hofman, Ludwig; Missouri, 1883 *5240.1 p20*
Hofmann, Baby 6 mos; America, 1854-1855 *9162.6 p104*
Hofmann, Baby 6 mos; America, 1854-1855 *9162.6 p105*
Hofmann, Adam 8; America, 1854-1855 *9162.6 p104*
Hofmann, Amanda Rosine 31 *SEE* Hofmann, Chr. Gottloh
Hofmann, C.; Wheeling, WV, 1852 *8582.3 p78*
Hofmann, Chr. Gottloh 40; New Orleans, 1839 *9420.2 p167*
   Wife:Amanda Rosine 31
Hofmann, Elizabetha 25; America, 1853 *9162.8 p36*
Hofmann, Eva Mgr. 3; America, 1854-1855 *9162.6 p104*
Hofmann, Ferdinand; St. Louis, 1849 *6013.19 p73*
Hofmann, Georg 45; America, 1854-1855 *9162.6 p105*
Hofmann, Heinrich 26; America, 1853 *9162.7 p14*
Hofmann, Johann 10; America, 1854-1855 *9162.6 p104*
Hofmann, Kathr. 5; America, 1854-1855 *9162.6 p104*

Hofmann, Mar. Elis. 20; America, 1854-1855 *9162.6 p105*
Hofmann, Mar. Elizab. 37; America, 1854-1855 *9162.6 p104*
Hofmann, Marg. 23; America, 1853 *9162.8 p36*
Hofmann, Martin; Died enroute, 1750-1752 *8125.6 p23*
Hofmann, Peter 1 mo; America, 1853 *9162.8 p36*
Hofmann, Peter 25; America, 1853 *9162.8 p36*
Hofmann, Phil. Jacob 37; America, 1854-1855 *9162.6 p104*
Hofmeister, Franz; Trenton, NJ, 1776 *8137 p9*
Hofmeister, Wilhelm; Illinois, 1846 *8582.2 p51*
Hofnicle, George; Indiana, 1847 *9117 p16*
Hofs, Frederich; Wisconsin, n.d. *9675.6 p51*
Hofsaess, Hans Jerg; Pennsylvania, 1749 *2444 p169*
   With wife
Hofstadter, Adam 2; Port uncertain, 1839 *778.5 p275*
Hofstadter, Adam 24; Port uncertain, 1839 *778.5 p275*
Hofstadter, Salome 40; Port uncertain, 1839 *778.5 p275*
Hofstetter, Joseph; America, 1870 *1450.2 p68A*
Hoft, Henry; Wisconsin, n.d. *9675.6 p51*
Hoft, William; Wisconsin, n.d. *9675.6 p51*
Hogan, A.F. 28; New York, NY, 1893 *9026.4 p41*
   With wife 25
Hogan, Bridget 35; Massachusetts, 1850 *5881.1 p45*
Hogan, Bryan; America, 1740 *4971 p32*
Hogan, Charles; Virginia, 1846 *4626.16 p13*
Hogan, Charles 20; Massachusetts, 1849 *5881.1 p45*
Hogan, Christopher; Illinois, 1864 *2896.5 p18*
Hogan, David; Arizona, 1897 *9228.30 p2*
Hogan, Dom.; America, 1736 *4971 p80*
Hogan, Dominick; America, 1743 *4971 p18*
Hogan, Dominick; Delaware, 1743 *4971 p105*
Hogan, Edouard; Montreal, 1825 *7603 p101*
Hogan, Edward 1; Massachusetts, 1849 *5881.1 p46*
Hogan, Edward 18; Massachusetts, 1847 *5881.1 p46*
Hogan, Johanna 30; Massachusetts, 1849 *5881.1 p47*
Hogan, John; Colorado, 1884 *9678.2 p24*
Hogan, John; New York, NY, 1838 *8208.4 p74*
Hogan, John 31; Massachusetts, 1850 *5881.1 p47*
Hogan, Mary 10; Massachusetts, 1850 *5881.1 p49*
Hogan, Mary 27; Massachusetts, 1849 *5881.1 p48*
Hogan, Michael; America, 1736-1743 *4971 p58*
Hogan, Michael; America, 1742 *4971 p29*
Hogan, Michael; Maryland, 1742 *4971 p106*
Hogan, Michael; New York, NY, 1837 *8208.4 p36*
Hogan, Nanny 2; Massachusetts, 1850 *5881.1 p49*
Hogan, Ned 5; Massachusetts, 1850 *5881.1 p49*
Hogan, Nicolas; Montreal, 1810 *7603 p91*
Hogan, Owen; America, 1739 *4971 p52*
Hogan, Patk; New York, NY, 1816 *2859.11 p33*
Hogan, Patrick 28; Massachusetts, 1849 *5881.1 p50*
Hogan, Richard; Arizona, 1897 *9228.30 p3*
Hogan, Thomas; America, 1736-1743 *4971 p58*
Hogan, Thomas; New York, NY, 1834 *8208.4 p31*
Hogan, Thomas; New York, NY, 1834 *8208.4 p50*
Hogan, Thomas; Virginia, 1856 *4626.16 p16*
Hogan, Timothy 21; Massachusetts, 1849 *5881.1 p50*
Hogan, William; America, 1742 *4971 p17*
Hogan, William; New York, NY, 1838 *8208.4 p72*
Hogarty, Bridget 23; Massachusetts, 1850 *5881.1 p45*
Hogarty, Catharine 20; Massachusetts, 1849 *5881.1 p45*
Hogarty, Margaret 17; Massachusetts, 1849 *5881.1 p48*
Hogden, John 49; Philadelphia, 1774 *1219.7 p216*
Hoge, E. M.; Washington, 1859-1920 *2872.1 p16*
Hoge, Helen; Washington, 1859-1920 *2872.1 p16*
Hoge, John; Washington, 1859-1920 *2872.1 p16*
Hoge, Patrick; Washington, 1859-1920 *2872.1 p16*
Hoge, William; Wisconsin, n.d. *9675.6 p51*
Hogelberger, H. Zacharias; Pennsylvania, 1752 *4779.3 p14*
Hogelton, Adam 30; Philadelphia, 1856 *5704.8 p128*
Hogelton, Joseph 9 mos; Philadelphia, 1856 *5704.8 p128*
Hogelton, Samuel 2; Philadelphia, 1856 *5704.8 p128*
Hogelton, Sarah 31; Philadelphia, 1856 *5704.8 p128*
Hogelton, Thomas 3; Philadelphia, 1856 *5704.8 p128*
Hogendorff, Baron von; America, 1777 *9786 p63*
Hogg, David 16; Newfoundland, 1789 *4915.24 p57*
Hogg, Elizabeth; North Carolina, 1764-1788 *1639.20 p94*
Hogg, George 57; Philadelphia, 1859 *5704.8 p141*
Hogg, Helen; North Carolina, 1768-1846 *1639.20 p94*
Hogg, James; America, 1798 *1639.20 p95*
Hogg, James; North Carolina, 1774 *1639.20 p95*
Hogg, John 16; Pennsylvania, 1722 *3690.1 p114*
Hogg, John 25; Philadelphia, 1859 *5704.8 p141*
Hogg, Margaret; North Carolina, 1775 *1639.20 p21*
Hogg, Margarey 22; Philadelphia, 1859 *5704.8 p141*
Hogg, Martha; Philadelphia, 1864 *5704.8 p184*
Hogg, Martha 53; Philadelphia, 1859 *5704.8 p141*
Hogg, Mary 18; Jamaica, 1727 *3690.1 p290*
Hogg, Michl; America, 1705 *2212 p45*
Hogg, Richard 15; Philadelphia, 1775 *1219.7 p274*
Hogg, Robert 21; Pennsylvania, 1735 *3690.1 p114*

Hogg, Robert 28; Maryland, 1774 ***1219.7*** *p192*
Hogg, Robina; North Carolina, 1772-1800 ***1639.20*** *p95*
Hogg, Thomas Birkett; New York, NY, 1834 ***8208.4*** *p28*
Hoggan, James; America, 1868 ***5704.8*** *p231*
Hoggart, Robert 21; Virginia, 1773 ***1219.7*** *p168*
Hoggatt, J. W.; Washington, 1859-1920 ***2872.1*** *p16*
Hoggatt, John W.; Washington, 1859-1920 ***2872.1*** *p16*
Hoggatt, Philip; North Carolina, 1687-1783 ***1639.20*** *p95*
Hoggett, Henry; New York, NY, 1836 ***8208.4*** *p10*
Hoggett, William; New York, NY, 1838 ***8208.4*** *p87*
Hoghegan, Thady; America, 1735-1743 ***4971*** *p78*
Hoghey, Neil 21; Quebec, 1858 ***5704.8*** *p138*
Hoglund, Herman G.; Arkansas, 1918 ***95.2*** *p57*
Hograve, Henry; Virginia, 1851 ***4626.16*** *p14*
Hogskins, John; Virginia, 1621 ***6219*** *p2*
Hogue, John; Washington, 1859-1920 ***2872.1*** *p16*
Hoh, . . .; Canada, 1776-1783 ***9786*** *p24*
Hoh, . . .; Pennsylvania, 1752 ***4525*** *p222*
Hoh, Hans Adam; Pennsylvania, 1752 ***4525*** *p222*
With wife
With 4 children
Hoh, Mrs. Hans Adam; Pennsylvania, 1752 ***4525*** *p222*
With 3 children
Hoh, Johan Gorg; Pennsylvania, 1752 ***4525*** *p222*
Hohansee, Reinhold 56; Arizona, 1921 ***9228.40*** *p25*
Hoheisel, Albert; America, 1891 ***1450.2*** *p68A*
Hohemut, Georg; Venezuela, n.d. ***8582.3*** *p79*
Hohenadel, Gertrud 18; America, 1853 ***9162.7*** *p14*
Hohenholz, Preacher; Illinois, 1834 ***8582.1*** *p55*
Hoher, Magdalene; New Orleans, 1837 ***5647.5*** *p4*
Hohle, John Gottl. 26; New Orleans, 1839 ***9420.2*** *p485*
Hohlen, Anna Barbara; America, 1754-1756 ***2444*** *p162*
Hohlen, Catharina; America, 1754-1756 ***2444*** *p162*
Hohlen, Christina; America, 1754-1756 ***2444*** *p162*
Hohlscheit, Catharina; Pennsylvania, 1749 ***2444*** *p201*
Hohlt, Fred; Illinois, 1889 ***2896.5*** *p18*
Hohmann, Carl Joh 27; America, 1854-1855 ***9162.6*** *p104*
Hohmann, Ernst Heinrich Friedrich; America, 1856 ***4610.10*** *p99*
Hohmann, George; Georgia, 1738 ***9332*** *p320*
Hohmann, Johannes; Lancaster, PA, 1780 ***8137*** *p10*
Hohmann, John Peter; New York, 1749 ***3652*** *p71*
Hohmann, Konrad; Philadelphia, 1779 ***8137*** *p10*
Hohmeister, Philipp; America, 1853 ***8582.3*** *p32*
Hohn, William; America, 1893 ***1450.2*** *p68A*
Hohne, Concordia Wilhm. 45 *SEE* Hohne, Joh. Gottl.
Hohne, Elias Furchtegott 10 *SEE* Hohne, Joh. Gottl.
Hohne, Joh. Constantine 8 *SEE* Hohne, Joh. Gottl.
Hohne, Joh. Gottl. 38; New Orleans, 1839 ***9420.2*** *p167*
*Wife:*Concordia Wilhm. 45
*Child:*Elias Furchtegott 10
*Child:*Joh. Constantine 8
Hoile, James; New York, NY, 1838 ***8208.4*** *p66*
Hoin, John K. 28; Harris Co., TX, 1898 ***6254*** *p4*
Hoinacki, Stefan; Arkansas, 1918 ***95.2*** *p57*
Hoiser, Jacob 29; America, 1836 ***778.5*** *p275*
Hojynacky, Kostanty; Arkansas, 1918 ***95.2*** *p57*
Hokanson, Edward Bror; Arkansas, 1918 ***95.2*** *p57*
Hokanson, Frans Gustaf; Illinois, 1886 ***5012.39*** *p52*
Hoke Family ; America, 1885 ***4610.10*** *p76*
Hoke, Friedrich 9; America, 1844 ***4610.10*** *p76*
Hokstad, Hans; Washington, 1859-1920 ***2872.1*** *p16*
Holaghan, Patt; Quebec, 1847 ***5704.8*** *p37*
Holaghan, Peter; Quebec, 1847 ***5704.8*** *p37*
Holagray, Emile 21; New Orleans, 1823 ***778.5*** *p275*
Holaman, Frederick; Washington, 1859-1920 ***2872.1*** *p16*
Holbeche, William; New York, NY, 1839 ***6013.19*** *p73*
Holberton, Walter; Virginia, 1642 ***6219*** *p191*
Holbird, Samuel 17; New England, 1724 ***3690.1*** *p114*
Holbrook, John 12; Philadelphia, 1775 ***1219.7*** *p248*
Holburg, Arvid Carl; Arkansas, 1918 ***95.2*** *p57*
Holden, Abraham 37; Maryland, 1775 ***1219.7*** *p254*
Holden, Charles Edwin; St. Louis, 1898 ***5240.1*** *p20*
Holden, Edward; Philadelphia, 1816 ***2859.11*** *p33*
Holden, John; Buffalo, NY, 1832 ***9892.11*** *p21*
Holden, Jon.; Virginia, 1637 ***6219*** *p180*
Holden, Joshua 16; Maryland or Virginia, 1699 ***2212*** *p21*
Holden, Perry 20; Massachusetts, 1849 ***5881.1*** *p50*
Holden, Ralph 24; Maryland, 1774 ***1219.7*** *p224*
Holden, Rich.; Virginia, 1652 ***6251*** *p19*
Holden, Robert; Jamaica, 1753 ***1219.7*** *p23*
Holden, Robert; Jamaica, 1753 ***3690.1*** *p114*
Holden, Robert; New York, NY, 1835 ***8208.4*** *p76*
Holden, Robert 24; Kansas, 1895 ***5240.1*** *p80*
Holden, Robert H. 24; Kansas, 1895 ***5240.1*** *p20*
Holden, Thomas 27; Maryland, 1775 ***1219.7*** *p255*
Holden, William; New York, NY, 1839 ***8208.4*** *p97*
Holden, William; Quebec, 1824 ***7603*** *p58*
Holder, Eliza. *SEE* Holder, John
Holder, Gottlieb; America, 1849 ***8582.2*** *p16*
Holder, Henry 20; Jamaica, 1738 ***3690.1*** *p114*
Holder, John; Virginia, 1639 ***6219*** *p150*
*Wife:*Eliza.
Holdermann, David; Ohio, 1798-1818 ***8582.2*** *p53*
Holdin, John; Virginia, 1635 ***6219*** *p70*
Holding, Edward; Boston, 1751 ***1219.7*** *p2*
Holding, Elizabeth; Virginia, 1698 ***2212*** *p15*
Holding, James; Virginia, 1638 ***6219*** *p120*
Holding, John 16; Maryland, 1724 ***3690.1*** *p114*
Holding, John 26; Maryland, 1774 ***1219.7*** *p184*
Holdman, Mr.; Jamaica, 1775 ***1219.7*** *p260*
Holdorf, John; Washington, 1859-1920 ***2872.1*** *p16*
Holdway, Mary 19; Jamaica, 1731 ***3690.1*** *p114*
Hole, Richard; Virginia, 1638 ***6219*** *p119*
Holeman, Thomas; Virginia, 1635 ***6219*** *p71*
Holford, Eleoner 15; America, 1706 ***2212*** *p45*
Holfries, Peter; New York, NY, 1840 ***8208.4*** *p111*
Holgel, August Friedr. 26; New Orleans, 1839 ***9420.2*** *p69*
Holgel, August Wm. 3; New Orleans, 1839 ***9420.2*** *p69*
Holgel, Christianne Wme. 26; New Orleans, 1839 ***9420.2*** *p69*
Holgel, Fredr. Adolph 1; New Orleans, 1839 ***9420.2*** *p69*
Holgrave, John 28; New England, 1699 ***2212*** *p18*
Holiday, John 46; Nova Scotia, 1774 ***1219.7*** *p210*
With wife
With 5 children
Holiday, Sarah 22; Virginia, 1775 ***1219.7*** *p246*
Holiday, William; South Carolina, 1781 ***1639.20*** *p95*
Holihan, Catharine 5; Massachusetts, 1848 ***5881.1*** *p45*
Holihan, Daniel 8; Massachusetts, 1848 ***5881.1*** *p46*
Holihan, Kate 11; Massachusetts, 1850 ***5881.1*** *p48*
Holihan, Margaret 35; Massachusetts, 1848 ***5881.1*** *p48*
Holihan, Mary 16; Massachusetts, 1849 ***5881.1*** *p49*
Holihan, Mary 20; Massachusetts, 1850 ***5881.1*** *p49*
Holihan, Michael 11; Massachusetts, 1848 ***5881.1*** *p48*
Holioake, John 26; Jamaica, 1736 ***3690.1*** *p114*
Holke, Conrad; Canada, 1783 ***9786*** *p38A*
Holkirk, William 19; Maryland, 1774 ***1219.7*** *p192*
Holkmann, Mrs. 23; Port uncertain, 1838 ***778.5*** *p275*
Holkmann, G. A. 35; Port uncertain, 1838 ***778.5*** *p275*
Holl, Anna Josephine 30; New Orleans, 1836 ***778.5*** *p275*
Holl, Apollonia; America, 1765 ***2444*** *p170*
Holl, Christian; America, 1854 ***1450.2*** *p68A*
Holl, Etienne 6 mos; New Orleans, 1836 ***778.5*** *p275*
Holl, Fredrick; Illinois, 1868 ***5012.38*** *p99*
Holl, John Pierre 27; New Orleans, 1836 ***778.5*** *p275*
Hollaghan, Philip; America, 1736-1743 ***4971*** *p58*
Hollam, Hen.; Virginia, 1635 ***6219*** *p69*
Hollan, John; Illinois, 1858 ***2896.5*** *p18*
Holland, . . .; Canada, 1776-1783 ***9786*** *p24*
Holland, Carl Johannes; Arkansas, 1918 ***95.2*** *p57*
Holland, Charles; Quebec, 1851 ***5704.8*** *p75*
Holland, Christopher; California, 1866 ***3840.2*** *p14*
Holland, Edw.; Virginia, 1636 ***6219*** *p75*
Holland, Edward; Virginia, 1635 ***6219*** *p74*
Holland, Edward; Virginia, 1636 ***6219*** *p75*
Holland, Ellen; Pennsylvania, 1682 ***4961*** *p6*
Holland, Francis; Virginia, 1643 ***6219*** *p202*
Holland, Geo. E.; Iowa, 1866-1943 ***123.54*** *p23*
Holland, George E.; Iowa, 1866-1943 ***123.54*** *p23*
Holland, Henry; New York, NY, 1811 ***2859.11*** *p13*
With family
Holland, Honor 19; St. John, N.B., 1864 ***5704.8*** *p157*
Holland, James; Maryland, 1750 ***3690.1*** *p114*
Holland, James; Maryland, 1751 ***1219.7*** *p2*
Holland, James 28; Kansas, 1871 ***5240.1*** *p51*
Holland, Jeremiah D.; Arizona, 1888 ***2764.35*** *p35*
Holland, Johann; Kentucky, 1797 ***8582.3*** *p95*
Holland, John; America, 1832 ***1450.2*** *p68A*
Holland, John; Iowa, 1866-1943 ***123.54*** *p23*
Holland, John George 22; Georgia, 1738 ***9332*** *p329*
Holland, Michael; America, 1742-1743 ***4971*** *p42*
Holland, Michael; New York, NY, 1840 ***8208.4*** *p107*
Holland, Michael; Wisconsin, n.d. ***9675.6*** *p51*
Holland, Patrick; California, 1875 ***2764.35*** *p30*
Holland, Patrick 5; Massachusetts, 1850 ***5881.1*** *p50*
Holland, Peter; Virginia, 1698 ***2212*** *p14*
Holland, Peter 26; America, 1699 ***2212*** *p25*
Holland, Richard; Iowa, 1866-1943 ***123.54*** *p23*
Holland, Richard; Virginia, 1855 ***4626.16*** *p15*
Holland, Robert; Philadelphia, 1867 ***5704.8*** *p220*
Holland, Rose; Philadelphia, 1848 ***53.26*** *p38*
Holland, Rose; Philadelphia, 1848 ***5704.8*** *p45*
Holland, Thomas 20; Virginia, 1775 ***1219.7*** *p261*
Holland, Tim; Washington, 1859-1920 ***2872.1*** *p16*
Holland, William; Virginia, 1639 ***6219*** *p150*
Holland, William; Washington, 1859-1920 ***2872.1*** *p16*
Holland, William 8; Massachusetts, 1850 ***5881.1*** *p51*
Holland, William 19; Massachusetts, 1849 ***5881.1*** *p51*
Holland, Wm.; Virginia, 1636 ***6219*** *p74*
Holland, Wm.; Virginia, 1637 ***6219*** *p108*
Hollaus, Veit; Georgia, 1738 ***9332*** *p320*
Holle, . . .; Canada, 1776-1783 ***9786*** *p24*
Holle, Friedrich 9; New York, NY, 1867 ***3702.7*** *p571*
*Relative:*Friedrich 58
*Relative:*Marie 69
*Relative:*Johann 19
*Relative:*Hermann 16
Holle, Friedrich 58 *SEE* Holle, Friedrich
Holle, Heinrich *SEE* Holle, Karl
Holle, Heinrich 17; New York, NY, 1867 ***3702.7*** *p571*
Holle, Hermann *SEE* Holle, Karl
Holle, Hermann 16 *SEE* Holle, Friedrich
Holle, Jean-Baptiste; Ontario, 1757 ***7603*** *p26*
Holle, Johann 19 *SEE* Holle, Friedrich
Holle, Karl; Indianapolis, 1860 ***3702.7*** *p571*
*Brother:*Heinrich
*Brother:*Hermann
Holle, Marie 69 *SEE* Holle, Friedrich
Holle, Theodor; America, 1845 ***8582.1*** *p16*
Holle, Wilhelm; Indianapolis, 1867 ***3702.7*** *p580*
Holleffe, Jon.; Virginia, 1642 ***6219*** *p191*
Holleman, Aaren; Washington, 1859-1920 ***2872.1*** *p17*
Holleman, Bertha; Washington, 1859-1920 ***2872.1*** *p17*
Holleman, Fritz; Washington, 1859-1920 ***2872.1*** *p17*
Holleman, Johan; Washington, 1859-1920 ***2872.1*** *p17*
Holleman, Pieter; Washington, 1859-1920 ***2872.1*** *p17*
Hollenback, Christian; Indiana, 1836 ***9117*** *p15*
Hollenbeck, Martin; Cincinnati, 1869-1887 ***8582*** *p14*
Hollenbeck, Wilhelm; Pennsylvania, 1800 ***8582.1*** *p48*
Holleney, Dyan; Virginia, 1642 ***6219*** *p193*
Hollenfals, William; Wisconsin, n.d. ***9675.6*** *p51*
Hollenkamp, Bernard; Baltimore, 1832 ***8582*** *p14*
Hollenkamp, F. W.; America, 1823 ***8582.2*** *p61*
Holler, Adam; Ohio, 1800 ***8582.2*** *p55*
Holler, George; America, 1853 ***1450.2*** *p68A*
Holler, George; Philadelphia, 1761 ***9973.7*** *p36*
Holler, Philip Henry; America, 1847 ***1450.2*** *p68A*
Holler, Reinhard; Baltimore, 1852 ***1450.2*** *p68A*
Holler, Theodore; America, 1865 ***1450.2*** *p69A*
Hollermann, Simon; New York, NY, 1838 ***8208.4*** *p64*
Holley, Lyonell; Virginia, 1642 ***6219*** *p193*
Holley, William; New York, NY, 1839 ***8208.4*** *p94*
Holliack, Roger; Virginia, 1635 ***6219*** *p73*
Holliday, Agnes 17; Massachusetts, 1847 ***5881.1*** *p44*
Holliday, Georg; Virginia, 1639 ***6219*** *p150*
Holliday, Jane; Massachusetts, 1847 ***5881.1*** *p47*
With child
Holliday, John; Virginia, 1638 ***6219*** *p159*
Holliday, John 40; Nova Scotia, 1774 ***1219.7*** *p210*
Holliday, Julia 25; Massachusetts, 1849 ***5881.1*** *p47*
Holliday, Robert 30; New York, 1775 ***1219.7*** *p246*
Holliday, Wm.; Virginia, 1637 ***6219*** *p85*
Hollier, C. F. 21; Port uncertain, 1836 ***778.5*** *p275*
Hollier, Julian; Virginia, 1623 ***6219*** *p20*
Hollier, Stephen 16; Jamaica, 1730 ***3690.1*** *p114*
Holling, Christian Friedrich; America, 1861 ***4610.10*** *p158*
Holling, Christian Heinrich; America, 1856 ***4610.10*** *p157*
Holling, Robert 37; Arizona, 1890 ***2764.35*** *p35*
Hollinger, Jakob; Ohio, 1817 ***8582.1*** *p48*
Hollingham, Thomas; Virginia, 1639 ***6219*** *p156*
Hollingshed, Francis 19; Virginia, 1733 ***3690.1*** *p114*
Hollingsworth, John; Virginia, 1638 ***6219*** *p122*
*Wife:*Sarah
Hollingsworth, Sarah *SEE* Hollingsworth, John
Hollingworth, George 21; Maryland, 1775 ***1219.7*** *p259*
Hollis, Daniel 24; Philadelphia, 1775 ***1219.7*** *p255*
Hollis, Jon.; Virginia, 1642 ***6219*** *p191*
Hollis, Thomas; Virginia, 1647 ***6219*** *p247*
Hollman, Arnold; Illinois, 1880 ***2896.5*** *p18*
Hollman, Henry; Illinois, 1880 ***2896.5*** *p18*
Hollmann Family ; Illinois, 1800-1899 ***4610.10*** *p66*
Hollohan, Mary 50; Massachusetts, 1849 ***5881.1*** *p49*
Holloway, J. L.; Quebec, 1815 ***9229.18*** *p80*
Holloway, James 26; Jamaica, 1736 ***3690.1*** *p115*
Holloway, John; Virginia, 1623-1700 ***6219*** *p182*
Holloway, John; Virginia, 1750 ***3690.1*** *p115*
Holloway, John; Virginia, 1751 ***1219.7*** *p2*
Holloway, Peter; Virginia, 1635 ***6219*** *p71*
Holloway, William 15; Pennsylvania, 1723 ***3690.1*** *p115*
Holloway, William 21; Maryland, 1775 ***1219.7*** *p252*
Holloway, William C. 36; Kansas, 1879 ***5240.1*** *p21*
Holloway, William C. 36; Kansas, 1879 ***5240.1*** *p60*
Hollrigel, Joseph; Wisconsin, n.d. ***9675.6*** *p51*
Hollwege, . . .; Canada, 1776-1783 ***9786*** *p24*
Holly, Jacob; America, 1852 ***1450.2*** *p69A*
Hollyday, Jane 21; St. John, N.B., 1855 ***5704.8*** *p126*
Hollyday, Margaret 23; St. John, N.B., 1855 ***5704.8*** *p127*
Hollypark, William; Philadelphia, 1852 ***5704.8*** *p89*
Holm, Andrew 21; Maryland, 1724 ***3690.1*** *p115*
Holm, Charly; Washington, 1859-1920 ***2872.1*** *p17*
Holm, Ferdinand 27; Kansas, 1873 ***5240.1*** *p21*
Holm, Ferdinand 27; Kansas, 1873 ***5240.1*** *p54*
Holm, Thomas 35; Maryland, 1739 ***3690.1*** *p115*
Holman, Elmer E.; Arkansas, 1918 ***95.2*** *p57*

Holman, George; San Francisco, 1850 *4914.15 p10*
Holman, John; South Carolina, 1788 *7119 p198*
Holman, Joseph; South Carolina, 1788 *7119 p198*
Holman, Melcher; South Carolina, 1788 *7119 p198*
Holman, Robert; Virginia, 1638 *6219 p14*
Holman, Thomas B.; Colorado, 1895 *9678.2 p24*
Holman, Wm.; Virginia, 1639 *6219 p150*
Holmann, Jakob; Kentucky, 1810 *8582.3 p97*
Holmberg, Frances L. L.; Kansas, 1888 *5240.1 p21*
Holmden, R. J. 23; Kansas, 1893 *5240.1 p78*
Holme, Ellen 19; America, 1705 *2212 p42*
Holme, James; America, 1699 *2212 p25*
Holme, Mary; Virginia, 1698 *2212 p17*
Holme, Thomas 35; Maryland, 1739 *3690.1 p115*
Holmes, Axel; Arkansas, 1918 *95.2 p57*
Holmes, Ben; Washington, 1859-1920 *2872.1 p17*
Holmes, Benjamin; Washington, 1859-1920 *2872.1 p17*
Holmes, Catherine 16; Philadelphia, 1854 *5704.8 p118*
Holmes, David; Virginia, 1643 *6219 p205*
Holmes, David; Virginia, 1648 *6219 p246*
Holmes, Eliz.; Virginia, 1648 *6219 p250*
Holmes, Ellen; Philadelphia, 1865 *5704.8 p191*
Holmes, Fanny; America, 1868 *5704.8 p231*
Holmes, Fran.; Virginia, 1648 *6219 p252*
Holmes, Frank; Arkansas, 1918 *95.2 p57*
Holmes, Mrs. G. 75; Washington, 1916-1919 *1728.4 p255*
Holmes, Georg; Virginia, 1636 *6219 p180*
  *Wife:*Rebecca
Holmes, Georg; Virginia, 1637 *6219 p108*
  *Wife:*Rebecca
Holmes, George; New York, NY, 1815 *2859.11 p33*
Holmes, George; Virginia, 1635 *6219 p70*
  *Wife:*Rebecca
Holmes, Henry 21; Jamaica, 1736 *3690.1 p115*
Holmes, James; New York, NY, 1815 *2859.11 p33*
Holmes, James; New York, NY, 1838 *8208.4 p73*
Holmes, James 21; Maryland, 1774 *1219.7 p211*
Holmes, John; New York, NY, 1815 *2859.11 p33*
Holmes, John; Virginia, 1622 *6219 p1*
Holmes, John 20; Jamaica, 1724 *3690.1 p115*
Holmes, John 29; Jamaica, 1733 *3690.1 p115*
Holmes, John 32; Virginia, 1773 *1219.7 p171*
Holmes, John 38; Kansas, 1901 *5240.1 p82*
Holmes, John George; Colorado, 1904 *9678.2 p24*
Holmes, Jon.; Virginia, 1636 *6219 p34*
Holmes, Joseph; Baltimore, 1816 *2859.11 p33*
Holmes, Joseph; Illinois, 1856 *7857 p4*
Holmes, Julia *SEE* Holmes, Richard
Holmes, Marg.; Virginia, 1648 *6219 p253*
Holmes, Margaret 20; Massachusetts, 1850 *5881.1 p49*
Holmes, Mary Jane 23; Quebec, 1856 *5704.8 p130*
Holmes, Mathew; Virginia, 1638 *6219 p116*
Holmes, P.; Quebec, 1815 *9229.18 p82*
Holmes, Rebecca *SEE* Holmes, Georg
Holmes, Rebecca *SEE* Holmes, Georg
Holmes, Rebecca *SEE* Holmes, George
Holmes, Richard; Boston, 1904 *3455.2 p99*
  *Wife:*Julia
Holmes, Richd; Virginia, 1698 *2212 p16*
Holmes, S. W.; Washington, 1859-1920 *2872.1 p17*
Holmes, Samuel; Georgia, 1733 *1639.20 p95*
Holmes, Samuel W.; Washington, 1859-1920 *2872.1 p17*
Holmes, Thomas; Virginia, 1639 *6219 p161*
Holmes, Thomas 27; Pennsylvania, 1728 *3690.1 p115*
Holmes, Thomas 29; Maryland, 1774 *1219.7 p180*
Holmes, Thomas 31; New York, 1775 *1219.7 p246*
Holmes, Thomas J.; New York, NY, 1840 *8208.4 p108*
Holmes, William; New York, NY, 1835 *8208.4 p6*
Holmes, William; Philadelphia, 1851 *5704.8 p81*
Holmes, William; Philadelphia, 1852 *5704.8 p97*
Holmes, William; Philadelphia, 1853 *5704.8 p112*
Holmes, William 17; Maryland, 1774 *1219.7 p229*
Holmgren, Alfred; Illinois, 1888 *5012.39 p52*
Holmgren, Alfred; Illinois, 1893 *5012.40 p53*
Holmgren, Olof; Illinois, 1888 *5012.39 p52*
Holmqvist, Carl Johan; Minneapolis, 1874-1885 *6410.35 p59*
Holms, Ezekiel 15; America, 1702 *2212 p38*
Holms, Robert; Savannah, GA, 1774 *1219.7 p227*
  With wife
Holmstadt, Adolph F.; Kansas, 1871 *5240.1 p21*
Holnagel, William; Wisconsin, n.d. *9675.6 p51*
Holne, Christiane Amalie 39 *SEE* Holne, Joh. Carl Aug.
Holne, Joh. Carl Aug. 44; New Orleans, 1839 *9420.2 p167*
  *Wife:*Christiane Amalie 39
Holomek, Charles Jacob; Arkansas, 1918 *95.2 p57*
Holowatyk, Vascil; Arkansas, 1918 *95.2 p57*
Holowinski, . . .; New York, 1831 *4606 p173*
Holrn, Denis; America, 1849 *1450.2 p69A*
Holsbrekken, Michael; Arkansas, 1918 *95.2 p57*
Holse, William; Virginia, 1648 *6219 p253*

Holshiser, Martin; Pennsylvania, 1752 *2444 p169*
Holsig, Laurenz 28; Kansas, 1878 *5240.1 p59*
Holske, William; America, 1840 *1450.2 p69A*
Holster, Wilhelm; Ohio, 1816 *8582.1 p47*
Holsworth, Abel; Quebec, 1713 *7603 p26*
Holt, Mr.; Quebec, 1815 *9229.18 p76*
Holt, Edward; Virginia, 1648 *6219 p250*
Holt, Eliza; Philadelphia, 1868 *5704.8 p230*
Holt, Ellen 27; Virginia, 1699 *2212 p20*
Holt, Francis; Virginia, 1639 *6219 p153*
Holt, George 17; America, 1699 *2212 p25*
Holt, Henry 11; Philadelphia, 1852 *5704.8 p88*
Holt, Lester 31; Kansas, 1896 *5240.1 p80*
Holt, Matt.; Virginia, 1645 *6219 p233*
Holt, Patrick; Philadelphia, 1852 *5704.8 p88*
Holt, Rebecca 9; Philadelphia, 1852 *5704.8 p88*
Holt, Robert; Virginia, 1638 *6219 p148*
Holt, Susan; Virginia, 1646 *6219 p240*
Holt, Thomas; Virginia, 1637 *6219 p82*
Holt, William; Maryland or Virginia, 1698 *2212 p5*
Holt, William 16; Jamaica, 1736 *3690.1 p250*
Holtby, Gustavus 34; Massachusetts, 1860 *6410.32 p113*
Holtdorp, Frederick; Wisconsin, n.d. *9675.6 p51*
Holten, William V.; Illinois, 1888 *5012.39 p121*
Holters, B.; Cincinnati, 1869-1887 *8582 p14*
Holtje, Henrich Heinrich Hermann; Kansas, 1896 *5240.1 p21*
Holtje, Herman D. Fritz 21; Kansas, 1891 *5240.1 p76*
Holtje, Herman Henry 22; Kansas, 1887 *5240.1 p21*
Holtje, Herman Henry 22; Kansas, 1887 *5240.1 p70*
Holtke, Henry F. 27; Kansas, 1881 *5240.1 p62*
Holtke, Louis D. 21; Kansas, 1888 *5240.1 p72*
Holtke, W. F.; Kansas, 1898 *5240.1 p21*
Holtman, John Henry; New Orleans, 1855 *1450.2 p16B*
Holtmann, Wilhelm; America, 1852 *8582.3 p32*
Holtogel, . . .; Canada, 1776-1783 *9786 p24*
Holton, George 21; Port uncertain, 1774 *1219.7 p177*
Holton, Jon.; Virginia, 1634 *6219 p32*
Holton, Pat; Philadelphia, 1852 *5704.8 p92*
Holton, Wm.; Virginia, 1634 *6219 p32*
Holtse, Hans P.; Arkansas, 1918 *95.2 p57*
Holtslag, William; Wisconsin, n.d. *9675.6 p51*
Holtz, Charles 55; California, 1873 *2769.10 p4*
Holtz, Frederick; Indiana, 1848 *9117 p16*
Holtz, George; Wisconsin, n.d. *9675.6 p51*
Holtz, William; Indiana, 1848 *9117 p16*
Holtzapfel, Erasmus; Philadelphia, 1763 *9973.7 p38*
Holtze, Conrad; Canada, 1783 *9786 p38A*
Holtzer, Catharina; Georgia, 1739 *9332 p324*
Holtzer, Catharina 15; Georgia, 1739 *9332 p327*
Holtzer, John; America, 1839 *1450.2 p69A*
Holtzer, Susannah; Georgia, 1734 *9332 p328*
Holtzermann, Jacob D.; Ohio, 1869-1887 *8582 p14*
Holtzhaeuser, Catharina D. Raetzler *SEE* Holtzhaeuser, Johann Martin
Holtzhaeuser, Johann Christoph *SEE* Holtzhaeuser, Johann Martin
Holtzhaeuser, Johann Martin *SEE* Holtzhaeuser, Johann Martin
Holtzhaeuser, Johann Martin; Port uncertain, 1750-1755 *2444 p169*
  *Wife:*Catharina D. Raetzler
  *Child:*Juliana Elisabetha
  *Child:*Johann Martin
  *Child:*Johann Christoph
Holtzhaeuser, Juliana Elisabetha *SEE* Holtzhaeuser, Johann Martin
Holtzhaeusser, Martin; Pennsylvania, 1752 *2444 p169*
Holtzhauser, Catharina D. Raetzler *SEE* Holtzhauser, Johann Martin
Holtzhauser, Johann Christoph *SEE* Holtzhauser, Johann Martin
Holtzhauser, Johann Martin *SEE* Holtzhauser, Johann Martin
Holtzhauser, Johann Martin; Port uncertain, 1750-1755 *2444 p169*
  *Wife:*Catharina D. Raetzler
  *Child:*Juliana Elisabetha
  *Child:*Johann Martin
  *Child:*Johann Christoph
Holtzhauser, Juliana Elisabetha *SEE* Holtzhauser, Johann Martin
Holtzkam, Christian; Philadelphia, 1777-1779 *8137 p10*
Holubicki, Fryderyk; New York, 1835 *4606 p179*
Holvik, Anne Forgerson; Arkansas, 1918 *95.2 p57*
Holy, Anton; Arkansas, 1918 *95.2 p57*
Holz, Charles H. 33; Arizona, 1890 *2764.35 p33*
Holzberger, . . .; Canada, 1776-1783 *9786 p24*
Holzer, . . .; Canada, 1776-1783 *9786 p24*
Holzhaeuser, Catharina D. Raetzler *SEE* Holzhaeuser, Johann Martin
Holzhaeuser, Johann Christoph *SEE* Holzhaeuser, Johann Martin

Holzhaeuser, Johann Martin *SEE* Holzhaeuser, Johann Martin
Holzhaeuser, Johann Martin; Port uncertain, 1750-1755 *2444 p169*
  *Wife:*Catharina D. Raetzler
  *Child:*Juliana Elisabetha
  *Child:*Johann Martin
  *Child:*Johann Christoph
Holzhaeuser, Juliana Elisabetha *SEE* Holzhaeuser, Johann Martin
Holzhauer, Anne M.C. Charlotte Kolling; America, 1871 *4610.10 p100*
  *Child:*Christ.
  *Child:*Dietrich
Holzhauer, Anne Marie L.C. Droste *SEE* Holzhauer, Carl Diedrich
Holzhauer, Carl 15 *SEE* Holzhauer, Carl Diedrich
Holzhauer, Carl Diedrich; America, 1871 *4610.10 p100*
  *Child:*Fritz 17
  *Child:*Carl 15
  *Child:*Johann 13
  *Child:*Hermann 11
  *Wife:*Anne Marie L.C. Droste
Holzhauer, Christ. *SEE* Holzhauer, Anne M.C. Charlotte Kollin
Holzhauer, Dietrich *SEE* Holzhauer, Anne M.C. Charlotte Kollin
Holzhauer, Fritz *SEE* Holzhauer, Karl Friedrich Moritz
Holzhauer, Fritz 17 *SEE* Holzhauer, Carl Diedrich
Holzhauer, Heinrich *SEE* Holzhauer, Karl Friedrich Moritz
Holzhauer, Hermann 11 *SEE* Holzhauer, Carl Diedrich
Holzhauer, Johann 13 *SEE* Holzhauer, Carl Diedrich
Holzhauer, Karl Friedrich Moritz; America, 1869 *4610.10 p100*
  *Child:*Karoline
  *Child:*Louise
  *Child:*Fritz
  *Child:*Heinrich
  *Child:*Wihelm
Holzhauer, Karoline *SEE* Holzhauer, Karl Friedrich Moritz
Holzhauer, Louise *SEE* Holzhauer, Karl Friedrich Moritz
Holzhauer, Mrs. S.; Milwaukee, 1875 *4719.30 p257*
  With child
Holzhauer, Wihelm *SEE* Holzhauer, Karl Friedrich Moritz
Holzhausen, . . .; Canada, 1776-1783 *9786 p24*
Holzman, Louis; Arkansas, 1918 *95.2 p57*
Holzman, Phillip 31; Kansas, 1891 *5240.1 p76*
Holzmeister, . . .; Canada, 1776-1783 *9786 p24*
Holzmeister, Mrs. L. V.; Milwaukee, 1875 *4719.30 p257*
Holzwart, Heinrich; Wisconsin, n.d. *9675.6 p51*
Holzwerter, . . .; Canada, 1776-1783 *9786 p24*
Homan, William 18; Maryland, 1720 *3690.1 p115*
Homann, . . .; Canada, 1776-1783 *9786 p24*
Homann, . . .; New Orleans, 1846 *3702.7 p84*
Homberger, Helwig; Philadelphia, 1779 *8137 p10*
Homberger, Johannes; Philadelphia, 1779 *8137 p10*
Homburg, Anne Catharine Charlotte 52; America, 1853 *4610.10 p151*
Homburg, August Heinrich Friedrich; America, 1883 *4610.10 p96*
Homburg, Carl; America, 1886 *4610.10 p153*
Homburg, Carl Christian; America, 1871 *4610.10 p152*
Homburg, Carl Friedrich *SEE* Homburg, Johann Carl August
Homburg, Christian Friedrich *SEE* Homburg, Christian Friedrich
Homburg, Christian Friedrich; America, 1852 *4610.10 p156*
  *Son:*Christian Friedrich
Homburg, Conradin; Wheeling, WV, 1852 *8582.3 p78*
Homburg, Ernst Friedrich Wilhelm; America, 1883 *4610.10 p96*
Homburg, Ernst H. Christian *SEE* Homburg, Johann Carl August
Homburg, Heinrich Christian Friedrich; America, 1854 *4610.10 p151*
Homburg, Heinrich P. Wilhelm *SEE* Homburg, Johann Carl August
Homburg, Heinrich Wilhelm; America, 1873 *4610.10 p152*
Homburg, Johann Carl August; America, 1844 *4610.10 p150*
  *Wife:*Marie S. M. Ilsabein
  *Child:*Ernst H. Christian
  *Child:*Heinrich P. Wilhelm
  *Child:*Carl Friedrich
Homburg, Louise; America, 1850 *4610.10 p139*
Homburg, Marie S. M. Ilsabein *SEE* Homburg, Johann Carl August
Home, Catharine 19; America, 1728 *3690.1 p115*

Home, Eleanora Elizabeth; Quebec, 1787 ***8894.2*** *p57*
Homel, John; Ohio, 1842 ***8365.25*** *p12*
Homer, Christian; Philadelphia, 1759 ***9973.7*** *p33*
Homermar, . . .; Canada, 1776-1783 ***9786*** *p24*
Homes, Jane; Philadelphia, 1864 ***5704.8*** *p176*
Homes, Margaret; Quebec, 1849 ***5704.8*** *p57*
Homes, Patrick; Philadelphia, 1865 ***5704.8*** *p190*
Homes, Richard; Jamaica, 1756 ***1219.7*** *p43*
Homes, Richard; Jamaica, 1756 ***3690.1*** *p115*
Homeyer, Carl Friedrich; America, 1864 ***4610.10*** *p117*
*Son:*Friedrich Wilhelm
Homeyer, Diedrich; America, 1886 ***4610.10*** *p150*
Homeyer, Fr.; America, 1869-1886 ***4610.10*** *p150*
Homeyer, Friedrich Wilhelm *SEE* Homeyer, Carl Friedrich
Homier, John Frederick; Illinois, 1860 ***2896.5*** *p18*
Hommelmann, . . .; Canada, 1776-1783 ***9786*** *p24*
Hommerich, . . .; Canada, 1776-1783 ***9786*** *p24*
Hompejo, . . .; Colorado, 1896 ***9678.2*** *p24*
Homsenn, George; New York, NY, 1834 ***8208.4*** *p29*
Homsey, Alexander; Arkansas, 1918 ***95.2*** *p57*
Hon, Adam 24; America, 1836 ***778.5*** *p276*
Honal, F. 29; America, 1836 ***778.5*** *p276*
Hone, Catharine; New York, NY, 1864 ***5704.8*** *p172*
Hone, Catherine; New York, NY, 1868 ***5704.8*** *p228*
Hone, Ellen 21; Philadelphia, 1860 ***5704.8*** *p146*
Hone, John; Virginia, 1642 ***6219*** *p189*
Hone, Mary; New York, NY, 1868 ***5704.8*** *p228*
Hone, Mary 20; Philadelphia, 1860 ***5704.8*** *p146*
Hone, Sarah 18; Philadelphia, 1861 ***5704.8*** *p147*
Hone, Thomas 18; Philadelphia, 1864 ***5704.8*** *p161*
Honeck, Michael; New England, 1753 ***4525*** *p222*
Honeck, Michael; Pennsylvania, 1753 ***4525*** *p222*
Honegger, Arnold; Iroquois Co., IL, 1892 ***3455.1*** *p11*
Honer, John B.; America, 1849 ***8582.3*** *p32*
Honer, Roger; Virginia, 1638 ***6219*** *p11*
Honeten, Keatty; Philadelphia, 1850 ***5704.8*** *p60*
Honetin, Keatty; Philadelphia, 1850 ***53.26*** *p38*
Honeywood, Arthur 22; Maryland, 1774 ***1219.7*** *p229*
Hongell, Andrew; Washington, 1859-1920 ***2872.1*** *p17*
Hongo, Arvo John; Arkansas, 1918 ***95.2*** *p57*
Honhorst, Joseph; America, 1837 ***8582.3*** *p32*
Honig, Werner; New York, NY, 1922 ***3455.3*** *p81*
Honine, Jane; Virginia, 1638 ***6219*** *p118*
Honing, Frank; Cincinnati, 1845 ***8582.1*** *p16*
Honnywood, Robert; Virginia, 1638 ***6219*** *p180*
Honold, Mr. 32; America, 1837 ***778.5*** *p276*
Honold, Dietrich; Ohio, 1798-1818 ***8582.2*** *p54*
Honold, Dietrich; Ohio, 1812-1814 ***8582.2*** *p59*
Honorina, Sister M.; Wisconsin, n.d. ***9675.5*** *p121*
Hons, Claus; New York, NY, 1836 ***8208.4*** *p13*
Honsdon, Henry 21; Virginia, 1774 ***1219.7*** *p239*
Honson, Ingvold Conrad; Arkansas, 1918 ***95.2*** *p57*
Hontete, Miss; New Orleans, 1839 ***778.5*** *p276*
Honyborne, Robert; Virginia, 1635 ***6219*** *p72*
Hoobs, Michael; South Carolina, 1788 ***7119*** *p200*
Hoock, Catharina Dorothea; Port uncertain, 1730-1800 ***2444*** *p169*
Hood, Ann; Philadelphia, 1851 ***5704.8*** *p80*
Hood, Ann; St. John, N.B., 1847 ***5704.8*** *p18*
Hood, Elizabeth 7; Philadelphia, 1851 ***5704.8*** *p76*
Hood, Elizabeth 30; Maryland, 1775 ***1219.7*** *p264*
Hood, Frederick 11; Philadelphia, 1851 ***5704.8*** *p76*
Hood, Henry; Philadelphia, 1851 ***5704.8*** *p76*
Hood, Henry; St. John, N.B., 1852 ***5704.8*** *p93*
Hood, Isabella; Quebec, 1847 ***5704.8*** *p16*
Hood, James; Quebec, 1847 ***5704.8*** *p38*
Hood, James; Quebec, 1850 ***5704.8*** *p69*
Hood, James; Quebec, 1851 ***5704.8*** *p75*
Hood, Jane; Quebec, 1851 ***5704.8*** *p75*
Hood, Jane; St. John, N.B., 1853 ***5704.8*** *p107*
Hood, John; Philadelphia, 1850 ***5704.8*** *p64*
Hood, Margaret; St. John, N.B., 1847 ***5704.8*** *p18*
Hood, Margaret; St. John, N.B., 1851 ***5704.8*** *p78*
Hood, Margaret 12; Philadelphia, 1851 ***5704.8*** *p76*
Hood, Martha; St. John, N.B., 1852 ***5704.8*** *p93*
Hood, Mary; Philadelphia, 1851 ***5704.8*** *p77*
Hood, Mary; Philadelphia, 1870 ***5704.8*** *p239*
Hood, Mary; Quebec, 1853 ***5704.8*** *p104*
Hood, Mary Anne; Philadelphia, 1851 ***5704.8*** *p76*
Hood, Oliver; Quebec, 1847 ***5704.8*** *p38*
Hood, Richard 19; Jamaica, 1725 ***3690.1*** *p116*
Hood, Robert 3; Philadelphia, 1851 ***5704.8*** *p76*
Hood, W.G.; Illinois, 1902 ***5012.39*** *p53*
Hood, W.G.; Illinois, 1902 ***5012.40*** *p80*
Hood, William; America, 1864 ***5704.8*** *p175*
Hood, William; Quebec, 1847 ***5704.8*** *p16*
Hood, William; Quebec, 1853 ***5704.8*** *p104*
Hood, William 29; Virginia, 1774 ***1219.7*** *p186*
Hooey, William 35; St. John, N.B., 1853 ***5704.8*** *p109*
Hoofman, George; Ohio, 1842 ***8365.25*** *p12*
Hoofman, John; South Carolina, 1788 ***7119*** *p198*
Hoofman, Wolf; America, 1888 ***1450.2*** *p69A*
Hoofmire, Henry; New Orleans, 1845 ***2896.5*** *p18*
Hoofnagle, Frantz Henrich; Pennsylvania, 1753 ***4779.3*** *p14*
*Relative:*Johan Christian
Hoofnagle, Johan Christian *SEE* Hoofnagle, Frantz Henrich
Hoofnagle, Johannes; Pennsylvania, 1752 ***4779.3*** *p14*
Hoofnaigle, John; Pennsylvania, 1762 ***4779.3*** *p14*
Hoofnocle, John; Indiana, 1848 ***9117*** *p16*
Hoogendorn, Eva; Iowa, 1866-1943 ***123.54*** *p23*
Hoogendorn, Jacob; Iowa, 1866-1943 ***123.54*** *p23*
Hoogstraat, John; New York, NY, 1923 ***3455.4*** *p50*
Hoogstraat, Tjaardt; New York, NY, 1923 ***3455.3*** *p85*
Hoogstraat, Tjaardt; New York, NY, 1923 ***3455.4*** *p51*
Hook, Peter 37; Arizona, 1890 ***2764.35*** *p35*
Hook, Samuel 38; Philadelphia, 1774 ***1219.7*** *p233*
Hookart, Jacob; Philadelphia, 1759 ***9973.7*** *p34*
Hooke, Edw.; Virginia, 1637 ***6219*** *p11*
Hooke, Nathaniel; Virginia, 1635 ***6219*** *p69*
Hooke, Wm.; Virginia, 1643 ***6219*** *p202*
Hooker, Tho.; Virginia, 1643 ***6219*** *p204*
Hooker, Thomas 15; Maryland, 1774 ***1219.7*** *p211*
Hooker, William; Pensacola, FL, 1767 ***1219.7*** *p130*
Hookes, Wm.; Virginia, 1629 ***6219*** *p31*
Hookes, Wm.; Virginia, 1637 ***6219*** *p13*
Hooley, Merry 60; Massachusetts, 1849 ***5881.1*** *p48*
Hoome, Jane 20; Philadelphia, 1858 ***5704.8*** *p139*
Hoons, Mary 18; Maryland, 1775 ***1219.7*** *p253*
Hooper, Adolph C. H.; Washington, 1859-1920 ***2872.1*** *p17*
Hooper, Henry; New York, NY, 1834 ***8208.4*** *p2*
Hooper, James 22; Philadelphia, 1774 ***1219.7*** *p233*
Hooper, Jeremiah 39; Maryland, 1774 ***1219.7*** *p181*
Hooper, John Whitford; California, 1869 ***2769.5*** *p4*
Hooper, Jon.; Virginia, 1643 ***6219*** *p202*
Hooper, Mary 18; Virginia, 1774 ***1219.7*** *p238*
Hooper, Peter; Virginia, 1635 ***6219*** *p12*
Hooper, Richard; Virginia, 1643 ***6219*** *p23*
Hooper, Robert 22; Maryland, 1774 ***1219.7*** *p192*
Hooper, Tho.; Virginia, 1635 ***6219*** *p72*
Hooper, William 20; Pennsylvania, 1735 ***3690.1*** *p116*
Hoople, Mr.; Quebec, 1815 ***9229.18*** *p76*
Hoops, John; Wisconsin, n.d. ***9675.6*** *p51*
Hoornhorst, Richard; Arkansas, 1918 ***95.2*** *p58*
Hoornhorst, Richard 26; Arkansas, 1918 ***95.2*** *p57*
Hoorquist, Elias; Maine, 1871-1880 ***6410.22*** *p119*
Hoos, Henrich; Trenton, NJ, 1776 ***8137*** *p10*
Hoot, Catherine; Philadelphia, 1850 ***53.26*** *p38*
Hooton, Christopher; Virginia, 1643 ***6219*** *p202*
Hoover, Heinrich; Kentucky, 1839-1840 ***8582.3*** *p98*
Hoover, John; America, 1827 ***1450.2*** *p69A*
Hoover, Theador; America, 1827 ***1450.2*** *p69A*
Hope, August; Illinois, 1838-1906 ***2896.5*** *p18*
Hope, Cuthbert Collingwood; West Virginia, 1860 ***9788.3*** *p12*
Hope, Joseph 42; Kansas, 1872 ***5240.1*** *p52*
Hope, Josiah 20; Jamaica, 1721 ***3690.1*** *p116*
Hope, Sarah 60; Massachusetts, 1848 ***5881.1*** *p50*
Hope, William Henry; West Virginia, 1860 ***9788.3*** *p12*
Hopf, Johan Caspar; Pennsylvania, 1753 ***2444*** *p169*
Hopf, Johannes; Pennsylvania, 1753 ***2444*** *p169*
Hopf, Leopold; Washington, 1859-1920 ***2872.1*** *p17*
Hopff, Johannes; Pennsylvania, 1751 ***2444*** *p169*
Hopff, Johannes; Port uncertain, 1751 ***2444*** *p169*
*Wife:*Margaretha Wendel
Hopff, Margaretha Wendel *SEE* Hopff, Johannes
Hopffenrath, . . .; Canada, 1776-1783 ***9786*** *p24*
Hopflinger, Anna Maria; Georgia, 1739 ***9332*** *p323*
Hoph, Jno.; Pennsylvania, 1751-1753 ***2444*** *p169*
Hopkin, Ann; Baltimore, 1837 ***8893*** *p265*
Hopkin, Ann 3 mos *SEE* Hopkin, Thomas
Hopkin, Ann 3 mos; Philadelphia, 1847 ***5704.8*** *p30*
Hopkin, Jane *SEE* Hopkin, Thomas
Hopkin, Jane; Philadelphia, 1847 ***5704.8*** *p30*
Hopkin, Matilda *SEE* Hopkin, Thomas
Hopkin, Matilda; Philadelphia, 1847 ***5704.8*** *p30*
Hopkin, Thomas; Philadelphia, 1847 ***53.26*** *p38*
*Wife:*Jane
*Relative:*Matilda
*Relative:*Ann 3 mos
Hopkin, Thomas; Philadelphia, 1847 ***5704.8*** *p30*
Hopkin, William; Virginia, 1641 ***6219*** *p185*
Hopkins, Ann 29; Baltimore, 1775 ***1219.7*** *p269*
Hopkins, Ann 33 *SEE* Hopkins, William
Hopkins, Betty; St. John, N.B., 1847 ***5704.8*** *p26*
Hopkins, David; Virginia, 1637 ***6219*** *p11*
Hopkins, E. G.; Arkansas, 1918 ***95.2*** *p107*
Hopkins, Elizabeth 18; Philadelphia, 1774 ***1219.7*** *p182*
Hopkins, Ernest George; Arkansas, 1918 ***95.2*** *p58*
Hopkins, James; Colorado, 1898 ***9678.2*** *p24*
Hopkins, John; Philadelphia, 1864 ***5704.8*** *p181*
Hopkins, John; Virginia, 1642 ***6219*** *p15*
Hopkins, John; Virginia, 1642 ***6219*** *p190*
Hopkins, John 5; Massachusetts, 1848 ***5881.1*** *p47*
Hopkins, John 19; Maryland, 1775 ***1219.7*** *p264*
Hopkins, Joseph; St. John, N.B., 1847 ***5704.8*** *p26*
Hopkins, Martha; Philadelphia, 1864 ***5704.8*** *p181*
Hopkins, Mary 17; Pennsylvania, 1723 ***3690.1*** *p116*
Hopkins, Mathew; Philadelphia, 1816 ***2859.11*** *p33*
Hopkins, Patrick 25; Maryland, 1774 ***1219.7*** *p229*
Hopkins, Phaebus; Virginia, 1621 ***6219*** *p67*
Hopkins, Richard; Virginia, 1647 ***6219*** *p244*
Hopkins, Robert; Virginia, 1635 ***6219*** *p69*
Hopkins, Robert; Virginia, 1642 ***6219*** *p190*
Hopkins, Robert 19; Jamaica, 1734 ***3690.1*** *p116*
Hopkins, Robert 21; Philadelphia, 1803 ***53.26*** *p38*
Hopkins, Samuel; New York, NY, 1816 ***2859.11*** *p33*
Hopkins, Samuel; St. John, N.B., 1847 ***5704.8*** *p26*
Hopkins, Sarah; Philadelphia, 1864 ***5704.8*** *p181*
Hopkins, Suzanne; Montreal, 1818 ***7603*** *p67*
Hopkins, Tho.; Virginia, 1643 ***6219*** *p204*
Hopkins, Thomas 21; Maryland, 1736 ***3690.1*** *p116*
Hopkins, William; St. John, N.B., 1847 ***5704.8*** *p26*
Hopkins, William 18; Virginia, 1719 ***3690.1*** *p116*
Hopkins, William 33; Port uncertain, 1774 ***1219.7*** *p176*
*Wife:*Ann 33
Hopkinson, Daniel; Virginia, 1637 ***6219*** *p13*
Hopp, Elfrieda Helene; Wisconsin, n.d. ***9675.6*** *p51*
Hopp, Ernst; Wisconsin, n.d. ***9675.6*** *p51*
Hopp, John; Wisconsin, n.d. ***9675.6*** *p51*
Hoppacher, Adam; Pennsylvania, 1753 ***2444*** *p169*
*Child:*Hans Michael
*Child:*Adam Friedrich
Hoppacher, Adam Friedrich *SEE* Hoppacher, Adam
Hoppacher, Hans Michael *SEE* Hoppacher, Adam
Hoppat, Robert 33; Jamaica, 1736 ***3690.1*** *p120*
Hoppe, . . .; Canada, 1776-1783 ***9786*** *p24*
Hoppe, Albert; Wisconsin, n.d. ***9675.6*** *p51*
Hoppe, August; Wisconsin, n.d. ***9675.6*** *p51*
Hoppe, Charles; Wisconsin, n.d. ***9675.6*** *p51*
Hoppe, Fritz 42; Harris Co., TX, 1897 ***6254*** *p3*
Hoppe, Herman; Wisconsin, n.d. ***9675.6*** *p51*
Hoppe, I.E.G.H.; Wisconsin, n.d. ***9675.6*** *p51*
Hoppel, Kaspar; Cincinnati, 1800-1876 ***8582.3*** *p81*
Hopper, Anthony 19; Maryland, 1775 ***1219.7*** *p260*
Hopper, John 23; Nova Scotia, 1774 ***1219.7*** *p209*
Hopper, Peter; America, 1741 ***4971*** *p16*
Hopper, Richard; Quebec, 1849 ***5704.8*** *p51*
Hopper, Thomas 32; Maryland, 1774 ***1219.7*** *p224*
Hopper, Thomas 32; Maryland, 1774 ***1219.7*** *p229*
Hopps, Robert; Virginia, 1642 ***6219*** *p195*
Hopton, William; Virginia, 1642 ***6219*** *p189*
Horace, Elizabeth 43; Massachusetts, 1860 ***6410.32*** *p99*
Horahan, Thomas; America, 1740 ***4971*** *p28*
Horan, Gordian; Quebec, 1811 ***7603*** *p81*
Horan, John; New York, NY, 1811 ***2859.11*** *p13*
Horan, John; Quebec, 1794 ***7603*** *p76*
Horan, Michael; Arizona, 1897 ***9228.30*** *p3*
Horan, Michael; Arizona, 1898 ***9228.30*** *p5*
Horan, Michael; New York, NY, 1835 ***8208.4*** *p7*
Horan, Simon; New York, NY, 1811 ***2859.11*** *p13*
Horask, Daniel; Philadelphia, 1864 ***5704.8*** *p181*
Horber, Anna Barbara; America, 1743-1800 ***2444*** *p193*
Horde, William; America, 1856 ***1450.2*** *p69A*
Hore, And.; Virginia, 1637 ***6219*** *p113*
Hored, Margaret; Annapolis, MD, 1742 ***4971*** *p92*
Horeghty, Ellen; Philadelphia, 1853 ***5704.8*** *p101*
Horenden, Thomas 17; Virginia, 1750 ***3690.1*** *p116*
Horenden, Thomas 17; Virginia, 1751 ***1219.7*** *p2*
Horer, Magdalena 22; New Orleans, 1837 ***5647.5*** *p3*
Horeysek, Emilie Weidig 56; America, 1903 ***1763*** *p40D*
Horgan, Mary 26; Massachusetts, 1847 ***5881.1*** *p48*
Horgan, Michael 24; Massachusetts, 1847 ***5881.1*** *p48*
Horigan, Matthew; Boston, 1847 ***6013.19*** *p73*
Horin, Alfred; Arkansas, 1918 ***95.2*** *p58*
Horinchuk, Roman; Arkansas, 1918 ***95.2*** *p58*
Horisk, William; Philadelphia, 1866 ***5704.8*** *p208*
Hork, Albert M.; Wisconsin, n.d. ***9675.6*** *p51*
Horlacher, Johann David; Pennsylvania, 1752 ***2444*** *p169*
Horlacher, Maria Elisabetha; Philadelphia, 1764 ***2444*** *p181*
Horle, Ad. 20; America, 1853 ***9162.8*** *p36*
Horman, Francois; Quebec, 1782 ***7603*** *p25*
Hormebrooke, Arthur; Virginia, 1642 ***6219*** *p188*
Hormer, James; Virginia, 1636 ***6219*** *p75*
Horn, . . .; Canada, 1776-1783 ***9786*** *p24*
Horn, Alexander; America, 1763 ***1639.20*** *p95*
Horn, Andrew; New York, 1744 ***3652*** *p63*
*Wife:*Dorothea
Horn, Anna Marie 70; Arizona, 1908 ***9228.40*** *p12*
Horn, Anna Rosina Wiessner *SEE* Horn, Sebastian
Horn, Barbara *SEE* Horn, Christoph, Sr.
Horn, Barbara 10; America, 1854-1855 ***9162.6*** *p104*
Horn, Catharine *SEE* Horn, Christoph, Sr.
Horn, Christoph; Pennsylvania, 1753 ***4525*** *p222*
Horn, Christoph; Pennsylvania, 1753 ***4525*** *p223*

Horn, Christoph, Jr.; Pennsylvania, 1752 ***4525*** *p223*
*Cousin:*Philipp
Horn, Christoph, Sr.; New England, 1753 ***4525*** *p222*
*Wife:*Catharine
*Child:*Eva
*Child:*Barbara
*Child:*Stephan
Horn, Dorothea *SEE* Horn, Andrew
Horn, Eva *SEE* Horn, Christoph, Sr.
Horn, Francois 36; America, 1836 ***778.5*** *p276*
Horn, Georg; Pennsylvania, 1753 ***2444*** *p170*
Horn, George; Pennsylvania, 1753 ***4525*** *p222*
Horn, George; Pennsylvania, 1753 ***4525*** *p223*
Horn, Gustaf; Illinois, 1879 ***2896.5*** *p18*
Horn, Gustav; Illinois, 1880 ***2896.5*** *p19*
Horn, Joachim; Wisconsin, n.d. ***9675.6*** *p51*
Horn, Johannes; Pennsylvania, 1753 ***4525*** *p222*
Horn, Johannes; Pennsylvania, 1753 ***4525*** *p223*
Horn, John; Illinois, 1880 ***2896.5*** *p19*
Horn, John; Wisconsin, n.d. ***9675.6*** *p51*
Horn, John 20; Pennsylvania, 1730 ***3690.1*** *p116*
Horn, Julius; Arkansas, 1918 ***95.2*** *p58*
Horn, Karl; New York, NY, 1900 ***1450.2*** *p16B*
Horn, M. Barbara; New York, 1763 ***3652*** *p89*
Horn, Maria Barbara; Pennsylvania, 1763 ***4525*** *p223*
Horn, Michael; Arizona, 1898 ***9228.30*** *p11*
Horn, Michael; Illinois, 1880 ***2896.5*** *p19*
Horn, Oscar Mike; Iowa, 1866-1943 ***123.54*** *p65*
Horn, Philipp *SEE* Horn, Christoph, Jr.
Horn, Philipp Jacob; Pennsylvania, 1752 ***4525*** *p223*
Horn, Sebastian; New England, 1753 ***4525*** *p223*
*Wife:*Anna Rosina Wiessner
Horn, Sebastian; Pennsylvania, 1753 ***4525*** *p223*
Horn, Sebastian; Wisconsin, n.d. ***9675.6*** *p51*
Horn, Stephan *SEE* Horn, Christoph, Sr.
Horn, Stephan; Philadelphia, 1752 ***4525*** *p223*
With wife
With 2 children
Hornberger, Friedrich; Cincinnati, 1869-1887 ***8582*** *p14*
Hornberger, John; Indiana, 1869-1887 ***8582*** *p14*
Hornburg, . . .; Canada, 1776-1783 ***9786*** *p25*
Hornburg, Auguste Albertine Friederike; America, 1890 ***4610.10*** *p137*
Hornby, Joseph; America, 1739 ***4971*** *p99*
Hornby, William; Washington, 1859-1920 ***2872.1*** *p17*
Horne, . . .; Pennsylvania, n.d. ***4525*** *p223*
Horne, Mr. 26; St. Kitts, 1773 ***1219.7*** *p174*
Horne, Daniel; Barbados, 1766 ***1219.7*** *p124*
Horne, Henry 22; Maryland, 1774 ***1219.7*** *p220*
Horne, John; Virginia, 1636 ***6219*** *p28*
Horne, John 20; Virginia, 1699 ***2212*** *p27*
Horne, Jon.; Virginia, 1635 ***6219*** *p17*
Horne, Stephan; Philadelphia, 1752 ***4525*** *p223*
Horne, Stephen; Pennsylvania, 1755 ***4525*** *p224*
Horne, Thomas; St. Christopher, 1756 ***1219.7*** *p45*
Horneber, . . .; Canada, 1776-1783 ***9786*** *p25*
Hornecker, Joh. M. 30; St. Louis, 1838 ***778.5*** *p276*
Horner, Anna *SEE* Horner, Geo
Horner, Anna *SEE* Horner, Geo
Horner, Conrad 14; America, 1838 ***778.5*** *p276*
Horner, Geo; Pennsylvania, 1785 ***4525*** *p224*
*Wife:*Anna
*Child:*Jno
*Child:*Jacob
*Child:*George, Jr.
*Child:*Anna
*Child:*Marg't
*Child:*Kunigunda
Horner, George, Jr. *SEE* Horner, Geo
Horner, Jacob *SEE* Horner, Geo
Horner, Jane Ann; Philadelphia, 1852 ***5704.8*** *p89*
Horner, Jno *SEE* Horner, Geo
Horner, John 29; Massachusetts, 1847 ***5881.1*** *p47*
Horner, Kunigunda *SEE* Horner, Geo
Horner, Marg't *SEE* Horner, Geo
Horner, Michael; New England, 1753 ***4525*** *p225*
Horner, Michael; Pennsylvania, 1753 ***4525*** *p225*
Horner, Samuel; America, 1739 ***4971*** *p99*
Horner, Thomas; Virginia, 1642 ***6219*** *p193*
Hornett, Daniel 42; California, 1867 ***3840.2*** *p14*
Hornickel, Caspar 72; America, 1895 ***1763*** *p40D*
Hornig, Christian; America, 1733-1812 ***2444*** *p219*
Hornig, Christian; New York, 1761 ***3652*** *p87*
Hornn, Heinerick; Canada, 1783 ***9786*** *p38A*
Hornoga, Pierre Auguste; Port uncertain, 1839 ***778.5*** *p276*
Hornsberger, Maria 60; New York, NY, 1897 ***1763*** *p40D*
Hornsell, Richard 25; New York, 1774 ***1219.7*** *p217*
Hornsham, Geo. 19; Port uncertain, 1849 ***4535.10*** *p198*
Hornug, Jakob; New York, NY, 1840 ***8208.4*** *p112*
Horodynski, Ludwik; New York, 1831 ***4606*** *p174*
Horouse, Peter; New York, NY, 1839 ***8208.4*** *p98*
Horowitz, Samuel E.; America, 1864 ***1450.2*** *p69A*
Horr, Jacob; South Carolina, 1788 ***7119*** *p198*
Horr, Ludwig 16; America, 1854-1855 ***9162.6*** *p105*
Horr, Nicolaus 27; America, 1854-1855 ***9162.6*** *p104*
Horrabin, Edward 22; Maryland, 1775 ***1219.7*** *p264*
Horrell, Francis 14; Philadelphia, 1775 ***1219.7*** *p248*
Horridge, James; Iowa, 1866-1943 ***123.54*** *p23*
Horrigan, Mary 20; Massachusetts, 1850 ***5881.1*** *p49*
Horrige, James; Iowa, 1866-1943 ***123.54*** *p23*
Horrisk, Catharine; Philadelphia, 1864 ***5704.8*** *p180*
Horrisk, James; Philadelphia, 1864 ***5704.8*** *p180*
Horrocks, Harry; Iowa, 1866-1943 ***123.54*** *p23*
Horrocks, John Robert; Iowa, 1866-1943 ***123.54*** *p65*
Horrogan, Michael; Illinois, 1860 ***2896.5*** *p19*
Horsbell, John 16; America, 1700 ***2212*** *p31*
Horsburgh, John 30; Jamaica, 1725 ***3690.1*** *p116*
Horsburgh, William; Carolina, 1761 ***1639.20*** *p95*
Horsch, Thomas; Milwaukee, 1857 ***8125.8*** *p437*
Horsey, George 21; Jamaica, 1736 ***3690.1*** *p116*
Horsfield, Joseph 24; Maryland, 1774 ***1219.7*** *p222*
Horsfield, Luke 36; Maryland, 1774 ***1219.7*** *p221*
Horsley, George 19; Virginia, 1720 ***3690.1*** *p116*
Horsly, Ralph; Virginia, 1652 ***6251*** *p19*
Horsman, Christopher 27; Nova Scotia, 1775 ***1219.7*** *p263*
Horspool, H. B. 32; Kansas, 1899 ***5240.1*** *p81*
Horst, Anton; Washington, 1859-1920 ***2872.1*** *p17*
Horsten, Fred; Arkansas, 1918 ***95.2*** *p58*
Horstkotte, Anna Catharine Elisabeth; America, 1867 ***4610.10*** *p158*
*Son:*Ernst Heinrich
Horstkotte, Anna Marie L. Trampe *SEE* Horstkotte, Carl Friedrich
Horstkotte, Carl Friedrich; America, 1841 ***4610.10*** *p154*
*Wife:*Anna Marie L. Trampe
*Son:*Carl Heinrich
Horstkotte, Carl Heinrich *SEE* Horstkotte, Carl Friedrich
Horstkotte, Carl Heinrich; America, 1854 ***4610.10*** *p135*
Horstkotte, Ernst Heinrich *SEE* Horstkotte, Anna Catharine Elisabeth
Horstkotte, Friedrich Wilhelm; America, 1856 ***4610.10*** *p157*
Horstmann, Carl Friedrich Ferdinand; America, 1881 ***4610.10*** *p149*
Horstmann, Heinrich; Kentucky, 1800-1877 ***8582.3*** *p99*
Horstmann, Heinrich; Kentucky, 1840 ***8582.3*** *p100*
Horstmann, Henry; America, 1848 ***6013.19*** *p73*
Horth, John 23; Jamaica, 1733 ***3690.1*** *p117*
Hortigan, John; New York, NY, 1834 ***8208.4*** *p2*
Hortness, David; Philadelphia, 1852 ***5704.8*** *p89*
Horton, Barth.; Virginia, 1638 ***6219*** *p11*
Horton, D. B.; Washington, 1859-1920 ***2872.1*** *p17*
Horton, George; New York, NY, 1838 ***8208.4*** *p82*
Horton, Isaac; Virginia, 1636 ***6219*** *p80*
Horton, Isaac; Virginia, 1639 ***6219*** *p161*
Horton, Jane; America, 1698 ***2212*** *p5*
Horton, Patrick 48; Massachusetts, 1849 ***5881.1*** *p50*
Horton, Robert; Virginia, 1648 ***6219*** *p246*
Horton, Tobias; Virginia, 1638 ***6219*** *p119*
Hortus, . . .; Canada, 1776-1783 ***9786*** *p25*
Horund, Frederick; America, 1857 ***1450.2*** *p70A*
Horvat, John; Washington, 1859-1920 ***2872.1*** *p17*
Horwitz, Abram 23; Arkansas, 1918 ***95.2*** *p30*
Horwitz, Abram 23; Arkansas, 1918 ***95.2*** *p58*
Hosack, Margaret; Canada, 1842 ***8893*** *p266*
Hosch, Jacob; Wisconsin, n.d. ***9675.6*** *p51*
Hoschel, Sophie 28; New Orleans, 1839 ***9420.2*** *p167*
Hose, Henry; Wisconsin, n.d. ***9675.6*** *p51*
Hosey, Patrick; America, 1740 ***4971*** *p32*
Hosier, Charles 21; Barbados, 1731 ***3690.1*** *p117*
Hoskins, Bartholomew; Virginia, 1624 ***6219*** *p14*
Hoskins, John; Quebec, 1815 ***7603*** *p29*
Hoskins, John 21; Virginia, 1774 ***1219.7*** *p225*
Hoskins, Richard; Virginia, 1645 ***6219*** *p253*
Hoskins, Thomas 25; Maryland, 1774 ***1219.7*** *p179*
Hoskins, William 17; Pennsylvania, 1719 ***3690.1*** *p117*
Hosquents, Edouard 37; Montreal, 1757 ***7603*** *p29*
Hoss, Agnes Catharina *SEE* Hoss, Johann
Hoss, Johann; Port uncertain, 1750-1800 ***2444*** *p170*
*Wife:*Agnes Catharina
*Child:*Maria Jacobina
Hoss, John; Pennsylvania, 1752 ***2444*** *p170*
Hoss, Maria Jacobina *SEE* Hoss, Johann
Hossac, Mr.; New Orleans, 1839 ***778.5*** *p276*
Hossack, Miss; Quebec, 1815 ***9229.18*** *p81*
Hossdentelfel, Marguerite 2; America, 1838 ***778.5*** *p276*
Hossdentelfel, Marguerite 23; America, 1838 ***778.5*** *p276*
Hosser, Rebecca 16; Maryland, 1775 ***1219.7*** *p260*
Hossfeld, Charles; America, 1857 ***1450.2*** *p70A*
Host, Frank; Iowa, 1866-1943 ***123.54*** *p23*
Hosters, William; Germantown, PA, 1684 ***2467.7*** *p5*
Hostetter, Louis; California, 1860 ***3840.2*** *p14*
Hot Eye ; America, 1743 ***4971*** *p18*
Hotchkis, William 31; Maryland, 1775 ***1219.7*** *p249*
Hotham, Richard 40; Philadelphia, 1774 ***1219.7*** *p201*
Hothersall, Francis *SEE* Hothersall, Thomas
Hothersall, Mary *SEE* Hothersall, Thomas
Hothersall, Richard *SEE* Hothersall, Thomas
Hothersall, Thomas; Virginia, 1621 ***6219*** *p14*
*Wife:*Francis
*Child:*Richard
*Child:*Mary
Hotkouski, Walter Stanley; Arkansas, 1918 ***95.2*** *p58*
Hotson, Mr. 25; Antigua (Antego), 1774 ***1219.7*** *p177*
Hottan, Alice; Philadelphia, 1847 ***53.26*** *p38*
*Relative:*Margaret 11
Hottan, Alice; Philadelphia, 1847 ***5704.8*** *p30*
Hottan, Margaret 11 *SEE* Hottan, Alice
Hottan, Margaret 11; Philadelphia, 1847 ***5704.8*** *p30*
Hotte, . . .; Canada, 1776-1783 ***9786*** *p25*
Hottelmann, . . .; Canada, 1776-1783 ***9786*** *p25*
Hotter, John; Colorado, 1888-1904 ***9678.2*** *p24*
Hotz, Michael; Pennsylvania, 1731-1769 ***4525*** *p226*
With wife
With children
Houchard, Joseph; Iowa, 1866-1943 ***123.54*** *p23*
Houchen, Sarah 26; Maryland, 1775 ***1219.7*** *p249*
Houchen, Susanna 30; Maryland, 1775 ***1219.7*** *p249*
Houchins, John; Antigua (Antego), 1773 ***1219.7*** *p161*
Houck, Philip; South Carolina, 1788 ***7119*** *p200*
Houden, John 20; Philadelphia, 1856 ***5704.8*** *p128*
Houden, Margaret; Philadelphia, 1852 ***5704.8*** *p87*
Houden, Margaret 55; Philadelphia, 1856 ***5704.8*** *p128*
Houe, Jean-Baptiste 35; Montreal, 1704 ***7603*** *p64*
Houff, . . .; Canada, 1776-1783 ***9786*** *p25*
Houfgh, Francis; Virginia, 1618 ***6219*** *p16*
Hough, John 28; Barbados, 1730 ***3690.1*** *p117*
Hough, Teigue; America, 1736-1743 ***4971*** *p58*
Hough, Thomas 14; America, 1705 ***2212*** *p42*
Houghtin, Mary 30; St. John, N.B., 1855 ***5704.8*** *p127*
Houghton, Charles; Washington, 1859-1920 ***2872.1*** *p17*
Houghton, Edward; Virginia, 1698 ***2212*** *p13*
Houghton, Ellen; St. John, N.B., 1852 ***5704.8*** *p95*
Houghton, John; Iowa, 1866-1943 ***123.54*** *p23*
Houghton, John; New York, 1820 ***1450.2*** *p70A*
Houghton, John 19; Jamaica, 1738 ***3690.1*** *p117*
Houghton, Robt.; Virginia, 1635 ***6219*** *p36*
Hougland, John 16; United States or West Indies, 1705 ***2212*** *p44*
Houille Bilfeldt, Mr. 35; Port uncertain, 1836 ***778.5*** *p276*
Hould, Christopher; Virginia, 1636 ***6219*** *p73*
Hoult, John 26; Virginia, 1774 ***1219.7*** *p243*
Houlton, John 6 *SEE* Houlton, Margaret
Houlton, John 6; Philadelphia, 1849 ***5704.8*** *p50*
Houlton, Margaret; Philadelphia, 1849 ***53.26*** *p38*
*Relative:*Mary
*Relative:*Thomas 8
*Relative:*John 6
*Relative:*Patrick 5
Houlton, Margaret; Philadelphia, 1849 ***5704.8*** *p50*
Houlton, Mary *SEE* Houlton, Margaret
Houlton, Mary; Philadelphia, 1849 ***5704.8*** *p50*
Houlton, Patrick 3; Philadelphia, 1849 ***5704.8*** *p50*
Houlton, Patrick 5 *SEE* Houlton, Margaret
Houlton, Thomas 8 *SEE* Houlton, Margaret
Houlton, Thomas 8; Philadelphia, 1849 ***5704.8*** *p50*
Hound, Dorias; Virginia, 1635 ***6219*** *p4*
Hounsby, John 30; Jamaica, 1775 ***1219.7*** *p279*
Houprius, Mr.; Port uncertain, 1839 ***778.5*** *p276*
Houpuris, Mr.; Port uncertain, 1839 ***778.5*** *p276*
Houpy, . . .; Port uncertain, 1839 ***778.5*** *p276*
Houpy, . . .; Port uncertain, 1839 ***778.5*** *p277*
Houpy, Louise; Port uncertain, 1839 ***778.5*** *p277*
Hourbigt, Alex. 10; New Orleans, 1839 ***778.5*** *p277*
Hourbigt, Melainie 30; New Orleans, 1839 ***778.5*** *p277*
Hourbigt, Octavie 7; New Orleans, 1839 ***778.5*** *p277*
Hourbigt, Pierre 41; New Orleans, 1839 ***778.5*** *p277*
House, E. E.; Washington, 1859-1920 ***2872.1*** *p17*
House, James 17; Jamaica, 1774 ***1219.7*** *p242*
Houseman, . . .; Pennsylvania, n.d. ***2444*** *p163*
Houseman, Henry 35; Carolina, 1774 ***1219.7*** *p231*
Houseman, Jno; America, 1697-1707 ***2212*** *p9*
Houseman, John; Pennsylvania, 1750 ***2444*** *p163*
Houseman, John 20; Virginia, 1699 ***2212*** *p26*
Housman, Frederick; Pennsylvania, 1771 ***9973.8*** *p32*
Houssy, Jean; Quebec, 1672 ***7603*** *p70*
Houstan, Anne 30; Philadelphia, 1861 ***5704.8*** *p148*
Houstan, John; New Orleans, 1849 ***5704.8*** *p59*
Houstan, John; Philadelphia, 1853 ***5704.8*** *p108*
Houstan, Mary 20; Philadelphia, 1861 ***5704.8*** *p148*
Houston, . . . 11 mos; Philadelphia, 1868 ***5704.8*** *p225*
Houston, Alexander 45; Philadelphia, 1803 ***53.26*** *p38*
Houston, Anne; St. John, N.B., 1850 ***5704.8*** *p62*
Houston, Bridget 24; Philadelphia, 1868 ***5704.8*** *p225*
Houston, Catharine 24; Philadelphia, 1868 ***5704.8*** *p225*
Houston, Ellen; Philadelphia, 1849 ***53.26*** *p38*

Houston, Ellen; Philadelphia, 1849 ***5704.8*** *p54*
Houston, Francis 20; Philadelphia, 1803 ***53.26*** *p38*
Houston, George 42; North Carolina, 1850 ***1639.20*** *p95*
Houston, Isabella 20; Wilmington, DE, 1831 ***6508.3*** *p101*
Houston, James; New York, NY, 1815 ***2859.11*** *p33*
Houston, James; New York, NY, 1839 ***8208.4*** *p96*
Houston, James 18; Wilmington, DE, 1831 ***6508.3*** *p100*
Houston, Jane 13; Wilmington, DE, 1831 ***6508.3*** *p100*
Houston, Jane 14; Philadelphia, 1857 ***5704.8*** *p132*
Houston, Jane 30; St. John, N.B., 1853 ***5704.8*** *p110*
Houston, John; St. John, N.B., 1852 ***5704.8*** *p92*
Houston, Joseph; Philadelphia, 1853 ***5704.8*** *p103*
Houston, Margaret; St. John, N.B., 1852 ***5704.8*** *p92*
Houston, Margaret 10; Wilmington, DE, 1831 ***6508.3*** *p100*
Houston, Mary 20; Wilmington, DE, 1831 ***6508.3*** *p100*
Houston, Mary Ann 20; Philadelphia, 1857 ***5704.8*** *p132*
Houston, Nelly; Philadelphia, 1851 ***5704.8*** *p78*
Houston, Peter 26; St. John, N.B., 1864 ***5704.8*** *p158*
Houston, Robert 16; Wilmington, DE, 1831 ***6508.3*** *p100*
Houston, Sarah Jane 12; Quebec, 1847 ***5704.8*** *p13*
Houston, Sarah Jane 20; Philadelphia, 1860 ***5704.8*** *p145*
Houston, Susana 11; Philadelphia, 1854 ***5704.8*** *p120*
Houston, Thomas 19; Philadelphia, 1854 ***5704.8*** *p120*
Houston, William; North Carolina, 1700-1799 ***1639.20*** *p96*
Houstone, Jane; Philadelphia, 1847 ***53.26*** *p39*
Houstone, Jane; Philadelphia, 1847 ***5704.8*** *p1*
Houstown, Alexander 22; Grenada, 1776 ***1219.7*** *p282*
Houstulakis, George Mechlen; Arkansas, 1918 ***95.2*** *p58*
Houstutakis, George; Arkansas, 1918 ***95.2*** *p58*
Houtan, Edward; St. John, N.B., 1847 ***5704.8*** *p4*
Houtan, Ellen; St. John, N.B., 1847 ***5704.8*** *p2*
Houtan, Patrick; St. John, N.B., 1848 ***5704.8*** *p39*
Houtan, Peggy; St. John, N.B., 1848 ***5704.8*** *p43*
Houtan, Richard; St. John, N.B., 1853 ***5704.8*** *p106*
Houtan, Susan; St. John, N.B., 1853 ***5704.8*** *p106*
Houtan, William; St. John, N.B., 1848 ***5704.8*** *p44*
Houten, Catherine 28; St. John, N.B., 1854 ***5704.8*** *p114*
Houten, Edward 3 mos; St. John, N.B., 1854 ***5704.8*** *p122*
Houten, James; Philadelphia, 1847 ***53.26*** *p39*
Houten, James; Philadelphia, 1847 ***5704.8*** *p13*
Houten, Mary 35; St. John, N.B., 1854 ***5704.8*** *p122*
Houten, Rose 6; St. John, N.B., 1854 ***5704.8*** *p122*
Houtin, Edward 40; St. John, N.B., 1855 ***5704.8*** *p127*
Houtin, Owen 10; St. John, N.B., 1855 ***5704.8*** *p127*
Houtin, Patrick 12; St. John, N.B., 1855 ***5704.8*** *p127*
Houton, James; St. John, N.B., 1847 ***5704.8*** *p24*
Houtton, . . . 2; Philadelphia, 1866 ***5704.8*** *p204*
Houtton, John 5; Philadelphia, 1866 ***5704.8*** *p204*
Houtton, Michael 9; Philadelphia, 1866 ***5704.8*** *p204*
Houtton, Owen 7; Philadelphia, 1866 ***5704.8*** *p204*
Houtton, Patrick; Philadelphia, 1866 ***5704.8*** *p204*
Houtton, Peggy 8; New York, NY, 1867 ***5704.8*** *p221*
Hovan, Anna; America, 1894 ***7137*** *p169*
Hovan, George; America, 1884 ***7137*** *p168*
*Wife:*Mary
Hovan, John; America, 1890 ***7137*** *p169*
Hovan, John; America, 1891 ***7137*** *p169*
Hovan, Mary *SEE* Hovan, George
Hove, John Johnson 30; Arkansas, 1918 ***95.2*** *p58*
Hoveller, Jeremiah; Virginia, 1637 ***6219*** *p24*
Hoveln, Bus; Illinois, 1895 ***5012.37*** *p63*
Hoven, C.; Washington, 1859-1920 ***2872.1*** *p17*
Hoven, Christ C.; Washington, 1859-1920 ***2872.1*** *p17*
Hoven, Emanuel Jansen; Washington, 1859-1920 ***2872.1*** *p17*
Hovermel, John; New York, NY, 1839 ***8208.4*** *p93*
Hovey, George F.; New York, NY, 1838 ***8208.4*** *p88*
Hovin, Jean 31; America, 1837 ***778.5*** *p277*
Hovlid, Johannes M.; Colorado, 1904 ***9678.2*** *p24*
How, Mr.; Jamaica, 1775 ***1219.7*** *p277*
How, Francis 30; Maryland, 1774 ***1219.7*** *p184*
How, Isaac 24; Virginia, 1773 ***1219.7*** *p169*
How, Jane; Virginia, 1648 ***6219*** *p246*
How, John; Quebec, 1786 ***7603*** *p85*
How, John; Virginia, 1638 ***6219*** *p17*
How, Matthew 17; Maryland, 1723 ***3690.1*** *p117*
How, Richard; Virginia, 1640 ***6219*** *p160*
How, Robert; North Carolina, 1743 ***1639.20*** *p96*
How, Robert Nesbit; Charleston, SC, 1821 ***1639.20*** *p96*
How, Thomas; South Carolina, 1822 ***1639.20*** *p96*
Howard, Albert; America, 1888 ***1450.2*** *p70A*
Howard, Anthony 46; Massachusetts, 1847 ***5881.1*** *p44*
Howard, Bessy 24; Massachusetts, 1849 ***5881.1*** *p45*
Howard, Bridget 3; Massachusetts, 1850 ***5881.1*** *p45*
Howard, C. A.; Minneapolis, 1873-1878 ***6410.35*** *p55*
Howard, D. F.; Washington, 1859-1920 ***2872.1*** *p17*
Howard, Elizabeth 23; Virginia, 1773 ***1219.7*** *p169*
Howard, Ellen 22; Massachusetts, 1849 ***5881.1*** *p46*
Howard, Francis; Virginia, 1648 ***6219*** *p237*
Howard, George; Antigua (Antego), 1737 ***3690.1*** *p117*
Howard, George 19; Maryland, 1724 ***3690.1*** *p117*
Howard, Hannah 26; Newport, RI, 1851 ***6508.5*** *p20*
Howard, Henry 30; Jamaica, 1738 ***3690.1*** *p117*
Howard, James; Illinois, 1855 ***2896.5*** *p19*
Howard, James 7; Quebec, 1850 ***5704.8*** *p69*
Howard, James 19; Virginia, 1729 ***3690.1*** *p117*
Howard, James 23; Jamaica, 1730 ***3690.1*** *p117*
Howard, James 25; Virginia, 1775 ***1219.7*** *p247*
Howard, Jane; Quebec, 1850 ***5704.8*** *p69*
Howard, Jno 28; Virginia, 1701 ***2212*** *p35*
Howard, Job; Virginia, 1698 ***2212*** *p15*
Howard, Johanna 19; Massachusetts, 1849 ***5881.1*** *p47*
Howard, Johanna 21; Massachusetts, 1850 ***5881.1*** *p48*
Howard, John; America, 1741 ***4971*** *p10*
Howard, John; America, 1741 ***4971*** *p94*
Howard, John; Virginia, 1641 ***6219*** *p187*
Howard, John 19; Pennsylvania, 1738 ***3690.1*** *p118*
Howard, John 20; Massachusetts, 1849 ***5881.1*** *p47*
Howard, John 20; Massachusetts, 1849 ***5881.1*** *p48*
Howard, John 20; Pennsylvania, Virginia or Maryland, 1723 ***3690.1*** *p117*
Howard, John 22; Maryland, 1775 ***1219.7*** *p251*
Howard, John 25; Virginia, 1773 ***1219.7*** *p168*
Howard, John J. 41; Arizona, 1890 ***2764.35*** *p31*
Howard, Joseph 21; Maryland, 1774 ***1219.7*** *p181*
Howard, Margaret 21; Philadelphia, 1774 ***1219.7*** *p219*
Howard, Martin 13; Massachusetts, 1850 ***5881.1*** *p49*
Howard, Mary; Annapolis, MD, 1742 ***4971*** *p92*
Howard, Mary 25; America, 1699 ***2212*** *p28*
Howard, Mary 30; Massachusetts, 1850 ***5881.1*** *p49*
Howard, Michael 17; Maryland, 1774 ***1219.7*** *p215*
Howard, Michael 27; Massachusetts, 1849 ***5881.1*** *p49*
Howard, Patrick; New York, NY, 1837 ***8208.4*** *p36*
Howard, Patrick 50; Massachusetts, 1849 ***5881.1*** *p50*
Howard, Polly; Quebec, 1850 ***5704.8*** *p69*
Howard, Robert 19; Maryland, 1720 ***3690.1*** *p118*
Howard, Samuel; Quebec, 1822 ***7603*** *p92*
Howard, Svan; Minneapolis, 1865-1881 ***6410.35*** *p55*
Howard, Thomas; America, 1848 ***1450.2*** *p70A*
Howard, Thomas 23; Jamaica, 1730 ***3690.1*** *p118*
Howard, Thomas 28; Maryland, 1774 ***1219.7*** *p187*
Howard, Thomas 28; Virginia, 1773 ***1219.7*** *p169*
Howard, Thomas 29; Maryland, 1775 ***1219.7*** *p249*
Howard, William; Illinois, 1861 ***2896.5*** *p19*
Howard, William; Quebec, 1847 ***5704.8*** *p29*
Howard, William 1; Massachusetts, 1850 ***5881.1*** *p51*
Howard, William 15; Maryland, 1775 ***1219.7*** *p264*
Howard, William 20; Maryland, 1722 ***3690.1*** *p118*
Howard, William 26; Virginia, 1773 ***1219.7*** *p168*
Howarth, Thomas 21; Maryland or Virginia, 1699 ***2212*** *p23*
Howatt, James; San Francisco, 1850 ***4914.15*** *p10*
Howatt, James; San Francisco, 1850 ***4914.15*** *p13*
Howe, . . .; Baltimore, 1837 ***3702.7*** *p71*
Howe, Charles; America, 1850 ***1450.2*** *p70A*
Howe, Ernst; America, 1842 ***8582.1*** *p16*
Howe, Janet 30; Massachusetts, 1849 ***5881.1*** *p47*
Howe, John; Virginia, 1635 ***6219*** *p28*
Howe, John; Virginia, 1642 ***6219*** *p189*
Howe, Marie 46; Kansas, 1893 ***5240.1*** *p77*
Howe, Mary; Montreal, 1824 ***7603*** *p23*
Howe, Rice; Virginia, 1636 ***6219*** *p73*
With wife
Howe, William; Virginia, 1636 ***6219*** *p23*
Howel, Edwd; America, 1697 ***2212*** *p8*
Howell, Abraham 20; Antigua (Antego), 1728 ***3690.1*** *p118*
Howell, Andrew; Virginia, 1636 ***6219*** *p16*
Howell, Andrew; Virginia, 1637 ***6219*** *p109*
Howell, Andrew; Virginia, 1639 ***6219*** *p154*
Howell, Charles; Virginia, 1637 ***6219*** *p84*
Howell, Cob.; Virginia, 1634 ***6219*** *p32*
Howell, Cobb; Virginia, 1638 ***6219*** *p120*
Howell, George W.; Kansas, 1893 ***5240.1*** *p21*
Howell, Henry; Virginia, 1637 ***6219*** *p11*
Howell, Humphrey; America, 1698 ***2212*** *p10*
Howell, Humphrey; Virginia, 1698 ***2212*** *p11*
Howell, John; New York, NY, 1816 ***2859.11*** *p33*
Howell, John; Virginia, 1637 ***6219*** *p13*
Howell, John 25; Jamaica, 1731 ***3690.1*** *p118*
Howell, Jonathan 15; St. Christopher, 1730 ***3690.1*** *p118*
Howell, Owen; Virginia, 1635 ***6219*** *p33*
Howell, Rebecca 21; Maryland, 1775 ***1219.7*** *p257*
Howell, Sarah 21; Maryland, 1775 ***1219.7*** *p257*
Howell, Susan; Philadelphia, 1869 ***5704.8*** *p236*
Howell, Walter; Virginia, 1635 ***6219*** *p35*
Howell, Watkin; Virginia, 1641 ***6219*** *p184*
Howgate, Jon; Virginia, 1636 ***6219*** *p19*
Howgate, Tho.; Virginia, 1641 ***6219*** *p185*
Howie, Mary 25; Wilmington, NC, 1774 ***1639.20*** *p87*
Howie, Robert 18; Wilmington, NC, 1774 ***1639.20*** *p96*
Howing, Mr. 25; New Orleans, 1821 ***778.5*** *p277*
Howkins, Richard; New York, NY, 1837 ***8208.4*** *p51*
Howler, Thomas; Virginia, 1639 ***6219*** *p161*
Howlett, Adolphus; New York, NY, 1838 ***8208.4*** *p83*
Howley, John; Montreal, 1817 ***7603*** *p88*
Howman, Jon.; Virginia, 1637 ***6219*** *p11*
Howrahan, Bridget 19; Massachusetts, 1850 ***5881.1*** *p45*
Howrahan, Catharine 20; Massachusetts, 1850 ***5881.1*** *p45*
Howrahan, Ellen 16; Massachusetts, 1850 ***5881.1*** *p46*
Howrahan, Ellen 42; Massachusetts, 1850 ***5881.1*** *p46*
Howrahan, Patrick 9; Massachusetts, 1850 ***5881.1*** *p50*
Howrahan, Timothy 22; Massachusetts, 1850 ***5881.1*** *p51*
Howran, William; America, 1737 ***4971*** *p55*
Howrigan, Thomas; Quebec, 1823 ***7603*** *p63*
Howse, Robert; Virginia, 1638 ***6219*** *p122*
Howtree, Mary; Virginia, 1642 ***6219*** *p194*
Hoy, John; Philadelphia, 1760 ***9973.7*** *p34*
Hoy, John 21; Baltimore, 1775 ***1219.7*** *p270*
Hoy, Sarah; Quebec, 1850 ***5704.8*** *p67*
Hoy, Thomas; America, 1741 ***4971*** *p9*
Hoye, James P. 30; Kansas, 1889 ***5240.1*** *p73*
Hoye, Patrick; New York, NY, 1815 ***2859.11*** *p33*
Hoye, Tarry; Quebec, 1849 ***5704.8*** *p52*
Hoyer, . . .; Canada, 1776-1783 ***9786*** *p25*
Hoyer, Lieut.; Quebec, 1776 ***9786*** *p105*
Hoyer, Johan; Wisconsin, n.d. ***9675.6*** *p51*
Hoyer, Mathias; Wisconsin, n.d. ***9675.6*** *p51*
Hoyer, Wenzel; Wisconsin, n.d. ***9675.6*** *p51*
Hoyer, Wilhelm; Quebec, 1776 ***9786*** *p256*
Hoyl, William 12; Maryland, 1702 ***2212*** *p36*
Hoyland, Benjamin 19; Jamaica, 1738 ***3690.1*** *p118*
Hoyle, Mr.; Quebec, 1815 ***9229.18*** *p80*
Hoyle, William Roofe; New York, NY, 1836 ***8208.4*** *p10*
Hoyles, Mr.; Quebec, 1815 ***9229.18*** *p82*
Hribar, Fred; Arkansas, 1918 ***95.2*** *p58*
Hrica, John; Arkansas, 1918 ***95.2*** *p58*
Hrudt, Herman; Arkansas, 1881 ***3688*** *p7*
Huard, Jean 31; Port uncertain, 1836 ***778.5*** *p277*
Huart, Aimable 27; America, 1839 ***778.5*** *p277*
Huart, Jane 35; America, 1839 ***778.5*** *p277*
Huavinen, Christo; Washington, 1859-1920 ***2872.1*** *p17*
Huavinen, Elma; Washington, 1859-1920 ***2872.1*** *p17*
Huavinen, Helmi; Washington, 1859-1920 ***2872.1*** *p17*
Huavinen, Ieno; Washington, 1859-1920 ***2872.1*** *p17*
Huavinen, Lempa; Washington, 1859-1920 ***2872.1*** *p17*
Huavinen, Tillie; Washington, 1859-1920 ***2872.1*** *p17*
Hubart, John; Ohio, 1843 ***8365.26*** *p12*
Hubat, Marie 23; Port uncertain, 1839 ***778.5*** *p277*
Hubball, Richard; Virginia, 1652 ***6251*** *p20*
Hubbard, Benj.; Virginia, 1639 ***6219*** *p159*
Hubbard, Edward, Jr. 18; Maryland, 1724 ***3690.1*** *p118*
Hubbard, John 20; Maryland, 1774 ***1219.7*** *p187*
Hubbard, John 31; Windward Islands, 1722 ***3690.1*** *p118*
Hubbart, Joseph 40; Maryland, 1774 ***1219.7*** *p178*
Hubbart, Wm 21; Maryland or Virginia, 1699 ***2212*** *p23*
Hubberd, John; Virginia, 1642 ***6219*** *p191*
Huben, Daniel von; Ohio, 1869-1887 ***8582*** *p14*
Huber, Adam 24; New Orleans, 1839 ***778.5*** *p277*
Huber, Andreas 15; America, 1738 ***9898*** *p28*
Huber, Blaiz 28; Savannah, GA, 1738 ***9332*** *p332*
Huber, Elisabeth; Illinois, 1839 ***8582.2*** *p50*
Huber, Eva 29; Port uncertain, 1839 ***778.5*** *p277*
Huber, Eva 29; Port uncertain, 1839 ***778.5*** *p278*
Huber, Franz; America, 1831 ***8582.1*** *p16*
Huber, Friederike; Philadelphia, 1860 ***2691.4*** *p168*
Huber, Hans; Georgia, 1734 ***9332*** *p328*
Huber, Heinrich; Kentucky, 1839-1840 ***8582.3*** *p98*
Huber, John; Philadelphia, 1762 ***9973.7*** *p37*
Huber, John Michael; Philadelphia, 1742 ***3652*** *p55*
Huber, Josef 27; New York, NY, 1893 ***9026.4*** *p41*
Huber, Joseph 84; San Francisco, 1869 ***8582*** *p14*
Huber, Joseph A.; Colorado, 1903 ***9678.2*** *p24*
Huber, Joseph H. 39; Arizona, 1890 ***2764.35*** *p35*
Huber, Lorentz 54; Georgia, 1734 ***9332*** *p327*
*Wife:*Maria 52
Huber, Magdalena 15; Georgia, 1734 ***9332*** *p328*
Huber, Margaretha; Georgia, 1739 ***9332*** *p325*
Huber, Maria; Georgia, 1734 ***9332*** *p328*
Huber, Maria 52 *SEE* Huber, Lorentz
Huber, Michael; Pennsylvania, 1772 ***9973.8*** *p33*
Huber, Peter; America, 1853 ***2853.7*** *p109*
Huber, Peter 65; Washington, 1916-1919 ***1728.4*** *p255*
Huber, Wilhelm; Cincinnati, 1869 ***8582*** *p14*
Huber, William; Baltimore, 1887 ***1450.2*** *p17B*
Huber, Xaver; Cincinnati, 1869-1887 ***8582*** *p14*
Huber, Xaver 19; New Orleans, 1832 ***8582.3*** *p32*
Huberson, A. 28; New Orleans, 1838 ***778.5*** *p278*
Hubersou, A. 28; New Orleans, 1838 ***778.5*** *p278*
Hubert, . . .; Canada, 1776-1783 ***9786*** *p25*
Hubert, Antoine; New York, NY, 1838 ***8208.4*** *p86*
Hubert, Auguste 26; America, 1839 ***778.5*** *p278*
Hubert, Eliza 18; St. John, N.B., 1856 ***5704.8*** *p131*
Hubert, Francis 30; New Orleans, 1827 ***778.5*** *p278*

Hubert, M. 30; America, 1837 ***778.5*** *p278*
Huberth, . . .; Canada, 1776-1783 ***9786*** *p25*
Hubinger, John F.; Kentucky, 1869-1887 ***8582*** *p14*
Hublard, Rich.; Virginia, 1642 ***6219*** *p191*
Hubler, Jacob; Illinois, 1871 ***2896.5*** *p19*
Hubner, Agathe; New York, NY, 1923 ***3455.3*** *p86*
*Husband:*Fred
Hubner, Fred *SEE* Hubner, Agathe
Hubner, Friedrich; Illinois, 1883 ***2896.5*** *p19*
Hubsel, John; Iowa, 1866-1943 ***123.54*** *p23*
Hubuk, . . .; Canada, 1776-1783 ***9786*** *p42*
Huby, Samll.; Virginia, 1643 ***6219*** *p203*
Hucheson, Elizabeth; Philadelphia, 1852 ***5704.8*** *p88*
Huchet, L. 46; New Orleans, 1835 ***778.5*** *p278*
Huck, . . .; Canada, 1776-1783 ***9786*** *p25*
Huck, Frederick; America, 1850 ***1450.2*** *p70A*
Huckaby, Nancy 79; South Carolina, 1850 ***1639.20*** *p96*
Huckle, Andrew; Virginia, 1643 ***6219*** *p203*
Huckleberry, H. Zacharias; Pennsylvania, 1752 ***4779.3*** *p14*
Huckley, John; Virginia, 1644 ***6219*** *p231*
Hucks, John; Virginia, 1637 ***6219*** *p85*
Hucks, Marie A. 24; America, 1839 ***778.5*** *p278*
Hucock, Jon.; Virginia, 1637 ***6219*** *p83*
Hudales, Frank; Wisconsin, n.d. ***9675.6*** *p51*
Hudd, Thomas 22; Philadelphia, 1774 ***1219.7*** *p183*
Huddleston, Joseph Henry; Barbados, 1755 ***1219.7*** *p37*
Huddy, Daniel 28?; Arizona, 1890 ***2764.35*** *p31*
Hudleston, Thomas 18; Maryland, 1775 ***1219.7*** *p272*
Hudon, Joseph Arthur; Wisconsin, n.d. ***9675.6*** *p51*
Hudry, J. Louis 29; New Orleans, 1838 ***778.5*** *p278*
Hudsey, Peter; Virginia, 1637 ***6219*** *p86*
Hudson, . . .; Virginia, 1642 ***6219*** *p198*
Hudson, Ann; St. John, N.B., 1852 ***5704.8*** *p84*
Hudson, Edw.; Virginia, 1637 ***6219*** *p11*
Hudson, Edw.; Virginia, 1637 ***6219*** *p114*
Hudson, Edward; Virginia, 1652 ***6251*** *p20*
Hudson, Elizabeth; Virginia, 1635 ***6219*** *p6*
Hudson, George; Virginia, 1645 ***6219*** *p252*
Hudson, James 16; Baltimore, 1775 ***1219.7*** *p270*
Hudson, Jeremiah 24; Jamaica, 1731 ***3690.1*** *p118*
Hudson, John; Jamaica, 1756 ***1219.7*** *p49*
Hudson, John; Jamaica, 1756 ***3690.1*** *p118*
Hudson, John; Pennsylvania, 1764 ***1219.7*** *p101*
Hudson, John; Virginia, 1638 ***6219*** *p159*
Hudson, John 20; Maryland, 1774 ***1219.7*** *p179*
Hudson, Joseph; Illinois, 1870 ***5012.38*** *p99*
Hudson, Mary 22; Baltimore, 1775 ***1219.7*** *p271*
Hudson, Mathew; Virginia, 1648 ***6219*** *p250*
Hudson, Patrick; St. John, N.B., 1852 ***5704.8*** *p84*
Hudson, Robert; Virginia, 1639 ***6219*** *p151*
Hudson, Robt.; Virginia, 1635 ***6219*** *p69*
Hudson, Samuel; Virginia, 1638 ***6219*** *p122*
Hudson, Susanna 22; Philadelphia, 1774 ***1219.7*** *p212*
Hudson, Tho 19; America, 1699 ***2212*** *p28*
Hudson, Thomas 19; Pennsylvania, Virginia or Maryland, 1719 ***3690.1*** *p118*
Hudson, Thomas 22; Maryland, 1774 ***1219.7*** *p179*
Hudson, Thomas 22; Virginia, 1774 ***1219.7*** *p201*
Hudson, William 20; Virginia, 1774 ***1219.7*** *p186*
Hudson, William 25; Maryland, 1775 ***1219.7*** *p247*
Hudson, William 30; Jamaica, 1730 ***3690.1*** *p119*
Hudson, William 32; Maryland, 1775 ***1219.7*** *p250*
Hudson, Wm; Maryland or Virginia, 1698 ***2212*** *p10*
Hue, Jean; New Orleans, 1839 ***778.5*** *p278*
Hueber, Abraham *SEE* Hueber, Abraham
Hueber, Abraham; New England, 1749 ***2444*** *p170*
*Wife:*Christina Springer
*Child:*Abraham
Hueber, Christina Springer *SEE* Hueber, Abraham
Hueber, Johann; America, 1749-1800 ***2444*** *p170*
Hueber, Johann Jacob; Pennsylvania, 1749 ***2444*** *p170*
Hueber, Peter; America, 1836 ***8582.3*** *p33*
Huebert, Helena; Quebec, 1876 ***9980.20*** *p48*
Huebner, Christian; Wisconsin, n.d. ***9675.6*** *p51*
Huebner, William; Arkansas, 1918 ***95.2*** *p58*
Huebner, William; Wisconsin, n.d. ***9675.6*** *p51*
Huedepohl, Louis; America, 1837 ***8582.2*** *p17*
Huek, Francis; Canada, 1776-1783 ***9786*** *p207A*
Huepsch, Joseph; New York, 1754 ***3652*** *p80*
Huer, August; Wisconsin, n.d. ***9675.6*** *p51*
Hueras, Joseph; Wisconsin, n.d. ***9675.6*** *p51*
Huerman, Konrad; Indiana, 1869-1887 ***8582*** *p14*
Huermann, Heinrich; America, 1848 ***8582.1*** *p16*
Huermann, Heinrich; Baltimore, 1848 ***8582.2*** *p17*
Huern, Anna Maria *SEE* Huern, Johann Georg
Huern, Anna Maria *SEE* Huern, Johann Georg
Huern, Catharina *SEE* Huern, Johann Georg
Huern, Johann Georg; New England, 1753 ***2444*** *p170*
*Wife:*Anna Maria
*Child:*Anna Maria
*Child:*Catharina
Hues, John; Virginia, 1638 ***6219*** *p146*
Hues, John; Virginia, 1647 ***6219*** *p247*
Hues, Jon.; Virginia, 1637 ***6219*** *p11*
Hues, Owen; Virginia, 1637 ***6219*** *p37*
Hues, Richard; Virginia, 1637 ***6219*** *p110*
Hues, Richard; Virginia, 1642 ***6219*** *p197*
Huesmann, Friedrich; Cincinnati, 1830-1849 ***8582*** *p14*
Hueston, James 14; Philadelphia, 1859 ***5704.8*** *p141*
Hueston, Margery 17; Philadelphia, 1859 ***5704.8*** *p142*
Hueston, Robert 20; Philadelphia, 1859 ***5704.8*** *p141*
Huet, Mr. 50; America, 1837 ***778.5*** *p278*
Huet, Charles 31; America, 1837 ***778.5*** *p278*
Huet, Eugene 18; America, 1837 ***778.5*** *p278*
Huet, M. 31; America, 1838 ***778.5*** *p278*
Huett, Edward 27; Quebec, 1862 ***5704.8*** *p152*
Huett, Francis; Virginia, 1642 ***6219*** *p193*
Huett, John; Virginia, 1639 ***6219*** *p161*
Huett, Morgon; Virginia, 1635 ***6219*** *p73*
Huett, Rich.; Virginia, 1629 ***6219*** *p8*
Huett, Robert; Virginia, 1638 ***6219*** *p150*
Huettenmueller, Wilhelm; America, 1850 ***8582.3*** *p33*
Huettenrauch, Elsie; Wisconsin, n.d. ***9675.6*** *p51*
Huettmann, John; Wisconsin, n.d. ***9675.6*** *p51*
Huewel, Edward; America, 1886 ***1450.2*** *p70A*
Huey, Betty; New York, NY, 1816 ***2859.11*** *p33*
Huey, Elizabeth; Philadelphia, 1868 ***5704.8*** *p230*
Huey, George; Philadelphia, 1867 ***5704.8*** *p223*
Huey, James; New York, NY, 1816 ***2859.11*** *p33*
Huey, James; St. John, N.B., 1847 ***5704.8*** *p18*
Huey, John 8; St. John, N.B., 1847 ***5704.8*** *p18*
Huey, Margaret; Philadelphia, 1851 ***5704.8*** *p80*
Huey, Margaret; Philadelphia, 1868 ***5704.8*** *p230*
Huey, Margaret 1 wk; St. John, N.B., 1847 ***5704.8*** *p18*
Huey, Robert 9 mos; St. John, N.B., 1847 ***5704.8*** *p18*
Huey, Rose; St. John, N.B., 1847 ***5704.8*** *p18*
Hufer, Frederich; Wisconsin, n.d. ***9675.6*** *p51*
Hufert, Franz; New York, NY, 1838 ***8208.4*** *p82*
Huff, James M.; Washington, 1859-1920 ***2872.1*** *p17*
Huffe, Mary; Virginia, 1636 ***6219*** *p80*
Huffer, John; Virginia, 1639 ***6219*** *p151*
Huffington, Eliza 24; Philadelphia, 1853 ***5704.8*** *p108*
Huffington, John 24; Philadelphia, 1853 ***5704.8*** *p108*
Huffmeier, A. Cath. Ilsabein; America, 1888 ***4610.10*** *p161*
Huffnagel, Johannes; Ohio, 1798-1818 ***8582.2*** *p17*
Huffnagle, Frantz Henrich; Pennsylvania, 1753 ***4779.3*** *p14*
*Relative:*Johan Christian
Huffnagle, Johan Christian *SEE* Huffnagle, Frantz Henrich
Huffnagle, Johannes; Pennsylvania, 1752 ***4779.3*** *p14*
Huffnail, Frantz Henrich; Pennsylvania, 1753 ***4779.3*** *p14*
*Relative:*Johan Christian
Huffnail, Johan Christian *SEE* Huffnail, Frantz Henrich
Huffnail, Johannes; Pennsylvania, 1752 ***4779.3*** *p14*
Huffnogle, Frantz Henrich; Pennsylvania, 1753 ***4779.3*** *p14*
*Relative:*Johan Christian
Huffnogle, Johan Christian *SEE* Huffnogle, Frantz Henrich
Huffnogle, Johannes; Pennsylvania, 1752 ***4779.3*** *p14*
Hufirtt, John; Wisconsin, n.d. ***9675.6*** *p51*
Hufnagel, Mr.; Ohio, 1826 ***8582.2*** *p59*
Hufnagel, Frantz Henrich; Pennsylvania, 1753 ***4779.3*** *p14*
*Relative:*Johan Christian
Hufnagel, Johan Christian *SEE* Hufnagel, Frantz Henrich
Hufnagel, Johannes; Pennsylvania, 1752 ***4779.3*** *p14*
Hufnagle, Frantz Henrich; Pennsylvania, 1753 ***4779.3*** *p14*
*Relative:*Johan Christian
Hufnagle, Johan Christian *SEE* Hufnagle, Frantz Henrich
Hufnagle, Johannes; Pennsylvania, 1752 ***4779.3*** *p14*
Hufschmidt, . . .; Canada, 1776-1783 ***9786*** *p25*
Hufschmidt, Francis; Canada, 1776-1783 ***9786*** *p207A*
Hufschmidt, Richard; Maryland, 1894 ***1450.2*** *p17B*
Hug, Edward; Iroquois Co., IL, 1892 ***3455.1*** *p11*
Hug, John; America, 1851 ***1450.2*** *p70A*
Hug, Martin; America, 1849 ***1450.2*** *p71A*
Hug, Michael; Pennsylvania, 1749 ***2444*** *p171*
Hug, Rudolph; America, 1849 ***8582.3*** *p33*
Hugel, Rudolf; Arkansas, 1918 ***95.2*** *p58*
Huges, John; New York, NY, 1811 ***2859.11*** *p13*
Huges, Robert; New York, NY, 1811 ***2859.11*** *p13*
With family
Huggard, John 24; Quebec, 1863 ***5704.8*** *p154*
Huggeson, Joane; Virginia, 1636 ***6219*** *p32*
Huggesson, James; Virginia, 1635 ***6219*** *p17*
Hugget, Sigmund; Canada, 1779 ***9786*** *p266*
Huggin, William 30; Maryland, 1775 ***1219.7*** *p257*
Huggins, John 19; Maryland, 1723 ***3690.1*** *p119*
Huggins, Robert; Jamaica, 1771 ***1219.7*** *p149*
Huggins, William; Jamaica, 1750 ***3690.1*** *p119*
Hugh, . . .; New England, 1816 ***2859.11*** *p33*
Hughes, Alexander; Philadelphia, 1849 ***53.26*** *p39*
Hughes, Alexander; Philadelphia, 1849 ***5704.8*** *p50*
Hughes, Ann; St. John, N.B., 1852 ***5704.8*** *p95*
Hughes, Ann 23; America, 1699 ***2212*** *p28*
Hughes, Anthony; Wisconsin, n.d. ***9675.6*** *p51*
Hughes, Arthur; New York, NY, 1811 ***2859.11*** *p13*
Hughes, Arthur; New York, NY, 1833 ***8208.4*** *p60*
Hughes, Arthur; Virginia, 1639 ***6219*** *p152*
Hughes, Arthur 17; Virginia, 1775 ***1219.7*** *p261*
Hughes, Barzillai 20; Maryland, 1724 ***3690.1*** *p119*
Hughes, Betty 21; Port uncertain, 1774 ***1219.7*** *p176*
Hughes, Bridget; Montreal, 1825 ***7603*** *p99*
Hughes, Bridget 5; Massachusetts, 1850 ***5881.1*** *p45*
Hughes, Bridget 40; Massachusetts, 1850 ***5881.1*** *p45*
Hughes, Brigitte; Montreal, 1821 ***7603*** *p89*
Hughes, Catharine 17; Massachusetts, 1847 ***5881.1*** *p45*
Hughes, Catherine; St. John, N.B., 1847 ***5704.8*** *p11*
Hughes, Catherine 20; Wilmington, DE, 1831 ***6508.7*** *p160*
Hughes, Charles; New York, NY, 1816 ***2859.11*** *p33*
Hughes, David; Pennsylvania, 1772 ***1219.7*** *p156*
Hughes, Diana 26; Maryland, 1774 ***1219.7*** *p208*
Hughes, Edward; Illinois, 1890 ***5012.40*** *p25*
Hughes, Edward 42; Virginia, 1729 ***3690.1*** *p119*
Hughes, Edwd; America, 1697 ***2212*** *p8*
Hughes, Eliz 21; America, 1703 ***2212*** *p38*
Hughes, Eliza; Philadelphia, 1853 ***5704.8*** *p108*
Hughes, Elizabeth 20; Virginia, 1700 ***2212*** *p30*
Hughes, Elizabeth 22 *SEE* Hughes, Joseph
Hughes, Ellen; America, 1697 ***2212*** *p7*
Hughes, Ellen 6; Massachusetts, 1850 ***5881.1*** *p46*
Hughes, Ellen 21; America, 1702 ***2212*** *p37*
Hughes, Evans 13; Maryland or Virginia, 1699 ***2212*** *p23*
Hughes, Felix; Colorado, 1880 ***9678.2*** *p25*
Hughes, Geo.; Virginia, 1646 ***6219*** *p236*
Hughes, George; New York, NY, 1839 ***8208.4*** *p102*
Hughes, Griffith 18; America, 1700 ***2212*** *p33*
Hughes, Henry; Philadelphia, 1851 ***5704.8*** *p71*
Hughes, Henry 18; Maryland, 1774 ***1219.7*** *p229*
Hughes, Henry 20; Jamaica, 1724 ***3690.1*** *p119*
Hughes, Hugh; Massachusetts, 1850 ***5881.1*** *p46*
Hughes, Hugh; New York, NY, 1816 ***2859.11*** *p33*
Hughes, J.; New York, NY, 1816 ***2859.11*** *p33*
Hughes, J. B.; Washington, 1859-1920 ***2872.1*** *p17*
Hughes, James; Colorado, 1905 ***9678.2*** *p25*
Hughes, James; New York, NY, 1835 ***8208.4*** *p42*
Hughes, James; New York, NY, 1836 ***8208.4*** *p25*
Hughes, James; New York, NY, 1838 ***8208.4*** *p62*
Hughes, Jane 4; St. John, N.B., 1847 ***5704.8*** *p21*
Hughes, Jas.; New York, NY, 1811 ***2859.11*** *p13*
Hughes, Jno; Barbados, 1698 ***2212*** *p5*
Hughes, Jno 14; America, 1705 ***2212*** *p42*
Hughes, John; America, 1698 ***2212*** *p8*
Hughes, John; Charleston, SC, 1772 ***1639.20*** *p96*
Hughes, John; New York, NY, 1811 ***2859.11*** *p13*
Hughes, John; New York, NY, 1816 ***2859.11*** *p33*
Hughes, John; New York, NY, 1835 ***8208.4*** *p76*
Hughes, John; New York, NY, 1838 ***8208.4*** *p75*
Hughes, John; St. John, N.B., 1847 ***5704.8*** *p26*
Hughes, John 20; Jamaica, 1721 ***3690.1*** *p119*
Hughes, John 45; Maryland, 1774 ***1219.7*** *p187*
Hughes, Joseph 28; Savannah, GA, 1733 ***4719.17*** *p311*
*Wife:*Elizabeth 22
Hughes, Julia 23; Massachusetts, 1849 ***5881.1*** *p47*
Hughes, Kath 22; America, 1703 ***2212*** *p40*
Hughes, Katherine; America, 1697 ***2212*** *p7*
Hughes, Margaret 7; Massachusetts, 1850 ***5881.1*** *p49*
Hughes, Margaret 11; St. John, N.B., 1854 ***5704.8*** *p119*
Hughes, Margaret 14; Massachusetts, 1850 ***5881.1*** *p49*
Hughes, Margarett 22; America, 1699 ***2212*** *p25*
Hughes, Margtte 13; America, 1701 ***2212*** *p35*
Hughes, Martha 17; Maryland or Virginia, 1699 ***2212*** *p23*
Hughes, Martin 3; Massachusetts, 1850 ***5881.1*** *p49*
Hughes, Mary 10; Massachusetts, 1850 ***5881.1*** *p49*
Hughes, Mary 15; Maryland, 1775 ***1219.7*** *p264*
Hughes, Matthew; New York, NY, 1838 ***8208.4*** *p62*
Hughes, Michael; America, 1864 ***5704.8*** *p187*
Hughes, Michael; Philadelphia, 1865 ***5704.8*** *p193*
Hughes, Michael 30; St. John, N.B., 1854 ***5704.8*** *p119*
Hughes, Michal 15; America, 1700 ***2212*** *p31*
Hughes, Owen; America, 1697 ***2212*** *p8*
Hughes, Owen; Ohio, 1870-1888 ***9892.11*** *p21*
Hughes, Owen; St. John, N.B., 1847 ***5704.8*** *p11*
Hughes, Owen 25; Massachusetts, 1849 ***5881.1*** *p49*
Hughes, Patrick; New York, NY, 1816 ***2859.11*** *p33*
Hughes, Patrick; Philadelphia, 1864 ***5704.8*** *p179*
Hughes, Peirce 15; Maryland or Virginia, 1699 ***2212*** *p23*
Hughes, Peter; New York, NY, 1811 ***2859.11*** *p13*
Hughes, Peter; New York, NY, 1816 ***2859.11*** *p33*
Hughes, Rees; New York, NY, 1834 ***8208.4*** *p42*
Hughes, Richard; New York, NY, 1811 ***2859.11*** *p13*
With family

Hughes, Richard; Virginia, 1637 ***6219*** *p115*
Hughes, Richard; Virginia, 1638 ***6219*** *p147*
Hughes, Richard; Virginia, 1639 ***6219*** *p157*
Hughes, Richard 30; Massachusetts, 1847 ***5881.1*** *p50*
Hughes, Richd; Barbados, 1698 ***2212*** *p4*
Hughes, Richd 14; Maryland or Virginia, 1699 ***2212*** *p23*
Hughes, Robert; Iowa, 1866-1943 ***123.54*** *p65*
Hughes, Robert; New Jersey, 1827 ***8208.4*** *p47*
Hughes, Robert 15; America, 1700 ***2212*** *p33*
Hughes, Robt; America, 1697 ***2212*** *p8*
Hughes, Robt; America, 1698 ***2212*** *p8*
Hughes, Robt; America, 1698 ***2212*** *p9*
Hughes, S.; New York, NY, 1816 ***2859.11*** *p33*
Hughes, Samuel 19; Maryland, 1774 ***1219.7*** *p226*
Hughes, Stephen 33; Maryland, 1774 ***1219.7*** *p179*
Hughes, Tho.; Virginia, 1642 ***6219*** *p194*
Hughes, Tho.; Virginia, 1643 ***6219*** *p200*
Hughes, Tho 14; Maryland or Virginia, 1699 ***2212*** *p23*
Hughes, Tho 25; Maryland or Virginia, 1699 ***2212*** *p25*
Hughes, Thomas; America, 1697 ***2212*** *p8*
Hughes, Thomas; Illinois, 1869 ***7857*** *p4*
Hughes, Thomas; Virginia, 1642 ***6219*** *p18*
Hughes, Thomas; Virginia, 1642 ***6219*** *p188*
Hughes, Thomas 15; America, 1704 ***2212*** *p40*
Hughes, Thomas 16; Jamaica, 1730 ***3690.1*** *p119*
Hughes, Thomas 21; Georgia, 1774 ***1219.7*** *p188*
Hughes, Thomas 21; Maryland, 1774 ***1219.7*** *p211*
Hughes, Thomas 25; Massachusetts, 1849 ***5881.1*** *p50*
Hughes, Walter; America, 1741 ***4971*** *p10*
Hughes, William; America, 1697 ***2212*** *p8*
Hughes, William; America, 1735-1743 ***4971*** *p7*
Hughes, William; California, 1860 ***2764.35*** *p34*
Hughes, William; St. John, N.B., 1847 ***5704.8*** *p26*
Hughes, William 34; Maryland, 1774 ***1219.7*** *p224*
Hughes, Wm; America, 1697 ***2212*** *p8*
Hughey, Bessey; Quebec, 1851 ***5704.8*** *p74*
Hughey, John; Quebec, 1851 ***5704.8*** *p73*
Hughey, John 20; St. John, N.B., 1859 ***5704.8*** *p140*
Hughey, Margaret 11; Quebec, 1851 ***5704.8*** *p74*
Hughey, Margaret 21; St. John, N.B., 1859 ***5704.8*** *p140*
Hughey, Sarah; Philadelphia, 1852 ***5704.8*** *p96*
Hughey, Sarah 6; Quebec, 1851 ***5704.8*** *p74*
Hughles, Hugh 19; New England, 1699 ***2212*** *p19*
Hughs, Daniel; America, 1743 ***4971*** *p95*
Hughs, Pat.; America, 1739 ***4971*** *p64*
Hughs, Pat.; America, 1741 ***4971*** *p63*
Hughs, Walter; America, 1741 ***4971*** *p94*
Hughs, William 20; Jamaica, 1731 ***3690.1*** *p119*
Hugill, John; West Virginia, 1854-1858 ***9788.3*** *p12*
Hugo, . . .; Canada, 1776-1783 ***9786*** *p42*
Hugo, Charles; America, 1845 ***1450.2*** *p71A*
Hugo, H. L.; America, 1842 ***8582.2*** *p17*
Hugo, Henry; New York, 1845 ***1450.2*** *p71A*
Hugon, Pierre 29; America, 1838 ***778.5*** *p278*
Hugonet, Alphonce 27; New Orleans, 1839 ***778.5*** *p278*
Huguenot, Pierre 19; Halifax, N.S., 1752 ***7074.6*** *p210*
Huguenot, Theodore 50; New Orleans, 1822 ***778.5*** *p279*
Hugues, James; Montreal, 1825 ***7603*** *p99*
Hugues, John; Montreal, 1823 ***7603*** *p55*
Huguet, Madame 27; New Orleans, 1820 ***778.5*** *p279*
Huhs, Carl Friedrich; America, 1836 ***4610.10*** *p97*
Huie, Jean 23; Wilmington, NC, 1774 ***1639.20*** *p203*
Huie, Martha 26; Wilmington, NC, 1774 ***1639.20*** *p262*
Huiker, Mrs. 22; New Orleans, 1835 ***778.5*** *p273*
Huiker, J. 25; New Orleans, 1835 ***778.5*** *p273*
Huiras, George; Wisconsin, n.d. ***9675.6*** *p51*
Huisman, Tennis; Arkansas, 1918 ***95.2*** *p58*
Hukiede, Ernest; New York, 1864 ***1450.2*** *p17B*
Huld, David; Washington, 1859-1920 ***2872.1*** *p17*
Huld, Ida; Washington, 1859-1920 ***2872.1*** *p17*
Huld, Reno; Washington, 1859-1920 ***2872.1*** *p17*
Huld, Una; Washington, 1859-1920 ***2872.1*** *p17*
Hulda, Joseph; Kansas, 1902 ***5240.1*** *p21*
Hulett, J. N.; Washington, 1859-1920 ***2872.1*** *p17*
Hulett, Thomas H.; Washington, 1859-1920 ***2872.1*** *p17*
Hulett, Thomas N.; Washington, 1859-1920 ***2872.1*** *p17*
Hulic, Antoine; New Orleans, 1839 ***778.5*** *p279*
Hull, David *SEE* Hull, George
Hull, David *SEE* Hull, George
Hull, Edm. *SEE* Hull, George
Hull, Edward *SEE* Hull, George
Hull, Eliza. *SEE* Hull, George
Hull, Eliza *SEE* Hull, George
Hull, George; Virginia, 1643 ***6219*** *p205*
*Wife:*Eliza.
*Son:*Edward
*Son:*David
Hull, George; Virginia, 1648 ***6219*** *p246*
*Wife:*Eliza
*Son:*Edm.
*Son:*David
Hull, Jefferie; Virginia, 1617 ***6219*** *p5*
Hull, John; Philadelphia, 1848 ***53.26*** *p39*
Hull, John; Philadelphia, 1848 ***5704.8*** *p40*
Hull, Tho.; Virginia, 1634 ***6219*** *p84*
Hull, William 15; Maryland, 1775 ***1219.7*** *p266*
Hullatt, John 22; Maryland, 1775 ***1219.7*** *p247*
Huller, Johann Melchior; South Carolina, 1788 ***7119*** *p200*
Hullet, Mrs.; Quebec, 1815 ***9229.18*** *p76*
Hulme, Arthur 23; Kansas, 1891 ***5240.1*** *p76*
Hulme, John; Pennsylvania, 1884 ***5240.1*** *p21*
Hulot, Jean-Baptiste 17; Port uncertain, 1838 ***778.5*** *p279*
Hulsman, Harmannus 28; New York, NY, 1847 ***3377.6*** *p16*
Hulsman, Willem 31; New York, NY, 1847 ***3377.6*** *p16*
Hulstrom, John; Washington, 1859-1920 ***2872.1*** *p17*
Hulstyn, Peter Jansz; Wisconsin, n.d. ***9675.6*** *p51*
Hult, Jonal Peter; Iowa, 1866-1943 ***123.54*** *p23*
Hultin, D. J.; Minneapolis, 1870-1877 ***6410.35*** *p55*
Hulton, Patrick; New York, NY, 1816 ***2859.11*** *p33*
Humbert, Fred 24; Kansas, 1887 ***5240.1*** *p69*
Humbert, George; Washington, 1859-1920 ***2872.1*** *p17*
Humbert, Jean 24; New Orleans, 1835 ***778.5*** *p279*
Humbert, Pierre 24; Halifax, N.S., 1752 ***7074.6*** *p207*
Humbert, Pierre 24; Halifax, N.S., 1752 ***7074.6*** *p210*
Humble, George H. 36; Kansas, 1890 ***5240.1*** *p75*
Humble, John 21; Philadelphia, 1775 ***1219.7*** *p258*
Humble, Roger; Virginia, 1637 ***6219*** *p24*
Humble, Thomas Isaac 26; Kansas, 1882 ***5240.1*** *p63*
Humblet, Melina Victoria *SEE* Humblet, Norbet Henry Joseph
Humblet, Norbet Henry Joseph; New York, NY, 1889 ***3455.1*** *p41*
*Wife:*Melina Victoria
Hume, John 28; Georgia, 1775 ***1219.7*** *p276*
Hume, Peter; South Carolina, 1738 ***1639.20*** *p96*
Hume, Robert 24; Philadelphia, 1854 ***5704.8*** *p118*
Humes, Catherine; St. John, N.B., 1852 ***5704.8*** *p84*
Humes, Charles 12; St. John, N.B., 1852 ***5704.8*** *p84*
Humes, Daniel 8; Quebec, 1849 ***5704.8*** *p57*
Humes, David 7; St. John, N.B., 1851 ***5704.8*** *p78*
Humes, Eleanor; Quebec, 1849 ***5704.8*** *p57*
Humes, Giles; St. John, N.B., 1852 ***5704.8*** *p84*
Humes, James 19; Philadelphia, 1855 ***5704.8*** *p123*
Humes, John 21; Philadelphia, 1856 ***5704.8*** *p128*
Humes, Margaret; St. John, N.B., 1852 ***5704.8*** *p84*
Humes, Margaret 18; Philadelphia, 1855 ***5704.8*** *p123*
Humes, Mary; St. John, N.B., 1851 ***5704.8*** *p78*
Humfeld, Herman S. 46; Kansas, 1903 ***5240.1*** *p82*
Humfrey, Thomas 13; Maryland, 1730 ***3690.1*** *p119*
Hummel, Anna Barbara *SEE* Hummel, Johannes
Hummel, Anna Barbara Binder *SEE* Hummel, Johannes
Hummel, David; America, 1846 ***8582.1*** *p16*
Hummel, Johann; Cincinnati, 1869-1887 ***8582*** *p14*
Hummel, Johannes; Pennsylvania, 1740-1800 ***2444*** *p170*
*Wife:*Anna Barbara Binder
*Child:*Anna Barbara
Hummel, Johannes; Pennsylvania, 1746 ***2444*** *p170*
Hummel, Johannis; Pennsylvania, 1749 ***2444*** *p170*
Hummel, John; Wisconsin, n.d. ***9675.6*** *p51*
Hummell, Elias; Philadelphia, 1760 ***9973.7*** *p35*
Hummerich, . . .; Canada, 1776-1783 ***9786*** *p25*
Hummertzhim, Gerhard; Minnesota, 1874 ***5240.1*** *p21*
Humpeler, August; Illinois, 1878 ***2896.5*** *p19*
Humpeler, Charles; Illinois, 1865 ***2896.5*** *p19*
Humpeler, Ferdinand; Illinois, 1874 ***2896.5*** *p19*
Humpeler, Ferdinand, Jr.; Illinois, 1882 ***2896.5*** *p19*
Humpeler, John P.; Illinois, 1882 ***2896.5*** *p19*
Humpheres, Thomas; Maryland, 1756 ***1219.7*** *p44*
Humpheres, Thomas; Maryland, 1756 ***3690.1*** *p119*
Humphrey, Amey; Virginia, 1634 ***6219*** *p84*
Humphrey, James; Ohio, 1867-1879 ***9892.11*** *p21*
Humphrey, James; Ohio, 1881 ***9892.11*** *p22*
Humphrey, Jno 12; America, 1702 ***2212*** *p37*
Humphrey, John; Virginia, 1636 ***6219*** *p78*
Humphrey, Joseph; Colorado, 1886 ***9678.2*** *p25*
Humphrey, Joseph; Ohio, 1867-1879 ***9892.11*** *p22*
Humphrey, Joseph; Ohio, 1882 ***9892.11*** *p22*
Humphrey, M.A. 20; Massachusetts, 1847 ***5881.1*** *p48*
Humphrey, Thomas; America, 1698 ***2212*** *p8*
Humphrey, Wm.; Virginia, 1643 ***6219*** *p204*
Humphrey, Wm 16; America, 1699 ***2212*** *p25*
Humphreys, Andrew; Quebec, 1847 ***5704.8*** *p8*
Humphreys, Francis; Philadelphia, 1816 ***2859.11*** *p33*
Humphreys, James; Quebec, 1847 ***5704.8*** *p8*
Humphreys, John 27; Jamaica, 1737 ***3690.1*** *p119*
Humphreys, Margaret; Quebec, 1847 ***5704.8*** *p8*
Humphreys, Richard; Illinois, 1872 ***5012.39*** *p26*
Humphries, John 21; Georgia, 1774 ***1219.7*** *p188*
Humphries, Leonard James; Arkansas, 1918 ***95.2*** *p58*
Humphries, Leonard James 31; Arkansas, 1918 ***95.2*** *p58*
Humphry, Charles 25; Virginia, 1774 ***1219.7*** *p238*
Humphry, Thomas 22; Maryland, 1775 ***1219.7*** *p255*
Humphrys, Anne 22; Virginia, 1700 ***2212*** *p32*
Humphrys, John 25; Maryland, 1739 ***3690.1*** *p120*
Humphrys, Richard 40; Maryland, 1774 ***1219.7*** *p179*
Humpries, Jo.; Virginia, 1644 ***6219*** *p231*
Hun, Rachel; New York, NY, 1811 ***2859.11*** *p13*
Hunan, Thomas; Shreveport, LA, 1879 ***7129*** *p44*
Huncke, O.M.; Illinois, 1869-1885 ***8582.2*** *p52*
Huncock, Grv.; Iowa, 1866-1943 ***123.54*** *p23*
Hund, . . .; Canada, 1776-1783 ***9786*** *p25*
Hundchen, Albert; Colorado, 1885 ***9678.2*** *p25*
Hundelach, Christian; Canada, 1783 ***9786*** *p38A*
Hundemer, Johann B.; America, 1854 ***8582.3*** *p33*
Hunder, Moses; Iowa, 1866-1943 ***123.54*** *p23*
Hundertpfund, Jacob; Illinois, 1872 ***5012.39*** *p26*
Hundertpfund, Jacob; Illinois, 1874 ***5012.39*** *p91*
Hundhausen, Friedrich; America, 1840 ***8582.1*** *p16*
Hundsicker, Nickel; America, 1753 ***4349*** *p46*
Hunn, Sebastian; New York, NY, 1840 ***8208.4*** *p107*
Hunold, Carl; Illinois, 1866-1906 ***2896.5*** *p19*
Hunsdal, Sam Olson; Arkansas, 1918 ***95.2*** *p58*
Hunsen, Jules; Arkansas, 1918 ***95.2*** *p58*
Hunsley, Henry W.; Illinois, 1888 ***5012.39*** *p121*
Hunstedt, . . .; Canada, 1776-1783 ***9786*** *p25*
Hunt, Charles; Virginia, 1784 ***4778.2*** *p142*
Hunt, Christopher; Virginia, 1636 ***6219*** *p27*
Hunt, Edward; Virginia, 1636 ***6219*** *p7*
Hunt, Elizabeth; Virginia, 1698 ***2212*** *p15*
Hunt, Francis 21; Kansas, 1886 ***5240.1*** *p68*
Hunt, Francis C. 21; Kansas, 1886 ***5240.1*** *p21*
Hunt, George 15; Maryland, 1775 ***1219.7*** *p264*
Hunt, James; Virginia, 1636 ***6219*** *p77*
Hunt, James; Virginia, 1638-1700 ***6219*** *p150*
Hunt, James 23; Kansas, 1877 ***5240.1*** *p21*
Hunt, James 23; Kansas, 1877 ***5240.1*** *p58*
Hunt, John; Charles Town, SC, 1760 ***1219.7*** *p75*
Hunt, John; Charleston, SC, 1803 ***1639.20*** *p96*
Hunt, John; Virginia, 1623-1648 ***6219*** *p252*
Hunt, John 16; Windward Islands, 1722 ***3690.1*** *p120*
Hunt, John 19; Virginia, 1774 ***1219.7*** *p242*
Hunt, Jon.; Virginia, 1635 ***6219*** *p36*
Hunt, Joseph 19; Maryland, 1731 ***3690.1*** *p120*
Hunt, Margery; America, 1697 ***2212*** *p7*
Hunt, Mary 12; Massachusetts, 1849 ***5881.1*** *p48*
Hunt, Owen 10; Massachusetts, 1849 ***5881.1*** *p49*
Hunt, Ralph; Virginia, 1632 ***6219*** *p180*
Hunt, Richard 21; Maryland, 1735 ***3690.1*** *p120*
Hunt, Rosa 31; Kansas, 1876 ***5240.1*** *p57*
Hunt, Samuel; New York, 1753 ***3652*** *p77*
Hunt, Samuel 22; Kansas, 1877 ***5240.1*** *p58*
Hunt, Tho.; Virginia, 1637 ***6219*** *p24*
Hunt, Tho.; Virginia, 1643 ***6219*** *p205*
Hunt, Thomas; New York, NY, 1837 ***8208.4*** *p24*
Hunt, Thomas; Virginia, 1636 ***6219*** *p76*
Hunt, Thomas 22; Kansas, 1870 ***5240.1*** *p51*
Hunt, Walter 25; Philadelphia, 1774 ***1219.7*** *p217*
Hunt, William; Virginia, 1638 ***6219*** *p120*
Hunt, William 14; Massachusetts, 1850 ***5881.1*** *p51*
Hunt, William 22; New York, 1774 ***1219.7*** *p203*
Hunt, William 23; Kansas, 1886 ***5240.1*** *p68*
Hunt, Wilson A.; Philadelphia, 1816 ***2859.11*** *p33*
Hunt, Wm. 19; Port uncertain, 1849 ***4535.10*** *p198*
Hunter, . . .; Canada, 1776-1783 ***9786*** *p25*
Hunter, . . . 1; Philadelphia, 1864 ***5704.8*** *p182*
Hunter, . . . 2; Philadelphia, 1864 ***5704.8*** *p182*
Hunter, . . . 7; Philadelphia, 1864 ***5704.8*** *p182*
Hunter, Abram 28; Wilmington, NC, 1774 ***1639.20*** *p96*
Hunter, Adam; St. John, N.B., 1853 ***5704.8*** *p106*
Hunter, Alexander; Arizona, 1886 ***2764.35*** *p35*
Hunter, Alexander; New York, NY, 1837 ***8208.4*** *p55*
Hunter, Ann; New York, NY, 1811 ***2859.11*** *p13*
Hunter, Catherine; New York, NY, 1816 ***2859.11*** *p33*
Hunter, Charles; New York, NY, 1816 ***2859.11*** *p33*
Hunter, Daniel 18; Quebec, 1857 ***5704.8*** *p135*
Hunter, David; New York, NY, 1811 ***2859.11*** *p13*
Hunter, David; New York, NY, 1870 ***5704.8*** *p237*
Hunter, David 6; Quebec, 1847 ***5704.8*** *p12*
Hunter, David 28; Philadelphia, 1803 ***53.26*** *p39*
Hunter, David K.; New York, NY, 1840 ***8208.4*** *p109*
Hunter, Edward 34; Philadelphia, 1803 ***53.26*** *p39*
*Relative:*George 14
Hunter, Eleanor; Philadelphia, 1811 ***53.26*** *p39*
Hunter, Eleanor; Philadelphia, 1811 ***2859.11*** *p13*
Hunter, Eliza 12; Maryland or Virginia, 1699 ***2212*** *p24*
Hunter, Eliza 13; St. John, N.B., 1861 ***5704.8*** *p147*
Hunter, Eliza Jane 16; Quebec, 1853 ***5704.8*** *p104*
Hunter, Elizabeth *SEE* Hunter, Scott
Hunter, Elizabeth; Philadelphia, 1847 ***5704.8*** *p31*
Hunter, Elizabeth; Philadelphia, 1867 ***5704.8*** *p222*
Hunter, Elizabeth; Quebec, 1851 ***5704.8*** *p73*
Hunter, Elleanor; Quebec, 1847 ***5704.8*** *p12*
Hunter, Ellen 20; St. John, N.B., 1857 ***5704.8*** *p135*
Hunter, George; Charleston, SC, 1755 ***1639.20*** *p96*
Hunter, George 7; Quebec, 1851 ***5704.8*** *p73*
Hunter, George 8; Quebec, 1854 ***5704.8*** *p119*
Hunter, George 14 *SEE* Hunter, Edward

Hunter, George 40; North America, 1774 ***1219.7*** *p199*
Hunter, Gerard; Philadelphia, 1811 ***53.26*** *p39*
*Relative:*Martha
*Relative:*John
*Relative:*Mary
Hunter, Gerard; Philadelphia, 1811 ***2859.11*** *p13*
Hunter, Hugh; Quebec, 1851 ***5704.8*** *p73*
Hunter, Hugh 9 mos; Philadelphia, 1853 ***5704.8*** *p113*
Hunter, Hugh 1; Philadelphia, 1854 ***5704.8*** *p117*
Hunter, Hugh 10; Quebec, 1851 ***5704.8*** *p73*
Hunter, Hugh 25; Philadelphia, 1864 ***5704.8*** *p156*
Hunter, Isabella; Philadelphia, 1864 ***5704.8*** *p182*
Hunter, Isabella; Quebec, 1851 ***5704.8*** *p73*
Hunter, Isabella 40; Quebec, 1853 ***5704.8*** *p104*
Hunter, James; America, 1854-1855 ***8893*** *p266*
*Wife:*Mary Morrisan
Hunter, James; Charleston, SC, 1810 ***1639.20*** *p97*
Hunter, James; Iowa, 1866-1943 ***123.54*** *p23*
Hunter, James; New York, NY, 1816 ***2859.11*** *p33*
Hunter, James; Philadelphia, 1811 ***53.26*** *p39*
*Relative:*William
Hunter, James; Philadelphia, 1811 ***2859.11*** *p13*
Hunter, James; Philadelphia, 1853 ***5704.8*** *p100*
Hunter, James 13; Quebec, 1854 ***5704.8*** *p119*
Hunter, James 27; Virginia, 1774 ***1219.7*** *p227*
Hunter, Jane; America, 1866 ***5704.8*** *p211*
Hunter, Jane; North Carolina, 1770 ***1639.20*** *p195*
Hunter, Jane; North Carolina, 1770 ***1639.20*** *p196*
Hunter, Jane; Philadelphia, 1852 ***5704.8*** *p84*
Hunter, Jane 4; Quebec, 1847 ***5704.8*** *p12*
Hunter, Jane 11; Quebec, 1854 ***5704.8*** *p119*
Hunter, Jane 19; Philadelphia, 1856 ***5704.8*** *p129*
Hunter, Jn 18; America, 1702 ***2212*** *p38*
Hunter, John *SEE* Hunter, Gerard
Hunter, John; New York, NY, 1811 ***2859.11*** *p13*
Hunter, John; New York, NY, 1816 ***2859.11*** *p33*
Hunter, John; New York, NY, 1835 ***8208.4*** *p79*
Hunter, John; New York, NY, 1838 ***8208.4*** *p83*
Hunter, John; New York, NY, 1869 ***5704.8*** *p232*
Hunter, John; Philadelphia, 1811 ***2859.11*** *p13*
Hunter, John; South Carolina, 1825 ***1639.20*** *p97*
Hunter, John 6 mos *SEE* Hunter, Scott
Hunter, John 6 mos; Philadelphia, 1847 ***5704.8*** *p31*
Hunter, John 6; St. John, N.B., 1849 ***5704.8*** *p56*
Hunter, John 14; Jamaica, 1753 ***1219.7*** *p19*
Hunter, John 14; Jamaica, 1753 ***3690.1*** *p120*
Hunter, John 18; St. John, N.B., 1861 ***5704.8*** *p147*
Hunter, John 19; St. John, N.B., 1856 ***5704.8*** *p131*
Hunter, John 21; Quebec, 1853 ***5704.8*** *p105*
Hunter, John 22; Philadelphia, 1857 ***5704.8*** *p133*
Hunter, Jon.; Virginia, 1642 ***6219*** *p192*
Hunter, Joseph; America, 1867 ***5704.8*** *p220*
Hunter, Joseph 6; Philadelphia, 1853 ***5704.8*** *p113*
Hunter, Joseph 7; Philadelphia, 1854 ***5704.8*** *p117*
Hunter, M.A. 28; Virginia, 1774 ***1219.7*** *p226*
Hunter, Margaret; Philadelphia, 1852 ***5704.8*** *p84*
Hunter, Margaret; Philadelphia, 1868 ***5704.8*** *p226*
Hunter, Margaret 6 mos; Quebec, 1847 ***5704.8*** *p12*
Hunter, Margaret 18; St. John, N.B., 1857 ***5704.8*** *p135*
Hunter, Margaret Jane; Quebec, 1847 ***5704.8*** *p12*
Hunter, Martha *SEE* Hunter, Gerard
Hunter, Martha; Philadelphia, 1811 ***2859.11*** *p13*
Hunter, Martha; Philadelphia, 1868 ***5704.8*** *p227*
Hunter, Martha 4; Philadelphia, 1853 ***5704.8*** *p113*
Hunter, Martha 5; Philadelphia, 1854 ***5704.8*** *p117*
Hunter, Mary *SEE* Hunter, Gerard
Hunter, Mary; New York, NY, 1816 ***2859.11*** *p33*
Hunter, Mary; New York, NY, 1870 ***5704.8*** *p239*
Hunter, Mary; Philadelphia, 1811 ***2859.11*** *p13*
Hunter, Mary 8; Quebec, 1847 ***5704.8*** *p12*
Hunter, Mary Ann; Philadelphia, 1849 ***53.26*** *p39*
Hunter, Mary Ann; Philadelphia, 1849 ***5704.8*** *p54*
Hunter, Mary Ann 4; Quebec, 1851 ***5704.8*** *p73*
Hunter, Mary Morrisan *SEE* Hunter, James
Hunter, Mathew; Quebec, 1847 ***5704.8*** *p12*
Hunter, Mathew 20; New York, 1774 ***1219.7*** *p202*
Hunter, Moses; Philadelphia, 1811 ***53.26*** *p39*
Hunter, Moses; Philadelphia, 1811 ***2859.11*** *p13*
Hunter, Nancy; Quebec, 1847 ***5704.8*** *p12*
Hunter, Nathaniel 24; Philadelphia, 1857 ***5704.8*** *p133*
Hunter, Peter; Cape Fear, NC, 1752-1753 ***1639.20*** *p97*
Hunter, Phebe 40; Quebec, 1854 ***5704.8*** *p119*
Hunter, Rebecca 9; Quebec, 1847 ***5704.8*** *p6*
Hunter, Rebecca 13; Quebec, 1853 ***5704.8*** *p104*
Hunter, Rebecca 25; Philadelphia, 1853 ***5704.8*** *p113*
Hunter, Rebecca 25; Philadelphia, 1854 ***5704.8*** *p116*
Hunter, Richard; Virginia, 1646 ***6219*** *p245*
Hunter, Richard 16; Philadelphia, 1854 ***5704.8*** *p117*
Hunter, Robert; New York, NY, 1811 ***2859.11*** *p13*
Hunter, Robert; Ohio, 1841 ***9892.11*** *p22*
Hunter, Robert; Ohio, 1851 ***9892.11*** *p22*
Hunter, Robert; Quebec, 1849 ***5704.8*** *p52*
Hunter, Robert 3; Quebec, 1854 ***5704.8*** *p119*
Hunter, Robert 8 *SEE* Hunter, Scott
Hunter, Robert 8; Philadelphia, 1847 ***5704.8*** *p31*
Hunter, Robert 8; Philadelphia, 1853 ***5704.8*** *p113*
Hunter, Robert 9; Philadelphia, 1854 ***5704.8*** *p116*
Hunter, Robert 40; Quebec, 1854 ***5704.8*** *p119*
Hunter, Samuel; New York, NY, 1811 ***2859.11*** *p13*
With family
Hunter, Samuel; Quebec, 1847 ***5704.8*** *p12*
Hunter, Samuel 6; Quebec, 1854 ***5704.8*** *p119*
Hunter, Samuel 13; Quebec, 1851 ***5704.8*** *p73*
Hunter, Samuel 20; Nevis, 1773 ***1219.7*** *p170*
Hunter, Samuel 41; Kansas, 1881 ***5240.1*** *p63*
Hunter, Sarah 6; Quebec, 1853 ***5704.8*** *p104*
Hunter, Sarah 30; Philadelphia, 1856 ***5704.8*** *p129*
Hunter, Sarah Ann 10; Philadelphia, 1853 ***5704.8*** *p113*
Hunter, Sarah Ann 10; Philadelphia, 1854 ***5704.8*** *p116*
Hunter, Scott; Philadelphia, 1847 ***53.26*** *p39*
*Relative:*Elizabeth
*Relative:*Robert 8
*Relative:*William 6
*Relative:*John 6 mos
Hunter, Scott; Philadelphia, 1847 ***5704.8*** *p31*
Hunter, Scott 26; Philadelphia, 1833-1834 ***53.26*** *p39*
Hunter, Susan 9; Quebec, 1854 ***5704.8*** *p119*
Hunter, Thomas; Charleston, SC, 1813 ***1639.20*** *p97*
Hunter, Thomas; New York, NY, 1811 ***2859.11*** *p13*
Hunter, Thomas; Quebec, 1850 ***5704.8*** *p67*
Hunter, Thomas; Quebec, 1854 ***5704.8*** *p119*
Hunter, William *SEE* Hunter, James
Hunter, William; America, 1742 ***4971*** *p65*
Hunter, William; Arkansas, 1918 ***95.2*** *p58*
Hunter, William; New York, NY, 1816 ***2859.11*** *p33*
Hunter, William; Philadelphia, 1866 ***5704.8*** *p209*
Hunter, William; Philadelphia, 1868 ***5704.8*** *p227*
Hunter, William; Quebec, 1850 ***5704.8*** *p67*
Hunter, William 6 mos; Quebec, 1851 ***5704.8*** *p73*
Hunter, William 3; Philadelphia, 1847 ***5704.8*** *p31*
Hunter, William 4; St. John, N.B., 1849 ***5704.8*** *p56*
Hunter, William 6 *SEE* Hunter, Scott
Hunter, William 15; Jamaica, 1751 ***1219.7*** *p7*
Hunter, William 15; Jamaica, 1751 ***3690.1*** *p120*
Hunter, William 20; Philadelphia, 1860 ***5704.8*** *p145*
Hunter, William 48; South Carolina, 1850 ***1639.20*** *p97*
Hunter, Wm.; Philadelphia, 1811 ***2859.11*** *p13*
Huntington, Andrew; Virginia, 1642 ***6219*** *p190*
Huntington, Chandler; Washington, 1859-1920 ***2872.1*** *p17*
Huntington, E. E.; Washington, 1859-1920 ***2872.1*** *p17*
Huntington, H. V.; Washington, 1859-1920 ***2872.1*** *p17*
Huntington, Harry W.; Washington, 1859-1920 ***2872.1*** *p17*
Huntington, Lydia; Virginia, 1642 ***6219*** *p190*
Huntington, Nels H.; Washington, 1859-1920 ***2872.1*** *p17*
Huntington, Wm 28; Maryland or Virginia, 1699 ***2212*** *p22*
Huntley, Hen.; Virginia, 1642 ***6219*** *p192*
Huntlong, Hugh 27; Philadelphia, 1774 ***1219.7*** *p212*
Huntmann, Johann Heinrich; Kentucky, 1843 ***8582.3*** *p100*
Huntsmann, Heinrich; Kentucky, 1840-1845 ***8582.3*** *p100*
Huopana, Alex; Arkansas, 1918 ***95.2*** *p58*
Huovenen, Antti; Washington, 1859-1920 ***2872.1*** *p18*
Hupart, Th.; New Orleans, 1839 ***778.5*** *p279*
Hupenden, . . .; Canada, 1776-1783 ***9786*** *p25*
Hupin, Mr. 25; New Orleans, 1836 ***778.5*** *p279*
Hupp, Henry 26; Kansas, 1885 ***5240.1*** *p68*
Huppert, . . .; Canada, 1776-1783 ***9786*** *p25*
Huppert, Frederick; Wisconsin, n.d. ***9675.6*** *p51*
Huppert, Robert 33; Jamaica, 1736 ***3690.1*** *p120*
Huptin, Hiram; Iowa, 1866-1943 ***123.54*** *p23*
Hupton, James; Iowa, 1866-1943 ***123.54*** *p23*
Huquenin, Robert Lindsey; Iowa, 1866-1943 ***123.54*** *p23*
Hurat, Ann; Quebec, 1850 ***5704.8*** *p69*
Hurback, John; Philadelphia, 1762 ***9973.7*** *p37*
Hurd, . . .; Canada, 1776-1783 ***9786*** *p25*
Hurd, John 14; Maryland, 1775 ***1219.7*** *p256*
Hurd, Nicholas 19; New England, 1699 ***2212*** *p19*
Hurd, Philip Zimmer; South Carolina, 1788 ***7119*** *p203*
Hurdis, Wm.; Virginia, 1635 ***6219*** *p69*
Hurdy, Jane 16; Nova Scotia, 1775 ***1219.7*** *p263*
Hurenka, John; Arkansas, 1918 ***95.2*** *p58*
Hurey, Harrel 18; America, 1827 ***778.5*** *p279*
Hurger, Catherine 56; America, 1836 ***778.5*** *p279*
Hurim, Nowell; Virginia, 1642 ***6219*** *p188*
Hurleman, Michael; Milwaukee, 1875 ***4719.30*** *p257*
Hurlemann, Michael; Milwaukee, 1875 ***4719.30*** *p257*
Hurley, Celia 10; Massachusetts, 1849 ***5881.1*** *p45*
Hurley, Daniel 21; Maryland, 1774 ***1219.7*** *p225*
Hurley, Dennis; Massachusetts, 1847 ***5881.1*** *p45*
Hurley, Edward; New York, NY, 1839 ***8208.4*** *p95*
Hurley, Ellen 8; Massachusetts, 1849 ***5881.1*** *p46*
Hurley, Ellen 15; Massachusetts, 1847 ***5881.1*** *p46*
Hurley, Ellen 31; Massachusetts, 1849 ***5881.1*** *p46*
Hurley, Honora 1; Massachusetts, 1849 ***5881.1*** *p46*
Hurley, Jeremiah 60; Massachusetts, 1849 ***5881.1*** *p47*
Hurley, John; New York, NY, 1838 ***8208.4*** *p82*
Hurley, John 11; Massachusetts, 1849 ***5881.1*** *p47*
Hurley, John 22; Newfoundland, 1789 ***4915.24*** *p56*
Hurley, Mary 19; Philadelphia, 1833 ***53.26*** *p39*
Hurley, Michael; New York, NY, 1837 ***8208.4*** *p52*
Hurley, Michael; Quebec, 1825 ***7603*** *p72*
Hurley, Patrick 22; Massachusetts, 1849 ***5881.1*** *p50*
Hurley, Patrick 30; Massachusetts, 1850 ***5881.1*** *p50*
Hurley, Patrick 46; Massachusetts, 1850 ***5881.1*** *p50*
Hurley, Paul 48; Maryland, 1775 ***1219.7*** *p259*
Hurley, Thomas; Wisconsin, n.d. ***9675.6*** *p51*
Hurley, Timothy 21; Massachusetts, 1848 ***5881.1*** *p50*
Hurley, Wm.; New York, NY, 1811 ***2859.11*** *p13*
Hurling, Fred; Iroquois Co., IL, 1894 ***3455.1*** *p11*
Hurling, Gottlieb; Iroquois Co., IL, 1892 ***3455.1*** *p11*
Hurling, Wilhelm; Iroquois Co., IL, 1895 ***3455.1*** *p11*
Hurly, Bryan; America, 1740 ***4971*** *p31*
Hurly, Daniel; New York, NY, 1838 ***8208.4*** *p86*
Hurly, Margaret; America, 1739 ***4971*** *p47*
Hurly, Margaret; America, 1741 ***4971*** *p49*
Hurm, Wendel; Cincinnati, 1869-1887 ***8582*** *p14*
Hurn, Mary 20; Quebec, 1853 ***5704.8*** *p104*
Hurnn, Sebastian; New York, NY, 1840 ***8208.4*** *p107*
Huroitz, M. 26; Harris Co., TX, 1898 ***6254*** *p4*
Hurrle, Ignatz; Indiana, 1850 ***1450.2*** *p71A*
Hurs, Andrew 30; Philadelphia, 1803 ***53.26*** *p39*
Hursmiller, Jacob; New York, NY, 1839 ***8208.4*** *p90*
Hurst, Alexander; Quebec, 1852 ***5704.8*** *p86*
Hurst, Alexander; Quebec, 1852 ***5704.8*** *p90*
Hurst, Ann; New York, 1800-1854 ***4535.11*** *p53*
Hurst, Ann 21; Philadelphia, 1774 ***1219.7*** *p212*
Hurst, David; St. John, N.B., 1847 ***5704.8*** *p15*
Hurst, Ellan; St. John, N.B., 1847 ***5704.8*** *p25*
Hurst, Geo. 13; New York, 1854 ***4535.11*** *p53*
*Brother:*Joseph 11
*Brother:*John 9
Hurst, George; Illinois, 1896 ***5012.40*** *p55*
Hurst, George; North Carolina, 1758-1844 ***1639.20*** *p97*
Hurst, Henry; Virginia, 1652 ***6251*** *p20*
Hurst, James 13; Quebec, 1855 ***5704.8*** *p124*
Hurst, Jane 8; St. John, N.B., 1847 ***5704.8*** *p25*
Hurst, Jane 11; Quebec, 1855 ***5704.8*** *p124*
Hurst, John 2; Quebec, 1852 ***5704.8*** *p90*
Hurst, John 9 *SEE* Hurst, Geo.
Hurst, John 11; St. John, N.B., 1847 ***5704.8*** *p15*
Hurst, Joseph; Quebec, 1852 ***5704.8*** *p86*
Hurst, Joseph; Quebec, 1852 ***5704.8*** *p90*
Hurst, Joseph 11 *SEE* Hurst, Geo.
Hurst, Margaret 10; St. John, N.B., 1847 ***5704.8*** *p25*
Hurst, Mary Ann 9; Quebec, 1855 ***5704.8*** *p124*
Hurst, Matilda 8; St. John, N.B., 1847 ***5704.8*** *p15*
Hurst, Rebecca; St. John, N.B., 1847 ***5704.8*** *p15*
Hurst, Rebecca 12; St. John, N.B., 1847 ***5704.8*** *p25*
Hurst, Robert 30; Philadelphia, 1774 ***1219.7*** *p228*
Hurst, Rose; Quebec, 1852 ***5704.8*** *p86*
Hurst, Rose; Quebec, 1852 ***5704.8*** *p90*
Hurst, Sarah 9 mos; Quebec, 1852 ***5704.8*** *p90*
Hurst, Stephen 15; Virginia, 1774 ***1219.7*** *p193*
Hurtaen, Stere; Washington, 1859-1920 ***2872.1*** *p18*
Hurtel, Mrs. 21; Alabama, 1823 ***778.5*** *p279*
Hurtel, Pierre 26; New Orleans, 1821 ***778.5*** *p279*
Hurth, Herman; Wisconsin, n.d. ***9675.6*** *p51*
Hurthans, Albert 33; America, 1832 ***778.5*** *p279*
Huse, Jno.; Pennsylvania, 1752 ***2444*** *p170*
Huse, John; Virginia, 1648 ***6219*** *p251*
Huseby, Christian Olaf; Arkansas, 1918 ***95.2*** *p58*
Husemann, F. W.; America, 1853 ***4610.10*** *p17*
Husemann, Wilhelm; New York, NY, 1899 ***1450.2*** *p17B*
Husey, David; Virginia, 1648 ***6219*** *p250*
Husin, Ann 26; Died enroute, 1838 ***778.5*** *p279*
Husing, A. M. F. Johanne *SEE* Husing, Ernst Philipp
Husing, August Heinrich Fr. *SEE* Husing, Ernst Philipp
Husing, Caroline L. L. Trampe *SEE* Husing, Ernst Philipp
Husing, Ernst Philipp; America, 1885 ***4610.10*** *p160*
*Wife:*Caroline L. L. Trampe
*Child:*Heinrich W. August
*Child:*Hermann H. Ernst
*Child:*A. M. F. Johanne
*Child:*August Heinrich Fr.
Husing, Fr. W. August; America, 1886 ***4610.10*** *p161*
Husing, Heinrich W. August *SEE* Husing, Ernst Philipp
Husing, Hermann H. Ernst *SEE* Husing, Ernst Philipp
Huske, Anna Obermeier *SEE* Huske, Heinrich
Huske, Elizabeth Hogg; North Carolina, 1764-1788 ***1639.20*** *p94*
Huske, Heinrich; America, 1884 ***4610.10*** *p161*

Huske, Heinrich; Nebraska, 1884-1885 *4610.10 p44*
  Wife: Anna Obermeier
  With 3 children
  With mother-in-law
Husley, Eliz.; Virginia, 1635 *6219 p3*
Husman, Andreas; Cincinnati, 1869-1887 *8582 p14*
Husmann, Andreas; New York, NY, 1841 *8582.1 p16*
Husmann, Gerhard; Ohio, 1798-1818 *8582.2 p54*
Huson, Elizabeth; Virginia, 1638 *6219 p119*
Huson, John; Virginia, 1639 *6219 p158*
Huson, Tho.; Virginia, 1637 *6219 p115*
Huss, Carl Heinrich Friedrich Wilhelm; America, 1841 *4610.10 p154*
Huss, Christian Friedrich Wilhelm; America, 1849 *4610.10 p142*
Huss, Johannes; Pennsylvania, 1752 *2444 p170*
Hussey, Alice 11; Massachusetts, 1849 *5881.1 p45*
Hussey, Benjamin 27; Pennsylvania, 1728 *3690.1 p120*
Hussey, Catharine 20; Massachusetts, 1850 *5881.1 p45*
Hussey, David; Virginia, 1648 *6219 p250*
Hussey, Ellen 2; Massachusetts, 1849 *5881.1 p46*
Hussey, Ellinor; America, 1735-1743 *4971 p8*
Hussey, James; America, 1736 *4971 p71*
Hussey, John; America, 1736 *4971 p81*
Hussey, John; North America, 1760 *1219.7 p79*
Hussey, Martha *SEE* Hussey, Robert
Hussey, Mary; America, 1741 *4971 p16*
Hussey, Robert; Philadelphia, 1742 *3652 p55*
  Wife: Martha
Hussey, William 21; Virginia, 1736 *3690.1 p120*
Hussman, John F.; Washington, 1859-1920 *2872.1 p18*
Hussner, J. 35; America, 1836 *778.5 p279*
Husson, James; New York, NY, 1816 *2859.11 p33*
Husson, Jean 34; America, 1839 *778.5 p279*
Husson, Ursul. 37; America, 1839 *778.5 p280*
Hussquy, Elisabetha 20; Port uncertain, 1839 *778.5 p280*
Hussy, Ann 9; Massachusetts, 1849 *5881.1 p45*
Hussy, Honora 19; Massachusetts, 1849 *5881.1 p46*
Hussy, Johanna 12; Massachusetts, 1849 *5881.1 p47*
Hussy, John 5; Massachusetts, 1849 *5881.1 p47*
Hussy, Wm 20; America, 1699 *2212 p28*
Hust, Henry; Cincinnati, 1869 *8582 p14*
Hust, Jacob; Cincinnati, 1869-1887 *8582 p14*
Hust, Jakob; Ohio, 1843 *8582.1 p71*
Husted, John; Canada, 1835 *4535.10 p198*
  With wife
Husted, John; New York, 1835 *4535.10 p198*
  With wife
Husted, Peter; Canada, 1835 *4535.10 p198*
  With wife
  With 9 children
Husted, Peter; New York, 1835 *4535.10 p198*
  With wife
  With 9 children
Husten, Lewis 28; New Orleans, 1831 *778.5 p280*
Husting, Anten; Wisconsin, n.d. *9675.6 p51*
Husting, Valentine; Wisconsin, n.d. *9675.6 p51*
Huston, Kennedy 20; St. John, N.B., 1863 *5704.8 p153*
Huston, Thomas 61; Quebec, 1856 *5704.8 p129*
Hutawa, Edward; Baltimore, 1832 *3702.7 p97*
Hutawa, Julius; Baltimore, 1832 *3702.7 p97*
Hutcheson, Alexander; New York, NY, 1864 *5704.8 p184*
Hutcheson, Elizabeth; Quebec, 1847 *5704.8 p13*
Hutcheson, Elizabeth 13; Quebec, 1847 *5704.8 p13*
Hutcheson, Ellan; Quebec, 1847 *5704.8 p13*
Hutcheson, George; Quebec, 1847 *5704.8 p7*
Hutcheson, John; Quebec, 1847 *5704.8 p13*
Hutcheson, Margaret; Quebec, 1847 *5704.8 p13*
Hutcheson, Margaret 20; Philadelphia, 1859 *5704.8 p142*
Hutcheson, Mary; St. John, N.B., 1852 *5704.8 p9*
Hutcheson, Mary A.; New York, NY, 1866 *5704.8 p213*
Hutcheson, Robert 22; Philadelphia, 1833-1834 *53.26 p39*
Hutcheson, Thomas; Quebec, 1847 *5704.8 p13*
Hutcheson, William; Quebec, 1847 *5704.8 p13*
Hutchin, John, Jr.; New York, NY, 1811 *2859.11 p13*
Hutchin, William 17; Antigua (Antego), 1737 *3690.1 p120*
Hutchingston, Andrew 57; South Carolina, 1850 *1639.20 p98*
Hutchins, Ann; Pennsylvania, 1682 *4962 p151*
Hutchins, Charles; Ohio, 1851 *9892.11 p22*
Hutchins, Eliz.; Virginia, 1642 *6219 p189*
Hutchins, Elizabeth 20; Massachusetts, 1848 *5881.1 p46*
Hutchins, Isaac; Virginia, 1637 *6219 p24*
Hutchins, Matthew; Boston, 1762 *1219.7 p89*

Hutchins, Noy Willey; Charles Town, SC, 1762 *1219.7 p89*
Hutchins, Thomas; Ohio, 1849 *9892.11 p22*
Hutchins, William; Ohio, 1843 *9892.11 p22*
Hutchinson, Ann 2 *SEE* Hutchinson, John
Hutchinson, Ann Jane *SEE* Hutchinson, William
Hutchinson, Daniel 21; Virginia, 1774 *1219.7 p226*
Hutchinson, Edward; Virginia, 1638 *6219 p119*
Hutchinson, Edward; Virginia, 1639 *6219 p182*
Hutchinson, Elenor; Annapolis, MD, 1742 *4971 p92*
Hutchinson, Eliz.; Virginia, 1638 *6219 p123*
Hutchinson, Ellenor; America, 1742 *4971 p17*
Hutchinson, Francis; Virginia, 1636 *6219 p21*
Hutchinson, Francis 10 *SEE* Hutchinson, John
Hutchinson, George; America, 1803 *1639.20 p97*
Hutchinson, James; Virginia, 1636 *6219 p21*
Hutchinson, James 20; Wilmington, DE, 1831 *6508.3 p101*
Hutchinson, John; Philadelphia, 1853 *5704.8 p100*
Hutchinson, John 21; Jamaica, 1736 *3690.1 p120*
Hutchinson, John 22; Halifax, N.S., 1774 *1219.7 p213*
Hutchinson, John 30; New York, 1774 *1219.7 p202*
  Wife: Margaret 30
  Child: Francis 10
  Child: Margaret 8
  Child: Ralph 7
  Child: Ann 2
  Child: Major 9
Hutchinson, Joseph 21; Pennsylvania, 1728 *3690.1 p120*
Hutchinson, Joseph 27; Virginia, 1774 *1219.7 p201*
Hutchinson, Major 9 *SEE* Hutchinson, John
Hutchinson, Margaret 8 *SEE* Hutchinson, John
Hutchinson, Margaret 30 *SEE* Hutchinson, John
Hutchinson, Mary; Annapolis, MD, 1742 *4971 p92*
Hutchinson, Rachael; Philadelphia, 1853 *5704.8 p100*
Hutchinson, Ralph 7 *SEE* Hutchinson, John
Hutchinson, Richard; Virginia, 1638 *6219 p153*
Hutchinson, Samuel 24; Maryland, 1775 *1219.7 p273*
Hutchinson, Thomas; New York, NY, 1811 *2859.11 p13*
Hutchinson, William; Philadelphia, 1847 *53.26 p39*
  Relative: Ann Jane
Hutchinson, William; Philadelphia, 1852 *5704.8 p92*
Hutchinson, Wm.; Virginia, 1636 *6219 p77*
Hutchison, Ann; St. John, N.B., 1847 *5704.8 p11*
Hutchison, Ann Jane; Philadelphia, 1847 *5704.8 p1*
Hutchison, Edward; St. John, N.B., 1850 *5704.8 p62*
Hutchison, Elinor; Maryland, 1742 *4971 p107*
Hutchison, Eliza; Philadelphia, 1848 *5704.8 p46*
Hutchison, Hugh; Quebec, 1851 *5704.8 p82*
Hutchison, Isabella; Philadelphia, 1853 *5704.8 p101*
Hutchison, James; Quebec, 1847 *5704.8 p36*
Hutchison, James 40; New York, 1775 *1219.7 p269*
  With wife
  With 4 children
Hutchison, Jane; St. John, N.B., 1852 *5704.8 p93*
Hutchison, John; Philadelphia, 1849 *53.26 p39*
  Relative: Mary
Hutchison, John; Philadelphia, 1849 *5704.8 p58*
Hutchison, John 63; South Carolina, 1850 *1639.20 p97*
Hutchison, Mary *SEE* Hutchison, John
Hutchison, Mary; America, 1742 *4971 p17*
Hutchison, Mary; Maryland, 1742 *4971 p107*
Hutchison, Mary; Philadelphia, 1849 *5704.8 p58*
Hutchison, Rose; St. John, N.B., 1847 *5704.8 p8*
Hutchison, Sarah; Philadelphia, 1869 *5704.8 p236*
Hutchison, William; Philadelphia, 1847 *5704.8 p1*
Hutchison, William John; Philadelphia, 1853 *5704.8 p101*
Hutchison, Wm.; New York, NY, 1811 *2859.11 p13*
Huth, Alvin; Wisconsin, n.d. *9675.6 p51*
Hutley, J.; New York, NY, 1811 *2859.11 p13*
Hutner, . . .; Canada, 1776-1783 *9786 p25*
Hutten, Philipp von; Venezuela, n.d. *8582.3 p79*
Hutting, . . .; Canada, 1776-1783 *9786 p25*
Huttinger, . . .; Canada, 1776-1783 *9786 p25*
Huttner, . . .; Canada, 1776-1783 *9786 p25*
Hutto, Henry; South Carolina, 1788 *7119 p197*
Hutton, Christopher 24; Maryland, 1774 *1219.7 p221*
Hutton, Daniell; Virginia, 1633 *6219 p32*
Hutton, James; Charleston, SC, 1796 *1639.20 p97*
Hutton, James; New York, NY, 1816 *2859.11 p33*
Hutton, James 15; Halifax, N.S., 1775 *1219.7 p262*
Hutton, John; New York, NY, 1811 *2859.11 p13*
Hutton, John; New York, NY, 1837 *8208.4 p32*
Hutton, John; St. John, N.B., 1847 *5704.8 p25*
Hutton, John 8; St. John, N.B., 1847 *5704.8 p25*
Hutton, Lea; St. John, N.B., 1847 *5704.8 p25*

Hutton, Lea 6; St. John, N.B., 1847 *5704.8 p25*
Hutton, Mary Ann 9 mos; St. John, N.B., 1847 *5704.8 p25*
Hutton, Patrick; New York, NY, 1816 *2859.11 p33*
Hutton, Robert 12; St. John, N.B., 1847 *5704.8 p25*
Hutton, Sally Jane 10; St. John, N.B., 1847 *5704.8 p25*
Hutton, Samuel 4; St. John, N.B., 1847 *5704.8 p25*
Huttow, Johanes; South Carolina, 1788 *7119 p204*
Huttson, Henry 21; Nova Scotia, 1774 *1219.7 p209*
Hutz Family ; New York, 1765 *8125.8 p436*
Hutz, Michael; Pennsylvania, 1731-1769 *4525 p226*
Hux, Alexr.; Virginia, 1648 *6219 p250*
Huy, Charles 35; America, 1838 *778.5 p280*
Huyn, von; New York, 1776 *9786 p278*
Hvarness, Bernhard Anton; Washington, 1859-1920 *2872.1 p18*
Hvarness, Helga; Washington, 1859-1920 *2872.1 p18*
Hyam, Joseph 17; Grenada, 1775 *1219.7 p280*
Hyatt, Campbell Douglass 63; California, 1873 *2769.10 p4*
Hyatt, George; New York, NY, 1835 *8208.4 p45*
Hyatt, John; New York, NY, 1839 *8208.4 p102*
Hyde, Daniel 42; Massachusetts, 1850 *5881.1 p46*
Hyde, Francis 33; Port uncertain, 1838 *778.5 p280*
Hyde, John 19; St. Christopher, 1722 *3690.1 p120*
Hyde, John C.; America, 1865 *5240.1 p21*
Hyde, Phillipp; Virginia, 1642 *6219 p196*
Hyde, Thomas; Quebec, 1823 *7603 p98*
Hyer, Peter 58; Port uncertain, 1838 *778.5 p280*
Hylahan, Morres; America, 1736-1743 *4971 p57*
Hylan, Darby; America, 1736-1743 *4971 p57*
Hyland, Elizabeth; America, 1741 *4971 p10*
Hyland, Elizabeth; America, 1741 *4971 p94*
Hyland, Henry; America, 1742 *4971 p37*
Hyland, Henry; Delaware, 1743 *4971 p105*
Hyland, Philadelphius 25; Massachusetts, 1848 *5881.1 p50*
Hyland, William; New York, NY, 1830 *8208.4 p56*
Hyman, J.; Shreveport, LA, 1878 *7129 p44*
Hymen, Colomb 51; New Orleans, 1823 *778.5 p280*
Hymoss, Caron 18; Jamaica, 1719 *3690.1 p121*
Hynde, Tho.; Virginia, 1642 *6219 p196*
Hyndman, Andrew 46; Wilmington, NC, 1774 *1639.20 p98*
  Wife: Catherine Campbell 46
  Child: Mary 18
  Child: Margaret 14
Hyndman, Ballantine 10; Quebec, 1852 *5704.8 p94*
Hyndman, Betty; Quebec, 1852 *5704.8 p94*
Hyndman, Catherine Campbell 46 *SEE* Hyndman, Andrew
Hyndman, Eliza 1; Quebec, 1852 *5704.8 p94*
Hyndman, John; Quebec, 1852 *5704.8 p94*
Hyndman, Margaret 14 *SEE* Hyndman, Andrew
Hyndman, Mary 6; Quebec, 1852 *5704.8 p94*
Hyndman, Mary 18 *SEE* Hyndman, Andrew
Hyndman, Nancy; St. John, N.B., 1847 *5704.8 p9*
Hyndman, Robert; Quebec, 1852 *5704.8 p94*
Hyndman, Sarah 3; Quebec, 1852 *5704.8 p94*
Hyndman, William 12; Quebec, 1852 *5704.8 p94*
Hynds, Robert 33; St. John, N.B., 1866 *5704.8 p167*
Hynds, Thomas 27; St. John, N.B., 1866 *5704.8 p167*
Hynes, Mr.; Quebec, 1815 *9229.18 p79*
Hynes, Alexander 23; Maryland, 1774 *1219.7 p221*
Hynes, Andrew 22; Massachusetts, 1849 *5881.1 p44*
Hynes, Bessy 35; Massachusetts, 1849 *5881.1 p45*
Hynes, Bridget 22; Massachusetts, 1849 *5881.1 p45*
Hynes, Bridget 25; Massachusetts, 1849 *5881.1 p45*
Hynes, Catherine 55; St. John, N.B., 1864 *5704.8 p159*
Hynes, Edward; New York, NY, 1816 *2859.11 p33*
Hynes, Edward 22; Maryland, 1775 *1219.7 p264*
Hynes, John; America, 1895 *1450.2 p71A*
Hynes, John; Montreal, 1818 *7603 p57*
Hynes, Marinus; Virginia, 1640 *6219 p188*
Hynes, Michael; America, 1741 *4971 p83*
Hynes, Michael; America, 1742 *4971 p83*
Hynes, Patrick 30; Massachusetts, 1848 *5881.1 p50*
Hynes, Sarah; Virginia, 1640 *6219 p188*
Hynes, Thomas; Virginia, 1637 *6219 p112*
Hynicky, Adam; Philadelphia, 1767 *9973.7 p40*
Hypolite, James 18; Port uncertain, 1838 *778.5 p280*
Hyram, Louis 28; Port uncertain, 1838 *778.5 p280*
Hyre, John; Virginia, 1638 *6219 p153*
Hyslop, Robert 30; Quebec, 1862 *5704.8 p152*
Hyssley, Conrad; Philadelphia, 1760 *9973.7 p34*
Hyves, Henry; Virginia, 1638 *6219 p125*
Hyz, Jan; New York, 1831 *4606 p174*

I

Iacovone, Francesco; Iowa, 1866-1943 *123.54 p23*
Iager, Valentin; Canada, 1783 *9786 p38A*
Ialango, Francesco; Arkansas, 1918 *95.2 p58*
Ianncei, Peter; Arkansas, 1918 *95.2 p59*
Iannictello, Alessandro; Colorado, 1904 *9678.2 p25*
Ibach Family ; New York, 1765 *8125.8 p436*
Iben, Frerich; New York, NY, 1923 *3455.3 p83*
Ibert, Konrad; Philadelphia, 1779 *8137 p10*
Ibingfield, Richard 26; Jamaica, 1738 *3690.1 p121*
Ibister, Hugh; Georgia, 1775 *1219.7 p274*
Ibos, Francois 36; Port uncertain, 1839 *778.5 p280*
Iburg, Ferdinand Bendix; America, 1864 *4610.10 p123*
Iburg, Gustav 18; America, 1872 *4610.10 p124*
Iburg, Gustav Adolph; America, 1881 *4610.10 p124*
Iburg, Hermann; America, 1873 *4610.10 p124*
Icaro, Robert; New York, NY, 1821 *8208.4 p36*
Ichinger, Annalis 9 *SEE* Ichinger, Jacob
Ichinger, Catherina 52 *SEE* Ichinger, Jacob
Ichinger, Hans Michael 14 *SEE* Ichinger, Jacob
Ichinger, Jacob 5 *SEE* Ichinger, Jacob
Ichinger, Jacob 48; Georgia, 1738 *9332 p332*
  *Wife:*Catherina 52
  *Daughter:*Sophia 18
  *Son:*Hans Michael 14
  *Daughter:*Annalis 9
  *Son:*Jacob 5
Ichinger, Sophia 18 *SEE* Ichinger, Jacob
Icleberger, Martin; Philadelphia, 1760 *9973.7 p34*
Id, Johan Magnus; Minneapolis, 1881-1886 *6410.35 p52*
Idam, Robert; Virginia, 1637 *6219 p11*
Idam, Robert; Virginia, 1637 *6219 p114*
Iden, Hen.; Virginia, 1643 *6219 p204*
Idess, Ulfert H. 25; Kansas, 1883 *5240.1 p64*
Idler, Rudolph W.; New York, 1882 *1450.2 p72A*
Iego, Nicho.; Virginia, 1646 *6219 p239*
Iffla, J. 40; Mexico, 1829 *778.5 p280*
Iffland, von; Canada, 1776-1783 *9786 p233*
Iffland, John; Canada, 1776-1783 *9786 p242*
Ifflandt, . . .; Canada, 1776-1783 *9786 p25*
Ifland, . . .; Canada, 1776-1783 *9786 p25*
Iglefritz, George; Philadelphia, 1761 *9973.7 p36*
Igo, . . .; Ohio, 1796 *8582.2 p54*
Igo, Ludwig; Pennsylvania, 1785 *8582.2 p54*
Ihben, Frerich; New York, NY, 1923 *3455.4 p50*
Ihlenfeld, Johann Gottlieb; Wisconsin, n.d. *9675.6 p51*
Ihlenfeld, William; Wisconsin, n.d. *9675.6 p51*
Ihrig, Theodor; America, 1854-1855 *9162.6 p104*
Ilenstein, Charles 33; California, 1872 *2769.5 p5*
Ilgen, . . .; New Orleans, 1839 *9420.2 p362*
Illaby, John 16; Maryland, 1723 *3690.1 p121*
Illig, Johannes; America, 1817 *8582.2 p60*
Illig, Johannes; Indiana, 1869-1887 *8582 p14*
Illing, Walter 19; Jamaica, 1736 *3690.1 p121*
Illingworth, James 31; Kansas, 1874 *5240.1 p55*
Illinski, Ksawery; New York, 1831 *4606 p174*
Illisch, Willfried; Illinois, 1850-1855 *8582.2 p50*
Illy, Andre; Wisconsin, n.d. *9675.6 p51*
Ilsley, Randal 17; New York, 1775 *1219.7 p246*
Imblard, P. 19; New Orleans, 1835 *778.5 p280*
Imbler, Lodowick; Philadelphia, 1759 *9973.7 p34*
Imbrie, W.; Charleston, SC, 1816 *1639.20 p98*
  With wife
Immel, Leonard; Philadelphia, 1761 *9973.7 p36*
Immenthal, . . .; Canada, 1776-1783 *9786 p25*
Immhoff, . . .; Canada, 1776-1783 *9786 p25*
Immink, Berendina 26; New York, NY, 1847 *3377.6 p13*
Immink, Gerradina 21; New York, NY, 1847 *3377.6 p13*

Immink, Gerrit John 18; New York, NY, 1847 *3377.6 p13*
Immink, Gerrit John 59; New York, NY, 1847 *3377.6 p13*
Immink, Harriet 35; New York, NY, 1847 *3377.6 p13*
Immink, Hendrika 30; New York, NY, 1847 *3377.6 p13*
Immink, Jantje 27; New York, NY, 1847 *3377.6 p13*
Immink, Jenneken 28; New York, NY, 1847 *3377.6 p13*
Immink, Johanna 13; New York, NY, 1847 *3377.6 p13*
Immink, Willemina 58; New York, NY, 1847 *3377.6 p13*
Immoberstake, Abraham; Philadelphia, 1759 *9973.7 p34*
Imort, Mr.; America, 1844 *4610.10 p133*
  *Wife:*Anna Marie W. Scholz
  *Child:*Carl Heinrich Wilhelm
  *Child:*M. Cath. Engel
Imort, Anna Marie W. Scholz *SEE* Imort, Mr.
Imort, Carl Friedrich Wilhelm; America, 1860 *4610.10 p136*
Imort, Carl Heinrich Wilhelm *SEE* Imort, Mr.
Imort, M. Cath. Engel *SEE* Imort, Mr.
Imrie, W. J.; Charleston, SC, 1817 *1639.20 p98*
Imries, Jane Graham; Charleston, SC, 1817 *1639.20 p84*
Imus, A. H.; Washington, 1859-1920 *2872.1 p18*
Imus, W. H.; Washington, 1859-1920 *2872.1 p18*
Inabnit, Christian; South Carolina, 1788 *7119 p198*
Inabnit, John; South Carolina, 1788 *7119 p198*
Inch, Chary; Philadelphia, 1847 *53.26 p39*
Inch, Chary; Philadelphia, 1847 *5704.8 p30*
Inch, Henry; Philadelphia, 1850 *5704.8 p64*
Inch, William; St. John, N.B., 1848 *5704.8 p44*
Inch, William Spencer; New York, NY, 1835 *8208.4 p6*
Inches, James; New Brunswick, 1832 *8893 p263*
Ineats, Guillaume 29; Port uncertain, 1839 *778.5 p280*
Ineff, Valdimir; Arkansas, 1918 *95.2 p59*
Ingaldsdottir, Palina 25; Quebec, 1879 *2557.1 p22*
Ingalsdottir, Johanna 50; Quebec, 1879 *2557.1 p22*
Ingam, Richd 30; America, 1703 *2212 p38*
Ingarson, Johan; Iowa, 1849 *2090 p609*
Ingebretsen, Eric; New York, 1750 *3652 p74*
Ingelo, Richard; Pennsylvania, 1682 *4960 p159*
Ingelo, Richard; Pennsylvania, 1682 *4962 p152*
Ingerdall, William; America, 1738 *4971 p33*
Ingerson, W. P.; Washington, 1859-1920 *2872.1 p18*
Ingham, Benjamin; Savannah, GA, 1736 *3652 p51*
Ingham, Isaac; Pennsylvania, 1682 *4960 p159*
Ingjaldsdottir, Johanna 50; Quebec, 1879 *2557.1 p22*
Ingjaldsson, August 12; Quebec, 1879 *2557.1 p22*
Ingjaldsson, Sveinbjorn 7; Quebec, 1879 *2557.1 p22*
Ingleston, Edward; Virginia, 1636 *6219 p7*
Ingleton, Jacob; Virginia, 1647 *6219 p239*
Inglis, James; New York, NY, 1838 *8208.4 p62*
Inglis, Jean 20; Maryland, 1738 *3690.1 p72*
Inglis, John; America, 1773 *1639.20 p98*
Ingo, Joseph 24; Montreal, 1775 *7603 p25*
Ingold, Otto; Kansas, 1887 *5240.1 p21*
Ingouf, Dominique 12; New Orleans, 1839 *778.5 p280*
Ingouf, Louis 39; New Orleans, 1839 *778.5 p280*
Ingouf, Madeleine 10; New Orleans, 1839 *778.5 p281*
Ingouf, Marie 44; New Orleans, 1839 *778.5 p281*
Ingouf, Marthe 5; New Orleans, 1839 *778.5 p281*
Ingraham, Thomas; New York, NY, 1816 *2859.11 p33*
  With wife & 9 children
Ingraham, William 23; New York, NY, 1850 *6013.19 p73*
Ingram, Andrew; Charleston, SC, 1803 *1639.20 p98*
Ingram, Daniel 25; Quebec, 1855 *5704.8 p126*

Ingram, Farmer; Philadelphia, 1816 *2859.11 p33*
Ingram, Florena; Philadelphia, 1816 *2859.11 p33*
Ingram, Floyd; Washington, 1859-1920 *2872.1 p18*
Ingram, Frank; Washington, 1859-1920 *2872.1 p18*
Ingram, Isaac; Pennsylvania, 1682 *4960 p159*
Ingram, John; Philadelphia, 1816 *2859.11 p33*
Ingram, John; Virginia, 1652 *6251 p20*
Ingram, Mary; Philadelphia, 1816 *2859.11 p33*
Ingram, Mary L.; Washington, 1859-1920 *2872.1 p18*
Ingram, Media; Washington, 1859-1920 *2872.1 p18*
Ingram, Nettie; Washington, 1859-1920 *2872.1 p18*
Ingram, Rich.; Virginia, 1642 *6219 p198*
Ingram, Sally; Philadelphia, 1816 *2859.11 p33*
Ingram, Walter; Washington, 1859-1920 *2872.1 p18*
Ingram, William; Grenada, 1770 *1219.7 p147*
Ingram, William; New York, NY, 1834 *8208.4 p51*
Ingram, William; Philadelphia, 1851 *5704.8 p80*
Ingram, William 22; Maryland, 1774 *1219.7 p221*
Ingran, Alexander 13; Philadelphia, 1854 *5704.8 p116*
Inhelder, Abraham; New York, NY, 1851 *2896.5 p19*
Inkel, . . .; Canada, 1776-1783 *9786 p25*
Inkel, Jacob; Canada, 1776-1783 *9786 p242*
Inkenbrand, Philip; Indiana, 1847 *9117 p17*
Inkenbrandt, Nicholas; Indiana, 1848 *9117 p19*
Inkson, William 22; Jamaica, 1736 *3690.1 p121*
Inman, James M. 42; Kansas, 1872 *5240.1 p52*
Inman, Mary; South Carolina, 1769 *1219.7 p140*
Innes, Alexander; Philadelphia, 1850 *53.26 p39*
Innes, Alexander; Philadelphia, 1850 *5704.8 p59*
Innes, Daniel; Charleston, SC, 1797 *1639.20 p98*
Innes, James; Cape Fear, NC, 1732 *1639.20 p98*
Innes, James; Cape Fear, NC, 1732 *4814 p92*
Innes, James; Ontario, 1853 *9775.5 p216*
Innes, John; St. John, N.B., 1866 *5704.8 p166*
Innis, Robert 23; Virginia, 1774 *1219.7 p186*
Innis, Simon 40; Maryland, 1774 *1219.7 p220*
Inse, Mathias; Kentucky, 1840 *8582.3 p100*
Inshaw, Richard B.; New York, NY, 1835 *8208.4 p76*
Ionger, John George; South Carolina, 1752-1753 *3689.17 p21*
Iovalde, Ambrose; Arkansas, 1918 *95.2 p59*
Ipuan, Mr. 31; Port uncertain, 1839 *778.5 p281*
Iredale, William J.; Colorado, 1904 *9678.2 p25*
Ireland, Christian; America, 1697 *2212 p8*
Ireland, George; Massachusetts, 1850 *5881.1 p51*
Ireland, John; Virginia, 1638 *6219 p15*
  *Wife:*Martha
  *Child:*John Mathew
  *Child:*Martha
Ireland, John; Virginia, 1640 *6219 p182*
Ireland, John Mathew *SEE* Ireland, John
Ireland, Jon.; Virginia, 1643 *6219 p202*
Ireland, Martha *SEE* Ireland, John
Ireland, Martha *SEE* Ireland, John
Ireland, Mary A. 24; Massachusetts, 1850 *5881.1 p51*
Ireland, Thomas 17; Maryland, 1774 *1219.7 p224*
Ireland, William 26; West Virginia, 1822 *9788.3 p12*
Irlweg, Frank John; Wisconsin, n.d. *9675.6 p51*
Irons, Edward; Kansas, 1875 *5240.1 p21*
Irons, Elisha; Iowa, 1868 *5240.1 p21*
Irons, William; New York, NY, 1864 *5704.8 p172*
Irrgang, Roderick; Baltimore, 1888 *1450.2 p72A*
Irvin, Charles; New York, NY, 1864 *5704.8 p187*
Irvin, Ellan; Philadelphia, 1847 *5704.8 p31*
Irvin, Ellen *SEE* Irvin, John
Irvin, George 52; North Carolina, 1850 *1639.20 p98*
  *Relative:*Jane 43

Irvin, Jane 43 *SEE* Irvin, George
Irvin, John; Philadelphia, 1847 ***53.26*** *p39*
*Relative:*Ellen
Irvin, John; Philadelphia, 1847 ***5704.8*** *p31*
Irvin, John 18; Philadelphia, 1859 ***5704.8*** *p141*
Irvin, Laurence 20; Jamaica, 1735 ***3690.1*** *p73*
Irvin, Sarah; Quebec, 1853 ***5704.8*** *p103*
Irvine, Mr.; New York, NY, 1815 ***2859.11*** *p33*
Irvine, Adam 38; Quebec, 1775 ***1219.7*** *p259*
*Wife:*Elizabeth 36
With 3 children
Irvine, Andrew; Philadelphia, 1811 ***53.26*** *p39*
Irvine, Andrew; Philadelphia, 1811 ***2859.11*** *p13*
Irvine, Ann Jane 8; Quebec, 1852 ***5704.8*** *p97*
Irvine, Anne; Quebec, 1851 ***5704.8*** *p74*
Irvine, Arthur; Quebec, 1852 ***5704.8*** *p97*
Irvine, Bridget; Quebec, 1851 ***5704.8*** *p74*
Irvine, Caroline 4; Quebec, 1852 ***5704.8*** *p97*
Irvine, Catherine; Philadelphia, 1852 ***5704.8*** *p92*
Irvine, Catherine; Quebec, 1852 ***5704.8*** *p97*
Irvine, Catherine 60; Quebec, 1857 ***5704.8*** *p135*
Irvine, Charles 20; St. John, N.B., 1854 ***5704.8*** *p114*
Irvine, Dary; New York, NY, 1815 ***2859.11*** *p33*
Irvine, David; Philadelphia, 1852 ***5704.8*** *p92*
Irvine, Eliza; St. John, N.B., 1847 ***5704.8*** *p21*
Irvine, Elizabeth; Quebec, 1852 ***5704.8*** *p86*
Irvine, Elizabeth; Quebec, 1852 ***5704.8*** *p90*
Irvine, Elizabeth 9 mos; Quebec, 1849 ***5704.8*** *p51*
Irvine, Elizabeth 30; St. John, N.B., 1854 ***5704.8*** *p115*
Irvine, Elizabeth 36 *SEE* Irvine, Adam
Irvine, George; New York, NY, 1835 ***8208.4*** *p39*
Irvine, Hugh; Quebec, 1852 ***5704.8*** *p86*
Irvine, Hugh; Quebec, 1852 ***5704.8*** *p90*
Irvine, Hugh 3; Quebec, 1849 ***5704.8*** *p51*
Irvine, Isabella; Quebec, 1852 ***5704.8*** *p86*
Irvine, Isabella; Quebec, 1852 ***5704.8*** *p90*
Irvine, James; Georgia, 1775 ***1219.7*** *p274*
Irvine, James; New York, NY, 1815 ***2859.11*** *p33*
Irvine, James 10; Quebec, 1849 ***5704.8*** *p51*
Irvine, James 10; Quebec, 1852 ***5704.8*** *p97*
Irvine, Jane; St. John, N.B., 1848 ***5704.8*** *p45*
Irvine, John; New York, NY, 1815 ***2859.11*** *p33*
Irvine, John; Philadelphia, 1811 ***53.26*** *p39*
Irvine, John; Philadelphia, 1811 ***2859.11*** *p13*
Irvine, John; Quebec, 1852 ***5704.8*** *p86*
Irvine, John; Quebec, 1852 ***5704.8*** *p90*
Irvine, John 10; Quebec, 1852 ***5704.8*** *p97*
Irvine, Lancelutt 62; Quebec, 1857 ***5704.8*** *p135*
Irvine, Margaret; Quebec, 1847 ***5704.8*** *p28*
Irvine, Margaret 2; Quebec, 1852 ***5704.8*** *p97*
Irvine, Mary; Quebec, 1849 ***5704.8*** *p51*
Irvine, Mary Ann 12; Quebec, 1852 ***5704.8*** *p97*
Irvine, Matilda 22; Quebec, 1863 ***5704.8*** *p154*
Irvine, Richard; St. John, N.B., 1847 ***5704.8*** *p9*
Irvine, Robert; New York, NY, 1815 ***2859.11*** *p33*
Irvine, Robert; Quebec, 1849 ***5704.8*** *p51*
Irvine, Samuel; New York, NY, 1811 ***2859.11*** *p13*
With family
Irvine, Sarah; St. John, N.B., 1847 ***5704.8*** *p9*
Irvine, Sarah; St. John, N.B., 1847 ***5704.8*** *p11*
Irvine, Thomas Henry 6; Quebec, 1852 ***5704.8*** *p97*
Irvine, Thomas John 21; Kansas, 1885 ***5240.1*** *p67*
Irvine, William; New York, NY, 1815 ***2859.11*** *p33*
Irvine, William; Quebec, 1852 ***5704.8*** *p86*
Irvine, William; Quebec, 1852 ***5704.8*** *p90*
Irvine, William 7; Quebec, 1849 ***5704.8*** *p51*
Irvine, William 13; Quebec, 1852 ***5704.8*** *p97*
Irvine, William N.; Illinois, 1869 ***7857*** *p4*
Irving, A. Campbell; San Francisco, 1850 ***4914.15*** *p10*
Irving, John; Savannah, GA, 1774 ***1219.7*** *p227*
Irving, Thomas; North Carolina, 1825 ***1639.20*** *p98*
Irving, Winifred; South Carolina, 1779 ***1639.20*** *p99*
Irwin, Anne Bella 6 mos; Quebec, 1851 ***5704.8*** *p73*
Irwin, Catherine; Philadelphia, 1847 ***53.26*** *p39*
Irwin, Catherine; Philadelphia, 1847 ***5704.8*** *p31*
Irwin, Catherine; St. John, N.B., 1847 ***5704.8*** *p34*
Irwin, Charles; New York, NY, 1870 ***5704.8*** *p239*
Irwin, Charolott; New York, NY, 1870 ***5704.8*** *p239*
Irwin, David; Illinois, 1853 ***7857*** *p4*
Irwin, David; St. John, N.B., 1848 ***5704.8*** *p44*
Irwin, Edward; St. John, N.B., 1847 ***5704.8*** *p34*
Irwin, Edward 7; Philadelphia, 1865 ***5704.8*** *p164*
Irwin, Edward 8; St. John, N.B., 1847 ***5704.8*** *p34*
Irwin, Eliza; Quebec, 1851 ***5704.8*** *p73*
Irwin, Eliza; St. John, N.B., 1848 ***5704.8*** *p44*
Irwin, Henry; Quebec, 1847 ***5704.8*** *p27*
Irwin, Henry 6 mos; Quebec, 1847 ***5704.8*** *p27*
Irwin, Henry 17; Quebec, 1862 ***5704.8*** *p151*
Irwin, Isabella; Philadelphia, 1849 ***53.26*** *p39*
*Relative:*Rebecca
Irwin, Isabella; Philadelphia, 1849 ***5704.8*** *p58*
Irwin, Isabella; Philadelphia, 1851 ***5704.8*** *p80*
Irwin, Isabella 2; St. John, N.B., 1851 ***5704.8*** *p77*
Irwin, Jacob 17; Philadelphia, 1865 ***5704.8*** *p164*
Irwin, James; New York, NY, 1816 ***2859.11*** *p33*
Irwin, James 5; St. John, N.B., 1847 ***5704.8*** *p34*
Irwin, James 12; Quebec, 1853 ***5704.8*** *p103*
Irwin, James 19; Quebec, 1862 ***5704.8*** *p151*
Irwin, James 20; Philadelphia, 1865 ***5704.8*** *p164*
Irwin, James 22; Antigua (Antego), 1773 ***1219.7*** *p171*
Irwin, Jane; New York, NY, 1870 ***5704.8*** *p239*
Irwin, Jane; St. John, N.B., 1847 ***5704.8*** *p34*
Irwin, Jane 10; St. John, N.B., 1848 ***5704.8*** *p44*
Irwin, Jarret 10; St. John, N.B., 1851 ***5704.8*** *p77*
Irwin, John; New York, NY, 1839 ***8208.4*** *p97*
Irwin, John; Philadelphia, 1850 ***53.26*** *p39*
Irwin, John; Philadelphia, 1850 ***5704.8*** *p69*
Irwin, John; St. John, N.B., 1847 ***5704.8*** *p34*
Irwin, John; St. John, N.B., 1848 ***5704.8*** *p44*
Irwin, John 8; Quebec, 1847 ***5704.8*** *p27*
Irwin, John 12; St. John, N.B., 1848 ***5704.8*** *p44*
Irwin, John 15; Philadelphia, 1865 ***5704.8*** *p164*
Irwin, John 19; Philadelphia, 1854 ***5704.8*** *p118*
Irwin, Joseph 7; St. John, N.B., 1847 ***5704.8*** *p10*
Irwin, Joseph W.; Colorado, 1906 ***9678.2*** *p25*
Irwin, Letty; Quebec, 1850 ***5704.8*** *p69*
Irwin, Lydia 8; Philadelphia, 1865 ***5704.8*** *p164*
Irwin, Margaret; Quebec, 1847 ***5704.8*** *p27*
Irwin, Margaret; St. John, N.B., 1848 ***5704.8*** *p44*
Irwin, Margaret 2; St. John, N.B., 1847 ***5704.8*** *p34*
Irwin, Margaret 11; Quebec, 1847 ***5704.8*** *p27*
Irwin, Mary 5; Philadelphia, 1865 ***5704.8*** *p164*
Irwin, Mary 6; Quebec, 1847 ***5704.8*** *p27*
Irwin, Mary 6; St. John, N.B., 1848 ***5704.8*** *p44*
Irwin, Mary Ann 8; St. John, N.B., 1851 ***5704.8*** *p77*
Irwin, Mary Ann 13; St. John, N.B., 1847 ***5704.8*** *p34*
Irwin, Matilda 13; St. John, N.B., 1851 ***5704.8*** *p77*
Irwin, Molly; St. John, N.B., 1851 ***5704.8*** *p77*
Irwin, Nancy *SEE* Irwin, William
Irwin, Nancy; Philadelphia, 1849 ***5704.8*** *p58*
Irwin, Nancy Jane; Philadelphia, 1848 ***53.26*** *p39*
Irwin, Nancy Jane; Philadelphia, 1848 ***5704.8*** *p45*
Irwin, Rebecca *SEE* Irwin, Isabella
Irwin, Rebecca; St. John, N.B., 1848 ***5704.8*** *p44*
Irwin, Rebecca 2; Philadelphia, 1849 ***5704.8*** *p58*
Irwin, Richard 13; Quebec, 1847 ***5704.8*** *p27*
Irwin, Robert; America, 1738 ***4971*** *p75*
Irwin, Robert; St. John, N.B., 1848 ***5704.8*** *p44*
Irwin, Robert 2; Quebec, 1851 ***5704.8*** *p73*
Irwin, Robert 8; St. John, N.B., 1848 ***5704.8*** *p44*
Irwin, Samuel; Philadelphia, 1852 ***5704.8*** *p89*
Irwin, Sarah 11; St. John, N.B., 1851 ***5704.8*** *p77*
Irwin, Thomas; Colorado, 1906 ***9678.2*** *p25*
Irwin, Thomas; New York, NY, 1870 ***5704.8*** *p239*
Irwin, Thomas John 21; Iowa, 1885 ***5240.1*** *p21*
Irwin, William; Philadelphia, 1849 ***53.26*** *p39*
*Relative:*Nancy
Irwin, William; Philadelphia, 1849 ***5704.8*** *p58*
Irwin, William; Quebec, 1847 ***5704.8*** *p38*
Irwin, William; Quebec, 1851 ***5704.8*** *p73*
Irwin, William; St. John, N.B., 1847 ***5704.8*** *p10*
Irwin, William; St. John, N.B., 1851 ***5704.8*** *p77*
Irwin, William 4; St. John, N.B., 1851 ***5704.8*** *p77*
Irwin, William 11; St. John, N.B., 1847 ***5704.8*** *p10*
Irwine, Andrew; Quebec, 1851 ***5704.8*** *p74*
Irwine, Charles 21; Quebec, 1856 ***5704.8*** *p130*
Irwine, Edward; Quebec, 1851 ***5704.8*** *p74*
Irwine, George; New York, NY, 1811 ***2859.11*** *p13*
Irwine, Hugh; Quebec, 1851 ***5704.8*** *p74*
Irwine, James; Quebec, 1851 ***5704.8*** *p74*
Irwine, Jane; Quebec, 1851 ***5704.8*** *p74*
Irwine, Martha; Quebec, 1851 ***5704.8*** *p74*
Irwine, Rachel; New York, NY, 1811 ***2859.11*** *p13*
Irwine, Rebecca 23; Quebec, 1857 ***5704.8*** *p135*
Irwine, Sarah Jane; Quebec, 1851 ***5704.8*** *p74*
Irwine, William 18; Philadelphia, 1857 ***5704.8*** *p133*
Isaac, Andrew; America, 1738 ***4971*** *p13*
Isaac, Christ.; Virginia, 1643 ***6219*** *p204*
Isaac, Frank; Illinois, 1900 ***5012.40*** *p79*
Isaac, Henry 14; Louisiana, 1827 ***778.5*** *p281*
Isaac, Jacob; Philadelphia, 1758 ***9973.7*** *p33*
Isaac, Joseph 19; Virginia, 1773 ***1219.7*** *p170*
Isaac, Joseph 20; Maryland, 1729 ***3690.1*** *p121*
Isaac, William 22; Grenada, 1776 ***1219.7*** *p282*
Isaacs, Samuel 21; Baltimore, 1775 ***1219.7*** *p270*
Isaacs, Solomon; New York, NY, 1837 ***8208.4*** *p53*
Isaacson, Jr.; Shreveport, LA, 1878 ***7129*** *p44*
Isacsson, Daniel; Minneapolis, 1870-1877 ***6410.35*** *p55*
Isacsson, Johan Emil; Minneapolis, 1882-1883 ***6410.35*** *p56*
Isberg, Alexander; Boston, 1850-1859 ***6410.32*** *p125*
Isbetto, Margaret; America, 1735-1743 ***4971*** *p8*
Isbister, Agathas; North America, 1808 ***8894.2*** *p57*
Isbister, John; Canada, 1822 ***8893*** *p266*
Isburg, Alexander; Boston, 1850-1859 ***6410.32*** *p125*
Ischler, Apollonia Holl *SEE* Ischler, Ludwig
Ischler, Ludwig; America, 1765 ***2444*** *p170*
*Wife:*Apollonia Holl
Ischler, Ludwig; Pennsylvania, 1765 ***2444*** *p170*
Isele, Georg York; New York, NY, 1838 ***8208.4*** *p70*
Isele, Martin; New York, NY, 1838 ***8208.4*** *p70*
Iseley, John; Ohio, 1837 ***9892.11*** *p22*
Iselin, Alexandrine *SEE* Iselin, Jean-Pierre
Iselin, Catherine *SEE* Iselin, Jean-Pierre
Iselin, Elisabeth *SEE* Iselin, Jean-Pierre
Iselin, Jean-Pierre 40; Halifax, N.S., 1752 ***7074.6*** *p210*
*Wife:*Elisabeth
*Son:*Pierre
*Sister-in-law:*Alexandrine
*Niece:*Catherine
With child
Iselin, Pierre *SEE* Iselin, Jean-Pierre
Isemann, Miss; America, 1854 ***4610.10*** *p151*
Isemann, Carl Heinrich; America, 1872 ***4610.10*** *p106*
Isemann, Ernst Heinrich; America, 1856 ***4610.10*** *p157*
Isemann, Friedrich 17; America, 1881 ***4610.10*** *p159*
Isemann, Philipp; Pennsylvania, 1773 ***2444*** *p152*
Iserhof, . . .; Canada, 1776-1783 ***9786*** *p25*
Isermeyer, Anne Marie Elisabeth; America, 1843 ***4610.10*** *p119*
Isherwood, Wm 16; America, 1703 ***2212*** *p38*
Isinberg, Alex 63; Massachusetts, 1860 ***6410.32*** *p115*
Isinbrey, Peter 27; Pennsylvania, 1753 ***2444*** *p132*
Isingbrid, Peter 27; Pennsylvania, 1753 ***2444*** *p132*
Iske, Friedrich; America, 1870 ***1450.2*** *p72A*
Iskl, Christoph; New York, NY, 1854 ***1450.2*** *p72A*
Isley, Mr.; Quebec, 1815 ***9229.18*** *p77*
Isley, Simon; Iroquois Co., IL, 1892 ***3455.1*** *p11*
Islister, James 19; Philadelphia, 1861 ***5704.8*** *p148*
Ison, Benjamin; West Virginia, 1854 ***9788.3*** *p12*
Ison, Edward; Virginia, 1642 ***6219*** *p188*
Ison, Nicholas; Virginia, 1638 ***6219*** *p119*
Isphording, A.; Cincinnati, 1848 ***8582.1*** *p16*
Israel, A.; Iowa, 1866-1943 ***123.54*** *p23*
Israel, Abe; Arkansas, 1918 ***95.2*** *p59*
Israel, Marks; Shreveport, LA, 1877 ***7129*** *p44*
Issek, Judith; New York, 1749 ***3652*** *p69*
Issler, Catharina 11 mos; New York, NY, 1889 ***7846*** *p40*
Issler, Catharina 27; New York, NY, 1889 ***7846*** *p40*
Issler, Gottlieb 25; New York, NY, 1889 ***7846*** *p40*
Isten, . . .; Canada, 1776-1783 ***9786*** *p25*
Isuard, Mr. 28; New Orleans, 1822 ***778.5*** *p281*
Isum, Math.; Virginia, 1643 ***6219*** *p200*
Iszler, Catharina 11 mos; New York, NY, 1889 ***7846*** *p40*
Iszler, Catharina 27; New York, NY, 1889 ***7846*** *p40*
Iszler, Gottlieb 25; New York, NY, 1889 ***7846*** *p40*
Italo, Antonelli; Arkansas, 1918 ***95.2*** *p59*
Itkin, Hyman; Iowa, 1866-1943 ***123.54*** *p65*
Ittlangsdottir, Bjorg 22; Quebec, 1879 ***2557.1*** *p22*
Itzenhaeuser, Georg; Philadelphia, 1779 ***8137*** *p10*
Itzenhaeuser, Johannes; Philadelphia, 1779 ***8137*** *p10*
Ivell, John; Virginia, 1637 ***6219*** *p113*
Ivers, Anne; New York, NY, 1816 ***2859.11*** *p33*
Ivers, Catherine; New York, NY, 1816 ***2859.11*** *p33*
Ivers, Elizabeth; America, 1743 ***4971*** *p43*
Ivers, John; New York, NY, 1816 ***2859.11*** *p33*
Ivers, Patrick; America, 1849 ***1450.2*** *p72A*
Ivers, R.; New York, NY, 1816 ***2859.11*** *p33*
Ivers, Samuel G.; New York, NY, 1816 ***2859.11*** *p33*
Ivers, William; New York, NY, 1816 ***2859.11*** *p33*
Iversen, Lars Christian; Washington, 1859-1920 ***2872.1*** *p18*
Iverson, Ole 52; Washington, 1916-1919 ***1728.4*** *p255*
Ives, Alexander; New York, NY, 1837 ***8208.4*** *p52*
Ives, John 19; Jamaica, 1723 ***3690.1*** *p121*
Ives, Robert; Virginia, 1643 ***6219*** *p200*
Iveson, Aba.; Virginia, 1636 ***6219*** *p34*
Ivey, John 18; Maryland or Virginia, 1721 ***3690.1*** *p121*
Ivil, Stephen; Port uncertain, 1849 ***4535.10*** *p198*
Ivist, John; Iowa, 1866-1943 ***123.54*** *p23*
Ivory, Andrew; New Brunswick, 1798-1806 ***7603*** *p76*
Ivory, Chr.; New York, NY, 1815 ***2859.11*** *p33*
With wife & child
Ivory, Edward; Annapolis, MD, 1742 ***4971*** *p93*
Ivory, Ellen 16; Massachusetts, 1848 ***5881.1*** *p51*
Ivory, John; New York, NY, 1836 ***8208.4*** *p12*
Ivory, Mary-Ann; Montreal, 1823 ***7603*** *p26*
Iwanowski, . . .; New York, 1831 ***4606*** *p174*
Izard, Sarah; Charleston, SC, 1763 ***1639.20*** *p99*
Izat, John; Charleston, SC, 1800 ***1639.20*** *p99*
Izmanowska, Bloeslaw 2 *SEE* Izmanowska, Stanislawa Dundzik
Izmanowska, Felix 25 *SEE* Izmanowska, Stanislawa Dundzik
Izmanowska, Hendryk 3 *SEE* Izmanowska, Stanislawa Dundzik
Izmanowska, Sabina 9 mos *SEE* Izmanowska, Stanislawa Dundzik
Izmanowska, Stanislaw; New York, 1912 ***9980.29*** *p74*

230 *FOR A COMPLETE EXPLANATION OF ENTRY, SEE "HOW TO READ A CITATION" SECTION*

Izmanowska, Stanislawa Dundzik 27; New York, 1912
9980.29 p74
  *Son:*Hendryk 3
  *Son:*Bloeslaw 2
  *Daughter:*Sabina 9 mos
  *Brother-in-law:*Felix 25
Izmanowski, Boleslaw 2 *SEE* Izmanowski, Stanislawa
Dundzik

Izmanowski, Felix 25 *SEE* Izmanowski, Stanislawa
Dundzik
Izmanowski, Hendryk 3 *SEE* Izmanowski, Stanislawa
Dundzik
Izmanowski, Sabina 9 mos *SEE* Izmanowski, Stanislawa
Dundzik
Izmanowski, Stanislaw; New York, 1912 *9980.29 p74*

Izmanowski, Stanislawa Dundzik 27; New York, 1912
9980.29 p74
  *Son:*Hendryk 3
  *Son:*Boleslaw 2
  *Daughter:*Sabina 9 mos
  *Brother-in-law:*Felix 25
Izzo, Carmino J.; Arkansas, 1918 *95.2 p59*

J

Jaax, Edward 24; Kansas, 1890 *5240.1 p21*
Jaax, Edward 24; Kansas, 1890 *5240.1 p75*
Jaberth, William; South Carolina, 1788 *7119 p203*
Jablonski, Jozef; New York, 1831 *4606 p174*
Jablouski, Frank; Wisconsin, n.d. *9675.6 p51*
Jabrich, Pasquale; Illinois, 1905 *5012.39 p54*
Jabrillat, Mr. 25; New Orleans, 1839 *778.5 p281*
Jabs, Ewald 21; Kansas, 1888 *5240.1 p22*
Jabs, Ewald 21; Kansas, 1888 *5240.1 p71*
Jabs, Herman; Illinois, 1879 *5240.1 p22*
Jacaitec, John A.; Arkansas, 1918 *95.2 p59*
Jacerdote, Simon 42; New Orleans, 1829 *778.5 p281*
Jache, Fred 36; Kansas, 1884 *5240.1 p66*
Jachoire, J. 27; America, 1829 *778.5 p281*
Jacin, . . .; Port uncertain, 1839 *778.5 p281*
Jacin, Mme.; Port uncertain, 1839 *778.5 p281*
Jacin, Mr.; Port uncertain, 1839 *778.5 p281*
Jack, Andy; Philadelphia, 1853 *5704.8 p101*
Jack, Ann 70; Massachusetts, 1849 *5881.1 p51*
Jack, Christoph; Wisconsin, n.d. *9675.6 p51*
Jack, James 20; Quebec, 1855 *5704.8 p125*
Jack, James 21; Philadelphia, 1857 *5704.8 p133*
Jack, Jane 20; Quebec, 1855 *5704.8 p125*
Jack, John; New York, NY, 1811 *2859.11 p14*
Jack, Robert; New York, NY, 1815 *2859.11 p33*
Jack, Samuel 21; Quebec, 1853 *5704.8 p105*
Jack, William 70; Massachusetts, 1849 *5881.1 p52*
Jackeno, Bert; Iowa, 1866-1943 *123.54 p24*
Jackgive, John; Virginia, 1639 *6219 p181*
Jackim, Jacob 15; America, 1705 *2212 p44*
Jackino, Bert; Iowa, 1866-1943 *123.54 p24*
Jackle, Christopher 20; Port uncertain, 1838 *778.5 p281*
Jacklin, Anne 3; Philadelphia, 1866 *5704.8 p211*
Jackman, James; Montreal, 1832-1833 *4535.12 p113*
   With family
Jackmann, Dominic; Wisconsin, n.d. *9675.6 p51*
Jackmann, Lorenz; Wisconsin, n.d. *9675.6 p51*
Jacks, James 19; Maryland, 1774 *1219.7 p204*
Jackson, Mr.; Quebec, 1815 *9229.18 p78*
   With wife
Jackson, A.J.; Minneapolis, 1881-1887 *6410.35 p55*
Jackson, Ann; Quebec, 1847 *5704.8 p38*
Jackson, Ann; Virginia, 1647 *6219 p244*
Jackson, Benjamin 40; Nova Scotia, 1774 *1219.7 p209*
   With wife
   With 3 sons
Jackson, David 2; St. John, N.B., 1867 *5704.8 p167*
Jackson, Mrs. David 25; St. John, N.B., 1867 *5704.8 p167*
Jackson, Edward 15; Georgia, 1775 *1219.7 p276*
Jackson, Edward 22; Philadelphia, 1775 *1219.7 p271*
Jackson, Eliza.; Virginia, 1642 *6219 p195*
Jackson, Eliza 24; Quebec, 1864 *5704.8 p160*
Jackson, Elizabeth 9; Philadelphia, 1851 *5704.8 p71*
Jackson, Elizabeth 44; Philadelphia, 1864 *5704.8 p160*
Jackson, Ellan 7; Philadelphia, 1851 *5704.8 p71*
Jackson, Fanny 22; Quebec, 1864 *5704.8 p160*
Jackson, Frances 17; Virginia, 1699 *2212 p27*
Jackson, George; New York, NY, 1840 *8208.4 p107*
Jackson, Hen.; Virginia, 1636 *6219 p19*
Jackson, Hen.; Virginia, 1642 *6219 p191*
Jackson, Mrs. Hugh 26; St. John, N.B., 1867 *5704.8 p167*
Jackson, Isabella 25; Virginia, 1774 *1219.7 p200*
Jackson, James; Illinois, 1888 *5012.39 p122*
Jackson, James; New York, NY, 1816 *2859.11 p33*
Jackson, James; Virginia, 1645 *6219 p233*

Jackson, James 1; Philadelphia, 1851 *5704.8 p71*
Jackson, James 19; Maryland, 1775 *1219.7 p264*
Jackson, James 20; Quebec, 1858 *5704.8 p138*
Jackson, Jane; Philadelphia, 1851 *5704.8 p71*
Jackson, Jane; Virginia, 1640 *6219 p208*
Jackson, Jane 16; Maryland, 1721 *3690.1 p121*
Jackson, Jane 62; Massachusetts, 1850 *5881.1 p51*
Jackson, John; America, 1703 *2212 p38*
Jackson, John; Arkansas, 1918 *95.2 p59*
Jackson, John; New York, NY, 1811 *2859.11 p14*
Jackson, John; Quebec, 1815 *9229.18 p80*
Jackson, John; Shreveport, LA, 1879 *7129 p44*
Jackson, John; Virginia, 1639 *6219 p182*
Jackson, John; Virginia, 1643 *6219 p23*
Jackson, John 4; St. John, N.B., 1867 *5704.8 p167*
Jackson, John 20; Jamaica, 1738 *3690.1 p122*
Jackson, John 29; Maryland, 1775 *1219.7 p257*
Jackson, John 32; Philadelphia, 1774 *1219.7 p216*
Jackson, John Joseph; New York, NY, 1836 *8208.4 p20*
Jackson, John Thomas 26; Kansas, 1892 *5240.1 p77*
Jackson, Jonah; Virginia, 1640 *6219 p208*
Jackson, Jonathon; Iowa, 1866-1943 *123.54 p24*
Jackson, Joseph; New York, NY, 1834 *8208.4 p27*
Jackson, Joseph 20; Virginia, 1719 *3690.1 p122*
Jackson, Katie; Washington, 1859-1920 *2872.1 p18*
Jackson, Laur.; Virginia, 1638 *6219 p118*
Jackson, Law.; Virginia, 1636 *6219 p78*
Jackson, Louis; Washington, 1859-1920 *2872.1 p18*
Jackson, Luke; New York, NY, 1811 *2859.11 p14*
Jackson, Mamie; Washington, 1859-1920 *2872.1 p18*
Jackson, Martha; Virginia, 1698 *2212 p16*
Jackson, Mary; Philadelphia, 1811 *2859.11 p14*
Jackson, Mary; Virginia, 1639 *6219 p22*
Jackson, Mary; Virginia, 1639 *6219 p151*
Jackson, Mary 16; Jamaica, 1730 *3690.1 p290*
Jackson, Mary 21; St. John, N.B., 1855 *5704.8 p127*
Jackson, Mary Ann 13; Quebec, 1847 *5704.8 p38*
Jackson, Matilda; Philadelphia, 1865 *5704.8 p191*
Jackson, Matt; Washington, 1859-1920 *2872.1 p18*
Jackson, Michael 39; Maryland, 1775 *1219.7 p253*
Jackson, Pard; Washington, 1859-1920 *2872.1 p18*
Jackson, Patrick; Virginia, 1640 *6219 p187*
Jackson, Randall; Virginia, 1637 *6219 p28*
Jackson, Rich.; Virginia, 1635 *6219 p33*
Jackson, Rich.; Virginia, 1635 *6219 p35*
Jackson, Rich.; Virginia, 1643 *6219 p206*
Jackson, Richard; Colorado, 1894 *9678.2 p58*
Jackson, Richard; Virginia, 1641 *6219 p186*
Jackson, Richard 20; Jamaica, 1729 *3690.1 p122*
Jackson, Robert; Virginia, 1637 *6219 p109*
Jackson, Robert 9; Quebec, 1847 *5704.8 p38*
Jackson, Robert 15; America, 1701 *2212 p34*
Jackson, Robert 20; Maryland, 1721 *3690.1 p122*
Jackson, Robert 39; Nova Scotia, 1774 *1219.7 p208*
   With wife
   With 3 children
Jackson, Robert 48; Nova Scotia, 1774 *1219.7 p208*
   With wife
   With 3 children
Jackson, Robt.; Virginia, 1636 *6219 p19*
Jackson, Robt.; Virginia, 1640 *6219 p208*
Jackson, Ruth; Philadelphia, 1869 *5704.8 p236*
Jackson, Samuel; New York, NY, 1839 *8208.4 p99*
Jackson, Samuel 23; Pennsylvania, 1728 *3690.1 p122*
Jackson, Sarah; Quebec, 1853 *5704.8 p105*
Jackson, Sarah 28; Maryland, 1775 *1219.7 p257*
Jackson, Stephen; Maryland, 1775 *1219.7 p265*

Jackson, Susanna 11; Quebec, 1775 *1219.7 p258*
Jackson, Tho.; Virginia, 1635 *6219 p17*
Jackson, Thomas; America, 1737 *4971 p35*
Jackson, Thomas; America, 1845 *1450.2 p73A*
Jackson, Thomas; New York, NY, 1837 *8208.4 p55*
Jackson, Thomas; Philadelphia, 1851 *5704.8 p71*
Jackson, Thomas; West Virginia, 1854-1858 *9788.3 p12*
Jackson, Thomas 18; America, 1706 *2212 p46*
Jackson, Thomas 19; Newfoundland, 1699-1700 *2212 p18*
Jackson, Thomas 21; Maryland, 1774 *1219.7 p230*
Jackson, Thomas 23; Maryland, 1775 *1219.7 p251*
Jackson, Thomas 26; Philadelphia, 1774 *1219.7 p219*
Jackson, Thomas 48; Philadelphia, 1774 *1219.7 p216*
Jackson, Walter; Virginia, 1643 *6219 p200*
Jackson, William; New York, NY, 1832 *8208.4 p78*
Jackson, William; Philadelphia, 1850 *53.26 p40*
Jackson, William; Philadelphia, 1850 *5704.8 p69*
Jackson, William; Quebec, 1851 *5704.8 p75*
Jackson, William; Virginia, 1642 *6219 p198*
Jackson, William; Virginia, 1646 *6219 p236*
Jackson, William; Washington, 1859-1920 *2872.1 p18*
Jackson, William 15; Maryland, 1718 *3690.1 p122*
Jackson, William 16; Georgia, 1775 *1219.7 p277*
Jackson, William 19; Jamaica, 1736 *3690.1 p122*
Jackson, William 22; Jamaica, 1731 *3690.1 p122*
Jackson, William 22; Maryland, 1735 *3690.1 p122*
Jackson, William 24; Maryland, 1775 *1219.7 p266*
Jackson, William 27; America, 1700 *2212 p29*
Jackson, William 30; Virginia, 1774 *1219.7 p241*
Jackson, William B. 29; Kansas, 1874 *5240.1 p55*
Jackson, William John 9 mos; St. John, N.B., 1867 *5704.8 p167*
Jackson, Wm.; Virginia, 1635 *6219 p27*
Jackson, Wm.; Virginia, 1638 *6219 p145*
Jackson, Wm.; Virginia, 1648 *6219 p244*
Jacment, Jacob 15; America, 1831 *778.5 p281*
Jacob, Andrew; Virginia, 1635 *6219 p71*
Jacob, Anne Jane; St. John, N.B., 1850 *5704.8 p65*
Jacob, Carl, Jr.; America, 1850 *8582.3 p33*
Jacob, Elias; California, 1866 *2769.5 p5*
Jacob, Eugene 8; New Orleans, 1822 *778.5 p281*
Jacob, Heinrich; Wisconsin, n.d. *9675.6 p51*
Jacob, Hendrik Drockhard 17; Halifax, N.S., 1752 *7074.6 p207*
Jacob, Henry SEE Jacob, William
Jacob, Henry 23; Kansas, 1871 *5240.1 p51*
Jacob, Jean-Baptiste 22; Quebec, 1753 *7603 p26*
Jacob, John; Pennsylvania, 1746 *2444 p184*
Jacob, John; Pennsylvania, 1746 *2444 p185*
Jacob, John H.; Kansas, 1885 *5240.1 p22*
Jacob, Joseph; America, 1848 *8582.3 p33*
Jacob, Louis, Sr.; Cincinnati, 1869-1887 *8582 p14*
Jacob, Louise 24; St. Louis, 1835 *778.5 p282*
Jacob, Margaret SEE Jacob, William
Jacob, Martha; Virginia, 1642 *6219 p188*
Jacob, Richard; Virginia, 1647 *6219 p244*
Jacob, Samuel 20; Maryland, 1774 *1219.7 p192*
Jacob, Thomas; Quebec, 1781 *7603 p47*
Jacob, William; Virginia, 1637 *6219 p16*
   *Wife:*Margaret
   *Son:*Henry
Jacob, William; Virginia, 1637 *6219 p29*
Jacob, Wm.; Virginia, 1636 *6219 p28*
Jacobe, Frank; Wisconsin, n.d. *9675.6 p51*
Jacobi, . . .; Canada, 1776-1783 *9786 p42*
Jacobi, Frank; Wisconsin, n.d. *9675.6 p52*

Jacobs, . . .; Canada, 1776-1783 ***9786*** *p25*
Jacobs, Charles C.; Cincinnati, 1830-1849 ***8582*** *p14*
Jacobs, Daniel; Cincinnati, 1869-1887 ***8582*** *p15*
Jacobs, Gottlieb; Ohio, 1881-1888 ***9892.11*** *p22*
Jacobs, Jules; Arkansas, 1918 ***95.2*** *p59*
Jacobs, L. H.; Washington, 1859-1920 ***2872.1*** *p18*
Jacobs, M.; Illinois, 1846 ***8582.2*** *p51*
Jacobs, Malhe 51; New York, NY, 1878 ***9253*** *p47*
Jacobs, Moses 22; Philadelphia, 1775 ***1219.7*** *p258*
Jacobs, Peter; Ohio, 1869-1887 ***8582*** *p15*
Jacobs, Thomas 25; Maryland, 1774 ***1219.7*** *p224*
Jacobs, William; Bangor, ME, 1855-1876 ***6410.22*** *p116*
Jacobs, William; Illinois, 1852 ***7857*** *p4*
Jacobs, William; New York, 1882 ***1450.2*** *p17B*
Jacobsen, Christian; New York, 1754 ***3652*** *p79*
Jacobsen, Henry; Colorado, 1903 ***9678.2*** *p58*
Jacobsen, Ingvald; Arkansas, 1918 ***95.2*** *p59*
Jacobsen, Jacob Corneilus; Washington, 1859-1920 ***2872.1*** *p18*
Jacobsen, Johannes; Wisconsin, n.d. ***9675.6*** *p52*
Jacobsen, John; Bangor, ME, 1897 ***6410.22*** *p127*
Jacobsen, Michal; Colorado, 1903 ***9678.2*** *p58*
Jacobsen, Nels; Colorado, 1903 ***9678.2*** *p58*
Jacobsen, O.A.; Arizona, 1898 ***9228.30*** *p10*
Jacobsen, Peter; Colorado, 1905 ***9678.2*** *p58*
Jacobsen, Viggo 36; Kansas, 1884 ***5240.1*** *p67*
Jacobsmeyer, Franz Heinrich; America, 1839 ***4610.10*** *p133*
Jacobson, Andrew Gustav; Iowa, 1866-1943 ***123.54*** *p24*
Jacobson, Carl August; Maine, 1870-1882 ***6410.22*** *p116*
Jacobson, G.P.; Wisconsin, n.d. ***9675.6*** *p52*
Jacobson, Hans; Minneapolis, 1880-1884 ***6410.35*** *p55*
Jacobson, Jacob; Wisconsin, n.d. ***9675.6*** *p52*
Jacobson, Joakim R.; Bangor, ME, 1892 ***6410.22*** *p126*
Jacobson, Joseph 21; Massachusetts, 1860 ***6410.32*** *p119*
Jacobson, Neels; Wisconsin, n.d. ***9675.6*** *p52*
Jacobson, O.; Wisconsin, n.d. ***9675.6*** *p52*
Jacobson, O.A. 33; Arizona, 1898 ***9228.40*** *p3*
Jacobson, Oscar; Arkansas, 1918 ***95.2*** *p59*
Jacobson, Oscar Wilhelm; Iowa, 1866-1943 ***123.54*** *p24*
Jacobson, Peter; Arkansas, 1918 ***95.2*** *p59*
Jacobson, Peter; Washington, 1859-1920 ***2872.1*** *p18*
Jacobson, Sigurd; Arkansas, 1918 ***95.2*** *p59*
Jacobson, Sven; Iowa, 1847 ***2090*** *p611*
Jacobson, Wm.; Virginia, 1642 ***6219*** *p199*
Jacobsson, Hans; Minneapolis, 1880-1884 ***6410.35*** *p55*
Jacoby, Carl 40; Kansas, 1887 ***5240.1*** *p70*
Jacoffet, Annette 30; Port uncertain, 1839 ***778.5*** *p282*
Jacoffet, Francois 40; Port uncertain, 1839 ***778.5*** *p282*
Jacomin, Domenico; Iowa, 1866-1943 ***123.54*** *p24*
Jacot, Catherine *SEE* Jacot, Jacob
Jacot, Catherine *SEE* Jacot, Jonas
Jacot, Daniel C.; New York, 1774 ***7074.6*** *p214*
Jacot, Jacob *SEE* Jacot, Jacob
Jacot, Jacob 30; Halifax, N.S., 1752 ***7074.6*** *p210*
*Wife:*Catherine
*Child:*Jacob
*Child:*Madeleine
Jacot, Jonas 38; Halifax, N.S., 1752 ***7074.6*** *p210*
*Wife:*Catherine
Jacot, Madeleine *SEE* Jacot, Jacob
Jacovetta, Pasquale; Colorado, 1903 ***9678.2*** *p58*
Jacque, Abraham 48; Halifax, N.S., 1752 ***7074.6*** *p210*
*Wife:*Eve
*Daughter:*Jeanne
*Daughter:*Marguerite
*Daughter:*Elisabeth
Jacque, Bernard 22; New Orleans, 1839 ***778.5*** *p282*
Jacque, Elisabeth *SEE* Jacque, Abraham
Jacque, Eve *SEE* Jacque, Abraham
Jacque, Jeanne *SEE* Jacque, Abraham
Jacque, Marguerite *SEE* Jacque, Abraham
Jacque, William 25; Maryland, 1774 ***1219.7*** *p192*
Jacquelin, Francis 21; Maryland, 1774 ***1219.7*** *p211*
Jacquelle, Antoine 17; New Orleans, 1837 ***778.5*** *p282*
Jacques, . . .; Canada, 1776-1783 ***9786*** *p25*
Jacques, Eleanor 28 *SEE* Jacques, Joseph
Jacques, Elisabeth; Halifax, N.S., 1752 ***7074.6*** *p216*
Jacques, Henry; America, 1736 ***4971*** *p45*
Jacques, Jean 24; New Orleans, 1836 ***778.5*** *p282*
Jacques, Jean Bapt. 28; New Orleans, 1838 ***778.5*** *p282*
Jacques, Joseph 28; North America, 1774 ***1219.7*** *p200*
*Wife:*Eleanor 28
Jacques, Mas. 32; New Orleans, 1836 ***778.5*** *p282*
Jacquesnau, Dominique 30; New Orleans, 1831 ***778.5*** *p282*
Jacquet, Jean 20; Louisiana, 1820 ***778.5*** *p282*
Jacquin, Christophe *SEE* Jacquin, Jacques-Frederic
Jacquin, Frederic *SEE* Jacquin, Jacques-Frederic
Jacquin, Jacques-Frederic 45; Halifax, N.S., 1752 ***7074.6*** *p210*
*Wife:*Marguerite
*Child:*Jean-George
*Child:*Frederic
*Child:*Christophe
*Child:*Marguerite
Jacquin, Jean-George *SEE* Jacquin, Jacques-Frederic
Jacquin, Marguerite *SEE* Jacquin, Jacques-Frederic
Jacquin, Marguerite *SEE* Jacquin, Jacques-Frederic
Jadaka, August 26; Kansas, 1884 ***5240.1*** *p65*
Jadaka, Christopher 56; Kansas, 1884 ***5240.1*** *p65*
Jadaka, Frederick 30; Kansas, 1884 ***5240.1*** *p65*
Jaeckell, . . .; Canada, 1776-1783 ***9786*** *p25*
Jaeckle, Christoph; Pennsylvania, 1749 ***2444*** *p171*
Jaeger, . . .; Canada, 1776-1783 ***9786*** *p25*
Jaeger, Bernard 25; New York, NY, 1889 ***7846*** *p40*
Jaeger, Catharina 6 mos; New York, NY, 1889 ***7846*** *p40*
Jaeger, Christina 25; New York, NY, 1889 ***7846*** *p40*
Jaeger, Edward; Wisconsin, n.d. ***9675.6*** *p52*
Jaeger, Friedrick; Wisconsin, n.d. ***9675.6*** *p52*
Jaeger, Georg; Kentucky, 1771 ***8582.3*** *p93*
Jaeger, Georg; Kentucky, 1771 ***8582.3*** *p96*
Jaeger, Georg Heinrich; New Orleans, 1843 ***8582*** *p15*
Jaeger, Herman; Wisconsin, n.d. ***9675.6*** *p52*
Jaeger, Johann Christoph; America, 1844 ***8582.3*** *p33*
Jaeger, Johannes; Philadelphia, 1779 ***8137*** *p10*
Jaeger, Peter; New York, NY, 1836 ***8208.4*** *p18*
Jaeger, Ralph 22; Kansas, 1894 ***5240.1*** *p22*
Jaeger, Ralph 22; Kansas, 1894 ***5240.1*** *p79*
Jaeger, Simon; Kentucky, 1840 ***8582.3*** *p100*
Jaegers, Albert; America, 1868-1925 ***8125.8*** *p437*
Jaehnert, Herman; Wisconsin, n.d. ***9675.6*** *p52*
Jaencke, Andrew; New York, 1750 ***3652*** *p74*
Jaequinet, John B.; Wisconsin, n.d. ***9675.6*** *p52*
Jaes, John; New York, NY, 1838 ***8208.4*** *p75*
Jaeschke, Juliana; Savannah, GA, 1736 ***3652*** *p51*
Jaffrey, Edward; Charleston, SC, 1795 ***1639.20*** *p99*
Jag, David; Savannah, GA, 1736 ***3652*** *p51*
Jag, John; New York, 1754 ***3652*** *p80*
Jagemann, John W.; New York, NY, 1836 ***8208.4*** *p13*
Jager Family ; New York, 1765 ***8125.8*** *p436*
Jager, Bernard 25; New York, NY, 1889 ***7846*** *p40*
Jager, Catharina 6 mos; New York, NY, 1889 ***7846*** *p40*
Jager, Christina 25; New York, NY, 1889 ***7846*** *p40*
Jager, George Christian Frederick; America, 1847 ***1450.2*** *p73A*
Jager, Harman; New York, NY, 1839 ***8208.4*** *p101*
Jager, Johann Carl Heinrich *SEE* Jager, Johanne F. Windmeyer Schilling
Jager, Johanne F. Windmeyer Schilling; America, 1846 ***4610.10*** *p115*
*Husband:*Johann Carl Heinrich
Jager, Phillip; New York, NY, 1838 ***8208.4*** *p89*
Jager, Simon Heinrich; America, 1841 ***4610.10*** *p114*
Jager, Valentin; Canada, 1783 ***9786*** *p38A*
Jagiello, . . .; New York, 1831 ***4606*** *p174*
Jagneaux, John 25; Port uncertain, 1836 ***778.5*** *p282*
Jago, Catharine 13; Massachusetts, 1849 ***5881.1*** *p51*
Jago, Catharine 13; Massachusetts, 1850 ***5881.1*** *p51*
Jago, Catharine 35; Massachusetts, 1850 ***5881.1*** *p51*
Jago, Hester 50; Massachusetts, 1849 ***5881.1*** *p51*
Jago, John 60; Massachusetts, 1849 ***5881.1*** *p51*
Jago, Jonathan 12; Massachusetts, 1850 ***5881.1*** *p51*
Jago, Patrick 27; Massachusetts, 1849 ***5881.1*** *p51*
Jaguszewski, Michal; New York, 1835 ***4606*** *p179*
Jahan, Louis 22; America, 1838 ***778.5*** *p282*
Jahi, Mlle. 18; New Orleans, 1839 ***778.5*** *p282*
Jahn, . . .; Canada, 1776-1783 ***9786*** *p25*
Jahn, Ferdinand; Illinois, 1884 ***2896.5*** *p19*
Jahn, Gottfried; Wisconsin, n.d. ***9675.6*** *p52*
Jahn, Mathias; Wisconsin, n.d. ***9675.6*** *p52*
Jahn, William; Wisconsin, n.d. ***9675.6*** *p52*
Jahnke, Albert; New York, NY, 1907 ***3455.3*** *p107*
Jahnke, Herman; Wisconsin, n.d. ***9675.6*** *p52*
Jahns, Martin; Saratoga, NY, 1777 ***8137*** *p10*
Jahraus, Jacob; Illinois, 1867 ***2896.5*** *p19*
Jaiger, Peter; New York, NY, 1836 ***8208.4*** *p18*
Jaihler, Isaac 28; America, 1839 ***778.5*** *p282*
Jaillet, Andre 26; Halifax, N.S., 1752 ***7074.6*** *p213*
*Wife:*Marguerite
*Daughter:*Suzanne
*Daughter:*Marie
With child
Jaillet, Marguerite *SEE* Jaillet, Andre
Jaillet, Marie *SEE* Jaillet, Andre
Jaillet, Suzanne *SEE* Jaillet, Andre
Jaiser, John; Virginia, 1855 ***4626.16*** *p15*
Jakaitis, Henry Michael; Arkansas, 1918 ***95.2*** *p59*
Jakeman, Richd 22; America, 1703 ***2212*** *p38*
Jakle, Johan Friedrich; New York, NY, 1836 ***8208.4*** *p18*
Jakob, Andreas; Kentucky, 1843 ***8582.3*** *p100*
Jakob, Johs. 27; America, 1853 ***9162.8*** *p36*
Jakob, Jost 46; Kansas, 1882 ***5240.1*** *p64*
Jakobs, Mr.; Cincinnati, 1863 ***8582.1*** *p5*
Jakobson, A.B.; Iowa, 1866-1943 ***123.54*** *p24*
Jakubowicz, . . .; New York, 1831 ***4606*** *p174*
Jakubowski, August; Mexico, 1831-1900 ***4606*** *p174*
Jakubowski, August; New York, 1831 ***4606*** *p174*
Jakubowski, Franciszek; New York, 1831 ***4606*** *p174*
Jalbert, Joseph Hildebert; Wisconsin, n.d. ***9675.6*** *p52*
Jally, Hugh; Ohio, 1843 ***8365.26*** *p12*
Jambon, Mr. 25; Port uncertain, 1839 ***778.5*** *p282*
Jameison, Alexander; New Orleans, 1849 ***5704.8*** *p58*
Jameison, James 41; Kansas, 1890 ***5240.1*** *p22*
Jamellier, . . .; Port uncertain, 1839 ***778.5*** *p283*
James, Mme. 22; America, 1839 ***778.5*** *p283*
James, Abraham 17; America, 1728 ***3690.1*** *p122*
James, Alfred; America, 1882 ***1450.2*** *p73A*
James, Alfred B. 26; Kansas, 1888 ***5240.1*** *p72*
James, Ann 21; Maryland, 1774 ***1219.7*** *p208*
James, Anthony; Virginia, 1646 ***6219*** *p242*
James, Benjamin Hammond; Nevada, 1882 ***2764.35*** *p36*
James, Charles T. 36; Kansas, 1888 ***5240.1*** *p72*
James, Daniel 22; Maryland, 1775 ***1219.7*** *p247*
James, David; Illinois, 1847 ***7857*** *p4*
James, Elizabeth; New York, NY, 1816 ***2859.11*** *p33*
James, Elizh; New York, NY, 1816 ***2859.11*** *p33*
James, Evan 22; Maryland, 1775 ***1219.7*** *p250*
James, George 18; Philadelphia, 1774 ***1219.7*** *p228*
James, George 30; America, 1839 ***778.5*** *p283*
James, Guillaume 21; Montreal, 1703 ***7603*** *p29*
James, Henrietta 18; Maryland, 1775 ***1219.7*** *p267*
James, Henry; Colorado, 1890 ***9678.2*** *p58*
James, Henry 20; Jamaica, 1733 ***3690.1*** *p122*
James, Henry 23; Jamaica, 1730 ***3690.1*** *p290*
James, Hugh; Virginia, 1629 ***6219*** *p8*
James, Isaac 20; Jamaica, 1725 ***3690.1*** *p123*
James, Jane; New York, NY, 1816 ***2859.11*** *p33*
James, John; Jamaica, 1754 ***1219.7*** *p31*
James, John; Jamaica, 1754 ***3690.1*** *p123*
James, John; New York, NY, 1816 ***2859.11*** *p33*
James, John; Virginia, 1639 ***6219*** *p155*
James, John 18; Virginia, 1733 ***3690.1*** *p123*
James, John 36; Barbados, 1774 ***1219.7*** *p202*
James, Jon.; Virginia, 1635 ***6219*** *p73*
James, Jon.; Virginia, 1637 ***6219*** *p113*
James, Joseph; Iowa, 1866-1943 ***123.54*** *p24*
James, Joseph; New York, NY, 1816 ***2859.11*** *p33*
James, Lewis; Virginia, 1636 ***6219*** *p26*
James, Margaret; Philadelphia, 1850 ***53.26*** *p40*
James, Margaret; Philadelphia, 1850 ***5704.8*** *p65*
James, Mary; New York, NY, 1816 ***2859.11*** *p34*
James, Mary; Virginia, 1637 ***6219*** *p109*
James, Michael; Virginia, 1644 ***6219*** *p231*
James, Peter Dimitri; Arkansas, 1918 ***95.2*** *p59*
James, Richard; Virginia, 1637 ***6219*** *p81*
James, Richard; Virginia, 1640 ***6219*** *p160*
James, Robert; New York, NY, 1816 ***2859.11*** *p34*
James, Robert; Virginia, 1636 ***6219*** *p23*
James, Robert; Virginia, 1637 ***6219*** *p24*
James, Robert; Virginia, 1642 ***6219*** *p15*
James, Robert; Virginia, 1642 ***6219*** *p190*
James, Samll.; Virginia, 1643 ***6219*** *p204*
James, Samuel; Washington, 1859-1920 ***2872.1*** *p18*
James, Samuel 20; Maryland, 1724 ***3690.1*** *p123*
James, Sarah; Virginia, 1636 ***6219*** *p16*
James, Thomas; New York, NY, 1816 ***2859.11*** *p34*
James, Thomas; Virginia, 1639 ***6219*** *p155*
James, William; Iowa, 1866-1943 ***123.54*** *p24*
James, William; New York, NY, 1816 ***2859.11*** *p34*
James, William 19; America, 1728 ***3690.1*** *p123*
James, William Thomas; Colorado, 1886 ***9678.2*** *p58*
James, Wm.; Virginia, 1636 ***6219*** *p34*
James, Wm.; Virginia, 1642 ***6219*** *p189*
Jamesison, John; St. John, N.B., 1847 ***5704.8*** *p21*
Jameson, Andrew; New York, NY, 1815 ***2859.11*** *p34*
Jameson, Ann Jane; New York, NY, 1865 ***5704.8*** *p203*
Jameson, B.; New York, NY, 1816 ***2859.11*** *p34*
Jameson, Eliza; New York, NY, 1865 ***5704.8*** *p203*
Jameson, Grace; New York, NY, 1865 ***5704.8*** *p203*
Jameson, Hugh; New York, NY, 1815 ***2859.11*** *p34*
Jameson, J.; New York, NY, 1816 ***2859.11*** *p34*
With brother
Jameson, James; America, 1698 ***2212*** *p10*
Jameson, James 21; Virginia, 1773 ***1219.7*** *p169*
Jameson, Jean Ewenson; Newfoundland, 1842 ***8893*** *p264*
Jameson, John; New York, NY, 1811 ***2859.11*** *p14*
Jameson, John 17; Philadelphia, 1856 ***5704.8*** *p129*
Jameson, John 23; Philadelphia, 1853 ***5704.8*** *p108*
Jameson, John 23; Virginia, 1775 ***1219.7*** *p247*
Jameson, John James 18; Quebec, 1856 ***5704.8*** *p130*
Jameson, Maria; New York, NY, 1865 ***5704.8*** *p203*
Jameson, Mary; New York, NY, 1864 ***5704.8*** *p175*
Jameson, Philip 23; Maryland, 1730 ***3690.1*** *p123*
Jameson, Robert James 11; New York, NY, 1865 ***5704.8*** *p203*
Jameson, Samuel William 9; New York, NY, 1865 ***5704.8*** *p203*
Jameson, Sarah 20; Philadelphia, 1856 ***5704.8*** *p129*

Jamesone, Philip 23; Maryland, 1730 *3690.1 p123*
Jamieson, David; Carolina, 1684 *1639.20 p99*
Jamieson, Edward; Quebec, 1852 *5704.8 p98*
Jamieson, Eliza; Philadelphia, 1864 *5704.8 p177*
Jamieson, James; Brunswick, NC, 1775 *1639.20 p99*
  With wife & 4 children
Jamieson, James 41; Kansas, 1890 *5240.1 p74*
Jamieson, Robert; Quebec, 1852 *5704.8 p98*
Jamieson, Thomas 36; Kansas, 1879 *5240.1 p61*
Jamieson, William; Philadelphia, 1850 *5704.8 p65*
Jamin, John; Wisconsin, n.d. *9675.6 p52*
Jamison, Agnes; New York, NY, 1811 *2859.11 p14*
Jamison, Allen 4; Quebec, 1848 *5704.8 p41*
Jamison, Eliza; New York, NY, 1866 *5704.8 p213*
Jamison, Elizabeth; Quebec, 1848 *5704.8 p41*
Jamison, Elizabeth 7; Quebec, 1848 *5704.8 p41*
Jamison, Jane 19; Philadelphia, 1834 *53.26 p40*
Jamison, Margaret 2; Quebec, 1848 *5704.8 p41*
Jamison, Margaret 12; St. John, N.B., 1847 *5704.8 p19*
Jamison, Mary Ann *SEE* Jamison, Sarah
Jamison, Mary Ann; Philadelphia, 1847 *5704.8 p14*
Jamison, Robert; Quebec, 1848 *5704.8 p41*
Jamison, Samuel; New York, NY, 1811 *2859.11 p14*
Jamison, Sarah; Philadelphia, 1847 *53.26 p40*
  *Relative:*Mary Ann
Jamison, Sarah; Philadelphia, 1847 *5704.8 p14*
Jamison, William; Philadelphia, 1850 *53.26 p40*
Jan, . . .; Milwaukee, 1875 *4719.30 p258*
Jandullet, Louis 21; Port uncertain, 1838 *778.5 p283*
Janes, Eliza 9 mos; St. John, N.B., 1848 *5704.8 p44*
Janes, Isabella; St. John, N.B., 1848 *5704.8 p44*
Janes, Mary 5; St. John, N.B., 1848 *5704.8 p44*
Janes, Roger; New York, NY, 1816 *2859.11 p34*
Janes, William; New York, NY, 1816 *2859.11 p34*
Janes, William; St. John, N.B., 1848 *5704.8 p44*
Janeway, James; Buffalo, NY, 1832 *9892.11 p22*
Janeway, James; Ohio, 1838 *9892.11 p22*
Janga, Neal; New York, NY, 1811 *2859.11 p14*
Jangolaski, John; Arkansas, 1918 *95.2 p59*
Jangula, Lorenz; Alberta, n.d. *5262 p58*
Janhiainen, Heikki; Washington, 1859-1920 *2872.1 p18*
Janicki, Zdislaw Frank; Arkansas, 1918 *95.2 p59*
Janin, Mr. 45; Louisiana, 1820 *778.5 p283*
Janke, Gustave John; Wisconsin, n.d. *9675.6 p52*
Janke, Herman; Wisconsin, n.d. *9675.6 p52*
Jankiai, Herman; Washington, 1859-1920 *2872.1 p18*
Jankus, Carl 30; Kansas, 1887 *5240.1 p69*
Jankus, John; Wisconsin, n.d. *9675.6 p52*
Jannaway, Susanna; Virginia, 1639 *6219 p151*
Jannin, Claude; Port uncertain, 1839 *778.5 p283*
Jannkowski, Antonia 55; New York, NY, 1862 *9831.18 p16*
Jannkowski, Jacob 50; New York, NY, 1862 *9831.18 p16*
Jannkowski, Michalina 14; New York, NY, 1862 *9831.18 p16*
Jannkowski, Vincenz 19; New York, NY, 1862 *9831.18 p16*
Janoch, Frank 27; Harris Co., TX, 1899 *6254 p5*
Janor, John; Arkansas, 1918 *95.2 p59*
Janowski, . . .; New York, 1831 *4606 p174*
Janse, Jesus Iqures 29; California, 1872 *2769.5 p5*
Jansen, . . .; Canada, 1776-1783 *9786 p42*
Jansen, Bernard; Kentucky, 1843 *8582.3 p100*
Jansen, Charles; Milwaukee, 1875 *4719.30 p258*
Jansen, Dirk J.; Iroquois Co., IL, 1894 *3455.1 p11*
Jansen, Friedrich Wilhelm; Illinois, 1835 *8125.8 p437*
Jansen, Heinrich K.; America, 1866-1930 *8125.8 p437*
Jansen, Hi.; Illinois, 1894 *5012.39 p53*
Jansen, Hie; Illinois, 1896 *5012.40 p54*
Jansen, Johann; New Netherland, 1630-1646 *8582.2 p51*
Jansen, Klas; Germantown, PA, 1684 *2467.7 p5*
Jansen, Martin; Bangor, ME, 1894 *6410.22 p127*
Jansen, Martin; Cincinnati, 1869-1887 *8582 p15*
Jansen, Oscar; Wisconsin, n.d. *9675.6 p52*
Jansen, Paulus; New Netherland, 1630-1646 *8582.2 p51*
Jansen, Peter; New York, NY, 1836 *8208.4 p19*
Jansen, Peter; St. Louis, 1833 *8582.1 p55*
Jansen, Peter; Washington, 1859-1920 *2872.1 p18*
Janski, Antoni; New York, 1831 *4606 p174*
Janson, Adam 30; America, 1838 *778.5 p283*
Janson, Andrew; Bangor, ME, 1893 *6410.22 p126*
Janson, Eliza 26; America, 1838 *778.5 p283*
Janson, Henry 24; America, 1838 *778.5 p283*
Janson, John 50; Kansas, 1890 *5240.1 p75*
Janson, Nels; Illinois, 1874 *7857 p4*
Janson, Peter; Washington, 1859-1920 *2872.1 p18*
Janson, Valentin 28; America, 1838 *778.5 p283*
Janssen, Frederick W.; Wisconsin, n.d. *9675.6 p52*
Janssen, Johann; New York, NY, 1924 *3455.4 p53*
Janssen, Johann Juddeke; New York, NY, 1910 *3455.3 p17*

Janssen, Lobbe T.; Wisconsin, n.d. *9675.6 p52*
Janssen, Remmer; Iroquois Co., IL, 1892 *3455.1 p11*
Janssen, Siebelt; Iroquois Co., IL, 1896 *3455.1 p11*
Jansson, Anders; Minneapolis, 1861-1877 *6410.35 p55*
Jansson, Anders Peter; Minneapolis, 1880-1886 *6410.35 p60*
Jansson, Gustaf; Minneapolis, 1869-1877 *6410.35 p57*
Jansson, Maria Josephina; America, 1851 *6410.32 p126*
Jansson, Sven August; Minneapolis, 1869-1883 *6410.35 p58*
Janty, Louis; Arkansas, 1918 *95.2 p59*
Jantzen, Nels; Washington, 1859-1920 *2872.1 p18*
Janucy, Vincent; Iowa, 1866-1943 *123.54 p24*
Janulos, Emanuel; Arkansas, 1918 *95.2 p59*
Januszkiewicz, Piotr 23; New York, 1912 *9980.29 p68*
Janvier, Mr. 40; New Orleans, 1839 *778.5 p283*
Janzen, Anna; America, 1880 *5240.1 p22*
Janzen, Herman; Kansas, 1873 *5240.1 p22*
Janzen, Jacob; Kansas, 1885 *5240.1 p22*
Janzen, John; America, 1800-1885 *5240.1 p22*
Janzen, John 70; Kansas, 1885 *5240.1 p67*
Janzen, Maria; Kansas, 1885 *5240.1 p22*
Jaqbosky, Will; Arkansas, 1918 *95.2 p59*
Jaqubusky, Will; Arkansas, 1918 *95.2 p59*
Jaquemet, Louis 48; America, 1838 *778.5 p283*
Jaques, John 26; Nova Scotia, 1774 *1219.7 p209*
  With wife
  With 3 children
Jardel, Mr. 27; America, 1838 *778.5 p283*
Jardette, P. E.; New Orleans, 1839 *778.5 p283*
Jardine, Sarah; Philadelphia, 1852 *5704.8 p89*
Jardine, Walter; Iowa, 1866-1943 *123.54 p24*
Jardine, William 22; Jamaica, 1731 *3690.1 p130*
Jarecki, Felix 25; New York, 1912 *9980.29 p74*
Jarecki, Vincent; Wisconsin, n.d. *9675.6 p52*
Jarenne, J. 32; New Orleans, 1836 *778.5 p485*
Jaret, Frederick; California, 1864 *3840.2 p14*
Jaritz, Lt.; Quebec, 1778 *9786 p168*
Jaritz, Lt.; Quebec, 1778 *9786 p267*
Jaritz, George; Indiana, 1848 *9117 p17*
Jaritz, George; Indiana, 1848 *9117 p19*
Jarl, Jan; New York, NY, 1858 *2896.5 p19*
Jarlan, Jean Simon 39; New Orleans, 1838 *778.5 p283*
Jarlant, Miss; New Orleans, 1839 *778.5 p284*
Jarlant, F.; New Orleans, 1839 *778.5 p284*
Jarmez, Craten 39; Port uncertain, 1838 *778.5 p284*
Jarnicke, Henry William Frederick; America, 1852 *1450.2 p73A*
Jarosh, . . .; Canada, 1776-1783 *9786 p42*
Jarosz, Helena 24; New York, 1912 *9980.29 p62*
Jaroszewski, January; Mexico, 1831-1900 *4606 p174*
Jaroszewski, January; New York, 1831 *4606 p174*
Jaroszynski, Bazyli; New York, 1834 *4606 p178*
Jarras, Mr. 28; Louisiana, 1820 *778.5 p284*
Jarratt, William 40; Nova Scotia, 1774 *1219.7 p209*
Jarre, John; Virginia, 1642 *6219 p188*
Jarreau, Mr. 20; New Orleans, 1827 *778.5 p284*
Jarrett, Elizabeth 16; Maryland, 1775 *1219.7 p249*
Jarrillot, Nicholas; Colorado, 1904 *9678.2 p58*
Jarrod, Mary 28; Maryland, 1775 *1219.7 p267*
Jartoux, Joseph 34; America, 1838 *778.5 p284*
Jartrux, Joseph 34; America, 1838 *778.5 p284*
Jaruszewska, Eduard 4 *SEE* Jaruszewska, Josef
Jaruszewska, Josef 25; New York, 1912 *9980.29 p72*
  *Wife:*Waleria 21
  *Son:*Eduard 4
Jaruszewska, Waleria 21 *SEE* Jaruszewska, Josef
Jaruszewski, Eduard 4 *SEE* Jaruszewski, Josef
Jaruszewski, Josef 25; New York, 1912 *9980.29 p72*
  *Wife:*Waleria 21
  *Son:*Eduard 4
Jaruszewski, Waleria 21 *SEE* Jaruszewski, Josef
Jarvi, William; Washington, 1859-1920 *2872.1 p18*
Jarvis, Abraham 25; Jamaica, 1730 *3690.1 p123*
Jarvis, Francis; Virginia, 1636 *6219 p80*
Jarvis, George 21; Virginia, 1775 *1219.7 p261*
Jarvis, Henry 17; West Indies, 1722 *3690.1 p123*
Jarvis, John; Quebec, 1849 *5704.8 p77*
Jarvis, Robert 19; Jamaica, 1729 *3690.1 p123*
Jarvis, Stephen M. 21; Kansas, 1874 *5240.1 p56*
Jarvis, Thomas 21; Jamaica, 1730 *3690.1 p123*
Jarvis, William; Indiana, 1850 *9117 p20*
Jarvis, William 19; Jamaica, 1736 *3690.1 p123*
Jarvnick, Frank; Wisconsin, n.d. *9675.6 p52*
Jarzombek, Adam; Wisconsin, n.d. *9675.6 p52*
Jarzombkowska, Jozefa 27 *SEE* Jarzombkowska, Julianna
Jarzombkowska, Julianna 19; New York, 1912 *9980.29 p61*
  *Sister:*Jozefa 27
Jasinski, Jan; New York, 1831 *4606 p174*
Jasinski, Kazimierz; New York, 1831 *4606 p174*
Jaskiewicz, Anna 18; New York, 1912 *9980.29 p50*

Jasko, John; Colorado, 1899 *9678.2 p58*
Jasmin, Mrs. 63; New Orleans, 1830 *778.5 p284*
Jasper, . . .; Canada, 1776-1783 *9786 p42*
Jasper, John; Virginia, 1634 *6219 p186*
Jaspers, Edwd 21; Maryland, 1702 *2212 p36*
Jasperson, Herman; Washington, 1859-1920 *2872.1 p18*
Jass, Charles; America, 1866 *1450.2 p73A*
Jastrzembska, Marcin; New York, 1912 *9980.29 p67*
Jastrzembska, Maria 2 *SEE* Jastrzembska, Wladislawa
Jastrzembska, Wladislawa 24; New York, 1912 *9980.29 p67*
  *Daughter:*Maria 2
Jastrzembski, Marcin; New York, 1912 *9980.29 p67*
Jastrzembski, Maria 2 *SEE* Jastrzembski, Wladislawa
Jastrzembski, Wladislawa 24; New York, 1912 *9980.29 p67*
  *Daughter:*Maria 2
Jaszewski, . . .; New York, 1831 *4606 p174*
Jatczak, Stanislawa 26; New York, 1912 *9980.29 p52*
Jatkowitz, Meyer 24; New York, NY, 1878 *9253 p47*
Jatous, P. 22; New Orleans, 1827 *778.5 p284*
Jatscheck, . . .; Canada, 1776-1783 *9786 p25*
Jaubert, J. F. 18; America, 1832 *778.5 p284*
Jauchzler, Jean; Cincinnati, 1848 *8582.1 p53*
Jaud, Andreas; Wisconsin, n.d. *9675.6 p52*
Jaudry, Jean Christoph 44; Halifax, N.S., 1752 *7074.6 p207*
  With family of 7
Jaukaitis, Tony; Wisconsin, n.d. *9675.6 p52*
Jauko, Sam; Iowa, 1866-1943 *123.54 p24*
Jaume, Honore 22; Louisiana, 1820 *778.5 p284*
Jaunet, Francois 38; New Orleans, 1836 *778.5 p284*
Jaunne, Pierre 32; Halifax, N.S., 1752 *7074.6 p207*
  With family of 6
Jaunsaph, Dan; Wisconsin, n.d. *9675.6 p52*
Jauson, Mr. 18; America, 1839 *778.5 p284*
Jausse, Mr. 22; New Orleans, 1822 *778.5 p284*
Jausse, Mrs. 20; New Orleans, 1822 *778.5 p284*
Javes, William 41; Baltimore, 1775 *1219.7 p270*
Javin, Augustus F.; New York, NY, 1839 *8208.4 p103*
Jaworski, Mikolay; New York, 1831 *4606 p174*
Jaworski, Tomasz; New York, 1831 *4606 p174*
Jax, Eliz.; Virginia, 1637 *6219 p8*
Jay, Patrick; Wisconsin, n.d. *9675.6 p52*
Jayes, Robt; America, 1699 *2212 p29*
Jean, . . .; Canada, 1776-1783 *9786 p25*
Jean, Mr. 18; New Orleans, 1837 *778.5 p285*
Jean, Baptiste Ursule 17; America, 1837 *778.5 p285*
Jean, Marguerite 18; America, 1837 *778.5 p285*
Jean Baptiste, Ursule 17; America, 1837 *778.5 p285*
Jean Batiste, R. 28; America, 1835 *778.5 p285*
Jean-Pierre, Cobardy 28; America, 1827 *778.5 p285*
Jeanbas, David 18; Halifax, N.S., 1752 *7074.6 p210*
  *Brother:*Jean-Jacques 25
  *Sister:*Judith
Jeanbas, Jean-Jacques 25 *SEE* Jeanbas, David
Jeanbas, Judith *SEE* Jeanbas, David
Jeangirard, Francois 21; New Orleans, 1835 *778.5 p285*
Jeankunas, Frank; Wisconsin, n.d. *9675.6 p52*
Jeanmarie, Joseph 27; Port uncertain, 1836 *778.5 p285*
Jeanmarie, Louis 27; Port uncertain, 1836 *778.5 p285*
Jeanmmon, Jean 23; Louisiana, 1820 *778.5 p285*
Jeanperin, . . .; Halifax, N.S., 1752 *7074.6 p230*
Jeanperine, . . .; Halifax, N.S., 1752 *7074.6 p230*
Jeanperine, Christophe; Halifax, N.S., 1752 *7074.6 p228*
Jeanperine, George; Halifax, N.S., 1752 *7074.6 p228*
Jeanperrain, Jean Urban 32; Halifax, N.S., 1752 *7074.6 p207*
Jeanperrin, Jean-Urbain 32; Halifax, N.S., 1752 *7074.6 p210*
Jeans, John; Milwaukee, 1875 *4719.30 p258*
Jeans, Mrs. John; Milwaukee, 1875 *4719.30 p258*
Jeans, Robert; St. John, N.B., 1852 *5704.8 p95*
Jeanson, Guillaume; Nova Scotia, 1715 *7603 p37*
Jeantien, John 32; America, 1830 *778.5 p285*
Jeanty, Mr. 45; New Orleans, 1823 *778.5 p285*
Jeanvoine, Mr. 40; New Orleans, 1826 *778.5 p285*
Jeaudry, Anne-Catherine *SEE* Jeaudry, Jean-Christophe
Jeaudry, Anne-Marie *SEE* Jeaudry, Jean
Jeaudry, Catherine *SEE* Jeaudry, Jean
Jeaudry, Catherine *SEE* Jeaudry, Jean-Christophe
Jeaudry, Frederic *SEE* Jeaudry, Jean-Christophe
Jeaudry, Jacques 27 *SEE* Jeaudry, Jean
Jeaudry, Jean 54; Halifax, N.S., 1752 *7074.6 p210*
  *Child:*Joseph
  *Child:*Catherine
  *Child:*Judith
  *Child:*Anne-Marie
  *Son:*Jacques 27
Jeaudry, Jean-Christophe 44; Halifax, N.S., 1752 *7074.6 p210*
  *Wife:*Anne-Catherine
  *Child:*Jean-George

*Child:*Catherine
*Child:*Pierre
*Child:*Jeanne
*Child:*Frederic
*Child:*Jean-Urbain
Jeaudry, Jean-George *SEE* Jeaudry, Jean-Christophe
Jeaudry, Jean-George 24; Halifax, N.S., 1752 ***7074.6*** *p211*
Jeaudry, Jean-Urbain *SEE* Jeaudry, Jean-Christophe
Jeaudry, Jeanne *SEE* Jeaudry, Jean-Christophe
Jeaudry, Joseph *SEE* Jeaudry, Jean
Jeaudry, Judith *SEE* Jeaudry, Jean
Jeaudry, Marc-Elie 26; Halifax, N.S., 1752 ***7074.6*** *p210*
Jeaudry, Pierre *SEE* Jeaudry, Jean-Christophe
Jeaunne, Charlotte *SEE* Jeaunne, Pierre
Jeaunne, Frederic *SEE* Jeaunne, Pierre
Jeaunne, Jacques *SEE* Jeaunne, Pierre
Jeaunne, Jean-George *SEE* Jeaunne, Pierre
Jeaunne, Pierre *SEE* Jeaunne, Pierre
Jeaunne, Pierre 32; Halifax, N.S., 1752 ***7074.6*** *p211*
*Wife:*Charlotte
*Son:*Frederic
*Son:*Pierre
*Son:*Jacques
*Son:*Samuel
*Son:*Jean-George
Jeaunne, Samuel *SEE* Jeaunne, Pierre
Jeckel, Heinrich; America, 1849 ***8582.3*** *p33*
Jeckel, Peter 31; America, 1853 ***9162.7*** *p14*
Jeffereys, C.; Philadelphia, 1756 ***8582.3*** *p95*
Jefferies, Tho.; Virginia, 1636 ***6219*** *p76*
Jeffers, Anthony; New York, NY, 1815 ***2859.11*** *p34*
Jeffers, John; Virginia, 1640 ***6219*** *p181*
Jeffers, Tho.; Virginia, 1642 ***6219*** *p192*
Jefferson, Alice; Virginia, 1648 ***6219*** *p252*
Jefferson, James; Virginia, 1638 ***6219*** *p2*
Jefferson, John; Virginia, 1635 ***6219*** *p4*
With stepfather & mother
Jefferson, John Petter; Boston, 1886 ***1450.2*** *p73A*
Jefferson, Robert; Virginia, 1639 ***6219*** *p158*
Jefferson, Robert 24; Nova Scotia, 1774 ***1219.7*** *p210*
Jefferson, Robert 38; Philadelphia, 1774 ***1219.7*** *p212*
Jeffery, James 21; Philadelphia, 1774 ***1219.7*** *p216*
Jeffery, John; New York, NY, 1832 ***8208.4*** *p48*
Jeffery, Joseph 18; Pennsylvania, 1738 ***3690.1*** *p124*
Jeffery, Josias 16; Maryland, 1723 ***3690.1*** *p124*
Jeffery, Richard; Nevada, 1874 ***2764.35*** *p37*
Jeffery, Richard 27; Kansas, 1886 ***5240.1*** *p22*
Jeffery, Richard 27; Kansas, 1886 ***5240.1*** *p69*
Jeffery, Samuell; Virginia, 1643 ***6219*** *p207*
Jeffery, Thomas 30; Kansas, 1876 ***5240.1*** *p22*
Jeffery, Thomas 30; Kansas, 1876 ***5240.1*** *p57*
Jefferyes, Thomas; Virginia, 1638 ***6219*** *p2*
Jefferyes, Thomas; Virginia, 1638 ***6219*** *p150*
Jefferys, Hen.; Virginia, 1636 ***6219*** *p34*
Jefferys, Jobe; Virginia, 1636 ***6219*** *p22*
Jefferys, John; Virginia, 1639 ***6219*** *p155*
Jefferys, William 15; Philadelphia, 1774 ***1219.7*** *p182*
Jefferys, William 20; Maryland, 1725 ***3690.1*** *p124*
Jeffoys, William 20; Maryland, 1725 ***3690.1*** *p124*
Jeffres, Charles 16; Maryland, 1724 ***3690.1*** *p124*
Jeffres, James 20; Massachusetts, 1848 ***5881.1*** *p51*
Jeffres, Mary 60; Massachusetts, 1849 ***5881.1*** *p51*
Jeffrey, James; America, 1808 ***1639.20*** *p99*
Jeffrey, Jane; South Carolina, 1767 ***1639.20*** *p99*
Jeffrey, Malcolm 28; Kansas, 1875 ***5240.1*** *p56*
Jeffrey, N.T.; Iowa, 1866-1943 ***123.54*** *p24*
Jeffrey, Thomas; Quebec, 1712 ***7603*** *p21*
Jeffrys, Charles 16; Maryland, 1724 ***3690.1*** *p124*
Jeffrys, Job.; Virginia, 1639 ***6219*** *p22*
Jeffrys, John; New York, NY, 1811 ***2859.11*** *p14*
With family
Jeffs, Alfred C. 23; Kansas, 1871 ***5240.1*** *p52*
Jeggins, Anth.; Virginia, 1635 ***6219*** *p10*
Jego, Richard; Virginia, 1628 ***6219*** *p31*
Jehle, Otto; Wisconsin, n.d. ***9675.6*** *p52*
Jehlin, Ulrich; Philadelphia, 1749 ***7829*** *p8*
Jehn, Nathaniel; New York, NY, 1847 ***6013.19*** *p29*
Jekutis, Anton; Wisconsin, n.d. ***9675.6*** *p52*
Jekyll, Harriet 46; Kansas, 1886 ***5240.1*** *p68*
Jelaca, Gyuro; Arkansas, 1918 ***95.2*** *p59*
Jelgerhois, John V.; America, 1882 ***1450.2*** *p73A*
Jelinska, Maryanna 29; New York, 1912 ***9980.29*** *p53*
Jellett, Snalter; Virginia, 1638 ***6219*** *p147*
Jelly, Hugh 35; Philadelphia, 1804 ***53.26*** *p40*
Jelmeur, Joseph 15; New Orleans, 1836 ***778.5*** *p551*
Jelmeur, Marianne 43; New Orleans, 1836 ***778.5*** *p551*
Jelovnik, Frank; Wisconsin, n.d. ***9675.6*** *p52*
Jelovnik, Joseph; Wisconsin, n.d. ***9675.6*** *p52*
Jeltuchowski, . . .; New York, 1831 ***4606*** *p174*
Jelvonik, Math; Wisconsin, n.d. ***9675.6*** *p52*
Jem, Rice 25; Jamaica, 1736 ***3690.1*** *p124*
Jemaison, Allen; Quebec, 1847 ***5704.8*** *p8*
Jemaison, Mary Ann 13; Quebec, 1847 ***5704.8*** *p8*
Jemaison, Sarah 11; Quebec, 1847 ***5704.8*** *p8*
Jemm, Rice 25; Jamaica, 1736 ***3690.1*** *p124*
Jenars, Eliza; Philadelphia, 1848 ***53.26*** *p40*
Jenars, Eliza; Philadelphia, 1848 ***5704.8*** *p46*
Jenerie, Rich.; Virginia, 1628 ***6219*** *p31*
Jening, Wm.; Virginia, 1635 ***6219*** *p36*
Jenings, John; Virginia, 1643 ***6219*** *p205*
Jenings, Richard; Virginia, 1636 ***6219*** *p78*
Jenkin, David; Virginia, 1642 ***6219*** *p198*
Jenkin, Thomas; Virginia, 1638 ***6219*** *p125*
Jenkins, Alice; Virginia, 1642 ***6219*** *p191*
Jenkins, B. F.; Washington, 1859-1920 ***2872.1*** *p18*
Jenkins, Danll.; Virginia, 1643 ***6219*** *p229*
Jenkins, Edward; Virginia, 1638 ***6219*** *p159*
Jenkins, Elizabeth 24; Maryland, 1775 ***1219.7*** *p267*
Jenkins, Francis 16; United States or West Indies, 1733 ***3690.1*** *p124*
Jenkins, George 17; Jamaica, 1729 ***3690.1*** *p124*
Jenkins, Henry 26?; Arizona, 1890 ***2764.35*** *p37*
Jenkins, James; New York, 1870 ***1450.2*** *p17B*
Jenkins, James 45; South Carolina, 1850 ***1639.20*** *p99*
Jenkins, John; Virginia, 1648 ***6219*** *p245*
Jenkins, John 17; Philadelphia, 1774 ***1219.7*** *p175*
Jenkins, Jon.; Virginia, 1637 ***6219*** *p10*
Jenkins, Joseph; New York, NY, 1839 ***8208.4*** *p93*
Jenkins, Katherine; Virginia, 1643 ***6219*** *p205*
Jenkins, Mary Ann 20; Massachusetts, 1850 ***5881.1*** *p51*
Jenkins, Nancy 24; St. John, N.B., 1853 ***5704.8*** *p109*
Jenkins, Richard; New York, NY, 1801 ***9892.11*** *p22*
Jenkins, Richard 34; Philadelphia, 1775 ***1219.7*** *p255*
Jenkins, Sabinia; Virginia, 1643 ***6219*** *p205*
Jenkins, Sibbella; Virginia, 1648 ***6219*** *p246*
Jenkins, Tho.; Virginia, 1638 ***6219*** *p11*
Jenkins, Tho.; Virginia, 1642 ***6219*** *p193*
Jenkins, Thomas; New York, NY, 1801 ***9892.11*** *p23*
Jenkins, Thomas; Quebec, 1822 ***7603*** *p71*
Jenkins, William 20; St. John, N.B., 1853 ***5704.8*** *p109*
Jenkins, William 34; Maryland, 1775 ***1219.7*** *p247*
Jenkins, William 39; Maryland, 1773 ***1219.7*** *p173*
Jenkins, Wm.; Virginia, 1642 ***6219*** *p199*
Jenkinson, Mrs.; New York, NY, 1811 ***2859.11*** *p14*
Jenkinson, Ann; New York, NY, 1811 ***2859.11*** *p14*
Jenkinson, Elizabeth; New York, NY, 1811 ***2859.11*** *p14*
Jenkinson, Isaac; New York, NY, 1811 ***2859.11*** *p14*
Jenkinson, James; New York, NY, 1811 ***2859.11*** *p14*
Jenkinson, Richard; Virginia, 1637 ***6219*** *p112*
Jenkinson, Robert 48; California, 1872 ***2769.5*** *p5*
Jenks, William J.; Illinois, 1854 ***7857*** *p4*
Jenner, von, Mr.; Cincinnati, 1788-1821 ***8582.3*** *p89*
Jenner, Peter; Cincinnati, 1869-1887 ***8582*** *p15*
Jenner, Thomas 38; New Orleans, 1839 ***778.5*** *p285*
Jenner, William 50; Maryland, 1774 ***1219.7*** *p230*
Jenney, Richard; Virginia, 1639 ***6219*** *p152*
Jenney, William; St. John, N.B., 1850 ***5704.8*** *p61*
Jennings, Edward; Virginia, 1643 ***6219*** *p201*
Jennings, Edwin; America, 1879 ***1450.2*** *p17B*
Jennings, George 22; Maryland, 1775 ***1219.7*** *p252*
Jennings, George 33; Maryland, 1774 ***1219.7*** *p180*
Jennings, John; Virginia, 1637 ***6219*** *p10*
Jennings, John 22; Jamaica, 1734 ***3690.1*** *p124*
Jennings, John 30; St. John, N.B., 1858 ***5704.8*** *p137*
Jennings, Jon.; Virginia, 1635 ***6219*** *p10*
Jennings, Jon.; Virginia, 1637 ***6219*** *p115*
Jennings, Joseph 24; Maryland, 1773 ***1219.7*** *p173*
Jennings, Mathew; Virginia, 1642 ***6219*** *p191*
Jennings, Nath.; Virginia, 1643 ***6219*** *p201*
Jennings, Richard; Virginia, 1636 ***6219*** *p74*
Jennings, Robert; Maryland, 1753 ***1219.7*** *p22*
Jennings, Robert; Maryland, 1753 ***3690.1*** *p124*
Jennings, Solomon George; New York, NY, 1839 ***8208.4*** *p97*
Jennings, Symon; Virginia, 1643 ***6219*** *p204*
Jennings, Theodore 40; Maryland, 1775 ***1219.7*** *p262*
Jennings, Tho.; Virginia, 1638 ***6219*** *p118*
Jennings, Thomas; Arizona, 1881 ***2764.35*** *p37*
Jennings, Thomas; Virginia, 1636 ***6219*** *p78*
Jennis, Edward; Virginia, 1640 ***6219*** *p160*
Jennison, Thomas; America, 1698 ***2212*** *p13*
Jenny, Friedr; Cincinnati, 1839 ***8582.1*** *p16*
Jennyon, Tho; Virginia, 1698 ***2212*** *p15*
Jenot, . . .; Canada, 1776-1783 ***9786*** *p25*
Jensel, Anna *SEE* Jensel, Friedrich
Jensel, Barbara *SEE* Jensel, Michael
Jensel, Friedrich 28; Philadelphia, 1753 ***2444*** *p171*
*Wife:*Anna
*Child:*Regina
*Child:*Maria Catharina
*Child:*Johann Martin
Jensel, Johann Martin *SEE* Jensel, Friedrich
Jensel, Maria Barbara *SEE* Jensel, Michael
Jensel, Maria Catharina *SEE* Jensel, Friedrich
Jensel, Michael; Pennsylvania, 1750 ***2444*** *p171*
*Wife:*Barbara
*Child:*Maria Barbara
Jensel, Regina *SEE* Jensel, Friedrich
Jensen, Aage V.; Arkansas, 1918 ***95.2*** *p59*
Jensen, Alfred Julius; Arkansas, 1918 ***95.2*** *p59*
Jensen, Anders; Washington, 1859-1920 ***2872.1*** *p18*
Jensen, Anna 55; Washington, 1918-1920 ***1728.5*** *p10*
Jensen, Carl; Washington, 1859-1920 ***2872.1*** *p18*
Jensen, Chris Berg; Arkansas, 1918 ***95.2*** *p60*
Jensen, Christ Keldsen; Arkansas, 1918 ***95.2*** *p60*
Jensen, Christian; Arkansas, 1918 ***95.2*** *p60*
Jensen, Christian 22; Kansas, 1873 ***5240.1*** *p54*
Jensen, Clara *SEE* Jensen, Fabian
Jensen, Clara *SEE* Jensen, Fabian
Jensen, Conrad; Washington, 1859-1920 ***2872.1*** *p18*
Jensen, Dagmar *SEE* Jensen, Soren Peter
Jensen, Edward Christian; Arkansas, 1918 ***95.2*** *p60*
Jensen, Elnore; Washington, 1859-1920 ***2872.1*** *p18*
Jensen, Fabian; New York, NY, 1911 ***3455.3*** *p52*
*Wife:*Clara
Jensen, Fabian; New York, NY, 1911 ***3455.3*** *p85*
*Wife:*Clara
Jensen, Frederick Martinus; Washington, 1859-1920 ***2872.1*** *p18*
Jensen, George; Arkansas, 1918 ***95.2*** *p60*
Jensen, George Henry; New York, NY, 1914 ***3455.2*** *p50*
Jensen, Hans; Illinois, 1882 ***5012.39*** *p52*
Jensen, Hans Mortensen; Arkansas, 1918 ***95.2*** *p60*
Jensen, Herman Kofeod; Arkansas, 1918 ***95.2*** *p60*
Jensen, Herman Kofoed; Arkansas, 1918 ***95.2*** *p60*
Jensen, J. 62; Washington, 1916 ***1728.5*** *p10*
Jensen, J. N.; Shreveport, LA, 1879 ***7129*** *p44*
Jensen, Jens Adrin 30; Arkansas, 1918 ***95.2*** *p60*
Jensen, Jens Carl; Washington, 1859-1920 ***2872.1*** *p18*
Jensen, Jens Peder; Arkansas, 1918 ***95.2*** *p60*
Jensen, Jens Peter; Arkansas, 1918 ***95.2*** *p60*
Jensen, John A.; Colorado, 1904 ***9678.2*** *p59*
Jensen, Jorgen; Washington, 1859-1920 ***2872.1*** *p18*
Jensen, Julius Rose 28; Arkansas, 1918 ***95.2*** *p60*
Jensen, Just Marius; Arkansas, 1918 ***95.2*** *p60*
Jensen, Lars Peter 25; Arkansas, 1918 ***95.2*** *p60*
Jensen, Mattie *SEE* Jensen, Rasonus
Jensen, Olga Christine; Washington, 1859-1920 ***2872.1*** *p18*
Jensen, Peder Martin; Arkansas, 1918 ***95.2*** *p60*
Jensen, Peter; Colorado, 1894 ***9678.2*** *p59*
Jensen, Peter; Washington, 1859-1920 ***2872.1*** *p18*
Jensen, Peter Chris; Arkansas, 1918 ***95.2*** *p60*
Jensen, Rasmus; New York, NY, 1904 ***3455.2*** *p94*
Jensen, Rasonus; New York, NY, 1904 ***3455.2*** *p101*
*Wife:*Mattie
Jensen, Soren; Arkansas, 1918 ***95.2*** *p60*
Jensen, Soren Angreas; New York, NY, 1913 ***3455.2*** *p49*
Jensen, Soren Peter; New York, NY, 1906 ***3455.1*** *p54*
*Wife:*Dagmar
Jensen, Sven; Arkansas, 1918 ***95.2*** *p60*
Jensen, Valdermar; New York, NY, 1917 ***3455.3*** *p109*
Jensen, Victor; Arkansas, 1918 ***95.2*** *p60*
Jensen, Waldemar; New York, NY, 1917 ***3455.2*** *p50*
Jensen, Waldemar Theodore Louie; Arkansas, 1918 ***95.2*** *p60*
Jensen, William; Arkansas, 1918 ***95.2*** *p60*
Jenson, Clara *SEE* Jenson, Fabian
Jenson, Clara Cristinia *SEE* Jenson, Fabian
Jenson, Clara Cristinia; New York, NY, 1911 ***3455.4*** *p78*
*Husband:*Fabian
Jenson, Clara Helena; New York, NY, 1911 ***3455.3*** *p86*
*Husband:*Fabian
Jenson, Fabian *SEE* Jenson, Clara Cristinia
Jenson, Fabian *SEE* Jenson, Clara Helena
Jenson, Fabian; New York, NY, 1911 ***3455.3*** *p85*
*Wife:*Clara
Jenson, Fabian; New York, NY, 1911 ***3455.4*** *p78*
*Wife:*Clara Cristinia
Jenson, Peter; Washington, 1859-1920 ***2872.1*** *p18*
Jensterle, Bartholomaies; Wisconsin, n.d. ***9675.6*** *p52*
Jensterle, Joseph; Wisconsin, n.d. ***9675.6*** *p52*
Jent, Tho.; Virginia, 1638 ***6219*** *p118*
Jenta, Jean Marie 37; New Orleans, 1838 ***778.5*** *p285*
Jentges, Henery; Wisconsin, n.d. ***9675.6*** *p52*
Jentges, Michael; Wisconsin, n.d. ***9675.6*** *p52*
Jentges, Peter; Wisconsin, n.d. ***9675.6*** *p52*
Jents, Mr. 18; New Orleans, 1837 ***778.5*** *p285*
Jeoffrys, Constant 16; Maryland or Virginia, 1699 ***2212*** *p21*
Jeoseppo, Kraco; Wisconsin, n.d. ***9675.6*** *p52*
Jeppesen, Frank; Colorado, 1904 ***9678.2*** *p59*
Jeppeson, Jens P.; Illinois, 1872 ***2896.5*** *p20*
Jeppesson, Mons; Maine, 1871-1880 ***6410.22*** *p119*
Jeray, Pongraz; Wisconsin, n.d. ***9675.6*** *p52*
Jeray, Simon; Wisconsin, n.d. ***9675.6*** *p52*
Jerdan, Thomas; Illinois, 1876 ***5012.39*** *p120*

236
FOR A COMPLETE EXPLANATION OF ENTRY, SEE "HOW TO READ A CITATION" SECTION

Jeremiah, . . .; Virginia, 1637 ***6219*** *p17*
Jerkman, Frank; Wisconsin, n.d. ***9675.6*** *p52*
Jermalowicz, Adam 22; New York, 1912 ***9980.29*** *p58*
Jerman, David; Virginia, 1648 ***6219*** *p237*
Jerner, E.; Iowa, 1866-1943 ***123.54*** *p24*
Jerome, Lee 23; Kansas, 1888 ***5240.1*** *p71*
Jerome, Samuel John; Iowa, 1866-1943 ***123.54*** *p24*
Jerome, Samuel Wilson Leslie; Iowa, 1866-1943 ***123.54*** *p65*
Jerome, Wlm. C. J. 22; Kentucky, 1820 ***778.5*** *p286*
Jeroranni, Jucco; Iowa, 1866-1943 ***123.54*** *p24*
Jervey, Thomas; America, 1705 ***1639.20*** *p99*
Jervis, Andrew; Illinois, 1874 ***5012.39*** *p26*
Jervis, James; Philadelphia, 1847 ***53.26*** *p40*
Jervis, James; Philadelphia, 1847 ***5704.8*** *p31*
Jervis, John; Philadelphia, 1851 ***5704.8*** *p71*
Jervis, Peter 21; Jamaica, 1735 ***3690.1*** *p124*
Jervis, Thomas; Virginia, 1642 ***6219*** *p189*
Jeschke, August; Wisconsin, n.d. ***9675.6*** *p52*
Jesionowski, Anastasibls; Arkansas, 1918 ***95.2*** *p60*
Jesperson, Knud Slesstrip; Arkansas, 1918 ***95.2*** *p60*
Jesse, Lenard William; Arkansas, 1918 ***95.2*** *p60*
Jesse, Lenard William 22; Arkansas, 1918 ***95.2*** *p61*
Jesselsen, Andrew; Illinois, 1888 ***5012.39*** *p122*
Jessen, Fred 73; Kansas, 1906 ***5240.1*** *p84*
Jessen, Henry N.; Kansas, 1896 ***5240.1*** *p22*
Jessen, J. C.; Washington, 1859-1920 ***2872.1*** *p18*
Jessen, Louis H.; Kansas, 1896 ***5240.1*** *p22*
Jesser, Frederic 43; New Orleans, 1838 ***778.5*** *p286*
Jesson, Ann *SEE* Jesson, Harriet
Jesson, Eliz. *SEE* Jesson, Harriet
Jesson, Harriet; Ontario, 1853 ***4535.10*** *p196*
*Sister:*Ann
*Sister:*Eliz.
Jessop, Samuel Brook; New York, NY, 1835 ***8208.4*** *p29*
Jessy, Mme.; New Orleans, 1839 ***778.5*** *p286*
Jessy, Mr.; New Orleans, 1839 ***778.5*** *p286*
Jest, Charles S. 66; Harris Co., TX, 1898 ***6254*** *p5*
Jestien, L. 24; America, 1829 ***778.5*** *p286*
Jestland, Thomas; Arkansas, 1918 ***95.2*** *p61*
Jetter, Andreas *SEE* Jetter, Johann
Jetter, Anna Barbara; Pennsylvania, 1752 ***2444*** *p140*
Jetter, Catharina *SEE* Jetter, Johann
Jetter, Christoph *SEE* Jetter, Johann
Jetter, Johann; Pennsylvania, 1748 ***2444*** *p171*
*Wife:*Catharina
*Child:*Christoph
*Child:*Andreas
Jetter, Ursula; Pennsylvania, 1750 ***2444*** *p196*
Jettinger, Lewis; Illinois, 1858 ***5012.39*** *p54*
Jeulicke, Ernestine 22; America, 1839 ***778.5*** *p286*
Jeulicke, Eugenie 3 mos; America, 1839 ***778.5*** *p286*
Jeullard, Mr. 21; America, 1838 ***778.5*** *p286*
Jeunee, Pierre; Halifax, N.S., 1752 ***7074.6*** *p216*
Jeunehomme, John; Colorado, 1904 ***9678.2*** *p59*
Jeunnat, Jean J. 27; Port uncertain, 1839 ***778.5*** *p286*
Jeurling, Emely 8; Massachusetts, 1860 ***6410.32*** *p98*
Jeurling, Emilia Charlotta *SEE* Jeurling, Hedvig Amelia
Jeurling, Hedvig Amelia; America, 1853 ***6410.32*** *p122*
*Daughter:*Emilia Charlotta
Jeutte, B. 21; New Orleans, 1830 ***778.5*** *p286*
Jeuville, Jean-Baptiste 59; New Orleans, 1836 ***778.5*** *p286*
Jevieu, Denis 33; America, 1831 ***778.5*** *p286*
Jewell, Robt.; Virginia, 1637 ***6219*** *p13*
Jibbeau, Baptiste 34; America, 1831 ***778.5*** *p286*
Jimas, James A.; Arkansas, 1918 ***95.2*** *p61*
Jimneskoy, Jacob; Arkansas, 1918 ***95.2*** *p61*
Jinines, Richard; Quebec, 1778 ***7603*** *p88*
Jinkins, Joseph; America, 1697 ***2212*** *p7*
Jinks, William; Illinois, 1856 ***7857*** *p4*
Jirschefski, Albert; Wisconsin, n.d. ***9675.6*** *p52*
Joachim, Captain; Ohio, 1812-1814 ***8582.2*** *p59*
Joachim, Wendel; Cincinnati, 1840-1845 ***8582.1*** *p16*
Joachin, Remonde Louis 46; Port uncertain, 1839 ***778.5*** *p286*
Joanes, Eliza.; Virginia, 1637 ***6219*** *p28*
Joanes, Tymothy; Virginia, 1635 ***6219*** *p12*
Joanes, Wm.; Virginia, 1637 ***6219*** *p82*
Joannon, Mikela; Iowa, 1866-1943 ***123.54*** *p65*
Joaslin, George 21; Maryland, 1725 ***3690.1*** *p124*
Job, Alzire; America, 1849 ***1450.2*** *p73A*
Job, James; Quebec, 1852 ***5704.8*** *p90*
Job, James 38; Quebec, 1854 ***5704.8*** *p121*
Job, Jane; Quebec, 1852 ***5704.8*** *p86*
Job, John Nicholas; Philadelphia, 1760 ***9973.7*** *p34*
Job, Matilda 5; Quebec, 1852 ***5704.8*** *p86*
Job, Matilda 5; Quebec, 1852 ***5704.8*** *p90*
Jobb, Joane; Virginia, 1637 ***6219*** *p82*
Jobbin, Captain; Quebec, 1815 ***9229.18*** *p81*
Jobe, Pierre 21; America, 1838 ***778.5*** *p287*
Jobert, Adela A. 24; America, 1823 ***778.5*** *p287*
Jobert, John B. 31; America, 1823 ***778.5*** *p287*
Jobert, Pierre P. 27; New Orleans, 1823 ***778.5*** *p287*
Jobs, Friedrich; Wisconsin, n.d. ***9675.6*** *p52*
Jobson, Robert 45; Jamaica, 1736 ***3690.1*** *p125*
Jochum, Elise 20; America, 1853 ***9162.7*** *p14*
Jochum, Marg. 23; America, 1853 ***9162.7*** *p14*
Jockel, . . .; Canada, 1776-1783 ***9786*** *p37*
Jockell, . . .; Canada, 1776-1783 ***9786*** *p25*
Jockers, Johannes; Cincinnati, 1869-1887 ***8582*** *p15*
Jocks, . . .; Canada, 1776-1783 ***9786*** *p25*
Jocob, Mary; America, 1736 ***4971*** *p12*
Jodard, J. 48; Port uncertain, 1838 ***778.5*** *p287*
Jodge, Mr. 29; New Orleans, 1838 ***778.5*** *p287*
Joeder, Peter; Ohio, 1800-1812 ***8582.2*** *p57*
Joerg, Johann; Ohio, 1811 ***8582.1*** *p48*
Joergen, Johann; Illinois, 1828 ***8582.1*** *p54*
Joerger, Elisabeth; America, 1832 ***8582.1*** *p36*
Joerss, Aug. H.L.W.; Arizona, 1883 ***2764.35*** *p37*
Jogodzinski, Johan; Michigan, 1892 ***9980.29*** *p58*
Johann, Herbert; Wisconsin, n.d. ***9675.6*** *p52*
Johann, Nicholas; Wisconsin, n.d. ***9675.6*** *p52*
Johannesdottir, Bjorg 6 mos; Quebec, 1879 ***2557.2*** *p37*
Johannesdottir, Kristin 28; Quebec, 1879 ***2557.2*** *p37*
Johanneson, Johannes Dortin; Arkansas, 1918 ***95.2*** *p61*
Johannesson, Adolf Fredrik; Minneapolis, 1880-1883 ***6410.35*** *p54*
Johannesson, Anders Johan; Minneapolis, 1871-1878 ***6410.35*** *p55*
Johannesson, Carl; Minneapolis, 1882-1883 ***6410.35*** *p54*
Johannesson, Carl Alfred Theodor; Minneapolis, 1882-1884 ***6410.35*** *p56*
Johannesson, Jan Jacob; Minneapolis, 1877-1880 ***6410.35*** *p57*
Johannesson, Johan; Minneapolis, 1873-1887 ***6410.35*** *p57*
Johannesson, Johan Adolf; Minneapolis, 1880-1884 ***6410.35*** *p57*
Johannesson, Johan Peter; Minneapolis, 1866-1880 ***6410.35*** *p57*
Johannesson, Jordan; Minneapolis, 1880-1884 ***6410.35*** *p57*
Johannesson, Justus Reinhold; Minneapolis, 1872-1884 ***6410.35*** *p53*
Johannesson, Magnus; Minneapolis, 1883-1886 ***6410.35*** *p57*
Johannesson, Olof; Minneapolis, 1881-1883 ***6410.35*** *p58*
Johannigmann, Mathias; Cincinnati, 1869-1887 ***8582*** *p15*
Johanning, Heinrich; Cincinnati, 1788-1848 ***8582.3*** *p89*
Johannnesson, Carl; Minneapolis, 1879-1880 ***6410.35*** *p50*
Johannot, Israel; Jamaica, 1759 ***1219.7*** *p67*
Johanns, Leon 22; America, 1836 ***778.5*** *p287*
Johannsen, Joh. Martin 25; New Orleans, 1839 ***9420.2*** *p71*
Johannsmeier, Anne M. Cath. Engel *SEE* Johannsmeier, Joh. Friedrich
Johannsmeier, Anne M. L. Friederike *SEE* Johannsmeier, Joh. Friedrich
Johannsmeier, Anne Marie W. Moller *SEE* Johannsmeier, Joh. Friedrich
Johannsmeier, Carl Heinrich; America, 1854 ***4610.10*** *p151*
Johannsmeier, Hermann H. Friedrich *SEE* Johannsmeier, Joh. Friedrich
Johannsmeier, Joh. Friedrich; America, 1857 ***4610.10*** *p135*
*Wife:*Anne Marie W. Moller
*Child:*Anne M. L. Friederike
*Child:*Anne M. Cath. Engel
*Child:*Hermann H. Friedrich
Johannsmeyer, Anna M. Ilsabein Kiso *SEE* Johannsmeyer, Johann Heinrich
Johannsmeyer, Anne Marie Louise *SEE* Johannsmeyer, Johann Peter
Johannsmeyer, Carl Heinrich *SEE* Johannsmeyer, Johann Heinrich
Johannsmeyer, Friedrich August *SEE* Johannsmeyer, Johann Heinrich
Johannsmeyer, Friedrich Wilhelm *SEE* Johannsmeyer, Johann Peter
Johannsmeyer, Johann Heinrich *SEE* Johannsmeyer, Johann Heinrich
Johannsmeyer, Johann Heinrich *SEE* Johannsmeyer, Johann Heinrich
Johannsmeyer, Johann Heinrich; America, 1843 ***4610.10*** *p141*
*Wife:*Anna M. Ilsabein Kiso
*Child:*Carl Heinrich
*Child:*Johann Heinrich
*Child:*Friedrich August
*Child:*Johann Heinrich
Johannsmeyer, Johann Peter; America, 1850 ***4610.10*** *p138*
*Wife:*Marie L. Reinkensmeyer 26
*Child:*Friedrich Wilhelm
*Child:*Anne Marie Louise
Johannsmeyer, Marie L. Reinkensmeyer 26 *SEE* Johannsmeyer, Johann Peter
Johansen, Johan 25; Arkansas, 1918 ***95.2*** *p61*
Johansen, Johannes; Kansas, 1913 ***6013.40*** *p16*
Johansen, John Edwin; Washington, 1859-1920 ***2872.1*** *p19*
Johansen, Katrina; Washington, 1859-1920 ***2872.1*** *p19*
Johansen, Mary; Washington, 1859-1920 ***2872.1*** *p19*
Johansen, Oscar Fredrik; Washington, 1859-1920 ***2872.1*** *p19*
Johansen, Peter; Washington, 1859-1920 ***2872.1*** *p19*
Johansen, Ragnvald; Arkansas, 1918 ***95.2*** *p61*
Johansen, Selina; Washington, 1859-1920 ***2872.1*** *p19*
Johansen, Viggo 23; Arkansas, 1918 ***95.2*** *p61*
Johanson, A. M.; Minneapolis, 1881-1883 ***6410.35*** *p55*
Johanson, Anthony 27; Kansas, 1887 ***5240.1*** *p70*
Johanson, August; Colorado, 1904 ***9678.2*** *p59*
Johanson, Bror D.; New York, NY, 1913 ***3455.2*** *p48*
Johanson, C. J.; Minneapolis, 1880-1883 ***6410.35*** *p56*
Johanson, Clarence; Minneapolis, 1868-1877 ***6410.35*** *p56*
Johanson, George; Arkansas, 1918 ***95.2*** *p61*
Johanson, George; Bangor, ME, 1894 ***6410.22*** *p127*
Johanson, Hans Theodore 24; Arkansas, 1918 ***95.2*** *p61*
Johanson, Johan; Arkansas, 1918 ***95.2*** *p61*
Johanson, Johan; New Hampshire, 1890 ***5240.1*** *p22*
Johanson, Johan W.; Maine, 1871-1873 ***6410.22*** *p117*
Johanson, Joseph; Iroquois Co., IL, 1896 ***3455.1*** *p11*
Johanson, Nils Johan; Maine, 1871-1880 ***6410.22*** *p117*
Johanson, Svan; Minneapolis, 1869-1883 ***6410.35*** *p58*
Johanssesdottir, Steinnun 29; Quebec, 1879 ***2557.1*** *p20*
Johansson, August; Minneapolis, 1869-1884 ***6410.35*** *p50*
Johansson, August; Washington, 1859-1920 ***2872.1*** *p19*
Johansson, Axel Malcolm; Minneapolis, 1881-1883 ***6410.35*** *p55*
Johansson, Carl August; Minneapolis, 1881-1887 ***6410.35*** *p57*
Johansson, Carl Johan; Minneapolis, 1867-1877 ***6410.35*** *p56*
Johansson, Frans Johan; Minneapolis, 1883 ***6410.35*** *p56*
Johansson, Johannes; Minneapolis, 1873-1888 ***6410.35*** *p65*
Johansson, Johannes David; Minneapolis, 1877-1883 ***6410.35*** *p57*
Johansson, Otto; Minneapolis, 1878-1883 ***6410.35*** *p58*
Johl, Emil; Wisconsin, n.d. ***9675.6*** *p52*
John, . . .; Canada, 1776-1783 ***9786*** *p25*
John, Mme. 22; Ohio, 1837 ***778.5*** *p287*
John, Mr. 30; Ohio, 1837 ***778.5*** *p287*
John the rover ; America, 1738 ***4971*** *p68*
John, Fredrich William; Wisconsin, n.d. ***9675.6*** *p52*
John, Hills; Virginia, 1648 ***6219*** *p252*
John, James; Virginia, 1636 ***6219*** *p7*
John, John Little; Iowa, 1866-1943 ***123.54*** *p24*
John, Karl; Reading, PA, 1780 ***8137*** *p10*
John, Margaret 7; Massachusetts, 1848 ***5881.1*** *p51*
John, Marie B. 21; New Orleans, 1823 ***778.5*** *p287*
John, Michael; Wisconsin, n.d. ***9675.6*** *p52*
John, Nick William 29; Arkansas, 1918 ***95.2*** *p61*
John, Samuel; New York, 1754 ***3652*** *p80*
John, William; New York, NY, 1839 ***8208.4*** *p93*
Johnannsen, Charles Carl 26; Arkansas, 1918 ***95.2*** *p61*
Johnes, Richard; Virginia, 1638 ***6219*** *p146*
Johnins, John; America, 1735-1743 ***4971*** *p79*
Johnins, John; America, 1742 ***4971*** *p81*
Johnne, Louis 19; Port uncertain, 1836 ***778.5*** *p287*
Johns, . . .; Canada, 1776-1783 ***9786*** *p25*
Johns, Jacob; Virginia, 1645 ***6219*** *p240*
Johns, James 21; Maryland, 1774 ***1219.7*** *p225*
Johns, John 24; Maryland, 1774 ***1219.7*** *p228*
Johns, John G.; Wisconsin, n.d. ***9675.6*** *p52*
Johns, Mathew; Iowa, 1866-1943 ***123.54*** *p24*
Johns, Phil S.; Washington, 1859-1920 ***2872.1*** *p19*
Johns, Richard; Virginia, 1645 ***6219*** *p240*
Johns, Roger; Virginia, 1645 ***6219*** *p240*
Johns, Solomon; Iowa, 1866-1943 ***123.54*** *p24*
Johns, William H.; Colorado, 1904 ***9678.2*** *p59*
Johnsdottir, Elizabet 18; Quebec, 1879 ***2557.1*** *p20*
Johnsdottir, Thiveig 33; Quebec, 1879 ***2557.1*** *p21*
Johnsen, Axel Theodore; Arkansas, 1918 ***95.2*** *p61*
Johnsen, John; New York, NY, 1836 ***8208.4*** *p18*
Johnsier, Ole; Wisconsin, n.d. ***9675.6*** *p52*
Johnson Family ; Iowa, 1853 ***2090*** *p611*
Johnson, Mr. 22; Jamaica, 1775 ***1219.7*** *p260*
Johnson, A.; Iowa, 1866-1943 ***123.54*** *p24*
Johnson, A.; Minneapolis, 1861-1877 ***6410.35*** *p55*
Johnson, A.; Minneapolis, 1871-1878 ***6410.35*** *p55*
Johnson, A.N.; Iowa, 1866-1943 ***123.54*** *p24*

Johnson, Aaron; Iowa, 1866-1943 ***123.54*** *p24*
Johnson, Aba.; Virginia, 1648 ***6219*** *p241*
Johnson, Albert; New York, NY, 1903 ***3455.1*** *p42* *Wife:*Alma
Johnson, Albert W.; Washington, 1859-1920 ***2872.1*** *p19*
Johnson, Alex; Washington, 1859-1920 ***2872.1*** *p19*
Johnson, Alexander; America, 1804 ***1639.20*** *p100*
Johnson, Alexander; South Carolina, 1830 ***1639.20*** *p100*
Johnson, Alfred; Arkansas, 1918 ***95.2*** *p61*
Johnson, Alfred; Colorado, 1894 ***9678.2*** *p59*
Johnson, Alfred; Washington, 1859-1920 ***2872.1*** *p19*
Johnson, Alice; Virginia, 1636 ***6219*** *p75*
Johnson, Alice; Virginia, 1638 ***6219*** *p181*
Johnson, Alice; Virginia, 1641 ***6219*** *p184*
Johnson, Alma *SEE* Johnson, Albert
Johnson, Anders; Iowa, 1851 ***2090*** *p610* *Son:*Fred
Johnson, Andrew; America, 1846 ***6410.32*** *p123*
Johnson, Andrew; Iowa, 1849-1860 ***2090*** *p613*
Johnson, Andrew; Iowa, 1866-1943 ***123.54*** *p24*
Johnson, Andrew; Iowa, 1880 ***2764.35*** *p38*
Johnson, Andrew; Maine, 1895 ***6410.22*** *p127*
Johnson, Andrew; Washington, 1859-1920 ***2872.1*** *p19*
Johnson, Andrew 30; Massachusetts, 1860 ***6410.32*** *p107*
Johnson, Andrew 31; Kansas, 1879 ***5240.1*** *p61*
Johnson, Andrew 43; Massachusetts, 1860 ***6410.32*** *p104*
Johnson, Andrew N.; Colorado, 1903 ***9678.2*** *p59*
Johnson, Andrew Wrick; Colorado, 1880 ***9678.2*** *p59*
Johnson, Andy 48; Arizona, 1909 ***9228.40*** *p12*
Johnson, Ann; St. John, N.B., 1852 ***5704.8*** *p83*
Johnson, Anton Albin; Arkansas, 1918 ***95.2*** *p61*
Johnson, Anton Sigfrid; Arkansas, 1918 ***95.2*** *p61*
Johnson, Attn; Iowa, 1866-1943 ***123.54*** *p24*
Johnson, August; Bangor, ME, 1888 ***6410.22*** *p126*
Johnson, August; Illinois, 1894 ***5012.37*** *p63*
Johnson, August; Iowa, 1866-1943 ***123.54*** *p24*
Johnson, August; Minneapolis, 1880-1883 ***6410.35*** *p55*
Johnson, August; Washington, 1859-1920 ***2872.1*** *p19*
Johnson, August 21; Kansas, 1896 ***5240.1*** *p80*
Johnson, August 24; Kansas, 1874 ***5240.1*** *p22*
Johnson, August 24; Kansas, 1874 ***5240.1*** *p55*
Johnson, August 29; Kansas, 1893 ***5240.1*** *p22*
Johnson, August 29; Kansas, 1893 ***5240.1*** *p78*
Johnson, August L.; Minneapolis, 1869-1878 ***6410.35*** *p56*
Johnson, August Werner; Arkansas, 1918 ***95.2*** *p61*
Johnson, August William; Iowa, 1866-1943 ***123.54*** *p24*
Johnson, Augusta *SEE* Johnson, John Adolf Cebrius
Johnson, Augusta *SEE* Johnson, John Adolf Ciberius
Johnson, Axel 25; Harris Co., TX, 1898 ***6254*** *p4*
Johnson, Axel Lambert 23; Arkansas, 1918 ***95.2*** *p61*
Johnson, Axel N.; Iowa, 1866-1943 ***123.54*** *p24*
Johnson, Axel Willard; Arkansas, 1918 ***95.2*** *p61*
Johnson, B.C. 47?; Arizona, 1890 ***2764.35*** *p38*
Johnson, Ben S.; Colorado, 1893 ***9678.2*** *p59*
Johnson, Benjamin; Iowa, 1866-1943 ***123.54*** *p24*
Johnson, Benjamin 38; California, 1872 ***2769.5*** *p5*
Johnson, Bristiana 31; Massachusetts, 1849 ***5881.1*** *p51*
Johnson, Bror D.; New York, NY, 1913 ***3455.3*** *p52*
Johnson, Burre; Wisconsin, n.d. ***9675.6*** *p52*
Johnson, C. H. 43; Arizona, 1911 ***9228.40*** *p16*
Johnson, C.L.; Iowa, 1866-1943 ***123.54*** *p24*
Johnson, C. L.; Washington, 1859-1920 ***2872.1*** *p19*
Johnson, C. P.; Minneapolis, 1871-1881 ***6410.35*** *p56*
Johnson, C. R.; Washington, 1859-1920 ***2872.1*** *p19*
Johnson, C. V. 21; Kansas, 1889 ***5240.1*** *p23*
Johnson, C. V. 21; Kansas, 1889 ***5240.1*** *p73*
Johnson, Carl; Illinois, 1890 ***5012.39*** *p53*
Johnson, Carl; Illinois, 1892 ***5012.40*** *p26*
Johnson, Carl; Iowa, 1853 ***2090*** *p611*
Johnson, Carl; Minneapolis, 1880 ***6410.35*** *p56*
Johnson, Carl; New York, NY, 1906 ***3455.1*** *p55*
Johnson, Carl A.; Colorado, 1896 ***9678.2*** *p59*
Johnson, Carl Alfred; Colorado, 1904 ***9678.2*** *p59*
Johnson, Carl Eric; Arkansas, 1918 ***95.2*** *p61*
Johnson, Catherine; Annapolis, MD, 1742 ***4971*** *p92*
Johnson, Catherine; Maryland, 1742 ***4971*** *p107*
Johnson, Catherine; Philadelphia, 1816 ***2859.11*** *p34*
Johnson, Catherine 64; North Carolina, 1850 ***1639.20*** *p100*
Johnson, Charles; Arizona, 1897 ***9228.30*** *p3*
Johnson, Charles; Illinois, 1888 ***5012.37*** *p60*
Johnson, Charles; Minneapolis, 1867-1877 ***6410.35*** *p56*
Johnson, Charles; Minneapolis, 1881-1885 ***6410.35*** *p56*
Johnson, Charles; Minneapolis, 1882-1884 ***6410.35*** *p56*
Johnson, Charles; Washington, 1859-1920 ***2872.1*** *p19*
Johnson, Charles 19; Jamaica, 1722 ***3690.1*** *p125*
Johnson, Charles 21; Maryland, 1774 ***1219.7*** *p215*
Johnson, Charles 41; Massachusetts, 1860 ***6410.32*** *p100*
Johnson, Charles Emil; Washington, 1859-1920 ***2872.1*** *p19*
Johnson, Charles Fredrick; Arkansas, 1918 ***95.2*** *p61*
Johnson, Charles G.; Illinois, 1874 ***5012.39*** *p26*
Johnson, Charles H.; Bangor, ME, 1883-1890 ***6410.22*** *p120*
Johnson, Charles J.; Bangor, ME, 1892 ***6410.22*** *p126*
Johnson, Charles Karl; Washington, 1859-1920 ***2872.1*** *p19*
Johnson, Charles L.; Washington, 1859-1920 ***2872.1*** *p19*
Johnson, Charles R.; Bangor, ME, 1898 ***6410.22*** *p128*
Johnson, Charley 22; Kansas, 1876 ***5240.1*** *p23*
Johnson, Charley 22; Kansas, 1876 ***5240.1*** *p57*
Johnson, Charlie E.; Colorado, 1896 ***9678.2*** *p59*
Johnson, Choyce; Virginia, 1635 ***6219*** *p73*
Johnson, Choyce; Virginia, 1637 ***6219*** *p113*
Johnson, Chris; Bangor, ME, 1898 ***6410.22*** *p128*
Johnson, Christen; Illinois, 1892 ***5012.37*** *p63*
Johnson, Claus; Iowa, 1866-1943 ***123.54*** *p24*
Johnson, Conrad; Arkansas, 1918 ***95.2*** *p61*
Johnson, Dan; Washington, 1859-1920 ***2872.1*** *p19*
Johnson, Danll.; Virginia, 1646 ***6219*** *p242*
Johnson, David; Minneapolis, 1881-1888 ***6410.35*** *p56*
Johnson, David; New York, NY, 1811 ***2859.11*** *p14*
Johnson, David 21; Kansas, 1891 ***5240.1*** *p76*
Johnson, David 48; Maryland, 1775 ***1219.7*** *p267*
Johnson, David G. 39; Kansas, 1887 ***5240.1*** *p70*
Johnson, Diana; Virginia, 1698 ***2212*** *p16*
Johnson, Duncan; America, 1802 ***1639.20*** *p100*
Johnson, Earl Edvin; Arkansas, 1918 ***95.2*** *p61*
Johnson, Ed; Arkansas, 1918 ***95.2*** *p61*
Johnson, Ed; Minneapolis, 1880-1884 ***6410.35*** *p56*
Johnson, Eda S.; Iroquois Co., IL, 1892 ***3455.1*** *p11*
Johnson, Edward; Virginia, 1639 ***6219*** *p151*
Johnson, Edward; Virginia, 1643 ***6219*** *p202*
Johnson, Edward 20; Maryland, 1774 ***1219.7*** *p206*
Johnson, Edward 22; Maryland, 1774 ***1219.7*** *p221*
Johnson, Edward 30; Maryland, 1774 ***1219.7*** *p206*
Johnson, Elias; Bangor, ME, 1897 ***6410.22*** *p127*
Johnson, Elijah; Illinois, 1891 ***5012.40*** *p26*
Johnson, Eliz.; Newfoundland, 1829 ***8893*** *p263*
Johnson, Eliz.; Virginia, 1638 ***6219*** *p181*
Johnson, Eliz 25; America, 1702 ***2212*** *p38*
Johnson, Eliza.; Virginia, 1636 ***6219*** *p75*
Johnson, Eliza 13; St. John, N.B., 1852 ***5704.8*** *p83*
Johnson, Elizabeth *SEE* Johnson, Richard
Johnson, Elizabeth; New York, NY, 1811 ***2859.11*** *p14*
Johnson, Elizabeth; Virginia, 1635 ***6219*** *p16*
Johnson, Elizabeth 30; Massachusetts, 1860 ***6410.32*** *p111*
Johnson, Elnor; New York, NY, 1811 ***2859.11*** *p14*
Johnson, Emanuel 16 *SEE* Johnson, William
Johnson, Emil; Iowa, 1866-1943 ***123.54*** *p24*
Johnson, Emil; Minneapolis, 1882-1883 ***6410.35*** *p56*
Johnson, Enoch; Ohio, 1840 ***9892.11*** *p23*
Johnson, Enoch; Ohio, 1844 ***9892.11*** *p23*
Johnson, Eric; Washington, 1859-1920 ***2872.1*** *p19*
Johnson, Erik; Colorado, 1901 ***9678.2*** *p59*
Johnson, Ernest Albin; Boston, 1914 ***3455.4*** *p24*
Johnson, Ernest Elbin; Boston, 1914 ***3455.3*** *p45*
Johnson, Ernst Iven; New York, NY, 1911 ***3455.2*** *p52*
Johnson, Francis *SEE* Johnson, Richard
Johnson, Frank A.; Minneapolis, 1871-1878 ***6410.35*** *p56*
Johnson, Frank E.; Illinois, 1876 ***5012.39*** *p52*
Johnson, Frank J.; Minneapolis, 1883 ***6410.35*** *p56*
Johnson, Frank L. 25; Kansas, 1873 ***5240.1*** *p54*
Johnson, Fred *SEE* Johnson, Anders
Johnson, Fred Leonard; Arkansas, 1918 ***95.2*** *p62*
Johnson, Fredrick; Iowa, 1866-1943 ***123.54*** *p24*
Johnson, G.G.; Iowa, 1866-1943 ***123.54*** *p25*
Johnson, Garrelt; Illinois, 1891 ***5012.37*** *p62*
Johnson, Geo.; Virginia, 1637 ***6219*** *p112*
Johnson, Georg; Virginia, 1636 ***6219*** *p80*
Johnson, George; Arkansas, 1918 ***95.2*** *p62*
Johnson, George; New York, 1825 ***9892.11*** *p23*
Johnson, George; New York, NY, 1815 ***2859.11*** *p34*
Johnson, George; New York, NY, 1838 ***8208.4*** *p61*
Johnson, George; Ohio, 1830 ***9892.11*** *p23*
Johnson, George; Wisconsin, n.d. ***9675.6*** *p52*
Johnson, George 15; Kingston, Jamaica, 1773 ***1219.7*** *p170*
Johnson, George 24; Maryland, 1775 ***1219.7*** *p249*
Johnson, George 25; Baltimore, 1775 ***1219.7*** *p270*
Johnson, George 26 *SEE* Johnson, William
Johnson, George 30; Kansas, 1887 ***5240.1*** *p71*
Johnson, George J.; Iroquois Co., IL, 1892 ***3455.1*** *p11*
Johnson, Grace *SEE* Johnson, Hen.
Johnson, Guillaume; Nova Scotia, 1715 ***7603*** *p37*
Johnson, Gumme; Colorado, 1904 ***9678.2*** *p60*
Johnson, Gust; Minneapolis, 1869-1877 ***6410.35*** *p57*
Johnson, Gust; Minneapolis, 1881-1887 ***6410.35*** *p57*
Johnson, Gust; Washington, 1859-1920 ***2872.1*** *p19*
Johnson, Gustaf; Iowa, 1852 ***2090*** *p611*
Johnson, Gustaf Adolf; Iowa, 1866-1943 ***123.54*** *p25*
Johnson, Gustav 35; Kansas, 1893 ***5240.1*** *p78*
Johnson, Gustave Martin 22; Kansas, 1896 ***5240.1*** *p80*
Johnson, Gustof Carl; Iowa, 1866-1943 ***123.54*** *p25*
Johnson, Hans; Bangor, ME, 1816-1840 ***6410.22*** *p115*
Johnson, Hans; Illinois, 1882 ***5012.39*** *p52*
Johnson, Hans; Minneapolis, 1875-1884 ***6410.35*** *p57*
Johnson, Harm; Illinois, 1888 ***5012.37*** *p61*
Johnson, Heinrich; Illinois, 1888 ***5012.39*** *p121*
Johnson, Hen.; Virginia, 1635 ***6219*** *p3* *Wife:*Grace
Johnson, Hen.; Virginia, 1635 ***6219*** *p69*
Johnson, Henning; Arkansas, 1918 ***95.2*** *p62*
Johnson, Henning; New York, NY, 1906 ***3455.1*** *p52*
Johnson, Henning Edward; Washington, 1859-1920 ***2872.1*** *p19*
Johnson, Henry; Colorado, 1905 ***9678.2*** *p60*
Johnson, Henry; Iroquois Co., IL, 1894 ***3455.1*** *p11*
Johnson, Henry; New York, NY, 1815 ***2859.11*** *p34*
Johnson, Henry; New York, NY, 1835 ***8208.4*** *p77*
Johnson, Henry; New York, NY, 1874 ***9678.2*** *p60*
Johnson, Henry; Washington, 1859-1920 ***2872.1*** *p19*
Johnson, Henry 15; Maryland, 1724 ***3690.1*** *p125*
Johnson, Hersford 21; Maryland, 1774 ***1219.7*** *p229*
Johnson, Hezekiah 22; Jamaica, 1774 ***1219.7*** *p231*
Johnson, Hjabmar; Iowa, 1866-1943 ***123.54*** *p25*
Johnson, Hjalmer; Iowa, 1866-1943 ***123.54*** *p25*
Johnson, Hugh; New York, NY, 1811 ***2859.11*** *p14*
Johnson, Isabella 68; North Carolina, 1850 ***1639.20*** *p100* *Relative:*Jane 40
Johnson, Israell; Virginia, 1636 ***6219*** *p74*
Johnson, J.; Minneapolis, 1877-1883 ***6410.35*** *p57*
Johnson, J.A.; Iowa, 1866-1943 ***123.54*** *p25*
Johnson, J. A.; Minneapolis, 1880-1884 ***6410.35*** *p57*
Johnson, J.H. 81; Arizona, 1920 ***9228.40*** *p24*
Johnson, J. P.; Minneapolis, 1866-1880 ***6410.35*** *p57*
Johnson, J. W.; Minneapolis, 1877-1879 ***6410.35*** *p57*
Johnson, Jacob 18; Maryland, 1774 ***1219.7*** *p220*
Johnson, James; Indiana, 1848 ***9117*** *p17*
Johnson, James; New York, NY, 1811 ***2859.11*** *p14*
Johnson, James; New York, NY, 1816 ***2859.11*** *p34*
Johnson, James; New York, NY, 1834 ***8208.4*** *p4*
Johnson, James; St. John, N.B., 1852 ***5704.8*** *p83*
Johnson, James; Virginia, 1638 ***6219*** *p146*
Johnson, James 18; America, 1703 ***2212*** *p39*
Johnson, James 21; Virginia, 1700 ***2212*** *p31*
Johnson, James 23; Pennsylvania, Virginia or Maryland, 1699 ***2212*** *p19*
Johnson, James 25; Jamaica, 1733 ***3690.1*** *p125*
Johnson, James 42; Virginia, 1774 ***1219.7*** *p240*
Johnson, James 60; Massachusetts, 1860 ***6410.32*** *p100*
Johnson, James Chris; Colorado, 1904 ***9678.2*** *p60*
Johnson, Jane; St. John, N.B., 1852 ***5704.8*** *p83*
Johnson, Jane; Virginia, 1698 ***2212*** *p12*
Johnson, Jane 27; Massachusetts, 1860 ***6410.32*** *p103*
Johnson, Jane 40 *SEE* Johnson, Isabella
Johnson, Janet; Ohio, 1852 ***8893*** *p266*
Johnson, Jennie Charlotta *SEE* Johnson, Otto
Johnson, Jno 22; America, 1699 ***2212*** *p28*
Johnson, Johan Alfred; Washington, 1859-1920 ***2872.1*** *p19*
Johnson, Johan Erik; New York, 1896 ***1450.2*** *p17B*
Johnson, Johannes; Washington, 1859-1920 ***2872.1*** *p19*
Johnson, John; Arkansas, 1918 ***95.2*** *p62*
Johnson, John; Boston, 1856 ***6410.32*** *p124*
Johnson, John; Buffalo, NY, 1817 ***9892.11*** *p23*
Johnson, John; Iowa, 1866-1943 ***123.54*** *p25*
Johnson, John; Iroquois Co., IL, 1892 ***3455.1*** *p11*
Johnson, John; Maine, 1884-1896 ***6410.22*** *p123*
Johnson, John; Minneapolis, 1873-1887 ***6410.35*** *p57*
Johnson, John; Minneapolis, 1877-1880 ***6410.35*** *p57*
Johnson, John; New York, NY, 1811 ***2859.11*** *p14*
Johnson, John; New York, NY, 1835 ***8208.4*** *p5*
Johnson, John; New York, NY, 1838 ***8208.4*** *p83*
Johnson, John; New York, NY, 1840 ***8208.4*** *p109*
Johnson, John; Ohio, 1840 ***9892.11*** *p23*
Johnson, John; Virginia, 1635 ***6219*** *p36*
Johnson, John; Virginia, 1636 ***6219*** *p80*
Johnson, John; Virginia, 1637 ***6219*** *p83*
Johnson, John; Virginia, 1638 ***6219*** *p121*
Johnson, John; Virginia, 1638 ***6219*** *p160*
Johnson, John; Virginia, 1639 ***6219*** *p157*
Johnson, John; Virginia, 1639 ***6219*** *p162*
Johnson, John; Virginia, 1644 ***6219*** *p208*
Johnson, John; Virginia, 1648 ***6219*** *p251*
Johnson, John; Virginia, 1698 ***2212*** *p13*
Johnson, John 14; New York, NY, 1828 ***6508.4*** *p143*
Johnson, John 17; Pennsylvania, Virginia or Maryland, 1719 ***3690.1*** *p125*
Johnson, John 19; Jamaica, 1731 ***3690.1*** *p125*
Johnson, John 19; Philadelphia, 1803 ***53.26*** *p40*
Johnson, John 20; Nova Scotia, 1774 ***1219.7*** *p209*
Johnson, John 22; Maryland, 1775 ***1219.7*** *p247*
Johnson, John 23; Maryland, 1775 ***1219.7*** *p257*
Johnson, John 25; Quebec, 1774 ***1219.7*** *p211*

Johnston, Edward 21; Quebec, 1853 ***5704.8*** *p105*
Johnston, Elisabeth; Quebec, 1824 ***7603*** *p66*
Johnston, Eliza; New York, NY, 1864 ***5704.8*** *p172*
Johnston, Eliza; New York, NY, 1868 ***5704.8*** *p229*
Johnston, Eliza; Quebec, 1847 ***5704.8*** *p27*
Johnston, Eliza; Quebec, 1847 ***5704.8*** *p36*
Johnston, Eliza; Quebec, 1851 ***5704.8*** *p82*
Johnston, Eliza 8; St. John, N.B., 1847 ***5704.8*** *p25*
Johnston, Eliza 10 *SEE* Johnston, William
Johnston, Eliza 10; Philadelphia, 1849 ***5704.8*** *p58*
Johnston, Eliza 12; St. John, N.B., 1847 ***5704.8*** *p20*
Johnston, Eliza 17; St. John, N.B., 1863 ***5704.8*** *p155*
Johnston, Eliza 22; St. John, N.B., 1866 ***5704.8*** *p167*
Johnston, Eliza Ann 15 mos; New York, NY, 1868 ***5704.8*** *p229*
Johnston, Eliza Jane; Philadelphia, 1849 ***53.26*** *p40*
Johnston, Eliza Jane; Philadelphia, 1849 ***5704.8*** *p49*
Johnston, Elizabeth; New York, NY, 1816 ***2859.11*** *p34*
Johnston, Elizabeth 6; Philadelphia, 1861 ***5704.8*** *p147*
Johnston, Elizabeth 7; Philadelphia, 1859 ***5704.8*** *p142*
Johnston, Elizabeth 36; Philadelphia, 1861 ***5704.8*** *p147*
Johnston, Ellan; Philadelphia, 1849 ***53.26*** *p40*
Johnston, Ellan; Philadelphia, 1849 ***5704.8*** *p58*
Johnston, Ellen 58; St. John, N.B., 1854 ***5704.8*** *p115*
Johnston, Fanny 16; Quebec, 1857 ***5704.8*** *p135*
Johnston, Fanny 25; Philadelphia, 1859 ***5704.8*** *p141*
Johnston, Francis; New York, NY, 1811 ***2859.11*** *p14*
Johnston, Francis; New York, NY, 1816 ***2859.11*** *p34*
Johnston, Francis; Quebec, 1852 ***5704.8*** *p86*
Johnston, Francis; Quebec, 1852 ***5704.8*** *p90*
Johnston, Francis 23; Quebec, 1854 ***5704.8*** *p119*
Johnston, Gabriel; North Carolina, 1734 ***1639.20*** *p101*
Johnston, George *SEE* Johnston, William
Johnston, George; Philadelphia, 1847 ***5704.8*** *p22*
Johnston, George; Quebec, 1852 ***5704.8*** *p89*
Johnston, George 9 mos; Quebec, 1847 ***5704.8*** *p28*
Johnston, George 18; Massachusetts, 1847 ***5881.1*** *p51*
Johnston, Gera; New York, NY, 1816 ***2859.11*** *p34*
Johnston, Gilbert; Cape Fear, NC, 1746 ***1639.20*** *p101*
Johnston, Henry; New York, NY, 1811 ***2859.11*** *p14*
With family
Johnston, Henry 20; St. John, N.B., 1858 ***5704.8*** *p137*
Johnston, Hugh; New York, NY, 1889 ***1450.2*** *p18B*
Johnston, Hugh; St. John, N.B., 1847 ***5704.8*** *p11*
Johnston, Hugh 9; Quebec, 1847 ***5704.8*** *p28*
Johnston, Isabella; St. John, N.B., 1847 ***5704.8*** *p25*
Johnston, Isabella 9 mos; St. John, N.B., 1847 ***5704.8*** *p25*
Johnston, Isabella 18; St. John, N.B., 1858 ***5704.8*** *p137*
Johnston, James *SEE* Johnston, William
Johnston, James; Philadelphia, 1847 ***5704.8*** *p22*
Johnston, James; Philadelphia, 1851 ***5704.8*** *p75*
Johnston, James; Philadelphia, 1851 ***5704.8*** *p79*
Johnston, James; Quebec, 1847 ***5704.8*** *p6*
Johnston, James; Quebec, 1847 ***5704.8*** *p27*
Johnston, James; Quebec, 1847 ***5704.8*** *p36*
Johnston, James; St. John, N.B., 1850 ***5704.8*** *p62*
Johnston, James; St. John, N.B., 1853 ***5704.8*** *p99*
Johnston, James 2 mos; Philadelphia, 1861 ***5704.8*** *p147*
Johnston, James 2; Quebec, 1856 ***5704.8*** *p129*
Johnston, James 5; Wilmington, DE, 1831 ***6508.3*** *p100*
Johnston, James 6; Quebec, 1847 ***5704.8*** *p36*
Johnston, James 7; Quebec, 1847 ***5704.8*** *p28*
Johnston, James 20; Wilmington, DE, 1831 ***6508.3*** *p101*
Johnston, James 22; Philadelphia, 1858 ***5704.8*** *p139*
Johnston, James 28; Kansas, 1890 ***5240.1*** *p75*
Johnston, James 44; Quebec, 1856 ***5704.8*** *p129*
Johnston, Jane; New York, NY, 1816 ***2859.11*** *p34*
Johnston, Jane; Philadelphia, 1851 ***5704.8*** *p79*
Johnston, Jane; Philadelphia, 1852 ***5704.8*** *p86*
Johnston, Jane; Philadelphia, 1867 ***5704.8*** *p216*
Johnston, Jane; Quebec, 1847 ***5704.8*** *p6*
Johnston, Jane; Quebec, 1847 ***5704.8*** *p27*
Johnston, Jane; Quebec, 1847 ***5704.8*** *p36*
Johnston, Jane; Quebec, 1851 ***5704.8*** *p74*
Johnston, Jane; St. John, N.B., 1847 ***5704.8*** *p20*
Johnston, Jane; St. John, N.B., 1848 ***5704.8*** *p39*
Johnston, Jane; St. John, N.B., 1853 ***5704.8*** *p106*
Johnston, Jane 2; Wilmington, DE, 1831 ***6508.3*** *p100*
Johnston, Jane 20; St. John, N.B., 1853 ***5704.8*** *p109*
Johnston, Jane 29; Quebec, 1856 ***5704.8*** *p129*
Johnston, Janet *SEE* Johnston, Nicholas
Johnston, Jean; Quebec, 1783 ***7603*** *p35*
Johnston, John; America, 1740 ***4971*** *p70*
Johnston, John; Montreal, 1792 ***9775.5*** *p202*
Johnston, John; New York, NY, 1811 ***2859.11*** *p14*
Johnston, John; New York, NY, 1864 ***5704.8*** *p172*
Johnston, John; North Carolina, 1771 ***1639.20*** *p101*
Johnston, John; Quebec, 1847 ***5704.8*** *p17*
Johnston, John; Quebec, 1847 ***5704.8*** *p28*
Johnston, John; Quebec, 1849 ***5704.8*** *p52*
Johnston, John; Quebec, 1851 ***5704.8*** *p82*
Johnston, John; St. John, N.B., 1847 ***5704.8*** *p14*
Johnston, John; South Carolina, 1716 ***1639.20*** *p101*
Johnston, John; South Carolina, 1744 ***1639.20*** *p101*
Johnston, John 1; Philadelphia, 1861 ***5704.8*** *p147*
Johnston, John 3; Massachusetts, 1848 ***5881.1*** *p51*
Johnston, John 4; Quebec, 1856 ***5704.8*** *p129*
Johnston, John 10; St. John, N.B., 1847 ***5704.8*** *p25*
Johnston, John 11; Quebec, 1847 ***5704.8*** *p28*
Johnston, John 12; Quebec, 1847 ***5704.8*** *p8*
Johnston, John 13; Quebec, 1847 ***5704.8*** *p36*
Johnston, John 18; Philadelphia, 1833-1834 ***53.26*** *p40*
Johnston, John 19; Jamaica, 1731 ***3690.1*** *p125*
Johnston, John 20; Philadelphia, 1853 ***5704.8*** *p108*
Johnston, John 23; Philadelphia, 1803 ***53.26*** *p40*
Johnston, John 28; St. John, N.B., 1854 ***5704.8*** *p115*
Johnston, John 29; Philadelphia, 1854 ***5704.8*** *p117*
Johnston, John 36 *SEE* Johnston, Mary
Johnston, John Cenneroy; Arkansas, 1918 ***95.2*** *p62*
Johnston, Joseph; New York, NY, 1864 ***5704.8*** *p172*
Johnston, Joseph; Quebec, 1853 ***5704.8*** *p105*
Johnston, Joseph; St. John, N.B., 1850 ***5704.8*** *p67*
Johnston, Joseph 6 mos; Quebec, 1847 ***5704.8*** *p36*
Johnston, Joseph 20; Quebec, 1864 ***5704.8*** *p159*
Johnston, Joseph 21; Quebec, 1854 ***5704.8*** *p118*
Johnston, Lavia; New Orleans, 1849 ***5704.8*** *p59*
Johnston, Margaret; America, 1739 ***4971*** *p25*
Johnston, Margaret; America, 1742 ***4971*** *p17*
Johnston, Margaret; Philadelphia, 1852 ***5704.8*** *p86*
Johnston, Margaret; Philadelphia, 1852 ***5704.8*** *p88*
Johnston, Margaret; Quebec, 1847 ***5704.8*** *p6*
Johnston, Margaret; Quebec, 1847 ***5704.8*** *p17*
Johnston, Margaret; Quebec, 1847 ***5704.8*** *p36*
Johnston, Margaret 9 mos; St. John, N.B., 1847 ***5704.8*** *p20*
Johnston, Margaret 4; St. John, N.B., 1847 ***5704.8*** *p14*
Johnston, Margaret 8; Quebec, 1847 ***5704.8*** *p36*
Johnston, Margaret 17; Philadelphia, 1859 ***5704.8*** *p142*
Johnston, Margaret 20; St. John, N.B., 1865 ***5704.8*** *p165*
Johnston, Margaret 29; Quebec, 1856 ***5704.8*** *p130*
Johnston, Margaret 30 *SEE* Johnston, Mary
Johnston, Margaret 30; Wilmington, DE, 1831 ***6508.3*** *p100*
Johnston, Maria 5; Quebec, 1847 ***5704.8*** *p36*
Johnston, Maria 16; St. John, N.B., 1854 ***5704.8*** *p115*
Johnston, Martha; Quebec, 1847 ***5704.8*** *p27*
Johnston, Martha 12; Massachusetts, 1847 ***5881.1*** *p51*
Johnston, Martha 50; Wilmington, DE, 1831 ***6508.3*** *p101*
Johnston, Martha Jane 11; Quebec, 1847 ***5704.8*** *p36*
Johnston, Mary; New York, NY, 1816 ***2859.11*** *p34*
Johnston, Mary; Philadelphia, 1848 ***53.26*** *p40*
Johnston, Mary; Philadelphia, 1848 ***5704.8*** *p46*
Johnston, Mary; Philadelphia, 1851 ***5704.8*** *p80*
Johnston, Mary; Quebec, 1847 ***5704.8*** *p36*
Johnston, Mary; Quebec, 1850 ***5704.8*** *p66*
Johnston, Mary; St. John, N.B., 1847 ***5704.8*** *p11*
Johnston, Mary 6 mos; St. John, N.B., 1847 ***5704.8*** *p14*
Johnston, Mary 6; St. John, N.B., 1847 ***5704.8*** *p25*
Johnston, Mary 9; Massachusetts, 1848 ***5881.1*** *p51*
Johnston, Mary 14; Quebec, 1857 ***5704.8*** *p136*
Johnston, Mary 15; Massachusetts, 1847 ***5881.1*** *p51*
Johnston, Mary 19; Virginia, 1749 ***3690.1*** *p126*
Johnston, Mary 24; Wilmington, DE, 1831 ***6508.3*** *p101*
Johnston, Mary 38 *SEE* Johnston, Mary
Johnston, Mary 65; North Carolina, 1850 ***1639.20*** *p102*
*Relative:*Nancy 44
*Relative:*Alexander 40
*Relative:*Mary 38
*Relative:*John 36
*Relative:*Margaret 30
Johnston, Mary A. 5; Philadelphia, 1859 ***5704.8*** *p142*
Johnston, Mary Ann 10; Quebec, 1847 ***5704.8*** *p36*
Johnston, Mary Ann 13; Quebec, 1847 ***5704.8*** *p27*
Johnston, Mary Jane 7; Quebec, 1847 ***5704.8*** *p6*
Johnston, Mary Jane 8; Quebec, 1852 ***5704.8*** *p86*
Johnston, Mary Jane 8; Quebec, 1852 ***5704.8*** *p90*
Johnston, Mary Jane 29; Quebec, 1853 ***5704.8*** *p105*
Johnston, Matilda 3; Quebec, 1847 ***5704.8*** *p28*
Johnston, Matty 18; St. John, N.B., 1853 ***5704.8*** *p109*
Johnston, Mentha; New York, NY, 1864 ***5704.8*** *p173*
Johnston, Nancy *SEE* Johnston, William
Johnston, Nancy; Philadelphia, 1847 ***5704.8*** *p22*
Johnston, Nancy 44 *SEE* Johnston, Mary
Johnston, Neil; America, 1802 ***1639.20*** *p102*
Johnston, Nicholas; Georgia, 1775 ***1219.7*** *p274*
*Wife:*Janet
Johnston, Oliver; New York, NY, 1816 ***2859.11*** *p34*
Johnston, Patrick; America, 1741 ***4971*** *p10*
Johnston, Patrick; New York, NY, 1815 ***2859.11*** *p34*
Johnston, Patrick; Philadelphia, 1851 ***5704.8*** *p80*
Johnston, Peter; Savannah, GA, 1819 ***1639.20*** *p102*
Johnston, Rachael; Philadelphia, 1867 ***5704.8*** *p216*
Johnston, Rachael 8; Philadelphia, 1847 ***5704.8*** *p22*
Johnston, Rachel 8 *SEE* Johnston, William
Johnston, Rebecca; Quebec, 1850 ***5704.8*** *p66*
Johnston, Richard; St. John, N.B., 1850 ***5704.8*** *p66*
Johnston, Robert *SEE* Johnston, Samuel
Johnston, Robert; New Orleans, 1849 ***5704.8*** *p59*
Johnston, Robert; New York, NY, 1811 ***2859.11*** *p14*
Johnston, Robert; New York, NY, 1815 ***2859.11*** *p34*
Johnston, Robert; New York, NY, 1838 ***8208.4*** *p84*
Johnston, Robert; Philadelphia, 1847 ***53.26*** *p40*
Johnston, Robert; Philadelphia, 1847 ***5704.8*** *p22*
Johnston, Robert; Philadelphia, 1848 ***5704.8*** *p46*
Johnston, Robert; Quebec, 1847 ***5704.8*** *p36*
Johnston, Robert 8; St. John, N.B., 1847 ***5704.8*** *p20*
Johnston, Robert 9; Quebec, 1847 ***5704.8*** *p36*
Johnston, Robert 12; Quebec, 1847 ***5704.8*** *p36*
Johnston, Robert 15; Philadelphia, 1804 ***53.26*** *p40*
Johnston, Robert 20; Philadelphia, 1865 ***5704.8*** *p164*
Johnston, Rose; America, 1736 ***4971*** *p71*
Johnston, Roseanna 30; St. John, N.B., 1853 ***5704.8*** *p110*
Johnston, Samuel; New York, NY, 1816 ***2859.11*** *p34*
Johnston, Samuel; North Carolina, 1735 ***1639.20*** *p102*
Johnston, Samuel; Philadelphia, 1848 ***53.26*** *p40*
*Relative:*Robert
Johnston, Samuel; Philadelphia, 1848 ***5704.8*** *p46*
Johnston, Samuel; Quebec, 1847 ***5704.8*** *p36*
Johnston, Samuel; St. John, N.B., 1847 ***5704.8*** *p11*
Johnston, Samuel 3; Wilmington, DE, 1831 ***6508.3*** *p100*
Johnston, Sarah; St. John, N.B., 1847 ***5704.8*** *p14*
Johnston, Sarah 16; Quebec, 1854 ***5704.8*** *p118*
Johnston, Sarah 18; Wilmington, DE, 1831 ***6508.3*** *p101*
Johnston, Sarah 40; Quebec, 1853 ***5704.8*** *p105*
Johnston, Silas; Quebec, 1847 ***5704.8*** *p36*
Johnston, Teresa; Quebec, 1852 ***5704.8*** *p90*
Johnston, Teressa; Quebec, 1852 ***5704.8*** *p86*
Johnston, Thomas; America, 1739 ***4971*** *p75*
Johnston, Thomas; New York, NY, 1864 ***5704.8*** *p174*
Johnston, Thomas; Philadelphia, 1852 ***5704.8*** *p91*
Johnston, Thomas; Quebec, 1851 ***5704.8*** *p75*
Johnston, Thomas; St. John, N.B., 1847 ***5704.8*** *p20*
Johnston, Thomas 3; Wilmington, DE, 1831 ***6508.3*** *p100*
Johnston, Thomas 10; St. John, N.B., 1847 ***5704.8*** *p14*
Johnston, Thomas 12; St. John, N.B., 1847 ***5704.8*** *p25*
Johnston, Thomas 22; St. John, N.B., 1865 ***5704.8*** *p165*
Johnston, Thomas 25; Wilmington, DE, 1831 ***6508.3*** *p100*
Johnston, Warnock; St. John, N.B., 1852 ***5704.8*** *p84*
Johnston, William; Jamaica, 1750 ***3690.1*** *p126*
Johnston, William; Jamaica, 1751 ***1219.7*** *p2*
Johnston, William; New York, NY, 1815 ***2859.11*** *p34*
Johnston, William; New York, NY, 1816 ***2859.11*** *p34*
Johnston, William; New York, NY, 1864 ***5704.8*** *p174*
Johnston, William; North Carolina, 1780 ***1639.20*** *p102*
Johnston, William; Philadelphia, 1847 ***53.26*** *p40*
*Relative:*Nancy
*Relative:*James
*Relative:*George
*Relative:*Rachel 8
Johnston, William; Philadelphia, 1847 ***5704.8*** *p22*
Johnston, William; Philadelphia, 1852 ***5704.8*** *p86*
Johnston, William; Quebec, 1847 ***5704.8*** *p36*
Johnston, William; St. John, N.B., 1847 ***5704.8*** *p25*
Johnston, William; St. John, N.B., 1848 ***5704.8*** *p45*
Johnston, William; St. John, N.B., 1853 ***5704.8*** *p99*
Johnston, William; St. John, N.B., 1853 ***5704.8*** *p100*
Johnston, William; Virginia, 1805 ***4778.2*** *p141*
Johnston, William 5; Quebec, 1847 ***5704.8*** *p28*
Johnston, William 7; Quebec, 1847 ***5704.8*** *p36*
Johnston, William 7; Wilmington, DE, 1831 ***6508.3*** *p100*
Johnston, William 8; St. John, N.B., 1847 ***5704.8*** *p14*
Johnston, William 12; Philadelphia, 1849 ***53.26*** *p40*
*Relative:*Eliza 10
Johnston, William 12; Philadelphia, 1849 ***5704.8*** *p58*
Johnston, William 17; Wilmington, DE, 1831 ***6508.3*** *p101*
Johnston, William 26; Philadelphia, 1774 ***1219.7*** *p233*
Johnston, William John 9 mos; New Orleans, 1849 ***5704.8*** *p59*
Johnston, William S.; Cincinnati, 1800-1877 ***8582.3*** *p86*
Johnston, William Thomas; Quebec, 1849 ***5704.8*** *p57*
Johnstone, Mrs.; St. John, N.B., 1866 ***5704.8*** *p166*
Johnstone, Elizabeth; Wilmington, NC, 1733 ***1639.20*** *p101*
Johnstone, James; St. John, N.B., 1866 ***5704.8*** *p166*
Johnstone, John; St. John, N.B., 1866 ***5704.8*** *p166*
Johnstone, John 10; St. John, N.B., 1866 ***5704.8*** *p167*
Johnstone, John 40; Philadelphia, 1858 ***5704.8*** *p138*
Johnstone, Thomas 20; Quebec, 1858 ***5704.8*** *p138*
Johnstone, William 25; Philadelphia, 1864 ***5704.8*** *p157*
Johoni, George 21; New Orleans, 1838 ***778.5*** *p287*
Joice, Michael 15; Massachusetts, 1850 ***5881.1*** *p51*
Joice, Micheal; Illinois, 1859 ***5012.38*** *p97*
Joice, Richard 18; Massachusetts, 1847 ***5881.1*** *p52*
Joice, Thomas 21; Massachusetts, 1847 ***5881.1*** *p52*

Join, Mr.; New Orleans, 1839 ***778.5*** *p287*
Jokab, Martin; Wisconsin, n.d. ***9675.6*** *p52*
Jokobouski, John; Wisconsin, n.d. ***9675.6*** *p52*
Jolas, Thomas Bill 26; Arkansas, 1918 ***95.2*** *p62*
Jolicoeur, Jean-Baptiste 35; Montreal, 1704 ***7603*** *p64*
Jolimois, . . .; Halifax, N.S., 1752 ***7074.6*** *p230*
Jolimois, Jacques; Halifax, N.S., 1752 ***7074.6*** *p228*
Jolimore, . . .; Halifax, N.S., 1752 ***7074.6*** *p230*
Jolivet, John; New York, NY, 1838 ***8208.4*** *p87*
Jolivie, Mr. 25; America, 1838 ***778.5*** *p287*
Jollia, Geo. 34; New Orleans, 1829 ***778.5*** *p287*
Jollier, A. 22; America, 1827 ***778.5*** *p288*
Jolliff, William 20; Maryland, 1719 ***3690.1*** *p126*
Jollimai, Pierre; Halifax, N.S., 1752 ***7074.6*** *p216*
Jollimore, George; Halifax, N.S., 1752 ***7074.6*** *p230*
Jollimore, Jacques; Halifax, N.S., 1752 ***7074.6*** *p230*
Jolly, Charles 40; America, 1835 ***778.5*** *p288*
Jolly, Fran.; Virginia, 1648 ***6219*** *p252*
Jolly, James; America, 1854 ***1450.2*** *p73A*
Jolly, James 40; Maryland, 1775 ***1219.7*** *p252*
Jolly, John; Virginia, 1642 ***6219*** *p197*
Jolly, John; Virginia, 1648 ***6219*** *p252*
Jolly, Jon.; Virginia, 1636 ***6219*** *p76*
Jolly, Joseph; Virginia, 1636 ***6219*** *p16*
*Wife:*Margery
Jolly, Joseph; Virginia, 1637 ***6219*** *p109*
*Wife:*Margery
Jolly, Joseph; Virginia, 1637 ***6219*** *p113*
Jolly, Joseph; Virginia, 1643 ***6219*** *p200*
Jolly, Licha; Virginia, 1648 ***6219*** *p252*
Jolly, Margaret; New York, NY, 1816 ***2859.11*** *p34*
Jolly, Margery *SEE* Jolly, Joseph
Jolly, Margery *SEE* Jolly, Joseph
Jolly, Martin 22; St. Vincent, 1775 ***1219.7*** *p251*
Jolly, Patterson; New York, NY, 1811 ***2859.11*** *p14*
Jolly, Robert; New York, NY, 1816 ***2859.11*** *p34*
Jolly, William; America, 1854 ***1450.2*** *p74A*
Jollymore, . . .; Halifax, N.S., 1752 ***7074.6*** *p230*
Joly, John A.; New York, NY, 1837 ***8208.4*** *p40*
Joly, L. 35; New Orleans, 1826 ***778.5*** *p288*
Jolymoy, Nicolas *SEE* Jolymoy, Pierre
Jolymoy, Pierre *SEE* Jolymoy, Pierre
Jolymoy, Pierre 50; Halifax, N.S., 1752 ***7074.6*** *p211*
*Son:*Pierre
*Son:*Nicolas
Jomick, Steve; Arkansas, 1918 ***95.2*** *p62*
Jomphe, . . .; Canada, 1776-1783 ***9786*** *p25*
Jomphe, Christian; Canada, 1776-1783 ***9786*** *p243*
Jompson, William 33; Virginia, 1725 ***3690.1*** *p126*
Jomson, William 33; Virginia, 1725 ***3690.1*** *p126*
Jonanovich, Angelo; Iowa, 1866-1943 ***123.54*** *p25*
Jonartis, Frank; Wisconsin, n.d. ***9675.6*** *p52*
Jonas, John; Virginia, 1844 ***4626.16*** *p12*
Jonasdottir, Onding 32; Quebec, 1879 ***2557.1*** *p21*
Jonasson, Arvid Uno; Minneapolis, 1880-1884 ***6410.35*** *p56*
Jonasson, August; Minneapolis, 1869-1878 ***6410.35*** *p56*
Jonasson, August; Minneapolis, 1873-1881 ***6410.35*** *p47*
Jonasson, Erik; Minneapolis, 1870-1880 ***6410.35*** *p65*
Joncherrie, Louise 26; New Orleans, 1838 ***778.5*** *p288*
Joncherrie, Pierre 29; New Orleans, 1838 ***778.5*** *p288*
Jondot, Mr. 21; New Orleans, 1827 ***778.5*** *p288*
Jone, Mrs. 32; Port uncertain, 1838 ***778.5*** *p288*
Jone, P. 40; Port uncertain, 1838 ***778.5*** *p288*
Jones, Mr. 25; Massachusetts, 1849 ***5881.1*** *p51*
Jones, Mrs.; Philadelphia, 1774 ***1219.7*** *p201*
Jones, Mrs. 25; Massachusetts, 1849 ***5881.1*** *p51*
Jones, Abraham 36; Jamaica, 1730 ***3690.1*** *p126*
Jones, Alexr 12; Virginia, 1699 ***2212*** *p26*
Jones, Alice; Virginia, 1636 ***6219*** *p32*
Jones, Alice; Virginia, 1638 ***6219*** *p153*
Jones, Ann; America, 1697 ***2212*** *p4*
Jones, Ann; America, 1697 ***2212*** *p7*
Jones, Ann; America, 1737 ***4971*** *p85*
Jones, Ann; America, 1737 ***4971*** *p95*
Jones, Ann; America, 1743 ***4971*** *p11*
Jones, Ann; America, 1868 ***5704.8*** *p229*
Jones, Ann; Montreal, 1824 ***7603*** *p72*
Jones, Ann; Virginia, 1647 ***6219*** *p247*
Jones, Annabella; Prince Edward Island, 1854 ***8893*** *p266*
Jones, Arthur J.; Kansas, 1880 ***5240.1*** *p23*
Jones, Barbara; America, 1743 ***4971*** *p10*
Jones, Barbary 13 *SEE* Jones, Ellis
Jones, Benjamin; Barbados, 1765 ***1219.7*** *p112*
Jones, Bridget; Philadelphia, 1865 ***5704.8*** *p204*
Jones, Catherine; Charleston, SC, 1828 ***1639.20*** *p102*
Jones, Catherine; New York, NY, 1816 ***2859.11*** *p34*
Jones, Catherine 20; St. John, N.B., 1858 ***5704.8*** *p137*
Jones, Charles; Milwaukee, 1875 ***4719.30*** *p258*
With wife
Jones, Charles; Virginia, 1636 ***6219*** *p108*
Jones, Charles 20; Maryland, 1774 ***1219.7*** *p214*
Jones, Charles 25; Maryland, 1775 ***1219.7*** *p268*
Jones, Charles Henry 21; Virginia, 1737 ***3690.1*** *p127*
Jones, Charles M. 44; Harris Co., TX, 1898 ***6254*** *p4*
Jones, Cornelius 18; Jamaica, 1731 ***3690.1*** *p127*
Jones, David; Arizona, 1897 ***9228.30*** *p1*
Jones, David; New York, NY, 1834 ***8208.4*** *p3*
Jones, David; Virginia, 1635 ***6219*** *p10*
Jones, David; Virginia, 1851 ***4626.16*** *p14*
Jones, David 17; Maryland, 1719 ***3690.1*** *p127*
Jones, David 19; America, 1700 ***2212*** *p33*
Jones, David 21; Pennsylvania, 1730 ***3690.1*** *p127*
Jones, David 25; Virginia, 1774 ***1219.7*** *p201*
Jones, David J. 30?; Arizona, 1890 ***2764.35*** *p37*
Jones, David J. 46; Arizona, 1890 ***2764.35*** *p38*
Jones, David W.; West Virginia, 1802-1844 ***9788.3*** *p12*
Jones, Diana 17; Jamaica, 1749 ***3690.1*** *p127*
Jones, Dorothy 10 *SEE* Jones, Ellis
Jones, E. E.; Washington, 1859-1920 ***2872.1*** *p19*
Jones, Edw.; Virginia, 1636 ***6219*** *p26*
Jones, Edward; America, 1697 ***2212*** *p4*
Jones, Edward; Colorado, 1891 ***9678.2*** *p61*
Jones, Edward; Illinois, 1857 ***7857*** *p4*
Jones, Edward; Virginia, 1629 ***6219*** *p31*
Jones, Edward; Virginia, 1637 ***6219*** *p86*
Jones, Edward; Virginia, 1639 ***6219*** *p158*
Jones, Edward 20; Jamaica, 1729 ***3690.1*** *p127*
Jones, Edward 20; Maryland or Virginia, 1699 ***2212*** *p22*
Jones, Edward 20; Pennsylvania, 1725 ***3690.1*** *p127*
Jones, Edward 21; Maryland, 1774 ***1219.7*** *p230*
Jones, Edward 25; Massachusetts, 1849 ***5881.1*** *p51*
Jones, Edward Oswald; Arkansas, 1918 ***95.2*** *p62*
Jones, Edwd; America, 1698 ***2212*** *p6*
Jones, Edwd; America, 1698 ***2212*** *p8*
Jones, Edwd; America, 1698 ***2212*** *p9*
Jones, Edwd 15; America, 1700 ***2212*** *p31*
Jones, Elias; Virginia, 1635 ***6219*** *p17*
Jones, Elisabeth 2; New York, NY, 1851 ***9555.10*** *p26*
Jones, Eliz.; America, 1698 ***2212*** *p9*
Jones, Eliza.; Virginia, 1640 ***6219*** *p185*
Jones, Eliza 17; St. John, N.B., 1857 ***5704.8*** *p135*
Jones, Elizabeth *SEE* Jones, Giles
Jones, Elizabeth *SEE* Jones, William
Jones, Elizabeth; America, 1697 ***2212*** *p7*
Jones, Elizabeth; Quebec, 1849 ***5704.8*** *p51*
Jones, Elizabeth 16; Virginia, 1727 ***3690.1*** *p127*
Jones, Elizabeth 23; Philadelphia, 1774 ***1219.7*** *p182*
Jones, Elizabeth 24; Quebec, 1864 ***5704.8*** *p162*
Jones, Ellis 23; Philadelphia, 1774 ***1219.7*** *p216*
Jones, Ellis 45; Pennsylvania, 1682 ***4962*** *p155*
*Relative:*Jane 40
*Relative:*Barbary 13
*Relative:*Dorothy 10
*Relative:*Mary 12
*Relative:*Isaac 4 mos
Jones, Evan; Virginia, 1635 ***6219*** *p69*
Jones, Evan; Virginia, 1639 ***6219*** *p151*
Jones, Evan; Virginia, 1642 ***6219*** *p197*
Jones, Evan 17; Maryland, 1738 ***3690.1*** *p127*
Jones, Evan 30; America, 1703 ***2212*** *p39*
Jones, Evan Edwds; New York, NY, 1849 ***6013.19*** *p73*
Jones, Foulke; Virginia, 1642 ***6219*** *p196*
Jones, Francis 19; Maryland, 1735 ***3690.1*** *p127*
Jones, Frederick G.; Illinois, 1872 ***7857*** *p4*
Jones, Geo. W. C. 31; Kansas, 1886 ***5240.1*** *p23*
Jones, Geo. W. C. 31; Kansas, 1886 ***5240.1*** *p69*
Jones, George 21; Philadelphia, 1774 ***1219.7*** *p232*
Jones, George 38; Jamaica, 1731 ***3690.1*** *p127*
Jones, Giles; Virginia, 1623-1638 ***6219*** *p1*
*Wife:*Elizabeth
Jones, Grace 30; Arizona, 1910 ***9228.40*** *p12*
Jones, Grace 30; Arizona, 1910 ***9228.40*** *p15*
Jones, Hannah *SEE* Jones, Jno
Jones, Hannah; Virginia, 1638 ***6219*** *p147*
Jones, Harry; Bangor, ME, 1895 ***6410.22*** *p127*
Jones, Hen.; Virginia, 1642 ***6219*** *p191*
Jones, Henry; America, 1698 ***2212*** *p9*
Jones, Henry; New York, NY, 1815 ***2859.11*** *p34*
Jones, Henry; New York, NY, 1840 ***8208.4*** *p105*
Jones, Henry; Virginia, 1638 ***6219*** *p120*
Jones, Henry; Virginia, 1646 ***6219*** *p240*
Jones, Henry 21; Philadelphia, 1774 ***1219.7*** *p183*
Jones, Henry 23; Baltimore, 1775 ***1219.7*** *p271*
Jones, Hester; Virginia, 1644 ***6219*** *p231*
Jones, Hester 18; Virginia, 1700 ***2212*** *p31*
Jones, Howell; Virginia, 1642 ***6219*** *p191*
Jones, Howell 23; Virginia, 1700 ***2212*** *p31*
Jones, Hugh; America, 1697 ***2212*** *p8*
Jones, Hugh; America, 1698 ***2212*** *p6*
Jones, Hugh; Virginia, 1635 ***6219*** *p36*
Jones, Hugh; Virginia, 1637 ***6219*** *p13*
Jones, Hugh; Virginia, 1637 ***6219*** *p82*
Jones, Hugh; Virginia, 1637 ***6219*** *p83*
Jones, Hugh 25; Port uncertain, 1774 ***1219.7*** *p176*
Jones, Humphrey; Virginia, 1636 ***6219*** *p74*
Jones, Humphrey; Virginia, 1637 ***6219*** *p108*
Jones, Isaac; Virginia, 1643 ***6219*** *p229*
Jones, Isaac; Virginia, 1648 ***6219*** *p246*
Jones, Isaac 4 mos *SEE* Jones, Ellis
Jones, Isaac 29; Pennsylvania, 1733 ***3690.1*** *p127*
Jones, Isabel 25; America, 1705 ***2212*** *p42*
Jones, J.E.; Iowa, 1866-1943 ***123.54*** *p25*
Jones, J.P.; Arizona, 1890 ***2764.35*** *p38*
Jones, James; Illinois, 1869 ***5012.38*** *p99*
Jones, James; New York, NY, 1816 ***2859.11*** *p34*
Jones, James; Virginia, 1641 ***6219*** *p187*
Jones, James; Virginia, 1643 ***6219*** *p200*
Jones, James; Washington, 1859-1920 ***2872.1*** *p19*
Jones, James 7; Quebec, 1849 ***5704.8*** *p51*
Jones, James 24; Philadelphia, 1775 ***1219.7*** *p255*
Jones, James 43; Philadelphia, 1774 ***1219.7*** *p228*
Jones, James 53; Massachusetts, 1849 ***5881.1*** *p51*
Jones, James L.; New Mexico, 1887 ***2764.35*** *p37*
Jones, Jane 11; Quebec, 1849 ***5704.8*** *p51*
Jones, Jane 21; Massachusetts, 1847 ***5881.1*** *p51*
Jones, Jane 40 *SEE* Jones, Ellis
Jones, Jeremiah; America, 1698 ***2212*** *p13*
Jones, Jno; America, 1698 ***2212*** *p6*
*Wife:*Hannah
With child
Jones, Jno 19; Maryland or Virginia, 1699 ***2212*** *p23*
Jones, John; America, 1697 ***2212*** *p8*
Jones, John; America, 1742 ***4971*** *p17*
Jones, John; Annapolis, MD, 1742 ***4971*** *p93*
Jones, John; Illinois, 1856 ***7857*** *p4*
Jones, John; Iowa, 1866-1943 ***123.54*** *p25*
Jones, John; Maryland, 1742 ***4971*** *p107*
Jones, John; New York, NY, 1811 ***2859.11*** *p14*
Jones, John; New York, NY, 1838 ***8208.4*** *p71*
Jones, John; New York, NY, 1839 ***8208.4*** *p95*
Jones, John; Philadelphia, 1849 ***53.26*** *p40*
Jones, John; Philadelphia, 1849 ***5704.8*** *p50*
Jones, John; Quebec, 1820 ***7603*** *p47*
Jones, John; South Carolina, 1754 ***1219.7*** *p29*
Jones, John; Virginia, 1638 ***6219*** *p123*
Jones, John; Virginia, 1639 ***6219*** *p156*
Jones, John; Virginia, 1639 ***6219*** *p161*
Jones, John; Virginia, 1642 ***6219*** *p190*
Jones, John; Virginia, 1647 ***6219*** *p247*
Jones, John; Virginia, 1648 ***6219*** *p246*
Jones, John 7; New York, NY, 1851 ***9555.10*** *p26*
Jones, John 9; Quebec, 1849 ***5704.8*** *p51*
Jones, John 13; Maryland or Virginia, 1699 ***2212*** *p24*
Jones, John 15; Maryland or Virginia, 1735 ***3690.1*** *p128*
Jones, John 15; New York, 1775 ***1219.7*** *p246*
Jones, John 16; West Indies, 1722 ***3690.1*** *p128*
Jones, John 17; Jamaica, 1735 ***3690.1*** *p128*
Jones, John 17; Maryland or Virginia, 1720 ***3690.1*** *p128*
Jones, John 17; New England, 1699 ***2212*** *p18*
Jones, John 18; Jamaica, 1733 ***3690.1*** *p128*
Jones, John 18; Maryland, 1738 ***3690.1*** *p128*
Jones, John 18; Windward Islands, 1722 ***3690.1*** *p128*
Jones, John 19; Maryland, 1721 ***3690.1*** *p128*
Jones, John 19; Maryland, 1775 ***1219.7*** *p273*
Jones, John 20; Pennsylvania, 1728 ***3690.1*** *p128*
Jones, John 22; Jamaica, 1735 ***3690.1*** *p128*
Jones, John 25; United States or West Indies, 1734 ***3690.1*** *p128*
Jones, John 26; Virginia, 1774 ***1219.7*** *p244*
Jones, John 27; Philadelphia, 1774 ***1219.7*** *p231*
Jones, John 27; Virginia, 1774 ***1219.7*** *p193*
Jones, John 28; Pennsylvania, Virginia or Maryland, 1699 ***2212*** *p20*
Jones, John 31; Maryland, 1774 ***1219.7*** *p187*
Jones, John 34; Jamaica, 1730 ***3690.1*** *p128*
Jones, John 36; Maryland, 1775 ***1219.7*** *p254*
Jones, John 45; New York, NY, 1851 ***9555.10*** *p26*
Jones, John P. 37?; Arizona, 1890 ***2764.35*** *p37*
Jones, John W.; Washington, 1859-1920 ***2872.1*** *p20*
Jones, Jon.; Virginia, 1635 ***6219*** *p27*
Jones, Jon.; Virginia, 1636 ***6219*** *p80*
Jones, Jon.; Virginia, 1638 ***6219*** *p122*
Jones, Jon.; Virginia, 1638 ***6219*** *p145*
Jones, Jon.; Virginia, 1642 ***6219*** *p191*
Jones, Jon.; Virginia, 1643 ***6219*** *p205*
Jones, Joseph; Quebec, 1830 ***4719.7*** *p21*
Jones, Joseph 23; Pennsylvania, 1728 ***3690.1*** *p128*
Jones, Joseph 30; Jamaica, 1750 ***3690.1*** *p129*
Jones, Joseph 35; Port uncertain, 1774 ***1219.7*** *p176*
Jones, Katherine; Virginia, 1639 ***6219*** *p157*
Jones, Lawrance 20; New York, 1774 ***1219.7*** *p223*
Jones, Lewis; New York, NY, 1838 ***8208.4*** *p60*
Jones, Lewis; Virginia, 1637 ***6219*** *p86*
Jones, Lewis 19; Jamaica, 1734 ***3690.1*** *p129*
Jones, Lewis 30; Maryland or Virginia, 1699 ***2212*** *p23*
Jones, Margaret; America, 1743 ***4971*** *p43*
Jones, Margaret 16; America, 1706 ***2212*** *p47*
Jones, Margaret 17; South Carolina, 1732 ***3690.1*** *p129*

Jones, Margaret 32; New England, 1699 2212 p19
Jones, Margarette 17; Maryland or Virginia, 1699 2212 p23
Jones, Martha; Philadelphia, 1847 53.26 p40
Jones, Martha; Philadelphia, 1847 5704.8 p1
Jones, Mary; America, 1698 2212 p9
Jones, Mary; America, 1742 4971 p17
Jones, Mary 3 *SEE* Jones, Noble
Jones, Mary 6; New York, NY, 1851 9555.10 p26
Jones, Mary 12 *SEE* Jones, Ellis
Jones, Mary 17; America, 1701 2212 p35
Jones, Mary 18; Maryland or Virginia, 1699 2212 p22
Jones, Mary 20; America, 1699 2212 p29
Jones, Mary 21; Maryland, 1775 1219.7 p267
Jones, Mary 22; Virginia, 1774 1219.7 p239
Jones, Mary 29; New York, NY, 1851 9555.10 p26
Jones, Mary Ann 9 mos; Quebec, 1849 5704.8 p51
Jones, Maudlen; Virginia, 1637 6219 p17
Jones, Maurice 17; Maryland or Virginia, 1699 2212 p23
Jones, Morgan; Virginia, 1639 6219 p159
Jones, Morian; Virginia, 1646 6219 p242
Jones, Morris; Virginia, 1637 6219 p29
Jones, Moses 18; Maryland, 1774 1219.7 p181
Jones, Nicholas; Virginia, 1642 6219 p198
Jones, Nobel W. 10 *SEE* Jones, Noble
Jones, Noble 32; Savannah, GA, 1733 4719.17 p311
*Daughter:*Mary 3
*Son:*Nobel W. 10
*Wife:*Sarah 32
Jones, Owen; America, 1697 2212 p8
Jones, Owen; Virginia, 1638 6219 p160
Jones, Owen 19; Maryland, 1724 3690.1 p129
Jones, Owen 20; Virginia, 1700 2212 p32
Jones, Owen 24; Kansas, 1873 5240.1 p53
Jones, Owen 27; Massachusetts, 1849 5881.1 p51
Jones, Patient Job 18; Virginia, 1720 3690.1 p129
Jones, Patrick; America, 1738 4971 p71
Jones, Peter; Barbados, 1698 2212 p4
Jones, Peter; Virginia, 1698 2212 p16
Jones, Peter; Wisconsin, n.d. 9675.6 p52
Jones, Peter 20; Jamaica, 1730 3690.1 p129
Jones, Philip 27; Maryland, 1775 1219.7 p255
Jones, Phillip; Virginia, 1640 6219 p185
Jones, Ralph 22; Jamaica, 1730 3690.1 p129
Jones, Reynold; Virginia, 1600-1642 6219 p193
Jones, Rice; Virginia, 1623 6219 p16
Jones, Rice; Virginia, 1637 6219 p114
Jones, Rich.; Virginia, 1635 6219 p10
Jones, Rich.; Virginia, 1635 6219 p33
Jones, Rich.; Virginia, 1635 6219 p71
Jones, Richard; America, 1697 2212 p4
Jones, Richard; New York, NY, 1838 8208.4 p74
Jones, Richard; Virginia, 1621 6219 p25
Jones, Richard; Virginia, 1637 6219 p10
Jones, Richard; Virginia, 1638 6219 p115
Jones, Richard; Virginia, 1638 6219 p146
Jones, Richard; Virginia, 1648 6219 p237
Jones, Richard 15; America, 1700 2212 p22
Jones, Richard 17; Port uncertain, 1774 1219.7 p176
Jones, Richard 18; Maryland, 1720 3690.1 p129
Jones, Richard 21; Philadelphia, 1774 1219.7 p232
Jones, Richard 22; Jamaica, 1730 3690.1 p290
Jones, Richard 22; Pennsylvania, 1730 3690.1 p129
Jones, Richard 23; Jamaica, 1731 3690.1 p129
Jones, Richard 23; Maryland, 1774 1219.7 p224
Jones, Richard 24; Philadelphia, 1803 53.26 p40
Jones, Richd; America, 1697 2212 p8
Jones, Richd; Maryland or Virginia, 1697 2212 p4
Jones, Richd 19; Maryland or Virginia, 1699 2212 p23
Jones, Robert; America, 1697 2212 p7
Jones, Robert; Iowa, 1866-1943 123.54 p25
Jones, Robert; Virginia, 1646 6219 p236
Jones, Robert 3; Quebec, 1849 5704.8 p51
Jones, Robert 19; Pennsylvania, Virginia or Maryland, 1723 3690.1 p129
Jones, Robert 22; Maryland, 1774 1219.7 p180
Jones, Robert 22; Philadelphia, 1774 1219.7 p233
Jones, Robert 23; Jamaica, 1738 3690.1 p129
Jones, Robt; America, 1698 2212 p9
Jones, Robt.; Virginia, 1634 6219 p84
Jones, Roger 18; South Carolina, 1737 3690.1 p129
Jones, Rowland; America, 1698 2212 p5
Jones, Samuel 14; West Indies, 1722 3690.1 p27A
Jones, Samuel 17; Jamaica, 1739 3690.1 p130
Jones, Samuel 18; Philadelphia, 1775 1219.7 p248
Jones, Samuel E.; Ohio, 1842 9892.11 p23
Jones, Samuel E.; Ohio, 1844 9892.11 p23
Jones, Samuell; Virginia, 1638 6219 p125
Jones, Sarah; Virginia, 1637 6219 p109
Jones, Sarah 32 *SEE* Jones, Noble
Jones, Scriven 22; Maryland, 1775 1219.7 p249
Jones, Shri.; Virginia, 1637 6219 p8
Jones, Stanley; Arkansas, 1918 95.2 p62
Jones, Stephen S.; New York, NY, 1834 8208.4 p2
Jones, T.H.; Arizona, 1897 9228.30 p4
Jones, Tho.; Pennsylvania, 1682 4961 p165
Jones, Tho.; Virginia, 1635 6219 p3
Jones, Tho.; Virginia, 1635 6219 p23
Jones, Tho.; Virginia, 1635 6219 p69
Jones, Tho.; Virginia, 1637 6219 p107
Jones, Tho.; Virginia, 1642 6219 p195
Jones, Tho., Jr.; Virginia, 1648 6219 p252
Jones, Thomas; America, 1742 4971 p63
Jones, Thomas; Colorado, 1891 9678.2 p61
Jones, Thomas; New York, NY, 1835 8208.4 p59
Jones, Thomas; Pennsylvania, 1682 4962 p153
Jones, Thomas; Quebec, 1849 5704.8 p51
Jones, Thomas; Virginia, 1635 6219 p16
Jones, Thomas; Virginia, 1635 6219 p36
Jones, Thomas; Virginia, 1636 6219 p78
Jones, Thomas; Virginia, 1642 6219 p188
Jones, Thomas; Virginia, 1642 6219 p191
Jones, Thomas 13; Philadelphia, 1774 1219.7 p197
Jones, Thomas 17; Maryland, 1775 1219.7 p260
Jones, Thomas 18; Maryland or Virginia, 1735 3690.1 p130
Jones, Thomas 18; Philadelphia, 1774 1219.7 p197
Jones, Thomas 19; Maryland, 1718 3690.1 p130
Jones, Thomas 19; Philadelphia, 1857 5704.8 p132
Jones, Thomas 20; Newfoundland, 1699-1700 2212 p18
Jones, Thomas 21; Maryland, 1774 1219.7 p224
Jones, Thomas 21; Maryland, 1775 1219.7 p257
Jones, Thomas 22; Jamaica, 1730 3690.1 p130
Jones, Thomas 22; Maryland, 1774 1219.7 p181
Jones, Thomas 22; Maryland, 1775 1219.7 p250
Jones, Thomas 22; Maryland, 1775 1219.7 p268
Jones, Thomas 25; Jamaica, 1738 3690.1 p130
Jones, Thomas 27; Maryland, 1775 1219.7 p260
Jones, Thomas 29; America, 1700 2212 p33
Jones, Thomas 29; Philadelphia, 1774 1219.7 p196
Jones, Thomas Alfred; Illinois, 1902 2896.5 p20
Jones, Thomas E.; Virginia, 1852 4626.16 p14
Jones, Thomas Mercer; Ontario, 1829 9775.5 p215
Jones, Walter; Virginia, 1639 6219 p152
Jones, Walter; Virginia, 1642 6219 p195
Jones, William; Illinois, 1870 5012.38 p99
Jones, William; New York, 1765 1219.7 p112
Jones, William; New York, NY, 1833 8208.4 p58
Jones, William; Philadelphia, 1851 5704.8 p80
Jones, William; Virginia, 1638 6219 p147
Jones, William; Virginia, 1639 6219 p161
Jones, William; Virginia, 1639 6219 p181
Jones, William; Virginia, 1640 6219 p182
*Wife:*Elizabeth
Jones, William; Virginia, 1642 6219 p193
Jones, William; Virginia, 1648 6219 p249
Jones, William; Virginia, 1772 1219.7 p154
Jones, William; Washington, 1859-1920 2872.1 p20
Jones, William 9; Nova Scotia, 1774 1219.7 p209
Jones, William 15; Maryland, 1775 1219.7 p266
Jones, William 16; Maryland, 1724 3690.1 p130
Jones, William 18; Virginia, 1774 1219.7 p201
Jones, William 20; Antigua (Antego), 1727 3690.1 p130
Jones, William 21; Maryland, 1775 1219.7 p267
Jones, William 22; Maryland, 1774 1219.7 p220
Jones, William 22; Virginia, 1774 1219.7 p243
Jones, William 23; Maryland, 1775 1219.7 p254
Jones, William 24; Maryland, 1735 3690.1 p130
Jones, William 24; Maryland, 1775 1219.7 p264
Jones, William 25; Maryland, 1775 1219.7 p266
Jones, William 25; Pennsylvania, 1728 3690.1 p130
Jones, William 28; Philadelphia, 1774 1219.7 p205
Jones, William 37; Kansas, 1887 5240.1 p23
Jones, William 37; Kansas, 1887 5240.1 p70
Jones, William 38; Philadelphia, 1774 1219.7 p232
Jones, William 50; Tobago, W. Indies, 1773 1219.7 p170
Jones, Winifrid; Virginia, 1646 6219 p241
Jones, Wm.; Virginia, 1618 6219 p72
Jones, Wm; Virginia, 1634 6219 p105
Jones, Wm.; Virginia, 1637 6219 p24
Jones, Wm.; Virginia, 1637 6219 p107
Jones, Wm.; Virginia, 1637 6219 p115
Jones, Wm.; Virginia, 1638 6219 p2
Jones, Wm.; Virginia, 1643 6219 p23
Jones, Wm.; Virginia, 1647 6219 p247
Jonge, Wilhelm; Savannah, GA, 1775 8582.2 p64
Jonginer, Johannes 8 *SEE* Jonginer, Martin
Jonginer, Martin; South Carolina, 1752-1753 3689.17 p21
With wife
*Relative:*Johannes 8
*Relative:*Simon 7
Jonginer, Simon 7 *SEE* Jonginer, Martin
Jonker, August 29; Kansas, 1880 5240.1 p62
Jonkman, Jennie H.; New York, NY, 1875 3455.2 p77
Jonsan, Henning; New York, NY, 1906 3455.1 p52
Jonsdottir, Adalbjorg 26; Quebec, 1879 2557.1 p38
Jonsdottir, Adalbjorg 43; Quebec, 1879 2557.1 p22
Jonsdottir, Albert 13; Quebec, 1879 2557.1 p38A
Jonsdottir, Arnfridur 54; Quebec, 1879 2557.1 p20
Jonsdottir, Eggert 16; Quebec, 1879 2557.1 p38A
Jonsdottir, Elizabet 18; Quebec, 1879 2557.1 p20
Jonsdottir, Gisli 13?; Quebec, 1879 2557.1 p38A
Jonsdottir, Gudni 12; Quebec, 1879 2557.1 p38A
Jonsdottir, Gudny 46; Quebec, 1879 2557.2 p37
Jonsdottir, Gudrun 59; Quebec, 1879 2557.1 p38
Jonsdottir, Helga 48; Quebec, 1879 2557.1 p38A
Jonsdottir, Ingunar 37; Quebec, 1879 2557.2 p36
Jonsdottir, Jarfridur 56; Quebec, 1879 2557.1 p38A
Jonsdottir, Kristin 68; Quebec, 1879 2557.1 p38
Jonsdottir, Magiborg 36; Quebec, 1879 2557.1 p39
Jonsdottir, Magnina 6 mos; Quebec, 1879 2557.2 p37
Jonsdottir, Marselina 12; Quebec, 1879 2557.1 p39
Jonsdottir, Olof 22; Quebec, 1879 2557.1 p22
Jonsdottir, Sigridur 54; Quebec, 1879 2557.1 p38A
Jonsdottir, Sigurbjorg 31; Quebec, 1879 2557.2 p37
Jonsdottir, Thorey 33; Quebec, 1879 2557.1 p21
Jonson, Erik Johan; Washington, 1859-1920 2872.1 p20
Jonson, Frank L. 25; Kansas, 1872 5240.1 p53
Jonson, John 21; Jamaica, 1736 3690.1 p130
Jonson, Jon; Iowa, 1850-1855 2090 p613
Jonson, Nels Gustof; Washington, 1859-1920 2872.1 p20
Jonson, Sven Johan; Washington, 1859-1920 2872.1 p20
Jonsson, Albert 13; Quebec, 1879 2557.1 p38A
Jonsson, Baldvin 59; Quebec, 1879 2557.1 p39
Jonsson, Benedikt 15; Quebec, 1879 2557.1 p21
Jonsson, Benj. 28; Quebec, 1879 2557.1 p38A
Jonsson, Bergur 26; Quebec, 1879 2557.2 p37
Jonsson, Bjorn 19; Quebec, 1879 2557.2 p37
Jonsson, Carl August; Minneapolis, 1882-1887 6410.35 p56
Jonsson, Carl Gustaf; Iowa, 1866-1943 123.54 p25
Jonsson, Carl Theodore 27; Arkansas, 1918 95.2 p62
Jonsson, Dignus 46; Quebec, 1879 2557.1 p39A
Jonsson, Eggert 16; Quebec, 1879 2557.1 p38A
Jonsson, Einar 27; Quebec, 1879 2557.1 p22
Jonsson, Einar 45; Quebec, 1879 2557.1 p39
Jonsson, George Cornelius; Arkansas, 1918 95.2 p62
Jonsson, Gudjon 25; Quebec, 1879 2557.2 p37
Jonsson, Gudmundur 31; Quebec, 1879 2557.2 p36
Jonsson, Gudni 12; Quebec, 1879 2557.1 p38A
Jonsson, Halldor 12; Quebec, 1879 2557.1 p38A
Jonsson, Hans; Minneapolis, 1875-1884 6410.35 p57
Jonsson, Johann 40; Quebec, 1879 2557.2 p37
Jonsson, Jon 60; Quebec, 1879 2557.2 p37
Jonsson, Jons; Maine, 1871-1873 6410.22 p117
Jonsson, Joseph 35; Quebec, 1879 2557.2 p36
Jonsson, Kristinn 17; Quebec, 1879 2557.1 p38A
Jonsson, Magnus 26; Quebec, 1879 2557.1 p22
Jonsson, Margret 52; Quebec, 1879 2557.1 p38A
Jonsson, Marteinn 24; Quebec, 1879 2557.1 p38A
Jonsson, Olof; Minneapolis, 1881-1882 6410.35 p58
Jonsson, Pehr; Minneapolis, 1883-1886 6410.35 p58
Jonsson, Sigurdur 56; Quebec, 1879 2557.1 p38A
Jonsson, Sigvaldi 58; Quebec, 1879 2557.1 p22
Jonsson, Stefan 25; Quebec, 1879 2557.1 p38A
Jonsson, Sveinn 70; Quebec, 1879 2557.1 p22
Jonsson, Thorsteinn 40; Quebec, 1879 2557.1 p38A
Jonsson, Tomas 9; Quebec, 1879 2557.1 p39A
Jonsurany, Mrs. 30; New Orleans, 1836 778.5 p288
Jonte, Peter; Cincinnati, 1822-1833 8582.1 p41
Jonte, Peter R.; Kentucky, 1839-1840 8582.3 p98
Joos, Johann Melcher; Port uncertain, 1749 2444 p171
Joos, Samuel; America, 1749 2444 p171
Joost, Alexandre 20; America, 1838 778.5 p288
Jopp, Hugh 22; Maryland, 1774 1219.7 p204
Jordain, Francis 30; South Carolina, 1725 3690.1 p131
Jordain, Thomas; Philadelphia, 1816 2859.11 p34
Jordan, . . .; Canada, 1776-1783 9786 p25
Jordan, Anna Maria Bechtol *SEE* Jordan, Jakob
Jordan, Anna Marie 8 *SEE* Jordan, Anna Marie
Jordan, Anna Marie 8; New Orleans, 1846 5647.5 p92
Jordan, Anna Marie 41; New Orleans, 1846 5647.5 p92
Jordan, Anna Marie 42; New Orleans, 1846 5647.5 p92
*Relative:*Christina 20
*Relative:*Elizabeth 15
*Relative:*Cath. 11
*Relative:*Anna Marie 8
*Relative:*Marg. 6
Jordan, Anth.; Virginia, 1635 6219 p20
Jordan, Barbara 25 *SEE* Jordan, John B.
Jordan, Cath. 11 *SEE* Jordan, Anna Marie
Jordan, Catharine 11; New Orleans, 1846 5647.5 p92
Jordan, Christina 20 *SEE* Jordan, Anna Marie
Jordan, Christina 20; New Orleans, 1846 5647.5 p92
Jordan, David; America, 1832-1834 1450.2 p74A
Jordan, David; South Carolina, 1772 1219.7 p159
Jordan, David 24; Massachusetts, 1850 5881.1 p51
Jordan, Dennis; Philadelphia, 1816 2859.11 p34

Juinque, . . .; Canada, 1776-1783 *9786 p25*
Juitte, Mr. 44; New Orleans, 1829 *778.5 p291*
Jukes, David 23; Nova Scotia, 1774 *1219.7 p209*
Jukes, Israel; America, 1853 *1450.2 p74A*
Julian, Sam; Washington, 1859-1920 *2872.1 p20*
Julian, William; Virginia, 1641 *6219 p15*
Julie, Ms. 45; America, 1836 *778.5 p291*
Julien, Mme. 25; New Orleans, 1839 *778.5 p291*
Julien, D. 36; America, 1826 *778.5 p291*
Julien, Francis 60; New Orleans, 1822 *778.5 p291*
Julien, Joseph 21; America, 1826 *778.5 p291*
Julien, M. A., Mlle. 18; America, 1823 *778.5 p291*
Jullian, Jean; America, 1833 *778.5 p292*
Jullien, Mr. 37; New Orleans, 1829 *778.5 p292*
July, Nicholas; Wisconsin, n.d. *9675.6 p52*
Juncker, Heinrich Damian; Cincinnati, 1788-1848 *8582.3 p89*
Jundt, Adam 29; New York, NY, 1898-1899 *7846 p39*
Jundt, Margaretha 22; New York, NY, 1898-1899 *7846 p39*
Jundt, Wilhelm 2; New York, NY, 1898-1899 *7846 p39*
Junek, John 35; America, 1831 *778.5 p292*
Jung, . . .; America, 1700-1877 *8582.3 p80*
Jung, . . .; Canada, 1776-1783 *9786 p25*
Jung, Mr.; New Orleans, 1846-1848 *8582.3 p34*
　　With 2 brothers
Jung, Carl 36; New York, NY, 1857 *9831.14 p86*
Jung, Catharina *SEE* Jung, Michael
Jung, Chon 17; Port uncertain, 1839 *778.5 p292*
Jung, Daniel; Cincinnati, 1855 *8582.2 p46*
Jung, Daniel; Cincinnati, 1869-1887 *8582 p15*
Jung, Daniel 15; New York, NY, 1837 *8582.3 p34*
Jung, Georg; Charleston, SC, 1775-1781 *8582.2 p52*
Jung, Georg 18; New York, NY, 1889 *7846 p40*
Jung, Jakob 29; Port uncertain, 1839 *778.5 p292*
Jung, Johann; Cincinnati, 1869-1887 *8582 p15*
Jung, Michael; Pennsylvania, 1749 *2444 p171*
　　Wife: Catharina
Jung, Nicholas 51; Kansas, 1882 *5240.1 p64*
Jung, Peter; Wisconsin, n.d. *9675.6 p52*
Jung, Philip; Philadelphia, 1776 *2444 p161*
Jung, Philipp; America, 1847 *8582.3 p34*
Jung, Philipp 15; New York, NY, 1889 *7846 p40*
Jung, Philippine; America, 1848 *8582.3 p34*
Jung, Thomas; Ohio, 1798-1818 *8582.2 p54*
Junge, Charles F.; America, 1869-1887 *8582 p15*
Junge, Franz Carl; Cincinnati, 1837 *8582.1 p17*
Junge, Johann David; Pennsylvania, 1750 *2444 p171*
Junge, Michael; Pennsylvania, 1750 *2444 p171*
Junge, Peter; Pennsylvania, 1750 *2444 p171*

Junger, Leonh. 26; America, 1853 *9162.7 p14*
Jungers, Jacob; Wisconsin, n.d. *9675.6 p52*
Junghauss, August; Wisconsin, n.d. *9675.6 p52*
Junginger, Jacob; South Carolina, 1788 *7119 p202*
Junginger, Simon; South Carolina, 1788 *7119 p201*
Jungk, Reinhard; Halifax, N.S., 1778 *9786 p270*
Jungk, Reinhard; New York, 1776 *9786 p270*
Jungkind, Bernhard; America, 1850 *8582.2 p18*
Jungling, Johan J.; South Carolina, 1788 *7119 p204*
Jungmann, . . .; America, 1700-1877 *8582.3 p80*
Jungmann, Mrs.; Died enroute, 1731 *8582 p15*
　　With stepchild & 2 children
Jungmann, Mrs.; Philadelphia, 1727 *8582 p15*
Jungmann, Johann Georg 11; Rhode Island, 1731 *8582 p15*
　　With father & sister
Jungquist, Charles; Minneapolis, 1867-1881 *6410.35 p58*
Juninger, Simon; South Carolina, 1788 *7119 p199*
Junior, Wm.; Virginia, 1641 *6219 p184*
Junk, Thomas; Ohio, 1798-1818 *8582.2 p54*
Junken, Henrich; Philadelphia, 1776 *8582.3 p83*
Junker, Henry D.; Cincinnati, 1833 *8582.1 p52*
Junkermann, Gustav Friederich; America, 1848 *8582.3 p34*
Junkermann, Julius; New Orleans, 1861 *8125.8 p437*
Junkin, Thomas; Quebec, 1853 *5704.8 p105*
Junkins, Easter 26; Quebec, 1854 *5704.8 p121*
Junkins, Elizabeth 9; Quebec, 1854 *5704.8 p121*
Junkins, Jane 4; Quebec, 1854 *5704.8 p121*
Junkins, John 11; Quebec, 1854 *5704.8 p121*
Junkins, Mary 13; Quebec, 1854 *5704.8 p121*
Junkins, Santy 15; Quebec, 1854 *5704.8 p121*
Juno, Julien; America, 1839 *778.5 p292*
Junot, Ella Sophia; Washington, 1859-1920 *2872.1 p20*
Junta, Luke; Arkansas, 1918 *95.2 p63*
Juntunen, Eli Eanri; Washington, 1859-1920 *2872.1 p20*
Juntunen, Emil; Washington, 1859-1920 *2872.1 p20*
Juntunen, Margaret; Washington, 1859-1920 *2872.1 p20*
Juntunen, Selma Ino Creta; Washington, 1859-1920 *2872.1 p20*
Juntunen, Thomas; Washington, 1859-1920 *2872.1 p20*
Juntunen, Thomas Lamati; Washington, 1859-1920 *2872.1 p20*
Juntunen, Weerus; Washington, 1859-1920 *2872.1 p20*
Juppenlatz, Mr.; Cincinnati, 1831 *8582.1 p51*
Juppenlatz, Georg; Cincinnati, 1788-1876 *8582.3 p81*
Juppenlatz, Georg; Cincinnati, 1828 *8582.1 p51*
Jurboroki, Moses 18; New York, NY, 1878 *9253 p47*
Jurboroki, Rachel 20; New York, NY, 1878 *9253 p47*
Jurcic, Eva; Iowa, 1866-1943 *123.54 p65*

Jurcic, Josip; Iowa, 1866-1943 *123.54 p25*
Jurcie, Josep; Iowa, 1866-1943 *123.54 p25*
Jurczak, Teresa 50; New York, 1912 *9980.29 p64*
Jurdan, Christina; Indiana, 1827-1848 *5647.5 p95*
Juregenssen, John Nic; Wisconsin, n.d. *9675.6 p52*
Jurgens, . . .; Canada, 1776-1783 *9786 p25*
Jurgens, Henry; New York, NY, 1836 *8208.4 p10*
Jurgens, Jurren; Illinois, 1864 *7857 p4*
Jurgensen, Jacob; New York, 1753 *3652 p77*
Jurgensmeier, Ernst Heinrich Ferdinand; America, 1886 *4610.10 p110*
Jurgensmeyer, Ernst Heinrich August; America, 1881 *4610.10 p109*
Jurguns, . . .; Canada, 1776-1783 *9786 p37*
Juricevch, Thomas; Iowa, 1866-1943 *123.54 p25*
Juricza, George; Wisconsin, n.d. *9675.6 p52*
Jurisic, John; Arkansas, 1918 *95.2 p63*
Jurkovick, Joseph; Iowa, 1866-1943 *123.54 p25*
Jurmu, Elmer; Washington, 1859-1920 *2872.1 p20*
Jurmu, Elmer A.; Washington, 1859-1920 *2872.1 p20*
Jurstak, Joseph; Wisconsin, n.d. *9675.6 p52*
Jushka, John; Wisconsin, n.d. *9675.6 p52*
Jusius, Dominick; Arkansas, 1918 *95.2 p63*
Juska, Joseph; Wisconsin, n.d. *9675.6 p52*
Juskovicz, Jusepas; Wisconsin, n.d. *9675.6 p52*
Jussan, Francois 34; New Orleans, 1839 *778.5 p292*
Just, . . .; Canada, 1776-1783 *9786 p25*
Just, Clara; Milwaukee, 1875 *4719.30 p257*
　　With 2 children
Just, Conrad; Canada, 1776-1783 *9786 p231*
Just, George; Canada, 1783 *9786 p38A*
Just, Joh. Gottl. 30; New Orleans, 1839 *9420.2 p168*
Just, Joh. Gottl. 33; New Orleans, 1839 *9420.2 p168*
Juste, Gagnear Pierre 31; Died enroute, 1836 *778.5 p292*
Justi, Wilhelm; Halifax, N.S., 1778 *9786 p270*
Justi, Wilhelm; New York, 1776 *9786 p270*
Justice, Henry 21; Virginia, 1700 *2212 p32*
Justin, Anton; Washington, 1859-1920 *2872.1 p20*
Justin, Francis 16; America, 1829 *778.5 p292*
Justin, M. 21; New Orleans, 1839 *778.5 p292*
Justin, Martin; New York, NY, 1811 *2859.11 p14*
Justin, Requillon; Illinois, 1888 *2896.5 p20*
Justorf, Georg; Saratoga, NY, 1777 *8137 p10*
Justycki, Stanislaw; New York, 1835 *4606 p179*
Juvan, Jacob; Wisconsin, n.d. *9675.6 p52*
Juvan, Joseph; Wisconsin, n.d. *9675.6 p52*
Juve, Mrs. 22; New Orleans, 1830 *778.5 p292*
Juve, M. 36; New Orleans, 1830 *778.5 p292*
Juzwikiewicz, Julian; New York, 1831 *4606 p174*

FOR A COMPLETE EXPLANATION OF ENTRY, SEE "HOW TO READ A CITATION" SECTION

K

Kabbes, Georg; America, 1836 *8582.1 p17*
Kabitsky, Henry Constantine; Colorado, 1904 *9678.2 p61*
Kabitzky, . . .; Canada, 1776-1783 *9786 p42*
Kable, Mary; Virginia, 1637 *6219 p108*
Kaccio, Bunji; Iowa, 1866-1943 *123.54 p25*
Kachel, . . .; New England, 1752 *4525 p209*
Kachel, Andreas; Pennsylvania, 1750 *4525 p226*
  With family
Kachel, Hans Andreas; Pennsylvania, 1750 *4525 p233*
Kachel, Michael; Pennsylvania, 1752 *4525 p226*
Kaczanowski, Tytus; New York, 1835 *4606 p179*
Kaczinska, Frans; Massachusetts, 1912 *9980.29 p67*
Kaczinska, Maryan 1 *SEE* Kaczinska, Teofila
Kaczinska, Teofila 20; New York, 1912 *9980.29 p67*
  Son:Maryan 1
Kaczinski, Frans; Massachusetts, 1912 *9980.29 p67*
Kaczinski, Maryan 1 *SEE* Kaczinski, Teofila
Kaczinski, Teofila 20; New York, 1912 *9980.29 p67*
  Son:Maryan 1
Kaczmarek, Jadwiga 28; New York, 1912 *9980.29 p74*
  Son:Jan 9
Kaczmarek, Jan 9 *SEE* Kaczmarek, Jadwiga
Kadatz, August; Wisconsin, n.d. *9675.6 p52*
Kadel, Christina 20; America, 1853 *9162.7 p14*
Kadel, Georg 56; America, 1853 *9162.8 p36*
Kadel, Gg. 11; America, 1853 *9162.7 p14*
Kadel, Maria S. 18; America, 1853 *9162.7 p14*
Kadel, Nikolaus 3 mos; America, 1853 *9162.7 p14*
Kadel, Nikolaus 20; America, 1853 *9162.7 p14*
Kadmer, Friedrich; Wisconsin, n.d. *9675.6 p52*
Kadner, Martha; Wisconsin, n.d. *9675.6 p52*
Kadums, . . .; New York, 1831 *4606 p175*
Kady, Martha; St. John, N.B., 1852 *5704.8 p93*
Kadysiewski, Frank; Arkansas, 1918 *95.2 p63*
Kaefer, John 27; West Virginia, 1905 *9788.3 p12*
Kaege, Christian 40; Kansas, 1887 *5240.1 p70*
Kaelin, Nicolaus; America, 1851 *8582.3 p35*
Kaemingk, Engelbert; Arkansas, 1918 *95.2 p63*
Kaemmerer, Heinrich; Philadelphia, 1764 *8582.2 p65*
Kaemmerling, Gustav; America, 1850 *8582.2 p18*
Kaempher, M.; Shreveport, LA, 1878 *7129 p44*
Kaenn, Benedict 34; New Orleans, 1837 *778.5 p292*
Kaer, Johann; Wisconsin, n.d. *9675.6 p52*
Kaercher, Elisabetha; America, 1752 *2444 p172*
Kaesemann, Friedrich Wilhelm; America, 1772 *8582 p15*
  With brother
Kaesewieter, August; Kansas, 1887 *5240.1 p23*
Kafel, Ernest; Wisconsin, n.d. *9675.6 p52*
Kaffeberger, Phil 21; America, 1854-1855 *9162.6 p104*
Kafoglu, George; Arkansas, 1918 *95.2 p63*
Kafoure, David; America, 1895 *1450.2 p18B*
Kafoure, John; America, 1895 *1450.2 p18B*
Kafoure, Nedder E.; New York, NY, 1899 *1450.2 p18B*
Kagakus, Andrew; Arkansas, 1918 *95.2 p63*
Kagher, Martin 28; Massachusetts, 1848 *5881.1 p55*
Kaghler, John; South Carolina, 1788 *7119 p199*
Kagler, Mickel; South Carolina, 1788 *7119 p199*
Kagy, Jacob; Philadelphia, 1760 *9973.7 p34*
Kahl, Henry; New York, NY, 1867 *9678.2 p61*
Kahl, Max 55; Indiana, 1838 *1450.2 p75A*
Kahlfeld, . . .; Minnesota, 1858-1864 *8582.3 p82*
Kahmann, . . .; Canada, 1776-1783 *9786 p25*
Kahmer, Reinhardt; Philadelphia, 1764 *8582.3 p84*
Kahn, Heinrich; America, 1847 *8582.3 p35*
Kahn, Julius; America, 1847 *8582.3 p35*
Kahn, M.; Milwaukee, 1875 *4719.30 p257*
Kahn, Raphael; Shreveport, LA, 1877 *7129 p44*

Kahn, Solomon W.; New York, 1860 *1450.2 p18B*
Kahney, Anton; Cincinnati, 1818 *8582.1 p17*
Kahni, Anton; Cincinnati, 1818 *8582.1 p17*
Kahni, Anton; Cincinnati, 1826 *8582.1 p51*
Kahni, Anton; Cincinnati, 1834 *8582.1 p52*
Kahny, Anton; Cincinnati, 1818 *8582.1 p17*
Kahny, Anton; Ohio, 1843 *8582.1 p51*
Kahre, . . .; Illinois, 1800-1900 *4610.10 p67*
Kahre, Johann Friedrich; America, 1857 *4610.10 p105*
Kain, Ann 26; Quebec, 1853 *5704.8 p105*
Kain, Dennis; Iowa, 1866-1943 *123.54 p26*
Kain, Francis; St. John, N.B., 1847 *5704.8 p18*
Kain, James; New York, NY, 1838 *8208.4 p72*
Kain, James 12; St. John, N.B., 1847 *5704.8 p18*
Kain, Jane 10; St. John, N.B., 1847 *5704.8 p18*
Kain, John; New York, NY, 1838 *8208.4 p65*
Kain, John; New York, NY, 1839 *8208.4 p94*
Kain, John 5; St. John, N.B., 1847 *5704.8 p18*
Kain, Martha; St. John, N.B., 1847 *5704.8 p18*
Kain, Michael; America, 1860 *6014.1 p2*
Kain, Michael; St. John, N.B., 1852 *5704.8 p83*
Kain, Patrick; America, 1868 *6014.1 p2*
Kain, Percival; New York, NY, 1811 *2859.11 p14*
Kain, Thomas 20; Philadelphia, 1853 *5704.8 p111*
Kain, William 7; St. John, N.B., 1847 *5704.8 p18*
Kain, William 13; Philadelphia, 1853 *5704.8 p111*
Kaine, Catherine 18; Philadelphia, 1864 *5704.8 p155*
Kainer, Nick; Iowa, 1866-1943 *123.54 p26*
Kainz, Magdalena; Wisconsin, n.d. *9675.6 p52*
Kair, Thomas 25; Jamaica, 1774 *1219.7 p207*
Kaire, Hubert 28; New Orleans, 1837 *778.5 p292*
Kairkman, Richard 19; Pennsylvania, 1725 *3690.1 p134*
Kaiser, Mr.; Missouri, 1836 *3702.7 p100*
Kaiser, Franz Xaver; Cincinnati, 1869-1887 *8582 p15*
Kaiser, Franz Xaver; New Orleans, 1836 *8582.3 p35*
Kaiser, Friedrich; Illinois, 1888 *5012.37 p60*
Kaiser, Geo. 21; Kansas, 1872 *5240.1 p53*
Kaiser, George; Wisconsin, n.d. *9675.6 p52*
Kaiser, Gustave A.; West Virginia, 1889 *9788.3 p13*
Kaiser, Jacobina 1; America, 1838 *778.5 p292*
Kaiser, Johann; Cincinnati, 1826 *8582.1 p51*
Kaiser, Johann; Ohio, 1800-1885 *8582.2 p59*
Kaiser, John; New York, NY, 1834 *8208.4 p27*
Kaiser, John; Wisconsin, n.d. *9675.6 p52*
Kaiser, Marie Friederike; New York, NY, 1857 *3702.7 p535*
Kaiser, Mathias; Wisconsin, n.d. *9675.6 p52*
Kaiser, Otto; America, 1893 *1450.2 p75A*
Kaiser, Philippina 30; America, 1836 *778.5 p293*
Kaiser, Wilhelmine Elisabeth; America, 1837 *4815.7 p92*
Kaisermann, Jacob; Died enroute, 1738 *9898 p44*
  With wife
Kaisig, Theodor; New York, NY, 1892 *1450.2 p75A*
Kaiter, Catharina Barbara *SEE* Kaiter, Michael
Kaiter, Michael; America, 1753 *2444 p172*
  Wife:Catharina Barbara
Kaitter, Saine; Iowa, 1866-1943 *123.54 p26*
Kajander, . . .; Washington, 1859-1920 *2872.1 p20*
Kakavas, George Peter; Arkansas, 1918 *95.2 p63*
Kaker, Frank; Wisconsin, n.d. *9675.6 p52*
Kaker, Martin; Wisconsin, n.d. *9675.6 p52*
Kakinis, Peter; Wisconsin, n.d. *9675.6 p52*
Kalafatic, Frank; Iowa, 1866-1943 *123.54 p26*
Kalahan, C.; Washington, 1859-1920 *2872.1 p20*
Kalahan, George; Washington, 1859-1920 *2872.1 p20*
Kalahan, George W.; Washington, 1859-1920 *2872.1 p20*

Kalb, . . .; Canada, 1776-1783 *9786 p25*
Kalb, Conrad; America, 1848 *1450.2 p75A*
Kalberer, Christ; Colorado, 1905 *9678.2 p61*
Kalberlahn, Hans Martin; New York, 1753 *3652 p77*
Kalbos, Nichalaos; Arkansas, 1918 *95.2 p63*
Kalbos, Nicholas; Arkansas, 1918 *95.2 p63*
Kalcher, Margaretha *SEE* Kalcher, Ruprecht
Kalcher, Margaretha Gunter *SEE* Kalcher, Ruprecht
Kalcher, Ruprecht; Georgia, 1738 *9332 p321*
Kalcher, Ruprecht; Georgia, 1739 *9332 p323*
  Wife:Margaretha Gunter
Kalcher, Ruprecht; Georgia, 1739 *9332 p326*
  Wife:Margaretha
Kalci, Witolis; Iowa, 1866-1943 *123.54 p26*
Kalcich, Mat; Iowa, 1866-1943 *123.54 p26*
Kalck, . . .; Canada, 1776-1783 *9786 p25*
Kalemneos, Mike Sam; Arkansas, 1918 *95.2 p64*
Kalies, Robert; Wisconsin, n.d. *9675.6 p52*
Kalimios, George Sofokles; Arkansas, 1918 *95.2 p64*
Kalin, Thomas 24; Halifax, N.S., 1775 *1219.7 p262*
Kalisch, Isidor; America, 1848 *8582.1 p17*
Kalk, Gustav; Illinois, 1890 *5012.40 p25*
Kalkhoff, John; Canada, 1776-1783 *9786 p207A*
Kalkhorst, Fritz H. M. 22; Kansas, 1904 *5240.1 p83*
Kalkoff, . . .; Canada, 1776-1783 *9786 p25*
Kallaway, Katherine; Virginia, 1642 *6219 p18*
Kallaway, Katherine; Virginia, 1642 *6219 p197*
Kallberg, Hannah; Washington, 1859-1920 *2872.1 p20*
Kallberg, John; Washington, 1859-1920 *2872.1 p20*
Kalle, Frank 39; Kansas, 1885 *5240.1 p67*
Kallen, Johan; Wisconsin, n.d. *9675.6 p52*
Kallendorf, Christian Dietrich; America, 1850 *8582.2 p18*
Kallendorf, Friedrich Wilhelm; Cincinnati, 1869-1887 *8582 p15*
Kallish, Isidor; America, 1848 *8582.1 p17*
Kallmann, Simon 13; New York, NY, 1878 *9253 p46*
Kallmeyer, Friedrich; America, 1843 *8582.1 p17*
Kalmes, Nicholas; Wisconsin, n.d. *9675.6 p131*
Kalogeropoulos, Theodore; Arkansas, 1918 *95.2 p64*
Kalteisen, Michael; Charleston, SC, 1766 *8582.2 p65*
Kalteisen, Michael; Charleston, SC, 1775 *8582.2 p51*
Kalthoff, Christian Friedrich; America, 1837 *8582.1 p18*
Kam, George Michael; Philadelphia, 1760 *9973.7 p34*
Kamann, Heinrich Philipp; Cincinnati, 1869-1887 *8582 p15*
Kambeitz, Michael; Alberta, n.d. *5262 p58*
Kameloris, Jean 26; Kansas, 1905 *5240.1 p83*
Kamencky, Joe 32; Kansas, 1896 *5240.1 p80*
Kameneck, Joe 32; Kansas, 1896 *5240.1 p23*
Kamenesky, Herman 24; Kansas, 1900 *5240.1 p81*
Kamenesky, Samuel; Kansas, 1902 *5240.1 p23*
Kamerla, . . .; Canada, 1776-1783 *9786 p42*
Kamey, Lawrence 23; Philadelphia, 1774 *1219.7 p233*
Kamin, Anton; Wisconsin, n.d. *9675.6 p131*
Kaminska, Aniela 25; New York, 1912 *9980.29 p59*
Kaminska, Julia 18; New York, 1912 *9980.29 p68*
Kaminski, . . .; New York, 1831 *4606 p175*
Kamm, Jacob; Illinois, 1886 *5012.39 p120*
Kamm, John; Illinois, 1886 *5012.39 p120*
Kammeling, Bernard 36; America, 1838 *778.5 p293*
Kammeling, Delmas 23; America, 1838 *778.5 p293*
Kammeling, Marty Pierre 36; America, 1838 *778.5 p293*
Kammeling, Rose 38; America, 1838 *778.5 p293*
Kammerer, Heinrich; Philadelphia, 1764 *8582.2 p18*
Kammerer, J.; America, 1848 *8582.1 p18*
Kamp, Karl Auf Dem; Ohio, 1869-1887 *8582 p15*

Kampe, F. C.; Cincinnati, 1869-1887 ***8582*** *p15*
Kampe, Georg; America, 1850 ***8582.3*** *p35*
Kamper, Mr.; America, 1851 ***4610.10*** *p138*
With wife
Kamper, Carl; America, 1844 ***4610.10*** *p95*
*Wife:*Louise Stuhmeyer
*Son:*Karl Friedrich
Kamper, Carl Friedrich Wilhelm; America, 1848 ***4610.10*** *p138*
Kamper, Karl Friedrich *SEE* Kamper, Carl
Kamper, Louise Stuhmeyer *SEE* Kamper, Carl
Kampf, John; Washington, 1859-1920 ***2872.1*** *p20*
Kampfe, Jane Christne. 22 *SEE* Kampfe, John Samuel
Kampfe, John Samuel 28; New Orleans, 1839 ***9420.2*** *p485*
*Wife:*Jane Christne. 22
*Child:*Samuel 3 mos
Kampfe, Samuel 3 mos *SEE* Kampfe, John Samuel
Kamph, John; Washington, 1859-1920 ***2872.1*** *p20*
Kampha, Hugo 38; Kansas, 1884 ***5240.1*** *p66*
Kampmeyer, Christine Louise; America, 1844 ***4610.10*** *p119*
Kampner, Mandel; Virginia, 1856 ***4626.16*** *p16*
Kamrad, Herman; Illinois, 1892 ***5012.40*** *p27*
Kamradt, August Rudolph; Illinois, 1882 ***5012.39*** *p52*
Kamrodt, Albert; Illinois, 1888 ***5012.39*** *p121*
Kanan, Christopher; Ohio, 1840 ***9892.11*** *p23*
Kananak, Langn; New York, NY, 1816 ***2859.11*** *p34*
Kanapek, John; America, 1896 ***7137*** *p169*
Kandrat, John; Wisconsin, n.d. ***9675.6*** *p131*
Kandrat, Peter; Wisconsin, n.d. ***9675.6*** *p131*
Kane, . . . 4; Philadelphia, 1851 ***5704.8*** *p81*
Kane, . . . 5; Philadelphia, 1851 ***5704.8*** *p81*
Kane, . . . 7; Philadelphia, 1851 ***5704.8*** *p81*
Kane, . . . 9; Philadelphia, 1851 ***5704.8*** *p81*
Kane, Ann; Philadelphia, 1866 ***5704.8*** *p206*
Kane, Ann 2 mos; St. John, N.B., 1863 ***5704.8*** *p152*
Kane, Ann 9; Philadelphia, 1865 ***5704.8*** *p202*
Kane, Ann 19; Quebec, 1859 ***5704.8*** *p143*
Kane, Ann 22; St. John, N.B., 1853 ***5704.8*** *p110*
Kane, Ann 27; Philadelphia, 1858 ***5704.8*** *p139*
Kane, Ann 30; St. John, N.B., 1863 ***5704.8*** *p152*
Kane, Arthur 7 *SEE* Kane, John
Kane, Arthur 7; Philadelphia, 1849 ***5704.8*** *p50*
Kane, Barbara 20; Massachusetts, 1849 ***5881.1*** *p52*
Kane, Bernard 5; Philadelphia, 1865 ***5704.8*** *p202*
Kane, Bridget; Philadelphia, 1865 ***5704.8*** *p190*
Kane, Bridget 20; St. John, N.B., 1853 ***5704.8*** *p110*
Kane, Catharine 23; Massachusetts, 1850 ***5881.1*** *p83*
Kane, Catharine 30; Massachusetts, 1849 ***5881.1*** *p52*
Kane, Catherine; Philadelphia, 1847 ***53.26*** *p40*
Kane, Catherine; Philadelphia, 1847 ***5704.8*** *p23*
Kane, Catherine; Philadelphia, 1849 ***53.26*** *p40*
Kane, Catherine; Philadelphia, 1849 ***5704.8*** *p54*
Kane, Catherine; Philadelphia, 1852 ***5704.8*** *p91*
Kane, Catherine 24; Quebec, 1855 ***5704.8*** *p126*
Kane, Cath'rine 23; Massachusetts, 1850 ***5881.1*** *p53*
Kane, Charles; New York, NY, 1811 ***2859.11*** *p14*
With family
Kane, Charles; Philadelphia, 1869 ***5704.8*** *p236*
Kane, Charles 18; Philadelphia, 1856 ***5704.8*** *p128*
Kane, Charles 24; Quebec, 1855 ***5704.8*** *p126*
Kane, Daniel 18; Philadelphia, 1857 ***5704.8*** *p134*
Kane, David 49; Kansas, 1879 ***5240.1*** *p60*
Kane, Denis; America, 1848 ***1450.2*** *p75A*
Kane, Eliza; Baltimore, 1811 ***2859.11*** *p14*
Kane, Ellen; America, 1865 ***5704.8*** *p201*
Kane, Ellen; Philadelphia, 1865 ***5704.8*** *p202*
Kane, Ellen; St. John, N.B., 1847 ***5704.8*** *p10*
Kane, Ellen 19; Philadelphia, 1858 ***5704.8*** *p138*
Kane, Ellen 19; Philadelphia, 1860 ***5704.8*** *p145*
Kane, Ellen 30; St. John, N.B., 1853 ***5704.8*** *p109*
Kane, Francis; New York, NY, 1811 ***2859.11*** *p14*
With family
Kane, Francis; Philadelphia, 1852 ***5704.8*** *p97*
Kane, Francis; Philadelphia, 1866 ***5704.8*** *p211*
Kane, Francis 20; Philadelphia, 1854 ***5704.8*** *p117*
Kane, George; America, 1739 ***4971*** *p14*
Kane, Henry; New York, NY, 1865 ***5704.8*** *p192*
Kane, Henry; St. John, N.B., 1852 ***5704.8*** *p92*
Kane, Honora 30; Massachusetts, 1849 ***5881.1*** *p53*
Kane, Hugh 18; Philadelphia, 1860 ***5704.8*** *p145*
Kane, Isabella 19; Philadelphia, 1853 ***5704.8*** *p112*
Kane, James; New York, NY, 1864 ***5704.8*** *p186*
Kane, James; New York, NY, 1866 ***5704.8*** *p208*
Kane, James; Philadelphia, 1852 ***5704.8*** *p87*
Kane, James 1; St. John, N.B., 1863 ***5704.8*** *p152*
Kane, Jane; New York, NY, 1864 ***5704.8*** *p169*
Kane, Jane 17; Quebec, 1855 ***5704.8*** *p126*
Kane, Jane 40; St. John, N.B., 1862 ***5704.8*** *p150*
Kane, John; New York, NY, 1816 ***2859.11*** *p34*
Kane, John; Philadelphia, 1847 ***53.26*** *p40*
Kane, John; Philadelphia, 1847 ***5704.8*** *p5*
Kane, John; Philadelphia, 1849 ***53.26*** *p40*
*Relative:*Nancy 8
*Relative:*Arthur 7
Kane, John; Philadelphia, 1849 ***5704.8*** *p50*
Kane, John; Philadelphia, 1865 ***5704.8*** *p202*
Kane, John; Philadelphia, 1866 ***5704.8*** *p206*
Kane, John 4; Philadelphia, 1853 ***5704.8*** *p112*
Kane, John 18; St. John, N.B., 1853 ***5704.8*** *p109*
Kane, John 30; California, 1867 ***3840.2*** *p16*
Kane, John 50; St. John, N.B., 1853 ***5704.8*** *p109*
Kane, John 55; Massachusetts, 1849 ***5881.1*** *p54*
Kane, Lesley 18; Jamaica, 1720 ***3690.1*** *p131*
Kane, Lucy 18; Philadelphia, 1864 ***5704.8*** *p161*
Kane, Manus; Philadelphia, 1865 ***5704.8*** *p202*
Kane, Marcus; Philadelphia, 1852 ***5704.8*** *p85*
Kane, Margaret; New York, NY, 1864 ***5704.8*** *p174*
Kane, Margaret; Philadelphia, 1847 ***53.26*** *p40*
Kane, Margaret; Philadelphia, 1847 ***5704.8*** *p5*
Kane, Margaret; St. John, N.B., 1851 ***5704.8*** *p77*
Kane, Mary; New York, NY, 1865 ***5704.8*** *p192*
Kane, Mary; Philadelphia, 1848 ***53.26*** *p40*
Kane, Mary; Philadelphia, 1848 ***5704.8*** *p45*
Kane, Mary; Philadelphia, 1865 ***5704.8*** *p188*
Kane, Mary; Philadelphia, 1865 ***5704.8*** *p190*
Kane, Mary; Philadelphia, 1865 ***5704.8*** *p202*
Kane, Mary; St. John, N.B., 1851 ***5704.8*** *p77*
Kane, Mary 18; Philadelphia, 1864 ***5704.8*** *p156*
Kane, Mary 19; Quebec, 1855 ***5704.8*** *p126*
Kane, Mary 20; Massachusetts, 1847 ***5881.1*** *p54*
Kane, Mary 23; Quebec, 1857 ***5704.8*** *p136*
Kane, Mary 50; Quebec, 1857 ***5704.8*** *p136*
Kane, Mary 50; St. John, N.B., 1853 ***5704.8*** *p109*
Kane, Mary Jane; St. John, N.B., 1851 ***5704.8*** *p72*
Kane, Mathew 56; Massachusetts, 1850 ***5881.1*** *p55*
Kane, Matthew; America, 1741 ***4971*** *p69*
Kane, Michael; Massachusetts, 1850 ***5881.1*** *p55*
Kane, Michael; Massachusetts, 1850 ***5881.1*** *p86*
Kane, Michael; Philadelphia, 1864 ***5704.8*** *p175*
Kane, Michael; Quebec, 1851 ***5704.8*** *p82*
Kane, Mike 17; Massachusetts, 1847 ***5881.1*** *p54*
Kane, Nancy; St. John, N.B., 1850 ***5704.8*** *p67*
Kane, Nancy 8 *SEE* Kane, John
Kane, Nancy 8; Philadelphia, 1849 ***5704.8*** *p50*
Kane, Patrick; New York, NY, 1816 ***2859.11*** *p34*
Kane, Patrick; Philadelphia, 1847 ***53.26*** *p41*
Kane, Patrick; Philadelphia, 1847 ***5704.8*** *p31*
Kane, Patrick; Philadelphia, 1866 ***5704.8*** *p204*
Kane, Patrick; Philadelphia, 1866 ***5704.8*** *p205*
Kane, Patrick 1; Massachusetts, 1849 ***5881.1*** *p56*
Kane, Patrick 18; Philadelphia, 1864 ***5704.8*** *p156*
Kane, Paul; Montreal, 1822 ***7603*** *p67*
Kane, Paul 18; Philadelphia, 1860 ***5704.8*** *p144*
Kane, Peggy 20; Quebec, 1855 ***5704.8*** *p126*
Kane, Peter; Montreal, 1825 ***7603*** *p100*
Kane, Peter; New York, NY, 1866 ***5704.8*** *p214*
Kane, Peter; Philadelphia, 1865 ***5704.8*** *p190*
Kane, Richard John; Arkansas, 1918 ***95.2*** *p64*
Kane, Robert; New York, NY, 1816 ***2859.11*** *p34*
Kane, Robert 19; Philadelphia, 1860 ***5704.8*** *p145*
Kane, Rose; New York, NY, 1865 ***5704.8*** *p196*
Kane, Sally; Philadelphia, 1847 ***53.26*** *p41*
Kane, Sally; Philadelphia, 1847 ***5704.8*** *p1*
Kane, Sarah; St. John, N.B., 1852 ***5704.8*** *p92*
Kane, Sarah 11; New York, NY, 1865 ***5704.8*** *p192*
Kane, Sarah Ann; New York, NY, 1870 ***5704.8*** *p239*
Kane, Susanna 15; St. John, N.B., 1853 ***5704.8*** *p109*
Kane, Timothy; Kansas, 1874 ***5240.1*** *p56*
Kane, Timothy 35; Massachusetts, 1849 ***5881.1*** *p56*
Kane, William; America, 1741 ***4971*** *p10*
Kane, William; New York, NY, 1865 ***5704.8*** *p195*
Kane, William 11; Philadelphia, 1851 ***5704.8*** *p81*
Kane, William 13; St. John, N.B., 1853 ***5704.8*** *p109*
Kanellis, George; Arkansas, 1918 ***95.2*** *p64*
Kanelos, Alex; Arkansas, 1918 ***95.2*** *p64*
Kanitz, Moritz; New York, NY, 1849 ***6013.19*** *p73*
Kanitzer, Charles; America, 1846 ***1450.2*** *p75A*
Kaniuka, Sofrony Matvey; Arkansas, 1918 ***95.2*** *p64*
Kann, Richard C.; Wisconsin, n.d. ***9675.6*** *p131*
Kannel, Nicholas; Lancaster, PA, 1747 ***8582.3*** *p84*
Kanos, George; Arkansas, 1918 ***95.2*** *p64*
Kanter, Edward; Detroit, 1869-1887 ***8582*** *p16*
Kanteres, Gust John; Arkansas, 1918 ***95.2*** *p64*
Kanther, Philipp Jacob; Cincinnati, 1869-1887 ***8582*** *p16*
Kapff, Eduard; New York, 1861-1865 ***8582.3*** *p35*
Kapff, Sixtus Ludwig; New York, NY, 1848-1869 ***8582.3*** *p35*
Kapfhamer, John 43; Kansas, 1900 ***5240.1*** *p81*
Kapfhamer, Max; Wisconsin, n.d. ***9675.6*** *p131*
Kapke, Martin; Wisconsin, n.d. ***9675.6*** *p131*
Kapp, Jakob; Cincinnati, 1807-1876 ***8582.3*** *p81*
Kappe, . . .; Canada, 1776-1783 ***9786*** *p25*
Kappel, Adam; Cincinnati, 1869-1887 ***8582*** *p16*
Kappel, Johann; America, 1854 ***8582.3*** *p35*
Kappes, . . .; Canada, 1776-1783 ***9786*** *p25*
Kappes, Jeremias; Philadelphia, 1779 ***8137*** *p10*
Kapphartwig, Carl Friedrich Wilhelm; America, 1853 ***4610.10*** *p116*
Kapraszewski, Josef 27; New York, 1912 ***9980.29*** *p59*
Kaprick, Josef; Iowa, 1866-1943 ***123.54*** *p26*
Kapsalakis, Mike; Arkansas, 1918 ***95.2*** *p64*
Karaeskos, Eilftheros; Arkansas, 1918 ***95.2*** *p64*
Karaeskos, Eliefthercos; Arkansas, 1918 ***95.2*** *p64*
Karantoonia, P. M.; Arkansas, 1918 ***95.2*** *p27*
Karantoonia, Panayiotis Mike; Arkansas, 1918 ***95.2*** *p64*
Karas, George 27; Arkansas, 1918 ***95.2*** *p64*
Karash, William; Wisconsin, n.d. ***9675.6*** *p131*
Karaskiewicz, Antonina 26 *SEE* Karaskiewicz, Felix
Karaskiewicz, Felix 25; New York, 1912 ***9980.29*** *p72*
*Wife:*Antonina 26
Karaszewski, Bruno; Arkansas, 1918 ***95.2*** *p64*
Karber, Carl; America, 1819 ***8582.2*** *p60*
Karber, Charles; Ohio, 1869-1887 ***8582*** *p16*
Karber, Maria 16; America, 1854-1855 ***9162.6*** *p104*
Karchar, Martin; Philadelphia, 1759 ***9973.7*** *p33*
Karcher, Michael; Philadelphia, 1759 ***9973.7*** *p33*
Karczewski, Jozef; Boston, 1834 ***4606*** *p179*
Kare, Christian; Pennsylvania, 1769 ***9973.8*** *p32*
Kare, Jno; South Carolina, 1788 ***7119*** *p198*
Karg, Georg Adam *SEE* Karg, Joseph
Karg, Georg Jacob *SEE* Karg, Joseph
Karg, Johann Andreas *SEE* Karg, Joseph
Karg, Joseph; Pennsylvania, 1751 ***2444*** *p172*
*Wife:*Margaretha
*Child:*Georg Jacob
*Child:*Georg Adam
*Child:*Johann Andreas
Karg, Margaretha *SEE* Karg, Joseph
Karhanen, August; Washington, 1859-1920 ***2872.1*** *p20*
Karhe, John; Indiana, 1848 ***9117*** *p19*
Karhs, Henry; New York, NY, 1870 ***2764.35*** *p39*
Karjalainen, Kalle; Washington, 1859-1920 ***2872.1*** *p20*
Karjalainen, Lulu; Washington, 1859-1920 ***2872.1*** *p20*
Karjalainen, Sophia; Washington, 1859-1920 ***2872.1*** *p20*
Karl, . . .; Canada, 1776-1783 ***9786*** *p18*
Karl, Michael; Philadelphia, 1760 ***9973.7*** *p34*
Karl, Patrick; Quebec, 1811 ***7603*** *p82*
Karle, Christian; New York, 1847 ***1450.2*** *p75A*
Karle, Frederick; New York, NY, 1896 ***3455.2*** *p44*
Karle, Joseph; New York, 1847 ***1450.2*** *p75A*
Karles, J.P.; Wisconsin, n.d. ***9675.6*** *p131*
Karlfastamatis, Mathias; Arkansas, 1918 ***95.2*** *p64*
Karlin, Patt 42; Philadelphia, 1804 ***53.26*** *p41*
Karlis, Peter Paul; Arkansas, 1918 ***95.2*** *p64*
Karlofski, James; Wisconsin, n.d. ***9675.6*** *p131*
Karlsberger, Lob 17; America, 1854-1855 ***9162.6*** *p105*
Karlson, Erland August; Arkansas, 1918 ***95.2*** *p64*
Karlson, Karl Vicktor; Iowa, 1866-1943 ***123.54*** *p26*
Karmann, Johann; Kentucky, 1843 ***8582.3*** *p100*
Karmeier, Ernst Dietrich Wilhelm; America, 1862 ***4610.10*** *p109*
Karmeier, Ernst Friedrich Wilhelm; America, 1864 ***4610.10*** *p109*
Karnatz, John; America, 1860 ***1450.2*** *p75A*
Karnavezo, Gainoula P. *SEE* Karnavezo, Peter
Karnavezo, Peter; New York, NY, 1910 ***3455.2*** *p75*
*Wife:*Gainoula P.
Karnavezos, Gainoula P. *SEE* Karnavezos, Peter
Karnavezos, Peter; New York, NY, 1910 ***3455.2*** *p75*
*Wife:*Gainoula P.
Karney, Edward; Virginia, 1856 ***4626.16*** *p16*
Karnoske, Anton; Colorado, 1904 ***9678.2*** *p61*
Karobis, Christ; Arkansas, 1918 ***95.2*** *p64*
Karolis, Crest; Arkansas, 1918 ***95.2*** *p64*
Karp, Ladislaw 30; New York, 1912 ***9980.29*** *p61*
Karpe, . . .; Canada, 1776-1783 ***9786*** *p25*
Karpey, . . .; Canada, 1776-1783 ***9786*** *p25*
Karpinski, Anton; Arkansas, 1918 ***95.2*** *p64*
Karpuk, Leon; Arkansas, 1918 ***95.2*** *p64*
Karr, David; Indiana, 1847 ***9117*** *p17*
Karr, Henry; Virginia, 1844 ***4626.16*** *p12*
Karr, Jacob; Virginia, 1844 ***4626.16*** *p12*
Karras, George Athanasion; Arkansas, 1918 ***95.2*** *p64*
Karreman, James 28; Arkansas, 1918 ***95.2*** *p64*
Karrer, William; Illinois, 1868 ***2896.5*** *p20*
Karrman, Nicolas 31; New Orleans, 1838 ***778.5*** *p293*
Karrmann, Ferdinand; America, 1831 ***8582.1*** *p18*
Karrmann, Wilhelm; America, 1831 ***8582.1*** *p18*
Karry, Antoine 57; America, 1838 ***778.5*** *p293*
Karry, Augustine 15; America, 1838 ***778.5*** *p293*
Karry, Francois 14; America, 1838 ***778.5*** *p293*
Karry, Josephine 8; America, 1838 ***778.5*** *p293*
Karry, Julie 4; America, 1838 ***778.5*** *p293*
Karry, Julien 12; America, 1838 ***778.5*** *p293*
Karry, Louis 10; America, 1838 ***778.5*** *p293*
Karry, Marie 42; America, 1838 ***778.5*** *p293*
Karsch, . . .; Canada, 1776-1783 ***9786*** *p25*

246
FOR A COMPLETE EXPLANATION OF ENTRY, SEE "HOW TO READ A CITATION" SECTION

Karsten, August; Wisconsin, n.d. ***9675.6*** *p131*
Kartaiser, Nicholas; Wisconsin, n.d. ***9675.6*** *p131*
Kartanas, John; Wisconsin, n.d. ***9675.6*** *p131*
Karthauser, Otto Ernst; Wisconsin, n.d. ***9675.6*** *p131*
Kartheiser, Heinrich; Wisconsin, n.d. ***9675.6*** *p131*
Kartheiser, Nicolas; Wisconsin, n.d. ***9675.6*** *p131*
Kartoran, Joseph; Iowa, 1866-1943 ***123.54*** *p26*
Kartrecht, Joseph; Cincinnati, 1827 ***8582.1*** *p51*
Karverlick, Andrew; Iowa, 1866-1943 ***123.54*** *p26*
Karwacki, Joseph; New York, NY, 1909 ***3455.4*** *p93*
Karweil, . . .; Canada, 1776-1783 ***9786*** *p25*
Kasal, Waslaw 48; Kansas, 1879 ***5240.1*** *p60*
Kasch, Frederick; Illinois, 1868 ***2896.5*** *p20*
Kasch, Nicolas; California, 1856 ***3840.2*** *p16*
Kasch, Wilhelm; Wisconsin, n.d. ***9675.6*** *p131*
Kascho, . . .; Canada, 1776-1783 ***9786*** *p25*
Kasel, Bernhard; Wisconsin, n.d. ***9675.6*** *p131*
Kasewurm, Michel; Georgia, 1738 ***9332*** *p320*
Kasewurm, Paulus; Georgia, 1738 ***9332*** *p320*
Kasey, Hester; Virginia, 1638 ***6219*** *p146*
Kash, William; Illinois, 1866 ***2896.5*** *p20*
Kaske, George; Philadelphia, 1742 ***3652*** *p55*
Kaslowski, Dominik; Wisconsin, n.d. ***9675.6*** *p131*
Kasluck, Stephan; America, 1884 ***7137*** *p169*
Kasper, Anna; Wisconsin, n.d. ***9675.6*** *p131*
Kasper, Fred; Arkansas, 1918 ***95.2*** *p64*
Kasper, William; Wisconsin, n.d. ***9675.6*** *p131*
Kass, Frederick; Illinois, 1872 ***5012.39*** *p25*
Kassel, . . .; Iowa, 1841 ***2090*** *p608*
Kassel, P.; Iowa, 1854 ***2090*** *p612*
Kassem, Memedd Salem; Arkansas, 1918 ***95.2*** *p65*
Kassing, William; Baltimore, 1871 ***1450.2*** *p18B*
Kassmann, . . .; Canada, 1776-1783 ***9786*** *p25*
Kast, George; Philadelphia, 1758 ***9973.7*** *p33*
Kastel, John; Wisconsin, n.d. ***9675.6*** *p131*
Kastel, Thomas; Illinois, 1872 ***5012.37*** *p59*
Kastelic, Anton; Iowa, 1866-1943 ***123.54*** *p26*
Kasten, Carl Bernhard; Wisconsin, n.d. ***9675.6*** *p131*
Kasten, Henrich; Philadelphia, 1777-1779 ***8137*** *p10*
Kasten, Henry; New Orleans, 1844 ***2896.5*** *p20*
Kasten, Theodore; Wisconsin, n.d. ***9675.6*** *p131*
Kasten, William; Illinois, 1875 ***2896.5*** *p20*
Kastendeick, Lewis; New York, NY, 1839 ***8208.4*** *p91*
Kastic, Ivan; Iowa, 1866-1943 ***123.54*** *p26*
Kastner, Adam; America, 1849 ***8582.2*** *p18*
Kastner, John; Wisconsin, n.d. ***9675.6*** *p131*
Kastner, William; New York, NY, 1847 ***2896.5*** *p20*
Kaszula, Jozef; Arkansas, 1918 ***95.2*** *p65*
Katainen, David; Arkansas, 1918 ***95.2*** *p65*
Kate, Edmund; Jamaica, 1736 ***3690.1*** *p131*
Kate, James; Virginia, 1643 ***6219*** *p200*
Kateforis, Spiros; Arkansas, 1918 ***95.2*** *p65*
Kately, Andrew 16; Philadelphia, 1860 ***5704.8*** *p145*
Katemis, Peter; Arkansas, 1918 ***95.2*** *p65*
Katemis, Peter; Arkansas, 1918 ***95.2*** *p121*
Katerinos, James; Wisconsin, n.d. ***9675.6*** *p131*
Katernos, James; Wisconsin, n.d. ***9675.6*** *p131*
Kates, Mrs.; Quebec, 1815 ***9229.18*** *p77*
Kates, James 21; Jamaica, 1734 ***3690.1*** *p131*
Kathan, John; Arkansas, 1918 ***95.2*** *p65*
Katherine, John; Virginia, 1640 ***6219*** *p160*
Kathmann, Johann C.; America, 1845 ***8582.1*** *p18*
Kathmann, Johann Clemenz; America, 1843 ***8582.1*** *p18*
Katich, Mat; Iowa, 1866-1943 ***123.54*** *p26*
Katienovskie, Alexander; Arkansas, 1918 ***95.2*** *p65*
Kating, Daniel; Virginia, 1858 ***4626.16*** *p17*
Katkamp, F.; Cincinnati, 1847 ***3702.7*** *p85*
Katkos, John; Arkansas, 1918 ***95.2*** *p65*
Katrapas, George; Arkansas, 1918 ***95.2*** *p65*
Katric, Anton; Iowa, 1866-1943 ***123.54*** *p26*
Katselides, Constantine; New York, NY, 1838 ***8208.4*** *p59*
Katt, Edward Juluis; Iowa, 1866-1943 ***123.54*** *p26*
Kattenhorn, Harman; New York, NY, 1833 ***8208.4*** *p60*
Kattenhorn, Johann Heinrich; Cincinnati, 1872-1874 ***8582.1*** *p18*
Kattenkamp, . . .; Cincinnati, 1826 ***8582.1*** *p51*
Katter, Mr.; Ohio, 1859 ***3702.7*** *p93*
Kattman, Herman; Baltimore, 1832 ***2896.5*** *p20*
Kattmann, Bernhard; Cincinnati, 1869-1887 ***8582*** *p16*
Katz, Barbara Rommann *SEE* Katz, Martin
Katz, Jacob; Illinois, 1894 ***2896.5*** *p20*
Katz, Johann Jacob *SEE* Katz, Martin
Katz, John Henry; Philadelphia, 1760 ***9973.7*** *p34*
Katz, Joseph 65; New York, NY, 1912 ***1763*** *p40D*
Katz, Martin; Pennsylvania, 1762 ***2444*** *p172*
*Wife:*Barbara Rommann
*Child:*Johann Jacob
Katzenmeyer, Peter 18; America, 1853 ***9162.8*** *p36*
Katzinger, Edward 24; Kansas, 1888 ***5240.1*** *p71*
Kau, Mrs. 27; Port uncertain, 1838 ***778.5*** *p294*
Kau, Joseph 25; Port uncertain, 1838 ***778.5*** *p293*
Kauble, Michael; Philadelphia, 1758 ***9973.7*** *p33*
Kaucher, Michael; Kentucky, 1796 ***8582.3*** *p94*
Kaucijau, Ivan; Iowa, 1866-1943 ***123.54*** *p26*
Kaucijic, Ivan; Iowa, 1866-1943 ***123.54*** *p26*
Kauder, Conrad; Illinois, 1875 ***8582.2*** *p51*
Kauer, John; Wisconsin, n.d. ***9675.6*** *p131*
Kauffman, Anna Eva Christian; Pennsylvania, 1732 ***3627*** *p16*
Kauffman, Eckhard; Philadelphia, 1779 ***8137*** *p10*
Kauffman, Louis; Kentucky, 1892 ***1450.2*** *p76A*
Kauffmann, . . .; Canada, 1776-1783 ***9786*** *p25*
Kauffmann, Salomon; America, 1840 ***8582.3*** *p35*
Kaufman, . . .; Canada, 1776-1783 ***9786*** *p25*
Kaufman, Adam; New York, NY, 1840 ***8208.4*** *p110*
Kaufman, Catharine; Philadelphia, 1759 ***9973.7*** *p33*
Kaufman, Davis 17; America, 1837 ***778.5*** *p294*
Kaufman, Gustar; Shreveport, LA, 1874 ***7129*** *p45*
Kaufman, Louis; Iroquois Co., IL, 1892 ***3455.1*** *p11*
Kaufman, Maurice; Virginia, 1858 ***4626.16*** *p17*
Kaufman, Nicholas; Wisconsin, n.d. ***9675.6*** *p131*
Kaufman, Sam; Arkansas, 1918 ***95.2*** *p65*
Kaufman, Sigismund; New York, 1852 ***3702.7*** *p356*
Kaufmann, David; Charleston, SC, 1775-1781 ***8582.2*** *p52*
Kaufmann, Johann; Cincinnati, 1869-1887 ***8582*** *p16*
Kaufmann, Joseph 30; Kansas, 1886 ***5240.1*** *p68*
Kaugh, Dennis; Ohio, 1843 ***8365.26*** *p12*
Kaugho, Morris 25; Maryland, 1774 ***1219.7*** *p206*
Kaul, Andreas; Wisconsin, n.d. ***9675.6*** *p131*
Kaul, Conrad; Ohio, 1836 ***8582.1*** *p47*
Kaul, Fried.; Wisconsin, n.d. ***9675.6*** *p131*
Kaul, Wilhelm; Wisconsin, n.d. ***9675.6*** *p131*
Kaul, William; Wisconsin, n.d. ***9675.6*** *p131*
Kaun, Richard C.; Wisconsin, n.d. ***9675.6*** *p131*
Kaune, . . .; Canada, 1776-1783 ***9786*** *p25*
Kaunhauser, Elizabeth; New York, 1761 ***3652*** *p88*
Kaunisto, Emanuel; Washington, 1859-1920 ***2872.1*** *p20*
Kauntz, Christian; Wisconsin, n.d. ***9675.6*** *p131*
Kauper, Joseph; Illinois, 1892 ***5012.40*** *p26*
Kausianich, Mirko; Iowa, 1866-1943 ***123.54*** *p26*
Kausiarich, Mirko; Iowa, 1866-1943 ***123.54*** *p26*
Kauss, Mr.; Minnesota, 1857 ***8582.3*** *p82*
Kaussler, Albert; Missouri, 1855 ***2896.5*** *p20*
Kaust, Joseph; Illinois, 1905 ***5012.37*** *p63*
Kaust, Martin; Philadelphia, 1758 ***9973.7*** *p33*
Kauth, Adam; Wisconsin, n.d. ***9675.6*** *p131*
Kauth, Peter; Wisconsin, n.d. ***9675.6*** *p131*
Kauther, Philipp Jacob; Cincinnati, 1869-1887 ***8582*** *p16*
Kautz, Philipp; America, 1848 ***8582.1*** *p18*
Kauzlaric, Anton; Iowa, 1866-1943 ***123.54*** *p26*
Kauzlaric, Elizabeth Thresa; Iowa, 1866-1943 ***123.54*** *p26*
Kauzlaric, Frank; Iowa, 1866-1943 ***123.54*** *p26*
Kauzlaric, Geolio; Iowa, 1866-1943 ***123.54*** *p26*
Kauzlaric, Georj; Iowa, 1866-1943 ***123.54*** *p26*
Kauzlaric, Grgo; Iowa, 1866-1943 ***123.54*** *p26*
Kauzlaric, Josep; Iowa, 1866-1943 ***123.54*** *p26*
Kauzlaric, Josip; Iowa, 1866-1943 ***123.54*** *p26*
Kauzlaric, Kazimir; Iowa, 1866-1943 ***123.54*** *p26*
Kauzlaric, Mate; Iowa, 1866-1943 ***123.54*** *p26*
Kauzlaric, Peter; Iowa, 1866-1943 ***123.54*** *p26*
Kauzlaric, Venz; Iowa, 1866-1943 ***123.54*** *p26*
Kauzlarich, Andrew; Iowa, 1866-1943 ***123.54*** *p26*
Kauzlarich, Andrew; Iowa, 1866-1943 ***123.54*** *p27*
Kauzlarich, Anton; Iowa, 1866-1943 ***123.54*** *p27*
Kauzlarich, Brnordo; Iowa, 1866-1943 ***123.54*** *p27*
Kauzlarich, Charley; Iowa, 1866-1943 ***123.54*** *p27*
Kauzlarich, Frank; Iowa, 1866-1943 ***123.54*** *p27*
Kauzlarich, George; Iowa, 1866-1943 ***123.54*** *p27*
Kauzlarich, Josip; Iowa, 1866-1943 ***123.54*** *p27*
Kauzlarich, Julian; Iowa, 1866-1943 ***123.54*** *p27*
Kauzlarich, Juray; Iowa, 1866-1943 ***123.54*** *p27*
Kauzlarich, Kazimir; Iowa, 1866-1943 ***123.54*** *p65*
Kauzlarich, Kozoninin; Iowa, 1866-1943 ***123.54*** *p27*
Kauzlarich, Mary; Iowa, 1866-1943 ***123.54*** *p65*
Kauzlarich, Phillip; Iowa, 1866-1943 ***123.54*** *p27*
Kauzlarich, Valentine; Iowa, 1866-1943 ***123.54*** *p27*
Kauzlarick, Joseph; Iowa, 1866-1943 ***123.54*** *p27*
Kauzlavic, Powas; Iowa, 1866-1943 ***123.54*** *p27*
Kauzleric, August; Iowa, 1866-1943 ***123.54*** *p27*
Kauzlerich, Vinko; Iowa, 1866-1943 ***123.54*** *p27*
Kauzliski, George; Iowa, 1866-1943 ***123.54*** *p27*
Kauzlovic, Ivan; Iowa, 1866-1943 ***123.54*** *p27*
Kauzlratis, Max; Iowa, 1866-1943 ***123.54*** *p27*
Kauzlurich, Anton; Iowa, 1866-1943 ***123.54*** *p27*
Kavalic, George; America, 1900 ***7137*** *p169*
Kavanagh, Charles; New York, NY, 1838 ***8208.4*** *p86*
Kavanagh, Dennis; New York, NY, 1838 ***8208.4*** *p85*
Kavanagh, James; Philadelphia, 1811 ***53.26*** *p41*
Kavanagh, Patrick; New York, NY, 1834 ***8208.4*** *p60*
Kavanagh, Thomas; Montreal, 1822 ***7603*** *p101*
Kavanah, Andrew; America, 1844 ***1450.2*** *p76A*
Kavanaugh, Catharine 19; Massachusetts, 1850 ***5881.1*** *p53*
Kavanaugh, Patrick; Illinois, 1870 ***5012.38*** *p99*
Kavaney, Patrick; Virginia, 1844 ***4626.16*** *p13*
Kavenaugh, Margaret; Massachusetts, 1850 ***5881.1*** *p55*
Kaveny, Cornelius; New York, NY, 1837 ***8208.4*** *p53*
Kawiecka, Walentyna 40; New York, 1912 ***9980.29*** *p50*
Kay, Ann 9 *SEE* Kay, Bryan
Kay, Brian 20; North America, 1774 ***1219.7*** *p199*
Kay, Bryan 38; North America, 1774 ***1219.7*** *p198*
*Wife:*Dorothy 42
*Brother:*Robert 42
*Child:*Elizabeth 16
*Child:*Hannah 14
*Child:*Sarah 12
*Child:*Ann 9
*Child:*Jane 7
Kay, Clifford Alaxander; Iowa, 1866-1943 ***123.54*** *p67*
Kay, Dorothy 42 *SEE* Kay, Bryan
Kay, Elizabeth 16 *SEE* Kay, Bryan
Kay, Essie Tucker; Iowa, 1866-1943 ***123.54*** *p67*
Kay, George; New York, NY, 1834 ***8208.4*** *p44*
Kay, Hannah 14 *SEE* Kay, Bryan
Kay, James; North Carolina, 1817 ***1639.20*** *p102*
Kay, Jane 7 *SEE* Kay, Bryan
Kay, John; Quebec, 1815 ***9229.18*** *p77*
Kay, John 1; St. John, N.B., 1866 ***5704.8*** *p167*
Kay, Margaret 21; St. John, N.B., 1866 ***5704.8*** *p167*
Kay, Peter; New York, 1833 ***8208.4*** *p59*
Kay, Robert; North Carolina, 1827 ***1639.20*** *p102*
Kay, Robert 42 *SEE* Kay, Bryan
Kay, Sally; Philadelphia, 1866 ***5704.8*** *p204*
Kay, Sarah 12 *SEE* Kay, Bryan
Kay, Simon; New York, NY, 1836 ***8208.4*** *p12*
Kay, Thomas 22; St. John, N.B., 1866 ***5704.8*** *p167*
Kay, Timothy 22; Massachusetts, 1849 ***5881.1*** *p56*
Kay, William 17; Maryland, 1724 ***3690.1*** *p131*
Kay, William 20; North America, 1774 ***1219.7*** *p198*
Kay, William 39; Jamaica, 1735 ***3690.1*** *p131*
Kay, William W.; Illinois, 1861 ***2896.5*** *p20*
Kaye, Charles 30; Maryland, 1774 ***1219.7*** *p224*
Kaye, Henry Burdon 29; Kansas, 1884 ***5240.1*** *p65*
Kaylaric, Peter; Iowa, 1866-1943 ***123.54*** *p27*
Kayman, Benedict; Philadelphia, 1759 ***9973.7*** *p33*
Kayser, . . .; Canada, 1776-1783 ***9786*** *p25*
Kayser, Anna Catharina *SEE* Kayser, Johann Ulrich
Kayser, Anna Catharina Frech *SEE* Kayser, Johann Ulrich
Kayser, Anna Margaretha *SEE* Kayser, Johann Ulrich
Kayser, Anna Maria *SEE* Kayser, Johann Ulrich
Kayser, Anna Maria; America, 1752-1800 ***2444*** *p176*
Kayser, Elisabetha *SEE* Kayser, Johann Ulrich
Kayser, Franz Xaver; Cincinnati, 1869-1887 ***8582*** *p16*
Kayser, Frederick William; California, 1868 ***2769.5*** *p6*
Kayser, Fritz 29; Kansas, 1901 ***5240.1*** *p82*
Kayser, Jacob Frederick; New York, NY, 1835 ***8208.4*** *p7*
Kayser, Johann Ulrich; West Indies, 1752 ***2444*** *p172*
*Wife:*Anna Catharina Frech
*Child:*Elisabetha
*Child:*Anna Catharina
*Child:*Anna Margaretha
*Child:*Anna Maria
*Child:*Maria
Kayser, Maria *SEE* Kayser, Johann Ulrich
Kayser, Michael; Wisconsin, n.d. ***9675.6*** *p131*
Kayser, Peter; Wisconsin, n.d. ***9675.6*** *p131*
Kayser, Peter 19; America, 1831 ***778.5*** *p294*
Kayser, Robert Ernest; San Francisco, 1857 ***2769.5*** *p6*
Kayupp, Kath.; Virginia, 1643 ***6219*** *p204*
Kazelarich, Joseph; Iowa, 1866-1943 ***123.54*** *p27*
Kazelarich, Matthew; Iowa, 1866-1943 ***123.54*** *p27*
Kazleric, Lwan; Iowa, 1866-1943 ***123.54*** *p27*
Kazlericz, Anton; Iowa, 1866-1943 ***123.54*** *p27*
Keach, Thomas 16; Maryland, 1720 ***3690.1*** *p131*
Keady, Sarah 20; St. John, N.B., 1857 ***5704.8*** *p136*
Keafer, Frederick; Pennsylvania, 1715-1795 ***2444*** *p179*
Kealiher, Ellenor; America, 1740 ***4971*** *p48*
Kealiner, Ellenor; America, 1740 ***4971*** *p48*
Keally, Ellinor; America, 1735-1743 ***4971*** *p7*
Keally, Patrick; New York, NY, 1811 ***2859.11*** *p14*
Kealy, Bridget; Illinois, 1841 ***7036*** *p126*
*Brother:*Michael
Kealy, Charles; America, 1741 ***4971*** *p35*
Kealy, Jane 11; St. John, N.B., 1847 ***5704.8*** *p18*
Kealy, John; America, 1742 ***4971*** *p30*
Kealy, John; Maryland, 1742 ***4971*** *p106*
Kealy, Mary; St. John, N.B., 1847 ***5704.8*** *p18*
Kealy, Mary 9; St. John, N.B., 1847 ***5704.8*** *p18*
Kealy, Michael *SEE* Kealy, Bridget
Kealy, Nancy 18; Philadelphia, 1858 ***5704.8*** *p139*
Kean, Ann; America, 1740 ***4971*** *p37*
Kean, Biddy 11; Massachusetts, 1850 ***5881.1*** *p52*
Kean, Catharine 16; Massachusetts, 1850 ***5881.1*** *p53*
Kean, Darby; America, 1741 ***4971*** *p83*

Kean, Darby; America, 1742 ***4971*** *p83*
Kean, Francis; St. John, N.B., 1848 ***5704.8*** *p44*
Kean, James; America, 1743 ***4971*** *p84*
Kean, John; America, 1735-1743 ***4971*** *p51*
Kean, Mary 5; Massachusetts, 1849 ***5881.1*** *p55*
Kean, Patrick 7; Massachusetts, 1849 ***5881.1*** *p56*
Keane, Edmond; America, 1742 ***4971*** *p49*
Keane, Edmond; America, 1742 ***4971*** *p50*
Keane, Judy 35; Massachusetts, 1849 ***5881.1*** *p54*
Keane, Margaret; New York, NY, 1811 ***2859.11*** *p14*
Keanen, Patrick; New York, NY, 1815 ***2859.11*** *p34*
Keanigh, Jacob; Pennsylvania, 1750 ***2444*** *p177*
Keanigh, Jacob; Pennsylvania, 1750 ***2444*** *p235*
Keaning, . . .; Canada, 1776-1783 ***9786*** *p25*
Keans, James; New York, NY, 1840 ***8208.4*** *p110*
Kearceay, John; New York, NY, 1811 ***2859.11*** *p14*
Kearceay, Margaret; New York, NY, 1811 ***2859.11*** *p14*
Kearceay, Thomas; New York, NY, 1811 ***2859.11*** *p14*
Kearcey, Mr.; New York, NY, 1811 ***2859.11*** *p6*
With wife & relatives
Keareen, James 20; Massachusetts, 1849 ***5881.1*** *p54*
Keareen, Mary 20; Massachusetts, 1849 ***5881.1*** *p55*
Keareen, Thomas; America, 1739 ***4971*** *p46*
Keareen, Thomas; America, 1739 ***4971*** *p47*
Keareen, Thomas; America, 1741 ***4971*** *p49*
Kearfoote, Margaret; Virginia, 1698 ***2212*** *p12*
Kearin, Daniel; America, 1740 ***4971*** *p59*
Kearins, Mary; Philadelphia, 1865 ***5704.8*** *p192*
Kearins, Michael; Philadelphia, 1865 ***5704.8*** *p192*
Kearn, Frederick 28; California, 1872 ***2769.5*** *p6*
Kearn, John 20; Philadelphia, 1858 ***5704.8*** *p139*
Kearnan, Miles; America, 1741 ***4971*** *p37*
Kearnan, Patrick; America, 1743 ***4971*** *p37*
Kearnan, Thomas; America, 1741 ***4971*** *p10*
Kearnan, Thomas; America, 1741 ***4971*** *p94*
Kearnes, John 25; Massachusetts, 1847 ***5881.1*** *p53*
Kearnes, Margaret 25; Massachusetts, 1849 ***5881.1*** *p55*
Kearney, Anastatia 28; Massachusetts, 1848 ***5881.1*** *p52*
Kearney, Ann 17; Philadelphia, 1857 ***5704.8*** *p134*
Kearney, Biddy; Quebec, 1847 ***5704.8*** *p6*
Kearney, Bridget 6; Massachusetts, 1849 ***5881.1*** *p52*
Kearney, Catharine; New York, NY, 1865 ***5704.8*** *p192*
Kearney, Catherine; New York, NY, 1864 ***5704.8*** *p170*
Kearney, Edward; New York, NY, 1839 ***8208.4*** *p97*
Kearney, Edward; Philadelphia, 1852 ***5704.8*** *p96*
Kearney, Francis; New York, NY, 1811 ***2859.11*** *p14*
Kearney, Francis; Philadelphia, 1864 ***5704.8*** *p181*
Kearney, Hamilton; Philadelphia, 1852 ***5704.8*** *p89*
Kearney, Henry; Philadelphia, 1816 ***2859.11*** *p34*
Kearney, James; New York, NY, 1816 ***2859.11*** *p34*
Kearney, James 11; Philadelphia, 1852 ***5704.8*** *p96*
Kearney, James 16; Philadelphia, 1860 ***5704.8*** *p145*
Kearney, Jane 25; Massachusetts, 1850 ***5881.1*** *p54*
Kearney, Jno.; Philadelphia, 1816 ***2859.11*** *p34*
Kearney, John; New York, NY, 1816 ***2859.11*** *p34*
Kearney, John 18; Philadelphia, 1860 ***5704.8*** *p145*
Kearney, John 30; Massachusetts, 1850 ***5881.1*** *p54*
Kearney, Johnston; Philadelphia, 1816 ***2859.11*** *p34*
Kearney, Joy; St. John, N.B., 1847 ***5704.8*** *p25*
Kearney, Margaret 20; Philadelphia, 1857 ***5704.8*** *p133*
Kearney, Mary; Philadelphia, 1864 ***5704.8*** *p188*
Kearney, Mary 20; Philadelphia, 1860 ***5704.8*** *p145*
Kearney, Michael; New York, NY, 1811 ***2859.11*** *p14*
Kearney, Patrick; New York, NY, 1834 ***8208.4*** *p44*
Kearney, Patrick 9; Philadelphia, 1852 ***5704.8*** *p96*
Kearney, Peter 47; Massachusetts, 1849 ***5881.1*** *p56*
Kearney, Rosey 12; Quebec, 1847 ***5704.8*** *p8*
Kearney, Sarah; New York, NY, 1865 ***5704.8*** *p192*
Kearney, Susan; Philadelphia, 1852 ***5704.8*** *p96*
Kearney, Teresa; Philadelphia, 1852 ***5704.8*** *p96*
Kearney, Timothy; New York, NY, 1838 ***8208.4*** *p84*
Kearns, Alice 11; Philadelphia, 1865 ***5704.8*** *p196*
Kearns, Betty 21; Massachusetts, 1850 ***5881.1*** *p52*
Kearns, Dennis; America, 1739 ***4971*** *p68*
Kearns, Elizabeth; New York, NY, 1811 ***2859.11*** *p14*
Kearns, James; New York, NY, 1811 ***2859.11*** *p14*
Kearns, John 30; Wilmington, DE, 1831 ***6508.3*** *p100*
Kearns, John W.; New York, NY, 1835 ***8208.4*** *p29*
Kearns, Patrick; New York, NY, 1815 ***2859.11*** *p34*
Kearns, Peter 30; Massachusetts, 1850 ***5881.1*** *p56*
Kearny, Michael; New York, NY, 1836 ***8208.4*** *p12*
Kearny, Nicholas; America, 1743 ***4971*** *p43*
Kearny, Patrick; New York, NY, 1811 ***2859.11*** *p14*
Kearny, Thomas; New York, NY, 1836 ***8208.4*** *p12*
Kearsley, Eliza; America, 1807 ***8894.2*** *p55*
Keartland, Ann 19; Leeward Islands, 1723 ***3690.1*** *p132*
Keary, Ann; America, 1742 ***4971*** *p17*
Keary, Ann; Maryland, 1742 ***4971*** *p107*
Keary, Loughlin; Maryland, 1742 ***4971*** *p106*
Keate, Edmund; Jamaica, 1736 ***3690.1*** *p131*
Keater, William 29; Maryland, 1774 ***1219.7*** *p226*
Keath, Christ.; Virginia, 1643 ***6219*** *p204*
Keating, Abraham; New York, NY, 1811 ***2859.11*** *p14*
Keating, Anne; New York, NY, 1816 ***2859.11*** *p34*
With child
Keating, Bridget 36; Massachusetts, 1849 ***5881.1*** *p52*
Keating, Catharine 11; Massachusetts, 1849 ***5881.1*** *p53*
Keating, Daniel 4; Massachusetts, 1849 ***5881.1*** *p53*
Keating, Edward; New York, NY, 1816 ***2859.11*** *p34*
Keating, Edward 30; Massachusetts, 1849 ***5881.1*** *p53*
Keating, Henry; America, 1743 ***4971*** *p10*
Keating, Hugh; Philadelphia, 1816 ***2859.11*** *p34*
Keating, Jacques; Quebec, 1818 ***7603*** *p96*
Keating, Johanna; Quebec, 1825 ***7603*** *p66*
Keating, Johanna 9; Massachusetts, 1849 ***5881.1*** *p54*
Keating, John; New York, NY, 1811 ***2859.11*** *p14*
Keating, John 14; Massachusetts, 1849 ***5881.1*** *p54*
Keating, John 37; Arizona, 1890 ***2764.35*** *p39*
Keating, Mary; New York, NY, 1811 ***2859.11*** *p14*
Keating, Mary 41; Massachusetts, 1849 ***5881.1*** *p55*
With child
Keating, Peggy 11; Massachusetts, 1849 ***5881.1*** *p56*
Keating, Thomas; Massachusetts, 1849 ***5881.1*** *p56*
Keating, Thomas; San Francisco, 1850 ***4914.15*** *p10*
Keating, William 19; Massachusetts, 1848 ***5881.1*** *p56*
Keating, William 30; Massachusetts, 1848 ***5881.1*** *p56*
Keatings, Michael; America, 1739 ***4971*** *p37*
Keatlan, Annie; Philadelphia, 1865 ***5704.8*** *p191*
Keatley, Josiah; Colorado, 1890 ***9678.2*** *p61*
Keaton, James 25; Philadelphia, 1775 ***1219.7*** *p256*
Keaugh, Nicholas; New York, NY, 1835 ***8208.4*** *p45*
Keaver, Thomas; New Orleans, 1849 ***1450.2*** *p76A*
Keavy, Mary 15; Massachusetts, 1848 ***5881.1*** *p55*
Keays, John; New York, NY, 1838 ***8208.4*** *p61*
Kebalbach, Joseph; Wisconsin, n.d. ***9675.6*** *p131*
Kebbon, Erik Henrik; America, 1853 ***6410.32*** *p123*
Kebelbeck, William; Wisconsin, n.d. ***9675.6*** *p131*
Keble, John; Pennsylvania, 1759 ***1219.7*** *p68*
Kebler, John; Cincinnati, 1869-1887 ***8582*** *p16*
Keck, Anna Barbara; America, 1726-1800 ***2444*** *p172*
Keck, Anna Barbara; Pennsylvania, 1726-1785 ***2444*** *p172*
Keck, George; Pennsylvania, 1736 ***4779.3*** *p14*
Kedbey, Thomas; Virginia, 1639 ***6219*** *p181*
Keddie, William; Wilmington, NC, 1756-1809 ***1639.20*** *p103*
Kedman, Thomas 28; Maryland, 1775 ***1219.7*** *p253*
Kedton, William 19; Maryland, 1774 ***1219.7*** *p221*
Kee, Ann; New Orleans, 1849 ***5704.8*** *p58*
Kee, Billy; New Orleans, 1849 ***5704.8*** *p58*
Kee, Charles; Philadelphia, 1847 ***53.26*** *p41*
*Relative:*Eliza
*Relative:*John
*Relative:*Mary
*Relative:*Thomas 3
*Relative:*George 1
Kee, Charles; Philadelphia, 1847 ***5704.8*** *p30*
Kee, Eliza *SEE* Kee, Charles
Kee, Eliza; Philadelphia, 1847 ***5704.8*** *p30*
Kee, George 1 *SEE* Kee, Charles
Kee, George 1; Philadelphia, 1847 ***5704.8*** *p30*
Kee, Isaac; New Orleans, 1849 ***5704.8*** *p58*
Kee, Isaac 6; New Orleans, 1849 ***5704.8*** *p58*
Kee, James; Quebec, 1849 ***5704.8*** *p57*
Kee, Jane 38; Philadelphia, 1864 ***5704.8*** *p156*
Kee, John *SEE* Kee, Charles
Kee, John; New Orleans, 1849 ***5704.8*** *p58*
Kee, John; Philadelphia, 1847 ***5704.8*** *p30*
Kee, John; St. John, N.B., 1853 ***5704.8*** *p98*
Kee, John 8; New Orleans, 1849 ***5704.8*** *p58*
Kee, Lavina 5; Philadelphia, 1864 ***5704.8*** *p156*
Kee, Mary *SEE* Kee, Charles
Kee, Mary; Philadelphia, 1847 ***5704.8*** *p30*
Kee, Mary 4; New Orleans, 1849 ***5704.8*** *p58*
Kee, Thomas; New Orleans, 1849 ***5704.8*** *p58*
Kee, Thomas; Philadelphia, 1851 ***5704.8*** *p81*
Kee, Thomas; Philadelphia, 1852 ***5704.8*** *p96*
Kee, Thomas 1; New Orleans, 1849 ***5704.8*** *p58*
Kee, Thomas 2; Philadelphia, 1864 ***5704.8*** *p156*
Kee, Thomas 3 *SEE* Kee, Charles
Kee, Thomas 3; Philadelphia, 1847 ***5704.8*** *p30*
Kee, Thomas 23; Philadelphia, 1853 ***5704.8*** *p112*
Kee, William John 6; Philadelphia, 1864 ***5704.8*** *p156*
Keeble, Henry 27; Maryland, 1775 ***1219.7*** *p254*
Keechline, Peter; Philadelphia, 1759 ***9973.7*** *p33*
Keeding, Ann; Virginia, 1639 ***6219*** *p154*
Keef, Jean; Quebec, 1824 ***7603*** *p82*
Keef, John; America, 1736 ***4971*** *p44*
Keef, Thomas; Ohio, 1844 ***9892.11*** *p23*
Keefaber, Conrad; Philadelphia, 1764 ***9973.7*** *p39*
Keefe, Ann 13; Massachusetts, 1850 ***5881.1*** *p52*
Keefe, Arthur 26; Massachusetts, 1850 ***5881.1*** *p52*
Keefe, Biddy 11; Massachusetts, 1850 ***5881.1*** *p52*
Keefe, Bridget 19; Massachusetts, 1849 ***5881.1*** *p52*
Keefe, Catharine 8; Massachusetts, 1849 ***5881.1*** *p53*
Keefe, Daniel; Wisconsin, n.d. ***9675.6*** *p131*
Keefe, Elizabeth; America, 1736 ***4971*** *p43*
Keefe, Ellen 3; Massachusetts, 1850 ***5881.1*** *p53*
Keefe, Jerry 34; Newport, RI, 1851 ***6508.5*** *p20*
Keefe, Joanna 55; Massachusetts, 1848 ***5881.1*** *p54*
Keefe, John 5; Massachusetts, 1849 ***5881.1*** *p54*
Keefe, John 43; Kansas, 1880 ***5240.1*** *p62*
Keefe, Julia 20; Massachusetts, 1850 ***5881.1*** *p54*
Keefe, Margaret 3; Massachusetts, 1849 ***5881.1*** *p55*
Keefe, Margaret 21; Massachusetts, 1850 ***5881.1*** *p55*
Keefe, Mary 18; Massachusetts, 1849 ***5881.1*** *p55*
Keefe, Owen 27; Virginia, 1774 ***1219.7*** *p239*
Keefe, Patrick 13; Massachusetts, 1849 ***5881.1*** *p56*
Keefe, Patrick 26; Massachusetts, 1850 ***5881.1*** *p56*
Keefe, Peggy 10; Massachusetts, 1848 ***5881.1*** *p56*
Keefe, William 6; Massachusetts, 1850 ***5881.1*** *p57*
Keefer, Frederick; Pennsylvania, 1715-1795 ***2444*** *p179*
Keeffe, Bridget; Montreal, 1822 ***7603*** *p82*
Keeffe, Cornelius; New York, NY, 1836 ***8208.4*** *p13*
Keegan, Bessy; St. John, N.B., 1853 ***5704.8*** *p106*
Keegan, Bryan; America, 1735-1743 ***4971*** *p7*
Keegan, Francis; St. John, N.B., 1853 ***5704.8*** *p106*
Keegan, Owen; New York, NY, 1835 ***8208.4*** *p4*
Keegan, Patrick 26; Massachusetts, 1850 ***5881.1*** *p56*
Keegan, William 12; St. John, N.B., 1853 ***5704.8*** *p106*
Keegan, William John; Arkansas, 1918 ***95.2*** *p65*
Keehoe, Edward 20; Massachusetts, 1849 ***5881.1*** *p53*
Keeland, Charles; Philadelphia, 1847 ***53.26*** *p41*
Keeland, Charles; Philadelphia, 1847 ***5704.8*** *p31*
Keeler, Joseph; New York, NY, 1835 ***8208.4*** *p49*
Keeler, Smith; New York, NY, 1837 ***8208.4*** *p49*
Keeley, Dennis 18; Massachusetts, 1849 ***5881.1*** *p53*
Keeley, Ellen 16; Massachusetts, 1849 ***5881.1*** *p53*
Keelin, Sarah; Virginia, 1638 ***6219*** *p14*
Keeling, Ellen 24; Philadelphia, 1853 ***5704.8*** *p111*
Keeling, Mathew 25; Maryland, 1775 ***1219.7*** *p256*
Keeling, Thomas; Virginia, 1628 ***6219*** *p31*
Keelman, John N.; Indiana, 1847 ***9117*** *p19*
Keely, Elias; Virginia, 1637 ***6219*** *p13*
Keely, Maurice; Montreal, 1824 ***7603*** *p98*
Keely, Sarah; America, 1737 ***4971*** *p13*
Keemele, John; Pennsylvania, 1763 ***2444*** *p173*
Keen, Ann 9 mos; St. John, N.B., 1847 ***5704.8*** *p10*
Keen, Catharine 20; Massachusetts, 1849 ***5881.1*** *p52*
Keen, Edward 23; Baltimore, 1775 ***1219.7*** *p270*
Keen, Francis; St. John, N.B., 1847 ***5704.8*** *p10*
Keen, James 22; Maryland, 1774 ***1219.7*** *p228*
Keen, Mary; St. John, N.B., 1847 ***5704.8*** *p10*
Keen, Samuel; New York, NY, 1815 ***2859.11*** *p34*
Keenan, . . . 7 mos; New York, NY, 1869 ***5704.8*** *p235*
Keenan, Alice 5; Quebec, 1847 ***5704.8*** *p28*
Keenan, Andy 28; Massachusetts, 1850 ***5881.1*** *p52*
Keenan, Brigitte; Quebec, 1822 ***7603*** *p88*
Keenan, Catharine; America, 1865 ***5704.8*** *p204*
Keenan, Daniel; New York, NY, 1816 ***2859.11*** *p34*
Keenan, Daniel 18 mos; New York, NY, 1869 ***5704.8*** *p235*
Keenan, Dennis; New York, NY, 1811 ***2859.11*** *p14*
Keenan, Dunkan; America, 1740 ***4971*** *p73*
Keenan, Edward 4; New York, NY, 1869 ***5704.8*** *p235*
Keenan, Eliza; New York, NY, 1865 ***5704.8*** *p182*
Keenan, Ellen; New York, NY, 1816 ***2859.11*** *p34*
With child
Keenan, Francis 7; Quebec, 1847 ***5704.8*** *p28*
Keenan, Francis 20; St. John, N.B., 1867 ***5704.8*** *p168*
Keenan, Henry; America, 1741 ***4971*** *p73*
Keenan, Hugh; New York, NY, 1811 ***2859.11*** *p14*
Keenan, Hugh 17; Philadelphia, 1853 ***5704.8*** *p112*
Keenan, James; Ohio, 1860 ***9892.11*** *p23*
Keenan, James 17; Massachusetts, 1847 ***5881.1*** *p53*
Keenan, James 23; St. John, N.B., 1864 ***5704.8*** *p159*
Keenan, Jane 9; Massachusetts, 1849 ***5881.1*** *p54*
Keenan, John; America, 1742 ***4971*** *p65*
Keenan, John; America, 1864 ***5704.8*** *p183*
Keenan, John; Philadelphia, 1849 ***53.26*** *p41*
*Relative:*Patrick 8
*Relative:*Mary 6
Keenan, John; Philadelphia, 1849 ***5704.8*** *p58*
Keenan, John; Philadelphia, 1866 ***5704.8*** *p205*
Keenan, John; Quebec, 1847 ***5704.8*** *p8*
Keenan, John 10; Massachusetts, 1849 ***5881.1*** *p54*
Keenan, John 11; Quebec, 1847 ***5704.8*** *p28*
Keenan, John 13; Quebec, 1847 ***5704.8*** *p28*
Keenan, John 20; St. John, N.B., 1854 ***5704.8*** *p119*
Keenan, Margaret; New York, NY, 1865 ***5704.8*** *p182*
Keenan, Margaret 20; Massachusetts, 1850 ***5881.1*** *p55*
Keenan, Mary; America, 1737 ***4971*** *p13*
Keenan, Mary; New York, NY, 1869 ***5704.8*** *p235*
Keenan, Mary; Philadelphia, 1850 ***53.26*** *p41*
Keenan, Mary; Philadelphia, 1850 ***5704.8*** *p69*
Keenan, Mary; Quebec, 1849 ***5704.8*** *p52*
Keenan, Mary 6 *SEE* Keenan, John
Keenan, Mary 6; Philadelphia, 1849 ***5704.8*** *p58*
Keenan, Mary 20; Massachusetts, 1850 ***5881.1*** *p56*

Kelly, Arthur; Philadelphia, 1847 ***53.26*** *p41*
Kelly, Arthur; Philadelphia, 1847 ***5704.8*** *p31*
Kelly, B. 26; Philadelphia, 1774 ***1219.7*** *p228*
Kelly, Barney; Philadelphia, 1865 ***5704.8*** *p197*
Kelly, Barthol.; America, 1742 ***4971*** *p50*
Kelly, Bernard; Quebec, 1823 ***7603*** *p67*
Kelly, Bernard; St. John, N.B., 1853 ***5704.8*** *p99*
Kelly, Bernard 10 mos; Philadelphia, 1866 ***5704.8*** *p207*
Kelly, Bernard 8 *SEE* Kelly, Francis
Kelly, Bernard 8; Philadelphia, 1847 ***5704.8*** *p22*
Kelly, Bernard 35; Philadelphia, 1864 ***5704.8*** *p161*
Kelly, Bernard 45; Massachusetts, 1850 ***5881.1*** *p52*
Kelly, Betty; St. John, N.B., 1848 ***5704.8*** *p45*
Kelly, Betty 24; Philadelphia, 1859 ***5704.8*** *p143*
Kelly, Biddy; St. John, N.B., 1848 ***5704.8*** *p44*
Kelly, Biddy 11; New York, NY, 1864 ***5704.8*** *p173*
Kelly, Biddy 16; St. John, N.B., 1861 ***5704.8*** *p149*
Kelly, Biddy 18; Philadelphia, 1854 ***5704.8*** *p118*
Kelly, Biddy 20; Massachusetts, 1850 ***5881.1*** *p52*
Kelly, Biddy 50; Massachusetts, 1849 ***5881.1*** *p52*
Kelly, Brian 7; Philadelphia, 1852 ***5704.8*** *p85*
Kelly, Bridget; New York, NY, 1864 ***5704.8*** *p170*
Kelly, Bridget; New York, NY, 1865 ***5704.8*** *p192*
Kelly, Bridget; New York, NY, 1866 ***5704.8*** *p206*
Kelly, Bridget; New York, NY, 1866 ***5704.8*** *p210*
Kelly, Bridget; New York, NY, 1868 ***5704.8*** *p229*
Kelly, Bridget; Philadelphia, 1852 ***5704.8*** *p92*
Kelly, Bridget; Philadelphia, 1864 ***5704.8*** *p188*
Kelly, Bridget 6; Massachusetts, 1849 ***5881.1*** *p52*
Kelly, Bridget 12; St. John, N.B., 1851 ***5704.8*** *p79*
Kelly, Bridget 13; Massachusetts, 1847 ***5881.1*** *p52*
Kelly, Bridget 15; New York, NY, 1864 ***5704.8*** *p176*
Kelly, Bridget 16; Massachusetts, 1849 ***5881.1*** *p52*
Kelly, Bridget 18; Philadelphia, 1853 ***5704.8*** *p111*
Kelly, Bridget 20; Massachusetts, 1850 ***5881.1*** *p52*
Kelly, Bridget 30; Massachusetts, 1847 ***5881.1*** *p52*
Kelly, Bridget 40; Massachusetts, 1849 ***5881.1*** *p52*
Kelly, Bryan; America, 1735-1743 ***4971*** *p78*
Kelly, Bryan; America, 1741 ***4971*** *p37*
Kelly, Bryan; America, 1742 ***4971*** *p80*
Kelly, Bryan; Virginia, 1636 ***6219*** *p21*
Kelly, Bryan; Virginia, 1638 ***6219*** *p146*
Kelly, Cath.; Philadelphia, 1864 ***5704.8*** *p185*
Kelly, Catharine; Philadelphia, 1866 ***5704.8*** *p207*
Kelly, Catharine; Philadelphia, 1866 ***5704.8*** *p209*
Kelly, Catharine 6; New York, NY, 1864 ***5704.8*** *p176*
Kelly, Catharine 11; Philadelphia, 1847 ***5704.8*** *p22*
Kelly, Catharine 12; Massachusetts, 1849 ***5881.1*** *p53*
Kelly, Catharine 13; Massachusetts, 1849 ***5881.1*** *p52*
Kelly, Catharine 20; Massachusetts, 1849 ***5881.1*** *p52*
Kelly, Catharine 30; Massachusetts, 1848 ***5881.1*** *p52*
Kelly, Catharine 36; Massachusetts, 1850 ***5881.1*** *p53*
Kelly, Catharine A.; America, 1868 ***5704.8*** *p227*
Kelly, Catherine *SEE* Kelly, Catherine
Kelly, Catherine; New York, NY, 1811 ***2859.11*** *p14*
Kelly, Catherine; North Carolina, 1780-1864 ***1639.20*** *p104*
Kelly, Catherine; Philadelphia, 1847 ***53.26*** *p41*
*Relative:*Neal
*Relative:*Dennis
*Relative:*Catherine
Kelly, Catherine; Philadelphia, 1847 ***5704.8*** *p5*
Kelly, Catherine; Philadelphia, 1853 ***5704.8*** *p112*
Kelly, Catherine; Quebec, 1851 ***5704.8*** *p75*
Kelly, Catherine 11 *SEE* Kelly, Francis
Kelly, Catherine 19; Philadelphia, 1854 ***5704.8*** *p121*
Kelly, Catherine 22; Philadelphia, 1860 ***5704.8*** *p144*
Kelly, Catherine 65; South Carolina, 1850 ***1639.20*** *p104*
Kelly, Catherine 70; North Carolina, 1850 ***1639.20*** *p104*
Kelly, Catherine Chisholm; North Carolina, 1783-1859 ***1639.20*** *p43*
Kelly, Cecilia; America, 1870 ***5704.8*** *p237*
Kelly, Charles; New York, NY, 1816 ***2859.11*** *p34*
Kelly, Charles; New York, NY, 1869 ***5704.8*** *p233*
Kelly, Charles 2 *SEE* Kelly, Francis
Kelly, Charles 2; Philadelphia, 1847 ***5704.8*** *p22*
Kelly, Charles 6; Quebec, 1847 ***5704.8*** *p16*
Kelly, Charles 6; St. John, N.B., 1851 ***5704.8*** *p79*
Kelly, Charles 9; Philadelphia, 1853 ***5704.8*** *p113*
Kelly, Charles 12 *SEE* Kelly, Dennis
Kelly, Charles 12; Philadelphia, 1847 ***5704.8*** *p22*
Kelly, Charles 17; Philadelphia, 1858 ***5704.8*** *p138*
Kelly, Charles 21; Philadelphia, 1804 ***53.26*** *p41*
*Relative:*Hugh 22
Kelly, Charles 35; Quebec, 1864 ***5704.8*** *p162*
Kelly, Christian 1; Massachusetts, 1848 ***5881.1*** *p52*
Kelly, Christopher 17; Philadelphia, 1861 ***5704.8*** *p148*
Kelly, Dan; Philadelphia, 1852 ***5704.8*** *p97*
Kelly, Daniel; America, 1739 ***4971*** *p28*
Kelly, Daniel; America, 1786 ***1639.20*** *p104*
Kelly, Daniel; New York, NY, 1864 ***5704.8*** *p176*
Kelly, Daniel; Philadelphia, 1849 ***53.26*** *p41*
Kelly, Daniel; Philadelphia, 1849 ***5704.8*** *p58*
Kelly, Daniel; St. John, N.B., 1849 ***5704.8*** *p49*
Kelly, Daniel; Washington, 1859-1920 ***2872.1*** *p20*
Kelly, Daniel 11; Massachusetts, 1849 ***5881.1*** *p53*
Kelly, Daniel 11; Massachusetts, 1850 ***5881.1*** *p53*
Kelly, Daniel 12; Massachusetts, 1849 ***5881.1*** *p53*
Kelly, Daniel 19; Massachusetts, 1848 ***5881.1*** *p53*
Kelly, Darby; America, 1742 ***4971*** *p29*
Kelly, Darby; Annapolis, MD, 1742 ***4971*** *p93*
Kelly, Darby; Maryland, 1742 ***4971*** *p106*
Kelly, Darby; New York, NY, 1811 ***2859.11*** *p14*
Kelly, David; America, 1737-1738 ***4971*** *p59*
Kelly, David; San Francisco, 1875 ***2764.35*** *p39*
Kelly, Denis 19; Philadelphia, 1860 ***5704.8*** *p144*
Kelly, Dennis *SEE* Kelly, Catherine
Kelly, Dennis; America, 1735-1743 ***4971*** *p78*
Kelly, Dennis; America, 1736 ***4971*** *p44*
Kelly, Dennis; America, 1737 ***4971*** *p45*
Kelly, Dennis; America, 1741 ***4971*** *p37*
Kelly, Dennis; Philadelphia, 1847 ***53.26*** *p41*
*Relative:*Patrick 14
*Relative:*Charles 12
*Relative:*Dennis 9
*Relative:*Francis 7
*Relative:*Mary 2
Kelly, Dennis; Philadelphia, 1847 ***5704.8*** *p5*
Kelly, Dennis; Philadelphia, 1847 ***5704.8*** *p22*
Kelly, Dennis; Philadelphia, 1864 ***5704.8*** *p179*
Kelly, Dennis; Wisconsin, n.d. ***9675.6*** *p131*
Kelly, Dennis 9 *SEE* Kelly, Dennis
Kelly, Dennis 9; Philadelphia, 1847 ***5704.8*** *p22*
Kelly, Donald; North Carolina, 1773-1855 ***1639.20*** *p104*
Kelly, Donald 72; North Carolina, 1850 ***1639.20*** *p104*
Kelly, Dorby; Quebec, 1847 ***5704.8*** *p27*
Kelly, Dudley; New York, NY, 1816 ***2859.11*** *p34*
Kelly, Edward *SEE* Kelly, Edward
Kelly, Edward; New York, NY, 1816 ***2859.11*** *p34*
Kelly, Edward; New York, NY, 1838 ***8208.4*** *p71*
Kelly, Edward; New York, NY, 1840 ***8208.4*** *p108*
Kelly, Edward; New York, NY, 1864 ***5704.8*** *p173*
Kelly, Edward; Philadelphia, 1847 ***53.26*** *p41*
*Relative:*Patrick
*Relative:*Edward
*Relative:*Magy
Kelly, Edward; Philadelphia, 1847 ***5704.8*** *p23*
Kelly, Edward; Philadelphia, 1864 ***5704.8*** *p177*
Kelly, Edward 11; New York, NY, 1864 ***5704.8*** *p176*
Kelly, Edward 20; Philadelphia, 1854 ***5704.8*** *p116*
Kelly, Edward 21; Maryland, 1774 ***1219.7*** *p220*
Kelly, Edward 25; Massachusetts, 1847 ***5881.1*** *p53*
Kelly, Edward 30; Philadelphia, 1854 ***5704.8*** *p115*
Kelly, Edward 36; Port uncertain, 1774 ***1219.7*** *p176*
Kelly, Elenor; America, 1738-1743 ***4971*** *p91*
Kelly, Eliza; Philadelphia, 1869 ***5704.8*** *p235*
Kelly, Eliza 13; Quebec, 1847 ***5704.8*** *p16*
Kelly, Eliza 23; Massachusetts, 1850 ***5881.1*** *p53*
Kelly, Elizabeth; Quebec, 1847 ***5704.8*** *p8*
Kelly, Elizabeth; St. John, N.B., 1849 ***5704.8*** *p55*
Kelly, Elleanor; Philadelphia, 1847 ***53.26*** *p41*
*Relative:*Mary Ann
Kelly, Elleanor; Philadelphia, 1847 ***5704.8*** *p23*
Kelly, Ellen; New York, NY, 1864 ***5704.8*** *p173*
Kelly, Ellen; New York, NY, 1869 ***5704.8*** *p230*
Kelly, Ellen; Philadelphia, 1852 ***5704.8*** *p91*
Kelly, Ellen; Philadelphia, 1865 ***5704.8*** *p201*
Kelly, Ellen; Philadelphia, 1866 ***5704.8*** *p211*
Kelly, Ellen 6; Philadelphia, 1866 ***5704.8*** *p207*
Kelly, Ellen 7; Massachusetts, 1849 ***5881.1*** *p53*
Kelly, Ellen 8; Massachusetts, 1849 ***5881.1*** *p53*
Kelly, Ellen 16; Massachusetts, 1849 ***5881.1*** *p53*
Kelly, Ellen 18; Massachusetts, 1849 ***5881.1*** *p53*
Kelly, Ellen 19; Massachusetts, 1849 ***5881.1*** *p53*
Kelly, Ellen 20; Philadelphia, 1859 ***5704.8*** *p142*
Kelly, Ellen 22; Massachusetts, 1847 ***5881.1*** *p53*
Kelly, Ellen 24; Massachusetts, 1849 ***5881.1*** *p53*
Kelly, Ellen 40; Massachusetts, 1848 ***5881.1*** *p53*
Kelly, Ellenor; America, 1738 ***4971*** *p13*
Kelly, Elly 21; Philadelphia, 1859 ***5704.8*** *p141*
Kelly, Ferdinand 20; Massachusetts, 1847 ***5881.1*** *p53*
Kelly, Francis; America, 1741 ***4971*** *p23*
Kelly, Francis; America, 1865 ***5704.8*** *p197*
Kelly, Francis; New York, NY, 1840 ***8208.4*** *p108*
Kelly, Francis; Philadelphia, 1847 ***53.26*** *p42*
*Relative:*Ann
*Relative:*Patrick
*Relative:*Catherine 11
*Relative:*Bernard 8
*Relative:*Francis 6
*Relative:*Charles 2
*Relative:*Ann 6 mos
Kelly, Francis; Philadelphia, 1847 ***5704.8*** *p22*
Kelly, Francis 6 *SEE* Kelly, Francis
Kelly, Francis 6; Philadelphia, 1847 ***5704.8*** *p22*
Kelly, Francis 7 *SEE* Kelly, Dennis
Kelly, Francis 7; Philadelphia, 1847 ***5704.8*** *p22*
Kelly, Francis 23; Massachusetts, 1848 ***5881.1*** *p53*
Kelly, Frank; Arkansas, 1918 ***95.2*** *p65*
Kelly, Frank; Philadelphia, 1852 ***5704.8*** *p91*
Kelly, George; America, 1741 ***4971*** *p34*
Kelly, George; New York, NY, 1865 ***5704.8*** *p191*
Kelly, George; St. John, N.B., 1851 ***5704.8*** *p79*
Kelly, George 20; Philadelphia, 1854 ***5704.8*** *p118*
Kelly, Giley 17; Philadelphia, 1853 ***5704.8*** *p111*
Kelly, Grace; Philadelphia, 1864 ***5704.8*** *p177*
Kelly, Grace 20; Philadelphia, 1860 ***5704.8*** *p144*
Kelly, Hannah; New York, NY, 1868 ***5704.8*** *p226*
Kelly, Hannah; Philadelphia, 1852 ***5704.8*** *p85*
Kelly, Hannah; Philadelphia, 1865 ***5704.8*** *p192*
Kelly, Hannah; St. John, N.B., 1848 ***5704.8*** *p39*
Kelly, Hannah; St. John, N.B., 1852 ***5704.8*** *p93*
Kelly, Henry; Quebec, 1847 ***5704.8*** *p27*
Kelly, Henry; Quebec, 1849 ***5704.8*** *p57*
Kelly, Henry 4; Philadelphia, 1853 ***5704.8*** *p113*
Kelly, Honora 20; Massachusetts, 1849 ***5881.1*** *p53*
Kelly, Hugh *SEE* Kelly, James
Kelly, Hugh; New York, NY, 1815 ***2859.11*** *p34*
Kelly, Hugh; New York, NY, 1816 ***2859.11*** *p34*
Kelly, Hugh; New York, NY, 1834 ***8208.4*** *p3*
Kelly, Hugh; North Carolina, 1784-1851 ***1639.20*** *p104*
Kelly, Hugh; Philadelphia, 1847 ***5704.8*** *p30*
Kelly, Hugh; Philadelphia, 1864 ***5704.8*** *p181*
Kelly, Hugh; St. John, N.B., 1847 ***5704.8*** *p26*
Kelly, Hugh 22 *SEE* Kelly, Charles
Kelly, Hugh 30; Philadelphia, 1804 ***53.26*** *p42*
Kelly, James; America, 1739 ***4971*** *p26*
Kelly, James; America, 1739 ***4971*** *p40*
Kelly, James; America, 1740 ***4971*** *p63*
Kelly, James; America, 1741 ***4971*** *p37*
Kelly, James; America, 1741 ***4971*** *p40*
Kelly, James; America, 1851 ***6014.1*** *p2*
Kelly, James; America, 1866 ***5704.8*** *p208*
Kelly, James; Arkansas, 1918 ***95.2*** *p65*
Kelly, James; Illinois, 1861 ***2896.5*** *p20*
Kelly, James; Illinois, 1892 ***5012.39*** *p53*
Kelly, James; Illinois, 1900 ***5012.40*** *p77*
Kelly, James; Massachusetts, 1839 ***7036*** *p125*
Kelly, James; New York, NY, 1816 ***2859.11*** *p34*
Kelly, James; New York, NY, 1834 ***8208.4*** *p4*
Kelly, James; New York, NY, 1837 ***8208.4*** *p51*
Kelly, James; Ohio, 1842 ***8365.25*** *p12*
Kelly, James; Philadelphia, 1847 ***53.26*** *p42*
Kelly, James; Philadelphia, 1847 ***53.26*** *p42*
*Relative:*Hugh
Kelly, James; Philadelphia, 1847 ***5704.8*** *p30*
Kelly, James; Philadelphia, 1847 ***5704.8*** *p32*
Kelly, James; Philadelphia, 1850 ***53.26*** *p42*
*Relative:*James 12
*Relative:*Mary 11
Kelly, James; Philadelphia, 1850 ***5704.8*** *p65*
Kelly, James; Philadelphia, 1852 ***5704.8*** *p89*
Kelly, James; Philadelphia, 1864 ***5704.8*** *p172*
Kelly, James; Philadelphia, 1864 ***5704.8*** *p176*
Kelly, James; Philadelphia, 1866 ***5704.8*** *p206*
Kelly, James; Quebec, 1825 ***7603*** *p55*
Kelly, James; Quebec, 1851 ***5704.8*** *p74*
Kelly, James; St. John, N.B., 1848 ***5704.8*** *p43*
Kelly, James; West Virginia, 1858 ***9788.3*** *p13*
Kelly, James 1; Massachusetts, 1849 ***5881.1*** *p54*
Kelly, James 3; Massachusetts, 1849 ***5881.1*** *p54*
Kelly, James 4; Philadelphia, 1866 ***5704.8*** *p207*
Kelly, James 10; New York, NY, 1864 ***5704.8*** *p176*
Kelly, James 11; St. John, N.B., 1866 ***5704.8*** *p166*
Kelly, James 12 *SEE* Kelly, James
Kelly, James 12; Philadelphia, 1850 ***5704.8*** *p65*
Kelly, James 18; Philadelphia, 1860 ***5704.8*** *p145*
Kelly, James 20; Philadelphia, 1854 ***5704.8*** *p115*
Kelly, James 21; St. John, N.B., 1862 ***5704.8*** *p150*
Kelly, James 25; Quebec, 1856 ***5704.8*** *p130*
Kelly, James 25; Virginia, 1774 ***1219.7*** *p243*
Kelly, James 36; Philadelphia, 1861 ***5704.8*** *p148*
Kelly, James M. 21; Kansas, 1884 ***5240.1*** *p66*
Kelly, James P. 30; Kansas, 1874 ***5240.1*** *p55*
Kelly, Jane; America, 1741 ***4971*** *p16*
Kelly, Jane; New York, NY, 1865 ***5704.8*** *p203*
Kelly, Jane; Philadelphia, 1850 ***5704.8*** *p64*
Kelly, Jane; Philadelphia, 1864 ***5704.8*** *p186*
Kelly, Jane; St. John, N.B., 1848 ***5704.8*** *p39*
Kelly, Jane; St. John, N.B., 1850 ***5704.8*** *p65*
Kelly, Jane 6 mos; Quebec, 1856 ***5704.8*** *p130*
Kelly, Jane 9; New York, NY, 1870 ***5704.8*** *p238*
Kelly, Jane 20; Philadelphia, 1858 ***5704.8*** *p139*
Kelly, Jas.; New York, NY, 1816 ***2859.11*** *p34*
Kelly, Jeremiah; America, 1837 ***7036*** *p127*
Kelly, Jeremiah; Newfoundland, 1837 ***7036*** *p127*
Kelly, Jermiah; Philadelphia, 1865 ***5704.8*** *p198*
Kelly, Jerry 4; Massachusetts, 1850 ***5881.1*** *p54*
Kelly, John *SEE* Kelly, Susan

250 *FOR A COMPLETE EXPLANATION OF ENTRY, SEE "HOW TO READ A CITATION" SECTION*

Kelly, John; America, 1735-1743 ***4971*** *p78*
Kelly, John; America, 1738 ***4971*** *p68*
Kelly, John; America, 1738 ***4971*** *p80*
Kelly, John; America, 1739 ***4971*** *p46*
Kelly, John; America, 1739 ***4971*** *p47*
Kelly, John; America, 1740 ***4971*** *p22*
Kelly, John; America, 1741 ***4971*** *p49*
Kelly, John; America, 1857 ***6014.1*** *p2*
Kelly, John; America, 1868 ***5704.8*** *p227*
Kelly, John; Annapolis, MD, 1742 ***4971*** *p93*
Kelly, John; Illinois, 1860 ***2896.5*** *p21*
Kelly, John; Indiana, 1873 ***2764.35*** *p39*
Kelly, John; Montreal, 1824 ***7603*** *p98*
Kelly, John; Montreal, 1825 ***7603*** *p81*
Kelly, John; New York, NY, 1815 ***2859.11*** *p34*
Kelly, John; New York, NY, 1816 ***2859.11*** *p34*
Kelly, John; New York, NY, 1838 ***8208.4*** *p67*
Kelly, John; New York, NY, 1864 ***5704.8*** *p176*
Kelly, John; New York, NY, 1864 ***5704.8*** *p179*
Kelly, John; New York, NY, 1864 ***5704.8*** *p188*
Kelly, John; New York, NY, 1870 ***5704.8*** *p238*
Kelly, John; North Carolina, 1769-1813 ***1639.20*** *p104*
Kelly, John; North Carolina, 1788-1836 ***1639.20*** *p104*
Kelly, John; North Carolina, 1789-1847 ***1639.20*** *p105*
Kelly, John; Philadelphia, 1847 ***53.26*** *p42*
Kelly, John; Philadelphia, 1847 ***5704.8*** *p2*
Kelly, John; Philadelphia, 1847 ***5704.8*** *p14*
Kelly, John; Philadelphia, 1852 ***5704.8*** *p84*
Kelly, John; Philadelphia, 1852 ***5704.8*** *p91*
Kelly, John; Philadelphia, 1864 ***5704.8*** *p181*
Kelly, John; Philadelphia, 1865 ***5704.8*** *p184*
Kelly, John; Philadelphia, 1866 ***5704.8*** *p201*
Kelly, John; Philadelphia, 1866 ***5704.8*** *p214*
Kelly, John; Philadelphia, 1867 ***5704.8*** *p223*
Kelly, John; Quebec, 1852 ***5704.8*** *p97*
Kelly, John; St. John, N.B., 1847 ***5704.8*** *p3*
Kelly, John; St. John, N.B., 1848 ***5704.8*** *p39*
Kelly, John; St. John, N.B., 1852 ***5704.8*** *p83*
Kelly, John; St. John, N.B., 1853 ***5704.8*** *p106*
Kelly, John 3; Massachusetts, 1849 ***5881.1*** *p47*
Kelly, John 3; Massachusetts, 1849 ***5881.1*** *p54*
Kelly, John 4; Philadelphia, 1866 ***5704.8*** *p207*
Kelly, John 5; Massachusetts, 1849 ***5881.1*** *p54*
Kelly, John 10; Massachusetts, 1848 ***5881.1*** *p54*
Kelly, John 10; St. John, N.B., 1864 ***5704.8*** *p159*
Kelly, John 13; St. John, N.B., 1850 ***5704.8*** *p65*
Kelly, John 19; St. John, N.B., 1866 ***5704.8*** *p166*
Kelly, John 20; Georgia, 1752 ***1219.7*** *p12*
Kelly, John 20; Georgia, 1752 ***3690.1*** *p132*
Kelly, John 21; Philadelphia, 1854 ***5704.8*** *p121*
Kelly, John 21; Quebec, 1859 ***5704.8*** *p143*
Kelly, John 30; Newfoundland, 1789 ***4915.24*** *p57*
Kelly, John 31; New Orleans, 1860 ***5704.8*** *p144*
Kelly, John 37; Kansas, 1889 ***5240.1*** *p73*
Kelly, John 50; Massachusetts, 1849 ***5881.1*** *p54*
Kelly, John Joseph Alphonsus; Arkansas, 1918 ***95.2*** *p65*
Kelly, Joseph; America, 1869 ***5704.8*** *p235*
Kelly, Joseph; New York, NY, 1838 ***8208.4*** *p84*
Kelly, Joseph 7 *SEE* Kelly, Rose
Kelly, Joseph 7; Philadelphia, 1848 ***5704.8*** *p46*
Kelly, Julia 12; Massachusetts, 1848 ***5881.1*** *p54*
Kelly, Julia 30; Massachusetts, 1849 ***5881.1*** *p54*
Kelly, Lakey 25; Philadelphia, 1774 ***1219.7*** *p232*
Kelly, Lawrance 39; Baltimore, 1775 ***1219.7*** *p270*
Kelly, Lawrence 18; Jamaica, 1739 ***3690.1*** *p132*
Kelly, Magy *SEE* Kelly, Edward
Kelly, Magy; Philadelphia, 1847 ***5704.8*** *p23*
Kelly, Margaret; America, 1739 ***4971*** *p14*
Kelly, Margaret; New York, NY, 1815 ***2859.11*** *p34*
Kelly, Margaret; New York, NY, 1816 ***2859.11*** *p34*
Kelly, Margaret; New York, NY, 1866 ***5704.8*** *p207*
Kelly, Margaret; Philadelphia, 1847 ***53.26*** *p42*
Kelly, Margaret; Philadelphia, 1847 ***5704.8*** *p32*
Kelly, Margaret; Philadelphia, 1864 ***5704.8*** *p171*
Kelly, Margaret; Philadelphia, 1868 ***5704.8*** *p230*
Kelly, Margaret; Quebec, 1849 ***5704.8*** *p57*
Kelly, Margaret 8; Quebec, 1847 ***5704.8*** *p16*
Kelly, Margaret 14; Philadelphia, 1853 ***5704.8*** *p108*
Kelly, Margaret 20; Philadelphia, 1864 ***5704.8*** *p156*
Kelly, Margaret 40; Philadelphia, 1853 ***5704.8*** *p111*
Kelly, Maria 6; Massachusetts, 1850 ***5881.1*** *p55*
Kelly, Maria 12; Quebec, 1847 ***5704.8*** *p16*
Kelly, Martha; America, 1739 ***4971*** *p14*
Kelly, Martha; Quebec, 1847 ***5704.8*** *p16*
Kelly, Martin; Quebec, 1821 ***7603*** *p85*
Kelly, Martin 4; Massachusetts, 1848 ***5881.1*** *p54*
Kelly, Martin 20; Newfoundland, 1789 ***4915.24*** *p55*
Kelly, Mary; America, 1737 ***4971*** *p12*
Kelly, Mary; America, 1738 ***4971*** *p13*
Kelly, Mary; America, 1743 ***4971*** *p65*
Kelly, Mary; America, 1865 ***5704.8*** *p194*
Kelly, Mary; New York, NY, 1816 ***2859.11*** *p34*
Kelly, Mary; New York, NY, 1864 ***5704.8*** *p176*
Kelly, Mary; Philadelphia, 1847 ***53.26*** *p42*
Kelly, Mary; Philadelphia, 1847 ***5704.8*** *p32*
Kelly, Mary; Philadelphia, 1852 ***5704.8*** *p89*
Kelly, Mary; Philadelphia, 1852 ***5704.8*** *p91*
Kelly, Mary; Philadelphia, 1864 ***5704.8*** *p184*
Kelly, Mary; Philadelphia, 1866 ***5704.8*** *p206*
Kelly, Mary; Philadelphia, 1866 ***5704.8*** *p209*
Kelly, Mary; Philadelphia, 1868 ***5704.8*** *p229*
Kelly, Mary; St. John, N.B., 1849 ***5704.8*** *p55*
Kelly, Mary; St. John, N.B., 1851 ***5704.8*** *p79*
Kelly, Mary 1 mo; Philadelphia, 1853 ***5704.8*** *p113*
Kelly, Mary 2 *SEE* Kelly, Dennis
Kelly, Mary 2; Philadelphia, 1847 ***5704.8*** *p22*
Kelly, Mary 3; St. John, N.B., 1851 ***5704.8*** *p78*
Kelly, Mary 6; St. John, N.B., 1864 ***5704.8*** *p159*
Kelly, Mary 8; St. John, N.B., 1851 ***5704.8*** *p79*
Kelly, Mary 11 *SEE* Kelly, James
Kelly, Mary 11; Philadelphia, 1850 ***5704.8*** *p65*
Kelly, Mary 18; New Orleans, 1860 ***5704.8*** *p144*
Kelly, Mary 19; Massachusetts, 1849 ***5881.1*** *p55*
Kelly, Mary 20; Massachusetts, 1849 ***5881.1*** *p55*
Kelly, Mary 21; Philadelphia, 1855 ***5704.8*** *p124*
Kelly, Mary 22; Massachusetts, 1850 ***5881.1*** *p55*
Kelly, Mary 22; Massachusetts, 1850 ***5881.1*** *p56*
Kelly, Mary 22; Philadelphia, 1861 ***5704.8*** *p148*
Kelly, Mary 22; Philadelphia, 1864 ***5704.8*** *p156*
Kelly, Mary 25; Massachusetts, 1849 ***5881.1*** *p55*
Kelly, Mary 30; Massachusetts, 1849 ***5881.1*** *p55*
Kelly, Mary 30; Philadelphia, 1857 ***5704.8*** *p132*
Kelly, Mary 35; Massachusetts, 1850 ***5881.1*** *p55*
Kelly, Mary 38; St. John, N.B., 1861 ***5704.8*** *p149*
Kelly, Mary Ann *SEE* Kelly, Elleanor
Kelly, Mary Ann; Philadelphia, 1847 ***5704.8*** *p23*
Kelly, Mary Ann; Philadelphia, 1864 ***5704.8*** *p179*
Kelly, Mary Ann; Quebec, 1847 ***5704.8*** *p8*
Kelly, Mary Ann 5; Philadelphia, 1857 ***5704.8*** *p132*
Kelly, Mary Ann 23; St. John, N.B., 1853 ***5704.8*** *p110*
Kelly, Mary Jane 17; Philadelphia, 1853 ***5704.8*** *p108*
Kelly, Mathew 26; Philadelphia, 1864 ***5704.8*** *p157*
Kelly, Matilda 6 mos; Quebec, 1847 ***5704.8*** *p16*
Kelly, Maurice; America, 1740 ***4971*** *p34*
Kelly, Michael; America, 1738 ***4971*** *p22*
Kelly, Michael; America, 1738 ***4971*** *p31*
Kelly, Michael; America, 1864 ***5704.8*** *p172*
Kelly, Michael; Illinois, 1864 ***2896.5*** *p21*
Kelly, Michael; New England, 1816 ***2859.11*** *p34*
Kelly, Michael; New York, NY, 1811 ***2859.11*** *p14*
Kelly, Michael; New York, NY, 1816 ***2859.11*** *p34*
Kelly, Michael; New York, NY, 1838 ***8208.4*** *p62*
Kelly, Michael; New York, NY, 1864 ***5704.8*** *p172*
Kelly, Michael; New York, NY, 1870 ***5704.8*** *p238*
Kelly, Michael; Philadelphia, 1864 ***5704.8*** *p172*
Kelly, Michael; Philadelphia, 1864 ***5704.8*** *p175*
Kelly, Michael; St. John, N.B., 1847 ***5704.8*** *p26*
Kelly, Michael; St. John, N.B., 1850 ***5704.8*** *p67*
Kelly, Michael 10; Massachusetts, 1849 ***5881.1*** *p55*
Kelly, Michael 12; Massachusetts, 1849 ***5881.1*** *p55*
Kelly, Michael 14; Massachusetts, 1849 ***5881.1*** *p55*
Kelly, Michael 20; Massachusetts, 1847 ***5881.1*** *p54*
Kelly, Michael 25; Massachusetts, 1848 ***5881.1*** *p54*
Kelly, Michael 32?; Arizona, 1890 ***2764.35*** *p39*
Kelly, Michael 35; Massachusetts, 1849 ***5881.1*** *p55*
Kelly, Michael 38; Massachusetts, 1850 ***5881.1*** *p55*
Kelly, Michael 50; Massachusetts, 1850 ***5881.1*** *p55*
Kelly, Michael 60; Massachusetts, 1849 ***5881.1*** *p55*
Kelly, Michael Joseph; Arkansas, 1918 ***95.2*** *p65*
Kelly, Mike 9; Massachusetts, 1849 ***5881.1*** *p55*
Kelly, Mike 12; Massachusetts, 1849 ***5881.1*** *p55*
Kelly, Molly; New York, NY, 1811 ***2859.11*** *p14*
Kelly, Myles; New York, NY, 1834 ***8208.4*** *p49*
Kelly, Nancy; North Carolina, 1784-1858 ***1639.20*** *p105*
Kelly, Nancy; St. John, N.B., 1851 ***5704.8*** *p78*
Kelly, Neal *SEE* Kelly, Catherine
Kelly, Neal; New York, NY, 1811 ***2859.11*** *p14*
Kelly, Neal; Philadelphia, 1847 ***5704.8*** *p5*
Kelly, Neal; Philadelphia, 1852 ***5704.8*** *p89*
Kelly, Neal; St. John, N.B., 1847 ***5704.8*** *p24*
Kelly, Neally; St. John, N.B., 1847 ***5704.8*** *p34*
Kelly, Neil; New York, NY, 1836 ***8208.4*** *p12*
Kelly, Neil; Wisconsin, n.d. ***9675.6*** *p131*
Kelly, Nelly; Philadelphia, 1852 ***5704.8*** *p95*
Kelly, Owen; America, 1841 ***7036*** *p126*
Kelly, Owen; Pictou, N.S., 1841 ***7036*** *p126*
Kelly, Owen; Philadelphia, 1870 ***5704.8*** *p239*
Kelly, Owen 1; Philadelphia, 1865 ***5704.8*** *p181*
Kelly, Owen 11; St. John, N.B., 1861 ***5704.8*** *p149*
Kelly, Patrick *SEE* Kelly, Edward
Kelly, Patrick *SEE* Kelly, Francis
Kelly, Patrick; America, 1738 ***4971*** *p31*
Kelly, Patrick; America, 1739 ***4971*** *p24*
Kelly, Patrick; America, 1741 ***4971*** *p16*
Kelly, Patrick; New York, NY, 1811 ***2859.11*** *p14*
Kelly, Patrick; New York, NY, 1816 ***2859.11*** *p34*
Kelly, Patrick; New York, NY, 1838 ***8208.4*** *p65*
Kelly, Patrick; New York, NY, 1840 ***8208.4*** *p106*
Kelly, Patrick; New York, NY, 1864 ***5704.8*** *p169*
Kelly, Patrick; New York, NY, 1865 ***5704.8*** *p194*
Kelly, Patrick; Ohio, 1844 ***9892.11*** *p24*
Kelly, Patrick; Ohio, 1846 ***9892.11*** *p24*
Kelly, Patrick; Philadelphia, 1847 ***5704.8*** *p22*
Kelly, Patrick; Philadelphia, 1847 ***5704.8*** *p23*
Kelly, Patrick; Philadelphia, 1865 ***5704.8*** *p197*
Kelly, Patrick; Quebec, 1852 ***5704.8*** *p97*
Kelly, Patrick 10; Massachusetts, 1850 ***5881.1*** *p56*
Kelly, Patrick 12; Massachusetts, 1849 ***5881.1*** *p56*
Kelly, Patrick 14 *SEE* Kelly, Dennis
Kelly, Patrick 14; Philadelphia, 1847 ***5704.8*** *p22*
Kelly, Patrick 18; Philadelphia, 1864 ***5704.8*** *p157*
Kelly, Patrick 19; Massachusetts, 1848 ***5881.1*** *p56*
Kelly, Patrick 20; Philadelphia, 1840 ***7036*** *p117*
Kelly, Patrick 20; St. John, N.B., 1865 ***5704.8*** *p165*
Kelly, Patrick 23; Philadelphia, 1855 ***5704.8*** *p124*
Kelly, Patrick 24; Massachusetts, 1847 ***5881.1*** *p56*
Kelly, Patrick 27; Massachusetts, 1848 ***5881.1*** *p56*
Kelly, Patrick 33; New Orleans, 1860 ***5704.8*** *p144*
Kelly, Patrick J. 26; Kansas, 1887 ***5240.1*** *p70*
Kelly, Peggy; America, 1834 ***8894.2*** *p57*
Kelly, Peggy; Philadelphia, 1852 ***5704.8*** *p91*
Kelly, Peter; America, 1739 ***4971*** *p36*
Kelly, Peter; Philadelphia, 1864 ***5704.8*** *p172*
Kelly, Peter 28; Philadelphia, 1857 ***5704.8*** *p132*
Kelly, Peter 31; Massachusetts, 1847 ***5881.1*** *p56*
Kelly, Peter 70; North Carolina, 1850 ***1639.20*** *p105*
Kelly, Rebecca; Quebec, 1851 ***5704.8*** *p75*
Kelly, Richard; America, 1737 ***4971*** *p13*
Kelly, Richard; New York, NY, 1816 ***2859.11*** *p34*
Kelly, Richard; New York, NY, 1839 ***8208.4*** *p91*
Kelly, Robert; New York, NY, 1811 ***2859.11*** *p14*
Kelly, Robert; New York, NY, 1816 ***2859.11*** *p34*
Kelly, Robert; St. John, N.B., 1849 ***5704.8*** *p49*
Kelly, Rose; New York, NY, 1865 ***5704.8*** *p193*
Kelly, Rose; Philadelphia, 1848 ***53.26*** *p42*
*Relative:*Joseph 7
Kelly, Rose; Philadelphia, 1848 ***5704.8*** *p46*
Kelly, Rose; Philadelphia, 1867 ***5704.8*** *p223*
Kelly, Rose; St. John, N.B., 1847 ***5704.8*** *p24*
Kelly, Rose 20; Quebec, 1857 ***5704.8*** *p136*
Kelly, Rose 24; Quebec, 1856 ***5704.8*** *p130*
Kelly, Rosey 20; Philadelphia, 1858 ***5704.8*** *p138*
Kelly, Sally; Philadelphia, 1852 ***5704.8*** *p89*
Kelly, Sally 22; Philadelphia, 1859 ***5704.8*** *p141*
Kelly, Sarah; New York, NY, 1864 ***5704.8*** *p172*
Kelly, Sarah; New York, NY, 1866 ***5704.8*** *p210*
Kelly, Sarah; New York, NY, 1867 ***5704.8*** *p222*
Kelly, Sarah; Philadelphia, 1864 ***5704.8*** *p185*
Kelly, Sarah; St. John, N.B., 1851 ***5704.8*** *p71*
Kelly, Sarah 18; Massachusetts, 1848 ***5881.1*** *p56*
Kelly, Sarah 26; Philadelphia, 1861 ***5704.8*** *p148*
Kelly, Stephen; Montreal, 1816 ***7603*** *p72*
Kelly, Susan; Philadelphia, 1847 ***53.26*** *p42*
Kelly, Susan; Philadelphia, 1847 ***53.26*** *p42*
*Relative:*John
Kelly, Susan; Philadelphia, 1847 ***5704.8*** *p14*
Kelly, Susan; Philadelphia, 1847 ***5704.8*** *p23*
Kelly, Susanna; Quebec, 1847 ***5704.8*** *p36*
Kelly, Terry; New York, NY, 1839 ***8208.4*** *p93*
Kelly, Thady; America, 1735-1743 ***4971*** *p79*
Kelly, Theophilus 5; Quebec, 1847 ***5704.8*** *p16*
Kelly, Thomas; America, 1735-1743 ***4971*** *p8*
Kelly, Thomas; Illinois, 1858 ***2896.5*** *p21*
Kelly, Thomas; New York, NY, 1811 ***2859.11*** *p14*
Kelly, Thomas; New York, NY, 1838 ***8208.4*** *p62*
Kelly, Thomas; New York, NY, 1838 ***8208.4*** *p84*
Kelly, Thomas; New York, NY, 1865 ***5704.8*** *p203*
Kelly, Thomas; Philadelphia, 1816 ***2859.11*** *p34*
Kelly, Thomas; Philadelphia, 1852 ***5704.8*** *p88*
Kelly, Thomas; Philadelphia, 1853 ***5704.8*** *p102*
Kelly, Thomas; Philadelphia, 1864 ***5704.8*** *p188*
Kelly, Thomas; Philadelphia, 1866 ***5704.8*** *p211*
Kelly, Thomas; Quebec, 1772 ***7603*** *p77*
Kelly, Thomas; Quebec, 1849 ***5704.8*** *p52*
Kelly, Thomas; St. John, N.B., 1851 ***5704.8*** *p78*
Kelly, Thomas 7; Massachusetts, 1849 ***5881.1*** *p56*
Kelly, Thomas 7; Philadelphia, 1857 ***5704.8*** *p132*
Kelly, Thomas 16; Massachusetts, 1847 ***5881.1*** *p56*
Kelly, Thomas 25; Massachusetts, 1847 ***5881.1*** *p56*
Kelly, Thomas 28; California, 1867 ***3840.2*** *p16*
Kelly, Thomas 30; Newfoundland, 1789 ***4915.24*** *p57*
Kelly, Thomas 36; Philadelphia, 1803 ***53.26*** *p42*
Kelly, William; America, 1737 ***4971*** *p28*
Kelly, William; America, 1739 ***4971*** *p66*
Kelly, William; New York, NY, 1816 ***2859.11*** *p34*
Kelly, William; Philadelphia, 1852 ***5704.8*** *p92*
Kelly, William; Quebec, 1847 ***5704.8*** *p16*
Kelly, William 8; New York, NY, 1864 ***5704.8*** *p176*
Kelly, William 20; Philadelphia, 1833-1834 ***53.26*** *p42*

Kelly, William 22; Philadelphia, 1859 ***5704.8*** *p141*
Kelly, William 23; Philadelphia, 1803 ***53.26*** *p42*
Kelly, William 26; Massachusetts, 1848 ***5881.1*** *p56*
Kelly, William 29; Massachusetts, 1847 ***5881.1*** *p56*
Kelly, Winifred; America, 1738 ***4971*** *p46*
Kelly, Winnefred; America, 1739 ***4971*** *p46*
Kelly, Winnifred 18; Massachusetts, 1849 ***5881.1*** *p57*
Kelly, Wm.; Arizona, 1897 ***9228.30*** *p3*
Kelm, James 22; Philadelphia, 1864 ***5704.8*** *p161*
Kelman, Geo.; Austin, TX, 1886 ***9777*** *p5*
Kelridge, William; Virginia, 1636 ***6219*** *p80*
Kelsch, Franz; Alberta, n.d. ***5262*** *p58*
Kelsch, Friederich 27; Kansas, 1893 ***5240.1*** *p78*
Kelsey, Benjamin 16; Maryland, 1775 ***1219.7*** *p264*
Kelsey, John 18; Jamaica, 1752 ***1219.7*** *p16*
Kelsey, John 18; Jamaica, 1752 ***3690.1*** *p132*
Kelsh, Charles; Quebec, 1849 ***5704.8*** *p57*
Kelsh, Mary; Quebec, 1849 ***5704.8*** *p57*
Kelsher, Michael 23; Massachusetts, 1849 ***5881.1*** *p55*
Kelsick, Isaac; America, 1737 ***4971*** *p99*
Kelsick, Isaac; America, 1739 ***4971*** *p99*
Kelso, Elizabeth 7; Quebec, 1847 ***5704.8*** *p28*
Kelso, Elizabeth 50; Wilmington, NC, 1774 ***1639.20*** *p206*
Kelso, Hugh; Quebec, 1847 ***5704.8*** *p28*
Kelso, Jane; Philadelphia, 1865 ***5704.8*** *p200*
Kelso, John 12; Quebec, 1847 ***5704.8*** *p28*
Kelso, John 20; Philadelphia, 1857 ***5704.8*** *p132*
Kelso, Margaret; Philadelphia, 1865 ***5704.8*** *p204*
Kelso, Margaret; Quebec, 1847 ***5704.8*** *p28*
Kelso, Mathew; South Carolina, 1821 ***1639.20*** *p105*
Kelso, Thomas P. 28; Kansas, 1899 ***5240.1*** *p81*
Kelsoe, Anne 20; Philadelphia, 1864 ***5704.8*** *p157*
Kelsoe, Esther 50; Philadelphia, 1864 ***5704.8*** *p157*
Kelsoe, Hugh 16; Philadelphia, 1864 ***5704.8*** *p157*
Kelsoe, John 55; Philadelphia, 1864 ***5704.8*** *p157*
Keltie, James 12; St. John, N.B., 1850 ***5704.8*** *p66*
Keltie, Patrick; St. John, N.B., 1850 ***5704.8*** *p66*
Kelting, Henry C.; New York, 1895 ***1450.2*** *p19B*
Kelvie, William 25; Maryland, 1739 ***3690.1*** *p132*
Kely, Jacob I.; Indiana, 1836 ***9117*** *p15*
Kem, Robert 18; Maryland, 1721 ***3690.1*** *p132*
Kem, Samuel 25; North Carolina, 1738 ***3690.1*** *p132*
Kembal, Marie-Louise; Quebec, 1715 ***7603*** *p21*
Kembell, Thomas; Virginia, 1642 ***6219*** *p192*
Kemena, Anne Marie Louise; America, 1850 ***4610.10*** *p143*
Kemena, Samuel Diedrich; America, 1854 ***4610.10*** *p148*
Kemerling, Jacob; Pennsylvania, 1753 ***2444*** *p180*
Kemmblin, Daniel; South Carolina, 1788 ***7119*** *p198*
Kemmeras, Christian; Wisconsin, n.d. ***9675.6*** *p131*
Kemmerly, Hans Martin; Philadelphia, 1751 ***2444*** *p180*
Kemmerly, Jacob; Pennsylvania, 1753 ***2444*** *p180*
Kemmeter, John; Cincinnati, 1869-1887 ***8582*** *p16*
Kemmler, Anna Maria; Port uncertain, 1754 ***2444*** *p172*
Kemmler, Hans Jacob; Pennsylvania, 1743 ***2444*** *p180*
Kemp, Archibald 56; South Carolina, 1850 ***1639.20*** *p105*
Kemp, Arthur A. 33; Arizona, 1890 ***2764.35*** *p38*
Kemp, Evans; Virginia, 1637 ***6219*** *p8*
Kemp, James 18; St. John, N.B., 1866 ***5704.8*** *p167*
Kemp, John; Philadelphia, 1852 ***5704.8*** *p84*
Kemp, John; Virginia, 1639 ***6219*** *p18*
Kemp, John; Wisconsin, n.d. ***9675.6*** *p131*
Kemp, John 15; Jamaica, 1731 ***3690.1*** *p133*
Kemp, Mary; Philadelphia, 1853 ***5704.8*** *p103*
Kemp, Mathew; Philadelphia, 1853 ***5704.8*** *p103*
Kemp, Mathias; Wisconsin, n.d. ***9675.6*** *p131*
Kemp, Matthew; Philadelphia, 1851 ***5704.8*** *p71*
Kemp, Richard; Virginia, 1637 ***6219*** *p17*
Kemp, Richard; Virginia, 1643 ***6219*** *p199*
Kemp, Tho.; Virginia, 1618 ***6219*** *p72*
Kemp, Tho.; Virginia, 1634 ***6219*** *p105*
Kemp, Tho.; Virginia, 1642 ***6219*** *p198*
Kemp, Thomas; Virginia, 1638 ***6219*** *p147*
Kempe, John; Virginia, 1639 ***6219*** *p157*
Kempe, Wm.; Virginia, 1634 ***6219*** *p32*
Kempel, Johanne 22; Died enroute, 1839 ***9420.2*** *p71*
Kemper, Charles; America, 1837 ***1450.2*** *p77A*
Kemper, Christoph Heinrich *SEE* Kemper, Johann Hermann
Kemper, Johann F. Wilhelm *SEE* Kemper, Johann Hermann
Kemper, Johann Heinrich *SEE* Kemper, Johann Hermann
Kemper, Johann Hermann; America, 1851 ***4610.10*** *p139*
With wife
*Child:*Johann F. Wilhelm
*Child:*Johann Heinrich
*Child:*Christoph Heinrich
Kemper, Marie 22; America, 1881 ***4610.10*** *p140*
Kemperlin, Mr.; Died enroute, 1751-1754 ***2444*** *p180*
Kemperlin, Jacob; Pennsylvania, 1753 ***2444*** *p180*
Kemperlin, John; Philadelphia, 1751 ***2444*** *p180*
Kempf, Barbara 16; America, 1853 ***9162.8*** *p36*
Kempf, Bernard; Ohio, 1843 ***8582.1*** *p51*
Kempf, Christina 7; America, 1853 ***9162.8*** *p37*
Kempf, Elis. Marg. 34; America, 1853 ***9162.8*** *p36*
Kempf, Georg. 11 mos; America, 1853 ***9162.8*** *p37*
Kempf, Henry; Arizona, 1886 ***2764.35*** *p40*
Kempf, John; Washington, 1859-1920 ***2872.1*** *p20*
Kempf, Johs. 37; America, 1853 ***9162.8*** *p36*
Kempf, Kath. 9; America, 1853 ***9162.8*** *p37*
Kempf, Margaretha 4; America, 1853 ***9162.8*** *p37*
Kempf, Philipp 12; America, 1853 ***9162.8*** *p37*
Kempfer, August; Wisconsin, n.d. ***9675.6*** *p131*
Kempfer, Ernst; Wisconsin, n.d. ***9675.6*** *p131*
Kempfert, August; Wisconsin, n.d. ***9675.6*** *p131*
Kempista, Antoni 18; New York, 1912 ***9980.29*** *p52*
Kemple, John; New York, NY, 1815 ***2859.11*** *p34*
Kempt, James; Nova Scotia, 1819-1833 ***9775.5*** *p208*
Kemptner, John; Cincinnati, 1869-1887 ***8582*** *p16*
Kemstedt, Wilhelm 26; Kansas, 1890 ***5240.1*** *p74*
Kemys, Samuel 14; Philadelphia, 1775 ***1219.7*** *p248*
Kemzura, Felisk; Wisconsin, n.d. ***9675.6*** *p131*
Kenady, Alexander 23; Virginia, 1727 ***3690.1*** *p133*
Kenady, James; America, 1842 ***1450.2*** *p77A*
Kenag, Mathew; Indiana, 1848 ***9117*** *p17*
Kenaghan, Charles; St. John, N.B., 1852 ***5704.8*** *p84*
Kenaghan, Charles 3; St. John, N.B., 1853 ***5704.8*** *p110*
Kenaghan, Mary 40; St. John, N.B., 1853 ***5704.8*** *p110*
Kenaghan, Michael 4; St. John, N.B., 1853 ***5704.8*** *p110*
Kenaghan, Philip 6 mos; St. John, N.B., 1853 ***5704.8*** *p110*
Kenaghan, Thomas 7; St. John, N.B., 1853 ***5704.8*** *p110*
Kenah, Percy Norman; Arkansas, 1918 ***95.2*** *p65*
Kenan, Catharine 20; Massachusetts, 1849 ***5881.1*** *p52*
Kenan, Elizabeth Johnstone; Wilmington, NC, 1733 ***1639.20*** *p101*
Kenan, Felix; Pennsylvania, 1855 ***1450.2*** *p77A*
Kenan, Peter 18; Massachusetts, 1849 ***5881.1*** *p56*
Kenaps, A. 24; New Orleans, 1835 ***778.5*** *p294*
Kenardy, Hugh 35; America, 1699 ***2212*** *p28*
Kench, Richard; New York, NY, 1811 ***2859.11*** *p14*
Kendal, Ann 21; Maryland, 1775 ***1219.7*** *p257*
Kendall, John; Virginia, 1638 ***6219*** *p118*
Kendall, Robt.; Virginia, 1636 ***6219*** *p1*
Kendall, Thomas 20; Maryland or Virginia, 1730 ***3690.1*** *p290*
Kendig, Martin; Pennsylvania, 1709-1710 ***4480*** *p311*
Kendra, Thomas; Quebec, 1754 ***7603*** *p26*
Kendrick, Edwd.; Virginia, 1644 ***6219*** *p229*
Kenedy, Bridget; New York, NY, 1816 ***2859.11*** *p34*
Kenedy, John; New York, NY, 1816 ***2859.11*** *p34*
Kenedy, John 41; Philadelphia, 1803 ***53.26*** *p42*
Kenedy, Michael 26; Ohio, 1841 ***1450.2*** *p77A*
Keney, John C.; New York, NY, 1840 ***8208.4*** *p107*
Kenig, Godfried; Philadelphia, 1762 ***9973.7*** *p37*
Kenig, Jacob Philip; Philadelphia, 1762 ***9973.7*** *p37*
Kenig, Joseph; Colorado, 1891 ***9678.2*** *p61*
Kenigan, John; Quebec, 1850 ***5704.8*** *p63*
Kenim, Richard; Annapolis, MD, 1742 ***4971*** *p93*
Kenin, Robert; Virginia, 1642 ***6219*** *p199*
Kenk, Johanna 28; New York, NY, 1893 ***9026.4*** *p41*
Kenmaer, Andrew; New York, NY, 1811 ***2859.11*** *p14*
Kenna, Jane 22; Massachusetts, 1847 ***5881.1*** *p53*
Kenna, Martin 35; Massachusetts, 1849 ***5881.1*** *p55*
Kenna, Nicholas; Wisconsin, n.d. ***9675.6*** *p131*
Kennady, Daniel; Massachusetts, 1831-1840 ***7036*** *p124*
Kennady, Daniel; St. John, N.B., 1831 ***7036*** *p124*
Kennady, Val; Philadelphia, 1816 ***2859.11*** *p34*
Kennan, Thomas 25; Philadelphia, 1803 ***53.26*** *p42*
Kenneday, Alexander 38; Virginia, 1774 ***1219.7*** *p186*
Kenneday, John 26; Philadelphia, 1774 ***1219.7*** *p228*
Kenneday, Mary 21; Maryland, 1774 ***1219.7*** *p215*
Kenneday, Michael 33; Maryland, 1774 ***1219.7*** *p184*
Kenneday, Thomas 23; Maryland, 1773 ***1219.7*** *p173*
Kenneday, Timothy 21; Virginia, 1774 ***1219.7*** *p243*
Kennede, Patrick; Virginia, 1637 ***6219*** *p17*
Kennedy, . . .; New York, NY, 1864 ***5704.8*** *p187*
Kennedy, . . . 6 mos; America, 1866 ***5704.8*** *p206*
Kennedy, A. C. 61; Washington, 1918-1920 ***1728.5*** *p10*
Kennedy, Agathas Isbister *SEE* Kennedy, Alexander
Kennedy, Alexander; New York, NY, 1816 ***2859.11*** *p34*
Kennedy, Alexander; North America, 1808 ***8894.2*** *p57*
*Wife:*Agathas Isbister
Kennedy, Alexander; Philadelphia, 1816 ***2859.11*** *p34*
Kennedy, Alexander; Philadelphia, 1849 ***53.26*** *p42*
*Relative:*Margaret
*Relative:*James
Kennedy, Alexander; Philadelphia, 1849 ***5704.8*** *p53*
Kennedy, Alexander 9 mos; St. John, N.B., 1853 ***5704.8*** *p109*
Kennedy, Alexander 2; St. John, N.B., 1848 ***5704.8*** *p39*
Kennedy, Alexander 23; Virginia, 1727 ***3690.1*** *p133*
Kennedy, Anabella 8; Philadelphia, 1858 ***5704.8*** *p138*
Kennedy, Andrew; Austin, TX, 1886 ***9777*** *p5*
Kennedy, Andrew; New York, NY, 1816 ***2859.11*** *p34*
Kennedy, Andrew; Quebec, 1822 ***7603*** *p95*
Kennedy, Ann; Montreal, 1823 ***7603*** *p101*
Kennedy, Ann; St. John, N.B., 1847 ***5704.8*** *p25*
Kennedy, Ann; St. John, N.B., 1852 ***5704.8*** *p84*
Kennedy, Anne; New York, NY, 1816 ***2859.11*** *p34*
Kennedy, Anne; St. John, N.B., 1851 ***5704.8*** *p72*
Kennedy, Belle; New York, NY, 1865 ***5704.8*** *p189*
Kennedy, Catharine 19; Massachusetts, 1848 ***5881.1*** *p52*
Kennedy, Catharine 20; Massachusetts, 1848 ***5881.1*** *p52*
Kennedy, Catherine; America, 1737 ***4971*** *p13*
Kennedy, Catherine; Montreal, 1823 ***7603*** *p101*
Kennedy, Catherine; St. John, N.B., 1847 ***5704.8*** *p25*
Kennedy, Catherine 20; Philadelphia, 1861 ***5704.8*** *p149*
Kennedy, Charles; Charleston, SC, 1805 ***1639.20*** *p105*
Kennedy, Charles; St. John, N.B., 1850 ***5704.8*** *p65*
Kennedy, Charles 9; Quebec, 1849 ***5704.8*** *p57*
Kennedy, Charles 11 *SEE* Kennedy, Patt
Kennedy, Charles 19; Quebec, 1855 ***5704.8*** *p125*
Kennedy, Christian 31; Massachusetts, 1847 ***5881.1*** *p52*
Kennedy, Cornelius 1; Philadelphia, 1867 ***5704.8*** *p215*
Kennedy, Daniel; America, 1737-1738 ***4971*** *p59*
Kennedy, Daniel; Quebec, 1778 ***7603*** *p39*
Kennedy, Daniel; St. John, N.B., 1851 ***5704.8*** *p77*
Kennedy, Darby; America, 1742 ***4971*** *p32*
Kennedy, David 8; Massachusetts, 1847 ***5881.1*** *p53*
Kennedy, Dennis; New York, NY, 1836 ***8208.4*** *p16*
Kennedy, Dennis 36; Massachusetts, 1849 ***5881.1*** *p53*
Kennedy, Edmund; America, 1736-1743 ***4971*** *p58*
Kennedy, Edmund; America, 1741 ***4971*** *p35*
Kennedy, Edmund A. 26; Kansas, 1881 ***5240.1*** *p63*
Kennedy, Edward; New York, NY, 1834 ***8208.4*** *p39*
Kennedy, Edward; New York, NY, 1864 ***5704.8*** *p175*
Kennedy, Edward; Philadelphia, 1815 ***2859.11*** *p34*
Kennedy, Edward 13; Massachusetts, 1849 ***5881.1*** *p53*
Kennedy, Edward 24 *SEE* Kennedy, Patt
Kennedy, Eliza; St. John, N.B., 1847 ***5704.8*** *p25*
Kennedy, Elizabeth 13; St. John, N.B., 1848 ***5704.8*** *p39*
Kennedy, Elizabeth 13; St. John, N.B., 1853 ***5704.8*** *p109*
Kennedy, Elizabeth 35; St. John, N.B., 1853 ***5704.8*** *p109*
Kennedy, Ellen 12; Massachusetts, 1850 ***5881.1*** *p53*
Kennedy, Francis E.; Philadelphia, 1852 ***5704.8*** *p85*
Kennedy, Fullerton 3 *SEE* Kennedy, Joseph
Kennedy, George 11; St. John, N.B., 1853 ***5704.8*** *p109*
Kennedy, Geroge 5 *SEE* Kennedy, Joseph
Kennedy, Gilbert 20; St. John, N.B., 1854 ***5704.8*** *p115*
Kennedy, H. Groves 73; Washington, 1918-1920 ***1728.5*** *p10*
Kennedy, Hannah 18; St. John, N.B., 1860 ***5704.8*** *p143*
Kennedy, Honorah; America, 1738 ***4971*** *p22*
Kennedy, Hugh; New York, NY, 1838 ***8208.4*** *p63*
Kennedy, Hugh; New York, NY, 1864 ***5704.8*** *p187*
Kennedy, Hugh 20; Philadelphia, 1857 ***5704.8*** *p132*
Kennedy, Isabella 14; Quebec, 1849 ***5704.8*** *p57*
Kennedy, Mrs. J.; New York, NY, 1811 ***2859.11*** *p14*
Kennedy, James *SEE* Kennedy, Alexander
Kennedy, James; Montreal, 1818 ***7603*** *p92*
Kennedy, James; New York, NY, 1811 ***2859.11*** *p14*
Kennedy, James; Ohio, 1840 ***9892.11*** *p24*
Kennedy, James; Philadelphia, 1849 ***5704.8*** *p53*
Kennedy, James; Philadelphia, 1852 ***5704.8*** *p88*
Kennedy, James 13 *SEE* Kennedy, Patt
Kennedy, James 15; St. John, N.B., 1853 ***5704.8*** *p109*
Kennedy, James 17; Massachusetts, 1849 ***5881.1*** *p54*
Kennedy, James 18; Quebec, 1864 ***5704.8*** *p160*
Kennedy, James 27; Kansas, 1884 ***5240.1*** *p66*
Kennedy, Jane; Quebec, 1851 ***5704.8*** *p73*
Kennedy, Jane; St. John, N.B., 1848 ***5704.8*** *p43*
Kennedy, Jane 12; St. John, N.B., 1847 ***5704.8*** *p10*
Kennedy, Jane 18; Massachusetts, 1847 ***5881.1*** *p53*
Kennedy, Jane 20; Philadelphia, 1864 ***5704.8*** *p161*
Kennedy, Jane 25; Philadelphia, 1860 ***5704.8*** *p146*
Kennedy, Jane 28 *SEE* Kennedy, Joseph
Kennedy, Joan; America, 1818 ***1639.20*** *p105*
Kennedy, Johanna 20; Massachusetts, 1849 ***5881.1*** *p54*
Kennedy, John; America, 1866 ***5704.8*** *p206*
Kennedy, John; Illinois, 1871 ***5012.39*** *p25*
Kennedy, John; New York, NY, 1816 ***2859.11*** *p34*
Kennedy, John; New York, NY, 1816 ***2859.11*** *p34*
With wife
Kennedy, John; New York, NY, 1835 ***8208.4*** *p36*
Kennedy, John; St. John, N.B., 1847 ***5704.8*** *p25*
Kennedy, John; St. John, N.B., 1848 ***5704.8*** *p39*
Kennedy, John 5; Philadelphia, 1867 ***5704.8*** *p215*
Kennedy, John 9; St. John, N.B., 1853 ***5704.8*** *p109*
Kennedy, John 19 *SEE* Kennedy, Patt
Kennedy, John 20; Massachusetts, 1847 ***5881.1*** *p53*
Kennedy, John 25; Massachusetts, 1847 ***5881.1*** *p53*
Kennedy, John 68; North Carolina, 1850 ***1639.20*** *p105*
Kennedy, Joseph; New York, NY, 1816 ***2859.11*** *p34*
Kennedy, Joseph; Quebec, 1851 ***5704.8*** *p73*
Kennedy, Joseph 30; Philadelphia, 1833-1834 ***53.26*** *p42*
*Relative:*Jane 28
*Relative:*Mary 7

Keresey, Mr.; New York, NY, 1811 ***2859.11*** *p6*
With wife & relatives
Kerevan, Michael; Quebec, 1825 ***7603*** *p84*
Kerewine, Andrew; Maryland, 1742 ***4971*** *p107*
Kerfoote, Eliz.; Virginia, 1637 ***6219*** *p110*
Kergozet, J. M.; Arkansas, 1918 ***95.2*** *p73*
Kergozet, James Manuel; Arkansas, 1918 ***95.2*** *p65*
Keridl, John; Colorado, 1891 ***9678.2*** *p122*
Kerigan, James; Trenton, NJ, 1838 ***8208.4*** *p76*
Kerigoyen, Mr. 30; America, 1838 ***778.5*** *p294*
Kerins, Michael 40; California, 1872 ***2769.5*** *p6*
Keriss, Philipp; South Carolina, 1788 ***7119*** *p203*
Kerivan, Richard; Maryland, 1742 ***4971*** *p106*
Kerkhof, Christian Frederick; America, 1838 ***1450.2*** *p78A*
Kerkhoff, Carl Friedrich Wilhelm; America, 1849-1850 ***4610.10*** *p112*
Kerkhoff, Carl Friedrich Wilhelm 17; America, 1849 ***4610.10*** *p31*
Kerkhoff, Christian Frederick; America, 1838 ***1450.2*** *p79A*
Kerkhoff, Ernst Heinrich Ludwig; America, 1851 ***4610.10*** *p31*
Kerkhoff, Johann; Illinois, n.d. ***4610.10*** *p74*
Kerkof, Frederick; America, 1838 ***1450.2*** *p79A*
Kerley, Biddy 20; Massachusetts, 1850 ***5881.1*** *p52*
Kerley, John; Wisconsin, n.d. ***9675.6*** *p131*
Kerline, Ellen 30; St. John, N.B., 1859 ***5704.8*** *p140*
Kerm, . . .; Canada, 1776-1783 ***9786*** *p26*
Kermack, Robert R.; Colorado, 1904 ***9678.2*** *p62*
Kermet, Barbara 21; Maryland, 1775 ***1219.7*** *p253*
Kern, Charles; California, 1850 ***3840.2*** *p16*
Kern, Christian; America, 1851 ***2896.5*** *p21*
Kern, F. G.; Milwaukee, 1875 ***4719.30*** *p257*
Kern, Franz A.; America, 1848 ***8582.3*** *p36*
Kern, Friedrich *SEE* Kern, Matthias
Kern, Georg *SEE* Kern, Matthias
Kern, Georg Adam; Pennsylvania, 1752 ***2444*** *p172*
With wife
Kern, Henry 55; Port uncertain, 1839 ***778.5*** *p294*
Kern, Jacob; Pennsylvania, 1754 ***2444*** *p173*
Kern, Jacob; Philadelphia, 1763 ***9973.7*** *p38*
Kern, Jak; Philadelphia, 1756 ***4525*** *p262*
Kern, Johannes; Kentucky, 1823 ***8582.3*** *p97*
Kern, John 32; New Orleans, 1831 ***778.5*** *p294*
Kern, Mathias; Philadelphia, 1760 ***9973.7*** *p34*
Kern, Math's; Pennsylvania, 1754 ***2444*** *p173*
Kern, Matthias; Pennsylvania, 1747 ***2444*** *p173*
Kern, Matthias; Pennsylvania, 1751 ***2444*** *p173*
Kern, Matthias; Pennsylvania, 1752 ***2444*** *p173*
*Child:*Georg
*Child:*Friedrich
*Child:*Michel
With wife
Kern, Michel *SEE* Kern, Matthias
Kern, Paul 34; Kansas, 1876 ***5240.1*** *p57*
Kernaghan, Betty; Quebec, 1852 ***5704.8*** *p90*
Kernaghan, Robert; New York, NY, 1815 ***2859.11*** *p34*
Kernaghan, William; Quebec, 1852 ***5704.8*** *p90*
Kernahan, John 34; Kansas, 1902 ***5240.1*** *p82*
Kernan, . . .; Quebec, 1847 ***5704.8*** *p37*
Kernan, Barholmew; Ohio, 1845 ***9892.11*** *p24*
Kernan, Barney; Quebec, 1847 ***5704.8*** *p37*
Kernan, Bartholmew; New York, 1822 ***9892.11*** *p24*
Kernan, Bernard; Quebec, 1847 ***5704.8*** *p37*
Kernan, Biddy; Quebec, 1847 ***5704.8*** *p37*
Kernan, Carry; Quebec, 1847 ***5704.8*** *p37*
Kernan, Francis; Quebec, 1847 ***5704.8*** *p37*
Kernan, Margaret; Quebec, 1847 ***5704.8*** *p37*
Kernan, Pat; Quebec, 1847 ***5704.8*** *p37*
Kernan, Peter; Quebec, 1847 ***5704.8*** *p37*
Kerne, Jon.; Virginia, 1635 ***6219*** *p19*
Kerner, Anna Rosina; New York, 1749 ***3652*** *p73*
Kerner, Josef; Alberta, n.d. ***5262*** *p58*
Kerner, Justinus; Cincinnati, 1788-1848 ***8582.3*** *p90*
Kerner, Lewis; Ohio, 1840 ***9892.11*** *p24*
Kerner, Mary Josephine; Wisconsin, n.d. ***9675.6*** *p131*
Kernes, James; America, 1737 ***4971*** *p13*
Kerney, Anna; Montreal, 1823 ***7603*** *p87*
Kerney, James; Quebec, 1803 ***7603*** *p77*
Kerney, John; Quebec, 1850 ***5704.8*** *p66*
Kernise, Michael; Philadelphia, 1760 ***9973.7*** *p35*
Kernlein, Christian; South Carolina, 1788 ***7119*** *p200*
Kernlein, John; South Carolina, 1788 ***7119*** *p200*
Kernohan, Andrew; Arkansas, 1918 ***95.2*** *p65*
Kerns, Bernhard; Ohio, 1798 ***8582.2*** *p55*
Kerns, Frank; Wisconsin, n.d. ***9675.6*** *p131*
Kerpi, Anton; Wisconsin, n.d. ***9675.6*** *p131*
Kerr, Mr.; Quebec, 1815 ***9229.18*** *p74*
Kerr, Mr.; Quebec, 1815 ***9229.18*** *p81*
Kerr, Alexander; New York, NY, 1815 ***2859.11*** *p34*
Kerr, Alexander; North Carolina, 1726-1810 ***1639.20*** *p106*
Kerr, Alexander 18; Philadelphia, 1856 ***5704.8*** *p128*
Kerr, Allen; Philadelphia, 1811 ***53.26*** *p43*
Kerr, Allen; Philadelphia, 1811 ***2859.11*** *p14*
Kerr, Ann; America, 1864 ***5704.8*** *p176*
Kerr, Ann; Philadelphia, 1847 ***53.26*** *p43*
Kerr, Ann; Philadelphia, 1847 ***5704.8*** *p30*
Kerr, Ann; Philadelphia, 1849 ***53.26*** *p43*
Kerr, Ann; Philadelphia, 1849 ***5704.8*** *p53*
Kerr, Ann; Quebec, 1850 ***5704.8*** *p70*
Kerr, Ann; St. John, N.B., 1848 ***5704.8*** *p39*
Kerr, Ann 12 *SEE* Kerr, Cornilius
Kerr, Ann 12; Philadelphia, 1847 ***5704.8*** *p1*
Kerr, Ann 65; Philadelphia, 1864 ***5704.8*** *p157*
Kerr, Ann Blair; Charleston, SC, 1810 ***1639.20*** *p106*
Kerr, Arthur; St. John, N.B., 1853 ***5704.8*** *p109*
Kerr, Becky; St. John, N.B., 1847 ***5704.8*** *p34*
Kerr, Bridget 9; Philadelphia, 1853 ***5704.8*** *p113*
Kerr, Catharine; New York, NY, 1870 ***5704.8*** *p239*
Kerr, Catherine; New York, NY, 1811 ***2859.11*** *p14*
With family
Kerr, Catherine; New York, NY, 1815 ***2859.11*** *p34*
Kerr, Catherine 7 *SEE* Kerr, Cornilius
Kerr, Catherine 7; Philadelphia, 1847 ***5704.8*** *p1*
Kerr, Catherine 10 *SEE* Kerr, Mary Ann
Kerr, Catherine 10; Philadelphia, 1849 ***5704.8*** *p50*
Kerr, Catherine 11; Philadelphia, 1853 ***5704.8*** *p111*
Kerr, Catherine 18; Quebec, 1855 ***5704.8*** *p126*
Kerr, Charles; Philadelphia, 1848 ***53.26*** *p43*
Kerr, Charles; Philadelphia, 1848 ***5704.8*** *p40*
Kerr, Charles; St. John, N.B., 1849 ***5704.8*** *p55*
Kerr, Charles 4; St. John, N.B., 1848 ***5704.8*** *p39*
Kerr, Charles 5 *SEE* Kerr, Cornilius
Kerr, Charles 5; Philadelphia, 1847 ***5704.8*** *p1*
Kerr, Charles 18; Philadelphia, 1865 ***5704.8*** *p164*
Kerr, Cornilius; Philadelphia, 1847 ***53.26*** *p43*
*Relative:*Fanny
*Relative:*Ann 12
*Relative:*William 9
*Relative:*Catherine 7
*Relative:*Charles 5
*Relative:*Julian 3
*Relative:*James 1
Kerr, Cornilius; Philadelphia, 1847 ***5704.8*** *p1*
Kerr, Daniel; Philadelphia, 1851 ***5704.8*** *p76*
Kerr, Daniel 2; St. John, N.B., 1848 ***5704.8*** *p39*
Kerr, David; America, 1864 ***5704.8*** *p176*
Kerr, David; Philadelphia, 1847 ***53.26*** *p43*
*Relative:*Margaret
With relative
*Relative:*Martha
Kerr, David; Philadelphia, 1847 ***5704.8*** *p30*
Kerr, David 22; St. John, N.B., 1866 ***5704.8*** *p166*
Kerr, David 30; Jamaica, 1775 ***1219.7*** *p279*
Kerr, Dennis; Philadelphia, 1847 ***53.26*** *p43*
*Relative:*John
Kerr, Dennis; Philadelphia, 1847 ***5704.8*** *p24*
Kerr, Edward 15; Quebec, 1855 ***5704.8*** *p126*
Kerr, Eliza; Quebec, 1850 ***5704.8*** *p70*
Kerr, Eliza; Quebec, 1851 ***5704.8*** *p73*
Kerr, Elizabeth 21; Philadelphia, 1853 ***5704.8*** *p111*
Kerr, Ellen C. 7; New York, NY, 1866 ***5704.8*** *p212*
Kerr, Esther-Joseph; Quebec, 1823 ***7603*** *p67*
Kerr, Fanny *SEE* Kerr, Cornilius
Kerr, Fanny; Philadelphia, 1847 ***5704.8*** *p1*
Kerr, Francis; Philadelphia, 1848 ***53.26*** *p43*
Kerr, Francis; Philadelphia, 1848 ***5704.8*** *p41*
Kerr, George; New York, NY, 1815 ***2859.11*** *p34*
Kerr, George 29; St. John, N.B., 1866 ***5704.8*** *p166*
Kerr, George P.; New York, NY, 1834 ***8208.4*** *p2*
Kerr, Hannah; St. John, N.B., 1848 ***5704.8*** *p47*
Kerr, Hannah 50; Philadelphia, 1853 ***5704.8*** *p111*
Kerr, Henry; New York, NY, 1816 ***2859.11*** *p34*
Kerr, Henry 5; Philadelphia, 1851 ***5704.8*** *p76*
Kerr, Hugh; St. John, N.B., 1848 ***5704.8*** *p42*
Kerr, Hugh 9 mos; St. John, N.B., 1848 ***5704.8*** *p39*
Kerr, Hyndman; Quebec, 1847 ***5704.8*** *p29*
Kerr, Hyndman 10; Quebec, 1850 ***5704.8*** *p63*
Kerr, Isabella; New York, NY, 1815 ***2859.11*** *p34*
Kerr, Isabella MacWhinnie; South Carolina, 1829 ***1639.20*** *p106*
Kerr, James; New York, NY, 1811 ***2859.11*** *p14*
Kerr, James; New York, NY, 1815 ***2859.11*** *p34*
Kerr, James; Philadelphia, 1853 ***5704.8*** *p102*
Kerr, James; St. John, N.B., 1848 ***5704.8*** *p39*
Kerr, James; St. John, N.B., 1848 ***5704.8*** *p42*
Kerr, James 3 mos; St. John, N.B., 1848 ***5704.8*** *p42*
Kerr, James 9 mos; Philadelphia, 1853 ***5704.8*** *p111*
Kerr, James 9 mos; St. John, N.B., 1848 ***5704.8*** *p39*
Kerr, James 1 *SEE* Kerr, Cornilius
Kerr, James 1; Philadelphia, 1847 ***5704.8*** *p2*
Kerr, James 4; St. John, N.B., 1848 ***5704.8*** *p39*
Kerr, James 8 *SEE* Kerr, Mary Ann
Kerr, James 8; Philadelphia, 1849 ***5704.8*** *p50*
Kerr, James 11; Philadelphia, 1853 ***5704.8*** *p113*
Kerr, James 11; St. John, N.B., 1848 ***5704.8*** *p39*
Kerr, James 19; Philadelphia, 1864 ***5704.8*** *p156*
Kerr, James 25; Philadelphia, 1864 ***5704.8*** *p156*
Kerr, James 60; Philadelphia, 1853 ***5704.8*** *p111*
Kerr, Jane; Philadelphia, 1847 ***53.26*** *p43*
Kerr, Jane; Philadelphia, 1847 ***5704.8*** *p14*
Kerr, Jane; Quebec, 1848 ***5704.8*** *p41*
Kerr, Jane; St. John, N.B., 1849 ***5704.8*** *p48*
Kerr, Jane 13; Quebec, 1850 ***5704.8*** *p63*
Kerr, Jane 20; St. John, N.B., 1856 ***5704.8*** *p131*
Kerr, John *SEE* Kerr, Dennis
Kerr, John; New York, NY, 1811 ***2859.11*** *p14*
Kerr, John; New York, NY, 1815 ***2859.11*** *p34*
Kerr, John; New York, NY, 1816 ***2859.11*** *p34*
Kerr, John; Philadelphia, 1811 ***53.26*** *p43*
Kerr, John; Philadelphia, 1811 ***2859.11*** *p14*
Kerr, John; Philadelphia, 1847 ***5704.8*** *p24*
Kerr, John; Philadelphia, 1848 ***5704.8*** *p45*
Kerr, John; Philadelphia, 1851 ***5704.8*** *p76*
Kerr, John 7; St. John, N.B., 1848 ***5704.8*** *p39*
Kerr, John 19; Philadelphia, 1856 ***5704.8*** *p128*
Kerr, John 22; Philadelphia, 1833-1834 ***53.26*** *p43*
Kerr, John Cessford; Charleston, SC, 1820 ***1639.20*** *p106*
Kerr, Julian 3 *SEE* Kerr, Cornilius
Kerr, Julian 3; Philadelphia, 1847 ***5704.8*** *p2*
Kerr, Margaret *SEE* Kerr, David
Kerr, Margaret; Philadelphia, 1847 ***5704.8*** *p30*
Kerr, Margaret; Philadelphia, 1851 ***5704.8*** *p76*
Kerr, Margaret 8; Philadelphia, 1851 ***5704.8*** *p76*
Kerr, Martha *SEE* Kerr, David
Kerr, Martha; Philadelphia, 1847 ***5704.8*** *p30*
Kerr, Mary; Quebec, 1850 ***5704.8*** *p63*
Kerr, Mary; Quebec, 1873 ***4537.30*** *p26*
Kerr, Mary 3; St. John, N.B., 1848 ***5704.8*** *p42*
Kerr, Mary 38; Philadelphia, 1853 ***5704.8*** *p111*
Kerr, Mary Ann; Philadelphia, 1849 ***53.26*** *p43*
*Relative:*Catherine 10
*Relative:*James 8
Kerr, Mary Ann; Philadelphia, 1849 ***5704.8*** *p50*
Kerr, Matilda; New York, NY, 1815 ***2859.11*** *p34*
Kerr, Matilda 29; Philadelphia, 1853 ***5704.8*** *p111*
Kerr, Matthew; Philadelphia, 1811 ***53.26*** *p43*
Kerr, Matthew; Philadelphia, 1811 ***2859.11*** *p14*
Kerr, Michael; St. John, N.B., 1847 ***5704.8*** *p34*
Kerr, Michael; St. John, N.B., 1848 ***5704.8*** *p39*
Kerr, Michael 5; Philadelphia, 1853 ***5704.8*** *p111*
Kerr, Michael J.; Colorado, 1904 ***9678.2*** *p62*
Kerr, Morgan; New York, NY, 1834 ***8208.4*** *p1*
Kerr, Nancy; New York, NY, 1816 ***2859.11*** *p34*
Kerr, Nancy; St. John, N.B., 1848 ***5704.8*** *p39*
Kerr, Nancy; St. John, N.B., 1848 ***5704.8*** *p42*
Kerr, Patrick; America, 1739 ***4971*** *p66*
Kerr, Patrick; Baltimore, 1816 ***2859.11*** *p34*
Kerr, Patrick; St. John, N.B., 1848 ***5704.8*** *p39*
Kerr, Patrick 9; St. John, N.B., 1848 ***5704.8*** *p39*
Kerr, Patrick J.; Colorado, 1900 ***9678.2*** *p62*
Kerr, Patterson; Philadelphia, 1866 ***5704.8*** *p206*
Kerr, Rachel; New York, NY, 1811 ***2859.11*** *p14*
With 4 children
Kerr, Robert; New York, NY, 1815 ***2859.11*** *p34*
Kerr, Robert; New York, NY, 1816 ***2859.11*** *p34*
Kerr, Rosanna 2; St. John, N.B., 1848 ***5704.8*** *p39*
Kerr, Sally; Quebec, 1850 ***5704.8*** *p63*
Kerr, Samuel; St. John, N.B., 1847 ***5704.8*** *p9*
Kerr, Samuel 8; Quebec, 1850 ***5704.8*** *p63*
Kerr, Sarah Ann; St. John, N.B., 1848 ***5704.8*** *p42*
Kerr, Susan; Philadelphia, 1851 ***5704.8*** *p76*
Kerr, Teresa; St. John, N.B., 1848 ***5704.8*** *p47*
Kerr, Thomas; America, 1739 ***4971*** *p68*
Kerr, Thomas; New York, NY, 1816 ***2859.11*** *p34*
Kerr, Thomas; New York, NY, 1828 ***8208.4*** *p49*
Kerr, Thomas; Quebec, 1823 ***7603*** *p88*
Kerr, Thomas; Washington, 1859-1920 ***2872.1*** *p20*
Kerr, Thomas 2; Philadelphia, 1851 ***5704.8*** *p76*
Kerr, Thomas 17; St. John, N.B., 1854 ***5704.8*** *p114*
Kerr, Thomas 27; St. John, N.B., 1866 ***5704.8*** *p166*
Kerr, Unity 8; Philadelphia, 1853 ***5704.8*** *p111*
Kerr, William; Colorado, 1904 ***9678.2*** *p62*
Kerr, William; New York, NY, 1868 ***5704.8*** *p229*
Kerr, William; Philadelphia, 1864 ***5704.8*** *p178*
Kerr, William 9 *SEE* Kerr, Cornilius
Kerr, William 9; Philadelphia, 1847 ***5704.8*** *p1*
Kerr, William 21; St. John, N.B., 1856 ***5704.8*** *p131*
Kerr, William James; Philadelphia, 1851 ***5704.8*** *p76*
Kerr, William John 9; St. John, N.B., 1853 ***5704.8*** *p109*
Kerrigan, Alicia; St. John, N.B., 1850 ***5704.8*** *p67*
Kerrigan, Catherine; St. John, N.B., 1847 ***5704.8*** *p21*
Kerrigan, Honour; St. John, N.B., 1850 ***5704.8*** *p67*
Kerrigan, Hugh 46; Philadelphia, 1854 ***5704.8*** *p121*
Kerrigan, Mary Ann; New York, NY, 1865 ***5704.8*** *p195*
Kerrigan, Matilda; Philadelphia, 1847 ***53.26*** *p43*
Kerrigan, Matilda; Philadelphia, 1847 ***5704.8*** *p22*

254 *FOR A COMPLETE EXPLANATION OF ENTRY, SEE "HOW TO READ A CITATION" SECTION*

Kerrigan, Nancy 20; St. John, N.B., 1854 ***5704.8*** *p119*
Kerrigan, Patrick; St. John, N.B., 1847 ***5704.8*** *p33*
Kerrigan, Peter; Quebec, 1850 ***5704.8*** *p63*
Kerrigan, William; Philadelphia, 1868 ***5704.8*** *p231*
Kerrisey, Daniel 29; Massachusetts, 1849 ***5881.1*** *p53*
Kerrvan, Henry; New York, NY, 1816 ***2859.11*** *p34*
Kerry, Adam; Wisconsin, n.d. ***9675.6*** *p131*
Kerry, Susan 20; St. John, N.B., 1855 ***5704.8*** *p126*
Kerry, Thomas; America, 1743 ***4971*** *p32*
Kerry, Unity 45; St. John, N.B., 1855 ***5704.8*** *p126*
Kerschen, Francois; Wisconsin, n.d. ***9675.6*** *p131*
Kerschen, Frank 22; Kansas, 1883 ***5240.1*** *p23*
Kerschen, Frank 22; Kansas, 1883 ***5240.1*** *p64*
Kerschen, Jacob 54; Kansas, 1902 ***5240.1*** *p24*
Kerschen, Jacob 54; Kansas, 1902 ***5240.1*** *p82*
Kerschen, John; Iroquois Co., IL, 1892 ***3455.1*** *p11*
Kerschen, John 25; Kansas, 1881 ***5240.1*** *p24*
Kerschen, John 25; Kansas, 1881 ***5240.1*** *p63*
Kersey, Alfred; Ohio, 1845-1870 ***9892.11*** *p24*
Kersey, Thomas 22; Maryland, 1775 ***1219.7*** *p264*
Kershaw, Jam 18; Maryland or Virginia, 1699 ***2212*** *p21*
Kershaw, Ralph 23; Virginia, 1699 ***2212*** *p26*
Kershe, Edward 16; Maryland, 1729 ***3690.1*** *p133*
Kersting, Dorothee S. Kunning *SEE* Kersting, Johann Christoph
Kersting, Heinrich; America, 1849 ***8582.1*** *p18*
Kersting, Johann Christoph; Texas, 1845 ***4815.7*** *p92*
*Wife:*Dorothee S. Kunning
With 4 children
Kerston, August; Illinois, 1902 ***5012.40*** *p77*
Kerth, . . .; Canada, 1776-1783 ***9786*** *p26*
Kerting, Martha; Wisconsin, n.d. ***9675.6*** *p131*
Kerting, Otto; Wisconsin, n.d. ***9675.6*** *p131*
Kerton, William 21; Maryland, 1774 ***1219.7*** *p187*
Kertzner, . . .; Canada, 1776-1783 ***9786*** *p26*
Kervan, Thos.; New England, 1816 ***2859.11*** *p34*
Kerwan, James; New York, NY, 1811 ***2859.11*** *p14*
Kerwan, Richard; America, 1742 ***4971*** *p35*
Kerwin, Catharine 7; Massachusetts, 1850 ***5881.1*** *p53*
Kerwin, Dennis 21; Massachusetts, 1849 ***5881.1*** *p53*
Kerwin, Michael 30; Massachusetts, 1850 ***5881.1*** *p55*
Kescho, . . .; Canada, 1776-1783 ***9786*** *p26*
Keser, John G.; Philadelphia, 1832 ***9892.11*** *p24*
Kesh, Mary 15; Quebec, 1856 ***5704.8*** *p130*
Kesler, . . .; Canada, 1776-1783 ***9786*** *p26*
Kesler, Jacob 32; Port uncertain, 1839 ***778.5*** *p294*
Kesler, Joseph 8; Port uncertain, 1839 ***778.5*** *p294*
Kesler, Madelaine 10; Port uncertain, 1839 ***778.5*** *p294*
Kesler, Marie 40; Port uncertain, 1839 ***778.5*** *p294*
Kesler, Munbald 3; Port uncertain, 1839 ***778.5*** *p294*
Kesler, Sebastien 6; Port uncertain, 1839 ***778.5*** *p294*
Kesner, Jakob L.; Chicago, 1868 ***8125.8*** *p437*
Kessalaveca, Alex; Arkansas, 1918 ***95.2*** *p65*
Kessing, Bernard 33; California, 1873 ***2769.10*** *p4*
Kessing, John Ferdniand 43; California, 1873 ***2769.10*** *p4*
Kessler, . . .; Canada, 1776-1783 ***9786*** *p26*
Kessler, Mr.; Cincinnati, 1843 ***8582.2*** *p32*
Kessler, August; Washington, 1859-1920 ***2872.1*** *p20*
Kessler, Carl; Illinois, 1841 ***8582.2*** *p50*
Kessler, Christian; Chicago, 1893 ***1450.2*** *p78A*
Kessler, Frank; New York, 1883 ***1450.2*** *p19B*
Kessler, Franz 18; America, 1839 ***778.5*** *p295*
Kessler, Frederick; America, 1839 ***1450.2*** *p78A*
Kessler, George; New York, NY, 1838 ***8208.4*** *p81*
Kessler, Herchel; Arkansas, 1918 ***95.2*** *p65*
Kessler, Jakob; Trenton, NJ, 1776 ***8137*** *p10*
Kessler, Joseph *SEE* Kessler, Kunigunde
Kessler, Joseph; Cincinnati, 1824 ***8582.1*** *p51*
Kessler, Joseph; New York, NY, 1838 ***8208.4*** *p81*
Kessler, Kunigunde; America, 1810 ***8582.1*** *p17*
*Father:*Joseph
With mother
Kesson, Henry 34; Quebec, 1857 ***5704.8*** *p136*
Kesson, Thomas; Austin, TX, 1886 ***9777*** *p5*
Kessune, Patrick 30; Massachusetts, 1850 ***5881.1*** *p56*
Kester, Gerhard; Wisconsin, n.d. ***9675.6*** *p131*
Ketchen, Thomas; America, 1810-1830 ***1639.20*** *p106*
Keth, George; Virginia, 1635 ***6219*** *p17*
*Wife:*Martha
*Son:*John
Keth, John *SEE* Keth, George
Keth, Martha *SEE* Keth, George
Ketle, Tho.; Virginia, 1635 ***6219*** *p4*
Ketler, . . .; Canada, 1776-1783 ***9786*** *p26*
Ketler, John Carl 21; Virginia, 1773 ***1219.7*** *p169*
Ketley, James 18; Massachusetts, 1847 ***5881.1*** *p53*
Ketley, William 21; Massachusetts, 1847 ***5881.1*** *p56*
Ketly, Matthew; New York, NY, 1811 ***2859.11*** *p14*
Ketnocker, Goodlive; Ohio, 1848 ***9892.11*** *p24*
Ketsinger, Anna Maria 15 wks *SEE* Ketsinger, Tayt
Ketsinger, Matthew 2 *SEE* Ketsinger, Tayt
Ketsinger, Tayt; South Carolina, 1752-1753 ***3689.17*** *p21*
With wife
*Relative:*Matthew 2
*Relative:*Anna Maria 15 wks
Kettelher, Joachim; New Netherland, 1630-1646 ***8582.2*** *p51*
Ketten, John; Wisconsin, n.d. ***9675.6*** *p131*
Ketten, Nicholas; Wisconsin, n.d. ***9675.6*** *p131*
Ketter, Andrew J.; Arkansas, 1918 ***95.2*** *p65*
Ketterer, Bernhard; Illinois, 1896 ***5012.40*** *p54*
Ketterer, George; Wisconsin, n.d. ***9675.6*** *p131*
Kettle, Ralph; America, 1698 ***2212*** *p6*
Kettle, Ralph; Virginia, 1698 ***2212*** *p11*
Kettle, William 30; Jamaica, 1774 ***1219.7*** *p238*
Kettles, Absalom; America, 1738 ***4971*** *p68*
Kettlewell, Thomas 23; Maryland, 1735 ***3690.1*** *p133*
Kettner, . . .; Canada, 1776-1783 ***9786*** *p26*
Ketty, Louisa 40; Massachusetts, 1849 ***5881.1*** *p54*
Keurlis, Pieter; Pennsylvania, 1683 ***2155*** *p2*
Keutz, Georg; Illinois, 1839 ***8582.1*** *p55*
Kevan, Johanna 13; Massachusetts, 1849 ***5881.1*** *p54*
Kevan, Thomas 20; Massachusetts, 1849 ***5881.1*** *p56*
Kevenagh, James; Philadelphia, 1811 ***2859.11*** *p14*
Keving, Thomas; Buffalo, NY, 1832 ***9892.11*** *p24*
Keving, Thomas; Ohio, 1836 ***9892.11*** *p24*
Kewans, William; Charleston, SC, 1796 ***1639.20*** *p106*
Kewbifer, Mike; Arkansas, 1918 ***95.2*** *p66*
Kewerz, Johann; Wisconsin, n.d. ***9675.6*** *p131*
Kewing, Andrew; Annapolis, MD, 1742 ***4971*** *p93*
Kewton, Frank; Arkansas, 1918 ***95.2*** *p66*
Key, Adam; Virginia, 1639 ***6219*** *p161*
Key, John 25; America, 1700 ***2212*** *p29*
Key, John 33; Jamaica, 1738 ***3690.1*** *p133*
Key, Martha; Virginia, 1628 ***6219*** *p16*
Key, Richard; Virginia, 1637 ***6219*** *p83*
Key, Thomas; Virginia, 1648 ***6219*** *p253*
Key, William; Philadelphia, 1811 ***53.26*** *p43*
Key, William 19; Jamaica, 1733 ***3690.1*** *p133*
Key, William 22; Philadelphia, 1857 ***5704.8*** *p134*
Key, Wm.; Philadelphia, 1811 ***2859.11*** *p14*
Keyder, Michel Ludwig; Pennsylvania, 1753 ***2444*** *p172*
Keye, Tho.; Virginia, 1642 ***6219*** *p188*
Keyes, Daniell; Virginia, 1638 ***6219*** *p117*
Keyes, Tho.; Virginia, 1638 ***6219*** *p148*
Keyle, Amelia Ernestine 22 *SEE* Keyle, Gerald Wm.
Keyle, Gerald Wm. 35; New Orleans, 1839 ***9420.2*** *p483*
*Wife:*Amelia Ernestine 22
*Child:*Stephenus 3 mos
Keyle, Stephenus 3 mos *SEE* Keyle, Gerald Wm.
Keymer, William 32; Maryland, 1774 ***1219.7*** *p208*
Keymester, John 39; Maryland, 1774 ***1219.7*** *p221*
Keyne, Margaret 21; Massachusetts, 1849 ***5881.1*** *p55*
Keys, Alexander; Quebec, 1848 ***5704.8*** *p42*
Keys, Andrew; Quebec, 1848 ***5704.8*** *p41*
Keys, Ann; Quebec, 1850 ***5704.8*** *p63*
Keys, Eliza Jane 7; Quebec, 1848 ***5704.8*** *p42*
Keys, Elizabeth; Philadelphia, 1816 ***2859.11*** *p34*
Keys, Elizabeth; Philadelphia, 1852 ***5704.8*** *p88*
Keys, Elizabeth 6; Quebec, 1849 ***5704.8*** *p51*
Keys, Ellen; Quebec, 1849 ***5704.8*** *p51*
Keys, Emma 4; Quebec, 1851 ***5704.8*** *p75*
Keys, Hannah 5; Quebec, 1848 ***5704.8*** *p42*
Keys, Henry 7; Quebec, 1850 ***5704.8*** *p63*
Keys, Irvin; Ohio, 1887 ***9892.11*** *p25*
Keys, Irvine; Ohio, 1882-1884 ***9892.11*** *p25*
Keys, Isabella; Philadelphia, 1850 ***53.26*** *p43*
Keys, Isabella; Philadelphia, 1850 ***5704.8*** *p59*
Keys, James; Philadelphia, 1852 ***5704.8*** *p88*
Keys, Jane; Quebec, 1848 ***5704.8*** *p42*
Keys, Jemima 22; Port uncertain, 1774 ***1219.7*** *p177*
Keys, John; Philadelphia, 1852 ***5704.8*** *p88*
Keys, John; Quebec, 1849 ***5704.8*** *p51*
Keys, John 20; Jamaica, 1725 ***3690.1*** *p134*
Keys, Margaret; Philadelphia, 1851 ***5704.8*** *p71*
Keys, Margaret 11; Quebec, 1849 ***5704.8*** *p51*
Keys, Mary 3; Quebec, 1848 ***5704.8*** *p42*
Keys, Mary 30; Philadelphia, 1853 ***5704.8*** *p113*
Keys, Mary Ann 2; Quebec, 1851 ***5704.8*** *p75*
Keys, Mathias 23; Port uncertain, 1774 ***1219.7*** *p177*
Keys, Robert; Philadelphia, 1852 ***5704.8*** *p88*
Keys, Rose; Philadelphia, 1852 ***5704.8*** *p88*
Keys, Samuel; Philadelphia, 1816 ***2859.11*** *p34*
Keys, Sarah; Quebec, 1848 ***5704.8*** *p42*
Keys, Sarah Ann 9 mos; Quebec, 1848 ***5704.8*** *p42*
Keys, Thomas; Quebec, 1850 ***5704.8*** *p63*
Keyser, Christian 12 *SEE* Keyser, John Ulrich
Keyser, Conrad Frederick 15 *SEE* Keyser, John Ulrich
Keyser, Elizabeth 10 *SEE* Keyser, John Ulrich
Keyser, John Ulrich; South Carolina, 1752-1753 ***3689.17*** *p21*
With wife
*Relative:*Conrad Frederick 15
*Relative:*Christian 12
*Relative:*Elizabeth 10
*Relative:*Mary 5
Keyser, Mary 5 *SEE* Keyser, John Ulrich
Keyser, Ulrich; Pennsylvania, 1731 ***2444*** *p172*
Keyser, Ulrich; Pennsylvania, 1771 ***2444*** *p172*
Keytin, Nicholas; Virginia, 1639 ***6219*** *p155*
Khan, Carl; Milwaukee, 1875 ***4719.30*** *p258*
Kibart, Walter; Arkansas, 1918 ***95.2*** *p66*
Kibbin, Aric 35; Massachusetts, 1860 ***6410.32*** *p107*
Kibbin, Charlotte 30; Massachusetts, 1860 ***6410.32*** *p107*
Kibble, Richard; Virginia, 1639 ***6219*** *p158*
Kibelbeck, Ferdinand; Wisconsin, n.d. ***9675.6*** *p131*
Kibelbeck, Robert; Wisconsin, n.d. ***9675.6*** *p131*
Kibilda, John; Arkansas, 1918 ***95.2*** *p66*
Kibler, Jacob; Pennsylvania, 1749 ***2444*** *p179*
Kibort, Anton; Wisconsin, n.d. ***9675.6*** *p131*
Kicherer, Elisabetha Catharina *SEE* Kicherer, Hans Jerg
Kicherer, Hans Jerg; America, 1729-1800 ***2444*** *p173*
*Wife:*Elisabetha Catharina
*Child:*Hens Jerg
Kicherer, Hens Jerg *SEE* Kicherer, Hans Jerg
Kichlar, Valentine; New York, NY, 1834 ***8208.4*** *p30*
Kichley, Thomas; Virginia, 1642 ***6219*** *p190*
Kichmowez, William; Arkansas, 1918 ***95.2*** *p66*
Kick, Gottfried; Wisconsin, n.d. ***9675.6*** *p131*
Kicke, Wm.; Virginia, 1643 ***6219*** *p202*
Kickelighter, Catherine 16 *SEE* Kickelighter, Thomas
Kickelighter, Elizabeth 12 *SEE* Kickelighter, Thomas
Kickelighter, John Frederick 10 *SEE* Kickelighter, Thomas
Kickelighter, Thomas; South Carolina, 1752-1753 ***3689.17*** *p22*
With wife
*Relative:*Catherine 16
*Relative:*Elizabeth 12
*Relative:*John Frederick 10
Kickett, Christ.; Virginia, 1600-1642 ***6219*** *p193*
Kickhefer, Henry; Wisconsin, n.d. ***9675.6*** *p131*
Kidd, J.; New York, NY, 1816 ***2859.11*** *p34*
Kidd, Sarah Ann; Philadelphia, 1864 ***5704.8*** *p182*
Kidd, Tho.; Virginia, 1623-1648 ***6219*** *p252*
Kidder, Benjamin 15; Baltimore, 1775 ***1219.7*** *p270*
Kidder, William 20; Maryland, 1774 ***1219.7*** *p230*
Kiderlen, Wilhelm J. L.; Cincinnati, 1788-1848 ***8582.3*** *p91*
Kiderlen, Wilhelm L. J.; Cincinnati, 1788-1848 ***8582.3*** *p89*
Kiderlen, Wilhelm L. J.; Philadelphia, 1836 ***8582.3*** *p36*
Kidman, Thomas 27; Maryland, 1775 ***1219.7*** *p249*
Kidney, Anne 4; St. John, N.B., 1853 ***5704.8*** *p99*
Kidney, Eliza; St. John, N.B., 1853 ***5704.8*** *p99*
Kidney, James; St. John, N.B., 1852 ***5704.8*** *p83*
Kidney, James 5; St. John, N.B., 1853 ***5704.8*** *p99*
Kidney, John 6 mos; St. John, N.B., 1853 ***5704.8*** *p99*
Kiebach, Ferdinand A. A. 38; Kansas, 1887 ***5240.1*** *p69*
Kieblebeck, Henry; Wisconsin, n.d. ***9675.6*** *p131*
Kiebonitz, . . .; Canada, 1776-1783 ***9786*** *p26*
Kieckhoefer, August; Wisconsin, n.d. ***9675.6*** *p131*
Kieffer, Frederick; Pennsylvania, 1715-1795 ***2444*** *p179*
Kieffer, Jerg; Pennsylvania, 1742 ***2444*** *p180*
Kieffer, John; Wisconsin, n.d. ***9675.6*** *p131*
Kieffer, Ludwick; Philadelphia, 1765 ***9973.7*** *p40*
Kieffer, Nicholas; Wisconsin, n.d. ***9675.6*** *p131*
Kieffer, Primus; Kentucky, 1839-1840 ***8582.3*** *p98*
Kiehnau, Frieda; Wisconsin, n.d. ***9675.6*** *p131*
Kiehron, . . .; Canada, 1776-1783 ***9786*** *p26*
Kieker, Louis; Wisconsin, n.d. ***9675.6*** *p131*
Kiel, A. M. Louise Caroline; America, 1881 ***4610.10*** *p152*
Kiel, Fred; Illinois, 1865 ***5012.38*** *p98*
Kielburg, . . .; Canada, 1776-1783 ***9786*** *p26*
Kielburg, Jean; Canada, 1776-1783 ***9786*** *p242*
Kield, Isaac; New York, NY, 1816 ***2859.11*** *p34*
Kielmann, Anna Maria Mayer *SEE* Kielmann, Philipp
Kielmann, Christina *SEE* Kielmann, Philipp
Kielmann, Jacob Friedrich *SEE* Kielmann, Philipp
Kielmann, Johannes *SEE* Kielmann, Philipp
Kielmann, Philipp; America, 1754 ***2444*** *p173*
*Wife:*Anna Maria Mayer
*Child:*Jacob Friedrich
*Child:*Christina
*Child:*Johannes
Kielt, Mary 18; Philadelphia, 1861 ***5704.8*** *p148*
Kiemlin, Mr.; Pennsylvania, 1700-1763 ***2444*** *p173*
Kiemlin, Johannes; Pennsylvania, 1763 ***2444*** *p173*
Kienle, Anna Margaretha *SEE* Kienle, Michael
Kienle, Anna Maria *SEE* Kienle, Michael
Kienle, Catharina Rohrer *SEE* Kienle, Michael
Kienle, Jacob *SEE* Kienle, Michael
Kienle, Jacob; Pennsylvania, 1750 ***2444*** *p173*
With wife & children
Kienle, Johannes *SEE* Kienle, Michael
Kienle, Maria Catharina *SEE* Kienle, Michael

Kienle, Michael; Pennsylvania, 1750 ***2444*** *p173*
*Brother:*Jacob
*Wife:*Catharina Rohrer
*Child:*Anna Margaretha
*Child:*Maria Catharina
*Child:*Anna Maria
*Child:*Johannes
*Child:*Sabina
Kienle, Sabina *SEE* Kienle, Michael
Kienzel, . . .; Cincinnati, 1848 ***8582.2*** *p63*
Kienzle, Jacob; Wisconsin, n.d. ***9675.6*** *p131*
Kienzlein, Anna Barbara; Pennsylvania, 1754 ***2444*** *p156*
Kienzlerin, Anna Barbara; Pennsylvania, 1754 ***2444*** *p156*
Kiepger, Pierre; Wisconsin, n.d. ***9675.6*** *p131*
Kieran, Barbara 10; St. John, N.B., 1847 ***5704.8*** *p33*
Kieran, Catharine Ann 8; St. John, N.B., 1847 ***5704.8*** *p33*
Kieran, Catherine; St. John, N.B., 1847 ***5704.8*** *p33*
Kieran, Ellan; St. John, N.B., 1847 ***5704.8*** *p33*
Kieran, Jane; St. John, N.B., 1847 ***5704.8*** *p33*
Kieran, Owen; New York, NY, 1836 ***8208.4*** *p12*
Kieran, William; St. John, N.B., 1847 ***5704.8*** *p33*
Kiernan, Bernard; New York, NY, 1839 ***8208.4*** *p97*
Kiernan, David 7; St. John, N.B., 1847 ***5704.8*** *p24*
Kiernan, John; New York, NY, 1836 ***8208.4*** *p22*
Kiernan, John; St. John, N.B., 1847 ***5704.8*** *p24*
Kiernan, John 5; St. John, N.B., 1847 ***5704.8*** *p24*
Kiernan, Joseph 9; St. John, N.B., 1847 ***5704.8*** *p24*
Kiernan, Margaret; St. John, N.B., 1847 ***5704.8*** *p24*
Kiernan, Roda; St. John, N.B., 1847 ***5704.8*** *p24*
Kiernan, Samuel 12; St. John, N.B., 1847 ***5704.8*** *p24*
Kiernan, Sarah; St. John, N.B., 1847 ***5704.8*** *p24*
Kiernan, Thomas 3; St. John, N.B., 1847 ***5704.8*** *p25*
Kierstedt, Hans; New Netherland, 1630-1646 ***8582.2*** *p51*
Kies, Frederick; West Virginia, 1855 ***9788.3*** *p13*
Kiesecker, Johan Ernst 20; Pennsylvania, 1748 ***4525*** *p228*
Kiesecker, Johann Ernst; New England, 1754 ***4525*** *p226*
Kiesecker, Johann Ernst; Pennsylvania, 1754 ***4525*** *p226*
Kiesecker, Johann Matthaeus; Pennsylvania, 1754 ***4525*** *p228*
Kiesecker, Johannes; New England, 1754 ***4525*** *p228*
With wife
With child
Kiesecker, Johannes; Pennsylvania, 1754 ***4525*** *p228*
With wife & child
Kiesecker, Philip; Pennsylvania, 1753 ***4525*** *p228*
Kiesel, Christine 25; New York, NY, 1857 ***9831.14*** *p153*
Kiesele, Georg; New York, NY, 1836 ***8208.4*** *p15*
Kieser, Henry; California, 1871 ***2769.5*** *p6*
Kieszkowski, Wlodzimierz; New York, 1835 ***4606*** *p179*
Kietig, David; Wisconsin, n.d. ***9675.6*** *p131*
Kiewski, Jan 4 *SEE* Kiewski, Kazimierz
Kiewski, Kazimierz; New Jersey, 1912 ***9980.29*** *p66*
Kiewski, Kazimierz 9; New York, 1912 ***9980.29*** *p66*
With aunt
*Brother:*Jan 4
Kiffin, David; Virginia, 1636 ***6219*** *p77*
Kigan, Karbery; Virginia, 1643 ***6219*** *p187*
Kiger, Frederick; Indiana, 1847 ***9117*** *p19*
Kight, Alexander; South Carolina, 1788 ***7119*** *p199*
Kightly, Francis; Indiana, 1850 ***9117*** *p17*
Kightly, Josial; Indiana, 1850 ***9117*** *p17*
Kihlbom, Ellen 27; Massachusetts, 1860 ***6410.32*** *p102*
Kihlbom, John 33; Massachusetts, 1860 ***6410.32*** *p102*
Kihpen, Hermann; Ohio, 1881 ***3702.7*** *p434*
Kik, Henry; Philadelphia, 1760 ***9973.7*** *p35*
Kikenny, Francis 8; Massachusetts, 1849 ***5881.1*** *p53*
Kikenny, John 6; Massachusetts, 1849 ***5881.1*** *p54*
Kilberg, C.; Iowa, 1847 ***2090*** *p611*
With wife & 5 children
Kilbreth, Mathew 20; St. John, N.B., 1860 ***5704.8*** *p143*
Kilbrick, Lawrence 13; Massachusetts, 1850 ***5881.1*** *p54*
Kilbrick, Margaret 40; Massachusetts, 1850 ***5881.1*** *p55*
Kilbrick, Patrick 10; Massachusetts, 1850 ***5881.1*** *p56*
Kilbride, Abby 2; Massachusetts, 1849 ***5881.1*** *p52*
Kilbride, Andrew 45; Massachusetts, 1849 ***5881.1*** *p52*
Kilbride, Barnard 6; Massachusetts, 1849 ***5881.1*** *p52*
Kilbride, John 8; Massachusetts, 1849 ***5881.1*** *p54*
Kilburn, Ann; St. John, N.B., 1849 ***5704.8*** *p56*
Kilburn, Isaac 21; Maryland, 1774 ***1219.7*** *p229*
Kilbye, Henry; Virginia, 1637 ***6219*** *p24*
Kilcary, Mary; Philadelphia, 1866 ***5704.8*** *p210*
Kilchenmann, Gottlieb; New York, 1885 ***1450.2*** *p78A*
Kilday, Mary; Philadelphia, 1852 ***5704.8*** *p91*
Kilday, Mary J.; New York, NY, 1869 ***5704.8*** *p231*
Kilday, Nancy; Philadelphia, 1868 ***5704.8*** *p230*
Kilday, Patrick; Philadelphia, 1849 ***53.26*** *p43*
Kilday, Patrick; Philadelphia, 1849 ***5704.8*** *p54*
Kildea, Ann 10; Quebec, 1853 ***5704.8*** *p105*
Kildea, Bridget 18; Philadelphia, 1860 ***5704.8*** *p145*
Kildea, Jane 20; Philadelphia, 1853 ***5704.8*** *p113*
Kildea, John 20; Quebec, 1853 ***5704.8*** *p105*
Kildea, Mary; Philadelphia, 1864 ***5704.8*** *p173*
Kildiszoff, Leokadia 11 mos; New York, 1912 ***9980.29*** *p71*
Kildiszoff, Maria 2?; New York, 1912 ***9980.29*** *p71*
Kildiszoff, Wasily 26; New York, 1912 ***9980.29*** *p71*
Kildiszoff, Zofia 24; New York, 1912 ***9980.29*** *p71*
Kilell, Sam Albert; Arkansas, 1918 ***95.2*** *p66*
Kiley, Philip M.; Philadelphia, 1881 ***1450.2*** *p19B*
Kiley, William F.; America, 1887 ***1450.2*** *p78A*
Kilfeather, Ann; Quebec, 1851 ***5704.8*** *p73*
Kilfeather, Bridget 18; St. John, N.B., 1854 ***5704.8*** *p122*
Kilfeather, Mary; Quebec, 1851 ***5704.8*** *p73*
Kilfeather, Robert; Quebec, 1851 ***5704.8*** *p73*
Kilferty, Hugh; Quebec, 1853 ***5704.8*** *p104*
Kilferty, Nancy; Quebec, 1853 ***5704.8*** *p104*
Kilferty, Tara; Quebec, 1853 ***5704.8*** *p104*
Kilferty, William; Quebec, 1853 ***5704.8*** *p104*
Kilfoyle, . . . 40; California, 1872 ***2769.6*** *p3*
Kilfoyle, Peter; New York, NY, 1816 ***2859.11*** *p34*
Kilgallin, Michael; Quebec, 1825 ***7603*** *p96*
Kilgore, Alexander; St. John, N.B., 1847 ***5704.8*** *p9*
Kilgore, Charles; New York, NY, 1865 ***5704.8*** *p188*
Kilgore, Jacob; Ohio, 1798 ***8582.2*** *p55*
Kilgore, John; New York, NY, 1865 ***5704.8*** *p188*
Kilgore, Nancy; St. John, N.B., 1847 ***5704.8*** *p10*
Kilgore, William; Quebec, 1850 ***5704.8*** *p66*
Kilhoffer, Michael; Colorado, 1888 ***9678.2*** *p62*
Kilian, Casper 31; America, 1831 ***778.5*** *p295*
Kilkelly, Patrick; America, 1741 ***4971*** *p94*
Kilkenny, Anthony; New York, NY, 1839 ***8208.4*** *p92*
Kilker, Christian; Illinois, 1853 ***7857*** *p4*
Kill, John; New York, NY, 1811 ***2859.11*** *p14*
Killager, Mathew 20; Massachusetts, 1847 ***5881.1*** *p54*
Killagher, . . .; Quebec, 1847 ***5704.8*** *p37*
Killagher, Bridget; Quebec, 1847 ***5704.8*** *p37*
Killagher, Mary; Quebec, 1847 ***5704.8*** *p37*
Killagher, Pat; Quebec, 1847 ***5704.8*** *p37*
Killagher, Tom; Quebec, 1847 ***5704.8*** *p37*
Killaird, James; New York, NY, 1864 ***5704.8*** *p170*
Killalagh, Peter; St. John, N.B., 1833 ***7036*** *p122*
Killane, John; Montreal, 1825 ***7603*** *p87*
Killarary, Patrick; Philadelphia, 1865 ***5704.8*** *p200*
Killday, Mary 1; Massachusetts, 1848 ***5881.1*** *p54*
Killday, Sarah 30; Massachusetts, 1848 ***5881.1*** *p56*
Killduff, Luke 22; Massachusetts, 1847 ***5881.1*** *p54*
Killeen, John; New York, NY, 1838 ***8208.4*** *p83*
Killeen, William J. 25; Kansas, 1887 ***5240.1*** *p69*
Killeghane, Daniel; America, 1739 ***4971*** *p56*
Killelea, Bessy 10; Massachusetts, 1850 ***5881.1*** *p52*
Killen, Thomas; New York, NY, 1815 ***2859.11*** *p34*
Killend, Matilda; New York, NY, 1868 ***5704.8*** *p229*
Killerkin, John 36; Massachusetts, 1849 ***5881.1*** *p54*
Killet, Samuel 20; St. Christopher, 1722 ***3690.1*** *p134*
Killett, Samuell 20; St. Christopher, 1722 ***3690.1*** *p134*
Killey, Thomas; Illinois, 1877 ***2896.5*** *p21*
Killicke, Jane; Virginia, 1648 ***6219*** *p249*
Killigott, Maurice; America, 1743 ***4971*** *p42*
Killin, Hugh; New York, NY, 1836 ***8208.4*** *p20*
Killingly, Robert; Quebec, 1797 ***7603*** *p26*
Killkelly, Patrick; America, 1741 ***4971*** *p10*
Killmer, Nicklaus; Illinois, 1858 ***7857*** *p4*
Killnas, Silvester; Arkansas, 1918 ***95.2*** *p66*
Killoon, Mrs. 50; Massachusetts, 1849 ***5881.1*** *p55*
Killoon, Michael 12; Massachusetts, 1849 ***5881.1*** *p55*
Killoon, Patrick 15; Massachusetts, 1849 ***5881.1*** *p56*
Killroy, Ann 27; Massachusetts, 1849 ***5881.1*** *p52*
Kills, George Fransis; Arkansas, 1918 ***95.2*** *p66*
Killum, Mary; Philadelphia, 1865 ***5704.8*** *p197*
Killy, Daniel; New York, NY, 1811 ***2859.11*** *p14*
Kilman, Anders; Maine, 1872-1882 ***6410.22*** *p118*
Kilman, William 23; Virginia, 1773 ***1219.7*** *p169*
Kilmartin, Charles; New York, NY, 1816 ***2859.11*** *p34*
Kilmartin, Dennis; America, 1742 ***4971*** *p81*
Kilmartin, Hugh; New York, NY, 1816 ***2859.11*** *p34*
Kilmartin, John; New York, NY, 1816 ***2859.11*** *p34*
Kilmartin, Mary; New York, NY, 1816 ***2859.11*** *p34*
Kilmartin, Patrick; New York, NY, 1816 ***2859.11*** *p35*
Kilpatrick, Alexander; Philadelphia, 1851 ***5704.8*** *p71*
Kilpatrick, Andrew 22; Quebec, 1857 ***5704.8*** *p135*
Kilpatrick, Ann; Philadelphia, 1851 ***5704.8*** *p71*
Kilpatrick, Ann 50; Quebec, 1864 ***5704.8*** *p164*
Kilpatrick, Anne 20; Philadelphia, 1853 ***5704.8*** *p111*
Kilpatrick, Charles; Philadelphia, 1851 ***5704.8*** *p71*
Kilpatrick, David 25; St. John, N.B., 1856 ***5704.8*** *p131*
Kilpatrick, Dolly 23; Philadelphia, 1864 ***5704.8*** *p161*
Kilpatrick, Dolly 60; Philadelphia, 1864 ***5704.8*** *p161*
Kilpatrick, Eliza Jane; Philadelphia, 1851 ***5704.8*** *p71*
Kilpatrick, Elizabeth 16; Philadelphia, 1858 ***5704.8*** *p138*
Kilpatrick, Ellen 15; Quebec, 1864 ***5704.8*** *p164*
Kilpatrick, Fanny; Quebec, 1850 ***5704.8*** *p62*
Kilpatrick, Henry 20; Philadelphia, 1860 ***5704.8*** *p146*
Kilpatrick, Hugh 20; St. John, N.B., 1866 ***5704.8*** *p165*
Kilpatrick, James; New York, NY, 1835 ***8208.4*** *p5*
Kilpatrick, James; Philadelphia, 1848 ***53.26*** *p44*
Kilpatrick, James; Philadelphia, 1848 ***5704.8*** *p45*
Kilpatrick, James; Philadelphia, 1851 ***5704.8*** *p71*
Kilpatrick, James; Philadelphia, 1866 ***5704.8*** *p208*
Kilpatrick, James; Quebec, 1850 ***5704.8*** *p62*
Kilpatrick, James 23; Quebec, 1855 ***5704.8*** *p126*
Kilpatrick, John; Philadelphia, 1851 ***5704.8*** *p71*
Kilpatrick, John; St. John, N.B., 1850 ***5704.8*** *p67*
Kilpatrick, John 25; St. John, N.B., 1866 ***5704.8*** *p165*
Kilpatrick, John 64; Philadelphia, 1864 ***5704.8*** *p161*
Kilpatrick, Margaret Ann 17; Philadelphia, 1860 ***5704.8*** *p146*
Kilpatrick, Mary; Philadelphia, 1851 ***5704.8*** *p71*
Kilpatrick, Mary 19; Philadelphia, 1864 ***5704.8*** *p161*
Kilpatrick, Rebecca 24; Quebec, 1858 ***5704.8*** *p138*
Kilpatrick, Robert; Philadelphia, 1851 ***5704.8*** *p81*
Kilpatrick, Ruth 19; Quebec, 1859 ***5704.8*** *p143*
Kilpatrick, Thomas; Philadelphia, 1851 ***5704.8*** *p71*
Kilpatrick, Thomas 37; Philadelphia, 1804 ***53.26*** *p44*
Kilpatrick, Thomas 60; Quebec, 1864 ***5704.8*** *p164*
Kilpatrick, William 11; St. John, N.B., 1861 ***5704.8*** *p147*
Kilpatrick, William 18; Philadelphia, 1858 ***5704.8*** *p138*
Kilpatrick, William 36; Quebec, 1857 ***5704.8*** *p135*
Kilroy, John; Quebec, 1825 ***7603*** *p91*
Kilsby, John W.; New York, NY, 1837 ***8208.4*** *p35*
Kilsenlander, Anna Barbara Brunner *SEE* Kilsenlander, Christian
Kilsenlander, Christian; Philadelphia, 1729 ***2854*** *p44*
*Wife:*Anna Barbara Brunner
With son 6
With daughter 5
Kilshaw, Martha 18; Virginia, 1700 ***2212*** *p30*
Kiltre, Jane; St. John, N.B., 1849 ***5704.8*** *p56*
Kilty, Joseph; Philadelphia, 1850 ***53.26*** *p44*
Kilty, Joseph; Philadelphia, 1850 ***5704.8*** *p60*
Kilty, Owen; America, 1741 ***4971*** *p48*
Kilyanski, Stanislaw; Arkansas, 1918 ***95.2*** *p66*
Kim, Charles 56; Arizona, 1932 ***9228.40*** *p40*
Kimber, George; Colorado, 1905 ***9678.2*** *p62*
Kimberlin, Jon.; Virginia, 1642 ***6219*** *p197*
Kimberling, Jacob; Pennsylvania, 1753 ***2444*** *p180*
Kimel, . . .; New York, 1831 ***4606*** *p175*
Kimera, Ludwick 21; Pennsylvania, 1736 ***4779.3*** *p13*
Kimerley, Mr.; Died enroute, 1751-1754 ***2444*** *p180*
Kimerley, John; Philadelphia, 1751 ***2444*** *p180*
Kimerline, Mr.; Died enroute, 1751-1754 ***2444*** *p180*
Kimerline, John; Philadelphia, 1751 ***2444*** *p180*
Kimerly, Christian; Kansas, 1874 ***5240.1*** *p24*
Kimm, Georg Christoph; Canada, 1780 ***9786*** *p268*
Kimm, Georg Christoph; New York, 1776 ***9786*** *p268*
Kimmel, Jacob; Philadelphia, 1765 ***4779.3*** *p13*
Kimmel, Joh; Charleston, SC, 1775-1781 ***8582.2*** *p52*
Kimmel, Joseph; Charleston, SC, 1775-1781 ***8582.2*** *p52*
Kimmel, Joseph; Savannah, GA, 1779 ***8582.2*** *p52*
Kimmell, Jacob; Philadelphia, 1765 ***4779.3*** *p13*
Kimmer, Jacob; Pennsylvania, 1743 ***2444*** *p180*
Kimmerle, Albert 26; Kansas, 1889 ***5240.1*** *p73*
Kimmerle, Ernest G.; Kansas, 1896 ***5240.1*** *p24*
Kimmerle, Johan 21; Kansas, 1882 ***5240.1*** *p24*
Kimmerle, John 21; Kansas, 1882 ***5240.1*** *p63*
Kimmerle, John 21; Kansas, 1883 ***5240.1*** *p24*
Kimmerle, John 25; Kansas, 1883 ***5240.1*** *p64*
Kimmerlen, Mr.; Died enroute, 1751-1754 ***2444*** *p180*
Kimmerlen, Johannes; Philadelphia, 1751 ***2444*** *p180*
Kimmerling, Mr.; Died enroute, 1751-1754 ***2444*** *p180*
Kimmerling, John; Philadelphia, 1751 ***2444*** *p180*
Kimmich, Anna *SEE* Kimmich, Matthias
Kimmich, Anna Catharina *SEE* Kimmich, Matthias
Kimmich, Anna Catharina Thumm *SEE* Kimmich, Matthias
Kimmich, Anna Maria *SEE* Kimmich, Matthias
Kimmich, Anna Maria Kuehner *SEE* Kimmich, Johannes
Kimmich, Hans Jerg *SEE* Kimmich, Matthias
Kimmich, Jacob *SEE* Kimmich, Johannes
Kimmich, Johann Martin *SEE* Kimmich, Matthias
Kimmich, Johannes; Pennsylvania, 1754 ***2444*** *p173*
*Wife:*Anna Maria Kuehner
*Child:*Jacob
Kimmich, Matthaus *SEE* Kimmich, Matthias
Kimmich, Matthias; Pennsylvania, 1754 ***2444*** *p173*
*Wife:*Anna Catharina Thumm
*Child:*Matthaus
*Child:*Anna
*Child:*Hans Jerg
*Child:*Anna Catharina
*Child:*Johann Martin
*Child:*Anna Maria
Kimmin, Samuel; America, 1738 ***4971*** *p66*
Kimmmerlin, Hans Martin; Philadelphia, 1751 ***2444*** *p180*
Kimsey, Benjamin; North Carolina, 1725-1827 ***1639.20*** *p106*

Kitchiner, Joseph 27; Jamaica, 1731 ***3690.1*** *p135*
Kite, Thomas 15; Philadelphia, 1774 ***1219.7*** *p185*
Kithley, Thomas; Virginia, 1642 ***6219*** *p15*
Kitnocker, Goodlive; Ohio, 1851 ***9892.11*** *p25*
Kitsenlander, Anna Barbara Brunner *SEE* Kitsenlander, Christian
Kitsenlander, Christian; Philadelphia, 1729 ***2854*** *p44*
*Wife:*Anna Barbara Brunner
With son 6
With daughter 5
Kitsintander, Anna Barbara Brunner *SEE* Kitsintander, Christian
Kitsintander, Christian; Philadelphia, 1729 ***2854*** *p44*
*Wife:*Anna Barbara Brunner
With son 6
With daughter 5
Kitson, Merina; Virginia, 1636 ***6219*** *p7*
Kittel, Barbara *SEE* Kittel, Hans Jerg
Kittel, Hans Jerg; Pennsylvania, 1754 ***2444*** *p174*
*Wife:*Barbara
*Child:*Rosina Magdalena
*Child:*Maria Barbara
Kittel, Maria Barbara *SEE* Kittel, Hans Jerg
Kittel, Rosina Magdalena *SEE* Kittel, Hans Jerg
Kittle, George; Pennsylvania, 1754 ***2444*** *p174*
Kittner, Carl 42?; Ohio, 1865 ***9892.11*** *p25*
Kitto, James; New York, 1890 ***9678.2*** *p62*
Kitts, Michael; Philadelphia, 1793 ***8582.3*** *p84*
Kitz, Adam; Philadelphia, 1782 ***8137*** *p10*
Kitz, Hermann; Philadelphia, 1779 ***8137*** *p10*
Kitzel, C. von; Halifax, N.S., 1778 ***9786*** *p270*
Kitzel, C. von; New York, 1776 ***9786*** *p270*
Kiuc, Sebastian; America, 1900 ***7137*** *p169*
Kivich, Poffen B.; Illinois, 1864 ***7857*** *p4*
Kizer, . . .; Canada, 1776-1783 ***9786*** *p26*
Kizer, Frank Joseph; Washington, 1859-1920 ***2872.1*** *p21*
Kjeldgaard, Anders Christian Svante; Arkansas, 1918 ***95.2*** *p66*
Kjellberg, Victor; Iowa, 1866-1943 ***123.54*** *p28*
Kjellgren, M.; Minneapolis, 1881-1886 ***6410.35*** *p58*
Klaassen, Abraham H.; America, 1884 ***5240.1*** *p24*
Klaassen, Cornelius; Illinois, 1894 ***5012.37*** *p63*
Klaassen, Herman; America, 1884 ***5240.1*** *p24*
Klaassen, Jacob; Kansas, 1890 ***5240.1*** *p24*
Klaberg, Abraham; Ohio, 1816 ***8582.1*** *p47*
Kladas, Joachim; Wisconsin, n.d. ***9675.6*** *p132*
Klaen, George Adam; Virginia, 1855 ***4626.16*** *p14*
Klahold, . . .; Canada, 1776-1783 ***9786*** *p26*
Klaiber, Louis; Ohio, 1850 ***1450.2*** *p80A*
Klais, Catharina *SEE* Klais, Johann
Klais, Friedrich *SEE* Klais, Johann
Klais, Johann; Pennsylvania, 1751-1800 ***2444*** *p174*
*Wife:*Catharina
*Child:*Friedrich
Klam, Math.; Wisconsin, n.d. ***9675.6*** *p132*
Klamitter, Fritz; Shreveport, LA, 1878 ***7129*** *p45*
Klamm, Paul Herman; New York, NY, 1923 ***3455.4*** *p28*
Klandernd, Olof; Arkansas, 1918 ***95.2*** *p66*
Klane, Hubert; New York, NY, 1839 ***8208.4*** *p97*
Klanjac, Matt; Iowa, 1866-1943 ***123.54*** *p67*
Klanveiller, Jean 22; New Orleans, 1838 ***778.5*** *p295*
Klapf, John; Ohio, 1869-1887 ***8582*** *p16*
Klapproth, . . .; Canada, 1776-1783 ***9786*** *p26*
Klare, William F.; America, 1880 ***1450.2*** *p80A*
Klaric, Gust; Iowa, 1866-1943 ***123.54*** *p28*
Klaric, Josep; Iowa, 1866-1943 ***123.54*** *p28*
Klaric, Stefan; Arkansas, 1918 ***95.2*** *p66*
Klas, Jacob; Wisconsin, n.d. ***9675.6*** *p132*
Klasen, Kasper; Michigan, 1860 ***3702.7*** *p186*
Klasovsky, Stephen; America, 1887 ***7137*** *p169*
Klass, Saul; Arkansas, 1918 ***95.2*** *p66*
Klatte, Hans; Arkansas, 1918 ***95.2*** *p66*
Klatte, Oscar 33; Arizona, 1902 ***9228.40*** *p7*
Klatterer, . . .; Canada, 1776-1783 ***9786*** *p26*
Klauber, . . .; Canada, 1776-1783 ***9786*** *p26*
Klauk, John; Wisconsin, n.d. ***9675.6*** *p132*
Klauprecht, . . .; Cincinnati, 1837-1838 ***8582.1*** *p45*
Klauprecht, Emil; Cincinnati, 1788-1848 ***8582.3*** *p89*
Klauprecht, Emil; Cincinnati, 1830-1835 ***8582.3*** *p91*
Klauser, Fred; Wisconsin, n.d. ***9675.6*** *p132*
Klautsch, Nicholas; Wisconsin, n.d. ***9675.6*** *p132*
Klaymeier, John; Baltimore, 1845 ***8582.1*** *p18*
Kleber, Carl; Wisconsin, n.d. ***9675.6*** *p132*
Kleber, Emil; Ohio, 1881 ***3702.7*** *p434*
Klebonitz, . . .; Canada, 1776-1783 ***9786*** *p26*
Klebust, Carl; Illinois, 1860 ***5012.39*** *p90*
Klecha, Thekla 27; New York, 1912 ***9980.29*** *p71*
Klecker, Emil; Washington, 1859-1920 ***2872.1*** *p21*
Kleckly, John; South Carolina, 1788 ***7119*** *p199*
Kleczkowski, Stanislaw 40; New York, 1912 ***9980.29*** *p72*
Klee, Theodore; Indiana, 1845 ***9117*** *p17*
Kleebauer, Martin; New York, 1881 ***1450.2*** *p80A*
Kleefisch, Colonel; New York, 1861-1865 ***8582.3*** *p91*
Kleemann, . . .; Canada, 1776-1783 ***9786*** *p26*
Kleemann, Philipp Ludwig; America, 1855 ***4610.10*** *p157*
Kleenmann, . . .; Canada, 1776-1783 ***9786*** *p26*
Klehammer, Blasius; America, 1854 ***8582.3*** *p36*
Klehwer, . . .; Ohio, 1881 ***3702.7*** *p436*
Klei, Johanes; Wisconsin, n.d. ***9675.6*** *p132*
Kleimann, Martin; Illinois, 1894 ***2896.5*** *p21*
Kleimeier, Mr.; America, 1841-1858 ***4610.10*** *p145*
Kleimeier, Carl Dieterich; America, 1854 ***4610.10*** *p144*
Kleimeier, Heinrich Wilhelm; America, 1858 ***4610.10*** *p145*
Klein, . . .; Canada, 1776-1783 ***9786*** *p26*
Klein, Mr.; North Carolina, 1683-1817 ***3702.7*** *p2*
Klein, Mr. 81; America, 1895 ***1763*** *p40D*
Klein, A.; Kansas, 1892 ***5240.1*** *p24*
Klein, A. 30; Kansas, 1892 ***5240.1*** *p76*
Klein, Adam; Canada, 1776-1783 ***9786*** *p207A*
Klein, Adam 26; America, 1853 ***9162.8*** *p37*
Klein, Amanda; Wisconsin, n.d. ***9675.6*** *p132*
Klein, Andreas; Pennsylvania, 1751 ***4525*** *p228*
Klein, Andreas; Pennsylvania, 1753 ***4525*** *p228*
Klein, Andreas Michael; Pennsylvania, 1752 ***4525*** *p228*
With wife
With 2 children
Klein, Anna Elisabetha; America, 1744 ***8125.6*** *p22*
Klein, Anna Maria Ruckaber *SEE* Klein, Johann Jacob
Klein, Bruno Ernst; Wisconsin, n.d. ***9675.6*** *p132*
Klein, Carl; Indiana, 1876 ***5240.1*** *p24*
Klein, Christian G.; Cincinnati, 1869-1887 ***8582*** *p16*
Klein, Christophe 25; America, 1836 ***778.5*** *p295*
Klein, Dominic; Wisconsin, n.d. ***9675.6*** *p132*
Klein, Frederick; Illinois, 1872 ***5012.39*** *p26*
Klein, Friedrich H.; Cincinnati, 1816 ***8582.1*** *p51*
Klein, Friedrick; Illinois, 1874 ***5012.39*** *p91*
Klein, Georg; America, 1847 ***8582.3*** *p36*
Klein, Gertrudis *SEE* Klein, Michael
Klein, Hans Adam; America, 1709 ***9982*** *p24*
Klein, Heinrich; Philadelphia, 1737 ***9982*** *p25*
Klein, Henry; Indiana, 1876 ***5240.1*** *p24*
Klein, Henry; Wisconsin, n.d. ***9675.6*** *p132*
Klein, Jacob 45; Kansas, 1880 ***5240.1*** *p62*
Klein, Johan Nickles; Pennsylvania, 1753 ***4525*** *p228*
Klein, Johan Nickles; Pennsylvania, 1754 ***4525*** *p228*
Klein, Johann Jacob *SEE* Klein, Johann Jacob
Klein, Johann Jacob; Pennsylvania, 1755-1800 ***2444*** *p174*
*Wife:*Anna Maria Ruckaber
*Child:*Johann Jacob
Klein, Johann Martin; Surinam, 1700-1739 ***9898*** *p28*
Klein, Johannes; America, 1846 ***8582.3*** *p36*
Klein, John; New York, 1754 ***3652*** *p80*
Klein, John; Washington, 1859-1920 ***2872.1*** *p21*
Klein, John; Wisconsin, n.d. ***9675.6*** *p132*
Klein, John 22; Kansas, 1895 ***5240.1*** *p24*
Klein, John 22; Kansas, 1895 ***5240.1*** *p80*
Klein, John N.; Washington, 1859-1920 ***2872.1*** *p21*
Klein, Joseph; Cincinnati, 1869-1887 ***8582*** *p16*
Klein, Martin; Charleston, SC, 1775-1779 ***8582.2*** *p19*
Klein, Matee 40; America, 1838 ***778.5*** *p295*
Klein, Michael; Indiana, 1869-1887 ***8582*** *p16*
Klein, Michael; Pennsylvania, 1754 ***2444*** *p174*
Klein, Michael; Philadelphia, 1760 ***9973.7*** *p34*
Klein, Michael; Port uncertain, 1746-1800 ***2444*** *p174*
*Wife:*Gertrudis
*Child:*Regina Barbara
Klein, Michael 18; America, 1837 ***778.5*** *p295*
Klein, Michel 20; America, 1838 ***778.5*** *p295*
Klein, Michel 28; America, 1838 ***778.5*** *p295*
Klein, Moses 21; Kansas, 1901 ***5240.1*** *p82*
Klein, Moses 27; New Orleans, 1839 ***778.5*** *p295*
Klein, Nick; America, 1898 ***5240.1*** *p24*
Klein, Nicolaus; Pennsylvania, 1752 ***4525*** *p228*
With wife
With 3 children
Klein, Peter; Illinois, 1872 ***5012.39*** *p25*
Klein, Peter; Illinois, 1874 ***5012.39*** *p91*
Klein, Peter; Pennsylvania, 1854-1855 ***3702.7*** *p388*
Klein, Peter 26; Kansas, 1877 ***5240.1*** *p58*
Klein, Peter 29; Kansas, 1895 ***5240.1*** *p24*
Klein, Philipp; America, 1842 ***8582.2*** *p59*
Klein, Pierre 23; America, 1838 ***778.5*** *p295*
Klein, Regina Barbara *SEE* Klein, Michael
Kleinbrg, Heinrich; Kentucky, 1843 ***8582.3*** *p100*
Kleine, A. M. C. Charlotte *SEE* Kleine, Ernst Fr. W.
Kleine, A. M. Johanne *SEE* Kleine, Ernst Fr. W.
Kleine, Anne M. W. Dreckmeyer *SEE* Kleine, Ernst Gottlieb Friedrich
Kleine, Anne Marie Bredenhagen *SEE* Kleine, Carl Friedrich
Kleine, Bernard; Ohio, 1798-1818 ***8582.2*** *p54*
Kleine, Carl Friedrich; America, 1869 ***4610.10*** *p95*
*Wife:*Anne Marie Bredenhagen
*Son:*Heinrich Friedrich P.
Kleine, Christian; New York, NY, 1838 ***8208.4*** *p61*
Kleine, Christian H. Gottfried *SEE* Kleine, Ernst Fr. W.
Kleine, Ernst Fr. W.; America, 1885 ***4610.10*** *p160*
*Wife:*Friederike W Stallmann
*Child:*A. M. C. Charlotte
*Child:*A. M. Johanne
*Child:*Friederike Ilsabein
*Child:*Christian H. Gottfried
Kleine, Ernst Gottlieb Friedrich; America, 1854 ***4610.10*** *p156*
*Wife:*Anne M. W. Dreckmeyer
*Son:*Ernst H. Christian
Kleine, Ernst H. Christian *SEE* Kleine, Ernst Gottlieb Friedrich
Kleine, Friederike Ilsabein *SEE* Kleine, Ernst Fr. W.
Kleine, Friederike W Stallmann *SEE* Kleine, Ernst Fr. W.
Kleine, Friedrich; Cincinnati, 1830-1849 ***8582*** *p16*
Kleine, Friedrich Wilhelm; America, 1868 ***4610.10*** *p95*
Kleine, Heinrich Friedrich P. *SEE* Kleine, Carl Friedrich
Kleine, Jacob; Ohio, 1816 ***8582.1*** *p47*
Kleine, Joseph; Ohio, 1869-1887 ***8582*** *p16*
Kleine, Karoline; America, 1905 ***4610.10*** *p103*
Kleine-Garl, Ernst Fr. W.; America, 1885 ***4610.10*** *p160*
Kleiner, Fridolin; Cincinnati, 1850-1873 ***8582.1*** *p19*
Kleiner, Meinrad; New Orleans, 1850 ***8582.1*** *p19*
Kleinert, . . .; Canada, 1776-1783 ***9786*** *p26*
Kleing, . . .; Canada, 1776-1783 ***9786*** *p26*
Kleing, Albert; Canada, 1776-1783 ***9786*** *p242*
Kleinhans, Martin; Wisconsin, n.d. ***9675.6*** *p132*
Kleinheksel, Jane 27; New York, NY, 1847 ***3377.6*** *p11*
Kleinheksel, Mannes 30; New York, NY, 1847 ***3377.6*** *p11*
Kleinheksel, William 17; New York, NY, 1847 ***3377.6*** *p11*
Kleinhenn, George 34; America, 1837 ***778.5*** *p295*
Kleinman, Josef 25; New York, 1912 ***9980.29*** *p68*
Kleinmann, Gittel 5; New York, NY, 1878 ***9253*** *p46*
Kleinmann, Jacob 7; New York, NY, 1878 ***9253*** *p46*
Kleinmann, Lea 11 mos; New York, NY, 1878 ***9253*** *p46*
Kleinmann, Nachin 1 mo; New York, NY, 1878 ***9253*** *p46*
Kleinmann, Rose 33; New York, NY, 1878 ***9253*** *p46*
Kleinmeyer, Samuel Heinrich Wilhelm; America, 1850 ***4610.10*** *p139*
Kleinoehle, Wilhelm; America, 1850 ***8582.3*** *p37*
Kleinschmidt, . . .; Canada, 1776-1783 ***9786*** *p26*
Kleinschmidt, Amalie 14; New York, NY, 1862 ***9831.18*** *p16*
Kleinschmidt, Carl 5; New York, NY, 1862 ***9831.18*** *p16*
Kleinschmidt, Caroline 21; New York, NY, 1862 ***9831.18*** *p16*
Kleinschmidt, Caroline 22; New York, NY, 1862 ***9831.18*** *p16*
Kleinschmidt, Christian 49; New York, NY, 1862 ***9831.18*** *p16*
Kleinschmidt, Christine 19; New York, NY, 1862 ***9831.18*** *p16*
Kleinschmidt, Dorothea 35; New York, NY, 1862 ***9831.18*** *p16*
Kleinschmidt, Emilie 3; New York, NY, 1862 ***9831.18*** *p16*
Kleinschmidt, Ernst F.; Cincinnati, 1869-1887 ***8582*** *p16*
Kleinschmidt, Jacob; Illinois, 1844 ***8582.2*** *p51*
Kleinschmidt, Johann 8; New York, NY, 1862 ***9831.18*** *p16*
Kleinschmidt, Johann 19; New York, NY, 1862 ***9831.18*** *p16*
Kleinschmidt, Johann 53; New York, NY, 1862 ***9831.18*** *p16*
Kleinschmidt, Sophie 11; New York, NY, 1862 ***9831.18*** *p16*
Kleinschmidt, Sophie 44; New York, NY, 1862 ***9831.18*** *p16*
Kleinschmidt, Wilhelm 7; New York, NY, 1862 ***9831.18*** *p16*
Kleist, Fritz; America, 1854 ***8582.3*** *p37*
Klemans, Johann; Ohio, 1801-1802 ***8582.2*** *p55*
Klemens, Joseph; Wisconsin, n.d. ***9675.6*** *p132*
Klemens, Peter; Wisconsin, n.d. ***9675.6*** *p132*
Klemenz, Peter; Wisconsin, n.d. ***9675.6*** *p132*
Klemick, John; Illinois, 1897 ***5012.40*** *p55*
Klemke, Ferdinand; Wisconsin, n.d. ***9675.6*** *p132*
Klemme, Margaret; Milwaukee, 1875 ***4719.30*** *p257*
Klemmer, Anna Margaretha; Pennsylvania, 1743 ***1034.18*** *p21*
Klemmer, Henrich; Philadelphia, 1730 ***1034.18*** *p11*
*Son:*Johannes
Klemmer, Johannes *SEE* Klemmer, Henrich
Klemmer, Ludewig; Philadelphia, 1751 ***1034.18*** *p11*
Klemmer, Ludwig; Pennsylvania, 1747 ***1034.18*** *p11*
Klemmers, Johann Henrick; Philadelphia, 1730 ***1034.18*** *p11*
*Son:*Johannes

Klemmers, Johannes *SEE* Klemmers, Johann Henrick
Klemp, Carl; Wisconsin, n.d. ***9675.6*** *p132*
Klemp, Emil Rudolph; Wisconsin, n.d. ***9675.6*** *p132*
Klenke, Heinrich; Kentucky, 1843 ***8582.3*** *p100*
Klenofsky, Meyer; Arkansas, 1918 ***95.2*** *p66*
Klentz, George; New York, 1868 ***5240.1*** *p25*
Klenzmann, . . .; Canada, 1776-1783 ***9786*** *p26*
Klepacki, William P.; Arkansas, 1918 ***95.2*** *p66*
Kleper, Emil; Ohio, 1881 ***3702.7*** *p434*
Kleppe, Justin; Illinois, 1860 ***5012.38*** *p98*
Klepponk, Anthony; Wisconsin, n.d. ***9675.6*** *p132*
Klessig, Heinrich; Wisconsin, n.d. ***9675.6*** *p132*
Kletcher, . . .; Canada, 1776-1783 ***9786*** *p26*
Kletscher, . . .; Canada, 1776-1783 ***9786*** *p26*
Klett, Hans Jacob; America, 1751 ***2444*** *p174*
Klett, Hans Jacob; Pennsylvania, 1751 ***2444*** *p174*
Klette, Louis; Kentucky, 1841 ***8582.3*** *p97*
Klette, Louis; Kentucky, 1848 ***8582.3*** *p99*
Klette, Torger; Arkansas, 1918 ***95.2*** *p66*
Klewer, Emil; New York, 1881 ***3702.7*** *p426*
Kliefith, John; Wisconsin, n.d. ***9675.6*** *p132*
Kliefith, Theodore; Wisconsin, n.d. ***9675.6*** *p132*
Kliefuth, Carl; Wisconsin, n.d. ***9675.6*** *p132*
Kliest, Daniel; New York, 1749 ***3652*** *p71*
Kliewer, G. J.; Kansas, 1890 ***5240.1*** *p25*
Klimowski, Kasimir 22; New York, 1912 ***9980.29*** *p60*
Klimper, Friedrich; America, 1839 ***8582.1*** *p19*
Klimrath, Benjamin 22; Louisiana, 1820 ***778.5*** *p295*
Klinck, Dwight; Milwaukee, 1875 ***4719.30*** *p257*
Klinck, Georg Ludwig *SEE* Klinck, Johann Jacob
Klinck, Johann Friedrich *SEE* Klinck, Johann Jacob
Klinck, Johann Jacob; Pennsylvania, 1754 ***2444*** *p175*
*Wife:*Margaretha Fichter
*Child:*Johann Michael
*Child:*Johann Friedrich
*Child:*Georg Ludwig
Klinck, Johann Michael *SEE* Klinck, Johann Jacob
Klinck, Margaretha Fichter *SEE* Klinck, Johann Jacob
Klindera, Waclaw 23; California, 1872 ***2769.6*** *p3*
Kline, Mr.; North Carolina, 1683-1817 ***3702.7*** *p2*
Kline, Frederick; New York, 1879 ***1450.2*** *p80A*
Kline, Jacob; New York, NY, 1835 ***8208.4*** *p47*
Kline, Peter; Pennsylvania, 1854-1855 ***3702.7*** *p387*
Kline, Peter 29; Kansas, 1895 ***5240.1*** *p80*
Kline, Samuel; Shreveport, LA, 1879 ***7129*** *p45*
Kline, Thomas; Illinois, 1860 ***5012.38*** *p98*
Kling, . . .; Canada, 1776-1783 ***9786*** *p26*
Kling, Adam; Cincinnati, 1839 ***8582*** *p16*
Kling, Anna 43; America, 1836 ***778.5*** *p296*
Kling, Francisca 21; America, 1836 ***778.5*** *p296*
Kling, Frederick; New Orleans, 1846 ***2896.5*** *p21*
Kling, Michel 28; America, 1836 ***778.5*** *p296*
Klinge, . . .; Canada, 1776-1783 ***9786*** *p26*
Klinge, Alois; Illinois, 1894 ***2896.5*** *p21*
Klinge, Conrad 23; Kansas, 1873 ***5240.1*** *p54*
Klingel, Francis; New York, NY, 1838 ***8208.4*** *p67*
Klingele, Margaretha; Pennsylvania, 1750 ***2444*** *p175*
Klingelstein, Margaret Catherine; New York, 1752 ***3652*** *p76*
Klingemeyer, Conrad; Pennsylvania, 1751 ***2444*** *p175*
Klingenbrunn, . . .; Canada, 1776-1783 ***9786*** *p26*
Klingenmayer, Anna Maria *SEE* Klingenmayer, Conrad
Klingenmayer, Conrad *SEE* Klingenmayer, Conrad
Klingenmayer, Conrad; America, 1751 ***2444*** *p175*
*Wife:*Anna Maria
*Child:*Conrad
Klingenmayr, Johann Georg; America, 1753 ***2444*** *p175*
Klingenmeyr, Anna Maria *SEE* Klingenmeyr, Conrad
Klingenmeyr, Conrad *SEE* Klingenmeyr, Conrad
Klingenmeyr, Conrad; America, 1751 ***2444*** *p175*
*Wife:*Anna Maria
*Child:*Conrad
Klingenschmit, Daniel; Pennsylvania, 1738 ***4779.3*** *p13*
*Relative:*Frantz Daniel
Klingenschmit, Frantz Daniel *SEE* Klingenschmit, Daniel
Klinger, . . .; Canada, 1776-1783 ***9786*** *p26*
Klinger, Anna Maria; New York, NY, 1849 ***3702.7*** *p536*
Klinger, Barbara 20; New York, NY, 1851 ***3702.7*** *p543*
Klinger, Daniel; New York, NY, 1857 ***3702.7*** *p535*
*Wife:*Marie F. Kaiser
With 2 children
Klinger, Gottlieb 20; New York, NY, 1854 ***3702.7*** *p547*
Klinger, Katharina 18; New York, NY, 1854 ***3702.7*** *p534*
Klinger, Marie F. Kaiser *SEE* Klinger, Daniel
Klinger, Rosina; Canada, 1861 ***3702.7*** *p560*
Klinger, Rosina 20; New York, NY, 1859 ***3702.7*** *p556*
Klingersmith, Philip; Pennsylvania, 1765 ***4779.3*** *p13*
Klingl, Michael; Wisconsin, n.d. ***9675.6*** *p132*
Klingler, Joseph; America, 1832 ***8582.2*** *p60*
Klingler, Joseph; Cincinnati, 1869-1887 ***8582*** *p16*
Klingner, Johann Friederich August; America, 1848 ***8582.3*** *p37*
Klingsoerh, . . .; Canada, 1776-1783 ***9786*** *p26*
Klingstein, Ewald; America, 1874 ***1450.2*** *p19B*
Klink, Michael; Pennsylvania, 1754 ***2444*** *p175*
Klinker, John; New York, NY, 1904 ***3455.2*** *p95*
Klinkhammer, Heinrich; America, 1849 ***8582.2*** *p19*
Klinsman, William; Illinois, 1866 ***2896.5*** *p21*
Klipper, George; Ohio, 1869 ***6014.2*** *p7*
Klipstine, Michael; America, 1834 ***1450.2*** *p80A*
Klob, Anton; Wisconsin, n.d. ***9675.6*** *p132*
Klob, William; America, 1853 ***1450.2*** *p82A*
Klobichar, George; Iowa, 1866-1943 ***123.54*** *p28*
Klock, Johann Caspar; Pennsylvania, 1744 ***2444*** *p157*
Klocke, Anne Marie Louise *SEE* Klocke, Friedrich
Klocke, Friedrich; America, 1850 ***4610.10*** *p139*
*Wife:*Louise Dedert
*Child:*Anne Marie Louise
*Child:*Zacharias C. Heinrich
*Child:*Friedrich W. Gottlieb
*Child:*Wilhelm
Klocke, Friedrich W. Gottlieb *SEE* Klocke, Friedrich
Klocke, J. H.; Cincinnati, 1869-1887 ***8582*** *p16*
Klocke, Louise Dedert *SEE* Klocke, Friedrich
Klocke, Wilhelm *SEE* Klocke, Friedrich
Klocke, Zacharias C. Heinrich *SEE* Klocke, Friedrich
Klockow, Fredrick; Illinois, 1860 ***2764.35*** *p39*
Kloeber, John; Virginia, 1844 ***4626.16*** *p12*
Kloehn, John; Wisconsin, n.d. ***9675.6*** *p132*
Kloenne, J. H.; Cincinnati, 1830-1849 ***8582*** *p16*
Kloepfer, Christina *SEE* Kloepfer, Jerg Adam
Kloepfer, Jacobina Danzer *SEE* Kloepfer, Jerg Adam
Kloepfer, Jerg Adam; Pennsylvania, 1752 ***2444*** *p175*
*Wife:*Jacobina Danzer
*Child:*Maria Catharina
*Child:*Christina
Kloepfer, Maria Catharina *SEE* Kloepfer, Jerg Adam
Kloepfli Family ; Illinois, 1824-1827 ***8582.1*** *p54*
Kloes, Adam 75; Milwaukee, 1908 ***1763*** *p40D*
Kloety, Joseph; Wisconsin, n.d. ***9675.6*** *p132*
Kloetz, Christopher; New York, 1754 ***3652*** *p80*
Klofkorn, Friederich 30; Kansas, 1876 ***5240.1*** *p57*
Klofkorn, William 28; Kansas, 1877 ***5240.1*** *p25*
Klofkorn, William 28; Kansas, 1877 ***5240.1*** *p58*
Klolzsch, August 38; New Orleans, 1839 ***9420.2*** *p486*
*Wife:*Jane Frederke 30
Klolzsch, Jane Frederke 30 *SEE* Klolzsch, August
Klomann, Andreas; Pennsylvania, 1858 ***3702.7*** *p480*
*Brother:*Anton
Klomann, Anton *SEE* Klomann, Andreas
Klonhammer, Mrs. C.; Milwaukee, 1875 ***4719.30*** *p257*
Klonheimer, Mrs. C.; Milwaukee, 1875 ***4719.30*** *p257*
Klonoski, Barney; Arkansas, 1918 ***95.2*** *p67*
Kloos, Nicholaus; Wisconsin, n.d. ***9675.6*** *p132*
Klop, John; Wisconsin, n.d. ***9675.6*** *p132*
Klopffer, Louis; New York, NY, 1838 ***8208.4*** *p87*
Klopfstein, John 45; Kansas, 1890 ***5240.1*** *p75*
Klopp, John P.; Wisconsin, n.d. ***9675.6*** *p132*
Klopp, William; Wisconsin, n.d. ***9675.6*** *p132*
Klopper, Benno; Shreveport, LA, 1878 ***7129*** *p45*
Klos, Louis; Wisconsin, n.d. ***9675.6*** *p132*
Klos, Nicholas; Wisconsin, n.d. ***9675.6*** *p132*
Kloss, George 32; America, 1838 ***778.5*** *p296*
Kloss, Max Francis; Arkansas, 1918 ***95.2*** *p67*
Klosterbauer, . . .; Canada, 1776-1783 ***9786*** *p26*
Klostermann, Ennecke; Germantown, PA, 1684 ***2467.7*** *p5*
Klostermann, Johann Bernhard; America, 1847 ***8582.3*** *p37*
Klostermann, John; America, 1848 ***1450.2*** *p80A*
Klostermeyer, Miss; America, 1851 ***4610.10*** *p139*
Klostermeyer, Gottlieb; America, 1882 ***4610.10*** *p140*
Klotshow, Lonners; Illinois, 1858 ***2896.5*** *p21*
Klotter, Georg; Cincinnati, 1845 ***8582.3*** *p62*
Klotter, Georg, Sr.; Cincinnati, 1869-1887 ***8582*** *p16*
Klotter, Georg Friedrich; Cincinnati, 1869-1887 ***8582*** *p16*
Klotter, Johann Philipp; New Orleans, 1832 ***8582*** *p17*
Klotter, Philipp; Cincinnati, 1869-1887 ***8582*** *p17*
Klotz, Abraham 26; New Orleans, 1838 ***778.5*** *p296*
Klotz, Andrew; New York, 1888 ***1450.2*** *p20B*
Klotz, Anna Barbara; Port uncertain, 1717 ***3627*** *p13*
Klotz, Carl; Wisconsin, n.d. ***9675.6*** *p132*
Klotz, Emil; America, 1849 ***1450.2*** *p80A*
Klotz, Ernst; Wisconsin, n.d. ***9675.6*** *p132*
Klotz, Friderich 41; America, 1838 ***778.5*** *p296*
Klotz, Johann Jacob *SEE* Klotz, Johann Jacob
Klotz, Johann Jacob *SEE* Klotz, Johann Jacob
Klotz, Johann Jacob; Pennsylvania, 1749 ***2444*** *p175*
*Wife:*Martha Feissler
*Child:*Johann Jacob
*Child:*Ursula
*Child:*Johann Leonhard
Klotz, Johann Jacob; Port uncertain, 1749 ***2444*** *p175*
*Wife:*Martha Feissler
*Child:*Johann Jacob
*Child:*Ursula
*Child:*Johann Leonhard
Klotz, Johann Leonhard *SEE* Klotz, Johann Jacob
Klotz, Johann Leonhard *SEE* Klotz, Johann Jacob
Klotz, Marguerite 56; America, 1838 ***778.5*** *p296*
Klotz, Martha Feissler *SEE* Klotz, Johann Jacob
Klotz, Martha Feissler *SEE* Klotz, Johann Jacob
Klotz, Sophia Catharina; Pennsylvania, 1717 ***3627*** *p11*
Klotz, Ursula *SEE* Klotz, Johann Jacob
Klotz, Ursula *SEE* Klotz, Johann Jacob
Klotzbuecher, Dorothea; Pennsylvania, 1729-1800 ***2444*** *p175*
Kloz, Johann Jacob; Pennsylvania, 1749 ***2444*** *p175*
Kloz, Johann Jacob; Port uncertain, 1749 ***2444*** *p175*
Klucar, Peter; Pennsylvania, 1900 ***7137*** *p169*
Kludius, . . .; Canada, 1776-1783 ***9786*** *p26*
Klueber, Joseph; Cincinnati, 1869-1887 ***8582*** *p17*
Kluemper, Joseph; America, 1844 ***8582.2*** *p19*
Klug, August; Wisconsin, n.d. ***9675.6*** *p132*
Klug, Charles; Wisconsin, n.d. ***9675.6*** *p132*
Klug, Frank; Wisconsin, n.d. ***9675.6*** *p132*
Klug, Frederick; Wisconsin, n.d. ***9675.6*** *p132*
Klug, Henry; Wisconsin, n.d. ***9675.6*** *p132*
Klug, John; Wisconsin, n.d. ***9675.6*** *p132*
Klug, William; Wisconsin, n.d. ***9675.6*** *p132*
Kluge, . . .; Canada, 1776-1783 ***9786*** *p26*
Kluge, Anna M. Wilhelmine *SEE* Kluge, Carl Friedrich
Kluge, Anne Marie Engel *SEE* Kluge, Carl Friedrich
Kluge, Carl Friedrich; America, 1850 ***4610.10*** *p143*
*Wife:*Anne Marie Engel
*Child:*Anna M. Wilhelmine
*Child:*Wilhelm Bruning
Kluge, Michael; Wisconsin, n.d. ***9675.6*** *p132*
Kluge, Wilhelm Bruning *SEE* Kluge, Carl Friedrich
Klugel, Eva Rosina 60; New Orleans, 1839 ***9420.1*** *p376*
Klugel, Georg 38; New Orleans, 1839 ***9420.1*** *p376*
Klugel, Georg 66; New Orleans, 1839 ***9420.1*** *p376*
Klugel, Gottb. 32; New Orleans, 1839 ***9420.2*** *p167*
Klugel, Gottlob 26; New Orleans, 1839 ***9420.1*** *p376*
Klugel, Wilh. 37; New Orleans, 1839 ***9420.1*** *p376*
Klugel, Xissine 22; New Orleans, 1839 ***9420.1*** *p376*
Klum, James; Washington, 1859-1920 ***2872.1*** *p21*
Klumb, Fredrich J.; Wisconsin, n.d. ***9675.6*** *p132*
Klumb, Friedrich Jacob; Wisconsin, n.d. ***9675.6*** *p132*
Klumb, Jacob; Wisconsin, n.d. ***9675.6*** *p132*
Klumok, Sam; Arkansas, 1918 ***95.2*** *p67*
Klump, Moritz; America, 1853 ***8582.3*** *p37*
Klumper, Diena; New York, NY, 1847 ***3377.6*** *p15*
Klumper, Frederick 11; New York, NY, 1847 ***3377.6*** *p15*
Klumper, Gerrit John; New York, NY, 1847 ***3377.6*** *p15*
Klumper, Hendrik 37; New York, NY, 1847 ***3377.6*** *p15*
Klumper, Johanna 35; New York, NY, 1847 ***3377.6*** *p15*
Klumpp, Andrew David Frederick; New York, 1854 ***1450.2*** *p80A*
Klunn, James; Washington, 1859-1920 ***2872.1*** *p21*
Kluntz, Georg; Philadelphia, 1831 ***8582.2*** *p19*
Klunz, Georg; Ohio, 1869-1887 ***8582*** *p17*
Klusgenbergen, Miss; America, 1854 ***4610.10*** *p144*
Klusman, Lewis; Baltimore, 1846 ***1450.2*** *p80A*
Klusmann, . . .; Canada, 1776-1783 ***9786*** *p26*
Kluss, Michael Bruno; New York, NY, 1835 ***8208.4*** *p59*
Klussmann, . . .; Canada, 1776-1783 ***9786*** *p26*
Klute, Carl Heinrich; America, 1886 ***4610.10*** *p110*
Klute, Carl Heinrich Ferdinand; America, 1872 ***4610.10*** *p109*
Kluth, J. Fred 44; Kansas, 1902 ***5240.1*** *p82*
Klutt, Adolf; Washington, 1859-1920 ***2872.1*** *p21*
Klutt, Edward; Washington, 1859-1920 ***2872.1*** *p21*
Klutt, Emil; Washington, 1859-1920 ***2872.1*** *p21*
Klutt, Evrald; Washington, 1859-1920 ***2872.1*** *p21*
Klutt, Hertha; Washington, 1859-1920 ***2872.1*** *p21*
Klutt, Hulda; Washington, 1859-1920 ***2872.1*** *p21*
Klutt, Matilda; Washington, 1859-1920 ***2872.1*** *p21*
Klutt, Reinhold; Washington, 1859-1920 ***2872.1*** *p21*
Kmilenskis, Paul; Wisconsin, n.d. ***9675.6*** *p132*
Kmith, Joseph; Wisconsin, n.d. ***9675.6*** *p132*
Knaack, Auguste 60; Kansas, 1874 ***5240.1*** *p55*
Knab, . . .; Canada, 1776-1783 ***9786*** *p26*
Knab, Fritz; South Carolina, 1788 ***7119*** *p203*
Knab, Peter; South Carolina, 1788 ***7119*** *p203*
Knab, Philip Peter; South Carolina, 1788 ***7119*** *p203*
Knabe, . . .; America, n.d. ***8582.3*** *p79*
Knabe, Albert; America, 1830 ***8582.2*** *p61*
Knabe, Albert; Indiana, 1869-1887 ***8582*** *p17*
Knabe, Maurice H.; Wisconsin, n.d. ***9675.6*** *p132*
Knabe, Wilhelm; Baltimore, 1833 ***8582*** *p17*
Knabenschube, . . .; Canada, 1776-1783 ***9786*** *p26*
Knadlar, Anton 28; Kansas, 1873 ***5240.1*** *p54*
Knae, Theodore Joseph; Arkansas, 1918 ***95.2*** *p67*

Knaebel, Aloys 22; America, 1838 ***778.5*** *p296*
Knaebel, Caspar 28; America, 1838 ***778.5*** *p296*
Knaebel, G. 22; America, 1838 ***778.5*** *p296*
Knaebel, Georg L.; New York, NY, 1847 ***8582.1*** *p19*
Knaebel, Simon; Kentucky, 1840-1845 ***8582.3*** *p100*
Knaff, John Peter; Wisconsin, n.d. ***9675.6*** *p132*
Knall, Simon; Kentucky, 1844 ***8582.3*** *p101*
Knap, . . .; Canada, 1776-1783 ***9786*** *p26*
Knapp, Adam 17; America, 1853 ***9162.8*** *p36*
Knapp, David; New York, NY, 1839 ***8208.4*** *p90*
Knapp, Elis. 55; America, 1853 ***9162.8*** *p36*
Knapp, Elisabetha 11 mos; America, 1853 ***9162.8*** *p36*
Knapp, Elizabeth; Washington, 1859-1920 ***2872.1*** *p21*
Knapp, Eva 27; America, 1853 ***9162.8*** *p36*
Knapp, Fred; Washington, 1859-1920 ***2872.1*** *p21*
Knapp, Frederick Wilhelm; Washington, 1859-1920 ***2872.1*** *p21*
Knapp, George M.; Illinois, 1860 ***7857*** *p4*
Knapp, Herman Fredrick; Washington, 1859-1920 ***2872.1*** *p21*
Knapp, John; Pennsylvania, 1752 ***4779.3*** *p14A*
Knapp, Karl Adolf; Washington, 1859-1920 ***2872.1*** *p21*
Knapp, Kath. 23; America, 1853 ***9162.8*** *p36*
Knapp, Louis 17; New Orleans, 1835 ***778.5*** *p296*
Knapp, Louise Marie; Washington, 1859-1920 ***2872.1*** *p21*
Knapp, Martha Pauline; Washington, 1859-1920 ***2872.1*** *p21*
Knapp, P. J.; Washington, 1859-1920 ***2872.1*** *p21*
Knapp, Rudolph; Washington, 1859-1920 ***2872.1*** *p21*
Knapp, Uzal; America, 1777-1778 ***8582.2*** *p67*
Knapp, William; Virginia, 1641 ***6219*** *p187*
Knapper, Frederick; South Carolina, 1752-1753 ***3689.17*** *p22*
With wife
Knapple, Frederick; Wisconsin, n.d. ***9675.6*** *p132*
Knappmeyer, Heinrich 23; America, 1877 ***4610.10*** *p106*
Knapton, Charles; Barbados, 1767 ***1219.7*** *p134*
Knapton, Thomas J.; America, 1852 ***1450.2*** *p81A*
Knaub, John; Wisconsin, n.d. ***9675.6*** *p132*
Knaub, Sophia; Wisconsin, n.d. ***9675.6*** *p132*
Knauber, Jacob; America, 1846 ***8582.1*** *p19*
Knaubes, Martin; New York, NY, 1840 ***8208.4*** *p110*
Knauer, . . .; Pennsylvania, 1753 ***4525*** *p229*
Knauer, Andreas; New England, 1751 ***4525*** *p228*
*Wife:*Magdalena
With 9 children
Knauer, Andreas; Pennsylvania, 1751 ***4525*** *p228*
Knauer, Hans; Pennsylvania, 1751 ***4525*** *p228*
Knauer, Hans Petter; Pennsylvania, 1751 ***4525*** *p228*
Knauer, Johann Caspar; Pennsylvania, 1754 ***4525*** *p229*
Knauer, Magdalena *SEE* Knauer, Andreas
Knauf, Adam; America, 1854 ***1450.2*** *p81A*
Knauff, . . .; Canada, 1776-1783 ***9786*** *p26*
Knauff, Georg Henrich; Philadelphia, 1779 ***8137*** *p10*
Knauff, Henrich; Philadelphia, 1779 ***8137*** *p10*
Knaus, Anna Maria *SEE* Knaus, Johann Jacob
Knaus, Georg Jacob *SEE* Knaus, Johann Jacob
Knaus, Johann Georg *SEE* Knaus, Johann Jacob
Knaus, Johann Jacob; Pennsylvania, 1736-1785 ***2444*** *p175*
*Wife:*Anna Maria
*Child:*Georg Jacob
*Child:*Johann Georg
Knaus, S.; Ohio, 1868 ***6014.2*** *p7*
Knauthe, Henreeh E.; Wisconsin, n.d. ***9675.6*** *p132*
Knavin, Catherine; America, 1739 ***4971*** *p52*
Knavin, Timothy; America, 1739 ***4971*** *p52*
Kncinig, Martin; Iowa, 1866-1943 ***123.54*** *p28*
Kneale, Thomas; Colorado, 1890 ***9678.2*** *p62*
Knebel, Harman; New York, NY, 1836 ***8208.4*** *p24*
Knebler, Michel 32; Kansas, 1876 ***5240.1*** *p58*
Knebusch, Theodore; Wisconsin, n.d. ***9675.6*** *p132*
Knecht, Albert; Illinois, 1896 ***5012.40*** *p55*
Knecht, Daniel; Illinois, 1877 ***2896.5*** *p21*
Knecht, Emanuel; South Dakota, 1889 ***1641*** *p41*
Knecht, Ferdinand; South Dakota, 1889 ***1641*** *p41*
Knecht, Gottfried; Philadelphia, 1806 ***8125.8*** *p437*
Knecht, Katharine; South Dakota, 1889 ***1641*** *p41*
Knedler, George; Pennsylvania, 1750 ***2444*** *p176*
Knee, John 20; Philadelphia, 1854 ***5704.8*** *p117*
Knee, John 25; Massachusetts, 1847 ***5881.1*** *p53*
Kneebone, George; Colorado, 1893 ***9678.2*** *p62*
Kneedler, Hans Jerg; Pennsylvania, 1750 ***2444*** *p176*
Kneese, Wilhelm 34; Kansas, 1879 ***5240.1*** *p60*
Kneeshan, William S.; Illinois, 1869 ***5012.38*** *p99*
Knefelskamp, Johann Heinrich; America, 1854 ***4610.10*** *p151*
Kneidler, Hans Yerick; Pennsylvania, 1750 ***2444*** *p176*
Kneipp, Henry; Shreveport, LA, 1874 ***7129*** *p45*
Knell, Nicolas; Wisconsin, n.d. ***9675.6*** *p132*
Knell, Simon; Kentucky, 1844 ***8582.3*** *p101*
Kneppel, Gottfried; Wisconsin, n.d. ***9675.6*** *p132*
Knepper, Edward; Wisconsin, n.d. ***9675.6*** *p132*
Knepper, John B.; Wisconsin, n.d. ***9675.6*** *p132*
Knerr, Johann Nikolaus, Family; America, 1810-1923 ***2691.4*** *p171*
Knesebeck, v.d., Lieut.; Quebec, 1776 ***9786*** *p105*
Knesebeck, Friedrich; Quebec, 1776 ***9786*** *p254*
Knesse, Fredrick 45; Kansas, 1875 ***5240.1*** *p56*
Knesser, C.; Canada, 1776-1783 ***9786*** *p207A*
Knet, Francis 15; Maryland, 1775 ***1219.7*** *p253*
Knetcht, H. 25; Port uncertain, 1838 ***778.5*** *p296*
Kneubuehler, Julius; Washington, 1859-1920 ***2872.1*** *p21*
Kneucker, Apollonia; New England, 1752 ***4525*** *p221*
Kneucker, Apollonia 33; Pennsylvania, 1752 ***4525*** *p229*
With child 2
Knich, Jozef 28; New York, 1912 ***9980.29*** *p56*
Knickelbein, Fred; Wisconsin, n.d. ***9675.6*** *p132*
Knieling, Johannes; Philadelphia, 1779 ***8137*** *p10*
Knieriem, Kaspar; Philadelphia, 1779 ***8137*** *p10*
Knies, Johannes; Halifax, N.S., 1778 ***9786*** *p270*
Knies, Johannes; New York, 1776 ***9786*** *p270*
Kniese, Konrad; Philadelphia, 1779 ***8137*** *p10*
Knight, Ann; Pennsylvania, 1682 ***4962*** *p149*
Knight, Christobell; Virginia, 1639 ***6219*** *p154*
Knight, Edmund; Virginia, 1638 ***6219*** *p150*
Knight, Edmund; Virginia, 1642 ***6219*** *p188*
Knight, Eliza; New York, NY, 1865 ***5704.8*** *p195*
Knight, Francis 24; Jamaica, 1724 ***3690.1*** *p135*
Knight, George; Iowa, 1866-1943 ***123.54*** *p28*
Knight, Giles; Pennsylvania, 1682 ***4962*** *p148*
*Wife:*Mary English
*Son:*Joseph
Knight, Griffin 26; Maryland, 1774 ***1219.7*** *p225*
Knight, Harry S.; Colorado, 1904 ***9678.2*** *p62*
Knight, Henry 22; Jamaica, 1730 ***3690.1*** *p135*
Knight, Jacob 21; Maryland, 1774 ***1219.7*** *p204*
Knight, James; America, 1735-1743 ***4971*** *p8*
Knight, James; Quebec, 1785 ***7603*** *p24*
Knight, James 17; Pennsylvania, Virginia or Maryland, 1728 ***3690.1*** *p135*
Knight, Jane 30; America, 1702 ***2212*** *p36*
Knight, John 16; Maryland, 1774 ***1219.7*** *p244*
Knight, John 19; Maryland, 1774 ***1219.7*** *p236*
Knight, John 25; Virginia, 1774 ***1219.7*** *p201*
Knight, John 26; Maryland, 1774 ***1219.7*** *p178*
Knight, John Conrad; Philadelphia, 1764 ***9973.7*** *p39*
Knight, Jon.; Virginia, 1642 ***6219*** *p197*
Knight, Joseph *SEE* Knight, Giles
Knight, Mary; New York, NY, 1865 ***5704.8*** *p195*
Knight, Mary English *SEE* Knight, Giles
Knight, Peter; Philadelphia, 1757 ***9973.7*** *p33*
Knight, Peter; Virginia, 1638 ***6219*** *p17*
Knight, Peter; Virginia, 1643 ***6219*** *p241*
Knight, Peter; Virginia, 1652 ***6251*** *p19*
Knight, Richard; Virginia, 1646 ***6219*** *p244*
Knight, Robert; Virginia, 1638 ***6219*** *p148*
Knight, Robert; Virginia, 1648 ***6219*** *p250*
Knight, Robert 19; Pennsylvania, Virginia or Maryland, 1719 ***3690.1*** *p135*
Knight, Robert 25; Philadelphia, 1775 ***1219.7*** *p255*
Knight, Robert 26; Carolina, 1774 ***1219.7*** *p179*
Knight, Thomas 21; Jamaica, 1730 ***3690.1*** *p135*
Knight, Tomasin; Virginia, 1643 ***6219*** *p201*
Knight, William; Illinois, 1845 ***7857*** *p4*
Knight, William; Virginia, 1642 ***6219*** *p194*
Knight, Wm.; Austin, TX, 1886 ***9777*** *p5*
Knight, Wm.; Virginia, 1648 ***6219*** *p250*
Knighton, John; Virginia, 1643 ***6219*** *p200*
Knighton, Walter; Illinois, 1892 ***5012.37*** *p62*
Knill, Thomas; Colorado, 1892 ***9678.2*** *p62*
Knipe, William; New York, NY, 1837 ***8208.4*** *p32*
Knipes, William; Port uncertain, 1834 ***778.5*** *p296*
Knippenberg, Gerhard; Wisconsin, n.d. ***9675.6*** *p132*
Knipping, Friedrich; Philadelphia, 1777-1779 ***8137*** *p10*
Knipschild, . . .; Canada, 1776-1783 ***9786*** *p26*
Kniratsch, . . .; Canada, 1776-1783 ***9786*** *p26*
Knispel, O.C.; Illinois, 1888 ***2896.5*** *p21*
Knittel, Johann Georg *SEE* Knittel, Joseph
Knittel, Joseph 40; Pennsylvania, 1753 ***2444*** *p176*
*Wife:*Regina M. Fueglin
*Child:*Johann Georg
Knittel, Regina M. Fueglin *SEE* Knittel, Joseph
Knivenhoven, Dirk 27; Kansas, 1904 ***5240.1*** *p83*
Knobel, Godfrey; America, 1851 ***6014.1*** *p2*
Knobelich, Adam; Pennsylvania, 1754 ***2444*** *p176*
Knobelick, Adam; Pennsylvania, 1754 ***2444*** *p176*
Knoblanch, Charles; Wisconsin, n.d. ***9675.6*** *p132*
Knoblanch, J. B., Jr.; Kansas, 1893 ***5240.1*** *p25*
Knoblanch, John; Minnesota, 1874 ***5240.1*** *p25*
Knoblanch, Joseph; Minnesota, 1874 ***5240.1*** *p25*
Knoblauch, Adam; Pennsylvania, 1767 ***2444*** *p176*
Knoblauch, Theresa 22; Kansas, 1879 ***5240.1*** *p60*
Knobloch, Anna Maria Kayser *SEE* Knobloch, Hans Adam
Knobloch, Hans Adam; America, 1752-1800 ***2444*** *p176*
*Wife:*Anna Maria Kayser
*Child:*Johann Martin
Knobloch, Joh Gorg; Philadelphia, 1756 ***4525*** *p262*
Knobloch, Johann Martin *SEE* Knobloch, Hans Adam
Knobloch, Johann Martin; Pennsylvania, 1764 ***2444*** *p176*
Knoblock, Adam; Pennsylvania, 1754-1767 ***2444*** *p176*
Knock, Richard; New York, NY, 1834 ***8208.4*** *p56*
Knockins, William; America, 1739 ***4971*** *p46*
Knockins, William; America, 1739 ***4971*** *p47*
Knodel, Georg; Ohio, 1811 ***8582.1*** *p48*
Knodel, Johann Friedrich; Pennsylvania, 1714-1785 ***2444*** *p176*
With wife & 6 children
Knodel, Johann Friedrich; Port uncertain, 1752 ***2444*** *p176*
With wife & 6 children
Knodlin, Catharina; Pennsylvania, 1751 ***2444*** *p136*
Knoedeler, Hans Jurg; Pennsylvania, 1750 ***2444*** *p176*
Knoedler, Andreas; Pennsylvania, 1750 ***2444*** *p176*
Knoedler, Hans Georg; America, 1750 ***2444*** *p176*
*Wife:*Maria E. Heussler
Knoedler, Maria E. Heussler *SEE* Knoedler, Hans Georg
Knoefler, Christian; Wisconsin, n.d. ***9675.6*** *p132*
Knoerr, Adam; Wisconsin, n.d. ***9675.6*** *p132*
Knoertzer, Balthazer; Philadelphia, 1751 ***9973.7*** *p31*
Knol, Jn. Baptiste 40; America, 1838 ***778.5*** *p296*
Knol, John; Iowa, 1866-1943 ***123.54*** *p28*
Knoll, Ann Maria 26; Port uncertain, 1836 ***778.5*** *p296*
Knoll, Charles 2; Port uncertain, 1836 ***778.5*** *p297*
Knoll, Eva Barbara *SEE* Knoll, George Ludwig
Knoll, Franz; America, 1846 ***8582.3*** *p37*
Knoll, Georg Ludwig *SEE* Knoll, George Ludwig
Knoll, George Ludwig; Pennsylvania, 1751 ***2444*** *p177*
*Wife:*Ursula Barbara
*Child:*Eva Barbara
*Child:*Georg Ludwig
Knoll, Margaretha *SEE* Knoll, Margaretha
Knoll, Margaretha; Pennsylvania, 1744-1800 ***2444*** *p176*
*Child:*Margaretha
Knoll, Peter Paul 36; Port uncertain, 1836 ***778.5*** *p297*
Knoll, Ursula Barbara *SEE* Knoll, George Ludwig
Knoller, Johan Philip; New York, NY, 1838 ***8208.4*** *p62*
Knolls, Albert Laurence; Kansas, 1914 ***6013.40*** *p16*
Knolton, Hannah *SEE* Knolton, William P.
Knolton, William P.; Philadelphia, 1745 ***3652*** *p67*
*Wife:*Hannah
Knoop, Anne Marie Louise; America, 1857 ***4610.10*** *p136*
Knoop, Henry; Illinois, 1886 ***5012.39*** *p120*
Knop, Carl; Wisconsin, n.d. ***9675.6*** *p132*
Knop, Fred; Wisconsin, n.d. ***9675.6*** *p132*
Knop, Julius; Arkansas, 1918 ***95.2*** *p67*
Knop, Ludwig; Wisconsin, n.d. ***9675.6*** *p132*
Knor, Johann; Pennsylvania, 1751 ***4525*** *p228*
Knor, Johann Melchior; Pennsylvania, 1751 ***4525*** *p228*
Knor, Johannes; Pennsylvania, 1751 ***4525*** *p228*
Knore, Johann Melchior; Pennsylvania, 1751 ***4525*** *p228*
Knore, Johannes; Pennsylvania, 1751 ***4525*** *p228*
Knornschild, Adam; Illinois, 1872 ***7857*** *p4*
Knorr, Christian Friedr. 3; New Orleans, 1839 ***9420.1*** *p378*
Knorr, Christian Friedr. 38; New Orleans, 1839 ***9420.1*** *p377*
Knorr, Georg; America, 1853 ***8582.3*** *p37*
Knorr, Joh. Eleonore 8; New Orleans, 1839 ***9420.1*** *p378*
Knorr, Johann; Pennsylvania, 1751 ***4525*** *p228*
Knorr, Johann C.; America, 1849 ***8582.3*** *p37*
Knorr, Johanne Rosine 36; New Orleans, 1839 ***9420.1*** *p377*
Knorr, Johanne Sophia 10; New Orleans, 1839 ***9420.1*** *p377*
Knorr, Johannes; Pennsylvania, 1751 ***4525*** *p228*
Knospe, Christian; New York, NY, 1856 ***2896.5*** *p21*
Knott, Elianor *SEE* Knott, James
Knott, James; Virginia, 1635 ***6219*** *p17*
*Wife:*Elianor
Knott, Jesse; Arkansas, 1918 ***95.2*** *p67*
Knott, Richard; Virginia, 1642 ***6219*** *p194*
Knott, Samuel G.; Colorado, 1892 ***9678.2*** *p122*
Knott, William; Illinois, 1872 ***7857*** *p4*
Knowart, Kunegunda 54; Georgia, 1738 ***9332*** *p330*
Knowells, Henry; Virginia, 1648 ***6219*** *p246*
Knowland, James; New York, NY, 1838 ***8208.4*** *p70*
Knowler, Thos.; Virginia, 1621 ***6219*** *p67*
Knowles, Edmd 15; America, 1700 ***2212*** *p31*
Knowles, George Wright; Montreal, 1769 ***1219.7*** *p139*
Knowles, John; New Bern, NC, 1811 ***1639.20*** *p108*
Knowles, Nich.; Virginia, 1642 ***6219*** *p191*
Knowles, Robert; Pennsylvania, 1761 ***1219.7*** *p81*
Knowles, Wm.; Virginia, 1645 ***6219*** *p253*
Knows, Jacob; Pennsylvania, 1736-1785 ***2444*** *p175*
Knox, Ann; Quebec, 1825 ***7603*** *p68*

Knox, Cunningham; Quebec, 1849 ***5704.8*** *p51*
Knox, David 28; Philadelphia, 1854 ***5704.8*** *p123*
Knox, Dean; New York, NY, 1811 ***2859.11*** *p14*
Knox, Eliza 16; Philadelphia, 1853 ***5704.8*** *p114*
Knox, Ellen; Quebec, 1850 ***5704.8*** *p70*
Knox, Ellen 9; Philadelphia, 1865 ***5704.8*** *p191*
Knox, George; Quebec, 1852 ***5704.8*** *p89*
Knox, Hugh; Quebec, 1847 ***5704.8*** *p16*
Knox, Hugh 24; Massachusetts, 1849 ***5881.1*** *p53*
Knox, James; America, 1740 ***1639.20*** *p108*
Knox, James; Kansas, 1891 ***5240.1*** *p25*
Knox, James; New Orleans, 1848 ***5704.8*** *p48*
Knox, James; New York, NY, 1811 ***2859.11*** *p14*
With family
Knox, James; New York, NY, 1815 ***2859.11*** *p35*
Knox, Jane; New York, NY, 1811 ***2859.11*** *p14*
Knox, Jane; Quebec, 1847 ***5704.8*** *p16*
Knox, Jane; Quebec, 1853 ***5704.8*** *p103*
Knox, Jane 20; Quebec, 1856 ***5704.8*** *p129*
Knox, Janet 57; St. John, N.B., 1862 ***5704.8*** *p150*
Knox, John; Philadelphia, 1853 ***5704.8*** *p101*
Knox, John; Philadelphia, 1865 ***5704.8*** *p191*
Knox, John; Quebec, 1850 ***5704.8*** *p70*
Knox, John; St. John, N.B., 1848 ***5704.8*** *p39*
Knox, John 9 mos; Quebec, 1850 ***5704.8*** *p70*
Knox, John 1; Philadelphia, 1865 ***5704.8*** *p191*
Knox, John James 18; Philadelphia, 1853 ***5704.8*** *p114*
Knox, Joseph; New York, NY, 1811 ***2859.11*** *p14*
Knox, Ledia 40; Philadelphia, 1853 ***5704.8*** *p114*
Knox, Marcus; Arkansas, 1918 ***95.2*** *p67*
Knox, Mary; Philadelphia, 1852 ***5704.8*** *p89*
Knox, Mary; Philadelphia, 1853 ***5704.8*** *p101*
Knox, Mary 13; Philadelphia, 1853 ***5704.8*** *p114*
Knox, Mary Jane; Philadelphia, 1848 ***53.26*** *p44*
Knox, Mary Jane; Philadelphia, 1848 ***5704.8*** *p45*
Knox, Matilda; Philadelphia, 1865 ***5704.8*** *p191*
Knox, Rebecca 20; Quebec, 1853 ***5704.8*** *p105*
Knox, Rose Ann; Philadelphia, 1865 ***5704.8*** *p187*
Knox, Thomas; New York, NY, 1811 ***2859.11*** *p14*
Knox, Thomas; Quebec, 1853 ***5704.8*** *p103*
Knox, Walter; Charleston, SC, 1806 ***1639.20*** *p108*
Knox, Walter; Philadelphia, 1853 ***5704.8*** *p101*
Knox, William; America, 1864 ***5240.1*** *p25*
Knox, William; New York, NY, 1811 ***2859.11*** *p14*
Knox, William; Philadelphia, 1811 ***53.26*** *p44*
Knox, William; Philadelphia, 1847 ***53.26*** *p44*
Knox, William; Philadelphia, 1847 ***5704.8*** *p31*
Knox, William 3; Philadelphia, 1865 ***5704.8*** *p191*
Knox, William 11; Philadelphia, 1853 ***5704.8*** *p114*
Knox, William 18; Philadelphia, 1860 ***5704.8*** *p145*
Knox, William 37; Maryland, 1775 ***1219.7*** *p267*
Knox, Wm.; Philadelphia, 1811 ***2859.11*** *p14*
Knuckey, Richard 57; Arizona, 1900 ***9228.40*** *p7*
Knudsen, Mads Madsen; Arkansas, 1918 ***95.2*** *p67*
Knudsen, Syvert; Washington, 1859-1920 ***2872.1*** *p21*
Knudsen, Thorwald 25; Arkansas, 1918 ***95.2*** *p67*
Knudson, Christiopher; Wisconsin, n.d. ***9675.6*** *p132*
Knudson, Ingebret 24; Arkansas, 1918 ***95.2*** *p67*
Knudson, Syvert; Washington, 1859-1920 ***2872.1*** *p21*
Knudson, Thomas; Washington, 1859-1920 ***2872.1*** *p21*
Knueppel, Anna; Wisconsin, n.d. ***9675.6*** *p132*
Knust, . . .; Canada, 1776-1783 ***9786*** *p26*
Knuth, Frank; New York, 1882 ***1450.2*** *p20B*
Knutson, Louis; Illinois, 1898 ***5012.40*** *p55*
Knutson, Ole; Arkansas, 1918 ***95.2*** *p67*
Knutzsen, Mads.; Wisconsin, n.d. ***9675.6*** *p132*
Knyphausen, von; America, 1775-1781 ***8582.2*** *p53*
Knyphausen, von; New York, 1776 ***9786*** *p278*
Knyphausen, W. von; Halifax, N.S., 1780 ***9786*** *p268*
Knyphausen, W. von; New York, 1776 ***9786*** *p268*
Knyphausen, Wilhelm von; New York, 1776 ***9786*** *p278*
Kobak, Joseph; Wisconsin, n.d. ***9675.6*** *p132*
Kobbe, William; New York, NY, 1833 ***8208.4*** *p45*
Kobel, Fred; Illinois, 1867 ***5012.38*** *p98*
Kobel, Fridrich; South Carolina, 1788 ***7119*** *p197*
Kobelenz, Anna Catharina *SEE* Kobelenz, Niclaus
Kobelenz, Anna Maria *SEE* Kobelenz, Niclaus
Kobelenz, Joh. Adam *SEE* Kobelenz, Niclaus
Kobelenz, Joh. Herman *SEE* Kobelenz, Niclaus
Kobelenz, Joh. Peter *SEE* Kobelenz, Niclaus
Kobelenz, Joh. Philip *SEE* Kobelenz, Niclaus
Kobelenz, Johanna Dorothea *SEE* Kobelenz, Niclaus
Kobelenz, Maria Margaretha *SEE* Kobelenz, Niclaus
Kobelenz, Niclaus 45; Pennsylvania, 1743 ***1034.18*** *p7*
*Wife:*Anna Catharina
*Child:*Joh. Adam
*Child:*Joh. Philip
*Child:*Joh. Peter
*Child:*Joh. Herman
*Child:*Maria Margaretha
*Child:*Anna Maria
*Child:*Johanna Dorothea
Koblen, Morris 26; Arkansas, 1918 ***95.2*** *p67*
Koblentz, Anna Catharina *SEE* Koblentz, Nicholas
Koblentz, Anna Maria *SEE* Koblentz, Nicholas
Koblentz, Joh. Adam *SEE* Koblentz, Nicholas
Koblentz, Joh. Herman *SEE* Koblentz, Nicholas
Koblentz, Joh. Peter *SEE* Koblentz, Nicholas
Koblentz, Joh. Philip *SEE* Koblentz, Nicholas
Koblentz, Johanna Dorothea *SEE* Koblentz, Nicholas
Koblentz, Maria Margaretha *SEE* Koblentz, Nicholas
Koblentz, Nicholas 45; Pennsylvania, 1743 ***1034.18*** *p6*
*Wife:*Anna Catharina
*Child:*Joh. Adam
*Child:*Joh. Philip
*Child:*Joh. Peter
*Child:*Joh. Herman
*Child:*Maria Margaretha
*Child:*Anna Maria
*Child:*Johanna Dorothea
Kobler, John; Illinois, 1868 ***2896.5*** *p21*
Kobler, Simon 29; Kansas, 1887 ***5240.1*** *p69*
Koblitz, Gottfried 23; Kansas, 1873 ***5240.1*** *p25*
Koblitz, Gottfried 23; Kansas, 1873 ***5240.1*** *p53*
Koboska, William; Arkansas, 1918 ***95.2*** *p67*
Kobrish, Frank; Arkansas, 1918 ***95.2*** *p67*
Kobylinski, Boleslaw 29; New York, 1912 ***9980.29*** *p50*
Kobylski, Albert; Arkansas, 1918 ***95.2*** *p67*
Koch, . . .; Canada, 1776-1783 ***9786*** *p26*
Koch, Adam; America, 1777-1778 ***8582.2*** *p68*
Koch, Anne M. Ilsabein Blase *SEE* Koch, Johann Carl Friedrich
Koch, Anne Marie H. Wehmeyer *SEE* Koch, Johann Friedrich
Koch, Anton; America, 1845 ***8582.1*** *p19*
Koch, Bernard; Illinois, 1837 ***8582.1*** *p55*
Koch, Carl Friedrich *SEE* Koch, Johann Carl Friedrich
Koch, Carl Friedrich Gottlieb; America, 1858 ***4610.10*** *p158*
Koch, Carl Heinrich; America, 1844 ***4610.10*** *p147*
Koch, Carl Wilhelm; America, 1844 ***4610.10*** *p147*
Koch, Catharine; Philadelphia, 1758 ***9973.7*** *p33*
Koch, Christian; Philadelphia, 1779 ***8137*** *p10*
Koch, Christoph; Canada, 1783 ***9786*** *p38A*
Koch, Frederich; Wisconsin, n.d. ***9675.6*** *p132*
Koch, Frederick 25; New Orleans, 1839 ***9420.2*** *p483*
Koch, Friedrich Wilhelm; America, 1842 ***4610.10*** *p114*
Koch, G. Fried. 10; America, 1854-1855 ***9162.6*** *p104*
Koch, Georg Adam; Pennsylvania, 1754 ***4525*** *p229*
Koch, George 32; Kansas, 1879 ***5240.1*** *p61*
Koch, Gustav; Wisconsin, n.d. ***9675.6*** *p132*
Koch, Heinr. 68; Cleveland, OH, 1906 ***1763*** *p40D*
Koch, Heinrich; Cincinnati, 1869-1887 ***8582*** *p17*
Koch, Heinrich Wilhelm; America, 1853 ***4610.10*** *p148*
Koch, Henry; America, 1850 ***1450.2*** *p81A*
Koch, Henry; Washington, 1859-1920 ***2872.1*** *p21*
Koch, Jacob 51; America, 1854-1855 ***9162.6*** *p104*
Koch, Jacob, Family; America, 1814-1923 ***2691.4*** *p172*
Koch, Jakob 30; America, 1853 ***9162.7*** *p15*
Koch, Johann; Akron, OH, 1839 ***8582.1*** *p49*
Koch, Johann; Kentucky, 1796 ***8582.3*** *p95*
Koch, Johann 19; America, 1854-1855 ***9162.6*** *p104*
Koch, Johann Carl Friedrich; America, 1877 ***4610.10*** *p122*
*Wife:*Anne M. Ilsabein Blase
*Son:*Carl Friedrich
Koch, Johann Friedrich; America, 1844 ***4610.10*** *p115*
*Wife:*Anne Marie H. Wehmeyer
Koch, Johann Georg; Philadelphia, 1779-1780 ***8137*** *p10*
Koch, Johann L.; Illinois, 1839 ***8582.1*** *p55*
Koch, John; Arkansas, 1918 ***95.2*** *p67*
Koch, John; Canada, 1776-1783 ***9786*** *p207A*
Koch, John; New York, NY, 1840 ***8208.4*** *p113*
Koch, John; Pennsylvania, 1835 ***1450.2*** *p81A*
Koch, John Adam; Ohio, 1869-1887 ***8582*** *p17*
Koch, John D.; Cincinnati, 1869-1887 ***8582*** *p17*
Koch, John Henry; New York, 1835 ***1450.2*** *p81A*
Koch, John M.; Wisconsin, n.d. ***9675.6*** *p132*
Koch, Karl Friedrich; Cincinnati, 1869-1887 ***8582*** *p17*
Koch, Karl Ludwig; America, 1842 ***4610.10*** *p146*
With parents
Koch, Karsten 29; Arkansas, 1918 ***95.2*** *p67*
Koch, Kathr. 44; America, 1854-1855 ***9162.6*** *p104*
Koch, Louis; Akron, OH, 1843 ***8582.1*** *p49*
Koch, Otto; Kansas, 1902 ***5240.1*** *p25*
Koch, Philip; Indiana, 1848 ***9117*** *p17*
Koch, Wanda; Wisconsin, n.d. ***9675.6*** *p132*
Koch, Wilhelm; America, 1893 ***1450.2*** *p81A*
Koch, William; America, 1838 ***1450.2*** *p81A*
Koch, William; Illinois, 1860 ***2896.5*** *p21*
Koch, William; Philadelphia, 1760 ***9973.7*** *p34*
Kocher, Henry Wm.; America, 1845 ***1450.2*** *p81A*
Kochesperger, Chas. 26; Louisiana, 1820 ***778.5*** *p297*
Kocis, John; America, 1895 ***7137*** *p169*
Kock, . . .; Canada, 1776-1783 ***9786*** *p26*
Kock, Jean 20; Port uncertain, 1839 ***778.5*** *p297*
Kockel, And; Pennsylvania, 1750 ***4525*** *p226*
Kockritz, H. W.; Washington, 1859-1920 ***2872.1*** *p21*
Kodrich, Martin; Wisconsin, n.d. ***9675.6*** *p132*
Koebbe, Clemens; America, 1840 ***8582.3*** *p37*
Koebbe, Clemens; Kentucky, 1840 ***8582.3*** *p99*
Koebbe, Clemens 12; Baltimore, 1840 ***8582.3*** *p37*
With parents
Koebel, Michael; America, 1846 ***8582.1*** *p19*
Koebeler, August; Philadelphia, 1892 ***1450.2*** *p20B*
Koebelin, Jacob Frederick; America, 1849 ***1450.2*** *p81A*
Koebler, August; Philadelphia, 1892 ***1450.2*** *p20B*
Koecher, William; America, 1843 ***1450.2*** *p81A*
Koeck, Christina; America, 1896 ***7137*** *p168*
Koeck, Simon; America, 1900 ***7137*** *p169*
Koeck, Stanislaus; America, 1885 ***7137*** *p168*
Koeder, Henry; Baltimore, 1871 ***1450.2*** *p20B*
Koegel, Andreas; Ohio, 1843 ***8582.1*** *p51*
Koehl, Pierre 24; America, 1838 ***778.5*** *p297*
Koehler, . . .; Canada, 1776-1783 ***9786*** *p26*
Koehler, Anna Eva; Pennsylvania, 1753 ***4525*** *p224*
Koehler, Anthony Philip; New York, NY, 1850 ***2896.5*** *p21*
Koehler, Christian; Cincinnati, 1869-1887 ***8582*** *p17*
Koehler, Christian; Illinois, 1872 ***2896.5*** *p22*
Koehler, Fried.; Wisconsin, n.d. ***9675.6*** *p132*
Koehler, Friederich, II; America, 1843 ***8582.3*** *p37*
Koehler, Friedrich; America, 1849 ***8582.1*** *p19*
Koehler, Georg B. F.; America, 1846 ***8582.3*** *p38*
Koehler, Gottfried; Cincinnati, 1869-1887 ***8582*** *p17*
Koehler, Henrich; Philadelphia, 1779 ***8137*** *p10*
Koehler, Henry; Maryland, 1891 ***1450.2*** *p20B*
Koehler, Henry 36; Kansas, 1893 ***5240.1*** *p79*
Koehler, Joseph; Kansas, 1882 ***5240.1*** *p25*
Koehler, Louis; New York, NY, 1881 ***1450.2*** *p20B*
Koehler, Nikolaus; New York, NY, 1780 ***8137*** *p10*
Koehler, Valentine; Wisconsin, n.d. ***9675.6*** *p132*
Koehler, William; America, 1895 ***1450.2*** *p82A*
Koehn, Cornelius 48; Harris Co., TX, 1899 ***6254*** *p6*
Koehn, Eusebius; America, 1700-1877 ***8582.3*** *p80*
Koehn, Johann; Iroquois Co., IL, 1892 ***3455.1*** *p11*
Koehne, Jacob; Ohio, 1869-1887 ***8582*** *p17*
Koehne, Johann; America, 1824 ***8582.2*** *p61*
Koehnen, Peter; New York, 1852 ***1450.2*** *p82A*
Koehnken, Johann Heinrich; Cincinnati, 1869-1887 ***8582*** *p17*
Koeller, William Henry; Wisconsin, n.d. ***9675.6*** *p132*
Koelling, John; Iroquois Co., IL, 1892 ***3455.1*** *p11*
Koellner, Maria Elizth 44; Pennsylvania, 1787 ***4525*** *p229*
Koelner, Peter; America, 1785-1795 ***4525*** *p229*
Koelscher, . . .; Canada, 1776-1783 ***9786*** *p26*
Koelt, Dicholde 27; America, 1838 ***778.5*** *p297*
Koelt, Elizabeth 21; America, 1838 ***778.5*** *p297*
Koempf, Ursula; Pennsylvania, 1751 ***2444*** *p222*
Koenig, . . .; Canada, 1776-1783 ***9786*** *p26*
Koenig, August; Wisconsin, n.d. ***9675.6*** *p132*
Koenig, Chas.; Wisconsin, n.d. ***9675.6*** *p132*
Koenig, Ernst H.; Cincinnati, 1842 ***8582.1*** *p19*
Koenig, F. C.; Peoria, IL, 1855 ***8582.3*** *p38*
Koenig, Jacob; Pennsylvania, 1750 ***2444*** *p177*
Koenig, Jacob; Pennsylvania, 1751 ***2444*** *p177*
Koenig, Jean 33; New Orleans, 1838 ***778.5*** *p297*
Koenig, Johann G.; Cincinnati, 1869-1887 ***8582*** *p17*
Koenig, Johann Ludwig; Pennsylvania, 1748-1750 ***2444*** *p177*
Koenig, John; Wisconsin, n.d. ***9675.6*** *p132*
Koenig, Matheus; Pennsylvania, 1751 ***2444*** *p177*
Koenig, Peter; Cincinnati, 1869-1887 ***8582*** *p17*
Koenig, Peter; Ohio, 1819 ***8582.1*** *p47*
Koenig, Valentin; Cincinnati, 1869-1887 ***8582*** *p17*
Koeniger, Ph; Cincinnati, 1841 ***8582.1*** *p19*
Koening, Christian 5; America, 1835 ***778.5*** *p297*
Koening, Christian 31; America, 1835 ***778.5*** *p297*
Koening, Jacob 2; America, 1835 ***778.5*** *p297*
Koening, Jacobine 28; America, 1835 ***778.5*** *p297*
Koening, Johann 4; America, 1835 ***778.5*** *p297*
Koening, John; Baltimore, 1891 ***1450.2*** *p20B*
Koening, Michel 6 mos; America, 1835 ***778.5*** *p297*
Koeninger, Philipp; America, 1830 ***8582.2*** *p61*
Koentz, D. 30; New Orleans, 1838 ***778.5*** *p297*
Koepel, August; Wisconsin, n.d. ***9675.6*** *p132*
Koepke, Hans; Illinois, 1899 ***5012.40*** *p76*
Koepp, Ludwig; Wisconsin, n.d. ***9675.6*** *p132*
Koepsel, August; Wisconsin, n.d. ***9675.6*** *p132*
Koerbel, Ferdinand 23; Kansas, 1884 ***5240.1*** *p66*
Koerber, August; America, 1846 ***1450.2*** *p82A*
Koerber, Johann David; Pennsylvania, 1754 ***2444*** *p177*
Koerber, Maria Elisabetha; America, 1754 ***2444*** *p141*
Koerker, Fredrich; Wisconsin, n.d. ***9675.6*** *p132*
Koerner, Veit; America, 1843 ***8582.1*** *p19*
Koerner, Veit 12; New York, NY, 1843 ***8582.3*** *p38*
With parents
Koersley, David 30; New York, NY, 1847 ***3377.6*** *p14*
Koersley, Jane 30; New York, NY, 1847 ***3377.6*** *p14*

262

FOR A COMPLETE EXPLANATION OF ENTRY, SEE "HOW TO READ A CITATION" SECTION

Kooler, Jacob; South Carolina, 1752-1753 ***3689.17*** *p21*
With wife
Kooler, John George; South Carolina, 1752-1753 ***3689.17*** *p22*
With wife
*Relative:*Catherine Margarita 11
Koons, Francis; Philadelphia, 1764 ***2444*** *p181*
Koons, Joseph; New York, NY, 1840 ***8208.4*** *p113*
Koontz, Philip 29; Pennsylvania, 1741 ***4779.3*** *p13*
Koop, Henry; New York, NY, 1838 ***8208.4*** *p56*
Koopmann, Gerhard; Wisconsin, n.d. ***9675.6*** *p199*
Koops, Rudolph; New York, NY, 1835 ***8208.4*** *p78*
Koortsen, Elert; New York, 1756 ***3652*** *p81*
Koos, John; Arkansas, 1918 ***95.2*** *p68*
Koosak, Konstanc; Wisconsin, n.d. ***9675.6*** *p199*
Kootman, Froym; Arkansas, 1918 ***95.2*** *p68*
Kooyman, Tunnis; Arkansas, 1918 ***95.2*** *p68*
Kopacz, Marya 18; New York, 1912 ***9980.29*** *p56*
Kopatic, Frank; Iowa, 1866-1943 ***123.54*** *p28*
Kopcak, Elias; America, 1898 ***7137*** *p169*
Kopchick, John; America, 1899 ***7137*** *p169*
Kopcik, John; America, 1899 ***7137*** *p169*
Kopecki, Eugen; New York, 1834 ***4606*** *p178*
Kopf, Math. 43; Kansas, 1895 ***5240.1*** *p80*
Kophela, Xaver; Kentucky, 1839-1840 ***8582.3*** *p98*
Kopka, Ellen; America, 1899 ***7137*** *p169*
Kopka, Peter; America, 1895 ***7137*** *p169*
Kopl, Elisabeth 9 mos; America, 1836 ***778.5*** *p298*
Kopller, Christian; America, 1848 ***3702.7*** *p130*
Kopowski, Jozef; New York, 1831 ***4606*** *p174*
Kopp, . . .; Canada, 1776-1783 ***9786*** *p26*
Kopp, Albert F.; America, 1872 ***1450.2*** *p83A*
Kopp, Georg; America, 1848 ***8582.2*** *p20*
Kopp, George; Wisconsin, n.d. ***9675.6*** *p199*
Kopp, George 1; Port uncertain, 1839 ***778.5*** *p298*
Kopp, Jean 28; Port uncertain, 1839 ***778.5*** *p298*
Kopp, Joseph; Colorado, 1904 ***9678.2*** *p122*
Kopp, Margu.rite 28; Port uncertain, 1839 ***778.5*** *p298*
Koppe, . . .; Canada, 1776-1783 ***9786*** *p26*
Koppe, Amelia; Wisconsin, n.d. ***9675.6*** *p199*
Koppe, Otto; Wisconsin, n.d. ***9675.6*** *p199*
Koppel, John Fredk. 47; New Orleans, 1839 ***9420.2*** *p358*
*Wife:*Mary Susana 57
Koppel, Mary Susana 57 *SEE* Koppel, John Fredk.
Kopper, John; Kansas, 1900 ***5240.1*** *p25*
Kopper, John J.; America, 1891 ***5240.1*** *p25*
Kopper, Peter; America, 1893 ***5240.1*** *p25*
Koppes, James; Illinois, 1899 ***5012.40*** *p79*
Kopplin, Constanze 22; Kansas, 1879 ***5240.1*** *p60*
Kopplin, Otto 23; Kansas, 1879 ***5240.1*** *p60*
Korba, Roman; Arkansas, 1918 ***95.2*** *p68*
Korber, . . .; Canada, 1776-1783 ***9786*** *p26*
Korczynski, . . .; New York, 1831 ***4606*** *p175*
Kordouon, Stefan; Iowa, 1866-1943 ***123.54*** *p28*
Kordus, Thomas; Arkansas, 1918 ***95.2*** *p68*
Kordyl, Jan 30; New York, 1912 ***9980.29*** *p50*
Korell, Johann; America, 1848 ***8582.1*** *p20*
Korf, Heinrich; America, 1849 ***8582.3*** *p38*
Korff, Carl Ernst Wilhelm; America, 1888 ***4610.10*** *p96*
Korfingthan, Mr.; Maryland, 1768 ***8582.3*** *p96*
Korfmacher, Anne Marie Engel; America, 1852 ***4610.10*** *p98*
Korgan, John 40; Newport, RI, 1851 ***6508.5*** *p20*
Korinek, Joe; Arkansas, 1918 ***95.2*** *p68*
Korle, Frederick; New York, NY, 1896 ***3455.3*** *p25*
Korn, . . .; Canada, 1776-1783 ***9786*** *p26*
Korn, Chaim 11 mos; New York, NY, 1878 ***9253*** *p47*
Korn, Sara 25; New York, NY, 1878 ***9253*** *p47*
Kornblum, Mrs. M.; Milwaukee, 1875 ***4719.30*** *p257*
With 3 children
Kornblum, Mr. M.; Milwaukee, 1875 ***4719.30*** *p257*
Kornmann, John Theobold; New York, 1750 ***3652*** *p74*
Kornrumpff, Caspar Heinrich; Canada, 1777 ***9786*** *p266*
Korp, A. E.; Minneapolis, 1882-1883 ***6410.35*** *p58*
Korp, Lewis; Illinois, 1854 ***7857*** *p4*
Korp, T.; Minneapolis, 1858-1880 ***6410.35*** *p58*
Korschari, Otte; Wisconsin, n.d. ***9675.6*** *p199*
Korsmeier, Louise 26; America, 1857 ***4610.10*** *p105*
Korsmeier, Wilhelmina; America, 1853 ***5647.5*** *p37*
With family
Korsvik, Gustav Julius; Arkansas, 1918 ***95.2*** *p68*
Korte, Franz Heinrich; Cincinnati, 1869-1887 ***8582*** *p18*
Korte, John Herman 26; Kansas, 1899 ***5240.1*** *p25*
Korte, John Hermann 26; Kansas, 1899 ***5240.1*** *p81*
Kortepeter, Ernst; America, 1839 ***1450.2*** *p83A*
Kortepeter, Frederick; America, 1837 ***1450.2*** *p83A*
Kortepeter, Herman; America, 1837 ***1450.2*** *p83A*
Kortmeyer, Anne C. Wilhelmine *SEE* Kortmeyer, Heinrich Wilhelm Adolph
Kortmeyer, Anne Marie Charlotte *SEE* Kortmeyer, Heinrich Wilhelm Adolph
Kortmeyer, Anne Marie Charlotte; America, 1844 ***4610.10*** *p154*
Kortmeyer, Heinrich Wilhelm Adolph; America, 1855 ***4610.10*** *p154*
*Wife:*Anne Marie Charlotte
*Daughter:*Anne C. Wilhelmine
Kortpeter, John William; America, 1856 ***1450.2*** *p83A*
Kortsch, August; Wisconsin, n.d. ***9675.6*** *p199*
Korvalenko, John; Arkansas, 1918 ***95.2*** *p68*
Korzenborn, Friedrich; New York, NY, 1846 ***8582.3*** *p39*
Korzienewski, Bronislaw 21; New York, 1912 ***9980.29*** *p59*
Korzybski, Sylvester; Arkansas, 1918 ***95.2*** *p68*
Koscialowski, Jan; New York, 1831 ***4606*** *p174*
Kosech, Charles William; New York, NY, 1865 ***2896.5*** *p22*
Kosehe, Otto 38; Harris Co., TX, 1899 ***6254*** *p6*
Koselicki, Frank; Iowa, 1866-1943 ***123.54*** *p28*
Koselicki, Vince; Iowa, 1866-1943 ***123.54*** *p28*
Kosenchuk, Frank 24; Arkansas, 1918 ***95.2*** *p68*
Koser, Leonhardt; Pennsylvania, 1709 ***2444*** *p177*
With wife
With 3 children
Kosivetzky, Helena 22; New York, 1912 ***9980.29*** *p50*
Koska, Julius A.; Nevada, 1868 ***2764.35*** *p38*
Koskemeier, Caroline Buchholz *SEE* Koskemeier, Ernst Friedrich Wilhelm
Koskemeier, Ernst Friedrich Wilhelm; America, 1872 ***4610.10*** *p109*
*Wife:*Caroline Buchholz
*Son:*Heinrich
Koskemeier, Heinrich *SEE* Koskemeier, Ernst Friedrich Wilhelm
Koski, Fred; Washington, 1859-1920 ***2872.1*** *p21*
Koski, Matt; Washington, 1859-1920 ***2872.1*** *p21*
Kosler, Jurgen Nanning; New York, NY, 1838 ***8208.4*** *p76*
Kospoth, von; Canada, 1776-1783 ***9786*** *p200*
Koss, August; Illinois, 1888 ***5012.37*** *p61*
Koss, Lewis; Illinois, 1873 ***5012.39*** *p26*
Kossler, John; Colorado, 1888 ***9678.2*** *p122*
Kossover, Jake; Arkansas, 1918 ***95.2*** *p68*
Kossover, Max; Arkansas, 1918 ***95.2*** *p68*
Kossow, Gustav; America, 1898 ***1450.2*** *p20B*
Kossowski, Wincenty; New York, 1834 ***4606*** *p178*
Kostelz, Franz; Wisconsin, n.d. ***9675.6*** *p199*
Kostenbader, Mr.; Died enroute, 1738 ***9898*** *p38*
Kostenbader, Catharina 50; Savannah, GA, 1738 ***9898*** *p38*
Kostencka, Wladyslawa 17; New York, 1912 ***9980.29*** *p57*
Koster, Mr.; America, 1850 ***4610.10*** *p147*
*Wife:*Christine Puls
*Child:*Christoph H. Lebrecht
*Child:*Carl C. Ciedrich
Koster, Carl C. Ciedrich *SEE* Koster, Mr.
Koster, Caroline Buchholz *SEE* Koster, Ernst Friedrich Wilhelm
Koster, Christ 28; Kansas, 1886 ***5240.1*** *p69*
Koster, Christen 28; Kansas, 1886 ***5240.1*** *p26*
Koster, Christine Puls *SEE* Koster, Mr.
Koster, Christoph H. Lebrecht *SEE* Koster, Mr.
Koster, Ernst Friedrich Wilhelm; America, 1872 ***4610.10*** *p109*
*Wife:*Caroline Buchholz
*Son:*Heinrich
Koster, Frederick H. 21; Kansas, 1892 ***5240.1*** *p26*
Koster, Frederick H. 21; Kansas, 1892 ***5240.1*** *p76*
Koster, Gerard; New York, NY, 1836 ***8208.4*** *p16*
Koster, Hans Heinrink 32; Kansas, 1892 ***5240.1*** *p77*
Koster, Heinrich *SEE* Koster, Ernst Friedrich Wilhelm
Koster, Henry 23; Kansas, 1896 ***5240.1*** *p26*
Koster, Henry 23; Kansas, 1896 ***5240.1*** *p80*
Koster, Hermann; New York, NY, 1838 ***8208.4*** *p80*
Koster, Johann Friedrich Wilhelm; America, 1850 ***4610.10*** *p147*
Koster, Johann Heinrich; America, 1854 ***4610.10*** *p151*
Koster, John 21; Kansas, 1888 ***5240.1*** *p26*
Koster, John 21; Kansas, 1888 ***5240.1*** *p72*
Koster, Marie Elisabeth; America, 1860-1900 ***4610.10*** *p99*
Koster, Peter N. 38; Kansas, 1903 ***5240.1*** *p26*
Koster, Peter N. 38; Kansas, 1903 ***5240.1*** *p82*
Kostering, Mr.; America, 1839-1855 ***4610.10*** *p145*
Kostering, Anne M. Louise Engel *SEE* Kostering, Friedrich Wilhelm
Kostering, Carl Friedrich; America, 1850 ***4610.10*** *p143*
Kostering, Christoph Heinrich *SEE* Kostering, Friedrich Wilhelm
Kostering, Friedrich Wilhelm; America, 1855 ***4610.10*** *p145*
*Brother:*Christoph Heinrich
*Sister:*Anne M. Louise Engel
Kosters, Frank; Baltimore, 1870 ***1450.2*** *p20B*
Kostner, Casper 27; Kansas, 1885 ***5240.1*** *p68*
Kostner, Friedrich 29; Kansas, 1883 ***5240.1*** *p64*
Kostring, Agnes C. Louise Henke *SEE* Kostring, Christian Heinrich Wilhelm
Kostring, Anne Marie Louise Wilhelmine; America, 1857 ***4610.10*** *p157*
Kostring, Carl H. Christian *SEE* Kostring, Christian Heinrich Wilhelm
Kostring, Christian Heinrich Wilhelm; America, 1857 ***4610.10*** *p157*
*Wife:*Agnes C. Louise Henke
*Child:*Carl H. Christian
*Child:*Johann Friedrich
Kostring, Johann Friedrich *SEE* Kostring, Christian Heinrich Wilhelm
Koswiski, Lure; Iowa, 1866-1943 ***123.54*** *p28*
Koszeisza, Michael; Illinois, 1890 ***2896.5*** *p22*
Koszio, Anton; Colorado, 1904 ***9678.2*** *p122*
Kotar, Johann; Iowa, 1866-1943 ***123.54*** *p28*
Kotchever, William; Wisconsin, n.d. ***9675.6*** *p199*
Kothe, Captain; Cincinnati, 1830-1839 ***8582.1*** *p51*
Kothe, Hinrick; New York, NY, 1839 ***8208.4*** *p92*
Kothe, Johann A.; Cincinnati, 1827 ***8582.1*** *p51*
Kotic, George; Iowa, 1866-1943 ***123.54*** *p28*
Kotowicz, . . .; New York, 1831 ***4606*** *p174*
Kotowski, Franciszek; New York, 1831 ***4606*** *p174*
Kotric, George; America, 1891 ***7137*** *p169*
Kotrick, George; America, 1891 ***7137*** *p169*
Kotschever, John 22; California, 1872 ***2769.6*** *p3*
Kotsonas, James J.; Arkansas, 1918 ***95.2*** *p68*
Kotte, . . .; Canada, 1776-1783 ***9786*** *p26*
Kotte, F.; Quebec, 1776 ***9786*** *p105*
Kotte, Johann Gottfried; Quebec, 1776 ***9786*** *p263*
Kottenbrock, Henry; Cincinnati, 1869-1887 ***8582*** *p18*
Kottkamp, Friedrich; Indianapolis, 1875 ***3702.7*** *p574*
Kotton, Alexander; Arkansas, 1918 ***95.2*** *p68*
Kotz, Christoph; Pennsylvania, 1751 ***2444*** *p178*
*Wife:*Elisabetha Spohn
*Child:*Maria Barbara
Kotz, Elisabetha Spohn *SEE* Kotz, Christoph
Kotz, Ferdinand 40; Kansas, 1880 ***5240.1*** *p62*
Kotz, Maria Barbara *SEE* Kotz, Christoph
Kotzuba, Chawe 18; New York, 1912 ***9980.29*** *p72*
Kouch, Gustave; Kansas, 1875 ***5240.1*** *p26*
Koude, Joseph; America, 1839 ***8582.1*** *p20*
Kouel, . . .; Canada, 1776-1783 ***9786*** *p26*
Koulikas, Stamatios; Arkansas, 1918 ***95.2*** *p68*
Koumparoulis, Constantine; Arkansas, 1918 ***95.2*** *p68*
Koumparoulis, Constantine; Arkansas, 1918 ***95.2*** *p103*
Kounelis, John Nicholas; Iowa, 1866-1943 ***123.54*** *p28*
Kouri, Mike J. 28; Kansas, 1903 ***5240.1*** *p82*
Kourlewisc, Belar; Iowa, 1866-1943 ***123.54*** *p28*
Koustash, . . .; Canada, 1776-1783 ***9786*** *p19*
Kout, Thomas 30; Arkansas, 1918 ***95.2*** *p68*
Kouva, Robert; Washington, 1859-1920 ***2872.1*** *p21*
Kouvicka, John; Iowa, 1866-1943 ***123.54*** *p28*
Kouzlaris, Frank; Iowa, 1866-1943 ***123.54*** *p28*
Kovacevich, Antony; Iowa, 1866-1943 ***123.54*** *p28*
Kovach, Frank; Wisconsin, n.d. ***9675.6*** *p199*
Kovach, Martin; Wisconsin, n.d. ***9675.6*** *p199*
Kovadchy, . . .; Canada, 1776-1783 ***9786*** *p19*
Kovascia, John; Iowa, 1866-1943 ***123.54*** *p28*
Kovash, . . .; Canada, 1776-1783 ***9786*** *p19*
Kovezlicki, Jasper; Iowa, 1866-1943 ***123.54*** *p28*
Kovickch, Mike; Iowa, 1866-1943 ***123.54*** *p28*
Kowal, Petro 18; New York, 1912 ***9980.29*** *p62*
Kowalczyk, Antoni 30; New York, 1912 ***9980.29*** *p68*
*Wife:*Helena Krzelak 29
*Son:*Roman 11
Kowalczyk, Helena Krzelak 29 *SEE* Kowalczyk, Antoni
Kowalczyk, Johan 37; New York, 1912 ***9980.29*** *p57*
Kowalczyk, Roman 11 *SEE* Kowalczyk, Antoni
Kowald, . . .; Canada, 1776-1783 ***9786*** *p26*
Kowalic, Stanley; Arkansas, 1918 ***95.2*** *p68*
Kowalkouski, Peter; Arkansas, 1918 ***95.2*** *p68*
Kowalska, Johanna 30; New York, 1912 ***9980.29*** *p72*
Kowalski, . . .; New York, 1831 ***4606*** *p174*
Kowalski, Helena 33; New York, 1912 ***9980.29*** *p57*
Kowalski, John; Wisconsin, n.d. ***9675.6*** *p199*
Koweg, A. M. Ilsabein; America, 1881 ***4610.10*** *p153*
Kowerz, Johann; Wisconsin, n.d. ***9675.6*** *p199*
Kowic, Martin; Wisconsin, n.d. ***9675.6*** *p199*
Kowiera, Frank; Wisconsin, n.d. ***9675.6*** *p199*
Kowlaski, Stanley; Arkansas, 1918 ***95.2*** *p69*
Kowles, Josef 29; Harris Co., TX, 1898 ***6254*** *p4*
Kownacki, Konstanty; New York, 1835 ***4606*** *p179*
Kowrlaric, Tom; Iowa, 1866-1943 ***123.54*** *p28*
Koyler, George; Georgia, 1738 ***9332*** *p321*
Kozakiewicz, Joe; America, 1899 ***1450.2*** *p21B*
Kozakiewicz, Zygmunt; America, 1899 ***1450.2*** *p21B*
Kozelicki, Jasper; Iowa, 1866-1943 ***123.54*** *p28*
Kozelickki, Antony; Iowa, 1866-1943 ***123.54*** *p28*
Kozelickki, John; Iowa, 1866-1943 ***123.54*** *p28*
Kozelicky, Antony; Iowa, 1866-1943 ***123.54*** *p28*

264 *FOR A COMPLETE EXPLANATION OF ENTRY, SEE "HOW TO READ A CITATION" SECTION*

Kozenewski, Bronislaw 21; New York, 1912 ***9980.29*** *p59*
Kozevic, George; Iowa, 1866-1943 ***123.54*** *p28*
Kozibroda, Jan 23; New York, 1912 ***9980.29*** *p72*
Kozibroda, Wicenty 39; New York, 1912 ***9980.29*** *p71*
Kozik, Andrew 71; Arizona, 1927 ***9228.40*** *p31*
Koziol, Agata Jaworecka Walsek; Iowa, 1866-1943 ***123.54*** *p67*
Koziol, Jozef; Iowa, 1866-1943 ***123.54*** *p67*
Koziol, Maria Angaran; Iowa, 1866-1943 ***123.54*** *p67*
Koziol, Michal; Iowa, 1866-1943 ***123.54*** *p67*
Kozioradzki, Jan; New York, 1835 ***4606*** *p179*
Kozlay, Colonel; New York, 1861-1865 ***8582.3*** *p91*
Kozlicke, George; Iowa, 1866-1943 ***123.54*** *p28*
Kozlicki, Vinko; Iowa, 1866-1943 ***123.54*** *p28*
Kozloe, Wesley; Arkansas, 1918 ***95.2*** *p69*
Kozlowska, Antanas 20; New York, 1912 ***9980.29*** *p51*
Kozlvoick, Anton; Iowa, 1866-1943 ***123.54*** *p28*
Koznar, Rafael; Wisconsin, n.d. ***9675.6*** *p199*
Kozuh, John; Wisconsin, n.d. ***9675.6*** *p199*
Kozuk, Louis; Wisconsin, n.d. ***9675.6*** *p199*
Kraas, Wilhelm; America, 1872 ***1450.2*** *p21B*
Kraatz, . . .; Canada, 1776-1783 ***9786*** *p26*
Krabbe, John; Illinois, 1888 ***5012.39*** *p121*
Kracht, A.M. Charl.; America, 1857 ***4610.10*** *p112*
Kracht, Christian Friedrich; America, 1865 ***4610.10*** *p158*
Kracke, Joseph 18; America, 1853 ***9162.7*** *p15*
Kraegenbring, Charles F. H.; New Jersey, 1872 ***2896.5*** *p22*
Kraegenbring, Frederick; Illinois, 1871 ***2896.5*** *p22*
Kraeger, Eva Kathr. 44; America, 1854-1855 ***9162.6*** *p104*
Kraeger, Georg 7; America, 1854-1855 ***9162.6*** *p104*
Kraeger, Heinrich 47; America, 1854-1855 ***9162.6*** *p104*
Kraeger, Karl 9; America, 1854-1855 ***9162.6*** *p104*
Kraeger, Margr. 18; America, 1854-1855 ***9162.6*** *p104*
Kraemer, Anna Barbara *SEE* Kraemer, Hans Jerg
Kraemer, Anne Marie Christine *SEE* Kraemer, David Heinrich
Kraemer, Anne Marie Wilhelmine *SEE* Kraemer, David Heinrich
Kraemer, August; Wisconsin, n.d. ***9675.6*** *p199*
Kraemer, Carl Friedrich; Wisconsin, n.d. ***9675.6*** *p199*
Kraemer, Carl Heinrich; America, 1850 ***4610.10*** *p139*
Kraemer, Carl Heinrich Friedr. Wilh.; America, 1845 ***4610.10*** *p134*
Kraemer, Christian *SEE* Kraemer, Hans Jerg
Kraemer, Christian; America, 1832 ***8582*** *p18*
Kraemer, Christian; Pennsylvania, 1754 ***2444*** *p178*
Kraemer, Christine Engel *SEE* Kraemer, David Heinrich
Kraemer, Christine Karoline *SEE* Kraemer, David Heinrich
Kraemer, Christopher; Georgia, 1775 ***8582.2*** *p64*
Kraemer, David Heinrich; America, 1850 ***4610.10*** *p139*
*Wife:*Marie Cath. C. Sander
*Child:*Christine Engel
*Child:*Johann Otto Heinrich
*Child:*Anne Marie Christine
*Child:*Otto Hermann Daniel
*Child:*Anne Marie Wilhelmine
*Child:*Christine Karoline
*Child:*Johann H. Christoph
Kraemer, Elisabetha Barbara *SEE* Kraemer, Hans Jerg
Kraemer, Gg. Jac. 17; America, 1854-1855 ***9162.6*** *p105*
Kraemer, Hans Jerg; Pennsylvania, 1754 ***2444*** *p178*
*Wife:*Anna Barbara
*Child:*Johannes
*Child:*Christian
*Child:*Johannes Conrad
*Child:*Elisabetha Barbara
Kraemer, Johann Daniel; America, 1849 ***4610.10*** *p138*
Kraemer, Johann H. Christoph *SEE* Kraemer, David Heinrich
Kraemer, Johann Otto Heinrich *SEE* Kraemer, David Heinrich
Kraemer, Johannes *SEE* Kraemer, Hans Jerg
Kraemer, Johannes Conrad *SEE* Kraemer, Hans Jerg
Kraemer, Marie Cath. C. Sander *SEE* Kraemer, David Heinrich
Kraemer, Otto Hermann Daniel *SEE* Kraemer, David Heinrich
Kraeutler, Georg Martin; Pennsylvania, 1735-1800 ***2444*** *p178*
Kraeutler, Johann Friedrich *SEE* Kraeutler, Johann Georg
Kraeutler, Johann Georg *SEE* Kraeutler, Johann Georg
Kraeutler, Johann Georg; Pennsylvania, 1751 ***2444*** *p179*
*Child:*Johann Georg
*Child:*Johann Friedrich
Kraeutler, Maria Catharina; Pennsylvania, 1753 ***2444*** *p201*
Krafft, . . .; Canada, 1776-1783 ***9786*** *p26*
Krafft, . . .; Canada, 1776-1783 ***9786*** *p42*
Krafft, Lt.; Canada, 1776-1783 ***9786*** *p185*
Krafft, Adam 41; America, 1854-1855 ***9162.6*** *p105*
Krafft, Anna Catharina *SEE* Krafft, Martin
Krafft, Anna Catharina *SEE* Krafft, Martin
Krafft, Anna Dorothea; Port uncertain, 1753-1800 ***2444*** *p196*
Krafft, Frederich 18; America, 1854-1855 ***9162.6*** *p105*
Krafft, Friedrich Wilhelm; Canada, 1780 ***9786*** *p268*
Krafft, Friedrich Wilhelm; New York, 1776 ***9786*** *p268*
Krafft, George; America, 1836 ***2769.5*** *p6*
Krafft, Maria Magdalena *SEE* Krafft, Martin
Krafft, Maria Magdalena *SEE* Krafft, Martin
Krafft, Martin; America, 1744-1800 ***2444*** *p178*
*Wife:*Maria Magdalena
*Child:*Anna Catharina
Krafft, Martin; Pennsylvania, 1744-1753 ***2444*** *p178*
*Wife:*Maria Magdalena
*Child:*Anna Catharina
Krafft, Wigand; Lancaster, PA, 1780 ***8137*** *p10*
Kraft, Barbara *SEE* Kraft, Christoph
Kraft, Catharina *SEE* Kraft, Christoph
Kraft, Christian *SEE* Kraft, Christoph
Kraft, Christoph; Pennsylvania, 1750 ***2444*** *p178*
*Wife:*Barbara
*Child:*Catharina
*Child:*Christian
Kraft, Franz; Cincinnati, 1872-1874 ***8582.1*** *p20*
Kraft, Fred; Illinois, 1872 ***5012.39*** *p26*
Kraft, Frederick; America, 1852 ***1450.2*** *p83A*
Kraft, Geo.; Pennsylvania, 1785 ***4525*** *p245*
Kraft, Georg 66; Ohio, 1897 ***1763*** *p40D*
Kraft, Henry; Iroquois Co., IL, 1892 ***3455.1*** *p11*
Kraft, Johannes; Ohio, 1869-1887 ***8582*** *p18*
Kraft, John; Illinois, 1872 ***5012.37*** *p59*
Kraft, Martin; America, 1744-1800 ***2444*** *p178*
Kraft, Martin; Pennsylvania, 1744-1753 ***2444*** *p178*
Kraft, Peter; America, 1832 ***8582.3*** *p39*
Kraft, Peter; Philadelphia, 1764 ***8582.2*** *p65*
Kraft, Thomas; Pennsylvania, 1785 ***4525*** *p229*
Krahane, . . .; Canada, 1776-1783 ***9786*** *p26*
Krahe, Alexander Friedrich Wilhelm; America, 1881 ***4610.10*** *p150*
Krahe, Heinrich 19; America, 1892 ***4610.10*** *p125*
Krahenbuhl, Peter; Pennsylvania, 1709-1710 ***4480*** *p311*
Kraher, Barbara; Georgia, 1734 ***9332*** *p327*
Krahl, von 33; New York, NY, 1893 ***9026.4*** *p41*
Krahmer, Anna Catharina *SEE* Krahmer, Hans Adam
Krahmer, Anna Catharina; Pennsylvania, 1731 ***1034.18*** *p20*
Krahmer, Christina Appolonia *SEE* Krahmer, Hans Adam
Krahmer, Hans Adam; Pennsylvania, 1731 ***1034.18*** *p12*
*Daughter:*Christina Appolonia
*Daughter:*Anna Catharina
With son-in-law
*Daughter:*Juliana
*Wife:*Maria Elisabetha
Krahmer, Juliana *SEE* Krahmer, Hans Adam
Krahmer, Juliana; Pennsylvania, 1731 ***1034.18*** *p13*
Krahmer, Maria Elisabetha *SEE* Krahmer, Hans Adam
Kraig, . . .; Canada, 1776-1783 ***9786*** *p26*
Kraigie, . . .; Canada, 1776-1783 ***9786*** *p26*
Krain, Johannes; Lancaster, PA, 1780 ***8137*** *p10*
Krain, Konrad; Philadelphia, 1779 ***8137*** *p10*
Krainc, Anton; Wisconsin, n.d. ***9675.6*** *p199*
Krainz, John; Wisconsin, n.d. ***9675.6*** *p199*
Krainz, Mathias; Wisconsin, n.d. ***9675.6*** *p199*
Krais, John; New Orleans, 1846 ***8582.1*** *p20*
Kraitsir, Dr.; America, n.d. ***4606*** *p180*
Krajacrich, Paul; Iowa, 1866-1943 ***123.54*** *p28*
Krajewski, . . .; New York, 1831 ***4606*** *p175*
Krajnc, John; Wisconsin, n.d. ***9675.6*** *p199*
Krakansky, Banet; America, 1888 ***1450.2*** *p83A*
Krakowiak, Zofia 21; New York, 1912 ***9980.29*** *p61*
Kral, Frank 22; Kansas, 1896 ***5240.1*** *p80*
Krall, Johann; Wisconsin, n.d. ***9675.6*** *p199*
Krall, John; Washington, 1859-1920 ***2872.1*** *p21*
Krall, William; Washington, 1859-1920 ***2872.1*** *p22*
Krallschuffer, Eduard; New York, NY, 1838 ***8208.4*** *p84*
Kramer, . . .; Canada, 1776-1783 ***9786*** *p26*
Kramer, . . .; Connecticut, 1856 ***3702.7*** *p357*
Kramer, Adam; Indiana, 1844 ***9117*** *p17*
Kramer, Adolph; Cincinnati, 1869-1887 ***8582*** *p18*
Kramer, Anna Catharina *SEE* Kramer, Hans Adam
Kramer, August; Wisconsin, n.d. ***9675.6*** *p199*
Kramer, August Ernst Friedrich *SEE* Kramer, Marie Wilhelmine Geismeyer
Kramer, C. J.; Shreveport, LA, 1876 ***7129*** *p45*
Kramer, Carl 27; New York, NY, 1857 ***9831.14*** *p154*
Kramer, Charles; Indiana, 1848 ***9117*** *p17*
Kramer, Charles; Wisconsin, n.d. ***9675.6*** *p199*
Kramer, Christina Appolonia *SEE* Kramer, Hans Adam
Kramer, Dveira; Iowa, 1866-1943 ***123.54*** *p67*
Kramer, Elisabetha *SEE* Kramer, Hans Adam
Kramer, Frederick; Indiana, 1848 ***9117*** *p19*
Kramer, Friedrich 18; America, 1880 ***4610.10*** *p101*
Kramer, George 28; Kansas, 1874 ***5240.1*** *p55*
Kramer, Gg. P. 24; America, 1853 ***9162.7*** *p15*
Kramer, Gottfried 62; New Orleans, 1839 ***9420.2*** *p69*
Kramer, Gottlob 28; New Orleans, 1839 ***9420.2*** *p69*
Kramer, Haim; Iowa, 1866-1943 ***123.54*** *p67*
Kramer, Hans Adam; Pennsylvania, 1731 ***1034.18*** *p12*
*Wife:*Elisabetha
*Daughter:*Christina Appolonia
*Daughter:*Anna Catharina
With son-in-law
*Daughter:*Juliana
Kramer, Heinrich; Kentucky, 1843 ***8582.3*** *p100*
Kramer, Heinrich; Ohio, 1812-1814 ***8582.2*** *p59*
Kramer, Heinrich Friedrich August; America, 1850 ***4610.10*** *p155*
Kramer, Henrich; Pennsylvania, 1731 ***1034.18*** *p12*
Kramer, Herman J.; Washington, 1859-1920 ***2872.1*** *p21*
Kramer, Jacob; Illinois, 1895 ***2896.5*** *p22*
Kramer, Jacob; Indiana, 1848 ***9117*** *p17*
Kramer, Jette 19; New York, NY, 1878 ***9253*** *p47*
Kramer, Johann H.; America, 1847 ***8582.2*** *p20*
Kramer, John; Pennsylvania, 1801 ***8582.1*** *p48*
Kramer, Joseph; America, 1889 ***1450.2*** *p83A*
Kramer, Joseph; New York, NY, 1846 ***8582.1*** *p20*
Kramer, Juliana *SEE* Kramer, Hans Adam
Kramer, Karl; America, 1847 ***8582.2*** *p20*
Kramer, Louise; America, 1850 ***4610.10*** *p142*
Kramer, Marie Wilhelmine Geismeyer; America, 1851 ***4610.10*** *p155*
*Son:*August Ernst Friedrich
Kramer, Sylvester; Illinois, 1867 ***2896.5*** *p22*
Kramer, Valentine; Indiana, 1848 ***9117*** *p17*
Kramer, W. C. F.; Washington, 1859-1920 ***2872.1*** *p21*
Kramer, Wilhelm Anton Walther 17; America, 1894 ***4610.10*** *p125*
Kramer, William; Wisconsin, n.d. ***9675.6*** *p199*
Kramer, William Jacob; California, 1869 ***1450.2*** *p83A*
Kramer, Wm. 24; Died enroute, 1839 ***9420.2*** *p69*
Kramig, Franz; Cincinnati, 1869-1887 ***8582*** *p18*
Kraml, Frank; Arkansas, 1918 ***95.2*** *p69*
Krammer, Gertrud; America, 1763 ***2854*** *p45*
Kran, Henry; New York, NY, 1833 ***8208.4*** *p54*
Kranck, Anna C. Daubenschmidt *SEE* Kranck, Johann Adam
Kranck, Elisabetha Catharina *SEE* Kranck, Johann Adam
Kranck, Hans; Pennsylvania, 1752 ***4525*** *p230*
Kranck, Johann Adam; Pennsylvania, 1752 ***4525*** *p230*
*Wife:*Anna C. Daubenschmidt
*Child:*Elisabetha Catharina
Kranewinter, Jacob; Georgia, 1738 ***9332*** *p319*
Krank, Charles; Illinois, 1872 ***5012.39*** *p26*
Krank, Georg; Pennsylvania, 1752 ***4525*** *p230*
Krank, Hans; Pennsylvania, 1752 ***4525*** *p230*
Krank, Johannes; Pennsylvania, 1752 ***4525*** *p230*
With wife
With child
Krannenberger, Moses; Indiana, 1848 ***9117*** *p17*
Kranse, Herman; Illinois, 1888 ***5012.39*** *p122*
Kranz, Hugo 68; Canada, 1902 ***1763*** *p40D*
Kranz, Mathias; Wisconsin, n.d. ***9675.6*** *p199*
Kranz, Nicholas; America, 1866 ***6014.1*** *p2*
Krapf, John; Nebraska, 1895 ***5240.1*** *p26*
Krapp, Johannes; Philadelphia, 1779 ***8137*** *p10*
Krappler, Dorrade 20; Port uncertain, 1839 ***778.5*** *p299*
Krashowitz, August; America, 1886-1889 ***1450.2*** *p83A*
Krason, Ignatz 17; New York, 1912 ***9980.29*** *p59*
With 2 cousins
Krasowska, Paulina 19; New York, 1912 ***9980.29*** *p62*
Krass, . . .; Canada, 1776-1783 ***9786*** *p26*
Krass, Lt.; Canada, 1776-1783 ***9786*** *p185*
Krass, Lorenz; Wisconsin, n.d. ***9675.6*** *p199*
Krass, Peter; Indiana, 1847 ***9117*** *p18*
Krassane, . . .; Canada, 1776-1783 ***9786*** *p26*
Kratikofsky, . . .; Canada, 1776-1783 ***9786*** *p26*
Kratz, . . .; Canada, 1776-1783 ***9786*** *p27*
Kratz, Andrew; Virginia, 1855 ***4626.16*** *p15*
Kratzer, George; Wisconsin, n.d. ***9675.6*** *p199*
Kratzer, Johann Adam; Kentucky, 1840-1845 ***8582.3*** *p100*
Kraukoff, Jacob; America, 1850 ***1450.2*** *p84A*
Krauntz, Cirstian; Wisconsin, n.d. ***9675.6*** *p199*
Kraus, Anna Margaretha Zeller *SEE* Kraus, Hans Joerg
Kraus, Christine *SEE* Kraus, Hans Joerg
Kraus, Christoph; Wisconsin, n.d. ***9675.6*** *p199*
Kraus, Hans Joerg; America, 1746-1800 ***2444*** *p179*
*Wife:*Anna Margaretha Zeller
*Child:*Hans Jorg
*Child:*Johann Jacob
*Child:*Maria Barbara
*Child:*Johann Friedrich

*Child:*Christine
*Child:*Matthaus
Kraus, Hans Jorg *SEE* Kraus, Hans Joerg
Kraus, Johann Friedrich *SEE* Kraus, Hans Joerg
Kraus, Johann Jacob *SEE* Kraus, Hans Joerg
Kraus, John; Wisconsin, n.d. *9675.6 p199*
Kraus, John 38; Kansas, 1895 *5240.1 p80*
Kraus, John J.; Wisconsin, n.d. *9675.6 p199*
Kraus, Lorenz; Wisconsin, n.d. *9675.6 p199*
Kraus, Maria Barbara *SEE* Kraus, Hans Joerg
Kraus, Matthaus *SEE* Kraus, Hans Joerg
Kraus, Peter; Wisconsin, n.d. *9675.6 p199*
Kraus, Traugott Carl, Jr.; Wisconsin, n.d. *9675.6 p199*
Kraus, Wilhelm; Toledo, OH, 1869-1887 *8582 p18*
Krause, Andrew; New York, 1749 *3652 p71*
Krause, Anna Maria; New York, 1749 *3652 p73*
Krause, Barbara; New York, 1749 *3652 p73*
Krause, Carl; Wisconsin, n.d. *9675.6 p199*
Krause, Christina B. *SEE* Krause, Matthew
Krause, David; Pennsylvania, 1845 *8582 p18*
Krause, Dominicus; New York, 1761 *3652 p87*
Krause, Eduard; Kentucky, 1844 *8582.3 p101*
Krause, Emil; Washington, 1859-1920 *2872.1 p21*
Krause, Emil. Lebrecht 17; New Orleans, 1839 *9420.2 p170*
Krause, Fr. C. Traugott; Wisconsin, n.d. *9675.6 p199*
Krause, Frederick Wilhelm; Arkansas, 1881 *3688 p7*
Krause, Henry; New York, 1753 *3652 p77*
Krause, Herman; Wisconsin, n.d. *9675.6 p199*
Krause, Johann; Ohio, 1847 *8582.1 p48*
Krause, John; Wisconsin, n.d. *9675.6 p199*
Krause, John J.; Wisconsin, n.d. *9675.6 p199*
Krause, Leberecht Friedrich Traugott; America, 1839 *3702.7 p308*
Krause, Matthew; New York, 1743 *3652 p59*
*Wife:*Christina B.
Krause, Max Wilhelm Paul; Washington, 1859-1920 *2872.1 p21*
Krause, Paul William; Wisconsin, n.d. *9675.6 p199*
Krause, Philip; Arkansas, 1918 *95.2 p69*
Krause, Rosina *SEE* Krause, Samuel
Krause, Samuel; New York, 1749 *3652 p71*
*Wife:*Rosina
Krause, Theodore; Wisconsin, n.d. *9675.6 p199*
Krause, Wilhelm; America, 1853 *8582.3 p39*
Krauskopf, Ludwig; Cincinnati, 1827 *8582.1 p51*
Krauss, . . .; Canada, 1776-1783 *9786 p27*
Krauss, Anna Margaretha Zeller *SEE* Krauss, Hans Joerg
Krauss, Christine *SEE* Krauss, Hans Joerg
Krauss, David; America, 1754 *2444 p179*
Krauss, David; Pennsylvania, 1754 *2444 p179*
Krauss, Hans Georg; Pennsylvania, 1754 *2444 p179*
Krauss, Hans Joerg; America, 1746-1800 *2444 p179*
*Wife:*Anna Margaretha Zeller
*Child:*Hans Jorg
*Child:*Johann Jacob
*Child:*Maria Barbara
*Child:*Johann Friedrich
*Child:*Christine
*Child:*Matthaus
Krauss, Hans Jorg *SEE* Krauss, Hans Joerg
Krauss, Jacob; Pennsylvania, 1749 *2444 p179*
Krauss, Joh. Georg; Pennsylvania, 1749 *2444 p179*
Krauss, Johann Friedrich *SEE* Krauss, Hans Joerg
Krauss, Johann Jacob *SEE* Krauss, Hans Joerg
Krauss, Maria Barbara *SEE* Krauss, Hans Joerg
Krauss, Matthaus *SEE* Krauss, Hans Joerg
Kraut, Christian; Port uncertain, 1749-1800 *2444 p179*
*Wife:*Dorothea
*Child:*Matthias
Kraut, Dorothea *SEE* Kraut, Christian
Kraut, Jakob; Kentucky, 1810 *8582.3 p97*
Kraut, Matthias *SEE* Kraut, Christian
Krautwurst, . . .; Canada, 1776-1783 *9786 p27*
Krautz, Adam 87; Ontario, 1904 *1763 p40D*
Krawczynski, . . .; New York, 1831 *4606 p174*
Kreamer, Anna Maria 14 *SEE* Kreamer, Christian
Kreamer, Catharina; Pennsylvania, 1731 *1034.18 p21*
Kreamer, Christian 49; Savannah, GA, 1738 *9332 p332*
*Wife:*Clara 43
*Daughter:*Anna Maria 14
*Son:*Christopher 12
Kreamer, Christopher 12 *SEE* Kreamer, Christian
Kreamer, Clara 43 *SEE* Kreamer, Christian
Kreamp, Anna Margaretta 2 *SEE* Kreamp, John
Kreamp, Catherina 10 *SEE* Kreamp, John
Kreamp, John 35; Georgia, 1738 *9332 p329*
*Wife:*Sophia 40
*Daughter:*Catherina 10
*Daughter:*Maria Magdalena 7
*Son:*John Ulrick 4
*Daughter:*Anna Margaretta 2
Kreamp, John Ulrick 4 *SEE* Kreamp, John

Kreamp, Maria Magdalena 7 *SEE* Kreamp, John
Kreamp, Sophia 40 *SEE* Kreamp, John
Kreaviger, Francis; Indiana, 1847 *9117 p18*
Kreber, Anthony; Philadelphia, 1762 *9973.7 p37*
Krebs, . . .; Canada, 1776-1783 *9786 p27*
Krebs, Adolph; America, 1847 *8582.1 p20*
Krebs, Peter; Pennsylvania, 1854-1855 *3702.7 p389*
Krebs, Rachel 19; Virginia, 1720 *3690.1 p135*
Krecht, Ernst; Tennessee, 1891 *2896.5 p22*
Kreck, Paul; Wisconsin, n.d. *9675.6 p199*
Kreczicz, Walentz; Iowa, 1866-1943 *123.54 p29*
Kredel, Anna Mg. 48; America, 1854-1855 *9162.6 p105*
Kredel, Heinrich 22; America, 1854-1855 *9162.6 p105*
Kredel, Jacob 16; America, 1854-1855 *9162.6 p105*
Kredel, Peter 13; America, 1854-1855 *9162.6 p105*
Kreeb, Carl; Iroquois Co., IL, 1893 *3455.1 p11*
Kreeb, Emilie *SEE* Kreeb, Ernest Paul
Kreeb, Ernest Paul; New York, NY, 1910 *3455.3 p48*
*Wife:*Emilie
Kreeb, Gottlieb; Iroquois Co., IL, 1896 *3455.1 p11*
Kreemer, Adam; Pennsylvania, 1731 *1034.18 p12*
Kreemer, Adam; Pennsylvania, 1768 *9973.8 p32*
Kreemer, Christian; Pennsylvania, 1731 *1034.18 p12*
Kreemer, Christina; Pennsylvania, 1731 *1034.18 p12*
Kreemer, Elisabeth; Pennsylvania, 1731 *1034.18 p12*
Kreemer, Eve; Pennsylvania, 1731 *1034.18 p12*
Kreemer, Maria; Pennsylvania, 1731 *1034.18 p12*
Kreft, Heinrich Ludwig; America, 1850 *4610.10 p155*
Kregal, Louis; Iroquois Co., IL, 1892 *3455.1 p12*
Kreger, Christophe; Canada, 1776-1783 *9786 p243*
Kreger, Moris; Iowa, 1866-1943 *123.54 p29*
Kreglinski, . . .; New York, 1831 *4606 p175*
Kreidel, Frank; Colorado, 1898 *9678.2 p122*
Kreider, Johannes *SEE* Kreider, Michael
Kreider, Michael; Ohio, 1796 *8582.2 p57*
*Brother:*Johannes
Kreidl, Gottfried; Colorado, 1896 *9678.2 p122*
Kreidler, Georg Martin 22; Pennsylvania, 1753 *2444 p178*
Kreidler, Georg Martin 22; Pennsylvania, 1753 *2444 p201*
Kreidler, Johann Friedrich *SEE* Kreidler, Johann Georg
Kreidler, Johann Georg *SEE* Kreidler, Johann Georg
Kreidler, Johann Georg; Pennsylvania, 1751 *2444 p179*
*Child:*Johann Georg
*Child:*Johann Friedrich
Kreig, Mary 4; Massachusetts, 1849 *5881.1 p71*
Kreiger, August; Illinois, 1870 *5012.38 p99*
Kreiger, August; Illinois, 1872 *5012.39 p91*
Kreiger, Frederick; America, 1840 *1450.2 p84A*
Kreilich, Franz; Kentucky, 1810 *8582.3 p97*
Kreiling, Louis 72; America, 1908 *1763 p40D*
Krein, Joh. 82; Ontario, 1902 *1763 p48D*
Kreiner, Joh. Dietrich; Pennsylvania, 1729 *3627 p9*
Kreinhop, Johann H.; Illinois, 1836 *8582.1 p55*
Kreisig, Frederick William; Wisconsin, n.d. *9675.6 p199*
Kreismayer, Simeon; Philadelphia, 1738 *9898 p43*
Kreisse, Johannes; Trenton, NJ, 1776 *8137 p10*
Kreisser, Stophel; Lancaster, PA, 1773 *9973.8 p33*
Kreissler, . . .; Canada, 1776-1783 *9786 p27*
Kreitz, Johann M.; Illinois, 1850 *8582.2 p51*
Kreitzer, Albert J.; Wisconsin, n.d. *9675.6 p199*
Krekel, Arnold; America, 1832 *8125.8 p437*
With parents
Krekeler, Eduard Georg Ludwig Adolf; America, 1893 *4610.10 p103*
Krekeler, Laurentius Hermann Konrad; America, 1900 *4610.10 p103*
Krell, Albert; America, 1849 *8582.3 p39*
Krell, Anna Elis. 24; America, 1854-1855 *9162.6 p105*
Krell, Eregott; Wisconsin, n.d. *9675.6 p199*
Kremer, . . .; Pennsylvania, n.d. *2444 p146*
Kremer, Ernst; New York, 1885 *8125.8 p437*
Kremer, Henri; Canada, 1776-1783 *9786 p243*
Kremser, Andrew *SEE* Kremser, Rosina Oberdorf
Kremser, Andrew; New York, 1743 *3652 p59*
*Wife:*Rosina
Kremser, Anna Mary *SEE* Kremser, George
Kremser, George; New York, 1743 *3652 p59*
*Wife:*Anna Mary
Kremser, Matthew; New York, 1752 *3652 p76*
Kremser, Rosina *SEE* Kremser, Andrew
Kremser, Rosina Oberdorf; Pennsylvania, 1742 *4525 p230*
*Husband:*Andrew
Krendel, . . .; Canada, 1776-1783 *9786 p27*
Krentler, George; New York, NY, 1839 *8208.4 p95*
Krentler, Louis; America, 1872 *1450.2 p84A*
Krenzer, John; Wisconsin, n.d. *9675.6 p199*
Kreos, Christian 70; Kansas, 1888 *5240.1 p72*
Kreoscck, John; Arkansas, 1918 *95.2 p69*

Kreps, Chatharina 23; Ohio, 1839 *3702.7 p75*
With father
With 8 siblings
Kress, Georg Henrich; Canada, 1780 *9786 p268*
Kress, Georg Henrich; New York, 1776 *9786 p268*
Kress, Johannes; America, 1837 *8582.3 p39*
Kreth, August Frederick; New York, NY, 1850 *2896.5 p22*
Kreth, Carl; Illinois, 1858 *2896.5 p22*
Kreth, Charles; New York, NY, 1851 *2896.5 p22*
Kreth, Godfreth; New York, NY, 1853 *2896.5 p22*
Kreth, Henry; New York, 1853 *2896.5 p22*
Kretshman, Otto; Washington, 1859-1920 *2872.1 p21*
Kretzsch, Jane Sophie 50; New Orleans, 1839 *9420.2 p487*
Kreuder, Mrs. Martin; Philadelphia, 1776 *8582.3 p83*
Kreuger, August; Wisconsin, n.d. *9675.6 p199*
Kreuger, Hans 24; Halifax, N.S., 1752 *7074.6 p207*
Kreuter, Fred; Milwaukee, 1875 *4719.30 p257*
Kreutz, Daniel; America, 1850 *8582.3 p39*
Kreutz, Ludwig; America, 1848 *8582.1 p20*
Kreutzbourg, Col.; Canada, 1776 *9786 p123*
Kreutzburg, Ignatz; Cincinnati, 1869-1887 *8582 p18*
Kreutzer, . . .; Canada, 1776-1783 *9786 p27*
Kreutzer, John; Wisconsin, n.d. *9675.6 p199*
Kreutzmuller, Caroline Charlotte; America, 1884 *4610.10 p106*
Kreuz, . . .; New York, NY, 1837 *8582.3 p34*
Krewar, John; Illinois, 1860 *5012.39 p89*
Kreytler, Yerrick 22; Pennsylvania, 1753 *2444 p178*
Kreytler, Yerrick 22; Pennsylvania, 1753 *2444 p201*
Krick, Bernhard; Wisconsin, n.d. *9675.6 p199*
Krick, Chas.; Wisconsin, n.d. *9675.6 p199*
Krick, John; Wisconsin, n.d. *9675.6 p199*
Krick, Peter; Wisconsin, n.d. *9675.6 p199*
Krieg, . . .; Canada, 1776-1783 *9786 p27*
Krieg, Albert; Washington, 1859-1920 *2872.1 p21*
Krieg, Andreas; Ohio, 1819 *8582.1 p47*
Krieg, Michael; Wisconsin, n.d. *9675.6 p199*
Kriegbaum, John George; New York, 1754 *3652 p80*
Krieger, August Friedrich Wilhelm; America, 1881 *4610.10 p101*
Krieger, Conrad; Iroquois Co., IL, 1894 *3455.1 p12*
Krieger, Ernst Heinrich Friedrich; America, 1885 *4610.10 p102*
Krieger, Fred A.; Washington, 1859-1920 *2872.1 p22*
Krieger, Friederike; America, 1893 *4610.10 p103*
Krieger, Johann F.; America, 1850 *8582.3 p39*
Krieger, John; America, 1848 *8582.1 p20*
Krieger, John; Wisconsin, n.d. *9675.6 p199*
Krieger, Karl Heinrich; America, 1857 *4610.10 p109*
Krieger, Louise; America, 1893 *4610.10 p103*
Kriehn, Charles; Wisconsin, n.d. *9675.6 p199*
Krienke, Edmund Otto; Wisconsin, n.d. *9675.6 p199*
Kriernmo, Nels; Arkansas, 1918 *95.2 p69*
Krietemeier, Heinrich; Illinois, 1834-1912 *4610.10 p66*
Krigel, Elias; Kansas, 1917 *6013.40 p16*
Krigel, William; Virginia, 1852 *4626.16 p14*
Krighbaum, George; Philadelphia, 1832 *9892.11 p25*
Krighbaum, Jacob; Philadelphia, 1832 *9892.11 p25*
Krimmel, Anna Barbara *SEE* Krimmel, Dorothea Christina
Krimmel, Christina Dorothea; Pennsylvania, 1753 *2444 p136*
Krimmel, Dorothea Christina; Pennsylvania, 1735-1800 *2444 p179*
*Child:*Anna Barbara
Krimmel, Johann Ludwig; Philadelphia, 1786-1821 *2444 p179*
Krimmer, Wilhelmine; America, 1847 *3702.7 p312*
Kring, Friedr. Wilh. 87; St. Louis, 1905 *1763 p40D*
Kringe, Henry; New York, NY, 1838 *8208.4 p87*
Kringel, Henrich; Philadelphia, 1779 *8137 p10*
Kripars, George; Wisconsin, n.d. *9675.6 p199*
Krisch, Paul; Washington, 1859-1920 *2872.1 p22*
Krisoen, Albert; Wisconsin, n.d. *9675.6 p131*
Kristensen, Kristian Alfred; Arkansas, 1918 *95.2 p69*
Kristensen, Mads Kristian; Arkansas, 1918 *95.2 p69*
Kristjansdottir, Gudrun 42; Quebec, 1879 *2557.1 p20*
Kristjansdottir, Holmfridur 30; Quebec, 1879 *2557.1 p39A*
Kristjansdottir, Sigurbjorn 4; Quebec, 1879 *2557.1 p39A*
Kristjansson, Benedikt 33; Quebec, 1879 *2557.1 p39A*
Kristopoulus, Austrides Paulo; Arkansas, 1918 *95.2 p69*
Kritsen, Christopher; South Carolina, 1752-1753 *3689.17 p22*
With wife
Kritz, Hendrick; New York, NY, 1836 *8208.4 p19*
Kritzer, Rudolph 76; Kansas, 1896 *5240.1 p80*
Kritzner, Frederick; Wisconsin, n.d. *9675.6 p199*
Kriveck, George; Wisconsin, n.d. *9675.6 p199*
Krivitz, George; Wisconsin, n.d. *9675.6 p199*
Krivokucha, John; Iowa, 1866-1943 *123.54 p29*

Krizsanitz, Elizabeth *SEE* Krizsanitz, Matyas
Krizsanitz, Matyas; New York, NY, 1914 *3455.3 p48*
  *Wife:*Elizabeth
Krobbe, Carl; Illinois, 1872 *5012.39 p91*
Krobel, John; Arkansas, 1918 *95.2 p69*
Kroeckel, Frederick; America, 1870 *1450.2 p84A*
Kroeger, Adolph E.; America, 1848 *8582.1 p44*
  With father & family
Kroeger, Anne Marie *SEE* Kroeger, Johann Friedrich
Kroeger, Carl *SEE* Kroeger, Johann Friedrich
Kroeger, Christine *SEE* Kroeger, Johann Friedrich
Kroeger, Christine Louise Charlotte; America, 1850
  4610.10 p142
Kroeger, Elsie Anna; Wisconsin, n.d. *9675.6 p199*
Kroeger, Engel *SEE* Kroeger, Johann Friedrich
Kroeger, Friederike Hildebrand *SEE* Kroeger, Johann
  Friedrich
Kroeger, Gottlieb *SEE* Kroeger, Johann Friedrich
Kroeger, Heinrich *SEE* Kroeger, Johann Friedrich
Kroeger, Johann Friedrich 48; America, 1850 *4610.10*
  p143
  *Wife:*Friederike Hildebrand
  *Child:*Engel
  *Child:*Wilhelm
  *Child:*Heinrich
  *Child:*Carl
  *Child:*Louise
  *Child:*Christine
  *Child:*Gottlieb
  *Sister:*Anne Marie
Kroeger, Johann Heinrich; Cincinnati, 1869-1887 *8582*
  p18
Kroeger, Louise *SEE* Kroeger, Johann Friedrich
Kroeger, Peter; Cincinnati, 1788-1848 *8582.3 p90*
Kroeger, Wilhelm *SEE* Kroeger, Johann Friedrich
Kroehnke, Herman N.; Wisconsin, n.d. *9675.6 p199*
Kroehr, Catharina; Georgia, 1739 *9332 p324*
Kroehr, Gertraud; Georgia, 1739 *9332 p324*
Kroehr, Maria; Georgia, 1739 *9332 p323*
Kroekel, . . .; Canada, 1776-1783 *9786 p27*
Kroeker, Peter; Kansas, 1884 *5240.1 p26*
Kroell, August; Baltimore, 1834 *8582.1 p53*
  *Wife:*Henriette Lahatt
Kroell, August; Cincinnati, 1788-1848 *8582.3 p89*
Kroell, August; Cincinnati, 1788-1848 *8582.3 p90*
Kroell, August; Cincinnati, 1869-1887 *8582 p18*
Kroell, Henriette Lahatt *SEE* Kroell, August
Kroemer, Franz 25; America, 1836 *778.5 p299*
Kroenberg, Jacob; Wisconsin, n.d. *9675.6 p199*
Kroening, Georg; Philadelphia, 1779 *8137 p10*
Kroeser, . . .; Canada, 1776-1783 *9786 p27*
Kroeze, Gerrit Jan 5; New York, NY, 1847 *3377.6 p15*
Kroeze, Hendrik; New York, NY, 1847 *3377.6 p15*
Kroeze, Hendrik 36; New York, NY, 1847 *3377.6 p15*
Kroeze, Jennigje 10; New York, NY, 1847 *3377.6 p15*
Kroeze, Kunnegien 36; New York, NY, 1847 *3377.6 p15*
Kroff, Elisabetha; Pennsylvania, 1727 *1034.18 p15*
Krog, Owe Ludwig; New York, NY, 1838 *8208.4 p72*
Kroger, . . .; Illinois, 1800-1900 *4610.10 p67*
Kroger, Anne M. L. C. Finke *SEE* Kroger, Carl Heinrich
Kroger, B.; Cincinnati, 1869-1887 *8582 p18*
Kroger, Carl Heinrich; America, 1841 *4610.10 p138*
  *Wife:*Anne M. L. C. Finke
  *Son:*Johann Carl Diedrich
Kroger, Carl Heinrich Friedrich; America, 1870 *4610.10*
  p152
Kroger, Christian Friedrich Wilhelm; America, 1865
  4610.10 p158
Kroger, Heinr. Fr.; America, 1881 *4610.10 p152*
  *Wife:*Sophie L. C. Schaper
Kroger, Johann Carl Diedrich *SEE* Kroger, Carl Heinrich
Kroger, Johann Daniel; America, 1854 *4610.10 p139*
Kroger, Louise Charlotte; America, 1850 *4610.10 p142*
Kroger, Sophie L. C. Schaper *SEE* Kroger, Heinr. Fr.
Krogler, Mr.; Died enroute, 1752-1753 *3689.17 p22*
Krogler, Conrad 15 *SEE* Krogler, Oursella
Krogler, Gaspar 13 *SEE* Krogler, Oursella
Krogler, Hans Ulrich 6 *SEE* Krogler, Oursella
Krogler, Oursella; South Carolina, 1752-1753 *3689.17*
  p22
  *Relative:*Conrad 15
  *Relative:*Gaspar 13
  *Relative:*Hans Ulrich 6
Krogstrup, Otto Christian; New York, 1753 *3652 p77*
Krohn, Charles; Wisconsin, n.d. *9675.6 p199*
Krois, Paula; Wisconsin, n.d. *9675.6 p199*
Kroiss, Johann; Wisconsin, n.d. *9675.6 p199*
Kroiss, John; Wisconsin, n.d. *9675.6 p199*
Krok, Jean-Baptiste 28; New Orleans, 1838 *778.5 p299*
Krol, Boleslaw 5 *SEE* Krol, Ursula Parus
Krol, Stefania 9 *SEE* Krol, Ursula Parus

Krol, Ursula Parus 30; New York, 1912 *9980.29 p73*
  *Daughter:*Stefania 9
  *Son:*Wladyslaw 7
  *Son:*Boleslaw 5
Krol, Wladyslaw; Buffalo, NY, 1912 *9980.29 p73*
Krol, Wladyslaw 7 *SEE* Krol, Ursula Parus
Krolink, John; Wisconsin, n.d. *9675.6 p199*
Kroll, Boleslaw 5 *SEE* Kroll, Ursula Parus
Kroll, Hans Jerg; Pennsylvania, 1743 *2444 p179*
  *Wife:*Margaretha
  *Child:*Maria Rosina
Kroll, John; Washington, 1859-1920 *2872.1 p21*
Kroll, Margaretha *SEE* Kroll, Hans Jerg
Kroll, Maria Rosina *SEE* Kroll, Hans Jerg
Kroll, Stefania 9 *SEE* Kroll, Ursula Parus
Kroll, Ursula Parus 30; New York, 1912 *9980.29 p73*
  *Daughter:*Stefania 9
  *Son:*Wladyslaw 7
  *Son:*Boleslaw 5
Kroll, William; Washington, 1859-1920 *2872.1 p22*
Kroll, Wladyslaw; Buffalo, NY, 1912 *9980.29 p73*
Kroll, Wladyslaw 7 *SEE* Kroll, Ursula Parus
Krolnik, Frank; Wisconsin, n.d. *9675.6 p199*
Krolnik, Johann; Wisconsin, n.d. *9675.6 p199*
Krolnik, Martin; Wisconsin, n.d. *9675.6 p199*
Krome, Augustus; America, 1851 *1450.2 p84A*
Kromer, Andrew 15 mos *SEE* Kromer, George
Kromer, George; South Carolina, 1752-1753 *3689.17*
  p21
  With wife
  *Relative:*John Michael 10
  *Relative:*George 6
  *Relative:*Andrew 15 mos
Kromer, George 6 *SEE* Kromer, George
Kromer, John Michael 10 *SEE* Kromer, George
Krommel, Dominique 32; Port uncertain, 1839 *778.5*
  p299
Kron, Jacob; Indiana, 1845 *9117 p17*
Kronabidder, Francis J.; Ohio, 1845 *9892.11 p25*
Kronabidder, Francis J.; Ohio, 1847 *9892.11 p25*
Kronauer, Johannes; America, 1850 *8582.2 p20*
Kronenberg, Joseph; Wisconsin, n.d. *9675.6 p199*
Kronenberg, Kath. 73; Pittsburgh, 1913 *1763 p40D*
Kronenberg, Wilhelmine Charlotte; America, 1869
  4610.10 p137
Kronenbold, Mr.; Cincinnati, 1831 *8582.1 p51*
Kroning, Carl; Wisconsin, n.d. *9675.6 p199*
Kronlage, Franz; America, 1849 *8582.3 p39*
Kronlage, Heinrich; Baltimore, 1833 *8582 p18*
Kroofin, Maria; South Carolina, 1752-1753 *3689.17 p22*
Kropinski, Egnatz; Arkansas, 1918 *95.2 p69*
Kropp, D.H.; Wisconsin, n.d. *9675.6 p199*
Kropp, Franz F.W.; America, 1879 *1450.2 p21B*
Kross, Eduard; Kentucky, 1844 *8582.3 p101*
Kross, J. 22; America, 1839 *778.5 p299*
Krough, Jens Jensen 28; Arkansas, 1918 *95.2 p69*
Krous, Nicholas; Virginia, 1851 *4626.16 p14*
Krousz, Frederick; New York, NY, 1834 *8208.4 p27*
Krowas, Carl; Iroquois Co., IL, 1892 *3455.1 p12*
Krozic, Andro; Iowa, 1866-1943 *123.54 p29*
Krueger, August; Wisconsin, n.d. *9675.6 p199*
Krueger, Charles; Wisconsin, n.d. *9675.6 p200*
Krueger, Frederick; Wisconsin, n.d. *9675.6 p200*
Krueger, Gustave; Wisconsin, n.d. *9675.6 p200*
Krueger, Johann Ferd.; Wisconsin, n.d. *9675.6 p200*
Krueger, Minnie; Wisconsin, n.d. *9675.6 p200*
Krueger, William; Wisconsin, n.d. *9675.6 p200*
Kruell, Gustav; New Jersey, 1843-1906 *8125.8 p437*
Kruemberg, Theodor; Cincinnati, 1869-1887 *8582 p18*
Krug, . . .; Canada, 1776-1783 *9786 p27*
Krug, Adam; America, 1834 *8582.1 p20*
Krug, Charles; Illinois, 1860 *2896.5 p22*
Krug, Christian; Illinois, 1868 *2896.5 p22*
Krug, Christian; Illinois, 1876 *2896.5 p22*
Krug, Fred; Illinois, 1868 *2896.5 p22*
Krug, Georg; Alberta, n.d. *5262 p58*
Krug, Henry; Illinois, 1879 *2896.5 p23*
Krug, Johannes; Ohio, 1799 *8582.2 p55*
Krug, Justus; Illinois, 1868 *2896.5 p22*
Krug, William; Illinois, 1875 *2896.5 p23*
Krug, William; Illinois, 1880 *2896.5 p23*
Kruger, . . .; Canada, 1776-1783 *9786 p27*
Kruger, . . .; Illinois, 1800-1900 *4610.10 p67*
Kruger, Mr.; America, n.d. *4610.10 p53*
Kruger, Anna M. E. Brockmeyer *SEE* Kruger, Friedrich
  Wilhelm
Kruger, Anne Marie *SEE* Kruger, Johann Friedrich
Kruger, Anne Marie Engel Backs *SEE* Kruger, Carl
Kruger, Anne Marie Louise Charlotte; America, 1857
  4610.10 p158
Kruger, August; Illinois, 1870 *5012.38 p99*
Kruger, August; Wisconsin, n.d. *9675.6 p200*
Kruger, C. Frederick; Illinois, 1882 *2896.5 p23*

Kruger, Carl *SEE* Kruger, Johann Friedrich
Kruger, Carl; America, 1856 *4610.10 p140*
  *Wife:*Anne Marie Engel Backs
  *Child:*Carl Heinrich
  *Child:*Louise Charlotte Engel
  *Child:*Carl H. Friedrich
Kruger, Carl H. Friedrich *SEE* Kruger, Carl
Kruger, Carl Heinrich *SEE* Kruger, Carl
Kruger, Carl Heinrich Friedrich; America, 1884 *4610.10*
  p146
Kruger, Christine *SEE* Kruger, Johann Friedrich
Kruger, Engel *SEE* Kruger, Johann Friedrich
Kruger, Ernst H.; Illinois, 1800-1900 *4610.10 p67*
Kruger, Ernst Heinrich Ludwig *SEE* Kruger, Friedrich
  Wilhelm
Kruger, Friederike Hildebrand *SEE* Kruger, Johann
  Friedrich
Kruger, Friedrich Wilhelm; America, 1846 *4610.10 p95*
  *Wife:*Anna M. E. Brockmeyer
  *Son:*Ernst Heinrich Ludwig
Kruger, Gottlieb *SEE* Kruger, Johann Friedrich
Kruger, Heinrich *SEE* Kruger, Johann Friedrich
Kruger, Heinrich; America, 1871 *4610.10 p159*
Kruger, Heinrich Friedrich Gottlieb; America, 1850
  4610.10 p143
Kruger, Henry; Wisconsin, n.d. *9675.6 p200*
Kruger, Johann Friedrich 48; America, 1850 *4610.10*
  p143
  *Wife:*Friederike Hildebrand
  *Child:*Engel
  *Child:*Wilhelm
  *Child:*Heinrich
  *Child:*Carl
  *Child:*Louise
  *Child:*Christine
  *Child:*Gottlieb
  *Sister:*Anne Marie
Kruger, Louise *SEE* Kruger, Johann Friedrich
Kruger, Louise Charlotte Engel *SEE* Kruger, Carl
Kruger, Wilhelm *SEE* Kruger, Johann Friedrich
Krukansky, Banet; America, 1888 *1450.2 p83A*
Kruke, Henry; Wisconsin, n.d. *9675.6 p200*
Kruke, William; Wisconsin, n.d. *9675.6 p200*
Krukenbeig, John 27; Kansas, 1873 *5240.1 p54*
Krukowski, Kazimir 19; New York, 1912 *9980.29 p51*
Krull, . . .; Canada, 1776-1783 *9786 p27*
Krum, August; Iowa, 1866-1943 *123.54 p29*
Krumbiegel, Gustave; Wisconsin, n.d. *9675.6 p200*
Krumert, Francis 31; Port uncertain, 1839 *778.5 p299*
Krumholtz, Frank; Wisconsin, n.d. *9675.6 p200*
Krumm, . . .; Canada, 1776-1783 *9786 p27*
Krumme, . . .; America, 1833-1871 *3702.7 p62*
Krumme, Wilhelm 28; Ohio, 1837 *3702.7 p62*
Krummel, L.; America, 1853 *3702.7 p325*
Krummen, Sophia; America, 1841 *3702.7 p77*
Krumpanitzky, Harman; Baltimore, 1856 *1450.2 p84A*
Krunegal, Carl; Illinois, 1874 *2896.5 p24*
Krupa, Andrzej 39; New York, 1912 *9980.29 p50*
Krupa, Joseph; Iowa, 1866-1943 *123.54 p29*
Kruper, John Stanley; Arkansas, 1918 *95.2 p69*
Krupliania, Saro; Arkansas, 1918 *95.2 p69*
Krupowna, Anna 22; New York, 1912 *9980.29 p49*
Kruschke, Albert; Wisconsin, n.d. *9675.6 p200*
Kruse, . . .; Canada, 1776-1783 *9786 p27*
Kruse, Adolph Theodore 37; Kansas, 1875 *5240.1 p56*
Kruse, Anna Margarete; America, 1841 *4815.7 p92*
Kruse, Anne Cath Louise Clara *SEE* Kruse, Johann
  Heinrich
Kruse, Anne Marie Cath. Engel *SEE* Kruse, Johann
  Heinrich
Kruse, Anne Marie Cath. Engel *SEE* Kruse, Johann
  Heinrich
Kruse, Anne Marie Luise 7 *SEE* Kruse, Carl Heinrich
  Philipp
Kruse, Bernard; America, 1843 *8582.2 p60*
Kruse, Bernhard; Cincinnati, 1869-1887 *8582 p18*
Kruse, Carl Heinrich *SEE* Kruse, Carl Heinrich Philipp
Kruse, Carl Heinrich Philipp; America, 1853 *4610.10*
  p156
  With wife
  *Child:*Carl Heinrich
  *Child:*Anne Marie Luise 7
  *Child:*Louise Wilhelmine 5
Kruse, Carl Heinrich Wilhelm *SEE* Kruse, Johann
  Heinrich
Kruse, Christian; America, 1847 *1450.2 p84A*
Kruse, Christine Louise Dorothea; America, 1851
  4610.10 p98
Kruse, H. J.; Illinois, 1884 *2896.5 p23*
Kruse, Henry; America, 1853 *1450.2 p84A*
Kruse, J. Friedrich; Cincinnati, 1869-1887 *8582 p18*
Kruse, Joh. Carl Heinrich *SEE* Kruse, Johann Heinrich
Kruse, Johann; Illinois, 1884 *2896.5 p23*

Kruse, Johann; Kentucky, 1843 *8582.3 p100*
Kruse, Johann F. Wilhelm *SEE* Kruse, Johann Heinrich
Kruse, Johann Heinrich; America, 1846 *4610.10 p134*
  *Wife:*Anne Marie Cath. Engel
  *Child:*Anne Cath Louise Clara
  *Child:*Sophie Cath. Louise
  *Child:*Anne Marie Cath. Engel
  *Child:*Joh. Carl Heinrich
  *Child:*Carl Heinrich Wilhelm
  *Child:*Johann F. Wilhelm
Kruse, John C.F.; Illinois, 1870 *5012.38 p99*
Kruse, Louise Wilhelmine 5 *SEE* Kruse, Carl Heinrich
  Philipp
Kruse, Margarete Lucise; Cincinnati, 1838 *4815.7 p92*
Kruse, Marie Christine Louise Dorothee; America, 1844
  4610.10 p97
Kruse, Sophie Cath. Louise *SEE* Kruse, Johann Heinrich
Kruse, Wilhelm; Illinois, 1884 *7857 p4*
Krusewitz, Isabella 18; New York, 1912 *9980.29 p63*
Kruszewski, Jan; New York, 1834 *4606 p178*
Kruszyna, Joseph; Arkansas, 1918 *95.2 p69*
Kruthaun, Johann Joseph Friederich; America, 1850
  8582.3 p39
Krutmeyer, August Georg Wilhelm; America, 1887
  4610.10 p107
Krutz, Carl 56; New York, NY, 1857 *9831.14 p154*
Krutz, Carl Adam 4; New York, NY, 1857 *9831.14 p154*
Krutz, Caroline 20; New York, NY, 1857 *9831.14 p154*
Krutz, Ernestine 18; New York, NY, 1857 *9831.14 p154*
Krutz, Eva Charlotte 49; New York, NY, 1857 *9831.14
  p154*
Kruyeat, Simane; Iowa, 1866-1943 *123.54 p29*
Kruzic, Andro; Iowa, 1866-1943 *123.54 p29*
Kruzic, Anton; Iowa, 1866-1943 *123.54 p29*
Kruzich, Anna; Iowa, 1866-1943 *123.54 p67*
Kruzich, Josep; Iowa, 1866-1943 *123.54 p29*
Kruzich, Rakela; Iowa, 1866-1943 *123.54 p67*
Krychowiak, Aniela 19; New York, 1912 *9980.29 p52*
Krysinski, Tomasz; New York, 1831 *4606 p175*
Krysti, Stenly; Arkansas, 1918 *95.2 p69*
Krysztalowicz, Maria 17; New York, 1912 *9980.29 p61*
Kryzanowsky, Colonel; New York, 1861-1865 *8582.3
  p91*
Krzelak, Helena 29; New York, 1912 *9980.29 p68*
Krzewinski, Jozef; Arkansas, 1918 *95.2 p23*
Krzewinski, Jozef; Arkansas, 1918 *95.2 p69*
Krznar, Anton; Wisconsin, n.d. *9675.6 p200*
Krzyzanowski, Piotr; New York, 1831 *4606 p174*
Ksiadz, Jerzykiewicz Ludwik; New York, 1831 *4606
  p174*
Kuam, Jacob; Colorado, 1897 *9678.2 p122*
Kuam, Ole L.; Colorado, 1897 *9678.2 p122*
Kubarezyk, George; Arkansas, 1918 *95.2 p69*
Kubas, George; Wisconsin, n.d. *9675.6 p200*
Kubelbeck, Adelaide; Wisconsin, n.d. *9675.6 p200*
Kubelbek, Robert; Wisconsin, n.d. *9675.6 p200*
Kubitz, Herman; New York, 1883 *1450.2 p21B*
Kubom, Nicholas; Wisconsin, n.d. *9675.6 p200*
Kubos, Frank; Wisconsin, n.d. *9675.6 p200*
Kucan, Ivan; Iowa, 1866-1943 *123.54 p29*
Kucan, Katarina; Iowa, 1866-1943 *123.54 p29*
Kucan, Vinko; Iowa, 1866-1943 *123.54 p29*
Kuch, Burckhardt; Pennsylvania, 1754 *4525 p230*
Kuch, Burkhard; Pennsylvania, 1755 *4525 p230*
  With wife
  With children
Kuchan, Mary; Iowa, 1866-1943 *123.54 p29*
Kucharski, . . .; New York, 1835 *4606 p179*
Kuchenmann, Rumen 18; New York, NY, 1878 *9253
  p46*
Kuchenthal, . . .; Canada, 1776-1783 *9786 p42*
Kuchler, Joh. Ludw. 24; America, 1854-1855 *9162.6
  p104*
Kudelski, Antoni 20; New York, 1912 *9980.29 p50*
Kuder, Frederick; Indiana, 1848 *9117 p17*
Kuebelbeck, Adelaide; Wisconsin, n.d. *9675.6 p200*
Kuebelbeck, Joseph; Wisconsin, n.d. *9675.6 p200*
Kuebelbeck, Mike; Wisconsin, n.d. *9675.6 p200*
Kuebler, Alexander; Arkansas, 1918 *95.2 p69*
Kuebler, Anna Catharina *SEE* Kuebler, Jacob
Kuebler, Christian 47; California, 1873 *2769.10 p4*
Kuebler, Gottlieb *SEE* Kuebler, Jacob
Kuebler, Jacob; Pennsylvania, 1749 *2444 p179*
  *Wife:*Anna Catharina
  *Child:*Johann Jacob
  *Child:*Rosina
  *Child:*Gottlieb
Kuebler, Johann Jacob *SEE* Kuebler, Jacob
Kuebler, Rosina *SEE* Kuebler, Jacob
Kuechenmeister, Ferdinand 29; Kansas, 1886 *5240.1 p26*
Kuechenmeister, Ferdinand 29; Kansas, 1886 *5240.1 p69*
Kuefer, Georg Friedrich; Pennsylvania, 1715-1795 *2444
  p179*

Kuefer, Hans Jerg; Port uncertain, 1721-1800 *2444 p180*
Kuefer, Jerg; Pennsylvania, 1742 *2444 p180*
Kuefer, John George; Pennsylvania, 1752 *2444 p180*
Kuefer, Philipp; America, 1840 *8582.3 p39*
Kuefer, Primus; Kentucky, 1839-1840 *8582.3 p98*
Kueffer, John George; Pennsylvania, 1752 *2444 p180*
Kuehbord, Conrad; Cincinnati, 1869-1887 *8582 p18*
Kuehl, Dietrich Henry; Wisconsin, n.d. *9675.6 p200*
Kuehn, Eusebius Franz; America, n.d. *8582.3 p79*
Kuehn, Georg; America, 1836 *8582.3 p39*
Kuehn, Georg; Cincinnati, 1840 *8582.3 p86*
  With parents
Kuehn, Jacob 40; Kansas, 1882 *5240.1 p26*
Kuehn, Jacob 40; Kansas, 1882 *5240.1 p63*
Kuehnast, Christopher; New York, 1749 *3652 p71*
Kuehner, Anna Maria; Pennsylvania, 1754 *2444 p173*
Kuehr, Ferdinand; America, 1840 *8582.3 p101*
Kuehr, Ferdinand; Cincinnati, 1806-1848 *8582.3 p89*
Kuehr, Ferdinand; Kentucky, 1840-1845 *8582.3 p100*
Kuehr, Ferdinand; Kentucky, 1842 *8582.3 p100*
Kuehr, Ferdinand; Kentucky, 1869-1887 *8582 p18*
Kuehr, Johann Ferdinand; Charleston, SC, 1836-1840
  8582 p18
Kuemmerle, Anna Margaretha *SEE* Kuemmerle, Johann
  Jacob
Kuemmerle, Johann Jacob *SEE* Kuemmerle, Johann
  Jacob
Kuemmerle, Johann Jacob; Pennsylvania, 1753 *2444
  p180*
  *Wife:*M. Heintzelmann
  *Child:*Anna Margaretha
  *Child:*Johann Jacob
Kuemmerle, M. Heintzelmann *SEE* Kuemmerle, Johann
  Jacob
Kuemmerlen, Johann Ulrich, Jr.; Philadelphia, 1818
  8582.2 p21
Kuemmerlie, Jacob; Pennsylvania, 1753 *2444 p180*
Kuemmerlin, Mr.; Died enroute, 1751-1754 *2444 p180*
Kuemmerlin, Anna *SEE* Kuemmerlin, Johannes
Kuemmerlin, Anna Margaretha *SEE* Kuemmerlin,
  Johann Jacob
Kuemmerlin, Anna Maria *SEE* Kuemmerlin, Hans
  Martin
Kuemmerlin, Anna Maria *SEE* Kuemmerlin, Hans
  Martin
Kuemmerlin, Anna Maria *SEE* Kuemmerlin, Johannes
Kuemmerlin, Christianus *SEE* Kuemmerlin, Hans Martin
Kuemmerlin, Eva Enzlin *SEE* Kuemmerlin, Johannes
Kuemmerlin, Hans Martin; Philadelphia, 1751 *2444
  p180*
  *Wife:*Anna Maria
  *Child:*Anna Maria
  *Child:*Matthaus Jacob
  *Child:*Christianus
Kuemmerlin, Johann Georg *SEE* Kuemmerlin, Johannes
Kuemmerlin, Johann Jacob *SEE* Kuemmerlin, Johann
  Jacob
Kuemmerlin, Johann Jacob *SEE* Kuemmerlin, Johannes
Kuemmerlin, Johann Jacob; Pennsylvania, 1753 *2444
  p180*
  *Wife:*M. Heintzelmann
  *Child:*Anna Margaretha
  *Child:*Johann Jacob
Kuemmerlin, Johann Michael *SEE* Kuemmerlin,
  Johannes
Kuemmerlin, Johannes; Philadelphia, 1751 *2444 p180*
  With mother
  *Wife:*Eva Enzlin
  *Child:*Johann Michael
  *Child:*Anna
  *Child:*Johann Georg
  *Child:*Anna Maria
  *Child:*Johann Jacob
Kuemmerlin, M. Heintzelmann *SEE* Kuemmerlin, Johann
  Jacob
Kuemmerlin, Maria Agnes; Pennsylvania, 1749-1800
  2444 p232
Kuemmerlin, Matthaus Jacob *SEE* Kuemmerlin, Hans
  Martin
Kuemmerling, Martin; Philadelphia, 1751 *2444 p180*
Kuemmerly, Mr.; Died enroute, 1751-1754 *2444 p180*
Kuemmerly, Hans; Philadelphia, 1751 *2444 p180*
Kuemmler, Hans Jacob; America, 1736-1800 *2444 p180*
  *Wife:*Rosina
  *Child:*Ursula
Kuemmler, Rosina *SEE* Kuemmler, Hans Jacob
Kuemmler, Ursula *SEE* Kuemmler, Hans Jacob
Kuenkele, Daniel; Pennsylvania, 1746 *2444 p174*
Kuenninger, Andreas; America, 1830 *8582.2 p61*
Kueppel, Ernest; Wisconsin, n.d. *9675.6 p200*
Kuepper, Karl; Milwaukee, 1849 *8125.8 p437*
Kuerschner, Nikolaus; Philadelphia, 1779 *8137 p11*
Kuershner, Christopher; New York, 1754 *3652 p80*

Kuessy, Roger; Acadia, 1668 *7603 p75*
Kuester, C. E.; New York, 1850 *8125.8 p437*
Kuester, Charles Edward; New York, 1850 *1450.2 p84A*
Kuestner, Friedrich; Philadelphia, 1779 *8137 p11*
Kuffener, . . .; Canada, 1776-1783 *9786 p27*
Kugeler, . . .; Canada, 1776-1783 *9786 p27*
Kughler, Johannes; Pennsylvania, 1752 *2444 p181*
Kuglar, John; Pennsylvania, 1752 *2444 p181*
Kuglar, John; South Carolina, 1788 *7119 p201*
Kugler, Christopher; Cincinnati, 1835 *8582.2 p60*
Kugler, Gottlob; New York, NY, 1895 *3455.2 p45*
Kugler, Gottlob; New York, NY, 1895 *3455.3 p105*
  *Wife:*Minnie Siegle
Kugler, Johannes; Pennsylvania, 1752 *2444 p181*
Kugler, Minnie Siegle *SEE* Kugler, Gottlob
Kuhartzij, George; Arkansas, 1918 *95.2 p69*
Kuhartzy, George; Arkansas, 1918 *95.2 p69*
Kuhl, Friedrich; Philadelphia, 1776 *8582.3 p85*
Kuhl, Peter; Wisconsin, n.d. *9675.6 p200*
Kuhle, Arnold 18; America, 1880 *4610.10 p137*
Kuhler Family ; New York, 1765 *8125.8 p436*
Kuhler, Henrich Gustave; Kansas, 1875 *5240.1 p26*
Kuhler, Karl; New York, NY, 1838 *8208.4 p80*
Kuhling, Carolina 10 *SEE* Kuhling, John Gottl.
Kuhling, Johanna 48 *SEE* Kuhling, John Gottl.
Kuhling, John Gottl. 38; New Orleans, 1839 *9420.2 p361*
  *Wife:*Johanna 48
  *Daughter:*Carolina 10
Kuhlman, . . .; Canada, 1776-1783 *9786 p27*
Kuhlman, Christian; America, 1840 *1450.2 p85A*
Kuhlman, Edd; New York, NY, 1923 *3455.3 p84*
Kuhlman, Frederick; America, 1838 *1450.2 p85A*
Kuhlman, Henry; America, 1840 *1450.2 p85A*
Kuhlman, Peter; Indiana, 1850 *9117 p20*
Kuhlmann, Anna Marie Cath.; America, 1857 *4610.10
  p136*
Kuhlmann, Anne M. C. E. Stucke *SEE* Kuhlmann,
  Johann Caspar Heinrich
Kuhlmann, Anne M. Johanne Engel *SEE* Kuhlmann,
  Johann Caspar Heinrich
Kuhlmann, Carl Heinrich Wilhelm; America, 1858
  4610.10 p136
Kuhlmann, Christian Friedrich Adolph; America, 1875
  4610.10 p106
Kuhlmann, Elisabeth Ruter *SEE* Kuhlmann, Hermann
  Johann
Kuhlmann, Ernst Friedr. Gottlieb; America, 1885
  4610.10 p107
Kuhlmann, Friederich; Kentucky, 1843 *8582.3 p100*
Kuhlmann, Friedrich Wilhelm *SEE* Kuhlmann, Hermann
  Johann
Kuhlmann, Georg; America, 1846 *8582.1 p20*
Kuhlmann, Gottlieb H. H. E. Friedrich; America, 1887
  4610.10 p107
Kuhlmann, Heinrich August *SEE* Kuhlmann, Hermann
  Johann
Kuhlmann, Heinrich F. Ludwig *SEE* Kuhlmann,
  Hermann Johann
Kuhlmann, Heinrich Gottlieb; America, 1860 *4610.10
  p136*
Kuhlmann, Hermann Johann; America, 1888 *4610.10
  p107*
  *Wife:*Elisabeth Ruter
  *Child:*Heinrich F. Ludwig
  *Child:*Friedrich Wilhelm
  *Child:*Heinrich August
Kuhlmann, Johann Caspar Heinrich; America, 1860
  4610.10 p136
  *Wife:*Anne M. C. E. Stucke
  *Child:*Louise W. Engel
  *Child:*Anne M. Johanne Engel
Kuhlmann, Johann Heinrich; America, 1833 *8582.1 p20*
Kuhlmann, Johann Heinrich Wilhelm; America, 1860
  4610.10 p136
Kuhlmann, Louise W. Engel *SEE* Kuhlmann, Johann
  Caspar Heinrich
Kuhlmeyer, Friedrich Wilhelm; America, 1853 *4610.10
  p156*
  With stepfather
Kuhlo, Arnold; America, 1880 *4610.10 p146*
Kuhlo, August 16; America, 1880 *4610.10 p146*
Kuhlo, Ernst 13; America, 1880 *4610.10 p146*
Kuhmis, Joseph; Washington, 1859-1920 *2872.1 p22*
Kuhn, . . .; Canada, 1776-1783 *9786 p27*
Kuhn, Amalia Friedke 17; New Orleans, 1839 *9420.2
  p67*
Kuhn, Anna Barbara Adam *SEE* Kuhn, Johannes
Kuhn, Anna Elisabetha; Carolina, 1741 *4349 p46*
  *Son:*Johannes 23
  *Son:*Johann Wilhelm 13
Kuhn, Carl; Milwaukee, 1875 *4719.30 p258*
Kuhn, Caroline 7; New Orleans, 1839 *9420.2 p67*
Kuhn, Charles; Illinois, 1888 *5012.37 p61*

Kuhn, Christoph; Pennsylvania, 1752 ***4525*** *p230*
Kuhn, Christoph; Philadelphia, 1753 ***4525*** *p263*
Kuhn, Eleonore 11; New Orleans, 1839 ***9420.2*** *p67*
Kuhn, Elsie May; Maryland, 1889 ***1450.2*** *p21B*
Kuhn, Emilie 5; New Orleans, 1839 ***9420.2*** *p67*
Kuhn, Franz; Philadelphia, 1764 ***2444*** *p181*
*Wife:*Maria E. Horlacher
With child 4
With child 2
With child 6 mos
Kuhn, Frederick; Philadelphia, 1764 ***9973.7*** *p39*
Kuhn, Georg; Cincinnati, 1869-1887 ***8582*** *p18*
Kuhn, Georg Michael; America, 1836 ***8582*** *p18*
Kuhn, George; New York, NY, 1838 ***8208.4*** *p84*
Kuhn, George Phillip; Wisconsin, n.d. ***9675.6*** *p200*
Kuhn, Henry; South Carolina, 1788 ***7119*** *p198*
Kuhn, Jacob; New York, NY, 1838 ***8208.4*** *p71*
Kuhn, Joh. Gottfried 21; New Orleans, 1839 ***9420.2*** *p169*
Kuhn, Johann Adam 1; New Orleans, 1839 ***9420.2*** *p67*
Kuhn, Johann Adam 44; New Orleans, 1839 ***9420.2*** *p67*
Kuhn, Johann Wilhelm 13 *SEE* Kuhn, Anna Elisabetha
Kuhn, Johanna Christne. 15; New Orleans, 1839 ***9420.2*** *p67*
Kuhn, Johanne Elisabeth 44; New Orleans, 1839 ***9420.2*** *p67*
Kuhn, Johanne Rosine 14; New Orleans, 1839 ***9420.2*** *p67*
Kuhn, Johannes; Pennsylvania, 1753 ***2444*** *p181*
*Wife:*Anna Barbara Adam
With father-in-law
With 3 children
Kuhn, Johannes; Philadelphia, 1741 ***4349*** *p46*
Kuhn, Johannes; Philadelphia, 1779 ***8137*** *p11*
Kuhn, Johannes 23 *SEE* Kuhn, Anna Elisabetha
Kuhn, Maria E. Horlacher *SEE* Kuhn, Franz
Kuhn, Michael; America, 1850 ***8582.3*** *p40*
Kuhn, Peter; Wisconsin, n.d. ***9675.6*** *p200*
Kuhn, Rudolph 47; Pittsburgh, 1871 ***8582*** *p18*
Kuhn, Susanna Plank 49; America, 1897 ***1763*** *p40D*
Kuhne, . . .; Canada, 1776-1783 ***9786*** *p27*
Kuhne, Carl Friedrich August; America, 1850 ***4610.10*** *p143*
Kuhne, Caroline *SEE* Kuhne, Christoph Heinrich
Kuhne, Christoph Heinrich 51; America, 1852 ***4610.10*** *p144*
With wife
*Child:*Caroline
*Child:*Franz Carl Heinrich
*Child:*Friederike
Kuhne, Franz Carl Heinrich *SEE* Kuhne, Christoph Heinrich
Kuhne, Friederike *SEE* Kuhne, Christoph Heinrich
Kuhne, Herman; Illinois, 1892 ***2896.5*** *p23*
Kuhne, Paul Gustav Adolf; Illinois, 1906 ***5012.39*** *p54*
Kuhner, Anna Dorothea *SEE* Kuhner, Philipp
Kuhner, Christina Catharina *SEE* Kuhner, Philipp
Kuhner, Philipp; Port uncertain, 1717 ***3627*** *p17*
With 3 children
*Wife:*Christina Catharina
*Child:*Anna Dorothea
Kuhnert, Christian 11; New Orleans, 1839 ***9420.1*** *p377*
Kuhnert, Gottlieb 43; New Orleans, 1839 ***9420.1*** *p377*
Kuhnert, Juliane 13; New Orleans, 1839 ***9420.1*** *p377*
Kuhnert, Rosine 41; New Orleans, 1839 ***9420.1*** *p377*
Kuhns, Michael; Philadelphia, 1760 ***9973.7*** *p34*
Kuhr, Ferdinand; Kentucky, 1842 ***8582.3*** *p100*
Kuhron, . . .; Canada, 1776-1783 ***9786*** *p27*
Kuic, Simon; America, 1900 ***7137*** *p169*
Kuie, Louis; California, 1867 ***3840.2*** *p16*
Kuin, Louise 24; New Orleans, 1838 ***778.5*** *p299*
Kuizman, Vince; Iowa, 1866-1943 ***123.54*** *p29*
Kujanpaa, John; Arkansas, 1918 ***95.2*** *p69*
Kuk, . . .; Cincinnati, 1847 ***3702.7*** *p84*
Kukan, Alexander 35; Dominica, 1774 ***1219.7*** *p205*
Kuklandsky, Frank; Oklahoma, 1891 ***5240.1*** *p26*
Kulenski, Frank; Wisconsin, n.d. ***9675.6*** *p200*
Kulesz, Mikolaj 5 *SEE* Kulesz, Stanislawa Jatczak
Kulesz, Stanislawa Jatczak 26; New York, 1912 ***9980.29*** *p52*
*Son:*Stefan 9
*Son:*Mikolaj 5
Kulesz, Stefan 9 *SEE* Kulesz, Stanislawa Jatczak
Kulesza, Peter; Arkansas, 1918 ***95.2*** *p69*
Kulilic, Joseph; Wisconsin, n.d. ***9675.6*** *p200*
Kulka, Anna 17; New York, 1912 ***9980.29*** *p66*
Kulle, David; Pennsylvania, 1751 ***2444*** *p181*
Kullen, David; Pennsylvania, 1751 ***2444*** *p181*
Kullenberg Family ; New York, 1765 ***8125.8*** *p436*
Kullilane, Mary 22; Wilmington, DE, 1831 ***6508.3*** *p101*
Kullin, Sybilla Catharine; Pennsylvania, 1744 ***2444*** *p165*
Kulling, David; Pennsylvania, 1751 ***2444*** *p144*
Kulling, David; Pennsylvania, 1751 ***2444*** *p181*
Kullman, Valentine; Indiana, 1848 ***9117*** *p17*
Kulmann, Fritz; Died enroute, 1853 ***4610.10*** *p40*
Kulong, . . .; Canada, 1776-1783 ***9786*** *p27*
Kulp, . . .; Canada, 1776-1783 ***9786*** *p27*
Kultgen, Dominic; Wisconsin, n.d. ***9675.6*** *p200*
Kulvany, Frank; Colorado, 1902 ***9678.2*** *p122*
Kuly, Jonas Petros; Arkansas, 1918 ***95.2*** *p69*
Kumbarski, Peter; Wisconsin, n.d. ***9675.6*** *p200*
Kumbear, Johan; Wisconsin, n.d. ***9675.6*** *p200*
Kuminski, Christoph; Wisconsin, n.d. ***9675.6*** *p200*
Kumlert, Martin; Virginia, 1775 ***1219.7*** *p275*
Kummel, . . .; Canada, 1776-1783 ***9786*** *p27*
Kummel, Henry I.; New York, NY, 1837 ***8208.4*** *p51*
Kummerle, . . .; Canada, 1776-1783 ***9786*** *p27*
Kummerlin, Anna; Port uncertain, 1754 ***2444*** *p132*
Kump, Frank; Arkansas, 1918 ***95.2*** *p70*
Kumpf, Christoph; Pennsylvania, 1785 ***2444*** *p181*
With wife
With niece
Kumpf, Christoph; Port uncertain, 1785 ***2444*** *p181*
With wife
With niece
Kumpff, . . .; Canada, 1776-1783 ***9786*** *p27*
Kunad, Andrew 40; New Orleans, 1839 ***9420.2*** *p485*
Kunber, William 18; Maryland, 1774 ***1219.7*** *p181*
Kunckell, . . .; Canada, 1776-1783 ***9786*** *p27*
Kunczius, Francis; Wisconsin, n.d. ***9675.6*** *p200*
Kunda, Juray; Iowa, 1866-1943 ***123.54*** *p29*
Kunda, Paul; Iowa, 1866-1943 ***123.54*** *p29*
Kundek, Joseph; Cincinnati, 1788-1848 ***8582.3*** *p89*
Kundelach, . . .; Canada, 1776-1783 ***9786*** *p27*
Kunders, Cunread *SEE* Kunders, Tonis
Kunders, Jan *SEE* Kunders, Tonis
Kunders, Lijntijen Teissen *SEE* Kunders, Tonis
Kunders, Matthias *SEE* Kunders, Tonis
Kunders, Tonis; Pennsylvania, 1683 ***2155*** *p1*
*Wife:*Lijntijen Teissen
*Child:*Cunread
*Child:*Matthias
*Child:*Jan
Kundert, Fridolin; Illinois, 1871 ***8582*** *p19*
Kundner, Gabrial; Colorado, 1890 ***9678.2*** *p122*
Kundzewicz, John; Arkansas, 1918 ***95.2*** *p70*
Kunecke, Friderick; Canada, 1783 ***9786*** *p38A*
Kunert, Edwin; Washington, 1859-1920 ***2872.1*** *p22*
Kunert, Gottfried; Washington, 1859-1920 ***2872.1*** *p22*
Kunert, Henry 27; Kansas, 1884 ***5240.1*** *p66*
Kunert, Lenord; Washington, 1859-1920 ***2872.1*** *p22*
Kunert, Olleilei; Washington, 1859-1920 ***2872.1*** *p22*
Kunert, Pauline; Washington, 1859-1920 ***2872.1*** *p22*
Kunicki, Alfons; New York, 1831 ***4606*** *p174*
Kunigers, . . .; Canada, 1776-1783 ***9786*** *p27*
Kunkel, Albert; Nebraska, 1886 ***5240.1*** *p26*
Kunkel, Johannes; Cincinnati, 1869-1887 ***8582*** *p19*
Kunkel, Theodor; America, 1845 ***8582.3*** *p40*
Kunkler, Anna Mary *SEE* Kunkler, Daniel
Kunkler, Daniel; New York, 1743 ***3652*** *p59*
*Wife:*Anna Mary
Kunkler, Mattias; South Carolina, 1788 ***7119*** *p201*
Kunni, Nicholas; Wisconsin, n.d. ***9675.6*** *p200*
Kunning, Dorothee Sophie; Texas, 1845 ***4815.7*** *p92*
Kunning, Hermann Friedrich; America, 1845 ***4815.7*** *p92*
*Wife:*Margarete D. Speckmann
With 3 children
Kunning, Margarete D. Speckmann *SEE* Kunning, Hermann Friedrich
Kunopky, Ben; Arkansas, 1918 ***95.2*** *p70*
Kunse, Oscar; Wisconsin, n.d. ***9675.6*** *p200*
Kunstler, . . .; Canada, 1776-1783 ***9786*** *p27*
Kuntuctas, John; Wisconsin, n.d. ***9675.6*** *p200*
Kuntz, Charles; Wisconsin, n.d. ***9675.6*** *p200*
Kuntz, Franz; Kentucky, 1840-1845 ***8582.3*** *p100*
Kuntz, Georg; Lancaster, PA, 1780 ***8137*** *p11*
Kuntz, Jacob; Philadelphia, 1765 ***9973.7*** *p40*
Kuntz, Konrad; Lancaster, PA, 1780 ***8137*** *p11*
Kuntz, Lucien; New York, NY, 1914 ***3455.2*** *p73*
Kuntz, Lucien; New York, NY, 1914 ***3455.3*** *p45*
Kuntz, Ludwig; New York, NY, 1838 ***8208.4*** *p75*
Kuntz, Martin C.; New York, 1874 ***1450.2*** *p21B*
Kuntz, Philip 29; Pennsylvania, 1741 ***4779.3*** *p13*
Kuntz, Pierre 17; New Orleans, 1838 ***778.5*** *p299*
Kuntzelman, Hans Jerg; Pennsylvania, 1749 ***2444*** *p145*
Kuntzelman, Hans Jerg; Pennsylvania, 1749 ***2444*** *p164*
Kuntzelman, Hans Jerg; Pennsylvania, 1749 ***2444*** *p202*
Kunz, . . .; Canada, 1776-1783 ***9786*** *p27*
Kunz, Christine 24; New Orleans, 1838 ***778.5*** *p299*
Kunz, David; New York, 1749 ***3652*** *p72*
Kunz, David; New York, 1754 ***3652*** *p80*
Kunz, Elisabetha 18; America, 1853 ***9162.7*** *p15*
Kunz, Jean 32; America, 1836 ***778.5*** *p299*
Kunz, Matthew; New York, 1748 ***3652*** *p68*
Kunze, Chaplain; Quebec, 1776 ***9786*** *p263*
Kunzel, Mr.; Missouri, 1836 ***3702.7*** *p100*
Kunzlin, J. Sigmund; New York, NY, 1837 ***8208.4*** *p32*
Kunzlin, Sigsmund; New York, NY, 1838 ***8208.4*** *p83*
Kunztmann, . . .; Canada, 1776-1783 ***9786*** *p27*
Kuohn, Johannes; Pennsylvania, 1753 ***2444*** *p181*
Kuoth, . . .; Canada, 1776-1783 ***9786*** *p42*
Kupec, John; America, 1885 ***7137*** *p169*
Kupec, Mary; America, 1887 ***7137*** *p169*
Kupetz, John; America, 1885 ***7137*** *p169*
Kupetz, Mary; America, 1887 ***7137*** *p169*
Kupferle, Johannes; Kentucky, 1840-1845 ***8582.3*** *p100*
Kupffer, . . .; Canada, 1776-1783 ***9786*** *p27*
Kupic, Joseph; America, 1898 ***7137*** *p169*
Kupke, Carl; Wisconsin, n.d. ***9675.6*** *p200*
Kuppner, Christian; Illinois, 1836 ***8582.1*** *p55*
Kuratha, Mary 45; Arizona, 1916 ***9228.40*** *p20*
Kurck, Adam; New York, NY, 1836 ***8208.4*** *p16*
Kurdzalek, Albert; Arkansas, 1918 ***95.2*** *p70*
Kurdzialak, Woichieh; Arkansas, 1918 ***95.2*** *p70*
Kure, Nicholas 28; Port uncertain, 1838 ***778.5*** *p299*
Kurella, . . .; America, n.d. ***4606*** *p180*
Kurfess, Anna M. Heintzmann *SEE* Kurfess, Jacob
Kurfess, Anna Maria *SEE* Kurfess, Jacob
Kurfess, Anna Maria Elisabetha *SEE* Kurfess, Joerg
Kurfess, Emma Catharina *SEE* Kurfess, Jacob
Kurfess, Georg *SEE* Kurfess, Joerg
Kurfess, Gottlieb *SEE* Kurfess, Joerg
Kurfess, Hans Jorg *SEE* Kurfess, Jacob
Kurfess, Jacob *SEE* Kurfess, Jacob
Kurfess, Jacob; Pennsylvania, 1750-1800 ***2444*** *p181*
*Wife:*Anna M. Heintzmann
*Child:*Emma Catharina
*Child:*Hans Jorg
*Child:*Anna Maria
*Child:*Johannes
*Child:*Jacob
*Child:*Michael
Kurfess, Joerg; Pennsylvania, 1751-1800 ***2444*** *p182*
*Wife:*Maria Roth
*Child:*Anna Maria Elisabetha
*Child:*Johannes
*Child:*Georg
*Child:*Gottlieb
Kurfess, Johannes *SEE* Kurfess, Jacob
Kurfess, Johannes *SEE* Kurfess, Joerg
Kurfess, Maria Roth *SEE* Kurfess, Joerg
Kurfess, Michael *SEE* Kurfess, Jacob
Kurfingthan, Mr.; Maryland, 1768 ***8582.3*** *p96*
Kurfiss, Mr.; Cincinnati, 1831 ***8582.1*** *p51*
Kurfiss, Ernst Friedrich; New Orleans, 1829 ***8582*** *p19*
Kurfiss, Friedrich; Ohio, 1843 ***8582.1*** *p51*
Kurkiewicz, Agnes Tatczak 25; New York, 1912 ***9980.29*** *p57*
*Daughter:*Franciszka 2
Kurkiewicz, Franciszka 2 *SEE* Kurkiewicz, Agnes Tatczak
Kurkiewicz, Jan; Detroit, 1912 ***9980.29*** *p57*
Kurle, Johann Bernard; Illinois, 1800-1874 ***8582.1*** *p55*
Kurleth, Adam 17; America, 1836 ***778.5*** *p88*
Kurleth, Johanna 23; America, 1836 ***778.5*** *p88*
Kurlis, Peter; Pennsylvania, 1683 ***2155*** *p2*
Kurnerle, . . .; Canada, 1776-1783 ***9786*** *p27*
Kurnitzsky, Abraham 9; New York, NY, 1878 ***9253*** *p46*
Kurnitzsky, Cheim 11 mos; New York, NY, 1878 ***9253*** *p46*
Kurnitzsky, Hosias 8; New York, NY, 1878 ***9253*** *p46*
Kurnitzsky, Lea 38; New York, NY, 1878 ***9253*** *p46*
Kurre, H. H.; Kentucky, 1869-1887 ***8582*** *p19*
Kurre, Heinrich; Kentucky, 1840-1845 ***8582.3*** *p100*
Kursh, Herman; Washington, 1859-1920 ***2872.1*** *p22*
Kurt, Carl William; Arkansas, 1918 ***95.2*** *p70*
Kurth, Pauline; Washington, 1859-1920 ***2872.1*** *p22*
Kurtts, Mikael; Arkansas, 1918 ***95.2*** *p70*
Kurtz, Andre 1; America, 1836 ***778.5*** *p299*
Kurtz, Andre 37; America, 1836 ***778.5*** *p299*
Kurtz, Anne Marie 6 mos; America, 1836 ***778.5*** *p299*
Kurtz, Anne Marie 38; America, 1836 ***778.5*** *p299*
Kurtz, Catharine 6; America, 1836 ***778.5*** *p300*
Kurtz, Christianus *SEE* Kurtz, Johannes
Kurtz, Christoph; Pennsylvania, 1752 ***2444*** *p182*
Kurtz, Cretina 16; America, 1836 ***778.5*** *p300*
Kurtz, Daniel; Pennsylvania, 1749 ***2444*** *p182*
Kurtz, Frederick; Illinois, 1859 ***2896.5*** *p23*
Kurtz, Jacques 30; America, 1836 ***778.5*** *p300*
Kurtz, Johann Christophel; Pennsylvania, 1765 ***2444*** *p182*
Kurtz, Johann Jacob *SEE* Kurtz, Johannes
Kurtz, Johannes; Pennsylvania, 1752 ***2444*** *p182*
*Wife:*Margaretha
*Child:*Maria Agnes
*Child:*Christianus
*Child:*Johann Jacob
With 3 children
Kurtz, Johannes; Pennsylvania, 1752 ***2444*** *p204*

Kurtz, John; New York, NY, 1836 *8208.4 p15*
Kurtz, John; Pennsylvania, 1752 *4779.3 p14A*
Kurtz, Kurt Henrich; Lancaster, PA, 1780 *8137 p11*
Kurtz, Madelena 18; America, 1836 *778.5 p300*
Kurtz, Margaretha *SEE* Kurtz, Johannes
Kurtz, Maria Agnes *SEE* Kurtz, Johannes
Kurtz, Marie 30; America, 1836 *778.5 p300*
Kurtz, Michal 10; America, 1836 *778.5 p300*
Kurtz, Nicolas 2; America, 1836 *778.5 p300*
Kurtzrock, Georg; Philadelphia, 1779 *8137 p11*
Kurylowicz, . . .; New York, 1831 *4606 p174*
Kurz, Anna Barbara; Philadelphia, 1764 *2444 p142*
Kurz, Ch. Henry; Wisconsin, n.d. *9675.6 p200*
Kurz, Christianus *SEE* Kurz, Johannes
Kurz, Christoph; Port uncertain, 1751 *2444 p182*
Kurz, Daniel; America, 1745 *2444 p182*
Kurz, George Frederick; New York, NY, 1851 *2896.5 p23*
Kurz, Johann Jacob *SEE* Kurz, Johannes
Kurz, Johannes; Pennsylvania, 1752 *2444 p182*
   *Wife:*Margaretha
   *Child:*Maria Agnes
   *Child:*Christianus
   *Child:*Johann Jacob
   With 3 children
Kurz, Margaretha *SEE* Kurz, Johannes
Kurz, Margaretha; Pennsylvania, 1752 *2444 p199*
Kurz, Margaretha; Port uncertain, 1752 *2444 p199*
Kurz, Maria Agnes *SEE* Kurz, Johannes
Kurz, Philipp Heinrich 18; America, 1853 *9162.8 p36*
Kurzbuch, Alfred; Wisconsin, n.d. *9675.6 p200*
Kurzerwich, Samuel; Arkansas, 1918 *95.2 p70*
Kurziski, Michael; Arkansas, 1918 *95.2 p70*
Kusanke, Hermann; Wisconsin, n.d. *9675.6 p200*
Kusche, William; New York, NY, 1848 *1450.2 p85A*
Kuse, Friedrich Carl Heinrich; America, 1872 *4610.10 p100*
Kuse, Heinrich Dietrich Gottlieb; America, 1880 *4610.10 p101*
Kuske, Carl August 8; New York, NY, 1857 *9831.14 p154*
Kuske, Carl Friedr. Wilh. 14; New York, NY, 1857 *9831.14 p154*
Kuske, Carl Friedrich 11; New York, NY, 1857 *9831.14 p154*
Kuske, Carl Ludwig 11 mos; New York, NY, 1857 *9831.14 p154*
Kuske, Ernestine Auguste 6; New York, NY, 1857 *9831.14 p154*
Kuske, Joh. Friedrich 2; New York, NY, 1857 *9831.14 p154*

Kuske, Julius Friedrich 13; New York, NY, 1857 *9831.14 p154*
Kuske, Justine 38; New York, NY, 1857 *9831.14 p154*
Kuske, Marie Louise 4; New York, NY, 1857 *9831.14 p154*
Kuske, Wilhelm 39; New York, NY, 1857 *9831.14 p154*
Kuske, Wilhelmine 16; New York, NY, 1857 *9831.14 p154*
Kusn, Charles 23; America, 1838 *778.5 p300*
Kuss, Michel 27; Port uncertain, 1839 *778.5 p300*
Kussner, L. 20; America, 1836 *778.5 p300*
Kuster, Paulus; Germantown, PA, 1684 *2467.7 p5*
Kustner, Edward 15; America, 1854-1855 *9162.6 p105*
Kustner, Leonh. 17; America, 1854-1855 *9162.6 p105*
Kusyak, Andrew; Iowa, 1866-1943 *123.54 p29*
Kutait, Camil Mahanna; Arkansas, 1918 *95.2 p70*
Kutasi, Julius; Wisconsin, n.d. *9675.6 p200*
Kutasiewicz, . . .; New York, 1831 *4606 p174*
Kutchever, Jacob; California, 1870 *2769.6 p3*
Kuten, . . .; Canada, 1776-1783 *9786 p27*
Kuther, Herman; Wisconsin, n.d. *9675.6 p200*
Kuther, John Henry; Wisconsin, n.d. *9675.6 p200*
Kutnar, Anton; Wisconsin, n.d. *9675.6 p200*
Kutnar, John; Wisconsin, n.d. *9675.6 p200*
Kutner, Martin; Wisconsin, n.d. *9675.6 p200*
Kutnink, Hermann 26; Kansas, 1890 *5240.1 p75*
Kutshker, William; Wisconsin, n.d. *9675.6 p200*
Kutter, Leonard; Wisconsin, n.d. *9675.6 p200*
Kuttman, . . .; Canada, 1776-1783 *9786 p27*
Kuwatsch, . . .; Canada, 1776-1783 *9786 p27*
Kuzbiak, Wladislaw 17; New York, 1912 *9980.29 p53*
Kuznik, Annie *SEE* Kuznik, Thomas
Kuznik, Thomas; America, 1889 *7137 p169*
   *Wife:*Annie
Kvale, Bert; Arkansas, 1918 *95.2 p70*
Kvannen, Andrew E.; Arkansas, 1918 *95.2 p70*
Kvist, Joel; Iowa, 1866-1943 *123.54 p29*
Kwapinski, Edmund; Arkansas, 1918 *95.2 p70*
Kwecis, John; Wisconsin, n.d. *9675.6 p200*
Kweder, Kazimir; Wisconsin, n.d. *9675.6 p200*
Kwiatkowska, Mrs.; New York, 1831 *4606 p175*
   With husband
Kwiatkowski, Andrzey; New York, 1831 *4606 p175*
   With wife
Kwiatkowski, Franciszek; New York, 1831 *4606 p175*
Kwiatkowski, Jan; New York, 1831 *4606 p175*
Kwiatkowski, Jozef; New York, 1831 *4606 p175*
Kwiatkowski, Woyciech; New York, 1831 *4606 p175*
Kwiecinski, . . .; New York, 1831 *4606 p175*
Kydd, Gabriel; Philadelphia, 1867 *5704.8 p219*
Kydd, Henry 18; Philadelphia, 1859 *5704.8 p142*

Kydd, Margaret; Philadelphia, 1867 *5704.8 p219*
Kydd, Thomas; Philadelphia, 1867 *5704.8 p219*
Kydland, Ole Williamson; Washington, 1859-1920 *2872.1 p22*
Kyle, Arthur 30; Philadelphia, 1855 *5704.8 p124*
Kyle, Catharine 4; New York, NY, 1867 *5704.8 p223*
Kyle, Catherine *SEE* Kyle, Rosanna
Kyle, Catherine; St. John, N.B., 1847 *5704.8 p34*
Kyle, Catherine 9; Philadelphia, 1847 *5704.8 p14*
Kyle, Charles; St. John, N.B., 1847 *5704.8 p24*
Kyle, David; New York, NY, 1865 *5704.8 p193*
Kyle, Dolly; St. John, N.B., 1849 *5704.8 p48*
Kyle, Dolly 9; St. John, N.B., 1849 *5704.8 p48*
Kyle, Elizabeth; New York, NY, 1815 *2859.11 p35*
Kyle, Elizabeth 7; New York, NY, 1867 *5704.8 p223*
Kyle, Henry 17; Philadelphia, 1864 *5704.8 p160*
Kyle, Isabella; Quebec, 1852 *5704.8 p98*
Kyle, James 20; Philadelphia, 1858 *5704.8 p138*
Kyle, Jane *SEE* Kyle, Rosanna
Kyle, Jane; Philadelphia, 1847 *5704.8 p14*
Kyle, John; New York, NY, 1864 *5704.8 p173*
Kyle, John 4; Philadelphia, 1855 *5704.8 p124*
Kyle, John 7; St. John, N.B., 1849 *5704.8 p48*
Kyle, Letty 13; St. John, N.B., 1847 *5704.8 p24*
Kyle, Margaret *SEE* Kyle, Rosanna
Kyle, Margaret; Philadelphia, 1847 *5704.8 p14*
Kyle, Margaret Jane 6; Philadelphia, 1855 *5704.8 p124*
Kyle, Mary Ann 25; Philadelphia, 1855 *5704.8 p124*
Kyle, Matilda 3; Philadelphia, 1855 *5704.8 p124*
Kyle, Matty; St. John, N.B., 1847 *5704.8 p24*
Kyle, Ness Peterson 27; Kansas, 1885 *5240.1 p67*
Kyle, Robert; New York, NY, 1815 *2859.11 p35*
Kyle, Rosanna; Philadelphia, 1847 *53.26 p44*
   *Relative:*Jane
   *Relative:*Margaret
   *Relative:*Catherine
Kyle, Rosanna; Philadelphia, 1847 *5704.8 p14*
Kyle, Rose Ann; Quebec, 1852 *5704.8 p94*
Kyle, Rose Eliza 11; St. John, N.B., 1849 *5704.8 p48*
Kyle, Sarah 6 mos; Philadelphia, 1855 *5704.8 p124*
Kyle, Susan 13; St. John, N.B., 1849 *5704.8 p48*
Kyle, William; Quebec, 1853 *5704.8 p104*
Kyle, William 22; Philadelphia, 1855 *5704.8 p124*
Kyler, John 40; Massachusetts, 1850 *5881.1 p54*
Kyley, John 40; Massachusetts, 1850 *5881.1 p85*
Kyll, Forbes 19; Maryland, 1774 *1219.7 p213*
Kyller, Charles; Wisconsin, n.d. *9675.6 p200*
Kyllonen, Abel; Arkansas, 1918 *95.2 p70*
Kynn, John; New York, NY, 1816 *2859.11 p35*
Kyser, Christian; South Carolina, 1788 *7119 p200*

L

Laabs, Albert; Wisconsin, n.d. *9675.6 p200*
Laacks, Johannes; South Carolina, 1788 *7119 p203*
Laag, Anne M. I. E. Tiemann *SEE* Laag, Carl Diedrich Samuel
Laag, Carl Daniel *SEE* Laag, Carl Diedrich Samuel
Laag, Carl Diedrich Samuel; America, 1845 *4610.10 p141*
  Wife: Anne M. I. E. Tiemann
  Son: Carl Daniel
Laag, Carl H. Friedrich *SEE* Laag, Johann Diedrich
Laag, Engel Tiemann *SEE* Laag, Johann Diedrich
Laag, Johann Diedrich; America, 1844 *4610.10 p141*
  Wife: Engel Tiemann
  Son: Carl H. Friedrich
Laag, Wilhelmine Engel; America, 1854 *4610.10 p144*
Laage, Georg J.; Illinois, 1842 *8582.2 p51*
Laamsen, Julian; Pennsylvania, 1731 *1034.18 p13*
Laati, Topias; Washington, 1859-1920 *2872.1 p22*
Laba, Jean 25; America, 1837 *778.5 p300*
Laba, Jele 18; Port uncertain, 1832 *778.5 p300*
Labadie, F. 18; America, 1835 *778.5 p300*
Labally, A.; New Orleans, 1839 *778.5 p300*
Labally, H. 32; Port uncertain, 1839 *778.5 p300*
Labarde, Bertrand 19; New Orleans, 1838 *778.5 p301*
La Barre, Georg; America, 1861-1865 *8582.3 p91*
La Barre, Georg; Cincinnati, 1840-1841 *8582.2 p52*
Labaruse, . . .; America, 1836 *778.5 p301*
Labaruse, Mr. 64; America, 1836 *778.5 p301*
Labaruse, Mad. 64; America, 1836 *778.5 p301*
Labat, Mr. 21; New Orleans, 1839 *778.5 p301*
Labat, Mr. 22; America, 1837 *778.5 p301*
Labat, Mr. 22; New Orleans, 1839 *778.5 p301*
Labat, Jean Bertrand 29; Port uncertain, 1837 *778.5 p301*
Labat, John 32; America, 1838 *778.5 p301*
Labatte, Charles 22; America, 1831 *778.5 p301*
Labattus, Jules 21; America, 1838 *778.5 p301*
Labatut, Alex. 19; New Orleans, 1839 *778.5 p301*
Labatut, Marie 60; New Orleans, 1822 *778.5 p301*
LaBaze, Jules 24; New Orleans, 1835 *778.5 p301*
Labbatier, Joseph 29; New Orleans, 1837 *778.5 p301*
Labbatir, Joseph 29; New Orleans, 1837 *778.5 p301*
Labecki, Wiktor; New York, 1835 *4606 p179*
Labedens, Louis 26; Port uncertain, 1839 *778.5 p302*
LaBee, Jacques 25; New Orleans, 1836 *778.5 p302*
Labella, Tony; Arkansas, 1918 *95.2 p70*
Labendz, Feliksa 17; New York, 1912 *9980.29 p52*
Labeonadier, Mr. 21; New Orleans, 1830 *778.5 p302*
Labert, Mr. 7; America, 1831 *778.5 p302*
Labert, Joseph 9; America, 1831 *778.5 p302*
Labert, Mary 21; America, 1831 *778.5 p302*
Labet, Renais 34; Port uncertain, 1837 *778.5 p302*
Labetour, P. C. 20; New Orleans, 1839 *778.5 p302*
Labinelle, Mr. 14; Port uncertain, 1839 *778.5 p302*
Labody, Robert 32; Philadelphia, 1803 *53.26 p45*
Laboni, Mr. 27; New Orleans, 1838 *778.5 p302*
Labord, Turon 27; New Orleans, 1835 *778.5 p302*
Laborde, Miss 27; America, 1839 *778.5 p303*
Laborde, Mr. 20; New Orleans, 1839 *778.5 p302*
Laborde, Bernard 28; New Orleans, 1836 *778.5 p302*
Laborde, C. 38; America, 1839 *778.5 p302*
Laborde, H. 28; America, 1837 *778.5 p303*
Laborde, J. 32; America, 1835 *778.5 p303*
Laborde, Marinette 22; New Orleans, 1839 *778.5 p303*
Labory, Mrs.; America, 1839 *778.5 p303*
Labourant, Francois 36; New Orleans, 1836 *778.5 p303*
Labourdine, Mr.; Port uncertain, 1839 *778.5 p303*
Laboys, Jean 25; Port uncertain, 1839 *778.5 p303*

Labra, Jean 25; America, 1839 *778.5 p303*
Labrande, Dominique 26; Mexico, 1832 *778.5 p303*
Labrelle, Mr. 28; New Orleans, 1836 *778.5 p303*
Labrond, Cesar 45; America, 1835 *778.5 p303*
Labrouche, Rose 28; Port uncertain, 1839 *778.5 p303*
Labrouse, Peter 50; America, 1829 *778.5 p303*
Labully, Henry 37; New Orleans, 1839 *778.5 p303*
Labusquierre, Mr.; America, 1839 *778.5 p304*
Lacalles, Mr. 22; New Orleans, 1837 *778.5 p304*
Lacase, Mr. 21; America, 1838 *778.5 p304*
Lacase, B.; America, 1839 *778.5 p304*
Lacase, Grace 24; New Orleans, 1830 *778.5 p304*
Lacase, Jules 22; America, 1835 *778.5 p304*
Lacaze, Mr. 16; New Orleans, 1820 *778.5 p304*
Lacaze, Jules 23; New Orleans, 1836 *778.5 p304*
Lacaze Frouquet, Mr. 29; New Orleans, 1839 *778.5 p304*
Lacazette, Pierre Joseph 19; Port uncertain, 1838 *778.5 p304*
Laccabue, Cheden; Iowa, 1866-1943 *123.54 p29*
Lace, Brigitte; Quebec, 1817 *7603 p93*
Lacepo, Juan 35; America, 1826 *778.5 p304*
Lacerdote, Joseph 32; America, 1825 *778.5 p304*
Lacey, Francis 41; Newfoundland, 1789 *4915.24 p57*
Lacey, Hugh; America, 1839 *778.5 p304*
Lacey, Jeremiah; Illinois, 1875 *2896.5 p23*
Lacey, Michael; Quebec, 1853 *5704.8 p104*
Lach, Fred; Illinois, 1897 *2896.5 p23*
Lachambre, Jean 23; Quebec, 1666 *4533 p130*
Lachaud, Mme.; New Orleans, 1839 *778.5 p304*
Lachaud, J. 26; New Orleans, 1839 *778.5 p304*
LaChaumette, Mr. 25; New Orleans, 1839 *778.5 p304*
Lachin, Victor; Arkansas, 1918 *95.2 p70*
Lachlan, William 20; St. John, N.B., 1865 *5704.8 p165*
Lachman, Mark 26; Maryland, 1774 *1219.7 p224*
Lack, John 21; Baltimore, 1775 *1219.7 p271*
Lackey, Bridget Moore; America, 1839 *7036 p121*
  Husband: James
  With sister
Lackey, Catharine; Philadelphia, 1864 *5704.8 p188*
Lackey, James *SEE* Lackey, Bridget Moore
Lackey, Jane 18; Pennsylvania, Virginia or Maryland, 1699 *2212 p20*
Lackey, Mary; Philadelphia, 1864 *5704.8 p188*
Lackey, Rebecca; Philadelphia, 1867 *5704.8 p217*
Lackey, Susan; Philadelphia, 1867 *5704.8 p217*
Lackmann, Hermann; America, 1847 *8582.1 p20*
Lackner, Martin; Georgia, 1738 *9332 p321*
Lackner, Martin; Georgia, 1739 *9332 p324*
Lackner, Martin; Georgia, 1739 *9332 p327*
Lackner, Tobias 40; Georgia, 1734 *9332 p327*
Lacknevin, Gertrand; Georgia, 1738 *9332 p319*
Lackonnette St. Ange, Mr. 27; New Orleans, 1838 *778.5 p305*
Laclan Lateuliere, Mr. 23; New Orleans, 1839 *778.5 p305*
Laclau Lateuliere, Mr. 23; New Orleans, 1839 *778.5 p305*
Laclavere, Jean 25; America, 1837 *778.5 p305*
Lacock, John; Iroquois Co., IL, 1894 *3455.1 p12*
Lacolia, Elena 71 *SEE* Lacolia, Ginseppe
Lacolia, Elisabetta 20 *SEE* Lacolia, Ginseppe
Lacolia, Ginseppe 71; New York, NY, 1893 *9026.4 p41*
  Relative: Elena 71
  Relative: Elisabetta 20
Lacolonge, Urbin 28; America, 1838 *778.5 p305*
Lacombe, A. 28; America, 1836 *778.5 p305*

Lacombe, J. 23; Port uncertain, 1839 *778.5 p305*
Lacombe, J. P. 38; New Orleans, 1839 *778.5 p305*
Lacombe, Marie 28; Texas, 1837 *778.5 p305*
Lacon, Thomas 16; Maryland, 1733 *3690.1 p135*
Lacondam, Ml. 23; Port uncertain, 1839 *778.5 p305*
Lacoste, . . .; New Orleans, 1829 *778.5 p305*
Lacoste, . . .; New Orleans, 1829 *778.5 p306*
Lacoste, Mme. 36; New Orleans, 1829 *778.5 p306*
Lacoste, Mr. 22; New Orleans, 1837 *778.5 p305*
Lacoste, Mr. 24; Louisiana, 1820 *778.5 p305*
Lacoste, Mr. 25; New Orleans, 1839 *778.5 p305*
Lacoste, Mr. 40; New Orleans, 1829 *778.5 p306*
Lacoste, Alfred; Port uncertain, 1839 *778.5 p306*
Lacoste, Etienne 41; Mexico, 1829 *778.5 p306*
Lacoste, Francois 24; New Orleans, 1839 *778.5 p306*
Lacoste, Laurent 21; America, 1820 *778.5 p306*
Lacoste, William 28; Louisiana, 1820 *778.5 p306*
Lacounin, A. 30; New Orleans, 1838 *778.5 p306*
Lacounin, J. 25; New Orleans, 1838 *778.5 p306*
Lacouture, Andre 50; New Orleans, 1836 *778.5 p306*
Lacraug, Victor 16; America, 1827 *778.5 p307*
Lacrique, F. 36; America, 1835 *778.5 p307*
Lacroir, Juan 26; Port uncertain, 1835 *778.5 p307*
Lacroix, Mr. 19; America, 1838 *778.5 p307*
Lacroix, Mr. 25; America, 1837 *778.5 p307*
Lacroix, Mr. 25; Port uncertain, 1836 *778.5 p307*
LaCroix, Mr. 36; Louisiana, 1820 *778.5 p307*
Lacroix, Jean 32; New Orleans, 1835 *778.5 p307*
Lacroix, Joseph; America, 1862 *1450.2 p85A*
Lacroix, Juan 26; Port uncertain, 1835 *778.5 p307*
LaCroix, L. 21; America, 1836 *778.5 p307*
Lacroix, Louis 33; New Orleans, 1829 *778.5 p307*
Lacy, Ann; America, 1741 *4971 p16*
Lacy, Edward; New York, NY, 1811 *2859.11 p14*
Lacy, Eliz.; America, 1737 *4971 p32*
Lacy, John 2; Massachusetts, 1849 *5881.1 p59*
Lacy, Patrick; Illinois, 1878 *2896.5 p23*
Lacy, Rich.; Virginia, 1635 *6219 p35*
Lacy, Rich.; Virginia, 1637 *6219 p114*
Laddy, John; America, 1848 *1450.2 p85A*
Lade, Charles; Iroquois Co., IL, 1896 *3455.1 p12*
Ladee, P. Q.; America, 1839 *778.5 p307*
Ladelat, J. 26; Port uncertain, 1839 *778.5 p307*
Laden, James; Charleston, SC, 1768 *1219.7 p137*
Laden, James 24; Philadelphia, 1860 *5704.8 p145*
Laden, Philippe; Montreal, 1817 *7603 p71*
Ladendorf, Julius; America, 1873 *1450.2 p85A*
Ladigne, J. R. 30; New Orleans, 1827 *778.5 p307*
Ladin, A.; New Orleans, 1829 *778.5 p307*
Ladley, Walter 20; Jamaica, 1730 *3690.1 p135*
Ladoucette, C. 25; America, 1837 *778.5 p307*
Ladoux, Eugenie 23; America, 1838 *778.5 p308*
LaDroute, George; Arkansas, 1918 *95.2 p70*
Laduc, Julian 26; America, 1837 *778.5 p308*
Lady, Barney; New York, NY, 1836 *8208.4 p22*
Laemler, Johann Gottlieb; America, 1744-1800 *2444 p182*
Lafar, Joseph 21; Philadelphia, 1774 *1219.7 p219*
Lafargue, Ayde 40; America, 1838 *778.5 p308*
Lafargue, Mr. 21; New Orleans, 1837 *778.5 p308*
Lafargue, Ayde 40; America, 1838 *778.5 p308*
Lafargue, Isidore 19; New Orleans, 1839 *778.5 p308*
Lafargues, Mr. 25; America, 1838 *778.5 p308*
La Faulangle, Marie Louise J. 36; Port uncertain, 1820 *778.5 p308*
La Faulangle, Pierre 47; Port uncertain, 1820 *778.5 p308*
Lafaye, Mme. 40; New Orleans, 1836 *778.5 p308*

Lafaye, Mr. 37; New Orleans, 1827 ***778.5*** *p308*
Lafaye, P. 44; New Orleans, 1825 ***778.5*** *p308*
Laferty, Jane; Philadelphia, 1852 ***5704.8*** *p96*
Laferty, Thomas; Philadelphia, 1852 ***5704.8*** *p96*
LaFevre, John 72; Arizona, 1922 ***9228.40*** *p26*
Laff, Adolph; Illinois, 1872 ***5012.39*** *p25*
Laffargue, Numa 24; New Orleans, 1837 ***778.5*** *p308*
Lafferty, Andrew 15; Quebec, 1858 ***5704.8*** *p140*
Lafferty, Ann 35; Philadelphia, 1864 ***5704.8*** *p155*
Lafferty, Anthony 36; Philadelphia, 1864 ***5704.8*** *p155*
Lafferty, Barney 3; St. John, N.B., 1847 ***5704.8*** *p4*
Lafferty, Bernard 10; St. John, N.B., 1849 ***5704.8*** *p55*
Lafferty, Bessy; St. John, N.B., 1853 ***5704.8*** *p98*
Lafferty, Betty; St. John, N.B., 1851 ***5704.8*** *p72*
Lafferty, Biddy; Philadelphia, 1849 ***53.26*** *p45*
Lafferty, Biddy; Philadelphia, 1849 ***5704.8*** *p50*
Lafferty, Biddy; St. John, N.B., 1853 ***5704.8*** *p106*
Lafferty, Biddy 9; St. John, N.B., 1849 ***5704.8*** *p55*
Lafferty, Catherine 26; St. John, N.B., 1864 ***5704.8*** *p158*
Lafferty, Cathr 24; Wilmington, DE, 1831 ***6508.7*** *p160*
Lafferty, Charles; Quebec, 1847 ***5704.8*** *p16*
Lafferty, Charles; St. John, N.B., 1849 ***5704.8*** *p55*
Lafferty, Charles; St. John, N.B., 1851 ***5704.8*** *p78*
Lafferty, Charles; St. John, N.B., 1853 ***5704.8*** *p98*
Lafferty, Charles 21; St. John, N.B., 1857 ***5704.8*** *p134*
Lafferty, Daniel; Philadelphia, 1848 ***53.26*** *p45*
Lafferty, Daniel; Philadelphia, 1848 ***5704.8*** *p45*
Lafferty, Daniel 4; St. John, N.B., 1864 ***5704.8*** *p158*
Lafferty, Dennis 7; St. John, N.B., 1849 ***5704.8*** *p55*
Lafferty, Dinnis; St. John, N.B., 1848 ***5704.8*** *p44*
Lafferty, Eliza 6; Quebec, 1858 ***5704.8*** *p140*
Lafferty, Elleanor; Philadelphia, 1849 ***53.26*** *p45*
Lafferty, Elleanor; Philadelphia, 1849 ***5704.8*** *p50*
Lafferty, Ellen; St. John, N.B., 1853 ***5704.8*** *p106*
Lafferty, Ellen 13; St. John, N.B., 1848 ***5704.8*** *p44*
Lafferty, Fanny 11; Quebec, 1858 ***5704.8*** *p140*
Lafferty, Hannah 9; St. John, N.B., 1864 ***5704.8*** *p158*
Lafferty, Hannah 26; Philadelphia, 1859 ***5704.8*** *p142*
Lafferty, Henry 11; Philadelphia, 1864 ***5704.8*** *p155*
Lafferty, Hugh 40; Philadelphia, 1861 ***5704.8*** *p148*
Lafferty, James; Philadelphia, 1847 ***5704.8*** *p32*
Lafferty, James 1; St. John, N.B., 1864 ***5704.8*** *p158*
Lafferty, James 13; Philadelphia, 1854 ***5704.8*** *p121*
Lafferty, John; Philadelphia, 1847 ***53.26*** *p45*
Lafferty, John; Philadelphia, 1847 ***5704.8*** *p31*
Lafferty, John 6; Philadelphia, 1864 ***5704.8*** *p155*
Lafferty, John 40; Quebec, 1858 ***5704.8*** *p140*
Lafferty, Martha 35; Quebec, 1858 ***5704.8*** *p140*
Lafferty, Martha F.; Philadelphia, 1865 ***5704.8*** *p191*
Lafferty, Mary; Philadelphia, 1851 ***5704.8*** *p71*
Lafferty, Mary 3; St. John, N.B., 1848 ***5704.8*** *p44*
Lafferty, Mary 7; Philadelphia, 1864 ***5704.8*** *p155*
Lafferty, Mary 15; Philadelphia, 1854 ***5704.8*** *p121*
Lafferty, Mary 25; Philadelphia, 1857 ***5704.8*** *p132*
Lafferty, Mary 26; Wilmington, DE, 1831 ***6508.7*** *p160*
Lafferty, Mary Ann; St. John, N.B., 1853 ***5704.8*** *p98*
Lafferty, Nancy 20; Philadelphia, 1860 ***5704.8*** *p145*
Lafferty, Nancy 24; Wilmington, DE, 1831 ***6508.7*** *p160*
Lafferty, Neal 17; Philadelphia, 1853 ***5704.8*** *p111*
Lafferty, Neal 25; Philadelphia, 1864 ***5704.8*** *p156*
Lafferty, Owen; St. John, N.B., 1847 ***5704.8*** *p4*
Lafferty, Owen 12; St. John, N.B., 1849 ***5704.8*** *p55*
Lafferty, Owen 24; St. John, N.B., 1862 ***5704.8*** *p150*
Lafferty, Patrick 7; St. John, N.B., 1864 ***5704.8*** *p158*
Lafferty, Patrick 18; Massachusetts, 1849 ***5881.1*** *p61*
Lafferty, Patrick 21; Philadelphia, 1858 ***5704.8*** *p139*
Lafferty, Patrick 44; St. John, N.B., 1864 ***5704.8*** *p158*
Lafferty, Rose 3 mos; St. John, N.B., 1847 ***5704.8*** *p4*
Lafferty, Sally 19; St. John, N.B., 1857 ***5704.8*** *p134*
Lafferty, Sarah; New York, NY, 1867 ***5704.8*** *p220*
Lafferty, Sarah 1; Philadelphia, 1864 ***5704.8*** *p155*
Lafferty, Shuey; St. John, N.B., 1847 ***5704.8*** *p4*
Lafferty, Unity 16; St. John, N.B., 1864 ***5704.8*** *p158*
Laffety, James; Philadelphia, 1847 ***53.26*** *p45*
Laffey, James; New York, NY, 1816 ***2859.11*** *p35*
Laffin, Lawrence; Montreal, 1817 ***7603*** *p74*
Laffin, Patrick; Boston, 1818 ***9892.11*** *p26*
Laffitte, Peter 50; America, 1820 ***778.5*** *p308*
Lafforgue, L. 19; New Orleans, 1837 ***778.5*** *p308*
Lafitte, Mr. 26; New Orleans, 1839 ***778.5*** *p309*
Lafitte, Mr. 34; New Orleans, 1839 ***778.5*** *p309*
Lafitte, Ed. 20; New Orleans, 1826 ***778.5*** *p309*
Lafitte, G. 20; New Orleans, 1839 ***778.5*** *p309*
Lafitte, G. H. 21; New Orleans, 1839 ***778.5*** *p309*
Lafitte, Jean 30; America, 1837 ***778.5*** *p309*
Lafitte, Jean P. 50; New Orleans, 1839 ***778.5*** *p309*
Lafitte, Peter 28; Louisiana, 1820 ***778.5*** *p309*
Lafitton, Mr. 18; Port uncertain, 1825 ***778.5*** *p309*
Laflyn, Jasper; Virginia, 1637 ***6219*** *p110*
Laflyn, Jasper; Virginia, 1639 ***6219*** *p158*
Lafoire, Mr. 25; America, 1839 ***778.5*** *p322*
Lafon, Miss 18; Louisiana, 1821 ***778.5*** *p310*
Lafon, Mme. 45; Louisiana, 1821 ***778.5*** *p310*
Lafon, Mr. 40; New Orleans, 1839 ***778.5*** *p309*
Lafon, Bd. 35; Louisiana, 1820 ***778.5*** *p309*
Lafon, G. 25; New Orleans, 1827 ***778.5*** *p309*
Lafon, G. 28; Port uncertain, 1838 ***778.5*** *p309*
Lafon, Jean 16; America, 1837 ***778.5*** *p309*
Lafon, M. 50; Louisiana, 1821 ***778.5*** *p309*
Lafon, R. 22; New Orleans, 1839 ***778.5*** *p310*
Lafond, Mlle. 25; America, 1837 ***778.5*** *p310*
Lafond, Mlle. 50; New Orleans, 1838 ***778.5*** *p310*
Lafond, Charles 30; Port uncertain, 1836 ***778.5*** *p310*
Lafond, Joseph 14; New Orleans, 1837 ***778.5*** *p310*
Lafond, Marie 18; New Orleans, 1837 ***778.5*** *p310*
Lafond, Marie 40; New Orleans, 1837 ***778.5*** *p310*
Lafont, Francois 34; America, 1838 ***778.5*** *p310*
Lafonta, Celina Vallet 21; Port uncertain, 1838 ***778.5*** *p310*
LaFonta, Louis 31; America, 1839 ***778.5*** *p310*
Lafontain, Amos 38; Kansas, 1881 ***5240.1*** *p62*
Lafontaine, Mr. 40; Port uncertain, 1836 ***778.5*** *p310*
Lafontaine, F. C. 22; Louisiana, 1820 ***778.5*** *p310*
Lafore, Mme. 24; New Orleans, 1839 ***778.5*** *p310*
La Forge, C. Grant 31; New York, NY, 1893 ***9026.4*** *p41*
Laforgne, P. 29; Port uncertain, 1839 ***778.5*** *p311*
Lafratte, Mario; Wisconsin, n.d. ***9675.6*** *p200*
LaGally, Joseph 40; Kansas, 1892 ***5240.1*** *p77*
Lagan, Anne; America, 1865 ***5704.8*** *p201*
Lagan, Catherine 17; Philadelphia, 1855 ***5704.8*** *p123*
Lagan, Martha 18; Philadelphia, 1854 ***5704.8*** *p118*
Lagan, Mary; Philadelphia, 1851 ***5704.8*** *p70*
Lagan, Mary 18; Philadelphia, 1854 ***5704.8*** *p117*
Lagan, Mary Ann 17; Philadelphia, 1854 ***5704.8*** *p117*
Lagan, Moses 24; Philadelphia, 1854 ***5704.8*** *p118*
Lagan, Peggy; St. John, N.B., 1847 ***5704.8*** *p18*
Lagan, William 22; Philadelphia, 1833-1834 ***53.26*** *p45*
Lagarce, Anne-Marie *SEE* Lagarce, Jean
Lagarce, Anne-Marie *SEE* Lagarce, Pierre
Lagarce, Elisabeth *SEE* Lagarce, Jean
Lagarce, Jean 33; Halifax, N.S., 1752 ***7074.6*** *p211*
*Wife:*Anne-Marie
*Daughter:*Elisabeth
Lagarce, Nanette *SEE* Lagarce, Pierre
Lagarce, Nicolas 23; Halifax, N.S., 1752 ***7074.6*** *p211*
Lagarce, Pierre 42; Halifax, N.S., 1752 ***7074.6*** *p211*
*Wife:*Nanette
*Daughter:*Anne-Marie
Lagarde, Mrs. 16; New Orleans, 1837 ***778.5*** *p311*
Lagarde, A. 26; New Orleans, 1837 ***778.5*** *p311*
Lagarrigue, M. 31; Port uncertain, 1827 ***778.5*** *p311*
Lagash, Donald 2; Quebec, 1862 ***5704.8*** *p152*
Lagash, Donald 25; Quebec, 1862 ***5704.8*** *p151*
Lagash, Marion Blue 30; Quebec, 1862 ***5704.8*** *p151*
Lagash, Mary 6 mos; Quebec, 1862 ***5704.8*** *p152*
Lagash, Peggy 4; Quebec, 1862 ***5704.8*** *p152*
Lagemann, Paul; Maryland, 1897 ***1450.2*** *p22B*
Lager, Barny 24; Kansas, 1893 ***5240.1*** *p26*
Lager, Barny 24; Kansas, 1893 ***5240.1*** *p78*
Lagerqvist, Samuel Gustaf; Minneapolis, 1879-1883 ***6410.35*** *p60*
Laget, Frcos. 22; America, 1838 ***778.5*** *p311*
Lagiewska, Stefania 19; New York, 1912 ***9980.29*** *p59*
With nephew
Lagiewski, Alexander 11 mos; New York, 1912 ***9980.29*** *p59*
Lagiresse, Jn. Dominique 30; America, 1838 ***778.5*** *p311*
Lagoin, J.; New Orleans, 1839 ***778.5*** *p311*
Lagon, Adam; Philadelphia, 1853 ***5704.8*** *p103*
Lagrandeur, Jean; Quebec, 1712 ***7603*** *p21*
Lagrane, Mr. 28; America, 1835 ***778.5*** *p311*
Lagrange, Auguste 50; New Orleans, 1823 ***778.5*** *p311*
Lagrange, Claude 28; Louisiana, 1837 ***778.5*** *p311*
Lagrange, Eugene 4; New Orleans, 1838 ***778.5*** *p311*
Lagrange, G. 35; New Orleans, 1823 ***778.5*** *p311*
Lagrange, G. 40; America, 1829 ***778.5*** *p311*
Lagrange, Sibella 29; New Orleans, 1838 ***778.5*** *p311*
Lague, John 40; Port uncertain, 1820 ***778.5*** *p311*
Lagueux, M.-Henriette; Quebec, 1822 ***7603*** *p28*
Lahaie, Jean; Quebec, 1697 ***7603*** *p99*
Lahaie, Sophia 24; New Orleans, 1836 ***778.5*** *p312*
Lahan, Michael 26; Massachusetts, 1847 ***5881.1*** *p60*
Lahatt, Henriette; Baltimore, 1834 ***8582.1*** *p53*
Lahey, Daniel; Philadelphia, 1849 ***53.26*** *p45*
Lahey, Daniel; Philadelphia, 1849 ***5704.8*** *p49*
Lahey, James 28; Massachusetts, 1849 ***5881.1*** *p59*
Lahey, William 23; Massachusetts, 1848 ***5881.1*** *p62*
Lahiff, Thomas 20; Massachusetts, 1849 ***5881.1*** *p61*
Lahin, Margaret 26; Massachusetts, 1849 ***5881.1*** *p60*
Lahin, Mary 1; Massachusetts, 1849 ***5881.1*** *p60*
Lahmann, Heinrich; America, 1850 ***8582.2*** *p21*
Lahn, El 40; Kansas, 1906 ***5240.1*** *p83*
Lahon, Mr. 26; America, 1838 ***778.5*** *p312*
Lahrbusch, Arnold von; Halifax, N.S., 1778 ***9786*** *p270*
Lahrbusch, Arnold von; New York, 1776 ***9786*** *p270*
Lahy, Edmond; America, 1735-1743 ***4971*** *p78*
Lahy, Judy 18; Massachusetts, 1849 ***5881.1*** *p59*
Laick, . . .; Canada, 1776-1783 ***9786*** *p27*
Laidlow, Mr.; Quebec, 1815 ***9229.18*** *p77*
Laieieger, Michael; America, 1846 ***1450.2*** *p85A*
Laignux, Mr. 30; Port uncertain, 1836 ***778.5*** *p312*
Laikie, Archibald 24; Maryland, 1774 ***1219.7*** *p229*
Lain, David; New York, NY, 1816 ***2859.11*** *p35*
Laine, A. 25; America, 1838 ***778.5*** *p312*
Laine, Marie 15; Port uncertain, 1836 ***778.5*** *p312*
Laine, Pierre 56; America, 1838 ***778.5*** *p312*
Laing, James; Austin, TX, 1886 ***9777*** *p5*
Laird, Andrew; New York, NY, 1815 ***2859.11*** *p35*
Laird, Ann; Philadelphia, 1853 ***5704.8*** *p100*
Laird, Charles; Quebec, 1850 ***5704.8*** *p66*
Laird, Fanny; Philadelphia, 1868 ***5704.8*** *p231*
Laird, George; Quebec, 1850 ***5704.8*** *p67*
Laird, Isabella 17; St. John, N.B., 1856 ***5704.8*** *p131*
Laird, James; Philadelphia, 1852 ***5704.8*** *p85*
Laird, James 24; New York, NY, 1828 ***6508.4*** *p143*
Laird, Jane; Philadelphia, 1867 ***5704.8*** *p216*
Laird, John; Quebec, 1847 ***5704.8*** *p7*
Laird, John 33; Arizona, 1900 ***9228.40*** *p7*
Laird, John G. 26; Philadelphia, 1864 ***5704.8*** *p156*
Laird, Mary; Quebec, 1847 ***5704.8*** *p7*
Laird, Nancy; Philadelphia, 1867 ***5704.8*** *p223*
Laird, Patrick; Charleston, SC, 1761 ***1639.20*** *p108*
Laird, Robert; New York, NY, 1864 ***5704.8*** *p186*
Laird, Samuel; New York, NY, 1864 ***5704.8*** *p185*
Laird, Samuel; Philadelphia, 1853 ***5704.8*** *p100*
Laird, Samuel; Philadelphia, 1867 ***5704.8*** *p216*
Laird, Samuel; Philadelphia, 1867 ***5704.8*** *p219*
Laird, William 17; Maryland, 1774 ***1219.7*** *p187*
Laishley, Simeon W.; West Virginia, 1829-1844 ***9788.3*** *p14*
Laith, Jon.; Virginia, 1642 ***6219*** *p197*
Laitre, . . .; Canada, 1776-1783 ***9786*** *p28*
Laizadiole, Mr. 25; New Orleans, 1839 ***778.5*** *p312*
Lajous, Francois 25; New Orleans, 1839 ***778.5*** *p312*
Lakae, Joe; Arkansas, 1918 ***95.2*** *p70*
Lake, . . .; Canada, 1776-1783 ***9786*** *p27*
Lake, Charles 46; Maryland, 1774 ***1219.7*** *p207*
Lake, Gilbert; Virginia, 1646 ***6219*** *p241*
Lake, Henry; New York, NY, 1838 ***8208.4*** *p88*
Lake, Walter 27; Jamaica, 1730 ***3690.1*** *p135*
Lakeman, Daniel 22; Virginia, 1774 ***1219.7*** *p186*
Lalaguy, Mr. 30; New Orleans, 1839 ***778.5*** *p312*
Lalais, Francois 35; America, 1837 ***778.5*** *p312*
Lalam, William 19; Maryland, 1720 ***3690.1*** *p136*
Lalande, A. 30; America, 1835 ***778.5*** *p312*
Lalanne, Mr. 38; New Orleans, 1829 ***778.5*** *p312*
Lalanne, Ch. 20; New Orleans, 1831 ***778.5*** *p312*
Lalanne, Eugene Magne; Arkansas, 1918 ***95.2*** *p70*
Lalarre, Mr. 43; New Orleans, 1826 ***778.5*** *p312*
Lalaurie, L. 20; America, 1825 ***778.5*** *p312*
Lale, Frances 16; Canada, 1838 ***4535.12*** *p113*
Lalek, Stanley 30; Arkansas, 1918 ***95.2*** *p70*
Lalemant, Mary 30; America, 1838 ***778.5*** *p313*
Lalieure, Etienne 40; Port uncertain, 1839 ***778.5*** *p313*
Lall, Abraham; Colorado, 1904 ***9678.2*** *p122*
Lallande, E. 22; Louisiana, 1831 ***778.5*** *p313*
Lallande, Jacques 35; New Orleans, 1829 ***778.5*** *p313*
Lallanne, Eugene Magne; Arkansas, 1918 ***95.2*** *p70*
Lallemand, F. 28; New Orleans, 1832 ***778.5*** *p313*
Lallemand, M. 56; New Orleans, 1827 ***778.5*** *p313*
Lallier, Antoine 30; New Orleans, 1838 ***778.5*** *p313*
Lally, Bridget 22; Massachusetts, 1849 ***5881.1*** *p57*
Lally, Catharine 20; Massachusetts, 1849 ***5881.1*** *p57*
Lally, George A.; New York, NY, 1838 ***8208.4*** *p82*
Lally, Honora 14; Massachusetts, 1849 ***5881.1*** *p58*
Lally, Martin; Colorado, 1904 ***9678.2*** *p122*
Lally, Mary 55; Massachusetts, 1849 ***5881.1*** *p60*
Lally, Michael; New York, NY, 1816 ***2859.11*** *p35*
Lally, Thady; America, 1735-1743 ***4971*** *p78*
Lally, Thady; America, 1738 ***4971*** *p80*
Lalombere, Cyprien 22; America, 1820 ***778.5*** *p313*
Lalor, Danl.; Philadelphia, 1816 ***2859.11*** *p35*
Lalore, Catherine de; Sorel, Que., 1672 ***7603*** *p26*
Lalouette, Antoine P. 45; New Orleans, 1821 ***778.5*** *p313*
Lalthouse, John; New York, NY, 1843 ***6013.19*** *p29*
Laly, Thomas; New York, NY, 1840 ***8208.4*** *p108*
Lamaison, Mme. 22; America, 1830 ***778.5*** *p313*
Lamaison, Sophie 3; America, 1830 ***778.5*** *p313*
La Maison Neuve, Mr. 33; New Orleans, 1823 ***778.5*** *p313*
Lamalade, Ph. 19; New Orleans, 1830 ***778.5*** *p313*
Laman, Sarah; St. John, N.B., 1849 ***5704.8*** *p56*
Lamantia, Francesco; Iowa, 1866-1943 ***123.54*** *p67*
Lamantia, Mariano; Iowa, 1866-1943 ***123.54*** *p67*
LaMantis, Gaetano; Iowa, 1866-1943 ***123.54*** *p67*
Lamar, . . .; Canada, 1776-1783 ***9786*** *p27*
Lamarliere, Antoine 57; New Orleans, 1826 ***778.5*** *p313*
Lamarque, Mlle. 20; New Orleans, 1839 ***778.5*** *p314*
Lamarque, Mr. 18; America, 1837 ***778.5*** *p314*

Lamarque, Mr. 25; New Orleans, 1839 ***778.5*** *p314*
Lamarque, Mr. 32; New Orleans, 1839 ***778.5*** *p313*
Lamarque, C. 50; New Orleans, 1837 ***778.5*** *p314*
Lamarque Cusor, Mr. 45; New Orleans, 1839 ***778.5*** *p314*
Lamarre, . . .; Canada, 1776-1783 ***9786*** *p27*
Lamarre, Jean; New Brunswick, 1798 ***7603*** *p49*
Lamb, Mr.; Quebec, 1815 ***9229.18*** *p77*
Lamb, Alfred; Washington, 1859-1920 ***2872.1*** *p22*
Lamb, Bryan 21; Baltimore, 1775 ***1219.7*** *p270*
Lamb, James 23; St. John, N.B., 1866 ***5704.8*** *p166*
Lamb, James 35; Massachusetts, 1847 ***5881.1*** *p58*
Lamb, John; America, 1698 ***2212*** *p10*
Lamb, John; Charleston, SC, 1797 ***1639.20*** *p108*
Lamb, John; Charleston, SC, 1804 ***1639.20*** *p108*
Lamb, John; New York, NY, 1811 ***2859.11*** *p14*
Lamb, John; Quebec, 1849 ***5704.8*** *p52*
Lamb, John; Virginia, 1698 ***2212*** *p13*
Lamb, John 21; Nova Scotia, 1774 ***1219.7*** *p209*
Lamb, John 39; Philadelphia, 1774 ***1219.7*** *p216*
Lamb, Joseph 21; Maryland, 1775 ***1219.7*** *p254*
Lamb, Judith; America, 1740 ***4971*** *p15*
Lamb, Laurent; Quebec, 1811 ***7603*** *p102*
Lamb, Margt 21; Maryland or Virginia, 1699 ***2212*** *p24*
Lamb, Robert; Virginia, 1642 ***6219*** *p189*
Lamb, Robert 30; Philadelphia, 1853 ***5704.8*** *p108*
Lamb, Wilhelm; Ohio, 1800 ***8582.2*** *p55*
Lamb, William 21; Jamaica, 1774 ***1219.7*** *p232*
Lamb, Wm.; Virginia, 1646 ***6219*** *p236*
Lambden, Nathaniel 21; Jamaica, 1774 ***1219.7*** *p178*
Lambdin, Martha; Virginia, 1638 ***6219*** *p120*
Lambdin, Robert; Virginia, 1638 ***6219*** *p120*
Lambdin, William; Virginia, 1638 ***6219*** *p120*
Lambenet, Gracieux 25; America, 1837 ***778.5*** *p314*
Lamber, Mr. 30; New Orleans, 1836 ***778.5*** *p315*
Lambert, . . .; Canada, 1776-1783 ***9786*** *p27*
Lambert, . . . 40; Grenada, 1774 ***1219.7*** *p185*
Lambert, Andrew 27; Quebec, 1859 ***5704.8*** *p143*
Lambert, Anne; New York, NY, 1815 ***2859.11*** *p35*
Lambert, Anthony 36; Maryland, 1775 ***1219.7*** *p249*
Lambert, Anthony 36; Maryland, 1775 ***1219.7*** *p253*
Lambert, Bernard; San Francisco, 1851 ***6013.19*** *p73*
Lambert, Cornelius; New Netherland, 1630-1646 ***8582.2*** *p51*
Lambert, Elizabeth 30; Quebec, 1859 ***5704.8*** *p143*
Lambert, George 25; Virginia, 1773 ***1219.7*** *p169*
Lambert, Jacob; Pennsylvania, 1768 ***9973.8*** *p32*
Lambert, Jacques 35; New Orleans, 1839 ***778.5*** *p314*
Lambert, James 21; Virginia, 1773 ***1219.7*** *p169*
Lambert, John; New York, NY, 1811 ***2859.11*** *p14*
Lambert, Joseph 3 mos; New Orleans, 1836 ***778.5*** *p314*
Lambert, Joseph 5; New Orleans, 1836 ***778.5*** *p314*
Lambert, Joseph 36; New Orleans, 1836 ***778.5*** *p314*
Lambert, M. 50; Mexico, 1829 ***778.5*** *p314*
Lambert, Margaret; New York, NY, 1816 ***2859.11*** *p35*
Lambert, Maria 3; New Orleans, 1836 ***778.5*** *p314*
Lambert, Maria 30; New Orleans, 1836 ***778.5*** *p314*
Lambert, Pierre 40; Port uncertain, 1836 ***778.5*** *p314*
Lambert, Rebecca 75; Kansas, 1891 ***5240.1*** *p26*
Lambert, Rebecca 75; Kansas, 1891 ***5240.1*** *p75*
Lambert, Thomas; America, 1889 ***1450.2*** *p85A*
Lambert, Thomas; New York, NY, 1838 ***8208.4*** *p73*
Lambert, Thomas; Virginia, 1648 ***6219*** *p247*
Lambert, Wilhelm; Illinois, 1833 ***8582.1*** *p54*
Lambert, William; New York, NY, 1816 ***2859.11*** *p35*
Lambert, William 21; Philadelphia, 1774 ***1219.7*** *p216*
Lamberton, David 24; St. John, N.B., 1866 ***5704.8*** *p166*
Lambrechts, John B. 39; Kansas, 1883 ***5240.1*** *p65*
Lambridge, George; New York, NY, 1838 ***8208.4*** *p62*
Lambright, Philip; South Carolina, 1788 ***7119*** *p198*
Lamburray, Peter; Iowa, 1866-1943 ***123.54*** *p29*
Lambus, Dominic; Wisconsin, n.d. ***9675.6*** *p200*
Lamdoberger, Aron 21; New York, NY, 1878 ***9253*** *p47*
Lame, Joseph Marie 33; America, 1835 ***778.5*** *p314*
Lameck, Franz Teofhel; New York, NY, 1906 ***3455.2*** *p46*
Lameck, Franz Toefhel; New York, 1906 ***3455.3*** *p105*
Lamendola, Salvatore; Kansas, 1911 ***6013.40*** *p16*
Lamerin, A. 25; New Orleans, 1832 ***778.5*** *p315*
Lamers, Theodore 39; Kansas, 1900 ***5240.1*** *p81*
Lamfrom, J.; Milwaukee, 1875 ***4719.30*** *p257*
Lamiere, P.; New Orleans, 1839 ***778.5*** *p320*
Lamin, Peter; America, 1740 ***4971*** *p72*
Lamke, Charles; Illinois, 1871 ***5012.39*** *p25*
Lamly, Jacob; South Carolina, 1788 ***7119*** *p198*
Lammel, Simon 26; Kansas, 1895 ***5240.1*** *p26*
Lammel, Simon 26; Kansas, 1895 ***5240.1*** *p80*
Lammers, John Frederick; New York, NY, 1835 ***8208.4*** *p8*
Lammert, . . . 10; America, 1853 ***9162.8*** *p37*
Lammert, Elis. 25; America, 1853 ***9162.8*** *p37*
Lammert, Elisabetha 14; America, 1853 ***9162.8*** *p37*
Lammert, Eva 16; America, 1853 ***9162.8*** *p37*
Lammert, Joseph; America, 1849 ***8582.2*** *p22*
Lammert, Kaspar 23; America, 1853 ***9162.8*** *p37*
Lamming, Thomas; Kansas, 1885 ***5240.1*** *p26*
Lammingern, Maria Agatha; New York, 1717 ***3627*** *p11*
Lammore, Marsey; Virginia, 1642 ***6219*** *p195*
Lamon, Andrew 18; Philadelphia, 1804 ***53.26*** *p45*
Lamon, John 16; New Orleans, 1832 ***778.5*** *p315*
Lamond, Daniel 47; North Carolina, 1850 ***1639.20*** *p108*
Lamond, James; New Orleans, 1848 ***5704.8*** *p48*
Lamond, Robert; Charleston, SC, 1763 ***1639.20*** *p109*
Lamont, Christian 60 *SEE* Lamont, Henry
Lamont, Flora 55; North Carolina, 1850 ***1639.20*** *p109*
*Relative:*Mary 31
Lamont, Henry 60; North Carolina, 1850 ***1639.20*** *p109*
*Relative:*Christian 60
Lamont, Mary 31 *SEE* Lamont, Flora
Lamorere, J.; Shreveport, LA, 1879 ***7129*** *p45*
Lamoret, A. 34; Port uncertain, 1835 ***778.5*** *p315*
Lamothe Signet, Mr. 27; New Orleans, 1839 ***778.5*** *p315*
Lamouche, Robert; Quebec, 1664 ***4533*** *p128*
Lamoure, P. 29; America, 1835 ***778.5*** *p315*
Lamoureux, Miss 7; New Orleans, 1820 ***778.5*** *p315*
Lamoureux, Mrs. 30; New Orleans, 1820 ***778.5*** *p315*
Lamoureux, Ms.; New Orleans, 1820 ***778.5*** *p315*
Lamoureux, Jean Francois 39; New Orleans, 1820 ***778.5*** *p315*
Lampard, Albert 3 *SEE* Lampard, Wm. John
Lampard, Alfred 5 *SEE* Lampard, Wm. John
Lampard, Ellen 6 *SEE* Lampard, Wm. John
Lampard, Frances; Canada, 1851 ***4535.11*** *p53*
Lampard, Frances 10 *SEE* Lampard, Wm. John
Lampard, William 19; South Carolina, 1751 ***1219.7*** *p4*
Lampard, William 19; South Carolina, 1751 ***3690.1*** *p136*
Lampard, Wm. 8 *SEE* Lampard, Wm. John
Lampard, Wm. John; Canada, 1846-1851 ***4535.11*** *p53*
*Child:*Frances 10
*Child:*Wm. 8
*Child:*Ellen 6
*Child:*Alfred 5
*Child:*Albert 3
Lampas, Steve; Arkansas, 1918 ***95.2*** *p70*
Lampe, Miss; America, 1854 ***4610.10*** *p156*
Lampe, Anna Engel Schwarze; America, 1835-1844 ***4610.10*** *p154*
Lampe, Carl Heinrich Gottlieb; America, 1844 ***4610.10*** *p154*
Lampe, Carl Wilhelm; America, 1855 ***4610.10*** *p157*
With family
Lampe, Ernst Friedrich Wilhelm; America, 1855 ***4610.10*** *p157*
With family
Lampe, Friedrich; Cincinnati, 1869-1887 ***8582*** *p19*
Lampe, Friedrich; New Orleans, 1842 ***8582.1*** *p21*
Lampe, Heinrich Friedrich Wilhelm; America, 1881 ***4610.10*** *p110*
Lampe, Wilhelm; Illinois, 1800-1899 ***4610.10*** *p66*
Lampen, Mathew 23; Maryland, 1775 ***1219.7*** *p255*
Lampert, Jacob; Wisconsin, n.d. ***9675.6*** *p200*
Lampertus, Christoph; Trenton, NJ, 1776 ***8137*** *p11*
Lamping, Hermann Heinrich; America, 1830 ***4815.7*** *p92*
With 2 children
*Wife:*Margarete D. W. Rabbe
Lamping, Margarete D. W. Rabbe *SEE* Lamping, Hermann Heinrich
Lampl, Louis; New York, NY, 1884 ***5240.1*** *p26*
Lampo, Louis Nick; Arkansas, 1918 ***95.2*** *p70*
Lampre, F. 24; America, 1831 ***778.5*** *p315*
Lampre, Francis 30; America, 1832 ***778.5*** *p315*
Lampros, Mike; Arkansas, 1918 ***95.2*** *p71*
Lampton, Rachael 23; Massachusetts, 1848 ***5881.1*** *p61*
Lamy, Thomas; Quebec, 1753 ***7603*** *p94*
Lanaber, Mr. 30; New Orleans, 1836 ***778.5*** *p315*
Lanagan, Biddy 10 mos; Massachusetts, 1847 ***5881.1*** *p57*
Lanagan, Patrick 4; Massachusetts, 1847 ***5881.1*** *p61*
Lanaghan, Mary Ann; Quebec, 1851 ***5704.8*** *p74*
Lanberg, J.M.; Ohio, 1798-1818 ***8582.2*** *p54*
Lanburg, Emma 26; Massachusetts, 1860 ***6410.32*** *p112*
Lancashire, John 30; Jamaica, 1738 ***3690.1*** *p136*
Lancaster, John 16; Maryland, 1774 ***1219.7*** *p215*
Lancaster, Owen; Virginia, 1639 ***6219*** *p151*
Lancaster, Thomas 23; Halifax, N.S., 1774 ***1219.7*** *p213*
Lancelin, John 22; New Orleans, 1838 ***778.5*** *p315*
Lancer, Jean Francois 50; Died enroute, 1822 ***778.5*** *p315*
Lanci, Josepha 30; Port uncertain, 1839 ***778.5*** *p316*
Lancon, Mr.; New Orleans, 1839 ***778.5*** *p316*
Lancton, Thomas; Virginia, 1639 ***6219*** *p162*
Land, Frank 30; Kansas, 1896 ***5240.1*** *p80*
Land, Sarah; Philadelphia, 1866 ***5704.8*** *p209*
Landa, Ben Nathan; Arkansas, 1918 ***95.2*** *p71*
Landagan, Mr.; Quebec, 1815 ***9229.18*** *p75*
Landais, Mr. 45; Port uncertain, 1838 ***778.5*** *p316*
Landart, Louis 30; Port uncertain, 1836 ***778.5*** *p316*
Landau, F. 18; New Orleans, 1835 ***778.5*** *p316*
Landau, Valentin; Philadelphia, 1779 ***8137*** *p11*
Landauer, Catharina Maria *SEE* Landauer, Johannes
Landauer, Eberhardina *SEE* Landauer, Johannes
Landauer, Johannes; Pennsylvania, 1742-1800 ***2444*** *p182*
*Wife:*Ursula C. Schott
*Child:*Eberhardina
*Child:*Catharina Maria
Landauer, Ursula C. Schott *SEE* Landauer, Johannes
Landeck, Melcher; Philadelphia, 1756 ***4525*** *p262*
Landenberger, Anna Maria Groz *SEE* Landenberger, Johann Jacob
Landenberger, Johann Jacob; Pennsylvania, 1740-1800 ***2444*** *p182*
*Wife:*Anna Maria Groz
*Child:*Johannes
Landenberger, Johannes *SEE* Landenberger, Johann Jacob
Lander, Henry 20; Pennsylvania, 1730 ***3690.1*** *p136*
Lander, Joanna 28; Maryland, 1775 ***1219.7*** *p267*
Lander, John 19; Philadelphia, 1774 ***1219.7*** *p234*
Landergan, Bridget 60; Massachusetts, 1847 ***5881.1*** *p57*
Landergan, Daniel 17; Massachusetts, 1847 ***5881.1*** *p58*
Landergan, Lawrence 23; Massachusetts, 1849 ***5881.1*** *p59*
Landergan, Mary 16; Massachusetts, 1847 ***5881.1*** *p60*
Landergan, Richard 10; Massachusetts, 1849 ***5881.1*** *p61*
Landers, James 23; St. John, N.B., 1861 ***5704.8*** *p149*
Landers, John 28; Maryland, 1774 ***1219.7*** *p192*
Landers, Samuel 25; Maryland, 1774 ***1219.7*** *p229*
Landes, P. 30; America, 1837 ***778.5*** *p316*
Landfelder, Agatha 7 *SEE* Landfelder, Veit
Landfelder, Ursula *SEE* Landfelder, Veit
Landfelder, Ursula Wassermann *SEE* Landfelder, Veit
Landfelder, Veit; Georgia, 1739 ***9332*** *p323*
*Wife:*Ursula Wassermann
Landfelder, Veit; Georgia, 1739 ***9332*** *p326*
*Wife:*Ursula
*Daughter:*Agatha 7
Landfried, Phillip; Wisconsin, n.d. ***9675.6*** *p200*
Landgrat, Christn. Fredk. 34; New Orleans, 1839 ***9420.2*** *p486*
*Wife:*Jane Christlieke 24
Landgrat, Jane Christlieke 24 *SEE* Landgrat, Christn. Fredk.
Landgraverin, Lenora Marie 8 *SEE* Landgraverin, Margaret
Landgraverin, Margaret; South Carolina, 1752-1753 ***3689.17*** *p22*
*Relative:*Lenora Marie 8
Landifield, William; Boston, 1776 ***1219.7*** *p282*
Landman, Jacob; Toledo, OH, 1869-1887 ***8582*** *p19*
Landois, Anthony; New York, NY, 1837 ***8208.4*** *p32*
Landolt, William H.; Wisconsin, n.d. ***9675.6*** *p200*
Landon, Thomas 24; Maryland, 1775 ***1219.7*** *p259*
Landonsky, Victor John; Wisconsin, n.d. ***9675.6*** *p200*
Landre, C. 34; America, 1836 ***778.5*** *p316*
Landreau, Antoine 31; New Orleans, 1836 ***778.5*** *p316*
Landregan, Joanna; Montreal, 1823 ***7603*** *p98*
Landrith, Eliza 18; St. John, N.B., 1858 ***5704.8*** *p137*
Landros, Thoralf King; Arkansas, 1918 ***95.2*** *p71*
Landry, Baptiste 35; Louisiana, 1820 ***778.5*** *p316*
Landry, Marie Dugas 40; Louisiana, 1820 ***778.5*** *p316*
Landry, Patrick 60; Massachusetts, 1849 ***5881.1*** *p61*
Landry, Paul; New York, NY, 1837 ***8208.4*** *p24*
Lands, Kat; Virginia, 1647 ***6219*** *p245*
Landsky, Mary 23; Massachusetts, 1850 ***5881.1*** *p61*
Landuyt, Cyril; Arkansas, 1918 ***95.2*** *p71*
Landvatter, Anna Elisabetha; Port uncertain, 1717 ***3627*** *p16*
Landwehr, . . .; Canada, 1776-1783 ***9786*** *p27*
Landwehr, Friedrich Wilhelm; America, 1848 ***8582.3*** *p40*
Landwher, George; New York, NY, 1834 ***8208.4*** *p31*
Landwood, Ja.; Virginia, 1644 ***6219*** *p231*
Landy, Bridget 19; Massachusetts, 1847 ***5881.1*** *p57*
Lane, Albert; Washington, 1859-1920 ***2872.1*** *p22*
Lane, Charles H.; Washington, 1859-1920 ***2872.1*** *p22*
Lane, Daniel; Massachusetts, 1847 ***5881.1*** *p58*
Lane, Daniell; Virginia, 1635 ***6219*** *p69*
Lane, David; New York, NY, 1839 ***8208.4*** *p98*
Lane, Denis; New York, NY, 1836 ***8208.4*** *p12*
Lane, Ellen; New York, NY, 1811 ***2859.11*** *p14*
Lane, F. M.; Washington, 1859-1920 ***2872.1*** *p22*
Lane, Fred M.; Washington, 1859-1920 ***2872.1*** *p22*
Lane, Hugh 23; Philadelphia, 1833-1834 ***53.26*** *p45*
Lane, J. 23; New Orleans, 1835 ***778.5*** *p323*
Lane, John; New York, NY, 1811 ***2859.11*** *p14*
Lane, John; New York, NY, 1840 ***8208.4*** *p109*
Lane, John; Quebec, 1822 ***7603*** *p53*
Lane, John; Virginia, 1635 ***6219*** *p3*

Lane, John; Virginia, 1643 ***6219*** *p203*
Lane, John 17; Maryland, 1774 ***1219.7*** *p236*
Lane, John 17; Maryland, 1774 ***1219.7*** *p244*
Lane, John 28; Barbados, 1773 ***1219.7*** *p172*
Lane, Jonathan 45; Jamaica, 1730 ***3690.1*** *p136*
Lane, Mark; Washington, 1859-1920 ***2872.1*** *p22*
Lane, Martha; North Carolina, 1756 ***1219.7*** *p49*
Lane, Mary; New York, NY, 1811 ***2859.11*** *p14*
Lane, Mary Anne; New York, NY, 1816 ***2859.11*** *p35*
Lane, Rachell; Virginia, 1628 ***6219*** *p31*
Lane, Richard 12; Massachusetts, 1847 ***5881.1*** *p61*
Lane, S. G.; Washington, 1859-1920 ***2872.1*** *p22*
Lane, Samuel 19; Jamaica, 1720 ***3690.1*** *p136*
Lane, Samuel 35; Jamaica, 1725 ***3690.1*** *p136*
Lane, Stephen 19; Virginia, 1720 ***3690.1*** *p136*
Lane, Thomas 19; St. Christopher, 1722 ***3690.1*** *p136*
Lane, William 19; Maryland, 1774 ***1219.7*** *p236*
Laneau, Francis; New York, NY, 1840 ***8208.4*** *p110*
Lanehan, Maria 11; Massachusetts, 1849 ***5881.1*** *p60*
Lanehan, Patrick 8; Massachusetts, 1849 ***5881.1*** *p61*
Lanen, Bridget; New Brunswick, 1822 ***7603*** *p102*
Lanfron, J.; Milwaukee, 1875 ***4719.30*** *p257*
Lang, . . .; Canada, 1776-1783 ***9786*** *p27*
Lang, Agnes *SEE* Lang, Johann Martin
Lang, Anna Barbara; New England, 1752 ***2444*** *p189*
Lang, Anna Maria *SEE* Lang, Johann Jacob
Lang, Catharina *SEE* Lang, Christoph
Lang, Christ; America, 1847 ***1450.2*** *p86A*
Lang, Christoph; New England, 1746-1756 ***2444*** *p182*
*Wife:*Ursula
*Child:*Catharina
Lang, Christophel; Pennsylvania, 1754 ***2444*** *p182*
Lang, David 19; St. John, N.B., 1866 ***5704.8*** *p166*
Lang, Elisabetha *SEE* Lang, Johann Jacob
Lang, Francis 20; New Orleans, 1838 ***778.5*** *p316*
Lang, Franz; Kentucky, 1848 ***8582.3*** *p101*
Lang, Heinrich, Family; Ohio, 1833 ***8582.1*** *p46*
Lang, Jacob; Pennsylvania, 1752 ***2444*** *p183*
Lang, Jacob Friedrich *SEE* Lang, Johann Martin
Lang, Johann; America, 1840 ***8582.1*** *p21*
Lang, Johann 30; St. Louis, 1838 ***778.5*** *p316*
Lang, Johann Christoph; Pennsylvania, 1754 ***2444*** *p182*
Lang, Johann Jacob *SEE* Lang, Johann Martin
Lang, Johann Jacob; Pennsylvania, 1752 ***2444*** *p183*
Lang, Johann Jacob; Port uncertain, 1752-1800 ***2444*** *p183*
*Wife:*Maria Elisabetha
*Child:*Maria Elisabetha
*Child:*Elisabetha
*Child:*Anna Maria
Lang, Johann Martin; Pennsylvania, 1751 ***2444*** *p183*
*Wife:*Agnes
*Child:*Jacob Friedrich
*Child:*Philipp Leoboldus
*Child:*Johann Jacob
Lang, Johann Martin; Pennsylvania, 1752 ***2444*** *p183*
Lang, Johann Martin; Pennsylvania, 1769 ***2444*** *p183*
Lang, Johannes; Ohio, 1798-1818 ***8582.2*** *p54*
Lang, John; Ohio, 1815 ***8582.1*** *p47*
Lang, John; Wisconsin, n.d. ***9675.6*** *p200*
Lang, Joseph; Wisconsin, n.d. ***9675.6*** *p200*
Lang, Karl; America, 1854 ***8582.3*** *p40*
Lang, Kristina 28; America, 1853 ***9162.7*** *p15*
Lang, Maria Elisabetha *SEE* Lang, Johann Jacob
Lang, Maria Elisabetha *SEE* Lang, Johann Jacob
Lang, Nicolas 28; St. Louis, 1838 ***778.5*** *p316*
Lang, Patrick 23; Massachusetts, 1849 ***5881.1*** *p61*
Lang, Peter 30; West Virginia, 1894 ***9788.3*** *p14*
Lang, Peter 32; West Virginia, 1896 ***9788.3*** *p14*
Lang, Philipp Leoboldus *SEE* Lang, Johann Martin
Lang, Richter; Ohio, 1833 ***8582.1*** *p46*
Lang, Richter Wilhelm; Ohio, 1833 ***8582.1*** *p46*
With parents
Lang, Ursula *SEE* Lang, Christoph
Lang, Wilhelm; America, 1833 ***8582.1*** *p21*
Langaard, Andrew; New York, 1761 ***3652*** *p88*
Langan, Andre; Quebec, 1798 ***7603*** *p100*
Langan, Bryan; Philadelphia, 1850 ***53.26*** *p45*
Langan, Bryan; Philadelphia, 1850 ***5704.8*** *p60*
Langan, John; New York, NY, 1838 ***8208.4*** *p68*
Langan, Laurence; America, 1743 ***4971*** *p18*
Langan, Wm.; Arizona, 1897 ***9228.30*** *p4*
Langbein, Joseph; America, 1849 ***1450.2*** *p85A*
Langbridge, Bertie A.; Colorado, 1902 ***9678.2*** *p123*
Langdon, Elam P.; Cincinnati, 1788-1848 ***8582.3*** *p88*
Langdon, Henry 25; Pennsylvania, 1728 ***3690.1*** *p136*
Langdon, Johanna; Colorado, 1887 ***9678.2*** *p123*
Langdon, John 18; Maryland, 1775 ***1219.7*** *p254*
Langdon, Kath 21; America, 1705 ***2212*** *p42*
Lange, . . .; Canada, 1776-1783 ***9786*** *p27*
Lange, . . .; Cincinnati, 1831 ***8582.1*** *p51*
Lange, A.; Pennsylvania, 1866 ***2764.35*** *p42*
Lange, Albert; Cincinnati, 1788-1848 ***8582.3*** *p89*
Lange, Alfred Carl; Baltimore, 1888 ***3455.1*** *p46*
Lange, Carl Wilhelm Christian; America, 1881 ***4610.10*** *p124*
Lange, Christian; Cincinnati, 1869-1887 ***8582*** *p19*
Lange, Christian Friedrich Ludwig; America, 1853 ***4610.10*** *p116*
Lange, F.H.; Wisconsin, n.d. ***9675.6*** *p200*
Lange, Frank John; Arkansas, 1918 ***95.2*** *p71*
Lange, Gustav Frederich Christian; America, 1868 ***1450.2*** *p86A*
Lange, Hans W. 34; Harris Co., TX, 1898 ***6254*** *p4*
Lange, Henry George; Kansas, 1910 ***6013.40*** *p16*
Lange, Hugo; Arkansas, 1918 ***95.2*** *p71*
Lange, Jn.-Bte. 27; America, 1838 ***778.5*** *p316*
Lange, Johann Anton; Cincinnati, 1869-1887 ***8582*** *p19*
Lange, Johannes; Lancaster, PA, 1780 ***8137*** *p11*
Lange, John Gottlieb; New York, 1750 ***3652*** *p74*
Lange, Joseph H.; Portsmouth, 1869-1887 ***8582*** *p19*
Lange, Kurt; Philadelphia, 1779 ***8137*** *p11*
Lange, Leonard; America, 1881 ***1450.2*** *p22B*
Lange, Richard 20; America, 1838 ***778.5*** *p316*
Lange, Wilhelm 36; New Orleans, 1839 ***9420.2*** *p170*
Lange, Wladyslaw; New York, 1831 ***4606*** *p175*
Langeland, Torbjorn Mandeus; Arkansas, 1918 ***95.2*** *p71*
Langeleh, Marie Friedderike Charlotte; America, 1840 ***4610.10*** *p95*
Langeleh, Marie Friederike Charlotte; America, 1844 ***4610.10*** *p95*
Langell, Arthur; Ohio, 1849 ***9892.11*** *p26*
Langemeyer, . . .; Canada, 1776-1783 ***9786*** *p27*
Langemeyer, Regr.; Quebec, 1776 ***9786*** *p104*
Langen, Laurence; Delaware, 1743 ***4971*** *p105*
Langenberg, William; America, 1850 ***1450.2*** *p86A*
Langenecker, Peter; Pennsylvania, 1738 ***9898*** *p27*
Langenegger, John A.; Kansas, 1887 ***5240.1*** *p26*
Langenheim, Wilhelm; Philadelphia, 1874 ***8582.1*** *p21*
Langenschwartz, Johann Georg; Halifax, N.S., 1778 ***9786*** *p270*
Langenschwartz, Johann Georg; New York, 1776 ***9786*** *p270*
Langer, Ferdinand; New York, NY, 1835 ***8208.4*** *p78*
Langer, Richard; New York, NY, 1811 ***2859.11*** *p14*
Langerjaan, F.; Quebec, 1776 ***9786*** *p105*
Langerjahn, . . .; Canada, 1776-1783 ***9786*** *p27*
Langerjahn, Siegfried Christian; Quebec, 1776 ***9786*** *p255*
Langers, Nicholas; Wisconsin, n.d. ***9675.6*** *p200*
Langester, John 29; Philadelphia, 1774 ***1219.7*** *p217*
Langeteau, J. 21; America, 1836 ***778.5*** *p317*
Langevicz, Walter; Arkansas, 1918 ***95.2*** *p71*
Langford, Archibald; Quebec, 1764 ***7603*** *p35*
Langford, Edward; Virginia, 1638 ***6219*** *p121*
Langford, Walter; Virginia, 1643 ***6219*** *p200*
Langford, William; St. Kitts, 1763 ***1219.7*** *p97*
Langford, William 32; Maryland, 1774 ***1219.7*** *p220*
Langhan, Catharine 20; Massachusetts, 1849 ***5881.1*** *p57*
Langheinrich, Edward; Wisconsin, n.d. ***9675.6*** *p200*
Langhelee, . . .; Port uncertain, 1839 ***778.5*** *p317*
Langhelee, Miss; Port uncertain, 1839 ***778.5*** *p317*
Langhelee, Joseph; Port uncertain, 1839 ***778.5*** *p317*
Langhoff, Adolf; Illinois, 1892 ***5012.37*** *p62*
Langill, J. H.; Washington, 1859-1920 ***2872.1*** *p22*
Langille, . . .; Halifax, N.S., 1752 ***7074.6*** *p230*
Langille, Catherine *SEE* Langille, Leopold
Langille, David *SEE* Langille, Leopold
Langille, David 31; Halifax, N.S., 1752 ***7074.6*** *p211*
Langille, David 34; Halifax, N.S., 1752 ***7074.6*** *p211*
*Wife:*Marie-Christine
*Child:*Jean-Jacques
*Child:*Marguerite
*Child:*Jacques
Langille, Jacques *SEE* Langille, David
Langille, Jean-Jacques *SEE* Langille, David
Langille, Jean-Jacques 16; Halifax, N.S., 1752 ***7074.6*** *p211*
Langille, Leopold; Port uncertain, 1752 ***7074.6*** *p203*
*Wife:*Marguerite Sandoz
*Brother:*David
Langille, Leopold 24; Halifax, N.S., 1752 ***7074.6*** *p211*
*Wife:*Marguerite
*Daughter:*Catherine
Langille, Marguerite *SEE* Langille, David
Langille, Marguerite *SEE* Langille, Leopold
Langille, Marguerite Sandoz *SEE* Langille, Leopold
Langille, Marie-Christine *SEE* Langille, David
Langille, Matthieu 26; Halifax, N.S., 1752 ***7074.6*** *p211*
Langin, William 24; Massachusetts, 1849 ***5881.1*** *p62*
Langins, . . .; Canada, 1776-1783 ***9786*** *p27*
Langkop, . . .; Canada, 1776-1783 ***9786*** *p27*
Langlade, Pierre 22; Port uncertain, 1838 ***778.5*** *p317*
Langlais, Guillaume 21; Montreal, 1703 ***7603*** *p29*
Langlais, Jean-Baptiste; Ontario, 1757 ***7603*** *p26*
Langlais, Joseph; Quebec, 1730 ***7603*** *p26*
Langlais, Philippe; Quebec, 1825 ***7603*** *p48*
Langley, Francis; New York, NY, 1837 ***8208.4*** *p55*
Langley, John; America, 1742 ***4971*** *p99*
Langley, John; America, 1743 ***4971*** *p100*
Langley, John 27; Philadelphia, 1774 ***1219.7*** *p216*
Langley, Josiah 25; Philadelphia, 1774 ***1219.7*** *p216*
Langley, Mathew; Virginia, 1638 ***6219*** *p145*
Langley, Michael; New York, NY, 1815 ***2859.11*** *p35*
Langley, Ralph 16; America, 1704 ***2212*** *p40*
Langley, Richard; Virginia, 1637 ***6219*** *p110*
Langley, Timothy 22; Philadelphia, 1774 ***1219.7*** *p216*
Langlois, Mr. 35; New Orleans, 1821 ***778.5*** *p317*
Langlois, Mr. 36; Kentucky, 1820 ***778.5*** *p317*
Langlois, G. 43; America, 1829 ***778.5*** *p317*
Langlois, Jean; Quebec, 1710 ***7603*** *p27*
Langly, John; Virginia, 1642 ***6219*** *p188*
Langnas, Frederick; Wisconsin, n.d. ***9675.6*** *p200*
Langnese, Christian William; Wisconsin, n.d. ***9675.6*** *p200*
Langohr, Elisabeth 83; America, 1897 ***1763*** *p48D*
Langpaap, C. 45?; Arizona, 1890 ***2764.35*** *p41*
Langrick, George Francis 39; California, 1872 ***2769.6*** *p4*
Langsenkamp, Frank; America, 1848 ***1450.2*** *p86A*
Langston, John; Virginia, 1635 ***6219*** *p4*
Langton, Daniel; New York, NY, 1816 ***2859.11*** *p35*
Langton, John; Jamaica, 1755 ***1219.7*** *p32*
Langton, John; Jamaica, 1755 ***3690.1*** *p136*
Langton, Patrick; New York, NY, 1837 ***8208.4*** *p32*
Langworth, Jonathan; Virginia, 1638 ***6219*** *p125*
Langworthy, J. H.; Washington, 1859-1920 ***2872.1*** *p22*
Langworthy, Robert; Illinois, 1894 ***5012.39*** *p53*
Lanigan, George; New York, NY, 1811 ***2859.11*** *p14*
Lanius, Jacob; Pennsylvania, 1731 ***1034.18*** *p13*
*Wife:*Juliana Krahmer
Lanius, Juliana Krahmer *SEE* Lanius, Jacob
Lanke, Ferdinand; Illinois, 1886 ***2896.5*** *p23*
Lankheet, Berendina 33; New York, NY, 1847 ***3377.6*** *p13*
Lankheet, Everdina 40; New York, NY, 1847 ***3377.6*** *p11*
Lankheet, Gerrit 23; New York, NY, 1847 ***3377.6*** *p11*
Lankheet, Gerrit Hendrik 60; New York, NY, 1847 ***3377.6*** *p11*
Lankheet, Hendrika 3 mos; New York, NY, 1847 ***3377.6*** *p13*
Lankheet, Hendrikus Jacobus 36; New York, NY, 1847 ***3377.6*** *p13*
Lankheet, Janna Berendina 20; New York, NY, 1847 ***3377.6*** *p11*
Lankheet, John 5; New York, NY, 1847 ***3377.6*** *p13*
Lankheet, John 30; New York, NY, 1847 ***3377.6*** *p11*
Lankheet, John Willem 7; New York, NY, 1847 ***3377.6*** *p13*
Lannagan, Mary; St. John, N.B., 1853 ***5704.8*** *p107*
Lannegan, Ann 30; Massachusetts, 1847 ***5881.1*** *p57*
Lannegan, Dennis 28; Massachusetts, 1850 ***5881.1*** *p58*
Lannegan, Michael 6; Massachusetts, 1847 ***5881.1*** *p60*
Lannert, Barbara 36; America, 1853 ***9162.7*** *p15*
Lannert, Eva 49; America, 1853 ***9162.8*** *p37*
Lannert, Georg 16; America, 1853 ***9162.7*** *p15*
Lannert, Joseph 11; America, 1853 ***9162.7*** *p15*
Lannert, Marg. 15; America, 1853 ***9162.7*** *p15*
Lannert, Nicklaus 9; America, 1853 ***9162.7*** *p15*
Lannert, Ph. 48; America, 1853 ***9162.8*** *p37*
Lannes, Mr. 27; Port uncertain, 1836 ***778.5*** *p317*
Lannes, Joseph; Indiana, 1848 ***9117*** *p19*
Lannius, Jacob; Pennsylvania, 1761 ***1034.18*** *p14*
Lannius, Jacob; Philadelphia, 1761 ***9973.7*** *p36*
Lannluc, Mr. 24; New Orleans, 1839 ***778.5*** *p317*
Lannon, Ann 18; St. John, N.B., 1865 ***5704.8*** *p165*
Lannon, Bridget 20; St. John, N.B., 1865 ***5704.8*** *p165*
Lano, Bernhard; Wisconsin, n.d. ***9675.6*** *p200*
Lanon, A. F.; Iowa, 1866-1943 ***123.54*** *p29*
Lanon, Lewis E.; Iowa, 1866-1943 ***123.54*** *p29*
Lanoy, J. 57; Port uncertain, 1838 ***778.5*** *p317*
Lanper, Samson 46; New York, NY, 1878 ***9253*** *p45*
Lans, . . .; Canada, 1776-1783 ***9786*** *p27*
Lanscak, John; Iowa, 1866-1943 ***123.54*** *p29*
Lanser, Franz; Wisconsin, n.d. ***9675.6*** *p200*
Lansin, John; Iowa, 1866-1943 ***123.54*** *p29*
Lanstones, Elady; Virginia, 1641 ***6219*** *p187*
Lanstorf, Nickolas; Wisconsin, n.d. ***9675.6*** *p200*
Lantial, Mr. 50; New Orleans, 1837 ***778.5*** *p317*
Lantial, Juan 39; New Orleans, 1835 ***778.5*** *p317*
Lantier, J. 19; New Orleans, 1839 ***778.5*** *p317*
Lantz, Andrew; Philadelphia, 1765 ***9973.7*** *p40*
Lantz, Erick Emanuel 24; Arkansas, 1918 ***95.2*** *p71*
Lantz, Johann; Ohio, 1808 ***8582.2*** *p56*
Lantzin, Jean 36; New Orleans, 1837 ***778.5*** *p318*
Lantzin, Jean Michel 36; New Orleans, 1837 ***778.5*** *p317*
Lanuet, Mr. 14; New Orleans, 1838 ***778.5*** *p318*
Lanuet, Ms. 41; New Orleans, 1838 ***778.5*** *p318*
Lanusse, Mr. 14; Port uncertain, 1836 ***778.5*** *p318*

Lassen
PASSENGER AND IMMIGRATION LISTS INDEX: 1996 SUPPLEMENT

Lassen, Samuel; Arkansas, 1918 ***95.2*** *p72*
Lassere, B. 30; Port uncertain, 1837 ***778.5*** *p322*
Lasserre, Bd. 25; New Orleans, 1837 ***778.5*** *p322*
Lasseyne, M. 35; New Orleans, 1835 ***778.5*** *p318*
Lassiac, Madelaine 26; America, 1838 ***778.5*** *p322*
Lassiac, Sebastien 22; America, 1838 ***778.5*** *p322*
Lassiac, Urbain Joseph 26; America, 1838 ***778.5*** *p322*
Lassides, Meyer 23; New York, NY, 1878 ***9253*** *p47*
Lassila, Gusti Alfred; Arkansas, 1918 ***95.2*** *p72*
Lassoire, Mr. 25; America, 1839 ***778.5*** *p322*
Lassusse, Mr. 28; America, 1838 ***778.5*** *p322*
Last, Charles; Wisconsin, n.d. ***9675.6*** *p200*
Last, John; Wisconsin, n.d. ***9675.6*** *p200*
Lastia, Mme. 32; Port uncertain, 1838 ***778.5*** *p322*
Lastia, J. 38; Port uncertain, 1838 ***778.5*** *p322*
Lasting, Jossy; Virginia, 1643 ***6219*** *p200*
Lastrapes, Jean-Henri; Louisiana, 1789-1819 ***778.5*** *p556*
Latapy, F. 36; Port uncertain, 1839 ***778.5*** *p323*
Latassie, Barth. 30; America, 1839 ***778.5*** *p323*
Lataste, V. 26; America, 1835 ***778.5*** *p323*
Latchett, Robert; Virginia, 1621 ***6219*** *p29*
Latchett, Robert; Virginia, 1637 ***6219*** *p180*
Later, Brian; Quebec, 1853 ***5704.8*** *p104*
Later, Hugh; Quebec, 1853 ***5704.8*** *p104*
Laterman, . . .; Canada, 1776-1783 ***9786*** *p27*
LaTerriere, Dr.; Quebec, 1815 ***9229.18*** *p76*
With wife
Latewood, William 21; Maryland, 1775 ***1219.7*** *p272*
Latham, Elias; New York, NY, 1815 ***2859.11*** *p35*
Latham, Hannah; Philadelphia, 1816 ***2859.11*** *p35*
Latham, Henry; New York, NY, 1815 ***2859.11*** *p35*
Latham, Hugh; New York, NY, 1815 ***2859.11*** *p35*
Latham, John 16; Virginia, 1774 ***1219.7*** *p242*
Latham, John 32; Halifax, N.S., 1774 ***1219.7*** *p213*
Latham, Martha; New York, NY, 1815 ***2859.11*** *p35*
Latham, Mary 20; Grenada, 1774 ***1219.7*** *p177*
Latham, Nathaniel; New York, NY, 1815 ***2859.11*** *p35*
Latham, Thomas; New York, NY, 1815 ***2859.11*** *p35*
With wife
Latham, Thomas 20; Maryland, 1774 ***1219.7*** *p208*
Latham, William; New York, NY, 1815 ***2859.11*** *p35*
Lathem, Thomas 20; Jamaica, 1739 ***3690.1*** *p137*
Lather, Peter; Virginia, 1637 ***6219*** *p115*
Lathropp, John; Virginia, 1638 ***6219*** *p146*
Latner, Francis; Virginia, 1637 ***6219*** *p83*
Laton, John 18; Virginia, 1720 ***3690.1*** *p137*
Latorra, Felix; Colorado, 1886 ***9678.2*** *p123*
Latorra, Joseph; Colorado, 1886 ***9678.2*** *p123*
Latouche, Mr. 38; New Orleans, 1839 ***778.5*** *p323*
Latour, Mr. 28; New Orleans, 1839 ***778.5*** *p323*
Latour, Grace 21; New Orleans, 1830 ***778.5*** *p323*
LaToureau, Mr. 24; Port uncertain, 1839 ***778.5*** *p323*
Latta, Anne 7; Philadelphia, 1871 ***5704.8*** *p241*
Latta, Mary Ann; Philadelphia, 1871 ***5704.8*** *p241*
Latter, John 27; Jamaica, 1727 ***3690.1*** *p137*
Latterade, Mr. 28; America, 1839 ***778.5*** *p323*
Lattimore, Clement; Virginia, 1642 ***6219*** *p197*
Lattmann, . . .; Canada, 1776-1783 ***9786*** *p27*
Latvaaho, Henry; Arkansas, 1918 ***95.2*** *p72*
Latvaaho, Hentrig; Arkansas, 1918 ***95.2*** *p72*
Latz, . . .; Canada, 1776-1783 ***9786*** *p27*
Latzel, John; Wisconsin, n.d. ***9675.6*** *p200*
Latzl, John; Wisconsin, n.d. ***9675.6*** *p200*
Lau, Charles; Wisconsin, n.d. ***9675.6*** *p200*
Lau, Hardwig; Wisconsin, n.d. ***9675.6*** *p200*
Lau, Philip; Philadelphia, 1763 ***9973.7*** *p38*
Laub, Anna *SEE* Laub, Michael
Laub, Anna Barbara *SEE* Laub, Balthasar
Laub, Anna Elisabetha *SEE* Laub, Balthasar
Laub, Anna Maria *SEE* Laub, Balthasar
Laub, Balthasar; Pennsylvania, 1751 ***2444*** *p183*
Laub, Balthasar; Pennsylvania, 1753 ***2444*** *p183*
*Wife:*Maria B. Moessner
*Child:*Johann Michael
*Child:*Catharina Dorothea
*Child:*Anna Barbara
*Child:*Johannes
*Child:*Anna Elisabetha
*Child:*Anna Maria
Laub, Barbara *SEE* Laub, Michael
Laub, Catharina Dorothea *SEE* Laub, Balthasar
Laub, Dorothea *SEE* Laub, Michael
Laub, Elisabetha *SEE* Laub, Michael
Laub, Johann Michael *SEE* Laub, Balthasar
Laub, Johann Michael; Pennsylvania, 1753 ***2444*** *p183*
Laub, Johannes *SEE* Laub, Balthasar
Laub, Johannes *SEE* Laub, Michael
Laub, Johannes 18; Pennsylvania, 1753 ***2444*** *p183*
Laub, Maria B. Moessner *SEE* Laub, Balthasar
Laub, Matthaus *SEE* Laub, Michael
Laub, Michael; Pennsylvania, 1749 ***2444*** *p183*
*Wife:*Anna
*Child:*Matthaus
*Child:*Elisabetha
*Child:*Johannes
*Child:*Dorothea
*Child:*Barbara
With child
Laub, Michel; Pennsylvania, 1753 ***2444*** *p215*
Laub, Philipp 31; America, 1854-1855 ***9162.6*** *p105*
Laube, J. R.; America, 1850 ***8582.2*** *p22*
Laubenstein, Andrew; Wisconsin, n.d. ***9675.6*** *p200*
Laubenstein, John; Wisconsin, n.d. ***9675.6*** *p200*
Lauber, Albert 23; Kansas, 1902 ***5240.1*** *p27*
Lauber, Albert 23; Kansas, 1902 ***5240.1*** *p82*
Lauber, Leopold 36; Kansas, 1882 ***5240.1*** *p27*
Lauber, Leopold 36; Kansas, 1882 ***5240.1*** *p64*
Lauber, Theodore; Wisconsin, n.d. ***9675.6*** *p200*
Laubert, Henry Gottlieb; New York, 1875 ***1450.2*** *p22B*
Laubhan, Ray; Arkansas, 1918 ***95.2*** *p72*
Laubscher, Christian; New York, NY, 1837 ***9117*** *p17*
Lauc, Gowin; Virginia, 1638 ***6219*** *p150*
Lauc, J. 23; New Orleans, 1835 ***778.5*** *p323*
Lauch, Georg 22; Kentucky, 1842 ***8582.3*** *p100*
Lauchland, Andrew 31; Kansas, 1871 ***5240.1*** *p27*
Lauchland, Andrew 31; Kansas, 1871 ***5240.1*** *p51*
Laucione, Nicola 30; West Virginia, 1904 ***9788.3*** *p14*
Lauck, Franz; America, 1850 ***8582.3*** *p40*
Lauck, John Samuel; New York, 1750 ***3652*** *p74*
Laucothe, Mr. 20; New Orleans, 1839 ***778.5*** *p323*
Laude, Anton; New York, NY, 1836 ***8208.4*** *p9*
Laudenbough, Conrad; Philadelphia, 1763 ***9973.7*** *p38*
Lauder, Alexander; North Carolina, 1850 ***1639.20*** *p109*
Lauders, Nic.; Wisconsin, n.d. ***9675.6*** *p200*
Laudfelder, Veit; Georgia, 1738 ***9332*** *p321*
Laudonniere, Rene; Florida, 1564 ***8582.3*** *p75*
Lauer, . . .; Canada, 1776-1783 ***9786*** *p27*
Lauer, Mr.; Pittsburgh, 1817 ***8582.2*** *p27*
Lauer, Christian; America, 1733 ***4349*** *p48*
Lauer, Christian; Philadelphia, 1733 ***4349*** *p48*
Lauer, Georg; America, 1850 ***8582.2*** *p22*
Lauer, Henry; New York, NY, 1847 ***6013.19*** *p73*
Lauer, Oscar Alvin Felix 21; Arkansas, 1918 ***95.2*** *p72*
Lauer, Peter; America, 1830 ***8582.2*** *p61*
Lauer, Peter; Cincinnati, 1869-1887 ***8582*** *p19*
Lauer, Philip; New York, NY, 1839 ***8208.4*** *p95*
Lauerborn, Katy; New York, NY, 1922 ***3455.4*** *p28*
Lauf, Fred; Illinois, 1897 ***2896.5*** *p23*
Lauffer, Conrad; Pennsylvania, 1749 ***2444*** *p184*
Laugbaugh, Christian; Philadelphia, 1759 ***9973.7*** *p34*
Laughan, Martha 17; Quebec, 1857 ***5704.8*** *p136*
Laughery, Isabella; New York, NY, 1816 ***2859.11*** *p35*
Laughlan, John 20; Massachusetts, 1850 ***5881.1*** *p59*
Laughlan, Lawrence 30; Massachusetts, 1849 ***5881.1*** *p60*
Laughlan, Mary 20; Massachusetts, 1850 ***5881.1*** *p60*
Laughlan, Michael 30; Massachusetts, 1849 ***5881.1*** *p60*
Laughland, George 4; St. John, N.B., 1866 ***5704.8*** *p166*
Laughland, James 19; St. John, N.B., 1866 ***5704.8*** *p166*
Laughland, John 9; St. John, N.B., 1866 ***5704.8*** *p166*
Laughland, Marion 14; St. John, N.B., 1866 ***5704.8*** *p166*
Laughland, Robert 7; St. John, N.B., 1866 ***5704.8*** *p166*
Laughlin, Ann 14; St. John, N.B., 1860 ***5704.8*** *p144*
Laughlin, Catharine; America, 1868 ***5704.8*** *p231*
Laughlin, Catharine 8; Massachusetts, 1849 ***5881.1*** *p57*
Laughlin, Catharine 26; Massachusetts, 1849 ***5881.1*** *p57*
Laughlin, Charles 25; St. John, N.B., 1854 ***5704.8*** *p114*
Laughlin, Elizabeth 22; Wilmington, DE, 1831 ***6508.3*** *p100*
Laughlin, George; New York, NY, 1816 ***2859.11*** *p35*
Laughlin, Isabella; Quebec, 1847 ***5704.8*** *p36*
Laughlin, James; America, 1742 ***4971*** *p86*
Laughlin, James; America, 1742 ***4971*** *p95*
Laughlin, James; America, 1743 ***4971*** *p11*
Laughlin, James 22; St. John, N.B., 1857 ***5704.8*** *p135*
Laughlin, James 24; Wilmington, DE, 1831 ***6508.3*** *p100*
Laughlin, James 26; Kansas, 1872 ***5240.1*** *p52*
Laughlin, Mary; Quebec, 1851 ***5704.8*** *p74*
Laughlin, Mary 16; St. John, N.B., 1860 ***5704.8*** *p144*
Laughlin, Pat 61; Arizona, 1907 ***9228.40*** *p12*
Laughlin, Patrick 20; St. John, N.B., 1860 ***5704.8*** *p144*
Laughlin, Patrick 50; Philadelphia, 1853 ***5704.8*** *p108*
Laughlin, William; America, 1868 ***5704.8*** *p231*
Laughlin, Wm.; Philadelphia, 1816 ***2859.11*** *p35*
Laughran, Jas.; Philadelphia, 1816 ***2859.11*** *p35*
Laughson, Edward; Virginia, 1638 ***6219*** *p117*
Laughten, Bridget 25; Massachusetts, 1849 ***5881.1*** *p57*
Laughten, Mary 23; Massachusetts, 1849 ***5881.1*** *p60*
Laughton, Leon.; Virginia, 1636 ***6219*** *p26*
Laughton, Robert; New York, NY, 1816 ***2859.11*** *p35*
Laughton, Robert; Virginia, 1637 ***6219*** *p83*
Laughton, William; Charleston, SC, 1796 ***1639.20*** *p109*
Laughy, Michael; New York, NY, 1834 ***8208.4*** *p39*
Laugilet, Nicolas 44; Texas, 1839 ***778.5*** *p323*
Lauhifer, Henry; Illinois, 1856 ***7857*** *p4*
Laulainen, Ailli; Washington, 1859-1920 ***2872.1*** *p22*
Laulainen, Aleksander; Washington, 1859-1920 ***2872.1*** *p22*
Laulainen, Anne; Washington, 1859-1920 ***2872.1*** *p22*
Laulainen, Einori; Washington, 1859-1920 ***2872.1*** *p22*
Laulainen, Otto; Washington, 1859-1920 ***2872.1*** *p22*
Laulainen, William; Washington, 1859-1920 ***2872.1*** *p22*
Lauler, Ernest; New York, 1898 ***1450.2*** *p22B*
Lauler, Joseph; New York, NY, 1893 ***1450.2*** *p22B*
Laumaster, Wendle; Pennsylvania, 1750-1751 ***4525*** *p231*
Laumeister, Wendall; Philadelphia, 1762 ***9973.7*** *p37*
Laumeister, Wendel; Pennsylvania, 1751 ***4525*** *p231*
Launcelette, Peter L. 37; Port uncertain, 1829 ***778.5*** *p323*
Launders, Daniel 34; Massachusetts, 1850 ***5881.1*** *p58*
Launhard, . . .; Canada, 1776-1783 ***9786*** *p27*
Launhard, Henry; Canada, 1776-1783 ***9786*** *p207A*
Launiau, Jean 23; Port uncertain, 1836 ***778.5*** *p323*
Launitz, E. 49; New York, NY, 1870 ***8582*** *p19*
Launy, Cornelius; America, 1742 ***4971*** *p56*
Laup, Johannes Mich'l 20; Pennsylvania, 1753 ***2444*** *p183*
Laupe, Johanne Rosine 36; New Orleans, 1839 ***9420.2*** *p71*
Laupen, John; Wisconsin, n.d. ***9675.6*** *p200*
Lauppe, John F. 32; Kansas, 1879 ***5240.1*** *p61*
Laurant, L. 40; Port uncertain, 1835 ***778.5*** *p324*
Laure, Antoine 40; New Orleans, 1839 ***778.5*** *p324*
Laure, Antonio; Arkansas, 1918 ***95.2*** *p72*
Laurell, Penelope; Virginia, 1641 ***6219*** *p185*
Laurence, Joyce; Illinois, 1873 ***2896.5*** *p23*
Laurences, P. 36; New Orleans, 1825 ***778.5*** *p324*
Laurendais, P. 31; Mexico, 1829 ***778.5*** *p324*
Laurens, Colonel; Savannah, GA, 1779 ***8582.2*** *p52*
Laurens, J. 30; New Orleans, 1823 ***778.5*** *p324*
Laurent, Ms. 30; Port uncertain, 1838 ***778.5*** *p324*
Laurent, Emile 24; New Orleans, 1831 ***778.5*** *p324*
Laurent, Francis 40; Grenada, 1774 ***1219.7*** *p185*
Laurent, H. 21; Kansas, 1876 ***5240.1*** *p57*
Laurent, Henry 21; Kansas, 1876 ***5240.1*** *p27*
Laurent, J. 22; America, 1836 ***778.5*** *p326*
Laurent, J. 33; New Orleans, 1823 ***778.5*** *p324*
Laurent, J. 35; New Orleans, 1825 ***778.5*** *p324*
Laurent, Jacinthe 32; Louisiana, 1820 ***778.5*** *p324*
Laurent, Jacinthe 32; Port uncertain, 1823 ***778.5*** *p324*
Laurent, Michel 35; America, 1831 ***778.5*** *p324*
Laurenz, August; New York, NY, 1884 ***1450.2*** *p22B*
Laurenz, Charles; New York, NY, 1892 ***1450.2*** *p22B*
Laurenzio, Giov 50; New York, NY, 1893 ***9026.4*** *p41*
Laurich, Joseph; Wisconsin, n.d. ***9675.6*** *p200*
Lauridsen, Charley S.; Arkansas, 1918 ***95.2*** *p72*
Lauridsen, Jakob Ingvart Kristian; New York, NY, 1910 ***3455.3*** *p21*
Lauridsen, Laurid; America, 1906 ***3455.2*** *p102*
*Wife:*Marie
Lauridsen, Marie *SEE* Lauridsen, Laurid
Lauridsen, Mary *SEE* Lauridsen, Simon
Lauridsen, Ole Kristian; New York, NY, 1912 ***3455.3*** *p22*
Lauridsen, Otto; Arkansas, 1918 ***95.2*** *p72*
Lauridsen, Simon; New York, NY, 1906 ***3455.3*** *p22*
*Wife:*Mary
Laurie, Francis W. 28; Kansas, 1872 ***5240.1*** *p52*
Laurie, Frank; Wisconsin, n.d. ***9675.6*** *p200*
Laurie, Henry A. 26; Kansas, 1872 ***5240.1*** *p52*
Laurie, James 20; Maryland, 1736 ***3690.1*** *p137*
Laurie, James 22; Kansas, 1870 ***5240.1*** *p51*
Laurie, John; America, 1871 ***1450.2*** *p86A*
Laurie, John 29; Kansas, 1870 ***5240.1*** *p27*
Laurie, John 29; Kansas, 1870 ***5240.1*** *p51*
Laurie, Martin 23; Kansas, 1878 ***5240.1*** *p59*
Laurie, Thomas 22; Kansas, 1872 ***5240.1*** *p52*
Laurillard, . . .; Halifax, N.S., 1749 ***7074.6*** *p230*
Laurilliard, . . .; Halifax, N.S., 1749 ***7074.6*** *p230*
Laurilliard, Anne *SEE* Laurilliard, Jean-Christophe
Laurilliard, Elisabeth *SEE* Laurilliard, Jean-Christophe
Laurilliard, George *SEE* Laurilliard, Jean-Christophe
Laurilliard, Jean-Christophe; Halifax, N.S., 1749 ***7074.6*** *p213*
*Wife:*Anne
*Child:*Elisabeth
*Child:*Jean-Henri
*Child:*George
Laurilliard, Jean-Henri *SEE* Laurilliard, Jean-Christophe
Lauritzen, Cathrina Louise; Washington, 1859-1920 ***2872.1*** *p22*
Lauritzen, Fred Carl Christian; Arkansas, 1918 ***95.2*** *p72*
Lauronen, Lauri; Washington, 1859-1920 ***2872.1*** *p22*
Laurouet, Jean 27; New Orleans, 1839 ***778.5*** *p325*
Laursen, Chris Marinus; Arkansas, 1918 ***95.2*** *p73*
Laurwell, John; Virginia, 1637 ***6219*** *p86*
Laury, Lorenz; America, 1820-1829 ***8582.2*** *p56*
Lausch, Albert; Arkansas, 1918 ***95.2*** *p73*
Lausetti, Marco; Arkansas, 1918 ***95.2*** *p73*

276
FOR A COMPLETE EXPLANATION OF ENTRY, SEE "HOW TO READ A CITATION" SECTION

Laydon, Virginia; Virginia, 1636 ***6219*** *p74*
Layer, John; Maryland, 1740 ***4971*** *p91*
Layer, John; Philadelphia, 1741 ***4971*** *p92*
Layfield, Robert; Illinois, 1874 ***5012.37*** *p59*
Layman, Aaron; America, 1843 ***1450.2*** *p87A*
Layne, John; Virginia, 1648 ***6219*** *p250*
Layne, Robert; Virginia, 1648 ***6219*** *p246*
Layne, Robt.; Virginia, 1643 ***6219*** *p205*
Laynes, Christopher 6; Massachusetts, 1849 ***5881.1*** *p57*
Laynes, Elizabeth 35; Massachusetts, 1849 ***5881.1*** *p58*
Laynes, Ellen 8; Massachusetts, 1849 ***5881.1*** *p58*
Laynes, Mary 10; Massachusetts, 1849 ***5881.1*** *p60*
Laynes, Richard 12; Massachusetts, 1849 ***5881.1*** *p61*
Layotte, Mr. 45; New Orleans, 1821 ***778.5*** *p326*
Lays, Mr.; Quebec, 1815 ***9229.18*** *p78*
Layser, Ms. 20; New Orleans, 1836 ***778.5*** *p326*
Laysinby, Thomas; Jamaica, 1753 ***1219.7*** *p19*
Laysinby, Thomas; Jamaica, 1753 ***3690.1*** *p138*
Layton, Elizabeth *SEE* Layton, William
Layton, Elizabeth 26 *SEE* Layton, Francis
Layton, Francis 18 mos *SEE* Layton, Francis
Layton, Francis 29; Nova Scotia, 1774 ***1219.7*** *p193*
*Wife:*Elizabeth 26
*Son:*Francis 18 mos
Layton, Francis V. 43; Arizona, 1890 ***2764.35*** *p41*
Layton, John 22; Nova Scotia, 1774 ***1219.7*** *p194*
Layton, Thomas 32; Jamaica, 1774 ***1219.7*** *p231*
Layton, William; Virginia, 1636 ***6219*** *p79*
*Wife:*Elizabeth
Layton, William; Virginia, 1637 ***6219*** *p85*
Layton, Wm.; Virginia, 1636 ***6219*** *p79*
Lazar, Mary; America, 1898 ***7137*** *p169*
Lazar, Michael; America, 1896 ***7137*** *p169*
Lazard, Mr. 30; New Orleans, 1836 ***778.5*** *p326*
Lazard, Edward 26; America, 1821 ***778.5*** *p326*
Lazaro, James 23; Arkansas, 1918 ***95.2*** *p73*
Lazarre, Fasi 37; America, 1832 ***778.5*** *p326*
Lazas, A.; Iowa, 1866-1943 ***123.54*** *p30*
Lazell, Clement 22; Maryland, 1735 ***3690.1*** *p138*
Lazere, Mary; America, 1898 ***7137*** *p169*
Lazere, Michael; America, 1896 ***7137*** *p169*
Lazetich, Dusan; Arkansas, 1918 ***95.2*** *p73*
Lazinby, William 21; Maryland, 1774 ***1219.7*** *p229*
Lazon, Jean Pierre 26; America, 1838 ***778.5*** *p327*
Lazor, Mary; America, 1898 ***7137*** *p169*
Lazor, Michael; America, 1896 ***7137*** *p169*
Lazouret, Andre; Port uncertain, 1839 ***778.5*** *p327*
Lazzare, Santa 45; New York, NY, 1893 ***9026.4*** *p41*
Lazzaretti, Giusseppe; Iowa, 1866-1943 ***123.54*** *p67*
Lazzaretti, Marco; Iowa, 1866-1943 ***123.54*** *p30*
Lazziri, Tco. 41; New York, NY, 1893 ***9026.4*** *p41*
L'catny, Patrick C.; Illinois, 1861 ***7857*** *p4*
Lea, Benjamin; New York, NY, 1838 ***8208.4*** *p67*
Lea, Edwin; Nevada, 1878 ***2764.35*** *p42*
Lea, Francis 23; Virginia, 1725 ***3690.1*** *p138*
Lea, Henry 14; America, 1702 ***2212*** *p39*
Lea, Robert; Philadelphia, 1815 ***2859.11*** *p35*
Lea, Susan 29; Virginia, 1700 ***2212*** *p32*
Lea, Thomas; New York, NY, 1827 ***8208.4*** *p36*
Leach, Alexander; North Carolina, 1784-1886 ***1639.20*** *p109*
Leach, Alexander 66; North Carolina, 1850 ***1639.20*** *p109*
Leach, Angus; North Carolina, 1846 ***1639.20*** *p109*
Leach, Archibald; America, 1804 ***1639.20*** *p109*
Leach, Archibald 55; North Carolina, 1850 ***1639.20*** *p110*
Leach, Arthur Thomas; Washington, 1859-1920 ***2872.1*** *p22*
Leach, Catherine 58 *SEE* Leach, John
Leach, Charles; Washington, 1859-1920 ***2872.1*** *p22*
Leach, Christian 50 *SEE* Leach, Neill
Leach, Daniel 60; South Carolina, 1850 ***1639.20*** *p110*
Leach, Donald 74; North Carolina, 1850 ***1639.20*** *p110*
*Relative:*Mary 70
Leach, Dugald; America, 1803 ***1639.20*** *p110*
Leach, Duncan 55 *SEE* Leach, Neill
Leach, Edith Mary; Washington, 1859-1920 ***2872.1*** *p23*
Leach, Emma; Washington, 1859-1920 ***2872.1*** *p23*
Leach, Fern Edith; Washington, 1859-1920 ***2872.1*** *p23*
Leach, Ida Alice; Washington, 1859-1920 ***2872.1*** *p23*
Leach, James 27; Nova Scotia, 1774 ***1219.7*** *p193*
Leach, John; America, 1804 ***1639.20*** *p110*
Leach, John; America, 1804 ***1639.20*** *p111*
Leach, John 17; Virginia, 1774 ***1219.7*** *p239*
Leach, John 60; North Carolina, 1850 ***1639.20*** *p111*
Leach, John 67; North Carolina, 1850 ***1639.20*** *p110*
*Relative:*Catherine 58
Leach, John 68; South Carolina, 1850 ***1639.20*** *p110*
Leach, Leonard Charles; Washington, 1859-1920 ***2872.1*** *p23*
Leach, Leonard Wilfred; Washington, 1859-1920 ***2872.1*** *p23*
Leach, Malcolm; America, 1804 ***1639.20*** *p111*
Leach, Mary; North Carolina, 1844 ***1639.20*** *p111*
Leach, Mary 21; Philadelphia, 1774 ***1219.7*** *p212*
Leach, Mary 55; North Carolina, 1850 ***1639.20*** *p111*
Leach, Mary 70 *SEE* Leach, Donald
Leach, Nancy 60 *SEE* Leach, Neill
Leach, Neill 52; North Carolina, 1850 ***1639.20*** *p111*
*Relative:*Duncan 55
Leach, Neill 57; North Carolina, 1850 ***1639.20*** *p111*
*Relative:*Christian 50
*Relative:*Nancy 60
*Relative:*Sallie 50
Leach, Rebecca; Virginia, 1639 ***6219*** *p151*
Leach, Roger; Virginia, 1635 ***6219*** *p72*
Leach, Sallie 50 *SEE* Leach, Neill
Leadbeater, William 23; Jamaica, 1736 ***3690.1*** *p138*
Leaden, Patrick; Philadelphia, 1850 ***53.26*** *p45*
Leaden, Patrick; Philadelphia, 1850 ***5704.8*** *p69*
Leaderd, Robert; Virginia, 1637 ***6219*** *p11*
Leading, James; Virginia, 1628 ***6219*** *p31*
Leaffry, Henry; Iowa, 1866-1943 ***123.54*** *p30*
Leafield, Elizabeth 20; Virginia, 1700 ***2212*** *p30*
Leafield, Rob; Virginia, 1698 ***2212*** *p14*
Leager, Tho.; Virginia, 1636 ***6219*** *p36*
Leagich, Ludwig; Arkansas, 1918 ***95.2*** *p73*
League, Mr.; Quebec, 1815 ***9229.18*** *p78*
With wife
Leahey, Biddy 20; Massachusetts, 1849 ***5881.1*** *p57*
Leahey, Johanna 22; Massachusetts, 1849 ***5881.1*** *p59*
Leahy, Henry; Philadelphia, 1816 ***2859.11*** *p35*
Leahy, Johanna 11; Massachusetts, 1849 ***5881.1*** *p59*
Leahy, Michael 9; Massachusetts, 1849 ***5881.1*** *p60*
Leahy, Michael 40; Massachusetts, 1850 ***5881.1*** *p60*
Leahy, Patrick 10; Massachusetts, 1850 ***5881.1*** *p61*
Leahy, Timothy; Quebec, 1828 ***7036*** *p124*
Leahy, Timothy; Rochester, NY, 1838 ***7036*** *p124*
Leahy, Timothy 8; Massachusetts, 1850 ***5881.1*** *p61*
Leak, Samuel; New York, NY, 1836 ***8208.4*** *p19*
Leak, William 21; Maryland, 1727 ***3690.1*** *p138*
Leake, Andrew; Virginia, 1642 ***6219*** *p193*
Leake, John; Virginia, 1642 ***6219*** *p189*
Leake, Jon.; Virginia, 1628 ***6219*** *p31*
Leake, Richard; Virginia, 1636 ***6219*** *p77*
Leake, Richard; Virginia, 1639 ***6219*** *p22*
Leake, Richard; Virginia, 1643 ***6219*** *p202*
Leaky, John; New York, NY, 1811 ***2859.11*** *p14*
Lealand, Hugh; America, 1698 ***2212*** *p6*
Lealand, Jno; America, 1697-1707 ***2212*** *p3*
Lealand, William 13; Antigua (Antego), 1701 ***2212*** *p34*
Lealer, Patrick 50; Philadelphia, 1803 ***53.26*** *p45*
Leamond, Hannah 22; Quebec, 1863 ***5704.8*** *p154*
Leanhop, Henry; New York, 1891 ***1450.2*** *p23B*
Lear, John; New York, NY, 1815 ***2859.11*** *p35*
Learche, Charles F.; Kansas, 1874 ***5240.1*** *p27*
Learmonth, Alexander; Charleston, SC, 1700-1800 ***1639.20*** *p111*
Leary, Bridget; Massachusetts, 1847 ***5881.1*** *p57*
Leary, Catharine 8; Massachusetts, 1848 ***5881.1*** *p57*
Leary, Catharine 22; Massachusetts, 1847 ***5881.1*** *p57*
Leary, Catherine; America, 1736-1743 ***4971*** *p57*
Leary, Cornelius 7; Massachusetts, 1847 ***5881.1*** *p57*
Leary, Cornelius 50; Massachusetts, 1849 ***5881.1*** *p57*
Leary, Daniel 11; Massachusetts, 1848 ***5881.1*** *p58*
Leary, Daniel 18; Massachusetts, 1848 ***5881.1*** *p58*
Leary, David 31; Massachusetts, 1849 ***5881.1*** *p58*
Leary, Dennis; Massachusetts, 1847 ***5881.1*** *p58*
Leary, Dennis 24; Massachusetts, 1848 ***5881.1*** *p58*
Leary, Eliza 22; Massachusetts, 1847 ***5881.1*** *p58*
Leary, Ellen 26; Massachusetts, 1850 ***5881.1*** *p58*
Leary, Hannah 55; Massachusetts, 1850 ***5881.1*** *p58*
Leary, James 27; Massachusetts, 1850 ***5881.1*** *p59*
Leary, Jemina 18; Canada, 1838 ***4535.12*** *p113*
Leary, Johanna 5; Massachusetts, 1849 ***5881.1*** *p59*
Leary, Johanna 15; Massachusetts, 1850 ***5881.1*** *p59*
Leary, Johanna 30; Massachusetts, 1848 ***5881.1*** *p58*
Leary, John 3; Massachusetts, 1850 ***5881.1*** *p59*
Leary, John 17; Massachusetts, 1849 ***5881.1*** *p59*
Leary, John 50; Massachusetts, 1848 ***5881.1*** *p58*
Leary, Lewis; America, 1740 ***4971*** *p48*
Leary, Lewis; America, 1741 ***4971*** *p49*
Leary, Marie-Anne; Montreal, 1824 ***7603*** *p89*
Leary, Mary 18; Massachusetts, 1848 ***5881.1*** *p60*
Leary, Mary 20; Massachusetts, 1850 ***5881.1*** *p61*
Leary, Mary 50; Massachusetts, 1850 ***5881.1*** *p61*
Leary, Mary 60; Massachusetts, 1848 ***5881.1*** *p60*
Leary, Matthew; New York, NY, 1816 ***2859.11*** *p35*
Leary, Michael; New York, NY, 1811 ***2859.11*** *p14*
Leary, Michael 20; Massachusetts, 1849 ***5881.1*** *p60*
Leary, Michael 25; Massachusetts, 1849 ***5881.1*** *p60*
Leary, Moses; Illinois, 1868 ***7857*** *p4*
Leary, Patrick; Quebec, 1809 ***7603*** *p65*
Leary, Patrick 18; Massachusetts, 1849 ***5881.1*** *p61*
Leary, Richard 40; Massachusetts, 1849 ***5881.1*** *p61*
Leary, Samuel 35; California, 1867 ***3840.2*** *p16*
Leary, Thomas; Sorel, Que., 1818 ***7603*** *p77*
Leary, Thomas 13; Massachusetts, 1849 ***5881.1*** *p61*
Leary, Thomas 30; Massachusetts, 1849 ***5881.1*** *p61*
Leary, Timothy; America, 1741 ***4971*** *p41*
Leasiter, Adam 15; Virginia, 1699 ***2212*** *p26*
Leasiter, John 22; Maryland or Virginia, 1699 ***2212*** *p24*
Leathercap, William; America, 1742 ***4971*** *p22*
Leathercap, William; America, 1742 ***4971*** *p86*
Leathercap, William; America, 1742 ***4971*** *p95*
Leathergough, John 19; New York, 1775 ***1219.7*** *p246*
Leatherland, Wm 20; America, 1706-1707 ***2212*** *p48*
Leaths, Edward; America, 1740 ***4971*** *p67*
Leator, Elizabeth; Montreal, 1821 ***7603*** *p61*
Leator, Margaret; Montreal, 1823 ***7603*** *p61*
Leau, Catherine *SEE* Leau, David
Leau, Catherine *SEE* Leau, Jean
Leau, David 46; Halifax, N.S., 1752 ***7074.6*** *p207*
With family of 1
Leau, David 46; Halifax, N.S., 1752 ***7074.6*** *p211*
*Wife:*Catherine
Leau, Eve *SEE* Leau, George
Leau, Frederic *SEE* Leau, George
Leau, George 30; Halifax, N.S., 1752 ***7074.6*** *p207*
With family of 3
Leau, George 30; Halifax, N.S., 1752 ***7074.6*** *p211*
*Wife:*Marie-Madeleine
*Child:*Eve
*Child:*Frederic
Leau, Jean 27; Halifax, N.S., 1752 ***7074.6*** *p211*
*Wife:*Catherine
Leau, Jean George 20; Halifax, N.S., 1752 ***7074.6*** *p207*
Leau, Jean-George 20; Halifax, N.S., 1752 ***7074.6*** *p211*
Leau, Marie-Madeleine *SEE* Leau, George
Leavitt, C.O. 25; Massachusetts, 1860 ***6410.32*** *p119*
Leavitt, Johanna 25; Massachusetts, 1849 ***5881.1*** *p59*
Leays, John; New York, NY, 1837 ***8208.4*** *p52*
Leazenbee, John; New York, NY, 1837 ***8208.4*** *p36*
Lebar de Lauin, Mr. 32; America, 1835 ***778.5*** *p327*
Lebarbur, . . .; Port uncertain, 1839 ***778.5*** *p327*
Lebarbur, Mr.; Port uncertain, 1839 ***778.5*** *p327*
Lebeaupin, Mme. 38; Port uncertain, 1825 ***778.5*** *p327*
Lebeaupin, Mr. 37; Port uncertain, 1825 ***778.5*** *p327*
Lebedowicz, . . .; New York, 1831 ***4606*** *p175*
LeBel, Flavius; Chicago, 1904 ***3455.3*** *p19*
*Wife:*Laura Kirouac
LeBel, Laura Kirouac *SEE* LeBel, Flavius
Leben, Roay 36; Kansas, 1906 ***5240.1*** *p83*
LeBenoit, Louis 26; America, 1836 ***778.5*** *p327*
Leberge, Louis 30; New Orleans, 1838 ***778.5*** *p327*
Lebert, Pierre; Louisiana, 1789-1819 ***778.5*** *p556*
Lebey, Jacob; New York, NY, 1836 ***8208.4*** *p15*
Lebin, Emile; Iroquois Co., IL, 1894 ***3455.1*** *p12*
Lebinder, Burnet; South Carolina, 1788 ***7119*** *p198*
Leblanc, . . .; Port uncertain, 1838 ***778.5*** *p327*
Leblanc, Mme. 25; Port uncertain, 1838 ***778.5*** *p327*
LeBlanc, Benoit 28; America, 1825 ***778.5*** *p327*
LeBlanc, J. 28; America, 1826 ***778.5*** *p327*
LeBlanc, John B. 31; Louisiana, 1820 ***778.5*** *p327*
LeBlanc, Joseph 38; America, 1838 ***778.5*** *p328*
LeBlanc, Josh 28; New Orleans, 1835 ***778.5*** *p327*
Leblanc, N.; New Orleans, 1839 ***778.5*** *p328*
Leblane, Pierre; New York, NY, 1836 ***8208.4*** *p23*
LeBlond, Mme. 45; America, 1830 ***778.5*** *p328*
LeBlond, Mme. 47; New Orleans, 1826 ***778.5*** *p328*
Lebman, Louis; Shreveport, LA, 1879 ***7129*** *p45*
Lebo, Joseph D.; Washington, 1859-1920 ***2872.1*** *p23*
Lebolt, Johannes; South Carolina, 1788 ***7119*** *p200*
Lebon, Francois; Louisiana, 1789-1819 ***778.5*** *p556*
Lebon, Peter Emile; Michigan, 1904 ***3455.2*** *p46*
LeBondidier, Leon 30; New Orleans, 1838 ***778.5*** *p328*
Le Boucher, Mr. 30; Louisiana, 1820 ***778.5*** *p328*
Lebrand, Cesar 50; America, 1835 ***778.5*** *p328*
LeBraud, Cesar 50; Port uncertain, 1835 ***778.5*** *p329*
Lebrecht, . . .; Canada, 1776-1783 ***9786*** *p27*
Lebret, Francoise 77; New Orleans, 1838 ***778.5*** *p328*
Lebrun, Jacques 24; America, 1836 ***778.5*** *p328*
Lebrun, Jacques 25; Quebec, 1693 ***4533*** *p129*
Lebrun, Ramon 26; New Orleans, 1835 ***778.5*** *p328*
Lec, Thomas 51; New York, NY, 1893 ***9026.4*** *p41*
Lecannes, F. 35; New Orleans, 1825 ***778.5*** *p328*
Lecerf, D. 39; New Orleans, 1822 ***778.5*** *p328*
Lecher, Catherine; Wisconsin, n.d. ***9675.6*** *p200*
Lecher, John; Wisconsin, n.d. ***9675.6*** *p200*
Lecher, Michael; Wisconsin, n.d. ***9675.6*** *p200*
Lecher, Nicholas; Wisconsin, n.d. ***9675.6*** *p200*
Lecher, Paul; Wisconsin, n.d. ***9675.6*** *p200*
Lechowitsky, Benjamin; Arkansas, 1918 ***95.2*** *p73*
Leckey, Thomas; New York, NY, 1816 ***2859.11*** *p35*
Leckner, Max; America, 1860 ***1450.2*** *p87A*
Lecky, Elizabeth; St. John, N.B., 1848 ***5704.8*** *p47*
Lecky, Jane; Philadelphia, 1852 ***5704.8*** *p88*
Lecky, Jane 20; Quebec, 1855 ***5704.8*** *p125*
Lecky, John 22; Quebec, 1855 ***5704.8*** *p125*
Lecky, Margaret 50; Philadelphia, 1855 ***5704.8*** *p124*

Lecky, Sarah 20; Philadelphia, 1855 5704.8 p124
Lecky, William; Philadelphia, 1852 5704.8 p88
LeClair, P. 52; Port uncertain, 1839 778.5 p329
Lecler, Marie Jeanne 60; America, 1838 778.5 p329
Leclerc, Charles 28; New Orleans, 1835 778.5 p329
Leclerc, Franc.; Port uncertain, 1839 778.5 p329
Leclerc, Marie 20; New Orleans, 1837 778.5 p329
Leclere, J. B. H. 44; New Orleans, 1823 778.5 p329
Lecock, Joseph; Philadelphia, 1850 53.26 p45
*Relative:*Mary Jane
Lecock, Joseph; Philadelphia, 1850 5704.8 p68
Lecock, Mary Jane *SEE* Lecock, Joseph
Lecock, Mary Jane; Philadelphia, 1850 5704.8 p68
Lecomberry, Mr.; Port uncertain, 1839 778.5 p329
Lecompte, August 43; Port uncertain, 1836 778.5 p335
Le Compte, Nicholas; New York, NY, 1839 8208.4 p94
Le Comte, Augustine; Colorado, 1904 9678.2 p123
Le Comte, Vincent; New York, NY, 1836 8208.4 p8
Leconte, Prosper; Iroquois Co., IL, 1884 3455.1 p12
Leconvreur, P. 28; New Orleans, 1835 778.5 p329
l'Ecossais, Abraham; Quebec, 1621 9775.5 p197
Le Count, Samuel 24; Philadelphia, 1775 1219.7 p258
Lecounteu, Mr. 23; Port uncertain, 1838 778.5 p329
Lecourt, Mr. 26; New Orleans, 1839 778.5 p329
LeCoutier, Mr. 31; America, 1837 778.5 p329
LeCoutoun, Lieut.; Quebec, 1815 9229.18 p82
LeCraud, Cesar 50; Port uncertain, 1835 778.5 p329
Lecuyer, Jeanne; Quebec, 1749 7603 p24
Ledat, Marius; Arkansas, 1918 95.2 p73
Leddy, Mrs.; New York, NY, 1816 2859.11 p35
With 2 children
Leddy, Andrew; New York, 1830 9892.11 p26
Leddy, James; Montreal, 1820 7603 p57
Leddy, Michael; New York, NY, 1816 2859.11 p35
Leddy, Patrick; New York, NY, 1837 8208.4 p32
Ledebrink, Christian Fr.; America, 1881 4610.10 p159
Ledebrink, Christian Heinrich; America, 1881 4610.10 p160
Ledeman, Francis 28; Arizona, 1911 9228.40 p15
Lederer, . . .; Canada, 1776-1783 9786 p27
Lederer, Johannes; America, 1669 8582.3 p93
Lederer, Johannes; America, 1669-1670 8582.3 p79
Lederer, John; Wisconsin, n.d. 9675.6 p200
Lederer, Philippus; Pennsylvania, 1744-1800 2444 p184
Lederer, Philippus; West Indies, 1744-1800 2444 p184
Lederman, Hans; New York, NY, 1915 3455.2 p77
Lederman, Hans; New York, NY, 1915 3455.3 p51
Ledon, Bartholmew 20; St. John, N.B., 1866 5704.8 p167
Ledont, Leon; Iowa, 1866-1943 123.54 p30
Leduc, Mr. 3; Port uncertain, 1836 778.5 p329
Leduc, Jean Marie 21; Port uncertain, 1836 778.5 p329
Ledwidge, Catharine 7; Massachusetts, 1849 5881.1 p57
Ledwidge, Ellen 5; Massachusetts, 1849 5881.1 p58
Ledwidge, John; New York, NY, 1845 2896.5 p24
Lee, Mr.; Quebec, 1815 9229.18 p80
Lee, Abraham 20; Maryland, 1724 3690.1 p138
Lee, Alexander; New York, NY, 1815 2859.11 p35
Lee, Alexander 21; Virginia, 1774 1219.7 p243
Lee, Andrew; St. John, N.B., 1849 5704.8 p55
Lee, Ann *SEE* Lee, Richard
Lee, Ann 16; Massachusetts, 1850 5881.1 p57
Lee, Anne; New York, NY, 1815 2859.11 p35
Lee, Anthony; Virginia, 1637 6219 p111
Lee, Anthony; Virginia, 1638 6219 p149
Lee, Ben; Washington, 1859-1920 2872.1 p23
Lee, C. J.; Washington, 1859-1920 2872.1 p23
Lee, Charles F.; San Francisco, 1876 2764.35 p41
Lee, Edward; New York, NY, 1815 2859.11 p35
Lee, Edward 23 *SEE* Lee, Ephriam
Lee, Elizabeth; America, 1864 5704.8 p186
Lee, Ephriam 26; Philadelphia, 1803 53.26 p45
*Relative:*Edward 23
Lee, Geo.; Virginia, 1623-1648 6219 p252
Lee, Georg; Virginia, 1636 6219 p77
Lee, George; New York, NY, 1815 2859.11 p35
Lee, George 18; Maryland, 1750 3690.1 p138
Lee, George 18; Maryland, 1751 1219.7 p3
Lee, Gilbert; Virginia, 1635 6219 p3
Lee, Goon 37; Kansas, 1887 5240.1 p70
Lee, Grace; Virginia, 1637 6219 p107
Lee, Hen.; Virginia, 1638 6219 p116
Lee, Henry; Virginia, 1636 6219 p76
Lee, Henry; Virginia, 1637 6219 p107
Lee, Hugh; Virginia, 1652 6251 p19
Lee, J. R.; Washington, 1859-1920 2872.1 p23
Lee, James 26; Philadelphia, 1774 1219.7 p232
Lee, James 28; Massachusetts, 1847 5881.1 p58
Lee, Jane; New York, NY, 1815 2859.11 p35
Lee, Jim 25; Kansas, 1888 5240.1 p71
Lee, John; America, 1740 4971 p48
Lee, John; America, 1741 4971 p49
Lee, John; America, 1864 5704.8 p186
Lee, John; Iowa, 1866-1943 123.54 p30
Lee, John; New York, NY, 1815 2859.11 p35
Lee, John; Washington, 1859-1920 2872.1 p23
Lee, John 16; Philadelphia, 1774 1219.7 p233
Lee, John 35; Maryland, 1774 1219.7 p181
Lee, John Luther; Washington, 1859-1920 2872.1 p23
Lee, Jon.; Virginia, 1635 6219 p3
Lee, Jon.; Virginia, 1637 6219 p86
Lee, Margaret 7; Massachusetts, 1849 5881.1 p60
Lee, Margaret 13; Massachusetts, 1849 5881.1 p60
Lee, Margaret 52; Massachusetts, 1849 5881.1 p60
Lee, Mary; Montreal, 1822 7603 p61
Lee, Mary; New York, NY, 1815 2859.11 p35
Lee, Mary; Philadelphia, 1850 5704.8 p64
Lee, Mary 19; Pennsylvania, Virginia or Maryland, 1699 2212 p19
Lee, Mary 24; Quebec, 1856 5704.8 p130
Lee, Mathew; Virginia, 1623-1648 6219 p252
Lee, Michel; Quebec, 1821 7603 p22
Lee, Nich.; Virginia, 1635 6219 p16
Lee, Patrick 24; Newfoundland, 1789 4915.24 p56
Lee, Richard; Virginia, 1635 6219 p16
Lee, Richard; Virginia, 1642 6219 p189
*Wife:*Ann
Lee, Richard; Virginia, 1643 6219 p205
Lee, Richard; Virginia, 1643 6219 p230
Lee, Robert; Quebec, 1849 5704.8 p51
Lee, Robert 3; Quebec, 1856 5704.8 p130
Lee, Robert 17; America, 1728 3690.1 p138
Lee, Robert 22; Virginia, 1774 1219.7 p243
Lee, Rodger; Colorado, 1886 9678.2 p123
Lee, Samuel 32; Maryland, 1774 1219.7 p207
Lee, Sarah; New York, NY, 1815 2859.11 p35
Lee, Sarah Jane 6 mos; Quebec, 1856 5704.8 p130
Lee, Sherwood 18; Maryland, 1723 3690.1 p138
Lee, Simon; New York, NY, 1815 2859.11 p35
Lee, Tho.; Virginia, 1648 6219 p246
Lee, Thomas; Arkansas, 1918 95.2 p73
Lee, Thomas; New York, NY, 1815 2859.11 p35
Lee, Thomas 17; Maryland or Virginia, 1719 3690.1 p139
Lee, Thomas 85; Massachusetts, 1849 5881.1 p61
Lee, Willi.; Virginia, 1636 6219 p78
Lee, William; New York, NY, 1835 8208.4 p46
Lee, William; New York, NY, 1840 8208.4 p104
Lee, William; North Carolina, 1761 1219.7 p82
Lee, William; Washington, 1859-1920 2872.1 p23
Lee, William 19; Jamaica, 1738 3690.1 p139
Lee, William 21; Maryland, 1775 1219.7 p257
Lee, William 25; Virginia, 1774 1219.7 p238
Lee, William 26; Maryland, 1774 1219.7 p222
Lee, William E.; Washington, 1859-1920 2872.1 p23
Lee, William Ellis; Washington, 1859-1920 2872.1 p23
Lee, Wm.; Virginia, 1637 6219 p113
Leech, A.; New York, NY, 1816 2859.11 p35
Leech, Alice; America, 1706-1707 2212 p48
Leech, Andrew; New York, NY, 1816 2859.11 p35
Leech, Henry 21; Jamaica, 1736 3690.1 p139
Leech, Jon.; Virginia, 1636 6219 p76
Leech, Malcolm; New York, NY, 1816 2859.11 p35
Leech, Margaret; Philadelphia, 1851 5704.8 p70
Leech, Mark; Virginia, 1639 6219 p162
Leech, Sarah; New York, NY, 1816 2859.11 p35
Leech, Stephen; Virginia, 1639 6219 p161
Leed, Ellen 26; America, 1705 2212 p44
Leed, Phebe 19; Virginia, 1699 2212 p20
Leedey, . . .; Ohio, 1819 8582.1 p47
Leek, Clinton D.; Wisconsin, n.d. 9675.6 p200
Leek, Jno; Maryland or Virginia, 1697 2212 p3
Leek, John 17; Virginia, 1773 1219.7 p169
Leek, Marshal B.; Wisconsin, n.d. 9675.6 p200
Leek, W.P.; Wisconsin, n.d. 9675.6 p200
Leek, Walter P.; Wisconsin, n.d. 9675.6 p267
Leek, Wilber; Wisconsin, n.d. 9675.6 p267
Leelmann, George; Wisconsin, n.d. 9675.6 p200
Leeming, Mr.; Quebec, 1815 9229.18 p77
Leeming, George W.; Iowa, 1866-1943 123.54 p30
Leemkuil, Berend Henry; Washington, 1859-1920 2872.1 p23
Le Eon, Charles 38; Port uncertain, 1839 778.5 p329
Leeper, Francis 21; Philadelphia, 1856 5704.8 p128
Leeper, William 17; Philadelphia, 1856 5704.8 p128
Lees, John 17; Jamaica, 1735 3690.1 p139
Lees, William 19; Jamaica, 1731 3690.1 p139
Leesdale, John; Ohio, 1840 9892.11 p26
Leesmann, Heinrich; America, 1848 8582.3 p40
Lefebvre, Mr. 20; Port uncertain, 1838 778.5 p330
Lefebvre, Jean; Quebec, 1819 7603 p49
Lefebvre, N. 25?; America, 1839 778.5 p330
Lefeloine, Herbert Pierre; Virginia, 1848 4626.16 p13
Lefeon, Mr. 26; America, 1836 778.5 p330
Lefevre, Mr. 30; Louisiana, 1820 778.5 p330
Lefevre, A. 17; New Orleans, 1832 778.5 p330
Lefevre, A. 25; Port uncertain, 1838 778.5 p330
Lefevre, A. 30; New Orleans, 1821 778.5 p330
Lefevre, A. 32; New Orleans, 1823 778.5 p330
Lefevre, A. 33; New Orleans, 1823 778.5 p330
Lefevre, Jacques 31; America, 1837 778.5 p330
Lefevre, John Mathurin 23; New Orleans, 1836 778.5 p330
Lefevre, L. 38; New Orleans, 1829 778.5 p330
Lefevre, Louis 17; Louisiana, 1820 778.5 p330
Leff, Rudolph; Illinois, 1873 5012.39 p26
Leffert, . . .; Canada, 1776-1783 9786 p27
Leffholz, Carl Friedrich *SEE* Leffholz, Engel Schomburg
Leffholz, Engel Schomburg; America, 1853 4610.10 p144
*Son:*Carl Friedrich
Lefholz, Anna M. Cath. Becker *SEE* Lefholz, Samuel Diedrich
Lefholz, Carl F. Gottlieb *SEE* Lefholz, Samuel Diedrich
Lefholz, Hermann Heinrich *SEE* Lefholz, Samuel Diedrich
Lefholz, Samuel Diedrich; America, 1837 4610.10 p146
*Wife:*Anna M. Cath. Becker
*Child:*Carl F. Gottlieb
*Child:*Hermann Heinrich
Lefiriner, Mrs. 23; New Orleans, 1838 778.5 p331
Lefiriner, A. 32; New Orleans, 1838 778.5 p330
Lefkowitz, Max; Arkansas, 1918 95.2 p73
Lefler, Dorothea; New York, 1763 3652 p89
Lefonta, Mme. 23; America, 1838 778.5 p331
LeFount, Mary 19; Maryland, 1774 1219.7 p235
LeFrancois, Peter Louis 20; Port uncertain, 1835 778.5 p331
Left, Adam; Philadelphia, 1816 2859.11 p35
Legalet, Pierre; New Brunswick, 1795 7603 p48
Legallon, Henri 48; New Orleans, 1839 778.5 p331
Leganet, Mr.; Port uncertain, 1839 778.5 p331
Legard, Joseph 21; Maryland, 1774 1219.7 p224
Legaret, Mr.; Port uncertain, 1839 778.5 p331
Legat, Ja.; Virginia, 1635 6219 p26
Legat, Louis 22; America, 1838 778.5 p331
Legeay, Captain; Nicaragua, 1856 8582.3 p31
Legence, Joseph; Milwaukee, 1875 4719.30 p258
Legendre, A. 30; New Orleans, 1829 778.5 p331
Legendre, Georges 19; New Orleans, 1821 778.5 p331
Legendre, Louis; Louisiana, 1789-1819 778.5 p556
Leger, Hirsch 9; New York, NY, 1878 9253 p45
Leger, Isaac 55; New York, NY, 1878 9253 p45
Leger, Janbe 22; New York, NY, 1878 9253 p45
Leger, Levy 18; New York, NY, 1878 9253 p45
Leger, Marcus 19; New York, NY, 1878 9253 p45
Leger, Romine 25; New York, NY, 1878 9253 p45
Legerin, Amelie 14; New Orleans, 1839 778.5 p331
Legerin, Jeanne 34; New Orleans, 1839 778.5 p331
Legerin, Louise 11; New Orleans, 1839 778.5 p331
Leggatt, Robert; New York, NY, 1836 8208.4 p11
Leggett, Thomas 36; California, 1872 2769.6 p4
Leghorn, Mary Ann 18; Philadelphia, 1864 5704.8 p157
Legier, Charles 33; New Orleans, 1838 778.5 p331
Legin, Herman 47; California, 1868 3840.2 p16
Legler, Landerlin 13; New Orleans, 1836 778.5 p331
Legler, Magdalena 8; New Orleans, 1836 778.5 p331
Legler, Valentin 19; New Orleans, 1836 778.5 p332
Legler, Valentin 47; New Orleans, 1836 778.5 p331
Legler, Victoria 10; New Orleans, 1836 778.5 p332
L'Eglise, Joseph 19; New Orleans, 1829 778.5 p332
Legois, Fabian 45; Kansas, 1876 5240.1 p57
Legrand, Mr. 28; Port uncertain, 1832 778.5 p332
Legrand, A. 30; New Orleans, 1835 778.5 p332
Legrand, Nicolas 21; Port uncertain, 1839 778.5 p332
Le Gross, Mr. 15; Louisiana, 1820 778.5 p332
Le Gross, Mr. 45; Louisiana, 1820 778.5 p332
Leguyer, Mr. 25; New Orleans, 1821 778.5 p332
Lehaff, Barbara 34; America, 1839 778.5 p332
Lehaff, Philippe 33; America, 1839 778.5 p332
Lehan, Daniel 23; Massachusetts, 1849 5881.1 p58
Lehan, John 5; Massachusetts, 1849 5881.1 p59
Lehan, Mary 10; Massachusetts, 1849 5881.1 p60
Lehan, Michael 7; Massachusetts, 1849 5881.1 p60
Lehane, Ellen 30; Massachusetts, 1849 5881.1 p58
Lehane, Mary 1; Massachusetts, 1849 5881.1 p60
Lehane, Morty 30; Massachusetts, 1849 5881.1 p60
Lehee, Joseph 16; America, 1831 778.5 p332
Lehee, Joseph 36; America, 1831 778.5 p332
Lehee, Louise 36; America, 1831 778.5 p332
Lehenmann, Philip Theodor; Pennsylvania, 1682 4961 p14
Lehey, Dennis 13; Massachusetts, 1849 5881.1 p58
Lehey, Joseph; New York, NY, 1836 8208.4 p9
Lehey, Julia 11; Massachusetts, 1849 5881.1 p59
Lehincter, . . .; Canada, 1776-1783 9786 p27
Lehman, . . .; Canada, 1776-1783 9786 p42
Lehman, Hermann; Ohio, 1857 8582.1 p36
Lehman, John Gus; Arkansas, 1918 95.2 p73

Lehman, Leopold; America, 1851 1450.2 p87A
Lehmann, Charles; Arkansas, 1886 3688 p7
Lehmann, Christoph W.; Wisconsin, n.d. 9675.6 p267
Lehmann, Gaston 26; Arkansas, 1918 95.2 p73
Lehmann, Hermann; Ohio, 1857 8582.1 p36
Lehmann, Johann; Wisconsin, 1900 9460 p646
Lehmann, Julius William; Wisconsin, n.d. 9675.6 p267
Lehmann, Wilhelm; Philadelphia, 1764 8582.2 p65
Lehmkuhl, William; Wisconsin, n.d. 9675.6 p267
Lehn, . . .; Canada, 1776-1783 9786 p27
Lehn, Axel; Iowa, 1866-1943 123.54 p30
Lehn, Charles Fredck; Canada, 1776-1783 9786 p207A
Lehna, John; Dakota, 1885 5240.1 p27
Lehnmann, Philip Theodor; Pennsylvania, 1682 4961 p14
Lehoudes, Peter; Arkansas, 1918 95.2 p73
Lehre, Johann; Charleston, SC, 1766 8582.2 p65
Lehrriter, John A.; America, 1863 1450.2 p87A
Leib, Georg; Philadelphia, 1776 8582.3 p85
Leibel, Eva; Alberta, 1909-1950 5262 p58
Leibenrider, . . .; Canada, 1776-1783 9786 p27
Leibenzeder, . . .; Canada, 1776-1783 9786 p27
Leibhardt, Anthony; America, 1835 1450.2 p87A
Leibold, Johann; Cincinnati, 1869-1887 8582 p19
Leibold, Johann; Cincinnati, 1873 8582.1 p21
Leich, Jane; Philadelphia, 1864 5704.8 p179
Leichd, Hans Jerg; Pennsylvania, 1753 2444 p184
Leicher, Marie 24; America, 1835 778.5 p333
Leicher, Nicolas 34; America, 1835 778.5 p333
Leichhardt, Albert 38; Kansas, 1874 5240.1 p55
Leichhardt, Doris 66; Kansas, 1874 5240.1 p55
Leichmann, Inda N.; Iowa, 1866-1943 123.54 p30
Leichnitz, Robert 32; Kansas, 1888 5240.1 p72
Leichs, Georg; South Carolina, 1788 7119 p201
Leicht, Anna Zoller SEE Leicht, Hans Jerg
Leicht, Barbara; Carolina, 1752 2444 p224
Leicht, Hans Jerg; Pennsylvania, 1753 2444 p184
*Wife:*Anna Zoller
With 4 children
Leichtle, Peter; Ohio, 1798-1818 8582.2 p54
Leickel, Magdalena 22; America, 1836 778.5 p333
Leidendeker, Henry J.; Illinois, 1866 5012.37 p59
Leider, John P.; Wisconsin, n.d. 9675.6 p267
Leider, Joseph; Wisconsin, n.d. 9675.6 p267
Leider, Michael; Wisconsin, n.d. 9675.6 p267
Leider, Valentine; Wisconsin, n.d. 9675.6 p267
Leider, William; Wisconsin, n.d. 9675.6 p267
Leidgen, Mathias; Wisconsin, n.d. 9675.6 p267
Leidig, John; Arizona, 1882 2764.35 p42
Leier, Anton; America, 1852 1450.2 p87A
Leigh, Georg; Virginia, 1637 6219 p85
Leigh, John; Colorado, 1904 9678.2 p123
Leigh, John; Virginia, 1647 6219 p241
Leigh, Jon.; Virginia, 1643 6219 p202
Leigh, Mary SEE Leigh, William
Leigh, Mary SEE Leigh, William
Leigh, Tho.; Virginia, 1647 6219 p245
Leigh, Thomas; Virginia, 1639 6219 p156
Leigh, William; Virginia, 1608 6219 p6
Leigh, William; Virginia, 1642 6219 p189
*Wife:*Mary
*Daughter:*Mary
Leighmans, Paul; America, 1697 2212 p3
Leighner, Leonard; Philadelphia, 1760 9973.7 p34
Leighton, John; New York, 1743 3652 p60
*Wife:*Sarah
Leighton, Sarah SEE Leighton, John
Leignot, Mauric; Virginia, 1853 4626.16 p14
Leihl, Feigel 1 mo; New York, NY, 1878 9253 p47
Leihl, Hinde 28; New York, NY, 1878 9253 p47
Leihl, Jacob 5; New York, NY, 1878 9253 p47
Leihl, Jenbe 11 mos; New York, NY, 1878 9253 p47
Leihoffer, Anna; Georgia, 1739 9332 p323
Leimbach, Bernhard; Philadelphia, 1779 8137 p11
Leimberger, Christian; Georgia, 1738 9332 p321
Leimberger, Christian; Georgia, 1739 9332 p324
Leimberger, Christian; Georgia, 1739 9332 p325
Leimeister, Wendel; Pennsylvania, 1751 4525 p231
Leimer, . . .; Canada, 1776-1783 9786 p42
Leindertse, Jacobus Marinus 27; Kansas, 1904 5240.1 p83
Leiner, Heinrich; Halifax, N.S., 1888 2691.4 p167
Leiner, Heinrich; Peoria, IL, 1888 2691.4 p171
Leiner, Heinrich; Philadelphia, 1888 2691.4 p167
Leining, Mr.; Connecticut, 1855 3702.7 p349
Leinke, Henry; Illinois, 1886 2896.5 p24
Leinonen, Abel; Washington, 1859-1920 2872.1 p23
Leiper, Catharine; Philadelphia, 1867 5704.8 p220
Leiper, John; Wisconsin, n.d. 9675.6 p267
Leiper, Mary; Philadelphia, 1870 5704.8 p238
Leipold, . . .; Canada, 1776-1783 9786 p42
Leipsitt, James; Philadelphia, 1852 5704.8 p85
Leisage, John; New York, NY, 1913 3455.3 p104
Leisel, Alfred; Washington, 1859-1920 2872.1 p23
Leiser, Helen 19; New York, NY, 1878 9253 p47
Leiser, Kath. 82; America, 1902 1763 p48D
Leiser, Lina 30; New York, NY, 1878 9253 p47
Leiser, Martha 11 mos; New York, NY, 1878 9253 p47
Leiser, Sara 1 mo; New York, NY, 1878 9253 p47
Leisering, Carl; Wisconsin, n.d. 9675.6 p267
Leisge, John; New York, NY, 1913 3455.2 p44
Leisler, Jacob; New Netherland, 1630-1646 8582.2 p51
Leiss, Elizab. 28; America, 1854-1855 9162.6 p104
Leiss, Heinnich 26; America, 1854-1855 9162.6 p104
Leiss, Kathr. 30; America, 1854-1855 9162.6 p104
Leiss, Maria 20; America, 1854-1855 9162.6 p104
Leiss, Maria 60; America, 1854-1855 9162.6 p104
Leiss, Michael 22; America, 1854-1855 9162.6 p104
Leister, Jakob; Ohio, 1798-1818 8582.2 p54
*Relative:*Wilhelm
Leister, Wilhelm SEE Leister, Jakob
Leiszring, William; Wisconsin, n.d. 9675.6 p267
Leitch, Elizabeth 8; Quebec, 1864 5704.8 p163
Leitch, Ellen 41; Quebec, 1864 5704.8 p163
Leitch, James 5; Quebec, 1864 5704.8 p163
Leitch, Janet 3; Quebec, 1864 5704.8 p163
Leitch, John 10; Quebec, 1864 5704.8 p163
Leitch, Malcolm 16; St. John, N.B., 1863 5704.8 p153
Leitch, William 44; Quebec, 1864 5704.8 p163
Leite, Johannes; Ohio, 1801-1802 8582.2 p55
Leitel, Elias; Iowa, 1866-1943 123.54 p30
Leitman, Louis; Arkansas, 1918 95.2 p73
Leitner, Gregor; Cincinnati, 1828 8582.1 p51
Leitner, John; Wisconsin, n.d. 9675.6 p267
Leitner, Josef; Georgia, 1739 9332 p327
Leitner, Joseph; Georgia, 1738 9332 p321
Leitner, Joseph; Georgia, 1739 9332 p324
Leitner, Leopold; Wisconsin, n.d. 9675.6 p267
Leivesley, Robert 31; Jamaica, 1735 3690.1 p139
Lelamand, J. 34; New Orleans, 1831 778.5 p333
Lelans, T. 24; America, 1838 778.5 p333
LeLardeux, Edmund 34; America, 1820 778.5 p333
Lelicon, Mr. 50; America, 1839 778.5 p333
Lelievre, F.; New Orleans, 1839 778.5 p333
Lelimpsis, Louis; Arkansas, 1918 95.2 p73
Lelker, George Phillip; New York, NY, 1852 2896.5 p24
Leller, Domenico; Iowa, 1866-1943 123.54 p30
Lelong, H. 24; America, 1835 778.5 p333
LeLong, Jean; New York, NY, 1839 8208.4 p101
Lelong, Joseph; New York, NY, 1839 8208.4 p94
Lemac, Miss 1; New Orleans, 1839 778.5 p333
Lemac, Miss 3; New Orleans, 1839 778.5 p333
Lemac, Mr. 5; New Orleans, 1839 778.5 p333
Lemac, Mrs. 22; New Orleans, 1839 778.5 p333
Lemain, Phil; Pennsylvania, 1682 4961 p14
Lemaire, . . .; Canada, 1776-1783 9786 p27
Lemaire, Charles; Quebec, 1707 7603 p97
Lemaire, Christoph; New York, NY, 1833 8208.4 p29
Lemaistre, Flora 33; Louisiana, 1837 778.5 p333
Lemaistre, Louis 30; America, 1836 778.5 p334
Lemaitre, Mr. 26; America, 1836 778.5 p334
Leman, Emanuel J.; Shreveport, LA, 1877 7129 p45
Leman, James; New York, NY, 1811 2859.11 p14
Leman, Margaret; New York, NY, 1811 2859.11 p14
Lemanel, C. 19; Port uncertain, 1838 778.5 p334
Lemanowsky, Colonel; Cincinnati, 1788-1848 8582.3 p90
Lemanski, . . .; New York, 1831 4606 p175
Lemasurier, I.E.; Virginia, 1858 4626.16 p17
Lematin, F. A. 35; America, 1835 778.5 p334
Lematin, M. A. 16; America, 1835 778.5 p334
Lembeck, Joseph; Kansas, 1909 6013.40 p16
Lemberger, . . .; Canada, 1776-1783 9786 p27
Lemberger, David; Arkansas, 1918 95.2 p73
Lembke, Francis Christian; New York, 1754 3652 p78
Lembke, Hannah 36; Massachusetts, 1860 6410.32 p102
Lembke, Johan Andreas; Boston, 1854 6410.32 p123
Lembke, John A. 36; Massachusetts, 1860 6410.32 p102
Lemesurier, Hellier; Quebec, 1795 7603 p47
LeMignon, Mr. 44; Louisiana, 1820 778.5 p334
Leming, Robert 51; North America, 1774 1219.7 p200
Leming, Robert, Jr. 17; North America, 1774 1219.7 p200
Leming, Thomas 27; Jamaica, 1773 1219.7 p171
Lemire, Miss 1; New Orleans, 1839 778.5 p333
Lemire, Miss 3; New Orleans, 1839 778.5 p333
Lemire, Mr. 5; New Orleans, 1839 778.5 p333
Lemire, Mrs. 22; New Orleans, 1839 778.5 p333
Lemke, Adolf; Washington, 1859-1920 2872.1 p23
Lemke, Anna; Wisconsin, n.d. 9675.6 p267
Lemke, Anna Marie; Wisconsin, n.d. 9675.6 p267
Lemke, Carl; Wisconsin, n.d. 9675.6 p267
Lemke, Ernst; Washington, 1859-1920 2872.1 p23
Lemke, Ferdinand; Illinois, 1884 2896.5 p24
Lemke, George; Washington, 1859-1920 2872.1 p23
Lemke, Henry; Illinois, 1884 2896.5 p24
Lemke, Herman; Illinois, 1892 2896.5 p24
Lemke, Herman; Wisconsin, n.d. 9675.6 p267
Lemke, Ottilie; Washington, 1859-1920 2872.1 p23
Lemke, Otto R.; Illinois, 1898 2896.5 p24
Lemke, Rosalia; Washington, 1859-1920 2872.1 p23
Lemke, Rudolf; Washington, 1859-1920 2872.1 p23
Lemke, Walter Alfred; Wisconsin, n.d. 9675.6 p267
Lemle, J. G.; Ohio, 1798-1818 8582.2 p54
Lemma, Antonio D.; Colorado, 1898 9678.2 p123
Lemman, George; New York, NY, 1811 2859.11 p14
Lemman, Mary; New York, NY, 1811 2859.11 p14
Lemmee, John; America, 1741 4971 p41
Lemmen, George; West Virginia, 1833-1840 9788.3 p14
*Son:*James
Lemmen, James SEE Lemmen, George
Lemmenhofer, Maria SEE Lemmenhofer, Veit
Lemmenhofer, Veit; Georgia, 1739 9332 p326
*Wife:*Maria
Lemmenhoffer, Maria Halbenthaler SEE Lemmenhoffer, Veit
Lemmenhoffer, Paul; Georgia, 1734 9332 p328
Lemmenhoffer, Veit; Georgia, 1739 9332 p323
*Wife:*Maria Halbenthaler
Lemmer, Johann; Wisconsin, n.d. 9675.6 p267
Lemmer, Mathias; Wisconsin, n.d. 9675.6 p267
Lemmer, Peter; Wisconsin, n.d. 9675.6 p267
Lemmert, . . .; Canada, 1776-1783 9786 p42
Lemmert, Joseph; New York, 1753 3652 p77
Lemmon, George; West Virginia, 1833-1840 9788.3 p14
*Son:*James
Lemmon, George; West Virginia, 1851 9788.3 p14
Lemmon, James SEE Lemmon, George
Lemmon, Jane; Quebec, 1849 5704.8 p52
Lemmon, Mary; New York, NY, 1864 5704.8 p181
Lemoine, Mr.; Port uncertain, 1839 778.5 p334
With brother
Lemon, Guillaume; Quebec, 1756 7603 p57
Lemon, J. 12; Philadelphia, 1853 5704.8 p103
Lemon, John; South Carolina, 1716 1639.20 p111
Lemon, Margaret 3; Philadelphia, 1853 5704.8 p103
Lemon, Matilda; Philadelphia, 1853 5704.8 p103
Lemon, Wm.; Virginia, 1647 6219 p247
Lemond, Arch.; America, 1741 4971 p67
Lemond, R. 26; America, 1829 778.5 p334
Lemond, Robert; America, 1741 4971 p67
Lemonet, F. 36; Port uncertain, 1838 778.5 p334
Lemonier, P. 27; New Orleans, 1830 778.5 p334
Lemonier, S. 29; New Orleans, 1830 778.5 p334
Lemonnier, Edouard 21; Port uncertain, 1839 778.5 p334
Lemonnier, Henry 24; Port uncertain, 1839 778.5 p334
Lemorain, Alex. 31; America, 1839 778.5 p334
Lemorain, Joseph 14; America, 1839 778.5 p335
Lemorain, Marie 28; America, 1839 778.5 p335
Lempares, J. M.; Arkansas, 1918 95.2 p65
Lempares, James Manuel; Arkansas, 1918 95.2 p73
Lempicki, Stanislaw; Arkansas, 1918 95.2 p73
Lempke, August; Illinois, 1880 2896.5 p24
Len, Christine; Milwaukee, 1875 4719.30 p257
Len, Elizabeth; Milwaukee, 1875 4719.30 p257
Len, John; New York, NY, 1851 2896.5 p24
Lenaghan, Terence; Arkansas, 1918 95.2 p73
Lenaghan, Thomas; America, 1742 4971 p80
Lenahan, Patrick 45; St. John, N.B., 1854 5704.8 p115
Lenahen, John; New York, NY, 1834-1841 7036 p124
Lenahon, Mary 20; Quebec, 1862 5704.8 p152
Lenardo, Joe; Arkansas, 1918 95.2 p73
Lenau, . . .; America, 1836-1877 8582.3 p36
Lenau, Nicolaus; Cincinnati, 1788-1848 8582.3 p90
Lenburg, Theodore; Iowa, 1866-1943 123.54 p30
Lenckus, John 25; Arkansas, 1918 95.2 p73
Lender, Friedrich; Cincinnati, 1869-1887 8582 p19
Lendon, Thomas 83; Massachusetts, 1847 5881.1 p61
Lendvick, Eric Alfrid; Arkansas, 1918 95.2 p73
Lener, Foeger Rosa; Wisconsin, n.d. 9675.6 p267
Leneveu, Lewis 26; Maryland, 1774 1219.7 p214
Leney, James; Philadelphia, 1865 5704.8 p195
L'Enfant, . . . 2; Port uncertain, 1838 778.5 p335
L'Enfant, Mrs. 38; Port uncertain, 1838 778.5 p335
L'Enfant, Jean 50; Port uncertain, 1838 778.5 p335
L'Enfant, Joseph 24; New Orleans, 1839 778.5 p335
L'Enfant, Marguerite 20; New Orleans, 1839 778.5 p335
Lenfle, Mr. 26; New Orleans, 1838 778.5 p335
Lengenfelder, Catharina SEE Lengenfelder, Pancratius
Lengenfelder, Johann Michael SEE Lengenfelder, Pancratius
Lengenfelder, Johannes SEE Lengenfelder, Pancratius
Lengenfelder, Pancratius; Pennsylvania, 1754 2444 p184
*Wife:*Catharina
*Child:*Johannes
*Child:*Johann Michael
Lengl, Barth; Illinois, 1900 5012.40 p77
Lenhaeuser, Johannes; Philadelphia, 1779 8137 p11
Lenhard, . . .; Canada, 1776-1783 9786 p27

Lenhard, Barbara 57; New Orleans, 1838 ***778.5*** *p335*
Lenhard, Maria 16; New Orleans, 1838 ***778.5*** *p335*
Lenhardt, George 23; America, 1838 ***778.5*** *p335*
Lenhart, Peter; New York, NY, 1853 ***2896.5*** *p24*
Lenheusser, Johannes; Philadelphia, 1779 ***8137*** *p11*
Lenihen, Michael; America, 1850 ***1450.2*** *p87A*
Lenius, Heinrich; Wisconsin, n.d. ***9675.6*** *p267*
Lenke, Fredrick 23; Kansas, 1873 ***5240.1*** *p53*
Lenman, George; Kansas, 1874 ***5240.1*** *p27*
Lennan, Mary 14; St. John, N.B., 1867 ***5704.8*** *p168*
Lennehan, Michael; New York, NY, 1838 ***8208.4*** *p81*
Lennihen, Michael; America, 1850 ***1450.2*** *p87A*
Lennon, Ann 9; Massachusetts, 1849 ***5881.1*** *p57*
Lennon, Betty 43; Massachusetts, 1849 ***5881.1*** *p57*
Lennon, Edmund; Virginia, 1642 ***6219*** *p208*
Lennon, Honora 20; Massachusetts, 1847 ***5881.1*** *p58*
Lennon, John 6; Massachusetts, 1849 ***5881.1*** *p59*
Lennon, Margaret; Delaware, 1743 ***4971*** *p105*
Lennon, Michael 11; Massachusetts, 1849 ***5881.1*** *p60*
Lennon, Patrick 27; Philadelphia, 1858 ***5704.8*** *p139*
Lennon, Peirce; Virginia, 1635 ***6219*** *p19*
*Wife:*Rebecca
Lennon, Pierce; Virginia, 1642 ***6219*** *p208*
*Wife:*Rebecca
Lennon, Rebecca *SEE* Lennon, Peirce
Lennon, Rebecca *SEE* Lennon, Pierce
Lennon, William; Virginia, 1648 ***6219*** *p241*
Lennott, Robert 18; Philadelphia, 1854 ***5704.8*** *p117*
Lennox, James; Charleston, SC, 1765 ***1639.20*** *p111*
Lennox, John; Edenton, NC, 1802 ***1639.20*** *p112*
Lennox, Robert; Edenton, NC, 1755 ***1639.20*** *p112*
Lenny, . . . 2 mos; New York, NY, 1867 ***5704.8*** *p223*
Lenny, Ann; New York, NY, 1867 ***5704.8*** *p223*
Lenny, Daniel; New York, NY, 1867 ***5704.8*** *p223*
Lenny, James 18 mos; New York, NY, 1867 ***5704.8*** *p223*
Lenoble, Mr. 40; New Orleans, 1837 ***778.5*** *p335*
Lenoble, M. P. 40; Port uncertain, 1838 ***778.5*** *p335*
Lenoble, Pauline 18; New Orleans, 1837 ***778.5*** *p335*
Lenon, Henry; New York, NY, 1811 ***2859.11*** *p14*
Lenormand, Emile; San Francisco, 1871 ***2764.35*** *p42*
Lenox, James; St. John, N.B., 1850 ***5704.8*** *p61*
Lensen, Jan; Pennsylvania, 1683 ***2155*** *p2*
Lensey, Barbury 20; Virginia, 1700 ***2212*** *p32*
Lensman, Gurdt Henry; New York, NY, 1835 ***8208.4*** *p5*
Lenson, Andrew 25; Massachusetts, 1860 ***6410.32*** *p119*
Lent, Peter; Philadelphia, 1762 ***9973.7*** *p36*
Lentall, Geo.; Virginia, 1637 ***6219*** *p85*
Lento, Geo.; Virginia, 1636 ***6219*** *p79*
Lenton, Anth.; Virginia, 1637 ***6219*** *p114*
Lentowski, Wladislaw 21; New York, 1912 ***9980.29*** *p57*
Lentz, . . .; Canada, 1776-1783 ***9786*** *p27*
Lentz, . . .; Pennsylvania, 1746 ***2444*** *p232*
Lentz, Christian; America, 1852 ***1450.2*** *p87A*
Lentz, Christian; Pennsylvania, 1746 ***2444*** *p184*
Lentz, Christian; Pennsylvania, 1746 ***2444*** *p185*
Lentz, Christian 24; America, 1848 ***3702.7*** *p137*
Lentz, Christoph; Pennsylvania, 1746 ***2444*** *p184*
Lentz, Christoph; Pennsylvania, 1746 ***2444*** *p185*
Lentz, Gottlieb; New York, NY, 1838 ***8208.4*** *p83*
Lentz, Johann Christophe; Quebec, 1776 ***9786*** *p265*
Lentz, Johann Jacob; Pennsylvania, 1769 ***2444*** *p185*
Lentz, William Frederick; America, 1854 ***1450.2*** *p87A*
Lentze, . . .; Canada, 1776-1783 ***9786*** *p27*
Lentze, Friedrich; Canada, 1776-1783 ***9786*** *p242*
Lentzen, Anna; America, 1748-1749 ***8125.6*** *p23*
Lentzinger, . . .; Canada, 1776-1783 ***9786*** *p27*
Lenz, Anna Maria *SEE* Lenz, Christian
Lenz, Anna Maria Widenmayer *SEE* Lenz, Christian
Lenz, Charles; Wisconsin, n.d. ***9675.6*** *p267*
Lenz, Christian *SEE* Lenz, Christian
Lenz, Christian; Died enroute, 1746 ***2444*** *p184*
Lenz, Christian; Pennsylvania, 1746 ***2444*** *p184*
*Wife:*Anna Maria Widenmayer
*Child:*Christian
*Child:*Johann Jacob
*Child:*Maria Barbara
*Child:*Anna Maria
Lenz, Christian 24; America, 1848 ***3702.7*** *p122*
Lenz, Christoph; Died enroute, 1746 ***2444*** *p185*
Lenz, Gottlieb; Wisconsin, n.d. ***9675.6*** *p267*
Lenz, Henry 43; Philadelphia, 1804 ***2444*** *p184*
With wife
With 4 children
Lenz, Jacob; Wisconsin, n.d. ***9675.6*** *p267*
Lenz, Johann; Wisconsin, n.d. ***9675.6*** *p267*
Lenz, Johann Jacob *SEE* Lenz, Christian
Lenz, Johann Jacob; America, 1769 ***2444*** *p185*
With 2 or 3 children
Lenz, John B.; Wisconsin, n.d. ***9675.6*** *p267*
Lenz, Ludwig; Illinois, 1868 ***2896.5*** *p24*
Lenz, Ludwig, Sr.; Illinois, 1868 ***2896.5*** *p24*
Lenz, Maria Barbara *SEE* Lenz, Christian
Lenz, William; Illinois, 1866 ***2896.5*** *p24*
Lenzen, Frank 24; Kansas, 1890 ***5240.1*** *p75*
Lenzer, Johann Jst; America, 1845 ***8582.1*** *p21*
Lenzi, Guido; Washington, 1859-1920 ***2872.1*** *p23*
Lenzner, John Henry; New York, 1754 ***3652*** *p80*
Leo, . . .; Canada, 1776-1783 ***9786*** *p42*
Leo, Samuel 19; Maryland, 1725 ***3690.1*** *p139*
Leo, Vincinzo; Arkansas, 1918 ***95.2*** *p74*
Leodel, Mr.; Quebec, 1815 ***9229.18*** *p81*
Leoick, Jane; Philadelphia, 1865 ***5704.8*** *p200*
Leompte, August 43; Port uncertain, 1836 ***778.5*** *p335*
Leon, Mr. 15; Port uncertain, 1838 ***778.5*** *p336*
Leon, A. 19; Port uncertain, 1838 ***778.5*** *p336*
Leon, V. 24; America, 1838 ***778.5*** *p336*
Leonard, . . .; Canada, 1776-1783 ***9786*** *p27*
Leonard, Dr.; Ohio, 1826 ***8582.2*** *p59*
Leonard, Ann 6; Massachusetts, 1849 ***5881.1*** *p57*
Leonard, Bridget 15; Massachusetts, 1849 ***5881.1*** *p57*
Leonard, Celia 10; Massachusetts, 1849 ***5881.1*** *p57*
Leonard, Celia 32; Massachusetts, 1849 ***5881.1*** *p57*
Leonard, Edward; Arizona, 1898 ***9228.30*** *p13*
Leonard, Eliza; St. John, N.B., 1852 ***5704.8*** *p83*
Leonard, Francis; New York, NY, 1811 ***2859.11*** *p14*
Leonard, G. 16; Louisiana, 1820 ***778.5*** *p336*
Leonard, Georg; Kentucky, 1869-1887 ***8582*** *p19*
Leonard, George; Died enroute, 1875 ***4719.30*** *p258*
Leonard, Hugh; Philadelphia, 1867 ***5704.8*** *p214*
Leonard, James; Illinois, 1889 ***5012.40*** *p25*
Leonard, James; Virginia, 1635 ***6219*** *p3*
Leonard, James; Virginia, 1637 ***6219*** *p86*
Leonard, John; Philadelphia, 1847 ***53.26*** *p45*
Leonard, John; Philadelphia, 1847 ***5704.8*** *p31*
Leonard, John 14; Massachusetts, 1850 ***5881.1*** *p59*
Leonard, John 15; Jamaica, 1720 ***3690.1*** *p139*
Leonard, John 19; Georgia, 1738 ***9332*** *p333*
Leonard, John Thomas; Arkansas, 1918 ***95.2*** *p74*
Leonard, Katherine; Virginia, 1635 ***6219*** *p10*
Leonard, Michael 8; Massachusetts, 1849 ***5881.1*** *p60*
Leonard, Mike 12; Massachusetts, 1850 ***5881.1*** *p61*
Leonard, Patrick 40; Newfoundland, 1789 ***4915.24*** *p56*
Leonard, Peter; New York, NY, 1839 ***8208.4*** *p91*
Leonard, Robert; New York, NY, 1840 ***8208.4*** *p103*
Leonard, Robert 21; Philadelphia, 1804 ***53.26*** *p45*
Leonard, Rose; St. John, N.B., 1849 ***5704.8*** *p48*
Leonard, Sally 20; Philadelphia, 1853 ***5704.8*** *p108*
Leonard, Thomas; Quebec, 1849 ***5704.8*** *p52*
Leonard, Thomas, Jr.; Illinois, 1887 ***5012.39*** *p120*
Leonard, Walter; Arkansas, 1918 ***95.2*** *p74*
Leonard, William 15; Philadelphia, 1774 ***1219.7*** *p233*
Leonards, Leonard; Virginia, 1635 ***6219*** *p5*
Leonhaeuser, Johannes; Philadelphia, 1779 ***8137*** *p11*
Leonhard, . . .; Canada, 1776-1783 ***9786*** *p27*
Leonhard, Christiane Amalia 36; New Orleans, 1839 ***9420.2*** *p67*
Leonhard, George 24; New Orleans, 1838 ***778.5*** *p336*
Leonhard, Johann Ehrenfried 38; New Orleans, 1839 ***9420.2*** *p67*
Leonhard, Wm. Bruno 15; New Orleans, 1839 ***9420.2*** *p67*
Leonhardt, G.G.; Milwaukee, 1875 ***4719.30*** *p257*
Leonhardt, Jennie; Milwaukee, 1875 ***4719.30*** *p257*
Leonhardt, Mary W.; Milwaukee, 1875 ***4719.30*** *p257*
Leonhauser, Henry; Virginia, 1856 ***4626.16*** *p16*
Leontsinis, Emmanuel; Arkansas, 1918 ***95.2*** *p74*
Leoparre, J. B. 28; Louisiana, 1829 ***778.5*** *p336*
Leopoldt, Johann Friedrich Wilhelm; Cincinnati, 1869-1887 ***8582*** *p19*
Leopoldt, Wilhelm; New York, NY, 1836 ***8582.1*** *p21*
With parents
Leornard, Margaret; St. John, N.B., 1852 ***5704.8*** *p93*
Leots, Ernest; Cincinnati, 1847 ***3702.7*** *p85*
Lepage, Charles 3; America, 1839 ***778.5*** *p336*
Lepage, Charles 29; America, 1839 ***778.5*** *p336*
Lepage, Marie 35; America, 1839 ***778.5*** *p336*
Lepare, V.; Cincinnati, 1869-1887 ***8582*** *p19*
Lepaullard, L.; New Orleans, 1839 ***778.5*** *p336*
LePeintre, F. 60; Havana, 1829 ***778.5*** *p336*
Lepel, Frank 23; Kansas, 1877 ***5240.1*** *p58*
Lepel, Hermann 57; Kansas, 1877 ***5240.1*** *p58*
Lepel, Otto 28; Kansas, 1877 ***5240.1*** *p58*
Lepelletier, Mme. 60; Port uncertain, 1839 ***778.5*** *p336*
Lepelletier, Adolph 15; Port uncertain, 1839 ***778.5*** *p336*
Lepesse, Gregoire 20; America, 1838 ***778.5*** *p336*
Le Pettit, John; New York, NY, 1838 ***8208.4*** *p61*
Lepin, . . .; New York, 1831 ***4606*** *p175*
Lepine, Jean-Baptiste 31; Montreal, 1722 ***7603*** *p28*
Leping, . . .; New York, 1831 ***4606*** *p175*
Lepington, Barber 20; America, 1728 ***3690.1*** *p139*
Lepkowski, Tomasz; New York, 1831 ***4606*** *p175*
Lepman, T. 25; America, 1829 ***778.5*** *p336*
Lepo, John 30; Maryland, 1775 ***1219.7*** *p249*
Lepoullard, Mme.; Port uncertain, 1839 ***778.5*** *p337*
Lepoullard, Mr.; Port uncertain, 1839 ***778.5*** *p337*
Lepper, Arthur 3; Quebec, 1850 ***5704.8*** *p63*
Lepper, Jane; Quebec, 1850 ***5704.8*** *p63*
Lepper, John; Quebec, 1850 ***5704.8*** *p63*
Lepper, John 22; Virginia, 1733 ***3690.1*** *p139*
Lepper, Meria; Quebec, 1850 ***5704.8*** *p63*
Lepper, Sarah 6; Quebec, 1850 ***5704.8*** *p63*
Leppert, Jacob; Illinois, 1889 ***5012.37*** *p62*
Leppert, Lorenz; Illinois, 1888 ***5012.39*** *p122*
Leppington, Barber 20; America, 1728 ***3690.1*** *p139*
LePrende, Jos. 25; New Orleans, 1827 ***778.5*** *p337*
Leprince, Anne 37; America, 1839 ***778.5*** *p337*
Leprince, Joseph 11; America, 1839 ***778.5*** *p337*
Lequesne, John Francis; New York, NY, 1840 ***8208.4*** *p113*
Leratakis, Emmanuel; Arkansas, 1918 ***95.2*** *p74*
Lerch, Conrad; Wisconsin, n.d. ***9675.6*** *p267*
Lerch, Fredrick; Washington, 1859-1920 ***2872.1*** *p23*
Lerch, Michael; South Carolina, 1788 ***7119*** *p201*
Lerche, . . .; Canada, 1776-1783 ***9786*** *p28*
Lerche, Henry; Canada, 1776-1783 ***9786*** *p207A*
Lerche, Oscar; New York, NY, 1912 ***3455.3*** *p111*
Lercher, Charles F.; Kansas, 1874 ***5240.1*** *p27*
Lerchner, Bartholomeus; Georgia, 1738 ***9332*** *p320*
Leret, Mr. 19; America, 1835 ***778.5*** *p337*
Lerets, Antony; Philadelphia, 1757 ***9973.7*** *p33*
Le Riche, Mr. 42; New Orleans, 1825 ***778.5*** *p337*
Lerner, Gabriel; Ohio, 1869-1874 ***9892.11*** *p26*
Lerner, Meyer; Arkansas, 1918 ***95.2*** *p74*
Leroi, John 26; New Orleans, 1836 ***778.5*** *p342*
Leromain, Agatha 5; America, 1835 ***778.5*** *p337*
Leromain, Alexandre 3; America, 1835 ***778.5*** *p337*
Leromain, Jean Baptiste 34; America, 1835 ***778.5*** *p337*
Leromain, Jn.-Bte. 37; America, 1838 ***778.5*** *p337*
Leromain, M. Josephine 25; America, 1835 ***778.5*** *p337*
Leromain, Marie 55; America, 1835 ***778.5*** *p337*
Leromain, Marie Rose 3 mos; America, 1835 ***778.5*** *p337*
Leromain, Marie Rose 34; America, 1835 ***778.5*** *p337*
Leromain, Rosalie 15; America, 1835 ***778.5*** *p338*
LeRoux, Jeanne 57; Louisiana, 1820 ***778.5*** *p338*
Lerowski, John; Wisconsin, n.d. ***9675.6*** *p267*
Leroy, Mlle. 61; America, 1826 ***778.5*** *p338*
Le Roy, Mlle. 61; New Orleans, 1829 ***778.5*** *p338*
Leroy, Mr. 22; Port uncertain, 1829 ***778.5*** *p338*
Leroy, Mr. 24; New Orleans, 1839 ***778.5*** *p338*
Leroy, Mr. 36; New Orleans, 1827 ***778.5*** *p338*
Leroy, Mr. 46; Port uncertain, 1821 ***778.5*** *p338*
Leroy, Mrs. 28; New Orleans, 1827 ***778.5*** *p338*
Le Roy, Edgar D.; Washington, 1859-1920 ***2872.1*** *p23*
Le Roy, Telles; Washington, 1859-1920 ***2872.1*** *p22*
Leroy, Til. 37; America, 1837 ***778.5*** *p338*
Lerrand, Mr. 42; New Orleans, 1838 ***778.5*** *p338*
Lersch, Frederick; Washington, 1859-1920 ***2872.1*** *p23*
Lesaint, Franz; Cincinnati, 1869-1887 ***8582*** *p19*
Lesak, Andrew; America, 1892 ***7137*** *p169*
Lesak, Susan; America, 1896 ***7137*** *p169*
Lesanne, Christophe 33; America, 1837 ***778.5*** *p338*
Lesch, Marie; Wisconsin, n.d. ***9675.6*** *p267*
Lescos, F. 26; America, 1838 ***778.5*** *p338*
Leshier, Henry; Philadelphia, 1757 ***9973.7*** *p33*
Lesieur, Clement; Quebec, 1716 ***7603*** *p49*
Lesire, Mr. 3; New Orleans, 1835 ***778.5*** *p338*
Lesjack, Joseph; Wisconsin, n.d. ***9675.6*** *p267*
Lesk, David 40; Kansas, 1891 ***5240.1*** *p76*
Lesk, John 48; Quebec, 1861 ***5704.8*** *p149*
Leskos, Frank; Arkansas, 1918 ***95.2*** *p74*
Leskovshek, Frank; Wisconsin, n.d. ***9675.6*** *p267*
Lesley, Fanny; Quebec, 1852 ***5704.8*** *p91*
Lesley, Sarah Jane; Quebec, 1852 ***5704.8*** *p91*
Lesley, Thomas; Quebec, 1852 ***5704.8*** *p91*
Leslie, Alexander; South Carolina, 1716 ***1639.20*** *p112*
Leslie, Charles 37; Virginia, 1774 ***1219.7*** *p186*
Leslie, David; Quebec, 1855 ***5704.8*** *p125*
Leslie, Ephriam 24; Quebec, 1855 ***5704.8*** *p125*
Leslie, Fanny; Quebec, 1852 ***5704.8*** *p86*
Leslie, George; South Carolina, 1798 ***1639.20*** *p112*
Leslie, George 20; Quebec, 1856 ***5704.8*** *p130*
Leslie, Henry; Quebec, 1853 ***5704.8*** *p103*
Leslie, John; Illinois, 1900 ***5012.40*** *p77*
Leslie, Mary 18; Philadelphia, 1861 ***5704.8*** *p148*
Leslie, Nancy 22; Quebec, 1855 ***5704.8*** *p125*
Leslie, Sarah Jane; Quebec, 1852 ***5704.8*** *p86*
Leslie, Thomas; Quebec, 1852 ***5704.8*** *p86*
Lesmann, Charles Conrad; America, 1844 ***1450.2*** *p88A*
Lesminger, Catharina 26; New Orleans, 1837 ***778.5*** *p338*
Lesminger, Frederic 17; New Orleans, 1837 ***778.5*** *p339*
Lesminger, Georges 10; New Orleans, 1837 ***778.5*** *p339*
Lesminger, Jacob 51; New Orleans, 1837 ***778.5*** *p339*
Lesminger, Johannes 17; New Orleans, 1837 ***778.5*** *p339*
Lesminger, Margaritha 26; New Orleans, 1837 ***778.5*** *p339*
Lesminger, Margaritha 52; New Orleans, 1837 ***778.5*** *p339*
Lesner, Johann H.; Kentucky, 1797 ***8582.3*** *p95*

Lesotte, Pierre 30; America, 1826 ***778.5*** *p339*
Lesowska, Anna 20; New York, 1912 ***9980.29*** *p54*
L'Espanet, Mr. 38; New Orleans, 1827 ***778.5*** *p339*
Lesparre, A. 35; America, 1835 ***778.5*** *p339*
Lesparre, Jean 23; New Orleans, 1822 ***778.5*** *p339*
Lessairre, Francois; America, 1827 ***778.5*** *p339*
Lessard, . . .; Canada, 1776-1783 ***9786*** *p28*
Lessart, . . .; Canada, 1776-1783 ***9786*** *p28*
Lessel, Peter; Baltimore, 1840 ***8582.1*** *p22*
Lessel, Peter; Cincinnati, 1869-1887 ***8582*** *p19*
Lesseps, A. 30; New Orleans, 1823 ***778.5*** *p339*
Lessert, . . .; Canada, 1776-1783 ***9786*** *p28*
Lessley, David 24; New York, 1774 ***1219.7*** *p223*
Lessley, Robert 17; Georgia, 1774 ***1219.7*** *p188*
Lessmann, Anna Margarete Kruse *SEE* Lessmann, Johann Heinrich
Lessmann, Johann Heinrich; America, 1841 ***4815.7*** *p92*
*Wife:*Anna Margarete Kruse
Lest, Walter; Virginia, 1636 ***6219*** *p78*
Lesta, Frank; Iowa, 1866-1943 ***123.54*** *p30*
Lester, Mr.; Quebec, 1815 ***9229.18*** *p81*
Lester, Anne; New York, NY, 1815 ***2859.11*** *p35*
Lester, Charles 21; Maryland, 1774 ***1219.7*** *p187*
Lester, Francis 18; Maryland, 1774 ***1219.7*** *p230*
Lester, J. W. 60; Washington, 1916 ***1728.5*** *p10*
Lester, James; Virginia, 1637 ***6219*** *p112*
Lester, John; New York, NY, 1815 ***2859.11*** *p35*
Lester, Joseph 21; Jamaica, 1724 ***3690.1*** *p139*
Lester, Judith; America, 1736 ***4971*** *p12*
Lester, Ralph; Virginia, 1643 ***6219*** *p204*
Lester, Samuel; Maryland, 1756 ***1219.7*** *p44*
Lester, Samuel; Maryland, 1756 ***3690.1*** *p139*
Lesting, Angell; Virginia, 1643 ***6219*** *p207*
Lestly, George 30; Philadelphia, 1833 ***53.26*** *p45*
Lestrade, Antoine 22; America, 1838 ***778.5*** *p339*
Lestrade, Etienne 18; America, 1838 ***778.5*** *p339*
Lestrade, Paul 26; New Orleans, 1836 ***778.5*** *p339*
Lestrem, Jean 26; New Orleans, 1836 ***778.5*** *p340*
Lestrina, John; Arkansas, 1918 ***95.2*** *p74*
Lestsrade, Mr. 23; Port uncertain, 1839 ***778.5*** *p340*
Letamer, Ann Jane 18; Quebec, 1864 ***5704.8*** *p160*
Letamer, Edward 14; Quebec, 1864 ***5704.8*** *p160*
Lete Dumont, N. A. 24; New Orleans, 1836 ***778.5*** *p340*
Letellier Malot, Leon 14?; America, 1838 ***778.5*** *p340*
Letermelier, Adr. Charles; Port uncertain, 1839 ***778.5*** *p340*
Letermelier, Pierre Philippe; Port uncertain, 1839 ***778.5*** *p340*
Letery, C. 33; America, 1832 ***778.5*** *p340*
Leth, von; Canada, 1776-1783 ***9786*** *p185*
Leth, Adolph Neuburg von; Canada, 1777 ***9786*** *p266*
Letham, Robert; North Carolina, 1813 ***1639.20*** *p112*
Lethberrie, Jno 22; America, 1699 ***2212*** *p25*
Lethberrie, Tho 25; America, 1699 ***2212*** *p25*
Lether, John; Virginia, 1639 ***6219*** *p151*
Lether, John; Virginia, 1642 ***6219*** *p188*
Lethermore, Elinor *SEE* Lethermore, Tho.
Lethermore, Tho.; Virginia, 1645 ***6219*** *p232*
*Wife:*Elinor
Lethermore, Wm.; Virginia, 1638 ***6219*** *p122*
Letkemann, Anna; Quebec, 1876 ***9980.20*** *p49*
Letkemann, Anna Fehr; Quebec, 1876 ***9980.20*** *p49*
Letkemann, Catharienа; Quebec, 1876 ***9980.20*** *p49*
Letkemann, Elisabeth; Quebec, 1876 ***9980.20*** *p49*
Letkemann, Helena; Quebec, 1876 ***9980.20*** *p49*
Letkemann, Jacob; Quebec, 1876 ***9980.20*** *p49*
Letkemann, Johann; Quebec, 1876 ***9980.20*** *p49*
Letkemann, Maria; Quebec, 1877 ***9980.20*** *p49*
Letkemann, Peter; Quebec, 1876 ***9980.20*** *p49*
Letra, Louis 22; New Orleans, 1829 ***778.5*** *p340*
Letrat, Mr. 27; New Orleans, 1839 ***778.5*** *p340*
Letsch, Anna Maria; Philadelphia, 1751 ***2444*** *p232*
Letsch, Anna Maria Hess *SEE* Letsch, Christoph
Letsch, Christoph; Port uncertain, 1735-1800 ***2444*** *p185*
*Wife:*Anna Maria Hess
*Child:*Johann Georg
Letsch, Johann Georg *SEE* Letsch, Christoph
Letson, James; St. Louis, 1876 ***2764.35*** *p41*
Letter, . . .; Canada, 1776-1783 ***9786*** *p28*
Letterman, Martin; Philadelphia, 1757 ***9973.7*** *p33*
Lettimer, John 8; Quebec, 1862 ***5704.8*** *p150*
Lettimer, Margaret 19; Quebec, 1862 ***5704.8*** *p150*
Lettimer, Mary 48; Quebec, 1862 ***5704.8*** *p150*
Lettimer, Sarah 10; Quebec, 1862 ***5704.8*** *p150*
Lettinear, Daniel 22; Jamaica, 1734 ***3690.1*** *p139*
Lettner, Joseph; Wisconsin, n.d. ***9675.6*** *p267*
Lettre, . . .; Canada, 1776-1783 ***9786*** *p28*
Letts, Eliza.; Virginia, 1648 ***6219*** *p246*
Letzmaki, Peter; Iowa, 1866-1943 ***123.54*** *p30*
Letzvicko, Peter; Iowa, 1866-1943 ***123.54*** *p30*
Leu, Ulysse; New York, NY, 1920 ***3455.4*** *p24*
Leubari, . . .; America, 1837 ***778.5*** *p340*
Leubari, . . .; America, 1837 ***778.5*** *p341*
Leubari, Mr. 39; America, 1837 ***778.5*** *p340*
Leubari, Mrs. 36; America, 1837 ***778.5*** *p341*
Leuch, Michael; Cincinnati, 1848 ***8582.1*** *p53*
Leucher, Gilbert 1; America, 1835 ***778.5*** *p341*
Leucht, Simon; Died enroute, 1750-1800 ***2444*** *p185*
Leuchtweiss, August; America, 1848 ***8582.1*** *p22*
Leuchtweiss, August; New York, NY, 1849 ***8582.2*** *p22*
Leucian, George; Arkansas, 1918 ***95.2*** *p74*
Leucian, George Nichifor; Arkansas, 1918 ***95.2*** *p74*
Leuerman, Fredrick 38; Kansas, 1888 ***5240.1*** *p72*
Leullier, Ange 26; America, 1823 ***778.5*** *p341*
Leuning, Mr.; Connecticut, 1855 ***3702.7*** *p346*
*Son:*Adam
With family
Leuning, Adam *SEE* Leuning, Mr.
Leur, Wm.; Virginia, 1647 ***6219*** *p241*
Leuthaeuser, Heinrich; Philadelphia, 1764 ***8582.2*** *p65*
Leutz, Colonel; Canada, 1776-1783 ***9786*** *p176*
Levacour, E. 23; America, 1836 ***778.5*** *p341*
Levain, Pierre Marie 43; New Orleans, 1838 ***778.5*** *p341*
Levan, Bastian; Philadelphia, 1759 ***9973.7*** *p34*
Levanier, Louis 17; Barbados, 1718 ***3690.1*** *p140*
Levaseur, Terence 17; New Orleans, 1838 ***778.5*** *p341*
Levassier, Mr. 26; America, 1838 ***778.5*** *p341*
Levay, Stephan Coloman; Arkansas, 1918 ***95.2*** *p74*
Leve, Mrs. 30; New Orleans, 1827 ***778.5*** *p341*
Leve, Francois 30; New Orleans, 1827 ***778.5*** *p341*
Levedant, Mr. 22; America, 1837 ***778.5*** *p341*
Levelin, Henry; New York, 1883 ***1450.2*** *p23B*
Leven, Theodore; New York, NY, 1838 ***8208.4*** *p85*
Levens, William; St. John, N.B., 1849 ***5704.8*** *p56*
L'Eveque, D. 36; Port uncertain, 1838 ***778.5*** *p341*
Lever, Ashton 21; Maryland, 1775 ***1219.7*** *p264*
Lever, John 35; Virginia, 1729 ***3690.1*** *p137*
Leverick, Sarah; Virginia, 1636 ***6219*** *p15*
Levering, Gerhard; Germantown, PA, 1684 ***2467.7*** *p5*
Levering, Gerhard; Pennsylvania, 1686 ***8125.8*** *p437*
Levering, Wigard; Germantown, PA, 1684 ***2467.7*** *p5*
Levering, Wigard; Pennsylvania, 1686 ***8125.8*** *p437*
Leverrier, Mr. 40; America, 1837 ***778.5*** *p341*
Leverston, Ann 22; Virginia, 1774 ***1219.7*** *p239*
Levet, Mr. 20; New Orleans, 1820 ***778.5*** *p341*
Levet, C. F. 45; New Orleans, 1823 ***778.5*** *p341*
Levet, Martin 32; America, 1838 ***778.5*** *p342*
Levett, John; America, 1853 ***2896.5*** *p24*
Levey, James; New York, NY, 1838 ***8208.4*** *p70*
Levi, Henry; Shreveport, LA, 1879 ***7129*** *p45*
Levi, Hester 18 *SEE* Levi, Moses
Levi, Moses 25; Jamaica, 1774 ***1219.7*** *p219*
*Wife:*Hester 18
Levi, Saml. 30; America, 1839 ***778.5*** *p342*
Levi, Zelie 2; New Orleans, 1827 ***778.5*** *p342*
Levich Delacourt, Mr. 24; Port uncertain, 1836 ***778.5*** *p342*
Levillier, Mr. 40; America, 1826 ***778.5*** *p342*
Levin, Abraham 18; Maryland, 1739 ***3690.1*** *p140*
Levin, Arl; Arkansas, 1918 ***95.2*** *p74*
Levin, Jake; Arkansas, 1918 ***95.2*** *p74*
Levin, Mashel; Arkansas, 1918 ***95.2*** *p74*
Levine, Catherine 35; Massachusetts, 1860 ***6410.32*** *p108*
Levine, Louis 22; Arkansas, 1918 ***95.2*** *p74*
Levine, Max; Arkansas, 1918 ***95.2*** *p74*
Levinger, Jonas 26; Kansas, 1885 ***5240.1*** *p68*
Levingston, Mary; St. John, N.B., 1849 ***5704.8*** *p55*
Levingston, Mary Ann 4; St. John, N.B., 1849 ***5704.8*** *p55*
Levingston, William 9 mos; St. John, N.B., 1849 ***5704.8*** *p55*
Levingstone, Chloe 27; Philadelphia, 1774 ***1219.7*** *p183*
Levins, Thomas 17; Maryland, 1722 ***3690.1*** *p140*
Levinski, Osep; Arkansas, 1918 ***95.2*** *p74*
Levinson, Abram Harry; Arkansas, 1918 ***95.2*** *p74*
Levinson, Max; Iowa, 1866-1943 ***123.54*** *p30*
Levinthal, Isaac; Iowa, 1866-1943 ***123.54*** *p30*
Levis, Eli; Iowa, 1866-1943 ***123.54*** *p30*
Leviston, Charles; New York, NY, 1811 ***2859.11*** *p14*
Leviston, James; New York, NY, 1811 ***2859.11*** *p14*
With family
Leviston, Mary; New York, NY, 1811 ***2859.11*** *p14*
Levitier, Jean 28; America, 1832 ***778.5*** *p342*
Levitt, Alice *SEE* Levitt, Georg
Levitt, Eliza.; Virginia, 1643 ***6219*** *p205*
*Son:*Robert
Levitt, Georg; Virginia, 1643 ***6219*** *p205*
*Wife:*Alice
Levitt, Robert *SEE* Levitt, Eliza.
Levitur, Jean 28; America, 1832 ***778.5*** *p342*
Levns, Joseph; Iowa, 1866-1943 ***123.54*** *p30*
Levoi, John 26; New Orleans, 1836 ***778.5*** *p342*
Levois, Mr. 23; America, 1839 ***778.5*** *p342*
Levois, C. 30; America, 1838 ***778.5*** *p342*
Levries, Catilla 28; America, 1831 ***778.5*** *p342*
Levy, D. Lazarre 30; Port uncertain, 1835 ***778.5*** *p342*
Levy, Edna; Wisconsin, n.d. ***9675.6*** *p267*
Levy, Frank; America, 1892 ***7137*** *p169*
Levy, Henry; Arkansas, 1918 ***95.2*** *p74*
Levy, Henry; New York, NY, 1827 ***8208.4*** *p27*
Levy, Isa.c 42; New Orleans, 1836 ***778.5*** *p342*
Levy, Isaac; America, 1848 ***8582.3*** *p41*
Levy, Isaac; Philadelphia, 1755 ***1219.7*** *p37*
Levy, Joseph; Arkansas, 1918 ***95.2*** *p74*
Levy, Julius; California, 1855 ***2769.6*** *p3*
Levy, Mary; America, 1896 ***7137*** *p169*
Levy, Phan 22; Kansas, 1899 ***5240.1*** *p81*
Levy, Sam; Arkansas, 1918 ***95.2*** *p74*
Levy, Samuel; California, 1871 ***2769.6*** *p4*
Levy, Samuel 32; New Orleans, 1836 ***778.5*** *p342*
Levystet, Francis 12; Texas, 1839 ***778.5*** *p342*
Levystet, Rafiel 5; Texas, 1839 ***778.5*** *p342*
Levystete, Augustin 20; Texas, 1839 ***778.5*** *p343*
Levystete, Mary 42; Texas, 1839 ***778.5*** *p343*
Lew, Betsey 13; Massachusetts, 1849 ***5881.1*** *p57*
Lew, James 20; Massachusetts, 1849 ***5881.1*** *p59*
Lewandowska, Bartlomiej 49; New York, 1912 ***9980.29*** *p52*
With cousin
*Daughter:*Salomea 21
Lewandowska, Ludwika 58; New York, 1912 ***9980.29*** *p60*
Lewandowska, Salomea 21 *SEE* Lewandowska, Bartlomiej
Lewandowski, Bartlomiej 49; New York, 1912 ***9980.29*** *p51*
With cousin
*Daughter:*Salomea 21
Lewandowski, Jan; New York, 1834 ***4606*** *p178*
Lewandowski, Salomea 21 *SEE* Lewandowski, Bartlomiej
Lewandowski, Stanislaw 19; New York, 1912 ***9980.29*** *p69*
Lewandowsky, Zygmund 22; New York, 1912 ***9980.29*** *p60*
Lewce, John 24; Baltimore, 1775 ***1219.7*** *p270*
Lewe, George; South Carolina, 1788 ***7119*** *p203*
Lewekamp, John Henry 30; California, 1866 ***3840.2*** *p16*
Lewellin, Daniell; Virginia, 1637 ***6219*** *p113*
Lewellin, Jon.; Virginia, 1637 ***6219*** *p113*
Lewellyn, Lewellyn 29; New York, NY, 1851 ***9555.10*** *p26*
Lewen, Abraham 33; Maryland, 1738 ***3690.1*** *p140*
Lewen, John; Virginia, 1636 ***6219*** *p19*
Lewenberger, Christian 32; Georgia, 1738 ***9332*** *p333*
*Wife:*Margaretta 35
Lewenberger, Margaretta 35 *SEE* Lewenberger, Christian
Lewendowski, Jozef; Arkansas, 1918 ***95.2*** *p74*
Lewig, Meyer 20; New York, NY, 1878 ***9253*** *p47*
Lewin, A. 43; Harris Co., TX, 1900 ***6254*** *p6*
Lewin, Abraham 33; Maryland, 1738 ***3690.1*** *p140*
Lewin, John; Virginia, 1638 ***6219*** *p121*
*Wife:*Mary Butler
Lewin, Louis; Shreveport, LA, 1882 ***7129*** *p45*
Lewin, Mary Butler *SEE* Lewin, John
Lewine, Louis; Arkansas, 1918 ***95.2*** *p74*
Lewing, Richard 15; Jamaica, 1739 ***3690.1*** *p140*
Lewinson, Franziska Singer; Iowa, 1866-1943 ***123.54*** *p67*
Lewinson, Morduch Ber; Iowa, 1866-1943 ***123.54*** *p67*
Lewinson, Morduch Bernhard; Iowa, 1866-1943 ***123.54*** *p67*
Lewis, Mr.; Quebec, 1815 ***9229.18*** *p80*
Lewis, Adam; South Carolina, 1745 ***1639.20*** *p112*
Lewis, Adolph 24; California, 1873 ***2769.10*** *p4*
Lewis, Andrew 20; Philadelphia, 1803 ***53.26*** *p45*
Lewis, Betsey 13; Massachusetts, 1849 ***5881.1*** *p57*
Lewis, Catharine 36; Maryland, 1775 ***1219.7*** *p267*
Lewis, Charles 17; Philadelphia, 1774 ***1219.7*** *p219*
Lewis, Christopher; Virginia, 1635 ***6219*** *p33*
Lewis, Christopher 18; Jamaica, 1731 ***3690.1*** *p140*
Lewis, Daniel; Iowa, 1866-1943 ***123.54*** *p30*
Lewis, David; Virginia, 1638 ***6219*** *p148*
Lewis, David 18; Maryland, 1751 ***1219.7*** *p3*
Lewis, David 18; Maryland, 1751 ***3690.1*** *p140*
Lewis, Eliz.; Virginia, 1635 ***6219*** *p20*
Lewis, Eliz 23; America, 1703 ***2212*** *p40*
Lewis, Eliza.; Virginia, 1637 ***6219*** *p112*
Lewis, Elizabeth; Iowa, 1866-1943 ***123.54*** *p67*
Lewis, Fanny 70; Philadelphia, 1803 ***53.26*** *p45*
*Relative:*Fanny, Jr. 15
*Relative:*George 33
*Relative:*John 33
*Relative:*Susan 36
Lewis, Fanny, Jr. 15 *SEE* Lewis, Fanny
Lewis, Francis; Virginia, 1846 ***4626.16*** *p13*
Lewis, George; Indiana, 1848 ***9117*** *p17*
Lewis, George 33 *SEE* Lewis, Fanny
Lewis, Godfrey; Virginia, 1637 ***6219*** *p24*

Lewis, Harry Lee; Washington, 1859-1920 *2872.1* p23
Lewis, James 18; Jamaica, 1730 *3690.1* p140
Lewis, James 20; Massachusetts, 1849 *5881.1* p59
Lewis, James 21; Jamaica, 1724 *3690.1* p140
Lewis, Jno.; Virginia, 1647 *6219* p241
Lewis, John; Halifax, N.S., 1759 *1219.7* p68
Lewis, John; Virginia, 1635 *6219* p70
Lewis, John; Virginia, 1636 *6219* p10
Lewis, John; Virginia, 1638 *6219* p119
Lewis, John; Virginia, 1638 *6219* p153
Lewis, John 15; Pennsylvania, 1723 *3690.1* p140
Lewis, John 16; Philadelphia, 1774 *1219.7* p219
Lewis, John 19; Pennsylvania, 1731 *3690.1* p140
Lewis, John 25; Philadelphia, 1774 *1219.7* p201
Lewis, John 30; Virginia, 1775 *1219.7* p252
Lewis, John 33 SEE Lewis, Fanny
Lewis, John D.; Iowa, 1866-1943 *123.54* p30
Lewis, John E. 29; Kansas, 1895 *5240.1* p27
Lewis, John E. 29; Kansas, 1895 *5240.1* p80
Lewis, Jon.; Virginia, 1637 *6219* p180
Lewis, Jon.; Virginia, 1642 *6219* p191
Lewis, Jon.; Virginia, 1643 *6219* p200
Lewis, Jon., Jr.; Virginia, 1643 *6219* p200
Lewis, Jonathan; Virginia, 1640 *6219* p160
Lewis, Joseph 17; Jamaica, 1725 *3690.1* p141
Lewis, Joseph 24; Maryland, 1774 *1219.7* p192
Lewis, Joshua 19; Philadelphia, 1774 *1219.7* p219
Lewis, Kath.; Virginia, 1642 *6219* p198
Lewis, Katherin; Virginia, 1645 *6219* p232
Lewis, Katherine; Virginia, 1638 *6219* p122
Lewis, Lewis; New York, NY, 1830 *8208.4* p43
Lewis, M. 26; New Orleans, 1835 *778.5* p343
Lewis, Maudlin 15; New England, 1699 *2212* p19
Lewis, Patrick; America, 1743 *4971* p42
Lewis, Pieron 38; Died enroute, 1835 *778.5* p343
Lewis, Richard; South Carolina, 1767 *1639.20* p112
Lewis, Richard; Virginia, 1638 *6219* p125
Lewis, Richard; Virginia, 1698 *2212* p14
Lewis, Richard 11; America, 1700 *2212* p33
Lewis, Richard 15; Philadelphia, 1774 *1219.7* p183
Lewis, Richard 33; Maryland, 1774 *1219.7* p220
Lewis, Robert; Virginia, 1636 *6219* p80
Lewis, Robert; Virginia, 1698 *2212* p14
Lewis, Roger; Virginia, 1636 *6219* p32
Lewis, Samuel; Ohio, 1819 *8582.1* p47
Lewis, Samuel 18; Virginia, 1774 *1219.7* p201
Lewis, Samuel 28; Maryland, 1775 *1219.7* p271
Lewis, Susan 36 SEE Lewis, Fanny
Lewis, Susanna 30; Maryland, 1774 *1219.7* p206
Lewis, Tho.; Virginia, 1635 *6219* p69
Lewis, Tho.; Virginia, 1646 *6219* p239
Lewis, Thomas; Quebec, 1771 *7603* p47
Lewis, Thomas; Virginia, 1637 *6219* p24
Lewis, Thomas; Virginia, 1638 *6219* p160
Lewis, Thos.; Virginia, 1635 *6219* p74
Lewis, W. H.; Washington, 1859-1920 *2872.1* p23
Lewis, William 16; Maryland, 1774 *1219.7* p229
Lewis, William 18; Jamaica, 1730 *3690.1* p141
Lewis, William 20; Antigua (Antego), 1737 *3690.1* p141
Lewis, William 20; Leeward Islands, 1729 *3690.1* p141
Lewis, William 20; Virginia, 1774 *1219.7* p225
Lewis, William 27; Jamaica, 1773 *1219.7* p172
Lewis, William 33; Maryland, 1774 *1219.7* p204
Lewisger, John 26; Baltimore, 1775 *1219.7* p270
Lewison, Israel 19; New York, NY, 1878 *9253* p47
Lewkowicz, . . .; New York, 1831 *4606* p175
Lewman, Lawrence 26; Massachusetts, 1849 *5881.1* p59
Lewnan, Gottieb; Wisconsin, n.d. *9675.6* p267
Lewthwaite, John 21; Virginia, 1775 *1219.7* p251
Lewza, Paul; Arkansas, 1918 *95.2* p75
Lex, Andreas; America, 1848 *1450.2* p88A
Lexa, Anthony 50; Kansas, 1878 *5240.1* p29
Lexow, Friedrich 45; America, 1872 *8582.1* p22
Lexter, Pierre 31; America, 1839 *778.5* p343
Ley, . . .; Canada, 1776-1783 *9786* p28
Ley, John; Virginia, 1635 *6219* p6
Leyden, James; America, 1866 *5704.8* p210
Leyden, John; Virginia, 1636 *6219* p18
With wife
Leyden, Michael J.; America, 1865 *6014.1* p2
Leydens, Matthew; New Jersey, 1902 *3455.1* p43
Leydolff, . . .; Canada, 1776-1783 *9786* p28
Leydon, Thomas 25; Massachusetts, 1849 *5881.1* p61
Leyen, Christiaan; Arkansas, 1918 *95.2* p75
Leyer, . . .; Canada, 1776-1783 *9786* p28
Leyhr, Anna Magdalena; America, 1735-1749 *2444* p185
Leyhr, Johann Georg; America, 1733-1749 *2444* p185
Leyhr, Magdalena; America, 1749 *2444* p226
Leyland, John; Virginia, 1698 *2212* p12
Leymeister, Johann Wilhelm 58; Pennsylvania, 1748 *4525* p231
Leynard, Martha; Philadelphia, 1850 *5704.8* p64
Leyon, Johann 24; New Orleans, 1839 *778.5* p343

Leypoldt, Friedrich; New York, NY, 1839 *8208.4* p93
Leyss, Johann Georg; Pennsylvania, 1750 *2444* p185
Leytz, Leonhardt; South Carolina, 1788 *7119* p200
Lezanne, Francoise 30; New Orleans, 1838 *778.5* p343
Lezin, A. 24; New Orleans, 1835 *778.5* p343
L'Fabuere, Rachael 40; Carolina, 1774 *1219.7* p231
Lhin, John; New York, NY, 1838 *8208.4* p57
Libben, Harm; Illinois, 1894 *5012.40* p53
Libby, Charles Edwin; Washington, 1859-1920 *2872.1* p23
Libby, M.F.; Colorado, 1906 *9678.2* p124
Libby, Patrick; Quebec, 1825 *7603* p93
Libeau, Mr.; Cincinnati, 1831 *8582.1* p51
Liber, Christian Magdal 42; New Orleans, 1839 *9420.2* p357
Liber, Gasshold Henry 41; New Orleans, 1839 *9420.2* p357
*Wife:*Wma. Sophie 40
*Son:*Henry 10
*Daughter:*Martha Marie 8
*Son:*Simeon 3
Liber, Henry 10 SEE Liber, Gasshold Henry
Liber, Martha Marie 8 SEE Liber, Gasshold Henry
Liber, Simeon 3 SEE Liber, Gasshold Henry
Liber, Wma. Sophie 40 SEE Liber, Gasshold Henry
Liberator, Audry; Wisconsin, n.d. *9675.6* p267
Liberatore, Antonio; Arkansas, 1918 *95.2* p75
Liberatore, Francesho; Wisconsin, n.d. *9675.6* p267
Liberatore, Joseph; Wisconsin, n.d. *9675.6* p267
Liberatore, Pasquale; Wisconsin, n.d. *9675.6* p267
Liberman, Julius; New York, NY, 1887 *2764.35* p43
Libermann, Simon 46; New York, NY, 1878 *9253* p45
Lible, Martin 33; Kansas, 1877 *5240.1* p27
Lible, Martin 33; Kansas, 1877 *5240.1* p58
Liburatore, Franco 31; West Virginia, 1904 *9788.3* p14
Licamas, A. 35; New Orleans, 1835 *778.5* p343
Liccora, Abramo; Iowa, 1866-1943 *123.54* p30
Lichenstein, Isaak; Cincinnati, 1869-1887 *8582* p19
Licheston, Jon.; Virginia, 1637 *6219* p8
Licht, Jacob Heinrich; Cincinnati, 1869-1887 *8582* p19
Lichte, Mr.; America, 1852-1854 *4610.10* p144
Lichte, Anna M. C. Friederike SEE Lichte, Christoph Heinrich
Lichte, Anne M. E. Ellermann SEE Lichte, Christoph Heinrich
Lichte, Anne Marie Engel 8 SEE Lichte, Christine Anne Marie
Lichte, Anne Marie L. Grimmert SEE Lichte, Christ Heinrich
Lichte, Carl Dietrich SEE Lichte, Christ Heinrich
Lichte, Caroline 3 SEE Lichte, Christine Anne Marie
Lichte, Caroline Louise SEE Lichte, Christoph Heinrich
Lichte, Christ Heinrich; America, 1858 *4610.10* p149
*Wife:*Anne Marie L. Grimmert
*Child:*Carl Dietrich
*Child:*Luise Engel
Lichte, Christian Heinrich SEE Lichte, Christoph Heinrich
Lichte, Christine Anne Marie; America, 1854 *4610.10* p144
*Child:*Johann Carl Friedrich
*Child:*Anne Marie Engel 8
*Child:*Caroline 3
*Child:*Marie 9 mos
Lichte, Christoph Heinrich SEE Lichte, Christoph Heinrich
Lichte, Christoph Heinrich; America, 1844 *4610.10* p146
*Wife:*Anne M. E. Ellermann
*Child:*Christoph Heinrich
*Child:*Hermann Heinrich
*Child:*Anna M. C. Friederike
*Child:*Caroline Louise
*Child:*Justine W. Henriette
*Child:*Christian Heinrich
*Child:*Joh. F. Christian
Lichte, Ernst Friedrich; America, 1854 *4610.10* p148
Lichte, Hermann Heinrich SEE Lichte, Christoph Heinrich
Lichte, Joh. F. Christian SEE Lichte, Christoph Heinrich
Lichte, Johann Carl Friedrich SEE Lichte, Christine Anne Marie
Lichte, Johann Carl Heinrich; America, 1850 *4610.10* p147
Lichte, Justine W. Henriette SEE Lichte, Christoph Heinrich
Lichte, Luise Engel SEE Lichte, Christ Heinrich
Lichte, Marie 9 mos SEE Lichte, Christine Anne Marie
Lichtemberg, Charles; America, 1849 *1450.2* p88A
Lichtenstein, Auguste 22; New York, NY, 1878 *9253* p46
Lichtenwalter, . . .; Canada, 1776-1783 *9786* p28
Lichter, V.; Colorado, 1897 *9678.2* p124
Lichtor, Ben Meyer; Arkansas, 1918 *95.2* p75

Lickewalner, Lorentz; Georgia, 1738 *9332* p320
Lickfues, Fredrick; America, 1855 *6014.1* p2
Lictson, Mary; New York, NY, 1811 *2859.11* p14
Lictson, Thomas; New York, NY, 1811 *2859.11* p14
Liddell, Alex. 24; West Virginia, 1904 *9788.3* p14
Liddle, Eliza Jane; Philadelphia, 1850 *53.26* p45
Liddle, Eliza Jane; Philadelphia, 1850 *5704.8* p60
Liddle, George 15; Georgia, 1775 *1219.7* p276
Liddle, Mary Ann; Philadelphia, 1852 *5704.8* p92
Liddy, Andrew; Ohio, 1840 *9892.11* p26
Lide, Richard; Virginia, 1642 *6219* p194
Lidlowe, Mr.; Quebec, 1815 *9229.18* p76
Lidnescey, Nathaniell 26; Virginia, 1700 *2212* p32
Liebau, . . .; Canada, 1776-1783 *9786* p28
Liebau, Carl; Wisconsin, n.d. *9675.6* p267
Liebecke, Christoph; Canada, 1783 *9786* p38A
Liebegott, . . .; Canada, 1776-1783 *9786* p28
Liebenhaar, . . .; Canada, 1776-1783 *9786* p28
Lieber, Francis; New York, NY, 1827 *8582.1* p42
Lieber, Hermann; America, 1853 *8125.8* p437
Lieber, Richard; America, 1891 *1450.2* p88A
Lieberknecht, Gertraud 31; America, 1853 *9162.8* p37
Lieberknecht, Gretchen 6; America, 1853 *9162.8* p37
Lieberknecht, Heinrich 11 mos; America, 1853 *9162.8* p37
Lieberknecht, Kath. 8; America, 1853 *9162.8* p37
Lieberknecht, Michel 4; America, 1853 *9162.8* p37
Lieberknecht, Ph. 34; America, 1853 *9162.8* p37
Lieberknecht, Wilh. 9; America, 1853 *9162.8* p37
Lieberman, Nathan; Arkansas, 1918 *95.2* p75
Liebernikel, Christiane 10; New Orleans, 1839 *9420.1* p378
Liebernikel, Ehregolt 3; New Orleans, 1839 *9420.1* p378
Liebernikel, Eleanore 8; New Orleans, 1839 *9420.1* p378
Liebernikel, Johann Daniel 37; New Orleans, 1839 *9420.1* p378
Liebernikel, Johanne Rosine 12; New Orleans, 1839 *9420.1* p378
Liebernikel, Juliane 36; New Orleans, 1839 *9420.1* p378
Liebich, August; Washington, 1859-1920 *2872.1* p23
Liebich, Ludweich; Washington, 1859-1920 *2872.1* p23
Liebig, Andreas; New York, NY, 1838 *8208.4* p62
Liebisch, Anna SEE Liebisch, Martin
Liebisch, Anna; Pennsylvania, 1742 *3652* p58
Liebisch, Martin; Pennsylvania, 1742 *3652* p58
*Wife:*Anna
Liebler, Miss; New England, 1752 *4525* p221
Liebler, Margarete 20; Pennsylvania, 1752 *4525* p231
Liebscher, Oswald; Wisconsin, n.d. *9675.6* p267
Liebschuetz, Max; America, 1849 *8582.1* p22
Liechtenthaeler, Johannes Christianus; Philadelphia, 1752 *8125.6* p23
Liechti, Carl 49; Kansas, 1891 *5240.1* p76
Liedel, . . .; America, 1836 *8582.1* p39
Liedell, . . .; Canada, 1776-1783 *9786* p28
Lieder, . . .; Canada, 1776-1783 *9786* p28
Lieffert, . . .; Canada, 1776-1783 *9786* p28
Liemon, . . .; Canada, 1776-1783 *9786* p42
Lien, Martin; Arkansas, 1918 *95.2* p75
Lier, Conrad; Wisconsin, n.d. *9675.6* p267
Lierle, Johannes; Illinois, 1829 *8582.1* p54
Lierman, August; Illinois, 1876 *5012.39* p120
Lierman, Christian; Illinois, 1859 *5012.39* p54
Liermann, Margaret; Wisconsin, n.d. *9675.6* p267
Liersch, Otto; Washington, 1859-1920 *2872.1* p23
Lies, John 27; Kansas, 1884 *5240.1* p66
Liese, Frederick C.; New York, NY, 1838 *8208.4* p62
Liesegang, William; New York, NY, 1835 *8208.4* p77
Liesenberg, William; Wisconsin, n.d. *9675.6* p267
Liesert, . . .; Canada, 1776-1783 *9786* p28
Liesner, Eduard August Wilhelm 30; America, 1843 *3702.7* p312
Liessberger, Henriette 19; America, 1854-1855 *9162.6* p104
Lietsch, David; Kentucky, 1795 *8582.3* p94
Lieux, J. P. 27; Port uncertain, 1839 *778.5* p343
Lievens, Theofiel; Arkansas, 1918 *95.2* p75
Lievsay, Jane 20; America, 1706 *2212* p46
Liewenstien, George; Philadelphia, 1763 *9973.7* p38
Lifholm, A.; Minneapolis, 1870-1879 *6410.35* p59
Lifholm, B.A.; Minneapolis, 1873-1883 *6410.35* p59
Lifley, Edmund 27; Jamaica, 1733 *3690.1* p141
Lifliy, Edmund 27; Jamaica, 1733 *3690.1* p141
Liggett, Alexander 14; Quebec, 1856 *5704.8* p130
Liggett, Martha 40; Quebec, 1856 *5704.8* p130
Liggett, Mary; Quebec, 1852 *5704.8* p94
Liggett, Rebecca 11; Quebec, 1856 *5704.8* p130
Liggett, Robert 20; Quebec, 1856 *5704.8* p130
Liggett, Robert 50; Quebec, 1856 *5704.8* p130
Liggins, Thomas 34; Maryland, 1774 *1219.7* p208
Light, Augustus 26; Texas, 1839 *778.5* p343
Light, Elias; Virginia, 1636 *6219* p79
Light, Elias; Virginia, 1637 *6219* p85

Light, George; Virginia, 1623-1648 ***6219*** *p252*
Light, John 14; West Indies, 1722 ***3690.1*** *p141*
Light, Joseph 19; Jamaica, 1733 ***3690.1*** *p141*
Light, Rich.; Virginia, 1637 ***6219*** *p85*
Light, Richard; Virginia, 1636 ***6219*** *p79*
Lighten, Ann Jane 11; Philadelphia, 1854 ***5704.8*** *p122*
Lighten, Eliza 34; Philadelphia, 1854 ***5704.8*** *p122*
Lighten, Sarah 8; Philadelphia, 1854 ***5704.8*** *p122*
Lightfoot, Samuel 25; Jamaica, 1774 ***1219.7*** *p178*
Lightfoot, Sarah 18; New York, 1774 ***1219.7*** *p222*
Lightfoote, Ann; Virginia, 1635 ***6219*** *p69*
Lightholder, Jane 10; Massachusetts, 1849 ***5881.1*** *p59*
Lightholder, John 12; Massachusetts, 1849 ***5881.1*** *p59*
Lightholder, Joseph 10; Massachusetts, 1849 ***5881.1*** *p59*
Lighthollier, Wm.; Virginia, 1637 ***6219*** *p24*
Lighton, Mr.; New York, 1754 ***3652*** *p79*
Lighton, William; New York, NY, 1816 ***2859.11*** *p35*
Ligre, Auguste 23; New Orleans, 1838 ***778.5*** *p343*
Liguiet, Ant. F. 32; New Orleans, 1838 ***778.5*** *p343*
Likkanen, Henry; Washington, 1859-1920 ***2872.1*** *p23*
Lilburn, Adam; New York, NY, 1839 ***8208.4*** *p98*
Lile, Daniell; Virginia, 1639 ***6219*** *p155*
Liley, William; Colorado, 1906 ***9678.2*** *p124*
Lilia, John 25; New Orleans, 1835 ***778.5*** *p343*
Lilienkamp, A M Louise Hammelmann *SEE* Lilienkamp, Ernst Heinrich Gottlieb
Lilienkamp, Ernst Heinrich Gottlieb; America, 1852 ***4610.10*** *p112*
*Wife:*A M Louise Hammelmann
*Son:*Friedrich Wilhelm
Lilienkamp, Ernst Heinrich Ludwig; America, 1885 ***4610.10*** *p102*
Lilienkamp, Friedrich Wilhelm *SEE* Lilienkamp, Ernst Heinrich Gottlieb
Liliensiek, Friederike C. Justine; America, 1891 ***4610.10*** *p103*
Liliensiek, Heinrich Friedrich Wilhelm; America, 1881 ***4610.10*** *p101*
Lilienthal, Carl; Washington, 1859-1920 ***2872.1*** *p23*
Lilienthal, Max; America, 1845 ***8582.2*** *p22*
Lilja, Nels Magnus; Maine, 1890-1896 ***6410.22*** *p122*
Lilje, William; Illinois, 1875 ***5240.1*** *p27*
Liljegren, Arvid; Minneapolis, 1882-1883 ***6410.35*** *p59*
Liljengren, Nils P.; Minneapolis, 1873-1876 ***6410.35*** *p59*
Liljeqvist, Carl Henrik; America, 1843 ***6410.32*** *p124*
Liljeqvist, Mathias; America, 1830 ***6410.32*** *p124*
Liljeson, Phillip W.; Minneapolis, 1878-1884 ***6410.35*** *p59*
Lill, George L. 30; Kansas, 1874 ***5240.1*** *p56*
Lill, Joseph T. 35; Kansas, 1880 ***5240.1*** *p27*
Lill, Joseph T. 35; Kansas, 1880 ***5240.1*** *p62*
Lillas, Thomas; Virginia, 1856 ***4626.16*** *p15*
Lillemoe, Johannis; Arkansas, 1918 ***95.2*** *p75*
Lillequist, Carl Henrik; America, 1843 ***6410.32*** *p124*
Lillequist, Charles H. 18; Massachusetts, 1860 ***6410.32*** *p112*
Lillequist, Mary 54; Massachusetts, 1860 ***6410.32*** *p112*
Lillequist, Mathias; America, 1830 ***6410.32*** *p124*
Lilley, Mrs.; Quebec, 1815 ***9229.18*** *p77*
Lilley, Henry; Virginia, 1638 ***6219*** *p119*
Lilley, James 23; Virginia, 1774 ***1219.7*** *p243*
Lilley, James 37; Virginia, 1774 ***1219.7*** *p243*
Lilley, Joseph 16; Maryland, 1775 ***1219.7*** *p254*
Lilley, Joseph 20; Jamaica, 1730 ***3690.1*** *p141*
Lilley, Mary 18; Massachusetts, 1849 ***5881.1*** *p60*
Lillgequist, Carl Henrik; America, 1843 ***6410.32*** *p124*
Lillgequist, Matthew; America, 1830 ***6410.32*** *p124*
Lillie, Otto 21; Kansas, 1890 ***5240.1*** *p74*
Lilliendahl, Christian Daniel William; New Jersey, 1821 ***8208.4*** *p46*
Lilly, . . .; Canada, 1776-1783 ***9786*** *p28*
Lilly, Edward; Virginia, 1637 ***6219*** *p110*
Lilly, John; New York, NY, 1816 ***2859.11*** *p35*
Lilly, John 18; Windward Islands, 1722 ***3690.1*** *p141*
Lilly, Joseph 20; Jamaica, 1730 ***3690.1*** *p141*
Lilly, Mary 16; St. John, N.B., 1864 ***5704.8*** *p159*
Lilly, Paul 23; Arkansas, 1918 ***95.2*** *p48*
Lilly, Paul 23; Arkansas, 1918 ***95.2*** *p75*
Lilly, Thomas 22; Jamaica, 1730 ***3690.1*** *p141*
Lilly, William 30; Maryland, 1774 ***1219.7*** *p224*
Lillystone, John; Philadelphia, 1751 ***1219.7*** *p5*
Limb, Christine; Illinois, 1836 ***8582.1*** *p55*
Limbke, Charley; Kansas, 1882 ***5240.1*** *p27*
Limbright, Charles; America, 1866 ***6014.1*** *p2*
Limburg, Johann; New York, 1854 ***3702.7*** *p371*
*Relative:*K.
Limburg, K. *SEE* Limburg, Johann
Lime, . . .; Canada, 1776-1783 ***9786*** *p42*
Limerick, Alexander; New York, NY, 1816 ***2859.11*** *p35*
Limerick, Thomas K.; St. John, N.B., 1848 ***5704.8*** *p48*
Limes, John 20; Jamaica, 1730 ***3690.1*** *p141*
Limford, Elizabeth 21; Maryland, 1775 ***1219.7*** *p257*
Limmenhoffer, Veit; Georgia, 1738 ***9332*** *p321*
Limmey, Peter; Ohio, 1841 ***9892.11*** *p26*
Limouzin, Antoine Delisle 21; New Orleans, 1832 ***778.5*** *p343*
Limpson, Wm.; Virginia, 1635 ***6219*** *p3*
Linacre, Ann 38; America, 1703 ***2212*** *p39*
Linaghane, Thomas; America, 1735-1743 ***4971*** *p78*
Linch, . . .; Canada, 1776-1783 ***9786*** *p28*
Linch, Charles 11; St. John, N.B., 1855 ***5704.8*** *p127*
Linch, Daniel 22; Maryland, 1775 ***1219.7*** *p253*
Linch, James 18; Philadelphia, 1854 ***5704.8*** *p115*
Linch, Jeremiah; New York, 1848 ***1450.2*** *p88A*
Linch, John; Indiana, 1848 ***9117*** *p19*
Linch, John; New York, NY, 1827 ***8208.4*** *p36*
Linch, John; Virginia, 1646 ***6219*** *p246*
Linch, Michael 18; Philadelphia, 1854 ***5704.8*** *p115*
Linch, Nicalaus; Wisconsin, n.d. ***9675.6*** *p267*
Linch, Nicholas 26; Philadelphia, 1775 ***1219.7*** *p255*
Linch, Thomas 13; St. John, N.B., 1855 ***5704.8*** *p127*
Linchey, James; Philadelphia, 1816 ***2859.11*** *p35*
Linchy, Charles; America, 1742 ***4971*** *p64*
Linchy, William; Maryland, 1742 ***4971*** *p106*
Lincis, William; Wisconsin, n.d. ***9675.6*** *p267*
Lincolne, Edward; Virginia, 1639 ***6219*** *p155*
Lind, Anna; Colorado, 1904 ***9678.2*** *p124*
Lind, George 20; Maryland, 1774 ***1219.7*** *p206*
Lind, Jacob A.; Arkansas, 1918 ***95.2*** *p75*
Lind, John 21; America, 1827 ***778.5*** *p344*
Lind, Nels; Colorado, 1904 ***9678.2*** *p124*
Lind, Oliver 31; California, 1867 ***3840.2*** *p16*
Lind, P.M.; Minneapolis, 1879-1888 ***6410.35*** *p59*
Lindahl, August; Arkansas, 1918 ***95.2*** *p75*
Lindahl, John; Iowa, 1866-1943 ***123.54*** *p30*
Lindau, . . .; Canada, 1776-1783 ***9786*** *p28*
Lindauer, Heinr; Charleston, SC, 1775-1781 ***8582.2*** *p52*
Lindberg, . . .; Colorado, 1894 ***9678.2*** *p124*
Lindberg, Andrew; Colorado, 1894 ***9678.2*** *p124*
Lindberg, Andrew; Minneapolis, 1876-1888 ***6410.35*** *p59*
Lindberg, August; Minneapolis, 1881-1885 ***6410.35*** *p59*
Lindberg, Erick S. 23; Harris Co., TX, 1896 ***6254*** *p3*
Lindberg, John; Iowa, 1849-1860 ***2090*** *p613*
Lindberg, John E.; Maine, 1883-1892 ***6410.22*** *p120*
Lindblad, Oscar Wilhelm; Arkansas, 1918 ***95.2*** *p75*
Lindblom, Oscar; Iowa, 1866-1943 ***123.54*** *p30*
Lindblum, John; Washington, 1859-1920 ***2872.1*** *p23*
Lindebok, Ole O.; Illinois, 1876 ***5012.39*** *p91*
Lindegren, Nils Peter; Boston, 1858 ***6410.32*** *p123*
Lindegren, Olof; Boston, 1856 ***6410.32*** *p123*
Lindeman, Charles; Wisconsin, n.d. ***9675.6*** *p267*
Lindemann, . . .; America, n.d. ***8582.3*** *p79*
Lindemann, Adam; Lancaster, PA, 1780 ***8137*** *p11*
Lindemann, Georg; America, 1850 ***8582.2*** *p23*
Lindemann, Henrich; Philadelphia, 1779 ***8137*** *p11*
Lindemann, Herrmann; America, 1835 ***8582.1*** *p22*
Lindemann, Johann Friedrich Conrad; America, 1853 ***4610.10*** *p139*
Lindemann, Philipp; Ohio, 1834-1871 ***8582*** *p19*
Lindemann, Wilhelm; New York, NY, 1834 ***8582.2*** *p23*
Lindemann, Wilhelm, Family; New York, NY, 1835 ***8582.2*** *p23*
Linden, Charles Oscar; Washington, 1859-1920 ***2872.1*** *p23*
Linden, Gus; Washington, 1859-1920 ***2872.1*** *p23*
Linden, Gustave; Washington, 1859-1920 ***2872.1*** *p23*
Linden, Per Martin; Iowa, 1866-1943 ***123.54*** *p30*
Lindenberg, Charles H.; Arizona, 1886 ***2764.35*** *p41*
Lindenmeyer, Henry; New York, 1750 ***3652*** *p74*
Linder, Fred; Wisconsin, n.d. ***9675.6*** *p267*
Linder, George; New York, NY, 1835 ***8208.4*** *p20*
Linder, John; Illinois, 1888 ***5012.39*** *p52*
Linder, John; Illinois, 1888 ***5012.39*** *p122*
Linder, John; Minneapolis, 1874-1885 ***6410.35*** *p59*
Linder, John Olaf; Arkansas, 1918 ***95.2*** *p75*
Linderass, Charles; Minneapolis, 1869-1877 ***6410.35*** *p59*
Lindergreen, Nils P. 28; Massachusetts, 1860 ***6410.32*** *p103*
Lindergreen, Olaff 34; Massachusetts, 1860 ***6410.32*** *p103*
Lindergreen, Sophia 28; Massachusetts, 1860 ***6410.32*** *p103*
Linderlof, Samuel J.; Minneapolis, 1871-1883 ***6410.35*** *p60*
Linderman, Jan; Germantown, PA, 1684 ***2467.7*** *p5*
Lindgreen, Fritz; Illinois, 1900 ***5012.40*** *p79*
Lindgren, Axel F.; Arkansas, 1918 ***95.2*** *p75*
Lindgren, Carl Axel Fritjof; Arkansas, 1918 ***95.2*** *p75*
Lindgren, Isaac; Iroquois Co., IL, 1892 ***3455.1*** *p12*
Lindgren, Nils; Maine, 1883-1892 ***6410.22*** *p120*
Lindgrun, . . .; Canada, 1776-1783 ***9786*** *p28*
Lindholm, Frank; Maine, 1899 ***6410.22*** *p128*
Lindholm, Thomas; Shreveport, LA, 1878 ***7129*** *p45*
Lindhorst, Frank; Illinois, 1866 ***2896.5*** *p24*
Lindner, George; Wisconsin, n.d. ***9675.6*** *p267*
Lindner, Gottleb 24; New Orleans, 1839 ***9420.2*** *p483*
Lindner, Richard; Wisconsin, n.d. ***9675.6*** *p267*
Lindner, Samuel 34; New Orleans, 1839 ***9420.2*** *p483*
Lindquist, Carl Herman; Arkansas, 1918 ***95.2*** *p75*
Lindquist, Waldenmar; Arkansas, 1918 ***95.2*** *p75*
Lindreman, A. 24; New Orleans, 1837 ***778.5*** *p344*
Lindren, Henry 23; Port uncertain, 1838 ***778.5*** *p344*
Lindsay, Agnes 3; Quebec, 1864 ***5704.8*** *p163*
Lindsay, Agnes 7; Philadelphia, 1864 ***5704.8*** *p156*
Lindsay, Alexander; St. John, N.B., 1852 ***5704.8*** *p93*
Lindsay, Andre-Gilbert 22; Quebec, 1828 ***7603*** *p41*
Lindsay, Andrew; New York, NY, 1811 ***2859.11*** *p15*
Lindsay, Andrew; Philadelphia, 1864 ***5704.8*** *p187*
Lindsay, Andrew; St. John, N.B., 1851 ***5704.8*** *p72*
Lindsay, Andrew; St. John, N.B., 1852 ***5704.8*** *p93*
Lindsay, Anne Jane 8; Philadelphia, 1852 ***5704.8*** *p91*
Lindsay, Archibald C.; North Carolina, 1809 ***1639.20*** *p112*
Lindsay, Archy; Philadelphia, 1852 ***5704.8*** *p91*
Lindsay, Catherine; Philadelphia, 1852 ***5704.8*** *p88*
Lindsay, Charles T. 28; Kansas, 1891 ***5240.1*** *p76*
Lindsay, Colin; America, 1761 ***1639.20*** *p112*
Lindsay, David; New York, NY, 1811 ***2859.11*** *p15*
Lindsay, David 12; St. John, N.B., 1852 ***5704.8*** *p83*
Lindsay, Edward 20; Philadelphia, 1860 ***5704.8*** *p144*
Lindsay, Eliza; Philadelphia, 1865 ***5704.8*** *p200*
Lindsay, Elizabeth; St. John, N.B., 1852 ***5704.8*** *p93*
Lindsay, Elizabeth 9; Quebec, 1864 ***5704.8*** *p163*
Lindsay, Ellen 1; Quebec, 1864 ***5704.8*** *p163*
Lindsay, Ellen 39; Quebec, 1864 ***5704.8*** *p163*
Lindsay, Euphemia; North Carolina, 1797-1883 ***1639.20*** *p113*
Lindsay, Fanny; Quebec, 1852 ***5704.8*** *p86*
Lindsay, Fanny; Quebec, 1852 ***5704.8*** *p90*
Lindsay, George; New York, NY, 1815 ***2859.11*** *p35*
Lindsay, Henry D. 33; West Virginia, 1896 ***9788.3*** *p14*
Lindsay, Isabella; New York, NY, 1811 ***2859.11*** *p15*
Lindsay, Isabella; New York, NY, 1816 ***2859.11*** *p35*
Lindsay, Isabella; Quebec, 1851 ***5704.8*** *p75*
Lindsay, James; New York, NY, 1811 ***2859.11*** *p15*
Lindsay, James; Philadelphia, 1852 ***5704.8*** *p91*
Lindsay, James 19; St. John, N.B., 1864 ***5704.8*** *p157*
Lindsay, John; Philadelphia, 1852 ***5704.8*** *p91*
Lindsay, John 5; Quebec, 1864 ***5704.8*** *p163*
Lindsay, John 6; Philadelphia, 1853 ***5704.8*** *p111*
Lindsay, John 17; Philadelphia, 1853 ***5704.8*** *p111*
Lindsay, John 21; Wilmington, DE, 1831 ***6508.7*** *p161*
Lindsay, Joseph; Philadelphia, 1852 ***5704.8*** *p89*
Lindsay, Joseph; Philadelphia, 1852 ***5704.8*** *p91*
Lindsay, Margaret; Philadelphia, 1852 ***5704.8*** *p91*
Lindsay, Margaret; Philadelphia, 1865 ***5704.8*** *p200*
Lindsay, Margaret 50; Philadelphia, 1853 ***5704.8*** *p111*
Lindsay, Mary; Quebec, 1852 ***5704.8*** *p86*
Lindsay, Mary; Quebec, 1852 ***5704.8*** *p90*
Lindsay, Mary 8; Quebec, 1864 ***5704.8*** *p163*
Lindsay, Mary 20; Wilmington, DE, 1831 ***6508.7*** *p161*
Lindsay, Mary Jane 14; Philadelphia, 1853 ***5704.8*** *p111*
Lindsay, Nancy; Philadelphia, 1852 ***5704.8*** *p91*
Lindsay, Pheby 13; St. John, N.B., 1852 ***5704.8*** *p93*
Lindsay, Rebecca 9; Wilmington, DE, 1831 ***6508.7*** *p161*
Lindsay, Richard; New York, NY, 1815 ***2859.11*** *p35*
Lindsay, Robert; New York, NY, 1815 ***2859.11*** *p35*
Lindsay, Robert; New York, NY, 1864 ***5704.8*** *p187*
Lindsay, Robert; St. John, N.B., 1852 ***5704.8*** *p83*
Lindsay, Robert 20; Philadelphia, 1864 ***5704.8*** *p156*
Lindsay, Robert 35; Quebec, 1864 ***5704.8*** *p163*
Lindsay, Ruth 13; St. John, N.B., 1851 ***5704.8*** *p72*
Lindsay, Susan; New York, NY, 1816 ***2859.11*** *p35*
Lindsay, Thomas; Charleston, SC, 1803 ***1639.20*** *p113*
Lindsay, Thomas 16; Virginia, 1699 ***2212*** *p20*
Lindsay, Washington; Philadelphia, 1865 ***5704.8*** *p200*
Lindsay, William; Charleston, SC, 1786 ***1639.20*** *p113*
Lindsay, William; Philadelphia, 1850 ***53.26*** *p46*
Lindsay, William; Philadelphia, 1850 ***5704.8*** *p68*
Lindsay, William; Philadelphia, 1851 ***5704.8*** *p80*
Lindsay, William 28; St. John, N.B., 1866 ***5704.8*** *p166*
Lindsay, William 51; South Carolina, 1850 ***1639.20*** *p113*
Lindsey, Edward 17; Jamaica, 1734 ***3690.1*** *p141*
Lindsey, John 18; Montserrat, 1699-1700 ***2212*** *p22*
Lindsey, John 23; Jamaica, 1774 ***1219.7*** *p232*
Lindsey, Joseph 33; Philadelphia, 1804 ***53.26*** *p46*
Lindsey, Thomas; Ohio, 1844 ***9892.11*** *p26*
Lindsley, Andrew 27; Massachusetts, 1848 ***5881.1*** *p57*
Lindstedt, Nels 49; Washington, 1918 ***1728.5*** *p10*
Lindsten, Otto H.; Washington, 1859-1920 ***2872.1*** *p23*
Lindstrom, Adolph; Kansas, 1885-1906 ***5240.1*** *p27*
Lindstrom, John 35; Kansas, 1877 ***5240.1*** *p27*
Lindstrom, John 35; Kansas, 1877 ***5240.1*** *p58*
Lindworm, . . .; Canada, 1776-1783 ***9786*** *p28*
Lindwurm, . . .; Canada, 1776-1783 ***9786*** *p28*
Line, Hen.; Virginia, 1642 ***6219*** *p199*
Lineer, Marke; Virginia, 1642 ***6219*** *p191*
Linehan, Edward; New York, NY, 1836 ***8208.4*** *p13*
Linehan, Wm 30; Newport, RI, 1851 ***6508.5*** *p20*

Little, Elizabeth 23; St. John, N.B., 1856 ***5704.8*** *p132*
Little, Elizabeth 31 *SEE* Little, William
Little, Fanny 3 mos; St. John, N.B., 1847 ***5704.8*** *p34*
Little, Isaac; New York, NY, 1835 ***8208.4*** *p44*
Little, James; New York, NY, 1811 ***2859.11*** *p15*
Little, James 16; Virginia, 1775 ***1219.7*** *p261*
Little, Jane; Philadelphia, 1865 ***5704.8*** *p201*
Little, Jane; St. John, N.B., 1847 ***5704.8*** *p33*
Little, Jane; St. John, N.B., 1849 ***5704.8*** *p49*
Little, Jane; Virginia, 1640 ***6219*** *p182*
Little, John; New York, NY, 1811 ***2859.11*** *p15*
With family
Little, John; Ohio, 1844 ***9892.11*** *p26*
Little, John; Ohio, 1847 ***9892.11*** *p26*
Little, John; St. John, N.B., 1849 ***5704.8*** *p49*
Little, John; Virginia, 1647 ***6219*** *p245*
Little, John 7; St. John, N.B., 1847 ***5704.8*** *p33*
Little, John 19; Antigua (Antego), 1721 ***3690.1*** *p142*
Little, John 25; Philadelphia, 1803 ***53.26*** *p46*
Little, John 30; Virginia, 1774 ***1219.7*** *p243*
Little, Lavinia Jane; St. John, N.B., 1849 ***5704.8*** *p49*
Little, Lindsay; Philadelphia, 1865 ***5704.8*** *p195*
Little, Lucinda 20; Philadelphia, 1853 ***5704.8*** *p109*
Little, Margaret; St. John, N.B., 1847 ***5704.8*** *p33*
Little, Martha; New York, NY, 1811 ***2859.11*** *p15*
Little, Mary; St. John, N.B., 1847 ***5704.8*** *p33*
Little, Mary 5 *SEE* Little, William
Little, Mary Ann; Quebec, 1847 ***5704.8*** *p29*
Little, Mary Ann; St. John, N.B., 1849 ***5704.8*** *p49*
Little, Mary Ann 5; Quebec, 1852 ***5704.8*** *p94*
Little, Mary J.; Philadelphia, 1869 ***5704.8*** *p235*
Little, Peter; Philadelphia, 1760 ***9973.7*** *p35*
Little, Richard 21; Maryland, 1774 ***1219.7*** *p204*
Little, Robert 7; St. John, N.B., 1847 ***5704.8*** *p33*
Little, Robert 17; St. John, N.B., 1856 ***5704.8*** *p131*
Little, Robert 26; Philadelphia, 1803 ***53.26*** *p46*
Little, Samuel *SEE* Little, Thomas
Little, Samuel; Philadelphia, 1847 ***5704.8*** *p32*
Little, Sarah; Philadelphia, 1865 ***5704.8*** *p201*
Little, Susan 8; St. John, N.B., 1847 ***5704.8*** *p33*
Little, Terence 1; St. John, N.B., 1847 ***5704.8*** *p34*
Little, Thomas; New York, 1825 ***9892.11*** *p26*
Little, Thomas; New York, NY, 1816 ***2859.11*** *p35*
Little, Thomas; New York, NY, 1835 ***8208.4*** *p5*
Little, Thomas; New York, NY, 1868 ***5704.8*** *p231*
Little, Thomas; Ohio, 1840 ***9892.11*** *p26*
Little, Thomas; Philadelphia, 1847 ***53.26*** *p46*
*Relative:*Samuel
*Relative:*Elizabeth 11
Little, Thomas; Philadelphia, 1847 ***5704.8*** *p32*
Little, Thomas 4; St. John, N.B., 1847 ***5704.8*** *p34*
Little, Thomas 22; New York, 1774 ***1219.7*** *p217*
Little, Thomas 27; North America, 1774 ***1219.7*** *p200*
*Wife:*Ann 24
Little, William; New York, 1825 ***9892.11*** *p26*
Little, William; Ohio, 1840 ***9892.11*** *p26*
Little, William; Philadelphia, 1865 ***5704.8*** *p201*
Little, William; St. John, N.B., 1847 ***5704.8*** *p33*
Little, William 2 *SEE* Little, William
Little, William 20; Pennsylvania, 1738 ***3690.1*** *p142*
Little, William 20; St. Kitts, 1774 ***1219.7*** *p184*
Little, William 31; Savannah, GA, 1733 ***4719.17*** *p311*
*Wife:*Elizabeth 31
*Daughter:*Mary 5
*Son:*William 2
Little, William 49; Kansas, 1884 ***5240.1*** *p65*
Littleboy, Lawr.; Virginia, 1638 ***6219*** *p147*
Littlehales, Clayton Haines; Jamaica, 1764 ***1219.7*** *p104*
Littlejohn, James; Virginia, 1635 ***6219*** *p1*
Littlejohn, William; America, 1760 ***1639.20*** *p114*
Littler, William; Boston, 1765 ***1219.7*** *p108*
Littleton, George; Jamaica, 1759 ***1219.7*** *p67*
Littlewood, Benjamin 21; Philadelphia, 1774 ***1219.7*** *p224*
Littlewood, Eliza; Virginia, 1643 ***6219*** *p199*
Litzke, Anna 72; Kansas, 1879 ***5240.1*** *p60*
Lively, Dennis 22; Kansas, 1872 ***5240.1*** *p52*
Livesey, Thomas; Ohio, 1840 ***9892.11*** *p26*
Livillion, Felix 30; Louisiana, 1820 ***778.5*** *p344*
Living, Jno; America, 1703 ***2212*** *p40*
Livingston, Alexander; New York, NY, 1835 ***8208.4*** *p37*
Livingston, Dynes 48; Kansas, 1879 ***5240.1*** *p60*
Livingston, Helen 26; Quebec, 1862 ***5704.8*** *p152*
Livingston, Hugh; Charleston, SC, 1819 ***1639.20*** *p114*
Livingston, John; Wilmington, NC, 1800 ***1639.20*** *p114*
Livingston, John W. 54; North Carolina, 1680-1830 ***1639.20*** *p114*
Livingston, Peter; America, 1804 ***1639.20*** *p114*
Livingston, Peter 59; North Carolina, 1850 ***1639.20*** *p114*
Livingston, William; New York, NY, 1834 ***8208.4*** *p57*
Livingstone, Duncan 76; North Carolina, 1850 ***1639.20*** *p258*
Livy, . . .; Canada, 1776-1783 ***9786*** *p28*
Lizius, Bernard; America, 1870 ***1450.2*** *p88A*
Lizius, Charles Bernart; America, 1870 ***1450.2*** *p88A*
Ljubisa, Milo Lazo; Arkansas, 1918 ***95.2*** *p75*
Llademan, Mr. 30; New Orleans, 1839 ***778.5*** *p344*
Llewellyn, Major; Iowa, 1866-1943 ***123.54*** *p31*
Lloyd, Alfred Edward; Arkansas, 1918 ***95.2*** *p75*
Lloyd, Bernard 30; Harris Co., TX, 1896 ***6254*** *p3*
Lloyd, David; Colorado, 1893 ***9678.2*** *p124*
Lloyd, David; Ohio, 1838 ***1450.2*** *p88A*
Lloyd, Henry 15; America, 1703 ***2212*** *p40*
Lloyd, Henry 21; Savannah, GA, 1733 ***4719.17*** *p312*
Lloyd, Jno; America, 1697 ***2212*** *p8*
Lloyd, Jno; America, 1698 ***2212*** *p5*
Lloyd, Jno; Virginia, 1698 ***2212*** *p15*
Lloyd, John; Virginia, 1643 ***6219*** *p230*
Lloyd, John 21; Jamaica, 1738 ***3690.1*** *p142*
Lloyd, Lucy 20; Maryland, 1773 ***1219.7*** *p173*
Lloyd, Margarette 20; Maryland or Virginia, 1699 ***2212*** *p23*
Lloyd, Martha; Virginia, 1698 ***2212*** *p12*
Lloyd, Martha 20; America, 1706 ***2212*** *p48*
Lloyd, Philip 22; Jamaica, 1725 ***3690.1*** *p142*
Lloyd, Robert; Virginia, 1637 ***6219*** *p111*
Lloyd, Sarah 22; Maryland, 1735 ***3690.1*** *p142*
Lloyd, Thomas; America, 1698 ***2212*** *p5*
Lloyd, Thomas; New York, NY, 1833 ***8208.4*** *p31*
Lloyd, Thomas; Quebec, 1822 ***7603*** *p28*
Lloyd, Thomas 13; Maryland or Virginia, 1699 ***2212*** *p24*
Lloyd, Thomas 27; Maryland, 1775 ***1219.7*** *p256*
Lloyd, William 19; Jamaica, 1734 ***3690.1*** *p142*
Lloyd, William 22; Jamaica, 1722 ***3690.1*** *p142*
Lloyd, Wm. G.; Virginia, 1856 ***4626.16*** *p15*
Lo, Genevieve 24; New Orleans, 1837 ***778.5*** *p345*
Loague, John 18; Philadelphia, 1854 ***5704.8*** *p120*
Loan, John A.; New York, NY, 1867 ***5704.8*** *p222*
Lobasko, Andy; Iowa, 1866-1943 ***123.54*** *p31*
Lobb, George; Virginia, 1771 ***1219.7*** *p149*
Lobbes, . . .; Canada, 1776-1783 ***9786*** *p42*
Lobenhofer, John; Wisconsin, n.d. ***9675.6*** *p267*
Lober, Pastor; New Orleans, 1839 ***9420.1*** *p373*
Lobey, Catharine 12; Massachusetts, 1850 ***5881.1*** *p57*
Lobey, Ellen 40; Massachusetts, 1850 ***5881.1*** *p58*
Lobmiller, Theodor; America, 1850 ***8582.2*** *p24*
Lobol, Jacob 21; New York, NY, 1878 ***9253*** *p46*
Lobris, Pierre L.; Wisconsin, n.d. ***9675.6*** *p267*
Lo Castro, Guiseppe; Arkansas, 1918 ***95.2*** *p75*
Locco, Pier.e 26; America, 1839 ***778.5*** *p345*
Lochbihlor, Casper; America, 1854 ***1450.2*** *p89A*
Lochhead, John McLean; New York, 1889 ***1450.2*** *p23B*
Lochrie, Martin; Illinois, 1858-1905 ***5012.38*** *p98*
Lochrie, Michael; Illinois, 1859 ***5012.38*** *p97*
Lochrie, William; Illinois, 1860 ***5012.38*** *p97*
Lock, . . .; Virginia, 1642 ***6219*** *p188*
Lock, John; Virginia, 1628 ***6219*** *p31*
Lock, Peter 19; Jamaica, 1729 ***3690.1*** *p142*
Lock, Tho.; Virginia, 1635 ***6219*** *p70*
Lock, Tho.; Virginia, 1638 ***6219*** *p116*
Lock, Thomasin; America, 1742 ***4971*** *p17*
Lock, William; Virginia, 1600-1642 ***6219*** *p193*
Lockart, Andrew; Philadelphia, 1852 ***5704.8*** *p87*
Lockart, Catherine 18; St. John, N.B., 1859 ***5704.8*** *p140*
Lockart, Eliza 7; Philadelphia, 1852 ***5704.8*** *p87*
Lockart, John 12; Philadelphia, 1852 ***5704.8*** *p87*
Lockart, Margaret 20; St. John, N.B., 1859 ***5704.8*** *p140*
Lockart, Nancy; Philadelphia, 1852 ***5704.8*** *p87*
Lockart, Robert 10; Philadelphia, 1852 ***5704.8*** *p87*
Lockart, William 25; St. John, N.B., 1857 ***5704.8*** *p134*
Lockat, John; New York, NY, 1811 ***2859.11*** *p15*
Locke, Ann 23; Massachusetts, 1850 ***5881.1*** *p57*
Locke, Anne 36; Massachusetts, 1850 ***5881.1*** *p57*
Locke, George; Massachusetts, 1850 ***5881.1*** *p58*
Locke, John; South Carolina, 1788 ***7119*** *p202*
Locke, John; Virginia, 1621 ***6219*** *p30*
Locke, Stephan; South Carolina, 1788 ***7119*** *p202*
Locke, William; Virginia, 1639 ***6219*** *p156*
Lockeit, Jean 22; America, 1838 ***778.5*** *p345*
Lockeit, Paul 20; America, 1838 ***778.5*** *p345*
Locker, Georg; Virginia, 1635 ***6219*** *p3*
Lockery, James; New York, NY, 1811 ***2859.11*** *p15*
Lockery, Margaret; New York, NY, 1811 ***2859.11*** *p15*
Lockhart, Anna Catherine 4; Philadelphia, 1864 ***5704.8*** *p155*
Lockhart, Anne; Philadelphia, 1865 ***5704.8*** *p189*
Lockhart, Eliza Mary 7; Philadelphia, 1864 ***5704.8*** *p155*
Lockhart, Elizabeth; Philadelphia, 1865 ***5704.8*** *p189*
Lockhart, James 10; Philadelphia, 1864 ***5704.8*** *p155*
Lockhart, John; New York, NY, 1815 ***2859.11*** *p35*
Lockhart, John; New York, NY, 1839 ***8208.4*** *p99*
Lockhart, John 14; Philadelphia, 1864 ***5704.8*** *p155*
Lockhart, Margaret; New York, NY, 1815 ***2859.11*** *p35*
Lockhart, Mary 29; Philadelphia, 1854 ***5704.8*** *p117*
Lockhart, Sarah 16; Philadelphia, 1864 ***5704.8*** *p155*
Lockhead, John McK. 41; Kansas, 1884 ***5240.1*** *p65*
Lockier, Captain; Quebec, 1815 ***9229.18*** *p80*
Locklay, Barbara 8; New Orleans, 1831 ***778.5*** *p345*
Locklay, Jane 30; New Orleans, 1831 ***778.5*** *p345*
Locklay, John 34; New Orleans, 1831 ***778.5*** *p345*
Locklay, Martha 1; New Orleans, 1831 ***778.5*** *p345*
Locklay, Mary 3; New Orleans, 1831 ***778.5*** *p345*
Lockley, Charles; Virginia, 1638 ***6219*** *p147*
Lockley, Charles; Virginia, 1639 ***6219*** *p150*
Lockly, Tho.; Virginia, 1639 ***6219*** *p150*
Lockwar, Samuel 17; New York, 1775 ***1219.7*** *p246*
Lockwood, George 31; Kansas, 1872 ***5240.1*** *p52*
Lockwood, John; New York, NY, 1816 ***2859.11*** *p35*
Lockyer, Richard Joseph; New York, NY, 1833 ***8208.4*** *p76*
Locoul, R. 37; America, 1832 ***778.5*** *p345*
Lodde, Anton Barend; Washington, 1859-1920 ***2872.1*** *p23*
Lodde, Barend; Washington, 1859-1920 ***2872.1*** *p23*
Lodde, Beulah Faith; Washington, 1859-1920 ***2872.1*** *p23*
Lodde, Telitha Verba; Washington, 1859-1920 ***2872.1*** *p24*
Lodde, Verba Barbara; Washington, 1859-1920 ***2872.1*** *p24*
Loddewyk, Marie Angeline; Iowa, 1866-1943 ***123.54*** *p69*
Loddewyk, Pierre Edoward; Iowa, 1866-1943 ***123.54*** *p69*
Lode, . . .; Canada, 1776-1783 ***9786*** *p28*
Lodell, . . .; Canada, 1776-1783 ***9786*** *p28*
Lodge, Adam 20; Pennsylvania, 1730 ***3690.1*** *p290*
Lodge, Georg; Virginia, 1638 ***6219*** *p122*
Lodge, James 30; Kansas, 1879 ***5240.1*** *p61*
Lodge, Jane 20; Pennsylvania, 1723 ***3690.1*** *p142*
Lodge, Mathew 20; Nova Scotia, 1775 ***1219.7*** *p263*
Lodge, Thomas; Virginia, 1637 ***6219*** *p109*
Lods, . . .; Halifax, N.S., 1752 ***7074.6*** *p232*
Lods, Claudine *SEE* Lods, Jean-Jacques
Lods, Etienne *SEE* Lods, Jean-Jacques
Lods, Jean-George *SEE* Lods, Jean-Jacques
Lods, Mrs. Jean-Jacques; Died enroute, 1752 ***7074.6*** *p211*
Lods, Jean-Jacques 38; Halifax, N.S., 1752 ***7074.6*** *p211*
*Child:*Jean-George
*Child:*Etienne
*Child:*Jeanne-Catherine
*Child:*Claudine
Lods, Jeanne-Catherine *SEE* Lods, Jean-Jacques
Lodwick, Michael; Philadelphia, 1759 ***9973.7*** *p34*
Loeb, Felix V.; Shreveport, LA, 1877 ***7129*** *p45*
Loeb, Issac; Shreveport, LA, 1879 ***7129*** *p45*
Loeb, Leopold; Cincinnati, 1842 ***8582*** *p19*
Loeb, Louis; Illinois, 1858 ***5012.39*** *p54*
Loeb, Max William; Illinois, 1874 ***5012.39*** *p91*
Loeb, Samuel; Illinois, 1906 ***5012.37*** *p63*
Loeber, Carl 72; Arizona, 1914 ***9228.40*** *p18*
Loedel, . . .; Canada, 1776-1783 ***9786*** *p28*
Loedel, Henry Nicholas Christopher; Canada, 1776-1783 ***9786*** *p219*
Loeder, . . .; Canada, 1776-1783 ***9786*** *p28*
Loeffler, Christian; Illinois, 1876 ***5012.37*** *p59*
Loeffler, Christina; Pennsylvania, 1754-1773 ***2444*** *p167*
Loeffler, Emil; Illinois, 1905 ***5012.37*** *p63*
Loeffler, Johanna Jourdan *SEE* Loeffler, Phillip
Loeffler, Margaretha; Pennsylvania, 1752 ***2444*** *p155*
Loeffler, Phillip; New York, 1851 ***5647.5*** *p123*
*Wife:*Johanna Jourdan
Loeges, Anna Barbara 9 *SEE* Loeges, George Paul
Loeges, Anna Maria 8 *SEE* Loeges, George Paul
Loeges, George Paul; South Carolina, 1752-1753 ***3689.17*** *p22*
With wife
*Relative:*Anna Barbara 9
*Relative:*Anna Maria 8
*Relative:*John George 7
*Relative:*John Michael 4 mos
Loeges, John George 7 *SEE* Loeges, George Paul
Loeges, John Michael 4 mos *SEE* Loeges, George Paul
Loehl, Mr.; Port uncertain, 1749 ***2444*** *p186*
With daughter
Loehmann, C. H.; America, 1839 ***8582.3*** *p41*
Loehr, Ferdinand; America, 1849 ***1450.2*** *p89A*
Loehr, Ferdinand von; California, 1852 ***8582.3*** *p41*
Loehr, Philipp; America, 1851 ***1450.2*** *p89A*
Loehrke, Fred Wilhelm; New York, NY, 1836-1918 ***3455.2*** *p52*
Loell, Mr.; Port uncertain, 1749 ***2444*** *p186*
With daughter
Loell, Henry; Wisconsin, n.d. ***9675.6*** *p267*
Loerich, J.; Ohio, 1798-1818 ***8582.2*** *p53*
Loerven, Nicholas; Wisconsin, n.d. ***9675.6*** *p267*
Loesch, Friederich; America, 1850 ***8582.3*** *p41*
Loesch, Johann Peter; America, 1849 ***8582.3*** *p42*
Loesch, Nicholas; Wisconsin, n.d. ***9675.6*** *p267*
Loeschke, Ferdinand; America, 1881 ***1450.2*** *p89A*
Loeschner, Fredk. 44; New Orleans, 1839 ***9420.2*** *p165*

Loeser, Louis; Wisconsin, n.d. ***9675.6*** *p267*
Loether, Christian Henry; New York, 1750 ***3652*** *p74*
Loevenich, John 37; Kansas, 1889 ***5240.1*** *p74*
Loewen, Helena *SEE* Loewen, Peter
Loewen, Henry R. 38; Harris Co., TX, 1899 ***6254*** *p5*
Loewen, Katharina *SEE* Loewen, Peter
Loewen, Peter; New York, 1855 ***3702.7*** *p182*
*Sister:*Katharina
With family & brother-in-law
*Niece:*Helena
Loewenstein, August; America, 1846 ***8582.2*** *p24*
Loewenstein, Georg Wilhelm von; Halifax, N.S., 1780 ***9786*** *p269*
Loewenstein, Georg Wilhelm von; New York, 1776 ***9786*** *p269*
Loewenstein, Julius H.; America, 1844 ***8582.3*** *p42*
Loezze, Franseseo; Wisconsin, n.d. ***9675.6*** *p267*
Loffendal, Augusta 38; Massachusetts, 1860 ***6410.32*** *p111*
Loffendal, Joseph 33; Massachusetts, 1860 ***6410.32*** *p111*
Lofferer, . . .; Canada, 1776-1783 ***9786*** *p28*
Loffler, Helena; New York, NY, 1855 ***3702.7*** *p194*
Loffler, Johanna Jourdan *SEE* Loffler, Phillip
Loffler, Phillip; New York, 1851 ***5647.5*** *p123*
*Wife:*Johanna Jourdan
Lofgreen, Olef; Iowa, 1866-1943 ***123.54*** *p31*
Lofgreen, Peter A.; St. Louis, 1869 ***2764.35*** *p41*
Lofgren, Alfred; Iowa, 1866-1943 ***123.54*** *p31*
Lofgren, Edwin; Iowa, 1866-1943 ***123.54*** *p31*
Lofgren, Nels; Iowa, 1866-1943 ***123.54*** *p31*
Lofgren, Nils; Minneapolis, 1883-1887 ***6410.35*** *p60*
Lofgren, P. M.; Minneapolis, 1879-1888 ***6410.35*** *p60*
Loftes, Patrick 23; Massachusetts, 1848 ***5881.1*** *p61*
Loftis, Willi.; Virginia, 1642 ***6219*** *p193*
Loftis, Wm.; Virginia, 1647 ***6219*** *p239*
Loftman, Benjamin 16; Maryland, 1774 ***1219.7*** *p230*
Lofvendahl, Joseph; Boston, 1862 ***6410.32*** *p124*
Logan, Mr.; Montreal, n.d. ***9775.5*** *p202*
Logan, Alexr. 1; Wilmington, DE, 1831 ***6508.7*** *p161*
Logan, Andrew 23; Tennessee, 1860 ***1450.2*** *p89A*
Logan, Bernard; Philadelphia, 1864 ***5704.8*** *p177*
Logan, Betty; Quebec, 1853 ***5704.8*** *p103*
Logan, Bridget; New York, NY, 1869 ***5704.8*** *p234*
Logan, Catharine; New York, NY, 1870 ***5704.8*** *p240*
Logan, Catherine; St. John, N.B., 1847 ***5704.8*** *p21*
Logan, Charles; New York, NY, 1811 ***2859.11*** *p15*
Logan, Daniel; America, 1897 ***1450.2*** *p23B*
Logan, Daniel; New York, NY, 1815 ***2859.11*** *p35*
Logan, Eliza 18; Wilmington, DE, 1831 ***6508.7*** *p161*
Logan, Elizabeth; New York, NY, 1864 ***5704.8*** *p172*
Logan, Elizabeth; Quebec, 1820 ***7603*** *p97*
Logan, Elizabeth 54; Wilmington, DE, 1831 ***6508.7*** *p161*
Logan, George 21; St. John, N.B., 1859 ***5704.8*** *p140*
Logan, George 25; Philadelphia, 1804 ***53.26*** *p46*
Logan, Gust; Minneapolis, 1879-1883 ***6410.35*** *p60*
Logan, Hugh; America, 1865 ***5704.8*** *p202*
Logan, James; New York, NY, 1839 ***8208.4*** *p92*
Logan, James; Philadelphia, 1866 ***5704.8*** *p206*
Logan, James; Quebec, 1853 ***5704.8*** *p103*
Logan, James 9; New York, NY, 1870 ***5704.8*** *p240*
Logan, James 22; Philadelphia, 1859 ***5704.8*** *p142*
Logan, James 23; St. John, N.B., 1859 ***5704.8*** *p140*
Logan, James 27; Maryland, 1774 ***1219.7*** *p211*
Logan, James M.; New York, NY, 1834 ***8208.4*** *p3*
Logan, John; Charleston, SC, 1761 ***1639.20*** *p114*
Logan, John; New York, NY, 1811 ***2859.11*** *p15*
Logan, John; Philadelphia, 1816 ***2859.11*** *p35*
Logan, John 3; New York, NY, 1870 ***5704.8*** *p240*
Logan, John 7; Quebec, 1853 ***5704.8*** *p103*
Logan, John 13; St. John, N.B., 1859 ***5704.8*** *p140*
Logan, John 19; Philadelphia, 1775 ***1219.7*** *p259*
Logan, Joseph 19; Philadelphia, 1859 ***5704.8*** *p142*
Logan, Margaret; America, 1865 ***5704.8*** *p193*
Logan, Margaret; St. John, N.B., 1850 ***5704.8*** *p66*
Logan, Margaret 12; Quebec, 1853 ***5704.8*** *p103*
Logan, Margt 13; Wilmington, DE, 1831 ***6508.7*** *p161*
Logan, Margt 18; Wilmington, DE, 1831 ***6508.7*** *p161*
Logan, Margt 40; Wilmington, DE, 1831 ***6508.7*** *p161*
Logan, Martha 46; Wilmington, DE, 1831 ***6508.7*** *p161*
Logan, Mary; New York, NY, 1811 ***2859.11*** *p15*
Logan, Mary; New York, NY, 1870 ***5704.8*** *p240*
Logan, Mary; Philadelphia, 1811 ***53.26*** *p46*
Logan, Mary; Philadelphia, 1811 ***2859.11*** *p15*
Logan, Mary; St. John, N.B., 1850 ***5704.8*** *p66*
Logan, Mary 16; St. John, N.B., 1859 ***5704.8*** *p140*
Logan, Mary 52; St. John, N.B., 1859 ***5704.8*** *p140*
Logan, Mary A.; America, 1865 ***5704.8*** *p193*
Logan, Nancy 30; Wilmington, DE, 1831 ***6508.7*** *p161*
Logan, Patrick; New York, NY, 1838 ***8208.4*** *p74*
Logan, Patrick; Philadelphia, 1864 ***5704.8*** *p175*
Logan, Rebecca *SEE* Logan, Thomas
Logan, Rebecca; Philadelphia, 1849 ***5704.8*** *p53*
Logan, Robert 20; Philadelphia, 1859 ***5704.8*** *p142*
Logan, Robert 60; St. John, N.B., 1859 ***5704.8*** *p140*
Logan, Robt. 1; Wilmington, DE, 1831 ***6508.7*** *p161*
Logan, Robt 30; Wilmington, DE, 1831 ***6508.7*** *p161*
Logan, Robt 54; Wilmington, DE, 1831 ***6508.7*** *p161*
Logan, Samuel; America, 1867 ***5704.8*** *p223*
Logan, Susan; New York, NY, 1864 ***5704.8*** *p172*
Logan, Thady; America, 1735-1743 ***4971*** *p78*
Logan, Thomas; New York, NY, 1815 ***2859.11*** *p35*
Logan, Thomas; Philadelphia, 1849 ***53.26*** *p46*
*Relative:*Rebecca
Logan, Thomas; Philadelphia, 1849 ***5704.8*** *p53*
Logan, Thomas 21; Massachusetts, 1848 ***5881.1*** *p61*
Logan, William; New York, NY, 1864 ***5704.8*** *p172*
Logan, William; Philadelphia, 1852 ***5704.8*** *p85*
Logan, William; Philadelphia, 1852 ***5704.8*** *p88*
Logan, William; St. John, N.B., 1850 ***5704.8*** *p66*
Logan, William 25; St. John, N.B., 1859 ***5704.8*** *p140*
Logemeier, William 30; Kentucky, 1859 ***1450.2*** *p89A*
Logenmann, John 25; Kansas, 1882 ***5240.1*** *p27*
Logenmann, John 25; Kansas, 1882 ***5240.1*** *p64*
Loghan, Bemard; America, 1850 ***1450.2*** *p89A*
Loghran, Patrick; Quebec, 1820 ***7603*** *p81*
Logney, Mary; New York, NY, 1866 ***5704.8*** *p213*
Logordia, Jose 48; Arizona, 1920 ***9228.40*** *p24*
Logue, Ann 14; Quebec, 1850 ***5704.8*** *p63*
Logue, Ann 31; Quebec, 1854 ***5704.8*** *p118*
Logue, Ann Jane 19; Philadelphia, 1864 ***5704.8*** *p157*
Logue, Anne 16; Philadelphia, 1859 ***5704.8*** *p141*
Logue, Bernard; New York, NY, 1866 ***5704.8*** *p210*
Logue, Bernard 15 *SEE* Logue, John
Logue, Biddy; Philadelphia, 1811 ***2859.11*** *p15*
Logue, Biddy; St. John, N.B., 1847 ***5704.8*** *p35*
Logue, Catharine; Philadelphia, 1864 ***5704.8*** *p178*
Logue, Catharine; St. John, N.B., 1847 ***5704.8*** *p15*
Logue, Daniel; Philadelphia, 1850 ***5704.8*** *p64*
Logue, Edward; St. John, N.B., 1849 ***5704.8*** *p56*
Logue, Eleanor; Quebec, 1850 ***5704.8*** *p63*
Logue, Elizabeth; New York, NY, 1869 ***5704.8*** *p234*
Logue, Ellan; Philadelphia, 1849 ***5704.8*** *p54*
Logue, Ellen; Philadelphia, 1849 ***53.26*** *p46*
*Relative:*Mary Jane
Logue, Fanny 18; St. John, N.B., 1863 ***5704.8*** *p153*
Logue, Felix; St. John, N.B., 1847 ***5704.8*** *p15*
Logue, Grace; New York, NY, 1871 ***5704.8*** *p240*
Logue, Hanah; Quebec, 1849 ***5704.8*** *p57*
Logue, Hannah; America, 1869 ***5704.8*** *p232*
Logue, Hugh; Philadelphia, 1867 ***5704.8*** *p212*
Logue, Hugh; St. John, N.B., 1847 ***5704.8*** *p33*
Logue, Isabella; New York, NY, 1864 ***5704.8*** *p173*
Logue, James; New York, NY, 1864 ***5704.8*** *p182*
Logue, James; New York, NY, 1869 ***5704.8*** *p234*
Logue, James; Philadelphia, 1811 ***53.26*** *p46*
Logue, James; Philadelphia, 1811 ***2859.11*** *p15*
Logue, James; Philadelphia, 1848 ***53.26*** *p46*
Logue, James; Philadelphia, 1853 ***5704.8*** *p100*
Logue, James; Philadelphia, 1853 ***5704.8*** *p101*
Logue, James; Quebec, 1849 ***5704.8*** *p57*
Logue, James; St. John, N.B., 1847 ***5704.8*** *p34*
Logue, James 6; Quebec, 1849 ***5704.8*** *p57*
Logue, Jane 8; Quebec, 1850 ***5704.8*** *p63*
Logue, John *SEE* Logue, William
Logue, John; Philadelphia, 1849 ***5704.8*** *p50*
Logue, John 9; Quebec, 1854 ***5704.8*** *p118*
Logue, John 12; Quebec, 1849 ***5704.8*** *p57*
Logue, John 18; Philadelphia, 1833-1834 ***53.26*** *p46*
*Relative:*Bernard 15
Logue, John 24; Philadelphia, 1860 ***5704.8*** *p144*
Logue, John 26; Philadelphia, 1860 ***5704.8*** *p146*
Logue, Kate; New York, NY, 1868 ***5704.8*** *p227*
Logue, Margaret; America, 1865 ***5704.8*** *p199*
Logue, Margaret; Philadelphia, 1867 ***5704.8*** *p212*
Logue, Margaret; Philadelphia, 1867 ***5704.8*** *p213*
Logue, Margaret; St. John, N.B., 1847 ***5704.8*** *p26*
Logue, Margaret 15; Quebec, 1854 ***5704.8*** *p118*
Logue, Mary; America, 1868 ***5704.8*** *p231*
Logue, Mary; New York, NY, 1864 ***5704.8*** *p173*
Logue, Mary; New York, NY, 1869 ***5704.8*** *p232*
Logue, Mary; Philadelphia, 1811 ***2859.11*** *p15*
Logue, Mary; St. John, N.B., 1847 ***5704.8*** *p26*
Logue, Mary Jane *SEE* Logue, Ellen
Logue, Mary Jane; Philadelphia, 1849 ***5704.8*** *p54*
Logue, Michael; America, 1869 ***5704.8*** *p232*
Logue, Michael; Quebec, 1850 ***5704.8*** *p63*
Logue, Nancy 9; Quebec, 1849 ***5704.8*** *p57*
Logue, Neal; St. John, N.B., 1852 ***5704.8*** *p83*
Logue, Neal 4; Quebec, 1849 ***5704.8*** *p57*
Logue, Patrick; New York, NY, 1864 ***5704.8*** *p173*
Logue, Patrick; Philadelphia, 1853 ***5704.8*** *p101*
Logue, Patrick; St. John, N.B., 1852 ***5704.8*** *p83*
Logue, Patrick 6; Quebec, 1850 ***5704.8*** *p63*
Logue, Patrick 21; St. John, N.B., 1858 ***5704.8*** *p137*
Logue, Philip; Philadelphia, 1866 ***5704.8*** *p210*
Logue, Rebecca; Philadelphia, 1853 ***5704.8*** *p100*
Logue, Robert; Philadelphia, 1848 ***53.26*** *p46*
Logue, Robert; Philadelphia, 1848 ***5704.8*** *p40*
Logue, Rosanna 6; Philadelphia, 1853 ***5704.8*** *p111*
Logue, Sarah; St. John, N.B., 1847 ***5704.8*** *p33*
Logue, Susan; New York, NY, 1865 ***5704.8*** *p193*
Logue, Thomas; Philadelphia, 1864 ***5704.8*** *p171*
Logue, William; New York, NY, 1868 ***5704.8*** *p227*
Logue, William; Philadelphia, 1811 ***53.26*** *p46*
Logue, William; Philadelphia, 1849 ***53.26*** *p46*
*Relative:*John
Logue, William; Philadelphia, 1849 ***53.26*** *p46*
Logue, William; Philadelphia, 1849 ***5704.8*** *p50*
Logue, William; Philadelphia, 1867 ***5704.8*** *p217*
Logue, William 11; Quebec, 1850 ***5704.8*** *p63*
Logue, William 12; Quebec, 1854 ***5704.8*** *p118*
Logue, Wm.; Philadelphia, 1811 ***2859.11*** *p15*
Lohheide, Heinrich Wilhelm; America, 1853 ***4610.10*** *p156*
Lohkamp, Marie Christine Hedwig; America, 1834 ***4610.10*** *p119*
Lohman, Charles; New York, NY, 1836 ***8208.4*** *p13*
Lohman, Frederick; America, 1838 ***1450.2*** *p89A*
Lohman, Job; Illinois, 1860 ***5012.39*** *p90*
Lohman, William; New York, NY, 1836 ***8208.4*** *p15*
Lohmann, . . .; Canada, 1776-1783 ***9786*** *p28*
Lohmeyer, Johann Friedrich *SEE* Lohmeyer, Karl Heinrich
Lohmeyer, Karl Heinrich; America, 1834 ***4610.10*** *p119*
*Father:*Johann Friedrich
*Mother:*Marie C. H. Lohkamp
Lohmeyer, Marie C. H. Lohkamp *SEE* Lohmeyer, Karl Heinrich
Lohmiller, Theodor; America, 1850 ***8582.2*** *p24*
Lohneisen, v., Capit.; Quebec, 1776 ***9786*** *p104*
Lohneysen, Albrecht Daniel; Quebec, 1776 ***9786*** *p261*
Lohoff, Ernst Friedrich Wilhelm; America, 1869 ***4610.10*** *p100*
Lohoff, Heinrich Friedrich Wilhelm; America, 1869 ***4610.10*** *p159*
Lohr, . . .; Canada, 1776-1783 ***9786*** *p42*
Lohr, Jakob 26; America, 1853 ***9162.8*** *p37*
Lohr, Magdalena 58; America, 1853 ***9162.8*** *p37*
Lohrman, Fred; Indiana, 1898 ***1450.2*** *p89A*
Lohrmann, Margareta Diether *SEE* Lohrmann, Peter
Lohrmann, Peter; Philadelphia, 1737 ***9898*** *p42*
*Wife:*Margareta Diether
Lohry, Joseph 29; West Virginia, 1898 ***9788.3*** *p14*
Lo Iacono, Frank; Arkansas, 1918 ***95.2*** *p75*
Loiseau, . . .; Canada, 1776-1783 ***9786*** *p28*
Loiseau, Mr. 26; America, 1838 ***778.5*** *p345*
Loisel, Marguerite; Quebec, 1790 ***7603*** *p37*
Loison, Frd. 27; America, 1839 ***778.5*** *p345*
Lokowski, Walter; Arkansas, 1918 ***95.2*** *p76*
Loley, Honora 20; Massachusetts, 1849 ***5881.1*** *p58*
Loll, William 31; Kansas, 1889 ***5240.1*** *p73*
Loly, Honora 20; Massachusetts, 1850 ***5881.1*** *p90*
Loman, Frederick; America, 1838 ***1450.2*** *p89A*
Loman, John; New York, NY, 1836 ***8208.4*** *p15*
Loman, Joshua 17; Maryland, 1719 ***3690.1*** *p143*
Loman, Louise; Indianapolis, 1867 ***3702.7*** *p578*
Lomas, Matthew Wainwright; Illinois, 1869 ***5012.38*** *p99*
Lomas, William 33; Jamaica, 1774 ***1219.7*** *p223*
Lomax, Stephen 17; Maryland, 1719 ***3690.1*** *p143*
Lomax, Thomas 18; Maryland, 1719 ***3690.1*** *p143*
Lombar, Antoine 30; New Orleans, 1826 ***778.5*** *p345*
Lombard, . . .; New Orleans, 1821 ***778.5*** *p346*
Lombard, Mme.; New Orleans, 1821 ***778.5*** *p346*
Lombard, Mr. 25; New Orleans, 1823 ***778.5*** *p345*
Lombard, Mr. 45; New Orleans, 1821 ***778.5*** *p345*
Lombard, Adolphe 24; America, 1826 ***778.5*** *p346*
Lombard, Ann; America, 1736 ***4971*** *p44*
Lombard, Ann; America, 1736 ***4971*** *p45*
Lombard, Etienne 39; New Orleans, 1836 ***778.5*** *p346*
Lombard, G. 28; New Orleans, 1826 ***778.5*** *p346*
Lombard, Leonard 29; Port uncertain, 1836 ***778.5*** *p346*
Lombard, Sebastino; Colorado, 1904 ***9678.2*** *p124*
Lombardi, Luigi 30?; Arizona, 1890 ***2764.35*** *p42*
Lombardo, Antoni; Arkansas, 1918 ***95.2*** *p76*
Lomel, Mr. 42; New Orleans, 1837 ***778.5*** *p346*
Lomes, Richard 21; Philadelphia, 1774 ***1219.7*** *p212*
Lommas, Ewen 21; Maryland or Virginia, 1699 ***2212*** *p21*
Lomseck, Simon; Wisconsin, n.d. ***9675.6*** *p267*
Lonagan, Catherine; Quebec, 1825 ***7603*** *p96*
Londe, Louis; Arkansas, 1918 ***95.2*** *p76*
London, Humphrey; Virginia, 1639 ***6219*** *p161*
London, John; Virginia, 1636 ***6219*** *p13*
London, John; Virginia, 1637 ***6219*** *p83*
London, Richard 14; Pennsylvania, 1719 ***3690.1*** *p143*
Londre, Joseph 27; Port uncertain, 1836 ***778.5*** *p346*
Lone, Elizabeth 21; Virginia, 1774 ***1219.7*** *p241*
Lonergan, John; Wisconsin, n.d. ***9675.6*** *p267*
Lonergan, Patrick; Wisconsin, n.d. ***9675.6*** *p267*

Lones, Nicolas; Illinois, 1894 *5012.40 p53*
Lonet, Bernard 32; Dominican Republic, 1822 *778.5 p346*
Long, Alexander 19; Philadelphia, 1857 *5704.8 p132*
Long, Andrew; St. John, N.B., 1847 *5704.8 p9*
Long, Aneslie Edward; Washington, 1859-1920 *2872.1 p24*
Long, Ann; Virginia, 1633 *6219 p31*
Long, Annti William; Washington, 1859-1920 *2872.1 p24*
Long, Bertha Helen; Washington, 1859-1920 *2872.1 p24*
Long, Betty 45; Quebec, 1855 *5704.8 p125*
Long, Catharine 48; Massachusetts, 1847 *5881.1 p57*
Long, Charles 9; Quebec, 1856 *5704.8 p129*
Long, Eliza; Philadelphia, 1866 *5704.8 p210*
Long, Eliza Jane; St. John, N.B., 1853 *5704.8 p109*
Long, Elizabeth; America, 1740 *4971 p15*
Long, Elizabeth; Maryland, 1740 *4971 p91*
Long, Elizabeth; Philadelphia, 1741 *4971 p92*
Long, Elizabeth 22; Maryland, 1775 *1219.7 p257*
Long, Fanny; Philadelphia, 1848 *53.26 p46*
Long, Fanny; Philadelphia, 1848 *5704.8 p45*
Long, George 22; Maryland, 1774 *1219.7 p187*
Long, Grace 8; New York, NY, 1864 *5704.8 p169*
Long, Heikki Wester; Washington, 1859-1920 *2872.1 p24*
Long, Henry; New York, NY, 1838 *8208.4 p85*
Long, Henry 23; Virginia, 1774 *1219.7 p201*
Long, Isabella; Quebec, 1850 *5704.8 p67*
Long, Jacob 26; Jamaica, 1730 *3690.1 p143*
Long, James; New Orleans, 1848 *5704.8 p48*
Long, James; Virginia, 1629 *6219 p8*
Long, James; Virginia, 1642 *6219 p188*
Long, James 8; Massachusetts, 1847 *5881.1 p58*
Long, James 15; Quebec, 1856 *5704.8 p129*
Long, James 20; Quebec, 1856 *5704.8 p130*
Long, James 25; Philadelphia, 1865 *5704.8 p164*
Long, James 30; Philadelphia, 1857 *5704.8 p132*
Long, Jane; Philadelphia, 1864 *5704.8 p173*
Long, Jane; St. John, N.B., 1847 *5704.8 p20*
Long, Jane 45; Quebec, 1856 *5704.8 p129*
Long, Jeremiah; Burlington, VT, 1836 *1450.2 p90A*
Long, John *SEE* Long, Robert
Long, John; America, 1737 *4971 p13*
Long, John; America, 1740 *4971 p28*
Long, John; America, 1741 *4971 p41*
Long, John; Virginia, 1858 *4626.16 p17*
Long, John 23; Maryland, 1774 *1219.7 p230*
Long, John 27; Jamaica, 1733 *3690.1 p143*
Long, John 47; Quebec, 1856 *5704.8 p129*
Long, John Conrad; America, 1848 *1450.2 p89A*
Long, Jon.; Virginia, 1629 *6219 p8*
Long, Jon.; Virginia, 1637 *6219 p113*
Long, Joseph; America, 1834 *1450.2 p90A*
Long, Joseph; New York, NY, 1816 *2859.11 p35*
Long, Lawrence 22; Massachusetts, 1849 *5881.1 p59*
Long, Lewis; Virginia, 1639 *6219 p152*
Long, Lydia Mary; Washington, 1859-1920 *2872.1 p24*
Long, Margaret; New York, NY, 1864 *5704.8 p173*
Long, Margaret 26; Quebec, 1855 *5704.8 p125*
Long, Mary; America, 1742 *4971 p17*
Long, Mary; St. John, N.B., 1847 *5704.8 p18*
Long, Mary 45; Massachusetts, 1847 *5881.1 p60*
Long, Mary Ann 8; Quebec, 1856 *5704.8 p129*
Long, Mathew 11; Quebec, 1856 *5704.8 p129*
Long, Matty; Philadelphia, 1853 *5704.8 p111*
Long, Michael; Philadelphia, 1762 *9973.7 p37*
Long, Michael; Philadelphia, 1832 *9892.11 p27*
Long, Michael 7; Massachusetts, 1847 *5881.1 p60*
Long, Michael 25; Massachusetts, 1849 *5881.1 p60*
Long, Michael 57; Massachusetts, 1849 *5881.1 p60*
Long, Murty; Nevada, 1879 *2764.35 p40*
Long, Nick; Washington, 1859-1920 *2872.1 p24*
Long, Patrick; America, 1738 *4971 p13*
Long, Ralph; Virginia, 1648 *6219 p122*
Long, Richard; St. John, N.B., 1851 *5704.8 p78*
Long, Richard; St. John, N.B., 1853 *5704.8 p107*
Long, Richard; Virginia, 1642 *6219 p186*
Long, Richard 9; Massachusetts, 1847 *5881.1 p61*
Long, Richard 14; Massachusetts, 1847 *5881.1 p61*
Long, Richard 20; Jamaica, 1723 *3690.1 p143*
Long, Robert *SEE* Long, Robert
Long, Robert; Virginia, 1643 *6219 p204*
  With wife
  *Son:*Robert
  *Son:*John
Long, Robert 21; Maryland, 1774 *1219.7 p191*
Long, Robert 23; Quebec, 1855 *5704.8 p125*
Long, Robert 45; Quebec, 1855 *5704.8 p125*
Long, Samuel 28; Maryland, 1774 *1219.7 p221*
Long, Susan 20; Philadelphia, 1859 *5704.8 p142*
Long, Tho.; Virginia, 1638 *6219 p147*

Long, Thomas; New York, NY, 1811 *2859.11 p15*
  With family
Long, Viola Sylvia; Washington, 1859-1920 *2872.1 p24*
Long, William; New York, NY, 1816 *2859.11 p35*
Long, William; Philadelphia, 1849 *53.26 p46*
Long, William; Philadelphia, 1849 *5704.8 p53*
Long, William; Washington, 1859-1920 *2872.1 p24*
Long, William 12; Massachusetts, 1847 *5881.1 p61*
Long, William C.; Washington, 1859-1920 *2872.1 p24*
Long, Wm.; Virginia, 1637 *6219 p13*
Long, Wm.; Virginia, 1644 *6219 p208*
Long, Wm.; Virginia, 1648 *6219 p251*
Longan, James; St. John, N.B., 1849 *5704.8 p56*
Longanne, Adolph D. 19; New Orleans, 1822 *778.5 p346*
Longbine, George; Indiana, 1836 *9117 p15*
Longbottom, Edwin 33; Kansas, 1873 *5240.1 p54*
Longe, Fanny *SEE* Longe, Michael
Longe, Fanny; Philadelphia, 1847 *5704.8 p23*
Longe, Grace *SEE* Longe, Neal
Longe, Grace; Philadelphia, 1847 *5704.8 p23*
Longe, Grace 5 *SEE* Longe, Michael
Longe, Grace 5; Philadelphia, 1847 *5704.8 p23*
Longe, James 13 *SEE* Longe, Michael
Longe, James 13; Philadelphia, 1847 *5704.8 p23*
Longe, Mary 10 *SEE* Longe, Michael
Longe, Mary 10; Philadelphia, 1847 *5704.8 p23*
Longe, Michael; Philadelphia, 1847 *53.26 p46*
  *Relative:*Fanny
  *Relative:*James 13
  *Relative:*Mary 10
  *Relative:*Patrick 8
  *Relative:*Grace 5
  *Relative:*Nelly 3
  *Relative:*Nancy 1
Longe, Michael; Philadelphia, 1847 *5704.8 p23*
Longe, Nancy 1 *SEE* Longe, Michael
Longe, Nancy 1; Philadelphia, 1847 *5704.8 p23*
Longe, Neal *SEE* Longe, Neal
Longe, Neal; Philadelphia, 1847 *53.26 p46*
  *Relative:*Paddy
  *Relative:*Grace
  *Relative:*Neal
  *Relative:*Thomas
Longe, Neal; Philadelphia, 1847 *5704.8 p23*
Longe, Nelly 3 *SEE* Longe, Michael
Longe, Nelly 3; Philadelphia, 1847 *5704.8 p23*
Longe, Paddy *SEE* Longe, Neal
Longe, Paddy; Philadelphia, 1847 *5704.8 p23*
Longe, Patrick 8 *SEE* Longe, Michael
Longe, Patrick 8; Philadelphia, 1847 *5704.8 p23*
Longe, Thomas *SEE* Longe, Neal
Longe, Thomas; Philadelphia, 1847 *5704.8 p23*
Longeneker, Ernst; Kansas, 1887 *5240.1 p28*
Longes, P. 31; America, 1838 *778.5 p346*
Longest, Daniel 40; Maryland, 1775 *1219.7 p254*
Longford, Joseph 23; North Carolina, 1736 *3690.1 p143*
Longheld, Philip; Virginia, 1636 *6219 p21*
Longhman, Anthony; America, 1838 *1450.2 p90A*
Longhurst, Elizabeth *SEE* Longhurst, John
Longhurst, John; New York, NY, 1838 *8208.4 p85*
Longhurst, John; Pennsylvania, 1682 *4961 p240*
  *Wife:*Mary
  *Daughter:*Elizabeth
  *Son:*John, Jr.
  *Child:*Sarah
  With son-in-law
Longhurst, John, Jr. *SEE* Longhurst, John
Longhurst, Mary *SEE* Longhurst, John
Longhurst, Sarah *SEE* Longhurst, John
Longile, . . .; Halifax, N.S., 1752 *7074.6 p230*
Longis, P. 31; America, 1838 *778.5 p346*
Longlands, Percy 21; Kansas, 1876 *5240.1 p57*
Longley, Andrew R.; New York, NY, 1839 *8208.4 p98*
Longman, Robert; New York, NY, 1815 *2859.11 p35*
Longmore, James; America, 1739 *4971 p66*
Longmore, Maud; Washington, 1859-1920 *2872.1 p24*
Longoni, Antonio; Arkansas, 1918 *95.2 p76*
Longrave, Winifrid; Virginia, 1636 *6219 p32*
Longust, Reuben 35; Virginia, 1774 *1219.7 p240*
Longwood, William 23; Philadelphia, 1775 *1219.7 p258*
Longworths, Mr.; Quebec, 1815 *9229.18 p78*
Longworthy, John; Virginia, 1648 *6219 p110*
Lonsdale, George 20; St. Christopher, 1722 *3690.1 p143*
Lonsdale, William 16; Massachusetts, 1850 *5881.1 p62*
Lontilhac, J. 24; Port uncertain, 1839 *778.5 p346*
Lonx, . . .; Canada, 1776-1783 *9786 p28*
Lony, Frederic 30; America, 1829 *778.5 p347*
Loober, Peter 20; Massachusetts, 1849 *5881.1 p61*
Looby, John; America, 1736-1743 *4971 p40*
Looch, Michael; South Carolina, 1788 *7119 p200*
Looker, Benjamin 24; Maryland, 1774 *1219.7 p208*
Lookin, Eliza 50; Massachusetts, 1849 *5881.1 p58*

Lookin, John; Arkansas, 1918 *95.2 p76*
Loomey, Mary 20; Massachusetts, 1849 *5881.1 p60*
Loon, Daniel 28; Massachusetts, 1848 *5881.1 p58*
Looney, Catharine; Philadelphia, 1849 *5704.8 p55*
Looney, Catherine *SEE* Looney, Christopher
Looney, Christopher; Philadelphia, 1849 *53.26 p47*
  *Relative:*Catherine
  *Relative:*Christopher 9
  *Relative:*Hugh 7
  *Relative:*Michael 5
  *Relative:*John 3
Looney, Christopher; Philadelphia, 1849 *5704.8 p55*
Looney, Christopher 9 *SEE* Looney, Christopher
Looney, Christopher 9; Philadelphia, 1849 *5704.8 p55*
Looney, Ellen 22; Massachusetts, 1849 *5881.1 p58*
Looney, Hugh 7 *SEE* Looney, Christopher
Looney, Hugh 7; Philadelphia, 1849 *5704.8 p55*
Looney, James; Massachusetts, 1849 *5881.1 p59*
Looney, James 60; Massachusetts, 1850 *5881.1 p59*
Looney, John 3 *SEE* Looney, Christopher
Looney, John 3; Philadelphia, 1849 *5704.8 p55*
Looney, John Thomas; Arkansas, 1918 *95.2 p76*
Looney, Michael 5 *SEE* Looney, Christopher
Looney, Michael 5; Philadelphia, 1849 *5704.8 p55*
Loonis, Charles 20; Quebec, 1856 *5704.8 p130*
Loony, Anne; New York, NY, 1815 *2859.11 p35*
Loos, Col.; New York, 1776 *9786 p278*
Loos, Alexander; America, 1852 *8582.3 p42*
Loos, Johann August von; Canada, 1780 *9786 p181*
Loos, Johann August von; Canada, 1780 *9786 p268*
Loos, Johann August von; New York, 1776 *9786 p268*
Loose, William; Wisconsin, n.d. *9675.6 p267*
Loots, Catharina *SEE* Loots, Matthaeus
Loots, Johannes *SEE* Loots, Matthaeus
Loots, Matthaeus; Pennsylvania, 1754 *2444 p186*
  *Wife:*Catharina
  *Child:*Johannes
Lopakka, Gustof; Washington, 1859-1920 *2872.1 p24*
Lopata, George; Pennsylvania, 1900 *7137 p169*
Lopes, Francis; Virginia, 1844 *4626.16 p12*
Lopes, John; Virginia, 1856 *4626.16 p15*
Lopez, Antonio 27; Arizona, 1924 *9228.40 p28*
Lopez, Candalads 23; Arizona, 1903 *9228.40 p7*
Lopez, Ignacio; Arkansas, 1918 *95.2 p76*
Lopez, Jesus 50; Arizona, 1922 *9228.40 p26*
Lopez, Jose M. 38; Arizona, 1914 *9228.40 p18*
Lopez, Manuel 70; Arizona, 1923 *9228.40 p27*
Lopez, Marie 22; Arizona, 1922 *9228.40 p26*
Lopez, Ramona 27; Arizona, 1926 *9228.40 p30*
Lopnow, John; Milwaukee, 1875 *2764.35 p42*
Lops, Ambrose 26; Maryland, 1775 *1219.7 p252*
Loram, Symon; Virginia, 1635 *6219 p20*
Lorang, Mr. 30; Louisiana, 1825 *778.5 p347*
Lorang, John; Wisconsin, n.d. *9675.6 p267*
Lorantos, George; Arkansas, 1918 *95.2 p76*
Lorcan, James; America, 1738 *4971 p75*
Lord, Dorothy; America, 1742 *4971 p17*
Lord, George 30; America, 1705 *2212 p43*
Lord, James; America, 1740 *4971 p15*
Lord, Richard 15; Maryland, 1775 *1219.7 p264*
Lorence, Joseph; Wisconsin, n.d. *9675.6 p267*
Lorensen, . . .; Canada, 1776-1783 *9786 p42*
Lorensen, Loren A. 28; Kansas, 1904 *5240.1 p83*
Lorenson, Martin P.; Kansas, 1874 *5240.1 p28*
Lorentz, Charles; Bangor, ME, 1868-1879 *6410.22 p115*
Lorentz, Joseph; Nevada, 1872 *2764.35 p42*
Lorenz, Emil; America, 1882 *5240.1 p28*
Lorenz, Johann Gottfried 31; New Orleans, 1839 *9420.2 p68*
Lorenz, Johann Heinrich 22; Kansas, 1873 *5240.1 p28*
Lorenz, Johann Henrich; Kansas, 1873 *5240.1 p28*
Lorenz, Johanne Christine 10; New Orleans, 1839 *9420.2 p68*
Lorenz, John; Illinois, 1876 *2896.5 p25*
Lorenz, John Henry 22; Kansas, 1873 *5240.1 p54*
Lorenz, Joseph; Wisconsin, n.d. *9675.6 p267*
Lorenz, Philipp; America, 1852 *8582.3 p42*
Lorenz, Rosine 28; New Orleans, 1839 *9420.2 p68*
Lorenz, Wally; Wisconsin, n.d. *9675.6 p267*
Lorenze, Joseph; Wisconsin, n.d. *9675.6 p267*
Lorenzen, . . .; Canada, 1776-1783 *9786 p42*
Lorethe, Mr. 40; America, 1838 *778.5 p347*
Lorge, John; Wisconsin, n.d. *9675.6 p267*
Lorge, Peter; Wisconsin, n.d. *9675.6 p267*
Lorianx, Joseph; Kansas, 1911 *6013.40 p16*
Lorillard, Anne *SEE* Lorillard, Jean-Christophe
Lorillard, Elisabeth *SEE* Lorillard, Jean-Christophe
Lorillard, George *SEE* Lorillard, Jean-Christophe
Lorillard, Jean-Christophe; Halifax, N.S., 1749 *7074.6 p213*
  *Wife:*Anne
  *Child:*Elisabeth

*Child:*Jean-Henri
*Child:*George
Lorillard, Jean-Henri *SEE* Lorillard, Jean-Christophe
Lorince, Mike Paul; Arkansas, 1918 ***95.2*** *p76*
Loris, Mad. 35; New Orleans, 1837 ***778.5*** *p347*
Loronio, Jesus 65; Arizona, 1926 ***9228.40*** *p30*
Lorontos, George 27; Arkansas, 1918 ***95.2*** *p76*
Lorran, Clementine 2; America, 1839 ***778.5*** *p347*
Lorran, Josephine 35; America, 1839 ***778.5*** *p347*
Lorran, Louis 30; America, 1839 ***778.5*** *p347*
Lorrimore, George 21; Maryland, 1773 ***1219.7*** *p173*
Lory, Mr. 50; America, 1839 ***778.5*** *p347*
Lory, John 32; Kansas, 1894 ***5240.1*** *p79*
Lorymore, Thomas; Virginia, 1646 ***6219*** *p238*
Los, Andrew; Arkansas, 1918 ***95.2*** *p76*
Losaker, Joseph; Wisconsin, n.d. ***9675.6*** *p267*
Loschen, Harm; Illinois, 1894 ***5012.40*** *p53*
Loser, Anna Margaretha; Port uncertain, 1754 ***2444*** *p153*
Loser, David M. 27; Kansas, 1879 ***5240.1*** *p60*
Losh, Stephen; Virginia, 1638 ***6219*** *p125*
Losin, Loder; New York, NY, 1836 ***8208.4*** *p23*
Losiph, Thomas 20; Texas, 1839 ***778.5*** *p347*
Loskiel, . . .; America, 1700-1877 ***8582.3*** *p80*
Lossberg, von; New York, 1776 ***9786*** *p278*
Lossetti, Louis; Colorado, 1904 ***9678.2*** *p124*
Losteray, Miss 26; Port uncertain, 1838 ***778.5*** *p347*
Lotarski, Charles; Colorado, 1887 ***9678.2*** *p124*
Lotherer, . . .; Canada, 1776-1783 ***9786*** *p28*
Lothmann, John Ferdinand; Arkansas, 1918 ***95.2*** *p76*
Lots, B. Otto; America, 1846 ***8582.3*** *p42*
Lots, Ernst; Cincinnati, 1847 ***3702.7*** *p85*
Lott, Friedrich; Ohio, 1869-1887 ***8582*** *p19*
Lottich, Conrad; Maryland, 1850-1865 ***3702.7*** *p205*
Lottich, Georg; America, 1851 ***3702.7*** *p205*
Lottich, Johannes; America, 1851 ***3702.7*** *p205*
Lottig, Conrad; Maryland, 1850-1865 ***3702.7*** *p205*
Lottig, Georg; America, 1851 ***3702.7*** *p205*
Lottig, Johannes; America, 1851 ***3702.7*** *p205*
Lotts, John 22; Maryland, 1725 ***3690.1*** *p143*
Lotz, . . .; Canada, 1776-1783 ***9786*** *p28*
Lotz, Anna Catharina; Pennsylvania, 1743 ***4525*** *p239*
Lotz, Fred William; Wisconsin, n.d. ***9675.6*** *p267*
Lotz, George; America, 1880 ***1450.2*** *p90A*
Lotz, Heinrich; Cincinnati, 1869-1887 ***8582*** *p19*
Lotz, Peter; Cincinnati, 1869-1887 ***8582*** *p20*
Lotze, Adolph; America, 1830 ***8582.2*** *p61*
Lotze, Adolphus; Cincinnati, 1869-1887 ***8582*** *p20*
Louailler, Madame 40; New Orleans, 1829 ***778.5*** *p347*
Louailler, Mr. 43; New Orleans, 1829 ***778.5*** *p347*
Louaillier, Mlle. 16; New Orleans, 1829 ***778.5*** *p347*
Loubart, J. 41; New Orleans, 1837 ***778.5*** *p347*
Loubet, Mme. 26; Port uncertain, 1839 ***778.5*** *p348*
Loubet, Mr. 32; Port uncertain, 1839 ***778.5*** *p347*
Louden, John; North Carolina, 1680-1830 ***1639.20*** *p114*
Louden, Leon; Iowa, 1866-1943 ***123.54*** *p31*
Louder, James; Virginia, 1648 ***6219*** *p250*
Louder, Rich.; Virginia, 1637 ***6219*** *p110*
Loudon, John Carl von; Philadelphia, 1756 ***8582.3*** *p95*
Loudon, Thomas 42; Arizona, 1890 ***2764.35*** *p40*
Louge, James; Philadelphia, 1848 ***5704.8*** *p40*
Louge, Thomas; Philadelphia, 1852 ***5704.8*** *p89*
Lough, Christian; Philadelphia, 1768 ***9973.7*** *p40*
Lough, Peter; Philadelphia, 1768 ***9973.7*** *p40*
Loughead, Cath.; Philadelphia, 1811 ***2859.11*** *p15*
Loughead, Catherine *SEE* Loughead, Edward
Loughead, Edward; Philadelphia, 1811 ***53.26*** *p47*
*Relative:*Catherine
Loughead, Edward; Philadelphia, 1811 ***2859.11*** *p15*
Loughead, Elizabeth 20; Philadelphia, 1854 ***5704.8*** *p117*
Loughead, Isabella 22; St. John, N.B., 1855 ***5704.8*** *p127*
Loughead, John; Philadelphia, 1852 ***5704.8*** *p85*
Loughead, Sophia; New York, NY, 1865 ***5704.8*** *p196*
Loughery, Ann 21; St. John, N.B., 1855 ***5704.8*** *p127*
Loughery, Bernard 21; St. John, N.B., 1860 ***5704.8*** *p143*
Loughery, Elizabeth 15; Philadelphia, 1854 ***5704.8*** *p117*
Loughery, Fanny 11; Philadelphia, 1854 ***5704.8*** *p117*
Loughery, James; Philadelphia, 1849 ***53.26*** *p47*
*Relative:*Margaret
Loughery, James 20; St. John, N.B., 1855 ***5704.8*** *p127*
Loughery, Jane; Philadelphia, 1870 ***5704.8*** *p239*
Loughery, Margaret *SEE* Loughery, James
Loughery, Mary; Philadelphia, 1870 ***5704.8*** *p239*
Loughery, Michael 24; Philadelphia, 1860 ***5704.8*** *p144*
Loughery, Sarah; New York, NY, 1869 ***5704.8*** *p233*
Loughlan, Mary; Quebec, 1851 ***5704.8*** *p75*
Loughlin, Eacy; Philadelphia, 1851 ***5704.8*** *p75*
Loughlin, Francis; New York, NY, 1870 ***5704.8*** *p238*
Loughlin, James; Maryland, 1742 ***4971*** *p107*
Loughlin, Jane 25; St. John, N.B., 1860 ***5704.8*** *p144*
Loughlin, John; New York, NY, 1836 ***8208.4*** *p24*
Loughlin, Margaret 25; Quebec, 1864 ***5704.8*** *p160*
Loughlin, Patrick; New York, NY, 1838 ***8208.4*** *p84*
Loughlin, William; New York, NY, 1870 ***5704.8*** *p238*
Loughnan, Martin; New York, NY, 1816 ***2859.11*** *p35*
Loughran, Catherine; St. John, N.B., 1853 ***5704.8*** *p107*
Loughran, Michael J.; Colorado, 1901 ***9678.2*** *p124*
Loughran, Owen; America, 1738 ***4971*** *p71*
Loughran, Patrick; Illinois, 1856 ***2896.5*** *p24*
Loughren, Michael; Wisconsin, n.d. ***9675.6*** *p267*
Loughrey, Ann; Philadelphia, 1852 ***5704.8*** *p97*
Loughrey, Edward; Philadelphia, 1851 ***5704.8*** *p76*
Loughrey, Eliza; Philadelphia, 1849 ***53.26*** *p47*
*Relative:*Jane
Loughrey, Eliza; Philadelphia, 1849 ***5704.8*** *p50*
Loughrey, Ellen; Philadelphia, 1851 ***5704.8*** *p76*
Loughrey, James; Philadelphia, 1849 ***5704.8*** *p49*
Loughrey, Jane *SEE* Loughrey, Eliza
Loughrey, Jane; Philadelphia, 1849 ***5704.8*** *p50*
Loughrey, Margaret; Philadelphia, 1849 ***5704.8*** *p49*
Loughrey, Mary; Philadelphia, 1851 ***5704.8*** *p71*
Loughrey, Mary; Quebec, 1848 ***5704.8*** *p42*
Loughrey, Thomas; Philadelphia, 1851 ***5704.8*** *p71*
Loughridge, Elizabeth 2 *SEE* Loughridge, William
Loughridge, James 5 *SEE* Loughridge, William
Loughridge, Jane 7 *SEE* Loughridge, William
Loughridge, Mg. 24 *SEE* Loughridge, William
Loughridge, William 30; Philadelphia, 1803 ***53.26*** *p47*
*Relative:*Mg. 24
*Relative:*Jane 7
*Relative:*Elizabeth 2
*Relative:*James 5
Loughry, Catherine; Philadelphia, 1852 ***5704.8*** *p87*
Loughry, Hugh; Philadelphia, 1852 ***5704.8*** *p87*
Loughry, Jane; Philadelphia, 1852 ***5704.8*** *p87*
Loughry, Louisa; Philadelphia, 1847 ***53.26*** *p47*
*Relative:*Mary Ann
Loughry, Louisa; Philadelphia, 1847 ***5704.8*** *p32*
Loughry, Mary; Philadelphia, 1852 ***5704.8*** *p87*
Loughry, Mary Ann *SEE* Loughry, Louisa
Loughry, Mary Ann; Philadelphia, 1847 ***5704.8*** *p32*
Loughry, Owen; Philadelphia, 1852 ***5704.8*** *p87*
Loughton, Leonard; Virginia, 1637 ***6219*** *p86*
Louing, Charles; Sorel, Que., 1774 ***7603*** *p25*
Louis, Mr. 40; New Orleans, 1837 ***778.5*** *p348*
Louis, Mr. 45; America, 1839 ***778.5*** *p348*
Louis, Andre 30; New Orleans, 1831 ***778.5*** *p348*
Louis, Bender; New York, NY, 1838 ***8208.4*** *p67*
Louis, Henry 50; Arizona, 1909 ***9228.40*** *p12*
Louis, Jacques 27; Port uncertain, 1835 ***778.5*** *p348*
Louis, Jean 5; America, 1832 ***778.5*** *p348*
Louis, Jean Florant 35; America, 1832 ***778.5*** *p348*
Louis, Margueritte 30; America, 1832 ***778.5*** *p348*
Louis, Marie 2; America, 1832 ***778.5*** *p348*
Louisa, Miss 1; Louisiana, 1822 ***778.5*** *p348*
Louisette, Peter L. 49; America, 1820 ***778.5*** *p348*
Louistaman, Jno.; Shreveport, LA, 1879 ***7129*** *p45*
Loukouen, John Gust; Colorado, 1895 ***9678.2*** *p124*
Loumaide, H. 33; New Orleans, 1837 ***778.5*** *p348*
Loumarche, Mr. 30; America, 1838 ***778.5*** *p349*
Loumide, H. 25; America, 1829 ***778.5*** *p349*
Lounsbury, Amelia Cath. 11; Massachusetts, 1850 ***5881.1*** *p57*
Lounsbury, Andrew 2; Massachusetts, 1850 ***5881.1*** *p57*
Lounsbury, Daniel 6; Massachusetts, 1850 ***5881.1*** *p58*
Lounsbury, Mary 28; Massachusetts, 1850 ***5881.1*** *p61*
Lounsbury, Sarah 4; Massachusetts, 1848 ***5881.1*** *p61*
Loupe, Anna Barbara 6 *SEE* Loupe, George
Loupe, George; South Carolina, 1752-1753 ***3689.17*** *p22*
*Relative:*Anna Barbara 6
Louq, Anna 51; America, 1831 ***778.5*** *p349*
Louq, Barbara 11; America, 1831 ***778.5*** *p349*
Louq, Catharine 22; America, 1831 ***778.5*** *p349*
Louq, John 22; America, 1838 ***778.5*** *p349*
Louq, Peter 16; America, 1831 ***778.5*** *p349*
Louq, Peter 54; America, 1831 ***778.5*** *p349*
Louquet, . . .; Port uncertain, 1839 ***778.5*** *p349*
Louquet, Jean; Port uncertain, 1839 ***778.5*** *p349*
Lour, Wm.; Virginia, 1647 ***6219*** *p241*
Loushan, Mr.; Port uncertain, 1839 ***778.5*** *p349*
Lousser, Mich; Philadelphia, 1756 ***4525*** *p262*
Loutit, Thomas; Savannah, GA, 1774 ***1219.7*** *p227*
Loutz, George; Philadelphia, 1759 ***9973.7*** *p33*
Loux, . . .; Canada, 1776-1783 ***9786*** *p28*
Love, Abraham 23; Jamaica, 1733 ***3690.1*** *p143*
Love, Alexander; New York, NY, 1816 ***2859.11*** *p35*
Love, Andrew; Quebec, 1852 ***5704.8*** *p97*
Love, Ann 18; Philadelphia, 1853 ***5704.8*** *p111*
Love, Ann 40; St. John, N.B., 1862 ***5704.8*** *p151*
Love, Anne; New York, NY, 1815 ***2859.11*** *p35*
Love, Anne 9; St. John, N.B., 1849 ***5704.8*** *p48*
Love, Catharine; Philadelphia, 1867 ***5704.8*** *p216*
Love, Edward; San Francisco, 1850 ***4914.15*** *p10*
Love, Edward; San Francisco, 1850 ***4914.15*** *p13*
Love, Eliza 13; Quebec, 1857 ***5704.8*** *p135*
Love, Elizabeth; Philadelphia, 1852 ***5704.8*** *p92*
Love, Hester; Philadelphia, 1864 ***5704.8*** *p176*
Love, Isabella 20; St. John, N.B., 1862 ***5704.8*** *p150*
Love, James; New York, NY, 1811 ***2859.11*** *p15*
Love, John 13; Quebec, 1853 ***5704.8*** *p105*
Love, Jon.; Virginia, 1637 ***6219*** *p107*
Love, Maggie; New York, NY, 1869 ***5704.8*** *p233*
Love, Margaret; Philadelphia, 1864 ***5704.8*** *p183*
Love, Margaret 22; Maryland, 1775 ***1219.7*** *p268*
Love, Margaret A.; Philadelphia, 1865 ***5704.8*** *p202*
Love, Martha; Quebec, 1850 ***5704.8*** *p63*
Love, Patrick 20; St. John, N.B., 1855 ***5704.8*** *p127*
Love, Patt; St. John, N.B., 1849 ***5704.8*** *p48*
Love, Rebecca 17; Philadelphia, 1864 ***5704.8*** *p161*
Love, Richard; Virginia, 1642 ***6219*** *p193*
Love, Robert; New York, NY, 1811 ***2859.11*** *p15*
Love, Robert; New York, NY, 1869 ***5704.8*** *p233*
Love, Samuel; New York, NY, 1815 ***2859.11*** *p35*
Love, Sarah; St. John, N.B., 1849 ***5704.8*** *p48*
Love, Tho.; Virginia, 1636 ***6219*** *p80*
Love, Tho.; Virginia, 1637 ***6219*** *p109*
Love, Thomas; Philadelphia, 1864 ***5704.8*** *p184*
Love, William 24; Maryland, 1775 ***1219.7*** *p251*
Lovee, Peter 20; Maryland, 1725 ***3690.1*** *p143*
Loveing, Tho.; Virginia, 1638 ***6219*** *p160*
Lovejoy, William; Jamaica, 1751 ***1219.7*** *p2*
Lovelane, Susan M.; Colorado, 1904 ***9678.2*** *p124*
Lovelidge, Thomas 20; Jamaica, 1734 ***3690.1*** *p144*
Lovell, Francis 2; Quebec, 1858 ***5704.8*** *p138*
Lovell, John 6 mos; Quebec, 1858 ***5704.8*** *p138*
Lovell, Mary 24; Quebec, 1858 ***5704.8*** *p138*
Lovell, Robt.; Virginia, 1635 ***6219*** *p10*
Lovell, Robt.; Virginia, 1637 ***6219*** *p10*
Lovell, William 34; Port uncertain, 1774 ***1219.7*** *p177*
Lovell, William King; Long Island, 1776 ***1219.7*** *p283*
Lovell, Winifred; Virginia, 1637 ***6219*** *p110*
Lovelock, Daniel 16; Pennsylvania, 1728 ***3690.1*** *p144*
Lovely, Mr.; Quebec, 1815 ***9229.18*** *p75*
Lovemore, Charles; Jamaica, 1754 ***1219.7*** *p30*
Lovemore, Charles; Jamaica, 1754 ***3690.1*** *p144*
Lover, James 15; Philadelphia, 1775 ***1219.7*** *p259*
Lovett, Benjamin; Quebec, 1821 ***7603*** *p28*
Lovett, Ellen 21; Philadelphia, 1854 ***5704.8*** *p120*
Lovett, John 19; Massachusetts, 1849 ***5881.1*** *p59*
Lovett, Joseph; Colorado, 1904 ***9678.2*** *p124*
Lovett, Mary 20; Massachusetts, 1849 ***5881.1*** *p60*
Lovett, Thomas; Illinois, 1880 ***2896.5*** *p25*
Lovett, William 18; Maryland, 1729 ***3690.1*** *p144*
Lovgren, Nels Ferdinand; Washington, 1859-1920 ***2872.1*** *p24*
Lovison, Maria Maddelina; Iowa, 1866-1943 ***123.54*** *p69*
Lovit, Mary; Quebec, 1851 ***5704.8*** *p75*
Lovoi, Rosario; Arkansas, 1918 ***95.2*** *p76*
Lovov, Jules 22; America, 1837 ***778.5*** *p349*
Low, . . .; Canada, 1776-1783 ***9786*** *p28*
Low, Ellen 16?; Maryland or Virginia, 1705 ***2212*** *p44*
Low, Frances Fred.k; Petersburg, VA, 1810 ***4778.2*** *p142*
Low, Georg; Virginia, 1698 ***2212*** *p11*
Low, James 15; America, 1702 ***2212*** *p38*
Low, Jno 30; America, 1699 ***2212*** *p28*
Low, John; New York, NY, 1815 ***2859.11*** *p35*
Low, John 16; Antigua (Antego), 1701 ***2212*** *p34*
Low, John 19; Maryland, 1774 ***1219.7*** *p191*
Low, John 23; Virginia, 1773 ***1219.7*** *p168*
Low, John 23; Virginia, 1774 ***1219.7*** *p193*
Low, John 24; Philadelphia, 1774 ***1219.7*** *p189*
Low, Mary; Virginia, 1643 ***6219*** *p205*
Low, Peter; Virginia, 1637 ***6219*** *p113*
Low, Robert; Virginia, 1638 ***6219*** *p122*
Low, Samuel; America, 1697 ***2212*** *p7*
Low, Thomas 17; Virginia, 1774 ***1219.7*** *p186*
Low, Wm.; Virginia, 1635 ***6219*** *p72*
Lowd, Rich.; Virginia, 1637 ***6219*** *p11*
Lowden, Edwin; Arkansas, 1918 ***95.2*** *p76*
Lowden, James; America, 1850 ***1450.2*** *p90A*
Lowden, James; Virginia, 1635 ***6219*** *p160*
Lowden, James 40; Philadelphia, 1833-1834 ***53.26*** *p47*
*Relative:*Jane 36
*Relative:*Mary 3
*Relative:*John 1
Lowden, Jane 36 *SEE* Lowden, James
Lowden, John; Virginia, 1636 ***6219*** *p146*
Lowden, John 1 *SEE* Lowden, James
Lowden, Mary 3 *SEE* Lowden, James
Lowden, Robert; New York, NY, 1815 ***2859.11*** *p35*
Lowder, Henry; Virginia, 1639 ***6219*** *p150*
Lowder, Wm.; Virginia, 1638 ***6219*** *p124*
Lowe, . . .; Canada, 1776-1783 ***9786*** *p28*
Lowe, . . .; Halifax, N.S., 1752 ***7074.6*** *p232*
Lowe, Mr.; Quebec, 1815 ***9229.18*** *p76*
Lowe, Andrew *SEE* Lowe, David
Lowe, Ann *SEE* Lowe, David
Lowe, David; West Virginia, 1818-1840 ***9788.3*** *p15*
With wife
*Child:*William

Child:George
Child:Andrew
Child:Ann
Child:Milley
Lowe, David; West Virginia, 1844 9788.3 p15
Lowe, George SEE Lowe, David
Lowe, Jon.; Virginia, 1635 6219 p26
Lowe, Joshua 19; Jamaica, 1722 3690.1 p144
Lowe, Mary; Virginia, 1648 6219 p246
Lowe, Milley SEE Lowe, David
Lowe, Robert; Virginia, 1637 6219 p111
Lowe, Sarah 29; Virginia, 1774 1219.7 p240
Lowe, Tho.; Virginia, 1639 6219 p161
Lowe, Thomas; South Carolina, 1767 1639.20 p114
Lowe, Warren; Washington, 1859-1920 2872.1 p24
Lowe, William SEE Lowe, David
Lowe, William; West Virginia, 1821-1859 9788.3 p15
Lowell, Henry; Washington, 1859-1920 2872.1 p24
Lowell, Thomas; Virginia, 1637 6219 p37
Lowen, Franz Joseph 19; New York, 1857 3702.7 p182
Lowen, Helena SEE Lowen, Peter
Lowen, Katharina SEE Lowen, Peter
Lowen, Peter; New York, 1855 3702.7 p182
Sister:Katharina
With family
With brother-in-law
Niece:Helena
Lowenstein, Nathan; Arkansas, 1918 95.2 p76
Lowenthal, Louis; America, 1895 1450.2 p90A
Lowenthal, William; America, 1889 1450.2 p90A
Lower, William; Shreveport, LA, 1878 7129 p45
Lowerman, John; South Carolina, 1788 7119 p199
Lowerson, Mary 27; Nova Scotia, 1775 1219.7 p263
Lowerson, Richard 32; North America, 1774 1219.7 p199
Lowery, Mr.; Quebec, 1815 9229.18 p81
Lowery, Lorenz; America, 1820-1829 8582.2 p56
Lowitz, Abraham Morris; Arkansas, 1918 95.2 p76
Lowitz, Johann; Wisconsin, n.d. 9675.6 p267
Lowitz, Louis; Wisconsin, n.d. 9675.6 p267
Lowman, Bernard; Philadelphia, 1751 9973.7 p31
Lownd, Alex.; Virginia, 1637 6219 p107
Lowndes, John; Charleston, SC, 1805 1639.20 p115
Lownee, Henry; Virginia, 1645 6219 p232
Lownes, Edward; Virginia, 1634 6219 p84
Lowney, Catharine 24; Massachusetts, 1849 5881.1 p57
Lownsdill, John 20; Jamaica, 1731 3690.1 p144
Lowrey, Elinor; Virginia, 1649 6219 p253
Lowrey, Ema.; Virginia, 1649 6219 p253
Lowrey, James 5; Massachusetts, 1848 5881.1 p59
Lowry, Arthur; Philadelphia, 1847 53.26 p47
Relative:Elizabeth
Relative:Isabella 12
Lowry, Arthur; Philadelphia, 1847 5704.8 p2
Lowry, Catherine; Philadelphia, 1851 5704.8 p79
Lowry, Catherine; Quebec, 1851 5704.8 p75
Lowry, Elizabeth SEE Lowry, Arthur
Lowry, Elizabeth; Philadelphia, 1847 5704.8 p2
Lowry, Elizabeth; Philadelphia, 1866 5704.8 p207
Lowry, Elizabeth 20; Philadelphia, 1857 5704.8 p132
Lowry, Henry 21; Philadelphia, 1857 5704.8 p132
Lowry, Henry 47; Arizona, 1890 2764.35 p42
Lowry, Isabella 12 SEE Lowry, Arthur
Lowry, Isabella 12; Philadelphia, 1847 5704.8 p2
Lowry, James; Philadelphia, 1847 53.26 p47
Relative:Jane
Lowry, James 25; Quebec, 1856 5704.8 p129
Lowry, Jane SEE Lowry, James
Lowry, Jane; Philadelphia, 1847 5704.8 p1
Lowry, Jane 11; Massachusetts, 1847 5881.1 p58
Lowry, John; St. John, N.B., 1847 5704.8 p18
Lowry, John; St. John, N.B., 1851 5704.8 p77
Lowry, John 32; Philadelphia, 1833-1834 53.26 p47
Relative:Mary 30
Lowry, Joseph; Philadelphia, 1847 5704.8 p1
Lowry, Joseph; West Virginia, 1807 9788.3 p15
Lowry, Martha; Philadelphia, 1852 5704.8 p84
Lowry, Mary 27; Nova Scotia, 1775 1219.7 p263
Lowry, Mary 30 SEE Lowry, John
Lowry, Peter 7; Massachusetts, 1848 5881.1 p61
Lowry, Robert; New York, NY, 1811 2859.11 p15
With family
Lowry, Robert; Philadelphia, 1850 53.26 p47
Lowry, Robert; Philadelphia, 1850 5704.8 p65
Lowry, Robert 23; Quebec, 1856 5704.8 p129
Lowry, Ruth 52; Quebec, 1858 5704.8 p138
Lowry, Samuel; New York, NY, 1816 2859.11 p35
Lowry, Sarah 9; Massachusetts, 1848 5881.1 p61
Lowry, Silly 20; Quebec, 1856 5704.8 p129
Lowry, Thomas; New York, NY, 1816 2859.11 p35
Lowry, William 29; Philadelphia, 1803 53.26 p47
Lowther, Charles; New York, NY, 1838 8208.4 p71
Lowther, George; West Virginia, 1886 9788.3 p15
Lowther, James; Illinois, 1886 5012.39 p52
Lowther, James; Illinois, 1888 5012.39 p122
Lowther, Mary 21; North America, 1774 1219.7 p200
Loxell, Joseph Wilhelm; Washington, 1859-1920 2872.1 p24
Loy, John 21; Massachusetts, 1847 5881.1 p58
Loyd, . . .; Canada, 1776-1783 9786 p28
Loyd, David; Virginia, 1638 6219 p147
Loyd, Hugh; Virginia, 1639 6219 p151
Loyd, John; Virginia, 1642 6219 p197
Loyd, John; Virginia, 1643 6219 p200
Loyd, John 11; America, 1700 2212 p31
Loyd, Joseph; Virginia, 1639 6219 p158
Loyd, Margaret 22; Massachusetts, 1848 5881.1 p60
Loyd, Mary; Virginia, 1639 6219 p156
Loyd, Morris; Virginia, 1642 6219 p191
Loyd, Thead.; Virginia, 1635 6219 p35
Loyd, Thomas 28; Maryland, 1774 1219.7 p230
Loyd, Wm.; Virginia, 1642 6219 p198
Loyell, Anthony 26; Antigua (Antego), 1730 3690.1 p144
Loyer, Brasenburne; Virginia, 1638 6219 p149
Loyn, Auguste 29; Ohio, 1820 778.5 p349
Loyn, Pelagie 33; Ohio, 1820 778.5 p350
Loyon, Cesar 33; America, 1838 778.5 p350
Loyon, Cesarine 5; America, 1838 778.5 p350
Loyon, Francois 11; America, 1838 778.5 p350
Loyon, Marie 32; America, 1838 778.5 p350
Loyse, John; Virginia, 1638 6219 p125
Loyte, William 17; Virginia, 1733 3690.1 p144
Loz, . . .; Canada, 1776-1783 9786 p28
Lozak, Max; Arkansas, 1918 95.2 p76
Loze, Anna Catharina; Pennsylvania, 1743 4525 p239
Lozers, A.; Iowa, 1866-1943 123.54 p31
Lozes, Jean Paul 27; Port uncertain, 1838 778.5 p350
Lozes, Toussaint 11; New Orleans, 1839 778.5 p350
Lozum, Charles 15; Philadelphia, 1774 1219.7 p183
Lubahn, William; Wisconsin, n.d. 9675.6 p267
Lubbe, Peter; New York, NY, 1834 8208.4 p79
Lubbe, Rients Janson; Illinois, 1872 5240.1 p28
Lubben, William; Iroquois Co., IL, 1892 3455.1 p12
Lubbing, A.M. Ilse; America, 1840 4610.10 p111
Lubbing, Christine Friederike Hedwig; America, 1853 4610.10 p116
Lubbing, Christine Louise Charlotte; America, 1883 4610.10 p113
Lubbing, Heinrich W.; America, 1886 4610.10 p153
Lubbing, Louise; America, 1877 4610.10 p113
Lube, Fred; Wisconsin, n.d. 9675.6 p267
Lubenelli, Alec.; Iowa, 1866-1943 123.54 p31
Lubenow, Kurt; Wisconsin, n.d. 9675.6 p267
Luber, Carl; Canada, 1783 9786 p38A
Luber, George; Wisconsin, n.d. 9675.6 p267
Lubicki, Franciszek 25; New York, 1912 9980.29 p59
Lubin, Joe 30; Kansas, 1906 5240.1 p83
Lubke, Anna 6 mos; New York, NY, 1857 9831.14 p153
Lubke, Carl 3; New York, NY, 1857 9831.14 p153
Lubke, Friederika 8; New York, NY, 1857 9831.14 p153
Lubke, Gottlieb 32; New York, NY, 1857 9831.14 p153
Lubking, Charles Henry; America, 1837 1450.2 p90A
Lubking, Charles Henry; America, 1845 1450.2 p90A
Lubking, Frederick Anthony; America, 1845 1450.2 p90A
Lubs, Friedrich; Wisconsin, n.d. 9675.6 p267
Lucas, . . .; Canada, 1776-1783 9786 p43
Lucas, Mr. 20; New Orleans, 1822 778.5 p350
Lucas, Adam; Philadelphia, 1849 53.26 p47
Lucas, Adam; Philadelphia, 1849 5704.8 p54
Lucas, Anton; America, 1885 4610.10 p125
Lucas, Betsy; New York, NY, 1811 2859.11 p15
Lucas, Eleanor; New York, NY, 1816 2859.11 p35
Lucas, Goerge; Iowa, 1866-1943 123.54 p31
Lucas, Hewill 23; Maryland, 1774 1219.7 p184
Lucas, Jno 17; Maryland, 1705 2212 p43
Lucas, John; New York, NY, 1838 8208.4 p74
Lucas, John 23; Maryland, 1774 1219.7 p230
Lucas, Rich.; Virginia, 1637 6219 p114
Lucas, Richard; Virginia, 1639 6219 p156
Lucas, Robert; St. John, N.B., 1853 5704.8 p107
Lucas, Robert; Virginia, 1639 6219 p152
Lucas, Roger; Virginia, 1636 6219 p8
Lucas, Samll.; Virginia, 1635 6219 p69
Lucas, Samuell; Virginia, 1638 6219 p148
Lucas, Tho.; Virginia, 1648 6219 p246
Lucas, William; Virginia, 1638 6219 p181
Lucas, William 18; Maryland or Virginia, 1720 3690.1 p144
Lucas, Wm 19; America, 1706 2212 p46
Lucchesi, Adolfo 21; New York, NY, 1893 9026.4 p41
Lucchesi, Guiseppi; Arkansas, 1918 95.2 p76
Lucci, Domick; Arkansas, 1918 95.2 p76
Luce, Betty 35; Massachusetts, 1849 5881.1 p57
Lucentie, Ozrazio; Wisconsin, n.d. 9675.6 p267
Lucht, . . .; Canada, 1776-1783 9786 p28
Luchterpand, Frederick; Massachusetts, 1860 6410.32 p125
Luck, Christian; Illinois, 1868 2896.5 p25
Luck, Edward 22; Maryland, 1775 1219.7 p247
Luck, Fredrich 54; Kansas, 1881 5240.1 p63
Luck, Joseph 21; Jamaica, 1736 3690.1 p144
Luck, William; New York, 1816 9892.11 p27
Luckard, Julia Kohler 83; America, 1895 1763 p48D
Lucke, . . .; Canada, 1776-1783 9786 p43
Lucke, de; Canada, 1776-1783 9786 p183
Lucke, Balthasar Bogislaus; Quebec, 1776 9786 p259
Lucke, Catherine F. Moller SEE Lucke, Johann Christoph
Lucke, Johann Christoph; America, 1842 4610.10 p119
Wife:Catherine F. Moller
Luckeer, Seibert 82; Canada, 1905 1763 p40D
Luckel, . . .; Canada, 1776-1783 9786 p28
Luckemeier, Catherine F. Moller SEE Luckemeier, Johann Christoph
Luckemeier, Johann Christoph; America, 1842 4610.10 p119
Wife:Catherine F. Moller
Lucken, Jan; Pennsylvania, 1683 2155 p2
With wife
Lucken, Maria; Pennsylvania, 1683 2155 p2
Luckenagel, A. M. Christine Wilhelmine; America, 1887 4610.10 p153
Luckens, Jan; Pennsylvania, 1683 2155 p2
With wife
Luckensmeyer, Carl Heinrich SEE Luckensmeyer, Heinrich
Luckensmeyer, Heinrich; America, 1852 4610.10 p147
Wife:Luise Marcks
Child:Marie Luise J. Amalie
Child:Carl Heinrich
Child:Zacharias Heinrich
Luckensmeyer, Luise Marcks SEE Luckensmeyer, Heinrich
Luckensmeyer, Marie Luise J. Amalie SEE Luckensmeyer, Heinrich
Luckensmeyer, Zacharias Heinrich SEE Luckensmeyer, Heinrich
Luckin, George; Virginia, 1635 6219 p5
Lucking, Charlotte 6 mos SEE Lucking, Fritz Johann Friedrich
Lucking, Friedrich 2 SEE Lucking, Fritz Johann Friedrich
Lucking, Fritz Johann Friedrich; America, 1872 4610.10 p100
Wife:Louise 26
Child:Friedrich 2
Child:Charlotte 6 mos
Lucking, Louise 26 SEE Lucking, Fritz Johann Friedrich
Luckins, Eliza.; Virginia, 1639 6219 p152
Luckman, Fred. Wm.; California, 1861 3840.2 p16
Luckman, James 37; Maryland, 1775 1219.7 p257
Luckston, Edward; Virginia, 1638 6219 p122
Luco, Anth.; Virginia, 1638 6219 p148
Lucowich, Joe; Colorado, 1904 9678.2 p125
Lucrelli, Rocco; Arkansas, 1918 95.2 p76
Lucus, Jone; Virginia, 1637 6219 p84
Lucy, Dennis 30; Massachusetts, 1849 5881.1 p58
Lucy, Ellen 30; Massachusetts, 1847 5881.1 p58
Lucy, James 20; Massachusetts, 1849 5881.1 p59
Luddington, Allen; Virginia, 1642 6219 p198
Luddy, Thos.; California, 1859 3840.2 p16
Luddy, Wm. 39; California, 1867 3840.2 p16
Ludecke, . . .; Canada, 1776-1783 9786 p28
Ludemann, Adolf 23; Kansas, 1885 5240.1 p68
Luder, Jacob; Cincinnati, 1848 8582.1 p53
Ludewig, Hermann G.; New York, NY, 1844 8582.1 p22
Ludewig, Lorentz; Pennsylvania, 1751 2444 p186
Ludiche, Albert 36; Kansas, 1884 5240.1 p65
Ludingsdorff, Emil Von Frankenburg; Wisconsin, n.d. 9675.6 p267
Ludke, August; Wisconsin, n.d. 9675.6 p267
Ludley, Eleanor 35; Maryland, 1775 1219.7 p266
Ludloe, Wm; Maryland or Virginia, 1697-1707 2212 p3
Ludlow, Joseph; America, 1864 2896.5 p25
Ludlow, Michael; America, 1743 4971 p18
Ludman, Thomas; Ohio, 1848 9892.11 p27
Ludolph, Theodor; Wisconsin, n.d. 9675.6 p267
Ludtke, Julius; Wisconsin, n.d. 9675.6 p267
Ludvigh, Samuel; Cincinnati, 1788-1848 8582.3 p89
Ludvigh, Samuel; Philadelphia, 1837 8582.3 p90
Ludwell, Tho.; Virginia, 1646 6219 p240
Ludwick, . . .; Canada, 1776-1783 9786 p28
Ludwick, Lorentz; Pennsylvania, 1751 2444 p186
Ludwig, . . .; Canada, 1776-1783 9786 p28
Ludwig, . . .; Philadelphia, 1775-1776 8582.3 p83
Ludwig, Anna Margaretha; America, 1752 2444 p186
Child:Maria Christina
Ludwig, Anton; Wisconsin, n.d. 9675.6 p267
Ludwig, Carl; New York, 1750 3652 p74

Ludwig, Christoph; Philadelphia, 1774 *8582.3 p85*
Ludwig, Christopher; Germantown, PA, 1775-1781 *8582.3 p81*
Ludwig, Christopher; Philadelphia, 1764 *8582.2 p65*
Ludwig, Gottfried; America, 1828 *8582.2 p61*
Ludwig, Gottfried; Cincinnati, 1869-1887 *8582 p20*
Ludwig, Hendrick; New York, NY, 1840 *8208.4 p110*
Ludwig, John; Wisconsin, n.d. *9675.6 p267*
Ludwig, John E.; Kentucky, 1869-1887 *8582 p20*
Ludwig, Lorentz; Pennsylvania, 1751 *2444 p186*
Ludwig, Maria Christina SEE Ludwig, Anna Margaretha
Ludwig, Nicholas; Wisconsin, n.d. *9675.6 p267*
Ludwig, Peter; Ohio, 1836 *8582.1 p47*
Ludwig, Philip; New Orleans, 1849 *1450.2 p91A*
Ludwig, Samuel; Ohio, 1819 *8582.1 p47*
Ludwikowski, . . .; New York, 1831 *4606 p175*
Ludwing, . . .; Canada, 1776-1783 *9786 p28*
Luebbe, A. J.; Illinois, 1846 *8582.2 p51*
Luebbermann, Gregorius; America, 1842 *8582.3 p42*
Luebke, August; Wisconsin, n.d. *9675.6 p267*
Luedig, . . .; Ohio, 1819 *8582.1 p47*
Luedke, Alfred Edmond; Arkansas, 1918 *95.2 p76*
Luedke, Daniel; Wisconsin, n.d. *9675.6 p267*
Luedtke, Alfred E.; Arkansas, 1918 *95.2 p76*
Luedtke, Alfred Edmund; Arkansas, 1918 *95.2 p76*
Luedtke, Marie; Wisconsin, n.d. *9675.6 p267*
Lueers, Johann Heinrich 13; New York, NY, 1833 *8582 p20*
Lueking, Wilhelm; Illinois, 1840-1890 *4610.10 p59*
Luening, Joseph; Cincinnati, 1846 *8582.1 p22*
  With brother
Luening, Joseph; Cincinnati, 1847 *8582.1 p22*
Luerehne, Rowne; Died enroute, 1875 *4719.30 p258*
Lueron, . . .; New Orleans, 1839 *778.5 p350*
Lueron, Miss; New Orleans, 1839 *778.5 p350*
Lueron, Mr.; New Orleans, 1839 *778.5 p350*
Luers, Johann Heinrich; Cincinnati, 1819-1848 *8582.3 p89*
Luers, John H. 13; New York, NY, 1833 *8582 p20*
Luethi, Heinrich; Cincinnati, 1848 *8582.1 p53*
Luettgen, Walter; New York, 1866 *8125.8 p437*
Luettich, Barbara; Port uncertain, 1751-1800 *2444 p219*
Lufelsmeyer, A. M. Louise Charlotte; America, 1884 *4610.10 p113*
Luffe, Mary; Virginia, 1639 *6219 p161*
Luft, Christoph; Cincinnati, 1869-1887 *8582 p20*
Luft, Fredrick; Wisconsin, n.d. *9675.6 p267*
Lufurrier, Anthony; Virginia, 1637 *6219 p16*
Lufurrier, Anthony; Virginia, 1637 *6219 p29*
Lugannie, Mr. 28; New Orleans, 1839 *778.5 p350*
Lugerne, Jean Francois 32; America, 1836 *778.5 p350*
Lugert, Joseph; Wisconsin, n.d. *9675.6 p267*
Luggett, Georg; Virginia, 1642 *6219 p191*
Lughterhead, Frederick; Massachusetts, 1860 *6410.32 p125*
Lughterhead, Frederick 27; Massachusetts, 1860 *6410.32 p117*
Lughterhead, Hannah 6; Massachusetts, 1860 *6410.32 p117*
Lughterhead, John 4; Massachusetts, 1860 *6410.32 p117*
Lughterhead, Sophia 30; Massachusetts, 1860 *6410.32 p117*
Luhn, J. H.; Cincinnati, 1869-1887 *8582 p20*
Luhn, Johann Heinrich 20; Baltimore, 1842 *8582.2 p24*
Luhn, Johann Wilhelm; Cincinnati, 1869-1887 *8582 p20*
Luhr, John Heinrich; Cincinnati, 1843 *8582.1 p22*
Luigg, Alvis 25; Kansas, 1884 *5240.1 p28*
Luigg, Alvis 25; Kansas, 1884 *5240.1 p67*
Luigi, Lazzaris 24; West Virginia, 1903 *9788.3 p15*
Luiji, Tiberi; Wisconsin, n.d. *9675.6 p267*
Luing, Elizabeth 23; Maryland, 1724 *3690.1 p144*
Luinny, Fredrick; Quebec, 1851 *5704.8 p75*
Luinstra, Peter; Arkansas, 1918 *95.2 p76*
Luippold, Agnes; Pennsylvania, 1750 *2444 p186*
Luippold, Anna; America, 1750 *2444 p161*
Luis, Henry; Indiana, 1847 *9117 p17*
Luis, Juan 45; New Orleans, 1835 *778.5 p351*
Lukas, Joseph; Arkansas, 1918 *95.2 p77*
Lukaskovcez, Walter Frank; Arkansas, 1918 *95.2 p77*
Lukaszwicz, Anthony; Arkansas, 1918 *95.2 p77*
Luke, Charles; New York, NY, 1835 *8208.4 p46*
Luke, James; New York, NY, 1811 *2859.11 p15*
Luke, Samuel; New York, NY, 1816 *2859.11 p35*
Luken, Jan; Pennsylvania, 1683 *2155 p2*
  With wife
Lukenheimer, Jacob; Indiana, 1848 *9117 p17*
Luking, Ann 39 SEE Luking, Joshua
Luking, Johann Friedrich Wilhelm; America, 1862 *4610.10 p99*
Luking, Joshua 41; Halifax, N.S., 1774 *1219.7 p213*
  Wife:Ann 39
  With child 11
Lulay, Georg 27; America, 1853 *9162.8 p37*

Lullor, Marguerite; Quebec, 1820 *7603 p77*
Lullore, Alfred C. 19; America, 1838 *778.5 p351*
Lumberland, Johannes; South Carolina, 1788 *7119 p200*
Lumbrey, Domnick; Virginia, 1600-1643 *6219 p200*
Lumley, Diana 14 SEE Lumley, Thomas
Lumley, Hannah; Philadelphia, 1850 *5704.8 p64*
Lumley, John 6 SEE Lumley, Thomas
Lumley, John 23; Nova Scotia, 1774 *1219.7 p194*
Lumley, Robert J.; Detroit, 1909 *3455.4 p55*
Lumley, Ruth 44 SEE Lumley, Thomas
Lumley, Thomas 45; North America, 1774 *1219.7 p199*
  Wife:Ruth 44
  Child:Diana 14
  Child:John 6
Lumpe, Fred Henry; Wisconsin, n.d. *9675.6 p267*
Lumpe, Henry; Wisconsin, n.d. *9675.6 p267*
Lumpert, Jacob 26; New Orleans, 1831 *778.5 p351*
Lumpey, Ambrose 26; Maryland, 1775 *1219.7 p249*
Lumsden, James 22; Virginia, 1774 *1219.7 p201*
Lumsden, James 38; North Carolina, 1850 *1639.20 p115*
Lumsden, John; New York, NY, 1835 *8208.4 p7*
Lumstuff, C. 55; New Orleans, 1837 *778.5 p351*
Lun, Mary; Quebec, 1823 *7603 p70*
Lunay, Ellen 22; Massachusetts, 1849 *5881.1 p58*
Lunchanan, Daniel; America, 1738 *4971 p77*
Lund, Albert; New York, NY, 1890 *9678.2 p125*
Lund, Frode; New York, NY, 1912 *3455.1 p53*
Lund, G. A.; Iroquois Co., IL, 1894 *3455.1 p12*
Lund, Gust; Colorado, 1906 *9678.2 p125*
Lund, John; Colorado, 1879 *9678.2 p125*
Lund, John; Minneapolis, 1881-1884 *6410.35 p60*
Lund, John; Portland, ME, 1868 *6410.22 p124*
Lund, Nelson P.; Maine, 1897 *6410.22 p127*
Lund, Niels; New York, 1761 *3652 p87*
Lundahl, Peter; Iowa, 1866-1943 *123.54 p31*
Lundamire, Ernest; Ohio, 1848 *9892.11 p27*
Lundback, Isaak 25; Kansas, 1873 *5240.1 p55*
Lundberg, Andrew; Kansas, 1878 *2764.35 p41*
Lundberg, Gustaf Adolf; Washington, 1859-1920 *2872.1 p24*
Lundblad, Anders; Maine, 1876-1881 *6410.22 p118*
Lundblad, Andrew; Iowa, 1849-1860 *2090 p613*
Lundblad, August; Maine, 1880-1885 *6410.22 p118*
Lundburg, C.; Minneapolis, 1870-1883 *6410.35 p60*
Lundell, Gust; Minneapolis, 1868-1876 *6410.35 p60*
Lunden, Andreas; New York, NY, 1832 *8208.4 p47*
Lundgreen, Tom; Iowa, 1866-1943 *123.54 p31*
Lundgren, George Henry; Arkansas, 1918 *95.2 p77*
Lundgren, Gustaf L.; Maine, 1871-1873 *6410.22 p117*
Lundgren, J.; Minneapolis, 1881-1883 *6410.35 p60*
Lundin, Olof; Maine, 1873-1881 *6410.22 p118*
Lundin, Peter; Illinois, 1871 *5012.39 p25*
Lundman, Carl; Iowa, 1866-1943 *123.54 p31*
Lundquist, Aaron Reynold; Boston, 1885 *6410.32 p124*
Lundquist, John; Minneapolis, 1880-1883 *6410.35 p60*
Lundquist, Matt; Arkansas, 1918 *95.2 p77*
Lundvall, John J. 41; Kansas, 1875 *5240.1 p56*
Lung, Jacob; New York, 1750 *3652 p74*
Lungan, Ann SEE Lungan, Catherine
Lungan, Ann; Philadelphia, 1847 *5704.8 p24*
Lungan, Catherine; Philadelphia, 1847 *53.26 p47*
  Relative:Ann
Lungan, Catherine; Philadelphia, 1847 *5704.8 p24*
Lungren, Nels; Washington, 1859-1920 *2872.1 p24*
Lungren, Nels J.; Washington, 1859-1920 *2872.1 p24*
Lungstras, Mme. 30; New Orleans, 1832 *778.5 p351*
Lungstras, Louis 3; New Orleans, 1832 *778.5 p351*
Lungstras, Louis 31; New Orleans, 1832 *778.5 p351*
Lungstras, Theodore 1; New Orleans, 1832 *778.5 p351*
Lunkenheimer, Friedrich; America, 1845 *8582.1 p23*
Lunmore, Mercy; Virginia, 1640 *6219 p185*
Lunn, Benjamin 21; Maryland, 1735 *3690.1 p144*
Lunn, Wm. 18; Port uncertain, 1849 *4535.10 p198*
Lunney, John; New York, NY, 1836 *8208.4 p11*
Lunningham, Alexander 41; Dominica, 1774 *1219.7 p177*
Lunny, Catherine; Quebec, 1847 *5704.8 p8*
Lunny, Charles H.; America, 1865 *5704.8 p188*
Lunny, Mary; Quebec, 1847 *5704.8 p27*
Lunny, Pat 20; Philadelphia, 1803 *53.26 p47*
Lunt, Edward 13; America, 1699 *2212 p21*
Lunt, Elizabeth 23; Virginia, 1700 *2212 p32*
Lunt, Lewis 40; Massachusetts, 1860 *6410.32 p107*
Lunt, Susan 26; Massachusetts, 1860 *6410.32 p107*
Lunte, A. M. Ilsabein; America, 1881 *4610.10 p159*
Lunte, Anne Marie; Illinois, 1800-1900 *4610.10 p67*
Lunte, Carl Friedrich Gottlieb; America, 1858 *4610.10 p158*
Lunz, George; Iroquois Co., IL, 1896 *3455.1 p12*
Lupo, Albiano; Virginia, 1624 *6219 p18*
  Wife:Elizabeth
Lupo, Elizabeth SEE Lupo, Albiano
Lupo, Wm.; Virginia, 1643 *6219 p204*

Luppen, Thomas 20; Quebec, 1856 *5704.8 p130*
Lupruses, Lorenz; Wisconsin, n.d. *9675.6 p267*
Lupton, John; Virginia, 1638 *6219 p18*
Luque, Mr. 28; America, 1839 *778.5 p351*
Lurkie, Jane; Philadelphia, 1811 *53.26 p47*
Lurkie, Jane; Philadelphia, 1811 *2859.11 p15*
Lurzckfassel, F.; Iowa, 1866-1943 *123.54 p31*
Lus, John; Wisconsin, n.d. *9675.6 p268*
Lusby, Henry 23; Maryland, 1774 *1219.7 p192*
Lusby, Robert 21; Maryland, 1774 *1219.7 p192*
Lusby, Thomas 16; Philadelphia, 1774 *1219.7 p175*
Luscombe, William 16; Maryland, 1773 *1219.7 p173*
Lush, Joseph; America, 1838 *4535.11 p52*
  With family
Lush, Richard, Jr.; New York, NY, 1839 *8208.4 p98*
Lusher, John 23; Maryland, 1775 *1219.7 p265*
Lushington, William; Pennsylvania, 1682 *4962 p153*
Lusin, Louis; Iowa, 1866-1943 *123.54 p31*
Lusk, Mary Ann; Quebec, 1852 *5704.8 p86*
Lusk, Mary Ann; Quebec, 1852 *5704.8 p90*
Lusk, Nancy; St. John, N.B., 1847 *5704.8 p19*
Lusk, Robert John 4; St. John, N.B., 1847 *5704.8 p19*
Lusk, Thomas; St. John, N.B., 1847 *5704.8 p19*
Lusk, Thomas 6 mos; St. John, N.B., 1847 *5704.8 p19*
Lusman, H.F.; Iowa, 1866-1943 *123.54 p31*
Luss, Susanna; Philadelphia, 1849 *53.26 p47*
Luss, Susanna; Philadelphia, 1849 *5704.8 p54*
Lussan du Blagnne Coulon, Jean 28; America, 1838 *778.5 p351*
Lussey, Thomas; Quebec, 1822 *7603 p80*
Lust, Christoph; Cincinnati, 1869-1887 *8582 p20*
Lustcomb, Thomas; Virginia, 1647 *6219 p241*
Lustig, Leopold 25; Missouri, 1872 *1450.2 p91A*
Lustsakis, George Elias; Arkansas, 1918 *95.2 p77*
Luszczynski, Pawel; New York, 1831 *4606 p175*
Luter, Tho.; Virginia, 1635 *6219 p3*
Luters, . . .; Canada, 1776-1783 *9786 p28*
Lutge, Ferdinand; Illinois, 1900 *5012.40 p77*
Luth, Jochim H.; Illinois, 1893 *5012.40 p53*
Luther, . . .; Canada, 1776-1783 *9786 p43*
Luther, Charles; Illinois, 1888 *5012.39 p121*
Luther, Frank; Colorado, 1904 *9678.2 p125*
Luther, George; Illinois, 1888 *5012.39 p121*
Luther, John; Illinois, 1862 *5012.38 p98*
Luther, John George; Illinois, 1888 *5012.39 p121*
Luther, John Otto; Wisconsin, n.d. *9675.6 p268*
Lutke, Albert 4; New York, NY, 1857 *9831.14 p154*
Lutke, August 8; New York, NY, 1857 *9831.14 p154*
Lutke, Dorothea 35; New York, NY, 1857 *9831.14 p154*
Lutke, Emilie 1; New York, NY, 1857 *9831.14 p154*
Lutke, Martin 35; New York, NY, 1857 *9831.14 p154*
Lutke, Martin 60; New York, NY, 1857 *9831.14 p154*
Lutke, Wilhelmine 6; New York, NY, 1857 *9831.14 p154*
Lutsow, Anthon Adolph August von; Halifax, N.S., 1780 *9786 p269*
Lutsow, Anthon Adolph August von; New York, 1776 *9786 p269*
Lutt, John; New York, NY, 1837 *2896.5 p25*
Lutter, . . .; Canada, 1776-1783 *9786 p43*
Lutterbeck, Friedrich 42; Ohio, 1837 *3702.7 p84*
Lutterer, Christ; Illinois, 1860 *5012.39 p90*
Lutterman, Frederick; Indiana, 1844 *9117 p18*
Luttermann, Hermann Friedrich; America, 1857 *4610.10 p121*
Luttermann, Karl Ludwig; America, 1857 *4610.10 p121*
Luttge, . . .; Canada, 1776-1783 *9786 p28*
Luttig, Philipp; New York, NY, 1837 *8208.4 p42*
Lutton, John 17; Philadelphia, 1774 *1219.7 p197*
Lutton, Sidney 20; Jamaica, 1738 *3690.1 p144*
Lutz, . . .; Canada, 1776-1783 *9786 p28*
Lutz, Anna Catharina; Pennsylvania, 1743 *4525 p239*
Lutz, Barbara Schlessmann SEE Lutz, Michael
Lutz, Catharina SEE Lutz, Matthaeus
Lutz, Conrad; New York, NY, 1834 *8208.4 p3*
Lutz, Georg Michael; Pennsylvania, 1752 *4525 p231*
  With wife
  With 2 children
Lutz, Johann; America, 1847 *8582.1 p23*
Lutz, Johann; New York, NY, 1847 *8582.1 p23*
  With family
Lutz, Johann Thomas; Pennsylvania, 1755 *4525 p231*
  With wife
  With child
Lutz, Johannes SEE Lutz, Matthaeus
Lutz, Martin; Wisconsin, n.d. *9675.6 p268*
Lutz, Matthaeus; Pennsylvania, 1754 *2444 p186*
  Wife:Catharina
  Child:Johannes
Lutz, Mattheis; Pennsylvania, 1751 *2444 p186*
Lutz, Michael; Pennsylvania, 1752 *4525 p231*
  Wife:Barbara Schlessmann
Lutz, Sybilla; Pennsylvania, 1752 *2444 p202*

Lutzen, Peter; Wisconsin, n.d. 9675.6 p268
Lutzow, August Conrad; Quebec, 1776 9786 p258
Lux, Guillaume 22; America, 1836 778.5 p351
Lux, Thomasin; Virginia, 1635 6219 p12
Luz, Mr. 25; America, 1838 778.5 p351
Lybrand, Christian 28 SEE Lybrand, Henrich
Lybrand, Henrich; South Carolina, 1752-1753 3689.17 p22
  Relative:Christian 28
  Relative:Simon 18
  Relative:Maria Margarita 16
  With wife
Lybrand, Maria Margarita 16 SEE Lybrand, Henrich
Lybrand, Simon 18 SEE Lybrand, Henrich
Lycett, Catherine; America, 1743 4971 p50
Lycett, John; Antigua (Antego), 1754 1219.7 p28
Lyddy, Mary 25; Massachusetts, 1849 5881.1 p60
Lyden, O. W.; Minneapolis, 1883-1885 6410.35 p60
Lydie, Jacob; Philadelphia, 1764 9973.7 p39
Lydon, Andrew Martin; Arkansas, 1918 95.2 p77
Lye, William 18; Philadelphia, 1774 1219.7 p233
Lyke, Anne; Virginia, 1642 6219 p191
Lyle, Alexander; New York, NY, 1834 8208.4 p50
Lyle, Elizabeth; America, 1864 5704.8 p189
Lyle, Elizabeth; Philadelphia, 1866 5704.8 p204
Lyle, James; Illinois, 1863 7857 p5
Lyle, Robert W.; Illinois, 1868 7857 p5
Lylley, John; Virginia, 1642 6219 p189
  With wife
Lylls, Martha; Virginia, 1646 6219 p241
Lymon, Henry; Kansas, 1870 5240.1 p51
Lynagh, Dennis; America, 1742 4971 p24
Lynagh, Edward; St. John, N.B., 1848 5704.8 p44
Lynagh, Grace 28; Philadelphia, 1854 5704.8 p123
Lynagh, James; America, 1742 4971 p17
Lynagh, James; Maryland, 1742 4971 p107
Lynagh, James 20; Philadelphia, 1858 5704.8 p138
Lynagh, Michael SEE Lynagh, Patrick
Lynagh, Michael; Philadelphia, 1847 5704.8 p5
Lynagh, Patrick SEE Lynagh, Patrick
Lynagh, Patrick; Philadelphia, 1847 53.26 p47
  Relative:Michael
  Relative:Sophia
  Relative:Patrick
Lynagh, Patrick; Philadelphia, 1847 5704.8 p5
Lynagh, Sophia SEE Lynagh, Patrick
Lynagh, Sophia; Philadelphia, 1847 5704.8 p5
Lynan, Laughlin; America, 1741 4971 p28
Lynard, Roger; Virginia, 1646 6219 p236
Lynaugh, John 27; Massachusetts, 1848 5881.1 p59
Lynaugh, Mary 27; Massachusetts, 1848 5881.1 p60
Lynch, Mr.; New York, NY, 1815 2859.11 p35
Lynch, Alexander 50; Quebec, 1857 5704.8 p135
Lynch, Andrew C.; New York, NY, 1836 8208.4 p13
Lynch, Ann; Philadelphia, 1849 53.26 p47
Lynch, Ann; Philadelphia, 1849 5704.8 p50
Lynch, Ann; St. John, N.B., 1850 5704.8 p61
Lynch, Ann 11 SEE Lynch, Catherine
Lynch, Ann 11; Philadelphia, 1847 5704.8 p32
Lynch, Arthur; Quebec, 1847 5704.8 p12
Lynch, Arthur; St. John, N.B., 1847 5704.8 p3
Lynch, Bartholemew 40; Massachusetts, 1849 5881.1 p57
Lynch, Bernard; New York, NY, 1838 8208.4 p66
Lynch, Bernard 37; Philadelphia, 1853 5704.8 p112
Lynch, Betty; St. John, N.B., 1848 5704.8 p39
Lynch, Betty 26; St. John, N.B., 1855 5704.8 p127
Lynch, Biddy; St. John, N.B., 1852 5704.8 p93
Lynch, Bidy 25; Philadelphia, 1856 5704.8 p129
Lynch, Bridget; Massachusetts, 1848 5881.1 p57
Lynch, Bridget 9; St. John, N.B., 1847 5704.8 p20
Lynch, Bridget 40; Massachusetts, 1849 5881.1 p57
Lynch, Bryan; New York, NY, 1815 2859.11 p35
Lynch, Catharine; Philadelphia, 1870 5704.8 p237
Lynch, Catharine; St. John, N.B., 1848 5704.8 p45
Lynch, Catharine 11; Massachusetts, 1849 5881.1 p57
Lynch, Catharine 14; Massachusetts, 1848 5881.1 p57
Lynch, Catharine 20; Massachusetts, 1850 5881.1 p58
Lynch, Catharine 30; Massachusetts, 1850 5881.1 p58
Lynch, Catharine Ann; Quebec, 1851 5704.8 p73
Lynch, Catherine; Philadelphia, 1847 53.26 p48
Lynch, Catherine; Philadelphia, 1847 53.26 p48
  Relative:John
  Relative:Hugh
  Relative:Ann 11
  Relative:Ellen 6
  Relative:Sarah 2
Lynch, Catherine; Philadelphia, 1847 5704.8 p31
Lynch, Catherine; Philadelphia, 1847 5704.8 p32
Lynch, Catherine; Quebec, 1820 7603 p100
Lynch, Catherine; St. John, N.B., 1847 5704.8 p3
Lynch, Catherine 4; St. John, N.B., 1848 5704.8 p47
Lynch, Catherine 11; St. John, N.B., 1847 5704.8 p20
Lynch, Catherine 18; Philadelphia, 1854 5704.8 p123
Lynch, Catherine 20; Philadelphia, 1857 5704.8 p134
Lynch, Catherine 20; St. John, N.B., 1858 5704.8 p137
Lynch, Catherine 48; Philadelphia, 1858 5704.8 p138
Lynch, Charles; Philadelphia, 1847 53.26 p48
Lynch, Charles; Philadelphia, 1847 5704.8 p1
Lynch, Charles 15; St. John, N.B., 1854 5704.8 p119
Lynch, Christopher; Michigan, 1837-1841 7036 p126
Lynch, Christopher; Philadelphia, 1850 53.26 p48
Lynch, Christopher; Philadelphia, 1850 5704.8 p60
Lynch, Daniel; Philadelphia, 1851 5704.8 p81
Lynch, Daniel; Quebec, 1851 5704.8 p73
Lynch, Daniel; St. John, N.B., 1847 5704.8 p21
Lynch, Daniel; Wisconsin, n.d. 9675.6 p268
Lynch, Daniel 18; St. John, N.B., 1854 5704.8 p120
Lynch, Daniel 22; Massachusetts, 1849 5881.1 p58
Lynch, Dennis; St. John, N.B., 1850 5704.8 p67
Lynch, Dennis 4; Massachusetts, 1850 5881.1 p36
Lynch, Dennis 4; Massachusetts, 1850 5881.1 p58
Lynch, Dennis 23; Massachusetts, 1849 5881.1 p58
Lynch, Dennis 25; Massachusetts, 1849 5881.1 p58
Lynch, Edmond; America, 1741-1742 4971 p60
Lynch, Edward; Illinois, 1900 5012.39 p53
Lynch, Edward; Illinois, 1901 5012.40 p79
Lynch, Edward; Wisconsin, n.d. 9675.6 p268
Lynch, Edward 28; Philadelphia, 1857 5704.8 p133
Lynch, Edward 70; Philadelphia, 1853 5704.8 p112
Lynch, Eleanor; Philadelphia, 1850 5704.8 p64
Lynch, Eleanor 18; Wilmington, DE, 1831 6508.7 p160
Lynch, Eleonor; Quebec, 1813 7603 p22
Lynch, Eliza; Philadelphia, 1850 5704.8 p64
Lynch, Elizabeth; Philadelphia, 1848 53.26 p48
  Relative:John
Lynch, Elizabeth; Philadelphia, 1848 5704.8 p46
Lynch, Elizabeth; Quebec, 1819 7603 p77
Lynch, Ellan 6; Philadelphia, 1847 5704.8 p32
Lynch, Elleanor; Philadelphia, 1849 53.26 p48
Lynch, Elleanor; Philadelphia, 1849 5704.8 p49
Lynch, Ellen; New York, NY, 1865 5704.8 p196
Lynch, Ellen; New York, NY, 1869 5704.8 p233
Lynch, Ellen 6 SEE Lynch, Catherine
Lynch, Ellen 22; Philadelphia, 1855 5704.8 p123
Lynch, Ellen 26; Massachusetts, 1849 5881.1 p58
Lynch, Fanny; St. John, N.B., 1850 5704.8 p61
Lynch, Felix; Quebec, 1851 5704.8 p74
Lynch, George 26; St. John, N.B., 1854 5704.8 p122
Lynch, Guillaume; Quebec, 1813 7603 p77
Lynch, Hannah; Philadelphia, 1849 53.26 p48
Lynch, Hannah; Philadelphia, 1849 5704.8 p50
Lynch, Henry; Illinois, 1861 2896.5 p25
Lynch, Hugh SEE Lynch, Catherine
Lynch, Hugh; Philadelphia, 1847 5704.8 p32
Lynch, Hugh; St. John, N.B., 1847 5704.8 p3
Lynch, Hugh 21; Philadelphia, 1857 5704.8 p133
Lynch, Humphrey; Iowa, 1866-1943 123.54 p31
Lynch, James; New York, NY, 1831 8208.4 p46
Lynch, James; New York, NY, 1869 5704.8 p234
Lynch, James; Philadelphia, 1847 53.26 p48
Lynch, James; Philadelphia, 1847 5704.8 p13
Lynch, James; Quebec, 1849 5704.8 p51
Lynch, James; St. John, N.B., 1847 5704.8 p3
Lynch, James; St. John, N.B., 1848 5704.8 p47
Lynch, James; St. John, N.B., 1851 5704.8 p77
Lynch, James 6; Philadelphia, 1858 5704.8 p138
Lynch, James 8; St. John, N.B., 1847 5704.8 p3
Lynch, James 19; Massachusetts, 1849 5881.1 p59
Lynch, James 19; Philadelphia, 1854 5704.8 p123
Lynch, James 24; Maryland, 1774 1219.7 p187
Lynch, James 26; Massachusetts, 1849 5881.1 p59
Lynch, Jane; New York, NY, 1866 5704.8 p213
Lynch, Jane; New York, NY, 1868 5704.8 p228
Lynch, Jane; Philadelphia, 1851 5704.8 p70
Lynch, Jane; Quebec, 1851 5704.8 p74
Lynch, Jane; St. John, N.B., 1847 5704.8 p21
Lynch, Jane 7; Massachusetts, 1850 5881.1 p59
Lynch, Jean; Quebec, 1789 7603 p58
Lynch, Jeremiah; Virginia, 1638 6219 p125
Lynch, Jeremiah 11; Massachusetts, 1849 5881.1 p59
Lynch, Jeremiah 45; Massachusetts, 1849 5881.1 p59
Lynch, Jeremiah 50; Massachusetts, 1849 5881.1 p59
Lynch, Joan; America, 1740 4971 p47
Lynch, Joan; America, 1741 4971 p49
Lynch, Johey 50; Massachusetts, 1849 5881.1 p59
Lynch, John SEE Lynch, Catherine
Lynch, John SEE Lynch, Elizabeth
Lynch, John; America, 1735-1743 4971 p78
Lynch, John; America, 1742 4971 p17
Lynch, John; Illinois, 1899 2896.5 p25
Lynch, John; Montreal, 1821 7603 p70
Lynch, John; New York, NY, 1811 2859.11 p15
Lynch, John; New York, NY, 1816 2859.11 p35
Lynch, John; New York, NY, 1836 8208.4 p21
Lynch, John; Ohio, 1839 9892.11 p27
Lynch, John; Philadelphia, 1847 53.26 p48
Lynch, John; Philadelphia, 1847 5704.8 p30
Lynch, John; Philadelphia, 1847 5704.8 p32
Lynch, John; Philadelphia, 1848 5704.8 p46
Lynch, John; Philadelphia, 1851 5704.8 p71
Lynch, John; Philadelphia, 1868 5704.8 p228
Lynch, John; Quebec, 1848 5704.8 p42
Lynch, John; St. John, N.B., 1847 5704.8 p11
Lynch, John; St. John, N.B., 1853 5704.8 p98
Lynch, John; Wisconsin, n.d. 9675.6 p268
Lynch, John 2; Massachusetts, 1850 5881.1 p59
Lynch, John 3; St. John, N.B., 1855 5704.8 p127
Lynch, John 8; St. John, N.B., 1848 5704.8 p47
Lynch, John 15; Massachusetts, 1849 5881.1 p59
Lynch, John 16; Maryland, 1774 1219.7 p229
Lynch, John 18; Jamaica, 1733 3690.1 p145
Lynch, John 19; Massachusetts, 1849 5881.1 p59
Lynch, John 19; Quebec, 1864 5704.8 p161
Lynch, John 21; Massachusetts, 1848 5881.1 p59
Lynch, John 21; Massachusetts, 1850 5881.1 p59
Lynch, John 26; Massachusetts, 1850 5881.1 p59
Lynch, John 26; Philadelphia, 1864 5704.8 p161
Lynch, John 36; Massachusetts, 1850 5881.1 p59
Lynch, John 37; Jamaica, 1774 1219.7 p223
Lynch, John 45; St. John, N.B., 1856 5704.8 p131
Lynch, John 58; Philadelphia, 1868 5704.8 p225
Lynch, John Joseph; Arkansas, 1918 95.2 p77
Lynch, Joseph; Philadelphia, 1850 53.26 p48
  Relative:Sally
Lynch, Joseph 2; Philadelphia, 1850 5704.8 p68
Lynch, Julia 24; Massachusetts, 1849 5881.1 p59
Lynch, Kate 7 mos; Massachusetts, 1849 5881.1 p59
Lynch, Lewis; New York, NY, 1867 5704.8 p223
Lynch, Manus 2; Quebec, 1856 5704.8 p129
Lynch, Margaret; Philadelphia, 1850 5704.8 p64
Lynch, Margaret 10; St. John, N.B., 1847 5704.8 p3
Lynch, Margaret 30; Massachusetts, 1849 5881.1 p60
Lynch, Margaret 45; Quebec, 1857 5704.8 p135
Lynch, Mary; Massachusetts, 1849 5881.1 p60
Lynch, Mary; Philadelphia, 1850 53.26 p48
Lynch, Mary; Philadelphia, 1850 5704.8 p60
Lynch, Mary; Philadelphia, 1865 5704.8 p196
Lynch, Mary; Philadelphia, 1867 5704.8 p217
Lynch, Mary; St. John, N.B., 1847 5704.8 p3
Lynch, Mary; St. John, N.B., 1847 5704.8 p21
Lynch, Mary; St. John, N.B., 1852 5704.8 p93
Lynch, Mary 2; Massachusetts, 1849 5881.1 p60
Lynch, Mary 3; St. John, N.B., 1848 5704.8 p47
Lynch, Mary 5; St. John, N.B., 1847 5704.8 p20
Lynch, Mary 35; Massachusetts, 1849 5881.1 p60
Lynch, Mary 45; St. John, N.B., 1856 5704.8 p131
Lynch, Mary A. 47; Quebec, 1864 5704.8 p161
Lynch, Mary Ann 2; St. John, N.B., 1855 5704.8 p127
Lynch, Mary Ann 13; St. John, N.B., 1847 5704.8 p21
Lynch, Mary Ann 20; Quebec, 1857 5704.8 p135
Lynch, Mary Jane; Philadelphia, 1851 5704.8 p76
Lynch, Mathew; Wisconsin, n.d. 9675.6 p268
Lynch, Matilda 8; Quebec, 1857 5704.8 p135
Lynch, Matilda 25; Philadelphia, 1860 5704.8 p146
Lynch, Michael; America, 1836 2896.5 p25
Lynch, Michael; Montreal, 1825 7603 p96
Lynch, Michael; New York, NY, 1838 8208.4 p69
Lynch, Michael; Quebec, 1825 7603 p56
Lynch, Michael; St. John, N.B., 1847 5704.8 p3
Lynch, Michael; Wisconsin, n.d. 9675.6 p268
Lynch, Michael 3; Massachusetts, 1850 5881.1 p60
Lynch, Michael 7; Massachusetts, 1850 5881.1 p40
Lynch, Michael 7; Massachusetts, 1850 5881.1 p61
Lynch, Michael 17; Philadelphia, 1868 5704.8 p225
Lynch, Morris 22; Ohio, 1867 6014.1 p2
Lynch, Nancy; Philadelphia, 1849 53.26 p48
Lynch, Nancy; Philadelphia, 1849 5704.8 p54
Lynch, Nancy; Philadelphia, 1865 5704.8 p196
Lynch, Neal; St. John, N.B., 1848 5704.8 p43
Lynch, Neil; Philadelphia, 1851 5704.8 p77
Lynch, Neil; Philadelphia, 1866 5704.8 p207
Lynch, Owen; St. John, N.B., 1847 5704.8 p20
Lynch, Pat; Quebec, 1847 5704.8 p12
Lynch, Patrick; Illinois, 1873 5012.37 p59
Lynch, Patrick; Massachusetts, 1849 5881.1 p61
Lynch, Patrick; New York, NY, 1815 2859.11 p35
Lynch, Patrick; New York, NY, 1837 8208.4 p53
Lynch, Patrick; New York, NY, 1839 6013.19 p73
Lynch, Patrick; St. John, N.B., 1847 5704.8 p20
Lynch, Patrick; Virginia, 1855 4626.16 p15
Lynch, Patrick; Wisconsin, n.d. 9675.6 p268
Lynch, Patrick 13; St. John, N.B., 1854 5704.8 p119
Lynch, Patrick 27; Philadelphia, 1803 53.26 p48
Lynch, Patrick D.; New York, NY, 1833 8208.4 p57
Lynch, Patrick M.; New York, NY, 1840 8208.4 p113
Lynch, Peggy; St. John, N.B., 1847 5704.8 p20
Lynch, Peggy 16; Massachusetts, 1849 5881.1 p61
Lynch, Peter; New York, NY, 1816 2859.11 p35
Lynch, Peter 23; Philadelphia, 1861 5704.8 p149

Lynch, Peyton; Petersburg, VA, 1810 *4778.2* p142
Lynch, Phillip 40; Massachusetts, 1849 *5881.1* p61
Lynch, Rachael; Quebec, 1851 *5704.8* p73
Lynch, Rebecca; St. John, N.B., 1850 *5704.8* p61
Lynch, Rebecca 11; Quebec, 1857 *5704.8* p135
Lynch, Richard; Philadelphia, 1848 *53.26* p48
Lynch, Richard; Philadelphia, 1848 *5704.8* p45
Lynch, Robert; New York, NY, 1836 *8208.4* p14
Lynch, Rosanna 19; Philadelphia, 1868 *5704.8* p225
Lynch, Rose; St. John, N.B., 1847 *5704.8* p3
Lynch, Sally *SEE* Lynch, Joseph
Lynch, Sally; Philadelphia, 1850 *5704.8* p68
Lynch, Sarah 2 *SEE* Lynch, Catherine
Lynch, Sarah 2; Philadelphia, 1847 *5704.8* p32
Lynch, Sarah 58; Philadelphia, 1868 *5704.8* p225
Lynch, Susan; New York, NY, 1816 *2859.11* p35
Lynch, Susan; New York, NY, 1869 *5704.8* p235
Lynch, Susan; Quebec, 1851 *5704.8* p74
Lynch, Thomas; America, 1737 *4971* p52
Lynch, Thomas; Annapolis, MD, 1742 *4971* p93
Lynch, Thomas; Montreal, 1811 *7603* p82
Lynch, Thomas; New York, NY, 1815 *2859.11* p35
Lynch, Thomas; New York, NY, 1834 *8208.4* p3
Lynch, Thomas; Wisconsin, n.d. *9675.6* p268
Lynch, Thomas 19; Massachusetts, 1848 *5881.1* p61
Lynch, Timothy 18; Massachusetts, 1850 *5881.1* p61
Lynch, Timothy 30; Massachusetts, 1849 *5881.1* p61
Lynch, William; America, 1735-1743 *4971* p51
Lynch, William; Annapolis, MD, 1742 *4971* p93
Lynch, William; New York, NY, 1836 *8208.4* p21
Lynch, William; Ohio, 1841 *8365.25* p12
Lynch, William; Quebec, 1847 *5704.8* p29
Lynch, William; St. John, N.B., 1850 *5704.8* p67
Lynch, William 10; Philadelphia, 1859 *5704.8* p141
Lynch, William 16; Quebec, 1857 *5704.8* p135
Lynch, William 16; St. John, N.B., 1854 *5704.8* p114
Lynch, William 19; Philadelphia, 1853 *5704.8* p112
Lynch, William 55; Massachusetts, 1848 *5881.1* p62
Lynchakin, Denis 20; Philadelphia, 1803 *53.26* p48
Lynchy, Elizabeth; America, 1736 *4971* p43
Lynchy, Joan; America, 1737 *4971* p45
Lynchy, John; America, 1742 *4971* p49
Lynchy, John; America, 1742 *4971* p70
Lynchy, John; America, 1743 *4971* p50
Lynchy, Patrick; America, 1743 *4971* p42
Lynchy, Will.; America, 1742 *4971* p30
Lynd, John; Illinois, 1877 *2896.5* p25
Lynd, Marion; New York, NY, 1869 *5704.8* p235
Lynd, William 19; St. John, N.B., 1863 *5704.8* p153
Lyndon, James; Philadelphia, 1816 *2859.11* p35
Lyndon, Mary; Philadelphia, 1816 *2859.11* p35
Lyndsley, Charlotte 22; Massachusetts, 1848 *5881.1* p57
Lyne, Arthur; Ohio, 1915-1917 *9892.11* p27
Lyne, Cornelius; America, 1742 *4971* p56
Lyne, Daniel; America, 1848 *1450.2* p91A
Lyne, Darby; America, 1736 *4971* p43
Lyne, Darby; America, 1736 *4971* p45
Lyne, James 18; Massachusetts, 1850 *5881.1* p59
Lyne, James 24; Massachusetts, 1849 *5881.1* p59
Lyne, John; Virginia, 1623-1648 *6219* p252
Lyne, William; America, 1736 *4971* p45
Lynge, Martinus 29; Arkansas, 1918 *95.2* p77
Lynham, Thomas; America, 1741 *4971* p29
Lynn, Charles; Indiana, 1836 *9117* p15
Lynn, Daniel; New York, NY, 1811 *2859.11* p15
  With family
Lynn, Edward; Philadelphia, 1847 *53.26* p48
Lynn, Edward; Philadelphia, 1847 *5704.8* p23
Lynn, Edward 21; Jamaica, 1736 *3690.1* p145
Lynn, Eliza; America, 1864 *5704.8* p188
Lynn, Elizabeth; Philadelphia, 1866 *5704.8* p215
Lynn, George; Quebec, 1852 *5704.8* p86
Lynn, George; Quebec, 1852 *5704.8* p90
Lynn, Henry; St. John, N.B., 1847 *5704.8* p35
Lynn, James 20; Philadelphia, 1774 *1219.7* p228
Lynn, Jane 9 *SEE* Lynn, Mary Jane
Lynn, Jane 9; Philadelphia, 1849 *5704.8* p53
Lynn, John; America, 1864 *5704.8* p187

Lynn, John 19; Massachusetts, 1849 *5881.1* p59
Lynn, John 26; Philadelphia, 1860 *5704.8* p146
Lynn, Margaret 35; Philadelphia, 1853 *5704.8* p111
Lynn, Mary; Philadelphia, 1864 *5704.8* p171
Lynn, Mary Jane; Philadelphia, 1849 *53.26* p48
  *Relative:*Jane 9
Lynn, Mary Jane; Philadelphia, 1849 *5704.8* p53
Lynn, Rebecca; Quebec, 1848 *5704.8* p42
Lynn, Robert Ross; Philadelphia, 1849 *5704.8* p53
Lynn, Samuel; Philadelphia, 1849 *53.26* p48
Lynn, Samuel; Philadelphia, 1849 *5704.8* p52
Lynn, Sarah Jane; Philadelphia, 1850 *5704.8* p64
Lynn, Susan; Philadelphia, 1866 *5704.8* p205
Lynn, Thomas; America, 1864 *5704.8* p188
Lynn, Thomas 17; Maryland, 1774 *1219.7* p202
Lynne, Connor; America, 1738 *4971* p80
Lynott, Edward 13; St. John, N.B., 1852 *5704.8* p93
Lynott, John; Oswego, NY, 1834-1844 *2896.5* p25
Lynott, Thomas; St. John, N.B., 1852 *5704.8* p93
Lynton, Mary 16; Massachusetts, 1848 *5881.1* p60
Lyon, Ms. 32; New Orleans, 1839 *778.5* p351
Lyon, Achile 26; New Orleans, 1839 *778.5* p351
Lyon, Ann; Carolina, 1771 *8894.1* p191
Lyon, Daniel; Virginia, 1698 *2212* p12
Lyon, George; Cape Fear, NC, 1690-1790 *1639.20* p115
Lyon, Hugh 24; St. John, N.B., 1862 *5704.8* p150
Lyon, Isaac; Maryland or Virginia, 1749 *3690.1* p145
Lyon, James; Annapolis, MD, 1742 *4971* p92
Lyon, James; North Carolina, 1734 *1639.20* p115
Lyon, James 18; Virginia, 1774 *1219.7* p242
Lyon, James 21 *SEE* Lyon, Matthew
Lyon, Jno; Virginia, 1698 *2212* p15
Lyon, John; New York, NY, 1835 *8208.4* p28
Lyon, John; North Carolina, 1814 *1639.20* p115
Lyon, John 23; Jamaica, 1731 *3690.1* p145
Lyon, John 25; Massachusetts, 1847 *5881.1* p58
Lyon, Joseph 16; Baltimore, 1775 *1219.7* p271
Lyon, Martha; St. John, N.B., 1847 *5704.8* p24
Lyon, Mary 50 *SEE* Lyon, Matthew
Lyon, Matthew 49; North Carolina, 1775 *1639.20* p115
  *Wife:*Mary 50
  *Son:*James 21
Lyon, Philip; South Carolina, 1716 *1639.20* p115
Lyon, William 30; Maryland, 1774 *1219.7* p230
Lyon, William Bridgman; Kansas, 1896 *5240.1* p28
Lyonnet, Francois; Colorado, 1904 *9678.2* p125
Lyonnis, Patrick; America, 1850 *6014.1* p2
Lyons, Mr.; Quebec, 1815 *9229.18* p74
Lyons, Ann 7; Quebec, 1862 *5704.8* p150
Lyons, Ann 25; Massachusetts, 1849 *5881.1* p57
Lyons, Anne; Philadelphia, 1852 *5704.8* p85
Lyons, Anne; Philadelphia, 1864 *5704.8* p179
Lyons, Anne 10; Philadelphia, 1852 *5704.8* p85
Lyons, Beatty 8; Philadelphia, 1852 *5704.8* p85
Lyons, Bridget 2; Massachusetts, 1847 *5881.1* p57
Lyons, Bridget 40; Massachusetts, 1847 *5881.1* p57
Lyons, Caroline 34; Massachusetts, 1860 *6410.32* p103
Lyons, Catharine 3; Massachusetts, 1847 *5881.1* p57
Lyons, Catharine 35; Massachusetts, 1850 *5881.1* p57
Lyons, Catherine; St. John, N.B., 1847 *5704.8* p25
Lyons, Charles; New York, NY, 1864 *5704.8* p170
Lyons, Charles; Quebec, 1823 *7603* p99
Lyons, Connor; America, 1738 *4971* p80
Lyons, Cornelius; New York, NY, 1811 *2859.11* p15
Lyons, Dennis 22; Massachusetts, 1849 *5881.1* p58
Lyons, Edward; Philadelphia, 1864 *5704.8* p179
Lyons, Eliza; Baltimore, 1811 *2859.11* p15
Lyons, Ellen 10; Massachusetts, 1847 *5881.1* p58
Lyons, Honora 8; Massachusetts, 1849 *5881.1* p58
Lyons, James; Baltimore, 1811 *2859.11* p15
Lyons, James 2; Massachusetts, 1847 *5881.1* p58
Lyons, James 2; Quebec, 1862 *5704.8* p150
Lyons, James 10; Massachusetts, 1849 *5881.1* p59
Lyons, James 11; Philadelphia, 1852 *5704.8* p85
Lyons, James 43; Quebec, 1862 *5704.8* p150
Lyons, Jane; Quebec, 1847 *5704.8* p17
Lyons, John; Baltimore, 1811 *2859.11* p15
Lyons, John 14; Massachusetts, 1847 *5881.1* p58

Lyons, John 29; Virginia, 1775 *1219.7* p246
Lyons, John 40; Quebec, 1862 *5704.8* p150
Lyons, John A. 35; Massachusetts, 1860 *6410.32* p103
Lyons, Joseph; Baltimore, 1811 *2859.11* p15
Lyons, Lawrence 44; Massachusetts, 1848 *5881.1* p60
Lyons, Malacha; New York, NY, 1839 *8208.4* p95
Lyons, Margaret; Philadelphia, 1852 *5704.8* p85
Lyons, Margaret 1; Massachusetts, 1849 *5881.1* p60
Lyons, Margaret 5; Quebec, 1862 *5704.8* p150
Lyons, Margaret 18; Massachusetts, 1849 *5881.1* p60
Lyons, Margaret 31; Quebec, 1862 *5704.8* p150
Lyons, Mary; Baltimore, 1811 *2859.11* p15
Lyons, Mary; New York, NY, 1864 *5704.8* p170
Lyons, Mary 16; Philadelphia, 1774 *1219.7* p182
Lyons, Mary 50; Massachusetts, 1850 *5881.1* p61
Lyons, Mary Jane 2; Quebec, 1862 *5704.8* p150
Lyons, Mathew; Philadelphia, 1864 *5704.8* p179
Lyons, Matilda; Philadelphia, 1852 *5704.8* p85
Lyons, Michael; Kentucky, 1843 *8582.3* p100
Lyons, Michael 11; Massachusetts, 1847 *5881.1* p60
Lyons, Michael 40; Massachusetts, 1847 *5881.1* p60
Lyons, Oliver; Philadelphia, 1849 *53.26* p48
Lyons, Oliver; Philadelphia, 1849 *5704.8* p53
Lyons, Patrick; Illinois, 1886 *5012.39* p120
Lyons, Patrick; New York, NY, 1837 *8208.4* p35
Lyons, Patrick; New York, NY, 1838 *8208.4* p83
Lyons, Patrick 4; Massachusetts, 1850 *5881.1* p61
Lyons, Patrick 8; Massachusetts, 1847 *5881.1* p61
Lyons, Patrick 21; Massachusetts, 1848 *5881.1* p61
Lyons, Peter; New York, NY, 1811 *2859.11* p15
Lyons, Robert; New York, NY, 1811 *2859.11* p15
Lyons, Samuel; America, 1740 *4971* p99
Lyons, Samuel; America, 1741 *4971* p99
Lyons, Samuel; Baltimore, 1811 *2859.11* p15
Lyons, Summer; Philadelphia, 1852 *5704.8* p85
Lyons, Thady; America, 1735-1743 *4971* p79
Lyons, Thady; America, 1740 *4971* p82
Lyons, Thomas; Illinois, 1886 *5012.39* p120
Lyons, Thomas; New York, NY, 1833 *8208.4* p44
Lyons, Thomas; New York, NY, 1837 *8208.4* p55
Lyons, Thomas; Virginia, 1856 *4626.16* p16
Lyons, Thomas 4; Quebec, 1862 *5704.8* p150
Lyons, Thomas 35; Massachusetts, 1849 *5881.1* p61
Lyons, William; America, 1736 *4971* p45
Lyons, William; New York, NY, 1816 *2859.11* p35
Lyons, William 22; Port uncertain, 1774 *1219.7* p176
Lyons, William 33; Massachusetts, 1848 *5881.1* p62
Lyouis, Elisabeth Gulide; Quebec, 1762 *7603* p47
Lysens, Louis; Washington, 1859-1920 *2872.1* p24
Lysiak, Piotr 30; New York, 1912 *9980.29* p54
Lysons, J. L.; Washington, 1859-1920 *2872.1* p24
Lysons, W. S.; Washington, 1859-1920 *2872.1* p24
Lysons, Walter; Washington, 1859-1920 *2872.1* p24
Lytefoote, John; Virginia, 1624 *6219* p18
Lytham, James 19; Port uncertain, 1774 *1219.7* p177
Lytle, Archibald; North Carolina, 1730-1790 *1639.20* p115
Lytle, Esther 7 *SEE* Lytle, Joseph
Lytle, Esther 7; Philadelphia, 1850 *5704.8* p60
Lytle, James; Quebec, 1851 *5704.8* p73
Lytle, Joseph; Philadelphia, 1850 *53.26* p48
  *Relative:*Sarah
  *Relative:*Margaret
  *Relative:*Mary
  *Relative:*Joseph 11
  *Relative:*Esther 7
Lytle, Joseph; Philadelphia, 1850 *5704.8* p60
Lytle, Joseph 11 *SEE* Lytle, Joseph
Lytle, Joseph 11; Philadelphia, 1850 *5704.8* p60
Lytle, Margaret *SEE* Lytle, Joseph
Lytle, Margaret; Philadelphia, 1850 *5704.8* p60
Lytle, Mary *SEE* Lytle, Joseph
Lytle, Mary; Philadelphia, 1850 *5704.8* p60
Lytle, Mary; Quebec, 1847 *5704.8* p16
Lytle, Sarah *SEE* Lytle, Joseph
Lytle, Sarah; Philadelphia, 1850 *5704.8* p60
Lytle, Sarah; Philadelphia, 1850 *5704.8* p64
Lyving, Mathew; Virginia, 1618 *6219* p4

M

Maag, . . .; Pennsylvania, n.d. **2444** *p193*
Maag, Henry; America, 1889 **1450.2** *p23B*
Maag, Jacob; Philadelphia, 1760 **9973.7** *p34*
Maag, Johann Friedrich Joseph; America, 1847 **8582.1** *p23*
Maak, . . .; Pennsylvania, n.d. **2444** *p193*
Maans, Martha; New York, 1749 **3652** *p73*
Maar, Henry; New York, NY, 1871 **1450.2** *p23B*
Maas, Carl; Wisconsin, n.d. **9675.6** *p268*
Maas, Fred; America, 1874 **1450.2** *p91A*
Maas, John; Wisconsin, n.d. **9675.6** *p268*
Maass, Friedrich; Illinois, 1900 **5012.40** *p77*
Maass, Herman Albert; Wisconsin, n.d. **9675.6** *p268*
Maass, Louis William; Wisconsin, n.d. **9675.6** *p268*
Maassen, Henry; Arkansas, 1918 **95.2** *p77*
Maassen, Teunis; Arkansas, 1918 **95.2** *p77*
Maathey, Ferdinand; Wisconsin, n.d. **9675.6** *p268*
Maatman, Gerrit 28; New York, NY, 1847 **3377.6** *p15*
Maatman, Harmina 54; New York, NY, 1847 **3377.6** *p15*
Maatman, Hendrika 20; New York, NY, 1847 **3377.6** *p15*
Maatman, Hendrikus 63; New York, NY, 1847 **3377.6** *p15*
Maatman, Janna 37; New York, NY, 1847 **3377.6** *p15*
Maatman, Mannes 25; New York, NY, 1847 **3377.6** *p15*
Mabb, Tho.; Virginia, 1643 **6219** *p204*
Maben, Robert 62; North Carolina, 1850 **1639.20** *p115*
Mabin, Mary 50; Philadelphia, 1860 **5704.8** *p144*
Mabletuft, Samuel 21; Maryland, 1774 **1219.7** *p181*
Macabe, Anne; Quebec, 1847 **5704.8** *p8*
Macabe, Anne 10; Quebec, 1847 **5704.8** *p8*
Macabe, Isabella 7; Quebec, 1847 **5704.8** *p8*
Macabe, Margaret; Quebec, 1847 **5704.8** *p8*
Macabe, Sarah 5; Quebec, 1847 **5704.8** *p8*
Macabe, Thomas; Quebec, 1847 **5704.8** *p8*
MacAdam, James; Charleston, SC, 1799 **1639.20** *p115*
MacAdam, John; Charleston, SC, 1823 **1639.20** *p116*
MacAffer, Andrew; New York, NY, 1816 **2859.11** *p35*
MacAlister, Anthony; New York, NY, 1816 **2859.11** *p35*
MacAlister, Daniel; New York, NY, 1816 **2859.11** *p35*
MacAllan, Agnes Thain *SEE* MacAllan, William
MacAllan, Agnes Thain *SEE* MacAllan, William
MacAllan, William; Canada, 1835 **8893** *p264*
  Wife: Agnes Thain
MacAllan, William; New York, 1833 **8893** *p264*
  Wife: Agnes Thain
MacAllignon, Rich; New York, NY, 1816 **2859.11** *p35*
MacAllisted, Felix; New York, NY, 1811 **2859.11** *p15*
MacAllisted, James; New York, NY, 1811 **2859.11** *p15*
MacAllister, R.; New York, NY, 1811 **2859.11** *p15*
MacAllister, Rose; New York, NY, 1811 **2859.11** *p15*
MacAloo, Daniel; New York, NY, 1816 **2859.11** *p35*
MacAlpin, Hugh; New York, NY, 1811 **2859.11** *p15*
MacAlpin, James; New York, NY, 1811 **2859.11** *p15*
MacAlpin, Jane; New York, NY, 1811 **2859.11** *p15*
MacAlvin, Alex.; New York, NY, 1811 **2859.11** *p15*
  With family
MacAnalty, Patrick; New York, NY, 1816 **2859.11** *p35*
MacAnnulty, James; New York, NY, 1811 **2859.11** *p15*
MacAnorney, Michael; New York, NY, 1811 **2859.11** *p15*
MacArand, Patrick; Philadelphia, 1816 **2859.11** *p35*
MacArdle, Anne; New York, NY, 1816 **2859.11** *p35*
MacArdle, John; New York, NY, 1816 **2859.11** *p35*
MacArdle, Mary Anne; New York, NY, 1816 **2859.11** *p35*

MacArdle, Owen; New York, NY, 1816 **2859.11** *p35*
MacArdle, Peter; New York, NY, 1816 **2859.11** *p35*
MacArnon, Mary; New York, NY, 1815 **2859.11** *p35*
MacArthur, Ann *SEE* MacArthur, Kirsty MacLeod
MacArthur, Ann MacAulay *SEE* MacArthur, Norman
MacArthur, Catherine *SEE* MacArthur, Kirsty MacLeod
MacArthur, John *SEE* MacArthur, Kirsty MacLeod
MacArthur, John; Philadelphia, 1811 **2859.11** *p15*
MacArthur, Kirsty *SEE* MacArthur, Kirsty MacLeod
MacArthur, Kirsty MacLeod; Quebec, 1853 **4537.30** *p46*
  Child: Kirsty
  Child: John
  Child: Norman
  Child: Ann
  Child: Catherine
MacArthur, Mary; Quebec, 1851 **4537.30** *p4*
MacArthur, Mary; Quebec, 1855 **4537.30** *p57*
MacArthur, Norman *SEE* MacArthur, Kirsty MacLeod
MacArthur, Norman; Quebec, 1851 **4537.30** *p46*
  Wife: Ann MacAulay
MacArthur, Robert; Philadelphia, 1811 **2859.11** *p15*
Macartney, Lady; Grenada, 1776 **1219.7** *p282*
Macartney, George 34; Grenada, 1776 **1219.7** *p282*
Macarty, V. 34; America, 1839 **778.5** *p351*
MacAskill, Siblings; Ontario, 1820-1900 **4537.30** *p47*
MacAskill, Alex; Quebec, 1843 **4537.30** *p47*
  Wife: Catherine MacLeod
  Child: Ann
  Child: Angus
  Child: Margaret
  Child: Kenneth
  Child: Roderick
MacAskill, Angus *SEE* MacAskill, Alex
MacAskill, Angus *SEE* MacAskill, Murdo
MacAskill, Ann *SEE* MacAskill, Alex
MacAskill, Ann *SEE* MacAskill, Donald
MacAskill, Ann MacKay *SEE* MacAskill, John
MacAskill, Annabella MacDonald *SEE* MacAskill, Donald
MacAskill, Catherine *SEE* MacAskill, John
MacAskill, Catherine MacLeod *SEE* MacAskill, Alex
MacAskill, Donald *SEE* MacAskill, Malcolm
MacAskill, Donald; Quebec, 1842 **4537.30** *p47*
  Wife: Annabella MacDonald
  Child: Ann
  Child: John
  Child: Malcolm
MacAskill, Dorothy; Quebec, 1852 **4537.30** *p104*
MacAskill, Dorothy MacDonald *SEE* MacAskill, Malcolm
MacAskill, Effie; Quebec, 1865 **4537.30** *p66*
MacAskill, Isabella *SEE* MacAskill, John
MacAskill, Isabella *SEE* MacAskill, Malcolm
MacAskill, Isabella *SEE* MacAskill, Murdo
MacAskill, John *SEE* MacAskill, Donald
MacAskill, John *SEE* MacAskill, Murdo
MacAskill, John; Quebec, 1843 **4537.30** *p48*
  Wife: Ann MacKay
  Child: Catherine
  Child: Isabella
  Child: Murdo
MacAskill, Kenneth *SEE* MacAskill, Alex
MacAskill, Kirsty; Quebec, 1863 **4537.30** *p21*
MacAskill, Kirsty Ann *SEE* MacAskill, Malcolm
MacAskill, Malcolm *SEE* MacAskill, Donald
MacAskill, Malcolm *SEE* MacAskill, Malcolm

MacAskill, Malcolm; Quebec, 1890-1892 **4537.30** *p48*
  Wife: Dorothy MacDonald
  Child: Margaret
  Child: William
  Child: Roderick
  Child: Norman
  Child: Donald
  Child: Kirsty Ann
  Child: Isabella
  Child: Malcolm
MacAskill, Margaret *SEE* MacAskill, Alex
MacAskill, Margaret *SEE* MacAskill, Malcolm
MacAskill, Margaret MacIver *SEE* MacAskill, Murdo
MacAskill, Murdo *SEE* MacAskill, John
MacAskill, Murdo; Quebec, 1851 **4537.30** *p47*
  Wife: Margaret MacIver
  Child: Angus
  Child: John
  Child: Isabella
  Child: William
MacAskill, Norman *SEE* MacAskill, Malcolm
MacAskill, Roderick *SEE* MacAskill, Alex
MacAskill, Roderick *SEE* MacAskill, Malcolm
MacAskill, William *SEE* MacAskill, Malcolm
MacAskill, William *SEE* MacAskill, Murdo
MacAskin, John; New York, NY, 1811 **2859.11** *p15*
MacAtier, James; New York, NY, 1815 **2859.11** *p35*
MacAtter, Betty; New York, NY, 1811 **2859.11** *p15*
MacAtter, Mark; New York, NY, 1811 **2859.11** *p15*
MacAttur, Ann; New York, NY, 1811 **2859.11** *p15*
MacAttur, James; New York, NY, 1811 **2859.11** *p15*
MacAulay, Alex; Quebec, 1870-1879 **4537.30** *p55*
  Wife: Marion MacLeod
  Child: Ann
  Child: John
  Child: Mary
  Child: Effie
  Child: Donald
  Child: Marion
  Child: Margaret
Macaulay, Aneas; Prince Edward Island, 1803 **9775.5** *p210*
MacAulay, Angus *SEE* MacAulay, Donald
MacAulay, Angus *SEE* MacAulay, Kenneth
MacAulay, Angus *SEE* MacAulay, Malcolm
MacAulay, Angus; Quebec, 1851 **4537.30** *p49*
  Wife: Mary MacInnes
  Child: Murdo
  Child: Mary
  Child: Malcolm
  Child: Norman
  Child: Donald
MacAulay, Angus; Quebec, 1855 **4537.30** *p49*
  Wife: Effie Morrison
  Child: Donald
  Child: Catherine
  Child: Ann
  Child: Malcolm
MacAulay, Ann *SEE* MacAulay, Alex
MacAulay, Ann *SEE* MacAulay, Angus
MacAulay, Ann *SEE* MacAulay, Donald
MacAulay, Ann *SEE* MacAulay, Malcolm
MacAulay, Ann *SEE* MacAulay, Malcolm
MacAulay, Ann; Quebec, 1851 **4537.30** *p2*
MacAulay, Ann; Quebec, 1851 **4537.30** *p46*
MacAulay, Ann; Quebec, 1872 **4537.30** *p18*
MacAulay, Ann Buchanan *SEE* MacAulay, Malcolm

MacAulay, Catherine *SEE* MacAulay, Angus
MacAulay, Catherine *SEE* MacAulay, Kenneth
MacAulay, Catherine *SEE* MacAulay, Malcolm
MacAulay, Catherine *SEE* MacAulay, Malcolm
MacAulay, Catherine; Quebec, 1851 *4537.30 p107*
MacAulay, Catherine MacLean *SEE* MacAulay, Donald
Macaulay, Daniel; America, 1770 *1219.7 p148*
MacAulay, Donald *SEE* MacAulay, Alex
MacAulay, Donald *SEE* MacAulay, Angus
MacAulay, Donald *SEE* MacAulay, Angus
MacAulay, Donald *SEE* MacAulay, Donald
MacAulay, Donald *SEE* MacAulay, Donald
MacAulay, Donald *SEE* MacAulay, Donald
MacAulay, Donald *SEE* MacAulay, John
MacAulay, Donald *SEE* MacAulay, Kenneth
MacAulay, Donald *SEE* MacAulay, Malcolm
MacAulay, Donald *SEE* MacAulay, Malcolm
MacAulay, Donald *SEE* MacAulay, Malcolm
MacAulay, Donald *SEE* MacAulay, Malcolm
MacAulay, Donald; Quebec, 1843 *4537.30 p50*
  Wife: Catherine MacLean
  Child: Donald
  Child: Mary
  Child: Ann
  Child: Kenneth
  Child: Malcolm
MacAulay, Donald; Quebec, 1851 *4537.30 p50*
  Wife: Isabella Smith
  With son
  Child: Malcolm
  Child: Donald
  Child: Norman
  Child: Angus
  Child: Kenneth
  Child: John
MacAulay, Donald; Quebec, 1851 *4537.30 p51*
  Wife: Mary MacDonald
MacAulay, Donald; Quebec, 1855 *4537.30 p54*
  Wife: Kate MacAulay
  Child: Donald
  Child: Margaret
  Child: John Z.
  Brother: John
  Brother: Malcolm
  Brother: William
  Sister-in-law: Mary MacIver
MacAulay, Donald; Quebec, 1863 *4537.30 p50*
  Wife: Kirsty MacRae
  Child: Mary
  Child: Donald
  Child: John Robert
  Child: Murdo
  Child: Joan
MacAulay, Effie *SEE* MacAulay, Alex
MacAulay, Effie Morrison *SEE* MacAulay, Angus
MacAulay, Isabella Smith *SEE* MacAulay, Donald
MacAulay, Jane *SEE* MacAulay, Malcolm
MacAulay, Jessie *SEE* MacAulay, Joan
MacAulay, Joan; Quebec, 1880-1889 *4537.30 p55*
  Sister: Jessie
MacAulay, John *SEE* MacAulay, Alex
MacAulay, John *SEE* MacAulay, Donald
MacAulay, John *SEE* MacAulay, Donald
MacAulay, John *SEE* MacAulay, John
MacAulay, John *SEE* MacAulay, Malcolm
MacAulay, John *SEE* MacAulay, Malcolm
MacAulay, John *SEE* MacAulay, Malcolm
MacAulay, John; Quebec, 1855 *4537.30 p51*
  Wife: Margaret MacLean
  Child: Donald
  Child: Murdo
  Child: Malcolm
  Child: John
  Child: Margaret
MacAulay, John Robert *SEE* MacAulay, Donald
MacAulay, John Z. *SEE* MacAulay, Donald
MacAulay, Kate; Quebec, 1855 *4537.30 p54*
MacAulay, Kate MacAulay *SEE* MacAulay, Donald
MacAulay, Kenneth *SEE* MacAulay, Donald
MacAulay, Kenneth *SEE* MacAulay, Donald
MacAulay, Kenneth *SEE* MacAulay, Malcolm
MacAulay, Kenneth; Quebec, 1851 *4537.30 p51*
  Wife: Mary Matheson
  Child: Murdo
  Child: Angus
  Child: Donald
  Child: Catherine
MacAulay, Kirsty *SEE* MacAulay, Malcolm
MacAulay, Kirsty *SEE* MacAulay, Malcolm
MacAulay, Kirsty; Quebec, 1851 *4537.30 p91*

MacAulay, Kirsty; Quebec, 1860-1900 *4537.30 p49*
MacAulay, Kirsty; Quebec, 1873 *4537.30 p34*
MacAulay, Kirsty MacRae *SEE* MacAulay, Donald
MacAulay, Kirsty MacRitchie *SEE* MacAulay, Malcolm
MacAulay, Malcolm *SEE* MacAulay, Angus
MacAulay, Malcolm *SEE* MacAulay, Angus
MacAulay, Malcolm *SEE* MacAulay, Donald
MacAulay, Malcolm *SEE* MacAulay, Donald
MacAulay, Malcolm *SEE* MacAulay, Donald
MacAulay, Malcolm *SEE* MacAulay, John
MacAulay, Malcolm *SEE* MacAulay, Malcolm
MacAulay, Malcolm *SEE* MacAulay, Malcolm
MacAulay, Malcolm; Quebec, 1851 *4537.30 p52*
  Wife: Ann Buchanan
  Child: John
  Child: Donald
  Child: Murdo
  Child: Margaret
  Child: Roderick
  Child: Catherine
  Child: Norman
MacAulay, Malcolm; Quebec, 1851 *4537.30 p52*
  Wife: Kirsty MacRitchie
  Child: Margaret
  Child: Ann
  Child: Donald
  Child: Angus
  Child: Kenneth
  Child: John
  Child: Jane
  Child: Donald
  Child: Malcolm
MacAulay, Malcolm; Quebec, 1851 *4537.30 p52*
  Wife: Margaret MacKenzie
  Child: Kirsty
MacAulay, Malcolm; Quebec, 1855 *4537.30 p54*
  Wife: Mary MacIver
  Brother: John
  Brother: William
  Brother: Donald
MacAulay, Malcolm; Quebec, 1869 *4537.30 p53*
  Wife: Mary
  Child: Catherine
  Child: Malcolm
  Child: Donald
  Child: Ann
  Child: Kirsty
  Child: Marion
MacAulay, Margaret *SEE* MacAulay, Alex
MacAulay, Margaret *SEE* MacAulay, Donald
MacAulay, Margaret *SEE* MacAulay, John
MacAulay, Margaret *SEE* MacAulay, Malcolm
MacAulay, Margaret *SEE* MacAulay, Malcolm
MacAulay, Margaret MacKenzie *SEE* MacAulay, Malcolm
MacAulay, Margaret MacLean *SEE* MacAulay, John
MacAulay, Marion *SEE* MacAulay, Alex
MacAulay, Marion *SEE* MacAulay, Malcolm
MacAulay, Marion MacLeod *SEE* MacAulay, Alex
MacAulay, Mary *SEE* MacAulay, Alex
MacAulay, Mary *SEE* MacAulay, Angus
MacAulay, Mary *SEE* MacAulay, Donald
MacAulay, Mary *SEE* MacAulay, Donald
MacAulay, Mary *SEE* MacAulay, Malcolm
MacAulay, Mary MacDonald *SEE* MacAulay, Donald
MacAulay, Mary MacInnes *SEE* MacAulay, Angus
MacAulay, Mary MacIver *SEE* MacAulay, Donald
MacAulay, Mary MacIver *SEE* MacAulay, Malcolm
MacAulay, Mary Matheson *SEE* MacAulay, Kenneth
MacAulay, Murdo *SEE* MacAulay, Angus
MacAulay, Murdo *SEE* MacAulay, Donald
MacAulay, Murdo *SEE* MacAulay, John
MacAulay, Murdo *SEE* MacAulay, Kenneth
MacAulay, Murdo *SEE* MacAulay, Malcolm
MacAulay, Norman *SEE* MacAulay, Angus
MacAulay, Norman *SEE* MacAulay, Donald
MacAulay, Norman *SEE* MacAulay, Malcolm
MacAulay, Rachel; Quebec, 1851 *4537.30 p65*
MacAulay, Rachel; Quebec, 1873 *4537.30 p74*
MacAulay, Roderick *SEE* MacAulay, Malcolm
MacAulay, William *SEE* MacAulay, Donald
MacAulay, William *SEE* MacAulay, Malcolm
MacAulay, William; Quebec, 1843 *4537.30 p53*
MacAuley, James; New York, NY, 1816 *2859.11 p35*
Macauley, James; New York, NY, 1839 *8208.4 p100*
MacAuslan, Jane; North Carolina, 1814 *1639.20 p119*
Macbeth, George; Georgia, 1775 *1219.7 p275*
MacBeth, Kirsty; Quebec, 1852 *4537.30 p100*
MacBraty, Chs.; New York, NY, 1816 *2859.11 p35*
MacBride, Bernard; New York, NY, 1816 *2859.11 p35*
MacBride, James; New York, NY, 1811 *2859.11 p15*
  With wife & family
MacBride, James; New York, NY, 1815 *2859.11 p35*

MacBride, John; New York, NY, 1816 *2859.11 p35*
MacBride, Patrick; Philadelphia, 1816 *2859.11 p36*
MacBride, William; New York, NY, 1816 *2859.11 p36*
MacBrien, John; New York, NY, 1815 *2859.11 p15*
MacBrine, Jane; Philadelphia, 1811 *2859.11 p15*
MacBurney, Mrs.; Philadelphia, 1811 *2859.11 p15*
MacCabe, Betsy; New York, NY, 1811 *2859.11 p15*
MacCabe, James; New York, NY, 1811 *2859.11 p15*
MacCabe, John; New York, NY, 1815 *2859.11 p36*
MacCabe, Pat.; Baltimore, 1816 *2859.11 p36*
MacCabe, Patrick; New York, NY, 1811 *2859.11 p15*
MacCabe, Terrence; New York, NY, 1816 *2859.11 p36*
MacCafferty, Edw.; Philadelphia, 1811 *2859.11 p15*
MacCafferty, Susan; New York, NY, 1811 *2859.11 p15*
MacCaghy, Nath.; New York, NY, 1811 *2859.11 p15*
  With family
MacCaird, William; New York, NY, 1811 *2859.11 p15*
MacCall, Alex; New York, NY, 1816 *2859.11 p36*
MacCall, Alice; New York, NY, 1816 *2859.11 p36*
MacCallaghan, Callaghan; America, 1741 *4971 p49*
MacCallan, James; New York, NY, 1816 *2859.11 p36*
MacCallum, Stephen; San Francisco, 1850 *4914.15 p9*
Maccally, James 17; Jamaica, 1737 *3690.1 p145*
MacCam, Felix; New York, NY, 1816 *2859.11 p36*
MacCambridge, Alexander; New York, NY, 1815
  2859.11 p36
MacCambridge, Jas.; New York, NY, 1816 *2859.11 p36*
MacCammar, Samuel; New York, NY, 1811 *2859.11
  p15*
MacCanaghty, James; New York, NY, 1816 *2859.11
  p36*
MacCanaghy, David; New York, NY, 1816 *2859.11 p36*
MacCanaghy, Mary; New York, NY, 1816 *2859.11 p36*
MacCanbrey, Rich.; New York, NY, 1816 *2859.11 p36*
MacCance, James; New York, NY, 1811 *2859.11 p15*
MacCane, Robert; New York, NY, 1811 *2859.11 p15*
MacCanly, Robert; New York, NY, 1816 *2859.11 p36*
MacCann, Bernard; New York, NY, 1816 *2859.11 p36*
MacCann, Daniel; New York, NY, 1815 *2859.11 p36*
MacCann, John; New York, NY, 1816 *2859.11 p36*
MacCann, Owen; New York, NY, 1816 *2859.11 p36*
MacCann, William; Philadelphia, 1815 *2859.11 p36*
MacCannell, Carry; Baltimore, 1816 *2859.11 p36*
MacCannell, Samuel; Baltimore, 1816 *2859.11 p36*
MacCarden, Edward; New York, NY, 1815 *2859.11 p36*
MacCarfin, T.; New York, NY, 1816 *2859.11 p36*
Maccari, Vittorio; Arkansas, 1918 *95.2 p77*
MacCarker, Patrick; New York, NY, 1816 *2859.11 p36*
MacCarter, James; New York, NY, 1815 *2859.11 p36*
MacCarthy, Bryan; New York, NY, 1816 *2859.11 p36*
MacCartney, Eliza; New York, NY, 1811 *2859.11 p15*
MacCartney, Ellen; New York, NY, 1811 *2859.11 p15*
MacCartney, Hannah; New York, NY, 1811 *2859.11
  p15*
MacCartney, John; New York, NY, 1811 *2859.11 p15*
MacCartney, Nancy; New York, NY, 1811 *2859.11 p15*
MacCartney, Patrick; New York, NY, 1811 *2859.11 p15*
MacCartney, Patrick; New York, NY, 1816 *2859.11 p36*
MacCartney, Samuel; New York, NY, 1811 *2859.11 p15*
MacCarton, Charles; New York, NY, 1811 *2859.11 p15*
MacCarton, James; New York, NY, 1811 *2859.11 p15*
MacCarty, Rose; New York, NY, 1815 *2859.11 p36*
MacCaskey, Eliza; Philadelphia, 1816 *2859.11 p36*
MacCaskey, John; Philadelphia, 1816 *2859.11 p36*
MacCasle, Thomas; Philadelphia, 1815 *2859.11 p36*
MacCathen, Adam; New York, NY, 1816 *2859.11 p36*
MacCaughall, Geo.; New York, NY, 1811 *2859.11 p15*
MacCaughan, Alex; Baltimore, 1811 *2859.11 p15*
MacCauley, Eliza; Philadelphia, 1816 *2859.11 p36*
MacCauley, Elizabeth; Philadelphia, 1816 *2859.11 p36*
MacCauley, Robert; Philadelphia, 1816 *2859.11 p36*
  With brother
MacCauly, Jane; Philadelphia, 1816 *2859.11 p36*
MacCauly, John; New York, NY, 1816 *2859.11 p36*
MacCauly, John; Philadelphia, 1816 *2859.11 p36*
MacCausland, Andrew; New York, NY, 1816 *2859.11
  p36*
MacCawley, James; Philadelphia, 1816 *2859.11 p36*
MacCawlley, Hugh; New York, NY, 1811 *2859.11 p15*
MacClane, John; New York, NY, 1811 *2859.11 p15*
MacClane, Mary; New York, NY, 1811 *2859.11 p15*
MacClaskey, Dennis; New York, NY, 1816 *2859.11 p36*
MacClaskey, Henry; New York, NY, 1816 *2859.11 p36*
MacClaskey, Hugh; New York, NY, 1816 *2859.11 p36*
MacClean, David; New York, NY, 1811 *2859.11 p15*
  With family
MacClean, James; New York, NY, 1816 *2859.11 p36*
MacClean, M.; New York, NY, 1816 *2859.11 p36*
Macclean, William 22; Maryland or Virginia, 1734
  3690.1 p145
MacCleary, Sam; New York, NY, 1815 *2859.11 p36*
MacClelland, Mr.; New York, NY, 1815 *2859.11 p36*
MacClelland, Mrs.; New York, NY, 1815 *2859.11 p36*

FOR A COMPLETE EXPLANATION OF ENTRY, SEE "HOW TO READ A CITATION" SECTION

MacClelland, James; New York, NY, 1815 *2859.11 p36*
MacClelland, Mary; New York, NY, 1815 *2859.11 p36*
MacClelland, Samuel; New York, NY, 1815 *2859.11 p36*
MacClellon, William; New York, NY, 1815 *2859.11 p36*
MacClenaghan, James; Philadelphia, 1811 *2859.11 p15*
MacCloskey, James; Philadelphia, 1811 *2859.11 p15*
MacCloud, Anne; New York, NY, 1816 *2859.11 p36*
MacCloud, Daniel; New York, NY, 1816 *2859.11 p36*
MacCloud, James; New York, NY, 1816 *2859.11 p36*
MacCloud, John; New York, NY, 1816 *2859.11 p36*
MacCloud, Mary Anne; New York, NY, 1816 *2859.11 p36*
MacCloud, Neile; New York, NY, 1816 *2859.11 p36*
MacCloy, Thomas; New York, NY, 1811 *2859.11 p15*
    With family
MacClure, Anne; New York, NY, 1811 *2859.11 p15*
MacClure, Thomas; New York, NY, 1811 *2859.11 p15*
MacClushey, Martha; New York, NY, 1816 *2859.11 p36*
MacClushey, Matilda; New York, NY, 1816 *2859.11 p36*
MacCoal, Charles; New York, NY, 1816 *2859.11 p36*
MacCoal, Patrick; New York, NY, 1816 *2859.11 p36*
MacColgan, George; New York, NY, 1816 *2859.11 p36*
MacColgan, John; Philadelphia, 1816 *2859.11 p36*
MacColgin, John; New York, NY, 1811 *2859.11 p15*
MacColim, Daniel; New York, NY, 1815 *2859.11 p36*
MacColim, Margaret; New York, NY, 1815 *2859.11 p36*
MacColley, John; New York, NY, 1811 *2859.11 p15*
MacColley, John; New York, NY, 1816 *2859.11 p36*
MacCollison, David; New York, NY, 1815 *2859.11 p36*
MacCollison, Thomas; New York, NY, 1815 *2859.11 p36*
MacCollough, Wm.; Philadelphia, 1816 *2859.11 p36*
MacComb, Ann; New York, NY, 1811 *2859.11 p15*
MacComb, Daniel; New York, NY, 1816 *2859.11 p36*
MacComb, Henry; New York, NY, 1811 *2859.11 p15*
MacComb, John; New York, NY, 1816 *2859.11 p36*
MacComb, Margaret; New York, NY, 1811 *2859.11 p15*
MacComb, Robert; New York, NY, 1811 *2859.11 p15*
    With family
MacComb, Thomas; New York, NY, 1811 *2859.11 p15*
MacConaghy, Alex; New York, NY, 1811 *2859.11 p15*
MacConley, George; New York, NY, 1816 *2859.11 p36*
MacConley, John; New York, NY, 1811 *2859.11 p15*
MacConnaghy, Jas.; New York, NY, 1811 *2859.11 p15*
MacConnell, James; New York, NY, 1811 *2859.11 p15*
MacConnell, James; New York, NY, 1816 *2859.11 p36*
MacConnell, James; Philadelphia, 1811 *2859.11 p15*
MacConnell, John; New York, NY, 1811 *2859.11 p15*
MacConnell, P.; New York, NY, 1811 *2859.11 p15*
    With family
MacConnell, Sarah; New York, NY, 1811 *2859.11 p15*
MacConstand, Esther; Baltimore, 1811 *2859.11 p15*
MacConway, Edw.; New York, NY, 1811 *2859.11 p15*
MacCool, James; New York, NY, 1816 *2859.11 p36*
MacCormac, Francis J.L.; Colorado, 1904 *9678.2 p125*
MacCormac, John Francis; Colorado, 1894 *9678.2 p125*
MacCormack, B.; New York, NY, 1815 *2859.11 p36*
MacCormick, Esther; New York, NY, 1816 *2859.11 p36*
MacCormick, James; New York, NY, 1816 *2859.11 p36*
MacCormick, Jno.; Philadelphia, 1816 *2859.11 p36*
MacCormick, John; New York, NY, 1816 *2859.11 p36*
MacCormick, Patrick; New York, NY, 1816 *2859.11 p36*
MacCormick, Thomas; New York, NY, 1811 *2859.11 p15*
Maccormick, William; Montreal, 1822 *7603 p87*
MacCosker, Bernard; New York, NY, 1811 *2859.11 p15*
MacCoskery, John; New York, NY, 1811 *2859.11 p15*
MacCoun, Charles; Philadelphia, 1811 *2859.11 p15*
MacCousland, Ann; Baltimore, 1811 *2859.11 p15*
MacCousland, Mar.; Baltimore, 1811 *2859.11 p15*
MacCousland, Mary; Baltimore, 1811 *2859.11 p15*
MacCoy, Alexander; New York, NY, 1816 *2859.11 p36*
MacCoy, Joseph; New York, NY, 1811 *2859.11 p15*
    With family
MacCracken, Alexander; New York, NY, 1816 *2859.11 p36*
MacCracken, Alexander, Jr.; New York, NY, 1816 *2859.11 p36*
MacCracken, Joseph; New York, NY, 1816 *2859.11 p36*
MacCracken, Robert; New York, NY, 1811 *2859.11 p15*
MacCrea, John; New York, NY, 1816 *2859.11 p36*
MacCready, Elinor; New York, NY, 1811 *2859.11 p15*
MacCready, John; New York, NY, 1811 *2859.11 p15*
MacCready, Wm.; New York, NY, 1811 *2859.11 p15*
MacCrecan, James; New York, NY, 1811 *2859.11 p15*
MacCreery, John; Baltimore, 1811 *2859.11 p15*
MacCrossin, John; New York, NY, 1816 *2859.11 p36*
MacCue, Daniel; Philadelphia, 1811 *2859.11 p15*
MacCue, Michael; Philadelphia, 1811 *2859.11 p15*
MacCue, Thomas; Baltimore, 1811 *2859.11 p15*

MacCullagh, Michael; New York, NY, 1815 *2859.11 p36*
MacCullaugh, John; New York, NY, 1811 *2859.11 p15*
    With family
MacCulloch, Geo.; Baltimore, 1811 *2859.11 p15*
MacCulloch, James; New York, NY, 1816 *2859.11 p36*
MacCulloch, Mary; New York, NY, 1811 *2859.11 p15*
MacCulloch, Wm.; New York, NY, 1811 *2859.11 p15*
MacCullough, Alex; New York, NY, 1811 *2859.11 p15*
MacCullough, Hamilton; New York, NY, 1811 *2859.11 p15*
MacCullum, Joseph; New York, NY, 1816 *2859.11 p36*
MacCully, Mathew; New York, NY, 1811 *2859.11 p15*
MacCune, Clem.; Philadelphia, 1811 *2859.11 p15*
MacCurdy, James; New York, NY, 1815 *2859.11 p36*
MacCurdy, Jane; New York, NY, 1815 *2859.11 p36*
MacCurdy, John; New York, NY, 1815 *2859.11 p36*
MacCurdy, Morgan; Philadelphia, 1811 *2859.11 p15*
MacCurdy, Neil; New York, NY, 1815 *2859.11 p36*
MacCurdy, William; New York, NY, 1815 *2859.11 p36*
MacCurdy, William; Philadelphia, 1811 *2859.11 p15*
MacCurry, Henry; New York, NY, 1811 *2859.11 p15*
MacCurtney, James; New York, NY, 1811 *2859.11 p15*
MacCusker, Terence; New York, NY, 1816 *2859.11 p36*
Maccutchon, John; Quebec, 1763 *7603 p42*
MacDaid, John; New York, NY, 1816 *2859.11 p36*
MacDaniel, Mrs.; New York, NY, 1816 *2859.11 p36*
    With child
MacDaniel, And'w; New York, NY, 1816 *2859.11 p36*
Macdaniel, Edward 16; Maryland, 1723 *3690.1 p145*
MacDaniel, John; New York, NY, 1816 *2859.11 p36*
MacDaniel, Less; New York, NY, 1816 *2859.11 p36*
MacDaniel, Mary; New York, NY, 1815 *2859.11 p36*
MacDaniel, Michael; New York, NY, 1815 *2859.11 p36*
MacDaniel, Owen; New York, NY, 1816 *2859.11 p36*
MacDaniel, T.; New York, NY, 1816 *2859.11 p36*
MacDaniel, Tho.; New York, NY, 1816 *2859.11 p36*
MacDemiott, Peter; Philadelphia, 1816 *2859.11 p36*
Macdennis, G.K.; Wisconsin, n.d. *9675.6 p268*
MacDermid, Archie *SEE* MacDermid, Donald
MacDermid, Charles *SEE* MacDermid, Donald
MacDermid, Donald; Quebec, 1865 *4537.30 p55*
    Wife: Marion Smith
    Child: Charles
    Child: Margaret
    Child: Neil
    Child: Archie
MacDermid, Margaret *SEE* MacDermid, Donald
MacDermid, Margaret; Quebec, 1870 *4537.30 p64*
MacDermid, Marion Smith *SEE* MacDermid, Donald
MacDermid, Neil *SEE* MacDermid, Donald
MacDermot, John; New York, NY, 1816 *2859.11 p36*
MacDermot, Susana; New York, NY, 1811 *2859.11 p15*
    With family
Macdermott, Anne; Quebec, 1791 *7603 p77*
MacDermott, Charles; New York, NY, 1816 *2859.11 p36*
MacDermott, Daniel; New York, NY, 1816 *2859.11 p36*
MacDermott, John; New England, 1816 *2859.11 p36*
MacDermott, Mary; New York, NY, 1816 *2859.11 p36*
MacDermott, Owen; New England, 1816 *2859.11 p36*
MacDermott, Patk; New York, NY, 1816 *2859.11 p36*
MacDermott, Patrick; New York, NY, 1816 *2859.11 p36*
MacDermott, Rose; New York, NY, 1816 *2859.11 p36*
MacDermott, Susannah; New York, NY, 1816 *2859.11 p36*
MacDermott, William; New York, NY, 1816 *2859.11 p36*
MacDevitt, P.; New York, NY, 1811 *2859.11 p15*
MacDhomhnuill, Alexander *SEE* MacDhomhnuill, Flora
MacDhomhnuill, Allen *SEE* MacDhomhnuill, Flora
MacDhomhnuill, Anne *SEE* MacDhomhnuill, Flora
MacDhomhnuill, Flora; Cape Fear, NC, 1774 *4814 p92*
    Husband: Allen
    Son: Alexander
    Son: James
    Daughter: Anne
MacDhomhnuill, James *SEE* MacDhomhnuill, Flora
MacDill, John; New York, NY, 1816 *2859.11 p36*
MacDonagh, James; New York, NY, 1816 *2859.11 p36*
Macdonald, Mr.; Montreal, n.d. *9775.5 p202*
Macdonald, Mrs.; Quebec, 1851 *4537.30 p69*
    Son: John
    Son: Donald
MacDonald, Alex *SEE* MacDonald, Alex
MacDonald, Alex *SEE* MacDonald, Finlay
MacDonald, Alex *SEE* MacDonald, John
MacDonald, Alex *SEE* MacDonald, Murdo
MacDonald, Alex *SEE* MacDonald, Murdo
MacDonald, Alex; Quebec, 1851 *4537.30 p56*
    Wife: Mary MacIver
    Child: Catherine
    Child: John

    Child: Mary
    Child: Margaret
    Child: Alex
    Child: Kirsty
MacDonald, Alexander *SEE* MacDonald, Flora
MacDonald, Alexander; America, 1766 *4814 p104*
MacDonald, Alexander; Cape Fear, NC, 1771 *4814 p92*
    Wife: Annabella
MacDonald, Alexander; Halifax, N.S., 1775 *4814 p104*
MacDonald, Alexander; North Carolina, 1771 *4814 p96*
    With wife & family
MacDonald, Alexander; Nova Scotia, 1778 *4814 p106*
Macdonald, Alexandre; Quebec, 1793 *7603 p40*
Macdonald, Allan *SEE* MacDonald, John
MacDonald, Allen *SEE* MacDonald, Flora
Macdonald, Allen; Nova Scotia, 1778 *4814 p106*
    Wife: Flora
MacDonald, Angus *SEE* MacDonald, Donald
MacDonald, Angus *SEE* MacDonald, Farquhar
MacDonald, Angus *SEE* MacDonald, Finlay
MacDonald, Angus *SEE* MacDonald, Isabella
MacDonald, Angus *SEE* MacDonald, John
MacDonald, Angus *SEE* MacDonald, John
MacDonald, Angus *SEE* MacDonald, John
MacDonald, Angus *SEE* MacDonald, John
MacDonald, Angus *SEE* MacDonald, Murdo
MacDonald, Angus *SEE* MacDonald, William
MacDonald, Angus; Cape Fear, NC, 1773 *4814 p92*
MacDonald, Angus; North Carolina, 1773 *4814 p97*
MacDonald, Angus; Nova Scotia, 1776-1785 *4814 p97*
    With wife & 5 children
MacDonald, Angus; Nova Scotia, 1783 *4814 p101*
MacDonald, Angus; Quebec, 1773 *7603 p37*
Macdonald, Angus; Quebec, 1821-1854 *4537.30 p56*
MacDonald, Angus; Quebec, 1821-1899 *4537.30 p56*
MacDonald, Angus; Quebec, 1821-1899 *4537.30 p57*
MacDonald, Angus; Quebec, 1847 *4537.30 p57*
MacDonald, Angus; Quebec, 1855 *4537.30 p57*
    Wife: Mary MacArthur
    Child: Donald A.
    Child: Ann
    Child: John A.
MacDonald, Angus; Quebec, 1870-1879 *4537.30 p72*
    Wife: Mary Campbell
    Child: Catherine
    Child: Donald
MacDonald, Ann *SEE* MacDonald, Angus
MacDonald, Ann *SEE* MacDonald, Donald
MacDonald, Ann *SEE* MacDonald, Donald
MacDonald, Ann *SEE* MacDonald, Donald
MacDonald, Ann *SEE* MacDonald, Donald
MacDonald, Ann *SEE* MacDonald, Finlay
MacDonald, Ann *SEE* MacDonald, John
MacDonald, Ann *SEE* MacDonald, John
MacDonald, Ann *SEE* MacDonald, John
MacDonald, Ann *SEE* MacDonald, John
MacDonald, Ann *SEE* MacDonald, Malcolm
MacDonald, Ann *SEE* MacDonald, Murdo
MacDonald, Ann *SEE* MacDonald, Murdo
MacDonald, Ann *SEE* MacDonald, Neil
MacDonald, Ann *SEE* MacDonald, Norman
MacDonald, Ann *SEE* MacDonald, Thomas
MacDonald, Ann; Quebec, 1838 *4537.30 p104*
MacDonald, Ann; Quebec, 1840 *4537.30 p2*
MacDonald, Ann; Quebec, 1845 *4537.30 p30*
MacDonald, Ann; Quebec, 1851 *4537.30 p75*
MacDonald, Ann; Quebec, 1870 *4537.30 p37*
MacDonald, Ann MacKenzie *SEE* MacDonald, John
MacDonald, Ann MacLeod *SEE* MacDonald, John Og
MacDonald, Ann MacLeod *SEE* MacDonald, Neil
MacDonald, Ann Matheson *SEE* MacDonald, Donald
MacDonald, Ann Thomson *SEE* MacDonald, John
MacDonald, Annabella *SEE* MacDonald, Alexander
MacDonald, Annabella; Quebec, 1842 *4537.30 p47*
MacDonald, Anne *SEE* MacDonald, Flora
MacDonald, Anne; North Carolina, 1774 *4814 p100*
MacDonald, Bess *SEE* MacDonald, Farquhar
MacDonald, Catherine *SEE* MacDonald, Alex
MacDonald, Catherine *SEE* MacDonald, Angus
MacDonald, Catherine *SEE* MacDonald, Donald
MacDonald, Catherine *SEE* MacDonald, Donald
MacDonald, Catherine *SEE* MacDonald, Donald
MacDonald, Catherine *SEE* MacDonald, Farquhar
MacDonald, Catherine *SEE* MacDonald, Isabella
MacDonald, Catherine *SEE* MacDonald, Janet Murray
MacDonald, Catherine *SEE* MacDonald, John
MacDonald, Catherine *SEE* MacDonald, John
MacDonald, Catherine *SEE* MacDonald, John
MacDonald, Catherine *SEE* MacDonald, Murdo
MacDonald, Catherine *SEE* MacDonald, Norman
MacDonald, Catherine *SEE* MacDonald, William

MacDonald, Catherine; Quebec, 1851 *4537.30 p13*
MacDonald, Catherine; Quebec, 1851 *4537.30 p33*
MacDonald, Catherine; Quebec, 1855 *4537.30 p24*
MacDonald, Catherine; Quebec, 1855 *4537.30 p88*
MacDonald, Catherine Graham *SEE* MacDonald, John
MacDonald, Catherine MacLeod *SEE* MacDonald, Murdo
MacDonald, Catherine Morrison *SEE* MacDonald, Norman
MacDonald, Catherine Smith *SEE* MacDonald, Kenneth
MacDonald, Catherine Smith *SEE* MacDonald, Malcolm
MacDonald, Charles *SEE* MacDonald, John
MacDonald, Charles; America, 1771-1776 *4814 p105*
MacDonald, Charles; Halifax, N.S., 1776 *4814 p105*
Macdonald, Christopher 21; Virginia, 1734 *3690.1 p145*
MacDonald, Donald *SEE* MacDonald, Mrs.
MacDonald, Donald *SEE* MacDonald, Angus
MacDonald, Donald *SEE* MacDonald, Donald
MacDonald, Donald *SEE* MacDonald, Finlay
MacDonald, Donald *SEE* MacDonald, Isabella MacIver
MacDonald, Donald *SEE* MacDonald, John
MacDonald, Donald *SEE* MacDonald, John
MacDonald, Donald *SEE* MacDonald, John
MacDonald, Donald *SEE* MacDonald, John
MacDonald, Donald *SEE* MacDonald, John
MacDonald, Donald *SEE* MacDonald, John
MacDonald, Donald *SEE* MacDonald, John
MacDonald, Donald *SEE* MacDonald, Malcolm
MacDonald, Donald *SEE* MacDonald, Thomas
MacDonald, Donald *SEE* MacDonald, William
Macdonald, Donald; America, 1853 *8893 p265*
MacDonald, Donald; Cape Fear, NC, 1774 *4814 p92*
MacDonald, Donald; North Carolina, 1773 *1639.20 p141*
MacDonald, Donald; North Carolina, 1773-1774 *4814 p98*
MacDonald, Donald; North Carolina, 1775-1776 *4814 p94*
MacDonald, Donald; Quebec, 1813-1899 *4537.30 p58*
MacDonald, Donald; Quebec, 1841 *4537.30 p58*
  *Wife:*Catherine
  *Child:*Mary
  *Child:*Ann
  *Child:*John
  *Child:*Catherine
  *Child:*Kirsty
  *Child:*William
MacDonald, Donald; Quebec, 1843 *4537.30 p60*
MacDonald, Donald; Quebec, 1843-1899 *4537.30 p72*
MacDonald, Donald; Quebec, 1851 *4537.30 p59*
  *Wife:*Kirsty MacDonald
  *Child:*Ann
  *Brother:*Murdo
  *Brother:*Angus
  *Child:*Malcolm
MacDonald, Donald; Quebec, 1851 *4537.30 p70*
  *Wife:*Ann Matheson
  *Child:*Catherine
  *Child:*Mary
  *Child:*Ann
  *Child:*Donald
  *Child:*John
  *Child:*Malcolm
MacDonald, Donald; Quebec, 1855 *4537.30 p58*
  *Wife:*Kirsty Campbell
  *Child:*Norman D.
  *Child:*Kirsty
  *Child:*John
  *Child:*Ann
MacDonald, Donald; Quebec, 1855 *4537.30 p60*
  *Wife:*Mary Morrison
  *Child:*Norman
  *Child:*Catherine
  *Child:*John
MacDonald, Donald, Sr.; Quebec, 1873 *4537.30 p70*
MacDonald, Donald A. *SEE* MacDonald, Angus
MacDonald, Dorothy; Quebec, 1890-1892 *4537.30 p48*
MacDonald, Effie *SEE* MacDonald, Finlay
MacDonald, Effie *SEE* MacDonald, John
MacDonald, Effie *SEE* MacDonald, Murdo
MacDonald, Effie; Quebec, 1841 *4537.30 p38*
MacDonald, Effie; Quebec, 1841 *4537.30 p41*
MacDonald, Effie; Quebec, 1842 *4537.30 p90*
MacDonald, Effie; Quebec, 1855 *4537.30 p17*
MacDonald, Effie MacAskill *SEE* MacDonald, Murdo
MacDonald, Effie MacIver *SEE* MacDonald, Murdo
MacDonald, Farquhar; Quebec, 1841 *4537.30 p60*
  *Wife:*Kirsty MacDonald
  *Child:*Angus
  *Child:*Bess
  *Child:*Catherine
MacDonald, Finlay *SEE* MacDonald, Murdo

MacDonald, Finlay; Quebec, 1851 *4537.30 p61*
  *Wife:*Effie
  *Child:*John
  *Child:*Kirsty
  *Child:*Alex
  *Child:*Marion
  *Child:*Angus
  *Child:*Donald
  *Child:*Ann
MacDonald, Flora *SEE* MacDonald, Allen
MacDonald, Flora *SEE* MacDonald, John
MacDonald, Flora; Cape Fear, NC, 1774 *4814 p92*
  *Husband:*Allen
  *Son:*Alexander
  *Son:*James
  *Daughter:*Anne
MacDonald, Hugh *SEE* MacDonald, Isabella
MacDonald, Hugh; Cape Fear, NC, 1771 *4814 p92*
Macdonald, Ignace; Quebec, 1793 *7603 p40*
MacDonald, Isabella *SEE* MacDonald, James
MacDonald, Isabella *SEE* MacDonald, John
MacDonald, Isabella *SEE* MacDonald, John Og
MacDonald, Isabella *SEE* MacDonald, Norman
MacDonald, Isabella; Quebec, 1829-1900 *4537.30 p71*
  *Child:*John
  *Child:*Angus
  *Child:*Catherine
  *Child:*Hugh
MacDonald, Isabella; Quebec, 1873 *4537.30 p36*
MacDonald, Isabella MacIver; Quebec, 1884 *4537.30 p70*
  *Son:*Donald
  *Son:*John
MacDonald, Isabella MacLeod *SEE* MacDonald, Murdo
MacDonald, James *SEE* MacDonald, Flora
MacDonald, James; North Carolina, 1776 *4814 p98*
  *Wife:*Isabella
  With family
MacDonald, Jane *SEE* MacDonald, Murdo
MacDonald, Jane MacLeod *SEE* MacDonald, John
MacDonald, Janet *SEE* MacDonald, Norman
MacDonald, Janet; Quebec, 1851 *4537.30 p1*
MacDonald, Janet Murray; Quebec, 1852 *4537.30 p39*
  *Child:*Catherine
MacDonald, Joan *SEE* MacDonald, John
MacDonald, Joan *SEE* MacDonald, John
MacDonald, John *SEE* MacDonald, Mrs.
MacDonald, John *SEE* MacDonald, Alex
MacDonald, John *SEE* MacDonald, Donald
MacDonald, John *SEE* MacDonald, Donald
MacDonald, John *SEE* MacDonald, Donald
MacDonald, John *SEE* MacDonald, Finlay
MacDonald, John *SEE* MacDonald, Isabella
MacDonald, John *SEE* MacDonald, Isabella MacIver
MacDonald, John *SEE* MacDonald, John
MacDonald, John *SEE* MacDonald, John
MacDonald, John *SEE* MacDonald, John
MacDonald, John *SEE* MacDonald, John
MacDonald, John *SEE* MacDonald, John
MacDonald, John *SEE* MacDonald, John
MacDonald, John *SEE* MacDonald, John
MacDonald, John *SEE* MacDonald, John
MacDonald, John *SEE* MacDonald, Malcolm
MacDonald, John *SEE* MacDonald, Malcolm
MacDonald, John *SEE* MacDonald, Murdo
MacDonald, John *SEE* MacDonald, Murdo
MacDonald, John *SEE* MacDonald, Norman
MacDonald, John *SEE* MacDonald, William
Macdonald, John; America, 1761 *4814 p99*
MacDonald, John; North Carolina, 1755 *4814 p99*
Macdonald, John; Pennsylvania, 1755 *4814 p99*
MacDonald, John; Quebec, 1783 *7603 p39*
Macdonald, John; Quebec, 1800-1860 *9775.5 p203*
MacDonald, John; Quebec, 1835-1899 *4537.30 p62*
MacDonald, John; Quebec, 1839-1879 *4537.30 p62*
MacDonald, John; Quebec, 1841 *4537.30 p64*
  *Wife:*Margaret MacIver
  *Child:*Kenneth
  *Child:*Malcolm
  *Child:*Effie
  *Child:*Angus
  *Child:*John
MacDonald, John; Quebec, 1842 *4537.30 p63*
  *Wife:*Kirsty
  *Child:*Ann
  *Child:*Catherine
  *Child:*Donald
MacDonald, John; Quebec, 1843 *4537.30 p64*
  *Wife:*Margaret MacRitchie
  *Child:*Norman
  *Child:*John
  *Child:*Donald
  *Child:*Kirsty

MacDonald, John; Quebec, 1851 *4537.30 p63*
  *Wife:*Kirsty MacKay
  *Child:*Mary
  *Child:*Margaret
  *Child:*William
  *Child:*Murdo
  *Child:*Kirsty
  *Child:*Joan
MacDonald, John; Quebec, 1851 *4537.30 p65*
  *Wife:*Rachel MacAulay
  *Child:*Catherine
  *Child:*Ann
  *Child:*Murdo
  *Child:*Margaret
  *Child:*Donald
  *Child:*Flora
  *Child:*Kirsty
  *Child:*Mary
MacDonald, John; Quebec, 1853 *4537.30 p61*
  *Wife:*Ann MacKenzie
  *Child:*Donald
  *Child:*Angus
  *Child:*John
  *Child:*William
  *Child:*Catherine
  *Child:*Norman
  *Child:*Allan
MacDonald, John; Quebec, 1853 *4537.30 p63*
  *Wife:*Jane MacLeod
  *Child:*Marion
  *Child:*Donald
  *Child:*John
  *Child:*Ann
  *Child:*Catherine
  *Child:*Mary
MacDonald, John; Quebec, 1855 *4537.30 p65*
  *Wife:*Mary Morrison
  *Child:*Donald
  *Child:*Kenneth
  *Child:*Angus
  *Child:*John
  *Child:*Roderick
  *Child:*Kirsty
MacDonald, John; Quebec, 1857 *4537.30 p62*
  *Wife:*Ann
  *Child:*John
  *Child:*Donald
  *Child:*Roderick
  *Child:*Kirsty
  *Child:*Margaret
  *Child:*Norman
MacDonald, John; Quebec, 1870 *4537.30 p64*
  *Wife:*Margaret MacDermid
  *Child:*John
  *Child:*Charles
  *Child:*Joan
  *Child:*Marion
MacDonald, John; Quebec, 1875 *4537.30 p71*
  *Wife:*Catherine Graham
  *Child:*Murdo
MacDonald, John; Quebec, 1875 *4537.30 p72*
  *Wife:*Ann Thomson
  *Child:*Angus
  *Child:*Murdo
  *Child:*Alex
  *Child:*Isabella
MacDonald, John A. *SEE* MacDonald, Angus
Macdonald, John A.; Ottawa, 1867 *9775.5 p215*
Macdonald, John Og; Quebec, 1851 *4537.30 p61*
  *Wife:*Ann MacLeod
  *Child:*Isabella
MacDonald, Kenneth *SEE* MacDonald, John
MacDonald, Kenneth *SEE* MacDonald, John
MacDonald, Kenneth; Quebec, 1851 *4537.30 p65*
  *Wife:*Catherine Smith
MacDonald, Kirsty *SEE* MacDonald, Alex
MacDonald, Kirsty *SEE* MacDonald, Donald
MacDonald, Kirsty *SEE* MacDonald, Donald
MacDonald, Kirsty *SEE* MacDonald, Finlay
MacDonald, Kirsty *SEE* MacDonald, John
MacDonald, Kirsty *SEE* MacDonald, John
MacDonald, Kirsty *SEE* MacDonald, John
MacDonald, Kirsty *SEE* MacDonald, John
MacDonald, Kirsty *SEE* MacDonald, John
MacDonald, Kirsty *SEE* MacDonald, Murdo
MacDonald, Kirsty *SEE* MacDonald, William
MacDonald, Kirsty; Quebec, 1820-1841 *4537.30 p17*
MacDonald, Kirsty; Quebec, 1841 *4537.30 p60*
MacDonald, Kirsty; Quebec, 1851 *4537.30 p59*
MacDonald, Kirsty; Quebec, 1851 *4537.30 p102*
MacDonald, Kirsty; Quebec, 1865 *4537.30 p101*
MacDonald, Kirsty; Quebec, 1883 *4537.30 p33*

MacDonald, Kirsty Campbell *SEE* MacDonald, Donald
MacDonald, Kirsty Campbell *SEE* MacDonald, Murdo
MacDonald, Kirsty MacDonald *SEE* MacDonald, Donald
MacDonald, Kirsty MacDonald *SEE* MacDonald, Farquhar
MacDonald, Kirsty MacKay *SEE* MacDonald, John
MacDonald, Kirsty MacRitchie *SEE* MacDonald, Thomas
MacDonald, Malcolm *SEE* MacDonald, Donald
MacDonald, Malcolm *SEE* MacDonald, Donald
MacDonald, Malcolm *SEE* MacDonald, John
MacDonald, Malcolm *SEE* MacDonald, Neil
MacDonald, Malcolm *SEE* MacDonald, Thomas
MacDonald, Malcolm *SEE* MacDonald, William
MacDonald, Malcolm; Quebec, 1851 *4537.30 p66*
  Wife: Margaret MacKay
  Child: William
  Child: Murdo
  Child: Mary
  Child: John
MacDonald, Malcolm; Quebec, 1851 *4537.30 p70*
  Wife: Catherine Smith
  Child: John
  Child: Donald
  Child: Margaret
  Child: Ann
MacDonald, Margaret *SEE* MacDonald, Alex
MacDonald, Margaret *SEE* MacDonald, John
MacDonald, Margaret *SEE* MacDonald, John
MacDonald, Margaret *SEE* MacDonald, John
MacDonald, Margaret *SEE* MacDonald, Malcolm
MacDonald, Margaret *SEE* MacDonald, Murdo
MacDonald, Margaret *SEE* MacDonald, Murdo
MacDonald, Margaret *SEE* MacDonald, Murdo
MacDonald, Margaret *SEE* MacDonald, Neil
MacDonald, Margaret *SEE* MacDonald, Thomas
MacDonald, Margaret; Quebec, 1793 *7603 p40*
MacDonald, Margaret; Quebec, 1845 *4537.30 p79*
MacDonald, Margaret; Quebec, 1858 *4537.30 p110*
MacDonald, Margaret; Quebec, 1863 *4537.30 p37*
MacDonald, Margaret; Quebec, 1863 *4537.30 p80*
MacDonald, Margaret MacDermid *SEE* MacDonald, John
MacDonald, Margaret MacIver *SEE* MacDonald, John
MacDonald, Margaret MacKay *SEE* MacDonald, Malcolm
MacDonald, Margaret MacRitchie *SEE* MacDonald, John
MacDonald, Marion *SEE* MacDonald, Finlay
MacDonald, Marion *SEE* MacDonald, John
MacDonald, Marion *SEE* MacDonald, John
MacDonald, Marion *SEE* MacDonald, Murdo
MacDonald, Mary *SEE* MacDonald, Alex
MacDonald, Mary *SEE* MacDonald, Donald
MacDonald, Mary *SEE* MacDonald, Donald
MacDonald, Mary *SEE* MacDonald, John
MacDonald, Mary *SEE* MacDonald, John
MacDonald, Mary *SEE* MacDonald, John
MacDonald, Mary *SEE* MacDonald, Malcolm
MacDonald, Mary *SEE* MacDonald, Murdo
MacDonald, Mary *SEE* MacDonald, Murdo
MacDonald, Mary *SEE* MacDonald, Murdo
MacDonald, Mary *SEE* MacDonald, Murdo
MacDonald, Mary; Quebec, 1851 *4537.30 p51*
MacDonald, Mary; Quebec, 1851 *4537.30 p80*
MacDonald, Mary; Quebec, 1851 *4537.30 p95*
MacDonald, Mary; Quebec, 1851 *4537.30 p119*
MacDonald, Mary; Quebec, 1855 *4537.30 p119*
MacDonald, Mary; Quebec, 1863 *4537.30 p14*
MacDonald, Mary; Quebec, 1887 *4537.30 p11*
MacDonald, Mary Campbell *SEE* MacDonald, Angus
MacDonald, Mary MacArthur *SEE* MacDonald, Angus
MacDonald, Mary MacIver *SEE* MacDonald, Alex
MacDonald, Mary MacRitchie *SEE* MacDonald, William
MacDonald, Mary Morrison *SEE* MacDonald, Donald
MacDonald, Mary Morrison *SEE* MacDonald, John
MacDonald, Moore; New York, NY, 1811 *2859.11 p15*
MacDonald, Murdo *SEE* MacDonald, Donald
MacDonald, Murdo *SEE* MacDonald, John
MacDonald, Murdo *SEE* MacDonald, John
MacDonald, Murdo *SEE* MacDonald, John
MacDonald, Murdo *SEE* MacDonald, John
MacDonald, Murdo *SEE* MacDonald, Malcolm
MacDonald, Murdo *SEE* MacDonald, William
MacDonald, Murdo; Quebec, 1845 *4537.30 p66*
  Wife: Effie MacIver
  Child: Peter
  Child: Mary
  Child: Ann
MacDonald, Murdo; Quebec, 1851 *4537.30 p67*
  Wife: Isabella MacLeod
  Child: John
  Child: Mary
  Child: Jane

Child: Angus
Child: Alex
Child: Ann
Child: Kirsty
MacDonald, Murdo; Quebec, 1851 *4537.30 p67*
  Child: Margaret
MacDonald, Murdo; Quebec, 1864 *4537.30 p67*
  Wife: Kirsty Campbell
  Child: Alex
  Child: Effie
  Child: Mary
  Child: Roderick
  Child: Catherine
  Child: Finlay
MacDonald, Murdo; Quebec, 1865 *4537.30 p66*
  Wife: Effie MacAskill
  Child: William
  Child: Marion
  Child: Margaret
  Child: Mary
MacDonald, Murdo; Quebec, 1873 *4537.30 p71*
  Wife: Catherine MacLeod
  Child: John
  Child: Margaret
MacDonald, Murdoch; America, 1775-1786 *4814 p99*
MacDonald, Neil *SEE* MacDonald, Norman
MacDonald, Neil; America, 1802 *1639.20 p145*
  With wife & 3 sons
MacDonald, Neil; Quebec, 1855 *4537.30 p68*
  Wife: Ann MacLeod
  Child: Ann
  Child: Malcolm
  Child: Margaret
MacDonald, Norman *SEE* MacDonald, Donald
MacDonald, Norman *SEE* MacDonald, John
MacDonald, Norman *SEE* MacDonald, John
MacDonald, Norman *SEE* MacDonald, John
MacDonald, Norman *SEE* MacDonald, Thomas
MacDonald, Norman; Quebec, 1847 *4537.30 p69*
MacDonald, Norman; Quebec, 1853 *4537.30 p68*
  Wife: Janet
  Child: Ann
  Child: John
  Child: Roderick
  Child: William
  Child: Neil
  Child: Catherine
  Child: Isabella
  Child: Sally
MacDonald, Norman; Quebec, 1855 *4537.30 p68*
  Wife: Catherine Morrison
MacDonald, Norman D. *SEE* MacDonald, Donald
MacDonald, Peter *SEE* MacDonald, Murdo
MacDonald, Rachel MacAulay *SEE* MacDonald, John
MacDonald, Ranald; Halifax, N.S., 1775 *4814 p104*
MacDonald, Robert; New York, NY, 1811 *2859.11 p15*
MacDonald, Roderick *SEE* MacDonald, John
MacDonald, Roderick *SEE* MacDonald, John
MacDonald, Roderick *SEE* MacDonald, Murdo
MacDonald, Roderick *SEE* MacDonald, Norman
MacDonald, Sally *SEE* MacDonald, Norman
Macdonald, Sally; Montreal, 1818 *7603 p77*
MacDonald, Soirle; North Carolina, 1786 *4814 p99*
MacDonald, Terence; America, 1773-1774 *2859.11 p7*
MacDonald, Thomas; Quebec, 1784 *7603 p77*
MacDonald, Thomas; Quebec, 1863 *4537.30 p69*
  Wife: Kirsty MacRitchie
  Child: Donald
  Child: Margaret
  Child: Malcolm
  Child: Ann
  Child: Norman
MacDonald, Thos; New York, NY, 1816 *2859.11 p36*
MacDonald, William *SEE* MacDonald, Donald
MacDonald, William *SEE* MacDonald, John
MacDonald, William *SEE* MacDonald, John
MacDonald, William *SEE* MacDonald, Malcolm
MacDonald, William *SEE* MacDonald, Murdo
MacDonald, William *SEE* MacDonald, Norman
MacDonald, William; New York, NY, 1811 *2859.11 p15*
MacDonald, William; Quebec, 1820-1839 *4537.30 p69*
  Wife: Mary MacRitchie
  Child: Kirsty
  Child: John
  Child: Malcolm
  Child: Catherine
  Child: Donald
  Child: Murdo
  Child: Angus
MacDonel, James; New York, NY, 1816 *2859.11 p36*
MacDonell, Alexander; Ontario, 1792 *9775.5 p211*
MacDonell, Alexander; Ontario, 1803 *9775.5 p212*
Macdonell, Angus-Eneas; Montreal, 1787 *7603 p41*

Macdonell, Eneas-John 38; Montreal, 1791 *7603 p40*
Macdonell, Onesime 28; Montreal, 1775 *7603 p37*
Macdonell, Patrick; Montreal, 1818 *7603 p94*
MacDonnel, . . .; New England, 1816 *2859.11 p36*
MacDonnell, James; New York, NY, 1811 *2859.11 p15*
  With family
Macdonnell, James 34; Montreal, 1786 *7603 p39*
MacDonnell, Judith; New York, NY, 1816 *2859.11 p36*
MacDonnell, Margaret; New York, NY, 1816 *2859.11 p36*
MacDonnell, Michael; New York, NY, 1816 *2859.11 p36*
MacDonnell, Robert; New York, NY, 1816 *2859.11 p36*
MacDonnell, Thomas; New York, NY, 1816 *2859.11 p36*
MacDougal, John; New York, NY, 1815 *2859.11 p36*
MacDougal, Mary; New York, NY, 1815 *2859.11 p36*
MacDougal, Mary; New York, NY, 1816 *2859.11 p36*
MacDougall, John; New York, NY, 1816 *2859.11 p36*
MacDowel, C.; New York, NY, 1816 *2859.11 p36*
MacDowel, John; New York, NY, 1816 *2859.11 p36*
MacDowel, M.; New York, NY, 1816 *2859.11 p36*
MacDowel, W.; New York, NY, 1816 *2859.11 p36*
MacDowell, Alexander; New York, NY, 1815 *2859.11 p36*
MacDowell, John; New York, NY, 1816 *2859.11 p36*
MacDowl, Alexander; New York, NY, 1811 *2859.11 p15*
MacDowl, Elizabeth; New York, NY, 1811 *2859.11 p16*
MacDowl, Ezibella; New York, NY, 1811 *2859.11 p16*
MacDowl, John; New York, NY, 1811 *2859.11 p16*
MacDowl, Mary Ann; New York, NY, 1811 *2859.11 p16*
MacDowl, Rachel; New York, NY, 1811 *2859.11 p16*
MacDowl, Thomas; New York, NY, 1811 *2859.11 p16*
Mace, Miss; America, 1839 *778.5 p352*
Mace, Mrs.; America, 1839 *778.5 p352*
Mace, George 19; Pennsylvania, 1728 *3690.1 p27A*
Mace, Jon.; Virginia, 1637 *6219 p113*
MacEliver, George; New York, NY, 1811 *2859.11 p16*
MacElkeney, Robert; New York, NY, 1811 *2859.11 p16*
MacElroy, Arch.; Philadelphia, 1811 *2859.11 p16*
  With family
MacElwin, Hugh; New York, NY, 1811 *2859.11 p16*
MacElwrath, Rob't.; New York, NY, 1811 *2859.11 p16*
  With wife & child
MacEver, William; Baltimore, 1811 *2859.11 p16*
MacEvory, John; New York, NY, 1811 *2859.11 p16*
MacEvoy, Edward; Philadelphia, 1816 *2859.11 p36*
MacEvoy, Owen; New York, NY, 1816 *2859.11 p36*
MacEwan, Patrick Campbell 22; Kansas, 1895 *5240.1 p80*
MacEwen, John; New York, NY, 1811 *2859.11 p16*
Macey, John; Virginia, 1638 *6219 p2*
MacFadden, Charles; New York, NY, 1816 *2859.11 p36*
MacFadden, Samuel; New York, NY, 1815 *2859.11 p36*
MacFaddin, Eleanor; Philadelphia, 1811 *2859.11 p16*
MacFaddin, Manus; Philadelphia, 1811 *2859.11 p16*
MacFade, Jane; New York, NY, 1811 *2859.11 p16*
MacFaden, John; New York, NY, 1811 *2859.11 p16*
MacFall, John; New York, NY, 1811 *2859.11 p16*
MacFarland, John; New York, NY, 1811 *2859.11 p16*
  With wife & family
MacFarland, Robert; New York, NY, 1816 *2859.11 p36*
MacFarland, Wm.; New York, NY, 1811 *2859.11 p16*
  With family
MacFarland, Wm.; Philadelphia, 1811 *2859.11 p16*
MacFarlane, Alex; Quebec, 1852 *4537.30 p73*
  Wife: Peggy
  Child: Margaret
  Child: Donald
  Child: Catherine
  Child: Norman
  Child: John
  Child: Kirsty
  With child
MacFarlane, Catherine *SEE* MacFarlane, Alex
MacFarlane, Catherine; Quebec, 1863 *4537.30 p5*
MacFarlane, Catherine; Quebec, 1863 *4537.30 p73*
  Sibling: Donald
  Sibling: Margaret
MacFarlane, Donald *SEE* MacFarlane, Alex
MacFarlane, Donald *SEE* MacFarlane, Catherine
MacFarlane, George; Maryland, 1756 *1219.7 p43*
Macfarlane, George; Maryland, 1756 *3690.1 p145*
MacFarlane, John *SEE* MacFarlane, Alex
MacFarlane, John; Philadelphia, 1816 *2859.11 p36*
MacFarlane, Kirsty *SEE* MacFarlane, Alex
MacFarlane, Margaret *SEE* MacFarlane, Alex
MacFarlane, Margaret *SEE* MacFarlane, Catherine
MacFarlane, Mary Morrison; Quebec, 1873 *4537.30 p73*
MacFarlane, Norman *SEE* MacFarlane, Alex
MacFarlane, Peggy *SEE* MacFarlane, Alex
MacFaul, Daniel; New York, NY, 1811 *2859.11 p16*
MacFeely, Charles; New York, NY, 1811 *2859.11 p16*
MacFie, Dugald; Charleston, SC, 1812 *1639.20 p154*

MacGanty, Edward; New York, NY, 1811 *2859.11 p16*
MacGaragher, J.; New York, NY, 1816 *2859.11 p36*
  With wife & 5 children
MacGaraghy, Bryan; New York, NY, 1816 *2859.11 p37*
MacGattiger, Daniel; New York, NY, 1816 *2859.11 p37*
MacGaughrin, Farguis; New York, NY, 1811 *2859.11 p16*
MacGavaran, John; New York, NY, 1816 *2859.11 p37*
MacGaw, John; New York, NY, 1811 *2859.11 p16*
  With family
MacGaw, Robert; New York, NY, 1811 *2859.11 p16*
MacGaw, Thomas; New York, NY, 1811 *2859.11 p16*
Macgee, Lawrence; Montreal, 1822 *7603 p96*
MacGellaghan, Pat; Philadelphia, 1811 *2859.11 p16*
MacGeoch, Ellen; New York, NY, 1816 *2859.11 p37*
MacGeoch, Grace; New York, NY, 1816 *2859.11 p37*
MacGeoch, Sam.; New York, NY, 1816 *2859.11 p37*
MacGibbon, Samuel; New York, NY, 1816 *2859.11 p37*
MacGill, Anthony; Baltimore, 1811 *2859.11 p16*
Macgill, Bridget; Montreal, 1824 *7603 p61*
MacGill, Robert; New York, NY, 1816 *2859.11 p37*
Macgillis, Daniel; Quebec, 1784 *7603 p37*
Macgillis, Donald; Montreal, 1805 *7603 p42*
MacGinley, Corn.; New York, NY, 1811 *2859.11 p16*
MacGinn, Rose; New York, NY, 1816 *2859.11 p37*
MacGinness, Danl.; New York, NY, 1811 *2859.11 p16*
MacGinnis, Bernard; Philadelphia, 1811 *2859.11 p16*
MacGinnis, Daniel; New York, NY, 1816 *2859.11 p37*
MacGinnis, Ellen; New York, NY, 1816 *2859.11 p37*
MacGinnis, Henry; New York, NY, 1816 *2859.11 p37*
MacGinnis, John; New York, NY, 1816 *2859.11 p37*
MacGinnis, Owen; New York, NY, 1816 *2859.11 p37*
MacGinnis, Thomas; New York, NY, 1816 *2859.11 p37*
MacGladery, Samuel; New York, NY, 1815 *2859.11 p37*
MacGlam, John; New York, NY, 1816 *2859.11 p37*
MacGlam, Patrick; New York, NY, 1816 *2859.11 p37*
MacGlaughlin, Robert; New York, NY, 1815 *2859.11 p37*
MacGleeve, James; New York, NY, 1811 *2859.11 p16*
MacGloin, Edward; New York, NY, 1816 *2859.11 p37*
MacGloin, Henry; New York, NY, 1816 *2859.11 p37*
MacGloin, John; New York, NY, 1816 *2859.11 p37*
MacGloin, Margaret; New York, NY, 1816 *2859.11 p37*
MacGloin, Mary; New York, NY, 1816 *2859.11 p37*
  With child
MacGlonan, Ann; New York, NY, 1811 *2859.11 p16*
MacGlonan, James; New York, NY, 1811 *2859.11 p16*
MacGlonan, Mary; New York, NY, 1811 *2859.11 p16*
MacGlonan, Nathaniel; New York, NY, 1811 *2859.11 p16*
MacGloughlin, Dennis; New York, NY, 1815 *2859.11 p37*
MacGloughlin, Mary; New York, NY, 1815 *2859.11 p37*
MacGloughlin, Patrick; New York, NY, 1815 *2859.11 p37*
MacGlyn, Catherine; New York, NY, 1816 *2859.11 p37*
Macgnard, Carl Christian; Arkansas, 1918 *95.2 p77*
MacGohey, Mary; New York, NY, 1811 *2859.11 p16*
MacGongle, Henry; New York, NY, 1816 *2859.11 p37*
MacGouran, Samuel; New York, NY, 1815 *2859.11 p37*
MacGovern, Charles; New York, NY, 1815 *2859.11 p37*
MacGowan, Andrew; New York, NY, 1816 *2859.11 p37*
MacGowan, Bernard; New York, NY, 1815 *2859.11 p37*
MacGowan, Dennis; New York, NY, 1816 *2859.11 p37*
MacGowan, James; New York, NY, 1815 *2859.11 p37*
MacGowan, John; New York, NY, 1816 *2859.11 p37*
MacGowan, Mary; New York, NY, 1816 *2859.11 p37*
MacGowan, Patrick; New York, NY, 1816 *2859.11 p37*
MacGowan, Philip; Philadelphia, 1811 *2859.11 p16*
MacGown, Andrew; New York, NY, 1816 *2859.11 p37*
MacGra, John; New York, NY, 1816 *2859.11 p37*
MacGranahan, Thomas; New York, NY, 1816 *2859.11 p37*
Macgrath, Henry 22; Virginia, 1734 *3690.1 p145*
MacGrath, James; New York, NY, 1815 *2859.11 p37*
MacGrath, James; Philadelphia, 1811 *2859.11 p16*
MacGrath, Marg.; Philadelphia, 1811 *2859.11 p16*
MacGrath, Patrick; New York, NY, 1811 *2859.11 p16*
MacGrath, Thos.; Philadelphia, 1811 *2859.11 p16*
MacGrath, William; Philadelphia, 1816 *2859.11 p37*
MacGrath, Wm.; New York, NY, 1811 *2859.11 p16*
MacGrave, Marg.; New York, NY, 1811 *2859.11 p16*
MacGraw, . . .; Canada, 1776-1783 *9786 p28*
MacGreedy, John; New York, NY, 1811 *2859.11 p16*
MacGreevy, Patrick; New York, NY, 1816 *2859.11 p37*
MacGreggor, James; Virginia, 1652 *6251 p20*
MacGregor, Alexander Simpson; Arkansas, 1918 *95.2 p77*
MacGrery, James; New York, NY, 1816 *2859.11 p37*
MacGrery, Margaret; New York, NY, 1816 *2859.11 p37*
MacGrier, Robert; New York, NY, 1815 *2859.11 p37*
MacGrim, Bryan; Philadelphia, 1816 *2859.11 p37*
MacGuinness, Edw.; New York, NY, 1811 *2859.11 p16*

MacGuire, Bridget; New York, NY, 1816 *2859.11 p37*
MacGuire, Ellen; Baltimore, 1816 *2859.11 p37*
MacGuire, Mary; New York, NY, 1816 *2859.11 p37*
Macguire, Peter 17; Maryland, 1775 *1219.7 p272*
MacGuire, Roger; New York, NY, 1811 *2859.11 p16*
MacGum, Patrick; New York, NY, 1816 *2859.11 p37*
MacGuragle, Robert; New York, NY, 1816 *2859.11 p37*
MacGurrah, John; New York, NY, 1811 *2859.11 p16*
  With family
MacGuskin, A.; New York, NY, 1816 *2859.11 p37*
Machado, Amaro; Virginia, 1844 *4626.16 p12*
MacHale, Thomas; New York, NY, 1816 *2859.11 p37*
Macham, John; Virginia, 1635 *6219 p73*
Machannah, Patrick; Montreal, 1824 *7603 p89*
Machart, Anastair 27; America, 1830 *778.5 p352*
Machiafave, Calogero; Iowa, 1866-1943 *123.54 p31*
Machikunas, Clemens S.; Arkansas, 1918 *95.2 p77*
Machin, Alfred E.; Illinois, 1905 *5012.37 p63*
Machin, Eliza.; Virginia, 1635 *6219 p73*
Machin, Johathan; Colorado, 1904 *9678.2 p125*
Machino, Angelo; Arkansas, 1918 *95.2 p77*
Machleit, Daniel; Pennsylvania, 1752 *2444 p186*
Machlen, Jacob; Pennsylvania, 1751 *4779.3 p14*
Machleyd, Adam Friedrich *SEE* Machleyd, Daniel
Machleyd, Anna *SEE* Machleyd, Daniel
Machleyd, Anna Catharina *SEE* Machleyd, Daniel
Machleyd, Anna Christina *SEE* Machleyd, Daniel
Machleyd, Anna Margaretha *SEE* Machleyd, Daniel
Machleyd, Daniel *SEE* Machleyd, Daniel
Machleyd, Daniel; Pennsylvania, 1752 *2444 p186*
  *Wife:*Euphrosina Beurer
  *Child:*Anna Catharina
  *Child:*Euphrosina
  *Child:*Anna Margaretha
  *Child:*Daniel
  *Child:*Anna Christina
  *Child:*Wilhelm
  *Child:*Adam Friedrich
  *Child:*Jacob
  *Child:*Anna
Machleyd, Euphrosina *SEE* Machleyd, Daniel
Machleyd, Euphrosina Beurer *SEE* Machleyd, Daniel
Machleyd, Jacob *SEE* Machleyd, Daniel
Machleyd, Wilhelm *SEE* Machleyd, Daniel
MacHolland, Mich.; New York, NY, 1811 *2859.11 p16*
Machtig, Anton; Wisconsin, n.d. *9675.6 p268*
Machtle, Deinrich; Wisconsin, n.d. *9675.6 p268*
MacHugh, Andrew; New York, NY, 1816 *2859.11 p37*
Macijanskas, Martin; Wisconsin, n.d. *9675.6 p268*
MacIldoon, Hugh; New York, NY, 1811 *2859.11 p16*
MacIlhames, John; New York, NY, 1816 *2859.11 p37*
MacIlheny, Robert; New York, NY, 1816 *2859.11 p37*
MacIlrath, King; New York, NY, 1815 *2859.11 p37*
MacIlroy, Mrs.; New York, NY, 1816 *2859.11 p37*
MacIlroy, Charles; Baltimore, 1811 *2859.11 p16*
MacIlroy, Charles; New York, NY, 1816 *2859.11 p37*
MacIlroy, Patrick; New York, NY, 1816 *2859.11 p37*
MacIndoo, Robert; New York, NY, 1811 *2859.11 p16*
  With wife
Macini, Pietro 30; West Virginia, 1904 *9788.3 p15*
MacInnes, Ann *SEE* MacInnes, Donald
MacInnes, Ann *SEE* MacInnes, John
MacInnes, Ann; Quebec, 1851 *4537.30 p83*
MacInnes, Ann Morrison *SEE* MacInnes, Donald
MacInnes, Betsy *SEE* MacInnes, Donald
MacInnes, Catherine *SEE* MacInnes, Donald
MacInnes, Donald *SEE* MacInnes, Donald
MacInnes, Donald; North Carolina, 1773 *4814 p101*
  With parents
MacInnes, Donald; Quebec, 1855 *4537.30 p74*
  *Wife:*Ann Morrison
  *Child:*Mary
  *Child:*Margaret
  *Child:*Ann
  *Child:*Catherine
  *Child:*Donald
  *Child:*Betsy
  *Child:*Isabella
MacInnes, Isabella *SEE* MacInnes, Donald
MacInnes, John; Quebec, 1873 *4537.30 p74*
  *Wife:*Rachel MacAulay
  With child
  *Child:*Ann
  *Child:*Rachel
  With child
  *Child:*Murdo
MacInnes, Margaret *SEE* MacInnes, Donald
MacInnes, Mary *SEE* MacInnes, Donald
MacInnes, Mary; Quebec, 1851 *4537.30 p49*
MacInnes, Miles; Cape Fear, NC, 1774 *4814 p92*
MacInnes, Miles; North Carolina, 1774 *4814 p100*
MacInnes, Miles; Nova Scotia, 1784 *4814 p100*
MacInnes, Miles; Nova Scotia, 1784 *4814 p107*

MacInnes, Murdo *SEE* MacInnes, John
MacInnes, Rachel *SEE* MacInnes, John
MacInnes, Rachel MacAulay *SEE* MacInnes, John
MacInnish, Donald; Wilmington, NC, 1792 *1639.20 p161*
MacIntire, Abrm.; Philadelphia, 1811 *2859.11 p16*
MacIntire, Donald 54; Wilmington, NC, 1775 *1639.20 p165*
  *Wife:*Katherine 41
  *Child:*Mary 12
  *Child:*Margaret 9
  *Child:*John 6
  *Child:*Duncan 5
MacIntire, Duncan 5 *SEE* MacIntire, Donald
MacIntire, James; New York, NY, 1815 *2859.11 p37*
MacIntire, John 6 *SEE* MacIntire, Donald
MacIntire, Katherine 41 *SEE* MacIntire, Donald
MacIntire, Margaret 9 *SEE* MacIntire, Donald
MacIntire, Mary 12 *SEE* MacIntire, Donald
MacIntire, Robert; New York, NY, 1815 *2859.11 p37*
MacIntire, Robt.; New York, NY, 1816 *2859.11 p37*
MacIntire, Samuel; New York, NY, 1815 *2859.11 p37*
MacIntosh, Jane; New York, NY, 1816 *2859.11 p37*
MacIntosh, William; New York, NY, 1816 *2859.11 p37*
MacIver, Alex *SEE* MacIver, Angus
MacIver, Alex *SEE* MacIver, Kenneth
MacIver, Alexander; Quebec, 1842 *4537.30 p74*
  *Wife:*Ann Smith
  *Child:*Kenneth
  *Child:*John
MacIver, Alexina *SEE* MacIver, Donald
MacIver, Angus *SEE* MacIver, Angus
MacIver, Angus *SEE* MacIver, Donald
MacIver, Angus *SEE* MacIver, Donald
MacIver, Angus *SEE* MacIver, Malcolm
MacIver, Angus; Quebec, 1841 *4537.30 p75*
  *Wife:*Margaret Murray
  *Child:*Kirsty
  *Child:*Murdo
MacIver, Angus; Quebec, 1851 *4537.30 p75*
  *Wife:*Ann MacDonald
  *Child:*Ann
  *Child:*Donald
  *Child:*Janet
  *Child:*Kirsty
  *Child:*John
  *Child:*Alex
  *Child:*Mary
  *Child:*Kenneth
MacIver, Angus; Quebec, 1851 *4537.30 p76*
  *Wife:*Mary Matheson
  *Child:*Annabella
  *Child:*Donald
  *Child:*Catherine
  *Child:*Colin
  *Child:*Marion
  *Child:*Angus
  *Child:*Ann
  *Child:*Murdo
  *Child:*Kirsty
  *Child:*Mary
MacIver, Ann *SEE* MacIver, Angus
MacIver, Ann *SEE* MacIver, Angus
MacIver, Ann *SEE* MacIver, Donald
MacIver, Ann *SEE* MacIver, Donald
MacIver, Ann *SEE* MacIver, Donald
MacIver, Ann *SEE* MacIver, Evander
MacIver, Ann *SEE* MacIver, John
MacIver, Ann *SEE* MacIver, John
MacIver, Ann *SEE* MacIver, Malcolm
MacIver, Ann *SEE* MacIver, Murdo
MacIver, Ann; Quebec, 1845 *4537.30 p109*
MacIver, Ann; Quebec, 1851 *4537.30 p106*
MacIver, Ann; Quebec, 1852 *4537.30 p3*
MacIver, Ann Finlayson *SEE* MacIver, Murdo
MacIver, Ann MacDonald *SEE* MacIver, Angus
MacIver, Ann MacLeod *SEE* MacIver, Murdo
MacIver, Ann Morrison *SEE* MacIver, Donald
MacIver, Ann Smith *SEE* MacIver, Alexander
MacIver, Annabella *SEE* MacIver, Angus
MacIver, Annabella *SEE* MacIver, Donald
MacIver, Annabella; Quebec, 1874 *4537.30 p15*
MacIver, Bess *SEE* MacIver, Evander
MacIver, Catherine *SEE* MacIver, Angus
MacIver, Catherine *SEE* MacIver, Donald
MacIver, Catherine *SEE* MacIver, Donald
MacIver, Catherine *SEE* MacIver, Donald
MacIver, Catherine *SEE* MacIver, John
MacIver, Catherine *SEE* MacIver, John
MacIver, Catherine *SEE* MacIver, John
MacIver, Catherine; Quebec, 1851 *4537.30 p5*
MacIver, Catherine; Quebec, 1851 *4537.30 p83*

MacKay, Betsy *SEE* MacKay, John
MacKay, Catherine *SEE* MacKay, Angus
MacKay, Catherine *SEE* MacKay, Donald
MacKay, Catherine *SEE* MacKay, Donald
MacKay, Catherine *SEE* MacKay, Donald
MacKay, Catherine *SEE* MacKay, Flora Matheson
MacKay, Catherine *SEE* MacKay, John
MacKay, Catherine *SEE* MacKay, Norman
MacKay, Catherine; Quebec, 1845 *4537.30 p107*
MacKay, Catherine; Quebec, 1855 *4537.30 p18*
MacKay, Catherine 3 mos; St. John, N.B., 1847 *5704.8 p9*
MacKay, Catherine MacIver *SEE* MacKay, Donald
MacKay, Catherine MacLeod *SEE* MacKay, John
MacKay, Charles; Philadelphia, 1811 *2859.11 p16*
Mackay, Daniel 17; Jamaica, 1730 *3690.1 p145*
MacKay, Donald *SEE* MacKay, Angus
MacKay, Donald *SEE* MacKay, Donald
MacKay, Donald *SEE* MacKay, Donald
MacKay, Donald *SEE* MacKay, John
MacKay, Donald *SEE* MacKay, Norman
MacKay, Donald; Quebec, 1838 *4537.30 p84*
  *Wife:*Catherine
  *Child:*Donald
  *Child:*Margaret M.
  *Child:*Catherine
MacKay, Donald; Quebec, 1842 *4537.30 p84*
  *Wife:*Kirsty MacKenzie
  *Child:*Ann
  *Child:*Mary
  *Child:*James
MacKay, Donald; Quebec, 1851 *4537.30 p83*
  *Wife:*Ann MacInnes
  *Child:*Catherine
  *Child:*Mary
  *Child:*Margaret
  *Child:*Ann
  *Child:*Kirsty
  *Child:*Donald
MacKay, Donald; Quebec, 1851 *4537.30 p83*
  *Wife:*Catherine MacIver
MacKay, Eliza; New York, NY, 1816 *2859.11 p37*
MacKay, Eliza 28; Philadelphia, 1854 *5704.8 p116*
MacKay, Finlay *SEE* MacKay, Flora Matheson
MacKay, Flora Matheson; Quebec, 1841 *4537.30 p85*
  *Child:*Ann
  *Child:*William
  *Child:*Mary
  *Child:*Kirsty
  *Child:*Neil
  *Child:*Murdo
  *Child:*John
  *Child:*Finlay
  *Child:*Catherine
MacKay, Francis; Philadelphia, 1815 *2859.11 p37*
MacKay, Hugh; Ohio, 1839 *9892.11 p34*
MacKay, Isabella *SEE* MacKay, Angus
MacKay, Isabella; Quebec, 1863 *4537.30 p35*
Mackay, Isabella 45; Quebec, 1859 *5704.8 p143*
MacKay, James *SEE* MacKay, Donald
MacKay, James; New York, NY, 1816 *2859.11 p37*
Mackay, James; St. John, N.B., 1847 *5704.8 p9*
MacKay, John *SEE* MacKay, Flora Matheson
MacKay, John *SEE* MacKay, John
Mackay, John; Illinois, 1860 *7857 p5*
Mackay, John; Ontario, 1851 *4537.30 p83*
  With wife
  With family
MacKay, John; Quebec, 1841 *4537.30 p85*
  *Wife:*Kirsty MacLean
  *Child:*Catherine
MacKay, John; Quebec, 1851 *4537.30 p84*
  *Wife:*Catherine MacLeod
  *Child:*Donald
  *Child:*Angus
  *Child:*Ann
  *Child:*John
  *Child:*Betsy
Mackay, John 15; Philadelphia, 1774 *1219.7 p175*
Mackay, John 23; Philadelphia, 1854 *5704.8 p116*
Mackay, John 25; Philadelphia, 1774 *1219.7 p216*
Mackay, John 25; Savannah, GA, 1733 *4719.17 p312*
Mackay, John 48; Quebec, 1859 *5704.8 p143*
Mackay, John Alexander 18; Maryland, 1774 *1219.7 p196*
MacKay, Kenneth *SEE* MacKay, Angus
MacKay, Kirsty *SEE* MacKay, Angus
MacKay, Kirsty *SEE* MacKay, Angus
MacKay, Kirsty *SEE* MacKay, Donald
MacKay, Kirsty *SEE* MacKay, Flora Matheson
MacKay, Kirsty *SEE* MacKay, Nora
MacKay, Kirsty; Quebec, 1841 *4537.30 p39*
MacKay, Kirsty; Quebec, 1851 *4537.30 p63*

MacKay, Kirsty Buchanan *SEE* MacKay, Norman
MacKay, Kirsty MacKenzie *SEE* MacKay, Donald
MacKay, Kirsty MacLean *SEE* MacKay, John
Mackay, Magy; St. John, N.B., 1847 *5704.8 p9*
MacKay, Malcolm *SEE* MacKay, Norman
MacKay, Malcolm; Quebec, 1841 *4537.30 p86*
MacKay, Margaret *SEE* MacKay, Angus
MacKay, Margaret *SEE* MacKay, Donald
MacKay, Margaret; Quebec, 1851 *4537.30 p66*
MacKay, Margaret M. *SEE* MacKay, Donald
MacKay, Marion *SEE* MacKay, Angus
MacKay, Mary *SEE* MacKay, Angus
MacKay, Mary *SEE* MacKay, Donald
MacKay, Mary *SEE* MacKay, Donald
MacKay, Mary *SEE* MacKay, Flora Matheson
MacKay, Mary *SEE* MacKay, Nora
MacKay, Mary *SEE* MacKay, Norman
MacKay, Mary; Quebec, 1838 *4537.30 p103*
MacKay, Mary; Quebec, 1851 *4537.30 p45*
MacKay, Mary; Quebec, 1851 *4537.30 p112*
MacKay, Murdo *SEE* MacKay, Flora Matheson
MacKay, Murdo *SEE* MacKay, Norman
MacKay, Neil *SEE* MacKay, Flora Matheson
MacKay, Neil *SEE* MacKay, Norman
MacKay, Nora; Quebec, 1860-1900 *4537.30 p49*
  *Relative:*Kirsty
  *Relative:*Mary
  *Relative:*Norman
MacKay, Norman *SEE* MacKay, Nora
MacKay, Norman; Quebec, 1838 *4537.30 p86*
  *Wife:*Kirsty Buchanan
  *Child:*Catherine
  *Child:*Donald
  *Child:*Mary
  *Child:*Malcolm
  *Child:*Murdo
  *Child:*Neil
  *Child:*Ann Morrison
MacKay, P.; New York, NY, 1816 *2859.11 p37*
Mackay, Robert; Virginia, 1772 *1219.7 p158*
Mackay, S.; New York, NY, 1816 *2859.11 p37*
Mackay, Vivian Pretor; Arkansas, 1918 *95.2 p77*
MacKay, William *SEE* MacKay, Flora Matheson
MacKay, William; New York, NY, 1816 *2859.11 p37*
Mackay, William 27; Philadelphia, 1854 *5704.8 p116*
Mackbene, Robert 16; Jamaica, 1736 *3690.1 p146*
Mackdonald, James 19; Pennsylvania, 1738 *3690.1 p153*
Macke, Alexander 22; Antigua (Antego), 1731 *3690.1 p146*
Macke, Franz Heinrich; Indiana, 1830-1849 *8582 p20*
Macke, H. H.; Ohio, 1869-1887 *8582 p20*
Macke, William 19; Antigua (Antego), 1731 *3690.1 p146*
MacKee, George; New York, NY, 1811 *2859.11 p16*
Mackee, James; New York, NY, 1811 *2859.11 p16*
MacKee, Jane; New York, NY, 1811 *2859.11 p16*
MacKee, John; New York, NY, 1811 *2859.11 p16*
MacKee, Margaret; New York, NY, 1811 *2859.11 p16*
MacKee, Patrick; New York, NY, 1811 *2859.11 p16*
MacKee, Robert; New York, NY, 1811 *2859.11 p16*
MacKee, Robert; New York, NY, 1815 *2859.11 p37*
  With wife
MacKee, Robert; New York, NY, 1816 *2859.11 p37*
MacKee, Thomas; New York, NY, 1811 *2859.11 p16*
MacKee, William; New York, NY, 1816 *2859.11 p37*
MacKeene, Peter; New York, NY, 1816 *2859.11 p37*
MacKeighan, . . .; New York, NY, 1816 *2859.11 p37*
Mackel, . . . 65; Quebec, 1855 *5704.8 p126*
Mackel, Ellen 58; Quebec, 1855 *5704.8 p126*
MacKelery, Jane; New York, NY, 1811 *2859.11 p16*
MacKelery, William; New York, NY, 1811 *2859.11 p16*
Macken, George; America, 1739 *4971 p37*
Macken, Patrick; America, 1742 *4971 p23*
Macken, William; Montreal, 1824 *7603 p68*
Mackeney, James 19; Pennsylvania, 1733 *3690.1 p146*
MacKennan, Bernart; New York, NY, 1815 *2859.11 p37*
MacKennan, Patrick; New York, NY, 1815 *2859.11 p37*
MacKenney, Alice; New York, NY, 1811 *2859.11 p16*
MacKenny, Alexander; New York, NY, 1811 *2859.11 p16*
Mackenny, Argyle 20; Maryland, 1724 *3690.1 p146*
Mackensey, Mary 22; North Carolina, 1736 *3690.1 p146*
Mackentepe, Bernard; America, 1830-1849 *8582.2 p25*
Mackentepe, Bernard; Cincinnati, 1830-1849 *8582 p20*
MacKenzie, Alex *SEE* MacKenzie, Charles
MacKenzie, Alex *SEE* MacKenzie, Colin
MacKenzie, Alex; New York, NY, 1811 *2859.11 p16*
MacKenzie, Alex; Quebec, 1842 *4537.30 p87*
  *Wife:*Kirsty MacKinnon
  *Child:*John
MacKenzie, Alex; Quebec, 1855 *4537.30 p87*
  *Wife:*Bess MacLeod
  *Child:*Kenneth
  *Child:*John

  *Child:*Donald
  *Child:*Catherine
  *Child:*Murdo
  *Child:*Jane
Mackenzie, Alexander; Canada, 1784-1789 *9775.5 p199*
  *Cousin:*Roderick
Mackenzie, Alexander; Ottawa, 1873 *9775.5 p216*
MacKenzie, Allan *SEE* MacKenzie, John
MacKenzie, Allan *SEE* MacKenzie, Murdo
MacKenzie, Angus *SEE* MacKenzie, Finlay
MacKenzie, Angus; Quebec, 1900 *4537.30 p90*
  *Wife:*Isabella MacLeod
  *Child:*John
MacKenzie, Ann *SEE* MacKenzie, Colin
MacKenzie, Ann *SEE* MacKenzie, James
MacKenzie, Ann *SEE* MacKenzie, John
MacKenzie, Ann; Quebec, 1853 *4537.30 p61*
MacKenzie, Ann; Quebec, 1877 *4537.30 p118*
MacKenzie, Anne; Charleston, SC, 1764 *1639.20 p173*
MacKenzie, Bess MacLeod *SEE* MacKenzie, Alex
MacKenzie, Catherine *SEE* MacKenzie, Alex
MacKenzie, Catherine *SEE* MacKenzie, John
MacKenzie, Catherine *SEE* MacKenzie, Murdo
MacKenzie, Catherine; Quebec, 1853 *4537.30 p30*
MacKenzie, Catherine MacDonald *SEE* MacKenzie, Finlay
MacKenzie, Catherine Thomson *SEE* MacKenzie, Colin
MacKenzie, Charles; Quebec, 1853 *4537.30 p87*
  *Wife:*Isabella Stewart
  *Child:*Alex
Mackenzie, Colin; Antigua (Antego), 1754 *3690.1 p153*
MacKenzie, Colin; Quebec, 1873 *4537.30 p90*
  *Wife:*Catherine Thomson
  *Child:*Alex
  *Child:*Margaret
  *Child:*Mary
  *Child:*Ann
MacKenzie, Donald *SEE* MacKenzie, Alex
MacKenzie, Donald *SEE* MacKenzie, James
MacKenzie, Effie *SEE* MacKenzie, Jessie
MacKenzie, Effie; Quebec, 1873 *4537.30 p34*
MacKenzie, Finlay; Quebec, 1855 *4537.30 p88*
  *Wife:*Catherine MacDonald
  *Child:*Angus
MacKenzie, Isabella *SEE* MacKenzie, John
MacKenzie, Isabella; Quebec, 1873 *4537.30 p43*
MacKenzie, Isabella MacLeod *SEE* MacKenzie, Angus
MacKenzie, Isabella Stewart *SEE* MacKenzie, Charles
MacKenzie, James *SEE* MacKenzie, Kirsty MacLeod
MacKenzie, James; Quebec, 1851 *4537.30 p88*
  *Wife:*Mary Matheson
  *Child:*John
  *Child:*Donald
  *Child:*Ann
MacKenzie, Jane *SEE* MacKenzie, Alex
MacKenzie, Jane; South Carolina, 1753 *1639.20 p174*
MacKenzie, Jessie; Quebec, 1865 *4537.30 p89*
  *Child:*Effie
  *Child:*Murdo
MacKenzie, John *SEE* MacKenzie, Alex
MacKenzie, John *SEE* MacKenzie, Alex
MacKenzie, John *SEE* MacKenzie, Angus
MacKenzie, John *SEE* MacKenzie, James
MacKenzie, John *SEE* MacKenzie, Kirsty MacLeod
MacKenzie, John; New York, NY, 1811 *2859.11 p16*
MacKenzie, John; Quebec, 1873 *4537.30 p89*
  *Wife:*Ann
  *Child:*Margaret
  *Child:*Catherine
  *Child:*Isabella
  *Child:*Allan
  *Child:*Kirsty
  *Child:*Murdo D.
MacKenzie, John; Quebec, 1873 *4537.30 p89*
  *Brother:*Malcolm
  *Sister:*Margaret
Mackenzie, John 16; Carolina, 1774 *1219.7 p242*
MacKenzie, John 16; Carolina, 1774 *1639.20 p174*
MacKenzie, Kenneth *SEE* MacKenzie, Alex
MacKenzie, Kirsty *SEE* MacKenzie, John
MacKenzie, Kirsty *SEE* MacKenzie, Murdo
MacKenzie, Kirsty; Quebec, 1842 *4537.30 p84*
MacKenzie, Kirsty; Quebec, 1851 *4537.30 p110*
MacKenzie, Kirsty; Quebec, 1855 *4537.30 p111*
MacKenzie, Kirsty MacKinnon *SEE* MacKenzie, Alex
MacKenzie, Kirsty MacLeod; Quebec, 1866 *4537.30 p88*
  *Son:*Roderick
  *Son:*James
  *Son:*Murdo
  *Son:*John
MacKenzie, Malcolm *SEE* MacKenzie, John
MacKenzie, Margaret *SEE* MacKenzie, Colin
MacKenzie, Margaret *SEE* MacKenzie, John

FOR A COMPLETE EXPLANATION OF ENTRY, SEE "HOW TO READ A CITATION" SECTION

MacKenzie, Margaret SEE MacKenzie, John
MacKenzie, Margaret SEE MacKenzie, Murdo
MacKenzie, Margaret; Quebec, 1851 *4537.30 p52*
MacKenzie, Marion MacRitchie SEE MacKenzie, Murdo
MacKenzie, Mary SEE MacKenzie, Colin
MacKenzie, Mary; Quebec, 1855 *4537.30 p31*
MacKenzie, Mary; Quebec, 1855 *4537.30 p108*
Mackenzie, Mary; South Carolina, 1750-1757 *1639.20 p175*
MacKenzie, Mary 22; North Carolina, 1736 *1639.20 p174*
MacKenzie, Mary Matheson SEE MacKenzie, James
MacKenzie, Murdo SEE MacKenzie, Alex
MacKenzie, Murdo SEE MacKenzie, Jessie
MacKenzie, Murdo SEE MacKenzie, Kirsty MacLeod
MacKenzie, Murdo; Quebec, 1851 *4537.30 p89*
  Wife:Marion MacRitchie
  Child:Kirsty
  Child:Allan
  Child:Sophia
  Child:Margaret
  Child:Catherine
MacKenzie, Murdo D. SEE MacKenzie, John
MacKenzie, Neil 21; Boston, 1791 *8894.1 p192*
MacKenzie, Norman; Quebec, 1863 *4537.30 p88*
MacKenzie, Philip; New York, NY, 1811 *2859.11 p16*
MacKenzie, Ralph; New York, NY, 1811 *2859.11 p16*
Mackenzie, Robert; New Jersey, 1764 *1219.7 p101*
MacKenzie, Roderick SEE Mackenzie, Alexander
MacKenzie, Roderick SEE MacKenzie, Kirsty MacLeod
MacKenzie, Roderick; Virginia, 1855 *4626.16 p15*
MacKenzie, Sibla; Quebec, 1819-1845 *4537.30 p24*
MacKenzie, Sophia SEE MacKenzie, Murdo
Mackenzie, Thomas; Savannah, GA, 1817 *1639.20 p175*
Mackenzie, William; Charleston, SC, 1639-1739 *1639.20 p175*
Mackenzie, William Lyon; Ontario, n.d. *9775.5 p216*
Mackenzy, Thomas 29; Maryland, 1774 *1219.7 p208*
Mackeon, Isabella; New York, NY, 1815 *2859.11 p37*
MacKeon, Robt.; Philadelphia, 1816 *2859.11 p37*
MacKeon, Rose; New York, NY, 1815 *2859.11 p37*
Mackeon, William; New York, NY, 1815 *2859.11 p37*
MacKeown, Anne; New York, NY, 1816 *2859.11 p37*
MacKeown, John, Jr.; New York, NY, 1816 *2859.11 p37*
MacKeown, John, Sr.; New York, NY, 1816 *2859.11 p37*
MacKeown, Margaret; New York, NY, 1816 *2859.11 p37*
MacKeown, Mary; New York, NY, 1816 *2859.11 p37*
MacKeown, Saml.; New York, NY, 1816 *2859.11 p37*
MacKeown, Samuel; New York, NY, 1816 *2859.11 p37*
MacKeown, Sarah; New York, NY, 1816 *2859.11 p37*
MacKeown, William; New York, NY, 1816 *2859.11 p37*
Macker, Adolph; Illinois, 1859 *5012.39 p89*
Macker, Owen; Virginia, 1637 *6219 p113*
Macker, Roger; Virginia, 1621 *6219 p25*
Mackerill, James; New York, NY, 1816 *2859.11 p37*
Mackerill, Jane; New York, NY, 1816 *2859.11 p37*
Mackerill, Thomas; New York, NY, 1816 *2859.11 p37*
MacKernan, Edward; New York, NY, 1815 *2859.11 p37*
MacKernan, Patrick; New York, NY, 1815 *2859.11 p37*
Mackeson; New York, NY, 1816 *2859.11 p37*
Mackett, Eliz. 6 SEE Mackett, Mary B.
Mackett, Ellen 3 SEE Mackett, Mary B.
Mackett, Elz. 28; Canada, 1838 *4535.12 p113*
Mackett, Mary B. 8; Canada, 1838 *4535.12 p113*
  Relative:Ellen 3
  Relative:Eliz. 6
Mackett, Thos. 32; Canada, 1838 *4535.12 p113*
MacKever, Edward; New York, NY, 1811 *2859.11 p16*
  With family
MacKevers, Peter; New York, NY, 1816 *2859.11 p37*
Mackey, Mr.; New York, 1850 *4535.11 p53*
MacKey, Daniel; New York, NY, 1811 *2859.11 p16*
  With family
MacKey, Eleanor; Philadelphia, 1816 *2859.11 p37*
MacKey, Ellen; New York, NY, 1811 *2859.11 p16*
Mackey, Geo. 7 SEE Mackey, Jane
Mackey, James; New York, NY, 1811 *2859.11 p16*
Mackey, James W.; Plymouth, NC, 1821 *1639.20 p176*
Mackey, Jane 28; New York, 1854 *4535.11 p53*
  Child:Wm. 9
  Child:Geo. 7
  Child:Richard 5
Mackey, John; America, 1735-1743 *4971 p79*
Mackey, Richard 5 SEE Mackey, Jane
Mackey, Sarah 30; Quebec, 1862 *5704.8 p151*
Mackey, Sinclair; Philadelphia, 1851 *5704.8 p70*
MacKey, Thomas; New York, NY, 1811 *2859.11 p16*
Mackey, Wm. 9 SEE Mackey, Jane
MacKichan, Dugald; Nova Scotia, 1831 *8893 p263*
Mackie, Alexander 22; Antigua (Antego), 1731 *3690.1 p146*

Mackie, Alexr.; America, 1832 *8893 p265*
Mackier, William 22; Jamaica, 1731 *3690.1 p146*
Mackiewicz, Sahar; Arkansas, 1918 *95.2 p77*
Mackiewicz, Zubow vel; America, n.d. *4606 p180*
MacKill, Thos.; New York, NY, 1816 *2859.11 p37*
Mackin, John 32; California, 1873 *2769.10 p5*
Mackin, Michael; St. John, N.B., 1847 *5704.8 p11*
Mackinen, Robert; Pensacola, FL, 1767 *1219.7 p127*
MacKinlay, Agnes; Wilmington, NC, 1798 *1639.20 p177*
MacKinlay, George; New York, NY, 1811 *2859.11 p16*
MacKinlay, John; New York, NY, 1811 *2859.11 p16*
MacKinley, Hugh; Philadelphia, 1811 *2859.11 p16*
MacKinne, John; New York, NY, 1816 *2859.11 p37*
MacKinney, Eliza; New York, NY, 1811 *2859.11 p16*
MacKinney, George; New York, NY, 1811 *2859.11 p16*
MacKinnon, Alex SEE MacKinnon, John
MacKinnon, Angus SEE MacKinnon, John
MacKinnon, Daniel; America, 1788 *1639.20 p178*
MacKinnon, Effie MacDonald SEE MacKinnon, John
MacKinnon, John; Quebec, 1842 *4537.30 p90*
  Wife:Effie MacDonald
  Child:Angus
  Child:Alex
Mackinnon, John Frazer; Arkansas, 1918 *95.2 p77*
MacKinnon, Kirsty; Quebec, 1842 *4537.30 p87*
MacKinstry, John; Philadelphia, 1816 *2859.11 p37*
Mackintosh, John; Georgia, 1736 *1639.20 p164*
Mackintosh, Miles; Charleston, SC, 1729 *1639.20 p164*
Mackkensey, Kenney 16; Jamaica, 1733 *3690.1 p146*
Macklaken, John 20; Jamaica, 1736 *3690.1 p146*
Mackle, Margaret; Quebec, 1847 *5704.8 p8*
Mackleland, James 18; Pennsylvania, 1731 *3690.1 p153*
Macklen, William 22; Maryland or Virginia, 1734 *3690.1 p145*
Macklin, Jacob SEE Macklin, Theobald
Macklin, James; New York, NY, 1838 *8208.4 p85*
Macklin, John 24; Carolina, 1774 *1219.7 p190*
  Wife:Mary 23
Macklin, Mary 23 SEE Macklin, John
Macklin, Theobald; Pennsylvania, 1728 *4779.3 p14*
  Relative:Jacob
Mackline, Jacob SEE Mackline, Theobald
Mackline, Theobald; Pennsylvania, 1728 *4779.3 p14*
  Relative:Jacob
Macknamara, John; America, 1743 *4971 p50*
MacKnight, Andrew; Philadelphia, 1811 *2859.11 p16*
MacKnight, Daniel; Philadelphia, 1811 *2859.11 p16*
MacKnight, David; Philadelphia, 1811 *2859.11 p16*
MacKnight, Jane; Philadelphia, 1811 *2859.11 p16*
MacKnight, Mary; Philadelphia, 1811 *2859.11 p16*
MacKnight, Thomas; Philadelphia, 1811 *2859.11 p16*
MacKninon, Hannah; New York, NY, 1816 *2859.11 p37*
MacKnott, Robert; New York, NY, 1811 *2859.11 p16*
  With family
MacKosker, Hugh; New York, NY, 1811 *2859.11 p16*
Mackqueen, Alexander 17; Jamaica, 1722 *3690.1 p147*
Mackreall, Jno.; Virginia, 1648 *6219 p246*
Mackrell, Edward 25; Virginia, 1775 *1219.7 p247*
Mackrell, James 21; Virginia, 1775 *1219.7 p247*
Mackus, Alex; Wisconsin, n.d. *9675.6 p268*
Mackway, William 20; Maryland, 1721 *3690.1 p146*
Mackworth, Arthur; Virginia, 1643 *6219 p200*
Macky, Abraham 18; Quebec, 1858 *5704.8 p138*
Macky, Catherine; Philadelphia, 1851 *5704.8 p78*
Macky, Charles 3; St. John, N.B., 1848 *5704.8 p38*
Macky, Jane; Philadelphia, 1851 *5704.8 p78*
Macky, Margaret; St. John, N.B., 1848 *5704.8 p38*
Macky, Robert; Philadelphia, 1849 *53.26 p48*
  Relative:Sarah
Macky, Robert; Philadelphia, 1849 *5704.8 p49*
Macky, Samuel; St. John, N.B., 1848 *5704.8 p38*
Macky, Samuel 2; St. John, N.B., 1848 *5704.8 p38*
Macky, Sarah SEE Macky, Robert
Macky, Sarah; Philadelphia, 1849 *5704.8 p49*
MacLachling, John; New York, NY, 1815 *2859.11 p37*
MacLain, John; Philadelphia, 1816 *2859.11 p37*
MacLaine, Archibald; North Carolina, 1750 *1639.20 p180*
MacLanna, John; New York, NY, 1811 *2859.11 p16*
Maclaran, John 31; Maryland, 1737 *3690.1 p146*
MacLaran, Lowry; South Carolina, 1739 *1639.20 p184*
MacLary, Benjamin; New York, NY, 1811 *2859.11 p16*
MacLaughlin, Ann; New York, NY, 1811 *2859.11 p16*
MacLaughlin, Benj.; New York, NY, 1811 *2859.11 p16*
MacLaughlin, Biddy; Philadelphia, 1811 *2859.11 p16*
MacLaughlin, Cornelius; New York, NY, 1816 *2859.11 p37*
MacLaughlin, Dennis; New York, NY, 1816 *2859.11 p37*
MacLaughlin, Edward; New York, NY, 1816 *2859.11 p37*
MacLaughlin, Elea.; Philadelphia, 1811 *2859.11 p16*

MacLaughlin, F.; New York, NY, 1811 *2859.11 p16*
  With family
MacLaughlin, Fran; Philadelphia, 1811 *2859.11 p16*
MacLaughlin, H.; Philadelphia, 1811 *2859.11 p16*
MacLaughlin, Hugh; New York, NY, 1816 *2859.11 p37*
MacLaughlin, James; New York, NY, 1816 *2859.11 p37*
MacLaughlin, John; New York, NY, 1816 *2859.11 p37*
MacLaughlin, Margaret; New York, NY, 1816 *2859.11 p37*
MacLaughlin, Mary; New York, NY, 1816 *2859.11 p37*
MacLaughlin, Peter; New York, NY, 1816 *2859.11 p37*
MacLaughlin, Philip; New York, NY, 1811 *2859.11 p16*
MacLaughlin, Philip; New York, NY, 1816 *2859.11 p37*
MacLaughlin, Sarah; New York, NY, 1816 *2859.11 p37*
MacLean, Alex SEE MacLean, Malcolm
MacLean, Angus SEE MacLean, Donald
MacLean, Angus SEE MacLean, Malcolm
MacLean, Angus; Quebec, 1838 *4537.30 p95*
MacLean, Angus; Quebec, 1851 *4537.30 p91*
  Wife:Margaret MacRitchie
MacLean, Ann SEE MacLean, Donald
MacLean, Ann SEE MacLean, John
MacLean, Ann SEE MacLean, Malcolm
MacLean, Ann; Quebec, 1838 *4537.30 p2*
MacLean, Ann; Quebec, 1841 *4537.30 p38*
MacLean, Ann MacKay SEE MacLean, Murdo
MacLean, Ann MacLeod SEE MacLean, John
MacLean, Ann Munro SEE MacLean, Malcolm
MacLean, Annabella SEE MacLean, Murdo
MacLean, Bridget; New York, NY, 1815 *2859.11 p37*
MacLean, Catherine SEE MacLean, Donald
MacLean, Catherine SEE MacLean, John
MacLean, Catherine SEE MacLean, John
MacLean, Catherine SEE MacLean, Murdo
MacLean, Catherine; Quebec, 1843 *4537.30 p50*
MacLean, Catherine Macleod SEE MacLean, John
MacLean, Catherine MacRitchie SEE MacLean, John
MacLean, Donald SEE MacLean, Donald
MacLean, Donald SEE MacLean, John
MacLean, Donald SEE MacLean, Malcolm
MacLean, Donald; Quebec, 1838 *4537.30 p91*
  Wife:Margaret MacLeod
  Child:John
MacLean, Donald; Quebec, 1851 *4537.30 p91*
  Wife:Kirsty MacAulay
  Child:Ann
  Child:Catherine
MacLean, Donald; Quebec, 1851 *4537.30 p92*
  Wife:Mary Morrison
  Child:Hugh
  Child:Donald
  Child:Peter
  Child:Angus
  Child:John
  Child:Kirsty
Maclean, Donald 28; Quebec, 1862 *5704.8 p152*
MacLean, Effie SEE MacLean, Malcolm
MacLean, Flora; Quebec, 1845 *4537.30 p97*
MacLean, Gormelia; Quebec, 1887 *4537.30 p29*
MacLean, Hugh SEE MacLean, Donald
MacLean, Isabella SEE MacLean, Malcolm
MacLean, Isabella; Quebec, 1853 *4537.30 p31*
Maclean, James; Philadelphia, 1852 *5704.8 p88*
MacLean, Janet SEE MacLean, Malcolm
MacLean, John SEE MacLean, Donald
MacLean, John SEE MacLean, Donald
MacLean, John SEE MacLean, John
MacLean, John SEE MacLean, Malcolm
MacLean, John; Canada, 1867 *9775.5 p221*
MacLean, John; Charleston, SC, 1796 *1639.20 p191*
MacLean, John; Quebec, 1820-1853 *4537.30 p94*
MacLean, John; Quebec, 1851 *4537.30 p92*
  Wife:Ann MacLeod
  Child:Murdo
  Child:Donald
  Child:Margaret
  Child:John
  Child:Catherine
  Child:Mary
  Child:Malcolm
MacLean, John; Quebec, 1851 *4537.30 p92*
  Wife:Catherine Macleod
  Child:Ann
  Child:Catherine
MacLean, John; Quebec, 1855 *4537.30 p93*
  Wife:Catherine MacRitchie
  Child:Kirsty
  Child:Margaret
MacLean, Kirsty SEE MacLean, Donald
MacLean, Kirsty SEE MacLean, John
MacLean, Kirsty SEE MacLean, Malcolm
MacLean, Kirsty; Quebec, 1841 *4537.30 p85*
MacLean, Kirsty; Quebec, 1851 *4537.30 p42*

FOR A COMPLETE EXPLANATION OF ENTRY, SEE "HOW TO READ A CITATION" SECTION

MacLeod, Donald; Quebec, 1838 *4537.30 p114*
  *Wife:*Eoridh Matheson
  *Child:*John
  *Child:*Murdo
  *Child:*Mary
  *Child:*Catherine
MacLeod, Donald; Quebec, 1845 *4537.30 p109*
  *Wife:*Ann MacIver
  *Child:*Mary
  *Child:*Ann
  *Child:*Murdo
  *Child:*Kirsty
  *Child:*Margaret
MacLeod, Donald; Quebec, 1851 *4537.30 p101*
  *Wife:*Catherine
  *Child:*Catherine
  *Child:*Norman
  *Child:*Kirsty
  *Child:*Margaret
  *Child:*John
  *Child:*Murdo
  *Child:*Hannah
MacLeod, Donald; Quebec, 1851 *4537.30 p102*
  *Wife:*Kirsty MacDonald
  *Child:*Murdo
MacLeod, Donald; Quebec, 1851 *4537.30 p103*
  *Wife:*Rachel
  *Child:*Effie
  *Child:*Donald
  *Child:*Angus
  *Child:*John
  *Child:*Murdo
MacLeod, Donald; Quebec, 1855 *4537.30 p102*
  *Wife:*Effie Ferguson
  *Child:*Mary
  *Child:*Donald
  *Child:*Jessie
MacLeod, Donald; Quebec, 1865 *4537.30 p101*
  *Wife:*Ann Smith
  *Child:*Murdo
  *Child:*Ann
  *Child:*Kirsty
  With child
  *Child:*Roderick
  *Child:*Donald
  *Child:*Malcolm
  *Child:*Mary
  *Child:*John
  *Child:*Angus
MacLeod, Donald; Quebec, 1873 *4537.30 p114*
  *Wife:*Mary Morrison
  *Child:*Isabella
  *Child:*Ann
  *Child:*John
  *Child:*Murdo
  *Child:*Margaret
MacLeod, Donald; Quebec, 1873 *4537.30 p114*
  *Wife:*Kirsty Michael
  *Child:*John
  *Child:*Hugh
  *Child:*Ann
  *Child:*William
  *Child:*Jessie
  *Child:*Robert
  *Child:*David
  *Child:*James
  *Child:*Donald
MacLeod, Donald Gordon *SEE* MacLeod, John
MacLeod, Donald N. *SEE* MacLeod, Norman
MacLeod, Dorothy MacAskill *SEE* MacLeod, John
MacLeod, Dougal *SEE* MacLeod, Angus
MacLeod, Duncan *SEE* MacLeod, John
MacLeod, Duncan; Quebec, 1817-1852 *4537.30 p103*
MacLeod, Effie *SEE* MacLeod, Donald
MacLeod, Effie *SEE* MacLeod, Malcolm
MacLeod, Effie *SEE* MacLeod, Mary MacKay
MacLeod, Effie *SEE* MacLeod, Norman
MacLeod, Effie Ferguson *SEE* MacLeod, Donald
MacLeod, Effie McInnis *SEE* MacLeod, William
MacLeod, Eoridh Matheson *SEE* MacLeod, Donald
MacLeod, Evander *SEE* MacLeod, Kenneth
MacLeod, Finlay *SEE* MacLeod, Alex
MacLeod, Finlay; Quebec, 1811-1852 *4537.30 p103*
MacLeod, Finlay; Quebec, 1863 *4537.30 p106*
  With wife
MacLeod, Flora Nicolson *SEE* MacLeod, John
MacLeod, Flora Nicolson *SEE* MacLeod, Malcolm
MacLeod, Gormelia *SEE* MacLeod, Murdo
MacLeod, Hannah *SEE* MacLeod, Donald
MacLeod, Hugh *SEE* MacLeod, Donald
MacLeod, Hugh *SEE* MacLeod, Donald
MacLeod, Isabella *SEE* MacLeod, Donald
MacLeod, Isabella *SEE* MacLeod, Mary MacKay

MacLeod, Isabella *SEE* MacLeod, Peter
MacLeod, Isabella; Quebec, 1838 *4537.30 p97*
MacLeod, Isabella; Quebec, 1851 *4537.30 p6*
MacLeod, Isabella; Quebec, 1851 *4537.30 p23*
MacLeod, Isabella; Quebec, 1851 *4537.30 p67*
MacLeod, Isabella; Quebec, 1863 *4537.30 p25*
MacLeod, Isabella; Quebec, 1900 *4537.30 p90*
MacLeod, Isabella Stewart *SEE* MacLeod, Alex
MacLeod, James *SEE* MacLeod, Donald
MacLeod, James *SEE* MacLeod, Murdo
MacLeod, Jane; Quebec, 1853 *4537.30 p63*
MacLeod, Jane Hunter *SEE* MacLeod, Daniel
MacLeod, Jane Hunter *SEE* MacLeod, John
MacLeod, Janet *SEE* MacLeod, Norman
MacLeod, Janet *SEE* MacLeod, Peter
MacLeod, Jessie *SEE* MacLeod, Angus
MacLeod, Jessie *SEE* MacLeod, Donald
MacLeod, Jessie *SEE* MacLeod, Donald
MacLeod, John *SEE* MacLeod, Angus
MacLeod, John *SEE* MacLeod, Ann
MacLeod, John *SEE* MacLeod, Ann Morrison
MacLeod, John *SEE* MacLeod, Daniel
MacLeod, John *SEE* MacLeod, Donald
MacLeod, John *SEE* MacLeod, Donald
MacLeod, John *SEE* MacLeod, Donald
MacLeod, John *SEE* MacLeod, Donald
MacLeod, John *SEE* MacLeod, Donald
MacLeod, John *SEE* MacLeod, Donald
MacLeod, John *SEE* MacLeod, Donald
MacLeod, John *SEE* MacLeod, John
MacLeod, John *SEE* MacLeod, John
MacLeod, John *SEE* MacLeod, John
MacLeod, John *SEE* MacLeod, John
MacLeod, John *SEE* MacLeod, John
MacLeod, John *SEE* MacLeod, Kenneth
MacLeod, John *SEE* MacLeod, Malcolm
MacLeod, John *SEE* MacLeod, Malcolm
MacLeod, John *SEE* MacLeod, Malcolm
MacLeod, John *SEE* MacLeod, Murdo
MacLeod, John *SEE* MacLeod, Murdo
MacLeod, John *SEE* MacLeod, Norman
MacLeod, John *SEE* MacLeod, Norman
MacLeod, John *SEE* MacLeod, William
MacLeod, John; North Carolina, 1770 *1639.20 p196*
  *Father:*John
  *Mother:*Jane Hunter
MacLeod, John; Quebec, 1811-1844 *4537.30 p104*
MacLeod, John; Quebec, 1833-1855 *4537.30 p105*
MacLeod, John; Quebec, 1845 *4537.30 p105*
  *Wife:*Mary
  *Child:*Kirsty
  *Child:*Donald
  *Child:*Ann
  *Child:*Malcolm
  *Child:*Angus
MacLeod, John; Quebec, 1852 *4537.30 p104*
  *Wife:*Dorothy MacAskill
  *Child:*Murdo
  *Child:*Mary Ann
  *Child:*Margaret
  *Child:*Ann
  *Child:*John
  *Child:*Duncan
  *Child:*Donald Gordon
MacLeod, John; Quebec, 1855 *4537.30 p111*
  *Wife:*Kirsty Morrison
  *Child:*Donald
  *Child:*John
MacLeod, John; Quebec, 1873 *4537.30 p112*
  *Wife:*Flora Nicolson
  *Child:*Betsy
  *Child:*Mary
  *Child:*Kenneth
  *Child:*Catherine
  *Child:*John
  *Child:*Louis
  *Child:*Kirsty
  *Child:*Malcolm
  *Child:*Marion
MacLeod, John; Quebec, 1878 *4537.30 p105*
  *Wife:*Kirsty Smith
  *Child:*Ann
  *Child:*Mary
  *Child:*John
  *Child:*Kirsty
  *Child:*Alex
  *Child:*Donald
  *Child:*Allan
  With child
Macleod, John; Wilmington, NC, 1745-1775 *1639.20 p196*
MacLeod, John N. *SEE* MacLeod, Norman
MacLeod, Joseph *SEE* MacLeod, Robert

MacLeod, Kenneth *SEE* MacLeod, John
MacLeod, Kenneth *SEE* MacLeod, Murdo
MacLeod, Kenneth; North Carolina, 1745-1776 *1639.20 p198*
MacLeod, Kenneth; Quebec, 1823-1900 *4537.30 p106*
MacLeod, Kenneth; Quebec, 1841 *4537.30 p106*
  *Wife:*Catherine MacRitchie
  *Child:*Evander
MacLeod, Kenneth; Quebec, 1851 *4537.30 p106*
  *Wife:*Ann MacIver
  *Child:*Margaret
MacLeod, Kenneth; Quebec, 1852 *4537.30 p113*
  *Wife:*Mary
  *Child:*Ann
  *Child:*Angus
  *Child:*John
  *Child:*Donald
  *Child:*Norman
  *Child:*Kirsty
MacLeod, Kent; Died enroute, 1802 *1639.20 p199*
MacLeod, Kirsty *SEE* MacLeod, Alex
MacLeod, Kirsty *SEE* MacLeod, Angus
MacLeod, Kirsty *SEE* MacLeod, Donald
MacLeod, Kirsty *SEE* MacLeod, Donald
MacLeod, Kirsty *SEE* MacLeod, Donald
MacLeod, Kirsty *SEE* MacLeod, John
MacLeod, Kirsty *SEE* MacLeod, John
MacLeod, Kirsty *SEE* MacLeod, John
MacLeod, Kirsty *SEE* MacLeod, Kenneth
MacLeod, Kirsty *SEE* MacLeod, Malcolm
MacLeod, Kirsty *SEE* MacLeod, Malcolm
MacLeod, Kirsty *SEE* MacLeod, Norman
MacLeod, Kirsty; Quebec, 1853 *4537.30 p46*
MacLeod, Kirsty; Quebec, 1866 *4537.30 p88*
MacLeod, Kirsty; Quebec, 1875 *4537.30 p15*
MacLeod, Kirsty Campbell *SEE* MacLeod, Angus
MacLeod, Kirsty MacBeth *SEE* MacLeod, Angus
MacLeod, Kirsty MacDonald *SEE* MacLeod, Angus
MacLeod, Kirsty MacDonald *SEE* MacLeod, Donald
MacLeod, Kirsty MacKenzie *SEE* MacLeod, Norman
MacLeod, Kirsty MacKenzie *SEE* MacLeod, Roderick
MacLeod, Kirsty Michael *SEE* MacLeod, Donald
MacLeod, Kirsty Morrison *SEE* MacLeod, John
MacLeod, Kirsty Smith *SEE* MacLeod, John
MacLeod, Louis *SEE* MacLeod, John
MacLeod, Malcolm *SEE* MacLeod, Ann
MacLeod, Malcolm *SEE* MacLeod, Ann Morrison
MacLeod, Malcolm *SEE* MacLeod, Donald
MacLeod, Malcolm *SEE* MacLeod, Donald
MacLeod, Malcolm *SEE* MacLeod, John
MacLeod, Malcolm *SEE* MacLeod, John
MacLeod, Malcolm *SEE* MacLeod, Malcolm
MacLeod, Malcolm *SEE* MacLeod, Malcolm
MacLeod, Malcolm *SEE* MacLeod, Malcolm
MacLeod, Malcolm *SEE* MacLeod, Mary MacKay
MacLeod, Malcolm *SEE* MacLeod, Peter
MacLeod, Malcolm; Quebec, 1821-1900 *4537.30 p108*
MacLeod, Malcolm; Quebec, 1841 *4537.30 p107*
  *Wife:*Catherine
  *Child:*Murdo
  *Child:*Ann
  *Child:*John
  *Child:*Margaret
  *Child:*Marion
MacLeod, Malcolm; Quebec, 1845 *4537.30 p107*
  *Wife:*Catherine MacKay
  *Child:*Murdo
  *Child:*Mary
  *Child:*Malcolm
  *Child:*John
  *Child:*Kirsty
MacLeod, Malcolm; Quebec, 1851 *4537.30 p107*
  *Wife:*Catherine MacAulay
  *Child:*John
  *Child:*Malcolm
  *Child:*Catherine
MacLeod, Malcolm; Quebec, 1875 *4537.30 p113*
MacLeod, Malcolm; Quebec, 1875 *4537.30 p115*
  *Wife:*Flora Nicolson
  *Child:*Catherine
  *Child:*Kirsty
  *Child:*Effie
  *Child:*Neil
  *Child:*Marion
  *Child:*Malcolm
MacLeod, Margaret *SEE* MacLeod, Angus
MacLeod, Margaret *SEE* MacLeod, Donald
MacLeod, Margaret *SEE* MacLeod, Donald
MacLeod, Margaret *SEE* MacLeod, Donald
MacLeod, Margaret *SEE* MacLeod, John
MacLeod, Margaret *SEE* MacLeod, Kenneth
MacLeod, Margaret *SEE* MacLeod, Malcolm
MacLeod, Margaret *SEE* MacLeod, Norman

MacPeak, Owen; New York, NY, 1811 *2859.11 p16*
MacPharland, Mrs.; New York, NY, 1811 *2859.11 p16*
  With 2 children
MacPharland, P.; New York, NY, 1811 *2859.11 p16*
MacPherson, Hugh; New Brunswick, 1819 *9775.5 p204*
  With family
MacPhilaney, Margaret; New York, NY, 1816 *2859.11 p38*
MacPhiloron, Dennis; New York, NY, 1816 *2859.11 p38*
MacQueen, Alexander *SEE* MacQueen, Margaret Martin
Macqueen, Alexander 17; Jamaica, 1722 *3690.1 p147*
MacQueen, Angus *SEE* MacQueen, Margaret Martin
MacQueen, Archibald; Cape Fear, NC, 1771 *4814 p92*
MacQueen, Donald *SEE* MacQueen, Margaret Martin
MacQueen, Flora *SEE* MacQueen, Margaret Martin
MacQueen, Margaret Martin; Wilmington, NC, 1802
  1639.20 p221
  *Daughter:*Flora
  *Son:*Alexander
  *Son:*Donald
  *Son:*Angus
MacQueen, Matthew; New York, NY, 1816 *2859.11 p38*
MacQueen, Murdoch; America, 1772 *1639.20 p221*
Macquelin, James 16; Maryland, 1720 *3690.1 p147*
Macquet, Peter 34; Virginia, 1773 *1219.7 p170*
MacQuig, William; New York, NY, 1816 *2859.11 p38*
MacQuillan, H.; Philadelphia, 1811 *2859.11 p16*
  With family
MacQuinn, Patrick; New York, NY, 1816 *2859.11 p38*
MacQuoid, James; New York, NY, 1815 *2859.11 p38*
MacRae, Alex *SEE* MacRae, Alex
MacRae, Alex *SEE* MacRae, Alexander
MacRae, Alex *SEE* MacRae, Neil
MacRae, Alex; Quebec, 1850 *4537.30 p117*
  *Wife:*Kirsty Martin
  *Child:*George
  *Child:*Alex
  *Child:*Neil
  *Child:*Jane
  *Child:*Catherine
  *Child:*Duncan
  *Child:*Margaret
  *Child:*Donald M.
MacRae, Alexander; Quebec, 1875 *4537.30 p118*
  *Wife:*Annabella MacLeod
  *Child:*Alex
  *Child:*John
  *Child:*Ann
  *Child:*Isabella
MacRae, Angus *SEE* MacRae, Angus
MacRae, Angus; Quebec, 1845 *4537.30 p117*
  *Wife:*Bess Stewart
  *Child:*John
  *Child:*George
  *Child:*Margaret
MacRae, Angus; Quebec, 1855 *4537.30 p117*
  *Wife:*Ann Murray
  *Child:*Donald
  *Child:*Ann
  *Child:*Margaret
  *Child:*Mary
  *Child:*Angus
  *Child:*Daniel
  *Child:*Murdo
MacRae, Ann *SEE* MacRae, Alexander
MacRae, Ann *SEE* MacRae, Angus
MacRae, Ann Cameron *SEE* MacRae, Duncan
MacRae, Ann Campbell *SEE* MacRae, Neil
MacRae, Ann MacKenzie *SEE* MacRae, Donald
MacRae, Ann Margaret *SEE* MacRae, Donald
MacRae, Ann Murray *SEE* MacRae, Angus
MacRae, Annabella *SEE* MacRae, Donald
MacRae, Annabella MacLeod *SEE* MacRae, Alexander
MacRae, Bess Stewart *SEE* MacRae, Angus
MacRae, Catherine *SEE* MacRae, Alex
MacRae, Catherine *SEE* MacRae, Donald
MacRae, Catherine *SEE* MacRae, Neil
Macrae, Charlotte Johana; Florida, 1830 *8893 p265*
MacRae, Daniel *SEE* MacRae, Angus
MacRae, Donald *SEE* MacRae, Angus
MacRae, Donald *SEE* MacRae, Donald
MacRae, Donald; Quebec, 1877 *4537.30 p118*
  *Wife:*Ann MacKenzie
  *Child:*Catherine
  *Child:*Mary
  *Child:*Flora
  *Child:*Kenneth
  *Child:*Annabella
  *Child:*Donald
  *Child:*Ann Margaret
MacRae, Donald M. *SEE* MacRae, Alex
MacRae, Dorothy *SEE* MacRae, Neil
MacRae, Duncan *SEE* MacRae, Alex

MacRae, Duncan; Norfolk, VA, 1773 *1639.20 p223*
  *Wife:*Ann Cameron
MacRae, Duncan; South Carolina, 1754-1776 *1639.20
  p223*
MacRae, Finlay Philip; Wilmington, NC, 1770 *1639.20
  p223*
MacRae, Flora *SEE* MacRae, Donald
MacRae, George *SEE* MacRae, Alex
MacRae, George *SEE* MacRae, Angus
MacRae, Isabella *SEE* MacRae, Alexander
MacRae, Isabella *SEE* MacRae, Neil
MacRae, Jane *SEE* MacRae, Alex
MacRae, John *SEE* MacRae, Alexander
MacRae, John *SEE* MacRae, Angus
MacRae, John; North Carolina, 1774 *1639.20 p224*
  With wife
MacRae, John; South Carolina, 1828 *1639.20 p224*
MacRae, Kenneth *SEE* MacRae, Donald
MacRae, Kirsty; Quebec, 1863 *4537.30 p50*
MacRae, Kirsty Martin *SEE* MacRae, Alex
MacRae, Margaret *SEE* MacRae, Alex
MacRae, Margaret *SEE* MacRae, Angus
MacRae, Margaret *SEE* MacRae, Angus
MacRae, Mary *SEE* MacRae, Angus
MacRae, Mary *SEE* MacRae, Donald
MacRae, Mary; Quebec, 1841 *4537.30 p16*
MacRae, Mary; Wilmington, NC, 1770 *1639.20 p225*
MacRae, Murdo *SEE* MacRae, Angus
MacRae, Murdoch; North Carolina, 1773 *1639.20 p225*
MacRae, Neil *SEE* MacRae, Alex
MacRae, Neil; Quebec, 1873 *4537.30 p118*
  *Wife:*Ann Campbell
  *Child:*Isabella
  *Child:*Catherine
  *Child:*Dorothy
  *Child:*Alex
MacRae, Roderick; Wilmington, NC, 1770 *1639.20 p225*
MacRalin, Roger; New York, NY, 1815 *2859.11 p38*
Macre, Charlotte Johana; Florida, 1830 *8893 p265*
MacRedden, James; New York, NY, 1816 *2859.11 p38*
Macredie, Janett 69; Kansas, 1875 *5240.1 p56*
MacRitchie, Ann *SEE* MacRitchie, Donald
MacRitchie, Ann *SEE* MacRitchie, Norman
MacRitchie, Catherine *SEE* MacRitchie, Donald
MacRitchie, Catherine; Quebec, 1841 *4537.30 p14*
MacRitchie, Catherine; Quebec, 1841 *4537.30 p106*
MacRitchie, Catherine; Quebec, 1855 *4537.30 p93*
MacRitchie, Catherine MacLeod *SEE* MacRitchie, John
MacRitchie, Donald *SEE* MacRitchie, Donald
MacRitchie, Donald *SEE* MacRitchie, John
MacRitchie, Donald; Quebec, 1855 *4537.30 p119*
  *Wife:*Mary MacDonald
  *Child:*Catherine
  *Child:*John
  *Child:*Donald
  *Child:*Ann
  *Child:*Isabella
MacRitchie, Finlay *SEE* MacRitchie, John
MacRitchie, Isabella *SEE* MacRitchie, Donald
MacRitchie, John *SEE* MacRitchie, Donald
MacRitchie, John; Quebec, 1843 *4537.30 p119*
  *Wife:*Catherine MacLeod
  *Child:*Donald
  *Child:*Margaret
  *Child:*Finlay
MacRitchie, Kirsty; Quebec, 1841 *4537.30 p40*
MacRitchie, Kirsty; Quebec, 1851 *4537.30 p52*
MacRitchie, Kirsty; Quebec, 1863 *4537.30 p69*
MacRitchie, Margaret *SEE* MacRitchie, John
MacRitchie, Margaret; Quebec, 1843 *4537.30 p64*
MacRitchie, Margaret; Quebec, 1851 *4537.30 p91*
MacRitchie, Marion; Quebec, 1853 *4537.30 p89*
MacRitchie, Mary; Quebec, 1820-1839 *4537.30 p69*
MacRitchie, Mary; Quebec, 1855 *4537.30 p21*
MacRitchie, Mary MacDonald *SEE* MacRitchie, Donald
MacRitchie, Mary MacDonald *SEE* MacRitchie, Norman
MacRitchie, Norman; Quebec, 1851 *4537.30 p119*
  *Wife:*Mary MacDonald
  *Child:*Ann
  *Child:*William
MacRitchie, Roderick; Quebec, 1841 *4537.30 p120*
MacRitchie, William *SEE* MacRitchie, Norman
MacSerley, James; New York, NY, 1816 *2859.11 p38*
MacShane, Daniel; New York, NY, 1815 *2859.11 p38*
MacShane, Thomas; Philadelphia, 1811 *2859.11 p16*
MacSheldon, James; Philadelphia, 1815 *2859.11 p38*
MacSherry, Patrick; New York, NY, 1816 *2859.11 p38*
MacSleeve, James; New York, NY, 1811 *2859.11 p17*
MacSuine, Donald; North Carolina, 1809 *1639.20 p226*
MacSwigon, Mary; New York, NY, 1816 *2859.11 p38*
MacSwigon, Philip; New York, NY, 1816 *2859.11 p38*
MacTahan, Henry; New York, NY, 1816 *2859.11 p38*
  With wife

MacTea, Arthur; New York, NY, 1816 *2859.11 p38*
MacTice, Andrew; New York, NY, 1816 *2859.11 p38*
MacTogert, Mrs.; Philadelphia, 1811 *2859.11 p17*
  With family
Macuga, John; Iowa, 1866-1943 *123.54 p31*
Maculan, Bernardo; Arkansas, 1918 *95.2 p77*
Macusker, Bridget; Quebec, 1847 *5704.8 p7*
MacVaid, James; New York, NY, 1816 *2859.11 p38*
MacVay, M.; New York, NY, 1811 *2859.11 p17*
  With family
MacVea, Jas.; Philadelphia, 1816 *2859.11 p38*
MacVeagh, Patrick; New York, NY, 1811 *2859.11 p17*
MacVeigh, Henry; New York, NY, 1816 *2859.11 p38*
Macvga, John; Iowa, 1866-1943 *123.54 p31*
MacVicker, Thos.; New York, NY, 1815 *2859.11 p38*
MacVoy, Dominick; New York, NY, 1816 *2859.11 p38*
Macwell, William 33; Georgia, 1775 *1219.7 p276*
MacWhatey, Jane; New York, NY, 1811 *2859.11 p17*
MacWhaty, John; New York, NY, 1811 *2859.11 p17*
MacWherter, Jane; New York, NY, 1811 *2859.11 p17*
MacWhinnie, Isabella; South Carolina, 1829 *1639.20
  p106*
Macwiney, Margaret; Philadelphia, 1864 *5704.8 p188*
Maczejewski, Mariana; Wisconsin, n.d. *9675.6 p268*
Madagin, Michel; Montreal, 1808 *7603 p86*
Madalinska, Helena 19 *SEE* Madalinska, Josef
Madalinska, Josef 26; New York, 1912 *9980.29 p53*
  *Sister:*Helena 19
Madalinski, Helena 19 *SEE* Madalinski, Josef
Madalinski, Josef 26; New York, 1912 *9980.29 p53*
  *Sister:*Helena 19
Madallozzo, Jack; Iowa, 1866-1943 *123.54 p32*
Madallozzo, John; Iowa, 1866-1943 *123.54 p32*
Madalozzo, Jacomo; Iowa, 1866-1943 *123.54 p32*
Maddalazzo, Valentino; Iowa, 1866-1943 *123.54 p69*
Maddalozzo, Angelo; Iowa, 1866-1943 *123.54 p31*
Madden, Bernard; Quebec, 1816 *7603 p96*
Madden, Betty Ann 12; Quebec, 1850 *5704.8 p62*
Madden, Catherine 7; Quebec, 1850 *5704.8 p62*
Madden, Cornelius; America, 1737 *4971 p33*
Madden, Darby; America, 1742 *4971 p49*
Madden, Darby; America, 1742 *4971 p50*
Madden, David 26; Philadelphia, 1856 *5704.8 p128*
Madden, Dennis; America, 1739 *4971 p31*
Madden, Elizabeth; Quebec, 1850 *5704.8 p62*
Madden, Elizabeth 25; Philadelphia, 1856 *5704.8 p128*
Madden, Frederick B.; Illinois, 1900 *5012.40 p77*
Madden, James; New York, NY, 1815 *2859.11 p38*
Madden, James; New York, NY, 1816 *2859.11 p38*
Madden, James 57; Massachusetts, 1849 *5881.1 p69*
Madden, John; New York, NY, 1811 *2859.11 p17*
Madden, John 17; Virginia, 1775 *1219.7 p261*
Madden, Malachi; America, 1741 *4971 p41*
Madden, Peggy 50; Massachusetts, 1849 *5881.1 p74*
Madden, Samuel N.; Illinois, 1896 *5012.40 p54*
Madden, Sarah 18; Massachusetts, 1847 *5881.1 p75*
Madden, Thomas 9; Quebec, 1850 *5704.8 p62*
Madden, William; Quebec, 1850 *5704.8 p62*
Madden, William 50; Massachusetts, 1849 *5881.1 p77*
Maddern, James Henry; Arkansas, 1918 *95.2 p77*
Maddey, Thomas; Jamaica, 1753 *1219.7 p25*
Maddin, Henry; Virginia, 1643 *6219 p23*
Maddis, Theodore; Arkansas, 1918 *95.2 p77*
Maddison, James 23; Jamaica, 1738 *3690.1 p147*
Maddison, Jon.; Virginia, 1642 *6219 p195*
Maddison, Rich.; Virginia, 1635 *6219 p71*
Maddock, James 30; Virginia, 1700 *2212 p32*
Maddock, Katherine 16; America, 1699 *2212 p25*
Maddock, Nicholas; Illinois, 1858 *7857 p5*
Maddock, Robert J.; Illinois, 1891 *5012.37 p62*
Maddock, S. H.; Washington, 1859-1920 *2872.1 p24*
Maddock, Samuel H.; Washington, 1859-1920 *2872.1
  p24*
Maddock, William 21; America, 1700 *2212 p31*
Maddocks, Thomas 21; Jamaica, 1724 *3690.1 p147*
Maddon, John 32; Massachusetts, 1849 *5881.1 p68*
Maddox, Mrs. 35; Massachusetts, 1850 *5881.1 p73*
Maddox, John; Jamaica, 1773 *1219.7 p167*
Maddox, Joseph-Daniel 25; Montreal, 1818 *7603 p23*
Maddox, Thomas; Massachusetts, 1850 *5881.1 p76*
Madenwald, Charles; Illinois, 1868 *5012.38 p98*
Mader, Ambrose; Virginia, 1636 *6219 p75*
Mader, Elisabetha; New England, 1738-1800 *2444 p187*
Mader, Joerg; Pennsylvania, 1751 *2444 p187*
Madereiter, Johann; Georgia, 1734 *9332 p327*
Madern, Catharine 25; America, 1836 *778.5 p352*
Madesce, Catharine 25; America, 1836 *778.5 p352*
Madigan, Ally; New York, NY, 1815 *2859.11 p38*
Madigan, Anne; New York, NY, 1815 *2859.11 p38*
Madigan, Edward; New York, NY, 1815 *2859.11 p38*
Madigan, James; New York, NY, 1815 *2859.11 p38*
Madigan, Judy; New York, NY, 1815 *2859.11 p38*
Madigan, Mary; New York, NY, 1815 *2859.11 p38*

Madigan, Michael; Montreal, 1825 ***7603*** *p86*
Madigan, Michael; New York, NY, 1835 ***8208.4*** *p26*
Madigan, Peggy; New York, NY, 1815 ***2859.11*** *p38*
Madigan, Thomas; New York, NY, 1836 ***8208.4*** *p80*
Madigan, Thomas; Quebec, 1823 ***7603*** *p86*
Madigan, Walter; New York, NY, 1815 ***2859.11*** *p38*
Madigan, William; New York, NY, 1815 ***2859.11*** *p38*
Madihan, Patrick; Wisconsin, n.d. ***9675.6*** *p268*
Madinas, Jose 40; Arizona, 1925 ***9228.40*** *p29*
Mading, Gottlob 38; New Orleans, 1839 ***9420.2*** *p68*
Mading, Leonhard 40; New Orleans, 1839 ***9420.2*** *p68*
Mading, Magdaline 70; New Orleans, 1839 ***9420.2*** *p68*
Madison, August; Iowa, 1866-1943 ***123.54*** *p32*
Madison, Charles; Shreveport, LA, 1879 ***7129*** *p45*
Madison, James; Shreveport, LA, 1878 ***7129*** *p45*
Madlener, Ursulina; Wisconsin, n.d. ***9675.6*** *p268*
Madlock, Robert; Virginia, 1638 ***6219*** *p125*
Madokovich, Mike; Arkansas, 1918 ***95.2*** *p77*
Madonne, James; Colorado, 1904 ***9678.2*** *p125*
Madonne, John; Colorado, 1904 ***9678.2*** *p125*
Madrin, Owin; Virginia, 1640 ***6219*** *p182*
Madsen, Frans Peter; New York, NY, 1913 ***3455.3*** *p52*
Madsen, Franz Peter Kristinan Thorvald; New York, NY, 1913 ***3455.2*** *p49*
Madsen, Fredrich; New York, NY, 1893 ***3455.3*** *p78*
Madsen, Fredrik; New York, NY, 1893 ***3455.2*** *p75*
Madsen, H.C.J.; Illinois, 1892 ***5012.40*** *p26*
Madsen, Jens Andneas Christian; Arkansas, 1918 ***95.2*** *p78*
Madsen, Lars Hensen; Arkansas, 1918 ***95.2*** *p78*
Madsen, Niels Gerhard Miller; New York, NY, 1913 ***3455.2*** *p44*
Madsen, Niels Gerhard Miller; New York, NY, 1913 ***3455.3*** *p104*
Madsen, Ole Peter Christ 31; Arkansas, 1918 ***95.2*** *p78*
Madsen, R. 34; Washington, 1919 ***1728.5*** *p12*
Madvey, Stanley; Arkansas, 1918 ***95.2*** *p78*
Madwell, William; Virginia, 1639 ***6219*** *p18*
Madwell, William; Virginia, 1639 ***6219*** *p157*
Madwell, Wm.; Virginia, 1637 ***6219*** *p112*
Madworth, Wm.; Virginia, 1637 ***6219*** *p13*
Maear, Frederick; Illinois, 1871 ***5012.39*** *p25*
Maechtle, Jacob; Wisconsin, n.d. ***9675.6*** *p268*
Maechtlen, Wm 30; Kansas, 1872 ***5240.1*** *p52*
Maene, Peter; Arkansas, 1918 ***95.2*** *p78*
Maestened, Jean J. 24; New Orleans, 1839 ***778.5*** *p352*
Maetzold, John Gottlieb; Wisconsin, n.d. ***9675.6*** *p268*
Maeule, Catharina Barbara Off 50 *SEE* Maeule, Matthias Friedrich
Maeule, Matthias Friedrich 47; Philadelphia, 1805 ***2444*** *p187*
*Wife:*Catharina Barbara Off 50
Maeurlin, Anna Barbara; Pennsylvania, 1751 ***2444*** *p204*
Maffett, James; New York, NY, 1811 ***2859.11*** *p17*
Magagros, Mrs. 36; Louisiana, 1823 ***778.5*** *p352*
Magagros, Adele 14; Louisiana, 1823 ***778.5*** *p352*
Magagros, Delphine 17; Louisiana, 1823 ***778.5*** *p352*
Magain, Mr. 30; Louisiana, 1825 ***778.5*** *p352*
Magalena, Mr.; Port uncertain, 1839 ***778.5*** *p352*
Magan, Patrick; Virginia, 1858 ***4626.16*** *p17*
Magano, Giovanni; Arkansas, 1918 ***95.2*** *p78*
Magar, John Wm.; Colorado, 1904 ***9678.2*** *p125*
Magauran, Thomas; America, 1740 ***4971*** *p22*
Magawley, Philip; Delaware Bay or River, 1743 ***4971*** *p104*
Magee, Mrs.; Philadelphia, 1865 ***5704.8*** *p194*
Magee, Alexander; Philadelphia, 1865 ***5704.8*** *p194*
Magee, Anabella; Philadelphia, 1866 ***5704.8*** *p207*
Magee, Andrew; Philadelphia, 1852 ***5704.8*** *p88*
Magee, Andrew 21; Quebec, 1857 ***5704.8*** *p136*
Magee, Ann 17; St. John, N.B., 1864 ***5704.8*** *p158*
Magee, Anne; St. John, N.B., 1851 ***5704.8*** *p72*
Magee, Anne 22; Philadelphia, 1854 ***5704.8*** *p120*
Magee, Annie; New York, NY, 1866 ***5704.8*** *p212*
Magee, Arthur 10; St. John, N.B., 1864 ***5704.8*** *p158*
Magee, Bernard; New York, NY, 1816 ***2859.11*** *p38*
Magee, Bernard F.; New York, NY, 1839 ***8208.4*** *p91*
Magee, Bernd.; New York, NY, 1816 ***2859.11*** *p38*
Magee, Bessie; America, 1864-1871 ***5704.8*** *p240*
Magee, Betty 44; St. John, N.B., 1864 ***5704.8*** *p158*
Magee, Bridget 9; Philadelphia, 1865 ***5704.8*** *p194*
Magee, Catherine; New York, NY, 1864 ***5704.8*** *p174*
Magee, Catherine; Philadelphia, 1851 ***5704.8*** *p80*
Magee, Catherine 18; St. John, N.B., 1864 ***5704.8*** *p158*
Magee, Catherine 19; St. John, N.B., 1864 ***5704.8*** *p158*
Magee, Catherine 60; St. John, N.B., 1864 ***5704.8*** *p158*
Magee, Columbus 19; Philadelphia, 1855 ***5704.8*** *p124*
Magee, Elizabeth 9 mos; Philadelphia, 1851 ***5704.8*** *p80*
Magee, Elizabeth J. 20; St. John, N.B., 1859 ***5704.8*** *p140*
Magee, Ellen; America, 1866 ***5704.8*** *p215*
Magee, Ellen 20; St. John, N.B., 1864 ***5704.8*** *p158*
Magee, Francis; Philadelphia, 1865 ***5704.8*** *p194*
Magee, Frank; Philadelphia, 1865 ***5704.8*** *p194*
Magee, George; New York, NY, 1836 ***8208.4*** *p22*
Magee, Henry 4; St. John, N.B., 1864 ***5704.8*** *p158*
Magee, Henry 16; St. John, N.B., 1854 ***5704.8*** *p121*
Magee, Hugh; New York, NY, 1866 ***5704.8*** *p212*
Magee, Hugh 11; Philadelphia, 1865 ***5704.8*** *p194*
Magee, James; New York, NY, 1816 ***2859.11*** *p38*
Magee, James; Philadelphia, 1852 ***5704.8*** *p91*
Magee, James; Quebec, 1847 ***5704.8*** *p36*
Magee, James 4; St. John, N.B., 1864 ***5704.8*** *p158*
Magee, James 21; St. John, N.B., 1854 ***5704.8*** *p115*
Magee, John; America, 1867 ***5704.8*** *p220*
Magee, John; New York, NY, 1816 ***2859.11*** *p38*
Magee, John 20; Philadelphia, 1859 ***5704.8*** *p142*
Magee, John 21; Quebec, 1857 ***5704.8*** *p136*
Magee, John 26; St. John, N.B., 1864 ***5704.8*** *p158*
Magee, Joseph; New York, NY, 1838 ***8208.4*** *p86*
Magee, Joseph; Philadelphia, 1864 ***5704.8*** *p177*
Magee, Mary; New York, NY, 1864 ***5704.8*** *p182*
Magee, Mary; Philadelphia, 1848 ***53.26*** *p48*
Magee, Mary; Philadelphia, 1848 ***5704.8*** *p45*
Magee, Mary; St. John, N.B., 1851 ***5704.8*** *p72*
Magee, Mary 18; Philadelphia, 1853 ***5704.8*** *p108*
Magee, Mary Ann; St. John, N.B., 1847 ***5704.8*** *p33*
Magee, Nancy; Philadelphia, 1852 ***5704.8*** *p91*
Magee, Patrick; New York, NY, 1816 ***2859.11*** *p38*
Magee, Patt 24; St. John, N.B., 1864 ***5704.8*** *p158*
Magee, Robert 12; St. John, N.B., 1864 ***5704.8*** *p158*
Magee, Robert 18; Philadelphia, 1860 ***5704.8*** *p145*
Magee, Robert 23; Philadelphia, 1856 ***5704.8*** *p128*
Magee, Rose; Philadelphia, 1865 ***5704.8*** *p194*
Magee, Susan; St. John, N.B., 1847 ***5704.8*** *p33*
Magee, William; New York, NY, 1816 ***2859.11*** *p38*
Magel, Heinr. 55; Pittsburgh, 1904 ***1763*** *p48D*
Magell, Ekiza; New York, NY, 1811 ***2859.11*** *p17*
Magell, John; New York, NY, 1811 ***2859.11*** *p17*
Magell, Samuel; New York, NY, 1811 ***2859.11*** *p17*
Magennis, Philip; America, 1739 ***4971*** *p9*
Magennis, Philip; America, 1739 ***4971*** *p103*
Mager, Hugo Alfred; Wisconsin, n.d. ***9675.6*** *p268*
Mager, Valentine; New York, NY, 1836 ***8208.4*** *p14*
Mages, Joseph; Philadelphia, 1811 ***2859.11*** *p17*
Maggee, Patrick; Philadelphia, 1864 ***5704.8*** *p174*
Maggid, Joseph; Iowa, 1866-1943 ***123.54*** *p32*
Maggid, Sam; Iowa, 1866-1943 ***123.54*** *p32*
Maggini, Gins 50; New York, NY, 1893 ***9026.4*** *p42*
Magguire, Elizabeth 17; Maryland, 1774 ***1219.7*** *p234*
Magher, . . .; New York, NY, 1816 ***2859.11*** *p38*
Magher, Ellenor; America, 1740 ***4971*** *p48*
Magher, Jeremy; Quebec, 1790 ***7603*** *p96*
Magher, John; Maryland, 1742 ***4971*** *p107*
Magher, Michael; Illinois, 1868 ***7857*** *p5*
Magher, Patrick; America, 1740 ***4971*** *p31*
Maghi, Lugi 36; West Virginia, 1898 ***9788.3*** *p15*
Magill, Daniel; New York, NY, 1816 ***2859.11*** *p38*
Magill, John; New York, NY, 1815 ***2859.11*** *p38*
Magill, Mary; New York, NY, 1870 ***5704.8*** *p237*
Magill, W. F.; Washington, 1859-1920 ***2872.1*** *p24*
Magimkin, Mary Jane; St. John, N.B., 1851 ***5704.8*** *p72*
Magin, Alice; St. John, N.B., 1847 ***5704.8*** *p34*
Magin, James; St. John, N.B., 1847 ***5704.8*** *p34*
Maginis, Charles; Wisconsin, n.d. ***9675.6*** *p268*
Maginley, John 25; Philadelphia, 1861 ***5704.8*** *p148*
Maginn, Ellen; Philadelphia, 1864 ***5704.8*** *p183*
Maginn, John; New York, NY, 1836 ***8208.4*** *p18*
Maginn, Rosa; St. John, N.B., 1851 ***5704.8*** *p72*
Maginn, Susan; Philadelphia, 1864 ***5704.8*** *p183*
Maginness, Biddy; Philadelphia, 1853 ***5704.8*** *p100*
Maginniss, Mary Ann; Philadelphia, 1850 ***5704.8*** *p64*
Maginot, Jean 27; America, 1838 ***778.5*** *p352*
Magior, John 20; Pennsylvania, 1728 ***3690.1*** *p147*
Magis, Joseph; Philadelphia, 1811 ***53.26*** *p48*
Magis, Joseph; Philadelphia, 1811 ***2859.11*** *p17*
Magly, John; America, 1855 ***1450.2*** *p91A*
Magnan, Charles 32; Jamaica, 1825 ***778.5*** *p353*
Magnane, Grace; Arkansas, 1918 ***95.2*** *p78*
Magne, Mr. 40; Port uncertain, 1837 ***778.5*** *p353*
Magne, S. 28; Mexico, 1835 ***778.5*** *p353*
Magnen, C. 40; New Orleans, 1829 ***778.5*** *p353*
Magneson, Emil Sigfrid 27; Arkansas, 1918 ***95.2*** *p78*
Magnin, Mme. 29; America, 1836 ***778.5*** *p353*
Magnin, Charles Joseph 30; Norfolk, VA, 1820 ***778.5*** *p353*
Magnin, Jean 48; America, 1838 ***778.5*** *p353*
Magnin, M. 32; America, 1836 ***778.5*** *p353*
Magnus, Carl Heinrich; America, 1845 ***4610.10*** *p97*
*Wife:*Sophie L Schockemoller
*Son:*Karl Ernst Heinrich
*Son:*Karl Friedrich Wilhelm
Magnus, Henry Frederick Wilhelm; Illinois, 1877 ***2896.5*** *p25*
Magnus, Karl Ernst Heinrich *SEE* Magnus, Carl Heinrich
Magnus, Karl Friedrich Wilhelm *SEE* Magnus, Carl Heinrich
Magnus, Sophie L Schockemoller *SEE* Magnus, Carl Heinrich
Magnusdottir, Anna 4; Quebec, 1879 ***2557.1*** *p22*
Magnusdottir, Einar 5; Quebec, 1879 ***2557.2*** *p37*
Magnusdottir, Gunnhildur 24; Quebec, 1879 ***2557.2*** *p37*
Magnusdottir, Jon 1; Quebec, 1879 ***2557.2*** *p37*
Magnusdottir, Jonatan 6 mos; Quebec, 1879 ***2557.2*** *p37*
Magnusdottir, Magnus 3; Quebec, 1879 ***2557.2*** *p37*
Magnusdottir, Matthilda 24; Quebec, 1879 ***2557.2*** *p37*
Magnusdottir, Solveig 50; Quebec, 1879 ***2557.1*** *p20*
Magnusdottir, Thorbjorg 19; Quebec, 1879 ***2557.2*** *p37*
Magnusdottir, Vilborg 44; Quebec, 1879 ***2557.1*** *p22*
Magnusjon, Niklase; Illinois, 1882 ***5012.39*** *p52*
Magnuski, Jan; New York, 1834 ***4606*** *p178*
Magnuson, Andrew; Iowa, 1866-1943 ***123.54*** *p32*
Magnuson, Charles A.; Iowa, 1866-1943 ***123.54*** *p32*
Magnuson, John Alfred; Arkansas, 1918 ***95.2*** *p78*
Magnuson, Nels; Colorado, 1900 ***9678.2*** *p125*
Magnusson, Elias; Minneapolis, 1883 ***6410.35*** *p60*
Magnusson, Jon 24; Quebec, 1879 ***2557.2*** *p37*
Magnusson, Nicholas; Illinois, 1882 ***5012.39*** *p52*
Magnusson, Peter Magnus; Minneapolis, 1879-1888 ***6410.35*** *p59*
Magnusson, Sveinn 13; Quebec, 1879 ***2557.1*** *p22*
Magnusson, Sven 36; Kansas, 1888 ***5240.1*** *p72*
Magny, Antoine 34; America, 1839 ***778.5*** *p353*
Magny, Denis 22; New Orleans, 1836 ***778.5*** *p353*
Magny, Xavier 34; America, 1838 ***778.5*** *p353*
Magoan, John 10; Philadelphia, 1861 ***5704.8*** *p149*
Magoan, Thomas 16; Philadelphia, 1861 ***5704.8*** *p149*
Magolrick, James; America, 1737 ***4971*** *p72*
Magouran, Mr. 22; New Orleans, 1821 ***778.5*** *p353*
Magowan, Elizabeth 20; St. John, N.B., 1862 ***5704.8*** *p151*
Magowan, Ellen 25; Philadelphia, 1864 ***5704.8*** *p155*
Magrath, Honnora 1; Newport, RI, 1851 ***6508.5*** *p20*
Magrath, John; America, 1736 ***4971*** *p44*
Magrath, John; America, 1736 ***4971*** *p45*
Magrath, John 35; Newport, RI, 1851 ***6508.5*** *p20*
Magrath, Sarah 35; Newport, RI, 1851 ***6508.5*** *p20*
Magrath, Thomas; America, 1742 ***4971*** *p32*
Magratli, Hugh; America, 1735-1743 ***4971*** *p79*
Magsann, Charles; Illinois, 1876 ***5012.39*** *p91*
Magson, Jon.; Virginia, 1600-1643 ***6219*** *p200*
Maguin, Mr. 30; Louisiana, 1825 ***778.5*** *p352*
Maguinis, Isabella; New York, NY, 1811 ***2859.11*** *p17*
Maguinis, John; New York, NY, 1811 ***2859.11*** *p17*
Maguire, Alice 14; Philadelphia, 1860 ***5704.8*** *p146*
Maguire, Andrew; New York, NY, 1838 ***8208.4*** *p84*
Maguire, Andrew 4; Quebec, 1863 ***5704.8*** *p153*
Maguire, Andrew 11; Quebec, 1851 ***5704.8*** *p82*
Maguire, Andrew 16; Quebec, 1862 ***5704.8*** *p150*
Maguire, Ann *SEE* Maguire, James
Maguire, Ann; Philadelphia, 1850 ***5704.8*** *p69*
Maguire, Ann; Quebec, 1822 ***7603*** *p83*
Maguire, Ann; Quebec, 1847 ***5704.8*** *p38*
Maguire, Ann; Quebec, 1850 ***5704.8*** *p70*
Maguire, Ann 5; St. John, N.B., 1847 ***5704.8*** *p35*
Maguire, Ann 7; St. John, N.B., 1847 ***5704.8*** *p34*
Maguire, Ann 18; Philadelphia, 1856 ***5704.8*** *p129*
Maguire, Anne; Philadelphia, 1866 ***5704.8*** *p208*
Maguire, Anne; Quebec, 1823 ***7603*** *p90*
Maguire, Anne; Quebec, 1847 ***5704.8*** *p38*
Maguire, Anne; Quebec, 1851 ***5704.8*** *p73*
Maguire, Anne 50; Quebec, 1863 ***5704.8*** *p153*
Maguire, Bernard; Quebec, 1847 ***5704.8*** *p37*
Maguire, Bernard; Quebec, 1847 ***5704.8*** *p38*
Maguire, Bernard 4; St. John, N.B., 1847 ***5704.8*** *p9*
Maguire, Bernard 5 *SEE* Maguire, Sarah
Maguire, Bernard 5; Philadelphia, 1849 ***5704.8*** *p54*
Maguire, Bernard 10; Massachusetts, 1849 ***5881.1*** *p63*
Maguire, Bessie; Philadelphia, 1865 ***5704.8*** *p186*
Maguire, Bessy; Philadelphia, 1851 ***5704.8*** *p81*
Maguire, Biddy; Quebec, 1851 ***5704.8*** *p74*
Maguire, Biddy; St. John, N.B., 1847 ***5704.8*** *p21*
Maguire, Biddy; St. John, N.B., 1847 ***5704.8*** *p34*
Maguire, Bridget; New York, NY, 1866 ***5704.8*** *p211*
Maguire, Bridget; Quebec, 1847 ***5704.8*** *p28*
Maguire, Bridget 6; Quebec, 1847 ***5704.8*** *p7*
Maguire, Bridget 22; Quebec, 1863 ***5704.8*** *p153*
Maguire, Bridget 36; Philadelphia, 1804 ***53.26*** *p48*
Maguire, Brigitte; Quebec, 1820 ***7603*** *p57*
Maguire, Catherine; Philadelphia, 1848 ***53.26*** *p49*
*Relative:*Charles 8
*Relative:*Francis 6
*Relative:*John 3
*Relative:*Hugh 1
Maguire, Catherine; Philadelphia, 1848 ***5704.8*** *p46*
Maguire, Catherine; Quebec, 1847 ***5704.8*** *p17*
Maguire, Catherine; Quebec, 1847 ***5704.8*** *p38*
Maguire, Catherine; Quebec, 1849 ***5704.8*** *p51*
Maguire, Catherine; Quebec, 1851 ***5704.8*** *p82*
Maguire, Catherine 9; Quebec, 1863 ***5704.8*** *p153*

Maguire, Catherine 13; Quebec, 1847 ***5704.8*** *p7*
Maguire, Cecilia; New York, NY, 1870 ***5704.8*** *p240*
Maguire, Charles; Quebec, 1820 ***7603*** *p69*
Maguire, Charles; Quebec, 1847 ***5704.8*** *p17*
Maguire, Charles 8 *SEE* Maguire, Catherine
Maguire, Charles 8; Philadelphia, 1848 ***5704.8*** *p46*
Maguire, Chas.; America, 1868 ***1450.2*** *p91A*
Maguire, Daniel 23; Philadelphia, 1854 ***5704.8*** *p118*
Maguire, Daniel 45; Philadelphia, 1854 ***5704.8*** *p117*
Maguire, Denis; Quebec, 1847 ***5704.8*** *p29*
Maguire, Dennis 7 *SEE* Maguire, Sarah
Maguire, Dennis 7; Philadelphia, 1849 ***5704.8*** *p54*
Maguire, Edward; Quebec, 1823 ***7603*** *p53*
Maguire, Elizabeth; Quebec, 1847 ***5704.8*** *p38*
Maguire, Ellan; Quebec, 1847 ***5704.8*** *p17*
Maguire, Esther; America, 1742 ***4971*** *p94*
Maguire, Feiry; Quebec, 1847 ***5704.8*** *p7*
Maguire, Felix 8; Quebec, 1847 ***5704.8*** *p7*
Maguire, Francis; St. John, N.B., 1847 ***5704.8*** *p21*
Maguire, Francis 6 *SEE* Maguire, Catherine
Maguire, Francis 6; Philadelphia, 1848 ***5704.8*** *p46*
Maguire, Francis 7; Quebec, 1849 ***5704.8*** *p51*
Maguire, Francis 38; Philadelphia, 1804 ***53.26*** *p49*
Maguire, Henry; New York, NY, 1815 ***2859.11*** *p38*
Maguire, Henry; Quebec, 1847 ***5704.8*** *p38*
Maguire, Hugh 1 *SEE* Maguire, Catherine
Maguire, Hugh 1; Philadelphia, 1848 ***5704.8*** *p46*
Maguire, Isabella; St. John, N.B., 1847 ***5704.8*** *p21*
Maguire, Isabella 13; St. John, N.B., 1847 ***5704.8*** *p21*
Maguire, James *SEE* Maguire, Sarah
Maguire, James; America, 1735-1743 ***4971*** *p8*
Maguire, James; America, 1742 ***4971*** *p94*
Maguire, James; New York, NY, 1840 ***8208.4*** *p106*
Maguire, James; Philadelphia, 1849 ***5704.8*** *p54*
Maguire, James; Philadelphia, 1850 ***53.26*** *p49*
*Relative:*William
*Relative:*Ann
*Relative:*Margaret
Maguire, James; Philadelphia, 1850 ***5704.8*** *p69*
Maguire, James; Quebec, 1847 ***5704.8*** *p36*
Maguire, James; Quebec, 1847 ***5704.8*** *p38*
Maguire, James; Quebec, 1850 ***5704.8*** *p67*
Maguire, James; Quebec, 1852 ***5704.8*** *p97*
Maguire, James; St. John, N.B., 1847 ***5704.8*** *p35*
Maguire, James 2; St. John, N.B., 1847 ***5704.8*** *p35*
Maguire, James 11; Quebec, 1863 ***5704.8*** *p153*
Maguire, James 57; Quebec, 1863 ***5704.8*** *p153*
Maguire, Jane; Quebec, 1847 ***5704.8*** *p28*
Maguire, Jane; Quebec, 1847 ***5704.8*** *p29*
Maguire, Jane; St. John, N.B., 1847 ***5704.8*** *p19*
Maguire, Jane 9 *SEE* Maguire, Sarah
Maguire, Jane 9; Philadelphia, 1849 ***5704.8*** *p54*
Maguire, John; America, 1742 ***4971*** *p94*
Maguire, John; Quebec, 1847 ***5704.8*** *p7*
Maguire, John; Quebec, 1847 ***5704.8*** *p28*
Maguire, John; Quebec, 1847 ***5704.8*** *p38*
Maguire, John; Quebec, 1851 ***5704.8*** *p75*
Maguire, John; St. John, N.B., 1847 ***5704.8*** *p21*
Maguire, John; St. John, N.B., 1852 ***5704.8*** *p93*
Maguire, John; St. John, N.B., 1853 ***5704.8*** *p109*
Maguire, John 6 mos; St. John, N.B., 1847 ***5704.8*** *p35*
Maguire, John 3 *SEE* Maguire, Catherine
Maguire, John 3; Philadelphia, 1848 ***5704.8*** *p46*
Maguire, John 9; Quebec, 1851 ***5704.8*** *p82*
Maguire, John 11; Quebec, 1847 ***5704.8*** *p36*
Maguire, John 20; Massachusetts, 1848 ***5881.1*** *p68*
Maguire, John 20; St. John, N.B., 1864 ***5704.8*** *p158*
Maguire, John 24; Philadelphia, 1854 ***5704.8*** *p118*
Maguire, John 25; Quebec, 1856 ***5704.8*** *p130*
Maguire, John 26; Massachusetts, 1849 ***5881.1*** *p68*
Maguire, John 40; St. John, N.B., 1864 ***5704.8*** *p158*
Maguire, John 45; Massachusetts, 1849 ***5881.1*** *p69*
Maguire, Judy 36; Massachusetts, 1848 ***5881.1*** *p68*
Maguire, Liddy; Quebec, 1851 ***5704.8*** *p82*
Maguire, Lucy; Quebec, 1847 ***5704.8*** *p36*
Maguire, Margaret *SEE* Maguire, James
Maguire, Margaret; Philadelphia, 1850 ***5704.8*** *p69*
Maguire, Margaret; Quebec, 1847 ***5704.8*** *p36*
Maguire, Margaret; Quebec, 1847 ***5704.8*** *p38*
Maguire, Margaret 18; Quebec, 1862 ***5704.8*** *p150*
Maguire, Margaret 20; Massachusetts, 1847 ***5881.1*** *p70*
Maguire, Margaret 24; St. John, N.B., 1856 ***5704.8*** *p132*
Maguire, Margaret 28; Philadelphia, 1858 ***5704.8*** *p139*
Maguire, Martha; Quebec, 1851 ***5704.8*** *p82*
Maguire, Mary; America, 1735-1743 ***4971*** *p7*
Maguire, Mary; America, 1741 ***4971*** *p10*
Maguire, Mary; America, 1741 ***4971*** *p94*
Maguire, Mary; America, 1742 ***4971*** *p17*
Maguire, Mary; Annapolis, MD, 1742 ***4971*** *p93*
Maguire, Mary; Maryland, 1742 ***4971*** *p107*
Maguire, Mary; Philadelphia, 1866 ***5704.8*** *p208*
Maguire, Mary; Philadelphia, 1866 ***5704.8*** *p210*
Maguire, Mary; Quebec, 1822 ***7603*** *p82*
Maguire, Mary; Quebec, 1847 ***5704.8*** *p7*
Maguire, Mary; Quebec, 1847 ***5704.8*** *p17*
Maguire, Mary; Quebec, 1847 ***5704.8*** *p37*
Maguire, Mary; Quebec, 1847 ***5704.8*** *p38*
Maguire, Mary; Quebec, 1852 ***5704.8*** *p98*
Maguire, Mary; St. John, N.B., 1847 ***5704.8*** *p21*
Maguire, Mary 2; Quebec, 1847 ***5704.8*** *p17*
Maguire, Mary 3; Quebec, 1847 ***5704.8*** *p7*
Maguire, Mary 7; St. John, N.B., 1847 ***5704.8*** *p35*
Maguire, Mary 10; St. John, N.B., 1852 ***5704.8*** *p93*
Maguire, Mary 11 *SEE* Maguire, Sarah
Maguire, Mary 11; Philadelphia, 1849 ***5704.8*** *p54*
Maguire, Mary 16; Quebec, 1863 ***5704.8*** *p153*
Maguire, Mary 20; Quebec, 1855 ***5704.8*** *p124*
Maguire, Mary 45; St. John, N.B., 1864 ***5704.8*** *p158*
Maguire, Mary Ann; Quebec, 1847 ***5704.8*** *p36*
Maguire, Mary Ann; Quebec, 1851 ***5704.8*** *p82*
Maguire, Mary Ann 17; Philadelphia, 1858 ***5704.8*** *p139*
Maguire, Michael; America, 1841 ***7036*** *p120*
Maguire, Michael; New York, NY, 1839 ***8208.4*** *p94*
Maguire, Michael 11; Quebec, 1847 ***5704.8*** *p17*
Maguire, Michael 25; Philadelphia, 1858 ***5704.8*** *p139*
Maguire, Mick; Quebec, 1847 ***5704.8*** *p7*
Maguire, Moses; New Orleans, 1849 ***5704.8*** *p59*
Maguire, Owen; Quebec, 1852 ***5704.8*** *p90*
Maguire, Patrick; Delaware Bay or River, 1743 ***4971*** *p104*
Maguire, Patrick; New York, NY, 1864 ***5704.8*** *p183*
Maguire, Patrick; Philadelphia, 1866 ***5704.8*** *p208*
Maguire, Patrick; Quebec, 1847 ***5704.8*** *p7*
Maguire, Patrick 5; St. John, N.B., 1847 ***5704.8*** *p34*
Maguire, Patrick 7 *SEE* Maguire, Sarah
Maguire, Patrick 7; Philadelphia, 1849 ***5704.8*** *p54*
Maguire, Patrick 19; Massachusetts, 1847 ***5881.1*** *p74*
Maguire, Patrick 20; Quebec, 1863 ***5704.8*** *p153*
Maguire, Patrick 20; Quebec, 1863 ***5704.8*** *p154*
Maguire, Peter; New York, NY, 1834 ***8208.4*** *p49*
Maguire, Peter; Quebec, 1847 ***5704.8*** *p38*
Maguire, Rody 6 mos; Quebec, 1847 ***5704.8*** *p17*
Maguire, Sarah; Philadelphia, 1849 ***53.26*** *p49*
*Relative:*James
*Relative:*Mary 11
*Relative:*Jane 9
*Relative:*Patrick 7
*Relative:*Bernard 5
*Relative:*Sarah 9 mos
*Relative:*Dennis 7
Maguire, Sarah; Philadelphia, 1849 ***5704.8*** *p54*
Maguire, Sarah; St. John, N.B., 1847 ***5704.8*** *p35*
Maguire, Sarah 9 mos *SEE* Maguire, Sarah
Maguire, Sarah 9 mos; Philadelphia, 1849 ***5704.8*** *p54*
Maguire, Susan 6; Quebec, 1847 ***5704.8*** *p36*
Maguire, Terance; New York, NY, 1835 ***8208.4*** *p49*
Maguire, Thomas; Quebec, 1847 ***5704.8*** *p36*
Maguire, Thomas 9 mos; Quebec, 1863 ***5704.8*** *p153*
Maguire, Thomas 6; St. John, N.B., 1847 ***5704.8*** *p9*
Maguire, William *SEE* Maguire, James
Maguire, William; Philadelphia, 1850 ***5704.8*** *p69*
Maguire, William; Quebec, 1847 ***5704.8*** *p38*
Maguire, William 10; St. John, N.B., 1847 ***5704.8*** *p21*
Maguire, William 21; Philadelphia, 1857 ***5704.8*** *p133*
Magwigan, William; Washington, 1859-1920 ***2872.1*** *p24*
Mahady, James; New York, NY, 1838 ***8208.4*** *p70*
Mahady, Michael; New York, NY, 1834 ***8208.4*** *p3*
Mahady, Michael; New York, NY, 1838 ***8208.4*** *p70*
Mahaffy, James; Philadelphia, 1811 ***2859.11*** *p17*
With family
Mahaffy, Jane; America, 1869 ***5704.8*** *p235*
Mahalovich, Philip; Iowa, 1866-1943 ***123.54*** *p32*
Mahan, Bridget 16; Massachusetts, 1847 ***5881.1*** *p63*
Mahan, Elizabeth; Quebec, 1818 ***7603*** *p71*
Mahan, John 25; Philadelphia, 1857 ***5704.8*** *p134*
Mahan, Michael; Virginia, 1856 ***4626.16*** *p15*
Mahan, Patrick; Philadelphia, 1865 ***5704.8*** *p189*
Mahanny, Jane 16; Philadelphia, 1860 ***5704.8*** *p146*
Mahany, Dennis; New York, NY, 1839 ***8208.4*** *p101*
Mahany, Dennis 27; Baltimore, 1775 ***1219.7*** *p269*
Mahany, John; New York, NY, 1816 ***2859.11*** *p38*
Mahany, Mary; New York, NY, 1816 ***2859.11*** *p38*
Mahany, Mary J.; New York, NY, 1816 ***2859.11*** *p38*
Mahar, Daniel; Iroquois Co., IL, 1868 ***3455.1*** *p12*
Mahar, Patrick; New York, NY, 1839 ***8208.4*** *p99*
Mahar, Thomas 9; Massachusetts, 1850 ***5881.1*** *p76*
Maharg, James; New York, NY, 1811 ***2859.11*** *p17*
Mahawrs, Nick Pete; Arkansas, 1918 ***95.2*** *p78*
Mahen, Mary 28; Massachusetts, 1849 ***5881.1*** *p71*
Maher, . . .; Canada, 1776-1783 ***9786*** *p28*
Maher, Abby 14; Massachusetts, 1850 ***5881.1*** *p62*
Maher, Anty 55; Massachusetts, 1849 ***5881.1*** *p62*
Maher, Edward J.; Arkansas, 1918 ***95.2*** *p78*
Maher, Eliza 13; Massachusetts, 1849 ***5881.1*** *p65*
Maher, Johanna 30; Massachusetts, 1850 ***5881.1*** *p69*
Maher, John; New York, NY, 1838 ***8208.4*** *p89*
Maher, Margaret 36; Massachusetts, 1850 ***5881.1*** *p73*
Maher, Mary 5; Massachusetts, 1849 ***5881.1*** *p72*
Maher, Mary 15; Massachusetts, 1850 ***5881.1*** *p73*
Maher, Mary 16; Massachusetts, 1849 ***5881.1*** *p72*
Maher, Matthew; America, 1740 ***4971*** *p15*
Maher, Michael; Wisconsin, n.d. ***9675.6*** *p268*
Maher, Michael 30; Massachusetts, 1850 ***5881.1*** *p72*
Maher, Patrick; New York, NY, 1839 ***8208.4*** *p97*
Maher, Patrick 8; Massachusetts, 1850 ***5881.1*** *p75*
Maher, Richard; Yamaska, Que., 1825 ***7603*** *p77*
Maher, Robert 10; Massachusetts, 1850 ***5881.1*** *p75*
Maher, Thomas; Massachusetts, 1850 ***5881.1*** *p76*
Maher, William; Quebec, 1824 ***7603*** *p63*
Maher, William 23; Massachusetts, 1849 ***5881.1*** *p77*
Maheu, . . .; Canada, 1776-1783 ***9786*** *p28*
Mahew, Joseph 19; Maryland, 1723 ***3690.1*** *p147*
Mahle, Jacob; America, 1863 ***6014.1*** *p2*
Mahler, . . .; Canada, 1776-1783 ***9786*** *p43*
Mahler, Colonel; Pennsylvania, 1861-1865 ***8582.3*** *p91*
Mahler, Charles G.; America, 1893 ***1450.2*** *p91A*
Mahler, Thomas; Ohio, 1843 ***9892.11*** *p27*
Mahlhorn, Herman; Wisconsin, n.d. ***9675.6*** *p268*
Mahlo, . . .; Canada, 1776-1783 ***9786*** *p43*
Mahlstedt, Wilhelm; New York, NY, 1926 ***3455.4*** *p80*
Mahnka, August C.; Illinois, 1868 ***2896.5*** *p25*
Mahogan, Margaret 30; Massachusetts, 1849 ***5881.1*** *p71*
Mahon, Catharine 20; Massachusetts, 1847 ***5881.1*** *p64*
Mahon, Catherine; Philadelphia, 1816 ***2859.11*** *p38*
Mahon, Charles; New York, NY, 1816 ***2859.11*** *p38*
Mahon, Dennis 50; Massachusetts, 1849 ***5881.1*** *p65*
Mahon, Eliza; Philadelphia, 1865 ***5704.8*** *p200*
Mahon, Ellen 50; Massachusetts, 1848 ***5881.1*** *p65*
Mahon, Joseph; Philadelphia, 1816 ***2859.11*** *p38*
Mahon, Margaret 22; Quebec, 1857 ***5704.8*** *p136*
Mahon, Sally 20; Massachusetts, 1850 ***5881.1*** *p76*
Mahon, Samuel 6 mos; Quebec, 1857 ***5704.8*** *p136*
Mahon, Thady; America, 1739 ***4971*** *p27*
Mahon, Thomas 19; Philadelphia, 1860 ***5704.8*** *p144*
Mahoney, Mr.; Quebec, 1815 ***9229.18*** *p81*
With family
Mahoney, Betty 20; Massachusetts, 1850 ***5881.1*** *p64*
Mahoney, Daniel; New York, NY, 1834 ***8208.4*** *p60*
Mahoney, Dennis; Wisconsin, n.d. ***9675.6*** *p268*
Mahoney, Jeremiah; Wisconsin, n.d. ***9675.6*** *p268*
Mahoney, John; Illinois, 1877 ***2896.5*** *p25*
Mahoney, John; Virginia, 1844 ***4626.16*** *p13*
Mahoney, John 44; Newfoundland, 1789 ***4915.24*** *p56*
Mahoney, Julia 25; Newport, RI, 1851 ***6508.5*** *p19*
Mahoney, Margaret; Quebec, 1794 ***7603*** *p77*
Mahoney, Mary; Quebec, 1824 ***7603*** *p77*
Mahoney, Patrick; California, 1867 ***3840.2*** *p18*
Mahoney, Peggy 6; Massachusetts, 1849 ***5881.1*** *p74*
Mahony, Bridget 25; Massachusetts, 1849 ***5881.1*** *p63*
Mahony, Cornelius; New York, NY, 1838 ***8208.4*** *p75*
Mahony, Daniel; America, 1736-1743 ***4971*** *p58*
Mahony, Darby; America, 1742-1743 ***4971*** *p42*
Mahony, Dennis; America, 1739 ***4971*** *p46*
Mahony, Dennis 30; Massachusetts, 1849 ***5881.1*** *p65*
Mahony, Edward 23; Virginia, 1774 ***1219.7*** *p243*
Mahony, Ellenor; America, 1739 ***4971*** *p47*
Mahony, F.; New York, NY, 1816 ***2859.11*** *p38*
Mahony, Florence; Ohio, 1841 ***8365.25*** *p12*
Mahony, James; America, 1741 ***4971*** *p41*
Mahony, James; Pennsylvania, 1851 ***1450.2*** *p91A*
Mahony, Jasper 16; Maryland, 1775 ***1219.7*** *p249*
Mahony, Jeremiah; America, 1742 ***4971*** *p49*
Mahony, Jeremiah; America, 1742 ***4971*** *p50*
Mahony, John; America, 1742 ***4971*** *p49*
Mahony, John; America, 1743 ***4971*** *p50*
Mahony, John; New York, NY, 1838 ***8208.4*** *p68*
Mahony, John 19; Massachusetts, 1847 ***5881.1*** *p67*
Mahony, Joseph 23; Virginia, 1774 ***1219.7*** *p243*
Mahony, Kitty 9; Massachusetts, 1849 ***5881.1*** *p70*
Mahony, Margaret 18; Massachusetts, 1847 ***5881.1*** *p70*
Mahony, Mary 14; Massachusetts, 1850 ***5881.1*** *p73*
Mahony, Mary 20; Massachusetts, 1849 ***5881.1*** *p71*
Mahony, Patrick 35; Massachusetts, 1849 ***5881.1*** *p74*
Mahony, Peggy 20; Massachusetts, 1849 ***5881.1*** *p75*
Mahony, Philip 22; Massachusetts, 1850 ***5881.1*** *p75*
Mahony, Pierre; Quebec, 1802 ***7603*** *p80*
Mahony, Robert 40; Massachusetts, 1850 ***5881.1*** *p75*
Mahony, Timothy; Boston, 1841 ***7036*** *p120*
Mahony, Timothy 17; Massachusetts, 1847 ***5881.1*** *p76*
Mahr, . . .; Canada, 1776-1783 ***9786*** *p28*
Mahrdt, John J.; Iowa, 1890 ***1450.2*** *p24B*
Mahyna, Stanislaw Izydor; Arkansas, 1918 ***95.2*** *p78*
Maiar, Charles; Baltimore, 1838 ***1450.2*** *p91A*
Maiben, Jane; New York, NY, 1815 ***2859.11*** *p38*
With child
Maibom, Carl Christoph; Quebec, 1776 ***9786*** *p257*
Maichszak, Stanislaw 18; New York, 1912 ***9980.29*** *p60*
Maidlow, James; Indiana, 1824 ***9117*** *p14*
Maier, Abraham; New York, 1900 ***1450.2*** *p24B*

Maier, Anna Maria *SEE* Maier, Johann Jacob
Maier, Anna Maria *SEE* Maier, Johann Jacob
Maier, Frederick; Wisconsin, n.d. ***9675.6*** *p268*
Maier, Gottlieb; Ohio, 1879 ***9892.11*** *p27*
Maier, Jacob *SEE* Maier, Johann Jacob
Maier, Johann Jacob; New England, 1747-1800 ***2444*** *p187*
*Wife:*Anna Maria
*Child:*Jacob
*Child:*Anna Maria
Maier, John; Cincinnati, 1869-1887 ***8582*** *p20*
Maier, John; Colorado, 1898 ***9678.2*** *p125*
Maier, John P.; New York, 1901 ***1450.2*** *p24B*
Maier, Michaila; Arkansas, 1918 ***95.2*** *p78*
Maier, Pilipp 26; Port uncertain, 1839 ***778.5*** *p353*
Maige, Clement 29; America, 1839 ***778.5*** *p354*
Maigher, Michael; New York, 1835 ***1450.2*** *p91A*
Maignan, Mr. 20; America, 1839 ***778.5*** *p354*
Maignol, Emmanuel 14; America, 1838 ***778.5*** *p354*
Mailanen, Pete; Washington, 1859-1920 ***2872.1*** *p24*
Maillard, . . .; Halifax, N.S., 1752 ***7074.6*** *p232*
Maillard, Catherine *SEE* Maillard, Frederic
Maillard, Elisabeth *SEE* Maillard, Frederic
Maillard, Elisabeth *SEE* Maillard, Jean-Frederic
Maillard, Frederic 45; Halifax, N.S., 1752 ***7074.6*** *p211*
*Wife:*Judith
*Mother:*Judith
*Child:*Catherine
*Child:*Elisabeth
*Child:*Jean
*Child:*Jeanne
*Child:*Suzanne
*Son:*Pierre 15
Maillard, Jean *SEE* Maillard, Frederic
Maillard, Jean-Frederic; Halifax, N.S., 1752 ***7074.6*** *p211*
*Wife:*Elisabeth
Maillard, Jeanne *SEE* Maillard, Frederic
Maillard, Judith *SEE* Maillard, Frederic
Maillard, Judith *SEE* Maillard, Frederic
Maillard, Pierre 15 *SEE* Maillard, Frederic
Maillard, Suzanne *SEE* Maillard, Frederic
Maille, . . .; Canada, 1776-1783 ***9786*** *p28*
Maille, Catharina Barbara 25 *SEE* Maille, Matthis Friederich
Maille, Catharina Barbara 50 *SEE* Maille, Matthis Friederich
Maille, Friederika 19 *SEE* Maille, Matthis Friederich
Maille, Jean-Marie 30; New Orleans, 1836 ***778.5*** *p354*
Maille, Johannes 21 *SEE* Maille, Matthis Friederich
Maille, Mathias Friederich 22 *SEE* Maille, Matthis Friederich
Maille, Matthis Friederich 47; Philadelphia, 1805 ***2444*** *p187*
*Wife:*Catharina Barbara 50
*Child:*Catharina Barbara 25
*Child:*Mathias Friederich 22
*Child:*Johannes 21
*Child:*Friederika 19
*Child:*Walburga 15
Maille, Walburga 15 *SEE* Maille, Matthis Friederich
Maillet, Baptiste 28; New Orleans, 1839 ***778.5*** *p354*
Maillet, Baptiste, Mme. 30; New Orleans, 1839 ***778.5*** *p354*
Mailly, Edouard; Sorel, Que., 1809 ***7603*** *p77*
Mailly, J. B. 42; Havana, 1825 ***778.5*** *p354*
Maily, Charles; Philadelphia, 1853 ***5704.8*** *p102*
Maily, Eleanor; Philadelphia, 1853 ***5704.8*** *p102*
Maimee Dauzette, Mr. 25; America, 1838 ***778.5*** *p354*
Main, J. 19; Port uncertain, 1838 ***778.5*** *p354*
Main, Pierre 41; New Orleans, 1837 ***778.5*** *p354*
Maine, John 30; Port uncertain, 1837 ***778.5*** *p354*
Maino, Antonio; Iowa, 1866-1943 ***123.54*** *p32*
Mains, John; New York, NY, 1838 ***8208.4*** *p68*
Mainson, Jon.; Virginia, 1643 ***6219*** *p200*
Mainwaring, William; Virginia, 1764 ***1219.7*** *p101*
Maior, Eliz.; Virginia, 1642 ***6219*** *p192*
Maior, Georg; Virginia, 1643 ***6219*** *p204*
Maior, Jane; Virginia, 1640 ***6219*** *p160*
Maior, John; Virginia, 1640 ***6219*** *p160*
Maior, Robert; Virginia, 1642 ***6219*** *p195*
Maior, Wm.; Virginia, 1643 ***6219*** *p202*
Mair, Peter 35; Port uncertain, 1774 ***1219.7*** *p176*
Mair, Thomas; Charleston, SC, 1798 ***1639.20*** *p228*
Maires, Josiah 19; New England, 1699 ***2212*** *p18*
Mairet, . . .; Halifax, N.S., 1752 ***7074.6*** *p230*
Mairs, Ann 43; Philadelphia, 1834 ***53.26*** *p49*
*Relative:*Margaret 18
*Relative:*Sarah 13
*Relative:*Jane 10
*Relative:*Matilda 3
Mairs, Jane 10 *SEE* Mairs, Ann
Mairs, Margaret 18 *SEE* Mairs, Ann
Mairs, Matilda 3 *SEE* Mairs, Ann
Mairs, Sarah 13 *SEE* Mairs, Ann
Mairs, Soba 40; Philadelphia, 1834 ***53.26*** *p49*
Maisch, . . .; Canada, 1776-1783 ***9786*** *p28*
Maisilane, H. 52; Havana, 1830 ***778.5*** *p354*
Maisonable, Mr. 22; America, 1837 ***778.5*** *p354*
Maister, Gregorius; Philadelphia, 1759 ***9973.7*** *p33*
Maithes, Mr. 19; Port uncertain, 1839 ***778.5*** *p355*
Maitland, Agnes; Chicago, 1851 ***8893*** *p266*
Maitland, Peregrine; Nova Scotia, 1819-1833 ***9775.5*** *p208*
Maitland, William; Quebec, 1788 ***7603*** *p41*
Maitland, Wm.; New York, NY, 1811 ***2859.11*** *p17*
Maize, Eliza 7; Quebec, 1853 ***5704.8*** *p104*
Maize, Ellen 13; Quebec, 1853 ***5704.8*** *p104*
Maize, George; New York, NY, 1836 ***8208.4*** *p12*
Maize, James 9; Quebec, 1853 ***5704.8*** *p104*
Maize, Jane; Quebec, 1853 ***5704.8*** *p103*
Maize, John; Quebec, 1853 ***5704.8*** *p103*
Maize, John 11; Quebec, 1853 ***5704.8*** *p104*
Maize, Robert; Quebec, 1853 ***5704.8*** *p104*
Majer, Anna *SEE* Majer, Johann Martin
Majer, Anna Maria *SEE* Majer, Johann Martin
Majer, Anna Maria; Pennsylvania, 1754 ***2444*** *p149*
Majer, Catharina; America, 1742-1800 ***2444*** *p201*
Majer, Catharina; Pennsylvania, 1751 ***2444*** *p203*
Majer, Daniel *SEE* Majer, Johann Martin
Majer, Dorothea Gutbrod *SEE* Majer, Johann Martin
Majer, Elisabetha; America, 1749 ***2444*** *p187*
Majer, Johann Martin; America, 1772 ***2444*** *p188*
*Wife:*Dorothea Gutbrod
*Child:*Anna Maria
*Child:*Anna
*Child:*Daniel
Majerus, Nicholas; Wisconsin, n.d. ***9675.6*** *p268*
Majeste, Mr. 27; Port uncertain, 1839 ***778.5*** *p355*
Majeste, Louis 26; New Orleans, 1836 ***778.5*** *p355*
Majewski, Joseph Walter; Arkansas, 1918 ***95.2*** *p78*
Majher, Steve; Arkansas, 1918 ***95.2*** *p78*
Majkowski, Wladislaw 27; New York, 1912 ***9980.29*** *p69*
Major, . . .; Canada, 1776-1783 ***9786*** *p28*
Major, Edward; Virginia, 1637 ***6219*** *p81*
Major, Edward; Virginia, 1645 ***6219*** *p245*
Major, Eliza.; Virginia, 1645 ***6219*** *p245*
Major, Fra.; Virginia, 1645 ***6219*** *p245*
Major, James 27; Virginia, 1773 ***1219.7*** *p168*
Major, John; New York, NY, 1834 ***8208.4*** *p1*
Major, John 18; Maryland, 1750 ***3690.1*** *p147*
Major, John 20; Pennsylvania, 1728 ***3690.1*** *p147*
Major, Nathaniel; New York, NY, 1838 ***8208.4*** *p82*
Major, Phi.; Virginia, 1637 ***6219*** *p113*
Major, Tho.; Virginia, 1645 ***6219*** *p245*
Majszejowa, Antonina 16; New York, 1912 ***9980.29*** *p64*
Majszejowa, Boleslaw; New York, 1912 ***9980.29*** *p64*
Majszys, Antonina 16; New York, 1912 ***9980.29*** *p64*
Majszys, Boleslaw; New York, 1912 ***9980.29*** *p64*
Makar, James 25; Maryland, 1775 ***1219.7*** *p253*
Make, Mr. 30; America, 1822 ***778.5*** *p355*
Makester, Rich.; Virginia, 1634 ***6219*** *p84*
Maki, Arthur; Washington, 1859-1920 ***2872.1*** *p24*
Maki, Emil; Washington, 1859-1920 ***2872.1*** *p24*
Maki, Jacob; Washington, 1859-1920 ***2872.1*** *p24*
Maki, Justina; Washington, 1859-1920 ***2872.1*** *p24*
Makilburn, Edward 23; Quebec, 1854 ***5704.8*** *p118*
Makilburn, Margaret 20; Quebec, 1854 ***5704.8*** *p118*
Makin, Charles W. L. 29; Kansas, 1884 ***5240.1*** *p65*
Making, Elias 30; Maryland, 1774 ***1219.7*** *p230*
Makle, Christian; America, 1900 ***1450.2*** *p24B*
Maklin, Jennie; Washington, 1859-1920 ***2872.1*** *p24*
Maklin, John Anton; Washington, 1859-1920 ***2872.1*** *p24*
Makusk, Jozas; Arkansas, 1918 ***95.2*** *p77*
Makusk, Jozas; Arkansas, 1918 ***95.2*** *p78*
Malam, Eliza.; Virginia, 1647 ***6219*** *p247*
Malan, Joseph; New York, 1895 ***1450.2*** *p24B*
Malarky, Cornelius 18; Massachusetts, 1849 ***5881.1*** *p64*
Malatin, Paul; America, 1891 ***7137*** *p169*
Malay, John; Illinois, 1871 ***5012.39*** *p25*
Malbec, Mr.; America, 1839 ***778.5*** *p355*
Malberg, Samuel; Arkansas, 1918 ***95.2*** *p78*
Malbern, Cornelius 17; Maryland, 1719 ***3690.1*** *p147*
Malbon, Anne-Marie *SEE* Malbon, Daniel
Malbon, Catherine *SEE* Malbon, Daniel
Malbon, Daniel 40; Halifax, N.S., 1752 ***7074.6*** *p211*
*Wife:*Jeanne-Marguerite
*Child:*Anne-Marie
*Child:*Suzanne-Elisabeth
*Child:*Jacques
*Child:*Catherine
Malbon, Jacques *SEE* Malbon, Daniel
Malbon, Jeanne-Marguerite *SEE* Malbon, Daniel
Malbon, Suzanne-Elisabeth *SEE* Malbon, Daniel
Malchow, Johann Frederick; Illinois, 1866 ***2896.5*** *p25*
Malcolm, Archibald 26; Kansas, 1873 ***5240.1*** *p54*
Malcolm, Francis; New York, NY, 1834 ***8208.4*** *p49*
Malcolm, Jennet 22; Kansas, 1875 ***5240.1*** *p56*
Malcolm, John S. 28; Kansas, 1877 ***5240.1*** *p58*
Malcolmson, Adam; New York, NY, 1816 ***2859.11*** *p38*
Malcom, Archie; Washington, 1859-1920 ***2872.1*** *p24*
Malcom, Bertha; Washington, 1859-1920 ***2872.1*** *p24*
Malcomsen, Ann; Newfoundland, 1851 ***8893*** *p264*
Malcomson, James 17; St. John, N.B., 1864 ***5704.8*** *p157*
Malcomson, John; New York, NY, 1811 ***2859.11*** *p17*
Malden, Frances 10; Port uncertain, 1838 ***778.5*** *p355*
Malden, Francis 45; Port uncertain, 1838 ***778.5*** *p355*
Malden, Jane 73; Port uncertain, 1838 ***778.5*** *p355*
Malden, Josephine 8; Port uncertain, 1838 ***778.5*** *p355*
Malden, Mary 7; Port uncertain, 1838 ***778.5*** *p355*
Malen, Georg; Virginia, 1639 ***6219*** *p158*
Malencik, Jacob; Arkansas, 1918 ***95.2*** *p78*
Malet, Charles 41; Port uncertain, 1839 ***778.5*** *p355*
Maletta, Antonia; Iowa, 1866-1943 ***123.54*** *p32*
Maletta, John; Iowa, 1866-1943 ***123.54*** *p32*
Maley, Bridget; America, 1742 ***4971*** *p95*
Maley, Bridget; America, 1743 ***4971*** *p11*
Maley, Bridget; Maryland, 1742 ***4971*** *p107*
Maley, Daniell; Virginia, 1647 ***6219*** *p243*
Maley, John; Illinois, 1871 ***5012.39*** *p25*
Malfatti, Virgilio; Washington, 1859-1920 ***2872.1*** *p24*
Malget, August; Wisconsin, n.d. ***9675.6*** *p268*
Malherbe, Francois 21; Kansas, 1883 ***5240.1*** *p64*
Malherbe, Joseph; Wisconsin, n.d. ***9675.6*** *p268*
Malherbeau, Jean 20?; Quebec, 1666-1667 ***4533*** *p130*
Malick, Louis 23; Port uncertain, 1839 ***778.5*** *p355*
Malicki, Ignatz; Arkansas, 1918 ***95.2*** *p78*
Malicki, Michal 18; New York, 1912 ***9980.29*** *p65*
Maliff, Franklin; Illinois, 1858 ***2896.5*** *p25*
Malin, Bridget 8 *SEE* Malin, Patrick
Malin, Bridget 8; Philadelphia, 1847 ***5704.8*** *p14*
Malin, Daniel 12 *SEE* Malin, Patrick
Malin, Daniel 12; Philadelphia, 1847 ***5704.8*** *p14*
Malin, Patrick *SEE* Malin, Patrick
Malin, Patrick; Philadelphia, 1847 ***53.26*** *p49*
*Relative:*Patrick
*Relative:*Daniel 12
*Relative:*Bridget 8
Malin, Patrick; Philadelphia, 1847 ***5704.8*** *p14*
Malin, Patrick 1; Philadelphia, 1847 ***5704.8*** *p14*
Malinar, Jacob; Iowa, 1866-1943 ***123.54*** *p32*
Malinar, Paul; Iowa, 1866-1943 ***123.54*** *p32*
Maline, John; Washington, 1859-1920 ***2872.1*** *p24*
Malisovsky, Julia; America, 1892 ***7137*** *p169*
Malkowski, Piote; Arkansas, 1918 ***95.2*** *p78*
Mallard, Mr. 20; New Orleans, 1838 ***778.5*** *p355*
Mallard, Tho.; Virginia, 1646 ***6219*** *p236*
Mallattn, Nicholis; Iowa, 1866-1943 ***123.54*** *p32*
Mallen, Michael; Ohio, 1840 ***9892.11*** *p27*
Mallen, Michael, Jr.; Ohio, 1840 ***9892.11*** *p27*
Mallen, Michael, Sr.; Ohio, 1840 ***9892.11*** *p27*
Maller, . . .; Canada, 1776-1783 ***9786*** *p43*
Maller, Bernhard 44; Port uncertain, 1839 ***778.5*** *p355*
Maller, Jean 17; Port uncertain, 1839 ***778.5*** *p356*
Maller, Louis 15; Port uncertain, 1839 ***778.5*** *p356*
Maller, Louis 43; Port uncertain, 1839 ***778.5*** *p356*
Maller, Marguerite 13; Port uncertain, 1839 ***778.5*** *p356*
Maller, Marie 19; Port uncertain, 1839 ***778.5*** *p356*
Maller, Marie 40; Port uncertain, 1839 ***778.5*** *p356*
Maller, Nicholas 5; Port uncertain, 1839 ***778.5*** *p356*
Maller, Rose 4; Port uncertain, 1839 ***778.5*** *p355*
Mallery, Henry; New York, NY, 1835 ***8208.4*** *p51*
Mallery, Mary 18; Massachusetts, 1849 ***5881.1*** *p71*
Mallet, Claude 22; Louisiana, 1820 ***778.5*** *p356*
Mallet, Jean 22; Louisiana, 1820 ***778.5*** *p356*
Mallett, Wm.; Virginia, 1635 ***6219*** *p71*
Malleun, Hannah; Philadelphia, 1864 ***5704.8*** *p181*
Malley, Ellen 40; Massachusetts, 1849 ***5881.1*** *p66*
Malley, George 57; Massachusetts, 1849 ***5881.1*** *p67*
Malley, Patrick 8; Massachusetts, 1849 ***5881.1*** *p74*
Malley, Sarah 5; Massachusetts, 1849 ***5881.1*** *p75*
Mallin, Bell; St. John, N.B., 1847 ***5704.8*** *p26*
Mallin, Ellen; Philadelphia, 1867 ***5704.8*** *p215*
Mallin, Ferdinand; New York, 1833 ***9892.11*** *p27*
Mallin, Ferdinand; Ohio, 1840 ***9892.11*** *p27*
Mallin, Henry; New York, NY, 1839 ***8208.4*** *p99*
Mallin, Mary; Philadelphia, 1867 ***5704.8*** *p215*
Mallin, Michael; New York, 1814 ***9892.11*** *p27*
Mallin, Michael; New York, 1831 ***9892.11*** *p27*
Mallin, Rose; Philadelphia, 1867 ***5704.8*** *p215*
Mallin, William; Philadelphia, 1867 ***5704.8*** *p215*
Malliner, John; Washington, 1859-1920 ***2872.1*** *p24*
Mallinger, Peter; Wisconsin, n.d. ***9675.6*** *p268*
Mallmayeu, Jacques 36; Halifax, N.S., 1752 ***7074.6*** *p207*
With family of 1
Mallon, Ann 21; Philadelphia, 1868 ***5704.8*** *p225*
Mallon, Charles; New York, NY, 1837 ***8208.4*** *p32*
Mallon, George; New York, NY, 1838 ***8208.4*** *p80*
Mallon, George 28; Massachusetts, 1849 ***5881.1*** *p67*
Mallon, Jane; Quebec, 1853 ***5704.8*** *p104*

310
FOR A COMPLETE EXPLANATION OF ENTRY, SEE "HOW TO READ A CITATION" SECTION

Mallon, John; Montreal, 1807 7603 p56
Mallon, John; New York, NY, 1838 8208.4 p80
Mallory, Edward G.; Washington, 1859-1920 2872.1 p24
Malloy, Archibald 55 *SEE* Malloy, Neill
Malloy, Duncan 53; North Carolina, 1850 1639.20 p229
Malloy, John; North Carolina, 1804 1639.20 p229
Malloy, Michael 25; Philadelphia, 1864 5704.8 p156
Malloy, Neill 50; North Carolina, 1850 1639.20 p229
*Relative:*Archibald 55
Malm, Andrew 23; Maryland, 1773 1219.7 p173
Malmahu, Jacques 36; Halifax, N.S., 1752 7074.6 p211
*Wife:*Nanette
Malmahu, Nanette *SEE* Malmahu, Jacques
Malmgren, August; Iowa, 1892 2896.5 p25
Malo, . . .; Canada, 1776-1783 9786 p43
Malobert, Mr. 35; Port uncertain, 1839 778.5 p356
Maloftas, Manuel; Arkansas, 1918 95.2 p78
Malon, Ann; Massachusetts, 1847 5881.1 p62
Malone, Alice; Quebec, 1851 5704.8 p82
Malone, Ann; America, 1742 4971 p17
Malone, Ann 15; Massachusetts, 1849 5881.1 p62
Malone, Catherine; America, 1736 4971 p12
Malone, Dennis; Illinois, 1858 2896.5 p25
Malone, Edward W.; Illinois, 1876 7857 p5
Malone, Francis; New York, NY, 1815 2859.11 p38
Malone, George; Illinois, 1862 5012.38 p98
Malone, Henry; New York, NY, 1815 2859.11 p38
Malone, James; America, 1736 4971 p12
Malone, James; New York, 1848 1450.2 p91A
Malone, James 4; Quebec, 1851 5704.8 p82
Malone, John; New York, NY, 1839 8208.4 p97
Malone, John 26; Jamaica, 1750 3690.1 p147
Malone, John 30; Maryland, 1775 1219.7 p257
Malone, John 50; Massachusetts, 1850 5881.1 p70
Malone, Lawrence; Illinois, 1858 2896.5 p25
Malone, Margaret 9; Quebec, 1851 5704.8 p82
Malone, Mark 27; Maryland, 1774 1219.7 p196
Malone, Michael; America, 1742 4971 p27
Malone, Michael; Quebec, 1851 5704.8 p82
Malone, Pat 11; Quebec, 1851 5704.8 p82
Malone, Peter 7; Quebec, 1851 5704.8 p82
Malone, Peter 26; Massachusetts, 1847 5881.1 p74
Malone, William 6 mos; Quebec, 1851 5704.8 p82
Maloney, Mr.; Quebec, 1815 9229.18 p82
Maloney, Edmund; Wisconsin, n.d. 9675.6 p268
Maloney, Edward; Wisconsin, n.d. 9675.6 p268
Maloney, James; Illinois, 1870 5012.38 p99
Maloney, John; Illinois, 1857 7857 p5
Maloney, John 21; Kansas, 1884 5240.1 p66
Maloney, Joseph; Quebec, 1825 7603 p74
Maloney, Margaret; New York, NY, 1811 2859.11 p17
Maloney, Minnie 25; Kansas, 1902 5240.1 p82
Maloney, Thomas; Illinois, 1854 7857 p5
Malony, Ann; New York, NY, 1866 5704.8 p211
Malony, Bridget 13; Massachusetts, 1850 5881.1 p64
Malony, Catharine; New York, NY, 1866 5704.8 p211
Malony, Ellen 9; Massachusetts, 1850 5881.1 p66
Malony, Hugh; St. John, N.B., 1853 5704.8 p99
Malony, James 30; Massachusetts, 1850 5881.1 p69
Malony, Johanna 17; Massachusetts, 1849 5881.1 p69
Malony, Margaret 30; Massachusetts, 1847 5881.1 p70
Malony, Mary 11; Massachusetts, 1850 5881.1 p73
Malony, Patrick; St. John, N.B., 1853 5704.8 p99
Malony, Timothy; Arkansas, 1918 95.2 p78
Malony, William; Quebec, 1787 7603 p77
Maloon, Daniel 19; Maryland, 1729 3690.1 p147
Malowney, Jerry; New York, NY, 1811 2859.11 p17
Malowney, John; New York, NY, 1811 2859.11 p17
Maloy, Betsey; Massachusetts, 1847 5881.1 p63
Maloy, Elizabeth; America, 1868 5704.8 p228
Maloy, Sarah; America, 1864-1871 5704.8 p240
Malpezzi, Dante; Arkansas, 1918 95.2 p78
Malsey, Mary; New York, NY, 1816 2859.11 p38
Malta, Mr. 32; New Orleans, 1839 778.5 p356
Malte, Wilhelm Karl; Illinois, 1879 2896.5 p26
Malterre, Aglae Blanche 8; New Orleans, 1838 778.5 p356
Malterre, Antoine 75; New Orleans, 1838 778.5 p356
Malterre, Blanche 29; New Orleans, 1838 778.5 p356
Maltiz, Rudolph Reichsfreiherr von; Cincinnati, 1788-1848 8582.3 p90
Maltiz, Rudolph von; Cincinnati, 1788-1848 8582.3 p89
Malvares, Domingo; New York, NY, 1836 8208.4 p17
Malvin, William; New York, NY, 1811 2859.11 p17
With wife 5 sons & 4 daughters
Maly, John; New York, NY, 1816 2859.11 p38
Maly, Thomas; America, 1685 4962 p152
Malys, John; Arkansas, 1918 95.2 p78
Mamchur, Nicholas; Arkansas, 1918 95.2 p79
Mamebouk, Carl 29; Kansas, 1888 5240.1 p72
Mamer, Nick D.; Wisconsin, n.d. 9675.6 p268
Mamer, Peter; Wisconsin, n.d. 9675.6 p268
Mamman, Dickery; Virginia, 1638 6219 p125
Mammer, Jacob; Wisconsin, n.d. 9675.6 p268
Mammer, Nicalaus; Wisconsin, n.d. 9675.6 p268
Mammer, Nicholaus; Wisconsin, n.d. 9675.6 p268
Mamroth, Samuel; Arkansas, 1918 95.2 p79
Man, Lieutenant; Grenada, 1775 1219.7 p280
Man, Gustav 28; Kansas, 1890 5240.1 p74
Man, Henry 16; Pennsylvania, 1731 3690.1 p148
Man, Jacob; Pennsylvania, 1753 2444 p188
Man, James 18; Jamaica, 1725 3690.1 p148
Man, Nich.; Virginia, 1636 6219 p77
Man, Robert; Virginia, 1636 6219 p76
Man, Robert; Virginia, 1637 6219 p108
Man, Thomas; Virginia, 1638 6219 p2
Man, Thomas; Virginia, 1638 6219 p150
Man, Thos.; Virginia, 1628 6219 p9
Man, William 16; Pennsylvania, 1734 3690.1 p148
Managan, James 15; Maryland, 1775 1219.7 p253
Managhan, Peter; New York, NY, 1838 8208.4 p71
Managheene, Timothy; America, 1742 4971 p56
Manahan, Michael; Illinois, 1866 7857 p5
Manahan, Richard; New York, NY, 1836 8208.4 p22
Manaut, E. 34; Port uncertain, 1839 778.5 p356
Manautin, Emile 17; Louisiana, 1820 778.5 p357
Manay, Ann 50; Philadelphia, 1854 5704.8 p116
Manay, Arthur 7; Philadelphia, 1854 5704.8 p116
Manay, Bernard 17; Philadelphia, 1854 5704.8 p116
Manay, Bridget 15; Philadelphia, 1854 5704.8 p116
Manay, Hugh 10; Philadelphia, 1854 5704.8 p116
Manay, Hugh 50; Philadelphia, 1854 5704.8 p116
Manbour, Auguste 27; New Orleans, 1838 778.5 p357
Manbourne, Mr. 24; New Orleans, 1839 778.5 p357
Manby, John; Virginia, 1636 6219 p21
Manca, Paolo; Wisconsin, n.d. 9675.6 p268
Manca, Raffaele; Wisconsin, n.d. 9675.6 p268
Manceni, Onofria 35; West Virginia, 1904 9788.3 p15
Manchest, John; Virginia, 1645 6219 p232
Mancini, Giovanni; New York, NY, 1837 8208.4 p24
Mancour, Auguste 27; New Orleans, 1838 778.5 p357
Mancuso, Vincent Salvado; Arkansas, 1918 95.2 p79
Mande, Mr. 28; New Orleans, 1822 778.5 p371
Mande, John; Wisconsin, n.d. 9675.6 p268
Mandelkow, John; Illinois, 1860 5012.38 p98
Manderbach, Mike 25; Kansas, 1888 5240.1 p73
Manderfield, Paul 18; Jamaica, 1729 3690.1 p148
Manderstried, Rosalie 28; New Orleans, 1839 778.5 p357
Mandery, Jacob; America, 1839 8582.1 p23
Mandery, Jacob; Cincinnati, 1869-1887 8582 p20
Mandevile, Miss 25; Barbados, 1774 1219.7 p190
Mandich, George; Arkansas, 1918 95.2 p79
Mandillon, Antoine 31; Port uncertain, 1838 778.5 p357
Mandler, Paul; Cincinnati, 1869-1887 8582 p20
Mandli, Josef; Wisconsin, n.d. 9675.6 p268
Mandrdot, A. 25; Port uncertain, 1832 778.5 p357
Mane, Patsey F.; Arkansas, 1918 95.2 p79
Manecke, . . .; Canada, 1776-1783 9786 p28
Maneily, John 22; Philadelphia, 1859 5704.8 p141
Manely, Henry; New York, NY, 1811 2859.11 p17
Manely, Michael; New York, NY, 1811 2859.11 p17
Manendez, Pablo 36; Arizona, 1890 2764.35 p46
Manes, Jean 25; America, 1838 778.5 p357
Manet, Wal.; Virginia, 1637 6219 p13
Maney, Mary 22; Massachusetts, 1849 5881.1 p72
Maney, Morris 23; Virginia, 1774 1219.7 p244
Maney, Patrick; New York, NY, 1811 2859.11 p17
Maney, Patrick 20; Massachusetts, 1849 5881.1 p74
Manfeet, Julius; America, 1853 1450.2 p92A
Mangal, Peter; Wisconsin, n.d. 9675.6 p268
Mangan, John 26; Kansas, 1888 5240.1 p72
Manganello, Salvatore; Iowa, 1866-1943 123.54 p32
Manganello, Salvorte; Iowa, 1866-1943 123.54 p32
Mangano, Francisco; Arkansas, 1918 95.2 p79
Mangeameli, Antonino; Arkansas, 1918 95.2 p79
Mangeard, Jacques 30; Port uncertain, 1836 778.5 p357
Mangel, John; Wisconsin, n.d. 9675.6 p268
Mangen, John; Wisconsin, n.d. 9675.6 p268
Manger, Peter 38; Port uncertain, 1838 778.5 p357
Mangin, William 34; Massachusetts, 1849 5881.1 p77
Manging, Thomas; America, 1853 6014.1 p2
Mangini, Allemantro 22; West Virginia, 1904 9788.3 p15
Mangnes, Elias; Minneapolis, 1883 6410.35 p60
Mangold, Adam; America, 1848 8582.2 p25
Mangold, Mathaeus; America, 1850 8582.3 p42
Mangold, Peter; New York, NY, 1839 8208.4 p90
Mangon, John 22; Maryland, 1735 3690.1 p148
Mangono, Joe Domenigo; Arkansas, 1918 95.2 p79
Manhaupt, Wilhelm; Philadelphia, 1779 8137 p11
Manhold, John; Kansas, 1887 5240.1 p29
Mania, Eugenie 40; America, 1836 778.5 p357
Manias, John George; Arkansas, 1918 95.2 p79
Manice, A.R. 21 *SEE* Manice, Miss K.M.
Manice, Miss K.M. 24; New York, NY, 1893 9026.4 p42
*Relative:*A.R. 21
Manike, . . .; Canada, 1776-1783 9786 p28
Maniles, James; New York, NY, 1864 5704.8 p185
Maning, Lazarus; Virginia, 1635 6219 p69
Manion, Peter; Arkansas, 1918 95.2 p79
Maniotte, Jean 19; New Orleans, 1837 778.5 p357
Maniotte, Louis 18; New Orleans, 1837 778.5 p357
Maniscalco, Giuseppe; Arkansas, 1918 95.2 p79
Manit, Nancy; St. John, N.B., 1847 5704.8 p4
Manitaras, George; Arkansas, 1918 95.2 p79
Manka, Georg; Kentucky, 1844 8582.3 p100
Manka, Otto; Illinois, 1890 5012.37 p62
Mankoff, Louis G.; Michigan, 1876 5240.1 p29
Manley, Catharine 28; Massachusetts, 1850 5881.1 p65
Manley, Mary 13; Massachusetts, 1850 5881.1 p72
Manley, William 31; Philadelphia, 1775 1219.7 p255
Manlufmore, Mary 15; Philadelphia, 1774 1219.7 p212
Manly, Jon.; Virginia, 1637 6219 p112
Manly, Michael; Philadelphia, 1864 5704.8 p175
Mann, Alec; Austin, TX, 1886 9777 p5
Mann, Anna; New York, 1752 3652 p76
Mann, Catharina Dorothea *SEE* Mann, Johann Jacob
Mann, Catherine 20; St. John, N.B., 1854 5704.8 p120
Mann, Christina *SEE* Mann, Johann Jacob
Mann, Christina C. Menold *SEE* Mann, Johann Jacob
Mann, Christopher Hans; Philadelphia, 1757 9973.7 p32
Mann, Miss F.; Milwaukee, 1875 4719.30 p257
Mann, George; Colorado, 1894 9678.2 p125
Mann, George 21; Maryland, 1774 1219.7 p221
Mann, George 40; Kansas, 1879 5240.1 p59
Mann, Hans Georg; Pennsylvania, 1753 2444 p188
Mann, Henry; Wisconsin, n.d. 9675.6 p268
Mann, Jacob 31; Pennsylvania, 1753 2444 p188
Mann, Jacob 41; Pennsylvania, 1753 2444 p188
Mann, James 31; Maryland, 1775 1219.7 p249
Mann, Johann Jacob; America, 1751-1800 2444 p188
*Wife:*Christina C. Menold
*Child:*Catharina Dorothea
*Child:*Christina
*Child:*Maria Barbara
Mann, Johann Michael *SEE* Mann, Johannes
Mann, Johannes; Pennsylvania, 1744 2444 p188
*Wife:*Margaretha
*Child:*Johann Michael
Mann, Johannes; Pennsylvania, 1753 2444 p188
Mann, John; Memphis, TN, 1848 2769.6 p5
Mann, John 30; Philadelphia, 1774 1219.7 p216
Mann, John F.; Wisconsin, n.d. 9675.6 p268
Mann, Magdalena; Port uncertain, 1754 2444 p139
Mann, Margaret; St. John, N.B., 1854 5704.8 p120
Mann, Margaretha *SEE* Mann, Johannes
Mann, Maria Barbara *SEE* Mann, Johann Jacob
Mann, Nicholas; Virginia, 1642 6219 p199
Manna, Luigi; Wisconsin, n.d. 9675.6 p268
Manna, Sylvester; Wisconsin, n.d. 9675.6 p268
Mannagan, Hugh 22; Massachusetts, 1849 5881.1 p67
Mannant, Bertrand 17; Louisiana, 1827 778.5 p357
Mannard, Mme. 60; New Orleans, 1837 778.5 p357
Manne, Edouard 34; America, 1838 778.5 p357
Mannebrot, Mike 25; Kansas, 1888 5240.1 p29
Mannehan, John 20; Massachusetts, 1849 5881.1 p69
Manneke, James Cason 18; Maryland, 1720 3690.1 p148
Manner, Erma Ann; Washington, 1859-1920 2872.1 p24
Manner, Mamie; Washington, 1859-1920 2872.1 p24
Manner, Tiovo Alexander; Washington, 1859-1920 2872.1 p25
Manners, Erma Ann; Washington, 1859-1920 2872.1 p24
Manners, Jos.; Virginia, 1635 6219 p71
Manners, Mamie; Washington, 1859-1920 2872.1 p24
Manners, Patrick 18; Massachusetts, 1847 5881.1 p74
Mannheimer, Mrs. E.; Milwaukee, 1875 4719.30 p257
With children
Manni, Pietro; Arkansas, 1918 95.2 p79
Mannihan, William 20; Massachusetts, 1849 5881.1 p77
Manninen, Herman; Washington, 1859-1920 2872.1 p25
Manninen, John Erik; Washington, 1859-1920 2872.1 p25
Manning, Benjamin; Antigua (Antego), 1758 1219.7 p61
Manning, Benjamin; Antigua (Antego), 1758 3690.1 p148
Manning, Daniel 26; Massachusetts, 1847 5881.1 p65
Manning, James; Colorado, 1904 9678.2 p126
Manning, Joseph; Maryland, 1756 1219.7 p43
Manning, Joseph; Maryland, 1756 3690.1 p148
Manning, Lawrence 24; Massachusetts, 1847 5881.1 p70
Manning, Patrick 15; Massachusetts, 1848 5881.1 p74
Manning, Peggy 25; Massachusetts, 1849 5881.1 p74
Manning, Robert 31; Maryland, 1775 1219.7 p266
Manning, Thomas; Maine, 1839-1840 7036 p117
Manning, Thomas; St. John, N.B., 1839 7036 p117
Manning, Thomas 30; Jamaica, 1775 1219.7 p279
Manning, William; New York, NY, 1816 2859.11 p38
Manning, William 16; Philadelphia, 1774 1219.7 p232
Mannion, John 3; Massachusetts, 1849 5881.1 p68

FOR A COMPLETE EXPLANATION OF ENTRY, SEE "HOW TO READ A CITATION" SECTION

Markes, Peter; Virginia, 1643 ***6219*** *p202*
Markes, Richard; Virginia, 1645 ***6219*** *p239*
Markey, James; New York, NY, 1816 ***2859.11*** *p38*
Markey, Pat; Illinois, 1872 ***5012.39*** *p26*
Markham, George 24; Maryland, 1775 ***1219.7*** *p266*
Markham, John; Virginia, 1638 ***6219*** *p147*
Markham, Susan Greenleafe *SEE* Markham, Thomas
Markham, Thomas; Virginia, 1636 ***6219*** *p21*
*Wife:*Susan Greenleafe
Markham, William 20; St. Kitts, 1774 ***1219.7*** *p205*
Marki, Henry; Iroquois Co., IL, 1896 ***3455.1*** *p12*
Markief, Raymond 35; Port uncertain, 1839 ***778.5*** *p363*
Markiewicz, Jan; New York, 1831 ***4606*** *p175*
Markiewicz, Janina 18; New York, 1912 ***9980.29*** *p52*
Markl, Jacob; New York, NY, 1835 ***8208.4*** *p6*
Markle, Mich'l; Pennsylvania, 1752-1794 ***2444*** *p191*
Markley, Abraham; Charleston, SC, 1775-1781 ***8582.2*** *p52*
Markley, Eliz; America, 1698 ***2212*** *p6*
Markley, Georg Paul; Pennsylvania, 1774 ***3627*** *p8*
Markowitz, Rolmeu 21; New York, NY, 1878 ***9253*** *p47*
Marks, Adolph; Wisconsin, n.d. ***9675.6*** *p268*
Marks, Anne Marie Wilhelmine *SEE* Marks, Christian Heinrich Wilhelm
Marks, Brice; Virginia, 1638 ***6219*** *p115*
Marks, Carl Friedrich; America, 1844 ***4610.10*** *p120*
*Wife:*Caroline W. F. Pape
*Son:*Carl Friedrich Wilhelm
Marks, Carl Friedrich Wilhelm *SEE* Marks, Carl Friedrich
Marks, Carl Heinrich *SEE* Marks, Christian Heinrich Wilhelm
Marks, Caroline Louise Wilh. *SEE* Marks, Wilhelm
Marks, Caroline W. F. Pape *SEE* Marks, Carl Friedrich
Marks, Christian Heinrich Wilhelm; America, 1854 ***4610.10*** *p156*
With wife
*Child:*Anne Marie Wilhelmine
*Child:*Carl Heinrich
Marks, Dorothea Ottilie 8; New York, NY, 1857 ***9831.14*** *p154*
Marks, E.; Cincinnati, 1869-1887 ***8582*** *p20*
Marks, Emil 27?; Arizona, 1890 ***2764.35*** *p45*
Marks, Friedrich Carl *SEE* Marks, Wilhelm
Marks, Heinrich Carl *SEE* Marks, Wilhelm
Marks, Hyman Aaron; Arkansas, 1918 ***95.2*** *p80*
Marks, Johann Carl Friedr. Wilh.; America, 1866 ***4610.10*** *p109*
Marks, John; Philadelphia, 1811 ***2859.11*** *p17*
With family
Marks, Karl Friedrich Wilhelm; America, 1849 ***4610.10*** *p104*
Marks, Louis; Shreveport, LA, 1879 ***7129*** *p45*
Marks, Louise Ruschmeier 36 *SEE* Marks, Wilhelm
Marks, Maria 43; New York, NY, 1857 ***9831.14*** *p154*
Marks, Martin 56; New York, NY, 1857 ***9831.14*** *p154*
Marks, Max.; California, 1874 ***2764.35*** *p43*
Marks, Sophia 23; New York, NY, 1857 ***9831.14*** *p154*
Marks, Wilhelm *SEE* Marks, Wilhelm
Marks, Wilhelm; America, 1865 ***4610.10*** *p105*
*Wife:*Louise Ruschmeier 36
*Child:*Wilhelm
*Child:*Heinrich Carl
*Child:*Friedrich Carl
*Child:*Caroline Louise Wilh.
Marksman, James; New York, NY, 1837 ***8208.4*** *p24*
Markulin, Louis; Wisconsin, n.d. ***9675.6*** *p268*
Markwort, Friedr. 26; New Orleans, 1839 ***9420.2*** *p71*
Marland, Tho; America, 1698 ***2212*** *p10*
Marland, Tho; Virginia, 1698 ***2212*** *p11*
Marlas, George Louis; Arkansas, 1918 ***95.2*** *p80*
Marley, Catharine; Philadelphia, 1864 ***5704.8*** *p186*
Marley, Cornelious 48; Philadelphia, 1859 ***5704.8*** *p141*
Marley, Elizabeth 5; Philadelphia, 1855 ***5704.8*** *p123*
Marley, Fanny 9; Philadelphia, 1864 ***5704.8*** *p187*
Marley, Hugh; Philadelphia, 1864 ***5704.8*** *p186*
Marley, James; Philadelphia, 1864 ***5704.8*** *p186*
Marley, John 3; Philadelphia, 1855 ***5704.8*** *p123*
Marley, John 14; Philadelphia, 1860 ***5704.8*** *p145*
Marley, Margaret 30; Philadelphia, 1855 ***5704.8*** *p123*
Marley, Michael 11; Philadelphia, 1864 ***5704.8*** *p186*
Marley, Patrick 20; Philadelphia, 1859 ***5704.8*** *p142*
Marley, Sarah; Philadelphia, 1864 ***5704.8*** *p186*
Marley, Susan; America, 1867 ***5704.8*** *p218*
Marlin, Fidel; Wisconsin, n.d. ***9675.6*** *p268*
Marlin, John; Virginia, 1639 ***6219*** *p161*
Marlot, N. 32; New Orleans, 1825 ***778.5*** *p363*
Marlow, Bridget; Philadelphia, 1851 ***5704.8*** *p71*
Marlow, Michael; Philadelphia, 1852 ***5704.8*** *p85*
Marlow, Owen; Philadelphia, 1849 ***53.26*** *p49*
Marlow, Owen; Philadelphia, 1849 ***5704.8*** *p50*
Marmaduke, Richard; Virginia, 1638 ***6219*** *p125*
Marmet, Otto; America, 1850 ***8582.3*** *p43*
Marmisse, Sylveste Guillaume 20; Port uncertain, 1838 ***778.5*** *p363*
Marmont, Hugo; America, 1852 ***1450.2*** *p92A*
Marmore, Eliz.; Virginia, 1638 ***6219*** *p147*
Marmottant, Lady 28; America, 1839 ***778.5*** *p363*
Marmottant, Joseph 32; America, 1839 ***778.5*** *p363*
Marner, Adrian; Virginia, 1638 ***6219*** *p147*
Marneval, Elisabetha; Pennsylvania, 1753 ***2444*** *p198*
Marnzo, Thomas; Iowa, 1866-1943 ***123.54*** *p32*
Maroglous, Mr. 19; New Orleans, 1839 ***778.5*** *p363*
Maron, Owen; New York, NY, 1811 ***2859.11*** *p17*
Marone, Giusippe M.; America, 1872 ***1450.2*** *p92A*
Marooney, Patrick 20; Massachusetts, 1848 ***5881.1*** *p74*
Marosa, Guiseppe; Iowa, 1866-1943 ***123.54*** *p32*
Maroski, Anthony; America, 1843 ***1450.2*** *p92A*
Maroso, Antonio; Iowa, 1866-1943 ***123.54*** *p69*
Maroso, Geo.; Iowa, 1866-1943 ***123.54*** *p32*
Marot, Reny 20; Maryland or Virginia, 1722 ***3690.1*** *p148*
Marow, Abraham 19; New York, NY, 1878 ***9253*** *p46*
Maroz, Kazemer; Wisconsin, n.d. ***9675.6*** *p268*
Marpenter, Patrick; America, 1742 ***4971*** *p17*
Marquard, Anna Magdalena; New England, 1749 ***2444*** *p134*
Marquard, Carl; Wisconsin, n.d. ***9675.6*** *p268*
Marquard, Henry; San Francisco, 1863 ***2764.35*** *p44*
Marquard, Ludwig H.C.; Wisconsin, n.d. ***9675.6*** *p268*
Marquardt, William; Wisconsin, n.d. ***9675.6*** *p268*
Marquart, Adam 30; America, 1853 ***9162.7*** *p15*
Marquehosse, Mr. 25; New Orleans, 1837 ***778.5*** *p363*
Marques, Lucas; Los Angeles, 1866 ***2764.35*** *p46*
Marquet, Francois 59; America, 1838 ***778.5*** *p363*
Marquet, Marie Therese 45; America, 1838 ***778.5*** *p363*
Marquetand, Lorenze; Philadelphia, 1760 ***9973.7*** *p34*
Marquette, William; Wisconsin, n.d. ***9675.6*** *p268*
Marquis, Mr. 25; New Orleans, 1839 ***778.5*** *p363*
Marquis, Mrs. 35; New Orleans, 1822 ***778.5*** *p363*
Marquis, A. 25; America, 1838 ***778.5*** *p363*
Marquis, E. 26; America, 1838 ***778.5*** *p363*
Marr, James 17; Virginia, 1774 ***1219.7*** *p243*
Marr, Johann; Wisconsin, 1871 ***8582*** *p20*
Marr, Peter A.; New York, NY, 1840 ***8208.4*** *p105*
Marrah, Peter; New York, NY, 1834 ***8208.4*** *p43*
Marran, George; New York, NY, 1839 ***8208.4*** *p97*
Marras, John 25; Port uncertain, 1757 ***3690.1*** *p149*
Marreck, . . .; Canada, 1776-1783 ***9786*** *p28*
Marreroe, P. 84; America, 1825 ***778.5*** *p372*
Marret, Elizabeth 35; Philadelphia, 1860 ***5704.8*** *p146*
Marrick, T.; Quebec, 1815 ***9229.18*** *p74*
Marriette, Marie; Halifax, N.S., 1752 ***7074.6*** *p216*
Marrin, Francis; New York, NY, 1834 ***8208.4*** *p27*
Marriner, John; New York, NY, 1834 ***8208.4*** *p4*
Marriott, . . .; Halifax, N.S., 1752 ***7074.6*** *p230*
Marriott, Henry; Virginia, 1646 ***6219*** *p240*
Marriott, Pierre; Halifax, N.S., 1752 ***7074.6*** *p230*
Marrow, Geo.; Virginia, 1647 ***6219*** *p245*
Marry, John; America, 1736-1743 ***4971*** *p58*
Mars, Michael; America, 1742 ***4971*** *p31*
Marsac, Mr. 40; America, 1837 ***778.5*** *p364*
Marsam, Edward; Virginia, 1642 ***6219*** *p188*
Marschalck, von; Saratoga, NY, 1775-1781 ***8582.3*** *p43*
Marschalk, Andreas; America, 1775-1781 ***8582.3*** *p43*
Marschall, Bernard; Kentucky, 1840-1845 ***8582.3*** *p100*
Marschall, Conrad; America, 1843 ***8582.3*** *p43*
Marschke, Frederick; America, 1880 ***1450.2*** *p92A*
Marschke, Wilhelm; New York, 1879 ***1450.2*** *p92A*
Marschke, William; Illinois, 1890 ***5012.40*** *p25*
Marsden, Christopher 20; Virginia, 1700 ***2212*** *p32*
Marsden, Christopher 22; Jamaica, 1722 ***3690.1*** *p149*
Marsden, George; New York, NY, 1839 ***8208.4*** *p94*
Marsden, Peter; Iowa, 1866-1943 ***123.54*** *p32*
Marse, Joseph; Wisconsin, n.d. ***9675.6*** *p268*
Marsen, Miekl; Arkansas, 1918 ***95.2*** *p80*
Marsey, Jon.; Virginia, 1637 ***6219*** *p113*
Marsh, Alexander; Virginia, 1698 ***2212*** *p14*
Marsh, Eliz 16; America, 1699 ***2212*** *p29*
Marsh, Francis; Virginia, 1643 ***6219*** *p230*
Marsh, Frederick H.; Illinois, 1861 ***7857*** *p5*
Marsh, George; Arkansas, 1918 ***95.2*** *p80*
Marsh, George L.; Washington, 1859-1920 ***2872.1*** *p25*
Marsh, James; New York, NY, 1838 ***8208.4*** *p63*
Marsh, John; New England, 1758 ***1219.7*** *p63*
Marsh, John; Virginia, 1643 ***6219*** *p230*
Marsh, Joseph; Boston, 1770 ***1219.7*** *p148*
Marsh, Joseph; Virginia, 1638 ***6219*** *p11*
Marsh, Lewis; Virginia, 1643 ***6219*** *p230*
Marsh, Page 28; Virginia, 1773 ***1219.7*** *p171*
Marsh, Stayfield 18; St. Christopher, 1730 ***3690.1*** *p149*
Marsh, Thomas; New York, NY, 1834 ***8208.4*** *p55*
Marsh, Thomas; Virginia, 1637 ***6219*** *p82*
Marsh, William 19; Jamaica, 1730 ***3690.1*** *p149*
Marshal, David 24; North Carolina, 1774 ***1219.7*** *p189*
Marshal, Leonora 21; Maryland, 1774 ***1219.7*** *p213*
Marshal, Thomas 15; Philadelphia, 1774 ***1219.7*** *p197*
Marshall, Mr.; New Orleans, 1839 ***778.5*** *p364*
Marshall, Mr.; Quebec, 1815 ***9229.18*** *p82*
Marshall, A. 22; America, 1838 ***778.5*** *p364*
Marshall, Alex; St. John, N.B., 1853 ***5704.8*** *p107*
Marshall, Alexander; Quebec, 1852 ***5704.8*** *p90*
Marshall, Alexander 31; Quebec, 1864 ***5704.8*** *p163*
Marshall, Andrew; South Carolina, 1826 ***1639.20*** *p229*
Marshall, Andrew W. 35; Kansas, 1886 ***5240.1*** *p68*
Marshall, Ann 7; Quebec, 1851 ***5704.8*** *p73*
Marshall, Anne; Virginia, 1642 ***6219*** *p198*
Marshall, Bastian; Wisconsin, n.d. ***9675.6*** *p268*
Marshall, David; St. John, N.B., 1848 ***5704.8*** *p47*
Marshall, David 23; Kansas, 1890 ***5240.1*** *p75*
Marshall, David 24; North Carolina, 1774 ***1639.20*** *p229*
Marshall, Edm.; Virginia, 1648 ***6219*** *p251*
Marshall, Edward; New York, NY, 1839 ***8208.4*** *p95*
Marshall, Edward; Virginia, 1639 ***6219*** *p150*
Marshall, Eliza; New York, NY, 1811 ***2859.11*** *p17*
Marshall, Eliza 1; Quebec, 1864 ***5704.8*** *p163*
Marshall, Eliza 30; Quebec, 1864 ***5704.8*** *p163*
Marshall, Elleanor 28; St. John, N.B., 1856 ***5704.8*** *p131*
Marshall, Francis; Virginia, 1847 ***4626.16*** *p13*
Marshall, George 27; Maryland or Virginia, 1736 ***3690.1*** *p149*
Marshall, George Francis; Illinois, 1892 ***5012.40*** *p26*
Marshall, H. M. 37; Washington, 1918-1920 ***1728.5*** *p10*
Marshall, Henry; New York, NY, 1838 ***8208.4*** *p86*
Marshall, Henry; Virginia, 1638 ***6219*** *p125*
Marshall, Henry; Virginia, 1638 ***6219*** *p147*
Marshall, Hugh; Quebec, 1851 ***5704.8*** *p75*
Marshall, Isabel; Charleston, SC, 1767 ***1639.20*** *p229*
Marshall, Isabella; New York, NY, 1815 ***2859.11*** *p38*
Marshall, Isabella; Quebec, 1851 ***5704.8*** *p82*
Marshall, Israel 28; North America, 1774 ***1219.7*** *p199*
Marshall, James; America, 1737 ***4971*** *p55*
Marshall, James; Charleston, SC, 1765 ***1639.20*** *p230*
Marshall, James 22; Maryland, 1735 ***3690.1*** *p149*
Marshall, James 24; Barbados, 1774 ***1219.7*** *p211*
With wife 22
Marshall, Jane; Philadelphia, 1853 ***5704.8*** *p102*
Marshall, Jane 21; St. John, N.B., 1859 ***5704.8*** *p140*
Marshall, Jeorge; New York, NY, 1811 ***2859.11*** *p17*
Marshall, Jno.; Virginia, 1644 ***6219*** *p231*
Marshall, Jno 15; America, 1702 ***2212*** *p36*
Marshall, John; Brunswick, NC, 1775 ***1639.20*** *p230*
Marshall, John; Charleston, SC, 1820 ***1639.20*** *p230*
Marshall, John; New York, NY, 1815 ***2859.11*** *p38*
Marshall, John; New York, NY, 1833 ***8208.4*** *p51*
Marshall, John; St. John, N.B., 1848 ***5704.8*** *p47*
Marshall, John; Virginia, 1642 ***6219*** *p197*
Marshall, John; Virginia, 1646 ***6219*** *p247*
Marshall, John 2; Quebec, 1852 ***5704.8*** *p93*
Marshall, John 11; St. John, N.B., 1848 ***5704.8*** *p47*
Marshall, John 20; Jamaica, 1732 ***3690.1*** *p149*
Marshall, John 29; St. John, N.B., 1856 ***5704.8*** *p131*
Marshall, John P.C.; New York, NY, 1840 ***8208.4*** *p106*
Marshall, John T. 48; Charleston, SC, 1850 ***1639.20*** *p230*
*Relative:*Ruth 36
Marshall, Jon.; Virginia, 1636 ***6219*** *p74*
Marshall, Joseph; New York, NY, 1811 ***2859.11*** *p17*
Marshall, Joseph; Wisconsin, n.d. ***9675.6*** *p268*
Marshall, Letty Ann; St. John, N.B., 1848 ***5704.8*** *p47*
Marshall, Margaret; New York, NY, 1815 ***2859.11*** *p38*
Marshall, Martha; Philadelphia, 1851 ***5704.8*** *p80*
Marshall, Mary; New York, NY, 1815 ***2859.11*** *p38*
Marshall, Mary; Quebec, 1852 ***5704.8*** *p93*
Marshall, Mary; St. John, N.B., 1847 ***5704.8*** *p11*
Marshall, Mary 3; Quebec, 1864 ***5704.8*** *p163*
Marshall, Mary 11; Quebec, 1851 ***5704.8*** *p73*
Marshall, Mary A.; Philadelphia, 1866 ***5704.8*** *p208*
Marshall, Mary Ann 21; Philadelphia, 1859 ***5704.8*** *p142*
Marshall, Patrick; Charleston, SC, 1761 ***1639.20*** *p230*
Marshall, Richard 20; Virginia, 1736 ***3690.1*** *p149*
Marshall, Robert; Ohio, 1845 ***9892.11*** *p27*
Marshall, Robert 18; Quebec, 1858 ***5704.8*** *p138*
Marshall, Rose; Philadelphia, 1852 ***5704.8*** *p97*
Marshall, Ruth 36 *SEE* Marshall, John T.
Marshall, Samuel; New York, NY, 1815 ***2859.11*** *p38*
Marshall, Samuel; Quebec, 1852 ***5704.8*** *p93*
Marshall, Sarah; St. John, N.B., 1847 ***5704.8*** *p8*
Marshall, Sarah; St. John, N.B., 1848 ***5704.8*** *p47*
Marshall, Sarah 4; Quebec, 1864 ***5704.8*** *p163*
Marshall, Susanah; Virginia, 1750 ***3690.1*** *p149*
Marshall, Susannah; Virginia, 1751 ***1219.7*** *p2*
Marshall, Teterick; Philadelphia, 1757 ***9973.7*** *p32*
Marshall, Thomas; New York, NY, 1838 ***8208.4*** *p89*
Marshall, W.; New York, NY, 1811 ***2859.11*** *p17*
With family
Marshall, Walter; Virginia, 1639 ***6219*** *p157*
Marshall, William; New York, NY, 1816 ***2859.11*** *p38*
Marshall, William; Quebec, 1851 ***5704.8*** *p75*

Marshall, William 6; Quebec, 1864 ***5704.8*** *p163*
Marshall, William 16; St. John, N.B., 1866 ***5704.8*** *p167*
Marshall, William 18; Massachusetts, 1849 ***5881.1*** *p77*
Marshall, William 50; Maryland, 1774 ***1219.7*** *p177*
With wife
With 10 children
Marshall, Wm.; Virginia, 1643 ***6219*** *p203*
Marshall, Wm.; Virginia, 1648 ***6219*** *p250*
Marshel, Jonathan 19; Jamaica, 1737 ***3690.1*** *p149*
Marshell, Mr. 22; New Orleans, 1839 ***778.5*** *p364*
Marsidoschek, Joseph; Wisconsin, n.d. ***9675.6*** *p268*
Marsiglio, Agostino; Iowa, 1866-1943 ***123.54*** *p32*
Marsiglio, Agustino; Iowa, 1866-1943 ***123.54*** *p33*
Marsiglio, Alex; Iowa, 1866-1943 ***123.54*** *p33*
Marsiglio, Angela Elisabeta; Iowa, 1866-1943 ***123.54*** *p69*
Marsiglio, Gerlando; New York, NY, 1837 ***8208.4*** *p24*
Marsischky, Wilhelm; New York, 1884 ***1450.2*** *p92A*
Marski, . . .; New York, 1831 ***4606*** *p175*
Marson, Thomas; Illinois, 1856 ***7857*** *p5*
Marsten, Wm.; Virginia, 1637 ***6219*** *p8*
Marston, F. G.; Washington, 1859-1920 ***2872.1*** *p25*
Marston, Frank; Washington, 1859-1920 ***2872.1*** *p25*
Marston, Frank G.; Washington, 1859-1920 ***2872.1*** *p25*
Marston, Gilbert 21; Windward Islands, 1722 ***3690.1*** *p149*
Marston, John; Washington, 1859-1920 ***2872.1*** *p25*
Martanhoff, Johann Hinrich; New York, NY, 1840 ***8208.4*** *p112*
Martel, D. 19; Port uncertain, 1839 ***778.5*** *p364*
Martell, F.; Shreveport, LA, 1874 ***7129*** *p45*
Martello, Anello; Arkansas, 1918 ***95.2*** *p80*
Martels, Baron von; Baltimore, 1832 ***3702.7*** *p96*
With 2 sons
*Son:*Heinrich von
Martels, Heinrich von *SEE* Martels, Baron von
Martels, Heinrich von; Cincinnati, 1869-1887 ***8582*** *p20*
Marten, Alexander 16; Jamaica, 1733 ***3690.1*** *p150*
Marten, Don Louis 40; Mexico, 1829 ***778.5*** *p364*
Marten, Fred; Wisconsin, n.d. ***9675.6*** *p268*
Marten, Gustav A.; Indiana, 1868 ***1450.2*** *p92A*
Marten, Henry 22; Philadelphia, 1864 ***5704.8*** *p161*
Marten, John; New York, NY, 1866 ***5704.8*** *p206*
Marten, Leonhard; Wisconsin, n.d. ***9675.6*** *p268*
Marten, Michael 20; Philadelphia, 1864 ***5704.8*** *p156*
Martens, Heinrich; Quebec, 1776 ***9786*** *p265*
Martens, Johann C. 45; Kansas, 1884 ***5240.1*** *p66*
Martens, Johann Christian 20; Kansas, 1887 ***5240.1*** *p70*
Martens, Matte J. A.; Washington, 1859-1920 ***2872.1*** *p25*
Martens, William; Wisconsin, n.d. ***9675.6*** *p268*
Martenson, James; Illinois, 1893 ***5012.39*** *p53*
Martenson, Svan 23; Kansas, 1878 ***5240.1*** *p59*
Marthal, Mrs. 28; Louisiana, 1826 ***778.5*** *p364*
Marthaller, Johann; Alberta, n.d. ***5262*** *p58*
Marthaller, Liborius; Alberta, n.d. ***5262*** *p58*
Marti, Pilipp 18; Port uncertain, 1839 ***778.5*** *p364*
Martiall, Jno.; Virginia, 1648 ***6219*** *p253*
Martian, Eliz. *SEE* Martian, Nicholas
Martian, Jane *SEE* Martian, Nicholas
Martian, Nicholas *SEE* Martian, Nicholas
Martian, Nicholas; Virginia, 1639 ***6219*** *p162*
*Wife:*Jane
*Son:*Nicholas
*Daughter:*Eliz.
With granddaughter
Martiere, Mad. 28; America, 1839 ***778.5*** *p364*
Martigny, Theodore de; Canada, 1776-1783 ***9786*** *p233*
Martin, . . .; Canada, 1776-1783 ***9786*** *p28*
Martin, . . .; New Orleans, 1838 ***778.5*** *p365*
Martin, . . .; New York, NY, 1811 ***2859.11*** *p17*
With family
Martin, . . .; Virginia, 1635 ***6219*** *p3*
Martin, . . . 9 mos; Philadelphia, 1866 ***5704.8*** *p214*
Martin, Miss 14; America, 1839 ***778.5*** *p367*
Martin, Mlle. 28; New Orleans, 1838 ***778.5*** *p367*
Martin, Mr.; Quebec, 1815 ***9229.18*** *p77*
Martin, Mr. 24; New Orleans, 1822 ***778.5*** *p364*
Martin, Mr. 24; New Orleans, 1822 ***778.5*** *p365*
Martin, Mr. 30; New Orleans, 1839 ***778.5*** *p364*
Martin, Mr. 32; New Orleans, 1825 ***778.5*** *p364*
Martin, Mr. 35; Louisiana, 1820 ***778.5*** *p364*
Martin, Mr. 41; Port uncertain, 1838 ***778.5*** *p364*
Martin, Mr. 42; America, 1836 ***778.5*** *p367*
Martin, Mrs. 36; America, 1836 ***778.5*** *p367*
Martin, A. 30; Port uncertain, 1825 ***778.5*** *p365*
Martin, Abraham; Quebec, 1621 ***9775.5*** *p197*
Martin, Abram L. 25; Kansas, 1872 ***5240.1*** *p53*
Martin, Adolphe 16; New Orleans, 1821 ***778.5*** *p365*
Martin, Agnes 30; Wilmington, DE, 1831 ***6508.7*** *p160*
Martin, Agnis; Virginia, 1639 ***6219*** *p156*
Martin, Albert; Washington, 1859-1920 ***2872.1*** *p25*
Martin, Albert Luther; Washington, 1859-1920 ***2872.1*** *p25*
Martin, Alex; Quebec, 1841 ***4537.30*** *p16*
*Wife:*Mary MacRae
*Child:*Donald
*Child:*Ann
*Child:*William
*Child:*Catherine
*Child:*Mary
*Child:*Margaret
Martin, Alex; Quebec, 1851 ***5704.8*** *p82*
Martin, Alexander; America, 1788 ***1639.20*** *p230*
Martin, Alexander; America, 1811 ***1639.20*** *p230*
Martin, Alexander; Colorado, 1903 ***9678.2*** *p126*
Martin, Alexander 18; St. John, N.B., 1862 ***5704.8*** *p150*
Martin, Alfred; Norfolk, VA, 1818 ***9892.11*** *p28*
Martin, Alice 19; Quebec, 1855 ***5704.8*** *p125*
Martin, Allan; America, 1854 ***1450.2*** *p92A*
Martin, And; Virginia, 1698 ***2212*** *p14*
Martin, Andrew; New York, NY, 1811 ***2859.11*** *p17*
Martin, Andrew; Philadelphia, 1816 ***2859.11*** *p38*
Martin, Andrew 1; Quebec, 1859 ***5704.8*** *p143*
Martin, Angus 20; St. John, N.B., 1862 ***5704.8*** *p150*
Martin, Ann *SEE* Martin, Alex
Martin, Ann; Quebec, 1851 ***5704.8*** *p73*
Martin, Ann 3; Massachusetts, 1848 ***5881.1*** *p62*
Martin, Ann 8; Philadelphia, 1848 ***5704.8*** *p40*
Martin, Ann 8; St. John, N.B., 1862 ***5704.8*** *p150*
Martin, Ann 11; Quebec, 1854 ***5704.8*** *p121*
Martin, Ann 18; Massachusetts, 1850 ***5881.1*** *p62*
Martin, Ann 19; Philadelphia, 1857 ***5704.8*** *p134*
Martin, Ann 24; St. John, N.B., 1857 ***5704.8*** *p134*
Martin, Ann 47; Quebec, 1854 ***5704.8*** *p121*
Martin, Ann Jane 15; Philadelphia, 1854 ***5704.8*** *p120*
Martin, Anna; New York, NY, 1811 ***2859.11*** *p17*
Martin, Anne 20; Philadelphia, 1803 ***53.26*** *p49*
Martin, Aug. Wm. 21; New Orleans, 1839 ***9420.2*** *p169*
Martin, Bernard; Quebec, 1820 ***7603*** *p90*
Martin, Bessy 20; Massachusetts, 1849 ***5881.1*** *p63*
Martin, Biddy 50; Philadelphia, 1864 ***5704.8*** *p160*
Martin, Bridget 24; Massachusetts, 1847 ***5881.1*** *p63*
Martin, Burgere 26; America, 1832 ***778.5*** *p365*
Martin, C.; Quebec, 1815 ***9229.18*** *p79*
Martin, Cartin 8; Massachusetts, 1847 ***5881.1*** *p64*
Martin, Catharine; Philadelphia, 1865 ***5704.8*** *p191*
Martin, Catharine 35; Massachusetts, 1847 ***5881.1*** *p64*
Martin, Catherine *SEE* Martin, Alex
Martin, Catherine; America, 1737 ***4971*** *p12*
Martin, Catherine 8; Philadelphia, 1864 ***5704.8*** *p161*
Martin, Catherine 25; Philadelphia, 1864 ***5704.8*** *p160*
Martin, Charles 8 mos; Philadelphia, 1864 ***5704.8*** *p161*
Martin, Charles 24; Philadelphia, 1859 ***5704.8*** *p141*
Martin, Christian; Charleston, SC, 1775-1781 ***8582.2*** *p52*
Martin, Christina 47; St. John, N.B., 1862 ***5704.8*** *p150*
Martin, Christopher 19; Quebec, 1857 ***5704.8*** *p136*
Martin, Christopher 40; Quebec, 1858 ***5704.8*** *p138*
Martin, Conrad; Wisconsin, n.d. ***9675.6*** *p268*
Martin, Daniel 5; Philadelphia, 1864 ***5704.8*** *p160*
Martin, Daniel 22; Philadelphia, 1833-1834 ***53.26*** *p49*
Martin, Daniel 71; North Carolina, 1850 ***1639.20*** *p230*
*Relative:*Sarah 71
*Relative:*Flora 40
*Relative:*Dorothea B. 38
Martin, Denis 27; Philadelphia, 1864 ***5704.8*** *p160*
Martin, Dolly 20; St. John, N.B., 1855 ***5704.8*** *p127*
Martin, Dominique 29; America, 1829 ***778.5*** *p365*
Martin, Donald *SEE* Martin, Alex
Martin, Donald; America, 1811 ***1639.20*** *p230*
Martin, Donald 36; Quebec, 1864 ***5704.8*** *p164*
Martin, Dorothea B. 38 *SEE* Martin, Daniel
Martin, Earnest Earl; Washington, 1859-1920 ***2872.1*** *p25*
Martin, Edward; Philadelphia, 1864 ***5704.8*** *p186*
Martin, Edward 5; St. John, N.B., 1851 ***5704.8*** *p79*
Martin, Elizabeth *SEE* Martin, Robert
Martin, Elizabeth; Quebec, 1849 ***5704.8*** *p51*
Martin, Elizabeth 9; Quebec, 1854 ***5704.8*** *p121*
Martin, Elizabeth 11; Quebec, 1858 ***5704.8*** *p138*
Martin, Elizabeth 12; Quebec, 1855 ***5704.8*** *p126*
Martin, Elizabeth 22; Philadelphia, 1864 ***5704.8*** *p161*
Martin, Elleanor 23; St. John, N.B., 1856 ***5704.8*** *p132*
Martin, Ellen; St. John, N.B., 1847 ***5704.8*** *p35*
Martin, Ellen; St. John, N.B., 1851 ***5704.8*** *p79*
Martin, Emil; America, 1867 ***1450.2*** *p93A*
Martin, Emilie 6 mos; New Orleans, 1838 ***778.5*** *p365*
Martin, Ethel May; Washington, 1859-1920 ***2872.1*** *p25*
Martin, Everhart; Philadelphia, 1758 ***9973.7*** *p33*
Martin, F. 35; Louisiana, 1829 ***778.5*** *p365*
Martin, Flora 28; Quebec, 1864 ***5704.8*** *p164*
Martin, Flora 40 *SEE* Martin, Daniel
Martin, Flora 65; North Carolina, 1850 ***1639.20*** *p231*
Martin, Francis 36; Port uncertain, 1836 ***778.5*** *p365*
Martin, Francois 31; Port uncertain, 1839 ***778.5*** *p365*
Martin, Francoise 26; New Orleans, 1838 ***778.5*** *p365*
Martin, Freeman; Illinois, 1844 ***7857*** *p5*
Martin, George; America, 1847 ***1450.2*** *p93A*
Martin, George; New York, NY, 1816 ***2859.11*** *p38*
Martin, George; Ohio, 1852 ***9892.11*** *p28*
Martin, George 35; Philadelphia, 1804 ***53.26*** *p49*
Martin, George 47; Arizona, 1890 ***2764.35*** *p45*
Martin, George H.; Illinois, 1876 ***2896.5*** *p26*
Martin, George Pickney; Ohio, 1825 ***9892.11*** *p28*
Martin, George Pinkney; Philadelphia, 1819 ***9892.11*** *p28*
Martin, George Raymond; Washington, 1859-1920 ***2872.1*** *p25*
Martin, Gilbert 40; Massachusetts, 1849 ***5881.1*** *p67*
Martin, Giles; Virginia, 1623 ***6219*** *p20*
Martin, Guillaume 6; New Orleans, 1838 ***778.5*** *p365*
Martin, Guillaume 33; Port uncertain, 1839 ***778.5*** *p365*
Martin, H.; Quebec, 1815 ***9229.18*** *p79*
With wife
Martin, H. L.; Washington, 1859-1920 ***2872.1*** *p25*
Martin, Harriett; Washington, 1859-1920 ***2872.1*** *p25*
Martin, Henry; Virginia, 1639 ***6219*** *p161*
Martin, Herman; Illinois, 1856 ***7857*** *p5*
Martin, Hugh; New York, NY, 1816 ***2859.11*** *p38*
Martin, Hugh; New York, NY, 1838 ***8208.4*** *p66*
Martin, Hugh 7; Philadelphia, 1864 ***5704.8*** *p160*
Martin, Hugh 18; Philadelphia, 1857 ***5704.8*** *p134*
Martin, Hugh 22; Philadelphia, 1864 ***5704.8*** *p160*
Martin, Hugh 28; Arkansas, 1918 ***95.2*** *p80*
Martin, Isaac; Ohio, 1819 ***8582.1*** *p47*
Martin, Isaac; Washington, 1859-1920 ***2872.1*** *p25*
Martin, Isaac 22; Maryland, 1775 ***1219.7*** *p253*
Martin, Isabella 7; Quebec, 1858 ***5704.8*** *p138*
Martin, Isabella 21; New Orleans, 1829 ***778.5*** *p366*
Martin, Isabella 36; Philadelphia, 1860 ***5704.8*** *p145*
Martin, J. 26; America, 1835 ***778.5*** *p366*
Martin, J. 47; New Orleans, 1827 ***778.5*** *p366*
Martin, Jacob 25; Kansas, 1893 ***5240.1*** *p29*
Martin, Jacob 25; Kansas, 1893 ***5240.1*** *p79*
Martin, Jacques 44; New Orleans, 1821 ***778.5*** *p366*
Martin, James; Montreal, 1825 ***7603*** *p72*
Martin, James; New York, NY, 1811 ***2859.11*** *p17*
Martin, James; New York, NY, 1816 ***2859.11*** *p38*
Martin, James; New York, NY, 1838 ***8208.4*** *p65*
Martin, James; New York, NY, 1838 ***8208.4*** *p75*
Martin, James; New York, NY, 1869 ***5704.8*** *p234*
Martin, James; Ohio, 1844 ***9892.11*** *p28*
Martin, James; Philadelphia, 1811 ***53.26*** *p49*
Martin, James; Philadelphia, 1811 ***2859.11*** *p17*
Martin, James; Philadelphia, 1816 ***2859.11*** *p38*
Martin, James; Philadelphia, 1852 ***5704.8*** *p89*
Martin, James; Philadelphia, 1867 ***5704.8*** *p216*
Martin, James 1; Philadelphia, 1864 ***5704.8*** *p160*
Martin, James 5; Quebec, 1858 ***5704.8*** *p138*
Martin, James 10; Quebec, 1855 ***5704.8*** *p126*
Martin, James 13; Quebec, 1852 ***5704.8*** *p86*
Martin, James 13; Quebec, 1852 ***5704.8*** *p90*
Martin, James 15; Quebec, 1853 ***5704.8*** *p105*
Martin, James 18; Philadelphia, 1864 ***5704.8*** *p160*
Martin, James 22; St. John, N.B., 1855 ***5704.8*** *p127*
Martin, James 23; Quebec, 1857 ***5704.8*** *p136*
Martin, James 25; Massachusetts, 1847 ***5881.1*** *p67*
Martin, James 30; Quebec, 1864 ***5704.8*** *p160*
Martin, James B.; New York, NY, 1840 ***8208.4*** *p104*
Martin, James D.; Nevada, 1876 ***2764.35*** *p46*
Martin, Jane; New York, NY, 1811 ***2859.11*** *p17*
Martin, Jane; Quebec, 1852 ***5704.8*** *p86*
Martin, Jane; Quebec, 1852 ***5704.8*** *p90*
Martin, Jane 1; Quebec, 1849 ***5704.8*** *p51*
Martin, Jane 30; Carolina, 1775 ***1219.7*** *p278*
Martin, Jane 57; Quebec, 1863 ***5704.8*** *p153*
Martin, Jean 40; Port uncertain, 1839 ***778.5*** *p366*
Martin, Jessie 24; Quebec, 1864 ***5704.8*** *p164*
Martin, Joannah 48; Massachusetts, 1860 ***6410.32*** *p99*
Martin, Johann Jost; Trenton, NJ, 1776 ***8137*** *p11*
Martin, Johanna 25; Massachusetts, 1848 ***5881.1*** *p68*
Martin, Johannes; Philadelphia, 1779 ***8137*** *p11*
Martin, John; America, 1737 ***4971*** *p99*
Martin, John; America, 1739 ***4971*** *p68*
Martin, John; America, 1742 ***4971*** *p99*
Martin, John; Arkansas, 1918 ***95.2*** *p79*
Martin, John; Illinois, 1856 ***7857*** *p5*
Martin, John; New York, 1833 ***1450.2*** *p93A*
Martin, John; New York, NY, 1811 ***2859.11*** *p17*
Martin, John; New York, NY, 1816 ***2859.11*** *p38*
Martin, John; New York, NY, 1865 ***5704.8*** *p194*
Martin, John; North Carolina, 1793 ***1639.20*** *p231*
Martin, John; Ohio, 1819-1899 ***9892.11*** *p28*
Martin, John; Philadelphia, 1864 ***5704.8*** *p175*
Martin, John; Philadelphia, 1865 ***5704.8*** *p191*
Martin, John; Quebec, 1849 ***5704.8*** *p51*
Martin, John; Quebec, 1851 ***5704.8*** *p82*
Martin, John; Virginia, 1622 ***6219*** *p6*
Martin, John 5; St. John, N.B., 1862 ***5704.8*** *p150*
Martin, John 6; Philadelphia, 1848 ***5704.8*** *p40*

Martin, John 8; St. John, N.B., 1851 ***5704.8*** *p79*
Martin, John 11; Quebec, 1859 ***5704.8*** *p143*
Martin, John 14; Quebec, 1858 ***5704.8*** *p138*
Martin, John 21; Philadelphia, 1803 ***53.26*** *p49*
Martin, John 21; Philadelphia, 1864 ***5704.8*** *p161*
Martin, John 24; Philadelphia, 1854 ***5704.8*** *p120*
Martin, John 26; Quebec, 1864 ***5704.8*** *p164*
Martin, John 28; Massachusetts, 1849 ***5881.1*** *p69*
Martin, John 43; Philadelphia, 1860 ***5704.8*** *p145*
Martin, John 63; South Carolina, 1850 ***1639.20*** *p231*
Martin, John 81; Arizona, 1897 ***9228.40*** *p3*
Martin, John Golrick; New York, NY, 1815 ***2859.11*** *p38*
Martin, John W.; Iowa, 1866-1943 ***123.54*** *p33*
Martin, Joseph; America, 1850 ***8582.3*** *p43*
Martin, Joseph; Illinois, 1870 ***1450.2*** *p93A*
Martin, Joseph 2; New Orleans, 1838 ***778.5*** *p366*
Martin, Joseph 16; Maryland, 1774 ***1219.7*** *p224*
Martin, Joseph 24; Maryland, 1775 ***1219.7*** *p256*
Martin, Joseph 30; Maryland, 1774 ***1219.7*** *p214*
Martin, Joseph 40; America, 1838 ***778.5*** *p366*
Martin, Jules 8; America, 1836 ***778.5*** *p366*
Martin, Kirsty; Quebec, 1850 ***4537.30*** *p117*
Martin, Larence 3 mos; Quebec, 1849 ***5704.8*** *p51*
Martin, Lawrence; Virginia, 1855 ***4626.16*** *p15*
Martin, Lawrence 62; Arizona, 1910 ***9228.40*** *p15*
Martin, Leonide 10; America, 1836 ***778.5*** *p366*
Martin, Lewis; New York, NY, 1838 ***8208.4*** *p82*
Martin, Lewis 34; Philadelphia, 1774 ***1219.7*** *p183*
Martin, Louis 22; New Orleans, 1830 ***778.5*** *p366*
Martin, Louis 37; New Orleans, 1838 ***778.5*** *p366*
Martin, Louis 38; New Orleans, 1830 ***778.5*** *p366*
Martin, Louis 40; New Orleans, 1823 ***778.5*** *p366*
Martin, Louis 40; New Orleans, 1826 ***778.5*** *p366*
Martin, Louis 40; Port uncertain, 1835 ***778.5*** *p366*
Martin, M. 23; Louisiana, 1820 ***778.5*** *p367*
Martin, Marcella; New York, NY, 1816 ***2859.11*** *p38*
Martin, Margaret *SEE* Martin, Alex
Martin, Margaret; Philadelphia, 1849 ***5704.8*** *p50*
Martin, Margaret; Philadelphia, 1866 ***5704.8*** *p214*
Martin, Margaret; Philadelphia, 1868 ***5704.8*** *p226*
Martin, Margaret; Quebec, 1851 ***4537.30*** *p80*
Martin, Margaret; Quebec, 1855 ***4537.30*** *p44*
Martin, Margaret; St. John, N.B., 1851 ***5704.8*** *p77*
Martin, Margaret 3; Quebec, 1858 ***5704.8*** *p138*
Martin, Margaret 4; Massachusetts, 1848 ***5881.1*** *p71*
Martin, Margaret 15; St. John, N.B., 1862 ***5704.8*** *p150*
Martin, Margaret 22; Quebec, 1853 ***5704.8*** *p105*
Martin, Margaret 54; Philadelphia, 1864 ***5704.8*** *p160*
Martin, Maria 32; New Orleans, 1838 ***778.5*** *p367*
Martin, Martha; New York, NY, 1815 ***2859.11*** *p38*
Martin, Martha; Philadelphia, 1811 ***53.26*** *p49*
Martin, Martha; Philadelphia, 1811 ***2859.11*** *p17*
Martin, Martha 1; Quebec, 1858 ***5704.8*** *p138*
Martin, Martha 70; Wilmington, DE, 1831 ***6508.7*** *p160*
Martin, Martin 22; St. John, N.B., 1862 ***5704.8*** *p150*
Martin, Martin 81; South Carolina, 1850 ***1639.20*** *p231*
Martin, Mary *SEE* Martin, Alex
Martin, Mary; America, 1742 ***4971*** *p17*
Martin, Mary; America, 1865 ***5704.8*** *p195*
Martin, Mary; Annapolis, MD, 1742 ***4971*** *p92*
Martin, Mary; Maryland, 1742 ***4971*** *p107*
Martin, Mary; Quebec, 1855 ***4537.30*** *p9*
Martin, Mary; St. John, N.B., 1851 ***5704.8*** *p77*
Martin, Mary; Virginia, 1623-1648 ***6219*** *p252*
Martin, Mary 6; Massachusetts, 1850 ***5881.1*** *p73*
Martin, Mary 10; Quebec, 1859 ***5704.8*** *p143*
Martin, Mary 11; St. John, N.B., 1862 ***5704.8*** *p150*
Martin, Mary 20; Philadelphia, 1861 ***5704.8*** *p148*
Martin, Mary 25; Philadelphia, 1864 ***5704.8*** *p160*
Martin, Mary 30; Quebec, 1859 ***5704.8*** *p143*
Martin, Mary 41; America, 1838 ***778.5*** *p367*
Martin, Mary 60; Massachusetts, 1850 ***5881.1*** *p73*
Martin, Mary A. 4; Massachusetts, 1849 ***5881.1*** *p71*
Martin, Mary Ann 17; Quebec, 1857 ***5704.8*** *p136*
Martin, Mary Ann 25; St. John, N.B., 1856 ***5704.8*** *p131*
Martin, Mary Jane 20; Quebec, 1854 ***5704.8*** *p121*
Martin, Mary MacRae *SEE* Martin, Alex
Martin, Mich.; America, 1740 ***4971*** *p30*
Martin, Michael; New York, NY, 1833 ***8208.4*** *p43*
Martin, Michael; New York, NY, 1835 ***8208.4*** *p6*
Martin, Michael 1; Massachusetts, 1847 ***5881.1*** *p70*
Martin, Nancy; New York, NY, 1811 ***2859.11*** *p17*
Martin, Nancy 12; Philadelphia, 1864 ***5704.8*** *p161*
Martin, Nancy 60; South Carolina, 1850 ***1639.20*** *p231*
Martin, Nathan; Virginia, 1636 ***6219*** *p20*
Martin, Nathaniel; New York, NY, 1838 ***8208.4*** *p86*
Martin, Nathaniel; Virginia, 1637 ***6219*** *p37*
Martin, Nich.; Virginia, 1636 ***6219*** *p26*
Martin, Nich.; Virginia, 1638 ***6219*** *p122*
Martin, Nich.; Virginia, 1642 ***6219*** *p191*
Martin, Nicholas; Virginia, 1638 ***6219*** *p121*
Martin, Nicholas 52; Kansas, 1884 ***5240.1*** *p67*
Martin, Nick 52; Kansas, 1884 ***5240.1*** *p29*
Martin, Nicolas; Acadia, 1799 ***7603*** *p47*
Martin, Nicolas 17; America, 1836 ***778.5*** *p367*
Martin, Nicolas 32; New Orleans, 1838 ***778.5*** *p367*
Martin, Nicolaus; Wisconsin, n.d. ***9675.6*** *p268*
Martin, Owen 15; Philadelphia, 1864 ***5704.8*** *p161*
Martin, Owen 60; Philadelphia, 1864 ***5704.8*** *p160*
Martin, P. 50; New Orleans, 1824 ***778.5*** *p367*
Martin, Pat. Golrick; New York, NY, 1815 ***2859.11*** *p38*
Martin, Patrick; Philadelphia, 1848 ***5704.8*** *p40*
Martin, Patrick; St. John, N.B., 1849 ***5704.8*** *p56*
Martin, Patrick 4; Quebec, 1849 ***5704.8*** *p51*
Martin, Paul B. 64; America, 1838 ***778.5*** *p367*
Martin, Peggy 12; Philadelphia, 1864 ***5704.8*** *p160*
Martin, Peter; Wisconsin, n.d. ***9675.6*** *p268*
Martin, Peter 35; Virginia, 1774 ***1219.7*** *p241*
Martin, Peter, Jr. 32; Kansas, 1876 ***5240.1*** *p58*
Martin, Philip; New York, NY, 1838 ***8208.4*** *p85*
Martin, Philip 21; Pennsylvania, 1738 ***3690.1*** *p150*
Martin, Phillip; Virginia, 1648 ***6219*** *p246*
Martin, Pierre Mathieu 22; Port uncertain, 1838 ***778.5*** *p367*
Martin, Rachel; New York, NY, 1815 ***2859.11*** *p38*
Martin, Rachel 36; Quebec, 1858 ***5704.8*** *p138*
Martin, Ralph 16; Maryland, 1736 ***3690.1*** *p150*
Martin, Richd.; Virginia, 1642 ***6219*** *p191*
Martin, Robert; Iowa, 1866-1943 ***123.54*** *p33*
Martin, Robert; New York, NY, 1816 ***2859.11*** *p38*
Martin, Robert; Virginia, 1635 ***6219*** *p72*
Martin, Robert; Virginia, 1638 ***6219*** *p118*
Martin, Robert; Virginia, 1638 ***6219*** *p124*
*Wife:*Elizabeth
Martin, Robert; Virginia, 1643 ***6219*** *p204*
Martin, Robert 8; Quebec, 1859 ***5704.8*** *p143*
Martin, Robert 10; Quebec, 1852 ***5704.8*** *p86*
Martin, Robert 10; Quebec, 1852 ***5704.8*** *p90*
Martin, Robert 20; Quebec, 1863 ***5704.8*** *p153*
Martin, Robert 21; Maryland, 1774 ***1219.7*** *p220*
Martin, Robert 23; Antigua (Antego), 1774 ***1219.7*** *p238*
Martin, Robert 26; Georgia, 1775 ***1219.7*** *p276*
Martin, Robert 40; Quebec, 1859 ***5704.8*** *p143*
Martin, Roderick 6; Quebec, 1849 ***5704.8*** *p51*
Martin, Roger 55; Philadelphia, 1864 ***5704.8*** *p160*
Martin, Rossine 4; New Orleans, 1838 ***778.5*** *p367*
Martin, Saddie May; Washington, 1859-1920 ***2872.1*** *p25*
Martin, Sam John; Arkansas, 1918 ***95.2*** *p80*
Martin, Sameul; Philadelphia, 1811 ***53.26*** *p49*
Martin, Samuel; New York, 1817 ***9892.11*** *p28*
Martin, Samuel; New York, NY, 1838 ***8208.4*** *p61*
Martin, Samuel; Ohio, 1825 ***9892.11*** *p28*
Martin, Samuel; Philadelphia, 1811 ***2859.11*** *p17*
Martin, Sarah 12; St. John, N.B., 1851 ***5704.8*** *p79*
Martin, Sarah 71 *SEE* Martin, Daniel
Martin, Sebastian; America, 1842 ***1450.2*** *p93A*
Martin, Seraphine 31; New Orleans, 1825 ***778.5*** *p367*
Martin, Sheelah 19; Philadelphia, 1864 ***5704.8*** *p160*
Martin, Susan 2; St. John, N.B., 1851 ***5704.8*** *p79*
Martin, Terissa 22; St. John, N.B., 1857 ***5704.8*** *p134*
Martin, Thady; America, 1735-1743 ***4971*** *p78*
Martin, Thady; America, 1742 ***4971*** *p80*
Martin, Tho.; America, 1737 ***4971*** *p32*
Martin, Tho.; Virginia, 1636 ***6219*** *p34*
Martin, Tho.; Virginia, 1637 ***6219*** *p8*
Martin, Thomas; Kansas, 1883 ***5240.1*** *p29*
Martin, Thomas; New York, NY, 1811 ***2859.11*** *p17*
With family
Martin, Thomas; New York, NY, 1811 ***2859.11*** *p17*
Martin, Thomas; New York, NY, 1815 ***2859.11*** *p38*
Martin, Thomas; New York, NY, 1816 ***2859.11*** *p38*
Martin, Thomas; New York, NY, 1839 ***8208.4*** *p102*
Martin, Thomas; St. John, N.B., 1853 ***5704.8*** *p107*
Martin, Thomas; West Virginia, 1831-1840 ***9788.3*** *p15*
Martin, Thomas; West Virginia, 1846 ***9788.3*** *p16*
Martin, Thomas 23; Philadelphia, 1775 ***1219.7*** *p258*
Martin, Thos.; New York, NY, 1816 ***2859.11*** *p38*
Martin, Tim; Colorado, 1904 ***9678.2*** *p126*
Martin, W. F.; Washington, 1859-1920 ***2872.1*** *p25*
Martin, W. S.; Washington, 1859-1920 ***2872.1*** *p25*
Martin, Walter 17; Maryland or Virginia, 1734 ***3690.1*** *p150*
Martin, William *SEE* Martin, Alex
Martin, William; New Orleans, 1853 ***2896.5*** *p26*
Martin, William; New York, 1860 ***2896.5*** *p26*
Martin, William; New York, NY, 1815 ***2859.11*** *p38*
Martin, William; New York, NY, 1816 ***2859.11*** *p38*
Martin, William; New York, NY, 1865 ***5704.8*** *p194*
Martin, William; Philadelphia, 1816 ***2859.11*** *p38*
Martin, William; Philadelphia, 1849 ***5704.8*** *p50*
Martin, William; Quebec, 1849 ***5704.8*** *p52*
Martin, William; Virginia, 1638 ***6219*** *p120*
Martin, William; Washington, 1859-1920 ***2872.1*** *p25*
Martin, William; Wisconsin, n.d. ***9675.6*** *p268*
Martin, William 9; Quebec, 1858 ***5704.8*** *p138*
Martin, William 13; Quebec, 1854 ***5704.8*** *p121*
Martin, William 16; Virginia, 1720 ***3690.1*** *p150*
Martin, William 17; Philadelphia, 1864 ***5704.8*** *p160*
Martin, William 21; Maryland, 1774 ***1219.7*** *p224*
Martin, William 21; Philadelphia, 1861 ***5704.8*** *p147*
Martin, William 30; Quebec, 1856 ***5704.8*** *p130*
Martin, William 33; Quebec, 1864 ***5704.8*** *p164*
Martin, William 36; Maryland, 1774 ***1219.7*** *p204*
Martin, William 50; St. John, N.B., 1862 ***5704.8*** *p150*
Martin, William 51; Philadelphia, 1864 ***5704.8*** *p161*
Martin, William Stewart 5; Quebec, 1859 ***5704.8*** *p143*
Martin, Willm.; Virginia, 1646 ***6219*** *p240*
Martine, Alexander 16; Jamaica, 1733 ***3690.1*** *p150*
Martine, Jas.; America, 1792 ***8894.2*** *p55*
Martine, Margaret *SEE* Martine, William
Martine, William; Philadelphia, 1849 ***53.26*** *p50*
*Relative:*Margaret
Martineau, Mr.; Quebec, 1815 ***9229.18*** *p77*
Martinelli, Constantino; California, 1876 ***2764.35*** *p45*
Martines, Joseph; Arkansas, 1918 ***95.2*** *p80*
Martines, P. A. 24; Port uncertain, 1839 ***778.5*** *p367*
Martinet, M. 27; Mobile, AL, 1837 ***778.5*** *p368*
Martinez, Francisco; Kansas, 1914 ***6013.40*** *p16*
Martinez, Juan Francisco 31; California, 1873 ***2769.10*** *p5*
Martinez, M. 40; Arizona, 1907 ***9228.40*** *p13*
Martinez, Mariano 25; Port uncertain, 1837 ***778.5*** *p368*
Martinez, William D.; Arizona, 1882 ***2764.35*** *p47*
Martini, Giovanni; Arkansas, 1918 ***95.2*** *p80*
Martini, Moritz; Wisconsin, n.d. ***9675.6*** *p268*
Martini, Morritz; Wisconsin, n.d. ***9675.6*** *p268*
Martini, Robert F.L.; Wisconsin, n.d. ***9675.6*** *p268*
Martinier, Annette 26; New Orleans, 1837 ***778.5*** *p368*
Martinier, Antoine 40; Port uncertain, 1836 ***778.5*** *p368*
Martinier, Jean 34; Port uncertain, 1836 ***778.5*** *p368*
Martinier, Jean 36; New Orleans, 1837 ***778.5*** *p368*
Martino, Sam 22; Arkansas, 1918 ***95.2*** *p80*
Martinopulos, Sam John; Arkansas, 1918 ***95.2*** *p80*
Martinovic, Nicola 48; New York, NY, 1893 ***9026.4*** *p42*
Martins, J.A.; Bangor, ME, 1888 ***6410.22*** *p126*
Martins, John A.; Bangor, ME, 1885-1894 ***6410.22*** *p121*
Martinsky, Peter; Arkansas, 1918 ***95.2*** *p80*
Martinson, Nels 33; Kansas, 1871 ***5240.1*** *p29*
Martinson, Nels 33; Kansas, 1871 ***5240.1*** *p51*
Martinson, Olma; Kansas, 1869 ***5240.1*** *p29*
Martis, Charli; Wisconsin, n.d. ***9675.6*** *p268*
Martlage, Henry; New York, 1892 ***1450.2*** *p24B*
Martledon, Math.; Virginia, 1635 ***6219*** *p26*
Martorell, Juan; California, 1871 ***2769.7*** *p3*
Martson, Andrew; Illinois, 1886 ***5012.39*** *p120*
Marty, Charles Joseph; Illinois, 1891 ***2896.5*** *p26*
Marty, John J.; Illinois, 1872 ***2896.5*** *p26*
Marty, John J.; Illinois, 1888 ***2896.5*** *p26*
Marty, Louis; Ohio, 1869-1887 ***8582*** *p20*
Martyn, Elizabeth *SEE* Martyn, Robert
Martyn, Patience; Virginia, 1641 ***6219*** *p185*
Martyn, Robert; Virginia, 1638 ***6219*** *p124*
*Wife:*Elizabeth
Martz, August Christian; Arkansas, 1918 ***95.2*** *p80*
Martz, William C. F.; Washington, 1859-1920 ***2872.1*** *p25*
Maruit, Mr. 32; New Orleans, 1839 ***778.5*** *p368*
Maruth, John Baptist 42; New Orleans, 1836 ***778.5*** *p368*
Marvelli, Rock; Arkansas, 1918 ***95.2*** *p80*
Marx, Abraham 18; America, 1854-1855 ***9162.6*** *p105*
Marx, Bruno; Arkansas, 1918 ***95.2*** *p80*
Marx, Carl 30; Kansas, 1900 ***5240.1*** *p81*
Marx, Carl J.; America, 1892 ***5240.1*** *p29*
Marx, Caroline Louise Wilh. *SEE* Marx, Wilhelm
Marx, Friedrich Carl *SEE* Marx, Wilhelm
Marx, Fritz 28; Kansas, 1892 ***5240.1*** *p77*
Marx, Guido; Toledo, OH, 1875 ***8582.2*** *p52*
Marx, Heinrich; America, 1851 ***8582.3*** *p43*
Marx, Heinrich Carl *SEE* Marx, Wilhelm
Marx, Issac; Shreveport, LA, 1876 ***7129*** *p45*
Marx, Louise Ruschmeier 36 *SEE* Marx, Wilhelm
Marx, Magdalena 24; Philadelphia, 1752 ***4525*** *p232*
*Sister:*Maria Catharina 22
Marx, Maria Catharina 22 *SEE* Marx, Magdalena
Marx, Salomon; America, 1849 ***8582.3*** *p43*
Marx, Wilhelm *SEE* Marx, Wilhelm
Marx, Wilhelm; America, 1865 ***4610.10*** *p105*
*Wife:*Louise Ruschmeier 36
*Child:*Wilhelm
*Child:*Heinrich Carl
*Child:*Friedrich Carl
*Child:*Caroline Louise Wilh.
Mary, Miss 10; New Orleans, 1829 ***778.5*** *p368*
Marz, David; Illinois, 1866 ***5012.38*** *p98*
Marz, Frederick; South Dakota, 1889 ***1641*** *p41*
Marz, Katharina; South Dakota, 1889 ***1641*** *p41*
Marzahn, Fred; Illinois, 1888 ***2896.5*** *p26*
Marzahn, Louis; Illinois, 1884 ***2896.5*** *p26*
Marzahn, Ludwig; Illinois, 1884 ***2896.5*** *p26*

Marzahn, Ludwig; Illinois, 1885 ***2896.5*** *p26*
Marzan, Herman; Illinois, 1884 ***2896.5*** *p26*
Marzini, John; Wisconsin, n.d. ***9675.6*** *p268*
Mas, Francis; New York, NY, 1836 ***8208.4*** *p9*
Masan, Jacob; Missouri, 1849 ***6013.19*** *p74*
Mascagin, Serafino 22; Arkansas, 1918 ***95.2*** *p80*
Mascagni, Gallieo; Iowa, 1866-1943 ***123.54*** *p33*
Mascall, Joseph; Jamaica, 1770 ***1219.7*** *p147*
Mascall, William; Virginia, 1642 ***6219*** *p197*
Mascari, Frank; New Orleans, 1882 ***1450.2*** *p93A*
Mascaro, Francesco; Iowa, 1866-1943 ***123.54*** *p33*
Maschhaupt, Anne Marie E. Nagel *SEE* Maschhaupt, Johann Friedrich
Maschhaupt, Ernst Heinrich Friedrich; America, 1849 ***4610.10*** *p98*
Maschhaupt, Johann Friedrich; America, 1853 ***4610.10*** *p98*
*Wife:*Anne Marie E. Nagel
Maschhoff, Heinrich; Illinois, 1840-1890 ***4610.10*** *p59*
Maschke, Frederick Wilhelm; Washington, 1859-1920 ***2872.1*** *p25*
Maschke, Martin; Washington, 1859-1920 ***2872.1*** *p25*
Maschke, Martin Louis; Washington, 1859-1920 ***2872.1*** *p25*
Maschke, Regina Gert; Washington, 1859-1920 ***2872.1*** *p25*
Maschkowitz, Fren 18; New York, NY, 1878 ***9253*** *p47*
Maschmeier, . . .; New York, NY, 1867 ***3702.7*** *p587*
Maschmeier, Wilhelm 18; New York, NY, 1867 ***3702.7*** *p571*
Maschweg, . . .; Canada, 1776-1783 ***9786*** *p28*
Mascoll, Rich.; Virginia, 1618 ***6219*** *p72*
Mascoll, Rich.; Virginia, 1634 ***6219*** *p105*
Mascoll, Richard; Virginia, 1638 ***6219*** *p147*
Mascow, John; Virginia, 1846 ***4626.16*** *p13*
Mascrow, Alice 21; Massachusetts, 1847 ***5881.1*** *p62*
Masdal, Tom; Arkansas, 1918 ***95.2*** *p80*
Mase, J. 34; America, 1838 ***778.5*** *p368*
Mase, Phillip; Iowa, 1866-1943 ***123.54*** *p33*
Maseckis, Barbara; Wisconsin, n.d. ***9675.6*** *p268*
Masen, Christopher 45; Kansas, 1878 ***5240.1*** *p59*
Maser, . . .; Pennsylvania, n.d. ***2444*** *p188*
Maser, Gallus *SEE* Maser, Jacob
Maser, Jacob; Port uncertain, 1736-1800 ***2444*** *p188*
*Wife:*Magdalena
*Child:*Gallus
*Child:*Matthaus
Maser, Magdalena *SEE* Maser, Jacob
Maser, Magdalena *SEE* Maser, Magdalena
Maser, Magdalena; Pennsylvania, 1750-1800 ***2444*** *p188*
*Child:*Magdalena
Maser, Matthaus *SEE* Maser, Jacob
Masgarke, Jaques; Virginia, 1642 ***6219*** *p186*
Mash, Joseph; Quebec, 1809 ***7603*** *p30*
Mash, Thomas; Virginia, 1638 ***6219*** *p125*
Mashman, Samuel 36; Maryland, 1774 ***1219.7*** *p235*
Masi, Petro; Arkansas, 1918 ***95.2*** *p80*
Maskal, George; America, 1895 ***7137*** *p169*
Maskal, Henry 19; Carolina, 1774 ***1219.7*** *p179*
Maske, Albert; Wisconsin, n.d. ***9675.6*** *p268*
Maske, Carl; Wisconsin, n.d. ***9675.6*** *p268*
Maske, Robert; Illinois, 1866 ***2896.5*** *p28*
Maskulka, John; America, 1893 ***7137*** *p169*
Maslanka, Wojciech 20; New York, 1912 ***9980.29*** *p60*
Maslerz, Adalbert; Iowa, 1866-1943 ***123.54*** *p69*
Masles, George; Iowa, 1866-1943 ***123.54*** *p69*
Masles, Mary; Iowa, 1866-1943 ***123.54*** *p69*
Maslowski, Marcel A.; Arkansas, 1918 ***95.2*** *p80*
Masner, John George; New York, 1750 ***3652*** *p74*
Masnin, Jean 25; America, 1838 ***778.5*** *p368*
Mason, . . .; Halifax, N.S., 1752 ***7074.6*** *p230*
Mason, Mr.; Quebec, 1815 ***9229.18*** *p80*
With wife
Mason, Abraham 43; Nova Scotia, 1774 ***1219.7*** *p194*
Mason, Albert; Colorado, 1894 ***9678.2*** *p126*
Mason, Ann; Virginia, 1621 ***6219*** *p25*
Mason, Ann; Virginia, 1642 ***6219*** *p191*
Mason, Caroline F. 21; Massachusetts, 1860 ***6410.32*** *p108*
Mason, Charles; Virginia, 1637 ***6219*** *p113*
Mason, Daniel; New York, NY, 1815 ***2859.11*** *p38*
Mason, Edward 18; Virginia, 1720 ***3690.1*** *p150*
Mason, Francis; Virginia, 1642 ***6219*** *p191*
*Wife:*Mary
Mason, Francis 33; Nova Scotia, 1774 ***1219.7*** *p209*
Mason, Francois 26; Halifax, N.S., 1752 ***7074.6*** *p207*
Mason, Frederick 31; Halifax, N.S., 1752 ***7074.6*** *p207*
With family of 5
Mason, George 28; Kansas, 1871 ***5240.1*** *p51*
Mason, Grace 21; Barbados, 1724 ***3690.1*** *p150*
Mason, Henry; Virginia, 1646 ***6219*** *p242*
Mason, James; Virginia, 1638 ***6219*** *p124*
Mason, James 19; Maryland, 1720 ***3690.1*** *p150*
Mason, Jane 25; Maryland, 1775 ***1219.7*** *p254*
Mason, Jno; Maryland or Virginia, 1698 ***2212*** *p5*
Mason, John; Nevis, 1753 ***1219.7*** *p23*
Mason, John; Virginia, 1641 ***6219*** *p187*
Mason, John; Virginia, 1642 ***6219*** *p192*
Mason, John 20; New England, 1721 ***3690.1*** *p150*
Mason, John 21; Philadelphia, 1774 ***1219.7*** *p232*
Mason, Jon.; Virginia, 1636 ***6219*** *p74*
Mason, Jon.; Virginia, 1637 ***6219*** *p108*
Mason, Jon.; Virginia, 1643 ***6219*** *p201*
Mason, Marmaduke 22; Virginia, 1774 ***1219.7*** *p242*
Mason, Mary *SEE* Mason, Francis
Mason, Peter; Virginia, 1628 ***6219*** *p9*
Mason, Peter; Virginia, 1751 ***1219.7*** *p1*
Mason, Peter; Washington, 1859-1920 ***2872.1*** *p25*
Mason, Richard 15; Maryland, 1775 ***1219.7*** *p253*
Mason, Robert; Charleston, SC, 1768 ***1639.20*** *p231*
Mason, Robert; Virginia, 1635 ***6219*** *p25*
Mason, Robert; Virginia, 1639 ***6219*** *p161*
Mason, Robert; Virginia, 1642 ***6219*** *p195*
Mason, Robert 17; Virginia, 1775 ***1219.7*** *p247*
Mason, Rose 23; Maryland, 1775 ***1219.7*** *p257*
Mason, Samuel; New York, NY, 1836 ***8208.4*** *p13*
Mason, Tho.; Virginia, 1646 ***6219*** *p236*
Mason, Thomas; New England, 1816 ***2859.11*** *p38*
With wife
Mason, Thomas 20; Jamaica, 1733 ***3690.1*** *p150*
Mason, Thomas 28; Maryland, 1735 ***3690.1*** *p150*
Mason, Thomas H.; New York, NY, 1836 ***8208.4*** *p13*
Mason, William; New York, NY, 1839 ***8208.4*** *p102*
Mason, William; Virginia, 1646 ***6219*** *p240*
Mason, Wm; America, 1698 ***2212*** *p5*
Masotos, Teddy Broun; Arkansas, 1918 ***95.2*** *p81*
Mass, Miss; New Orleans, 1839 ***778.5*** *p368*
Massa, Domenik; Iowa, 1866-1943 ***123.54*** *p33*
Massa, Joseph; Arkansas, 1918 ***95.2*** *p81*
Massabro, Mikelle; Arkansas, 1918 ***95.2*** *p81*
Massard, . . .; Cincinnati, 1816 ***8582.3*** *p89*
Massard, Johann M.; Cincinnati, 1824 ***8582.1*** *p51*
Massat, Joseph 18; New Orleans, 1836 ***778.5*** *p368*
Masschmeier, Wilhelm; New York, NY, 1867 ***3702.7*** *p579*
Masse, Mr.; New Orleans, 1839 ***778.5*** *p368*
Masse, Mr. 31; Port uncertain, 1836 ***778.5*** *p369*
Masse, Francois 30; Port uncertain, 1821 ***778.5*** *p369*
Masseo, Rizzolo; Iowa, 1866-1943 ***123.54*** *p33*
Masser, Anna Maria *SEE* Masser, Christian
Masser, Anna Maria *SEE* Masser, Jacob
Masser, Anna Maria Brodbeck *SEE* Masser, Christian
Masser, Catharina *SEE* Masser, Jacob
Masser, Christian; Port uncertain, 1743-1800 ***2444*** *p188*
*Wife:*Anna Maria Brodbeck
*Child:*Anna Maria
Masser, Jacob; Pennsylvania, 1748-1800 ***2444*** *p188*
*Wife:*Anna Maria
*Child:*Catharina
Masserback, Felix; Virginia, 1775 ***1219.7*** *p275*
Masserly, Daniel; Philadelphia, 1762 ***9973.7*** *p36*
Massey, Albert; Iowa, 1866-1943 ***123.54*** *p33*
Massey, Elizabeth 21; Maryland, 1733 ***3690.1*** *p151*
Massey, John 45; Maryland, 1730 ***3690.1*** *p151*
Massey, Richard; Ohio, 1845 ***9892.11*** *p28*
Massey, Richard; Ohio, 1848 ***9892.11*** *p28*
Massey, Walter; Iowa, 1866-1943 ***123.54*** *p33*
Massey, William; New York, NY, 1839 ***8208.4*** *p96*
Massey, Wm.; Iowa, 1866-1943 ***123.54*** *p33*
Masshmeier, Wilhelm; Indianapolis, 1868 ***3702.7*** *p582*
Massimelliano, Pellin; Iowa, 1866-1943 ***123.54*** *p33*
Massin, Agnes 22; America, 1837 ***778.5*** *p369*
Massmann, Louis; Cincinnati, 1869-1887 ***8582*** *p20*
Masson, . . .; Halifax, N.S., 1752 ***7074.6*** *p230*
Masson, Mr. 24; America, 1836 ***778.5*** *p369*
Masson, A. 23; New Orleans, 1837 ***778.5*** *p369*
Masson, Andrew; America, 1816 ***8893*** *p265*
Masson, Catherine *SEE* Masson, Frederic
Masson, Catherine *SEE* Masson, Frederic
Masson, Francois 26; Halifax, N.S., 1752 ***7074.6*** *p211*
Masson, Frederic 31; Halifax, N.S., 1752 ***7074.6*** *p211*
*Wife:*Catherine
*Child:*Pierre
*Child:*Catherine
*Child:*Henriette
*Child:*Nanette
Masson, Henriette *SEE* Masson, Frederic
Masson, Mary 20; Virginia, 1700 ***2212*** *p30*
Masson, Nanette *SEE* Masson, Frederic
Masson, Nicolas 37; America, 1839 ***778.5*** *p369*
Masson, Pierre *SEE* Masson, Frederic
Masstin, Robert 28; Maryland, 1774 ***1219.7*** *p212*
Mast, Jacob, Jr.; Ohio, 1840 ***9892.11*** *p28*
Mast, John; Ohio, 1840 ***9892.11*** *p28*
Mast, Joseph; Illinois, 1834 ***8582.1*** *p55*
Mast, Michael; Illinois, 1828 ***8582.1*** *p54*
Mast, Peter; New York, 1833 ***9892.11*** *p28*
Mast, Peter; Ohio, 1839 ***9892.11*** *p28*
Mastello, Antonio; Colorado, 1904 ***9678.2*** *p126*
Masterman, Ellen 20; Maryland or Virginia, 1699 ***2212*** *p22*
Masters, Robert; Virginia, 1638 ***6219*** *p124*
Masters, Thomas; Virginia, 1639 ***6219*** *p159*
Masterson, Ann; New York, NY, 1811 ***2859.11*** *p17*
Masterson, Bernard; Quebec, 1824 ***7603*** *p83*
Masterson, Bridget 49; Massachusetts, 1848 ***5881.1*** *p63*
Masterson, Charles; New York, 1820 ***9892.11*** *p28*
Masterson, Charles; New York, NY, 1816 ***2859.11*** *p38*
Masterson, Edward; New York, NY, 1811 ***2859.11*** *p17*
Masterson, Hannah 20; Massachusetts, 1849 ***5881.1*** *p67*
Masterson, Hugh; New York, NY, 1815 ***2859.11*** *p38*
Masterson, James; New York, NY, 1838 ***8208.4*** *p87*
Masterson, James 9; Massachusetts, 1849 ***5881.1*** *p68*
Masterson, James 36; Maryland, 1774 ***1219.7*** *p235*
Masterson, John; America, 1743 ***4971*** *p18*
Masterson, John 10; America, 1866 ***5704.8*** *p210*
Masterson, Mary 29; Philadelphia, 1858 ***5704.8*** *p139*
Masterson, Patrick; Albany, NY, 1831 ***9892.11*** *p29*
Masterson, Patrick; New York, NY, 1816 ***2859.11*** *p38*
Masterson, Patrick; New York, NY, 1828 ***9892.11*** *p29*
Masterson, Patrick; New York, NY, 1835 ***8208.4*** *p7*
Masterson, Patrick; Ohio, 1833 ***9892.11*** *p29*
Masterson, Patrick; Ohio, 1840 ***9892.11*** *p29*
Masterson, Thomas; Ohio, 1856 ***9892.11*** *p29*
Masterton, William 29; Kansas, 1870 ***5240.1*** *p51*
Mastin, Frederick R.; Illinois, 1860 ***7857*** *p5*
Maston, Wm.; Virginia, 1642 ***6219*** *p196*
Mastoras, Sparo; Arkansas, 1918 ***95.2*** *p81*
Mastron, Philipp; Ohio, 1798-1818 ***8582.2*** *p54*
Masuilis, Petras; Arkansas, 1918 ***95.2*** *p81*
Mat, John; Wisconsin, n.d. ***9675.6*** *p268*
Mataija, Tony; Iowa, 1866-1943 ***123.54*** *p33*
Matassi, Caroline 32; Port uncertain, 1836 ***778.5*** *p369*
Matcovich, Stef; Iowa, 1866-1943 ***123.54*** *p33*
Matczak, Josef 27; New York, 1912 ***9980.29*** *p68*
*Wife:*Maryanna 24
*Son:*Maryan 2
Matczak, Maryan 2 *SEE* Matczak, Josef
Matczak, Maryanna 24 *SEE* Matczak, Josef
Mateer, Michael; Wisconsin, n.d. ***9675.6*** *p268*
Matejovic, Adam; Iowa, 1866-1943 ***123.54*** *p33*
Matena, Henry; Illinois, 1893 ***5012.40*** *p53*
Mater, Charles 26; Virginia, 1774 ***1219.7*** *p201*
Materski, . . .; New York, 1831 ***4606*** *p175*
Mathai, Joseph; Wisconsin, n.d. ***9675.6*** *p268*
Matharan, J. P. 24; Port uncertain, 1839 ***778.5*** *p369*
Matharan, Louis 25; Port uncertain, 1839 ***778.5*** *p369*
Mathason, Alexander 27; Philadelphia, 1774 ***1219.7*** *p216*
Mathede, Louis 46; America, 1831 ***778.5*** *p369*
Mathemeier, Caroline Justine Charlotte; America, 1890 ***4610.10*** *p103*
Mathemeyer, Ernst Friedrich Wilhelm; America, 1869 ***4610.10*** *p100*
Mather, Mme. 35; America, 1820 ***778.5*** *p369*
Mather, Eliza 25; Philadelphia, 1774 ***1219.7*** *p212*
Mather, Isabella 76; North Carolina, 1850 ***1639.20*** *p231*
Mather, John; America, 1854 ***1450.2*** *p93A*
Mather, Maria 10; America, 1820 ***778.5*** *p369*
Mather, Richard; Pittsburgh, 1763 ***1219.7*** *p92*
Mather, Thursden; Virginia, 1698 ***2212*** *p12*
Matherell, William; Virginia, 1637 ***6219*** *p110*
Matherne, Joseph 49; America, 1839 ***778.5*** *p369*
Matheron, Mr. 26; America, 1838 ***778.5*** *p369*
Mathershaw, Joseph 21; Virginia, 1774 ***1219.7*** *p240*
Mathes, Nicholas; Illinois, 1848 ***7857*** *p5*
Matheson, Alexander; Carolina, 1750-1799 ***1639.20*** *p231*
Matheson, Allan *SEE* Matheson, Norman
Matheson, Angus; Quebec, 1855 ***4537.30*** *p17*
*Wife:*Effie MacDonald
*Child:*Kirsty
*Child:*John
*Child:*Peter
Matheson, Ann *SEE* Matheson, Donald
Matheson, Ann; Quebec, 1851 ***4537.30*** *p70*
Matheson, Ann MacAulay *SEE* Matheson, John
Matheson, Archie *SEE* Matheson, Donald
Matheson, C. 54; South Carolina, 1850 ***1639.20*** *p232*
Matheson, Catherine *SEE* Matheson, Donald
Matheson, Catherine *SEE* Matheson, Donald
Matheson, Catherine *SEE* Matheson, Norman
Matheson, Catherine MacKay *SEE* Matheson, Norman
Matheson, Daniel; Asheville, NC, 1764-1812 ***1639.20*** *p232*
Matheson, Daniel; Colorado, 1894 ***9678.2*** *p126*
Matheson, Donald *SEE* Matheson, Donald
Matheson, Donald *SEE* Matheson, Norman
Matheson, Donald; America, 1825 ***1639.20*** *p233*
Matheson, Donald; Charleston, SC, 1825 ***1639.20*** *p232*

Matheson, Donald; Colorado, 1905 ***9678.2*** *p126*
Matheson, Donald; Quebec, 1820-1841 ***4537.30*** *p17*
*Wife:*Kirsty MacDonald
Matheson, Donald; Quebec, 1860-1869 ***4537.30*** *p19*
Matheson, Donald; Quebec, 1863 ***4537.30*** *p17*
*Wife:*Mary MacMillan
*Child:*Catherine
*Child:*Archie
*Child:*John
Matheson, Donald; Quebec, 1873 ***4537.30*** *p19*
*Wife:*Mary Smith
*Child:*Murdo
*Child:*Ann
*Child:*Catherine
*Child:*Donald
*Child:*Norman
*Child:*Kirsty
Matheson, Duncan; Carolina, 1812 ***1639.20*** *p233*
Matheson, Effie MacDonald *SEE* Matheson, Angus
Matheson, Eoridh; Quebec, 1838 ***4537.30*** *p114*
Matheson, Flora; Quebec, 1841 ***4537.30*** *p85*
Matheson, Hugh 32; Wilmington, NC, 1774 ***1639.20*** *p232*
With wife
With child 8
With child 2
With child
*Sister:*Katherine 16
Matheson, James 38; North Carolina, 1775 ***1639.20*** *p232*
*Wife:*Jean McQuiston 27
*Child:*Margaret 4
Matheson, Jean McQuiston 27 *SEE* Matheson, James
Matheson, John *SEE* Matheson, Angus
Matheson, John *SEE* Matheson, Donald
Matheson, John *SEE* Matheson, John
Matheson, John *SEE* Matheson, Norman
Matheson, John; Quebec, 1872 ***4537.30*** *p18*
*Wife:*Ann MacAulay
*Child:*Norman
*Child:*John
*Child:*Mary
Matheson, John; South Carolina, 1822 ***1639.20*** *p232*
Matheson, Katherine 16 *SEE* Matheson, Hugh
Matheson, Kirsty *SEE* Matheson, Angus
Matheson, Kirsty *SEE* Matheson, Donald
Matheson, Kirsty; Quebec, 1851 ***4537.30*** *p98*
Matheson, Kirsty MacDonald *SEE* Matheson, Donald
Matheson, Malcolm *SEE* Matheson, Norman
Matheson, Malcolm; Quebec, 1848-1875 ***4537.30*** *p19*
Matheson, Margaret 4 *SEE* Matheson, James
Matheson, Mary *SEE* Matheson, John
Matheson, Mary; America, 1812 ***8893*** *p266*
Matheson, Mary; Quebec, 1851 ***4537.30*** *p51*
Matheson, Mary; Quebec, 1851 ***4537.30*** *p76*
Matheson, Mary; Quebec, 1851 ***4537.30*** *p88*
Matheson, Mary MacMillan *SEE* Matheson, Donald
Matheson, Mary Smith *SEE* Matheson, Donald
Matheson, Murdo *SEE* Matheson, Donald
Matheson, Norman *SEE* Matheson, Donald
Matheson, Norman *SEE* Matheson, John
Matheson, Norman; Quebec, 1855 ***4537.30*** *p18*
*Wife:*Catherine MacKay
*Child:*Catherine
*Child:*Donald
*Child:*John
*Child:*Malcolm
*Child:*Allan
With child
Matheson, Peter *SEE* Matheson, Angus
Matheson, Peter; Quebec, 1845 ***4537.30*** *p16*
Matheson, Roderick; Carolina, 1811 ***1639.20*** *p233*
Matheu, Aug..tin 18; Port uncertain, 1839 ***778.5*** *p369*
Matheuson, Alexander 11; St. John, N.B., 1862 ***5704.8*** *p150*
Matheuson, Alexander 27; St. John, N.B., 1862 ***5704.8*** *p150*
Matheuson, Ann 9; St. John, N.B., 1862 ***5704.8*** *p150*
Matheuson, Cristina 22; St. John, N.B., 1862 ***5704.8*** *p150*
Matheuson, Janet 4; St. John, N.B., 1862 ***5704.8*** *p150*
Matheuson, Lachcan 18; St. John, N.B., 1862 ***5704.8*** *p150*
Matheuson, Mary 47; St. John, N.B., 1862 ***5704.8*** *p150*
Matheuson, Peggy 7; St. John, N.B., 1862 ***5704.8*** *p150*
Matheuson, Peter 25; St. John, N.B., 1862 ***5704.8*** *p150*
Matheuson, William 54; St. John, N.B., 1862 ***5704.8*** *p150*
Mathew, Jon.; Virginia, 1637 ***6219*** *p11*
Mathew, Jon.; Virginia, 1637 ***6219*** *p114*
Mathew, Jon.; Virginia, 1639 ***6219*** *p154*
Mathew, Patrick; New York, NY, 1811 ***2859.11*** *p17*
Mathew, Peter 22; Maryland, 1774 ***1219.7*** *p220*
Mathewes, Jeane; Pennsylvania, 1682 ***4961*** *p165*
Mathews, Anth.; Virginia, 1638 ***6219*** *p117*
Mathews, Anth.; Virginia, 1638 ***6219*** *p150*
Mathews, Benjamin 15; Maryland, 1723 ***3690.1*** *p151*
Mathews, Elizabeth 5; New Orleans, 1849 ***5704.8*** *p59*
Mathews, Elizabeth 25 *SEE* Mathews, Thomas
Mathews, Ever; America, 1737 ***4971*** *p24*
Mathews, George; Colorado, 1903 ***9678.2*** *p126*
Mathews, Jacob; Virginia, 1647 ***6219*** *p244*
Mathews, James; America, 1737 ***4971*** *p24*
Mathews, Jane; America, 1738 ***4971*** *p36*
Mathews, Jno.; Virginia, 1648 ***6219*** *p250*
Mathews, John; Virginia, 1642 ***6219*** *p198*
Mathews, John 15; Jamaica, 1730 ***3690.1*** *p151*
Mathews, John 17; Virginia, 1700 ***2212*** *p30*
Mathews, John 25; Maryland, 1774 ***1219.7*** *p180*
Mathews, John 26; Philadelphia, 1775 ***1219.7*** *p255*
Mathews, Jon.; Virginia, 1635 ***6219*** *p70*
Mathews, Jon.; Virginia, 1637 ***6219*** *p180*
Mathews, Mary; America, 1867 ***5704.8*** *p215*
Mathews, Mary 12; Massachusetts, 1848 ***5881.1*** *p71*
Mathews, Mary 26; Philadelphia, 1774 ***1219.7*** *p212*
Mathews, Mary A.; New York, NY, 1868 ***5704.8*** *p228*
Mathews, Mary Ann 9 mos; New Orleans, 1849 ***5704.8*** *p59*
Mathews, Mic.; America, 1737 ***4971*** *p68*
Mathews, Michael; New York, NY, 1816 ***2859.11*** *p38*
Mathews, Patrick; America, 1739 ***4971*** *p14*
Mathews, Rich.; Virginia, 1637 ***6219*** *p114*
Mathews, Richard; Virginia, 1643 ***6219*** *p207*
Mathews, Richard 21; Maryland, 1774 ***1219.7*** *p192*
Mathews, Robert; Virginia, 1643 ***6219*** *p204*
Mathews, Robert 16; Jamaica, 1749 ***3690.1*** *p151*
Mathews, Robert 20; Quebec, 1854 ***5704.8*** *p121*
Mathews, Roger; Virginia, 1639 ***6219*** *p152*
Mathews, Rose; New Orleans, 1849 ***5704.8*** *p59*
Mathews, Sally 7; New Orleans, 1849 ***5704.8*** *p59*
Mathews, Stephen; New York, NY, 1811 ***2859.11*** *p17*
With wife
Mathews, Tho 9; America, 1700 ***2212*** *p31*
Mathews, Thomas; New York, NY, 1811 ***2859.11*** *p17*
With family
Mathews, Thomas; New York, NY, 1815 ***2859.11*** *p38*
Mathews, Thomas; Virginia, 1639 ***6219*** *p152*
Mathews, Thomas 25; Philadelphia, 1774 ***1219.7*** *p212*
Mathews, Thomas 27; Philadelphia, 1803 ***53.26*** *p50*
*Relative:*Elizabeth 25
Mathews, William; Virginia, 1638 ***6219*** *p120*
Mathews, William 25; Maryland, 1775 ***1219.7*** *p257*
Mathewson, Clark; New York, NY, 1816 ***2859.11*** *p38*
Mathewson, David; New York, NY, 1816 ***2859.11*** *p38*
Mathewson, Margaret; St. John, N.B., 1847 ***5704.8*** *p35*
Mathewson, Wil.; New York, NY, 1811 ***2859.11*** *p17*
Mathey, Frederick 21; Maryland, 1774 ***1219.7*** *p230*
Mathey, Louis; New York, NY, 1834 ***8208.4*** *p57*
Mathias, David; America, 1857 ***1450.2*** *p93A*
Mathias, Hermann; Illinois, 1893 ***5012.40*** *p53*
Mathias, Johannes; Ohio, 1798-1818 ***8582.2*** *p54*
Mathias, Louis 16; New Orleans, 1836 ***778.5*** *p370*
Mathier, John 30; America, 1836 ***778.5*** *p370*
Mathiesen, Ivar Viggo Jensen; Arkansas, 1918 ***95.2*** *p81*
Mathieson, Alexander; Charleston, SC, 1830 ***1639.20*** *p232*
Mathieson, Duncan; Charleston, SC, 1744-1830 ***1639.20*** *p233*
Mathieson, Iver Viggo Jensen; Arkansas, 1918 ***95.2*** *p81*
Mathieu, Mme. 35; America, 1820 ***778.5*** *p369*
Mathieu, Mr. 27; New Orleans, 1839 ***778.5*** *p370*
Mathieu, Mr. 34; Port uncertain, 1836 ***778.5*** *p370*
Mathieu, Mr. 50; America, 1820 ***778.5*** *p370*
Mathieu, Mrs. 40; Port uncertain, 1836 ***778.5*** *p370*
Mathieu, Adrien; Arkansas, 1918 ***95.2*** *p81*
Mathieu, Ferdinan; Baltimore, 1870 ***8125.8*** *p437*
Mathieu, Francoise *SEE* Mathieu, Jerome
Mathieu, Jeanne *SEE* Mathieu, Jerome
Mathieu, Jerome 21; Halifax, N.S., 1752 ***7074.6*** *p211*
*Mother:*Jeanne
*Sister:*Marguerite
*Sister:*Francoise
Mathieu, Marguerite *SEE* Mathieu, Jerome
Mathieu, Maria 10; America, 1820 ***778.5*** *p369*
Mathin, Eliz.; Virginia, 1640 ***6219*** *p160*
Mathiott, George G.; New York, NY, 1836 ***8208.4*** *p17*
Mathis, Ann; Virginia, 1636 ***6219*** *p75*
Mathis, Ann; Virginia, 1638 ***6219*** *p181*
Mathis, Mary 68; North Carolina, 1850 ***1639.20*** *p234*
Mathisen, Jens 30; Arkansas, 1918 ***95.2*** *p81*
Mathison, John Bull; Jamaica, 1773 ***1219.7*** *p167*
Mathison, Thore; Arkansas, 1918 ***95.2*** *p81*
Mathiu, Louis 48; America, 1835 ***778.5*** *p370*
Matien, Santiago 30; New York, 1829 ***778.5*** *p370*
Maties, Alexander; Virginia, 1638 ***6219*** *p118*
Matilla, Oscar; Washington, 1859-1920 ***2872.1*** *p25*
Matison, John; Illinois, 1861 ***2896.5*** *p26*
Matka, Frank; Wisconsin, n.d. ***9675.6*** *p268*
Matka, Math.; Wisconsin, n.d. ***9675.6*** *p268*
Matka, Mathias; Wisconsin, n.d. ***9675.6*** *p268*
Matkiewicz, Joseph; Arkansas, 1918 ***95.2*** *p81*
Matkovic, Ivan; Iowa, 1866-1943 ***123.54*** *p69*
Matkovic, Stephan; Iowa, 1866-1943 ***123.54*** *p33*
Matkovich, Georj; Iowa, 1866-1943 ***123.54*** *p33*
Matkovich, John; Iowa, 1866-1943 ***123.54*** *p69*
Matkovich, Josip; Iowa, 1866-1943 ***123.54*** *p33*
Matkovich, Louise; Iowa, 1866-1943 ***123.54*** *p69*
Matkovich, Matt; Iowa, 1866-1943 ***123.54*** *p33*
Matkovich, Stef; Iowa, 1866-1943 ***123.54*** *p33*
Matli, Victor; Arizona, 1898 ***9228.30*** *p8*
Matolish, Joseph; Arkansas, 1918 ***95.2*** *p81*
Maton, Nicholas; Virginia, 1638 ***6219*** *p122*
Matrasko, Steve; New York, NY, 1901 ***9892.11*** *p29*
Matrau, . . . 14; New Orleans, 1836 ***778.5*** *p370*
Matrau, Mme. 39; New Orleans, 1836 ***778.5*** *p370*
Matrau, Ambroste 16; New Orleans, 1836 ***778.5*** *p370*
Matre, Philip; Cincinnati, 1844 ***8582.1*** *p23*
Matrim, Betty 66; Massachusetts, 1847 ***5881.1*** *p63*
Matrisciano, Vingenzo; Arkansas, 1918 ***95.2*** *p81*
Matrun, Wm.; Virginia, 1635 ***6219*** *p69*
Matson, Alida; Washington, 1859-1920 ***2872.1*** *p25*
Matson, Astrid Elida; Washington, 1859-1920 ***2872.1*** *p25*
Matson, Charles; Washington, 1859-1920 ***2872.1*** *p25*
Matson, Eliza; Philadelphia, 1847 ***53.26*** *p50*
Matson, Eliza; Philadelphia, 1847 ***5704.8*** *p30*
Matson, Eric; Maine, 1871-1884 ***6410.22*** *p119*
Matson, James; Washington, 1859-1920 ***2872.1*** *p25*
Matson, Jennie Violet; Washington, 1859-1920 ***2872.1*** *p25*
Matson, John; Quebec, 1852 ***5704.8*** *p86*
Matson, Nels N.; Illinois, 1894 ***5240.1*** *p29*
Matson, Otto Wilhelm; Washington, 1859-1920 ***2872.1*** *p25*
Matson, Rasmus; Bangor, ME, 1881-1892 ***6410.22*** *p121*
Matson, Ruth Margaret; Washington, 1859-1920 ***2872.1*** *p25*
Matson, Samuel 22; Kansas, 1904 ***5240.1*** *p83*
Mattaei, F. W. 23; Kansas, 1876 ***5240.1*** *p58*
Mattaglito, Louis; Arkansas, 1918 ***95.2*** *p81*
Mattar, Emile 30; Arizona, 1901 ***9228.40*** *p7*
Mattatal, . . .; Halifax, N.S., 1752 ***7074.6*** *p232*
Mattei, John; Wisconsin, n.d. ***9675.6*** *p268*
Mattelein, Marie 35; New Orleans, 1839 ***778.5*** *p370*
Matter, A. Alexander 30; Kansas, 1887 ***5240.1*** *p70*
Matter, Valtin; Pennsylvania, 1751 ***2444*** *p187*
Mattern, Charles O.; Washington, 1859-1920 ***2872.1*** *p25*
Mattern, Hulda; Washington, 1859-1920 ***2872.1*** *p25*
Matterson, Bridget 24; Massachusetts, 1847 ***5881.1*** *p63*
Mattesewick, Agathe 20; New York, NY, 1878 ***9253*** *p47*
Matthaes, . . .; Canada, 1776-1783 ***9786*** *p28*
Mattheis, George; Maine, 1868-1882 ***6410.22*** *p117*
Mattheis, Margaretha; Pennsylvania, 1752 ***2444*** *p210*
Mattheisen, Peter 41; Kansas, 1883 ***5240.1*** *p64*
Mattheison, Peter 41; Kansas, 1883 ***5240.1*** *p30*
Matthes, Clemens; America, 1855 ***1450.2*** *p94A*
Mattheson, Alexander; South Carolina, 1773-1826 ***1639.20*** *p231*
Matthew, David; New York, NY, 1836 ***8208.4*** *p13*
Matthew, John, Jr.; New York, NY, 1836 ***8208.4*** *p13*
Matthew, Margaret 72 *SEE* Matthew, Nancy
Matthew, Nancy 51; North Carolina, 1850 ***1639.20*** *p233*
*Relative:*Margaret 72
Matthew, Peter; Barbados, 1698 ***2212*** *p5*
Matthew, Robert; America, 1697 ***2212*** *p7*
Matthew, Thomas; New York, NY, 1836 ***8208.4*** *p13*
Matthews, Arnold 38; Jamaica, 1736 ***3690.1*** *p151*
Matthews, Benjamin 16; South Carolina, 1723 ***3690.1*** *p151*
Matthews, Demetreos; Arkansas, 1918 ***95.2*** *p81*
Matthews, Edward T.; Illinois, 1876 ***7857*** *p5*
Matthews, Effie 50; North Carolina, 1850 ***1639.20*** *p233*
Matthews, George; Carolina, 1772 ***1219.7*** *p155*
Matthews, James; New Jersey, 1834 ***8208.4*** *p47*
Matthews, James 19; Maryland, 1724 ***3690.1*** *p151*
Matthews, Jeane; Pennsylvania, 1682 ***4962*** *p153*
Matthews, John; Iowa, 1866-1943 ***123.54*** *p33*
Matthews, John 17; South Carolina, 1732 ***3690.1*** *p151*
Matthews, Sarah 19; Virginia, 1720 ***3690.1*** *p151*
Matthews, Thomas; New York, NY, 1840 ***8208.4*** *p113*
Matthews, Thomas Steel; Illinois, 1864 ***5012.38*** *p98*
Matthews, William 19; Jamaica, 1736 ***3690.1*** *p151*
Matthews, William 20; Maryland, 1723 ***3690.1*** *p151*
Matthews, William 20; St. Christopher, 1722 ***3690.1*** *p151*
Matthewson, John; South Carolina, 1716 ***1639.20*** *p233*
Matthiesen, Christopher; New York, 1750 ***3652*** *p74*
Matthiesen, Nicholas; New York, 1750 ***3652*** *p74*
Matthieson, John; Carolina, 1684 ***1639.20*** *p232*
Mattia, Teresa 64; New York, NY, 1893 ***9026.4*** *p42*

Mattioda, Fiorenzo; Iowa, 1866-1943 ***123.54*** *p33*
Mattioda, Maria; Iowa, 1866-1943 ***123.54*** *p71*
Mattis, Georg Clemens; Illinois, 1866 ***2896.5*** *p26*
Mattis, George; America, 1899 ***7137*** *p169*
Mattison, John A. 23; New York, NY, 1847 ***6410.32*** *p126*
Mattison, John A. 28; Massachusetts, 1860 ***6410.32*** *p118*
Mattison, William; America, 1863 ***5240.1*** *p30*
Mattison, William E.; Oklahoma, 1894 ***5240.1*** *p30*
Mattrevers, William 22; Jamaica, 1733 ***3690.1*** *p152*
Mattson, A.; Minneapolis, 1870-1882 ***6410.35*** *p60*
Mattson, John; Minneapolis, 1856-1886 ***6410.35*** *p60*
Mattson, Louis; Arkansas, 1918 ***95.2*** *p81*
Mattsson, Johan Aron 23; New York, NY, 1847 ***6410.32*** *p126*
Mattuz, Friederich; Charleston, SC, 1766 ***8582.2*** *p65*
Maturin, Edward; New York, NY, 1832 ***8208.4*** *p49*
Matz, Christian 29; New Orleans, 1839 ***778.5*** *p370*
Matzger, Julius; Illinois, 1884 ***2896.5*** *p26*
Matzka, Emil 24; Kansas, 1906 ***5240.1*** *p83*
Matzka, Moritz Albert 35; Kansas, 1879 ***5240.1*** *p60*
Matzner, Edward; Missouri, 1857 ***2896.5*** *p26*
Mau, John; Illinois, 1860 ***5012.38*** *p98*
Mauban, Marie 17; America, 1835 ***778.5*** *p370*
Maubar, Maria Apollonia; Port uncertain, 1717 ***3627*** *p16*
Maube, Mr. 30; America, 1839 ***778.5*** *p370*
Maube, Jean Arnaud 28; Port uncertain, 1838 ***778.5*** *p371*
Mauberret, Mr.; New Orleans, 1822 ***778.5*** *p371*
Mauberret, Ms.; New Orleans, 1822 ***778.5*** *p371*
Mauberret, Jeanne 34; New Orleans, 1822 ***778.5*** *p371*
Maubinet, Claude 40; Louisiana, 1820 ***778.5*** *p371*
Mauch, Maria Catharina; New England, 1753 ***2444*** *p231*
Mauck, . . .; Canada, 1776-1783 ***9786*** *p29*
Mauckes, Gilbert; Virginia, 1637 ***6219*** *p113*
Maud, William; Jamaica, 1757 ***1219.7*** *p57*
Maude, Mr. 28; New Orleans, 1822 ***778.5*** *p371*
Maude, Elizabeth Parr; Pennsylvania, 1682 ***4961*** *p5*
Maude, Jane 15 *SEE* Maude, Marjory
Maude, Marjory 11; Pennsylvania, 1682 ***4961*** *p5*
*Sister:*Jane 15
Maudor, Randall; Virginia, 1647 ***6219*** *p248*
Maudoz, Mr. 24; New Orleans, 1839 ***778.5*** *p371*
Maue, Friedrich; Cincinnati, 1869-1887 ***8582*** *p20*
Maugaridge, Hannah; Pennsylvania, 1682 ***4962*** *p154*
Mauger, Jean; Quebec, 1823 ***7603*** *p49*
Mauger, Philippe; Quebec, 1824 ***7603*** *p48*
Mauger, Richard; Quebec, 1809 ***7603*** *p48*
Maugher, Edward 26; Philadelphia, 1803 ***53.26*** *p50*
Maugher, John; America, 1742 ***4971*** *p17*
Maugon, Peter 20; America, 1829 ***778.5*** *p371*
Maugon, Peter 27; America, 1829 ***778.5*** *p371*
Maugridge, Hannah; Pennsylvania, 1682 ***4962*** *p154*
Mauk, . . .; Canada, 1776-1783 ***9786*** *p29*
Maul, Anna M. Schnaufer *SEE* Maul, Hans
Maul, Hans; America, 1751 ***2444*** *p188*
*Wife:*Anna M. Schnaufer
Maul, J. Jacob; Pennsylvania, 1751 ***2444*** *p188*
Maul, Johann Georg; America, 1727-1800 ***2444*** *p189*
Maul, John George; Pennsylvania, 1754 ***2444*** *p189*
Maul, Philip; Illinois, 1854 ***7857*** *p5*
Maul, Philip; Illinois, 1858 ***7857*** *p5*
Maulden, Francis; Virginia, 1636 ***6219*** *p21*
*Wife:*Katherine
Maulden, Katherine *SEE* Maulden, Francis
Maulden, Wm.; Virginia, 1635 ***6219*** *p70*
Maule, James 18; Jamaica, 1736 ***3690.1*** *p152*
Maule, Nathaniel 26; Maryland, 1724 ***3690.1*** *p152*
Maumus, Jean 31; New Orleans, 1835 ***778.5*** *p371*
Maunders, Thomas 33; Maryland, 1775 ***1219.7*** *p259*
Maupriver, Mr. 35; New Orleans, 1837 ***778.5*** *p371*
Maurain, Louisa; America, 1827 ***778.5*** *p371*
Maurath, Rudolph; New York, 1884 ***1450.2*** *p24B*
Maurepas, Mr. 20; New Orleans, 1821 ***778.5*** *p371*
Maurer, . . .; Canada, 1776-1783 ***9786*** *p43*
Maurer, Adam 21; America, 1836 ***778.5*** *p371*
Maurer, Barbara; Georgia, 1739 ***9332*** *p327*
Maurer, Barbara 7; America, 1853 ***9162.8*** *p37*
Maurer, Bendicht; Pennsylvania, 1709-1710 ***4480*** *p311*
Maurer, Catharina *SEE* Maurer, Hans
Maurer, Catharina; America, 1764 ***2854*** *p45*
Maurer, Catharina Mayr *SEE* Maurer, Hans
Maurer, Franz Mathias 30; America, 1853 ***9162.8*** *p37*
Maurer, Gabriel; Georgia, 1738 ***9332*** *p321*
Maurer, Gabriel; Georgia, 1739 ***9332*** *p324*
Maurer, Gabriel; Georgia, 1739 ***9332*** *p326*
Maurer, Georg 5; America, 1853 ***9162.8*** *p37*
Maurer, Gg. Franz 30; America, 1853 ***9162.8*** *p37*
Maurer, Hans; Georgia, 1739 ***9332*** *p323*
*Wife:*Catharina Mayr
Maurer, Hans; Georgia, 1739 ***9332*** *p326*
*Wife:*Catharina
Maurer, Joh. 27; America, 1853 ***9162.8*** *p37*
Maurer, Joh. Nikl. 25; America, 1853 ***9162.8*** *p37*
Maurer, Johannes; Pennsylvania, 1742-1800 ***2444*** *p189*
*Wife:*Maria Agnes Beck
*Child:*Susanna Catharina
Maurer, Johannes; Pennsylvania, 1749 ***2444*** *p189*
Maurer, John; Georgia, 1738 ***9332*** *p321*
Maurer, Johs. 32; America, 1853 ***9162.8*** *p37*
Maurer, Kath. 10; America, 1853 ***9162.8*** *p37*
Maurer, Marg. 23; America, 1853 ***9162.8*** *p37*
Maurer, Maria 30; America, 1853 ***9162.8*** *p37*
Maurer, Maria Agnes Beck *SEE* Maurer, Johannes
Maurer, Michael 24; America, 1853 ***9162.8*** *p37*
Maurer, Peter 18; America, 1853 ***9162.8*** *p37*
Maurer, Susanna Catharina *SEE* Maurer, Johannes
Maurfield, Thomas 24; Massachusetts, 1847 ***5881.1*** *p76*
Mauric, Mme. 60; Mexico, 1829 ***778.5*** *p371*
Maurice, Mr.; Quebec, 1815 ***9229.18*** *p75*
Maurice, Mr. 22; America, 1831 ***778.5*** *p372*
Maurice, Cathe 50; Wilmington, DE, 1831 ***6508.7*** *p161*
Maurice, James; New York, NY, 1816 ***2859.11*** *p38*
Maurice, Louise C. 4; New Orleans, 1821 ***778.5*** *p372*
Maurice, Marie A. 29; New Orleans, 1821 ***778.5*** *p372*
Maurice, P. 84; America, 1825 ***778.5*** *p372*
Maurice, Peter; New Orleans, 1831 ***778.5*** *p372*
Maurice, Pierre Francois 37; New Orleans, 1821 ***778.5*** *p372*
Maurice, Rober 20; Virginia, 1699 ***2212*** *p26*
Maurice, Willi.; Virginia, 1637 ***6219*** *p84*
Maurice, William; Virginia, 1637 ***6219*** *p114*
Maurin, Miss 23; New Orleans, 1825 ***778.5*** *p372*
Maurinas, Ivan; Iowa, 1866-1943 ***123.54*** *p33*
Maurreau, Mr. 19; New Orleans, 1837 ***778.5*** *p372*
Maurrer, Christian 23; Port uncertain, 1839 ***778.5*** *p372*
Maury, Jean; Quebec, 1673 ***4533*** *p130*
Maus, Joseph; America, 1837 ***8582.1*** *p23*
Maus, Wendel; America, 1837 ***8582.1*** *p23*
Mauser, Agatha Gomminger *SEE* Mauser, Hans Michael
Mauser, Agnes *SEE* Mauser, Hans Michael
Mauser, Anna Maria *SEE* Mauser, Hans Michael
Mauser, Hans Michael; America, 1751 ***2444*** *p189*
*Wife:*Agatha Gomminger
*Child:*Johannes
*Child:*Agnes
*Child:*Johann Friedrich
*Child:*Johann Jacob
*Child:*Anna Maria
*Child:*Nicolaus
Mauser, Johann Friedrich *SEE* Mauser, Hans Michael
Mauser, Johann Jacob *SEE* Mauser, Hans Michael
Mauser, Johannes *SEE* Mauser, Hans Michael
Mauser, Johannes; Pennsylvania, 1751 ***2444*** *p189*
Mauser, Michel; Pennsylvania, 1751 ***2444*** *p189*
Mauser, Nicolaus *SEE* Mauser, Hans Michael
Mausom, Habeeb; Arkansas, 1918 ***95.2*** *p81*
Maut, Mattheis; Pennsylvania, 1747 ***2444*** *p190*
Maute, Anna Maria Letsch; Philadelphia, 1751 ***2444*** *p232*
*Child:*Maria Magdalena
*Child:*Rosina
*Child:*Maria Margaretha
*Child:*Johann David
*Child:*Regina
Maute, Balthas; Pennsylvania, 1752 ***2444*** *p189*
Maute, Johann David *SEE* Maute, Anna Maria Letsch
Maute, Maria Magdalena *SEE* Maute, Anna Maria Letsch
Maute, Maria Margaretha *SEE* Maute, Anna Maria Letsch
Maute, Regina *SEE* Maute, Anna Maria Letsch
Maute, Rosina *SEE* Maute, Anna Maria Letsch
Mauthe, Anna Barbara Lang *SEE* Mauthe, Balthas
Mauthe, Balthas; New England, 1752 ***2444*** *p189*
*Wife:*Anna Barbara Lang
*Child:*Catharina
Mauthe, Catharina *SEE* Mauthe, Balthas
Mautte, Matthaeus; Pennsylvania, 1746 ***2444*** *p189*
Mauty, Mathias; Pennsylvania, 1747 ***2444*** *p190*
Mauxion, Henri 19; New Orleans, 1839 ***778.5*** *p372*
Mauz, Anna C. Greiner *SEE* Mauz, Friedrich
Mauz, Friedrich; Port uncertain, 1749 ***2444*** *p190*
*Wife:*Anna C. Greiner
Mauzley, John 31; Quebec, 1820 ***7603*** *p22*
Mavel, Fanny 16; New Orleans, 1836 ***778.5*** *p372*
Maves, Jean 25; America, 1838 ***778.5*** *p357*
Mavrimic, Yovakin; Iowa, 1866-1943 ***123.54*** *p33*
Mavrono, Michel 25; West Virginia, 1892 ***9788.3*** *p16*
Mawd, John 18; Virginia, 1720 ***3690.1*** *p152*
Mawe, Hanna; Virginia, 1638 ***6219*** *p124*
Mawhinney, Samson 20; St. John, N.B., 1855 ***5704.8*** *p126*
Mawhinny, Ellen 10; St. John, N.B., 1852 ***5704.8*** *p83*
Mawhinny, James 6; St. John, N.B., 1852 ***5704.8*** *p83*
Mawhinny, Jane; St. John, N.B., 1852 ***5704.8*** *p83*
Mawhinny, Sarah 8; St. John, N.B., 1852 ***5704.8*** *p83*
Max, Louis; New Jersey, 1893 ***1450.2*** *p94A*
Maxe, Robert; Virginia, 1635 ***6219*** *p17*
Maxey, Joseph; Charleston, SC, 1768 ***1219.7*** *p137*
Maxfeild, John; Virginia, 1638 ***6219*** *p121*
Maxilien, Henry 47; New Orleans, 1825 ***778.5*** *p372*
Maxney, Charles; Virginia, 1636 ***6219*** *p78*
Maxton, John; Charleston, SC, 1825 ***1639.20*** *p234*
Maxwell, . . . 4 mos; Philadelphia, 1865 ***5704.8*** *p203*
Maxwell, Alexander 4; St. John, N.B., 1853 ***5704.8*** *p110*
Maxwell, Ann 3; Philadelphia, 1865 ***5704.8*** *p203*
Maxwell, Bridget 1; Massachusetts, 1848 ***5881.1*** *p63*
Maxwell, Catherine 6; St. John, N.B., 1853 ***5704.8*** *p110*
Maxwell, David; Quebec, 1850 ***5704.8*** *p69*
Maxwell, David 19; Georgia, 1775 ***1219.7*** *p276*
Maxwell, Eliza; New York, NY, 1815 ***2859.11*** *p38*
Maxwell, Eliza 27; Philadelphia, 1854 ***5704.8*** *p117*
Maxwell, Elizabeth; Philadelphia, 1865 ***5704.8*** *p203*
Maxwell, Elizabeth 27; Philadelphia, 1857 ***5704.8*** *p132*
Maxwell, Ellen; Philadelphia, 1867 ***5704.8*** *p219*
Maxwell, Ellen 28; St. John, N.B., 1853 ***5704.8*** *p110*
Maxwell, Finley; Iowa, 1866-1943 ***123.54*** *p33*
Maxwell, George; St. John, N.B., 1851 ***5704.8*** *p78*
Maxwell, George 24; Philadelphia, 1804 ***53.26*** *p50*
Maxwell, Isabella; Philadelphia, 1816 ***2859.11*** *p38*
Maxwell, James; Charleston, SC, 1790-1830 ***1639.20*** *p234*
Maxwell, James; Philadelphia, 1816 ***2859.11*** *p38*
Maxwell, James; Shreveport, LA, 1879 ***7129*** *p45*
Maxwell, James 9 mos; St. John, N.B., 1853 ***5704.8*** *p110*
Maxwell, James 11; Quebec, 1852 ***5704.8*** *p86*
Maxwell, James 11; Quebec, 1852 ***5704.8*** *p90*
Maxwell, Jane 3; Philadelphia, 1865 ***5704.8*** *p203*
Maxwell, John; Iowa, 1866-1943 ***123.54*** *p33*
Maxwell, John; New York, NY, 1815 ***2859.11*** *p38*
Maxwell, John; Quebec, 1851 ***5704.8*** *p75*
Maxwell, John 25; Jamaica, 1735 ***3690.1*** *p152*
Maxwell, John 25; Maryland, 1775 ***1219.7*** *p267*
Maxwell, John 26; St. John, N.B., 1866 ***5704.8*** *p166*
Maxwell, John 39; Wilmington, DE, 1831 ***6508.3*** *p100*
Maxwell, John 39; Wilmington, DE, 1831 ***6508.3*** *p101*
Maxwell, Letitia 18; Philadelphia, 1860 ***5704.8*** *p144*
Maxwell, Margaret; America, 1815 ***1639.20*** *p234*
Maxwell, Margaret; New York, NY, 1815 ***2859.11*** *p38*
Maxwell, Margaret; Quebec, 1851 ***5704.8*** *p75*
Maxwell, Margaret 18; Philadelphia, 1854 ***5704.8*** *p120*
Maxwell, Mary; Quebec, 1852 ***5704.8*** *p86*
Maxwell, Mary; Quebec, 1852 ***5704.8*** *p90*
Maxwell, Mary 16; Philadelphia, 1853 ***5704.8*** *p111*
Maxwell, Mary 25; St. John, N.B., 1853 ***5704.8*** *p110*
Maxwell, Mathias 3; Massachusetts, 1848 ***5881.1*** *p71*
Maxwell, Matilda; Quebec, 1852 ***5704.8*** *p86*
Maxwell, Matilda; Quebec, 1852 ***5704.8*** *p90*
Maxwell, Nancy 30; Philadelphia, 1803 ***53.26*** *p50*
*Relative:*Robert 10
Maxwell, Peter; North Carolina, 1763-1812 ***1639.20*** *p234*
Maxwell, Peter 35; Tobago, W. Indies, 1774 ***1219.7*** *p224*
Maxwell, Robert 8; St. John, N.B., 1853 ***5704.8*** *p110*
Maxwell, Robert 10 *SEE* Maxwell, Nancy
Maxwell, Robert 18; Carolina, 1774 ***1219.7*** *p234*
Maxwell, Robert 18; Carolina, 1774 ***1639.20*** *p234*
Maxwell, Robert 20; St. John, N.B., 1860 ***5704.8*** *p143*
Maxwell, Rosina 21; Massachusetts, 1848 ***5881.1*** *p75*
Maxwell, Samuel; Philadelphia, 1864 ***5704.8*** *p183*
Maxwell, Samuel 19; Philadelphia, 1857 ***5704.8*** *p132*
Maxwell, Sarah Jane 13; Quebec, 1852 ***5704.8*** *p86*
Maxwell, Sarah Jane 13; Quebec, 1852 ***5704.8*** *p90*
Maxwell, Mrs. T.; New York, NY, 1815 ***2859.11*** *p38*
Maxwell, Thomas; New York, NY, 1816 ***2859.11*** *p38*
Maxwell, Thomas; North Carolina, 1827 ***1639.20*** *p234*
Maxwell, William; Cincinnati, 1793 ***8582.3*** *p88*
Maxwell, William; South Carolina, 1723 ***1639.20*** *p234*
Maxwell, William 32; St. John, N.B., 1853 ***5704.8*** *p110*
Maxwell, Wm.; New York, NY, 1811 ***2859.11*** *p17*
May, Anna Maria *SEE* May, Martin
May, Anna Maria Herold *SEE* May, Martin
May, Charles 22; Virginia, 1774 ***1219.7*** *p238*
May, Edward; Virginia, 1637 ***6219*** *p86*
May, Edward; Virginia, 1643 ***6219*** *p204*
May, Edward 35; Philadelphia, 1774 ***1219.7*** *p217*
May, Etienne; Quebec, 1820 ***7603*** *p26*
May, Florian Karl; Charleston, SC, 1775-1781 ***8582.2*** *p52*
May, Francis 21; Philadelphia, 1774 ***1219.7*** *p233*
May, Frank; Arkansas, 1918 ***95.2*** *p81*
May, Gerhard; Minnesota, 1886 ***5240.1*** *p30*
May, Hannah; Virginia, 1637 ***6219*** *p24*
May, Jacob; Jamaica, 1764 ***1219.7*** *p104*
May, James 17; Maryland, 1724 ***3690.1*** *p152*
May, Johannes; Ohio, 1798-1818 ***8582.2*** *p53*
May, John; New York, NY, 1839 ***8208.4*** *p102*
May, John; North Carolina, 1700-1735 ***1639.20*** *p235*
May, John; Virginia, 1642 ***6219*** *p193*
May, John 20; Jamaica, 1724 ***3690.1*** *p152*
May, John 37; Virginia, 1774 ***1219.7*** *p243*

McAleece, Francis 19; St. John, N.B., 1856 *5704.8 p131*
McAleer, Biddy 11; Quebec, 1847 *5704.8 p29*
McAleer, Catharine; New York, NY, 1866 *5704.8 p211*
McAleer, Catharine; New York, NY, 1866 *5704.8 p213*
McAleer, Catherine 13; Quebec, 1847 *5704.8 p29*
McAleer, Denis; Philadelphia, 1867 *5704.8 p219*
McAleer, Edward; Quebec, 1847 *5704.8 p29*
McAleer, Eliza 5; New York, NY, 1866 *5704.8 p211*
McAleer, Elleanor; Quebec, 1847 *5704.8 p29*
McAleer, James; New Orleans, 1849 *5704.8 p59*
McAleer, James 5; St. John, N.B., 1850 *5704.8 p65*
McAleer, James 9; Quebec, 1847 *5704.8 p29*
McAleer, John; Philadelphia, 1849 *53.26 p50*
McAleer, John; Philadelphia, 1849 *5704.8 p58*
McAleer, John; Philadelphia, 1865 *5704.8 p197*
McAleer, John; Quebec, 1847 *5704.8 p12*
McAleer, John; St. John, N.B., 1847 *5704.8 p15*
McAleer, John 7; St. John, N.B., 1850 *5704.8 p65*
McAleer, Marcus; New York, NY, 1866 *5704.8 p211*
McAleer, Margaret; New York, NY, 1867 *5704.8 p220*
McAleer, Margaret; Quebec, 1849 *5704.8 p57*
McAleer, Margaret 1; Quebec, 1847 *5704.8 p12*
McAleer, Mary; New York, NY, 1867 *5704.8 p220*
McAleer, Mary; Philadelphia, 1849 *53.26 p50*
McAleer, Mary; Philadelphia, 1849 *5704.8 p49*
McAleer, Mary; St. John, N.B., 1850 *5704.8 p65*
McAleer, Mary 7; Quebec, 1847 *5704.8 p12*
McAleer, Mary 24; Philadelphia, 1860 *5704.8 p144*
McAleer, Mary Ann 9; St. John, N.B., 1850 *5704.8 p65*
McAleer, Michael; Philadelphia, 1848 *53.26 p50*
McAleer, Michael; Philadelphia, 1848 *5704.8 p45*
McAleer, Michael; Philadelphia, 1865 *5704.8 p192*
McAleer, Pat 9; Quebec, 1847 *5704.8 p12*
McAleer, Patrick; Philadelphia, 1864 *5704.8 p179*
McAleer, Patrick; Philadelphia, 1865 *5704.8 p197*
McAleer, Rose; Quebec, 1847 *5704.8 p12*
McAleer, Sally 1; Quebec, 1847 *5704.8 p29*
McAlees, Ann Jane 4; St. John, N.B., 1849 *5704.8 p48*
McAlees, Benjamin 9; St. John, N.B., 1849 *5704.8 p48*
McAlees, Elizabeth 13; St. John, N.B., 1849 *5704.8 p48*
McAlees, John; St. John, N.B., 1849 *5704.8 p48*
McAlees, John 6 mos; St. John, N.B., 1849 *5704.8 p48*
McAlees, John 18; Philadelphia, 1853 *5704.8 p108*
McAlees, Matilda 6; St. John, N.B., 1849 *5704.8 p48*
McAlees, Nancy; St. John, N.B., 1849 *5704.8 p48*
McAlees, William; St. John, N.B., 1849 *5704.8 p48*
McAleese, Rose Ann; Philadelphia, 1864 *5704.8 p187*
McAleney, George 20; Quebec, 1855 *5704.8 p125*
McAleney, George 30; Quebec, 1855 *5704.8 p125*
McAlenney, Patrick; America, 1864 *5704.8 p189*
McAleny, Susan; St. John, N.B., 1848 *5704.8 p48*
McAlester, Angus; Carolina, 1774 *1639.20 p116*
  With wife 2 sons & daughter
McAlester, Catherine; Wilmington, NC, 1774 *1639.20 p204*
McAlester, Catherine 30; Wilmington, NC, 1774 *1639.20 p117*
McAlester, Coll 24; Wilmington, NC, 1774 *1639.20 p116*
McAlester, Hector; Brunswick, NC, 1739 *1639.20 p116*
McAlester, John; Brunswick, NC, 1739 *1639.20 p117*
McAlester, Mary 31; Wilmington, NC, 1774 *1639.20 p117*
McAlester, Mary 64; Wilmington, NC, 1774 *1639.20 p292*
McAlice, Edward; Quebec, 1851 *5704.8 p73*
McAlice, Margaret 18; Quebec, 1864 *5704.8 p160*
McAlinny, Bridget 13; St. John, N.B., 1867 *5704.8 p168*
McAlister, Alexander; North Carolina, 1771 *1639.20 p116*
McAlister, Alexander; St. John, N.B., 1852 *5704.8 p95*
McAlister, Alexandra; North Carolina, 1771 *1639.20 p116*
McAlister, Angus; New York, NY, 1738 *1639.20 p116*
McAlister, Angus; North Carolina, 1771 *1639.20 p116*
McAlister, Biddy SEE McAlister, Margaret
McAlister, Biddy; Philadelphia, 1850 *5704.8 p69*
McAlister, Biddy; St. John, N.B., 1847 *5704.8 p19*
McAlister, Coll; North Carolina, 1739 *1639.20 p116*
McAlister, Daniel; Quebec, 1847 *5704.8 p8*
McAlister, Elizabeth SEE McAlister, William
McAlister, Elizabeth; Philadelphia, 1848 *5704.8 p46*
McAlister, James; North Carolina, 1739 *1639.20 p117*
McAlister, James 6; Quebec, 1847 *5704.8 p36*
McAlister, John; Quebec, 1847 *5704.8 p36*
McAlister, John 24; Philadelphia, 1859 *5704.8 p143*
McAlister, Margaret; Philadelphia, 1850 *53.26 p50*
  *Relative:*William
  *Relative:*Biddy
McAlister, Margaret; Philadelphia, 1850 *5704.8 p69*
McAlister, Mary; Quebec, 1847 *5704.8 p36*
McAlister, Mary; St. John, N.B., 1848 *5704.8 p38*
McAlister, Mary; St. John, N.B., 1851 *5704.8 p78*

McAlister, Mary 4; Quebec, 1847 *5704.8 p36*
McAlister, Nancy SEE McAlister, William
McAlister, Nancy; Philadelphia, 1848 *5704.8 p46*
McAlister, Peter 9 mos; Quebec, 1847 *5704.8 p36*
McAlister, Sarah 74; North Carolina, 1850 *1639.20 p117*
McAlister, Thomas 22; Philadelphia, 1859 *5704.8 p143*
McAlister, William SEE McAlister, Margaret
McAlister, William; Philadelphia, 1848 *53.26 p50*
  *Relative:*Nancy
  *Relative:*Elizabeth
McAlister, William; Philadelphia, 1848 *5704.8 p46*
McAlister, William; Philadelphia, 1850 *5704.8 p69*
McAlleer, Henry; Philadelphia, 1864 *5704.8 p178*
McAlleese, John 11; Philadelphia, 1869 *5704.8 p236*
McAlleese, Mary A. 7; Philadelphia, 1869 *5704.8 p236*
McAlleese, Nancy; Philadelphia, 1869 *5704.8 p236*
McAllester, Anne 20; St. John, N.B., 1866 *5704.8 p167*
McAllester, David 21; St. John, N.B., 1866 *5704.8 p167*
McAllester, Joseph 42; St. John, N.B., 1866 *5704.8 p167*
McAllion, Anna Maria; St. John, N.B., 1848 *5704.8 p43*
McAllion, Margaret; St. John, N.B., 1848 *5704.8 p43*
M'Callister, Mr.; Quebec, 1815 *9229.18 p74*
McAllister, Agnes 23; St. John, N.B., 1864 *5704.8 p157*
McAllister, Alexander; Wilmington, NC, 1736 *1639.20 p116*
McAllister, Betsy; New York, NY, 1864 *5704.8 p175*
McAllister, Hector; North Carolina, 1771 *1639.20 p117*
McAllister, Hugh; Iowa, 1866-1943 *123.54 p31*
McAllister, Hugh 26; Philadelphia, 1833-1834 *53.26 p50*
McAllister, James; New York, NY, 1835 *8208.4 p7*
McAllister, James P.; Nevada, 1886 *2764.35 p47*
McAllister, John; New York, NY, 1864 *5704.8 p175*
McAllister, John 24; St. John, N.B., 1855 *5704.8 p127*
McAllister, John 24; St. John, N.B., 1866 *5704.8 p167*
McAllister, Margaret; New York, NY, 1864 *5704.8 p175*
McAllister, Nancy; New York, NY, 1864 *5704.8 p175*
McAllister, Patrick; Iowa, 1846 *6013.19 p29*
McAllister, Robert 35; St. John, N.B., 1866 *5704.8 p167*
McAllister, Rose 20; St. John, N.B., 1864 *5704.8 p157*
McAllister, Samuel 28; Kansas, 1873 *5240.1 p53*
McAllister, Sarah Jane SEE McAllister, William
McAllister, Susan; Philadelphia, 1864 *5704.8 p177*
McAllister, William SEE McAllister, William
McAllister, William; New York, NY, 1864 *5704.8 p175*
McAllister, William; Philadelphia, 1847 *53.26 p50*
  *Relative:*William
  *Relative:*Sarah Jane
McAllum, Archibald; North Carolina, 1800 *1639.20 p117*
McAllum, Catherine McAlester 30 SEE McAllum, Duncan
McAllum, Duncan 22; Wilmington, NC, 1774 *1639.20 p117*
  *Wife:*Catherine McAlester 30
M'Callum, J.; Quebec, 1815 *9229.18 p75*
McAloon, Patrick 10; Massachusetts, 1850 *5881.1 p75*
McAloon, Thomas; St. John, N.B., 1848 *5704.8 p44*
McAloran, Alexander 12; St. John, N.B., 1847 *5704.8 p21*
McAloran, Archy 2; St. John, N.B., 1847 *5704.8 p21*
McAloran, Daniel; St. John, N.B., 1847 *5704.8 p21*
McAloran, Ellen; St. John, N.B., 1847 *5704.8 p21*
McAloran, James; St. John, N.B., 1847 *5704.8 p21*
McAloran, John 5; St. John, N.B., 1847 *5704.8 p21*
McAloran, Robert 8; St. John, N.B., 1847 *5704.8 p21*
McAloran, Sarah 7; St. John, N.B., 1847 *5704.8 p21*
McAlowen, Bernard; Philadelphia, 1869 *5704.8 p236*
McAlowen, Catharine 8; Philadelphia, 1869 *5704.8 p236*
McAlowen, Elizabeth; Philadelphia, 1869 *5704.8 p236*
McAlowen, Elizabeth 9; Philadelphia, 1869 *5704.8 p236*
McAlowen, Ellen; Philadelphia, 1869 *5704.8 p236*
McAlowen, Margaret 11; Philadelphia, 1869 *5704.8 p236*
McAlowen, Mary 15; Philadelphia, 1869 *5704.8 p236*
McAlowen, Rosanna; Philadelphia, 1869 *5704.8 p236*
McAlpin, Archibald; Georgia, 1772-1822 *1639.20 p117*
McAlpin, Dennis; New York, 1821 *9892.11 p33*
McAlpine, Colin; South Carolina, 1772 *1639.20 p117*
McAlpine, John; North Carolina, 1777-1807 *1639.20 p117*
McAlpine, Malcolm; North Carolina, 1755-1825 *1639.20 p118*
McAlwee, Thomas 20; St. John, N.B., 1856 *5704.8 p131*
McAna, Barry 24; Philadelphia, 1803 *53.26 p50*
McAnaller, Bridget 3; Quebec, 1858 *5704.8 p138*
McAnaller, Bridget 40; Quebec, 1858 *5704.8 p138*
McAnaller, Catherine 8; Quebec, 1858 *5704.8 p138*
McAnaller, Ellen 4; Quebec, 1858 *5704.8 p138*
McAnaller, John 1; Quebec, 1858 *5704.8 p138*
McAnaller, Mary 11; Quebec, 1858 *5704.8 p138*
McAnaller, Michael 6; Quebec, 1858 *5704.8 p138*
McAnaller, Michael 40; Quebec, 1858 *5704.8 p138*
McAnaller, Sarah 10; Quebec, 1858 *5704.8 p138*
McAnally, Bernard; Philadelphia, 1865 *5704.8 p199*
McAnally, Bernard; Quebec, 1847 *5704.8 p38*

McAnally, Bernard 17; Philadelphia, 1864 *5704.8 p157*
McAnally, Catherine; St. John, N.B., 1847 *5704.8 p5*
McAnally, Catherine 22; Philadelphia, 1858 *5704.8 p139*
McAnally, Edward; New York, NY, 1865 *5704.8 p192*
McAnally, Hugh; New York, NY, 1867 *5704.8 p223*
McAnally, James; Philadelphia, 1868 *5704.8 p226*
McAnally, Margaret 20; St. John, N.B., 1854 *5704.8 p120*
McAnally, Owen; Quebec, 1822 *7603 p56*
McAnally, Patrick; Quebec, 1847 *5704.8 p38*
McAnally, Susan; Philadelphia, 1864 *5704.8 p184*
McAnally, Thomas; America, 1738 *4971 p13*
McAnalty, Pat.; America, 1743 *4971 p65*
McAnamny, Margaret; Philadelphia, 1866 *5704.8 p207*
McAnamny, Sally; America, 1866 *5704.8 p207*
McAnamy, Margaret 24; Philadelphia, 1854 *5704.8 p121*
McAnaney, John; Montreal, 1824 *7603 p89*
McAnanly, Patrick; Quebec, 1825 *7603 p62*
McAnany, Bernard; Philadelphia, 1866 *5704.8 p203*
McAnany, Catharine; Philadelphia, 1868 *5704.8 p230*
McAnary, Bridget 19; Massachusetts, 1850 *5881.1 p63*
McAnaspie, James; Philadelphia, 1849 *53.26 p50*
McAnaspie, James; Philadelphia, 1849 *5704.8 p53*
McAncey, Judy 30; Massachusetts, 1849 *5881.1 p69*
McAndre, Sarah 2; Massachusetts, 1847 *5881.1 p75*
McAndre, Sarah 27; Massachusetts, 1847 *5881.1 p75*
McAndrew, Alexander 18; Georgia, 1775 *1219.7 p277*
McAndrew, Bridget 25; Philadelphia, 1864 *5704.8 p161*
McAndrew, Mary 22; Philadelphia, 1864 *5704.8 p161*
McAndrew, Michael; Philadelphia, 1864 *5704.8 p179*
McAndrew, William 22; Philadelphia, 1864 *5704.8 p161*
McAneely, Barnard 28; St. John, N.B., 1853 *5704.8 p111*
McAneiley, Margaret 22; St. John, N.B., 1859 *5704.8 p140*
McAnelly, Catherine; Quebec, 1851 *5704.8 p74*
McAnelly, John; Quebec, 1851 *5704.8 p74*
McAneny, Ann; New York, NY, 1868 *5704.8 p229*
McAneny, Catherine 10 SEE McAneny, Margaret
McAneny, Catherine 10; Philadelphia, 1849 *5704.8 p58*
McAneny, Catherine 19; Philadelphia, 1858 *5704.8 p139*
McAneny, Charles; New York, NY, 1868 *5704.8 p229*
McAneny, James SEE McAneny, Margaret
McAneny, James; Philadelphia, 1849 *5704.8 p58*
McAneny, Margaret SEE McAneny, Margaret
McAneny, Margaret; Philadelphia, 1849 *53.26 p50*
  *Relative:*James
  *Relative:*Margaret
  *Relative:*Catherine 10
  *Relative:*Peter 8
McAneny, Margaret; Philadelphia, 1849 *5704.8 p58*
McAneny, Matilda; New Orleans, 1849 *5704.8 p59*
McAneny, Peter 8 SEE McAneny, Margaret
McAneny, Peter 8; Philadelphia, 1849 *5704.8 p58*
McAneny, Rosey SEE McAneny, Thomas
McAneny, Rosey 9 mos; Philadelphia, 1848 *5704.8 p45*
McAneny, Sarah SEE McAneny, Thomas
McAneny, Sarah; Philadelphia, 1848 *5704.8 p45*
McAneny, Thomas; Philadelphia, 1848 *53.26 p50*
  *Relative:*Sarah
  *Relative:*Rosey
McAneny, Thomas; Philadelphia, 1848 *5704.8 p45*
McAnespie, Arthur; Philadelphia, 1851 *5704.8 p81*
McAnespy, John; Philadelphia, 1850 *53.26 p51*
McAnespy, John; Philadelphia, 1850 *5704.8 p60*
McAnilly, Ann 8; Quebec, 1857 *5704.8 p135*
McAnilly, Eliza 40; Quebec, 1857 *5704.8 p135*
McAnilly, Elizabeth 18; Quebec, 1857 *5704.8 p135*
McAnilly, James 20; Quebec, 1862 *5704.8 p151*
McAnilly, James 21; Quebec, 1857 *5704.8 p135*
McAnilly, Patrick 40; Quebec, 1857 *5704.8 p135*
McAnilly, Thomas 10; Quebec, 1857 *5704.8 p135*
McAnliff, Ellen 20; Massachusetts, 1849 *5881.1 p66*
McAnnanly, Mary; Quebec, 1825 *7603 p62*
McAnnulty, William 60; Massachusetts, 1850 *5881.1 p77*
McAnully, Daniel; Quebec, 1847 *5704.8 p16*
McAnully, Dennis; Quebec, 1847 *5704.8 p16*
McAnully, Dennis 10; Quebec, 1847 *5704.8 p16*
McAnully, Magary 12; Quebec, 1847 *5704.8 p16*
McAnully, Mary; Quebec, 1847 *5704.8 p16*
McAnulty, Bernard 11; Philadelphia, 1852 *5704.8 p88*
McAnulty, Biddy SEE McAnulty, George
McAnulty, Biddy; Philadelphia, 1847 *5704.8 p22*
McAnulty, Biddy; Philadelphia, 1851 *5704.8 p70*
McAnulty, Catherine; Quebec, 1822 *7603 p99*
McAnulty, Catherine; St. John, N.B., 1851 *5704.8 p77*
McAnulty, Catherine 7 SEE McAnulty, George
McAnulty, Catherine 7; Philadelphia, 1847 *5704.8 p22*
McAnulty, Cicily; Philadelphia, 1853 *5704.8 p108*
McAnulty, Edward 10 SEE McAnulty, George
McAnulty, Edward 10; Philadelphia, 1847 *5704.8 p22*

McAnulty, George; Philadelphia, 1847 ***53.26*** *p51*
*Relative:*Biddy
*Relative:*Edward 10
*Relative:*Catherine 7
*Relative:*George 4
McAnulty, George; Philadelphia, 1847 ***5704.8*** *p22*
McAnulty, George 4 *SEE* McAnulty, George
McAnulty, George 4; Philadelphia, 1847 ***5704.8*** *p22*
McAnulty, James; Philadelphia, 1852 ***5704.8*** *p89*
McAnulty, John; Quebec, 1850 ***5704.8*** *p66*
McAnulty, Margaret; Philadelphia, 1850 ***53.26*** *p51*
McAnulty, Margaret; Philadelphia, 1850 ***5704.8*** *p59*
McAnulty, Margaret; Philadelphia, 1852 ***5704.8*** *p88*
McAnulty, Margaret 9; Philadelphia, 1852 ***5704.8*** *p88*
McAnulty, Mary; St. John, N.B., 1847 ***5704.8*** *p35*
McAnulty, Mary 24; Philadelphia, 1860 ***5704.8*** *p144*
McAnulty, Peter 22; Quebec, 1856 ***5704.8*** *p130*
McAnulty, Rose Ann; Quebec, 1847 ***5704.8*** *p28*
McAnulty, Thomas; New Orleans, 1849 ***5704.8*** *p59*
McAnulty, William; Philadelphia, 1847 ***53.26*** *p51*
McAnulty, William; Philadelphia, 1847 ***5704.8*** *p24*
McAnulty, William 5; Quebec, 1850 ***5704.8*** *p66*
McAnurlan, Peter; America, 1737 ***4971*** *p77*
McAnvy, John 22; Kansas, 1884 ***5240.1*** *p65*
McAny, James; Philadelphia, 1864 ***5704.8*** *p172*
McArdle, Barney; New York, NY, 1856 ***2764.35*** *p48*
McArdle, Dolly 50; Massachusetts, 1847 ***5881.1*** *p65*
McArdle, James; America, 1740 ***4971*** *p25*
McArdle, James 24; Massachusetts, 1847 ***5881.1*** *p67*
McAreary, Bridget 5; Quebec, 1864 ***5704.8*** *p161*
McAreary, Ellen 33; Quebec, 1864 ***5704.8*** *p161*
McAreary, John 7; Quebec, 1864 ***5704.8*** *p161*
McAreary, Mary 9 mos; Quebec, 1864 ***5704.8*** *p162*
McAreary, Patt 9; Quebec, 1864 ***5704.8*** *p161*
McAreary, Thomas 3; Quebec, 1864 ***5704.8*** *p161*
McAree, Brine; Quebec, 1850 ***5704.8*** *p62*
McAree, Sarah 60; North Carolina, 1850 ***1639.20*** *p118*
McAremny, William 20; Philadelphia, 1857 ***5704.8*** *p134*
McArn, Margaret 51; South Carolina, 1850 ***1639.20*** *p118*
McArthur, Ann 38 *SEE* McArthur, Peter
McArthur, Catherine 84; North Carolina, 1850 ***1639.20*** *p118*
McArthur, Christian Bride 52 *SEE* McArthur, Peter
McArthur, Daniel; North Carolina, 1745-1819 ***1639.20*** *p118*
McArthur, Eleanor; Philadelphia, 1851 ***5704.8*** *p79*
McArthur, Janet; North Carolina, 1764-1852 ***1639.20*** *p118*
McArthur, Joan 20 *SEE* McArthur, Peter
McArthur, John *SEE* McArthur, Robert
McArthur, John 16 *SEE* McArthur, Peter
McArthur, John 28 *SEE* McArthur, Peter
McArthur, Neil; North Carolina, 1764 ***1639.20*** *p118*
McArthur, Peter 58; Wilmington, NC, 1774 ***1639.20*** *p118*
*Wife:*Christian Bride 52
*Child:*John 28
*Child:*Ann 38
*Child:*Joan 20
*Child:*John 16
McArthur, Peter 80; North Carolina, 1850 ***1639.20*** *p118*
McArthur, Robert; Philadelphia, 1811 ***53.26*** *p51*
*Relative:*John
McArtor, Thomas; Wisconsin, n.d. ***9675.7*** *p51*
M'Carty, Jno; Ohio, 1839 ***9892.11*** *p32*
McAshee, Francis; Philadelphia, 1847 ***53.26*** *p51*
*Relative:*Thomas
McAshee, Francis; Philadelphia, 1847 ***5704.8*** *p22*
McAshee, Thomas *SEE* McAshee, Francis
McAshee, Thomas; Philadelphia, 1847 ***5704.8*** *p22*
McAskill, Jane *SEE* McAskill, Kenneth
McAskill, Kenneth; North Carolina, 1725-1825 ***1639.20*** *p126*
*Wife:*Nancy McKinnon
McAskill, Kenneth; North Carolina, 1725-1825 ***1639.20*** *p127*
*Wife:*Mary Campbell
*Child:*Jane
McAskill, Mary Campbell *SEE* McAskill, Kenneth
McAskill, Nancy McKinnon *SEE* McAskill, Kenneth
McAtagart, Phillip 21; Quebec, 1853 ***5704.8*** *p105*
McAtaggart, Patrick; Philadelphia, 1850 ***5704.8*** *p65*
McAtamney, Bridget; New York, NY, 1864 ***5704.8*** *p171*
McAtamney, Jane; Philadelphia, 1865 ***5704.8*** *p200*
McAtear, John; St. John, N.B., 1848 ***5704.8*** *p39*
McAtee, Pat.; America, 1741 ***4971*** *p63*
McAtee, Patrick; America, 1741 ***4971*** *p35*
McAteen, John; Philadelphia, 1866 ***5704.8*** *p204*
McAteen, Michael; Philadelphia, 1866 ***5704.8*** *p204*
McAteer, Bridget 22; Philadelphia, 1865 ***5704.8*** *p164*
McAteer, Catharine; Philadelphia, 1867 ***5704.8*** *p223*
McAteer, Charles 9; Philadelphia, 1867 ***5704.8*** *p223*
McAteer, Elizabeth 30; Philadelphia, 1854 ***5704.8*** *p122*
McAteer, Francis 1; Philadelphia, 1865 ***5704.8*** *p164*
McAteer, Hannah 25; Philadelphia, 1865 ***5704.8*** *p164*
McAteer, John; Philadelphia, 1867 ***5704.8*** *p223*
McAteer, John 42; Quebec, 1856 ***5704.8*** *p130*
McAteer, Michael; Philadelphia, 1847 ***53.26*** *p51*
McAteer, Michael; Philadelphia, 1847 ***5704.8*** *p1*
McAteer, Thomas 10; Philadelphia, 1867 ***5704.8*** *p223*
McAtier, Isabella; Philadelphia, 1852 ***5704.8*** *p89*
McAtier, Thomas; Philadelphia, 1852 ***5704.8*** *p89*
McAtire, Bryan; America, 1741 ***4971*** *p9*
McAtire, Bryan; America, 1741 ***4971*** *p94*
McAttaggart, Margaret; Philadelphia, 1864 ***5704.8*** *p184*
McAulay, Angus; Arkansas, 1918 ***95.2*** *p81*
McAulay, Angus; Wilmington, NC, 1773 ***1639.20*** *p119*
*Wife:*Margaret McLeod
McAulay, Donald; Quebec, 1790 ***9775.5*** *p198A*
With family of 7
McAulay, Farquhar; Wilmington, NC, 1773 ***1639.20*** *p119*
McAulay, John; Quebec, 1790 ***9775.5*** *p198A*
McAulay, Margaret McLeod *SEE* McAulay, Angus
McAulay, Nancy 49; North Carolina, 1850 ***1639.20*** *p119*
McAuley, Anne; Philadelphia, 1852 ***5704.8*** *p85*
McAuley, Bridget; St. John, N.B., 1850 ***5704.8*** *p62*
McAuley, Daniel; Montreal, 1824 ***7603*** *p54*
McAuley, Daniel; Quebec, 1851 ***5704.8*** *p74*
McAuley, Edward; New Jersey, 1882 ***5240.1*** *p28*
McAuley, John; Montreal, 1825 ***7603*** *p54*
McAuley, John; New York, NY, 1835 ***8208.4*** *p43*
McAuley, Patrick; Philadelphia, 1852 ***5704.8*** *p92*
McAuley, Richard; Montreal, 1821 ***7603*** *p54*
McAuley, Richard; Quebec, 1819 ***7603*** *p101*
McAuliff, James 25; Massachusetts, 1849 ***5881.1*** *p68*
McAuliff, Johanna 47; Massachusetts, 1849 ***5881.1*** *p68*
McAuliff, Margaret 30; Massachusetts, 1849 ***5881.1*** *p71*
McAuliff, Norry 13; Massachusetts, 1848 ***5881.1*** *p73*
McAuly, Bryan-buy; America, 1741 ***4971*** *p67*
McAuly, Charles; America, 1740 ***4971*** *p67*
McAuly, Neall; America, 1740 ***4971*** *p67*
McAuly, Richard; Quebec, 1819 ***7603*** *p101*
McAuslin, John; Wilmington, NC, 1761-1836 ***1639.20*** *p119*
McAvally, Henry 17; Philadelphia, 1854 ***5704.8*** *p123*
McAvay, John *SEE* McAvay, Margaret
McAvay, John; Philadelphia, 1849 ***5704.8*** *p54*
McAvay, Margaret; Philadelphia, 1849 ***53.26*** *p51*
*Relative:*John
McAvay, Margaret; Philadelphia, 1849 ***5704.8*** *p54*
McAverny, Honora 38; Massachusetts, 1850 ***5881.1*** *p67*
McAvey, Charles; Philadelphia, 1867 ***5704.8*** *p221*
McAvey, Daniel; St. John, N.B., 1853 ***5704.8*** *p98*
McAvey, Dennis; St. John, N.B., 1853 ***5704.8*** *p98*
McAvey, Easter; St. John, N.B., 1853 ***5704.8*** *p98*
McAvey, Ellen; Philadelphia, 1865 ***5704.8*** *p199*
McAvey, Joseph; St. John, N.B., 1853 ***5704.8*** *p98*
McAvey, Neal 6; St. John, N.B., 1853 ***5704.8*** *p98*
McAvey, Peggy; St. John, N.B., 1853 ***5704.8*** *p98*
McAvey, Shane; St. John, N.B., 1853 ***5704.8*** *p98*
McAvoy, Arthur 19; Massachusetts, 1850 ***5881.1*** *p62*
McAvoy, Catharine 40; Massachusetts, 1850 ***5881.1*** *p65*
McAvoy, Edward 12; Massachusetts, 1850 ***5881.1*** *p66*
McAvoy, James 45; Philadelphia, 1854 ***5704.8*** *p115*
McAvoy, John; America, 1738 ***4971*** *p36*
McAvoy, Mary 5; Massachusetts, 1850 ***5881.1*** *p73*
McAvoy, Michael 9; Massachusetts, 1850 ***5881.1*** *p73*
McAvoy, Owen 16; Massachusetts, 1850 ***5881.1*** *p73*
McAvoy, Patrick 21; Massachusetts, 1850 ***5881.1*** *p75*
McAvoy, William 11; Philadelphia, 1854 ***5704.8*** *p117*
McAward, Ann; Philadelphia, 1854 ***5704.8*** *p116*
McAward, Ann; St. John, N.B., 1852 ***5704.8*** *p95*
McAward, Ferrol 21; Philadelphia, 1803 ***53.26*** *p51*
McAward, James; Philadelphia, 1851 ***5704.8*** *p81*
McAward, Mary 11; Philadelphia, 1854 ***5704.8*** *p116*
McAward, Pat; Philadelphia, 1854 ***5704.8*** *p116*
McAward, Rebecca; Philadelphia, 1866 ***5704.8*** *p214*
McAward, William; Philadelphia, 1866 ***5704.8*** *p214*
McAwly, Alexander; Philadelphia, 1850 ***53.26*** *p51*
McAwly, Alexander; Philadelphia, 1850 ***5704.8*** *p60*
McBane, Daniel; North Carolina, 1680-1830 ***1639.20*** *p119*
McBarron, Francis; New York, NY, 1834 ***8208.4*** *p58*
McBarron, Michael; New York, NY, 1864 ***5704.8*** *p171*
McBarron, Patrick, Jr.; New York, NY, 1836 ***8208.4*** *p11*
McBay, James; Quebec, 1850 ***5704.8*** *p62*
McBay, Margaret; Quebec, 1850 ***5704.8*** *p62*
McBean, Lachlan; South Carolina, 1716 ***1639.20*** *p119*
McBeath, John 37; Wilmington, NC, 1774 ***1639.20*** *p119*
With wife & 3 children
With child 13
With child 9 mos
McBenn, John; Quebec, 1773 ***7603*** *p40*
McBeth, James 15; Antigua (Antego), 1731 ***3690.1*** *p153*
McBeth, John 26; West Virginia, 1904 ***9788.3*** *p16*
McBey, Mary 9; Philadelphia, 1852 ***5704.8*** *p84*
McBone, Thomas 26; Maryland, 1775 ***1219.7*** *p264*
McBrady, Thomas 19; St. John, N.B., 1866 ***5704.8*** *p167*
McBraine, Murdoch; North Carolina, 1739 ***1639.20*** *p120*
McBrairty, Ann 60; St. John, N.B., 1865 ***5704.8*** *p165*
McBrairty, Margaret 30; St. John, N.B., 1865 ***5704.8*** *p165*
McBraith, John; New York, NY, 1840 ***8208.4*** *p111*
McBrarty, Ann; Philadelphia, 1865 ***5704.8*** *p199*
McBrearty, Catherine 17; Philadelphia, 1860 ***5704.8*** *p146*
McBrearty, Cornelius; Philadelphia, 1864 ***5704.8*** *p184*
McBrearty, Ellen 23; St. John, N.B., 1865 ***5704.8*** *p165*
McBrearty, Mary 20; Philadelphia, 1854 ***5704.8*** *p123*
McBriarty, Ann 22; St. John, N.B., 1861 ***5704.8*** *p147*
McBriarty, Bridget *SEE* McBriarty, James
McBriarty, Bridget; Philadelphia, 1847 ***5704.8*** *p23*
McBriarty, Francis 3 *SEE* McBriarty, James
McBriarty, Francis 3; Philadelphia, 1847 ***5704.8*** *p23*
McBriarty, James; Philadelphia, 1847 ***53.26*** *p51*
*Relative:*Bridget
*Relative:*Francis 3
*Relative:*Rose Ann 1
McBriarty, James; Philadelphia, 1847 ***5704.8*** *p23*
McBriarty, Patrick; Philadelphia, 1847 ***53.26*** *p51*
McBriarty, Patrick; Philadelphia, 1847 ***5704.8*** *p32*
McBriarty, Rose Ann 1 *SEE* McBriarty, James
McBriarty, Rose Ann 1; Philadelphia, 1847 ***5704.8*** *p23*
McBride, . . . 1 mo; America, 1864 ***5704.8*** *p188*
McBride, Alexander 18; Philadelphia, 1856 ***5704.8*** *p129*
McBride, Alexander 21; Philadelphia, 1854 ***5704.8*** *p116*
McBride, Andrew 20; St. John, N.B., 1862 ***5704.8*** *p150*
McBride, Ann; Philadelphia, 1865 ***5704.8*** *p198*
McBride, Ann 9; St. John, N.B., 1853 ***5704.8*** *p99*
McBride, Anne *SEE* McBride, Neal
McBride, Anne; America, 1864 ***5704.8*** *p188*
McBride, Anne; Philadelphia, 1849 ***5704.8*** *p49*
McBride, Anne 2; America, 1864 ***5704.8*** *p188*
McBride, Anne 18; New York, NY, 1868 ***5704.8*** *p225*
McBride, Auten 22; Philadelphia, 1854 ***5704.8*** *p123*
McBride, Bernard; Philadelphia, 1853 ***5704.8*** *p100*
McBride, Betty; Philadelphia, 1847 ***53.26*** *p51*
McBride, Betty; Philadelphia, 1847 ***5704.8*** *p30*
McBride, Biddy; Philadelphia, 1851 ***5704.8*** *p81*
McBride, Biddy 8; Quebec, 1847 ***5704.8*** *p36*
McBride, Biddy 11 *SEE* McBride, Neal
McBride, Biddy 11; Philadelphia, 1849 ***5704.8*** *p49*
McBride, Bridget; Philadelphia, 1865 ***5704.8*** *p190*
McBride, Bridget; Philadelphia, 1870 ***5704.8*** *p239*
McBride, Bridget 13; St. John, N.B., 1853 ***5704.8*** *p99*
McBride, Bridget 20; Philadelphia, 1864 ***5704.8*** *p156*
McBride, Bridget 24; Quebec, 1863 ***5704.8*** *p153*
McBride, Catharine; New York, NY, 1866 ***5704.8*** *p211*
McBride, Catharine; Philadelphia, 1864 ***5704.8*** *p175*
McBride, Catharine; Philadelphia, 1865 ***5704.8*** *p201*
McBride, Catherine; Philadelphia, 1847 ***53.26*** *p51*
McBride, Catherine; Philadelphia, 1847 ***5704.8*** *p1*
McBride, Catherine; Philadelphia, 1851 ***5704.8*** *p81*
McBride, Catherine 21; Quebec, 1863 ***5704.8*** *p153*
McBride, Catherine 26; Philadelphia, 1864 ***5704.8*** *p161*
McBride, Charles; Philadelphia, 1851 ***5704.8*** *p81*
McBride, Charles; Philadelphia, 1853 ***5704.8*** *p100*
McBride, Charles; Philadelphia, 1865 ***5704.8*** *p190*
McBride, Charles; Philadelphia, 1865 ***5704.8*** *p197*
McBride, Daniel; Philadelphia, 1852 ***5704.8*** *p89*
McBride, Daniel 21; Quebec, 1853 ***5704.8*** *p105*
McBride, Denis; St. John, N.B., 1847 ***5704.8*** *p15*
McBride, Dennis 16; Philadelphia, 1854 ***5704.8*** *p123*
McBride, Dolly; Philadelphia, 1865 ***5704.8*** *p198*
McBride, Domnick; New York, NY, 1869 ***5704.8*** *p232*
McBride, Eanus; Philadelphia, 1867 ***5704.8*** *p223*
McBride, Eliza; New York, NY, 1864 ***5704.8*** *p172*
McBride, Elizabeth; St. John, N.B., 1853 ***5704.8*** *p106*
McBride, Elleanor; New Orleans, 1848 ***5704.8*** *p48*
McBride, Ellen; New York, NY, 1868 ***5704.8*** *p223*
McBride, Ellen; New York, NY, 1869 ***5704.8*** *p233*
McBride, Ellen; Philadelphia, 1867 ***5704.8*** *p219*
McBride, Ellen 19; Philadelphia, 1855 ***5704.8*** *p124*
McBride, Eunice; New York, NY, 1869 ***5704.8*** *p232*
McBride, Felix; St. John, N.B., 1847 ***5704.8*** *p11*
McBride, Flora; Wilmington, NC, 1774 ***1639.20*** *p8*
McBride, Francis; Philadelphia, 1864 ***5704.8*** *p176*
McBride, Francis 2; Quebec, 1847 ***5704.8*** *p36*
McBride, Grace; New York, NY, 1867 ***5704.8*** *p222*
McBride, Grace; Philadelphia, 1851 ***5704.8*** *p81*
McBride, Hannah; New York, NY, 1868 ***5704.8*** *p223*
McBride, Hannah; Philadelphia, 1851 ***5704.8*** *p70*
McBride, Hannah; Philadelphia, 1866 ***5704.8*** *p208*
McBride, Hannah 23; Philadelphia, 1854 ***5704.8*** *p123*
McBride, Henry; St. John, N.B., 1847 ***5704.8*** *p11*
McBride, Hugh; Arizona, 1897-1898 ***9228.30*** *p12*
McBride, Hugh 26; Philadelphia, 1803 ***53.26*** *p51*
*Relative:*William 25

McBride, Hugh 31; Arizona, 1898 *9228.40 p3*
McBride, James; New York, NY, 1864 *5704.8 p184*
McBride, James; New York, NY, 1866 *5704.8 p211*
McBride, James; Philadelphia, 1852 *5704.8 p85*
McBride, James; Philadelphia, 1867 *5704.8 p219*
McBride, James; Quebec, 1847 *5704.8 p8*
McBride, James 22; St. John, N.B., 1864 *5704.8 p158*
McBride, Jane; Philadelphia, 1852 *5704.8 p88*
McBride, Jane 24; St. John, N.B., 1862 *5704.8 p150*
McBride, John; America, 1737 *4971 p66*
McBride, John; America, 1864 *5704.8 p188*
McBride, John; America, 1865 *5704.8 p195*
McBride, John; New York, NY, 1865 *5704.8 p191*
McBride, John; New York, NY, 1865 *5704.8 p193*
McBride, John; New York, NY, 1865 *5704.8 p199*
McBride, John; New York, NY, 1866 *5704.8 p209*
McBride, John; New York, NY, 1867 *5704.8 p224*
McBride, John; Philadelphia, 1851 *5704.8 p81*
McBride, John; Quebec, 1847 *5704.8 p36*
McBride, John; St. John, N.B., 1847 *5704.8 p11*
McBride, John 5; New York, NY, 1869 *5704.8 p235*
McBride, John 6; Quebec, 1847 *5704.8 p36*
McBride, John 11; St. John, N.B., 1853 *5704.8 p99*
McBride, John 25; Philadelphia, 1854 *5704.8 p123*
McBride, John 30; Philadelphia, 1854 *5704.8 p123*
McBride, John 54; Philadelphia, 1861 *5704.8 p148*
McBride, Joseph; St. John, N.B., 1850 *5704.8 p61*
McBride, Margaret; St. John, N.B., 1850 *5704.8 p61*
McBride, Margaret; St. John, N.B., 1853 *5704.8 p99*
McBride, Margaret 18; St. John, N.B., 1855 *5704.8 p127*
McBride, Margery 17; Philadelphia, 1859 *5704.8 p141*
McBride, Martha 16; Baltimore, 1775 *1219.7 p271*
McBride, Mary; America, 1869 *5704.8 p236*
McBride, Mary; New York, NY, 1866 *5704.8 p212*
McBride, Mary; Philadelphia, 1849 *53.26 p51*
McBride, Mary; Philadelphia, 1849 *5704.8 p50*
McBride, Mary; Philadelphia, 1851 *5704.8 p81*
McBride, Mary; Philadelphia, 1853 *5704.8 p113*
McBride, Mary; Philadelphia, 1865 *5704.8 p198*
McBride, Mary; Philadelphia, 1868 *5704.8 p222*
McBride, Mary; Philadelphia, 1868 *5704.8 p230*
McBride, Mary; Quebec, 1847 *5704.8 p36*
McBride, Mary; St. John, N.B., 1853 *5704.8 p99*
McBride, Mary 17; Quebec, 1863 *5704.8 p153*
McBride, Mary 19; Philadelphia, 1854 *5704.8 p116*
McBride, Mary 22; St. John, N.B., 1864 *5704.8 p159*
McBride, Mary A.; Philadelphia, 1864 *5704.8 p172*
McBride, Mary Ann 25; Philadelphia, 1860 *5704.8 p145*
McBride, Mary Jane 21; St. John, N.B., 1864 *5704.8 p158*
McBride, Michael; New York, NY, 1836 *8208.4 p22*
McBride, Michael; New York, NY, 1868 *5704.8 p223*
McBride, Michael; Ohio, 1848 *1450.2 p95A*
McBride, Michael; Philadelphia, 1854 *5704.8 p123*
McBride, Michael; Quebec, 1847 *5704.8 p36*
McBride, Michael 9 mos; Quebec, 1847 *5704.8 p36*
McBride, Michael 10; Philadelphia, 1852 *5704.8 p85*
McBride, Nancy 22; Quebec, 1853 *5704.8 p105*
McBride, Neal; Massachusetts, 1847 *5881.1 p73*
McBride, Neal; Philadelphia, 1849 *53.26 p51*
  *Relative:*Anne
  *Relative:*Biddy 11
McBride, Neal; Philadelphia, 1849 *5704.8 p49*
McBride, Neal; Philadelphia, 1852 *5704.8 p85*
McBride, Neil; New York, NY, 1869 *5704.8 p235*
McBride, Owen; New York, NY, 1838 *8208.4 p70*
McBride, Pat; Philadelphia, 1851 *5704.8 p81*
McBride, Pat 18; Philadelphia, 1855 *5704.8 p124*
McBride, Patrick; New York, NY, 1869 *5704.8 p235*
McBride, Patrick; St. John, N.B., 1853 *5704.8 p108*
McBride, Patrick 9 mos; St. John, N.B., 1850 *5704.8 p61*
McBride, Patrick 4; Quebec, 1847 *5704.8 p36*
McBride, Patrick 18; Philadelphia, 1854 *5704.8 p123*
McBride, Peggy 18; Philadelphia, 1853 *5704.8 p112*
McBride, Peggy 18; Philadelphia, 1854 *5704.8 p123*
McBride, Peggy 24; Philadelphia, 1854 *5704.8 p123*
McBride, Peter; St. John, N.B., 1847 *5704.8 p11*
McBride, Peter 9; St. John, N.B., 1850 *5704.8 p61*
McBride, Peter 19; Philadelphia, 1854 *5704.8 p117*
McBride, Peter 20; Philadelphia, 1854 *5704.8 p116*
McBride, Rodger 20; Philadelphia, 1854 *5704.8 p123*
McBride, Roger; America, 1740 *4971 p67*
McBride, Rose; New York, NY, 1866 *5704.8 p205*
McBride, Rose; Philadelphia, 1865 *5704.8 p198*
McBride, Sally; Philadelphia, 1851 *5704.8 p81*
McBride, Sally; St. John, N.B., 1853 *5704.8 p99*
McBride, Samuel; St. John, N.B., 1851 *5704.8 p78*
McBride, Samuel 28; Philadelphia, 1803 *53.26 p51*
McBride, Sarah; America, 1864 *5704.8 p187*
McBride, Sarah; New York, NY, 1865 *5704.8 p193*
McBride, Sarah; Philadelphia, 1867 *5704.8 p215*
McBride, Sarah; Philadelphia, 1867 *5704.8 p216*
McBride, Susan; New York, NY, 1869 *5704.8 p235*

McBride, Thomas; Charleston, SC, 1695-1795 *1639.20 p120*
McBride, Towel; Philadelphia, 1851 *5704.8 p81*
McBride, William; Illinois, 1865 *7857 p5*
McBride, William; New York, NY, 1838 *8208.4 p61*
McBride, William; Philadelphia, 1852 *5704.8 p85*
McBride, William; Washington, 1859-1920 *2872.1 p27*
McBride, William 7; New York, NY, 1869 *5704.8 p235*
McBride, William 25 SEE McBride, Hugh
McBride, William 50; Philadelphia, 1803 *53.26 p51*
McBrien, Alexander 13; Quebec, 1851 *5704.8 p74*
McBrien, Ann; Philadelphia, 1847 *5704.8 p31*
McBrien, David; St. John, N.B., 1850 *5704.8 p66*
McBrien, Mary; Philadelphia, 1847 *5704.8 p31*
McBrien, Phillip 6; Quebec, 1851 *5704.8 p74*
McBrien, Sarah Jane; Quebec, 1851 *5704.8 p74*
McBrien, Susan; Quebec, 1851 *5704.8 p74*
McBrine, Ann 24; St. John, N.B., 1856 *5704.8 p131*
McBrine, Hugh 30; Kansas, 1888 *5240.1 p72*
McBrine, Jane; Philadelphia, 1811 *53.26 p51*
McBrine, Mary; St. John, N.B., 1847 *5704.8 p21*
McBrine, Patrick; Philadelphia, 1847 *53.26 p51*
McBrine, Patrick; Philadelphia, 1847 *5704.8 p1*
McBrine, Prudy; Philadelphia, 1853 *5704.8 p102*
McBrine, Rebecca 50; St. John, N.B., 1854 *5704.8 p115*
McBrurty, Catherine; St. John, N.B., 1853 *5704.8 p106*
McBrurty, James; St. John, N.B., 1853 *5704.8 p106*
McBrurty, William; St. John, N.B., 1853 *5704.8 p106*
McBryan, Patrick; America, 1742 *4971 p23*
McBryde, Alexander; America, 1804 *1639.20 p120*
McBryde, Alexander 22; North Carolina, 1775 *1639.20 p120*
McBryde, Alexander 63; North Carolina, 1850 *1639.20 p120*
McBryde, Archibald; America, 1766-1836 *1639.20 p120*
  With parents
McBryde, Archibald 7 SEE McBryde, James
McBryde, Elizabeth 5 SEE McBryde, James
McBryde, Isabella 2; Quebec, 1864 *5704.8 p163*
McBryde, Isabella 28; Quebec, 1864 *5704.8 p163*
McBryde, James 38; North Carolina, 1775 *1639.20 p120*
  *Wife:*Janet McMiken 39
  *Child:*Archibald 7
  *Child:*Elizabeth 5
  *Child:*Jenny 4
McBryde, Janet McMiken 39 SEE McBryde, James
McBryde, Jenny 4 SEE McBryde, James
McBryde, John; Augusta, GA, 1819 *1639.20 p120*
McBryde, John 4; Quebec, 1864 *5704.8 p163*
McBryde, Margaret 66; North Carolina, 1850 *1639.20 p120*
McBryde, Mary 6; Quebec, 1864 *5704.8 p163*
McBryde, Mary 45; South Carolina, 1850 *1639.20 p120*
McBryde, Miles 30; Quebec, 1864 *5704.8 p163*
McCabe, . . . 6 mos; Philadelphia, 1867 *5704.8 p218*
McCabe, Ally; Quebec, 1847 *5704.8 p37*
McCabe, Ann 32; Massachusetts, 1848 *5881.1 p62*
McCabe, Ann Maria; St. John, N.B., 1852 *5704.8 p93*
McCabe, Anne; Quebec, 1847 *5704.8 p37*
McCabe, Bernard; Ohio, 1843 *9892.11 p32*
McCabe, Biddy 20; Massachusetts, 1849 *5881.1 p63*
McCabe, Bridget 5; Philadelphia, 1864 *5704.8 p173*
McCabe, Bridget 8; Massachusetts, 1848 *5881.1 p63*
McCabe, Bryan; America, 1741 *4971 p23*
McCabe, Ed.; Austin, TX, 1886 *9777 p5*
McCabe, Edm.; America, 1740 *4971 p30*
McCabe, Eliza; Philadelphia, 1867 *5704.8 p218*
McCabe, Eliza 10; Massachusetts, 1848 *5881.1 p65*
McCabe, Elizabeth 50; Philadelphia, 1854 *5704.8 p120*
McCabe, Ellen; America, 1840 *7036 p117*
McCabe, Harry 25; Kansas, 1890 *5240.1 p28*
McCabe, Harry 25; Kansas, 1890 *5240.1 p74*
McCabe, Jacques; Quebec, 1823 *7603 p88*
McCabe, James; America, 1737 *4971 p74*
McCabe, James; America, 1739 *4971 p25*
McCabe, James; America, 1741 *4971 p23*
McCabe, James; New York, NY, 1837 *8208.4 p53*
McCabe, James; Quebec, 1847 *5704.8 p37*
McCabe, Jane 24; Philadelphia, 1854 *5704.8 p120*
McCabe, John; Quebec, 1847 *5704.8 p37*
McCabe, John James 13; St. John, N.B., 1854 *5704.8 p121*
McCabe, Mary SEE McCabe, Patrick
McCabe, Mary; America, 1840 *7036 p117*
McCabe, Mary; Quebec, 1847 *5704.8 p37*
McCabe, Mary 23; Massachusetts, 1849 *5881.1 p72*
McCabe, Mary Ann 8; Philadelphia, 1854 *5704.8 p120*
McCabe, Owen; America, 1738 *4971 p38*
McCabe, Owen; Quebec, 1847 *5704.8 p37*
McCabe, Patrick; New York, NY, 1840 *7036 p117*
  *Relative:*Mary
McCabe, Patrick 50; Massachusetts, 1849 *5881.1 p74*
McCabe, Terrance 25; Massachusetts, 1848 *5881.1 p76*

McCabe, Thomas 10; Philadelphia, 1854 *5704.8 p120*
McCad, John 29; Philadelphia, 1803 *53.26 p51*
McCadam, John; Ohio, 1846 *9892.11 p32*
McCaddin, Henry; St. John, N.B., 1852 *5704.8 p95*
McCaddin, James; New York, NY, 1839 *8208.4 p100*
McCade, Jane 9; Massachusetts, 1848 *5881.1 p68*
McCaden, John 24; St. John, N.B., 1854 *5704.8 p119*
McCafferty, Bernard; Montreal, 1825 *7603 p54*
McCafferty, Bernard; Philadelphia, 1848 *53.26 p51*
McCafferty, Bernard; Philadelphia, 1848 *5704.8 p46*
McCafferty, Biddy 20; Philadelphia, 1804 *53.26 p51*
McCafferty, Bridget 16; Philadelphia, 1856 *5704.8 p129*
McCafferty, Bridget 17; Philadelphia, 1853 *5704.8 p111*
McCafferty, Cain 19; Philadelphia, 1854 *5704.8 p118*
McCafferty, Catherine SEE McCafferty, John
McCafferty, Catherine; Philadelphia, 1847 *5704.8 p22*
McCafferty, Catherine; St. John, N.B., 1847 *5704.8 p15*
McCafferty, Catherine 17; Philadelphia, 1859 *5704.8 p141*
McCafferty, David; St. John, N.B., 1847 *5704.8 p18*
McCafferty, Edward; Philadelphia, 1811 *53.26 p52*
McCafferty, Elisha 18; Quebec, 1856 *5704.8 p130*
McCafferty, Elizabeth SEE McCafferty, John
McCafferty, Elizabeth; Philadelphia, 1847 *5704.8 p22*
McCafferty, Ellen 7; Philadelphia, 1856 *5704.8 p129*
McCafferty, Fanny; Philadelphia, 1849 *5704.8 p54*
McCafferty, Giley 17; Philadelphia, 1853 *5704.8 p108*
McCafferty, John; New York, NY, 1869 *5704.8 p232*
McCafferty, John; Philadelphia, 1847 *53.26 p52*
  *Relative:*Elizabeth
  *Relative:*Catherine
McCafferty, John; Philadelphia, 1847 *5704.8 p22*
McCafferty, John; St. John, N.B., 1847 *5704.8 p5*
McCafferty, John 10; Philadelphia, 1856 *5704.8 p129*
McCafferty, John 21; Philadelphia, 1854 *5704.8 p118*
McCafferty, John 21; St. John, N.B., 1854 *5704.8 p114*
McCafferty, John 25; Philadelphia, 1854 *5704.8 p116*
McCafferty, Margaret; New York, NY, 1869 *5704.8 p232*
McCafferty, Margery; Philadelphia, 1868 *5704.8 p226*
McCafferty, Mary; America, 1869 *5704.8 p232*
McCafferty, Mary; America, 1869 *5704.8 p236*
McCafferty, Mary 12; Philadelphia, 1856 *5704.8 p129*
McCafferty, Mary 18; Philadelphia, 1856 *5704.8 p128*
McCafferty, Neal; Quebec, 1848 *5704.8 p41*
McCafferty, Neal 23; St. John, N.B., 1854 *5704.8 p114*
McCafferty, Nelly; Quebec, 1848 *5704.8 p41*
McCafferty, Patrick; America, 1868 *5704.8 p231*
McCafferty, Patrick; Philadelphia, 1852 *5704.8 p91*
McCafferty, Patrick 20; Philadelphia, 1859 *5704.8 p141*
McCafferty, Susan 11; Philadelphia, 1849 *5704.8 p54*
McCafferty, Thomas 18; Philadelphia, 1854 *5704.8 p122*
McCafferty, William 22; Quebec, 1857 *5704.8 p136*
McCaffery, Andy; St. John, N.B., 1851 *5704.8 p77*
McCaffery, Catherine 19; Quebec, 1855 *5704.8 p125*
McCaffery, Ellen 23; Philadelphia, 1853 *5704.8 p109*
McCaffery, John 21; Quebec, 1855 *5704.8 p125*
McCaffery, John 40; Quebec, 1856 *5704.8 p130*
McCaffery, Patrick; St. John, N.B., 1851 *5704.8 p77*
McCaffray, Bessy 4; Massachusetts, 1849 *5881.1 p63*
McCaffrey, Ellen 1; Massachusetts, 1849 *5881.1 p66*
McCaffrey, James 10; Massachusetts, 1849 *5881.1 p68*
McCaffrey, Jane 6; Massachusetts, 1849 *5881.1 p68*
McCaffrey, John; New York, NY, 1838 *8208.4 p68*
McCaffrey, John; New York, NY, 1838 *8208.4 p84*
McCaffrey, Michael; New York, NY, 1838 *8208.4 p68*
McCaffrey, Nancy 50; Massachusetts, 1849 *5881.1 p73*
McCaffrey, William; Montreal, 1823 *7603 p55*
McCaffry, Ailes 11; Quebec, 1847 *5704.8 p12*
McCaffry, Ann; Quebec, 1823 *7603 p53*
McCaffry, Ann; St. John, N.B., 1849 *5704.8 p48*
McCaffry, Anne; St. John, N.B., 1849 *5704.8 p48*
McCaffry, Bernard; New York, NY, 1839 *8208.4 p100*
McCaffry, Biddy; Philadelphia, 1850 *53.26 p52*
McCaffry, Biddy; Philadelphia, 1850 *5704.8 p68*
McCaffry, Bridget; Quebec, 1847 *5704.8 p28*
McCaffry, Bridget 9; Philadelphia, 1864 *5704.8 p171*
McCaffry, Catherine; St. John, N.B., 1849 *5704.8 p48*
McCaffry, Charles; Quebec, 1847 *5704.8 p12*
McCaffry, Denis 6; St. John, N.B., 1849 *5704.8 p48*
McCaffry, Ellen; Philadelphia, 1864 *5704.8 p171*
McCaffry, Henry; Philadelphia, 1864 *5704.8 p180*
McCaffry, James 8; St. John, N.B., 1849 *5704.8 p48*
McCaffry, John; Philadelphia, 1866 *5704.8 p212*
McCaffry, John; Quebec, 1847 *5704.8 p28*
McCaffry, John; St. John, N.B., 1849 *5704.8 p48*
McCaffry, John 2; St. John, N.B., 1849 *5704.8 p48*
McCaffry, Knogh.; America, 1737 *4971 p63*
McCaffry, Latt; Quebec, 1847 *5704.8 p29*
McCaffry, Lotty; Quebec, 1851 *5704.8 p75*
McCaffry, Margaret 9 mos; St. John, N.B., 1849 *5704.8 p48*
McCaffry, Margaret 11; Quebec, 1847 *5704.8 p16*

McCaffry, Mary; Quebec, 1847 ***5704.8*** *p12*
McCaffry, Mary; St. John, N.B., 1847 ***5704.8*** *p24*
McCaffry, Mary Anne 4; St. John, N.B., 1849 ***5704.8*** *p48*
McCaffry, Nancy; Quebec, 1847 ***5704.8*** *p12*
McCaffry, Owen; America, 1740 ***4971*** *p72*
McCaffry, Patrick; Philadelphia, 1864 ***5704.8*** *p171*
McCaffry, Peter; Quebec, 1847 ***5704.8*** *p16*
McCaffry, Rose; Quebec, 1847 ***5704.8*** *p12*
McCaffry, Rose 7; Philadelphia, 1864 ***5704.8*** *p171*
McCaffry, Sally 13; Quebec, 1847 ***5704.8*** *p12*
McCaffry, Teragh; Philadelphia, 1849 ***53.26*** *p52*
McCaffry, Teragh; Philadelphia, 1849 ***5704.8*** *p53*
McCaffry, Thomas; Philadelphia, 1864 ***5704.8*** *p171*
McCaffry, Thomas; Quebec, 1847 ***5704.8*** *p28*
McCage, Hannah; St. John, N.B., 1850 ***5704.8*** *p61*
McCaghen, Eliza; Philadelphia, 1851 ***5704.8*** *p81*
McCahen, James 20; Philadelphia, 1864 ***5704.8*** *p157*
McCahen, Robert; Philadelphia, 1864 ***5704.8*** *p157*
McCahill, Alice 21; Philadelphia, 1855 ***5704.8*** *p124*
McCahill, Ann 23; Philadelphia, 1855 ***5704.8*** *p124*
McCahill, Conoly; Philadelphia, 1849 ***53.26*** *p52*
*Relative:*Dennis
*Relative:*Magy
McCahill, Conoly; Philadelphia, 1849 ***5704.8*** *p53*
McCahill, Denis; Philadelphia, 1849 ***5704.8*** *p53*
McCahill, Dennis *SEE* McCahill, Conoly
McCahill, Ellen; America, 1863-1871 ***5704.8*** *p199*
McCahill, Ellen 20; Philadelphia, 1865 ***5704.8*** *p165*
McCahill, Hannah; Philadelphia, 1864 ***5704.8*** *p184*
McCahill, John; America, 1866 ***5704.8*** *p212*
McCahill, Magy *SEE* McCahill, Conoly
McCahill, Magy; Philadelphia, 1849 ***5704.8*** *p53*
McCahill, Mary; Philadelphia, 1851 ***5704.8*** *p78*
McCahill, Patrick; New York, NY, 1839 ***8208.4*** *p91*
McCahon, John; Baltimore, 1831 ***9892.11*** *p32*
McCaister, Elizabeth 21; Philadelphia, 1857 ***5704.8*** *p133*
McCalaugh, John 16; Quebec, 1855 ***5704.8*** *p125*
McCalaugh, Moses 10; Quebec, 1855 ***5704.8*** *p125*
McCale, Mary; New York, NY, 1864 ***5704.8*** *p172*
McCalester, Daniel 23; Philadelphia, 1860 ***5704.8*** *p145*
McCalig, James 22; St. John, N.B., 1854 ***5704.8*** *p114*
McCaligh, John 21; St. John, N.B., 1857 ***5704.8*** *p135*
McCalister, Keatty; Philadelphia, 1849 ***53.26*** *p52*
McCalister, Keatty 13; Philadelphia, 1849 ***5704.8*** *p58*
McCalister, Sarah Jane; Philadelphia, 1847 ***5704.8*** *p24*
McCalister, William; Philadelphia, 1847 ***5704.8*** *p24*
McCall, Catharine 6; Massachusetts, 1849 ***5881.1*** *p64*
McCall, Catherine 79 *SEE* McCall, Duncan
McCall, Christian 35 *SEE* McCall, Duncan
McCall, Daniel; America, 1793 ***1639.20*** *p130*
McCall, Daniel 55; North Carolina, 1850 ***1639.20*** *p130*
McCall, Daniel 62; South Carolina, 1850 ***1639.20*** *p130*
McCall, Duncan 74; South Carolina, 1850 ***1639.20*** *p131*
*Relative:*Catherine 79
*Relative:*Christian 35
McCall, Eliza; Philadelphia, 1850 ***53.26*** *p52*
McCall, Eliza; Philadelphia, 1850 ***5704.8*** *p59*
McCall, Emma; Philadelphia, 1864 ***5704.8*** *p178*
McCall, Fanny; Philadelphia, 1864 ***5704.8*** *p173*
McCall, Fred; Arkansas, 1918 ***95.2*** *p82*
McCall, John; Charleston, SC, 1808 ***1639.20*** *p132*
McCall, John; New York, NY, 1835 ***8208.4*** *p41*
McCall, John; Philadelphia, 1864 ***5704.8*** *p185*
McCall, John; Wilmington, NC, 1775 ***1639.20*** *p131*
*Wife:*Margaret
With children
McCall, Margaret *SEE* McCall, John
McCall, Mary; Philadelphia, 1864 ***5704.8*** *p177*
McCall, Nancy; South Carolina, 1850 ***1639.20*** *p132*
McCall, Patrick; Philadelphia, 1864 ***5704.8*** *p177*
McCallag, Francis 24; St. John, N.B., 1854 ***5704.8*** *p114*
McCallaghan, Call.; America, 1740 ***4971*** *p47*
McCallam, Matthew; New York, NY, 1834 ***8208.4*** *p31*
McCallan, John 20; Philadelphia, 1853 ***5704.8*** *p111*
McCallen, Catherine 21; Philadelphia, 1864 ***5704.8*** *p160*
McCallen, Eliza Jane 2 mos; Philadelphia, 1864 ***5704.8*** *p160*
McCallen, Mathew 25; Philadelphia, 1864 ***5704.8*** *p160*
McCallen, Patrick 33; Philadelphia, 1803 ***53.26*** *p52*
McCallester, Anne; New York, NY, 1870 ***5704.8*** *p237*
McCallester, Sarah; New York, NY, 1870 ***5704.8*** *p237*
McCallester, Thomas; New York, NY, 1870 ***5704.8*** *p237*
McCalley, George 20; Quebec, 1858 ***5704.8*** *p138*
McCallig, John; Philadelphia, 1852 ***5704.8*** *p85*
McCallig, Mary; Philadelphia, 1852 ***5704.8*** *p85*
McCallig, Unity; Philadelphia, 1852 ***5704.8*** *p85*
McCallin, Cicily; St. John, N.B., 1847 ***5704.8*** *p19*
McCallin, Nancy; St. John, N.B., 1849 ***5704.8*** *p48*
McCallin, Patrick; St. John, N.B., 1847 ***5704.8*** *p19*
McCallin, Rosey; St. John, N.B., 1847 ***5704.8*** *p19*
McCallion, Ann; New York, NY, 1866 ***5704.8*** *p213*
McCallion, Ann; St. John, N.B., 1850 ***5704.8*** *p67*
McCallion, Bernard; St. John, N.B., 1847 ***5704.8*** *p2*
McCallion, Betty 2; St. John, N.B., 1853 ***5704.8*** *p107*
McCallion, Bridget; New York, NY, 1870 ***5704.8*** *p237*
McCallion, Catharine; Philadelphia, 1867 ***5704.8*** *p221*
McCallion, Catharine; Philadelphia, 1871 ***5704.8*** *p241*
McCallion, Ceclia 18; Philadelphia, 1868 ***5704.8*** *p225*
McCallion, Charles; St. John, N.B., 1853 ***5704.8*** *p107*
McCallion, Charlott 19; Quebec, 1856 ***5704.8*** *p130*
McCallion, Daniel 9; St. John, N.B., 1850 ***5704.8*** *p67*
McCallion, Dennis; St. John, N.B., 1850 ***5704.8*** *p67*
McCallion, Donald; St. John, N.B., 1850 ***5704.8*** *p67*
McCallion, Ellan; St. John, N.B., 1847 ***5704.8*** *p34*
McCallion, Ellen; Philadelphia, 1851 ***5704.8*** *p70*
McCallion, Ellen; St. John, N.B., 1850 ***5704.8*** *p67*
McCallion, Fanny; Philadelphia, 1868 ***5704.8*** *p225*
McCallion, James; Philadelphia, 1851 ***5704.8*** *p70*
McCallion, James; St. John, N.B., 1853 ***5704.8*** *p107*
McCallion, Jane 13; Quebec, 1856 ***5704.8*** *p130*
McCallion, John; Philadelphia, 1870 ***5704.8*** *p239*
McCallion, John 10; St. John, N.B., 1847 ***5704.8*** *p2*
McCallion, John 12; St. John, N.B., 1850 ***5704.8*** *p67*
McCallion, John 19; St. John, N.B., 1854 ***5704.8*** *p115*
McCallion, John 21; Philadelphia, 1858 ***5704.8*** *p138*
McCallion, John 43; St. John, N.B., 1855 ***5704.8*** *p127*
McCallion, Margaret; New York, NY, 1868 ***5704.8*** *p228*
McCallion, Margaret; Philadelphia, 1851 ***5704.8*** *p70*
McCallion, Margaret 17; St. John, N.B., 1854 ***5704.8*** *p115*
McCallion, Margaret 45; St. John, N.B., 1855 ***5704.8*** *p127*
McCallion, Mary; Philadelphia, 1847 ***53.26*** *p52*
McCallion, Mary; Philadelphia, 1847 ***5704.8*** *p31*
McCallion, Mary 8; St. John, N.B., 1847 ***5704.8*** *p2*
McCallion, Mary 17; Philadelphia, 1861 ***5704.8*** *p149*
McCallion, Michael; New York, NY, 1865 ***5704.8*** *p195*
McCallion, Michael; St. John, N.B., 1847 ***5704.8*** *p2*
McCallion, Michael 5; St. John, N.B., 1847 ***5704.8*** *p2*
McCallion, Michael 14; St. John, N.B., 1850 ***5704.8*** *p67*
McCallion, Nancy; St. John, N.B., 1853 ***5704.8*** *p107*
McCallion, Neally 2; St. John, N.B., 1847 ***5704.8*** *p2*
McCallion, Patrick; St. John, N.B., 1847 ***5704.8*** *p34*
McCallion, Phillip; Philadelphia, 1867 ***5704.8*** *p218*
McCallion, Phillip; St. John, N.B., 1847 ***5704.8*** *p2*
McCallion, Rosanna 24; St. John, N.B., 1855 ***5704.8*** *p127*
McCallion, Rose; Philadelphia, 1870 ***5704.8*** *p239*
McCallion, Rosey 13; St. John, N.B., 1847 ***5704.8*** *p2*
McCallion, Sarah; Philadelphia, 1868 ***5704.8*** *p225*
McCallion, Stewart; Philadelphia, 1851 ***5704.8*** *p70*
McCallion, Susan 9 mos; St. John, N.B., 1847 ***5704.8*** *p34*
McCallion, Susey; St. John, N.B., 1847 ***5704.8*** *p2*
McCallion, Thomas; St. John, N.B., 1853 ***5704.8*** *p107*
McCallion, William; New York, NY, 1868 ***5704.8*** *p229*
McCallion, William 9; St. John, N.B., 1847 ***5704.8*** *p2*
McCallister, Catharine; Philadelphia, 1864 ***5704.8*** *p187*
McCallister, James; Philadelphia, 1864 ***5704.8*** *p187*
McCallister, Mary; Philadelphia, 1866 ***5704.8*** *p206*
McCallister, Mary; Philadelphia, 1867 ***5704.8*** *p219*
McCallister, Michael 16; Philadelphia, 1855 ***5704.8*** *p124*
McCallister, Susan; Philadelphia, 1865 ***5704.8*** *p201*
McCalls, David; America, 1737 ***4971*** *p68*
McCalls, Mary; America, 1739 ***4971*** *p68*
McCalls, Robert; America, 1737 ***4971*** *p68*
McCallum, Archibald; America, 1804 ***1639.20*** *p121*
McCallum, Donald; South Carolina, 1716 ***1639.20*** *p121*
McCallum, Duncan; America, 1792 ***1639.20*** *p121*
McCallum, Duncan; North Carolina, 1824 ***1639.20*** *p121*
McCallum, Duncan; South Carolina, 1716 ***1639.20*** *p121*
McCallum, Duncan 30; Wilmington, NC, 1775 ***1639.20*** *p121*
McCallum, Duncan 66; South Carolina, 1850 ***1639.20*** *p121*
McCallum, Flora 80; North Carolina, 1850 ***1639.20*** *p121*
McCallum, John; New York, NY, 1834 ***8208.4*** *p38*
McCallum, John; South Carolina, 1716 ***1639.20*** *p122*
McCallum, John 12; St. John, N.B., 1847 ***5704.8*** *p21*
McCallum, John 58; North Carolina, 1850 ***1639.20*** *p122*
McCallum, Katie; North Carolina, 1700-1799 ***1639.20*** *p207*
McCallum, Margaret 70; North Carolina, 1850 ***1639.20*** *p122*
McCallum, Mary 84; North Carolina, 1850 ***1639.20*** *p122*
McCallum, Stephen; San Francisco, 1850 ***4914.15*** *p10*
McCally, Bridget 24; Philadelphia, 1854 ***5704.8*** *p122*
McCally, Michael 24; Philadelphia, 1854 ***5704.8*** *p122*
McCally, Sally 20; Philadelphia, 1854 ***5704.8*** *p122*
McCally, Susan 16; Philadelphia, 1854 ***5704.8*** *p122*
McCalsa, Catherine; St. John, N.B., 1853 ***5704.8*** *p99*
McCalsa, James; St. John, N.B., 1853 ***5704.8*** *p99*
McCambridge, Michael; America, 1866 ***5704.8*** *p213*
McCamis, Pat 20; Philadelphia, 1857 ***5704.8*** *p132*
McCan, James; Ohio, 1842 ***8365.25*** *p12*
McCan, Me. 30; Port uncertain, 1836 ***778.5*** *p103*
McCandchie, John; Illinois, 1859 ***2896.5*** *p26*
McCandless, Alexander S.; New York, NY, 1867 ***5704.8*** *p220*
McCandless, Ann; St. John, N.B., 1851 ***5704.8*** *p80*
McCandless, David; St. John, N.B., 1851 ***5704.8*** *p78*
McCandless, Eliz. Ann *SEE* McCandless, Hugh
McCandless, Eliza; New York, NY, 1867 ***5704.8*** *p220*
McCandless, Eliza Ann; Philadelphia, 1849 ***5704.8*** *p53*
McCandless, Elizabeth 24; St. John, N.B., 1854 ***5704.8*** *p119*
McCandless, George 2; St. John, N.B., 1856 ***5704.8*** *p131*
McCandless, George 18; Philadelphia, 1855 ***5704.8*** *p123*
McCandless, Hugh; Philadelphia, 1849 ***53.26*** *p52*
*Relative:*Eliz. Ann
McCandless, Hugh; Philadelphia, 1849 ***5704.8*** *p53*
McCandless, Hugh; Philadelphia, 1851 ***5704.8*** *p80*
McCandless, Hugh 55; Philadelphia, 1853 ***5704.8*** *p109*
McCandless, James 3; New York, NY, 1867 ***5704.8*** *p220*
McCandless, Jane; St. John, N.B., 1850 ***5704.8*** *p65*
McCandless, John; Philadelphia, 1851 ***5704.8*** *p78*
McCandless, Joseph 18; Philadelphia, 1853 ***5704.8*** *p109*
McCandless, Martha; St. John, N.B., 1848 ***5704.8*** *p44*
McCandless, Mary Ann 26; St. John, N.B., 1856 ***5704.8*** *p131*
McCandless, Nancy 8; New York, NY, 1867 ***5704.8*** *p220*
McCandless, Nancy 53; Philadelphia, 1853 ***5704.8*** *p109*
McCandless, Ruth 9; Philadelphia, 1853 ***5704.8*** *p109*
McCandless, Samuel 16; Philadelphia, 1853 ***5704.8*** *p109*
McCandless, Thomas; St. John, N.B., 1852 ***5704.8*** *p84*
McCandless, Thomas 11; New York, NY, 1867 ***5704.8*** *p220*
McCanley, Bridget 21; Massachusetts, 1849 ***5881.1*** *p63*
McCanlis, John 25; Philadelphia, 1833-1834 ***53.26*** *p52*
McCann, . . .; Massachusetts, 1847 ***5881.1*** *p70*
McCann, Alexander; New York, NY, 1864 ***5704.8*** *p171*
McCann, Ann 20; Massachusetts, 1849 ***5881.1*** *p62*
McCann, Ann 20; Philadelphia, 1861 ***5704.8*** *p148*
McCann, Archangel Marie; Washington, 1859-1920 ***2872.1*** *p27*
McCann, Brian; St. John, N.B., 1847 ***5704.8*** *p21*
McCann, Bridget; Quebec, 1853 ***5704.8*** *p103*
McCann, Bridget; St. John, N.B., 1850 ***5704.8*** *p61*
McCann, Bridget 26; Philadelphia, 1859 ***5704.8*** *p141*
McCann, Catherine; St. John, N.B., 1850 ***5704.8*** *p61*
McCann, Catherine 13; St. John, N.B., 1847 ***5704.8*** *p5*
McCann, Daniel; Montreal, 1824 ***7603*** *p55*
McCann, David 21; St. John, N.B., 1855 ***5704.8*** *p127*
McCann, Edward; New York, NY, 1839 ***8208.4*** *p98*
McCann, Edward; New York, NY, 1864 ***5704.8*** *p179*
McCann, Eliza 45; Massachusetts, 1849 ***5881.1*** *p66*
McCann, Ellen 24; Quebec, 1855 ***5704.8*** *p126*
McCann, Ellen 60; Quebec, 1855 ***5704.8*** *p126*
McCann, Fanny; Philadelphia, 1847 ***53.26*** *p52*
McCann, Fanny; Philadelphia, 1847 ***5704.8*** *p32*
McCann, Francis; Montreal, 1823 ***7603*** *p54*
McCann, George; California, 1869 ***2769.6*** *p6*
McCann, Grace 20; Philadelphia, 1855 ***5704.8*** *p123*
McCann, Hannah; New York, NY, 1866 ***5704.8*** *p214*
McCann, Hannah 19; St. John, N.B., 1863 ***5704.8*** *p153*
McCann, Henry; Philadelphia, 1865 ***5704.8*** *p192*
McCann, Hugh; Philadelphia, 1864 ***5704.8*** *p186*
McCann, James; California, 1869 ***2769.6*** *p6*
McCann, James; Philadelphia, 1849 ***53.26*** *p52*
McCann, James; Philadelphia, 1849 ***5704.8*** *p58*
McCann, James; Philadelphia, 1866 ***5704.8*** *p207*
McCann, James 30; Quebec, 1855 ***5704.8*** *p126*
McCann, John; Illinois, 1859 ***7857*** *p5*
McCann, John; Nevada, 1874 ***2764.35*** *p50*
McCann, John; New York, NY, 1840 ***8208.4*** *p104*
McCann, John; St. John, N.B., 1853 ***5704.8*** *p99*
McCann, John; Washington, 1859-1920 ***2872.1*** *p27*
McCann, John 11; St. John, N.B., 1847 ***5704.8*** *p5*
McCann, John L.; Washington, 1859-1920 ***2872.1*** *p27*
McCann, Margaret; New York, NY, 1864 ***5704.8*** *p174*
McCann, Margaret; Philadelphia, 1849 ***53.26*** *p52*
McCann, Margaret; Philadelphia, 1849 ***5704.8*** *p54*
McCann, Margaret; Philadelphia, 1866 ***5704.8*** *p215*
McCann, Margaret 8; Massachusetts, 1849 ***5881.1*** *p72*
McCann, Margaret 28; Massachusetts, 1847 ***5881.1*** *p70*
McCann, Mary *SEE* McCann, Michael
McCann, Mary; Montreal, 1824 ***7603*** *p55*
McCann, Mary; Philadelphia, 1847 ***5704.8*** *p6*
McCann, Mary 1; Quebec, 1855 ***5704.8*** *p126*
McCann, Mary 9; St. John, N.B., 1847 ***5704.8*** *p5*
McCann, Mary 28; Quebec, 1855 ***5704.8*** *p126*
McCann, Michael; Philadelphia, 1847 ***53.26*** *p52*
*Relative:*Mary
McCann, Michael; Philadelphia, 1847 ***5704.8*** *p6*

McCann, Nicholas; America, 1866 ***5704.8*** *p214*
McCann, Nicholas 5; Massachusetts, 1849 ***5881.1*** *p73*
McCann, Patrick; America, 1741 ***4971*** *p35*
McCann, Patrick; America, 1845-1847 ***1450.2*** *p95A*
McCann, Patrick; Illinois, 1870 ***5012.38*** *p99*
McCann, Patrick; Illinois, 1872 ***5012.39*** *p91*
McCann, Patrick; New York, NY, 1864 ***5704.8*** *p175*
McCann, Patrick 25; Massachusetts, 1847 ***5881.1*** *p74*
McCann, Rosa 8; Massachusetts, 1849 ***5881.1*** *p75*
McCann, Rose; Philadelphia, 1850 ***53.26*** *p52*
McCann, Rose; Philadelphia, 1850 ***5704.8*** *p59*
McCann, Sarah; Philadelphia, 1852 ***5704.8*** *p88*
McCann, Sarah 16; St. John, N.B., 1855 ***5704.8*** *p127*
McCann, William; New York, NY, 1836 ***8208.4*** *p14*
McCann, William; Quebec, 1853 ***5704.8*** *p103*
McCanna, Barny 43; Philadelphia, 1804 ***53.26*** *p52*
McCanna, Catherine; Quebec, 1847 ***5704.8*** *p6*
McCanna, Catherine 7; Quebec, 1847 ***5704.8*** *p6*
McCanna, Catherine 14; Quebec, 1847 ***5704.8*** *p6*
McCanna, Daniel; Quebec, 1847 ***5704.8*** *p6*
McCanna, Eliza; Quebec, 1847 ***5704.8*** *p6*
McCanna, Henry; Quebec, 1847 ***5704.8*** *p6*
McCanna, James 11; Quebec, 1847 ***5704.8*** *p6*
McCanna, John; Quebec, 1847 ***5704.8*** *p6*
McCanna, Margaret; Quebec, 1847 ***5704.8*** *p6*
McCanna, Mary; Quebec, 1847 ***5704.8*** *p6*
McCanna, Mary 12; Quebec, 1847 ***5704.8*** *p6*
McCanna, Patrick; Quebec, 1847 ***5704.8*** *p6*
McCanna, Patrick 13; Quebec, 1847 ***5704.8*** *p6*
McCanna, Phillip 5; Quebec, 1847 ***5704.8*** *p6*
McCanna, Sarah 18; Philadelphia, 1856 ***5704.8*** *p128*
McCanney, . . . 1; Philadelphia, 1865 ***5704.8*** *p193*
McCanney, Ellen 5; Philadelphia, 1865 ***5704.8*** *p193*
McCanney, James 7; Philadelphia, 1865 ***5704.8*** *p193*
McCanney, Mary A. 2; Philadelphia, 1865 ***5704.8*** *p193*
McCanney, Thomas 4; Philadelphia, 1865 ***5704.8*** *p193*
McCanney, Unity; Philadelphia, 1865 ***5704.8*** *p193*
McCannigan, Mary; St. John, N.B., 1853 ***5704.8*** *p106*
McCanny, Ann 11; Quebec, 1864 ***5704.8*** *p159*
McCanny, Bridget; Quebec, 1850 ***5704.8*** *p62*
McCanny, Charles 9; Quebec, 1864 ***5704.8*** *p159*
McCanny, Francis 9 *SEE* McCanny, Margaret
McCanny, Francis 9; Philadelphia, 1847 ***5704.8*** *p22*
McCanny, James 18; Philadelphia, 1861 ***5704.8*** *p149*
McCanny, John; Philadelphia, 1848 ***53.26*** *p52*
*Relative:*Nathaniel
McCanny, John; Philadelphia, 1848 ***5704.8*** *p46*
McCanny, Margaret; Philadelphia, 1847 ***53.26*** *p52*
*Relative:*Francis 9
McCanny, Margaret; Philadelphia, 1847 ***5704.8*** *p22*
McCanny, Nancy; Philadelphia, 1850 ***53.26*** *p52*
McCanny, Nancy; Philadelphia, 1850 ***5704.8*** *p60*
McCanny, Nathaniel *SEE* McCanny, John
McCanny, Nathaniel; Philadelphia, 1848 ***5704.8*** *p46*
McCanny, Susan; Philadelphia, 1852 ***5704.8*** *p97*
McCanon, Mary 19; Quebec, 1855 ***5704.8*** *p125*
McCappin, John; St. John, N.B., 1847 ***5704.8*** *p19*
McCaraher, Eliza; Philadelphia, 1847 ***53.26*** *p52*
*Relative:*Sarah 12
*Relative:*Neil 9
McCaraher, Eliza; Philadelphia, 1847 ***5704.8*** *p2*
McCaraher, Neil 9 *SEE* McCaraher, Eliza
McCaraher, Neil 9; Philadelphia, 1847 ***5704.8*** *p2*
McCaraher, Sarah 12 *SEE* McCaraher, Eliza
McCaraher, Sarah 12; Philadelphia, 1847 ***5704.8*** *p2*
McCard, James; St. John, N.B., 1851 ***5704.8*** *p78*
McCard, Sarah; St. John, N.B., 1851 ***5704.8*** *p78*
McCaren, Elizabeth 20; Wilmington, DE, 1831 ***6508.7*** *p161*
McCaren, Isabella 21; Wilmington, DE, 1831 ***6508.7*** *p161*
McCarey, Bridget; New York, NY, 1866 ***5704.8*** *p212*
McCarey, Catherine; Philadelphia, 1854 ***5704.8*** *p116*
McCarey, Ellen; Philadelphia, 1864 ***5704.8*** *p178*
McCariston, Biddy 16; St. John, N.B., 1856 ***5704.8*** *p131*
McCarlen, Michael; New York, 1828 ***1450.2*** *p96A*
McCarmack, Thomas; America, 1836 ***1450.2*** *p96A*
McCarmal, Hugh 20; Philadelphia, 1857 ***5704.8*** *p133*
McCarn, Sarah 17; Massachusetts, 1847 ***5881.1*** *p75*
McCarne, Patrick; America, 1866 ***5704.8*** *p211*
McCarney, Bridget *SEE* McCarney, Patrick
McCarney, Bridget; Philadelphia, 1850 ***5704.8*** *p60*
McCarney, Patrick; Philadelphia, 1850 ***53.26*** *p52*
*Relative:*Bridget
McCarney, Patrick; Philadelphia, 1850 ***5704.8*** *p60*
McCarny, John 27; Philadelphia, 1858 ***5704.8*** *p139*
McCarny, Sophia 20; Philadelphia, 1858 ***5704.8*** *p139*
McCaroll, John; Quebec, 1830 ***4719.7*** *p21*
McCarra, Augustine; America, 1735-1743 ***4971*** *p78*
McCarra, Augustine; America, 1742 ***4971*** *p80*
McCarren, Brigitte; Montreal, 1820 ***7603*** *p61*
McCarren, Daniel; America, 1738 ***4971*** *p36*
McCarren, Edward 45; Philadelphia, 1853 ***5704.8*** *p109*
McCarren, Mary; St. John, N.B., 1848 ***5704.8*** *p43*
McCarroll, Mary; Philadelphia, 1851 ***5704.8*** *p71*
McCarroll, Patrick 26; Philadelphia, 1804 ***53.26*** *p52*
McCarroll, Susanna; Philadelphia, 1847 ***53.26*** *p52*
McCarroll, Susanna; Philadelphia, 1847 ***5704.8*** *p32*
McCarron, Alexander 3; Quebec, 1847 ***5704.8*** *p6*
McCarron, Andrew; Philadelphia, 1868 ***5704.8*** *p226*
McCarron, Ann; Quebec, 1851 ***5704.8*** *p82*
McCarron, Ann; St. John, N.B., 1847 ***5704.8*** *p34*
McCarron, Ann 8; St. John, N.B., 1847 ***5704.8*** *p34*
McCarron, Ann 19; St. John, N.B., 1854 ***5704.8*** *p120*
McCarron, Anne; America, 1864-1871 ***5704.8*** *p240*
McCarron, Anne 18; New York, NY, 1868 ***5704.8*** *p225*
McCarron, Anthony; Philadelphia, 1853 ***5704.8*** *p100*
McCarron, Biddy 6; St. John, N.B., 1847 ***5704.8*** *p34*
McCarron, Bridget 16; Quebec, 1854 ***5704.8*** *p119*
McCarron, Catherine; St. John, N.B., 1848 ***5704.8*** *p39*
McCarron, Charles; New York, NY, 1867 ***5704.8*** *p218*
McCarron, Charles; Philadelphia, 1851 ***5704.8*** *p81*
McCarron, Charles 4; St. John, N.B., 1854 ***5704.8*** *p120*
McCarron, Charles 22; Philadelphia, 1860 ***5704.8*** *p145*
McCarron, Charles 32; St. John, N.B., 1854 ***5704.8*** *p120*
McCarron, Cicily; St. John, N.B., 1852 ***5704.8*** *p83*
McCarron, Daniel; America, 1866 ***5704.8*** *p209*
McCarron, Daniel 12; St. John, N.B., 1854 ***5704.8*** *p120*
McCarron, Daniel 25; Philadelphia, 1861 ***5704.8*** *p148*
McCarron, Edward; America, 1864-1871 ***5704.8*** *p240*
McCarron, Eliza 5; Quebec, 1847 ***5704.8*** *p6*
McCarron, Eliza 12; Quebec, 1847 ***5704.8*** *p12*
McCarron, Ellan 11; St. John, N.B., 1847 ***5704.8*** *p34*
McCarron, Ellen; Quebec, 1847 ***5704.8*** *p6*
McCarron, Ellen 2; St. John, N.B., 1854 ***5704.8*** *p120*
McCarron, Fanny; New York, NY, 1864 ***5704.8*** *p172*
McCarron, Fanny; St. John, N.B., 1853 ***5704.8*** *p99*
McCarron, Grace 8; St. John, N.B., 1854 ***5704.8*** *p121*
McCarron, Hanna; Quebec, 1847 ***5704.8*** *p6*
McCarron, Hugh; New York, NY, 1864 ***5704.8*** *p172*
McCarron, Hugh; St. John, N.B., 1847 ***5704.8*** *p9*
McCarron, Hugh; St. John, N.B., 1851 ***5704.8*** *p80*
McCarron, Hugh 11; Philadelphia, 1860 ***5704.8*** *p146*
McCarron, Isabella 20; Quebec, 1857 ***5704.8*** *p135*
McCarron, James; Quebec, 1847 ***5704.8*** *p6*
McCarron, James; St. John, N.B., 1850 ***5704.8*** *p61*
McCarron, James; St. John, N.B., 1853 ***5704.8*** *p107*
McCarron, James 1; Quebec, 1847 ***5704.8*** *p12*
McCarron, James 9; Quebec, 1847 ***5704.8*** *p6*
McCarron, James 13; Quebec, 1851 ***5704.8*** *p82*
McCarron, James 13; Quebec, 1854 ***5704.8*** *p119*
McCarron, Jane; Philadelphia, 1853 ***5704.8*** *p101*
McCarron, Jane 8; Quebec, 1847 ***5704.8*** *p12*
McCarron, Jane 13; Quebec, 1847 ***5704.8*** *p6*
McCarron, Jane 18; Quebec, 1857 ***5704.8*** *p135*
McCarron, Jane 32; St. John, N.B., 1854 ***5704.8*** *p120*
McCarron, Jermiah; St. John, N.B., 1849 ***5704.8*** *p48*
McCarron, John; New York, NY, 1864 ***5704.8*** *p172*
McCarron, John; New York, NY, 1865 ***5704.8*** *p193*
McCarron, John; Quebec, 1847 ***5704.8*** *p6*
McCarron, John; Quebec, 1847 ***5704.8*** *p12*
McCarron, John 18; St. John, N.B., 1854 ***5704.8*** *p114*
McCarron, Margaret; Philadelphia, 1851 ***5704.8*** *p80*
McCarron, Margaret; Philadelphia, 1866 ***5704.8*** *p205*
McCarron, Margaret 20; Philadelphia, 1859 ***5704.8*** *p141*
McCarron, Margaret 25; St. John, N.B., 1866 ***5704.8*** *p166*
McCarron, Margery; Quebec, 1851 ***5704.8*** *p82*
McCarron, Mary; Philadelphia, 1851 ***5704.8*** *p80*
McCarron, Mary; St. John, N.B., 1853 ***5704.8*** *p99*
McCarron, Mary 9; St. John, N.B., 1847 ***5704.8*** *p34*
McCarron, Mary 10; St. John, N.B., 1853 ***5704.8*** *p110*
McCarron, Mary 11; Quebec, 1854 ***5704.8*** *p119*
McCarron, Mary 11; St. John, N.B., 1848 ***5704.8*** *p39*
McCarron, Mary 20; Philadelphia, 1860 ***5704.8*** *p146*
McCarron, Mary A.; Philadelphia, 1868 ***5704.8*** *p226*
McCarron, Matty 6; Quebec, 1847 ***5704.8*** *p12*
McCarron, Michael; Quebec, 1850 ***5704.8*** *p66*
McCarron, Michael; St. John, N.B., 1847 ***5704.8*** *p34*
McCarron, Miller; Quebec, 1847 ***5704.8*** *p6*
McCarron, Nancy; Quebec, 1847 ***5704.8*** *p12*
McCarron, Owen; St. John, N.B., 1848 ***5704.8*** *p39*
McCarron, Patrick; St. John, N.B., 1847 ***5704.8*** *p21*
McCarron, Robert 7; Quebec, 1847 ***5704.8*** *p6*
McCarron, Robert 25; Quebec, 1856 ***5704.8*** *p130*
McCarron, Rosanna 18; Philadelphia, 1860 ***5704.8*** *p146*
McCarron, Rose 5; St. John, N.B., 1853 ***5704.8*** *p110*
McCarron, Sarah; St. John, N.B., 1852 ***5704.8*** *p83*
McCarron, Sarah 4; St. John, N.B., 1847 ***5704.8*** *p34*
McCarron, Sarah 11; Quebec, 1847 ***5704.8*** *p6*
McCarron, Susan 9 mos; St. John, N.B., 1847 ***5704.8*** *p34*
McCarron, Susan 22; St. John, N.B., 1866 ***5704.8*** *p166*
McCarron, Thomas; Philadelphia, 1864 ***5704.8*** *p180*
McCarron, William; Philadelphia, 1849 ***53.26*** *p52*
McCarron, William; Philadelphia, 1849 ***5704.8*** *p58*
McCarron, William; Philadelphia, 1852 ***5704.8*** *p92*
McCarron, William; Quebec, 1847 ***5704.8*** *p6*
McCarron, William 10; Quebec, 1847 ***5704.8*** *p12*
McCarry, Michael; Philadelphia, 1853 ***5704.8*** *p101*
McCarson, Harriett 9; St. John, N.B., 1847 ***5704.8*** *p25*
McCarson, John 11; St. John, N.B., 1847 ***5704.8*** *p25*
McCart, Henry; Ohio, 1819 ***8582.1*** *p47*
McCart, Mary 22; St. John, N.B., 1864 ***5704.8*** *p159*
McCarten, Patrick; Wisconsin, n.d. ***9675.7*** *p51*
McCarter, Ann; New York, NY, 1864 ***5704.8*** *p169*
McCarter, Ann 27; Philadelphia, 1864 ***5704.8*** *p160*
McCarter, Anne; St. John, N.B., 1852 ***5704.8*** *p92*
McCarter, Catharine; Philadelphia, 1865 ***5704.8*** *p199*
McCarter, Daniel; Philadelphia, 1850 ***53.26*** *p52*
*Relative:*Thomas
McCarter, Daniel; Philadelphia, 1850 ***5704.8*** *p69*
McCarter, Edward; Quebec, 1847 ***5704.8*** *p37*
McCarter, James; Philadelphia, 1852 ***5704.8*** *p84*
McCarter, James 3 mos; Philadelphia, 1864 ***5704.8*** *p160*
McCarter, Jane; Philadelphia, 1851 ***5704.8*** *p76*
McCarter, Jane; Philadelphia, 1865 ***5704.8*** *p199*
McCarter, John; Quebec, 1847 ***5704.8*** *p37*
McCarter, John 3; Philadelphia, 1864 ***5704.8*** *p160*
McCarter, Margaret; Philadelphia, 1851 ***5704.8*** *p78*
McCarter, Martha; Philadelphia, 1865 ***5704.8*** *p199*
McCarter, Mary; Philadelphia, 1865 ***5704.8*** *p199*
McCarter, Mary; Quebec, 1847 ***5704.8*** *p37*
McCarter, Michael 24; Quebec, 1858 ***5704.8*** *p138*
McCarter, Pat; Quebec, 1847 ***5704.8*** *p37*
McCarter, Patrick; Quebec, 1847 ***5704.8*** *p37*
McCarter, Rebecca; Philadelphia, 1865 ***5704.8*** *p199*
McCarter, Rebecca Jane 2; Philadelphia, 1864 ***5704.8*** *p160*
McCarter, Thomas *SEE* McCarter, Daniel
McCarter, Thomas; Philadelphia, 1850 ***5704.8*** *p69*
McCarter, Thomas; Quebec, 1847 ***5704.8*** *p37*
McCarter, William; Philadelphia, 1853 ***5704.8*** *p100*
McCarter, William 21; Philadelphia, 1861 ***5704.8*** *p149*
McCarter, William 26; Philadelphia, 1864 ***5704.8*** *p160*
McCarthy, Alice 40; Massachusetts, 1847 ***5881.1*** *p62*
McCarthy, Bridget 2; Massachusetts, 1850 ***5881.1*** *p63*
McCarthy, Bridget 36; Massachusetts, 1849 ***5881.1*** *p63*
McCarthy, Catharine 3; Massachusetts, 1850 ***5881.1*** *p65*
McCarthy, Catharine 4; Massachusetts, 1850 ***5881.1*** *p65*
McCarthy, Catharine 14; Massachusetts, 1849 ***5881.1*** *p64*
McCarthy, Catharine 15; Massachusetts, 1849 ***5881.1*** *p64*
McCarthy, Charles 55; Newfoundland, 1789 ***4915.24*** *p57*
McCarthy, Daniel; New York, NY, 1838 ***8208.4*** *p64*
McCarthy, Daniel 40; Massachusetts, 1849 ***5881.1*** *p65*
McCarthy, Daniel 53; Arizona, 1925 ***9228.40*** *p29*
McCarthy, Daniel 60; North Carolina, 1850 ***1639.20*** *p122*
McCarthy, David 30; Massachusetts, 1849 ***5881.1*** *p65*
McCarthy, Dennis; America, 1742 ***4971*** *p49*
McCarthy, Dennis; America, 1742 ***4971*** *p50*
McCarthy, Dennis; Virginia, 1856 ***4626.16*** *p16*
McCarthy, Dennis; Wisconsin, n.d. ***9675.7*** *p51*
McCarthy, Dennis 24; West Virginia, 1896 ***9788.3*** *p16*
McCarthy, Dennis 33; Massachusetts, 1849 ***5881.1*** *p65*
McCarthy, Elizabeth 32; Newport, RI, 1851 ***6508.5*** *p19*
McCarthy, Ellen 6; Massachusetts, 1849 ***5881.1*** *p65*
McCarthy, Ellen 15; Newport, RI, 1851 ***6508.5*** *p20*
McCarthy, Ellen 40; Massachusetts, 1847 ***5881.1*** *p65*
McCarthy, Felix; Wisconsin, n.d. ***9675.7*** *p51*
McCarthy, Florence 12; Massachusetts, 1850 ***5881.1*** *p66*
McCarthy, Florence 23; Newport, RI, 1851 ***6508.5*** *p19*
McCarthy, Florence 32; Massachusetts, 1849 ***5881.1*** *p66*
McCarthy, James; Montreal, 1824 ***7603*** *p65*
McCarthy, James; Wisconsin, n.d. ***9675.7*** *p51*
McCarthy, James 25; Montreal, 1796 ***7603*** *p80*
McCarthy, Jeremy; Quebec, 1780 ***7603*** *p63*
McCarthy, John; New York, NY, 1834 ***8208.4*** *p1*
McCarthy, John; New York, NY, 1836 ***8208.4*** *p12*
McCarthy, John; New York, NY, 1837 ***8208.4*** *p51*
McCarthy, John; Quebec, 1814 ***7603*** *p77*
McCarthy, John; Quebec, 1821 ***7603*** *p65*
McCarthy, John 4; Newport, RI, 1851 ***6508.5*** *p19*
McCarthy, John 10; Massachusetts, 1849 ***5881.1*** *p69*
McCarthy, John 10; Massachusetts, 1850 ***5881.1*** *p69*
McCarthy, John 13; Massachusetts, 1849 ***5881.1*** *p69*
McCarthy, John 30; Newport, RI, 1851 ***6508.5*** *p20*
McCarthy, John 36; Massachusetts, 1849 ***5881.1*** *p69*
McCarthy, Judy 20; Massachusetts, 1849 ***5881.1*** *p68*
McCarthy, Margaret 6; Massachusetts, 1849 ***5881.1*** *p71*
McCarthy, Margaret 7; Massachusetts, 1850 ***5881.1*** *p72*
McCarthy, Margt 5; Newport, RI, 1851 ***6508.5*** *p19*
McCarthy, Mary 20; Massachusetts, 1849 ***5881.1*** *p71*
McCarthy, Mary 30; Massachusetts, 1849 ***5881.1*** *p71*
McCarthy, Mary 39; Massachusetts, 1849 ***5881.1*** *p72*

McCarthy, Mary 40; Newport, RI, 1851 *6508.5 p20*
McCarthy, Mary 50; Massachusetts, 1849 *5881.1 p71*
McCarthy, Maurice 33; Newport, RI, 1851 *6508.5 p19*
McCarthy, Michael; Arkansas, 1918 *95.2 p82*
McCarthy, Michael; Wisconsin, n.d. *9675.7 p51*
McCarthy, Mick 1; Newport, RI, 1851 *6508.5 p19*
McCarthy, Nicolas; Quebec, 1822 *7603 p89*
McCarthy, Patrick 14; Massachusetts, 1849 *5881.1 p74*
McCarthy, Thomas 8; Massachusetts, 1849 *5881.1 p76*
McCarthy, Timothy; Philadelphia, 1841 *6013.19 p74*
McCartin, Bridget; Philadelphia, 1865 *5704.8 p194*
McCartin, Charles; Philadelphia, 1865 *5704.8 p194*
McCartin, Frank; Philadelphia, 1865 *5704.8 p194*
McCartney, Bridget 25; Quebec, 1853 *5704.8 p105*
McCartney, Dorothy; Quebec, 1851 *5704.8 p82*
McCartney, Hugh; Philadelphia, 1865 *5704.8 p189*
McCartney, James 1; Quebec, 1851 *5704.8 p82*
McCartney, James 26; Philadelphia, 1858 *5704.8 p139*
McCartney, John 6; Quebec, 1851 *5704.8 p82*
McCartney, Johnston 3; Quebec, 1851 *5704.8 p82*
McCartney, Margaret 8; Quebec, 1851 *5704.8 p82*
McCartney, Owen; New York, NY, 1864 *5704.8 p186*
McCartney, Owen; Philadelphia, 1865 *5704.8 p200*
McCartney, Patrick 25; Massachusetts, 1849 *5881.1 p75*
McCartney, Robert; Quebec, 1851 *5704.8 p82*
McCartney, Samuel; Charleston, SC, 1805 *1639.20 p122*
McCartney, Susan; New York, NY, 1869 *5704.8 p233*
McCartney, Thomas; Philadelphia, 1865 *5704.8 p200*
McCartney, William 12; Quebec, 1851 *5704.8 p82*
McCarton, Bridget; New York, NY, 1867 *5704.8 p221*
McCarton, Thomas; New York, NY, 1867 *5704.8 p221*
McCarton, Thomas 11; New York, NY, 1867 *5704.8 p221*
McCarty, Ann; Montreal, 1824 *7603 p98*
McCarty, Bridget 25; Massachusetts, 1849 *5881.1 p63*
McCarty, Bridget 54; Massachusetts, 1850 *5881.1 p64*
McCarty, Daniel; Quebec, 1788 *7603 p64*
McCarty, Daniel 30; Massachusetts, 1849 *5881.1 p65*
McCarty, Ellen 6; Massachusetts, 1850 *5881.1 p66*
McCarty, Ellen 50; Massachusetts, 1849 *5881.1 p66*
McCarty, Eugene 9; Massachusetts, 1849 *5881.1 p66*
McCarty, Eugene 25; Massachusetts, 1849 *5881.1 p66*
McCarty, Honora 30; Massachusetts, 1849 *5881.1 p67*
McCarty, James 4; Massachusetts, 1847 *5881.1 p67*
McCarty, James 24; Massachusetts, 1847 *5881.1 p67*
McCarty, Jeremiah; California, 1865 *3840.2 p18*
McCarty, Jeremiah; Wisconsin, n.d. *9675.7 p51*
McCarty, Jerry 7; Massachusetts, 1849 *5881.1 p69*
McCarty, Jerry 75; Massachusetts, 1847 *5881.1 p67*
McCarty, Johanna 11; Massachusetts, 1850 *5881.1 p69*
McCarty, John; Arizona, 1883 *2764.35 p49*
McCarty, John; Boston, 1837 *1450.2 p96A*
McCarty, John; Ohio, 1843 *9892.11 p32*
McCarty, John 8; Massachusetts, 1850 *5881.1 p69*
McCarty, Judy 40; Massachusetts, 1847 *5881.1 p67*
McCarty, Kitty 18; Massachusetts, 1847 *5881.1 p70*
McCarty, Mable; America, 1735-1743 *4971 p78*
McCarty, Mable; America, 1742 *4971 p80*
McCarty, Margaret 26; Massachusetts, 1849 *5881.1 p71*
McCarty, Mary; Quebec, 1823 *7603 p65*
McCarty, Mary 7; Massachusetts, 1849 *5881.1 p72*
McCarty, Nancy 9; Massachusetts, 1849 *5881.1 p73*
McCarty, Patrick 11; Massachusetts, 1847 *5881.1 p74*
McCarty, Philip 3; Massachusetts, 1847 *5881.1 p74*
McCarty, Thomas; New York, NY, 1838 *8208.4 p87*
McCarty, Thomas 22; Maryland, 1774 *1219.7 p178*
McCarty, William; Washington, 1859-1920 *2872.1 p27*
McCash, Hugh 22 SEE McCash, John
McCash, Jane 56 SEE McCash, John
McCash, John 60; Philadelphia, 1833-1834 *53.26 p52*
  *Relative:*Jane 56
  *Relative:*William 30
  *Relative:*Joseph 24
  *Relative:*Hugh 22
McCash, Joseph 24 SEE McCash, John
McCash, William 30 SEE McCash, John
McCashen, Francis 20; Massachusetts, 1849 *5881.1 p66*
McCashland, Henry; America, 1737 *4971 p66*
McCaskey, Anne; Quebec, 1851 *5704.8 p82*
McCaskey, Jane 4; Quebec, 1851 *5704.8 p82*
McCaskey, Robert 9; Quebec, 1851 *5704.8 p82*
McCaskey, William 7; Quebec, 1851 *5704.8 p82*
McCaskie, Donald; America, 1791 *1639.20 p122*
McCaskie, John; America, 1802 *1639.20 p122*
McCaskie, Malcolm 50; South Carolina, 1850 *1639.20 p122*
McCaskie, Margaret 48; South Carolina, 1850 *1639.20 p122*
McCaskill, Alexander; America, 1802 *1639.20 p123*
McCaskill, Alexander 55; North Carolina, 1850 *1639.20 p123*
  *Relative:*Margaret 52

McCaskill, Allan; North Carolina, 1727-1775 *1639.20 p123*
McCaskill, Allan; North Carolina, 1760-1850 *1639.20 p123*
McCaskill, Allen; America, 1811 *1639.20 p123*
McCaskill, Allen; North Carolina, 1765-1847 *1639.20 p123*
McCaskill, Allen; North Carolina, 1768-1868 *1639.20 p123*
McCaskill, Angus; North Carolina, 1737-1837 *1639.20 p123*
McCaskill, Angus 47 SEE McCaskill, Nancy
McCaskill, Angus Alexander; North Carolina, 1769-1807 *1639.20 p123*
McCaskill, Ann; North Carolina, 1747-1819 *1639.20 p124*
McCaskill, Christian; North Carolina, 1750-1850 *1639.20 p124*
McCaskill, Christian 56 SEE McCaskill, Hector
McCaskill, Daniel; America, 1811 *1639.20 p124*
McCaskill, Daniel; North Carolina, 1769-1853 *1639.20 p124*
McCaskill, Daniel; North Carolina, 1775 *1639.20 p124*
McCaskill, Daniel; North Carolina, 1792-1882 *1639.20 p125*
McCaskill, Daniel; North Carolina, 1793-1821 *1639.20 p125*
McCaskill, Daniel 56; North Carolina, 1850 *1639.20 p125*
McCaskill, Daniel 81; North Carolina, 1850 *1639.20 p124*
McCaskill, Daniel D. M.; North Carolina, 1775 *1639.20 p124*
McCaskill, Effie; North Carolina, 1745-1819 *1639.20 p125*
McCaskill, Effie 58 SEE McCaskill, Norman
McCaskill, Elizabeth; North Carolina, 1750-1850 *1639.20 p125*
McCaskill, Finlay; North Carolina, 1754-1854 *1639.20 p125*
McCaskill, Finley; North Carolina, 1730-1774 *1639.20 p125*
McCaskill, Flora; South Carolina, 1750-1850 *1639.20 p126*
McCaskill, Hector 60; North Carolina, 1850 *1639.20 p126*
  *Relative:*Christian 56
McCaskill, John; America, 1770 *1639.20 p126*
McCaskill, John; America, 1802 *1639.20 p126*
McCaskill, John; North Carolina, 1742-1811 *1639.20 p126*
McCaskill, John; North Carolina, 1742-1818 *1639.20 p126*
McCaskill, K.; America, 1811 *1639.20 p127*
McCaskill, Kenneth; North Carolina, 1740-1790 *1639.20 p126*
McCaskill, Kenneth 50; South Carolina, 1850 *1639.20 p127*
  *Relative:*Mary 45
McCaskill, Malcolm; North Carolina, 1730-1793 *1639.20 p127*
McCaskill, Margaret; North Carolina, 1756-1817 *1639.20 p127*
McCaskill, Margaret 52 SEE McCaskill, Alexander
McCaskill, Mary; North Carolina, 1750-1850 *1639.20 p127*
McCaskill, Mary 45 SEE McCaskill, Kenneth
McCaskill, Murdoch; North Carolina, 1738-1770 *1639.20 p127*
McCaskill, Nancy 46 SEE McCaskill, Norman
McCaskill, Nancy 65; South Carolina, 1850 *1639.20 p128*
  *Relative:*Sarah 40
McCaskill, Nancy 74; South Carolina, 1850 *1639.20 p127*
  *Relative:*Angus 47
McCaskill, Norman 50; North Carolina, 1850 *1639.20 p128*
  *Relative:*Effie 58
  *Relative:*Sarah 52
  *Relative:*Nancy 46
McCaskill, Peter; America, 1802 *1639.20 p128*
McCaskill, Peter; America, 1811 *1639.20 p128*
McCaskill, Peter; North Carolina, 1770-1861 *1639.20 p128*
McCaskill, Sallie; North Carolina, 1769-1859 *1639.20 p128*
McCaskill, Sarah; North Carolina, 1750-1850 *1639.20 p128*
McCaskill, Sarah 40 SEE McCaskill, Nancy
McCaskill, Sarah 52 SEE McCaskill, Norman
McCaskill, Taskill; North Carolina, 1750-1806 *1639.20 p128*

McCatt, John 30; Massachusetts, 1850 *5881.1 p69*
McCaughan, John; Montreal, 1820 *7603 p77*
McCaughel, Patrick; Massachusetts, 1841 *7036 p123*
McCaughey, George; Philadelphia, 1865 *5704.8 p197*
McCaughey, Harey; New York, NY, 1867 *5704.8 p221*
McCaughey, John; St. John, N.B., 1847 *5704.8 p3*
McCaughey, Samuel; Philadelphia, 1865 *5704.8 p197*
McCaughty, Jane 20 SEE McCaughty, Robert
McCaughty, Robert 25; Philadelphia, 1804 *53.26 p53*
  *Relative:*Jane 20
McCaul, William; Charleston, SC, 1796 *1639.20 p132*
McCaulay, Margaret 39 SEE McCaulay, White
McCaulay, White 43; Charleston, SC, 1850 *1639.20 p128*
  *Relative:*Margaret 39
McCauley, Catharine; New York, NY, 1870 *5704.8 p238*
McCauley, Daniel; Montreal, 1823 *7603 p54*
McCauley, Edward; Philadelphia, 1864 *5704.8 p174*
McCauley, Hannah; Philadelphia, 1866 *5704.8 p208*
McCauley, Isabella; Philadelphia, 1866 *5704.8 p209*
McCauley, Jane; Philadelphia, 1865 *5704.8 p194*
McCauley, John; New York, NY, 1836 *8208.4 p14*
McCauley, John; Philadelphia, 1850 *53.26 p53*
McCauley, John; Philadelphia, 1850 *5704.8 p68*
McCauley, Lilly; Philadelphia, 1865 *5704.8 p197*
McCauley, Mary; Philadelphia, 1864 *5704.8 p174*
McCauley, Mary; Philadelphia, 1866 *5704.8 p209*
McCauley, Michael; New York, NY, 1833 *8208.4 p44*
McCauley, Michael 22; Philadelphia, 1865 *5704.8 p164*
McCauley, Nancy; New York, NY, 1867 *5704.8 p222*
McCauley, Neal; America, 1868 *5704.8 p226*
McCauley, Neal; America, 1869 *5704.8 p231*
McCauley, Philip 30; Allegany Co., MD, 1840 *1450.2 p96A*
McCauley, Rebecca; Philadelphia, 1865 *5704.8 p197*
McCauley, Robert 30; Philadelphia, 1833-1834 *53.26 p53*
McCauley, Thomas; Philadelphia, 1864 *5704.8 p174*
McCauley, Thomas; St. John, N.B., 1847 *5704.8 p15*
McCauley, William; Philadelphia, 1866 *5704.8 p208*
McCaulley, Biddy; St. John, N.B., 1852 *5704.8 p95*
McCaulley, Patrick; St. John, N.B., 1852 *5704.8 p95*
McCauly, Rose; New York, NY, 1867 *5704.8 p217*
McCauly, Patrick; New York, NY, 1838 *8208.4 p74*
McCauly, Thomas 21; St. John, N.B., 1863 *5704.8 p155*
McCausland, Andrew; Quebec, 1847 *5704.8 p16*
McCausland, Anne; New York, NY, 1869 *5704.8 p233*
McCausland, Eliza Jane 6; Quebec, 1847 *5704.8 p16*
McCausland, James; Philadelphia, 1849 *53.26 p53*
McCausland, James; Philadelphia, 1849 *5704.8 p50*
McCausland, James 9 mos SEE McCausland, John
McCausland, James 9 mos; Philadelphia, 1849 *5704.8 p49*
McCausland, James 24; Philadelphia, 1855 *5704.8 p124*
McCausland, John; Philadelphia, 1847 *53.26 p53*
McCausland, John; Philadelphia, 1847 *5704.8 p1*
McCausland, John; Philadelphia, 1849 *53.26 p53*
  *Relative:*Mary Eiza
  *Relative:*James 9 mos
McCausland, John; Philadelphia, 1849 *5704.8 p49*
McCausland, John; Philadelphia, 1867 *5704.8 p211*
McCausland, John 13; Quebec, 1847 *5704.8 p16*
McCausland, Margaret; St. John, N.B., 1847 *5704.8 p25*
McCausland, Mary; America, 1867 *5704.8 p223*
McCausland, Mary; Quebec, 1847 *5704.8 p16*
McCausland, Mary Eiza SEE McCausland, John
McCausland, Mary Eliza; America, 1867 *5704.8 p223*
McCausland, Mary Eliza; Philadelphia, 1849 *5704.8 p49*
McCausland, Michael 26; Philadelphia, 1854 *5704.8 p118*
McCausland, William; Philadelphia, 1852 *5704.8 p89*
McCavill, Pat.; America, 1742 *4971 p65*
McCavine, Michael; New York, NY, 1837 *8208.4 p52*
McCaviskin, Patrick 20; St. John, N.B., 1855 *5704.8 p127*
McCaw, Peter; Charleston, SC, 1797 *1639.20 p133*
McCawell, John; Quebec, 1851 *5704.8 p73*
McCawell, William 22; Philadelphia, 1854 *5704.8 p117*
McCawley, James; Maryland, 1740 *4971 p91*
McCawly, John 18; St. John, N.B., 1857 *5704.8 p135*
McCay, Annie; Philadelphia, 1848 *53.26 p53*
McCay, Annie; Philadelphia, 1848 *5704.8 p45*
McCay, Catherine 18; Philadelphia, 1854 *5704.8 p115*
McCay, Christopher 21; Philadelphia, 1855 *5704.8 p124*
McCay, Eliza; Philadelphia, 1864 *5704.8 p179*
McCay, Eliza 11; Philadelphia, 1849 *53.26 p53*
  *Relative:*Prudence 6
McCay, Eliza 11; Philadelphia, 1849 *5704.8 p58*
McCay, Elleanor; Philadelphia, 1853 *5704.8 p112*
McCay, Francis; St. John, N.B., 1849 *5704.8 p56*
McCay, Henry 18; Philadelphia, 1854 *5704.8 p120*
McCay, Hugh; Philadelphia, 1847 *53.26 p53*
McCay, Hugh; Philadelphia, 1847 *5704.8 p1*

McCay, Hugh; Philadelphia, 1864 ***5704.8*** *p179*
McCay, Isabella 40; Quebec, 1855 ***5704.8*** *p125*
McCay, James 10; New York, NY, 1866 ***5704.8*** *p214*
McCay, James 17; Philadelphia, 1857 ***5704.8*** *p133*
McCay, John 20; Quebec, 1855 ***5704.8*** *p126*
McCay, Margaret; Philadelphia, 1853 ***5704.8*** *p101*
McCay, Mary; Philadelphia, 1847 ***53.26*** *p53*
McCay, Mary; Philadelphia, 1847 ***5704.8*** *p1*
McCay, Mary; Philadelphia, 1853 ***5704.8*** *p100*
McCay, Mary; Philadelphia, 1853 ***5704.8*** *p101*
McCay, Mary; Philadelphia, 1867 ***5704.8*** *p221*
McCay, Michael 22; St. John, N.B., 1857 ***5704.8*** *p134*
McCay, Peter; New York, NY, 1838 ***8208.4*** *p88*
McCay, Prudence 6 *SEE* McCay, Eliza
McCay, Prudence 6; Philadelphia, 1849 ***5704.8*** *p58*
McCay, Rose 42; Quebec, 1855 ***5704.8*** *p126*
McCay, Rosey; Philadelphia, 1847 ***53.26*** *p53*
McCay, Rosey; St. John, N.B., 1850 ***5704.8*** *p67*
McCay, Sally 24; Philadelphia, 1857 ***5704.8*** *p133*
McCay, William; St. John, N.B., 1849 ***5704.8*** *p49*
McCellan, Hugh; St. John, N.B., 1847 ***5704.8*** *p15*
McCellan, Isabella 6; St. John, N.B., 1847 ***5704.8*** *p15*
McCellan, Jane 9; St. John, N.B., 1847 ***5704.8*** *p15*
McCellan, Mary; St. John, N.B., 1847 ***5704.8*** *p15*
McCellan, Rosanna 7; St. John, N.B., 1847 ***5704.8*** *p15*
McCellan, Thomas; St. John, N.B., 1847 ***5704.8*** *p15*
McCeue, Catherine 20; Philadelphia, 1864 ***5704.8*** *p156*
McCeun, Capt. 30; New York, 1774 ***1219.7*** *p189*
McCharnay, John; Montreal, 1823 ***7603*** *p99*
McChisholm, John; Carolina, 1684 ***1639.20*** *p129*
McChon, Thomas; America, 1856 ***6014.1*** *p2*
McChristal, Mary; Philadelphia, 1869 ***5704.8*** *p232*
McChristal, Mary 18; Philadelphia, 1864 ***5704.8*** *p161*
McChristal, Patrick 21; Philadelphia, 1864 ***5704.8*** *p155*
McChristle, Bridget; New York, NY, 1871 ***5704.8*** *p241*
McChristle, Catharine; New York, NY, 1871 ***5704.8*** *p241*
McChristle, Jane; New York, NY, 1871 ***5704.8*** *p241*
McChristle, Peter; St. John, N.B., 1847 ***5704.8*** *p33*
McChristle, Rose; New York, NY, 1871 ***5704.8*** *p241*
McChrystal, Ann; St. John, N.B., 1852 ***5704.8*** *p84*
McChrystal, Catherine 20; Quebec, 1863 ***5704.8*** *p154*
McChrystal, James 18; Quebec, 1863 ***5704.8*** *p154*
McChrystall, Bridget; Philadelphia, 1866 ***5704.8*** *p206*
McChrystall, James; Philadelphia, 1866 ***5704.8*** *p206*
McClafferty, Biddy 35; Philadelphia, 1864 ***5704.8*** *p161*
McClafferty, Bryan; Philadelphia, 1847 ***53.26*** *p53*
*Relative:*Rosey
McClafferty, Bryan; Philadelphia, 1847 ***5704.8*** *p5*
McClafferty, Charles; Philadelphia, 1867 ***5704.8*** *p219*
McClafferty, Dennis 6; Philadelphia, 1864 ***5704.8*** *p161*
McClafferty, Ellen; New York, NY, 1866 ***5704.8*** *p210*
McClafferty, Hannah 3; Philadelphia, 1864 ***5704.8*** *p161*
McClafferty, Isabella; Philadelphia, 1847 ***53.26*** *p53*
McClafferty, Isabella; Philadelphia, 1847 ***5704.8*** *p5*
McClafferty, James 4; Philadelphia, 1864 ***5704.8*** *p161*
McClafferty, John; New York, NY, 1869 ***5704.8*** *p232*
McClafferty, John; Philadelphia, 1865 ***5704.8*** *p192*
McClafferty, John 8; Philadelphia, 1864 ***5704.8*** *p161*
McClafferty, Manus; Philadelphia, 1851 ***5704.8*** *p81*
McClafferty, Manus 25; Philadelphia, 1853 ***5704.8*** *p109*
McClafferty, Margaret; Philadelphia, 1851 ***5704.8*** *p80*
McClafferty, Margary 10; Philadelphia, 1864 ***5704.8*** *p161*
McClafferty, Mary; America, 1870 ***5704.8*** *p240*
McClafferty, Mary 1; Philadelphia, 1864 ***5704.8*** *p161*
McClafferty, Patrick 22; Philadelphia, 1853 ***5704.8*** *p108*
McClafferty, Rosey *SEE* McClafferty, Bryan
McClafferty, Rosey; Philadelphia, 1847 ***5704.8*** *p5*
McClafferty, Steven; Philadelphia, 1851 ***5704.8*** *p80*
McClafferty, Susan; Philadelphia, 1865 ***5704.8*** *p192*
McClafferty, Susan 24; Philadelphia, 1853 ***5704.8*** *p108*
McClafferty, William; Philadelphia, 1848 ***53.26*** *p53*
McClafferty, William; Philadelphia, 1848 ***5704.8*** *p40*
McClafferty, William 22; Philadelphia, 1859 ***5704.8*** *p142*
McClain, Anne; Quebec, 1850 ***5704.8*** *p63*
McClain, Anne 6 mos; Quebec, 1850 ***5704.8*** *p63*
McClain, James; Philadelphia, 1848 ***53.26*** *p53*
McClain, James; Philadelphia, 1848 ***5704.8*** *p40*
McClain, James; Philadelphia, 1864 ***5704.8*** *p178*
McClain, James; Philadelphia, 1867 ***5704.8*** *p222*
McClain, Jane; Philadelphia, 1867 ***5704.8*** *p222*
McClain, John; Philadelphia, 1864 ***5704.8*** *p178*
McClain, Margaret 11; New York, NY, 1865 ***5704.8*** *p193*
McClain, Mary; America, 1866 ***5704.8*** *p212*
McClaine, Jane; Quebec, 1850 ***5704.8*** *p66*
McClancy, Patrick; Philadelphia, 1864 ***5704.8*** *p170*
McClaren, Alexander 24; Jamaica, 1731 ***3690.1*** *p153*
McClaren, Edward; Philadelphia, 1848 ***53.26*** *p53*
McClaren, Edward; Philadelphia, 1848 ***5704.8*** *p40*
McClary, Bernard; New York, NY, 1840 ***8208.4*** *p110*
McClasky, Catharine 18; Massachusetts, 1849 ***5881.1*** *p64*
McClasky, Philip 28; Massachusetts, 1847 ***5881.1*** *p74*
McClay, Allen; Philadelphia, 1849 ***53.26*** *p53*
McClay, Allen; Philadelphia, 1849 ***5704.8*** *p50*
McClay, Andy; St. John, N.B., 1851 ***5704.8*** *p77*
McClay, Archy; New Orleans, 1848 ***5704.8*** *p48*
McClay, Arthur; Philadelphia, 1849 ***53.26*** *p53*
*Relative:*Margaret
McClay, Arthur; Philadelphia, 1849 ***5704.8*** *p50*
McClay, Daniel *SEE* McClay, Elleanor
McClay, Daniel; Philadelphia, 1847 ***5704.8*** *p23*
McClay, Edward; Philadelphia, 1851 ***5704.8*** *p77*
McClay, Eliz; Philadelphia, 1850 ***53.26*** *p53*
McClay, Eliza; Philadelphia, 1850 ***5704.8*** *p69*
McClay, Eliza; St. John, N.B., 1851 ***5704.8*** *p77*
McClay, Elleanor; Philadelphia, 1847 ***53.26*** *p53*
*Relative:*Daniel
*Relative:*Patrick
*Relative:*Margaret
*Relative:*Philip
McClay, Elleanor; Philadelphia, 1847 ***5704.8*** *p23*
McClay, Giles; Philadelphia, 1851 ***5704.8*** *p77*
McClay, Isabella; America, 1865 ***5704.8*** *p192*
McClay, James; St. John, N.B., 1851 ***5704.8*** *p77*
McClay, James 10; Philadelphia, 1851 ***5704.8*** *p77*
McClay, Jane; St. John, N.B., 1853 ***5704.8*** *p106*
McClay, John 12; Philadelphia, 1851 ***5704.8*** *p77*
McClay, Margaret *SEE* McClay, Arthur
McClay, Margaret *SEE* McClay, Elleanor
McClay, Margaret; Philadelphia, 1847 ***5704.8*** *p23*
McClay, Margaret Ann; Philadelphia, 1849 ***5704.8*** *p50*
McClay, Mary; Philadelphia, 1853 ***5704.8*** *p100*
McClay, Mary; St. John, N.B., 1851 ***5704.8*** *p77*
McClay, Mary Ann; Philadelphia, 1864 ***5704.8*** *p183*
McClay, Nancy 20; Philadelphia, 1856 ***5704.8*** *p129*
McClay, Patrick *SEE* McClay, Elleanor
McClay, Patrick; Philadelphia, 1847 ***5704.8*** *p23*
McClay, Philip *SEE* McClay, Elleanor
McClay, Philip; Philadelphia, 1847 ***5704.8*** *p23*
McClay, Robert; St. John, N.B., 1852 ***5704.8*** *p93*
McClean, Alex; Philadelphia, 1851 ***5704.8*** *p76*
McClean, Andrew; St. John, N.B., 1847 ***5704.8*** *p15*
McClean, Anna; Philadelphia, 1851 ***5704.8*** *p76*
McClean, Archibald; Philadelphia, 1847 ***5704.8*** *p13*
McClean, Archibold; Philadelphia, 1847 ***53.26*** *p53*
*Relative:*Mary Jane
*Relative:*Martha 3
*Relative:*Robert 3 mos
McClean, Catherine 23; Quebec, 1863 ***5704.8*** *p154*
McClean, Eliza; St. John, N.B., 1847 ***5704.8*** *p15*
McClean, Ellen Jane; Philadelphia, 1851 ***5704.8*** *p78*
McClean, James; New Orleans, 1848 ***5704.8*** *p48*
McClean, James; Philadelphia, 1851 ***5704.8*** *p76*
McClean, John; Philadelphia, 1852 ***5704.8*** *p88*
McClean, Margaret; Philadelphia, 1847 ***53.26*** *p53*
McClean, Margaret; Philadelphia, 1847 ***5704.8*** *p1*
McClean, Martha 2; Philadelphia, 1847 ***5704.8*** *p13*
McClean, Martha 3 *SEE* McClean, Archibold
McClean, Martha Jane; Philadelphia, 1851 ***5704.8*** *p76*
McClean, Mary Jane *SEE* McClean, Archibold
McClean, Mary Jane; Philadelphia, 1847 ***5704.8*** *p13*
McClean, Mary L.; Philadelphia, 1852 ***5704.8*** *p96*
McClean, Robert 3 mos *SEE* McClean, Archibold
McClean, Robert 3 mos; Philadelphia, 1847 ***5704.8*** *p13*
McClean, William; Illinois, 1854 ***7857*** *p5*
McClean, William; Philadelphia, 1851 ***5704.8*** *p76*
McCleary, Ann 16; Quebec, 1856 ***5704.8*** *p130*
McCleary, Archibald; New York, NY, 1838 ***8208.4*** *p61*
McCleary, Eliza 48; Quebec, 1856 ***5704.8*** *p130*
McCleary, Hugh 35; Harris Co., TX, 1898 ***6254*** *p4*
McCleary, Isabella 11; Quebec, 1856 ***5704.8*** *p130*
McCleary, James 19; Quebec, 1856 ***5704.8*** *p130*
McCleary, Jane 48; Quebec, 1856 ***5704.8*** *p130*
McCleary, John 28; Philadelphia, 1853 ***5704.8*** *p108*
McCleary, Margaret 11; Quebec, 1856 ***5704.8*** *p130*
McCleary, Mary 21; Quebec, 1856 ***5704.8*** *p130*
McCleary, Robert 6; Quebec, 1856 ***5704.8*** *p130*
McCleary, Sarah 8; Quebec, 1856 ***5704.8*** *p130*
McCleary, Sarah 20; Philadelphia, 1853 ***5704.8*** *p108*
McCleery, Isabella; Philadelphia, 1866 ***5704.8*** *p207*
McCleery, John; Philadelphia, 1854 ***5704.8*** *p116*
McCleery, Mary; Quebec, 1847 ***5704.8*** *p28*
McCleery, Mary 23; Quebec, 1856 ***5704.8*** *p130*
McCleery, Sally; Quebec, 1847 ***5704.8*** *p28*
McCleery, William; Quebec, 1847 ***5704.8*** *p28*
McClefferty, . . .; Philadelphia, 1865 ***5704.8*** *p192*
McClefferty, Belle; Philadelphia, 1865 ***5704.8*** *p192*
McClefferty, Mary; Philadelphia, 1865 ***5704.8*** *p192*
McClefferty, Patrick; Philadelphia, 1865 ***5704.8*** *p192*
McClellan, William; Illinois, 1855 ***7857*** *p5*
McClelland, Andrew 22; St. John, N.B., 1863 ***5704.8*** *p153*
McClelland, Ann 38; Philadelphia, 1853 ***5704.8*** *p113*
McClelland, Biddy *SEE* McClelland, Mary
McClelland, Biddy; Philadelphia, 1848 ***5704.8*** *p46*
McClelland, Cochran *SEE* McClelland, James
McClelland, Cochran; Philadelphia, 1849 ***5704.8*** *p53*
McClelland, Eliz. Ann *SEE* McClelland, James
McClelland, Eliza; St. John, N.B., 1847 ***5704.8*** *p9*
McClelland, Eliza 15; Philadelphia, 1853 ***5704.8*** *p113*
McClelland, Elizabeth Ann; Philadelphia, 1849 ***5704.8*** *p53*
McClelland, Gabrial 18; Philadelphia, 1857 ***5704.8*** *p132*
McClelland, James; Philadelphia, 1849 ***53.26*** *p53*
*Relative:*William
*Relative:*Margaret
*Relative:*John
*Relative:*Eliz. Ann
*Relative:*Robert
*Relative:*Cochran
*Relative:*Thomas
McClelland, James; Philadelphia, 1849 ***5704.8*** *p53*
McClelland, James 17; Philadelphia, 1853 ***5704.8*** *p113*
McClelland, John *SEE* McClelland, James
McClelland, John; New York, NY, 1839 ***8208.4*** *p99*
McClelland, John; Philadelphia, 1849 ***5704.8*** *p53*
McClelland, John 13; Philadelphia, 1853 ***5704.8*** *p113*
McClelland, Joseph *SEE* McClelland, William
McClelland, Joseph; Philadelphia, 1849 ***5704.8*** *p53*
McClelland, Margaret *SEE* McClelland, James
McClelland, Margaret *SEE* McClelland, William
McClelland, Margaret; Philadelphia, 1847 ***53.26*** *p54*
*Relative:*Ross 10
McClelland, Margaret; Philadelphia, 1847 ***5704.8*** *p30*
McClelland, Margaret; Philadelphia, 1848 ***53.26*** *p54*
McClelland, Margaret; Philadelphia, 1848 ***5704.8*** *p40*
McClelland, Margaret; Philadelphia, 1849 ***5704.8*** *p53*
McClelland, Margaret 20; Philadelphia, 1856 ***5704.8*** *p128*
McClelland, Martha *SEE* McClelland, William
McClelland, Martha; Philadelphia, 1849 ***5704.8*** *p53*
McClelland, Martha; St. John, N.B., 1853 ***5704.8*** *p100*
McClelland, Mary; Philadelphia, 1848 ***53.26*** *p54*
*Relative:*Biddy
McClelland, Mary; Philadelphia, 1848 ***5704.8*** *p45*
McClelland, Mary 4; Philadelphia, 1853 ***5704.8*** *p113*
McClelland, Nancy *SEE* McClelland, William
McClelland, Nancy; Philadelphia, 1849 ***5704.8*** *p53*
McClelland, Nancy; St. John, N.B., 1853 ***5704.8*** *p100*
McClelland, Rebecca 3 mos; St. John, N.B., 1863 ***5704.8*** *p153*
McClelland, Rebecca 50; St. John, N.B., 1864 ***5704.8*** *p157*
McClelland, Richard 9; Philadelphia, 1853 ***5704.8*** *p113*
McClelland, Robert *SEE* McClelland, James
McClelland, Robert; Philadelphia, 1849 ***5704.8*** *p53*
McClelland, Robert 9 mos; Philadelphia, 1853 ***5704.8*** *p113*
McClelland, Ross 10 *SEE* McClelland, Margaret
McClelland, Ross 10; Philadelphia, 1847 ***5704.8*** *p30*
McClelland, Samuel 11; Philadelphia, 1853 ***5704.8*** *p113*
McClelland, Samuel 26; Philadelphia, 1856 ***5704.8*** *p128*
McClelland, Sarah 19; St. John, N.B., 1863 ***5704.8*** *p153*
McClelland, Thomas *SEE* McClelland, James
McClelland, Thomas; Philadelphia, 1849 ***53.26*** *p54*
McClelland, Thomas; Philadelphia, 1849 ***5704.8*** *p52*
McClelland, Thomas; Philadelphia, 1849 ***5704.8*** *p53*
McClelland, Thomas 6; Philadelphia, 1853 ***5704.8*** *p113*
McClelland, Thomas 40; Philadelphia, 1853 ***5704.8*** *p113*
McClelland, William *SEE* McClelland, James
McClelland, William; Philadelphia, 1849 ***53.26*** *p54*
*Relative:*Margaret
*Relative:*Martha
*Relative:*Joseph
*Relative:*Nancy
McClelland, William; Philadelphia, 1849 ***5704.8*** *p53*
McClelland, William 19; Philadelphia, 1853 ***5704.8*** *p113*
McClement, Hugh; America, 1740 ***4971*** *p69*
McClenaghan, Andrew; St. John, N.B., 1847 ***5704.8*** *p8*
McClenaghan, David; St. John, N.B., 1847 ***5704.8*** *p8*
McClenaghan, Isabella 20; Philadelphia, 1857 ***5704.8*** *p132*
McClenaghan, James; Philadelphia, 1851 ***5704.8*** *p77*
McClenaghan, John; St. John, N.B., 1847 ***5704.8*** *p8*
McClenaghan, Keatty 12; St. John, N.B., 1847 ***5704.8*** *p8*
McClenaghan, Margaret; St. John, N.B., 1847 ***5704.8*** *p8*
McClenaghan, Martha; St. John, N.B., 1847 ***5704.8*** *p8*
McClenaghan, Matilda; St. John, N.B., 1847 ***5704.8*** *p8*
McClenahan, Eliza 11 *SEE* McClenahan, Margaret
McClenahan, Eliza 11; Philadelphia, 1849 ***5704.8*** *p58*
McClenahan, Hugh 2 *SEE* McClenahan, Margaret
McClenahan, Hugh 2; Philadelphia, 1849 ***5704.8*** *p58*
McClenahan, Margaret *SEE* McClenahan, Margaret

McClenahan, Margaret; Philadelphia, 1849 *53.26 p54*
  *Relative:*Eliza 11
  *Relative:*Margaret 8
  *Relative:*Nancy 6
  *Relative:*Hugh 2
  *Relative:*Margaret
McClenahan, Margaret; Philadelphia, 1849 *5704.8 p58*
McClenahan, Margaret 8 *SEE* McClenahan, Margaret
McClenahan, Margaret 8; Philadelphia, 1849 *5704.8 p58*
McClenahan, Nancy 6 *SEE* McClenahan, Margaret
McClenahan, Nancy 6; Philadelphia, 1849 *5704.8 p58*
McClenhill, James; Ohio, 1851 *9892.11 p32*
McClenneghan, Horatio 48; South Carolina, 1850 *1639.20 p129*
McClernan, John 20; Philadelphia, 1853 *5704.8 p113*
McClimore, George; Quebec, 1850 *5704.8 p63*
McClintock, Catherine 11; St. John, N.B., 1847 *5704.8 p10*
McClintock, Eliza; Philadelphia, 1850 *53.26 p54*
  *Relative:*Sarah
  *Relative:*John 2
  *Relative:*William 6 mos
McClintock, Eliza; Philadelphia, 1850 *5704.8 p68*
McClintock, Elizabeth 8; Philadelphia, 1853 *5704.8 p102*
McClintock, Elizabeth 9 *SEE* McClintock, James
McClintock, Elizabeth 9; Philadelphia, 1847 *5704.8 p30*
McClintock, James; Philadelphia, 1847 *53.26 p54*
  *Relative:*Mary
  *Relative:*Susanna
  *Relative:*John
  *Relative:*Rebecca
  *Relative:*Mary 11
  *Relative:*Elizabeth 9
McClintock, James; Philadelphia, 1847 *5704.8 p30*
McClintock, James 11 *SEE* McClintock, William
McClintock, James 11; Philadelphia, 1849 *5704.8 p49*
McClintock, Jane *SEE* McClintock, William
McClintock, Jane; Philadelphia, 1849 *5704.8 p49*
McClintock, John *SEE* McClintock, James
McClintock, John; New York, NY, 1864 *5704.8 p171*
McClintock, John; Philadelphia, 1847 *5704.8 p30*
McClintock, John 2 *SEE* McClintock, Eliza
McClintock, John 2; Philadelphia, 1850 *5704.8 p68*
McClintock, John 20; Philadelphia, 1857 *5704.8 p134*
McClintock, Margaret; Philadelphia, 1849 *53.26 p54*
McClintock, Margaret; Philadelphia, 1849 *5704.8 p49*
McClintock, Margaret 3 mos *SEE* McClintock, William
McClintock, Margaret 3 mos; Philadelphia, 1849 *5704.8 p49*
McClintock, Mary *SEE* McClintock, James
McClintock, Mary; Philadelphia, 1847 *5704.8 p30*
McClintock, Mary 11 *SEE* McClintock, James
McClintock, Mary 11; Philadelphia, 1847 *5704.8 p30*
McClintock, Nancy; St. John, N.B., 1847 *5704.8 p10*
McClintock, Rebecca *SEE* McClintock, James
McClintock, Rebecca; Philadelphia, 1847 *5704.8 p30*
McClintock, Rebecca; Philadelphia, 1849 *53.26 p54*
McClintock, Rebecca; Philadelphia, 1849 *5704.8 p49*
McClintock, Robert 2 *SEE* McClintock, William
McClintock, Robert 2; Philadelphia, 1849 *5704.8 p49*
McClintock, Sarah *SEE* McClintock, Eliza
McClintock, Sarah; Philadelphia, 1850 *5704.8 p68*
McClintock, Susanna *SEE* McClintock, James
McClintock, Susanna; Philadelphia, 1847 *5704.8 p30*
McClintock, William; New York, 1864 *1450.2 p25B*
McClintock, William; Philadelphia, 1849 *53.26 p54*
  *Relative:*Jane
  *Relative:*James 11
  *Relative:*William 3
  *Relative:*Robert 2
  *Relative:*Margaret 3 mos
McClintock, William; Philadelphia, 1849 *5704.8 p49*
McClintock, William; Philadelphia, 1852 *5704.8 p92*
McClintock, William 6 mos *SEE* McClintock, Eliza
McClintock, William 6 mos; Philadelphia, 1850 *5704.8 p68*
McClintock, William 3 *SEE* McClintock, William
McClintock, William 3; Philadelphia, 1849 *5704.8 p49*
McClisky, Neil; Illinois, 1854 *7857 p5*
McClonan, Martha; Philadelphia, 1865 *5704.8 p192*
McClone, Rose; Montreal, 1820 *7603 p90*
McCloskey, Miss; Philadelphia, 1866 *5704.8 p204*
McCloskey, Andrew 20; Philadelphia, 1855 *5704.8 p123*
McCloskey, Ann; St. John, N.B., 1851 *5704.8 p77*
McCloskey, Anne 11; Philadelphia, 1864 *5704.8 p180*
McCloskey, Anne 12; St. John, N.B., 1850 *5704.8 p65*
McCloskey, Anne 40; Philadelphia, 1864 *5704.8 p180*
McCloskey, Annie; New York, NY, 1865 *5704.8 p192*
McCloskey, Bernard; Philadelphia, 1864 *5704.8 p178*
McCloskey, Bernard 12; Philadelphia, 1852 *5704.8 p89*
McCloskey, Bernard 16; Philadelphia, 1857 *5704.8 p132*
McCloskey, Betty; New York, NY, 1865 *5704.8 p198*
McCloskey, Betty; Philadelphia, 1851 *5704.8 p76*

McCloskey, Biddy; St. John, N.B., 1847 *5704.8 p19*
McCloskey, Biddy 9; New York, NY, 1864 *5704.8 p175*
McCloskey, Biddy 13; Philadelphia, 1856 *5704.8 p129*
McCloskey, Bridget; New York, NY, 1864 *5704.8 p175*
McCloskey, Bridget; Philadelphia, 1864 *5704.8 p185*
McCloskey, Bridget; Philadelphia, 1868 *5704.8 p229*
McCloskey, Bridget 17; Philadelphia, 1859 *5704.8 p142*
McCloskey, Bridget 20; Philadelphia, 1860 *5704.8 p145*
McCloskey, Bridget 21; Philadelphia, 1860 *5704.8 p145*
McCloskey, Bryan; Philadelphia, 1847 *53.26 p55*
  *Relative:*Ellen
  *Relative:*Michael 6 mos
  *Relative:*James
  *Relative:*Rose
McCloskey, Bryan; Philadelphia, 1847 *5704.8 p1*
McCloskey, Catharine; New York, NY, 1865 *5704.8 p193*
McCloskey, Catherine 22; Philadelphia, 1864 *5704.8 p161*
McCloskey, Charles; Philadelphia, 1864 *5704.8 p185*
McCloskey, David 22; Philadelphia, 1854 *5704.8 p121*
McCloskey, Dennis; Philadelphia, 1864 *5704.8 p178*
McCloskey, Dennis; Philadelphia, 1866 *5704.8 p207*
McCloskey, Dennis; St. John, N.B., 1847 *5704.8 p10*
McCloskey, Dennis 10; St. John, N.B., 1848 *5704.8 p43*
McCloskey, Edward; Quebec, 1852 *5704.8 p94*
McCloskey, Eliza 11; St. John, N.B., 1850 *5704.8 p65*
McCloskey, Elizabeth; Philadelphia, 1865 *5704.8 p200*
McCloskey, Elizabeth; Philadelphia, 1867 *5704.8 p221*
McCloskey, Elizabeth; Quebec, 1853 *5704.8 p103*
McCloskey, Elizabeth 9; Philadelphia, 1852 *5704.8 p89*
McCloskey, Elizabeth 35; Philadelphia, 1858 *5704.8 p138*
McCloskey, Ellen *SEE* McCloskey, Bryan
McCloskey, Ellen; New York, NY, 1869 *5704.8 p234*
McCloskey, Ellen; Philadelphia, 1847 *5704.8 p1*
McCloskey, Ellen 6; St. John, N.B., 1859 *5704.8 p140*
McCloskey, Emily; St. John, N.B., 1850 *5704.8 p65*
McCloskey, Fanny; Philadelphia, 1852 *5704.8 p96*
McCloskey, Grace; New York, NY, 1869 *5704.8 p234*
McCloskey, Grace 26; Philadelphia, 1864 *5704.8 p160*
McCloskey, Hannah; New York, NY, 1867 *5704.8 p218*
McCloskey, Hannah; Philadelphia, 1852 *5704.8 p88*
McCloskey, Henry; Philadelphia, 1868 *5704.8 p226*
McCloskey, Henry; Philadelphia, 1868 *5704.8 p231*
McCloskey, Hugh; New York, NY, 1864 *5704.8 p179*
McCloskey, Hugh; New York, NY, 1865 *5704.8 p193*
McCloskey, Hugh; Philadelphia, 1852 *5704.8 p88*
McCloskey, Hugh 9 mos; St. John, N.B., 1859 *5704.8 p140*
McCloskey, Hugh 11; Philadelphia, 1864 *5704.8 p180*
McCloskey, Hugh 25; St. John, N.B., 1861 *5704.8 p149*
McCloskey, Hugh 50; St. John, N.B., 1864 *5704.8 p159*
McCloskey, James *SEE* McCloskey, Bryan
McCloskey, James; Ohio, 1849 *9892.11 p32*
McCloskey, James; Philadelphia, 1811 *53.26 p55*
McCloskey, James; Philadelphia, 1847 *5704.8 p1*
McCloskey, James; Philadelphia, 1852 *5704.8 p89*
McCloskey, James 7; Philadelphia, 1852 *5704.8 p89*
McCloskey, James 17; Philadelphia, 1859 *5704.8 p141*
McCloskey, James 22; Philadelphia, 1859 *5704.8 p143*
McCloskey, James 26; Philadelphia, 1833-1834 *53.26 p55*
  *Relative:*Jane 28
McCloskey, Jane; Philadelphia, 1853 *5704.8 p103*
McCloskey, Jane; St. John, N.B., 1847 *5704.8 p2*
McCloskey, Jane 28 *SEE* McCloskey, James
McCloskey, John; New York, NY, 1867 *5704.8 p217*
McCloskey, John; Philadelphia, 1847 *53.26 p55*
McCloskey, John; Philadelphia, 1847 *5704.8 p1*
McCloskey, John; Philadelphia, 1852 *5704.8 p97*
McCloskey, John; Philadelphia, 1864 *5704.8 p171*
McCloskey, John; Philadelphia, 1864 *5704.8 p178*
McCloskey, John; Philadelphia, 1865 *5704.8 p203*
McCloskey, John; St. John, N.B., 1850 *5704.8 p65*
McCloskey, John 5; Philadelphia, 1852 *5704.8 p89*
McCloskey, John 7; New York, NY, 1864 *5704.8 p175*
McCloskey, John 9; St. John, N.B., 1847 *5704.8 p10*
McCloskey, John 22; St. John, N.B., 1854 *5704.8 p122*
McCloskey, John 24; Philadelphia, 1860 *5704.8 p146*
McCloskey, Joseph 20; St. John, N.B., 1853 *5704.8 p109*
McCloskey, Lizzie; America, 1869 *5704.8 p233*
McCloskey, Magy; Philadelphia, 1852 *5704.8 p91*
McCloskey, Margaret; America, 1866 *5704.8 p215*
McCloskey, Margaret; Philadelphia, 1864 *5704.8 p170*
McCloskey, Margaret; Philadelphia, 1868 *5704.8 p230*
McCloskey, Margaret 9 mos; St. John, N.B., 1847 *5704.8 p10*
McCloskey, Margaret 10; New York, NY, 1864 *5704.8 p175*
McCloskey, Margery 20; Philadelphia, 1857 *5704.8 p134*
McCloskey, Mariah 26; St. John, N.B., 1859 *5704.8 p140*

McCloskey, Mary; America, 1866 *5704.8 p211*
McCloskey, Mary; New York, NY, 1865 *5704.8 p195*
McCloskey, Mary; Philadelphia, 1852 *5704.8 p89*
McCloskey, Mary; Philadelphia, 1864 *5704.8 p178*
McCloskey, Mary; Philadelphia, 1865 *5704.8 p200*
McCloskey, Mary; Quebec, 1852 *5704.8 p94*
McCloskey, Mary; St. John, N.B., 1848 *5704.8 p44*
McCloskey, Mary 5; New York, NY, 1864 *5704.8 p175*
McCloskey, Mary 19; Philadelphia, 1859 *5704.8 p141*
McCloskey, Mary 21; Philadelphia, 1854 *5704.8 p122*
McCloskey, Mary 26; Philadelphia, 1854 *5704.8 p117*
McCloskey, Mary 28; Philadelphia, 1854 *5704.8 p117*
McCloskey, Mary 67; Philadelphia, 1854 *5704.8 p117*
McCloskey, Mary Ann 19; Philadelphia, 1854 *5704.8 p117*
McCloskey, Mary Ann 25; St. John, N.B., 1866 *5704.8 p167*
McCloskey, Mary Jane 3; St. John, N.B., 1859 *5704.8 p140*
McCloskey, Matilda; St. John, N.B., 1847 *5704.8 p10*
McCloskey, Michael; Philadelphia, 1852 *5704.8 p89*
McCloskey, Michael; St. John, N.B., 1847 *5704.8 p8*
McCloskey, Michael 6 mos *SEE* McCloskey, Bryan
McCloskey, Michael 6 mos; Philadelphia, 1847 *5704.8 p1*
McCloskey, Michael 18; Philadelphia, 1854 *5704.8 p117*
McCloskey, Michael 18; St. John, N.B., 1853 *5704.8 p109*
McCloskey, Michael 22; Philadelphia, 1860 *5704.8 p144*
McCloskey, Michael 30; Philadelphia, 1854 *5704.8 p117*
McCloskey, Nancy 12; St. John, N.B., 1847 *5704.8 p10*
McCloskey, Nancy 24; St. John, N.B., 1859 *5704.8 p143*
McCloskey, Owen; New York, NY, 1867 *5704.8 p216*
McCloskey, Owen 40; Philadelphia, 1861 *5704.8 p148*
McCloskey, Pat 7 mos; Philadelphia, 1864 *5704.8 p160*
McCloskey, Patrick; New York, NY, 1864 *5704.8 p175*
McCloskey, Patrick; New York, NY, 1865 *5704.8 p194*
McCloskey, Patrick; Philadelphia, 1847 *53.26 p55*
McCloskey, Patrick; Philadelphia, 1847 *5704.8 p1*
McCloskey, Patrick; Quebec, 1851 *5704.8 p73*
McCloskey, Patrick; St. John, N.B., 1847 *5704.8 p10*
McCloskey, Peggy; St. John, N.B., 1847 *5704.8 p10*
McCloskey, Peggy; St. John, N.B., 1852 *5704.8 p84*
McCloskey, Rebecca; Philadelphia, 1865 *5704.8 p193*
McCloskey, Rebecca 32; Philadelphia, 1853 *5704.8 p114*
McCloskey, Richard; St. John, N.B., 1847 *5704.8 p10*
McCloskey, Richard 4; St. John, N.B., 1847 *5704.8 p10*
McCloskey, Rose *SEE* McCloskey, Bryan
McCloskey, Rose; Philadelphia, 1847 *5704.8 p1*
McCloskey, Rose 15; Philadelphia, 1860 *5704.8 p145*
McCloskey, Sarah; America, 1865 *5704.8 p204*
McCloskey, Sarah; Philadelphia, 1848 *53.26 p55*
McCloskey, Sarah; Philadelphia, 1848 *5704.8 p46*
McCloskey, Sarah; Philadelphia, 1852 *5704.8 p92*
McCloskey, Sarah; Philadelphia, 1866 *5704.8 p207*
McCloskey, Sarah; Philadelphia, 1868 *5704.8 p230*
McCloskey, Sarah; Quebec, 1852 *5704.8 p94*
McCloskey, Susan 21; Philadelphia, 1860 *5704.8 p146*
McCloskey, Thomas; New York, NY, 1864 *5704.8 p170*
McCloskey, Thomas; New York, NY, 1867 *5704.8 p217*
McCloskey, Unity; St. John, N.B., 1847 *5704.8 p10*
McCloskey, William; Philadelphia, 1848 *53.26 p55*
McCloskey, William; Philadelphia, 1848 *5704.8 p45*
McCloskey, William 9 mos; St. John, N.B., 1850 *5704.8 p65*
McCloskey, William 20; Wilmington, DE, 1831 *6508.7 p161*
McClosky, Ann; St. John, N.B., 1847 *5704.8 p25*
McClosky, Charles 12; Massachusetts, 1849 *5881.1 p64*
McClosky, Eliza; Quebec, 1847 *5704.8 p29*
McClosky, Ellen; St. John, N.B., 1849 *5704.8 p49*
McClosky, Hugh; Philadelphia, 1852 *5704.8 p88*
McClosky, Isabella; Philadelphia, 1847 *53.26 p55*
  *Relative:*Owen 2
McClosky, Isabella; Philadelphia, 1847 *5704.8 p23*
McClosky, James; St. John, N.B., 1847 *5704.8 p10*
McClosky, James; St. John, N.B., 1849 *5704.8 p55*
McClosky, John 25; Philadelphia, 1804 *53.26 p55*
  *Relative:*Rose 19
McClosky, Mary; Philadelphia, 1847 *53.26 p55*
  *Relative:*Rose
McClosky, Mary; Philadelphia, 1847 *5704.8 p31*
McClosky, Mary; St. John, N.B., 1847 *5704.8 p15*
McClosky, Michael; St. John, N.B., 1847 *5704.8 p15*
McClosky, Michael; St. John, N.B., 1849 *5704.8 p49*
McClosky, Owen 2 *SEE* McClosky, Isabella
McClosky, Own 2; Philadelphia, 1847 *5704.8 p23*
McClosky, Robert; St. John, N.B., 1847 *5704.8 p15*
McClosky, Rose *SEE* McClosky, Mary
McClosky, Rose; Philadelphia, 1847 *5704.8 p31*
McClosky, Rose 19 *SEE* McClosky, John
McCloud, John 28; Virginia, 1773 *1219.7 p169*

McCloud, Roderick 17; Tobago, W. Indies, 1775 ***1219.7*** *p247*
McCloy, John; Philadelphia, 1853 ***5704.8*** *p102*
McClung, James; New York, NY, 1839 ***8208.4*** *p97*
McClung, John; New York, NY, 1837 ***8208.4*** *p55*
McClure, . . . 9 mos; Philadelphia, 1853 ***5704.8*** *p102*
McClure, Alexander; Charleston, SC, 1796 ***1639.20*** *p129*
McClure, Alexander; St. John, N.B., 1853 ***5704.8*** *p98*
McClure, Ann Jane; Philadelphia, 1853 ***5704.8*** *p102*
McClure, Archibald; Iowa, 1866-1943 ***123.54*** *p31*
McClure, Catherine 18; St. John, N.B., 1854 ***5704.8*** *p114*
McClure, David; Philadelphia, 1853 ***5704.8*** *p111*
McClure, David 12; Philadelphia, 1850 ***53.26*** *p55*
McClure, John; Philadelphia, 1853 ***5704.8*** *p103*
McClure, John; Philadelphia, 1864 ***5704.8*** *p183*
McClure, Margaret; Philadelphia, 1864 ***5704.8*** *p183*
McClure, Margaret 10; Philadelphia, 1853 ***5704.8*** *p102*
McClure, Nancy 3; Philadelphia, 1853 ***5704.8*** *p102*
McClure, Samuel 19; Quebec, 1856 ***5704.8*** *p130*
McCluskey, Betty 20; Philadelphia, 1860 ***5704.8*** *p145*
McCluskey, Bridget 18; Philadelphia, 1860 ***5704.8*** *p145*
McCluskey, Catharine 4; Massachusetts, 1849 ***5881.1*** *p65*
McCluskey, Catherine 18; St. John, N.B., 1857 ***5704.8*** *p135*
McCluskey, George; New York, NY, 1835 ***8208.4*** *p4*
McCluskey, Henry; Montreal, 1825 ***7603*** *p67*
McCluskey, James 22; Philadelphia, 1860 ***5704.8*** *p144*
McCluskey, John 19; St. John, N.B., 1866 ***5704.8*** *p165*
McCluskie, Michael 23; Philadelphia, 1864 ***5704.8*** *p156*
McClusky, Mrs. 28; Massachusetts, 1848 ***5881.1*** *p70*
McClusky, Charles; St. John, N.B., 1852 ***5704.8*** *p95*
McClusky, Charles 8; Massachusetts, 1849 ***5881.1*** *p64*
McClusky, Francis 22; Massachusetts, 1849 ***5881.1*** *p66*
McClusky, Mary 6; Massachusetts, 1849 ***5881.1*** *p72*
McClusky, Mary 35; Massachusetts, 1849 ***5881.1*** *p72*
McClusky, Patrick 10; Massachusetts, 1849 ***5881.1*** *p75*
McClyment, Agnes 4; Quebec, 1864 ***5704.8*** *p163*
McClyment, James 34; Quebec, 1864 ***5704.8*** *p163*
McClyment, Margaret 1; Quebec, 1864 ***5704.8*** *p163*
McClyment, Mary 31; Quebec, 1864 ***5704.8*** *p163*
McClyment, Sarah 6; Quebec, 1864 ***5704.8*** *p163*
McClyment, William 10; Quebec, 1864 ***5704.8*** *p163*
McCoach, Eliza 16; Philadelphia, 1860 ***5704.8*** *p146*
McCoach, Ellen *SEE* McCoach, Mary
McCoach, Ellen; Philadelphia, 1847 ***5704.8*** *p31*
McCoach, James; Philadelphia, 1865 ***5704.8*** *p203*
McCoach, Magy; Philadelphia, 1853 ***5704.8*** *p102*
McCoach, Margaret; America, 1865 ***5704.8*** *p200*
McCoach, Margaret; America, 1866 ***5704.8*** *p213*
McCoach, Margaret; Philadelphia, 1865 ***5704.8*** *p203*
McCoach, Mary; Philadelphia, 1847 ***53.26*** *p55*
*Relative:*Ellen
McCoach, Mary; Philadelphia, 1847 ***5704.8*** *p31*
McCoart, Fergal; America, 1740 ***4971*** *p75*
McCoart, Michael; America, 1740 ***4971*** *p75*
McCobb, William; New York, NY, 1866 ***5704.8*** *p212*
McCole, Alexander 4 *SEE* McCole, John
McCole, Ann 3 *SEE* McCole, Duncan
McCole, Ann 38 *SEE* McCole, Dugal
McCole, Christian 2 *SEE* McCole, Duncan
McCole, Christian 10 *SEE* McCole, Duncan
McCole, Christian 35 *SEE* McCole, Duncan
McCole, Christine 40 *SEE* McCole, Duncan
McCole, David 30; Wilmington, NC, 1775 ***1639.20*** *p129*
McCole, Donald 12 *SEE* McCole, John
McCole, Donald 34; Wilmington, NC, 1775 ***1639.20*** *p129*
*Wife:*Katherine 40
*Son:*Ewan 6
McCole, Douglas 8 *SEE* McCole, John
McCole, Dugal 38; Wilmington, NC, 1775 ***1639.20*** *p129*
*Wife:*Ann 38
*Child:*Margaret 10
*Child:*Mary 8
*Child:*Sarah 2
With baby
McCole, Dugald 20 *SEE* McCole, Duncan
McCole, Duncan 21 *SEE* McCole, Duncan
McCole, Duncan 35; Wilmington, NC, 1775 ***1639.20*** *p129*
*Wife:*Christian 35
*Child:*Dugald 20
*Child:*Christian 2
*Child:*Katherine 3
McCole, Duncan 45; Wilmington, NC, 1775 ***1639.20*** *p129*
*Wife:*Christine 40
*Child:*Duncan 21
*Child:*Mary 18
*Child:*Sarah 15
*Child:*Christian 10
*Child:*Mildred 6
*Child:*Ann 3
McCole, Ewan 6 *SEE* McCole, Donald
McCole, John 16 *SEE* McCole, John
McCole, John 49; Wilmington, NC, 1775 ***1639.20*** *p130*
*Wife:*Mildred 40
*Child:*John 16
*Child:*Samuel 15
*Child:*Donald 12
*Child:*Douglas 8
*Child:*Alexander 4
*Child:*Katherine 2
McCole, Katherine 2 *SEE* McCole, John
McCole, Katherine 3 *SEE* McCole, Duncan
McCole, Katherine 40 *SEE* McCole, Donald
McCole, Margaret 10 *SEE* McCole, Dugal
McCole, Mary 8 *SEE* McCole, Dugal
McCole, Mary 18 *SEE* McCole, Duncan
McCole, Michael; Arkansas, 1918 ***95.2*** *p82*
McCole, Mildred 6 *SEE* McCole, Duncan
McCole, Mildred 40 *SEE* McCole, John
McCole, Nelly; St. John, N.B., 1847 ***5704.8*** *p3*
McCole, Samuel 15 *SEE* McCole, John
McCole, Sarah 2 *SEE* McCole, Dugal
McCole, Sarah 15 *SEE* McCole, Duncan
McColgan, Biddy; St. John, N.B., 1850 ***5704.8*** *p65*
McColgan, Catherine; St. John, N.B., 1847 ***5704.8*** *p26*
McColgan, Catherine; St. John, N.B., 1851 ***5704.8*** *p77*
McColgan, Caty; St. John, N.B., 1853 ***5704.8*** *p106*
McColgan, Daniel; St. John, N.B., 1848 ***5704.8*** *p39*
McColgan, Daniel 22; St. John, N.B., 1856 ***5704.8*** *p131*
McColgan, Edward 12; St. John, N.B., 1847 ***5704.8*** *p26*
McColgan, Edward 20; St. John, N.B., 1854 ***5704.8*** *p114*
McColgan, Elizabeth 13; Philadelphia, 1858 ***5704.8*** *p139*
McColgan, Ellan; St. John, N.B., 1851 ***5704.8*** *p79*
McColgan, Ellen; Philadelphia, 1864 ***5704.8*** *p176*
McColgan, Ellen; Philadelphia, 1865 ***5704.8*** *p192*
McColgan, Ellen 17; Philadelphia, 1860 ***5704.8*** *p145*
McColgan, Fanny; St. John, N.B., 1850 ***5704.8*** *p67*
McColgan, Francis; New Orleans, 1848 ***5704.8*** *p48*
McColgan, Grace; St. John, N.B., 1850 ***5704.8*** *p65*
McColgan, James; New York, NY, 1837 ***8208.4*** *p55*
McColgan, James; Philadelphia, 1847 ***53.26*** *p55*
*Relative:*Sally
McColgan, James; Philadelphia, 1847 ***5704.8*** *p30*
McColgan, James 10; St. John, N.B., 1847 ***5704.8*** *p26*
McColgan, John; St. John, N.B., 1853 ***5704.8*** *p100*
McColgan, Margery 16; St. John, N.B., 1854 ***5704.8*** *p122*
McColgan, Mary; Philadelphia, 1851 ***5704.8*** *p70*
McColgan, Mary; St. John, N.B., 1849 ***5704.8*** *p56*
McColgan, Mary; St. John, N.B., 1853 ***5704.8*** *p100*
McColgan, Mary Ann; New York, NY, 1867 ***5704.8*** *p219*
McColgan, Mary Ann; Philadelphia, 1849 ***53.26*** *p55*
*Relative:*Peggy
McColgan, Mary Ann; Philadelphia, 1849 ***5704.8*** *p49*
McColgan, Michael; St. John, N.B., 1848 ***5704.8*** *p38*
McColgan, Michael; St. John, N.B., 1853 ***5704.8*** *p99*
McColgan, Nancy; Philadelphia, 1865 ***5704.8*** *p192*
McColgan, Nancy 13; St. John, N.B., 1849 ***5704.8*** *p55*
McColgan, Pat 6; St. John, N.B., 1847 ***5704.8*** *p26*
McColgan, Patrick 9; St. John, N.B., 1851 ***5704.8*** *p77*
McColgan, Patrick 20; St. John, N.B., 1858 ***5704.8*** *p137*
McColgan, Peggy *SEE* McColgan, Mary Ann
McColgan, Peggy; Philadelphia, 1849 ***5704.8*** *p49*
McColgan, Peggy; St. John, N.B., 1851 ***5704.8*** *p79*
McColgan, Phillip 11; St. John, N.B., 1851 ***5704.8*** *p77*
McColgan, Richard; St. John, N.B., 1853 ***5704.8*** *p106*
McColgan, Rose; New York, NY, 1870 ***5704.8*** *p236*
McColgan, Rosey 8; St. John, N.B., 1847 ***5704.8*** *p26*
McColgan, Sally *SEE* McColgan, James
McColgan, Sally; Philadelphia, 1847 ***5704.8*** *p30*
McColgan, Sheelagh; Philadelphia, 1864 ***5704.8*** *p186*
McColgan, Susan; St. John, N.B., 1852 ***5704.8*** *p93*
McColgan, Susan 1 mo; St. John, N.B., 1853 ***5704.8*** *p106*
McColgan, Thomas; Philadelphia, 1864 ***5704.8*** *p176*
McColgan, William; Philadelphia, 1850 ***5704.8*** *p68*
McColgan, William; Philadelphia, 1865 ***5704.8*** *p191*
McColgan, William 19; St. John, N.B., 1856 ***5704.8*** *p131*
McColgan, Willian; Philadelphia, 1850 ***53.26*** *p55*
McColgen, Elizabeth 15; Quebec, 1856 ***5704.8*** *p130*
McColgen, Elizabeth 48; Quebec, 1856 ***5704.8*** *p130*
McColgen, James 19; Quebec, 1856 ***5704.8*** *p130*
McColgen, Robert 50; Quebec, 1856 ***5704.8*** *p130*
McColgen, Sarah 17; Quebec, 1856 ***5704.8*** *p130*
McColgen, William John 21; Quebec, 1856 ***5704.8*** *p130*
McColl, D.; America, 1792 ***1639.20*** *p130*
McColl, Daniel; America, 1787 ***1639.20*** *p130*
McColl, Dolly 72 *SEE* McColl, John
McColl, Dugald 48; South Carolina, 1850 ***1639.20*** *p130*
McColl, Duncan; America, 1791 ***1639.20*** *p131*
McColl, Duncan; North Carolina, 1774-1850 ***1639.20*** *p131*
McColl, Duncan; South Carolina, 1803 ***1639.20*** *p130*
McColl, Elenor 40; Philadelphia, 1865 ***5704.8*** *p164*
McColl, H.; America, 1803 ***1639.20*** *p131*
McColl, Hugh; America, 1790 ***1639.20*** *p131*
McColl, Hugh; America, 1791 ***1639.20*** *p131*
McColl, John; America, 1792 ***1639.20*** *p132*
McColl, John; America, 1802 ***1639.20*** *p132*
McColl, John; America, 1803 ***1639.20*** *p131*
McColl, John; North Carolina, 1761-1815 ***1639.20*** *p132*
McColl, John; South Carolina, 1790 ***1639.20*** *p131*
McColl, John 75; South Carolina, 1850 ***1639.20*** *p132*
*Relative:*Dolly 72
McColl, John 77; South Carolina, 1850 ***1639.20*** *p131*
McColl, Lauchlen; America, 1790 ***1639.20*** *p132*
McColl, Mary 28; North Carolina, 1850 ***1639.20*** *p132*
McColl, Peter Hugh 5; Philadelphia, 1865 ***5704.8*** *p164*
McColl, Soloman; South Carolina, 1790 ***1639.20*** *p132*
McColl, William 37; Maryland, 1774 ***1219.7*** *p235*
McCollan, William; St. John, N.B., 1847 ***5704.8*** *p19*
McColley, Alcia Ann; Philadelphia, 1849 ***5704.8*** *p53*
McColley, Alicia Ann; Philadelphia, 1849 ***53.26*** *p55*
*Relative:*Thomas 11
McColley, Benjamin 33; Maryland, 1774 ***1219.7*** *p204*
McColley, Biddy 20; St. John, N.B., 1853 ***5704.8*** *p109*
McColley, Ellan; St. John, N.B., 1849 ***5704.8*** *p56*
McColley, John; St. John, N.B., 1851 ***5704.8*** *p80*
McColley, Thomas 11 *SEE* McColley, Alicia Ann
McColley, Thomas 11; Philadelphia, 1849 ***5704.8*** *p53*
McCollin, Margaret 24; Philadelphia, 1865 ***5704.8*** *p165*
McCollister, Archibald 24; Philadelphia, 1853 ***5704.8*** *p108*
McCollom, Eliza; Quebec, 1849 ***5704.8*** *p52*
McCollough, Sally; New York, NY, 1864 ***5704.8*** *p170*
McCollough, Thomas; America, 1862 ***6014.1*** *p3*
McCollow, Edward 16; Philadelphia, 1856 ***5704.8*** *p128*
McCollum, Alexander; Philadelphia, 1866 ***5704.8*** *p214*
McCollum, Ann; America, 1866 ***5704.8*** *p206*
McCollum, Ann Eliza 10; Quebec, 1850 ***5704.8*** *p62*
McCollum, Anne; New York, NY, 1864 ***5704.8*** *p169*
McCollum, Archibald; Philadelphia, 1796 ***9892.11*** *p32*
McCollum, Archibald 11; Quebec, 1850 ***5704.8*** *p62*
McCollum, Archy; Quebec, 1850 ***5704.8*** *p66*
McCollum, Bernard; New York, NY, 1864 ***5704.8*** *p169*
McCollum, Biddy 3; Quebec, 1847 ***5704.8*** *p28*
McCollum, Bryan 10; St. John, N.B., 1847 ***5704.8*** *p15*
McCollum, Dennis; New York, NY, 1864 ***5704.8*** *p169*
McCollum, Dennis; St. John, N.B., 1847 ***5704.8*** *p5*
McCollum, George 13; St. John, N.B., 1847 ***5704.8*** *p15*
McCollum, Hugh 7; Philadelphia, 1865 ***5704.8*** *p164*
McCollum, Isabella; Philadelphia, 1866 ***5704.8*** *p214*
McCollum, James; America, 1866 ***5704.8*** *p206*
McCollum, James 3 mos; Quebec, 1847 ***5704.8*** *p28*
McCollum, James 46; Philadelphia, 1865 ***5704.8*** *p164*
McCollum, John; America, 1750 ***1639.20*** *p121*
McCollum, John; Philadelphia, 1866 ***5704.8*** *p214*
McCollum, John; St. John, N.B., 1847 ***5704.8*** *p5*
McCollum, Margaret; Philadelphia, 1849 ***53.26*** *p55*
*Relative:*Martha
McCollum, Margaret; Philadelphia, 1849 ***5704.8*** *p49*
McCollum, Margaret 46; Philadelphia, 1865 ***5704.8*** *p164*
McCollum, Martha *SEE* McCollum, Margaret
McCollum, Martha; Philadelphia, 1849 ***5704.8*** *p49*
McCollum, Mary 5; Philadelphia, 1865 ***5704.8*** *p164*
McCollum, Mary 5; Quebec, 1850 ***5704.8*** *p62*
McCollum, Mary J.; America, 1866 ***5704.8*** *p206*
McCollum, Patrick; St. John, N.B., 1847 ***5704.8*** *p5*
McCollum, Rachel; Quebec, 1850 ***5704.8*** *p62*
McCollum, Rose 4; Philadelphia, 1865 ***5704.8*** *p164*
McCollum, Sally; Quebec, 1847 ***5704.8*** *p28*
McCollum, Thomas; Quebec, 1847 ***5704.8*** *p28*
McCollum, William; New York, NY, 1866 ***5704.8*** *p212*
McCollum, William; St. John, N.B., 1847 ***5704.8*** *p15*
McCollum, William; St. John, N.B., 1847 ***5704.8*** *p21*
McColman, Malcolm 65; North Carolina, 1850 ***1639.20*** *p133*
McComay, Duncan; America, 1792 ***1639.20*** *p133*
McComb, David 22; St. John, N.B., 1864 ***5704.8*** *p158*
McComb, Isabella 21; St. John, N.B., 1864 ***5704.8*** *p158*
McComb, James; New York, NY, 1839 ***8208.4*** *p102*
McComb, Mary; America, 1739 ***4971*** *p68*
McComb, Mathew; Quebec, 1847 ***5704.8*** *p8*
McComb, Robert; New York, NY, 1840 ***8208.4*** *p110*
McComb, Robert 13; Quebec, 1847 ***5704.8*** *p8*
McComb, Wilfred R. 44; Arizona, 1890 ***2764.35*** *p49*
McCombs, Frances; Quebec, 1822 ***7603*** *p85*
McComiskey, Whitman D.; America, 1895 ***1450.2*** *p96A*
McCompt, Catharine 5; Massachusetts, 1849 ***5881.1*** *p64*
McCompt, Catharine 40; Massachusetts, 1849 ***5881.1*** *p64*
McCompt, Charles 3; Massachusetts, 1849 ***5881.1*** *p64*

McCompt, Eliza 9; Massachusetts, 1849 ***5881.1*** *p66*
McCompt, Jane 11; Massachusetts, 1849 ***5881.1*** *p69*
McCompt, John 17; Massachusetts, 1849 ***5881.1*** *p69*
McCompt, Mary 16; Massachusetts, 1849 ***5881.1*** *p72*
McCompt, William 7; Massachusetts, 1849 ***5881.1*** *p77*
McCompt, William 45; Massachusetts, 1849 ***5881.1*** *p77*
McCon, Sarah; Philadelphia, 1852 ***5704.8*** *p96*
McConachy, Richard; Washington, 1859-1920 ***2872.1*** *p27*
McConacley, Richard; Washington, 1859-1920 ***2872.1*** *p27*
McConaghan, Charles 20; Philadelphia, 1858 ***5704.8*** *p138*
McConaghty, Sarah 21; Quebec, 1857 ***5704.8*** *p135*
McConaghy, Catharine 20; Massachusetts, 1849 ***5881.1*** *p64*
McConaghy, David 30; Philadelphia, 1803 ***53.26*** *p55*
McConaghy, Eliza 20; Philadelphia, 1865 ***5704.8*** *p164*
McConaghy, Jane; Philadelphia, 1852 ***5704.8*** *p97*
McConaghy, Jane 26; St. John, N.B., 1858 ***5704.8*** *p140*
McConaghy, John; Quebec, 1847 ***5704.8*** *p13*
McConaghy, John; St. John, N.B., 1849 ***5704.8*** *p56*
McConaghy, John 16; Quebec, 1855 ***5704.8*** *p126*
McConaghy, Martha; St. John, N.B., 1848 ***5704.8*** *p44*
McConaghy, Mary; St. John, N.B., 1847 ***5704.8*** *p26*
McConaghy, Mary; St. John, N.B., 1848 ***5704.8*** *p44*
McConaghy, Patrick 25; Philadelphia, 1859 ***5704.8*** *p141*
McConaghy, Robert; St. John, N.B., 1848 ***5704.8*** *p44*
McConaghy, Robert 20; Philadelphia, 1859 ***5704.8*** *p141*
McConahie, A. H. 25; Kansas, 1873 ***5240.1*** *p54*
McConamy, Susan; St. John, N.B., 1847 ***5704.8*** *p20*
McConchie, Samuel; Charleston, SC, 1807 ***1639.20*** *p133*
McConghen, Margaret; Philadelphia, 1850 ***5704.8*** *p64*
McConghen, Mary Jane; Philadelphia, 1850 ***5704.8*** *p64*
McConghen, Matty Ann; Philadelphia, 1850 ***5704.8*** *p64*
McConghen, Nancy; Philadelphia, 1850 ***5704.8*** *p64*
McConghen, Robert; Philadelphia, 1850 ***5704.8*** *p64*
McConghen, William; Philadelphia, 1850 ***5704.8*** *p64*
McConkey, James; New York, NY, 1835 ***8208.4*** *p8*
McConlogue, Bernard 11; St. John, N.B., 1851 ***5704.8*** *p72*
McConlogue, Biddy; St. John, N.B., 1848 ***5704.8*** *p38*
McConlogue, Catherine 10; St. John, N.B., 1851 ***5704.8*** *p72*
McConlogue, Daniel 9; St. John, N.B., 1851 ***5704.8*** *p72*
McConlogue, Edward; St. John, N.B., 1850 ***5704.8*** *p61*
McConlogue, George; St. John, N.B., 1852 ***5704.8*** *p84*
McConlogue, Henry; Philadelphia, 1853 ***5704.8*** *p100*
McConlogue, Hugh 9 mos; St. John, N.B., 1851 ***5704.8*** *p72*
McConlogue, John; Philadelphia, 1853 ***5704.8*** *p100*
McConlogue, John; St. John, N.B., 1853 ***5704.8*** *p107*
McConlogue, John 4; St. John, N.B., 1851 ***5704.8*** *p72*
McConlogue, Margaret; St. John, N.B., 1853 ***5704.8*** *p107*
McConlogue, Michael 6; St. John, N.B., 1851 ***5704.8*** *p72*
McConlogue, Nancy; St. John, N.B., 1848 ***5704.8*** *p45*
McConlogue, Patrick; St. John, N.B., 1851 ***5704.8*** *p72*
McConlogue, Patrick; St. John, N.B., 1853 ***5704.8*** *p107*
McConlogue, Peggy; St. John, N.B., 1851 ***5704.8*** *p72*
McConlogue, William; St. John, N.B., 1853 ***5704.8*** *p99*
McConlouge, Catherine 10; St. John, N.B., 1851 ***5704.8*** *p72*
McConlouge, Ellen 6; St. John, N.B., 1851 ***5704.8*** *p72*
McConlouge, James 11; St. John, N.B., 1851 ***5704.8*** *p72*
McConn, Alex 15; Philadelphia, 1853 ***5704.8*** *p112*
McConnamy, Dennis 20; St. John, N.B., 1854 ***5704.8*** *p114*
McConnel, Mary; Montreal, 1822 ***7603*** *p54*
McConnel, Nancy 9 mos; St. John, N.B., 1847 ***5704.8*** *p10*
McConnel, Peggy; St. John, N.B., 1847 ***5704.8*** *p10*
McConnel, Peter; St. John, N.B., 1847 ***5704.8*** *p10*
McConnell, Adam; San Francisco, 1864 ***2769.6*** *p6*
McConnell, Alex 21; Quebec, 1864 ***5704.8*** *p162*
McConnell, Alexander 3; Quebec, 1848 ***5704.8*** *p42*
McConnell, Alexander 25; Philadelphia, 1868 ***5704.8*** *p225*
McConnell, Allan; Quebec, 1848 ***5704.8*** *p42*
McConnell, Andrew 19; Philadelphia, 1860 ***5704.8*** *p145*
McConnell, Ann; Quebec, 1847 ***5704.8*** *p6*
McConnell, Ann 3; Philadelphia, 1865 ***5704.8*** *p201*
McConnell, Ann 17; Quebec, 1853 ***5704.8*** *p105*
McConnell, Anne; New York, NY, 1864 ***5704.8*** *p169*
McConnell, Anne; Philadelphia, 1852 ***5704.8*** *p92*
McConnell, Anne; Philadelphia, 1864 ***5704.8*** *p184*
McConnell, Bernard 21; Philadelphia, 1854 ***5704.8*** *p116*
McConnell, Bridget; Philadelphia, 1865 ***5704.8*** *p201*
McConnell, Bridget 10 mos; Philadelphia, 1865 ***5704.8*** *p201*
McConnell, Catharine; New York, NY, 1867 ***5704.8*** *p222*
McConnell, Catharine 50; Philadelphia, 1868 ***5704.8*** *p225*
McConnell, Catherine; Philadelphia, 1852 ***5704.8*** *p96*
McConnell, Catherine 1; Philadelphia, 1852 ***5704.8*** *p96*
McConnell, Catherine 23; St. John, N.B., 1866 ***5704.8*** *p167*
McConnell, Charles 21; Quebec, 1853 ***5704.8*** *p105*
McConnell, Crissy 62; Wilmington, DE, 1831 ***6508.7*** *p161*
McConnell, Daniel 4; Philadelphia, 1852 ***5704.8*** *p96*
McConnell, Eliza 4 *SEE* McConnell, William
McConnell, Eliza Mary 4; Philadelphia, 1848 ***5704.8*** *p45*
McConnell, Ellen; Philadelphia, 1852 ***5704.8*** *p92*
McConnell, Ellen; Quebec, 1848 ***5704.8*** *p42*
McConnell, Ellen 20; St. John, N.B., 1861 ***5704.8*** *p147*
McConnell, Fanny; New York, NY, 1868 ***5704.8*** *p227*
McConnell, George; New York, NY, 1837 ***8208.4*** *p35*
McConnell, George; Quebec, 1847 ***5704.8*** *p6*
McConnell, George; St. John, N.B., 1847 ***5704.8*** *p19*
McConnell, George 6; St. John, N.B., 1847 ***5704.8*** *p19*
McConnell, Gibson 21; Philadelphia, 1858 ***5704.8*** *p139*
McConnell, Hannah 17; Philadelphia, 1857 ***5704.8*** *p134*
McConnell, Hugh 20; Philadelphia, 1857 ***5704.8*** *p134*
McConnell, Isabella; New York, NY, 1868 ***5704.8*** *p225*
McConnell, Isabella; Quebec, 1852 ***5704.8*** *p87*
McConnell, Isabella; Quebec, 1852 ***5704.8*** *p91*
McConnell, Isabella 14; Philadelphia, 1868 ***5704.8*** *p225*
McConnell, James; Philadelphia, 1811 ***53.26*** *p55*
McConnell, James; Philadelphia, 1852 ***5704.8*** *p88*
McConnell, James; Quebec, 1853 ***5704.8*** *p105*
McConnell, James; St. John, N.B., 1852 ***5704.8*** *p83*
McConnell, James 6; Philadelphia, 1865 ***5704.8*** *p201*
McConnell, Jane *SEE* McConnell, William
McConnell, Jane; Philadelphia, 1848 ***5704.8*** *p45*
McConnell, Jane; Quebec, 1851 ***5704.8*** *p82*
McConnell, Jane 2 *SEE* McConnell, Rebecca
McConnell, Jane 2; Philadelphia, 1849 ***5704.8*** *p54*
McConnell, Jane 18; Philadelphia, 1859 ***5704.8*** *p142*
McConnell, Jane 42; Quebec, 1853 ***5704.8*** *p105*
McConnell, John; Philadelphia, 1850 ***53.26*** *p55*
*Relative:*Mary
*Relative:*Mary Ann
*Relative:*Sarah 5
*Relative:*Nancy 1
McConnell, John; Philadelphia, 1850 ***5704.8*** *p68*
McConnell, John; Philadelphia, 1864 ***5704.8*** *p184*
McConnell, John; Quebec, 1847 ***5704.8*** *p6*
McConnell, John 4; St. John, N.B., 1847 ***5704.8*** *p19*
McConnell, John 5 *SEE* McConnell, William
McConnell, John 5; Philadelphia, 1848 ***5704.8*** *p45*
McConnell, John 7 *SEE* McConnell, Rebecca
McConnell, John 7; Philadelphia, 1849 ***5704.8*** *p54*
McConnell, John 11; Philadelphia, 1865 ***5704.8*** *p201*
McConnell, John 18; St. John, N.B., 1866 ***5704.8*** *p167*
McConnell, John 45; Quebec, 1853 ***5704.8*** *p105*
McConnell, Joseph; Quebec, 1852 ***5704.8*** *p87*
McConnell, Joseph; Quebec, 1852 ***5704.8*** *p91*
McConnell, Lawrance; New York, NY, 1864 ***5704.8*** *p185*
McConnell, Manus; Philadelphia, 1852 ***5704.8*** *p85*
McConnell, Marg. Jane 8 *SEE* McConnell, William
McConnell, Margaret; Philadelphia, 1850 ***53.26*** *p55*
McConnell, Margaret; Philadelphia, 1850 ***5704.8*** *p60*
McConnell, Margaret 8; St. John, N.B., 1847 ***5704.8*** *p19*
McConnell, Margaret 15; St. John, N.B., 1861 ***5704.8*** *p147*
McConnell, Margaret 45; Philadelphia, 1860 ***5704.8*** *p146*
McConnell, Margaret Jane 8; Philadelphia, 1848 ***5704.8*** *p45*
McConnell, Martha; Quebec, 1847 ***5704.8*** *p6*
McConnell, Martha 18; Quebec, 1864 ***5704.8*** *p160*
McConnell, Mary *SEE* McConnell, John
McConnell, Mary *SEE* McConnell, Rebecca
McConnell, Mary; America, 1867 ***5704.8*** *p224*
McConnell, Mary; Philadelphia, 1849 ***53.26*** *p56*
McConnell, Mary; Philadelphia, 1849 ***5704.8*** *p50*
McConnell, Mary; Philadelphia, 1849 ***5704.8*** *p54*
McConnell, Mary; Philadelphia, 1850 ***5704.8*** *p68*
McConnell, Mary; Philadelphia, 1867 ***5704.8*** *p220*
McConnell, Mary 17; Philadelphia, 1861 ***5704.8*** *p148*
McConnell, Mary Ann *SEE* McConnell, John
McConnell, Mary Ann; Philadelphia, 1850 ***5704.8*** *p68*
McConnell, Mary Ann; Philadelphia, 1852 ***5704.8*** *p96*
McConnell, Mary Ann 11 *SEE* McConnell, Rebecca
McConnell, Mary Ann 11; Philadelphia, 1849 ***5704.8*** *p54*
McConnell, Mary Jane 10; St. John, N.B., 1847 ***5704.8*** *p19*
McConnell, Nancy 1 *SEE* McConnell, John
McConnell, Nancy 1; Philadelphia, 1850 ***5704.8*** *p68*
McConnell, Patrick 8; Philadelphia, 1865 ***5704.8*** *p201*
McConnell, Rachael; Philadelphia, 1867 ***5704.8*** *p220*
McConnell, Rebecca; Philadelphia, 1849 ***53.26*** *p55*
*Relative:*Mary
*Relative:*Mary Ann 11
*Relative:*John 7
*Relative:*Thomas 5
*Relative:*Jane 2
McConnell, Rebecca; Philadelphia, 1849 ***5704.8*** *p54*
McConnell, Rebecca; Philadelphia, 1852 ***5704.8*** *p96*
McConnell, Rebecca; St. John, N.B., 1847 ***5704.8*** *p19*
McConnell, Richard; America, 1866 ***5704.8*** *p209*
McConnell, Richard Alexander; New York, NY, 1836 ***8208.4*** *p10*
McConnell, Ruth 50; St. John, N.B., 1866 ***5704.8*** *p167*
McConnell, Samuel 3 mos *SEE* McConnell, William
McConnell, Samuel 9 mos; Philadelphia, 1848 ***5704.8*** *p45*
McConnell, Sarah; Quebec, 1852 ***5704.8*** *p87*
McConnell, Sarah 6 mos; Quebec, 1852 ***5704.8*** *p91*
McConnell, Sarah 5 *SEE* McConnell, John
McConnell, Sarah 5; Philadelphia, 1850 ***5704.8*** *p68*
McConnell, Sarah 20; Philadelphia, 1868 ***5704.8*** *p225*
McConnell, Sarah Ann 2; Quebec, 1848 ***5704.8*** *p42*
McConnell, Stephen; America, 1841 ***1450.2*** *p96A*
McConnell, Susan; New York, NY, 1865 ***5704.8*** *p203*
McConnell, Susan; Quebec, 1851 ***5704.8*** *p82*
McConnell, Thomas; Philadelphia, 1864 ***5704.8*** *p184*
McConnell, Thomas 1; Philadelphia, 1850 ***5704.8*** *p60*
McConnell, Thomas 5 *SEE* McConnell, Rebecca
McConnell, Thomas 5; Philadelphia, 1849 ***5704.8*** *p54*
McConnell, Thomas 20; Philadelphia, 1854 ***5704.8*** *p122*
McConnell, Thomas 22; St. John, N.B., 1862 ***5704.8*** *p151*
McConnell, Thomas 40; Quebec, 1853 ***5704.8*** *p105*
McConnell, William; New York, NY, 1865 ***5704.8*** *p195*
McConnell, William; Philadelphia, 1848 ***53.26*** *p56*
*Relative:*Jane
*Relative:*William 11
*Relative:*Marg. Jane 8
*Relative:*Eliza 4
*Relative:*John 5
*Relative:*Samuel 3 mos
McConnell, William; Philadelphia, 1848 ***5704.8*** *p45*
McConnell, William; Philadelphia, 1866 ***5704.8*** *p206*
McConnell, William 11 *SEE* McConnell, William
McConnell, William 11; Philadelphia, 1848 ***5704.8*** *p45*
McConnell, William J.; Illinois, 1890 ***5012.40*** *p25*
McConnogh, William; America, 1735-1743 ***4971*** *p79*
McConnoway, John; St. John, N.B., 1847 ***5704.8*** *p26*
McConologhe, Unity; Philadelphia, 1849 ***53.26*** *p56*
McConologue, James; Philadelphia, 1849 ***53.26*** *p56*
*Relative:*William
McConologue, James; Philadelphia, 1849 ***5704.8*** *p54*
McConologue, Patrick; Philadelphia, 1867 ***5704.8*** *p217*
McConologue, Peggy 50; St. John, N.B., 1855 ***5704.8*** *p126*
McConologue, Thomas; Philadelphia, 1867 ***5704.8*** *p222*
McConologue, Unity; Philadelphia, 1849 ***5704.8*** *p50*
McConologue, William *SEE* McConologue, James
McConologue, William; Philadelphia, 1849 ***5704.8*** *p54*
McConomy, Daniel *SEE* McConomy, Magg
McConomy, Daniel; Philadelphia, 1849 ***53.26*** *p56*
McConomy, Daniel; Philadelphia, 1849 ***5704.8*** *p50*
McConomy, Daniel; Philadelphia, 1850 ***5704.8*** *p60*
McConomy, Fanny *SEE* McConomy, Magg
McConomy, Fanny; Philadelphia, 1850 ***5704.8*** *p60*
McConomy, Henry 25; Quebec, 1857 ***5704.8*** *p136*
McConomy, Keatty *SEE* McConomy, Magg
McConomy, Keatty; Philadelphia, 1850 ***5704.8*** *p60*
McConomy, Magg; Philadelphia, 1850 ***53.26*** *p56*
*Relative:*Keatty
*Relative:*Fanny
*Relative:*Daniel
McConomy, Magg; Philadelphia, 1850 ***5704.8*** *p60*
McConoway, Biddy; St. John, N.B., 1847 ***5704.8*** *p18*
McConvill, Edward; Iowa, 1866-1943 ***123.54*** *p31*
McConville, Barney; Arkansas, 1918 ***95.2*** *p82*
McConway, John 28; Philadelphia, 1804 ***53.26*** *p56*
*Relative:*Mary 26
McConway, Mary 26 *SEE* McConway, John
McCook, Alex; Philadelphia, 1851 ***5704.8*** *p76*
McCook, James 22; Philadelphia, 1833-1834 ***53.26*** *p56*
*Relative:*John 20
McCook, John 20 *SEE* McCook, James
McCook, Matthew; Philadelphia, 1851 ***5704.8*** *p76*
McCool, Ann; St. John, N.B., 1848 ***5704.8*** *p39*
McCool, Anne 22; St. John, N.B., 1854 ***5704.8*** *p115*
McCool, Bernard; St. John, N.B., 1847 ***5704.8*** *p4*
McCool, Catherine; Quebec, 1852 ***5704.8*** *p94*
McCool, Charles; Quebec, 1850 ***5704.8*** *p63*
McCool, Charles; St. John, N.B., 1847 ***5704.8*** *p4*
McCool, Elenor; America, 1865 ***5704.8*** *p199*
McCool, Elizabeth 5; Quebec, 1863 ***5704.8*** *p154*
McCool, George 8; Quebec, 1863 ***5704.8*** *p154*

McCool, Hugh; Philadelphia, 1864 5704.8 p179
McCool, James; Quebec, 1847 5704.8 p17
McCool, James; St. John, N.B., 1853 5704.8 p107
McCool, James 6; St. John, N.B., 1853 5704.8 p107
McCool, James 7; Quebec, 1863 5704.8 p154
McCool, John; Philadelphia, 1852 5704.8 p91
McCool, John 11; Quebec, 1863 5704.8 p154
McCool, John 20; St. John, N.B., 1860 5704.8 p144
McCool, John 21; Philadelphia, 1833-1834 53.26 p56
McCool, Magy; St. John, N.B., 1853 5704.8 p107
McCool, Margaret; Philadelphia, 1865 5704.8 p192
McCool, Martha 28; Quebec, 1857 5704.8 p135
McCool, Mary; Philadelphia, 1864 5704.8 p179
McCool, Mary Ann 10; Quebec, 1863 5704.8 p154
McCool, Matilda; Quebec, 1863 5704.8 p154
McCool, Michael; New York, NY, 1836 8208.4 p11
McCool, Nancy; St. John, N.B., 1853 5704.8 p107
McCool, Nancy 3; Quebec, 1863 5704.8 p154
McCool, Nancy 33; Quebec, 1863 5704.8 p154
McCool, Nelly; St. John, N.B., 1847 5704.8 p3
McCool, Owen; St. John, N.B., 1853 5704.8 p107
McCool, Owney; St. John, N.B., 1848 5704.8 p39
McCool, Patrick; St. John, N.B., 1847 5704.8 p3
McCool, Patrick; St. John, N.B., 1847 5704.8 p4
McCool, Patrick; St. John, N.B., 1847 5704.8 p9
McCool, Patrick; St. John, N.B., 1848 5704.8 p43
McCool, Patrick; St. John, N.B., 1853 5704.8 p107
McCool, Patrick 18; St. John, N.B., 1860 5704.8 p143
McCool, Rose; St. John, N.B., 1853 5704.8 p99
McCool, Sarah; Philadelphia, 1864 5704.8 p179
McCool, Sarah; Philadelphia, 1865 5704.8 p192
McCool, Sarah Jane 15; Quebec, 1863 5704.8 p154
McCool, William 42; Quebec, 1863 5704.8 p154
McCoole, Bridget 23; St. John, N.B., 1854 5704.8 p114
McCoory, . . . 4; Philadelphia, 1865 5704.8 p198
McCoory, William; Philadelphia, 1865 5704.8 p198
McCord, Jane; Philadelphia, 1852 5704.8 p96
McCord, Margaret; Philadelphia, 1847 53.26 p56
McCord, Margaret; Philadelphia, 1847 5704.8 p1
McCord, Mary; Philadelphia, 1853 5704.8 p113
McCorgary, Daniel; Kansas, 1884 5240.1 p28
McCorgary, James 32; Kansas, 1900 5240.1 p28
McCorgary, James 32; Kansas, 1900 5240.1 p81
McCoristine, Marguerite; Montreal, 1799 7603 p77
McCoristine, Terence 30; Montreal, 1780 7603 p59
McCorkell, Andrew; Quebec, 1853 5704.8 p104
McCorkell, Andrew 61; Quebec, 1857 5704.8 p136
McCorkell, Anne; Philadelphia, 1869 5704.8 p235
McCorkell, Anne 15; Quebec, 1857 5704.8 p136
McCorkell, Augusta 4; Quebec, 1850 5704.8 p63
McCorkell, David; Philadelphia, 1852 5704.8 p89
McCorkell, Ian; St. John, N.B., 1852 5704.8 p84
McCorkell, John; Philadelphia, 1851 5704.8 p79
McCorkell, John 23; St. John, N.B., 1854 5704.8 p122
McCorkell, Lydia 20; Quebec, 1857 5704.8 p136
McCorkell, Lydia 56; Quebec, 1857 5704.8 p136
McCorkell, Martha 22; Quebec, 1857 5704.8 p136
McCorkell, Mary; St. John, N.B., 1852 5704.8 p83
McCorkell, Robert; Quebec, 1850 5704.8 p63
McCorkell, Thomas; Philadelphia, 1851 5704.8 p70
McCorkell, William 10; Quebec, 1857 5704.8 p136
McCorkie, Alexander; Pennsylvania, 1722-1745 1639.20 p133
McCorkill, Easter; St. John, N.B., 1847 5704.8 p19
McCorkill, John; St. John, N.B., 1853 5704.8 p98
McCorkill, Mary Ann; St. John, N.B., 1853 5704.8 p98
McCorkle, Catherine 11; Quebec, 1847 5704.8 p38
McCorkle, Francis, Sr.; North Carolina, 1745-1802 1639.20 p133
McCorkle, Mary; Quebec, 1847 5704.8 p38
McCorkle, Samuel; Quebec, 1847 5704.8 p38
McCormac, Flora 80; North Carolina, 1850 1639.20 p133
McCormack, Bridget 8 mos; Massachusetts, 1847 5881.1 p63
McCormack, John; Wilmington, NC, 1791 1639.20 p134
McCormack, John 26; Massachusetts, 1847 5881.1 p67
McCormack, John 40; Massachusetts, 1849 5881.1 p69
McCormack, John 41; Massachusetts, 1850 5881.1 p69
McCormack, Mary; North Carolina, 1751-1826 1639.20 p134
McCormack, Mary 18; Massachusetts, 1849 5881.1 p72
McCormack, Michael 45; Massachusetts, 1849 5881.1 p72
McCormack, William; North Carolina, 1821 1639.20 p134
McCormack, William 19; Massachusetts, 1849 5881.1 p77
McCormack, William 24; Massachusetts, 1847 5881.1 p77
McCormaig, Mary; Canada, 1825 8894.2 p57
McCormaig, Mary 64; North Carolina, 1850 1639.20 p134
McCormell, John 21; Wilmington, DE, 1831 6508.7 p160
McCormick, Alexander 36; Kansas, 1879 5240.1 p28
McCormick, Alexander 36; Kansas, 1879 5240.1 p61
McCormick, Allice; Philadelphia, 1865 5704.8 p197
McCormick, Ann 18; Philadelphia, 1854 5704.8 p121
McCormick, Bernard *SEE* McCormick, John
McCormick, Bernard *SEE* McCormick, John
McCormick, Bernard; Philadelphia, 1847 5704.8 p31
McCormick, Biddy 7 *SEE* McCormick, John
McCormick, Biddy 7 *SEE* McCormick, John
McCormick, Biddy 7; Philadelphia, 1847 5704.8 p31
McCormick, Biddy 23; St. John, N.B., 1862 5704.8 p150
McCormick, Bridget; Philadelphia, 1864 5704.8 p179
McCormick, Catharine; Philadelphia, 1867 5704.8 p221
McCormick, Catharine 9; Massachusetts, 1849 5881.1 p64
McCormick, Catherine 20; Quebec, 1864 5704.8 p162
McCormick, Charles; Philadelphia, 1866 5704.8 p207
McCormick, Christopher 20; Massachusetts, 1849 5881.1 p64
McCormick, Daniel; Philadelphia, 1847 53.26 p56
McCormick, Daniel; Philadelphia, 1847 5704.8 p2
McCormick, Daniel 11; Philadelphia, 1853 5704.8 p108
McCormick, Daniel 40; St. John, N.B., 1862 5704.8 p150
McCormick, Dennis 11; Quebec, 1847 5704.8 p36
McCormick, Donald; Quebec, 1790 9775.5 p198A
With family of 1
McCormick, Donald; Quebec, 1790 9775.5 p198A
McCormick, Dugald 28; Kansas, 1889 5240.1 p74
McCormick, Duncan; Wilmington, NC, 1791 1639.20 p133
McCormick, Eleanor; Quebec, 1847 5704.8 p7
McCormick, Eleanor 6 mos; Quebec, 1847 5704.8 p7
McCormick, Elizabeth; Philadelphia, 1851 5704.8 p76
McCormick, Elizabeth 24; Wilmington, DE, 1831 6508.3 p101
McCormick, Ellanor; Philadelphia, 1847 53.26 p56
McCormick, Ellanor; Philadelphia, 1847 5704.8 p23
McCormick, Elleanor; St. John, N.B., 1847 5704.8 p26
McCormick, Ellen; Philadelphia, 1864 5704.8 p179
McCormick, Ellen 19; Philadelphia, 1864 5704.8 p157
McCormick, Francis 27; Kansas, 1889 5240.1 p28
McCormick, Francis 27; Kansas, 1889 5240.1 p73
McCormick, Francis, Sr. 68; Kansas, 1879 5240.1 p61
McCormick, Helen; Quebec, 1822 7603 p59
McCormick, Henry; Quebec, 1851 5704.8 p75
McCormick, Henry 2; Quebec, 1847 5704.8 p7
McCormick, Henry 18; Philadelphia, 1854 5704.8 p120
McCormick, Hugh; Quebec, 1847 5704.8 p36
McCormick, Isabella; Philadelphia, 1864 5704.8 p177
McCormick, Isabella; Quebec, 1847 5704.8 p7
McCormick, James; New York, NY, 1836 8208.4 p21
McCormick, James; New York, NY, 1864 5704.8 p186
McCormick, James; New York, NY, 1866 5704.8 p208
McCormick, James; Quebec, 1847 5704.8 p12
McCormick, James; St. John, N.B., 1847 5704.8 p26
McCormick, James; St. John, N.B., 1853 5704.8 p100
McCormick, James 14; Philadelphia, 1861 5704.8 p148
McCormick, James 25; Wilmington, DE, 1831 6508.3 p101
McCormick, James 27; St. John, N.B., 1853 5704.8 p110
McCormick, James 40; West Virginia, 1800 9788.3 p16
McCormick, Jane 12; Quebec, 1847 5704.8 p7
McCormick, John; America, 1768 1639.20 p133
McCormick, John; New York, NY, 1834 8208.4 p1
McCormick, John; Philadelphia, 1847 53.26 p56
*Relative:*Bernard
*Relative:*Mary 10
*Relative:*Margaret 10
*Relative:*Biddy 7
McCormick, John; Philadelphia, 1847 53.26 p56
*Relative:*Bernard
*Relative:*Mary 12
*Relative:*Margaret 10
*Relative:*Biddy 7
McCormick, John; Philadelphia, 1847 5704.8 p31
McCormick, John; Philadelphia, 1865 5704.8 p195
McCormick, John; Philadelphia, 1867 5704.8 p220
McCormick, John; Quebec, 1847 5704.8 p7
McCormick, John; Quebec, 1851 5704.8 p75
McCormick, John; St. John, N.B., 1848 5704.8 p39
McCormick, Joseph; America, 1737 4971 p85
McCormick, Joseph; Quebec, 1847 5704.8 p12
McCormick, Katty; Philadelphia, 1849 53.26 p56
McCormick, Katty; Philadelphia, 1849 5704.8 p54
McCormick, Margaret; New York, NY, 1865 5704.8 p197
McCormick, Margaret; Quebec, 1847 5704.8 p36
McCormick, Margaret; St. John, N.B., 1847 5704.8 p18
McCormick, Margaret 8; Quebec, 1847 5704.8 p7
McCormick, Margaret 10 *SEE* McCormick, John
McCormick, Margaret 10 *SEE* McCormick, John
McCormick, Margaret 10; Philadelphia, 1847 5704.8 p3
McCormick, Mary; Philadelphia, 1864 5704.8 p185
McCormick, Mary 10 *SEE* McCormick, John
McCormick, Mary 12 *SEE* McCormick, John
McCormick, Mary 12; Philadelphia, 1847 5704.8 p31
McCormick, Mary 20; Massachusetts, 1849 5881.1 p71
McCormick, Mary Ann; St. John, N.B., 1847 5704.8 p1
McCormick, Mary Ann Moore 30; Montreal, 1775 7603 p68
McCormick, Mary Jane; St. John, N.B., 1852 5704.8 p93
McCormick, Michael; New York, NY, 1869 5704.8 p235
McCormick, Michael 17; Philadelphia, 1864 5704.8 p157
McCormick, Patrick; New York, NY, 1834 8208.4 p38
McCormick, Patrick; New York, NY, 1839 8208.4 p96
McCormick, Patrick; New York, NY, 1870 5704.8 p238
McCormick, Patrick; Philadelphia, 1847 53.26 p56
*Relative:*Sally
McCormick, Patrick; Philadelphia, 1847 5704.8 p31
McCormick, Patrick 20; St. John, N.B., 1856 5704.8 p132
McCormick, Patrick 25; Philadelphia, 1833-1834 53.26 p56
*Relative:*William 23
McCormick, Peggy 25; Massachusetts, 1849 5881.1 p74
McCormick, Peter; New York, NY, 1836 8208.4 p20
McCormick, Peter; Philadelphia, 1864 5704.8 p179
McCormick, Peter 30; Massachusetts, 1849 5881.1 p74
McCormick, Rachael; New York, NY, 1864 5704.8 p17
McCormick, Robert; New York, NY, 1865 5704.8 p195
McCormick, Rosanna; Philadelphia, 1850 5704.8 p64
McCormick, Rose; Quebec, 1847 5704.8 p36
McCormick, Sally *SEE* McCormick, Patrick
McCormick, Sally; Philadelphia, 1847 5704.8 p31
McCormick, Seba 21; Massachusetts, 1847 5881.1 p75
McCormick, Susan 7; Philadelphia, 1856 5704.8 p128
McCormick, William; America, 1737 4971 p12
McCormick, William; Charleston, SC, 1822 1639.20 p134
McCormick, William; West Virginia, 1831 9788.3 p16
McCormick, William; West Virginia, 1834 9788.3 p16
McCormick, William 17; St. John, N.B., 1864 5704.8 p158
McCormick, William 18; Quebec, 1859 5704.8 p143
McCormick, William 20; St. John, N.B., 1856 5704.8 p131
McCormick, William 23 *SEE* McCormick, Patrick
McCormick, William 39; West Virginia, 1800-1906 9788.3 p2
McCormick, William 39; West Virginia, 1829 9788.3 p16
McCornish, Honora 26; Massachusetts, 1849 5881.1 p67
McCornish, James 9; Massachusetts, 1849 5881.1 p68
McCorqudale, John 80; North Carolina, 1850 1639.20 p134
McCorreston, Catherine; St. John, N.B., 1849 5704.8 p48
McCorriston, Cicily; St. John, N.B., 1848 5704.8 p43
McCorry, Charles; America, 1864 5704.8 p189
McCorry, John; America, 1864 5704.8 p189
McCorry, John; Quebec, 1847 5704.8 p38
McCorry, Mary; America, 1864 5704.8 p189
McCorry, Mary; Quebec, 1847 5704.8 p38
McCort, Ann; St. John, N.B., 1848 5704.8 p44
McCort, Jane; St. John, N.B., 1848 5704.8 p44
McCort, Patrick 21; St. John, N.B., 1856 5704.8 p131
McCoskar, Francis; New York, NY, 1834 8208.4 p4
McCosker, Ann; Philadelphia, 1852 5704.8 p85
McCosker, Bridget 20; Philadelphia, 1854 5704.8 p117
McCosker, John; New York, NY, 1833 8208.4 p79
McCosker, John 13; Philadelphia, 1860 5704.8 p144
McCosker, Philip; Ohio, 1840 9892.11 p32
McCoster, Hugh; New York, NY, 1836 8208.4 p22
McCotter, Wiliam; Philadelphia, 1850 53.26 p56
McCotter, William; Philadelphia, 1850 5704.8 p68
McCottry, Ellis; New York, NY, 1839 8208.4 p98
McCottry, Thomas; New York, NY, 1838 8208.4 p90
McCougan, Angus 53; North Carolina, 1850 1639.20 p134
*Relative:*Donald 51
McCougan, Donald 51 *SEE* McCougan, Angus
McCoun, Charles; Philadelphia, 1811 53.26 p56
McCourt, Arthur; America, 1742 4971 p72
McCourt, Bell; Quebec, 1851 5704.8 p74
McCourt, Bridget 9; Philadelphia, 1868 5704.8 p223
McCourt, Ellan; St. John, N.B., 1848 5704.8 p47
McCourt, Hannah; St. John, N.B., 1855 5704.8 p127
McCourt, James 9; Philadelphia, 1868 5704.8 p223

330
FOR A COMPLETE EXPLANATION OF ENTRY, SEE "HOW TO READ A CITATION" SECTION

McCourt, John 21; St. John, N.B., 1865 ***5704.8*** *p165*
McCourt, Margaret; Quebec, 1847 ***5704.8*** *p29*
McCourt, Mary Jane; Quebec, 1852 ***5704.8*** *p86*
McCourt, Mary Jane; Quebec, 1852 ***5704.8*** *p91*
McCourt, Matilda; Quebec, 1851 ***5704.8*** *p74*
McCourt, Rebecca; Quebec, 1851 ***5704.8*** *p74*
McCourt, Robert; Quebec, 1851 ***5704.8*** *p74*
McCourt, Rosey; St. John, N.B., 1855 ***5704.8*** *p127*
McCourt, William 27; West Virginia, 1890 ***9788.3*** *p16*
McCowden, Mary; Quebec, 1779 ***7603*** *p99*
McCowell, Charles; America, 1742 ***4971*** *p73*
McCowell, Edmund; America, 1742 ***4971*** *p73*
McCowell, Michael; America, 1741 ***4971*** *p73*
McCowley, James; Philadelphia, 1741 ***4971*** *p92*
McCowly, James; America, 1735-1743 ***4971*** *p8*
McCown, John 17; Philadelphia, 1857 ***5704.8*** *p133*
McCoy, Alexander; North Carolina, 1754-1830 ***1639.20*** *p134*
McCoy, Ann 23; Philadelphia, 1858 ***5704.8*** *p139*
McCoy, Catharine; America, 1866 ***5704.8*** *p211*
McCoy, Daniel; Illinois, 1894 ***5012.40*** *p53*
McCoy, Daniel 40; Massachusetts, 1849 ***5881.1*** *p65*
McCoy, Donald; South Carolina, 1716 ***1639.20*** *p135*
McCoy, Edward; Philadelphia, 1864 ***5704.8*** *p174*
McCoy, Isabella 12; St. John, N.B., 1849 ***5704.8*** *p49*
McCoy, James; Philadelphia, 1849 ***53.26*** *p56*
McCoy, James; Philadelphia, 1849 ***5704.8*** *p54*
McCoy, James Walter; Arkansas, 1918 ***95.2*** *p82*
McCoy, Jane; St. John, N.B., 1847 ***5704.8*** *p32*
McCoy, John; Montreal, 1814 ***7603*** *p66*
McCoy, John; South Carolina, 1716 ***1639.20*** *p135*
McCoy, John 11; St. John, N.B., 1847 ***5704.8*** *p32*
McCoy, John 20; Philadelphia, 1803 ***53.26*** *p56*
McCoy, Joseph; St. John, N.B., 1849 ***5704.8*** *p49*
McCoy, Kelsey; Washington, 1859-1920 ***2872.1*** *p27*
McCoy, Margaret; Philadelphia, 1868 ***5704.8*** *p230*
McCoy, Margaret 22; St. John, N.B., 1860 ***5704.8*** *p144*
McCoy, Matilda; Philadelphia, 1868 ***5704.8*** *p230*
McCoy, Neil; St. John, N.B., 1847 ***5704.8*** *p32*
McCoy, Neill; St. John, N.B., 1849 ***5704.8*** *p49*
McCoyage, Ellen 18; Philadelphia, 1861 ***5704.8*** *p148*
McCrab, Alexander 17; St. John, N.B., 1854 ***5704.8*** *p122*
McCrabb, Eliza Jane 10; Philadelphia, 1851 ***5704.8*** *p77*
McCrabb, Elleanor 8; Philadelphia, 1851 ***5704.8*** *p77*
McCrabb, Mathew; Philadelphia, 1851 ***5704.8*** *p77*
McCrackan, John; New Haven, CT, 1769 ***1219.7*** *p139*
McCracken, Henry *SEE* McCracken, James
McCracken, Henry; Philadelphia, 1847 ***5704.8*** *p14*
McCracken, James; Philadelphia, 1847 ***53.26*** *p56*
*Relative:*Mary
*Relative:*Henry
*Relative:*Jane 3 mos
McCracken, James; Philadelphia, 1847 ***5704.8*** *p14*
McCracken, Jane 3 mos *SEE* McCracken, James
McCracken, Jane 3 mos; Philadelphia, 1847 ***5704.8*** *p14*
McCracken, John; Pennsylvania, 1768 ***1639.20*** *p135*
McCracken, John; Philadelphia, 1849 ***53.26*** *p57*
McCracken, John; Philadelphia, 1849 ***5704.8*** *p50*
McCracken, John 18; St. John, N.B., 1863 ***5704.8*** *p152*
McCracken, Mary *SEE* McCracken, James
McCracken, Mary; Philadelphia, 1847 ***5704.8*** *p14*
McCracken, Mary; Quebec, 1851 ***5704.8*** *p82*
McCracken, Robert; Quebec, 1818 ***7603*** *p77*
McCracken, Robert; Quebec, 1851 ***5704.8*** *p82*
McCracken, William; Quebec, 1847 ***5704.8*** *p28*
McCrackin, Ann; St. John, N.B., 1850 ***5704.8*** *p66*
McCrackin, Elizabeth 19; Philadelphia, 1864 ***5704.8*** *p161*
McCrackin, Jane; Quebec, 1850 ***5704.8*** *p67*
McCrackin, Margaret; St. John, N.B., 1850 ***5704.8*** *p66*
McCrackin, Nancy Jane 9; Philadelphia, 1864 ***5704.8*** *p161*
McCrackin, William 20; Philadelphia, 1856 ***5704.8*** *p128*
McCrady, Margaret; New York, NY, 1869 ***5704.8*** *p233*
McCrady, William 22; Massachusetts, 1849 ***5881.1*** *p77*
McCrae, William 22; Kansas, 1890 ***5240.1*** *p74*
McCraig, Ann 5; Philadelphia, 1856 ***5704.8*** *p128*
McCraig, Ellen 25; Philadelphia, 1856 ***5704.8*** *p128*
McCrain, Kenneth; America, 1787 ***1639.20*** *p135*
McCraine, . . .; North Carolina, 1764 ***1639.20*** *p135*
McCraine, Hugh; North Carolina, 1739 ***1639.20*** *p135*
McCraine, Murdoch; Brunswick, NC, 1739 ***1639.20*** *p135*
McCrainey, Kenneth; America, 1788 ***1639.20*** *p135*
McCrainey, Malcolm; America, 1802 ***1639.20*** *p135*
McCrainey, Neill; America, 1788 ***1639.20*** *p136*
McCraw, Duncan; Quebec, 1790 ***9775.5*** *p198A*
McCray, George; Philadelphia, 1864 ***5704.8*** *p180*
McCrea, . . .; Philadelphia, 1847 ***53.26*** *p57*
McCrea, . . .; Philadelphia, 1847 ***5704.8*** *p22*
McCrea, Andrew; New York, NY, 1869 ***5704.8*** *p234*
McCrea, Anne; New York, NY, 1868 ***5704.8*** *p229*
McCrea, Anne; Quebec, 1847 ***5704.8*** *p27*
McCrea, Anne 8; New York, NY, 1868 ***5704.8*** *p229*
McCrea, Catharine; New York, NY, 1869 ***5704.8*** *p234*
McCrea, Eliza; Philadelphia, 1865 ***5704.8*** *p200*
McCrea, Elizabeth; Quebec, 1848 ***5704.8*** *p42*
McCrea, Ellan; Quebec, 1847 ***5704.8*** *p27*
McCrea, Ellen; Philadelphia, 1868 ***5704.8*** *p228*
McCrea, Fanny 12; Quebec, 1847 ***5704.8*** *p27*
McCrea, George; New York, NY, 1832 ***8208.4*** *p27*
McCrea, George; Quebec, 1847 ***5704.8*** *p27*
McCrea, Henry; New York, NY, 1868 ***5704.8*** *p230*
McCrea, Henry; Philadelphia, 1865 ***5704.8*** *p200*
McCrea, James; Philadelphia, 1847 ***53.26*** *p57*
*Relative:*William
McCrea, James; Philadelphia, 1847 ***5704.8*** *p22*
McCrea, James 7; Quebec, 1848 ***5704.8*** *p42*
McCrea, Jane 18; St. John, N.B., 1864 ***5704.8*** *p158*
McCrea, John; Quebec, 1847 ***5704.8*** *p27*
McCrea, John 13; New York, NY, 1868 ***5704.8*** *p229*
McCrea, John 24; Philadelphia, 1804 ***53.26*** *p57*
McCrea, Margaret 10; New York, NY, 1868 ***5704.8*** *p229*
McCrea, Rebecca; Quebec, 1847 ***5704.8*** *p27*
McCrea, Robert 28; Kansas, 1886 ***5240.1*** *p69*
McCrea, Robert 30; Philadelphia, 1803 ***53.26*** *p57*
McCrea, Samuel 16; St. John, N.B., 1864 ***5704.8*** *p158*
McCrea, Sarah 6; New York, NY, 1868 ***5704.8*** *p229*
McCrea, William *SEE* McCrea, James
McCrea, William; Philadelphia, 1847 ***5704.8*** *p22*
McCrea, William; Philadelphia, 1864 ***5704.8*** *p181*
McCrea, William 4; Quebec, 1848 ***5704.8*** *p42*
McCrea, William 10; Quebec, 1847 ***5704.8*** *p27*
McCrea, William 34; Kansas, 1906 ***5240.1*** *p84*
McCready, Andrew 23; Philadelphia, 1855 ***5704.8*** *p124*
McCready, Ann 20; Philadelphia, 1854 ***5704.8*** *p116*
McCready, Archibald 9; Philadelphia, 1854 ***5704.8*** *p116*
McCready, Arthur; New York, NY, 1840 ***8208.4*** *p106*
McCready, Charles 5; Philadelphia, 1854 ***5704.8*** *p116*
McCready, Charles 10; Philadelphia, 1853 ***5704.8*** *p112*
McCready, Cornelius 22; St. John, N.B., 1864 ***5704.8*** *p159*
McCready, Daniel 20; St. John, N.B., 1854 ***5704.8*** *p114*
McCready, Edward 29; St. John, N.B., 1854 ***5704.8*** *p114*
McCready, Elizabeth 27; Philadelphia, 1857 ***5704.8*** *p133*
McCready, Hannah 60; Philadelphia, 1854 ***5704.8*** *p116*
McCready, James; St. John, N.B., 1853 ***5704.8*** *p99*
McCready, James 25; St. John, N.B., 1854 ***5704.8*** *p115*
McCready, John 7; Philadelphia, 1854 ***5704.8*** *p116*
McCready, Margaret 22; St. John, N.B., 1854 ***5704.8*** *p114*
McCready, Margaret 30; Philadelphia, 1854 ***5704.8*** *p116*
McCready, Martha 11; Philadelphia, 1854 ***5704.8*** *p116*
McCready, Patrick 19; St. John, N.B., 1854 ***5704.8*** *p114*
McCready, Sarah 20; St. John, N.B., 1855 ***5704.8*** *p126*
McCready, Susan 2; Philadelphia, 1854 ***5704.8*** *p116*
McCready, Thomas 19; St. John, N.B., 1854 ***5704.8*** *p114*
McCready, William; St. John, N.B., 1852 ***5704.8*** *p93*
McCready, William 18; Philadelphia, 1854 ***5704.8*** *p116*
McCreary, Margaret; Quebec, 1847 ***5704.8*** *p8*
McCreble, James; Boston, 1834-1841 ***7036*** *p123*
McCreedy, Alexander 20; Philadelphia, 1864 ***5704.8*** *p156*
McCreedy, James 19; Philadelphia, 1864 ***5704.8*** *p156*
McCreedy, Jane; New York, NY, 1869 ***5704.8*** *p232*
McCreeny, Charles 7; Philadelphia, 1864 ***5704.8*** *p155*
McCreeny, Elizabeth 11; Philadelphia, 1864 ***5704.8*** *p155*
McCreeny, Elizabeth 38; Philadelphia, 1864 ***5704.8*** *p155*
McCreeny, Harriet 14; Philadelphia, 1864 ***5704.8*** *p155*
McCreeny, James 3; Philadelphia, 1864 ***5704.8*** *p155*
McCreeny, Margaret 5; Philadelphia, 1864 ***5704.8*** *p155*
McCreeny, Robert 6 mos; Philadelphia, 1864 ***5704.8*** *p155*
McCreeny, Thomas 8; Philadelphia, 1864 ***5704.8*** *p155*
McCreery, Charles 24; Philadelphia, 1864 ***5704.8*** *p155*
McCrees, William; Quebec, 1853 ***5704.8*** *p105*
McCreey, F.C. 39; New York, NY, 1893 ***9026.4*** *p42*
McCreig, Susan 28; Massachusetts, 1849 ***5881.1*** *p75*
McCreky, Samll; Virginia, 1698 ***2212*** *p15*
McCrenner, William; Philadelphia, 1851 ***5704.8*** *p79*
McCrew, Catharine 18; Massachusetts, 1849 ***5881.1*** *p64*
McCrickle, Nancy; Philadelphia, 1851 ***5704.8*** *p81*
McCrighton, Catharine 1; Massachusetts, 1849 ***5881.1*** *p64*
McCrighton, Mary 40; Massachusetts, 1849 ***5881.1*** *p72*
McCrillis, James 23; St. John, N.B., 1859 ***5704.8*** *p140*
McCrimmon, Catherine *SEE* McCrimmon, Malcolm
McCrimmon, Isabella 74 *SEE* McCrimmon, Rodric
McCrimmon, Malcolm; America, 1787 ***1639.20*** *p136*
McCrimmon, Malcolm; North Carolina, 1858 ***1639.20*** *p136*
*Relative:*Catherine
McCrimmon, Roderick; North Carolina, 1774-1856 ***1639.20*** *p136*
McCrimmon, Rodric 74; North Carolina, 1850 ***1639.20*** *p136*
*Relative:*Isabella 74
McCristal, Bridget 18; Philadelphia, 1858 ***5704.8*** *p138*
McCristal, Charles; St. John, N.B., 1849 ***5704.8*** *p55*
McCristal, Mary 16; Philadelphia, 1858 ***5704.8*** *p138*
McCristal, Mary 18; Philadelphia, 1853 ***5704.8*** *p112*
McCristal, Pat; Philadelphia, 1852 ***5704.8*** *p85*
McCristal, Patrick 1; St. John, N.B., 1862 ***5704.8*** *p151*
McCristal, Peggy 30; St. John, N.B., 1862 ***5704.8*** *p151*
McCristal, Rose 2; St. John, N.B., 1862 ***5704.8*** *p151*
McCristal, Thomas 4; St. John, N.B., 1862 ***5704.8*** *p151*
McCristal, Thomas 30; St. John, N.B., 1862 ***5704.8*** *p151*
McCristle, Mary; St. John, N.B., 1847 ***5704.8*** *p21*
McCroddan, John; America, 1740 ***4971*** *p63*
McCrohan, Barthol 14; Massachusetts, 1849 ***5881.1*** *p63*
McCrohan, Eugene 48; Massachusetts, 1849 ***5881.1*** *p66*
McCrohan, Margaret 45; Massachusetts, 1849 ***5881.1*** *p72*
McCrohan, Patrick 21; Massachusetts, 1849 ***5881.1*** *p74*
McCrorey, Miles; Philadelphia, 1847 ***53.26*** *p57*
McCrorey, Miles; Philadelphia, 1847 ***5704.8*** *p1*
McCrorie, William; North Carolina, 1827 ***1639.20*** *p136*
McCrory, Ann 9 *SEE* McCrory, Biddy
McCrory, Ann 9; Philadelphia, 1848 ***5704.8*** *p40*
McCrory, Biddy; Philadelphia, 1848 ***53.26*** *p57*
*Relative:*Margaret
*Relative:*Ann 9
*Relative:*Hugh 7
*Relative:*Bridget 5
McCrory, Biddy; Philadelphia, 1848 ***5704.8*** *p40*
McCrory, Biddy; St. John, N.B., 1848 ***5704.8*** *p47*
McCrory, Bridget; Philadelphia, 1852 ***5704.8*** *p87*
McCrory, Bridget 3; Philadelphia, 1852 ***5704.8*** *p87*
McCrory, Bridget 5 *SEE* McCrory, Biddy
McCrory, Bridget 5; Philadelphia, 1848 ***5704.8*** *p40*
McCrory, Hugh *SEE* McCrory, Hugh
McCrory, Hugh; Philadelphia, 1847 ***53.26*** *p57*
*Relative:*Hugh
McCrory, Hugh; Philadelphia, 1847 ***5704.8*** *p31*
McCrory, Hugh 7 *SEE* McCrory, Biddy
McCrory, Hugh 7; Philadelphia, 1848 ***5704.8*** *p40*
McCrory, James 3 mos; Philadelphia, 1852 ***5704.8*** *p89*
McCrory, James 10; Quebec, 1847 ***5704.8*** *p27*
McCrory, Jane; Quebec, 1847 ***5704.8*** *p27*
McCrory, John; Philadelphia, 1847 ***5704.8*** *p31*
McCrory, Margaret *SEE* McCrory, Biddy
McCrory, Margaret; Philadelphia, 1848 ***5704.8*** *p40*
McCrory, Margaret; Philadelphia, 1852 ***5704.8*** *p89*
McCrory, Mary 5; Philadelphia, 1852 ***5704.8*** *p87*
McCrory, Mary 11; Quebec, 1847 ***5704.8*** *p27*
McCrory, Mary Anne 1; Philadelphia, 1852 ***5704.8*** *p89*
McCrory, Neal; Philadelphia, 1852 ***5704.8*** *p87*
McCrory, Neal 4; Philadelphia, 1852 ***5704.8*** *p89*
McCrory, Peter 13; Quebec, 1847 ***5704.8*** *p27*
McCrory, Sarah 1; Philadelphia, 1852 ***5704.8*** *p87*
McCrory, Terence; Philadelphia, 1852 ***5704.8*** *p89*
McCrory, Terence 7; Philadelphia, 1852 ***5704.8*** *p87*
McCrory, William; Quebec, 1847 ***5704.8*** *p27*
McCrossan, Ann; Philadelphia, 1852 ***5704.8*** *p92*
McCrossan, Bernard; St. John, N.B., 1848 ***5704.8*** *p47*
McCrossan, Bridget; America, 1864 ***5704.8*** *p172*
McCrossan, Bridget; St. John, N.B., 1849 ***5704.8*** *p56*
McCrossan, Charles; Philadelphia, 1847 ***53.26*** *p57*
*Relative:*William
McCrossan, Charles; Philadelphia, 1847 ***5704.8*** *p22*
McCrossan, Charles 12; Philadelphia, 1852 ***5704.8*** *p92*
McCrossan, Ellen; St. John, N.B., 1851 ***5704.8*** *p72*
McCrossan, Ellen 12; St. John, N.B., 1853 ***5704.8*** *p106*
McCrossan, Hannah; Philadelphia, 1851 ***5704.8*** *p76*
McCrossan, Hariet; St. John, N.B., 1853 ***5704.8*** *p106*
McCrossan, Hugh 3; St. John, N.B., 1851 ***5704.8*** *p72*
McCrossan, Isac; Philadelphia, 1850 ***5704.8*** *p64*
McCrossan, James; Philadelphia, 1851 ***5704.8*** *p70*
McCrossan, Jane; Philadelphia, 1850 ***5704.8*** *p64*
McCrossan, Jane; Philadelphia, 1851 ***5704.8*** *p76*
McCrossan, John; Philadelphia, 1849 ***53.26*** *p57*
McCrossan, John; Philadelphia, 1849 ***5704.8*** *p55*
McCrossan, John; Philadelphia, 1852 ***5704.8*** *p96*
McCrossan, John 13; St. John, N.B., 1851 ***5704.8*** *p72*
McCrossan, Mannasser; Ohio, 1841 ***9892.11*** *p32*
McCrossan, Margaret; Philadelphia, 1852 ***5704.8*** *p96*
McCrossan, Margaret 9; St. John, N.B., 1853 ***5704.8*** *p106*
McCrossan, Margaret 11; Philadelphia, 1852 ***5704.8*** *p96*
McCrossan, Mary; Philadelphia, 1850 ***5704.8*** *p64*
McCrossan, Mary; Philadelphia, 1851 ***5704.8*** *p70*
McCrossan, Mary; Philadelphia, 1851 ***5704.8*** *p79*
McCrossan, Thomas; Philadelphia, 1852 ***5704.8*** *p96*
McCrossan, William *SEE* McCrossan, Charles
McCrossan, William; Philadelphia, 1847 ***5704.8*** *p22*

McCrosson, John; St. John, N.B., 1850 *5704.8 p62*
McCrosson, Sarah; Philadelphia, 1868 *5704.8 p225*
McCrtel, Thomas; Wisconsin, n.d. *9675.7 p51*
McCrudy, James; Philadelphia, 1853 *5704.8 p100*
McCue, Anne 14; Philadelphia, 1857 *5704.8 p133*
McCue, Bernard; St. John, N.B., 1853 *5704.8 p107*
McCue, Catharine; Philadelphia, 1868 *5704.8 p225*
McCue, Catherine 19; Philadelphia, 1853 *5704.8 p111*
McCue, Charles; St. John, N.B., 1852 *5704.8 p83*
McCue, Daniel; Philadelphia, 1811 *53.26 p57*
McCue, Edward 25; Kansas, 1889 *5240.1 p73*
McCue, Hannah; New York, NY, 1866 *5704.8 p213*
McCue, Hannah; Philadelphia, 1852 *5704.8 p85*
McCue, Hannah; St. John, N.B., 1847 *5704.8 p33*
McCue, Hugh; Philadelphia, 1847 *53.26 p57*
McCue, Hugh; Philadelphia, 1847 *5704.8 p22*
McCue, Joseph; St. John, N.B., 1847 *5704.8 p33*
McCue, Margaret 21; Philadelphia, 1855 *5704.8 p124*
McCue, Martin 30; Wilmington, DE, 1831 *6508.7 p161*
McCue, Mary; Massachusetts, 1847 *5881.1 p70*
McCue, Michael; America, 1867 *5704.8 p223*
McCue, Michael; Philadelphia, 1811 *53.26 p57*
McCue, Michael; Philadelphia, 1868 *5704.8 p226*
McCue, Michael 20; Massachusetts, 1850 *5881.1 p73*
McCue, Nancy; New York, NY, 1868 *5704.8 p231*
McCue, Rose Ann; New York, NY, 1866 *5704.8 p213*
McCue, Sarah 30; Wilmington, DE, 1831 *6508.7 p161*
McCuiston, James; New Castle, DE, 1735 *1639.20 p136*
McCuiston, Thomas; New Castle, DE, 1735 *1639.20 p137*
McCull, William; America, 1739 *4971 p33*
McCullagh, Alice; Philadelphia, 1847 *53.26 p57*
McCullagh, Alice; Philadelphia, 1847 *5704.8 p30*
McCullagh, Benjamin; Philadelphia, 1866 *5704.8 p210*
McCullagh, Bridget; St. John, N.B., 1849 *5704.8 p55*
McCullagh, Catherine 12 *SEE* McCullagh, John
McCullagh, Catherine 12; Philadelphia, 1850 *5704.8 p68*
McCullagh, Daniel; Philadelphia, 1847 *53.26 p57*
McCullagh, Daniel; Philadelphia, 1847 *5704.8 p22*
McCullagh, Eliza; Quebec, 1851 *5704.8 p73*
McCullagh, Henry; St. John, N.B., 1852 *5704.8 p93*
McCullagh, Henry 40; Philadelphia, 1857 *5704.8 p133*
McCullagh, Hugh 20; Philadelphia, 1857 *5704.8 p133*
McCullagh, James; America, 1737 *4971 p74*
McCullagh, James; America, 1741 *4971 p73*
McCullagh, James; St. John, N.B., 1849 *5704.8 p55*
McCullagh, Jane; Philadelphia, 1847 *53.26 p57*
McCullagh, Jane; Philadelphia, 1847 *5704.8 p31*
McCullagh, John; Philadelphia, 1850 *53.26 p57*
  *Relative:*Mary
  *Relative:*Catherine 12
  *Relative:*Pat 7
  *Relative:*William 5
McCullagh, John; Philadelphia, 1850 *5704.8 p68*
McCullagh, Mary *SEE* McCullagh, John
McCullagh, Mary; Philadelphia, 1850 *5704.8 p68*
McCullagh, Mary 30; Philadelphia, 1857 *5704.8 p133*
McCullagh, Michael; America, 1742 *4971 p24*
McCullagh, Michael 12; St. John, N.B., 1853 *5704.8 p110*
McCullagh, Nancy 24; Philadelphia, 1857 *5704.8 p133*
McCullagh, Pat 7 *SEE* McCullagh, John
McCullagh, Pat 7; Philadelphia, 1850 *5704.8 p68*
McCullagh, Rosy *SEE* McCullagh, Sally
McCullagh, Rosy; Philadelphia, 1847 *5704.8 p13*
McCullagh, Sally; Philadelphia, 1847 *53.26 p57*
  *Relative:*Rosy
McCullagh, Sally; Philadelphia, 1847 *5704.8 p13*
McCullagh, Sally 28; Philadelphia, 1857 *5704.8 p133*
McCullagh, William 5 *SEE* McCullagh, John
McCullagh, William 5; Philadelphia, 1850 *5704.8 p68*
McCullam, Edward; America, 1738 *4971 p25*
McCullen, James; Philadelphia, 1852 *5704.8 p88*
McCullen, James; Philadelphia, 1866 *5704.8 p210*
McCullen, John; Quebec, 1825 *7603 p63*
McCullen, Rose Ann 30; Philadelphia, 1865 *5704.8 p164*
McCulley, Ann; St. John, N.B., 1847 *5704.8 p19*
McCulley, Frank; Arkansas, 1918 *95.2 p82*
McCulloch, Charles; New York, 1818 *1639.20 p137*
McCulloch, Hugh 25; Maryland, 1774 *1219.7 p207*
McCulloch, Thomas; Pictou, N.S., 1804 *9775.5 p208*
McCulloch, William 50; Kansas, 1871 *5240.1 p52*
McCullock, Barbara 24 *SEE* McCullock, William
McCullock, Catherine 20; Philadelphia, 1860 *5704.8 p146*
McCullock, James 23; St. John, N.B., 1866 *5704.8 p166*
McCullock, Mary 17; Port uncertain, 1774 *1219.7 p177*
McCullock, William 24; Georgia, 1775 *1219.7 p276*
  *Wife:*Barbara 24
McCullogh, Ann 4; St. John, N.B., 1847 *5704.8 p4*
McCullogh, Bernard 6; St. John, N.B., 1847 *5704.8 p4*
McCullogh, Bridget; St. John, N.B., 1847 *5704.8 p4*
McCullogh, Bridget 15; Philadelphia, 1856 *5704.8 p128*

McCullogh, Catherine; St. John, N.B., 1847 *5704.8 p4*
McCullogh, Dimnock; St. John, N.B., 1847 *5704.8 p4*
McCullogh, Patrick 2; St. John, N.B., 1847 *5704.8 p4*
McCullogh, Susanna 8; St. John, N.B., 1847 *5704.8 p4*
McCullogh, Thomas 10; St. John, N.B., 1847 *5704.8 p4*
McCullough, . . .; Philadelphia, 1865 *5704.8 p199*
McCullough, Alice; Philadelphia, 1867 *5704.8 p222*
McCullough, Ann; Philadelphia, 1865 *5704.8 p199*
McCullough, Bernard; America, 1865 *5704.8 p198*
McCullough, Bessie; New York, NY, 1864 *5704.8 p169*
McCullough, Biddy; Philadelphia, 1865 *5704.8 p199*
McCullough, Bridget; Philadelphia, 1868 *5704.8 p222*
McCullough, Catharine; Philadelphia, 1865 *5704.8 p201*
McCullough, Cecilia; New York, NY, 1867 *5704.8 p219*
McCullough, Elizabeth *SEE* McCullough, James
McCullough, Elizabeth; Philadelphia, 1849 *5704.8 p54*
McCullough, Hannah; Philadelphia, 1864 *5704.8 p188*
McCullough, Hers. 27; Philadelphia, 1803 *53.26 p57*
McCullough, Hugh; Philadelphia, 1864 *5704.8 p181*
McCullough, Isabella; New York, NY, 1864 *5704.8 p169*
McCullough, James; Philadelphia, 1849 *53.26 p57*
  *Relative:*Elizabeth
McCullough, James; Philadelphia, 1849 *5704.8 p54*
McCullough, Jane 11; Philadelphia, 1864 *5704.8 p188*
McCullough, John; America, 1866 *5704.8 p213*
McCullough, John; America, 1883 *1450.2 p96A*
McCullough, John; Philadelphia, 1864 *5704.8 p171*
McCullough, John; Philadelphia, 1868 *5704.8 p222*
McCullough, Margaret; Philadelphia, 1865 *5704.8 p199*
McCullough, Mary; Philadelphia, 1868 *5704.8 p222*
McCullough, Patrick; New York, NY, 1867 *5704.8 p219*
McCullough, Peter; New York, NY, 1864 *5704.8 p170*
McCullough, Peter; Philadelphia, 1868 *5704.8 p229*
McCullough, Robert; New York, NY, 1864 *5704.8 p169*
McCullough, Rose; Philadelphia, 1864 *5704.8 p170*
McCullough, Sarah; Philadelphia, 1868 *5704.8 p225*
McCullough, William; Philadelphia, 1864 *5704.8 p188*
McCullough, William; Philadelphia, 1866 *5704.8 p211*
McCullow, Bernard; New Orleans, 1849 *5704.8 p59*
McCullow, Biddy 13; Philadelphia, 1856 *5704.8 p128*
McCullow, Daniel; Quebec, 1853 *5704.8 p104*
McCullow, Hugh 11; Philadelphia, 1856 *5704.8 p128*
McCullow, Jane; Quebec, 1852 *5704.8 p89*
McCullow, Patrick; Philadelphia, 1851 *5704.8 p70*
McCullow, Patrick 9; Philadelphia, 1856 *5704.8 p128*
McCullum, Alexander 25; Quebec, 1864 *5704.8 p160*
McCullum, John; New York, NY, 1839 *8208.4 p103*
McCully, Andrew 50; Philadelphia, 1833-1834 *53.26 p57*
  *Relative:*Catherine 48
McCully, Catherine 48 *SEE* McCully, Andrew
McCully, Eleanor 22; Philadelphia, 1853 *5704.8 p112*
McCully, Ellen; New York, NY, 1865 *5704.8 p193*
McCully, James 6; St. John, N.B., 1852 *5704.8 p83*
McCully, John 11; St. John, N.B., 1852 *5704.8 p83*
McCully, Joseph; St. John, N.B., 1852 *5704.8 p83*
McCully, Margaret 4; St. John, N.B., 1852 *5704.8 p83*
McCully, Mary; St. John, N.B., 1852 *5704.8 p83*
McCully, Mary 9 mos; St. John, N.B., 1852 *5704.8 p83*
McCully, Michael 23; Massachusetts, 1848 *5881.1 p71*
McCully, Nancy 9; St. John, N.B., 1852 *5704.8 p83*
McCully, Newman; St. John, N.B., 1849 *5704.8 p49*
McCully, Patrick 13; St. John, N.B., 1852 *5704.8 p83*
McCully, Peter 2; St. John, N.B., 1852 *5704.8 p83*
McCully, Philip 2; Philadelphia, 1853 *5704.8 p112*
McCune, Samuel; New York, NY, 1838 *8208.4 p72*
McCune, Terrens; Ohio, 1812-1840 *9892.11 p32*
McCunn, John 22; Philadelphia, 1775 *1219.7 p258*
McCunn, Mathew 15; Philadelphia, 1774 *1219.7 p197*
McCurday, John 30; Kansas, 1874 *5240.1 p56*
McCurdy, Archibald; St. John, N.B., 1847 *5704.8 p10*
McCurdy, Betty 22; Massachusetts, 1849 *5881.1 p63*
McCurdy, Charles; Philadelphia, 1853 *5704.8 p101*
McCurdy, Don; St. John, N.B., 1847 *5704.8 p11*
McCurdy, Eliza 12; Philadelphia, 1849 *53.26 p57*
  *Relative:*Jane 10
McCurdy, Eliza 12; Philadelphia, 1849 *5704.8 p58*
McCurdy, Francis; Philadelphia, 1851 *5704.8 p76*
McCurdy, Francis; Philadelphia, 1864 *5704.8 p179*
McCurdy, James; St. John, N.B., 1847 *5704.8 p11*
McCurdy, James 22; Wilmington, DE, 1831 *6508.3 p100*
McCurdy, Jane 10 *SEE* McCurdy, Eliza
McCurdy, Jane 10; Philadelphia, 1849 *5704.8 p58*
McCurdy, John; St. John, N.B., 1847 *5704.8 p11*
McCurdy, John 3; Massachusetts, 1849 *5881.1 p68*
McCurdy, Keatty 3; St. John, N.B., 1847 *5704.8 p11*
McCurdy, Margaret; Philadelphia, 1847 *53.26 p57*
  *Relative:*Margaret 9
  *Relative:*Nancy 8
McCurdy, Margaret; Philadelphia, 1847 *5704.8 p30*
McCurdy, Margaret 9 *SEE* McCurdy, Margaret
McCurdy, Margaret 9; Philadelphia, 1849 *5704.8 p53*
McCurdy, Mary; America, 1864 *5704.8 p190*

McCurdy, Mary 6 mos; St. John, N.B., 1847 *5704.8 p11*
McCurdy, Mary 20; Massachusetts, 1849 *5881.1 p71*
McCurdy, Mary Hill 2; Philadelphia, 1854 *5704.8 p122*
McCurdy, Morgan *SEE* McCurdy, William
McCurdy, Nancy; St. John, N.B., 1847 *5704.8 p11*
McCurdy, Nancy 8 *SEE* McCurdy, Margaret
McCurdy, Nancy 8; Philadelphia, 1849 *5704.8 p53*
McCurdy, Nancy 50; Massachusetts, 1849 *5881.1 p73*
McCurdy, Nelly; St. John, N.B., 1847 *5704.8 p11*
McCurdy, Peggy; St. John, N.B., 1847 *5704.8 p11*
McCurdy, Robert; Virginia, 1844 *4626.16 p12*
McCurdy, William; Philadelphia, 1811 *53.26 p58*
  *Relative:*Morgan
McCurr, Daniell 12; Jamaica, 1736 *3690.1 p153*
McCurra, William; New York, NY, 1867 *5704.8 p222*
McCurrister, Catherine 20; St. John, N.B., 1858 *5704.8 p137*
McCurry, Ann 22; Philadelphia, 1853 *5704.8 p112*
McCurry, Ann 22; Quebec, 1854 *5704.8 p121*
McCurry, Biddy; Quebec, 1851 *5704.8 p74*
McCurry, Jane; Quebec, 1851 *5704.8 p74*
McCurry, Manus 15; Quebec, 1854 *5704.8 p121*
McCurry, Mary; Quebec, 1851 *5704.8 p74*
McCurry, Mary 12; Philadelphia, 1853 *5704.8 p112*
McCurry, Sarah Ann; Quebec, 1851 *5704.8 p74*
McCusker, Catharine; Philadelphia, 1867 *5704.8 p216*
McCusker, Hugh; Philadelphia, 1852 *5704.8 p89*
McCusker, Isabella; Philadelphia, 1867 *5704.8 p216*
McCusker, James; Philadelphia, 1864 *5704.8 p176*
McCusker, Mary 22; St. John, N.B., 1864 *5704.8 p159*
McCusker, Patrick; New York, NY, 1867 *5704.8 p223*
McCusker, Philip; Philadelphia, 1849 *53.26 p58*
McCusker, Philip; Philadelphia, 1849 *5704.8 p54*
McCuskey, James; Quebec, 1822 *7603 p81*
McCutchen, John; Indiana, 1843 *9117 p17*
McCutcheon, Agnes 15; Quebec, 1864 *5704.8 p163*
McCutcheon, Alexr. 22; Wilmington, DE, 1831 *6508.7 p161*
McCutcheon, Charlotte; Quebec, 1864 *5704.8 p163*
McCutcheon, Eliza *SEE* McCutcheon, George
McCutcheon, Eliza; Philadelphia, 1847 *5704.8 p14*
McCutcheon, Elizabeth 4; Quebec, 1864 *5704.8 p163*
McCutcheon, George *SEE* McCutcheon, George
McCutcheon, George; Philadelphia, 1847 *53.26 p58*
  *Relative:*Eliza
  *Relative:*Marg. Jane
  *Relative:*Martha
  *Relative:*Mary
  *Relative:*George
McCutcheon, George; Philadelphia, 1847 *5704.8 p14*
McCutcheon, George 4; Philadelphia, 1847 *5704.8 p14*
McCutcheon, Isabella 30; Quebec, 1857 *5704.8 p136*
McCutcheon, James 1; Quebec, 1864 *5704.8 p163*
McCutcheon, Jane 11; Quebec, 1864 *5704.8 p163*
McCutcheon, Jane 18; St. John, N.B., 1863 *5704.8 p153*
McCutcheon, John 40; Quebec, 1864 *5704.8 p163*
McCutcheon, Marg. Jane *SEE* McCutcheon, George
McCutcheon, Margaret 3; Quebec, 1857 *5704.8 p136*
McCutcheon, Margaret Jane; Philadelphia, 1847 *5704.8 p14*
McCutcheon, Martha *SEE* McCutcheon, George
McCutcheon, Martha 10; Philadelphia, 1847 *5704.8 p14*
McCutcheon, Mary *SEE* McCutcheon, George
McCutcheon, Mary; Quebec, 1851 *5704.8 p75*
McCutcheon, Mary 7; Philadelphia, 1847 *5704.8 p14*
McCutcheon, Mary Ann 9 mos; Quebec, 1857 *5704.8 p136*
McCutcheon, Robert; Quebec, 1851 *5704.8 p74*
McCutcheon, Robert 5; Quebec, 1857 *5704.8 p136*
McCutcheon, Sarah 35; Quebec, 1864 *5704.8 p163*
McCutcheson, Susan; America, 1867 *5704.8 p216*
McCutchion, Ann 17; Quebec, 1853 *5704.8 p104*
McCutchion, Ann 40; Quebec, 1853 *5704.8 p104*
McCutchion, Ian; St. John, N.B., 1850 *5704.8 p66*
McCutchion, Jane 20; Quebec, 1853 *5704.8 p104*
McCutchion, Robert 40; Quebec, 1853 *5704.8 p104*
McCutchson, William; New York, NY, 1868 *5704.8 p226*
McDade, Alice; Philadelphia, 1850 *53.26 p58*
  *Relative:*Patrick 2
  *Relative:*Margaret
McDade, Alice; Philadelphia, 1850 *5704.8 p60*
McDade, Ann; St. John, N.B., 1851 *5704.8 p78*
McDade, Ann 20; Massachusetts, 1850 *5881.1 p62*
McDade, Ann Jane; Quebec, 1851 *5704.8 p73*
McDade, Anne 7; Philadelphia, 1853 *5704.8 p113*
McDade, Bell; St. John, N.B., 1847 *5704.8 p25*
McDade, Betty; Philadelphia, 1851 *5704.8 p78*
McDade, Biddy; Philadelphia, 1847 *53.26 p58*
McDade, Biddy; Philadelphia, 1847 *5704.8 p5*
McDade, Biddy; St. John, N.B., 1847 *5704.8 p35*
McDade, Biddy; St. John, N.B., 1852 *5704.8 p95*
McDade, Biddy 13; St. John, N.B., 1849 *5704.8 p55*

McDade, Biddy 22; St. John, N.B., 1861 ***5704.8*** *p147*
McDade, Charles; Philadelphia, 1849 ***53.26*** *p58*
McDade, Charles; Philadelphia, 1849 ***5704.8*** *p54*
McDade, Charles; St. John, N.B., 1847 ***5704.8*** *p9*
McDade, Elleanor; Philadelphia, 1847 ***53.26*** *p58*
McDade, Elleanor; Philadelphia, 1847 ***5704.8*** *p5*
McDade, Fanny; Philadelphia, 1848 ***53.26*** *p58*
*Relative:*Mary
McDade, Fanny; Philadelphia, 1848 ***5704.8*** *p40*
McDade, Grace; New York, NY, 1868 ***5704.8*** *p228*
McDade, Grace 4; St. John, N.B., 1848 ***5704.8*** *p40*
McDade, Hady 2; St. John, N.B., 1848 ***5704.8*** *p40*
McDade, Henry 20; Philadelphia, 1853 ***5704.8*** *p112*
McDade, James; Philadelphia, 1849 ***53.26*** *p58*
*Relative:*Mary
*Relative:*Thomas 12
McDade, James; Philadelphia, 1849 ***5704.8*** *p58*
McDade, James; St. John, N.B., 1848 ***5704.8*** *p39*
McDade, James; St. John, N.B., 1848 ***5704.8*** *p44*
McDade, James 22; Philadelphia, 1804 ***53.26*** *p58*
McDade, John; America, 1741 ***4971*** *p72*
McDade, Margaret *SEE* McDade, Alice
McDade, Margaret; Philadelphia, 1850 ***5704.8*** *p60*
McDade, Margaret; St. John, N.B., 1850 ***5704.8*** *p66*
McDade, Mary *SEE* McDade, Fanny
McDade, Mary *SEE* McDade, James
McDade, Mary; Philadelphia, 1848 ***5704.8*** *p40*
McDade, Mary; Philadelphia, 1849 ***5704.8*** *p58*
McDade, Mary; St. John, N.B., 1847 ***5704.8*** *p9*
McDade, Mary; St. John, N.B., 1847 ***5704.8*** *p35*
McDade, Mary; St. John, N.B., 1853 ***5704.8*** *p107*
McDade, Mary 11; Philadelphia, 1853 ***5704.8*** *p113*
McDade, Mary 25; Philadelphia, 1853 ***5704.8*** *p114*
McDade, Mary Ann; Philadelphia, 1847 ***53.26*** *p58*
McDade, Mary Ann; Philadelphia, 1847 ***5704.8*** *p31*
McDade, Nelly; St. John, N.B., 1848 ***5704.8*** *p40*
McDade, Owen 28; Philadelphia, 1803 ***53.26*** *p58*
McDade, Patrick 1; St. John, N.B., 1848 ***5704.8*** *p40*
McDade, Patrick 2 *SEE* McDade, Alice
McDade, Patrick 2; Philadelphia, 1850 ***5704.8*** *p60*
McDade, Patrick 30; Philadelphia, 1853 ***5704.8*** *p114*
McDade, Rosey; St. John, N.B., 1847 ***5704.8*** *p19*
McDade, Sally 16; St. John, N.B., 1854 ***5704.8*** *p122*
McDade, Sally 28; St. John, N.B., 1861 ***5704.8*** *p147*
McDade, Susan; Philadelphia, 1851 ***5704.8*** *p79*
McDade, Susan; St. John, N.B., 1847 ***5704.8*** *p35*
McDade, Thomas 12 *SEE* McDade, James
McDade, Thomas 12; Philadelphia, 1849 ***5704.8*** *p58*
McDade, Unity; Philadelphia, 1850 ***53.26*** *p58*
McDade, Unity; Philadelphia, 1850 ***5704.8*** *p60*
McDade, William; Philadelphia, 1851 ***5704.8*** *p76*
McDade, William; St. John, N.B., 1847 ***5704.8*** *p25*
McDaid, Ann 20; Philadelphia, 1854 ***5704.8*** *p120*
McDaid, Bernard 9; St. John, N.B., 1864 ***5704.8*** *p158*
McDaid, Betty; St. John, N.B., 1847 ***5704.8*** *p24*
McDaid, Biddy; St. John, N.B., 1853 ***5704.8*** *p107*
McDaid, Biddy 6 mos; St. John, N.B., 1847 ***5704.8*** *p24*
McDaid, Catherine 6 mos; St. John, N.B., 1864 ***5704.8*** *p158*
McDaid, Charles; Quebec, 1853 ***5704.8*** *p103*
McDaid, Daniel 4; St. John, N.B., 1864 ***5704.8*** *p158*
McDaid, Daniel 27; St. John, N.B., 1854 ***5704.8*** *p114*
McDaid, Daniel 40; Philadelphia, 1854 ***5704.8*** *p120*
McDaid, Domnick 5; Philadelphia, 1864 ***5704.8*** *p156*
McDaid, Domnick 46; Philadelphia, 1864 ***5704.8*** *p156*
McDaid, Edward; Philadelphia, 1852 ***5704.8*** *p92*
McDaid, Elenor; St. John, N.B., 1850 ***5704.8*** *p65*
McDaid, Ellen 12; St. John, N.B., 1849 ***5704.8*** *p55*
McDaid, Ellen 13; Philadelphia, 1864 ***5704.8*** *p156*
McDaid, Hannah 11; Philadelphia, 1864 ***5704.8*** *p156*
McDaid, Hannah 30; Philadelphia, 1864 ***5704.8*** *p156*
McDaid, Henry; St. John, N.B., 1848 ***5704.8*** *p44*
McDaid, Henry; St. John, N.B., 1853 ***5704.8*** *p107*
McDaid, Hugh; St. John, N.B., 1847 ***5704.8*** *p24*
McDaid, Hugh 25; St. John, N.B., 1864 ***5704.8*** *p158*
McDaid, James; Quebec, 1848 ***5704.8*** *p42*
McDaid, James; St. John, N.B., 1847 ***5704.8*** *p25*
McDaid, James 45; St. John, N.B., 1864 ***5704.8*** *p158*
McDaid, Jane 25; St. John, N.B., 1864 ***5704.8*** *p158*
McDaid, John 1; Philadelphia, 1864 ***5704.8*** *p156*
McDaid, John 2; St. John, N.B., 1864 ***5704.8*** *p158*
McDaid, John 20; St. John, N.B., 1854 ***5704.8*** *p115*
McDaid, Kitty; St. John, N.B., 1847 ***5704.8*** *p20*
McDaid, Margaret; Philadelphia, 1864 ***5704.8*** *p184*
McDaid, Margaret 3; Philadelphia, 1864 ***5704.8*** *p156*
McDaid, Mary; New York, NY, 1868 ***5704.8*** *p228*
McDaid, Mary 7; Philadelphia, 1854 ***5704.8*** *p120*
McDaid, Mary 9; Philadelphia, 1864 ***5704.8*** *p156*
McDaid, Mary 11; Philadelphia, 1853 ***5704.8*** *p111*
McDaid, Mary 11; St. John, N.B., 1864 ***5704.8*** *p158*
McDaid, Mary 44; St. John, N.B., 1864 ***5704.8*** *p158*
McDaid, Michael 25; St. John, N.B., 1863 ***5704.8*** *p153*
McDaid, Patrick 7; Philadelphia, 1864 ***5704.8*** *p156*
McDaid, Peggy 13; St. John, N.B., 1848 ***5704.8*** *p44*
McDaid, Phillip 17; Philadelphia, 1864 ***5704.8*** *p156*
McDaid, Robert 7; St. John, N.B., 1864 ***5704.8*** *p158*
McDaid, Rody; Philadelphia, 1854 ***5704.8*** *p120*
McDaid, Rosanna 20; Philadelphia, 1860 ***5704.8*** *p146*
McDaid, Rose 35; Philadelphia, 1854 ***5704.8*** *p120*
McDaid, Susan; New York, NY, 1865 ***5704.8*** *p194*
McDaid, Unity 2; St. John, N.B., 1864 ***5704.8*** *p158*
McDaide, William 20; Philadelphia, 1859 ***5704.8*** *p142*
McDale, Isabella 18; Quebec, 1858 ***5704.8*** *p137*
McDale, John 36; Philadelphia, 1803 ***53.26*** *p58*
McDanal, William 22; Quebec, 1853 ***5704.8*** *p105*
McDaniel, Alexander; America, 1741 ***4971*** *p28*
McDaniel, Alexander 26; Virginia, 1774 ***1219.7*** *p238*
McDaniel, Ann; America, 1739 ***4971*** *p46*
McDaniel, Asa; North Carolina, 1776-1802 ***1639.20*** *p137*
McDaniel, Constant; America, 1738-1743 ***4971*** *p91*
McDaniel, John; New York, NY, 1840 ***8208.4*** *p104*
McDaniel, Malcolm 65; South Carolina, 1850 ***1639.20*** *p137*
McDaniell, Alice; America, 1742 ***4971*** *p17*
McDaniell, Constance; America, 1738 ***4971*** *p13*
McDaniell, Hugh; America, 1742 ***4971*** *p32*
McDaniell, James; America, 1737 ***4971*** *p34*
McDaniell, James; America, 1740 ***4971*** *p15*
McDaniell, John; America, 1737 ***4971*** *p27*
McDaniell, Owen; America, 1741 ***4971*** *p35*
McDaniell, Patrick; America, 1737 ***4971*** *p34*
McDaniell, Thomas; America, 1741 ***4971*** *p28*
McDaniell, Timothy; America, 1737 ***4971*** *p33*
McDavett, Patrick 16; Philadelphia, 1860 ***5704.8*** *p145*
McDavitt, Ann; St. John, N.B., 1853 ***5704.8*** *p107*
McDavitt, Edward; Illinois, 1858 ***2896.5*** *p26*
McDavitt, James; Philadelphia, 1850 ***5704.8*** *p64*
McDavitt, James; St. John, N.B., 1853 ***5704.8*** *p107*
McDead, James; America, 1737 ***4971*** *p77*
McDearmid, William 47; North Carolina, 1850 ***1639.20*** *p138*
McDermend, Hugh; New York, 1768 ***8894.2*** *p56*
McDermid, Catherine; Canada, 1833 ***9775.5*** *p222*
McDermid, John 16; St. John, N.B., 1865 ***5704.8*** *p165*
McDermid, John R. 21; Kansas, 1890 ***5240.1*** *p75*
McDermit, Margaret *SEE* McDermit, Neil
McDermit, Neil; Nova Scotia, 1830 ***7085.4*** *p44*
*Wife:*Margaret
McDermitt, Henry 18; Philadelphia, 1853 ***5704.8*** *p108*
McDermitt, John; St. John, N.B., 1847 ***5704.8*** *p11*
McDermot, Isabella; America, 1737 ***4971*** *p71*
McDermott, . . .; St. John, N.B., 1854 ***5704.8*** *p119*
McDermott, Ann 6 *SEE* McDermott, Catherine
McDermott, Ann 6; Philadelphia, 1850 ***5704.8*** *p60*
McDermott, Ann 21; Massachusetts, 1848 ***5881.1*** *p62*
McDermott, Anne; Philadelphia, 1868 ***5704.8*** *p230*
McDermott, Bridget 11; Massachusetts, 1850 ***5881.1*** *p63*
McDermott, Bridget 28; Philadelphia, 1855 ***5704.8*** *p123*
McDermott, Bridget 36; Philadelphia, 1864 ***5704.8*** *p161*
McDermott, Catharine; Philadelphia, 1850 ***5704.8*** *p60*
McDermott, Catherine; Philadelphia, 1850 ***53.26*** *p58*
*Relative:*Ellen 10
*Relative:*Ann 6
McDermott, Catherine; Philadelphia, 1853 ***5704.8*** *p100*
McDermott, Catherine; St. John, N.B., 1850 ***5704.8*** *p66*
McDermott, Catherine; St. John, N.B., 1852 ***5704.8*** *p95*
McDermott, Catherine 9; St. John, N.B., 1862 ***5704.8*** *p151*
McDermott, Catherine 11; Philadelphia, 1864 ***5704.8*** *p183*
McDermott, Catherine 16; Philadelphia, 1858 ***5704.8*** *p138*
McDermott, Celia 20; Massachusetts, 1850 ***5881.1*** *p65*
McDermott, Charles; Philadelphia, 1864 ***5704.8*** *p182*
McDermott, Connor; America, 1738 ***4971*** *p36*
McDermott, Cornelius 16; Massachusetts, 1847 ***5881.1*** *p64*
McDermott, Edward; Philadelphia, 1847 ***53.26*** *p58*
*Relative:*John
McDermott, Edward; Philadelphia, 1847 ***5704.8*** *p31*
McDermott, Eliza 30; St. John, N.B., 1854 ***5704.8*** *p119*
McDermott, Elizabeth; New York, NY, 1869 ***5704.8*** *p232*
McDermott, Elizabeth; St. John, N.B., 1847 ***5704.8*** *p21*
McDermott, Ellan; St. John, N.B., 1847 ***5704.8*** *p21*
McDermott, Elleanor 20; Philadelphia, 1856 ***5704.8*** *p128*
McDermott, Ellen; Philadelphia, 1868 ***5704.8*** *p230*
McDermott, Ellen 6; Philadelphia, 1864 ***5704.8*** *p183*
McDermott, Ellen 10 *SEE* McDermott, Catherine
McDermott, Ellen 10; Philadelphia, 1850 ***5704.8*** *p60*
McDermott, Ellen 12; Massachusetts, 1849 ***5881.1*** *p66*
McDermott, Francis 45; Massachusetts, 1849 ***5881.1*** *p66*
McDermott, George 13; St. John, N.B., 1853 ***5704.8*** *p106*
McDermott, Hannah; Philadelphia, 1864 ***5704.8*** *p174*
McDermott, Hannah; Philadelphia, 1864 ***5704.8*** *p183*
McDermott, Hugh; St. John, N.B., 1850 ***5704.8*** *p61*
McDermott, Hugh 30; St. John, N.B., 1854 ***5704.8*** *p119*
McDermott, James; America, 1869 ***5704.8*** *p233*
McDermott, James; New York, NY, 1839 ***8208.4*** *p95*
McDermott, James; St. John, N.B., 1850 ***5704.8*** *p61*
McDermott, James 20; Quebec, 1863 ***5704.8*** *p154*
McDermott, James 65; Arizona, 1890 ***2764.35*** *p48*
McDermott, Jane; St. John, N.B., 1847 ***5704.8*** *p21*
McDermott, Jane 24; Philadelphia, 1853 ***5704.8*** *p112*
McDermott, John *SEE* McDermott, Edward
McDermott, John; New York, NY, 1866 ***5704.8*** *p203*
McDermott, John; St. John, N.B., 1850 ***5704.8*** *p61*
McDermott, John; St. John, N.B., 1853 ***5704.8*** *p99*
McDermott, John 4; Philadelphia, 1864 ***5704.8*** *p183*
McDermott, John 5; St. John, N.B., 1855 ***5704.8*** *p127*
McDermott, John 12; Philadelphia, 1847 ***5704.8*** *p31*
McDermott, John 20; St. John, N.B., 1855 ***5704.8*** *p127*
McDermott, John 21; Kansas, 1898 ***5240.1*** *p81*
McDermott, Letitia; St. John, N.B., 1850 ***5704.8*** *p61*
McDermott, Margaret; New York, NY, 1867 ***5704.8*** *p222*
McDermott, Margaret 20; Philadelphia, 1858 ***5704.8*** *p138*
McDermott, Martha 1; St. John, N.B., 1862 ***5704.8*** *p151*
McDermott, Mary; New York, NY, 1869 ***5704.8*** *p232*
McDermott, Mary; Philadelphia, 1849 ***53.26*** *p58*
McDermott, Mary; Philadelphia, 1849 ***5704.8*** *p50*
McDermott, Mary; Philadelphia, 1867 ***5704.8*** *p216*
McDermott, Mary 18; Philadelphia, 1858 ***5704.8*** *p138*
McDermott, Mary 20; Philadelphia, 1859 ***5704.8*** *p143*
McDermott, Mary A.; New York, NY, 1865 ***5704.8*** *p203*
McDermott, Mary Ann 11; St. John, N.B., 1862 ***5704.8*** *p151*
McDermott, Neal; St. John, N.B., 1848 ***5704.8*** *p38*
McDermott, Patrick; America, 1738 ***4971*** *p36*
McDermott, Patrick; Iowa, 1866-1943 ***123.54*** *p31*
McDermott, Patrick; New York, NY, 1840 ***8208.4*** *p105*
McDermott, Patrick; Philadelphia, 1848 ***53.26*** *p58*
McDermott, Patrick; Philadelphia, 1848 ***5704.8*** *p40*
McDermott, Patrick; Philadelphia, 1865 ***5704.8*** *p189*
McDermott, Patrick; St. John, N.B., 1851 ***5704.8*** *p72*
McDermott, Patrick; St. John, N.B., 1853 ***5704.8*** *p99*
McDermott, Patrick 40; Kansas, 1884 ***5240.1*** *p65*
McDermott, Philip; New York, NY, 1865 ***5704.8*** *p192*
McDermott, Rose 16; Massachusetts, 1847 ***5881.1*** *p75*
McDermott, Sally 16; Philadelphia, 1864 ***5704.8*** *p156*
McDermott, Sally 24; Philadelphia, 1856 ***5704.8*** *p128*
McDermott, Samuel 56; St. John, N.B., 1862 ***5704.8*** *p151*
McDermott, Sophia 18; Philadelphia, 1857 ***5704.8*** *p133*
McDermott, Susan; New York, NY, 1865 ***5704.8*** *p194*
McDermott, Susan; St. John, N.B., 1853 ***5704.8*** *p100*
McDermott, Susan 3; St. John, N.B., 1855 ***5704.8*** *p127*
McDermott, Theresa 9; Philadelphia, 1864 ***5704.8*** *p183*
McDermott, Thomas; America, 1883 ***5240.1*** *p28*
McDermott, Thomas; St. John, N.B., 1853 ***5704.8*** *p99*
McDermott, Thomas 20; Newfoundland, 1789 ***4915.24*** *p58*
McDermott, Thomas 32; Kansas, 1888 ***5240.1*** *p72*
McDermott, William; New York, NY, 1836 ***8208.4*** *p22*
McDermott, William 19; Quebec, 1862 ***5704.8*** *p151*
McDevett, John; Philadelphia, 1864 ***5704.8*** *p175*
McDevett, John; Philadelphia, 1870 ***5704.8*** *p238*
McDevett, Margaret; Philadelphia, 1868 ***5704.8*** *p226*
McDevett, Mary; Philadelphia, 1870 ***5704.8*** *p238*
McDevett, Sarah; Philadelphia, 1870 ***5704.8*** *p238*
McDevett, Sarah 2; Philadelphia, 1870 ***5704.8*** *p238*
McDevett, Susan; America, 1868 ***5704.8*** *p231*
McDevette, Daniel; America, 1870 ***5704.8*** *p239*
McDevette, Grace; Philadelphia, 1868 ***5704.8*** *p225*
McDevette, Hannah; New York, NY, 1870 ***5704.8*** *p240*
McDevette, Sarah; New York, NY, 1870 ***5704.8*** *p240*
McDevitt, . . . 4 mos; Philadelphia, 1866 ***5704.8*** *p215*
McDevitt, Alexander; Philadelphia, 1866 ***5704.8*** *p205*
McDevitt, Andrew; Philadelphia, 1866 ***5704.8*** *p205*
McDevitt, Ann; Philadelphia, 1864 ***5704.8*** *p176*
McDevitt, Ann 9; Philadelphia, 1864 ***5704.8*** *p176*
McDevitt, Anne; Philadelphia, 1864 ***5704.8*** *p170*
McDevitt, Annie 9; Philadelphia, 1866 ***5704.8*** *p205*
McDevitt, Barney; Philadelphia, 1865 ***5704.8*** *p196*
McDevitt, Bridget; St. John, N.B., 1850 ***5704.8*** *p65*
McDevitt, Bridget 20; Philadelphia, 1857 ***5704.8*** *p134*
McDevitt, Catharine; Philadelphia, 1866 ***5704.8*** *p205*
McDevitt, Catharine 5; Philadelphia, 1866 ***5704.8*** *p205*
McDevitt, Catherine; New York, NY, 1864 ***5704.8*** *p174*
McDevitt, Catherine; Philadelphia, 1849 ***53.26*** *p58*
*Relative:*Margaret 12
*Relative:*Francis 4
McDevitt, Catherine; Philadelphia, 1849 ***5704.8*** *p55*
McDevitt, Catherine 18; Philadelphia, 1865 ***5704.8*** *p164*
McDevitt, Charles 10; Philadelphia, 1866 ***5704.8*** *p205*
McDevitt, Daniel; America, 1864 ***5704.8*** *p181*

McDowall, Daniel 51; South Carolina, 1850 ***1639.20*** *p150*
McDowall, John; Charleston, SC, 1830 ***1639.20*** *p150*
McDowell, Alexander 23; Kansas, 1880 ***5240.1*** *p62*
McDowell, Christopher; New York, NY, 1836 ***8208.4*** *p19*
McDowell, Isabella 18; Quebec, 1857 ***5704.8*** *p136*
McDuff, Charles; Quebec, 1787 ***7603*** *p77*
McDuffie, Abigail 75; North Carolina, 1850 ***1639.20*** *p150*
McDuffie, Alexander 63; North Carolina, 1850 ***1639.20*** *p150*
McDuffie, Angus; America, 1803 ***1639.20*** *p150*
McDuffie, Catherine 61; North Carolina, 1850 ***1639.20*** *p150*
McDuffie, Catherine 68; North Carolina, 1850 ***1639.20*** *p151*
McDuffie, Daniel; Brunswick, NC, 1739 ***1639.20*** *p151*
McDuffie, Margaret 90; North Carolina, 1850 ***1639.20*** *p151*
McDuffie, Murdo; America, 1802 ***1639.20*** *p151*
McDuffie, Murdoch 58; North Carolina, 1850 ***1639.20*** *p151*
McDuffie, Neil; America, 1802 ***1639.20*** *p151*
McDuffie, Sally 70; North Carolina, 1850 ***1639.20*** *p151*
McDugal, Alexander; America, 1792 ***1639.20*** *p147*
McDugald, Alexander 45; North Carolina, 1850 ***1639.20*** *p147*
McDugald, Allan 60; North Carolina, 1850 ***1639.20*** *p147*
*Relative:*John 21
*Relative:*Mary 15
McDugald, Angus 66; North Carolina, 1850 ***1639.20*** *p147*
McDugald, Dugald 62; North Carolina, 1850 ***1639.20*** *p148*
McDugald, Duncan; America, 1795 ***1639.20*** *p148*
McDugald, Isabel 57 *SEE* McDugald, John
McDugald, James; North Carolina, 1739 ***1639.20*** *p149*
McDugald, John 21 *SEE* McDugald, Allan
McDugald, John 52; North Carolina, 1850 ***1639.20*** *p149*
*Relative:*Isabel 57
McDugald, John 80; North Carolina, 1850 ***1639.20*** *p149*
*Relative:*Margaret 81
McDugald, Margaret 66; North Carolina, 1850 ***1639.20*** *p149*
McDugald, Margaret 81 *SEE* McDugald, John
McDugald, Mary 15 *SEE* McDugald, Allan
McDugald, Samuel; America, 1793 ***1639.20*** *p150*
McDugall, James 18; Philadelphia, 1858 ***5704.8*** *p138*
McDugil, Hannah Bell 18; Philadelphia, 1860 ***5704.8*** *p144*
McEachen, Daniel; America, 1804 ***1639.20*** *p151*
McEachen, Effy 46; South Carolina, 1850 ***1639.20*** *p152*
McEachen, Malcolm 66; North Carolina, 1850 ***1639.20*** *p152*
McEachen, Mary 50; South Carolina, 1850 ***1639.20*** *p152*
McEachern, Angus; Charleston, SC, 1811 ***1639.20*** *p151*
McEachern, Herbert D. 38; Washington, 1919 ***1728.5*** *p12*
McEachern, Mary; North Carolina, 1740-1837 ***1639.20*** *p152*
McEachern, Mary 74; North Carolina, 1850 ***1639.20*** *p215*
McEachin, Alexander; North Carolina, 1790-1881 ***1639.20*** *p151*
McEachin, Patrick; North Carolina, 1750-1828 ***1639.20*** *p152*
McEachin, Patrick; North Carolina, 1776 ***1639.20*** *p152*
McEawon, James 26; Philadelphia, 1864 ***5704.8*** *p155*
McElain, Margaret 9; Philadelphia, 1849 ***5704.8*** *p54*
McElain, Margeret; Philadelphia, 1849 ***53.26*** *p59*
McEldoon, Michael; Philadelphia, 1852 ***5704.8*** *p92*
McEldown, William 14; Philadelphia, 1857 ***5704.8*** *p132*
McEleaney, Catherine; St. John, N.B., 1849 ***5704.8*** *p48*
McEleney, James; St. John, N.B., 1848 ***5704.8*** *p38*
McElere, Ann 7; St. John, N.B., 1847 ***5704.8*** *p11*
McElere, Bernard 3; St. John, N.B., 1847 ***5704.8*** *p11*
McElere, John 5; St. John, N.B., 1847 ***5704.8*** *p11*
McElere, Mary; St. John, N.B., 1847 ***5704.8*** *p11*
McElere, Patrick; St. John, N.B., 1847 ***5704.8*** *p11*
McElery, Mary; America, 1742 ***4971*** *p67*
McElfatrick, David; Arkansas, 1918 ***95.2*** *p82*
McElgrew, Patrick; St. John, N.B., 1848 ***5704.8*** *p47*
McElgrew, William 13; St. John, N.B., 1848 ***5704.8*** *p47*
McElhadden, Jane 18; Philadelphia, 1864 ***5704.8*** *p156*
McElhaton, Mary; St. John, N.B., 1847 ***5704.8*** *p11*
McElhatten, Mary Jane; Philadelphia, 1852 ***5704.8*** *p91*
McElhatten, William; Philadelphia, 1851 ***5704.8*** *p70*
McElhattin, Daniel; Philadelphia, 1850 ***5704.8*** *p64*
McElhattin, James 11; Philadelphia, 1850 ***5704.8*** *p64*
McElhatton, Archy; New Orleans, 1849 ***5704.8*** *p58*
McElhatton, Eliza 8; Philadelphia, 1854 ***5704.8*** *p118*
McElhatton, Elizabeth 40; Philadelphia, 1854 ***5704.8*** *p118*
McElhatton, Martha; St. John, N.B., 1848 ***5704.8*** *p47*
McElhatton, Nancy 10; Philadelphia, 1854 ***5704.8*** *p118*
McElhatton, Patrick; New Orleans, 1849 ***5704.8*** *p58*
McElhatton, Samuel 5; Philadelphia, 1854 ***5704.8*** *p118*
McElhatton, Thomas; Quebec, 1853 ***5704.8*** *p104*
McElhenny, Catherine; St. John, N.B., 1851 ***5704.8*** *p72*
McElhenny, Jane; Philadelphia, 1850 ***53.26*** *p59*
McElhenny, Jane; Philadelphia, 1850 ***5704.8*** *p65*
McElhenny, Margaret; St. John, N.B., 1847 ***5704.8*** *p26*
McElhenny, Sicily; St. John, N.B., 1847 ***5704.8*** *p26*
McElhenny, Susan; St. John, N.B., 1847 ***5704.8*** *p26*
McElhenny, Thomas; Philadelphia, 1848 ***53.26*** *p59*
McElhenny, Thomas; Philadelphia, 1848 ***5704.8*** *p40*
McElhill, Jane 20; Philadelphia, 1853 ***5704.8*** *p111*
McElhill, John 8; St. John, N.B., 1854 ***5704.8*** *p115*
McElhill, Nancy; Philadelphia, 1852 ***5704.8*** *p96*
McElhill, Rose 50; St. John, N.B., 1854 ***5704.8*** *p115*
McElhiney, Patrick 20; Philadelphia, 1860 ***5704.8*** *p145*
McElhinney, Andrew; New York, NY, 1864 ***5704.8*** *p174*
McElhinney, Cicily; St. John, N.B., 1852 ***5704.8*** *p83*
McElhinney, Ellen; St. John, N.B., 1851 ***5704.8*** *p78*
McElhinney, Hugh; St. John, N.B., 1851 ***5704.8*** *p78*
McElhinney, Jane; St. John, N.B., 1852 ***5704.8*** *p83*
McElhinney, Thomas; St. John, N.B., 1851 ***5704.8*** *p71*
McElhinney, William 19; Philadelphia, 1859 ***5704.8*** *p141*
McElhinney, William 25; Philadelphia, 1856 ***5704.8*** *p128*
McElhinny, Catherine; Philadelphia, 1847 ***53.26*** *p59*
McElhinny, Catherine; Philadelphia, 1847 ***5704.8*** *p32*
McElhinny, Hugh; St. John, N.B., 1847 ***5704.8*** *p24*
McElhinny, James; St. John, N.B., 1847 ***5704.8*** *p4*
McElhinny, John; St. John, N.B., 1847 ***5704.8*** *p26*
McElhinny, John 12; Philadelphia, 1848 ***5704.8*** *p46*
McElhinny, Mary; St. John, N.B., 1847 ***5704.8*** *p18*
McElhinny, Patrick 20; St. John, N.B., 1854 ***5704.8*** *p114*
McElhinny, Patrick 45; St. John, N.B., 1854 ***5704.8*** *p114*
McElhinny, Phillip; St. John, N.B., 1847 ***5704.8*** *p4*
McElhinny, Sally; Philadelphia, 1848 ***5704.8*** *p46*
McElhone, Catharine; America, 1864 ***5704.8*** *p188*
McElhone, Neil; America, 1864 ***5704.8*** *p188*
McElien, Elizabeth; St. John, N.B., 1850 ***5704.8*** *p61*
McElien, Ellan; St. John, N.B., 1850 ***5704.8*** *p61*
McEligott, Jeremiah; Illinois, 1856 ***7857*** *p5*
McEliney, James; Philadelphia, 1847 ***53.26*** *p59*
McEliney, James; Philadelphia, 1847 ***5704.8*** *p1*
McElkel, Ann; Philadelphia, 1852 ***5704.8*** *p88*
McElkil, Catherine; St. John, N.B., 1852 ***5704.8*** *p84*
McElmayle, Robert; Philadelphia, 1852 ***5704.8*** *p88*
McElmurry, Mary 14; Quebec, 1855 ***5704.8*** *p126*
McElroy, Ann; Philadelphia, 1848 ***53.26*** *p59*
*Relative:*Isabella
McElroy, Ann; Philadelphia, 1848 ***5704.8*** *p40*
McElroy, Ann 18; Quebec, 1855 ***5704.8*** *p126*
McElroy, Anne; Quebec, 1851 ***5704.8*** *p73*
McElroy, Annie; St. John, N.B., 1863 ***5704.8*** *p153*
McElroy, Arthur 7; St. John, N.B., 1863 ***5704.8*** *p153*
McElroy, Arthur 40; St. John, N.B., 1863 ***5704.8*** *p153*
McElroy, Benjamin; Philadelphia, 1851 ***5704.8*** *p81*
McElroy, Biddy; St. John, N.B., 1847 ***5704.8*** *p20*
McElroy, Bridget; Philadelphia, 1852 ***5704.8*** *p96*
McElroy, Catherine 5; St. John, N.B., 1847 ***5704.8*** *p33*
McElroy, Catherine 5; St. John, N.B., 1863 ***5704.8*** *p153*
McElroy, Daniel 13; St. John, N.B., 1852 ***5704.8*** *p95*
McElroy, Edward 2; Philadelphia, 1852 ***5704.8*** *p96*
McElroy, Ellen 13; St. John, N.B., 1847 ***5704.8*** *p33*
McElroy, Francis; New York, NY, 1840 ***8208.4*** *p107*
McElroy, Francis; New York, NY, 1868 ***5704.8*** *p227*
McElroy, George; Philadelphia, 1811 ***53.26*** *p59*
With family
McElroy, Grace; Philadelphia, 1852 ***5704.8*** *p96*
McElroy, Hannah 16; Philadelphia, 1864 ***5704.8*** *p157*
McElroy, Hugh 14; Philadelphia, 1864 ***5704.8*** *p157*
McElroy, Isabella *SEE* McElroy, Ann
McElroy, Isabella; Philadelphia, 1848 ***5704.8*** *p40*
McElroy, James; New York, NY, 1867 ***5704.8*** *p222*
McElroy, James; Quebec, 1850 ***5704.8*** *p63*
McElroy, James 5; St. John, N.B., 1863 ***5704.8*** *p153*
McElroy, James 9; St. John, N.B., 1854 ***5704.8*** *p120*
McElroy, James 13; Massachusetts, 1847 ***5881.1*** *p67*
McElroy, James 23; Wilmington, DE, 1831 ***6508.7*** *p161*
McElroy, Jane 29; St. John, N.B., 1854 ***5704.8*** *p120*
McElroy, Jeremiah; Philadelphia, 1864 ***5704.8*** *p183*
McElroy, John; New York, NY, 1868 ***5704.8*** *p227*
McElroy, John; Philadelphia, 1851 ***5704.8*** *p81*
McElroy, John 6 mos; St. John, N.B., 1847 ***5704.8*** *p33*
McElroy, Margaret 3; St. John, N.B., 1863 ***5704.8*** *p153*
McElroy, Margaret 12; St. John, N.B., 1847 ***5704.8*** *p33*
McElroy, Margaret 40; St. John, N.B., 1863 ***5704.8*** *p153*
McElroy, Mary; America, 1742 ***4971*** *p67*
McElroy, Mary; Philadelphia, 1851 ***5704.8*** *p80*
McElroy, Mary; St. John, N.B., 1847 ***5704.8*** *p20*
McElroy, Mary; St. John, N.B., 1847 ***5704.8*** *p33*
McElroy, Mary; St. John, N.B., 1852 ***5704.8*** *p93*
McElroy, Mary 2; St. John, N.B., 1847 ***5704.8*** *p33*
McElroy, Mary 4; St. John, N.B., 1852 ***5704.8*** *p95*
McElroy, Mary 9; St. John, N.B., 1863 ***5704.8*** *p153*
McElroy, Michael; Philadelphia, 1867 ***5704.8*** *p220*
McElroy, Nancy 7; St. John, N.B., 1852 ***5704.8*** *p95*
McElroy, Neil; Philadelphia, 1851 ***5704.8*** *p81*
McElroy, Nelly; St. John, N.B., 1851 ***5704.8*** *p79*
McElroy, Patrick 11; Massachusetts, 1849 ***5881.1*** *p74*
McElroy, Patrick 50; Massachusetts, 1847 ***5881.1*** *p74*
McElroy, Peter; Quebec, 1851 ***5704.8*** *p73*
McElroy, Phelix; St. John, N.B., 1847 ***5704.8*** *p33*
McElroy, Rachel; St. John, N.B., 1852 ***5704.8*** *p95*
McElroy, Robert; St. John, N.B., 1852 ***5704.8*** *p84*
McElroy, Robert; St. John, N.B., 1852 ***5704.8*** *p95*
McElroy, Roddy; St. John, N.B., 1849 ***5704.8*** *p55*
McElroy, Rose; Philadelphia, 1867 ***5704.8*** *p219*
McElroy, Thomas; St. John, N.B., 1847 ***5704.8*** *p20*
McElroy, Thomas 25; Philadelphia, 1864 ***5704.8*** *p156*
McElroy, William; New York, NY, 1866 ***5704.8*** *p212*
McElroy, William; St. John, N.B., 1852 ***5704.8*** *p95*
McElroy, William 20; Wilmington, DE, 1831 ***6508.7*** *p161*
McElroy, Wright; Quebec, 1851 ***5704.8*** *p73*
McElshinder, Betty 24; St. John, N.B., 1859 ***5704.8*** *p141*
McElshinder, Robert 28; St. John, N.B., 1859 ***5704.8*** *p141*
McElshinder, Thomas 2; St. John, N.B., 1859 ***5704.8*** *p141*
McElvenny, James 20; Quebec, 1854 ***5704.8*** *p121*
McElveny, Thomas; New York, NY, 1834 ***8208.4*** *p40*
McElvoy, Jane; Philadelphia, 1865 ***5704.8*** *p190*
McElwain, Albert; Quebec, 1851 ***5704.8*** *p75*
McElwain, David; St. John, N.B., 1851 ***5704.8*** *p72*
McElwain, Jane; Philadelphia, 1851 ***5704.8*** *p79*
McElwain, John; New York, NY, 1835 ***8208.4*** *p77*
McElwain, Maty; St. John, N.B., 1851 ***5704.8*** *p72*
McElwain, Nail 20; Philadelphia, 1859 ***5704.8*** *p142*
McElwaine, Biddy 18; St. John, N.B., 1854 ***5704.8*** *p119*
McElwaine, Catherine; Philadelphia, 1853 ***5704.8*** *p102*
McElwaine, Catherine 23; St. John, N.B., 1853 ***5704.8*** *p110*
McElwaine, Charles 8; Philadelphia, 1852 ***5704.8*** *p87*
McElwaine, Daniel 12; Philadelphia, 1854 ***5704.8*** *p123*
McElwaine, Eliza 11; Philadelphia, 1852 ***5704.8*** *p87*
McElwaine, Elleanor; St. John, N.B., 1851 ***5704.8*** *p72*
McElwaine, James 21; Philadelphia, 1859 ***5704.8*** *p142*
McElwaine, James 26; Philadelphia, 1855 ***5704.8*** *p124*
McElwaine, Jane 6; Philadelphia, 1852 ***5704.8*** *p87*
McElwaine, Joseph; Philadelphia, 1852 ***5704.8*** *p87*
McElwaine, Margaret; Philadelphia, 1851 ***5704.8*** *p76*
McElwaine, Maria; Philadelphia, 1851 ***5704.8*** *p76*
McElwaine, Martha 4; Philadelphia, 1852 ***5704.8*** *p87*
McElwaine, Neal 22; Philadelphia, 1854 ***5704.8*** *p118*
McElwaine, Richard; Philadelphia, 1852 ***5704.8*** *p87*
McElwaine, Samuel; Philadelphia, 1850 ***5704.8*** *p69*
McElwaine, Sarah; Philadelphia, 1852 ***5704.8*** *p87*
McElwaine, William; Philadelphia, 1850 ***5704.8*** *p69*
McElwee, Andrew 18; Philadelphia, 1853 ***5704.8*** *p109*
McElwee, Catharine; Philadelphia, 1866 ***5704.8*** *p214*
McElwee, Catherine *SEE* McElwee, Charles
McElwee, Catherine; Philadelphia, 1847 ***5704.8*** *p23*
McElwee, Charles; Philadelphia, 1847 ***53.26*** *p59*
*Relative:*Catherine
McElwee, Charles; Philadelphia, 1847 ***5704.8*** *p23*
McElwee, Cornelis 22; Philadelphia, 1853 ***5704.8*** *p113*
McElwee, Cornelius 23; Philadelphia, 1854 ***5704.8*** *p123*
McElwee, Daniel; Philadelphia, 1853 ***5704.8*** *p100*
McElwee, Ellen; Philadelphia, 1866 ***5704.8*** *p205*
McElwee, Ellen; Philadelphia, 1866 ***5704.8*** *p214*
McElwee, George; St. John, N.B., 1852 ***5704.8*** *p93*
McElwee, Hannah; Philadelphia, 1864 ***5704.8*** *p178*
McElwee, Isabella; Philadelphia, 1864 ***5704.8*** *p184*
McElwee, John; Philadelphia, 1864 ***5704.8*** *p181*
McElwee, John 11; Philadelphia, 1853 ***5704.8*** *p102*
McElwee, Letitia; New York, NY, 1869 ***5704.8*** *p233*
McElwee, Letitia; New York, NY, 1870 ***5704.8*** *p238*
McElwee, Margaret; New York, NY, 1865 ***5704.8*** *p193*
McElwee, Margaret; New York, NY, 1869 ***5704.8*** *p233*
McElwee, Margaret; Philadelphia, 1864 ***5704.8*** *p173*
McElwee, Margaret 9; Philadelphia, 1853 ***5704.8*** *p102*
McElwee, Margaret 20; St. John, N.B., 1854 ***5704.8*** *p121*
McElwee, Martha; New York, NY, 1869 ***5704.8*** *p233*
McElwee, Mary; Philadelphia, 1864 ***5704.8*** *p180*
McElwee, Mary; Philadelphia, 1865 ***5704.8*** *p198*
McElwee, Mary; Philadelphia, 1866 ***5704.8*** *p214*
McElwee, Mary; St. John, N.B., 1852 ***5704.8*** *p93*
McElwee, Michael; Philadelphia, 1864 ***5704.8*** *p178*
McElwee, Michael; Philadelphia, 1864 ***5704.8*** *p180*
McElwee, Patrick; Philadelphia, 1866 ***5704.8*** *p214*

336
FOR A COMPLETE EXPLANATION OF ENTRY, SEE "HOW TO READ A CITATION" SECTION

McElwee, Rodger; Philadelphia, 1853 ***5704.8*** *p102*
McElwee, Samuel; Philadelphia, 1852 ***5704.8*** *p91*
McElwee, Sarah; Philadelphia, 1864 ***5704.8*** *p180*
McElwee, Sarah; St. John, N.B., 1847 ***5704.8*** *p5*
McElwee, Sarah 18; Philadelphia, 1856 ***5704.8*** *p128*
McElwee, Stephen; Philadelphia, 1865 ***5704.8*** *p189*
McElwee, Susan; Philadelphia, 1853 ***5704.8*** *p102*
McElwee, Thomas 8; New York, NY, 1869 ***5704.8*** *p233*
McElwee, William 4; New York, NY, 1869 ***5704.8*** *p233*
McElwee, William 13; Philadelphia, 1853 ***5704.8*** *p102*
McElwee, William 18; St. John, N.B., 1854 ***5704.8*** *p121*
McElwy, Sarah 20; Philadelphia, 1854 ***5704.8*** *p118*
McEnerny, Catharine 6; Massachusetts, 1850 ***5881.1*** *p65*
McEnerny, John 8; Massachusetts, 1850 ***5881.1*** *p70*
McEnerny, Mary 10; Massachusetts, 1850 ***5881.1*** *p73*
McEnerny, Thomas 1; Massachusetts, 1850 ***5881.1*** *p76*
McEnery, George; Washington, 1859-1920 ***2872.1*** *p27*
McEnhill, James; Ohio, 1851 ***9892.11*** *p32*
McEnhill, Margaret; America, 1864 ***5704.8*** *p188*
McEnnis, Edward 15; Maryland, 1775 ***1219.7*** *p254*
McEnorland, James; America, 1741 ***4971*** *p76*
McEnoy, Patrick 30; Kansas, 1871 ***5240.1*** *p51*
McEntee, Andrew; New York, NY, 1838 ***8208.4*** *p73*
McEntee, Catharine 6; Massachusetts, 1848 ***5881.1*** *p64*
McEntee, John; America, 1737 ***4971*** *p63*
McEntee, Mary 4; Massachusetts, 1848 ***5881.1*** *p70*
McEntee, Mary 30; Massachusetts, 1848 ***5881.1*** *p70*
McEntee, Owen; New York, NY, 1837 ***8208.4*** *p31*
McEntyre, Robert 28; Philadelphia, 1833-1834 ***53.26*** *p59*
McErlain, Catherine; Philadelphia, 1850 ***53.26*** *p59*
McErlain, Catherine; Philadelphia, 1850 ***5704.8*** *p68*
McErlean, Patrick; New York, 1850 ***6013.19*** *p74*
McErlin, Patrick; New York, 1850 ***6013.19*** *p74*
McEuroy, Margaret 23; St. John, N.B., 1857 ***5704.8*** *p135*
McEuroy, Michael 22; St. John, N.B., 1857 ***5704.8*** *p135*
McEvary, Edm.; America, 1742 ***4971*** *p30*
McEvay, Andrew 5 *SEE* McEvay, James
McEvay, Andrew 5; Philadelphia, 1850 ***5704.8*** *p60*
McEvay, Ann 1 *SEE* McEvay, James
McEvay, Ann 1; Philadelphia, 1850 ***5704.8*** *p60*
McEvay, Barney *SEE* McEvay, Sally
McEvay, Barney; Philadelphia, 1850 ***5704.8*** *p60*
McEvay, Bridget 3 *SEE* McEvay, James
McEvay, Bridget 3; Philadelphia, 1850 ***5704.8*** *p60*
McEvay, Daniel *SEE* McEvay, Sally
McEvay, Daniel; Philadelphia, 1850 ***5704.8*** *p60*
McEvay, Ellan 9; Philadelphia, 1850 ***5704.8*** *p60*
McEvay, Ellen 9 *SEE* McEvay, James
McEvay, Hugh *SEE* McEvay, Sally
McEvay, Hugh; Philadelphia, 1850 ***5704.8*** *p60*
McEvay, James 11; Philadelphia, 1803-1850 ***53.26*** *p59*
*Relative:*Ellen 9
*Relative:*Patrick 7
*Relative:*Andrew 5
*Relative:*Bridget 3
*Relative:*Ann 1
McEvay, James 11; Philadelphia, 1850 ***5704.8*** *p60*
McEvay, Patrick 7 *SEE* McEvay, James
McEvay, Patrick 7; Philadelphia, 1850 ***5704.8*** *p60*
McEvay, Sally; Philadelphia, 1850 ***53.26*** *p59*
*Relative:*Barney
*Relative:*Daniel
*Relative:*Hugh
McEvay, Sally; Philadelphia, 1850 ***5704.8*** *p60*
McEvenin, Jane; Montreal, 1819 ***7603*** *p66*
McEverny, Bridget 20; Massachusetts, 1848 ***5881.1*** *p63*
McEvoy, John; New York, NY, 1833 ***8208.4*** *p31*
McEvoy, Michael; Quebec, 1823 ***7603*** *p59*
McEvoy, Nancy; Philadelphia, 1852 ***5704.8*** *p85*
McEwan, Dinah 35 *SEE* McEwan, James
McEwan, Dinah 61 *SEE* McEwan, James
McEwan, James 71; South Carolina, 1850 ***1639.20*** *p152*
*Relative:*Dinah 61
*Relative:*Dinah 35
McEwen, John; New York, NY, 1836 ***8208.4*** *p21*
McEwing, John; Charleston, SC, 1804 ***1639.20*** *p152*
McFadden, Ann; Philadelphia, 1847 ***53.26*** *p59*
McFadden, Ann; Philadelphia, 1847 ***5704.8*** *p32*
McFadden, Ann 19; Philadelphia, 1853 ***5704.8*** *p112*
McFadden, Ann 20; Philadelphia, 1864 ***5704.8*** *p161*
McFadden, Biddy 1 mo; Philadelphia, 1864 ***5704.8*** *p160*
McFadden, Biddy 12; Philadelphia, 1851 ***5704.8*** *p71*
McFadden, Bidy 18; Philadelphia, 1857 ***5704.8*** *p132*
McFadden, Bridget 3; Philadelphia, 1854 ***5704.8*** *p118*
McFadden, Bridget 9; St. John, N.B., 1853 ***5704.8*** *p106*
McFadden, Bridget 30; Philadelphia, 1854 ***5704.8*** *p118*
McFadden, Brine; St. John, N.B., 1847 ***5704.8*** *p35*
McFadden, Bryan; Philadelphia, 1853 ***5704.8*** *p100*
McFadden, Catharine; New York, NY, 1866 ***5704.8*** *p209*
McFadden, Catharine; Philadelphia, 1864 ***5704.8*** *p182*
McFadden, Catharine 20; Massachusetts, 1847 ***5881.1*** *p64*
McFadden, Catherine; St. John, N.B., 1847 ***5704.8*** *p9*
McFadden, Catherine; St. John, N.B., 1853 ***5704.8*** *p106*
McFadden, Catherine 10; Philadelphia, 1851 ***5704.8*** *p71*
McFadden, Catherine 10; Quebec, 1849 ***5704.8*** *p57*
McFadden, Catherine 19; Philadelphia, 1857 ***5704.8*** *p133*
McFadden, Charles; New York, NY, 1868 ***5704.8*** *p229*
McFadden, Charles; St. John, N.B., 1847 ***5704.8*** *p33*
McFadden, Charles 17; Philadelphia, 1861 ***5704.8*** *p148*
McFadden, Cormick; New York, NY, 1865 ***5704.8*** *p183*
McFadden, Cornielius 22; Philadelphia, 1854 ***5704.8*** *p116*
McFadden, Daniel; America, 1864 ***5704.8*** *p181*
McFadden, Daniel; New York, NY, 1865 ***5704.8*** *p191*
McFadden, Daniel 11; St. John, N.B., 1847 ***5704.8*** *p35*
McFadden, David; New York, NY, 1838 ***8208.4*** *p89*
McFadden, David; Philadelphia, 1864 ***5704.8*** *p180*
McFadden, Dennis; New York, NY, 1869 ***5704.8*** *p234*
McFadden, Dennis; Philadelphia, 1853 ***5704.8*** *p100*
McFadden, Dominick; Philadelphia, 1847 ***53.26*** *p59*
McFadden, Dominick; Philadelphia, 1847 ***5704.8*** *p5*
McFadden, Donnel 3; Quebec, 1848 ***5704.8*** *p41*
McFadden, Edward 17; Philadelphia, 1854 ***5704.8*** *p116*
McFadden, Elizabeth; St. John, N.B., 1851 ***5704.8*** *p80*
McFadden, Elizabeth 13; St. John, N.B., 1852 ***5704.8*** *p83*
McFadden, Fanny 26; Philadelphia, 1865 ***5704.8*** *p164*
McFadden, George; St. John, N.B., 1850 ***5704.8*** *p66*
McFadden, Giley; Philadelphia, 1870 ***5704.8*** *p237*
McFadden, Gilley; Philadelphia, 1866 ***5704.8*** *p204*
McFadden, Grace; Quebec, 1849 ***5704.8*** *p57*
McFadden, Hugh; St. John, N.B., 1847 ***5704.8*** *p35*
McFadden, Hugh 1; St. John, N.B., 1847 ***5704.8*** *p33*
McFadden, Isabella; New York, NY, 1865 ***5704.8*** *p194*
McFadden, Isabella 18; St. John, N.B., 1855 ***5704.8*** *p127*
McFadden, James; Philadelphia, 1851 ***5704.8*** *p71*
McFadden, James; Philadelphia, 1865 ***5704.8*** *p203*
McFadden, James; Philadelphia, 1867 ***5704.8*** *p218*
McFadden, James 1; Philadelphia, 1865 ***5704.8*** *p164*
McFadden, John; Philadelphia, 1847 ***53.26*** *p59*
McFadden, John; Philadelphia, 1847 ***5704.8*** *p14*
McFadden, John; Philadelphia, 1850 ***53.26*** *p59*
McFadden, John; Philadelphia, 1850 ***5704.8*** *p60*
McFadden, John; Philadelphia, 1854 ***5704.8*** *p116*
McFadden, John; Philadelphia, 1866 ***5704.8*** *p204*
McFadden, John; Quebec, 1849 ***5704.8*** *p57*
McFadden, John 7; Quebec, 1848 ***5704.8*** *p41*
McFadden, John 20; Quebec, 1854 ***5704.8*** *p119*
McFadden, John 22; Philadelphia, 1856 ***5704.8*** *p128*
McFadden, Julia 14; Philadelphia, 1858 ***5704.8*** *p139*
McFadden, Madge 4; America, 1864 ***5704.8*** *p188*
McFadden, Madge 25; Philadelphia, 1864 ***5704.8*** *p160*
McFadden, Magey; Philadelphia, 1853 ***5704.8*** *p100*
McFadden, Magy 4; St. John, N.B., 1847 ***5704.8*** *p33*
McFadden, Margaret; Philadelphia, 1851 ***5704.8*** *p81*
McFadden, Margaret; St. John, N.B., 1852 ***5704.8*** *p83*
McFadden, Margaret 11; St. John, N.B., 1853 ***5704.8*** *p106*
McFadden, Mary; New York, NY, 1866 ***5704.8*** *p210*
McFadden, Mary; New York, NY, 1866 ***5704.8*** *p213*
McFadden, Mary; New York, NY, 1869 ***5704.8*** *p233*
McFadden, Mary; Philadelphia, 1849 ***53.26*** *p59*
McFadden, Mary; Philadelphia, 1849 ***5704.8*** *p58*
McFadden, Mary; Philadelphia, 1865 ***5704.8*** *p203*
McFadden, Mary 8; St. John, N.B., 1847 ***5704.8*** *p33*
McFadden, Mary 17; Philadelphia, 1856 ***5704.8*** *p129*
McFadden, Mary A.; Philadelphia, 1866 ***5704.8*** *p208*
McFadden, Maundy 22; St. John, N.B., 1855 ***5704.8*** *p127*
McFadden, Michael; New York, NY, 1865 ***5704.8*** *p194*
McFadden, Michael; Philadelphia, 1864 ***5704.8*** *p176*
McFadden, Michael 28; Philadelphia, 1864 ***5704.8*** *p160*
McFadden, Nancy; New York, NY, 1870 ***5704.8*** *p237*
McFadden, Nancy; St. John, N.B., 1847 ***5704.8*** *p35*
McFadden, Nancy 12; St. John, N.B., 1847 ***5704.8*** *p33*
McFadden, Nancy 19; Philadelphia, 1858 ***5704.8*** *p139*
McFadden, Neal; Philadelphia, 1847 ***53.26*** *p60*
*Relative:*Uny
*Relative:*Paddy 4
McFadden, Neal; Philadelphia, 1847 ***5704.8*** *p30*
McFadden, Neal; St. John, N.B., 1852 ***5704.8*** *p83*
McFadden, Paddy 4 *SEE* McFadden, Neal
McFadden, Paddy 4; Philadelphia, 1847 ***5704.8*** *p30*
McFadden, Pat; Philadelphia, 1852 ***5704.8*** *p92*
McFadden, Pat 4; Quebec, 1849 ***5704.8*** *p57*
McFadden, Patrick; Philadelphia, 1865 ***5704.8*** *p203*
McFadden, Patrick 8; St. John, N.B., 1847 ***5704.8*** *p35*
McFadden, Patrick 9; Philadelphia, 1854 ***5704.8*** *p118*
McFadden, Patrick 11; New York, NY, 1864 ***5704.8*** *p186*
McFadden, Rose; New York, NY, 1869 ***5704.8*** *p232*
McFadden, Rose; St. John, N.B., 1847 ***5704.8*** *p33*
McFadden, Rose; St. John, N.B., 1847 ***5704.8*** *p35*
McFadden, Rose 5; Quebec, 1848 ***5704.8*** *p41*
McFadden, Rose 13; Quebec, 1849 ***5704.8*** *p57*
McFadden, Rose 48; Massachusetts, 1847 ***5881.1*** *p75*
McFadden, Rosey 6; St. John, N.B., 1852 ***5704.8*** *p83*
McFadden, Sarah; Philadelphia, 1867 ***5704.8*** *p218*
McFadden, Sarah; Quebec, 1849 ***5704.8*** *p57*
McFadden, Sarah 6; Quebec, 1849 ***5704.8*** *p57*
McFadden, Sophia 20; Philadelphia, 1854 ***5704.8*** *p118*
McFadden, Susan; St. John, N.B., 1848 ***5704.8*** *p39*
McFadden, Susan 19; Philadelphia, 1865 ***5704.8*** *p164*
McFadden, Thomas 20; Philadelphia, 1857 ***5704.8*** *p132*
McFadden, Uny *SEE* McFadden, Neal
McFadden, Uny; Philadelphia, 1847 ***5704.8*** *p30*
McFadden, William; Quebec, 1848 ***5704.8*** *p41*
McFadden, William; Quebec, 1849 ***5704.8*** *p57*
McFadden, William; St. John, N.B., 1853 ***5704.8*** *p106*
McFaddin, Eleanor *SEE* McFaddin, Manus
McFaddin, Manus; Philadelphia, 1811 ***53.26*** *p60*
*Relative:*Eleanor
McFaden, Catherine; St. John, N.B., 1848 ***5704.8*** *p39*
McFading, Edward 24; Maryland, 1775 ***1219.7*** *p253*
McFadyen, Archibald; America, 1785 ***1639.20*** *p153*
McFadyen, Archibald; North Carolina, 1754-1830 ***1639.20*** *p152*
McFadyen, John 53; North Carolina, 1850 ***1639.20*** *p153*
McFadyen, Margaret 61; North Carolina, 1850 ***1639.20*** *p153*
McFadyen, Robert 20; St. John, N.B., 1866 ***5704.8*** *p167*
McFail, James 24; Philadelphia, 1857 ***5704.8*** *p133*
McFail, Patrick 50; Philadelphia, 1857 ***5704.8*** *p133*
McFail, Rosanna 30; Philadelphia, 1857 ***5704.8*** *p133*
McFall, Bernard 20; Philadelphia, 1854 ***5704.8*** *p123*
McFall, Betty; St. John, N.B., 1848 ***5704.8*** *p44*
McFall, Catharine 11; Philadelphia, 1865 ***5704.8*** *p198*
McFall, Elleanor; Quebec, 1851 ***5704.8*** *p82*
McFall, Lizzie; Philadelphia, 1864 ***5704.8*** *p183*
McFall, Mary; Philadelphia, 1865 ***5704.8*** *p198*
McFall, Mary; St. John, N.B., 1847 ***5704.8*** *p11*
McFall, Mary; St. John, N.B., 1848 ***5704.8*** *p44*
McFally, John 18; St. John, N.B., 1860 ***5704.8*** *p144*
McFarland, Alexander; St. John, N.B., 1847 ***5704.8*** *p24*
McFarland, Alexander; St. John, N.B., 1847 ***5704.8*** *p34*
McFarland, Andrew; Philadelphia, 1847 ***53.26*** *p60*
McFarland, Andrew; Philadelphia, 1847 ***5704.8*** *p21*
McFarland, Andrew; Quebec, 1851 ***5704.8*** *p73*
McFarland, Ann 18; Quebec, 1855 ***5704.8*** *p125*
McFarland, Anne 13 *SEE* McFarland, Isabella
McFarland, Anne 13; Philadelphia, 1849 ***5704.8*** *p49*
McFarland, Archibald 65; South Carolina, 1850 ***1639.20*** *p153*
McFarland, Bill 9 *SEE* McFarland, John
McFarland, Bill 9; Philadelphia, 1850 ***5704.8*** *p68*
McFarland, Catherine *SEE* McFarland, John
McFarland, Catherine; Philadelphia, 1850 ***5704.8*** *p68*
McFarland, Catherine 21; Philadelphia, 1860 ***5704.8*** *p145*
McFarland, Daniel; Boston, 1860 ***6410.32*** *p125*
McFarland, Daniel 3; Quebec, 1853 ***5704.8*** *p104*
McFarland, Daniel 33; Massachusetts, 1860 ***6410.32*** *p114*
McFarland, Eliza; St. John, N.B., 1852 ***5704.8*** *p95*
McFarland, Eliza 11 *SEE* McFarland, John
McFarland, Eliza 11; Philadelphia, 1850 ***5704.8*** *p68*
McFarland, Eliza Ann; Philadelphia, 1852 ***5704.8*** *p87*
McFarland, Eliza Jane 9; Quebec, 1847 ***5704.8*** *p13*
McFarland, Eliza Jane 16; Philadelphia, 1860 ***5704.8*** *p146*
McFarland, Elizabeth *SEE* McFarland, John
McFarland, Elizabeth; Philadelphia, 1850 ***5704.8*** *p68*
McFarland, Elizabeth; Philadelphia, 1851 ***5704.8*** *p78*
McFarland, Elizabeth 10; New Orleans, 1858 ***5704.8*** *p140*
McFarland, Elleanor; St. John, N.B., 1847 ***5704.8*** *p24*
McFarland, Ellen; St. John, N.B., 1851 ***5704.8*** *p79*
McFarland, George; Quebec, 1853 ***5704.8*** *p104*
McFarland, George 38; New Orleans, 1858 ***5704.8*** *p140*
McFarland, Henry 12; Quebec, 1854 ***5704.8*** *p121*
McFarland, Ian; Philadelphia, 1852 ***5704.8*** *p87*
McFarland, Isabella; Philadelphia, 1849 ***53.26*** *p60*
*Relative:*Anne 13
McFarland, Isabella; Philadelphia, 1849 ***5704.8*** *p49*
McFarland, Isabella; Philadelphia, 1852 ***5704.8*** *p87*
McFarland, Isabella; Quebec, 1851 ***5704.8*** *p73*
McFarland, Isabella 40; Philadelphia, 1860 ***5704.8*** *p146*
McFarland, James *SEE* McFarland, John
McFarland, James; Philadelphia, 1850 ***5704.8*** *p68*
McFarland, James; Philadelphia, 1851 ***5704.8*** *p79*
McFarland, James; Quebec, 1847 ***5704.8*** *p12*
McFarland, James 25; Massachusetts, 1849 ***5881.1*** *p68*
McFarland, James 33; Quebec, 1857 ***5704.8*** *p135*

McFarland, Jane *SEE* McFarland, John
McFarland, Jane; Philadelphia, 1850 *5704.8 p68*
McFarland, Jane; Philadelphia, 1852 *5704.8 p89*
McFarland, Jane; Quebec, 1853 *5704.8 p104*
McFarland, Jane 7; Quebec, 1854 *5704.8 p121*
McFarland, Jane 19; Quebec, 1855 *5704.8 p126*
McFarland, Jane 40; Quebec, 1854 *5704.8 p121*
McFarland, John; North Carolina, 1767 *1639.20 p153*
McFarland, John; Philadelphia, 1847 *53.26 p60*
McFarland, John; Philadelphia, 1847 *53.26 p60*
   *Relative:*Margaret
McFarland, John; Philadelphia, 1847 *5704.8 p13*
McFarland, John; Philadelphia, 1847 *5704.8 p30*
McFarland, John; Philadelphia, 1850 *53.26 p60*
   *Relative:*Elizabeth
   *Relative:*James
   *Relative:*Catherine
   *Relative:*Jane
   *Relative:*Eliza 11
   *Relative:*Bill 9
   *Relative:*William 6
McFarland, John; Philadelphia, 1850 *5704.8 p68*
McFarland, John; Philadelphia, 1851 *5704.8 p81*
McFarland, John; Philadelphia, 1853 *5704.8 p100*
McFarland, John; Quebec, 1853 *5704.8 p104*
McFarland, John; St. John, N.B., 1847 *5704.8 p20*
McFarland, John 3; New Orleans, 1858 *5704.8 p140*
McFarland, John 13; Quebec, 1853 *5704.8 p104*
McFarland, John 28; Massachusetts, 1849 *5881.1 p68*
McFarland, John 50; Philadelphia, 1860 *5704.8 p146*
McFarland, Joseph; America, 1739 *4971 p75*
McFarland, Joseph; Philadelphia, 1849 *53.26 p60*
McFarland, Joseph; Philadelphia, 1849 *5704.8 p54*
McFarland, Joseph 16; Philadelphia, 1860 *5704.8 p145*
McFarland, Joseph 18; Philadelphia, 1860 *5704.8 p146*
McFarland, Joseph 20; St. John, N.B., 1853 *5704.8 p110*
McFarland, Lucinda 21; Philadelphia, 1858 *5704.8 p139*
McFarland, Margaret *SEE* McFarland, John
McFarland, Margaret; America, 1866 *5704.8 p210*
McFarland, Margaret; Philadelphia, 1847 *5704.8 p13*
McFarland, Margaret; Philadelphia, 1851 *5704.8 p80*
McFarland, Margaret; St. John, N.B., 1847 *5704.8 p34*
McFarland, Margaret 6; New Orleans, 1858 *5704.8 p140*
McFarland, Margaret 9; Philadelphia, 1860 *5704.8 p146*
McFarland, Margaret 10; Quebec, 1854 *5704.8 p121*
McFarland, Margaret 38; New Orleans, 1858 *5704.8 p140*
McFarland, Martha; Philadelphia, 1851 *5704.8 p76*
McFarland, Mary; Philadelphia, 1851 *5704.8 p79*
McFarland, Mary; Quebec, 1847 *5704.8 p12*
McFarland, Mary; Quebec, 1853 *5704.8 p104*
McFarland, Mary 5; Quebec, 1854 *5704.8 p121*
McFarland, Mary 20; Philadelphia, 1859 *5704.8 p141*
McFarland, Mary 20; St. John, N.B., 1861 *5704.8 p149*
McFarland, Mathew; America, 1866 *5704.8 p210*
McFarland, Neall; America, 1738 *4971 p66*
McFarland, Peggy 20; St. John, N.B., 1861 *5704.8 p149*
McFarland, Rebecca 11; Quebec, 1853 *5704.8 p104*
McFarland, Robert; Philadelphia, 1852 *5704.8 p87*
McFarland, Robert; Philadelphia, 1853 *5704.8 p100*
McFarland, Robert; Philadelphia, 1864 *5704.8 p182*
McFarland, Robert; St. John, N.B., 1847 *5704.8 p20*
McFarland, Robert 6 mos; St. John, N.B., 1861 *5704.8 p149*
McFarland, Robert 7; Quebec, 1853 *5704.8 p104*
McFarland, Samuel; New Orleans, 1849 *5704.8 p59*
McFarland, Samuel; Philadelphia, 1849 *53.26 p60*
McFarland, Samuel; Philadelphia, 1849 *5704.8 p58*
McFarland, Susan 14; Quebec, 1854 *5704.8 p121*
McFarland, Susanna 2; Quebec, 1847 *5704.8 p12*
McFarland, Thomas; Ohio, 1840 *9892.11 p33*
McFarland, Walter 20; North Carolina, 1775 *1639.20 p154*
McFarland, William; Philadelphia, 1851 *5704.8 p76*
McFarland, William; Philadelphia, 1852 *5704.8 p89*
McFarland, William; Philadelphia, 1853 *5704.8 p101*
McFarland, William; Quebec, 1853 *5704.8 p104*
McFarland, William; St. John, N.B., 1852 *5704.8 p93*
McFarland, William 6 *SEE* McFarland, John
McFarland, William 6; Philadelphia, 1850 *5704.8 p68*
McFarlane, Alexander 20; St. John, N.B., 1863 *5704.8 p152*
McFarlane, Alexander 20; St. John, N.B., 1866 *5704.8 p167*
McFarlane, Allen 30; South Carolina, 1850 *1639.20 p153*
   *Relative:*Janet 67
   *Relative:*Catherine 28
   *Relative:*Janet 32
   *Relative:*Marjory 25
McFarlane, Catherine 28 *SEE* McFarlane, Allen
McFarlane, Donald 6 *SEE* McFarlane, Donald

McFarlane, Donald 26; Wilmington, NC, 1774 *1639.20 p153*
   *Son:*Donald 6
McFarlane, Eliza 22; St. John, N.B., 1863 *5704.8 p152*
McFarlane, Flora 60; North Carolina, 1850 *1639.20 p153*
McFarlane, Janet 32 *SEE* McFarlane, Allen
McFarlane, Janet 67 *SEE* McFarlane, Allen
McFarlane, John 30; Kansas, 1877 *5240.1 p58*
McFarlane, Joseph 21; Quebec, 1863 *5704.8 p154*
McFarlane, Malcolm; Charleston, SC, 1813 *1639.20 p153*
McFarlane, Marjory 25 *SEE* McFarlane, Allen
McFarlane, Martha 20; St. John, N.B., 1863 *5704.8 p152*
McFarlane, Mary 19; Quebec, 1863 *5704.8 p154*
McFarlane, Robert; New York, NY, 1835 *8208.4 p48*
McFarlane, Sarah; North Carolina, 1850 *1639.20 p153*
McFarlane, Sarah; St. John, N.B., 1847 *5704.8 p26*
McFarlane, Sarah 48; St. John, N.B., 1863 *5704.8 p152*
McFarlane, William 16; St. John, N.B., 1863 *5704.8 p152*
McFarlane, William 48; St. John, N.B., 1863 *5704.8 p152*
McFasson, Daniel 38; New York, 1774 *1219.7 p242*
McFate, Jane; Philadelphia, 1852 *5704.8 p92*
McFate, Letitia; Philadelphia, 1852 *5704.8 p92*
McFate, Margaret; Philadelphia, 1852 *5704.8 p92*
McFate, Robert; Philadelphia, 1852 *5704.8 p92*
McFaul, Madge; New York, NY, 1867 *5704.8 p219*
McFauls, Margaret; Philadelphia, 1848 *53.26 p60*
McFauls, Margaret Ann; Philadelphia, 1848 *5704.8 p41*
McFawn, George 15; Massachusetts, 1849 *5881.1 p67*
McFawn, Margaret; Philadelphia, 1867 *5704.8 p224*
McFeeley, Edward 18; Massachusetts, 1849 *5881.1 p66*
McFeely, Biddy 12; St. John, N.B., 1854 *5704.8 p119*
McFeely, Bridget; Philadelphia, 1853 *5704.8 p102*
McFeely, Catherine 60; Philadelphia, 1853 *5704.8 p112*
McFeely, Daniel 27; St. John, N.B., 1854 *5704.8 p114*
McFeely, Edward 24; Philadelphia, 1855 *5704.8 p123*
McFeely, Eliza 46 *SEE* McFeely, James
McFeely, Hannah 20; St. John, N.B., 1862 *5704.8 p150*
McFeely, James 9 mos; St. John, N.B., 1862 *5704.8 p150*
McFeely, James 24; Philadelphia, 1865 *5704.8 p164*
McFeely, James 52; Charleston, SC, 1850 *1639.20 p154*
   *Relative:*Eliza 46
McFeely, Jane 22; Philadelphia, 1865 *5704.8 p164*
McFeely, John 35; St. John, N.B., 1862 *5704.8 p150*
McFeely, Margery; St. John, N.B., 1852 *5704.8 p83*
McFeely, Neal; Philadelphia, 1852 *5704.8 p85*
McFeeters, Catherine 45; Philadelphia, 1860 *5704.8 p146*
McFeeters, Eliza Jane; Philadelphia, 1850 *53.26 p60*
McFeeters, Eliza Jane; Philadelphia, 1850 *5704.8 p60*
McFeeters, James 21; Philadelphia, 1860 *5704.8 p144*
McFeeters, Margaret 20; Philadelphia, 1860 *5704.8 p146*
McFeeters, William; Philadelphia, 1852 *5704.8 p85*
McFeeters, William J.; Philadelphia, 1864 *5704.8 p181*
McFeetridge, Henry 21; St. John, N.B., 1864 *5704.8 p157*
McFeily, Mary 21; Wilmington, DE, 1831 *6508.7 p161*
McFerran, Robert; Sacramento Co., CA, 1855 *3840.2 p18*
McFeters, Ann Jane 10; Philadelphia, 1854 *5704.8 p115*
McFeters, John 7; Philadelphia, 1854 *5704.8 p115*
McFeters, Mary 30; Philadelphia, 1854 *5704.8 p115*
McFeters, William 5; Philadelphia, 1854 *5704.8 p115*
McFetrick, David *SEE* McFetrick, Jane
McFetrick, David; Philadelphia, 1848 *5704.8 p46*
McFetrick, Jane; Philadelphia, 1848 *53.26 p60*
   *Relative:*David
McFetrick, Jane; Philadelphia, 1848 *5704.8 p46*
McFetridge, Daniel; Philadelphia, 1853 *5704.8 p102*
McFetridge, Eliza; Philadelphia, 1852 *5704.8 p95*
McFetridge, Isabella; Philadelphia, 1848 *53.26 p60*
McFetridge, Isabella; Philadelphia, 1848 *5704.8 p45*
McFetridge, John 24; Philadelphia, 1834 *53.26 p60*
McFetridge, Joseph; Philadelphia, 1847 *53.26 p60*
McFetridge, Joseph; Philadelphia, 1847 *5704.8 p30*
McFetridge, Joseph; Philadelphia, 1851 *5704.8 p80*
McFetridge, Margaret; New York, NY, 1867 *5704.8 p224*
McFetridge, Robert 18; Philadelphia, 1833-1834 *53.26 p60*
McFetridge, William 22; Philadelphia, 1833-1834 *53.26 p60*
McFittrig, Michael; Philadelphia, 1853 *5704.8 p113*
McFrederick, John; Philadelphia, 1871 *5704.8 p240*
McGachin, James; Carolina, 1684 *1639.20 p154*
McGafferty, Pat 19; Philadelphia, 1803 *53.26 p60*
McGaghen, John; Quebec, 1851 *5704.8 p73*
McGaghey, Catherine; St. John, N.B., 1847 *5704.8 p34*
McGaghey, James 13; Quebec, 1852 *5704.8 p98*
McGaghey, John; St. John, N.B., 1851 *5704.8 p72*
McGaghey, John 4; St. John, N.B., 1851 *5704.8 p72*

McGaghey, Margaret; St. John, N.B., 1847 *5704.8 p10*
McGaghey, Mary; St. John, N.B., 1851 *5704.8 p72*
McGaghey, Mary Ann; Philadelphia, 1851 *5704.8 p81*
McGaghey, Patrick 2; St. John, N.B., 1851 *5704.8 p72*
McGahan, John 45; Quebec, 1855 *5704.8 p124*
McGahan, Margaret 13; Quebec, 1855 *5704.8 p124*
McGahan, Sally 11; Quebec, 1855 *5704.8 p124*
McGahan, Susan 17; Quebec, 1855 *5704.8 p124*
McGahey, Ellen M.; Philadelphia, 1850 *53.26 p60*
McGahey, Ellen Margaret; Philadelphia, 1850 *5704.8 p68*
McGahey, Mary; Philadelphia, 1868 *5704.8 p225*
McGailey, Michael; New York, NY, 1866 *5704.8 p208*
McGainty, Bessy 19; St. John, N.B., 1858 *5704.8 p137*
McGalloway, John; New York, NY, 1834 *8208.4 p25*
McGan, Elinor 1 *SEE* McGan, John
McGan, Elizabeth 30 *SEE* McGan, John
McGan, John 34; Philadelphia, 1803 *53.26 p60*
   *Relative:*Elizabeth 30
   *Relative:*Sarah 2
   *Relative:*Elinor 1
McGan, Sarah 2 *SEE* McGan, John
McGanary, Catharine; New York, NY, 1869 *5704.8 p234*
McGanary, Nancy; New York, NY, 1869 *5704.8 p234*
McGandy, Ellen 25; Philadelphia, 1860 *5704.8 p144*
McGandy, Margaret 21; Philadelphia, 1860 *5704.8 p144*
McGann, John; New York, NY, 1839 *8208.4 p95*
McGaraty, John 27; Massachusetts, 1849 *5881.1 p69*
McGarigle, Cormick 22; Quebec, 1853 *5704.8 p105*
McGarigle, Mary 26; St. John, N.B., 1866 *5704.8 p167*
McGarity, Ann 26; Philadelphia, 1861 *5704.8 p148*
McGarity, Mary; Philadelphia, 1847 *53.26 p60*
McGarity, Mary; Philadelphia, 1847 *5704.8 p13*
McGarity, Mary; Philadelphia, 1848 *53.26 p60*
McGarity, Mary; Philadelphia, 1848 *5704.8 p46*
McGaroon, Rose 22; Massachusetts, 1850 *5881.1 p75*
McGarr, James 3; Quebec, 1847 *5704.8 p6*
McGarr, Margaret; Quebec, 1847 *5704.8 p6*
McGarr, Mary 5; Quebec, 1847 *5704.8 p6*
McGarrety, Arthur; America, 1739 *4971 p25*
McGarrey, James; America, 1864 *5704.8 p189*
McGarrey, John; Philadelphia, 1865 *5704.8 p194*
McGarrigal, William; St. John, N.B., 1850 *5704.8 p67*
McGarrigan, Jane 28; St. John, N.B., 1854 *5704.8 p114*
McGarrigle, . . . 4 mos; Philadelphia, 1865 *5704.8 p199*
McGarrigle, Bridget 18; St. John, N.B., 1854 *5704.8 p115*
McGarrigle, Catherine 30; Philadelphia, 1864 *5704.8 p160*
McGarrigle, Edward; Philadelphia, 1852 *5704.8 p96*
McGarrigle, Edward; St. John, N.B., 1850 *5704.8 p66*
McGarrigle, Ellen; New York, NY, 1867 *5704.8 p224*
McGarrigle, Ellen; St. John, N.B., 1852 *5704.8 p93*
McGarrigle, John; St. John, N.B., 1852 *5704.8 p93*
McGarrigle, John 22; St. John, N.B., 1866 *5704.8 p167*
McGarrigle, Mary; Philadelphia, 1865 *5704.8 p199*
McGarrigle, Mary; St. John, N.B., 1852 *5704.8 p93*
McGarrigle, Pat; St. John, N.B., 1850 *5704.8 p66*
McGarrigle, Patrick; New York, NY, 1853 *2896.5 p27*
McGarrity, Ellen; Philadelphia, 1850 *53.26 p60*
   *Relative:*Sophia
McGarrity, Ellen; Philadelphia, 1850 *5704.8 p65*
McGarrity, Magy; Quebec, 1851 *5704.8 p82*
McGarrity, Margaret 20; St. John, N.B., 1857 *5704.8 p135*
McGarrity, Sophia *SEE* McGarrity, Ellen
McGarrity, Sophia; Philadelphia, 1850 *5704.8 p65*
McGarry, David; New Jersey, 1815 *9892.11 p33*
McGarry, Eliza; New York, NY, 1866 *5704.8 p208*
McGarry, Francis; Quebec, 1822 *7603 p62*
McGarry, Jane; New York, NY, 1866 *5704.8 p208*
McGarry, Margaret; Quebec, 1822 *7603 p62*
McGarry, Mary; Philadelphia, 1849 *53.26 p60*
McGarry, Mary; Philadelphia, 1849 *5704.8 p50*
McGartland, James; Philadelphia, 1868 *5704.8 p226*
McGarty, John; Quebec, 1847 *5704.8 p37*
McGarty, Michael 12; Quebec, 1847 *5704.8 p37*
McGarvey, Andrew; St. John, N.B., 1852 *5704.8 p94*
McGarvey, Anne 18; Philadelphia, 1860 *5704.8 p146*
McGarvey, Anthony 12; Philadelphia, 1859 *5704.8 p142*
McGarvey, Betty 18; Philadelphia, 1853 *5704.8 p111*
McGarvey, Biddy 4; Philadelphia, 1859 *5704.8 p142*
McGarvey, Bridget; New York, NY, 1866 *5704.8 p210*
McGarvey, Catherine; Quebec, 1847 *5704.8 p36*
McGarvey, Catherine 20; Philadelphia, 1859 *5704.8 p142*
McGarvey, Charles; New York, NY, 1867 *5704.8 p216*
McGarvey, Cormick; Philadelphia, 1870 *5704.8 p238*
McGarvey, Edward; Philadelphia, 1867 *5704.8 p217*
McGarvey, Elizabeth *SEE* McGarvey, William
McGarvey, Elizabeth; Philadelphia, 1847 *5704.8 p1*
McGarvey, Ellan; Philadelphia, 1849 *5704.8 p50*

McGarvey, Ellen; Philadelphia, 1849 ***53.26*** *p61*
McGarvey, Grace 20; Philadelphia, 1865 ***5704.8*** *p164*
McGarvey, Hannah 14; Philadelphia, 1859 ***5704.8*** *p142*
McGarvey, Hugh; St. John, N.B., 1848 ***5704.8*** *p39*
McGarvey, Hugh 20; St. John, N.B., 1854 ***5704.8*** *p119*
McGarvey, James; Philadelphia, 1847 ***53.26*** *p61*
McGarvey, James; Philadelphia, 1847 ***5704.8*** *p24*
McGarvey, James 45; Philadelphia, 1859 ***5704.8*** *p141*
McGarvey, Jane; New York, NY, 1867 ***5704.8*** *p216*
McGarvey, John; Philadelphia, 1867 ***5704.8*** *p218*
McGarvey, Joseph; Iowa, 1866-1943 ***123.54*** *p31*
McGarvey, Madge; Philadelphia, 1864 ***5704.8*** *p181*
McGarvey, Margaret; New York, NY, 1869 ***5704.8*** *p235*
McGarvey, Margaret; Philadelphia, 1864 ***5704.8*** *p181*
McGarvey, Mary; Montreal, 1822 ***7603*** *p61*
McGarvey, Mary; New York, NY, 1869 ***5704.8*** *p235*
McGarvey, Mary; Philadelphia, 1867 ***5704.8*** *p221*
McGarvey, Mary; Philadelphia, 1868 ***5704.8*** *p230*
McGarvey, Mary; Quebec, 1852 ***5704.8*** *p94*
McGarvey, Mary 25; Philadelphia, 1859 ***5704.8*** *p141*
McGarvey, Mathew 6; Philadelphia, 1870 ***5704.8*** *p238*
McGarvey, Mathew 15; Philadelphia, 1859 ***5704.8*** *p142*
McGarvey, Michael 28; Philadelphia, 1857 ***5704.8*** *p133*
McGarvey, Nancy; Philadelphia, 1867 ***5704.8*** *p223*
McGarvey, Nancy; St. John, N.B., 1852 ***5704.8*** *p94*
McGarvey, Nelly 16; Philadelphia, 1859 ***5704.8*** *p142*
McGarvey, Nelly 40; Philadelphia, 1859 ***5704.8*** *p141*
McGarvey, Patrick; America, 1864 ***5704.8*** *p188*
McGarvey, Patrick 5; Philadelphia, 1859 ***5704.8*** *p142*
McGarvey, Rebecca; Philadelphia, 1866 ***5704.8*** *p206*
McGarvey, Rose 19; Quebec, 1853 ***5704.8*** *p105*
McGarvey, Rosy 7; Philadelphia, 1859 ***5704.8*** *p142*
McGarvey, Sarah 17; Philadelphia, 1859 ***5704.8*** *p142*
McGarvey, Susan 13; Philadelphia, 1859 ***5704.8*** *p142*
McGarvey, Susan 20; Philadelphia, 1860 ***5704.8*** *p146*
McGarvey, Susanna; Philadelphia, 1849 ***53.26*** *p61*
McGarvey, Susanna; Philadelphia, 1849 ***5704.8*** *p54*
McGarvey, Thomas; Philadelphia, 1853 ***5704.8*** *p101*
McGarvey, Thomas; Philadelphia, 1867 ***5704.8*** *p217*
McGarvey, Thomas 12; Philadelphia, 1859 ***5704.8*** *p142*
McGarvey, William; New York, NY, 1869 ***5704.8*** *p235*
McGarvey, William; Philadelphia, 1847 ***53.26*** *p61*
*Relative:*Elizabeth
McGarvey, William; Philadelphia, 1847 ***5704.8*** *p1*
McGarvey, William; Philadelphia, 1851 ***5704.8*** *p79*
McGarvey, William; Philadelphia, 1852 ***5704.8*** *p87*
McGarvey, Wm.; California, 1863 ***3840.2*** *p18*
McGarvy, Daniel; Montreal, 1825 ***7603*** *p61*
McGarvy, Patrick; Montreal, 1823 ***7603*** *p61*
McGaughem, Mary; St. John, N.B., 1848 ***5704.8*** *p38*
McGaughey, Elizabeth 24; Philadelphia, 1864 ***5704.8*** *p157*
McGaughey, Jane 19; Quebec, 1856 ***5704.8*** *p129*
McGaughey, Martha; Quebec, 1856 ***5704.8*** *p129*
McGaughey, Rebecca 17; Quebec, 1856 ***5704.8*** *p129*
McGaughy, Mary; Philadelphia, 1852 ***5704.8*** *p92*
McGaughy, Sarah; Philadelphia, 1852 ***5704.8*** *p92*
McGaughy, William; Philadelphia, 1852 ***5704.8*** *p92*
McGauran, Thomas; New York, NY, 1837 ***8208.4*** *p47*
McGaven, Bridget; Quebec, 1847 ***5704.8*** *p17*
McGaven, Catherine 4; Quebec, 1847 ***5704.8*** *p17*
McGaven, Cicily; Quebec, 1847 ***5704.8*** *p17*
McGaven, Lawrance; Quebec, 1847 ***5704.8*** *p17*
McGaven, Mary 9 mos; Quebec, 1847 ***5704.8*** *p17*
McGaven, Mary 28; Massachusetts, 1849 ***5881.1*** *p72*
McGavine, Mary 13; Massachusetts, 1850 ***5881.1*** *p73*
McGaw, Eliza Jane; New York, NY, 1864 ***5704.8*** *p187*
McGaw, Ellen 30; Massachusetts, 1849 ***5881.1*** *p66*
McGaw, John A.; America, 1857 ***1450.2*** *p96A*
McGaw, Michael 2; Massachusetts, 1849 ***5881.1*** *p72*
McGaw, Samuel; Brunswick, NC, 1739 ***1639.20*** *p154*
McGeachy, Alexander; America, 1783-1844 ***1639.20*** *p154*
McGeady, Ann 22; Philadelphia, 1864 ***5704.8*** *p155*
McGeady, Bell; Philadelphia, 1851 ***5704.8*** *p70*
McGeady, Fanny *SEE* McGeady, Hugh
McGeady, Fanny; Philadelphia, 1847 ***5704.8*** *p2*
McGeady, Hugh; Philadelphia, 1847 ***53.26*** *p61*
*Relative:*Fanny
*Relative:*William 10
McGeady, Hugh; Philadelphia, 1847 ***5704.8*** *p2*
McGeady, Jermiah; St. John, N.B., 1847 ***5704.8*** *p20*
McGeady, John; Philadelphia, 1851 ***5704.8*** *p70*
McGeady, John 16; Philadelphia, 1856 ***5704.8*** *p128*
McGeady, Margaret; Quebec, 1849 ***5704.8*** *p52*
McGeady, William; Philadelphia, 1851 ***5704.8*** *p70*
McGeady, William 10 *SEE* McGeady, Hugh
McGeady, William 10; Philadelphia, 1847 ***5704.8*** *p2*
McGeag, Mary; St. John, N.B., 1847 ***5704.8*** *p10*
McGee, Ann; Quebec, 1823 ***7603*** *p96*
McGee, Ann 20; Quebec, 1857 ***5704.8*** *p135*
McGee, Ann Jane 25; Quebec, 1853 ***5704.8*** *p105*
McGee, Anne 20; Philadelphia, 1868 ***5704.8*** *p225*
McGee, Arthur; Montreal, 1823 ***7603*** *p54*
McGee, Bernard; St. John, N.B., 1847 ***5704.8*** *p33*
McGee, Betsey; St. John, N.B., 1850 ***5704.8*** *p61*
McGee, Cicily; Philadelphia, 1852 ***5704.8*** *p89*
McGee, Eustache; Quebec, 1781 ***7603*** *p39*
McGee, Fanny; Philadelphia, 1852 ***5704.8*** *p85*
McGee, Fanny 24; Philadelphia, 1854 ***5704.8*** *p117*
McGee, Giles 22; Philadelphia, 1855 ***5704.8*** *p123*
McGee, Hanna; St. John, N.B., 1849 ***5704.8*** *p56*
McGee, Hannah; St. John, N.B., 1852 ***5704.8*** *p83*
McGee, Henry; St. John, N.B., 1853 ***5704.8*** *p107*
McGee, Hugh; Austin, TX, 1886 ***9777*** *p5*
McGee, Hugh; St. John, N.B., 1853 ***5704.8*** *p107*
McGee, James; St. John, N.B., 1853 ***5704.8*** *p107*
McGee, James 4; Quebec, 1864 ***5704.8*** *p163*
McGee, James 22; Philadelphia, 1854 ***5704.8*** *p118*
McGee, Jane 2; Quebec, 1864 ***5704.8*** *p163*
McGee, John; St. John, N.B., 1847 ***5704.8*** *p35*
McGee, John 15; America, 1705 ***2212*** *p44*
McGee, John 19; Philadelphia, 1854 ***5704.8*** *p118*
McGee, Margaret; Philadelphia, 1854 ***5704.8*** *p116*
McGee, Margaret; Quebec, 1851 ***5704.8*** *p74*
McGee, Margery; Quebec, 1849 ***5704.8*** *p57*
McGee, Mary; St. John, N.B., 1851 ***5704.8*** *p77*
McGee, Matilda 3; Quebec, 1853 ***5704.8*** *p105*
McGee, Michael; St. John, N.B., 1853 ***5704.8*** *p99*
McGee, Neal 5; Quebec, 1851 ***5704.8*** *p74*
McGee, Neal 20; Philadelphia, 1855 ***5704.8*** *p123*
McGee, Patrick 18; Philadelphia, 1854 ***5704.8*** *p123*
McGee, Patrick 30; Massachusetts, 1849 ***5881.1*** *p74*
McGee, Robert 9 mos; St. John, N.B., 1850 ***5704.8*** *p61*
McGee, Robert 22; Quebec, 1857 ***5704.8*** *p135*
McGee, Sarah; Philadelphia, 1852 ***5704.8*** *p96*
McGee, Susan 24; Quebec, 1864 ***5704.8*** *p163*
McGee, Thomas 30; Quebec, 1864 ***5704.8*** *p163*
McGee, William; Massachusetts, 1849 ***5881.1*** *p77*
McGee, William; Quebec, 1851 ***5704.8*** *p73*
McGee, William 2; St. John, N.B., 1850 ***5704.8*** *p61*
McGeeghan, Annie 1; St. John, N.B., 1853 ***5704.8*** *p109*
McGeeghan, George 10; St. John, N.B., 1853 ***5704.8*** *p109*
McGeeghan, Harriet 7; St. John, N.B., 1853 ***5704.8*** *p109*
McGeeghan, James; Philadelphia, 1849 ***53.26*** *p61*
McGeeghan, James; Philadelphia, 1849 ***5704.8*** *p54*
McGeeghan, John 12; St. John, N.B., 1853 ***5704.8*** *p109*
McGeeghan, Martha 3; St. John, N.B., 1853 ***5704.8*** *p109*
McGeeghan, Mary 44; St. John, N.B., 1853 ***5704.8*** *p109*
McGeeghan, Rebecca 13; St. John, N.B., 1853 ***5704.8*** *p109*
McGeeghan, Robert; St. John, N.B., 1849 ***5704.8*** *p56*
McGeehan, Biddy 21; Philadelphia, 1864 ***5704.8*** *p160*
McGeehan, Biddy 40; Quebec, 1856 ***5704.8*** *p130*
McGeehan, Hannah 20; Quebec, 1856 ***5704.8*** *p130*
McGeehan, Margaret; Philadelphia, 1867 ***5704.8*** *p221*
McGeehan, Sally 3; Philadelphia, 1864 ***5704.8*** *p160*
McGeevan, Hugh 4; Philadelphia, 1853 ***5704.8*** *p108*
McGeevan, James 8; Philadelphia, 1853 ***5704.8*** *p108*
McGeevan, Sarah 6; Philadelphia, 1853 ***5704.8*** *p108*
McGeever, Hugh 45; Philadelphia, 1853 ***5704.8*** *p109*
McGeever, Susan 19; Philadelphia, 1853 ***5704.8*** *p108*
McGeffert, John; New York, NY, 1833 ***8208.4*** *p80*
McGeighan, Dennis; Philadelphia, 1849 ***53.26*** *p61*
McGeighan, Dennis; Philadelphia, 1849 ***5704.8*** *p54*
McGellaghan, Patrick; Philadelphia, 1811 ***53.26*** *p61*
McGennis, Bernard 20; Massachusetts, 1849 ***5881.1*** *p63*
McGennis, Cornelius 20; Massachusetts, 1849 ***5881.1*** *p64*
McGeogan, Catherine; St. John, N.B., 1847 ***5704.8*** *p10*
McGeogan, James; St. John, N.B., 1847 ***5704.8*** *p10*
McGeogan, John; Philadelphia, 1853 ***5704.8*** *p101*
McGeogh, Anne; Philadelphia, 1864 ***5704.8*** *p183*
McGeogh, John; America, 1742 ***4971*** *p76*
McGeogh, Patrick; Philadelphia, 1864 ***5704.8*** *p183*
McGeoghagan, Nelly; St. John, N.B., 1847 ***5704.8*** *p9*
McGeoghan, Margaret; Philadelphia, 1852 ***5704.8*** *p89*
McGeoghan, Mary; Philadelphia, 1847 ***53.26*** *p61*
McGeoghan, Mary; Philadelphia, 1847 ***5704.8*** *p5*
McGeoghegan, Mary; St. John, N.B., 1851 ***5704.8*** *p72*
McGeoghigan, Bryan; St. John, N.B., 1853 ***5704.8*** *p106*
McGeoghigan, Edward; St. John, N.B., 1853 ***5704.8*** *p107*
McGeoghigan, Elleanor; Philadelphia, 1852 ***5704.8*** *p97*
McGeoghigan, Mary; St. John, N.B., 1853 ***5704.8*** *p107*
McGeown, John; New Jersey, 1892 ***5240.1*** *p28*
McGerrigan, Hugh; Philadelphia, 1848 ***53.26*** *p61*
McGerrigan, Hugh; Philadelphia, 1848 ***5704.8*** *p46*
McGerrigle, Ann 18; Philadelphia, 1859 ***5704.8*** *p142*
McGerrigle, Bridget; New Orleans, 1849 ***5704.8*** *p59*
McGerrigle, James; New Orleans, 1849 ***5704.8*** *p59*
McGerrigle, James 3; New Orleans, 1849 ***5704.8*** *p59*
McGerrigle, Phillip 3 mos; New Orleans, 1849 ***5704.8*** *p59*
McGetigan, Elleanor; Philadelphia, 1847 ***5704.8*** *p22*
McGettigan, Ann; Philadelphia, 1864 ***5704.8*** *p176*
McGettigan, Ann; Philadelphia, 1866 ***5704.8*** *p203*
McGettigan, Anne; America, 1869 ***5704.8*** *p236*
McGettigan, Bernard; St. John, N.B., 1847 ***5704.8*** *p33*
McGettigan, Bernard 20; Philadelphia, 1860 ***5704.8*** *p145*
McGettigan, Biddy; Philadelphia, 1853 ***5704.8*** *p100*
McGettigan, Biddy; Philadelphia, 1867 ***5704.8*** *p219*
McGettigan, Bridget; New York, NY, 1865 ***5704.8*** *p203*
McGettigan, Bridget; Philadelphia, 1865 ***5704.8*** *p198*
McGettigan, Bridget; Philadelphia, 1865 ***5704.8*** *p204*
McGettigan, Catherine; Philadelphia, 1853 ***5704.8*** *p101*
McGettigan, Elleanor *SEE* McGettigan, Grace
McGettigan, Ellen; Philadelphia, 1867 ***5704.8*** *p221*
McGettigan, Ellen; Philadelphia, 1868 ***5704.8*** *p226*
McGettigan, Francis 3; Philadelphia, 1867 ***5704.8*** *p221*
McGettigan, Grace; Philadelphia, 1847 ***53.26*** *p61*
*Relative:*Elleanor
McGettigan, Grace; Philadelphia, 1847 ***5704.8*** *p22*
McGettigan, Grant; New York, NY, 1866 ***5704.8*** *p207*
McGettigan, Hannah 20; Philadelphia, 1854 ***5704.8*** *p120*
McGettigan, Hugh; New York, NY, 1864 ***5704.8*** *p171*
McGettigan, Hugh; New York, NY, 1866 ***5704.8*** *p209*
McGettigan, Hugh; Philadelphia, 1853 ***5704.8*** *p100*
McGettigan, James; Philadelphia, 1852 ***5704.8*** *p88*
McGettigan, James 4 mos; Philadelphia, 1867 ***5704.8*** *p221*
McGettigan, Madge; Philadelphia, 1864 ***5704.8*** *p177*
McGettigan, Patrick; New York, NY, 1864 ***5704.8*** *p171*
McGettigan, Patrick; New York, NY, 1864 ***5704.8*** *p185*
McGettigan, Ralp 20; Philadelphia, 1854 ***5704.8*** *p117*
McGettigan, Robert; Philadelphia, 1849 ***53.26*** *p61*
McGettigan, Robert; Philadelphia, 1849 ***5704.8*** *p54*
McGettigan, Sally 12; Philadelphia, 1853 ***5704.8*** *p112*
McGettigan, William 2; Philadelphia, 1867 ***5704.8*** *p221*
McGever, Patrick 50; Philadelphia, 1853 ***5704.8*** *p113*
McGhee, Catharine; America, 1866 ***5704.8*** *p211*
McGhee, Dennis 5; Philadelphia, 1853 ***5704.8*** *p109*
McGhee, Hannah 28; Philadelphia, 1853 ***5704.8*** *p109*
McGhee, John; St. John, N.B., 1850 ***5704.8*** *p65*
McGhee, Margaret 20; Philadelphia, 1853 ***5704.8*** *p111*
McGhee, Mary; Philadelphia, 1847 ***53.26*** *p61*
McGhee, Mary; Philadelphia, 1847 ***5704.8*** *p23*
McGhee, Patrick 7; Philadelphia, 1853 ***5704.8*** *p109*
McGhee, Robert 19; Philadelphia, 1853 ***5704.8*** *p109*
McGhee, Roseanna; St. John, N.B., 1850 ***5704.8*** *p65*
McGhee, Samuel 60; Quebec, 1864 ***5704.8*** *p162*
McGhee, Sarah 18; Quebec, 1857 ***5704.8*** *p136*
McGhee, Thomas; Quebec, 1851 ***5704.8*** *p75*
McGheeghan, James; Philadelphia, 1847 ***53.26*** *p61*
McGheeghan, James; Philadelphia, 1847 ***5704.8*** *p32*
McGheeghan, John; Quebec, 1849 ***5704.8*** *p52*
McGhie, Daniel 15; Philadelphia, 1774 ***1219.7*** *p216*
McGhin, Biddy; Philadelphia, 1852 ***5704.8*** *p96*
McGibbon, Hugh; South Carolina, 1767 ***1639.20*** *p154*
McGibbon, Robert 17; Jamaica, 1753 ***1219.7*** *p22*
McGibbon, Robert 17; Jamaica, 1753 ***3690.1*** *p153*
McGilaway, Magy; St. John, N.B., 1847 ***5704.8*** *p33*
McGilbray, Daniel; America, 1803 ***1639.20*** *p155*
McGilbray, Daniel; America, 1805 ***1639.20*** *p155*
McGilbray, Donald; America, 1803 ***1639.20*** *p154*
McGilbray, James; America, 1803 ***1639.20*** *p155*
McGilbray, Malcolm; America, 1803 ***1639.20*** *p155*
McGilchrist, Malcolm; North Carolina, 1771 ***1639.20*** *p155*
McGilchrist, William; South Carolina, 1741 ***1639.20*** *p155*
McGilcuddy, Catharine 20; Massachusetts, 1849 ***5881.1*** *p64*
McGildowney, Thomas 19; Quebec, 1858 ***5704.8*** *p137*
McGilery, Charles; St. John, N.B., 1851 ***5704.8*** *p78*
McGill, A. C. 49; South Carolina, 1850 ***1639.20*** *p155*
McGill, Andrew 25; Virginia, 1774 ***1219.7*** *p225*
McGill, Angus; North Carolina, 1749-1827 ***1639.20*** *p155*
McGill, Archibald; North Carolina, 1739 ***1639.20*** *p155*
McGill, Archibald 34 *SEE* McGill, Effie
McGill, Bernard; New York, NY, 1834 ***8208.4*** *p9*
McGill, Bridget; Quebec, 1847 ***5704.8*** *p28*
McGill, Catharine; New York, NY, 1870 ***5704.8*** *p237*
McGill, Daniel 20 *SEE* McGill, Isabel
McGill, Daniel 50 *SEE* McGill, Effie
McGill, Donald; America, 1804 ***1639.20*** *p156*
McGill, Duncan 30 *SEE* McGill, Isabel
McGill, Effie 79; North Carolina, 1850 ***1639.20*** *p156*
*Relative:*Daniel 50
*Relative:*Archibald 34
McGill, Eliza; St. John, N.B., 1851 ***5704.8*** *p72*
McGill, Elizabeth; Quebec, 1847 ***5704.8*** *p28*
McGill, Ester 10; Quebec, 1847 ***5704.8*** *p28*
McGill, Flora 65; North Carolina, 1850 ***1639.20*** *p156*
McGill, Garrett 36; Massachusetts, 1849 ***5881.1*** *p67*
McGill, Henry; St. John, N.B., 1852 ***5704.8*** *p93*
McGill, Henry 12; Quebec, 1847 ***5704.8*** *p28*

McGill, Isabel 60; North Carolina, 1850 ***1639.20*** *p156*
*Relative:*Duncan 30
*Relative:*Daniel 20
McGill, James; Montreal, 1792 ***9775.5*** *p202*
McGill, John; St. John, N.B., 1853 ***5704.8*** *p107*
McGill, John 29; Philadelphia, 1774 ***1219.7*** *p185*
McGill, John 57; Arizona, 1890 ***2764.35*** *p48*
McGill, John 65; North Carolina, 1850 ***1639.20*** *p156*
*Relative:*Mary 50
McGill, Malcolm; North Carolina, 1771 ***1639.20*** *p156*
McGill, Mary 21; Philadelphia, 1864 ***5704.8*** *p161*
McGill, Mary 50 *SEE* McGill, John
McGill, Mary 89; North Carolina, 1850 ***1639.20*** *p156*
McGill, Mary Jane; Quebec, 1847 ***5704.8*** *p28*
McGill, Neill; Brunswick, NC, 1739 ***1639.20*** *p156*
McGill, Roger; Montreal, 1823 ***7603*** *p54*
McGill, Samuel; Ohio, 1840 ***9892.11*** *p33*
McGill, Samuel; Ohio, 1843 ***9892.11*** *p33*
McGill, Sarah; Quebec, 1847 ***5704.8*** *p28*
McGill, Thomas 23; Kansas, 1871 ***5240.1*** *p51*
McGill, William; Quebec, 1847 ***5704.8*** *p28*
McGill, William J. 45; Arizona, 1890 ***2764.35*** *p49*
McGillan, Eliza; Philadelphia, 1864 ***5704.8*** *p184*
McGillan, Mary; Philadelphia, 1852 ***5704.8*** *p96*
McGillaway, Elizabeth; Philadelphia, 1866 ***5704.8*** *p215*
McGillaway, George; Philadelphia, 1866 ***5704.8*** *p215*
McGillaway, Sallie; Philadelphia, 1866 ***5704.8*** *p215*
McGillcally, Dennis 21; Massachusetts, 1847 ***5881.1*** *p65*
McGillcally, Joanna 14; Massachusetts, 1847 ***5881.1*** *p67*
McGillcally, John 50; Massachusetts, 1847 ***5881.1*** *p67*
McGilleally, Catharine 17; Massachusetts, 1847 ***5881.1*** *p64*
McGillen, Ann; Philadelphia, 1853 ***5704.8*** *p103*
McGillen, Bell 46; St. John, N.B., 1853 ***5704.8*** *p109*
McGillen, Elizabeth 5; Philadelphia, 1864 ***5704.8*** *p178*
McGillen, James; Quebec, 1852 ***5704.8*** *p89*
McGillen, James 3; Philadelphia, 1864 ***5704.8*** *p178*
McGillen, John; Quebec, 1852 ***5704.8*** *p89*
McGillen, Mary; Quebec, 1852 ***5704.8*** *p89*
McGillen, Patrick 20; St. John, N.B., 1853 ***5704.8*** *p109*
McGillen, Sarah A. 15; Philadelphia, 1864 ***5704.8*** *p178*
McGillen, Sarah Jane; Quebec, 1852 ***5704.8*** *p89*
McGilley, Ellen 14; Quebec, 1856 ***5704.8*** *p129*
McGillian, . . . 4; New York, NY, 1865 ***5704.8*** *p203*
McGillian, . . . 6; New York, NY, 1865 ***5704.8*** *p203*
McGillian, . . . 8; New York, NY, 1865 ***5704.8*** *p203*
McGillian, Barney; New York, NY, 1865 ***5704.8*** *p193*
McGillian, Barney 16; Philadelphia, 1864 ***5704.8*** *p157*
McGillian, Catharine; New York, NY, 1865 ***5704.8*** *p203*
McGillian, James; New York, NY, 1865 ***5704.8*** *p199*
McGillian, James 20; Philadelphia, 1864 ***5704.8*** *p157*
McGillian, Mary 18; Philadelphia, 1864 ***5704.8*** *p157*
McGillian, Michael 18; Philadelphia, 1864 ***5704.8*** *p157*
McGilligan, John 19; Philadelphia, 1855 ***5704.8*** *p124*
McGillin, John 24; Philadelphia, 1864 ***5704.8*** *p161*
McGillion, John; St. John, N.B., 1848 ***5704.8*** *p45*
McGillioray, Walter 26; Kansas, 1872 ***5240.1*** *p53*
McGillis, John; Quebec, 1815 ***7603*** *p37*
McGilliveray, Donald; South Carolina, 1716 ***1639.20*** *p157*
McGillivray, Fergus; South Carolina, 1716 ***1639.20*** *p157*
McGillivray, James; South Carolina, 1716 ***1639.20*** *p157*
McGillivray, John; South Carolina, 1716 ***1639.20*** *p157*
McGillivray, Loughlan; South Carolina, 1716 ***1639.20*** *p157*
McGillivray, Owen; South Carolina, 1716 ***1639.20*** *p157*
McGillivray, William; Canada, 1784-1789 ***9775.5*** *p199*
McGilloway, John 20; Philadelphia, 1859 ***5704.8*** *p142*
McGillway, James 21; Philadelphia, 1859 ***5704.8*** *p141*
McGilp, Sarah; Cape Fear, NC, 1805 ***1639.20*** *p203*
McGilray, Jane 47; North Carolina, 1850 ***1639.20*** *p158*
McGilray, Mary 48; North Carolina, 1850 ***1639.20*** *p158*
McGilroy, Angus 87; North Carolina, 1850 ***1639.20*** *p157*
McGilroy, Archibald 87; North Carolina, 1850 ***1639.20*** *p157*
McGilten, Adam; St. John, N.B., 1847 ***5704.8*** *p19*
McGilvay, Bernard; New York, NY, 1835 ***8208.4*** *p5*
McGilvery, A.; America, 1792 ***1639.20*** *p156*
McGilvery, Alexander; America, 1805 ***1639.20*** *p156*
McGilvray, Ann 76 *SEE* McGilvray, Daniel
McGilvray, Daniel 77; North Carolina, 1850 ***1639.20*** *p158*
*Relative:*Ann 76
McGimpsey, David 24; Kansas, 1884 ***5240.1*** *p65*
McGinchy, Hannah 18; Philadelphia, 1853 ***5704.8*** *p108*
McGinlan, James; St. John, N.B., 1847 ***5704.8*** *p21*
McGinlan, Ketty 13; St. John, N.B., 1847 ***5704.8*** *p21*
McGinlan, Mary; St. John, N.B., 1847 ***5704.8*** *p21*
McGinlay, James 19; Philadelphia, 1854 ***5704.8*** *p117*
McGinlay, Peter 20; Philadelphia, 1855 ***5704.8*** *p124*
McGinley, Alice; New York, NY, 1865 ***5704.8*** *p193*
McGinley, Andrew 11; St. John, N.B., 1850 ***5704.8*** *p61*
McGinley, Ann; Philadelphia, 1865 ***5704.8*** *p191*
McGinley, Ann; Philadelphia, 1865 ***5704.8*** *p197*
McGinley, Ann Jane 7; St. John, N.B., 1850 ***5704.8*** *p61*
McGinley, Anne; St. John, N.B., 1850 ***5704.8*** *p61*
McGinley, Bernard; New York, NY, 1864 ***5704.8*** *p181*
McGinley, Biddy 16; Philadelphia, 1865 ***5704.8*** *p164*
McGinley, Biddy 21; Philadelphia, 1864 ***5704.8*** *p155*
McGinley, Bridget; New York, NY, 1869 ***5704.8*** *p233*
McGinley, Bridget 5; New York, NY, 1865 ***5704.8*** *p191*
McGinley, Bridget 18; Philadelphia, 1864 ***5704.8*** *p161*
McGinley, Catharine; New York, NY, 1865 ***5704.8*** *p203*
McGinley, Catherine 11; St. John, N.B., 1862 ***5704.8*** *p150*
McGinley, Catherine 16; Philadelphia, 1859 ***5704.8*** *p142*
McGinley, Charles 8; Philadelphia, 1853 ***5704.8*** *p112*
McGinley, Charles 8; St. John, N.B., 1864 ***5704.8*** *p159*
McGinley, Charles 14; Philadelphia, 1854 ***5704.8*** *p118*
McGinley, Charles 48; St. John, N.B., 1864 ***5704.8*** *p159*
McGinley, Cornelius; Philadelphia, 1847 ***53.26*** *p61*
McGinley, Cornelius; Philadelphia, 1847 ***5704.8*** *p5*
McGinley, Daniel; St. John, N.B., 1847 ***5704.8*** *p18*
McGinley, David 16; Quebec, 1853 ***5704.8*** *p105*
McGinley, Dennis; New York, NY, 1868 ***5704.8*** *p228*
McGinley, Dennis 21; Philadelphia, 1854 ***5704.8*** *p116*
McGinley, Edward; Philadelphia, 1864 ***5704.8*** *p178*
McGinley, Ellen 10; St. John, N.B., 1864 ***5704.8*** *p159*
McGinley, Ellen 50; Philadelphia, 1865 ***5704.8*** *p164*
McGinley, Fanny 22; Philadelphia, 1859 ***5704.8*** *p142*
McGinley, George 13; St. John, N.B., 1850 ***5704.8*** *p61*
McGinley, Grace; Philadelphia, 1847 ***53.26*** *p61*
McGinley, Grace; Philadelphia, 1847 ***5704.8*** *p5*
McGinley, Hannah; New York, NY, 1865 ***5704.8*** *p194*
McGinley, Hannah; Philadelphia, 1866 ***5704.8*** *p210*
McGinley, Hannah; Philadelphia, 1868 ***5704.8*** *p224*
McGinley, Hannah 20; Philadelphia, 1859 ***5704.8*** *p143*
McGinley, Hugh 8; Philadelphia, 1853 ***5704.8*** *p112*
McGinley, James; Philadelphia, 1847 ***53.26*** *p61*
McGinley, James; Philadelphia, 1847 ***5704.8*** *p22*
McGinley, Jane; New York, NY, 1864 ***5704.8*** *p176*
McGinley, John; America, 1867 ***5704.8*** *p216*
McGinley, John; America, 1890 ***1450.2*** *p96A*
McGinley, John; New York, NY, 1864 ***5704.8*** *p186*
McGinley, John; Philadelphia, 1865 ***5704.8*** *p189*
McGinley, John 7; New York, NY, 1865 ***5704.8*** *p191*
McGinley, John 9; St. John, N.B., 1850 ***5704.8*** *p61*
McGinley, John 20; Philadelphia, 1861 ***5704.8*** *p148*
McGinley, Magy; Philadelphia, 1852 ***5704.8*** *p96*
McGinley, Margaret; New York, NY, 1865 ***5704.8*** *p191*
McGinley, Margaret 3; St. John, N.B., 1850 ***5704.8*** *p61*
McGinley, Martha 2; St. John, N.B., 1850 ***5704.8*** *p61*
McGinley, Mary; New York, NY, 1864 ***5704.8*** *p176*
McGinley, Mary; New York, NY, 1869 ***5704.8*** *p233*
McGinley, Mary; Philadelphia, 1854 ***5704.8*** *p117*
McGinley, Mary; Philadelphia, 1864 ***5704.8*** *p185*
McGinley, Mary; Philadelphia, 1868 ***5704.8*** *p226*
McGinley, Mary 15; St. John, N.B., 1862 ***5704.8*** *p150*
McGinley, Mary 18; Philadelphia, 1858 ***5704.8*** *p138*
McGinley, Mary 20; Philadelphia, 1865 ***5704.8*** *p164*
McGinley, Mary 50; Philadelphia, 1853 ***5704.8*** *p112*
McGinley, Mary Ann; Philadelphia, 1849 ***5704.8*** *p49*
McGinley, Michael; Philadelphia, 1867 ***5704.8*** *p218*
McGinley, Michael 16; Philadelphia, 1854 ***5704.8*** *p117*
McGinley, Mickey; Philadelphia, 1848 ***53.26*** *p61*
McGinley, Mickey; Philadelphia, 1848 ***5704.8*** *p45*
McGinley, Minnie 3; New York, NY, 1865 ***5704.8*** *p191*
McGinley, Nancy; New York, NY, 1867 ***5704.8*** *p218*
McGinley, Patrick; America, 1865 ***5704.8*** *p192*
McGinley, Patrick; Montreal, 1819 ***7603*** *p84*
McGinley, Patrick; Philadelphia, 1864 ***5704.8*** *p182*
McGinley, Patrick; Philadelphia, 1867 ***5704.8*** *p218*
McGinley, Patrick 22; Philadelphia, 1865 ***5704.8*** *p164*
McGinley, Rosey; Philadelphia, 1868 ***5704.8*** *p223*
McGinley, Sarah; Philadelphia, 1853 ***5704.8*** *p102*
McGinley, Sarah; Philadelphia, 1864 ***5704.8*** *p181*
McGinley, Sarah 5; St. John, N.B., 1850 ***5704.8*** *p61*
McGinley, Sarah 20; Philadelphia, 1865 ***5704.8*** *p164*
McGinley, Sophia; Philadelphia, 1852 ***5704.8*** *p96*
McGinley, Susan 19; Philadelphia, 1859 ***5704.8*** *p142*
McGinley, William; Philadelphia, 1852 ***5704.8*** *p85*
McGinley, William; Quebec, 1851 ***5704.8*** *p75*
McGinley, William; St. John, N.B., 1850 ***5704.8*** *p61*
McGinly, Hugh 28; St. John, N.B., 1854 ***5704.8*** *p114*
McGinly, Rose 22; Philadelphia, 1855 ***5704.8*** *p123*
McGinn, Ann; Philadelphia, 1864 ***5704.8*** *p176*
McGinn, Annie; New York, NY, 1865 ***5704.8*** *p193*
McGinn, Bernard; St. John, N.B., 1847 ***5704.8*** *p21*
McGinn, Biddy; St. John, N.B., 1847 ***5704.8*** *p35*
McGinn, Charles 9; Quebec, 1851 ***5704.8*** *p74*
McGinn, Edward; Quebec, 1851 ***5704.8*** *p74*
McGinn, Eliz 48; Kansas, 1872 ***5240.1*** *p52*
McGinn, Francis; St. John, N.B., 1848 ***5704.8*** *p45*
McGinn, James; Illinois, 1860 ***7857*** *p5*
McGinn, James; St. John, N.B., 1847 ***5704.8*** *p35*
McGinn, John 13; Quebec, 1851 ***5704.8*** *p74*
McGinn, Nancy; Quebec, 1851 ***5704.8*** *p74*
McGinn, Owen; New York, NY, 1838 ***8208.4*** *p62*
McGinnes, John; Philadelphia, 1849 ***5704.8*** *p53*
McGinnes, Mary; Philadelphia, 1849 ***5704.8*** *p53*
McGinness, Alexander; Quebec, 1847 ***5704.8*** *p13*
McGinness, Alexander 6 mos; St. John, N.B., 1847 ***5704.8*** *p3*
McGinness, Ann; St. John, N.B., 1851 ***5704.8*** *p72*
McGinness, Ann 20; Philadelphia, 1853 ***5704.8*** *p108*
McGinness, Ann Jane 10; Quebec, 1847 ***5704.8*** *p13*
McGinness, Barny; St. John, N.B., 1847 ***5704.8*** *p15*
McGinness, Bernard; Philadelphia, 1851 ***5704.8*** *p76*
McGinness, Bridget; St. John, N.B., 1851 ***5704.8*** *p72*
McGinness, Bridget 20; St. John, N.B., 1856 ***5704.8*** *p131*
McGinness, Catherine; St. John, N.B., 1852 ***5704.8*** *p92*
McGinness, Catherine 4; St. John, N.B., 1847 ***5704.8*** *p3*
McGinness, Catherine 8; Quebec, 1847 ***5704.8*** *p13*
McGinness, Catherine 8; St. John, N.B., 1847 ***5704.8*** *p15*
McGinness, Charles; Quebec, 1849 ***5704.8*** *p52*
McGinness, Eleanor 18; Philadelphia, 1853 ***5704.8*** *p108*
McGinness, Elizabeth 12; Quebec, 1847 ***5704.8*** *p13*
McGinness, Ellen; New York, NY, 1867 ***5704.8*** *p219*
McGinness, Ellen; New York, NY, 1871 ***5704.8*** *p240*
McGinness, Ellen; Philadelphia, 1851 ***5704.8*** *p78*
McGinness, Fanny; Philadelphia, 1852 ***5704.8*** *p96*
McGinness, George 1; St. John, N.B., 1858 ***5704.8*** *p137*
McGinness, Hannah; Philadelphia, 1852 ***5704.8*** *p96*
McGinness, Hannah 9 mos; Philadelphia, 1852 ***5704.8*** *p96*
McGinness, Henry 21; St. John, N.B., 1858 ***5704.8*** *p137*
McGinness, Hugh 28; Philadelphia, 1855 ***5704.8*** *p124*
McGinness, James; New York, NY, 1836 ***8208.4*** *p20*
McGinness, James; New York, NY, 1865 ***5704.8*** *p195*
McGinness, James; St. John, N.B., 1847 ***5704.8*** *p3*
McGinness, James; St. John, N.B., 1847 ***5704.8*** *p15*
McGinness, James; St. John, N.B., 1847 ***5704.8*** *p21*
McGinness, James 7; St. John, N.B., 1858 ***5704.8*** *p137*
McGinness, James 21; Quebec, 1855 ***5704.8*** *p126*
McGinness, Jane; Quebec, 1847 ***5704.8*** *p13*
McGinness, Jane; Quebec, 1849 ***5704.8*** *p52*
McGinness, John; Philadelphia, 1848 ***53.26*** *p61*
McGinness, John; Philadelphia, 1848 ***5704.8*** *p45*
McGinness, John; Philadelphia, 1852 ***5704.8*** *p85*
McGinness, John; St. John, N.B., 1847 ***5704.8*** *p15*
McGinness, John 9; St. John, N.B., 1858 ***5704.8*** *p137*
McGinness, John 28; Philadelphia, 1855 ***5704.8*** *p123*
McGinness, Joseph; Quebec, 1847 ***5704.8*** *p13*
McGinness, Joseph 30; Philadelphia, 1864 ***5704.8*** *p161*
McGinness, Lucinda 6 mos; Quebec, 1847 ***5704.8*** *p13*
McGinness, Margaret; Philadelphia, 1851 ***5704.8*** *p76*
McGinness, Margaret; St. John, N.B., 1847 ***5704.8*** *p3*
McGinness, Margaret 2; St. John, N.B., 1847 ***5704.8*** *p3*
McGinness, Margaret 6; Quebec, 1847 ***5704.8*** *p13*
McGinness, Margaret 32; Philadelphia, 1864 ***5704.8*** *p161*
McGinness, Mary; Philadelphia, 1851 ***5704.8*** *p79*
McGinness, Mary; Quebec, 1847 ***5704.8*** *p13*
McGinness, Mary; St. John, N.B., 1847 ***5704.8*** *p2*
McGinness, Mary 30; St. John, N.B., 1858 ***5704.8*** *p137*
McGinness, Mary Ann 6; St. John, N.B., 1847 ***5704.8*** *p3*
McGinness, Mary Ann 10; St. John, N.B., 1847 ***5704.8*** *p15*
McGinness, Michael 7; Philadelphia, 1852 ***5704.8*** *p96*
McGinness, Michael 45; St. John, N.B., 1858 ***5704.8*** *p137*
McGinness, Nancy; St. John, N.B., 1847 ***5704.8*** *p15*
McGinness, Patrick; New York, NY, 1837 ***8208.4*** *p54*
McGinness, Peter 5; Philadelphia, 1852 ***5704.8*** *p96*
McGinness, Rosan; St. John, N.B., 1848 ***5704.8*** *p39*
McGinness, Sarah; Philadelphia, 1851 ***5704.8*** *p81*
McGinness, Sarah 13; St. John, N.B., 1848 ***5704.8*** *p39*
McGinness, Thomas 9; St. John, N.B., 1847 ***5704.8*** *p3*
McGinness, William; Quebec, 1847 ***5704.8*** *p13*
McGinness, William; Quebec, 1850 ***5704.8*** *p66*
McGinney, Ann; Quebec, 1852 ***5704.8*** *p90*
McGinney, Catherine; Quebec, 1852 ***5704.8*** *p90*
McGinney, Mary; Quebec, 1852 ***5704.8*** *p90*
McGinnis, A.A.; New Mexico, 1887 ***2764.35*** *p49*
McGinnis, Abraham 40; California, 1872 ***2769.6*** *p6*
McGinnis, Andrew 18; Philadelphia, 1865 ***5704.8*** *p164*
McGinnis, Ann 18; Massachusetts, 1849 ***5881.1*** *p62*
McGinnis, Ann 19; Philadelphia, 1857 ***5704.8*** *p134*
McGinnis, Anne; Montreal, 1823 ***7603*** *p87*
McGinnis, Daniel; Montreal, 1805 ***7603*** *p68*
McGinnis, James; America, 1742 ***4971*** *p76*
McGinnis, John; Massachusetts, 1846 ***3840.2*** *p18*
McGinnis, John; Philadelphia, 1849 ***53.26*** *p61*
*Relative:*Mary
McGinnis, Joseph 87; Charleston, SC, 1850 ***1639.20*** *p158*
McGinnis, Mary *SEE* McGinnis, John

340
FOR A COMPLETE EXPLANATION OF ENTRY, SEE "HOW TO READ A CITATION" SECTION

McGinnis, Nancy; New York, NY, 1868 ***5704.8*** *p227*
McGinnis, Owen; Rochester, NY, 1835 ***1450.2*** *p97A*
McGinnis, Patrick 20; Philadelphia, 1857 ***5704.8*** *p133*
McGinnis, Pierre; Quebec, 1492-1825 ***7603*** *p37*
McGinnis, Rodger 26; St. John, N.B., 1859 ***5704.8*** *p140*
McGinnis, Unity 24; St. John, N.B., 1859 ***5704.8*** *p140*
McGinniss, Arthur 22; California, 1872 ***2769.7*** *p3*
McGinnus, Mary 18; Philadelphia, 1854 ***5704.8*** *p118*
McGintey, William; New York, NY, 1866 ***5704.8*** *p212*
McGinty, Ann 7; Philadelphia, 1849 ***5704.8*** *p53*
McGinty, Anne *SEE* McGinty, Patrick
McGinty, Anne; Philadelphia, 1849 ***5704.8*** *p53*
McGinty, Anne 7 *SEE* McGinty, Patrick
McGinty, Biddy 18; Quebec, 1856 ***5704.8*** *p130*
McGinty, Bridget 5; New York, NY, 1865 ***5704.8*** *p202*
McGinty, Bryan; New York, NY, 1869 ***5704.8*** *p234*
McGinty, Catharine; Philadelphia, 1864 ***5704.8*** *p179*
McGinty, Catherine 3 mos *SEE* McGinty, Patrick
McGinty, Catherine 3 mos; Philadelphia, 1849 ***5704.8*** *p53*
McGinty, Charles 13 *SEE* McGinty, Patrick
McGinty, Charles 13; Philadelphia, 1849 ***5704.8*** *p53*
McGinty, Charles 24; Quebec, 1856 ***5704.8*** *p130*
McGinty, Edward; St. John, N.B., 1852 ***5704.8*** *p95*
McGinty, Ellen; New York, NY, 1867 ***5704.8*** *p221*
McGinty, Fanny; Philadelphia, 1864 ***5704.8*** *p178*
McGinty, Giley; Quebec, 1852 ***5704.8*** *p86*
McGinty, Giley; Quebec, 1852 ***5704.8*** *p90*
McGinty, James 9 *SEE* McGinty, Patrick
McGinty, James 9; Philadelphia, 1849 ***5704.8*** *p53*
McGinty, John; Philadelphia, 1852 ***5704.8*** *p89*
McGinty, John 4 *SEE* McGinty, Patrick
McGinty, John 4; Philadelphia, 1849 ***5704.8*** *p53*
McGinty, John 22; St. John, N.B., 1854 ***5704.8*** *p122*
McGinty, Manus; Philadelphia, 1864 ***5704.8*** *p179*
McGinty, Manus 18; Philadelphia, 1856 ***5704.8*** *p128*
McGinty, Maria 25; Quebec, 1854 ***5704.8*** *p119*
McGinty, Mary; Philadelphia, 1864 ***5704.8*** *p177*
McGinty, Mary; Philadelphia, 1864 ***5704.8*** *p178*
McGinty, Mary; Philadelphia, 1864 ***5704.8*** *p179*
McGinty, Mary 6 *SEE* McGinty, Patrick
McGinty, Mary 6; Philadelphia, 1849 ***5704.8*** *p53*
McGinty, Michael; Philadelphia, 1864 ***5704.8*** *p177*
McGinty, Patrick; Philadelphia, 1849 ***53.26*** *p61*
*Relative:*Anne
*Relative:*Charles 13
*Relative:*Patrick 11
*Relative:*James 9
*Relative:*Anne 7
*Relative:*John 4
*Relative:*Mary 6
*Relative:*Catherine 3 mos
McGinty, Patrick; Philadelphia, 1849 ***5704.8*** *p53*
McGinty, Patrick 11 *SEE* McGinty, Patrick
McGinty, Patrick 11; Philadelphia, 1849 ***5704.8*** *p53*
McGinty, Patrick 18; Quebec, 1854 ***5704.8*** *p119*
McGinty, Peter 20; Philadelphia, 1856 ***5704.8*** *p128*
McGinty, Sarah 7; New York, NY, 1865 ***5704.8*** *p202*
McGinty, Susan; New York, NY, 1865 ***5704.8*** *p202*
McGirgan, Mary; Quebec, 1847 ***5704.8*** *p36*
McGirk, John; Philadelphia, 1847 ***53.26*** *p61*
McGirk, John; Philadelphia, 1847 ***5704.8*** *p1*
McGirk, Robert; Quebec, 1847 ***5704.8*** *p13*
McGirr, Ann; St. John, N.B., 1852 ***5704.8*** *p93*
McGirr, Bridget; St. John, N.B., 1852 ***5704.8*** *p93*
McGirr, James; Philadelphia, 1867 ***5704.8*** *p216*
McGirr, James; Quebec, 1847 ***5704.8*** *p38*
McGirr, James A. 5; Philadelphia, 1867 ***5704.8*** *p216*
McGirr, Mary; Philadelphia, 1867 ***5704.8*** *p216*
McGirr, Mary; St. John, N.B., 1847 ***5704.8*** *p24*
McGirr, Neely; America, 1737 ***4971*** *p74*
McGirr, Robert 9; Philadelphia, 1867 ***5704.8*** *p216*
McGirr, Rosanna; Philadelphia, 1851 ***5704.8*** *p76*
McGirr, Ruth 7; Philadelphia, 1867 ***5704.8*** *p216*
McGirr, Sarah; Quebec, 1849 ***5704.8*** *p51*
McGirr, Susan; Philadelphia, 1851 ***5704.8*** *p76*
McGirr, Thomas; Quebec, 1849 ***5704.8*** *p51*
McGirr, William G.; Philadelphia, 1867 ***5704.8*** *p216*
McGirvey, John; Philadelphia, 1853 ***5704.8*** *p100*
McGirvey, Patrick; St. John, N.B., 1847 ***5704.8*** *p9*
McGittigan, Neil; America, 1737 ***4971*** *p73*
McGiven, Hugh; New Jersey, 1828 ***8208.4*** *p26*
McGivern, Daniel; New York, NY, 1837 ***8208.4*** *p53*
McGivine, James 56; Massachusetts, 1849 ***5881.1*** *p68*
McGivine, Margaret 46; Massachusetts, 1849 ***5881.1*** *p71*
McGivney, Peter; New York, NY, 1838 ***8208.4*** *p89*
McGivney, Thomas Anthony; Arkansas, 1918 ***95.2*** *p82*
McGivney, William; New York, NY, 1839 ***8208.4*** *p102*
McGivrin, James; New York, NY, 1836 ***8208.4*** *p24*
McGlaghlin, Catherine 35; St. John, N.B., 1854 ***5704.8*** *p122*
McGlaghlin, Francis 16; St. John, N.B., 1854 ***5704.8*** *p122*
McGlaghlin, James 11; St. John, N.B., 1854 ***5704.8*** *p122*
McGlaghlin, William 18; St. John, N.B., 1854 ***5704.8*** *p122*
McGlaughlin, Bridget 35; Massachusetts, 1849 ***5881.1*** *p63*
McGlaughlin, Patrick 33; Massachusetts, 1849 ***5881.1*** *p74*
McGleich, George; Ohio, 1842 ***8365.25*** *p12*
McGlenaghan, James; Philadelphia, 1852 ***5704.8*** *p97*
McGlenn, Thomas; New York, NY, 1840 ***8208.4*** *p105*
McGlensay, Margaret; Philadelphia, 1847 ***53.26*** *p61*
McGlensay, Margaret; Philadelphia, 1847 ***5704.8*** *p14*
McGlensey, Catherine; Philadelphia, 1852 ***5704.8*** *p89*
McGlensey, Cecelia; Philadelphia, 1852 ***5704.8*** *p89*
McGlensey, Charles 22; Philadelphia, 1854 ***5704.8*** *p117*
McGlensey, Mary 17; Philadelphia, 1854 ***5704.8*** *p117*
McGlensey, Patrick; Quebec, 1848 ***5704.8*** *p42*
McGlensey, Sarah; Philadelphia, 1852 ***5704.8*** *p85*
McGlin, Bartly; Philadelphia, 1853 ***5704.8*** *p100*
McGlin, Hugh; Philadelphia, 1853 ***5704.8*** *p100*
McGlin, Margaret; New York, NY, 1868 ***5704.8*** *p227*
McGlin, Mary; New York, NY, 1868 ***5704.8*** *p227*
McGlincey, Hannah 12; St. John, N.B., 1848 ***5704.8*** *p44*
McGlincey, Nancy; St. John, N.B., 1848 ***5704.8*** *p44*
McGlinchey, Anne; New York, NY, 1867 ***5704.8*** *p216*
McGlinchey, Ellen; Philadelphia, 1864 ***5704.8*** *p179*
McGlinchey, James; Philadelphia, 1866 ***5704.8*** *p205*
McGlinchey, James 24; Philadelphia, 1864 ***5704.8*** *p157*
McGlinchey, Margaret; Philadelphia, 1865 ***5704.8*** *p200*
McGlinchey, Mary; New York, NY, 1870 ***5704.8*** *p240*
McGlinchey, Mary; Philadelphia, 1865 ***5704.8*** *p201*
McGlinchey, Peter; New York, NY, 1866 ***5704.8*** *p208*
McGlinchey, Thomas 18; Philadelphia, 1864 ***5704.8*** *p157*
McGlinchy, Anne 25; Philadelphia, 1861 ***5704.8*** *p148*
McGlinchy, Charles 25; Philadelphia, 1854 ***5704.8*** *p115*
McGlinchy, Daniel 19; Philadelphia, 1854 ***5704.8*** *p115*
McGlinchy, Elizabeth; St. John, N.B., 1850 ***5704.8*** *p62*
McGlinchy, Jane; St. John, N.B., 1847 ***5704.8*** *p14*
McGlinchy, John 3 mos; St. John, N.B., 1847 ***5704.8*** *p14*
McGlinchy, Margaret; Philadelphia, 1851 ***5704.8*** *p70*
McGlinchy, Mary Anne; St. John, N.B., 1847 ***5704.8*** *p2*
McGlinchy, Neal; America, 1864 ***5704.8*** *p183*
McGlinchy, Patrick; Philadelphia, 1852 ***5704.8*** *p91*
McGlinchy, Patrick; St. John, N.B., 1847 ***5704.8*** *p33*
McGlinchy, William; St. John, N.B., 1847 ***5704.8*** *p14*
McGlincy, Catherine 17; Philadelphia, 1853 ***5704.8*** *p111*
McGlincy, Edward 18; Philadelphia, 1853 ***5704.8*** *p111*
McGlincy, Hannah 16; Philadelphia, 1853 ***5704.8*** *p111*
McGlincy, Mary 16; Philadelphia, 1853 ***5704.8*** *p111*
McGlinn, Allice 22; Philadelphia, 1861 ***5704.8*** *p148*
McGlinn, Andrew; New York, NY, 1840 ***8208.4*** *p105*
McGlinn, Ann; Philadelphia, 1851 ***5704.8*** *p80*
McGlinn, Bryan; America, 1737 ***4971*** *p77*
McGlinn, Catherine; America, 1736 ***4971*** *p81*
McGlinn, Daniel; New York, NY, 1869 ***5704.8*** *p232*
McGlinn, Henry 23; Quebec, 1854 ***5704.8*** *p119*
McGlinn, Mary; New York, NY, 1870 ***5704.8*** *p237*
McGlinn, Neal; America, 1863-1871 ***5704.8*** *p199*
McGlinn, Patrick; America, 1735-1743 ***4971*** *p78*
McGlinn, Patrick; America, 1742 ***4971*** *p80*
McGlinn, Peter; Philadelphia, 1864 ***5704.8*** *p177*
McGlinn, Sarah 65; Philadelphia, 1861 ***5704.8*** *p148*
McGlinnen, Patrick; Quebec, 1824 ***7603*** *p95*
McGlinsey, Michael; Philadelphia, 1852 ***5704.8*** *p84*
McGlinshy, Catherine 20; St. John, N.B., 1857 ***5704.8*** *p136*
McGloin, Bridget; Philadelphia, 1851 ***5704.8*** *p71*
McGlone, Bridget *SEE* McGlone, John
McGlone, Bridget; Philadelphia, 1849 ***5704.8*** *p54*
McGlone, James *SEE* McGlone, John
McGlone, James; Philadelphia, 1849 ***5704.8*** *p54*
McGlone, John; Philadelphia, 1849 ***53.26*** *p61*
*Relative:*James
*Relative:*Bridget
McGlone, John; Philadelphia, 1849 ***5704.8*** *p54*
McGlone, Mary; Philadelphia, 1864 ***5704.8*** *p183*
McGlone, Michael 6 mos; Philadelphia, 1864 ***5704.8*** *p183*
McGlone, Thomas; New York, NY, 1837 ***8208.4*** *p54*
McGlooin, Ann; St. John, N.B., 1850 ***5704.8*** *p66*
McGlooin, Patrick; St. John, N.B., 1850 ***5704.8*** *p66*
McGloon, James; St. John, N.B., 1847 ***5704.8*** *p33*
McGlosky, John; America, 1742 ***4971*** *p76*
McGloughlin, Nelly 30 *SEE* McGloughlin, Owen
McGloughlin, Owen 29; Philadelphia, 1804 ***53.26*** *p62*
*Relative:*Nelly 30
With child 5
McGlyn, Ann 50; St. John, N.B., 1860 ***5704.8*** *p143*
McGlyn, Ann 56; St. John, N.B., 1865 ***5704.8*** *p165*
McGlyn, John; New York, NY, 1838 ***8208.4*** *p65*
McGlynn, Bartholomew; California, 1859 ***2764.35*** *p48*
McGlynn, Fanny; America, 1865 ***5704.8*** *p196*
McGlynn, John; Philadelphia, 1847 ***53.26*** *p62*
McGlynn, John; Philadelphia, 1847 ***5704.8*** *p31*
McGlynn, Margaret; America, 1841 ***7036*** *p126*
McGoh, Bridget 18; Massachusetts, 1850 ***5881.1*** *p63*
McGoldrick, Anne; St. John, N.B., 1848 ***5704.8*** *p39*
McGoldrick, Bridget; Philadelphia, 1867 ***5704.8*** *p219*
McGoldrick, Bridget; St. John, N.B., 1853 ***5704.8*** *p106*
McGoldrick, Edward 26; St. John, N.B., 1864 ***5704.8*** *p159*
McGoldrick, Ellen 18; St. John, N.B., 1863 ***5704.8*** *p155*
McGoldrick, Ellen 50; St. John, N.B., 1863 ***5704.8*** *p155*
McGoldrick, Hannah; Philadelphia, 1864 ***5704.8*** *p180*
McGoldrick, Isabella; Quebec, 1825 ***7603*** *p69*
McGoldrick, John; Philadelphia, 1864 ***5704.8*** *p180*
McGoldrick, John 11; St. John, N.B., 1863 ***5704.8*** *p155*
McGoldrick, John 15; St. John, N.B., 1853 ***5704.8*** *p110*
McGoldrick, Margaret; Philadelphia, 1864 ***5704.8*** *p176*
McGoldrick, Mary; New York, NY, 1865 ***5704.8*** *p195*
McGoldrick, Mary 30; St. John, N.B., 1863 ***5704.8*** *p155*
McGoldrick, Mary A.; Philadelphia, 1864 ***5704.8*** *p180*
McGoldrick, Patrick 21; St. John, N.B., 1863 ***5704.8*** *p155*
McGoldrick, Sarah; Philadelphia, 1864 ***5704.8*** *p173*
McGoldrick, Thomas; St. John, N.B., 1848 ***5704.8*** *p39*
McGoldrick, Thomas 60; St. John, N.B., 1863 ***5704.8*** *p155*
McGoldrick, Unity; Philadelphia, 1864 ***5704.8*** *p184*
McGoldrick, William 22; Quebec, 1857 ***5704.8*** *p136*
McGolrick, Ann 8; St. John, N.B., 1847 ***5704.8*** *p3*
McGolrick, Felix 3; St. John, N.B., 1849 ***5704.8*** *p56*
McGolrick, James 5; St. John, N.B., 1849 ***5704.8*** *p56*
McGolrick, Jane 10; Philadelphia, 1858 ***5704.8*** *p139*
McGolrick, John; Philadelphia, 1853 ***5704.8*** *p103*
McGolrick, Margaret; St. John, N.B., 1847 ***5704.8*** *p3*
McGolrick, Mary; Quebec, 1847 ***5704.8*** *p6*
McGolrick, Patrick; Quebec, 1847 ***5704.8*** *p6*
McGolrick, Rose 6; St. John, N.B., 1847 ***5704.8*** *p3*
McGomery, Mary 17; Philadelphia, 1804 ***53.26*** *p62*
McGonagall, James 36; Philadelphia, 1803 ***53.26*** *p62*
McGonagle, Catharine; New York, NY, 1868 ***5704.8*** *p229*
McGonagle, Daniel; Philadelphia, 1864 ***5704.8*** *p184*
McGonagle, Edward; St. John, N.B., 1847 ***5704.8*** *p11*
McGonagle, Ellen 12; St. John, N.B., 1849 ***5704.8*** *p55*
McGonagle, Eugene; St. John, N.B., 1852 ***5704.8*** *p84*
McGonagle, John 11; St. John, N.B., 1849 ***5704.8*** *p55*
McGonagle, Mary; New York, NY, 1868 ***5704.8*** *p229*
McGonagle, Mary; Philadelphia, 1864 ***5704.8*** *p178*
McGonagle, Mary; Philadelphia, 1864 ***5704.8*** *p186*
McGonagle, Mary 14; Philadelphia, 1861 ***5704.8*** *p149*
McGonagle, Mary A. 2; America, 1868 ***5704.8*** *p231*
McGonagle, Peggy; St. John, N.B., 1849 ***5704.8*** *p55*
McGonagle, William; America, 1865 ***5704.8*** *p197*
McGonegal, Mary 26; St. John, N.B., 1863 ***5704.8*** *p153*
McGonegall, James 25; Philadelphia, 1803 ***53.26*** *p62*
McGonegle, Bridget; Philadelphia, 1850 ***53.26*** *p62*
*Relative:*Peggy 8
*Relative:*Edward 4
McGonegle, Bridget; Philadelphia, 1850 ***5704.8*** *p60*
McGonegle, Charles; Philadelphia, 1850 ***53.26*** *p62*
McGonegle, Charles; Philadelphia, 1850 ***5704.8*** *p68*
McGonegle, Edward 4 *SEE* McGonegle, Bridget
McGonegle, Edward 4; Philadelphia, 1850 ***5704.8*** *p60*
McGonegle, Jane; St. John, N.B., 1850 ***5704.8*** *p65*
McGonegle, Peggy 8 *SEE* McGonegle, Bridget
McGonegle, Peggy 8; Philadelphia, 1850 ***5704.8*** *p60*
McGonegle, Phil; St. John, N.B., 1847 ***5704.8*** *p25*
McGongle, Owen; St. John, N.B., 1853 ***5704.8*** *p106*
McGonigal, John; America, 1737 ***4971*** *p77*
McGonigle, . . . 23; St. John, N.B., 1856 ***5704.8*** *p131*
McGonigle, Alexander; Philadelphia, 1852 ***5704.8*** *p88*
McGonigle, Alexander 24; St. John, N.B., 1863 ***5704.8*** *p155*
McGonigle, Ann; St. John, N.B., 1853 ***5704.8*** *p107*
McGonigle, Ann 18; Philadelphia, 1857 ***5704.8*** *p133*
McGonigle, Barny 10; St. John, N.B., 1851 ***5704.8*** *p71*
McGonigle, Betty 5; St. John, N.B., 1847 ***5704.8*** *p9*
McGonigle, Biddy; St. John, N.B., 1847 ***5704.8*** *p4*
McGonigle, Biddy; St. John, N.B., 1852 ***5704.8*** *p95*
McGonigle, Biddy 6; St. John, N.B., 1851 ***5704.8*** *p71*
McGonigle, Bridget; St. John, N.B., 1847 ***5704.8*** *p9*
McGonigle, Catherine 3; St. John, N.B., 1847 ***5704.8*** *p9*
McGonigle, Catherine 20; Philadelphia, 1860 ***5704.8*** *p145*
McGonigle, Daniel; Philadelphia, 1849 ***53.26*** *p62*
McGonigle, Daniel; Philadelphia, 1849 ***5704.8*** *p50*
McGonigle, Dennis; Philadelphia, 1848 ***53.26*** *p62*
McGonigle, Dennis; Philadelphia, 1848 ***5704.8*** *p46*
McGonigle, Eliza 23; Philadelphia, 1864 ***5704.8*** *p160*
McGonigle, Elizabeth; Philadelphia, 1852 ***5704.8*** *p88*
McGonigle, Elizabeth 20; Philadelphia, 1854 ***5704.8*** *p118*

McGonigle, Elleanor 7; St. John, N.B., 1847 5704.8 p9
McGonigle, George; Quebec, 1822 7603 p71
McGonigle, George; St. John, N.B., 1852 5704.8 p93
McGonigle, Hugh; Philadelphia, 1852 5704.8 p88
McGonigle, James 3; Philadelphia, 1861 5704.8 p147
McGonigle, Jane; Philadelphia, 1852 5704.8 p88
McGonigle, John 3 *SEE* McGonigle, Margaret
McGonigle, John 7; Philadelphia, 1861 5704.8 p147
McGonigle, John 24; St. John, N.B., 1853 5704.8 p110
McGonigle, John 36; St. John, N.B., 1866 5704.8 p166
McGonigle, Margaret 3 mos; Philadelphia, 1861 5704.8 p147
McGonigle, Margaret 5; Philadelphia, 1834 53.26 p62
*Relative:*John 3
McGonigle, Margaret 18; Philadelphia, 1864 5704.8 p156
McGonigle, Margaret 20; Philadelphia, 1864 5704.8 p160
McGonigle, Martha 4; Philadelphia, 1861 5704.8 p147
McGonigle, Mary; Philadelphia, 1851 5704.8 p81
McGonigle, Mary 9 mos; St. John, N.B., 1847 5704.8 p9
McGonigle, Mary 8; Philadelphia, 1852 5704.8 p88
McGonigle, Mary 20; Philadelphia, 1854 5704.8 p116
McGonigle, Mary Jane 2; Philadelphia, 1861 5704.8 p147
McGonigle, Matilda 25; Philadelphia, 1861 5704.8 p147
McGonigle, Michael; St. John, N.B., 1853 5704.8 p107
McGonigle, Neal; St. John, N.B., 1847 5704.8 p5
McGonigle, Neal; St. John, N.B., 1847 5704.8 p9
McGonigle, Neal; St. John, N.B., 1847 5704.8 p25
McGonigle, Owen; St. John, N.B., 1847 5704.8 p4
McGonigle, Patrick 27; Philadelphia, 1853 5704.8 p108
McGonigle, Robert 30; Philadelphia, 1864 5704.8 p161
McGonigle, Rose 16; St. John, N.B., 1854 5704.8 p114
McGonigle, Rose 18; Quebec, 1855 5704.8 p126
McGonigle, Sally 8; St. John, N.B., 1851 5704.8 p71
McGonigle, Shane; St. John, N.B., 1847 5704.8 p9
McGonigle, William; St. John, N.B., 1853 5704.8 p106
McGonigle, William 22; Philadelphia, 1860 5704.8 p144
McGonigle, William 30; Philadelphia, 1861 5704.8 p147
McGonley, Mathew 25; Massachusetts, 1849 5881.1 p72
McGonnigle, Daniel 21; Philadelphia, 1854 5704.8 p123
McGoogan, Daniel; America, 1804 1639.20 p158
McGoogan, Daniel 72; North Carolina, 1850 1639.20 p158
*Relative:*Mary 65
McGoogan, Duncan 51; North Carolina, 1850 1639.20 p158
McGoogan, Mary 65 *SEE* McGoogan, Daniel
McGoolan, Thomas 12; Massachusetts, 1850 5881.1 p76
McGoory, John; Philadelphia, 1866 5704.8 p205
McGordlick, Catherine 11; Quebec, 1847 5704.8 p7
McGordlick, Daniel; Quebec, 1847 5704.8 p7
McGordlick, Edward; St. John, N.B., 1848 5704.8 p39
McGordlick, Hugh 9; Quebec, 1847 5704.8 p7
McGordlick, James 7; Quebec, 1847 5704.8 p7
McGordlick, John; Quebec, 1847 5704.8 p7
McGordlick, Margaret Ann; Quebec, 1847 5704.8 p7
McGordlick, Mary; Quebec, 1847 5704.8 p7
McGordlick, Mary; St. John, N.B., 1848 5704.8 p39
McGordlick, Patrick 13; Quebec, 1847 5704.8 p7
McGordlick, Thomas 5; Quebec, 1847 5704.8 p7
McGorlick, Judy 60; Massachusetts, 1848 5881.1 p68
McGorm, Terence; Quebec, 1820 7603 p82
McGorman, Catherine 4; Quebec, 1847 5704.8 p6
McGorman, Elizabeth 7; Quebec, 1847 5704.8 p6
McGorman, Henry; Quebec, 1847 5704.8 p6
McGorman, Isabella; Quebec, 1847 5704.8 p6
McGorman, John; Philadelphia, 1850 53.26 p62
McGorman, John; Philadelphia, 1850 5704.8 p68
McGorman, Margaret; America, 1869 5704.8 p235
McGorman, Pat; St. John, N.B., 1850 5704.8 p62
McGorman, Samuel; Quebec, 1847 5704.8 p6
McGorman, Sarah 9; Quebec, 1847 5704.8 p6
McGorman, William; Quebec, 1847 5704.8 p6
McGorory, Bridget; America, 1864 5704.8 p184
McGorory, James; America, 1864 5704.8 p184
McGorrin, Stanislaus Andrew; Arkansas, 1918 95.2 p82
McGorry, Margaret; St. John, N.B., 1848 5704.8 p39
McGorry, Michael; St. John, N.B., 1848 5704.8 p39
McGoserry, Patrick; New York, NY, 1864 5704.8 p180
McGotegan, Unity; Philadelphia, 1851 5704.8 p81
McGougan, Malcolm; San Francisco, 1850 4914.15 p10
McGougan, Malcolm; San Francisco, 1850 4914.15 p13
McGough, Samuel; Philadelphia, 1849 5704.8 p54
McGoughey, James; St. John, N.B., 1849 5704.8 p55
McGourey, . . . 20; St. John, N.B., 1857 5704.8 p135
McGourk, Francis; America, 1738 4971 p73
McGourk, Hugh; America, 1738 4971 p73
McGourk, James; America, 1738 4971 p73
McGouskin, John 27; St. John, N.B., 1857 5704.8 p135
McGovan, Thomas 11; Massachusetts, 1849 5881.1 p76
McGovern, Anthony; Philadelphia, 1867 5704.8 p219
McGovern, Bernard; New York, NY, 1840 8208.4 p109
McGovern, Catherine; New York, NY, 1864 5704.8 p173
McGovern, Charles; Ohio, 1848 9892.11 p33
McGovern, Ellen; America, 1870 5704.8 p237
McGovern, Hugh; New York, NY, 1864 5704.8 p173
McGovern, Hugh 21; Massachusetts, 1848 5881.1 p67
McGovern, Mathew; Quebec, 1822 7603 p70
McGovern, Matthew; Ohio, 1812-1840 9892.11 p33
McGovern, Matthew; Ohio, 1848 9892.11 p33
McGovern, Michael; New York, NY, 1839 8208.4 p102
McGovern, Patrick; Philadelphia, 1864 5704.8 p174
McGovern, Patrick; Virginia, 1855 4626.16 p15
McGovern, Susan 30; Massachusetts, 1850 5881.1 p76
McGovern, Thomas; America, 1866 5704.8 p210
McGovern, Thomas; New York, NY, 1838 8208.4 p73
McGowan, Affie; America, 1866 5704.8 p208
McGowan, Andrew; North Carolina, 1811 1639.20 p158
McGowan, Andy 9 mos; Philadelphia, 1850 5704.8 p69
McGowan, Ann; Quebec, 1847 5704.8 p29
McGowan, Ann; St. John, N.B., 1847 5704.8 p4
McGowan, Ann 10; St. John, N.B., 1847 5704.8 p4
McGowan, Ann 23; St. John, N.B., 1854 5704.8 p120
McGowan, Anne; New York, NY, 1864 5704.8 p173
McGowan, Bartly; Quebec, 1847 5704.8 p29
McGowan, Biddy; St. John, N.B., 1847 5704.8 p4
McGowan, Biddy 6; Philadelphia, 1850 5704.8 p69
McGowan, Biddy 6; St. John, N.B., 1847 5704.8 p19
McGowan, Bridget 20; St. John, N.B., 1853 5704.8 p110
McGowan, Catharine; Philadelphia, 1866 5704.8 p212
McGowan, Catherine; New York, NY, 1864 5704.8 p176
McGowan, Catherine; Philadelphia, 1850 5704.8 p69
McGowan, Catherine; St. John, N.B., 1847 5704.8 p35
McGowan, Catherine 18; St. John, N.B., 1855 5704.8 p127
McGowan, Catherine 20; St. John, N.B., 1862 5704.8 p151
McGowan, Daniel; St. John, N.B., 1847 5704.8 p20
McGowan, Daniel 10; St. John, N.B., 1855 5704.8 p127
McGowan, Daniel 30; St. John, N.B., 1865 5704.8 p165
McGowan, Edward; New York, NY, 1864 5704.8 p173
McGowan, Edward; New York, NY, 1865 5704.8 p193
McGowan, Eliza 2; New Orleans, 1849 5704.8 p59
McGowan, Elizabeth 19; St. John, N.B., 1862 5704.8 p151
McGowan, Ellen; St. John, N.B., 1847 5704.8 p4
McGowan, Francis 2; Quebec, 1848 5704.8 p42
McGowan, George; Quebec, 1848 5704.8 p42
McGowan, George 3 mos; Quebec, 1848 5704.8 p42
McGowan, George 6 mos; New Orleans, 1849 5704.8 p59
McGowan, Gracey; St. John, N.B., 1847 5704.8 p19
McGowan, Hugh 20; St. John, N.B., 1861 5704.8 p149
McGowan, Hugh 56; St. John, N.B., 1855 5704.8 p127
McGowan, Isabella; America, 1868 5704.8 p231
McGowan, James; New York, NY, 1864 5704.8 p176
McGowan, James; New York, NY, 1865 5704.8 p197
McGowan, James; Philadelphia, 1851 5704.8 p76
McGowan, James; St. John, N.B., 1847 5704.8 p4
McGowan, James; St. John, N.B., 1853 5704.8 p109
McGowan, James 45; St. John, N.B., 1853 5704.8 p110
McGowan, Jno; Ohio, 1840 9892.11 p33
McGowan, John; America, 1866 5704.8 p209
McGowan, John; New Orleans, 1849 5704.8 p59
McGowan, John; St. John, N.B., 1847 5704.8 p4
McGowan, John 6; Philadelphia, 1851 5704.8 p81
McGowan, Johny 3; St. John, N.B., 1847 5704.8 p19
McGowan, Letitia; New York, NY, 1864 5704.8 p175
McGowan, Manasses 24; Philadelphia, 1859 5704.8 p142
McGowan, Margaret; New York, NY, 1866 5704.8 p212
McGowan, Margaret; Quebec, 1848 5704.8 p42
McGowan, Margaret; St. John, N.B., 1847 5704.8 p4
McGowan, Margaret; St. John, N.B., 1847 5704.8 p11
McGowan, Margaret; St. John, N.B., 1847 5704.8 p19
McGowan, Margaret 6; St. John, N.B., 1847 5704.8 p4
McGowan, Mary; Philadelphia, 1851 5704.8 p81
McGowan, Mary; Quebec, 1847 5704.8 p29
McGowan, Mary; St. John, N.B., 1847 5704.8 p4
McGowan, Mary 9 mos; Philadelphia, 1850 5704.8 p69
McGowan, Mary 4; Quebec, 1848 5704.8 p42
McGowan, Mary 7; St. John, N.B., 1849 5704.8 p56
McGowan, Mary 11; St. John, N.B., 1855 5704.8 p127
McGowan, Mary 30; Massachusetts, 1850 5881.1 p73
McGowan, Mary 35; St. John, N.B., 1855 5704.8 p127
McGowan, Michael; America, 1864 5704.8 p177
McGowan, Michael; New York, NY, 1864 5704.8 p173
McGowan, Michael 40; St. John, N.B., 1854 5704.8 p120
McGowan, Nancy; Philadelphia, 1850 53.26 p62
McGowan, Nancy; Philadelphia, 1850 5704.8 p68
McGowan, Neal; St. John, N.B., 1852 5704.8 p84
McGowan, Own 50; Philadelphia, 1859 5704.8 p141
McGowan, Pat 4; Philadelphia, 1850 5704.8 p69
McGowan, Patrick; Quebec, 1847 5704.8 p29
McGowan, Patrick; Quebec, 1851 5704.8 p75
McGowan, Patrick; St. John, N.B., 1847 5704.8 p19
McGowan, Patrick 8; St. John, N.B., 1847 5704.8 p4
McGowan, Patrick 40; St. John, N.B., 1853 5704.8 p109
McGowan, Peter 18; Philadelphia, 1861 5704.8 p148
McGowan, Philip; Philadelphia, 1811 53.26 p62
McGowan, Robert 20; Philadelphia, 1860 5704.8 p144
McGowan, Rose; America, 1866 5704.8 p209
McGowan, Rose 6 mos; St. John, N.B., 1855 5704.8 p127
McGowan, Rose 18; Philadelphia, 1856 5704.8 p129
McGowan, Sally; New Orleans, 1849 5704.8 p59
McGowan, Sarah; America, 1869 5704.8 p233
McGowan, Sarah; Quebec, 1852 5704.8 p89
McGowan, Sarah Ann; Philadelphia, 1864 5704.8 p187
McGowan, Teddy 3; St. John, N.B., 1855 5704.8 p127
McGowan, Terence 7; St. John, N.B., 1855 5704.8 p127
McGowan, Thomas; Philadelphia, 1867 5704.8 p215
McGowan, Thomas 12; St. John, N.B., 1849 5704.8 p56
McGowan, Timothy; New York, NY, 1836 8208.4 p13
McGowan, William; New York, NY, 1864 5704.8 p170
McGowan, William; Philadelphia, 1850 5704.8 p69
McGowan, William; St. John, N.B., 1850 5704.8 p65
McGowan, William 20; Philadelphia, 1859 5704.8 p142
McGowan, William 35; Philadelphia, 1804 53.26 p62
McGowen, Alice 20; Massachusetts, 1849 5881.1 p62
McGowen, Ellen 20; Massachusetts, 1849 5881.1 p66
McGowen, James; Philadelphia, 1853 5704.8 p103
McGowen, Jane; Philadelphia, 1853 5704.8 p103
McGowen, John; New York, NY, 1828 8208.4 p55
McGowen, John 20; Massachusetts, 1847 5881.1 p67
McGowen, Margaret; Quebec, 1825 7603 p68
McGowen, Patrick; Illinois, 1866 7857 p5
McGown, Ann; Quebec, 1823 7603 p96
McGowran, John; America, 1743 4971 p25
McGra, Dennis; Ohio, 1843 8365.26 p12
McGrah, Roger; Illinois, 1860 5012.39 p90
McGranagan, James 30; Massachusetts, 1848 5881.1 p68
McGranaghan, Charles; Philadelphia, 1847 53.26 p62
McGranaghan, Charles; Philadelphia, 1847 5704.8 p5
McGranaghan, Daniel 3; St. John, N.B., 1848 5704.8 p47
McGranaghan, John 6; St. John, N.B., 1848 5704.8 p47
McGranaghan, Mary; St. John, N.B., 1847 5704.8 p26
McGranaghan, Mary Ann 9 mos; St. John, N.B., 1848 5704.8 p47
McGranaghan, Patrick; Philadelphia, 1847 5704.8 p5
McGranaghan, Rose 15; Philadelphia, 1857 5704.8 p132
McGranaghan, Susan; St. John, N.B., 1848 5704.8 p47
McGranahan, Bridget; Philadelphia, 1866 5704.8 p207
McGranahan, Margaret; Philadelphia, 1866 5704.8 p207
McGranahan, Margaret; St. John, N.B., 1853 5704.8 p99
McGranahan, Patrick; Philadelphia, 1847 53.26 p62
McGranahan, Patrick; St. John, N.B., 1847 5704.8 p25
McGrane, Peter; Illinois, 1858 5012.39 p54
McGrath, Ann 1; Massachusetts, 1848 5881.1 p62
McGrath, Ann 21; Philadelphia, 1858 5704.8 p139
McGrath, Bridget; New York, NY, 1869 5704.8 p231
McGrath, Bridget; Philadelphia, 1865 5704.8 p200
McGrath, Bridget; Quebec, 1847 5704.8 p17
McGrath, Bridget 22; Massachusetts, 1849 5881.1 p63
McGrath, Bridget 28; Philadelphia, 1854 5704.8 p117
McGrath, Catharine; America, 1866 5704.8 p212
McGrath, Catharine; New York, NY, 1866 5704.8 p214
McGrath, Catherine; St. John, N.B., 1848 5704.8 p44
McGrath, Catherine 24; Philadelphia, 1854 5704.8 p120
McGrath, Cicily; New York, NY, 1864 5704.8 p185
McGrath, Daniel; New York, NY, 1840 8208.4 p108
McGrath, Dennis 50; Massachusetts, 1849 5881.1 p65
McGrath, Edward; New Brunswick, 1821 7603 p77
McGrath, Eleanor; Quebec, 1849 5704.8 p57
McGrath, Elizabeth; Quebec, 1850 5704.8 p63
McGrath, Ellan 3 mos; Quebec, 1847 5704.8 p17
McGrath, Ellen; New York, NY, 1865 5704.8 p194
McGrath, Ellen 16; Massachusetts, 1847 5881.1 p65
McGrath, Eugene; New York, NY, 1838 8208.4 p84
McGrath, Honor; Carolina, 1767 1639.20 p158
McGrath, Hugh; New York, NY, 1869 5704.8 p231
McGrath, James *SEE* McGrath, Thomas
McGrath, James; New York, NY, 1866 5704.8 p213
McGrath, James; Quebec, 1847 5704.8 p17
McGrath, James 24; Massachusetts, 1849 5881.1 p68
McGrath, James 27; St. John, N.B., 1856 5704.8 p131
McGrath, Jane 17; Philadelphia, 1860 5704.8 p145
McGrath, John; New York, NY, 1832 8208.4 p30
McGrath, John; New York, NY, 1836 8208.4 p9
McGrath, John; New York, NY, 1869 5704.8 p231
McGrath, John 10; Massachusetts, 1850 5881.1 p69
McGrath, John 11; New York, NY, 1866 5704.8 p214
McGrath, John 21; St. John, N.B., 1859 5704.8 p140
McGrath, John 25; Massachusetts, 1850 5881.1 p69
McGrath, John 26; Massachusetts, 1849 5881.1 p68

McGrath, Margaret *SEE* McGrath, Thomas
McGrath, Margaret; St. John, N.B., 1848 ***5704.8*** *p47*
McGrath, Margaret 22; Massachusetts, 1849 ***5881.1*** *p71*
McGrath, Mary; America, 1742 ***4971*** *p83*
McGrath, Mary; St. John, N.B., 1853 ***5704.8*** *p99*
McGrath, Mary 18; Massachusetts, 1849 ***5881.1*** *p72*
McGrath, Mary 35; Massachusetts, 1849 ***5881.1*** *p72*
McGrath, Michael; New York, NY, 1834 ***8208.4*** *p28*
McGrath, Michael; Quebec, 1820 ***7603*** *p98*
McGrath, Michael 22; Massachusetts, 1849 ***5881.1*** *p71*
McGrath, Michael 24; Massachusetts, 1850 ***5881.1*** *p73*
McGrath, Rosey; St. John, N.B., 1847 ***5704.8*** *p25*
McGrath, Rosie; New York, NY, 1867 ***5704.8*** *p216*
McGrath, Thomas; America, 1742 ***4971*** *p83*
McGrath, Thomas; Philadelphia, 1811 ***53.26*** *p62*
*Relative:*Margaret
*Relative:*James
McGrath, Thomas 60; Arizona, 1922 ***9228.40*** *p26*
McGrath, Tim Frank 30; Arkansas, 1918 ***95.2*** *p82*
McGravey, Eleanor; St. John, N.B., 1848 ***5704.8*** *p47*
McGraw, Daniel; America, 1849 ***1450.2*** *p97A*
McGraw, James; Quebec, 1788 ***7603*** *p102*
McGraw, John; Philadelphia, 1850 ***53.26*** *p62*
McGraw, John; Philadelphia, 1850 ***5704.8*** *p69*
McGraw, Margaret; Montreal, 1825 ***7603*** *p87*
McGraw, Mary Ann; St. John, N.B., 1847 ***5704.8*** *p5*
McGrawh, Daniel; Illinois, 1872 ***7857*** *p5*
McGrean, Mary 23; Philadelphia, 1861 ***5704.8*** *p147*
McGrearty, Patrick 25; St. John, N.B., 1854 ***5704.8*** *p115*
McGreary, Jane 7; Massachusetts, 1850 ***5881.1*** *p70*
McGreary, Margaret 9; Massachusetts, 1850 ***5881.1*** *p73*
McGreary, Michael 5; Massachusetts, 1850 ***5881.1*** *p73*
McGreen, Madeleine; Quebec, 1825 ***7603*** *p77*
McGreenary, Margaret; New York, NY, 1867 ***5704.8*** *p219*
McGreenary, Mary; New York, NY, 1867 ***5704.8*** *p219*
McGreenery, Daniel; New York, NY, 1865 ***5704.8*** *p191*
McGreenery, Neil; New York, NY, 1865 ***5704.8*** *p191*
McGreery, Ann 16; Philadelphia, 1854 ***5704.8*** *p116*
McGreevy, Teigue; America, 1735-1743 ***4971*** *p79*
McGregor, Mr.; Quebec, 1815 ***9229.18*** *p75*
McGregor, Alexander; Charleston, SC, 1827 ***1639.20*** *p159*
McGregor, Alexander; North Carolina, 1793 ***1639.20*** *p87*
McGregor, Ann 28; St. John, N.B., 1867 ***5704.8*** *p168*
McGregor, Archibald; America, 1804 ***1639.20*** *p159*
McGregor, Archibald 70; North Carolina, 1850 ***1639.20*** *p159*
*Relative:*Effie 65
*Relative:*Flora 40
McGregor, Duncan; South Carolina, 1716 ***1639.20*** *p159*
McGregor, Effie 65 *SEE* McGregor, Archibald
McGregor, Eliza; Philadelphia, 1866 ***5704.8*** *p214*
McGregor, Flora 40 *SEE* McGregor, Archibald
McGregor, James; New York, NY, 1837 ***8208.4*** *p54*
McGregor, James; Nova Scotia, 1786 ***9775.5*** *p208*
McGregor, James; Philadelphia, 1853 ***5704.8*** *p103*
McGregor, James 27; St. John, N.B., 1867 ***5704.8*** *p167*
McGregor, Jane; Philadelphia, 1851 ***5704.8*** *p80*
McGregor, John; Quebec, 1847 ***5704.8*** *p29*
McGregor, John; Texas, 1836 ***9777*** *p4*
McGregor, John 1; St. John, N.B., 1867 ***5704.8*** *p168*
McGregor, Malcolm; Charleston, SC, 1793 ***1639.20*** *p159*
McGregor, Malcolm; South Carolina, 1716 ***1639.20*** *p159*
McGregor, Malcolm 58; North Carolina, 1850 ***1639.20*** *p159*
McGregor, Neil; Charleston, SC, 1813 ***1639.20*** *p159*
McGregor, Richard; Washington, D.C., 1866 ***2764.35*** *p50*
McGregor, Rosina 3; St. John, N.B., 1867 ***5704.8*** *p168*
McGregor, William; Havana, 1766 ***1219.7*** *p117*
McGregor, William 25; St. John, N.B., 1862 ***5704.8*** *p150*
McGrenan, John 18; Philadelphia, 1803 ***53.26*** *p62*
McGrener, John 33; Philadelphia, 1859 ***5704.8*** *p143*
McGrener, Susanna 30; Philadelphia, 1859 ***5704.8*** *p143*
McGrenery, Ellen; America, 1866 ***5704.8*** *p208*
McGrenery, Hannah; America, 1866 ***5704.8*** *p208*
McGrenery, Hugh; Philadelphia, 1866 ***5704.8*** *p208*
McGrenery, Patrick; America, 1866 ***5704.8*** *p208*
McGrenor, John 50; Philadelphia, 1853 ***5704.8*** *p111*
McGrillis, Mary; Quebec, 1852 ***5704.8*** *p94*
McGrillis, Rose; Quebec, 1852 ***5704.8*** *p94*
McGrinder, James; Philadelphia, 1853 ***5704.8*** *p100*
McGrinder, James; St. John, N.B., 1847 ***5704.8*** *p11*
McGrinder, Joseph; Philadelphia, 1853 ***5704.8*** *p100*
McGroarty, John; New York, NY, 1840 ***8208.4*** *p105*
McGroarty, Mary; Philadelphia, 1853 ***5704.8*** *p101*
McGroarty, Neal; New York, 1868 ***1450.2*** *p25B*
McGroarty, Patrick; New York, NY, 1866 ***5704.8*** *p211*
McGroly, Nicholas 23; Massachusetts, 1849 ***5881.1*** *p73*
McGrong, John 18; Massachusetts, 1849 ***5881.1*** *p68*
McGrooey, Fanny; St. John, N.B., 1850 ***5704.8*** *p67*
McGrorey, Mary; Philadelphia, 1852 ***5704.8*** *p89*
McGrorty, Ann; America, 1867 ***5704.8*** *p219*
McGrorty, Bridget; Philadelphia, 1864 ***5704.8*** *p179*
McGrorty, Catherine; St. John, N.B., 1847 ***5704.8*** *p33*
McGrorty, Daniel; Philadelphia, 1847 ***53.26*** *p62*
McGrorty, Daniel; Philadelphia, 1847 ***5704.8*** *p5*
McGrorty, Dennis 3; St. John, N.B., 1847 ***5704.8*** *p33*
McGrorty, Ellen 20; Philadelphia, 1857 ***5704.8*** *p133*
McGrorty, Francis; Philadelphia, 1853 ***5704.8*** *p101*
McGrorty, James; St. John, N.B., 1847 ***5704.8*** *p14*
McGrorty, Mary; America, 1864 ***5704.8*** *p185*
McGrorty, Mary; Philadelphia, 1865 ***5704.8*** *p197*
McGrorty, Michael; St. John, N.B., 1847 ***5704.8*** *p33*
McGrorty, Nancy; Philadelphia, 1864 ***5704.8*** *p174*
McGrorty, Patrick 12; St. John, N.B., 1847 ***5704.8*** *p33*
McGrorty, Rose Ann; Philadelphia, 1868 ***5704.8*** *p230*
McGrory, Ann; Philadelphia, 1849 ***53.26*** *p62*
McGrory, Ann; Philadelphia, 1849 ***5704.8*** *p53*
McGrory, Biddy 50; Philadelphia, 1860 ***5704.8*** *p144*
McGrory, Bridget; St. John, N.B., 1851 ***5704.8*** *p80*
McGrory, Charles; Philadelphia, 1851 ***5704.8*** *p70*
McGrory, Edward; St. John, N.B., 1848 ***5704.8*** *p47*
McGrory, Edward 26; Philadelphia, 1860 ***5704.8*** *p144*
McGrory, Grace; St. John, N.B., 1851 ***5704.8*** *p80*
McGrory, James; Philadelphia, 1852 ***5704.8*** *p89*
McGrory, James; Quebec, 1853 ***5704.8*** *p104*
McGrory, John 20; Philadelphia, 1857 ***5704.8*** *p132*
McGrory, Mary; St. John, N.B., 1847 ***5704.8*** *p5*
McGrory, Patrick 30; Philadelphia, 1858 ***5704.8*** *p139*
McGrotty, Biddy 28; Quebec, 1863 ***5704.8*** *p153*
McGrotty, John; Philadelphia, 1849 ***53.26*** *p62*
McGrotty, John; Philadelphia, 1849 ***5704.8*** *p58*
McGrotty, Mary Jane 20; St. John, N.B., 1861 ***5704.8*** *p149*
McGroud, Ann 11; St. John, N.B., 1849 ***5704.8*** *p56*
McGroud, Ellan; St. John, N.B., 1849 ***5704.8*** *p56*
McGroud, Mary 9; St. John, N.B., 1849 ***5704.8*** *p56*
McGroud, William; St. John, N.B., 1849 ***5704.8*** *p56*
McGrough, Michael 30; Massachusetts, 1849 ***5881.1*** *p71*
McGrovery, Patrick; New York, NY, 1866 ***5704.8*** *p208*
McGrudden, Thomas; Philadelphia, 1851 ***5704.8*** *p81*
McGrury, Catherine; Philadelphia, 1853 ***5704.8*** *p100*
McGrury, Joan; Philadelphia, 1853 ***5704.8*** *p100*
McGuckian, Rose; America, 1865 ***5704.8*** *p200*
McGuggan, Duncan; America, 1801 ***1639.20*** *p159*
McGuggan, John 67; South Carolina, 1850 ***1639.20*** *p160*
*Relative:*Mary 55
McGuggan, Mary 55 *SEE* McGuggan, John
McGuigan, Anne; Philadelphia, 1864 ***5704.8*** *p183*
McGuigan, Bidy 22; Philadelphia, 1860 ***5704.8*** *p145*
McGuigan, Catherine; Montreal, 1821 ***7603*** *p55*
McGuigan, Catherine; St. John, N.B., 1852 ***5704.8*** *p83*
McGuigan, Christy *SEE* McGuigan, James
McGuigan, Christy; Philadelphia, 1847 ***5704.8*** *p1*
McGuigan, Edward; Philadelphia, 1866 ***5704.8*** *p206*
McGuigan, Ellen; St. John, N.B., 1853 ***5704.8*** *p99*
McGuigan, Francis 20; St. John, N.B., 1864 ***5704.8*** *p159*
McGuigan, James; New York, NY, 1868 ***5704.8*** *p228*
McGuigan, James; Philadelphia, 1847 ***53.26*** *p62*
*Relative:*Christy
*Relative:*Nancy
*Relative:*Pat
McGuigan, James; Philadelphia, 1847 ***5704.8*** *p1*
McGuigan, James; Philadelphia, 1870 ***5704.8*** *p239*
McGuigan, Jane; Montreal, 1823 ***7603*** *p55*
McGuigan, Jane 50; St. John, N.B., 1854 ***5704.8*** *p119*
McGuigan, Margaret 28; St. John, N.B., 1854 ***5704.8*** *p119*
McGuigan, Mary 20; Philadelphia, 1860 ***5704.8*** *p145*
McGuigan, Mary 21; St. John, N.B., 1864 ***5704.8*** *p159*
McGuigan, Michael; New York, NY, 1867 ***5704.8*** *p222*
McGuigan, Nancy *SEE* McGuigan, James
McGuigan, Nancy; Philadelphia, 1847 ***5704.8*** *p1*
McGuigan, Pat *SEE* McGuigan, James
McGuigan, Pat; Philadelphia, 1847 ***5704.8*** *p1*
McGuigan, Patrick; Philadelphia, 1847 ***53.26*** *p62*
McGuigan, Patrick; Philadelphia, 1847 ***5704.8*** *p2*
McGuigan, Patrick; Philadelphia, 1852 ***5704.8*** *p85*
McGuigan, Patrick 19; St. John, N.B., 1854 ***5704.8*** *p119*
McGuigan, Patrick 20; Philadelphia, 1857 ***5704.8*** *p132*
McGuigan, Rose; St. John, N.B., 1852 ***5704.8*** *p83*
McGuiggan, Hugh; New York, NY, 1866 ***5704.8*** *p208*
McGuiness, Emily; Philadelphia, 1853 ***5704.8*** *p101*
McGuiness, Henry; Philadelphia, 1853 ***5704.8*** *p101*
McGuiness, Terence; Virginia, 1858 ***4626.16*** *p17*
McGuinness, James; St. John, N.B., 1852 ***5704.8*** *p84*
McGuinness, John; St. John, N.B., 1853 ***5704.8*** *p100*
McGuire, Mrs. 24; Massachusetts, 1849 ***5881.1*** *p72*
McGuire, Alice 15; Massachusetts, 1850 ***5881.1*** *p62*
McGuire, Ann 35; Quebec, 1855 ***5704.8*** *p125*
McGuire, Ann 50; Philadelphia, 1865 ***5704.8*** *p165*
McGuire, Bridget 20; St. John, N.B., 1863 ***5704.8*** *p155*
McGuire, Bryan; America, 1738 ***4971*** *p31*
McGuire, Bryan; America, 1738 ***4971*** *p72*
McGuire, Catharine 25; Massachusetts, 1849 ***5881.1*** *p64*
McGuire, Catharine 50; Massachusetts, 1850 ***5881.1*** *p65*
McGuire, Catherine; St. John, N.B., 1847 ***5704.8*** *p11*
McGuire, Catherine; St. John, N.B., 1850 ***5704.8*** *p67*
McGuire, Catherine 15; Philadelphia, 1858 ***5704.8*** *p139*
McGuire, Charles; Philadelphia, 1847 ***53.26*** *p62*
McGuire, Charles; Philadelphia, 1847 ***5704.8*** *p23*
McGuire, Charles; St. John, N.B., 1847 ***5704.8*** *p11*
McGuire, Charles 24; Quebec, 1856 ***5704.8*** *p129*
McGuire, Daniel; America, 1741 ***4971*** *p70*
McGuire, Daniel 22; Philadelphia, 1774 ***1219.7*** *p216*
McGuire, Edward; America, 1839 ***7036*** *p120*
McGuire, Ellen; St. John, N.B., 1847 ***5704.8*** *p11*
McGuire, Ellen 9 mos; Massachusetts, 1849 ***5881.1*** *p66*
McGuire, Ellen 20; Philadelphia, 1855 ***5704.8*** *p124*
McGuire, Francis 35; St. John, N.B., 1867 ***5704.8*** *p168*
McGuire, George P.; New York, 1849 ***2764.35*** *p49*
McGuire, Helena; Montreal, 1823 ***7603*** *p61*
McGuire, Hester; America, 1743 ***4971*** *p86*
McGuire, Hugh; St. John, N.B., 1853 ***5704.8*** *p99*
McGuire, James; America, 1743 ***4971*** *p86*
McGuire, James; New York, NY, 1835 ***8208.4*** *p38*
McGuire, James 16; St. John, N.B., 1856 ***5704.8*** *p131*
McGuire, James 21; Philadelphia, 1864 ***5704.8*** *p156*
McGuire, James 25; Newfoundland, 1789 ***4915.24*** *p56*
McGuire, John; America, 1743 ***4971*** *p86*
McGuire, John; Fredericton, N.B., 1820 ***7603*** *p77*
McGuire, John; Quebec, 1852 ***5704.8*** *p94*
McGuire, Margaret 18; Massachusetts, 1850 ***5881.1*** *p72*
McGuire, Mary 15; Quebec, 1855 ***5704.8*** *p125*
McGuire, Mary 50; Massachusetts, 1850 ***5881.1*** *p73*
McGuire, Michael *SEE* McGuire, Pat
McGuire, Michael; New York, NY, 1839 ***8208.4*** *p100*
McGuire, Michael; Philadelphia, 1847 ***5704.8*** *p32*
McGuire, Michael; St. John, N.B., 1847 ***5704.8*** *p11*
McGuire, Nancy 96; Kansas, 1879 ***5240.1*** *p61*
McGuire, Owen; America, 1742 ***4971*** *p23*
McGuire, Owen; Quebec, 1852 ***5704.8*** *p86*
McGuire, Pat; Philadelphia, 1847 ***53.26*** *p63*
*Relative:*Michael
McGuire, Pat; Philadelphia, 1847 ***5704.8*** *p32*
McGuire, Patrick; Quebec, 1850 ***5704.8*** *p63*
McGuire, Patrick 24; Massachusetts, 1849 ***5881.1*** *p74*
McGuire, Rose; America, 1740 ***4971*** *p75*
McGuire, Rose; Montreal, 1823 ***7603*** *p55*
McGuire, Rose 23; Quebec, 1856 ***5704.8*** *p129*
McGuire, Susan 10; Philadelphia, 1858 ***5704.8*** *p139*
McGuire, Terence 33; St. John, N.B., 1867 ***5704.8*** *p168*
McGuire, Thomas; New York, NY, 1838 ***8208.4*** *p89*
McGuire, Thomas; St. John, N.B., 1848 ***5704.8*** *p45*
McGuire, Thomas 18; Massachusetts, 1847 ***5881.1*** *p76*
McGuire, Thomas 18; Quebec, 1855 ***5704.8*** *p125*
McGuire, Timothy; New York, NY, 1840 ***8208.4*** *p108*
McGuire, William J.; New York, NY, 1838 ***8208.4*** *p82*
McGuirk, Mary 19; St. John, N.B., 1864 ***5704.8*** *p159*
McGuirk, Michael; Arizona, 1890 ***2764.35*** *p50*
McGuly, Patrick; New York, NY, 1838 ***8208.4*** *p69*
McGurdy, James 22; St. John, N.B., 1856 ***5704.8*** *p131*
McGurk, . . . 6 mos; Quebec, 1847 ***5704.8*** *p7*
McGurk, Alexander; Philadelphia, 1866 ***5704.8*** *p209*
McGurk, Allice 35; Philadelphia, 1864 ***5704.8*** *p160*
McGurk, Arthur; Quebec, 1847 ***5704.8*** *p7*
McGurk, Bernard; America, 1864 ***5704.8*** *p187*
McGurk, Catherine; Quebec, 1847 ***5704.8*** *p7*
McGurk, Francis; Philadelphia, 1866 ***5704.8*** *p209*
McGurk, Hugh 8; Quebec, 1847 ***5704.8*** *p7*
McGurk, James; Quebec, 1847 ***5704.8*** *p7*
McGurk, James 11; Quebec, 1847 ***5704.8*** *p7*
McGurk, James 20; Philadelphia, 1853 ***5704.8*** *p113*
McGurk, Jane 17; Philadelphia, 1853 ***5704.8*** *p113*
McGurk, John; Quebec, 1851 ***5704.8*** *p75*
McGurk, John 10; Quebec, 1847 ***5704.8*** *p7*
McGurk, Mary 7; Quebec, 1847 ***5704.8*** *p7*
McGurk, Michael; Quebec, 1851 ***5704.8*** *p73*
McGurk, Mickey 13; Quebec, 1847 ***5704.8*** *p7*
McGurk, Moses; Philadelphia, 1866 ***5704.8*** *p210*
McGurk, Nelly 4; Quebec, 1847 ***5704.8*** *p7*
McGurk, Patrick; New York, NY, 1839 ***8208.4*** *p95*
McGurk, Patrick; Quebec, 1847 ***5704.8*** *p7*
McGurr, William 25; St. John, N.B., 1865 ***5704.8*** *p165*
McGuyn, Mary 15; Philadelphia, 1856 ***5704.8*** *p129*
McGuyn, Moses 12; Philadelphia, 1856 ***5704.8*** *p129*
McGwee, Michael; Philadelphia, 1866 ***5704.8*** *p206*
McGwigan, Margaret 19; Philadelphia, 1856 ***5704.8*** *p128*
McGwinn, Bridget 50; Massachusetts, 1848 ***5881.1*** *p63*
McGwire, Hester; America, 1741 ***4971*** *p21*
McGwire, Jane; America, 1741 ***4971*** *p21*
McGwire, John; America, 1741 ***4971*** *p21*
McHaig, Mary; Philadelphia, 1851 ***5704.8*** *p81*
McHale, Michael; Colorado, 1894 ***9678.2*** *p128*

McHall, Robert; Philadelphia, 1851 *5704.8 p70*
Mchany, B. 75; Kansas, 1875 *5240.1 p56*
McHar, John; Annapolis, MD, 1742 *4971 p92*
McHarey, Edward; New York, NY, 1864 *5704.8 p172*
McHarey, Michael; New York, NY, 1864 *5704.8 p172*
McHarg, Joseph 39; Kansas, 1888 *5240.1 p28*
McHarg, Joseph 39; Kansas, 1888 *5240.1 p71*
McHarg, Martha Jane 29; Kansas, 1888 *5240.1 p71*
McHarg, Samuel 21; Kansas, 1896 *5240.1 p28*
McHarg, Samuel 21; Kansas, 1896 *5240.1 p29*
McHarg, Samuel 21; Kansas, 1896 *5240.1 p80*
McHean, Maria 23 *SEE* McHean, Stewart
McHean, Stewart 30; Philadelphia, 1774 *1219.7 p217*
*Wife:*Maria 23
McHenny, William 28; St. John, N.B., 1862 *5704.8 p150*
McHenry, Ann 22; Philadelphia, 1859 *5704.8 p141*
McHenry, Catharine; Philadelphia, 1866 *5704.8 p207*
McHenry, Charles S. 40; Arizona, 1890 *2764.35 p48*
McHenry, Michael 48; Philadelphia, 1857 *5704.8 p134*
McHenry, Sarah; Philadelphia, 1866 *5704.8 p207*
McHenry, William 24; Philadelphia, 1855 *5704.8 p123*
McHinnie, Peter 38; St. John, N.B., 1862 *5704.8 p150*
McHomes, James; New York, NY, 1839 *8208.4 p100*
Mchovie, George 60; Kansas, 1872 *5240.1 p53*
McHugh, . . .; Philadelphia, 1864 *5704.8 p186*
McHugh, Andrew; America, 1735-1743 *4971 p79*
McHugh, Andrew; Philadelphia, 1865 *5704.8 p194*
McHugh, Andrew 10; St. John, N.B., 1853 *5704.8 p110*
McHugh, Ann; St. John, N.B., 1847 *5704.8 p34*
McHugh, Ann 13; Quebec, 1854 *5704.8 p119*
McHugh, Ann 17; Philadelphia, 1854 *5704.8 p123*
McHugh, Ann 26; Philadelphia, 1853 *5704.8 p111*
McHugh, Ann 26; St. John, N.B., 1854 *5704.8 p119*
McHugh, Anthony 20; Philadelphia, 1854 *5704.8 p123*
McHugh, Bridget 16; Philadelphia, 1853 *5704.8 p112*
McHugh, Bridget 23; Philadelphia, 1861 *5704.8 p148*
McHugh, Catharine; New York, NY, 1867 *5704.8 p223*
McHugh, Catharine; Philadelphia, 1865 *5704.8 p192*
McHugh, Catherine; St. John, N.B., 1850 *5704.8 p61*
McHugh, Catherine 7; Quebec, 1847 *5704.8 p38*
McHugh, Catherine 18; Quebec, 1864 *5704.8 p160*
McHugh, Catherine 20; St. John, N.B., 1856 *5704.8 p131*
McHugh, Charles; Quebec, 1847 *5704.8 p17*
McHugh, Daniel; Philadelphia, 1866 *5704.8 p211*
McHugh, Daniel 27; St. John, N.B., 1854 *5704.8 p120*
McHugh, Edward; Philadelphia, 1853 *5704.8 p102*
McHugh, Edward; Philadelphia, 1864 *5704.8 p175*
McHugh, Edward 4; St. John, N.B., 1850 *5704.8 p61*
McHugh, Eleanor 10; St. John, N.B., 1850 *5704.8 p61*
McHugh, Eliza 25; St. John, N.B., 1854 *5704.8 p119*
McHugh, Eliza A.; New York, NY, 1869 *5704.8 p232*
McHugh, Elleanor; St. John, N.B., 1847 *5704.8 p26*
McHugh, Francis 2; St. John, N.B., 1850 *5704.8 p61*
McHugh, Francis 25; Quebec, 1864 *5704.8 p160*
McHugh, Hannah; Philadelphia, 1868 *5704.8 p226*
McHugh, Hugh 10; Quebec, 1854 *5704.8 p119*
McHugh, Hugh 26; Philadelphia, 1865 *5704.8 p164*
McHugh, Isabella; New York, NY, 1865 *5704.8 p203*
McHugh, James; Ohio, 1851 *9892.11 p33*
McHugh, James; Quebec, 1852 *5704.8 p90*
McHugh, James 8; St. John, N.B., 1850 *5704.8 p61*
McHugh, James 21; Philadelphia, 1857 *5704.8 p132*
McHugh, James 32?; Arizona, 1890 *2764.35 p50*
McHugh, Jane; Philadelphia, 1865 *5704.8 p190*
McHugh, Jane; Quebec, 1847 *5704.8 p17*
McHugh, Jane; Quebec, 1852 *5704.8 p90*
McHugh, Jane 19; Philadelphia, 1854 *5704.8 p123*
McHugh, Jane 25; St. John, N.B., 1864 *5704.8 p159*
McHugh, John; New York, NY, 1865 *5704.8 p178*
McHugh, John; Philadelphia, 1851 *5704.8 p79*
McHugh, John; Philadelphia, 1868 *5704.8 p220*
McHugh, John 12; St. John, N.B., 1850 *5704.8 p61*
McHugh, John 23; Philadelphia, 1856 *5704.8 p128*
McHugh, Joseph 6; St. John, N.B., 1854 *5704.8 p120*
McHugh, Keatty; Quebec, 1847 *5704.8 p29*
McHugh, Margaret; New York, NY, 1865 *5704.8 p203*
McHugh, Margaret; Philadelphia, 1851 *5704.8 p79*
McHugh, Margaret; Philadelphia, 1870 *5704.8 p238*
McHugh, Margaret 50; St. John, N.B., 1853 *5704.8 p110*
McHugh, Margery; Philadelphia, 1865 *5704.8 p195*
McHugh, Margery; Philadelphia, 1868 *5704.8 p224*
McHugh, Mary; Philadelphia, 1868 *5704.8 p220*
McHugh, Mary; Philadelphia, 1870 *5704.8 p239*
McHugh, Mary; Quebec, 1847 *5704.8 p17*
McHugh, Mary; Quebec, 1847 *5704.8 p29*
McHugh, Mary; St. John, N.B., 1847 *5704.8 p26*
McHugh, Mary 7; Philadelphia, 1870 *5704.8 p238*
McHugh, Mary 12; Philadelphia, 1853 *5704.8 p112*
McHugh, Mary Ann 4; St. John, N.B., 1854 *5704.8 p120*
McHugh, Mathew; Illinois, 1898 *5012.40 p55*
McHugh, Michael; Philadelphia, 1864 *5704.8 p170*
McHugh, Michael; Quebec, 1847 *5704.8 p17*
McHugh, Michael; Quebec, 1849 *5704.8 p51*
McHugh, Michael; Quebec, 1852 *5704.8 p87*
McHugh, Michael; Quebec, 1852 *5704.8 p91*
McHugh, Michael; St. John, N.B., 1850 *5704.8 p66*
McHugh, Michael 3; Philadelphia, 1864 *5704.8 p186*
McHugh, Miles 6; St. John, N.B., 1850 *5704.8 p61*
McHugh, Neil; America, 1736 *4971 p81*
McHugh, Nixon James; New York, NY, 1838 *8208.4 p62*
McHugh, Patrick; New York, NY, 1867 *5704.8 p218*
McHugh, Patrick; Philadelphia, 1864 *5704.8 p169*
McHugh, Patrick; Quebec, 1847 *5704.8 p17*
McHugh, Philip 18; Philadelphia, 1859 *5704.8 p142*
McHugh, Rosy; Quebec, 1847 *5704.8 p29*
McHugh, Sally; Philadelphia, 1870 *5704.8 p238*
McHugh, Sarah; New York, NY, 1868 *5704.8 p226*
McHugh, Sarah; New York, NY, 1870 *5704.8 p239*
McHugh, Sarah; Philadelphia, 1866 *5704.8 p211*
McHugh, Sarah; Philadelphia, 1870 *5704.8 p239*
McHugh, Sarah 2; St. John, N.B., 1854 *5704.8 p120*
McHugh, Sophia 20; Philadelphia, 1861 *5704.8 p147*
McHugh, Susan; Quebec, 1847 *5704.8 p29*
McHugh, Teage; Philadelphia, 1866 *5704.8 p215*
McHugh, Thomas 8; Quebec, 1847 *5704.8 p29*
McHugh, Unity; Philadelphia, 1866 *5704.8 p204*
McHugh, William James 6 mos; St. John, N.B., 1864 *5704.8 p159*
McHugh, Winnie; America, 1864 *5704.8 p186*
McHughey, Isabella; Philadelphia, 1868 *5704.8 p226*
McHutcheson, Alexander 4; Quebec, 1864 *5704.8 p162*
McHutcheson, Euphemia 8; Quebec, 1864 *5704.8 p162*
McHutcheson, Jane 40; Quebec, 1864 *5704.8 p162*
McHutcheson, Janet 1; Quebec, 1864 *5704.8 p162*
McHutcheson, John 11; Quebec, 1864 *5704.8 p162*
McHutcheson, Thomas 18; Quebec, 1864 *5704.8 p162*
McHutcheson, Walter 42; Quebec, 1864 *5704.8 p162*
McHutcheson, William 9; Quebec, 1864 *5704.8 p162*
McIlbride, Archibald; North Carolina, 1771 *1639.20 p160*
McIles, Gregory; America, 1735-1743 *4971 p78*
McIlhargy, Alexander; New York, NY, 1836 *8208.4 p17*
McIlhavey, Andrew; Quebec, 1851 *5704.8 p75*
McIlhenny, Alexander; Philadelphia, 1850 *53.26 p63*
McIlhenny, Alexander; Philadelphia, 1850 *5704.8 p69*
McIlhenny, Biddy; St. John, N.B., 1851 *5704.8 p72*
McIlhenny, Daniel 17; St. John, N.B., 1854 *5704.8 p120*
McIlhenny, John; St. John, N.B., 1848 *5704.8 p43*
McIlhenny, John 1 *SEE* McIlhenny, Sarah
McIlhenny, John 1; Philadelphia, 1847 *5704.8 p13*
McIlhenny, Margaret; Philadelphia, 1847 *53.26 p63*
McIlhenny, Margaret; Philadelphia, 1847 *5704.8 p14*
McIlhenny, Margaret 12; St. John, N.B., 1850 *5704.8 p61*
McIlhenny, Mary; St. John, N.B., 1848 *5704.8 p39*
McIlhenny, Mary; St. John, N.B., 1849 *5704.8 p49*
McIlhenny, Robert; Philadelphia, 1851 *5704.8 p70*
McIlhenny, Robert 45; Philadelphia, 1864 *5704.8 p157*
McIlhenny, Ruth 18; Philadelphia, 1859 *5704.8 p141*
McIlhenny, Sarah; Philadelphia, 1847 *53.26 p63*
*Relative:*John 1
McIlhenny, Sarah; Philadelphia, 1847 *5704.8 p13*
McIlhenny, Walter 21; Philadelphia, 1864 *5704.8 p157*
McIlhill, Ann *SEE* McIlhill, Michael
McIlhill, Ann; Philadelphia, 1847 *5704.8 p22*
McIlhill, Michael; Philadelphia, 1847 *53.26 p63*
*Relative:*Ann
McIlhill, Michael; Philadelphia, 1847 *5704.8 p22*
McIlhiney, Anne 17; Philadelphia, 1860 *5704.8 p145*
McIlhiney, John 19; Philadelphia, 1860 *5704.8 p145*
McIlhinney, Ann 10; Philadelphia, 1864 *5704.8 p155*
McIlhinney, Bridget; Philadelphia, 1867 *5704.8 p216*
McIlhinney, Catharine; New York, NY, 1864 *5704.8 p184*
McIlhinney, Fanny A. 4; Philadelphia, 1866 *5704.8 p215*
McIlhinney, Jane; Philadelphia, 1866 *5704.8 p215*
McIlhinney, John; Philadelphia, 1864 *5704.8 p185*
McIlhinney, John; Philadelphia, 1866 *5704.8 p206*
McIlhinney, John 2; Philadelphia, 1866 *5704.8 p215*
McIlhinney, Margaret J.; New York, NY, 1867 *5704.8 p219*
McIlhinney, Mary 6; Philadelphia, 1866 *5704.8 p215*
McIlhinney, Nancy 50; Philadelphia, 1864 *5704.8 p155*
McIlhinney, Robert 19; Philadelphia, 1864 *5704.8 p155*
McIlhinney, William; New York, NY, 1869 *5704.8 p235*
McIlhinney, William; Philadelphia, 1866 *5704.8 p206*
McIlhone, Andrew; New York, NY, 1865 *5704.8 p199*
McIllhinny, Jane 14; Philadelphia, 1864 *5704.8 p156*
McIlhinny, Joseph; Philadelphia, 1864 *5704.8 p156*
McIlrea, Archibald 26; Wilmington, DE, 1831 *6508.3 p101*
McIlrea, Jane 28; Wilmington, DE, 1831 *6508.3 p101*
McIlrea, Martha 40; Wilmington, DE, 1831 *6508.3 p101*
McIlrea, William 20; Wilmington, DE, 1831 *6508.3 p100*
McIlroy, John 18; Jamaica, 1731 *3690.1 p153*
McIlroy, William; Quebec, 1847 *5704.8 p28*
McIlvay, Duncan; Carolina, 1684 *1639.20 p160*
McIlwain, Catherine 9; Philadelphia, 1860 *5704.8 p146*
McIlwain, Ellen 16; Philadelphia, 1860 *5704.8 p146*
McIlwaine, Catherine; Philadelphia, 1851 *5704.8 p70*
McIlwaine, Charles; Philadelphia, 1851 *5704.8 p71*
McIlwaine, James; Philadelphia, 1851 *5704.8 p70*
McIlwaine, Jane; Philadelphia, 1851 *5704.8 p70*
McIlwaine, John 6; Philadelphia, 1858 *5704.8 p138*
McIlwaine, John 8; Philadelphia, 1851 *5704.8 p71*
McIlwaine, John 40; Philadelphia, 1858 *5704.8 p138*
McIlwaine, John H.; Philadelphia, 1851 *5704.8 p76*
McIlwaine, Manasses; Philadelphia, 1851 *5704.8 p71*
McIlwaine, Margaret; New York, NY, 1865 *5704.8 p191*
McIlwaine, Margaret 25; Philadelphia, 1865 *5704.8 p164*
McIlwaine, Margery 40; Philadelphia, 1858 *5704.8 p138*
McIlwaine, Mary; Philadelphia, 1852 *5704.8 p97*
McIlwaine, Neal 7; Philadelphia, 1858 *5704.8 p138*
McIlwaine, Owen 6; Philadelphia, 1851 *5704.8 p71*
McIlwaine, Pat 12; Philadelphia, 1851 *5704.8 p71*
McIlwaine, Peter; Philadelphia, 1866 *5704.8 p205*
McIlwaine, Sarah 10; Philadelphia, 1858 *5704.8 p138*
McIlwaine, William; Philadelphia, 1866 *5704.8 p205*
McIlwane, Mary J.; Philadelphia, 1864 *5704.8 p169*
McIlwee, Alexander; Philadelphia, 1851 *5704.8 p71*
McInerney, Michael 26; Kansas, 1879 *5240.1 p60*
McInnery, John; Indiana, 1850 *9117 p20*
McInnes, Angus *SEE* McInnes, Angus
McInnes, Angus; Nova Scotia, 1830 *7085.4 p44*
*Wife:*Margaret
*Child:*Mary
*Child:*Angus
McInnes, Ann 15 *SEE* McInnes, Malcolm
McInnes, Archibald 4 *SEE* McInnes, Malcolm
McInnes, Catherine 11 *SEE* McInnes, Malcolm
McInnes, Christy *SEE* McInnes, Miles
McInnes, Donald 8 *SEE* McInnes, Malcolm
McInnes, Flora *SEE* McInnes, John
McInnes, Flora *SEE* McInnes, Miles
McInnes, Janet 36 *SEE* McInnes, Malcolm
McInnes, John *SEE* McInnes, Miles
McInnes, John; Colorado, 1903 *9678.2 p128*
McInnes, John; Nova Scotia, 1830 *7085.4 p44*
*Wife:*Flora
McInnes, John; South Carolina, 1716 *1639.20 p161*
McInnes, John 20 *SEE* McInnes, Malcolm
McInnes, Joseph 22; St. John, N.B., 1866 *5704.8 p166*
McInnes, Ket *SEE* McInnes, Malcolm
McInnes, Malcolm; Nova Scotia, 1830 *7085.4 p44*
*Wife:*Marion
*Child:*Marion
*Child:*Neil
*Child:*Ket
McInnes, Malcolm 40; Wilmington, NC, 1775 *1639.20 p162*
*Wife:*Janet 36
*Child:*John 20
*Child:*Ann 15
*Child:*Catherine 11
*Child:*Donald 8
*Child:*Archibald 4
McInnes, Margaret *SEE* McInnes, Angus
McInnes, Marion *SEE* McInnes, Malcolm
McInnes, Marion *SEE* McInnes, Malcolm
McInnes, Mary *SEE* McInnes, Angus
McInnes, Mary *SEE* McInnes, Miles
McInnes, Mary *SEE* McInnes, Miles
McInnes, Miles; Nova Scotia, 1830 *7085.4 p45*
*Wife:*Mary
*Child:*Mary
*Child:*Christy
*Child:*John
*Child:*Flora
McInnes, Neil *SEE* McInnes, Malcolm
McInnis, A. 65; South Carolina, 1850 *1639.20 p160*
McInnis, Angus; America, 1802 *1639.20 p160*
McInnis, Angus; North Carolina, 1785-1849 *1639.20 p160*
McInnis, Angus 60; North Carolina, 1850 *1639.20 p160*
*Relative:*Christian 62
McInnis, Catherine 65; North Carolina, 1850 *1639.20 p161*
McInnis, Catherine 96; North Carolina, 1850 *1639.20 p160*
McInnis, Christian 62 *SEE* McInnis, Angus
McInnis, Daniel; America, 1792 *1639.20 p161*
McInnis, Duncan; America, 1792 *1639.20 p161*
McInnis, Duncan; America, 1802 *1639.20 p161*
McInnis, Effie; North Carolina, 1802 *1639.20 p199*
McInnis, Hellen 25; Massachusetts, 1849 *5881.1 p67*

McInnis, James; America, 1792 ***1639.20*** *p161*
McInnis, John; America, 1792 ***1639.20*** *p162*
McInnis, Murdoch; North Carolina, 1790 ***1639.20*** *p162*
McInnis, Thomas 10; Massachusetts, 1849 ***5881.1*** *p76*
McInnis, William 5; Massachusetts, 1849 ***5881.1*** *p77*
McIntagart, Daniel; America, 1792 ***1639.20*** *p162*
McIntagart, Gilbert; America, 1791 ***1639.20*** *p162*
McIntire, Miss; New York, NY, 1864 ***5704.8*** *p171*
McIntire, Abraham; Philadelphia, 1811 ***53.26*** *p63*
McIntire, Alexander; America, 1802 ***1639.20*** *p165*
McIntire, Ann 60; Wilmington, NC, 1775 ***1639.20*** *p165*
McIntire, Betty; St. John, N.B., 1847 ***5704.8*** *p18*
McIntire, Bridget 20; St. John, N.B., 1854 ***5704.8*** *p114*
McIntire, Catharine; New York, NY, 1864 ***5704.8*** *p169*
McIntire, Con 50; Quebec, 1859 ***5704.8*** *p143*
McIntire, Daniel; Quebec, 1847 ***5704.8*** *p29*
McIntire, Daniel 10; Philadelphia, 1853 ***5704.8*** *p112*
McIntire, Daniel 10; Philadelphia, 1854 ***5704.8*** *p115*
McIntire, Daniel 19; St. John, N.B., 1857 ***5704.8*** *p134*
McIntire, Duncan; Pennsylvania, 1844 ***2764.35*** *p49*
McIntire, Eliza; Quebec, 1855 ***5704.8*** *p125*
McIntire, Elleanor 14; Quebec, 1856 ***5704.8*** *p130*
McIntire, Ellen 8; Massachusetts, 1849 ***5881.1*** *p66*
McIntire, Ellen 9; Philadelphia, 1853 ***5704.8*** *p112*
McIntire, Ellen 9; Philadelphia, 1854 ***5704.8*** *p115*
McIntire, Fanny 23; Quebec, 1855 ***5704.8*** *p125*
McIntire, George; St. John, N.B., 1847 ***5704.8*** *p18*
McIntire, George 10; St. John, N.B., 1847 ***5704.8*** *p18*
McIntire, Hugh; New York, NY, 1864 ***5704.8*** *p169*
McIntire, Isabella 28; Quebec, 1855 ***5704.8*** *p125*
McIntire, James 26; Quebec, 1855 ***5704.8*** *p125*
McIntire, John 40; St. John, N.B., 1851 ***5704.8*** *p72*
McIntire, Margaret; Philadelphia, 1864 ***5704.8*** *p180*
McIntire, Margaret; St. John, N.B., 1850 ***5704.8*** *p62*
McIntire, Margaret 28; Quebec, 1858 ***5704.8*** *p140*
McIntire, Margaret 30; Philadelphia, 1853 ***5704.8*** *p112*
McIntire, Margaret 30; Philadelphia, 1854 ***5704.8*** *p115*
McIntire, Margaret Jane; Quebec, 1847 ***5704.8*** *p29*
McIntire, Mary; New York, NY, 1864 ***5704.8*** *p169*
McIntire, Mary 45; St. John, N.B., 1863 ***5704.8*** *p152*
McIntire, Peter; New York, NY, 1830-1841 ***7036*** *p121*
McIntire, Robert 21; Quebec, 1856 ***5704.8*** *p130*
McIntire, Rosa 9 mos; Massachusetts, 1849 ***5881.1*** *p75*
McIntire, Rosey 20; St. John, N.B., 1857 ***5704.8*** *p134*
McIntire, Sally 45; Massachusetts, 1849 ***5881.1*** *p76*
McIntire, Thomas 11; Philadelphia, 1853 ***5704.8*** *p112*
McIntire, Thomas 35; Massachusetts, 1849 ***5881.1*** *p76*
McIntosh, . . . 5; Pictou, N.S., 1801 ***9775.5*** *p207A*
McIntosh, Ale...; Pictou, N.S., 1801 ***9775.5*** *p207A*
McIntosh, Alexander 35; Quebec, 1864 ***5704.8*** *p162*
McIntosh, Ann 8; Quebec, 1861 ***5704.8*** *p149*
McIntosh, Cath; Pictou, N.S., 1801 ***9775.5*** *p207A*
McIntosh, D.; Illinois, 1892 ***5012.40*** *p27*
McIntosh, Daniel 86; North Carolina, 1850 ***1639.20*** *p162*
McIntosh, Donald; Charleston, SC, 1830 ***1639.20*** *p162*
McIntosh, Donald; Pictou, N.S., 1801 ***9775.5*** *p207A*
McIntosh, Duncan; South Carolina, 1716 ***1639.20*** *p162*
McIntosh, Duncan; South Carolina, 1716 ***1639.20*** *p163*
McIntosh, Ewan; South Carolina, 1716 ***1639.20*** *p163*
McIntosh, James; South Carolina, 1716 ***1639.20*** *p163*
McIntosh, James 3; Quebec, 1864 ***5704.8*** *p162*
McIntosh, Janet; Pictou, N.S., 1801 ***9775.5*** *p207A*
McIntosh, John; Charleston, SC, 1810 ***1639.20*** *p164*
McIntosh, John; Charleston, SC, 1813 ***1639.20*** *p164*
McIntosh, John; New York, NY, 1838 ***8208.4*** *p66*
McIntosh, John; Pictou, N.S., 1801 ***9775.5*** *p207A*
McIntosh, John; South Carolina, 1716 ***1639.20*** *p163*
McIntosh, John 3; Pictou, N.S., 1801 ***9775.5*** *p207A*
McIntosh, John 32; Georgia, 1775 ***1219.7*** *p276*
McIntosh, John 60; Philadelphia, 1858 ***5704.8*** *p138*
McIntosh, Kenneth 1; Quebec, 1864 ***5704.8*** *p162*
McIntosh, Lauchlin; New York, 1804 ***1639.20*** *p164*
McIntosh, Lauchlin; Nova Scotia, 1800 ***1639.20*** *p164*
McIntosh, Letitia 16; Philadelphia, 1858 ***5704.8*** *p138*
McIntosh, Lucy 82; North Carolina, 1850 ***1639.20*** *p164*
McIntosh, Margaret 14; Philadelphia, 1858 ***5704.8*** *p138*
McIntosh, Margt 14; Pictou, N.S., 1801 ***9775.5*** *p207A*
McIntosh, Mary 28; Quebec, 1864 ***5704.8*** *p162*
McIntosh, Nicholas 35; New York, 1775 ***1219.7*** *p268*
McIntosh, Robert 22; Philadelphia, 1858 ***5704.8*** *p138*
McIntosh, Sarah Ann 20; Philadelphia, 1858 ***5704.8*** *p138*
McIntosh, Walter; Raleigh, NC, 1808-1850 ***1639.20*** *p164*
McIntosh, William; South Carolina, 1716 ***1639.20*** *p164*
McIntosh, William; South Carolina, 1822 ***1639.20*** *p164*
McIntyer, Mary McCormaig *SEE* McIntyer, Peter
McIntyer, Peter; Canada, 1825 ***8894.2*** *p57*
*Wife:*Mary McCormaig
With child
McIntyre, Alexander 12 *SEE* McIntyre, George
McIntyre, Alexander 12; Philadelphia, 1849 ***5704.8*** *p54*
McIntyre, Andrew 12; St. John, N.B., 1854 ***5704.8*** *p114*
McIntyre, Angus; Charleston, SC, 1822 ***1639.20*** *p165*
McIntyre, Ann 32 *SEE* McIntyre, John
McIntyre, Ann 36 *SEE* McIntyre, Gilbert
McIntyre, Archibald 4 *SEE* McIntyre, John
McIntyre, Archibald 79; North Carolina, 1850 ***1639.20*** *p165*
McIntyre, Bess; Quebec, 1848 ***5704.8*** *p42*
McIntyre, Bridget; Quebec, 1825 ***7603*** *p82*
McIntyre, Bridget; St. John, N.B., 1847 ***5704.8*** *p25*
McIntyre, Catharine; Philadelphia, 1865 ***5704.8*** *p197*
McIntyre, Catherine 63; North Carolina, 1850 ***1639.20*** *p165*
McIntyre, Charles 11 *SEE* McIntyre, Gilbert
McIntyre, Christian Carmichael; South Carolina, 1821 ***1639.20*** *p37*
McIntyre, Daniel 11; New York, NY, 1865 ***5704.8*** *p193*
McIntyre, Daniel 50; South Carolina, 1850 ***1639.20*** *p165*
McIntyre, Donald 3 *SEE* McIntyre, John
McIntyre, Donald 28; Wilmington, NC, 1774 ***1639.20*** *p165*
*Wife:*Mary 25
McIntyre, Dougal 52; South Carolina, 1850 ***1639.20*** *p166*
*Relative:*Lilly 48
*Relative:*Elizabeth 27
McIntyre, Dougald; South Carolina, 1820 ***1639.20*** *p166*
McIntyre, Duncan; New York, NY, 1836 ***8208.4*** *p22*
McIntyre, Duncan 40; Wilmington, NC, 1774 ***1639.20*** *p166*
*Wife:*Katherine 28
McIntyre, Duncan 55; Wilmington, NC, 1775 ***1639.20*** *p166*
*Wife:*Katherine 55
*Child:*Mary 24
*Child:*Katherine 17
*Child:*Elizabeth 14
McIntyre, Edward; Quebec, 1777 ***7603*** *p77*
McIntyre, Eliza *SEE* McIntyre, George
McIntyre, Eliza; Philadelphia, 1849 ***5704.8*** *p54*
McIntyre, Elizabeth 14 *SEE* McIntyre, Duncan
McIntyre, Elizabeth 27 *SEE* McIntyre, Dougal
McIntyre, Ellen; Philadelphia, 1864 ***5704.8*** *p184*
McIntyre, Ellen; Philadelphia, 1865 ***5704.8*** *p198*
McIntyre, Ennice; Philadelphia, 1864 ***5704.8*** *p184*
McIntyre, Ewan 5 *SEE* McIntyre, Gilbert
McIntyre, Genevieve; Quebec, 1791 ***7603*** *p36*
McIntyre, George; Philadelphia, 1849 ***53.26*** *p63*
*Relative:*Eliza
*Relative:*Alexander 12
*Relative:*Margaret 10
*Relative:*Jane 8
*Relative:*Isabella 6
*Relative:*Mary 4
McIntyre, George; Philadelphia, 1849 ***5704.8*** *p54*
McIntyre, Gilbert 34; Wilmington, NC, 1775 ***1639.20*** *p166*
*Wife:*Ann 36
*Child:*Charles 11
*Child:*Margaret 9
*Child:*Ewan 5
*Child:*Malcolm 1
McIntyre, Isabella; Philadelphia, 1849 ***53.26*** *p63*
McIntyre, Isabella; Philadelphia, 1849 ***5704.8*** *p54*
McIntyre, Isabella 6 *SEE* McIntyre, George
McIntyre, Isabella 6; Philadelphia, 1849 ***5704.8*** *p54*
McIntyre, Isobel 24; Wilmington, NC, 1774 ***1639.20*** *p287*
McIntyre, James; St. John, N.B., 1847 ***5704.8*** *p25*
McIntyre, James 9; Philadelphia, 1864 ***5704.8*** *p184*
McIntyre, Jane; Philadelphia, 1847 ***53.26*** *p63*
McIntyre, Jane; Philadelphia, 1847 ***5704.8*** *p24*
McIntyre, Jane 8 *SEE* McIntyre, George
McIntyre, Jane 8; Philadelphia, 1849 ***5704.8*** *p54*
McIntyre, Jane 24; Philadelphia, 1856 ***5704.8*** *p129*
McIntyre, John *SEE* McIntyre, John
McIntyre, John; America, 1864 ***5704.8*** *p188*
McIntyre, John; North Carolina, 1764-1829 ***1639.20*** *p167*
McIntyre, John; North Carolina, 1767-1854 ***1639.20*** *p167*
McIntyre, John; North Carolina, 1850 ***1639.20*** *p168*
McIntyre, John; Wilmington, NC, 1791 ***1639.20*** *p167*
McIntyre, John 1 *SEE* McIntyre, John
McIntyre, John 9; New York, NY, 1865 ***5704.8*** *p193*
McIntyre, John 32; Wilmington, NC, 1775 ***1639.20*** *p167*
*Wife:*Katherine 30
*Child:*Donald 3
*Child:*John 1
McIntyre, John 35; Wilmington, NC, 1774 ***1639.20*** *p166*
*Wife:*Margaret 30
McIntyre, John 35; Wilmington, NC, 1775 ***1639.20*** *p167*
*Wife:*Ann 32
*Child:*Margaret 6
*Child:*Archibald 4
*Child:*John
McIntyre, John 45; Wilmington, NC, 1774 ***1639.20*** *p166*
*Wife:*Mary Downie 35
McIntyre, John 55; North Carolina, 1850 ***1639.20*** *p150*
McIntyre, John 83; North Carolina, 1850 ***1639.20*** *p167*
McIntyre, John R. 28; North Carolina, 1850 ***1639.20*** *p168*
McIntyre, Katherine; Wilmington, NC, 1774 ***1639.20*** *p70*
McIntyre, Katherine 17 *SEE* McIntyre, Duncan
McIntyre, Katherine 28 *SEE* McIntyre, Duncan
McIntyre, Katherine 30 *SEE* McIntyre, John
McIntyre, Katherine 55 *SEE* McIntyre, Duncan
McIntyre, Lilly 48 *SEE* McIntyre, Dougal
McIntyre, Malcolm 1 *SEE* McIntyre, Gilbert
McIntyre, Margaret 6 *SEE* McIntyre, John
McIntyre, Margaret 9 *SEE* McIntyre, Gilbert
McIntyre, Margaret 10 *SEE* McIntyre, George
McIntyre, Margaret 10; Philadelphia, 1849 ***5704.8*** *p54*
McIntyre, Margaret 13; Philadelphia, 1851 ***5704.8*** *p78*
McIntyre, Margaret 18; St. John, N.B., 1854 ***5704.8*** *p114*
McIntyre, Margaret 30 *SEE* McIntyre, John
McIntyre, Marie McNeil; Quebec, 1778 ***7603*** *p35*
McIntyre, Mary; Philadelphia, 1865 ***5704.8*** *p199*
McIntyre, Mary 4 *SEE* McIntyre, George
McIntyre, Mary 4; Philadelphia, 1849 ***5704.8*** *p54*
McIntyre, Mary 24 *SEE* McIntyre, Duncan
McIntyre, Mary 25 *SEE* McIntyre, Donald
McIntyre, Mary Downie 35 *SEE* McIntyre, John
McIntyre, Mary J.; Philadelphia, 1868 ***5704.8*** *p226*
McIntyre, Nicholas; America, 1792 ***1639.20*** *p168*
McIntyre, Robert; America, 1868 ***5704.8*** *p229*
McIntyre, Thomas; New York, NY, 1867 ***5704.8*** *p223*
McIntyre, Thomas; Quebec, 1824 ***7603*** *p66*
McIntyre, William 7; New York, NY, 1865 ***5704.8*** *p193*
McIrny, William; Quebec, 1814 ***7603*** *p82*
McIver, Bella Jane 3 mos; St. John, N.B., 1862 ***5704.8*** *p149*
McIver, Colin; North Carolina, 1809 ***1639.20*** *p168*
McIver, Dorothy; North Carolina, 1802-1857 ***1639.20*** *p168*
McIver, Edley 22; St. John, N.B., 1862 ***5704.8*** *p149*
McIver, Evander; North Carolina, 1744-1830 ***1639.20*** *p168*
McIver, Flora 61; North Carolina, 1850 ***1639.20*** *p168*
McIver, Jane 60; North Carolina, 1850 ***1639.20*** *p169*
McIver, John; Colombia, SC, 1829 ***1639.20*** *p169*
McIver, John 78; North Carolina, 1850 ***1639.20*** *p169*
*Relative:*Neill 51
McIver, Joseph; New York, NY, 1839 ***8208.4*** *p102*
McIver, Margaret; Quebec, 1852 ***5704.8*** *p94*
McIver, Mary; North Carolina, 1802-1856 ***1639.20*** *p169*
McIver, Mary Ann 20; St. John, N.B., 1862 ***5704.8*** *p149*
McIver, Neill 51 *SEE* McIver, John
McIver, Thomas 18; Philadelphia, 1864 ***5704.8*** *p161*
McIvor, Evander 56; North Carolina, 1850 ***1639.20*** *p168*
McIvor, John; Philadelphia, 1864 ***5704.8*** *p186*
McJernkin, Mary; Quebec, 1852 ***5704.8*** *p97*
McJernkin, Mary Ann; Quebec, 1852 ***5704.8*** *p97*
McJernkin, Robert; Quebec, 1852 ***5704.8*** *p97*
McJernkin, Samuel 10; Quebec, 1852 ***5704.8*** *p97*
McJimkin, Catherine; St. John, N.B., 1851 ***5704.8*** *p72*
McJohn, Teigue; America, 1736-1743 ***4971*** *p57*
McKaan, James; Quebec, 1788 ***7603*** *p41*
McKaig, Mary; Philadelphia, 1867 ***5704.8*** *p224*
McKaigney, Bridget 60; Philadelphia, 1854 ***5704.8*** *p118*
McKaigney, Peter 13; Philadelphia, 1854 ***5704.8*** *p118*
McKane, Henry 20; Quebec, 1863 ***5704.8*** *p154*
McKane, James; New York, NY, 1866 ***5704.8*** *p206*
McKane, James; Philadelphia, 1850 ***5704.8*** *p64*
McKane, John; Quebec, 1851 ***5704.8*** *p73*
McKane, Mary; New York, NY, 1866 ***5704.8*** *p213*
McKane, Mary; Quebec, 1823 ***7603*** *p67*
McKannon, James; Quebec, 1851 ***5704.8*** *p82*
McKannon, James 9 mos; Quebec, 1851 ***5704.8*** *p82*
McKannon, Margaret Jane 4; Quebec, 1851 ***5704.8*** *p82*
McKannon, Mary Jane; Quebec, 1851 ***5704.8*** *p82*
McKannon, Robert 8; Quebec, 1851 ***5704.8*** *p82*
McKannon, Tristrum 6; Quebec, 1851 ***5704.8*** *p82*
McKany, Catharine; Philadelphia, 1847 ***5704.8*** *p31*
McKany, Catherine; Philadelphia, 1847 ***53.26*** *p63*
*Relative:*Ellen
*Relative:*Owen 10
McKany, Ellen *SEE* McKany, Catherine
McKany, Ellen; Philadelphia, 1847 ***5704.8*** *p31*
McKany, Owen 10 *SEE* McKany, Catherine
McKany, Owen 10; Philadelphia, 1847 ***5704.8*** *p31*
McKarry, Ales; Philadelphia, 1847 ***5704.8*** *p32*
McKarry, Alex; Philadelphia, 1847 ***53.26*** *p63*
McKary, Johnston; St. John, N.B., 1864 ***5704.8*** *p159*
McKasper, Mary; Philadelphia, 1853 ***5704.8*** *p103*

McKay, Alexander; America, 1802 ***1639.20*** *p169*
McKay, Alexander; Brunswick, NC, 1739 ***1639.20*** *p169*
McKay, Alexander 49; North Carolina, 1850 ***1639.20*** *p169*
McKay, Archbald; Quebec, 1850 ***5704.8*** *p62*
McKay, Benjamin; Quebec, 1787 ***7603*** *p77*
McKay, Catherine; Quebec, 1819 ***7603*** *p57*
McKay, Catherine 50; North Carolina, 1850 ***1639.20*** *p170*
McKay, Catherine 60; North Carolina, 1850 ***1639.20*** *p170*
McKay, Catherine 71; North Carolina, 1850 ***1639.20*** *p170*
McKay, Charles; Philadelphia, 1811 ***53.26*** *p63*
McKay, Charles 22; St. John, N.B., 1864 ***5704.8*** *p157*
McKay, Christian 60; North Carolina, 1850 ***1639.20*** *p170*
*Relative:*Jennett 55
McKay, Daniel; America, 1792 ***1639.20*** *p170*
McKay, Daniel; New York, NY, 1837 ***8208.4*** *p34*
McKay, Daniel 17; Jamaica, 1730 ***3690.1*** *p145*
McKay, Daniel C. 24; West Virginia, 1902 ***9788.3*** *p16*
McKay, Donald; America, 1803 ***1639.20*** *p170*
McKay, Donald 20; Wilmington, NC, 1774 ***1639.20*** *p170*
McKay, Duncan; Cape Fear, NC, 1803 ***1639.20*** *p170*
McKay, Duncan, Sr.; America, 1802 ***1639.20*** *p171*
McKay, Elizabeth; Quebec, 1850 ***5704.8*** *p62*
McKay, Elizabeth 80; North Carolina, 1850 ***1639.20*** *p171*
McKay, Ellan; Quebec, 1850 ***5704.8*** *p62*
McKay, George 40; Wilmington, NC, 1774 ***1639.20*** *p171*
With wife & child
McKay, Hugh; America, 1792 ***1639.20*** *p171*
McKay, James 60; Wilmington, NC, 1774 ***1639.20*** *p171*
With wife & child
McKay, Jennett 55 *SEE* McKay, Christian
McKay, John; California, 1861 ***2769.6*** *p5*
McKay, John; Quebec, 1790 ***9775.5*** *p198A*
McKay, John; Quebec, 1850 ***5704.8*** *p63*
McKay, John; South Carolina, 1768 ***1639.20*** *p171*
McKay, John; Yamaska, Que., 1766 ***7603*** *p36*
McKay, John 25; Massachusetts, 1847 ***5881.1*** *p67*
McKay, Letitia 26; Massachusetts, 1850 ***5881.1*** *p70*
McKay, Mabella 14 mos; Massachusetts, 1850 ***5881.1*** *p73*
McKay, Malcolm; Charleston, SC, 1805 ***1639.20*** *p171*
McKay, Margaret Ann; Quebec, 1850 ***5704.8*** *p62*
McKay, Mary; Montreal, 1822 ***7603*** *p57*
McKay, Mary 73; North Carolina, 1850 ***1639.20*** *p171*
McKay, Mary Ann 22; Massachusetts, 1847 ***5881.1*** *p70*
McKay, Mungo Campbell; Charleston, SC, 1798 ***1639.20*** *p171*
McKay, Murdoch; Georgia, 1775 ***1219.7*** *p275*
McKay, Nancy; Quebec, 1850 ***5704.8*** *p62*
McKay, Neil; North Carolina, 1813 ***1639.20*** *p171*
McKay, Rosey; Philadelphia, 1847 ***5704.8*** *p23*
McKay, Terence; New York, NY, 1835 ***8208.4*** *p5*
McKay, William; Illinois, 1861 ***2896.5*** *p27*
McKay, William 26; Wilmington, NC, 1774 ***1639.20*** *p172*
McKay, William 30; Wilmington, NC, 1774 ***1639.20*** *p172*
With wife
With child
With child 8
With child 2
McKay, William 37; Wilmington, NC, 1774 ***1639.20*** *p172*
With wife & 2 children
With child 8
With child 18 mos
McKeag, Alexander; St. John, N.B., 1852 ***5704.8*** *p94*
McKeag, Ann; St. John, N.B., 1852 ***5704.8*** *p94*
McKeag, Jane; Philadelphia, 1865 ***5704.8*** *p192*
McKeage, Mary; Montreal, 1812 ***7603*** *p54*
McKeagen, Elizabeth 6; St. John, N.B., 1847 ***5704.8*** *p20*
McKeagen, John; St. John, N.B., 1847 ***5704.8*** *p20*
McKeagen, Kitty; St. John, N.B., 1847 ***5704.8*** *p20*
McKeagen, Mary; St. John, N.B., 1847 ***5704.8*** *p20*
McKeagen, Robert 3 mos; St. John, N.B., 1847 ***5704.8*** *p20*
McKeagen, Sally 11; St. John, N.B., 1847 ***5704.8*** *p20*
McKeagen, Sean 13; St. John, N.B., 1847 ***5704.8*** *p20*
McKeagen, William; St. John, N.B., 1847 ***5704.8*** *p20*
McKeagney, Bridget; Philadelphia, 1868 ***5704.8*** *p226*
McKeagney, Margaret; Philadelphia, 1868 ***5704.8*** *p226*
McKeague, Daniel; St. John, N.B., 1848 ***5704.8*** *p43*
McKeague, George 18; Massachusetts, 1848 ***5881.1*** *p66*
McKeague, Sally 11; St. John, N.B., 1848 ***5704.8*** *p43*
McKeal, Saad Joseph; Washington, 1859-1920 ***2872.1*** *p27*
McKean, James; America, 1835 ***1450.2*** *p97A*
McKean, James; Philadelphia, 1866 ***5704.8*** *p215*
McKean, Letitia; Philadelphia, 1866 ***5704.8*** *p215*
McKean, Rose; New York, NY, 1866 ***5704.8*** *p214*
McKean, Sarah; Philadelphia, 1866 ***5704.8*** *p215*
McKean, William George; Washington, 1859-1920 ***2872.1*** *p27*
McKeany, Andrew; America, 1837 ***7036*** *p116*
McKeany, Catherine; St. John, N.B., 1852 ***5704.8*** *p95*
McKearnan, Dennis; America, 1739 ***4971*** *p68*
McKearnan, Nancy 20; Wilmington, DE, 1831 ***6508.3*** *p101*
McKearnard, James 35; Massachusetts, 1849 ***5881.1*** *p68*
McKechine, Neil 26; St. John, N.B., 1866 ***5704.8*** *p166*
McKee, Andrew 6 mos *SEE* McKee, Henry
McKee, Andrew 6 mos; Philadelphia, 1850 ***5704.8*** *p69*
McKee, Anton; Philadelphia, 1847 ***53.26*** *p63*
McKee, Anton; Philadelphia, 1847 ***5704.8*** *p30*
McKee, David; Buffalo, NY, 1832 ***9892.11*** *p33*
McKee, Davis; Ohio, 1840 ***9892.11*** *p33*
McKee, Ellen 8; Philadelphia, 1851 ***5704.8*** *p80*
McKee, George 3; St. John, N.B., 1848 ***5704.8*** *p47*
McKee, Henry; New York, NY, 1838 ***8208.4*** *p85*
McKee, Henry; Philadelphia, 1850 ***53.26*** *p63*
*Relative:*Margaret
*Relative:*Sarah 10
*Relative:*James 7
*Relative:*Andrew 6 mos
McKee, Henry; Philadelphia, 1850 ***5704.8*** *p69*
McKee, James; New York, NY, 1838 ***8208.4*** *p80*
McKee, James; Philadelphia, 1851 ***5704.8*** *p80*
McKee, James; Philadelphia, 1852 ***5704.8*** *p97*
McKee, James; Quebec, 1847 ***5704.8*** *p38*
McKee, James; St. John, N.B., 1848 ***5704.8*** *p47*
McKee, James 7 *SEE* McKee, Henry
McKee, James 7; Philadelphia, 1850 ***5704.8*** *p69*
McKee, James 24; St. John, N.B., 1857 ***5704.8*** *p135*
McKee, James 56; Quebec, 1864 ***5704.8*** *p160*
McKee, John; Quebec, 1847 ***5704.8*** *p8*
McKee, John; San Francisco, 1879 ***2764.35*** *p50*
McKee, John 9; Quebec, 1862 ***5704.8*** *p152*
McKee, Margaret *SEE* McKee, Henry
McKee, Margaret; Philadelphia, 1850 ***5704.8*** *p69*
McKee, Margaret 6; Philadelphia, 1851 ***5704.8*** *p80*
McKee, Mary; Philadelphia, 1852 ***5704.8*** *p88*
McKee, Mary; St. John, N.B., 1848 ***5704.8*** *p47*
McKee, Mary Ann; Quebec, 1847 ***5704.8*** *p36*
McKee, Neil; New York, NY, 1867 ***5704.8*** *p217*
McKee, Owen; New York, NY, 1836 ***8208.4*** *p20*
McKee, Robert 7; Quebec, 1862 ***5704.8*** *p152*
McKee, Samuel; Quebec, 1847 ***5704.8*** *p36*
McKee, Sarah 10 *SEE* McKee, Henry
McKee, Sarah 10; Philadelphia, 1850 ***5704.8*** *p69*
McKee, Thomas; St. John, N.B., 1848 ***5704.8*** *p47*
McKee, Thomas 6; St. John, N.B., 1848 ***5704.8*** *p47*
McKee, Thomas 23; Quebec, 1864 ***5704.8*** *p160*
McKee, Thomas 37; Quebec, 1862 ***5704.8*** *p152*
McKee, William; New Orleans, 1833 ***9892.11*** *p33*
McKee, William; Ohio, 1840 ***9892.11*** *p33*
McKee, William; Philadelphia, 1852 ***5704.8*** *p88*
McKeegan, Anne 35; St. John, N.B., 1863 ***5704.8*** *p152*
McKeegan, Ellen 11; Philadelphia, 1865 ***5704.8*** *p190*
McKeegan, Hugh 10; St. John, N.B., 1863 ***5704.8*** *p152*
McKeegan, Mathew; Philadelphia, 1865 ***5704.8*** *p189*
McKeels, Daniel; South Carolina, 1716 ***1639.20*** *p172*
McKeeman, Alexander 23; St. John, N.B., 1863 ***5704.8*** *p152*
McKeeman, Charlotte; Quebec, 1823 ***7603*** *p80*
McKeeman, Daniel 16; St. John, N.B., 1863 ***5704.8*** *p152*
McKeeman, Mary 55; St. John, N.B., 1863 ***5704.8*** *p152*
McKeeman, Nancy 25; St. John, N.B., 1863 ***5704.8*** *p152*
McKeeman, Sally 18; St. John, N.B., 1863 ***5704.8*** *p152*
McKeenan, Moses; Philadelphia, 1847 ***53.26*** *p63*
McKeenan, Moses; Philadelphia, 1847 ***5704.8*** *p23*
McKeenan, William J.; New York, NY, 1867 ***5704.8*** *p220*
McKeeney, Cathy; Philadelphia, 1852 ***5704.8*** *p91*
McKeever, Alexander; New York, NY, 1838 ***8208.4*** *p89*
McKeever, Bernard 7; St. John, N.B., 1856 ***5704.8*** *p131*
McKeever, Bridget 14; St. John, N.B., 1856 ***5704.8*** *p131*
McKeever, Bridget 45; St. John, N.B., 1856 ***5704.8*** *p131*
McKeever, Brine 56; St. John, N.B., 1856 ***5704.8*** *p131*
McKeever, Charles 13; St. John, N.B., 1847 ***5704.8*** *p25*
McKeever, Charles 25; Philadelphia, 1853 ***5704.8*** *p109*
McKeever, Daniel 28; St. John, N.B., 1853 ***5704.8*** *p110*
McKeever, Hugh; Philadelphia, 1865 ***5704.8*** *p191*
McKeever, James 18; St. John, N.B., 1856 ***5704.8*** *p131*
McKeever, James 21; St. John, N.B., 1853 ***5704.8*** *p109*
McKeever, Jane; St. John, N.B., 1847 ***5704.8*** *p25*
McKeever, Jane 19; St. John, N.B., 1853 ***5704.8*** *p109*
McKeever, John; New York, NY, 1864 ***5704.8*** *p170*
McKeever, John; Philadelphia, 1848 ***53.26*** *p63*
McKeever, John; Philadelphia, 1848 ***5704.8*** *p46*
McKeever, John 10; St. John, N.B., 1847 ***5704.8*** *p25*
McKeever, John 11; St. John, N.B., 1856 ***5704.8*** *p131*
McKeever, John 21; St. John, N.B., 1856 ***5704.8*** *p131*
McKeever, Margaret; Philadelphia, 1870 ***5704.8*** *p239*
McKeever, Mary; Montreal, 1824 ***7603*** *p54*
McKeever, Mary; Philadelphia, 1865 ***5704.8*** *p191*
McKeever, Mary 18; Philadelphia, 1853 ***5704.8*** *p108*
McKeever, Matilda 9; St. John, N.B., 1856 ***5704.8*** *p131*
McKeever, Nancy 45; Philadelphia, 1804 ***53.26*** *p63*
McKeever, Patt 22; Philadelphia, 1856 ***5704.8*** *p129*
McKeever, Sarah; Philadelphia, 1865 ***5704.8*** *p204*
McKeever, Sarah 28; Quebec, 1858 ***5704.8*** *p138*
McKeever, William 12; St. John, N.B., 1847 ***5704.8*** *p25*
McKeever, William 17; St. John, N.B., 1856 ***5704.8*** *p131*
McKegue, Hamish 16; St. John, N.B., 1854 ***5704.8*** *p114*
McKeichan, Nancy; North Carolina, 1765-1838 ***1639.20*** *p176*
McKeir, William 22; Jamaica, 1731 ***3690.1*** *p146*
McKeithan, Neill; North Carolina, 1752-1785 ***1639.20*** *p172*
McKeithen, Neill; North Carolina, 1752-1785 ***1639.20*** *p176*
McKeiven, Ann; Montreal, 1822 ***7603*** *p54*
McKellar, Arthur Scott; Illinois, 1897 ***2896.5*** *p27*
McKellar, Dugald; South Carolina, 1816 ***1639.20*** *p172*
McKellar, John; Augusta, GA, 1771-1812 ***1639.20*** *p172*
McKellar, Mary 49; South Carolina, 1850 ***1639.20*** *p172*
McKellar, Peter 40; South Carolina, 1850 ***1639.20*** *p172*
McKelvey, David 55; Kansas, 1875 ***5240.1*** *p56*
McKelvey, Hannah; Philadelphia, 1865 ***5704.8*** *p195*
McKelvey, Jane; Philadelphia, 1864 ***5704.8*** *p171*
McKelvey, John; Philadelphia, 1864 ***5704.8*** *p171*
McKelvey, Joseph; New York, NY, 1864 ***5704.8*** *p183*
McKelvey, Margaret; Philadelphia, 1850 ***53.26*** *p63*
McKelvey, Margaret; Philadelphia, 1850 ***5704.8*** *p60*
McKelvey, Margaret 17; Philadelphia, 1855 ***5704.8*** *p124*
McKelvey, Mary; New York, NY, 1864 ***5704.8*** *p171*
McKelvey, Patrick 19; Philadelphia, 1855 ***5704.8*** *p124*
McKelvey, Robert 21; Quebec, 1859 ***5704.8*** *p143*
McKelvey, Sally; Philadelphia, 1850 ***53.26*** *p63*
McKelvey, Sally; Philadelphia, 1850 ***5704.8*** *p60*
McKelvey, Susanna; New York, NY, 1864 ***5704.8*** *p170*
McKelvey, William 22; Quebec, 1855 ***5704.8*** *p126*
McKelvy, George, Sr.; Pennsylvania, 1805-1872 ***2769.6*** *p6*
McKelvy, John; Quebec, 1849 ***5704.8*** *p52*
McKelvy, Patrick; Quebec, 1849 ***5704.8*** *p52*
McKelvy, William; New Orleans, 1849 ***5704.8*** *p59*
McKen, Bridget 25; St. John, N.B., 1862 ***5704.8*** *p150*
McKendric, Joseph 20; Wilmington, DE, 1831 ***6508.7*** *p161*
McKendrick, Ann; Philadelphia, 1865 ***5704.8*** *p199*
McKendrick, Janet 24; Wilmington, NC, 1774 ***1639.20*** *p176*
McKendrick, Patrick; America, 1739 ***4971*** *p14*
McKenerny, Matthew; Quebec, 1823 ***7603*** *p81*
McKenly, James; America, 1865 ***5704.8*** *p201*
McKenna, . . . 6; America, 1864 ***5704.8*** *p179*
McKenna, Widow; Quebec, 1847 ***5704.8*** *p38*
McKenna, Agnes 42; St. John, N.B., 1867 ***5704.8*** *p168*
McKenna, Alexander 7; Quebec, 1851 ***5704.8*** *p75*
McKenna, Alexandre; New Brunswick, 1823 ***7603*** *p36*
McKenna, Alice 11; St. John, N.B., 1867 ***5704.8*** *p168*
McKenna, Andrew 40; St. John, N.B., 1867 ***5704.8*** *p168*
McKenna, Ann; Philadelphia, 1851 ***5704.8*** *p70*
McKenna, Ann; Quebec, 1847 ***5704.8*** *p38*
McKenna, Ann 7; St. John, N.B., 1867 ***5704.8*** *p168*
McKenna, Anne 31; Quebec, 1863 ***5704.8*** *p154*
McKenna, Archy 3; Massachusetts, 1847 ***5881.1*** *p62*
McKenna, Archy 3; Massachusetts, 1849 ***5881.1*** *p62*
McKenna, Bernard; New York, NY, 1838 ***8208.4*** *p74*
McKenna, Bridget 3; St. John, N.B., 1867 ***5704.8*** *p168*
McKenna, Bridget 10; Philadelphia, 1860 ***5704.8*** *p146*
McKenna, Catharine; Philadelphia, 1867 ***5704.8*** *p220*
McKenna, Catharine 32; Massachusetts, 1847 ***5881.1*** *p64*
McKenna, Catherine 9 mos; Quebec, 1851 ***5704.8*** *p75*
McKenna, Catherine 1; St. John, N.B., 1867 ***5704.8*** *p168*
McKenna, Catherine 19; Philadelphia, 1855 ***5704.8*** *p124*
McKenna, Charles; Philadelphia, 1851 ***5704.8*** *p81*
McKenna, Edward 19; Quebec, 1855 ***5704.8*** *p126*
McKenna, Eliza 17; Massachusetts, 1849 ***5881.1*** *p66*
McKenna, Eliza 19; Philadelphia, 1856 ***5704.8*** *p128*
McKenna, Elizabeth; New York, NY, 1868 ***5704.8*** *p227*
McKenna, Ellen; New York, NY, 1864 ***5704.8*** *p188*
McKenna, Ellen; Philadelphia, 1864 ***5704.8*** *p172*
McKenna, Fanny 11; Quebec, 1851 ***5704.8*** *p75*
McKenna, Felix; Quebec, 1847 ***5704.8*** *p38*
McKenna, Francis 18; Philadelphia, 1860 ***5704.8*** *p145*
McKenna, Francis 30; Massachusetts, 1850 ***5881.1*** *p66*
McKenna, Hugh; Philadelphia, 1864 ***5704.8*** *p176*
McKenna, Hugh 10; Quebec, 1863 ***5704.8*** *p154*
McKenna, James; America, 1739 ***4971*** *p64*
McKenna, James; America, 1850 ***1450.2*** *p97A*
McKenna, James; Montreal, 1821 ***7603*** *p90*

*Relative:*Elizabeth 6
*Relative:*Margaret 5
McKinley, Jane; Philadelphia, 1848 ***5704.8*** *p46*
McKinley, Jane 30; Philadelphia, 1860 ***5704.8*** *p146*
McKinley, John; Quebec, 1852 ***5704.8*** *p91*
McKinley, John 2; Philadelphia, 1860 ***5704.8*** *p146*
McKinley, John 35; St. John, N.B., 1859 ***5704.8*** *p140*
McKinley, Margaret; Philadelphia, 1850 ***53.26*** *p64*
McKinley, Margaret; Philadelphia, 1850 ***5704.8*** *p68*
McKinley, Margaret; St. John, N.B., 1848 ***5704.8*** *p43*
McKinley, Margaret 5 *SEE* McKinley, Jane
McKinley, Margaret 5; Philadelphia, 1848 ***5704.8*** *p46*
McKinley, Mary 4; Philadelphia, 1860 ***5704.8*** *p146*
McKinley, Matty *SEE* McKinley, Jane
McKinley, Matty; Philadelphia, 1848 ***5704.8*** *p46*
McKinley, Patrick; New York, NY, 1864 ***5704.8*** *p173*
McKinley, Peter; Kansas, 1908 ***6013.40*** *p16*
McKinley, Rebecca; New York, NY, 1867 ***5704.8*** *p224*
McKinley, Samuel; Philadelphia, 1860 ***5704.8*** *p146*
McKinley, Samuel 33; Philadelphia, 1804 ***53.26*** *p64*
McKinley, Sarah; New York, NY, 1864 ***5704.8*** *p173*
McKinley, William George 3; St. John, N.B., 1848 ***5704.8*** *p43*
McKinlwy, Hugh; Philadelphia, 1811 ***53.26*** *p64*
McKinly, Catherine 30; Philadelphia, 1865 ***5704.8*** *p164*
McKinly, John 32; Philadelphia, 1865 ***5704.8*** *p164*
McKinn, Edward; New York, NY, 1835 ***8208.4*** *p5*
McKinna, Margaret *SEE* McKinna, Mary
McKinna, Margaret; Philadelphia, 1850 ***5704.8*** *p68*
McKinna, Mary; Philadelphia, 1850 ***53.26*** *p64*
*Relative:*Margaret
McKinna, Mary; Philadelphia, 1850 ***5704.8*** *p68*
McKinnal, Daniel; Quebec, 1768 ***7603*** *p38*
McKinnan, M. 28; Kansas, 1876 ***5240.1*** *p57*
McKinnedy, Bella; New York, NY, 1869 ***5704.8*** *p235*
McKinnedy, James; New York, NY, 1869 ***5704.8*** *p235*
McKinner, Ann *SEE* McKinner, James
McKinner, Ann; Philadelphia, 1850 ***5704.8*** *p60*
McKinner, James; Philadelphia, 1850 ***53.26*** *p64*
*Relative:*Ann
McKinner, James; Philadelphia, 1850 ***5704.8*** *p60*
McKinney, Alexander 1; St. John, N.B., 1864 ***5704.8*** *p158*
McKinney, Anne; St. John, N.B., 1853 ***5704.8*** *p99*
McKinney, Bridget; New York, NY, 1867 ***5704.8*** *p216*
McKinney, Bryan 6 mos; St. John, N.B., 1847 ***5704.8*** *p9*
McKinney, Catharine; Philadelphia, 1865 ***5704.8*** *p193*
McKinney, Edward; Philadelphia, 1850 ***5704.8*** *p64*
McKinney, Edward; Philadelphia, 1866 ***5704.8*** *p209*
McKinney, Elenor 2; St. John, N.B., 1847 ***5704.8*** *p9*
McKinney, Elizabeth; St. John, N.B., 1853 ***5704.8*** *p99*
McKinney, Hugh; St. John, N.B., 1847 ***5704.8*** *p9*
McKinney, Isabella 65; St. John, N.B., 1864 ***5704.8*** *p158*
McKinney, James; Philadelphia, 1851 ***5704.8*** *p70*
McKinney, James; Philadelphia, 1852 ***5704.8*** *p85*
McKinney, James; Quebec, 1852 ***5704.8*** *p87*
McKinney, James; Quebec, 1852 ***5704.8*** *p91*
McKinney, James 13; St. John, N.B., 1853 ***5704.8*** *p99*
McKinney, James 17; St. John, N.B., 1856 ***5704.8*** *p131*
McKinney, James William 25; St. John, N.B., 1864 ***5704.8*** *p158*
McKinney, Jane; Philadelphia, 1866 ***5704.8*** *p205*
McKinney, Jane; St. John, N.B., 1848 ***5704.8*** *p47*
McKinney, Jane 20; Philadelphia, 1857 ***5704.8*** *p132*
McKinney, Jermiah; Philadelphia, 1865 ***5704.8*** *p197*
McKinney, John; Philadelphia, 1850 ***53.26*** *p64*
McKinney, John; Philadelphia, 1850 ***5704.8*** *p60*
McKinney, John; St. John, N.B., 1852 ***5704.8*** *p95*
McKinney, John; St. John, N.B., 1853 ***5704.8*** *p99*
McKinney, John 20; St. John, N.B., 1854 ***5704.8*** *p122*
McKinney, John H.; Illinois, 1868 ***2896.5*** *p27*
McKinney, Margaret; New York, NY, 1869 ***5704.8*** *p235*
McKinney, Margaret; Philadelphia, 1852 ***5704.8*** *p92*
McKinney, Margaret; St. John, N.B., 1852 ***5704.8*** *p95*
McKinney, Martha 25; St. John, N.B., 1864 ***5704.8*** *p158*
McKinney, Mary; New York, NY, 1864 ***5704.8*** *p183*
McKinney, Mary; Philadelphia, 1850 ***5704.8*** *p64*
McKinney, Mary; St. John, N.B., 1848 ***5704.8*** *p39*
McKinney, Mary 24; Philadelphia, 1868 ***5704.8*** *p225*
McKinney, Mary J.; New York, NY, 1864 ***5704.8*** *p175*
McKinney, Mathew; Philadelphia, 1865 ***5704.8*** *p185*
McKinney, Michael; New York, NY, 1869 ***5704.8*** *p233*
McKinney, Patrick; Philadelphia, 1867 ***5704.8*** *p216*
McKinney, Peggy; St. John, N.B., 1847 ***5704.8*** *p4*
McKinney, Peggy 3; St. John, N.B., 1847 ***5704.8*** *p9*
McKinney, Rachel 25; Philadelphia, 1860 ***5704.8*** *p145*
McKinney, Rose; Philadelphia, 1867 ***5704.8*** *p223*
McKinney, Sarah; America, 1868 ***5704.8*** *p225*
McKinney, Sarah; Philadelphia, 1847 ***53.26*** *p64*
McKinney, Sarah; Philadelphia, 1847 ***5704.8*** *p23*
McKinney, Sarah; St. John, N.B., 1847 ***5704.8*** *p9*
McKinney, Sarah Ann 20; Philadelphia, 1858 ***5704.8*** *p138*
McKinnon, Alexander *SEE* McKinnon, John
McKinnon, Alexander; America, 1802 ***1639.20*** *p177*
McKinnon, Alexander 64; North Carolina, 1850 ***1639.20*** *p177*
McKinnon, Alexander 68; North Carolina, 1850 ***1639.20*** *p177*
McKinnon, Ann 30; St. John, N.B., 1862 ***5704.8*** *p150*
McKinnon, Anna Belle 23; Kansas, 1876 ***5240.1*** *p57*
McKinnon, Catherine; North Carolina, 1766-1826 ***1639.20*** *p178*
McKinnon, Catherine 51; North Carolina, 1850 ***1639.20*** *p178*
McKinnon, Charles; North Carolina, 1778-1816 ***1639.20*** *p178*
McKinnon, Christian; North Carolina, 1745-1824 ***1639.20*** *p178*
McKinnon, Christina 27; St. John, N.B., 1862 ***5704.8*** *p150*
McKinnon, Christy *SEE* McKinnon, Donald
McKinnon, Christy *SEE* McKinnon, John
McKinnon, Daniel; America, 1787 ***1639.20*** *p178*
McKinnon, Daniel 55; St. John, N.B., 1862 ***5704.8*** *p150*
McKinnon, Daniel H. 32; Kansas, 1876 ***5240.1*** *p57*
McKinnon, Donald; North Carolina, 1703-1803 ***1639.20*** *p178*
McKinnon, Donald; Nova Scotia, 1830 ***7085.4*** *p45*
*Wife:*Christy
McKinnon, Duncan C. 39; Kansas, 1879 ***5240.1*** *p60*
McKinnon, Effie 58 *SEE* McKinnon, Roderick
McKinnon, Flora *SEE* McKinnon, John
McKinnon, Gilbert; Wilmington, NC, 1782-1819 ***1639.20*** *p178*
McKinnon, John *SEE* McKinnon, John
McKinnon, John; North Carolina, 1750-1819 ***1639.20*** *p178*
McKinnon, John; North Carolina, 1768-1812 ***1639.20*** *p178*
McKinnon, John; Nova Scotia, 1830 ***7085.4*** *p44*
*Wife:*Flora
*Child:*John
*Child:*Christy
*Child:*Alexander
McKinnon, John; Washington, 1859-1920 ***2872.1*** *p27*
McKinnon, John, Sr. 62; North Carolina, 1850 ***1639.20*** *p179*
McKinnon, John H.; Washington, 1859-1920 ***2872.1*** *p27*
McKinnon, Ket *SEE* McKinnon, Neil
McKinnon, Malcolm *SEE* McKinnon, Neil
McKinnon, Malcolm 28; St. John, N.B., 1862 ***5704.8*** *p150*
McKinnon, Margaret *SEE* McKinnon, Neil
McKinnon, Margaret 80; North Carolina, 1850 ***1639.20*** *p179*
McKinnon, Marion *SEE* McKinnon, Neil
McKinnon, Mary *SEE* McKinnon, Neil
McKinnon, Mary 30; Kansas, 1877 ***5240.1*** *p58*
McKinnon, Mary 62; North Carolina, 1850 ***1639.20*** *p209*
McKinnon, Mary Ann 23; Kansas, 1876 ***5240.1*** *p57*
McKinnon, Murdoch; America, 1802 ***1639.20*** *p179*
McKinnon, Nancy; North Carolina, 1725-1825 ***1639.20*** *p126*
McKinnon, Neil; America, 1791 ***1639.20*** *p179*
McKinnon, Neil; Nova Scotia, 1830 ***7085.4*** *p44*
*Wife:*Marion
*Child:*Malcolm
*Child:*Mary
*Child:*Ket
*Child:*Margaret
McKinnon, Neill; America, 1803 ***1639.20*** *p179*
McKinnon, Peter; San Francisco, 1850 ***4914.15*** *p10*
McKinnon, Peter; San Francisco, 1850 ***4914.15*** *p12*
McKinnon, Peter; Washington, 1859-1920 ***2872.1*** *p27*
McKinnon, Roderick 60; South Carolina, 1850 ***1639.20*** *p179*
*Relative:*Effie 58
McKinnon, Roy; America, 1802 ***1639.20*** *p179*
McKinny, James; Philadelphia, 1852 ***5704.8*** *p88*
McKinny, Margery; Philadelphia, 1852 ***5704.8*** *p88*
McKinny, William 33; Massachusetts, 1848 ***5881.1*** *p77*
McKinon, Donald 26; Montreal, 1765 ***7603*** *p40*
McKinstry, . . .; Iroquois Co., IL, 1892 ***3455.1*** *p12*
McKinzey, John; New York, NY, 1834 ***8208.4*** *p2*
McKinzie, Colin; Colorado, 1903 ***9678.2*** *p128*
McKinziey, Argyle 20; Maryland, 1724 ***3690.1*** *p146*
McKirlen, John; Philadelphia, 1866 ***5704.8*** *p208*
McKirnan, Alexander 2; Philadelphia, 1856 ***5704.8*** *p128*
McKirnan, Elizabeth 25; Philadelphia, 1856 ***5704.8*** *p128*
McKissock, Elizabeth 4; Quebec, 1864 ***5704.8*** *p163*
McKissock, Isabella 26; Quebec, 1864 ***5704.8*** *p163*
McKissock, John 30; Quebec, 1864 ***5704.8*** *p163*
McKissock, Mary 2; Quebec, 1864 ***5704.8*** *p163*
McKnally, Michael 18; Philadelphia, 1774 ***1219.7*** *p183*
McKnight, Andrew *SEE* McKnight, David
McKnight, Daniel *SEE* McKnight, David
McKnight, David; Philadelphia, 1811 ***53.26*** *p64*
*Relative:*Mary
*Relative:*Andrew
*Relative:*Jane
*Relative:*Thomas
*Relative:*Daniel
McKnight, Jane *SEE* McKnight, David
McKnight, Mary *SEE* McKnight, David
McKnight, Samuel; Charleston, SC, 1825 ***1639.20*** *p179*
McKnight, Susanna; Philadelphia, 1866 ***5704.8*** *p207*
McKnight, Thomas *SEE* McKnight, David
McKoag, Mary 4; Massachusetts, 1849 ***5881.1*** *p71*
McKoag, Thomas 20; Massachusetts, 1849 ***5881.1*** *p76*
McKoin, Thomas; America, 1773-1774 ***2859.11*** *p7*
McKoin, Thomas 28; Virginia, 1773 ***1219.7*** *p169*
McKoon, Thomas 20; Massachusetts, 1847 ***5881.1*** *p76*
McKowen, Alice 22; Philadelphia, 1864 ***5704.8*** *p155*
McKowen, Jane 11; Philadelphia, 1864 ***5704.8*** *p155*
McKowen, Patrick 20; Philadelphia, 1864 ***5704.8*** *p155*
McKown, . . . 5 mos; New York, NY, 1868 ***5704.8*** *p227*
McKown, Jane; New York, NY, 1868 ***5704.8*** *p227*
McKown, Mary Jane 3; New York, NY, 1868 ***5704.8*** *p227*
McKown, Robert 3; New York, NY, 1868 ***5704.8*** *p227*
McKown, Robert John 4; New York, NY, 1868 ***5704.8*** *p227*
McKown, Sarah; New York, NY, 1868 ***5704.8*** *p227*
McKown, Thomas 2; New York, NY, 1868 ***5704.8*** *p227*
McKray, Sarah; Quebec, 1825 ***7603*** *p88*
McKreig, James 10 mos; Massachusetts, 1849 ***5881.1*** *p68*
McKreig, James 33; Massachusetts, 1849 ***5881.1*** *p68*
McKreig, John 8; Massachusetts, 1849 ***5881.1*** *p68*
McKuirson, John; Quebec, 1790 ***9775.5*** *p198A*
McKuirson, Lachlan; Quebec, 1790 ***9775.5*** *p198A*
With family of 10
McKune, David; New York, NY, 1835 ***8208.4*** *p6*
McKutchen, Mary 22; Wilmington, DE, 1831 ***6508.3*** *p101*
McKutien, Ann; Quebec, 1824 ***7603*** *p95*
McLachlan, Peter; North Carolina, 1823 ***1639.20*** *p180*
McLachlan, Robert; North Carolina, 1814 ***1639.20*** *p180*
McLachlen, James; North Carolina, 1739 ***1639.20*** *p180*
McLafferty, Anne; Philadelphia, 1867 ***5704.8*** *p217*
McLagash, Archibald 69; Quebec, 1862 ***5704.8*** *p151*
McLaggan, Archibald; North Carolina, 1771 ***1639.20*** *p180*
McLain, Daniel; America, 1802 ***1639.20*** *p189*
McLain, Duncan; Virginia, 1798 ***4778.2*** *p141*
McLain, John; America, 1802 ***1639.20*** *p192*
McLaine, John; North Carolina, 1814 ***1639.20*** *p180*
McLairen, Donald; New England, 1729 ***8894.1*** *p192*
McLamont, Eliza Ann; Philadelphia, 1849 ***53.26*** *p64*
McLamont, Eliza Ann; Philadelphia, 1849 ***5704.8*** *p53*
McLanberg, John; Ohio, 1798-1818 ***8582.2*** *p25*
McLanburg, John; Ohio, 1798-1818 ***8582.2*** *p54*
McLancy, Cormick 5; Philadelphia, 1850 ***53.26*** *p64*
*Relative:*Daniel 3
McLancy, Cormick 5; Philadelphia, 1850 ***5704.8*** *p69*
McLancy, Daniel 3 *SEE* McLancy, Cormick
McLancy, Daniel 3; Philadelphia, 1850 ***5704.8*** *p69*
McLandburgh, John; Ohio, 1798-1818 ***8582.2*** *p54*
McLanghlan, Susan; St. John, N.B., 1850 ***5704.8*** *p66*
McLarchy, James; St. John, N.B., 1847 ***5704.8*** *p21*
McLaren, . . . 79; South Carolina, 1850 ***1639.20*** *p180*
*Relative:*Janet 76
McLaren, Alexander 8; St. John, N.B., 1863 ***5704.8*** *p152*
McLaren, Charlotte 1; St. John, N.B., 1863 ***5704.8*** *p152*
McLaren, Daniel; North Carolina, 1713-1813 ***1639.20*** *p182*
McLaren, Donald 12; Wilmington, NC, 1775 ***1639.20*** *p182*
McLaren, Duncan 30; Wilmington, NC, 1775 ***1639.20*** *p182*
McLaren, Janet 76 *SEE* McLaren, . . .
McLaren, John; Illinois, 1890 ***2896.5*** *p27*
McLaren, John; South Carolina, 1716 ***1639.20*** *p183*
McLaren, John 10; St. John, N.B., 1863 ***5704.8*** *p152*
McLaren, Lachlen 25; Wilmington, NC, 1775 ***1639.20*** *p183*
McLaren, Lawrence 20; Wilmington, NC, 1775 ***1639.20*** *p183*
McLaren, Margaret 20; St. John, N.B., 1863 ***5704.8*** *p152*
McLaren, Margaret 44; St. John, N.B., 1863 ***5704.8*** *p152*
McLaren, Mary Anderson; New York, 1791 ***8894.1*** *p192*
McLaren, Patrick; South Carolina, 1716 ***1639.20*** *p185*
McLargan, Catharine; Philadelphia, 1865 ***5704.8*** *p197*
McLarkey, Charles; New York, NY, 1869 ***5704.8*** *p233*
McLarkey, Charles; Philadelphia, 1871 ***5704.8*** *p240*

McLarkey, Mary; New York, NY, 1869 ***5704.8*** *p233*
McLarkey, Mary; Philadelphia, 1871 ***5704.8*** *p240*
McLarkey, Patrick; Philadelphia, 1871 ***5704.8*** *p240*
McLarren, Jane 16; St. John, N.B., 1855 ***5704.8*** *p127*
McLarren, William; St. John, N.B., 1848 ***5704.8*** *p48*
McLarty, Alexander; America, 1773 ***1639.20*** *p185*
McLarty, Alexander; North Carolina, 1757-1824 ***1639.20*** *p185*
McLarty, Archibald; North Carolina, 1756-1814 ***1639.20*** *p185*
McLauchlan, John; America, 1791 ***1639.20*** *p187*
McLauchlan, John; America, 1811 ***1639.20*** *p187*
McLauchlan, Lauchlan; America, 1805 ***1639.20*** *p187*
McLauchlan, Robert; America, 1802 ***1639.20*** *p187*
McLauchlen, John; America, 1803 ***1639.20*** *p187*
McLauchlin, Archibald; North Carolina, 1805 ***1639.20*** *p186*
McLauchlin, Dugald; North Carolina, 1757-1830 ***1639.20*** *p186*
McLauchlin, Duncan; North Carolina, 1796-1822 ***1639.20*** *p186*
McLauchlin, Duncan; North Carolina, 1805 ***1639.20*** *p186*
McLauchlin, Duncan 53 *SEE* McLauchlin, Sarah
McLauchlin, Flora 85; North Carolina, 1850 ***1639.20*** *p111*
McLauchlin, Jennett 66; North Carolina, 1850 ***1639.20*** *p186*
McLauchlin, Neil; North Carolina, 1805 ***1639.20*** *p187*
McLauchlin, Peter 66; North Carolina, 1850 ***1639.20*** *p187*
*Relative:*Sarah 28
McLauchlin, Sarah 28 *SEE* McLauchlin, Peter
McLauchlin, Sarah 85; North Carolina, 1850 ***1639.20*** *p188*
*Relative:*Duncan 53
McLaughlan, Biddy; Philadelphia, 1851 ***5704.8*** *p81*
McLaughlan, Catherine; St. John, N.B., 1850 ***5704.8*** *p61*
McLaughlan, Cicily; St. John, N.B., 1850 ***5704.8*** *p62*
McLaughlan, Daniel; St. John, N.B., 1850 ***5704.8*** *p62*
McLaughlan, Elizabeth; Philadelphia, 1851 ***5704.8*** *p76*
McLaughlan, Fanny; St. John, N.B., 1847 ***5704.8*** *p19*
McLaughlan, Margaret; Philadelphia, 1851 ***5704.8*** *p79*
McLaughlan, Margaret; Philadelphia, 1851 ***5704.8*** *p81*
McLaughlan, Margaret; St. John, N.B., 1850 ***5704.8*** *p61*
McLaughlan, Michael; Philadelphia, 1851 ***5704.8*** *p81*
McLaughlan, Nancy; St. John, N.B., 1851 ***5704.8*** *p78*
McLaughlan, Patrick; St. John, N.B., 1847 ***5704.8*** *p25*
McLaughlan, Patrick; St. John, N.B., 1851 ***5704.8*** *p77*
McLaughlan, Rosanna; St. John, N.B., 1850 ***5704.8*** *p61*
McLaughlan, Sarah; Philadelphia, 1847 ***53.26*** *p64*
McLaughlan, Sarah; Philadelphia, 1847 ***5704.8*** *p24*
McLaughlan, William; Philadelphia, 1850 ***5704.8*** *p64*
McLaughlan, William; Philadelphia, 1851 ***5704.8*** *p76*
McLaughlin, Alex; St. John, N.B., 1850 ***5704.8*** *p62*
McLaughlin, Alexander; Quebec, 1847 ***5704.8*** *p8*
McLaughlin, Alexander 12; Philadelphia, 1850 ***5704.8*** *p64*
McLaughlin, Alexander 46; North Carolina, 1850 ***1639.20*** *p185*
McLaughlin, Andrew; Philadelphia, 1852 ***5704.8*** *p85*
McLaughlin, Andrew; Philadelphia, 1852 ***5704.8*** *p89*
McLaughlin, Andrew 4; Philadelphia, 1865 ***5704.8*** *p190*
McLaughlin, Angus 23; Massachusetts, 1850 ***5881.1*** *p62*
McLaughlin, Ann *SEE* McLaughlin, James
McLaughlin, Ann; America, 1865 ***5704.8*** *p203*
McLaughlin, Ann; Philadelphia, 1847 ***5704.8*** *p22*
McLaughlin, Ann; Philadelphia, 1853 ***5704.8*** *p100*
McLaughlin, Ann; St. John, N.B., 1847 ***5704.8*** *p24*
McLaughlin, Ann; St. John, N.B., 1850 ***5704.8*** *p62*
McLaughlin, Ann 9 mos; Philadelphia, 1853 ***5704.8*** *p111*
McLaughlin, Ann 9; Massachusetts, 1849 ***5881.1*** *p62*
McLaughlin, Ann 16; Massachusetts, 1849 ***5881.1*** *p62*
McLaughlin, Ann 17; St. John, N.B., 1863 ***5704.8*** *p153*
McLaughlin, Ann 19; Philadelphia, 1859 ***5704.8*** *p141*
McLaughlin, Ann 23; Philadelphia, 1860 ***5704.8*** *p145*
McLaughlin, Ann 30; Philadelphia, 1859 ***5704.8*** *p141*
McLaughlin, Anne; New York, NY, 1868 ***5704.8*** *p228*
McLaughlin, Anne; St. John, N.B., 1847 ***5704.8*** *p25*
McLaughlin, Anne; St. John, N.B., 1850 ***5704.8*** *p68*
McLaughlin, Anne; St. John, N.B., 1853 ***5704.8*** *p106*
McLaughlin, Anne 9; St. John, N.B., 1849 ***5704.8*** *p56*
McLaughlin, Anne 17; Philadelphia, 1857 ***5704.8*** *p132*
McLaughlin, Anne 27; St. John, N.B., 1863 ***5704.8*** *p155*
McLaughlin, Anney 20; St. John, N.B., 1864 ***5704.8*** *p158*
McLaughlin, Archibald; America, 1804 ***1639.20*** *p186*
McLaughlin, Barney; Philadelphia, 1864 ***5704.8*** *p180*
McLaughlin, Barney; St. John, N.B., 1853 ***5704.8*** *p98*
McLaughlin, Barney 3 mos; Philadelphia, 1852 ***5704.8*** *p89*
McLaughlin, Barney 14; Philadelphia, 1856 ***5704.8*** *p128*
McLaughlin, Beddy 5; Philadelphia, 1853 ***5704.8*** *p101*
McLaughlin, Bernard; New York, NY, 1838 ***8208.4*** *p74*
McLaughlin, Bernard; Philadelphia, 1847 ***53.26*** *p64*
*Relative:*Catherine
McLaughlin, Bernard; Philadelphia, 1847 ***5704.8*** *p30*
McLaughlin, Bernard; Philadelphia, 1849 ***53.26*** *p64*
McLaughlin, Bernard; Philadelphia, 1849 ***5704.8*** *p50*
McLaughlin, Bernard; Philadelphia, 1850 ***5704.8*** *p64*
McLaughlin, Bernard; St. John, N.B., 1852 ***5704.8*** *p95*
McLaughlin, Bernard; St. John, N.B., 1853 ***5704.8*** *p106*
McLaughlin, Bernard 13; St. John, N.B., 1850 ***5704.8*** *p68*
McLaughlin, Bernard 18; St. John, N.B., 1853 ***5704.8*** *p110*
McLaughlin, Betsey; Philadelphia, 1852 ***5704.8*** *p88*
McLaughlin, Betty; Philadelphia, 1868 ***5704.8*** *p225*
McLaughlin, Betty; Quebec, 1849 ***5704.8*** *p52*
McLaughlin, Betty; St. John, N.B., 1851 ***5704.8*** *p72*
McLaughlin, Betty 20; Philadelphia, 1857 ***5704.8*** *p132*
McLaughlin, Betty 48; St. John, N.B., 1858 ***5704.8*** *p137*
McLaughlin, Betty Ann; St. John, N.B., 1851 ***5704.8*** *p77*
McLaughlin, Biddy *SEE* McLaughlin, Francis
McLaughlin, Biddy; New York, NY, 1864 ***5704.8*** *p171*
McLaughlin, Biddy; Philadelphia, 1853 ***5704.8*** *p100*
McLaughlin, Biddy; St. John, N.B., 1848 ***5704.8*** *p39*
McLaughlin, Biddy; St. John, N.B., 1852 ***5704.8*** *p93*
McLaughlin, Biddy; St. John, N.B., 1853 ***5704.8*** *p106*
McLaughlin, Biddy 4 *SEE* McLaughlin, John
McLaughlin, Biddy 4; Philadelphia, 1847 ***5704.8*** *p5*
McLaughlin, Biddy 9; St. John, N.B., 1851 ***5704.8*** *p72*
McLaughlin, Biddy 11; Philadelphia, 1852 ***5704.8*** *p89*
McLaughlin, Biddy 11; St. John, N.B., 1854 ***5704.8*** *p121*
McLaughlin, Biddy 12; St. John, N.B., 1853 ***5704.8*** *p99*
McLaughlin, Bridget; Philadelphia, 1848 ***53.26*** *p64*
*Relative:*Dennis 2
*Relative:*Catherine 6 mos
McLaughlin, Bridget; Philadelphia, 1848 ***5704.8*** *p40*
McLaughlin, Bridget; Philadelphia, 1850 ***53.26*** *p64*
McLaughlin, Bridget; Philadelphia, 1850 ***5704.8*** *p60*
McLaughlin, Bridget 20; St. John, N.B., 1862 ***5704.8*** *p150*
McLaughlin, Catharine; New York, NY, 1865 ***5704.8*** *p195*
McLaughlin, Catharine; New York, NY, 1866 ***5704.8*** *p205*
McLaughlin, Catharine; New York, NY, 1868 ***5704.8*** *p228*
McLaughlin, Catharine; Philadelphia, 1847 ***5704.8*** *p22*
McLaughlin, Catharine; Philadelphia, 1864 ***5704.8*** *p183*
McLaughlin, Catharine; Philadelphia, 1864 ***5704.8*** *p185*
McLaughlin, Catharine; Philadelphia, 1865 ***5704.8*** *p190*
McLaughlin, Catharine; Philadelphia, 1867 ***5704.8*** *p218*
McLaughlin, Catherine *SEE* McLaughlin, Bernard
McLaughlin, Catherine *SEE* McLaughlin, James
McLaughlin, Catherine; Philadelphia, 1847 ***5704.8*** *p30*
McLaughlin, Catherine; Philadelphia, 1850 ***53.26*** *p64*
McLaughlin, Catherine; Quebec, 1848 ***5704.8*** *p41*
McLaughlin, Catherine; St. John, N.B., 1847 ***5704.8*** *p9*
McLaughlin, Catherine; St. John, N.B., 1848 ***5704.8*** *p38*
McLaughlin, Catherine; St. John, N.B., 1849 ***5704.8*** *p48*
McLaughlin, Catherine; St. John, N.B., 1851 ***5704.8*** *p71*
McLaughlin, Catherine; St. John, N.B., 1853 ***5704.8*** *p100*
McLaughlin, Catherine 6 mos *SEE* McLaughlin, Bridget
McLaughlin, Catherine 6 mos; Philadelphia, 1848 ***5704.8*** *p40*
McLaughlin, Catherine 8; St. John, N.B., 1864 ***5704.8*** *p158*
McLaughlin, Catherine 12; St. John, N.B., 1850 ***5704.8*** *p67*
McLaughlin, Catherine 14; Philadelphia, 1858 ***5704.8*** *p139*
McLaughlin, Catherine 16; St. John, N.B., 1859 ***5704.8*** *p143*
McLaughlin, Catherine 19; St. John, N.B., 1854 ***5704.8*** *p115*
McLaughlin, Catherine 24; Philadelphia, 1855 ***5704.8*** *p123*
McLaughlin, Catherine 24; St. John, N.B., 1856 ***5704.8*** *p131*
McLaughlin, Catherine 47; Philadelphia, 1854 ***5704.8*** *p123*
McLaughlin, Catherine Ann; Philadelphia, 1850 ***5704.8*** *p59*
McLaughlin, Caty 21; St. John, N.B., 1857 ***5704.8*** *p134*
McLaughlin, Cecilia; New York, NY, 1869 ***5704.8*** *p232*
McLaughlin, Cecilia; Philadelphia, 1869 ***5704.8*** *p236*
McLaughlin, Charles; Philadelphia, 1850 ***53.26*** *p64*
*Relative:*Susan
McLaughlin, Charles; Philadelphia, 1850 ***5704.8*** *p65*
McLaughlin, Charles; Philadelphia, 1866 ***5704.8*** *p207*
McLaughlin, Charles; St. John, N.B., 1847 ***5704.8*** *p26*
McLaughlin, Charles; St. John, N.B., 1848 ***5704.8*** *p38*
McLaughlin, Charles; St. John, N.B., 1852 ***5704.8*** *p84*
McLaughlin, Charles 2; New York, NY, 1870 ***5704.8*** *p237*
McLaughlin, Charles 4; Philadelphia, 1854 ***5704.8*** *p123*
McLaughlin, Charles 17; Philadelphia, 1857 ***5704.8*** *p133*
McLaughlin, Charlotte 3; Philadelphia, 1853 ***5704.8*** *p112*
McLaughlin, Christina 20; St. John, N.B., 1857 ***5704.8*** *p135*
McLaughlin, Cicily; St. John, N.B., 1849 ***5704.8*** *p56*
McLaughlin, Cicily; St. John, N.B., 1853 ***5704.8*** *p107*
McLaughlin, Cicily 13; St. John, N.B., 1848 ***5704.8*** *p39*
McLaughlin, Cicily 18; St. John, N.B., 1863 ***5704.8*** *p152*
McLaughlin, Cicily 21; St. John, N.B., 1854 ***5704.8*** *p115*
McLaughlin, Claudius 40; Philadelphia, 1853 ***5704.8*** *p111*
McLaughlin, Cornelius; Philadelphia, 1864 ***5704.8*** *p185*
McLaughlin, Dan; Quebec, 1847 ***5704.8*** *p16*
McLaughlin, Daniel; New York, 1836 ***7036*** *p122*
McLaughlin, Daniel; Philadelphia, 1864 ***5704.8*** *p183*
McLaughlin, Daniel; St. John, N.B., 1847 ***5704.8*** *p9*
McLaughlin, Daniel; St. John, N.B., 1849 ***5704.8*** *p56*
McLaughlin, Daniel; St. John, N.B., 1851 ***5704.8*** *p72*
McLaughlin, Daniel; St. John, N.B., 1853 ***5704.8*** *p99*
McLaughlin, Daniel 12 *SEE* McLaughlin, Sally
McLaughlin, Daniel 12; Philadelphia, 1850 ***5704.8*** *p65*
McLaughlin, David; Philadelphia, 1867 ***5704.8*** *p218*
McLaughlin, Dennis; Philadelphia, 1868 ***5704.8*** *p225*
McLaughlin, Dennis; St. John, N.B., 1851 ***5704.8*** *p72*
McLaughlin, Dennis 2 *SEE* McLaughlin, Bridget
McLaughlin, Dennis 2; Philadelphia, 1848 ***5704.8*** *p40*
McLaughlin, Dennis 12; St. John, N.B., 1853 ***5704.8*** *p106*
McLaughlin, Dennis 20; St. John, N.B., 1860 ***5704.8*** *p144*
McLaughlin, Donnil; St. John, N.B., 1847 ***5704.8*** *p9*
McLaughlin, Edward; New York, NY, 1869 ***5704.8*** *p233*
McLaughlin, Edward; Philadelphia, 1852 ***5704.8*** *p85*
McLaughlin, Edward; Philadelphia, 1867 ***5704.8*** *p217*
McLaughlin, Edward; St. John, N.B., 1847 ***5704.8*** *p9*
McLaughlin, Edward 11; New York, NY, 1869 ***5704.8*** *p233*
McLaughlin, Edward 19; Philadelphia, 1854 ***5704.8*** *p117*
McLaughlin, Edward 20; Philadelphia, 1855 ***5704.8*** *p123*
McLaughlin, Edward 20; St. John, N.B., 1860 ***5704.8*** *p143*
McLaughlin, Edward 22; Philadelphia, 1857 ***5704.8*** *p132*
McLaughlin, Edward 50; St. John, N.B., 1861 ***5704.8*** *p149*
McLaughlin, Eleanor; Philadelphia, 1811 ***53.26*** *p64*
McLaughlin, Eleanor; St. John, N.B., 1851 ***5704.8*** *p72*
McLaughlin, Eleanor; St. John, N.B., 1853 ***5704.8*** *p106*
McLaughlin, Eliza; New York, NY, 1867 ***5704.8*** *p219*
McLaughlin, Eliza; Philadelphia, 1867 ***5704.8*** *p221*
McLaughlin, Eliza 6; Philadelphia, 1853 ***5704.8*** *p111*
McLaughlin, Elizabeth; Philadelphia, 1851 ***5704.8*** *p70*
McLaughlin, Elizabeth 13; Quebec, 1853 ***5704.8*** *p103*
McLaughlin, Elizabeth 20; Wilmington, DE, 1831 ***6508.3*** *p100*
McLaughlin, Elizabeth 22; Philadelphia, 1859 ***5704.8*** *p142*
McLaughlin, Elleanor *SEE* McLaughlin, John
McLaughlin, Elleanor; Philadelphia, 1847 ***5704.8*** *p5*
McLaughlin, Elleanor; St. John, N.B., 1847 ***5704.8*** *p5*
McLaughlin, Elleanor; St. John, N.B., 1847 ***5704.8*** *p15*
McLaughlin, Elleanor; St. John, N.B., 1847 ***5704.8*** *p24*
McLaughlin, Elleanor; St. John, N.B., 1847 ***5704.8*** *p25*
McLaughlin, Elleanor 6 *SEE* McLaughlin, Sally
McLaughlin, Elleanor 6; Philadelphia, 1850 ***5704.8*** *p65*
McLaughlin, Elleanor 21; Philadelphia, 1854 ***5704.8*** *p117*
McLaughlin, Ellen; Philadelphia, 1850 ***53.26*** *p64*
McLaughlin, Ellen; Philadelphia, 1850 ***5704.8*** *p68*
McLaughlin, Ellen; Philadelphia, 1851 ***5704.8*** *p81*
McLaughlin, Ellen; Philadelphia, 1866 ***5704.8*** *p205*
McLaughlin, Ellen; Philadelphia, 1867 ***5704.8*** *p221*
McLaughlin, Ellen; Quebec, 1847 ***5704.8*** *p16*
McLaughlin, Ellen; Quebec, 1849 ***5704.8*** *p57*
McLaughlin, Ellen; St. John, N.B., 1847 ***5704.8*** *p9*
McLaughlin, Ellen; St. John, N.B., 1851 ***5704.8*** *p72*
McLaughlin, Ellen; St. John, N.B., 1853 ***5704.8*** *p107*
McLaughlin, Ellen 16; Philadelphia, 1855 ***5704.8*** *p123*
McLaughlin, Ellen 18; St. John, N.B., 1856 ***5704.8*** *p131*
McLaughlin, Ellen 21; St. John, N.B., 1863 ***5704.8*** *p153*
McLaughlin, Ellen 35; Philadelphia, 1855 ***5704.8*** *p123*
McLaughlin, Ellen 45; Philadelphia, 1855 ***5704.8*** *p123*
McLaughlin, Fanny 19; St. John, N.B., 1856 ***5704.8*** *p131*

McLaughlin, Francis; Philadelphia, 1811 *53.26 p64*
  *Relative:*Biddy
McLaughlin, Francis 9 mos; New York, NY, 1870
  5704.8 p237
McLaughlin, Frank 34; St. John, N.B., 1858 *5704.8 p137*
McLaughlin, George; Philadelphia, 1847 *53.26 p64*
  *Relative:*Rosan
McLaughlin, George; Philadelphia, 1847 *5704.8 p13*
McLaughlin, George; Philadelphia, 1853 *5704.8 p101*
McLaughlin, George; Philadelphia, 1853 *5704.8 p102*
McLaughlin, George; St. John, N.B., 1847 *5704.8 p9*
McLaughlin, Grace; Quebec, 1852 *5704.8 p94*
McLaughlin, Grace 7; Philadelphia, 1854 *5704.8 p123*
McLaughlin, Grace 19; Philadelphia, 1861 *5704.8 p148*
McLaughlin, Grace 20; Philadelphia, 1856 *5704.8 p128*
McLaughlin, H.; Philadelphia, 1811 *53.26 p64*
McLaughlin, Hannah; St. John, N.B., 1852 *5704.8 p93*
McLaughlin, Hannah 18; Philadelphia, 1860 *5704.8 p146*
McLaughlin, Henry 10; Philadelphia, 1864 *5704.8 p188*
McLaughlin, Henry 22; Philadelphia, 1864 *5704.8 p156*
McLaughlin, Henry 24; Philadelphia, 1864 *5704.8 p156*
McLaughlin, Henry 60; Massachusetts, 1849 *5881.1 p67*
McLaughlin, Hugh; Brunswick, NC, 1739 *1639.20 p180*
McLaughlin, Hugh; Philadelphia, 1847 *53.26 p64*
McLaughlin, Hugh; Philadelphia, 1847 *5704.8 p5*
McLaughlin, Hugh; St. John, N.B., 1848 *5704.8 p48*
McLaughlin, Hugh; St. John, N.B., 1849 *5704.8 p56*
McLaughlin, Hugh 2; Philadelphia, 1865 *5704.8 p190*
McLaughlin, Hugh 8; St. John, N.B., 1854 *5704.8 p119*
McLaughlin, Isabella; Quebec, 1847 *5704.8 p8*
McLaughlin, Isabella; St. John, N.B., 1847 *5704.8 p26*
McLaughlin, Isabella 1; Philadelphia, 1865 *5704.8 p190*
McLaughlin, James *SEE* McLaughlin, James
McLaughlin, James; New York, NY, 1838 *8208.4 p65*
McLaughlin, James; New York, NY, 1864 *5704.8 p171*
McLaughlin, James; New York, NY, 1864 *5704.8 p174*
McLaughlin, James; Philadelphia, 1847 *53.26 p65*
  *Relative:*Nancy
  *Relative:*James
  *Relative:*Ann
  *Relative:*Catherine
McLaughlin, James; Philadelphia, 1847 *5704.8 p22*
McLaughlin, James; Philadelphia, 1848 *53.26 p65*
  *Relative:*Sarah
  *Relative:*Sarah 9 mos
McLaughlin, James; Philadelphia, 1848 *5704.8 p45*
McLaughlin, James; Philadelphia, 1852 *5704.8 p85*
McLaughlin, James; Philadelphia, 1853 *5704.8 p101*
McLaughlin, James; Philadelphia, 1865 *5704.8 p190*
McLaughlin, James; St. John, N.B., 1847 *5704.8 p5*
McLaughlin, James; St. John, N.B., 1851 *5704.8 p72*
McLaughlin, James; St. John, N.B., 1853 *5704.8 p107*
McLaughlin, James 9 mos; St. John, N.B., 1851 *5704.8
  p72*
McLaughlin, James 10; Philadelphia, 1853 *5704.8 p111*
McLaughlin, James 13; St. John, N.B., 1851 *5704.8 p72*
McLaughlin, James 14; St. John, N.B., 1864 *5704.8
  p158*
McLaughlin, James 15; Philadelphia, 1858 *5704.8 p138*
McLaughlin, James 16; St. John, N.B., 1867 *5704.8
  p167*
McLaughlin, James 20; Philadelphia, 1855 *5704.8 p124*
McLaughlin, James 20; Philadelphia, 1864 *5704.8 p157*
McLaughlin, James 20; St. John, N.B., 1856 *5704.8
  p131*
McLaughlin, James 22; Quebec, 1854 *5704.8 p119*
McLaughlin, James 22; Wilmington, DE, 1831 *6508.3
  p100*
McLaughlin, James 22; Wilmington, DE, 1831 *6508.3
  p101*
McLaughlin, James 23; Philadelphia, 1861 *5704.8 p148*
McLaughlin, James 25; Wilmington, DE, 1831 *6508.3
  p101*
McLaughlin, James 35; Philadelphia, 1857 *5704.8 p132*
McLaughlin, James 48; St. John, N.B., 1864 *5704.8
  p158*
McLaughlin, James Henry 1; Quebec, 1848 *5704.8 p41*
McLaughlin, Jane; Philadelphia, 1864 *5704.8 p188*
McLaughlin, Jane; Philadelphia, 1865 *5704.8 p190*
McLaughlin, Jane; Philadelphia, 1867 *5704.8 p222*
McLaughlin, Jane; Quebec, 1852 *5704.8 p98*
McLaughlin, Jane; St. John, N.B., 1853 *5704.8 p99*
McLaughlin, Jane 3 mos; Philadelphia, 1853 *5704.8
  p112*
McLaughlin, Jane 9; Philadelphia, 1851 *5704.8 p76*
McLaughlin, Jane 9; Philadelphia, 1852 *5704.8 p85*
McLaughlin, Jane 12; Philadelphia, 1853 *5704.8 p111*
McLaughlin, Jane 17; St. John, N.B., 1855 *5704.8 p127*
McLaughlin, Jane 26; Philadelphia, 1858 *5704.8 p138*
McLaughlin, John *SEE* McLaughlin, John
McLaughlin, John; America, 1865 *5704.8 p194*
McLaughlin, John; New York, NY, 1837 *8208.4 p53*

McLaughlin, John; Philadelphia, 1847 *53.26 p65*
  *Relative:*Elleanor
  *Relative:*Biddy 4
McLaughlin, John; Philadelphia, 1847 *53.26 p65*
  *Relative:*John
McLaughlin, John; Philadelphia, 1847 *5704.8 p5*
McLaughlin, John; Philadelphia, 1847 *5704.8 p23*
McLaughlin, John; Philadelphia, 1850 *53.26 p65*
McLaughlin, John; Philadelphia, 1850 *5704.8 p60*
McLaughlin, John; Philadelphia, 1850 *5704.8 p68*
McLaughlin, John; Philadelphia, 1852 *5704.8 p97*
McLaughlin, John; Philadelphia, 1864 *5704.8 p170*
McLaughlin, John; Philadelphia, 1864 *5704.8 p183*
McLaughlin, John; Philadelphia, 1864 *5704.8 p185*
McLaughlin, John; Philadelphia, 1865 *5704.8 p190*
McLaughlin, John; Philadelphia, 1865 *5704.8 p197*
McLaughlin, John; Philadelphia, 1866 *5704.8 p205*
McLaughlin, John; Philadelphia, 1866 *5704.8 p209*
McLaughlin, John; Philadelphia, 1871 *5704.8 p240*
McLaughlin, John; Quebec, 1847 *5704.8 p28*
McLaughlin, John; Quebec, 1852 *5704.8 p94*
McLaughlin, John; Quebec, 1852 *5704.8 p98*
McLaughlin, John; Quebec, 1853 *5704.8 p104*
McLaughlin, John; St. John, N.B., 1847 *5704.8 p21*
McLaughlin, John; St. John, N.B., 1847 *5704.8 p24*
McLaughlin, John; St. John, N.B., 1847 *5704.8 p25*
McLaughlin, John; St. John, N.B., 1847 *5704.8 p26*
McLaughlin, John; St. John, N.B., 1848 *5704.8 p38*
McLaughlin, John; St. John, N.B., 1848 *5704.8 p43*
McLaughlin, John; St. John, N.B., 1850 *5704.8 p62*
McLaughlin, John; St. John, N.B., 1851 *5704.8 p72*
McLaughlin, John; St. John, N.B., 1851 *5704.8 p80*
McLaughlin, John; St. John, N.B., 1852 *5704.8 p92*
McLaughlin, John 5; Philadelphia, 1851 *5704.8 p76*
McLaughlin, John 5; Philadelphia, 1853 *5704.8 p109*
McLaughlin, John 5; St. John, N.B., 1853 *5704.8 p99*
McLaughlin, John 6; St. John, N.B., 1864 *5704.8 p158*
McLaughlin, John 8; St. John, N.B., 1858 *5704.8 p137*
McLaughlin, John 12; St. John, N.B., 1851 *5704.8 p72*
McLaughlin, John 13; New York, NY, 1869 *5704.8
  p233*
McLaughlin, John 16; Philadelphia, 1857 *5704.8 p133*
McLaughlin, John 18; Philadelphia, 1854 *5704.8 p117*
McLaughlin, John 19; Massachusetts, 1850 *5881.1 p70*
McLaughlin, John 19; Philadelphia, 1854 *5704.8 p118*
McLaughlin, John 19; St. John, N.B., 1854 *5704.8 p120*
McLaughlin, John 20; Philadelphia, 1853 *5704.8 p109*
McLaughlin, John 20; St. John, N.B., 1854 *5704.8 p122*
McLaughlin, John 20; St. John, N.B., 1857 *5704.8 p135*
McLaughlin, John 21; St. John, N.B., 1855 *5704.8 p127*
McLaughlin, John 22; Philadelphia, 1860 *5704.8 p146*
McLaughlin, John 22; St. John, N.B., 1854 *5704.8 p115*
McLaughlin, John 24; Philadelphia, 1854 *5704.8 p115*
McLaughlin, John 40; St. John, N.B., 1856 *5704.8 p132*
McLaughlin, John 45; Quebec, 1858 *5704.8 p138*
McLaughlin, John 50; Quebec, 1856 *5704.8 p130*
McLaughlin, Joseph; St. John, N.B., 1849 *5704.8 p56*
McLaughlin, Joseph 5; Philadelphia, 1853 *5704.8 p112*
McLaughlin, Joseph 20; St. John, N.B., 1856 *5704.8
  p131*
McLaughlin, Kitty; New Orleans, 1852 *5704.8 p98*
McLaughlin, Laughlin; New York, NY, 1865 *5704.8
  p195*
McLaughlin, Laughlin; Philadelphia, 1867 *5704.8 p218*
McLaughlin, Letty 25; St. John, N.B., 1857 *5704.8 p134*
McLaughlin, Lizzie; Philadelphia, 1867 *5704.8 p218*
McLaughlin, Madge 15; Philadelphia, 1860 *5704.8 p146*
McLaughlin, Magy; St. John, N.B., 1847 *5704.8 p20*
McLaughlin, Magy 4 *SEE* McLaughlin, Sally
McLaughlin, Magy 4; Philadelphia, 1850 *5704.8 p65*
McLaughlin, Manny; Philadelphia, 1849 *53.26 p65*
McLaughlin, Manny; Philadelphia, 1849 *5704.8 p53*
McLaughlin, Manus; New York, NY, 1870 *5704.8 p237*
McLaughlin, Margaret; New York, NY, 1868 *5704.8
  p227*
McLaughlin, Margaret; New York, NY, 1871 *5704.8
  p240*
McLaughlin, Margaret; Philadelphia, 1836 *7036 p116*
McLaughlin, Margaret; Philadelphia, 1852 *5704.8 p85*
McLaughlin, Margaret; Philadelphia, 1852 *5704.8 p92*
McLaughlin, Margaret; Philadelphia, 1853 *5704.8 p109*
McLaughlin, Margaret; Philadelphia, 1864 *5704.8 p185*
McLaughlin, Margaret; Philadelphia, 1865 *5704.8 p190*
McLaughlin, Margaret; Philadelphia, 1865 *5704.8 p201*
McLaughlin, Margaret; St. John, N.B., 1847 *5704.8 p19*
McLaughlin, Margaret 9 mos; New Orleans, 1852
  5704.8 p98
McLaughlin, Margaret 6; St. John, N.B., 1854 *5704.8
  p119*
McLaughlin, Margaret 10; St. John, N.B., 1864 *5704.8
  p158*
McLaughlin, Margaret 11; St. John, N.B., 1849 *5704.8
  p49*

McLaughlin, Margaret 11; St. John, N.B., 1861 *5704.8
  p149*
McLaughlin, Margaret 16; St. John, N.B., 1859 *5704.8
  p143*
McLaughlin, Margaret 18; St. John, N.B., 1864 *5704.8
  p158*
McLaughlin, Margaret 19; Philadelphia, 1856 *5704.8
  p128*
McLaughlin, Margaret 19; St. John, N.B., 1863 *5704.8
  p155*
McLaughlin, Margaret 20; Philadelphia, 1853 *5704.8
  p113*
McLaughlin, Margaret 20; St. John, N.B., 1854 *5704.8
  p121*
McLaughlin, Margaret 25; Philadelphia, 1858 *5704.8
  p139*
McLaughlin, Margaret 35; St. John, N.B., 1853 *5704.8
  p110*
McLaughlin, Margery 11; St. John, N.B., 1853 *5704.8
  p106*
McLaughlin, Martha; New York, NY, 1869 *5704.8 p233*
McLaughlin, Martha; New York, NY, 1870 *5704.8 p238*
McLaughlin, Martha; Philadelphia, 1865 *5704.8 p197*
McLaughlin, Mary; America, 1864 *5704.8 p189*
McLaughlin, Mary; America, 1867 *5704.8 p217*
McLaughlin, Mary; New Orleans, 1849 *5704.8 p58*
McLaughlin, Mary; New York, NY, 1864 *5704.8 p174*
McLaughlin, Mary; Philadelphia, 1847 *53.26 p65*
McLaughlin, Mary; Philadelphia, 1847 *5704.8 p1*
McLaughlin, Mary; Philadelphia, 1847 *5704.8 p23*
McLaughlin, Mary; Philadelphia, 1849 *53.26 p65*
McLaughlin, Mary; Philadelphia, 1849 *5704.8 p53*
McLaughlin, Mary; Philadelphia, 1850 *53.26 p65*
McLaughlin, Mary; Philadelphia, 1850 *5704.8 p64*
McLaughlin, Mary; Philadelphia, 1850 *5704.8 p69*
McLaughlin, Mary; Philadelphia, 1851 *5704.8 p77*
McLaughlin, Mary; Philadelphia, 1851 *5704.8 p78*
McLaughlin, Mary; Philadelphia, 1853 *5704.8 p101*
McLaughlin, Mary; Philadelphia, 1864 *5704.8 p180*
McLaughlin, Mary; Philadelphia, 1865 *5704.8 p197*
McLaughlin, Mary; Philadelphia, 1866 *5704.8 p205*
McLaughlin, Mary; Philadelphia, 1866 *5704.8 p206*
McLaughlin, Mary; Philadelphia, 1867 *5704.8 p218*
McLaughlin, Mary; Philadelphia, 1868 *5704.8 p226*
McLaughlin, Mary; Philadelphia, 1871 *5704.8 p240*
McLaughlin, Mary; St. John, N.B., 1847 *5704.8 p3*
McLaughlin, Mary; St. John, N.B., 1847 *5704.8 p9*
McLaughlin, Mary; St. John, N.B., 1847 *5704.8 p20*
McLaughlin, Mary; St. John, N.B., 1847 *5704.8 p25*
McLaughlin, Mary; St. John, N.B., 1847 *5704.8 p26*
McLaughlin, Mary; St. John, N.B., 1849 *5704.8 p49*
McLaughlin, Mary; St. John, N.B., 1849 *5704.8 p55*
McLaughlin, Mary; St. John, N.B., 1850 *5704.8 p61*
McLaughlin, Mary; St. John, N.B., 1850 *5704.8 p62*
McLaughlin, Mary; St. John, N.B., 1850 *5704.8 p67*
McLaughlin, Mary; St. John, N.B., 1851 *5704.8 p79*
McLaughlin, Mary; St. John, N.B., 1851 *5704.8 p80*
McLaughlin, Mary; St. John, N.B., 1852 *5704.8 p83*
McLaughlin, Mary; St. John, N.B., 1852 *5704.8 p84*
McLaughlin, Mary; St. John, N.B., 1852 *5704.8 p92*
McLaughlin, Mary; St. John, N.B., 1852 *5704.8 p95*
McLaughlin, Mary 1; St. John, N.B., 1864 *5704.8 p158*
McLaughlin, Mary 7; Philadelphia, 1851 *5704.8 p76*
McLaughlin, Mary 7; St. John, N.B., 1851 *5704.8 p72*
McLaughlin, Mary 7; St. John, N.B., 1862 *5704.8 p151*
McLaughlin, Mary 8; Philadelphia, 1853 *5704.8 p109*
McLaughlin, Mary 10; Philadelphia, 1859 *5704.8 p141*
McLaughlin, Mary 10; St. John, N.B., 1849 *5704.8 p56*
McLaughlin, Mary 11; Massachusetts, 1849 *5881.1 p71*
McLaughlin, Mary 12; St. John, N.B., 1854 *5704.8 p115*
McLaughlin, Mary 13; St. John, N.B., 1847 *5704.8 p26*
McLaughlin, Mary 18; Philadelphia, 1854 *5704.8 p117*
McLaughlin, Mary 18; Philadelphia, 1855 *5704.8 p123*
McLaughlin, Mary 18; St. John, N.B., 1859 *5704.8 p143*
McLaughlin, Mary 20; Philadelphia, 1853 *5704.8 p111*
McLaughlin, Mary 20; Philadelphia, 1857 *5704.8 p134*
McLaughlin, Mary 20; Philadelphia, 1859 *5704.8 p141*
McLaughlin, Mary 20; St. John, N.B., 1862 *5704.8 p150*
McLaughlin, Mary 30; Philadelphia, 1853 *5704.8 p111*
McLaughlin, Mary 30; St. John, N.B., 1855 *5704.8 p127*
McLaughlin, Mary 40; Philadelphia, 1853 *5704.8 p111*
McLaughlin, Mary A.; Philadelphia, 1867 *5704.8 p221*
McLaughlin, Mary A. 6; Philadelphia, 1865 *5704.8 p190*
McLaughlin, Mary Ann 8; Philadelphia, 1853 *5704.8
  p111*
McLaughlin, Mary Ann 8; St. John, N.B., 1849 *5704.8
  p56*
McLaughlin, Matilda; Philadelphia, 1871 *5704.8 p241*
McLaughlin, Matilda 15; Philadelphia, 1860 *5704.8 p146*
McLaughlin, Michael; New York, NY, 1839 *8208.4 p93*
McLaughlin, Michael; New York, NY, 1865 *5704.8
  p197*
McLaughlin, Michael; Philadelphia, 1847 *53.26 p65*

McLaughlin, Michael; Philadelphia, 1847 *5704.8 p32*
McLaughlin, Michael; Philadelphia, 1852 *5704.8 p92*
McLaughlin, Michael; Philadelphia, 1864 *5704.8 p171*
McLaughlin, Michael; Quebec, 1841 *7036 p124*
McLaughlin, Michael; St. John, N.B., 1847 *5704.8 p20*
McLaughlin, Michael; St. John, N.B., 1851 *5704.8 p71*
McLaughlin, Michael; St. John, N.B., 1851 *5704.8 p72*
McLaughlin, Michael; St. John, N.B., 1852 *5704.8 p83*
McLaughlin, Michael 10; St. John, N.B., 1861 *5704.8 p149*
McLaughlin, Michael 14; Philadelphia, 1858 *5704.8 p139*
McLaughlin, Michael 15; Philadelphia, 1859 *5704.8 p141*
McLaughlin, Michael 17; St. John, N.B., 1853 *5704.8 p110*
McLaughlin, Michael 20; St. John, N.B., 1859 *5704.8 p141*
McLaughlin, Michael 20; St. John, N.B., 1860 *5704.8 p144*
McLaughlin, Michael 30; St. John, N.B., 1853 *5704.8 p110*
McLaughlin, Michael 50; Philadelphia, 1854 *5704.8 p123*
McLaughlin, Miles 23; St. John, N.B., 1857 *5704.8 p134*
McLaughlin, Nancy *SEE* McLaughlin, James
McLaughlin, Nancy; New York, NY, 1864 *5704.8 p174*
McLaughlin, Nancy; Philadelphia, 1847 *53.26 p65*
McLaughlin, Nancy; Philadelphia, 1847 *5704.8 p22*
McLaughlin, Nancy; Philadelphia, 1847 *5704.8 p23*
McLaughlin, Nancy; Philadelphia, 1850 *53.26 p65*
McLaughlin, Nancy; Philadelphia, 1850 *5704.8 p59*
McLaughlin, Nancy; Philadelphia, 1852 *5704.8 p89*
McLaughlin, Nancy; Philadelphia, 1852 *5704.8 p92*
McLaughlin, Nancy; St. John, N.B., 1850 *5704.8 p66*
McLaughlin, Nancy; St. John, N.B., 1852 *5704.8 p83*
McLaughlin, Nancy 52; North Carolina, 1850 *1639.20 p187*
McLaughlin, Nancy 58; Massachusetts, 1849 *5881.1 p73*
McLaughlin, Neal; Philadelphia, 1847 *53.26 p65*
McLaughlin, Neal; Philadelphia, 1847 *5704.8 p5*
McLaughlin, Neal; Philadelphia, 1852 *5704.8 p97*
McLaughlin, Neal; St. John, N.B., 1853 *5704.8 p99*
McLaughlin, Neal; St. John, N.B., 1853 *5704.8 p106*
McLaughlin, Neal 6 mos; St. John, N.B., 1853 *5704.8 p99*
McLaughlin, Neal 5; St. John, N.B., 1853 *5704.8 p106*
McLaughlin, Neil; America, 1866 *5704.8 p209*
McLaughlin, Neil 18; Philadelphia, 1856 *5704.8 p129*
McLaughlin, Neil 21; Philadelphia, 1856 *5704.8 p128*
McLaughlin, Owen; New York, NY, 1838 *8208.4 p68*
McLaughlin, Owen; Philadelphia, 1852 *5704.8 p89*
McLaughlin, Owen; Philadelphia, 1852 *5704.8 p96*
McLaughlin, Owen; St. John, N.B., 1849 *5704.8 p48*
McLaughlin, Owen 22; Philadelphia, 1857 *5704.8 p133*
McLaughlin, Owen 22; St. John, N.B., 1854 *5704.8 p114*
McLaughlin, Owen 25; St. John, N.B., 1854 *5704.8 p114*
McLaughlin, Paddy; St. John, N.B., 1853 *5704.8 p106*
McLaughlin, Pat; Quebec, 1847 *5704.8 p16*
McLaughlin, Patrick; America, 1866 *5704.8 p208*
McLaughlin, Patrick; Illinois, 1892 *2896.5 p27*
McLaughlin, Patrick; New York, NY, 1864 *5704.8 p173*
McLaughlin, Patrick; Philadelphia, 1850 *53.26 p65*
McLaughlin, Patrick; Philadelphia, 1850 *5704.8 p60*
McLaughlin, Patrick; Philadelphia, 1850 *5704.8 p64*
McLaughlin, Patrick; Philadelphia, 1852 *5704.8 p88*
McLaughlin, Patrick; Philadelphia, 1853 *5704.8 p100*
McLaughlin, Patrick; Philadelphia, 1866 *5704.8 p205*
McLaughlin, Patrick; Philadelphia, 1867 *5704.8 p220*
McLaughlin, Patrick; Quebec, 1853 *5704.8 p103*
McLaughlin, Patrick; St. John, N.B., 1847 *5704.8 p3*
McLaughlin, Patrick; St. John, N.B., 1849 *5704.8 p56*
McLaughlin, Patrick; St. John, N.B., 1853 *5704.8 p106*
McLaughlin, Patrick 17; Philadelphia, 1857 *5704.8 p133*
McLaughlin, Patrick 22; Philadelphia, 1854 *5704.8 p117*
McLaughlin, Patrick 22; St. John, N.B., 1857 *5704.8 p134*
McLaughlin, Patrick 24; St. John, N.B., 1854 *5704.8 p114*
McLaughlin, Patrick 24; St. John, N.B., 1854 *5704.8 p122*
McLaughlin, Patrick 35; Sacramento Co., CA, 1867 *3840.2 p18*
McLaughlin, Patrick 64; Philadelphia, 1859 *5704.8 p142*
McLaughlin, Peggy; St. John, N.B., 1847 *5704.8 p24*
McLaughlin, Peggy; St. John, N.B., 1851 *5704.8 p72*
McLaughlin, Peggy; St. John, N.B., 1852 *5704.8 p84*
McLaughlin, Peggy 18; Philadelphia, 1857 *5704.8 p133*
McLaughlin, Peggy 30; Philadelphia, 1853 *5704.8 p112*
McLaughlin, Philip; St. John, N.B., 1852 *5704.8 p84*
McLaughlin, Rebecca; Philadelphia, 1851 *5704.8 p70*

McLaughlin, Richard; New York, NY, 1836 *8208.4 p23*
McLaughlin, Richard; Philadelphia, 1850 *5704.8 p64*
McLaughlin, Richard 10; Quebec, 1847 *5704.8 p28*
McLaughlin, Robert; Philadelphia, 1852 *5704.8 p84*
McLaughlin, Robert 22; Philadelphia, 1855 *5704.8 p124*
McLaughlin, Rosa 45; St. John, N.B., 1861 *5704.8 p149*
McLaughlin, Rosan *SEE* McLaughlin, George
McLaughlin, Rosan; Philadelphia, 1847 *5704.8 p13*
McLaughlin, Rosanna; New York, NY, 1865 *5704.8 p195*
McLaughlin, Rosanna 20; Philadelphia, 1860 *5704.8 p146*
McLaughlin, Rose; New York, NY, 1869 *5704.8 p235*
McLaughlin, Rose; St. John, N.B., 1852 *5704.8 p83*
McLaughlin, Rose 12; Philadelphia, 1861 *5704.8 p148*
McLaughlin, Rose 12; St. John, N.B., 1851 *5704.8 p72*
McLaughlin, Rose 19; Philadelphia, 1854 *5704.8 p116*
McLaughlin, Rose Ann 16; St. John, N.B., 1864 *5704.8 p158*
McLaughlin, Rose Ann 18; St. John, N.B., 1858 *5704.8 p140*
McLaughlin, Roseann; Philadelphia, 1852 *5704.8 p85*
McLaughlin, Rosey *SEE* McLaughlin, Thomas
McLaughlin, Rosey; Philadelphia, 1847 *5704.8 p5*
McLaughlin, Rosy; St. John, N.B., 1851 *5704.8 p72*
McLaughlin, Sally; New York, NY, 1867 *5704.8 p219*
McLaughlin, Sally; Philadelphia, 1850 *53.26 p65*
  *Relative:*Daniel 12
  *Relative:*Elleanor 6
  *Relative:*Magy 4
McLaughlin, Sally; Philadelphia, 1850 *5704.8 p65*
McLaughlin, Sally; St. John, N.B., 1847 *5704.8 p10*
McLaughlin, Sally; St. John, N.B., 1848 *5704.8 p38*
McLaughlin, Sally; St. John, N.B., 1851 *5704.8 p72*
McLaughlin, Sally; St. John, N.B., 1852 *5704.8 p93*
McLaughlin, Sally; St. John, N.B., 1853 *5704.8 p99*
McLaughlin, Sally 6; St. John, N.B., 1849 *5704.8 p56*
McLaughlin, Saml 30; Wilmington, DE, 1831 *6508.7 p161*
McLaughlin, Samuel; St. John, N.B., 1853 *5704.8 p98*
McLaughlin, Sarah *SEE* McLaughlin, James
McLaughlin, Sarah; New York, NY, 1869 *5704.8 p236*
McLaughlin, Sarah; Philadelphia, 1847 *53.26 p65*
McLaughlin, Sarah; Philadelphia, 1847 *5704.8 p31*
McLaughlin, Sarah; Philadelphia, 1848 *5704.8 p45*
McLaughlin, Sarah; Philadelphia, 1852 *5704.8 p97*
McLaughlin, Sarah; Philadelphia, 1864 *5704.8 p185*
McLaughlin, Sarah; Philadelphia, 1865 *5704.8 p197*
McLaughlin, Sarah; Philadelphia, 1866 *5704.8 p205*
McLaughlin, Sarah; St. John, N.B., 1848 *5704.8 p39*
McLaughlin, Sarah; St. John, N.B., 1851 *5704.8 p72*
McLaughlin, Sarah 9 mos *SEE* McLaughlin, James
McLaughlin, Sarah 9 mos; Philadelphia, 1848 *5704.8 p45*
McLaughlin, Sarah 18; Philadelphia, 1854 *5704.8 p123*
McLaughlin, Shelah 10; Philadelphia, 1853 *5704.8 p109*
McLaughlin, Susan *SEE* McLaughlin, Charles
McLaughlin, Susan; Philadelphia, 1850 *5704.8 p65*
McLaughlin, Susan; Philadelphia, 1851 *5704.8 p80*
McLaughlin, Susan; Philadelphia, 1852 *5704.8 p85*
McLaughlin, Susan; St. John, N.B., 1847 *5704.8 p25*
McLaughlin, Susan 20; Philadelphia, 1853 *5704.8 p113*
McLaughlin, Susanah 14; St. John, N.B., 1854 *5704.8 p121*
McLaughlin, Susanna; St. John, N.B., 1851 *5704.8 p71*
McLaughlin, Susanna 17; St. John, N.B., 1856 *5704.8 p131*
McLaughlin, Thomas; America, 1852 *1450.2 p97A*
McLaughlin, Thomas; New York, NY, 1837 *8208.4 p53*
McLaughlin, Thomas; New York, NY, 1868 *5704.8 p228*
McLaughlin, Thomas; Philadelphia, 1847 *53.26 p65*
  *Relative:*Rosey
McLaughlin, Thomas; Philadelphia, 1847 *5704.8 p5*
McLaughlin, Thomas; Quebec, 1847 *5704.8 p8*
McLaughlin, Thomas; St. John, N.B., 1860 *5704.8 p144*
McLaughlin, Thomas 10; St. John, N.B., 1855 *5704.8 p127*
McLaughlin, Thomas 19; St. John, N.B., 1853 *5704.8 p109*
McLaughlin, Thomas 20; St. John, N.B., 1856 *5704.8 p131*
McLaughlin, Unity; New York, NY, 1870 *5704.8 p237*
McLaughlin, Unity; St. John, N.B., 1851 *5704.8 p72*
McLaughlin, William; America, 1866 *5704.8 p207*
McLaughlin, William; America, 1868 *5704.8 p227*
McLaughlin, William; Philadelphia, 1852 *5704.8 p85*
McLaughlin, William; Philadelphia, 1867 *5704.8 p218*
McLaughlin, William; St. John, N.B., 1849 *5704.8 p55*
McLaughlin, William; St. John, N.B., 1851 *5704.8 p71*
McLaughlin, William 10; St. John, N.B., 1851 *5704.8 p72*

McLaughlin, William 10; St. John, N.B., 1854 *5704.8 p119*
McLaughlin, William 15; Philadelphia, 1857 *5704.8 p133*
McLaughlin, William 18; Philadelphia, 1856 *5704.8 p128*
McLaughlin, William 21; St. John, N.B., 1863 *5704.8 p153*
McLaughlin, William 22; St. John, N.B., 1854 *5704.8 p121*
McLaughlin, William 23; Philadelphia, 1860 *5704.8 p146*
McLaughlin, William 40; Philadelphia, 1853 *5704.8 p111*
McLaughlin, William 48; St. John, N.B., 1858 *5704.8 p137*
McLaughlin, William Richard 9; Quebec, 1848 *5704.8 p41*
McLaughlon, Mary; St. John, N.B., 1850 *5704.8 p61*
McLauren, Christian 63; North Carolina, 1850 *1639.20 p181*
McLauren, Donald; America, 1792 *1639.20 p182*
McLaurin, Angus; America, 1790 *1639.20 p181*
McLaurin, Angus; America, 1792 *1639.20 p181*
McLaurin, Carabell 47 *SEE* McLaurin, James
McLaurin, Catherine 65; North Carolina, 1850 *1639.20 p181*
McLaurin, Catherine 84; North Carolina, 1850 *1639.20 p181*
McLaurin, Catherine Calhoun; America, 1790 *1639.20 p24*
McLaurin, Catherine Colquhoun; North Carolina, 1762-1841 *1639.20 p181*
McLaurin, Daniel; America, 1790 *1639.20 p182*
McLaurin, Duncan; North Carolina, 1741-1828 *1639.20 p182*
McLaurin, Effie 39 *SEE* McLaurin, John
McLaurin, Effie Stalker; North Carolina, 1804-1881 *1639.20 p295*
McLaurin, Hugh; America, 1802 *1639.20 p183*
McLaurin, Hugh; North Carolina, 1790 *1639.20 p182*
McLaurin, Hugh 62; North Carolina, 1850 *1639.20 p183*
McLaurin, James 43; Charleston, SC, 1850 *1639.20 p183*
  *Relative:*Carabell 47
McLaurin, John 59; North Carolina, 1850 *1639.20 p183*
  *Relative:*Effie 39
McLaurin, Laurin; North Carolina, 1817 *1639.20 p183*
McLaurin, Mary; North Carolina, 1745-1827 *1639.20 p184*
McLaurin, Mary 73; North Carolina, 1850 *1639.20 p184*
McLaurin, Maurice; America, 1790 *1639.20 p184*
McLaurin, Nancy; North Carolina, 1780-1860 *1639.20 p184*
McLaurin, Nancy 58; North Carolina, 1850 *1639.20 p184*
McLaurin, Nancy 69; North Carolina, 1850 *1639.20 p184*
McLaurin, Neil; Wilmington, NC, 1775-1853 *1639.20 p185*
McLaurin, Neill; North Carolina, 1772-1827 *1639.20 p184*
McLaurin, Neill; North Carolina, 1778-1853 *1639.20 p185*
McLaurin, Neill; North Carolina, 1779-1840 *1639.20 p185*
McLaviston, Hugh; St. John, N.B., 1847 *5704.8 p18*
McLaviston, James; St. John, N.B., 1847 *5704.8 p18*
McLaviston, Jane; St. John, N.B., 1847 *5704.8 p18*
McLaviston, John; St. John, N.B., 1847 *5704.8 p18*
McLaviston, Margaret; St. John, N.B., 1847 *5704.8 p18*
McLaviston, William; St. John, N.B., 1847 *5704.8 p18*
McLaviston, William 12; St. John, N.B., 1847 *5704.8 p18*
McLaws, Beatrix Sharp *SEE* McLaws, William
McLaws, William; Philadelphia, 1796 *8894.2 p56*
  *Wife:*Beatrix Sharp
McLean, Alexander; Philadelphia, 1725-1729 *1639.20 p188*
McLean, Alexander; South Carolina, 1716 *1639.20 p188*
McLean, Alexander; Washington, 1859-1920 *2872.1 p27*
McLean, Allan; California, 1865 *3840.2 p18*
McLean, Angus 66; America, 1804 *1639.20 p188*
  *Relative:*Nancy 60
McLean, Ann 60; St. John, N.B., 1864 *5704.8 p159*
McLean, Archibald; America, 1802 *1639.20 p188*
McLean, Archibald; North Carolina, 1741-1822 *1639.20 p188*
McLean, Benjamin F. 27; Kansas, 1886 *5240.1 p69*
McLean, Catherine 78 *SEE* McLean, Daniel
McLean, Charles; America, 1750 *1639.20 p188*

McMahan, Mary 24; Massachusetts, 1849 ***5881.1*** *p71*
McMahan, Michael 49; Arizona, 1902 ***9228.40*** *p7*
McMahan, Miles; New Orleans, 1848 ***1450.2*** *p97A*
McMahill, Betty 50; Philadelphia, 1858 ***5704.8*** *p139*
McMahon, Ann 14; St. John, N.B., 1849 ***5704.8*** *p55*
McMahon, Arthur; America, 1743 ***4971*** *p11*
McMahon, Catharine 49; Massachusetts, 1849 ***5881.1*** *p64*
McMahon, Con.; America, 1737 ***4971*** *p63*
McMahon, Daniel; America, 1743 ***4971*** *p74*
McMahon, Eliza; America, 1864 ***5704.8*** *p188*
McMahon, Eliza; America, 1866 ***5704.8*** *p213*
McMahon, Ellen; Philadelphia, 1851 ***5704.8*** *p79*
McMahon, Hugh 55; Massachusetts, 1849 ***5881.1*** *p67*
McMahon, James; Philadelphia, 1864 ***5704.8*** *p177*
McMahon, John; New York, NY, 1838 ***8208.4*** *p89*
McMahon, John; Philadelphia, 1865 ***5704.8*** *p200*
McMahon, Mary; America, 1741 ***4971*** *p63*
McMahon, Mary 6; Massachusetts, 1849 ***5881.1*** *p72*
McMahon, Mic.; America, 1737 ***4971*** *p68*
McMahon, Michael; America, 1859 ***6014.1*** *p3*
McMahon, Michael 20; Massachusetts, 1848 ***5881.1*** *p71*
McMahon, Micky 12; St. John, N.B., 1849 ***5704.8*** *p55*
McMahon, Owen 1; Massachusetts, 1849 ***5881.1*** *p73*
McMahon, Patrick; America, 1741 ***4971*** *p23*
McMahon, Patrick; America, 1866 ***5704.8*** *p211*
McMahon, Patrick; New York, NY, 1837 ***8208.4*** *p32*
McMahon, Patrick; Philadelphia, 1865 ***5704.8*** *p193*
McMahon, Patrick 13; Massachusetts, 1849 ***5881.1*** *p74*
McMahon, Patrick 55; Massachusetts, 1850 ***5881.1*** *p75*
McMaillin, Daniel; Quebec, 1784 ***7603*** *p38*
McMain, William 23; St. John, N.B., 1866 ***5704.8*** *p167*
McMaken, Rosa 62; Kansas, 1874 ***5240.1*** *p56*
McMalaney, Patrick 40; Kansas, 1874 ***5240.1*** *p56*
McMamnon, Dennis; Baltimore, 1883 ***1450.2*** *p97A*
McManamin, Elizabeth; Philadelphia, 1847 ***53.26*** *p65*
McManey, Elizabeth; Philadelphia, 1850 ***5704.8*** *p64*
McManey, John; Montreal, 1824 ***7603*** *p78*
McManion, Sarah 16; Massachusetts, 1849 ***5881.1*** *p76*
McManmee, Frances 45; Philadelphia, 1845 ***6508.6*** *p115*
McManners, Bessy 16; Massachusetts, 1847 ***5881.1*** *p63*
McManners, Charles; Montreal, 1822 ***7603*** *p87*
McManners, Patrick 10; Massachusetts, 1849 ***5881.1*** *p74*
McManns, Owen; New York, 1830 ***1450.2*** *p97A*
McMannus, Nathaniel; New York, NY, 1864 ***5704.8*** *p185*
McMannus, Terrance; Massachusetts, 1848 ***5881.1*** *p76*
McMannus, Thomas; Ohio, 1840 ***9892.11*** *p34*
McManus, Ann; Philadelphia, 1866 ***5704.8*** *p205*
McManus, Ann; Quebec, 1849 ***5704.8*** *p56*
McManus, Ann 10; Massachusetts, 1850 ***5881.1*** *p62*
McManus, Ann 24; Massachusetts, 1849 ***5881.1*** *p62*
McManus, Anne; Philadelphia, 1867 ***5704.8*** *p219*
McManus, Annie; Philadelphia, 1866 ***5704.8*** *p204*
McManus, Arthur; Quebec, 1847 ***5704.8*** *p12*
McManus, Barney 18; Wilmington, DE, 1831 ***6508.7*** *p160*
McManus, Barthol.; America, 1735-1743 ***4971*** *p8*
McManus, Bernard; Philadelphia, 1852 ***5704.8*** *p92*
McManus, Bess 6; Massachusetts, 1850 ***5881.1*** *p64*
McManus, Biddy; Quebec, 1847 ***5704.8*** *p37*
McManus, Bridget 16; Massachusetts, 1847 ***5881.1*** *p63*
McManus, Catharine; Philadelphia, 1866 ***5704.8*** *p204*
McManus, Catherine; Quebec, 1847 ***5704.8*** *p7*
McManus, Catherine; Quebec, 1847 ***5704.8*** *p37*
McManus, Catherine; St. John, N.B., 1847 ***5704.8*** *p11*
McManus, Catherine 18 *SEE* McManus, Mary
McManus, Charles; America, 1740 ***4971*** *p72*
McManus, Charles; New York, NY, 1838 ***8208.4*** *p70*
McManus, Charles 16; Philadelphia, 1853 ***5704.8*** *p108*
McManus, Edward; Montreal, 1820 ***7603*** *p72*
McManus, Edward; New York, NY, 1836 ***8208.4*** *p20*
McManus, Edward; New York, NY, 1865 ***5704.8*** *p203*
McManus, Edward 13; Quebec, 1847 ***5704.8*** *p7*
McManus, Eleanor; Quebec, 1847 ***5704.8*** *p7*
McManus, Elizabeth; Quebec, 1852 ***5704.8*** *p98*
McManus, Elizabeth 3 mos; Quebec, 1852 ***5704.8*** *p98*
McManus, Elizabeth 17; St. John, N.B., 1854 ***5704.8*** *p114*
McManus, Ellen; St. John, N.B., 1852 ***5704.8*** *p95*
McManus, Ellen 27; Philadelphia, 1861 ***5704.8*** *p148*
McManus, Ellen 55; Massachusetts, 1850 ***5881.1*** *p66*
McManus, Fanny 18; Philadelphia, 1845 ***6508.6*** *p115*
McManus, Francis; New York, NY, 1839 ***8208.4*** *p91*
McManus, Francis; Philadelphia, 1865 ***5704.8*** *p201*
McManus, Francis; St. John, N.B., 1847 ***5704.8*** *p26*
McManus, Frank; Quebec, 1847 ***5704.8*** *p37*
McManus, Hugh; America, 1866 ***5704.8*** *p213*
McManus, Hugh; Quebec, 1847 ***5704.8*** *p7*
McManus, Hugh 21; Massachusetts, 1848 ***5881.1*** *p67*
McManus, James; Philadelphia, 1852 ***5704.8*** *p92*
McManus, James; St. John, N.B., 1847 ***5704.8*** *p25*
McManus, James 16; St. John, N.B., 1861 ***5704.8*** *p147*
McManus, James 20; St. John, N.B., 1864 ***5704.8*** *p158*
McManus, John; Quebec, 1847 ***5704.8*** *p37*
McManus, John; St. John, N.B., 1847 ***5704.8*** *p15*
McManus, John 8; Massachusetts, 1850 ***5881.1*** *p70*
McManus, John 11; Quebec, 1847 ***5704.8*** *p7*
McManus, John 15; Massachusetts, 1847 ***5881.1*** *p67*
McManus, John 19; St. John, N.B., 1861 ***5704.8*** *p147*
McManus, Kitty; St. John, N.B., 1847 ***5704.8*** *p34*
McManus, Margaret; Quebec, 1847 ***5704.8*** *p12*
McManus, Margaret 16; Philadelphia, 1861 ***5704.8*** *p148*
McManus, Mary; Philadelphia, 1867 ***5704.8*** *p219*
McManus, Mary; Quebec, 1847 ***5704.8*** *p37*
McManus, Mary 13; St. John, N.B., 1847 ***5704.8*** *p34*
McManus, Mary 16; Massachusetts, 1848 ***5881.1*** *p71*
McManus, Mary 20; Philadelphia, 1833-1834 ***53.26*** *p66*
*Relative:*Catherine 18
McManus, Mary 22; St. John, N.B., 1857 ***5704.8*** *p134*
McManus, Michael; New York, NY, 1839 ***8208.4*** *p91*
McManus, Michael; Quebec, 1832 ***7036*** *p120*
McManus, Nabby 50; Massachusetts, 1849 ***5881.1*** *p73*
McManus, Owen; New York, NY, 1839 ***8208.4*** *p94*
McManus, Pat; Quebec, 1847 ***5704.8*** *p37*
McManus, Patrick; Philadelphia, 1866 ***5704.8*** *p205*
McManus, Patrick 9; Quebec, 1847 ***5704.8*** *p7*
McManus, Phil 25; Philadelphia, 1853 ***5704.8*** *p113*
McManus, Rose; St. John, N.B., 1847 ***5704.8*** *p34*
McManus, Rose 30; Massachusetts, 1848 ***5881.1*** *p75*
McManus, Terance 6; Philadelphia, 1864 ***5704.8*** *p173*
McManus, Terence; New York, NY, 1838 ***8208.4*** *p70*
McManus, Thady; America, 1742 ***4971*** *p37*
McManus, Thomas 21; Massachusetts, 1847 ***5881.1*** *p76*
McMany, Catherine; St. John, N.B., 1848 ***5704.8*** *p45*
McMany, Hugh; St. John, N.B., 1848 ***5704.8*** *p45*
McMar, Honora 12; Massachusetts, 1849 ***5881.1*** *p67*
McMaster, Andrew; South Carolina, 1764 ***1639.20*** *p200*
McMaster, Angus; New Brunswick, 1840 ***9775.5*** *p204*
McMaster, Catherine; Philadelphia, 1851 ***5704.8*** *p81*
McMaster, Catherine 2; Philadelphia, 1851 ***5704.8*** *p81*
McMaster, Charles; New Brunswick, 1840-1900 ***9775.5*** *p204*
McMaster, Edward 9; Philadelphia, 1851 ***5704.8*** *p81*
McMaster, George 11; Philadelphia, 1851 ***5704.8*** *p81*
McMaster, Jane 68; Charleston, SC, 1850 ***1639.20*** *p200*
McMaster, John 11; Philadelphia, 1851 ***5704.8*** *p81*
McMaster, John, Jr.; New York, NY, 1836 ***8208.4*** *p8*
McMaster, Mary; Montreal, 1823 ***7603*** *p41*
McMaster, Mary 13; Philadelphia, 1851 ***5704.8*** *p81*
McMaster, Nancy; Philadelphia, 1851 ***5704.8*** *p81*
McMaster, William; Philadelphia, 1851 ***5704.8*** *p81*
McMasters, Thomas; North Carolina, 1809 ***1639.20*** *p200*
McMeans, Andrew 21; Philadelphia, 1864 ***5704.8*** *p156*
McMearty, Fanny; Philadelphia, 1852 ***5704.8*** *p88*
McMeekin, Alexander 21; Philadelphia, 1803 ***53.26*** *p66*
McMeekin, James 26; Philadelphia, 1856 ***5704.8*** *p129*
McMelty, Francis; America, 1741 ***4971*** *p72*
McMenaman, Isabella 16; Philadelphia, 1853 ***5704.8*** *p108*
McMenamin, Agnes 16; Philadelphia, 1865 ***5704.8*** *p164*
McMenamin, Ann; Philadelphia, 1848 ***53.26*** *p66*
McMenamin, Ann; Philadelphia, 1848 ***5704.8*** *p40*
McMenamin, Ann 4; St. John, N.B., 1847 ***5704.8*** *p19*
McMenamin, Ann 17; Philadelphia, 1857 ***5704.8*** *p134*
McMenamin, Bern; St. John, N.B., 1850 ***5704.8*** *p67*
McMenamin, Bridget 22; Philadelphia, 1861 ***5704.8*** *p147*
McMenamin, Catharine; New York, NY, 1864 ***5704.8*** *p173*
McMenamin, Catharine; New York, NY, 1864 ***5704.8*** *p185*
McMenamin, Catherine; Philadelphia, 1850 ***53.26*** *p66*
McMenamin, Catherine; Philadelphia, 1850 ***5704.8*** *p69*
McMenamin, Catherine 9 mos; St. John, N.B., 1847 ***5704.8*** *p19*
McMenamin, Cornelius 10; St. John, N.B., 1847 ***5704.8*** *p19*
McMenamin, Edward; Philadelphia, 1864 ***5704.8*** *p180*
McMenamin, Elizabeth; Philadelphia, 1847 ***5704.8*** *p5*
McMenamin, Esther 20; St. John, N.B., 1866 ***5704.8*** *p166*
McMenamin, Fanny; St. John, N.B., 1852 ***5704.8*** *p95*
McMenamin, Grace; Philadelphia, 1850 ***53.26*** *p66*
McMenamin, Grace; Philadelphia, 1850 ***5704.8*** *p69*
McMenamin, Grace 18; Philadelphia, 1864 ***5704.8*** *p161*
McMenamin, Hannah; New York, NY, 1864 ***5704.8*** *p172*
McMenamin, Henry 18; St. John, N.B., 1854 ***5704.8*** *p114*
McMenamin, Hugh *SEE* McMenamin, James
McMenamin, Hugh; New Orleans, 1848 ***5704.8*** *p48*
McMenamin, Hugh; Philadelphia, 1864 ***5704.8*** *p175*
McMenamin, Hugh; St. John, N.B., 1847 ***5704.8*** *p5*
McMenamin, Hugh 1; Philadelphia, 1847 ***5704.8*** *p23*
McMenamin, James; Philadelphia, 1847 ***53.26*** *p66*
McMenamin, James; Philadelphia, 1847 ***53.26*** *p66*
*Relative:*Sarah 5
*Relative:*John 3
*Relative:*Margaret 1
*Relative:*Hugh
McMenamin, James; Philadelphia, 1847 ***5704.8*** *p23*
McMenamin, James; Philadelphia, 1847 ***5704.8*** *p30*
McMenamin, James; St. John, N.B., 1847 ***5704.8*** *p19*
McMenamin, James; St. John, N.B., 1852 ***5704.8*** *p83*
McMenamin, James 32; St. John, N.B., 1866 ***5704.8*** *p166*
McMenamin, Jane 20; Philadelphia, 1854 ***5704.8*** *p116*
McMenamin, Jane 45; Philadelphia, 1853 ***5704.8*** *p108*
McMenamin, John; New York, NY, 1864 ***5704.8*** *p172*
McMenamin, John; Philadelphia, 1847 ***53.26*** *p66*
McMenamin, John; Philadelphia, 1847 ***5704.8*** *p30*
McMenamin, John; Philadelphia, 1850 ***53.26*** *p66*
McMenamin, John; Philadelphia, 1850 ***5704.8*** *p69*
McMenamin, John; Quebec, 1847 ***5704.8*** *p29*
McMenamin, John 3 *SEE* McMenamin, James
McMenamin, John 5; Philadelphia, 1847 ***5704.8*** *p23*
McMenamin, John 23; St. John, N.B., 1855 ***5704.8*** *p126*
McMenamin, Margaret; Philadelphia, 1866 ***5704.8*** *p209*
McMenamin, Margaret; St. John, N.B., 1847 ***5704.8*** *p19*
McMenamin, Margaret 1 *SEE* McMenamin, James
McMenamin, Margaret 3; Philadelphia, 1847 ***5704.8*** *p23*
McMenamin, Margaret 8; St. John, N.B., 1847 ***5704.8*** *p19*
McMenamin, Margaret 21; Philadelphia, 1864 ***5704.8*** *p161*
McMenamin, Margaret 24; Philadelphia, 1856 ***5704.8*** *p129*
McMenamin, Mary; New York, NY, 1865 ***5704.8*** *p185*
McMenamin, Mary; Philadelphia, 1866 ***5704.8*** *p208*
McMenamin, Mary; Philadelphia, 1868 ***5704.8*** *p223*
McMenamin, Mary; Quebec, 1847 ***5704.8*** *p7*
McMenamin, Mary; Quebec, 1853 ***5704.8*** *p104*
McMenamin, Mary; St. John, N.B., 1852 ***5704.8*** *p95*
McMenamin, Mary A.; New York, NY, 1864 ***5704.8*** *p171*
McMenamin, Mary Jane 7; Philadelphia, 1853 ***5704.8*** *p108*
McMenamin, Michael; St. John, N.B., 1849 ***5704.8*** *p49*
McMenamin, Michael 59; Philadelphia, 1859 ***5704.8*** *p141*
McMenamin, Nancy; St. John, N.B., 1847 ***5704.8*** *p19*
McMenamin, Nancy; St. John, N.B., 1852 ***5704.8*** *p84*
McMenamin, Pat; St. John, N.B., 1852 ***5704.8*** *p95*
McMenamin, Patrick 19; Philadelphia, 1857 ***5704.8*** *p134*
McMenamin, Patrick 20; Philadelphia, 1855 ***5704.8*** *p124*
McMenamin, Rose; Philadelphia, 1850 ***53.26*** *p66*
McMenamin, Rose; Philadelphia, 1850 ***5704.8*** *p69*
McMenamin, Rose; Philadelphia, 1853 ***5704.8*** *p113*
McMenamin, Rose Ann 13; Quebec, 1851 ***5704.8*** *p74*
McMenamin, Rosey; St. John, N.B., 1852 ***5704.8*** *p95*
McMenamin, Sarah; New York, NY, 1866 ***5704.8*** *p212*
McMenamin, Sarah; New York, NY, 1866 ***5704.8*** *p213*
McMenamin, Sarah; Philadelphia, 1847 ***5704.8*** *p23*
McMenamin, Sarah; Quebec, 1851 ***5704.8*** *p74*
McMenamin, Sarah 5 *SEE* McMenamin, James
McMenamin, Susan 6; St. John, N.B., 1847 ***5704.8*** *p19*
McMenamin, William; Philadelphia, 1847 ***53.26*** *p66*
McMenamin, William; Philadelphia, 1847 ***5704.8*** *p5*
McMenamin, William 36; Philadelphia, 1853 ***5704.8*** *p108*
McMenamin, William James 5; Philadelphia, 1853 ***5704.8*** *p108*
McMenarny, Robt. Jno. 31; Kansas, 1872 ***5240.1*** *p53*
McMenemin, Ane 24; Philadelphia, 1864 ***5704.8*** *p157*
McMenemin, Bridget 8; Philadelphia, 1864 ***5704.8*** *p157*
McMenemy, Pat 21; Philadelphia, 1857 ***5704.8*** *p132*
McMenomin, Ann; New York, NY, 1865 ***5704.8*** *p190*
McMenomin, Anne; America, 1864 ***5704.8*** *p188*
McMenomin, Catharine; Philadelphia, 1868 ***5704.8*** *p227*
McMenomin, Daniel; New York, NY, 1869 ***5704.8*** *p234*
McMenomin, John; America, 1868 ***5704.8*** *p230*
McMenomin, Mary; America, 1868 ***5704.8*** *p229*
McMenomin, Patrick; Philadelphia, 1865 ***5704.8*** *p201*
McMenomy, Sarah; Philadelphia, 1868 ***5704.8*** *p225*
McMenonoy, Hannah; New York, NY, 1869 ***5704.8*** *p232*
McMeurty, Catherine 11; Philadelphia, 1861 ***5704.8*** *p148*
McMeurty, Grace 15; Philadelphia, 1861 ***5704.8*** *p148*
McMichael, Daniel; New York, NY, 1867 ***5704.8*** *p224*
McMichael, Hugh; Philadelphia, 1864 ***5704.8*** *p170*
McMichael, James; Philadelphia, 1847 ***53.26*** *p66*
McMichael, James; Philadelphia, 1847 ***5704.8*** *p31*
McMichael, Joseph; Philadelphia, 1853 ***5704.8*** *p102*
McMichael, Martha; New York, NY, 1867 ***5704.8*** *p224*
McMichael, Mary; Philadelphia, 1853 ***5704.8*** *p101*
McMichael, Paul; New York, NY, 1867 ***5704.8*** *p224*
McMichael, Robert; Philadelphia, 1851 ***5704.8*** *p80*

Child:Mary 17
Child:Elizabeth 14
Child:Robert 9
McMurchie, Mary 17 SEE McMurchie, Hugh
McMurchie, Neil 3 SEE McMurchie, Finlay
McMurchie, Patrick 17 SEE McMurchie, Hugh
McMurchie, Robert 9 SEE McMurchie, Hugh
McMurchy, Donald; Kansas, 1871 5240.1 p29
McMurchy, Ivor; America, 1770 1639.20 p206
With wife
McMurchy, John 23; Kansas, 1871 5240.1 p29
McMurchy, John 23; Kansas, 1871 5240.1 p52
McMurphy, Barbara 65; Wilmington, NC, 1850 1639.20 p206
McMurray, . . . 13; Philadelphia, 1857 5704.8 p134
McMurray, Bridget 3; Philadelphia, 1857 5704.8 p134
McMurray, Bryan 9; Massachusetts, 1849 5881.1 p63
McMurray, Catharine 16; Massachusetts, 1849 5881.1 p64
McMurray, Donald 83; North Carolina, 1850 1639.20 p206
McMurray, Mary 11; Massachusetts, 1849 5881.1 p72
McMurray, Mary 16; Philadelphia, 1857 5704.8 p133
McMurray, William 16; Philadelphia, 1860 5704.8 p145
McMurry, Alexander; Philadelphia, 1853 5704.8 p103
McMurry, Catherine; Philadelphia, 1853 5704.8 p103
McMurtry, Ann; St. John, N.B., 1847 5704.8 p18
McMurtry, Betty 12; St. John, N.B., 1847 5704.8 p18
McMurtry, Hugh; St. John, N.B., 1847 5704.8 p21
McMurtry, Hugh 9; St. John, N.B., 1847 5704.8 p18
McMurtry, James; St. John, N.B., 1847 5704.8 p18
McMurtry, John; St. John, N.B., 1847 5704.8 p18
McMurtry, Martha 5; St. John, N.B., 1847 5704.8 p18
McMurtry, Nancy; St. John, N.B., 1847 5704.8 p18
McMurtry, Nancy 3; St. John, N.B., 1847 5704.8 p18
McMurtry, Rachel 9 mos; St. John, N.B., 1847 5704.8 p18
McMurtry, Samuel 7; St. John, N.B., 1847 5704.8 p18
McNab, Alexander; America, 1771 8894.1 p192
McNab, Andrew SEE McNab, John
McNab, Anne SEE McNab, John
McNab, Archibald; Montreal, 1825 9775.5 p213
McNab, Archibald; New York, 1767 1219.7 p129
McNab, Charles Henry; Washington, 1859-1920 2872.1 p27
McNab, John SEE McNab, John
McNab, John; Nova Scotia, 1830 7085.4 p45
Wife:Ket
Child:Mary
Child:Anne
Child:Andrew
Child:John
Child:Marion
McNab, Ket SEE McNab, John
McNab, Marion SEE McNab, John
McNab, Mary SEE McNab, John
McNab, Robert 45; North Carolina, 1850 1639.20 p206
McNabb, Duncan; Charleston, SC, 1798-1830 1639.20 p206
McNabb, James; New York, NY, 1838 8208.4 p71
McNabb, Jean 19 SEE McNabb, John
McNabb, John 24; North Carolina, 1775 1639.20 p206
Wife:Jean 19
McNabb, Malcolm; New York, NY, 1837 8208.4 p54
McNabb, Mary SEE McNabb, Mathew
McNabb, Mary; Philadelphia, 1848 5704.8 p40
McNabb, Mathew; Philadelphia, 1848 53.26 p66
Relative:Mary
McNabb, Mathew; Philadelphia, 1848 5704.8 p40
McNabb, Rachael; America, 1868 5704.8 p227
McNabb, Robert 23; Philadelphia, 1854 5704.8 p116
McNabb, Tibby 20; North Carolina, 1775 1639.20 p206
McNabney, David; America, 1826 1450.2 p98A
McNaboll, Barnard 18; Massachusetts, 1849 5881.1 p63
McNaboll, Ellen 9 mos; Massachusetts, 1849 5881.1 p66
McNaboll, Winnefred 24; Massachusetts, 1849 5881.1 p77
McNaghten, Margaret Ann; St. John, N.B., 1850 5704.8 p66
McNahoe, James; America, 1738 4971 p38
McNail, George; Philadelphia, 1851 5704.8 p80
McNair, Bernard; America, 1786 1639.20 p207
McNair, Betsy 52; North Carolina, 1850 1639.20 p207
McNair, Daniel, Sr.; North Carolina, 1731-1800 1639.20 p207
McNair, Duncan; North Carolina, 1700-1799 1639.20 p207
Wife:Katie McCallum
McNair, Edward 45; North Carolina, 1850 1639.20 p207
McNair, Janet; North Carolina, 1781-1826 1639.20 p207
McNair, John; America, 1770 1639.20 p207
Son:Roderick
With daughter
McNair, John 63; North Carolina, 1850 1639.20 p208
McNair, Katie McCallum SEE McNair, Duncan
McNair, Mary; North Carolina, 1745-1807 1639.20 p208
McNair, Roderick SEE McNair, John
McNair, Roderick; North Carolina, 1764-1839 1639.20 p208
McNally, Alice 26; Massachusetts, 1849 5881.1 p62
McNally, Honora; America, 1740 4971 p15
McNally, Honora; America, 1741 4971 p98
McNally, Hugh; Quebec, 1824 7603 p69
McNally, Patrick 20; Philadelphia, 1861 5704.8 p149
McNally, William 19; Quebec, 1856 5704.8 p129
McNamara, Ann 15; Quebec, 1864 5704.8 p164
McNamara, Anne; Quebec, 1821 7603 p71
McNamara, Bartholomew; Ohio, 1841 8365.25 p12
McNamara, Bridget 8; Massachusetts, 1849 5881.1 p63
McNamara, Bridget 50; Massachusetts, 1850 5881.1 p63
McNamara, Catherine; Quebec, 1864 5704.8 p164
McNamara, Daniel; New York, NY, 1840 8208.4 p106
McNamara, Elizabeth 13; Massachusetts, 1850 5881.1 p66
McNamara, John; America, 1742 4971 p83
McNamara, John; America, 1743 4971 p35
McNamara, John; Arkansas, 1918 95.2 p82
McNamara, John; Massachusetts, 1849 5881.1 p69
McNamara, John; Quebec, 1786 7603 p86
McNamara, John 34; Massachusetts, 1849 5881.1 p69
McNamara, John 45; Massachusetts, 1850 5881.1 p69
McNamara, Margaret; Quebec, 1822 7603 p83
McNamara, Margaret 9; Massachusetts, 1849 5881.1 p72
McNamara, Maria 20; Massachusetts, 1850 5881.1 p72
McNamara, Mary 36; Massachusetts, 1849 5881.1 p72
McNamara, Mary Louise 39; Kansas, 1900 5240.1 p81
McNamara, Matt. 5; Massachusetts, 1850 5881.1 p73
McNamara, Matthew; New York, NY, 1852 3840.2 p18
McNamara, Michael; Illinois, 1861 2896.5 p27
McNamara, Michael 35; Quebec, 1818 7603 p62
McNamara, Patrick; America, 1742 4971 p83
McNamara, Peggy 16; Massachusetts, 1849 5881.1 p75
McNamara, Thady 50; Massachusetts, 1850 5881.1 p76
McNamara, Thady, Jr. 11; Massachusetts, 1850 5881.1 p76
McNamara, Thomas Joseph; Iowa, 1866-1943 123.54 p69
McNamara, Thomas P.; New York, NY, 1838 8208.4 p81
McNamard, William; Philadelphia, 1850 5704.8 p64
McNamee, Ann; Philadelphia, 1851 5704.8 p77
McNamee, Ann; Philadelphia, 1853 5704.8 p101
McNamee, Anne 12; St. John, N.B., 1848 5704.8 p44
McNamee, Annie 25; Philadelphia, 1864 5704.8 p155
McNamee, Bernard; Philadelphia, 1851 5704.8 p76
McNamee, Bernard; St. John, N.B., 1853 5704.8 p99
McNamee, Elleanor; St. John, N.B., 1847 5704.8 p35
McNamee, Francis 30; Philadelphia, 1864 5704.8 p155
McNamee, Helene; Quebec, 1823 7603 p69
McNamee, Hugh; America, 1741 4971 p74
McNamee, James; Philadelphia, 1847 53.26 p66
McNamee, James; Philadelphia, 1847 5704.8 p22
McNamee, Jane 9; St. John, N.B., 1848 5704.8 p44
McNamee, John; St. John, N.B., 1847 5704.8 p26
McNamee, John 26; Philadelphia, 1853 5704.8 p108
McNamee, Margaret; Philadelphia, 1867 5704.8 p217
McNamee, Margaret 7; St. John, N.B., 1848 5704.8 p44
McNamee, Mary; America, 1868 5704.8 p226
McNamee, Mary; Philadelphia, 1851 5704.8 p76
McNamee, Mary; St. John, N.B., 1853 5704.8 p99
McNamee, Mary 10; St. John, N.B., 1853 5704.8 p99
McNamee, Michael; Philadelphia, 1853 5704.8 p101
McNamee, Michael; Philadelphia, 1870 5704.8 p238
McNamee, Pat 3; St. John, N.B., 1853 5704.8 p99
McNamee, Rose; Philadelphia, 1867 5704.8 p217
McNamee, Rose 21; Philadelphia, 1860 5704.8 p145
McNamee, Sandy; St. John, N.B., 1848 5704.8 p44
McNamee, Sarah 8; St. John, N.B., 1853 5704.8 p99
McNamee, Teague; Philadelphia, 1847 53.26 p66
McNamee, Teague; Philadelphia, 1847 5704.8 p31
McNamee, William 6 mos; St. John, N.B., 1853 5704.8 p99
McNames, Jeremiah; Illinois, 1854 7857 p5
McNarin, Joseph; South Carolina, 1794 1639.20 p208
McNaughlin, Helen 3; New York, NY, 1828 6508.4 p143
McNaughlin, Helen 49; New York, NY, 1828 6508.4 p143
McNaughlin, Margt 1; New York, NY, 1828 6508.4 p143
McNaughlin, Mary 5; New York, NY, 1828 6508.4 p143
McNaught, Archibald; Philadelphia, 1853 5704.8 p102
McNaught, Glen SEE McNaught, John
McNaught, Glen; Philadelphia, 1850 5704.8 p68
McNaught, James; New York, NY, 1869 5704.8 p234
McNaught, James; Philadelphia, 1853 5704.8 p103
McNaught, Jane; New York, NY, 1866 5704.8 p213
McNaught, John; Philadelphia, 1850 53.26 p66
Relative:Glen
McNaught, John; Philadelphia, 1850 5704.8 p68
McNaught, Mary; Philadelphia, 1853 5704.8 p102
McNaught, William 30; Wilmington, DE, 1831 6508.7 p160
McNaughtan, Anne; America, 1776 8894.1 p192
McNaughton, Duncan; South Carolina, 1716 1639.20 p208
McNeal, Archibald 50; California, 1873 2769.10 p5
McNeal, Margaret 20; Philadelphia, 1861 5704.8 p148
McNeal, Mary Ann 22; Massachusetts, 1847 5881.1 p70
McNeal, Roger; Philadelphia, 1811 53.26 p66
McNeal, William; Philadelphia, 1850 53.26 p66
McNeal, William; Philadelphia, 1850 5704.8 p65
McNeary, Margaret; New York, NY, 1865 5704.8 p194
McNeary, Mathew; New York, NY, 1865 5704.8 p194
McNeely, Ann 21; Quebec, 1863 5704.8 p154
McNeely, Ann 65; Quebec, 1863 5704.8 p154
McNeely, Ann Jane 7; Quebec, 1863 5704.8 p154
McNeely, Catherine 4; Quebec, 1863 5704.8 p154
McNeely, James 19; Quebec, 1863 5704.8 p154
McNeely, James 40; Quebec, 1863 5704.8 p154
McNeely, Jane 25; Quebec, 1863 5704.8 p154
McNeely, John 1 mo; Quebec, 1863 5704.8 p154
McNeely, John 4; Quebec, 1863 5704.8 p154
McNeely, John 30; Quebec, 1863 5704.8 p154
McNeely, Margaret 30; Quebec, 1863 5704.8 p154
McNeely, Robert 6; Quebec, 1863 5704.8 p154
McNeely, Thomas 1; Quebec, 1863 5704.8 p154
McNeely, William 3; Quebec, 1863 5704.8 p154
McNeely, William 18; Quebec, 1864 5704.8 p162
McNeight, Robert; America, 1737 4971 p66
McNeil, Alice; North Carolina, 1791 1639.20 p208
McNeil, Alice Clunie; Wilmington, NC, 1791 1639.20 p47
McNeil, Andrew; St. John, N.B., 1866 5704.8 p166
McNeil, Barbara; Philadelphia, 1853 5704.8 p113
McNeil, Catherine; St. John, N.B., 1866 5704.8 p166
McNeil, Daniel; North Carolina, 1739 1639.20 p209
McNeil, Daniel; North Carolina, 1760 1639.20 p209
McNeil, Daniel 28 SEE McNeil, Neil
McNeil, Hector; North Carolina, 1739 1639.20 p210
McNeil, Hector 24 SEE McNeil, Neil
McNeil, Ignace; Quebec, 1764 7603 p38
McNeil, Isobel Simpson 64 SEE McNeil, Neil
McNeil, James; New York, NY, 1837 8208.4 p29
McNeil, John; America, 1792 1639.20 p211
McNeil, John; Quebec, 1825 7603 p66
McNeil, John 4; St. John, N.B., 1866 5704.8 p166
McNeil, Katherine; St. John, N.B., 1852 5704.8 p83
McNeil, Malcolm; North Carolina, 1739 1639.20 p211
McNeil, Marie; Quebec, 1778 7603 p35
McNeil, Mary 9 SEE McNeil, Neil
McNeil, Neil; North Carolina, 1739 1639.20 p211
McNeil, Neil; North Carolina, 1739 1639.20 p212
McNeil, Neil; North Carolina, 1792 1639.20 p212
McNeil, Neil 18 SEE McNeil, Neil
McNeil, Neil 64; Wilmington, NC, 1774 1639.20 p212
Wife:Isobel Simpson 64
Child:Daniel 28
Child:Hector 24
Child:Peter 22
Child:Neil 18
Child:William 15
Child:Mary 9
McNeil, Neil 70; Charleston, SC, 1850 1639.20 p212
McNeil, Peter 22 SEE McNeil, Neil
McNeil, Robert; Illinois, 1875 5012.39 p26
McNeil, Robert 2; St. John, N.B., 1866 5704.8 p166
McNeil, Rory; Quebec, 1779 7603 p35
McNeil, Samuel; Charleston, SC, 1812 1639.20 p213
McNeil, William; North Carolina, 1792 1639.20 p213
McNeil, William 15 SEE McNeil, Neil
McNeill, Mrs.; North Carolina, 1771 1639.20 p214
With family
McNeill, Angus; North Carolina, 1762-1835 1639.20 p208
McNeill, Ann; Quebec, 1853 5704.8 p105
McNeill, Ann Talbot SEE McNeill, Thomas
McNeill, Archibald; Brunswick, NC, 1739 1639.20 p208
McNeill, Archibald; St. John, N.B., 1849 5704.8 p56
McNeill, Archibald; South Carolina, 1772 1639.20 p208
McNeill, Christian 59; North Carolina, 1850 1639.20 p209
McNeill, Daniel; America, 1797 1639.20 p209
McNeill, Daniel; North Carolina, 1770-1830 1639.20 p209
McNeill, Daniel 72; North Carolina, 1850 1639.20 p209
McNeill, Duncan; North Carolina, 1728-1791 1639.20 p210
McNeill, Edward 19; St. John, N.B., 1858 5704.8 p140

McNeill, Eliza; Philadelphia, 1851 *5704.8 p81*
McNeill, Eliza A.; New York, NY, 1868 *5704.8 p229*
McNeill, Elizabeth 5; St. John, N.B., 1849 *5704.8 p56*
McNeill, Francis; America, 1737 *4971 p72*
McNeill, Grisell; North Carolina, 1771 *1639.20 p210*
McNeill, Hector; America, 1746-1830 *1639.20 p210*
McNeill, Hector; North Carolina, 1750-1830 *1639.20 p210*
McNeill, Isabella; St. John, N.B., 1847 *5704.8 p10*
McNeill, James; St. John, N.B., 1851 *5704.8 p77*
McNeill, James 1; Quebec, 1859 *5704.8 p143*
McNeill, James 4; St. John, N.B., 1847 *5704.8 p10*
McNeill, James 42; Kansas, 1888 *5240.1 p29*
McNeill, James 42; Kansas, 1888 *5240.1 p72*
McNeill, Jane; St. John, N.B., 1851 *5704.8 p77*
McNeill, Jean 32; Wilmington, NC, 1774 *1639.20 p27*
McNeill, John; America, 1788 *1639.20 p210*
McNeill, John; North Carolina, 1747-1810 *1639.20 p210*
McNeill, John; St. John, N.B., 1847 *5704.8 p10*
McNeill, John; Washington, 1859-1920 *2872.1 p27*
McNeill, John 8; St. John, N.B., 1847 *5704.8 p10*
McNeill, John 54; North Carolina, 1850 *1639.20 p211*
McNeill, John 74; North Carolina, 1850 *1639.20 p211*
McNeill, Lachlan; Brunswick, NC, 1739 *1639.20 p211*
McNeill, Margaret; North Carolina, 1759-1849 *1639.20 p211*
McNeill, Margaret 30; Quebec, 1859 *5704.8 p143*
McNeill, Margaret 31 *SEE* McNeill, Neill
McNeill, Mary 8; Quebec, 1859 *5704.8 p143*
McNeill, Mary 76; North Carolina, 1850 *1639.20 p211*
McNeill, Mary J.; Philadelphia, 1867 *5704.8 p218*
McNeill, Neill; Cape Fear, NC, 1747 *1639.20 p212*
McNeill, Neill; Charleston, SC, 1806 *1639.20 p212*
McNeill, Neill; North Carolina, 1784-1857 *1639.20 p213*
McNeill, Neill 65; North Carolina, 1850 *1639.20 p213*
McNeill, Neill 68; North Carolina, 1850 *1639.20 p213*
  *Relative:*Sarah 65
  *Relative:*Margaret 31
McNeill, Robert; Philadelphia, 1867 *5704.8 p220*
McNeill, Sarah 51; North Carolina, 1850 *1639.20 p213*
McNeill, Sarah 65 *SEE* McNeill, Neill
McNeill, Susan; St. John, N.B., 1847 *5704.8 p10*
McNeill, Susan 58; Charleston, SC, 1850 *1639.20 p213*
McNeill, Thomas; North Carolina, 1777 *1639.20 p213*
  *Wife:*Ann Talbot
McNeill, Torquil; Brunswick, NC, 1739 *1639.20 p213*
McNeill, William; St. John, N.B., 1847 *5704.8 p9*
McNeish, Nancy 77; North Carolina, 1850 *1639.20 p214*
McNelas, Wm.; California, 1865 *3840.2 p18*
McNelis, Margaret Ann; Philadelphia, 1851 *5704.8 p81*
McNell, Daniel 19; Maryland, 1731 *3690.1 p147*
McNelly, Rose; St. John, N.B., 1847 *5704.8 p33*
McNemara, James; Ohio, 1843 *8365.26 p12*
McNemara, Joan; Delaware Bay or River, 1743 *4971 p104*
McNemara, Lawrence; Ohio, 1843 *8365.26 p12*
McNemara, Timothy; Virginia, 1855 *4626.16 p15*
McNenny, Isabella 18; Philadelphia, 1861 *5704.8 p148*
McNenny, Thomas; New York, NY, 1837 *8208.4 p34*
McNeny, Phil.; America, 1738 *4971 p63*
McNerlin, Eliza; Philadelphia, 1864 *5704.8 p181*
McNerny, Mary 20; Massachusetts, 1849 *5881.1 p71*
McNerny, Michael 24; Massachusetts, 1849 *5881.1 p71*
McNes, Charles-John; Quebec, 1824 *7603 p78*
McNichol, Bridget; Philadelphia, 1865 *5704.8 p201*
McNichol, Elizabeth; New York, NY, 1869 *5704.8 p235*
McNichol, Ellen; Philadelphia, 1865 *5704.8 p187*
McNichol, Felix; Philadelphia, 1865 *5704.8 p187*
McNichol, James 60; Philadelphia, 1860 *5704.8 p146*
McNichol, Patrick; Philadelphia, 1867 *5704.8 p217*
McNichol, Susan; Philadelphia, 1865 *5704.8 p187*
McNicholl, James; Philadelphia, 1847 *53.26 p66*
McNicholl, James; Philadelphia, 1847 *5704.8 p31*
McNicholl, James 24; Philadelphia, 1857 *5704.8 p133*
McNicholl, Margaret 22; St. John, N.B., 1855 *5704.8 p127*
McNicholl, Mary; Philadelphia, 1850 *5704.8 p64*
McNicholl, Patrick; Philadelphia, 1849 *53.26 p66*
McNicholl, Patrick; Philadelphia, 1849 *5704.8 p54*
McNichols, Bridget 46; Massachusetts, 1847 *5881.1 p63*
McNichols, Mary 18; Massachusetts, 1847 *5881.1 p70*
McNichols, Thomas 13; Massachusetts, 1847 *5881.1 p76*
McNickel, Mary; Philadelphia, 1853 *5704.8 p103*
McNickle, Daniel 7; Quebec, 1850 *5704.8 p62*
McNickle, Eliza; Quebec, 1850 *5704.8 p62*
McNickle, James 11; Quebec, 1850 *5704.8 p62*
McNickle, John 13; Quebec, 1850 *5704.8 p62*
McNickle, John 20; Quebec, 1854 *5704.8 p119*
McNickle, John 22; Quebec, 1854 *5704.8 p119*
McNickle, Mary Jane 5; Quebec, 1850 *5704.8 p62*
McNickle, Robert 3; Quebec, 1850 *5704.8 p62*
McNickle, William 9; Quebec, 1850 *5704.8 p62*
McNicol, Alexander; New York, NY, 1838 *8208.4 p70*

McNicol, Angus 30; Wilmington, NC, 1775 *1639.20 p214*
  *Wife:*Ann 20
McNicol, Ann 20 *SEE* McNicol, Angus
McNicol, Annabel *SEE* McNicol, Robert
McNicol, Annabell *SEE* McNicol, Duncan
McNicol, Catherine 31; Quebec, 1864 *5704.8 p163*
McNicol, Charles 10; Quebec, 1864 *5704.8 p163*
McNicol, Colin; New Jersey, 1764 *1219.7 p101*
McNicol, Daniel; South Carolina, 1825 *1639.20 p214*
McNicol, Duncan; North Carolina, 1774 *1639.20 p214*
  With wife
  With 2 children
  *Child:*Patrick
  *Child:*Annabell
  *Child:*Elizabeth
McNicol, Duncan Alexander 26; Kansas, 1889 *5240.1 p74*
McNicol, Elizabeth *SEE* McNicol, Duncan
McNicol, James 24; Kansas, 1873 *5240.1 p54*
McNicol, Jean Campbell 24 *SEE* McNicol, Robert
McNicol, John 8; Quebec, 1864 *5704.8 p163*
McNicol, John 24; Wilmington, NC, 1774 *1639.20 p214*
McNicol, John 32; Quebec, 1864 *5704.8 p163*
McNicol, Mary 5; Quebec, 1864 *5704.8 p163*
McNicol, Patrick *SEE* McNicol, Duncan
McNicol, Peter 20; St. John, N.B., 1866 *5704.8 p167*
McNicol, Robert 30; Wilmington, NC, 1774 *1639.20 p214*
  *Wife:*Jean Campbell 24
  *Daughter:*Annabel
McNicol, Thomas 2; Quebec, 1864 *5704.8 p163*
McNicoll, Agnes; Quebec, 1790 *7603 p38*
McNiff, John 12; Massachusetts, 1847 *5881.1 p67*
McNight, Margaret; St. John, N.B., 1847 *5704.8 p10*
McNinny, Thomas; New York, NY, 1837 *8208.4 p34*
McNish, Thomas; Washington, 1859-1920 *2872.1 p27*
McNolty, Charles; Montreal, 1823 *7603 p68*
McNully, Sarah; New York, NY, 1865 *5704.8 p192*
McNulty, Ann 18; Massachusetts, 1847 *5881.1 p62*
McNulty, Bridget; St. John, N.B., 1847 *5704.8 p15*
McNulty, Bridget 50; Massachusetts, 1849 *5881.1 p63*
McNulty, Edward; Quebec, 1825 *7603 p71*
McNulty, Elizabeth; New Orleans, 1849 *5704.8 p58*
McNulty, Grace 18; Philadelphia, 1861 *5704.8 p148*
McNulty, Hugh 24; Massachusetts, 1847 *5881.1 p67*
McNulty, Isabella; Quebec, 1847 *5704.8 p36*
McNulty, James; America, 1891 *1450.2 p98A*
McNulty, James; Massachusetts, 1848 *5881.1 p68*
McNulty, James 22; Philadelphia, 1864 *5704.8 p156*
McNulty, Jane 19; St. John, N.B., 1857 *5704.8 p134*
McNulty, Jane 24; St. John, N.B., 1854 *5704.8 p115*
McNulty, John 11; St. John, N.B., 1847 *5704.8 p11*
McNulty, John 17; St. John, N.B., 1856 *5704.8 p131*
McNulty, Margaret 16; Massachusetts, 1847 *5881.1 p70*
McNulty, Margaret 21; Philadelphia, 1860 *5704.8 p145*
McNulty, Margaret 24; Philadelphia, 1864 *5704.8 p156*
McNulty, Mary; Philadelphia, 1853 *5704.8 p100*
McNulty, Michael; America, 1867 *6014.1 p3*
McNulty, Michael; New York, NY, 1836 *8208.4 p12*
McNulty, Michael; St. John, N.B., 1849 *5704.8 p56*
McNulty, Michael 9; St. John, N.B., 1847 *5704.8 p11*
McNulty, Neal 10; Massachusetts, 1847 *5881.1 p73*
McNulty, Patrick; New York, NY, 1866 *5704.8 p206*
McNulty, Patrick 34; Quebec, 1864 *5704.8 p160*
McNulty, Patrick 50; Massachusetts, 1849 *5881.1 p74*
McNulty, Susan 50; Massachusetts, 1847 *5881.1 p75*
McNulty, Thomas 20; St. John, N.B., 1857 *5704.8 p134*
McNulty, William; New York, NY, 1866 *5704.8 p213*
McNulty, William 18; Massachusetts, 1847 *5881.1 p77*
McNurtry, Jane 23; St. John, N.B., 1863 *5704.8 p153*
McNutt, . . .; New York, NY, 1869 *5704.8 p235*
McNutt, Ann; New York, NY, 1869 *5704.8 p235*
McNutt, Anne; New York, NY, 1869 *5704.8 p235*
McNutt, Daniel; Philadelphia, 1864 *5704.8 p185*
McNutt, Elleanor 15; St. John, N.B., 1854 *5704.8 p120*
McNutt, Francis; Philadelphia, 1864 *5704.8 p185*
McNutt, George 22; St. John, N.B., 1854 *5704.8 p120*
McNutt, Henry 11; New York, NY, 1869 *5704.8 p235*
McNutt, James; New York, NY, 1865 *5704.8 p189*
McNutt, James 13; St. John, N.B., 1849 *5704.8 p56*
McNutt, James 18; Philadelphia, 1857 *5704.8 p133*
McNutt, John; New York, NY, 1865 *5704.8 p189*
McNutt, John 6; New York, NY, 1869 *5704.8 p235*
McNutt, Katey; Philadelphia, 1864 *5704.8 p185*
McNutt, Margaret; America, 1866 *5704.8 p212*
McNutt, Martha; St. John, N.B., 1849 *5704.8 p56*
McNutt, Mary Ann 11; St. John, N.B., 1854 *5704.8 p120*
McNutt, Matty; Philadelphia, 1847 *53.26 p66*
McNutt, Matty; Philadelphia, 1847 *5704.8 p30*
McNutt, Thomas; New York, NY, 1865 *5704.8 p189*
McNutty, James; Wisconsin, n.d. *9675.7 p51*
McOran, Hugh 24; Quebec, 1857 *5704.8 p135*

McOran, Patrick 24; Quebec, 1857 *5704.8 p135*
McOuat, Margaret; Indiana, 1832 *1450.2 p98A*
McOuat, William; America, 1832 *1450.2 p98A*
McOwens, Peter 22; Massachusetts, 1849 *5881.1 p75*
McPadden, Patrick; America, 1735-1743 *4971 p79*
McPartlan, Hugh 23; Philadelphia, 1804 *53.26 p66*
  *Relative:*Mary 22
McPartlan, Mary 22 *SEE* McPartlan, Hugh
McPartland, Mary; St. John, N.B., 1840 *7036 p123*
McPartlin, Thomas; Arkansas, 1918 *95.2 p82*
McPeak, Henry; New York, NY, 1866 *5704.8 p211*
McPeak, John 14; Philadelphia, 1854 *5704.8 p120*
McPeak, Mary; Quebec, 1851 *5704.8 p75*
McPeak, Sarah; Philadelphia, 1865 *5704.8 p198*
McPeak, Thomas; New York, NY, 1864 *5704.8 p170*
McPeake, Biddy; St. John, N.B., 1852 *5704.8 p95*
McPeake, Catherine 8; St. John, N.B., 1852 *5704.8 p95*
McPeake, Ellen 2; Quebec, 1856 *5704.8 p130*
McPeake, Francis 10; St. John, N.B., 1852 *5704.8 p95*
McPeake, John 12; St. John, N.B., 1852 *5704.8 p95*
McPeake, Mary 6; St. John, N.B., 1852 *5704.8 p95*
McPeake, Philip 3; St. John, N.B., 1852 *5704.8 p95*
McPeake, Rose 20; Philadelphia, 1861 *5704.8 p148*
McPeake, Rosey 6 mos; St. John, N.B., 1852 *5704.8 p95*
McPhail, Elizabeth 20 *SEE* McPhail, John
McPhail, Flora 67; North Carolina, 1850 *1639.20 p215*
McPhail, Hugh 23 *SEE* McPhail, John
McPhail, John 36; St. John, N.B., 1866 *5704.8 p166*
McPhail, John 62; South Carolina, 1850 *1639.20 p215*
  *Relative:*Maranetta 56
McPhail, John 72; North Carolina, 1850 *1639.20 p215*
  *Relative:*Mary 60
  *Relative:*Neill 30
  *Relative:*Mary 28
  *Relative:*Hugh 23
  *Relative:*Elizabeth 20
McPhail, Malcolm; America, 1741-1769 *1639.20 p215*
McPhail, Malcolm 78; North Carolina, 1850 *1639.20 p215*
McPhail, Maranetta 56 *SEE* McPhail, John
McPhail, Mary 15; St. John, N.B., 1866 *5704.8 p166*
McPhail, Mary 23; St. John, N.B., 1866 *5704.8 p166*
McPhail, Mary 28 *SEE* McPhail, John
McPhail, Mary 60 *SEE* McPhail, John
McPhail, Mary 70; North Carolina, 1850 *1639.20 p215*
McPhail, Neill 30 *SEE* McPhail, John
McPhail, Peter 38; South Carolina, 1850 *1639.20 p216*
McPhaill, John; North Carolina, 1770-1852 *1639.20 p215*
McPharland, Bernard; New York, NY, 1838 *8208.4 p74*
McPhatter, Mary 75; North Carolina, 1850 *1639.20 p216*
McPhearson, Colin; New York, 1765 *1219.7 p109*
McPhee, Angus; America, 1802 *1639.20 p216*
McPhee, Daniel 21; Maryland, 1775 *1219.7 p264*
McPhelimy, Peter; Philadelphia, 1851 *5704.8 p81*
McPhersin, Agnes 23; St. John, N.B., 1856 *5704.8 p131*
McPherson, Adam 18; St. John, N.B., 1856 *5704.8 p131*
McPherson, Alexander *SEE* McPherson, Donald
McPherson, Alexander; South Carolina, 1716 *1639.20 p216*
McPherson, Alexander 50; South Carolina, 1850 *1639.20 p216*
  *Relative:*Nancy 50
McPherson, Amelia 20; St. John, N.B., 1856 *5704.8 p131*
McPherson, Angus; South Carolina, 1716 *1639.20 p216*
McPherson, Annie; Pictou, N.S., 1846 *8893 p265*
McPherson, Archibald 78; North Carolina, 1850 *1639.20 p216*
McPherson, Archibald 78; North Carolina, 1850 *1639.20 p216*
  *Relative:*Sarah 75
McPherson, Catharine 60 *SEE* McPherson, Dugald
McPherson, Catherine 42; South Carolina, 1850 *1639.20 p217*
  *Relative:*Mary 45
McPherson, Christian 60; North Carolina, 1850 *1639.20 p217*
McPherson, Christian Downie 30 *SEE* McPherson, Malcolm
McPherson, David; St. John, N.B., 1847 *5704.8 p21*
McPherson, Donald *SEE* McPherson, Donald
McPherson, Donald; America, 1811 *1639.20 p217*
McPherson, Donald; America, 1822 *8893 p265*
  *Wife:*Mary
McPherson, Donald; Nova Scotia, 1830 *7085.4 p44*
  *Wife:*Marion
  *Child:*Donald
  *Child:*John
  *Child:*Alexander
  *Child:*Mary
  *Child:*Margaret
McPherson, Donald; South Carolina, 1716 *1639.20 p217*

McPherson, Dugald 60; South Carolina, 1850 *1639.20* p217
 Relative: Catharine 60
McPherson, Duncan; America, 1803 *1639.20* p217
McPherson, Duncan; South Carolina, 1716 *1639.20* p217
McPherson, George; New York, NY, 1839 *8208.4* p98
McPherson, Hugh 50; North Carolina, 1850 *1639.20* p218
 Relative: Nancy 52
McPherson, James; Philadelphia, 1853 *5704.8* p102
McPherson, James 19; Jamaica, 1727 *3690.1* p154
McPherson, James 30; Philadelphia, 1864 *5704.8* p156
McPherson, James 37; South Carolina, 1850 *1639.20* p218
McPherson, Jane; Philadelphia, 1852 *5704.8* p87
McPherson, Janet 10 SEE McPherson, Malcolm
McPherson, Janet 39; North Carolina, 1850 *1639.20* p218
McPherson, John SEE McPherson, Donald
McPherson, John; North Carolina, 1739 *1639.20* p218
McPherson, John; Philadelphia, 1853 *5704.8* p102
McPherson, John; South Carolina, 1716 *1639.20* p218
McPherson, John 20; Philadelphia, 1853 *5704.8* p113
McPherson, John 21; Philadelphia, 1854 *5704.8* p120
McPherson, M.; America, 1803 *1639.20* p218
McPherson, Malcolm 40; Wilmington, NC, 1774 *1639.20* p218
 Wife: Christian Downie 30
 Child: Janet 10
 Child: William 9
McPherson, Margaret SEE McPherson, Donald
McPherson, Margaret 70; Philadelphia, 1861 *5704.8* p148
McPherson, Marion SEE McPherson, Donald
McPherson, Mary SEE McPherson, Donald
McPherson, Mary SEE McPherson, Donald
McPherson, Mary 45 SEE McPherson, Catherine
McPherson, Nancy 50 SEE McPherson, Alexander
McPherson, Nancy 52 SEE McPherson, Hugh
McPherson, Nancy 70; North Carolina, 1850 *1639.20* p218
McPherson, Nancy 75; North Carolina, 1850 *1639.20* p218
McPherson, Neil; America, 1788 *1639.20* p219
McPherson, Peter; South Carolina, 1811 *1639.20* p219
McPherson, Samuel; Virginia, 1857 *4626.16* p16
McPherson, Sarah; Philadelphia, 1853 *5704.8* p102
McPherson, Sarah 75 SEE McPherson, Archibald
McPherson, Thomas 28; Philadelphia, 1859 *5704.8* p141
McPherson, Tom; Quebec, 1851 *5704.8* p73
McPherson, W. A.; Detroit, 1892 *1450.2* p98A
McPherson, William 9 SEE McPherson, Malcolm
McPherson, William 22; Philadelphia, 1774 *1219.7* p201
McPhil, Catherine 23; St. John, N.B., 1863 *5704.8* p152
McPhil, Catherine 56; St. John, N.B., 1863 *5704.8* p152
McPhilamey, Francis; Philadelphia, 1865 *5704.8* p204
McPhilamey, Susanna; Philadelphia, 1865 *5704.8* p204
McPhilamy, James 19; St. John, N.B., 1854 *5704.8* p121
McPhilamy, Mary 17; St. John, N.B., 1854 *5704.8* p121
McPhilim, Bridget; New Orleans, 1852 *5704.8* p98
McPhilim, Bridget 14; New Orleans, 1852 *5704.8* p98
McPhilim, Catherine 11; New Orleans, 1852 *5704.8* p98
McPhilim, Con; New Orleans, 1852 *5704.8* p98
McPhilim, John; New Orleans, 1852 *5704.8* p98
McPhilim, John 8; New Orleans, 1852 *5704.8* p98
McPhilim, Mary; New Orleans, 1852 *5704.8* p98
McPhilim, Susan; New Orleans, 1852 *5704.8* p98
McPhilimy, Isabella 45; Quebec, 1855 *5704.8* p125
McPhilimy, John 13; Quebec, 1855 *5704.8* p125
McPhillam, Ann; St. John, N.B., 1853 *5704.8* p106
McPhillamy, Catherine; Philadelphia, 1851 *5704.8* p71
McPhillamy, Sarah; St. John, N.B., 1853 *5704.8* p106
McPhillimy, Catherine; St. John, N.B., 1847 *5704.8* p35
McPhillimy, James; St. John, N.B., 1847 *5704.8* p35
McPhillimy, James 3 mos; St. John, N.B., 1847 *5704.8* p35
McPhillimy, Jane; St. John, N.B., 1847 *5704.8* p35
McPhillips, John; America, 1852 *6014.1* p3
McPike, Anthony 7; Quebec, 1853 *5704.8* p105
McPike, Bridget; Philadelphia, 1847 *53.26* p66
McPike, Bridget; Philadelphia, 1847 *5704.8* p2
McPike, Catherine 48; Quebec, 1853 *5704.8* p105
McPike, Edward 13; St. John, N.B., 1852 *5704.8* p93
McPike, James; St. John, N.B., 1852 *5704.8* p93
McPike, John; Quebec, 1852 *5704.8* p98
McPike, John 10; Quebec, 1853 *5704.8* p105
McPike, Neal 1; Massachusetts, 1847 *5881.1* p73
McPike, Patrick; St. John, N.B., 1852 *5704.8* p93
McPike, Richard 28; Massachusetts, 1847 *5881.1* p75
McPike, Thomas; Quebec, 1852 *5704.8* p98
McPoland, Betsey 16; Massachusetts, 1850 *5881.1* p64
McQuade, Anna; Quebec, 1825 *7603* p63
McQuade, Arthur; Philadelphia, 1847 *53.26* p66

McQuade, Arthur; Philadelphia, 1847 *5704.8* p32
McQuade, Arthur; Philadelphia, 1848 *53.26* p67
McQuade, Arthur; Philadelphia, 1848 *5704.8* p46
McQuade, Biddy; Philadelphia, 1847 *53.26* p67
McQuade, Biddy; Philadelphia, 1847 *5704.8* p31
McQuade, Bryan; America, 1740 *4971* p63
McQuade, Bryan; America, 1741 *4971* p73
McQuade, Catherine; Philadelphia, 1851 *5704.8* p79
McQuade, Catherine; St. John, N.B., 1848 *5704.8* p44
McQuade, Charles; Philadelphia, 1851 *5704.8* p79
McQuade, Charles; St. John, N.B., 1848 *5704.8* p44
McQuade, Edward; Philadelphia, 1847 *53.26* p67
McQuade, Edward; Philadelphia, 1847 *5704.8* p22
McQuade, Henry; America, 1741 *4971* p73
McQuade, James; Philadelphia, 1852 *5704.8* p89
McQuade, James 4; Massachusetts, 1849 *5881.1* p69
McQuade, John; Massachusetts, 1849 *5881.1* p69
McQuade, John; Philadelphia, 1852 *5704.8* p91
McQuade, Mary; St. John, N.B., 1847 *5704.8* p35
McQuade, Mary 8; Massachusetts, 1849 *5881.1* p72
McQuade, Nancy 60; Philadelphia, 1861 *5704.8* p147
McQuade, Nelis; Philadelphia, 1849 *53.26* p67
McQuade, Nelis; Philadelphia, 1849 *5704.8* p58
McQuade, Owen; St. John, N.B., 1847 *5704.8* p35
McQuade, Patrick; America, 1741 *4971* p73
McQuade, Patrick; St. John, N.B., 1847 *5704.8* p35
McQuade, Peter; Philadelphia, 1851 *5704.8* p79
McQuade, Peter 6 mos; St. John, N.B., 1848 *5704.8* p44
McQuade, Roger; America, 1741 *4971* p73
McQuade, Sarah Jane; Philadelphia, 1851 *5704.8* p77
McQuaid, Catherine 9 SEE McQuaid, John
McQuaid, Catherine 9; Philadelphia, 1848 *5704.8* p41
McQuaid, Edward; New York, NY, 1811 *2859.11* p16
McQuaid, Francis; Philadelphia, 1851 *5704.8* p79
McQuaid, James SEE McQuaid, John
McQuaid, James; Philadelphia, 1848 *5704.8* p41
McQuaid, John; Philadelphia, 1848 *53.26* p67
 Relative: Mary
 Relative: James
 Relative: Sarah 11
 Relative: Catherine 9
 Relative: Michael
McQuaid, John; Philadelphia, 1848 *5704.8* p41
McQuaid, John; Philadelphia, 1848 *5704.8* p79
McQuaid, Mary SEE McQuaid, John
McQuaid, Mary; Philadelphia, 1848 *5704.8* p41
McQuaid, Mary 20; Quebec, 1867 *5704.8* p168
McQuaid, Michael SEE McQuaid, John
McQuaid, Michael; Philadelphia, 1848 *5704.8* p41
McQuaid, Rose; America, 1864 *5704.8* p177
McQuaid, Sarah 11 SEE McQuaid, John
McQuaid, Sarah 11; Philadelphia, 1848 *5704.8* p41
McQueen, Alexander; South Carolina, 1716 *1639.20* p219
McQueen, Alexander; South Carolina, 1771-1828 *1639.20* p219
McQueen, Angus; North Carolina, 1764-1848 *1639.20* p219
McQueen, Angus 70; North Carolina, 1850 *1639.20* p67
McQueen, Ann 3; St. John, N.B., 1863 *5704.8* p152
McQueen, Anny 80; North Carolina, 1850 *1639.20* p219
McQueen, David; South Carolina, 1716 *1639.20* p219
McQueen, Donald; America, 1802 *1639.20* p220
McQueen, Donald 28; St. John, N.B., 1863 *5704.8* p152
McQueen, Donald 63; North Carolina, 1850 *1639.20* p220
McQueen, Donald 67; North Carolina, 1850 *1639.20* p220
McQueen, Duncan; South Carolina, 1716 *1639.20* p220
McQueen, Elizabeth 53; North Carolina, 1850 *1639.20* p220
McQueen, Flora 5; St. John, N.B., 1863 *5704.8* p152
McQueen, James; Wilmington, NC, 1772 *1639.20* p220
McQueen, Janet 28; St. John, N.B., 1863 *5704.8* p152
McQueen, John; South Carolina, 1716 *1639.20* p220
McQueen, Margaret; North Carolina, 1757-1837 *1639.20* p221
McQueen, Mary 1; St. John, N.B., 1863 *5704.8* p152
McQueen, Mary 80; North Carolina, 1850 *1639.20* p221
McQueen, Murdo; North Carolina, 1743-1828 *1639.20* p221
McQueen, Murdoch; Wilmington, NC, 1772 *1639.20* p221
McQueen, Nancy 42; North Carolina, 1850 *1639.20* p221
McQueen, Neill 50; North Carolina, 1850 *1639.20* p222
McQueen, Peter; Wilmington, NC, 1802 *1639.20* p222
McQueen, Thomas; Ontario, 1848 *9775.5* p216
McQueeney, Mary 60; Massachusetts, 1848 *5881.1* p70
McQuig, Elizabeth 2; Quebec, 1847 *5704.8* p28
McQuig, Jane; Quebec, 1847 *5704.8* p28
McQuig, Jane 7; Quebec, 1847 *5704.8* p28
McQuig, John 3 mos; Quebec, 1847 *5704.8* p28
McQuig, Malcolm; Quebec, 1847 *5704.8* p28

McQuig, Mary 9; Quebec, 1847 *5704.8* p28
McQuig, Rose 30; Massachusetts, 1849 *5881.1* p75
McQuilan, Mary 34; Wilmington, DE, 1831 *6508.7* p161
McQuilkan, Alexander 24; Philadelphia, 1853 *5704.8* p113
McQuilkan, Alexander 24; Philadelphia, 1855 *5704.8* p124
McQuilkan, Margaret; Philadelphia, 1847 *5704.8* p32
McQuilken, Elizabeth; Philadelphia, 1865 *5704.8* p197
McQuilken, Letitia; New York, NY, 1869 *5704.8* p232
McQuilken, Mary; Philadelphia, 1865 *5704.8* p197
McQuilken, Samuel; New York, NY, 1869 *5704.8* p232
McQuilken, William; Philadelphia, 1865 *5704.8* p197
McQuilkin, Ellen; New York, NY, 1864 *5704.8* p174
McQuilkin, Mary; America, 1864 *5704.8* p188
McQuilkin, William; America, 1864 *5704.8* p188
McQuillan, Margaret; Philadelphia, 1847 *53.26* p67
McQuillan, Martha; Philadelphia, 1850 *53.26* p67
McQuillan, Martha; Philadelphia, 1850 *5704.8* p59
McQuillan, Patrick 14; Massachusetts, 1847 *5881.1* p74
McQuin, Alexander; South Carolina, 1716 *1639.20* p222
McQuin, John; South Carolina, 1716 *1639.20* p222
McQuin, Patrick; New York, NY, 1838 *8208.4* p69
McQuinlan, Margaret 12; Massachusetts, 1849 *5881.1* p72
McQuinn, John; California, 1867 *2769.6* p5
McQuinn, Thomas W.; New York, NY, 1840 *8208.4* p104
McQuiston, Jean 27; North Carolina, 1775 *1639.20* p232
McQuiston, John; North Carolina, 1775 *1639.20* p222
McQuiston, Robert 26; Philadelphia, 1803 *53.26* p67
McRacken, Margaret; North Carolina, 1744-1829 *1639.20* p222
McRae, Ann; Charleston, SC, 1772 *1639.20* p222
McRae, Christian 55 SEE McRae, Robert
McRae, Christian 82; South Carolina, 1850 *1639.20* p223
McRae, Duncan; America, 1826 *8893* p265
McRae, Duncan; Carolina, 1780 *1639.20* p223
McRae, Finlay; Wilmington, NC, 1780 *1639.20* p223
 With wife
McRae, Flora 75; North Carolina, 1850 *1639.20* p224
McRae, Janet; North Carolina, 1799-1888 *1639.20* p224
McRae, John; North Carolina, 1700-1799 *1639.20* p224
 Wife: Mary
McRae, John L.; Colorado, 1904 *9678.2* p128
McRae, Katherine; North Carolina, 1765-1847 *1639.20* p224
McRae, Malcolm; America, 1791 *1639.20* p224
McRae, Margaret; North Carolina, 1787-1856 *1639.20* p224
McRae, Mary SEE McRae, John
McRae, Murdoch 84; North Carolina, 1850 *1639.20* p225
McRae, Norman; North Carolina, 1850 *1639.20* p225
McRae, Peter; America, 1788 *1639.20* p225
McRae, Philip; North Carolina, 1785 *1639.20* p225
McRae, Robert 54; South Carolina, 1850 *1639.20* p225
 Relative: Christian 55
McRae, Sarah 65; North Carolina, 1850 *1639.20* p226
McRael, Thomas 19; Maryland, 1775 *1219.7* p260
McRainey, Malcolm 66; North Carolina, 1850 *1639.20* p226
McRanald, Catherine 7 SEE McRanald, John
McRanald, Catherine 7; Philadelphia, 1850 *5704.8* p60
McRanald, John SEE McRanald, John
McRanald, John; Philadelphia, 1850 *53.26* p67
 Relative: Mary
 Relative: John
 Relative: Michael 12
 Relative: Nancy 10
 Relative: Catherine 7
 Relative: Patrick 4
McRanald, John; Philadelphia, 1850 *5704.8* p60
McRanald, Mary SEE McRanald, John
McRanald, Mary; Philadelphia, 1850 *5704.8* p60
McRanald, Michael 12 SEE McRanald, John
McRanald, Michael 12; Philadelphia, 1850 *5704.8* p60
McRanald, Nancy 10 SEE McRanald, John
McRanald, Nancy 10; Philadelphia, 1850 *5704.8* p60
McRanald, Patrick 4 SEE McRanald, John
McRanald, Patrick 4; Philadelphia, 1850 *5704.8* p60
McRaw, Isabell Paterson SEE McRaw, Peter
McRaw, Peter; South Carolina, 1780 *8894.1* p191
 Wife: Isabell Paterson
McRedden, Andrew; St. John, N.B., 1847 *5704.8* p21
McRob, Duncan 26; Wilmington, NC, 1774 *1639.20* p226
McRoberts, William; New York, NY, 1833 *8208.4* p31
McRoddin, Edmond; America, 1737 *4971* p74
McRoory, Michael; St. John, N.B., 1851 *5704.8* p79
McRorty, Michael 45; St. John, N.B., 1864 *5704.8* p159
McRory, Patrick; America, 1741 *4971* p76
McRory, Patrick; St. John, N.B., 1847 *5704.8* p5
McRosey, Daniel 18; Philadelphia, 1853 *5704.8* p113

McRye, Margaret; Philadelphia, 1850 ***53.26*** *p67*
McRye, Margaret; Philadelphia, 1850 ***5704.8*** *p60*
McShaferry, Ann 17; St. John, N.B., 1859 ***5704.8*** *p140*
McShaferry, Ann 20; St. John, N.B., 1859 ***5704.8*** *p140*
McShaferry, Bernard 10; St. John, N.B., 1859 ***5704.8*** *p140*
McShaferry, John 16; St. John, N.B., 1859 ***5704.8*** *p140*
McShaferry, Mary 6 mos; St. John, N.B., 1859 ***5704.8*** *p140*
McShaferry, Mary 18; St. John, N.B., 1859 ***5704.8*** *p140*
McShaferry, Mary 40; St. John, N.B., 1859 ***5704.8*** *p140*
McShain, Joseph; Philadelphia, 1851 ***5704.8*** *p77*
McShane, Alice; New York, NY, 1866 ***5704.8*** *p214*
McShane, Ann; Philadelphia, 1851 ***5704.8*** *p70*
McShane, Ann; St. John, N.B., 1847 ***5704.8*** *p26*
McShane, Catharine; Philadelphia, 1868 ***5704.8*** *p230*
McShane, Condy; Wisconsin, n.d. ***9675.7*** *p51*
McShane, Cormick; St. John, N.B., 1853 ***5704.8*** *p107*
McShane, Isabella; St. John, N.B., 1847 ***5704.8*** *p25*
McShane, John 20; Philadelphia, 1855 ***5704.8*** *p124*
McShane, John 25; Philadelphia, 1861 ***5704.8*** *p149*
McShane, Mary; St. John, N.B., 1847 ***5704.8*** *p26*
McShane, Mary 3; St. John, N.B., 1847 ***5704.8*** *p25*
McShane, Mary 18; Philadelphia, 1861 ***5704.8*** *p149*
McShane, Sarah; Philadelphia, 1868 ***5704.8*** *p230*
McShane, Thomas; Philadelphia, 1811 ***53.26*** *p67*
McShane, William; New York, NY, 1864 ***5704.8*** *p187*
McShany, Edward 3; St. John, N.B., 1852 ***5704.8*** *p83*
McShany, John 5; St. John, N.B., 1852 ***5704.8*** *p83*
McShany, Mary; St. John, N.B., 1852 ***5704.8*** *p83*
McShany, Mary Jane 7; St. John, N.B., 1852 ***5704.8*** *p83*
McShany, Patrick; St. John, N.B., 1852 ***5704.8*** *p83*
McShany, Rose Ann 6 mos; St. John, N.B., 1852 ***5704.8*** *p84*
McSharry, Bryan; America, 1735-1743 ***4971*** *p78*
McSharry, Bryan; America, 1736 ***4971*** *p80*
McSharry, Terence 33; St. John, N.B., 1855 ***5704.8*** *p127*
McSharry, Thomas; America, 1735-1743 ***4971*** *p78*
McSharry, Thomas; America, 1736 ***4971*** *p80*
McShary, John 50; St. John, N.B., 1861 ***5704.8*** *p149*
McShary, Margaret 14; St. John, N.B., 1861 ***5704.8*** *p149*
McShary, Patrick 12; St. John, N.B., 1861 ***5704.8*** *p149*
McShea, James *SEE* McShea, Mary
McShea, James; Philadelphia, 1848 ***5704.8*** *p46*
McShea, James; St. John, N.B., 1850 ***5704.8*** *p66*
McShea, Mary; Philadelphia, 1848 ***53.26*** *p67*
*Relative:*James
McShea, Mary; Philadelphia, 1848 ***5704.8*** *p46*
McSheely, John; America, 1847 ***1450.2*** *p98A*
McSheffry, Ann; St. John, N.B., 1847 ***5704.8*** *p25*
McSheffry, Betty; St. John, N.B., 1847 ***5704.8*** *p3*
McSheffry, Bridget 20; St. John, N.B., 1862 ***5704.8*** *p150*
McSheffry, Daniel; St. John, N.B., 1853 ***5704.8*** *p99*
McSheffry, Daniel 13; St. John, N.B., 1853 ***5704.8*** *p99*
McSheffry, Elizabeth 11; St. John, N.B., 1853 ***5704.8*** *p99*
McSheffry, Hugh; Philadelphia, 1847 ***53.26*** *p67*
McSheffry, Hugh; Philadelphia, 1847 ***5704.8*** *p5*
McSheffry, Hugh; Philadelphia, 1850 ***5704.8*** *p64*
McSheffry, John; St. John, N.B., 1847 ***5704.8*** *p9*
McSheffry, John; St. John, N.B., 1850 ***5704.8*** *p61*
McSheffry, Maria; St. John, N.B., 1853 ***5704.8*** *p99*
McSheffry, Mary; St. John, N.B., 1850 ***5704.8*** *p61*
McSheffry, Mary; St. John, N.B., 1853 ***5704.8*** *p99*
McSheffry, Patrick; St. John, N.B., 1847 ***5704.8*** *p25*
McSheffry, Rebecca 8; St. John, N.B., 1853 ***5704.8*** *p99*
McSheffry, William; St. John, N.B., 1851 ***5704.8*** *p78*
McShefry, Margery 3 mos; St. John, N.B., 1863 ***5704.8*** *p152*
McShefry, Mary 18; St. John, N.B., 1854 ***5704.8*** *p114*
McShefry, Mary 30; St. John, N.B., 1863 ***5704.8*** *p152*
McShefry, Neal 33; St. John, N.B., 1863 ***5704.8*** *p152*
McShefry, Rose 20; St. John, N.B., 1854 ***5704.8*** *p114*
McSherry, Ann 9; Quebec, 1847 ***5704.8*** *p17*
McSherry, Bridget; Quebec, 1847 ***5704.8*** *p17*
McSherry, Catherine 19; St. John, N.B., 1860 ***5704.8*** *p144*
McSherry, Ellan 7; Quebec, 1847 ***5704.8*** *p18*
McSherry, Elleanor; St. John, N.B., 1848 ***5704.8*** *p45*
McSherry, John 17; St. John, N.B., 1860 ***5704.8*** *p144*
McSherry, Margaret; St. John, N.B., 1848 ***5704.8*** *p45*
McSherry, Mary; St. John, N.B., 1848 ***5704.8*** *p45*
McSherry, Mary 4; Quebec, 1847 ***5704.8*** *p18*
McSherry, Patrick; Quebec, 1847 ***5704.8*** *p17*
McSherry, Patrick 2; Quebec, 1847 ***5704.8*** *p18*
McSherry, Terence; St. John, N.B., 1847 ***5704.8*** *p33*
McSherry, Tom 59; Arizona, 1924 ***9228.40*** *p28*
McShiffry, Magy; St. John, N.B., 1851 ***5704.8*** *p79*
McSorlay, Bridget; New York, NY, 1864 ***5704.8*** *p175*
McSorlay, Michael; New York, NY, 1864 ***5704.8*** *p175*
McSorlay, Nancy; New York, NY, 1866 ***5704.8*** *p211*
McSorlay, Patrick; Philadelphia, 1867 ***5704.8*** *p217*
McSorley, Arthur 22; Philadelphia, 1857 ***5704.8*** *p132*
McSorley, Catherine; New York, NY, 1864 ***5704.8*** *p171*
McSorley, David 28; Philadelphia, 1854 ***5704.8*** *p121*
McSorley, Eliza; New York, NY, 1867 ***5704.8*** *p218*
McSorley, Eliza 23; St. John, N.B., 1858 ***5704.8*** *p137*
McSorley, Elizabeth; St. John, N.B., 1848 ***5704.8*** *p47*
McSorley, Elleanor 50; St. John, N.B., 1856 ***5704.8*** *p131*
McSorley, Isabella; Philadelphia, 1865 ***5704.8*** *p201*
McSorley, James; New York, NY, 1864 ***5704.8*** *p171*
McSorley, James 22; St. John, N.B., 1856 ***5704.8*** *p131*
McSorley, John; Philadelphia, 1852 ***5704.8*** *p96*
McSorley, John 21; St. John, N.B., 1854 ***5704.8*** *p121*
McSorley, John 22; Philadelphia, 1865 ***5704.8*** *p164*
McSorley, Joseph; New York, NY, 1864 ***5704.8*** *p170*
McSorley, Joseph; New York, NY, 1867 ***5704.8*** *p218*
McSorley, Margaret 8; New York, NY, 1867 ***5704.8*** *p218*
McSorley, Mary; Quebec, 1849 ***5704.8*** *p57*
McSorley, Mary 20; St. John, N.B., 1856 ***5704.8*** *p131*
McSorley, Michael; Philadelphia, 1851 ***5704.8*** *p70*
McSorley, Sally; New York, NY, 1867 ***5704.8*** *p218*
McSorley, Sarah; New York, NY, 1864 ***5704.8*** *p169*
McSorley, William 25; Philadelphia, 1865 ***5704.8*** *p164*
McSorlie, James; St. John, N.B., 1847 ***5704.8*** *p9*
McSourlay, Charles; America, 1868 ***5704.8*** *p231*
McSparran, Arch. 40; Philadelphia, 1833-1834 ***53.26*** *p67*
*Relative:*M.H. 35
McSparran, M.H. 35 *SEE* McSparran, Arch.
McStay, William Vincent 22; Kansas, 1886 ***5240.1*** *p69*
McSuiggin, Catherine 11; Philadelphia, 1853 ***5704.8*** *p103*
McSuiggin, Jane; Philadelphia, 1853 ***5704.8*** *p103*
McSuiggin, Margaret 9; Philadelphia, 1853 ***5704.8*** *p103*
McSuiggin, Mary; Philadelphia, 1853 ***5704.8*** *p103*
McSuiggin, Rosanna 11; Philadelphia, 1853 ***5704.8*** *p103*
McSuiggin, Sophia; Philadelphia, 1853 ***5704.8*** *p103*
McSurley, Hugh 10; Massachusetts, 1849 ***5881.1*** *p67*
McSurley, Patrick 13; Massachusetts, 1849 ***5881.1*** *p74*
McSwain, Daniel; America, 1790 ***1639.20*** *p226*
McSwain, Daniel; America, 1802 ***1639.20*** *p226*
McSwain, David; America, 1731 ***1639.20*** *p227*
McSwain, Finlay; America, 1790 ***1639.20*** *p227*
McSween, Angus; America, 1802 ***1639.20*** *p226*
McSween, Donald Murdoch; North Carolina, 1725-1825 ***1639.20*** *p227*
McSween, Finlay; America, 1803 ***1639.20*** *p227*
McSween, Finley; South Carolina, 1746-1829 ***1639.20*** *p227*
McSween, Sarah; North Carolina, 1748-1822 ***1639.20*** *p227*
McSweeney, Anastatia 60; Massachusetts, 1847 ***5881.1*** *p62*
McSweeney, Catharine 36; Massachusetts, 1849 ***5881.1*** *p64*
McSweeney, Edward 62; Massachusetts, 1847 ***5881.1*** *p65*
McSweeney, John 40; Massachusetts, 1849 ***5881.1*** *p68*
McSwegan, Jane 11; Philadelphia, 1853 ***5704.8*** *p112*
McSwegan, Mary 14; Philadelphia, 1853 ***5704.8*** *p112*
McSwegan, Phillip; Philadelphia, 1849 ***5704.8*** *p54*
McSwigan, Bernard; Philadelphia, 1848 ***53.26*** *p67*
McSwigan, Bernard; Philadelphia, 1848 ***5704.8*** *p41*
McSwigan, Ellen; Philadelphia, 1849 ***53.26*** *p67*
McSwigan, Ellen; Philadelphia, 1849 ***5704.8*** *p54*
McSwigan, Ellen; Quebec, 1850 ***5704.8*** *p66*
McSwigan, Mary; Quebec, 1851 ***5704.8*** *p75*
McSwiggan, Bridget; New York, NY, 1869 ***5704.8*** *p232*
McSwiggan, Catharine; Philadelphia, 1868 ***5704.8*** *p230*
McSwiggan, Eliza; America, 1867 ***5704.8*** *p224*
McSwiggan, Hugh; New York, NY, 1865 ***5704.8*** *p199*
McSwiggan, Hugh; Philadelphia, 1865 ***5704.8*** *p196*
McSwiggan, James; Philadelphia, 1865 ***5704.8*** *p196*
McSwiggan, John; Philadelphia, 1865 ***5704.8*** *p196*
McSwiggan, Margaret; New York, NY, 1865 ***5704.8*** *p193*
McSwine, Biddy 6; Quebec, 1848 ***5704.8*** *p41*
McSwine, Edward 40; Philadelphia, 1854 ***5704.8*** *p117*
McSwine, Elleanor 4; Quebec, 1848 ***5704.8*** *p41*
McSwine, Hannah 3; Philadelphia, 1865 ***5704.8*** *p164*
McSwine, Hannah 36; Philadelphia, 1865 ***5704.8*** *p164*
McSwine, Hugh; Philadelphia, 1847 ***53.26*** *p67*
McSwine, Hugh; Philadelphia, 1847 ***5704.8*** *p32*
McSwine, Isabella; St. John, N.B., 1847 ***5704.8*** *p18*
McSwine, James; St. John, N.B., 1847 ***5704.8*** *p26*
McSwine, Jamy 2; Quebec, 1848 ***5704.8*** *p41*
McSwine, John; St. John, N.B., 1848 ***5704.8*** *p39*
McSwine, John 11; Philadelphia, 1865 ***5704.8*** *p164*
McSwine, John 12; Quebec, 1848 ***5704.8*** *p41*
McSwine, Keatty; Quebec, 1848 ***5704.8*** *p41*
McSwine, Mary; Philadelphia, 1852 ***5704.8*** *p96*
McSwine, Mary 1; Philadelphia, 1865 ***5704.8*** *p164*
McSwine, Nancy 6; Philadelphia, 1865 ***5704.8*** *p164*
McSwine, Neal Mergagh; America, 1739 ***4971*** *p75*
McSwine, Patrick; Quebec, 1848 ***5704.8*** *p41*
McSwine, Rosey 17; Philadelphia, 1865 ***5704.8*** *p164*
McTagart, Mary J.; Philadelphia, 1867 ***5704.8*** *p222*
McTaget, Robert; America, 1776 ***8894.1*** *p191*
McTaggart, Edward; St. John, N.B., 1847 ***5704.8*** *p3*
McTaggart, James 18; Philadelphia, 1860 ***5704.8*** *p146*
McTaggart, Mary; St. John, N.B., 1847 ***5704.8*** *p24*
McTaggart, Mary 18; Philadelphia, 1858 ***5704.8*** *p139*
McTaggart, Patrick; Philadelphia, 1850 ***53.26*** *p67*
McTaggart, Patrick; St. John, N.B., 1847 ***5704.8*** *p24*
McTaggart, Rose; St. John, N.B., 1848 ***5704.8*** *p44*
McTaggart, Sally; St. John, N.B., 1849 ***5704.8*** *p55*
McTammany, William; New York, NY, 1838 ***8208.4*** *p67*
McTate, Anne; New York, NY, 1864 ***5704.8*** *p181*
McTavish, Isabella 22; Massachusetts, 1849 ***5881.1*** *p67*
McTavish, Simon; Canada, 1764-1784 ***9775.5*** *p199*
McTavish, Simon; New York, 1764 ***9775.5*** *p199*
McTeague, Betty; St. John, N.B., 1847 ***5704.8*** *p34*
McTeague, Daniel; Philadelphia, 1852 ***5704.8*** *p96*
McTeague, Hugh; St. John, N.B., 1847 ***5704.8*** *p34*
McTeague, Hugh 10; St. John, N.B., 1847 ***5704.8*** *p34*
McTeague, John 8; St. John, N.B., 1847 ***5704.8*** *p34*
McTeague, Odey 6; St. John, N.B., 1847 ***5704.8*** *p34*
McTearnin, Maggy 20; Massachusetts, 1847 ***5881.1*** *p70*
McTogart, Mrs.; Philadelphia, 1816 ***53.26*** *p67*
With family
M'Cutcheon, Mr.; Quebec, 1815 ***9229.18*** *p77*
McVane, John; South Carolina, 1716 ***1639.20*** *p227*
McVane, Katherine 30; Wilmington, NC, 1775 ***1639.20*** *p227*
With daughter 4
With son
McVane, Malcolm; South Carolina, 1716 ***1639.20*** *p228*
McVay, Alexander 45; St. John, N.B., 1864 ***5704.8*** *p157*
McVay, Eliza 11; St. John, N.B., 1864 ***5704.8*** *p157*
McVay, Elizabeth 45; St. John, N.B., 1864 ***5704.8*** *p157*
McVay, Isabella 8; St. John, N.B., 1864 ***5704.8*** *p157*
McVay, Joseph 17; St. John, N.B., 1864 ***5704.8*** *p157*
McVay, Mary 10; St. John, N.B., 1864 ***5704.8*** *p157*
McVeagh, James; Illinois, 1856 ***7857*** *p5*
McVeagh, Mary; St. John, N.B., 1847 ***5704.8*** *p20*
McVeety, Susan; Philadelphia, 1865 ***5704.8*** *p189*
McVey, . . .; New York, NY, 1870 ***5704.8*** *p237*
McVey, Charles; Philadelphia, 1848 ***53.26*** *p67*
*Relative:*Susan
*Relative:*John 11
*Relative:*George 9
*Relative:*Sarah 7
*Relative:*Susan 5
*Relative:*Mary Jane 2
*Relative:*Charles 6 mos
McVey, Charles; Philadelphia, 1848 ***5704.8*** *p46*
McVey, Charles 6 mos *SEE* McVey, Charles
McVey, Charles 6 mos; Philadelphia, 1848 ***5704.8*** *p46*
McVey, Douglas 30; North Carolina, 1775 ***1639.20*** *p228*
McVey, Edward; New York, NY, 1864 ***5704.8*** *p171*
McVey, Elizabeth; New York, NY, 1870 ***5704.8*** *p237*
McVey, George 9 *SEE* McVey, Charles
McVey, George 9; Philadelphia, 1848 ***5704.8*** *p46*
McVey, Jane; New York, NY, 1864 ***5704.8*** *p171*
McVey, John; Montreal, 1822 ***7603*** *p68*
McVey, John; New York, NY, 1870 ***5704.8*** *p237*
McVey, John; Quebec, 1825 ***7603*** *p67*
McVey, John 11 *SEE* McVey, Charles
McVey, John 11; Philadelphia, 1848 ***5704.8*** *p46*
McVey, John 18; Philadelphia, 1853 ***5704.8*** *p108*
McVey, Mary; New York, NY, 1869 ***5704.8*** *p236*
McVey, Mary Jane 2 *SEE* McVey, Charles
McVey, Mary Jane 2; Philadelphia, 1848 ***5704.8*** *p46*
McVey, Nancy; New York, NY, 1864 ***5704.8*** *p171*
McVey, Patrick; Philadelphia, 1864 ***5704.8*** *p157*
McVey, Sarah 7 *SEE* McVey, Charles
McVey, Sarah 7; Philadelphia, 1848 ***5704.8*** *p46*
McVey, Susan *SEE* McVey, Charles
McVey, Susan; Philadelphia, 1848 ***5704.8*** *p46*
McVey, Susan 5 *SEE* McVey, Charles
McVey, Susan 5; Philadelphia, 1848 ***5704.8*** *p46*
McVey, William; New York, NY, 1869 ***5704.8*** *p236*
McVey, William; Philadelphia, 1864 ***5704.8*** *p186*
McVicar, Archibald; Charleston, SC, 1813 ***1639.20*** *p228*
McVicar, Archibald; Kansas, 1870 ***5240.1*** *p29*
McVicar, Archibald 34; Kansas, 1870 ***5240.1*** *p51*
McVicar, Barnabas 22; Virginia, 1775 ***1219.7*** *p261*
McVicar, John 36; Wilmington, NC, 1774 ***1639.20*** *p228*
McVicar, Neil; Charleston, SC, 1824 ***1639.20*** *p228*
McVicker, Robert; Philadelphia, 1851 ***5704.8*** *p80*
McWalters, James 16; St. John, N.B., 1865 ***5704.8*** *p165*
McWar, James; Philadelphia, 1850 ***53.26*** *p68*
McWar, James; Philadelphia, 1850 ***5704.8*** *p69*
McWard, Elizabeth; Philadelphia, 1851 ***5704.8*** *p71*
McWeeny, Bryan; America, 1735-1743 ***4971*** *p78*
McWeeny, Bryan; America, 1742 ***4971*** *p80*

McWhinnie, William; Charleston, SC, 1828 ***1639.20*** *p228*
McWilliam, William; South Carolina, 1825 ***1639.20*** *p228*
McWilliams, Ann 20; Philadelphia, 1855 ***5704.8*** *p124*
McWilliams, Archibald; Charleston, SC, 1797 ***1639.20*** *p228*
McWilliams, Bernard; Quebec, 1825 ***7603*** *p67*
McWilliams, Catherine; Philadelphia, 1849 ***5704.8*** *p54*
McWilliams, Cathrine; Philadelphia, 1849 ***53.26*** *p68*
McWilliams, Daniel; Quebec, 1849 ***5704.8*** *p51*
McWilliams, Eliza 28; Quebec, 1856 ***5704.8*** *p130*
McWilliams, Francis; Philadelphia, 1851 ***5704.8*** *p71*
McWilliams, James; St. John, N.B., 1847 ***5704.8*** *p21*
McWilliams, James; St. John, N.B., 1850 ***5704.8*** *p66*
McWilliams, James 18; Philadelphia, 1855 ***5704.8*** *p123*
McWilliams, James 24; Philadelphia, 1864 ***5704.8*** *p161*
McWilliams, Mary 13; St. John, N.B., 1847 ***5704.8*** *p21*
McWilliams, Michael 25; St. John, N.B., 1861 ***5704.8*** *p147*
McWilliams, Richard 18; Philadelphia, 1864 ***5704.8*** *p161*
McWilliams, Rose; New York, NY, 1864 ***5704.8*** *p171*
McWilliams, William 26; Quebec, 1856 ***5704.8*** *p130*
M'Donald, Mr.; Quebec, 1815 ***9229.18*** *p76*
Meachy, James 30; Massachusetts, 1847 ***5881.1*** *p67*
Mead, Ellen 26; Massachusetts, 1849 ***5881.1*** *p65*
Mead, Garrit; New York, NY, 1838 ***8208.4*** *p61*
Mead, James 27; Maryland, 1775 ***1219.7*** *p250*
Mead, John; New York, NY, 1816 ***2859.11*** *p38*
Mead, John; New York, NY, 1836 ***8208.4*** *p12*
Mead, John 6; Massachusetts, 1850 ***5881.1*** *p69*
Mead, John 17; Virginia, 1774 ***1219.7*** *p243*
Mead, John 39; Philadelphia, 1774 ***1219.7*** *p216*
Mead, Jon.; Virginia, 1643 ***6219*** *p199*
Mead, Joseph; Carolina, 1757 ***1219.7*** *p55*
Mead, Joseph 37; Maryland, 1774 ***1219.7*** *p230*
Mead, Julia 22; Massachusetts, 1849 ***5881.1*** *p68*
Mead, Matthew 21; Maryland, 1722 ***3690.1*** *p154*
Mead, Owen 17; Massachusetts, 1847 ***5881.1*** *p73*
Mead, Peter 30; Massachusetts, 1850 ***5881.1*** *p75*
Mead, Richard; New York, NY, 1838 ***8208.4*** *p67*
Mead, Samuel 15; Pennsylvania, 1733 ***3690.1*** *p154*
Mead, Thomas 41; Massachusetts, 1850 ***5881.1*** *p76*
Mead, William 15; Baltimore, 1775 ***1219.7*** *p269*
Meader, Ambrose; Virginia, 1636 ***6219*** *p75*
With wife
Meader, Nich.; Virginia, 1638 ***6219*** *p119*
Meades, Thomas; Virginia, 1636 ***6219*** *p12*
Meagher, Edmund; America, 1736-1743 ***4971*** *p58*
Meagher, James 18; Jamaica, 1731 ***3690.1*** *p154*
Meagher, Richard; America, 1844 ***1450.2*** *p98A*
Meagher, William; America, 1736-1743 ***4971*** *p58*
Meagher, William; Quebec, 1823 ***7603*** *p78*
Meahan, Mary; Philadelphia, 1847 ***53.26*** *p68*
Meahan, Mary; Philadelphia, 1847 ***5704.8*** *p14*
Meakes, John; Virginia, 1642 ***6219*** *p190*
Meakin, Elizabeth 16; America, 1704 ***2212*** *p40*
Meakins, Samuel 29; Maryland, 1774 ***1219.7*** *p181*
Mealey, Martin 25; Virginia, 1774 ***1219.7*** *p244*
Mealy, Bridget; America, 1742 ***4971*** *p86*
Mealy, Bridget; Annapolis, MD, 1742 ***4971*** *p92*
Mealy, John; America, 1742 ***4971*** *p81*
Mealy, Margaret 30; Massachusetts, 1849 ***5881.1*** *p71*
Mealy, Mary; America, 1738 ***4971*** *p13*
Mealy, Rose; America, 1740 ***4971*** *p15*
Meane, Hugh; America, 1739 ***4971*** *p73*
Means, Catherine; Quebec, 1849 ***5704.8*** *p50*
Means, Catherine 13; Quebec, 1849 ***5704.8*** *p50*
Means, Dederick; Illinois, 1862 ***7857*** *p5*
Means, Eliza; Quebec, 1849 ***5704.8*** *p51*
Means, Eliza 5; Quebec, 1849 ***5704.8*** *p50*
Means, John 3; Quebec, 1849 ***5704.8*** *p50*
Means, Mary Ann 17; Philadelphia, 1864 ***5704.8*** *p156*
Means, Michael 15; Philadelphia, 1864 ***5704.8*** *p156*
Means, Samuel; Quebec, 1849 ***5704.8*** *p50*
Means, Samuel 11; Quebec, 1849 ***5704.8*** *p50*
Means, William; Quebec, 1849 ***5704.8*** *p50*
Means, William; Quebec, 1849 ***5704.8*** *p51*
Meany, Edward J.; West Virginia, 1846 ***9788.3*** *p16*
Meany, Mary; America, 1740 ***4971*** *p48*
Meares, Hen.; Virginia, 1635 ***6219*** *p70*
Meares, Hen.; Virginia, 1638 ***6219*** *p116*
Mearn, Mary; Philadelphia, 1852 ***5704.8*** *p89*
Mears, James; Jamaica, 1754 ***1219.7*** *p27*
Mears, James; Jamaica, 1754 ***3690.1*** *p154*
Mears, Martin; America, 1742 ***4971*** *p83*
Meath, Helene; Quebec, 1821 ***7603*** *p101*
Meath, John; Illinois, 1898 ***5012.40*** *p55*
Meathfield, Mr.; Quebec, 1815 ***9229.18*** *p82*
Meau, Andrea 42; America, 1836 ***778.5*** *p374*
Mebbison, John 16; Jamaica, 1734 ***3690.1*** *p154*
Mebius, . . .; Canada, 1776-1783 ***9786*** *p29*
Mecali, Augsto; Arkansas, 1918 ***95.2*** *p82*
Mechan, Catherine; New York, NY, 1815 ***2859.11*** *p38*
Mechan, James; New York, NY, 1816 ***2859.11*** *p38*
Mechan, John; America, 1736-1737 ***4971*** *p26*
Mechlan, Mary; New York, NY, 1816 ***2859.11*** *p38*
Mechlan, William; New York, NY, 1816 ***2859.11*** *p38*
Mechlin, Henry; Philadelphia Co., PA, 1765 ***4779.3*** *p14*
Mechling, Jacob *SEE* Mechling, Theobald
Mechling, Theobald; Pennsylvania, 1728 ***4779.3*** *p14*
*Relative:*Jacob
Meckelein, Hans; Pennsylvania, 1753 ***4525*** *p232*
Meckelein, Hans; Pennsylvania, 1753 ***4779.3*** *p14*
*Relative:*Johann Heinrich
Meckelein, Johan Heinrich; Pennsylvania, 1753 ***4525*** *p232*
Meckelein, Johann Heinrich *SEE* Meckelein, Hans
Meckelein, Johannes; New England, 1753 ***4525*** *p232*
Meckels Family ; New York, 1765 ***8125.8*** *p436*
Mecker, . . .; Canada, 1776-1783 ***9786*** *p29*
Meckin, Jos.; New York, NY, 1811 ***2859.11*** *p17*
Mecklein, . . .; Pennsylvania, n.d. ***4525*** *p232*
Mecklenburg, Johann; Ohio, 1798-1818 ***8582.2*** *p54*
Mecklenburg, John; Ohio, 1798-1818 ***8582.2*** *p54*
Mecklien, John; Philadelphia Co., PA, 1763 ***4779.3*** *p14*
Mecklin, John; Pennsylvania, 1753 ***4525*** *p232*
Mecklin, John; Philadelphia Co., PA, 1765 ***4779.3*** *p14*
Meckline, John George; Philadelphia Co., PA, 1765 ***4779.3*** *p14*
Meckling, Johann George; Pennsylvania, 1752 ***4779.3*** *p14*
Medan, Jean Bertrand 28; America, 1838 ***778.5*** *p374*
Medan, Pierre 28; America, 1838 ***778.5*** *p374*
Medant, J. 30; New Orleans, 1839 ***778.5*** *p374*
Medcalfe, Christopher; Virginia, 1635 ***6219*** *p160*
Medcalfe, Henry; Virginia, 1636 ***6219*** *p77*
Medcalfe, Jeffery; Virginia, 1645 ***6219*** *p232*
Medcalfe, William; Virginia, 1639 ***6219*** *p155*
Medcalfe, William; Virginia, 1652 ***6251*** *p19*
Medcalfe, Xtopr.; Virginia, 1648 ***6219*** *p250*
Medecine, John 13?; America, 1701 ***2212*** *p35*
Medget, Joseph 16; Philadelphia, 1774 ***1219.7*** *p233*
Medias, Charles; New York, 1888 ***1450.2*** *p98A*
Mediata, Rocco; Arkansas, 1918 ***95.2*** *p82*
Mediate, Rosco 25; Arkansas, 1918 ***95.2*** *p82*
Medigovich, Vaso G.; Arizona, 1890 ***2764.35*** *p44*
Medile, David; New York, NY, 1815 ***2859.11*** *p38*
Medlam, Agnis; Virginia, 1636 ***6219*** *p77*
Medland, Geo.; Virginia, 1642 ***6219*** *p198*
Medland, Robert; Iowa, 1866-1943 ***123.54*** *p33*
Medle, Robt.; Virginia, 1637 ***6219*** *p117*
Medlecoe, Joseph; Virginia, 1643 ***6219*** *p203*
Medley, Harriet Fanny Ann; Wisconsin, 1852 ***8893*** *p263*
Medley, John 19; Virginia, 1700 ***2212*** *p30*
Medley, Robert; Virginia, 1641 ***6219*** *p184*
Medlicot, George; America, 1735-1743 ***4971*** *p7*
Medor, Jane 23; America, 1837 ***778.5*** *p374*
Medrano, Cervito 26; Arizona, 1921 ***9228.40*** *p25*
Medruer, Mr. 38; New Orleans, 1839 ***778.5*** *p374*
Medway, Elizabeth 8 *SEE* Medway, Robert
Medway, Lydia 5 *SEE* Medway, Robert
Medway, Lydia 33 *SEE* Medway, Robert
Medway, Robert 2 *SEE* Medway, Robert
Medway, Robert 35; Norfolk, VA, 1774 ***1219.7*** *p222*
*Wife:*Lydia 33
*Child:*Susanna 10
*Child:*Elizabeth 8
*Child:*Lydia 5
*Child:*Robert 2
Medway, Susanna 10 *SEE* Medway, Robert
Medwit, Joe; Wisconsin, n.d. ***9675.7*** *p51*
Medworth, Hannah 42; Kansas, 1879 ***5240.1*** *p30*
Medworth, Hannah 42; Kansas, 1879 ***5240.1*** *p60*
Medynska, Felix 3 *SEE* Medynska, Maria Glowacki
Medynska, Kazimier 4 *SEE* Medynska, Maria Glowacki
Medynska, Maria Glowacki 30; New York, 1912 ***9980.29*** *p67*
*Child:*Wincent 9
*Child:*Kazimier 4
*Child:*Felix 3
Medynska, Tomas; Pennsylvania, 1912 ***9980.29*** *p67*
Medynska, Wincent 9 *SEE* Medynska, Maria Glowacki
Medynski, Felix 3 *SEE* Medynski, Maria Glowacki
Medynski, Kazimier 4 *SEE* Medynski, Maria Glowacki
Medynski, Maria Glowacki 30; New York, 1912 ***9980.29*** *p67*
*Child:*Wincent 9
*Child:*Kazimier 4
*Child:*Felix 3
Medynski, Tomas; Pennsylvania, 1912 ***9980.29*** *p67*
Medynski, Wincent 9 *SEE* Medynski, Maria Glowacki
Mee, Dominico 20; Massachusetts, 1849 ***5881.1*** *p65*
Mee, Georg; Virginia, 1633 ***6219*** *p32*
Mee, William 24; Baltimore, 1775 ***1219.7*** *p270*
Meean, Bridget; Philadelphia, 1868 ***5704.8*** *p226*
Meech, John 17; Philadelphia, 1774 ***1219.7*** *p232*
Meed, John 20; Jamaica, 1721 ***3690.1*** *p154*
Meede, John 20; Jamaica, 1721 ***3690.1*** *p154*
Meedel, Geo. 45; Kansas, 1885 ***5240.1*** *p30*
Meeghan, Hugh 28; St. John, N.B., 1854 ***5704.8*** *p114*
Meeghan, Patrick; New York, NY, 1811 ***2859.11*** *p17*
Meeghon, Ellen 47; Quebec, 1858 ***5704.8*** *p140*
Meeh, John; Pennsylvania, 1752 ***2444*** *p193*
Meehan, Catherine; New York, NY, 1811 ***2859.11*** *p17*
Meehan, Hannah; Philadelphia, 1866 ***5704.8*** *p207*
Meehan, James; New York, NY, 1838 ***8208.4*** *p86*
Meehan, James; Philadelphia, 1865 ***5704.8*** *p198*
Meehan, James John; Kansas, 1916 ***6013.40*** *p16*
Meehan, John; New York, 1866 ***1450.2*** *p99A*
Meehan, John 10; Philadelphia, 1852 ***5704.8*** *p96*
Meehan, Mary Ann 7; Philadelphia, 1852 ***5704.8*** *p96*
Meehan, Mathew 18; Philadelphia, 1858 ***5704.8*** *p139*
Meehan, Owen; New York, NY, 1811 ***2859.11*** *p17*
Meehan, Patrick; America, 1742 ***4971*** *p23*
Meehan, Patrick; New York, NY, 1834 ***8208.4*** *p78*
Meehan, Patrick; New York, NY, 1850 ***2896.5*** *p27*
Meehan, Patrick; Quebec, 1850 ***5704.8*** *p69*
Meehan, Philip; New York, NY, 1864 ***5704.8*** *p171*
Meehan, Sarah 20; Philadelphia, 1861 ***5704.8*** *p148*
Meehan, Thomas 32; West Virginia, 1895 ***9788.3*** *p16*
Meehan, Thomas 34; West Virginia, 1897 ***9788.3*** *p16*
Meek, Euphemea 26; St. John, N.B., 1866 ***5704.8*** *p166*
Meek, Isabella; Philadelphia, 1852 ***5704.8*** *p88*
Meek, John 21; Virginia, 1736 ***3690.1*** *p154*
Meek, William; Philadelphia, 1852 ***5704.8*** *p92*
Meek, William 24; St. John, N.B., 1866 ***5704.8*** *p166*
Meekham, Samuel 15; Philadelphia, 1774 ***1219.7*** *p232*
Meekulski, Flerion; Wisconsin, n.d. ***9675.7*** *p51*
Meenagh, Owen; America, 1741 ***4971*** *p23*
Meenan, Catharine; New York, NY, 1870 ***5704.8*** *p238*
Meenan, Catharine; Philadelphia, 1867 ***5704.8*** *p216*
Meenan, Catherine; Philadelphia, 1852 ***5704.8*** *p87*
Meenan, Eleanor; New Orleans, 1852 ***5704.8*** *p98*
Meenan, Ellen; New York, NY, 1870 ***5704.8*** *p238*
Meenan, Isabella; Philadelphia, 1867 ***5704.8*** *p221*
Meenan, James; New York, NY, 1868 ***5704.8*** *p227*
Meenan, James; Philadelphia, 1865 ***5704.8*** *p192*
Meenan, John; New York, NY, 1864 ***5704.8*** *p170*
Meenan, John; New York, NY, 1866 ***5704.8*** *p205*
Meenan, Manus; New Orleans, 1852 ***5704.8*** *p98*
Meenan, Margaret; New York, NY, 1840 ***7036*** *p117*
Meenan, Mary; New York, NY, 1865 ***5704.8*** *p194*
Meenan, Michael; New York, NY, 1868 ***5704.8*** *p227*
Meenan, Neal; Philadelphia, 1851 ***5704.8*** *p78*
Meenan, Peggy; Philadelphia, 1849 ***53.26*** *p68*
Meenan, Sally; New York, NY, 1868 ***5704.8*** *p227*
Meenin, Peggy; Philadelphia, 1849 ***5704.8*** *p52*
Meentemeier, Gustav E. Wilhelm Ludwig; America, 1868 ***4610.10*** *p100*
Meents, Cornelius; New York, NY, 1905 ***3455.1*** *p48*
Meents, John Becker; Philadelphia, 1897 ***3455.2*** *p53*
Meents, John Becker; Philadelphia, 1897 ***3455.3*** *p113*
Meerkin, Catharine 6; Massachusetts, 1849 ***5881.1*** *p64*
Meerwald, Anna Margaretha; Port uncertain, 1696-1800 ***2444*** *p191*
Mees, Jacob; America, 1788 ***8582.2*** *p57*
Meester, Margreeta Wollauf Wimmer; New York, 1709 ***3627*** *p7*
*Child:*Susan Cath
With 2 children
Meester, Susan Cath *SEE* Meester, Margreeta Wollauf Wimmer
Meeth, Philip; Philadelphia, 1760 ***9973.7*** *p34*
Meffert, . . .; Canada, 1776-1783 ***9786*** *p29*
Mege, J. 36; Louisiana, 1820 ***778.5*** *p374*
Megerle, Christian; America, 1852 ***8582.3*** *p44*
Megerlin, Johannes; New England, 1753 ***4525*** *p232*
Megie, Jean 23; New Orleans, 1838 ***778.5*** *p374*
Meginiss, Anthony 23; Jamaica, 1730 ***3690.1*** *p154*
Meguin, Charles; Port uncertain, 1834 ***778.5*** *p374*
Mehaffy, Charles 6 *SEE* Mehaffy, Margaret
Mehaffy, Charles 6; Philadelphia, 1849 ***5704.8*** *p50*
Mehaffy, Edward 4 *SEE* Mehaffy, Margaret
Mehaffy, Edward 4; Philadelphia, 1849 ***5704.8*** *p50*
Mehaffy, Isabella; Philadelphia, 1865 ***5704.8*** *p198*
Mehaffy, James 12 *SEE* Mehaffy, Margaret
Mehaffy, James 12; Philadelphia, 1849 ***5704.8*** *p50*
Mehaffy, John 10 *SEE* Mehaffy, Margaret
Mehaffy, John 10; Philadelphia, 1849 ***5704.8*** *p50*
Mehaffy, Margaret; Philadelphia, 1849 ***53.26*** *p68*
*Relative:*James 12
*Relative:*John 10
*Relative:*Patrick 8
*Relative:*Charles 6
*Relative:*Edward 4
Mehaffy, Margaret; Philadelphia, 1849 ***5704.8*** *p50*
Mehaffy, Patrick 8 *SEE* Mehaffy, Margaret
Mehaffy, Patrick 8; Philadelphia, 1849 ***5704.8*** *p50*
Mehagn, Themathe; Wisconsin, n.d. ***9675.7*** *p51*

Mehan, Bessy 59; Massachusetts, 1848 ***5881.1*** *p63*
Mehan, Betsey 23; Massachusetts, 1850 ***5881.1*** *p64*
Mehan, Biddy 12; St. John, N.B., 1847 ***5704.8*** *p10*
Mehan, Catharine; Philadelphia, 1866 ***5704.8*** *p211*
Mehan, Catherine; St. John, N.B., 1847 ***5704.8*** *p10*
Mehan, Charles; St. John, N.B., 1847 ***5704.8*** *p10*
Mehan, Cicily; St. John, N.B., 1847 ***5704.8*** *p10*
Mehan, Cicily 7; Quebec, 1851 ***5704.8*** *p82*
Mehan, Daniel; St. John, N.B., 1852 ***5704.8*** *p93*
Mehan, Daniel 20; Massachusetts, 1849 ***5881.1*** *p65*
Mehan, Ellen; Quebec, 1851 ***5704.8*** *p82*
Mehan, Ellen; St. John, N.B., 1852 ***5704.8*** *p93*
Mehan, George; Arkansas, 1918 ***95.2*** *p82*
Mehan, Henry; St. John, N.B., 1847 ***5704.8*** *p10*
Mehan, Hugh 53; Massachusetts, 1849 ***5881.1*** *p67*
Mehan, James; Philadelphia, 1866 ***5704.8*** *p208*
Mehan, James; St. John, N.B., 1847 ***5704.8*** *p10*
Mehan, James 6 mos; St. John, N.B., 1847 ***5704.8*** *p10*
Mehan, James 25; Philadelphia, 1858 ***5704.8*** *p139*
Mehan, John 23; Massachusetts, 1848 ***5881.1*** *p68*
Mehan, John 24; Massachusetts, 1850 ***5881.1*** *p70*
Mehan, Kitty; St. John, N.B., 1847 ***5704.8*** *p10*
Mehan, Lawrence 24; Massachusetts, 1848 ***5881.1*** *p70*
Mehan, Margaret; Quebec, 1851 ***5704.8*** *p74*
Mehan, Margaret 13; St. John, N.B., 1847 ***5704.8*** *p10*
Mehan, Mathew 19; Massachusetts, 1848 ***5881.1*** *p71*
Mehan, Mathew 62; Massachusetts, 1848 ***5881.1*** *p71*
Mehan, Rosanna 7; St. John, N.B., 1847 ***5704.8*** *p10*
Mehan, Sarah; Philadelphia, 1866 ***5704.8*** *p211*
Mehan, Unity; St. John, N.B., 1847 ***5704.8*** *p10*
Mehane, Jane 22; Massachusetts, 1848 ***5881.1*** *p68*
Mehatrich, Lorenz; Iowa, 1866-1943 ***123.54*** *p33*
Mehl, Ernst; America, 1890 ***1450.2*** *p99A*
Mehler, Elisabetha Hayn *SEE* Mehler, Johann Martin
Mehler, Johann Martin; Pennsylvania, 1754 ***2444*** *p192*
*Wife:*Elisabetha Hayn
Mehlhaefin, Maria Clara; Pennsylvania, 1753 ***2444*** *p154*
Mehlhafen, Maria Clara; Pennsylvania, 1753 ***2444*** *p154*
Mehlinger, Joseph 28; West Virginia, 1900 ***9788.3*** *p16*
Mehnert, Paul; America, 1893 ***1450.2*** *p99A*
Mehres, John; Wisconsin, n.d. ***9675.7*** *p51*
Mehrhoff, Christian H.; Iowa, 1866-1943 ***123.54*** *p71*
Mehrhoff, Christian Henry; Iowa, 1866-1943 ***123.54*** *p71*
Mehrling, Georg; Philadelphia, 1756 ***4525*** *p261*
Mehrmann, Peter; America, 1853 ***2853.7*** *p109*
Mehrtens, Herman Henry; New York, NY, 1836 ***8208.4*** *p24*
Mehrtens, William 31; California, 1872 ***2769.7*** *p3*
Mehus, Tarkel; Arkansas, 1918 ***95.2*** *p82*
Meibers, Johann Bernard; America, 1852 ***8582.3*** *p44*
Meickhart, Peter; Mississippi, 1724 ***2854*** *p45*
With family
Meier, Mr.; America, 1764-1808 ***8582.1*** *p6*
Meier, Albert 2; New York, NY, 1857 ***9831.14*** *p154*
Meier, August; Illinois, 1855 ***7857*** *p5*
Meier, August 36; New York, NY, 1857 ***9831.14*** *p154*
Meier, Bertha 6; New York, NY, 1857 ***9831.14*** *p154*
Meier, Carl 3; New York, NY, 1857 ***9831.14*** *p154*
Meier, Charles; Illinois, 1860 ***5012.38*** *p98*
Meier, Christian Frederick; America, 1840 ***1450.2*** *p99A*
Meier, Friedrich Wilhelm; Texas, 1866 ***4610.10*** *p13*
Meier, George; New York, NY, 1873 ***2896.5*** *p27*
Meier, Gerhard; Virginia, 1852 ***4626.16*** *p14*
Meier, Gottlieb 23; Kansas, 1887 ***5240.1*** *p69*
Meier, Heinrich Wilhelm; Cincinnati, 1869-1887 ***8582*** *p20*
Meier, Henry Alberts; America, 1854 ***1450.2*** *p99A*
Meier, Herman; Illinois, 1875 ***2896.5*** *p27*
Meier, Herman; New York, 1848 ***2896.5*** *p27*
Meier, Herman H.W.; Illinois, 1876 ***2896.5*** *p27*
Meier, Johan Michael; America, 1846 ***1450.2*** *p99A*
Meier, Johann Heinrich; America, 1881 ***4610.10*** *p160*
Meier, Johann Vallentin; Pennsylvania, 1754 ***2444*** *p190*
Meier, John; New York, NY, 1836 ***8208.4*** *p24*
Meier, John 45; Kansas, 1874 ***5240.1*** *p55*
Meier, John Henry; America, 1866 ***1450.2*** *p99A*
Meier, Lambert; Wisconsin, n.d. ***9675.7*** *p51*
Meier, Louise; America, 1872 ***4610.10*** *p109*
Meier, Michael; Cincinnati, 1869-1887 ***8582*** *p20*
Meier, Reinald 32; Kansas, 1886 ***5240.1*** *p68*
Meier, Rudolph; Illinois, 1877 ***2896.5*** *p27*
Meier, Wilhelmine 27; New York, NY, 1857 ***9831.14*** *p154*
Meier, William; America, 1840 ***1450.2*** *p99A*
Meieres, Michel; Wisconsin, n.d. ***9675.7*** *p51*
Meiggitzer, . . .; Georgia, 1738 ***9332*** *p321*
Meighan, Anne; Philadelphia, 1851 ***5704.8*** *p80*
Meighan, Catherine; Philadelphia, 1851 ***5704.8*** *p80*
Meighan, Christopher; New York, NY, 1830 ***8208.4*** *p55*
Meighan, James; Philadelphia, 1851 ***5704.8*** *p80*
Meighan, Mary 3; Philadelphia, 1855 ***5704.8*** *p124*
Meighan, Mary 30; Philadelphia, 1855 ***5704.8*** *p124*
Meighan, Mary 53; St. John, N.B., 1855 ***5704.8*** *p126*
Meighan, Matty 18; St. John, N.B., 1855 ***5704.8*** *p126*
Meighan, Patrick; St. John, N.B., 1851 ***5704.8*** *p77*
Meighan, Rodger; Philadelphia, 1851 ***5704.8*** *p80*
Meijer, Andrew; Canada, 1783 ***9786*** *p38A*
Meikel, Charles; America, 1835 ***1450.2*** *p101A*
Meikle, John 46; Kansas, 1879 ***5240.1*** *p61*
Meilisjerg, Hans Jerg; Pennsylvania, 1749 ***2444*** *p163*
Meilleur, Jean; Louisiana, 1789-1819 ***778.5*** *p556*
Meimel, Mr. 28; Port uncertain, 1838 ***778.5*** *p374*
Mein, John; New York, NY, 1816 ***2859.11*** *p38*
Meinders, Annetje; New York, 1662 ***8125.8*** *p436*
Meinders, Behrend; Iroquois Co., IL, 1893 ***3455.1*** *p12*
Meindzi, Johann 24; New York, 1912 ***9980.29*** *p75*
Meinecke, . . .; Canada, 1776-1783 ***9786*** *p29*
Meineke, Fred; Washington, 1859-1920 ***2872.1*** *p26*
Meineke, Frederick; Washington, 1859-1920 ***2872.1*** *p26*
Meinen, . . .; Canada, 1776-1783 ***9786*** *p29*
Meiners, . . .; Canada, 1776-1783 ***9786*** *p43*
Meiners, Hermann; Cincinnati, 1869-1887 ***8582*** *p20*
Meinert, Ernst Heinrich F. Ludwig; America, 1872 ***4610.10*** *p100*
Meiney, Laurent 50; America, 1839 ***778.5*** *p374*
Meinguth, Johannes; Philadelphia, 1779 ***8137*** *p11*
Meinholz, Caroline Louise Charlotte; America, 1883 ***4610.10*** *p102*
Meinholz, Ernst Heinrich Friedrich; America, 1882 ***4610.10*** *p101*
Meininger, Carl; America, 1849 ***8582.2*** *p25*
Meinone, . . .; Canada, 1776-1783 ***9786*** *p29*
Meins, Karl; Wisconsin, n.d. ***9675.7*** *p51*
Meinung, Abraham; Philadelphia, 1741 ***3652*** *p53*
*Relative:*Judith
Meinung, Judith *SEE* Meinung, Abraham
Meir, George; Illinois, 1892 ***5012.40*** *p27*
Meis, Gerhard; Minnesota, 1870 ***5240.1*** *p30*
Meis, Robert; Ohio, 1812 ***8582.1*** *p49*
Meisker, Christopher; Illinois, 1867 ***2896.5*** *p27*
Meisker, Herman; Illinois, 1867 ***2896.5*** *p27*
Meiski, Johs; Died enroute, 1854 ***3702.7*** *p341*
Meiss, Theodor; Chicago, 1910 ***2691.4*** *p167*
Meisser, Henry George; New York, 1754 ***3652*** *p80*
Meissner, Anton 42; Kansas, 1881 ***5240.1*** *p30*
Meissner, Anton 42; Kansas, 1881 ***5240.1*** *p63*
Meister, Johann; America, 1848 ***8582.3*** *p44*
Meister, Peter; Wisconsin, n.d. ***9675.7*** *p51*
Meister, Peter 28; America, 1853 ***9162.7*** *p15*
Meistrich, Sam; America, 1889 ***1450.2*** *p99A*
Meitez, Cathrine 21; America, 1839 ***778.5*** *p375*
Meitez, Cathrine 30; America, 1839 ***778.5*** *p375*
Meitez, Jean 33; America, 1839 ***778.5*** *p375*
Meitez, Wilhelm 39; America, 1839 ***778.5*** *p375*
Meixner, . . .; Canada, 1776-1783 ***9786*** *p29*
Meixner, Theodore; America, 1883 ***1450.2*** *p25B*
Mejer, Frank; Arkansas, 1918 ***95.2*** *p82*
Mekenny, Eliza 4; St. John, N.B., 1855 ***5704.8*** *p127*
Mekenny, John 7; St. John, N.B., 1855 ***5704.8*** *p127*
Mekenny, Mary 35; St. John, N.B., 1855 ***5704.8*** *p127*
Meland, Johannes Marseluis; Arkansas, 1918 ***95.2*** *p82*
Meland, Mary; Virginia, 1647 ***6219*** *p244*
Melany, John; St. John, N.B., 1852 ***5704.8*** *p93*
Melany, Sarah; St. John, N.B., 1852 ***5704.8*** *p93*
Melar, Frank; Wisconsin, n.d. ***9675.7*** *p51*
Melaragno, Cherubino; Arkansas, 1918 ***95.2*** *p82*
Melarkey, Bridget; New York, NY, 1866 ***5704.8*** *p214*
Melasevic, Blar; Iowa, 1866-1943 ***123.54*** *p33*
Melchan, Jane; America, 1738 ***4971*** *p13*
Melcher, . . .; Canada, 1776-1783 ***9786*** *p43*
Melcher, Johann; Pennsylvania, 1752 ***4525*** *p224*
Melcher, Lewis; Iowa, 1866-1943 ***123.54*** *p33*
Melchers, . . .; Canada, 1776-1783 ***9786*** *p43*
Melchers, Friederich; America, 1846 ***8582.3*** *p44*
Melchers, Jacob Hendrick; Arkansas, 1918 ***95.2*** *p82*
Melchior, Eduard; Chicago, 1866 ***8125.8*** *p438*
*Brother:*Ernst
*Brother:*Hugo
*Brother:*Fritz
Melchior, Ernst *SEE* Melchior, Eduard
Melchior, Fritz *SEE* Melchior, Eduard
Melchior, Hugo *SEE* Melchior, Eduard
Melchior, Leonard; Philadelphia, 1776 ***8582.3*** *p83*
Melchior, Leonhard; Philadelphia, 1776 ***8582.3*** *p84*
Melchor, Isaac; Philadelphia, 1775 ***8582.3*** *p85*
Melck, Jacob; Wisconsin, n.d. ***9675.7*** *p51*
Melder, John; Virginia, 1636 ***6219*** *p78*
Meldhein, John 33; America, 1827 ***778.5*** *p375*
Meldrum, Isabella; Quebec, 1851 ***5704.8*** *p75*
Meldrum, James; Quebec, 1852 ***5704.8*** *p87*
Meldrum, John; Quebec, 1851 ***5704.8*** *p75*
Meldrum, Mary; Quebec, 1851 ***5704.8*** *p75*
Meldrum, Robert; Quebec, 1852 ***5704.8*** *p87*
Meleva, Lawrence; Arkansas, 1918 ***95.2*** *p83*
Melham, James; Virginia, 1643 ***6219*** *p202*
Melick, Steve; Colorado, 1904 ***9678.2*** *p126*
Melioto, Nicole; Arkansas, 1918 ***95.2*** *p83*
Mellaerts, G. 27; Mexico, 1827 ***778.5*** *p375*
Mellanefy, Patrick 25; Philadelphia, 1861 ***5704.8*** *p149*
Mellanefy, Thomas 40; Philadelphia, 1861 ***5704.8*** *p149*
Mellanson, Charles; Acadia, 1663 ***7603*** *p22*
Mellanson, Pierre; Acadia, 1664 ***7603*** *p22*
Mellarts, Mr. 28; New Orleans, 1829 ***778.5*** *p375*
Mellen, George 25; Massachusetts, 1850 ***5881.1*** *p67*
Meller, Chas 62; Arizona, 1916 ***9228.40*** *p20*
Mellers, George 21; Virginia, 1774 ***1219.7*** *p193*
Mellers, James 28; Maryland, 1774 ***1219.7*** *p196*
Melling, John 32; New York, 1774 ***1219.7*** *p217*
Melling, William; Virginia, 1636 ***6219*** *p21*
Mellon, Ann; Quebec, 1848 ***5704.8*** *p41*
Mellon, Ann 6; Quebec, 1848 ***5704.8*** *p41*
Mellon, Eliza; St. John, N.B., 1848 ***5704.8*** *p44*
Mellon, Elizabeth *SEE* Mellon, John
Mellon, Elizabeth; Philadelphia, 1848 ***5704.8*** *p40*
Mellon, Elizabeth; Philadelphia, 1853 ***5704.8*** *p101*
Mellon, Ellen 19; Philadelphia, 1857 ***5704.8*** *p133*
Mellon, George 17; Philadelphia, 1853 ***5704.8*** *p113*
Mellon, Henry; New York, NY, 1836 ***8208.4*** *p21*
Mellon, Isabella 19; Philadelphia, 1860 ***5704.8*** *p146*
Mellon, James 23; Philadelphia, 1833-1834 ***53.26*** *p68*
Mellon, James 37; Philadelphia, 1858 ***5704.8*** *p138*
Mellon, Jane; Quebec, 1847 ***5704.8*** *p6*
Mellon, Jane 13; Quebec, 1847 ***5704.8*** *p6*
Mellon, John; Philadelphia, 1848 ***53.26*** *p68*
*Relative:*Elizabeth
Mellon, John; Philadelphia, 1848 ***5704.8*** *p40*
Mellon, John; Quebec, 1848 ***5704.8*** *p41*
Mellon, Keatty 13; Quebec, 1848 ***5704.8*** *p41*
Mellon, Magy; Quebec, 1848 ***5704.8*** *p41*
Mellon, Margaret; Quebec, 1847 ***5704.8*** *p6*
Mellon, Margaret 1 *SEE* Mellon, Susan
Mellon, Margaret 1; Philadelphia, 1847 ***5704.8*** *p21*
Mellon, Mary; New York, NY, 1866 ***5704.8*** *p214*
Mellon, Michael; Philadelphia, 1864 ***5704.8*** *p186*
Mellon, Owen; Quebec, 1848 ***5704.8*** *p41*
Mellon, Own 11; Quebec, 1848 ***5704.8*** *p41*
Mellon, Pat; Quebec, 1848 ***5704.8*** *p41*
Mellon, Patrick; Quebec, 1847 ***5704.8*** *p6*
Mellon, Peter 8; Quebec, 1848 ***5704.8*** *p41*
Mellon, Robert; Quebec, 1847 ***5704.8*** *p6*
Mellon, Roddy; Quebec, 1848 ***5704.8*** *p41*
Mellon, Sarah; Quebec, 1847 ***5704.8*** *p6*
Mellon, Susan; Philadelphia, 1847 ***53.26*** *p68*
*Relative:*Margaret 1
Mellon, Susan; Philadelphia, 1847 ***5704.8*** *p21*
Mellor, George; Ohio, 1798-1822 ***9892.11*** *p29*
Mellor, John; Ohio, 1798-1822 ***9892.11*** *p29*
Mellor, Michael; Ohio, 1837 ***9892.11*** *p29*
Mellor, Samuel; Ohio, 1798-1822 ***9892.11*** *p29*
Mellord, David; Georgia, 1775 ***1219.7*** *p275*
Mellord, Isabella; Georgia, 1775 ***1219.7*** *p275*
Mellot, Francois 49; America, 1838 ***778.5*** *p375*
Mellot, Joseph 28; Port uncertain, 1839 ***778.5*** *p375*
Melloy, Francis; Quebec, 1825 ***7603*** *p55*
Mellquist, C. J.; Minneapolis, 1884-1887 ***6410.35*** *p60*
Melly, Bridget; St. John, N.B., 1850 ***5704.8*** *p62*
Melly, Catherine 12; St. John, N.B., 1850 ***5704.8*** *p62*
Melon, Mary 26; Quebec, 1854 ***5704.8*** *p121*
Melonguet, Mr. 23; New Orleans, 1831 ***778.5*** *p375*
Melonore, George; Arkansas, 1918 ***95.2*** *p83*
Melonus, George; Arkansas, 1918 ***95.2*** *p83*
Melor, Edward; Ohio, 1823 ***9892.11*** *p29*
Meloy, Jno.; Philadelphia, 1816 ***2859.11*** *p38*
Melsch, . . .; Canada, 1776-1783 ***9786*** *p29*
Melsheimer, Chaplain; Quebec, 1776 ***9786*** *p104*
Melsheimer, Carl; Quebec, 1776 ***9786*** *p253*
Melson, William 24; Virginia, 1774 ***1219.7*** *p240*
Meltans, Gustaf Robert; Washington, 1859-1920 ***2872.1*** *p26*
Melton, Hannah *SEE* Melton, Thomas
Melton, Richard 20; Maryland, 1720 ***3690.1*** *p154*
Melton, Thomas; Virginia, 1628 ***6219*** *p31*
Melton, Thomas; Virginia, 1638 ***6219*** *p150*
*Wife:*Hannah
Meltzer, Heinrich; Cincinnati, 1869-1887 ***8582*** *p20*
Melvil, James 29; Philadelphia, 1774 ***1219.7*** *p197*
Melville, Mr.; Grenada, 1774 ***1219.7*** *p210*
Melvin, David; North Carolina, 1804 ***1639.20*** *p235*
Melvin, John; Quebec, 1766 ***7603*** *p38*
Melvin, Patrick; New York, NY, 1840 ***8208.4*** *p105*
Melvin, Patrick; New York, NY, 1840 ***8208.4*** *p111*
Membery, Charles 18; Philadelphia, 1750 ***3690.1*** *p154*
Memler, Louis; Wisconsin, n.d. ***9675.7*** *p51*
Memmel, J. M.; Cincinnati, 1869-1887 ***8582*** *p20*
Memminger, Christopher Gustav 3; Charleston, SC, 1806 ***8582.2*** *p25*
With parents
Memminger, Maria; Philadelphia, 1776 ***8582.3*** *p83*

Memmler, Friederich Gottlob; Wisconsin, n.d. ***9675.7*** *p51*
Mena, J. 32; America, 1826 ***778.5*** *p375*
Menagh, Alexander; Philadelphia, 1848 ***53.26*** *p68*
*Relative:*Rebecca
*Relative:*Marg. Eliza. 9 mos
Menagh, Alexander; Philadelphia, 1848 ***5704.8*** *p40*
Menagh, Ann 13 *SEE* Menagh, Michael
Menagh, Ann 13; Philadelphia, 1847 ***5704.8*** *p31*
Menagh, Biddy *SEE* Menagh, Michael
Menagh, Biddy; Philadelphia, 1847 ***5704.8*** *p31*
Menagh, Biddy 9 mos *SEE* Menagh, Michael
Menagh, Biddy 9 mos; Philadelphia, 1847 ***5704.8*** *p31*
Menagh, Daniel 8 *SEE* Menagh, Michael
Menagh, Daniel 8; Philadelphia, 1847 ***5704.8*** *p31*
Menagh, Elliot 6 *SEE* Menagh, Michael
Menagh, Elliott 6; Philadelphia, 1847 ***5704.8*** *p31*
Menagh, Marg. Eliza. 9 mos *SEE* Menagh, Alexander
Menagh, Margaret 10 *SEE* Menagh, Michael
Menagh, Margaret 10; Philadelphia, 1847 ***5704.8*** *p31*
Menagh, Margaret Elizabeth 9 mos; Philadelphia, 1848 ***5704.8*** *p40*
Menagh, Michael; Philadelphia, 1847 ***53.26*** *p68*
*Relative:*Biddy
*Relative:*Ann 13
*Relative:*Margaret 10
*Relative:*Daniel 8
*Relative:*Elliot 6
*Relative:*Pat 3
*Relative:*Biddy 9 mos
Menagh, Michael; Philadelphia, 1847 ***5704.8*** *p31*
Menagh, Pat 3 *SEE* Menagh, Michael
Menagh, Pat 3; Philadelphia, 1847 ***5704.8*** *p31*
Menagh, Rebecca *SEE* Menagh, Alexander
Menagh, Rebecca; Philadelphia, 1848 ***5704.8*** *p40*
Menaman, Ann 5; St. John, N.B., 1853 ***5704.8*** *p110*
Menaman, Bridget 45; St. John, N.B., 1853 ***5704.8*** *p110*
Menaman, Patrick 12; St. John, N.B., 1853 ***5704.8*** *p110*
Menan, Ann 8; St. John, N.B., 1847 ***5704.8*** *p11*
Menan, Bridget; St. John, N.B., 1847 ***5704.8*** *p11*
Menan, Catharine; Philadelphia, 1865 ***5704.8*** *p189*
Menan, Michael; St. John, N.B., 1847 ***5704.8*** *p11*
Menan, Michael 2; St. John, N.B., 1847 ***5704.8*** *p11*
Menard, Mr. 28; New Orleans, 1821 ***778.5*** *p375*
Menard, Jean 40; America, 1831 ***778.5*** *p375*
Menard, Marguerite 38; New Orleans, 1839 ***778.5*** *p375*
Menas, John; Arkansas, 1918 ***95.2*** *p83*
Menaugh, William 22; Quebec, 1857 ***5704.8*** *p135*
Mendal, George 45; Kansas, 1885 ***5240.1*** *p68*
Mendam, Charles 19; America, 1699 ***2212*** *p28*
Menday, Albert Henry; Washington, 1859-1920 ***2872.1*** *p26*
Menday, Frederick Percy; Washington, 1859-1920 ***2872.1*** *p26*
Mende, Christiane 43; New Orleans, 1839 ***9420.2*** *p70*
Mende, Christiane Gottlieb 41; New Orleans, 1839 ***9420.2*** *p70*
Mende, Friedke. 5; New Orleans, 1839 ***9420.2*** *p71*
Mende, Gottlob 9; New Orleans, 1839 ***9420.2*** *p70*
Mende, Henriette 17; New Orleans, 1839 ***9420.2*** *p70*
Mende, Hermann 7; New Orleans, 1839 ***9420.2*** *p71*
Mende, Johanne 11; New Orleans, 1839 ***9420.2*** *p70*
Mende, Wilhelmine 13; New Orleans, 1839 ***9420.2*** *p70*
Mender, Jos. N. 23; America, 1838 ***778.5*** *p375*
Mendez, J. 26; New Orleans, 1822 ***778.5*** *p376*
Mendolia, Mariano; Arkansas, 1918 ***95.2*** *p83*
Menefy, George; Virginia, 1622 ***6219*** *p19*
Menegal, . . .; Halifax, N.S., 1752 ***7074.6*** *p232*
Menegau, Jean Frederick 38; Halifax, N.S., 1752 ***7074.6*** *p207*
With family of 7
Menegau, Jean George 44; Halifax, N.S., 1752 ***7074.6*** *p207*
With family of 6
Menegaux, . . .; Halifax, N.S., 1752 ***7074.6*** *p230*
Menegaux, Ms.; Died enroute, 1752 ***7074.6*** *p208*
Menegaux, Anne *SEE* Menegaux, Jean-Frederic
Menegaux, Anne-Marie *SEE* Menegaux, Jean-Frederic
Menegaux, Anne-Marie *SEE* Menegaux, Jean-George
Menegaux, Elisabeth *SEE* Menegaux, Jean-Frederic
Menegaux, Francoise *SEE* Menegaux, Jean-George
Menegaux, Jean-Frederic 38; Halifax, N.S., 1752 ***7074.6*** *p212*
*Wife:*Anne
*Child:*Anne-Marie
*Child:*Elisabeth
*Child:*Jean-George
*Child:*Suzanne
With son
Menegaux, Jean-George *SEE* Menegaux, Jean-Frederic
Menegaux, Jean-George 44; Halifax, N.S., 1752 ***7074.6*** *p211*
*Child:*Marie-Catherine
*Child:*Francoise
*Child:*Jean-Jacques
*Child:*Suzanne
*Child:*Anne-Marie
*Child:*Jean-Nicolas
Menegaux, Jean-Jacques *SEE* Menegaux, Jean-George
Menegaux, Jean-Nicolas *SEE* Menegaux, Jean-George
Menegaux, Marie-Catherine *SEE* Menegaux, Jean-George
Menegaux, Suzanne *SEE* Menegaux, Jean-Frederic
Menegaux, Suzanne *SEE* Menegaux, Jean-George
Menegus, Antonio; Colorado, 1902 ***9678.2*** *p126*
Menengot, Goerge; Arkansas, 1918 ***95.2*** *p83*
Menftye, Georg; Virginia, 1638 ***6219*** *p150*
Menge, Carl Henrick; Iowa, 1866-1943 ***123.54*** *p33*
Menge, Carl Henry; Iowa, 1866-1943 ***123.54*** *p33*
Menge, Charles; Wisconsin, n.d. ***9675.7*** *p51*
Mengelino, Vincenzo; Iowa, 1866-1943 ***123.54*** *p33*
Mengen, v., Major; Quebec, 1776 ***9786*** *p105*
Mengen, Otto Carl Anton; Quebec, 1776 ***9786*** *p256*
Menges, George; Kansas, 1890 ***5240.1*** *p75*
Menges, Henrich; Philadelphia, 1779 ***8137*** *p11*
Menia, Charles; Indiana, 1848 ***9117*** *p17*
Menieur, Dennis; New York, NY, 1811 ***2859.11*** *p17*
Menifie, William; Virginia, 1639 ***6219*** *p161*
Menin, Christopher; St. John, N.B., 1853 ***5704.8*** *p107*
Menke, Miss; America, 1856 ***4610.10*** *p157*
Menke, Johann Bernard; America, 1839 ***8582.3*** *p44*
Menke, Rudolph; Kentucky, 1839-1840 ***8582.3*** *p98*
Menkhaus, Johann Friederich 8; Baltimore, 1834 ***8582.2*** *p26*
With parents
Menkhaus, John F.; Cincinnati, 1869-1887 ***8582*** *p21*
Menle, J. 18; Port uncertain, 1838 ***778.5*** *p376*
Menmann, Henry; America, 1848 ***1450.2*** *p99A*
Mennard, George 21; Nova Scotia, 1774 ***1219.7*** *p209*
With wife
With child
Mennard, Robert 27; Nova Scotia, 1774 ***1219.7*** *p209*
Mennenga, Charles; Illinois, 1892 ***5012.37*** *p62*
Mennenga, Frank C.; Illinois, 1892 ***5012.40*** *p26*
Mennenga, Fred.; Illinois, 1892 ***5012.37*** *p62*
Mennenga, Henry; Illinois, 1892 ***5012.40*** *p27*
Mennesier, Mr.; Cincinnati, 1789-1800 ***8582.3*** *p87*
Mennger, Katherina 24; Port uncertain, 1839 ***778.5*** *p376*
Menniger, Albert; Kentucky, 1848 ***8582.3*** *p101*
Mennilli, Eugene; Arkansas, 1918 ***95.2*** *p83*
Menninger, Franz X.; Cincinnati, 1788-1848 ***8582.3*** *p89*
Menninger, John G.; America, 1839 ***8582.3*** *p44*
Menninger, Wilhelm Adam; America, 1843 ***8582.3*** *p44*
Menold, Catharina Barbara *SEE* Menold, Georg Melchior
Menold, Christina Catharina; America, 1751-1800 ***2444*** *p188*
Menold, Georg Melchior; Pennsylvania, 1753 ***2444*** *p191*
*Wife:*Maria Barbara Doerrer
*Child:*Georg Melchior 22
*Child:*Catharina Barbara
*Child:*Regina Catharina
*Child:*Johann Michael
*Child:*Johann Martin
*Child:*Maria Elisabetha
Menold, Georg Melchior 22 *SEE* Menold, Georg Melchior
Menold, Johann Martin *SEE* Menold, Georg Melchior
Menold, Johann Michael *SEE* Menold, Georg Melchior
Menold, Maria Barbara Doerrer *SEE* Menold, Georg Melchior
Menold, Maria Elisabetha *SEE* Menold, Georg Melchior
Menold, Regina Catharina *SEE* Menold, Georg Melchior
Menozzi, G. 43; New York, NY, 1893 ***9026.4*** *p42*
Menpen, Simon; Illinois, 1863 ***7857*** *p5*
Menske, . . .; Canada, 1776-1783 ***9786*** *p29*
Menston, John; Illinois, 1855 ***7857*** *p5*
Mentel, V.; Cincinnati, 1869-1887 ***8582*** *p21*
Menth, John; Wisconsin, n.d. ***9675.7*** *p51*
Mention, Agnes; New York, NY, 1811 ***2859.11*** *p17*
Mention, Alexander; New York, NY, 1811 ***2859.11*** *p17*
Mentuccia, P.; Wisconsin, n.d. ***9675.7*** *p51*
Mentue, Augusto; Wisconsin, n.d. ***9675.7*** *p51*
Mentz, Jacob; Kentucky, 1839-1840 ***8582.3*** *p98*
Mentz, Jean; Wisconsin, n.d. ***9675.7*** *p51*
Mentz, Johan Christoph; South Carolina, 1788 ***7119*** *p203*
Mentz, William 50; Kansas, 1893 ***5240.1*** *p78*
Mentzel, . . .; Canada, 1776-1783 ***9786*** *p29*
Mentzel, Charles; Wisconsin, n.d. ***9675.7*** *p51*
Mentzer, . . .; Canada, 1776-1783 ***9786*** *p29*
Mentzinger, George Ernst; New York, 1756 ***3652*** *p81*
Menz, August; Cincinnati, 1788-1848 ***8582.3*** *p90*
Menz, Frederick; New York, 1875 ***5240.1*** *p30*
Menzel, Adolph; Cincinnati, 1788-1848 ***8582.3*** *p91*
Menzel, Engelbert; Ohio, 1869-1887 ***8582*** *p21*
Menzel, Gustav Adolph; Cincinnati, 1869-1887 ***8582*** *p21*
Menzel, Jacob; America, 1846 ***8582.1*** *p24*
Menzies, John; Virginia, 1772 ***1639.20*** *p235*
Menzies, Mary 25; North Carolina, 1775 ***1639.20*** *p235*
Meorcy, George 31; Jamaica, 1730 ***3690.1*** *p154*
Meosgrave, Hugh; Illinois, 1860 ***7857*** *p5*
Meral, Ant. 23; America, 1839 ***778.5*** *p376*
Meral, Guillaume 19; America, 1836 ***778.5*** *p376*
Merament, Jean 20; New Orleans, 1827 ***778.5*** *p376*
Mercer, Eliza; St. John, N.B., 1853 ***5704.8*** *p107*
Mercer, Elizabeth; America, 1742 ***4971*** *p65*
Mercer, George 22; Maryland, 1775 ***1219.7*** *p253*
Mercer, Helena; Pennsylvania, 1683 ***4961*** *p13*
Mercer, James; Albany, NY, 1759 ***1219.7*** *p67*
Mercer, James Francis; New York, 1760 ***1219.7*** *p77*
Mercer, Jno 15; America, 1702 ***2212*** *p37*
Mercer, John; Virginia, 1642 ***6219*** *p191*
Mercer, John 20; Jamaica, 1733 ***3690.1*** *p155*
Mercer, Richard; Virginia, 1643 ***6219*** *p230*
Mercer, Robt.; Virginia, 1637 ***6219*** *p113*
Mercere, J. P. 27; New Orleans, 1839 ***778.5*** *p376*
Mercet, August 39; Kansas, 1880 ***5240.1*** *p62*
Mercey, M.; Shreveport, LA, 1878 ***7129*** *p45*
Merchant, Charles; Washington, 1859-1920 ***2872.1*** *p26*
Merchant, David; Philadelphia, 1853 ***5704.8*** *p101*
Merchant, Frederick Harold; Washington, 1859-1920 ***2872.1*** *p26*
Merchant, Gideon; New York, NY, 1838 ***8208.4*** *p87*
Merchant, Jeffery; Virginia, 1637 ***6219*** *p85*
Merchant, Wm.; Austin, TX, 1886 ***9777*** *p5*
Mercier, Mr. 23; America, 1838 ***778.5*** *p376*
Mercier, Mr. 45; New Orleans, 1829 ***778.5*** *p376*
Mercier, Adolph 29; America, 1835 ***778.5*** *p376*
Mercier, Thomas; America, 1759 ***1219.7*** *p70*
Merciol, Jn. Baptiste 31; America, 1838 ***778.5*** *p376*
Merck, Baldaster; South Carolina, 1788 ***7119*** *p203*
Merck, John Henry; New York, 1750 ***3652*** *p75*
Merckel, . . .; Canada, 1776-1783 ***9786*** *p29*
Merckle, . . .; Canada, 1776-1783 ***9786*** *p29*
Merckle, Abraham; New York, 1717 ***3627*** *p8*
*Wife:*Anna Veronika
*Child:*Anna Maria
*Child:*Anna Felizitas
*Child:*Anna Katharine
*Child:*Regina Christine
*Child:*Anna Rosina
With son-in-law
Merckle, Anna Felicitas; New York, 1717 ***3627*** *p8*
Merckle, Anna Felizitas *SEE* Merckle, Abraham
Merckle, Anna Katharine *SEE* Merckle, Abraham
Merckle, Anna Maria *SEE* Merckle, Abraham
Merckle, Anna Maria *SEE* Merckle, Johann Michael, Jr.
Merckle, Anna Rosina *SEE* Merckle, Abraham
Merckle, Anna Veronika *SEE* Merckle, Abraham
Merckle, Balthasar; Pennsylvania, 1717 ***3627*** *p16*
*Wife:*Elisabetha
*Child:*Maria Catharina
*Child:*Hans Jerg
*Child:*Maria Elisabetha
Merckle, Barbara *SEE* Merckle, Johann Michael, Jr.
Merckle, Dorothea *SEE* Merckle, Johann Michael, Jr.
Merckle, Elisabetha *SEE* Merckle, Balthasar
Merckle, Georg Paul; Pennsylvania, 1774 ***3627*** *p8*
Merckle, Hans Jerg *SEE* Merckle, Balthasar
Merckle, Johann Michael *SEE* Merckle, Johann Michael, Jr.
Merckle, Johann Michael, Jr.; Pennsylvania, 1752-1794 ***2444*** *p191*
*Wife:*Margaretha
*Child:*Dorothea
*Child:*Anna Maria
*Child:*Johann Michael
*Child:*Barbara
Merckle, Margaretha *SEE* Merckle, Johann Michael, Jr.
Merckle, Maria Catharina *SEE* Merckle, Balthasar
Merckle, Maria Elisabetha *SEE* Merckle, Balthasar
Merckle, Regina Christine *SEE* Merckle, Abraham
Merckley, Balthasar; Pennsylvania, 1717 ***3627*** *p16*
*Wife:*Elisabetha
*Child:*Maria Catharina
*Child:*Hans Jerg
*Child:*Maria Elisabetha
Merckley, Elisabetha *SEE* Merckley, Balthasar
Merckley, Hans Jerg *SEE* Merckley, Balthasar
Merckley, Maria Catharina *SEE* Merckley, Balthasar
Merckley, Maria Elisabetha *SEE* Merckley, Balthasar
Mercklin, Anna Felicitas; Germantown, PA, 1717 ***3627*** *p12*
Mercklin, Anna Maria *SEE* Mercklin, Johann Michael, Jr.
Mercklin, Anna Maria; New York, 1709 ***3627*** *p5*
Mercklin, Barbara *SEE* Mercklin, Johann Michael, Jr.
Mercklin, Dorothea *SEE* Mercklin, Johann Michael, Jr.

Mercklin, Johann Michael SEE Mercklin, Johann Michael, Jr.
Mercklin, Johann Michael, Jr.; Pennsylvania, 1752-1794 *2444* p191
   Wife:Margaretha
   Child:Dorothea
   Child:Anna Maria
   Child:Johann Michael
   Child:Barbara
Mercklin, Margaretha SEE Mercklin, Johann Michael, Jr.
Mercurio, Raffael; Arkansas, 1918 *95.2* p83
Mercy, Elizabeth; America, 1740 *4971* p15
Mercy, George 28; Maryland, 1774 *1219.7* p214
Mercy, John; America, 1736 *4971* p12
Mercy, Peter; Charleston, SC, 1775-1781 *8582.2* p26
Merdith, Easter 20; Maryland, 1718 *3690.1* p155
Merdith, John; Maryland, 1751 *3690.1* p155
Mere, Thomas 5; United States or West Indies, 1705 *2212* p42
Merecoeur, Baptisto; Colorado, 1904 *9678.2* p126
Meredith, Joannah 21; America, 1705 *2212* p42
Meredith, Joannah 22; America, 1706 *2212* p47
Meredith, John; Maryland, 1751 *1219.7* p3
Meredith, Thomas; West Virginia, 1802-1844 *9788.3* p16
Merefield, Robert 19; Jamaica, 1724 *3690.1* p155
Mereles, Santiago 36; Harris Co., TX, 1898 *6254* p4
Meret, Pierre 41; America, 1839 *778.5* p376
Mereta, A. C.; Shreveport, LA, 1874 *7129* p45
Merfee, James; Virginia, 1637 *6219* p82
Mergenthaler, Christian; America, 1836 *8582.1* p24
Meric, Mr. 20; New Orleans, 1839 *778.5* p376
Meric, Mr. 36; America, 1837 *778.5* p376
Meric, Mrs. 26; America, 1837 *778.5* p377
Meric, Gm. 32; Port uncertain, 1839 *778.5* p376
Merideth, Ann 70; Massachusetts, 1848 *5881.1* p62
Meridith, Elizabeth 16; Virginia, 1720 *3690.1* p155
Meridith, Hestor 20; Maryland, 1718 *3690.1* p155
Merifield, Abra.; Virginia, 1646 *6219* p246
Merigden, Patrick; Yamaska, Que., 1823 *7603* p78
Merigut, Mr. 25; New Orleans, 1839 *778.5* p377
Meriton, Thomas 19; Maryland, 1718 *3690.1* p155
Merity, Andrew 29; St. John, N.B., 1857 *5704.8* p135
Merity, Fanny 40; St. John, N.B., 1857 *5704.8* p135
Merk, Fritz; America, 1849 *8582.1* p24
Merkel, Josephine Emilie 12; New Orleans, 1820 *778.5* p377
Merkel, Konrad; Kentucky, 1844 *8582.3* p101
Merkhofer, Georg; New York, NY, 1840 *8582.1* p24
Merkle, Adam; Akron, OH, 1826-1833 *8582.1* p49
Merkle, Georg Paul; Pennsylvania, 1774 *3627* p8
Merkle, Johann 42; New York, NY, 1889 *7846* p39
Merklin, Abraham; New York, 1717 *3627* p8
   Wife:Anna Veronika
   Child:Anna Maria
   Child:Anna Felizitas
   Child:Anna Katharine
   Child:Regina Christine
   Child:Anna Rosina
   With son-in-law
Merklin, Anna Felizitas SEE Merklin, Abraham
Merklin, Anna Katharine SEE Merklin, Abraham
Merklin, Anna Maria SEE Merklin, Abraham
Merklin, Anna Rosina SEE Merklin, Abraham
Merklin, Anna Veronika SEE Merklin, Abraham
Merklin, Regina Christine SEE Merklin, Abraham
Merkly, Christopher; New York, 1750 *3652* p74
Merlan, Henry Adam; America, 1846 *1450.2* p100A
Merland, R. 24; New Orleans, 1821 *778.5* p377
Merle, Mme. 21; New Orleans, 1829 *778.5* p377
Merle, Mr. 33; New Orleans, 1837 *778.5* p377
Merle, J. 16; Louisiana, 1820 *778.5* p377
Merle, J. 26; America, 1832 *778.5* p377
Merle, Jules 39; Port uncertain, 1838 *778.5* p377
Merlin, Mr. 24; America, 1838 *778.5* p377
Merlo, Guiseppe; Arkansas, 1918 *95.2* p83
Merrard, Deborah; Virginia, 1635 *6219* p16
Merrel, John J.; Arkansas, 1918 *95.2* p46
Merrel, John J.; Arkansas, 1918 *95.2* p83
Merrell, F. 37; New Orleans, 1837 *778.5* p377
Merrett, William; Virginia, 1637 *6219* p107
Merrick, Mr. 32; New Orleans, 1839 *778.5* p377
Merrick, Hen.; Virginia, 1635 *6219* p17
Merrick, Thomas; Virginia, 1643 *6219* p203
Merrick, Thomas 21; Baltimore, 1775 *1219.7* p270
Merrick, Thomas 22; Maryland, 1775 *1219.7* p254
Merrideth, Francis; Virginia, 1636 *6219* p12
Merrideth, Joseph 70; Massachusetts, 1848 *5881.1* p68
Merrideth, Thomas; Virginia, 1636 *6219* p12
Merrie, Savage; Virginia, 1635 *6219* p33
Merrihy, John; America, 1741 *4971* p40
Merrill, John 36; Maryland, 1775 *1219.7* p272
Merrill, R. M.; Washington, 1859-1920 *2872.1* p26

Merriman, Edward; Virginia, 1635 *6219* p20
   Wife:Sarah
Merriman, Henry; New Orleans, 1841 *7036* p122
Merriman, James; Virginia, 1635 *6219* p71
   Wife:Sarah
Merriman, Sarah SEE Merriman, Edward
Merriman, Sarah SEE Merriman, James
Merring, Frederich; Illinois, 1853 *7857* p5
Merriott, Midleton 20; Maryland, 1775 *1219.7* p249
Merrison, Henry 16; Jamaica, 1725 *3690.1* p155
Merritt, Ann 20; Virginia, 1775 *1219.7* p246
Merror, Nicho.; Virginia, 1623-1648 *6219* p252
Merroyer, Maurice 38; Port uncertain, 1839 *778.5* p377
Merry, Isaac; Virginia, 1636 *6219* p28
Merry, Jon.; Virginia, 1643 *6219* p200
Merryfield, John 19; Virginia, 1774 *1219.7* p201
Merryfield, John H. 24; Kansas, 1884 *5240.1* p65
Merryfield, Robert 15; Philadelphia, 1774 *1219.7* p233
Merryman, Ann; Virginia, 1643 *6219* p206
Merryman, James; Virginia, 1643 *6219* p206
Mers, August 44; Kansas, 1890 *5240.1* p30
Mers, August 44; Kansas, 1890 *5240.1* p74
Mers, Ludwig; Wisconsin, n.d. *9675.7* p51
Mersch, Barb. 22; America, 1853 *9162.8* p37
Merssey, William 23; Virginia, 1773 *1219.7* p169
Mersten, Casten; New York, NY, 1836 *8208.4* p15
Merten, Casten; New York, NY, 1836 *8208.4* p15
Mertens, . . .; Canada, 1776-1783 *9786* p29
Mertens, Daniel; Canada, 1783 *9786* p38A
Mertens, Jacob; Canada, 1783 *9786* p38A
Mertes, Bernard; Wisconsin, n.d. *9675.7* p51
Mertes, John 36; Kansas, 1880 *5240.1* p62
Mertes, Peter Jacob; Michigan, 1882 *5240.1* p30
Mertins, Behrend Henry; New York, NY, 1836 *8208.4* p22
Mertins, Frederick Albert; America, 1876 *1450.2* p25B
Merton, Richd; Barbados, 1698 *2212* p5
Mertz, Anna Margaretha SEE Mertz, Anna Margaretha
Mertz, Anna Margaretha; Pennsylvania, 1743 *2444* p192
   Child:Anna Margaretha
   Child:Maria Juditha
Mertz, Jacob; Wisconsin, n.d. *9675.7* p51
Mertz, Maria Juditha SEE Mertz, Anna Margaretha
Mertz, Victor; Wisconsin, n.d. *9675.7* p51
Mertz, Wilhelm; Philadelphia, 1779 *8137* p11
Mertzig, Gerard; Wisconsin, n.d. *9675.7* p51
Mervar, Joseph; America, 1899 *1450.2* p25B
Merven, Nicholas 29; Jamaica, 1736 *3690.1* p155
Merwin, H. C.; Washington, 1859-1920 *2872.1* p26
Merwin, Nicholas 29; Jamaica, 1736 *3690.1* p155
Mery, Etienne 23; America, 1837 *778.5* p377
Merz, Anna Margaretha SEE Merz, Anna Margaretha
Merz, Anna Margaretha; Pennsylvania, 1743 *2444* p192
   Child:Anna Margaretha
   Child:Maria Juditha
Merz, Gustav 33; Iowa, 1884 *1450.2* p25B
Merz, Maria Juditha SEE Merz, Anna Margaretha
Merz, Mathias; Wisconsin, n.d. *9675.7* p51
Mesel, A. 56; Kansas, 1889 *5240.1* p74
Mesell, Jos.; Virginia, 1643 *6219* p207
Meser, Margaret Wollauf Wimmer; New York, 1709 *3627* p7
   Child:Susan Cath
   With 2 children
Meser, Susan Cath SEE Meser, Margaret Wollauf Wimmer
Meshaw, Catherine 65; North Carolina, 1850 *1639.20* p235
Meskill, Kate 9; Massachusetts, 1850 *5881.1* p70
Meskin, James 9; Massachusetts, 1849 *5881.1* p68
Meskin, Patrick 1; Massachusetts, 1849 *5881.1* p74
Meskin, William 3; Massachusetts, 1849 *5881.1* p77
Meslier, Jean Baptiste 26; America, 1837 *778.5* p377
Mesner, Margreeta Wollauf Wimmer; New York, 1709 *3627* p7
   Child:Susan Cath
   With 2 children
Mesner, Susan Cath SEE Mesner, Margreeta Wollauf Wimmer
Mesplex, John Bte. 25; Louisiana, 1820 *778.5* p378
Mespoulets, A. 50; New Orleans, 1822 *778.5* p378
Messan, Jean; Quebec, 1756 *7603* p26
Messant, Rene 22; New Orleans, 1820 *778.5* p378
Messe, Mr. 19; America, 1838 *778.5* p378
Messe, Christine 24; America, 1831 *778.5* p378
Messe, John Mitchel 19; America, 1836 *778.5* p378
Messegnur, Mr. 22; New Orleans, 1829 *778.5* p378
Messen, Jean 32; New Orleans, 1838 *778.5* p378
Messenberg, George 19; Virginia, 1774 *1219.7* p228
Messener, Johann Michael; Pennsylvania, 1749 *2444* p234
Messenger, . . .; Canada, 1776-1783 *9786* p29
Messenger, Hercules; Virginia, 1638 *6219* p181

Messenger, Richard 31; Montserrat, 1700 *2212* p22
Messequt, Mr. 28; America, 1839 *778.5* p378
Messer, Henry; Illinois, 1890 *5012.40* p25
Messer, Mathilde; Baltimore, 1819 *8582* p28
Messer, Theodore 18; Maryland, 1730 *3690.1* p155
Messerley, Charles G.; Kansas, 1888 *5240.1* p30
Messerschmidt, Georg; New York, NY, 1838 *8208.4* p88
Messerschmidt, Rudolph; Arkansas, 1918 *95.2* p83
Messignat, Jn. 40; New Orleans, 1839 *778.5* p378
Messing, . . .; Canada, 1776-1783 *9786* p29
Messinger, Joseph; America, 1845 *8582.3* p44
Messmann, Michael; Illinois, 1871 *5012.39* p25
Messmen, John C.; Illinois, 1867 *5012.38* p98
Messojed, . . .; New York, 1831 *4606* p175
Messrah, Kelley Nekola; Arkansas, 1918 *95.2* p83
Messrey, Joseph 27; Kansas, 1900 *5240.1* p81
Met, Leroy; Wisconsin, n.d. *9675.7* p51
Metadall, Jean George 20; Halifax, N.S., 1752 *7074.6* p207
Metadall, Jean Nicolas 30; Halifax, N.S., 1752 *7074.6* p207
   With family of 4
Metatall, Jacques Christoph 50; Halifax, N.S., 1752 *7074.6* p207
   With family of 4
Metayer, F. 25; New Orleans, 1837 *778.5* p378
Metayer, Felix 8; Louisiana, 1820 *778.5* p378
Metayer, Louis 14; Louisiana, 1820 *778.5* p379
Metayer, Thomas 35; Louisiana, 1820 *778.5* p379
Metcalf, Mr.; Quebec, 1815 *9229.18* p82
Metcalf, Alexander; Washington, 1859-1920 *2872.1* p26
Metcalf, George A. 32; Kansas, 1879 *5240.1* p60
Metcalf, George Elsworth; Arkansas, 1918 *95.2* p83
Metcalf, William 16; New York, 1774 *1219.7* p203
Metcalf, William 25; Virginia, 1775 *1219.7* p252
Metcalf, Wm.; Iowa, 1866-1943 *123.54* p33
Metch, . . .; Canada, 1776-1783 *9786* p29
Metchell, Tho.; Virginia, 1635 *6219* p73
Metchon, John; New York, NY, 1811 *2859.11* p17
Methias, Johannes; Ohio, 1798-1818 *8582.2* p54
Methold, Tho.; Virginia, 1643 *6219* p200
Metin, Jean-Nicolas 17; Halifax, N.S., 1752 *7074.6* p212
Metivier, Jean; Quebec, 1701 *4533* p131
Metizer, Mr. 17; New Orleans, 1839 *778.5* p379
Metsch, . . .; Canada, 1776-1783 *9786* p29
Metscher, Michael; New York, NY, 1835 *8208.4* p27
Mettais, Mr. 40; Cuba, 1820 *778.5* p379
Mettetal, . . .; Halifax, N.S., 1752 *7074.6* p232
Mettetal, Ms.; Died enroute, 1752 *7074.6* p208
   With baby
Mettetal, Anne-Catherine SEE Mettetal, Jean-Nicolas
Mettetal, Catherine SEE Mettetal, Jean-Nicolas
Mettetal, Jacques-Christophe 50; Halifax, N.S., 1752 *7074.6* p212
   Wife:Judith
   Daughter:Suzanne
   Daughter:Marguerite
Mettetal, Jean-George 20; Halifax, N.S., 1752 *7074.6* p212
Mettetal, Jean-Nicolas 30; Halifax, N.S., 1752 *7074.6* p212
   Wife:Judith
   Daughter:Catherine
   Daughter:Anne-Catherine
   With child
Mettetal, Judith SEE Mettetal, Jacques-Christophe
Mettetal, Judith SEE Mettetal, Jean-Nicolas
Mettetal, Marguerite SEE Mettetal, Jacques-Christophe
Mettetal, Suzanne SEE Mettetal, Jacques-Christophe
Metto, Frank Corta; Shreveport, LA, 1878 *7129* p45
Metz, Adam; Cincinnati, 1869-1887 *8582* p21
Metz, Adam; South Carolina, 1788 *7119* p201
Metz, Albert 31; Kansas, 1900 *5240.1* p81
Metz, Christoph; South Carolina, 1788 *7119* p197
Metz, Friedrich M.; Ohio, 1869-1887 *8582* p21
Metz, Jacob; Ohio, 1869-1887 *8582* p21
Metz, Jakob; Illinois, 1836 *8582.1* p55
   With family
Metz, Jakob; Kentucky, 1840-1845 *8582.3* p100
Metz, Johann Jacob; Pennsylvania, 1743-1772 *2444* p192
Metz, John; South Carolina, 1788 *7119* p200
Metz, John; South Carolina, 1788 *7119* p201
Metz, M.; New Orleans, 1841 *8582.1* p24
Metz, Martin; Illinois, 1894 *5012.40* p54
Metz, William; Illinois, 1859 *5012.39* p89
Metzcher, Michael; New York, NY, 1835 *8208.4* p27
Metzdorff, . . .; Canada, 1776-1783 *9786* p29
Metze, Georg; America, 1848 *8582.1* p24
Metzer, Michael; Wisconsin, n.d. *9675.7* p51
Metzger, . . .; Canada, 1776-1783 *9786* p29
Metzger, . . .; Iroquois Co., IL, 1892 *3455.1* p12
Metzger, Alexander; New York, 1847-1849 *1450.2* p100A

Metzger, Anna; America, 1746-1800 *2444 p214*
Metzger, Barbara Dast *SEE* Metzger, Johann Jacob
Metzger, Daniel; Illinois, 1852 *7857 p5*
Metzger, Jacob *SEE* Metzger, Johann Jacob
Metzger, Jacob; Illinois, 1868 *2896.5 p27*
Metzger, Jacob; Pennsylvania, 1749 *2444 p192*
Metzger, Johann; America, 1852 *8582.3 p44*
Metzger, Johann J.; Illinois, 1875 *8582.2 p51*
Metzger, Johann Jacob; America, 1749 *2444 p192*
  *Wife:*Barbara Dast
  *Child:*Jacob
Metzger, John; Illinois, 1866 *2896.5 p27*
Metzger, John U.; Illinois, 1868 *2896.5 p27*
Metzger, Margaret Wollauf Wimmer; New York, 1709
  3627 p7
  *Child:*Susan Cath
  With 2 children
Metzger, Michael; Cincinnati, 1869-1887 *8582 p21*
Metzger, Susan Cath *SEE* Metzger, Margaret Wollauf
  Wimmer
Metzger, W.; Milwaukee, 1875 *4719.30 p257*
Metzke, W.; Milwaukee, 1875 *4719.30 p257*
Metzler, . . .; Canada, 1776-1783 *9786 p29*
Metzner, Johann Dietrich; Philadelphia, 1776 *8582.3 p83*
Meubert, T. 30; Port uncertain, 1839 *778.5 p379*
Meule, Ms.; Port uncertain, 1839 *778.5 p379*
Meule, Adele Saunier; Port uncertain, 1839 *778.5 p379*
Meulenkamp, Cornelis Nicolas 29; Kansas, 1905 *5240.1
  p83*
Meuner, Mr. 30; Port uncertain, 1836 *778.5 p379*
Meunier, Jean 26; New Orleans, 1821 *778.5 p379*
Meurer, John Philip; Philadelphia, 1742 *3652 p56*
Meurice, Joseph 26; New Orleans, 1838 *778.5 p379*
Meuro, M. 19; New Orleans, 1830 *778.5 p379*
Meurset, Peter; Charleston, SC, 1775-1781 *8582.2 p52*
Meusebach, von; Texas, 1774-1874 *8582.1 p21*
Meuser, George 52; Kansas, 1873 *5240.1 p53*
Meuser, William; Illinois, 1872 *5012.39 p25*
Meville, Alice; Quebec, 1851 *5704.8 p75*
Mevius, Henrich; Philadelphia, 1779 *8137 p11*
Mexcy, James; New York, NY, 1835 *8208.4 p58*
Mexlow, Edward; Illinois, 1860 *5012.38 p98*
Mexom, Adonizah; Boston, 1776 *1219.7 p278*
Mey, Anna Maria *SEE* Mey, Martin
Mey, Anna Maria Herold *SEE* Mey, Martin
Mey, Friedrich; Wisconsin, n.d. *9675.7 p51*
Mey, Maria Agnes *SEE* Mey, Martin
Mey, Maria Elisabetha *SEE* Mey, Martin
Mey, Maria Felicitas *SEE* Mey, Martin
Mey, Martin; New York, 1717 *3627 p12*
  *Wife:*Anna Maria Herold
  *Child:*Maria Elisabetha
  *Child:*Anna Maria
  *Child:*Maria Agnes
  *Child:*Maria Felicitas
Mey, William; Wisconsin, n.d. *9675.7 p51*
Meybom, v., May; Quebec, 1776 *9786 p104*
Meybom, F. v.; Quebec, 1776 *9786 p105*
Meyboom, v., Maj.; Quebec, 1776 *9786 p104*
Meyer, . . .; Canada, 1776-1783 *9786 p29*
Meyer, Miss; America, 1854 *4610.10 p144*
Meyer, Mr.; America, 1873-1895 *4610.10 p114*
  With brother
Meyer, Ms. 26; America, 1839 *778.5 p379*
Meyer, Miss A.; Milwaukee, 1875 *4719.30 p257*
Meyer, A.A.; Iowa, 1866-1943 *123.54 p34*
Meyer, A. Caroline Gertrud *SEE* Meyer, Georg August
Meyer, A.M.L.K. Behrensmeyer *SEE* Meyer, Christian
  Friedrich
Meyer, Abe; Shreveport, LA, 1879 *7129 p45*
Meyer, Adolph; Philadelphia, 1742 *3652 p55*
Meyer, Adolph; Philadelphia, 1757 *9973.7 p32*
Meyer, Agnes; New York, 1752 *3652 p76*
Meyer, Agnes Gretzing *SEE* Meyer, Johannes
Meyer, Albert W.; Illinois, 1863 *7857 p5*
Meyer, Aluis; Virginia, 1844 *4626.16 p12*
Meyer, Andreas; Quebec, 1776 *9786 p263*
Meyer, Andrew C.; Illinois, 1897 *2896.5 p27*
Meyer, Anna Friederike Engel *SEE* Meyer, Carl Heinrich
  Wilhelm
Meyer, Anna Marie Marg. Engel; America, 1846 *4610.10
  p134*
Meyer, Anne Marie C. C. Ruter *SEE* Meyer, Carl
  Diedrich
Meyer, Anne Marie Christine *SEE* Meyer, Carl Friedrich
Meyer, Anne Marie Engel; America, 1847 *4610.10 p134*
Meyer, Anne Marie W. Engel *SEE* Meyer, Carl Heinrich
Meyer, Antoine 28; New Orleans, 1838 *778.5 p379*
Meyer, Anton; Wisconsin, n.d. *9675.7 p51*
Meyer, Anton Friedrich; America, 1836 *4610.10 p97*
Meyer, Anton Friedrich August; America, 1836 *4610.10
  p97*
Meyer, Anton Moritz *SEE* Meyer, Carl Diedrich

Meyer, Barbara *SEE* Meyer, Johann
Meyer, Barbara; America, 1745-1800 *2444 p196*
Meyer, Bernhard; Wisconsin, n.d. *9675.7 p51*
Meyer, Carl; Wisconsin, n.d. *9675.7 p51*
Meyer, Carl Christoph H. F. Friedrich; America, 1886
  4610.10 p118
Meyer, Carl Diedrich; America, 1858 *4610.10 p99*
  *Wife:*Anne Marie C. C. Ruter
  *Son:*Anton Moritz
Meyer, Carl Friedrich *SEE* Meyer, Carl Friedrich
Meyer, Carl Friedrich 28; America, 1852 *4610.10 p147*
  With wife
  *Child:*Christine C. Louise
  *Child:*Carl Friedrich
  *Child:*Ernst Heinrich
  *Child:*Anne Marie Christine
Meyer, Carl Friedrich Wilhelm *SEE* Meyer, Carl
  Heinrich Wilhelm
Meyer, Carl Friedrich Wilhelm; America, 1858 *4610.10
  p136*
Meyer, Carl Heinrich *SEE* Meyer, Carl Heinrich
Meyer, Carl Heinrich; America, 1850 *4610.10 p143*
  *Wife:*Marie M. I. Griemert
  *Child:*Anne Marie W. Engel
  *Child:*Christoph Heinrich
  *Child:*Carl Heinrich
Meyer, Carl Heinrich Wilhelm; America, 1844 *4610.10
  p134*
  With mother-in-law
  *Child:*Anna Friederike Engel
  *Child:*Carl Friedrich Wilhelm
Meyer, Carl Heinrich Wilhelm; America, 1886 *4610.10
  p118*
Meyer, Carl Wilhelm Frederick; New York, NY, 1901
  3455.1 p54
  *Wife:*Hemer
Meyer, Cath. Ilsabein Friederike; America, 1838-1854
  4610.10 p148
Meyer, Catharina; Pennsylvania, 1747 *2444 p192*
Meyer, Catherine; Philadelphia, 1738 *9898 p44*
Meyer, Charles; Wisconsin, n.d. *9675.7 p51*
Meyer, Charles Frederick Theodore; America, 1851
  1450.2 p100A
Meyer, Christian Frederick Gottlieb; America, 1851
  1450.2 p100A
Meyer, Christian Friedrich; America, 1857 *4610.10 p105*
  *Child:*Marie Friederike
  *Child:*Friederike K. Louise
  *Wife:*A.M.L.K. Behrensmeyer
Meyer, Christian Heinrich; America, 1847 *8582.3 p44*
Meyer, Christine C. Louise *SEE* Meyer, Carl Friedrich
Meyer, Christine Louise Dorothea Kruse; America, 1851
  4610.10 p98
  *Son:*Ernst H. Carl Eduard
Meyer, Christoph Heinrich *SEE* Meyer, Carl Heinrich
Meyer, Christopher 28; Kansas, 1878 *5240.1 p59*
Meyer, Conrad; Iroquois Co., IL, 1896 *3455.1 p12*
Meyer, Cord; Wisconsin, n.d. *9675.7 p51*
Meyer, D.; Shreveport, LA, 1878 *7129 p45*
Meyer, Daniel; New York, NY, 1849 *6013.19 p74*
Meyer, David; Wisconsin, n.d. *9675.7 p51*
Meyer, Detrick; Philadelphia, 1762 *9973.7 p37*
Meyer, Diedrich; Illinois, 1888 *5012.39 p52*
Meyer, Diedrich 20; Kansas, 1887 *5240.1 p30*
Meyer, Diedrich 20; Kansas, 1887 *5240.1 p70*
Meyer, Dominic; Wisconsin, n.d. *9675.7 p51*
Meyer, Dominic H.; Wisconsin, n.d. *9675.7 p51*
Meyer, Eduard Adolph; America, 1854 *4610.10 p148*
Meyer, Elisabeth Michel; America, 1751-1752 *4349 p47*
  *Husband:*Georg
Meyer, Ernst H. Carl Eduard *SEE* Meyer, Christine
  Louise Dorothea Krus
Meyer, Ernst Heinrich *SEE* Meyer, Carl Friedrich
Meyer, Eve Mary; Philadelphia, 1745 *3652 p67*
Meyer, Fr Wm; Philadelphia, 1768 *9973.7 p40*
Meyer, Frederick; Philadelphia, 1768 *9973.7 p40*
Meyer, Friederich; Kentucky, 1839-1840 *8582.3 p98*
Meyer, Friederike 58; America, 1856 *4610.10 p157*
Meyer, Friederike K. Louise *SEE* Meyer, Christian
  Friedrich
Meyer, Friedrich Christian Wilhelm; America, 1880
  4610.10 p101
Meyer, Friedrich Leopold Engelhard; Quebec, 1776 *9786
  p260*
Meyer, Friedrich Wilhelm; America, 1881 *4610.10 p113*
Meyer, Friedrich Wilhelm Adolph; America, 1856
  4610.10 p112
Meyer, Georg *SEE* Meyer, Elisabeth Michel
Meyer, Georg; Philadelphia, 1752 *4349 p47*
Meyer, Georg August; America, 1881 *4610.10 p150*
  *Wife:*M. Louise Engel Rohde
  *Child:*M. Sophie Louise
  *Child:*A. Caroline Gertrud

Meyer, Georg Ludwig; America, 1845 *8582.3 p44*
Meyer, George; Indiana, 1886 *5240.1 p30*
Meyer, George Franz; Wisconsin, n.d. *9675.7 p51*
Meyer, Gottlieb; America, 1887 *4610.10 p114*
Meyer, Gottlieb; Cincinnati, 1831 *8582.1 p51*
Meyer, Hans Martin; Pennsylvania, 1772 *2444 p188*
Meyer, Heinrich; Illinois, 1856 *7857 p5*
Meyer, Heinrich F.W. Theodor *SEE* Meyer, Marie
  Christine Louise D. Krus
Meyer, Hemer *SEE* Meyer, Carl Wilhelm Frederick
Meyer, Henry; America, 1850 *1450.2 p100A*
Meyer, Henry; Illinois, 1876 *5012.39 p91*
Meyer, Henry; Philadelphia, 1756 *9973.7 p32*
Meyer, Henry; Shreveport, LA, 1878 *7129 p45*
Meyer, Henry; Wisconsin, n.d. *9675.7 p51*
Meyer, Henry 25; Kansas, 1888 *5240.1 p71*
Meyer, Henry 59; Kansas, 1888 *5240.1 p30*
Meyer, Henry 59; Kansas, 1888 *5240.1 p73*
Meyer, Henry F.; Wisconsin, n.d. *9675.7 p51*
Meyer, Henry John; Arkansas, 1918 *95.2 p83*
Meyer, Herman; Kansas, 1884 *5240.1 p30*
Meyer, Herman; New York, 1848 *2896.5 p27*
Meyer, Herman; Washington, 1859-1920 *2872.1 p26*
Meyer, Hermann; America, 1844 *8582.2 p27*
Meyer, Hermann Friedrich Karl; America, 1866 *4610.10
  p136*
Meyer, Hermann Heinrich; America, 1860 *4610.10 p158*
Meyer, Jacob; America, 1847 *8582.1 p24*
Meyer, Jacob; Indiana, 1847 *9117 p19*
Meyer, Jacob; New York, 1750 *3652 p74*
Meyer, Jacob; Pennsylvania, 1749 *2444 p190*
Meyer, Jacob; Philadelphia, 1761 *9973.7 p35*
Meyer, Jacob Bernard; Arkansas, 1918 *95.2 p83*
Meyer, Jacob Fredrick; Pennsylvania, 1754 *2444 p190*
Meyer, Jakob; Cincinnati, 1869-1887 *8582 p21*
Meyer, Jakob; New York, NY, 1847 *8582.3 p44*
Meyer, Joerg; Died enroute, 1804 *8582.2 p27*
  With son & 2 daughters
Meyer, Johann; America, 1764 *2854 p45*
  *Brother:*Julius
Meyer, Johann; America, 1804 *8582.2 p60*
Meyer, Johann; Baltimore, 1804 *8582.2 p27*
  With sister & brother
  *Mother:*Barbara
Meyer, Johann; Cincinnati, 1788-1876 *8582.3 p81*
Meyer, Johann Andreas; Quebec, 1776 *9786 p262*
Meyer, Johann Dietrich; Baltimore, 1837 *8582.3 p45*
Meyer, Johann Friedrich; America, 1852 *4610.10 p98*
Meyer, Johann H.; Iroquois Co., IL, 1894 *3455.1 p12*
Meyer, Johann Heinrich; America, 1837 *8582.3 p45*
Meyer, Johann Heinrich; Kentucky, 1838 *8582.3 p99*
Meyer, Johann Heinrich; Quebec, 1776 *9786 p258*
Meyer, Johann Konrad; America, 1849 *8582.1 p24*
Meyer, Johann Vincent; Died enroute, 1738 *9898 p44*
Meyer, Johanne 50 *SEE* Meyer, Louis
Meyer, Johannes *SEE* Meyer, Johannes
Meyer, Johannes; America, 1835 *8582.2 p27*
Meyer, Johannes; Pennsylvania, 1752 *2444 p192*
  *Wife:*Agnes Gretzing
  *Child:*Johannes
Meyer, Johannes, Family; America, 1815-1923 *2691.4
  p172*
Meyer, John; Cincinnati, 1831 *8582.1 p51*
Meyer, John; Indiana, 1844 *9117 p17*
Meyer, John; Ohio, 1844 *2769.6 p5*
Meyer, John; Philadelphia, 1763 *9973.7 p38*
Meyer, John 51; Kansas, 1878 *5240.1 p59*
Meyer, John D.; America, 1837 *8582.1 p24*
Meyer, John F.; New York, NY, 1840 *8208.4 p109*
Meyer, John F. W. 21; Kansas, 1883 *5240.1 p30*
Meyer, John F. W. 21; Kansas, 1883 *5240.1 p30*
Meyer, John Michael; Savannah, GA, 1736 *3652 p51*
Meyer, John Stephen; New York, 1750 *3652 p74*
Meyer, Jonas 11 mos; America, 1853 *9162.8 p37*
Meyer, Joseph; America, 1847 *8582.1 p24*
Meyer, Julius *SEE* Meyer, Johann
Meyer, Karl Dietrich; America, 1841 *4610.10 p97*
  *Wife:*Marie Kathrine Ruter
  *Son:*Karl Heinrich
Meyer, Karl Heinrich *SEE* Meyer, Karl Dietrich
Meyer, Karl Heinrich Ferdinand; America, 1895 *4610.10
  p114*
Meyer, L.; Wheeling, WV, 1852 *8582.3 p78*
Meyer, Leopold; America, 1847 *8582.2 p28*
Meyer, Leopold; Wisconsin, n.d. *9675.7 p51*
Meyer, Levi; America, 1847 *8582.3 p45*
Meyer, Louis; New York, NY, 1849 *6013.19 p74*
Meyer, Louis 50; New York, 1901 *4610.10 p125*
  *Wife:*Johanne 50
Meyer, Louis 83; America, 1908 *1763 p40D*
Meyer, Ludwig; America, 1843 *1450.2 p100A*
Meyer, Ludwig; Philadelphia, 1779 *8137 p11*
Meyer, Ludwig Ferdinand; America, 1854 *4610.10 p148*

Meyer, M. Louise Engel Rohde *SEE* Meyer, Georg August
Meyer, M. Sophie Louise *SEE* Meyer, Georg August
Meyer, Maria Dorothea; Died enroute, 1742 ***3652*** *p58*
Meyer, Marie 45; Kansas, 1893 ***5240.1*** *p78*
Meyer, Marie Christine Louise D. Kruse; America, 1844 ***4610.10*** *p97*
*Son:*Heinrich F.W. Theodor
Meyer, Marie Friederike *SEE* Meyer, Christian Friedrich
Meyer, Marie Kathrine Ruter *SEE* Meyer, Karl Dietrich
Meyer, Marie M. I. Griemert *SEE* Meyer, Carl Heinrich
Meyer, Martin; America, 1857 ***1450.2*** *p100A*
Meyer, Mary Ann 62; Kansas, 1880 ***5240.1*** *p61*
Meyer, Mary Magdalena; New York, 1761 ***3652*** *p88*
Meyer, Michel; Pennsylvania, 1747 ***2444*** *p165*
Meyer, Michel; Philadelphia, 1747 ***2444*** *p191*
Meyer, Mine 32; America, 1853 ***9162.8*** *p37*
Meyer, Morris; Wisconsin, n.d. ***9675.7*** *p51*
Meyer, Nicholas H.; Ohio, 1869-1887 ***8582*** *p21*
Meyer, Nikolaus Heinrich; America, 1832 ***8582.1*** *p24*
Meyer, Peter; Wisconsin, n.d. ***9675.7*** *p51*
Meyer, Philip; New York, 1750 ***3652*** *p74*
Meyer, Philipp Jacob; America, 1828 ***8582.2*** *p28*
Meyer, Richard 39; Kansas, 1890 ***5240.1*** *p74*
Meyer, Rudolph; America, 1848 ***8582.3*** *p45*
Meyer, Rudolph; Illinois, 1877 ***2896.5*** *p27*
Meyer, S.; Ohio, 1816 ***8582.1*** *p47*
Meyer, Solomon 38; America, 1853 ***9162.8*** *p37*
Meyer, Valentine; New Orleans, 1850 ***1450.2*** *p100A*
Meyer, Wilhelm; Illinois, 1877 ***2896.5*** *p28*
Meyer, Wilhelm; Illinois, 1888 ***2896.5*** *p28*
Meyer, Wilhelm Carl Friedrich; America, 1882 ***4610.10*** *p101*
Meyer, William; America, 1854 ***1450.2*** *p100A*
Meyer, William; Illinois, 1864 ***2896.5*** *p28*
Meyer, William; Washington, 1859-1920 ***2872.1*** *p25*
Meyer, William; Wisconsin, n.d. ***9675.7*** *p51*
Meyerfreund, Anton Friedrich; America, 1881 ***4610.10*** *p117*
Meyerhoff, Magdalena; New York, 1749 ***3652*** *p73*
Meyerholz, Harman H.; New York, 1851 ***2896.5*** *p28*
Meyerholz, Henrich; New York, NY, 1836 ***8208.4*** *p18*
Meyern, v.; Quebec, 1776 ***9786*** *p105*
Meyern, Johann Jacob; Quebec, 1776 ***9786*** *p262*
Meyern, Ludwig Gottlieb; Quebec, 1776 ***9786*** *p257*
Meyers, . . .; Canada, 1776-1783 ***9786*** *p29*
Meyers, Albert; California, 1867 ***3840.2*** *p18*
Meyers, Albert Frederick 27; California, 1872 ***2769.6*** *p5*
Meyers, Anthony; Ohio, 1843 ***9892.11*** *p29*
Meyers, Baltzer; Philadelphia, 1749 ***2444*** *p191*
Meyers, Charles 67; Arizona, 1898 ***9228.40*** *p3*
Meyers, Frederich 42; Kansas, 1889 ***5240.1*** *p74*
Meyers, Frederick 42; Kansas, 1889 ***5240.1*** *p30*
Meyers, Johann; Cincinnati, 1824 ***8582.1*** *p51*
Meyers, Wilhelm; Kentucky, 1700-1796 ***8582.2*** *p57*
Meyle, Eugen 28; Kansas, 1884 ***5240.1*** *p65*
Meyn, . . .; Canada, 1776-1783 ***9786*** *p29*
Meynards, Annetje; New York, 1662 ***8125.8*** *p436*
Meynert, Friedrich Ernst Adolf; America, 1876 ***4610.10*** *p101*
Meysenbug, Richard, Freiherr von; Cincinnati, 1844 ***8582.3*** *p90*
Meysenburg, Richard, Freiherr von; Cincinnati, 1844 ***8582.3*** *p90*
Meytinger, Jakob; America, 1775-1781 ***8582.3*** *p81*
Meytinger, Jakob; America, 1777-1778 ***8582.2*** *p67*
Mezanguet, Mr.; Port uncertain, 1839 ***778.5*** *p379*
Mezler, Edward; Wisconsin, n.d. ***9675.7*** *p51*
Mezzomo, Luigi; Iowa, 1866-1943 ***123.54*** *p34*
Mgillis, Augustin 22; Montreal, 1794 ***7603*** *p39*
M'Halpin, Dennis; New York, 1821 ***9892.11*** *p33*
M'Hugh, Barnard; Ohio, 1839 ***9892.11*** *p33*
Miahani, P. 34; Port uncertain, 1839 ***778.5*** *p379*
Mialhe, M. 28; New Orleans, 1837 ***778.5*** *p379*
Miano, John B.; Santa Clara Co., CA, 1878 ***2764.35*** *p43*
Miaulir, Mr. 23; America, 1838 ***778.5*** *p380*
Mibross, Jane 30; Georgia, 1775 ***1219.7*** *p277*
Micali, Jasper; Iowa, 1866-1943 ***123.54*** *p34*
Micea, Entorno; Wisconsin, n.d. ***9675.7*** *p51*
Micer, Frans 24; Arizona, 1907 ***9228.40*** *p13*
Micetic, Peter; Iowa, 1866-1943 ***123.54*** *p71*
Mich, Bernard 22; America, 1836 ***778.5*** *p380*
Michael, . . .; Canada, 1776-1783 ***9786*** *p29*
Michael, Charles; America, 1835 ***1450.2*** *p101A*
Michael, Jane; Philadelphia, 1853 ***5704.8*** *p113*
Michael, Johann H.; America, 1842 ***8582.3*** *p45*
Michael, John Philip; America, 1835 ***1450.2*** *p101A*
Michael, Kirsty; Quebec, 1873 ***4537.30*** *p114*
Michael, Philip; Baltimore, 1834 ***1450.2*** *p101A*
Michael, Thomas; Philadelphia, 1853 ***5704.8*** *p103*
Michaelis, . . .; Canada, 1776-1783 ***9786*** *p29*
Michaelis, Carl Aug. Herm. 11; New York, NY, 1857 ***9831.14*** *p154*
Michaelis, Caroline Wilhelmine 9; New York, NY, 1857 ***9831.14*** *p154*
Michaelis, Friedr. Wilh. 38; New York, NY, 1857 ***9831.14*** *p154*
Michaelis, Julius Ferdinand 4; New York, NY, 1857 ***9831.14*** *p154*
Michaelis, Konrad; Trenton, NJ, 1776 ***8137*** *p11*
Michaelis, Marie 35; New York, NY, 1857 ***9831.14*** *p154*
Michaell, Edwd.; Virginia, 1648 ***6219*** *p246*
Michaell, Richard; Virginia, 1645 ***6219*** *p239*
Michaell, Wm.; Virginia, 1635 ***6219*** *p70*
Michaels, Christ; Wisconsin, n.d. ***9675.7*** *p51*
Michaels, Henry; Wisconsin, n.d. ***9675.7*** *p51*
Michaels, Karl Friederich Theodor; America, 1849 ***8582.3*** *p45*
Michaelson, Magnus 51; Quebec, 1879 ***2557.2*** *p37*
Michaleirtz, Ivan; Iowa, 1866-1943 ***123.54*** *p34*
Michall, Moses; Arkansas, 1918 ***95.2*** *p83*
Michand, Francois 45; Port uncertain, 1832 ***778.5*** *p380*
Michaud, Mr. 28; New Orleans, 1822 ***778.5*** *p380*
Michaud, Claude 25; Port uncertain, 1836 ***778.5*** *p380*
Michaud, F. 31; America, 1823 ***778.5*** *p380*
Michaud, Francois 30; New Orleans, 1827 ***778.5*** *p380*
Michaud, Francois 45; Port uncertain, 1832 ***778.5*** *p380*
Michaud, Francois J. 32; New Orleans, 1826 ***778.5*** *p380*
Michaud, Jean-Baptiste 36; New Orleans, 1835 ***778.5*** *p380*
Michaw, James; New York, NY, 1816 ***2859.11*** *p38*
Micheal, John H.; America, 1834 ***1450.2*** *p101A*
Michel, . . .; Canada, 1776-1783 ***9786*** *p43*
Michel, Miss 27; Port uncertain, 1839 ***778.5*** *p381*
Michel, Mme. 28; Port uncertain, 1839 ***778.5*** *p381*
Michel, Mr. 27; America, 1838 ***778.5*** *p380*
Michel, Mr. 50; New Orleans, 1827 ***778.5*** *p380*
Michel, Ad. 27; America, 1853 ***9162.8*** *p37*
Michel, Ad. 52; America, 1853 ***9162.8*** *p37*
Michel, Albin 52; New Orleans, 1829 ***778.5*** *p380*
Michel, Antoine 20; Port uncertain, 1825 ***778.5*** *p380*
Michel, August; Illinois, 1878 ***2896.5*** *p28*
Michel, C. 25; New Orleans, 1838 ***778.5*** *p380*
Michel, Charles Alexander 45; Kentucky, 1820 ***778.5*** *p380*
Michel, Constance 17; Port uncertain, 1835 ***778.5*** *p381*
Michel, Elis. 16; America, 1853 ***9162.8*** *p37*
Michel, Elis. 50; America, 1853 ***9162.8*** *p37*
Michel, Elisabeth; America, 1751-1752 ***4349*** *p47*
Michel, Elise 10; America, 1853 ***9162.8*** *p37*
Michel, Etienne 54; Port uncertain, 1835 ***778.5*** *p381*
Michel, Eva 14; America, 1853 ***9162.8*** *p37*
Michel, Francis 43; Port uncertain, 1835 ***778.5*** *p381*
Michel, Franz; Illinois, 1876 ***2896.5*** *p28*
Michel, George; New York, NY, 1836 ***8208.4*** *p12*
Michel, Henry 11; Port uncertain, 1835 ***778.5*** *p381*
Michel, J. 28; Port uncertain, 1835 ***778.5*** *p381*
Michel, Jacob; Philadelphia, 1767 ***9973.7*** *p40*
Michel, John; Illinois, 1874 ***2896.5*** *p28*
Michel, Joseph; New York, NY, 1811 ***2859.11*** *p17*
Michel, Karolina 14; Port uncertain, 1839 ***778.5*** *p381*
Michel, Karolina 39; Port uncertain, 1839 ***778.5*** *p381*
Michel, Mag 1; Port uncertain, 1839 ***778.5*** *p381*
Michel, Mathias; Wisconsin, n.d. ***9675.7*** *p51*
Michel, Peter 20; America, 1853 ***9162.8*** *p37*
Michel, Phillipp; Wisconsin, n.d. ***9675.7*** *p51*
Michel, Pilipp 13; Port uncertain, 1839 ***778.5*** *p381*
Michel, Victorine 15; Port uncertain, 1835 ***778.5*** *p381*
Michele, Chiara; Arkansas, 1918 ***95.2*** *p83*
Michell, Barnard 19; Maryland or Virginia, 1730 ***3690.1*** *p155*
Michell, George; New York, NY, 1833 ***8208.4*** *p27*
Michell, Joanna; Virginia, 1637 ***6219*** *p83*
Michell, Tho.; Virginia, 1636 ***6219*** *p21*
Michell, Thomas; Philadelphia, 1864 ***5704.8*** *p184*
Michelotti, Alexander; Arkansas, 1918 ***95.2*** *p83*
Michels, Geo.; Wisconsin, n.d. ***9675.7*** *p51*
Michels, Jon.; Virginia, 1636 ***6219*** *p75*
Michels, Mathias; Illinois, 1860 ***5012.38*** *p98*
Michenfelder, Johann Caspar; Lancaster, PA, 1768 ***2854*** *p45*
Micheve, George 45; New York, NY, 1893 ***9026.4*** *p42*
Michie, William; Charleston, SC, 1772 ***1639.20*** *p235*
Michler, Barbara *SEE* Michler, John
Michler, John; New York, 1743 ***3652*** *p59*
*Wife:*Barbara
Michlik, Michael; America, 1898 ***7137*** *p169*
Michoelis, Henry; America, 1847 ***1450.2*** *p101A*
Michon, Marya 24; New York, 1912 ***9980.29*** *p67*
Michoux, G. M. 26; New Orleans, 1821 ***778.5*** *p381*
Mickanney, Timothy 16; Windward Islands, 1722 ***3690.1*** *p155*
Mickel, Eassa; Arkansas, 1918 ***95.2*** *p83*
Mickell, Ephraim Christian 34; Maryland, 1774 ***1219.7*** *p230*
Mickelson, John; Washington, 1859-1920 ***2872.1*** *p26*
Mickelson, William; Washington, 1859-1920 ***2872.1*** *p26*
Mickewiczj, Stanislaw; Wisconsin, n.d. ***9675.7*** *p51*
Mickewitz, Henry; Wisconsin, n.d. ***9675.7*** *p51*
Micklejohn, Robert 23; Massachusetts, 1849 ***5881.1*** *p75*
Mickler, Peter; South Carolina, 1788 ***7119*** *p202*
Mickles, John; Illinois, 1892 ***5012.40*** *p26*
Mickus, Peter; Arkansas, 1918 ***95.2*** *p83*
Miclea, Charles Niculaic; Arkansas, 1918 ***95.2*** *p83*
Micucci, Vita; Arkansas, 1918 ***95.2*** *p83*
Midal, M. 28; New Orleans, 1831 ***778.5*** *p381*
Midclare, Mary 24; Virginia, 1699 ***2212*** *p26*
Middendorf, Johann Hermann; America, 1847 ***8582.3*** *p45*
Middendorf, Wilhelm; America, 1851 ***8582.3*** *p45*
Middep, John; Virginia, 1636 ***6219*** *p26*
Middlebrook, Theophilus 21; Maryland, 1733 ***3690.1*** *p155*
Middleton, Catherine; Virginia, 1647 ***6219*** *p239*
Middleton, Eliza; Philadelphia, 1852 ***5704.8*** *p88*
Middleton, Elizabeth; Montreal, 1823 ***7603*** *p26*
Middleton, George 18; Jamaica, 1724 ***3690.1*** *p155*
Middleton, Margaret; America, 1742 ***4971*** *p50*
Middleton, Marry; Virginia, 1644 ***6219*** *p231*
Middleton, Mary 48; Massachusetts, 1850 ***5881.1*** *p73*
Middleton, Nich.; Virginia, 1635 ***6219*** *p70*
Middleton, Owen; Virginia, 1647 ***6219*** *p241*
Middleton, Robert; Virginia, 1698 ***2212*** *p17*
Middleton, Sarah; South Carolina, 1683-1765 ***1639.20*** *p235*
Middleton, William 21; Maryland, 1775 ***1219.7*** *p272*
Middleton, William 23; Jamaica, 1774 ***1219.7*** *p232*
Middleton, William 32; St. John, N.B., 1862 ***5704.8*** *p150*
Middleton, William 46; Massachusetts, 1849 ***5881.1*** *p77*
Middowes, Henry; Virginia, 1638 ***6219*** *p122*
Midghy, Margaret 18; Philadelphia, 1861 ***5704.8*** *p148*
Midleton, James; Virginia, 1637 ***6219*** *p86*
Midleton, James; Virginia, 1638 ***6219*** *p123*
Midleton, John; Virginia, 1639 ***6219*** *p181*
Midleton, John; Virginia, 1642 ***6219*** *p191*
Midleton, Nich.; Virginia, 1638 ***6219*** *p116*
Midleton, Wm.; Virginia, 1638 ***6219*** *p124*
Midolet, Nicolas Vincente 28; America, 1838 ***778.5*** *p382*
Midul, M. 28; New Orleans, 1831 ***778.5*** *p381*
Midwinter, George 32; Jamaica, 1724 ***3690.1*** *p156*
Miear, Vincent; Illinois, 1896 ***5012.40*** *p54*
Miechalowski, Teodor 18; New York, 1912 ***9980.29*** *p61*
Mieczkowska, Feliksa 18; New York, 1912 ***9980.29*** *p74*
Miedzielski, . . .; America, n.d. ***4606*** *p180*
Mieer, Henry; Washington, 1859-1920 ***2872.1*** *p26*
Miegel, Gustave 21; America, 1839 ***778.5*** *p382*
Mields, Fredrick; Wisconsin, n.d. ***9675.7*** *p51*
Mields, Wilhelm; Wisconsin, n.d. ***9675.7*** *p51*
Mieling, Frederich William; Arkansas, 1918 ***95.2*** *p83*
Mielke, Carl; Wisconsin, n.d. ***9675.7*** *p51*
Mielke, Chas H.; Wisconsin, n.d. ***9675.7*** *p51*
Mielke, Fred; Wisconsin, n.d. ***9675.7*** *p51*
Mielke, Mathilda; Wisconsin, n.d. ***9675.7*** *p51*
Miendlar, Sebastyan 17; New York, 1912 ***9980.29*** *p71*
Mier, Diedrich; Wisconsin, n.d. ***9675.7*** *p51*
Miers, Easter 20; America, 1701 ***2212*** *p34*
Miers, Frank 35; New Orleans, 1838 ***778.5*** *p382*
Miers, Joseph 33; New Orleans, 1838 ***778.5*** *p382*
Mierzwinski, . . .; Mexico, 1831-1900 ***4606*** *p175*
Mierzwinski, . . .; New York, 1831 ***4606*** *p175*
Miess, Maria 38; America, 1836 ***778.5*** *p382*
Mieugard, Jean 25; America, 1838 ***778.5*** *p382*
Migent, Michael 22; Virginia, 1774 ***1219.7*** *p240*
Migey, Mr. 28; New Orleans, 1838 ***778.5*** *p382*
Mignerai, Jacques; Halifax, N.S., 1752 ***7074.6*** *p208*
*Sibling:*Jean-George
Mignerai, Jacques; Halifax, N.S., 1753 ***7074.6*** *p217*
Mignerai, Jean-George *SEE* Mignerai, Jacques
Mignerai, Jean-Pierre; Halifax, N.S., 1753 ***7074.6*** *p217*
Mignon, Bernard 26; Port uncertain, 1836 ***778.5*** *p382*
Mignon, John 30; Louisiana, 1826 ***778.5*** *p382*
Mignotte, Jean Alexandre 1; America, 1835 ***778.5*** *p382*
Mignotte, Petronille 26; America, 1835 ***778.5*** *p382*
Mignotte, Pierre 27; America, 1835 ***778.5*** *p382*
Migoulet, Pierre 25; America, 1837 ***778.5*** *p382*
Mihalevic, Lynac; Iowa, 1866-1943 ***123.54*** *p34*
Mihalgevic, Grgo; Iowa, 1866-1943 ***123.54*** *p34*
Mihalik, Michael; America, 1898 ***7137*** *p169*
Mihaljevic, Karlo; Iowa, 1866-1943 ***123.54*** *p34*
Mihalko, John; America, 1888 ***7137*** *p169*
Mihalovic, John; Iowa, 1866-1943 ***123.54*** *p34*
Mihalovic, Phillip; Iowa, 1866-1943 ***123.54*** *p34*
Mihalovich, Franjo; Iowa, 1866-1943 ***123.54*** *p34*
Mihalovich, Frank; Iowa, 1866-1943 ***123.54*** *p34*
Mihalovich, Ignac; Iowa, 1866-1943 ***123.54*** *p34*
Mihalovich, John; Iowa, 1866-1943 ***123.54*** *p34*
Mihalovich, Joseph; Iowa, 1866-1943 ***123.54*** *p34*
Mihalovich, William; Iowa, 1866-1943 ***123.54*** *p34*

Mihalyovich, John; Iowa, 1866-1943 ***123.54*** *p34*
Mihalzvich, John; Iowa, 1866-1943 ***123.54*** *p34*
Mihazevic, George; Iowa, 1866-1943 ***123.54*** *p34*
Mihin, Nicholas; America, 1742 ***4971*** *p28*
Mihoilovia, Luie; Iowa, 1866-1943 ***123.54*** *p34*
Mihollovic, Gregosian; Iowa, 1866-1943 ***123.54*** *p34*
Miicoud, T. 40; New Orleans, 1830 ***778.5*** *p382*
Mike, Ann; Virginia, 1642 ***6219*** *p194*
Mike, Anthony; Arkansas, 1918 ***95.2*** *p84*
Mikele, Giordono Francesco Fu 28; West Virginia, 1902 ***9788.3*** *p17*
Mikenas, Martin; Arkansas, 1918 ***95.2*** *p84*
Miklaices, Ignac; Wisconsin, n.d. ***9675.7*** *p51*
Mikoc, Toni; Iowa, 1866-1943 ***123.54*** *p34*
Mikorak, Maryanna 26; New York, 1912 ***9980.29*** *p62*
Miksch, Infant; Died enroute, 1742 ***3652*** *p55*
Miksch, Anna Johanna *SEE* Miksch, Michael
Miksch, John Matthew; New York, 1754 ***3652*** *p80*
Miksch, Michael; Philadelphia, 1742 ***3652*** *p55*
*Wife:*Anna Johanna
Mikula, John; America, 1899 ***7137*** *p169*
Mikulsky, Ardadi Keprean; Arkansas, 1918 ***95.2*** *p84*
Mikusch, Val; Wisconsin, n.d. ***9675.7*** *p51*
Miland, James *SEE* Miland, James
Miland, James 29; Port uncertain, 1849 ***4535.10*** *p198*
*Wife:*Susan 26
*Child:*James
Miland, Susan 26 *SEE* Miland, James
Milane, Cosimo; Iowa, 1866-1943 ***123.54*** *p34*
Milani, Augusto; Iowa, 1866-1943 ***123.54*** *p34*
Milani, Gust; Iowa, 1866-1943 ***123.54*** *p34*
Milani, Joe; Iowa, 1866-1943 ***123.54*** *p34*
Milani, Pietro; Iowa, 1866-1943 ***123.54*** *p34*
Milbert, Anna Maria 25; America, 1853 ***9162.8*** *p37*
Milbert, Elisabetha 22; America, 1853 ***9162.8*** *p37*
Milborn, Andrew 7; Carolina, 1774 ***1219.7*** *p242*
Milborn, Christopher 2; Carolina, 1774 ***1219.7*** *p242*
Milborne, Rich; Virginia, 1635 ***6219*** *p71*
Milbourn, John 27; Pennsylvania, 1728 ***3690.1*** *p156*
Milbrat, John; Wisconsin, n.d. ***9675.7*** *p51*
Milburn, Elizabeth 20; Georgia, 1775 ***1219.7*** *p277*
Milch, Johann 28; Philadelphia, 1808 ***2854*** *p45*
Milche, Frederick; Wisconsin, n.d. ***9675.7*** *p51*
Mildebrandt, Paul A.; Arkansas, 1918 ***95.2*** *p84*
Mildrum, James; Quebec, 1852 ***5704.8*** *p91*
Mildrum, Robert; Quebec, 1852 ***5704.8*** *p91*
Milener, John; Virginia, 1698 ***2212*** *p16*
Mileris, Frank; Arkansas, 1918 ***95.2*** *p84*
Miles, Andrew 4; St. John, N.B., 1854 ***5704.8*** *p122*
Miles, Barbara; Virginia, 1642 ***6219*** *p15*
Miles, Barbara; Virginia, 1642 ***6219*** *p190*
Miles, Benjamin 21; Maryland, 1775 ***1219.7*** *p251*
Miles, Christopher 56; Kansas, 1874 ***5240.1*** *p56*
Miles, David; New York, NY, 1836 ***8208.4*** *p78*
Miles, Eliza 19; St. John, N.B., 1855 ***5704.8*** *p127*
Miles, Fanny; Quebec, 1852 ***5704.8*** *p87*
Miles, Francis 21; Maryland, 1775 ***1219.7*** *p250*
Miles, Francis Ann 11; St. John, N.B., 1854 ***5704.8*** *p122*
Miles, James; St. John, N.B., 1847 ***5704.8*** *p35*
Miles, John; Quebec, 1822 ***7603*** *p82*
Miles, John; Virginia, 1647 ***6219*** *p239*
Miles, John 25; Massachusetts, 1850 ***5881.1*** *p69*
Miles, Josiph; Iowa, 1866-1943 ***123.54*** *p34*
Miles, Margaret 9; St. John, N.B., 1854 ***5704.8*** *p122*
Miles, Richard 18; Maryland, 1729 ***3690.1*** *p156*
Miles, Robert; Quebec, 1852 ***5704.8*** *p87*
Miles, Robert, Jr.; Virginia, 1642 ***6219*** *p15*
Miles, Robert, Jr.; Virginia, 1642 ***6219*** *p190*
Miles, Thomas 17; Philadelphia, 1774 ***1219.7*** *p212*
Miles, William 16; Philadelphia, 1774 ***1219.7*** *p212*
Miles, William 19; Virginia, 1722 ***3690.1*** *p156*
Miles, William 22; St. John, N.B., 1855 ***5704.8*** *p126*
Miles, Wm.; Virginia, 1642 ***6219*** *p191*
Miletich, Mike; Iowa, 1866-1943 ***123.54*** *p71*
Miley, George; Philadelphia, 1761 ***9973.7*** *p36*
Miley, Hannah 19; Massachusetts, 1848 ***5881.1*** *p67*
Miley, John 45; Philadelphia, 1803 ***53.26*** *p68*
Miley, Jules 43; America, 1837 ***778.5*** *p382*
Milham, David; New York, 1817 ***9892.11*** *p29*
Milheim, Christian; Philadelphia, 1760 ***9973.7*** *p34*
Milhernen, Cornelius; St. John, N.B., 1847 ***5704.8*** *p10*
Miliet, Abraham 31; Halifax, N.S., 1752 ***7074.6*** *p212*
*Sister:*Clemence
*Sister:*Suzanne-Marguerite
Miliet, Clemence *SEE* Miliet, Abraham
Miliet, Suzanne-Marguerite *SEE* Miliet, Abraham
Miligan, Elizabeth; New York, NY, 1811 ***2859.11*** *p17*
Milinski, . . .; New York, 1831 ***4606*** *p175*
Militich, Mile; Iowa, 1866-1943 ***123.54*** *p71*
Milius, Johann August; Quebec, 1776 ***9786*** *p257*
Milkau, Christian Friedrich; Quebec, 1776 ***9786*** *p258*
Milke, John Fredrick; Wisconsin, n.d. ***9675.7*** *p51*
Milkie, Julius; Illinois, 1870 ***5012.38*** *p99*
Milko, John; America, 1888 ***7137*** *p169*
Mill, Mr.; Grenada, 1774 ***1219.7*** *p210*
Millacha, Ja.; Virginia, 1649 ***6219*** *p253*
Milladon, Philippe; America, 1833 ***778.5*** *p383*
Millan, James 24; St. John, N.B., 1861 ***5704.8*** *p146*
Millar, Andrew; America, 1775 ***8894.2*** *p57*
Millar, James; Wilmington, NC, 1815 ***1639.20*** *p236*
Millar, John; New York, NY, 1816 ***2859.11*** *p38*
Millar, Mary; Quebec, 1852 ***5704.8*** *p98*
Millar, Robert; New York, NY, 1816 ***2859.11*** *p38*
Millar, Robert 26; Philadelphia, 1804 ***53.26*** *p68*
Millar, William; Charleston, SC, 1807 ***1639.20*** *p237*
Millar, William; North Carolina, 1773 ***1639.20*** *p237*
Millard, . . .; Halifax, N.S., 1752 ***7074.6*** *p232*
Millard, George; Iowa, 1866-1943 ***123.54*** *p34*
Millard, Henry 16; Maryland, 1720 ***3690.1*** *p156*
Millard, Jn 14; America, 1705 ***2212*** *p43*
Millard, Richard; Virginia, 1638 ***6219*** *p148*
Millaudon, Philip 40; America, 1839 ***778.5*** *p383*
Millbourn, John 27; Pennsylvania, 1728 ***3690.1*** *p156*
Mille, Luke; Virginia, 1638 ***6219*** *p149*
Milledge, Elizabeth 40 *SEE* Milledge, Thomas
Milledge, Frances 5 *SEE* Milledge, Thomas
Milledge, James 2 *SEE* Milledge, Thomas
Milledge, John 11 *SEE* Milledge, Thomas
Milledge, Richard 8 *SEE* Milledge, Thomas
Milledge, Sarah 9 *SEE* Milledge, Thomas
Milledge, Thomas 42; Savannah, GA, 1733 ***4719.17*** *p312*
*Wife:*Elizabeth 40
*Daughter:*Frances 5
*Son:*James 2
*Son:*John 11
*Son:*Richard 8
*Daughter:*Sarah 9
Milleman, Debold; New York, NY, 1838 ***8208.4*** *p67*
Millen, Barthol.; Virginia, 1642 ***6219*** *p195*
Millen, Eliza *SEE* Millen, Magy
Millen, Eliza; Philadelphia, 1849 ***5704.8*** *p58*
Millen, James; New York, NY, 1838 ***8208.4*** *p66*
Millen, Jane; Philadelphia, 1849 ***53.26*** *p68*
*Relative:*Samuel
Millen, Jane; Philadelphia, 1849 ***5704.8*** *p53*
Millen, Magy; Philadelphia, 1849 ***53.26*** *p68*
*Relative:*Eliza
Millen, Magy; Philadelphia, 1849 ***5704.8*** *p58*
Millen, Mary Jane; St. John, N.B., 1847 ***5704.8*** *p18*
Millen, Samuel *SEE* Millen, Jane
Millen, Samuel 11; Philadelphia, 1849 ***5704.8*** *p53*
Miller, . . .; Canada, 1776-1783 ***9786*** *p29*
Miller, . . .; Pennsylvania, 1748 ***2444*** *p194*
Miller, . . . 10 mos; New York, NY, 1866 ***5704.8*** *p212*
Miller, A. M. 85; Washington, 1918-1920 ***1728.5*** *p12*
Miller, Adam; Iowa, 1866-1943 ***123.54*** *p34*
Miller, Adam 9; America, 1839 ***778.5*** *p383*
Miller, Agnes; New York, NY, 1866 ***5704.8*** *p212*
Miller, Agnes 57; Quebec, 1863 ***5704.8*** *p154*
Miller, Alexander; New York, NY, 1816 ***2859.11*** *p38*
Miller, Alexander; New York, NY, 1864 ***5704.8*** *p171*
Miller, Alexander; North Carolina, 1831 ***1639.20*** *p235*
Miller, Alexander 6 mos; Quebec, 1847 ***5704.8*** *p30*
Miller, Alexander 12; Quebec, 1847 ***5704.8*** *p28*
Miller, Alexander 19; Barbados, 1774 ***1219.7*** *p178*
Miller, Allen; Ohio, 1859-1867 ***9892.11*** *p29*
Miller, Andrew; Philadelphia, 1850 ***53.26*** *p68*
*Relative:*Rebecca
Miller, Andrew; Philadelphia, 1850 ***5704.8*** *p59*
Miller, Andrew; Washington, 1859-1920 ***2872.1*** *p26*
Miller, Ann *SEE* Miller, Mary Jane
Miller, Ann; Philadelphia, 1847 ***5704.8*** *p1*
Miller, Ann; Philadelphia, 1866 ***5704.8*** *p205*
Miller, Ann 18; St. John, N.B., 1864 ***5704.8*** *p158*
Miller, Ann Eliza 2; Quebec, 1847 ***5704.8*** *p28*
Miller, Anna; Charles Town, SC, 1791 ***8894.1*** *p191*
Miller, Anne; New York, NY, 1811 ***2859.11*** *p17*
Miller, Annie 1; America, 1866 ***5704.8*** *p204*
Miller, Antke Marie 37; Kansas, 1889 ***5240.1*** *p73*
Miller, Anton; Wisconsin, n.d. ***9675.7*** *p51*
Miller, Archibald 27; Virginia, 1774 ***1219.7*** *p240*
Miller, Armour; Quebec, 1849 ***5704.8*** *p56*
Miller, August A.; Illinois, 1867 ***2896.5*** *p28*
Miller, Bella; Philadelphia, 1866 ***5704.8*** *p205*
Miller, Benjamin; New York, NY, 1816 ***2859.11*** *p38*
Miller, C.A.; Illinois, 1898 ***5012.40*** *p55*
Miller, Caroline 23; Quebec, 1864 ***5704.8*** *p160*
Miller, Carrie S.; Washington, 1859-1920 ***2872.1*** *p26*
Miller, Catherine; Philadelphia, 1847 ***53.26*** *p68*
Miller, Catherine; Philadelphia, 1847 ***5704.8*** *p30*
Miller, Catherine; Philadelphia, 1848 ***53.26*** *p68*
Miller, Catherine 18; Quebec, 1855 ***5704.8*** *p126*
Miller, Catherine Ann; Philadelphia, 1848 ***5704.8*** *p40*
Miller, Charles; America, 1846 ***1450.2*** *p101A*
Miller, Charles F.; America, 1844 ***1450.2*** *p101A*
Miller, Charles G.; America, 1852 ***1450.2*** *p101A*
Miller, Charles J.; New York, NY, 1866 ***5704.8*** *p213*
Miller, Charley A.; Colorado, 1901 ***9678.2*** *p126*
Miller, Christian Frederick William; America, 1844 ***1450.2*** *p101A*
Miller, Christiana 30 *SEE* Miller, John Adam
Miller, Christopher; Pennsylvania, 1772 ***9973.8*** *p33*
Miller, Christopher A.; Illinois, 1860 ***5012.39*** *p90*
Miller, Conrad 14; America, 1839 ***778.5*** *p383*
Miller, Crawford; St. John, N.B., 1848 ***5704.8*** *p47*
Miller, Daniel; America, 1844 ***1450.2*** *p102A*
Miller, Daniel; New York, NY, 1840 ***8208.4*** *p110*
Miller, Daniel; Philadelphia, 1751 ***2854*** *p45*
Miller, David; New York, NY, 1866 ***5704.8*** *p212*
Miller, David; Quebec, 1847 ***5704.8*** *p16*
Miller, Dorethea; Quebec, 1848 ***5704.8*** *p42*
Miller, Edith 17; Jamaica, 1731 ***3690.1*** *p156*
Miller, Edward; Ohio, 1859-1867 ***9892.11*** *p30*
Miller, Edward; Virginia, 1643 ***6219*** *p23*
Miller, Edward 45; Arizona, 1890 ***2764.35*** *p46*
Miller, Elenora Beggs *SEE* Miller, John
Miller, Elisabeth 49; America, 1839 ***778.5*** *p383*
Miller, Eliza; New York, NY, 1864 ***5704.8*** *p175*
Miller, Eliza; Philadelphia, 1851 ***5704.8*** *p79*
Miller, Eliza; Quebec, 1847 ***5704.8*** *p28*
Miller, Eliza; Quebec, 1847 ***5704.8*** *p29*
Miller, Eliza; Quebec, 1847 ***5704.8*** *p36*
Miller, Eliza 10; Philadelphia, 1854 ***5704.8*** *p122*
Miller, Eliza 40; Philadelphia, 1854 ***5704.8*** *p122*
Miller, Elizabeth; New York, NY, 1811 ***2859.11*** *p17*
Miller, Elizabeth; Philadelphia, 1864 ***5704.8*** *p187*
Miller, Elizabeth 1; Quebec, 1847 ***5704.8*** *p30*
Miller, Elizabeth 1; Quebec, 1864 ***5704.8*** *p160*
Miller, Elizabeth 4; New York, NY, 1866 ***5704.8*** *p212*
Miller, Ellen; Iowa, 1866-1943 ***123.54*** *p71*
Miller, Emil; Arkansas, 1918 ***95.2*** *p84*
Miller, Ernest; Kansas, 1911 ***6013.40*** *p16*
Miller, Falkert G. 39; Kansas, 1875 ***5240.1*** *p56*
Miller, Fanny; Quebec, 1847 ***5704.8*** *p29*
Miller, Fr.; Virginia, 1637 ***6219*** *p11*
Miller, Fr.; Virginia, 1637 ***6219*** *p114*
Miller, Francis; Charleston, SC, 1797 ***1639.20*** *p236*
Miller, Francis 20; Maryland, 1720 ***3690.1*** *p156*
Miller, Frank; America, 1882 ***5240.1*** *p30*
Miller, Frank; Wisconsin, n.d. ***9675.7*** *p51*
Miller, Fred; Kansas, 1879 ***5240.1*** *p30*
Miller, Fred; Washington, 1859-1920 ***2872.1*** *p26*
Miller, Frederick; Baltimore, 1835 ***1450.2*** *p102A*
Miller, Frederick; New York, NY, 1836 ***8208.4*** *p21*
Miller, Fredrick; Wisconsin, n.d. ***9675.7*** *p51*
Miller, Gabriel; South Carolina, 1788 ***7119*** *p202*
Miller, Georg; Virginia, 1638 ***6219*** *p122*
Miller, George; Indiana, 1844 ***9117*** *p17*
Miller, George; Philadelphia, 1851 ***5704.8*** *p75*
Miller, George; South Carolina, 1788 ***7119*** *p197*
Miller, George; Virginia, 1858 ***4626.16*** *p17*
Miller, George 84; Massachusetts, 1860 ***6410.32*** *p117*
Miller, George P.; Washington, 1859-1920 ***2872.1*** *p26*
Miller, Gottfried; Illinois, 1866 ***2896.5*** *p28*
Miller, Graham 10; Quebec, 1847 ***5704.8*** *p28*
Miller, Gust; Arkansas, 1918 ***95.2*** *p84*
Miller, H. D.; Washington, 1859-1920 ***2872.1*** *p26*
Miller, Harry; Arkansas, 1918 ***95.2*** *p84*
Miller, Harry; Quebec, 1847 ***5704.8*** *p36*
Miller, Heinrich; Philadelphia, 1740 ***8582.3*** *p84*
Miller, Heinrich; Wisconsin, n.d. ***9675.7*** *p51*
Miller, Henrich; California, 1860 ***3702.7*** *p400*
Miller, Henry; America, 1851 ***1450.2*** *p102A*
Miller, Henry; Arizona, 1898 ***9228.30*** *p11*
Miller, Henry; Philadelphia, 1864 ***5704.8*** *p187*
Miller, Henry 20; New York, 1865 ***3702.7*** *p203*
Miller, Henry 55; Kansas, 1884 ***5240.1*** *p66*
Miller, Henry, Jr.; America, 1844 ***1450.2*** *p102A*
Miller, Henry William; New York, NY, 1836 ***8208.4*** *p10*
Miller, Herman; Philadelphia, 1764 ***9973.7*** *p39*
Miller, Isaac; America, 1894 ***1450.2*** *p102A*
Miller, Isabella *SEE* Miller, William
Miller, Isabella; America, 1866 ***5704.8*** *p204*
Miller, Isabella 17; Massachusetts, 1849 ***5881.1*** *p67*
Miller, J. 38; New Orleans, 1821 ***778.5*** *p383*
Miller, Jacob; Ohio, 1843 ***9892.11*** *p30*
Miller, Jacob; Ohio, 1845 ***9892.11*** *p30*
Miller, Jacob 23; Pennsylvania, 1748 ***2444*** *p194*
Miller, Jacques; Quebec, 1812 ***7603*** *p102*
Miller, James; Charleston, SC, 1796 ***1639.20*** *p236*
Miller, James; Iowa, 1866-1943 ***123.54*** *p71*
Miller, James; Ohio, 1857-1875 ***9892.11*** *p30*
Miller, James; Ohio, 1877 ***9892.11*** *p30*
Miller, James; Philadelphia, 1847 ***53.26*** *p68*
Miller, James; Philadelphia, 1847 ***5704.8*** *p1*
Miller, James; Quebec, 1849 ***5704.8*** *p51*
Miller, James; St. John, N.B., 1866 ***5704.8*** *p166*
Miller, James; Virginia, 1637 ***6219*** *p110*
*Wife:*Mary

Miller, James 3 mos; Quebec, 1849 *5704.8 p56*
Miller, James 6 SEE Miller, Thomas
Miller, James 6; Philadelphia, 1847 *5704.8 p21*
Miller, James 7; New York, NY, 1864 *5704.8 p171*
Miller, James 7; St. John, N.B., 1851 *5704.8 p79*
Miller, James 15; Baltimore, 1775 *1219.7 p271*
Miller, James 16; St. John, N.B., 1862 *5704.8 p150*
Miller, James 20; Philadelphia, 1853 *5704.8 p114*
Miller, James 21; Maryland, 1733 *3690.1 p156*
Miller, James 22; St. John, N.B., 1864 *5704.8 p158*
Miller, Jan; Arkansas, 1918 *95.2 p84*
Miller, Jane; New York, NY, 1866 *5704.8 p212*
Miller, Jane; Philadelphia, 1864 *5704.8 p187*
Miller, Jane; Philadelphia, 1866 *5704.8 p205*
Miller, Jane 8; America, 1866 *5704.8 p204*
Miller, Jane 22; America, 1704 *2212 p40*
Miller, Jane 25; Halifax, N.S., 1774 *1219.7 p213*
Miller, Jane Ann 22; St. John, N.B., 1866 *5704.8 p166*
Miller, Jarvis 22; Wilmington, DE, 1831 *6508.3 p100*
Miller, Jenny 4; St. John, N.B., 1851 *5704.8 p79*
Miller, Jno.; Virginia, 1643 *6219 p207*
Miller, Johan Jacob 21; Pennsylvania, 1748 *2444 p194*
Miller, Johanna Dorothea; New York, 1752 *3652 p76*
Miller, John; Georgia, 1775 *1219.7 p274*
Miller, John; Indiana, 1848 *9117 p17*
Miller, John; Iowa, 1866-1943 *123.54 p34*
Miller, John; Iroquois Co., IL, 1892 *3455.1 p12*
Miller, John; Kansas, 1907 *6013.40 p16*
Miller, John; New Orleans, 1849 *5704.8 p59*
Miller, John; New York, NY, 1815 *2859.11 p38*
Miller, John; New York, NY, 1816 *2859.11 p38*
Miller, John; New York, NY, 1840 *8208.4 p104*
Miller, John; Ohio, 1840 *9892.11 p30*
Miller, John; Philadelphia, 1850 *53.26 p68*
Miller, John; Philadelphia, 1850 *5704.8 p68*
Miller, John; Quebec, 1847 *5704.8 p28*
Miller, John; Quebec, 1847 *5704.8 p36*
Miller, John; Quebec, 1848 *5704.8 p42*
Miller, John; St. John, N.B., 1847 *5704.8 p9*
Miller, John; Savannah, GA, 1821 *8893 p264*
  Wife:Elenora Beggs
Miller, John; South Carolina, 1752-1753 *3689.17 p22*
  With wife
Miller, John 4 SEE Miller, Thomas
Miller, John 4; Philadelphia, 1847 *5704.8 p21*
Miller, John 4; Quebec, 1864 *5704.8 p160*
Miller, John 8; Quebec, 1847 *5704.8 p28*
Miller, John 8; Quebec, 1847 *5704.8 p30*
Miller, John 18; America, 1728 *3690.1 p156*
Miller, John 20; Port uncertain, 1838 *778.5 p383*
Miller, John 21; Maryland, 1774 *1219.7 p215*
Miller, John 21; Philadelphia, 1833 *53.26 p69*
Miller, John 21; Philadelphia, 1833-1834 *53.26 p69*
  Relative:Margaret 18
Miller, John 22; Kansas, 1884 *5240.1 p66*
Miller, John 26; Maryland, 1774 *1219.7 p206*
Miller, John 31; America, 1839 *778.5 p383*
Miller, John 40; West Virginia, 1800 *9788.3 p17*
Miller, John Adam 48; Savannah, GA, 1738 *9332 p332*
  Wife:Christiana 30
  Daughter:Veronica 16
  Son:Philip 14
  Son:John Nicholas 12
  Daughter:Mary Catherina 10
Miller, John Alexander; New York, NY, 1835 *8208.4 p28*
Miller, John H.; Virginia, 1856 *4626.16 p15*
Miller, John H. 42; Massachusetts, 1860 *6410.32 p104*
Miller, John Henry; Boston, 1835 *6410.32 p123*
Miller, John Henry; Illinois, 1869 *2896.5 p28*
Miller, John Henry; Philadelphia, 1741 *3652 p53*
Miller, John Jacob; Philadelphia, 1741 *3652 p53*
Miller, John Michael; New York, NY, 1832 *8208.4 p40*
Miller, John Michael; Wisconsin, n.d. *9675.7 p51*
Miller, John Nicholas 12 SEE Miller, John Adam
Miller, Jonathan Adam; Philadelphia, 1758 *9973.7 p33*
Miller, Josef 20; New York, NY, 1878 *9253 p45*
Miller, Joseph; America, 1792 *1639.20 p236*
Miller, Joseph; Quebec, 1847 *5704.8 p30*
Miller, Joseph 6; Quebec, 1847 *5704.8 p30*
Miller, Joseph 16; Windward Islands, 1722 *3690.1 p156*
Miller, Joseph 29; Maryland, 1775 *1219.7 p266*
Miller, Lavina; St. John, N.B., 1848 *5704.8 p47*
Miller, Lawrence; Virginia, 1851 *4626.16 p14*
Miller, Leonard 22; Maryland, 1775 *1219.7 p251*
Miller, Ludewic; Philadelphia, 1762 *9973.7 p37*
Miller, Margaret; New York, NY, 1816 *2859.11 p39*
Miller, Margaret; Philadelphia, 1850 *5704.8 p64*
Miller, Margaret; Quebec, 1849 *5704.8 p56*
Miller, Margaret 2; New York, NY, 1866 *5704.8 p212*
Miller, Margaret 6; Philadelphia, 1854 *5704.8 p122*
Miller, Margaret 9; Quebec, 1847 *5704.8 p29*
Miller, Margaret 9; St. John, N.B., 1851 *5704.8 p79*

Miller, Margaret 18 SEE Miller, John
Miller, Margaret 20; Philadelphia, 1855 *5704.8 p124*
Miller, Margaret 20; St. John, N.B., 1866 *5704.8 p166*
Miller, Margaret 40; Quebec, 1864 *5704.8 p160*
Miller, Margerett; Virginia, 1638 *6219 p120*
Miller, Maria 38; America, 1839 *778.5 p383*
Miller, Marselle 27; America, 1839 *778.5 p383*
Miller, Martha SEE Miller, Thomas
Miller, Martha; Philadelphia, 1847 *5704.8 p21*
Miller, Martha; Quebec, 1847 *5704.8 p28*
Miller, Martha 9 mos; Quebec, 1847 *5704.8 p28*
Miller, Martha 20; St. John, N.B., 1864 *5704.8 p159*
Miller, Martin; America, 1880 *6014.1 p3*
Miller, Martin; Charleston, SC, 1766 *8582.2 p65*
Miller, Martin; Charleston, SC, 1775-1781 *8582.2 p52*
Miller, Martin; Indiana, 1848 *9117 p17*
Miller, Mary SEE Miller, James
Miller, Mary; St. John, N.B., 1848 *5704.8 p47*
Miller, Mary; St. John, N.B., 1851 *5704.8 p79*
Miller, Mary 2; St. John, N.B., 1848 *5704.8 p47*
Miller, Mary 23; Quebec, 1856 *5704.8 p129*
Miller, Mary 23; St. John, N.B., 1864 *5704.8 p159*
Miller, Mary Ann; Philadelphia, 1865 *5704.8 p191*
Miller, Mary Ann 10; St. John, N.B., 1853 *5704.8 p100*
Miller, Mary Catherina 10 SEE Miller, John Adam
Miller, Mary Jane; Philadelphia, 1847 *53.26 p69*
  Relative:Ann
Miller, Mary Jane; Philadelphia, 1847 *5704.8 p1*
Miller, Matilda 20; St. John, N.B., 1864 *5704.8 p158*
Miller, Matilda 38; Kansas, 1873 *5240.1 p54*
Miller, Matty; New York, NY, 1811 *2859.11 p17*
Miller, Max; Arkansas, 1918 *95.2 p84*
Miller, Michael; Ohio, 1839 *9892.11 p30*
Miller, Michael 24; Pennsylvania, 1748 *2444 p194*
Miller, Michael 24; Pennsylvania, 1748 *2444 p195*
Miller, Michel; Quebec, 1821 *7603 p78*
Miller, Nancy 6; New York, NY, 1866 *5704.8 p212*
Miller, Nancy 21; St. John, N.B., 1855 *5704.8 p127*
Miller, Nicholas 34; Maryland, 1775 *1219.7 p260*
Miller, Oliver 2; Quebec, 1847 *5704.8 p30*
Miller, Peder Chris Pedersen; Arkansas, 1918 *95.2 p84*
Miller, Peggy; St. John, N.B., 1847 *5704.8 p9*
Miller, Peter; New York, 1832 *9892.11 p30*
Miller, Peter; New York, NY, 1837 *8582.1 p25*
Miller, Peter; Ohio, 1838 *9892.11 p30*
Miller, Peter; Wisconsin, n.d. *9675.7 p51*
Miller, Philip; North Carolina, 1818 *1639.20 p236*
Miller, Philip; Philadelphia, 1762 *9973.7 p37*
Miller, Philip 14 SEE Miller, John Adam
Miller, Phillip; Illinois, 1888 *5012.37 p60*
Miller, Rebecca SEE Miller, Andrew
Miller, Rebecca; Philadelphia, 1850 *5704.8 p59*
Miller, Rebecca 16; Philadelphia, 1857 *5704.8 p133*
Miller, Rebecca 19; Philadelphia, 1854 *5704.8 p117*
Miller, Richard; Virginia, 1638 *6219 p120*
Miller, Richard 15; West Indies, 1722 *3690.1 p156*
Miller, Richard 21; Jamaica, 1774 *1219.7 p184*
Miller, Richard 26; Philadelphia, 1774 *1219.7 p216*
Miller, Robert; New York, NY, 1811 *2859.11 p17*
Miller, Robert; Philadelphia, 1853 *5704.8 p108*
Miller, Robert; Quebec, 1847 *5704.8 p36*
Miller, Robert 3; Philadelphia, 1866 *5704.8 p209*
Miller, Robert 10; Quebec, 1864 *5704.8 p160*
Miller, Robert 19; St. John, N.B., 1855 *5704.8 p127*
Miller, Robert 50; St. John, N.B., 1866 *5704.8 p166*
Miller, Robert Johnstone; America, 1758-1784 *1639.20 p236*
Miller, Rody; Philadelphia, 1852 *5704.8 p96*
Miller, Rudolf 39; Kansas, 1883 *5240.1 p64*
Miller, Ruth; Quebec, 1847 *5704.8 p28*
Miller, S. H.; Washington, 1859-1920 *2872.1 p26*
Miller, Sally; New Orleans, 1849 *5704.8 p59*
Miller, Samuel; America, 1884 *1450.2 p102A*
Miller, Samuel; Austin, TX, 1886 *9777 p5*
Miller, Samuel; Charleston, SC, 1795 *1639.20 p236*
Miller, Samuel; South Carolina, 1788 *7119 p199*
Miller, Samuel 4; Quebec, 1847 *5704.8 p30*
Miller, Samuel 6; Quebec, 1847 *5704.8 p28*
Miller, Samuel 35; Kansas, 1899 *5240.1 p30*
Miller, Samuel 35; Kansas, 1899 *5240.1 p81*
Miller, Sarah; America, 1864 *5704.8 p188*
Miller, Sarah; Quebec, 1847 *5704.8 p30*
Miller, Sarah; Quebec, 1849 *5704.8 p56*
Miller, Sarah 15; St. John, N.B., 1855 *5704.8 p127*
Miller, Theophilus 19; Maryland, 1736 *3690.1 p156*
Miller, Thomas; Carolina, 1697 *1639.20 p236*
Miller, Thomas; Cincinnati, 1824 *8582.1 p51*
Miller, Thomas; Illinois, 1861 *2896.5 p28*
Miller, Thomas; New York, NY, 1816 *2859.11 p39*
Miller, Thomas; Philadelphia, 1847 *53.26 p69*
  Relative:Martha
  Relative:James 6

  Relative:John 4
  Relative:William 1
Miller, Thomas; Philadelphia, 1847 *5704.8 p21*
Miller, Thomas 9; New York, NY, 1866 *5704.8 p212*
Miller, Thomas 15; Quebec, 1864 *5704.8 p160*
Miller, Thomas 20; Jamaica, 1731 *3690.1 p156*
Miller, Thomas 26; Halifax, N.S., 1774 *1219.7 p213*
Miller, Thomas 31; Kansas, 1871 *5240.1 p51*
Miller, Valentin 17; America, 1839 *778.5 p383*
Miller, Valentine 60; America, 1839 *778.5 p383*
Miller, Veronica 16 SEE Miller, John Adam
Miller, Wilhelm M.; Indiana, 1869-1887 *8582 p21*
Miller, William; Georgia, 1775 *1219.7 p274*
  Wife:Isabella
Miller, William; Georgia, 1775 *1219.7 p274*
Miller, William; Illinois, 1892 *5012.40 p27*
Miller, Mrs. William; New York, NY, 1811 *2859.11 p17*
Miller, William; New York, NY, 1816 *2859.11 p39*
Miller, William; Ohio, 1842 *9892.11 p30*
Miller, William; Philadelphia, 1851 *5704.8 p80*
Miller, William; Philadelphia, 1866 *5704.8 p209*
Miller, William; Quebec, 1847 *5704.8 p29*
Miller, William; Washington, 1859-1920 *2872.1 p26*
Miller, William 1 SEE Miller, Thomas
Miller, William 1; Philadelphia, 1847 *5704.8 p21*
Miller, William 6; America, 1866 *5704.8 p204*
Miller, William 7; Philadelphia, 1866 *5704.8 p205*
Miller, William 18; St. John, N.B., 1862 *5704.8 p150*
Miller, William 21; Kansas, 1872 *5240.1 p53*
Miller, William 21; Quebec, 1856 *5704.8 p129*
Miller, William 24; Maryland, 1774 *1219.7 p211*
Miller, William 28; Massachusetts, 1860 *6410.32 p119*
Miller, William 29; Maryland, 1774 *1219.7 p230*
Miller, William 31; New Orleans, 1831 *778.5 p383*
Miller, William 45; St. John, N.B., 1867 *5704.8 p167*
Miller, William 60; St. John, N.B., 1855 *5704.8 p127*
Miller, William A.; Illinois, 1879 *2896.5 p28*
Miller, William S.; St. Louis, 1898 *5240.1 p31*
Milleson, Thomas 20; Jamaica, 1730 *3690.1 p157*
Millet, Mr. 24; Louisiana, 1820 *778.5 p383*
Millet, A. 26; Port uncertain, 1839 *778.5 p383*
Millet, Philippe 28; America, 1837 *778.5 p384*
Milley, Margaret 15; Massachusetts, 1849 *5881.1 p72*
Millgan, Bernard; New York, NY, 1815 *2859.11 p39*
Millican, Mary; New York, NY, 1864 *5704.8 p183*
Millich, Johann; Philadelphia, 1805 *2854 p45*
Millidge, John; Wisconsin, n.d. *9675.7 p51*
Millie, Mr. 22; New Orleans, 1837 *778.5 p384*
Milliet, Abraham 31; Halifax, N.S., 1752 *7074.6 p207*
  With family of 2
Milligan, Alexander D.; Ohio, 1845-1866 *9892.11 p30*
Milligan, Daniel; Philadelphia, 1852 *5704.8 p84*
Milligan, Elizabeth 4; Quebec, 1864 *5704.8 p162*
Milligan, Elizabeth 50; Quebec, 1864 *5704.8 p162*
Milligan, Henry G. 45; Kansas, 1885 *5240.1 p31*
Milligan, Henry G. 47; Kansas, 1885 *5240.1 p67*
Milligan, Jane 24; Quebec, 1864 *5704.8 p162*
Milligan, Margaret; St. John, N.B., 1852 *5704.8 p83*
Milligan, Margaret 26; Quebec, 1864 *5704.8 p162*
Milligan, Martin 29; Massachusetts, 1849 *5881.1 p71*
Milligan, Robert 20; Quebec, 1864 *5704.8 p162*
Milligan, Samuel 52; Quebec, 1864 *5704.8 p162*
Millikan, John; Philadelphia, 1850 *5704.8 p64*
Milliken, James; New York, NY, 1838 *8208.4 p85*
Milliken, Mary A.; New York, NY, 1864 *5704.8 p171*
Milliken, W.; New York, NY, 1816 *2859.11 p39*
Milliner, Francis 31; Maryland, 1774 *1219.7 p191*
Millington, Nathaniel 23; Maryland, 1774 *1219.7 p206*
Milliron, Chrisopp SEE Milliron, Christian
Milliron, Christian; Pennsylvania, 1747 *4779.3 p14*
  Relative:Chrisopp
Milliron, Jacob; Pennsylvania, 1765 *4779.3 p14*
Millison, John; New Jersey, 1834 *8208.4 p47*
Millner, Carl Albert 31; Harris Co., TX, 1898 *6254 p4*
Millner, James; San Francisco, 1850 *4914.15 p10*
Millner, James; San Francisco, 1850 *4914.15 p14*
Millon, . . .; Canada, 1776-1783 *9786 p29*
Millon, Jane; Philadelphia, 1847 *53.26 p69*
Millon, Jane; Philadelphia, 1847 *5704.8 p31*
Millone, Thomas; America, 1742 *4971 p56*
Millot, Daniel 19; Pennsylvania, 1738 *3690.1 p157*
Milloz, P. 35; New Orleans, 1829 *778.5 p384*
Mills, Alice; Virginia, 1634 *6219 p84*
Mills, Andrew; America, 1740 *4971 p73*
Mills, Andrew; Philadelphia, 1811 *53.26 p69*
Mills, Andrew; Philadelphia, 1811 *2859.11 p17*
Mills, Ann; Jamaica, 1731 *3690.1 p157*
Mills, Charles; Quebec, 1852 *5704.8 p98*
Mills, Charles 16; America, 1699 *2212 p25*
Mills, Daniel 18; Pennsylvania, 1731 *3690.1 p157*
Mills, David; Pennsylvania, 1750 *3690.1 p157*
Mills, David; Quebec, 1852 *5704.8 p87*
Mills, David; Quebec, 1852 *5704.8 p91*

Mills, Edward; New York, NY, 1840 ***8208.4*** *p108*
Mills, Elizabeth; South Carolina, 1775 ***1639.20*** *p237*
Mills, Esther 23; Maryland, 1774 ***1219.7*** *p206*
Mills, Fanny; Quebec, 1852 ***5704.8*** *p91*
Mills, Francis 19; Jamaica, 1730 ***3690.1*** *p157*
Mills, George; Philadelphia, 1852 ***5704.8*** *p88*
Mills, James 23; St. John, N.B., 1853 ***5704.8*** *p110*
Mills, James 48; Quebec, 1857 ***5704.8*** *p135*
Mills, Jane; Philadelphia, 1848 ***53.26*** *p69*
Mills, Jane; Philadelphia, 1848 ***5704.8*** *p46*
Mills, Jane; Quebec, 1850 ***5704.8*** *p63*
Mills, John; South Carolina, 1775 ***1639.20*** *p237*
Mills, John; Virginia, 1637 ***6219*** *p84*
Mills, John 12; New England, 1699 ***2212*** *p19*
Mills, John 12; Virginia, 1700 ***2212*** *p31*
Mills, John F.; Illinois, 1896 ***5012.40*** *p54*
Mills, Jon.; Virginia, 1642 ***6219*** *p192*
Mills, Jon.; Virginia, 1642 ***6219*** *p198*
Mills, Leonard 17; Maryland, 1751 ***1219.7*** *p3*
Mills, Leonard 17; Maryland, 1751 ***3690.1*** *p157*
Mills, Lewis; Virginia, 1642 ***6219*** *p195*
Mills, Martha; St. John, N.B., 1853 ***5704.8*** *p99*
Mills, Mary 16; America, 1704 ***2212*** *p41*
Mills, Mary 19; Jamaica, 1731 ***3690.1*** *p157*
Mills, Mary 19; Quebec, 1857 ***5704.8*** *p135*
Mills, Mary 23; Virginia, 1700 ***2212*** *p32*
Mills, Mary Ann 48; Quebec, 1857 ***5704.8*** *p135*
Mills, Maten 22; Virginia, 1774 ***1219.7*** *p238*
Mills, P. Benjamin; Iowa, 1866-1943 ***123.54*** *p34*
Mills, Peter 16; Windward Islands, 1722 ***3690.1*** *p157*
Mills, Richard 23; Philadelphia, 1774 ***1219.7*** *p217*
Mills, Robert; America, 1740 ***4971*** *p73*
Mills, Robert; New Orleans, 1848 ***5704.8*** *p48*
Mills, Robert; Quebec, 1825 ***7603*** *p88*
Mills, Robert; Quebec, 1852 ***5704.8*** *p91*
Mills, Robert 20; Maryland, 1729 ***3690.1*** *p157*
Mills, Robert 22; Maryland, 1730 ***3690.1*** *p157*
Mills, Robert 22; Maryland, 1774 ***1219.7*** *p221*
Mills, Robert 40; Philadelphia, 1803 ***53.26*** *p69*
Mills, Samuel 17; Quebec, 1857 ***5704.8*** *p135*
Mills, Simon 18; Jamaica, 1736 ***3690.1*** *p157*
Mills, Susan; Virginia, 1629 ***6219*** *p8*
Mills, Thomas 18; Maryland, 1774 ***1219.7*** *p213*
Mills, Thomas 22; Maryland, 1775 ***1219.7*** *p257*
Mills, Thomas 28; Jamaica, 1774 ***1219.7*** *p180*
Mills, William; America, 1738 ***4971*** *p13*
Millward, John; Arkansas, 1918 ***95.2*** *p84*
Millward, Joseph 30; Jamaica, 1735 ***3690.1*** *p157*
Millwood, Mr.; Quebec, 1815 ***9229.18*** *p80*
With wife
Milly, Margaret 35; Wilmington, DE, 1831 ***6508.3*** *p101*
Milly, Mary 22; Philadelphia, 1853 ***5704.8*** *p108*
Milne, Alec; Austin, TX, 1886 ***9777*** *p5*
Milne, Andrew 55; Charleston, SC, 1850 ***1639.20*** *p237*
Milne, Charles; South Carolina, 1772 ***1639.20*** *p237*
Milne, George; Illinois, 1894 ***5012.40*** *p54*
Milne, George; Kansas, 1880 ***5240.1*** *p31*
Milne, James; Illinois, 1889 ***2896.5*** *p28*
Milne, James; Pittsburgh, 1765 ***1219.7*** *p107*
Milne, James W.; Kansas, 1883 ***5240.1*** *p31*
Milne, John 55; South Carolina, 1850 ***1639.20*** *p237*
Milne, Peter 28; Jamaica, 1774 ***1219.7*** *p179*
Milne, Robert; Austin, TX, 1886 ***9777*** *p5*
Milner, Elizabeth 30; Nova Scotia, 1774 ***1219.7*** *p210*
Milner, Elizabeth 50; Nova Scotia, 1774 ***1219.7*** *p210*
Milner, James; America, 1759 ***1639.20*** *p237*
Milner, Jonathan 26; Nova Scotia, 1774 ***1219.7*** *p210*
Milner, Robert 33; Nova Scotia, 1774 ***1219.7*** *p210*
Milon, Charles 34; New Orleans, 1826 ***778.5*** *p384*
Milonas, Constantine; Arkansas, 1918 ***95.2*** *p84*
Milosavic, Stephen; Iowa, 1866-1943 ***123.54*** *p34*
Milosich, Laurence; Iowa, 1866-1943 ***123.54*** *p35*
Mils, Andrew; St. John, N.B., 1850 ***5704.8*** *p66*
Mils, Francis Ann; St. John, N.B., 1850 ***5704.8*** *p66*
Mils, William; St. John, N.B., 1850 ***5704.8*** *p66*
Milsteed, John 22; Virginia, 1774 ***1219.7*** *p201*
Milstrum, A. P.; Minneapolis, 1880-1886 ***6410.35*** *p60*
Miltner, Maria; Milwaukee, 1875 ***4719.30*** *p257*
With child
Milton, . . .; Canada, 1776-1783 ***9786*** *p29*
Milton, George 22; Baltimore, 1775 ***1219.7*** *p269*
Milton, George Abraham; Arkansas, 1918 ***95.2*** *p84*
Milton, Thomas 28; Baltimore, 1775 ***1219.7*** *p269*
Milton, Wm.; Virginia, 1638 ***6219*** *p122*
Miltsor, Louis; Iowa, 1866-1943 ***123.54*** *p35*
Milwright, Cheshir 23; America, 1699 ***2212*** *p29*
Mina, Jacob; Indiana, 1848 ***9117*** *p19*
Minck, Adam 28; America, 1839 ***778.5*** *p384*
Minden, Ernst Heinrich Christian; America, 1881 ***4610.10*** *p101*
Minegrand, Marie R. 25; New Orleans, 1821 ***778.5*** *p384*
Miner, Lawrence P.; New York, NY, 1840 ***8208.4*** *p109*
Mines, . . .; Canada, 1776-1783 ***9786*** *p29*
Minetes, Biddy; New York, NY, 1811 ***2859.11*** *p17*
Minetes, Francis; New York, NY, 1811 ***2859.11*** *p17*
Miney, George; Indiana, 1845 ***9117*** *p17*
Ming, Philipp; Wisconsin, n.d. ***9675.7*** *p51*
Mingay, John 44; Philadelphia, 1774 ***1219.7*** *p233*
Mingeaud, Francois 31; New Orleans, 1837 ***778.5*** *p384*
Minges, Simon 39; Kansas, 1884 ***5240.1*** *p65*
Mingo, . . .; Halifax, N.S., 1752 ***7074.6*** *p230*
Mingo, George; Halifax, N.S., 1752 ***7074.6*** *p226*
Mingo, Jean; Halifax, N.S., 1752 ***7074.6*** *p226*
Mingo, Jean; Halifax, N.S., 1752 ***7074.6*** *p230*
Mingo, Magdalena; New York, 1749 ***3652*** *p73*
Minick, Adam; Charleston, SC, 1775-1781 ***8582.2*** *p52*
Minicke, . . .; Canada, 1776-1783 ***9786*** *p29*
Minier, Ernst 20; America, 1854-1855 ***9162.6*** *p105*
Minifie, Charles; Virginia, 1643 ***6219*** *p206*
Minis, Catherine; New York, NY, 1816 ***2859.11*** *p39*
Minister, Mary; America, 1736 ***4971*** *p44*
Minister, Mary; America, 1736 ***4971*** *p45*
Minnabroker, Henry; New York, 1881 ***1450.2*** *p25B*
Minnehan, Ann 12; Massachusetts, 1849 ***5881.1*** *p62*
Minnehan, Johanna 60; Massachusetts, 1849 ***5881.1*** *p68*
Minnehan, Mary 16; Massachusetts, 1849 ***5881.1*** *p71*
Minnehan, Mary 22; Massachusetts, 1849 ***5881.1*** *p72*
Minners, Geo.; Virginia, 1647 ***6219*** *p241*
Minnette, Franz; Wisconsin, n.d. ***9675.7*** *p51*
Minnich, Georg; Kentucky, 1845 ***8582.3*** *p101*
Minnichio, Theodore 25; Arkansas, 1918 ***95.2*** *p84*
Minnigerode, Friedrich Ludwig von; Halifax, N.S., 1780 ***9786*** *p269*
Minnigerode, Friedrich Ludwig von; New York, 1776 ***9786*** *p269*
Minnilley, Robert 19; Virginia, 1720 ***3690.1*** *p158*
Minnis, Evlin 13; St. John, N.B., 1853 ***5704.8*** *p110*
Minnis, Fras.; New York, NY, 1816 ***2859.11*** *p39*
Minnis, J.P.; Illinois, 1861 ***7857*** *p5*
Minnis, William; Illinois, 1859 ***7857*** *p5*
Minnivan, Garrett 45; Massachusetts, 1849 ***5881.1*** *p67*
Minnokes, William; Virginia, 1639 ***6219*** *p151*
Minns, James 60; Boston, 1774 ***1219.7*** *p206*
Minns, James, Jr. 30; Boston, 1774 ***1219.7*** *p206*
Minolt, Melcher 22; Pennsylvania, 1753 ***2444*** *p188*
Minolt, Melcher 22; Pennsylvania, 1753 ***2444*** *p191*
Minoni, . . .; Canada, 1776-1783 ***9786*** *p29*
Minoni, Michel; Canada, 1776-1783 ***9786*** *p207A*
Minor, Katherine; Virginia, 1643 ***6219*** *p205*
Minos, George; Arkansas, 1918 ***95.2*** *p84*
Minosoler, Guiseppe; Iowa, 1866-1943 ***123.54*** *p35*
Minota, Tomas; Kansas, n.d. ***6013.40*** *p16*
Minphey, Samuel 15; Maryland, 1775 ***1219.7*** *p254*
Minsky, Aaron; Arkansas, 1918 ***95.2*** *p84*
Minst, Friedreich; South Carolina, 1788 ***7119*** *p200*
Minster, Wm.; Virginia, 1855 ***4626.16*** *p15*
Minten, George; Illinois, 1856 ***7857*** *p5*
Minten, William; Illinois, 1856 ***7857*** *p5*
Minter, Ann *SEE* Minter, Edward
Minter, David; Virginia, 1635 ***6219*** *p10*
Minter, Edward *SEE* Minter, Edward
Minter, Edward; Virginia, 1635 ***6219*** *p20*
*Wife:*Ann
*Son:*Edward
*Son:*John
Minter, Grace; Virginia, 1636 ***6219*** *p20*
Minter, John *SEE* Minter, Edward
Minter, Jon.; Virginia, 1635 ***6219*** *p27*
Minter, Jon.; Virginia, 1638 ***6219*** *p145*
Mintner, Maria; Milwaukee, 1875 ***4719.30*** *p257*
With child
Minton, David; Virginia, 1637 ***6219*** *p10*
Mintus, Antonina; America, 1895 ***7137*** *p169*
Mintus, Clement; America, 1891 ***7137*** *p169*
Mintzeng, Philipp; Charleston, SC, 1775-1781 ***8582.2*** *p52*
Mintzing, Philipp; Charleston, SC, 1766 ***8582.2*** *p65*
Mintzlaff, Chas F.; Wisconsin, n.d. ***9675.7*** *p51*
Mintzlaff, Herman; Wisconsin, n.d. ***9675.7*** *p51*
Minuit, Francoise 28; America, 1838 ***778.5*** *p384*
Minuit, Peter; New Netherland, 1630-1646 ***8582.2*** *p51*
Minvielle, Jean 23; Port uncertain, 1839 ***778.5*** *p384*
Minvielle, Jean 25; Port uncertain, 1839 ***778.5*** *p384*
Minvielle, Jean 44; New Orleans, 1839 ***778.5*** *p384*
Miok, Loues; Arkansas, 1918 ***95.2*** *p84*
Mirachane, Bryan; America, 1739 ***4971*** *p82*
Miraghan, Bryan; America, 1735-1743 ***4971*** *p79*
Miral, Guills 28; America, 1836 ***778.5*** *p384*
Miramond, Mr. 20; New Orleans, 1829 ***778.5*** *p384*
Miramond, Anne 23; New Orleans, 1829 ***778.5*** *p384*
Miramond, J. 35; New Orleans, 1829 ***778.5*** *p384*
Miranda, Donald Peter; Arkansas, 1918 ***95.2*** *p84*
Miranda, Francisco 40; Arizona, 1922 ***9228.40*** *p26*
Mire, Mathias; Pennsylvania, 1753 ***2444*** *p191*
Mirek, Jan 27; New York, 1912 ***9980.29*** *p62*
Miremont, Pierre 17; New Orleans, 1822 ***778.5*** *p385*
Mires, Andrew; Ohio, 1840 ***9892.11*** *p30*
Mires, Frederick; Illinois, 1866 ***2896.5*** *p28*
Mischky, . . .; Canada, 1776-1783 ***9786*** *p43*
Misegades, Fritz; New York, NY, 1926 ***3455.4*** *p81*
Mishel, Konstanti 22; New York, 1912 ***9980.29*** *p64*
Mishew, Henry; Virginia, 1637 ***6219*** *p113*
Misiak, Karol 26; New York, 1912 ***9980.29*** *p63*
Misle, Luke; Virginia, 1635 ***6219*** *p12*
Missi, Giralomo 28; America, 1836 ***778.5*** *p385*
Mission, Jno.; Virginia, 1646 ***6219*** *p239*
Missuk, John; Arkansas, 1918 ***95.2*** *p84*
Mistre, Mr. 52; America, 1838 ***778.5*** *p385*
Mistrot, Jacques 19; New Orleans, 1839 ***778.5*** *p385*
Mitaud, Vespre 23; New Orleans, 1826 ***778.5*** *p385*
Mitcham, Christopher 25; Maryland, 1775 ***1219.7*** *p273*
Mitchel, David 38; Jamaica, 1776 ***1219.7*** *p281*
Mitchel, James; Maryland, 1767 ***8894.2*** *p55*
Mitchel, James; New York, NY, 1816 ***2859.11*** *p39*
Mitchel, John 21; Maryland, 1775 ***1219.7*** *p257*
Mitchel, John 23; Virginia, 1774 ***1219.7*** *p186*
Mitchel, Samuel 24; Virginia, 1774 ***1219.7*** *p186*
Mitchell, Abraham; Ohio, 1840 ***9892.11*** *p30*
Mitchell, Alexander; Philadelphia, 1865 ***5704.8*** *p191*
Mitchell, Alexander 19; St. John, N.B., 1854 ***5704.8*** *p121*
Mitchell, Alexander 32; St. John, N.B., 1865 ***5704.8*** *p165*
Mitchell, Alexander B.; Iowa, 1866-1943 ***123.54*** *p35*
Mitchell, Alexr.; America, 1807 ***8894.2*** *p55*
*Wife:*Eliza Kearsley
Mitchell, Andrew; Charleston, SC, 1796 ***1639.20*** *p237*
Mitchell, Andrew; Quebec, 1847 ***5704.8*** *p38*
Mitchell, Andrew 13; St. John, N.B., 1847 ***5704.8*** *p20*
Mitchell, Ann; St. John, N.B., 1847 ***5704.8*** *p10*
Mitchell, Ann Campbell 26 *SEE* Mitchell, Robert
Mitchell, Ann Hopkin *SEE* Mitchell, James
Mitchell, Ann Jane; Philadelphia, 1852 ***5704.8*** *p88*
Mitchell, Anne *SEE* Mitchell, Thomas
Mitchell, Anne; Philadelphia, 1849 ***5704.8*** *p52*
Mitchell, Annie; Philadelphia, 1865 ***5704.8*** *p190*
Mitchell, Antonjja; Iowa, 1866-1943 ***123.54*** *p71*
Mitchell, Archibald; New York, NY, 1850 ***6013.19*** *p74*
Mitchell, Bell 4; St. John, N.B., 1847 ***5704.8*** *p25*
Mitchell, Catherine; Quebec, 1847 ***5704.8*** *p38*
Mitchell, Catherine 6; Quebec, 1864 ***5704.8*** *p162*
Mitchell, Catherine 20; St. John, N.B., 1860 ***5704.8*** *p144*
Mitchell, Catherine 40; Quebec, 1864 ***5704.8*** *p162*
Mitchell, Charles; New York, NY, 1816 ***2859.11*** *p39*
Mitchell, Christian 3 *SEE* Mitchell, Thomas
Mitchell, Christian 3; Philadelphia, 1849 ***5704.8*** *p52*
Mitchell, Colin; South Carolina, 1805 ***1639.20*** *p238*
Mitchell, David; St. John, N.B., 1853 ***5704.8*** *p99*
Mitchell, David; South Carolina, 1767 ***1639.20*** *p238*
Mitchell, David 48; Philadelphia, 1855 ***5704.8*** *p124*
Mitchell, Edw.; Virginia, 1643 ***6219*** *p205*
Mitchell, Eliza; St. John, N.B., 1847 ***5704.8*** *p19*
Mitchell, Eliza 7; St. John, N.B., 1847 ***5704.8*** *p20*
Mitchell, Eliza Kearsley *SEE* Mitchell, Alexr.
Mitchell, Elizabeth 10; Quebec, 1853 ***5704.8*** *p104*
Mitchell, Elizabeth 35; Philadelphia, 1860 ***5704.8*** *p145*
Mitchell, Ellen 8 *SEE* Mitchell, Thomas
Mitchell, Ellen 8; Philadelphia, 1849 ***5704.8*** *p52*
Mitchell, George; Philadelphia, 1768 ***9973.7*** *p40*
Mitchell, George; St. John, N.B., 1847 ***5704.8*** *p10*
Mitchell, George; South Carolina, 1749 ***1639.20*** *p238*
Mitchell, George 8; St. John, N.B., 1847 ***5704.8*** *p25*
Mitchell, George 13; St. John, N.B., 1847 ***5704.8*** *p19*
Mitchell, Hanora 40; Kansas, 1873 ***5240.1*** *p54*
Mitchell, Henry; Quebec, 1847 ***5704.8*** *p28*
Mitchell, Henry 11; St. John, N.B., 1847 ***5704.8*** *p10*
Mitchell, Henry 18; Antigua (Antego), 1734 ***3690.1*** *p158*
Mitchell, Hugh; America, 1863-1871 ***5704.8*** *p199*
Mitchell, Isabella 11; St. John, N.B., 1847 ***5704.8*** *p19*
Mitchell, James *SEE* Mitchell, John
Mitchell, James; Austin, TX, 1886 ***9777*** *p5*
Mitchell, James; Baltimore, 1837 ***8893*** *p265*
*Wife:*Ann Hopkin
Mitchell, James; Iowa, 1866-1943 ***123.54*** *p35*
Mitchell, James; Philadelphia, 1847 ***5704.8*** *p13*
Mitchell, James; Quebec, 1849 ***5704.8*** *p50*
Mitchell, James; St. John, N.B., 1847 ***5704.8*** *p10*
Mitchell, James; St. John, N.B., 1847 ***5704.8*** *p20*
Mitchell, James; Virginia, 1638 ***6219*** *p147*
Mitchell, James 4; St. John, N.B., 1847 ***5704.8*** *p19*
Mitchell, James 22; Philadelphia, 1803 ***53.26*** *p69*
Mitchell, Jane; Philadelphia, 1851 ***5704.8*** *p70*
Mitchell, Jane; St. John, N.B., 1847 ***5704.8*** *p8*
Mitchell, Jane; St. John, N.B., 1847 ***5704.8*** *p25*
Mitchell, Jane 8; Quebec, 1864 ***5704.8*** *p162*
Mitchell, Jane 10; St. John, N.B., 1847 ***5704.8*** *p25*
Mitchell, Jane 13; Quebec, 1853 ***5704.8*** *p104*
Mitchell, Jas.; Philadelphia, 1816 ***2859.11*** *p39*
Mitchell, John; America, 1871 ***1450.2*** *p102A*

Mitchell, John; New York, NY, 1834 8208.4 p50
Mitchell, John; Ohio, 1844 9892.11 p30
Mitchell, John; Philadelphia, 1847 53.26 p69
*Relative:*James
Mitchell, John; Philadelphia, 1847 5704.8 p13
Mitchell, John; St. John, N.B., 1847 5704.8 p10
Mitchell, John; St. John, N.B., 1847 5704.8 p19
Mitchell, John; St. John, N.B., 1847 5704.8 p20
Mitchell, John; St. John, N.B., 1847 5704.8 p25
Mitchell, John 4; Quebec, 1864 5704.8 p162
Mitchell, John 4; St. John, N.B., 1847 5704.8 p20
Mitchell, John 6; St. John, N.B., 1847 5704.8 p25
Mitchell, John 15; Jamaica, 1739 3690.1 p158
Mitchell, John 19; Philadelphia, 1853 5704.8 p113
Mitchell, John 20; Maryland, 1727 3690.1 p158
Mitchell, John 29; St. John, N.B., 1866 5704.8 p167
Mitchell, John E.; Iowa, 1866-1943 123.54 p35
Mitchell, John O. 28; Kansas, 1884 5240.1 p65
Mitchell, Jon.; Virginia, 1636 6219 p32
Mitchell, Jonas; Wisconsin, n.d. 9675.7 p51
Mitchell, Joseph 8; St. John, N.B., 1847 5704.8 p10
Mitchell, Josiah; Colorado, 1880 9678.2 p126
Mitchell, Lawrence 36; Massachusetts, 1849 5881.1 p70
Mitchell, Levi 40; California, 1872 2769.6 p5
Mitchell, Lilly; St. John, N.B., 1848 5704.8 p43
Mitchell, Margaret; Quebec, 1850 5704.8 p63
Mitchell, Margaret; St. John, N.B., 1847 5704.8 p20
Mitchell, Margaret 2; Quebec, 1847 5704.8 p38
Mitchell, Margaret 16; Quebec, 1864 5704.8 p162
Mitchell, Mark 19; Virginia, 1774 1219.7 p186
Mitchell, Marshall; St. John, N.B., 1847 5704.8 p20
Mitchell, Martin; New York, NY, 1816 2859.11 p39
Mitchell, Mary; America, 1737 4971 p74
Mitchell, Mary; Philadelphia, 1847 53.26 p69
Mitchell, Mary; Philadelphia, 1847 5704.8 p1
Mitchell, Mary; Philadelphia, 1848 53.26 p69
Mitchell, Mary; Philadelphia, 1848 5704.8 p45
Mitchell, Mary; Quebec, 1850 5704.8 p63
Mitchell, Mary; St. John, N.B., 1847 5704.8 p19
Mitchell, Mary 9; St. John, N.B., 1847 5704.8 p19
Mitchell, Mary 11; Quebec, 1864 5704.8 p162
Mitchell, Mary 25; Quebec, 1858 5704.8 p140
Mitchell, Mary Ann; Philadelphia, 1849 5704.8 p52
Mitchell, Mary Anne *SEE* Mitchell, Thomas
Mitchell, Mary Jane 6 *SEE* Mitchell, Thomas
Mitchell, Mary Jane 6; Philadelphia, 1849 5704.8 p52
Mitchell, Matilda 9 mos; St. John, N.B., 1847 5704.8 p25
Mitchell, Michael; Ohio, 1843 9892.11 p30
Mitchell, Rebecca; St. John, N.B., 1847 5704.8 p19
Mitchell, Rebecca 10; St. John, N.B., 1847 5704.8 p20
Mitchell, Richard; New York, NY, 1839 8208.4 p91
Mitchell, Richard 15; Philadelphia, 1774 1219.7 p232
Mitchell, Richard 19; Jamaica, 1736 3690.1 p158
Mitchell, Robert; Quebec, 1850 5704.8 p63
Mitchell, Robert; St. John, N.B., 1847 5704.8 p10
Mitchell, Robert; Washington, 1859-1920 2872.1 p26
Mitchell, Robert 19; Maryland, 1723 3690.1 p158
Mitchell, Robert 26; Wilmington, NC, 1774 1639.20 p238
*Wife:*Ann Campbell 26
Mitchell, Samuel; New Orleans, 1849 5704.8 p59
Mitchell, Samuel; New York, NY, 1816 2859.11 p39
Mitchell, Samuel, Jr.; New York, NY, 1840 8208.4 p105
Mitchell, Sarah *SEE* Mitchell, William
Mitchell, Sarah; Philadelphia, 1847 5704.8 p13
Mitchell, Sarah 6; St. John, N.B., 1847 5704.8 p10
Mitchell, Sarah 12 *SEE* Mitchell, Thomas
Mitchell, Sarah 12; Philadelphia, 1849 5704.8 p52
Mitchell, Sarah 25; Philadelphia, 1804 53.26 p69
Mitchell, Susan; Philadelphia, 1853 5704.8 p108
Mitchell, Tho.; Virginia, 1637 6219 p113
Mitchell, Tho.; Virginia, 1638 6219 p118
Mitchell, Thomas; Charleston, SC, 1827 1639.20 p238
Mitchell, Thomas; New York, NY, 1834 8208.4 p30
Mitchell, Thomas; North Carolina, 1803 1639.20 p238
Mitchell, Thomas; Philadelphia, 1849 53.26 p69
*Relative:*Mary Anne
*Relative:*Sarah 12
*Relative:*Ellen 8
*Relative:*Mary Jane 6
*Relative:*Christian 3
*Relative:*Anne
Mitchell, Thomas; Philadelphia, 1849 5704.8 p52
Mitchell, Thomas; Philadelphia, 1851 5704.8 p80
Mitchell, Thomas; Quebec, 1850 5704.8 p63
Mitchell, Thomas 13; St. John, N.B., 1847 5704.8 p10
Mitchell, Thomas 19; Quebec, 1864 5704.8 p162
Mitchell, Thomas 23; Dominica, 1773 1219.7 p170
Mitchell, Thomas 27; Jamaica, 1739 3690.1 p158
Mitchell, Thomas 36; Pennsylvania, 1731 3690.1 p158
Mitchell, Thomas 40; Quebec, 1864 5704.8 p162
Mitchell, William; Arkansas, 1918 95.2 p84
Mitchell, William; Brunswick, NC, 1775 1639.20 p238
With wife
With children
Mitchell, William; Charleston, SC, 1820 1639.20 p238
Mitchell, William; New York, NY, 1834 8208.4 p43
Mitchell, William; Philadelphia, 1847 53.26 p69
*Relative:*Sarah
Mitchell, William; Philadelphia, 1847 5704.8 p13
Mitchell, William; Philadelphia, 1852 5704.8 p85
Mitchell, William; Quebec, 1850 5704.8 p63
Mitchell, William; St. John, N.B., 1847 5704.8 p25
Mitchell, William 9 mos; Quebec, 1847 5704.8 p38
Mitchell, William 20; Philadelphia, 1803 53.26 p69
Mitchell, William 21; Philadelphia, 1775 1219.7 p258
Mitchell, William 22; Maryland, 1731 3690.1 p158
Mitchell, William 28; Maryland, 1773 1219.7 p172
Mitchell, William 28; St. John, N.B., 1862 5704.8 p150
Mitchell, William John; St. John, N.B., 1847 5704.8 p19
Mitchell, Wm.; Virginia, 1636 6219 p74
Mitchell, Wm.; Virginia, 1637 6219 p180
Mitchener, Mary 33; Jamaica, 1730 3690.1 p158
Mitchinson, William 30; Norfolk, VA, 1774 1219.7 p222
Mite, Samuel; New York, NY, 1816 2859.11 p39
Mithcell, Mary 13; Quebec, 1847 5704.8 p6
Mithoffe, Henry; America, 1852 1450.2 p102A
Mitner, Robert 20; Philadelphia, 1774 1219.7 p223
Mitsch, Marg. 15; America, 1853 9162.7 p15
Mitson, John 21; Virginia, 1774 1219.7 p244
Mittage, John Christian; America, 1836 1450.2 p102A
Mittchell, . . .; Canada, 1776-1783 9786 p29
Mittelberger, Gottlieb; Pennsylvania, 1750 2444 p139
Mittelberger, Gottlieb; Pennsylvania, 1750 2444 p219
Mittendorf, Max; America, 1900 8125.8 p438
Mittensteiner, Matthias 41; Georgia, 1734 9332 p327
Mitterecker, Joseph; Georgia, 1738 9332 p319
Mittmann, Charles; New York, 1890 1450.2 p25B
Mitton, John 22; Nova Scotia, 1774 1219.7 p209
Mitz, Solomon; Arkansas, 1918 95.2 p84
Mitzel, Karl; Alberta, n.d. 5262 p58
Miun, George 29; Port uncertain, 1838 778.5 p385
M'Kenaor, Lieut.; Quebec, 1815 9229.18 p77
M'Kenzie, Mr.; Quebec, 1815 9229.18 p74
M'Kenzie, Mr.; Quebec, 1815 9229.18 p81
Mkoz, Alexander; Arkansas, 1918 95.2 p84
Mladan, Milos; Arkansas, 1918 95.2 p84
M'Lean, Mr.; Quebec, 1815 9229.18 p76
M'Lean, Mr.; Quebec, 1815 9229.18 p77
Mlodzianowski, Edward; New York, 1831 4606 p175
M'Murray, Henry; Ohio, 1839 9892.11 p34
Mniszek, . . .; New York, 1831 4606 p175
Moad, James 22; Barbados, 1735 3690.1 p158
Moairn, Lewis 19; America, 1832 778.5 p385
Moairn, Peter 18; America, 1832 778.5 p385
Moakley, Edward; West Virginia, 1871 9788.3 p17
Moan, Ann; Quebec, 1847 5704.8 p18
Moan, Catherine 8; Quebec, 1847 5704.8 p18
Moan, Felix; Baltimore, 1828 1450.2 p102A
Moan, James; New York, NY, 1834 8208.4 p48
Moan, James; Quebec, 1847 5704.8 p18
Moan, Michael 3; Quebec, 1847 5704.8 p18
Moan, Patrick 12; Quebec, 1847 5704.8 p18
Moarain, M. 32; Port uncertain, 1836 778.5 p385
Moascomi, James 22; Arkansas, 1918 95.2 p84
Moawad, Abraham; Washington, 1859-1920 2872.1 p26
Moawad, Ely; Washington, 1859-1920 2872.1 p26
Moawad, John; Washington, 1859-1920 2872.1 p26
Moawad, Joseph; Washington, 1859-1920 2872.1 p26
Moawad, Moawad; Washington, 1859-1920 2872.1 p26
Moawad, Rosa; Washington, 1859-1920 2872.1 p26
Moawad, Sarah; Washington, 1859-1920 2872.1 p26
Moberry, Sarah; Quebec, 1850 5704.8 p66
Moblet, . . .; Port uncertain, 1839 778.5 p385
Moblet, Mme.; Port uncertain, 1839 778.5 p385
Moblet, Mr.; Port uncertain, 1839 778.5 p385
Moch, Peter; Alberta, n.d. 5262 p58
Mochan, Elizabeth; New York, NY, 1816 2859.11 p39
Moche, . . .; Canada, 1776-1783 9786 p43
Mochel, Susanna; Cincinnati, 1844-1855 8582.2 p45
Mochinfost, Anna Maria 6 *SEE* Mochinfost, Michael
Mochinfost, Christina 4 *SEE* Mochinfost, Michael
Mochinfost, John George 17 *SEE* Mochinfost, Michael
Mochinfost, Joseph 14 *SEE* Mochinfost, Michael
Mochinfost, Michael; South Carolina, 1752-1753 3689.17 p22
With wife
*Relative:*Michael 23
*Relative:*John George 17
*Relative:*Joseph 14
*Relative:*Thomas 11
*Relative:*Anna Maria 6
*Relative:*Christina 4
Mochinfost, Michael 23 *SEE* Mochinfost, Michael
Mochinfost, Thomas 11 *SEE* Mochinfost, Michael
Mock, Ernest; New York, NY, 1891 1450.2 p26B
Mock, Hans Jorg; Pennsylvania, 1752 2444 p187
Mockes, Walter; Wisconsin, n.d. 9675.7 p51
Mockiewicz, John; Wisconsin, n.d. 9675.7 p51
Mockley, Garret; Wisconsin, n.d. 9675.7 p51
Mockus, Anton; Wisconsin, n.d. 9675.7 p51
Mockus, John; Wisconsin, n.d. 9675.7 p51
Mockus, Joseph; Wisconsin, n.d. 9675.7 p51
Mockus, Paul; Wisconsin, n.d. 9675.7 p51
Mode, Elizabeth Parr; Pennsylvania, 1682 4961 p5
Mode, Jane 15 *SEE* Mode, Marjory
Mode, Marjory 11; Pennsylvania, 1682 4961 p5
*Sister:*Jane 15
Modell, . . .; Canada, 1776-1783 9786 p43
Moderen, James; Charleston, SC, 1808 1639.20 p239
Modrach, Christian Heinrich; Quebec, 1776 9786 p260
Modrow, David; Washington, 1859-1920 2872.1 p26
Moe, Einar; Arkansas, 1918 95.2 p85
Moe, Einar; Arkansas, 1918 95.2 p123
Moe, Martin Andreas; Arkansas, 1918 95.2 p85
Moe, Sverre; Colorado, 1904 9678.2 p126
Moeck, George H. 26; Arkansas, 1918 95.2 p85
Moedtke, Baron von; America, 1777-1778 8582.2 p67
Moegenburg, Fredinand; Wisconsin, n.d. 9675.7 p51
Moegenburg, Fredrick; Wisconsin, n.d. 9675.7 p51
Moehler, Elisabetha Hayn *SEE* Moehler, Johann Martin
Moehler, Johann Martin; Pennsylvania, 1754 2444 p192
*Wife:*Elisabetha Hayn
Moehlmann, Wilhelm; Trenton, NJ, 1776 8137 p11
Moehring, Friederich; Kentucky, 1840-1845 8582.3 p100
Moehring, John Michael; New York, 1761 3652 p87
Moehring, M. E.; America, 1828 8582.2 p60
Moehring, M. E.; New York, NY, 1869-1887 8582 p21
Moehrmann, John B.; America, 1831 8582.2 p28
Moelk, Fred; Wisconsin, n.d. 9675.7 p51
Moelk, Jacob; Wisconsin, n.d. 9675.7 p51
Moeller, Bernhard; America, 1847 8582.3 p46
Moeller, Bernhard; America, 1872-1874 8582.1 p24
Moeller, Charles; Wisconsin, n.d. 9675.7 p51
Moeller, Ernst; Illinois, 1870 2896.5 p28
Moeller, Fred; Baltimore, 1893 1450.2 p26B
Moeller, Henry 20; New York, 1865 3702.7 p212
Moeller, John; Illinois, 1871 5012.39 p25
Moeller, John Henry; New York, 1743 3652 p59
*Wife:*Rosina
Moeller, Joseph; Philadelphia, 1742 3652 p56
Moeller, Marten; Pennsylvania, 1767 2444 p192
Moeller, Rosina *SEE* Moeller, John Henry
Moeller, Wilhelm Christian; Canada, 1780 9786 p268
Moeller, Wilhelm Christian; New York, 1776 9786 p268
Moeller, William; Illinois, 1870 2896.5 p28
Moellhaus, Johannes; Ohio, 1798 8582.2 p54
Moellmann, Wilhelm; Cincinnati, 1873 8582.1 p53
Moen, Imbert; Colorado, 1905 9678.2 p127
Moen, James; New York, NY, 1834 8208.4 p48
Moench, Heinrich; Pennsylvania, 1751 4525 p232
Moench, Johan Henrich; Pennsylvania, 1752 4525 p232
Moenkedick, Heinrich; America, 1849 8582.3 p46
Moenning, Franz; America, 1846 8582.3 p46
Moering, Nicholas 53; Kansas, 1892 5240.1 p77
Moerlein, Christian; Cincinnati, 1869-1887 8582 p21
Moerlein, Christian; Cincinnati, 1870 8582.3 p87
Moesch, Henry W.; New York, 1883 1450.2 p26B
Moeschler, John, Jr.; Wisconsin, n.d. 9675.7 p51
Moeser, Heinrich; America, 1852 8582.3 p46
Moeser, Johann Christian; America, 1836 8582.3 p46
Moeser, William; New York, NY, 1838 8208.4 p66
Moesle, Johann Jacob; Cincinnati, 1848 8582.1 p53
Moessner, Elisabetha *SEE* Moessner, Hans Jacob
Moessner, Hans Jacob; Pennsylvania, 1746-1780 2444 p192
*Wife:*Elisabetha
*Child:*Mattheus
Moessner, Maria Barbara; Pennsylvania, 1753 2444 p183
Moessner, Mattheus *SEE* Moessner, Hans Jacob
Moessner, Rosina; Pennsylvania, 1752 2444 p219
Moffat, Mr.; Quebec, 1815 9229.18 p81
Moffat, Andrew; Charleston, SC, 1820 1639.20 p239
Moffat, Edward; New York, NY, 1816 2859.11 p39
Moffat, James; Carolina, 1684 1639.20 p239
Moffat, Janet 70; South Carolina, 1850 1639.20 p239
*Relative:*Keith S. 30
Moffat, John; New York, NY, 1815 2859.11 p39
Moffat, Keith S. 30 *SEE* Moffat, Janet
Moffat, Robert 14; Quebec, 1858 5704.8 p140
Moffat, William; New York, NY, 1815 2859.11 p39
Moffatt, James 20; Massachusetts, 1848 5881.1 p70
Moffatt, James 24; Massachusetts, 1848 5881.1 p68
Moffatt, Margaret; Philadelphia, 1853 5704.8 p101
Moffatt, Samuel J.; Washington, 1859-1920 2872.1 p26
Moffet, Andrew 10; Quebec, 1847 5704.8 p17
Moffet, James 7; Quebec, 1847 5704.8 p17
Moffet, Martha; Quebec, 1847 5704.8 p17

Moffet, William; Quebec, 1847 5704.8 p17
Moffiee, Mr. 28; New Orleans, 1839 778.5 p385
Moffiee, Mrs. 18; New Orleans, 1839 778.5 p385
Moffit, John; New York, NY, 1811 2859.11 p17
Moffit, Margaret; New York, NY, 1811 2859.11 p17
Moffitt, Charles; Philadelphia, 1867 5704.8 p216
Moffitt, Eliza 22; Massachusetts, 1849 5881.1 p66
Moffitt, John; Colorado, 1904 9678.2 p127
Moffitt, John; Philadelphia, 1864 5704.8 p174
Moffitt, John; Philadelphia, 1866 5704.8 p205
Moffitt, Sterling; Arkansas, 1918 95.2 p85
Mog, Marg. 76; America, 1895 1763 p40D
Mogarty, Tho's 25; Massachusetts, 1849 5881.1 p76
Mogdridge, Hannah; Pennsylvania, 1682 4962 p153
Mogensen, Peter; Illinois, 1896 5012.40 p54
Moggia, Bartholomew; New York, NY, 1836 8208.4 p12
Moghes, Miss 6; New Orleans, 1839 778.5 p386
Moghes, Miss 12; New Orleans, 1839 778.5 p386
Moghes, Mr. 16; New Orleans, 1839 778.5 p386
Moghes, Ms. 28; New Orleans, 1839 778.5 p386
Mogie, Jane; Philadelphia, 1847 53.26 p69
Mogie, Jane; Philadelphia, 1847 5704.8 p24
Mogl, . . .; Canada, 1776-1783 9786 p29
Mogniau, C. 18; New Orleans, 1831 778.5 p386
Mohan, Ann 6; Massachusetts, 1848 5881.1 p62
Mohan, Bridget 12; Massachusetts, 1848 5881.1 p63
Mohan, James Joseph; Arkansas, 1918 95.2 p85
Mohan, Joseph 1; Massachusetts, 1848 5881.1 p68
Mohan, Judith 34; Massachusetts, 1848 5881.1 p68
Mohan, Mac 50; Massachusetts, 1849 5881.1 p71
Mohan, Mary; St. John, N.B., 1847 5704.8 p26
Mohan, Mary 3; Massachusetts, 1848 5881.1 p70
Mohan, Michael; St. John, N.B., 1852 5704.8 p95
Mohan, Patrick; America, 1739 4971 p25
Mohan, Rose 9; Massachusetts, 1848 5881.1 p75
Moher, David 25; Massachusetts, 1849 5881.1 p65
Mohill, Ellenor; America, 1742 4971 p56
Mohler, Martin; Pennsylvania, 1767 2444 p192
Mohlin, August; Minneapolis, 1882-1887 6410.35 p60
Mohlin, B. R.; Minneapolis, 1885-1887 6410.35 p61
Mohlmann, Mr.; Illinois, 1800-1854 4610.10 p66
Mohlmann, Caroline; Illinois, 1854 4610.10 p66
With 3 children
Mohlmann, Heinrich 15; America, 1872 4610.10 p96
Mohlmann, Louise 19; America, 1872 4610.10 p96
Mohlmeyer, Ernst Heinrich August; America, 1857 4610.10 p117
Mohn, Frederick; New York, NY, 1836 8208.4 p18
Mohonney, Dennis; Virginia, 1635 6219 p4
Mohony, Ellenor; America, 1739 4971 p47
Mohr, . . .; Ohio, 1843 8582.1 p51
Mohr, Anna Barbara Horber *SEE* Mohr, Jacob
Mohr, Carl 25; New York, NY, 1857 9831.14 p154
Mohr, Clemens; Wisconsin, n.d. 9675.7 p51
Mohr, Gustavus 28?; California, 1866 3840.2 p18
Mohr, Harman; Philadelphia, 1760 9973.7 p35
Mohr, Jacob; America, 1743-1800 2444 p193
*Wife:*Anna Barbara Horber
*Child:*Johanna
Mohr, Jacob; America, 1848 1450.2 p103A
Mohr, Jacob; Pennsylvania, 1749 2444 p193
Mohr, Jacob; Pennsylvania, 1754 2444 p193
Mohr, Jacob; Pennsylvania, 1765 2444 p193
Mohr, Johan George; Virginia, 1775 1219.7 p275
Mohr, Johanna *SEE* Mohr, Jacob
Mohr, John; Washington, 1859-1920 2872.1 p26
Mohr, Michel 24; Kansas, 1893 5240.1 p31
Mohr, Michel 24; Kansas, 1893 5240.1 p79
Mohr, Paul; America, 1848 8582.3 p46
Mohr, Rudolph; Wisconsin, n.d. 9675.7 p52
Mohring, von; Quebec, 1778 9786 p267
Mohrmann, Anna M. E. Diekmann *SEE* Mohrmann, Berend Heinrich
Mohrmann, Berend Heinrich; America, 1831 4815.7 p92
*Wife:*Anna M. E. Diekmann
Mohrmann, Henry; Wisconsin, n.d. 9675.7 p52
Moia, John; Iowa, 1866-1943 123.54 p35
Moilanen, Simon; Washington, 1859-1920 2872.1 p26
Moilot, Grigoru; Arkansas, 1918 95.2 p85
Moir, Alec; Austin, TX, 1886 9777 p5
Moir, Andrew 21; Maryland, 1774 1219.7 p193
Moir, Geo.; Austin, TX, 1886 9777 p5
Moir, James; North Carolina, 1766 1639.20 p239
Moir, James 22; Maryland, 1774 1219.7 p193
Moir, Jane 15; Tortola, 1773 1219.7 p172
Moirison, Margaret; St. John, N.B., 1848 5704.8 p43
Moiser, . . .; Pennsylvania, n.d. 2444 p189
Molan, James 17; Maryland, 1774 1219.7 p208
Moland, William 21; Maryland, 1774 1219.7 p224
Moldenhauer, Carl F.; Wisconsin, n.d. 9675.7 p52
Moldenhauer, Carl Freiderich; Wisconsin, n.d. 9675.7 p52
Moldenhauer, Fredrick; Wisconsin, n.d. 9675.7 p52
Moldenhauer, Michael; Wisconsin, n.d. 9675.7 p52
Mole, William; Wisconsin, n.d. 9675.7 p52
Molesson, . . .; New York, 1831 4606 p175
Moley, Carlo; Arkansas, 1918 95.2 p85
Molicnick, Martin; Wisconsin, n.d. 9675.7 p52
Molier, Mr. 30; New Orleans, 1839 778.5 p386
Molin, Axel Theodore 24; Arkansas, 1918 95.2 p85
Molin, J. P.; Minneapolis, 1879-1880 6410.35 p61
Molinaro, Domenico; Arkansas, 1918 95.2 p85
Moline, R.W.; Iowa, 1866-1943 123.54 p35
Molineau, James; New York, NY, 1811 2859.11 p17
Molineaux, John; California, 1863 3840.2 p18
Molino, Mirano 38; Arizona, 1890 2764.35 p47
Molins, Peter C. 25; Louisiana, 1820 778.5 p386
Molison, Thomas 21; Maryland, 1730 3690.1 p291
Molithor, . . .; Canada, 1776-1783 9786 p29
Molitor, . . .; Cincinnati, 1837-1838 8582.1 p45
Molitor, Mr.; Pennsylvania, 1749 2444 p193
Molitor, Adam; Pennsylvania, 1771 2444 p193
Molitor, Anna Hochwegger; New York, NY, 1831-1833 8582.3 p46
*Husband:*Stephan
Molitor, Jean; Wisconsin, n.d. 9675.7 p52
Molitor, John T.; Wisconsin, n.d. 9675.7 p52
Molitor, Peter; Wisconsin, n.d. 9675.7 p52
Molitor, Stephan *SEE* Molitor, Anna Hochwegger
Molitor, Stephan; Cincinnati, 1788-1848 8582.3 p89
Molitor, Stephan; Cincinnati, 1788-1848 8582.3 p90
Molitor, Stephan; Ohio, 1843 8582.1 p51
Molitor, Stephen; America, 1830 8582.1 p24
Moll, John; Philadelphia, 1759 9973.7 p34
Moll, Wendolin; Colorado, 1886 9678.2 p127
Mollan, Hugh; New York, NY, 1816 2859.11 p39
Mollaun, Anton; Indiana, 1869-1887 8582 p21
Molle, . . .; Canada, 1776-1783 9786 p29
Mollenhauer, Heinrich; Illinois, 1846 8582.2 p51
Mollenkopf, John Jacob; America, 1826 1450.2 p103A
Moller, . . .; Canada, 1776-1783 9786 p29
Moller, A. M. Friederike Louise; America, 1892 4610.10 p161
Moller, A. M. Wilhelmine; America, 1881 4610.10 p160
Moller, Anne Marie Wilh.; America, 1857 4610.10 p135
Moller, Carl Friedrich Wilhelm; America, 1862 4610.10 p158
Moller, Carl Heinrich Gottlieb; America, 1885 4610.10 p160
Moller, Carl Justus Heinrich; America, 1881 4610.10 p160
Moller, Catherine Florine; America, 1842 4610.10 p119
Moller, Charles; Wisconsin, n.d. 9675.7 p52
Moller, Ernst Gottlieb; America, 1868 4610.10 p159
Moller, Ernst Heinrich; America, 1855 4610.10 p157
Moller, Ernst Heinrich Wilhelm; America, 1892 4610.10 p161
Moller, Heinrich 20; New York, 1865 3702.7 p205
Moller, John; Illinois, 1871 5012.39 p25
Mollet, Mr. 28; Port uncertain, 1836 778.5 p386
Mollet, Elizabeth 21; Philadelphia, 1774 1219.7 p212
Molley, Mrs. 30; Carolina, 1774 1219.7 p215
Molliere, Mr. 27; America, 1836 778.5 p386
Mollin, Patrick; New York, NY, 1811 2859.11 p17
With wife & 4 children
Molling, Nicholas; Wisconsin, n.d. 9675.7 p52
Molling, William 19; Virginia, 1774 1219.7 p239
Molloghan, Patrick; New York, NY, 1816 2859.11 p39
Mollony, John; New York, NY, 1811 2859.11 p17
Molloy, Annie; Philadelphia, 1867 5704.8 p224
Molloy, Bridget; Quebec, 1810 7603 p78
Molloy, Daniel 11; St. John, N.B., 1863 5704.8 p152
Molloy, Elizabeth; New York, NY, 1869 5704.8 p235
Molloy, Ellen 19; St. John, N.B., 1854 5704.8 p114
Molloy, George 11; St. John, N.B., 1863 5704.8 p152
Molloy, Honor; America, 1739 4971 p37
Molloy, Jane; Quebec, 1798 7603 p78
Molloy, Jane 40; Philadelphia, 1853 5704.8 p113
Molloy, John 40; St. John, N.B., 1863 5704.8 p152
Molloy, Luke; Quebec, 1795 7603 p78
Molloy, Martin; America, 1735-1743 4971 p78
Molloy, Mary; Philadelphia, 1864 5704.8 p182
Molloy, Mary 35; St. John, N.B., 1863 5704.8 p152
Molloy, Owen 21; St. John, N.B., 1864 5704.8 p158
Molloy, Patrick; America, 1735-1743 4971 p8
Molloy, Patrick; New York, NY, 1815 2859.11 p39
Molloy, Patrick; Quebec, 1817 7603 p64
Molloy, Patrick 24; St. John, N.B., 1854 5704.8 p114
Molloy, Peter 40; Philadelphia, 1853 5704.8 p113
Molloy, Roger; Quebec, 1821 7603 p69
Molloy, William; Quebec, 1820 7603 p91
Molloy, William 17; Philadelphia, 1861 5704.8 p148
Molnar, Mike; Arkansas, 1918 95.2 p85
Molnar, Nicholas; America, 1893 7137 p169
*Wife:*Susan
Molnar, Susan *SEE* Molnar, Nicholas
Molner, Andrew; America, 1896 7137 p169
Molner, Nicholas; America, 1893 7137 p169
*Wife:*Susan
Molner, Susan *SEE* Molner, Nicholas
Mologhan, Daniel; New York, NY, 1838 8208.4 p64
Moloney, John 20; Jamaica, 1749 3690.1 p158
Moloy, Michael; New York, NY, 1838 8208.4 p64
Moloy, Thomas; New York, NY, 1837 8208.4 p26
Molska, Paulina 22; New York, NY, 1912 9980.29 p66
With 2 nephews
Molson, Mr.; Quebec, 1815 9229.18 p79
With wife
With sister
Molter, Margaretha C. Clos *SEE* Molter, Peter
Molter, Peter; Pennsylvania, 1766 4349 p48
*Wife:*Margaretha C. Clos
Molther, Johanna Sophia; Philadelphia, 1740 3652 p52
Molton, Jasper; Virginia, 1636 6219 p80
Molton, Jasper; Virginia, 1637 6219 p110
Molyneux, Diana 20; Virginia, 1700 2212 p32
Mom, John; America, 1846 1450.2 p103A
Momellini, Frank Hugo; New York, NY, 1920 3455.3 p79
Mommier, Adalphe; Iowa, 1866-1943 123.54 p35
Momroth, Philip; Arkansas, 1918 95.2 p85
Momus, Mr. 25; Port uncertain, 1836 778.5 p386
Momus, P. 27; New Orleans, 1838 778.5 p386
Monaghan, Alexander; Philadelphia, 1865 5704.8 p192
Monaghan, Ann; Philadelphia, 1849 53.26 p69
Monaghan, Ann; Philadelphia, 1849 5704.8 p50
Monaghan, Ann; St. John, N.B., 1853 5704.8 p100
Monaghan, Ann 9 mos; Quebec, 1864 5704.8 p161
Monaghan, Ann Jane; Quebec, 1852 5704.8 p86
Monaghan, Ann Jane; Quebec, 1852 5704.8 p90
Monaghan, Bailley; Philadelphia, 1853 5704.8 p108
Monaghan, Barney; Philadelphia, 1866 5704.8 p205
Monaghan, Biddy; Quebec, 1847 5704.8 p16
Monaghan, Biddy 4; Quebec, 1847 5704.8 p16
Monaghan, Bridget 5; St. John, N.B., 1847 5704.8 p21
Monaghan, Bryan; America, 1735-1743 4971 p79
Monaghan, Bryan; America, 1738 4971 p81
Monaghan, Bryan; America, 1739 4971 p82
Monaghan, Cath.; America, 1864 5704.8 p185
Monaghan, Catharine; Philadelphia, 1867 5704.8 p221
Monaghan, Catharine; Quebec, 1847 5704.8 p29
Monaghan, Catharine 28; Massachusetts, 1850 5881.1 p65
Monaghan, Catherine 30; Philadelphia, 1857 5704.8 p133
Monaghan, Charles 9; St. John, N.B., 1853 5704.8 p100
Monaghan, Charles 12; Quebec, 1847 5704.8 p16
Monaghan, Edward; St. John, N.B., 1851 5704.8 p80
Monaghan, Eliza 12; Quebec, 1854 5704.8 p119
Monaghan, Elizabeth; Philadelphia, 1851 5704.8 p71
Monaghan, Elizabeth 1; St. John, N.B., 1847 5704.8 p21
Monaghan, Elizabeth 7; St. John, N.B., 1853 5704.8 p100
Monaghan, Ellan 9 mos; Quebec, 1847 5704.8 p16
Monaghan, Ellen; Philadelphia, 1864 5704.8 p180
Monaghan, Ellen; St. John, N.B., 1848 5704.8 p43
Monaghan, Fanny; America, 1864 5704.8 p185
Monaghan, Hannagh 6; St. John, N.B., 1853 5704.8 p100
Monaghan, Hannah; New York, NY, 1868 5704.8 p226
Monaghan, Hugh; St. John, N.B., 1851 5704.8 p72
Monaghan, Isabella 26; Quebec, 1864 5704.8 p161
Monaghan, James; Quebec, 1847 5704.8 p16
Monaghan, James; Quebec, 1847 5704.8 p29
Monaghan, John; America, 1864 5704.8 p177
Monaghan, John; New York, NY, 1868 5704.8 p226
Monaghan, John; Philadelphia, 1867 5704.8 p221
Monaghan, John; Quebec, 1847 5704.8 p16
Monaghan, John 7; St. John, N.B., 1847 5704.8 p21
Monaghan, John 10; Quebec, 1854 5704.8 p119
Monaghan, John 11; St. John, N.B., 1853 5704.8 p100
Monaghan, John 26; Quebec, 1864 5704.8 p161
Monaghan, John William 7; Quebec, 1847 5704.8 p16
Monaghan, Mable; St. John, N.B., 1847 5704.8 p35
Monaghan, Margaret; New York, NY, 1865 5704.8 p203
Monaghan, Margaret; St. John, N.B., 1847 5704.8 p21
Monaghan, Margaret 3; St. John, N.B., 1847 5704.8 p21
Monaghan, Margaret 7; Massachusetts, 1849 5881.1 p72
Monaghan, Mary; Quebec, 1847 5704.8 p16
Monaghan, Mary; St. John, N.B., 1853 5704.8 p100
Monaghan, Mary 9; St. John, N.B., 1847 5704.8 p21
Monaghan, Mary 13; Quebec, 1847 5704.8 p29
Monaghan, Michael; Quebec, 1852 5704.8 p86
Monaghan, Michael; Quebec, 1852 5704.8 p90
Monaghan, Nelly; St. John, N.B., 1848 5704.8 p45
Monaghan, Own 10; Quebec, 1847 5704.8 p16
Monaghan, Pat; Quebec, 1847 5704.8 p29
Monaghan, Pat; Quebec, 1847 5704.8 p38
Monaghan, Patrick; St. John, N.B., 1853 5704.8 p100

FOR A COMPLETE EXPLANATION OF ENTRY, SEE "HOW TO READ A CITATION" SECTION

Montgomery, Henry; St. John, N.B., 1847 ***5704.8*** *p10*
Montgomery, Hugh; St. John, N.B., 1847 ***5704.8*** *p10*
Montgomery, Hugh 12; Quebec, 1851 ***5704.8*** *p82*
Montgomery, Isabella 16; St. John, N.B., 1856 ***5704.8*** *p132*
Montgomery, J.; New York, NY, 1811 ***2859.11*** *p17*
Montgomery, James 18; Philadelphia, 1854 ***5704.8*** *p120*
Montgomery, James 31; St. John, N.B., 1866 ***5704.8*** *p166*
Montgomery, James 50; South Carolina, 1850 ***1639.20*** *p242*
Montgomery, Jane; St. John, N.B., 1847 ***5704.8*** *p10*
Montgomery, Jane 10; Quebec, 1851 ***5704.8*** *p82*
Montgomery, Jane 52; Philadelphia, 1854 ***5704.8*** *p120*
Montgomery, John; New York, NY, 1815 ***2859.11*** *p39*
Montgomery, John; South Carolina, 1723-1743 ***1639.20*** *p242*
Montgomery, John 13; St. John, N.B., 1856 ***5704.8*** *p132*
Montgomery, Joseph; Philadelphia, 1811 ***2859.11*** *p17*
With family
Montgomery, Joseph 12; Philadelphia, 1856 ***5704.8*** *p129*
Montgomery, Margaret *SEE* Montgomery, William
Montgomery, Margaret; New York, NY, 1868 ***5704.8*** *p228*
Montgomery, Margaret; Philadelphia, 1847 ***5704.8*** *p23*
Montgomery, Margaret; St. John, N.B., 1850 ***5704.8*** *p65*
Montgomery, Margaret 42; St. John, N.B., 1856 ***5704.8*** *p132*
Montgomery, Mary; Quebec, 1851 ***5704.8*** *p82*
Montgomery, Mary 22; St. John, N.B., 1856 ***5704.8*** *p132*
Montgomery, May 41; Philadelphia, 1803 ***53.26*** *p70*
Montgomery, Michael 20; Philadelphia, 1858 ***5704.8*** *p139*
Montgomery, Moses; New York, NY, 1811 ***2859.11*** *p17*
With wife & 3 children
Montgomery, Rebecca 10; Philadelphia, 1803 ***53.26*** *p70*
Montgomery, Robert; North Carolina, 1795 ***1639.20*** *p242*
Montgomery, Robert; Philadelphia, 1868 ***5704.8*** *p226*
Montgomery, Robert 6; St. John, N.B., 1856 ***5704.8*** *p132*
Montgomery, Robert 8; Quebec, 1851 ***5704.8*** *p82*
Montgomery, Robert 12; Philadelphia, 1854 ***5704.8*** *p120*
Montgomery, Robert 18; Massachusetts, 1850 ***5881.1*** *p75*
Montgomery, Robert 42; St. John, N.B., 1856 ***5704.8*** *p132*
Montgomery, Samuel; Quebec, 1847 ***5704.8*** *p28*
Montgomery, Samuel 12; Philadelphia, 1803 ***53.26*** *p70*
Montgomery, Sarah; Philadelphia, 1852 ***5704.8*** *p96*
Montgomery, Sarah; Quebec, 1851 ***5704.8*** *p82*
Montgomery, Sarah 12; Philadelphia, 1847 ***53.26*** *p70*
Montgomery, Sarah Jane; Philadelphia, 1847 ***5704.8*** *p30*
Montgomery, Sarah Jane 9; St. John, N.B., 1856 ***5704.8*** *p132*
Montgomery, Susan; Quebec, 1851 ***5704.8*** *p82*
Montgomery, Susanna 63 *SEE* Montgomery, Amos
Montgomery, Thomas; Quebec, 1850 ***5704.8*** *p63*
Montgomery, Thomas; Quebec, 1851 ***5704.8*** *p82*
Montgomery, Walter George; Arkansas, 1918 ***95.2*** *p85*
Montgomery, William; Philadelphia, 1847 ***53.26*** *p70*
*Relative:*Margaret
Montgomery, William; Philadelphia, 1847 ***5704.8*** *p23*
Montgomery, William; St. John, N.B., 1847 ***5704.8*** *p10*
Montgomery, William; South Carolina, 1590-1690 ***1639.20*** *p243*
Montgomery, William 19; Philadelphia, 1860 ***5704.8*** *p145*
Montgomery, William 22; Philadelphia, 1803 ***53.26*** *p70*
Montgomery, William 30; St. John, N.B., 1863 ***5704.8*** *p152*
Montgomery, William 45; Philadelphia, 1854 ***5704.8*** *p120*
Montgomery, Wm.; Philadelphia, 1811 ***2859.11*** *p17*
With family
Montgomery of Grevock, Mr.; South Carolina, 1684 ***1639.20*** *p242*
With son
Montgomery of Skelmorlie, Robert; Carolina, 1717 ***1639.20*** *p242*
Montgommery, Ann; Montreal, 1824 ***7603*** *p68*
Montiach, Jean 31; New Orleans, 1836 ***778.5*** *p390*
Montiaeh, Jean 31; New Orleans, 1836 ***778.5*** *p390*
Montieth, Catherine 30; Quebec, 1857 ***5704.8*** *p136*
Montieth, James; New York, NY, 1869 ***5704.8*** *p234*
Montieth, James; St. John, N.B., 1847 ***5704.8*** *p20*
Montieth, Jane; St. John, N.B., 1847 ***5704.8*** *p20*
Montieth, John; St. John, N.B., 1847 ***5704.8*** *p20*
Montieth, Mary 6 mos; Quebec, 1857 ***5704.8*** *p136*
Montieth, Robert 2; Quebec, 1857 ***5704.8*** *p136*
Montieth, Robert 13; St. John, N.B., 1847 ***5704.8*** *p20*
Montieth, Robert 30; Quebec, 1857 ***5704.8*** *p136*
Montieth, Samuel; St. John, N.B., 1847 ***5704.8*** *p20*
Montieth, Sarah; St. John, N.B., 1853 ***5704.8*** *p106*
Montieth, Susan; St. John, N.B., 1847 ***5704.8*** *p20*
Montieth, William 12; St. John, N.B., 1847 ***5704.8*** *p20*
Montigue, Mr. 30; America, 1838 ***778.5*** *p390*
Montin, Silvestre 35; New Orleans, 1823 ***778.5*** *p390*
Montonnier, Elizabeth 26; New Orleans, 1826 ***778.5*** *p390*
Montooth, James 22; Philadelphia, 1860 ***5704.8*** *p146*
Montoussay, Mr. 27; America, 1836 ***778.5*** *p390*
Montousse, Jacques 19; New Orleans, 1839 ***778.5*** *p390*
Montousse, N. 33; New Orleans, 1831 ***778.5*** *p390*
Montousse, Pierre 24; New Orleans, 1839 ***778.5*** *p390*
Montouth, Margaret; Quebec, 1825 ***7603*** *p87*
Montrag, Valentin 26; America, 1838 ***778.5*** *p390*
Montreal, . . .; Canada, 1776-1783 ***9786*** *p29*
Montreal, Comte de Seigneur de; Quebec, 1745 ***9775.5*** *p197*
Montrose, Captain; Quebec, 1815 ***9229.18*** *p82*
Montz, Jakob; Kentucky, 1844 ***8582.3*** *p101*
Moobat, Joseph 40; Baltimore, 1775 ***1219.7*** *p269*
Mood, Philander; Illinois, 1857 ***7857*** *p5*
Moodie, John; Ontario, 1832 ***9775.5*** *p213*
*Wife:*Susanna Strickland
Moodie, Susanna Strickland *SEE* Moodie, John
Moody, Catherine; Philadelphia, 1851 ***5704.8*** *p79*
Moody, James; New York, NY, 1816 ***2859.11*** *p39*
Moody, James 22; Philadelphia, 1861 ***5704.8*** *p148*
Moody, John; Philadelphia, 1851 ***5704.8*** *p79*
Moody, John; Quebec, 1851 ***5704.8*** *p74*
Moody, John; Quebec, 1851 ***5704.8*** *p82*
Moody, John 18; Philadelphia, 1774 ***1219.7*** *p182*
Moody, John 21; Jamaica, 1774 ***1219.7*** *p219*
Moody, John T.; New York, NY, 1835 ***8208.4*** *p5*
Moody, Margaret; Philadelphia, 1853 ***5704.8*** *p101*
Moody, Mary; Virginia, 1641 ***6219*** *p37*
Moody, Mary; Virginia, 1641 ***6219*** *p160*
Moody, Robert Henry; Washington, 1859-1920 ***2872.1*** *p26*
Moody, Sam; Washington, 1859-1920 ***2872.1*** *p26*
Moody, William 19; Montserrat, 1729 ***3690.1*** *p159*
Moog, Johannes; Pennsylvania, 1750 ***2444*** *p193*
*Wife:*Rosina Bricker
Moog, Rosina Bricker *SEE* Moog, Johannes
Moogh, Hans 38; Pennsylvania, 1739 ***2444*** *p193*
Moohan, John 24; St. John, N.B., 1857 ***5704.8*** *p134*
Moold, Francis; Virginia, 1643 ***6219*** *p200*
Moon, Ed; Iowa, 1866-1943 ***123.54*** *p71*
Moon, Edward; Iowa, 1866-1943 ***123.54*** *p71*
Moon, Edward 20; Philadelphia, 1834 ***53.26*** *p70*
Moon, James 9; New York, 1774 ***1219.7*** *p203*
Moon, John 24; Philadelphia, 1834 ***53.26*** *p70*
Moon, John 40; New York, 1774 ***1219.7*** *p203*
Moon, Jonathan 24; Philadelphia, 1834 ***53.26*** *p70*
Moon, Meredith William; Charleston, SC, 1794 ***1639.20*** *p243*
Moon, Samuel 23; Jamaica, 1730 ***3690.1*** *p159*
Moon, William 25; Nova Scotia, 1774 ***1219.7*** *p209*
Moonan, Bridget 5; Massachusetts, 1849 ***5881.1*** *p63*
Moonan, Mick 5; Massachusetts, 1850 ***5881.1*** *p73*
Moonan, Patrick 40; Massachusetts, 1849 ***5881.1*** *p74*
Moone, Abraham; Virginia, 1639 ***6219*** *p155*
Moone, Abraham; Virginia, 1642 ***6219*** *p192*
Moone, Hen.; Virginia, 1637 ***6219*** *p114*
Moone, J.; New York, NY, 1816 ***2859.11*** *p39*
Moone, John; Virginia, 1635 ***6219*** *p20*
*Wife:*Susan
Moone, Susan *SEE* Moone, John
Mooney, Alexander; New York, NY, 1816 ***2859.11*** *p39*
Mooney, Barney 33; St. John, N.B., 1862 ***5704.8*** *p150*
Mooney, Bart 29; Newfoundland, 1789 ***4915.24*** *p57*
Mooney, Catharine 3; Massachusetts, 1849 ***5881.1*** *p64*
Mooney, Catharine 28; Massachusetts, 1850 ***5881.1*** *p65*
Mooney, Charles; Philadelphia, 1853 ***5704.8*** *p101*
Mooney, Daniel; America, 1736-1743 ***4971*** *p58*
Mooney, Edward; Wisconsin, n.d. ***9675.7*** *p52*
Mooney, Edward 3; St. John, N.B., 1862 ***5704.8*** *p150*
Mooney, Elizabeth; America, 1740 ***4971*** *p15*
Mooney, Hannah *SEE* Mooney, William
Mooney, Hannah *SEE* Mooney, William
Mooney, Hannah; Philadelphia, 1847 ***5704.8*** *p23*
Mooney, James; New Brunswick, 1822 ***7603*** *p85*
Mooney, James; New York, NY, 1837 ***8208.4*** *p27*
Mooney, James; Philadelphia, 1867 ***5704.8*** *p222*
Mooney, James; Quebec, 1851 ***5704.8*** *p74*
Mooney, James 16; Philadelphia, 1803 ***53.26*** *p70*
Mooney, Jane; Philadelphia, 1853 ***5704.8*** *p101*
Mooney, John; New York, NY, 1816 ***2859.11*** *p39*
Mooney, John; Philadelphia, 1849 ***53.26*** *p70*
Mooney, John; Philadelphia, 1849 ***5704.8*** *p49*
Mooney, John 40; Massachusetts, 1849 ***5881.1*** *p69*
Mooney, Martha; Philadelphia, 1849 ***53.26*** *p70*
Mooney, Martha; Philadelphia, 1849 ***5704.8*** *p54*
Mooney, Mary; New York, NY, 1816 ***2859.11*** *p39*
Mooney, Mary; St. John, N.B., 1851 ***5704.8*** *p78*
Mooney, Mary; St. John, N.B., 1852 ***5704.8*** *p95*
Mooney, Mary 18; Massachusetts, 1849 ***5881.1*** *p72*
Mooney, Mary 21; St. John, N.B., 1864 ***5704.8*** *p159*
Mooney, Mary 35; Massachusetts, 1849 ***5881.1*** *p72*
Mooney, Mary 40; Massachusetts, 1849 ***5881.1*** *p71*
Mooney, Mathew; America, 1741 ***4971*** *p23*
Mooney, Matilda; Philadelphia, 1851 ***5704.8*** *p76*
Mooney, Michael; New York, NY, 1816 ***2859.11*** *p39*
Mooney, Michael; Quebec, 1851 ***5704.8*** *p75*
Mooney, Michael; St. John, N.B., 1848 ***5704.8*** *p39*
Mooney, Michael 5; St. John, N.B., 1862 ***5704.8*** *p150*
Mooney, Michael 39; California, 1872 ***2769.6*** *p6*
Mooney, Mortagh; America, 1735-1743 ***4971*** *p78*
Mooney, Murtogh; America, 1742 ***4971*** *p80*
Mooney, Patrick; America, 1737 ***4971*** *p75*
Mooney, Patrick 8; St. John, N.B., 1862 ***5704.8*** *p150*
Mooney, Peggy Anne; America, 1866 ***5704.8*** *p210*
Mooney, Peter Joseph; Arkansas, 1918 ***95.2*** *p85*
Mooney, Philip; Philadelphia, 1866 ***5704.8*** *p209*
Mooney, Rebecca 11 *SEE* Mooney, William
Mooney, Rebecca 11; Philadelphia, 1847 ***5704.8*** *p23*
Mooney, Richard; Wisconsin, n.d. ***9675.7*** *p52*
Mooney, Sarah 28; St. John, N.B., 1862 ***5704.8*** *p150*
Mooney, Terrence; Illinois, 1870 ***5012.38*** *p99*
Mooney, Thomas 55; St. John, N.B., 1862 ***5704.8*** *p150*
Mooney, William *SEE* Mooney, William
Mooney, William; Philadelphia, 1847 ***53.26*** *p70*
*Relative:*Hannah
*Relative:*William
*Relative:*Hannah
*Relative:*Rebecca 11
Mooney, William; Philadelphia, 1847 ***5704.8*** *p23*
Mooney, William John; Arkansas, 1918 ***95.2*** *p85*
Moor, . . .; Ohio, 1843 ***8582.1*** *p51*
Moor, Alexander; Georgia, 1775 ***1219.7*** *p274*
Moor, Anne; Quebec, 1850 ***5704.8*** *p66*
Moor, August; Cincinnati, 1869-1887 ***8582*** *p21*
Moor, Edward 18; St. Christopher, 1722 ***3690.1*** *p159*
Moor, Elizabeth 5; Quebec, 1864 ***5704.8*** *p162*
Moor, Friedrich; Died enroute, 1738 ***9898*** *p31*
Moor, Hannah 8; Quebec, 1850 ***5704.8*** *p66*
Moor, Isabella; Quebec, 1850 ***5704.8*** *p66*
Moor, James; Quebec, 1850 ***5704.8*** *p66*
Moor, Jane; Quebec, 1850 ***5704.8*** *p66*
Moor, Jno.; Virginia, 1645 ***6219*** *p232*
Moor, John; America, 1738 ***4971*** *p68*
Moor, John; America, 1743 ***4971*** *p10*
Moor, John 21; Philadelphia, 1774 ***1219.7*** *p183*
Moor, John 24; New York, 1775 ***1219.7*** *p268*
With wife
With child
Moor, Lewis 19; Jamaica, 1730 ***3690.1*** *p159*
Moor, Margaret 3; Quebec, 1864 ***5704.8*** *p162*
Moor, Margaret 11; Quebec, 1850 ***5704.8*** *p66*
Moor, Margaret 26; Quebec, 1864 ***5704.8*** *p162*
Moor, Mary 25; America, 1702 ***2212*** *p39*
Moor, Mathew 22; Maryland, 1774 ***1219.7*** *p221*
Moor, Michael; South Carolina, 1752 ***1639.20*** *p243*
Moor, Miles; South Carolina, 1716 ***1639.20*** *p243*
Moor, Patrick; Quebec, 1850 ***5704.8*** *p66*
Moor, Richard 19; Pennsylvania, 1724 ***3690.1*** *p159*
Moor, Robert 19; Pennsylvania, 1728 ***3690.1*** *p159*
Moor, Robert 23; Jamaica, 1724 ***3690.1*** *p159*
Moor, Samuel 38; Maryland, 1774 ***1219.7*** *p230*
Moor, Sarah; Quebec, 1850 ***5704.8*** *p66*
Moor, Thomas; America, 1698 ***2212*** *p8*
Moor, William 1; Quebec, 1864 ***5704.8*** *p162*
Moor, William 28; Quebec, 1864 ***5704.8*** *p162*
Moor, Wm; America, 1697 ***2212*** *p9*
Mooratyl, Daniel; America, 1837 ***1450.2*** *p103A*
Moore, . . . 1; New York, NY, 1866 ***5704.8*** *p213*
Moore, Abdala; Virginia, 1646 ***6219*** *p235*
Moore, Alex; Quebec, 1851 ***5704.8*** *p82*
Moore, Alexander; Illinois, 1872 ***5012.39*** *p91*
Moore, Alexander; New York, NY, 1815 ***2859.11*** *p39*
Moore, Alexander; Philadelphia, 1847 ***53.26*** *p70*
*Relative:*Catherine
*Relative:*Peter
*Relative:*Matty 2
Moore, Alexander; Philadelphia, 1847 ***53.26*** *p70*
*Relative:*Jane
*Relative:*William
*Relative:*Rebecca
Moore, Alexander; Philadelphia, 1847 ***5704.8*** *p23*
Moore, Alexander; St. John, N.B., 1847 ***5704.8*** *p18*
Moore, Alexander 27; Philadelphia, 1855 ***5704.8*** *p124*
Moore, Andrew; New York, NY, 1816 ***2859.11*** *p39*
Moore, Ann *SEE* Moore, Margaret
Moore, Ann; New York, NY, 1866 ***5704.8*** *p213*
Moore, Ann; Philadelphia, 1847 ***5704.8*** *p1*
Moore, Ann; Philadelphia, 1850 ***5704.8*** *p64*

Moore, Ann J.; Philadelphia, 1850 ***5704.8*** *p64*
Moore, Archibald; Quebec, 1847 ***5704.8*** *p36*
Moore, Bell; Philadelphia, 1848 ***5704.8*** *p46*
Moore, Benjamin 20; Philadelphia, 1853 ***5704.8*** *p113*
Moore, Bessy 10; Wilmington, DE, 1831 ***6508.3*** *p101*
Moore, Bridget; America, 1839 ***7036*** *p121*
*Sister:*Margaret
Moore, Catharine; Massachusetts, 1847 ***5881.1*** *p64*
Moore, Catharine; Philadelphia, 1847 ***5704.8*** *p23*
Moore, Catharine; Philadelphia, 1865 ***5704.8*** *p190*
Moore, Catharine 29; Massachusetts, 1860 ***6410.32*** *p113*
Moore, Catharine 55; Massachusetts, 1849 ***5881.1*** *p64*
Moore, Catherine *SEE* Moore, Alexander
Moore, Catherine; St. John, N.B., 1847 ***5704.8*** *p18*
Moore, Catherine Jane 3; Quebec, 1847 ***5704.8*** *p16*
Moore, Charles 36; Maryland, 1734 ***3690.1*** *p159*
Moore, Charles E.; America, 1885 ***1450.2*** *p103A*
Moore, David; Philadelphia, 1850 ***53.26*** *p70*
Moore, David; Philadelphia, 1850 ***5704.8*** *p60*
Moore, David 20; Quebec, 1859 ***5704.8*** *p143*
Moore, Edmund; New York, NY, 1838 ***8208.4*** *p87*
Moore, Edward; San Francisco, 1850 ***4914.15*** *p10*
Moore, Edward; San Francisco, 1850 ***4914.15*** *p13*
Moore, Eliz.; Virginia, 1637 ***6219*** *p113*
Moore, Eliza; New York, NY, 1811 ***2859.11*** *p17*
Moore, Eliza; Philadelphia, 1850 ***5704.8*** *p64*
Moore, Eliza 5; Philadelphia, 1866 ***5704.8*** *p204*
Moore, Eliza Ann 3 mos; Quebec, 1847 ***5704.8*** *p16*
Moore, Elizabeth; St. John, N.B., 1847 ***5704.8*** *p32*
Moore, Ellan; Quebec, 1851 ***5704.8*** *p82*
Moore, Elleanor; St. John, N.B., 1847 ***5704.8*** *p32*
Moore, Elleanor; St. John, N.B., 1848 ***5704.8*** *p43*
Moore, Elleanor 12; Quebec, 1847 ***5704.8*** *p36*
Moore, F. A.; Washington, 1859-1920 ***2872.1*** *p26*
Moore, Fanny 6; New York, NY, 1866 ***5704.8*** *p213*
Moore, Florinda; Philadelphia, 1865 ***5704.8*** *p201*
Moore, George; Philadelphia, 1865 ***5704.8*** *p190*
Moore, George; San Francisco, 1850 ***4914.15*** *p10*
Moore, George; San Francisco, 1850 ***4914.15*** *p13*
Moore, George; San Francisco, 1850 ***4914.15*** *p14*
Moore, George 5; Massachusetts, 1847 ***5881.1*** *p66*
Moore, George 16; Virginia, 1774 ***1219.7*** *p193*
Moore, George R.; Colorado, 1899 ***9678.2*** *p127*
Moore, Henry; America, 1844 ***1450.2*** *p103A*
Moore, Henry; New York, NY, 1811 ***2859.11*** *p17*
Moore, Henry; Virginia, 1643 ***6219*** *p201*
Moore, Herbert 28; Arkansas, 1918 ***95.2*** *p85*
Moore, Isabella; Quebec, 1852 ***5704.8*** *p86*
Moore, Isabella; Quebec, 1852 ***5704.8*** *p91*
Moore, Isabella; St. John, N.B., 1847 ***5704.8*** *p11*
Moore, James; America, 1738 ***4971*** *p9*
Moore, James; New York, NY, 1811 ***2859.11*** *p17*
Moore, James; New York, NY, 1815 ***2859.11*** *p39*
Moore, James; New York, NY, 1816 ***2859.11*** *p39*
Moore, James; Philadelphia, 1868 ***5704.8*** *p224*
Moore, James; Quebec, 1851 ***5704.8*** *p75*
Moore, James 3; Quebec, 1847 ***5704.8*** *p36*
Moore, James 4; St. John, N.B., 1847 ***5704.8*** *p11*
Moore, James 7; New York, NY, 1866 ***5704.8*** *p213*
Moore, James 19; Philadelphia, 1803 ***53.26*** *p70*
Moore, James 20; Quebec, 1853 ***5704.8*** *p104*
Moore, James 20; Quebec, 1855 ***5704.8*** *p125*
Moore, James 21; Philadelphia, 1803 ***53.26*** *p70*
Moore, James 23; Philadelphia, 1853 ***5704.8*** *p108*
Moore, James 25; Massachusetts, 1849 ***5881.1*** *p68*
Moore, James 29; Maryland, 1774 ***1219.7*** *p192*
Moore, Jane *SEE* Moore, Alexander
Moore, Jane; New York, NY, 1815 ***2859.11*** *p39*
Moore, Jane; Philadelphia, 1847 ***5704.8*** *p23*
Moore, Jane; Philadelphia, 1853 ***5704.8*** *p101*
Moore, Jane; Quebec, 1852 ***5704.8*** *p97*
Moore, Jane; Virginia, 1637 ***6219*** *p85*
Moore, Jane; Virginia, 1639 ***6219*** *p18*
Moore, Jane; Virginia, 1639 ***6219*** *p157*
Moore, Jane 5; Quebec, 1847 ***5704.8*** *p36*
Moore, Jane 12; St. John, N.B., 1854 ***5704.8*** *p122*
Moore, Jane 20; Philadelphia, 1859 ***5704.8*** *p141*
Moore, John; America, 1737 ***4971*** *p85*
Moore, John; America, 1737 ***4971*** *p95*
Moore, John; America, 1864 ***5704.8*** *p185*
Moore, John; New York, NY, 1811 ***2859.11*** *p17*
Moore, John; New York, NY, 1815 ***2859.11*** *p39*
Moore, John; New York, NY, 1816 ***2859.11*** *p39*
Moore, John; New York, NY, 1836 ***8208.4*** *p59*
Moore, John; Philadelphia, 1853 ***5704.8*** *p100*
Moore, John; Philadelphia, 1866 ***5704.8*** *p211*
Moore, John; Quebec, 1847 ***5704.8*** *p28*
Moore, John; St. John, N.B., 1847 ***5704.8*** *p24*
Moore, John; Virginia, 1638 ***6219*** *p123*
Moore, John; Virginia, 1638 ***6219*** *p124*
Moore, John; Virginia, 1643 ***6219*** *p204*
Moore, John; Virginia, 1646 ***6219*** *p241*
Moore, John 3; New York, NY, 1866 ***5704.8*** *p213*
Moore, John 7; St. John, N.B., 1847 ***5704.8*** *p11*
Moore, John 15; Maryland, 1775 ***1219.7*** *p254*
Moore, John 16; Baltimore, 1775 ***1219.7*** *p269*
Moore, John 18; Virginia, 1723 ***3690.1*** *p159*
Moore, John 19; Philadelphia, 1803 ***53.26*** *p70*
Moore, John 19; Quebec, 1863 ***5704.8*** *p154*
Moore, John 20; Philadelphia, 1833-1834 ***53.26*** *p70*
Moore, John 21; Virginia, 1774 ***1219.7*** *p201*
Moore, John 22; Philadelphia, 1803 ***53.26*** *p70*
Moore, John 22; St. John, N.B., 1856 ***5704.8*** *p131*
Moore, John 23; Virginia, 1775 ***1219.7*** *p247*
Moore, John 25; Baltimore, 1775 ***1219.7*** *p269*
Moore, John 31; Arizona, 1890 ***2764.35*** *p45*
Moore, John 32; Maryland, 1774 ***1219.7*** *p191*
Moore, John 45; Arizona, 1903 ***9228.40*** *p7*
Moore, Jon.; Virginia, 1643 ***6219*** *p200*
Moore, Joseph; Virginia, 1622 ***6219*** *p27*
Moore, Joseph; Virginia, 1642 ***6219*** *p193*
Moore, Joseph; Virginia, 1852 ***4626.16*** *p14*
Moore, Joseph 27; Virginia, 1774 ***1219.7*** *p244*
Moore, Letitia 11; Philadelphia, 1865 ***5704.8*** *p190*
Moore, Letitia 21; St. John, N.B., 1856 ***5704.8*** *p131*
Moore, Letty; New York, NY, 1815 ***2859.11*** *p39*
Moore, Lewis 19; Jamaica, 1730 ***3690.1*** *p159*
Moore, Louisa Catherine; New York, NY, 1836 ***8208.4*** *p79*
Moore, Margaret *SEE* Moore, Bridget
Moore, Margaret; America, 1865 ***5704.8*** *p198*
Moore, Margaret; New York, NY, 1811 ***2859.11*** *p17*
Moore, Margaret; New York, NY, 1815 ***2859.11*** *p39*
Moore, Margaret; Philadelphia, 1847 ***53.26*** *p70*
*Relative:*William
*Relative:*Ann
*Relative:*Mary
*Relative:*Thomas 10
Moore, Margaret; Philadelphia, 1847 ***5704.8*** *p1*
Moore, Margaret; Philadelphia, 1850 ***5704.8*** *p64*
Moore, Margaret; Philadelphia, 1851 ***5704.8*** *p81*
Moore, Margaret; Quebec, 1847 ***5704.8*** *p16*
Moore, Margaret; Quebec, 1851 ***5704.8*** *p82*
Moore, Margaret 9 mos; Quebec, 1852 ***5704.8*** *p97*
Moore, Margaret 21; New York, 1775 ***1219.7*** *p268*
Moore, Margaret 21; Port uncertain, 1774 ***1219.7*** *p176*
Moore, Margaret 22; St. John, N.B., 1853 ***5704.8*** *p109*
Moore, Margaret Ann 22; Philadelphia, 1859 ***5704.8*** *p141*
Moore, Martha *SEE* Moore, Peggy
Moore, Martha; Philadelphia, 1847 ***5704.8*** *p1*
Moore, Martha; Philadelphia, 1865 ***5704.8*** *p190*
Moore, Mary *SEE* Moore, Margaret
Moore, Mary; New York, NY, 1811 ***2859.11*** *p17*
Moore, Mary; Philadelphia, 1847 ***5704.8*** *p1*
Moore, Mary; Philadelphia, 1866 ***5704.8*** *p204*
Moore, Mary; Quebec, 1850 ***5704.8*** *p63*
Moore, Mary 20; Philadelphia, 1864 ***5704.8*** *p156*
Moore, Mary 20; Quebec, 1856 ***5704.8*** *p130*
Moore, Mary 55; Quebec, 1855 ***5704.8*** *p124*
Moore, Mary Ann; Philadelphia, 1851 ***5704.8*** *p78*
Moore, Mary Ann 19; Quebec, 1855 ***5704.8*** *p125*
Moore, Mary Ann 22; Wilmington, DE, 1831 ***6508.7*** *p161*
Moore, Mary Ann 30; Montreal, 1775 ***7603*** *p68*
Moore, Mary Anne 19; Philadelphia, 1861 ***5704.8*** *p148*
Moore, Mary Jane 8; Quebec, 1850 ***5704.8*** *p63*
Moore, Mathew; New York, NY, 1811 ***2859.11*** *p17*
With wife & 3 children
Moore, Mathew; Philadelphia, 1850 ***5704.8*** *p64*
Moore, Matty 2 *SEE* Moore, Alexander
Moore, Matty 2; Philadelphia, 1847 ***5704.8*** *p23*
Moore, Michael 40; Massachusetts, 1849 ***5881.1*** *p71*
Moore, Molly; Quebec, 1851 ***5704.8*** *p82*
Moore, Molly 9 mos; Quebec, 1851 ***5704.8*** *p82*
Moore, Nancy; Quebec, 1847 ***5704.8*** *p28*
Moore, Nancy 7; Quebec, 1847 ***5704.8*** *p36*
Moore, Nath.; Virginia, 1618 ***6219*** *p72*
Moore, Nath; Virginia, 1634 ***6219*** *p105*
Moore, Nath.; Virginia, 1638 ***6219*** *p147*
Moore, Nathaniel 26; Maryland, 1730 ***3690.1*** *p159*
Moore, Nich.; Virginia, 1637 ***6219*** *p11*
Moore, Nich.; Virginia, 1637 ***6219*** *p114*
Moore, Patrick; America, 1742 ***4971*** *p29*
Moore, Patrick; Delaware, 1743 ***4971*** *p105*
Moore, Patrick; Ohio, 1868 ***6014.2*** *p7*
Moore, Patrick; St. John, N.B., 1853 ***5704.8*** *p99*
Moore, Patrick 24; Massachusetts, 1850 ***5881.1*** *p75*
Moore, Patrick 40; Massachusetts, 1849 ***5881.1*** *p74*
Moore, Peggy; Philadelphia, 1847 ***53.26*** *p71*
*Relative:*Martha
Moore, Peggy; Philadelphia, 1847 ***5704.8*** *p1*
Moore, Peter *SEE* Moore, Alexander
Moore, Peter; America, 1742-1743 ***4971*** *p62*
Moore, Peter; Philadelphia, 1847 ***5704.8*** *p23*
Moore, Peter; Washington, 1859-1920 ***2872.1*** *p26*
Moore, Philip; New York, NY, 1838 ***8208.4*** *p87*
Moore, Rarde 5; Philadelphia, 1866 ***5704.8*** *p204*
Moore, Rebecca *SEE* Moore, Alexander
Moore, Rebecca *SEE* Moore, Verner
Moore, Rebecca; Philadelphia, 1847 ***5704.8*** *p23*
Moore, Rebecca; Philadelphia, 1850 ***53.26*** *p71*
Moore, Rebecca; Philadelphia, 1850 ***5704.8*** *p60*
Moore, Rebecca; Philadelphia, 1850 ***5704.8*** *p64*
Moore, Rebecca; Philadelphia, 1851 ***5704.8*** *p78*
Moore, Rebecca; Philadelphia, 1852 ***5704.8*** *p87*
Moore, Richard; Philadelphia, 1849 ***53.26*** *p71*
Moore, Richard; Philadelphia, 1849 ***5704.8*** *p53*
Moore, Richard; Virginia, 1639 ***6219*** *p152*
Moore, Richard; Virginia, 1639 ***6219*** *p158*
Moore, Richard; Virginia, 1646 ***6219*** *p242*
Moore, Richard 19; Pennsylvania, 1724 ***3690.1*** *p159*
Moore, Robert; New York, NY, 1811 ***2859.11*** *p17*
Moore, Robert; New York, NY, 1815 ***2859.11*** *p39*
Moore, Robert; Philadelphia, 1847 ***53.26*** *p71*
Moore, Robert; Philadelphia, 1847 ***5704.8*** *p5*
Moore, Robert; Philadelphia, 1851 ***5704.8*** *p81*
Moore, Robert; St. John, N.B., 1849 ***5704.8*** *p49*
Moore, Robert 15; St. John, N.B., 1853 ***5704.8*** *p110*
Moore, Robert 19; Pennsylvania, 1728 ***3690.1*** *p159*
Moore, Robert 37; Maryland, 1774 ***1219.7*** *p224*
Moore, Robert 37; Maryland, 1774 ***1219.7*** *p228*
Moore, Robert A.; Philadelphia, 1866 ***5704.8*** *p207*
Moore, Robt.; Virginia, 1635 ***6219*** *p3*
Moore, Robt 22; Philadelphia, 1845 ***6508.6*** *p115*
Moore, Roger; Boston, 1776 ***1219.7*** *p277*
Moore, Roger; New York, NY, 1838 ***8208.4*** *p61*
Moore, Sally; Quebec, 1847 ***5704.8*** *p36*
Moore, Salvatore; Iowa, 1866-1943 ***123.54*** *p35*
Moore, Samuel; Indiana, 1831 ***1450.2*** *p103A*
Moore, Samuel; New York, NY, 1815 ***2859.11*** *p39*
Moore, Samuel; Philadelphia, 1851 ***5704.8*** *p78*
Moore, Samuel 9 mos; St. John, N.B., 1853 ***5704.8*** *p109*
Moore, Samuel 8; Philadelphia, 1866 ***5704.8*** *p204*
Moore, Samuel D.; New York, NY, 1815 ***2859.11*** *p39*
Moore, Sarah; Quebec, 1851 ***5704.8*** *p82*
Moore, Sarah 9 mos; Quebec, 1847 ***5704.8*** *p36*
Moore, Stephen 60; Quebec, 1855 ***5704.8*** *p124*
Moore, Tho.; Virginia, 1638 ***6219*** *p124*
Moore, Thomas; New York, NY, 1811 ***2859.11*** *p17*
With family
Moore, Thomas; Ohio, 1840 ***9892.11*** *p31*
Moore, Thomas; Quebec, 1690 ***7603*** *p23*
Moore, Thomas; Virginia, 1637 ***6219*** *p108*
Moore, Thomas; Virginia, 1646 ***6219*** *p242*
Moore, Thomas 10 *SEE* Moore, Margaret
Moore, Thomas 10; Philadelphia, 1847 ***5704.8*** *p1*
Moore, Thomas 10; Quebec, 1850 ***5704.8*** *p63*
Moore, Thomas 11; Philadelphia, 1865 ***5704.8*** *p190*
Moore, Thomas 20; Philadelphia, 1865 ***5704.8*** *p164*
Moore, Turbett; St. John, N.B., 1847 ***5704.8*** *p18*
Moore, Verner; Philadelphia, 1847 ***53.26*** *p71*
*Relative:*Rebecca
Moore, William *SEE* Moore, Alexander
Moore, William *SEE* Moore, Margaret
Moore, William; New York, NY, 1815 ***2859.11*** *p39*
Moore, William; New York, NY, 1836 ***8208.4*** *p20*
Moore, William; New York, NY, 1843 ***6410.32*** *p125*
Moore, William; New York, NY, 1864 ***5704.8*** *p187*
Moore, William; Philadelphia, 1811 ***53.26*** *p71*
Moore, William; Philadelphia, 1811 ***2859.11*** *p17*
Moore, William; Philadelphia, 1816 ***2859.11*** *p39*
Moore, William; Philadelphia, 1847 ***53.26*** *p71*
Moore, William; Philadelphia, 1847 ***5704.8*** *p1*
Moore, William; Philadelphia, 1847 ***5704.8*** *p23*
Moore, William; Philadelphia, 1851 ***5704.8*** *p76*
Moore, William; Philadelphia, 1865 ***5704.8*** *p201*
Moore, William; Quebec, 1847 ***5704.8*** *p16*
Moore, William; San Francisco, 1850 ***4914.15*** *p10*
Moore, William; San Francisco, 1850 ***4914.15*** *p13*
Moore, William 3; Quebec, 1852 ***5704.8*** *p97*
Moore, William 10; Quebec, 1847 ***5704.8*** *p36*
Moore, William 20; St. John, N.B., 1853 ***5704.8*** *p109*
Moore, William 30; Massachusetts, 1860 ***6410.32*** *p113*
Moore, William H.; Colorado, 1887 ***9678.2*** *p127*
Moore, William John; Philadelphia, 1864 ***5704.8*** *p171*
Moore, Wm.; Virginia, 1635 ***6219*** *p35*
Moore, Wm.; Virginia, 1855 ***4626.16*** *p15*
Moorefield, Joseph 16; Maryland, 1720 ***3690.1*** *p160*
Moorehead, Eliza J. 17; Philadelphia, 1861 ***5704.8*** *p148*
Mooreland, Mary; Virginia, 1637 ***6219*** *p9*
Mooreland, Thomas; Virginia, 1642 ***6219*** *p189*
Moores, Jno; America, 1697-1707 ***2212*** *p3*
Moores, Rich.; Virginia, 1637 ***6219*** *p110*
Moorescroft, Henry; Virginia, 1640 ***6219*** *p18*
Mooreton, Mathew 20; New England, 1699 ***2212*** *p18*
Moorhead, Alexander; Philadelphia, 1850 ***53.26*** *p71*
Moorhead, Alexander; Philadelphia, 1850 ***5704.8*** *p65*

Moorhead, Charlotte 9 mos; Philadelphia, 1852 ***5704.8*** *p96*
Moorhead, Jane; New York, NY, 1868 ***5704.8*** *p230*
Moorhead, John; New York, NY, 1835 ***8208.4*** *p38*
Moorhead, Margaret; Philadelphia, 1847 ***53.26*** *p71*
Moorhead, Margaret; Philadelphia, 1847 ***5704.8*** *p23*
Moorhead, Martha; Philadelphia, 1852 ***5704.8*** *p96*
Moorhead, Rebecca 20; Philadelphia, 1853 ***5704.8*** *p111*
Moorhead, Samuel; New York, NY, 1811 ***2859.11*** *p17*
Moorhouse, Stephen 28; New York, 1774 ***1219.7*** *p217*
Mooring, Andrew 29; Maryland, 1775 ***1219.7*** *p271*
Mooring, James 17; Philadelphia, 1774 ***1219.7*** *p233*
Mooring, Thomas 23; Nova Scotia, 1774 ***1219.7*** *p209*
Moormann, Ferdinand Heinrich; America, 1847 ***8582.1*** *p25*
Moormann, Friedrich Wilhelm; America, 1847 ***4610.10*** *p66*
Moormann, J. H.; Indiana, 1869-1887 ***8582*** *p21*
Moormann, Johann B.; Ohio, 1869-1887 ***8582*** *p21*
Moormann, John B.; America, 1831 ***8582.2*** *p28*
Moormann, Theodor; America, 1847 ***8582.3*** *p47*
Moos, Niels; New York, 1761 ***3652*** *p88*
Mooshake, F.; California, 1849 ***8582*** *p21*
Mootry, Ellen 20; St. John, N.B., 1857 ***5704.8*** *p135*
Mootz, Henry; America, 1892 ***1450.2*** *p26B*
Mootz, Jacob; Wisconsin, n.d. ***9675.7*** *p52*
Mootz, John Baptist; Wisconsin, n.d. ***9675.7*** *p52*
Moquelin, Mme. 27; New Orleans, 1825 ***778.5*** *p391*
Mor, Jacob; Illinois, 1863 ***7857*** *p5*
Mora, John; Iowa, 1866-1943 ***123.54*** *p35*
Morachini, Charles F. 28; New Orleans, 1835 ***778.5*** *p391*
Moracy, Michel; Quebec, 1818 ***7603*** *p98*
Moragh, Michel; Quebec, 1822 ***7603*** *p70*
Moran, . . .; New York, NY, 1811 ***2859.11*** *p17*
With family
Moran, Anne; America, 1864 ***5704.8*** *p189*
Moran, Bernard 11; Massachusetts, 1850 ***5881.1*** *p63*
Moran, Biddy 20; Massachusetts, 1850 ***5881.1*** *p64*
Moran, Catharine 8; Massachusetts, 1850 ***5881.1*** *p65*
Moran, Catharine 20; Massachusetts, 1849 ***5881.1*** *p64*
Moran, Dennis; America, 1735-1743 ***4971*** *p7*
Moran, Dennis; Massachusetts, 1840 ***7036*** *p122*
*Brother:*James
*Brother:*Michael
*Brother:*Patrick
Moran, Dennis 24; Massachusetts, 1849 ***5881.1*** *p65*
Moran, Edward; America, 1735-1743 ***4971*** *p7*
Moran, Edward; America, 1864 ***5704.8*** *p189*
Moran, Ellen 22; Massachusetts, 1849 ***5881.1*** *p66*
Moran, George; Philadelphia, 1864 ***5704.8*** *p175*
Moran, George 17; Philadelphia, 1858 ***5704.8*** *p139*
Moran, Honora 13; Massachusetts, 1850 ***5881.1*** *p67*
Moran, Honora 20; Massachusetts, 1849 ***5881.1*** *p67*
Moran, James *SEE* Moran, Dennis
Moran, James; New York, NY, 1815 ***2859.11*** *p39*
Moran, James; New York, NY, 1846 ***2896.5*** *p28*
Moran, James; Philadelphia, 1850 ***53.26*** *p71*
Moran, James; Philadelphia, 1850 ***5704.8*** *p61*
Moran, James 3; Massachusetts, 1847 ***5881.1*** *p68*
Moran, James 22; Massachusetts, 1849 ***5881.1*** *p68*
Moran, James 35; Massachusetts, 1847 ***5881.1*** *p67*
Moran, James 40; Massachusetts, 1847 ***5881.1*** *p67*
Moran, Jane 20; Philadelphia, 1857 ***5704.8*** *p134*
Moran, John; America, 1735-1743 ***4971*** *p78*
Moran, John; America, 1742 ***4971*** *p80*
Moran, John; New York, NY, 1833 ***8208.4*** *p46*
Moran, John; Pennsylvania, 1895 ***1450.2*** *p26B*
Moran, Joseph; America, 1740 ***4971*** *p31*
Moran, Mary 18; Massachusetts, 1849 ***5881.1*** *p72*
Moran, Mary 35; Massachusetts, 1847 ***5881.1*** *p70*
Moran, Mary 45; Massachusetts, 1850 ***5881.1*** *p72*
Moran, Michael *SEE* Moran, Dennis
Moran, Michael 20; Massachusetts, 1848 ***5881.1*** *p71*
Moran, Michael 22; Massachusetts, 1850 ***5881.1*** *p72*
Moran, Norry 20; Massachusetts, 1849 ***5881.1*** *p73*
Moran, Patrick *SEE* Moran, Dennis
Moran, Patrick; America, 1737 ***4971*** *p27*
Moran, Patrick; America, 1738 ***4971*** *p22*
Moran, Patrick; New York, NY, 1840 ***8208.4*** *p109*
Moran, Patrick; Wisconsin, n.d. ***9675.7*** *p52*
Moran, Patrick 3; Massachusetts, 1849 ***5881.1*** *p74*
Moran, Richard; Quebec, 1798 ***7603*** *p78*
Moran, Sarah; America, 1864 ***5704.8*** *p189*
Moran, Thomas; America, 1742 ***4971*** *p22*
Moran, Thomas; America, 1742 ***4971*** *p86*
Moran, Thomas; America, 1742 ***4971*** *p95*
Moran, Thomas 35; Massachusetts, 1847 ***5881.1*** *p76*
Moran, William; New York, NY, 1839 ***8208.4*** *p101*
Moran, Winnefred 28; Massachusetts, 1847 ***5881.1*** *p77*
Moran, Wm.; Illinois, 1876 ***5012.39*** *p91*
Morand, John; Montreal, 1820 ***7603*** *p89*
Morano, Dominco 30; Arkansas, 1918 ***95.2*** *p85*
Morano, Francisco 28; Arkansas, 1918 ***95.2*** *p86*
Morarity, Michael; America, 1852-1856 ***1450.2*** *p104A*
Morarty, Mat; America, 1849 ***1450.2*** *p103A*
Moras, Niko; Iowa, 1866-1943 ***123.54*** *p35*
Moraulis, Anton; Wisconsin, n.d. ***9675.7*** *p52*
Morawski, . . .; New York, 1831 ***4606*** *p175*
Morbach, Andreas, Family; America, 1804-1923 ***2691.4*** *p172*
Morbach, Catharine 59; America, 1838 ***778.5*** *p391*
Morbach, Dominique 19; America, 1838 ***778.5*** *p391*
Morbach, Marie 28; America, 1838 ***778.5*** *p391*
Morbach, Nicolas 56; America, 1838 ***778.5*** *p391*
Morbach, Rosa 22; America, 1838 ***778.5*** *p391*
Morcarty, Robert; America, 1739 ***4971*** *p40*
Mord, Mr.; America, 1839 ***778.5*** *p391*
Mordecai, Jonah; New York, NY, 1836 ***8208.4*** *p59*
Morden, James; Virginia, 1698 ***2212*** *p16*
Mordick, Peter; New York, 1749 ***3652*** *p72*
Mordt, . . .; Canada, 1776-1783 ***9786*** *p29*
More, Doro; Virginia, 1647 ***6219*** *p248*
More, John; Virginia, 1643 ***6219*** *p199*
More, Nathll.; Virginia, 1648 ***6219*** *p252*
More, William; Virginia, 1647 ***6219*** *p247*
More, William; Virginia, 1647 ***6219*** *p248*
Morearty, Margaret 30; Massachusetts, 1849 ***5881.1*** *p71*
Moreau, Mr. 21; America, 1839 ***778.5*** *p391*
Moreau, Mr. 25; New Orleans, 1835 ***778.5*** *p391*
Moreau, C. 50; New Orleans, 1821 ***778.5*** *p391*
Moreau, J. B.; New Orleans, 1839 ***778.5*** *p391*
Moreau, L. T. 31; New Orleans, 1836 ***778.5*** *p391*
Moreau, Nicolas 48; America, 1839 ***778.5*** *p391*
Moreau, Pierre; Louisiana, 1789-1819 ***778.5*** *p556*
Moreau, Rene; Montreal, 1672 ***4533*** *p127*
Morecock, John; Virginia, 1634 ***6219*** *p84*
Morefield, Joseph 16; Maryland, 1720 ***3690.1*** *p160*
Morehead, John; New York, NY, 1835 ***8208.4*** *p38*
Morehead, Mary Ann; St. John, N.B., 1847 ***5704.8*** *p26*
Morehead, William; St. John, N.B., 1847 ***5704.8*** *p26*
Morehead, William; West Virginia, 1878 ***9788.3*** *p17*
Morel, Mr.; New Orleans, 1839 ***778.5*** *p391*
Morel, Mr. 21; America, 1838 ***778.5*** *p392*
Morel, Charles Emanuel; New York, NY, 1875 ***3455.3*** *p108*
*Wife:*Theresa
Morel, Charles Emanul; New York, NY, 1875 ***3455.2*** *p45*
Morel, Jacques Maxime; New York, NY, 1835 ***8208.4*** *p6*
Morel, Jean; Quebec, 1819 ***7603*** *p85*
Morel, Jean Pierre *SEE* Morel, Matthieu
Morel, Jeanne Marie Ozias *SEE* Morel, Matthieu
Morel, Joseph 19; Port uncertain, 1836 ***778.5*** *p392*
Morel, Julio 35; New Orleans, 1839 ***778.5*** *p392*
Morel, Lucresse *SEE* Morel, Matthieu
Morel, Marie Madeleine *SEE* Morel, Matthieu
Morel, Matthieu; America, 1751 ***2444*** *p193*
*Wife:*Jeanne Marie Ozias
*Child:*Jean Pierre
*Child:*Marie Madeleine
*Child:*Lucresse
Morel, Nicholas; New York, NY, 1838 ***8208.4*** *p88*
Morel, Theresa *SEE* Morel, Charles Emanuel
Moreland, Christopher 20; Maryland, 1737 ***3690.1*** *p160*
Morell, Jean Pierre *SEE* Morell, Matthieu
Morell, Jeanne Marie Ozias *SEE* Morell, Matthieu
Morell, Louis 27; Died enroute, 1822 ***778.5*** *p392*
Morell, Lucresse *SEE* Morell, Matthieu
Morell, Marie Madeleine *SEE* Morell, Matthieu
Morell, Matthieu; America, 1751 ***2444*** *p193*
*Wife:*Jeanne Marie Ozias
*Child:*Jean Pierre
*Child:*Marie Madeleine
*Child:*Lucresse
Morelle, Nicolas 33; New Orleans, 1837 ***778.5*** *p392*
Morelly, Charles; West Virginia, 1856 ***9788.3*** *p17*
Morely, Fra. Fra.; Virginia, 1647 ***6219*** *p248*
Moren, Ann *SEE* Moren, Philip
Moren, Ann; Philadelphia, 1850 ***5704.8*** *p69*
Moren, Catherine *SEE* Moren, Philip
Moren, Catherine; Philadelphia, 1850 ***5704.8*** *p69*
Moren, James *SEE* Moren, Philip
Moren, James; Philadelphia, 1850 ***5704.8*** *p69*
Moren, Knute Axel; Arkansas, 1918 ***95.2*** *p86*
Moren, Philip; Philadelphia, 1850 ***53.26*** *p71*
*Relative:*Catherine
*Relative:*Ann
*Relative:*James
Moren, Philip; Philadelphia, 1850 ***5704.8*** *p69*
Moren, Pierre 32; New Orleans, 1836 ***778.5*** *p392*
Moreno, N. 69; Arizona, 1906 ***9228.40*** *p13*
Morenz, August F.; Illinois, 1888 ***5012.37*** *p61*
Morer, James; New York, NY, 1816 ***2859.11*** *p39*
Moreran, William 21; Baltimore, 1775 ***1219.7*** *p270*
Mores, Simione; Iowa, 1866-1943 ***123.54*** *p35*
Moret, A. 30; America, 1839 ***778.5*** *p392*
Moret, Matthieu; Pennsylvania, 1751 ***2444*** *p193*
Morethorpe, Thomas; Virginia, 1636 ***6219*** *p75*
Moreton, Margaret; America, 1738 ***4971*** *p68*
Moreton, Mathew; Virginia, 1698 ***2212*** *p11*
Moretown, Matthew; America, 1698 ***2212*** *p10*
Morey, Adolfe 35; America, 1838 ***778.5*** *p392*
Morey, Alex.; Virginia, 1638 ***6219*** *p118*
Morey, Timothy; New York, NY, 1841 ***7036*** *p123*
Morfett, Hannah 14 *SEE* Morfett, William
Morfett, Mary 9 *SEE* Morfett, William
Morfett, Mary 48 *SEE* Morfett, William
Morfett, William 12 *SEE* Morfett, William
Morfett, William 44; Norfolk, VA, 1774 ***1219.7*** *p222*
*Wife:*Mary 48
*Child:*Hannah 14
*Child:*William 12
*Child:*Mary 9
Morfey, Silas; Illinois, 1888 ***5012.39*** *p122*
Morfey, William; Illinois, 1888 ***5012.39*** *p121*
Morgan, Mr.; Quebec, 1815 ***9229.18*** *p82*
Morgan, Alice; Virginia, 1643 ***6219*** *p205*
Morgan, Andrew; New York, NY, 1839 ***8208.4*** *p92*
Morgan, Andrew 40; Massachusetts, 1849 ***5881.1*** *p62*
Morgan, Ann 20; Quebec, 1862 ***5704.8*** *p151*
Morgan, Biddy 2; Massachusetts, 1850 ***5881.1*** *p64*
Morgan, Bridget 24; Massachusetts, 1849 ***5881.1*** *p63*
Morgan, Catharine 16; Massachusetts, 1848 ***5881.1*** *p64*
Morgan, Charles; New York, NY, 1837 ***8208.4*** *p53*
Morgan, Charles 31; Philadelphia, 1775 ***1219.7*** *p255*
Morgan, David; Iowa, 1866-1943 ***123.54*** *p35*
Morgan, David 32; Kansas, 1896 ***5240.1*** *p80*
Morgan, Ed.; America, 1740 ***4971*** *p66*
Morgan, Edw.; Virginia, 1637 ***6219*** *p13*
Morgan, Edward; Virginia, 1636 ***6219*** *p13*
Morgan, Edward; Virginia, 1636 ***6219*** *p146*
Morgan, Edward; Virginia, 1637 ***6219*** *p83*
Morgan, Edward; Virginia, 1638 ***6219*** *p121*
Morgan, Edwd.; New York, NY, 1816 ***2859.11*** *p39*
Morgan, Elizabeth 22; Baltimore, 1775 ***1219.7*** *p271*
Morgan, Evan; Virginia, 1637 ***6219*** *p113*
Morgan, Fra.; Virginia, 1648 ***6219*** *p246*
Morgan, Francis; Virginia, 1637 ***6219*** *p109*
Morgan, George 37; Wilmington, NC, 1774 ***1639.20*** *p243*
With wife
With child 7
With child 1
Morgan, Henry; Virginia, 1648 ***6219*** *p241*
Morgan, Henry 22; Quebec, 1862 ***5704.8*** *p151*
Morgan, Isaac; New York, NY, 1838 ***8208.4*** *p89*
Morgan, James; New York, NY, 1811 ***2859.11*** *p17*
With family
Morgan, James; Philadelphia, 1865 ***5704.8*** *p200*
Morgan, James; Quebec, 1852 ***5704.8*** *p98*
Morgan, James J.; Illinois, 1869 ***5012.38*** *p99*
Morgan, Jane 14; America, 1702 ***2212*** *p36*
Morgan, Jane 24; Quebec, 1863 ***5704.8*** *p153*
Morgan, Jno; America, 1697 ***2212*** *p8*
Morgan, John; America, 1851 ***1450.2*** *p104A*
Morgan, John; Jamaica, 1751 ***1219.7*** *p7*
Morgan, John; Jamaica, 1751 ***3690.1*** *p160*
Morgan, John; New York, NY, 1815 ***2859.11*** *p39*
Morgan, John; New York, NY, 1838 ***8208.4*** *p75*
Morgan, John; Virginia, 1635 ***6219*** *p1*
Morgan, John; Virginia, 1635 ***6219*** *p25*
Morgan, John; Virginia, 1637 ***6219*** *p145*
Morgan, John; Virginia, 1638 ***6219*** *p123*
Morgan, John; Virginia, 1639 ***6219*** *p158*
Morgan, John; Virginia, 1698 ***2212*** *p14*
Morgan, John 13; Virginia, 1700 ***2212*** *p31*
Morgan, John 24; Maryland, 1735 ***3690.1*** *p160*
Morgan, John 30; Massachusetts, 1850 ***5881.1*** *p69*
Morgan, Jon.; Virginia, 1636 ***6219*** *p79*
Morgan, Jon.; Virginia, 1642 ***6219*** *p195*
Morgan, Lewis 15; Maryland, 1775 ***1219.7*** *p250*
Morgan, Luke; New York, NY, 1811 ***2859.11*** *p17*
Morgan, Margaret 24; Philadelphia, 1860 ***5704.8*** *p145*
Morgan, Margarett Sanders *SEE* Morgan, William
Morgan, Mary; America, 1737 ***4971*** *p12*
Morgan, Mary; Philadelphia, 1865 ***5704.8*** *p178*
Morgan, Mary Ann 9; Jamaica, 1774 ***1219.7*** *p189*
Morgan, Mathew; Virginia, 1638 ***6219*** *p122*
Morgan, Maurice 22; Massachusetts, 1849 ***5881.1*** *p72*
Morgan, Mercer 20; Maryland, 1729 ***3690.1*** *p160*
Morgan, Meredith; Virginia, 1641 ***6219*** *p184*
Morgan, Michael; America, 1740 ***4971*** *p15*
Morgan, Michael; New York, NY, 1835 ***8208.4*** *p6*
Morgan, Michel; Quebec, 1830 ***4719.7*** *p21*
Morgan, Richard; Illinois, 1860 ***5012.38*** *p97*
Morgan, Richard; Illinois, 1861 ***5012.38*** *p98*
Morgan, Richard; Massachusetts, 1850 ***5881.1*** *p75*
Morgan, Richard; Virginia, 1642 ***6219*** *p195*

Morgan, Richard 16; Jamaica, 1731 ***3690.1*** *p160*
Morgan, Robert; Virginia, 1621 ***6219*** *p30*
Morgan, Roger 17; Maryland, 1723 ***3690.1*** *p160*
Morgan, Rolland; Iowa, 1866-1943 ***123.54*** *p35*
Morgan, Simon 19; Jamaica, 1730 ***3690.1*** *p160*
Morgan, Stephen J. 39; Kansas, 1893 ***5240.1*** *p79*
Morgan, Tho.; Virginia, 1618 ***6219*** *p72*
Morgan, Tho.; Virginia, 1634 ***6219*** *p105*
Morgan, Tho.; Virginia, 1642 ***6219*** *p195*
Morgan, Thomas; Virginia, 1636 ***6219*** *p80*
Morgan, Thomas; Virginia, 1638 ***6219*** *p147*
Morgan, Thomas; Virginia, 1638-1700 ***6219*** *p150*
Morgan, Thomas 16; Maryland, 1775 ***1219.7*** *p264*
Morgan, Thomas 20; Maryland, 1724 ***3690.1*** *p160*
Morgan, Thomas 25; Baltimore, 1775 ***1219.7*** *p270*
Morgan, Thomas 27; Maryland, 1774 ***1219.7*** *p235*
Morgan, William; America, 1740 ***4971*** *p24*
Morgan, William; America, 1773-1774 ***2859.11*** *p7*
Morgan, William; Jamaica, 1736 ***3690.1*** *p160*
Morgan, William; Virginia, 1638 ***6219*** *p122*
*Wife:*Margarett Sanders
Morgan, William; Virginia, 1639 ***6219*** *p149*
Morgan, William; Virginia, 1639 ***6219*** *p154*
Morgan, William 21; Maryland, 1774 ***1219.7*** *p192*
Morgan, William 26; Maryland or Virginia, 1735 ***3690.1*** *p160*
Morgan, William 31; Virginia, 1773 ***1219.7*** *p168*
Morgan, Wm.; Virginia, 1645 ***6219*** *p233*
Morganstam, Adam; Ohio, 1847 ***9892.11*** *p31*
Morganstern, Adam; Ohio, 1840 ***9892.11*** *p31*
Morgate, Peter; Virginia, 1638 ***6219*** *p149*
Morgenstern, Capit.; Quebec, 1776 ***9786*** *p105*
Morgenstern, Lieut.; Quebec, 1776 ***9786*** *p105*
Morgenstern, Carl Friedrich; Quebec, 1776 ***9786*** *p256*
Morgenstern, Johann Carl; Quebec, 1776 ***9786*** *p256*
Morggon, Allen; Virginia, 1642 ***6219*** *p191*
Morgin, Tho.; Virginia, 1645 ***6219*** *p233*
Morgin, Thomas; Virginia, 1637 ***6219*** *p110*
Morgrave, Adam; Virginia, 1643 ***6219*** *p203*
Morgrave, Morcas; Virginia, 1645 ***6219*** *p252*
Morhardt, Christina; New York, 1752 ***3652*** *p76*
Moriac, Mr. 30; Louisiana, 1820 ***778.5*** *p392*
Morial, Fage 28; New Orleans, 1838 ***778.5*** *p392*
Moriarty, Ellen 20; Massachusetts, 1849 ***5881.1*** *p66*
Moriarty, Eugene 13; Massachusetts, 1849 ***5881.1*** *p66*
Moriarty, Margaret 26; Massachusetts, 1850 ***5881.1*** *p73*
Moriarty, Michael 15; Massachusetts, 1848 ***5881.1*** *p71*
Moriarty, Michael 20; Massachusetts, 1849 ***5881.1*** *p72*
Moriarty, Robert; America, 1741 ***4971*** *p41*
Moriarty, Tho's 25; Massachusetts, 1849 ***5881.1*** *p76*
Moriarty, William; Chicago, 1841 ***7036*** *p122*
Moriaux, Joseph 29; America, 1838 ***778.5*** *p392*
Moriaux, Rosalie 28; America, 1838 ***778.5*** *p392*
Moribeto, Gragorio; Arkansas, 1918 ***95.2*** *p86*
Morici, Vincenzo; Iowa, 1866-1943 ***123.54*** *p35*
Morie, J. F. 32; Port uncertain, 1837 ***778.5*** *p392*
Morien, John 23; Maryland, 1773 ***1219.7*** *p172*
Moril, Jn. 33; New Orleans, 1835 ***778.5*** *p392*
Morin, Amante 40; New Orleans, 1829 ***778.5*** *p392*
Morin, Charles; New York, NY, 1838 ***8208.4*** *p62*
Morin, Emanuel Dieudonne 42; West Virginia, 1902 ***9788.3*** *p17*
Morin, F. 20; New Orleans, 1839 ***778.5*** *p393*
Morin, J. 25; Port uncertain, 1836 ***778.5*** *p393*
Morin, Jean Baptiste 41; America, 1836 ***778.5*** *p393*
Morin, Laurent; Montreal, 1873 ***7603*** *p78*
Morine, Miss; Quebec, 1815 ***9229.18*** *p81*
Morine, Mrs.; Quebec, 1815 ***9229.18*** *p81*
Morine, John; New York, NY, 1816 ***2859.11*** *p39*
Morine, Judith; New York, NY, 1816 ***2859.11*** *p39*
With 2 children
Morinet, Alphonse 18; America, 1835 ***778.5*** *p393*
Moring, Jean; Sorel, Que., 1764 ***7603*** *p36*
Morinnet, Mr. 22; America, 1837 ***778.5*** *p393*
Morino, Carlos; Arkansas, 1918 ***95.2*** *p86*
Moris, Mary 20; St. John, N.B., 1865 ***5704.8*** *p165*
Morison, Alexander; California, 1853 ***8893*** *p266*
Morison, Alexander 60; Wilmington, NC, 1774 ***1639.20*** *p243*
With wife
With son
Morison, Jemima Oliphant; Charleston, SC, 1804 ***1639.20*** *p256*
Morison, John; Charleston, SC, 1807 ***1639.20*** *p245*
Morison, Simon; Charleston, SC, 1830 ***1639.20*** *p247*
Morison, William; America, 1807 ***8893*** *p264*
Morissy, Mary; America, 1737 ***4971*** *p32*
Moritsch, Carl; Wisconsin, n.d. ***9675.7*** *p52*
Moritz, Jacob; Wisconsin, n.d. ***9675.7*** *p52*
Mork, Thor J.; Colorado, 1898 ***9678.2*** *p127*
Morleau, Anne-Catherine *SEE* Morleau, Jean-Pierre
Morleau, Daniel *SEE* Morleau, Jean-Pierre
Morleau, Daniel *SEE* Morleau, Jean-Pierre
Morleau, Hedwige Grosrenault *SEE* Morleau, Jean-Pierre
Morleau, Jean-George *SEE* Morleau, Jean-Pierre
Morleau, Jean-George *SEE* Morleau, Jean-Pierre
Morleau, Jean-Pierre *SEE* Morleau, Jean-Pierre
Morleau, Jean-Pierre *SEE* Morleau, Jean-Pierre
Morleau, Jean-Pierre; Halifax, N.S., 1752 ***7074.6*** *p213*
*Wife:*Hedwige Grosrenault
*Son:*Jean-George
*Son:*Daniel
*Son:*Jean-Pierre
Morleau, Jean-Pierre 48; Halifax, N.S., 1752 ***7074.6*** *p212*
*Wife:*Anne-Catherine
*Son:*Jean-George
*Son:*Daniel
*Son:*Jean-Pierre
Morleaux, Jean Pierre 48; Halifax, N.S., 1752 ***7074.6*** *p207*
With family of 4
Morley, James 14; Pennsylvania, Virginia or Maryland, 1719 ***3690.1*** *p161*
Morley, Rudolph 40; Kansas, 1885 ***5240.1*** *p68*
Morley, Sym.; Virginia, 1636 ***6219*** *p80*
Morley, Symon; Virginia, 1639 ***6219*** *p161*
Morley, Tho 16; America, 1706 ***2212*** *p47*
Morlin, Jon.; Virginia, 1636 ***6219*** *p80*
Morlot, Mr. 30; New Orleans, 1822 ***778.5*** *p393*
Morlot, Mr. 34; New Orleans, 1821 ***778.5*** *p393*
Morlot, Mr. 41; New Orleans, 1837 ***778.5*** *p393*
Morlot, Daniel *SEE* Morlot, Jean-Pierre
Morlot, Hedwige Grosrenault *SEE* Morlot, Jean-Pierre
Morlot, Jean-George *SEE* Morlot, Jean-Pierre
Morlot, Jean-Pierre *SEE* Morlot, Jean-Pierre
Morlot, Jean-Pierre; Halifax, N.S., 1752 ***7074.6*** *p213*
*Wife:*Hedwige Grosrenault
*Son:*Jean-George
*Son:*Daniel
*Son:*Jean-Pierre
Morlot, Nicolas 32; New Orleans, 1822 ***778.5*** *p393*
Morning, Richard; New Brunswick, 1798 ***7603*** *p78*
Moro, . . .; Canada, 1776-1783 ***9786*** *p29*
Moro, Julius 69; Arizona, 1913 ***9228.40*** *p18*
Morolle, Guissepe; Arkansas, 1918 ***95.2*** *p86*
Moron, Edward; Philadelphia, 1866 ***5704.8*** *p206*
Moroney, William; Quebec, 1779 ***7603*** *p84*
Morost, Jean Martin 31; Port uncertain, 1838 ***778.5*** *p393*
Moroz, Julius; Arkansas, 1918 ***95.2*** *p86*
Morozowski, . . .; New York, 1831 ***4606*** *p175*
Morpeth, Thomas 15; Philadelphia, 1774 ***1219.7*** *p183*
Morphew, Michaell; Virginia, 1641 ***6219*** *p185*
Morr, . . .; Canada, 1776-1783 ***9786*** *p29*
Morran, Andrew; New York, NY, 1811 ***2859.11*** *p17*
With wife
Morrarhin, Jospeh 36; Port uncertain, 1839 ***778.5*** *p393*
Morrel, Anthony 20; Jamaica, 1738 ***3690.1*** *p161*
Morrell, Anthony 20; Jamaica, 1738 ***3690.1*** *p161*
Morrell, Tho.; Virginia, 1638 ***6219*** *p147*
Morrell, Thomas; Philadelphia, 1865 ***5704.8*** *p202*
Morren, Mary Ann 24; Philadelphia, 1854 ***5704.8*** *p122*
Morres, John 30; Virginia, 1774 ***1219.7*** *p239*
Morres, June; New York, NY, 1871 ***5704.8*** *p240*
Morres, Richard; America, 1742 ***4971*** *p27*
Morres, Simon; New York, NY, 1871 ***5704.8*** *p240*
Morrey, Elizabeth *SEE* Morrey, Thomas
Morrey, Thomas; Virginia, 1641 ***6219*** *p184*
*Wife:*Elizabeth
Morrey, Thomas; Virginia, 1643 ***6219*** *p204*
Morrice, James; Virginia, 1645 ***6219*** *p232*
Morrice, Jno 16; Maryland or Virginia, 1699 ***2212*** *p23*
Morrice, Richard; Virginia, 1641 ***6219*** *p184*
Morrice, William; Virginia, 1638 ***6219*** *p153*
Morriday, John; Virginia, 1638 ***6219*** *p36*
Morrin, Mr.; Quebec, 1815 ***9229.18*** *p78*
Morrin, Andrew; America, 1739 ***4971*** *p28*
Morrin, Edward; Philadelphia, 1848 ***53.26*** *p71*
*Relative:*Sarah
Morrin, Edward; Philadelphia, 1848 ***5704.8*** *p46*
Morrin, Sarah *SEE* Morrin, Edward
Morrin, Sarah; Philadelphia, 1848 ***5704.8*** *p46*
Morris, Ann 17; Quebec, 1858 ***5704.8*** *p137*
Morris, Arthur 36; Maryland, 1775 ***1219.7*** *p254*
Morris, Bernard; America, 1864 ***5704.8*** *p185*
Morris, Bernard; New York, NY, 1864 ***5704.8*** *p169*
Morris, Bernard; Philadelphia, 1847 ***53.26*** *p71*
*Relative:*Isabella
Morris, Bernard; Philadelphia, 1847 ***5704.8*** *p1*
Morris, Bernard 18; Quebec, 1853 ***5704.8*** *p104*
Morris, Bridget; Philadelphia, 1864 ***5704.8*** *p181*
Morris, Bridget 6; Massachusetts, 1848 ***5881.1*** *p63*
Morris, Bridget 28; Philadelphia, 1864 ***5704.8*** *p161*
Morris, Carthy 30; Massachusetts, 1847 ***5881.1*** *p64*
Morris, Catherine; Philadelphia, 1847 ***53.26*** *p71*
*Relative:*Mary
Morris, Catherine; Philadelphia, 1847 ***5704.8*** *p32*
Morris, Catherine; St. John, N.B., 1848 ***5704.8*** *p44*
Morris, Catherine 20; Philadelphia, 1853 ***5704.8*** *p109*
Morris, Celia 60; Massachusetts, 1847 ***5881.1*** *p64*
Morris, Charley; Arkansas, 1918 ***95.2*** *p86*
Morris, Christopher 22; Baltimore, 1775 ***1219.7*** *p269*
Morris, Daniel; Philadelphia, 1864 ***5704.8*** *p169*
Morris, Daniel 3 mos; Philadelphia, 1864 ***5704.8*** *p161*
Morris, Daniel 28; Philadelphia, 1864 ***5704.8*** *p161*
Morris, David R. 21; Kansas, 1872 ***5240.1*** *p52*
Morris, Domnick; Philadelphia, 1864 ***5704.8*** *p173*
Morris, Edward; Virginia, 1648 ***6219*** *p245*
Morris, Eleanor; St. John, N.B., 1852 ***5704.8*** *p83*
Morris, Eleanor 11; St. John, N.B., 1852 ***5704.8*** *p83*
Morris, Eliz 25; America, 1701 ***2212*** *p35*
Morris, Eliza; Virginia, 1638 ***6219*** *p148*
Morris, Elizabeth 16; Maryland, 1774 ***1219.7*** *p207*
Morris, Elizabeth 22; Philadelphia, 1774 ***1219.7*** *p201*
Morris, Ellen; America, 1864 ***5704.8*** *p185*
Morris, Ellen; New York, NY, 1868 ***5704.8*** *p228*
Morris, Ellen 8; Massachusetts, 1848 ***5881.1*** *p65*
Morris, Ellen 40; Massachusetts, 1848 ***5881.1*** *p65*
Morris, Evan; Virginia, 1643 ***6219*** *p205*
Morris, Evan; Virginia, 1648 ***6219*** *p246*
Morris, Finlh; America, 1697 ***2212*** *p8*
Morris, George; Ohio, 1825 ***9892.11*** *p31*
Morris, George 23; Virginia, 1774 ***1219.7*** *p240*
Morris, Hannah; Philadelphia, 1864 ***5704.8*** *p173*
Morris, Helene; Quebec, 1822 ***7603*** *p83*
Morris, Henry; St. John, N.B., 1852 ***5704.8*** *p84*
Morris, Henry 7; Massachusetts, 1849 ***5881.1*** *p67*
Morris, Henry 27; Virginia, 1774 ***1219.7*** *p193*
Morris, Hugh; America, 1739 ***4971*** *p14*
Morris, Hugh 11; Philadelphia, 1864 ***5704.8*** *p161*
Morris, Hugh 14; Maryland or Virginia, 1699 ***2212*** *p23*
Morris, Isabella *SEE* Morris, Bernard
Morris, Isabella; Philadelphia, 1847 ***5704.8*** *p1*
Morris, James; Philadelphia, 1784 ***8893*** *p266*
Morris, James; St. John, N.B., 1847 ***5704.8*** *p9*
Morris, James; Virginia, 1636 ***6219*** *p32*
Morris, James 3; St. John, N.B., 1852 ***5704.8*** *p83*
Morris, James 21; Maryland, 1775 ***1219.7*** *p254*
Morris, James D.; Colorado, 1905 ***9678.2*** *p127*
Morris, James H. 37; Kansas, 1874 ***5240.1*** *p56*
Morris, Jno 20; Maryland or Virginia, 1699 ***2212*** *p24*
Morris, John; Iowa, 1866-1943 ***123.54*** *p35*
Morris, John; New York, NY, 1815 ***2859.11*** *p39*
Morris, John; St. John, N.B., 1852 ***5704.8*** *p83*
Morris, John; Virginia, 1636 ***6219*** *p19*
Morris, John; Virginia, 1642 ***6219*** *p189*
Morris, John; Virginia, 1643 ***6219*** *p205*
Morris, John; Wisconsin, n.d. ***9675.7*** *p52*
Morris, John 6 mos; St. John, N.B., 1847 ***5704.8*** *p9*
Morris, John 6; Philadelphia, 1864 ***5704.8*** *p161*
Morris, John 6; St. John, N.B., 1852 ***5704.8*** *p83*
Morris, John 16; Philadelphia, 1854 ***5704.8*** *p118*
Morris, John 45; Philadelphia, 1864 ***5704.8*** *p161*
Morris, John Arthur; New York, NY, 1837 ***8208.4*** *p51*
Morris, John B.; New York, 1868 ***1450.2*** *p104A*
Morris, John D.; New York, NY, 1835 ***8208.4*** *p59*
Morris, Jon.; Virginia, 1636 ***6219*** *p74*
Morris, Joshua; Pennsylvania, 1682 ***4962*** *p154*
Morris, Julia 20; Massachusetts, 1848 ***5881.1*** *p68*
Morris, L. H.; Washington, 1859-1920 ***2872.1*** *p26*
Morris, Lawrence 7; Massachusetts, 1849 ***5881.1*** *p70*
Morris, Margaret; Philadelphia, 1851 ***5704.8*** *p70*
Morris, Margaret; St. John, N.B., 1847 ***5704.8*** *p9*
Morris, Maria 45; Massachusetts, 1850 ***5881.1*** *p72*
Morris, Martin; Iowa, 1866-1943 ***123.54*** *p35*
Morris, Martin 60; Newfoundland, 1774 ***1219.7*** *p196*
Morris, Mary *SEE* Morris, Catherine
Morris, Mary; America, 1737 ***4971*** *p12*
Morris, Mary; America, 1869 ***5704.8*** *p232*
Morris, Mary; New York, NY, 1816 ***2859.11*** *p39*
Morris, Mary; Philadelphia, 1847 ***5704.8*** *p32*
Morris, Mary; Philadelphia, 1851 ***5704.8*** *p76*
Morris, Mary; Philadelphia, 1852 ***5704.8*** *p96*
Morris, Mary; Quebec, 1847 ***5704.8*** *p38*
Morris, Mary; St. John, N.B., 1848 ***5704.8*** *p44*
Morris, Mary 18; America, 1702 ***2212*** *p36*
Morris, Mary 18; Massachusetts, 1848 ***5881.1*** *p71*
Morris, Mary 30; Virginia, 1700 ***2212*** *p32*
Morris, Mary 45; Philadelphia, 1864 ***5704.8*** *p161*
Morris, Mary Jane 6; Massachusetts, 1847 ***5881.1*** *p70*
Morris, Matilda 11; Quebec, 1858 ***5704.8*** *p137*
Morris, Michael; America, 1735-1743 ***4971*** *p8*
Morris, Michael; Philadelphia, 1864 ***5704.8*** *p169*
Morris, Michael 9; St. John, N.B., 1852 ***5704.8*** *p83*
Morris, Nancy; Philadelphia, 1849 ***53.26*** *p71*
Morris, Nancy; Philadelphia, 1849 ***5704.8*** *p50*
Morris, Nicholas; Arkansas, 1918 ***95.2*** *p86*
Morris, Nicholas; Virginia, 1652 ***6251*** *p19*
Morris, Owen 10; Massachusetts, 1849 ***5881.1*** *p73*

374

FOR A COMPLETE EXPLANATION OF ENTRY, SEE "HOW TO READ A CITATION" SECTION

Morris, Owen 40; Massachusetts, 1849 *5881.1 p73*
Morris, Patrick; Philadelphia, 1851 *5704.8 p76*
Morris, Patrick 3; Philadelphia, 1864 *5704.8 p161*
Morris, Patrick 8; Massachusetts, 1847 *5881.1 p74*
Morris, Patrick 12; Massachusetts, 1848 *5881.1 p74*
Morris, Philip 25; Massachusetts, 1847 *5881.1 p74*
Morris, Rich.; Virginia, 1635 *6219 p3*
Morris, Richard; California, 1866 *3840.2 p18*
Morris, Richard; Virginia, 1638 *6219 p9*
Morris, Richard; Virginia, 1638 *6219 p120*
Morris, Richard; Virginia, 1643 *6219 p204*
Morris, Richard 26; Jamaica, 1738 *3690.1 p161*
Morris, Richd.; Virginia, 1642 *6219 p191*
Morris, Robert; Virginia, 1635 *6219 p71*
Morris, Robert 22; America, 1700 *2212 p33*
Morris, Rosa Gardiner; America, 1816 *8894.2 p56*
Morris, Samuel 24; Kansas, 1888 *5240.1 p71*
Morris, Sarah; Virginia, 1643 *6219 p206*
Morris, Sarah 10; Philadelphia, 1864 *5704.8 p161*
Morris, Stanley; Wisconsin, n.d. *9675.7 p52*
Morris, Stephen 36; Maryland, 1775 *1219.7 p250*
Morris, Tho.; Virginia, 1637 *6219 p8*
Morris, Thomas; America, 1698 *2212 p8*
Morris, Thomas; New York, NY, 1834 *8208.4 p76*
Morris, Thomas; Quebec, 1781 *7603 p78*
Morris, Thomas; Quebec, 1781 *7603 p102*
Morris, Thomas 13; Massachusetts, 1847 *5881.1 p76*
Morris, Thomas 14; Massachusetts, 1848 *5881.1 p76*
Morris, Thomas 17; Pennsylvania, 1731 *3690.1 p161*
Morris, Thomas 19; Georgia, 1733 *3690.1 p161*
Morris, Thomas 21; Jamaica, 1730 *3690.1 p161*
Morris, William; New York, NY, 1834 *8208.4 p27*
Morris, William; Philadelphia, 1849 *53.26 p71*
Morris, William; Philadelphia, 1849 *5704.8 p54*
Morris, William; Virginia, 1638 *6219 p115*
Morris, William 16; Jamaica, 1734 *3690.1 p161*
Morris, William 17; Maryland, 1775 *1219.7 p253*
Morris, William 20; Jamaica, 1721 *3690.1 p161*
Morris, William 36; Virginia, 1700 *2212 p32*
Morris, William 38; Massachusetts, 1849 *5881.1 p77*
Morris, William E.; New Jersey, 1872 *2764.35 p44*
Morris, Wm.; Virginia, 1621 *6219 p4*
Morris, Wm.; Virginia, 1643 *6219 p203*
Morris, Wm.; Virginia, 1643 *6219 p204*
Morris, Woolaston 21; Maryland, 1774 *1219.7 p211*
Morrisan, Mary; America, 1854-1855 *8893 p266*
Morrisey, John; New York, 1752 *1219.7 p11*
Morrison, . . . 4 mos; New York, NY, 1866 *5704.8 p214*
Morrison, . . . 6 mos; America, 1864 *5704.8 p190*
Morrison, Mr.; Quebec, 1885 *4537.30 p26*
    With sons
Morrison, Alex *SEE* Morrison, John
Morrison, Alex; Quebec, 1843 *4537.30 p25*
    *Wife:*Margaret MacIver
    *Child:*Flora
    *Child:*John
    *Child:*Margaret
    *Child:*Murdo
Morrison, Alex; Quebec, 1856 *4537.30 p20*
Morrison, Alex D. *SEE* Morrison, Donald
Morrison, Alex G. *SEE* Morrison, Donald
Morrison, Alex S. *SEE* Morrison, John S.
Morrison, Alexander; North Carolina, 1717-1777 *1639.20 p243*
Morrison, Alexander; Philadelphia, 1868 *5704.8 p230*
Morrison, Andrew; Philadelphia, 1851 *5704.8 p77*
Morrison, Angus *SEE* Morrison, Angus
Morrison, Angus *SEE* Morrison, Angus
Morrison, Angus *SEE* Morrison, Angus
Morrison, Angus *SEE* Morrison, Donald
Morrison, Angus *SEE* Morrison, John S.
Morrison, Angus; Quebec, 1855 *4537.30 p21*
    *Wife:*Mary MacRitchie
    *Child:*Kirsty
    *Child:*Malcolm
    *Child:*Angus
    *Child:*Murdo
    *Child:*Catherine
    *Child:*Donald
Morrison, Angus; Quebec, 1863 *4537.30 p20*
    *Wife:*Catherine Campbell
    *Child:*Angus
Morrison, Angus; Quebec, 1863 *4537.30 p20*
    *Wife:*Flora Morrison
    *Child:*Angus
    *Child:*John
    *Child:*Donald
    *Child:*Roderick
    *Child:*Ann
Morrison, Angus; Quebec, 1863 *4537.30 p21*
    *Wife:*Kirsty MacAskill
    *Child:*Catherine
    *Child:*Mary

*Child:*Ann
*Child:*John
Morrison, Angus; Quebec, 1873 *4537.30 p28*
    *Wife:*Kirsty Murray
Morrison, Angus; Quebec, 1887 *4537.30 p29*
    *Wife:*Gormelia MacLean
    *Child:*Donald
    *Child:*Murdo
    *Child:*Ann
    *Child:*Effie
    With child
Morrison, Ann *SEE* Morrison, Angus
Morrison, Ann *SEE* Morrison, Angus
Morrison, Ann *SEE* Morrison, Angus
Morrison, Ann *SEE* Morrison, Donald
Morrison, Ann *SEE* Morrison, Donald
Morrison, Ann *SEE* Morrison, Donald
Morrison, Ann *SEE* Morrison, John
Morrison, Ann *SEE* Morrison, John S.
Morrison, Ann *SEE* Morrison, Margaret Murray
Morrison, Ann *SEE* Morrison, Murdo
Morrison, Ann *SEE* Morrison, Roderick
Morrison, Ann; Quebec, 1838 *4537.30 p113*
Morrison, Ann; Quebec, 1842 *4537.30 p96*
Morrison, Ann; Quebec, 1845 *4537.30 p82*
Morrison, Ann; Quebec, 1855 *4537.30 p74*
Morrison, Ann; Quebec, 1863 *4537.30 p45*
Morrison, Ann MacLeod *SEE* Morrison, John
Morrison, Barbara 82; North Carolina, 1850 *1639.20 p244*
Morrison, Bessie; New York, NY, 1865 *5704.8 p196*
Morrison, Betty Munro *SEE* Morrison, Donald
Morrison, Catherine *SEE* Morrison, Angus
Morrison, Catherine *SEE* Morrison, Angus
Morrison, Catherine *SEE* Morrison, John
Morrison, Catherine *SEE* Morrison, John
Morrison, Catherine *SEE* Morrison, John
Morrison, Catherine *SEE* Morrison, Murdo
Morrison, Catherine *SEE* Morrison, Norman
Morrison, Catherine *SEE* Morrison, Roderick
Morrison, Catherine; Philadelphia, 1853 *5704.8 p103*
Morrison, Catherine; Quebec, 1852 *4537.30 p23*
    *Child:*Malcolm
Morrison, Catherine; Quebec, 1855 *4537.30 p68*
Morrison, Catherine 65; North Carolina, 1850 *1639.20 p244*
Morrison, Catherine Campbell *SEE* Morrison, Angus
Morrison, Catherine MacDonald *SEE* Morrison, Murdo
Morrison, Catherine Stewart *SEE* Morrison, Donald
Morrison, Charles; Arkansas, 1878 *3688 p7*
Morrison, Charles; St. John, N.B., 1847 *5704.8 p26*
Morrison, Charles; St. John, N.B., 1848 *5704.8 p47*
Morrison, Cicily 35; St. John, N.B., 1853 *5704.8 p110*
Morrison, Colin *SEE* Morrison, Duncan
Morrison, D.H.; Iowa, 1866-1943 *123.54 p35*
Morrison, Daniel; New York, NY, 1866 *5704.8 p214*
Morrison, David 67; North Carolina, 1850 *1639.20 p244*
Morrison, Donald *SEE* Morrison, Angus
Morrison, Donald *SEE* Morrison, Angus
Morrison, Donald *SEE* Morrison, Angus
Morrison, Donald *SEE* Morrison, Donald
Morrison, Donald *SEE* Morrison, Duncan
Morrison, Donald *SEE* Morrison, John
Morrison, Donald *SEE* Morrison, John
Morrison, Donald *SEE* Morrison, John
Morrison, Donald *SEE* Morrison, John S.
Morrison, Donald *SEE* Morrison, Norman
Morrison, Donald; Quebec, 1855 *4537.30 p22*
Morrison, Donald; Quebec, 1873 *4537.30 p21*
    *Wife:*Betty Munro
    *Child:*Alex G.
    *Child:*Kirsty
    *Child:*Ann
    *Child:*Alex D.
    *Child:*John D.
    *Child:*Mary
Morrison, Donald; Quebec, 1873 *4537.30 p26*
    *Wife:*Mary Kerr
    *Child:*Ewen
    *Child:*Roderick
    *Child:*Marion
    *Child:*Peter
    *Child:*Sam
Morrison, Donald; Quebec, 1873 *4537.30 p28*
    *Wife:*Margaret MacIver
    *Child:*Angus
    *Child:*Ann
    *Child:*Donald
    *Child:*Malcolm
    *Child:*John
    *Child:*Norman

Morrison, Donald; Quebec, 1875 *4537.30 p26*
    *Wife:*Catherine Stewart
    *Child:*Ann
    *Child:*Murdo
    *Child:*Kirsty
    *Child:*Mary Ann
    *Child:*Jessie
Morrison, Duncan *SEE* Morrison, John
Morrison, Duncan; Quebec, 1852 *4537.30 p22*
    *Wife:*Lily Cameron
    *Child:*Donald
    *Child:*Kenneth
    *Child:*John
    *Child:*Colin
    *Child:*Hector
    *Child:*Peter
Morrison, Edward; St. John, N.B., 1853 *5704.8 p99*
Morrison, Effie *SEE* Morrison, Angus
Morrison, Effie *SEE* Morrison, John
Morrison, Effie; Quebec, 1855 *4537.30 p49*
Morrison, Effie 60; North Carolina, 1850 *1639.20 p244*
    *Relative:*Sally 58
Morrison, Effie Smith *SEE* Morrison, John S.
Morrison, Effy 57; South Carolina, 1850 *1639.20 p244*
Morrison, Eliza; America, 1864 *5704.8 p190*
Morrison, Eliza 7; St. John, N.B., 1847 *5704.8 p4*
Morrison, Eliza 12; St. John, N.B., 1854 *5704.8 p122*
Morrison, Elizabeth; Philadelphia, 1811 *53.26 p71*
Morrison, Elizabeth; Philadelphia, 1811 *2859.11 p17*
Morrison, Ellen; Quebec, 1852 *5704.8 p86*
Morrison, Ewen *SEE* Morrison, Donald
Morrison, Flora *SEE* Morrison, Alex
Morrison, Flora; North Carolina, 1796-1881 *1639.20 p244*
Morrison, Flora; Quebec, 1863 *4537.30 p20*
Morrison, Flora 51; North Carolina, 1850 *1639.20 p244*
Morrison, Flora Morrison *SEE* Morrison, Angus
Morrison, Francis; America, 1742 *4971 p80*
Morrison, George *SEE* Morrison, Roderick
Morrison, Gormelia MacLean *SEE* Morrison, Angus
Morrison, Hannah; St. John, N.B., 1847 *5704.8 p4*
Morrison, Hector *SEE* Morrison, Duncan
Morrison, Henry; Virginia, 1648 *6219 p247*
Morrison, Hugh; Philadelphia, 1850 *53.26 p71*
Morrison, Hugh; Philadelphia, 1850 *5704.8 p69*
Morrison, Isabella *SEE* Morrison, Margaret Murray
Morrison, Isabella; New York, NY, 1865 *5704.8 p192*
Morrison, Isabella; Quebec, 1851 *4537.30 p116*
Morrison, Isabella; Quebec, 1852 *5704.8 p86*
Morrison, Isabella; Quebec, 1852 *5704.8 p90*
Morrison, Isabella 9; St. John, N.B., 1847 *5704.8 p4*
Morrison, Isabella MacIver *SEE* Morrison, Murdo
Morrison, Isabella MacLeod *SEE* Morrison, Roderick
Morrison, Isabella MacLeod *SEE* Morrison, Roderick
Morrison, J.; New York, NY, 1816 *2859.11 p39*
Morrison, J. White 18 *SEE* Morrison, T. White
Morrison, Jacob; New York, NY, 1864 *5704.8 p186*
Morrison, James *SEE* Morrison, John
Morrison, James; Charleston, SC, 1798 *1639.20 p244*
Morrison, James; New York, NY, 1811 *2859.11 p17*
    With family
Morrison, James; New York, NY, 1864 *5704.8 p186*
Morrison, James; Quebec, 1852 *5704.8 p90*
Morrison, James; St. John, N.B., 1848 *5704.8 p39*
Morrison, James; South Carolina, 1810 *1639.20 p244*
Morrison, James 8; Quebec, 1852 *5704.8 p86*
Morrison, Jane; Philadelphia, 1851 *5704.8 p77*
Morrison, Jane; Quebec, 1852 *5704.8 p86*
Morrison, Jane; Quebec, 1852 *5704.8 p90*
Morrison, Jane; St. John, N.B., 1847 *5704.8 p18*
Morrison, Jessie *SEE* Morrison, Donald
Morrison, John *SEE* Morrison, Alex
Morrison, John *SEE* Morrison, Angus
Morrison, John *SEE* Morrison, Angus
Morrison, John *SEE* Morrison, Donald
Morrison, John *SEE* Morrison, Duncan
Morrison, John *SEE* Morrison, John
Morrison, John *SEE* Morrison, John
Morrison, John *SEE* Morrison, Roderick
Morrison, John *SEE* Morrison, Roderick
Morrison, John; America, 1788 *1639.20 p245*
Morrison, John; America, 1802 *1639.20 p244*
Morrison, John; America, 1802 *1639.20 p245*
Morrison, John; New Brunswick, 1809 *7603 p38*
Morrison, John; New York, NY, 1811 *2859.11 p17*
Morrison, John; Quebec, 1851 *4537.30 p22*
    *Wife:*Ann MacLeod
    *Child:*Mary
    *Child:*Donald
    *Child:*Kirsty

Morrison, John; Quebec, 1863 *4537.30 p23*
  *Wife:*Mary MacLeod
  *Child:*Norman
  *Child:*Ann
  *Child:*Margaret
  *Child:*Catherine
  *Child:*John
Morrison, John; Quebec, 1872 *4537.30 p26*
  *Wife:*Mary Campbell
  *Child:*Catherine
  *Child:*Marion
  *Child:*Roderick
Morrison, John; Quebec, 1873 *4537.30 p27*
  *Wife:*Margaret MacMillan
  *Child:*John
  *Child:*Norman
  *Child:*Donald
  *Child:*Duncan
  *Child:*John
  *Child:*Alex
  *Child:*Margaret
  *Child:*Mary
Morrison, John; Quebec, 1887 *4537.30 p29*
  *Wife:*Margaret Murray
  *Child:*James
  *Child:*Catherine
  *Child:*Mary Ann
  *Child:*William
  *Child:*Effie
  *Child:*Donald
  With child
Morrison, John 2; St. John, N.B., 1847 *5704.8 p4*
Morrison, John 28; Massachusetts, 1849 *5881.1 p68*
Morrison, John 67; North Carolina, 1850 *1639.20 p245*
Morrison, John 80; North Carolina, 1850 *1639.20 p245*
Morrison, John D. *SEE* Morrison, Donald
Morrison, John D. *SEE* Morrison, Murdo
Morrison, John McD.; America, 1802 *1639.20 p245*
Morrison, John S.; Quebec, 1855 *4537.30 p23*
  *Wife:*Effie Smith
  *Child:*Angus
  *Child:*Mary
  *Child:*Kirsty
  *Child:*Rachel
  *Child:*Margaret
  *Child:*Alex S.
  *Child:*Donald
  *Child:*Ann
Morrison, Joseph; New York, NY, 1838 *8208.4 p80*
Morrison, Joseph, Jr.; New York, NY, 1838 *8208.4 p72*
Morrison, Kenneth *SEE* Morrison, Duncan
Morrison, Kenneth *SEE* Morrison, Margaret Murray
Morrison, Kenneth *SEE* Morrison, Murdo
Morrison, Kenneth *SEE* Morrison, Norman
Morrison, Kenneth 79; South Carolina, 1850 *1639.20 p245*
Morrison, Kirsty *SEE* Morrison, Angus
Morrison, Kirsty *SEE* Morrison, Donald
Morrison, Kirsty *SEE* Morrison, Donald
Morrison, Kirsty *SEE* Morrison, John
Morrison, Kirsty *SEE* Morrison, John S.
Morrison, Kirsty *SEE* Morrison, Murdo
Morrison, Kirsty *SEE* Morrison, Norman
Morrison, Kirsty *SEE* Morrison, Roderick
Morrison, Kirsty; Quebec, 1851 *4537.30 p42*
Morrison, Kirsty; Quebec, 1855 *4537.30 p111*
Morrison, Kirsty; Quebec, 1861-1881 *4537.30 p32*
Morrison, Kirsty MacAskill *SEE* Morrison, Angus
Morrison, Kirsty Murray *SEE* Morrison, Angus
Morrison, Letitia; Philadelphia, 1868 *5704.8 p230*
Morrison, Lily Cameron *SEE* Morrison, Duncan
Morrison, Malcolm *SEE* Morrison, Angus
Morrison, Malcolm *SEE* Morrison, Catherine
Morrison, Malcolm *SEE* Morrison, Donald
Morrison, Malcolm *SEE* Morrison, Roderick
Morrison, Malcolm; America, 1802 *1639.20 p246*
Morrison, Margaret *SEE* Morrison, Alex
Morrison, Margaret *SEE* Morrison, John
Morrison, Margaret *SEE* Morrison, John
Morrison, Margaret *SEE* Morrison, John S.
Morrison, Margaret *SEE* Morrison, Murdo
Morrison, Margaret *SEE* Morrison, Roderick
Morrison, Margaret *SEE* Morrison, Roderick
Morrison, Margaret *SEE* Morrison, Roderick
Morrison, Margaret 11; St. John, N.B., 1847 *5704.8 p4*
Morrison, Margaret 48; North Carolina, 1850 *1639.20 p246*
Morrison, Margaret 65; North Carolina, 1850 *1639.20 p246*
Morrison, Margaret J.; New York, NY, 1864 *5704.8 p186*
Morrison, Margaret MacIver *SEE* Morrison, Alex
Morrison, Margaret MacIver *SEE* Morrison, Donald

Morrison, Margaret MacMillan *SEE* Morrison, John
Morrison, Margaret Murray *SEE* Morrison, John
Morrison, Margaret Murray; Quebec, 1920 *4537.30 p29*
  *Child:*Norman
  *Child:*Kenneth
  *Child:*Roderick
  *Child:*Isabella
  *Child:*Ann
  *Child:*Mary
Morrison, Margt 18; Newport, RI, 1851 *6508.5 p19*
Morrison, Margt 50; Newport, RI, 1851 *6508.5 p19*
Morrison, Marion *SEE* Morrison, Donald
Morrison, Marion *SEE* Morrison, John
Morrison, Marion *SEE* Morrison, Roderick
Morrison, Marion; Quebec, 1886-1889 *4537.30 p37*
Morrison, Martha; Philadelphia, 1811 *2859.11 p17*
Morrison, Martin; St. John, N.B., 1847 *5704.8 p4*
Morrison, Mary *SEE* Morrison, Angus
Morrison, Mary *SEE* Morrison, Donald
Morrison, Mary *SEE* Morrison, John
Morrison, Mary *SEE* Morrison, John
Morrison, Mary *SEE* Morrison, John S.
Morrison, Mary *SEE* Morrison, Margaret Murray
Morrison, Mary *SEE* Morrison, Murdo
Morrison, Mary *SEE* Morrison, Roderick
Morrison, Mary; New York, NY, 1866 *5704.8 p214*
Morrison, Mary; Quebec, 1851 *4537.30 p25*
Morrison, Mary; Quebec, 1851 *4537.30 p92*
Morrison, Mary; Quebec, 1855 *4537.30 p60*
Morrison, Mary; Quebec, 1855 *4537.30 p65*
Morrison, Mary; Quebec, 1863 *4537.30 p7*
Morrison, Mary; Quebec, 1873 *4537.30 p73*
Morrison, Mary; Quebec, 1873 *4537.30 p114*
Morrison, Mary; St. John, N.B., 1847 *5704.8 p5*
Morrison, Mary 24; Massachusetts, 1849 *5881.1 p71*
Morrison, Mary 24; Philadelphia, 1854 *5704.8 p123*
Morrison, Mary 65; North Carolina, 1850 *1639.20 p246*
Morrison, Mary A.; America, 1864 *5704.8 p190*
Morrison, Mary Ann *SEE* Morrison, Donald
Morrison, Mary Ann *SEE* Morrison, John
Morrison, Mary Ann; Philadelphia, 1851 *5704.8 p77*
Morrison, Mary Campbell *SEE* Morrison, John
Morrison, Mary Jane; Philadelphia, 1852 *5704.8 p96*
Morrison, Mary Kerr *SEE* Morrison, Donald
Morrison, Mary MacIver *SEE* Morrison, Norman
Morrison, Mary MacLennan *SEE* Morrison, Murdo
Morrison, Mary MacLeod *SEE* Morrison, John
Morrison, Mary MacRitchie *SEE* Morrison, Angus
Morrison, Mary Morrison *SEE* Morrison, Roderick
Morrison, Mathew 12; St. John, N.B., 1847 *5704.8 p4*
Morrison, Matilda; Philadelphia, 1849 *53.26 p71*
Morrison, Matilda; Philadelphia, 1849 *5704.8 p55*
Morrison, Matthew; New York, NY, 1816 *2859.11 p39*
Morrison, Michael; New York, NY, 1835 *8208.4 p6*
Morrison, Michael; Quebec, 1852 *5704.8 p86*
Morrison, Michael; Quebec, 1852 *5704.8 p90*
Morrison, Morris 25; Baltimore, 1775 *1219.7 p270*
Morrison, Murdo *SEE* Morrison, Alex
Morrison, Murdo *SEE* Morrison, Angus
Morrison, Murdo *SEE* Morrison, Angus
Morrison, Murdo *SEE* Morrison, Donald
Morrison, Murdo *SEE* Morrison, Murdo
Morrison, Murdo *SEE* Morrison, Murdo
Morrison, Murdo *SEE* Morrison, Norman
Morrison, Murdo; America, 1788 *1639.20 p246*
Morrison, Murdo; Quebec, 1842 *4537.30 p24*
Morrison, Murdo; Quebec, 1855 *4537.30 p24*
  *Wife:*Catherine MacDonald
  *Child:*John D.
  *Child:*Mary
Morrison, Murdo; Quebec, 1873 *4537.30 p27*
  *Wife:*Isabella MacIver
  *Child:*Kenneth
  *Child:*Catherine
  *Child:*Margaret
  *Child:*Murdo
Morrison, Murdo; Quebec, 1873 *4537.30 p27*
  *Wife:*Mary MacLennan
  *Child:*Ann
  *Child:*Murdo
  *Child:*Kirsty
Morrison, Nancy 48; North Carolina, 1850 *1639.20 p246*
Morrison, Neil; South Carolina, 1825 *1639.20 p246*
Morrison, Norman *SEE* Morrison, Donald
Morrison, Norman *SEE* Morrison, John
Morrison, Norman *SEE* Morrison, John
Morrison, Norman *SEE* Morrison, Margaret Murray
Morrison, Norman; America, 1790 *1639.20 p246*
Morrison, Norman; America, 1802 *1639.20 p247*
Morrison, Norman; North Carolina, 1773 *1639.20 p247*
Morrison, Norman; Quebec, 1851 *4537.30 p24*
  *Wife:*Mary MacIver
  *Child:*Kenneth

  *Child:*Donald
  *Child:*Kirsty
  *Child:*Catherine
  *Child:*Murdo
  With child
Morrison, Patt 55; Newport, RI, 1851 *6508.5 p19*
Morrison, Peter *SEE* Morrison, Donald
Morrison, Peter *SEE* Morrison, Duncan
Morrison, Peter; New York, NY, 1839 *8208.4 p100*
Morrison, Phillip; Arkansas, 1887 *3688 p7*
Morrison, R.; New York, NY, 1816 *2859.11 p39*
Morrison, Rachel *SEE* Morrison, John S.
Morrison, Rebecca; Philadelphia, 1851 *5704.8 p77*
Morrison, Richard; Virginia, 1648 *6219 p247*
  *Wife:*Winifred
Morrison, Richard; Virginia, 1648 *6219 p248*
Morrison, Robert 10; Philadelphia, 1851 *5704.8 p77*
Morrison, Robert 43; Quebec, 1858 *5704.8 p138*
Morrison, Roderick *SEE* Morrison, Angus
Morrison, Roderick *SEE* Morrison, Donald
Morrison, Roderick *SEE* Morrison, John
Morrison, Roderick *SEE* Morrison, Margaret Murray
Morrison, Roderick; Quebec, 1851 *4537.30 p23*
  *Wife:*Isabella MacLeod
  *Child:*Margaret
  *Child:*John
Morrison, Roderick; Quebec, 1851 *4537.30 p25*
  *Wife:*Mary Morrison
  *Child:*Kirsty
  *Child:*Margaret
  *Child:*Mary
  *Child:*Ann
  *Child:*John
  *Child:*Malcolm
Morrison, Roderick; Quebec, 1863 *4537.30 p25*
  *Wife:*Isabella MacLeod
  *Child:*Marion
  *Child:*Margaret
  *Child:*Catherine
  *Child:*George
Morrison, Sally 58 *SEE* Morrison, Effie
Morrison, Sam *SEE* Morrison, Donald
Morrison, Samuel 21; Philadelphia, 1856 *5704.8 p128*
Morrison, Sarah; Philadelphia, 1852 *5704.8 p88*
Morrison, Sarah; St. John, N.B., 1848 *5704.8 p47*
Morrison, Sarah 63; North Carolina, 1850 *1639.20 p247*
Morrison, T. White 20; Philadelphia, 1833-1834 *53.26 p71*
  *Relative:*J. White 18
Morrison, Thomas; New York, NY, 1864 *5704.8 p171*
Morrison, Thomas; New York, NY, 1865 *5704.8 p196*
Morrison, Thomas 27; Philadelphia, 1774 *1219.7 p216*
Morrison, William *SEE* Morrison, John
Morrison, William; America, 1788 *1639.20 p247*
Morrison, William; New York, NY, 1865 *5704.8 p190*
Morrison, William; Philadelphia, 1851 *5704.8 p77*
Morrison, William; Quebec, 1852 *5704.8 p90*
Morrison, William 4; St. John, N.B., 1847 *5704.8 p4*
Morrison, William 11; Quebec, 1852 *5704.8 p86*
Morrison, William 26; Maryland, 1774 *1219.7 p222*
Morrison, William 35; St. John, N.B., 1853 *5704.8 p109*
Morrison, William 36; St. John, N.B., 1859 *5704.8 p143*
Morrison, Winifred *SEE* Morrison, Richard
Morriss, Bridget; Philadelphia, 1864 *5704.8 p170*
Morriss, Catherine; Philadelphia, 1864 *5704.8 p170*
Morrissey, Walter; Illinois, 1874 *5012.37 p59*
Morrissy, Lawrence; Illinois, 1870 *7857 p5*
Morrissy, Margaret 24; Massachusetts, 1849 *5881.1 p72*
Morrissy, Patrick; Illinois, 1856 *7857 p5*
Morron, John; New York, NY, 1811 *2859.11 p6*
Morron, John; New York, NY, 1811 *2859.11 p17*
Morros, Tom; Iowa, 1866-1943 *123.54 p35*
Morrough, Nicholas 21; Maryland, 1775 *1219.7 p272*
Morrow, . . .; Philadelphia, 1850 *5704.8 p64*
Morrow, Aaron 60; Quebec, 1853 *5704.8 p105*
Morrow, Andrew 40; Quebec, 1853 *5704.8 p159*
Morrow, Ann; Philadelphia, 1852 *5704.8 p96*
Morrow, Anne; New Orleans, 1848 *5704.8 p48*
Morrow, Archibald; America, 1864 *5704.8 p189*
Morrow, Barbara 19; Quebec, 1853 *5704.8 p105*
Morrow, Catherine 21; Quebec, 1864 *5704.8 p159*
Morrow, Eliza; Philadelphia, 1864 *5704.8 p197*
Morrow, Eliza 5; Quebec, 1850 *5704.8 p63*
Morrow, Elleanor; St. John, N.B., 1847 *5704.8 p11*
Morrow, Ellen; New York, NY, 1811 *2859.11 p17*
Morrow, George; New York, NY, 1847 *6013.19 p74*
Morrow, George 3; Quebec, 1864 *5704.8 p160*
Morrow, George 28; Philadelphia, 1803 *53.26 p71*
Morrow, Henry; Philadelphia, 1849 *53.26 p71*
Morrow, Henry; Philadelphia, 1849 *5704.8 p54*
Morrow, Henry; Quebec, 1847 *5704.8 p27*
Morrow, Hugh; St. John, N.B., 1852 *5704.8 p95*
Morrow, Hugh 22; Philadelphia, 1859 *5704.8 p142*

Morrow, James; New York, NY, 1811 ***2859.11*** *p17*
With family
Morrow, James; New York, NY, 1864 ***5704.8*** *p177*
Morrow, James; Philadelphia, 1852 ***5704.8*** *p87*
Morrow, James; Philadelphia, 1864 ***5704.8*** *p187*
Morrow, Jane; New York, NY, 1811 ***2859.11*** *p17*
Morrow, Jane; Quebec, 1850 ***5704.8*** *p63*
Morrow, Jane 18; St. John, N.B., 1861 ***5704.8*** *p147*
Morrow, Jane 19; Quebec, 1864 ***5704.8*** *p159*
Morrow, John; New York, NY, 1811 ***2859.11*** *p17*
Morrow, John; Philadelphia, 1850 ***5704.8*** *p64*
Morrow, John 3; St. John, N.B., 1849 ***5704.8*** *p56*
Morrow, Joseph; Philadelphia, 1816 ***2859.11*** *p39*
Morrow, Joseph 2; Philadelphia, 1864 ***5704.8*** *p160*
Morrow, Lyle 45; California, 1867 ***3840.2*** *p18*
Morrow, Margaret; New York, NY, 1868 ***5704.8*** *p226*
Morrow, Margaret; St. John, N.B., 1847 ***5704.8*** *p11*
Morrow, Margaret; St. John, N.B., 1849 ***5704.8*** *p56*
Morrow, Margaret 3; Philadelphia, 1864 ***5704.8*** *p160*
Morrow, Margaret 7; Quebec, 1850 ***5704.8*** *p63*
Morrow, Margaret 8; Quebec, 1864 ***5704.8*** *p160*
Morrow, Margaret 30; Philadelphia, 1861 ***5704.8*** *p147*
Morrow, Martha; New York, NY, 1864 ***5704.8*** *p177*
Morrow, Mary; Philadelphia, 1865 ***5704.8*** *p190*
Morrow, Mary Jane 27; Philadelphia, 1864 ***5704.8*** *p160*
Morrow, Mathew 20; Philadelphia, 1854 ***5704.8*** *p118*
Morrow, Nancy; Philadelphia, 1853 ***5704.8*** *p100*
Morrow, Richard; Quebec, 1847 ***5704.8*** *p38*
Morrow, Robert; New York, NY, 1816 ***2859.11*** *p39*
Morrow, Sarah 18; Philadelphia, 1859 ***5704.8*** *p142*
Morrow, Susan; America, 1868 ***5704.8*** *p227*
Morrow, Susan 17; Quebec, 1864 ***5704.8*** *p159*
Morrow, Thomas; New York, NY, 1815 ***2859.11*** *p39*
Morrow, Thomas; Philadelphia, 1853 ***5704.8*** *p101*
Morrow, Thomas 9 mos; Philadelphia, 1861 ***5704.8*** *p147*
Morrow, Thomas 19; Quebec, 1856 ***5704.8*** *p130*
Morrow, Thomas 21; Quebec, 1853 ***5704.8*** *p105*
Morrow, Thos.; New York, NY, 1816 ***2859.11*** *p39*
Mors, Tho.; Virginia, 1646 ***6219*** *p241*
Morse, Jane 30; Massachusetts, 1848 ***5881.1*** *p68*
Morse, Sarah 46; North Carolina, 1850 ***1639.20*** *p247*
Morse, William 24; Massachusetts, 1847 ***5881.1*** *p77*
Morsey, Friederich; Missouri, 1832 ***3702.7*** *p97*
Morstod, Peder; Arkansas, 1918 ***95.2*** *p86*
Morte, Jesper; Virginia, 1642 ***6219*** *p191*
Mortensen, Andrew; Arkansas, 1918 ***95.2*** *p86*
Mortensen, Jens Kristian; Arkansas, 1918 ***95.2*** *p86*
Mortensen, Otto; Arkansas, 1918 ***95.2*** *p86*
Mortenson, Lars; Illinois, 1867 ***5240.1*** *p31*
Mortenson, Niels; Illinois, 1887 ***5012.39*** *p121*
Morter, Thomas; Virginia, 1639 ***6219*** *p161*
Mortimer, Robert; Philadelphia, 1864 ***5704.8*** *p180*
Mortimer, Rowland; Virginia, 1639 ***6219*** *p156*
Mortimore, John; America, 1737 ***4971*** *p45*
Mortin, Wm. 70; Washington, 1918-1920 ***1728.5*** *p10*
Mortinsen, Morten Henry; Arkansas, 1918 ***95.2*** *p86*
Mortisch, Carl; Wisconsin, n.d. ***9675.7*** *p52*
Mortisch, Joseph; Wisconsin, n.d. ***9675.7*** *p52*
Mortlye, Jon.; Virginia, 1635 ***6219*** *p10*
Morton, Alexander; Charleston, SC, 1807 ***1639.20*** *p247*
Morton, Francis; New York, NY, 1816 ***2859.11*** *p39*
Morton, George 29; Kansas, 1873 ***5240.1*** *p55*
Morton, Isiah; Arkansas, 1918 ***95.2*** *p86*
Morton, James 25; Port uncertain, 1774 ***1219.7*** *p176*
Morton, John; Colorado, 1894 ***9678.2*** *p127*
Morton, John; St. John, N.B., 1847 ***5704.8*** *p25*
Morton, Margaret; St. John, N.B., 1847 ***5704.8*** *p34*
Morton, Mark; Georgia, 1775 ***1219.7*** *p275*
*Wife:*Mary
With 3 children
Morton, Mark 42; Savannah, GA, 1775 ***1219.7*** *p274*
With wife
With 3 children
Morton, Mary *SEE* Morton, Mark
Morton, Mary; St. John, N.B., 1853 ***5704.8*** *p106*
Morton, Mathew; Virginia, 1639 ***6219*** *p152*
Morton, Richard 20; Jamaica, 1725 ***3690.1*** *p161*
Morton, Robert 19; Jamaica, 1731 ***3690.1*** *p161*
Morton, Thomas 31; Kansas, 1883 ***5240.1*** *p64*
Morton, Thomas 40; South Carolina, 1850 ***1639.20*** *p247*
Morton, William; New York, NY, 1838 ***8208.4*** *p82*
Morton, William; St. John, N.B., 1853 ***5704.8*** *p106*
Morton, Wm.; Virginia, 1636 ***6219*** *p21*
Mory, . . .; Canada, 1776-1783 ***9786*** *p43*
Moryepier, Mr. 23; New Orleans, 1839 ***778.5*** *p393*
Moryepier, Mrs. 29; New Orleans, 1839 ***778.5*** *p393*
Moryow, Henry; Virginia, 1647 ***6219*** *p249*
Morz, Tone; Wisconsin, n.d. ***9675.7*** *p52*
Mose, Andrew M.; Ohio, 1842 ***8365.25*** *p12*
Moselage, Heinrich; America, 1857 ***8582.3*** *p47*
Moseley, Jos.; Virginia, 1637 ***6219*** *p13*
Moseley, Thomas 19; Maryland, 1720-1721 ***3690.1*** *p161*
Moselle, Pierre 18; America, 1838 ***778.5*** *p393*
Mosely, Robert; Virginia, 1640 ***6219*** *p183*
Mosely, William; Virginia, 1642 ***6219*** *p195*
Moseman, Christian; Kansas, 1884 ***5240.1*** *p31*
Mosenmeier, Bernhard; Cincinnati, 1869-1887 ***8582*** *p21*
Moser, Jacob; Pennsylvania, 1747 ***2444*** *p188*
Moser, Jacob; Pennsylvania, 1754 ***2444*** *p188*
Moser, Jacob; Pennsylvania, 1772 ***2444*** *p188*
Moser, Jacob 27; Kansas, 1884 ***5240.1*** *p65*
Moser, Johann F.; America, 1847 ***8582.3*** *p47*
Moser, Karl 50; America, 1895 ***1763*** *p40D*
Moser, M. J.; Washington, 1859-1920 ***2872.1*** *p26*
Moser, Robert 36; Washington, 1918-1920 ***1728.5*** *p10*
Moser, Wilhelm Jonathan; America, 1738 ***9898*** *p27*
With wife
Moses, . . .; Canada, 1776-1783 ***9786*** *p29*
Moses, Albert; Washington, 1859-1920 ***2872.1*** *p26*
Moses, Edward; Washington, 1859-1920 ***2872.1*** *p26*
Moses, Elias; Washington, 1859-1920 ***2872.1*** *p26*
Moses, George; Arkansas, 1918 ***95.2*** *p86*
Moses, George; Kansas, 1899 ***5240.1*** *p31*
Moses, John; Washington, 1859-1920 ***2872.1*** *p26*
Moses, John Abdollha; Washington, 1859-1920 ***2872.1*** *p26*
Moses, Joseph; Washington, 1859-1920 ***2872.1*** *p26*
Moses, Julia; Washington, 1859-1920 ***2872.1*** *p26*
Moses, Lyon 24; Philadelphia, 1774 ***1219.7*** *p212*
Moses, Mary; Washington, 1859-1920 ***2872.1*** *p27*
Moses, Minnie; Washington, 1859-1920 ***2872.1*** *p27*
Moses, Nathan; America, 1841 ***8582.3*** *p47*
Moses, Richard 24; Maryland, 1733 ***3690.1*** *p161*
Moses, Tom; Washington, 1859-1920 ***2872.1*** *p27*
Mosgrove, Sarah; Quebec, 1853 ***5704.8*** *p104*
Moske, Robert; Illinois, 1866 ***2896.5*** *p28*
Moskedal, Andreas 24; Kansas, 1874 ***5240.1*** *p55*
Mosko, Fred; Arkansas, 1918 ***95.2*** *p86*
Mosko, John; Wisconsin, n.d. ***9675.7*** *p52*
Mosler, Gustav; America, 1849 ***8582.1*** *p25*
Mosler, Gustav; New York, NY, 1849 ***8582.1*** *p25*
With family
Mosley, Adam 15; America, 1706 ***2212*** *p44*
Mosley, Elizabeth 20; Maryland, 1773 ***1219.7*** *p173*
Mosley, Henry; Virginia, 1652 ***6251*** *p20*
Mosrah, Alex 36; Kansas, 1901 ***5240.1*** *p82*
Moss, Catherine *SEE* Moss, John
Moss, Catherine; Philadelphia, 1850 ***5704.8*** *p68*
Moss, Edward; Jamaica, 1763 ***1219.7*** *p91*
Moss, Grace; Quebec, 1847 ***5704.8*** *p29*
Moss, James; Quebec, 1847 ***5704.8*** *p29*
Moss, John; Philadelphia, 1850 ***53.26*** *p71*
*Relative:*Catherine
*Relative:*John 12
*Relative:*Sally 10
*Relative:*Mary Ann 8
Moss, John; Philadelphia, 1850 ***5704.8*** *p68*
Moss, John; St. John, N.B., 1853 ***5704.8*** *p106*
Moss, John 12 *SEE* Moss, John
Moss, John 12; Philadelphia, 1850 ***5704.8*** *p68*
Moss, Joseph; Illinois, 1877 ***2896.5*** *p28*
Moss, Joseph 21; Virginia, 1775 ***1219.7*** *p246*
Moss, Mary; Virginia, 1698 ***2212*** *p12*
Moss, Mary Ann 8 *SEE* Moss, John
Moss, Mary Ann 8; Philadelphia, 1850 ***5704.8*** *p68*
Moss, Otto; Washington, 1859-1920 ***2872.1*** *p27*
Moss, Reuben 38; Kansas, 1892 ***5240.1*** *p76*
Moss, Robert 40; Maryland, 1775 ***1219.7*** *p253*
Moss, Rueben 38; Kansas, 1892 ***5240.1*** *p31*
Moss, Sally 10 *SEE* Moss, John
Moss, Sally 10; Philadelphia, 1850 ***5704.8*** *p68*
Moss, Thomas; New York, NY, 1836 ***8208.4*** *p23*
Moss, Wilhelm; Savannah, GA, 1775 ***8582.2*** *p64*
Mosse, Eliz.; Virginia, 1639 ***6219*** *p157*
Mosse, Tho 16; America, 1699 ***2212*** *p29*
Mosser, Christian; Pennsylvania, 1744 ***2444*** *p188*
Mossey, Mary; Philadelphia, 1847 ***53.26*** *p71*
Mossey, Mary; Philadelphia, 1847 ***5704.8*** *p13*
Mosshammer, Hans; Georgia, 1734 ***9332*** *p327*
Mosshammer, Maria; Georgia, 1739 ***9332*** *p325*
Mossmann, Jakob; Savannah, GA, 1775 ***8582.2*** *p64*
Mosson, William; Maryland or Virginia, 1697 ***2212*** *p3*
Most, . . .; Canada, 1776-1783 ***9786*** *p29*
Most, Thomas 19; Virginia, 1700 ***2212*** *p32*
Mosteica, Frank; Wisconsin, n.d. ***9675.7*** *p52*
Mostowski, . . .; New York, 1831 ***4606*** *p175*
Mosung, John; Wisconsin, n.d. ***9675.7*** *p52*
Moszewski, . . .; New York, 1831 ***4606*** *p175*
Motekat, Mike; Washington, 1859-1920 ***2872.1*** *p27*
Motel, Christophe; New York, NY, 1836 ***8208.4*** *p8*
Moteres, Alex 41; Arizona, 1907 ***9228.40*** *p13*
Motgovih, Stipan; Iowa, 1866-1943 ***123.54*** *p35*
Motly, John; Virginia, 1637 ***6219*** *p10*
Motral, Thomas 26; Jamaica, 1775 ***1219.7*** *p265*
Motsch, Heinrich; Cincinnati, 1869-1887 ***8582*** *p21*
Mott, John, Jr.; Virginia, 1621 ***6219*** *p2*
Mott, John, Sr.; Virginia, 1621 ***6219*** *p2*
Mott, Tony 24; West Virginia, 1892 ***9788.3*** *p17*
Motta, Angelo 25; West Virginia, 1896 ***9788.3*** *p17*
Motterhold, John George 2 *SEE* Motterhold, Paulus
Motterhold, John Paul 6 *SEE* Motterhold, Paulus
Motterhold, Paulus; South Carolina, 1752-1753 ***3689.17*** *p22*
With wife
*Relative:*John Paul 6
*Relative:*John George 2
Mottershed, Adam; Virginia, 1698 ***2212*** *p16*
Mottery, Ferdinand; New York, NY, 1854 ***1450.2*** *p104A*
Mottet, Dorothy Valerie; Iowa, 1866-1943 ***123.54*** *p71*
Motto, John; Iowa, 1866-1943 ***123.54*** *p35*
Mottoli, Victor; Arkansas, 1918 ***95.2*** *p86*
Mottrom, John; Virginia, 1652 ***6251*** *p19*
Mottrom, John, Jr.; Virginia, 1652 ***6251*** *p19*
Motts, Jacques 32; New Orleans, 1831 ***778.5*** *p394*
Motts, Wm.; Virginia, 1635 ***6219*** *p71*
Motz, Hans; Port uncertain, 1717 ***3627*** *p15*
*Wife:*Maria Apollonia Maubar
Motz, Johannes; America, 1842 ***8582.2*** *p28*
Motz, Maria Apollonia Maubar *SEE* Motz, Hans
Motzkus, Anton; Wisconsin, n.d. ***9675.7*** *p52*
Mou, E. R.; Illinois, 1860 ***5012.38*** *p98*
Mou, Eugene 36; America, 1838 ***778.5*** *p394*
Mouard, Eugene Joseph; Wisconsin, n.d. ***9675.7*** *p52*
Mouat, Elizabeth; Savannah, GA, 1774 ***1219.7*** *p227*
Mouat, James; Savannah, GA, 1774 ***1219.7*** *p227*
Mouche, . . .; Canada, 1776-1783 ***9786*** *p29*
Mouchet, Achille 15; New Orleans, 1836 ***778.5*** *p394*
Mouchet, Francois 44; New Orleans, 1836 ***778.5*** *p394*
Mouchon, Veronique 6; New Orleans, 1836 ***778.5*** *p394*
Moudix, Mr.; Port uncertain, 1839 ***778.5*** *p394*
Mougnaud, Eugene 17; Port uncertain, 1838 ***778.5*** *p394*
Mougneau, Jean 65; New Orleans, 1838 ***778.5*** *p394*
Moui, Elize 21; America, 1838 ***778.5*** *p394*
Mouillac, Mr. 22; New Orleans, 1831 ***778.5*** *p394*
Mouillae, Mr. 22; New Orleans, 1831 ***778.5*** *p394*
Mouillon, Charles 18; Port uncertain, 1825 ***778.5*** *p394*
Mouillon, Pierre 42; Port uncertain, 1825 ***778.5*** *p394*
Moulard, Louis 25; New Orleans, 1838 ***778.5*** *p394*
Mould, Hester 25; Jamaica, 1730 ***3690.1*** *p162*
Mould, John Tom.; Colorado, 1894 ***9678.2*** *p127*
Moulder, Jon.; Virginia, 1643 ***6219*** *p199*
Moulds, Robert 26; Kansas, 1876 ***5240.1*** *p57*
Moulds, Suzanne; Quebec, 1821 ***7603*** *p72*
Mouletdous, Mr.; New Orleans, 1839 ***778.5*** *p394*
Moulin, Esprit; America, 1833 ***778.5*** *p394*
Moulin, Felicite 38; New Orleans, 1836 ***778.5*** *p395*
Moulin, Pierre; America, 1833 ***778.5*** *p395*
Moulin, Virginia 13; New Orleans, 1836 ***778.5*** *p395*
Moult, Wm.; Virginia, 1638 ***6219*** *p115*
Moulton, Thomas; Virginia, 1637 ***6219*** *p110*
Moultrie, John; Charleston, SC, 1729 ***1639.20*** *p248*
Mouncey, Thomas 20; United States or West Indies, 1721 ***3690.1*** *p162*
Mounckton, William 17; Jamaica, 1739 ***3690.1*** *p162*
Mount, Eliza; Philadelphia, 1853 ***5704.8*** *p108*
Mount, Laurent; Montreal, 1823 ***7603*** *p68*
Mountain, William; Quebec, 1814 ***7603*** *p78*
Mountair, Dorothy 26; New York, 1774 ***1219.7*** *p218*
Mountair, Francis 25; New York, 1774 ***1219.7*** *p218*
Mountgomery, Jonathan 25; Jamaica, 1731 ***3690.1*** *p159*
Moup, Eugene 36; America, 1838 ***778.5*** *p394*
Moura, Mr. 27; New Orleans, 1829 ***778.5*** *p395*
Mouradian, Marderos; Arkansas, 1918 ***95.2*** *p86*
Mouras, Jacques 27; New Orleans, 1831 ***778.5*** *p395*
Mouret, Bertrand 27; America, 1839 ***778.5*** *p395*
Mourgois, T. 30; Louisiana, 1820 ***778.5*** *p395*
Mouse, Robt.; Virginia, 1639 ***6219*** *p22*
Mouser, . . .; Pennsylvania, n.d. ***2444*** *p189*
Mouseron, Eurchose 52; America, 1839 ***778.5*** *p395*
Moussier, Mr. 31; America, 1838 ***778.5*** *p395*
Moussil, M. 30; Port uncertain, 1839 ***778.5*** *p395*
Moussion, Robert; Quebec, 1664 ***4533*** *p128*
Moussouk, Eugene 24; New Orleans, 1837 ***778.5*** *p395*
Moustes, Charles 51; New Orleans, 1839 ***778.5*** *p395*
Moustier, Raymond 20; America, 1838 ***778.5*** *p395*
Moutine, Louis 40; America, 1825 ***778.5*** *p395*
Mouts, Lawrence; Baltimore, 1833 ***9892.11*** *p31*
Mouts, Lawrence; Ohio, 1840 ***9892.11*** *p31*
Moutz, Gotleib; Ohio, 1840 ***9892.11*** *p31*
Mouvet, V. 23; America, 1829 ***778.5*** *p395*
Mouyard, C. 28; New Orleans, 1837 ***778.5*** *p396*
Movrich, Peter; Iowa, 1866-1943 ***123.54*** *p35*
Mowatt, John; New York, NY, 1836 ***8208.4*** *p19*
Mowbray, Arthur; South Carolina, 1746 ***1639.20*** *p248*
Mowbray, Lilias; South Carolina, 1765 ***1639.20*** *p248*
Mowbray, Robert; Arkansas, 1918 ***95.2*** *p86*
Mowily, Harry 18; Philadelphia, 1854 ***5704.8*** *p118*
Mowren, Ann; Quebec, 1847 ***5704.8*** *p37*
Mowren, Eliza; Quebec, 1847 ***5704.8*** *p37*

Mowren, Ellen; Quebec, 1847 ***5704.8*** *p37*
Mowren, Mary; Quebec, 1847 ***5704.8*** *p37*
Mowren, Mick; Quebec, 1847 ***5704.8*** *p37*
Mowren, Rose; Quebec, 1847 ***5704.8*** *p37*
Mowren, Terry; Quebec, 1847 ***5704.8*** *p37*
Mowrer, Joseph; New York, 1831-1832 ***9892.11*** *p31*
Mowry, Frederick Herbert; Colorado, 1905 ***9678.2*** *p127*
Mowser, John; Virginia, 1635 ***6219*** *p160*
Mowwe, Henry; America, 1867-1868 ***1450.2*** *p104A*
Moxham, James 46; California, 1867 ***3840.2*** *p18*
Moye, Alice; Virginia, 1648 ***6219*** *p245*
Moye, Dorothy *SEE* Moye, John
Moye, John; Virginia, 1638 ***6219*** *p120*
*Wife:*Dorothy
Moyer, George 32; West Virginia, 1902 ***9788.3*** *p17*
Moyer, H. 21; America, 1838 ***778.5*** *p396*
Moyer, John; America, 1856 ***6014.1*** *p3*
Moyer, John; America, 1858 ***6014.1*** *p2*
Moyer, John; Virginia, 1628 ***6219*** *p9*
Moyes, John; Virginia, 1637 ***6219*** *p37*
Moyle, Thomas 25; California, 1872 ***2769.6*** *p6*
Moyn, Catharine; Philadelphia, 1847 ***5704.8*** *p22*
Moyn, William; Philadelphia, 1847 ***5704.8*** *p22*
Moyne, Catherine *SEE* Moyne, William
Moyne, William; Philadelphia, 1847 ***53.26*** *p71*
*Relative:*Catherine
Moynihan, Timothy; New York, NY, 1837 ***8208.4*** *p36*
Moyon, P. P. 20; Port uncertain, 1822 ***778.5*** *p396*
Moyse, Jon.; Virginia, 1628 ***6219*** *p31*
Moyses, Chri.; Virginia, 1638 ***6219*** *p115*
Moyses, Theodor; Virginia, 1643 ***6219*** *p205*
Moyses, Wm.; Virginia, 1637 ***6219*** *p11*
Mozer, John; New York, 1743 ***3652*** *p60*
*Wife:*Mary Philippina
Mozer, Mary Philippina *SEE* Mozer, John
Mozery, Fanny 18; St. Louis, 1835 ***778.5*** *p396*
Mpakuros, Panagotis; Arkansas, 1918 ***95.2*** *p86*
M'Quay, Mr.; Quebec, 1815 ***9229.18*** *p74*
Mras, Joseph 38; West Virginia, 1898 ***9788.3*** *p17*
Mras, Joseph 42; West Virginia, 1902 ***9788.3*** *p17*
M'Tagert, Mr.; Quebec, 1815 ***9229.18*** *p78*
MttDonell, Jno 19; America, 1699 ***2212*** *p28*
Mubrea, H.; New York, NY, 1811 ***2859.11*** *p17*
Muchford, Jno.; Virginia, 1648 ***6219*** *p250*
Muchlen, Anthony; New York, 1840 ***1450.2*** *p104A*
Muckart, William Stewart; Arkansas, 1918 ***95.2*** *p86*
Muckenberger, Maria Barbara; Pennsylvania, 1751 ***2444*** *p193*
Muckensretren, Joseph 19; America, 1838 ***778.5*** *p396*
Muckleroy, Catherine; America, 1742 ***4971*** *p27*
Mucklewraith, Mr.; Quebec, 1815 ***9229.18*** *p78*
Mudd, Peter; Virginia, 1640 ***6219*** *p182*
Muddiford, William 27; America, 1700 ***2212*** *p27*
Mudie, George; South Carolina, 1820 ***1639.20*** *p248*
Mudie, Jean; South Carolina, 1769 ***1639.20*** *p248*
Mudra, Frank; Arkansas, 1918 ***95.2*** *p86*
Mudry, Michael; America, 1891 ***7137*** *p169*
Mudzinski, Jozef Jozel; Arkansas, 1918 ***95.2*** *p86*
Muecke, Catherine *SEE* Muecke, John Michael
Muecke, John Michael; New York, 1743 ***3652*** *p60*
*Wife:*Catherine
Muegel, Peter; Cincinnati, 1869-1887 ***8582*** *p21*
Muegel, Peter; New Orleans, 1841 ***8582.1*** *p25*
Mueh, Agatha *SEE* Mueh, Johannes
Mueh, Agatha *SEE* Mueh, Johannes
Mueh, Anna *SEE* Mueh, Johannes
Mueh, Anna *SEE* Mueh, Johannes
Mueh, Christina *SEE* Mueh, Johannes
Mueh, Christina *SEE* Mueh, Johannes
Mueh, Johannes; America, 1752 ***2444*** *p193*
*Wife:*Anna
*Child:*Peter Christian
*Child:*Christina
*Child:*Agatha
Mueh, Johannes; Pennsylvania, 1752 ***2444*** *p193*
*Wife:*Anna
*Child:*Peter Christian
*Child:*Christina
*Child:*Agatha
Mueh, Peter Christian *SEE* Mueh, Johannes
Mueh, Peter Christian *SEE* Mueh, Johannes
Muehl, Eduard; Cincinnati, 1788-1848 ***8582.3*** *p90*
Muehleisen, Catharina *SEE* Muehleisen, Hans Jerg
Muehleisen, Hans Jerg; Pennsylvania, 1743-1800 ***2444*** *p193*
*Wife:*Catharina
*Child:*Johann Michael
Muehleisen, Johann Michael *SEE* Muehleisen, Hans Jerg
Muehlenberg, Ernst; Philadelphia, 1776 ***8582.3*** *p85*
With father
Muehlenberg, Ernst Heinrich; America, 1776-1877 ***8582.3*** *p80*
Muehlenberg, Friedrich August; New York, NY, 1776 ***8582.3*** *p85*
Muehlenberg, Heinrich August; America, 1776-1877 ***8582.3*** *p80*
Muehler, Peter 36; Port uncertain, 1839 ***778.5*** *p396*
Muehlforth, Johann Jost; Philadelphia, 1779 ***8137*** *p11*
Muehlhaeuser, Gottlieb; America, 1850 ***8582.3*** *p47*
Muehlhausen, Nikolaus; Philadelphia, 1779 ***8137*** *p11*
Muehliesen, Christian; Washington, 1859-1920 ***2872.1*** *p27*
Muehlner, Abraham; Illinois, 1888 ***2896.5*** *p28*
Muelke, Justine Caroline Charlotte; America, 1881 ***4610.10*** *p101*
Mueller, Adam; Saratoga, NY, 1777 ***8137*** *p11*
Mueller, Albrecht; Wisconsin, n.d. ***9675.7*** *p52*
Mueller, Alex; America, 1884 ***1450.2*** *p26B*
Mueller, Andreas; Wisconsin, n.d. ***9675.7*** *p52*
Mueller, Anna; Wisconsin, n.d. ***9675.7*** *p52*
Mueller, Anna Catharina; Pennsylvania, 1752 ***4525*** *p232*
Mueller, Anna Maria *SEE* Mueller, Jacob
Mueller, August; Ohio, 1800-1885 ***8582.2*** *p59*
Mueller, Barbara; Indiana, 1861 ***5647.5*** *p102*
Mueller, Bernard; America, 1844 ***8582.2*** *p28*
Mueller, Carl; Wisconsin, n.d. ***9675.7*** *p52*
Mueller, Carl R.; Maryland, 1892 ***1450.2*** *p26B*
Mueller, Catharina; Pennsylvania, 1754 ***2444*** *p225*
Mueller, Catharina; Port uncertain, 1752 ***2444*** *p194*
Mueller, Charles; America, 1894 ***1450.2*** *p104A*
Mueller, Christian; Ohio, 1843 ***8582.1*** *p51*
Mueller, Christianus; Pennsylvania, 1723-1800 ***2444*** *p194*
Mueller, Conrad; Cincinnati, 1869-1887 ***8582*** *p21*
Mueller, Daniel; Philadelphia, 1779 ***8137*** *p11*
Mueller, David; Ohio, 1869-1885 ***8582.2*** *p56*
Mueller, Echard; Philadelphia, 1779 ***8137*** *p11*
Mueller, Friederich; Illinois, 1842 ***8582.2*** *p51*
Mueller, Friedrich; Cincinnati, 1869-1887 ***8582*** *p21*
Mueller, Friedrich Wilhelm; America, 1842 ***8582.1*** *p25*
Mueller, Gabriel; Cincinnati, 1869-1887 ***8582*** *p21*
Mueller, Georg Friedrich; New Orleans, 1832 ***8582*** *p21*
Mueller, George; America, 1896 ***1450.2*** *p26B*
Mueller, Gerhard J.; Illinois, 1892 ***5012.40*** *p27*
Mueller, Gottfried Cjristian; Wisconsin, n.d. ***9675.7*** *p52*
Mueller, Gottlieb; Wisconsin, n.d. ***9675.7*** *p52*
Mueller, Heinrich; America, 1834 ***8582.1*** *p25*
Mueller, Henrich; Philadelphia, 1779 ***8137*** *p11*
Mueller, Henry; America, 1881 ***1450.2*** *p27B*
Mueller, Henry; Wisconsin, n.d. ***9675.7*** *p52*
Mueller, J.; Wheeling, WV, 1852 ***8582.3*** *p78*
Mueller, Jacob; America, 1829 ***8582.3*** *p47*
Mueller, Jacob; Pennsylvania, 1748 ***2444*** *p194*
Mueller, Jacob; Pennsylvania, 1750-1800 ***2444*** *p194*
*Wife:*Anna Maria
*Child:*Johann Georg
Mueller, Jacob Henry; Cincinnati, 1869-1887 ***8582*** *p21*
Mueller, Jerk *SEE* Mueller, Johannes
Mueller, Johann; Cincinnati, 1869-1887 ***8582*** *p21*
Mueller, Johann; Cincinnati, 1869-1887 ***8582*** *p22*
Mueller, Johann Georg *SEE* Mueller, Jacob
Mueller, Johann Heinrich; Pennsylvania, 1786 ***2444*** *p194*
Mueller, Johanna Babette; Wisconsin, n.d. ***9675.7*** *p52*
Mueller, Johannes; Lancaster, PA, 1780 ***8137*** *p11*
Mueller, Johannes; Pennsylvania, 1742-1800 ***2444*** *p194*
*Wife:*Rosina
*Child:*Jerk
Mueller, Johannes; Pennsylvania, 1754 ***2444*** *p194*
*Wife:*Maria Arnold
Mueller, Johannes; Philadelphia, 1779 ***8137*** *p11*
Mueller, Johannes; Trenton, NJ, 1776 ***8137*** *p11*
Mueller, John; America, 1854 ***1450.2*** *p104A*
Mueller, John; New York, 1756 ***3652*** *p81*
Mueller, John; Wisconsin, n.d. ***9675.7*** *p52*
Mueller, John Bernhard; New York, 1749 ***3652*** *p72*
Mueller, John C.; Wisconsin, n.d. ***9675.7*** *p52*
Mueller, John M.; America, 1848 ***8582.3*** *p47*
Mueller, Joseph; New York, 1749 ***3652*** *p71*
*Wife:*Verona
Mueller, Joseph; Ohio, 1812-1814 ***8582.2*** *p59*
Mueller, Klaus Henrich; Lancaster, PA, 1780 ***8137*** *p11*
Mueller, Louis; Wisconsin, n.d. ***9675.7*** *p52*
Mueller, Louis H.; America, 1860 ***1450.2*** *p104A*
Mueller, Ludwig; Wisconsin, n.d. ***9675.7*** *p52*
Mueller, M. L.; Ohio, 1848 ***8582.1*** *p48*
Mueller, Margaretha; Pennsylvania, 1748 ***2444*** *p195*
Mueller, Maria Arnold *SEE* Mueller, Johannes
Mueller, Michael; Pennsylvania, 1748 ***2444*** *p195*
Mueller, Niclas; America, 1869-1885 ***8582.2*** *p69*
Mueller, Niclas; New York, NY, 1853 ***8582.2*** *p28*
Mueller, Nikolaus; New York, NY, 1800-1877 ***8582.3*** *p92*
Mueller, Nikolaus; Philadelphia, 1779 ***8137*** *p11*
Mueller, Otto Griedrich; Wisconsin, n.d. ***9675.7*** *p52*
Mueller, Peter; America, 1867 ***1450.2*** *p105A*
Mueller, Peter; Cincinnati, 1869-1887 ***8582*** *p22*
Mueller, Peter; New York, NY, 1837 ***8582.1*** *p25*
Mueller, Peter; Philadelphia, 1776 ***8582.3*** *p83*
Mueller, Phillip; Wisconsin, n.d. ***9675.7*** *p52*
Mueller, Rosina *SEE* Mueller, Johannes
Mueller, Sophia; Wisconsin, n.d. ***9675.7*** *p52*
Mueller, Thomas; Cincinnati, 1824 ***8582.1*** *p25*
Mueller, Valentin; Ohio, 1869-1887 ***8582*** *p22*
Mueller, Verona *SEE* Mueller, Joseph
Mueller, Wessel; Kentucky, 1798 ***8582.3*** *p95*
Mueller, Wilhelm; America, 1849 ***8582.3*** *p47*
Mueller, Wilhelm; Ohio, 1812-1814 ***8582.2*** *p59*
Mueller, Wilhelm; Trenton, NJ, 1776 ***8137*** *p12*
Mueller, Wilhelm M.; Baltimore, 1834 ***8582.3*** *p47*
With parents
Muelter, Charles 32; New Orleans, 1839 ***778.5*** *p396*
Muench, Christian Jacob; Halifax, N.S., 1778 ***9786*** *p270*
Muench, Christian Jacob; New York, 1776 ***9786*** *p270*
Muench, Johannes; Philadelphia, 1779 ***8137*** *p12*
Muenchen, John P.; Wisconsin, n.d. ***9675.7*** *p52*
Muensch, John; New York, 1750 ***3652*** *p74*
Muensinger, Johann Jacob; America, 1743-1800 ***2444*** *p193*
Muenster, Anna *SEE* Muenster, Paul
Muenster, Melchior; New York, 1750 ***3652*** *p74*
Muenster, Michael; New York, 1749 ***3652*** *p72*
Muenster, Paul; New York, 1761 ***3652*** *p87*
*Wife:*Anna
Mueser, Wilhelm; America, n.d. ***8125.8*** *p438*
Muess, . . .; Canada, 1776-1783 ***9786*** *p29*
Muffett, Francis; Virginia, 1637 ***6219*** *p23*
Muffley, Nichs.; Pennsylvania, 1765 ***4779.3*** *p14*
Muffley, Nicklaus; Pennsylvania, 1737 ***4779.3*** *p14*
Muffli, Nicklaus; Pennsylvania, 1737 ***4779.3*** *p14*
Mugel, Christina; America, 1851-1900 ***2691.4*** *p168*
Mugford, Thomas; New York, NY, 1866 ***9678.2*** *p127*
Mugier, Mr. 28; New Orleans, 1839 ***778.5*** *p396*
Mugler, Barbara; Pennsylvania, 1750-1800 ***2444*** *p195*
*Child:*Johann Georg
Mugler, Johann Georg *SEE* Mugler, Barbara
Mugride, Francis 39; Savannah, GA, 1733 ***4719.17*** *p312*
Muheisen, Jacob; Pennsylvania, 1765 ***4779.3*** *p14*
Muheran, James 6; Massachusetts, 1850 ***5881.1*** *p70*
Muhl, Peter; Lancaster, PA, 1780 ***8137*** *p12*
Muhlbacher, Johan; New York, NY, 1838 ***8208.4*** *p70*
Muhle, Marie Adelheid; America, 1831 ***4815.7*** *p92*
Muhleisen, Chrisopp *SEE* Muhleisen, Christian
Muhleisen, Christian; Pennsylvania, 1747 ***4779.3*** *p14*
*Relative:*Chrisopp
Muhlenfeldt, Carl Anton Ludwig; Quebec, 1776 ***9786*** *p263*
Muhleon, Valentin 30; America, 1838 ***778.5*** *p396*
Muhlmaester, Henry; New York, NY, 1837 ***8208.4*** *p27*
Muhr, Jacob; America, 1848 ***1450.2*** *p103A*
Muidian, Honore 30; America, 1836 ***778.5*** *p396*
Muiller, Pierre 31; Port uncertain, 1839 ***778.5*** *p396*
Muir, Alexander; Canada, 1833 ***9775.5*** *p222*
*Mother:*Catherine McDermid
*Father:*John
Muir, Alexander 21; Virginia, 1773 ***1219.7*** *p169*
Muir, Andrew 10; Quebec, 1864 ***5704.8*** *p162*
Muir, Ann 7; Quebec, 1864 ***5704.8*** *p162*
Muir, Barbara 4; Quebec, 1864 ***5704.8*** *p162*
Muir, Catherine McDermid *SEE* Muir, Alexander
Muir, Ellen 38 *SEE* Muir, James
Muir, Francis 39; Quebec, 1864 ***5704.8*** *p162*
Muir, Helen 17; Quebec, 1864 ***5704.8*** *p162*
Muir, Helen 34; Quebec, 1864 ***5704.8*** *p162*
Muir, James; America, 1849 ***1450.2*** *p105A*
Muir, James 38; Georgia, 1733 ***1639.20*** *p248*
Muir, James 38; Savannah, GA, 1733 ***4719.17*** *p312*
*Son:*John 2
*Wife:*Ellen 38
Muir, John *SEE* Muir, Alexander
Muir, John; Providence, RI, 1844 ***2896.5*** *p29*
Muir, John 2 *SEE* Muir, James
Muir, Malcholm; New York, 1850 ***2896.5*** *p29*
Muir, Mary 1; Quebec, 1864 ***5704.8*** *p162*
Muir, Murie 25; Kansas, 1873 ***5240.1*** *p53*
Muir, William; America, 1840 ***1450.2*** *p105A*
Muirhead, Alexander 19; Pennsylvania, 1731 ***3690.1*** *p162*
Muirhead, James; Carolina, 1684 ***1639.20*** *p248*
Muirhead, James; Charleston, SC, 1813 ***1639.20*** *p249*
Muirhead, Margaret; Carolina, 1684 ***1639.20*** *p249*
Muirhead, Richard M.; Charleston, SC, 1819 ***1639.20*** *p249*
Muirhead, Robert 50; South Carolina, 1850 ***1639.20*** *p249*
Muirs, Catherine 20; Philadelphia, 1853 ***5704.8*** *p112*
Muirs, Mary Jane 18; Philadelphia, 1853 ***5704.8*** *p112*
Muitusewieze, Jonas; Wisconsin, n.d. ***9675.7*** *p52*
Muladore, . . .; Pennsylvania, n.d. ***2444*** *p193*

378 *FOR A COMPLETE EXPLANATION OF ENTRY, SEE "HOW TO READ A CITATION" SECTION*

Mularkey, John; Philadelphia, 1867 ***5704.8*** *p217*
Mulberry, Eliza 3 mos *SEE* Mulberry, Robert
Mulberry, Eliza 3 mos; Philadelphia, 1849 ***5704.8*** *p54*
Mulberry, James 10 *SEE* Mulberry, Robert
Mulberry, James 10; Philadelphia, 1849 ***5704.8*** *p54*
Mulberry, Jane *SEE* Mulberry, Robert
Mulberry, Jane; Philadelphia, 1849 ***5704.8*** *p54*
Mulberry, Martha *SEE* Mulberry, Robert
Mulberry, Martha; Philadelphia, 1849 ***5704.8*** *p54*
Mulberry, Martha 2 *SEE* Mulberry, Robert
Mulberry, Martha 2; Philadelphia, 1849 ***5704.8*** *p54*
Mulberry, Mary Jane 8 *SEE* Mulberry, Robert
Mulberry, Mary Jane 8; Philadelphia, 1849 ***5704.8*** *p54*
Mulberry, Rebecca 4 *SEE* Mulberry, Robert
Mulberry, Rebecca 4; Philadelphia, 1849 ***5704.8*** *p54*
Mulberry, Robert; Philadelphia, 1849 ***53.26*** *p72*
*Relative:*Martha
*Relative:*James 10
*Relative:*Mary Jane 8
*Relative:*Rebecca 4
*Relative:*Martha 2
*Relative:*Eliza 3 mos
*Relative:*Jane
Mulberry, Robert; Philadelphia, 1849 ***5704.8*** *p54*
Mulcahy, Darby; America, 1740 ***4971*** *p59*
Mulcahy, Edmund; America, 1741 ***4971*** *p41*
Mulcahy, Eliza 26; Massachusetts, 1849 ***5881.1*** *p66*
Mulcahy, John; America, 1740 ***4971*** *p59*
Mulcahy, John; Wisconsin, n.d. ***9675.7*** *p52*
Mulcahy, John 28; Massachusetts, 1849 ***5881.1*** *p68*
Mulcahy, Mary 20; Massachusetts, 1849 ***5881.1*** *p71*
Mulcahy, Mary 24; Massachusetts, 1849 ***5881.1*** *p71*
Mulcahy, Michael; America, 1741 ***4971*** *p59*
Mulcahy, Patrick 9; Massachusetts, 1849 ***5881.1*** *p75*
Mulcane, James; America, 1741 ***4971*** *p56*
Mulcara, Patrick; Ohio, 1843 ***8365.26*** *p12*
Muldary, Thomas; Philadelphia, 1816 ***2859.11*** *p39*
Muldawney, Michael; New York, NY, 1815 ***2859.11*** *p39*
Mulden, Anthony; Philadelphia, 1811 ***53.26*** *p72*
Mulden, Anthony; Philadelphia, 1811 ***2859.11*** *p17*
Mulder, William; Arkansas, 1918 ***95.2*** *p86*
Mulderry, Patrick 50; Massachusetts, 1849 ***5881.1*** *p74*
Muldoon, Ally; Quebec, 1847 ***5704.8*** *p8*
Muldoon, Andrew; St. John, N.B., 1847 ***5704.8*** *p26*
Muldoon, Ann 7; Quebec, 1847 ***5704.8*** *p8*
Muldoon, Ann 20; Massachusetts, 1847 ***5881.1*** *p62*
Muldoon, Anne; St. John, N.B., 1852 ***5704.8*** *p83*
Muldoon, Arthur 40; Massachusetts, 1850 ***5881.1*** *p62*
Muldoon, Bridget 22; Massachusetts, 1847 ***5881.1*** *p63*
Muldoon, Ellen 5; Massachusetts, 1849 ***5881.1*** *p66*
Muldoon, Ellen 30; St. John, N.B., 1856 ***5704.8*** *p131*
Muldoon, Hugh; St. John, N.B., 1847 ***5704.8*** *p15*
Muldoon, James; Quebec, 1847 ***5704.8*** *p8*
Muldoon, James; Quebec, 1852 ***5704.8*** *p86*
Muldoon, James; Quebec, 1852 ***5704.8*** *p90*
Muldoon, James 12; Massachusetts, 1847 ***5881.1*** *p67*
Muldoon, James 20; St. John, N.B., 1858 ***5704.8*** *p137*
Muldoon, John 12; Quebec, 1847 ***5704.8*** *p8*
Muldoon, Margaret; Quebec, 1851 ***5704.8*** *p82*
Muldoon, Mary; St. John, N.B., 1847 ***5704.8*** *p25*
Muldoon, Mary 7; Massachusetts, 1849 ***5881.1*** *p71*
Muldoon, Michael 17; Massachusetts, 1847 ***5881.1*** *p70*
Muldoon, Patrick 10; Massachusetts, 1849 ***5881.1*** *p74*
Muldoon, Patrick 10; Quebec, 1847 ***5704.8*** *p8*
Muldoon, Thomas; St. John, N.B., 1847 ***5704.8*** *p21*
Muldoon, Thomas 2; Quebec, 1847 ***5704.8*** *p8*
Muldoon, Thomas 10; Massachusetts, 1847 ***5881.1*** *p76*
Muldoon, William; St. John, N.B., 1847 ***5704.8*** *p11*
Muldoon, William 4; Quebec, 1847 ***5704.8*** *p8*
Mulenburg, Catterina 21; Kansas, 1873 ***5240.1*** *p53*
Mulet, Pierre 26; America, 1831 ***778.5*** *p396*
Mulford, Thomas 23; Jamaica, 1730 ***3690.1*** *p162*
Mulhaire, Margaret; New York, NY, 1870 ***5704.8*** *p238*
Mulhaire, Mary 7; New York, NY, 1870 ***5704.8*** *p238*
Mulhaire, Patrick 2; New York, NY, 1870 ***5704.8*** *p238*
Mulhaire, Sarah 5; New York, NY, 1870 ***5704.8*** *p238*
Mulhall, Mary; New York, NY, 1816 ***2859.11*** *p39*
Mulhall, William 30; Massachusetts, 1850 ***5881.1*** *p77*
Mulharrin, Ann; St. John, N.B., 1847 ***5704.8*** *p21*
Mulharrin, Arthur; St. John, N.B., 1847 ***5704.8*** *p21*
Mulharrin, Bridget; St. John, N.B., 1847 ***5704.8*** *p21*
Mulharrin, Charles 4; St. John, N.B., 1847 ***5704.8*** *p21*
Mulharrin, James 2; St. John, N.B., 1847 ***5704.8*** *p21*
Mulharrin, John 12; St. John, N.B., 1847 ***5704.8*** *p21*
Mulharrin, Michael 10; St. John, N.B., 1847 ***5704.8*** *p21*
Mulharrin, Patrick 8; St. John, N.B., 1847 ***5704.8*** *p21*
Mulharrin, Susan; St. John, N.B., 1847 ***5704.8*** *p21*
Mulharrin, Susan 6; St. John, N.B., 1847 ***5704.8*** *p21*
Mulhartagh, Daniel 19; Quebec, 1853 ***5704.8*** *p105*
Mulhartagh, Edward; Quebec, 1852 ***5704.8*** *p97*
Mulhartagh, Neal 12; Quebec, 1853 ***5704.8*** *p105*
Mulhatagh, Catherine 22; St. John, N.B., 1862 ***5704.8*** *p151*
Mulhaus, Johannes; Ohio, 1798 ***8582.2*** *p29*
Mulhein, James 14; Massachusetts, 1849 ***5881.1*** *p69*
Mulhein, John 7; Massachusetts, 1849 ***5881.1*** *p69*
Mulheny, Patrick 32; St. John, N.B., 1853 ***5704.8*** *p110*
Mulher, John; New York, NY, 1840 ***8208.4*** *p105*
Mulheran, Daniel; New York, NY, 1838 ***8208.4*** *p71*
Mulherle, Pierre; Wisconsin, n.d. ***9675.7*** *p52*
Mulhern, John 15; Philadelphia, 1861 ***5704.8*** *p147*
Mulhern, Mary 20; Philadelphia, 1861 ***5704.8*** *p147*
Mulhern, Michael 10; Philadelphia, 1861 ***5704.8*** *p147*
Mulhern, Sarah 22; Philadelphia, 1861 ***5704.8*** *p147*
Mulheron, Catharine; Philadelphia, 1870 ***5704.8*** *p238*
Mulheron, Catherine; Quebec, 1852 ***5704.8*** *p97*
Mulheron, John; New York, NY, 1816 ***2859.11*** *p39*
Mulheron, Johnson; Philadelphia, 1865 ***5704.8*** *p192*
Mulheron, Michael 18; Philadelphia, 1854 ***5704.8*** *p116*
Mulheron, Patrick; New York, NY, 1866 ***5704.8*** *p212*
Mulheron, William 23; Philadelphia, 1859 ***5704.8*** *p143*
Mulherran, John 21; St. John, N.B., 1857 ***5704.8*** *p135*
Mulherran, Michael; Quebec, 1848 ***5704.8*** *p42*
Mulherren, Ellen 7; Quebec, 1850 ***5704.8*** *p63*
Mulherren, John 4; Quebec, 1850 ***5704.8*** *p63*
Mulherren, Mary; Quebec, 1850 ***5704.8*** *p63*
Mulherren, Terrence 10; Quebec, 1850 ***5704.8*** *p63*
Mulherrin, Catherine 56; St. John, N.B., 1863 ***5704.8*** *p155*
Mulherrin, Charles; Philadelphia, 1850 ***53.26*** *p72*
Mulherrin, Charles; Philadelphia, 1850 ***5704.8*** *p65*
Mulherrin, Edward 25; Philadelphia, 1858 ***5704.8*** *p139*
Mulherrin, Jane; Philadelphia, 1853 ***5704.8*** *p102*
Mulherrin, Jane; St. John, N.B., 1848 ***5704.8*** *p47*
Mulherrin, Michael; St. John, N.B., 1848 ***5704.8*** *p47*
Mulherrin, Robert 23; St. John, N.B., 1862 ***5704.8*** *p150*
Mulherrin, Thomas 20; St. John, N.B., 1853 ***5704.8*** *p110*
Mulherron, Ellen; Philadelphia, 1864 ***5704.8*** *p184*
Mulherron, James; Philadelphia, 1852 ***5704.8*** *p96*
Mulhollan, Owen; America, 1742 ***4971*** *p17*
Mulhollan, Patrick; America, 1737 ***4971*** *p77*
Mulhollan, Suzanne; Montreal, 1823 ***7603*** *p55*
Mulholland, Ann; Philadelphia, 1865 ***5704.8*** *p199*
Mulholland, Betty; St. John, N.B., 1848 ***5704.8*** *p44*
Mulholland, Biddy 3; St. John, N.B., 1848 ***5704.8*** *p44*
Mulholland, Biddy 5; St. John, N.B., 1847 ***5704.8*** *p19*
Mulholland, Bridget; Quebec, 1851 ***5704.8*** *p73*
Mulholland, Charles 34; St. John, N.B., 1866 ***5704.8*** *p166*
Mulholland, Daniel; Philadelphia, 1864 ***5704.8*** *p181*
Mulholland, David; Philadelphia, 1851 ***5704.8*** *p71*
Mulholland, Dennis 8; St. John, N.B., 1847 ***5704.8*** *p19*
Mulholland, George; New York, NY, 1811 ***2859.11*** *p17*
Mulholland, Henry; New York, NY, 1816 ***2859.11*** *p39*
Mulholland, Jamy 6; St. John, N.B., 1848 ***5704.8*** *p44*
Mulholland, John; New York, NY, 1816 ***2859.11*** *p39*
Mulholland, John 10; St. John, N.B., 1847 ***5704.8*** *p19*
Mulholland, Keatty 4; St. John, N.B., 1848 ***5704.8*** *p44*
Mulholland, Lissy 10; St. John, N.B., 1848 ***5704.8*** *p44*
Mulholland, Margaret; Quebec, 1851 ***5704.8*** *p73*
Mulholland, Mary; Philadelphia, 1864 ***5704.8*** *p181*
Mulholland, Nancy; St. John, N.B., 1847 ***5704.8*** *p19*
Mulholland, Nancy 11; St. John, N.B., 1847 ***5704.8*** *p19*
Mulholland, Ned 8; St. John, N.B., 1848 ***5704.8*** *p44*
Mulholland, Patrick; America, 1741 ***4971*** *p26*
Mulholland, Patrick; America, 1864 ***5704.8*** *p179*
Mulholland, Patrick; America, 1865 ***5704.8*** *p201*
Mulholland, Rodrick; Quebec, 1822 ***7603*** *p57*
Mulholland, Rosanah 21; Philadelphia, 1854 ***5704.8*** *p123*
Mulholland, Sally 13; St. John, N.B., 1848 ***5704.8*** *p44*
Mulholland, William; St. John, N.B., 1847 ***5704.8*** *p19*
Mulhollen, Catherine; St. John, N.B., 1848 ***5704.8*** *p45*
Mulhollen, Hannah; St. John, N.B., 1848 ***5704.8*** *p45*
Mulke, Carl August Ludwig; America, 1864 ***4610.10*** *p100*
Mulke, Ernst Heinrich; America, 1864 ***4610.10*** *p100*
Mulke, Friedrich Wilhelm; America, 1849 ***4610.10*** *p155*
Mullagh, James; St. John, N.B., 1847 ***5704.8*** *p18*
Mullally, Catharine 28; Massachusetts, 1849 ***5881.1*** *p64*
Mullally, Thady; America, 1735-1743 ***4971*** *p78*
Mullally, William; New York, NY, 1840 ***8208.4*** *p108*
Mullan, Ann; Philadelphia, 1851 ***5704.8*** *p80*
Mullan, Ann; Philadelphia, 1864 ***5704.8*** *p182*
Mullan, Ann 19; Philadelphia, 1853 ***5704.8*** *p112*
Mullan, Ann 20; St. John, N.B., 1856 ***5704.8*** *p131*
Mullan, Ann 21; Philadelphia, 1860 ***5704.8*** *p146*
Mullan, Anne; New York, NY, 1864 ***5704.8*** *p174*
Mullan, Anne; St. John, N.B., 1847 ***5704.8*** *p2*
Mullan, Arthur; New York, NY, 1815 ***2859.11*** *p39*
Mullan, Bernard; New York, NY, 1864 ***5704.8*** *p172*
Mullan, Bernard; St. John, N.B., 1847 ***5704.8*** *p2*
Mullan, Biddy; Philadelphia, 1847 ***53.26*** *p72*
Mullan, Biddy; Philadelphia, 1847 ***5704.8*** *p31*
Mullan, Biddy; St. John, N.B., 1847 ***5704.8*** *p2*
Mullan, Biddy 12; St. John, N.B., 1865 ***5704.8*** *p165*
Mullan, Bridget; New York, NY, 1816 ***2859.11*** *p39*
Mullan, Catharine 7; St. John, N.B., 1848 ***5704.8*** *p47*
Mullan, Catherine 19; St. John, N.B., 1867 ***5704.8*** *p168*
Mullan, Cicey; New York, NY, 1815 ***2859.11*** *p39*
Mullan, Daniel 5; New York, NY, 1864 ***5704.8*** *p174*
Mullan, Edward; America, 1738 ***4971*** *p14*
Mullan, Edward; St. John, N.B., 1847 ***5704.8*** *p34*
Mullan, Edward 8; New York, NY, 1864 ***5704.8*** *p174*
Mullan, Elizabeth; Philadelphia, 1864 ***5704.8*** *p182*
Mullan, Elizabeth 1; Philadelphia, 1860 ***5704.8*** *p145*
Mullan, Elleanor; St. John, N.B., 1847 ***5704.8*** *p2*
Mullan, Ellen; New York, NY, 1864 ***5704.8*** *p174*
Mullan, Ellen 12; St. John, N.B., 1851 ***5704.8*** *p72*
Mullan, Henry 20; Wilmington, DE, 1831 ***6508.7*** *p160*
Mullan, James; New York, NY, 1864 ***5704.8*** *p185*
Mullan, James; Philadelphia, 1816 ***2859.11*** *p39*
Mullan, James; St. John, N.B., 1847 ***5704.8*** *p2*
Mullan, James 2; Philadelphia, 1860 ***5704.8*** *p145*
Mullan, James 5; New York, NY, 1864 ***5704.8*** *p174*
Mullan, James 8; St. John, N.B., 1848 ***5704.8*** *p44*
Mullan, James 16; St. John, N.B., 1865 ***5704.8*** *p165*
Mullan, James 52; St. John, N.B., 1865 ***5704.8*** *p165*
Mullan, Jane 5; St. John, N.B., 1848 ***5704.8*** *p44*
Mullan, Jane 22; Philadelphia, 1860 ***5704.8*** *p145*
Mullan, John; New York, NY, 1815 ***2859.11*** *p39*
Mullan, John; St. John, N.B., 1848 ***5704.8*** *p47*
Mullan, John; St. John, N.B., 1853 ***5704.8*** *p98*
Mullan, John 10; St. John, N.B., 1847 ***5704.8*** *p15*
Mullan, John 20; Philadelphia, 1864 ***5704.8*** *p155*
Mullan, Lucy; Philadelphia, 1864 ***5704.8*** *p183*
Mullan, Margaret; Philadelphia, 1864 ***5704.8*** *p175*
Mullan, Margaret 20; Philadelphia, 1860 ***5704.8*** *p145*
Mullan, Marie; Montreal, 1822 ***7603*** *p87*
Mullan, Mary; Philadelphia, 1849 ***53.26*** *p72*
Mullan, Mary; Philadelphia, 1849 ***5704.8*** *p58*
Mullan, Mary; St. John, N.B., 1847 ***5704.8*** *p24*
Mullan, Mary; St. John, N.B., 1848 ***5704.8*** *p47*
Mullan, Mary 10; St. John, N.B., 1848 ***5704.8*** *p44*
Mullan, Mary 12; St. John, N.B., 1847 ***5704.8*** *p15*
Mullan, Mary 13; St. John, N.B., 1848 ***5704.8*** *p47*
Mullan, Mary 17; Philadelphia, 1853 ***5704.8*** *p112*
Mullan, Mary 27; Philadelphia, 1860 ***5704.8*** *p145*
Mullan, Mary 46; Philadelphia, 1859 ***5704.8*** *p142*
Mullan, Mary A.; New York, NY, 1865 ***5704.8*** *p201*
Mullan, Mary Ann 14; St. John, N.B., 1865 ***5704.8*** *p165*
Mullan, Michael 9 mos; New York, NY, 1864 ***5704.8*** *p174*
Mullan, Nancy; Philadelphia, 1850 ***53.26*** *p72*
Mullan, Nancy; Philadelphia, 1850 ***5704.8*** *p60*
Mullan, Nancy 22; St. John, N.B., 1866 ***5704.8*** *p167*
Mullan, Neil; St. John, N.B., 1847 ***5704.8*** *p3*
Mullan, Patrick; America, 1738 ***4971*** *p14*
Mullan, Patrick; New York, NY, 1865 ***5704.8*** *p201*
Mullan, Patrick; Philadelphia, 1864 ***5704.8*** *p175*
Mullan, Patrick 21; Philadelphia, 1803 ***53.26*** *p72*
Mullan, Peter; America, 1743 ***4971*** *p18*
Mullan, Richard; St. John, N.B., 1847 ***5704.8*** *p15*
Mullan, Richd.; Baltimore, 1816 ***2859.11*** *p39*
Mullan, Robert; America, 1743 ***4971*** *p72*
Mullan, Robert 17; St. John, N.B., 1865 ***5704.8*** *p165*
Mullan, Rose 8; St. John, N.B., 1848 ***5704.8*** *p47*
Mullan, Sally; St. John, N.B., 1848 ***5704.8*** *p44*
Mullan, Susan; Philadelphia, 1864 ***5704.8*** *p177*
Mullan, Susan; St. John, N.B., 1853 ***5704.8*** *p107*
Mullan, Thomas; Philadelphia, 1849 ***53.26*** *p72*
Mullan, Thomas; Philadelphia, 1849 ***5704.8*** *p53*
Mullan, Thomas; Philadelphia, 1851 ***5704.8*** *p80*
Mullan, Thomas; Philadelphia, 1852 ***5704.8*** *p85*
Mullan, Thomas; St. John, N.B., 1847 ***5704.8*** *p24*
Mullan, William; New York, NY, 1815 ***2859.11*** *p39*
Mullan, William; New York, NY, 1865 ***5704.8*** *p201*
Mullan, Winie 18; St. John, N.B., 1861 ***5704.8*** *p149*
Mullane, Dennis; America, 1741 ***4971*** *p42*
Mullaney, Edward; Illinois, 1871 ***5012.39*** *p25*
Mullaney, Michael; St. John, N.B., 1849 ***5704.8*** *p49*
Mullany, Patrick; New York, NY, 1838 ***8208.4*** *p75*
Mullarkey, Rose; St. John, N.B., 1852 ***5704.8*** *p93*
Mullatto, Nicholas; Iowa, 1866-1943 ***123.54*** *p35*
Mullaven, James; Quebec, 1823 ***7603*** *p91*
Mullay, James; New York, NY, 1811 ***2859.11*** *p17*
With family
Mullay, William; New York, NY, 1815 ***2859.11*** *p39*
Mulldoon, James 26; St. John, N.B., 1864 ***5704.8*** *p158*
Mulledy, Patrick; America, 1741 ***4971*** *p38*
Mullegan, John; America, 1741 ***4971*** *p98*
Mullein, Bridget 21; Massachusetts, 1850 ***5881.1*** *p64*
Mulleines, Alice; Virginia, 1617 ***6219*** *p6*
Mullen, Father; Cincinnati, 1833 ***8582.1*** *p51*
Mullen, Ann 10 *SEE* Mullen, James
Mullen, Ann 18; Massachusetts, 1847 ***5881.1*** *p62*
Mullen, Ann 18; Philadelphia, 1864 ***5704.8*** *p157*
Mullen, Anne 10; St. John, N.B., 1853 ***5704.8*** *p110*

Muller, William; Wisconsin, n.d. ***9675.7*** *p52*
Muller, William A.; Illinois, 1879 ***2896.5*** *p29*
Mullery, Edward; Washington, 1859-1920 ***2872.1*** *p27*
Mullican, Daniel; America, 1742 ***4971*** *p81*
Mullican, John; America, 1735-1743 ***4971*** *p79*
Mullidore, Adam; Pennsylvania, 1771 ***2444*** *p193*
Mulligan, Alexander 3 mos; Quebec, 1854 ***5704.8*** *p121*
Mulligan, Andre 21; Montreal, 1756 ***7603*** *p67*
Mulligan, Ann 20; Massachusetts, 1847 ***5881.1*** *p62*
Mulligan, Bartholmew; Ohio, 1839 ***9892.11*** *p31*
Mulligan, Bartholmew; Ohio, 1844 ***9892.11*** *p31*
Mulligan, Cornelius; New York, NY, 1838 ***8208.4*** *p61*
Mulligan, Elizabeth 15; Quebec, 1854 ***5704.8*** *p121*
Mulligan, Fanny 6; Quebec, 1854 ***5704.8*** *p121*
Mulligan, Fanny 43; Quebec, 1854 ***5704.8*** *p121*
Mulligan, James; America, 1737 ***4971*** *p36*
Mulligan, James; Philadelphia, 1864 ***5704.8*** *p181*
Mulligan, James 11; Quebec, 1854 ***5704.8*** *p121*
Mulligan, James 44; Arizona, 1890 ***2764.35*** *p45*
Mulligan, James 50; Massachusetts, 1847 ***5881.1*** *p67*
Mulligan, James C.; Philadelphia, 1816 ***2859.11*** *p39*
Mulligan, John; America, 1740 ***4971*** *p70*
Mulligan, John; New York, NY, 1839 ***8208.4*** *p95*
Mulligan, John; Quebec, 1853 ***5704.8*** *p103*
Mulligan, John 53; Quebec, 1854 ***5704.8*** *p121*
Mulligan, Joseph; St. John, N.B., 1850 ***5704.8*** *p68*
Mulligan, Mary 18; Massachusetts, 1849 ***5881.1*** *p71*
Mulligan, Mary A. 20; Quebec, 1863 ***5704.8*** *p154*
Mulligan, Michael; New York, NY, 1816 ***2859.11*** *p39*
Mulligan, Michael; New York, NY, 1835 ***8208.4*** *p52*
Mulligan, Michael; New York, NY, 1838 ***8208.4*** *p73*
Mulligan, Michael; Ohio, 1844 ***9892.11*** *p31*
Mulligan, Nancy 50; Massachusetts, 1847 ***5881.1*** *p73*
Mulligan, Oliver; Quebec, 1853 ***5704.8*** *p103*
Mulligan, Owen; New York, NY, 1839 ***8208.4*** *p98*
Mulligan, Patrick; New York, NY, 1837 ***8208.4*** *p55*
Mulligan, Peter; Illinois, 1860 ***5012.39*** *p89*
Mulligan, Robert 3; Quebec, 1854 ***5704.8*** *p121*
Mulligan, Robert 18; St. John, N.B., 1856 ***5704.8*** *p131*
Mulligan, Rose 35; Massachusetts, 1847 ***5881.1*** *p75*
Mulligan, Sarah 9; Quebec, 1854 ***5704.8*** *p121*
Mulligan, Sarah 23; Philadelphia, 1853 ***5704.8*** *p114*
Mulligan, Susan 21; Philadelphia, 1854 ***5704.8*** *p118*
Mulligan, Thomas; New York, NY, 1836 ***8208.4*** *p76*
Mulligan, Thomas 4; Massachusetts, 1847 ***5881.1*** *p76*
Mulligan, Thomas 17; Quebec, 1854 ***5704.8*** *p121*
Mulligan, William; America, 1737 ***4971*** *p36*
Mulligan, William; New York, NY, 1836 ***8208.4*** *p20*
Mulligan, William 13; Quebec, 1854 ***5704.8*** *p121*
Mulliken, Martin 20; Massachusetts, 1849 ***5881.1*** *p71*
Mulliken, Robert 18; Pennsylvania, 1720 ***3690.1*** *p162*
Mullikind, Robert 18; Pennsylvania, 1720 ***3690.1*** *p162*
Mullin, Ann; Quebec, 1847 ***5704.8*** *p29*
Mullin, Ann 22; Philadelphia, 1864 ***5704.8*** *p160*
Mullin, Anne; Philadelphia, 1866 ***5704.8*** *p211*
Mullin, Biddy 18; Philadelphia, 1857 ***5704.8*** *p133*
Mullin, Catharine; Philadelphia, 1864 ***5704.8*** *p177*
Mullin, Catharine 11; New York, NY, 1865 ***5704.8*** *p195*
Mullin, Edward 7; Quebec, 1847 ***5704.8*** *p29*
Mullin, Elena; Philadelphia, 1851 ***5704.8*** *p76*
Mullin, Francois; Montreal, 1824 ***7603*** *p64*
Mullin, Hugh; Philadelphia, 1869 ***5704.8*** *p236*
Mullin, James; New York, NY, 1838 ***8208.4*** *p89*
Mullin, Jane 20; Philadelphia, 1857 ***5704.8*** *p133*
Mullin, John; Philadelphia, 1853 ***5704.8*** *p101*
Mullin, John 9; Quebec, 1847 ***5704.8*** *p29*
Mullin, John 23; St. John, N.B., 1854 ***5704.8*** *p119*
Mullin, Josiah; Philadelphia, 1864 ***5704.8*** *p176*
Mullin, Margaret; New York, NY, 1865 ***5704.8*** *p195*
Mullin, Margaret 3; Quebec, 1847 ***5704.8*** *p29*
Mullin, Margaret Jane; Philadelphia, 1851 ***5704.8*** *p76*
Mullin, Mary; Montreal, 1818 ***7603*** *p83*
Mullin, Mary; Philadelphia, 1869 ***5704.8*** *p236*
Mullin, Mary 2; Quebec, 1847 ***5704.8*** *p29*
Mullin, Mary 3; Quebec, 1847 ***5704.8*** *p29*
Mullin, Michael; Quebec, 1850 ***5704.8*** *p67*
Mullin, Pat; Quebec, 1847 ***5704.8*** *p29*
Mullin, Pat; Quebec, 1850 ***5704.8*** *p67*
Mullin, Patrick; New York, NY, 1838 ***8208.4*** *p89*
Mullin, Patrick; New York, NY, 1865 ***5704.8*** *p195*
Mullin, Rose; Quebec, 1847 ***5704.8*** *p29*
Mullin, Sarah; Quebec, 1850 ***5704.8*** *p67*
Mullin, Susanna; Philadelphia, 1864 ***5704.8*** *p176*
Mullin, Thomas; Quebec, 1847 ***5704.8*** *p29*
Mullin, William; Quebec, 1851 ***5704.8*** *p75*
Mulliner, William R.; New York, NY, 1839 ***8208.4*** *p101*
Mullings, John; Charleston, SC, 1824 ***1639.20*** *p249*
Mullins, Andrew *SEE* Mullins, John
Mullins, Andrew; Philadelphia, 1850 ***5704.8*** *p59*
Mullins, Biddy *SEE* Mullins, John
Mullins, Biddy; Philadelphia, 1850 ***5704.8*** *p59*
Mullins, Biddy 10 *SEE* Mullins, John
Mullins, Biddy 10; Philadelphia, 1850 ***5704.8*** *p59*
Mullins, Catherine *SEE* Mullins, John
Mullins, Catherine; Philadelphia, 1850 ***5704.8*** *p59*
Mullins, Elizabeth 24; Philadelphia, 1854 ***5704.8*** *p117*
Mullins, Ellen 8 *SEE* Mullins, John
Mullins, Ellen 8; Philadelphia, 1850 ***5704.8*** *p59*
Mullins, Grace 6 *SEE* Mullins, John
Mullins, Grace 6; Philadelphia, 1850 ***5704.8*** *p59*
Mullins, James 3 mos *SEE* Mullins, John
Mullins, James 9 mos; Philadelphia, 1850 ***5704.8*** *p59*
Mullins, John; Philadelphia, 1850 ***53.26*** *p72*
*Relative:*Biddy
*Relative:*Andrew
*Relative:*Catherine
*Relative:*Nancy 12
*Relative:*Biddy 10
*Relative:*Ellen 8
*Relative:*Grace 6
*Relative:*Mary 3
*Relative:*James 3 mos
Mullins, John; Philadelphia, 1850 ***5704.8*** *p59*
Mullins, Manus; St. John, N.B., 1853 ***5704.8*** *p100*
Mullins, Margaret; St. John, N.B., 1853 ***5704.8*** *p100*
Mullins, Mary 3 *SEE* Mullins, John
Mullins, Mary 3; Philadelphia, 1850 ***5704.8*** *p59*
Mullins, Nancy 12 *SEE* Mullins, John
Mullins, Nancy 12; Philadelphia, 1850 ***5704.8*** *p59*
Mullins, Thomas 19; South Carolina, 1733 ***3690.1*** *p162*
Mulller, John 26; New Orleans, 1836 ***778.5*** *p399*
Mullon, Timothy J.; Arkansas, 1918 ***95.2*** *p86*
Mullony, Ann 18; Massachusetts, 1849 ***5881.1*** *p62*
Mullord, L. 27; America, 1838 ***778.5*** *p399*
Mullowney, John; America, 1740 ***4971*** *p15*
Mulloy, Ann 30; Massachusetts, 1850 ***5881.1*** *p62*
Mulloy, Anne; Philadelphia, 1864 ***5704.8*** *p183*
Mulloy, Betty 12; St. John, N.B., 1851 ***5704.8*** *p77*
Mulloy, Biddy; St. John, N.B., 1851 ***5704.8*** *p79*
Mulloy, Dennis 22; St. John, N.B., 1854 ***5704.8*** *p122*
Mulloy, Francis 5; Massachusetts, 1850 ***5881.1*** *p66*
Mulloy, Hugh 50; St. John, N.B., 1854 ***5704.8*** *p122*
Mulloy, Jack; Philadelphia, 1853 ***5704.8*** *p101*
Mulloy, James 9; Massachusetts, 1850 ***5881.1*** *p69*
Mulloy, John; Philadelphia, 1864 ***5704.8*** *p182*
Mulloy, Martin; America, 1742 ***4971*** *p80*
Mulloy, Mary; New York, NY, 1867 ***5704.8*** *p222*
Mulloy, Mary 10; St. John, N.B., 1851 ***5704.8*** *p77*
Mulloy, Mary 26; Philadelphia, 1854 ***5704.8*** *p123*
Mulloy, Nancy 21; Philadelphia, 1853 ***5704.8*** *p114*
Mulloy, Peter 7; Massachusetts, 1850 ***5881.1*** *p75*
Mulloy, Rose 50; St. John, N.B., 1854 ***5704.8*** *p119*
Mulloy, Susan 20; Philadelphia, 1853 ***5704.8*** *p114*
Mulloy, Thomas; New York, NY, 1838 ***8208.4*** *p72*
Mulloy, William 30; Massachusetts, 1847 ***5881.1*** *p77*
Mulloyne, Edward 13; St. John, N.B., 1848 ***5704.8*** *p47*
Mulloyne, James 8; St. John, N.B., 1848 ***5704.8*** *p47*
Mulloyne, Margaret 10; St. John, N.B., 1848 ***5704.8*** *p47*
Mulloyne, Mary; St. John, N.B., 1848 ***5704.8*** *p47*
Mulloyne, Peter 4; St. John, N.B., 1848 ***5704.8*** *p47*
Mulloyne, Sarah Ann 12; St. John, N.B., 1848 ***5704.8*** *p47*
Mullunly, Margdin 25; Maryland, 1774 ***1219.7*** *p230*
Mulnane, Ellen 20; Massachusetts, 1849 ***5881.1*** *p66*
Mulone, Catharine; New York, NY, 1867 ***5704.8*** *p224*
Mulony, James; New York, NY, 1811 ***2859.11*** *p17*
Mulqueen, Thomas; New York, NY, 1840 ***8208.4*** *p104*
Mulrennan, Patrick; St. John, N.B., 1847 ***5704.8*** *p26*
Mulrine, James; Ohio, 1842 ***9892.11*** *p31*
Mulrone, Catherine 19; Philadelphia, 1859 ***5704.8*** *p142*
Mulrooney, Edmond; Quebec, 1819 ***7603*** *p82*
Mulroy, Daniel; St. John, N.B., 1850 ***5704.8*** *p61*
Mulroy, Felix 50; Massachusetts, 1850 ***5881.1*** *p66*
Mulroy, Rachael 30; Massachusetts, 1850 ***5881.1*** *p75*
Mulroy, Winnefred 50; Massachusetts, 1850 ***5881.1*** *p77*
Mulshena, Moses; New York, NY, 1840 ***8208.4*** *p108*
Mulshine, John 40; Kansas, 1876 ***5240.1*** *p57*
Mulvany, Patrick; Philadelphia, 1816 ***2859.11*** *p39*
Mulvany, Thomas; New York, NY, 1815 ***2859.11*** *p39*
Mulvay, Jane 18; Massachusetts, 1849 ***5881.1*** *p69*
Mulvay, Mary 17; Massachusetts, 1848 ***5881.1*** *p70*
Mulvehill, Ann 23; Massachusetts, 1849 ***5881.1*** *p62*
Mulvey, Catherine; Quebec, 1847 ***5704.8*** *p37*
Mulvey, Ellen; Quebec, 1847 ***5704.8*** *p37*
Mulvey, Isabella; New York, NY, 1816 ***2859.11*** *p39*
Mulvey, John; America, 1739 ***4971*** *p14*
Mulvey, John; New York, NY, 1816 ***2859.11*** *p39*
Mulvey, Mary; Quebec, 1847 ***5704.8*** *p37*
Mulvihill, Patrick; New York, NY, 1840 ***8208.4*** *p108*
Mulvoy, John 43; Massachusetts, 1850 ***5881.1*** *p70*
Mulvoy, Peter 18; Massachusetts, 1849 ***5881.1*** *p74*
Mulvoy, Thomas 16; Massachusetts, 1850 ***5881.1*** *p77*
Mulvurnagh, Turlagh; America, 1742 ***4971*** *p71*
Mulvy, Edward; Philadelphia, 1833 ***8208.4*** *p37*
Mumert, Jakob; Cincinnati, 1869-1887 ***8582*** *p22*
Mumgaard, Antonius; Arkansas, 1918 ***95.2*** *p87*
Mumm, William; Illinois, 1870 ***5012.38*** *p99*
Mummenhoff, Frank; America, 1872 ***1450.2*** *p105A*
Mums, William; Virginia, 1639 ***6219*** *p154*
Munachina, Noziato; Arkansas, 1918 ***95.2*** *p87*
Munay, Catherine 6; Philadelphia, 1854 ***5704.8*** *p120*
Munay, Charles 22; Philadelphia, 1854 ***5704.8*** *p115*
Munay, Margaret; Philadelphia, 1848 ***53.26*** *p73*
*Relative:*Rebecca
Munay, Margaret; Philadelphia, 1848 ***5704.8*** *p45*
Munay, Rebecca *SEE* Munay, Margaret
Munay, Rebecca; Philadelphia, 1848 ***5704.8*** *p45*
Munch, Friedrich; Missouri, 1830-1834 ***3702.7*** *p8*
Munch, Friedrich; Missouri, 1834 ***3702.7*** *p96*
Munchhoff, Chaplain; Quebec, 1776 ***9786*** *p259*
Munck, Adam Henrich; Philadelphia, 1779 ***8137*** *p12*
Munck, Andreas; Philadelphia, 1779 ***8137*** *p12*
Munck, John; Virginia, 1648 ***6219*** *p250*
Munck, Joseph 22; America, 1697-1707 ***2212*** *p25*
Munckton, William 17; Jamaica, 1739 ***3690.1*** *p162*
Mund, . . .; Canada, 1776-1783 ***9786*** *p29*
Mund, John; Minnesota, 1863 ***5240.1*** *p31*
Munday, Denis 1; New Orleans, 1852 ***5704.8*** *p98*
Munday, Hugh; New Orleans, 1849 ***5704.8*** *p59*
Munday, Robert; Virginia, 1638 ***6219*** *p150*
Munday, Susan; New Orleans, 1852 ***5704.8*** *p98*
Munday, William; Virginia, 1639 ***6219*** *p161*
Munders, Johan; New Orleans, 1846 ***3702.7*** *p84*
*Wife:*Wilhelmiene Henschen
Munders, Wilhelmiene Henschen *SEE* Munders, Johan
Mundhenk, Heinrich; Cincinnati, 1807-1876 ***8582.3*** *p81*
Mundloch, Peter; Wisconsin, n.d. ***9675.7*** *p52*
Mundrello, Rudolph H.; America, 1881 ***5240.1*** *p31*
Mundrello, Rudolph H. 41; Kansas, 1893 ***5240.1*** *p79*
Munds, John; Illinois, 1888 ***5012.39*** *p122*
Mundt, Frederick; Colorado, 1904 ***9678.2*** *p128*
Mundt, John; Colorado, 1893 ***5240.1*** *p31*
Muneoke, Gottlieb 33; New Orleans, 1839 ***9420.2*** *p71*
Munger, John; Virginia, 1638 ***6219*** *p149*
Mungersdorf, Theodor; Colorado, 1890 ***9678.2*** *p128*
Mungin, Ellen 30; Massachusetts, 1849 ***5881.1*** *p66*
Mungin, Jeremiah 7; Massachusetts, 1849 ***5881.1*** *p69*
Mungin, Patrick 40; Massachusetts, 1849 ***5881.1*** *p75*
Mungle, Mary 9; Massachusetts, 1849 ***5881.1*** *p72*
Mungo, James 18; St. John, N.B., 1864 ***5704.8*** *p157*
Munich, . . .; Canada, 1776-1783 ***9786*** *p29*
Munich, Fred; Canada, 1776-1783 ***9786*** *p207A*
Munier, Mme. 30; New Orleans, 1831 ***778.5*** *p399*
Munier, Jos. 4; New Orleans, 1831 ***778.5*** *p399*
Munier, Jos. 34; New Orleans, 1831 ***778.5*** *p399*
Munigle, Ann 22; Philadelphia, 1864 ***5704.8*** *p156*
Munigle, William 25; Philadelphia, 1864 ***5704.8*** *p156*
Munis, Jacob; Wisconsin, n.d. ***9675.7*** *p52*
Munk, Alwin A.; Washington, 1859-1920 ***2872.1*** *p27*
Munk, Frank; Washington, 1859-1920 ***2872.1*** *p27*
Munkholm, Nels Peter Hansen; Arkansas, 1918 ***95.2*** *p87*
Munkvitz, Frederick H.; Wisconsin, n.d. ***9675.7*** *p52*
Munn, Catherine; Philadelphia, 1850 ***53.26*** *p73*
Munn, Catherine; Philadelphia, 1850 ***5704.8*** *p68*
Munn, Daniel 75; North Carolina, 1850 ***1639.20*** *p249*
*Relative:*Mary 57
Munn, John 21; Maryland, 1774 ***1219.7*** *p224*
Munn, Mary 57 *SEE* Munn, Daniel
Munn, Nancy 75; North Carolina, 1850 ***1639.20*** *p249*
Munn, William; New York, NY, 1811 ***2859.11*** *p17*
With family
Munnich, Henrich; Pennsylvania, 1751-1752 ***4525*** *p232*
Munns, Charles; Antigua (Antego), 1751 ***1219.7*** *p1*
Munns, James 30; Kansas, 1872 ***5240.1*** *p52*
Munns, Louisa 40; Kansas, 1889 ***5240.1*** *p73*
Munro, Ann; Quebec, 1851 ***4537.30*** *p93*
Munro, Betty; Quebec, 1873 ***4537.30*** *p21*
Munro, Catharine; America, 1840 ***8893*** *p266*
Munro, Catherine; Charleston, SC, 1828 ***1639.20*** *p102*
Munro, George; Quebec, 1770 ***7603*** *p39*
Munro, Hugh; Austin, TX, 1886 ***9777*** *p5*
Munro, Malcolm; Long Island, 1766 ***1219.7*** *p119*
Munro, Robert; South Carolina, 1823 ***1639.20*** *p241*
Munroe, Alexander; America, 1803 ***1639.20*** *p240*
Munroe, Daniel; America, 1790 ***1639.20*** *p240*
Munroe, Daniel; America, 1802 ***1639.20*** *p240*
Munroe, Donald; America, 1802 ***1639.20*** *p240*
Munroe, Effie 50; North Carolina, 1850 ***1639.20*** *p240*
Munroe, James; Charleston, SC, 1796 ***1639.20*** *p241*
Munroe, Philippe; Quebec, 1772 ***7603*** *p40*
Munroe, Robert; America, 1803 ***1639.20*** *p241*
Munroe, William; Charleston, SC, 1805 ***1639.20*** *p241*
Munson, Erick; Arkansas, 1918 ***95.2*** *p87*
Munson, James 25; Kansas, 1878 ***5240.1*** *p59*
Munster, John; New York, 1743 ***3652*** *p60*
*Wife:*Rosina
Munster, Rosina *SEE* Munster, John
Munstmann, Theadore; Missouri, 1876 ***5240.1*** *p31*
Munter, . . .; Illinois, 1800-1900 ***4610.10*** *p67*

Munter, August; Milwaukee, 1875 4719.30 p257
Munter, Mrs. August; Milwaukee, 1875 4719.30 p257
Munter, John 27; Jamaica, 1736 3690.1 p162
Munton, William 21; Maryland, 1775 1219.7 p267
Muntz, Bernhart; South Carolina, 1788 7119 p199
Munyun, Charles 40; New Orleans, 1831 778.5 p399
Munz, Anna Maria; America, 1766-1816 2444 p195
Munz, Johann Christian; America, 1766-1816 2444 p195
Murchison, Alexander; North Carolina, 1818 1639.20 p249
Murchison, Alexander 84; North Carolina, 1850 1639.20 p249
Murchison, John; Colorado, 1904 9678.2 p128
Murchison, Kenneth McKenzie; America, 1773 1639.20 p250
Murchison, Margaret 40; North Carolina, 1850 1639.20 p250
Murchison, Margaret 86; North Carolina, 1850 1639.20 p250
Murcia, Abram 31; Kansas, 1892 5240.1 p76
Murcocke, Georg.; Virginia, 1642 6219 p194
Murdick, George 21; Quebec, 1858 5704.8 p138
Murdoch, Edward 29; St. John, N.B., 1862 5704.8 p150
Murdoch, John; New York, NY, 1816 2859.11 p39
Murdoch, Obediah; New York, NY, 1815 2859.11 p39
Murdock, Esther; Baltimore, 1811 2859.11 p17
Murdock, John; Baltimore, 1811 2859.11 p17
Murdock, John 21; Virginia, 1774 1219.7 p218
Murdock, Johnston; Quebec, 1847 5704.8 p36
Murdock, M. Anne; Baltimore, 1811 2859.11 p17
Murdock, Margaret; Philadelphia, 1864 5704.8 p178
Murdock, Nancy; New York, NY, 1866 5704.8 p214
Murdock, Samuel 19; Virginia, 1774 1219.7 p218
Murdock, Thomas 17; Virginia, 1774 1219.7 p218
Murdough, Matthew; New York, NY, 1811 2859.11 p17
Mure, Jean; Quebec, 1798 7603 p39
Mures, Catherine 57; New Orleans, 1837 778.5 p399
Murette, Mr. 23; New Orleans, 1837 778.5 p399
Murf, John; New Orleans, 1837 778.5 p399
Murfeild, Edward; Virginia, 1638 6219 p125
Murfin, Griffin; Virginia, 1637 6219 p13
Murhahy, John; America, 1739 4971 p40
Murk, Alwin A.; Washington, 1859-1920 2872.1 p27
Murk, Frank; Washington, 1859-1920 2872.1 p27
Murkley, Christian 37; Quebec, 1857 5704.8 p136
Murkley, William 33; Quebec, 1857 5704.8 p136
Murney, Daniel 3; Massachusetts, 1849 5881.1 p65
Murney, Mary 1; Massachusetts, 1849 5881.1 p71
Murney, Patrick; New York, NY, 1816 2859.11 p39
Murney, Patrick 7; Massachusetts, 1849 5881.1 p74
Murney, Teady 9; Massachusetts, 1849 5881.1 p76
Murouskis, Jonas; Wisconsin, n.d. 9675.7 p52
Murowski, Paul; Kansas, 1887 5240.1 p31
Murphay, Thomas 27; Quebec, 1862 5704.8 p151
Murphey, Catharine 10; New York, NY, 1866 5704.8 p209
Murphey, Felix; Philadelphia, 1865 5704.8 p201
Murphey, Francis; New York, NY, 1866 5704.8 p209
Murphey, Margaret; New York, NY, 1866 5704.8 p209
Murphey, Margaret 20; Quebec, 1862 5704.8 p152
Murphy, . . . 1 mo; Philadelphia, 1864 5704.8 p178
Murphy, . . . 3; Philadelphia, 1864 5704.8 p178
Murphy, Abby 20; Massachusetts, 1850 5881.1 p62
Murphy, Abraham; America, 1736-1737 4971 p26
Murphy, Alex; Quebec, 1847 5704.8 p36
Murphy, Alice; Quebec, 1847 5704.8 p37
Murphy, Andre; Montreal, 1822 7603 p82
Murphy, Andrew 12 *SEE* Murphy, Lawrence
Murphy, Andrew 12; Philadelphia, 1847 5704.8 p23
Murphy, Ann; America, 1736 4971 p44
Murphy, Ann; America, 1736 4971 p45
Murphy, Ann; St. John, N.B., 1850 5704.8 p61
Murphy, Ann 10 *SEE* Murphy, Lawrence
Murphy, Ann 10; Philadelphia, 1847 5704.8 p23
Murphy, Ann 11; Philadelphia, 1853 5704.8 p111
Murphy, Ann 12; Massachusetts, 1847 5881.1 p62
Murphy, Ann 18; St. John, N.B., 1867 5704.8 p168
Murphy, Ann 21; Massachusetts, 1849 5881.1 p62
Murphy, Ann 30; Massachusetts, 1847 5881.1 p62
Murphy, Ann 40; Philadelphia, 1853 5704.8 p111
Murphy, Anthony; America, 1739 4971 p63
Murphy, Arthur; America, 1735-1743 4971 p8
Murphy, Arthur 49; Philadelphia, 1804 53.26 p73
Murphy, B. 26; Maryland, 1774 1219.7 p236
Murphy, Bernard 22; Massachusetts, 1848 5881.1 p63
Murphy, Betty 22; Massachusetts, 1850 5881.1 p63
Murphy, Biddy; Philadelphia, 1851 5704.8 p80
Murphy, Biddy 50; Massachusetts, 1850 5881.1 p64
Murphy, Bridget; New York, NY, 1816 2859.11 p39
Murphy, Bridget; Philadelphia, 1816 2859.11 p39
Murphy, Bridget; Quebec, 1847 5704.8 p8
Murphy, Bridget 30; Massachusetts, 1848 5881.1 p63
Murphy, C. 80; North Carolina, 1850 1639.20 p250
Murphy, Catharine 20; Massachusetts, 1848 5881.1 p64
Murphy, Catherine; America, 1737 4971 p45
Murphy, Catherine; America, 1738 4971 p46
Murphy, Catherine; New York, NY, 1816 2859.11 p39
Murphy, Catherine; Quebec, 1823 7603 p74
Murphy, Charles; America, 1849 1450.2 p105A
Murphy, Charles 27; Maryland, 1775 1219.7 p247
Murphy, Charles 60; Philadelphia, 1851 5704.8 p71
Murphy, Cicily; New York, NY, 1816 2859.11 p39
Murphy, Cornelius 32; Massachusetts, 1847 5881.1 p64
Murphy, Cul.; Massachusetts, 1841 7036 p119
Murphy, Daniel; America, 1738 4971 p33
Murphy, Daniel; America, 1738-1739 4971 p59
Murphy, Daniel; America, 1741 4971 p41
Murphy, Daniel; New York, 1828 1450.2 p105A
Murphy, Daniel 11; Massachusetts, 1849 5881.1 p65
Murphy, Darby; America, 1741 4971 p41
Murphy, David; New York, NY, 1844 6013.19 p74
Murphy, Dennis; New York, NY, 1816 2859.11 p39
Murphy, Dennis; New York, NY, 1837 8208.4 p46
Murphy, Dennis 5; Massachusetts, 1849 5881.1 p65
Murphy, Dennis 20; Massachusetts, 1849 5881.1 p65
Murphy, Dennis 23; Massachusetts, 1847 5881.1 p65
Murphy, Dennis 28; Massachusetts, 1847 5881.1 p65
Murphy, Edmund 28; Massachusetts, 1849 5881.1 p66
Murphy, Edward; America, 1738 4971 p14
Murphy, Edward; New York, NY, 1836 8208.4 p20
Murphy, Edward; St. John, N.B., 1847 5704.8 p11
Murphy, Edward 40; Massachusetts, 1850 5881.1 p66
Murphy, Edward 61; Massachusetts, 1849 5881.1 p66
Murphy, Edward F.; Illinois, 1872 5012.39 p26
Murphy, Eleanor; New York, NY, 1816 2859.11 p39
Murphy, Eleanor 6; Philadelphia, 1853 5704.8 p112
Murphy, Eliza 6; Quebec, 1857 5704.8 p135
Murphy, Elizabeth *SEE* Murphy, Lawrence
Murphy, Elizabeth; America, 1740 4971 p48
Murphy, Elizabeth; Philadelphia, 1847 5704.8 p23
Murphy, Ellen; Canada, 1823-1841 7036 p122
Murphy, Ellen; New York, NY, 1866 5704.8 p213
Murphy, Ellen 3; Massachusetts, 1850 5881.1 p66
Murphy, Ellen 8; Massachusetts, 1849 5881.1 p66
Murphy, Ellen 12; Massachusetts, 1850 5881.1 p66
Murphy, Ellen 20; Massachusetts, 1849 5881.1 p66
Murphy, Ellen 21; Massachusetts, 1848 5881.1 p65
Murphy, Ellen 25; Massachusetts, 1848 5881.1 p65
Murphy, Ellen Jane 2; Quebec, 1847 5704.8 p36
Murphy, Frances; New York, NY, 1816 2859.11 p39
Murphy, Francis; Philadelphia, 1816 2859.11 p39
Murphy, Francis; Philadelphia, 1864 5704.8 p180
Murphy, George 18; Philadelphia, 1855 5704.8 p124
Murphy, Hannah; America, 1739 4971 p33
Murphy, Helen; Quebec, 1825 7603 p78
Murphy, Honora 28; Massachusetts, 1849 5881.1 p67
Murphy, Honora 49; Massachusetts, 1849 5881.1 p67
Murphy, Hugh; North Carolina, 1752-1835 1639.20 p250
Murphy, Hugh 9; Massachusetts, 1850 5881.1 p67
Murphy, Hugh 18; Philadelphia, 1803 53.26 p73
Murphy, James; America, 1736 4971 p44
Murphy, James; America, 1740 4971 p25
Murphy, James; Iowa, 1866-1943 123.54 p35
Murphy, James; New Orleans, 1843 2769.6 p5
Murphy, James; New York, NY, 1811 2859.11 p17
Murphy, James; New York, NY, 1816 2859.11 p39
Murphy, James; New York, NY, 1866 5704.8 p213
Murphy, James; Quebec, 1847 5704.8 p8
Murphy, James 4; Quebec, 1847 5704.8 p36
Murphy, James 9; Massachusetts, 1849 5881.1 p69
Murphy, James 11; Massachusetts, 1850 5881.1 p69
Murphy, James 14; Philadelphia, 1853 5704.8 p111
Murphy, James 20; St. John, N.B., 1858 5704.8 p137
Murphy, James 25; Newport, RI, 1851 6508.5 p20
Murphy, James 25; Philadelphia, 1774 1219.7 p196
Murphy, James 28; St. John, N.B., 1866 5704.8 p165
Murphy, Jane; Quebec, 1847 5704.8 p36
Murphy, Jane; St. John, N.B., 1847 5704.8 p11
Murphy, Jane 8; Philadelphia, 1853 5704.8 p112
Murphy, Jeremiah 23; Virginia, 1774 1219.7 p240
Murphy, Jerry 18; Massachusetts, 1849 5881.1 p69
Murphy, Jerry 34; Massachusetts, 1849 5881.1 p68
Murphy, Joan; America, 1736 4971 p44
Murphy, Johanna; Philadelphia, 1816 2859.11 p39
Murphy, Johanna 25; Massachusetts, 1849 5881.1 p69
Murphy, Johanna 28; Massachusetts, 1849 5881.1 p68
Murphy, Johanna 28; Massachusetts, 1850 5881.1 p70
With child
Murphy, John; America, 1736 4971 p44
Murphy, John; America, 1737 4971 p45
Murphy, John; America, 1739 4971 p40
Murphy, John; America, 1741 4971 p40
Murphy, John; America, 1743 4971 p50
Murphy, John; Illinois, 1853 7857 p5
Murphy, John; Illinois, 1899 5012.40 p76
Murphy, John; Iowa, 1866-1943 123.54 p35
Murphy, John; Montreal, 1822 7603 p70
Murphy, John; New York, 1807 9892.11 p31
Murphy, John; New York, NY, 1810 7036 p118
Murphy, John; New York, NY, 1811 2859.11 p17
Murphy, John; New York, NY, 1815 2859.11 p39
Murphy, John; New York, NY, 1816 2859.11 p39
Murphy, John; New York, NY, 1834 8208.4 p1
Murphy, John; New York, NY, 1838 8208.4 p64
Murphy, John; New York, NY, 1840 8208.4 p111
Murphy, John; Philadelphia, 1816 2859.11 p39
Murphy, John; Philadelphia, 1849 53.26 p72
Murphy, John; Philadelphia, 1849 5704.8 p50
Murphy, John; Philadelphia, 1864 5704.8 p178
Murphy, John; Quebec, 1802 7603 p78
Murphy, John; Quebec, 1817 7603 p96
Murphy, John; Quebec, 1823 7603 p59
Murphy, John; Quebec, 1847 5704.8 p37
Murphy, John 4; Philadelphia, 1853 5704.8 p112
Murphy, John 9; Massachusetts, 1850 5881.1 p70
Murphy, John 10; Massachusetts, 1849 5881.1 p69
Murphy, John 13; Newfoundland, 1789 4915.24 p57
Murphy, John 14; Quebec, 1855 5704.8 p125
Murphy, John 20; Massachusetts, 1850 5881.1 p69
Murphy, John 24; Massachusetts, 1847 5881.1 p67
Murphy, John 24; Massachusetts, 1849 5881.1 p68
Murphy, John 26; New Orleans, 1858 5704.8 p140
Murphy, John 30; Massachusetts, 1849 5881.1 p69
Murphy, John 50; Massachusetts, 1850 5881.1 p69
Murphy, Joseph; New York, NY, 1839 8208.4 p99
Murphy, Joseph; Philadelphia, 1849 53.26 p73
Murphy, Joseph; Philadelphia, 1849 5704.8 p58
Murphy, Joseph; Washington, 1859-1920 2872.1 p27
Murphy, Julia 25; Massachusetts, 1849 5881.1 p69
Murphy, Julian; America, 1743 4971 p43
Murphy, Julie; Quebec, 1812 7603 p102
Murphy, Kitty 7; Massachusetts, 1848 5881.1 p70
Murphy, Kitty 22; Massachusetts, 1849 5881.1 p70
Murphy, Laughlin; America, 1735-1743 4971 p8
Murphy, Laughlin; America, 1738-1743 4971 p91
Murphy, Lavey *SEE* Murphy, Mary Ann
Murphy, Lavey; Philadelphia, 1850 5704.8 p69
Murphy, Lawrence; New York, NY, 1834 8208.4 p1
Murphy, Lawrence; Philadelphia, 1816 2859.11 p39
Murphy, Lawrence; Philadelphia, 1847 53.26 p73
*Relative:*Margaret
*Relative:*Elizabeth
*Relative:*Sarah
*Relative:*Andrew 12
*Relative:*Ann 10
Murphy, Lawrence; Philadelphia, 1847 5704.8 p23
Murphy, Lewis; Annapolis, MD, 1742 4971 p93
Murphy, Lewis; Maryland, 1742 4971 p106
Murphy, M.; New York, NY, 1811 2859.11 p17
With wife
Murphy, Magy; Philadelphia, 1852 5704.8 p96
Murphy, Marg.; New York, NY, 1816 2859.11 p39
With 2 children
Murphy, Margaret *SEE* Murphy, Lawrence
Murphy, Margaret; Canada, 1823 7036 p123
Murphy, Margaret; Philadelphia, 1847 5704.8 p23
Murphy, Margaret; Philadelphia, 1852 5704.8 p85
Murphy, Margaret 1; Massachusetts, 1847 5881.1 p70
Murphy, Margaret 7; Massachusetts, 1850 5881.1 p73
Murphy, Margaret 12; Massachusetts, 1850 5881.1 p73
Murphy, Margaret 19; Massachusetts, 1847 5881.1 p70
Murphy, Margaret 40; Massachusetts, 1850 5881.1 p73
Murphy, Marguerite; Montreal, 1814 7603 p29
Murphy, Martin; Montreal, 1819 7603 p73
Murphy, Martin; New York, NY, 1816 2859.11 p39
Murphy, Martin; Pennsylvania, 1892 1450.2 p27B
Murphy, Martin; Philadelphia, 1816 2859.11 p39
Murphy, Mary; America, 1737 4971 p26
Murphy, Mary; America, 1739 4971 p14
Murphy, Mary; New York, NY, 1811 2859.11 p17
Murphy, Mary; New York, NY, 1816 2859.11 p39
Murphy, Mary; Philadelphia, 1816 2859.11 p39
Murphy, Mary; Philadelphia, 1864 5704.8 p180
Murphy, Mary 9 days; Massachusetts, 1849 5881.1 p71
Murphy, Mary 11; Philadelphia, 1853 5704.8 p112
Murphy, Mary 12; Massachusetts, 1849 5881.1 p71
Murphy, Mary 17; Massachusetts, 1850 5881.1 p73
Murphy, Mary 20; Massachusetts, 1849 5881.1 p72
Murphy, Mary 23; Massachusetts, 1847 5881.1 p70
Murphy, Mary 24; Massachusetts, 1849 5881.1 p71
Murphy, Mary 50; Massachusetts, 1849 5881.1 p70
Murphy, Mary 62; Philadelphia, 1851 5704.8 p71
Murphy, Mary Ann; Philadelphia, 1850 53.26 p73
*Relative:*Lavey
Murphy, Mary Ann; Philadelphia, 1850 5704.8 p69
Murphy, Maryann 18; Philadelphia, 1845 6508.6 p115
Murphy, Matthew; America, 1740 4971 p15
Murphy, Matthew; New York, NY, 1811 2859.11 p17
Murphy, Michael; America, 1740 4971 p64

Murphy, Michael; America, 1741 4971 p42
Murphy, Michael; New York, NY, 1811 2859.11 p17
With family
Murphy, Michael; New York, NY, 1835 8208.4 p42
Murphy, Michael; New York, NY, 1838 8208.4 p69
Murphy, Michael 8; Massachusetts, 1849 5881.1 p72
Murphy, Michael 19; Massachusetts, 1849 5881.1 p72
Murphy, Michael 22; Maryland, 1775 1219.7 p273
Murphy, Michael 33; Massachusetts, 1849 5881.1 p72
Murphy, Morris; New York, NY, 1815 2859.11 p39
Murphy, Morris; New York, NY, 1816 2859.11 p39
Murphy, Nicholas; Ohio, 1840 9892.11 p31
Murphy, Nicholas; Ohio, 1843 9892.11 p31
Murphy, Norah; Montreal, 1818 7603 p64
Murphy, Norry 8; Massachusetts, 1849 5881.1 p73
Murphy, Owen; America, 1741 4971 p10
Murphy, Owen; America, 1741 4971 p94
Murphy, Owen; Quebec, 1847 5704.8 p37
Murphy, Patrick; America, 1774 1639.20 p250
Murphy, Patrick; Arkansas, 1918 95.2 p87
Murphy, Patrick; Isle aux Noix, Que., 1813 7603 p93
Murphy, Patrick; New Orleans, 1850 1450.2 p106A
Murphy, Patrick; New York, 1833 1450.2 p105A
Murphy, Patrick; New York, 1884 5240.1 p31
Murphy, Patrick; New York, NY, 1815 2859.11 p39
Murphy, Patrick; New York, NY, 1816 2859.11 p39
Murphy, Patrick; New York, NY, 1835 8208.4 p45
Murphy, Patrick; Quebec, 1852 5704.8 p86
Murphy, Patrick; Quebec, 1852 5704.8 p90
Murphy, Patrick 7; Massachusetts, 1849 5881.1 p74
Murphy, Patrick 12; Massachusetts, 1849 5881.1 p74
Murphy, Patrick 18; St. John, N.B., 1866 5704.8 p167
Murphy, Patrick 20; Massachusetts, 1850 5881.1 p75
Murphy, Patrick 26; Massachusetts, 1849 5881.1 p74
Murphy, Patrick 30; Massachusetts, 1847 5881.1 p73
Murphy, Patrick 30; Philadelphia, 1803 53.26 p73
Murphy, Patrick 54; Massachusetts, 1847 5881.1 p74
Murphy, Pete; America, 1741 4971 p40
Murphy, Peter; New York, NY, 1836 8208.4 p11
Murphy, Peter; New York, NY, 1838 8208.4 p65
Murphy, Peter 10; Massachusetts, 1850 5881.1 p75
Murphy, Peter 22; St. John, N.B., 1854 5704.8 p114
Murphy, Peter 26; Philadelphia, 1845 6508.6 p115
Murphy, Peter 40; Massachusetts, 1848 5881.1 p74
Murphy, Peter 45; Massachusetts, 1849 5881.1 p74
Murphy, Phelim; America, 1736-1737 4971 p26
Murphy, Philip; America, 1741 4971 p41
Murphy, Philip 7; Massachusetts, 1849 5881.1 p75
Murphy, Richard; America, 1743 4971 p23
Murphy, Richard; Iowa, 1866-1943 123.54 p35
Murphy, Robert; America, 1739 4971 p14
Murphy, Rosanna; Philadelphia, 1864 5704.8 p178
Murphy, Sally 45; Massachusetts, 1849 5881.1 p76
Murphy, Sarah *SEE* Murphy, Lawrence
Murphy, Sarah; Philadelphia, 1847 5704.8 p23
Murphy, Sarah 12; Massachusetts, 1847 5881.1 p75
Murphy, Sarah 21; Philadelphia, 1804 53.26 p73
Murphy, Simon; Philadelphia, 1816 2859.11 p39
Murphy, Stephen 10; Massachusetts, 1849 5881.1 p75
Murphy, Susan; New York, NY, 1816 2859.11 p39
Murphy, Teigue; America, 1741 4971 p41
Murphy, Terence; America, 1742 4971 p35
Murphy, Terence; Annapolis, MD, 1742 4971 p93
Murphy, Terence; Maryland, 1742 4971 p106
Murphy, Thomas; America, 1739 4971 p14
Murphy, Thomas; America, 1742 4971 p22
Murphy, Thomas; America, 1742 4971 p86
Murphy, Thomas; America, 1742 4971 p95
Murphy, Thomas; Annapolis, MD, 1742 4971 p93
Murphy, Thomas; Maryland, 1742 4971 p107
Murphy, Thomas; Quebec, 1819 7603 p102
Murphy, Thomas; Quebec, 1823 7603 p84
Murphy, Thomas; St. John, N.B., 1847 5704.8 p33
Murphy, Thomas 2; Massachusetts, 1847 5881.1 p76
Murphy, Thomas 11; Massachusetts, 1849 5881.1 p76
Murphy, Thomas 20; Massachusetts, 1849 5881.1 p76
Murphy, Thomas 21; Massachusetts, 1848 5881.1 p76
Murphy, Thomas 23; Massachusetts, 1849 5881.1 p76
Murphy, Thomas 25; Massachusetts, 1850 5881.1 p76
Murphy, Thomas 26; Philadelphia, 1803 53.26 p73
Murphy, Thomas 27; Maryland, 1774 1219.7 p192
Murphy, Thomas 28; Massachusetts, 1849 5881.1 p76
Murphy, Timothy; America, 1741 4971 p41
Murphy, Timothy; America, 1839 1450.2 p106A
Murphy, Timothy; New York, NY, 1811 2859.11 p17
Murphy, Timothy 12; Massachusetts, 1850 5881.1 p76
Murphy, Timothy 19; Massachusetts, 1849 5881.1 p76
Murphy, Walter; Annapolis, MD, 1742 4971 p93
Murphy, Walter; Maryland, 1742 4971 p106
Murphy, William; America, 1741 4971 p9
Murphy, William; America, 1741 4971 p94
Murphy, William; New York, NY, 1811 2859.11 p17
Murphy, William; New York, NY, 1840 8208.4 p105
Murphy, William 14; Philadelphia, 1853 5704.8 p112
Murphy, William 18; Massachusetts, 1847 5881.1 p77
Murr, Daniell; Virginia, 1637 6219 p108
Murr, Louis; America, 1872 1450.2 p106A
Murrah, David; Georgia, 1775 1219.7 p274
Murray, Agnes 10; St. John, N.B., 1867 5704.8 p167
Murray, Alex *SEE* Murray, John
Murray, Alex *SEE* Murray, Norman
Murray, Alex 36; St. John, N.B., 1867 5704.8 p167
Murray, Alexander; Charleston, SC, 1650-1750 1639.20 p250
Murray, Alexander; Charleston, SC, 1746 1639.20 p250
Murray, Alexander; Colorado, 1880 9678.2 p128
Murray, Alexander; New York, NY, 1838 8208.4 p62
Murray, Alexander Hunter; Northwest Terr., 1843 9775.5 p219
Murray, Andrew; Philadelphia, 1866 5704.8 p208
Murray, Angus *SEE* Murray, Donald
Murray, Angus *SEE* Murray, John
Murray, Angus; Quebec, 1855 4537.30 p30
*Wife:*Mary MacLean
*Child:*Margaret
*Child:*Norman
*Child:*Ann
*Child:*Isabella
Murray, Angus; Quebec, 1873 4537.30 p33
*Wife:*Ann Graham
*Child:*Norman
*Child:*Catherine
*Child:*John
Murray, Ann *SEE* Murray, Angus
Murray, Ann *SEE* Murray, John
Murray, Ann *SEE* Murray, Kenneth
Murray, Ann *SEE* Murray, Murdo
Murray, Ann *SEE* Murray, Roderick
Murray, Ann; Canada, 1832 8893 p263
Murray, Ann; Philadelphia, 1847 53.26 p73
*Relative:*Catherine 7
*Relative:*Rosannah 4
Murray, Ann; Philadelphia, 1847 5704.8 p2
Murray, Ann; Quebec, 1855 4537.30 p10
Murray, Ann; Quebec, 1855 4537.30 p117
Murray, Ann Graham *SEE* Murray, Angus
Murray, Ann MacDonald *SEE* Murray, Murdo
Murray, Anne; Charleston, SC, 1768 1639.20 p251
Murray, Anne; Philadelphia, 1868 5704.8 p226
Murray, Barney; New York, NY, 1835 8208.4 p4
Murray, Belle *SEE* Murray, Donald
Murray, Belle *SEE* Murray, John
Murray, Benjamin 16; Virginia, 1751 1219.7 p3
Murray, Benjamin 16; Virginia, 1751 3690.1 p162
Murray, Bernard; New York, NY, 1816 2859.11 p39
Murray, Betty; Philadelphia, 1851 5704.8 p71
Murray, Biddy; Quebec, 1851 5704.8 p73
Murray, Bridget; New York, NY, 1816 2859.11 p39
Murray, Bridget 19; Philadelphia, 1857 5704.8 p132
Murray, Catharine; Philadelphia, 1865 5704.8 p192
Murray, Catharine 9 mos; Philadelphia, 1866 5704.8 p211
Murray, Catharine 18; Massachusetts, 1848 5881.1 p64
Murray, Catherine *SEE* Murray, Angus
Murray, Catherine *SEE* Murray, John
Murray, Catherine *SEE* Murray, Kenneth
Murray, Catherine *SEE* Murray, Murdo
Murray, Catherine *SEE* Murray, Roderick
Murray, Catherine; Montreal, 1818 7603 p82
Murray, Catherine; Quebec, 1841 4537.30 p9
Murray, Catherine 7 *SEE* Murray, Ann
Murray, Catherine 7; Philadelphia, 1847 5704.8 p2
Murray, Catherine 20; Philadelphia, 1860 5704.8 p145
Murray, Catherine MacDonald *SEE* Murray, Kenneth
Murray, Catherine MacKenzie *SEE* Murray, Donald
Murray, Charles; New York, NY, 1838 8208.4 p70
Murray, Charles; Quebec, 1851 5704.8 p73
Murray, Charles 32; Philadelphia, 1858 5704.8 p139
Murray, Cormick; America, 1737 4971 p36
Murray, Daniel; New York, NY, 1870 5704.8 p239
Murray, Daniel; Philadelphia, 1816 2859.11 p39
Murray, Daniel; Philadelphia, 1847 5704.8 p32
Murray, Daniel 6 mos; St. John, N.B., 1847 5704.8 p34
Murray, David; Arkansas, 1918 95.2 p87
Murray, David 18; Maryland, 1737 3690.1 p162
Murray, David 23; Georgia, 1775 1219.7 p276
Murray, Dennis; New York, NY, 1839 8208.4 p94
Murray, Donald *SEE* Murray, Donald
Murray, Donald *SEE* Murray, Kenneth
Murray, Donald *SEE* Murray, Murdo
Murray, Donald *SEE* Murray, Norman
Murray, Donald *SEE* Murray, Roderick
Murray, Donald; Quebec, 1853 4537.30 p30
*Wife:*Catherine MacKenzie
*Child:*Norman
*Child:*Kirsty
*Child:*Belle
Murray, Donald; Quebec, 1853 4537.30 p31
*Wife:*Isabella MacLean
*Child:*Margaret
*Child:*Donald
*Child:*John
*Child:*Angus
*Child:*Mary
Murray, Donald; Quebec, 1883 4537.30 p33
*Wife:*Kirsty MacDonald
*Child:*Kenneth
*Child:*Kirsty
*Child:*Effie
With child
*Child:*Kenina
*Child:*Margaret
Murray, Edward; America, 1739 4971 p68
Murray, Edward; Montreal, 1821 7603 p78
Murray, Effie *SEE* Murray, Donald
Murray, Effie MacKenzie *SEE* Murray, Murdo
Murray, Eliza 24; Massachusetts, 1850 5881.1 p66
Murray, Elizabeth; Philadelphia, 1864 5704.8 p178
Murray, Ellen; Philadelphia, 1868 5704.8 p229
Murray, Ellen 13; Massachusetts, 1847 5881.1 p65
Murray, Ellen 24; Massachusetts, 1847 5881.1 p65
Murray, Francis A.; New York, NY, 1838 8208.4 p85
Murray, Grace 28; Philadelphia, 1858 5704.8 p139
Murray, Hannah; America, 1869 5704.8 p233
Murray, Hannah; New York, NY, 1870 5704.8 p239
Murray, Hannah; Quebec, 1834 7036 p123
Murray, Henry; America, 1741 4971 p65
Murray, Henry; America, 1741 4971 p76
Murray, Hugh; New York, NY, 1840 8208.4 p105
Murray, Hugh 4 mos; Massachusetts, 1849 5881.1 p67
Murray, Isabella *SEE* Murray, Angus
Murray, Isabella *SEE* Murray, John
Murray, Isabella *SEE* Murray, Kenneth
Murray, Isabella *SEE* Murray, Kirsty
Murray, Isabella *SEE* Murray, Murdo
Murray, Isabella *SEE* Murray, Norman
Murray, Isabella; Philadelphia, 1865 5704.8 p198
Murray, Isabella MacIver *SEE* Murray, John
Murray, Isabella MacLean *SEE* Murray, Donald
Murray, James; America, 1738 4971 p13
Murray, James; Cape Fear, NC, 1739 1639.20 p277
With cousin
Murray, James; Charleston, SC, 1735 1639.20 p251
Murray, James; Illinois, 1875 7857 p5
Murray, James; New York, NY, 1816 2859.11 p39
Murray, James; New York, NY, 1834 8208.4 p38
Murray, James; Philadelphia, 1847 5704.8 p32
Murray, James; Philadelphia, 1864 5704.8 p169
Murray, James 18; Massachusetts, 1850 5881.1 p69
Murray, James 20; Philadelphia, 1803 53.26 p73
Murray, James 21; Philadelphia, 1854 5704.8 p117
Murray, James 23; Newfoundland, 1789 4915.24 p57
Murray, Janet; Quebec, 1852 4537.30 p39
Murray, Jas.; New York, NY, 1816 2859.11 p39
Murray, Johanna 2; Massachusetts, 1850 5881.1 p69
Murray, John *SEE* Murray, Angus
Murray, John *SEE* Murray, Donald
Murray, John *SEE* Murray, John
Murray, John *SEE* Murray, Kenneth
Murray, John *SEE* Murray, Kenneth
Murray, John *SEE* Murray, Murdo
Murray, John *SEE* Murray, Murdo
Murray, John *SEE* Murray, Norman
Murray, John *SEE* Murray, Roderick
Murray, John; America, 1737 4971 p66
Murray, John; America, 1738 4971 p33
Murray, John; Charleston, SC, 1764 1639.20 p251
Murray, John; Montreal, 1818 7603 p68
Murray, John; New York, NY, 1815 2859.11 p39
Murray, John; New York, NY, 1839 8208.4 p98
Murray, John; New York, NY, 1869 5704.8 p235
Murray, John; North America, 1759 1219.7 p69
Murray, John; Philadelphia, 1816 2859.11 p39
With wife & 2 children
Murray, John; Philadelphia, 1851 5704.8 p70
Murray, John; Quebec, 1855 4537.30 p31
*Wife:*Mary MacKenzie
*Child:*Mary
*Child:*Ann
*Child:*Norman
*Child:*Malcolm
*Child:*Alex
*Child:*Belle
Murray, John; Quebec, 1855 4537.30 p31
*Wife:*Mary Nicolson
*Child:*John N.

Muting, Joe; Arkansas, 1918 *95.2 p87*
Mutkovic, Mat; Iowa, 1866-1943 *123.54 p35*
Muto, Antonio 35; West Virginia, 1896 *9788.3 p17*
Mutschler, Anna; Pennsylvania, 1754 *2444 p195*
Mutschler, Anna; Port uncertain, 1754 *2444 p195*
Muttery, James 23; Maryland, 1774 *1219.7 p187*
Mutton, James; Iroquois Co., IL, 1894 *3455.1 p12*
Mutton, Mary; Virginia, 1648 *6219 p251*
Mutz, Jost; South Carolina, 1788 *7119 p200*
Mutzel, . . .; Quebec, 1776 *9786 p104*
Mutzenberg, A.; America, 1829 *778.5 p400*
Muxford, John; Virginia, 1643 *6219 p203*
Muxford, Robt.; Virginia, 1638 *6219 p117*
Muyere, Francois Louis 46; Louisiana, 1820 *778.5 p400*
Muys, Peter 28; Arkansas, 1918 *95.2 p87*
Muzell, Ludwig Casimir; Quebec, 1776 *9786 p262*
MxLinn, Mrs. E.M. 69; Arizona, 1909 *9228.40 p12*
Myer, Barbara *SEE* Myer, John
Myer, Frederick; Illinois, 1871 *5012.39 p25*
Myer, George 25; America, 1835 *778.5 p400*
Myer, Joerg; Died enroute, 1804 *8582.2 p27*
    With son & 2 daughters
Myer, Johannes 37; Pennsylvania, 1753 *2444 p190*
Myer, Johannis Martin 18; Pennsylvania, 1753 *2444 p190*
Myer, John; Baltimore, 1804 *8582.2 p27*
    *Mother:*Barbara
    With sister & brother

Myer, Martin; Philadelphia, 1764 *9973.7 p39*
Myer, Mathias; Washington, 1859-1920 *2872.1 p27*
Myer, Mathias; Washington, 1859-1920 *2872.1 p44*
Myer, Matthew; Washington, 1859-1920 *2872.1 p27*
Myer, Myer H.; New York, NY, 1837 *8208.4 p54*
Myer, Valentine; Indiana, 1848 *9117 p17*
Myerly, David; Philadelphia, 1759 *9973.7 p34*
Myerly, John George; Philadelphia, 1759 *9973.7 p34*
Myers, Baltzer; Philadelphia, 1749 *2444 p191*
Myers, Barbara *SEE* Myers, Candy
Myers, Candy; America, 1804 *8582.2 p60*
Myers, Candy; Baltimore, 1804 *8582.2 p27*
    *Mother:*Barbara
    With sister & brother
Myers, Charles; Arizona, 1898 *9228.30 p5*
Myers, Egbert 45; New York, NY, 1847 *3377.6 p12*
Myers, Frederick; America, 1832 *1450.2 p100A*
Myers, Jacob; New York, NY, 1834 *8208.4 p4*
Myers, Joerg; Died enroute, 1804 *8582.2 p27*
    With son & 2 daughters
Myers, John; Cincinnati, 1869-1887 *8582 p22*
Myers, John; Ohio, 1869-1887 *8582 p22*
Myers, Lilly 60; Philadelphia, 1865 *5704.8 p164*
Myers, Lionel; New York, NY, 1838 *8208.4 p88*
Myers, Maargretta 20; New York, NY, 1847 *3377.6 p12*
Myers, Marie-Anne; Quebec, 1818 *7603 p26*
Myers, Martha 20; Philadelphia, 1865 *5704.8 p164*
Myers, Mary; Montreal, 1825 *7603 p102*

Myles, Ann 60; St. John, N.B., 1864 *5704.8 p159*
Myles, Bridget; Philadelphia, 1866 *5704.8 p207*
Myles, Elizabeth 20; St. John, N.B., 1864 *5704.8 p159*
Myles, George; South Carolina, 1745 *1639.20 p252*
Myles, James; St. John, N.B., 1852 *5704.8 p94*
Myles, James 17; St. John, N.B., 1864 *5704.8 p159*
Myles, Jane; St. John, N.B., 1852 *5704.8 p94*
Myles, John; Virginia, 1638 *6219 p148*
Myles, Margaret 25; Quebec, 1858 *5704.8 p137*
Myles, Robert 60; St. John, N.B., 1864 *5704.8 p159*
Myles, Susanna 26; Quebec, 1857 *5704.8 p136*
Mylet, James 45; Massachusetts, 1849 *5881.1 p68*
Mylius, Feldschr.; Quebec, 1776 *9786 p105*
Mylius, Traugott 47; New Orleans, 1839 *9420.2 p359*
Mylon, Nicholas; New York, 1831-1841 *7036 p124*
Mylon, Nicholas; St. John, N.B., 1831 *7036 p124*
Mynarsch, Piotr 26; New York, 1912 *9980.29 p68*
Mynat, Richard 20; Virginia, 1749 *3690.1 p163*
Mynatt, Richard 20; Virginia, 1749 *3690.1 p163*
Myner, Ann; Virginia, 1637 *6219 p108*
Myren, Thure Einar; Arkansas, 1918 *95.2 p87*
Myries, Miss; Jamaica, 1775 *1219.7 p277*
Myrvall, Peter J.; Maine, 1889-1896 *6410.22 p122*
Myszin, Leon 18; New York, 1912 *9980.29 p63*

N

Naacke, . . .; Canada, 1776-1783 *9786 p29*
Nabbs, Jonathan; Antigua (Antego), 1754 *1219.7 p27*
Naber, Jean 60; New Orleans, 1838 *778.5 p400*
Nablett, Mary; Virginia, 1636 *6219 p76*
Nabonne, Bernard 30; New Orleans, 1837 *778.5 p400*
Nabor, Madame 30; New Orleans, 1829 *778.5 p400*
Nabor, Mr. 55; New Orleans, 1829 *778.5 p400*
Naccarato, Angelo; Arkansas, 1918 *95.2 p87*
Naccarato, Guiseppe 22; West Virginia, 1904 *9788.3 p17*
Nacewicz, Anna 18; New York, 1912 *9980.29 p73*
Nack, . . .; Canada, 1776-1783 *9786 p29*
Nackley, Ad; Washington, 1859-1920 *2872.1 p27*
Nackley, Charley; Washington, 1859-1920 *2872.1 p27*
Nadle, J. M. 35; New Orleans, 1823 *778.5 p400*
Nadrowska, Adam 5 *SEE* Nadrowska, Walentina
Nadrowska, Janina 11 *SEE* Nadrowska, Walentina
Nadrowska, Maryan 9 *SEE* Nadrowska, Walentina
Nadrowska, Walentina 35; New York, 1912 *9980.29 p50*
   *Child:*Janina 11
   *Child:*Maryan 9
   *Child:*Wincenty 7
   *Child:*Adam 5
Nadrowska, Wincenty 7 *SEE* Nadrowska, Walentina
Naegele, John; Cincinnati, 1869-1887 *8582 p22*
Naegele, Hans Georg; America, 1744 *2444 p195*
Naegle, Nikolaus; America, 1845 *8582.3 p48*
Naegli, Johannes; Philadelphia, 1820 *8582.3 p87*
Naeve, Hinrich; Colorado, 1894 *9678.2 p128*
Naffseger, Peter; Pennsylvania, 1771 *9973.8 p32*
Nafin, John; Canada, 1841 *7036 p121*
Nagan, Philemon; Wisconsin, n.d. *9675.7 p52*
Nage, John 29; Maryland, 1775 *1219.7 p264*
Nagel, Lieutenant; Nicaragua, 1856 *8582.3 p31*
Nagel, Anna Gottschall *SEE* Nagel, Christian
Nagel, Anna Maria *SEE* Nagel, Christian
Nagel, Anne Marie Blobaum *SEE* Nagel, Carl Heinrich Friedrich
Nagel, Anne Marie Elisabeth; America, 1853 *4610.10 p98*
Nagel, Anne Marie Louise; America, 1839 *4610.10 p154*
Nagel, Anne Marie Rasche *SEE* Nagel, Wilhelm August
Nagel, August; Wisconsin, n.d. *9675.7 p52*
Nagel, Carl Friedrich; America, 1841 *4610.10 p154*
   *Wife:*Wilhelmine Blobaum
   *Son:*Carl Friedrich Wilhelm
Nagel, Carl Friedrich Wilhelm *SEE* Nagel, Carl Friedrich
Nagel, Carl H. F. Wilhelm *SEE* Nagel, Carl Heinrich Friedrich
Nagel, Carl Heinrich Friedrich; America, 1839 *4610.10 p154*
   *Wife:*Anne Marie Blobaum
   *Son:*Carl H. F. Wilhelm
Nagel, Caroline H. Engel *SEE* Nagel, Wilhelm August
Nagel, Charles; Wisconsin, n.d. *9675.7 p52*
Nagel, Charles Praisgod 22; New Orleans, 1839 *9420.2 p487*
Nagel, Christian *SEE* Nagel, Christian
Nagel, Christian; Pennsylvania, 1751 *2444 p137*
Nagel, Christian; Pennsylvania, 1751 *2444 p195*
   *Wife:*Anna Gottschall
   *Child:*Gottlieb
   *Child:*Anna Maria
   *Child:*Christian
   *Child:*Maria Agnes
Nagel, Christine; Died enroute, 1751 *2444 p195*
Nagel, Claus John 59; Kansas, 1880 *5240.1 p62*
Nagel, Dorothea Elise Konig *SEE* Nagel, Ernst Ludwig

Nagel, Ernst Heinrich Gottlieb; America, 1839 *4610.10 p154*
   With wife
   With 2 daughters
Nagel, Ernst Ludwig; America, 1838-1854 *4610.10 p149*
   *Wife:*Dorothea Elise Konig
Nagel, Fredrick; Wisconsin, n.d. *9675.7 p52*
Nagel, Friedrich W. Gottlieb *SEE* Nagel, Wilhelm August
Nagel, Georg 28; Port uncertain, 1839 *778.5 p400*
Nagel, Gottlieb *SEE* Nagel, Christian
Nagel, Gottlieb 26; Pennsylvania, 1754 *2444 p196*
Nagel, Hans Jerg; Pennsylvania, 1750 *2444 p196*
Nagel, Henry; Ohio, 1819 *8582.1 p47*
Nagel, Jean 18; Port uncertain, 1839 *778.5 p401*
Nagel, Johann; Pennsylvania, 1787 *2444 p196*
Nagel, Johann Wilhelm August; America, 1854 *4610.10 p149*
Nagel, John Baptist; Cincinnati, 1841 *8582.1 p25*
Nagel, Maria Agnes *SEE* Nagel, Christian
Nagel, Martin 25; Port uncertain, 1839 *778.5 p401*
Nagel, Wilhelm August; America, 1872 *4610.10 p159*
   *Wife:*Anne Marie Rasche
   *Child:*Friedrich W. Gottlieb
   *Child:*Caroline H. Engel
Nagel, Wilhelmine Blobaum *SEE* Nagel, Carl Friedrich
Naghten, Laughlin; America, 1739 *4971 p82*
Nagle, C. R. 59; Kansas, 1880 *5240.1 p31*
Nagle, Claus John; Illinois, 1872 *5240.1 p31*
Nagle, David; New York, NY, 1835 *8208.4 p56*
Nagle, Franz Joseph; Illinois, 1882 *2896.5 p29*
Nagle, John; Illinois, 1860 *2896.5 p29*
Nagle, John Jacob; New York, 1750 *3652 p74*
Nagle, Rose; America, 1739 *4971 p46*
Nagle, Rose; America, 1739 *4971 p47*
Naglee, Rudolph; Philadelphia, 1760 *9973.7 p35*
Nagler, Herman; Kansas, 1896 *5240.1 p31*
Nagrocki, Adam; Wisconsin, n.d. *9675.7 p52*
Nahally, Catharine 25; Massachusetts, 1849 *5881.1 p77*
Nahlik, Leopold; New York, NY, 1902 *3455.1 p40*
Nahm, Nicolaus; Pennsylvania, 1754 *4525 p232*
Nail, Henry; Ohio, 1819 *8582.1 p47*
Naile, John 16; Philadelphia, 1774 *1219.7 p183*
Naillier, Mr. 45; New Orleans, 1837 *778.5 p401*
Nailor, Wm.; New York, NY, 1811 *2859.11 p17*
   With family
Nainby, William 16; Maryland, 1774 *1219.7 p228*
Nairn, Elizabeth Edward Quintine; South Carolina, 1658-1721 *1639.20 p252*
Nairn, Thomas; South Carolina, 1715 *1639.20 p252*
Nairn, Thomas F.; Austin, TX, 1886 *9777 p6*
Naismith, R.; South Carolina, 1739 *1639.20 p252*
Nakaerts, Nestor; Iroquois Co., IL, 1894 *3455.1 p12*
Nalin, Patrick 40; Massachusetts, 1849 *5881.1 p78*
Nally, James; California, 1858 *3840.2 p18*
Nalty, Bridget; New York, NY, 1816 *2859.11 p39*
Nalty, Margaret; New York, NY, 1816 *2859.11 p39*
Nalty, Mary; New York, NY, 1816 *2859.11 p39*
Nalty, Patrick; New York, NY, 1816 *2859.11 p39*
Nalty, Thomas; New York, NY, 1816 *2859.11 p39*
Nalziger, Anna 29; New Orleans, 1837 *778.5 p401*
Nalziger, Catherine 2; New Orleans, 1837 *778.5 p401*
Nalziger, Catherine 19; New Orleans, 1837 *778.5 p401*
Nalziger, Jean 35; New Orleans, 1837 *778.5 p401*
Nalziger, Madeleine 25; New Orleans, 1837 *778.5 p401*
Nalziger, Pierre 4; New Orleans, 1837 *778.5 p401*
Namer, Anton; New York, NY, 1898 *1450.2 p27B*
Namerofsky, Loe; Wisconsin, n.d. *9675.7 p52*

Nammer, Caroline 2; America, 1836 *778.5 p401*
Nammer, Charles 21; America, 1836 *778.5 p401*
Nammer, Elisabeth 29; America, 1836 *778.5 p401*
Nance, Alice *SEE* Nance, Richard
Nance, Richard; Virginia, 1639 *6219 p23*
   *Wife:*Alice
Nanendi, Bernard 31; America, 1825 *778.5 p401*
Nangle, Elizabeth; America, 1740 *4971 p15*
Nangle, William 20; Maryland, 1774 *1219.7 p244*
Nankivel, William; San Francisco, 1850 *4914.15 p10*
Nanni, Aurelio; Arkansas, 1918 *95.2 p87*
Nanson, Mathew; Philadelphia, 1811 *53.26 p74*
Nanson, Mathew; Philadelphia, 1811 *2859.11 p17*
Nantel, . . .; Canada, 1776-1783 *9786 p43*
Nanzel, Michael; Virginia, 1844 *4626.16 p12*
Napeleon, Giacomo; Arkansas, 1918 *95.2 p87*
Napier, Thomas; South Carolina, 1778-1800 *1639.20 p252*
Napier, William; South Carolina, 1732 *1639.20 p252*
Naplor, Eliesa 19; Port uncertain, 1839 *778.5 p402*
Naplor, Perie 21; Port uncertain, 1839 *778.5 p402*
Napoleon, Ms. 66; New Orleans, 1839 *778.5 p402*
Napoleon, Samuel; New York, NY, 1839 *8208.4 p100*
Napoliello, Grazio 12; New York, NY, 1893 *9026.4 p42*
Nappinger, Andrew; Philadelphia, 1757 *9973.7 p32*
Narbonne, Mr. 26; New Orleans, 1823 *778.5 p402*
Narbutowitch, Joseph J.; Arkansas, 1918 *95.2 p87*
Nardin, Anne-Judith *SEE* Nardin, Jacques
Nardin, Anne-Judith *SEE* Nardin, Jean-Jacques
Nardin, Francoise *SEE* Nardin, Jean-Jacques
Nardin, Isaac *SEE* Nardin, Jacques
Nardin, Jacques 40; Halifax, N.S., 1752 *7074.6 p212*
   *Wife:*Anne-Judith
   *Daughter:*Jeanne
   *Daughter:*Marie
   With child
Nardin, Jacques 56; Halifax, N.S., 1752 *7074.6 p207*
   With son
   With family of 4
Nardin, Jacques 56; Halifax, N.S., 1752 *7074.6 p212*
   *Wife:*Madeleine
   *Child:*Isaac
   *Child:*Pierre
   *Child:*Suzette
   *Child:*Jean-Pierre
Nardin, Jean-Christophe *SEE* Nardin, Jean-Jacques
Nardin, Jean Jacques 36; Halifax, N.S., 1752 *7074.6 p207*
   With family of 3
Nardin, Jean-Jacques 36; Halifax, N.S., 1752 *7074.6 p212*
   *Wife:*Anne-Judith
   *Child:*Jean-Christophe
   *Child:*Francoise
Nardin, Jean-Pierre *SEE* Nardin, Jacques
Nardin, Jeanne *SEE* Nardin, Jacques
Nardin, Madeleine *SEE* Nardin, Jacques
Nardin, Marie *SEE* Nardin, Jacques
Nardin, Pierre *SEE* Nardin, Jacques
Nardin, Suzette *SEE* Nardin, Jacques
Nardini, G.; Arizona, 1890 *2764.35 p51*
Narey, Peter; New York, NY, 1816 *2859.11 p39*
Narr, David; New York, NY, 1836 *8208.4 p23*
Narroway, Anthony; Pennsylvania, 1764 *1219.7 p101*
Narry, Barnet 32; Virginia, 1775 *1219.7 p261*
Naruszewicz, . . .; New York, 1831 *4606 p176*
Nary, Patrick; America, 1741 *4971 p37*

Naser, Philipp; Charleston, SC, 1775-1781 ***8582.2*** *p52*
Nash, Bridget 25; Maryland, 1774 ***1219.7*** *p187*
Nash, Donald 26; Philadelphia, 1803 ***53.26*** *p74*
Nash, Edward; Wisconsin, n.d. ***9675.7*** *p52*
Nash, Henry 30; Maryland, 1774 ***1219.7*** *p211*
Nash, James 18; Maryland, 1774 ***1219.7*** *p236*
Nash, James 18; Maryland, 1774 ***1219.7*** *p244*
Nash, John 19; Jamaica, 1733 ***3690.1*** *p163*
Nash, John 52; Kansas, 1887 ***5240.1*** *p70*
Nash, John William; Arkansas, 1918 ***95.2*** *p87*
Nash, Joseph 20; Maryland, 1736 ***3690.1*** *p163*
Nash, Martin; New York, NY, 1838 ***8208.4*** *p65*
Nash, Michael 22; Kansas, 1884 ***5240.1*** *p66*
Nash, Partrick 30; Kansas, 1872 ***5240.1*** *p52*
Nash, Patrick 30; Kansas, 1872 ***5240.1*** *p31*
Nash, Robert; Virginia, 1637 ***6219*** *p10*
Nash, Robt.; Virginia, 1635 ***6219*** *p10*
Nash, Samuel 40; Maryland, 1775 ***1219.7*** *p264*
Nash, Sarah 24; Canada, 1838 ***4535.12*** *p113*
Nash, Thomas 28; Maryland, 1774 ***1219.7*** *p220*
Nash, William 26; Maryland, 1775 ***1219.7*** *p249*
Nash, William 26; Maryland, 1775 ***1219.7*** *p253*
Nasida, Catherine; New York, NY, 1816 ***2859.11*** *p40*
Nast, Mr.; New York, NY, 1849 ***8582*** *p22*
Nast, Thomas; America, 1846 ***8582*** *p22*
With mother & sister
Nast, Wilhelm; America, 1828 ***8582.3*** *p90*
Nast, William; Cincinnati, 1835 ***3702.7*** *p89*
Naterlow, Joseph 16; Virginia, 1775 ***1219.7*** *p258*
Natsis, George; Arkansas, 1918 ***95.2*** *p87*
Natvej, George; America, 1889 ***7137*** *p169*
Natvej, Mary; America, 1892 ***7137*** *p169*
Natzmer, Bruno von; Nicaragua, 1856 ***8582.3*** *p31*
Nau, J. 32; New Orleans, 1822 ***778.5*** *p402*
Nau, Johannes 25; Kansas, 1882 ***5240.1*** *p63*
Nauclin, . . . 45; America, 1839 ***778.5*** *p402*
Naudin, Charles; Washington, 1859-1920 ***2872.1*** *p27*
Naudin, Ernestine; Washington, 1859-1920 ***2872.1*** *p27*
Nauerofsky, Leo; Wisconsin, n.d. ***9675.7*** *p52*
Nauerth, Johann B.; Dayton, OH, 1869-1887 ***8582*** *p22*
Naughten, Bridget 20; Massachusetts, 1849 ***5881.1*** *p77*
Naughten, John 25; Massachusetts, 1849 ***5881.1*** *p78*
Naughten, John J.; Kansas, 1898 ***5240.1*** *p31*
Naughten, Mary 30; Massachusetts, 1848 ***5881.1*** *p78*
With child 1
Naughten, Patrick; New York, NY, 1816 ***2859.11*** *p40*
Naughten, Patrick 11; Massachusetts, 1850 ***5881.1*** *p78*
Naughten, Peter 23; Massachusetts, 1849 ***5881.1*** *p78*
Naughton, Ellenor; America, 1739 ***4971*** *p37*
Naughton, John; America, 1735-1743 ***4971*** *p79*
Naughton, Margaret; America, 1739 ***4971*** *p37*
Nauholz, George; Wisconsin, n.d. ***9675.7*** *p52*
Naulin, Michael; Wisconsin, n.d. ***9675.7*** *p52*
Naumann, Chaplain; Quebec, 1778 ***9786*** *p267*
Naumann, Fraugott 24; New Orleans, 1839 ***9420.2*** *p484*
Naus, John; Wisconsin, n.d. ***9675.7*** *p52*
Navalesi, Andrea 23; New York, NY, 1893 ***9026.4*** *p42*
*Relative:*Cehetti 25
Navalesi, Cehetti 25 *SEE* Navalesi, Andrea
Navarre, Mr. 27; New Orleans, 1821 ***778.5*** *p402*
Navarru, Angelo; Arkansas, 1918 ***95.2*** *p87*
Nave, Peter; Illinois, 1864 ***2896.5*** *p29*
Nave, William; New Orleans, 1846 ***2896.5*** *p29*
Navell, Mary; Quebec, 1824 ***7603*** *p100*
Naviel, Joseph 30; Port uncertain, 1820 ***778.5*** *p402*
Navieu, M. 32; America, 1836 ***778.5*** *p402*
Navin, Rose; Quebec, 1821 ***7603*** *p85*
Navino, John; Arkansas, 1918 ***95.2*** *p87*
Navy, Alley 15; Massachusetts, 1849 ***5881.1*** *p77*
Nawrocki, Stanislaw 22; New York, 1912 ***9980.29*** *p64*
Naylor, Ann 21; Philadelphia, 1775 ***1219.7*** *p257*
*Sister:*Elizabeth 12
Naylor, Elizabeth 12 *SEE* Naylor, Ann
Naylor, Elizabeth 18; Virginia, 1700 ***2212*** *p30*
Naylor, Elizabeth 26; Virginia, 1700 ***2212*** *p32*
Naylor, John; New York, NY, 1837 ***8208.4*** *p36*
Naylor, William; Virginia, 1639 ***6219*** *p155*
Nazaraua, Geramala; Wisconsin, n.d. ***9675.7*** *p52*
Nazzarena, Londena; Wisconsin, n.d. ***9675.7*** *p52*
Nazzareno, Juliano; Wisconsin, n.d. ***9675.7*** *p52*
Nazzoli, Fred; Arkansas, 1918 ***95.2*** *p87*
Nbotzki, Wladislaw 20; New York, 1912 ***9980.29*** *p73*
Neabal, John; Ohio, 1848 ***9892.11*** *p34*
Neagle, Johannes; Philadelphia, 1820 ***8582.3*** *p87*
Neagle, John; Louisiana, 1835 ***8208.4*** *p45*
Neagle, Pierce; Illinois, 1854 ***7857*** *p6*
Neagley, George; America, 1744 ***2444*** *p195*
Neaile, Robert 18; Maryland, 1720 ***3690.1*** *p163*
Neal, Betty 20; Massachusetts, 1849 ***5881.1*** *p77*
Neal, Betty 40; Massachusetts, 1850 ***5881.1*** *p77*
Neal, Caroline 7; Massachusetts, 1847 ***5881.1*** *p77*
Neal, Dennis 35; Massachusetts, 1849 ***5881.1*** *p77*
Neal, Edward 60; Massachusetts, 1849 ***5881.1*** *p77*
Neal, Elizabeth 6 mos; Massachusetts, 1849 ***5881.1*** *p78*
Neal, Francis; America, 1741 ***4971*** *p9*
Neal, Francis; America, 1741 ***4971*** *p94*
Neal, Gordan; America, 1741 ***4971*** *p33*
Neal, Henry; America, 1740 ***4971*** *p28*
Neal, James; America, 1742 ***4971*** *p27*
Neal, Joan 25; Massachusetts, 1848 ***5881.1*** *p78*
Neal, John; America, 1738 ***4971*** *p52*
Neal, John; America, 1743 ***4971*** *p11*
Neal, John; Illinois, 1857 ***7857*** *p6*
Neal, John 20; Massachusetts, 1849 ***5881.1*** *p78*
Neal, John 45; South Carolina, 1850 ***1639.20*** *p252*
Neal, Margaret 40; Massachusetts, 1849 ***5881.1*** *p78*
Neal, Mary; America, 1738 ***4971*** *p52*
Neal, Michael; Philadelphia, 1816 ***2859.11*** *p40*
Neal, Patrick 27; Newfoundland, 1789 ***4915.24*** *p56*
Neal, Peter 75; South Carolina, 1850 ***1639.20*** *p253*
Neal, Reuben 29; Kansas, 1880 ***5240.1*** *p62*
Neal, Sarah 45; Massachusetts, 1849 ***5881.1*** *p78*
Neal, Thomas 20; Massachusetts, 1850 ***5881.1*** *p78*
Neal, William; America, 1741 ***4971*** *p16*
Neal, William; Charleston, SC, 1804 ***1639.20*** *p253*
Neal, William 20; Jamaica, 1731 ***3690.1*** *p163*
Nealan, Daniel; America, 1742 ***4971*** *p53*
Nealan, Daniel 28; Massachusetts, 1849 ***5881.1*** *p77*
Nealan, Frank 26; Massachusetts, 1849 ***5881.1*** *p78*
Nealan, Thomas; America, 1742 ***4971*** *p53*
Neale, Francis 17; Jamaica, 1730 ***3690.1*** *p163*
Neale, George J.; New York, NY, 1840 ***8208.4*** *p103*
Neale, Gideon 16; Port uncertain, 1718-1759 ***3690.1*** *p163*
Neale, Henry; Virginia, 1643 ***6219*** *p23*
Neale, Honora; America, 1741 ***4971*** *p83*
Neale, Jeremiah 36; Quebec, 1864 ***5704.8*** *p163*
Neale, Jon.; Virginia, 1635 ***6219*** *p20*
Neale, Jon.; Virginia, 1643 ***6219*** *p23*
Neale, Pearce; Virginia, 1636 ***6219*** *p21*
Neale, Robert 18; Maryland, 1720 ***3690.1*** *p163*
Neale, Robert 20; Jamaica, 1754 ***1219.7*** *p28*
Neale, Robert 20; Jamaica, 1754 ***3690.1*** *p163*
Neale, Sarah 17; Maryland, 1775 ***1219.7*** *p260*
Neale, Thomas; Virginia, 1636 ***6219*** *p75*
Neale, Thomas 18; Philadelphia, 1774 ***1219.7*** *p182*
Neale, William; Virginia, 1642 ***6219*** *p191*
Nealen, John 8; St. John, N.B., 1849 ***5704.8*** *p56*
Nealen, Mary Ann 6; St. John, N.B., 1849 ***5704.8*** *p56*
Nealen, Susan 4; St. John, N.B., 1849 ***5704.8*** *p56*
Nealis, George; Philadelphia, 1865 ***5704.8*** *p201*
Nealis, Henry 21; Philadelphia, 1860 ***5704.8*** *p146*
Neall, John; Philadelphia, 1865 ***5704.8*** *p190*
Neall, John 48; North Carolina, 1850 ***1639.20*** *p253*
Neall, Mathew; New York, NY, 1811 ***2859.11*** *p17*
With wife
Neall, Nicholas 23; Virginia, 1727 ***3690.1*** *p163*
Neall, William 54; North Carolina, 1850 ***1639.20*** *p253*
Nealy, James; St. John, N.B., 1847 ***5704.8*** *p5*
Nealy, Rebica; Philadelphia, 1853 ***5704.8*** *p103*
Nealy, Sarah; Philadelphia, 1864 ***5704.8*** *p176*
Nealy, Thomas; Philadelphia, 1864 ***5704.8*** *p176*
Nealy, William; New York, NY, 1836 ***8208.4*** *p21*
Neary, Thaddeus; Quebec, 1824 ***7603*** *p83*
Neat, Ambrose; America, 1869 ***6014.1*** *p3*
Neate, William; Barbados, 1767 ***1219.7*** *p127*
Neatherwood, Joseph 19; Jamaica, 1774 ***1219.7*** *p219*
Neave, John 25; Maryland, 1774 ***1219.7*** *p230*
Nebble, Patrick 1; Massachusetts, 1849 ***5881.1*** *p78*
Nebel, . . .; Canada, 1776-1783 ***9786*** *p29*
Neberger, Simon 29; America, 1836 ***778.5*** *p402*
Neborgall, Jakob; Ohio, 1808 ***8582.2*** *p56*
Necco, Mrs. 36; St. Louis, 1827 ***778.5*** *p402*
Necco, J. 38; St. Louis, 1827 ***778.5*** *p402*
Neckler, Girard 32; America, 1835 ***778.5*** *p402*
Neckmann, Arnold; Wisconsin, n.d. ***9675.7*** *p52*
Neddessen, Christian 35; Kansas, 1875 ***5240.1*** *p56*
Nedenger, John; Baltimore, 1819 ***9892.11*** *p34*
*Relative:*Samuel 18
*Relative:*John 15
Nedenger, John 15 *SEE* Nedenger, John
Nedenger, Samuel 18 *SEE* Nedenger, John
Nedved, John Anthony; Arkansas, 1918 ***95.2*** *p87*
Nedved, John Anthony 23; Arkansas, 1918 ***95.2*** *p87*
Needham, Catherine; New York, NY, 1811 ***2859.11*** *p18*
Needham, Eliza; New York, NY, 1811 ***2859.11*** *p18*
Needham, Jno.; Virginia, 1621 ***6219*** *p67*
Needham, Joseph 29; Massachusetts, 1850 ***5881.1*** *p78*
Needham, Sarah 19?; Maryland or Virginia, 1705 ***2212*** *p44*
Needham, Thomas; America, 1741 ***4971*** *p38*
Needham, Thomas; Maryland, 1742 ***4971*** *p107*
Needham, Thomas; Virginia, 1638 ***6219*** *p146*
Needham, Thomas; Virginia, 1639 ***6219*** *p161*
Needham, Valient; New York, NY, 1811 ***2859.11*** *p18*
Needle, Johann Georg *SEE* Needle, Joseph
Needle, Joseph 40; Pennsylvania, 1753 ***2444*** *p176*
*Wife:*Regina M. Fueglin
*Child:*Johann Georg
Needle, Regina M. Fueglin *SEE* Needle, Joseph
Needs, James 21; Maryland, 1774 ***1219.7*** *p187*
Neef, Frederick; Illinois, 1888 ***5012.39*** *p121*
Neehan, Honora 29; Massachusetts, 1849 ***5881.1*** *p78*
Neehan, Patrick 1; Massachusetts, 1849 ***5881.1*** *p78*
Neelan, Henry; Quebec, 1848 ***5704.8*** *p42*
Neeley, . . .; New York, NY, 1865 ***5704.8*** *p194*
Neeley, Mary; New York, NY, 1865 ***5704.8*** *p194*
Neelson, Delos; Wisconsin, n.d. ***9675.7*** *p52*
Neely, Eliza; New York, NY, 1868 ***5704.8*** *p229*
Neely, Eliza; Philadelphia, 1853 ***5704.8*** *p100*
Neely, Eliza 20; Philadelphia, 1865 ***5704.8*** *p164*
Neely, Eliza Jane 18; Philadelphia, 1864 ***5704.8*** *p160*
Neely, Elizabeth; Philadelphia, 1852 ***5704.8*** *p96*
Neely, Ellen 20; Philadelphia, 1854 ***5704.8*** *p117*
Neely, Hugh 7; St. John, N.B., 1847 ***5704.8*** *p33*
Neely, James 4; St. John, N.B., 1847 ***5704.8*** *p33*
Neely, James 20 *SEE* Neely, Williiam
Neely, Jane 40 *SEE* Neely, Williiam
Neely, John; New York, NY, 1864 ***5704.8*** *p174*
Neely, John 21; Wilmington, DE, 1831 ***6508.7*** *p160*
Neely, John 25 *SEE* Neely, Williiam
Neely, Margaret; New Orleans, 1849 ***5704.8*** *p59*
Neely, Margaret; St. John, N.B., 1847 ***5704.8*** *p20*
Neely, Margaret; St. John, N.B., 1847 ***5704.8*** *p33*
Neely, Margaret 2; St. John, N.B., 1847 ***5704.8*** *p33*
Neely, Mary; St. John, N.B., 1847 ***5704.8*** *p20*
Neely, Mary 6; St. John, N.B., 1847 ***5704.8*** *p33*
Neely, Mary Ann 22 *SEE* Neely, Williiam
Neely, Mary Jane; Philadelphia, 1852 ***5704.8*** *p96*
Neely, Mathew 25; Philadelphia, 1855 ***5704.8*** *p124*
Neely, Nancy; Philadelphia, 1865 ***5704.8*** *p202*
Neely, Rebecca; New York, NY, 1864 ***5704.8*** *p174*
Neely, Robert; Philadelphia, 1852 ***5704.8*** *p95*
Neely, Robt 20; Wilmington, DE, 1831 ***6508.7*** *p160*
Neely, Samuel; New York, NY, 1864 ***5704.8*** *p174*
Neely, Thomas; St. John, N.B., 1847 ***5704.8*** *p33*
Neely, William 15 *SEE* Neely, Williiam
Neely, William 22; Philadelphia, 1854 ***5704.8*** *p117*
Neely, Williiam 55; Philadelphia, 1833-1834 ***53.26*** *p74*
*Relative:*Jane 40
*Relative:*James 20
*Relative:*William 15
*Relative:*John 25
*Relative:*Mary Ann 22
Neelycrofft, J. 24; America, 1838 ***778.5*** *p402*
Neesen, Henry; New York, 1866 ***1450.2*** *p27B*
Neff, Barbara Ebin *SEE* Neff, Franz
Neff, Franz; Pennsylvania, 1717 ***3627*** *p13*
*Wife:*Barbara Ebin
With children & brother
Neff, Heinrich; Pennsylvania, 1717 ***3627*** *p14*
With wife
With children
With brother
Neff, Peter 28; America, 1853 ***9162.7*** *p15*
Neff, William 23; Ohio, 1873 ***1450.2*** *p107A*
Negernelli, Tomaso; Iowa, 1866-1943 ***123.54*** *p71*
Negle, Anna Sara; Pennsylvania, 1750 ***2444*** *p163*
Negley, George; America, 1744 ***2444*** *p195*
Negro, Julius 58; Washington, 1918-1920 ***1728.5*** *p12*
Negus, Thomas 21; Philadelphia, 1774 ***1219.7*** *p216*
Nehegan, Timothy; Wisconsin, n.d. ***9675.7*** *p52*
Neher, Agnes *SEE* Neher, Hans Martin
Neher, Anna Maria *SEE* Neher, Hans Martin
Neher, George; Pennsylvania, 1852 ***2896.5*** *p29*
Neher, Hans Jerg *SEE* Neher, Hans Martin
Neher, Hans Martin *SEE* Neher, Hans Martin
Neher, Hans Martin; Pennsylvania, 1750 ***2444*** *p196*
*Wife:*Ursula Jetter
*Child:*Anna Maria
*Child:*Hans Martin
*Child:*Agnes
*Child:*Hans Jerg
Neher, Ursula Jetter *SEE* Neher, Hans Martin
Nehf, Andrew; Wisconsin, n.d. ***9675.7*** *p52*
Nehf, Geo.; Wisconsin, n.d. ***9675.7*** *p52*
Nehf, John L.; Wisconsin, n.d. ***9675.7*** *p52*
Nehf, William; Wisconsin, n.d. ***9675.7*** *p52*
Nehlig, Katharina; New Orleans, 1906 ***2691.4*** *p167*
Nehlig, Philipp; New Orleans, 1850-1883 ***2691.4*** *p167*
With sibling
Nehmann, William; America, 1854 ***1450.2*** *p108A*
Nehrengardt, . . .; Canada, 1776-1783 ***9786*** *p29*
Neib, John; Pennsylvania, 1754 ***2444*** *p196*
Neible, Christian; Ohio, 1848 ***9892.11*** *p34*
Neible, Christian; Ohio, 1850 ***9892.11*** *p34*
Neidel, Ernest Wielhelm; Mississippi, 1909 ***3455.2*** *p45*
Neidel, Ernest Wilhelm; Mississippi, 1909 ***3455.3*** *p110*
Neidel, Rudolf Max; New York, NY, 1910 ***3455.2*** *p101*

Neidenger, John; Baltimore, 1819 ***9892.11*** *p34*
*Relative:*Samuel 18
*Relative:*John 15
Neidenger, John 15 *SEE* Neidenger, John
Neidenger, Samuel 18 *SEE* Neidenger, John
Neiderfler, Joseph; Wisconsin, n.d. ***9675.7*** *p52*
Neiderhouser, John 29; Kansas, 1900 ***5240.1*** *p81*
Neiderkorn, John; Wisconsin, n.d. ***9675.7*** *p52*
Neiderkorn, P. Joseph; Wisconsin, n.d. ***9675.7*** *p52*
Neidikorn, Nicholas; Wisconsin, n.d. ***9675.7*** *p129*
Neidzwiedz, Martin; Arkansas, 1918 ***95.2*** *p87*
Neiens, George; Wisconsin, n.d. ***9675.7*** *p129*
Neiff, Barbara Ebin *SEE* Neiff, Francis
Neiff, Francis; Pennsylvania, 1717 ***3627*** *p14*
*Wife:*Barbara Ebin
With children & brother
Neigum, Matthaus; Alberta, n.d. ***5262*** *p58*
Neil, Hugh; New York, NY, 1811 ***2859.11*** *p18*
Neil, James; New York, NY, 1815 ***2859.11*** *p40*
Neil, Margaret; New York, NY, 1815 ***2859.11*** *p40*
Neil, Thomas; New York, NY, 1811 ***2859.11*** *p18*
Neilan, Eliza 30; Massachusetts, 1849 ***5881.1*** *p78*
Neilan, Luke; America, 1735-1743 ***4971*** *p78*
Neilan, Luke; America, 1742 ***4971*** *p80*
Neilan, Michael 10; Massachusetts, 1849 ***5881.1*** *p78*
Neiland, Peter; Wisconsin, n.d. ***9675.7*** *p129*
Neilhock, . . .; New York, 1750 ***3652*** *p74*
Neill, Ann 30; St. John, N.B., 1864 ***5704.8*** *p158*
Neill, Anne; St. John, N.B., 1852 ***5704.8*** *p93*
Neill, Dennis 22; Newport, RI, 1851 ***6508.5*** *p19*
Neill, Eliza *SEE* Neill, Martha
Neill, Eliza; Philadelphia, 1849 ***5704.8*** *p49*
Neill, Ellen 40; Newport, RI, 1851 ***6508.5*** *p19*
Neill, Henry D.; New York, NY, 1816 ***2859.11*** *p40*
Neill, Joseph; America, 1741 ***4971*** *p67*
Neill, Joseph 26; St. John, N.B., 1864 ***5704.8*** *p158*
Neill, Kate 10; Newport, RI, 1851 ***6508.5*** *p19*
Neill, Madge D.; New York, NY, 1816 ***2859.11*** *p40*
Neill, Margaret *SEE* Neill, William
Neill, Margaret; Philadelphia, 1847 ***5704.8*** *p1*
Neill, Martha; Philadelphia, 1849 ***53.26*** *p74*
*Relative:*Eliza
Neill, Martha; Philadelphia, 1849 ***5704.8*** *p49*
Neill, Mary; America, 1737 ***4971*** *p12*
Neill, Maurice 7; Newport, RI, 1851 ***6508.5*** *p19*
Neill, Nancy; St. John, N.B., 1851 ***5704.8*** *p72*
Neill, Samuel 22; St. John, N.B., 1864 ***5704.8*** *p158*
Neill, Sarah Ann 1; St. John, N.B., 1864 ***5704.8*** *p158*
Neill, Thomas 22; Maryland, 1774 ***1219.7*** *p184*
Neill, William; Philadelphia, 1847 ***53.26*** *p74*
*Relative:*Margaret
Neill, William; Philadelphia, 1847 ***5704.8*** *p1*
Neill, William 18; St. John, N.B., 1856 ***5704.8*** *p131*
Neill, William James; St. John, N.B., 1847 ***5704.8*** *p18*
Neilly, Joseph 24; Philadelphia, 1833-1834 ***53.26*** *p74*
Neilson, Eliza'h.; New York, NY, 1811 ***2859.11*** *p18*
With child
Neilson, Gerard; New York, NY, 1811 ***2859.11*** *p18*
Neilson, James; New York, NY, 1811 ***2859.11*** *p18*
Neilson, James; Philadelphia, 1811 ***53.26*** *p74*
Neilson, James; Philadelphia, 1811 ***2859.11*** *p18*
Neilson, James How; Charleston, SC, 1807 ***1639.20*** *p253*
Neilson, John; New York, NY, 1811 ***2859.11*** *p18*
With family
Neilson, John; Quebec, 1764 ***9775.5*** *p203*
Neilson, Thomas; New York, NY, 1811 ***2859.11*** *p18*
Neilson, William; New York, NY, 1811 ***2859.11*** *p18*
Neilson, William; Virginia, 1748-1816 ***1639.20*** *p253*
Neily, Eacy 20; Philadelphia, 1833-1834 ***53.26*** *p74*
Neiman, Fred; Washington, 1859-1920 ***2872.1*** *p28*
Neiman, G.; Washington, 1859-1920 ***2872.1*** *p28*
Neiman, Gunther; Washington, 1859-1920 ***2872.1*** *p28*
Neimeyer, Gottlieb 30; America, 1863 ***4610.10*** *p145*
Nein, Joseph; Ohio, 1798-1818 ***8582.2*** *p54*
Neipp, Agatha *SEE* Neipp, Johannes
Neipp, Barbara *SEE* Neipp, Johannes
Neipp, Johannes; Pennsylvania, 1754 ***2444*** *p196*
*Wife:*Agatha
*Child:*Barbara
Neiraghane, Patrick; America, 1735-1743 ***4971*** *p79*
Neis, Prter J.; Wisconsin, n.d. ***9675.7*** *p129*
Neisel, Jakob; Philadelphia, 1779 ***8137*** *p12*
Neisele, . . .; Canada, 1776-1783 ***9786*** *p29*
Neises, Theodor 32; Kansas, 1893 ***5240.1*** *p79*
Neisser, Augustine; Savannah, GA, 1736 ***3652*** *p51*
*Relative:*George
Neisser, George *SEE* Neisser, Augustine
Neisser, George; New York, 1744 ***3652*** *p63*
Neitmann, F.; New York, NY, 1853 ***4610.10*** *p34*
Neitmann, F.; New York, NY, 1853 ***4610.10*** *p38*
Neitz, . . .; Canada, 1776-1783 ***9786*** *p29*
Neitzer, Bernhart; Philadelphia, 1744 ***8125.6*** *p22*
Neitzert, Heinrich; America, 1748-1749 ***8125.6*** *p23*
Neitzert, Heinrich; Philadelphia, 1748 ***8125.6*** *p23*
Neizart, Henry; Philadelphia, 1748 ***8125.6*** *p23*
Nekring, Fredric J. 20; Kansas, 1876 ***5240.1*** *p57*
Nelan, Humphry; America, 1735-1743 ***4971*** *p78*
Nelis, Ann; Philadelphia, 1848 ***53.26*** *p74*
Nelis, Ann; Philadelphia, 1848 ***5704.8*** *p46*
Nelis, Bill; Quebec, 1847 ***5704.8*** *p38*
Nelis, Catherine 9; St. John, N.B., 1851 ***5704.8*** *p78*
Nelis, Catherine 28; St. John, N.B., 1858 ***5704.8*** *p140*
Nelis, Charles 13; St. John, N.B., 1851 ***5704.8*** *p78*
Nelis, Elleanor 12 *SEE* Nelis, Henry
Nelis, Elleanor 12; Philadelphia, 1849 ***5704.8*** *p50*
Nelis, Henry; Philadelphia, 1849 ***53.26*** *p74*
*Relative:*Margaret
*Relative:*Hugh
*Relative:*Elleanor 12
*Relative:*Matilda 10
*Relative:*John 5
*Relative:*Timothy 2
Nelis, Henry; Philadelphia, 1849 ***5704.8*** *p50*
Nelis, Hugh *SEE* Nelis, Henry
Nelis, Hugh; Philadelphia, 1849 ***5704.8*** *p50*
Nelis, Hugh; St. John, N.B., 1851 ***5704.8*** *p78*
Nelis, James; St. John, N.B., 1847 ***5704.8*** *p33*
Nelis, John; Philadelphia, 1847 ***53.26*** *p74*
Nelis, John; Philadelphia, 1847 ***5704.8*** *p13*
Nelis, John 5 *SEE* Nelis, Henry
Nelis, John 5; Philadelphia, 1849 ***5704.8*** *p50*
Nelis, Margaret *SEE* Nelis, Henry
Nelis, Margaret; Philadelphia, 1849 ***5704.8*** *p50*
Nelis, Margaret; St. John, N.B., 1851 ***5704.8*** *p78*
Nelis, Margy; Philadelphia, 1850 ***53.26*** *p74*
Nelis, Margy; Philadelphia, 1850 ***5704.8*** *p68*
Nelis, Mary; St. John, N.B., 1851 ***5704.8*** *p78*
Nelis, Mary Ann; St. John, N.B., 1851 ***5704.8*** *p78*
Nelis, Matilda 10 *SEE* Nelis, Henry
Nelis, Matilda 10; Philadelphia, 1849 ***5704.8*** *p50*
Nelis, Natl; St. John, N.B., 1851 ***5704.8*** *p78*
Nelis, Patrick; Philadelphia, 1851 ***5704.8*** *p71*
Nelis, Sarah 11; St. John, N.B., 1851 ***5704.8*** *p78*
Nelis, Susan; Philadelphia, 1848 ***5704.8*** *p46*
Nelis, Timothy 2 *SEE* Nelis, Henry
Nelis, Timothy 2; Philadelphia, 1849 ***5704.8*** *p50*
Nell, Mr. 40; New Orleans, 1837 ***778.5*** *p403*
Nell, Casper; Pennsylvania, 1753 ***2444*** *p197*
Nellegan, Mr. 40; Dominica, 1774 ***1219.7*** *p223*
Neller, Franz; Indiana, 1847 ***9117*** *p19*
Nelles, Janet 54; Charleston, SC, 1850 ***1639.20*** *p253*
Nellis, John; Philadelphia, 1851 ***5704.8*** *p78*
Nellis, Mary; America, 1869 ***5704.8*** *p236*
Nelly, Margaret 22; Massachusetts, 1847 ***5881.1*** *p78*
Nelsen, Christian Sorensen; Arkansas, 1918 ***95.2*** *p87*
Nelsen, Iner; Arkansas, 1918 ***95.2*** *p87*
Nelsen, John Bake; Washington, 1859-1920 ***2872.1*** *p28*
Nelsen, Louis; Colorado, 1902 ***9678.2*** *p129*
Nelson, A. O.; Washington, 1859-1920 ***2872.1*** *p28*
Nelson, Aadne; Wisconsin, n.d. ***9675.7*** *p129*
Nelson, Adolf Emil; Arkansas, 1918 ***95.2*** *p88*
Nelson, Alexander 26; St. John, N.B., 1867 ***5704.8*** *p168*
Nelson, Alfred 22; Massachusetts, 1860 ***6410.32*** *p113*
Nelson, Andrew; Illinois, 1860 ***5012.38*** *p98*
Nelson, Andrew; Iowa, 1866-1943 ***123.54*** *p36*
Nelson, Andrew; Philadelphia, 1852 ***5704.8*** *p88*
Nelson, Andrew G. 5; Massachusetts, 1849 ***5881.1*** *p77*
Nelson, Andrew J.; Colorado, 1891 ***9678.2*** *p129*
Nelson, Andrew John; Arkansas, 1918 ***95.2*** *p88*
Nelson, Andru; New York, NY, 1906 ***3455.2*** *p44*
Nelson, Andru; New York, NY, 1906 ***3455.3*** *p47*
Nelson, Ann 9 mos; St. John, N.B., 1847 ***5704.8*** *p25*
Nelson, Anna; Washington, 1859-1920 ***2872.1*** *p28*
Nelson, Anne J.; New York, NY, 1864 ***5704.8*** *p172*
Nelson, Archy; New York, NY, 1869 ***5704.8*** *p232*
Nelson, August; Colorado, 1886 ***9678.2*** *p129*
Nelson, August; Colorado, 1904 ***9678.2*** *p129*
Nelson, August Gottfrid 23; Kansas, 1891 ***5240.1*** *p75*
Nelson, August John; Colorado, 1904 ***9678.2*** *p129*
Nelson, C. A.; Iowa, 1866-1943 ***123.54*** *p36*
Nelson, C.S. 36; Arizona, 1890 ***2764.35*** *p52*
Nelson, Carl; Colorado, 1902 ***9678.2*** *p129*
Nelson, Carl J.; Maine, 1869-1884 ***6410.22*** *p120*
Nelson, Carl Oskar; Washington, 1859-1920 ***2872.1*** *p28*
Nelson, Caroline T. 31; Massachusetts, 1849 ***5881.1*** *p77*
Nelson, Catherine; Washington, 1859-1920 ***2872.1*** *p28*
Nelson, Catherine 3; St. John, N.B., 1847 ***5704.8*** *p25*
Nelson, Catherine 20; Philadelphia, 1861 ***5704.8*** *p148*
Nelson, Catherine 27; Philadelphia, 1858 ***5704.8*** *p139*
Nelson, Charles; Illinois, 1871 ***5012.39*** *p25*
Nelson, Charles; Washington, 1859-1920 ***2872.1*** *p28*
Nelson, Charles Oliver; Iroquois Co., IL, 1894 ***3455.1*** *p12*
Nelson, David; America, 1825 ***1639.20*** *p253*
Nelson, Mrs. E. N. 31; Washington, 1918-1920 ***1728.5*** *p12*
Nelson, Earl W.; Iowa, 1866-1943 ***123.54*** *p36*
Nelson, Eiler; Arkansas, 1918 ***95.2*** *p88*
Nelson, Elias; Arkansas, 1918 ***95.2*** *p88*
Nelson, Eliza 18; St. John, N.B., 1858 ***5704.8*** *p137*
Nelson, Elizabeth; Philadelphia, 1851 ***5704.8*** *p81*
Nelson, Elizabeth 2; St. John, N.B., 1854 ***5704.8*** *p119*
Nelson, Elizabeth 18; St. John, N.B., 1861 ***5704.8*** *p149*
Nelson, Elizabeth Mary; Quebec, 1851 ***5704.8*** *p75*
Nelson, Ella *SEE* Nelson, John
Nelson, Ellen; New York, NY, 1869 ***5704.8*** *p232*
Nelson, Ellen Catherine; Washington, 1859-1920 ***2872.1*** *p28*
Nelson, Ellen Monk; Iowa, 1866-1943 ***123.54*** *p71*
Nelson, Erick Robert; Arkansas, 1918 ***95.2*** *p88*
Nelson, Falloff; Wisconsin, n.d. ***9675.7*** *p129*
Nelson, Frank Oscar 28; Arkansas, 1918 ***95.2*** *p88*
Nelson, Fred T.; Illinois, 1895 ***5012.40*** *p54*
Nelson, George; Washington, 1859-1920 ***2872.1*** *p28*
Nelson, George; Wisconsin, n.d. ***9675.7*** *p129*
Nelson, George 50; Philadelphia, 1858 ***5704.8*** *p139*
Nelson, George Melvin; Washington, 1859-1920 ***2872.1*** *p28*
Nelson, Gerard; New York, NY, 1811 ***2859.11*** *p18*
Nelson, Gerda; Washington, 1859-1920 ***2872.1*** *p28*
Nelson, Gus Warner; Arkansas, 1918 ***95.2*** *p88*
Nelson, Gust; Iowa, 1866-1943 ***123.54*** *p36*
Nelson, H. M. 25; Kansas, 1874 ***5240.1*** *p31*
Nelson, H. M. 25; Kansas, 1874 ***5240.1*** *p55*
Nelson, Hannah 10; St. John, N.B., 1854 ***5704.8*** *p119*
Nelson, Hans; Colorado, 1900 ***9678.2*** *p129*
Nelson, Hans; Colorado, 1904 ***9678.2*** *p129*
Nelson, Hesekiah 6; St. John, N.B., 1854 ***5704.8*** *p119*
Nelson, J. G.; Iowa, 1866-1943 ***123.54*** *p36*
Nelson, J. H. 35; Washington, 1918-1920 ***1728.5*** *p12*
Nelson, J. P.; Washington, 1859-1920 ***2872.1*** *p28*
Nelson, Jacob; Iowa, 1846 ***2090*** *p610*
With 2 daughters
Nelson, Jacob; Iowa, 1866-1943 ***123.54*** *p36*
Nelson, James; Maine, 1857 ***6410.22*** *p124*
Nelson, James 9; St. John, N.B., 1858 ***5704.8*** *p137*
Nelson, James 17; St. John, N.B., 1864 ***5704.8*** *p157*
Nelson, James 21; Virginia, 1775 ***1219.7*** *p246*
Nelson, James 28; Philadelphia, 1803 ***53.26*** *p74*
Nelson, James 31; Antigua (Antego), 1722 ***3690.1*** *p163*
Nelson, James Peter; Fort Wayne, IN, 1893 ***3455.2*** *p104*
Nelson, James William 29; California, 1872 ***2769.7*** *p4*
Nelson, Jane; St. John, N.B., 1853 ***5704.8*** *p106*
Nelson, Joe; Washington, 1859-1920 ***2872.1*** *p28*
Nelson, Johan; Minneapolis, 1880-1885 ***6410.35*** *p61*
Nelson, Johannes; Detroit, 1870 ***9678.2*** *p129*
Nelson, John; America, 1890 ***3455.3*** *p78*
*Wife:*Ella
Nelson, John; Arkansas, 1918 ***95.2*** *p88*
Nelson, John; Boston, 1853 ***6410.32*** *p123*
Nelson, John; Colorado, 1901 ***9678.2*** *p129*
Nelson, John; Illinois, 1871 ***5012.39*** *p25*
Nelson, John; Iowa, 1846 ***2090*** *p610*
Nelson, John; Iowa, 1849-1860 ***2090*** *p613*
Nelson, John; Iowa, 1866-1943 ***123.54*** *p36*
Nelson, John; Iroquois Co., IL, 1895 ***3455.1*** *p12*
Nelson, John; New Orleans, 1848 ***6410.32*** *p122*
Nelson, John; New York, NY, 1811 ***2859.11*** *p18*
Nelson, John; New York, NY, 1850 ***6013.19*** *p74*
Nelson, John; Philadelphia, 1811 ***2859.11*** *p18*
With family
Nelson, John; Washington, 1859-1920 ***2872.1*** *p28*
Nelson, John 13; St. John, N.B., 1858 ***5704.8*** *p137*
Nelson, John 29; Massachusetts, 1860 ***6410.32*** *p100*
Nelson, John 36; Massachusetts, 1860 ***6410.32*** *p102*
Nelson, John Edward; Arkansas, 1918 ***95.2*** *p88*
Nelson, John Walfred; Arkansas, 1918 ***95.2*** *p88*
Nelson, Joseph 22; Massachusetts, 1860 ***6410.32*** *p113*
Nelson, Joshua 19; Virginia, 1720 ***3690.1*** *p164*
Nelson, L.W.; Colorado, 1896 ***9678.2*** *p129*
Nelson, Lars 67; Massachusetts, 1849 ***5881.1*** *p78*
Nelson, Laurids Orum; Arkansas, 1918 ***95.2*** *p88*
Nelson, Letitia 26; St. John, N.B., 1859 ***5704.8*** *p140*
Nelson, Margaret; Philadelphia, 1848 ***53.26*** *p74*
*Relative:*Sarah
Nelson, Margaret; Philadelphia, 1848 ***5704.8*** *p40*
Nelson, Margaret 45; St. John, N.B., 1854 ***5704.8*** *p119*
Nelson, Martha Jane 14; St. John, N.B., 1865 ***5704.8*** *p165*
Nelson, Martin; Iowa, 1866-1943 ***123.54*** *p36*
Nelson, Martin; Washington, 1859-1920 ***2872.1*** *p28*
Nelson, Martin Herbert; Arkansas, 1918 ***95.2*** *p88*
Nelson, Martin Ludvig; Illinois, 1888 ***5012.39*** *p121*
Nelson, Mary; St. John, N.B., 1847 ***5704.8*** *p25*
Nelson, Mary; Virginia, 1636 ***6219*** *p76*
Nelson, Mary; Virginia, 1637 ***6219*** *p108*
Nelson, Mary 4; St. John, N.B., 1858 ***5704.8*** *p137*
Nelson, Mary 20; St. John, N.B., 1865 ***5704.8*** *p165*
Nelson, Mary 28; Massachusetts, 1860 ***6410.32*** *p100*

Nelson, Mary 45; St. John, N.B., 1858 ***5704.8*** *p137*
Nelson, Mary Ann 5; St. John, N.B., 1847 ***5704.8*** *p25*
Nelson, Matthias; New York, NY, 1844 ***6410.32*** *p126*
Nelson, Matthias 38; Massachusetts, 1860 ***6410.32*** *p121*
Nelson, Melver; Wisconsin, n.d. ***9675.7*** *p129*
Nelson, Michael; St. John, N.B., 1847 ***5704.8*** *p26*
Nelson, N. G.; Minneapolis, 1873-1877 ***6410.35*** *p61*
Nelson, Nel; New York, NY, 1836 ***8208.4*** *p16*
Nelson, Nels; Arkansas, 1918 ***95.2*** *p88*
Nelson, Nels; Galveston, TX, 1871-1878 ***6410.22*** *p117*
Nelson, Nels Anker; Arkansas, 1918 ***95.2*** *p88*
Nelson, Nels Peter; Arkansas, 1918 ***95.2*** *p88*
Nelson, Nels W. 37; Arizona, 1890 ***2764.35*** *p51*
Nelson, Nicholas; New York, NY, 1834 ***8208.4*** *p27*
Nelson, O.A. Carlemann; Wisconsin, n.d. ***9675.7*** *p129*
Nelson, Ole; Washington, 1859-1920 ***2872.1*** *p28*
Nelson, Ole; Wisconsin, n.d. ***9675.7*** *p129*
Nelson, Olof; Colorado, 1890 ***9678.2*** *p129*
Nelson, Olof; Illinois, 1888 ***5012.39*** *p52*
Nelson, Olof; Maine, 1871-1887 ***6410.22*** *p120*
Nelson, Olof; Maine, 1887 ***6410.22*** *p126*
Nelson, Oscar; Iowa, 1866-1943 ***123.54*** *p36*
Nelson, Oscar Albin; Arkansas, 1918 ***95.2*** *p88*
Nelson, Oscar Fridolf; Illinois, 1902 ***5012.40*** *p77*
Nelson, Oscar Necander; Arkansas, 1918 ***95.2*** *p88*
Nelson, Otto; Bangor, ME, 1883-1895 ***6410.22*** *p121*
Nelson, Otto; Bangor, ME, 1892 ***6410.22*** *p126*
Nelson, Paul Arvid; Arkansas, 1918 ***95.2*** *p88*
Nelson, Peter; Iowa, 1866-1943 ***123.54*** *p36*
Nelson, Rasmas; Iroquois Co., IL, 1892 ***3455.1*** *p12*
Nelson, Rasmus; Arkansas, 1918 ***95.2*** *p88*
Nelson, Rasmus; Iowa, 1866-1943 ***123.54*** *p36*
Nelson, Rasmus; Wisconsin, 1868 ***5240.1*** *p31*
Nelson, Rebecca; Montreal, 1824 ***7603*** *p68*
Nelson, Richard; Illinois, 1890 ***5012.40*** *p25*
Nelson, Samuel 7; St. John, N.B., 1858 ***5704.8*** *p137*
Nelson, Sarah *SEE* Nelson, Margaret
Nelson, Sarah; Philadelphia, 1848 ***5704.8*** *p40*
Nelson, Sophia 2; Massachusetts, 1849 ***5881.1*** *p78*
Nelson, Swen; Maine, 1871-1882 ***6410.22*** *p117*
Nelson, Walter Martin; Arkansas, 1918 ***95.2*** *p88*
Nelson, William; Maine, 1882-1892 ***6410.22*** *p120*
Nelson, William; New York, NY, 1811 ***2859.11*** *p18*
Nelson, William; New York, NY, 1838 ***8208.4*** *p87*
Nelson, William; Philadelphia, 1811 ***2859.11*** *p18*
With family
Nelson, William; Philadelphia, 1848 ***5704.8*** *p45*
Nelson, William 13; St. John, N.B., 1853 ***5704.8*** *p106*
Nelson, William 37; Norfolk, VA, 1774 ***1219.7*** *p222*
Nelson, William H.; New York, NY, 1835 ***8208.4*** *p5*
Nelson, Wilson; Philadelphia, 1848 ***53.26*** *p74*
Neltner, Aegedeus; New York, 1847 ***1450.2*** *p107A*
Nemiro, Leo Rudolph; Arkansas, 1918 ***95.2*** *p88*
Nemitz, Herman; Wisconsin, n.d. ***9675.7*** *p129*
Nemitz, William H.; Arkansas, 1918 ***95.2*** *p88*
Nemo, John; Virginia, 1642 ***6219*** *p198*
Nemorin, Q. 25; New Orleans, 1838 ***778.5*** *p403*
Nemsee, Frank; Arkansas, 1918 ***95.2*** *p89*
Nendel, Caspar; Ohio, 1869-1887 ***8582*** *p22*
Nenzell, . . .; Canada, 1776-1783 ***9786*** *p29*
Neo, Mrs. E.; Milwaukee, 1875 ***4719.30*** *p257*
With 2 children
Neovius, George E.; Arkansas, 1918 ***95.2*** *p89*
Nepper, E. S.; America, 1839 ***8582.1*** *p25*
Nepper, G. F.; Cincinnati, 1839 ***8582.1*** *p26*
Nepper, Gustav F.; America, 1836 ***8582.2*** *p60*
Neps, Barbara Meyer *SEE* Neps, Friedrich
Neps, Christianus *SEE* Neps, Friedrich
Neps, Christina *SEE* Neps, Friedrich
Neps, Dorothea *SEE* Neps, Friedrich
Neps, Friedrich; America, 1745-1800 ***2444*** *p196*
*Wife:*Barbara Meyer
*Child:*Dorothea
*Child:*Christianus
*Child:*Justina
*Child:*Christina
Neps, Justina *SEE* Neps, Friedrich
Neque, Cyprien Jules 24; America, 1822 ***778.5*** *p403*
Nerac, E. A.; Cuba, 1829 ***778.5*** *p403*
Nerenberg, Jacob; Portland, ME, 1884 ***1450.2*** *p27B*
Nerger, Johan D.; Wisconsin, n.d. ***9675.7*** *p129*
Nerger, Peter C. 60; America, 1830 ***778.5*** *p403*
Nerhus, John; Arkansas, 1918 ***95.2*** *p89*
Nerichan, Claude 29; New Orleans, 1827 ***778.5*** *p403*
Nern, Johann Philipp; Pennsylvania, 1753 ***4525*** *p233*
Nero, Diedrich; Wisconsin, n.d. ***9675.7*** *p129*
Nero, Enneougud 43; Port uncertain, 1836 ***778.5*** *p403*
Nerode, John; Wisconsin, n.d. ***9675.7*** *p129*
Nerode, William; Wisconsin, n.d. ***9675.7*** *p129*
Nerr, Johann Philipp; Pennsylvania, 1753 ***4525*** *p233*
Nerra, Emanuel 22; New York, NY, 1898-1899 ***7846*** *p39*
Nertz, Jacob; South Carolina, 1788 ***7119*** *p203*
Nerve, John; Virginia, 1646 ***6219*** *p239*
Nesbet, George; Quebec, 1830 ***4719.7*** *p21*
Nesbit, Francis; America, 1790 ***1639.20*** *p255*
Nesbit, Hugh; New York, NY, 1816 ***2859.11*** *p40*
Nesbit, James; South Carolina, 1812 ***1639.20*** *p255*
Nesbit, John; America, 1743 ***4971*** *p64*
Nesbit, Robert; South Carolina, 1808 ***1639.20*** *p255*
Nesbitt, Elizabeth; St. John, N.B., 1853 ***5704.8*** *p107*
Nesbitt, John 21; Maryland, 1774 ***1219.7*** *p208*
Nesbitt, John-James; Quebec, 1825 ***7603*** *p27*
Nesheim, Sven John; Arkansas, 1918 ***95.2*** *p89*
Ness, George; Philadelphia, 1761 ***9973.7*** *p35*
Ness, Peter 35; Maryland, 1739 ***3690.1*** *p164*
Nesser, Alex; Arkansas, 1918 ***95.2*** *p89*
Nessler, John Joseph; Cincinnati, 1869-1887 ***8582*** *p22*
Nested, Andrew; Arkansas, 1918 ***95.2*** *p89*
Nestel, Anna Dorothea Krafft *SEE* Nestel, Johann Michel
Nestel, Anna Margaretha *SEE* Nestel, Johann Michel
Nestel, Anna Maria *SEE* Nestel, Johann Michel
Nestel, Anna Maria Seel *SEE* Nestel, Martin
Nestel, Christina *SEE* Nestel, Johann Michel
Nestel, Jacob Ulrich *SEE* Nestel, Martin
Nestel, Johann Gottlieb *SEE* Nestel, Martin
Nestel, Johann Michael *SEE* Nestel, Johann Michel
Nestel, Johann Michel; Port uncertain, 1753-1800 ***2444*** *p196*
*Wife:*Anna Dorothea Krafft
*Child:*Anna Margaretha
*Child:*Johann Michael
*Child:*Anna Maria
*Child:*Christina
Nestel, Martin; America, 1751 ***2444*** *p196*
*Wife:*Anna Maria Seel
*Child:*Johann Gottlieb
*Child:*Jacob Ulrich
Nestell, Martin; New York, 1774 ***2444*** *p196*
Nethery, Alexander; Quebec, 1851 ***5704.8*** *p74*
Nethery, Elizabeth; Quebec, 1851 ***5704.8*** *p74*
Nethery, James; Quebec, 1851 ***5704.8*** *p74*
Nethery, John 4; Quebec, 1851 ***5704.8*** *p74*
Nethery, Lanclott; Quebec, 1851 ***5704.8*** *p74*
Nethery, Margaret 4; Quebec, 1851 ***5704.8*** *p74*
Nethery, Sarah 1; Quebec, 1851 ***5704.8*** *p74*
Nethery, Sydney 11; Quebec, 1851 ***5704.8*** *p74*
Nethery, William 8; Quebec, 1851 ***5704.8*** *p74*
Nethry, Bessey; Quebec, 1850 ***5704.8*** *p62*
Nethry, James; Quebec, 1850 ***5704.8*** *p62*
Nethry, James 4; Quebec, 1850 ***5704.8*** *p62*
Netkensmeyer, Johann Andreas Friedrich; America, 1844 ***4610.10*** *p150*
Netlefeild, Georg; Virginia, 1642 ***6219*** *p197*
Nett, Elizabeth 36 *SEE* Nett, Frederick
Nett, Frederick 31; Georgia, 1738 ***9332*** *p333*
*Wife:*Elizabeth 36
Nett, Nicholas; Virginia, 1639 ***6219*** *p154*
Nettelton, Amos, Jr.; Illinois, 1857 ***7857*** *p6*
Nettingsmeyer, Anne C. Wilhelmine *SEE* Nettingsmeyer, Heinrich Wilhelm Adolp
Nettingsmeyer, Anne M. C. Kortmeyer *SEE* Nettingsmeyer, Heinrich Wilhelm Adolp
Nettingsmeyer, Heinrich Wilhelm Adolph; America, 1844 ***4610.10*** *p154*
*Wife:*Anne M. C. Kortmeyer
*Daughter:*Anne C. Wilhelmine
Nettlebeck, Herman; Missouri, 1861 ***2896.5*** *p29*
Nettleton, Freeman; Illinois, 1851 ***7857*** *p6*
Nettmann, Albrecht; St. Louis, 1886 ***3702.7*** *p493*
Neu, Daniel, Family; America, 1816-1923 ***2691.4*** *p172*
Neu, Joseph Adolph; America, 1852 ***8582.3*** *p48*
Neubauer, Christian; Arkansas, 1918 ***95.2*** *p89*
Neubeld, Anna Mgr. 19; America, 1854-1855 ***9162.6*** *p104*
Neuber, Georg; Cincinnati, 1869-1887 ***8582*** *p22*
Neuber, Johann Georg; America, 1840 ***8582.3*** *p48*
Neuberger, . . .; Canada, 1776-1783 ***9786*** *p27*
Neuberger, August; Philadelphia, 1781-1782 ***8137*** *p12*
Neuberger, Simon 18; Port uncertain, 1839 ***778.5*** *p403*
Neubert, Daniel; Pennsylvania, 1742 ***3652*** *p58*
*Wife:*Hannah
With child
Neubert, Hannah *SEE* Neubert, Daniel
Neuberth, Maria Barbara; America, 1742-1800 ***2444*** *p157*
Neubig, Kunigunda; Wisconsin, n.d. ***9675.7*** *p129*
Neuburger, . . .; Canada, 1776-1783 ***9786*** *p29*
Neuburger, August; Canada, 1776-1783 ***9786*** *p207A*
Neuemfeldt, Herman; Wisconsin, n.d. ***9675.7*** *p129*
Neuens, Heinrich; Wisconsin, n.d. ***9675.7*** *p129*
Neuens, Johann; Wisconsin, n.d. ***9675.7*** *p129*
Neuens, Michael; Wisconsin, n.d. ***9675.7*** *p129*
Neuens, Peter; Wisconsin, n.d. ***9675.7*** *p129*
Neuenschwander, Elizabeth; Pennsylvania, 1709-1710 ***4480*** *p311*
Neuenschwander, John 42; Kansas, 1906 ***5240.1*** *p84*
Neuer, Charles; Wisconsin, n.d. ***9675.7*** *p129*
Neufarth, Jacob; Cincinnati, 1839 ***8582.1*** *p26*
Neufeld, Agatha; Quebec, 1876 ***9980.20*** *p48*
Neufeld, Elizabeth S.; Kansas, 1899 ***5240.1*** *p32*
Neufeld, Eva; Quebec, 1876 ***9980.20*** *p49*
Neufert, . . .; Pennsylvania, n.d. ***2444*** *p196*
Neuff, Barbara Ebin *SEE* Neuff, Francis
Neuff, Francis; Pennsylvania, 1717 ***3627*** *p14*
*Wife:*Barbara Ebin
With children & brother
Neuffer, Georg *SEE* Neuffer, Johann Michael
Neuffer, Johann David *SEE* Neuffer, Johann Michael
Neuffer, Johann Michael *SEE* Neuffer, Johann Michael
Neuffer, Johann Michael; America, 1753-1800 ***2444*** *p196*
*Wife:*Margaretha Gehrung
*Child:*Johann Michael
*Child:*Johann David
*Child:*Georg
*Child:*Philipp Jacob
Neuffer, Margaretha Gehrung *SEE* Neuffer, Johann Michael
Neuffer, Philipp Jacob *SEE* Neuffer, Johann Michael
Neuhaus, . . .; Illinois, 1800-1900 ***4610.10*** *p67*
Neuhaus, Robert; Wisconsin, n.d. ***9675.7*** *p129*
Neuhause, Robert; Wisconsin, n.d. ***9675.7*** *p129*
Neuhauser, Francis A.; Virginia, 1858 ***4626.16*** *p17*
Neuheimer, . . .; Canada, 1776-1783 ***9786*** *p29*
Neuhoff, William 25; Kansas, 1893 ***5240.1*** *p78*
Neuholt, Frank 25; Kansas, 1890 ***5240.1*** *p32*
Neuholt, Frank 25; Kansas, 1890 ***5240.1*** *p75*
Neuhuld, Ed; Kansas, 1900 ***5240.1*** *p32*
Neukam, Kaspar 21; Kansas, 1890 ***5240.1*** *p75*
Neukom, Samuel; America, 1847 ***8582.1*** *p26*
Neukomm, Daniel; Pennsylvania, 1709-1710 ***4480*** *p311*
Neukomm, Johann; Iroquois Co., IL, 1895 ***3455.1*** *p12*
Neuman, Regina; New York, 1752 ***3652*** *p76*
Neumann, . . .; Ohio, 1819 ***8582.1*** *p26*
Neumann, Adolph Edward; Wisconsin, n.d. ***9675.7*** *p129*
Neumann, Carly 32; Kansas, 1888 ***5240.1*** *p71*
Neumann, George A.; Wisconsin, n.d. ***9675.7*** *p129*
Neumann, Gustav Theodore; New York, NY, 1871 ***1450.2*** *p107A*
Neumann, Herman; Wisconsin, n.d. ***9675.7*** *p129*
Neumann, Johannes; Halifax, N.S., 1778 ***9786*** *p270*
Neumann, Johannes; New York, 1776 ***9786*** *p270*
Neumann, Karlheinz; Wisconsin, n.d. ***9675.7*** *p129*
Neumann, Oskar Clemens; America, 1875 ***4610.10*** *p106*
Neumann, Paul Chas. 49; Kansas, 1893 ***5240.1*** *p32*
Neumann, Paul Chas. 49; Kansas, 1893 ***5240.1*** *p77*
Neumann, Rudolph; New York, NY, 1881 ***1450.2*** *p27B*
Neumann, Wilhelm Alexander; Wisconsin, n.d. ***9675.7*** *p129*
Neumark, Heinrich 24; New York, NY, 1878 ***9253*** *p47*
Neumark, Helene 23; New York, NY, 1878 ***9253*** *p47*
Neumeister, . . .; Canada, 1776-1783 ***9786*** *p29*
Neumuller, Christian; California, 1900 ***2691.4*** *p168*
Neumuller, Joh. Gottlob 27; New Orleans, 1839 ***9420.2*** *p170*
Neunubel, Michael; Wisconsin, n.d. ***9675.7*** *p129*
Neuport, Joseph; Kentucky, 1839-1840 ***8582.3*** *p98*
Neurhor, Henry; Virginia, 1855 ***4626.16*** *p15*
Neurhor, Joseph; Virginia, 1855 ***4626.16*** *p15*
Neuschwander, Peter; New York, NY, 1836 ***8208.4*** *p16*
Neusz, Jan; Germantown, PA, 1684 ***2467.7*** *p5*
Neuville, Arlo 20; America, 1838 ***778.5*** *p403*
Neuwald, . . .; Canada, 1776-1783 ***9786*** *p29*
Neuweger, Elisabeth 26; New York, NY, 1857 ***9831.14*** *p86*
Neuweiler, Louis F.; New York, NY, 1838 ***8208.4*** *p82*
Neveu, Jean; Quebec, 1687 ***4533*** *p127*
Nevil, Philip 24; Maryland, 1774 ***1219.7*** *p180*
Neville, Danl 32; Newport, RI, 1851 ***6508.5*** *p19*
Neville, Julia 60; Newport, RI, 1851 ***6508.5*** *p20*
Neville, Margaret 20; Newport, RI, 1851 ***6508.5*** *p19*
Neville, Robert 25; St. Christopher, 1725 ***3690.1*** *p164*
Nevin, F. J.; Washington, 1859-1920 ***2872.1*** *p28*
Nevin, James; New York, NY, 1840 ***8208.4*** *p111*
Nevin, John; Philadelphia, 1864 ***5704.8*** *p184*
Nevin, Joseph 16; St. John, N.B., 1865 ***5704.8*** *p165*
Nevin, Margaret 6 mos; Quebec, 1858 ***5704.8*** *p138*
Nevin, Margaret 30; Quebec, 1858 ***5704.8*** *p137*
Nevin, Mary 36; Massachusetts, 1850 ***5881.1*** *p78*
Nevin, Patrick; Philadelphia, 1816 ***2859.11*** *p40*
Nevin, Thomas 4; Quebec, 1858 ***5704.8*** *p138*
Nevin, Thomas 21; Kansas, 1872 ***5240.1*** *p53*
Nevin, William 3; Quebec, 1858 ***5704.8*** *p138*
Nevin, William 30; Quebec, 1858 ***5704.8*** *p137*
Nevins, Thomas; America, 1888 ***1450.2*** *p27B*
Nevinski, Boleslav Alick; Arkansas, 1918 ***95.2*** *p89*
Nevitt, William 20; Maryland, 1724 ***3690.1*** *p164*
New, George 15; Maryland, 1735 ***3690.1*** *p164*
New, John 16; Maryland, 1724 ***3690.1*** *p164*

390 *FOR A COMPLETE EXPLANATION OF ENTRY, SEE "HOW TO READ A CITATION" SECTION*

New, Martin 38; Virginia, 1774 ***1219.7*** *p201*
New, Richard; Virginia, 1637 ***6219*** *p115*
Newall, Matthew; Virginia, 1698 ***2212*** *p13*
Newan, Thomas; New York, NY, 1811 ***2859.11*** *p18*
Newarke, Jon.; Virginia, 1628 ***6219*** *p31*
Newberke, Robert; Virginia, 1637 ***6219*** *p83*
Newberke, Robt.; Virginia, 1635 ***6219*** *p36*
Newberry, John 19; New York, 1775 ***1219.7*** *p246*
Newberry, Robert; New York, NY, 1816 ***2859.11*** *p40*
Newberry, William 20; Maryland, 1729 ***3690.1*** *p164*
Newburgh, Oscar; Arkansas, 1918 ***95.2*** *p89*
Newby, Edward 15; Maryland, 1723 ***3690.1*** *p164*
Newby, John; Virginia, 1643 ***6219*** *p207*
Newcome, William 18; Maryland, 1774 ***1219.7*** *p204*
Neweham, Denis 19; Newfoundland, 1789 ***4915.24*** *p55*
Newell, James; New York, NY, 1839 ***8208.4*** *p100*
Newell, Richard; Virginia, 1637 ***6219*** *p17*
Newell, Richd; Pennsylvania, 1698 ***2212*** *p10*
Newer, Jon.; Virginia, 1637 ***6219*** *p115*
Newett, Winifrid; Virginia, 1636 ***6219*** *p7*
Newgent, Christ.; Virginia, 1634 ***6219*** *p32*
Newhalt, Samuel-Charles; Quebec, 1753 ***7603*** *p30*
Newham, James; Maryland, 1742 ***4971*** *p107*
Newhard, Jean 19; America, 1837 ***778.5*** *p403*
Newhart, Michael; Philadelphia, 1759 ***9973.7*** *p33*
Newhouse, Emil; Wisconsin, n.d. ***9675.7*** *p129*
Newhouse, Fred 59; Arizona, 1922 ***9228.40*** *p26*
Newhowse, John; Virginia, 1638 ***6219*** *p148*
Newlan, Patrick; New England, 1816 ***2859.11*** *p40*
Newland, Andrew 73; Massachusetts, 1860 ***6410.32*** *p117*
Newland, Charles F.; Washington, 1859-1920 ***2872.1*** *p28*
Newland, Henry 22; Virginia, 1774 ***1219.7*** *p186*
Newland, John 21; Maryland, 1774 ***1219.7*** *p208*
Newland, Richard; Virginia, 1639 ***6219*** *p152*
Newland, Thomas 32; Maryland, 1775 ***1219.7*** *p250*
Newley, Wm.; Indiana, 1850 ***9117*** *p20*
Newman, . . .; Ohio, 1819 ***8582.1*** *p47*
Newman, Alice; Virginia, 1638 ***6219*** *p146*
Newman, Alice; Virginia, 1641 ***6219*** *p184*
Newman, Andrew; Wisconsin, n.d. ***9675.7*** *p129*
Newman, Ann; St. John, N.B., 1847 ***5704.8*** *p33*
Newman, Biddy 16; Massachusetts, 1850 ***5881.1*** *p77*
Newman, C.F. 24; Maryland, 1775 ***1219.7*** *p250*
Newman, Charles A.; America, 1873 ***6014.1*** *p3*
Newman, David; New York, NY, 1840 ***8208.4*** *p108*
Newman, Edward 19; Georgia, 1774 ***1219.7*** *p188*
Newman, Fred; Arkansas, 1918 ***95.2*** *p89*
Newman, James; America, 1742 ***4971*** *p17*
Newman, James; Annapolis, MD, 1742 ***4971*** *p93*
Newman, James; New York, NY, 1839 ***8208.4*** *p93*
Newman, John; Virginia, 1635 ***6219*** *p26*
Newman, John; Virginia, 1643 ***6219*** *p203*
Newman, John; Virginia, 1648 ***6219*** *p241*
Newman, John; Virginia, 1648 ***6219*** *p251*
Newman, Jon.; Virginia, 1635 ***6219*** *p26*
Newman, Jon.; Virginia, 1636 ***6219*** *p34*
Newman, Jon.; Virginia, 1642 ***6219*** *p195*
Newman, Martha 23; Baltimore, 1775 ***1219.7*** *p271*
Newman, Matthew 19; Jamaica, 1736 ***3690.1*** *p164*
Newman, Patrick; St. John, N.B., 1847 ***5704.8*** *p33*
Newman, Richard; Virginia, 1642 ***6219*** *p186*
Newman, Robert; Virginia, 1637 ***6219*** *p22*
Newman, Robert; Virginia, 1645 ***6219*** *p233*
Newman, Robert; Virginia, 1652 ***6251*** *p20*
Newman, Robt.; Virginia, 1636 ***6219*** *p19*
Newman, Samuel 24; Philadelphia, 1774 ***1219.7*** *p185*
Newman, Tho.; Virginia, 1638 ***6219*** *p159*
Newman, Thomas; Ohio, 1843 ***9892.11*** *p34*
Newman, Thomas; Ohio, 1848 ***9892.11*** *p34*
Newman, Thomas 16; Virginia, 1774 ***1219.7*** *p240*
Newman, William 15; Maryland, 1724 ***3690.1*** *p164*
Newman, William 25; Philadelphia, 1775 ***1219.7*** *p274*
Newmann, . . .; Canada, 1776-1783 ***9786*** *p29*
Newmeister, Emil C.; Colorado, 1893 ***9678.2*** *p129*
Newminster, N. E.; Indiana, 1848 ***9117*** *p17*
Newons, Robert 16; St. John, N.B., 1856 ***5704.8*** *p131*
Newport, James 19; Maryland, 1775 ***1219.7*** *p271*
Newport, John; Arkansas, 1918 ***95.2*** *p89*
Newsam, James; Virginia, 1642 ***6219*** *p15*
Newsom, Thos.; Virginia, 1628 ***6219*** *p9*
Newsome, Mark 25; Maryland, 1774 ***1219.7*** *p214*
Newson, Isabella; Quebec, 1849 ***5704.8*** *p56*
Newson, John; Quebec, 1849 ***5704.8*** *p56*
Newson, Richard 19; Virginia, 1774 ***1219.7*** *p201*
Newson, Roseanna; Quebec, 1849 ***5704.8*** *p56*
Newstead, Mary 20; New England, 1724 ***3690.1*** *p164*
Newstead, Robert 28; Jamaica, 1775 ***1219.7*** *p253*
Newsted, Mary 20; New England, 1724 ***3690.1*** *p164*
Newstream, Charles; Minneapolis, 1880-1885 ***6410.35*** *p62*
Newstrom, Frank; Washington, 1859-1920 ***2872.1*** *p28*
Newsum, James; Virginia, 1642 ***6219*** *p190*
Newter, John 21; Virginia, 1774 ***1219.7*** *p239*
Newth, Samuel 23; Maryland, 1775 ***1219.7*** *p252*
Newton, Mr.; Quebec, 1815 ***9229.18*** *p74*
Newton, Ann; America, 1742 ***4971*** *p64*
Newton, Annabelle; Washington, 1859-1920 ***2872.1*** *p28*
Newton, Arthur Angello; Washington, 1859-1920 ***2872.1*** *p28*
Newton, Arthur Frederick; Washington, 1859-1920 ***2872.1*** *p28*
Newton, Augusta June; Washington, 1859-1920 ***2872.1*** *p28*
Newton, Ellen 24; Newport, RI, 1851 ***6508.5*** *p19*
Newton, Fergus 24; Port uncertain, 1774 ***1219.7*** *p177*
Newton, Fra.; Virginia, 1623-1648 ***6219*** *p252*
Newton, Francis; Virginia, 1628 ***6219*** *p31*
Newton, James; California, 1867 ***2769.7*** *p3*
Newton, Jn; America, 1698 ***2212*** *p13*
Newton, John; Philadelphia, 1853 ***5704.8*** *p103*
Newton, John; Virginia, 1643 ***6219*** *p33*
Newton, John; Virginia, 1648 ***6219*** *p252*
Newton, Jonathan; South Carolina, 1716 ***1639.20*** *p253*
Newton, Lilly May; Washington, 1859-1920 ***2872.1*** *p28*
Newton, Martha; Virginia, 1698 ***2212*** *p17*
Newton, Mary 21; Maryland, 1775 ***1219.7*** *p262*
Newton, Mathew 30; Halifax, N.S., 1775 ***1219.7*** *p265*
Newton, Nancy; Philadelphia, 1852 ***5704.8*** *p97*
Newton, Ph.; Virginia, 1647 ***6219*** *p247*
Newton, Rich.; Virginia, 1635 ***6219*** *p69*
Newton, Robert; Virginia, 1638 ***6219*** *p117*
Newton, Samuel 15; Jamaica, 1729 ***3690.1*** *p164*
Newton, Tom 22; Newport, RI, 1851 ***6508.5*** *p19*
Newton, William; Washington, 1859-1920 ***2872.1*** *p28*
Ney, Peter Stewart; South Carolina, 1787-1820 ***1639.20*** *p254*
Neylan, Mr.; Port uncertain, 1839 ***778.5*** *p403*
Neylou, Mr.; Port uncertain, 1839 ***778.5*** *p403*
Neys, Conrate; South Carolina, 1752-1753 ***3689.17*** *p22*
With wife
*Relative:*Paulus 25
*Relative:*Thorus 20
*Relative:*Dorothy 20
Neys, Dorothy 20 *SEE* Neys, Conrate
Neys, Paulus 25 *SEE* Neys, Conrate
Neys, Thorus 20 *SEE* Neys, Conrate
Neytzert, Johan Peter; Philadelphia, 1744 ***8125.6*** *p22*
Nibling, Johannes; Pennsylvania, 1749 ***2444*** *p197*
Nicamp, Christine Wilhelmine Louise; America, 1845 ***4610.10*** *p120*
Nicastro, Onifrio 24; Arkansas, 1918 ***95.2*** *p89*
Nice, Jan; Germantown, PA, 1684 ***2467.7*** *p5*
Nicedret, George 26; New Orleans, 1831 ***778.5*** *p403*
Nichane, Joan; America, 1741 ***4971*** *p41*
Nichleson, Mary 20; St. John, N.B., 1861 ***5704.8*** *p147*
Nichol, . . .; New York, NY, 1867 ***5704.8*** *p219*
Nichol, Isobella; America, 1832 ***8893*** *p265*
Nichol, Jane; Philadelphia, 1864 ***5704.8*** *p183*
Nichol, Miron 6; Philadelphia, 1864 ***5704.8*** *p183*
Nichol, Rachael; New York, NY, 1867 ***5704.8*** *p219*
Nicholai, Julius; Indiana, 1840 ***1450.2*** *p107A*
Nicholas, Andrew 36; America, 1835 ***778.5*** *p403*
Nicholas, Emmanuel; Arkansas, 1918 ***95.2*** *p89*
Nicholas, John; America, 1895 ***1450.2*** *p107A*
Nicholas, John; Philadelphia, 1811 ***2859.11*** *p18*
With family
Nicholas, John H. 34; Kansas, 1880 ***5240.1*** *p62*
Nicholas, Mathew Henry; Colorado, 1894 ***9678.2*** *p129*
Nicholas, Nick; Arkansas, 1918 ***95.2*** *p89*
Nicholas, Richard; Virginia, 1639 ***6219*** *p157*
Nicholas, Richard 22; Maryland, 1774 ***1219.7*** *p229*
Nicholas, William; Virginia, 1643 ***6219*** *p241*
Nicholes, Mr. 27; New Orleans, 1826 ***778.5*** *p404*
Nicholis, Peggy; St. John, N.B., 1847 ***5704.8*** *p25*
Nicholis, Sally 13; St. John, N.B., 1849 ***5704.8*** *p48*
Nicholl, David; Philadelphia, 1847 ***53.26*** *p74*
Nicholl, David; Philadelphia, 1847 ***5704.8*** *p14*
Nicholl, David A.; Austin, TX, 1886 ***9777*** *p5*
Nicholl, Eliza 24; Quebec, 1856 ***5704.8*** *p130*
Nicholl, Jenny; Philadelphia, 1853 ***5704.8*** *p101*
Nicholl, John; Philadelphia, 1760 ***9973.7*** *p35*
Nicholl, Margaret 28; Philadelphia, 1855 ***5704.8*** *p124*
Nicholl, Margaret Jane; St. John, N.B., 1852 ***5704.8*** *p95*
Nicholl, Robert; St. John, N.B., 1848 ***5704.8*** *p47*
Nicholl, Robert James 2; Philadelphia, 1855 ***5704.8*** *p124*
Nicholl, Sarah 22; Quebec, 1856 ***5704.8*** *p130*
Nicholl, Thomas 3; Philadelphia, 1855 ***5704.8*** *p124*
Nicholl, William 9 mos; Philadelphia, 1855 ***5704.8*** *p124*
Nicholls, Ann 17; South Carolina, 1723 ***3690.1*** *p165*
Nicholls, Goodfre.nd 16; West Indies, 1722 ***3690.1*** *p89*
Nicholls, Hannah 20; New England, 1721 ***3690.1*** *p165*
Nicholls, John 16; Jamaica, 1731 ***3690.1*** *p165*
Nicholls, Margarett 26; America, 1700 ***2212*** *p33*
Nicholls, Richard 16; Jamaica, 1733 ***3690.1*** *p165*
Nicholls, Richard 17; Virginia, 1727 ***3690.1*** *p165*
Nicholls, Samuell; Virginia, 1647 ***6219*** *p239*
Nicholls, Sands; Virginia, 1645 ***6219*** *p253*
Nicholo, Charles 18; Jamaica, 1720 ***3690.1*** *p165*
Nicholos, Gust; Arkansas, 1918 ***95.2*** *p89*
Nichols, Mrs. 65; New Orleans, 1821 ***778.5*** *p404*
Nichols, Andrew *SEE* Nichols, Andrew
Nichols, Andrew; Virginia, 1648 ***6219*** *p253*
*Wife:*Elizabeth
*Child:*Andrew
*Child:*William
*Child:*Elizabeth
Nichols, Elizabeth *SEE* Nichols, Andrew
Nichols, Elizabeth *SEE* Nichols, Andrew
Nichols, Elizabeth 30; Virginia, 1699 ***2212*** *p26*
Nichols, Fr.; Virginia, 1641 ***6219*** *p184*
Nichols, George; New York, NY, 1833 ***8208.4*** *p39*
Nichols, Isabella 17; Massachusetts, 1847 ***5881.1*** *p78*
Nichols, James; New York, NY, 1834 ***8208.4*** *p60*
Nichols, James 24; Carolina, 1774 ***1219.7*** *p227*
Nichols, John; America, 1698 ***2212*** *p10*
Nichols, John 22; Jamaica, 1733 ***3690.1*** *p165*
Nichols, John 23; Maryland, 1774 ***1219.7*** *p180*
Nichols, John 26; Maryland, 1774 ***1219.7*** *p204*
Nichols, Nathaniel 16; Maryland, 1751 ***1219.7*** *p3*
Nichols, Nathaniel 16; Maryland, 1751 ***3690.1*** *p165*
Nichols, Roger; Virginia, 1635 ***6219*** *p35*
Nichols, Roger 40; Virginia, 1774 ***1219.7*** *p186*
Nichols, Thomas 20; Philadelphia, 1751 ***1219.7*** *p6*
Nichols, Thomas 20; Philadelphia, 1751 ***3690.1*** *p165*
Nichols, Thomas 25; Maryland, 1774 ***1219.7*** *p187*
Nichols, Walter; Virginia, 1637 ***6219*** *p113*
Nichols, William *SEE* Nichols, Andrew
Nichols, William; Virginia, 1642 ***6219*** *p186*
Nichols, Zachariah 20; Virginia, 1751 ***1219.7*** *p4*
Nichols, Zachariah 20; Virginia, 1751 ***3690.1*** *p165*
Nicholsen, Hans Peter; Washington, 1859-1920 ***2872.1*** *p28*
Nicholsen, Jens; Washington, 1859-1920 ***2872.1*** *p28*
Nicholson, Alex. *SEE* Nicholson, Samuel
Nicholson, Alex.; Nova Scotia, 1830 ***7085.4*** *p44*
*Wife:*Margaret
*Child:*John
*Child:*Donald
Nicholson, Angus 26; St. John, N.B., 1863 ***5704.8*** *p152*
Nicholson, Anne *SEE* Nicholson, Duncan
Nicholson, Anne *SEE* Nicholson, James
Nicholson, Archibald 22; St. John, N.B., 1863 ***5704.8*** *p152*
Nicholson, Catherine 86; North Carolina, 1850 ***1639.20*** *p254*
Nicholson, Christian Theodore; Washington, 1859-1920 ***2872.1*** *p28*
Nicholson, Christy 48; St. John, N.B., 1863 ***5704.8*** *p152*
Nicholson, David; New York, 1851 ***1450.2*** *p107A*
Nicholson, Donald *SEE* Nicholson, Alex.
Nicholson, Donald *SEE* Nicholson, Samuel
Nicholson, Donald; America, 1802 ***1639.20*** *p254*
Nicholson, Donald; Ohio, 1881-1889 ***9892.11*** *p34*
Nicholson, Donald W.; Ohio, 1891 ***9892.11*** *p35*
Nicholson, Duncan; Nova Scotia, 1830 ***7085.4*** *p45*
*Wife:*Anne
Nicholson, Eliz.; Virginia, 1637 ***6219*** *p180*
Nicholson, Elizabeth; Virginia, 1635 ***6219*** *p70*
Nicholson, Georg; Virginia, 1635 ***6219*** *p35*
Nicholson, Georg; Virginia, 1638 ***6219*** *p146*
Nicholson, George 27; Grenada, 1774 ***1219.7*** *p238*
Nicholson, Henry; America, 1758 ***1219.7*** *p65*
Nicholson, James; Nova Scotia, 1830 ***7085.4*** *p45*
*Wife:*Margaret
*Child:*Anne
*Child:*John
Nicholson, Jens Peter; Washington, 1859-1920 ***2872.1*** *p28*
Nicholson, Jeremy 19; Antigua (Antego), 1729 ***3690.1*** *p165*
Nicholson, John *SEE* Nicholson, Alex.
Nicholson, John *SEE* Nicholson, James
Nicholson, John *SEE* Nicholson, Samuel
Nicholson, John; Iowa, 1866-1943 ***123.54*** *p36*
Nicholson, John; North Carolina, 1769-1814 ***1639.20*** *p254*
Nicholson, John; St. John, N.B., 1851 ***5704.8*** *p78*
Nicholson, John; South Carolina, 1716 ***1639.20*** *p254*
Nicholson, John 20; New England, 1699 ***2212*** *p20*
Nicholson, Ket *SEE* Nicholson, Samuel
Nicholson, Malcolm; America, 1802 ***1639.20*** *p254*
Nicholson, Margaret *SEE* Nicholson, Alex.
Nicholson, Margaret *SEE* Nicholson, James
Nicholson, Margaret 49 *SEE* Nicholson, Mary
Nicholson, Mary *SEE* Nicholson, Samuel
Nicholson, Mary 53 *SEE* Nicholson, Mary
Nicholson, Mary 75; North Carolina, 1850 ***1639.20*** *p254*
*Relative:*Mary 53
*Relative:*Margaret 49

Nicholson, Norman *SEE* Nicholson, Samuel
Nicholson, Peter; America, 1802 *1639.20 p255*
Nicholson, Pycroft 28; Jamaica, 1731 *3690.1 p165*
Nicholson, Richard 14; Virginia, 1720 *3690.1 p166*
Nicholson, S.; America, 1801 *1639.20 p255*
Nicholson, Samuel; Prince Edward Island, 1829-1830
  7085.4 p45
  *Wife:*Ket
  *Child:*John
  *Child:*Donald
  *Child:*Alex.
  *Child:*Mary
  *Child:*Norman
Nicholson, Samuel 55; St. John, N.B., 1863 *5704.8 p152*
Nicholson, Simon 41; Maryland, 1774 *1219.7 p178*
Nicholson, William; New York, 1851 *1450.2 p107A*
Nicholus, Dennis 9 mos; St. John, N.B., 1847 *5704.8 p10*
Nicholus, Elleanor; St. John, N.B., 1847 *5704.8 p10*
Nicholus, William; St. John, N.B., 1847 *5704.8 p10*
Nichter, Jacob; Wisconsin, n.d. *9675.7 p129*
Nichter, Martin; Wisconsin, n.d. *9675.7 p129*
Nick, . . .; Canada, 1776-1783 *9786 p43*
Nickalson, John 28; Maryland, 1730 *3690.1 p166*
Nickel, Adalbert; America, 1895 *1763 p40D*
Nickel, Eva Kathr. 18; America, 1854-1855 *9162.6 p104*
Nickel, G. R.; Kansas, 1894 *5240.1 p32*
Nickel, Herman 26; Kansas, 1883 *5240.1 p32*
Nickel, Hermann 26; Kansas, 1883 *5240.1 p64*
Nickel, Konrad; Philadelphia, 1779 *8137 p12*
Nickel, P. H.; Kansas, 1877 *5240.1 p32*
Nickelson, John 28; Maryland, 1730 *3690.1 p166*
Nickerson, Alexander; Bangor, ME, 1890 *6410.22 p126*
Nickey, Alex; Arkansas, 1918 *95.2 p89*
Nickhols, Steve; Arkansas, 1918 *95.2 p89*
Nickle, Betty 40; Philadelphia, 1853 *5704.8 p111*
Nickle, Margaret 20; Philadelphia, 1853 *5704.8 p111*
Nickle, Mary; Philadelphia, 1853 *5704.8 p101*
Nickle, Mathew 45; Philadelphia, 1853 *5704.8 p111*
Nickle, Sarah Jane; Philadelphia, 1853 *5704.8 p101*
Nickle, Thomas; New York, NY, 1815 *2859.11 p40*
Nickle, William; New York, NY, 1816 *2859.11 p40*
Nickle, William 19; Quebec, 1857 *5704.8 p136*
Nicklesworth, Wm.; Virginia, 1637 *6219 p24*
Nickner, . . .; Canada, 1776-1783 *9786 p29*
Nickolls, Elizabeth 18; Pennsylvania, 1719 *3690.1 p166*
Nickolopulos, Athanaseos George; Arkansas, 1918 *95.2*
  p89
Nickolosos, James; Iowa, 1866-1943 *123.54 p71*
Nickols, Goodfre.nd 16; West Indies, 1722 *3690.1 p89*
Nickolson, John; Arkansas, 1918 *95.2 p89*
Nickolson, Ness Andreas 27; Kansas, 1889 *5240.1 p73*
Nicks, John; Washington, 1859-1920 *2872.1 p28*
Niclo, Martin 18; Jamaica, 1730 *3690.1 p166*
Nicol, Robert; New York, 1848 *1450.2 p107A*
Nicol, Walter 21; St. John, N.B., 1867 *5704.8 p168*
Nicola, Wadie; Arkansas, 1918 *95.2 p89*
Nicolai, . . .; Canada, 1776-1783 *9786 p43*
Nicolai, Carl Wm. L.; America, 1843 *1450.2 p107A*
Nicolaisen, Gust; Arkansas, 1918 *95.2 p89*
Nicolas, . . .; Canada, 1776-1783 *9786 p43*
Nicolas, Mr. 2; America, 1836 *778.5 p404*
Nicolas, Frank; Wisconsin, n.d. *9675.7 p129*
Nicolas, Jean 31; America, 1836 *778.5 p404*
Nicolas, Jean M. 21; America, 1836 *778.5 p404*
Nicolas, Ludwig; Wisconsin, n.d. *9675.7 p129*
Nicolas, Madelene 46; America, 1836 *778.5 p404*
Nicolaus, Detter; Pennsylvania, 1749 *4525 p205*
Nicolaus, Jean; Iowa, 1866-1943 *123.54 p36*
Nicolaus, John; New York, NY, 1837 *8208.4 p55*
Nicolay, Heinrich; Cincinnati, 1869-1887 *8582 p22*
Nicolazzi, Geuseppe; Iowa, 1866-1943 *123.54 p36*
Nicolazzi, Giuseppe; Iowa, 1866-1943 *123.54 p71*
Nicolazzi, Guiseppe; Iowa, 1866-1943 *123.54 p36*
Nicole, Henry; Quebec, 1789 *7603 p27*
Nicolet, Mme. 25; Port uncertain, 1839 *778.5 p404*
Nicolet, Mr. 27; Port uncertain, 1839 *778.5 p404*
Nicolet, Mr. 50; New Orleans, 1838 *778.5 p404*
Nicoletto, Angelo; Iowa, 1866-1943 *123.54 p36*
Nicoletto, Clandio; Iowa, 1866-1943 *123.54 p36*
Nicoletto, Vitorio; Iowa, 1866-1943 *123.54 p36*
Nicolic, Mar.a 47; New York, NY, 1893 *9026.4 p42*
Nicolio, Antonia Grosso 23; New York, NY, 1893 *9026.4*
  p42
Nicoll, Alexander 46; South Carolina, 1850 *1639.20 p254*
Nicoll, Lewis 20; Jamaica, 1730 *3690.1 p166*
Nicollet, Henry; Wisconsin, n.d. *9675.7 p129*
Nicolls, Henry; Quebec, 1789 *7603 p27*
Nicoloussos, Demetrios; Iowa, 1866-1943 *123.54 p71*
Nicolozzi, Giovanni; Iowa, 1866-1943 *123.54 p36*
Nicols, Mr.; Quebec, 1815 *9229.18 p79*
Nicholson, Andrew *SEE* Nicolson, John
Nicholson, Angus *SEE* Nicolson, Kenneth

Nicolson, Ann *SEE* Nicolson, Kenneth
Nicolson, Ann *SEE* Nicolson, Malcolm
Nicolson, Catherine *SEE* Nicolson, Donald
Nicolson, Catherine *SEE* Nicolson, John
Nicolson, Catherine *SEE* Nicolson, Malcolm
Nicolson, Catherine Buchanan *SEE* Nicolson, Kenneth
Nicolson, Donald *SEE* Nicolson, John
Nicolson, Donald *SEE* Nicolson, Kenneth
Nicolson, Donald; Quebec, 1863 *4537.30 p35*
  *Wife:*Isabella MacKay
  *Child:*Murdo
  *Child:*Marion
  *Child:*Louis
  *Child:*Kenneth
  *Child:*Kirsty
Nicolson, Donald; Quebec, 1873 *4537.30 p36*
  *Sister:*Catherine
Nicolson, Flora; Quebec, 1873 *4537.30 p112*
Nicolson, Flora; Quebec, 1875 *4537.30 p115*
Nicolson, Isabella MacDonald *SEE* Nicolson, Malcolm
Nicolson, Isabella MacKay *SEE* Nicolson, Donald
Nicolson, Jane Finlayson *SEE* Nicolson, John
Nicolson, John *SEE* Nicolson, John
Nicolson, John; Quebec, 1855 *4537.30 p35*
  *Child:*John
  *Child:*Mary
  *Child:*Kenneth
  *Child:*Catherine
  *Child:*Donald
Nicolson, John; Quebec, 1873 *4537.30 p36*
  *Wife:*Jane Finlayson
  *Child:*Andrew
  *Child:*Mary
Nicolson, Kenneth *SEE* Nicolson, Donald
Nicolson, Kenneth *SEE* Nicolson, John
Nicolson, Kenneth; Quebec, 1841 *4537.30 p35*
  *Wife:*Catherine Buchanan
  *Child:*Malcolm
  *Child:*Murdo
  *Child:*Marion
  *Child:*Angus
  *Child:*Mary
  *Child:*Donald
  *Child:*Ann
  *Child:*Kirsty
  *Child:*Nicol
Nicolson, Kirsty *SEE* Nicolson, Donald
Nicolson, Kirsty *SEE* Nicolson, Kenneth
Nicolson, Louis *SEE* Nicolson, Donald
Nicolson, Malcolm *SEE* Nicolson, Kenneth
Nicolson, Malcolm; Quebec, 1873 *4537.30 p36*
  *Wife:*Isabella MacDonald
  *Child:*Ann
  *Child:*Catherine
  *Child:*Mary
Nicolson, Margaret; Quebec, 1855 *4537.30 p4*
Nicolson, Margaret; Quebec, 1873 *4537.30 p115*
Nicolson, Marion *SEE* Nicolson, Donald
Nicolson, Marion *SEE* Nicolson, Kenneth
Nicolson, Mary *SEE* Nicolson, John
Nicolson, Mary *SEE* Nicolson, John
Nicolson, Mary *SEE* Nicolson, Kenneth
Nicolson, Mary *SEE* Nicolson, Malcolm
Nicolson, Mary; Quebec, 1855 *4537.30 p31*
Nicolson, Murdo *SEE* Nicolson, Donald
Nicolson, Murdo *SEE* Nicolson, Kenneth
Nicolson, Nicol *SEE* Nicolson, Kenneth
Nicolucci, Pasquale; Arkansas, 1918 *95.2 p89*
Nicot, Paul M. 17; New Orleans, 1821 *778.5 p404*
Nieaise, Leon Ferdinand; Arkansas, 1918 *95.2 p89*
Niebler, Florent 22; America, 1835 *778.5 p404*
Niebler, Leonhard; Wisconsin, n.d. *9675.7 p129*
Nieblers, Mrs. G.; America, 1853 *2853.7 p109*
Niebling, Elisabetha; Port uncertain, 1749 *2444 p197*
Niebling, Johannes; Pennsylvania, 1749 *2444 p197*
  With wife
Nieburg, Friederike H L Nolting *SEE* Nieburg, Johann
  Friedrich
Nieburg, Johann Friedrich; America, 1855 *4610.10 p116*
  *Mother:*Friederike H L Nolting
Niedergerke, Anne Marie Christine; America, 1838
  4610.10 p119
Niedergerke, Carl Dietrich Wilhelm; America, 1881
  4610.10 p122
  *Wife:*Friederike 21
  *Daughter:*Louise 3 mos
Niedergerke, Friederike 21 *SEE* Niedergerke, Carl
  Dietrich Wilhelm
Niedergerke, Johann Carl Ludwig; America, 1843
  4610.10 p119
Niedergerke, Johann Friedrich Wilhelm; America, 1852
  4610.10 p121

Niedergerke, Louise 3 mos *SEE* Niedergerke, Carl
  Dietrich Wilhelm
Niederkorn, Henry; Wisconsin, n.d. *9675.7 p129*
Niederlucke, Anne Marie Hedwig; America, 1849
  4610.10 p115
Niederprim, John 26; Kansas, 1887 *5240.1 p32*
Niederprim, John 26; Kansas, 1887 *5240.1 p71*
Niederpruem, Peter 23; Kansas, 1890 *5240.1 p75*
Niederstadt, Gustav; Wisconsin, n.d. *9675.7 p129*
Niederstucke, Anne C. Marie E. Viehe *SEE*
  Niederstucke, Johann Hermann Heinrich
Niederstucke, Anne Marie W. Justine *SEE* Niederstucke,
  Johann Hermann Heinrich
Niederstucke, Carl F. W. Gottlieb *SEE* Niederstucke,
  Johann Hermann Heinrich
Niederstucke, Caspar Heinrich *SEE* Niederstucke, Johann
  Hermann Heinrich
Niederstucke, Cord Heinrich *SEE* Niederstucke, Johann
  Hermann Heinrich
Niederstucke, Ernst August Wilhelm *SEE* Niederstucke,
  Johann Hermann Heinrich
Niederstucke, Friedrich Wilhelm *SEE* Niederstucke,
  Johann Hermann Heinrich
Niederstucke, Johann Hermann Heinrich; America, 1844
  4610.10 p155
  *Wife:*Anne C. Marie E. Viehe
  *Child:*Cord Heinrich
  *Child:*Friedrich Wilhelm
  *Child:*Anne Marie W. Justine
  *Child:*Caspar Heinrich
  *Child:*Carl F. W. Gottlieb
  *Child:*Marie W. Caroline
  *Child:*Ernst August Wilhelm
  *Child:*Johanne W. Caroline
Niederstucke, Johanne W. Caroline *SEE* Niederstucke,
  Johann Hermann Heinrich
Niederstucke, Marie W. Caroline *SEE* Niederstucke,
  Johann Hermann Heinrich
Niedeur, Henriette 49; New Orleans, 1839 *9420.2 p483*
  *Daughter:*Laura 11
Niedeur, Laura 11 *SEE* Niedeur, Henriette
Nieding, . . .; Canada, 1776-1783 *9786 p29*
Niedner, Alice 23; New Orleans, 1839 *9420.2 p483*
Niedner, Charls. Aug. 30; New Orleans, 1839 *9420.2*
  p487
Niedner, Emma 17; New Orleans, 1839 *9420.2 p483*
Niedzwiecki, . . .; New York, 1831 *4606 p175*
Niehaus, Frederick; Illinois, 1876 *2896.5 p29*
Niehaus, Friedrich Wilhelm; America, 1853 *4610.10*
  p156
Niehaus, Heinrich; America, 1827 *8582.1 p26*
Niehaus, Joseph; Cincinnati, 1869-1887 *8582 p22*
Niehaus, Joseph H.; Illinois, 1880 *2896.5 p29*
Niehus, Carl *SEE* Niehus, Carl Friedrich Wilhelm Adolph
Niehus, Carl Friedrich Wilhelm Adolph; America, 1881
  4610.10 p106
  *Wife:*Charlotte Bartling
  *Child:*Johanne 7
  *Child:*Marie Franziska
  *Child:*Carl
Niehus, Caroline Kolling 64; America, 1881 *4610.10*
  p106
Niehus, Charlotte 31; America, 1881 *4610.10 p106*
Niehus, Charlotte Bartling *SEE* Niehus, Carl Friedrich
  Wilhelm Adolph
Niehus, Johanne 7 *SEE* Niehus, Carl Friedrich Wilhelm
  Adolph
Niehus, Marie Franziska *SEE* Niehus, Carl Friedrich
  Wilhelm Adolph
Niekamp, Christine Wilhelmine Louise; America, 1845
  4610.10 p120
Nieke, George; New York, 1743 *3652 p60*
  *Wife:*Johanna E.
Nieke, Johanna E. *SEE* Nieke, George
Niekranz, Christian; Illinois, 1878 *2896.5 p29*
Niel, Mr. 18; Grenada, 1774 *1219.7 p231*
Nielsen, Alfred; Arkansas, 1918 *95.2 p89*
Nielsen, Annie Marie *SEE* Nielsen, Niels Peter Dulby
Nielsen, Axel Alfred Viggo; Arkansas, 1918 *95.2 p89*
Nielsen, Chris; Illinois, 1891 *5012.40 p26*
Nielsen, Hans Fredrick; Arkansas, 1918 *95.2 p90*
Nielsen, Jens; New York, NY, 1904 *3455.1 p44*
Nielsen, Jens. 42; Kansas, 1886 *5240.1 p68*
Nielsen, Nels Peter; Arkansas, 1918 *95.2 p90*
Nielsen, Nick Christensen 29; Arkansas, 1918 *95.2 p90*
Nielsen, Niels 21; Kansas, 1873 *5240.1 p54*
Nielsen, Niels 22; Kansas, 1874 *5240.1 p55*
Nielsen, Niels Peter; Arkansas, 1918 *95.2 p90*
Nielsen, Niels Peter Dulby; New York, NY, 1911 *3455.2*
  p102
  *Wife:*Annie Marie
Nielsen, Peter 29; Kansas, 1893 *5240.1 p77*
Nielsen, Peter Olaf Alexius; Arkansas, 1918 *95.2 p90*

Nielsen, Reidai V.; Arkansas, 1918 ***95.2*** *p90*
Nielsen, Sayer; Arkansas, 1918 ***95.2*** *p90*
Nielsen, Steffen Viggo; Arkansas, 1918 ***95.2*** *p90*
Nielson, Albert; Arkansas, 1918 ***95.2*** *p90*
Nielson, Alfred Johnannes; Arkansas, 1918 ***95.2*** *p90*
Nielson, Carl Peter 28; Arkansas, 1918 ***95.2*** *p90*
Nielson, Herman 29; Arkansas, 1918 ***95.2*** *p90*
Nielson, James; Philadelphia, 1816 ***2859.11*** *p40*
Nielson, Jens; Wisconsin, n.d. ***9675.7*** *p129*
Nielson, Lorenz; New York, 1754 ***3652*** *p80*
Nielson, Nels Christian; Washington, 1859-1920 ***2872.1*** *p28*
Nielson, Niels Christian; Arkansas, 1918 ***95.2*** *p90*
Nielson, Niels Peter Fromberg; Arkansas, 1918 ***95.2*** *p90*
Nielson, Peter; Arkansas, 1918 ***95.2*** *p90*
Niely, Elizabeth 21; Philadelphia, 1803 ***53.26*** *p74*
Nieman, Anna Gertrude; Wisconsin, n.d. ***9675.7*** *p129*
Nieman, Frederick; America, 1853 ***1450.2*** *p108A*
Nieman, H. H.; Cincinnati, 1869-1887 ***8582*** *p22*
Nieman, Philipp; Cincinnati, 1869-1887 ***8582*** *p22*
Niemann, Anne Marie Louise Charlotte; America, 1860 ***4610.10*** *p99*
Niemann, Caspar Heinrich; America, 1854 ***4610.10*** *p144*
Niemann, Catharine Anna Ilsabein; America, 1849 ***4610.10*** *p98*
Niemann, Christ. Henriette 34 *SEE* Niemann, Johitr.
Niemann, Friedr. Martin 1 *SEE* Niemann, Johitr.
Niemann, Georg; Kentucky, 1839-1840 ***8582.3*** *p99*
Niemann, Heinrich Frederick; New York, NY, 1833 ***8208.4*** *p60*
Niemann, Herman; Wisconsin, n.d. ***9675.7*** *p129*
Niemann, Hermann Heinrich; Baltimore, 1834 ***8582.3*** *p48*
Niemann, Johitr. 34; New Orleans, 1839 ***9420.2*** *p168*
*Wife:*Christ. Henriette 34
*Child:*Marie Elisabeth 6
*Child:*Friedr. Martin 1
Niemann, John Henry; West Virginia, 1858 ***9788.3*** *p17*
Niemann, John Henry; West Virginia, 1868 ***9788.3*** *p17*
Niemann, Joseph; Wisconsin, n.d. ***9675.7*** *p129*
Niemann, Louise 40; America, 1873 ***4610.10*** *p159*
Niemann, Marie Elisabeth 6 *SEE* Niemann, Johitr.
Niemann, William; America, 1854 ***1450.2*** *p108A*
Niemann, William; Illinois, 1888 ***5012.39*** *p121*
Niemann, William; Wisconsin, n.d. ***9675.7*** *p129*
Niemeier, Heinrich; Ohio, 1869-1887 ***8582*** *p22*
Niemeier, Johann Heinrich; America, 1843 ***8582.1*** *p26*
Niemeier, Otto; America, 1869-1887 ***8582*** *p22*
Niemeyer, Carl Friedrich *SEE* Niemeyer, Johann Arnold
Niemeyer, Caroline Friederike Justine; America, 1881 ***4610.10*** *p96*
Niemeyer, Hanna J. H. Hansmeyer *SEE* Niemeyer, Johann Arnold
Niemeyer, Heinrich 17; New Orleans, 1842 ***8582.3*** *p48*
With parents
Niemeyer, Johann Arnold; America, 1865 ***4610.10*** *p122*
*Wife:*Hanna J. H. Hansmeyer
*Child:*Johann F. Wilhelm
*Child:*Carl Friedrich
Niemeyer, Johann F. Wilhelm *SEE* Niemeyer, Johann Arnold
Niemeyer, Johann Heinrich; Baltimore, 1843 ***8582.1*** *p26*
Niemi, Anna; Washington, 1859-1920 ***2872.1*** *p28*
Niemi, Atet; Washington, 1859-1920 ***2872.1*** *p28*
Niemi, Henry; Washington, 1859-1920 ***2872.1*** *p28*
Niemi, Kalle; Washington, 1859-1920 ***2872.1*** *p28*
Niemi, Omie Olkka; Washington, 1859-1920 ***2872.1*** *p28*
Niemi, Peter; Washington, 1859-1920 ***2872.1*** *p28*
Niemi, Ukko Eino; Washington, 1859-1920 ***2872.1*** *p28*
Niemi, Waino; Washington, 1859-1920 ***2872.1*** *p28*
Niemi, Wasla Lili; Washington, 1859-1920 ***2872.1*** *p28*
Niemi, Wast Ossi; Washington, 1859-1920 ***2872.1*** *p28*
Niemoenhuizen, Cornelis Van; Washington, 1859-1920 ***2872.1*** *p42*
Nienaber, Ferdinand; America, 1851 ***8582.3*** *p48*
Nienaver, Ahrend Henry; New York, NY, 1836 ***8208.4*** *p12*
Niendorff, Adolph Fredrick; Wisconsin, n.d. ***9675.7*** *p129*
Niendorff, Ursula Anna; Wisconsin, n.d. ***9675.7*** *p129*
Niermann, Caspar Carl Heinrich; America, 1892 ***4610.10*** *p153*
Niermann, Christoph; America, 1891 ***1450.2*** *p108A*
Niermann, Heinrich Fr. W.; America, 1885 ***4610.10*** *p153*
Nierode, Frederick; Wisconsin, n.d. ***9675.7*** *p129*
Nieroote, Fred; Wisconsin, n.d. ***9675.7*** *p129*
Nierth, Curt 22; Kansas, 1887 ***5240.1*** *p69*
Nies, Fredericka Dollinger; Dakota, 1867-1967 ***1641*** *p43*
Niesen, Frank E.; Wisconsin, n.d. ***9675.7*** *p129*
Niess, Joseph; New York, NY, 1836 ***8208.4*** *p9*
Niessen, Anna; Quebec, 1876 ***9980.20*** *p48*
Nietert, Heinrich; Cincinnati, 1869-1887 ***8582*** *p22*
Nietupski, . . .; New York, 1831 ***4606*** *p175*
Nietupski, Faustyn 20; New York, 1912 ***9980.29*** *p67*
Nietz, . . .; Canada, 1776-1783 ***9786*** *p30*
Niewadoma, Alexander; Pennsylvania, 1912 ***9980.29*** *p74*
Niewadoma, Antonina Winczewski 25; New York, 1912 ***9980.29*** *p74*
Niewadoma, Witold 1; New York, 1912 ***9980.29*** *p74*
Niewadomy, Alexander; Pennsylvania, 1912 ***9980.29*** *p74*
Niewadomy, Antonina Winczewski 25; New York, 1912 ***9980.29*** *p74*
Niewasoski, Alexander; Arkansas, 1918 ***95.2*** *p90*
Nigal, Catharine 14; Massachusetts, 1849 ***5881.1*** *p77*
Nigal, John 13; Massachusetts, 1849 ***5881.1*** *p78*
Nigent, Robert; Virginia, 1646 ***6219*** *p244*
Night, Robt.; Virginia, 1648 ***6219*** *p250*
Nightengale, Elias; Indiana, 1844 ***9117*** *p17*
Nightengale, John; Indiana, 1837 ***9117*** *p15*
Nigoulais, Js. 15; New Orleans, 1831 ***778.5*** *p404*
Nigro, Pasquale; California, 1871 ***2764.35*** *p51*
Nigum, Matthaus; Alberta, n.d. ***5262*** *p58*
Nijea, Vicente Samaila; Arkansas, 1918 ***95.2*** *p90*
Nijhuis, Gerrit 34; New York, NY, 1847 ***3377.6*** *p13*
Nijhuis, Hendrikus 1; New York, NY, 1847 ***3377.6*** *p13*
Nijhuis, Jenneke 61; New York, NY, 1847 ***3377.6*** *p13*
Nijhuis, Jenneken 33; New York, NY, 1847 ***3377.6*** *p13*
Nijhuis, Mannes 3; New York, NY, 1847 ***3377.6*** *p13*
Nijhuis, Mannes 67; New York, NY, 1847 ***3377.6*** *p13*
Nikkel, John D. 46; Harris Co., TX, 1899 ***6254*** *p5*
Nikolosus, Celesta; Iowa, 1866-1943 ***123.54*** *p36*
Nilis, Ann 25; St. John, N.B., 1856 ***5704.8*** *p131*
Nilis, Francis 11; St. John, N.B., 1856 ***5704.8*** *p131*
Nilis, Margaret 8; St. John, N.B., 1856 ***5704.8*** *p131*
Nill, Agnes *SEE* Nill, Johann Caspar
Nill, Anna *SEE* Nill, Johann Caspar
Nill, Anna Maria *SEE* Nill, Johann Caspar
Nill, Johann Caspar 33; Pennsylvania, 1753 ***2444*** *p197*
*Wife:*Anna
*Child:*Anna Maria
*Child:*Agnes
Nilledy, Mr. 22; New Orleans, 1837 ***778.5*** *p404*
Nillemin, Georg 19; Port uncertain, 1839 ***778.5*** *p404*
Nilly, Bridget; St. John, N.B., 1850 ***5704.8*** *p62*
Nilly, Ellen; St. John, N.B., 1850 ***5704.8*** *p62*
Nilly, William; St. John, N.B., 1850 ***5704.8*** *p62*
Nilon, Catharine; Philadelphia, 1865 ***5704.8*** *p196*
Nilsen, Jonas; New York, 1743 ***3652*** *p60*
*Wife:*Margaret
Nilsen, Karl Bernhart; Arkansas, 1918 ***95.2*** *p90*
Nilsen, Margaret *SEE* Nilsen, Jonas
Nilsen, Sven Gustaf 28; Arkansas, 1918 ***95.2*** *p90*
Nilson, Bengt J.; Illinois, 1888 ***5012.39*** *p122*
Nilson, Berger; Washington, 1859-1920 ***2872.1*** *p28*
Nilson, C. E.; Minneapolis, 1883-1887 ***6410.35*** *p61*
Nilson, C. R.; Minneapolis, 1880-1885 ***6410.35*** *p61*
Nilson, Daniel; Philadelphia, 1850 ***53.26*** *p74*
Nilson, Daniel; Philadelphia, 1850 ***5704.8*** *p60*
Nilson, Enoch G.; Minneapolis, 1881-1886 ***6410.35*** *p61*
Nilson, Frank O.; Minneapolis, 1882-1887 ***6410.35*** *p61*
Nilson, J. A.; Minneapolis, 1881-1888 ***6410.35*** *p61*
Nilson, John; Colorado, 1904 ***9678.2*** *p130*
Nilson, Margaret; America, 1866 ***5704.8*** *p206*
Nilson, Martin; Minneapolis, 1880-1886 ***6410.35*** *p61*
Nilson, Martin G.; Minneapolis, 1869-1877 ***6410.35*** *p61*
Nilson, Nils; Minneapolis, 1880-1885 ***6410.35*** *p61*
Nilson, Nils; Minneapolis, 1882-1885 ***6410.35*** *p61*
Nilson, Nils D.; Minneapolis, 1882-1883 ***6410.35*** *p61*
Nilson, Olof H.; Maine, 1871-1882 ***6410.22*** *p119*
Nilson, Ture; Maine, 1871-1882 ***6410.22*** *p119*
Nilssen, Johannes; Colorado, 1878 ***9678.2*** *p130*
Nilsson, Andreas; Illinois, 1860 ***5012.38*** *p98*
Nilsson, Ben; Minneapolis, 1872-1879 ***6410.35*** *p61*
Nilsson, Carl Johan; Maine, 1869-1884 ***6410.22*** *p120*
Nilsson, Carl Rudolf; Minneapolis, 1880-1885 ***6410.35*** *p61*
Nilsson, Claes Edvard; Minneapolis, 1883-1887 ***6410.35*** *p61*
Nilsson, Johan; Minneapolis, 1880-1885 ***6410.35*** *p61*
Nilsson, Johan Alfred; Minneapolis, 1869-1878 ***6410.35*** *p53*
Nilsson, Mathias; Minneapolis, 1880-1886 ***6410.35*** *p61*
Nilsson, Nils; Minneapolis, 1880-1885 ***6410.35*** *p61*
Nilsson, Nils; Minneapolis, 1882-1887 ***6410.35*** *p65*
Nilsson, Nils Goran; Minneapolis, 1873-1877 ***6410.35*** *p61*
Nilsson, Ola; Minneapolis, 1882-1887 ***6410.35*** *p61*
Nilsson, Pehr; Minneapolis, 1870-1886 ***6410.35*** *p52*
Nilsson, Tue; Maine, 1871-1882 ***6410.22*** *p119*
Nimal, William; America, 1868 ***1450.2*** *p108A*
Nimel, William; America, 1868 ***1450.2*** *p108A*
Nimfe, Charles; Virginia, 1642 ***6219*** *p197*
Nimmo, David 21; Quebec, 1859 ***5704.8*** *p143*
Nimmo, Thomas; Arkansas, 1918 ***95.2*** *p90*
Nimmock, Eliza; Philadelphia, 1849 ***53.26*** *p74*
Nimmock, Eliza; Philadelphia, 1849 ***5704.8*** *p52*
Ninghton, Margaret; Quebec, 1825 ***7603*** *p93*
Nino, Luigi Bianco 28; New York, NY, 1893 ***9026.4*** *p42*
Nipper, Bernard Heinrich; America, 1851 ***8582.3*** *p48*
Nipper, Bernhard Heinrich; Cincinnati, 1845 ***8582.1*** *p26*
Nipper, Bernhard Heinrich; Cincinnati, 1869-1887 ***8582*** *p22*
Nis, Charles; Virginia, 1855 ***4626.16*** *p15*
Nisbet, David 30; St. John, N.B., 1866 ***5704.8*** *p166*
Nisbet of Dean, Alexander; South Carolina, 1721 ***1639.20*** *p255*
Nish, James 46; St. John, N.B., 1866 ***5704.8*** *p167*
Nish, William 19; St. John, N.B., 1866 ***5704.8*** *p166*
Nislerin, Catherine; South Carolina, 1752-1753 ***3689.17*** *p22*
Nissen, Lauritz; Washington, 1859-1920 ***2872.1*** *p28*
Nissen, Niels Andersen; New York, 1892 ***1450.2*** *p27B*
Nissen, Peter 34; California, 1867 ***3840.3*** *p8*
Nisski, . . .; Canada, 1776-1783 ***9786*** *p30*
Nissky, . . .; Canada, 1776-1783 ***9786*** *p30*
Nitingale, Eliza.; Virginia, 1643 ***6219*** *p229*
Nitke, Nathan; Colorado, 1889 ***9678.2*** *p130*
Nitsche, Anna Maria; New York, 1749 ***3652*** *p73*
Nitsche, Michael 20; New Orleans, 1839 ***9420.2*** *p71*
Nitschmann, Anna; New York, 1761 ***3652*** *p88*
Nitschmann, Anna; Philadelphia, 1740 ***3652*** *p52*
Nitschmann, David; New York, 1749 ***3652*** *p71*
*Wife:*Rosina
Nitschmann, David; Savannah, GA, 1736 ***3652*** *p51*
Nitschmann, David, Sr.; New York, 1754 ***3652*** *p78*
Nitschmann, David, Sr.; Philadelphia, 1740 ***3652*** *p52*
Nitschmann, Emanuel; New York, 1761 ***3652*** *p88*
Nitschmann, John; New York, 1749 ***3652*** *p71*
*Wife:*Juliana
Nitschmann, Juliana *SEE* Nitschmann, John
Nitschmann, Martin; New York, 1749 ***3652*** *p72*
Nitschmann, Rosina *SEE* Nitschmann, David
Nitschmann, Rosina; Philadelphia, 1741 ***3652*** *p52*
Nitshke, Frank 34; Kansas, 1878 ***5240.1*** *p32*
Nitshke, Frank 34; Kansas, 1878 ***5240.1*** *p59*
Nitzschke, Julius 33; New Orleans, 1839 ***9420.2*** *p166*
Niven, Alexander; Arkansas, 1918 ***95.2*** *p90*
Niven, Duncan 63; North Carolina, 1850 ***1639.20*** *p255*
*Relative:*Flora 63
Niven, Flora 63 *SEE* Niven, Duncan
Niven, Patrick; New York, NY, 1816 ***2859.11*** *p40*
Niven, Robert; St. John, N.B., 1866 ***5704.8*** *p167*
Nix, . . .; Canada, 1776-1783 ***9786*** *p30*
Nix, Elizabeth; America, 1755-1828 ***1639.20*** *p37*
Nixdorf, John G.; New York, 1743 ***3652*** *p60*
Nixon, . . . 4 mos; New York, NY, 1868 ***5704.8*** *p228*
Nixon, Alexander; Philadelphia, 1867 ***5704.8*** *p215*
Nixon, Andrew; St. John, N.B., 1847 ***5704.8*** *p3*
Nixon, Anne J.; New York, NY, 1868 ***5704.8*** *p228*
Nixon, Charles; New York, NY, 1868 ***5704.8*** *p228*
Nixon, Eliza; New York, NY, 1866 ***5704.8*** *p205*
Nixon, Eliza; Quebec, 1849 ***5704.8*** *p51*
Nixon, Eliza; St. John, N.B., 1847 ***5704.8*** *p3*
Nixon, Ellen; New York, NY, 1870 ***5704.8*** *p239*
Nixon, Fanny 40; Philadelphia, 1861 ***5704.8*** *p148*
Nixon, George; New York, NY, 1811 ***2859.11*** *p18*
With family
Nixon, Hugh; Philadelphia, 1792 ***9892.11*** *p35*
Nixon, Isabella; Philadelphia, 1853 ***5704.8*** *p100*
Nixon, James; Philadelphia, 1853 ***5704.8*** *p100*
Nixon, James; Philadelphia, 1853 ***5704.8*** *p108*
Nixon, Jane; St. John, N.B., 1847 ***5704.8*** *p3*
Nixon, John; Philadelphia, 1864 ***5704.8*** *p188*
Nixon, Joseph; Philadelphia, 1852 ***5704.8*** *p88*
Nixon, Margaret; Quebec, 1849 ***5704.8*** *p51*
Nixon, Martha; St. John, N.B., 1847 ***5704.8*** *p3*
Nixon, Martha; St. John, N.B., 1853 ***5704.8*** *p107*
Nixon, Mary; New York, NY, 1811 ***2859.11*** *p18*
Nixon, Mary Ann; Quebec, 1849 ***5704.8*** *p52*
Nixon, Mary Jane; Philadelphia, 1853 ***5704.8*** *p100*
Nixon, Rebecca; New York, NY, 1868 ***5704.8*** *p228*
Nixon, Rebecca J.; New York, NY, 1868 ***5704.8*** *p228*
Nixon, Richard 25; New York, 1775 ***1219.7*** *p268*
With wife
Nixon, Samuel; Philadelphia, 1853 ***5704.8*** *p100*
Nixon, Samuel 22; Kansas, 1880 ***5240.1*** *p62*
Nixon, Thomas; St. John, N.B., 1852 ***5704.8*** *p95*
Nixon, William; Philadelphia, 1792 ***9892.11*** *p35*
Nixon, William 3; New York, NY, 1868 ***5704.8*** *p228*
Nizetich, Visko; Wisconsin, n.d. ***9675.7*** *p129*
No, Adele 32; Port uncertain, 1839 ***778.5*** *p404*
No, Adele 32; Port uncertain, 1839 ***778.5*** *p405*
No, Antoine 37; Port uncertain, 1839 ***778.5*** *p405*
Noal, Andy 60; Arizona, 1913 ***9228.40*** *p17*
Nobbe, Herman; America, 1848 ***8582.1*** *p26*
Nobbs, Henry 18; Jamaica, 1733 ***3690.1*** *p166*
Nobes, John; Quebec, 1841 ***4535.10*** *p198*
With family
Nobile, Ambrogio; Iowa, 1866-1943 ***123.54*** *p71*

Nobile, Carlo; Iowa, 1866-1943 ***123.54*** *p36*
Nobile, Guido; Iowa, 1866-1943 ***123.54*** *p71*
Nobile, John; Nevada, 1876 ***2764.35*** *p50*
Nobile, Liugi; Iowa, 1866-1943 ***123.54*** *p71*
Nobile, Nick; Nevada, 1868 ***2764.35*** *p51*
Nobille, Guido; Iowa, 1866-1943 ***123.54*** *p71*
Noble, Alex; Quebec, 1852 ***5704.8*** *p90*
Noble, Alexander; Quebec, 1852 ***5704.8*** *p86*
Noble, Anne; Philadelphia, 1866 ***5704.8*** *p210*
Noble, Catharine; Philadelphia, 1852 ***5704.8*** *p88*
Noble, Charles; Quebec, 1852 ***5704.8*** *p90*
Noble, Daniel 44; Quebec, 1864 ***5704.8*** *p163*
Noble, Eliza; Quebec, 1842 ***4537.30*** *p96*
Noble, Eliza 11; Quebec, 1847 ***5704.8*** *p16*
Noble, Henry; Quebec, 1851 ***5704.8*** *p75*
Noble, James 7; Quebec, 1864 ***5704.8*** *p163*
Noble, James 20; Georgia, 1734 ***3690.1*** *p166*
Noble, James Alexander; Philadelphia, 1853 ***5704.8*** *p103*
Noble, Jane; Quebec, 1852 ***5704.8*** *p86*
Noble, Jane; Quebec, 1852 ***5704.8*** *p90*
Noble, John; Illinois, 1876 ***5012.37*** *p60*
Noble, John; Philadelphia, 1852 ***5704.8*** *p88*
Noble, John; Philadelphia, 1865 ***5704.8*** *p202*
Noble, John; Quebec, 1852 ***5704.8*** *p86*
Noble, John; Quebec, 1852 ***5704.8*** *p90*
Noble, John 1; Quebec, 1864 ***5704.8*** *p163*
Noble, John 17; St. John, N.B., 1856 ***5704.8*** *p131*
Noble, Margaret 18; Philadelphia, 1861 ***5704.8*** *p147*
Noble, Mark 19; Maryland or Virginia, 1720 ***3690.1*** *p166*
Noble, Mary 5; Quebec, 1864 ***5704.8*** *p163*
Noble, Mary 38; Quebec, 1864 ***5704.8*** *p163*
Noble, Mary Ann; Quebec, 1851 ***5704.8*** *p74*
Noble, Mary Ann 9; Quebec, 1847 ***5704.8*** *p16*
Noble, Michaell; Virginia, 1643 ***6219*** *p203*
Noble, Peter; Boston, 1776 ***1219.7*** *p277*
Noble, Robert 11; Quebec, 1864 ***5704.8*** *p163*
Noble, Sarah 10; Quebec, 1864 ***5704.8*** *p163*
Noble, Sarah Jane; Philadelphia, 1853 ***5704.8*** *p103*
Noble, William; New York, NY, 1837 ***8208.4*** *p33*
Noble, William; Quebec, 1852 ***5704.8*** *p86*
Noble, William; St. John, N.B., 1848 ***5704.8*** *p39*
Noble, William; Virginia, 1640 ***6219*** *p160*
Noble, William John 5; Quebec, 1864 ***5704.8*** *p163*
Noble, Wm.; Virginia, 1637 ***6219*** *p116*
Noblesse, Mr. 34; New Orleans, 1836 ***778.5*** *p405*
Noblesse, Mrs. 22; New Orleans, 1835 ***778.5*** *p405*
Noblett, Robt; Virginia, 1698 ***2212*** *p14*
Noblig, Adam; Pennsylvania, 1754 ***2444*** *p176*
Nobmann, Friedrich; Wisconsin, n.d. ***9675.7*** *p129*
Noddin, Michael; Nova Scotia, 1774 ***1219.7*** *p210*
Noddings, George; Charleston, SC, 1768 ***1219.7*** *p137*
Noe, . . .; Canada, 1776-1783 ***9786*** *p30*
Noedel, Jost; New Jersey, 1777 ***8137*** *p12*
Noel, . . .; Canada, 1776-1783 ***9786*** *p43*
Noel, Mr. 17; Port uncertain, 1838 ***778.5*** *p405*
Noel, Mr. 36; America, 1838 ***778.5*** *p405*
Noel, Alonge 25; America, 1836 ***778.5*** *p405*
Noel, Edouard; Quebec, 1797 ***7603*** *p49*
Noel, Ernst Heinrich Friedrich; America, 1860 ***4610.10*** *p99*
Noelke, Frederick; America, 1866 ***1450.2*** *p108A*
Noell, Henry; Ohio, 1819 ***8582.1*** *p47*
Noerenberg, Fredrick; Wisconsin, n.d. ***9675.7*** *p129*
Noesen, Martin; Wisconsin, n.d. ***9675.7*** *p129*
Noesen, Theodore; Wisconsin, n.d. ***9675.7*** *p129*
Noffke, Frank; New York, NY, 1881 ***1450.2*** *p28B*
Noffke, Otto H.; Baltimore, 1889 ***1450.2*** *p28B*
Nofftz, Charles; Illinois, 1859 ***5012.38*** *p97*
Nogera, Aliche; Arkansas, 1918 ***95.2*** *p90*
Nogleo, John 76; Arizona, 1925 ***9228.40*** *p29*
Nohe, Michael; Illinois, 1848 ***7857*** *p6*
Nohra, . . .; Canada, 1776-1783 ***9786*** *p43*
Noigh, . . .; Canada, 1776-1783 ***9786*** *p30*
Noilhan, Mr. 26; Port uncertain, 1836 ***778.5*** *p405*
Nol, . . .; Canada, 1776-1783 ***9786*** *p30*
Nolan, Edward; California, 1866 ***2769.7*** *p3*
Nolan, Eleanor 12; Maryland, 1736 ***3690.1*** *p166*
Nolan, James; Nebraska, 1886 ***5240.1*** *p32*
Nolan, John; America, 1890 ***1450.2*** *p28B*
Nolan, M. H.; Shreveport, LA, 1876 ***7129*** *p45*
Nolan, Martin; Nevada, 1873 ***2764.35*** *p50*
Nolan, P.; New York, NY, 1816 ***2859.11*** *p40*
Nolan, P. W. 30; Kansas, 1887 ***5240.1*** *p32*
Nolan, P. W. 30; Kansas, 1887 ***5240.1*** *p70*
Nolan, Robert; Quebec, 1851 ***5704.8*** *p73*
Nolan, Thomas; Illinois, 1894 ***5012.40*** *p53*
Noland, Miss; America, 1869 ***5704.8*** *p234*
Noland, Edward 65; Arizona, 1885 ***9228.40*** *p1*
Noland, William 28; Kansas, 1902 ***5240.1*** *p82*
Nolbrow, William 28; Maryland, 1774 ***1219.7*** *p221*
Nolde, Adam; Wisconsin, n.d. ***9675.7*** *p129*
Noldener, George; Indiana, 1835 ***1450.2*** *p108A*
Noll, Anton; Philadelphia, 1744 ***8125.6*** *p22*
Noll, Francis; Philadelphia, 1761 ***9973.7*** *p35*
Noll, Johann 2; America, 1838 ***778.5*** *p405*
Noll, Johannetta 1; America, 1838 ***778.5*** *p405*
Noll, Johannetta 26; America, 1838 ***778.5*** *p405*
Noll, Justus P.; New York, NY, 1818 ***8208.4*** *p26*
Noll, Mattias; Philadelphia, 1744 ***8125.6*** *p22*
Noll, Peter; Cincinnati, 1869-1887 ***8582*** *p22*
Noll, Philippe 29; America, 1838 ***778.5*** *p405*
Noll, William; Kansas, 1896 ***5240.1*** *p32*
Noll, William 27; Philadelphia, 1774 ***1219.7*** *p232*
Noller, Joseph; Wisconsin, n.d. ***9675.7*** *p129*
Nolner, John; Petersburg, VA, 1812 ***4778.2*** *p142*
Nolon, Nancy; New York, NY, 1865 ***5704.8*** *p195*
Nolonier, Mr. 40; Grenada, 1774 ***1219.7*** *p245*
Nolte, . . .; Canada, 1776-1783 ***9786*** *p43*
Nolte, Georg Ludwig; America, 1847 ***8582.3*** *p48*
Nolte, Gurvais 30; New Orleans, 1831 ***778.5*** *p405*
Nolte, Johann B. H.; America, 1839 ***8582.3*** *p48*
Nolting, Mr.; America, 1844 ***4610.10*** *p134*
*Wife:*Anna M Engel Eickmeyer
*Child:*A. M. Wilhelmine Engel 15
*Child:*A. M. Catharina Engel 2
Nolting, A. M. Catharina Engel 2 *SEE* Nolting, Mr.
Nolting, A. M. Wilhelmine Engel 15 *SEE* Nolting, Mr.
Nolting, Anna M Engel Eickmeyer *SEE* Nolting, Mr.
Nolting, Anna Marie Engel *SEE* Nolting, Johann Daniel Heinrich
Nolting, Anna Marie Engel *SEE* Nolting, Johann Heinrich
Nolting, Anne Marie L. Kemena *SEE* Nolting, Johann Daniel Heinrich
Nolting, Anne Marie Louise *SEE* Nolting, Johann Daniel Heinrich
Nolting, Anne Marie W. Engel *SEE* Nolting, Carl Heinrich
Nolting, Anne Marie Wilhelmine *SEE* Nolting, Johann Daniel Heinrich
Nolting, Car. Friedrich; America, 1844 ***4610.10*** *p134*
*Wife:*Wilh. C. Friederike
*Child:*Heinrich C. Friedrich
*Child:*Carl Friedrich August
*Child:*Marie L. Engel Wilh.
*Child:*Marie Wilh. Engel
Nolting, Carl Friedrich August *SEE* Nolting, Car. Friedrich
Nolting, Carl Heinrich *SEE* Nolting, Carl Heinrich
Nolting, Carl Heinrich; America, 1850 ***4610.10*** *p143*
*Wife:*Marie M. I. Griemert
*Child:*Anne Marie W. Engel
*Child:*Christoph Heinrich
*Child:*Carl Heinrich
Nolting, Carl Heinrich F. *SEE* Nolting, Johann Heinrich
Nolting, Christine; America, 1843 ***4610.10*** *p141*
Nolting, Christoph H. Carl Camuel 35; America, 1854 ***4610.10*** *p144*
With wife
*Child:*Wilhelmine
*Child:*Louise
*Child:*Hermann Heinrich Carl
Nolting, Christoph Heinrich *SEE* Nolting, Carl Heinrich
Nolting, Christoph Heinrich *SEE* Nolting, Johann Daniel Heinrich
Nolting, Emil Adolph; America, 1859 ***4610.10*** *p123*
Nolting, Friederike Henriette Louise; America, 1855 ***4610.10*** *p116*
Nolting, Heinrich C. Friedrich *SEE* Nolting, Car. Friedrich
Nolting, Henry Christian; America, 1847 ***1450.2*** *p108A*
Nolting, Hermann Heinrich Carl *SEE* Nolting, Christoph H. Carl Camuel
Nolting, Johann Daniel Heinrich 47; America, 1850 ***4610.10*** *p143*
*Wife:*Anne Marie L. Kemena
*Child:*Anne Marie Louise
*Child:*Anna Marie Engel
*Child:*Johann Friedrich
*Child:*Johann Heinrich
*Child:*Christoph Heinrich
*Child:*Anne Marie Wilhelmine
Nolting, Johann Friedrich *SEE* Nolting, Johann Daniel Heinrich
Nolting, Johann Heinrich *SEE* Nolting, Johann Daniel Heinrich
Nolting, Johann Heinrich; America, 1844 ***4610.10*** *p141*
*Wife:*Anna Marie Engel
*Child:*Carl Heinrich F.
*Child:*Peter Friedrich W.
Nolting, John; New York, NY, 1869 ***1450.2*** *p28B*
Nolting, John; Virginia, 1855 ***4626.16*** *p15*
Nolting, Louise *SEE* Nolting, Christoph H. Carl Camuel
Nolting, Margaretha; Wisconsin, n.d. ***9675.7*** *p129*
Nolting, Marie L. Engel Wilh. *SEE* Nolting, Car. Friedrich
Nolting, Marie M. I. Griemert *SEE* Nolting, Carl Heinrich
Nolting, Marie Wilh. Engel *SEE* Nolting, Car. Friedrich
Nolting, Peter Friedrich W. *SEE* Nolting, Johann Heinrich
Nolting, Wilh. C. Friederike *SEE* Nolting, Car. Friedrich
Nolting, Wilhelmine *SEE* Nolting, Christoph H. Carl Camuel
Nolton, James; Philadelphia, 1855 ***1450.2*** *p108A*
Nomann, John 24; Kansas, 1883 ***5240.1*** *p64*
Nomasin, Marie 25; Louisiana, 1833 ***778.5*** *p405*
Nomellini, Carlo; New York, NY, 1906 ***3455.3*** *p47*
*Wife:*Rose
Nomellini, Frank Hugo; New York, NY, 1920 ***3455.4*** *p27*
Nomellini, Rose *SEE* Nomellini, Carlo
Nominacker, J. 32; New Orleans, 1831 ***778.5*** *p406*
Nonan, Patrick; America, 1741 ***4971*** *p38*
Nondre, M.-Barbe; Quebec, 1761 ***7603*** *p22*
Nonemaker, Ludwig; Pennsylvania, 1751 ***2444*** *p197*
Nongesser, . . .; Canada, 1776-1783 ***9786*** *p30*
Nonis, George 23; Philadelphia, 1775 ***1219.7*** *p274*
Nonnamaker, Lodwick; Pennsylvania, 1751 ***2444*** *p197*
Nonne, Mike; Arkansas, 1918 ***95.2*** *p90*
Nonnenmacher, Anna Margaretha *SEE* Nonnenmacher, Hans Ludwig
Nonnenmacher, Anna Maria *SEE* Nonnenmacher, Hans Ludwig
Nonnenmacher, Hans Ludwig; Pennsylvania, 1751 ***2444*** *p174*
Nonnenmacher, Hans Ludwig; Pennsylvania, 1751 ***2444*** *p197*
*Wife:*Anna Maria
*Child:*Heinrich
*Child:*Johann Adam
*Child:*Anna Margaretha
Nonnenmacher, Heinrich *SEE* Nonnenmacher, Hans Ludwig
Nonnenmacher, Johann Adam *SEE* Nonnenmacher, Hans Ludwig
Nonsette, Peter 16; Pennsylvania, 1728 ***3690.1*** *p166*
Noon, Daniel 22; Philadelphia, 1858 ***5704.8*** *p139*
Noon, Edward 14; Massachusetts, 1849 ***5881.1*** *p78*
Noon, Margaret; New York, NY, 1867 ***5704.8*** *p223*
Noon, Mary A.; Philadelphia, 1870 ***5704.8*** *p239*
Noon, Patrick 20; Massachusetts, 1849 ***5881.1*** *p78*
Noonan, Andrew 17; Massachusetts, 1848 ***5881.1*** *p77*
Noonan, Cornelius; New York, NY, 1838 ***8208.4*** *p84*
Noonan, Daniel; America, 1741 ***4971*** *p61*
Noonan, Edward 17; Massachusetts, 1849 ***5881.1*** *p78*
Noonan, James Patrick 36; California, 1868 ***3840.3*** *p8*
Noonan, John 20; Massachusetts, 1849 ***5881.1*** *p78*
Noonan, Judy 18; Massachusetts, 1850 ***5881.1*** *p78*
Noonan, Martin 18; Massachusetts, 1849 ***5881.1*** *p78*
Noonan, Mary 16; Massachusetts, 1848 ***5881.1*** *p78*
Noonan, Mary Ann 24; Massachusetts, 1849 ***5881.1*** *p78*
Noonan, Maurice 22; Massachusetts, 1849 ***5881.1*** *p78*
Noonane, Ally; America, 1739 ***4971*** *p56*
Noone, John; New York, NY, 1816 ***2859.11*** *p40*
Nooney, Patrick; Illinois, 1855 ***7857*** *p6*
Norakovic, Embro; Iowa, 1866-1943 ***123.54*** *p36*
Noray, Julien 25; New Orleans, 1825 ***778.5*** *p406*
Norbut, Peter; Wisconsin, n.d. ***9675.7*** *p129*
Norby, Henry Rudolph; Arkansas, 1918 ***95.2*** *p90*
Norcott, Wm.; Virginia, 1637 ***6219*** *p114*
Norcutt, Wm.; Virginia, 1637 ***6219*** *p11*
Nordberg, Otto; Washington, 1859-1920 ***2872.1*** *p28*
Nordeck, Lieutenant; Nicaragua, 1856 ***8582.3*** *p31*
Nordello, Luigi; Arkansas, 1918 ***95.2*** *p90*
Nordemann, Francis; Virginia, 1855 ***4626.16*** *p15*
Norden, Nils M.; Minneapolis, 1880 ***6410.35*** *p62*
Norden, Walton; Virginia, 1637 ***6219*** *p112*
Nordenberg, Oliver; Illinois, 1888 ***5012.39*** *p121*
Norder, Himke *SEE* Norder, Reinhardt
Norder, Reinhardt; Baltimore, 1892 ***3455.3*** *p19*
*Wife:*Himke
Nordgren, John A.; Minneapolis, 1882-1885 ***6410.35*** *p62*
Nordhaus, Henry; Iroquois Co., IL, 1892 ***3455.1*** *p12*
Nordkvist, W.A.; Iowa, 1866-1943 ***123.54*** *p36*
Nordlohne, Johannes; America, 1846 ***8582.3*** *p49*
Nordman, Alfred Hoenry; Arkansas, 1918 ***95.2*** *p91*
Nordmann, Wilhelm H.; Ohio, 1869-1887 ***8582*** *p22*
Nordquist, Wentzel Albin; Iowa, 1866-1943 ***123.54*** *p36*
Nordsick, Frederick; New York, NY, 1898 ***1450.2*** *p28B*
Nordstrom, C.; Minneapolis, 1883-1886 ***6410.35*** *p62*
Nordstrom, C. H.; Washington, 1859-1920 ***2872.1*** *p28*
Nordstrom, Frank; Minneapolis, 1880-1886 ***6410.35*** *p62*
Nordstrom, J. W.; Minneapolis, 1880-1887 ***6410.35*** *p62*
Nordstrom, N.; Minneapolis, 1872-1886 ***6410.35*** *p62*
Nordstrom, Nils J.; New York, NY, 1835 ***8208.4*** *p45*
Nordvik, J. J.; Washington, 1859-1920 ***2872.1*** *p29*
Nordvik, Jake Jakobsen; Washington, 1859-1920 ***2872.1*** *p29*

Noreika, Kazimier; Wisconsin, n.d. ***9675.7*** *p129*
Noreika, Ludwig; Wisconsin, n.d. ***9675.7*** *p129*
Norelli, Minna; Washington, 1859-1920 ***2872.1*** *p29*
Noren, August; Minneapolis, 1881-1884 ***6410.35*** *p62*
Noren, Iver J.; Illinois, 1892 ***5012.40*** *p27*
Norenberg, Carl Gottlieb; Wisconsin, n.d. ***9675.7*** *p129*
Nores, Hypolite 22; America, 1838 ***778.5*** *p406*
Noresco, Ginseppe 30; New York, NY, 1893 ***9026.4*** *p42*
*Relative:*Luigia 25
Noresco, Luigia 25 *SEE* Noresco, Ginseppe
Norey, Alex.; Virginia, 1636 ***6219*** *p21*
Norgaard, Andrew Andersen; Arkansas, 1918 ***95.2*** *p91*
Norgard, Catherina; Washington, 1859-1920 ***2872.1*** *p29*
Norgard, Matt; Washington, 1859-1920 ***2872.1*** *p29*
Norgard, Rosa Hazel; Washington, 1859-1920 ***2872.1*** *p29*
Norgard, Ruth Agnes; Washington, 1859-1920 ***2872.1*** *p29*
Norgate, Thomas 27; Barbados, 1730 ***3690.1*** *p166*
Norgate, Thomas 27; Jamaica, 1730 ***3690.1*** *p166*
Norkus, Frank; Arkansas, 1918 ***95.2*** *p91*
Norkus, Ignac; Wisconsin, n.d. ***9675.7*** *p129*
Norkus, Powel; Wisconsin, n.d. ***9675.7*** *p129*
Normaly, John; Illinois, 1888 ***5012.39*** *p121*
Norman, . . .; Canada, 1776-1783 ***9786*** *p43*
Norman, Ann 1; Massachusetts, 1847 ***5881.1*** *p77*
Norman, Ann 40; Massachusetts, 1847 ***5881.1*** *p77*
Norman, Austice; Virginia, 1637 ***6219*** *p13*
Norman, Charlotte 21; Massachusetts, 1860 ***6410.32*** *p116*
Norman, Edward 40; Massachusetts, 1847 ***5881.1*** *p77*
Norman, Hen.; Virginia, 1637 ***6219*** *p13*
Norman, Henry; Virginia, 1642 ***6219*** *p190*
Norman, James 21; Kansas, 1873 ***5240.1*** *p53*
Norman, John; Minneapolis, 1869-1877 ***6410.35*** *p62*
Norman, John; New York, NY, 1838 ***8208.4*** *p89*
Norman, John 18; Maryland, 1774 ***1219.7*** *p220*
Norman, John 22; Philadelphia, 1774 ***1219.7*** *p216*
Norman, Joseph; America, 1829 ***1450.2*** *p108A*
Norman, L.J. 24; Harris Co., TX, 1896 ***6254*** *p3*
Norman, Mary; America, 1697 ***2212*** *p9*
Norman, Mary; Virginia, 1636 ***6219*** *p13*
Norman, Mary; Virginia, 1636 ***6219*** *p146*
Norman, Peter; Virginia, 1636 ***6219*** *p13*
Norman, Peter; Virginia, 1636 ***6219*** *p146*
Norman, Peter; Virginia, 1637 ***6219*** *p13*
Norman, Vincent 37; New Orleans, 1829 ***778.5*** *p406*
Normand, Eugene 28; New Orleans, 1838 ***778.5*** *p406*
Normand, F. M. F. 23; New Orleans, 1823 ***778.5*** *p406*
Normandin, Clara 29; America, 1839 ***778.5*** *p406*
Normandin, J. 38; America, 1839 ***778.5*** *p406*
Normandin, V. 41; America, 1838 ***778.5*** *p406*
Normandly, Patrick; Illinois, 1888 ***5012.39*** *p122*
Normanly, John; Illinois, 1888 ***5012.39*** *p121*
Normann, . . .; Canada, 1776-1783 ***9786*** *p43*
Normann, Benjamin; Illinois, 1888 ***5012.39*** *p52*
Normmand, Mr. 37; America, 1835 ***778.5*** *p406*
Norquette, Jean; Quebec, 1791 ***7603*** *p24*
Norquist, Erland Amandus; Iowa, 1866-1943 ***123.54*** *p36*
Norrell, Peeter; Virginia, 1648 ***6219*** *p250*
Norrice, Thomas; Virginia, 1643 ***6219*** *p206*
Norris, Alexander 1; Quebec, 1848 ***5704.8*** *p41*
Norris, Andrew; Boston, 1753 ***1219.7*** *p22*
Norris, Ann 17; Baltimore, 1775 ***1219.7*** *p269*
Norris, Arthur 16; Maryland, 1729 ***3690.1*** *p167*
Norris, Catherine; America, 1743 ***4971*** *p18*
Norris, David; America, 1741 ***4971*** *p60*
Norris, Elizabeth; Quebec, 1852 ***5704.8*** *p89*
Norris, Hugh 8; Quebec, 1848 ***5704.8*** *p41*
Norris, Hugh 17; Maryland, 1775 ***1219.7*** *p272*
Norris, Jacob; Virginia, 1639 ***6219*** *p153*
Norris, James; New York, NY, 1836 ***8208.4*** *p21*
Norris, James; Quebec, 1848 ***5704.8*** *p41*
Norris, John 5; Quebec, 1848 ***5704.8*** *p41*
Norris, John 16; Philadelphia, 1803 ***53.26*** *p74*
Norris, John 17; Jamaica, 1736 ***3690.1*** *p167*
Norris, John 20; Philadelphia, 1865 ***5704.8*** *p165*
Norris, John 26; Jamaica, 1731 ***3690.1*** *p167*
Norris, Joseph 11; Quebec, 1848 ***5704.8*** *p41*
Norris, Margaret; Quebec, 1848 ***5704.8*** *p41*
Norris, Martha; Philadelphia, 1851 ***5704.8*** *p78*
Norris, Mary *SEE* Norris, Robert
Norris, Mary; Philadelphia, 1811 ***53.26*** *p74*
Norris, Mary; Philadelphia, 1811 ***2859.11*** *p18*
Norris, Mary; St. John, N.B., 1847 ***5704.8*** *p26*
Norris, Maurice; America, 1741 ***4971*** *p60*
Norris, Rebecca; Quebec, 1848 ***5704.8*** *p41*
Norris, Richard; Virginia, 1643 ***6219*** *p199*
Norris, Robert; Philadelphia, 1811 ***53.26*** *p74*
*Relative:*Mary
Norris, Robert; Philadelphia, 1811 ***2859.11*** *p18*
Norris, Robert; Quebec, 1848 ***5704.8*** *p41*
Norris, Sarah 13; Quebec, 1848 ***5704.8*** *p41*
Norris, Thomas; Virginia, 1647 ***6219*** *p241*
Norris, Thomas 4; St. John, N.B., 1847 ***5704.8*** *p26*
Norris, William; St. John, N.B., 1847 ***5704.8*** *p26*
Norris, William 3; Quebec, 1848 ***5704.8*** *p41*
Norris, William 19; Maryland, 1729 ***3690.1*** *p167*
Norrison, John 36; Maryland, 1775 ***1219.7*** *p264*
Norrman, Anders; Iowa, 1847 ***2090*** *p609*
With wife
Norrman, Andrew Bernhard; Bangor, ME, 1871-1876 ***6410.22*** *p115*
Norry, Alexander 7; Philadelphia, 1851 ***5704.8*** *p80*
Norry, David 16; Philadelphia, 1853 ***5704.8*** *p111*
Norry, Elizabeth 3 mos; Philadelphia, 1851 ***5704.8*** *p80*
Norry, Fanny; New York, NY, 1869 ***5704.8*** *p234*
Norry, James; Philadelphia, 1850 ***5704.8*** *p69*
Norry, James 11; Philadelphia, 1851 ***5704.8*** *p80*
Norry, Margaret 20; Philadelphia, 1853 ***5704.8*** *p111*
Norry, Margaret Ann; Philadelphia, 1851 ***5704.8*** *p80*
Norry, Matilda; Philadelphia, 1851 ***5704.8*** *p80*
Norry, May 2; Philadelphia, 1851 ***5704.8*** *p80*
Norry, Robert 9; Philadelphia, 1851 ***5704.8*** *p80*
Norry, Samuel; Philadelphia, 1851 ***5704.8*** *p80*
Norry, Sarah; St. John, N.B., 1847 ***5704.8*** *p26*
Norry, William 5; Philadelphia, 1851 ***5704.8*** *p80*
Norse, Leopold; Boston, 1800-1877 ***8582.3*** *p92*
North, Edward; Virginia, 1637 ***6219*** *p117*
North, George 22; Maryland or Virginia, 1733 ***3690.1*** *p167*
North, Henry 18; Maryland, 1733 ***3690.1*** *p167*
North, John; Virginia, 1636 ***6219*** *p21*
North, John; Virginia, 1642 ***6219*** *p188*
North, Sarah 27; Maryland, 1775 ***1219.7*** *p261*
Northall, William Knight; New York, NY, 1837 ***8208.4*** *p54*
Northerne, John; Virginia, 1636 ***6219*** *p80*
Northey, William 37; Maryland, 1775 ***1219.7*** *p273*
Northgraves, Guillaume; Quebec, 1817 ***7603*** *p29*
Northon, Toby; Virginia, 1647 ***6219*** *p244*
Northumb, Martin; Illinois, 1874 ***7857*** *p6*
Norton, Major; Quebec, 1815 ***9229.18*** *p81*
With wife
Norton, Ann *SEE* Norton, John
Norton, Bridget 11; Massachusetts, 1849 ***5881.1*** *p77*
Norton, Bryan 30; Massachusetts, 1847 ***5881.1*** *p77*
Norton, Catharine 15; Massachusetts, 1847 ***5881.1*** *p77*
Norton, Catherine; St. John, N.B., 1847 ***5704.8*** *p26*
Norton, Daniel; Illinois, 1861 ***2896.5*** *p29*
Norton, Harry B.; Illinois, 1892 ***5012.37*** *p62*
Norton, Jean; Quebec, 1823 ***7603*** *p28*
Norton, John; San Francisco, 1850 ***4914.15*** *p10*
Norton, John; Virginia, 1643 ***6219*** *p23*
*Wife:*Ann
Norton, John 19; Pennsylvania, 1731 ***3690.1*** *p161*
Norton, John 21; Georgia, 1774 ***1219.7*** *p188*
Norton, John 25; Massachusetts, 1860 ***6410.32*** *p113*
Norton, John 30; Maryland, 1774 ***1219.7*** *p180*
Norton, Joseph; America, 1735-1743 ***4971*** *p8*
Norton, Margaret; Virginia, 1647 ***6219*** *p244*
Norton, Martin; New York, NY, 1838 ***8208.4*** *p69*
Norton, Mary; America, 1737 ***4971*** *p13*
Norton, Mary 18; Massachusetts, 1847 ***5881.1*** *p78*
Norton, Mary 55; Massachusetts, 1847 ***5881.1*** *p78*
Norton, Nathaniel 26; Maryland, 1774 ***1219.7*** *p235*
Norton, Patrick; New York, NY, 1836 ***8208.4*** *p11*
Norton, Patrick 15; Massachusetts, 1847 ***5881.1*** *p78*
Norton, Robert 23; Grenada, 1774 ***1219.7*** *p178*
Norton, Stephen A.; Illinois, 1887 ***5012.39*** *p52*
Norton, Stephen A.; Illinois, 1888 ***5012.37*** *p60*
Norton, Thomas Frederick 27; Philadelphia, 1774 ***1219.7*** *p176*
Norton, William 22; Pennsylvania, 1728 ***3690.1*** *p167*
Norton, Wm.; Virginia, 1635 ***6219*** *p26*
Norton, Wm.; Virginia, 1637 ***6219*** *p83*
Norton, Xtopr.; Virginia, 1648 ***6219*** *p241*
Norts, Ma.; Virginia, 1647 ***6219*** *p248*
Norvaski, Alexander; Kentucky, 1839-1840 ***8582.3*** *p99*
Norway, John; Virginia, 1638 ***6219*** *p159*
Norwell, Wm.; Virginia, 1639 ***6219*** *p22*
Norwood, Charles; West Indies, 1770 ***1219.7*** *p144*
Norwood, John; New Orleans, 1836 ***778.5*** *p406*
Norwood, Richard; Virginia, 1643 ***6219*** *p204*
Noser, Joseph; New York, NY, 1838 ***8208.4*** *p67*
Nosse, Wm.; Virginia, 1636 ***6219*** *p77*
Noster, . . .; Canada, 1776-1783 ***9786*** *p43*
Nosworthy, Ann *SEE* Nosworthy, Tristrum
Nosworthy, Tristrum; Virginia, 1656 ***6219*** *p22*
*Wife:*Ann
Noth, . . .; Canada, 1776-1783 ***9786*** *p30*
Notley, Peter 27; Maryland, 1774 ***1219.7*** *p180*
Noto, Luizi 30; Arkansas, 1918 ***95.2*** *p91*
Nott, James; New York, NY, 1835 ***8208.4*** *p40*
Notter, Robert 20; Maryland, 1722 ***3690.1*** *p167*
Notting, Bernard; Wisconsin, n.d. ***9675.7*** *p129*
Notting, Michael; Wisconsin, n.d. ***9675.7*** *p129*
Nottmeir, Charles; America, 1837-1840 ***1450.2*** *p108A*
Notton, Jon.; Virginia, 1637 ***6219*** *p83*
Nouby, Marie; Quebec, 1770 ***7603*** *p29*
Noulin, William; Wisconsin, n.d. ***9675.7*** *p129*
Noulis, Peter; Arkansas, 1918 ***95.2*** *p91*
Noullatt, Joseph; New York, NY, 1838 ***8208.4*** *p84*
Nourot, Dominique 22; New Orleans, 1838 ***778.5*** *p406*
Nourot, Thiebault 25; New Orleans, 1838 ***778.5*** *p406*
Nousiainen, Onni; Washington, 1859-1920 ***2872.1*** *p29*
Nousson, Peter; Washington, 1859-1920 ***2872.1*** *p29*
Nouvet, Mr. 30; New Orleans, 1832 ***778.5*** *p406*
Novak, Franciszka 37; New York, 1912 ***9980.29*** *p51*
*Child:*Maryanna 14
*Child:*Jadwika 7
*Child:*Helena 4
Novak, Helena 4 *SEE* Novak, Franciszka
Novak, Jadwika 7 *SEE* Novak, Franciszka
Novak, John; Arkansas, 1918 ***95.2*** *p91*
Novak, Martin; Colorado, 1903 ***9678.2*** *p130*
Novak, Maryanna 14 *SEE* Novak, Franciszka
Novelli, Carlo 36; West Virginia, 1904 ***9788.3*** *p17*
Novello, Nicola; Arkansas, 1918 ***95.2*** *p91*
Novicki, John; Arkansas, 1918 ***95.2*** *p91*
Novshek, Anton; Wisconsin, n.d. ***9675.7*** *p129*
Nowacki, Frank Stanley; Arkansas, 1918 ***95.2*** *p91*
Nowacki, Stanislaw 19; New York, 1912 ***9980.29*** *p52*
Nowak, Herman; America, 1890 ***1450.2*** *p28B*
Nowak, Josef 30; New York, 1912 ***9980.29*** *p70*
Nowak, Stanislaw 22; New York, 1912 ***9980.29*** *p50*
Nowakouski, Antoni Stanislaw; Arkansas, 1918 ***95.2*** *p91*
Nowakowski, Michal; New York, 1831 ***4606*** *p175*
Nowbull, William 19; Maryland, 1719 ***3690.1*** *p167*
Nowell, Peeter; Virginia, 1647 ***6219*** *p244*
Nowells, Jon.; Virginia, 1629 ***6219*** *p8*
Nowicka, Stefania 20; New York, 1912 ***9980.29*** *p56*
Nowill, Joseph; New York, NY, 1840 ***8208.4*** *p109*
Nowlan, Charles; New England, 1816 ***2859.11*** *p40*
Nowlan, Christopher; New York, NY, 1815 ***2859.11*** *p40*
Nowlan, Daniel 17; Massachusetts, 1849 ***5881.1*** *p77*
Nowlan, Edmund; America, 1741 ***4971*** *p35*
Nowlan, Edouard; New Brunswick, 1822 ***7603*** *p59*
Nowlan, James; Montreal, 1823 ***7603*** *p65*
Nowlan, John; America, 1742 ***4971*** *p30*
Nowlan, Margaret; America, 1743 ***4971*** *p35*
Nowlan, Mary 18; Massachusetts, 1850 ***5881.1*** *p78*
Nowlan, Stephen; America, 1735-1743 ***4971*** *p7*
Nowlan, Thomas; America, 1736-1743 ***4971*** *p58*
Nowland, Daniel; America, 1741 ***4971*** *p16*
Nowland, James; New York, NY, 1816 ***2859.11*** *p40*
Nowland, James 38; Virginia, 1774 ***1219.7*** *p186*
Nowland, John; Annapolis, MD, 1742 ***4971*** *p93*
Nowland, John; Maryland, 1742 ***4971*** *p106*
Nowland, John; New York, NY, 1838 ***8208.4*** *p67*
Nowland, Margaret; Delaware, 1743 ***4971*** *p105*
Nowomieyski, . . .; New York, 1831 ***4606*** *p175*
Nowry, Alexander 8 *SEE* Nowry, James
Nowry, Alexander 8; Philadelphia, 1849 ***5704.8*** *p58*
Nowry, Eliza 34; Philadelphia, 1853 ***5704.8*** *p113*
Nowry, Elizabeth 6 *SEE* Nowry, James
Nowry, Elizabeth 6; Philadelphia, 1849 ***5704.8*** *p58*
Nowry, James; Philadelphia, 1849 ***53.26*** *p74*
*Relative:*Alexander 8
*Relative:*Elizabeth 6
Nowry, James; Philadelphia, 1849 ***5704.8*** *p58*
Nowry, Robert; Philadelphia, 1851 ***5704.8*** *p80*
Nox, Fanny 11; Quebec, 1855 ***5704.8*** *p125*
Nox, Jane 6; Quebec, 1855 ***5704.8*** *p125*
Nox, Robert 9; Quebec, 1855 ***5704.8*** *p125*
Nox, Thomas; Brunswick, NC, 1768 ***1219.7*** *p135*
Noxon, Richard 25; Philadelphia, 1775 ***1219.7*** *p258*
Noyce, Andrew; Virginia, 1634 ***6219*** *p84*
Noyes, Mrs. L.A. 53; Arizona, 1919 ***9228.40*** *p23*
Noyett, Mr.; Quebec, 1815 ***9229.18*** *p80*
Noyrend, Lewis 45; America, 1837 ***778.5*** *p406*
Nudham, Thomas; Annapolis, MD, 1742 ***4971*** *p93*
Nueckel, Konrad; Philadelphia, 1779 ***8137*** *p12*
Nuelsen, Anton; Cincinnati, 1869-1887 ***8582*** *p22*
Nuernberg, Dorothea; New York, 1749 ***3652*** *p73*
Nufenbacker, Peter 27; Port uncertain, 1839 ***778.5*** *p407*
Nufer, Christopher; Pennsylvania, 1751 ***2444*** *p197*
Nuffer, Christina *SEE* Nuffer, Christoph
Nuffer, Christoph; Pennsylvania, 1751 ***2444*** *p197*
*Child:*Eleanora Catharina
*Wife:*Christina
Nuffer, Eleanora Catharina *SEE* Nuffer, Christoph
Nufftz, Frederick; Illinois, 1858 ***5012.39*** *p54*
Nugent, . . .; Philadelphia, 1864 ***5704.8*** *p182*
Nugent, Ann; America, 1740 ***4971*** *p15*
Nugent, Ann; Maryland, 1740 ***4971*** *p91*
Nugent, Ann; Philadelphia, 1741 ***4971*** *p92*
Nugent, Arthur; Illinois, 1852 ***7857*** *p6*
Nugent, Catherine; America, 1736-1743 ***4971*** *p57*

Nugent, Christopher; Virginia, 1638 *6219 p120*
Nugent, Daniel; New York, NY, 1838 *8208.4 p70*
Nugent, Ellen 13; Massachusetts, 1847 *5881.1 p77*
Nugent, Ellenor; America, 1738 *4971 p36*
Nugent, James; New York, NY, 1838 *8208.4 p66*
Nugent, James 22; Philadelphia, 1861 *5704.8 p147*
Nugent, Jane; Philadelphia, 1852 *5704.8 p89*
Nugent, John 9; Massachusetts, 1847 *5881.1 p78*
Nugent, Laurence; Philadelphia, 1815 *2859.11 p40*
Nugent, Margaret 3; Philadelphia, 1861 *5704.8 p147*
Nugent, Margaret 6; Massachusetts, 1847 *5881.1 p78*
Nugent, Mary 24; Philadelphia, 1861 *5704.8 p147*
Nugent, Mary 25; Massachusetts, 1849 *5881.1 p78*
Nugent, Mary Ann 1; Philadelphia, 1861 *5704.8 p147*
Nugent, Michael; Philadelphia, 1852 *5704.8 p89*
Nugent, Michael 8; Massachusetts, 1847 *5881.1 p78*
Nugent, Michael C.; New York, NY, 1836 *8208.4 p12*
Nugent, Patrick; Philadelphia, 1847 *53.26 p75*
Nugent, Patrick; Philadelphia, 1847 *5704.8 p14*
Nugent, Patrick; St. John, N.B., 1847 *5704.8 p35*
Nugent, Patrick 40; Newfoundland, 1789 *4915.24 p56*
Nugent, Patrick 55; Massachusetts, 1849 *5881.1 p78*
Nugent, Richard 20; Jamaica, 1774 *1219.7 p189*
Nugent, Robert; America, 1742 *4971 p31*
Nuisi, Augustine; Colorado, 1904 *9678.2 p131*
Nuisi, Joseph; Colorado, 1904 *9678.2 p130*
Nulan, Michel; Wisconsin, n.d. *9675.7 p129*
Nulick, Joseph 36; Kansas, 1893 *5240.1 p78*
Nunan, Dennis; Ohio, 1842 *8365.25 p12*
Nunane, Michael; America, 1738 *4971 p39*
Nunberger, . . .; Canada, 1776-1783 *9786 p30*
Nunemacher, Hans Ludwig; Pennsylvania, 1751 *2444 p197*
Nunes, Elvena; Washington, 1859-1920 *2872.1 p29*
Nunes, Esther; Washington, 1859-1920 *2872.1 p29*
Nunes, Florence; Washington, 1859-1920 *2872.1 p29*

Nunes, Francis; Washington, 1859-1920 *2872.1 p29*
Nunes, Frank; Washington, 1859-1920 *2872.1 p29*
Nunes, Hazel; Washington, 1859-1920 *2872.1 p29*
Nunes, Lillie; Washington, 1859-1920 *2872.1 p29*
Nunes, Raymond; Washington, 1859-1920 *2872.1 p29*
Nungesser, Frederick; Philadelphia, 1760 *9973.7 p34*
Nungster, Martin; Ohio, 1798-1818 *8582.2 p53*
Nunnemaker, Hans Ludwig; Pennsylvania, 1751 *2444 p197*
Nunner, John; Washington, 1859-1920 *2872.1 p29*
Nunney, Alfred G.; Iowa, 1866-1943 *123.54 p36*
Nunninger, Ignatius; America, 1839 *8582.3 p49*
Nunny, David; Philadelphia, 1851 *5704.8 p76*
Nunumacher, Ludwick; Pennsylvania, 1751 *2444 p197*
Nuppanen, Henry; Illinois, 1868 *7857 p6*
Nuppenau, Capt.; Quebec, 1778 *9786 p167*
Nurnberg, Jacob; Portland, ME, 1884 *1450.2 p27B*
Nurnberger, . . .; Canada, 1776-1783 *9786 p30*
Nurse, Peter 19; Maryland, 1718 *3690.1 p167*
Nurserie, Daniell; Virginia, 1635 *6219 p35*
Nurton, John; Virginia, 1643 *6219 p23*
Nurton, Jon.; Virginia, 1638 *6219 p18*
Nusam, Penelope; Virginia, 1636 *6219 p22*
Nusam, Sarah; Virginia, 1636 *6219 p22*
Nusam, William; Virginia, 1636 *6219 p22*
Nusbaum, Carl; Arkansas, 1918 *95.2 p91*
Nuse, Wm.; Virginia, 1648 *6219 p250*
Nuseler, Domonic; Wisconsin, n.d. *9675.7 p129*
Nusier, Louis 24; New Orleans, 1837 *778.5 p407*
Nuspse, Jacob; New York, NY, 1838 *8208.4 p71*
Nussbaum, . . .; New York, 1854 *3702.7 p371*
Nussbaum, Leha 19; New York, NY, 1878 *9253 p47*
Nusz, Helena; New York, 1749 *3652 p73*
Nuszle, Mrs. 28; Port uncertain, 1838 *778.5 p407*
Nuszle, H. 28; Port uncertain, 1838 *778.5 p407*
Nute, Winifrid; Virginia, 1637 *6219 p110*

Nuten, Tho.; Virginia, 1637 *6219 p110*
Nuthall, Eliza. *SEE* Nuthall, John
Nuthall, John; Virginia, 1645 *6219 p233* Wife:Eliza.
Nutt, Darcus; Philadelphia, 1851 *5704.8 p81*
Nutt, Wm.; Virginia, 1635 *6219 p10*
Nuttall, Joseph 36; Maryland, 1774 *1219.7 p179*
Nuttall, Robt.; Virginia, 1637 *6219 p82*
Nutter, Johh 14; America, 1700 *2212 p30*
Nutter, Robert 20; Maryland, 1722 *3690.1 p167*
Nuttes, James 18; New England, 1699 *2212 p18*
Nutting, Joseph 17; Maryland, 1774 *1219.7 p224*
Nuttmier, Christian; America, 1847 *1450.2 p109A*
Nuttong, John 12; America, 1699 *2212 p20*
Nweeya, Samuel K.; Iowa, 1898 *1450.2 p109A*
Nyblom, J. E. A.; Minneapolis, 1870-1877 *6410.35 p62*
Nye, Frederick 21; America, 1869 *2896.5 p29*
Nye, John; Illinois, 1854 *7857 p6*
Nye, Joseph; Illinois, 1854 *7857 p6*
Nye, Nick 55; West Virginia, 1899 *9788.3 p17*
Nye, Nick 58; West Virginia, 1902 *9788.3 p18*
Nygaard, Helmuth Arnold Marens Edward; Arkansas, 1918 *95.2 p91*
Nykerk, Egbert 26; New York, NY, 1847 *3377.6 p11*
Nykerk, Hendrika; New York, NY, 1847 *3377.6 p11*
Nykerk, Hendrina 28; New York, NY, 1847 *3377.6 p11*
Nykerk, Jenneken 23; New York, NY, 1847 *3377.6 p11*
Nyko, Karol; New York, 1834 *4606 p178*
Nylander, Nils; Minneapolis, 1881-1886 *6410.35 p62*
Nyman, Carl B.; America, 1849 *6410.32 p123*
Nyman, Charles 28; Massachusetts, 1860 *6410.32 p107*
Nymann, Jens Christian 29; Arkansas, 1918 *95.2 p91*
Nyquist, Louis; Washington, 1859-1920 *2872.1 p29*
Nyschler, Joseph Lewis; New York, NY, 1836 *8208.4 p23*
Nystrom, C. G.; Minneapolis, 1883 *6410.35 p62*

O

Oaffel, Michael; Cincinnati, 1830-1835 *8582.3 p98*
Oaffel, Michael; Kentucky, 1840 *8582.3 p100*
Oakeley, John 19; Virginia, 1773 *1219.7 p169*
Oakes, Eliz 18; America, 1701 *2212 p34*
Oakes, Greg.; Virginia, 1637 *6219 p113*
Oakes, Janes Wallace 32; California, 1872 *2769.7 p4*
Oakes, William 23; Maryland, 1774 *1219.7 p192*
Oakley, John E.; Colorado, 1886 *9678.2 p130*
Oakley, William 40; Quebec, 1864 *5704.8 p159*
Oakman, Mrs. 76; Arizona, 1906 *9228.40 p13*
Oal, Sinclair; Halifax, N.S., 1817-1840 *8893 p263*
Oaltwalt, Christopher 26 SEE Oaltwalt, John
Oaltwalt, John; South Carolina, 1752-1753 *3689.17 p22*
  With wife
  *Relative:*Christopher 26
  *Relative:*John George 22
  *Relative:*Mathias 20
  *Relative:*Michael 17
Oaltwalt, John George 22 SEE Oaltwalt, John
Oaltwalt, Mathias 20 SEE Oaltwalt, John
Oaltwalt, Michael 17 SEE Oaltwalt, John
Oatelep, Phillipp; Virginia, 1636 *6219 p10*
Oates, Mary Jane; Colorado, 1904 *9678.2 p130*
Oates, Thomas 18; Jamaica, 1749 *3690.1 p167*
Obb, Peter; Philadelphia, 1761 *9973.7 p35*
Obebedorff, Andrew; Pennsylvania, 1773 *4525 p233*
O'Beirn, Michael; New York, NY, 1815 *2859.11 p40*
Obeley, John Peter 25; Maryland, 1774 *1219.7 p211*
Obenberger, Joseph; Wisconsin, n.d. *9675.7 p129*
Ober, John 40; Massachusetts, 1860 *6410.32 p106*
Oberdor, Dr.; Cincinnati, 1837-1838 *8582.1 p45*
Oberdorf, . . .; New England, 1777 *4525 p235*
  With siblings
Oberdorf, . . .; Pennsylvania, 1777 *4525 p235*
  With siblings
Oberdorf, Adam; New England, 1753 *4525 p233*
  *Wife:*Anna Magdalena
  With 3 children
Oberdorf, Adam; Pennsylvania, 1753 *4525 p233*
  *Wife:*Anna Magdalena
  With 3 children
Oberdorf, Andreas; New England, 1773 *4525 p250*
Oberdorf, Andreas; Pennsylvania, 1773 *4525 p233*
  With 6 children
Oberdorf, Andreas; Pennsylvania, 1773 *4525 p250*
Oberdorf, Anna Magdalena SEE Oberdorf, Adam
Oberdorf, Anna Magdalena SEE Oberdorf, Adam
Oberdorf, Baltasar; Pennsylvania, 1752 *4525 p233*
  With wife
Oberdorf, Barbara; Pennsylvania, 1752 *4525 p234*
Oberdorf, Caspar; Pennsylvania, 1754 *4525 p234*
Oberdorf, Caspar 12 SEE Oberdorf, Johann Jacob
Oberdorf, Catharina 7 SEE Oberdorf, Johann Jacob
Oberdorf, Franz J. C.; Baltimore, 1816 *8582 p22*
Oberdorf, Johann Christoph 5 SEE Oberdorf, Johann Jacob
Oberdorf, Johann Jacob; Pennsylvania, 1752 *4525 p234*
  With wife
  *Child:*Margaretha 13
  *Child:*Caspar 12
  *Child:*Catharina 7
  *Child:*Johann Christoph 5
Oberdorf, Johannes; Pennsylvania, 1782 *4525 p234*
Oberdorf, Margaretha 13 SEE Oberdorf, Johann Jacob
Oberdorf, Philipp Jacob; Pennsylvania, 1753 *4525 p234*
  With wife
  With child

Oberdorf, Rosina; Pennsylvania, 1742 *4525 p230*
Oberdorfer, Jacob; Pennsylvania, 1752 *4525 p234*
Oberdorff, Andreas; Pennsylvania, 1750 *4525 p233*
Oberdorff, Antterreas; Pennsylvania, 1773 *4525 p233*
Oberdorff, Andterreas; Pennsylvania, 1773 *4525 p237*
Oberdorff, Baltz; Pennsylvania, 1753 *4525 p233*
Oberdorff, Jacob; Pennsylvania, 1752 *4525 p234*
Oberdorff, Jacob; Pennsylvania, 1753 *4525 p233*
Oberdorff, Jacob; Pennsylvania, 1753 *4525 p234*
Oberdorff, Johan Gorg; Pennsylvania, 1753 *4525 p233*
Oberdorff, Johann Michel; Pennsylvania, 1773 *4525 p233*
Oberdorff, Johann Michel; Pennsylvania, 1773 *4525 p237*
Oberdorff, John Simon; Pennsylvania, 1750 *4525 p233*
Oberdorff, Kasper; Pennsylvania, 1750 *4525 p234*
Oberg, Edwin John; Arkansas, 1918 *95.2 p91*
Oberg, Gatfield; Arkansas, 1918 *95.2 p91*
Oberg, Hans; Iowa, 1849-1860 *2090 p613*
Oberg, John; Iowa, 1866-1943 *123.54 p36*
Oberg, John; New York, NY, 1840 *6410.32 p123*
Oberg, John E.; Arkansas, 1918 *95.2 p91*
Oberg, Wilhelm; Washington, 1859-1920 *2872.1 p29*
Obergfel, Frederick; New York, NY, 1893 *3455.3 p114*
  *Wife:*Katie
Obergfel, Katie SEE Obergfel, Frederick
Obergfell, Robert; New York, 1887 *1450.2 p28B*
Obergnas, P. 26; New Orleans, 1829 *778.5 p407*
Oberhaultz, Christine 26; Port uncertain, 1835 *778.5 p407*
Oberhaultz, Peter 34; Port uncertain, 1835 *778.5 p407*
Oberhellmann, Wilhelm; America, 1846 *8582.3 p49*
Oberheu, Fred; Wisconsin, n.d. *9675.7 p129*
Oberheu, Fried.; Wisconsin, n.d. *9675.7 p129*
Oberholtz, Pierre 32; America, 1838 *778.5 p407*
Oberhotz, Therese 25; America, 1836 *778.5 p407*
Oberlaender, Christian; New York, NY, 1836 *8208.4 p19*
Oberle, August H.; America, 1851 *8582.3 p49*
Oberle, Friederich; Ohio, 1797 *8582.2 p57*
Oberlender, Peter; Ohio, 1843 *8582.1 p51*
Oberlin, Ant..ne 25; New Orleans, 1838 *778.5 p407*
Oberlin, Antoine 7; New Orleans, 1838 *778.5 p407*
Oberlin, Aubert 8; New Orleans, 1838 *778.5 p407*
Oberlin, Danis 9; New Orleans, 1838 *778.5 p407*
Oberlin, John Francis; New York, 1761 *3652 p88*
Oberlin, Therese 29; New Orleans, 1838 *778.5 p408*
Oberling, Georg; Illinois, 1829 *8582.1 p54*
Oberling, Rudolph; Philadelphia, 1757 *9973.7 p33*
Oberlink, D.; Illinois, 1862 *2896.5 p30*
Oberly, Victor; America, 1846 *8582.3 p49*
Obermann, Henrich; Philadelphia, 1779 *8137 p12*
Obermeier, Anna; Nebraska, 1884-1885 *4610.10 p44*
  *Mother:*Luise
Obermeier, Luise SEE Obermeier, Anna
Obermeyer, Rudolph; Wisconsin, n.d. *9675.7 p129*
Oberry, John; Virginia, 1635 *6219 p23*
  *Wife:*Rose Stretchey
Oberry, Rose Stretchey SEE Oberry, John
Oberst, John; Wisconsin, n.d. *9675.7 p129*
Obert, John Lienert; Arkansas, 1918 *95.2 p91*
Obert, Wilhelm 17; America, 1880 *4610.10 p101*
Oberto, Andrew; Iowa, 1866-1943 *123.54 p36*
Oberto, John; Iowa, 1866-1943 *123.54 p36*
Obertorff, Vallentin; Pennsylvania, 1753 *4525 p233*
Oberweis, Mr.; New York, 1868 *3702.7 p379*
Oberyfel, Frederich; New York, NY, 1893 *3455.2 p72*

Obladen, Francis H.G.; Wisconsin, n.d. *9675.7 p129*
Obliger, Henriette 20; America, 1837 *778.5 p408*
O'Blinn, John; New York, 1818 *9892.11 p35*
Oborne, Thomas Watts 35; Maryland, 1774 *1219.7 p193*
O'Bourke, Shane; America, 1735-1743 *4971 p78*
O'Boy, Toal; America, 1741 *4971 p74*
O'Boyle, Charles; America, 1740 *4971 p75*
O'Boyle, Neal; New York, NY, 1816 *2859.11 p40*
Obradevick, Iso 28; Arkansas, 1918 *95.2 p91*
O'Bream, John; New York, NY, 1816 *2859.11 p40*
O'Brian, Arch.; America, 1773-1774 *2859.11 p7*
Obrian, Archibald 24; Virginia, 1773 *1219.7 p169*
O'Brian, Brian 24; Maryland, 1775 *1219.7 p268*
O'Brian, James; Ohio, 1840 *9892.11 p35*
O'Brian, Jeremiah; Ohio, 1843 *8365.26 p12*
O'Brian, John; Quebec, 1824 *7603 p53*
O'Brian, Patrick; Illinois, 1870 *5012.38 p99*
O'Brian, Patrick 25; Philadelphia, 1774 *1219.7 p175*
O'Brian, Thomas 27; Philadelphia, 1774 *1219.7 p175*
O'Brian, Timothy 29; Massachusetts, 1850 *5881.1 p80*
O'Brian, William; Quebec, 1819 *7603 p102*
Obrick, . . .; Canada, 1776-1783 *9786 p30*
O'Brien, Ann; Philadelphia, 1851 *5704.8 p80*
O'Brien, Ann 4 mos; Massachusetts, 1849 *5881.1 p78*
O'Brien, Ann 11; Massachusetts, 1849 *5881.1 p78*
O'Brien, Ann 27; Massachusetts, 1849 *5881.1 p78*
O'Brien, Anne; America, 1869 *5704.8 p236*
O'Brien, Barny; Philadelphia, 1847 *53.26 p75*
  *Relative:*Henry
O'Brien, Barny; Philadelphia, 1847 *5704.8 p22*
O'Brien, Bridget 2; Philadelphia, 1851 *5704.8 p80*
O'Brien, Bridget 8; Massachusetts, 1850 *5881.1 p78*
O'Brien, Bridget 30; Massachusetts, 1849 *5881.1 p78*
O'Brien, Catharine; Philadelphia, 1865 *5704.8 p198*
O'Brien, Catharine 4; Massachusetts, 1849 *5881.1 p79*
O'Brien, Catharine 4; Massachusetts, 1850 *5881.1 p79*
O'Brien, Catharine 32; Massachusetts, 1849 *5881.1 p79*
O'Brien, Catherine; America, 1735-1743 *4971 p78*
O'Brien, Charles 26; Newfoundland, 1789 *4915.24 p56*
O'Brien, Charles 35; Philadelphia, 1853 *5704.8 p114*
O'Brien, Christiana 3; Massachusetts, 1850 *5881.1 p79*
O'Brien, Cormick; Philadelphia, 1852 *5704.8 p96*
O'Brien, Daniel; New York, 1867 *1450.2 p28B*
O'Brien, Denis; Montreal, 1825 *7603 p65*
O'Brien, Denis; New York, NY, 1837 *8208.4 p35*
O'Brien, Dennis; New York, NY, 1811 *2859.11 p18*
O'Brien, Denis 46; California, 1867 *3840.3 p8*
O'Brien, Edward; New York, NY, 1865 *5704.8 p193*
O'Brien, Edward 4; Philadelphia, 1851 *5704.8 p80*
O'Brien, Edward 25; Massachusetts, 1850 *5881.1 p79*
O'Brien, Emily; New York, NY, 1864 *5704.8 p171*
O'Brien, George; New York, NY, 1866 *5704.8 p212*
O'Brien, George 1 SEE O'Brien, Margaret
O'Brien, George 1; Philadelphia, 1850 *5704.8 p60*
O'Brien, Harry SEE O'Brien, Sophia
O'Brien, Harry; Philadelphia, 1847 *5704.8 p22*
O'Brien, Henry SEE O'Brien, Barny
O'Brien, Henry; New York, NY, 1811 *2859.11 p18*
O'Brien, Henry; Philadelphia, 1847 *5704.8 p22*
O'Brien, Henry 25; Philadelphia, 1854 *5704.8 p122*
O'Brien, Honora 19; Massachusetts, 1849 *5881.1 p79*
O'Brien, Hugh; America, 1742 *4971 p73*
O'Brien, Hugh; Philadelphia, 1852 *5704.8 p96*
O'Brien, J.J. 47; Arizona, 1890 *2764.35 p53*
O'Brien, James; America, 1869 *5704.8 p236*
O'Brien, James; New York, NY, 1811 *2859.11 p18*
O'Brien, James; New York, NY, 1836 *8208.4 p12*

O'Brien, James; Quebec, 1815 ***9229.18*** *p76*
O'Brien, James Henry; New York, NY, 1833 ***8208.4*** *p37*
O'Brien, Jane 9; Massachusetts, 1849 ***5881.1*** *p79*
O'Brien, Johanna 17; Massachusetts, 1848 ***5881.1*** *p79*
O'Brien, John; America, 1840 ***7036*** *p118*
*Wife:*Mary Walsh
O'Brien, John; Arkansas, 1918 ***95.2*** *p91*
O'Brien, John; Illinois, 1858 ***2896.5*** *p29*
O'Brien, John; Illinois, 1896 ***5012.40*** *p55*
O'Brien, John; New York, NY, 1815 ***2859.11*** *p40*
O'Brien, John; New York, NY, 1838 ***8208.4*** *p75*
O'Brien, John; New York, NY, 1839 ***8208.4*** *p93*
O'Brien, John; Philadelphia, 1816 ***2859.11*** *p40*
With wife & child
O'Brien, John; Philadelphia, 1853 ***5704.8*** *p100*
O'Brien, John; Philadelphia, 1866 ***5704.8*** *p211*
O'Brien, John 1; Massachusetts, 1847 ***5881.1*** *p79*
O'Brien, John 21; Philadelphia, 1856 ***5704.8*** *p128*
O'Brien, John 55; Massachusetts, 1850 ***5881.1*** *p79*
O'Brien, John 65; Massachusetts, 1850 ***5881.1*** *p79*
O'Brien, Joseph; New York, NY, 1836 ***8208.4*** *p12*
O'Brien, Joseph 6; Massachusetts, 1849 ***5881.1*** *p79*
O'Brien, Lawrence; New York, NY, 1816 ***2859.11*** *p40*
O'Brien, Manus; Philadelphia, 1852 ***5704.8*** *p96*
O'Brien, Margaret; Baltimore, 1811 ***2859.11*** *p18*
O'Brien, Margaret; New York, NY, 1815 ***2859.11*** *p40*
O'Brien, Margaret; Philadelphia, 1850 ***53.26*** *p75*
*Relative:*Martha 12
*Relative:*Matthew 9
*Relative:*George 1
O'Brien, Margaret; Philadelphia, 1850 ***5704.8*** *p60*
O'Brien, Margaret; Quebec, 1849 ***5704.8*** *p51*
O'Brien, Margaret 16; Massachusetts, 1847 ***5881.1*** *p80*
O'Brien, Margaret 20; Massachusetts, 1850 ***5881.1*** *p80*
O'Brien, Martha 12 *SEE* O'Brien, Margaret
O'Brien, Martha 12; Philadelphia, 1850 ***5704.8*** *p60*
O'Brien, Mary; New York, NY, 1816 ***2859.11*** *p40*
O'Brien, Mary; Philadelphia, 1852 ***5704.8*** *p96*
O'Brien, Mary 2; Massachusetts, 1849 ***5881.1*** *p80*
O'Brien, Mary 8; Philadelphia, 1851 ***5704.8*** *p80*
O'Brien, Mary 18; Massachusetts, 1849 ***5881.1*** *p80*
O'Brien, Mary 20; Massachusetts, 1849 ***5881.1*** *p80*
O'Brien, Mary 21; Massachusetts, 1849 ***5881.1*** *p80*
O'Brien, Mary 22; Philadelphia, 1864 ***5704.8*** *p161*
O'Brien, Mary 26; Massachusetts, 1847 ***5881.1*** *p80*
O'Brien, Mary Walsh *SEE* O'Brien, John
O'Brien, Matthew 9 *SEE* O'Brien, Margaret
O'Brien, Matthew 9; Philadelphia, 1850 ***5704.8*** *p60*
O'Brien, Maurice 6; Philadelphia, 1851 ***5704.8*** *p80*
O'Brien, Michael; Montreal, 1825 ***7603*** *p89*
O'Brien, Michael; New York, 1885 ***1450.2*** *p29B*
O'Brien, Michael; New York, NY, 1815 ***2859.11*** *p40*
O'Brien, Michael; New York, NY, 1836 ***8208.4*** *p21*
O'Brien, Michael; New York, NY, 1837 ***8208.4*** *p47*
O'Brien, Michael; New York, NY, 1840 ***8208.4*** *p112*
O'Brien, Michael 3; Massachusetts, 1849 ***5881.1*** *p80*
O'Brien, Nicholson P. 32; Kansas, 1880 ***5240.1*** *p62*
O'Brien, Owen; Baltimore, 1811 ***2859.11*** *p18*
O'Brien, Owen 30; Massachusetts, 1850 ***5881.1*** *p80*
O'Brien, Patrick 28; Massachusetts, 1847 ***5881.1*** *p80*
O'Brien, Robert; Maryland, 1742 ***4971*** *p108*
O'Brien, Sarah; Philadelphia, 1848 ***53.26*** *p75*
O'Brien, Sarah; Philadelphia, 1848 ***5704.8*** *p40*
O'Brien, Sophia; Philadelphia, 1847 ***53.26*** *p75*
*Relative:*Harry
O'Brien, Sophia; Philadelphia, 1847 ***5704.8*** *p22*
O'Brien, Thomas; New York, NY, 1838 ***8208.4*** *p69*
O'Brien, Thomas; New York, NY, 1838 ***8208.4*** *p88*
O'Brien, Thomas 20; Massachusetts, 1847 ***5881.1*** *p80*
O'Brien, Thomas 20; Massachusetts, 1849 ***5881.1*** *p80*
O'Brien, Thomas 40; Massachusetts, 1850 ***5881.1*** *p80*
O'Brien, Thomas, Jr. 10; Massachusetts, 1850 ***5881.1*** *p80*
O'Brien, Unity 10; Philadelphia, 1851 ***5704.8*** *p80*
O'Brien, William; Wisconsin, n.d. ***9675.7*** *p129*
O'Brillaghan, Paul; America, 1742 ***4971*** *p72*
O'Brine, Ann; Philadelphia, 1853 ***5704.8*** *p102*
O'Brine, Biddy; Philadelphia, 1853 ***5704.8*** *p102*
O'Brine, Catherine; Philadelphia, 1853 ***5704.8*** *p102*
O'Brine, Charles; Philadelphia, 1853 ***5704.8*** *p102*
O'Brine, Daniel; Philadelphia, 1852 ***5704.8*** *p92*
O'Brine, Ellen 22; St. John, N.B., 1866 ***5704.8*** *p167*
O'Brine, Francis 21; Philadelphia, 1854 ***5704.8*** *p116*
O'Brine, James 20; Philadelphia, 1854 ***5704.8*** *p116*
O'Brine, Mary 10; Quebec, 1855 ***5704.8*** *p126*
O'Brine, Michael 22; Philadelphia, 1859 ***5704.8*** *p141*
O'Brine, Patrick; Philadelphia, 1853 ***5704.8*** *p102*
O'Brine, Tiny 24; Quebec, 1863 ***5704.8*** *p154*
O'Bryan, Denis; New York, NY, 1837 ***8208.4*** *p35*
O'Bryan, James; New York, NY, 1835 ***8208.4*** *p78*
O'Bryan, Patrick; New York, NY, 1834 ***8208.4*** *p1*
Obryan, Thomas 18; Jamaica, 1731 ***3690.1*** *p168*
O'Bryan, William; New York, NY, 1834 ***8208.4*** *p1*
Obryne, Adam 25; Jamaica, 1774 ***1219.7*** *p181*
Obryne, John; Illinois, 1853 ***7857*** *p6*
Obsatz, Harry Benjamin; Arkansas, 1918 ***95.2*** *p92*
Oburg, John; New York, NY, 1840 ***6410.32*** *p123*
O'Burne, Margaret 25; Massachusetts, 1849 ***5881.1*** *p80*
O'Byrne, James; New York, NY, 1836 ***8208.4*** *p10*
Obyrne, Patrick; Wisconsin, n.d. ***9675.7*** *p129*
O'Caddin, Terence; America, 1737 ***4971*** *p72*
O'Cahan, Barnet 20; Maryland, 1719 ***3690.1*** *p168*
O'Cahan, Patrick; America, 1740 ***4971*** *p76*
O'Cahane, Derby; America, 1738 ***4971*** *p66*
O'Cahane, Richard; America, 1738 ***4971*** *p66*
O'Cahen, Shane Braddagh; America, 1741 ***4971*** *p76*
O'Cain, Mrs. 20; Massachusetts, 1847 ***5881.1*** *p80*
O'Cain, John 13; Massachusetts, 1847 ***5881.1*** *p79*
O'Cain, Thos. H.; New York, NY, 1816 ***2859.11*** *p40*
O'Callaghan, Susan; New York, NY, 1869 ***5704.8*** *p236*
O'Callaghan, Thomas; New York, NY, 1869 ***5704.8*** *p236*
Ochatelle, Mr. 36; New Orleans, 1839 ***778.5*** *p408*
Ochiltree, Lord; Nova Scotia, 1629 ***9775.5*** *p205*
Ochs, Heinrich; America, 1839 ***8582.3*** *p49*
Ochs, John S.; America, 1847 ***8582.1*** *p26*
Ochs, Maier; New York, NY, 1847 ***6013.19*** *p74*
Ochse, Christoph; Philadelphia, 1779 ***8137*** *p12*
Ochse, Henrich; Philadelphia, 1779 ***8137*** *p12*
Ochse, Johannes; Lancaster, PA, 1780 ***8137*** *p12*
Ochsmer, Henry; Arkansas, 1918 ***95.2*** *p92*
Ocker, Anna *SEE* Ocker, Johann Michael
Ocker, Barbara Benzer *SEE* Ocker, Johann Michael
Ocker, Christina Margaretha *SEE* Ocker, Johann Michael
Ocker, Christina Sara *SEE* Ocker, Johann Michael
Ocker, Elisabetha *SEE* Ocker, Johann Michael
Ocker, Johann Michael *SEE* Ocker, Johann Michael
Ocker, Johann Michael; Pennsylvania, 1749 ***2444*** *p197*
*Wife:*Barbara Benzer
*Child:*Christina Margaretha
*Child:*Anna
*Child:*Christina Sara
*Child:*Elisabetha
*Child:*Johann Michael
Ockers, John Michael; Pennsylvania, 1749 ***2444*** *p197*
Ockershanson, John 25; Virginia, 1773 ***1219.7*** *p169*
Ockford, William 19; Virginia, 1720 ***3690.1*** *p168*
O'Connel, Laurentius; Canada, 1776-1783 ***9786*** *p252*
O'Connel, Lawrence 8 mos; Massachusetts, 1849 ***5881.1*** *p80*
O'Connell, Ann; New York, NY, 1815 ***2859.11*** *p40*
O'Connell, Biddy 6 mos; St. John, N.B., 1847 ***5704.8*** *p3*
O'Connell, Catherine 22; Philadelphia, 1864 ***5704.8*** *p156*
O'Connell, Cornelius; Virginia, 1844 ***4626.16*** *p13*
O'Connell, Daniel; Georgia, 1840 ***7036*** *p117*
O'Connell, Daniel 8 mos; Massachusetts, 1849 ***5881.1*** *p79*
O'Connell, Elleanor; St. John, N.B., 1847 ***5704.8*** *p3*
O'Connell, Honora 9; Massachusetts, 1849 ***5881.1*** *p79*
O'Connell, Jane; Philadelphia, 1865 ***5704.8*** *p201*
O'Connell, Johanna 11; Massachusetts, 1849 ***5881.1*** *p79*
O'Connell, John; Virginia, 1858 ***4626.16*** *p17*
O'Connell, Mary 12; Massachusetts, 1849 ***5881.1*** *p80*
O'Connell, Noah; Washington, 1859-1920 ***2872.1*** *p29*
O'Connell, Sarah 24; Philadelphia, 1864 ***5704.8*** *p156*
O'Connelly, John; Montreal, 1821 ***7603*** *p96*
O'Conner, Connor; America, 1742 ***4971*** *p53*
O'Conner, James; Buffalo, NY, 1836 ***2896.5*** *p30*
O'Conner, James; Illinois, 1861 ***2896.5*** *p30*
O'Conner, John; New York, NY, 1838 ***8208.4*** *p69*
O'Conner, John 32; California, 1873 ***2769.10*** *p5*
O'Conner, Michael 29; Philadelphia, 1859 ***5704.8*** *p143*
O'Conner, Thomas; Illinois, 1859 ***2896.5*** *p30*
O'Conner, Timothy; Illinois, 1877 ***2896.5*** *p30*
O'Connor, Charles 28; Dominica, 1774 ***1219.7*** *p177*
O'Connor, Daniel; New York, NY, 1837 ***8208.4*** *p33*
O'Connor, Daniel 8; Massachusetts, 1849 ***5881.1*** *p79*
O'Connor, Denis; Illinois, 1896 ***5012.37*** *p63*
O'Connor, Henry Higgins; New York, NY, 1838 ***8208.4*** *p63*
O'Connor, James; Quebec, 1823 ***7603*** *p93*
O'Connor, John; New York, NY, 1838 ***8208.4*** *p83*
O'Connor, John 7; Massachusetts, 1849 ***5881.1*** *p79*
O'Connor, John 51; Arizona, 1890 ***2764.35*** *p52*
O'Connor, Mary; Quebec, 1824 ***7603*** *p91*
O'Connor, Patrick; New York, NY, 1834 ***8208.4*** *p45*
O'Connor, Patrick; Quebec, 1821 ***7603*** *p78*
O'Connor, Patrick James; Arkansas, 1918 ***95.2*** *p91*
O'Connor, Sarah; New York, NY, 1869 ***5704.8*** *p234*
O'Connor, Taty; Montreal, 1821 ***7603*** *p54*
O'Connor, Thomas; New York, NY, 1838 ***8208.4*** *p73*
O'Connor, Thomas; Philadelphia, 1816 ***2859.11*** *p40*
O'Connor, Thomas; Virginia, 1855 ***4626.16*** *p15*
O'Connor, Thomas 7; Massachusetts, 1849 ***5881.1*** *p80*
O'Connor, Timothy; Illinois, 1896 ***5012.37*** *p63*
O'Connor, Timothy; Quebec, 1784 ***7603*** *p60*
O'Connor, William; Montreal, 1821 ***7603*** *p102*
O'Conolly, Patrick; America, 1737 ***4971*** *p75*
Octall, Mary 18; Philadelphia, 1854 ***5704.8*** *p123*
Oddy, John 16; Maryland, 1752 ***1219.7*** *p16*
Oddy, John 16; Maryland, 1752 ***3690.1*** *p168*
O'Dea, Mary 50; Massachusetts, 1849 ***5881.1*** *p80*
Oden, Meuthn; America, 1867 ***6014.1*** *p3*
Odenwald, John Michael; New York, 1750 ***3652*** *p74*
Odichon, J. 18; Louisiana, 1820 ***778.5*** *p408*
Odiffret, J.; New Orleans, 1839 ***778.5*** *p408*
Odin, Mr. 24; New Orleans, 1822 ***778.5*** *p408*
Odin, John H. 35; St. Louis, 1835 ***778.5*** *p408*
O'Divin, Bryan; America, 1737 ***4971*** *p74*
Odober, P. A. 35; New Orleans, 1837 ***778.5*** *p408*
O'Dogherty, Charles; America, 1740 ***4971*** *p75*
O'Dogherty, Edmond; America, 1741 ***4971*** *p74*
O'Doherty, John 19; Philadelphia, 1864 ***5704.8*** *p156*
O'Donaghy, Henry; America, 1741 ***4971*** *p76*
O'Donald, Bridget; Massachusetts, 1850 ***5881.1*** *p78*
O'Donald, Edmund 4; Massachusetts, 1850 ***5881.1*** *p79*
O'Donald, John 3; Massachusetts, 1850 ***5881.1*** *p79*
O'Donald, Mary; Philadelphia, 1852 ***5704.8*** *p85*
O'Donaly, Edward; Ohio, 1867 ***6014.2*** *p7*
O'Donavan, Ann; Montreal, 1825 ***7603*** *p86*
O'Donell, Mr.; Quebec, 1815 ***9229.18*** *p81*
With wife
O'Donlan, Johanna 8; Massachusetts, 1849 ***5881.1*** *p79*
O'Donlan, Margaret 10; Massachusetts, 1849 ***5881.1*** *p80*
O'Donlan, Maria 4; Massachusetts, 1849 ***5881.1*** *p80*
O'Donlan, Maria 40; Massachusetts, 1849 ***5881.1*** *p80*
O'Donlan, Michael 6; Massachusetts, 1849 ***5881.1*** *p80*
O'Donn, Michael 26; Ohio, 1867 ***6014.1*** *p3*
O'Donnel, M.; New York, NY, 1816 ***2859.11*** *p40*
With wife
O'Donnel, Mary 11; Massachusetts, 1849 ***5881.1*** *p80*
O'Donnel, Michael; Philadelphia, 1847 ***53.26*** *p75*
*Relative:*Sarah
O'Donnel, Michael; Philadelphia, 1847 ***5704.8*** *p31*
O'Donnel, Neil; Philadelphia, 1851 ***5704.8*** *p70*
O'Donnel, Patrick; America, 1737 ***4971*** *p75*
O'Donnel, Sarah *SEE* O'Donnel, Michael
O'Donnel, Sarah; Philadelphia, 1847 ***5704.8*** *p31*
O'Donnell, . . .; New York, NY, 1864 ***5704.8*** *p170*
O'Donnell, . . .; Philadelphia, 1865 ***5704.8*** *p202*
O'Donnell, . . . 8 mos; New York, NY, 1866 ***5704.8*** *p214*
O'Donnell, Alexander 4; Philadelphia, 1867 ***5704.8*** *p223*
O'Donnell, Ann; Philadelphia, 1866 ***5704.8*** *p204*
O'Donnell, Ann 11; America, 1864 ***5704.8*** *p181*
O'Donnell, Ann 55; St. John, N.B., 1853 ***5704.8*** *p110*
O'Donnell, Anthony; New York, NY, 1831 ***8208.4*** *p46*
O'Donnell, Anthony; New York, NY, 1835 ***8208.4*** *p30*
O'Donnell, Anthony; Philadelphia, 1852 ***5704.8*** *p95*
O'Donnell, Antony; St. John, N.B., 1849 ***5704.8*** *p56*
O'Donnell, Bernard; New York, NY, 1864 ***5704.8*** *p169*
O'Donnell, Bernard; St. John, N.B., 1849 ***5704.8*** *p48*
O'Donnell, Biddy; St. John, N.B., 1852 ***5704.8*** *p92*
O'Donnell, Biddy 9; St. John, N.B., 1847 ***5704.8*** *p4*
O'Donnell, Bryan; Virginia, 1856 ***4626.16*** *p16*
O'Donnell, C. 35; Arizona, 1924 ***9228.40*** *p28*
O'Donnell, Catharine 9; St. John, N.B., 1847 ***5704.8*** *p35*
O'Donnell, Catherine; Philadelphia, 1853 ***5704.8*** *p102*
O'Donnell, Catherine; St. John, N.B., 1847 ***5704.8*** *p20*
O'Donnell, Catherine; St. John, N.B., 1848 ***5704.8*** *p43*
O'Donnell, Catherine; St. John, N.B., 1850 ***5704.8*** *p65*
O'Donnell, Catherine; St. John, N.B., 1851 ***5704.8*** *p77*
O'Donnell, Catherine 1; St. John, N.B., 1867 ***5704.8*** *p168*
O'Donnell, Catherine 2; Philadelphia, 1852 ***5704.8*** *p96*
O'Donnell, Catherine 13; St. John, N.B., 1852 ***5704.8*** *p92*
O'Donnell, Catherine 18; Quebec, 1854 ***5704.8*** *p121*
O'Donnell, Charles; America, 1741 ***4971*** *p74*
O'Donnell, Charles; New York, NY, 1864 ***5704.8*** *p173*
O'Donnell, Charles; Philadelphia, 1847 ***53.26*** *p75*
*Relative:*Lily
*Relative:*John 4
*Relative:*James 2
O'Donnell, Charles; Philadelphia, 1847 ***5704.8*** *p2*
O'Donnell, Charles; Quebec, 1852 ***5704.8*** *p89*
O'Donnell, Charles; St. John, N.B., 1847 ***5704.8*** *p18*
O'Donnell, Charles 3; Philadelphia, 1861 ***5704.8*** *p147*
O'Donnell, Charles 4 *SEE* O'Donnell, John
O'Donnell, Charles 4; Philadelphia, 1847 ***5704.8*** *p2*
O'Donnell, Charles 4; St. John, N.B., 1847 ***5704.8*** *p4*
O'Donnell, Charles 21; Philadelphia, 1865 ***5704.8*** *p164*
O'Donnell, Cicely 28; Philadelphia, 1857 ***5704.8*** *p132*
O'Donnell, Con; St. John, N.B., 1847 ***5704.8*** *p35*
O'Donnell, Constantine; America, 1740 ***4971*** *p75*
O'Donnell, Daniel 13; Quebec, 1851 ***5704.8*** *p82*
O'Donnell, Dominick 12 *SEE* O'Donnell, John
O'Donnell, Dominick 12; Philadelphia, 1847 ***5704.8*** *p2*

O'Donnell, Dominico 30; Massachusetts, 1849 5881.1 p79
O'Donnell, Domnick; Philadelphia, 1866 5704.8 p210
O'Donnell, Donald; St. John, N.B., 1848 5704.8 p38
O'Donnell, Edward; Philadelphia, 1865 5704.8 p198
O'Donnell, Edward; Quebec, 1851 5704.8 p82
O'Donnell, Edward; St. John, N.B., 1848 5704.8 p38
O'Donnell, Edward 5; St. John, N.B., 1847 5704.8 p35
O'Donnell, Edward 10 *SEE* O'Donnell, John
O'Donnell, Edward 10; Philadelphia, 1847 5704.8 p2
O'Donnell, Edward 22; Philadelphia, 1857 5704.8 p133
O'Donnell, Eleanor; St. John, N.B., 1847 5704.8 p4
O'Donnell, Eleanor 11; St. John, N.B., 1847 5704.8 p4
O'Donnell, Elizabeth; Philadelphia, 1867 5704.8 p216
O'Donnell, Elizabeth 7; Philadelphia, 1853 5704.8 p112
O'Donnell, Ellan; Philadelphia, 1847 5704.8 p30
O'Donnell, Ellan; Philadelphia, 1866 5704.8 p207
O'Donnell, Ellan 11; St. John, N.B., 1847 5704.8 p35
O'Donnell, Ellen; Philadelphia, 1852 5704.8 p95
O'Donnell, Ellen; Philadelphia, 1865 5704.8 p198
O'Donnell, Ellen 21; Philadelphia, 1857 5704.8 p134
O'Donnell, Felix 3; St. John, N.B., 1847 5704.8 p35
O'Donnell, Francis 3 mos; Philadelphia, 1852 5704.8 p96
O'Donnell, Francis 13; Quebec, 1852 5704.8 p98
O'Donnell, George 7; St. John, N.B., 1847 5704.8 p4
O'Donnell, George 22; Philadelphia, 1861 5704.8 p147
O'Donnell, George 25; Quebec, 1864 5704.8 p160
O'Donnell, Grace; Philadelphia, 1852 5704.8 p91
O'Donnell, Grace 3 mos; St. John, N.B., 1847 5704.8 p4
O'Donnell, Hanna 24; Philadelphia, 1853 5704.8 p111
O'Donnell, Hannah; New York, NY, 1866 5704.8 p214
O'Donnell, Hannah; Philadelphia, 1864 5704.8 p180
O'Donnell, Hannah 22; St. John, N.B., 1864 5704.8 p158
O'Donnell, Helen; Quebec, 1825 7603 p92
O'Donnell, Henry; New Orleans, 1852 5704.8 p98
O'Donnell, Hugh; New York, NY, 1838 8208.4 p83
O'Donnell, Hugh; Philadelphia, 1866 5704.8 p208
O'Donnell, Hugh; St. John, N.B., 1847 5704.8 p4
O'Donnell, Hugh 3; Massachusetts, 1849 5881.1 p79
O'Donnell, Hugh 7; St. John, N.B., 1847 5704.8 p35
O'Donnell, Hugh 20; Quebec, 1862 5704.8 p151
O'Donnell, Isabella; New York, NY, 1815 2859.11 p40
O'Donnell, James; America, 1866 5704.8 p209
O'Donnell, James; New York, NY, 1811 2859.11 p18
O'Donnell, James; Philadelphia, 1865 5704.8 p199
O'Donnell, James 2 *SEE* O'Donnell, Charles
O'Donnell, James 2 *SEE* O'Donnell, John
O'Donnell, James 2; Philadelphia, 1847 5704.8 p2
O'Donnell, James 4; America, 1866 5704.8 p214
O'Donnell, James 16; Philadelphia, 1854 5704.8 p123
O'Donnell, James 20; Philadelphia, 1856 5704.8 p129
O'Donnell, James 28; St. John, N.B., 1864 5704.8 p158
O'Donnell, Jane *SEE* O'Donnell, John
O'Donnell, Jane; Philadelphia, 1847 5704.8 p2
O'Donnell, Jane; Philadelphia, 1850 5704.8 p60
O'Donnell, Jane 16; Massachusetts, 1849 5881.1 p79
O'Donnell, Jeremiah 26; Massachusetts, 1849 5881.1 p79
O'Donnell, John; America, 1741 4971 p16
O'Donnell, John; Illinois, 1850 7857 p6
O'Donnell, John; New York, NY, 1836 8208.4 p12
O'Donnell, John; New York, NY, 1869 5704.8 p234
O'Donnell, John; Philadelphia, 1847 53.26 p75
*Relative:*Jane
*Relative:*Dominick 12
*Relative:*Edward 10
*Relative:*John 8
*Relative:*Margaret 6
*Relative:*Charles 4
*Relative:*James 2
O'Donnell, John; Philadelphia, 1847 5704.8 p2
O'Donnell, John; Philadelphia, 1866 5704.8 p206
O'Donnell, John; Quebec, 1852 5704.8 p91
O'Donnell, John; St. John, N.B., 1848 5704.8 p39
O'Donnell, John; St. John, N.B., 1851 5704.8 p77
O'Donnell, John; Virginia, 1856 4626.16 p16
O'Donnell, John 9 mos; Philadelphia, 1865 5704.8 p164
O'Donnell, John 4 *SEE* O'Donnell, Charles
O'Donnell, John 4; Philadelphia, 1847 5704.8 p2
O'Donnell, John 5; Quebec, 1852 5704.8 p87
O'Donnell, John 8 *SEE* O'Donnell, John
O'Donnell, John 8; Massachusetts, 1849 5881.1 p79
O'Donnell, John 8; Philadelphia, 1847 5704.8 p2
O'Donnell, John 10; Philadelphia, 1857 5704.8 p134
O'Donnell, John 11; Philadelphia, 1855 5704.8 p124
O'Donnell, John 18; Philadelphia, 1853 5704.8 p112
O'Donnell, John 18; Philadelphia, 1853 5704.8 p113
O'Donnell, John 20; Philadelphia, 1854 5704.8 p118
O'Donnell, John 30; St. John, N.B., 1858 5704.8 p137
O'Donnell, John 38; West Virginia, 1905 9788.3 p18
O'Donnell, John 41; St. John, N.B., 1867 5704.8 p168
O'Donnell, John 60; Massachusetts, 1849 5881.1 p79
O'Donnell, Julia; America, 1869 5704.8 p235
O'Donnell, Lily *SEE* O'Donnell, Charles
O'Donnell, Lily; Philadelphia, 1847 5704.8 p2
O'Donnell, Magy; St. John, N.B., 1848 5704.8 p39
O'Donnell, Manas; Quebec, 1848 5704.8 p41
O'Donnell, Manus; Philadelphia, 1852 5704.8 p91
O'Donnell, Margaret; Philadelphia, 1865 5704.8 p202
O'Donnell, Margaret; Quebec, 1848 5704.8 p41
O'Donnell, Margaret; St. John, N.B., 1847 5704.8 p35
O'Donnell, Margaret 6 *SEE* O'Donnell, John
O'Donnell, Margaret 6; Philadelphia, 1847 5704.8 p2
O'Donnell, Margaret 18; Philadelphia, 1861 5704.8 p148
O'Donnell, Margaret 30; Massachusetts, 1849 5881.1 p80
O'Donnell, Marie; Quebec, 1818 7603 p58
O'Donnell, Martha; Philadelphia, 1848 53.26 p75
O'Donnell, Martha; Philadelphia, 1848 5704.8 p45
O'Donnell, Mary; New York, NY, 1815 2859.11 p40
O'Donnell, Mary; Philadelphia, 1852 5704.8 p95
O'Donnell, Mary; Philadelphia, 1852 5704.8 p96
O'Donnell, Mary; Quebec, 1852 5704.8 p87
O'Donnell, Mary; Quebec, 1852 5704.8 p91
O'Donnell, Mary; St. John, N.B., 1853 5704.8 p107
O'Donnell, Mary 3; Philadelphia, 1867 5704.8 p223
O'Donnell, Mary 5; Philadelphia, 1853 5704.8 p112
O'Donnell, Mary 20; Philadelphia, 1855 5704.8 p124
O'Donnell, Mary 22; Philadelphia, 1861 5704.8 p147
O'Donnell, Mary 25; Philadelphia, 1803 53.26 p75
O'Donnell, Mary 30; Quebec, 1863 5704.8 p154
O'Donnell, Mary 40; St. John, N.B., 1867 5704.8 p168
O'Donnell, Mary A.; New York, NY, 1866 5704.8 p214
O'Donnell, Mary Ann 3 mos; St. John, N.B., 1847 5704.8 p35
O'Donnell, Michael; St. John, N.B., 1847 5704.8 p3
O'Donnell, Michael 1; Massachusetts, 1849 5881.1 p80
O'Donnell, Nancy; Philadelphia, 1853 5704.8 p102
O'Donnell, Neal; St. John, N.B., 1851 5704.8 p77
O'Donnell, Nelly; St. John, N.B., 1847 5704.8 p3
O'Donnell, Niel; Colorado, 1893 9678.2 p130
O'Donnell, Owen; St. John, N.B., 1850 5704.8 p61
O'Donnell, Pat; Quebec, 1852 5704.8 p91
O'Donnell, Patk.; New York, NY, 1816 2859.11 p40
O'Donnell, Patrick; Illinois, 1878 5012.37 p60
O'Donnell, Patrick; New York, NY, 1838 8208.4 p65
O'Donnell, Patrick; New York, NY, 1839 8208.4 p96
O'Donnell, Patrick; Philadelphia, 1852 5704.8 p97
O'Donnell, Patrick; Philadelphia, 1865 5704.8 p198
O'Donnell, Patrick; Quebec, 1852 5704.8 p87
O'Donnell, Patrick; St. John, N.B., 1847 5704.8 p4
O'Donnell, Patrick; St. John, N.B., 1847 5704.8 p18
O'Donnell, Patrick; St. John, N.B., 1847 5704.8 p19
O'Donnell, Patrick 6 mos; Quebec, 1852 5704.8 p87
O'Donnell, Patt 9 mos; Quebec, 1852 5704.8 p91
O'Donnell, Peter; New York, NY, 1866 5704.8 p206
O'Donnell, Peter 21; Philadelphia, 1857 5704.8 p133
O'Donnell, Rebecca; New York, NY, 1866 5704.8 p214
O'Donnell, Richard; America, 1781 7036 p121
O'Donnell, Richard; Quebec, 1825 7603 p70
O'Donnell, Rosanna; Philadelphia, 1867 5704.8 p223
O'Donnell, Rose; New York, NY, 1866 5704.8 p214
O'Donnell, Rose; St. John, N.B., 1847 5704.8 p19
O'Donnell, Rose 20; Philadelphia, 1860 5704.8 p145
O'Donnell, Sally 20; Philadelphia, 1853 5704.8 p113
O'Donnell, Sarah; Philadelphia, 1848 5704.8 p45
O'Donnell, Susan 21; Philadelphia, 1865 5704.8 p164
O'Donnell, Thomas 20; Quebec, 1855 5704.8 p125
O'Donnell, Unity; America, 1869 5704.8 p236
O'Donnell, Vincent; Arkansas, 1918 95.2 p91
O'Donnell, William; Philadelphia, 1864 5704.8 p179
O'Donnell, William; Philadelphia, 1867 5704.8 p214
O'Donnell, William; Quebec, 1825 7603 p95
O'Donnell, William; St. John, N.B., 1853 5704.8 p106
O'Donnell, William 20; Philadelphia, 1858 5704.8 p139
O'Donnell, William 26; Philadelphia, 1861 5704.8 p148
O'Donnell, Wm.; New York, NY, 1815 2859.11 p40
With wife
O'Donnely, Owen; Quebec, 1812 7603 p78
O'Dougherty, Catherine; Quebec, 1822 7603 p97
O'Driscoll, Dennis; New York, NY, 1834 8208.4 p41
Oebel, Martin 29; Kansas, 1887 5240.1 p32
Oebel, Morton 29; Kansas, 1887 5240.1 p69
Oeffinger, Agnes *SEE* Oeffinger, Georg Heinrich
Oeffinger, Georg Heinrich; Pennsylvania, 1745-1779 2444 p198
*Wife:*Agnes
*Child:*Johann Melchior
*Child:*Regina
Oeffinger, Johann Melchior *SEE* Oeffinger, Georg Heinrich
Oeffinger, Regina *SEE* Oeffinger, Georg Heinrich
Oeh, Konrad; America, 1848 8582.1 p26
Oehlenschlager, Ad. 34; America, 1853 9162.7 p15
Oehlenschlager, Elis. 9; America, 1853 9162.7 p15
Oehlenschlager, Joh. 29; America, 1853 9162.7 p15
Oehlenschlager, Marg. 32; America, 1853 9162.7 p15
Oehlenschlager, Marg. 58; America, 1853 9162.7 p15
Oehlenschlager, Marie 11 mos; America, 1853 9162.7 p15
Oehlenschlager, Nicol 11 mos; America, 1853 9162.7 p15
Oehlenschlager, Valentin 10; America, 1853 9162.7 p15
Oehler, Philipp; America, 1828 8582.1 p26
Oehler, Philipp; America, 1828 8582.2 p61
Oehlmann, . . .; Cincinnati, 1826 8582.1 p51
Oehlmann, Frederick H.; Ohio, 1869-1887 8582 p23
Oehlmann, Friederich Heinrich; Baltimore, 1831 8582.2 p30
With parents
Oehme, Frederick; Wisconsin, n.d. 9675.7 p129
Oehmke, Charles; Illinois, 1870 5012.38 p99
Oehmke, Fritz; Illinois, 1869 5012.38 p99
Oehrle, Christina *SEE* Oehrle, Hans Jacob
Oehrle, Hans Jacob; Pennsylvania, 1750 2444 p198
*Wife:*Christina
*Child:*Lucia
*Child:*Johannes
Oehrle, Johannes *SEE* Oehrle, Hans Jacob
Oehrle, Lucia *SEE* Oehrle, Hans Jacob
Oelhans, Andreas; Halifax, N.S., 1778 9786 p270
Oelhans, Andreas; New York, 1776 9786 p270
Oelrichs, Eilert; Iroquois Co., IL, 1892 3455.1 p12
Oelrichs, Eilert; Iroquois Co., IL, 1896 3455.1 p12
Oelschlager, . . .; Canada, 1776-1783 9786 p30
Oelschlager, Mrs.; America, 1854 4610.10 p135
*Child:*Anne C. W. Ilsabein
*Child:*Heinrich F. Wilhelm
Oelschlager, Anne C. W. Ilsabein *SEE* Oelschlager, Mrs.
Oelschlager, Heinrich F. Wilhelm *SEE* Oelschlager, Mrs.
Oerke, Fredrike 44; Kansas, 1880 5240.1 p62
Oertel, . . .; Canada, 1776-1783 9786 p30
Oertel, Elizabeth; New York, 1749 3652 p73
Oertel, Maximilian; Cincinnati, 1788-1848 8582.3 p89
Oerter, Christian Frederic; New York, 1743 3652 p60
Oertler, Anna Barbara; America, 1753 2444 p164
Oertwig, Carl F. O.; Illinois, 1878 2896.5 p30
Oertwig, Ernest; Illinois, 1886 2896.5 p11
Oertwig, Ernst; Illinois, 1883 2896.5 p30
Oertwig, Frederick; Illinois, 1867 2896.5 p30
Oertwig, Michael; Illinois, 1866 2896.5 p30
Oertwig, Michael 13; America, 1864 2896.5 p30
With father
Oertwig, Michael, Jr.; Illinois, 1880 2896.5 p30
Oesch, Marie; Wisconsin, n.d. 9675.7 p129
Oesch, Nicholas Wm.; Wisconsin, n.d. 9675.7 p129
Oesch, William; Wisconsin, n.d. 9675.7 p129
Oesker, Anne M. Friederike Charlotte 40; America, 1882 4610.10 p123
Oesterlein, Jeremias; Pennsylvania, 1752 4525 p235
Oesterlein, Jeremias; Pennsylvania, 1753 4525 p235
With wife
With child
Oesterley, Sophia; Baltimore, 1832 3702.7 p95
Oeters, Johann Hermann; New York, NY, 1837 8208.4 p33
Oetert, Karl; Cincinnati, 1869-1887 8582 p23
Oetil, Schedvill. 19; America, 1836 778.5 p408
Oetzel, Andreas; Pennsylvania, 1750 4525 p233
Oetzel, Andreas; Pennsylvania, 1750 4525 p235
With wife
Oetzel, Jakob; New England, 1773 4525 p235
With wife
With 3 children
Oetzel, Jakob; Pennsylvania, 1773 4525 p235
With wife & 3 children
Oetzel, Michel; Pennsylvania, 1752 4525 p235
With child
Oexemann, Justine Louise Charlotte; America, 1848 4610.10 p97
Oexmann, Heinrich Ferdinand Karl; America, 1880 4610.10 p96
With 2 brothers
Of, Catharina Barbara 50; Philadelphia, 1805 2444 p187
O'Farrell, John 40; Massachusetts, 1849 5881.1 p79
O'Fegan, Arthur; America, 1742 4971 p65
Off, Catharina Barbara 50; Philadelphia, 1805 2444 p187
Offal, Michael; Cincinnati, 1830-1835 8582.3 p98
Offeney, . . .; Canada, 1776-1783 9786 p30
Offhansen, Therese 25; Kansas, 1890 5240.1 p74
Offhausen, Adolf Charles; Kansas, 1882 5240.1 p32
Offhausen, Ernest 30; Kansas, 1890 5240.1 p75
Offley, Nicho.; Virginia, 1642 6219 p190
O'Finn, John; New York, NY, 1838 8208.4 p64
O'Flinn, John; Ohio, 1832 9892.11 p35
O'Flinn, Patrick; St. John, N.B., 1847 5704.8 p11
O'Friel, Bernard 18; Philadelphia, 1853 5704.8 p108
Ogalby, David 29; Maryland, 1729 3690.1 p168
O'Gallagher, Charles; America, 1738 4971 p75
O'Gallagher, Hugh-buy; America, 1737 4971 p75
Ogas, Cedronio 69; Arizona, 1925 9228.40 p29

Ogden, David; Pennsylvania, 1682 4962 p148
Ogden, John 46; Massachusetts, 1847 5881.1 p79
Ogden, Thomas; New York, NY, 1838 8208.4 p82
Ogden, William N.; Colorado, 1894 9678.2 p130
Ogelvie, Robert 19; Virginia, 1773 1219.7 p169
Oger, Charles Rene Gatien; Louisiana, 1789-1819 778.5 p555
Oger, P. 30; New Orleans, 1836 778.5 p408
Oger, Pierre M. 35; America, 1839 778.5 p408
Ogeron, Louis; Louisiana, 1789-1819 778.5 p555
Oggero, Charles; Iowa, 1866-1943 123.54 p36
Oggero, Joseph; Iowa, 1866-1943 123.54 p37
Oghnard, Marie 26; Port uncertain, 1836 778.5 p408
Ogier, Mr. 29; New Orleans, 1829 778.5 p408
Ogier, Catherine 16; Carolina, 1774 1219.7 p190
Ogier, Catherine 40 *SEE* Ogier, Lewis
Ogier, Charlotte 9; Carolina, 1774 1219.7 p190
Ogier, George 15; Carolina, 1774 1219.7 p179
Ogier, John 8; Carolina, 1774 1219.7 p190
Ogier, Lewis 19; Carolina, 1774 1219.7 p190
Ogier, Lewis 47; Carolina, 1774 1219.7 p190
*Wife:*Catherine 40
Ogier, Lucy 13; Carolina, 1774 1219.7 p190
Ogier, Mary 6; Carolina, 1774 1219.7 p190
Ogier, Peter 5; Carolina, 1774 1219.7 p190
Ogier, Thomas 20; Carolina, 1774 1219.7 p190
Ogilby, Mrs.; New York, NY, 1816 2859.11 p40
Ogilby, David 29; Maryland, 1729 3690.1 p168
Ogilby, Frederick; New York, NY, 1816 2859.11 p40
Ogilby, John; New York, NY, 1816 2859.11 p40
Ogilby, Robert; New York, NY, 1816 2859.11 p40
Ogilvia, John; Iowa, 1866-1943 123.54 p37
Ogilvie, James; Charleston, SC, 1744 1639.20 p256
Ogilvie, Jane Elizabeth; America, 1847 8893 p264
Ogilvie, William; Nevada, 1874 2764.35 p52
Ogilvie, William; New York, 1763 1219.7 p96
Ogilvy, Henry; Pensacola, FL, 1779 1639.20 p256
Ogilvy, William; North Carolina, 1674-1774 1639.20 p256
Ogle, Ann 50; Quebec, 1855 5704.8 p125
Ogle, Benjamin 23; Virginia, 1774 1219.7 p186
Ogle, James; Ohio, 1840 9892.11 p35
Ogle, Jane; Quebec, 1855 5704.8 p125
Ogle, John 16; Quebec, 1855 5704.8 p125
Ogle, Mary Ann 22; Quebec, 1855 5704.8 p125
Ogle, Ruth 20; Quebec, 1855 5704.8 p125
Ogle, William 27; Quebec, 1855 5704.8 p125
Ogle, William 50; Quebec, 1855 5704.8 p125
Oglebie, John 19; America, 1700 2212 p31
Oglebie, Robert 17; America, 1700 2212 p34
Ogleston, Harry; Washington, 1859-1920 2872.1 p29
Oglethorpe, General; Savannah, GA, 1736 3652 p51
O'Gorman, Elleanor 11; St. John, N.B., 1854 5704.8 p120
O'Gorman, Jane; St. John, N.B., 1849 5704.8 p49
O'Gorman, Michael; St. John, N.B., 1849 5704.8 p49
O'Gorman, Sarah 50; St. John, N.B., 1854 5704.8 p120
O'Gorman, Susanah 8; St. John, N.B., 1854 5704.8 p120
O'Grady, John D.; New York, NY, 1836 8208.4 p19
O'Grady, Mary 16; Massachusetts, 1850 5881.1 p80
O'Grady, Susan 25; Massachusetts, 1850 5881.1 p80
Ogren, John Oscar; Arkansas, 1918 95.2 p92
Ogrinc, Joseph; Wisconsin, n.d. 9675.7 p129
O'Hagan, Henry; America, 1741 4971 p76
O'Hagan, John; Philadelphia, 1864 5704.8 p175
O'Haghy, Philip; America, 1740 4971 p73
O'Hairs, Jane 14; St. John, N.B., 1851 5704.8 p73
O'Hall, William; Quebec, 1810 7603 p64
Ohanian, Manoog; Arkansas, 1918 95.2 p92
O'Hara, Mr.; Quebec, 1815 9229.18 p75
With daughter
O'Hara, Alice; Philadelphia, 1865 5704.8 p192
O'Hara, Anne; Philadelphia, 1864 5704.8 p173
O'Hara, Annie 5; New York, NY, 1866 5704.8 p212
O'Hara, Arthur; New York, NY, 1838 8208.4 p65
O'Hara, Arthur; New York, NY, 1838 8208.4 p67
O'Hara, Barney 25; Massachusetts, 1847 5881.1 p78
O'Hara, Bridget; Quebec, 1824 7603 p94
O'Hara, Celia 14; Massachusetts, 1850 5881.1 p79
O'Hara, Elizabeth; Philadelphia, 1864 5704.8 p184
O'Hara, Elizabeth 10; New York, NY, 1866 5704.8 p212
O'Hara, Ellen 8; New York, NY, 1866 5704.8 p212
O'Hara, Francis 10; Massachusetts, 1848 5881.1 p79
O'Hara, James; Philadelphia, 1865 5704.8 p192
O'Hara, James; Philadelphia, 1866 5704.8 p207
O'Hara, Jane 35; Massachusetts, 1850 5881.1 p79
O'Hara, John; Quebec, 1812 7603 p54
O'Hara, John 18; Massachusetts, 1847 5881.1 p79
O'Hara, John 20; Philadelphia, 1857 5704.8 p132
O'Hara, Margaret; Philadelphia, 1866 5704.8 p207
O'Hara, Margaret 11; New York, NY, 1864 5704.8 p173
O'Hara, Martha; Philadelphia, 1852 5704.8 p95
O'Hara, Mary; St. John, N.B., 1851 5704.8 p79
O'Hara, Mary 5; Massachusetts, 1849 5881.1 p80
O'Hara, Mary 11; St. John, N.B., 1852 5704.8 p92
O'Hara, Mary J. 7; New York, NY, 1866 5704.8 p212
O'Hara, Michael; Montreal, 1825 7603 p61
O'Hara, Michael 16; Massachusetts, 1847 5881.1 p80
O'Hara, Patrick; New York, NY, 1838 8208.4 p80
O'Hara, Peter; New York, NY, 1864 5704.8 p173
O'Hara, Rebecca 20; Massachusetts, 1850 5881.1 p80
O'Hara, Sarah 7; St. John, N.B., 1852 5704.8 p92
O'Hara, William; New England, 1816 2859.11 p40
O'Hara, William; New York, NY, 1816 2859.11 p40
O'Hare, Ann 4; Massachusetts, 1849 5881.1 p78
O'Hare, Bernard 29; Kansas, 1891 5240.1 p76
O'Hare, Henry; New York, NY, 1834 8208.4 p79
O'Hare, Henry; Ohio, 1842 8365.25 p12
O'Hare, John; New York, NY, 1816 2859.11 p40
O'Hare, Martin; San Francisco, 1872 2764.35 p53
O'Hare, Peter; Montreal, 1825 7603 p68
O'Harny, Charles; America, 1738 4971 p76
O Harry, Anna 1; New York, NY, 1828 6508.4 p143
O Harry, Mary 30; New York, NY, 1828 6508.4 p143
Ohe, Anna Catharina; America, 1831 4815.7 p92
Ohear, Francis; America, 1742 4971 p25
O'Hearan, Bartholomew; Massachusetts, 1849 5881.1 p78
O'Hearan, Mary 23; Massachusetts, 1849 5881.1 p80
Ohel, Jacques 21?; America, 1838 778.5 p408
O'Higgin, Dunkan; America, 1738 4971 p76
Ohl, Barbara 33; Port uncertain, 1839 778.5 p408
Ohl, Chretien 38; America, 1835 778.5 p409
Ohl, Christine 39; America, 1835 778.5 p409
Ohl, Johann 1; Port uncertain, 1839 778.5 p409
Ohl, Luis 8; Port uncertain, 1839 778.5 p409
Ohl, Marguerite 7; America, 1835 778.5 p409
Ohl, Michael; Philadelphia, 1760 9973.7 p34
Ohle, . . .; Canada, 1776-1783 9786 p30
Ohlen, Henry George 16; New York, 1775 1219.7 p246
Ohlendorff, H.A. Wm.; Wisconsin, n.d. 9675.7 p129
Ohler, Johann Wilhelm; Pennsylvania, 1737 1034.18 p14
*Wife:*Ursula
*Child:*Marx Simon
Ohler, Marx Simon *SEE* Ohler, Johann Wilhelm
Ohler, Peter; Pennsylvania, 1730 1034.18 p14
Ohler, Ursula *SEE* Ohler, Johann Wilhelm
Ohlfalt, Carl; Minneapolis, 1883 6410.35 p62
Ohliger, Anne Marie 10; America, 1838 778.5 p409
Ohliger, Anne Marie 38; America, 1838 778.5 p409
Ohliger, Balthazard 12; America, 1838 778.5 p409
Ohliger, Jean 14; America, 1838 778.5 p409
Ohliger, Jeanne 18; America, 1838 778.5 p409
Ohlin, Vernon; Arkansas, 1918 95.2 p92
Ohlman, . . .; Canada, 1776-1783 9786 p43
Ohlman, William H.; Illinois, 1896 5012.40 p55
Ohlseen, Acsell Carl; Arkansas, 1918 95.2 p92
Ohlson, Amond; Wisconsin, n.d. 9675.7 p129
Ohlson, William 29; Maryland, 1774 1219.7 p229
Ohm, Herman; Wisconsin, n.d. 9675.7 p129
Ohm, Ida; Wisconsin, n.d. 9675.7 p129
Ohm, John; Wisconsin, n.d. 9675.7 p129
Ohme, . . .; Canada, 1776-1783 9786 p30
Ohme, Hans; Arkansas, 1918 95.2 p92
Ohmstad, Sjur; Arkansas, 1918 95.2 p92
Ohneberg, George; New York, 1743 3652 p60
*Wife:*Susan
Ohneberg, Susan *SEE* Ohneberg, George
Ohnemiller, John; America, 1884 5240.1 p32
Ohnemuller, John 44; Kansas, 1887 5240.1 p69
Ohnesorgen, William 41; Arizona, 1890 2764.35 p52
O'Houghian, John; America, 1740 4971 p67
O'Houghian, Oli.; America, 1740 4971 p67
Ohrle, Johannes; Pennsylvania, 1750 2444 p198
Ohrmund, Gustav; Wisconsin, n.d. 9675.7 p129
Ohrt, Christoffer; New York, NY, 1923 3455.4 p29
Ohst, Herman; Wisconsin, n.d. 9675.7 p129
Ohtterman, Georg 23; Port uncertain, 1839 778.5 p409
Ojile, Sam 50; Kansas, 1905 5240.1 p83
O'Kain, Catherine; St. John, N.B., 1847 5704.8 p15
O'Kain, Catherine Ann 4; St. John, N.B., 1847 5704.8 p15
O'Kain, Eliza 10; St. John, N.B., 1847 5704.8 p15
O'Kain, Henry; St. John, N.B., 1847 5704.8 p15
O'Kain, Patrick; America, 1740 4971 p73
O'Kain, Patrick; St. John, N.B., 1847 5704.8 p15
O'Kain, Sarah 12; St. John, N.B., 1847 5704.8 p15
Okal, William E.; Arkansas, 1918 95.2 p92
O'Kane, Bernard; St. John, N.B., 1852 5704.8 p93
O'Kane, Bridget; Philadelphia, 1851 5704.8 p76
O'Kane, Bridget; Philadelphia, 1864 5704.8 p182
O'Kane, Dennis 3 *SEE* O'Kane, Dennis
O'Kane, Dennis 33; Philadelphia, 1844 53.26 p75
*Relative:*Jane
*Relative:*Jane 13
*Relative:*Rosa 11
*Relative:*John 9
*Relative:*Dennis 3
O'Kane, Eliza; Philadelphia, 1851 5704.8 p76
O'Kane, Ellen; Philadelphia, 1851 5704.8 p76
O'Kane, James 17; Philadelphia, 1861 5704.8 p148
O'Kane, James 55; Philadelphia, 1865 5704.8 p165
O'Kane, Jane *SEE* O'Kane, Dennis
O'Kane, Jane 13 *SEE* O'Kane, Dennis
O'Kane, John; Philadelphia, 1851 5704.8 p76
O'Kane, John; Philadelphia, 1852 5704.8 p91
O'Kane, John 9 *SEE* O'Kane, Dennis
O'Kane, Patrick; St. John, N.B., 1852 5704.8 p93
O'Kane, Rosa 11 *SEE* O'Kane, Dennis
O'Kane, Rosanna; Philadelphia, 1868 5704.8 p225
O'Kane, Rose 17; Philadelphia, 1865 5704.8 p165
O'Kane, Sarah; Philadelphia, 1851 5704.8 p76
O'Keefe, Bridget 10; Massachusetts, 1849 5881.1 p78
O'Keefe, John 11; Massachusetts, 1849 5881.1 p79
O'Keefe, Mary; Quebec, 1795 7603 p78
O'Keefe, Richard; Montreal, 1814 7603 p100
Okeley, Robert; Virginia, 1642 6219 p191
Okell, George 24; Maryland, 1775 1219.7 p257
O'Kelly, Teigue; America, 1741 4971 p74
Okely, John; Philadelphia, 1742 3652 p56
Okely, William; New York, 1754 3652 p79
Okely, William; Philadelphia, 1742 3652 p55
Oker, John; Virginia, 1635 6219 p72
Okher, Michal; Pennsylvania, 1749 2444 p197
Okland, John; Arkansas, 1918 95.2 p92
Oladowski, . . .; New York, 1831 4606 p176
Olafsdottir, Gudrun 22; Quebec, 1879 2557.1 p20
Olafsdottir, Lillias 4; Quebec, 1879 2557.1 p21
Olafsdottir, Margret 8; Quebec, 1879 2557.1 p21
Olafsdottir, Oddny 8; Quebec, 1879 2557.1 p20
Olafsdottir, Olavia 25; Quebec, 1879 2557.1 p38
Olafsdottir, Thorey; Quebec, 1879 2557.1 p21
Olafsen, Oscar Martin; Arkansas, 1918 95.2 p92
Olafson, Martin; Washington, 1859-1920 2872.1 p29
Olafsson, Einar 23; Quebec, 1879 2557.1 p20
Olafsson, Einar 23; Quebec, 1879 2557.2 p37
Olafsson, Gudmundur 5; Quebec, 1879 2557.1 p20
Olafsson, Jon 49; Quebec, 1879 2557.1 p38A
Olafsson, Jonas 11; Quebec, 1879 2557.1 p21
Olafsson, Margret 8; Quebec, 1879 2557.1 p21
Olafsson, Stefan 18; Quebec, 1879 2557.1 p20
Olamer, Michael; South Carolina, 1752-1753 3689.17 p22
With wife
Olander, Carl Verner; Arkansas, 1918 95.2 p92
Olander, Eva; Colorado, 1903 9678.2 p130
Olander, Matilda 24; Massachusetts, 1860 6410.32 p103
Olander, Paul J.; America, 1854 6410.32 p123
Olander, Paul J. 30; Massachusetts, 1860 6410.32 p103
O'Lane, Patrick 9; Massachusetts, 1848 5881.1 p80
O'Larkin, Art; America, 1741 4971 p76
Olaski, Joseph Eddie; Arkansas, 1918 95.2 p92
O'Laughlin, John 29; Massachusetts, 1850 5881.1 p79
O'Laughlin, Patrick 20; Massachusetts, 1847 5881.1 p80
Olaveson, John; Maine, 1886-1891 6410.22 p120
Old, John 16; Maryland, 1774 1219.7 p204
Old, John 30; Halifax, N.S., 1774 1219.7 p213
Oldaker, William 22; Philadelphia, 1774 1219.7 p233
Oldani, Barbera 18; New York, NY, 1893 9026.4 p42
Oldekopf, Friedrich Ernst; Quebec, 1776 9786 p258
Oldeloren, Luce; Quebec, 1816 7603 p79
Oldendorf, . . .; Canada, 1776-1783 9786 p30
Oldfield, Edward 20; Jamaica, 1730 3690.1 p168
Oldfield, Leonard 21; Jamaica, 1735 3690.1 p168
Oldham, Richard; New York, NY, 1837 8208.4 p48
Oldham, William; Quebec, 1793 7603 p27
Oldis, John; Virginia, 1637 6219 p37
Oldman, Claus H.; Wisconsin, n.d. 9675.7 p129
Oldman, Sidney; Washington, 1859-1920 2872.1 p29
Oldring, William; New York, NY, 1837 8208.4 p33
Oldum, Eliz.; Virginia, 1643 6219 p206
Oldum, James; Virginia, 1643 6219 p206
*Wife:*Pearcy
Oldum, Pearcy *SEE* Oldum, James
Olear, Joseph; America, 1900 7137 p169
O'Leary, Daniel; New York, NY, 1838 8208.4 p66
O'Leary, Daniel 40; Massachusetts, 1850 5881.1 p79
O'Leary, James; Arkansas, 1918 95.2 p91
O'Leary, James; New York, NY, 1815 2859.11 p40
O'Leary, James; Quebec, 1818 7603 p64
O'Leary, Jerry 40; Kansas, 1884 5240.1 p66
O'Leary, John J. 40; Arizona, 1922 9228.40 p26
O'Leary, Mary; Montreal, 1825 7603 p65
O'Leary, Timothy J.; Arkansas, 1918 95.2 p91
Olejar, Joseph; America, 1900 7137 p169
Olejnik, Jospeh; Arkansas, 1918 95.2 p92
Oler, Marx Simon *SEE* Oler, William
Oler, Ursula *SEE* Oler, William

Oler, William; Pennsylvania, 1737 ***1034.18*** *p14*
*Wife:*Ursula
*Child:*Marx Simon
Olers, Captain; Canada, 1776-1783 ***9786*** *p189*
Olesin, Evern; Wisconsin, n.d. ***9675.7*** *p129*
Oleson, Carl; Iowa, 1866-1943 ***123.54*** *p37*
Olewniczak, Joseph; Arkansas, 1918 ***95.2*** *p92*
Olfalt, C.; Minneapolis, 1883 ***6410.35*** *p62*
Olgeirsson, Bjarni 42; Quebec, 1879 ***2557.1*** *p39*
Olianio, Francisco 29; Arizona, 1913 ***9228.40*** *p18*
Olibois, Mr.; Port uncertain, 1839 ***778.5*** *p409*
Oliffe, Edgar; Arkansas, 1918 ***95.2*** *p92*
Olinger, John; Wisconsin, n.d. ***9675.7*** *p129*
Oliphant, Andrew; New England, 1762 ***1639.20*** *p256*
Oliphant, David; Charleston, SC, 1828 ***1639.20*** *p256*
Oliphant, David; South Carolina, 1746-1805 ***1639.20*** *p256*
Oliphant, James 34; Georgia, 1775 ***1219.7*** *p276*
Oliphant, Jemima; Charleston, SC, 1804 ***1639.20*** *p256*
Oliphant, Robert 16; Jamaica, 1733 ***3690.1*** *p168*
Olipher, Nancy 17; Philadelphia, 1858 ***5704.8*** *p139*
Oliva, Mr.; Quebec, 1815 ***9229.18*** *p78*
Oliva, Friedrich Wilhelm; Canada, 1776-1783 ***9786*** *p217*
Olivari, Agostino J.; Arkansas, 1918 ***95.2*** *p92*
Oliver, A.W.; Illinois, 1888 ***5012.37*** *p62*
Oliver, Adam; Virginia, 1637 ***6219*** *p112*
Oliver, Ann 22; Quebec, 1855 ***5704.8*** *p126*
Oliver, Boagg; Arkansas, 1918 ***95.2*** *p92*
Oliver, Catharine; New York, NY, 1864 ***5704.8*** *p187*
Oliver, Catherine; Philadelphia, 1851 ***5704.8*** *p70*
Oliver, Catherine 50; North Carolina, 1850 ***1639.20*** *p256*
Oliver, David *SEE* Oliver, Evan
Oliver, Edmund 20; Barbados, 1724 ***3690.1*** *p168*
Oliver, Edward; Arkansas, 1918 ***95.2*** *p92*
Oliver, Edward; Virginia, 1638 ***6219*** *p122*
Oliver, Eliza.; Virginia, 1643 ***6219*** *p206*
Oliver, Elizabeth *SEE* Oliver, Evan
Oliver, Ellen; Philadelphia, 1864 ***5704.8*** *p179*
Oliver, Evan *SEE* Oliver, Evan
Oliver, Evan; Pennsylvania, 1682 ***4961*** *p239*
*Wife:*Jean
*Child:*David
*Child:*Elizabeth
*Child:*John
*Child:*Hannah
*Child:*Mary
*Child:*Evan
*Child:*Seaborn
Oliver, Frances 18; Maryland, 1731 ***3690.1*** *p168*
Oliver, Garner; New York, NY, 1851 ***3455.2*** *p99*
Oliver, Hannah *SEE* Oliver, Evan
Oliver, Henry W.; New York, NY, 1839 ***8208.4*** *p101*
Oliver, Jack; Arkansas, 1918 ***95.2*** *p92*
Oliver, James; Ohio, 1867-1878 ***9892.11*** *p35*
Oliver, James; Ohio, 1880 ***9892.11*** *p35*
Oliver, James 18; Maryland, 1775 ***1219.7*** *p267*
Oliver, James 20; Philadelphia, 1854 ***5704.8*** *p116*
Oliver, Jane; New York, NY, 1864 ***5704.8*** *p187*
Oliver, Jean *SEE* Oliver, Evan
Oliver, John *SEE* Oliver, Evan
Oliver, John; Arkansas, 1918 ***95.2*** *p92*
Oliver, John; New York, NY, 1840 ***8208.4*** *p105*
Oliver, John; Ohio, 1867-1875 ***9892.11*** *p35*
Oliver, John; Ohio, 1878 ***9892.11*** *p35*
Oliver, John; Virginia, 1642 ***6219*** *p198*
Oliver, John; Virginia, 1648 ***6219*** *p250*
Oliver, John 17; Maryland, 1774 ***1219.7*** *p235*
Oliver, John 33; Maryland, 1775 ***1219.7*** *p272*
Oliver, Mary *SEE* Oliver, Evan
Oliver, Mary; Virginia, 1642 ***6219*** *p190*
Oliver, Matthew 32; Virginia, 1774 ***1219.7*** *p243*
Oliver, N. R.; Washington, 1859-1920 ***2872.1*** *p29*
Oliver, Nich.; Virginia, 1636 ***6219*** *p78*
Oliver, Nich.; Virginia, 1636 ***6219*** *p80*
Oliver, Nicholas; Virginia, 1639 ***6219*** *p161*
Oliver, Noble 17; St. John, N.B., 1854 ***5704.8*** *p122*
Oliver, Rebecca; Philadelphia, 1852 ***5704.8*** *p88*
Oliver, Richard; Virginia, 1642 ***6219*** *p196*
Oliver, Richard 19; Nova Scotia, 1774 ***1219.7*** *p210*
Oliver, Richard 31; Jamaica, 1736 ***3690.1*** *p168*
Oliver, Robert; New York, NY, 1864 ***5704.8*** *p187*
Oliver, Robert; Virginia, 1639 ***6219*** *p153*
Oliver, Samuel 19; Maryland, 1722 ***3690.1*** *p168*
Oliver, Sarah 16; Jamaica, 1736 ***3690.1*** *p169*
Oliver, Seaborn *SEE* Oliver, Evan
Oliver, Tho.; Virginia, 1640 ***6219*** *p160*
Oliver, Thomas; Ohio, 1844 ***9892.11*** *p35*
Oliver, Thomas; Philadelphia, 1865 ***5704.8*** *p202*
Oliver, Thomas; Savannah, GA, 1774 ***1219.7*** *p227*
With wife
Oliver, Thomas 29; Savannah, GA, 1774 ***1219.7*** *p226*
With wife
With 2 children
Oliver, Walter W.; Iowa, 1866-1943 ***123.54*** *p37*
Oliver, William; New York, NY, 1864 ***5704.8*** *p187*
Oliver, William; Ohio, 1854-1864 ***9892.11*** *p35*
Oliver, William; Ohio, 1865 ***9892.11*** *p35*
Oliver, William; Virginia, 1642 ***6219*** *p190*
Oliver, Wm. P. 32; Kansas, 1892 ***5240.1*** *p32*
Oliver, Wm. P. 32; Kansas, 1892 ***5240.1*** *p77*
Olivie, A.; New Orleans, 1839 ***778.5*** *p409*
Olivier, . . .; Canada, 1776-1783 ***9786*** *p30*
Olivier, Mr. 25; New Orleans, 1822 ***778.5*** *p409*
Olivier, Mrs. 20; New Orleans, 1822 ***778.5*** *p410*
Olivier, Abel; Quebec, 1718 ***7603*** *p27*
Olivier, H. 38; New Orleans, 1822 ***778.5*** *p409*
Olivier, J. 24; America, 1835 ***778.5*** *p410*
Olivier, J. 35; America, 1835 ***778.5*** *p410*
Olivier, Noel 23; Port uncertain, 1839 ***778.5*** *p410*
Olivier, Remi 37; California, 1871 ***2769.7*** *p4*
Olivieri, Ant. 48; New York, NY, 1893 ***9026.4*** *p42*
Olkowska, Wladyslaw 25; New York, 1912 ***9980.29*** *p60*
*Wife:*Zofia 28
Olkowska, Zofia 28 *SEE* Olkowska, Wladyslaw
Olkowski, Wladyslaw 25; New York, 1912 ***9980.29*** *p60*
*Wife:*Zofia 28
Olkowski, Zofia 28 *SEE* Olkowski, Wladyslaw
Ollaver, Wm.; Virginia, 1645 ***6219*** *p232*
Ollendorf, Carl; New York, 1754 ***3652*** *p80*
Ollerhead, Will 21; Virginia, 1699 ***2212*** *p27*
Olleris, Jean 40; New Orleans, 1823 ***778.5*** *p410*
Ollier, Joseph; America, 1852 ***8582.3*** *p49*
Olliffe, Robert; Virginia, 1642 ***6219*** *p199*
Olliotte, Mr. 24; New Orleans, 1839 ***778.5*** *p410*
Olliver, George; Virginia, 1636 ***6219*** *p28*
Ollringshaw, Henry; New York, 1756 ***3652*** *p81*
Olmsmeyer, Carl 45; America, 1850 ***4610.10*** *p143*
*Child:*Carl Heinrich
*Child:*Friedrich Gottlieb
Olmsmeyer, Carl Heinrich *SEE* Olmsmeyer, Carl
Olmsmeyer, Friedrich Gottlieb *SEE* Olmsmeyer, Carl
Olney, Syvenus; Ohio, 1812-1840 ***9892.11*** *p36*
Oloff, Frank; Arkansas, 1918 ***95.2*** *p92*
Olofson, Lars; Washington, 1859-1920 ***2872.1*** *p29*
Olofsson, Jonas; Minneapolis, 1868-1877 ***6410.35*** *p50*
O'Lone, Anne; Philadelphia, 1869 ***5704.8*** *p236*
O'Lone, Catharine; Philadelphia, 1869 ***5704.8*** *p236*
O'Lone, Ellen; Philadelphia, 1869 ***5704.8*** *p236*
O'Lone, John; Philadelphia, 1869 ***5704.8*** *p236*
O'Lone, Lawrence; Quebec, 1824 ***7603*** *p71*
O'Lone, Rose; Philadelphia, 1869 ***5704.8*** *p236*
O'Loone, Henry; New York, NY, 1816 ***2859.11*** *p40*
O'Loughlin, Laughlin; America, 1735-1743 ***4971*** *p78*
O'Loughre, John; New York, NY, 1848 ***9788.3*** *p18*
O'Loughre, John; West Virginia, 1855 ***9788.3*** *p18*
O'Love, Biddy; Philadelphia, 1867 ***5704.8*** *p223*
O'Love, Sarah; Philadelphia, 1867 ***5704.8*** *p223*
Olph, Barnard; Pennsylvania, 1752 ***2444*** *p198*
Olpp, Catharina Christina *SEE* Olpp, Hans Bernhard
Olpp, Catharina Reis *SEE* Olpp, Hans Bernhard
Olpp, Hans Bernhard; Pennsylvania, 1752 ***2444*** *p198*
*Wife:*Catharina Reis
*Child:*Catharina Christina
Olrich, . . .; Canada, 1776-1783 ***9786*** *p43*
Olsan, Olaf 28; Kansas, 1889 ***5240.1*** *p74*
Olsen, Alvin Norman; Washington, 1859-1920 ***2872.1*** *p29*
Olsen, Andrew; Washington, 1859-1920 ***2872.1*** *p29*
Olsen, Carl L.; Maine, 1871-1885 ***6410.22*** *p118*
Olsen, Christian Marinus; Arkansas, 1918 ***95.2*** *p92*
Olsen, Christopher Ole; Arkansas, 1885 ***3688*** *p7*
Olsen, Edward; New York, 1872 ***1450.2*** *p29B*
Olsen, Elmer; Arkansas, 1918 ***95.2*** *p92*
Olsen, Emel; Washington, 1859-1920 ***2872.1*** *p29*
Olsen, Gena S.; Washington, 1859-1920 ***2872.1*** *p29*
Olsen, Gunder; Wisconsin, n.d. ***9675.7*** *p129*
Olsen, H.C.; Illinois, 1876 ***5012.39*** *p91*
Olsen, Helen Ruth; Washington, 1859-1920 ***2872.1*** *p29*
Olsen, Hilja; Washington, 1859-1920 ***2872.1*** *p29*
Olsen, Hilmer Milford; Washington, 1859-1920 ***2872.1*** *p29*
Olsen, James 35; Arizona, 1890 ***2764.35*** *p52*
Olsen, John; Wisconsin, n.d. ***9675.7*** *p129*
Olsen, John P.; Illinois, 1876 ***5012.39*** *p91*
Olsen, Knud Thagaard 30; Arkansas, 1918 ***95.2*** *p92*
Olsen, Marius; Arkansas, 1918 ***95.2*** *p93*
Olsen, Martin; Arkansas, 1918 ***95.2*** *p93*
Olsen, Martin; Washington, 1859-1920 ***2872.1*** *p29*
Olsen, Mattie; Washington, 1859-1920 ***2872.1*** *p29*
Olsen, Nels; Washington, 1859-1920 ***2872.1*** *p29*
Olsen, Nels Matt; Washington, 1859-1920 ***2872.1*** *p29*
Olsen, Olaf Waldemar; Arkansas, 1918 ***95.2*** *p93*
Olsen, Ole; Maine, 1871-1881 ***6410.22*** *p118*
Olsen, Ole; Wisconsin, n.d. ***9675.7*** *p129*
Olsen, Oscar; Maine, 1897 ***6410.22*** *p127*
Olsen, Oscar Wilbur; Washington, 1859-1920 ***2872.1*** *p29*
Olsen, Salmer George; Washington, 1859-1920 ***2872.1*** *p29*
Olsen, Wilhelm; Arkansas, 1918 ***95.2*** *p93*
Olshausen, Arthur; America, 1837 ***8582.3*** *p49*
Olson, A. G.; Iowa, 1852 ***2090*** *p615*
Olson, A. G.; Minneapolis, 1882-1885 ***6410.35*** *p62*
Olson, Alban John; Arkansas, 1918 ***95.2*** *p93*
Olson, Alex; Iowa, 1866-1943 ***123.54*** *p37*
Olson, Alfred; Minneapolis, 1881-1884 ***6410.35*** *p63*
Olson, Amanda 23; Massachusetts, 1860 ***6410.32*** *p98*
Olson, Anders; New York, NY, 1908 ***3455.2*** *p95*
*Wife:*Justina Lovia
Olson, Andrew; Iowa, 1854 ***2090*** *p615*
*Wife:*Bertha
Olson, Aron; Colorado, 1904 ***9678.2*** *p130*
Olson, Axel Ray; Arkansas, 1918 ***95.2*** *p93*
Olson, B. O.; Washington, 1859-1920 ***2872.1*** *p29*
Olson, Bertha *SEE* Olson, Andrew
Olson, C. M.; Minneapolis, 1882-1883 ***6410.35*** *p63*
Olson, Carl Johan Olaf; Arkansas, 1918 ***95.2*** *p93*
Olson, Charles 27; Kansas, 1893 ***5240.1*** *p79*
Olson, Charles Niles; Bangor, ME, 1869-1880 ***6410.22*** *p116*
Olson, Christian 27; Massachusetts, 1860 ***6410.32*** *p98*
Olson, Conrad; Arkansas, 1918 ***95.2*** *p93*
Olson, Edmund; Wisconsin, n.d. ***9675.7*** *p129*
Olson, Elda; Washington, 1859-1920 ***2872.1*** *p29*
Olson, Elmer Ferdinand; Arkansas, 1918 ***95.2*** *p93*
Olson, Emil; New York, NY, 1908 ***3455.2*** *p95*
Olson, Erick; Minneapolis, 1881-1887 ***6410.35*** *p63*
Olson, Fred Herman; Arkansas, 1918 ***95.2*** *p93*
Olson, Gustaf Elof 25; Arkansas, 1918 ***95.2*** *p93*
Olson, Helmer Olaf; Arkansas, 1918 ***95.2*** *p93*
Olson, Henry; Iowa, 1866-1943 ***123.54*** *p37*
Olson, Ivan Gideon; Washington, 1859-1920 ***2872.1*** *p29*
Olson, J. E.; Minneapolis, 1850-1878 ***6410.35*** *p63*
Olson, John; Colorado, 1904 ***9678.2*** *p130*
Olson, John; Maine, 1883-1892 ***6410.22*** *p120*
Olson, John; Washington, 1859-1920 ***2872.1*** *p29*
Olson, John; Wisconsin, n.d. ***9675.7*** *p129*
Olson, John L.; Washington, 1859-1920 ***2872.1*** *p29*
Olson, John W.; Colorado, 1894 ***9678.2*** *p130*
Olson, Justina Lovia *SEE* Olson, Anders
Olson, L.; Washington, 1859-1920 ***2872.1*** *p29*
Olson, L. J.; Iowa, 1866-1943 ***123.54*** *p37*
Olson, Leonard; Iowa, 1866-1943 ***123.54*** *p37*
Olson, Lewis; Washington, 1859-1920 ***2872.1*** *p29*
Olson, Louis; Washington, 1859-1920 ***2872.1*** *p29*
Olson, Martin; Washington, 1859-1920 ***2872.1*** *p30*
Olson, Martin Andrew; Washington, 1859-1920 ***2872.1*** *p30*
Olson, Mathias; Washington, 1859-1920 ***2872.1*** *p30*
Olson, Morris; Arkansas, 1918 ***95.2*** *p93*
Olson, N. M.; Washington, 1859-1920 ***2872.1*** *p30*
Olson, Nels; Washington, 1859-1920 ***2872.1*** *p29*
Olson, Nels; Washington, 1859-1920 ***2872.1*** *p30*
Olson, Nicolaus; Minneapolis, 1874-1883 ***6410.35*** *p63*
Olson, O. Christian; New York, NY, 1852 ***6410.32*** *p122*
Olson, Peter; Bangor, ME, 1886 ***6410.22*** *p125*
Olson, Peter; Washington, 1859-1920 ***2872.1*** *p30*
Olson, Peter; Wisconsin, n.d. ***9675.7*** *p130*
Olson, Peter John; Maine, 1872-1876 ***6410.22*** *p116*
Olson, Sam; Arkansas, 1918 ***95.2*** *p93*
Olson, Sam; Minneapolis, 1880-1883 ***6410.35*** *p63*
Olson, Swan Justus; Arkansas, 1918 ***95.2*** *p93*
Olson, Thomas; Iowa, 1859 ***2090*** *p613*
Olson, Torkel 31; Arkansas, 1918 ***95.2*** *p93*
Olsson, Anders Gustaf; Minneapolis, 1882-1885 ***6410.35*** *p62*
Olsson, Lars G.; Minneapolis, 1887-1888 ***6410.35*** *p63*
Olsson, Nils; Bangor, ME, 1874 ***6410.22*** *p124*
Olsson, Nils; Minneapolis, 1883-1887 ***6410.35*** *p60*
Olsson, Otto; Minneapolis, 1881-1887 ***6410.35*** *p63*
Olsson, Otto; Minneapolis, 1885-1888 ***6410.35*** *p63*
Olsson, P. J.; Minneapolis, 1881-1883 ***6410.35*** *p63*
Olsson, Paul M. 21; Kansas, 1884 ***5240.1*** *p65*
Olsson, Petter Gust.; Bangor, ME, 1895 ***6410.22*** *p127*
Olszanski, . . .; New York, 1831 ***4606*** *p176*
Olszewski, . . .; New York, 1831 ***4606*** *p176*
Oltagh, John; America, 1738 ***4971*** *p55*
Olthoff, Charles; Kansas, 1892 ***5240.1*** *p32*
Olthoff, Henry; Wisconsin, 1874 ***5240.1*** *p32*
Oltmanns, Gebhard; Iroquois Co., IL, 1892 ***3455.1*** *p12*
Oltmans, Johann; New York, NY, 1925 ***3455.4*** *p56*
Olzewski, Joe; Arkansas, 1918 ***95.2*** *p93*
O'Madigan, Owen; America, 1741 ***4971*** *p76*
O'Maley, Bridget 11; Philadelphia, 1853 ***5704.8*** *p108*
O'Maley, Bridget 55; Philadelphia, 1853 ***5704.8*** *p108*
O'Maley, Conely 17; Philadelphia, 1853 ***5704.8*** *p108*
O'Maley, Ellan 15; Philadelphia, 1853 ***5704.8*** *p108*
O'Mallay, John 20; Massachusetts, 1848 ***5881.1*** *p79*
O'Malley, Constantine; Philadelphia, 1852 ***5704.8*** *p92*
O'Mallory, Catharine 4; Massachusetts, 1849 ***5881.1*** *p79*

O'Mallory, Catharine 38; Massachusetts, 1849 ***5881.1*** *p79*
O'Mallory, Edward 8; Massachusetts, 1849 ***5881.1*** *p79*
O'Mallory, Eleanor 6; Massachusetts, 1849 ***5881.1*** *p79*
O'Mallory, Hannah 2; Massachusetts, 1849 ***5881.1*** *p79*
Oman, Andrew; Boston, 1849 ***6410.32*** *p123*
Oman, Andrew 27; Massachusetts, 1860 ***6410.32*** *p103*
Oman, Andrew 28; Massachusetts, 1860 ***6410.32*** *p118*
Oman, Margaret 23; Massachusetts, 1860 ***6410.32*** *p103*
Oman, Margaret 23; Massachusetts, 1860 ***6410.32*** *p118*
O'Mara, Martin; America, 1741 ***4971*** *p83*
O'Mara, Michael; New York, 1867 ***2764.35*** *p52*
O'Mara, Michel; Montreal, 1819 ***7603*** *p80*
O'Meally, Mary; New York, NY, 1870 ***5704.8*** *p237*
O'Meara, John; New York, NY, 1837 ***8208.4*** *p52*
Omeara, Martin; Quebec, 1789 ***7603*** *p56*
O'Meara, Patrick; New York, NY, 1834 ***8208.4*** *p3*
Omietanski, William; Arkansas, 1918 ***95.2*** *p93*
O'Mullan, Arthur; America, 1742 ***4971*** *p76*
O'Mullan, Pat.; America, 1740 ***4971*** *p63*
O'Mullan, Phelemy; America, 1737 ***4971*** *p77*
Omyat, Josef 18; New York, 1912 ***9980.29*** *p72*
O'Naill, James; Philadelphia, 1853 ***5704.8*** *p103*
Onchard, John 31; Baltimore, 1775 ***1219.7*** *p270*
Oncken, Hajo H.; Illinois, 1889 ***5012.40*** *p25*
Ondale, John; Virginia, 1642 ***6219*** *p193*
O'Neal, Ann 60; Kansas, 1874 ***5240.1*** *p55*
O'Neal, Anne; Philadelphia, 1816 ***2859.11*** *p40*
O'Neal, Bridget 14; Massachusetts, 1847 ***5881.1*** *p78*
O'Neal, Catherine 18; Philadelphia, 1864 ***5704.8*** *p156*
O'Neal, Daniel; Indiana, 1848 ***9117*** *p17*
O'Neal, Dennis 1; Massachusetts, 1849 ***5881.1*** *p79*
O'Neal, Eliza 15; Philadelphia, 1861 ***5704.8*** *p147*
O'Neal, Ellen 26; Massachusetts, 1849 ***5881.1*** *p79*
O'Neal, Ellen 50; Massachusetts, 1848 ***5881.1*** *p79*
O'Neal, Eugene 40; Massachusetts, 1848 ***5881.1*** *p79*
O'Neal, Felix; New York, NY, 1811 ***2859.11*** *p18*
O'Neal, Hugh; Ohio, 1845 ***9892.11*** *p36*
O'Neal, Jaine; Philadelphia, 1850 ***5704.8*** *p68*
O'Neal, James Henry; Quebec, 1848 ***5704.8*** *p41*
O'Neal, John; America, 1834-1835 ***7036*** *p121*
O'Neal, John; New York, NY, 1816 ***2859.11*** *p40*
O'Neal, John; Ohio, 1852 ***9892.11*** *p36*
O'Neal, John 40; Massachusetts, 1850 ***5881.1*** *p79*
O'Neal, Kate 50; Massachusetts, 1850 ***5881.1*** *p79*
O'Neal, Margaret 24; Massachusetts, 1850 ***5881.1*** *p80*
O'Neal, Mary; St. John, N.B., 1848 ***5704.8*** *p44*
O'Neal, Nancy 3; Massachusetts, 1849 ***5881.1*** *p80*
O'Neal, Nicholas; Philadelphia, 1816 ***2859.11*** *p40*
O'Neal, Patrick 40; Kansas, 1873 ***5240.1*** *p55*
O'Neal, Sarah 16; Philadelphia, 1864 ***5704.8*** *p156*
O'Neal, Thomas; New York, NY, 1838 ***8208.4*** *p73*
O'Neal, William; Massachusetts, 1841 ***7036*** *p127*
O'Neal, William 25; Massachusetts, 1848 ***5881.1*** *p80*
O'Neale, David; Indiana, 1848 ***9117*** *p19*
O'Neall, Alexander; Philadelphia, 1816 ***2859.11*** *p40*
O'Neil, Ann; America, 1740 ***4971*** *p66*
O'Neil, Anne; New York, NY, 1864 ***5704.8*** *p186*
O'Neil, Charles; New York, NY, 1815 ***2859.11*** *p40*
O'Neil, Charles 9; St. John, N.B., 1853 ***5704.8*** *p106*
O'Neil, Cornelius; Quebec, 1713 ***7603*** *p87*
O'Neil, David; Colorado, 1904 ***9678.2*** *p130*
O'Neil, Denis; Quebec, 1810 ***7603*** *p78*
O'Neil, Duncan 24; Maryland, 1774 ***1219.7*** *p185*
O'Neil, Frances; Wisconsin, n.d. ***9675.7*** *p130*
O'Neil, Francis; Philadelphia, 1852 ***5704.8*** *p89*
O'Neil, Francis 5; St. John, N.B., 1851 ***5704.8*** *p72*
O'Neil, Henry; St. John, N.B., 1852 ***5704.8*** *p83*
O'Neil, Honor 12; St. John, N.B., 1853 ***5704.8*** *p106*
O'Neil, Hugh; Quebec, 1852 ***5704.8*** *p90*
O'Neil, J.; New York, NY, 1816 ***2859.11*** *p40*
O'Neil, James; Montreal, 1821 ***7603*** *p102*
O'Neil, James; New York, NY, 1816 ***2859.11*** *p40*
O'Neil, James 3; St. John, N.B., 1851 ***5704.8*** *p72*
Oneil, John; America, 1737 ***4971*** *p72*
O'Neil, John; Baltimore, 1816 ***2859.11*** *p40*
O'Neil, John; Montreal, 1825 ***7603*** *p73*
O'Neil, John; New York, NY, 1816 ***2859.11*** *p40*
With wife & child
O'Neil, John; New York, NY, 1834 ***8208.4*** *p2*
O'Neil, John 10; St. John, N.B., 1851 ***5704.8*** *p72*
O'Neil, John 17; Massachusetts, 1849 ***5881.1*** *p79*
O'Neil, John 20; Newfoundland, 1789 ***4915.24*** *p55*
O'Neil, Katie 66; Arizona, 1909 ***9228.40*** *p11*
O'Neil, Margaret; Quebec, 1852 ***5704.8*** *p90*
O'Neil, Martin 52; Arizona, 1903 ***9228.40*** *p7*
O'Neil, Mary; America, 1738 ***4971*** *p77*
O'Neil, Mary; St. John, N.B., 1851 ***5704.8*** *p72*
O'Neil, Michael; Illinois, 1872 ***2896.5*** *p30*
O'Neil, Michael; New York, NY, 1838 ***8208.4*** *p63*
O'Neil, Michal 30; Kansas, 1876 ***5240.1*** *p57*
O'Neil, Owen; Montreal, 1818 ***7603*** *p61*
O'Neil, Owen; Montreal, 1823 ***7603*** *p102*
O'Neil, Owen; Montreal, 1824 ***7603*** *p89*
O'Neil, Owen; New York, NY, 1816 ***2859.11*** *p40*
With wife & child
O'Neil, Owen; New York, NY, 1839 ***8208.4*** *p96*
O'Neil, Pat; St. John, N.B., 1848 ***5704.8*** *p39*
O'Neil, Richard; Montreal, 1817 ***7603*** *p58*
O'Neil, Roger; America, 1741 ***4971*** *p73*
O'Neil, Sally; Quebec, 1850 ***5704.8*** *p63*
O'Neil, Sally; St. John, N.B., 1851 ***5704.8*** *p72*
O'Neil, Terence; New York, NY, 1836 ***8208.4*** *p17*
O'Neil, Terence 20; Wilmington, DE, 1831 ***6508.7*** *p161*
O'Neil, Thomas; Illinois, 1876 ***2896.5*** *p30*
O'Neil, Thomas; New York, NY, 1852 ***2896.5*** *p30*
O'Neil, Thomas; Quebec, 1820 ***7603*** *p92*
O'Neil, William 23; Quebec, 1854 ***5704.8*** *p119*
O'Neile, Arthur; America, 1740 ***4971*** *p15*
O'Neill, Alice; Philadelphia, 1865 ***5704.8*** *p191*
O'Neill, Ann; Philadelphia, 1865 ***5704.8*** *p202*
O'Neill, Ann; Quebec, 1851 ***5704.8*** *p74*
O'Neill, Ann 19; St. John, N.B., 1854 ***5704.8*** *p114*
O'Neill, Ann 20; Philadelphia, 1858 ***5704.8*** *p139*
O'Neill, Ann 23; Philadelphia, 1864 ***5704.8*** *p157*
O'Neill, Anne 24; St. John, N.B., 1863 ***5704.8*** *p153*
O'Neill, Arthur; Philadelphia, 1851 ***5704.8*** *p80*
O'Neill, Arthur 12; Quebec, 1851 ***5704.8*** *p73*
O'Neill, Biddy 12; St. John, N.B., 1847 ***5704.8*** *p21*
O'Neill, Bridget 25; St. John, N.B., 1854 ***5704.8*** *p114*
O'Neill, Bridget 50; St. John, N.B., 1856 ***5704.8*** *p131*
O'Neill, Catharine; America, 1865 ***5704.8*** *p200*
O'Neill, Catharine; Philadelphia, 1865 ***5704.8*** *p201*
O'Neill, Catherine; Philadelphia, 1852 ***5704.8*** *p97*
O'Neill, Daniel 12; Philadelphia, 1853 ***5704.8*** *p101*
O'Neill, Edward; New York, NY, 1837 ***8208.4*** *p54*
O'Neill, Edward; New York, NY, 1838 ***8208.4*** *p57*
O'Neill, Edward 21; St. John, N.B., 1854 ***5704.8*** *p114*
O'Neill, Edward 50; St. John, N.B., 1856 ***5704.8*** *p131*
O'Neill, Eliza; St. John, N.B., 1853 ***5704.8*** *p99*
O'Neill, Eliza Ann 9; Quebec, 1856 ***5704.8*** *p129*
O'Neill, Elizabeth; Philadelphia, 1853 ***5704.8*** *p101*
O'Neill, Elleanor 13; St. John, N.B., 1847 ***5704.8*** *p19*
O'Neill, Ellen 20; Philadelphia, 1859 ***5704.8*** *p142*
O'Neill, Ellen 24; Philadelphia, 1845 ***6508.6*** *p115*
O'Neill, Emd 19; Philadelphia, 1845 ***6508.6*** *p115*
O'Neill, Emilia 22 *SEE* O'Neill, Francis
O'Neill, Francis 27; Philadelphia, 1804 ***53.26*** *p75*
*Relative:*Emilia 22
O'Neill, Henry 5; Quebec, 1856 ***5704.8*** *p129*
O'Neill, Hugh; America, 1741 ***4971*** *p65*
O'Neill, Hugh; Philadelphia, 1868 ***5704.8*** *p226*
O'Neill, Hugh; Quebec, 1851 ***5704.8*** *p73*
O'Neill, Hugh; Quebec, 1852 ***5704.8*** *p86*
O'Neill, James; America, 1865 ***5704.8*** *p199*
O'Neill, James; Quebec, 1853 ***5704.8*** *p104*
O'Neill, James 3; Quebec, 1856 ***5704.8*** *p129*
O'Neill, James 7; St. John, N.B., 1849 ***5704.8*** *p48*
O'Neill, James 10; Philadelphia, 1853 ***5704.8*** *p101*
O'Neill, James 28; Philadelphia, 1864 ***5704.8*** *p157*
O'Neill, Jane 8; Philadelphia, 1853 ***5704.8*** *p101*
O'Neill, John; New York, NY, 1811 ***2859.11*** *p18*
O'Neill, John; New York, NY, 1866 ***5704.8*** *p211*
O'Neill, John; Philadelphia, 1847 ***53.26*** *p75*
*Relative:*Mary
O'Neill, John; Philadelphia, 1847 ***5704.8*** *p14*
O'Neill, John; Quebec, 1852 ***5704.8*** *p94*
O'Neill, John; St. John, N.B., 1853 ***5704.8*** *p99*
O'Neill, John 1; Philadelphia, 1859 ***5704.8*** *p142*
O'Neill, John 20; Philadelphia, 1855 ***5704.8*** *p123*
O'Neill, John 22; Quebec, 1855 ***5704.8*** *p125*
O'Neill, John 25; St. John, N.B., 1863 ***5704.8*** *p153*
O'Neill, John 30; Philadelphia, 1853 ***5704.8*** *p113*
O'Neill, Joseph; Washington, 1859-1920 ***2872.1*** *p30*
O'Neill, Manus; Quebec, 1851 ***5704.8*** *p73*
O'Neill, Margaret; Quebec, 1852 ***5704.8*** *p86*
O'Neill, Margaret 21; Quebec, 1859 ***5704.8*** *p143*
O'Neill, Margaret 22; Quebec, 1855 ***5704.8*** *p126*
O'Neill, Mary *SEE* O'Neill, John
O'Neill, Mary; Philadelphia, 1847 ***5704.8*** *p14*
O'Neill, Mary; Quebec, 1851 ***5704.8*** *p73*
O'Neill, Mary; St. John, N.B., 1847 ***5704.8*** *p19*
O'Neill, Mary 7; Quebec, 1856 ***5704.8*** *p129*
O'Neill, Mary 22; Philadelphia, 1854 ***5704.8*** *p122*
O'Neill, Mary 34; Quebec, 1856 ***5704.8*** *p129*
O'Neill, Michael; New York, NY, 1840 ***8208.4*** *p106*
O'Neill, Michael; Philadelphia, 1865 ***5704.8*** *p195*
O'Neill, Patrick 20; Philadelphia, 1854 ***5704.8*** *p122*
O'Neill, Patrick 25; Quebec, 1863 ***5704.8*** *p154*
O'Neill, Robert; New York, NY, 1811 ***2859.11*** *p18*
With family
O'Neill, Robert 16; St. John, N.B., 1856 ***5704.8*** *p131*
O'Neill, Rosanna; Quebec, 1856 ***5704.8*** *p129*
O'Neill, Rose; Philadelphia, 1852 ***5704.8*** *p97*
O'Neill, Rose 13; St. John, N.B., 1863 ***5704.8*** *p153*
O'Neill, Rose 16; Philadelphia, 1861 ***5704.8*** *p149*
O'Neill, Roseana 18; St. John, N.B., 1856 ***5704.8*** *p131*
O'Neill, Sarah; New York, NY, 1816 ***2859.11*** *p40*
O'Neill, Sarah; Philadelphia, 1865 ***5704.8*** *p200*
O'Neill, Susan; Philadelphia, 1865 ***5704.8*** *p198*
Oneillon, Ludovoc Francois 23; America, 1839 ***778.5*** *p410*
Onelle, Cornelius; Quebec, 1713 ***7603*** *p87*
Oneta, Angela 26; New York, NY, 1893 ***9026.4*** *p42*
Oney, Benjamin 20; Maryland, 1719 ***3690.1*** *p169*
Onezime, Mme. 20; New Orleans, 1830 ***778.5*** *p410*
Onfroy, Mr. 26; America, 1837 ***778.5*** *p410*
Onfroy, P. J. 37; America, 1825 ***778.5*** *p410*
O'Niel, Charles; New York, NY, 1838 ***8208.4*** *p87*
O'Niel, John; New York, NY, 1838 ***8208.4*** *p85*
Oniell, Wm.; Quebec, 1830 ***4719.7*** *p21*
Onillon, Theodore 17; Ohio, 1837 ***778.5*** *p411*
Onion, John; Virginia, 1639 ***6219*** *p155*
Onken, John; Illinois, 1892 ***5012.40*** *p27*
Onken, Onno Henry; Illinois, 1901 ***5012.40*** *p77*
Onnen, Johann; New York, NY, 1923 ***3455.4*** *p78*
Onnen, Johann; New York, NY, 1926 ***3455.4*** *p80*
Onnen, Onno 26; Kansas, 1882 ***5240.1*** *p32*
Onnen, Onno 26; Kansas, 1882 ***5240.1*** *p64*
Onneston, Rebecca 25; Philadelphia, 1854 ***5704.8*** *p122*
Onorato, Antonio; Colorado, 1903 ***9678.2*** *p130*
Onsman, Thomas 19; Maryland, 1774 ***1219.7*** *p180*
Onsum, Bert; Arkansas, 1918 ***95.2*** *p93*
Onwin, John 17; Virginia, 1773 ***1219.7*** *p169*
Onyon, Robert 18; Jamaica, 1722 ***3690.1*** *p169*
Oor, Thomas; Petersburg, VA, 1809 ***4778.2*** *p141*
Opedahl, John; Colorado, 1904 ***9678.2*** *p131*
Opedal, Andrew T.; Colorado, 1904 ***9678.2*** *p131*
Opfer, Ernst; Illinois, 1866 ***2896.5*** *p30*
Opfer, Ernst; Illinois, 1870 ***2896.5*** *p30*
Opfer, Henry; Illinois, 1868 ***2896.5*** *p30*
Opfer, Henry; Illinois, 1871 ***2896.5*** *p30*
Opitz, . . .; Canada, 1776-1783 ***9786*** *p30*
Opitz, Carl; New York, 1749 ***3652*** *p72*
Opitz, Ella Blanche; Wisconsin, n.d. ***9675.7*** *p130*
Opitz, Ernst Frederick Wilhelm; New York, NY, 1856 ***2896.5*** *p30*
Opitz, Irene Margaret; Iowa, 1866-1943 ***123.54*** *p73*
Opitz, Maria Elizabeth; New York, 1749 ***3652*** *p73*
Opitz, Richard Clemens; Iowa, 1866-1943 ***123.54*** *p73*
Oppenheimer, Amalie 20; America, 1854-1855 ***9162.6*** *p105*
Oppenheimer, Salomon; Cincinnati, 1869-1887 ***8582*** *p23*
O'Quin, Knogher; America, 1737 ***4971*** *p73*
O'Quin, Michael; America, 1741 ***4971*** *p74*
O'Quin, Shane; America, 1738 ***4971*** *p73*
Oragehead, Mary 20; America, 1701 ***2212*** *p34*
Orain, Mr. 24; Port uncertain, 1825 ***778.5*** *p410*
Oran, Robert; Virginia, 1642 ***6219*** *p194*
O'Ray, Hugh; New York, NY, 1811 ***2859.11*** *p18*
Orbach, Henrich; Vermont, 1777 ***8137*** *p12*
Orbel, . . .; Canada, 1776-1783 ***9786*** *p30*
Orchard, Anne *SEE* Orchard, John
Orchard, Anne; Virginia, 1637 ***6219*** *p23*
Orchard, Hugh; Virginia, 1642 ***6219*** *p191*
Orchard, Isaac; New York, NY, 1837 ***8208.4*** *p53*
Orchard, John; Virginia, 1636 ***6219*** *p23*
*Wife:*Anne
Orchard, John; Virginia, 1637 ***6219*** *p23*
*Wife:*Mary
Orchard, Mary *SEE* Orchard, John
Orchard, Thomas; America, 1738 ***4971*** *p52*
Orchard, Thomas; Virginia, 1640 ***6219*** *p160*
Orczolecki, Michal 37; New York, 1912 ***9980.29*** *p52*
Orde, Margaret; Virginia, 1648 ***6219*** *p246*
Ordrienne, Jicaire 29; America, 1829 ***778.5*** *p410*
Ore, Samuel; New York, NY, 1838 ***8208.4*** *p89*
O'Regan, Hugh 28; New Orleans, 1860 ***5704.8*** *p144*
O'Regan, Patrick 27; Massachusetts, 1847 ***5881.1*** *p80*
O'Reilly, Daniel; Illinois, 1884 ***5012.39*** *p52*
O'Reilly, Edward; New York, NY, 1816 ***2859.11*** *p40*
O'Reilly, Eliza; New York, NY, 1816 ***2859.11*** *p40*
O'Reilly, Hugh; New York, NY, 1816 ***2859.11*** *p40*
O'Reilly, Margaret; New York, NY, 1816 ***2859.11*** *p40*
O'Reilly, Miles E.; New York, NY, 1815 ***2859.11*** *p40*
O'Reilly, Patrick; New York, NY, 1835 ***8208.4*** *p57*
O'Reilly, Philip John Marrk; New York, NY, 1837 ***8208.4*** *p26*
Orendolf, Christian; Philadelphia, 1758 ***9973.7*** *p33*
Oresnick, Frank; Wisconsin, n.d. ***9675.7*** *p130*
Orforst, Henry 28; America, 1835 ***778.5*** *p410*
Organ, James D.; Washington, 1859-1920 ***2872.1*** *p30*
Orie, Mr. 36; New Orleans, 1839 ***778.5*** *p410*
Orieux, Jeanne 25; Port uncertain, 1820 ***778.5*** *p410*
Orieux, Rene 39; Louisiana, 1820 ***778.5*** *p411*
Orillac, Mrs. 30; New Orleans, 1839 ***778.5*** *p411*
Orillon, Louis Francois 20; Ohio, 1837 ***778.5*** *p411*
Orillon, Theodore 17; Ohio, 1837 ***778.5*** *p411*
Orimoic, Philip; Iowa, 1866-1943 ***123.54*** *p37*

Oriori, Mr. 30; America, 1837 ***778.5*** *p411*
Orkird, John 30; Nova Scotia, 1774 ***1219.7*** *p210*
Orkney, Mr.; Quebec, 1815 ***9229.18*** *p75*
Orkney, John; North Carolina, 1787-1850 ***1639.20*** *p257*
Orlando, Felix; Arkansas, 1918 ***95.2*** *p93*
Orlando, Guisippe; Arkansas, 1918 ***95.2*** *p93*
Orlansky, Abram; Arkansas, 1918 ***95.2*** *p93*
Orlekowski, Walter; Wisconsin, n.d. ***9675.7*** *p130*
Orlowska, Aniela 20; New York, 1912 ***9980.29*** *p51*
Orlowski, Zofia 20; New York, 1912 ***9980.29*** *p54*
  With sister
  With cousin
Orman, John; New York, NY, 1837 ***8208.4*** *p36*
Ormiston, Jno; Ohio, 1840 ***9892.11*** *p36*
Ormiston, John; Ohio, 1844 ***9892.11*** *p36*
Ormond, Joseph 24; Virginia, 1774 ***1219.7*** *p186*
Ormsby, Eubule; Florida, 1768 ***1219.7*** *p136*
Ornal, . . .; Canada, 1776-1783 ***9786*** *p30*
Ornelik, Bartold; Iowa, 1866-1943 ***123.54*** *p37*
O'Rorke, Bernard; New York, NY, 1815 ***2859.11*** *p40*
O'Rorke, Patrick; New York, NY, 1815 ***2859.11*** *p40*
Orosco, Jose M. 28; Arizona, 1890 ***2764.35*** *p52*
Orosz, Louis; Arkansas, 1918 ***95.2*** *p93*
O'Rouke, Thomas John; Arkansas, 1918 ***95.2*** *p91*
O'Rourke, Owen; New York, NY, 1828 ***8208.4*** *p77*
Orp, William 20; Virginia, 1720 ***3690.1*** *p169*
Orpet, . . .; Canada, 1776-1783 ***9786*** *p30*
Orpwood, John 25; Virginia, 1773 ***1219.7*** *p169*
Orr, . . .; Philadelphia, 1871 ***5704.8*** *p240*
Orr, Ann; Philadelphia, 1851 ***5704.8*** *p76*
Orr, Ann; St. John, N.B., 1852 ***5704.8*** *p93*
Orr, Ann 5 *SEE* Orr, James
Orr, Ann J.; America, 1867 ***5704.8*** *p222*
Orr, Anne; New York, NY, 1816 ***2859.11*** *p40*
Orr, Charles; North Carolina, 1788 ***1639.20*** *p257*
Orr, Daniel 3; St. John, N.B., 1853 ***5704.8*** *p110*
Orr, Eliza *SEE* Orr, Matty
Orr, Eliza; Philadelphia, 1847 ***5704.8*** *p31*
Orr, Eliza; Quebec, 1849 ***5704.8*** *p51*
Orr, Eliza 6 mos; St. John, N.B., 1852 ***5704.8*** *p93*
Orr, Elizabeth; New York, NY, 1816 ***2859.11*** *p40*
Orr, Elizabeth 3; Philadelphia, 1864 ***5704.8*** *p155*
Orr, Elizabeth 6; St. John, N.B., 1853 ***5704.8*** *p110*
Orr, Elizabeth 9 *SEE* Orr, James
Orr, Ellen; Philadelphia, 1871 ***5704.8*** *p240*
Orr, George; New York, NY, 1816 ***2859.11*** *p40*
Orr, George; Philadelphia, 1851 ***5704.8*** *p70*
Orr, George; Philadelphia, 1864 ***5704.8*** *p181*
Orr, George; Philadelphia, 1871 ***5704.8*** *p240*
Orr, Hannah *SEE* Orr, Robert
Orr, Hannah; Philadelphia, 1847 ***5704.8*** *p21*
Orr, Hannah 3 *SEE* Orr, James
Orr, Isabella; Philadelphia, 1851 ***5704.8*** *p70*
Orr, Isabella 7 *SEE* Orr, James
Orr, James; America, 1742 ***4971*** *p69*
Orr, James; New York, NY, 1816 ***2859.11*** *p40*
Orr, James; Philadelphia, 1851 ***5704.8*** *p70*
Orr, James 7; St. John, N.B., 1852 ***5704.8*** *p93*
Orr, James 27; St. John, N.B., 1866 ***5704.8*** *p167*
Orr, James 30; Philadelphia, 1834 ***53.26*** *p75*
  *Relative:*Jane 32
  *Relative:*Margaret 11
  *Relative:*Elizabeth 9
  *Relative:*Ann 5
  *Relative:*Isabella 7
  *Relative:*Hannah 3
Orr, James 68; South Carolina, 1823 ***1639.20*** *p257*
  *Relative:*Martha 54
Orr, James William; Philadelphia, 1847 ***5704.8*** *p1*
Orr, Jane; New York, NY, 1816 ***2859.11*** *p40*
Orr, Jane 9; Philadelphia, 1851 ***5704.8*** *p70*
Orr, Jane 23; St. John, N.B., 1866 ***5704.8*** *p167*
Orr, Jane 32 *SEE* Orr, James
Orr, Jane 33; St. John, N.B., 1853 ***5704.8*** *p110*
Orr, John; New York, NY, 1811 ***2859.11*** *p18*
  With family
Orr, John; San Francisco, 1850 ***4914.15*** *p10*
Orr, John 20; Philadelphia, 1854 ***5704.8*** *p115*
Orr, John 28; St. John, N.B., 1864 ***5704.8*** *p159*
Orr, John 30; Philadelphia, 1861 ***5704.8*** *p148*
Orr, Joshua; Philadelphia, 1811 ***53.26*** *p76*
Orr, Joshua; Philadelphia, 1811 ***2859.11*** *p18*
Orr, Letitia; New York, NY, 1870 ***5704.8*** *p240*
Orr, Margaret; Philadelphia, 1851 ***5704.8*** *p70*
Orr, Margaret 11 *SEE* Orr, James
Orr, Martha 54 *SEE* Orr, James
Orr, Mary; New York, NY, 1811 ***2859.11*** *p18*
Orr, Mary Ann 4; St. John, N.B., 1852 ***5704.8*** *p93*
Orr, Mary Ann 8; St. John, N.B., 1853 ***5704.8*** *p110*
Orr, Mary Jane; Philadelphia, 1849 ***53.26*** *p76*
  *Relative:*Nancy
Orr, Mary Jane; Philadelphia, 1849 ***5704.8*** *p58*
Orr, Mathew; New York, NY, 1811 ***2859.11*** *p18*
Orr, Matty; Philadelphia, 1847 ***53.26*** *p76*
  *Relative:*Eliza
Orr, Matty; Philadelphia, 1847 ***5704.8*** *p31*
Orr, Moses 11; Philadelphia, 1851 ***5704.8*** *p70*
Orr, Nancy *SEE* Orr, Mary Jane
Orr, Nancy; Philadelphia, 1849 ***5704.8*** *p58*
Orr, Nancy; St. John, N.B., 1852 ***5704.8*** *p95*
Orr, Patrick; New York, NY, 1816 ***2859.11*** *p40*
Orr, Robert; Philadelphia, 1811 ***53.26*** *p76*
Orr, Robert; Philadelphia, 1811 ***2859.11*** *p18*
Orr, Robert; Philadelphia, 1847 ***53.26*** *p76*
  *Relative:*Hannah
Orr, Robert; Philadelphia, 1847 ***5704.8*** *p21*
Orr, Rose; Quebec, 1852 ***5704.8*** *p94*
Orr, Sarah; Philadelphia, 1851 ***5704.8*** *p77*
Orr, Thomas; New York, NY, 1816 ***2859.11*** *p40*
Orr, William; New York, NY, 1811 ***2859.11*** *p18*
Orr, William; New York, NY, 1811 ***2859.11*** *p18*
  With family
Orr, William; New York, NY, 1816 ***2859.11*** *p40*
Orr, William; Philadelphia, 1851 ***5704.8*** *p78*
Orr, William; Philadelphia, 1866 ***5704.8*** *p211*
Orr, William; Quebec, 1849 ***5704.8*** *p52*
Orrage, George 29; Virginia, 1774 ***1219.7*** *p242*
Orred, Aaron 18; Jamaica, 1733 ***3690.1*** *p169*
Orrell, Alex; America, 1705 ***2212*** *p45*
Orrell, Mary 20; Philadelphia, 1864 ***5704.8*** *p160*
Orry, Jane; Savannah, GA, 1774 ***1219.7*** *p227*
Orry, John; Savannah, GA, 1774 ***1219.7*** *p227*
Orry, William; Savannah, GA, 1774 ***1219.7*** *p227*
Orser, George; New York, NY, 1839 ***8208.4*** *p102*
Orsor, David; Washington, 1859-1920 ***2872.1*** *p30*
Orst, Hubert 64; Kansas, 1884 ***5240.1*** *p65*
Orstadt, Eckhard; Philadelphia, 1779 ***8137*** *p12*
Orszulak, Franciszek 31; New York, 1912 ***9980.29*** *p64*
Ort, Michael; America, 1842 ***8582.1*** *p26*
Orth, . . .; Canada, 1776-1783 ***9786*** *p30*
Orth, Anthony; America, 1871 ***6014.1*** *p3*
Orth, Frank 24; Kansas, 1888 ***5240.1*** *p71*
Orth, John 26; Kansas, 1885 ***5240.1*** *p32*
Orth, John 26; Kansas, 1885 ***5240.1*** *p68*
Orth, Mathias 23; Kansas, 1884 ***5240.1*** *p33*
Orth, Mathias 23; Kansas, 1884 ***5240.1*** *p67*
Orth, Mike 26; Kansas, 1893 ***5240.1*** *p78*
Orth, Nick; Kansas, 1892 ***5240.1*** *p33*
Orth, Peter 21; Kansas, 1891 ***5240.1*** *p76*
Orthmann, Johann; Wisconsin, n.d. ***9675.7*** *p130*
Orthner, . . .; Canada, 1776-1783 ***9786*** *p30*
Orthogean, Mr. 30; America, 1826 ***778.5*** *p411*
Orthwein, Friedrich 4 mos; New York, NY, 1889 ***7846*** *p39*
Orthwein, Ludwig 29; New York, NY, 1889 ***7846*** *p39*
Orthwein, Rosina 28; New York, NY, 1889 ***7846*** *p39*
Ortiz, Pedro 36; Kansas, 1900 ***5240.1*** *p81*
Ortlieb, John; New York, 1750 ***3652*** *p74*
Ortman, Fritz; Kansas, 1894 ***5240.1*** *p33*
Ortmann, Christoph; Georgia, 1739 ***9332*** *p325*
  *Wife:*Juliana
Ortmann, Johann; Ohio, 1800-1885 ***8582.2*** *p58*
Ortmann, Juliana *SEE* Ortmann, Christoph
Ortner, . . .; Canada, 1776-1783 ***9786*** *p30*
Ortolan, Felix 5; New Orleans, 1838 ***778.5*** *p411*
Ortolan, Louisa 7; New Orleans, 1838 ***778.5*** *p411*
Ortolan, Sernein 29; New Orleans, 1838 ***778.5*** *p411*
Orton, William; Carolina, 1772 ***1219.7*** *p152*
Ortwine, Friedrich 4 mos; New York, NY, 1889 ***7846*** *p39*
Ortwine, Ludwig 29; New York, NY, 1889 ***7846*** *p39*
Ortwine, Rosina 28; New York, NY, 1889 ***7846*** *p39*
Orvedal, Peter 27; Arkansas, 1918 ***95.2*** *p93*
Orzechowski, Stanislaw; New York, 1835 ***4606*** *p180*
Osagr, Gord; New York, NY, 1839 ***8208.4*** *p102*
Osaland, John Gabriel; Arkansas, 1918 ***95.2*** *p93*
Osander, Peter; Minneapolis, 1869-1876 ***6410.35*** *p63*
Osang, E.F.; Wisconsin, n.d. ***9675.7*** *p130*
Osar, Frank; Wisconsin, n.d. ***9675.7*** *p130*
Osben, Tho.; Virginia, 1638 ***6219*** *p122*
Osberg, John 17; Philadelphia, 1833-1834 ***53.26*** *p76*
Osberton, Alex.; Virginia, 1636 ***6219*** *p8*
Osborn, Abraham 16; Virginia, 1775 ***1219.7*** *p246*
Osborn, Edward; Washington, 1859-1920 ***2872.1*** *p30*
Osborn, Henry 22; Pennsylvania, 1728 ***3690.1*** *p169*
Osborn, John; Jamaica, 1736 ***3690.1*** *p169*
Osborn, John O.; New York, NY, 1836 ***8208.4*** *p16*
Osborne, Alexander 6; Quebec, 1851 ***5704.8*** *p82*
Osborne, Andrew 2; Quebec, 1851 ***5704.8*** *p82*
Osborne, Bridgett; Virginia, 1639 ***6219*** *p151*
Osborne, Edward; Virginia, 1636 ***6219*** *p23*
Osborne, George; Nevada, 1880 ***2764.35*** *p52*
Osborne, George; New York, NY, 1815 ***2859.11*** *p40*
Osborne, Henry; St. John, N.B., 1852 ***5704.8*** *p83*
Osborne, Henry 22; Pennsylvania, 1728 ***3690.1*** *p169*
Osborne, James 12; Quebec, 1851 ***5704.8*** *p82*
Osborne, James 27; Jamaica, 1736 ***3690.1*** *p169*
Osborne, John *SEE* Osborne, John
Osborne, John; Virginia, 1639 ***6219*** *p24*
  *Wife:*Margarett
  *Son:*John
Osborne, John 12; Quebec, 1851 ***5704.8*** *p82*
Osborne, John 25; Jamaica, 1736 ***3690.1*** *p169*
Osborne, John T.; Virginia, 1852 ***4626.16*** *p14*
Osborne, Joseph; St. John, N.B., 1849 ***5704.8*** *p48*
Osborne, Margaret; Quebec, 1851 ***5704.8*** *p82*
Osborne, Margarett *SEE* Osborne, John
Osborne, Mary; Virginia, 1637 ***6219*** *p112*
Osborne, Mary 8; Quebec, 1851 ***5704.8*** *p82*
Osborne, Nancy 10; Quebec, 1851 ***5704.8*** *p82*
Osborne, Richard; Virginia, 1637 ***6219*** *p113*
Osbrey, Frederick L.; New York, NY, 1838 ***8208.4*** *p85*
Osburg, John A.; Boston, 1868 ***6410.32*** *p126*
Osburg, John A. 24; Massachusetts, 1860 ***6410.32*** *p118*
Osburg, Mary F. 27; Massachusetts, 1860 ***6410.32*** *p118*
Osburn, George; Annapolis, MD, 1742 ***4971*** *p93*
Osburn, William 20; Virginia, 1774 ***1219.7*** *p213*
Osburne, James 4 *SEE* Osburne, Margaret
Osburne, Jane 6 *SEE* Osburne, Margaret
Osburne, Margaret 27; Philadelphia, 1804 ***53.26*** *p76*
  *Relative:*Jane 6
  *Relative:*James 4
O'Shaughnessy, . . .; New York, NY, 1816 ***2859.11*** *p40*
O'Shaughnessy, John; Washington, 1859-1920 ***2872.1*** *p30*
O'Shaughnessy, Margaret; New York, NY, 1816 ***2859.11*** *p40*
O'Sheil, Edward; New York, NY, 1835 ***8208.4*** *p31*
Osiander, Christina Barbara; Pennsylvania, 1749 ***2444*** *p164*
Osinski, Martin; Arkansas, 1918 ***95.2*** *p94*
Oskamp, Clemens; Cincinnati, 1869-1887 ***8582*** *p23*
Osladil, Frank 24; Kansas, 1905 ***5240.1*** *p83*
Osmond, Thomas 40; Virginia, 1774 ***1219.7*** *p241*
Osmont, William 18; Jamaica, 1731 ***3690.1*** *p169*
Osmotherly, William; Virginia, 1637 ***6219*** *p112*
Ossenecker, Thomas; Georgia, 1734 ***9332*** *p328*
Ossley, Nicho.; Virginia, 1642 ***6219*** *p15*
Ossmann, Jakob; Ohio, 1813 ***8582.1*** *p48*
Osswald, Anna Maria Rebstock *SEE* Osswald, Jacob Friedrich
Osswald, Friederica Barbara *SEE* Osswald, Jacob Friedrich
Osswald, Friederich 27; Pennsylvania, 1753 ***2444*** *p198*
Osswald, George; Wisconsin, n.d. ***9675.7*** *p130*
Osswald, Jacob Friedrich; Nova Scotia, 1752 ***2444*** *p198*
  *Wife:*Anna Maria Rebstock
  *Child:*Friederica Barbara
  *Child:*Johann Jacob
Osswald, Johann Jacob *SEE* Osswald, Jacob Friedrich
Osswald, Rupert; Illinois, 1885 ***2896.5*** *p31*
Ostapowski, . . .; New York, 1831 ***4606*** *p176*
Ostberg, C.; Minneapolis, 1882-1883 ***6410.35*** *p62*
Ostburg, J.A.; Boston, 1868 ***6410.32*** *p126*
Ostendorf, Henry 31; Kansas, 1887 ***5240.1*** *p69*
Oster, Christoph; Port uncertain, 1749 ***2444*** *p198*
Oster, Peter; Wisconsin, n.d. ***9675.7*** *p130*
Osterbind, Anton G.; Virginia, 1851 ***4626.16*** *p14*
Osterbind, Borend A.; Virginia, 1848 ***4626.16*** *p13*
Osterbur, F.T.; Illinois, 1892 ***5012.40*** *p27*
Osterbur, Henry T.; Illinois, 1892 ***5012.40*** *p27*
Osterhage, Anne M. Engel Louise *SEE* Osterhage, Johann Carl Heinrich Caspa
Osterhage, Anne M. L. Wilhelmine 19 *SEE* Osterhage, Johann Ernst H. Gottlieb
Osterhage, Carl H. B. Gottlieb *SEE* Osterhage, Johann Carl Heinrich Caspa
Osterhage, Carl H. F. Gottlieb *SEE* Osterhage, Johann Carl Heinrich Caspa
Osterhage, Johann Carl Heinrich Caspar; America, 1857 ***4610.10*** *p135*
  With wife
  *Child:*Anne M. Engel Louise
  *Child:*Carl H. F. Gottlieb
  *Child:*Carl H. B. Gottlieb
  *Child:*Wilhelmine Engel
Osterhage, Johann E. H. Gottlieb *SEE* Osterhage, Johann Ernst H. Gottlieb
Osterhage, Johann Ernst H. Gottlieb 45; America, 1855 ***4610.10*** *p139*
  With wife
  *Child:*Anne M. L. Wilhelmine 19
  *Child:*Johann E. H. Gottlieb
Osterhage, Wilhelmine Engel *SEE* Osterhage, Johann Carl Heinrich Caspa
Osterhoff, Leenert; Iroquois Co., IL, 1894 ***3455.1*** *p12*
Osterhoff, Willem; Iroquois Co., IL, 1894 ***3455.1*** *p12*
Osterholt, Ehler; New York, NY, 1835 ***8208.4*** *p5*
Osterholtz, Friederich; New York, NY, 1836 ***8208.4*** *p9*

Osterholz, A. M. Wilhelmine C. *SEE* Osterholz, Carl Heinrich
Osterholz, A.M. Wilhelmine Moller *SEE* Osterholz, Carl Heinrich
Osterholz, Carl Heinrich; America, 1881 ***4610.10*** *p160*
*Wife:*A.M. Wilhelmine Moller
*Daughter:*A. M. Wilhelmine C.
Osterlein, Jeremias; Pennsylvania, 1752-1753 ***4525*** *p235*
Osterloh, Elisabeth Ruter *SEE* Osterloh, Hermann Johann
Osterloh, Friedrich Wilhelm *SEE* Osterloh, Hermann Johann
Osterloh, Gottlieb H. H. E. Friedrich; America, 1887 ***4610.10*** *p107*
Osterloh, Heinrich 24; America, 1888 ***4610.10*** *p107*
Osterloh, Heinrich August *SEE* Osterloh, Hermann Johann
Osterloh, Heinrich F. Ludwig *SEE* Osterloh, Hermann Johann
Osterloh, Hermann 27; America, 1888 ***4610.10*** *p107*
Osterloh, Hermann Johann; America, 1888 ***4610.10*** *p107*
*Wife:*Elisabeth Ruter
*Child:*Heinrich F. Ludwig
*Child:*Friedrich Wilhelm
*Child:*Heinrich August
Ostermeier, Mr.; America, 1866-1883 ***4610.10*** *p160*
Ostermeier, Ernst Heinrich; America, 1886 ***4610.10*** *p161*
Ostermeier, Fr. W.; America, 1881 ***4610.10*** *p160*
Ostermeier, Heinrich W.; America, 1883 ***4610.10*** *p160*
Osterodt, . . .; Canada, 1776-1783 ***9786*** *p30*
Osterott, . . .; Canada, 1776-1783 ***9786*** *p30*
Osterwald, . . .; Canada, 1776-1783 ***9786*** *p30*
Ostino, Eugene; Iowa, 1866-1943 ***123.54*** *p37*
Ostlund, Adolph; Iowa, 1866-1943 ***123.54*** *p37*
Ostlund, David Emanuel; Washington, 1859-1920 ***2872.1*** *p30*
Ostroff, Henry; New York, NY, 1881 ***1450.2*** *p29B*
Ostrom, Axel; New York, NY, 1839 ***8208.4*** *p96*
Ostrom, Charles; Boston, 1840 ***6410.32*** *p126*
Ostrom, Charles G. 52; Massachusetts, 1860 ***6410.32*** *p119*
Ostrum, Andrew; New York, 1743 ***3652*** *p60*
*Wife:*Jane
Ostrum, Jane *SEE* Ostrum, Andrew
Osuch, Frank; Arkansas, 1918 ***95.2*** *p94*
O'Sullivan, D.; Springfield, MA, 1839 ***7036*** *p127*
O'Sullivan, Daniel; New York, NY, 1835 ***8208.4*** *p79*
O'Sullivan, Dennis 30; Massachusetts, 1849 ***5881.1*** *p79*
O'Sullivan, George Henry; Arkansas, 1918 ***95.2*** *p91*
O'Sullivan, John 20; Massachusetts, 1848 ***5881.1*** *p79*
O'Sullivan, Mary 23; Massachusetts, 1849 ***5881.1*** *p80*
O'Sullivan, Michael; Montreal, 1809 ***7603*** *p98*
O'Sullivan, Morty 30; Kansas, 1874 ***5240.1*** *p56*
Oswald, Christoph; South Carolina, 1788 ***7119*** *p200*
Oswald, Conrad; Wisconsin, n.d. ***9675.7*** *p130*
Oswald, Friederich 27; Pennsylvania, 1753 ***2444*** *p198*
Oswald, George; Illinois, 1899 ***5012.40*** *p56*
Oswald, Heinrich; South Carolina, 1788 ***7119*** *p200*
Oswald, Johann Philipp; Philadelphia, 1756 ***4525*** *p261*
Oswald, Matthaus; South Carolina, 1788 ***7119*** *p200*
Oswald, Michael; Illinois, 1894 ***5012.40*** *p53*
Oswald, Michael; South Carolina, 1788 ***7119*** *p200*
Oswald, Wilhelm; Wisconsin, n.d. ***9675.7*** *p130*
Oswald, William; Wisconsin, n.d. ***9675.7*** *p130*
Oswaldt, Mr.; Cincinnati, 1866 ***8582.1*** *p15*
Oswaldt, August; America, 1848 ***8582.1*** *p26*
Oswalt, Christoph; South Carolina, 1788 ***7119*** *p200*
Oswalt, Friederich 27; Pennsylvania, 1753 ***2444*** *p198*
Oswalt, John; South Carolina, 1788 ***7119*** *p200*
Other, Thomas; Virginia, 1638 ***6219*** *p146*
Otheys, Marie-Madeleine Warren; Montreal, 1693 ***7603*** *p22*
Othmann, . . .; Canada, 1776-1783 ***9786*** *p30*
O'Toole, Daniel; Philadelphia, 1880 ***2764.35*** *p53*
Otremba, Karol; Arkansas, 1918 ***95.2*** *p94*
Ott, Albert; Illinois, 1888 ***5012.39*** *p121*
Ott, August; Wisconsin, n.d. ***9675.7*** *p130*
Ott, Carl Siegmund; Georgia, 1739 ***9332*** *p324*
Ott, Carl Sigismund; Georgia, 1739 ***9332*** *p326*
Ott, David; Pennsylvania, 1770 ***4525*** *p211*
Ott, Friedr; Philadelphia, 1756 ***4525*** *p262*
Ott, Jacob; South Carolina, 1788 ***7119*** *p197*
Ott, Johann Heinrich; Pennsylvania, 1754 ***4525*** *p236*
Ott, Johann Nicolaus; New England, 1752 ***4525*** *p236*
Ott, Johann Nicolaus; Pennsylvania, 1752 ***4525*** *p236*
Ott, John; America, 1852 ***7137*** *p169*
*Wife:*Julia
Ott, Joseph 23; Kansas, 1885 ***5240.1*** *p68*
Ott, Julia *SEE* Ott, John
Ott, Leonhard; Pennsylvania, 1754 ***4525*** *p236*
With wife
With 3 children
With child 1
With child 15
Ott, Nicholas; Philadelphia, 1762 ***9973.7*** *p37*
Otte, Fritz; Kansas, 1892 ***5240.1*** *p33*
Otte, Hermann Friedrich; Cincinnati, 1869-1887 ***8582*** *p23*
Otte, Johan Herman Heinrich 21; Kansas, 1893 ***5240.1*** *p78*
Otte, Johan Herman Henrich 21; Kansas, 1893 ***5240.1*** *p33*
Ottens, Otto; Colorado, 1900 ***9678.2*** *p131*
Ottensmeier, Anne M. F. Charlotte *SEE* Ottensmeier, Christian Friedrich
Ottensmeier, Anne M. L. C. Kruger *SEE* Ottensmeier, Christian Friedrich
Ottensmeier, Christian Friedrich; America, 1857 ***4610.10*** *p158*
*Wife:*Anne M. L. C. Kruger
*Daughter:*Anne M. F. Charlotte
Ottensmeyer, Anton Dietrich Chr. F.; America, 1850 ***4610.10*** *p155*
Ottensmeyer, Carl Friedrich; America, 1883 ***4610.10*** *p106*
Ottensmeyer, Carl Heinrich Johann; America, 1881 ***4610.10*** *p113*
Ottensmeyer, Friedrich 23; America, 1883 ***4610.10*** *p124*
Ottensmeyer, Friedrich 27; America, 1876 ***4610.10*** *p101*
Otterbach, Louis; America, 1887 ***1450.2*** *p29B*
Ottermann, Johann W.; West Virginia, 1838 ***3702.7*** *p74*
With sister
With mother
Ottey, John; Pennsylvania, 1682 ***4960*** *p157*
Ottey, John; Pennsylvania, 1682 ***4963*** *p40*
Ottin, Maria; Philadelphia, 1776 ***8582.3*** *p83*
Otting, Gerhard Heinrich; America, 1842 ***8582.3*** *p49*
Ottinger, John Jacob; Philadelphia, 1761 ***9973.7*** *p35*
Ottman, . . .; Canada, 1776-1783 ***9786*** *p30*
Otto, . . .; Canada, 1776-1783 ***9786*** *p30*
Otto, Albert C.; New York, NY, 1870 ***1450.2*** *p29B*
Otto, Carl 23; Kansas, 1894 ***5240.1*** *p33*
Otto, Carl 23; Kansas, 1894 ***5240.1*** *p79*
Otto, Christian; New York, NY, 1835 ***8208.4*** *p57*
Otto, Christian 23; Kansas, 1890 ***5240.1*** *p75*
Otto, Ernest F.; Illinois, 1888 ***2896.5*** *p31*
Otto, Henrich; New Jersey, 1777 ***8137*** *p12*
Otto, Henry; Illinois, 1888 ***5012.37*** *p60*
Otto, John Gottfreid 43; New Orleans, 1839 ***9420.2*** *p358*
Otto, John Matthew; New York, 1750 ***3652*** *p74*
Otto, Justina 50; New Orleans, 1839 ***9420.2*** *p358*
Otto, Walter S.; Arkansas, 1918 ***95.2*** *p94*
Ottobusch, . . .; Canada, 1776-1783 ***9786*** *p30*
Ottoh, Francis Herman; New York, NY, 1835 ***8208.4*** *p78*
Otton, Cordt; New York, NY, 1835 ***8208.4*** *p7*
Otwell, Thomas P.; Washington, 1859-1920 ***2872.1*** *p30*
Otz, Hans Baltes; Pennsylvania, 1750 ***2444*** *p224*
Ouabard, Jean-Baptiste; Quebec, 1730 ***7603*** *p22*
Oubanjer, G. 25; America, 1839 ***778.5*** *p411*
Oubauger, G. 25; America, 1839 ***778.5*** *p411*
Oubre, Mr. 24; New Orleans, 1839 ***778.5*** *p411*
Oucken, Hajo H.; Illinois, 1889 ***5012.40*** *p25*
Oudin, Alex. J. 7; New Orleans, 1823 ***778.5*** *p411*
Ouellie, Louis 34; New Orleans, 1839 ***778.5*** *p411*
Ouilem, Joseph-Thomas; Quebec, 1715 ***7603*** *p48*
Ould, James 15; New York, 1775 ***1219.7*** *p246*
Ouler, Marx Simon *SEE* Ouler, William
Ouler, Peter; Pennsylvania, 1730 ***1034.18*** *p14*
Ouler, Ursula *SEE* Ouler, William
Ouler, William; Pennsylvania, 1737 ***1034.18*** *p14*
*Wife:*Ursula
*Child:*Marx Simon
Oulet, Jean; Quebec, 1765 ***7603*** *p95*
Oultagh, Brian; America, 1739 ***4971*** *p52*
Oultman, Frederick J.; Illinois, 1896 ***5012.40*** *p55*
Ourdan, Joseph J.P.; New York, NY, 1836 ***8208.4*** *p8*
Ourton, Tymothy; Virginia, 1643 ***6219*** *p200*
Ousset, Simon 19; New Orleans, 1839 ***778.5*** *p411*
Outelas, Jean; Quebec, 1692 ***7603*** *p27*
Outerhart, . . .; Canada, 1776-1783 ***9786*** *p30*
Ouvrard, Mr.; Port uncertain, 1839 ***778.5*** *p411*
Ovard, Christophe; Quebec, 1714 ***7603*** *p22*
Ovenkamp, Kaspar; New York, 1662 ***8125.8*** *p436*
Ovens, James 23; Quebec, 1867 ***5704.8*** *p168*
Over, Thomas 20; Maryland, 1720 ***3690.1*** *p169*
Overbeck, J. H.; Cincinnati, 1846 ***8582.1*** *p26*
Overbeck, Jane 39; New York, NY, 1847 ***3377.6*** *p15*
Overbeck, John 13; New York, NY, 1847 ***3377.6*** *p15*
Overbeck, John 47; New York, NY, 1847 ***3377.6*** *p15*
Overbeck, Sutirde 11; New York, NY, 1847 ***3377.6*** *p15*
Overend, Joshua 40; Savannah, GA, 1733 ***4719.17*** *p312*
Overmann, C. H.; Kentucky, 1839-1840 ***8582.3*** *p99*
Overmann, Heinrich; Kentucky, 1842 ***8582.3*** *p100*
Overmann, Heinrich; Kentucky, 1844 ***8582.3*** *p101*
Overmark, August; Illinois, 1885-1985 ***4610.10*** *p68*
Overson, Ole; Arkansas, 1918 ***95.2*** *p94*
Overy, John 20; Virginia, 1721 ***3690.1*** *p169*
Ovesen, Michael Christian 23; Arkansas, 1918 ***95.2*** *p94*
Ovesen, Oscar Marselius; Washington, 1859-1920 ***2872.1*** *p30*
Ovest, August; Iowa, 1866-1943 ***123.54*** *p37*
Ovington, Thomas; Colorado, 1895 ***9678.2*** *p131*
Owberry, John; Virginia, 1636 ***6219*** *p28*
Owen, Ann 38; Maryland or Virginia, 1699 ***2212*** *p24*
Owen, Edward; Virginia, 1636 ***6219*** *p15*
Owen, Edwd.; Virginia, 1635 ***6219*** *p70*
Owen, Ellen 20; America, 1702 ***2212*** *p39*
Owen, Ellinor *SEE* Owen, Griffith
Owen, Evan 20; America, 1699 ***2212*** *p29*
Owen, Evan 20; Newfoundland, 1699-1700 ***2212*** *p18*
Owen, George; San Francisco, 1850 ***4914.15*** *p10*
Owen, George; San Francisco, 1850 ***4914.15*** *p14*
Owen, Griffith; Pennsylvania, 1684 ***4961*** *p8*
*Wife:*Sarah
*Son:*Robert
*Daughter:*Sarah
*Daughter:*Ellinor
Owen, Henry 38; Maryland or Virginia, 1699 ***2212*** *p24*
Owen, Hugh; Virginia, 1698 ***2212*** *p16*
Owen, James 21; Maryland, 1774 ***1219.7*** *p181*
Owen, James 21; Virginia, 1774 ***1219.7*** *p186*
Owen, John; America, 1698 ***2212*** *p6*
Owen, Matilda; Philadelphia, 1864 ***5704.8*** *p177*
Owen, Richard; Virginia, 1642 ***6219*** *p186*
Owen, Richard 40; Georgia, 1774 ***1219.7*** *p188*
Owen, Richd; America, 1698 ***2212*** *p6*
Owen, Richd; America, 1698 ***2212*** *p10*
Owen, Robert *SEE* Owen, Griffith
Owen, Robert 18; Virginia, 1699 ***2212*** *p20*
Owen, Robert Dale; Cincinnati, 1788-1848 ***8582.3*** *p89*
Owen, Rowland; Virginia, 1636 ***6219*** *p1*
Owen, Sarah *SEE* Owen, Griffith
Owen, Sarah *SEE* Owen, Griffith
Owen, T. H.; Washington, 1859-1920 ***2872.1*** *p30*
Owen, Tho.; Virginia, 1632 ***6219*** *p10*
Owen, Tho.; Virginia, 1637 ***6219*** *p112*
Owen, Tho 25; Maryland or Virginia, 1699 ***2212*** *p23*
Owen, Thomas; America, 1697 ***2212*** *p7*
Owen, Thomas 33; Jamaica, 1738 ***3690.1*** *p169*
Owen, William; Virginia, 1698 ***2212*** *p16*
Owens, Allen; St. John, N.B., 1850 ***5704.8*** *p67*
Owens, Andrew; America, 1739 ***4971*** *p14*
Owens, Ann; America, 1738 ***4971*** *p14*
Owens, Anstace; America, 1742 ***4971*** *p50*
Owens, Biddy; St. John, N.B., 1847 ***5704.8*** *p34*
Owens, Bridget; Philadelphia, 1864 ***5704.8*** *p178*
Owens, Bridget; Philadelphia, 1866 ***5704.8*** *p207*
Owens, Bridget 1 mo; St. John, N.B., 1847 ***5704.8*** *p34*
Owens, Bridget 8; Massachusetts, 1849 ***5881.1*** *p78*
Owens, Catharine 30; Massachusetts, 1848 ***5881.1*** *p79*
Owens, Catherine 17; St. John, N.B., 1853 ***5704.8*** *p110*
Owens, Edward; New York, NY, 1837 ***8208.4*** *p54*
Owens, Elizabeth 18; Massachusetts, 1850 ***5881.1*** *p79*
Owens, Evan 11; Virginia, 1700 ***2212*** *p30*
Owens, Hugh 42; Massachusetts, 1849 ***5881.1*** *p79*
Owens, Isabella; Philadelphia, 1851 ***5704.8*** *p79*
Owens, James; New York, NY, 1815 ***2859.11*** *p40*
Owens, James; St. John, N.B., 1847 ***5704.8*** *p32*
Owens, James 3; Quebec, 1864 ***5704.8*** *p159*
Owens, James 17; Quebec, 1855 ***5704.8*** *p126*
Owens, James 17; St. John, N.B., 1853 ***5704.8*** *p110*
Owens, Jno; America, 1697 ***2212*** *p8*
Owens, John; New York, NY, 1811 ***2859.11*** *p18*
Owens, John; Philadelphia, 1864 ***5704.8*** *p178*
Owens, John 13; St. John, N.B., 1847 ***5704.8*** *p32*
Owens, Margaret; Montreal, 1824 ***7603*** *p87*
Owens, Mary; New York, NY, 1864 ***5704.8*** *p180*
Owens, Mary 9; St. John, N.B., 1847 ***5704.8*** *p32*
Owens, Mary 34 *SEE* Owens, Stephen
Owens, Nicholas 4; St. John, N.B., 1847 ***5704.8*** *p32*
Owens, Patrick; St. John, N.B., 1850 ***5704.8*** *p67*
Owens, Patrick 11; St. John, N.B., 1847 ***5704.8*** *p32*
Owens, Peter 10; Massachusetts, 1849 ***5881.1*** *p80*
Owens, Richard 16; Pennsylvania, 1735 ***3690.1*** *p170*
Owens, Richd 18; Virginia, 1700 ***2212*** *p30*
Owens, Rose 4; Massachusetts, 1849 ***5881.1*** *p80*
Owens, Rosey 6; St. John, N.B., 1847 ***5704.8*** *p34*
Owens, Sarah 17; Philadelphia, 1856 ***5704.8*** *p129*
Owens, Sarah 26; Quebec, 1864 ***5704.8*** *p159*
Owens, Stephen 45; Charleston, SC, 1850 ***1639.20*** *p257*
*Relative:*Mary 34
Owens, Susan 11; Massachusetts, 1850 ***5881.1*** *p80*
Owens, Tho 17; America, 1700 ***2212*** *p31*
Owens, Thomas 6; Massachusetts, 1849 ***5881.1*** *p80*
Owery, Mary 15; America, 1700 ***2212*** *p33*
Owins, James; Baltimore, 1811 ***2859.11*** *p18*
Owins, Margaret; Baltimore, 1811 ***2859.11*** *p18*
Owles, Robt.; Virginia, 1622 ***6219*** *p1*
Oxeham, William 20; Maryland, 1725 ***3690.1*** *p170*

Oxford, Christopher; Virginia, 1635 *6219 p28*
Oxford, Wm.; Virginia, 1636 *6219 p23*
Oxford, Wm.; Virginia, 1637 *6219 p23*
Oxman, William H.; Washington, 1859-1920 *2872.1 p30*
Oxon, Richard; Virginia, 1646 *6219 p239*
Oye, John; Illinois, 1886 *5012.39 p120*
Oyer, Aime. 10; America, 1838 *778.5 p412*
Oyer, Dlaite 17; America, 1838 *778.5 p412*
Oyer, Elisa 39; America, 1838 *778.5 p412*

Oyer, Louis 12; America, 1838 *778.5 p412*
Oyer, Pierre 44; America, 1838 *778.5 p412*
Oyle, Frederick 22; Maryland, 1774 *1219.7 p191*
Oyster, Riley; Washington, 1859-1920 *2872.1 p30*
Ozanick, Paval; Iowa, 1866-1943 *123.54 p37*
Ozeas, Elisabetha Marneval; Pennsylvania, 1753 *2444 p198*
Ozeas, Peter; Philadelphia, 1764 *8582.2 p65*
Ozeas, Peter; Philadelphia, 1776 *8582.3 p83*

Ozens, Mr. 26; New Orleans, 1821 *778.5 p412*
Ozias, Elisabetha Marneval; Pennsylvania, 1753 *2444 p198*
Ozias, Jeanne Marie; America, 1751 *2444 p193*
Ozimek, Antoni 16 *SEE* Ozimek, Jan
Ozimek, Jan 20; New York, 1912 *9980.29 p71*
   *Brother:*Antoni 16
Ozyryla, Joseph 23; Arkansas, 1918 *95.2 p94*

P

Paar, . . .; Canada, 1776-1783 *9786 p30*
Pabisch, Franz; Cincinnati, 1788-1848 *8582.3 p89*
Pabst, Fredolen 21; West Virginia, 1902 *9788.3 p18*
Pacatte, Nicholas; Illinois, 1868 *2896.5 p31*
Paccagrini, Ulisse; Iowa, 1866-1943 *123.54 p37*
Pace, Henry; Virginia, 1638 *6219 p146*
Pace, Isabella; Virginia, 1628 *6219 p25*
Pace, Rich.; Virginia, 1628 *6219 p25*
Pace, Tasquale 38; New York, NY, 1893 *9026.4 p42*
Pace, William 31; Jamaica, 1738 *3690.1 p170*
Pacey, John G. 23; Kansas, 1884 *5240.1 p65*
Pach, Beate Lowis 28; Virginia, 1773 *1219.7 p170*
Pacheco, Refujo; Arizona, 1868 *2764.35 p54*
Pacheritz, Joseph; Wisconsin, n.d. *9675.7 p130*
Pachillon, L. 26; New Orleans, 1832 *778.5 p412*
Pacifici, Nonzo; Wisconsin, n.d. *9675.7 p130*
Pack, Christ.; Virginia, 1642 *6219 p194*
Packeisen, Fredrick Wilhelm; Washington, 1859-1920 *2872.1 p30*
Packer, James 20; Virginia, 1774 *1219.7 p186*
Packer, John 19; New York, 1774 *1219.7 p222*
Packer, Richard 27; Maryland, 1733 *3690.1 p170*
Packett, Joane; Virginia, 1637 *6219 p13*
Packett, Wm.; Virginia, 1634 *6219 p84*
Packford, Wm.; Virginia, 1637 *6219 p82*
Packhurst, Antho.; Virginia, 1642 *6219 p187*
Packman, Geo.; Virginia, 1642 *6219 p190*
Pacon, Mathew; Virginia, 1639 *6219 p151*
Pacquet, E. 28; Louisiana, 1820 *778.5 p412*
Pacton, James 20; Maryland, 1727 *3690.1 p170*
Pacye, Henry; Virginia, 1623-1700 *6219 p182*
Padavic, Adela; Iowa, 1866-1943 *123.54 p37*
Padavic, Yakov; Iowa, 1866-1943 *123.54 p37*
Padavic, Yuraj; Iowa, 1866-1943 *123.54 p73*
Padavich, Jack; Iowa, 1866-1943 *123.54 p37*
Padavich, Kata; Iowa, 1866-1943 *123.54 p73*
Padavich, Louis; Iowa, 1866-1943 *123.54 p73*
Padavich, Matija; Iowa, 1866-1943 *123.54 p37*
Padavich, Nicholas; Iowa, 1866-1943 *123.54 p37*
Paddison, Tho.; Virginia, 1642 *6219 p188*
Padjen, Philip; Iowa, 1866-1943 *123.54 p37*
Padmore, J. 15; St. Kitts, 1774 *1219.7 p184*
Padmore, John Spencer; St. Christopher, 1774 *1219.7 p178*
Padmore, Joseph 20; Philadelphia, 1775 *1219.7 p248*
Padnani, Ant. 35; Louisiana, 1829 *778.5 p412*
Padouan, Secondo; Iowa, 1866-1943 *123.54 p37*
Padovic, Anton; Iowa, 1866-1943 *123.54 p37*
Paege, William 22; Kansas, 1890 *5240.1 p33*
Paege, William 22; Kansas, 1890 *5240.1 p75*
Paerly, Sarah; Philadelphia, 1853 *5704.8 p101*
Paetow, Emily; Wisconsin, n.d. *9675.7 p130*
Pafos, Nicholas Andrew; Arkansas, 1918 *95.2 p94*
Pagadakis, James Peter; Arkansas, 1918 *95.2 p94*
Paganelli, John Alfred; Arkansas, 1918 *95.2 p94*
Page, . . .; Canada, 1776-1783 *9786 p30*
Page, Annis; Virginia, 1640 *6219 p183*
Page, Edward; Virginia, 1635 *6219 p16*
Page, Eliz. 17; America, 1848 *4535.10 p197*
Page, Eliza 8; St. John, N.B., 1857 *5704.8 p136*
Page, George; Raleigh, NC, 1813-1836 *1639.20 p257*
Page, Henry; America, 1867 *1450.2 p109A*
Page, John 20; Philadelphia, 1775 *1219.7 p248*
Page, John 26; Maryland, 1775 *1219.7 p271*
Page, Mary Jane 14; St. John, N.B., 1857 *5704.8 p136*
Page, Nath.; Virginia, 1638 *6219 p147*
Page, Richard; Virginia, 1646 *6219 p241*

Page, Sarah 10; St. John, N.B., 1857 *5704.8 p136*
Page, Tho.; Virginia, 1645 *6219 p232*
Page, Thomas; New York, NY, 1835 *8208.4 p8*
Page, Thomas; Raleigh, NC, 1805-1834 *1639.20 p257*
Page, Thomas 17; West Indies, 1722 *3690.1 p170*
Page, Thomas 18; St. John, N.B., 1857 *5704.8 p136*
Page, Thomas 23; St. Christopher, 1725 *3690.1 p170*
Page, William 15; Philadelphia, 1774 *1219.7 p175*
Page, William 22; Kansas, 1890 *5240.1 p33*
Page, William 55; St. John, N.B., 1857 *5704.8 p136*
Pagella, Alfredo; Arkansas, 1918 *95.2 p94*
Pages, J. 40; Louisiana, 1820 *778.5 p412*
Paget, Mr. 24; Port uncertain, 1838 *778.5 p412*
Paget, Mary Jane 24; St. John, N.B., 1863 *5704.8 p155*
Pagett, Thomas; Virginia, 1639 *6219 p162*
Paginet, Miss 3; America, 1837 *778.5 p412*
Paginet, Mrs. 30; America, 1837 *778.5 p413*
Paginet, Augustin 35; America, 1837 *778.5 p412*
Pagles, John R.; Illinois, 1870 *7857 p6*
Paglia, Mike; Arkansas, 1918 *95.2 p94*
Pagne, A. 23; New Orleans, 1823 *778.5 p413*
Pagram, Gregory; Virginia, 1637 *6219 p82*
Pagram, William 30; Maryland, 1775 *1219.7 p257*
Pahl, Christian; Wisconsin, n.d. *9675.7 p130*
Pahle, Louis Micke; Wisconsin, n.d. *9675.7 p130*
Pahle, Louis Mike; Wisconsin, n.d. *9675.7 p130*
Pahle, Mathew Henry; Wisconsin, n.d. *9675.7 p130*
Pahlej, Mathew Henry; Wisconsin, n.d. *9675.7 p130*
Pahlman, John H.; New York, NY, 1836 *8208.4 p18*
Pahls, John; Cincinnati, 1869-1887 *8582 p23*
Pahmeier, Catharine M. Charlotte *SEE* Pahmeier, Ernst Heinrich Ferdinand
Pahmeier, Ernst Heinrich Ferdinand; America, 1858 *4610.10 p152*
   *Child:*Ernst Wilhelm Gottlieb
   *Child:*Catharine M. Charlotte
Pahmeier, Ernst Wilhelm Gottlieb *SEE* Pahmeier, Ernst Heinrich Ferdinand
Pahmeier, Friedrich 36; America, 1882 *4610.10 p118*
Pahmeyer, Anna M. Mouise Althof 53 *SEE* Pahmeyer, Friedrich Gottlieb
Pahmeyer, Carl Heinrich Christian; America, 1839 *4610.10 p138*
Pahmeyer, Carl Wilhelm August *SEE* Pahmeyer, Friedrich Gottlieb
Pahmeyer, Caroline C. Louise *SEE* Pahmeyer, Friedrich Gottlieb
Pahmeyer, Franziska Dreschmeier 37 *SEE* Pahmeyer, Friedrich Wilhelm
Pahmeyer, Friederike 9 *SEE* Pahmeyer, Friedrich Wilhelm
Pahmeyer, Friedrich Gottlieb; America, 1871 *4610.10 p113*
   *Wife:*Anna M. Mouise Althof 53
   *Child:*Caroline C. Louise
   *Child:*Carl Wilhelm August
Pahmeyer, Friedrich Heinrich August; America, 1865 *4610.10 p158*
Pahmeyer, Friedrich Wilhelm; America, 1868 *4610.10 p159*
Pahmeyer, Friedrich Wilhelm 38; America, 1882 *4610.10 p118*
   *Wife:*Franziska Dreschmeier 37
   *Child:*Friederike 9
   *Child:*Heinrich
   *Child:*Johanne 4
   *Child:*Wilhelm 9 mos

Pahmeyer, Heinrich *SEE* Pahmeyer, Friedrich Wilhelm
Pahmeyer, Hermann Heinrich; America, 1840 *4610.10 p138*
Pahmeyer, Johann Heinrich 58; America, 1852 *4610.10 p148*
   *Wife:*Luise Wegener
Pahmeyer, Johanne 4 *SEE* Pahmeyer, Friedrich Wilhelm
Pahmeyer, Justine Caroline Charlotte; America, 1885 *4610.10 p102*
Pahmeyer, Luise Wegener *SEE* Pahmeyer, Johann Heinrich
Pahmeyer, Wilhelm 9 mos *SEE* Pahmeyer, Friedrich Wilhelm
Pahnier, Mr.; Quebec, 1778 *9786 p267*
Paht, Mr. 26; New Orleans, 1836 *778.5 p413*
Paice, William 31; Jamaica, 1738 *3690.1 p170*
Paile, Louis 30; America, 1826 *778.5 p413*
Pailler, Felix 20; America, 1823 *778.5 p413*
Paillet, Mr. 40; America, 1827 *778.5 p413*
Pain, J. P. 54; Port uncertain, 1838 *778.5 p413*
Pain, John 18; Pennsylvania, 1731 *3690.1 p170*
Pain, S. 21; America, 1835 *778.5 p413*
Pain, William 16; Jamaica, 1729 *3690.1 p171*
Paine, Anthony 23; Maryland, 1774 *1219.7 p235*
Paine, Elizabeth 21; Maryland, 1775 *1219.7 p260*
Paine, George 19; Jamaica, 1740 *3690.1 p170*
Paine, John; Virginia, 1638 *6219 p122*
Paine, John; Virginia, 1642 *6219 p195*
Paine, John 18; Jamaica, 1723 *3690.1 p170*
Paine, Low 21; Maryland, 1775 *1219.7 p260*
Paine, Sarah 18; Pennsylvania, 1719 *3690.1 p171*
Paine, William; Virginia, 1642 *6219 p195*
Paine, William; Virginia, 1642 *6219 p197*
Paine, William 16; Jamaica, 1729 *3690.1 p171*
Paine, William 22; Jamaica, 1731 *3690.1 p171*
Paine, William 24; Boston, 1775 *1219.7 p258*
Paine, Wm.; New York, NY, 1811 *2859.11 p18*
   With family
Painter, John; Virginia, 1639 *6219 p161*
Painter, John 27; Jamaica, 1738 *3690.1 p171*
Painter, Thomas 18; Maryland, 1722 *3690.1 p171*
Paintin, William 17; Maryland, 1774 *1219.7 p185*
Paise, William 20; Maryland, 1720 *3690.1 p171*
Paisley, Andrew; Montreal, 1824 *7603 p65*
Paisley, Christopher; New York, NY, 1816 *2859.11 p40*
Paisley, Mary; Philadelphia, 1850 *53.26 p76*
Paisley, Mary; Philadelphia, 1850 *5704.8 p60*
Paisly, James 26; Charleston, SC, 1774 *1639.20 p257*
Paisly, John 23; Charleston, SC, 1774 *1639.20 p257*
   With wife 26
Paitan, Michael; Illinois, 1868 *7857 p6*
Paive, Jos. Fred. 25; Port uncertain, 1839 *778.5 p413*
Pake, Ann 40; Rhode Island, 1774 *1219.7 p189*
Pakendorff, Dr.; Quebec, 1778 *9786 p267*
Pakes, Walter; Virginia, 1639 *6219 p156*
Pal, Ludwig; Wisconsin, n.d. *9675.7 p130*
Palaces, Harry George; Arkansas, 1918 *95.2 p94*
Palache, Alexander; New York, NY, 1832 *8208.4 p40*
Palache, Mordecai; New York, NY, 1832 *8208.4 p26*
Palacias, Ysidro; California, 1871 *2769.7 p5*
Palamar, Ignacy 26; New York, 1912 *9980.29 p63*
Palangue, Mr. 21; New Orleans, 1829 *778.5 p413*
Palaologos, James; Arkansas, 1918 *95.2 p94*
Palaski, Charles; Illinois, 1888 *5012.39 p121*
Palatka, Frank; Arkansas, 1918 *95.2 p94*
Palbury, Anthony 49; Arizona, 1904 *9228.40 p8*
Palchum, Joseph; Arkansas, 1918 *95.2 p94*

Palczewski, Korneli 29; New York, 1912 ***9980.29*** *p69*
Palding, Robert; Quebec, 1822 ***7603*** *p25*
Pale, William; Virginia, 1636 ***6219*** *p77*
Palet, Mr. 26; New Orleans, 1836 ***778.5*** *p413*
Palhouzie, E.; New Orleans, 1839 ***778.5*** *p413*
Palhouzie, P.; New Orleans, 1839 ***778.5*** *p413*
Palice, John; Iowa, 1866-1943 ***123.54*** *p37*
Palina, Emily 13; New York, NY, 1847 ***3377.6*** *p12*
Palister, Joseph 25; North America, 1774 ***1219.7*** *p198*
Pallansch, John Peter; Wisconsin, n.d. ***9675.7*** *p130*
Palleh, Abraham 20; Newfoundland, 1789 ***4915.24*** *p57*
Pallesen, Christian; Arkansas, 1918 ***95.2*** *p94*
Pallet, William 16; Pennsylvania, 1722 ***3690.1*** *p171*
Pallett, James 19; Maryland, 1774 ***1219.7*** *p220*
Pallington, Rebecca; Virginia, 1639 ***6219*** *p22*
Palliser, Patrick; America, 1740 ***4971*** *p34*
Pallister, William H.; New York, NY, 1839 ***8208.4*** *p98*
Palloc, Louis 20; New Orleans, 1836 ***778.5*** *p413*
Palloe, Mr. 21; America, 1835 ***778.5*** *p413*
Pallotau, John Baptist 19; Pennsylvania, 1723 ***3690.1*** *p171*
Palm, John 35; Pennsylvania, 1753 ***2444*** *p135*
Palmasano, Frank; Illinois, 1904 ***5012.39*** *p53*
Palmasano, Joseph; Illinois, 1902 ***5012.39*** *p53*
Palmasano, Joseph; Illinois, 1902 ***5012.40*** *p79*
Palmer, Adolf; Minneapolis, 1880-1887 ***6410.35*** *p63*
Palmer, Benjamin 25; Philadelphia, 1774 ***1219.7*** *p233*
Palmer, Charles Butler; Ohio, 1918 ***9892.11*** *p36*
Palmer, Charles Komolsy; Arkansas, 1918 ***95.2*** *p94*
Palmer, Charlotte 18; Maryland, 1775 ***1219.7*** *p249*
Palmer, Daniel; Virginia, 1621 ***6219*** *p18*
Palmer, Edward; Virginia, 1629 ***6219*** *p31*
Palmer, Edward; Virginia, 1638 ***6219*** *p123*
Palmer, Edward; Virginia, 1642 ***6219*** *p197*
Palmer, Edward 44; Baltimore, 1775 ***1219.7*** *p270*
Palmer, Edwin; Iowa, 1866-1943 ***123.54*** *p37*
Palmer, Elizabeth *SEE* Palmer, George
Palmer, Elizabeth; New York, 1748 ***3652*** *p68*
Palmer, Esther; Philadelphia, 1816 ***2859.11*** *p40*
Palmer, Francis R.; New York, NY, 1840 ***8208.4*** *p112*
Palmer, George; Pennsylvania, 1600-1684 ***4961*** *p168*
*Wife:*Elizabeth
Palmer, George W.; Illinois, 1856 ***7857*** *p6*
Palmer, Henry; Virginia, 1638 ***6219*** *p124*
Palmer, Howell; Virginia, 1638 ***6219*** *p118*
Palmer, Hugh; St. John, N.B., 1847 ***5704.8*** *p10*
Palmer, J. W.; Washington, 1859-1920 ***2872.1*** *p30*
Palmer, James 27; Virginia, 1774 ***1219.7*** *p225*
Palmer, John; Jamaica, 1775 ***1219.7*** *p277*
Palmer, John 16; Maryland, 1775 ***1219.7*** *p252*
Palmer, John 27; Quebec, 1855 ***5704.8*** *p126*
Palmer, Jon.; Virginia, 1642 ***6219*** *p192*
Palmer, Joseph; New York, NY, 1815 ***2859.11*** *p40*
Palmer, Joseph; Wisconsin, n.d. ***9675.7*** *p130*
Palmer, Joseph 16; Philadelphia, 1774 ***1219.7*** *p232*
Palmer, Joseph E.; New York, NY, 1839 ***8208.4*** *p96*
Palmer, Margaret; Philadelphia, 1816 ***2859.11*** *p40*
Palmer, Mary 19; Pennsylvania, 1719 ***3690.1*** *p171*
Palmer, Mary 40; Massachusetts, 1849 ***5881.1*** *p81*
Palmer, Nathaniel 22; Maryland, 1775 ***1219.7*** *p247*
Palmer, Pete; Arkansas, 1918 ***95.2*** *p94*
Palmer, Rebecca; Virginia, 1642 ***6219*** *p194*
Palmer, Sarah; Virginia, 1636 ***6219*** *p79*
Palmer, Sarah; Virginia, 1637 ***6219*** *p85*
Palmer, Stephen 26; Virginia, 1774 ***1219.7*** *p243*
Palmer, Thomas 21; Baltimore, 1775 ***1219.7*** *p270*
Palmer, Thomas 28; Maryland, 1775 ***1219.7*** *p272*
Palmer, Thomas William, Jr.; New York, NY, 1840 ***8208.4*** *p112*
Palmer, Tom; Quebec, 1848 ***5704.8*** *p42*
Palmer, William; St. Christopher, 1755 ***1219.7*** *p38*
Palmer, William; Virginia, 1639 ***6219*** *p156*
Palmer, Wm.; Virginia, 1635 ***6219*** *p35*
Palmer, Wm.; Virginia, 1646 ***6219*** *p240*
Palmes, Guy 24; Jamaica, 1730 ***3690.1*** *p171*
Palmiotti, Vincenzo; Arkansas, 1918 ***95.2*** *p94*
Palmisano, Antonio; Illinois, 1900 ***5012.39*** *p53*
Palmisano, Antonio; Illinois, 1902 ***5012.40*** *p77*
Palmisano, Paul; Arkansas, 1918 ***95.2*** *p94*
Palogier, Mr. 20; New Orleans, 1839 ***778.5*** *p413*
Palpeman, Aaron 29; Virginia, 1773 ***1219.7*** *p168*
Palrim, John 21; Virginia, 1773 ***1219.7*** *p171*
Palsman, B. 41; America, 1838 ***778.5*** *p414*
Palson, John; Iowa, 1853 ***2090*** *p611*
Paltzer, Adam; South Carolina, 1788 ***7119*** *p204*
Paluto, John Baptist 19; Pennsylvania, 1723 ***3690.1*** *p171*
Pambrun, . . .; Canada, 1776-1783 ***9786*** *p30*
Pampe, Frederick 22; Virginia, 1774 ***1219.7*** *p186*
Pamplin, William 27; Antigua (Antego), 1739 ***3690.1*** *p171*
Pamplin, William Albert; Iowa, 1866-1943 ***123.54*** *p37*
Pamwitt, Elizabeth 22; Virginia, 1700 ***2212*** *p32*
Panagarakis, George; Arkansas, 1918 ***95.2*** *p94*
Panarouski, Veronica; Wisconsin, n.d. ***9675.7*** *p130*
Panavox, Alexander; Arkansas, 1918 ***95.2*** *p94*
Pancak, Antonina; America, 1889 ***7137*** *p169*
*Relative:*Joseph
*Relative:*Casimer
Pancak, Casimer *SEE* Pancak, Antonina
Pancak, Joseph *SEE* Pancak, Antonina
Pancell, Edward; Virginia, 1648 ***6219*** *p246*
Pancera, Anton; America, 1849 ***8582.2*** *p30*
Pancero, Anton; New Orleans, 1847 ***8582.3*** *p49*
Pancrazio, Giani; Iowa, 1866-1943 ***123.54*** *p37*
Panczak, Antonina; America, 1889 ***7137*** *p169*
*Relative:*Joseph
*Relative:*Casimer
Panczak, Casimer *SEE* Panczak, Antonina
Panczak, Joseph *SEE* Panczak, Antonina
Pandel, Martin 21; Maryland, 1774 ***1219.7*** *p230*
Pandelait, Mr. 28; New Orleans, 1836 ***778.5*** *p414*
Pandell, William 28; America, 1835 ***778.5*** *p414*
Pandino, Philip; Arkansas, 1918 ***95.2*** *p94*
Pandle, Henry; Virginia, 1639 ***6219*** *p161*
Panewczinsky, Stanislaw 18; New York, 1912 ***9980.29*** *p56*
Pangart, . . .; Canada, 1776-1783 ***9786*** *p30*
Panier, Jon.; Virginia, 1638 ***6219*** *p118*
Panis, William; Arkansas, 1918 ***95.2*** *p94*
Pankalos, Antonie K.; New York, NY, 1839 ***8208.4*** *p96*
Pankau, Andrew; Illinois, 1876 ***5012.39*** *p52*
Pankau, John; Illinois, 1858 ***5012.39*** *p54*
Pankhurst, Francis 20; Virginia, 1774 ***1219.7*** *p243*
Pankhurst, John; Illinois, 1856 ***7857*** *p6*
Pankhurst, Stephen; Illinois, 1856 ***7857*** *p6*
Pankowski, Joseph; Colorado, 1904 ***9678.2*** *p131*
Pannier, . . .; Canada, 1776-1783 ***9786*** *p43*
Panning, Mr.; Cincinnati, 1831 ***8582.1*** *p51*
Pannwitz, Arthur Max von; America, 1866 ***8582.3*** *p49*
Pannwitz, Erich von; New Jersey, 1861-1865 ***8582.3*** *p50*
Panonous, James; Arkansas, 1918 ***95.2*** *p95*
Panopoulos, George Eustathies; Arkansas, 1918 ***95.2*** *p95*
Panos, Emil John; Arkansas, 1918 ***95.2*** *p95*
Panstecki, . . .; New York, 1831 ***4606*** *p176*
Pantazis, Theodore; Wisconsin, n.d. ***9675.7*** *p130*
Pantenburg, Michael; Wisconsin, n.d. ***9675.7*** *p130*
Panthurst, Abra.; Virginia, 1636 ***6219*** *p21*
Panton, Alexander 19; Jamaica, 1733 ***3690.1*** *p171*
Pantschuh, Josef 6 mos; New York, NY, 1878 ***9253*** *p46*
Pantz, Carl; Wisconsin, n.d. ***9675.7*** *p130*
Pantz, John; Wisconsin, n.d. ***9675.7*** *p130*
Panverlin, John 17; Pennsylvania, 1722 ***3690.1*** *p171*
Panvif, Mr. 38; America, 1838 ***778.5*** *p414*
Panvif, Jean 23; America, 1837 ***778.5*** *p414*
Panwilzer, Marcus; Milwaukee, 1875 ***4719.30*** *p258*
Pany, Mr. 15; New Orleans, 1829 ***778.5*** *p414*
Panysga, Bertilio 35; Arizona, 1918 ***9228.40*** *p22*
Panzetto, Giuseppe; Iowa, 1866-1943 ***123.54*** *p73*
Paoli, Elbana 25; New York, NY, 1893 ***9026.4*** *p42*
Paorsich, Joseph; Iowa, 1866-1943 ***123.54*** *p37*
Papadakos, Aristedes 25; Harris Co., TX, 1900 ***6254*** *p6*
Papadatos, Peter; Arkansas, 1918 ***95.2*** *p95*
Papadike, Gus John 28; Arkansas, 1918 ***95.2*** *p95*
Papai, Feri; New York, NY, 1901 ***3455.4*** *p93*
Papai, Frank; Illinois, 1897-1974 ***3455.4*** *p94*
Papajian, Mardiros; Arkansas, 1918 ***95.2*** *p95*
Papanastasio, John; Arkansas, 1918 ***95.2*** *p95*
Papas, Angelo; Arkansas, 1918 ***95.2*** *p95*
Papas, Nick; Wisconsin, n.d. ***9675.7*** *p130*
Papash, Joseph; Colorado, 1904 ***9678.2*** *p131*
Papathanasen, George; Arkansas, 1918 ***95.2*** *p95*
Pape, . . .; Canada, 1776-1783 ***9786*** *p30*
Pape, B.H.; Ohio, 1843 ***8582.1*** *p51*
Pape, Caroline Wilhelmine Friederike; America, 1844 ***4610.10*** *p120*
Pape, Christoph; Philadelphia, 1777-1779 ***8137*** *p12*
Pape, Christoph; Wisconsin, n.d. ***9675.7*** *p130*
Pape, Frederick; Wisconsin, n.d. ***9675.7*** *p130*
Pape, Friederich; Illinois, 1846 ***8582.2*** *p51*
Pape, Henry Frederick; America, 1835 ***1450.2*** *p112A*
Pape, Johann Ernst Friedrich; America, 1841 ***4610.10*** *p119*
With parents
Papes, Tony; Arkansas, 1918 ***95.2*** *p95*
Papes, Tony 30; Arkansas, 1918 ***95.2*** *p95*
Papet, August Wilhelm, I; Quebec, 1776 ***9786*** *p258*
Papet, Friedrich Julius, II; Quebec, 1776 ***9786*** *p260*
Papez, Joseph; Wisconsin, n.d. ***9675.7*** *p130*
Papich, Frederick; Iowa, 1866-1943 ***123.54*** *p37*
Papich, Steve; Iowa, 1866-1943 ***123.54*** *p37*
Papich, Stjepan; Iowa, 1866-1943 ***123.54*** *p37*
Papimie, Theodore; Wisconsin, n.d. ***9675.7*** *p130*
Papist, Christoph; Philadelphia, 1777-1779 ***8137*** *p12*
Papoine, Joseph; Texas, 1865 ***2764.35*** *p55*
Papp, Margaretha; Pennsylvania, 1750 ***2444*** *p135*
Pappadakis, George Dimetrois; Arkansas, 1918 ***95.2*** *p95*
Pappademas, George; Arkansas, 1918 ***95.2*** *p95*
Pappagelopoules, Dimitrios; Arkansas, 1918 ***95.2*** *p95*
Pappagregoren, Steleanos George; Arkansas, 1918 ***95.2*** *p95*
Pappas, James; Arkansas, 1918 ***95.2*** *p95*
Pappas, John; Arkansas, 1918 ***95.2*** *p95*
Pappas, Lawrence George; Arkansas, 1918 ***95.2*** *p95*
Pappas, Louis; Arkansas, 1918 ***95.2*** *p95*
Pappas, Philip Emmanuel; Arkansas, 1918 ***95.2*** *p95*
Paputsakis, George Mike; Arkansas, 1918 ***95.2*** *p95*
Paque, Joseph 23; New Orleans, 1837 ***778.5*** *p414*
Paquet, Philippe 30?; Quebec, 1666 ***4533*** *p127*
Paquette, Sephen O. A.; Washington, 1859-1920 ***2872.1*** *p30*
Para, F. B. 19; New Orleans, 1839 ***778.5*** *p414*
Parade, N. 23; New Orleans, 1829 ***778.5*** *p414*
Paradine, Thomas; America, 1741 ***4971*** *p56*
Paragau, Peter 37; Port uncertain, 1837 ***778.5*** *p414*
Paragnas, Pierre 26; America, 1836 ***778.5*** *p414*
Paramelle, Jean 35; Louisiana, 1820 ***778.5*** *p414*
Paras, Gus Nick; Arkansas, 1918 ***95.2*** *p95*
Parbois, Desire; Colorado, 1894 ***9678.2*** *p131*
Parbs, Carl; Iroquois Co., IL, 1892 ***3455.1*** *p12*
Parcell, Ellen; New York, NY, 1816 ***2859.11*** *p40*
With child
Parchmore, Peter; Virginia, 1623-1648 ***6219*** *p252*
Parcost, Tho.; Virginia, 1636 ***6219*** *p80*
Parcroft, Thomas; Virginia, 1639 ***6219*** *p161*
Parda, Piotr 35; New York, 1912 ***9980.29*** *p69*
Pare, Charles; Quebec, 1819 ***7603*** *p22*
Pareira, Salomon; America, 1842 ***8582.3*** *p50*
Pareno, Toney; Arkansas, 1918 ***95.2*** *p95*
Parent, Esther 24 *SEE* Parent, T.P.
Parent, T.P. 25; Virginia, 1774 ***1219.7*** *p243*
*Wife:*Esther 24
Parents, John 20; Jamaica, 1730 ***3690.1*** *p172*
Paresi, Antonio; Arkansas, 1918 ***95.2*** *p96*
Paret, Jean 43; America, 1839 ***778.5*** *p414*
Parfianowicz, Antoni; America, 1912 ***9980.29*** *p73*
Parfianowicz, Eleanora Andukowicz 28; New York, 1912 ***9980.29*** *p73*
*Daughter:*Helena 8
Parfianowicz, Helena 8 *SEE* Parfianowicz, Eleanora Andukowicz
Parfitt, Henry 21; Port uncertain, 1849 ***4535.10*** *p198*
Parfitt, Sarah; Port uncertain, 1849 ***4535.10*** *p198*
Pargaud, H. 28; New Orleans, 1827 ***778.5*** *p414*
Pargiter, John; Virginia, 1639 ***6219*** *p149*
Parguay, Miss 7; Kentucky, 1820 ***778.5*** *p415*
Parguay, Mr. 4; Kentucky, 1820 ***778.5*** *p415*
Parguay, Mr. 35; Kentucky, 1820 ***778.5*** *p414*
Parguay, Mrs. 22; Kentucky, 1820 ***778.5*** *p415*
Parigoras, Demeter Michael; Arkansas, 1918 ***95.2*** *p96*
Parigot, F. 20; Port uncertain, 1839 ***778.5*** *p415*
Paris, Anne Marie Rachel *SEE* Paris, Isaac
Paris, Benjamin 37; Maryland, 1774 ***1219.7*** *p181*
Paris, Daniel *SEE* Paris, Isaac
Paris, David 50; Barbados, 1774 ***1219.7*** *p202*
Paris, David 50; Barbados, 1775 ***1219.7*** *p278*
Paris, E.; Arizona, 1898 ***9228.30*** *p13*
Paris, Etienne 26; America, 1838 ***778.5*** *p415*
Paris, Isaac; Pennsylvania, 1750 ***2444*** *p199*
Paris, Isaac; Pennsylvania, 1751 ***2444*** *p199*
*Child:*Isaac Barthelemi
*Child:*Pierre
*Child:*Jean Martin
*Child:*Daniel
*Child:*Anne Marie Rachel
*Wife:*Rachel Cochet
Paris, Isaac Barthelemi *SEE* Paris, Isaac
Paris, Jean Martin *SEE* Paris, Isaac
Paris, Peter; Philadelphia, 1760 ***9973.7*** *p34*
Paris, Peter; Philadelphia, 1776 ***8582.3*** *p83*
Paris, Pierre *SEE* Paris, Isaac
Paris, Pierre; Pennsylvania, 1750 ***2444*** *p199*
Paris, Rachel Cochet *SEE* Paris, Isaac
Parish, Edward; Virginia, 1628 ***6219*** *p31*
Parish, Frederick George; Chicago, 1889 ***1450.2*** *p109A*
Parisi, Mr. 24; New Orleans, 1839 ***778.5*** *p415*
Parisi, Vito; Arkansas, 1918 ***95.2*** *p96*
Parisse, Louis; Arkansas, 1918 ***95.2*** *p96*
Paritker, Marcus; Milwaukee, 1875 ***4719.30*** *p258*
Park, Annie; Philadelphia, 1865 ***5704.8*** *p200*
Park, Arthur; St. John, N.B., 1849 ***5704.8*** *p55*
Park, Charles; Quebec, 1850 ***5704.8*** *p63*
Park, David; New York, NY, 1811 ***2859.11*** *p18*
Park, David; New York, NY, 1816 ***2859.11*** *p40*
Park, Eliza Ann; St. John, N.B., 1848 ***5704.8*** *p38*
Park, Eliza J.; Philadelphia, 1865 ***5704.8*** *p200*
Park, Elizabeth; St. John, N.B., 1847 ***5704.8*** *p2*
Park, Elizabeth; Savannah, GA, 1770 ***1219.7*** *p145*
Park, Geo.; Quebec, 1830 ***4719.7*** *p21*
Park, George; Shreveport, LA, 1878 ***7129*** *p45*

408
FOR A COMPLETE EXPLANATION OF ENTRY, SEE "HOW TO READ A CITATION" SECTION

Pasa, Angelo; Iowa, 1866-1943 ***123.54*** *p38*
Pasa, John; Iowa, 1866-1943 ***123.54*** *p38*
Pasa, Louis; Iowa, 1866-1943 ***123.54*** *p38*
Pasa, Parquale; Iowa, 1866-1943 ***123.54*** *p38*
Pasa, Tony; Iowa, 1866-1943 ***123.54*** *p38*
Pasa, Victor Gabrielelle; Iowa, 1866-1943 ***123.54*** *p38*
Pasalinake, Adolf; Arkansas, 1918 ***95.2*** *p96*
Pascal, Mr. 22; America, 1839 ***778.5*** *p416*
Pascal, Mr. 28; New Orleans, 1837 ***778.5*** *p416*
Pascal, Mr. 28; New Orleans, 1839 ***778.5*** *p416*
Pascal, Mr. 32; America, 1839 ***778.5*** *p416*
Pascal, Mr. 32; New Orleans, 1839 ***778.5*** *p416*
Pascal, Jaques J. 23; New Orleans, 1835 ***778.5*** *p416*
Pascal, Samuel; Arkansas, 1918 ***95.2*** *p96*
Pascall, Robert 17; Windward Islands, 1722 ***3690.1*** *p173*
Paschalis, Panagiotes; Arkansas, 1918 ***95.2*** *p96*
Paschall, Thomas *SEE* Paschall, Thomas
Paschall, Thomas; Pennsylvania, 1682 ***4961*** *p8*
*Son:*Thomas
Pasche, . . .; Canada, 1776-1783 ***9786*** *p30*
Pascholy, Joseph; Santa Clara Co., CA, 1872 ***2764.35*** *p54*
Pascholy, Joseph; Santa Clara Co., CA, 1872 ***2764.35*** *p56*
Pasco, William 29; Virginia, 1774 ***1219.7*** *p244*
Pascoe, John; New York, NY, 1839 ***8208.4*** *p99*
Pascoe, Thomas; New York, NY, 1839 ***8208.4*** *p99*
Pasheloup, Mr. 21; America, 1838 ***778.5*** *p417*
Pashler, John 19; Windward Islands, 1722 ***3690.1*** *p173*
Pashley, William 70; Halifax, N.S., 1774 ***1219.7*** *p213*
Paskell, Thomas *SEE* Paskell, Thomas
Paskell, Thomas; Pennsylvania, 1682 ***4961*** *p8*
*Son:*Thomas
Paskiewicz, Alfons; Pennsylvania, 1912 ***9980.29*** *p60*
Paskiewicz, Amilia 17; New York, 1912 ***9980.29*** *p60*
Paskins, Edward; Virginia, 1636 ***6219*** *p21*
Paskuan, Petar; Iowa, 1866-1943 ***123.54*** *p38*
Paslley, Jane; New York, NY, 1865 ***5704.8*** *p203*
Pasmore, John; Virginia, 1638 ***6219*** *p118*
*Wife:*Mary
Pasmore, Mary *SEE* Pasmore, John
Pasquala, Lucie; Wisconsin, n.d. ***9675.7*** *p130*
Pasquet, Maius 29; America, 1827 ***778.5*** *p417*
Pasquier, Collombe 36; Port uncertain, 1837 ***778.5*** *p417*
Pasquier, Jeanbaptiste; America, 1854 ***1450.2*** *p109A*
Pasquier, Philippe 30?; Quebec, 1666 ***4533*** *p127*
Pasquil, John; Iowa, 1866-1943 ***123.54*** *p38*
Pass, Frank 37; West Virginia, 1898 ***9788.3*** *p18*
Passement, Miss 12; Louisiana, 1821 ***778.5*** *p417*
Passement, Miss 16; Louisiana, 1821 ***778.5*** *p417*
Passement, J. B. 25; New Orleans, 1823 ***778.5*** *p417*
Passement, J. B. 28; New Orleans, 1822 ***778.5*** *p417*
Passement, J. B. 28; New Orleans, 1823 ***778.5*** *p417*
Passement, John B. 30; New Orleans, 1821 ***778.5*** *p417*
Passement, M. 55; Louisiana, 1821 ***778.5*** *p417*
Passerant, J. B. 28; New Orleans, 1822 ***778.5*** *p417*
Passern, Luis von; Quebec, 1776 ***9786*** *p265*
Past, William 20; Jamaica, 1736 ***3690.1*** *p173*
Paster, . . .; Canada, 1776-1783 ***9786*** *p30*
Pasth, . . .; Milwaukee, 1875 ***4719.30*** *p258*
Pastisson, Mr. 22; America, 1838 ***778.5*** *p417*
Pastonell, Valentin; Wisconsin, n.d. ***9675.7*** *p130*
Pastoret, Michael; Wisconsin, n.d. ***9675.7*** *p130*
Pastorett, Phillip; Wisconsin, n.d. ***9675.7*** *p130*
Pastuzeau, J. 21; New Orleans, 1839 ***778.5*** *p417*
Pasty, Page; Arkansas, 1918 ***95.2*** *p96*
Pasunnas, Victor Toni; Arkansas, 1918 ***95.2*** *p96*
Pataszius, Benedict; Wisconsin, n.d. ***9675.7*** *p130*
Patchall, Alexander 11; Philadelphia, 1851 ***5704.8*** *p71*
Patchall, Anne; Philadelphia, 1851 ***5704.8*** *p71*
Patchall, David; Philadelphia, 1851 ***5704.8*** *p71*
Patchall, Edward; Philadelphia, 1851 ***5704.8*** *p71*
Patchall, Edward 9; Philadelphia, 1851 ***5704.8*** *p71*
Patchall, James 10; Philadelphia, 1851 ***5704.8*** *p71*
Patchall, Jane; Philadelphia, 1851 ***5704.8*** *p71*
Patchall, John; Philadelphia, 1851 ***5704.8*** *p71*
Patchall, Letitia; Philadelphia, 1851 ***5704.8*** *p71*
Patchall, William; Philadelphia, 1851 ***5704.8*** *p71*
Patchell, James; Philadelphia, 1852 ***5704.8*** *p89*
Patchell, John 14; Quebec, 1858 ***5704.8*** *p138*
Patchell, Margaret; Philadelphia, 1852 ***5704.8*** *p89*
Patchell, Mary 28; Philadelphia, 1864 ***5704.8*** *p157*
Patchell, Mary Ann 3; Philadelphia, 1864 ***5704.8*** *p157*
Patchell, Robert 5; Philadelphia, 1864 ***5704.8*** *p157*
Patchell, William 7; Philadelphia, 1864 ***5704.8*** *p157*
Pate, Richard; Virginia, 1636 ***6219*** *p78*
Pate, Richard 18; Antigua (Antego), 1739 ***3690.1*** *p173*
Pate, Wm.; Virginia, 1637 ***6219*** *p10*
Patenly, Patrick 44; Massachusetts, 1849 ***5881.1*** *p81*
Paterakis, Andreas; Arkansas, 1918 ***95.2*** *p96*
Paterlange, John 21; Maryland, 1774 ***1219.7*** *p230*
Paterni, Arturo; Iowa, 1866-1943 ***123.54*** *p38*
Paternotre, C. 33; New Orleans, 1826 ***778.5*** *p417*
Paterson, Mr.; Quebec, 1815 ***9229.18*** *p82*
Paterson, Agnes 25; St. John, N.B., 1866 ***5704.8*** *p166*
Paterson, Donald; North Carolina, 1764 ***1639.20*** *p258*
Paterson, Frederick; New York, NY, 1839 ***8208.4*** *p100*
Paterson, George; Quebec, 1847 ***5704.8*** *p12*
Paterson, Grace Dinholm; Quebec, 1822 ***8894.2*** *p57*
Paterson, Isabell; South Carolina, 1780 ***8894.1*** *p191*
Paterson, James; Carolina, 1684 ***1639.20*** *p259*
Paterson, James 20; Jamaica, 1736 ***3690.1*** *p173*
Paterson, Jane 22; Virginia, 1774 ***1219.7*** *p239*
Paterson, Mary; Quebec, 1863 ***4537.30*** *p13*
Paterson, Robert 25; St. John, N.B., 1866 ***5704.8*** *p166*
Paterson, Robert, Family; Nova Scotia, 1767 ***9775.5*** *p206*
Paterson, Thomas; Maryland, 1740 ***4971*** *p91*
Paterson, Thomas; Philadelphia, 1741 ***4971*** *p92*
Paterson, Thomas 1; St. John, N.B., 1866 ***5704.8*** *p166*
Paterson, Thomas 23; Maryland, 1774 ***1219.7*** *p230*
Paterson, William 21; Maryland, 1774 ***1219.7*** *p187*
Paterson, William 34; Halifax, N.S., 1774 ***1219.7*** *p213*
Patience, John 34?; America, 1701 ***2212*** *p35*
Patient, Arthur; Virginia, 1637 ***6219*** *p83*
Patient, James; Illinois, 1888 ***2896.5*** *p31*
Patison, Jonathan 19; North America, 1774 ***1219.7*** *p197*
Patmore, Richard 17; Maryland, 1774 ***1219.7*** *p208*
Paton, George 24; Kansas, 1871 ***5240.1*** *p52*
Paton, John 22; Kansas, 1874 ***5240.1*** *p55*
Paton, Joseph 30; Jamaica, 1735 ***3690.1*** *p173*
Paton, Mary Ann 19; St. John, N.B., 1853 ***5704.8*** *p109*
Paton, Thomas 15; Philadelphia, 1864 ***5704.8*** *p156*
Patoszius, Gorgis; Wisconsin, n.d. ***9675.7*** *p130*
Patou, Isidore 7; New Orleans, 1829 ***778.5*** *p418*
Patou, Louis 12; New Orleans, 1829 ***778.5*** *p418*
Patou, Pauline 6 mos; New Orleans, 1829 ***778.5*** *p418*
Patou, Pauline 23; New Orleans, 1829 ***778.5*** *p418*
Patou, Philip 5; New Orleans, 1829 ***778.5*** *p418*
Patou, Simeon 1; New Orleans, 1829 ***778.5*** *p418*
Patou, Simeon 37; New Orleans, 1829 ***778.5*** *p418*
Patras, Mr. 45; New Orleans, 1821 ***778.5*** *p418*
Patraz, Edward Richard; Arkansas, 1918 ***95.2*** *p96*
Patrick, Casimir; Charleston, SC, 1775-1781 ***8582.2*** *p52*
Patrick, Catharine Ann; Philadelphia, 1864 ***5704.8*** *p182*
Patrick, Christophr 20; New England, 1699 ***2212*** *p18*
Patrick, Eleanor 21; Maryland, 1774 ***1219.7*** *p206*
Patrick, Hen.; Virginia, 1636 ***6219*** *p20*
Patrick, James; New York, 1815 ***8894.2*** *p56*
Patrick, James; New York, NY, 1865 ***5704.8*** *p188*
Patrick, Jane; Philadelphia, 1851 ***5704.8*** *p80*
Patrick, John; Virginia, 1638 ***6219*** *p122*
Patrick, Leo.; Virginia, 1646 ***6219*** *p236*
Patrick, Manuel; Arkansas, 1918 ***95.2*** *p96*
Patrick, N. J. 26; Kansas, 1873 ***5240.1*** *p54*
Patrick, Paul; South Carolina, 1788 ***7119*** *p197*
Patrick, Robert; New York, NY, 1811 ***2859.11*** *p18*
Patrick, Seath; Virginia, 1646 ***6219*** *p241*
Patrick, Thomas; Virginia, 1643 ***6219*** *p202*
Patrick, William; Virginia, 1637 ***6219*** *p85*
Patridge, William 70; Arizona, 1899 ***9228.40*** *p3*
Patrignano, Bernardino; Wisconsin, n.d. ***9675.7*** *p130*
Patriquin, . . .; Halifax, N.S., 1752 ***7074.6*** *p232*
Patrojiz, Stanley; Wisconsin, n.d. ***9675.7*** *p130*
Patry, George 31; Kansas, 1884 ***5240.1*** *p66*
Patry, John B.; Minnesota, 1876 ***5240.1*** *p33*
Patry, John B. 26; Kansas, 1881 ***5240.1*** *p63*
Patry, Louis; Minnesota, 1874 ***5240.1*** *p33*
Patten, Edward 18; Philadelphia, 1858 ***5704.8*** *p139*
Patten, Eliza; Philadelphia, 1866 ***5704.8*** *p206*
Patten, James 18; St. John, N.B., 1858 ***5704.8*** *p137*
Patten, John; Havana, 1765 ***1219.7*** *p107*
Patten, John; New York, NY, 1837 ***8208.4*** *p24*
Patten, John 16; Philadelphia, 1858 ***5704.8*** *p139*
Patten, Maurice 14; Philadelphia, 1858 ***5704.8*** *p139*
Patten, William; Philadelphia, 1866 ***5704.8*** *p205*
Pattenson, John 30; New York, 1775 ***1219.7*** *p269*
With wife
With 3 children
Pattenson, Thomas 27; New York, 1775 ***1219.7*** *p268*
With wife
With child
Patterson, Miss; Quebec, 1815 ***9229.18*** *p78*
Patterson, Alexander; America, 1786 ***1639.20*** *p258*
Patterson, Alexander; New York, NY, 1840 ***8208.4*** *p104*
Patterson, Alexander; St. John, N.B., 1852 ***5704.8*** *p93*
Patterson, Alexander 3; St. John, N.B., 1851 ***5704.8*** *p77*
Patterson, Allen 5; Quebec, 1864 ***5704.8*** *p163*
Patterson, Ann; New York, NY, 1811 ***2859.11*** *p18*
Patterson, Archibald; America, 1802 ***1639.20*** *p258*
Patterson, Catharine; Quebec, 1847 ***5704.8*** *p17*
Patterson, Charles; Quebec, 1847 ***5704.8*** *p8*
Patterson, Daniel; America, 1803 ***1639.20*** *p258*
Patterson, Daniel 48; North Carolina, 1850 ***1639.20*** *p258*
*Relative:*Nancy 40
*Relative:*Euphemia 68
*Relative:*Mary 55
Patterson, David; New York, NY, 1811 ***2859.11*** *p18*
With family
Patterson, David; New York, NY, 1815 ***2859.11*** *p40*
Patterson, Duncan; North Carolina, 1680-1830 ***1639.20*** *p259*
Patterson, Edward; New York, NY, 1816 ***2859.11*** *p40*
Patterson, Eliza; New York, NY, 1811 ***2859.11*** *p18*
Patterson, Eliza; Quebec, 1847 ***5704.8*** *p8*
Patterson, Eliza; Quebec, 1851 ***5704.8*** *p74*
Patterson, Eliza; Quebec, 1851 ***5704.8*** *p82*
Patterson, Eliza; Quebec, 1852 ***5704.8*** *p94*
Patterson, Eliza Jane 6; Quebec, 1854 ***5704.8*** *p121*
Patterson, Eliza Jane 23; Philadelphia, 1853 ***5704.8*** *p109*
Patterson, Elizabeth 5; St. John, N.B., 1851 ***5704.8*** *p77*
Patterson, Elizabeth 25; Philadelphia, 1833-1834 ***53.26*** *p76*
Patterson, Elizabeth 25; Quebec, 1864 ***5704.8*** *p163*
Patterson, Ellan; Quebec, 1847 ***5704.8*** *p17*
Patterson, Ellan 9; Quebec, 1847 ***5704.8*** *p17*
Patterson, Ellen; St. John, N.B., 1853 ***5704.8*** *p99*
Patterson, Ellen 28; Quebec, 1854 ***5704.8*** *p121*
Patterson, Emilia 79; North Carolina, 1850 ***1639.20*** *p259*
Patterson, Euphemia 68 *SEE* Patterson, Daniel
Patterson, George; New York, NY, 1811 ***2859.11*** *p18*
Patterson, George 25; Quebec, 1855 ***5704.8*** *p126*
Patterson, Gilbert; Brunswick, NC, 1739 ***1639.20*** *p259*
Patterson, Grace; America, 1866 ***5704.8*** *p210*
Patterson, Henry; St. John, N.B., 1853 ***5704.8*** *p108*
Patterson, Henry 20; Massachusetts, 1849 ***5881.1*** *p81*
Patterson, Herbert; America, 1698 ***2212*** *p13*
Patterson, Herbert; Virginia, 1698 ***2212*** *p15*
Patterson, Hughey; Philadelphia, 1852 ***5704.8*** *p88*
Patterson, James; America, 1740 ***4971*** *p66*
Patterson, James; Charleston, SC, 1806 ***1639.20*** *p259*
Patterson, James; Quebec, 1847 ***5704.8*** *p8*
Patterson, James 10; St. John, N.B., 1851 ***5704.8*** *p77*
Patterson, James 25; Philadelphia, 1859 ***5704.8*** *p141*
Patterson, James 30; Quebec, 1853 ***5704.8*** *p104*
Patterson, James 60; Quebec, 1853 ***5704.8*** *p104*
Patterson, Jane; Quebec, 1847 ***5704.8*** *p17*
Patterson, Jane; Quebec, 1847 ***5704.8*** *p36*
Patterson, Jean 1 mo; Quebec, 1864 ***5704.8*** *p163*
Patterson, John; America, 1740 ***4971*** *p66*
Patterson, John; America, 1741 ***4971*** *p16*
Patterson, John; America, 1804 ***1639.20*** *p259*
Patterson, John; Austin, TX, 1886 ***9777*** *p5*
Patterson, John; New York, NY, 1811 ***2859.11*** *p18*
Patterson, John; Philadelphia, 1816 ***2859.11*** *p40*
Patterson, John; Philadelphia, 1852 ***5704.8*** *p92*
Patterson, John; Quebec, 1847 ***5704.8*** *p17*
Patterson, John; Quebec, 1847 ***5704.8*** *p36*
Patterson, John; Quebec, 1852 ***5704.8*** *p94*
Patterson, John 3; Quebec, 1864 ***5704.8*** *p163*
Patterson, John 18; Pennsylvania, 1738 ***3690.1*** *p173*
Patterson, John 20; Philadelphia, 1858 ***5704.8*** *p139*
Patterson, John 22; Virginia, 1773 ***1219.7*** *p169*
Patterson, John 30 *SEE* Patterson, Peter
Patterson, John 31; Quebec, 1864 ***5704.8*** *p163*
Patterson, Joseph; New York, NY, 1811 ***2859.11*** *p18*
Patterson, Joseph; New York, NY, 1815 ***2859.11*** *p40*
Patterson, Joseph; Quebec, 1847 ***5704.8*** *p8*
Patterson, Joseph; Quebec, 1848 ***5704.8*** *p41*
Patterson, Joseph; St. John, N.B., 1850 ***5704.8*** *p66*
Patterson, Joseph; St. John, N.B., 1851 ***5704.8*** *p77*
Patterson, Joseph 25; Philadelphia, 1858 ***5704.8*** *p139*
Patterson, Joseph 62; Philadelphia, 1833-1834 ***53.26*** *p76*
Patterson, Lilly 20; Philadelphia, 1859 ***5704.8*** *p141*
Patterson, Margaret; Philadelphia, 1866 ***5704.8*** *p210*
Patterson, Margaret; Quebec, 1851 ***5704.8*** *p74*
Patterson, Margaret; St. John, N.B., 1847 ***5704.8*** *p4*
Patterson, Margaret 8; Quebec, 1854 ***5704.8*** *p121*
Patterson, Margaret 60; Quebec, 1853 ***5704.8*** *p104*
Patterson, Margaret 64; North Carolina, 1850 ***1639.20*** *p259*
Patterson, Martha; St. John, N.B., 1847 ***5704.8*** *p2*
Patterson, Martha 3; Philadelphia, 1853 ***5704.8*** *p102*
Patterson, Mary; Montreal, 1823 ***7603*** *p89*
Patterson, Mary; New York, NY, 1811 ***2859.11*** *p18*
Patterson, Mary; New York, NY, 1868 ***5704.8*** *p229*
Patterson, Mary; Quebec, 1847 ***5704.8*** *p36*
Patterson, Mary; Quebec, 1851 ***5704.8*** *p75*
Patterson, Mary; St. John, N.B., 1849 ***5704.8*** *p56*
Patterson, Mary; St. John, N.B., 1852 ***5704.8*** *p93*
Patterson, Mary 6 mos; Quebec, 1847 ***5704.8*** *p17*
Patterson, Mary 10; Quebec, 1847 ***5704.8*** *p36*
Patterson, Mary 25; Quebec, 1856 ***5704.8*** *p130*
Patterson, Mary 26; Philadelphia, 1833-1834 ***53.26*** *p76*
Patterson, Mary 55 *SEE* Patterson, Daniel

Patterson, Mary 70; North Carolina, 1850 ***1639.20*** *p259*
*Relative:*Peter 45
Patterson, Mary 76; North Carolina, 1850 ***1639.20*** *p259*
Patterson, Mary Ann; St. John, N.B., 1852 ***5704.8*** *p93*
Patterson, Mary Ann 6 mos; Quebec, 1854 ***5704.8*** *p121*
Patterson, Mary Jane; St. John, N.B., 1851 ***5704.8*** *p77*
Patterson, Nancy 40 *SEE* Patterson, Daniel
Patterson, Nancy Jane 8; St. John, N.B., 1851 ***5704.8*** *p77*
Patterson, Neill; North Carolina, 1771 ***1639.20*** *p260*
Patterson, Peter; America, 1802 ***1639.20*** *p260*
Patterson, Peter 45 *SEE* Patterson, Mary
Patterson, Peter 60; North Carolina, 1850 ***1639.20*** *p260*
*Relative:*John 30
Patterson, Rachel 6 mos; St. John, N.B., 1851 ***5704.8*** *p77*
Patterson, Richard 43; Philadelphia, 1833-1834 ***53.26*** *p76*
Patterson, Robert; Philadelphia, 1852 ***5704.8*** *p91*
Patterson, Robert; West Virginia, 1819 ***9788.3*** *p18*
Patterson, Robert 56; Quebec, 1857 ***5704.8*** *p135*
Patterson, Samuel; Philadelphia, 1811 ***53.26*** *p76*
Patterson, Samuel; Philadelphia, 1811 ***2859.11*** *p18*
Patterson, Samuel; St. John, N.B., 1847 ***5704.8*** *p4*
Patterson, Samuel; West Virginia, 1819 ***9788.3*** *p18*
Patterson, Samuel 11; Quebec, 1847 ***5704.8*** *p36*
Patterson, Samuel 12; St. John, N.B., 1851 ***5704.8*** *p77*
Patterson, Samuel 33; Philadelphia, 1833-1834 ***53.26*** *p76*
Patterson, Sarah; St. John, N.B., 1847 ***5704.8*** *p2*
Patterson, Thomas; America, 1740 ***4971*** *p15*
Patterson, Thomas; Illinois, 1892 ***5012.40*** *p27*
Patterson, Thomas; Quebec, 1847 ***5704.8*** *p17*
Patterson, Thomas M.; Iowa, 1866-1943 ***123.54*** *p38*
Patterson, Will.; America, 1740 ***4971*** *p66*
Patterson, William; New York, NY, 1815 ***2859.11*** *p40*
Patterson, William; Quebec, 1847 ***5704.8*** *p36*
Patterson, William; Quebec, 1850 ***5704.8*** *p66*
Patterson, William; Quebec, 1856 ***5704.8*** *p130*
Patterson, William 3; Quebec, 1854 ***5704.8*** *p121*
Patterson, William 11; Quebec, 1847 ***5704.8*** *p17*
Patterson, William 24; Maryland, 1775 ***1219.7*** *p250*
Patterson, William 30; Arkansas, 1918 ***95.2*** *p96*
Patterson, William B.; Illinois, 1873 ***5012.39*** *p26*
Patterson, Wilson 13; Quebec, 1847 ***5704.8*** *p36*
Patterson, Wm.; New York, NY, 1811 ***2859.11*** *p18*
Pattingall, . . .; Canada, 1776-1783 ***9786*** *p30*
Pattison, Bridget 40; New York, 1775 ***1219.7*** *p268*
With child
Pattison, Edward 15; Pennsylvania, 1731 ***3690.1*** *p173*
Pattison, Gilbert; North Carolina, 1739 ***1639.20*** *p260*
Pattison, Hen.; Virginia, 1635 ***6219*** *p71*
Pattison, James; Virginia, 1636 ***6219*** *p21*
Pattison, John 18; Maryland, 1719 ***3690.1*** *p173*
Pattison, John 18; Pennsylvania, 1738 ***3690.1*** *p173*
Pattison, Rachell 19; Virginia, 1700 ***2212*** *p33*
Pattison, Thomas; New York, NY, 1836 ***8208.4*** *p20*
Pattison, Thos.; Virginia, 1629 ***6219*** *p8*
Pattman, Tho.; Virginia, 1640 ***6219*** *p160*
Patton, Alexander; Quebec, 1847 ***5704.8*** *p28*
Patton, Alexander 21; St. John, N.B., 1866 ***5704.8*** *p166*
Patton, Betty; Philadelphia, 1853 ***5704.8*** *p101*
Patton, Catharine; America, 1867 ***5704.8*** *p224*
Patton, Catherine 18; Philadelphia, 1854 ***5704.8*** *p116*
Patton, Catherine 22; Philadelphia, 1864 ***5704.8*** *p160*
Patton, David; Quebec, 1847 ***5704.8*** *p28*
Patton, David 25; Philadelphia, 1865 ***5704.8*** *p164*
Patton, Edward; New York, NY, 1811 ***2859.11*** *p18*
Patton, Eliza; Quebec, 1847 ***5704.8*** *p28*
Patton, Elizabeth; Philadelphia, 1852 ***5704.8*** *p84*
Patton, Elizabeth; Quebec, 1847 ***5704.8*** *p28*
Patton, Elleanor; Philadelphia, 1853 ***5704.8*** *p102*
Patton, Ellen *SEE* Patton, James
Patton, Ellen; Philadelphia, 1849 ***5704.8*** *p49*
Patton, Ellen; Philadelphia, 1864 ***5704.8*** *p183*
Patton, Francis 26; St. John, N.B., 1854 ***5704.8*** *p115*
Patton, George; Ohio, 1840 ***9892.11*** *p36*
Patton, George; Philadelphia, 1853 ***5704.8*** *p101*
Patton, Henry; Quebec, 1847 ***5704.8*** *p28*
Patton, Isabella; Philadelphia, 1853 ***5704.8*** *p101*
Patton, James; America, 1816 ***1639.20*** *p260*
Patton, James; New York, NY, 1864 ***5704.8*** *p172*
Patton, James; Philadelphia, 1849 ***53.26*** *p76*
*Relative:*Ellen
Patton, James; Philadelphia, 1849 ***5704.8*** *p49*
Patton, James; Quebec, 1847 ***5704.8*** *p7*
Patton, James 17; Philadelphia, 1860 ***5704.8*** *p145*
Patton, James 61; North Carolina, 1850 ***1639.20*** *p260*
*Relative:*Nicolas B. 38
Patton, Jane 3; Quebec, 1847 ***5704.8*** *p28*
Patton, Jean 49; Montreal, 1777 ***7603*** *p70*
Patton, Jinnett 13; Quebec, 1847 ***5704.8*** *p28*
Patton, John *SEE* Patton, Mathew
Patton, John; Philadelphia, 1849 ***5704.8*** *p58*
Patton, John; Philadelphia, 1853 ***5704.8*** *p101*
Patton, John; South Carolina, 1815 ***1639.20*** *p260*
Patton, John 9 mos; Philadelphia, 1853 ***5704.8*** *p102*
Patton, John 9 mos; St. John, N.B., 1850 ***5704.8*** *p62*
Patton, Joseph; Philadelphia, 1853 ***5704.8*** *p101*
Patton, Joseph 36 *SEE* Patton, Samuel
Patton, Margaret; New York, NY, 1864 ***5704.8*** *p172*
Patton, Margaret 15; Philadelphia, 1855 ***5704.8*** *p123*
Patton, Margaret Jane; Quebec, 1849 ***5704.8*** *p51*
Patton, Martha Jane *SEE* Patton, Mary
Patton, Martha Jane 3; Philadelphia, 1850 ***5704.8*** *p65*
Patton, Mary; Philadelphia, 1850 ***53.26*** *p76*
Patton, Mary; Philadelphia, 1850 ***53.26*** *p76*
*Relative:*Martha Jane
Patton, Mary; Philadelphia, 1850 ***5704.8*** *p65*
Patton, Mary; Philadelphia, 1850 ***5704.8*** *p68*
Patton, Mary; Philadelphia, 1852 ***5704.8*** *p85*
Patton, Mary; St. John, N.B., 1850 ***5704.8*** *p62*
Patton, Mary 24; Philadelphia, 1864 ***5704.8*** *p160*
Patton, Mathew; Philadelphia, 1849 ***53.26*** *p76*
*Relative:*John
Patton, Mathew; Philadelphia, 1849 ***5704.8*** *p58*
Patton, Matilda 7; Quebec, 1847 ***5704.8*** *p28*
Patton, Matthew 40; California, 1867 ***3840.3*** *p8*
Patton, Matty; Quebec, 1849 ***5704.8*** *p51*
Patton, Nancy 11; Quebec, 1847 ***5704.8*** *p28*
Patton, Neal; Philadelphia, 1853 ***5704.8*** *p101*
Patton, Neal 11; Philadelphia, 1852 ***5704.8*** *p85*
Patton, Nicolas B. 38 *SEE* Patton, James
Patton, Patrick 19; Philadelphia, 1859 ***5704.8*** *p142*
Patton, Robert; Quebec, 1830 ***4719.7*** *p21*
Patton, Robert; Quebec, 1847 ***5704.8*** *p28*
Patton, Samuel 32; Philadelphia, 1803 ***53.26*** *p76*
*Relative:*Joseph 36
Patton, Sarah; Philadelphia, 1853 ***5704.8*** *p108*
Patton, Susan 23; Philadelphia, 1853 ***5704.8*** *p112*
Patton, Thomas; St. John, N.B., 1850 ***5704.8*** *p61*
Patton, Thomas; St. John, N.B., 1853 ***5704.8*** *p99*
Patton, William 9; Quebec, 1847 ***5704.8*** *p28*
Patton, William 17; Philadelphia, 1854 ***5704.8*** *p116*
Patton, William 18; Virginia, 1723 ***3690.1*** *p174*
Patton, William 30; Massachusetts, 1849 ***5881.1*** *p81*
Patton, Winford 5; St. John, N.B., 1850 ***5704.8*** *p62*
Pattullo, Henry; Virginia, 1726-1801 ***1639.20*** *p260*
Patzel, . . .; Canada, 1776-1783 ***9786*** *p30*
Patzwitz, Adolf; Illinois, 1891 ***5012.39*** *p53*
Patzwitz, Adolf; Illinois, 1894 ***5012.40*** *p53*
Patzwitz, Frederick; Illinois, 1891 ***5012.39*** *p53*
Patzwitz, Frederick; Illinois, 1894 ***5012.40*** *p53*
Pauchon, Fidele 25; Port uncertain, 1836 ***778.5*** *p418*
Pauilly, Charles; Iowa, 1866-1943 ***123.54*** *p38*
Paul, . . .; Canada, 1776-1783 ***9786*** *p30*
Paul, Dr.; America, 1836 ***8582.1*** *p39*
Paul, Mr. 30; New Orleans, 1829 ***778.5*** *p418*
Paul, Alexander; Iowa, 1866-1943 ***123.54*** *p38*
Paul, Andrew; South Carolina, 1806 ***1639.20*** *p260*
Paul, Andrew 40; St. John, N.B., 1864 ***5704.8*** *p157*
Paul, Ann; Georgia, 1680-1770 ***1639.20*** *p261*
Paul, Antoine 36; America, 1822 ***778.5*** *p418*
Paul, Bernard; Wisconsin, n.d. ***9675.7*** *p130*
Paul, Conrad; America, 1853 ***8582.3*** *p50*
Paul, Conrad; Illinois, 1857 ***7857*** *p6*
Paul, D. 32; America, 1838 ***778.5*** *p418*
Paul, Dunbar; America, 1810 ***1639.20*** *p261*
Paul, Eliza; New York, NY, 1811 ***2859.11*** *p18*
Paul, Felix 25; New Orleans, 1829 ***778.5*** *p418*
Paul, Frederika 40 *SEE* Paul, John
Paul, G. H.; Cincinnati, 1869-1887 ***8582*** *p23*
Paul, Harriet 22; Canada, 1838 ***4535.12*** *p113*
Paul, Henrietta; St. John, N.B., 1848 ***5704.8*** *p43*
Paul, Henry; Wisconsin, n.d. ***9675.7*** *p130*
Paul, Herman; Virginia, 1854 ***4626.16*** *p14*
Paul, Isabella; St. John, N.B., 1847 ***5704.8*** *p21*
Paul, Jane 4; St. John, N.B., 1848 ***5704.8*** *p43*
Paul, Johann D.; Kentucky, 1843 ***8582.3*** *p100*
Paul, John; Charleston, SC, 1812 ***1639.20*** *p261*
Paul, John; Charleston, SC, 1829 ***1639.20*** *p261*
Paul, John 7; St. John, N.B., 1848 ***5704.8*** *p43*
Paul, John 27; Jamaica, 1738 ***3690.1*** *p174*
Paul, John 50; New Orleans, 1839 ***9420.2*** *p485*
*Wife:*Frederika 40
Paul, Joseph 24; America, 1835 ***778.5*** *p418*
Paul, L. 27; New Orleans, 1820 ***778.5*** *p418*
Paul, Lorenz; Virginia, 1844 ***4626.16*** *p12*
Paul, M. W.; Cincinnati, 1834 ***8582.1*** *p40*
Paul, Margaret; Philadelphia, 1868 ***5704.8*** *p230*
Paul, Margaret 2; St. John, N.B., 1848 ***5704.8*** *p43*
Paul, Mary Ann 29; St. John, N.B., 1864 ***5704.8*** *p157*
Paul, Mathew; St. John, N.B., 1848 ***5704.8*** *p43*
Paul, Michael 30; Canada, 1838 ***4535.12*** *p113*
Paul, Pat; Virginia, 1648 ***6219*** *p250*
Paul, Valentine; Wisconsin, n.d. ***9675.7*** *p130*
Paulding, Hiram; Washington, 1859-1920 ***2872.1*** *p30*
Paule, Frances *SEE* Paule, Thomas
Paule, Francis; Virginia, 1623-1637 ***6219*** *p83*
Paule, Mathew *SEE* Paule, Thomas
Paule, Stephen; Virginia, 1643 ***6219*** *p202*
Paule, Thomas; Virginia, 1637 ***6219*** *p83*
*Mother:*Mathew
*Sister:*Frances
Paulet, Mr. 22; New Orleans, 1826 ***778.5*** *p419*
Paulet, Onesime; Arkansas, 1918 ***95.2*** *p96*
Paulett, Chiddock *SEE* Paulett, Thomas
Paulett, Thomas; Virginia, 1637 ***6219*** *p113*
*Brother:*Chiddock
Pauletti, Guiseppe; Iowa, 1866-1943 ***123.54*** *p73*
Pauley, John; Philadelphia, 1849 ***53.26*** *p76*
Pauley, John; Philadelphia, 1849 ***5704.8*** *p55*
Pauli, Henry; America, 1852 ***1450.2*** *p109A*
Paulin, Theodore; Wisconsin, n.d. ***9675.7*** *p130*
Pauline, Ms.; New Orleans, 1820 ***778.5*** *p419*
Paulioglon, Stavres 29; Arkansas, 1918 ***95.2*** *p96*
Paulo, Michael A. 32; West Virginia, 1900 ***9788.3*** *p18*
Paulsen, . . .; Canada, 1776-1783 ***9786*** *p30*
Paulsen, Alfred; Arkansas, 1918 ***95.2*** *p96*
Paulsen, Catharine; New York, 1749 ***3652*** *p73*
Paulsen, Jens Viggo; Arkansas, 1918 ***95.2*** *p96*
Paulsen, P. A.; Milwaukee, 1875 ***4719.30*** *p257*
Paulsen, Paul; New York, 1748 ***3652*** *p68*
Paulsiek, Karl Friedrich Wilhelm; America, 1851-1852 ***4610.10*** *p112*
Paulsmeyer, Carl Friedrich; America, 1849 ***4610.10*** *p104*
*Wife:*Caroline L. Rolfsmeyer
*Son:*Johann Ernst Heinrich
Paulsmeyer, Caroline L. Rolfsmeyer *SEE* Paulsmeyer, Carl Friedrich
Paulsmeyer, Heinrich Diedrich Gottlieb; America, 1848 ***4610.10*** *p104*
Paulsmeyer, Johann Ernst Heinrich *SEE* Paulsmeyer, Carl Friedrich
Paulson, Erick; Maine, 1883-1896 ***6410.22*** *p122*
Paulson, George Heinrich Peter; New York, NY, 1838 ***8208.4*** *p56*
Paulson, James 43; Virginia, 1775 ***1219.7*** *p261*
Paulus, Christoph; Wisconsin, n.d. ***9675.7*** *p130*
Paulus, Emil Walter; Wisconsin, n.d. ***9675.7*** *p130*
Paulus, Henry Peter; Wisconsin, n.d. ***9675.7*** *p130*
Paulus, Luis; Canada, 1783 ***9786*** *p38A*
Paulus, Mathias; Wisconsin, n.d. ***9675.7*** *p130*
Paulus, Peter; Wisconsin, n.d. ***9675.7*** *p130*
Paur, Anton; Illinois, 1858 ***5012.39*** *p54*
Pausch, Georg; Canada, 1776 ***9786*** *p110*
Pausch, Georg; Quebec, 1776 ***9786*** *p98*
Pausch, Georg; Quebec, 1776 ***9786*** *p265*
Pause, . . .; Canada, 1776-1783 ***9786*** *p30*
Pause, Jean Georges; Canada, 1776-1783 ***9786*** *p237*
Pautz, Carl; Wisconsin, n.d. ***9675.7*** *p130*
Pauwels, Jean Francis; Iowa, 1866-1943 ***123.54*** *p38*
Pauwels, Marie Louise; Iowa, 1866-1943 ***123.54*** *p38*
Pauze, . . .; Canada, 1776-1783 ***9786*** *p30*
Pauze, Jean Georges; Canada, 1776-1783 ***9786*** *p237*
Paverell, Georg; Virginia, 1639 ***6219*** *p157*
Pavesich, Romano; Iowa, 1866-1943 ***123.54*** *p38*
Pavlic, Frank; America, 1898 ***7137*** *p169*
Pavlic, Mary; America, 1899 ***7137*** *p169*
Pavlick, Frank; America, 1898 ***7137*** *p169*
Pavlick, Mary; America, 1899 ***7137*** *p169*
Pavlovich, John; Arkansas, 1918 ***95.2*** *p96*
Pavy, William; Virginia, 1647 ***6219*** *p247*
Pawer, Leonard; Wisconsin, n.d. ***9675.7*** *p130*
Pawford, Thomas; Virginia, 1635 ***6219*** *p27*
Pawlik, Christine; Wisconsin, n.d. ***9675.7*** *p130*
Pawlinski, . . .; New York, 1831 ***4606*** *p176*
Pawlowski, Walter; Arkansas, 1918 ***95.2*** *p96*
Pawly, Jon.; Virginia, 1635 ***6219*** *p26*
Paxton, Wentworth; Boston, 1751 ***1219.7*** *p2*
Paya, Mr. 24; New Orleans, 1820 ***778.5*** *p419*
Payekin, Andrew; San Francisco, 1881 ***2764.35*** *p56*
Payen, Charles; New York, NY, 1840 ***8208.4*** *p103*
Payer, . . .; Canada, 1776-1783 ***9786*** *p30*
Payer, M. 30; Louisiana, 1821 ***778.5*** *p419*
Payes, Bertrand 31; America, 1837 ***778.5*** *p419*
Payeur, . . .; Canada, 1776-1783 ***9786*** *p30*
Payeur, Conrad Christophe; Canada, 1776-1783 ***9786*** *p243*
Payla, Frank 35?; Arizona, 1890 ***2764.35*** *p54*
Paylopoulos, Spyros Thanos; Arkansas, 1918 ***95.2*** *p96*
Payne, Alice; America, 1741 ***4971*** *p62*
Payne, David 38; Philadelphia, 1774 ***1219.7*** *p237*
Payne, Elizabeth *SEE* Payne, Jasper
Payne, Francis 25; Philadelphia, 1774 ***1219.7*** *p216*
Payne, George 21; Maryland, 1774 ***1219.7*** *p212*
Payne, Harlen Howard; Iowa, 1866-1943 ***123.54*** *p38*
Payne, Jasper; New York, 1743 ***3652*** *p60*
*Wife:*Elizabeth

Payne, John; New York, NY, 1835 ***8208.4*** *p7*
Payne, Philip; Quebec, 1852 ***5704.8*** *p94*
Payne, Richard 27; Maryland, 1774 ***1219.7*** *p181*
Payne, Samuel 25; Montreal, 1725 ***7603*** *p27*
Payne, Thomas 17; Antigua (Antego), 1755 ***1219.7*** *p39*
Payne, Thomas 17; Antigua (Antego), 1755 ***3690.1*** *p174*
Payne, Thomas 22; Philadelphia, 1774 ***1219.7*** *p234*
Payne, Thomas 28; Maryland, 1774 ***1219.7*** *p181*
Payne, Walter; Virginia, 1637 ***6219*** *p37*
Payne, William; New York, NY, 1840 ***8208.4*** *p109*
Payne, William 21; Virginia, 1774 ***1219.7*** *p185*
Payne, William 33; Virginia, 1774 ***1219.7*** *p193*
Payne, William Wisdom; New York, NY, 1833 ***8208.4*** *p28*
Payou, Mme.; Port uncertain, 1839 ***778.5*** *p419*
Payou, Mr.; Port uncertain, 1839 ***778.5*** *p419*
Paysan, J. S. 36; New Orleans, 1826 ***778.5*** *p419*
Payton, Hamilton; New Orleans, 1848 ***5704.8*** *p48*
Payton, Peter; Virginia, 1636 ***6219*** *p15*
Payu, Paul 19; America, 1835 ***778.5*** *p419*
Pazick, John; Arkansas, 1918 ***95.2*** *p97*
Pczetakewicz, Josef 20; New York, 1912 ***9980.29*** *p73*
Pea, J. W.; Washington, 1859-1920 ***2872.1*** *p30*
Pea, O. P.; Washington, 1859-1920 ***2872.1*** *p30*
Peach, Charles 70; Kansas, 1880 ***5240.1*** *p61*
Peach, Thomas 19; Jamaica, 1723 ***3690.1*** *p174*
Peach, Wm.; Virginia, 1643 ***6219*** *p201*
Peachey, Joseph 49; Kansas, 1881 ***5240.1*** *p63*
Peachey, Joseph W. 26; Kansas, 1882 ***5240.1*** *p64*
Peacock, . . .; America, 1869-1885 ***8582.2*** *p30*
Peacock, David 5; St. John, N.B., 1848 ***5704.8*** *p43*
Peacock, Edward 24; Jamaica, 1736 ***3690.1*** *p174*
Peacock, Elizabeth 34 *SEE* Peacock, John
Peacock, George; New York, NY, 1837 ***8208.4*** *p54*
Peacock, Isabella; Philadelphia, 1866 ***5704.8*** *p215*
Peacock, James; Maryland, 1753 ***1219.7*** *p22*
Peacock, James; Maryland, 1753 ***3690.1*** *p174*
Peacock, James; New York, NY, 1816 ***2859.11*** *p40*
Peacock, James; St. John, N.B., 1848 ***5704.8*** *p43*
Peacock, James 10; St. John, N.B., 1848 ***5704.8*** *p43*
Peacock, James 18; Maryland, 1723 ***3690.1*** *p174*
Peacock, Jane; St. John, N.B., 1848 ***5704.8*** *p43*
Peacock, John 18; Philadelphia, 1856 ***5704.8*** *p129*
Peacock, John 24; Philadelphia, 1856 ***5704.8*** *p128*
Peacock, John 39; Maryland, 1774 ***1219.7*** *p235*
*Wife:*Elizabeth 34
Peacock, Joseph 17; West Indies, 1722 ***3690.1*** *p174*
Peacock, Martha 7; St. John, N.B., 1848 ***5704.8*** *p43*
Peacock, Michaell; Virginia, 1642 ***6219*** *p195*
Peacock, Nathaniel 1; St. John, N.B., 1848 ***5704.8*** *p43*
Peacock, Richard; Virginia, 1642 ***6219*** *p191*
Peacock, Richard 18; Maryland, 1729 ***3690.1*** *p174*
Peacock, Robert 24; Maryland, 1774 ***1219.7*** *p230*
Peacock, Tho.; Virginia, 1635 ***6219*** *p27*
Peacock, Tho.; Virginia, 1646 ***6219*** *p242*
Peacock, Thomas 20; Jamaica, 1720 ***3690.1*** *p174*
Peacock, W.; South Carolina, 1790 ***1639.20*** *p261*
Peacock, William John 12; St. John, N.B., 1848 ***5704.8*** *p43*
Pead, Jon.; Virginia, 1637 ***6219*** *p11*
Peadle, Corbett; Virginia, 1643 ***6219*** *p200*
Peadle, Henry; Virginia, 1639 ***6219*** *p158*
Peadon, Robert; New York, NY, 1811 ***2859.11*** *p18*
Peagler, John; Virginia, 1646 ***6219*** *p244*
Peak, Martha; Virginia, 1698 ***2212*** *p13*
Peak, Mathias 19; Maryland, 1723 ***3690.1*** *p174*
Peake, Mathew; Virginia, 1636 ***6219*** *p77*
Peake, Miles; America, 1738 ***4971*** *p33*
Peake, Tho.; Virginia, 1642 ***6219*** *p195*
Peake, Wm.; Virginia, 1643 ***6219*** *p200*
Peakstone, Eleanor 26; Georgia, 1775 ***1219.7*** *p277*
Peal, Henry; America, 1846 ***1450.2*** *p111A*
Peale, Fr.; Virginia, 1635 ***6219*** *p71*
Peale, Thos.; Virginia, 1635 ***6219*** *p5*
Pealle, Chaplain; Quebec, 1776 ***9786*** *p257*
Pealstrine, Justine 28; Massachusetts, 1860 ***6410.32*** *p110*
Pean, Mr. 26; New Orleans, 1822 ***778.5*** *p419*
Pean, A. 45; New Orleans, 1827 ***778.5*** *p419*
Pearce, Edward; Virginia, 1635 ***6219*** *p36*
Pearce, Ellen 27; St. John, N.B., 1865 ***5704.8*** *p165*
Pearce, George 3; St. John, N.B., 1865 ***5704.8*** *p165*
Pearce, George 16; St. John, N.B., 1865 ***5704.8*** *p165*
Pearce, George 17; Maryland, 1774 ***1219.7*** *p211*
Pearce, Hugh 18; St. John, N.B., 1864 ***5704.8*** *p159*
Pearce, John 5; St. John, N.B., 1865 ***5704.8*** *p165*
Pearce, John 20; Maryland, 1729 ***3690.1*** *p174*
Pearce, Katherine; Virginia, 1635 ***6219*** *p70*
Pearce, Katherine; Virginia, 1637 ***6219*** *p180*
Pearce, Mary 1; St. John, N.B., 1865 ***5704.8*** *p165*
Pearce, Mary 14; St. John, N.B., 1865 ***5704.8*** *p165*
Pearce, Patrick; Quebec, 1825 ***7603*** *p94*
Pearce, Robert; Virginia, 1636 ***6219*** *p21*
Pearce, Robert 15; Virginia, 1774 ***1219.7*** *p238*
Pearce, William; Arizona, 1890 ***2764.35*** *p54*
Pearce, William 21; Maryland, 1722 ***3690.1*** *p174*
Pearce, William 28; St. John, N.B., 1864 ***5704.8*** *p159*
Pearce, Wm.; Virginia, 1636 ***6219*** *p21*
Pearcy, J. N.; Washington, 1859-1920 ***2872.1*** *p30*
Pearepoint, Wm.; Virginia, 1643 ***6219*** *p202*
Peares, John 18; America, 1700 ***2212*** *p33*
Peares, William 12; America, 1701 ***2212*** *p34*
Pearl, Frank 29; Kansas, 1889 ***5240.1*** *p73*
Pearl, Michael 22; Kansas, 1889 ***5240.1*** *p73*
Pearle, Franc.; Virginia, 1635 ***6219*** *p70*
Pearle, Francis; Virginia, 1637 ***6219*** *p180*
Pearlstrine, Justine; America, 1850-1859 ***6410.32*** *p124*
Pearsall, Joseph 18; Maryland or Virginia, 1737 ***3690.1*** *p175*
Pearse, Edward; Virginia, 1637 ***6219*** *p83*
Pearse, Mary; New York, NY, 1864 ***5704.8*** *p170*
Pearse, Robert; Virginia, 1637 ***6219*** *p82*
Pearse, Samuel; New York, NY, 1864 ***5704.8*** *p170*
Pearse, Samuel 12; Philadelphia, 1774 ***1219.7*** *p185*
Pearse, William 23; Maryland, 1774 ***1219.7*** *p230*
Pearse, William 33; Philadelphia, 1774 ***1219.7*** *p197*
With wife
With 2 children
Pearson, Mr.; Tobago, W. Indies, 1775 ***1219.7*** *p265*
Pearson, A. 50; North Carolina, 1850 ***1639.20*** *p261*
*Relative:*Eliza 48
Pearson, Anders; Iowa, 1853 ***2090*** *p611*
Pearson, Ann 19; Georgia, 1775 ***1219.7*** *p277*
Pearson, August Pear; Bangor, ME, 1876 ***6410.22*** *p124*
Pearson, August Per; Bangor, ME, 1871-1876 ***6410.22*** *p116*
Pearson, Carl A.; Bangor, ME, 1899 ***6410.22*** *p128*
Pearson, Christopher 20; Nova Scotia, 1774 ***1219.7*** *p210*
Pearson, E. A.; Washington, 1859-1920 ***2872.1*** *p30*
Pearson, Eliza 48 *SEE* Pearson, A.
Pearson, Esther 36 *SEE* Pearson, Nicholas
Pearson, George 27; Philadelphia, 1774 ***1219.7*** *p196*
Pearson, Gust; Iroquois Co., IL, 1896 ***3455.1*** *p12*
Pearson, John; Illinois, 1887 ***5012.39*** *p121*
Pearson, John 40; Baltimore, 1775 ***1219.7*** *p270*
Pearson, Ludwig; Iowa, 1866-1943 ***123.54*** *p38*
Pearson, Mamie Gordon; Colorado, 1904 ***9678.2*** *p131*
Pearson, Margaret 52; Philadelphia, 1804 ***53.26*** *p76*
Pearson, Mary; Virginia, 1646 ***6219*** *p236*
Pearson, Michael 18; Maryland, 1718 ***3690.1*** *p175*
Pearson, Nels; Illinois, 1892 ***5012.39*** *p53*
Pearson, Nels; Illinois, 1894 ***5012.40*** *p53*
Pearson, Nels; Iowa, 1854 ***2090*** *p611*
With wife
Pearson, Nels Antone; Arkansas, 1918 ***95.2*** *p97*
Pearson, Nicholas 40; Halifax, N.S., 1774 ***1219.7*** *p213*
*Wife:*Esther 36
With child 10
With child 6
With child 1
Pearson, Nils Fridolf; Washington, 1859-1920 ***2872.1*** *p30*
Pearson, Olaf; Arkansas, 1918 ***95.2*** *p97*
Pearson, Otto William 27; Arkansas, 1918 ***95.2*** *p97*
Pearson, Palmer; Arkansas, 1918 ***95.2*** *p97*
Pearson, Richard 26; America, 1701 ***2212*** *p34*
Pearson, Tho.; Virginia, 1636 ***6219*** *p80*
Pearson, Thomas; New York, NY, 1836 ***8208.4*** *p17*
Pearson, Thomas; New York, NY, 1839 ***8208.4*** *p99*
Pearson, Thomas 21; Virginia, 1700 ***2212*** *p33*
Pearson, Thomas 23; Maryland, 1774 ***1219.7*** *p229*
Pearson, Thomas 27; Tobago, W. Indies, 1775 ***1219.7*** *p268*
Pearson, Whitney; Bangor, ME, 1892 ***6410.22*** *p126*
Pearson, William 28; Nova Scotia, 1774 ***1219.7*** *p210*
Peasant, William; Virginia, 1636 ***6219*** *p146*
Peasey, Edmund 17; Maryland, 1718 ***3690.1*** *p175*
Peason, Elizabeth 60; St. John, N.B., 1861 ***5704.8*** *p146*
Peat, John; Virginia, 1649 ***6219*** *p253*
Peate, William 20; Maryland, 1774 ***1219.7*** *p220*
Peatiason, Ellen; Virginia, 1698 ***2212*** *p12*
Peatziak, Gan; Arkansas, 1918 ***95.2*** *p97*
Peaudeau, Mr. 24; America, 1837 ***778.5*** *p419*
Peauvert, Frances 36; America, 1838 ***778.5*** *p419*
Peauvert, Olive 4; America, 1838 ***778.5*** *p420*
Peayler, Joane; Virginia, 1623-1648 ***6219*** *p252*
Pechet, Marie Victoire 34; Louisiana, 1820 ***778.5*** *p420*
Pechstein, Johannes; Philadelphia, 1779 ***8137*** *p6*
Peciulis, Stanly; Wisconsin, n.d. ***9675.7*** *p130*
Peck, Aminadab; West Indies, 1770 ***1219.7*** *p144*
Peck, Elizabeth 17; Pennsylvania, 1719 ***3690.1*** *p175*
Peck, Elizabeth 19; Antigua (Antego), 1721 ***3690.1*** *p175*
Peck, Elizabeth 19; Maryland or Virginia, 1721 ***3690.1*** *p175*
Peck, Helen 15 *SEE* Peck, Richard
Peck, Isaac 13 *SEE* Peck, Richard
Peck, Jacob; Philadelphia, 1760 ***9973.7*** *p35*
Peck, Jane 17 *SEE* Peck, Richard
Peck, Jane 42 *SEE* Peck, Richard
Peck, Joseph 2 *SEE* Peck, Richard
Peck, Joshua 18; Maryland, 1774 ***1219.7*** *p222*
Peck, Mary 20 *SEE* Peck, Richard
Peck, Richard 5 *SEE* Peck, Richard
Peck, Richard 46; Nova Scotia, 1774 ***1219.7*** *p194*
Peck, Richard 47; Halifax, N.S., 1775 ***1219.7*** *p263*
*Wife:*Jane 42
*Child:*Mary 20
*Child:*Jane 17
*Child:*Helen 15
*Child:*Isaac 13
*Child:*Robert 10
*Child:*Rose 7
*Child:*Richard 5
*Child:*Joseph 2
Peck, Robert 10 *SEE* Peck, Richard
Peck, Rose 7 *SEE* Peck, Richard
Peck, Thomas 18; Antigua (Antego), 1721 ***3690.1*** *p175*
Pecket, James 50; Barbados, 1775 ***1219.7*** *p279*
Peckett, Edward 11; North America, 1774 ***1219.7*** *p198*
Peckett, Giles 41; North America, 1774 ***1219.7*** *p199*
*Wife:*Mary 38
*Child:*James 16
*Child:*John 7
*Child:*Margaret 5
*Child:*William 1
Peckett, James 16 *SEE* Peckett, Giles
Peckett, John 7 *SEE* Peckett, Giles
Peckett, Margaret 5 *SEE* Peckett, Giles
Peckett, Mary 38 *SEE* Peckett, Giles
Peckett, William 1 *SEE* Peckett, Giles
Pecmik, Anton; Wisconsin, n.d. ***9675.7*** *p130*
Pecnik, Andreas; Wisconsin, n.d. ***9675.7*** *p130*
Pecnik, Frank; Wisconsin, n.d. ***9675.7*** *p130*
Pecola, Johannes; Washington, 1859-1920 ***2872.1*** *p30*
Pecontel, Samson; Port uncertain, 1839 ***778.5*** *p420*
Pecoud, F. 32; New Orleans, 1823 ***778.5*** *p420*
Pecoud, Joseph 28; Louisiana, 1822 ***778.5*** *p420*
Pecoud, Scipion 25; Louisiana, 1822 ***778.5*** *p420*
Pecoutel, Mr. 25; America, 1837 ***778.5*** *p420*
Pedarre, J. 29; America, 1835 ***778.5*** *p420*
Pedder, William 24; Virginia, 1774 ***1219.7*** *p201*
Peddie, John; Austin, TX, 1858-1896 ***9777*** *p6*
Peddie, Robert; Charleston, SC, 1776-1801 ***1639.20*** *p261*
Peddy, Mr.; Quebec, 1815 ***9229.18*** *p77*
With wife
Peden, Alexander; Wilmington, NC, 1800 ***1639.20*** *p262*
Peden, James; New York, NY, 1816 ***2859.11*** *p40*
Peden, William; America, 1737 ***4971*** *p68*
Pedenden, Hen.; Virginia, 1646 ***6219*** *p246*
Pedenden, Mary; Virginia, 1646 ***6219*** *p239*
Peder, Frederick; Illinois, 1871 ***5012.39*** *p25*
Pederlaque, Peter 31; America, 1838 ***778.5*** *p420*
Pedersen, Bernt John; Washington, 1859-1920 ***2872.1*** *p30*
Pedersen, Carl Digennas; Arkansas, 1918 ***95.2*** *p97*
Pedersen, Jens Laurits; Arkansas, 1918 ***95.2*** *p97*
Pedersen, Jens Taft; Arkansas, 1918 ***95.2*** *p97*
Pedersen, Laurs; Arkansas, 1918 ***95.2*** *p97*
Pedersen, Mikkel Kristen; Arkansas, 1918 ***95.2*** *p97*
Pederson, Anton; Arkansas, 1918 ***95.2*** *p97*
Pederson, Charles; Washington, 1859-1920 ***2872.1*** *p30*
Pederson, Hagbart Edor; Arkansas, 1918 ***95.2*** *p97*
Pederson, James; Kansas, 1890 ***5240.1*** *p33*
Pederson, Laurens Bach 26; Arkansas, 1918 ***95.2*** *p97*
Pederson, Martin; Wisconsin, n.d. ***9675.7*** *p130*
Pedin, Martin E.; Minneapolis, 1872-1878 ***6410.35*** *p63*
Pedlo, James; New York, 1848 ***1450.2*** *p109A*
Pedocclie, Peter; Iowa, 1866-1943 ***123.54*** *p38*
Pedretti, Peter; Iowa, 1866-1943 ***123.54*** *p38*
Pedro, Mr. 30; New Orleans, 1830 ***778.5*** *p420*
Pedro, Jose 30; New Orleans, 1839 ***778.5*** *p420*
Pee, Laurens 19; New Orleans, 1837 ***778.5*** *p420*
Peebles, Hugh 36; Nova Scotia, 1774 ***1219.7*** *p210*
Peebles, John; New York, NY, 1837 ***8208.4*** *p41*
Peebles, Robert; New York, NY, 1838 ***8208.4*** *p63*
Peech, Thomas 19; Jamaica, 1723 ***3690.1*** *p174*
Peecone, Isidor; Wisconsin, n.d. ***9675.7*** *p130*
Peefe, Mary; Virginia, 1635 ***6219*** *p26*
Peel, Frederick; America, 1851 ***1450.2*** *p109A*
Peel, John 30; New York, 1775 ***1219.7*** *p269*
Peers, Lesley 7; Philadelphia, 1858 ***5704.8*** *p139*
Peers, Mary 40; Philadelphia, 1858 ***5704.8*** *p139*
Peers, Samuel 2; Philadelphia, 1858 ***5704.8*** *p139*
Peers, Samuel 40; Philadelphia, 1858 ***5704.8*** *p139*
Peeters, Jon.; Virginia, 1635 ***6219*** *p3*
Peeters, Lawrence; Virginia, 1646 ***6219*** *p240*
Peeters, Tho.; Virginia, 1643 ***6219*** *p200*
Pefhoske, Anton; Wisconsin, n.d. ***9675.7*** *p130*
Pegden, Henry 60; Kansas, 1885 ***5240.1*** *p67*
Pegg, William 19; Maryland, 1719 ***3690.1*** *p175*

Pegler, Herman; Arkansas, 1918 95.2 p97
Pegot, J. 21; New Orleans, 1825 778.5 p420
Pegot, Jean 23; New Orleans, 1837 778.5 p420
Pegournay, Francois 55; America, 1835 778.5 p420
Pehl, Gust 33; Kansas, 1888 5240.1 p72
Pehrson, Anders; Iowa, 1853 2090 p611
Pehrsson, Claes Peter; Minneapolis, 1868-1878 6410.35 p50
Pehrsson, Edvard; Minneapolis, 1868-1878 6410.35 p64
Pehrsson, Nils; Minneapolis, 1877-1883 6410.35 p64
Pehrsson, Nils; Minneapolis, 1880 6410.35 p62
Pehrsson, Nils; Minneapolis, 1881-1886 6410.35 p62
Pehrsson, Pehr; Minneapolis, 1881-1883 6410.35 p65
Pehrsson, Pehr Olof; Minneapolis, 1880-1884 6410.35 p64
Peifer, Henry; Cincinnati, 1869-1887 8582 p23
Peiffer, Frank; Wisconsin, n.d. 9675.7 p130
Peiffer, Henry; Wisconsin, n.d. 9675.7 p130
Peignie, James 17; Jamaica, 1736 3690.1 p175
Peikins, John; Virginia, 1648 6219 p249
Peile, Robert M.; Illinois, 1859 7857 p6
Pein, Marie 25; Port uncertain, 1839 778.5 p421
Peinerone, Baptist; Iowa, 1866-1943 123.54 p38
Peirach, Samel 18; New York, NY, 1878 9253 p47
Peirce, Chr.; Virginia, 1645 6219 p245
Peirce, Daniel; Virginia, 1637 6219 p11
Peirce, Daniell; Virginia, 1637 6219 p114
Peirce, David; Virginia, 1637 6219 p114
Peirce, Eliza; Virginia, 1643 6219 p33
Peirce, John; Virginia, 1639 6219 p154
Peirce, John; Virginia, 1643 6219 p206
Peirce, Mary; Virginia, 1638 6219 p150
Peirce, Mary; Virginia, 1647 6219 p243
Peirce, Peter; Virginia, 1647 6219 p249
Peirce, Richard; Virginia, 1623-1700 6219 p150
Peirce, Richard; Virginia, 1636 6219 p77
Peirce, Robert; Virginia, 1643 6219 p206
Peirce, Tho.; Virginia, 1642 6219 p188
Peirce, Thomas; Virginia, 1639 6219 p155
Peirce, William; Virginia, 1637 6219 p83
Peirce, William; Virginia, 1637 6219 p85
Peirce, William; Virginia, 1642 6219 p189
Peirce, William; Virginia, 1643 6219 p33
Peirce, William; Virginia, 1648 6219 p251
Peirce, Wm.; Virginia, 1635 6219 p69
Peirce, Wm.; Virginia, 1640 6219 p208
Peircifull, Robert; Virginia, 1642 6219 p190
Peircy, Katherine; Virginia, 1635 6219 p68
Peirie, Hugh; New York, NY, 1816 2859.11 p40
Peirot, Jaques; Pennsylvania, 1752 2444 p199
*Wife:*Louise Channet
*Child:*Michel
*Child:*Jean Pierre
*Child:*Susanne Catherine
*Child:*Jean Charles
Peirot, Jean Charles *SEE* Peirot, Jaques
Peirot, Jean Pierre *SEE* Peirot, Jaques
Peirot, Louise Channet *SEE* Peirot, Jaques
Peirot, Michel *SEE* Peirot, Jaques
Peirot, Susanne Catherine *SEE* Peirot, Jaques
Peirson, A. J.; Minneapolis, 1871-1885 6410.35 p63
Peirson, John; Illinois, 1892 5012.40 p27
Peitsch, . . .; Canada, 1776-1783 9786 p30
Peitsmeyer, Anton Friedrich; America, 1848 4610.10 p104
Peitz, Martin 43; Kansas, 1890 5240.1 p33
Peitz, Martin 43; Kansas, 1890 5240.1 p75
Peitzmeier, Ernst Heinrich Friedrich; America, 1853 4610.10 p156
Peitzmeyer, Miss; America, 1854 4610.10 p156
Peitzmeyer, August 30; America, 1869 4610.10 p123
Peivet, Mr. 24; New Orleans, 1837 778.5 p421
Pekarska, Stanislawa 20; New York, 1912 9980.29 p60
Pekrul, Albert; Arkansas, 1918 95.2 p97
Pelant, Mr. 26; Port uncertain, 1836 778.5 p421
Pelard, James; Virginia, 1648 6219 p246
Pelarrey, Bernard 21; New Orleans, 1839 778.5 p421
Pelarrey, Jean 28; New Orleans, 1839 778.5 p421
Pelaut, Mr. 26; Port uncertain, 1836 778.5 p421
Pelch, Mr.; Quebec, 1815 9229.18 p75
Pelcino, Frank; Arkansas, 1918 95.2 p97
Pelcock, Barthol.; Virginia, 1640 6219 p182
Pele, John 21; Virginia, 1774 1219.7 p238
Pelechek, John; Arkansas, 1918 95.2 p97
Pelelond, Mlle. 24; New Orleans, 1838 778.5 p421
Pelenus, Vicenti 19; New York, 1912 9980.29 p54
Pelerin, A. 14; America, 1831 778.5 p421
Pelerin, Antonio 17; America, 1831 778.5 p421
Pelerin, Bernard 20 mos; America, 1831 778.5 p421
Pelerin, Francois 6; America, 1831 778.5 p421
Pelerin, Jean.. 6; America, 1831 778.5 p421
Pelerin, Margret 9; America, 1831 778.5 p421
Pelerin, Margret 38; America, 1831 778.5 p421
Pelham, Mary 31 *SEE* Pelham, William
Pelham, William 34; Virginia, 1774 1219.7 p241
*Wife:*Mary 31
Pelhire, Abraham; Virginia, 1636 6219 p32
Peling, Richard 16; Barbados, 1702 2212 p36
Pelissier, Mr. 23; New Orleans, 1827 778.5 p421
Pelkanen, Evert; Washington, 1859-1920 2872.1 p30
Pelkington, William; Virginia, 1698 2212 p17
Pell, Charles 38; Jamaica, 1736 3690.1 p175
Pell, Peter J.; New York, 1750 3652 p74
Pellegrin, Germain 25; New Orleans, 1839 778.5 p421
Pellens, Georg W.; New York, NY, 1833 8582.2 p30
Pellens, Georg Wilhelm; Cincinnati, 1869-1887 8582 p23
Pelleros, Mr. 28; Louisiana, 1821 778.5 p422
Pellett, Rosetta 20; Philadelphia, 1774 1219.7 p212
Pellham, Nicholas 19; Maryland, 1725 3690.1 p175
Pellier, Mr. 30; New Orleans, 1825 778.5 p422
Pelligrino, Simi; Arkansas, 1918 95.2 p97
Pellin, Florindo; Iowa, 1866-1943 123.54 p38
Pellin, Frank; Iowa, 1866-1943 123.54 p38
Pellin, Mary; Iowa, 1866-1943 123.54 p73
Pellin, Vittore; Iowa, 1866-1943 123.54 p73
Pellin, Vittorio; Iowa, 1866-1943 123.54 p38
Pellissier, Francois 17; America, 1839 778.5 p422
Pellores, Mr.; Port uncertain, 1839 778.5 p422
Pels, Nick; Arkansas, 1918 95.2 p97
Pelt, Peter; Wisconsin, n.d. 9675.7 p130
Peltekis, Christos Anastasious; Kansas, 1917 6013.40 p16
Pelton, John 13; America, 1703 2212 p38
Peltree, Abraham; Virginia, 1638 6219 p147
Peltriman, Robert; Virginia, 1642 6219 p194
Peltz, Michel 65; Kansas, 1887 5240.1 p70
Pelucas, John; America, 1827 778.5 p422
Peluce, Adolfo; Arkansas, 1918 95.2 p97
Pelz, . . .; Canada, 1776-1783 9786 p30
Pelz, Miss; America, 1851-1868 8582.3 p51
Pelz, Mrs. 55; America, 1851-1868 8582.3 p50
*Son:*Johann Paul 16
Pelz, Eberhardt; New Netherland, 1630-1646 8582.2 p51
With wife
Pelz, Eduard; America, 1850-1868 8582.3 p50
Pelz, Johann Paul 16 *SEE* Pelz, Mrs.
Pelz, John 27; Kansas, 1894 5240.1 p33
Pelz, John 27; Kansas, 1894 5240.1 p79
Pelz, John 34; Kansas, 1885 5240.1 p67
Pelz, Mat 25; Kansas, 1894 5240.1 p79
Pelz, Mathias 22; Kansas, 1894 5240.1 p33
Pelz, Nick 22; Kansas, 1886 5240.1 p33
Pelz, Nik 22; Kansas, 1886 5240.1 p69
Pelzer, Joseph; Kansas, 1872 5240.1 p33
Pemberton, Charles 16; Philadelphia, 1774 1219.7 p232
Pemberton, Edward 30; Virginia, 1773 1219.7 p168
Pemberton, Phineas; Pennsylvania, 1682 4960 p163
Pemberton, Thomas 20; Virginia, 1773 1219.7 p169
Pembridge, Tho.; Virginia, 1643 6219 p202
Pembroke, John 24; Philadelphia, 1775 1219.7 p256
Pemlington, Henry 40; Kansas, 1876 5240.1 p57
Pemy, John; Virginia, 1637 6219 p86
Pen, William 21; Pennsylvania, 1730 3690.1 p176
Pena, Mauro 29; Harris Co., TX, 1898 6254 p5
Penard, Mr. 37; Port uncertain, 1827 778.5 p422
Penard, Joseph 23; America, 1838 778.5 p422
Penard, Mary Ann 52; America, 1838 778.5 p422
Penard, Remmi 49; America, 1838 778.5 p422
Penberry, Jno; Virginia, 1698 2212 p14
Pender, Bridget 9; Massachusetts, 1850 5881.1 p80
Pender, John 40; Massachusetts, 1850 5881.1 p81
Pendergast, Mr.; Quebec, 1815 9229.18 p78
Pendergast, Anastasie; Quebec, 1822 7603 p59
Pendergast, Edward; Montreal, 1823 7603 p98
Pendergast, Michael 13; Newfoundland, 1789 4915.24 p56
Pendergast, Phillipp; Virginia, 1643 6219 p204
Pendergrass, Michael; New York, NY, 1816 2859.11 p40
Pendergrass, Patrick 21; Massachusetts, 1847 5881.1 p81
Pendergrast, Catharine; Massachusetts, 1847 5881.1 p81
Pendergrast, Sylvester; Massachusetts, 1847 5881.1 p81
Pendleton, Samuel 22; Philadelphia, 1774 1219.7 p216
Pene, Pedro 20; New Orleans, 1837 778.5 p422
Pengel, Fred; Illinois, 1884 2896.5 p31
Penifold, Thomas 16; Maryland, 1775 1219.7 p272
Penill, Rich.; Virginia, 1634 6219 p84
Penkell, . . . 20; America, 1703 2212 p38
Penkell, Peter 12; America, 1703 2212 p38
Penman, Edward; Charleston, SC, 1784 1639.20 p262
Penman, James; Charleston, SC, 1789 1639.20 p262
Penman, Robert; Virginia, 1856 4626.16 p16
Penn, Amos; Arkansas, 1918 95.2 p97
Penn, Louis 26; America, 1838 778.5 p422
Penn, Samuel 24; Philadelphia, 1774 1219.7 p237
Penn, William; Pennsylvania, 1682 4960 p152
Penn, William; Pennsylvania, 1682 4962 p154
Pennant, John; Virginia, 1698 2212 p16
Penne, Richd.; Virginia, 1648 6219 p250
Pennell, Carfinch 20; Jamaica, 1736 3690.1 p176
Pennelot, Charles 42; New Orleans, 1832 778.5 p422
Penner, Gerhard; Kansas, 1885 5240.1 p34
Penner, Henry; Kansas, 1884 5240.1 p34
Penner, John; Kansas, 1882 5240.1 p34
Penner, Rudolph W.; Kansas, 1882 5240.1 p34
Penner, Veit; Philadelphia, 1762 9973.7 p37
Penney, John S.; Iowa, 1866-1943 123.54 p38
Penney, Solomon 18; Maryland, 1733 3690.1 p176
Pennie, James; St. John, N.B., 1866 5704.8 p167
Penning, John Peter; Wisconsin, n.d. 9675.7 p130
Penning, Mathias; Wisconsin, n.d. 9675.7 p130
Pennington, George 33; Maryland, 1739 3690.1 p176
Pennington, Jno 25; America, 1699 2212 p28
Pennington, John 35; Baltimore, 1775 1219.7 p269
Pennington, Sarah 23; Philadelphia, 1774 1219.7 p195
Pennock, William 20; Pennsylvania, 1728 3690.1 p176
Penny, Charles 15; Maryland, 1775 1219.7 p250
Penny, Charles Frederick; Arkansas, 1918 95.2 p97
Penny, James; New York, NY, 1837 8208.4 p39
Penny, John; Virginia, 1628 6219 p9
Penny, John 28; Philadelphia, 1774 1219.7 p183
Penny, Samuel 19; Maryland, 1775 1219.7 p264
Penny, Wm.; Virginia, 1643 6219 p203
Penrose, Elizabeth 46 *SEE* Penrose, John
Penrose, John 35; Savannah, GA, 1733 4719.17 p312
*Wife:*Elizabeth 46
Penry, Ann 18; America, 1699 2212 p28
Penser, . . .; Canada, 1776-1783 9786 p43
Pensint, William; Virginia, 1637 6219 p83
Pensint, Wm.; Virginia, 1636 6219 p13
Pensint, Wm.; Virginia, 1637 6219 p13
Penson, William; New York, NY, 1835 8208.4 p5
Pentcorne, Christo.; Virginia, 1637 6219 p11
Pentland, Mr.; Quebec, 1815 9229.18 p78
Penton, Ann 20 *SEE* Penton, Jesse
Penton, Jesse 26; Port uncertain, 1849 4535.10 p198
*Wife:*Ann 20
*Child:*John 2
Penton, John; Virginia, 1628 6219 p31
Penton, John 2 *SEE* Penton, Jesse
Penton, Tho.; Virginia, 1640 6219 p160
Penttinen, Aili Halvin; Washington, 1859-1920 2872.1 p30
Penttinen, Asaria; Washington, 1859-1920 2872.1 p30
Penttinen, Hilda Catherina; Washington, 1859-1920 2872.1 p30
Pentz, Jacob; Indiana, 1848 9117 p17
Pentz, John Philip; Philadelphia, 1765 9973.7 p40
Penz, . . .; Canada, 1776-1783 9786 p30
Penze, Peter; Saratoga, NY, 1777 8137 p12
People, Mary; America, 1865 5704.8 p197
Peoples, Daniel; New York, NY, 1837 8208.4 p55
Peoples, Eliza 13; Philadelphia, 1852 5704.8 p96
Peoples, Eliza Martha 2; Philadelphia, 1853 5704.8 p111
Peoples, Elizabeth; Philadelphia, 1852 5704.8 p96
Peoples, James; Philadelphia, 1849 53.26 p76
Peoples, James; Philadelphia, 1849 5704.8 p50
Peoples, James 14; Philadelphia, 1859 5704.8 p142
Peoples, James 18; Philadelphia, 1853 5704.8 p111
Peoples, James 20; Philadelphia, 1857 5704.8 p132
Peoples, James 23; Philadelphia, 1803 53.26 p76
Peoples, Jane 30; Philadelphia, 1858 5704.8 p139
Peoples, Joana; Philadelphia, 1847 53.26 p76
Peoples, Joana; Philadelphia, 1847 5704.8 p30
Peoples, John; New York, NY, 1867 5704.8 p221
Peoples, Joseph 11; Philadelphia, 1852 5704.8 p96
Peoples, Madge; Philadelphia, 1865 5704.8 p192
Peoples, Madge 20; Philadelphia, 1865 5704.8 p165
Peoples, Margaret; Philadelphia, 1849 53.26 p76
*Relative:*Samuel
Peoples, Margaret; Philadelphia, 1849 5704.8 p55
Peoples, Margaret; Philadelphia, 1852 5704.8 p96
Peoples, Margaret; Philadelphia, 1865 5704.8 p202
Peoples, Martha; Philadelphia, 1867 5704.8 p216
Peoples, Mary; New York, NY, 1867 5704.8 p221
Peoples, Mary; Philadelphia, 1852 5704.8 p96
Peoples, Mary 19; Philadelphia, 1859 5704.8 p141
Peoples, Patrick; New York, NY, 1865 5704.8 p192
Peoples, Patrick; New York, NY, 1868 5704.8 p230
Peoples, Patrick; Philadelphia, 1865 5704.8 p196
Peoples, Samuel *SEE* Peoples, Margaret
Peoples, Samuel; Philadelphia, 1849 5704.8 p55
Peoples, Samuel; Philadelphia, 1852 5704.8 p96
Peoples, Sarah; Philadelphia, 1851 5704.8 p71
Peoples, Sarah; Philadelphia, 1868 5704.8 p230
Peoples, Sarah 30; Philadelphia, 1853 5704.8 p111
Peoples, Susan; New York, NY, 1864 5704.8 p169
Peoples, William John 8; Philadelphia, 1853 5704.8 p111
Peoron, Peter; New York, 1831-1832 9892.11 p36
Peoron, Peter; New York, 1832 9892.11 p36

Peper, Joseph 21; Maryland, 1775 ***1219.7*** *p251*
Peplow, Richard 18; Philadelphia, 1775 ***1219.7*** *p259*
Peplow, Thomas; Jamaica, 1763 ***1219.7*** *p91*
Peppard, Patrick; Philadelphia, 1815 ***2859.11*** *p40*
With wife
Peppelmann, H.; Cincinnati, 1869-1887 ***8582*** *p23*
Pepper, David; Illinois, 1886 ***5012.39*** *p120*
Pepper, Edmund M.; Detroit, 1896 ***1450.2*** *p109A*
Pepper, Edward; New York, NY, 1811 ***2859.11*** *p18*
With family
Pepper, Francis; Virginia, 1600-1642 ***6219*** *p192*
Pepper, Henry; Virginia, 1643 ***6219*** *p203*
Pepper, John; Illinois, 1849 ***7857*** *p6*
Pepper, Thomas; Illinois, 1869 ***5012.38*** *p99*
Peralta, Jose 53; Arizona, 1901 ***9228.40*** *p8*
Perard, Auguste 23; America, 1836 ***778.5*** *p422*
Perasich, Michael; New York, NY, 1855 ***2764.35*** *p53*
Peraz, Shamcheir; New York, NY, 1839 ***8208.4*** *p101*
Perce, Miss 22; Port uncertain, 1839 ***778.5*** *p422*
Perce, P. 26; Port uncertain, 1839 ***778.5*** *p422*
Perce, William; Virginia, 1694 ***6219*** *p162*
Percel, de, Mme. 38; America, 1837 ***778.5*** *p423*
Percel, Her.ais 23; America, 1837 ***778.5*** *p423*
Percell, Edward 9; Massachusetts, 1847 ***5881.1*** *p81*
Percell, Eliza 30; Massachusetts, 1847 ***5881.1*** *p81*
Percell, John 18; Massachusetts, 1847 ***5881.1*** *p81*
Percell, Mary 14; Massachusetts, 1849 ***5881.1*** *p81*
Perches, William 32; Maryland, 1775 ***1219.7*** *p250*
Percie, John; Virginia, 1628 ***6219*** *p31*
Percival, D. W.; Milwaukee, 1875 ***4719.30*** *p257*
Percival, John; New York, NY, 1815 ***2859.11*** *p40*
Percival, John 25; Maryland, 1775 ***1219.7*** *p266*
Percival, Robert; San Francisco, 1850 ***4914.15*** *p10*
Percocks, Tho.; Virginia, 1638 ***6219*** *p145*
Percot, V., Mme. 36; America, 1838 ***778.5*** *p423*
Percy, Charles Henry; Milwaukee, 1875 ***4719.30*** *p258*
Percy, Edward; Virginia, 1637 ***6219*** *p113*
Percy, Robert 16; Jamaica, 1730 ***3690.1*** *p291*
Percye, Abraham; Virginia, 1624 ***6219*** *p31*
Perdeszet, Friederich; Kentucky, 1839-1840 ***8582.3*** *p99*
Perdeszet, Friederich; Kentucky, 1841-1849 ***8582.3*** *p98*
Perdrauville, Adelle 52; America, 1838 ***778.5*** *p423*
Perdreauville, R. 19; America, 1829 ***778.5*** *p423*
Perdreauville, R. 50; Port uncertain, 1827 ***778.5*** *p423*
Perdroville, M. 60; America, 1836 ***778.5*** *p423*
Perdu, Mr. 40; New Orleans, 1837 ***778.5*** *p423*
Perduit, Catherine 21; Port uncertain, 1839 ***778.5*** *p423*
Pere, Eugene 29; Port uncertain, 1837 ***778.5*** *p423*
Pereira, Francis; Virginia, 1846 ***4626.16*** *p13*
Perennes, Mr. 40; New Orleans, 1837 ***778.5*** *p423*
Peres, Antonio 28; Port uncertain, 1835 ***778.5*** *p423*
Peres, J. 24; Port uncertain, 1839 ***778.5*** *p423*
Peres, Jean E. H. 19; America, 1838 ***778.5*** *p423*
Peres, Leon 25; Port uncertain, 1839 ***778.5*** *p423*
Peres, Peter; Philadelphia, 1762 ***9973.7*** *p37*
Perez, Anrelia 28; Arizona, 1926 ***9228.40*** *p30*
Perez, Marie 34; Arizona, 1926 ***9228.40*** *p30*
Perez, Ramon 38; Arizona, 1923 ***9228.40*** *p27*
Perfect, Mr.; Quebec, 1815 ***9229.18*** *p76*
Perfitt, Noba; Virginia, 1636 ***6219*** *p75*
Pergakis, Nicholas Peter 29; Arkansas, 1918 ***95.2*** *p97*
Pergande, Julius; Wisconsin, n.d. ***9675.7*** *p130*
Pericoli, Mr. 25; New Orleans, 1839 ***778.5*** *p424*
Pericoli, Mrs.; New Orleans, 1839 ***778.5*** *p424*
Periew, Gilbert 15; America, 1706 ***2212*** *p47*
Peris, E. 60; Port uncertain, 1839 ***778.5*** *p424*
Peristeris, Polivios; Arkansas, 1918 ***95.2*** *p97*
Perk, Lewis; New York, 1894 ***1450.2*** *p29B*
Perker, Mr.; America, 1857 ***2896.5*** *p31*
Perker, Andreas; New York, 1717 ***3627*** *p11*
*Wife:*Maria A. Lammingern
*Child:*Maria Apollonia
*Child:*Johann Andreas
*Child:*Johann Michael
With child
Perker, Johann Andreas *SEE* Perker, Andreas
Perker, Johann Michael *SEE* Perker, Andreas
Perker, Maria A. Lammingern *SEE* Perker, Andreas
Perker, Maria Apollonia *SEE* Perker, Andreas
Perkes, Edward; Virginia, 1635 ***6219*** *p68*
Perkins, Andrew; Virginia, 1638 ***6219*** *p33*
Perkins, Ellin; Virginia, 1635 ***6219*** *p69*
Perkins, Guillaume 45; Montreal, 1710 ***7603*** *p25*
Perkins, James; Virginia, 1642 ***6219*** *p195*
Perkins, John 20; Maryland, 1729 ***3690.1*** *p176*
Perkins, Joseph 21; Jamaica, 1730 ***3690.1*** *p176*
Perkins, Nicholas; Virginia, 1641 ***6219*** *p187*
Perkins, Robert; Virginia, 1642 ***6219*** *p196*
Perkins, Samuel 15; Maryland, 1724 ***3690.1*** *p176*
Perkins, Tho.; Virginia, 1642 ***6219*** *p195*
Perkiss, Meyer; Arkansas, 1918 ***95.2*** *p98*
Perkle, James 22; Maryland, 1774 ***1219.7*** *p229*
Perlet, Henry Louis; New York, NY, 1836 ***8208.4*** *p18*
Perlinda, John; San Francisco, 1880 ***2764.35*** *p53*
Perlinger, . . .; Canada, 1776-1783 ***9786*** *p30*
Perlschke, Frederick; Illinois, 1859 ***5012.38*** *p97*
Permeter, John; Virginia, 1623-1648 ***6219*** *p252*
Pernat, Clair 73; America, 1838 ***778.5*** *p424*
Pernet, Johann Dietrich; Kentucky, 1839-1840 ***8582.3*** *p99*
Pernett, Louis 23; New Orleans, 1835 ***778.5*** *p424*
Peroneil, Bronet 28; New Orleans, 1836 ***778.5*** *p424*
Peroteau, Mr. 50; New Orleans, 1823 ***778.5*** *p424*
Perotte, Arthur Joseph; Iowa, 1866-1943 ***123.54*** *p38*
Perouille, Mr.; Port uncertain, 1839 ***778.5*** *p424*
Perouslt, Mr.; New Orleans, 1839 ***778.5*** *p424*
Peroutka, Ella; Washington, 1859-1920 ***2872.1*** *p30*
Peroutka, John, Jr.; Washington, 1859-1920 ***2872.1*** *p31*
Peroutka, John, Sr.; Washington, 1859-1920 ***2872.1*** *p31*
Peroutka, Louis; Washington, 1859-1920 ***2872.1*** *p31*
Peroutka, Ludwig; Washington, 1859-1920 ***2872.1*** *p31*
Peroutka, Rudolph; Washington, 1859-1920 ***2872.1*** *p31*
Peroz, Jean Baptiste; New York, NY, 1836 ***8208.4*** *p8*
Perquilhem, Mr. 19; New Orleans, 1839 ***778.5*** *p424*
Perrault, A. 18; New Orleans, 1835 ***778.5*** *p424*
Perrault, Eugene 29; America, 1820 ***778.5*** *p424*
Perreault, Simeon; Arkansas, 1918 ***95.2*** *p98*
Perreene, Thomas; Virginia, 1639 ***6219*** *p156*
Perren, James; Virginia, 1639 ***6219*** *p152*
Perrenot, Jean Battiste 7; America, 1836 ***778.5*** *p424*
Perrenot, Jean J. 20; America, 1836 ***778.5*** *p424*
Perreri, Edwardo; Arkansas, 1918 ***95.2*** *p98*
Perret, F. J. 20; New Orleans, 1823 ***778.5*** *p424*
Perrey, Ambrose 20; Maryland, 1719 ***3690.1*** *p176*
Perrey, Luke; America, 1702 ***2212*** *p36*
Perrey, Thomas; America, 1697 ***2212*** *p8*
Perrien, J. 55; New Orleans, 1821 ***778.5*** *p425*
Perrier, Mrs. 50; Mexico, 1830 ***778.5*** *p425*
Perrier, Adolphe 27; America, 1836 ***778.5*** *p425*
Perrier, Felip 50; New Orleans, 1836 ***778.5*** *p425*
Perrier, M. 46; New Orleans, 1829 ***778.5*** *p425*
Perrieu, Mr. 17; America, 1839 ***778.5*** *p425*
Perrillias, Michael 23; Louisiana, 1820 ***778.5*** *p425*
Perriman, Henry 22; Maryland, 1774 ***1219.7*** *p235*
Perriman, Richard 33; Maryland, 1774 ***1219.7*** *p222*
Perrin, . . .; Halifax, N.S., 1752 ***7074.6*** *p232*
Perrin, Mr. 57; New Orleans, 1822 ***778.5*** *p425*
Perrin, Andre 35; America, 1837 ***778.5*** *p425*
Perrin, Arthur; Virginia, 1638 ***6219*** *p160*
Perrin, John; Virginia, 1642 ***6219*** *p189*
Perrin, John 28; New Orleans, 1837 ***778.5*** *p425*
Perrin, Richard; Virginia, 1637 ***6219*** *p24*
Perrine, Ms. 19; Port uncertain, 1836 ***778.5*** *p425*
Perrinet, Francois 30; America, 1839 ***778.5*** *p425*
Perring, John 22; Philadelphia, 1774 ***1219.7*** *p196*
Perringes, John 18; Maryland, 1727 ***3690.1*** *p172*
Perris, Francis; Virginia, 1637 ***6219*** *p112*
Perris, Thomas 21; Philadelphia, 1774 ***1219.7*** *p217*
Perron, Magdalena 7; New Orleans, 1836 ***778.5*** *p425*
Perrot, Mr. 28; America, 1838 ***778.5*** *p425*
Perry, Alexander 25; Jamaica, 1774 ***1219.7*** *p179*
Perry, Ambrose 20; Maryland, 1719 ***3690.1*** *p176*
Perry, Ann; Virginia, 1643 ***6219*** *p230*
Perry, Ann 19; Jamaica, 1773 ***1219.7*** *p172*
Perry, Betty; Philadelphia, 1847 ***53.26*** *p76*
*Relative:*Matilda
Perry, Betty; Philadelphia, 1847 ***5704.8*** *p31*
Perry, Edwd; Virginia, 1698 ***2212*** *p11*
Perry, Ezekiell; Virginia, 1643 ***6219*** *p202*
Perry, George 18; Windward Islands, 1722 ***3690.1*** *p176*
Perry, George 23; Maryland, 1774 ***1219.7*** *p177*
Perry, Henry; America, 1697 ***2212*** *p8*
Perry, Henry Wedmore; New York, 1766 ***1219.7*** *p117*
Perry, Hugh; New York, NY, 1811 ***2859.11*** *p18*
Perry, Isaac 17; Philadelphia, 1774 ***1219.7*** *p212*
Perry, Isabella; Charleston, SC, 1805 ***1639.20*** *p262*
Perry, Isabella 18; Philadelphia, 1853 ***5704.8*** *p114*
Perry, Isabella 18; Philadelphia, 1854 ***5704.8*** *p120*
Perry, Isabella Pace; Virginia, 1628 ***6219*** *p25*
Perry, James 19; Pennsylvania, 1728 ***3690.1*** *p176*
Perry, John 16; Maryland, 1774 ***1219.7*** *p226*
Perry, Katherine; America, 1697 ***2212*** *p4*
Perry, Lawrence; Washington, 1859-1920 ***2872.1*** *p31*
Perry, Margaret; New York, NY, 1811 ***2859.11*** *p18*
Perry, Margaret 22; Quebec, 1857 ***5704.8*** *p136*
Perry, Mary Jane 17; Quebec, 1859 ***5704.8*** *p143*
Perry, Matilda *SEE* Perry, Betty
Perry, Matilda; Philadelphia, 1847 ***5704.8*** *p31*
Perry, Rich.; Virginia, 1635 ***6219*** *p71*
Perry, Robert; Virginia, 1637 ***6219*** *p17*
Perry, Robert 20; Virginia, 1774 ***1219.7*** *p240*
Perry, Robert 50; Quebec, 1853 ***5704.8*** *p105*
Perry, Robt.; Virginia, 1639 ***6219*** *p23*
Perry, Roger; New Orleans, 1849 ***1450.2*** *p110A*
Perry, Thomas 21; Jamaica, 1736 ***3690.1*** *p177*
Perry, William 13; Maryland, 1719 ***3690.1*** *p177*
Perry, William 20; Maryland, 1719 ***3690.1*** *p177*
Perry, William 60; Quebec, 1859 ***5704.8*** *p143*
Pers, Wm 21; Virginia, 1700 ***2212*** *p33*
Persat, A. 28; America, 1826 ***778.5*** *p445*
Persett, Ciro; Arkansas, 1918 ***95.2*** *p98*
Pershe, Mike Bohnr; Arkansas, 1918 ***95.2*** *p98*
Persil, Mme.; New Orleans, 1839 ***778.5*** *p426*
Persil, A.; New Orleans, 1839 ***778.5*** *p425*
Persil, Jn.; New Orleans, 1839 ***778.5*** *p426*
Perske, Albert Louis; Wisconsin, 1898 ***9460*** *p647*
Persoma, John B.; Washington, 1859-1920 ***2872.1*** *p31*
Person, Anton Sigfred; Arkansas, 1918 ***95.2*** *p98*
Person, Eric 21; Kansas, 1884 ***5240.1*** *p67*
Person, John; Arkansas, 1918 ***95.2*** *p98*
Person, Kath.; Virginia, 1636 ***6219*** *p108*
Person, N. P.; Minneapolis, 1877-1883 ***6410.35*** *p64*
Person, Oscar; Minneapolis, 1882-1887 ***6410.35*** *p64*
Person, Ralph; Virginia, 1637 ***6219*** *p110*
Person, Thomas; Virginia, 1639 ***6219*** *p158*
Person, Thomas; Virginia, 1639 ***6219*** *p161*
Personnett, Dorothea 30; America, 1835 ***778.5*** *p426*
Personnett, Jacques 30; America, 1835 ***778.5*** *p426*
Personnier, Charles 27; America, 1837 ***778.5*** *p426*
Persons, Henry; Virginia, 1648 ***6219*** *p250*
Persson, Andrew; Bangor, ME, 1868-1883 ***6410.22*** *p120*
Persson, Andrew; Bangor, ME, 1883 ***6410.22*** *p125*
Persson, Clara Helena; New York, NY, 1911 ***3455.3*** *p86*
*Husband:*Fabian
Persson, Dan; Iowa, 1866-1943 ***123.54*** *p38*
Persson, Edmund; Washington, 1859-1920 ***2872.1*** *p31*
Persson, Erik Andreas; Washington, 1859-1920 ***2872.1*** *p31*
Persson, Fabian *SEE* Persson, Clara Helena
Persson, Frank Edmund; Washington, 1859-1920 ***2872.1*** *p31*
Persson, Gerda; Washington, 1859-1920 ***2872.1*** *p31*
Persson, Haken; Maine, 1882-1884 ***6410.22*** *p119*
Persson, Hazel Elizabeth; Washington, 1859-1920 ***2872.1*** *p31*
Persson, John Erik Petrus H. Erikson; Washington, 1859-1920 ***2872.1*** *p31*
Persson, Per Erich; Illinois, 1891 ***5012.39*** *p53*
Persson, Per Erich; Illinois, 1893 ***5012.40*** *p53*
Persson, Peter A.; Bangor, ME, 1878-1886 ***6410.22*** *p120*
Persson, Peter E.; Washington, 1859-1920 ***2872.1*** *p31*
Pert, Mrs. 50; Port uncertain, 1836 ***778.5*** *p426*
Pert, J. 37; Port uncertain, 1836 ***778.5*** *p426*
Perte, Pierre 20; New Orleans, 1838 ***778.5*** *p426*
Pertiner, Joseph; Wisconsin, n.d. ***9675.7*** *p130*
Pertrellese, Aniello; Arkansas, 1918 ***95.2*** *p98*
Perzarcz, Fibif; Iowa, 1866-1943 ***123.54*** *p38*
Perzello, Paul 24; Arkansas, 1918 ***95.2*** *p98*
Pesavento, Pietro; Iowa, 1866-1943 ***123.54*** *p38*
Pescador, Andrew; Iowa, 1866-1943 ***123.54*** *p73*
Peschier, Madam 25; Grenada, 1774 ***1219.7*** *p245*
Peschier, John 31; Grenada, 1774 ***1219.7*** *p245*
Pescod, Joseph 48; New York, 1775 ***1219.7*** *p268*
With wife
With 5 children
Pesechis, Kazimer; Arkansas, 1918 ***95.2*** *p98*
Pesetsky, Sam; Wisconsin, n.d. ***9675.7*** *p130*
Pesh, Mathias; Wisconsin, n.d. ***9675.7*** *p130*
Peshina, Joseph James; Arkansas, 1918 ***95.2*** *p98*
Peshong, Peter; Wisconsin, n.d. ***9675.7*** *p130*
Peske, Charles; Illinois, 1860 ***5012.38*** *p97*
Pesky, John; America, 1854 ***1450.2*** *p109A*
Pessard, John 38; New Orleans, 1835 ***778.5*** *p426*
Pessie, P. 23; New Orleans, 1837 ***778.5*** *p426*
Pestana, Samuel 21; Jamaica, 1735 ***3690.1*** *p177*
Pestmer, Blasins; Colorado, 1904 ***9678.2*** *p131*
Pete, Ant. Rowlonte 19; Port uncertain, 1838 ***778.5*** *p426*
Pete, Tony; Arkansas, 1918 ***95.2*** *p98*
Peter, Amandus; America, 1849 ***8582.1*** *p27*
Peter, August; America, 1874 ***6014.1*** *p3*
Peter, Emil; Illinois, 1894 ***2896.5*** *p31*
Peter, Frederick; New York, 1761 ***3652*** *p88*
Peter, Henrich; Philadelphia, 1779 ***8137*** *p12*
Peter, Henry; Philadelphia, 1762 ***9973.7*** *p37*
Peter, Jacob 88; Ohio, 1872 ***8582*** *p23*
Peter, Jakob; Trenton, NJ, 1776 ***8137*** *p12*
Peter, John 19; Jamaica, 1722 ***3690.1*** *p177*
Peter, John 26; America, 1837 ***778.5*** *p426*
Peter, John Fred; Illinois, 1891 ***2896.5*** *p31*
Peterding, A.; New York, NY, 1853 ***4610.10*** *p34*
With wife
Peterkin, Alexander; Jamaica, 1775 ***1219.7*** *p277*
Peterman, Felix; Arkansas, 1918 ***95.2*** *p98*
Peterman, Henrietta; New York, 1752 ***3652*** *p76*
Petermann, Georg; Cincinnati, 1869-1887 ***8582*** *p23*
Peters, . . .; Canada, 1776-1783 ***9786*** *p30*
Peters, Mr. 30; America, 1836 ***778.5*** *p426*
Peters, Abraham; Quebec, 1876 ***9980.20*** *p48*
Peters, Aganetha 18; Quebec, 1876 ***9980.20*** *p48*

Peters, Agatha Neufeld; Quebec, 1876 ***9980.20*** *p48*
Peters, Carsten; New York, 1853 ***3840.3*** *p8*
Peters, Charles; Illinois, 1862 ***5012.38*** *p98*
Peters, Charles A.; Washington, 1859-1920 ***2872.1*** *p31*
Peters, Christian; Indiana, 1848 ***9117*** *p17*
Peters, David; Quebec, 1876 ***9980.20*** *p48*
Peters, Dorothea *SEE* Peters, Heinrich
Peters, Fred; Washington, 1859-1920 ***2872.1*** *p31*
Peters, Friedrich; New York, NY, 1923 ***3455.4*** *p25*
Peters, Heinrich; New York, NY, 1910 ***3455.2*** *p103*
*Wife:*Dorothea
Peters, Heinrich; Wisconsin, n.d. ***9675.7*** *p130*
Peters, Helena; Quebec, 1876 ***9980.20*** *p48*
Peters, Henry; New York, 1863 ***1450.2*** *p29B*
Peters, Henry; Wisconsin, n.d. ***9675.7*** *p130*
Peters, Henry 38; Kansas, 1876 ***5240.1*** *p57*
Peters, Herman; Wisconsin, n.d. ***9675.7*** *p130*
Peters, Heronan; New York, NY, 1909 ***3455.2*** *p104*
Peters, Herrmann; Quebec, 1876 ***9980.20*** *p48*
Peters, Jacob; Quebec, 1876 ***9980.20*** *p48*
Peters, James; Arkansas, 1918 ***95.2*** *p98*
Peters, Johann; Quebec, 1876 ***9980.20*** *p48*
Peters, Joseph; New York, 1891 ***1450.2*** *p29B*
Peters, Julius; Canada, 1776-1783 ***9786*** *p207A*
Peters, Katharien a; Quebec, 1876 ***9980.20*** *p48*
Peters, Maria; Quebec, 1876 ***9980.20*** *p48*
Peters, Masten 41; California, 1869 ***3840.3*** *p8*
Peters, Nathaniel 19; Maryland or Virginia, 1733 ***3690.1*** *p177*
Peters, Peter; Quebec, 1876 ***9980.20*** *p48*
Peters, Susanna; Quebec, 1876 ***9980.20*** *p48*
Peters, William; Arkansas, 1918 ***95.2*** *p98*
Peters, William; Arkansas, 1918 ***95.2*** *p100*
Peters, William 15; Virginia, 1774 ***1219.7*** *p240*
Peters, William 20; Pennsylvania, 1737 ***3690.1*** *p177*
Peters, Wm.; Virginia, 1635 ***6219*** *p69*
Petersan, Andre; Died enroute, 1875 ***4719.30*** *p258*
Petersdorff, . . .; Canada, 1776-1783 ***9786*** *p30*
Petersen, . . .; Canada, 1776-1783 ***9786*** *p30*
Petersen, Andrew; Washington, 1859-1920 ***2872.1*** *p31*
Petersen, Carl Ludwig; Quebec, 1776 ***9786*** *p260*
Petersen, Christian P.L.; Illinois, 1900 ***5012.40*** *p79*
Petersen, Hans; New York, 1750 ***3652*** *p74*
Petersen, Hans; New York, 1754 ***3652*** *p80*
Petersen, Harold Hjalmar; Washington, 1859-1920 ***2872.1*** *p31*
Petersen, John; New York, NY, 1835 ***8208.4*** *p78*
Petersen, Niels T.; Bangor, ME, 1895 ***6410.22*** *p127*
Petersen, Reinholdt; Arkansas, 1918 ***95.2*** *p98*
Petersmeier, Christine C. Louise; America, 1893 ***4610.10*** *p107*
Peterson, . . .; Canada, 1776-1783 ***9786*** *p30*
Peterson, A. G.; Minneapolis, 1881-1883 ***6410.35*** *p63*
Peterson, Alfred; Colorado, 1903 ***9678.2*** *p163*
Peterson, Alfred; Iowa, 1866-1943 ***123.54*** *p38*
Peterson, Andre 51; Arizona, 1905 ***9228.40*** *p13*
Peterson, Andrew; Virginia, 1635 ***6219*** *p22*
Peterson, Andrew; Washington, 1859-1920 ***2872.1*** *p31*
Peterson, Andrew 26; Kansas, 1879 ***5240.1*** *p60*
Peterson, Ann; Virginia, 1638 ***6219*** *p118*
Peterson, Anton; Washington, 1859-1920 ***2872.1*** *p31*
Peterson, Axel; Washington, 1859-1920 ***2872.1*** *p31*
Peterson, C. M.; Minneapolis, 1880-1888 ***6410.35*** *p64*
Peterson, Carl; Wisconsin, n.d. ***9675.7*** *p130*
Peterson, Carl Christian; Arkansas, 1918 ***95.2*** *p98*
Peterson, Charles; Iowa, 1866-1943 ***123.54*** *p39*
Peterson, Charles 40; Massachusetts, 1860 ***6410.32*** *p103*
Peterson, Charles J. 22; Kansas, 1906 ***5240.1*** *p83*
Peterson, Charles W.; Maine, 1880-1895 ***6410.22*** *p121*
Peterson, Christ; Illinois, 1884 ***2896.5*** *p31*
Peterson, Claes; Minneapolis, 1880-1884 ***6410.35*** *p64*
Peterson, Daniel; Kansas, 1870 ***5240.1*** *p34*
Peterson, David Otto Enoch; Arkansas, 1918 ***95.2*** *p98*
Peterson, Edward; Arkansas, 1918 ***95.2*** *p98*
Peterson, Edward; Minneapolis, 1868-1878 ***6410.35*** *p64*
Peterson, Erasmus; Colorado, 1888 ***9678.2*** *p163*
Peterson, Frank; Washington, 1859-1920 ***2872.1*** *p31*
Peterson, Fred; Minneapolis, 1868-1876 ***6410.35*** *p64*
Peterson, Fredrik Emil; Minneapolis, 1882-1884 ***6410.35*** *p64*
Peterson, Frithiof; Minneapolis, 1883-1884 ***6410.35*** *p64*
Peterson, George 27; Arkansas, 1918 ***95.2*** *p98*
Peterson, George 54; Washington, 1918-1920 ***1728.5*** *p12*
Peterson, George N.; America, 1877 ***5240.1*** *p34*
Peterson, Gust; Iowa, 1866-1943 ***123.54*** *p39*
Peterson, Gust; Minneapolis, 1880-1883 ***6410.35*** *p64*
Peterson, Gust; Minneapolis, 1880-1887 ***6410.35*** *p64*
Peterson, Gust; Minneapolis, 1881-1887 ***6410.35*** *p64*
Peterson, Gustav; Oklahoma City, 1915 ***9892.11*** *p36*
Peterson, Gustav V.; Washington, 1859-1920 ***2872.1*** *p31*
Peterson, Hans William 31; Arkansas, 1918 ***95.2*** *p98*
Peterson, Hicks 41?; Arizona, 1890 ***2764.35*** *p55*
Peterson, Hugo; Iowa, 1866-1943 ***123.54*** *p39*
Peterson, Hugo; Iowa, 1866-1943 ***123.54*** *p73*
Peterson, Isaac; Baltimore, 1830 ***8208.4*** *p36*
Peterson, Jacob; Illinois, 1876 ***5012.37*** *p60*
Peterson, James; Iowa, 1866-1943 ***123.54*** *p39*
Peterson, Jan; Illinois, 1874 ***7857*** *p6*
Peterson, John; Boston, 1843 ***6410.32*** *p124*
Peterson, John; Colorado, 1894 ***9678.2*** *p163*
Peterson, John; New York, NY, 1834 ***8208.4*** *p42*
Peterson, John; Washington, 1859-1920 ***2872.1*** *p31*
Peterson, John 38; Kansas, 1873 ***5240.1*** *p54*
Peterson, John B.; Iroquois Co., IL, 1896 ***3455.1*** *p12*
Peterson, John B.; New York, NY, 1836 ***8208.4*** *p9*
Peterson, John D.; Baltimore, 1835 ***1450.2*** *p110A*
Peterson, John F.; Minneapolis, 1864-1888 ***6410.35*** *p64*
Peterson, John Frederick; America, 1836 ***1450.2*** *p110A*
Peterson, John L.; Kansas, 1871 ***5240.1*** *p34*
Peterson, John M. 41; Massachusetts, 1860 ***6410.32*** *p110*
Peterson, John P.; Nevada, 1874 ***2764.35*** *p54*
Peterson, Jonas; Maine, 1870-1876 ***6410.22*** *p117*
Peterson, Jorgen; America, 1913 ***3455.3*** *p55*
*Wife:*Tora
Peterson, Jorgen; New York, NY, 1913 ***3455.2*** *p51*
Peterson, L. P.; Arkansas, 1918 ***95.2*** *p98*
Peterson, Louis; Illinois, 1874 ***5012.39*** *p26*
Peterson, Louis; Minneapolis, 1868-1886 ***6410.35*** *p64*
Peterson, Louis; Washington, 1859-1920 ***2872.1*** *p31*
Peterson, Louis 27; Arkansas, 1918 ***95.2*** *p98*
Peterson, Magnus 22; Arkansas, 1918 ***95.2*** *p98*
Peterson, Manne; Iroquois Co., IL, 1894 ***3455.1*** *p12*
Peterson, Mary J. 31; Massachusetts, 1860 ***6410.32*** *p110*
Peterson, Morris; New York, NY, 1913 ***9892.11*** *p36*
Peterson, Nels Nichcolas; Iowa, 1866-1943 ***123.54*** *p39*
Peterson, Nicholas; Iowa, 1850-1855 ***2090*** *p613*
Peterson, Nicklas; Illinois, 1900 ***5012.40*** *p77*
Peterson, Nickolai; Arkansas, 1918 ***95.2*** *p98*
Peterson, Niels Christian; Arkansas, 1918 ***95.2*** *p99*
Peterson, Ole; Minneapolis, 1880-1884 ***6410.35*** *p64*
Peterson, Olof; New York, NY, 1834 ***8208.4*** *p49*
Peterson, Oscar; Washington, 1859-1920 ***2872.1*** *p31*
Peterson, P. D.; Iowa, 1866-1943 ***123.54*** *p39*
Peterson, P. J.; Iowa, 1849-1860 ***2090*** *p613*
Peterson, Paul Thomas Ehrhorn; Arkansas, 1918 ***95.2*** *p99*
Peterson, Peter; Bangor, ME, 1870-1879 ***6410.22*** *p118*
Peterson, Peter; Bangor, ME, 1879 ***6410.22*** *p125*
Peterson, Peter; Illinois, 1888 ***5012.39*** *p122*
Peterson, Peter; Iowa, 1866-1943 ***123.54*** *p17*
Peterson, Peter; Minneapolis, 1868-1878 ***6410.35*** *p65*
Peterson, Peter; Minneapolis, 1881-1883 ***6410.35*** *p65*
Peterson, Peter; New York, NY, 1834 ***8208.4*** *p17*
Peterson, Peter K.; Washington, 1859-1920 ***2872.1*** *p31*
Peterson, Peter M.; New York, NY, 1839 ***8208.4*** *p91*
Peterson, Samuel; Iowa, 1849-1860 ***2090*** *p613*
Peterson, Staffan; Iowa, 1851 ***2090*** *p615*
Peterson, Svan Jno; Iowa, 1866-1943 ***123.54*** *p39*
Peterson, Thorvald; Arkansas, 1918 ***95.2*** *p99*
Peterson, Tora *SEE* Peterson, Jorgen
Peterson, Victor; Wisconsin, n.d. ***9675.7*** *p130*
Peterson, William; Virginia, 1638 ***6219*** *p119*
Peterson, William; West Virginia, 1855 ***9788.3*** *p18*
Petersson, Anders Gustaf; Minneapolis, 1881-1887 ***6410.35*** *p64*
Petersson, Dynes; Bangor, ME, 1894 ***6410.22*** *p127*
Petersson, Frans Johan; Minneapolis, 1880-1886 ***6410.35*** *p62*
Petersson, Fredrik; Minneapolis, 1882-1884 ***6410.35*** *p64*
Petersson, Gustaf Emil; Minneapolis, 1880-1883 ***6410.35*** *p64*
Petersson, Johan August; Minneapolis, 1880-1887 ***6410.35*** *p64*
Petersson, Nils Johan; Minneapolis, 1872-1886 ***6410.35*** *p62*
Petersson, P. M.; Minneapolis, 1884-1886 ***6410.35*** *p64*
Petersson, Pehr Fredrik; Minneapolis, 1871-1885 ***6410.35*** *p63*
Petesch, Michael; Wisconsin, n.d. ***9675.7*** *p130*
Petetjean, Albert; Kansas, 1890 ***5240.1*** *p34*
Petetjean, Jules; Kansas, 1892 ***5240.1*** *p34*
Petetson, Andrew; Iowa, 1866-1943 ***123.54*** *p39*
Petetz, Elias Morris; Arkansas, 1918 ***95.2*** *p99*
Pether, Mary 21; Port uncertain, 1774 ***1219.7*** *p177*
Pether, William; New York, NY, 1816 ***2859.11*** *p40*
Petick, Eliza.; Virginia, 1641 ***6219*** *p187*
Petick, Leonard; Virginia, 1641 ***6219*** *p187*
Petil, Auguste 28; New Orleans, 1837 ***778.5*** *p426*
Petisch, John; Wisconsin, n.d. ***9675.7*** *p130*
Petit, . . .; New Orleans, 1839 ***778.5*** *p427*
Petit, . . . 11; Port uncertain, 1838 ***778.5*** *p427*
Petit, . . . 14; Port uncertain, 1838 ***778.5*** *p427*
Petit, Miss; New Orleans, 1839 ***778.5*** *p427*
Petit, Miss 13; New Orleans, 1827 ***778.5*** *p427*
Petit, Mr.; New Orleans, 1839 ***778.5*** *p427*
Petit, Mr.; Port uncertain, 1839 ***778.5*** *p426*
Petit, Mr. 11; New Orleans, 1827 ***778.5*** *p427*
Petit, Mr. 30; America, 1839 ***778.5*** *p427*
Petit, Mrs. 28; New Orleans, 1827 ***778.5*** *p427*
Petit, A. 36; Port uncertain, 1835 ***778.5*** *p427*
Petit, Adolphus; New York, NY, 1838 ***8208.4*** *p57*
Petit, Berrard; New York, NY, 1816 ***2859.11*** *p40*
Petit, Caroline 21; New Orleans, 1837 ***778.5*** *p427*
Petit, Francois 26; New Orleans, 1826 ***778.5*** *p427*
Petit, Francoise 19; New Orleans, 1839 ***778.5*** *p427*
Petit, Jeanne 54; New Orleans, 1839 ***778.5*** *p428*
Petit, Joseph 45; America, 1838 ***778.5*** *p427*
Petit, M. 29; America, 1838 ***778.5*** *p427*
Petit, Pierre 30; America, 1837 ***778.5*** *p428*
Petit, Rose 17; New Orleans, 1839 ***778.5*** *p428*
Petitbien, Adolfe Bernard 23; Port uncertain, 1836 ***778.5*** *p428*
Petitjean, Archie; Kansas, 1898 ***5240.1*** *p34*
Petitjean, Emile; Kansas, 1896 ***5240.1*** *p34*
Petko, Sparo; Arkansas, 1918 ***95.2*** *p99*
Petne, Frederick G.; Illinois, 1847 ***7857*** *p6*
Petora, Mike; Arkansas, 1918 ***95.2*** *p99*
Petranowski, . . .; New York, 1831 ***4606*** *p176*
Petraud, Ms. 18; America, 1837 ***778.5*** *p428*
Petraud, Widow 48; America, 1837 ***778.5*** *p428*
Petre, Francis; New York, NY, 1835 ***8208.4*** *p59*
Petrella, Peter; Arkansas, 1918 ***95.2*** *p99*
Petrelli, Lindo; Arkansas, 1918 ***95.2*** *p99*
Petrequin, . . .; Halifax, N.S., 1752 ***7074.6*** *p232*
Petrequin, Anne-Marie *SEE* Petrequin, Jean
Petrequin, Jean 21; Halifax, N.S., 1752 ***7074.6*** *p212*
Petrequin, Jean 28; Halifax, N.S., 1752 ***7074.6*** *p212*
*Wife:*Anne-Marie
Petri, . . .; Canada, 1776-1783 ***9786*** *p43*
Petri, Johann Jost; Wisconsin, n.d. ***9675.7*** *p130*
Petrie, . . .; Canada, 1776-1783 ***9786*** *p43*
Petrie, Alexander S.; New York, NY, 1836 ***8208.4*** *p11*
Petrie, Frederick; Illinois, 1847 ***7857*** *p6*
Petrie, John 30; Tobago, W. Indies, 1775 ***1219.7*** *p251*
Petrie, John Innes; Arkansas, 1918 ***95.2*** *p99*
Petrie, Peter; Savannah, GA, 1774 ***1219.7*** *p227*
Petrie, William W.; New York, NY, 1834-1840 ***8208.4*** *p8*
Petrinovich, Mate; Iowa, 1866-1943 ***123.54*** *p39*
Petrokas, Joseph; Wisconsin, n.d. ***9675.7*** *p130*
Petrokas, Rapolas; Wisconsin, n.d. ***9675.7*** *p130*
Petrokos, Vincent; Wisconsin, n.d. ***9675.7*** *p130*
Petroks, Matausas; Wisconsin, n.d. ***9675.7*** *p130*
Petrolia, Salvatore; Iowa, 1866-1943 ***123.54*** *p73*
Petrones, Clemence; Arkansas, 1918 ***95.2*** *p99*
Petropoulous, Pericles Nicholas; Arkansas, 1918 ***95.2*** *p99*
Petropulous, Andrew Pietros; Arkansas, 1918 ***95.2*** *p99*
Petros, Tom; Arkansas, 1918 ***95.2*** *p99*
Petrou, Cellon 33; West Virginia, 1901 ***9788.3*** *p19*
Petrucci, A.; Wisconsin, n.d. ***9675.7*** *p130*
Petrucci, Ardainio; Wisconsin, n.d. ***9675.7*** *p130*
Petsch, Adam; Charleston, SC, 1775-1781 ***8582.2*** *p52*
Pett, Math.; Virginia, 1642 ***6219*** *p188*
Pett, Robert; Arkansas, 1918 ***95.2*** *p99*
Pett, Wm.; Virginia, 1637 ***6219*** *p82*
Petta, Gaetano; Arkansas, 1918 ***95.2*** *p99*
Pettay, Daniel; Buffalo, NY, 1819 ***9892.11*** *p36*
*Daughter:*Rebecca 2
Pettay, Rebecca 2 *SEE* Pettay, Daniel
Petters, William 20; Pennsylvania, 1737 ***3690.1*** *p177*
Petterson, A.; Minneapolis, 1882-1887 ***6410.35*** *p63*
Petterson, A. B.; Iowa, 1866-1943 ***123.54*** *p39*
Petterson, Anna Charlotte; Washington, 1859-1920 ***2872.1*** *p31*
Petterson, Carl Gustaf; Washington, 1859-1920 ***2872.1*** *p31*
Petterson, Carl J.; Colorado, 1904 ***9678.2*** *p163*
Petterson, Ebba Lorain; Washington, 1859-1920 ***2872.1*** *p31*
Petterson, Ivan Oscar Gotfred; Arkansas, 1918 ***95.2*** *p99*
Petterson, John; Washington, 1859-1920 ***2872.1*** *p31*
Petterson, Judith Noraine; Washington, 1859-1920 ***2872.1*** *p31*
Petterson, Pear John; Colorado, 1886 ***9678.2*** *p163*
Petterson, Stephen; New York, NY, 1836 ***8208.4*** *p21*
Pettibone, Richard; Virginia, 1641 ***6219*** *p185*
Pettier, Elzear; Canada, 1852 ***2896.5*** *p31*
Pettier, Elzear; Illinois, 1852 ***2896.5*** *p31*
Pettigrew, William; New York, NY, 1816 ***2859.11*** *p40*
Pettinato, Clement; Arkansas, 1918 ***95.2*** *p99*
Pettinen, Tini May; Washington, 1859-1920 ***2872.1*** *p30*
Pettis, Step.; Virginia, 1637 ***6219*** *p8*
Pettit, Bernard; New York, NY, 1816 ***2859.11*** *p40*
Pettit, Francis; Virginia, 1851 ***4626.16*** *p14*
Pettit, Patrick; Philadelphia, 1816 ***2859.11*** *p40*
Pettit, William; New York, NY, 1835 ***8208.4*** *p59*
Pettitt, Rich.; Virginia, 1636 ***6219*** *p77*
Pettret, Henry 31; America, 1839 ***778.5*** *p428*

Philips, Thomas; Iowa, 1866-1943 ***123.54*** *p39*
Philips, Wm 48; America, 1702 ***2212*** *p37*
Phillimore, Jacob 16; Virginia, 1727 ***3690.1*** *p177*
Phillip, Andrew; Illinois, 1863 ***2896.5*** *p31*
Phillip, David 21; St. John, N.B., 1866 ***5704.8*** *p166*
Phillip, Joshua Samuel; California, 1869 ***2769.7*** *p5*
Philliphan, Biddy 10 mos; Massachusetts, 1849 ***5881.1*** *p80*
Philliphan, Mary 26; Massachusetts, 1849 ***5881.1*** *p81*
Phillipi, John; Wisconsin, n.d. ***9675.7*** *p130*
Phillippi, Nicholas; Wisconsin, n.d. ***9675.7*** *p130*
Phillipps, Edward; Virginia, 1638 ***6219*** *p122*
Phillipps, Eliz.; Virginia, 1635 ***6219*** *p27*
Phillipps, Eliz.; Virginia, 1636 ***6219*** *p74*
Phillipps, Eliz.; Virginia, 1638 ***6219*** *p145*
Phillipps, Eliza.; Virginia, 1639 ***6219*** *p158*
Phillipps, Elizabeth *SEE* Phillipps, Thomas
Phillipps, Elizabeth *SEE* Phillipps, Thomas
Phillipps, Frederick; Wisconsin, n.d. ***9675.7*** *p130*
Phillipps, Georg; Virginia, 1638 ***6219*** *p8*
Phillipps, John; Virginia, 1628 ***6219*** *p9*
Phillipps, John; Virginia, 1636 ***6219*** *p73*
Phillipps, John; Virginia, 1638 ***6219*** *p121*
Phillipps, John; Virginia, 1643 ***6219*** *p200*
Phillipps, Jon.; Virginia, 1635 ***6219*** *p73*
Phillipps, Jon.; Virginia, 1637 ***6219*** *p113*
Phillipps, Lewis; Virginia, 1635 ***6219*** *p33*
Phillipps, Richard; Virginia, 1635 ***6219*** *p70*
Phillipps, Richard; Virginia, 1637 ***6219*** *p110*
Phillipps, Robert; Virginia, 1640 ***6219*** *p182*
Phillipps, Robt.; Virginia, 1637 ***6219*** *p13*
Phillipps, Robt.; Virginia, 1643 ***6219*** *p205*
Phillipps, Thomas; Virginia, 1635 ***6219*** *p25*
*Wife:*Elizabeth
*Daughter:*Elizabeth
Phillipps, Thos.; Virginia, 1637 ***6219*** *p13*
Phillipps, Wm.; Virginia, 1643 ***6219*** *p204*
Phillips, . . .; Canada, 1776-1783 ***9786*** *p31*
Phillips, Mr.; Quebec, 1815 ***9229.18*** *p74*
Phillips, Abraham; Quebec, 1847 ***5704.8*** *p28*
Phillips, Alexander 4; St. John, N.B., 1847 ***5704.8*** *p34*
Phillips, Alexander 15; Philadelphia, 1855 ***5704.8*** *p124*
Phillips, Andrew; Quebec, 1852 ***5704.8*** *p87*
Phillips, Andrew; Quebec, 1852 ***5704.8*** *p90*
Phillips, Ann 13; Philadelphia, 1853 ***5704.8*** *p113*
Phillips, Batiste; New York, NY, 1836 ***8208.4*** *p25*
Phillips, Bernard; New York, NY, 1815 ***2859.11*** *p40*
Phillips, Biddy 40; Philadelphia, 1853 ***5704.8*** *p113*
Phillips, Charles; Illinois, 1884 ***2896.5*** *p31*
Phillips, Charles; Illinois, 1892 ***5012.40*** *p27*
Phillips, Dav.; Virginia, 1648 ***6219*** *p250*
Phillips, Edward; New York, NY, 1835 ***8208.4*** *p27*
Phillips, Effie; Washington, 1859-1920 ***2872.1*** *p31*
Phillips, Elisabeth Bach; Michigan, 1911 ***2691.4*** *p166*
With husband
Phillips, Elisabeth Bach; Minnesota, 1911 ***2691.4*** *p166*
With husband
Phillips, Eliz.; Virginia, 1637 ***6219*** *p108*
Phillips, Eliza; New York, NY, 1811 ***2859.11*** *p18*
Phillips, Elizabeth; Quebec, 1847 ***5704.8*** *p28*
Phillips, Elizabeth 13; Quebec, 1847 ***5704.8*** *p28*
Phillips, Elizabeth 19; St. John, N.B., 1862 ***5704.8*** *p151*
Phillips, Elizabeth 20; Philadelphia, 1864 ***5704.8*** *p161*
Phillips, Elizabeth 49; Maryland, 1730 ***3690.1*** *p178*
Phillips, Elmer; Virginia, 1622-1633 ***6219*** *p25*
Phillips, G. W.; Washington, 1859-1920 ***2872.1*** *p31*
Phillips, George; California, 1852 ***2764.35*** *p56*
Phillips, George 3 mos; Philadelphia, 1864 ***5704.8*** *p161*
Phillips, George 22; Philadelphia, 1774 ***1219.7*** *p190*
Phillips, Giles; Pensacola, FL, 1766 ***1219.7*** *p117*
Phillips, Henry 17; Maryland, 1723 ***3690.1*** *p178*
Phillips, James; Illinois, 1892 ***5012.40*** *p27*
Phillips, James; Iowa, 1866-1943 ***123.54*** *p39*
Phillips, Jane 3; St. John, N.B., 1847 ***5704.8*** *p34*
Phillips, John 50; Quebec, 1775 ***1219.7*** *p268*
*Wife:*Sarah 45
Phillips, Margaret; St. John, N.B., 1852 ***5704.8*** *p95*
Phillips, Martha 16; Maryland, 1718 ***3690.1*** *p178*
Phillips, Mary A. 40; Philadelphia, 1855 ***5704.8*** *p124*
Phillips, Mary Jane 7; Quebec, 1847 ***5704.8*** *p28*
Phillips, Matilda 3; Quebec, 1847 ***5704.8*** *p28*
Phillips, Michael; New York, NY, 1840 ***8208.4*** *p108*
Phillips, Morgan; Virginia, 1637 ***6219*** *p13*
Phillips, Nancy; Quebec, 1847 ***5704.8*** *p28*
Phillips, Patrick 40; Philadelphia, 1853 ***5704.8*** *p113*
Phillips, Robert; America, 1738 ***4971*** *p25*
Phillips, Robert; St. John, N.B., 1847 ***5704.8*** *p33*
Phillips, Robert; St. John, N.B., 1853 ***5704.8*** *p99*
Phillips, Robert; Virginia, 1648 ***6219*** *p246*
Phillips, Robert 11; Philadelphia, 1855 ***5704.8*** *p124*
Phillips, Samuel; Iowa, 1866-1943 ***123.54*** *p39*
Phillips, Samuel; St. John, N.B., 1847 ***5704.8*** *p34*
Phillips, Samuel 24; Baltimore, 1775 ***1219.7*** *p269*
Phillips, Sarah 45 *SEE* Phillips, John
Phillips, Stephen 23; Maryland, 1774 ***1219.7*** *p220*
Phillips, Thomas; Illinois, 1888 ***2896.5*** *p31*
Phillips, Thomas; New York, NY, 1811 ***2859.11*** *p18*
Phillips, Thomas 13; Philadelphia, 1855 ***5704.8*** *p124*
Phillips, Thomas 17; Jamaica, 1719 ***3690.1*** *p178*
Phillips, William 7; St. John, N.B., 1847 ***5704.8*** *p34*
Phillips, William 21; Virginia, 1774 ***1219.7*** *p244*
Phillips, William 41; Virginia, 1774 ***1219.7*** *p186*
Phillips, William 50; Philadelphia, 1855 ***5704.8*** *p124*
Phillips, William James 5; Quebec, 1847 ***5704.8*** *p28*
Phillips, Wm.; Virginia, 1648 ***6219*** *p250*
Phillipson, Robert; Virginia, 1638 ***6219*** *p148*
Philpeck, George 86; North Carolina, 1850 ***1639.20*** *p262*
Philpeck, William 70; North Carolina, 1850 ***1639.20*** *p262*
Philpitt, James; New York, NY, 1838 ***8208.4*** *p84*
Philpot, Richard; Virginia, 1648 ***6219*** *p251*
Philps, Mary 22; Maryland, 1774 ***1219.7*** *p211*
Philps, Thomas 16; Maryland, 1774 ***1219.7*** *p244*
Philson, Robert; New York, NY, 1811 ***2859.11*** *p18*
Phinby, Edw.; Virginia, 1637 ***6219*** *p110*
With wife & child
Phinstaag, Mich'l 32; Pennsylvania, 1737 ***2444*** *p200*
Phipps, Edward; America, 1735-1743 ***4971*** *p79*
Phipps, John; Virginia, 1621 ***6219*** *p4*
Phipps, Thomas 21; Philadelphia, 1774 ***1219.7*** *p237*
Phipps, Thomas Henry 24; Kansas, 1871 ***5240.1*** *p52*
Phipps, William 20; Jamaica, 1739 ***3690.1*** *p178*
Phithian, Thomas 28; America, 1699 ***2212*** *p25*
Phiun, Parrick; Illinois, 1860 ***2896.5*** *p31*
Phoenix, John; New York, NY, 1816 ***2859.11*** *p40*
Photopulous, William George; Arkansas, 1918 ***95.2*** *p99*
Phouts, John; Baltimore, 1819 ***9892.11*** *p36*
Physick, Charles 8; Virginia, 1699 ***2212*** *p27*
Physick, Ellen 37; Virginia, 1699 ***2212*** *p27*
Physick, Tho 11; Virginia, 1699 ***2212*** *p27*
Physick, Wm 17; Virginia, 1699 ***2212*** *p27*
Pial, Christian; New York, 1840 ***1450.2*** *p110A*
Pianalto, Jean; Arkansas, 1918 ***95.2*** *p99*
Piantanida, Joe; Arkansas, 1918 ***95.2*** *p99*
Piarshinting, Joseph; Shreveport, LA, 1876 ***7129*** *p45*
Piazza, Dominico; Arkansas, 1918 ***95.2*** *p99*
Picard, Gustave 37; New Orleans, 1829 ***778.5*** *p429*
Picard, Josephine 29; New Orleans, 1829 ***778.5*** *p429*
Picaud, . . .; Louisiana, 1820 ***778.5*** *p429*
Picaud, . . .; Louisiana, 1820 ***778.5*** *p430*
Picaud, Mme.; Louisiana, 1820 ***778.5*** *p430*
Picaud, Francois 46; Louisiana, 1820 ***778.5*** *p430*
Piccalo, Carmelo; Iowa, 1866-1943 ***123.54*** *p39*
Piccioni, Giovanni; Arkansas, 1918 ***95.2*** *p99*
Piccola, Frank; Arkansas, 1918 ***95.2*** *p99*
Piccolo, Dominico; Iowa, 1866-1943 ***123.54*** *p39*
Pichard, Henry 22; New Orleans, 1820 ***778.5*** *p430*
Piche, F. 26; Port uncertain, 1836 ***778.5*** *p430*
Piche, F. 28; Port uncertain, 1838 ***778.5*** *p430*
Picheloup, Mr. 18; America, 1839 ***778.5*** *p430*
Picheloup, Mr. 35; America, 1839 ***778.5*** *p430*
Picheloup, Antoine 25; New Orleans, 1839 ***778.5*** *p430*
Picheloup, Rd. 29; New Orleans, 1837 ***778.5*** *p430*
Pichler, Margaretha *SEE* Pichler, Thomas
Pichler, Maria; Georgia, 1734 ***9332*** *p328*
Pichler, Thomas; Georgia, 1738 ***9332*** *p321*
Pichler, Thomas; Georgia, 1739 ***9332*** *p323*
Pichler, Thomas; Georgia, 1739 ***9332*** *p326*
*Wife:*Margaretha
Pichon, A. 32; America, 1826 ***778.5*** *p430*
Pichon, Eugene 26; New Orleans, 1838 ***778.5*** *p430*
Pichon, Nicolas 19; Port uncertain, 1836 ***778.5*** *p430*
Pichony, Mr. 45; Port uncertain, 1823 ***778.5*** *p431*
Pichot, Mr. 23; New Orleans, 1839 ***778.5*** *p431*
Picio, Valentin 26; New Orleans, 1827 ***778.5*** *p431*
Pickard, Francis John 30; Carolina, 1774 ***1219.7*** *p180*
Pickard, Joseph; Washington, 1859-1920 ***2872.1*** *p31*
Pickell, . . .; Canada, 1776-1783 ***9786*** *p31*
Picken, Martha Huie 26 *SEE* Picken, William
Picken, William 32; Wilmington, NC, 1774 ***1639.20*** *p262*
*Wife:*Martha Huie 26
Pickens, James 34; Kansas, 1875 ***5240.1*** *p56*
Pickering, James 20; Virginia, 1699 ***2212*** *p26*
Pickering, Joane; Virginia, 1623-1700 ***6219*** *p189*
Pickering, John 19; Windward Islands, 1722 ***3690.1*** *p178*
Pickering, John E.; Washington, 1859-1920 ***2872.1*** *p31*
Pickering, Richard 19; Antigua (Antego), 1729 ***3690.1*** *p178*
Pickering, Samuel 23; Nova Scotia, 1774 ***1219.7*** *p193*
Pickering, Thomt 29; Montserrat, 1700 ***2212*** *p22*
Pickering, William 14; Virginia, 1699 ***2212*** *p26*
Pickerskill, John 20; Jamaica, 1733 ***3690.1*** *p178*
Picket, . . .; Canada, 1776-1783 ***9786*** *p31*
Picket, Eliza Jane 9 mos; Quebec, 1855 ***5704.8*** *p125*
Picket, Elizabeth 22; Quebec, 1855 ***5704.8*** *p125*
Picket, Jane 11; Massachusetts, 1850 ***5881.1*** *p81*
Picket, Marcus 23; Quebec, 1855 ***5704.8*** *p125*
Picket, Mark; New England, 1816 ***2859.11*** *p40*
Picket, Sarah 2; Quebec, 1855 ***5704.8*** *p125*
Pickett, James; America, 1739 ***4971*** *p40*
Pickett, William; New York, NY, 1838 ***8208.4*** *p61*
Pickhardt, William; Indiana, 1850 ***9117*** *p20*
Pickin, John 16; Pennsylvania, Virginia or Maryland, 1719 ***3690.1*** *p178*
Pickle, Balthasar; New Jersey, 1680 ***8125.8*** *p438*
Pickler, Fanny 36; New York, 1774 ***1219.7*** *p202*
Pickler, Grace 1 *SEE* Pickler, Sarah
Pickler, Mary 9 *SEE* Pickler, Sarah
Pickler, Nancy 11 *SEE* Pickler, Sarah
Pickler, Sarah 6 *SEE* Pickler, Sarah
Pickler, Sarah 36; New York, 1774 ***1219.7*** *p202*
*Child:*Nancy 11
*Child:*Mary 9
*Child:*Sarah 6
*Child:*Grace 1
Picklie, Agnes 40 *SEE* Picklie, Hans George
Picklie, Hans George 43; Georgia, 1738 ***9332*** *p333*
*Wife:*Agnes 40
*Son:*John 17
*Son:*Thomas 13
*Son:*Jacob 8
Picklie, Jacob 8 *SEE* Picklie, Hans George
Picklie, John 17 *SEE* Picklie, Hans George
Picklie, Thomas 13 *SEE* Picklie, Hans George
Picknell, Frederick W.; Illinois, 1896 ***5012.40*** *p54*
Picknell, Harry; Illinois, 1896 ***5012.40*** *p54*
Picknell, Owen; Illinois, 1897 ***5012.40*** *p55*
Picollo, Antonio 24; West Virginia, 1904 ***9788.3*** *p19*
Picone, Guiseppe; Arkansas, 1918 ***95.2*** *p99*
Picot, Charles; Quebec, 1809 ***7603*** *p48*
Picot, Johann Christian; Kentucky, 1843 ***8582.3*** *p100*
Picot, Toussaint 34; New Orleans, 1826 ***778.5*** *p431*
Picott, Jean 44; America, 1835 ***778.5*** *p431*
Picotte, Mr.; Quebec, 1815 ***9229.18*** *p80*
Pidcock, John; Baltimore, 1818 ***9892.11*** *p37*
Pidcock, John; Ohio, 1829 ***9892.11*** *p37*
Piddington, Christopher; Virginia, 1638 ***6219*** *p125*
Piden, James; New York, NY, 1811 ***2859.11*** *p18*
Pidwell, John; San Francisco, 1850 ***4914.15*** *p10*
Pidwell, Thomas; San Francisco, 1876 ***2764.35*** *p53*
Pie, Catherine 20; St. John, N.B., 1854 ***5704.8*** *p120*
Pie, Eliza 22; St. John, N.B., 1854 ***5704.8*** *p120*
Piechowski, . . .; New York, 1831 ***4606*** *p176*
Piecuch, Franciszek 17; New York, 1912 ***9980.29*** *p62*
Piedler, Catharina; Georgia, 1739 ***9332*** *p324*
Piedro, Fred; Arkansas, 1918 ***95.2*** *p100*
Piehl, John; Wisconsin, n.d. ***9675.7*** *p130*
Piekarska, Wiktorya 33; New York, 1912 ***9980.29*** *p53*
Piekarski, . . .; New York, 1831 ***4606*** *p176*
Piekowska, Janina 7 *SEE* Piekowska, Marianna Tomacziewska
Piekowska, Marianna Tomacziewska 25; New York, 1912 ***9980.29*** *p69*
*Daughter:*Janina 7
Piel, Ernst Henry; America, 1845 ***1450.2*** *p111A*
Piel, Henry; America, 1846 ***1450.2*** *p111A*
Piel, Jacob; Canada, 1780 ***9786*** *p268*
Piel, Jacob; New York, 1776 ***9786*** *p268*
Piel, William Frederick; America, 1846 ***1450.2*** *p111A*
Pielarcheck, Mike; Wisconsin, n.d. ***9675.7*** *p199*
Pienskowski, . . .; New York, 1831 ***4606*** *p176*
Piepenbrink, Children; America, 1835-1890 ***4610.10*** *p103*
Piepenbrink, Caroline J C Vohsmeier *SEE* Piepenbrink, Christian F. Wilhelm
Piepenbrink, Christian F. Wilhelm; America, 1890 ***4610.10*** *p103*
*Wife:*Caroline J C Vohsmeier
*Child:*Friederike C. Louise
*Child:*Marie Justine Luise
Piepenbrink, Christine Caroline Luise; America, 1887 ***4610.10*** *p103*
Piepenbrink, Friederike C. Louise *SEE* Piepenbrink, Christian F. Wilhelm
Piepenbrink, Heinrich F. Wilhelm; America, 1885 ***4610.10*** *p102*
Piepenbrink, Marie Justine Luise *SEE* Piepenbrink, Christian F. Wilhelm
Pieper, . . .; Canada, 1776-1783 ***9786*** *p31*
Pieper, Friedrich; America, 1861 ***4610.10*** *p105*
Pieper, Wilhelm; America, 1847 ***8582.1*** *p27*
Pierage, Pablo 31; New Orleans, 1829 ***778.5*** *p431*
Pierce, Alex; New York, NY, 1816 ***2859.11*** *p40*
Pierce, Alexander 17; St. John, N.B., 1859 ***5704.8*** *p140*
Pierce, Hugh 35; Maryland or Virginia, 1699 ***2212*** *p23*
Pierce, James; Arizona, 1883 ***2764.35*** *p56*
Pierce, John; New York, NY, 1816 ***2859.11*** *p40*
Pierce, John 21; Massachusetts, 1850 ***5881.1*** *p81*

Pierce, John 28; Massachusetts, 1849 ***5881.1*** *p81*
Pierce, Patrick; New York, NY, 1811 ***2859.11*** *p18*
Pierce, William; Virginia, 1648 ***6219*** *p250*
Pierce, William 25; Massachusetts, 1847 ***5881.1*** *p81*
Pieretti, Mr. 22; New Orleans, 1822 ***778.5*** *p431*
Piernik, Lina 17; New York, 1912 ***9980.29*** *p49*
Piernikowski, Ignacy 20; New York, 1912 ***9980.29*** *p49*
Pierre, Mr. 34; New Orleans, 1837 ***778.5*** *p431*
Pierre, Angelique 18; America, 1837 ***778.5*** *p431*
Pierre, Auguste 4; New Orleans, 1837 ***778.5*** *p431*
Pierre, Cath. 48; America, 1839 ***778.5*** *p431*
Pierre, Catherine 67; New Orleans, 1837 ***778.5*** *p431*
Pierre, Charles-Georges; Quebec, 1816 ***7603*** *p47*
Pierre, Edouard 8 mos; New Orleans, 1837 ***778.5*** *p431*
Pierre, Ferges 28; America, 1829 ***778.5*** *p431*
Pierre, Franz 15; America, 1839 ***778.5*** *p431*
Pierre, Guillaume 30; Port uncertain, 1838 ***778.5*** *p432*
Pierre, J. 27; New Orleans, 1839 ***778.5*** *p432*
Pierre, John; Wisconsin, n.d. ***9675.7*** *p199*
Pierre, Jules Jen 35; New Orleans, 1836 ***778.5*** *p432*
Pierre, Julie 15; America, 1839 ***778.5*** *p432*
Pierre, Louis 21; America, 1836 ***778.5*** *p432*
Pierre, Marie 4; New Orleans, 1837 ***778.5*** *p432*
Pierre, Pauline 19; America, 1839 ***778.5*** *p432*
Pierreon, Marie 3; Port uncertain, 1839 ***778.5*** *p432*
Pierreon, Marie 14; Port uncertain, 1839 ***778.5*** *p432*
Pierret, John 25; Kansas, 1888 ***5240.1*** *p72*
Pierri, . . .; Canada, 1776-1783 ***9786*** *p43*
Pierron, Adelaide 6; Port uncertain, 1839 ***778.5*** *p432*
Pierron, Joseph 46; Port uncertain, 1839 ***778.5*** *p432*
Pierron, Marie 46; Port uncertain, 1839 ***778.5*** *p432*
Pierron, Nicolas 19; Port uncertain, 1839 ***778.5*** *p432*
Pierron, Peter; Wisconsin, n.d. ***9675.7*** *p199*
Pierrot, Mr. 50; New Orleans, 1822 ***778.5*** *p432*
Pierson, Carl G.; Colorado, 1891 ***9678.2*** *p163*
Pierson, Charles 24; Jamaica, 1736 ***3690.1*** *p178*
Pierson, Edward; Colorado, 1901 ***9678.2*** *p163*
Pierson, Ellen; America, 1705 ***2212*** *p45*
Pierson, Emil; Iroquois Co., IL, 1892 ***3455.1*** *p12*
Pierson, Jacob; New York, NY, 1811 ***2859.11*** *p18*
Pierson, Jane; New York, NY, 1811 ***2859.11*** *p18*
Pierson, Joseph 34; Halifax, N.S., 1774 ***1219.7*** *p213*
Piesch, George; Philadelphia, 1742 ***3652*** *p54*
Piescinski, John; Arkansas, 1918 ***95.2*** *p100*
Piet, Gennae 28; New Orleans, 1839 ***778.5*** *p432*
Pieters, Aaron 26; New York, NY, 1847 ***3377.6*** *p14*
Pieters, Fredrika 23; New York, NY, 1847 ***3377.6*** *p14*
Pieters, Gerrit; New York, NY, 1847 ***3377.6*** *p14*
Pieters, Gerrit 28; New York, NY, 1847 ***3377.6*** *p14*
Pieters, John 60; New York, NY, 1847 ***3377.6*** *p14*
Pietila, John Henry; Washington, 1859-1920 ***2872.1*** *p31*
Pietrawicie, Joseph; Wisconsin, n.d. ***9675.7*** *p199*
Pietrini, . . .; Arkansas, 1918 ***95.2*** *p100*
Pietro, Cecconello; Iowa, 1866-1943 ***123.54*** *p39*
Pietrocerro, Domenick; Colorado, 1904 ***9678.2*** *p163*
Pietrowicz, . . .; New York, 1831 ***4606*** *p176*
Pietrowska, Barbara 40; New York, 1912 ***9980.29*** *p55*
Pietrzak, Maryanna Stammachak 27; New York, 1912 ***9980.29*** *p69*
Pietrzak, Stanislaw 9 mos; New York, 1912 ***9980.29*** *p69*
Pietzsch, Frederick H.; Indiana, 1882 ***2896.5*** *p31*
Pietzsoh, Euphrosine 62 *SEE* Pietzsoh, Gottl.
Pietzsoh, Gottl. 55; New Orleans, 1839 ***9420.2*** *p169*
*Wife:*Euphrosine 62
Pigat, Jose A. 25; America, 1838 ***778.5*** *p433*
Pigaud, G. 23; New Orleans, 1826 ***778.5*** *p433*
Pigeon, Andrew; New York, NY, 1816 ***2859.11*** *p40*
Pigeon, Frederic 25; America, 1839 ***778.5*** *p433*
Pigeon, Peter; Illinois, 1878 ***2896.5*** *p31*
Piggott, John Butler; Charleston, SC, 1768 ***1219.7*** *p137*
Pigion, Jon.; Virginia, 1636 ***6219*** *p32*
Pignigny, Mr. 44; America, 1838 ***778.5*** *p433*
Pigott, Mark; New York, NY, 1811 ***2859.11*** *p18*
Pigott, Robin; New York, NY, 1811 ***2859.11*** *p18*
Pigotti, Pitro; Arkansas, 1918 ***95.2*** *p100*
Piguet, Adrien 32; Kansas, 1884 ***5240.1*** *p65*
Pihlstrand, Justine; America, 1850-1859 ***6410.32*** *p124*
Pihon, John; Pennsylvania, 1900 ***7137*** *p169*
Pike, Francis Newell 47; California, 1872 ***2769.7*** *p6*
Pike, Jean; Quebec, 1822 ***7603*** *p28*
Pike, Margaret; Quebec, 1822 ***7603*** *p62*
Pike, Moses; New York, NY, 1835 ***8208.4*** *p45*
Piland, Alexandra *SEE* Piland, James
Piland, Alexandria; Virginia, 1642 ***6219*** *p197*
Piland, James; Virginia, 1642 ***6219*** *p197*
*Wife:*Alexandra
Piland, Joane; Virginia, 1642 ***6219*** *p197*
Pilat, Joe; Washington, 1859-1920 ***2872.1*** *p31*
Pilat, Rudolph; Washington, 1859-1920 ***2872.1*** *p31*
Pilborough, Daniel 14; Maryland or Virginia, 1719 ***3690.1*** *p178*
Pilcher, Heinrich Ernst; Kentucky, 1840 ***8582.3*** *p101*
Pilcher, M.; Nicaragua, 1856 ***8582.3*** *p31*
Pilcison, Charles; Iowa, 1866-1943 ***123.54*** *p39*
Pilger, Elizab. 30; America, 1854-1855 ***9162.6*** *p105*
Pilgerim, William; Kansas, 1902 ***5240.1*** *p34*
Pilgrim, Amos 16; Maryland, 1724 ***3690.1*** *p178*
Pilikos, James; Arkansas, 1918 ***95.2*** *p100*
Pilkin, Henry 25; Maryland, 1733 ***3690.1*** *p179*
Pilkington, Edward; New York, NY, 1815 ***2859.11*** *p40*
Pilkington, Edward 26; Maryland, 1724 ***3690.1*** *p179*
Pilkington, George; Arkansas, 1918 ***95.2*** *p100*
Pilkington, Margarett *SEE* Pilkington, William
Pilkington, Roland; Ohio, 1840 ***9892.11*** *p37*
Pilkington, Roland; Ohio, 1843 ***9892.11*** *p37*
Pilkington, William; Virginia, 1635 ***6219*** *p26*
*Wife:*Margarett
Pilkinton, Edward 26; Maryland, 1724 ***3690.1*** *p179*
Pillar, Charles 25; Baltimore, 1775 ***1219.7*** *p270*
Pillard, Benj.; Virginia, 1642 ***6219*** *p196*
Pillary, Jasper; Virginia, 1648 ***6219*** *p251*
Pillas, Mr. 35; America, 1823 ***778.5*** *p433*
Pillas, Mrs. 27; America, 1823 ***778.5*** *p433*
Pille, Friederich; America, 1844 ***8582.3*** *p52*
Pillegrim, Paul; Arkansas, 1918 ***95.2*** *p100*
Pillet, V. 35; Port uncertain, 1838 ***778.5*** *p433*
Pilliturі, Gabrielle 28; Arkansas, 1918 ***95.2*** *p100*
Pillot, C. 20; Port uncertain, 1837 ***778.5*** *p433*
Pillotier, J.B. 22; America, 1827 ***778.5*** *p433*
Pillow, Isidor 27; Arkansas, 1918 ***95.2*** *p100*
Piltz, August; Wisconsin, n.d. ***9675.7*** *p199*
Pilz, Julius 13; New Orleans, 1839 ***9420.2*** *p167*
Pim, Dorothy; Virginia, 1637 ***6219*** *p114*
Pimble, William 21; Jamaica, 1736 ***3690.1*** *p179*
Pimm, John; Jamaica, 1753 ***1219.7*** *p20*
Pimm, John 19; Jamaica, 1721 ***3690.1*** *p179*
Pinard, J.; Port uncertain, 1839 ***778.5*** *p433*
Pinard, John 33; America, 1832 ***778.5*** *p433*
Pinard, Pierre 20; America, 1836 ***778.5*** *p433*
Pinau, Mr. 25; America, 1839 ***778.5*** *p433*
Pinaud, John 33; New Orleans, 1830 ***778.5*** *p433*
Pinaud, Joseph 40; New Orleans, 1837 ***778.5*** *p52*
Pinaud, Louis; Port uncertain, 1829 ***778.5*** *p433*
Pinch, John 18; Windward Islands, 1722 ***3690.1*** *p179*
Pincher, Wm.; Virginia, 1635 ***6219*** *p33*
Pinches, Jon.; Virginia, 1635 ***6219*** *p35*
Pincier, v.; Quebec, 1776 ***9786*** *p105*
Pincier, Christian Theodore; Quebec, 1776 ***9786*** *p256*
Pincier, Theodore de; Canada, 1776-1783 ***9786*** *p233*
Pincock, John 27; Maryland, 1774 ***1219.7*** *p192*
Pinder, George 21; Maryland, 1775 ***1219.7*** *p254*
Pinder, Thomas 16; Maryland, 1775 ***1219.7*** *p273*
Pindleton, Thomas 15; Maryland or Virginia, 1720 ***3690.1*** *p179*
Pine, Clement; New York, 1819 ***9892.11*** *p37*
Pine, Jane; Quebec, 1850 ***5704.8*** *p66*
Pine, Margaret; Quebec, 1850 ***5704.8*** *p66*
Pineau, F. J. 34; Port uncertain, 1839 ***778.5*** *p434*
Pineau, Louis Rene 33; New Orleans, 1836 ***778.5*** *p434*
Pinecki, Pawel; New York, 1835 ***4606*** *p180*
Pinel, Philippe; Quebec, 1819 ***7603*** *p48*
Pinette, A. 64; Washington, 1918-1920 ***1728.5*** *p12*
Pinette, Sarah A. 63; Washington, 1918-1920 ***1728.5*** *p12*
Pinger, Adam; New Orleans, 1833 ***8582*** *p23*
Pinger, Christian; Cincinnati, 1840 ***8582*** *p23*
Pinion, William; Virginia, 1643 ***6219*** *p201*
Pinitti, Panacca; Iowa, 1866-1943 ***123.54*** *p73*
Pink, Edward 32; Virginia, 1774 ***1219.7*** *p244*
Pinkert, Charles; Wisconsin, n.d. ***9675.7*** *p199*
Pinkert, Johann Gotthelf; Wisconsin, n.d. ***9675.7*** *p199*
Pinkerton, James; New York, NY, 1811 ***2859.11*** *p18*
Pinkerton, John; New York, NY, 1837 ***8208.4*** *p54*
Pinkman, James; Montreal, 1818 ***7603*** *p72*
Pinkney, James; Virginia, 1635 ***6219*** *p26*
Pinkny, Michael 42; Nova Scotia, 1774 ***1219.7*** *p209*
Pinkston, Sarah; Virginia, 1698 ***2212*** *p15*
Pinkvoos, Louis Heinrich; America, 1848 ***8582.3*** *p52*
Pinner, James; Virginia, 1643 ***6219*** *p202*
Pinnock, William; Virginia, 1637 ***6219*** *p83*
Pinquet, Mr. 39; New Orleans, 1839 ***778.5*** *p434*
Pinsent, John 16; Philadelphia, 1774 ***1219.7*** *p182*
Pinte, Joseph 15; Maryland, 1774 ***1219.7*** *p192*
Pinto, August 42; Kansas, 1889 ***5240.1*** *p73*
Pio, Donoto; Arkansas, 1918 ***95.2*** *p100*
Piotrowska, Anton 23 *SEE* Piotrowska, Anton
Piotrowska, Anton 53; New York, 1912 ***9980.29*** *p57*
*Wife:*Josephine 55
*Son:*Anton 23
Piotrowska, Josephine 55 *SEE* Piotrowska, Anton
Piotrowski, Anton 23 *SEE* Piotrowski, Anton
Piotrowski, Anton 53; New York, 1912 ***9980.29*** *p57*
*Wife:*Josephine 55
*Son:*Anton 23
Piotrowski, Antoni; New York, 1835 ***4606*** *p180*
Piotrowski, Boleslow; Arkansas, 1918 ***95.2*** *p98*
Piotrowski, Boleslow; Arkansas, 1918 ***95.2*** *p100*
Piotrowski, Josephine 55 *SEE* Piotrowski, Anton
Piotrowski, Tytus; Mexico, 1831-1900 ***4606*** *p176*
Piotrowski, Tytus; New York, 1831 ***4606*** *p176*
Piowaty, Oskar; New York, NY, 1901 ***1450.2*** *p30B*
Piper, Edward 20; Jamaica, 1728 ***3690.1*** *p179*
Piper, Frank; Kansas, 1892 ***5240.1*** *p34*
Piper, Johannes; Georgia, 1742 ***8582.3*** *p97*
With parents
Piper, Jon.; Virginia, 1635 ***6219*** *p17*
Piper, Rebecca Ann 20; Philadelphia, 1857 ***5704.8*** *p132*
Piper, Samuel; New York, NY, 1811 ***2859.11*** *p18*
Piper, William 22; Philadelphia, 1833-1834 ***53.26*** *p77*
Pipes, Jonathan 20; North America, 1774 ***1219.7*** *p199*
Pipes, William 22; North America, 1774 ***1219.7*** *p199*
Pipes, William 49; North America, 1774 ***1219.7*** *p199*
Pipolo, Michael; Arkansas, 1918 ***95.2*** *p100*
Pipon, Captain; Quebec, 1815 ***9229.18*** *p80*
With wife
Pippert, Johannes; Philadelphia, 1779 ***8137*** *p12*
Pippin, Wm.; Virginia, 1638 ***6219*** *p124*
Piquet, . . .; Canada, 1776-1783 ***9786*** *p31*
Piquet, von; Quebec, 1778 ***9786*** *p167*
Piquet, Carl Friedrich von; Quebec, 1778 ***9786*** *p267*
Piquet, Chs. 38; Port uncertain, 1839 ***778.5*** *p434*
Piquette, . . .; Canada, 1776-1783 ***9786*** *p31*
Pirano, Gioseppe; Wisconsin, n.d. ***9675.7*** *p199*
Piraro, Guiseppe; Arkansas, 1918 ***95.2*** *p100*
Piratte, John; Iowa, 1866-1943 ***123.54*** *p39*
Pirel, P.; New Orleans, 1839 ***778.5*** *p434*
Pirgime, Marie 5; America, 1836 ***778.5*** *p434*
Pirgime, Marie 32; America, 1836 ***778.5*** *p434*
Pirnie, Duncan; New York, NY, 1836 ***8208.4*** *p21*
Piro, Joseph 23; Arkansas, 1918 ***95.2*** *p100*
Pirone, George; Arkansas, 1918 ***95.2*** *p100*
Pirotte, Arthur; Iowa, 1866-1943 ***123.54*** *p39*
Pirotte, Augustine; Iowa, 1866-1943 ***123.54*** *p73*
Pirotte, Camille; Iowa, 1866-1943 ***123.54*** *p39*
Pirotte, Felicie; Iowa, 1866-1943 ***123.54*** *p39*
Pirotte, Victor; Iowa, 1866-1943 ***123.54*** *p39*
Pirotte, Victor Emil; Iowa, 1866-1943 ***123.54*** *p39*
Pirotte, Victor Joseph; Iowa, 1866-1943 ***123.54*** *p39*
Pirrung, John N.; Wisconsin, n.d. ***9675.7*** *p199*
Pirsmane, Elizabeth 60; America, 1831 ***778.5*** *p434*
Piryouzak, John; Arkansas, 1918 ***95.2*** *p100*
Pisand, . . .; Canada, 1776-1783 ***9786*** *p31*
Piscand, . . .; Canada, 1776-1783 ***9786*** *p31*
Pise, Wm.; Virginia, 1635 ***6219*** *p69*
Piskadlo, Katarzyna 33; New York, 1912 ***9980.29*** *p66*
Piske, Charles; Illinois, 1860 ***5012.38*** *p97*
Pisnik, Antonia; America, 1897 ***7137*** *p169*
Pisnik, Peter; America, 1889 ***7137*** *p169*
Pistner, Christopher; America, 1836 ***8582.2*** *p31*
Pistner, Christopher; Baltimore, 1832-1836 ***8582.3*** *p52*
Pistole, Eliz.; Virginia, 1636 ***6219*** *p21*
Pistole, Robt.; Virginia, 1636 ***6219*** *p21*
Piston, Joseph; America, 1886 ***1450.2*** *p111A*
Pistor, Carl; America, 1851 ***8582.3*** *p52*
Pitaud, Auguste 22; New Orleans, 1823 ***778.5*** *p434*
Pitcher, Edward E.; America, 1865 ***5240.1*** *p34*
Pitcher, Thomas 20; Virginia, 1731 ***3690.1*** *p179*
Pitcherd, Thomas; Virginia, 1642 ***6219*** *p198*
Pitchford, Edwin; Colorado, 1897 ***9678.2*** *p163*
Pitchland, Isaac 15; Virginia, 1751 ***3690.1*** *p179*
Pitchlin, Isaac 15; Virginia, 1751 ***1219.7*** *p3*
Pitchton, Isaac 15; Virginia, 1751 ***3690.1*** *p179*
Pitkin, Thomas 15; New York, 1775 ***1219.7*** *p246*
Pitman, Peter; New York, NY, 1816 ***2859.11*** *p40*
Pitman, William 24; Maryland, 1774 ***1219.7*** *p229*
Pitschmann, George; New York, 1749 ***3652*** *p72*
Pitt, Edith; Pennsylvania, 1679 ***4961*** *p167*
Pitt, James 18; Canada, 1838 ***4535.12*** *p113*
Pitt, James 23; Philadelphia, 1775 ***1219.7*** *p255*
Pitt, Robert 29; Kansas, 1891 ***5240.1*** *p76*
Pitt, Stephen 15; Maryland, 1775 ***1219.7*** *p254*
Pitt, Thomas; Virginia, 1641 ***6219*** *p185*
Pitt, William; New York, NY, 1839 ***8208.4*** *p98*
Pittenger, Benjamin; Washington, 1859-1920 ***2872.1*** *p31*
Pittenger, Peter; Ohio, 1815 ***8582.1*** *p47*
Pittfield, Charles R.; New York, NY, 1837 ***8208.4*** *p33*
Pittigrew, James 28; Charleston, SC, 1774 ***1639.20*** *p262*
Pittlekan, August J.; Washington, 1859-1920 ***2872.1*** *p31*
Pittlekan, August Julius; Washington, 1859-1920 ***2872.1*** *p31*
Pitts, Edward; Virginia, 1628 ***6219*** *p31*
Pitts, Henry 20; Jamaica, 1729 ***3690.1*** *p179*
Pitts, Robert; Virginia, 1637 ***6219*** *p117*
Pitts, William 32; Maryland, 1775 ***1219.7*** *p249*
Pittway, Edward *SEE* Pittway, Robert
Pittway, Mary *SEE* Pittway, Robert
Pittway, Mary *SEE* Pittway, Robert
Pittway, Robert; Virginia, 1637 ***6219*** *p115*

Pittway, Robert; Virginia, 1638 ***6219*** *p147*
*Wife:*Mary
*Child:*Edward
*Child:*Mary
Pittway, Robert; Virginia, 1639 ***6219*** *p151*
Pittz, Andrear; Georgia, 1738 ***9332*** *p319*
Pitway, Edward *SEE* Pitway, Robert
Pitway, Mary *SEE* Pitway, Robert
Pitway, Mary *SEE* Pitway, Robert
Pitway, Robert; Virginia, 1638 ***6219*** *p147*
*Wife:*Mary
*Child:*Edward
*Child:*Mary
Pitwell, Robert; Virginia, 1636 ***6219*** *p77*
Pitz, Wm. O.; Virginia, 1856 ***4626.16*** *p16*
Pitzman, John Michael; New York, 1750 ***3652*** *p74*
Piuze, . . .; Canada, 1776-1783 ***9786*** *p43*
Pivetti, Amerigo; Iowa, 1866-1943 ***123.54*** *p39*
Piveyer, Samuel 22; Baltimore, 1775 ***1219.7*** *p270*
Piworska, Helena 18; New York, 1912 ***9980.29*** *p58*
Pix, Thomas 19; Pennsylvania, 1731 ***3690.1*** *p179*
Pixley, Benjamine; Virginia, 1639 ***6219*** *p161*
Place, Elizabeth Ward Boates *SEE* Place, James
Place, James; Virginia, 1636 ***6219*** *p75*
Place, James; Virginia, 1636 ***6219*** *p79*
*Wife:*Elizabeth Ward Boates
Place, James 22; Maryland, 1774 ***1219.7*** *p181*
Place, John; Virginia, 1636 ***6219*** *p26*
*Wife:*Mary
Place, Mary *SEE* Place, John
Plachy, Rudolph Charles; Arkansas, 1918 ***95.2*** *p100*
Plag, Adam; Ohio, 1867 ***6014.1*** *p3*
Plageman, Bernard; Virginia, 1856 ***4626.16*** *p16*
Plagemann, Christian; Wisconsin, n.d. ***9675.7*** *p199*
Plain, Perlin; Illinois, 1848 ***7857*** *p6*
Plain, Perlin; Illinois, 1850 ***7857*** *p6*
Plaine, Jean de la; Germantown, PA, 1684 ***2467.7*** *p5*
Plaine, Robert; Virginia, 1638 ***6219*** *p153*
Plaise, Margt 20; Pennsylvania, Virginia or Maryland, 1699 ***2212*** *p20*
Plakke, Gerad Henry; America, 1840 ***1450.2*** *p111A*
Planche, P. 23; New Orleans, 1839 ***778.5*** *p434*
Plane, George V.; Colorado, 1889 ***9678.2*** *p163*
Plank, Anthony; New Orleans, 1847 ***1450.2*** *p111A*
Plank, Susanna 49; America, 1897 ***1763*** *p40D*
Plant, George; New York, 1831 ***1450.2*** *p111A*
Plant, John; Arkansas, 1918 ***95.2*** *p100*
Plant, Rich.; Virginia, 1638 ***6219*** *p119*
Plant, William 58; New York, 1775 ***1219.7*** *p260*
Plantage, Evert Jan; Arkansas, 1918 ***95.2*** *p100*
Plantevigne, Aantonette 18; America, 1821 ***778.5*** *p434*
Plantevigne, Ant. 45; Louisiana, 1839 ***778.5*** *p434*
Plantevigne, Antoine 30; America, 1821 ***778.5*** *p435*
Plantevigne, J. 38; New Orleans, 1829 ***778.5*** *p435*
Plantvin, Mr. 20; New Orleans, 1822 ***778.5*** *p435*
Planzer, Louis; Arkansas, 1918 ***95.2*** *p100*
Plasse, . . .; Canada, 1776-1783 ***9786*** *p31*
Plassmeyer, Wilhelm Friedrich; America, 1890 ***4610.10*** *p123*
Plaszinsky, Czeslaw 19; New York, 1912 ***9980.29*** *p60*
Plaszynski, Czeslaw 19; New York, 1912 ***9980.29*** *p60*
Plate, . . .; Canada, 1776-1783 ***9786*** *p31*
Plate, Johan Jakop; Colorado, 1904 ***9678.2*** *p163*
Platel, Jean 40; America, 1838 ***778.5*** *p435*
Platenka, Frantisek; Arkansas, 1918 ***95.2*** *p100*
Platner, . . .; Canada, 1776-1783 ***9786*** *p31*
Platt, Edward; Quebec, 1764 ***7603*** *p95*
Platt, Gilbert; Virginia, 1635 ***6219*** *p26*
Platt, James 12; America, 1705-1706 ***2212*** *p45*
Platt, Jane 18; America, 1705-1706 ***2212*** *p45*
Platt, John; New York, NY, 1811 ***2859.11*** *p18*
Platt, John 17; Quebec, 1858 ***5704.8*** *p137*
Platt, John 21; Philadelphia, 1774 ***1219.7*** *p217*
Platt, Martha 14; America, 1705-1706 ***2212*** *p45*
Platt, Mary 23; America, 1703 ***2212*** *p40*
Platt, Richard 19; Pennsylvania, 1725 ***3690.1*** *p179*
Platt, Thomas 20; Maryland, 1774 ***1219.7*** *p214*
Platte, . . .; Canada, 1776-1783 ***9786*** *p31*
Platte, Friedrich; Halifax, N.S., 1778 ***9786*** *p270*
Platte, Friedrich; New York, 1776 ***9786*** *p270*
Platten, Jesse; Washington, 1859-1920 ***2872.1*** *p31*
Platter, Christian; Ohio, 1800 ***8582.2*** *p55*
Platz, . . .; Canada, 1776-1783 ***9786*** *p31*
Platz, Adam Nichs; Pennsylvania, 1752 ***4525*** *p236*
Platz, Anna Maria *SEE* Platz, Johann Jacob
Platz, Christina *SEE* Platz, Johann Jacob
Platz, Christina Rentz *SEE* Platz, Johann Jacob
Platz, Christoph *SEE* Platz, Johann Jacob
Platz, Frank 43?; Arizona, 1890 ***2764.35*** *p55*
Platz, Johann Jacob *SEE* Platz, Johann Jacob
Platz, Johann Jacob; Pennsylvania, 1751 ***2444*** *p200*
*Wife:*Christina Rentz
*Child:*Maria Barbara
*Child:*Christina
*Child:*Anna Maria
*Child:*Johann Jacob
*Child:*Johanna
*Child:*Christoph
*Child:*Maria Magdalena
*Child:*Martin
Platz, Johann Paul; Pennsylvania, 1753 ***4525*** *p236*
With 2 sons
Platz, Johann Paulus; Pennsylvania, 1752 ***4525*** *p236*
Platz, Johanna *SEE* Platz, Johann Jacob
Platz, Maria Barbara *SEE* Platz, Johann Jacob
Platz, Maria Magdalena *SEE* Platz, Johann Jacob
Platz, Martin *SEE* Platz, Johann Jacob
Platzer, Karl; Wisconsin, n.d. ***9675.7*** *p199*
Plauche, M. 33; America, 1836 ***778.5*** *p435*
Plauck, Jacob Albert; New Netherland, 1630-1646 ***8582.2*** *p51*
Plaus, Isabell; New York, NY, 1811 ***2859.11*** *p18*
Playstow, Ann, Sr.; Virginia, 1642 ***6219*** *p196*
Playstowe, Ann, Jr.; Virginia, 1642 ***6219*** *p196*
Pleas, Theobald; New York, NY, 1838 ***8208.4*** *p63*
Pleden, John 29; Maryland, 1774 ***1219.7*** *p204*
Pledge, Mary 21; Maryland, 1775 ***1219.7*** *p266*
Pledge, Nich.; Virginia, 1636 ***6219*** *p78*
Pleier, Dominic; Wisconsin, n.d. ***9675.7*** *p199*
Pleikken, Menne Albus; Illinois, 1869 ***7857*** *p6*
Plein, Peter; Wisconsin, n.d. ***9675.7*** *p199*
Pleiner, Anton; Illinois, 1896 ***5012.40*** *p55*
Pleisteiner, Johann; Cincinnati, 1869-1887 ***8582*** *p23*
Pleitner, Herman; Illinois, 1880 ***2896.5*** *p32*
Plenchenot, Mrs. 26; Port uncertain, 1838 ***778.5*** *p435*
Plenchenot, Leonie 9; Port uncertain, 1838 ***778.5*** *p435*
Plenchenot, Louis 9; Port uncertain, 1838 ***778.5*** *p435*
Plenchenot, M. 34; Port uncertain, 1838 ***778.5*** *p435*
Plenninger, Matheas; Pennsylvania, 1749 ***2444*** *p164*
Plenninger, Matheas; Pennsylvania, 1749 ***2444*** *p201*
Plenninger, Matheas; Pennsylvania, 1749 ***2444*** *p202*
Plenta, Charles; Arkansas, 1918 ***95.2*** *p100*
Plenta, Charles; Arkansas, 1918 ***95.2*** *p130*
Plentin, Jean 38; America, 1839 ***778.5*** *p435*
Plesec, Franz; Wisconsin, n.d. ***9675.7*** *p199*
Plesec, Jacob; Wisconsin, n.d. ***9675.7*** *p199*
Plesec, Stefan; Wisconsin, n.d. ***9675.7*** *p199*
Plesez, Anton; Wisconsin, n.d. ***9675.7*** *p199*
Plessen, von; Canada, 1776-1783 ***9786*** *p170*
Plessen, Leopold Franz Friedrich B.; Quebec, 1776 ***9786*** *p257*
Plessier, F. 22; Havana, 1826 ***778.5*** *p435*
Pletscher, Frederica; New York, 1763 ***3652*** *p89*
Pletter, Elisabeth Wassermann *SEE* Pletter, Johann
Pletter, Johann; Georgia, 1739 ***9332*** *p323*
*Wife:*Elisabeth Wassermann
Pletter, Johann; Georgia, 1739 ***9332*** *p327*
Pletter, John; Georgia, 1738 ***9332*** *p321*
Plettner, . . .; Canada, 1776-1783 ***9786*** *p31*
Plettner, Georg H.; America, 1848 ***8582.1*** *p27*
Pletts, Joseph 33; Kansas, 1892 ***5240.1*** *p77*
Pletzer, Joh. 78; Ontario, 1908 ***1763*** *p48D*
Pletzger, Christoph Heinrich *SEE* Pletzger, Johann Georg
Pletzger, Christoph Heinrich; Pennsylvania, 1752 ***2444*** *p200*
With parents
Pletzger, Johann Georg; Port uncertain, 1752 ***2444*** *p200*
*Wife:*Magdalena Catharina
*Child:*Christoph Heinrich
Pletzger, Magdalena Catharina *SEE* Pletzger, Johann Georg
Plewinski, . . .; New York, 1831 ***4606*** *p176*
Plewnia, Simon 45; California, 1872 ***2769.7*** *p6*
Plieninger, Catharina Hohlscheit *SEE* Plieninger, Matthaeus
Plieninger, Maria Barbara; Pennsylvania, 1753 ***2444*** *p161*
Plieninger, Matthaeus; Pennsylvania, 1749 ***2444*** *p201*
*Wife:*Catharina Hohlscheit
Pliffe, Edgar; Arkansas, 1918 ***95.2*** *p100*
Plilevard, J. 34; Port uncertain, 1835 ***778.5*** *p435*
Plinta, Karol; New York, 1831 ***4606*** *p176*
Ploch, Frederick; New York, 1881 ***1450.2*** *p30B*
Ploch, Fritz; Ohio, 1869-1887 ***8582*** *p23*
Ploch, Hartmann; Ohio, 1869-1887 ***8582*** *p23*
Ploch, John; America, 1850 ***1450.2*** *p111A*
Ploch, Kath. Leiser 82; America, 1902 ***1763*** *p48D*
Plocher, Michael; Pennsylvania, 1753 ***2444*** *p139*
Plock, Frederick; Illinois, 1859 ***5012.39*** *p54*
Ploeger, August; Wisconsin, n.d. ***9675.7*** *p199*
Ploeger, Christian Heinrich; America, 1853 ***4610.10*** *p116*
Ploeger, Friedrich August; America, 1854 ***4610.10*** *p116*
Ploeger, John; New York, NY, 1881 ***1450.2*** *p30B*
Ploger, Lorenz 39; America, 1888 ***4610.10*** *p107*
Plona, Otto; Arkansas, 1918 ***95.2*** *p100*
Plonkowska, Janina 6; New York, 1912 ***9980.29*** *p70*
Plonkowska, Josefa Redzinska 45; New York, 1912 ***9980.29*** *p70*
Plonkowska, Marianna 18; New York, 1912 ***9980.29*** *p70*
Plonkowska, Stanislawa 10; New York, 1912 ***9980.29*** *p70*
Plonkowski, Jan 16; New York, 1912 ***9980.29*** *p70*
Ploughman, John; New York, NY, 1815 ***2859.11*** *p40*
Ploughton, Alexander 27; Virginia, 1774 ***1219.7*** *p226*
Plowman, Edward; Virginia, 1638 ***6219*** *p18*
Plowman, Henry; America, 1867 ***1450.2*** *p111A*
Plowman, Jonathan 12; Virginia, 1700 ***2212*** *p33*
Pluche, M. 38; New Orleans, 1839 ***778.5*** *p435*
Plukker, Wesley; Illinois, 1870 ***7857*** *p6*
Plumann, Hermann Heinrich; Kentucky, 1843 ***8582.3*** *p97*
Plumb, Wm 16; America, 1699 ***2212*** *p29*
Plumber, John 33; Maryland, 1775 ***1219.7*** *p273*
Plumblye, Phillip; Virginia, 1638 ***6219*** *p150*
Plumblye, Phillipp; Virginia, 1638 ***6219*** *p117*
Plume, Frederick Wilhelm; West Virginia, 1856 ***9788.3*** *p4*
Plummer, Addison; Boston, 1854 ***6410.32*** *p123*
Plummer, Addison 44; Massachusetts, 1860 ***6410.32*** *p106*
Plummer, Bernard; Colorado, 1903 ***9678.2*** *p163*
Plummer, John; New York, NY, 1835 ***8208.4*** *p58*
Plummer, John; Virginia, 1642 ***6219*** *p196*
Plummer, Susan 45; Massachusetts, 1860 ***6410.32*** *p106*
Plunckett, James; Virginia, 1638 ***6219*** *p11*
Plunket, I.F. 6 mos; Massachusetts, 1850 ***5881.1*** *p81*
Plunket, John; New York, NY, 1865 ***5704.8*** *p193*
Plunket, Joseph 22; Massachusetts, 1850 ***5881.1*** *p81*
Plunkett, . . . 18; Tortola, 1773 ***1219.7*** *p172*
Plunkett, George; L'Assomption, Que., 1781 ***7603*** *p79*
Plunkett, Patrick; New York, NY, 1850 ***2896.5*** *p32*
Plunknett, Edward; Virginia, 1642 ***6219*** *p199*
Pluta, Albert; Arkansas, 1918 ***95.2*** *p100*
Poague, John; America, 1738 ***4971*** *p66*
Poaug, John; Charleston, SC, 1768 ***1219.7*** *p137*
Poche, F. 32; New Orleans, 1827 ***778.5*** *p435*
Pochet, Claude 40; New Orleans, 1838 ***778.5*** *p435*
Pochet, F. 30; Mexico, 1829 ***778.5*** *p436*
Pochon, Batiste 17; New Orleans, 1836 ***778.5*** *p436*
Pock, Herman; Washington, 1859-1920 ***2872.1*** *p31*
Pockock, John 19; Maryland, 1738 ***3690.1*** *p180*
Pocock, William 17; Jamaica, 1731 ***3690.1*** *p180*
Pocock, William 21; Maryland, 1775 ***1219.7*** *p272*
Pocuch, Mile; Arkansas, 1918 ***95.2*** *p101*
Pod, Thomas; Quebec, 1800 ***7603*** *p23*
Poddey, William 27; Pennsylvania, 1728 ***3690.1*** *p180*
Podosowski, . . .; New York, 1831 ***4606*** *p176*
Podvin, John 21; Maryland, 1774 ***1219.7*** *p206*
Poeboulet, Francoise 72; Port uncertain, 1839 ***778.5*** *p436*
Poehner, Adam; America, 1885 ***5240.1*** *p34*
Poehner, Adam 52; Kansas, 1887 ***5240.1*** *p69*
Poehner, John; America, 1885 ***5240.1*** *p34*
Poehner, John H.; Cincinnati, 1869-1887 ***8582*** *p23*
Poenisch, Barney 24; Kansas, 1879 ***5240.1*** *p60*
Poenitz, Robert F.; America, 1882 ***1450.2*** *p30B*
Poepp, Joerg; New England, 1766 ***4525*** *p237*
Poepp, Joerg; Pennsylvania, 1766 ***4525*** *p237*
Poeppel, Abraham; Ohio, 1798-1818 ***8582.2*** *p54*
Poeppelmann, Heinrich; Cincinnati, 1840-1841 ***8582.2*** *p52*
Poessoit, Jacques 23; New Orleans, 1821 ***778.5*** *p442*
Poetner, . . .; Canada, 1776-1783 ***9786*** *p31*
Poggemeyer, Anne Marie W. Engel; America, 1857 ***4610.10*** *p157*
Poggemeyer, Christian F. Wilhelm; America, 1850 ***4610.10*** *p155*
Poggemeyer, Heinrich Friedrich Wilhelm; America, 1846 ***4610.10*** *p155*
Poggemoller, . . .; Illinois, 1800-1900 ***4610.10*** *p67*
Poggemoller, Christian Friedrich; America, 1849 ***4610.10*** *p98*
Poggenburg, Christian; Wisconsin, n.d. ***9675.7*** *p199*
Poggendorf, John; Illinois, 1870 ***5012.38*** *p99*
Pogue, Alexander; New York, NY, 1816 ***2859.11*** *p40*
Pohemvau, Mr. 24; New Orleans, 1837 ***778.5*** *p436*
Pohle, Julius; Wisconsin, n.d. ***9675.7*** *p199*
Pohler, Henry; America, 1861 ***1450.2*** *p112A*
Pohlmayer, Theodor; America, 1845 ***8582.1*** *p27*
Pohlmeyer, Theodor; New York, NY, 1846 ***8582.1*** *p27*
Pohmeyer, Louise 20; America, 1869 ***4610.10*** *p113*
Poiasecz, Simon; Iowa, 1866-1943 ***123.54*** *p39*
Poiden, Rose; Virginia, 1643 ***6219*** *p200*
Poillian, Jean 38; Louisiana, 1820 ***778.5*** *p436*
Poillou, M. 48; America, 1836 ***778.5*** *p436*
Poincy, E. 6 mos; New Orleans, 1827 ***778.5*** *p436*
Pointeau, James; Virginia, 1637 ***6219*** *p29*
Pointel, Mr. 45; New Orleans, 1836 ***778.5*** *p436*
Poirier, Joseph; Montreal, 1709 ***4533*** *p128*
Poirson, Madame 40; America, 1835 ***778.5*** *p436*

Poisir, James 74; Arizona, 1921 ***9228.40*** *p25*
Poisley, Thomas; Virginia, 1652 ***6251*** *p19*
Poizer, Thomas; Mobile, AL, 1767 ***1219.7*** *p129*
Poklasni, Aloyis; Wisconsin, n.d. ***9675.7*** *p199*
Poklasni, Mathias; Wisconsin, n.d. ***9675.7*** *p199*
Poklasny, Louis; Wisconsin, n.d. ***9675.7*** *p199*
Pokrop, John; Arkansas, 1918 ***95.2*** *p101*
Pokryczynski, Stanislaw 48; New York, 1912 ***9980.29*** *p64*
Pol, Bernhard; California, 1866-1869 ***6410.22*** *p115*
Polallis, Nick; Arkansas, 1918 ***95.2*** *p101*
Poland, Charles; Philadelphia, 1848 ***2896.5*** *p32*
Poland, George; Washington, 1859-1920 ***2872.1*** *p31*
Poland, Penrigin; Virginia, 1642 ***6219*** *p199*
Poland, Peter; New York, NY, 1816 ***2859.11*** *p40*
Polden, Richard; Virginia, 1646 ***6219*** *p236*
Pole, W.; New York, NY, 1816 ***2859.11*** *p40*
Polegreen, George; New York, NY, 1838 ***8208.4*** *p85*
Polehromas, John; Arkansas, 1918 ***95.2*** *p101*
Poler, Quintin; Georgia, 1776 ***8582.2*** *p64*
Polesse, Mr. 28; New Orleans, 1830 ***778.5*** *p436*
Polet, Claude 32; Port uncertain, 1839 ***778.5*** *p436*
Poletes, Constantinos Peter; Arkansas, 1918 ***95.2*** *p101*
Polewheele, Wm.; Virginia, 1643 ***6219*** *p206*
Polfer, Mathias; Wisconsin, n.d. ***9675.7*** *p199*
Poli, Angelo; Iowa, 1866-1943 ***123.54*** *p39*
Poli, Attilio; Iowa, 1866-1943 ***123.54*** *p39*
Polic, Bonaventura; Iowa, 1866-1943 ***123.54*** *p39*
Polic, George; Iowa, 1866-1943 ***123.54*** *p39*
Polic, Pauval; Iowa, 1866-1943 ***123.54*** *p39*
Polic, Radoslav; Iowa, 1866-1943 ***123.54*** *p39*
Polic, Torrey; Iowa, 1866-1943 ***123.54*** *p40*
Polic, Vatroslav; Iowa, 1866-1943 ***123.54*** *p73*
Polich, Felix Srecko; Iowa, 1866-1943 ***123.54*** *p73*
Polich, Mary; Iowa, 1866-1943 ***123.54*** *p73*
Polich, Wazmoslav; Iowa, 1866-1943 ***123.54*** *p40*
Polichnik, Sebastian; Wisconsin, n.d. ***9675.7*** *p199*
Policius, L. 40; Kansas, 1906 ***5240.1*** *p84*
Polick, Bartol; Iowa, 1866-1943 ***123.54*** *p40*
Polijan, Josip; Iowa, 1866-1943 ***123.54*** *p73*
Polijan, Mary; Iowa, 1866-1943 ***123.54*** *p73*
Polijan, Marya; Iowa, 1866-1943 ***123.54*** *p73*
Polis, Felip; Iowa, 1866-1943 ***123.54*** *p40*
Polisch, Adolphus 10 *SEE* Polisch, John Gottl.
Polisch, Amelia Wilhelm 8 *SEE* Polisch, John Gottl.
Polisch, Augusta Thersa 3 *SEE* Polisch, John Gottl.
Polisch, Chas. Lovegod 11 *SEE* Polisch, John Gottl.
Polisch, Emma Mary 5 *SEE* Polisch, John Gottl.
Polisch, Ernestine 6 *SEE* Polisch, John Gottl.
Polisch, Jane Christa 32 *SEE* Polisch, John Gottl.
Polisch, John Gottl. 33; New Orleans, 1839 ***9420.2*** *p485*
*Wife:*Jane Christa 32
*Son:*Chas. Lovegod 11
*Child:*Adolphus 10
*Daughter:*Ernestine 6
*Daughter:*Emma Mary 5
*Daughter:*Augusta Thersa 3
*Daughter:*Amelia Wilhelm 8
Politsch, Henrich; Illinois, 1841 ***8582.2*** *p50*
Poljak, Andrevi; Iowa, 1866-1943 ***123.54*** *p40*
Polkowski, . . .; New York, 1831 ***4606*** *p176*
Poll, Peter; New York, NY, 1834 ***8208.4*** *p26*
Polla, Tony; Arkansas, 1918 ***95.2*** *p101*
Pollara, John; Arkansas, 1918 ***95.2*** *p101*
Pollard, John; Virginia, 1642 ***6219*** *p190*
Pollard, Michael; New York, NY, 1835 ***8208.4*** *p5*
Pollard, William 21; Virginia, 1699 ***2212*** *p27*
Pollard, William 28; Philadelphia, 1774 ***1219.7*** *p183*
Poller, Martin 18; New Orleans, 1838 ***778.5*** *p436*
Pollet, Robert; America, 1698 ***2212*** *p10*
Polli, Assinita 14; New York, NY, 1893 ***9026.4*** *p42*
Pollion, Mr. 14; America, 1837 ***778.5*** *p436*
Pollmacher, Frank; New York, NY, 1914 ***3455.2*** *p71*
Pollnitz, v., C.; Quebec, 1776 ***9786*** *p105*
Pollnitz, Julius Ludwig August; Quebec, 1776 ***9786*** *p256*
Pollock, Ann; Philadelphia, 1850 ***53.26*** *p77*
Pollock, Ann; Philadelphia, 1850 ***5704.8*** *p60*
Pollock, Annie; Quebec, 1852 ***5704.8*** *p98*
Pollock, Catherine; Philadelphia, 1852 ***5704.8*** *p85*
Pollock, David; America, 1829-1835 ***1450.2*** *p112A*
Pollock, David; New York, NY, 1840 ***8208.4*** *p103*
Pollock, Eliza; Quebec, 1852 ***5704.8*** *p97*
Pollock, Eliza 4; Quebec, 1847 ***5704.8*** *p6*
Pollock, Elleanor 5; Quebec, 1847 ***5704.8*** *p6*
Pollock, Frank; Arkansas, 1918 ***95.2*** *p101*
Pollock, Hamill; Baltimore, 1811 ***2859.11*** *p18*
Pollock, Hamilton 2; Quebec, 1847 ***5704.8*** *p6*
Pollock, James 6 mos; Quebec, 1847 ***5704.8*** *p6*
Pollock, James 9; Quebec, 1852 ***5704.8*** *p97*
Pollock, James 35; St. John, N.B., 1866 ***5704.8*** *p166*
Pollock, Jane; Quebec, 1852 ***5704.8*** *p98*
Pollock, John; New York, NY, 1816 ***2859.11*** *p40*
Pollock, John 8; Quebec, 1847 ***5704.8*** *p6*
Pollock, John 13; Quebec, 1852 ***5704.8*** *p97*
Pollock, Joseph 22; St. John, N.B., 1860 ***5704.8*** *p144*
Pollock, Mary; Philadelphia, 1849 ***53.26*** *p77*
Pollock, Mary; Philadelphia, 1849 ***5704.8*** *p54*
Pollock, Mary; Philadelphia, 1850 ***5704.8*** *p64*
Pollock, Mary 12; Philadelphia, 1850 ***5704.8*** *p64*
Pollock, Robert; Illinois, 1859 ***7857*** *p6*
Pollock, Robert; Philadelphia, 1850 ***5704.8*** *p64*
Pollock, Robert; Quebec, 1852 ***5704.8*** *p97*
Pollock, Samuel; New York, NY, 1811 ***2859.11*** *p18*
Pollock, Samuel; Quebec, 1847 ***5704.8*** *p6*
Pollock, Samuel 11; Quebec, 1852 ***5704.8*** *p97*
Pollock, Sarah Jane; Quebec, 1847 ***5704.8*** *p6*
Pollock, Susan; Philadelphia, 1851 ***5704.8*** *p71*
Pollock, Thomas; North Carolina, 1683-1722 ***1639.20*** *p263*
Pollock, Thomas; Philadelphia, 1849 ***53.26*** *p77*
Pollock, Thomas; Philadelphia, 1849 ***5704.8*** *p53*
Pollock, Thomas; West Indies, 1683 ***1639.20*** *p263*
Pollock, William; Carolina, 1706 ***1639.20*** *p263*
Pollock, William; New York, NY, 1811 ***2859.11*** *p18*
Pollock, William 7; Quebec, 1852 ***5704.8*** *p97*
Pollock, William 22; St. John, N.B., 1861 ***5704.8*** *p146*
Pollok, Sarah; Philadelphia, 1850 ***5704.8*** *p64*
Polly, Ebenezer 23; Antigua (Antego), 1728 ***3690.1*** *p180*
Polly, Isabella Jane 7; St. John, N.B., 1852 ***5704.8*** *p93*
Polly, James 1; St. John, N.B., 1852 ***5704.8*** *p93*
Polly, Mary; St. John, N.B., 1852 ***5704.8*** *p93*
Polly, William; St. John, N.B., 1852 ***5704.8*** *p93*
Polly, William 5; St. John, N.B., 1852 ***5704.8*** *p93*
Poloos-Van Amstel, John; Arkansas, 1918 ***95.2*** *p101*
Polovich, Jake; Arkansas, 1918 ***95.2*** *p101*
Polson, Frank; Iowa, 1866-1943 ***123.54*** *p40*
Polson, P. A.; Iowa, 1866-1943 ***123.54*** *p40*
Polson, Peter; Illinois, 1896 ***5012.40*** *p55*
Polson, Peter; Maine, 1882 ***6410.22*** *p125*
Polson, Peter; Maine, 1882-1884 ***6410.22*** *p118*
Polster, Carl Gottlob; Wisconsin, n.d. ***9675.7*** *p199*
Poltormann, Herman; Wisconsin, n.d. ***9675.7*** *p199*
Polts, John Fraugott 25; New Orleans, 1839 ***9420.2*** *p485*
Polusna, Anna 34; New York, 1912 ***9980.29*** *p62*
Pomarede, L. 23; America, 1832 ***778.5*** *p437*
Pomeditis, Domonic; Wisconsin, n.d. ***9675.7*** *p199*
Pomeriet, Mr. 20; America, 1837 ***778.5*** *p437*
Pomeroy, James; New York, NY, 1816 ***2859.11*** *p40*
Pomeroy, W. J.; Washington, 1859-1920 ***2872.1*** *p31*
Pomeroy, William J.; Washington, 1859-1920 ***2872.1*** *p31*
Pomery, Henry; Virginia, 1636 ***6219*** *p79*
Pomfrey, William 38; Maryland, 1775 ***1219.7*** *p259*
Pomlin, John 23; Maryland or Virginia, 1737 ***3690.1*** *p180*
Pommerening, August; New York, NY, 1878 ***1450.2*** *p30B*
Pommerle, G. 30; America, 1835 ***778.5*** *p437*
Pommier, Julius 34; Harris Co., TX, 1896 ***6254*** *p3*
Pomplitz, Frederick; Wisconsin, n.d. ***9675.7*** *p199*
Ponay, George 27; Maryland, 1774 ***1219.7*** *p206*
Poncejio, Tonto; Wisconsin, n.d. ***9675.7*** *p199*
Ponchak, Mike; New York, NY, 1902 ***9892.11*** *p37*
Ponciar, Haurent 25; Port uncertain, 1839 ***778.5*** *p437*
Pond, John; Virginia, 1643 ***6219*** *p203*
Ponder, Thomas; Virginia, 1638 ***6219*** *p8*
Poniatowski, . . .; New York, 1831 ***4606*** *p176*
Ponkonski, Welem; Wisconsin, n.d. ***9675.7*** *p199*
Ponkouski, Michael; Wisconsin, n.d. ***9675.7*** *p199*
Ponnier, Jean 30; New Orleans, 1838 ***778.5*** *p437*
Pons, Mr. 22; New Orleans, 1838 ***778.5*** *p437*
Pons, August 25; Port uncertain, 1836 ***778.5*** *p437*
Ponsetto, John; Iowa, 1866-1943 ***123.54*** *p40*
Ponsetto, Michel Pietro; Iowa, 1866-1943 ***123.54*** *p73*
Ponsetto, Michel Pietro; Iowa, 1866-1943 ***123.54*** *p75*
Ponsoh, Jos.; Virginia, 1647 ***6219*** *p248*
Ponsonby, John; America, 1737 ***4971*** *p13*
Ponsonby, Mary; America, 1739 ***4971*** *p14*
Pont, Noel 20; New Orleans, 1826 ***778.5*** *p437*
Ponte, Louis 47; America, 1825 ***778.5*** *p437*
Pontian, . . .; Virginia, 1648 ***6219*** *p252*
Pontier, Angelie 50; New Orleans, 1838 ***778.5*** *p437*
Pontius, Andreas; Ohio, 1799 ***8582.2*** *p54*
Pontius, Friederich; Ohio, 1798-1818 ***8582.2*** *p53*
Pontoch, P.; Washington, 1859-1920 ***2872.1*** *p31*
Poobjoy, Walter 16; Jamaica, 1729 ***3690.1*** *p180*
Pool, Hannah 24; Montreal, 1775 ***1219.7*** *p261*
Pool, Hugh; Wisconsin, n.d. ***9675.7*** *p199*
Poole Family ; Boston, 1840-1847 ***4914.15*** *p9*
Poole, George; Illinois, 1871 ***7857*** *p6*
Poole, Henry; Virginia, 1637 ***6219*** *p85*
Poole, Henry 21; Maryland, 1775 ***1219.7*** *p257*
Poole, John *SEE* Poole, Robert
Poole, John; Virginia, 1638 ***6219*** *p125*
Poole, John 17; Pennsylvania, 1728 ***3690.1*** *p180*
Poole, Richard; Virginia, 1634 ***6219*** *p32*
Poole, Robert; New York, NY, 1816 ***2859.11*** *p40*
Poole, Robert; Virginia, 1623-1627 ***6219*** *p25*
*Brother:*John
Poole, Robert; Virginia, 1627 ***6219*** *p25*
Poole, Robert; Virginia, 1642 ***6219*** *p194*
Poole, Tho.; Virginia, 1635 ***6219*** *p20*
Poole, Tho.; Virginia, 1646 ***6219*** *p240*
Poole, Thomas; San Francisco, 1850 ***4914.15*** *p10*
Poole, William; Illinois, 1841 ***7857*** *p6*
Pooler, John; New York, NY, 1811 ***2859.11*** *p18*
Poolkuznick, Lawrence; Wisconsin, n.d. ***9675.7*** *p199*
Pooly, Elianor; Virginia, 1600-1643 ***6219*** *p200*
Pooly, Jon.; Virginia, 1643 ***6219*** *p200*
Poor, James; Quebec, 1821 ***7603*** *p100*
Poor, Mathew; Quebec, 1822 ***7603*** *p100*
Poor, Richard; Quebec, 1821 ***7603*** *p79*
Poor, Thomas; Quebec, 1823 ***7603*** *p100*
Poorey, Ann; Virginia, 1648 ***6219*** *p251*
Pop, Bernhart; Pennsylvania, 1754 ***4525*** *p237*
*Relative:*Johan Georg
Pop, Johan Georg *SEE* Pop, Bernhart
Popavich, Nikola; Iowa, 1866-1943 ***123.54*** *p40*
Pope, Henry; Antigua (Antego), 1762 ***1219.7*** *p85*
Pope, Henry; New York, NY, 1840 ***8208.4*** *p110*
Pope, Henry; Quebec, 1815 ***9229.18*** *p82*
Pope, Henry Frederick; America, 1835 ***1450.2*** *p112A*
Pope, James C.; San Francisco, 1850 ***4914.15*** *p10*
Pope, John 14; Maryland, 1774 ***1219.7*** *p244*
Pope, John 21; Maryland, 1774 ***1219.7*** *p184*
Pope, R.; Quebec, 1815 ***9229.18*** *p82*
Pope, Tho.; Virginia, 1648 ***6219*** *p252*
Pope, Thomas 20; Virginia, 1700 ***2212*** *p30*
Pope, William 18; Maryland, 1774 ***1219.7*** *p236*
Popelka, Joseph; Wisconsin, n.d. ***9675.7*** *p199*
Popeplewell, Jon.; Virginia, 1635 ***6219*** *p17*
Popic, John; Iowa, 1866-1943 ***123.54*** *p40*
Popkin, Thomas; Virginia, 1621 ***6219*** *p24*
Poplawski, Teofil; Arkansas, 1918 ***95.2*** *p101*
Poplett, Elizabeth 28; Virginia, 1774 ***1219.7*** *p240*
Popovitz, John 25; Indiana, 1880 ***1450.2*** *p112A*
Popp, Anna Felicitas Merckle *SEE* Popp, Hans Jurg
Popp, Edward 28; Kansas, 1872 ***5240.1*** *p53*
Popp, Frederick; Kansas, 1871 ***5240.1*** *p35*
Popp, Fredrich 27; Kansas, 1876 ***5240.1*** *p57*
Popp, Friederick 27; Kansas, 1876 ***5240.1*** *p35*
Popp, Friedrich 54; Kansas, 1871 ***5240.1*** *p51*
Popp, Hans Joerg; Pennsylvania, 1768 ***4525*** *p236*
With child 14
With child 4
Popp, Hans Jurg; New York, 1717 ***3627*** *p9*
*Wife:*Anna Felicitas Merckle
Popp, John 43; Kansas, 1893 ***5240.1*** *p35*
Popp, John 43; Kansas, 1893 ***5240.1*** *p78*
Poppe, Gerhard Heinrich; America, 1831 ***4815.7*** *p92*
*Wife:*Marie Adelheid Muhle
With 2 children
Poppe, Marie Adelheid Muhle *SEE* Poppe, Gerhard Heinrich
Poppen, John; Illinois, 1905 ***5012.39*** *p54*
Poppensieker, Engel; America, 1844 ***4610.10*** *p134*
Poppie, Frank; Illinois, 1897-1974 ***3455.4*** *p94*
Poppie, Frank; New York, NY, 1901 ***3455.4*** *p93*
Poppity, Chrislieb 25; New Orleans, 1839 ***9420.1*** *p376*
Poppity, Christian 56; New Orleans, 1839 ***9420.1*** *p376*
Poppity, Maroa 22; New Orleans, 1839 ***9420.1*** *p376*
Poppity, Rosina 26; New Orleans, 1839 ***9420.1*** *p376*
Poppity, Sophie 53; New Orleans, 1839 ***9420.1*** *p376*
Poppity, William 17; New Orleans, 1839 ***9420.1*** *p376*
Poppitz, Fred E.; Wisconsin, n.d. ***9675.7*** *p199*
Poppler, Henriette 71; America, 1911 ***1763*** *p40D*
Popplewell, Richard; Pennsylvania, 1749 ***3652*** *p73*
Porbeck, F. von; Halifax, N.S., 1778 ***9786*** *p269*
Porbeck, F. von; New York, 1776 ***9786*** *p269*
Porche, Azema 28; Port uncertain, 1836 ***778.5*** *p437*
Porczynski, . . .; New York, 1831 ***4606*** *p176*
Poret, Auguste 20; New Orleans, 1838 ***778.5*** *p437*
Poret, Eleonore 36; New Orleans, 1838 ***778.5*** *p437*
Poret, Leopold 18; New Orleans, 1838 ***778.5*** *p437*
Poris, Mr. 24; Port uncertain, 1836 ***778.5*** *p437*
Porither, Marcus; Milwaukee, 1875 ***4719.30*** *p258*
Porko, Eenori; Washington, 1859-1920 ***2872.1*** *p32*
Porko, Helen; Washington, 1859-1920 ***2872.1*** *p32*
Porko, Hilga; Washington, 1859-1920 ***2872.1*** *p32*
Porko, Hilma; Washington, 1859-1920 ***2872.1*** *p32*
Porko, Ida; Washington, 1859-1920 ***2872.1*** *p32*
Porko, John; Washington, 1859-1920 ***2872.1*** *p5*
Porko, John; Washington, 1859-1920 ***2872.1*** *p32*
Porko, Julia; Washington, 1859-1920 ***2872.1*** *p32*
Porko, Tillie; Washington, 1859-1920 ***2872.1*** *p32*
Porles, August 23; Havana, 1831 ***778.5*** *p438*
Porn, Mr. 27; New Orleans, 1838 ***778.5*** *p438*
Porra, Joseph 40; South America, 1825 ***778.5*** *p438*
Porri, Gregor; Ohio, 1804 ***8582.1*** *p48*
Porris, Thomas 22; South Carolina, 1733 ***3690.1*** *p180*

Port, Mrs. 50; Port uncertain, 1836 ***778.5*** *p426*
Port, J. 37; Port uncertain, 1836 ***778.5*** *p426*
Port, John; Wisconsin, n.d. ***9675.7*** *p199*
Port, Nick; Wisconsin, n.d. ***9675.7*** *p199*
Port, Peter; Jamaica, 1750 ***3690.1*** *p180*
Port, Peter; Wisconsin, n.d. ***9675.7*** *p199*
Porta, Antonio; Colorado, 1904 ***9678.2*** *p164*
Porta, Ida 14; New York, NY, 1893 ***9026.4*** *p42*
Porta, John; Colorado, 1904 ***9678.2*** *p164*
Portaway, Abraham 18; South Carolina, 1733 ***3690.1*** *p180*
Porte, Peter; Jamaica, 1750 ***3690.1*** *p180*
Porter, Mrs. 52; New York, NY, 1893 ***9026.4*** *p42*
Porter, Aaron 19; Leeward Islands, 1729 ***3690.1*** *p180*
Porter, Aaron 19; Maryland, 1729 ***3690.1*** *p180*
Porter, Abby 10; Philadelphia, 1855 ***5704.8*** *p123*
Porter, Agnes 6 mos; Philadelphia, 1855 ***5704.8*** *p123*
Porter, Alexander; Philadelphia, 1853 ***5704.8*** *p102*
Porter, Alexander 8; Philadelphia, 1855 ***5704.8*** *p123*
Porter, Alexander 18 *SEE* Porter, John
Porter, Andrew; Ohio, 1844 ***9892.11*** *p37*
Porter, Ann; Baltimore, 1811 ***2859.11*** *p18*
Porter, Arthur Everette; Washington, 1859-1920 ***2872.1*** *p32*
Porter, Bell; Baltimore, 1811 ***2859.11*** *p18*
Porter, Bridget; St. John, N.B., 1851 ***5704.8*** *p78*
Porter, Catharine 18; South Carolina, 1733 ***3690.1*** *p181*
Porter, Catherine 17; St. John, N.B., 1862 ***5704.8*** *p150*
Porter, Catherine 22 *SEE* Porter, John
Porter, Daniel; St. John, N.B., 1848 ***5704.8*** *p47*
Porter, Daniel 11; St. John, N.B., 1848 ***5704.8*** *p47*
Porter, David; Philadelphia, 1851 ***5704.8*** *p80*
Porter, David; Quebec, 1849 ***5704.8*** *p51*
Porter, Edmd.; Virginia, 1642 ***6219*** *p198*
With wife
Porter, Edmd., Jr.; Virginia, 1642 ***6219*** *p198*
Porter, Edmond, Jr.; Virginia, 1639 ***6219*** *p157*
*Father:*Edmond, Sr.
Porter, Edmond, Sr. *SEE* Porter, Edmond, Jr.
Porter, Elitia 44 *SEE* Porter, John
Porter, Eliza; Quebec, 1851 ***5704.8*** *p73*
Porter, Elizabeth; Baltimore, 1811 ***2859.11*** *p18*
Porter, Elizabeth; Philadelphia, 1851 ***5704.8*** *p70*
Porter, Elizabeth; Philadelphia, 1870 ***5704.8*** *p239*
Porter, Elizabeth 32; Philadelphia, 1855 ***5704.8*** *p123*
Porter, Fanny; America, 1867 ***5704.8*** *p222*
Porter, George 5; Philadelphia, 1853 ***5704.8*** *p102*
Porter, H.H. 52; New York, NY, 1893 ***9026.4*** *p42*
Porter, Harvey; Philadelphia, 1850 ***53.26*** *p77*
Porter, Harvey; Philadelphia, 1850 ***5704.8*** *p60*
Porter, Henry; Virginia, 1640 ***6219*** *p182*
Porter, Henry 35; St. John, N.B., 1866 ***5704.8*** *p166*
Porter, Hugh; Baltimore, 1816 ***2859.11*** *p40*
With wife & 4 children
Porter, Hugh; Ohio, 1840 ***9892.11*** *p37*
Porter, Hugh; Ohio, 1842 ***9892.11*** *p37*
Porter, Hugh 24; Philadelphia, 1803 ***53.26*** *p77*
Porter, Isaac 36; Jamaica, 1733 ***3690.1*** *p181*
Porter, James; New York, NY, 1870 ***5704.8*** *p237*
Porter, James; Ohio, 1840 ***9892.11*** *p37*
Porter, James; St. John, N.B., 1848 ***5704.8*** *p47*
Porter, James; Virginia, 1643 ***6219*** *p206*
Porter, James 35; Philadelphia, 1804 ***53.26*** *p77*
Porter, Jesse; New York, NY, 1837 ***8208.4*** *p42*
Porter, John; Baltimore, 1811 ***2859.11*** *p18*
Porter, John; New York, NY, 1811 ***2859.11*** *p18*
Porter, John; Ohio, 1839 ***9892.11*** *p37*
Porter, John; Ohio, 1840 ***9892.11*** *p37*
Porter, John; Virginia, 1698 ***2212*** *p16*
Porter, John 7; St. John, N.B., 1848 ***5704.8*** *p47*
Porter, John 14; Philadelphia, 1855 ***5704.8*** *p123*
Porter, John 21; St. John, N.B., 1865 ***5704.8*** *p165*
Porter, John 43; Philadelphia, 1804 ***53.26*** *p77*
*Relative:*Elitia 44
*Relative:*Catherine 22
*Relative:*William 20
*Relative:*Alexander 18
Porter, Jon., Jr.; Virginia, 1642 ***6219*** *p198*
Porter, Jon., Sr.; Virginia, 1642 ***6219*** *p198*
Porter, Manassa; Virginia, 1642 ***6219*** *p198*
Porter, Margaret; New York, NY, 1868 ***5704.8*** *p227*
Porter, Margaret; Philadelphia, 1870 ***5704.8*** *p239*
Porter, Margaret 12; Philadelphia, 1855 ***5704.8*** *p123*
Porter, Margaret 18; St. John, N.B., 1854 ***5704.8*** *p122*
Porter, Maria; New York, NY, 1868 ***5704.8*** *p229*
Porter, Martha 6; Philadelphia, 1855 ***5704.8*** *p123*
Porter, Martha Jane 9 mos; Philadelphia, 1853 ***5704.8*** *p102*
Porter, Mary; New York, NY, 1869 ***5704.8*** *p233*
Porter, Mary; New York, NY, 1870 ***5704.8*** *p237*
Porter, Mary; St. John, N.B., 1851 ***5704.8*** *p80*
Porter, Mary Ann; Philadelphia, 1853 ***5704.8*** *p102*
Porter, Mary Ann 22; St. John, N.B., 1854 ***5704.8*** *p122*
Porter, Mary Eliza 12; Philadelphia, 1855 ***5704.8*** *p123*
Porter, Nancy; St. John, N.B., 1848 ***5704.8*** *p39*
Porter, Nancy 7; St. John, N.B., 1854 ***5704.8*** *p122*
Porter, Nicholas; Virginia, 1636 ***6219*** *p16*
Porter, Nicholas; Virginia, 1637 ***6219*** *p109*
Porter, Patrick 2; St. John, N.B., 1848 ***5704.8*** *p47*
Porter, Phillip 4; St. John, N.B., 1854 ***5704.8*** *p122*
Porter, Rachel; St. John, N.B., 1847 ***5704.8*** *p25*
Porter, Robert; Quebec, 1848 ***5704.8*** *p42*
Porter, Robert; Virginia, 1647 ***6219*** *p247*
Porter, Robert 40; Philadelphia, 1855 ***5704.8*** *p123*
Porter, Rosannah 9; St. John, N.B., 1848 ***5704.8*** *p47*
Porter, Rose Ann; Philadelphia, 1868 ***5704.8*** *p231*
Porter, Sally; St. John, N.B., 1848 ***5704.8*** *p47*
Porter, Samuel; New York, NY, 1839 ***8208.4*** *p98*
Porter, Samuel; Ohio, 1847 ***9892.11*** *p37*
Porter, Samuel; St. John, N.B., 1847 ***5704.8*** *p33*
Porter, Samuel 20; Quebec, 1857 ***5704.8*** *p136*
Porter, Sandy; Quebec, 1850 ***5704.8*** *p63*
Porter, Sarah; New York, NY, 1870 ***5704.8*** *p237*
Porter, Sarah 19; Quebec, 1856 ***5704.8*** *p130*
Porter, Sarah Maria 2; Philadelphia, 1853 ***5704.8*** *p102*
Porter, Susan; St. John, N.B., 1848 ***5704.8*** *p47*
Porter, Susan 5; St. John, N.B., 1848 ***5704.8*** *p47*
Porter, Thomas; Baltimore, 1811 ***2859.11*** *p18*
Porter, Thomas 17; Maryland, 1724 ***3690.1*** *p181*
Porter, William; New York, NY, 1811 ***2859.11*** *p18*
Porter, William; New York, NY, 1839 ***8208.4*** *p100*
Porter, William; New York, NY, 1868 ***5704.8*** *p229*
Porter, William; Philadelphia, 1847 ***53.26*** *p77*
Porter, William; Philadelphia, 1847 ***5704.8*** *p31*
Porter, William 8; Philadelphia, 1853 ***5704.8*** *p102*
Porter, William 10; Philadelphia, 1855 ***5704.8*** *p123*
Porter, William 13; St. John, N.B., 1848 ***5704.8*** *p47*
Porter, William 18; St. John, N.B., 1853 ***5704.8*** *p110*
Porter, William 20 *SEE* Porter, John
Porter, William 20; Wilmington, DE, 1831 ***6508.7*** *p160*
Porterfield, Fanny; St. John, N.B., 1847 ***5704.8*** *p20*
Porteus, Alexander 3; Quebec, 1862 ***5704.8*** *p151*
Porteus, Margaret 1; Quebec, 1862 ***5704.8*** *p151*
Porteus, Margaret 25; Quebec, 1862 ***5704.8*** *p151*
Porteus, Simon 49; Georgia, 1775 ***1219.7*** *p276*
Porth, . . .; Canada, 1776-1783 ***9786*** *p31*
Portier, Carl Eberhard; America, 1848 ***8582.3*** *p52*
Portier, J. M. 25; Mobile, AL, 1837 ***778.5*** *p438*
Portman, Frank 29; West Virginia, 1898 ***9788.3*** *p19*
Portmann, Frank 33; West Virginia, 1903 ***9788.3*** *p19*
Portner, F.; Ohio, 1849 ***8582.1*** *p48*
Portram, Guilaume 28; America, 1838 ***778.5*** *p438*
Portsmouth, William; Carolina, 1756 ***1219.7*** *p45*
Portz, Mr. 48; America, 1839 ***778.5*** *p438*
Portzhut, Frederick; New York, NY, 1851 ***1450.2*** *p17A*
Porzelius, Adolph 30; Kansas, 1884 ***5240.1*** *p65*
Posch, Anton 44; Kansas, 1904 ***5240.1*** *p83*
Posch, Charles 38; Kansas, 1898 ***5240.1*** *p35*
Posch, Charles 38; Kansas, 1898 ***5240.1*** *p81*
Poser, . . .; Canada, 1776-1783 ***9786*** *p31*
Poser, Jean Georges; Canada, 1776-1783 ***9786*** *p237*
Posey, Fr.; Virginia, 1637 ***6219*** *p11*
Posit, Pierre 30; America, 1836 ***778.5*** *p438*
Poskin, Auguste; Iroquois Co., IL, 1894 ***3455.1*** *p12*
Posnanska, Bertha 11 mos; New York, NY, 1878 ***9253*** *p47*
Posnanska, Herman 7; New York, NY, 1878 ***9253*** *p47*
Posnanska, Pauline 4; New York, NY, 1878 ***9253*** *p47*
Posnanska, Theophilia 30; New York, NY, 1878 ***9253*** *p47*
Posse, Mr. 67; Port uncertain, 1835 ***778.5*** *p438*
Possell, Wm.; Virginia, 1635 ***6219*** *p73*
Possin, Rich.; Virginia, 1635 ***6219*** *p35*
Post, . . .; America, 1700-1877 ***8582.3*** *p80*
Post, Christian F.; Philadelphia, 1742 ***3652*** *p55*
Post, Christian Frederick; New York, 1754 ***3652*** *p80*
Post, Frederick; Philadelphia, 1760 ***9973.7*** *p35*
Post, John; Illinois, 1854 ***7857*** *p6*
Post, John B.; Cincinnati, 1869-1887 ***8582*** *p23*
Postel, John; New York, NY, 1832 ***8582*** *p23*
Postel, Karl; America, 1823-1826 ***8582.1*** *p44*
Posthous, John; Virginia, 1698 ***2212*** *p16*
Postilli, Augusto; Arkansas, 1918 ***95.2*** *p101*
Postlewaite, Mr.; Quebec, 1815 ***9229.18*** *p77*
Postol, Harry George; Arkansas, 1918 ***95.2*** *p101*
Poston, Henry 20; West Indies, 1722 ***3690.1*** *p181*
Poston, Jno 17; America, 1703 ***2212*** *p39*
Poszkus, Anton Josef; Arkansas, 1918 ***95.2*** *p101*
Poszkus, Charles; Wisconsin, n.d. ***9675.7*** *p199*
Poszkus, Nicholas; Wisconsin, n.d. ***9675.7*** *p199*
Potberg, Fritz 32; Kansas, 1888 ***5240.1*** *p71*
Poteete, Ann *SEE* Poteete, John
Poteete, John; Virginia, 1639 ***6219*** *p155*
*Wife:*Ann
Potenberg, Charles F.; America, 1871 ***1450.2*** *p112A*
Potery, Ann; Virginia, 1642 ***6219*** *p197*
Potet, Mr. 29; New Orleans, 1836 ***778.5*** *p438*
Potete, John 22; Jamaica, 1730 ***3690.1*** *p181*
Pothst, August; America, 1855 ***1450.2*** *p112A*
Potier, Mrs. 28; Louisiana, 1820 ***778.5*** *p438*
Potier, Charles 35; Louisiana, 1820 ***778.5*** *p438*
Potos, Mike; Arkansas, 1918 ***95.2*** *p101*
Potron, L. D. 28; New Orleans, 1837 ***778.5*** *p438*
Pott, John; Philadelphia, 1759 ***9973.7*** *p34*
Pott, John; Virginia, 1624 ***6219*** *p24*
Pott, John; Virginia, 1646 ***6219*** *p246*
Pottage, Benjamin; Philadelphia, 1820 ***1450.2*** *p112A*
Potteete, Georg; Virginia, 1640 ***6219*** *p160*
Potten, John; Havana, 1765 ***1219.7*** *p107*
Potter, Baldwin; America, 1739 ***4971*** *p36*
Potter, David; Illinois, 1843 ***7857*** *p6*
Potter, E. W.; Washington, 1859-1920 ***2872.1*** *p32*
Potter, Eliza.; Virginia, 1644 ***6219*** *p231*
Potter, Elizabeth; Virginia, 1648 ***6219*** *p246*
Potter, George; Washington, 1859-1920 ***2872.1*** *p32*
Potter, Herbert Ero 29; Harris Co., TX, 1899 ***6254*** *p5*
Potter, John; Virginia, 1635 ***6219*** *p4*
Potter, John; Virginia, 1638 ***6219*** *p2*
Potter, John; Virginia, 1638 ***6219*** *p150*
Potter, John 18; Maryland, 1719 ***3690.1*** *p181*
Potter, Phillip; Illinois, 1845 ***7857*** *p6*
Potter, Richard 50; Massachusetts, 1850 ***5881.1*** *p81*
Potter, Samuel, Jr.; New York, NY, 1839 ***8208.4*** *p102*
Potter, Thomas 21; Virginia, 1774 ***1219.7*** *p201*
Potter, Thomas 30; California, 1873 ***2769.10*** *p5*
Potter, William 17; Maryland, 1724 ***3690.1*** *p181*
Potterell, George 17; Jamaica, 1733 ***3690.1*** *p181*
Pottinger, James; Ticonderoga, NY, 1764 ***1219.7*** *p99*
Pottinger, James 15; Philadelphia, 1774 ***1219.7*** *p233*
Potts, John C.; New York, NY, 1839 ***8208.4*** *p99*
Potts, Robert; New York, NY, 1811 ***2859.11*** *p18*
With family
Potts, Robert; New York, NY, 1838 ***8208.4*** *p85*
Potts, Thomas; America, 1740 ***4971*** *p26*
Potts, Wade Hampton 49; California, 1872 ***2769.7*** *p6*
Potts, Walter 25; Philadelphia, 1803 ***53.26*** *p77*
Potukord, Stanislaw; Arkansas, 1918 ***95.2*** *p101*
Potzsoh, Ernestine 21; New Orleans, 1839 ***9420.2*** *p168*
Potzsohin, Auguste 31; New Orleans, 1839 ***9420.2*** *p166*
Pouan, Bd. 32; Havana, 1839 ***778.5*** *p246*
Poucel, Antoine 33; New Orleans, 1823 ***778.5*** *p438*
Pouchet, Arnaud 4; America, 1838 ***778.5*** *p439*
Pouchet, Arnaud 38; America, 1838 ***778.5*** *p438*
Pouchet, Mary 5; America, 1838 ***778.5*** *p439*
Pouchet, Verginia 30; America, 1838 ***778.5*** *p439*
Poucin, Mr.; Port uncertain, 1839 ***778.5*** *p439*
Poucy, Ann; Quebec, 1787 ***7603*** *p79*
Pouger, Jos; Philadelphia, 1754 ***2444*** *p140*
Pouget, F. 35; America, 1838 ***778.5*** *p439*
Pouget, Francois 29; America, 1837 ***778.5*** *p439*
Pouicki, Marguerite 60; Port uncertain, 1839 ***778.5*** *p439*
Pouicki, Michel 19; Port uncertain, 1839 ***778.5*** *p439*
Pouicki, Pierre 55; Port uncertain, 1839 ***778.5*** *p439*
Pouicki, Valentin 17; Port uncertain, 1839 ***778.5*** *p439*
Pouilley, Mr. 45; New Orleans, 1837 ***778.5*** *p439*
Pouillot, Mr. 7; America, 1831 ***778.5*** *p439*
Pouillot, Mr. 10; America, 1831 ***778.5*** *p439*
Pouillot, Jules 36; America, 1831 ***778.5*** *p439*
Poulain, A. 32; New Orleans, 1823 ***778.5*** *p439*
Poulain, Augustin; New Orleans, 1829 ***778.5*** *p440*
Poulat, Mathurin 41; Port uncertain, 1836 ***778.5*** *p440*
Poulet, Mr. 28; Port uncertain, 1836 ***778.5*** *p440*
Poulet, Jean 24; America, 1838 ***778.5*** *p440*
Pouletich, Robpetch; Iowa, 1866-1943 ***123.54*** *p40*
Poulioglou, Stavpos; Arkansas, 1918 ***95.2*** *p101*
Poull, Peter; Wisconsin, n.d. ***9675.7*** *p199*
Poullail, Mr. 32; New Orleans, 1822 ***778.5*** *p440*
Poullault, P. 26; Louisiana, 1826 ***778.5*** *p440*
Poulopoulos, James Stephen; Arkansas, 1918 ***95.2*** *p101*
Poulot, Leopold 22; New Orleans, 1822 ***778.5*** *p440*
Poulsen, Adolph; Arkansas, 1918 ***95.2*** *p101*
Poulter, Abraham 19; Jamaica, 1723 ***3690.1*** *p181*
Poulter, Henry 16; Port uncertain, 1849 ***4535.10*** *p198*
Poulter, Samuel 39; Virginia, 1774 ***1219.7*** *p238*
Poulton, Wm.; Virginia, 1643 ***6219*** *p199*
Poumos, Pausia 40; New Orleans, 1829 ***778.5*** *p440*
Pouncheval, E. 26; America, 1838 ***778.5*** *p440*
Pound, Edward 19; Maryland, 1774 ***1219.7*** *p204*
Pound, Edward 32; Maryland, 1774 ***1219.7*** *p187*
Pound, Susanna; Virginia, 1698 ***2212*** *p16*
Poupart, Mr.; America, 1839 ***778.5*** *p440*
Poupenee, Jeanne 25; Port uncertain, 1839 ***778.5*** *p440*
Poupenee, Marie 2; Port uncertain, 1839 ***778.5*** *p440*
Pousko, Bartelmes; Wisconsin, n.d. ***9675.7*** *p199*
Poussardin, John; New Orleans, 1832 ***2896.5*** *p32*
Poussin, Mr. 24; Port uncertain, 1839 ***778.5*** *p440*
Poussin, Joseph 30; New Orleans, 1826 ***778.5*** *p440*
Poussoir, Jacques 26; America, 1827 ***778.5*** *p440*
Povey, James 29; Philadelphia, 1774 ***1219.7*** *p237*

Povey, John; Virginia, 1643 ***6219*** *p229*
Povey, Thomas 31; Jamaica, 1730 ***3690.1*** *p181*
Povis, Mr. 24; Port uncertain, 1836 ***778.5*** *p437*
Povy, William; Virginia, 1638 ***6219*** *p146*
Powell, Ann; Virginia, 1635 ***6219*** *p26*
Powell, Ann; Virginia, 1637 ***6219*** *p83*
Powell, Ann; Virginia, 1642 ***6219*** *p189*
Powell, Ann 21; Baltimore, 1775 ***1219.7*** *p271*
Powell, Anne; Virginia, 1645 ***6219*** *p232*
Powell, Bridget; Philadelphia, 1867 ***5704.8*** *p217*
Powell, David; Virginia, 1640 ***6219*** *p183*
Powell, Edmund 19; Jamaica, 1730 ***3690.1*** *p181*
Powell, Eliza; Philadelphia, 1867 ***5704.8*** *p217*
Powell, Eliza 10; Philadelphia, 1867 ***5704.8*** *p217*
Powell, Ellen; Philadelphia, 1867 ***5704.8*** *p217*
Powell, Ellen; Virginia, 1642 ***6219*** *p188*
Powell, George 18; Pennsylvania, 1722 ***3690.1*** *p181*
Powell, George 25; Jamaica, 1727 ***3690.1*** *p181*
Powell, H. J.; Washington, 1859-1920 ***2872.1*** *p32*
Powell, Hen.; Virginia, 1635 ***6219*** *p70*
Powell, Hen.; Virginia, 1637 ***6219*** *p114*
Powell, Henry; Virginia, 1637 ***6219*** *p86*
Powell, Henry; Virginia, 1640 ***6219*** *p185*
Powell, Henry 21; Newfoundland, 1699-1700 ***2212*** *p18*
Powell, Howell; Virginia, 1642 ***6219*** *p198*
Powell, Hugh; America, 1698 ***2212*** *p5*
Powell, Hugh; Philadelphia, 1771 ***1219.7*** *p151*
Powell, Hugh; Virginia, 1635 ***6219*** *p71*
Powell, James; Maryland, 1755 ***1219.7*** *p37*
Powell, James; New York, NY, 1838 ***8208.4*** *p81*
Powell, James 21; Maryland, 1774 ***1219.7*** *p225*
Powell, James 22; Maryland, 1774 ***1219.7*** *p221*
Powell, Jo.; Virginia, 1652 ***6251*** *p19*
Powell, Job; Detroit, 1858 ***1450.2*** *p112A*
Powell, John; Iowa, 1866-1943 ***123.54*** *p40*
Powell, John; Ohio, 1840 ***9892.11*** *p37*
Powell, John; Virginia, 1624 ***6219*** *p24*
Powell, John; Virginia, 1636 ***6219*** *p78*
Powell, John; Virginia, 1642 ***6219*** *p196*
Powell, John; Virginia, 1644 ***6219*** *p231*
Powell, John; Virginia, 1648 ***6219*** *p246*
Powell, John 20; Pennsylvania, 1728 ***3690.1*** *p182*
Powell, John 25; Jamaica, 1775 ***1219.7*** *p278*
Powell, John 36; Virginia, 1774 ***1219.7*** *p186*
Powell, Jon.; Virginia, 1636 ***6219*** *p75*
Powell, Jon.; Virginia, 1637 ***6219*** *p82*
Powell, Joseph; Philadelphia, 1742 ***3652*** *p55*
*Wife:*Martha
Powell, Joseph 25; Maryland, 1773 ***1219.7*** *p173*
Powell, Lydia 21; Philadelphia, 1774 ***1219.7*** *p182*
Powell, Madelew; Virginia, 1646 ***6219*** *p240*
Powell, Margaret; Virginia, 1636 ***6219*** *p80*
Powell, Margaret 22; Massachusetts, 1850 ***5881.1*** *p81*
Powell, Margarett; Virginia, 1639 ***6219*** *p161*
Powell, Martha *SEE* Powell, Joseph
Powell, Martha *SEE* Powell, Samuel
Powell, Mary; Philadelphia, 1867 ***5704.8*** *p217*
Powell, Mary 6; Massachusetts, 1848 ***5881.1*** *p81*
Powell, Mary 33; Jamaica, 1774 ***1219.7*** *p237*
Powell, Penelope 23; Maryland, 1775 ***1219.7*** *p249*
Powell, Phi.; Virginia, 1635 ***6219*** *p20*
Powell, Phillipp; Virginia, 1637 ***6219*** *p112*
Powell, Ratl.; Virginia, 1645 ***6219*** *p233*
Powell, Rich.; Virginia, 1635 ***6219*** *p35*
Powell, Rich.; Virginia, 1637 ***6219*** *p114*
Powell, Richard; America, 1736-1743 ***4971*** *p57*
Powell, Richard; Virginia, 1635 ***6219*** *p69*
Powell, Richard; Virginia, 1642 ***6219*** *p188*
Powell, Richard 19; Jamaica, 1731 ***3690.1*** *p182*
Powell, Richard 21; Maryland, 1774 ***1219.7*** *p178*
Powell, Robert; Virginia, 1639 ***6219*** *p156*
Powell, Robert; Virginia, 1642 ***6219*** *p186*
Powell, Robt.; Virginia, 1638 ***6219*** *p119*
Powell, Robt 20; America, 1699 ***2212*** *p20*
Powell, Sallie 6; Philadelphia, 1867 ***5704.8*** *p217*
Powell, Samuel; Philadelphia, 1742 ***3652*** *p55*
*Wife:*Martha
Powell, Samuel; Virginia, 1637 ***6219*** *p110*
Powell, Sarah 21; Maryland, 1775 ***1219.7*** *p262*
Powell, T. L.; Washington, 1859-1920 ***2872.1*** *p32*
Powell, Tho; America, 1698 ***2212*** *p6*
Powell, Tho.; Virginia, 1635 ***6219*** *p70*
Powell, Tho.; Virginia, 1637 ***6219*** *p180*
Powell, Thomas; Jamaica, 1766 ***1219.7*** *p119*
Powell, Thomas; New York, NY, 1836 ***8208.4*** *p14*
Powell, Thomas; Virginia, 1636 ***6219*** *p78*
Powell, Thomas; Virginia, 1637 ***6219*** *p111*
Powell, Walter; Virginia, 1643 ***6219*** *p200*
Powell, William; Illinois, 1847 ***7857*** *p6*
Powell, William; Virginia, 1639 ***6219*** *p153*
Powell, William; Virginia, 1639 ***6219*** *p155*
Powell, William; Virginia, 1639 ***6219*** *p161*
Powell, William; Virginia, 1643 ***6219*** *p202*
Powell, William 15; Philadelphia, 1774 ***1219.7*** *p182*
Powell, William 18; Maryland, 1733 ***3690.1*** *p182*
Powelson, H. H.; Washington, 1859-1920 ***2872.1*** *p32*
Power, Mrs.; Quebec, 1815 ***9229.18*** *p76*
Power, Alice 20; Massachusetts, 1849 ***5881.1*** *p80*
Power, Andrew 15; Maryland, 1775 ***1219.7*** *p272*
Power, Ann; Quebec, 1787 ***7603*** *p79*
Power, Ann 6; Massachusetts, 1849 ***5881.1*** *p80*
Power, Ann 30; Massachusetts, 1849 ***5881.1*** *p80*
Power, Bridget; Montreal, 1824 ***7603*** *p87*
Power, Catherine; South Carolina, 1767 ***1639.20*** *p263*
Power, Daniel; Montreal, 1824 ***7603*** *p98*
Power, David; America, 1741-1742 ***4971*** *p60*
Power, Edmond; America, 1736-1743 ***4971*** *p57*
Power, Edmond; America, 1739 ***4971*** *p53*
Power, Ellinor; America, 1737 ***4971*** *p38*
Power, Guillaume; Quebec, 1818 ***7603*** *p100*
Power, Inocent; Virginia, 1622 ***6219*** *p4*
Power, James; Montreal, 1825 ***7603*** *p102*
Power, James 8; Massachusetts, 1849 ***5881.1*** *p81*
Power, Johanna; Quebec, 1823 ***7603*** *p101*
Power, John; America, 1742 ***4971*** *p94*
Power, John; America, 1743 ***4971*** *p86*
Power, John; Montreal, 1811 ***7603*** *p66*
Power, John; New York, NY, 1834 ***8208.4*** *p4*
Power, John; New York, NY, 1839 ***8208.4*** *p100*
Power, John; Quebec, 1797 ***7603*** *p70*
Power, Martin; Quebec, 1811 ***7603*** *p100*
Power, Mary 20; Massachusetts, 1849 ***5881.1*** *p81*
Power, Mary 60; Massachusetts, 1850 ***5881.1*** *p81*
Power, Maurice; New York, NY, 1815 ***2859.11*** *p40*
Power, Michael; New York, NY, 1838 ***8208.4*** *p62*
Power, Richard; America, 1741 ***4971*** *p59*
Power, Richard; Quebec, 1821 ***7603*** *p79*
Power, Thomas; Wisconsin, n.d. ***9675.7*** *p199*
Power, William 18; Philadelphia, 1774 ***1219.7*** *p228*
Power, William 24; Maryland, 1775 ***1219.7*** *p259*
Powers, Ann; Massachusetts, 1847 ***5881.1*** *p80*
Powers, Bridget 20; Massachusetts, 1850 ***5881.1*** *p80*
Powers, Catharine 14; Massachusetts, 1847 ***5881.1*** *p81*
Powers, Francis Edward; New York, NY, 1835 ***8208.4*** *p28*
Powers, Gregor; Ohio, 1804 ***8582.1*** *p48*
Powers, Jeffery; Virginia, 1638 ***6219*** *p120*
Powers, John 35; Massachusetts, 1850 ***5881.1*** *p81*
Powers, John 40; Philadelphia, 1853 ***5704.8*** *p109*
Powers, Mary 9; Massachusetts, 1850 ***5881.1*** *p81*
Powers, P.M.; Colorado, 1904 ***9678.2*** *p164*
Powers, Thomas; New London, CT, 1847 ***1450.2*** *p112A*
Powers, W.P. 21; Harris Co., TX, 1898 ***6254*** *p4*
Powett, Richard; Virginia, 1642 ***6219*** *p188*
Powis, Joseph 20; Pennsylvania, 1730 ***3690.1*** *p182*
Powis, Richard; New York, NY, 1834 ***8208.4*** *p26*
Powis, Thos.; Virginia, 1628 ***6219*** *p9*
Powley, Charles J.; Illinois, 1890 ***2896.5*** *p32*
Powlter, Andrew; Virginia, 1642 ***6219*** *p192*
Powlus, Adam; Philadelphia, 1763 ***9973.7*** *p38*
Powlus, Michael; Philadelphia, 1763 ***9973.7*** *p38*
Powndle, Henry; Virginia, 1636 ***6219*** *p80*
Powney, James 20; Jamaica, 1736 ***3690.1*** *p195*
Powolski, Andreas; Kansas, 1887 ***5240.1*** *p35*
Powrie, Peter 20; Jamaica, 1735 ***3690.1*** *p182*
Poy, Ong Jeony; Arkansas, 1918 ***95.2*** *p101*
Poyade, Bernard 30; America, 1839 ***778.5*** *p441*
Poyade, Bernard, Mme. 25; America, 1839 ***778.5*** *p441*
Poyner, Ambrose; Virginia, 1639 ***6219*** *p151*
Poyner, David 19; Virginia, 1728 ***3690.1*** *p182*
Poyntel, William 21; Baltimore, 1775 ***1219.7*** *p269*
Poyntell, William 21; Maryland, 1775 ***1219.7*** *p254*
Poynter, Tho.; Virginia, 1643 ***6219*** *p204*
Poyter, William; Virginia, 1646 ***6219*** *p240*
Poythers, Francis; Virginia, 1637 ***6219*** *p84*
Poythres, Francis; Virginia, 1642 ***6219*** *p187*
Poyton, James 40; Philadelphia, 1774 ***1219.7*** *p232*
Pozer, Jean Georges; Canada, 1776-1783 ***9786*** *p237*
Prach, . . .; Canada, 1776-1783 ***9786*** *p31*
Pracht, George Christian; Wisconsin, n.d. ***9675.7*** *p199*
Practor, Thomas; Virginia, 1623 ***6219*** *p25*
Praden, Guillaume 26; New Orleans, 1837 ***778.5*** *p441*
Praden, Laurent 24; New Orleans, 1837 ***778.5*** *p441*
Prader, Mr. 25; Port uncertain, 1836 ***778.5*** *p441*
Prados, Mrs. 23; Louisiana, 1826 ***778.5*** *p441*
Prados, Jose 25; Louisiana, 1826 ***778.5*** *p441*
Praet, Theophiel; Arkansas, 1918 ***95.2*** *p101*
Praetorius, Obstl.; Quebec, 1776 ***9786*** *p105*
Praetorius, C.J.; Quebec, 1776 ***9786*** *p102*
Praetorius, Christian Julius; Quebec, 1776 ***9786*** *p254*
Prager, Janny 28; New York, NY, 1878 ***9253*** *p46*
Prager, Robert; St. Louis, 1914 ***3702.7*** *p489*
Praget, P. 25; America, 1830 ***778.5*** *p441*
Praget, P. 26; New Orleans, 1831 ***778.5*** *p441*
Prahl, Carl F.; Wisconsin, n.d. ***9675.7*** *p199*
Prailes, Eugene; America, 1853 ***1450.2*** *p113A*
Praise, Wm.; Virginia, 1644 ***6219*** *p229*
Praket, Michael; New York, NY, 1838 ***8208.4*** *p65*
Pralle, Reg.-Feldscher; Quebec, 1776 ***9786*** *p105*
Prange, Captain; Nicaragua, 1856 ***8582.3*** *p31*
Prange, Mr.; Washington, 1913 ***3702.7*** *p278*
With wife
Prange, Anthony; America, 1864 ***1450.2*** *p113A*
Prange, Anton H.; New York, 1889 ***1450.2*** *p30B*
Prange, Charles; America, 1854 ***1450.2*** *p113A*
Prange, Frederick; America, 1883 ***1450.2*** *p30B*
Pranke, Christian; America, 1845 ***1450.2*** *p113A*
Praschag, Mathias; Colorado, 1902 ***9678.2*** *p164*
Praschag, Paul; Colorado, 1902 ***9678.2*** *p164*
Prat, John 21; Louisiana, 1820 ***778.5*** *p441*
Prat, Louis 30; Port uncertain, 1839 ***778.5*** *p441*
Prates, Peter 36; Port uncertain, 1838 ***778.5*** *p441*
Pratt, Andrew; Virginia, 1637 ***6219*** *p86*
Pratt, Christopher 29; Quebec, 1863 ***5704.8*** *p154*
Pratt, Elizabeth; Quebec, 1850 ***5704.8*** *p66*
Pratt, George 22; Virginia, 1774 ***1219.7*** *p228*
Pratt, Jno.; Virginia, 1643 ***6219*** *p207*
Pratt, John 18; Maryland, 1719 ***3690.1*** *p182*
Pratt, Jon.; Virginia, 1637 ***6219*** *p11*
Pratt, Thomas 21; Maryland or Virginia, 1737 ***3690.1*** *p182*
Pratt, Thomas 21; Savannah, GA, 1733 ***4719.17*** *p312*
Pravdica, Elisa; Iowa, 1866-1943 ***123.54*** *p75*
Pravdica, Irain; Iowa, 1866-1943 ***123.54*** *p40*
Prcodick, John; Iowa, 1866-1943 ***123.54*** *p40*
Preashoff, Paul; Washington, 1859-1920 ***2872.1*** *p32*
Preaushof, Paul; Washington, 1859-1920 ***2872.1*** *p32*
Prebedy, Geo.; Virginia, 1639 ***6219*** *p23*
Prechal, Jan; America, n.d. ***4606*** *p180*
Pree, Herman J.; Iroquois Co., IL, 1894 ***3455.1*** *p12*
Preese, Tho.; Virginia, 1639 ***6219*** *p154*
Preestley, Jonath; Virginia, 1698 ***2212*** *p14*
Prefe, Mr. 36; America, 1838 ***778.5*** *p441*
Preftakes, Cosmos; Arkansas, 1918 ***95.2*** *p101*
Pregowski, Wladyslaw; Arkansas, 1918 ***95.2*** *p101*
Preifmer, Carol 34; New Orleans, 1839 ***9420.2*** *p167*
Preining, Joseph; Illinois, 1859 ***5012.38*** *p97*
Preis, Wilh. 88; Louisiana, 1900 ***1763*** *p48D*
Preiss, Barbara Hermann *SEE* Preiss, Johannes
Preiss, Elisabetha Barbara *SEE* Preiss, Johannes
Preiss, Johannes; Pennsylvania, 1753 ***2444*** *p201*
*Wife:*Maria C. Kraeutler
*Child:*Elisabetha Barbara
Preiss, Johannes; Pennsylvania, 1753 ***2444*** *p201*
*Wife:*Barbara Hermann
*Child:*Salome
Preiss, Maria C. Kraeutler *SEE* Preiss, Johannes
Preiss, Salome *SEE* Preiss, Johannes
Prelier, F.; New Orleans, 1839 ***778.5*** *p441*
Preller, . . .; Canada, 1776-1783 ***9786*** *p31*
Pren, John; Virginia, 1638 ***6219*** *p181*
Prendergast, Cat.; America, 1742 ***4971*** *p49*
Prendergast, Catherine; America, 1742 ***4971*** *p50*
Prendergast, Edmond; America, 1740 ***4971*** *p34*
Prendergast, Ellenor; America, 1736 ***4971*** *p12*
Prendergast, James; America, 1736-1743 ***4971*** *p58*
Prendergast, Patrick; America, 1737 ***4971*** *p36*
Prendergast, Phillip; Virginia, 1647 ***6219*** *p243*
Prendeville, Honora 40; Massachusetts, 1850 ***5881.1*** *p81*
Prendeville, Julia 10; Massachusetts, 1850 ***5881.1*** *p81*
Prendeville, Richard 3; Massachusetts, 1850 ***5881.1*** *p81*
Prensch, J. Fred; America, 1865 ***1450.2*** *p113A*
Prerea, . . .; Canada, 1776-1783 ***9786*** *p31*
Presbetia, Anton; Iowa, 1866-1943 ***123.54*** *p40*
Presbetiro, Anton; Iowa, 1866-1943 ***123.54*** *p40*
Presbury, Wm.; Virginia, 1636 ***6219*** *p12*
Prescot, John; Virginia, 1698 ***2212*** *p12*
Prescott, Henry; America, 1697 ***2212*** *p7*
Prescott, Henry; Ohio, 1840 ***9892.11*** *p37*
Prescott, Henry 39; Maryland, 1775 ***1219.7*** *p254*
Prescott, James 1; St. John, N.B., 1864 ***5704.8*** *p159*
Prescott, Jno; America, 1698 ***2212*** *p6*
Prescott, Margaret 25; St. John, N.B., 1864 ***5704.8*** *p159*
Prescott, Mary 4; St. John, N.B., 1864 ***5704.8*** *p159*
Prescott, Nathaniel; Ohio, 1840 ***9892.11*** *p37*
Prescott, Robert; Ohio, 1840 ***9892.11*** *p38*
Prescott, Thomas 3; St. John, N.B., 1864 ***5704.8*** *p159*
Prescott, William 22; Jamaica, 1736 ***3690.1*** *p182*
Presly, Peter; Virginia, 1652 ***6251*** *p20*
Presly, William; Virginia, 1652 ***6251*** *p19*
Presly, William, Jr.; Virginia, 1652 ***6251*** *p19*
Press, Hugh; Virginia, 1637 ***6219*** *p112*
Presse, . . .; Canada, 1776-1783 ***9786*** *p43*
Presser, . . .; Canada, 1776-1783 ***9786*** *p31*
Presser, Martin; New York, 1750 ***3652*** *p75*
Pressett, John 20; Maryland, 1774 ***1219.7*** *p185*
Presson, . . .; Canada, 1776-1783 ***9786*** *p31*
Presson, Jacques 23; New Orleans, 1821 ***778.5*** *p442*
Prestee, Richard; Virginia, 1638 ***6219*** *p124*

Prestianne, Joseph; Arkansas, 1918 95.2 p101
Prestidg, Thom 15; America, 1703 2212 p40
Prestidge, Roger 15; America, 1705 2212 p42
Prestin, Theodor; Illinois, 1877 5012.39 p52
Prestine, Theodore; Illinois, 1877 5012.39 p52
Preston, Cherry; Philadelphia, 1849 53.26 p77
Preston, Cherry; Philadelphia, 1849 5704.8 p50
Preston, Edward 38; Maryland, 1774 1219.7 p222
Preston, George 21; Maryland, 1773 1219.7 p173
Preston, Hen.; Virginia, 1642 6219 p198
Preston, Johanna 16; Massachusetts, 1850 5881.1 p81
Preston, John; Virginia, 1648 6219 p251
Preston, Joseph; Boston, 1767 1219.7 p132
Preston, Mary Ann 16; Massachusetts, 1850 5881.1 p81
Preston, Richard; Virginia, 1636 6219 p80
With wife
Preston, Richard 19; Jamaica, 1720 3690.1 p182
Preston, Robert; Philadelphia, 1849 53.26 p77
Preston, Robert; Philadelphia, 1849 5704.8 p49
Preston, Sam.; Virginia, 1642 6219 p191
Preston, Samuel 34; Virginia, 1730 3690.1 p291
Preston, Thomas; New York, NY, 1811 2859.11 p18
Preston, Thomas; New York, NY, 1834 8208.4 p30
Preston, Thomas; Virginia, 1635 6219 p36
Preston, Thomas; Virginia, 1637 6219 p83
Preston, Wm 22; Maryland or Virginia, 1699 2212 p24
Preswicke, Roger 20; America, 1702 2212 p37
Pretto, Giosue; Arkansas, 1918 95.2 p102
Pretty, Charles 27; Harris Co., TX, 1896 6254 p3
Pretty, Harry 21; Harris Co., TX, 1896 6254 p3
Preuschof, Paul; Washington, 1859-1920 2872.1 p32
Prevat, Pierre 28; Port uncertain, 1836 778.5 p442
Prevost, Miss; America, 1829 778.5 p442
Prevost, Mr. 25; America, 1829 778.5 p442
Prevost, Mr. 26; America, 1838 778.5 p442
Prevost, Mr. 30; New Orleans, 1836 778.5 p442
Prevost, Mrs. 30; America, 1829 778.5 p442
Prevost, A.; America, 1839 778.5 p441
Prevost, Augustin; Philadelphia, 1756 8582.3 p95
Prevost, Jean 31; New Orleans, 1837 778.5 p442
Prevot, Henry 40?; Port uncertain, 1838 778.5 p442
Prewitt, Tho.; Virginia, 1636 6219 p74
Prey, August; Wisconsin, n.d. 9675.7 p199
Prey, David; New York, NY, 1816 2859.11 p40
Preyss, Johannes 30; Pennsylvania, 1753 2444 p201
Preyss, Johannes 33; Pennsylvania, 1753 2444 p201
Price, Abednego 21; Pennsylvania, 1731 3690.1 p182
Price, Ann; Philadelphia, 1849 53.26 p77
Price, Ann; Philadelphia, 1849 5704.8 p58
Price, Catherine; St. John, N.B., 1847 5704.8 p4
Price, Charles; America, 1737 4971 p66
Price, Edward; West Virginia, 1843-1844 9788.3 p19
Price, Edward 33; Virginia, 1773 1219.7 p171
Price, Edward Alexander; Arkansas, 1918 95.2 p102
Price, Ellan; St. John, N.B., 1847 5704.8 p21
Price, Geo.; Virginia, 1647 6219 p245
Price, H. N.; Washington, 1859-1920 2872.1 p32
Price, Henry; Virginia, 1637 6219 p13
Price, Henry; Virginia, 1648 6219 p250
Price, Hercules; Virginia, 1639 6219 p155
Price, Hugh; Virginia, 1618 6219 p200
Price, Hugh; Virginia, 1638 6219 p153
Price, Hugh 15; Philadelphia, 1774 1219.7 p232
Price, Humphry; Virginia, 1639 6219 p155
Price, James; New York, NY, 1840 8208.4 p103
Price, Jane; Virginia, 1639 6219 p154
Price, Jane; Virginia, 1645 6219 p232
Price, Jno.; Virginia, 1646 6219 p246
Price, Joe; Washington, 1859-1920 2872.1 p32
Price, Johanna 23; Massachusetts, 1849 5881.1 p81
Price, Johannes 30; Pennsylvania, 1753 2444 p201
Price, John; America, 1698 2212 p10
Price, John; California, 1860 2769.7 p4
Price, John; South Carolina, 1753 1219.7 p22
Price, John; Virginia, 1639 6219 p152
Price, John; Virginia, 1642 6219 p191
Price, John 17; Maryland, 1731 3690.1 p183
Price, John 18; Philadelphia, 1774 1219.7 p175
Price, John 22; Maryland, 1775 1219.7 p264
Price, John 26; Jamaica, 1730 3690.1 p182
Price, Jon.; Virginia, 1635 6219 p20
Price, Jon.; Virginia, 1637 6219 p11
Price, Jon.; Virginia, 1637 6219 p86
Price, Joseph 20; Jamaica, 1730 3690.1 p183
Price, Lucas; South Carolina, 1788 7119 p202
Price, Lucy 25; Massachusetts, 1849 5881.1 p81
Price, Lydian; Virginia, 1635 6219 p20
Price, Margaret; New York, NY, 1816 2859.11 p40
With 3 children
Price, Margery; Virginia, 1637 6219 p23
Price, Maurice; Virginia, 1643 6219 p203
Price, Nathaniel 22; Maryland, 1774 1219.7 p179
Price, Peter P.; Illinois, 1852 7857 p6
Price, Reuben; America, 1820 1450.2 p113A
Price, Rice 30; Maryland, 1775 1219.7 p260
Price, Richard; Virginia, 1637 6219 p109
Price, Richard; Washington, 1859-1920 2872.1 p32
Price, Robert; Virginia, 1647 6219 p241
Price, Robert 13; Maryland or Virginia, 1699 2212 p23
Price, Robert 19; Maryland, 1724 3690.1 p183
Price, Rose; St. John, N.B., 1852 5704.8 p95
Price, Rose Ann; St. John, N.B., 1852 5704.8 p95
Price, Samuel 25; Maryland, 1775 1219.7 p259
Price, Silas; America, 1821 1450.2 p113A
Price, Stephen; St. John, N.B., 1851 5704.8 p80
Price, Tho.; Virginia, 1643 6219 p206
Price, Tho.; Virginia, 1646 6219 p240
Price, Thomas; New York, NY, 1837 8208.4 p52
Price, Thomas; Virginia, 1636 6219 p80
Price, Thomas 17; Jamaica, 1731 3690.1 p183
Price, Thomas 18; Pennsylvania, 1722 3690.1 p183
Price, Thomas 22; Maryland, 1774 1219.7 p225
Price, Thomas 27; Jamaica, 1731 3690.1 p183
Price, Thomas 40; Maryland, 1774 1219.7 p208
Price, Thomas 50; Philadelphia, 1854 5704.8 p117
Price, Walter; Virginia, 1648 6219 p250
Price, William; Illinois, 1860 5012.39 p89
Price, William; Virginia, 1641 6219 p185
Price, William; Virginia, 1642 6219 p193
Price, William; West Virginia, 1857 9788.3 p19
Price, William 18; Pennsylvania, Virginia or Maryland, 1718 3690.1 p183
Price, William 19; Maryland, 1774 1219.7 p180
Price, William 32; Maryland, 1725 3690.1 p183
Prichard, Alice; Virginia, 1647 6219 p241
Prichard, Rice 17; Jamaica, 1731 3690.1 p183
Prichard, Richard; Virginia, 1639 6219 p154
Prichard, Robert; Virginia, 1637 6219 p107
Prichard, Rowland; Virginia, 1638 6219 p125
Prichard, Tho., Sr.; Virginia, 1643 6219 p204
Prichard, Thom; Barbados, 1698 2212 p4
Prichard, William 22; Jamaica, 1731 3690.1 p183
Pricker, John 22; Maryland, 1775 1219.7 p247
Pricklove, Geo.; Virginia, 1637 6219 p8
Pride, Hannah; South Carolina, 1767 1639.20 p263
Pride, Shadrack 20; Maryland, 1731 3690.1 p183
Pridgen, Thomas 19; Jamaica, 1725 3690.1 p183
Pridgen, Thomas 19; Jamaica, 1731 3690.1 p183
Pridmore, John; Quebec, 1820 7603 p27
Priebe, Albert 26; Kansas, 1888 5240.1 p72
Priedre, Bernard 27; America, 1837 778.5 p442
Priehs, Heinrich Ernst Wilhelm; America, 1882 4610.10 p101
Prier, Kath 21; America, 1702-1703 2212 p39
Prier, Peter; Barbados, 1698 2212 p5
Prier, Watkin; America, 1698 2212 p5
Priessing, Jacob; New York, 1750 3652 p74
Priest, Angus; America, 1804 1639.20 p263
Priest, Catherine 74 *SEE* Priest, David
Priest, David 71; North Carolina, 1850 1639.20 p263
*Relative:*Catherine 74
Priest, Joseph 19; Maryland, 1775 1219.7 p272
Priest, Mary 63; North Carolina, 1850 1639.20 p263
Priest, Ruth 18; Georgia, 1735 3690.1 p184
Priester, Henrich; Lancaster, PA, 1780 8137 p12
Prigg, Thomas 21; Virginia, 1727 3690.1 p184
Prigge, Dederick; New York, NY, 1839 8208.4 p102
Primas, Theophis; Wisconsin, n.d. 9675.7 p199
Primmer, William 23; America, 1724 3690.1 p184
Primrose, John; North Carolina, 1821 1639.20 p263
Primrose, John 47; Raleigh, NC, 1850 1639.20 p263
Primrose, Nicol; Charleston, SC, 1780 1639.20 p264
Primrose, Robert; Charleston, SC, 1824 1639.20 p264
Primrose, Robert; North Carolina, 1813 1639.20 p264
Primrose, Robert 53; North Carolina, 1850 1639.20 p264
Primrose, Robert Stuart; New Bern, NC, 1782-1825 1639.20 p264
Primrose, William 39; Maryland, 1775 1219.7 p252
Primrose, William 43; Maryland, 1775 1219.7 p249
Prince, Adelle 23; New Orleans, 1839 778.5 p442
Prince, Bernard 32; New Orleans, 1830 778.5 p442
Prince, Edmund; Virginia, 1640 6219 p208
Prince, Edward; Virginia, 1635 6219 p70
Prince, Edward; Virginia, 1646 6219 p241
Prince, James; Virginia, 1638 6219 p160
Prince, Jean 24; New Orleans, 1839 778.5 p442
Prince, Matthew; Wisconsin, n.d. 9675.7 p199
Prince, Samuel; America, 1738 4971 p39
Prince, Thomas; Virginia, 1639 6219 p161
Prince, William 21; Maryland, 1724 3690.1 p184
Prince August Wilhelm ; Quebec, 1778 9786 p267
Prince Friedrich August ; Quebec, 1776 9786 p254
Princekoffer, Christopher; Pennsylvania, 1803 2444 p201
Prindiville, John; Ohio, 1876 2764.35 p53
Pring, Captain; Quebec, 1815 9229.18 p81
Pringle, Ann; Charleston, SC, 1680-1830 1639.20 p264
Pringle, Charles; Quebec, 1820 7603 p70
Pringle, George 28; Philadelphia, 1774 1219.7 p182
Pringle, James; New York, NY, 1840 8208.4 p113
Pringle, James 16; Jamaica, 1774 1219.7 p237
Pringle, John; New York, NY, 1834 8208.4 p60
Pringle, John 27; Maryland, 1775 1219.7 p266
Pringle, John 30; Maryland, 1774 1219.7 p220
Pringle, Robert; Charleston, SC, 1725 1639.20 p264
Pringle, Sarah I. 11 mos; Massachusetts, 1849 5881.1 p81
Pringley, William 32; Maryland, 1774 1219.7 p215
Prinoch, Jonathan 21; Maryland, 1774 1219.7 p204
Print, John 21; Maryland, 1774 1219.7 p221
Printzighofer, Anna Maria Rieger *SEE* Printzighofer, Hans Georg
Printzighofer, Hans Georg; Port uncertain, 1752 2444 p201
*Wife:*Anna Maria Rieger
Prinz, John David; America, 1854 1450.2 p113A
Priola, Andrew; Arkansas, 1918 95.2 p102
Priona, G. 30; New Orleans, 1829 778.5 p442
Prior, Mr.; Quebec, 1815 9229.18 p76
Prior, Andrew; Quebec, 1847 5704.8 p37
Prior, Ann; Quebec, 1847 5704.8 p37
Prior, Benjamin 22; Maryland, 1774 1219.7 p222
Prior, Brian; Quebec, 1847 5704.8 p37
Prior, Catherine; Quebec, 1847 5704.8 p37
Prior, Henry; Arkansas, 1918 95.2 p102
Prior, Jane; Quebec, 1847 5704.8 p37
Prior, Jno; Barbados, 1698 2212 p4
Prior, John; Quebec, 1847 5704.8 p37
Prior, John 17; Antigua (Antego), 1728 3690.1 p184
Prior, Margaret; Quebec, 1847 5704.8 p37
Prior, Margarett *SEE* Prior, William
Prior, Mary; Quebec, 1847 5704.8 p37
Prior, Thomas; Quebec, 1847 5704.8 p37
Prior, Walter 32; Maryland, 1774 1219.7 p236
Prior, William; America, 1697 2212 p9
Prior, William; New York, NY, 1836 8208.4 p16
Prior, William; Virginia, 1637 6219 p85
*Wife:*Margarett
Prior, William; Virginia, 1642 6219 p189
With wife
Prior, Wm.; Virginia, 1635 6219 p26
Priour, Francois 22; Port uncertain, 1836 778.5 p442
Priour, Francoise 30; New Orleans, 1838 778.5 p443
Priour, Jean 21; New Orleans, 1838 778.5 p443
Priour, Jean-Marie 35; Port uncertain, 1836 778.5 p443
Prisby, Thomas; Virginia, 1652 6251 p19
Prischenk, Ike; Pennsylvania, 1895 1450.2 p30B
Prischnowski, Salomon 18; New York, NY, 1878 9253 p46
Prisello, Andrew; Arkansas, 1918 95.2 p102
Prislan, Frank; Wisconsin, n.d. 9675.7 p199
Prispana, Jalmar; Washington, 1859-1920 2872.1 p32
Priston, William; New York, NY, 1816 2859.11 p40
Pritchard, Amie 23; America, 1699 2212 p28
Pritchard, Charles Robert; Arkansas, 1918 95.2 p102
Pritchard, John 17; Jamaica, 1733 3690.1 p184
Pritchard, John G.; New York, 1872 2764.35 p54
Pritchard, Thomas 21; Jamaica, 1728 3690.1 p184
Pritchett, Andrew 23; Maryland or Virginia, 1699 2212 p22
Pritchett, Jno; America, 1698 2212 p6
Priterre, Napoleon; New York, NY, 1836 8208.4 p9
Pritmer, Joseph; Wisconsin, n.d. 9675.7 p199
Pritzlaff, August; Milwaukee, 1870 3702.7 p318
With wife 48
With 4 children
With child 7
With child 27
Pritzlaff, Johann Carl Wilhelm; New York, 1839 3702.7 p299
Pritzlow, August 52; Milwaukee, 1870 3702.7 p318
With wife 48
With 4 children
With child 7
With child 27
Privett, Mrs.; America, 1818-1846 4535.10 p195
Privett, Ann 29 *SEE* Privett, Jas.
Privett, Jas. 28; America, 1846 4535.10 p195
*Wife:*Ann 29
With son 1
Probat, Jno.; Virginia, 1635 6219 p19
Probst, A.; Cincinnati, 1788-1848 8582.3 p89
Probst, Adam; Philadelphia, 1760 9973.7 p34
Probst, Christian; Illinois, 1879 2896.5 p32
Probst, Jacob; Pennsylvania, 1771 9973.8 p32
Probstfeld, Mr.; New York, 1861 3702.7 p225
With 2 brothers
With 2 cousins
Probstfeld, Michael 20; America, 1852-1853 3702.7 p223

Probstfield, Mr.; New York, 1861 ***3702.7*** *p225*
With 2 brothers & 2 cousins
Probstfield, Randolph M. 20; America, 1852-1853 ***3702.7*** *p223*
Proby, Geo.; Virginia, 1647 ***6219*** *p245*
Procipio, Samuel; Arkansas, 1918 ***95.2*** *p102*
Procter, John; America, 1864 ***5704.8*** *p183*
Procter, Robert; New York, NY, 1868 ***5704.8*** *p229*
Proctor, Alexander 40; Philadelphia, 1833 ***53.26*** *p77*
Proctor, Ambrose; Virginia, 1637 ***6219*** *p11*
Proctor, Anth.; Virginia, 1638 ***6219*** *p122*
Proctor, Henry; Philadelphia, 1760 ***9973.7*** *p34*
Proctor, Henry 16; Maryland or Virginia, 1699 ***2212*** *p24*
Proctor, John; America, 1736-1743 ***4971*** *p57*
Produck, John 26; Jamaica, 1724 ***3690.1*** *p184*
Proemapki, Joseph; Arkansas, 1918 ***95.2*** *p102*
Progers, Thomas 23; Virginia, 1774 ***1219.7*** *p186*
Prohl, Heinr. 21; New Orleans, 1839 ***9420.2*** *p170*
Prokop, Julius; Pennsylvania, 1892 ***5240.1*** *p35*
Prolon, Jean 29; America, 1838 ***778.5*** *p443*
Prom, Mathias; Wisconsin, n.d. ***9675.7*** *p199*
Prom, Nicolas; Wisconsin, n.d. ***9675.7*** *p199*
Promse, Johann Friedrich Wilhelm; America, 1851 ***4610.10*** *p120*
Promse, Karl Heinrich; America, 1847 ***4610.10*** *p120*
Prondeville, Mary 40; Massachusetts, 1850 ***5881.1*** *p81*
Prondeville, Richard 60; Massachusetts, 1850 ***5881.1*** *p81*
Pronga, William; America, 1850 ***1450.2*** *p113A*
Proniewski, . . .; New York, 1831 ***4606*** *p176*
Proom, William 21; Maryland, 1774 ***1219.7*** *p184*
Proper, Tho.; Virginia, 1643 ***6219*** *p229*
Propp, Johann; Wisconsin, n.d. ***9675.7*** *p199*
Proschke, Charles Edward 23; New Orleans, 1839 ***9420.2*** *p486*
Prosig, . . .; Canada, 1776-1783 ***9786*** *p31*
Prosinger, Martin 47; Kansas, 1877 ***5240.1*** *p58*
Prosn, J. 25; America, 1837 ***778.5*** *p443*
Prosper, Mr. 21; New Orleans, 1838 ***778.5*** *p443*
Prosper, Leroy Louis 21; America, 1837 ***778.5*** *p443*
Prosper, Paul 39; America, 1837 ***778.5*** *p443*
Prosser, Ann; Virginia, 1636 ***6219*** *p21*
Prosser, Daniel; Ohio, 1816 ***8582.1*** *p47*
Prosser, Daniel; South Carolina, 1767 ***1639.20*** *p265*
Prosser, Georg; Virginia, 1637 ***6219*** *p180*
Prosser, Jane; Virginia, 1628 ***6219*** *p31*
Prosser, Mary 17; Virginia, 1719 ***3690.1*** *p184*
Prosser, Morris; Virginia, 1638 ***6219*** *p125*
Prosser, Richard 20; Jamaica, 1720 ***3690.1*** *p184*
Prosser, Wm.; Virginia, 1638 ***6219*** *p116*
Prossmann, . . .; Canada, 1776-1783 ***9786*** *p31*
Prostien, Lawrence; Arkansas, 1918 ***95.2*** *p102*
Prosu, J. 25; America, 1837 ***778.5*** *p443*
Prosy, . . .; Canada, 1776-1783 ***9786*** *p31*
Protecka, Stanislawa 17; New York, 1912 ***9980.29*** *p58*
Proth, . . .; Canada, 1776-1783 ***9786*** *p31*
Protherick, Sarah; Quebec, 1847 ***5704.8*** *p6*
Prothers, Thomas 24; Jamaica, 1730 ***3690.1*** *p184*
Prothoro, Thomas 18; Maryland or Virginia, 1719 ***3690.1*** *p184*
Prott, John; Wisconsin, n.d. ***9675.7*** *p199*
Protz, Wilhelm; St. Louis, 1875 ***2896.5*** *p32*
Proud, William 22; Maryland, 1774 ***1219.7*** *p220*
Proudfort, John 24; Virginia, 1774 ***1219.7*** *p239*
Proudlow, Pemberton 15; America, 1703 ***2212*** *p39*
Prous, J. 32; Port uncertain, 1836 ***778.5*** *p443*
Prouse, Emblence; Virginia, 1638 ***6219*** *p158*
Provose, Marke; Virginia, 1642 ***6219*** *p191*
Provost, Esther Cook; Quebec, 1738 ***7603*** *p26*
Prower, Geo.; Virginia, 1635 ***6219*** *p70*
Prowse, John; Virginia, 1639 ***6219*** *p157*
Prowse, John; Virginia, 1639 ***6219*** *p159*
Prowse, Wm.; Virginia, 1624 ***6219*** *p25*
Proyer, Michel 38; America, 1837 ***778.5*** *p443*
Prudat, Jean 27; Port uncertain, 1839 ***778.5*** *p443*
Prudel, Albert 35; America, 1836 ***778.5*** *p443*
Prudn, Bernard 27; America, 1837 ***778.5*** *p443*
Prudon, Victor 20; Mexico, 1827 ***778.5*** *p443*
Prudot, Mrs. 24; America, 1837 ***778.5*** *p444*
Prudot, Amelie 5; America, 1837 ***778.5*** *p443*
Prudot, Arsene 3; America, 1837 ***778.5*** *p444*
Prudot, Zoe 18 mos; America, 1837 ***778.5*** *p444*
Prudu, Bernard 27; America, 1837 ***778.5*** *p443*
Prue, Paul 28; New Orleans, 1836 ***778.5*** *p444*
Prue, Paulin 25; New Orleans, 1838 ***778.5*** *p444*
Pruesse, George; Canada, 1783 ***9786*** *p38A*
Prufer, Otto 30; Kansas, 1889 ***5240.1*** *p73*
Pruhard, Francois 35; America, 1837 ***778.5*** *p444*
Prumond, Mr. 30; New Orleans, 1838 ***778.5*** *p444*
Prunder, Catharina E. Thomas *SEE* Prunder, Josef
Prunder, Heinrich Elias 6 *SEE* Prunder, Josef
Prunder, Johannes 18 *SEE* Prunder, Josef
Prunder, Josef; Philadelphia, 1729 ***2854*** *p43*
*Wife:*Catharina E. Thomas
*Child:*Maria Catharina 19
*Child:*Johannes 18
*Child:*Heinrich Elias 6
Prunder, Maria Catharina 19 *SEE* Prunder, Josef
Pruno, Mr.; New York, NY, 1834 ***8582.2*** *p23*
Pruset, Paul 35; America, 1838 ***778.5*** *p444*
Prushoff, Paul; Washington, 1859-1920 ***2872.1*** *p32*
Prussner, Carl Heinrich Adolph; America, 1843 ***4610.10*** *p115*
Prussner, Johann Friedrich *SEE* Prussner, Julius Friedrich August
Prussner, Johanne S. Borghardt *SEE* Prussner, Julius Friedrich August
Prussner, Julius Friedrich August; America, 1867 ***4610.10*** *p117*
*Father:*Johann Friedrich
*Mother:*Johanne S. Borghardt
Pruszkewicz, Maryan 18; New York, 1912 ***9980.29*** *p70*
Pruszkewicz, Wladislaw; Ohio, 1912 ***9980.29*** *p70*
Pruys, John 21; Jamaica, 1736 ***3690.1*** *p184*
Pryde, Harry Fisher; Iowa, 1866-1943 ***123.54*** *p40*
Prye, Oliver; Virginia, 1636 ***6219*** *p26*
Prynn, Edmund; Virginia, 1641 ***6219*** *p186*
Pryor, John; Jamaica, 1753 ***1219.7*** *p20*
Pryor, John; Jamaica, 1753 ***3690.1*** *p185*
Pryor, Thomas; America, 1864 ***5704.8*** *p183*
Prysevick, Steuli; Wisconsin, n.d. ***9675.7*** *p199*
Prysicki, . . .; Arkansas, 1918 ***95.2*** *p102*
Prysing, Christina 8 *SEE* Prysing, Christopher
Prysing, Christopher; South Carolina, 1752-1753 ***3689.17*** *p22*
With wife
*Relative:*Christina 8
*Relative:*Melchior 6
*Relative:*Margaret 4
Prysing, Margaret 4 *SEE* Prysing, Christopher
Prysing, Melchior 6 *SEE* Prysing, Christopher
Przeborowski, Jozef; New York, 1835 ***4606*** *p180*
Przespolewska, Jozefa Gerschau 21; New York, 1912 ***9980.29*** *p56*
Przespolewska, Marianna 8; New York, 1912 ***9980.29*** *p56*
Przespolewski, Franciszek 6 mos; New York, 1912 ***9980.29*** *p56*
Przespolewski, Franz 19; New York, 1912 ***9980.29*** *p54*
Przeworska, Rozalia 20; New York, 1912 ***9980.29*** *p55*
Przybylowicz, Adam 17; New York, 1912 ***9980.29*** *p55*
Przytala, Adam; Arkansas, 1918 ***95.2*** *p102*
Psalter, Sam; Arkansas, 1918 ***95.2*** *p102*
Psaltes, Sam; Arkansas, 1918 ***95.2*** *p102*
Pschere, Fred *SEE* Pschere, Marie Vedovell
Pschere, Marie Vedovell; New York, NY, 1886 ***3455.3*** *p79*
*Husband:*Fred
Pscherer, Fred; Philadelphia, 1912 ***3455.2*** *p76*
Pscherer, Fred; Philadelphia, 1912 ***3455.3*** *p49*
*Wife:*Marie
Pscherer, Henry; New York, NY, 1922 ***3455.2*** *p79*
Pscherer, Marie *SEE* Pscherer, Fred
Pszolla, Fred; Washington, 1859-1920 ***2872.1*** *p32*
Ptolemy, Thomas; America, 1743 ***4971*** *p11*
Puccia, Steve; Arkansas, 1918 ***95.2*** *p102*
Puchalski, . . .; New York, 1831 ***4606*** *p176*
Puchen, Mme. 25; America, 1838 ***778.5*** *p444*
Puchen, Mr. 29; America, 1838 ***778.5*** *p444*
Puchereau, Jeanne 23; America, 1837 ***778.5*** *p444*
Puchot, J. 35; New Orleans, 1838 ***778.5*** *p444*
Pucinotti, Francesco; Iowa, 1866-1943 ***123.54*** *p75*
Puckel, . . .; Canada, 1776-1783 ***9786*** *p31*
Puckett, Nicholas; Illinois, 1868 ***2896.5*** *p32*
Puckridge, Moses 29; Virginia, 1774 ***1219.7*** *p243*
Puda, Joseph; Iowa, 1866-1943 ***123.54*** *p75*
Puda, Zofia; Iowa, 1866-1943 ***123.54*** *p75*
Puderford, Jane 21; Georgia, 1774 ***1219.7*** *p188*
Pudivatt, Jane *SEE* Pudivatt, William
Pudivatt, William; Virginia, 1642 ***6219*** *p198*
*Wife:*Jane
Pudsey, Ambrose 23; Maryland, 1733 ***3690.1*** *p185*
Puettman, Heinrich; Illinois, 1829 ***8582.1*** *p55*
Puetz, Henry; Wisconsin, n.d. ***9675.7*** *p199*
Puetz, Henry Joseph 39; Kansas, 1889 ***5240.1*** *p35*
Puetz, Henry Joseph 39; Kansas, 1889 ***5240.1*** *p73*
Puetz, John; Wisconsin, n.d. ***9675.7*** *p199*
Pugh, Ann 20; America, 1701 ***2212*** *p35*
Pugh, Edward; New Jersey, 1834 ***8208.4*** *p47*
Pugh, John G.; Colorado, 1893 ***9678.2*** *p164*
Pugh, Richard; Ohio, 1869-1874 ***9892.11*** *p38*
Pugh, Richard; Ohio, 1876 ***9892.11*** *p38*
Pughe, Charles; Colorado, 1904 ***9678.2*** *p164*
Pugly, Wm.; Virginia, 1648 ***6219*** *p250*
Pugo, Robert 29; New Orleans, 1823 ***778.5*** *p444*
Pugsley, John; Virginia, 1637 ***6219*** *p82*
Puhler, Henry; America, 1861 ***1450.2*** *p112A*
Puidack, Kazimer; Wisconsin, n.d. ***9675.7*** *p199*
Puis, Antonio 40; New Orleans, 1835 ***778.5*** *p444*
Puiss, Amedee 22; America, 1838 ***778.5*** *p444*
Puissant, A. 25; America, 1826 ***778.5*** *p445*
Pujdak, Adolph; Wisconsin, n.d. ***9675.7*** *p199*
Pujo, Jacques 27; New Orleans, 1839 ***778.5*** *p445*
Pujo, Paul 40; America, 1837 ***778.5*** *p445*
Pujo, Paul 42; New Orleans, 1839 ***778.5*** *p445*
Pujol, J. Joseph 31; New Orleans, 1837 ***778.5*** *p445*
Pujol, Pierre 36; America, 1838 ***778.5*** *p445*
Pujos, Mr. 38; America, 1838 ***778.5*** *p445*
Pulen, Hennrich; Indiana, 1848 ***9117*** *p17*
Pull, George; Illinois, 1868 ***7857*** *p6*
Pull, William 26; Antigua (Antego), 1730-1731 ***3690.1*** *p185*
Pullapin, Jon.; Virginia, 1635 ***6219*** *p12*
Pulle, Bennett; Virginia, 1621 ***6219*** *p25*
Pullen, Charles; Colorado, 1890 ***9678.2*** *p164*
Pullen, Robert; Virginia, 1652 ***6251*** *p20*
Pullen, Thomas 21; Philadelphia, 1774 ***1219.7*** *p212*
Pulley, Edward 30; Baltimore, 1775 ***1219.7*** *p269*
Pullin, Robert; Illinois, 1856 ***7857*** *p6*
Pullipen, Richard; Virginia, 1621 ***6219*** *p30*
Pullman, Michael; New York, NY, 1839 ***8208.4*** *p93*
Pullman, Thomas; New York, NY, 1832 ***8208.4*** *p55*
Pullock, David; Virginia, 1640 ***6219*** *p187*
Pullum, Edmund; Virginia, 1636 ***6219*** *p78*
Pulmer, Catharina Majer *SEE* Pulmer, Johannes
Pulmer, Johannes; America, 1742-1800 ***2444*** *p201*
*Mother:*Catharina Majer
With stepfather
Puloff, Samuel; Arkansas, 1918 ***95.2*** *p102*
Puls, Caspar Heinrich Gottlieb; America, 1858 ***4610.10*** *p140*
Puls, Christine; America, 1850 ***4610.10*** *p147*
Pulte, Josef H.; Cincinnati, 1869-1887 ***8582*** *p23*
Pulver, . . .; Canada, 1776-1783 ***9786*** *p43*
Pumfrey, John; Virginia, 1635 ***6219*** *p7*
Pummery, Robert 20; Pennsylvania, Virginia or Maryland, 1719 ***3690.1*** *p185*
Pump, William; San Francisco, 1881 ***2764.35*** *p53*
Pumphrey, F. M.; Washington, 1859-1920 ***2872.1*** *p32*
Pumphy, John 29; Philadelphia, 1803 ***53.26*** *p77*
Puncele, Joseph; Wisconsin, n.d. ***9675.7*** *p199*
Pungartnik, John; Wisconsin, n.d. ***9675.7*** *p199*
Puque, Francois 26; New Orleans, 1835 ***778.5*** *p445*
Purce, Mary 40; St. John, N.B., 1867 ***5704.8*** *p168*
Purce, Robert 11; St. John, N.B., 1867 ***5704.8*** *p168*
Purcel, Charles; New York, NY, 1816 ***2859.11*** *p40*
Purcel, Nicholas 23; Tortola, 1774 ***1219.7*** *p237*
Purcel, Patrick; America, 1743 ***4971*** *p22*
Purcel, Sarah; New York, NY, 1816 ***2859.11*** *p40*
Purcell, Alexandre; Montreal, 1821 ***7603*** *p82*
Purcell, Fanny; New York, NY, 1816 ***2859.11*** *p40*
Purcell, J.F.; Illinois, 1903 ***5012.40*** *p80*
Purcell, John 50; Arizona, 1900 ***9228.40*** *p8*
Purcell, Julian; America, 1740 ***4971*** *p48*
Purcell, Matth.; America, 1740 ***4971*** *p30*
Purcell, Patrick; America, 1743 ***4971*** *p95*
Purcell, Patrick; New York, NY, 1836 ***8208.4*** *p20*
Purcell, Patrick; Virginia, 1844 ***4626.16*** *p12*
Purcell, Peter, Jr. 19; Jamaica, 1730 ***3690.1*** *p185*
Purcell, Peter, Jr. 19; Jamaica, 1731 ***3690.1*** *p185*
Purcell, Pierce; America, 1738 ***4971*** *p31*
Purcell, Pierce; New York, NY, 1839 ***8208.4*** *p94*
Purches, Robt.; Virginia, 1635 ***6219*** *p10*
Purdie, Archibald; South Carolina, 1786 ***1639.20*** *p265*
Purdie, Grace 2; Quebec, 1859 ***5704.8*** *p143*
Purdie, James 45; Quebec, 1859 ***5704.8*** *p143*
Purdie, Jane 9; Quebec, 1859 ***5704.8*** *p143*
Purdie, John 26; New York, NY, 1828 ***6508.4*** *p143*
Purdie, Joseph 1; Quebec, 1859 ***5704.8*** *p143*
Purdie, Margaret 7; Quebec, 1859 ***5704.8*** *p143*
Purdie, Marion 39; Quebec, 1859 ***5704.8*** *p143*
Purdie, Richard; Virginia, 1646 ***6219*** *p236*
Purdon, Thomas; New York, NY, 1815 ***2859.11*** *p40*
Purdy, Harry; St. John, N.B., 1848 ***5704.8*** *p39*
Purdy, James; Iowa, 1866-1943 ***123.54*** *p40*
Purdy, Nancy; Philadelphia, 1850 ***53.26*** *p77*
Purdy, Nancy; Philadelphia, 1850 ***5704.8*** *p60*
Purdy, Robert 31; Kansas, 1894 ***5240.1*** *p35*
Purdy, Robert 31; Kansas, 1894 ***5240.1*** *p79*
Purdy, Thomas 17; Georgia, 1775 ***1219.7*** *p276*
Purellio, Camlin 18; Maryland, 1775 ***1219.7*** *p249*
Purfusbt, Fr. 29; New Orleans, 1839 ***9420.2*** *p169*
Purgand, Kaspar; Lancaster, PA, 1780 ***8137*** *p7*
Purgues, Mr. 29; New Orleans, 1839 ***778.5*** *p445*
Puricelli, Luigi; Arkansas, 1918 ***95.2*** *p102*
Purkeys, Robt.; Virginia, 1637 ***6219*** *p10*
Purnell, Arthur; Virginia, 1637 ***6219*** *p81*
Purnell, William; Virginia, 1638 ***6219*** *p147*

Purnell, Wm.; Virginia, 1618 *6219 p72*
Purnell, Wm; Virginia, 1634 *6219 p105*
Purois, Peter 32; Virginia, 1774 *1219.7 p201*
Purscinski, Franciszek 17; New York, 1912 *9980.29 p66*
Purse, Jennet; Charleston, SC, 1803-1826 *1639.20 p265*
Purser, Geo.; Virginia, 1635 *6219 p23*
Purser, James; Virginia, 1753 *1219.7 p21*
Purser, James 21; Virginia, 1774 *1219.7 p201*
Purtell, John Joseph; Arkansas, 1918 *95.2 p102*
Purves, John; New York, NY, 1866 *5704.8 p213*
Purves, Peter; New York, NY, 1834 *8208.4 p37*
Purvey, Ann; Virginia, 1639 *6219 p154*
Purvis, Bernard; New York, NY, 1869 *5704.8 p234*
Purvis, David 22; St. John, N.B., 1867 *5704.8 p168*
Purvis, John; Colombia, SC, 1825 *1639.20 p265*
Purvis, Margaret; New York, NY, 1869 *5704.8 p234*
Purvis, Sarah; New York, NY, 1869 *5704.8 p234*
Purvis, Teresa; New York, NY, 1869 *5704.8 p234*
Pusat, A. 28; America, 1826 *778.5 p445*
Pusatero, Vincenzo 29; New York, NY, 1893 *9026.4 p42*
Puschard, Karl; Philadelphia, 1779 *8137 p7*
Puschner, Christ. Gottl. 38; New Orleans, 1839 *9420.2 p168*
Puse, Richard; Virginia, 1642 *6219 p191*
Puspana, Jalmar; Washington, 1859-1920 *2872.1 p32*
Pussell, John 21; Maryland, 1775 *1219.7 p267*
Puszer, Amalie 2 *SEE* Puszer, Tragott

Puszer, Dorothea 39 *SEE* Puszer, Tragott
Puszer, Eleanore 14 *SEE* Puszer, Tragott
Puszer, Fredk. Traugote 11 *SEE* Puszer, Tragott
Puszer, Pauline 6 *SEE* Puszer, Tragott
Puszer, Tragott 46; New Orleans, 1839 *9420.2 p362*
    *Wife:*Dorothea 39
    *Child:*Eleanore 14
    *Child:*Fredk. Traugote 11
    *Child:*Pauline 6
    *Child:*Amalie 2
Puszkewicz, Maryan 18; New York, 1912 *9980.29 p70*
Puszkewicz, Wladislaw; Ohio, 1912 *9980.29 p70*
Putaala, Charley Edward; Washington, 1859-1920 *2872.1 p32*
Putaala, John; Washington, 1859-1920 *2872.1 p32*
Putelski, John; Wisconsin, n.d. *9675.7 p199*
Puthoff, Herman Heinrich Joseph; Kentucky, 1839 *8582.3 p99*
Puthoff, Hermann Heinrich Joseph; America, 1839 *8582.3 p52*
Putlovic, Frances; America, 1894 *7137 p169*
Putlovic, John; America, 1893 *7137 p169*
Putman, Heinrich; Illinois, 1829 *8582.1 p27*
Putman, Johann; Salem, MA, 1626 *8582.2 p58*
Putman, John; San Francisco, 1850 *4914.15 p10*
Putmann, . . .; America, 1869-1885 *8582.2 p31*
Putmann, Johann; Salem, MA, 1626 *8582.2 p58*
Putnam, Johann; Salem, MA, 1626 *8582.2 p58*

Putnam, Raymond; Arkansas, 1918 *95.2 p102*
Putnam, Reimi Christian; Arkansas, 1918 *95.2 p102*
Putrament, Barnaba; New York, 1834 *4606 p178*
Putt, William 26; Antigua (Antego), 1730-1731 *3690.1 p185*
Putterbach, Johann Peter; Philadelphia, 1752 *8125.6 p23*
Puxedda, Pasquale; New York, NY, 1834 *8208.4 p44*
Puyo, Paul 40; America, 1837 *778.5 p445*
Pye, Jam; Virginia, 1698 *2212 p15*
Pye, John 24; Philadelphia, 1774 *1219.7 p237*
Pye, Marcella; St. John, N.B., 1848 *5704.8 p44*
Pye, Mary 30; America, 1700 *2212 p30*
Pye, Noble 40; St. John, N.B., 1853 *5704.8 p110*
Pye, Thomas 11; St. John, N.B., 1853 *5704.8 p110*
Pyerden, John 32; Philadelphia, 1774 *1219.7 p237*
Pykett, David; Illinois, 1867 *2896.5 p32*
Pykett, David; Illinois, 1870 *2896.5 p32*
Pykonen, Elmer; Washington, 1859-1920 *2872.1 p32*
Pykonen, Henry; Washington, 1859-1920 *2872.1 p32*
Pykonen, Martin; Washington, 1859-1920 *2872.1 p32*
Pykonen, Ono; Washington, 1859-1920 *2872.1 p32*
Pykonen, Witla; Washington, 1859-1920 *2872.1 p32*
Pyll, Eliza.; Virginia, 1647 *6219 p243*
Pyner, Alfred; Iowa, 1866-1943 *123.54 p40*
Pynion, Lawrence; Virginia, 1638 *6219 p147*
Pyrlaeus, John C.; Philadelphia, 1741 *3652 p52*
Pyzikiewicz, Helena 18; New York, 1912 *9980.29 p66*

Q

Quade, Carl 40; New York, NY, 1862 **9831.18** *p16*
Quade, Pauline 24; New York, NY, 1862 **9831.18** *p16*
Quade, William; Wisconsin, n.d. **9675.7** *p199*
Quadeau, Mr. 35; America, 1837 **778.5** *p445*
Quader, Charles; Wisconsin, n.d. **9675.7** *p199*
Quaehl, Henrich; Philadelphia, 1779 **8137** *p12*
Quaglino, Barney; Arkansas, 1918 **95.2** *p102*
Quail, Henry 7; Massachusetts, 1848 **5881.1** *p81*
Quail, Margaret 4; Massachusetts, 1849 **5881.1** *p82*
Quail, Patrick 9; Massachusetts, 1849 **5881.1** *p82*
Quail, William; New York, NY, 1811 **2859.11** *p18*
  With family
Quaill, Jean 14; America, 1839 **778.5** *p445*
Quaing, Heinrich; America, 1846 **8582.1** *p27*
Quale, William; New York, NY, 1811 **2859.11** *p18*
Quane, Honora; America, 1738 **4971** *p80*
Quant, Robert 15; Jamaica, 1725 **3690.1** *p28A*
Quante, Heinrich; Cincinnati, 1869-1887 **8582** *p23*
Quario, Vito; Arkansas, 1918 **95.2** *p102*
Quarle, Andrew; Wisconsin, n.d. **9675.7** *p199*
Quaroni, John; America, 1892 **1450.2** *p114A*
Quarrell, Ellen; Virginia, 1638 **6219** *p150*
Quarrie, Frederick; Washington, 1859-1920 **2872.1** *p32*
Quarrie, Marie Gertrude; Washington, 1859-1920 **2872.1** *p32*
Quarryer, Charles 25; Maryland or Virginia, 1699 **2212** *p21*
Quartaroli, Antenore; Iowa, 1866-1943 **123.54** *p40*
Quartier, J. 21; New Orleans, 1827 **778.5** *p445*
Quary, John; Ohio, 1845 **9892.11** *p38*
Quary, John; Ohio, 1847 **9892.11** *p38*
Quash, Francis; Virginia, 1642 **6219** *p194*
Quast, Herman Friedrich; Wisconsin, n.d. **9675.7** *p199*
Quast, John Martin 20; New Orleans, 1839 **9420.2** *p486*
Quatmann, Heinrich; Ohio, 1832 **8582.2** *p49*
  With family
Quatreveaux, Madame 43; America, 1838 **778.5** *p445*
Quatreveaux, Clemence 2; America, 1838 **778.5** *p445*
Quattelbaum, Johanes; South Carolina, 1788 **7119** *p203*
Quayle, Thomas J.; Illinois, 1888 **5012.39** *p121*
Quayle, William; New York, NY, 1835 **8208.4** *p7*
Quayles, Richard; Virginia, 1639 **6219** *p159*
Queen, Andrew 3; Quebec, 1864 **5704.8** *p162*
Queen, Edward 40; Quebec, 1864 **5704.8** *p162*
Queen, Jean; Quebec, 1791 **7603** *p73*
Queen, Margaret 35; Quebec, 1864 **5704.8** *p162*
Queen, Sarah 5; Quebec, 1864 **5704.8** *p162*
Queen, William 11; Quebec, 1864 **5704.8** *p162*
Queenan, Bryan; New York, NY, 1816 **2859.11** *p41*
Queenan, Martin; New York, NY, 1816 **2859.11** *p41*
Queisser, Julius; America, 1853 **1450.2** *p114A*
Quelche, William; Virginia, 1639 **6219** *p155*
Quelle, Antoine 33; New Orleans, 1826 **778.5** *p446*
Quelle, Mde. 33; New Orleans, 1826 **778.5** *p446*
Quellmalz, Amalie Wme. 40 *SEE* Quellmalz, Chr. Gottfr.
Quellmalz, Anna Amalia 5 *SEE* Quellmalz, Chr. Gottfr.
Quellmalz, Carl Fr. 15 *SEE* Quellmalz, Chr. Gottfr.
Quellmalz, Chr. Gottfr. 50; New Orleans, 1839 **9420.2** *p168*
  *Wife:*Amalie Wme. 40
  *Child:*Carl Fr. 15
  *Child:*Wm. Cornelius 13
  *Child:*Ernst Wm. 10
  *Child:*Anna Amalia 5
Quellmalz, Ernst Wm. 10 *SEE* Quellmalz, Chr. Gottfr.
Quellmalz, Wm. Cornelius 13 *SEE* Quellmalz, Chr. Gottfr.

Quentin, Eugene 31; New Orleans, 1839 **778.5** *p446*
Quentin, Eugene, Mme. 25; New Orleans, 1839 **778.5** *p446*
Quentin, Martin Charles 26; New Orleans, 1836 **778.5** *p446*
Querel, Mr.; Port uncertain, 1839 **778.5** *p446*
Querl, . . .; Canada, 1776-1783 **9786** *p31*
Quernheim, Fr. W. Bernh.; America, 1890 **4610.10** *p137*
Quert, . . .; Canada, 1776-1783 **9786** *p31*
Quertier, Helier; Quebec, 1782 **7603** *p47*
Quesac, Eugene 30; Port uncertain, 1836 **778.5** *p446*
Quesne, Jean; Quebec, 1783 **7603** *p88*
Quessy, Edmond; Quebec, 1789 **7603** *p80*
Quessy, Roger; Acadia, 1668 **7603** *p75*
Queyrouse, Mr. 15; New Orleans, 1835 **778.5** *p446*
Quezac, E. 25; America, 1831 **778.5** *p446*
Quibelle, Js. 25; Port uncertain, 1839 **778.5** *p522*
Quick, A. R.; Washington, 1859-1920 **2872.1** *p32*
Quick, Alexander D.; Washington, 1859-1920 **2872.1** *p32*
Quick, Alice; Washington, 1859-1920 **2872.1** *p32*
Quick, Elis. 30; America, 1853 **9162.8** *p37*
Quick, George; Washington, 1859-1920 **2872.1** *p32*
Quick, John; Colorado, 1902 **9678.2** *p164*
Quick, Joseph; New York, NY, 1840 **8208.4** *p108*
Quidore, Baby; Died enroute, 1752 **7074.6** *p208*
Quidore, Clemence *SEE* Quidore, Jean-George
Quidore, Jean-George *SEE* Quidore, Jean-George
Quidore, Jean George 36; Halifax, N.S., 1752 **7074.6** *p207*
  With family of 3
Quidore, Jean-George 36; Halifax, N.S., 1752 **7074.6** *p212*
  *Wife:*Clemence
  *Child:*Jean-George
  *Child:*Jeanne
  With child
Quidore, Jeanne *SEE* Quidore, Jean-George
Quidort, George; Halifax, N.S., 1752 **7074.6** *p216*
Quiequario, Pietro; Wisconsin, n.d. **9675.7** *p199*
Quig, Andrew; Philadelphia, 1865 **5704.8** *p191*
Quig, John; New York, NY, 1836 **8208.4** *p14*
Quig, Richard 60; St. John, N.B., 1854 **5704.8** *p122*
Quig, William; Philadelphia, 1866 **5704.8** *p206*
Quigg, Catherine; St. John, N.B., 1850 **5704.8** *p67*
Quigg, Ellen 33; St. John, N.B., 1864 **5704.8** *p158*
Quigg, George H.; Philadelphia, 1826 **1450.2** *p114A*
Quigg, John; Philadelphia, 1847 **53.26** *p77*
Quigg, John; Philadelphia, 1848 **5704.8** *p6*
Quigg, Neal 33; St. John, N.B., 1864 **5704.8** *p158*
Quigley, Andrew; Philadelphia, 1849 **53.26** *p77*
  *Relative:*Roseann
Quigley, Andrew; Philadelphia, 1849 **5704.8** *p53*
Quigley, Ann; Philadelphia, 1851 **5704.8** *p81*
Quigley, Anne; St. John, N.B., 1851 **5704.8** *p77*
Quigley, Anne 18; Philadelphia, 1861 **5704.8** *p148*
Quigley, Biddy 5; St. John, N.B., 1849 **5704.8** *p56*
Quigley, Bridget; Philadelphia, 1867 **5704.8** *p217*
Quigley, Bridget; St. John, N.B., 1851 **5704.8** *p77*
Quigley, Bridget 20; Philadelphia, 1854 **5704.8** *p117*
Quigley, Catherine 10; Philadelphia, 1852 **5704.8** *p88*
Quigley, Catherine 10; Philadelphia, 1853 **5704.8** *p112*
Quigley, Catherine 44; St. John, N.B., 1854 **5704.8** *p120*
Quigley, Cecily 3; St. John, N.B., 1849 **5704.8** *p56*
Quigley, Charles; Philadelphia, 1867 **5704.8** *p217*
Quigley, David; New York, NY, 1816 **2859.11** *p41*
Quigley, David; Quebec, 1851 **5704.8** *p73*
Quigley, David; St. John, N.B., 1848 **5704.8** *p43*

Quigley, David 18; St. John, N.B., 1854 **5704.8** *p120*
Quigley, Dennis; America, 1741 **4971** *p76*
Quigley, Elizabeth; St. John, N.B., 1847 **5704.8** *p33*
Quigley, Ellen; Philadelphia, 1864 **5704.8** *p179*
Quigley, Fanny; New York, NY, 1869 **5704.8** *p235*
Quigley, Fanny; Philadelphia, 1870 **5704.8** *p238*
Quigley, George 22; Philadelphia, 1854 **5704.8** *p117*
Quigley, George R. 2; St. John, N.B., 1854 **5704.8** *p120*
Quigley, Hugh; Philadelphia, 1852 **5704.8** *p84*
Quigley, Hugh; Philadelphia, 1866 **5704.8** *p206*
Quigley, Isabella 5; St. John, N.B., 1854 **5704.8** *p120*
Quigley, James; Massachusetts, 1847 **5881.1** *p82*
Quigley, James; Philadelphia, 1851 **5704.8** *p70*
Quigley, James; Philadelphia, 1853 **5704.8** *p101*
Quigley, James; St. John, N.B., 1851 **5704.8** *p78*
Quigley, James; St. John, N.B., 1853 **5704.8** *p99*
Quigley, James 12; Philadelphia, 1852 **5704.8** *p88*
Quigley, John; Philadelphia, 1852 **5704.8** *p85*
Quigley, John; Philadelphia, 1852 **5704.8** *p88*
Quigley, John; Philadelphia, 1852 **5704.8** *p89*
Quigley, John; Philadelphia, 1853 **5704.8** *p102*
Quigley, John; Philadelphia, 1864 **5704.8** *p178*
Quigley, John; Philadelphia, 1865 **5704.8** *p190*
Quigley, John; Philadelphia, 1866 **5704.8** *p206*
Quigley, John; Quebec, 1851 **5704.8** *p74*
Quigley, John; Quebec, 1853 **5704.8** *p104*
Quigley, John; St. John, N.B., 1849 **5704.8** *p48*
Quigley, John 21; Philadelphia, 1854 **5704.8** *p116*
Quigley, Margaret; Quebec, 1851 **5704.8** *p73*
Quigley, Margaret 1; Philadelphia, 1852 **5704.8** *p88*
Quigley, Margaret 1; Quebec, 1850 **5704.8** *p63*
Quigley, Margaret 17; Philadelphia, 1858 **5704.8** *p139*
Quigley, Margary 20; Philadelphia, 1857 **5704.8** *p132*
Quigley, Martha; Philadelphia, 1811 **53.26** *p77*
Quigley, Martha; Philadelphia, 1811 **2859.11** *p18*
Quigley, Martha; St. John, N.B., 1853 **5704.8** *p99*
Quigley, Mary; Philadelphia, 1852 **5704.8** *p88*
Quigley, Mary; Quebec, 1850 **5704.8** *p63*
Quigley, Mary; St. John, N.B., 1850 **5704.8** *p65*
Quigley, Mary 16; St. John, N.B., 1854 **5704.8** *p120*
Quigley, Mary 20; Philadelphia, 1861 **5704.8** *p148*
Quigley, Mary 25; Massachusetts, 1847 **5881.1** *p82*
Quigley, Mary 25; Massachusetts, 1853 **5704.8** *p112*
Quigley, Mary Ann; St. John, N.B., 1849 **5704.8** *p55*
Quigley, Matilda; New York, NY, 1864 **5704.8** *p174*
Quigley, Michael 8; Philadelphia, 1852 **5704.8** *p88*
Quigley, Nancy; Philadelphia, 1852 **5704.8** *p96*
Quigley, Nelly; St. John, N.B., 1851 **5704.8** *p71*
Quigley, Patrick; America, 1866 **5704.8** *p208*
Quigley, Patrick; New York, NY, 1835 **8208.4** *p76*
Quigley, Peter 19; Philadelphia, 1864 **5704.8** *p155*
Quigley, Philip 20; Philadelphia, 1858 **5704.8** *p139*
Quigley, Rebecca; Philadelphia, 1850 **53.26** *p77*
Quigley, Rebecca; Philadelphia, 1850 **5704.8** *p59*
Quigley, Robert 10; St. John, N.B., 1854 **5704.8** *p120*
Quigley, Rose Ann 4; Philadelphia, 1852 **5704.8** *p88*
Quigley, Roseann *SEE* Quigley, Andrew
Quigley, Roseann; Philadelphia, 1849 **5704.8** *p53*
Quigley, Sally; Philadelphia, 1852 **5704.8** *p96*
Quigley, Samuel 20; Philadelphia, 1854 **5704.8** *p117*
Quigley, Sarah; Philadelphia, 1850 **53.26** *p77*
Quigley, Sarah; Philadelphia, 1850 **5704.8** *p69*
Quigley, Sarah 22; St. John, N.B., 1854 **5704.8** *p120*
Quigley, Sarah 24; Philadelphia, 1860 **5704.8** *p145*
Quigley, Susan; Philadelphia, 1866 **5704.8** *p209*
Quigley, Susan; St. John, N.B., 1849 **5704.8** *p56*
Quigley, Thomas 22; Philadelphia, 1860 **5704.8** *p145*

Quigley, William; Philadelphia, 1866 *5704.8 p207*
Quigley, William 19; Philadelphia, 1857 *5704.8 p132*
Quigley, William 20; St. John, N.B., 1854 *5704.8 p120*
Quigley, William 60; St. John, N.B., 1854 *5704.8 p120*
Quigly, Bridget; Philadelphia, 1852 *5704.8 p92*
Quigly, Laurent; Quebec, 1822 *7603 p102*
Quilmead, Wm.; Virginia, 1635 *6219 p3*
Quimblar, Mr. 54; New Orleans, 1837 *778.5 p446*
Quimper, Paul 30; America, 1829 *778.5 p446*
Quin, Agnes; Philadelphia, 1816 *2859.11 p41*
Quin, Arthur; New York, NY, 1816 *2859.11 p41*
Quin, Barney; Quebec, 1849 *5704.8 p51*
Quin, Catharine; New York, NY, 1866 *5704.8 p211*
Quin, Catherine 66; St. John, N.B., 1862 *5704.8 p151*
Quin, Charles; New York, NY, 1834 *8208.4 p4*
Quin, Charles; New York, NY, 1836 *8208.4 p20*
Quin, Charles; Philadelphia, 1811 *53.26 p77*
Quin, Connor; America, 1736-1743 *4971 p57*
Quin, Daniel; New York, NY, 1811 *2859.11 p18*
Quin, Henry; New York, NY, 1811 *2859.11 p18*
Quin, Hugh; New York, NY, 1811 *2859.11 p18*
Quin, James; America, 1735-1743 *4971 p7*
Quin, James; America, 1738 *4971 p38*
Quin, James; America, 1740 *4971 p26*
Quin, James; America, 1742 *4971 p17*
Quin, James; Annapolis, MD, 1742 *4971 p92*
Quin, James; Maryland, 1742 *4971 p108*
Quin, James; New Orleans, 1849 *5704.8 p59*
Quin, James; Philadelphia, 1851 *5704.8 p70*
Quin, James 6 mos; New Orleans, 1849 *5704.8 p59*
Quin, Jane; New York, NY, 1811 *2859.11 p18*
Quin, John; America, 1740 *4971 p28*
Quin, John; New York, NY, 1811 *2859.11 p18*
Quin, John; New York, NY, 1811 *2859.11 p18*
   With family
Quin, John; New York, NY, 1815 *2859.11 p41*
Quin, Margaret; New York, NY, 1811 *2859.11 p18*
Quin, Margaret; Philadelphia, 1848 *53.26 p77*
   *Relative:*Susannah
Quin, Margaret; Philadelphia, 1848 *5704.8 p46*
Quin, Margaret; Quebec, 1852 *5704.8 p94*
Quin, Mary; Philadelphia, 1851 *5704.8 p71*
Quin, Mary 13; St. John, N.B., 1854 *5704.8 p120*
Quin, Mary 25; St. John, N.B., 1862 *5704.8 p151*
Quin, Mary 35; St. John, N.B., 1862 *5704.8 p150*
Quin, Mary Jane; New Orleans, 1849 *5704.8 p59*
Quin, P.; New York, NY, 1811 *2859.11 p18*
Quin, Patrick; New York, NY, 1811 *2859.11 p18*
Quin, Patrick; New York, NY, 1838 *8208.4 p68*
Quin, Peter 18; Philadelphia, 1855 *5704.8 p123*
Quin, Susanna; Quebec, 1849 *5704.8 p51*
Quin, Susannah *SEE* Quin, Margaret
Quin, Susannah; Philadelphia, 1848 *5704.8 p46*
Quin, Terence 45; St. John, N.B., 1863 *5704.8 p153*
Quin, Thomas; Illinois, 1896 *5012.40 p94*
Quin, Thomas; New York, NY, 1838 *8208.4 p68*
Quinan, Robert; New York, NY, 1839 *8208.4 p94*
Quince, Thomas; New York, NY, 1816 *2859.11 p41*
Quinins, Frederick Hermann; New York, 1853 *1450.2 p114A*
Quinlan, Catharine 27; Massachusetts, 1849 *5881.1 p81*
Quinlan, Darby; America, 1741 *4971 p60*
Quinlan, Ellinor; America, 1740 *4971 p69*
Quinlan, James; Massachusetts, 1848 *5881.1 p81*
Quinlan, John; America, 1738 *4971 p13*
Quinlan, John; America, 1738-1743 *4971 p91*
Quinlan, John; Massachusetts, 1848 *5881.1 p81*
Quinlan, John 21; Massachusetts, 1849 *5881.1 p82*
Quinlan, John 24; Massachusetts, 1847 *5881.1 p82*
Quinlan, Kitty 28; Massachusetts, 1849 *5881.1 p82*
Quinlan, Mary 8; Massachusetts, 1850 *5881.1 p82*
Quinlan, Michael 30; Massachusetts, 1848 *5881.1 p82*
Quinlan, Patrick 17; Massachusetts, 1847 *5881.1 p82*
Quinlan, Philip; New York, NY, 1836 *8208.4 p10*
Quinlan, Thomas 11; Massachusetts, 1850 *5881.1 p82*
Quinlan, Thomas 30; Massachusetts, 1848 *5881.1 p82*
Quinlan, William; Illinois, 1861 *2896.5 p32*
Quinlan, William 18; Massachusetts, 1849 *5881.1 p82*

Quinlin, Patrick; New York, 1853 *1450.2 p114A*
Quinn, Alice; Philadelphia, 1870 *5704.8 p237*
Quinn, Alice 19; Massachusetts, 1848 *5881.1 p81*
Quinn, Ann; America, 1868 *5704.8 p231*
Quinn, Ann 20; Massachusetts, 1847 *5881.1 p81*
Quinn, Ann 20; Philadelphia, 1859 *5704.8 p141*
Quinn, Ann 22; St. John, N.B., 1865 *5704.8 p165*
Quinn, Anne 13; New York, NY, 1868 *5704.8 p229*
Quinn, Anne 22; Philadelphia, 1853 *5704.8 p111*
Quinn, Anne 36; St. John, N.B., 1863 *5704.8 p152*
Quinn, Anthony; Philadelphia, 1868 *5704.8 p231*
Quinn, Arthur; New York, NY, 1816 *2859.11 p41*
Quinn, Arthur 13; Massachusetts, 1848 *5881.1 p81*
Quinn, Arthur 45; Massachusetts, 1848 *5881.1 p81*
Quinn, Bernard; Philadelphia, 1865 *5704.8 p200*
Quinn, Bernard; Quebec, 1852 *5704.8 p94*
Quinn, Bridget; Philadelphia, 1847 *53.26 p77*
Quinn, Bridget; Philadelphia, 1847 *5704.8 p30*
Quinn, Bridget; Philadelphia, 1868 *5704.8 p225*
Quinn, Catharine; New York, NY, 1867 *5704.8 p219*
Quinn, Catharine; Philadelphia, 1864 *5704.8 p172*
Quinn, Catherine; Quebec, 1847 *5704.8 p16*
Quinn, Catherine; Quebec, 1851 *5704.8 p74*
Quinn, Catherine 9; Quebec, 1847 *5704.8 p16*
Quinn, Charles; New York, NY, 1816 *2859.11 p41*
Quinn, Charles; Philadelphia, 1811 *2859.11 p18*
Quinn, Charles 6; Philadelphia, 1857 *5704.8 p133*
Quinn, Charles 23; Philadelphia, 1861 *5704.8 p147*
Quinn, Cornelius; America, 1740 *4971 p64*
Quinn, Dan 12; Quebec, 1847 *5704.8 p16*
Quinn, Daniel; New York, NY, 1835 *8208.4 p5*
Quinn, Daniel 19; Massachusetts, 1849 *5881.1 p81*
Quinn, David; Philadelphia, 1864 *5704.8 p175*
Quinn, Edward; St. John, N.B., 1847 *5704.8 p34*
Quinn, Edward W. 41; Kansas, 1879 *5240.1 p61*
Quinn, Eliza; Philadelphia, 1866 *5704.8 p215*
Quinn, Elizabeth; Philadelphia, 1864 *5704.8 p175*
Quinn, Ellen; New York, NY, 1871 *5704.8 p240*
Quinn, Ellen; Philadelphia, 1870 *5704.8 p237*
Quinn, Ellen; Quebec, 1853 *5704.8 p104*
Quinn, Ellen 2; Massachusetts, 1848 *5881.1 p81*
Quinn, Ennis; America, 1738 *4971 p14*
Quinn, Ferdinand; Wisconsin, n.d. *9675.7 p199*
Quinn, Francis; New York, NY, 1816 *2859.11 p41*
Quinn, Grace; Quebec, 1851 *5704.8 p73*
Quinn, Henry; New York, NY, 1816 *2859.11 p41*
Quinn, Hugh; Quebec, 1851 *5704.8 p75*
Quinn, Isaac 13; Quebec, 1853 *5704.8 p105*
Quinn, Isabella; Quebec, 1852 *5704.8 p94*
Quinn, Jacques; Quebec, 1791 *7603 p79*
Quinn, James; New York, NY, 1816 *2859.11 p41*
Quinn, James; Philadelphia, 1865 *5704.8 p181*
Quinn, James; Quebec, 1847 *5704.8 p16*
Quinn, James 6; Quebec, 1847 *5704.8 p16*
Quinn, James 20; Massachusetts, 1848 *5881.1 p81*
Quinn, Jane 19; Massachusetts, 1850 *5881.1 p82*
Quinn, Jane 40; Massachusetts, 1848 *5881.1 p82*
Quinn, Jane 40; Quebec, 1853 *5704.8 p104*
Quinn, Jeremiah 20; Massachusetts, 1848 *5881.1 p81*
Quinn, John; Colorado, 1904 *9678.2 p164*
Quinn, John; New York, NY, 1816 *2859.11 p41*
Quinn, John; New York, NY, 1868 *5704.8 p229*
Quinn, John; New York, NY, 1871 *5704.8 p240*
Quinn, John; Philadelphia, 1866 *5704.8 p215*
Quinn, John 8; Massachusetts, 1848 *5881.1 p82*
Quinn, John 12; St. John, N.B., 1848 *5704.8 p45*
Quinn, John 18; Quebec, 1853 *5704.8 p105*
Quinn, Letita; Philadelphia, 1816 *2859.11 p41*
Quinn, Margaret; New York, NY, 1867 *5704.8 p224*
Quinn, Margaret; Philadelphia, 1865 *5704.8 p198*
Quinn, Margaret 6; Massachusetts, 1848 *5881.1 p82*
Quinn, Margaret 9; Massachusetts, 1850 *5881.1 p82*
Quinn, Margaret 16; Quebec, 1853 *5704.8 p105*
Quinn, Maria 16; Massachusetts, 1848 *5881.1 p82*
Quinn, Mary; Philadelphia, 1866 *5704.8 p203*
Quinn, Mary; Philadelphia, 1869 *5704.8 p236*
Quinn, Mary; Quebec, 1822 *7603 p90*
Quinn, Mary 2; Quebec, 1847 *5704.8 p16*

Quinn, Mary 9; New York, NY, 1868 *5704.8 p229*
Quinn, Mary 9; Quebec, 1853 *5704.8 p105*
Quinn, Mary 18; Philadelphia, 1864 *5704.8 p157*
Quinn, Mary 20; St. John, N.B., 1859 *5704.8 p143*
Quinn, Mary 24; Massachusetts, 1849 *5881.1 p82*
Quinn, Mary 25; Massachusetts, 1850 *5881.1 p82*
Quinn, Mary 25; Philadelphia, 1857 *5704.8 p133*
Quinn, Mary Ann 20; Philadelphia, 1859 *5704.8 p141*
Quinn, Mathew; Quebec, 1852 *5704.8 p94*
Quinn, Matthew; New York, 1872 *1450.2 p114A*
Quinn, Michael; Philadelphia, 1853 *5704.8 p103*
Quinn, Michael; St. John, N.B., 1847 *5704.8 p34*
Quinn, Michael 19; Massachusetts, 1848 *5881.1 p82*
Quinn, Michael 29; Kansas, 1877 *5240.1 p58*
Quinn, Michael 30; Massachusetts, 1848 *5881.1 p82*
Quinn, Nancy; Philadelphia, 1865 *5704.8 p200*
Quinn, Neall; America, 1740 *4971 p64*
Quinn, Nelson 28; Arizona, 1902 *9228.40 p8*
Quinn, Owen; New York, NY, 1866 *5704.8 p212*
Quinn, Owen; St. John, N.B., 1847 *5704.8 p15*
Quinn, Pat; Philadelphia, 1853 *5704.8 p103*
Quinn, Pat 18; St. John, N.B., 1863 *5704.8 p155*
Quinn, Patrick; Arkansas, 1918 *95.2 p102*
Quinn, Patrick; Montreal, 1821 *7603 p100*
Quinn, Patrick; Philadelphia, 1869 *5704.8 p236*
Quinn, Patrick 7; New York, NY, 1871 *5704.8 p240*
Quinn, Peter; America, 1735-1743 *4971 p7*
Quinn, Peter 17; Massachusetts, 1848 *5881.1 p82*
Quinn, Peter 58; Massachusetts, 1849 *5881.1 p82*
Quinn, Roger; New York, NY, 1868 *5704.8 p227*
Quinn, Rose; St. John, N.B., 1848 *5704.8 p45*
Quinn, Rose 17; Massachusetts, 1848 *5881.1 p82*
Quinn, Samuel 12; Quebec, 1853 *5704.8 p105*
Quinn, Sarah; New York, NY, 1868 *5704.8 p229*
Quinn, Sarah; Philadelphia, 1864 *5704.8 p185*
Quinn, Sarah; Philadelphia, 1866 *5704.8 p215*
Quinn, Sarah; Quebec, 1851 *5704.8 p75*
Quinn, Sarah 20; Philadelphia, 1857 *5704.8 p132*
Quinn, Susan; Philadelphia, 1869 *5704.8 p236*
Quinn, Susan; Quebec, 1852 *5704.8 p94*
Quinn, Susan 17; Massachusetts, 1849 *5881.1 p82*
Quinn, Thomas; New York, NY, 1836 *8208.4 p22*
Quinn, Thomas 40; Quebec, 1853 *5704.8 p104*
Quinn, Tobias; Philadelphia, 1865 *5704.8 p197*
Quinn, William; New York, NY, 1865 *5704.8 p195*
Quinne, Felix; St. John, N.B., 1851 *5704.8 p80*
Quinnie, Daniel 26; Massachusetts, 1849 *5881.1 p81*
Quino, Samuel 21; Maryland, 1724 *3690.1 p28A*
Quintana y Alarid, Felisiana; Santa Fe, NM, 1848 *3702.7 p113*
Quintin, James 19; Maryland or Virginia, 1735 *3690.1 p28A*
Quintine, Elizabeth Edward; South Carolina, 1658-1721 *1639.20 p252*
Quinto, Laccaro; Iowa, 1866-1943 *123.54 p40*
Quinton, Robert; New York, NY, 1815 *2859.11 p41*
Quinwell, John 67; Kansas, 1875 *5240.1 p56*
Quirk, Daniel; America, 1742 *4971 p56*
Quirk, Edward M.; Arizona, 1883 *2764.35 p57*
Quirk, Ellen; America, 1742 *4971 p60*
Quirk, Ellenor; America, 1742 *4971 p56*
Quirk, Johanna 20; Massachusetts, 1849 *5881.1 p82*
Quirry, Stephen 20; Jamaica, 1722 *3690.1 p28A*
Quist, Anna; Washington, 1859-1920 *2872.1 p32*
Quist, Anna Emilia; Iowa, 1866-1943 *123.54 p40*
Quist, Charles A.; Iowa, 1866-1943 *123.54 p40*
Quist, Knut Robert; Washington, 1859-1920 *2872.1 p32*
Quist, Knut Wallentin; Washington, 1859-1920 *2872.1 p32*
Quizic, John; America, 1847 *1450.2 p114A*
Quliza, Anton; America, 1890 *1450.2 p114A*
Quong, Toy Man; Arkansas, 1918 *95.2 p102*
Quoriskey, Biddy 24; Philadelphia, 1864 *5704.8 p160*
Qusten, Anne 5; Quebec, 1856 *5704.8 p129*
Qusten, James 54; Quebec, 1856 *5704.8 p129*
Qusten, Robert 19; Quebec, 1856 *5704.8 p129*

R

Raab, Sebastian; America, 1852 *1450.2 p115A*
Raabe, . . .; Canada, 1776-1783 *9786 p31*
Raabe, Carl Heinrich; America, 1902 *4610.10 p123*
Raabe, Herman 24; Kansas, 1879 *5240.1 p61*
Raaf, Andreas *SEE* Raaf, Michael
Raaf, Johannes *SEE* Raaf, Michael
Raaf, Margaretha Baumann *SEE* Raaf, Michael
Raaf, Maria Barbara *SEE* Raaf, Michael
Raaf, Michael; Pennsylvania, 1751 *2444 p201*
  *Wife:*Margaretha Baumann
  *Child:*Johannes
  *Child:*Andreas
  *Child:*Maria Barbara
Raake, Christian; New York, NY, 1836 *8208.4 p17*
Raappana, Aleksander; Washington, 1859-1920 *2872.1 p32*
Raasch, Frederick; Wisconsin, n.d. *9675.7 p199*
Raball, Juan 25; New Orleans, 1839 *778.5 p446*
Rabbe, Margarete Dorothee Wilhelmine; America, 1830 *4815.7 p92*
Rabbe, Wilhelm; America, 1848 *8582.1 p28*
Rabbermann, Anne Marie C. Bullmann *SEE* Rabbermann, Heinrich
Rabbermann, Ernst Heinrich Wilhelm; America, 1846 *4610.10 p155*
Rabbermann, Heinrich; America, 1838-1846 *4610.10 p155*
  *Wife:*Anne Marie C. Bullmann
Rabbish, James; Virginia, 1642 *6219 p191*
Rabe, Albrecht Christian; Quebec, 1776 *9786 p263*
Rabe, Anthony Frederick; America, 1836 *1450.2 p115A*
Rabe, Johannes; Saratoga, NY, 1777 *8137 p12*
Rabel, T. 24; America, 1838 *778.5 p446*
Raber, Georg; Ohio, 1869-1887 *8582 p23*
Rabick, Mary *SEE* Rabick, Michael
Rabick, Michael; America, 1890 *7137 p169*
  *Wife:*Mary
Rabie, P. 28; New Orleans, 1831 *778.5 p446*
Rabik, Mary *SEE* Rabik, Michael
Rabik, Michael; America, 1890 *7137 p169*
  *Wife:*Mary
Rabin, Mr. 25; America, 1839 *778.5 p447*
Rabke, William; America, 1845 *1450.2 p115A*
Rabmowitz, Abraham 30; New York, NY, 1878 *9253 p47*
Rabmowitz, Debora 25; New York, NY, 1878 *9253 p47*
Rabmowitz, Lina 11 mos; New York, NY, 1878 *9253 p47*
Rabourden, G. J. 16; New Orleans, 1835 *778.5 p447*
Rabuteaux, Ms. 37; America, 1838 *778.5 p447*
Raby, Robert; Virginia, 1637 *6219 p86*
Rabye, Robert; Virginia, 1635 *6219 p3*
Racanelli, Vitonicole; Arkansas, 1918 *95.2 p102*
Racca, Louis Henry; Louisiana, 1789-1819 *778.5 p556*
Racchione, Guiseppe 44; West Virginia, 1904 *9788.3 p19*
Rach, . . .; Canada, 1776-1783 *9786 p31*
Rach, Catha'ne 22; Massachusetts, 1849 *5881.1 p83*
Rach, Ellen 18; Massachusetts, 1849 *5881.1 p83*
Rachel, Phillip; Illinois, 1860 *2896.5 p32*
Rachki, Louis; Iowa, 1866-1943 *123.54 p40*
Rachmel, August 40; New Orleans, 1832 *778.5 p447*
Rack, Joseph; Wisconsin, n.d. *9675.7 p199*
Racka, Josef Vok; Arkansas, 1918 *95.2 p103*
Racki, Andrew C.; Iowa, 1866-1943 *123.54 p40*
Rackly, Rich.; Virginia, 1639 *6219 p154*
Rackstrow, Thomas 38; Virginia, 1774 *1219.7 p186*

Racon, Mr. 12; New Orleans, 1822 *778.5 p447*
Racon, Mrs. 28; New Orleans, 1822 *778.5 p447*
Racon, V. 30; New Orleans, 1822 *778.5 p447*
Radas, Donat 45; America, 1827 *778.5 p447*
Radaux, Johann Franziscus; Philadelphia, 1779 *8137 p12*
Radaz, Donat 50; America, 1836 *778.5 p447*
Radcliff, Jane 20; New England, 1699 *2212 p18*
Radcliff, Tho 21; Virginia, 1699 *2212 p26*
Radcliffe, George; Illinois, 1870 *2896.5 p32*
Radcliffe, John 24; Philadelphia, 1775 *1219.7 p255*
Raddish, David; Virginia, 1642 *6219 p193*
Rade, John 17; Maryland, 1730 *3690.1 p185*
Rade, Michael; Quebec, 1847 *5704.8 p27*
Radeback, Henry; Philadelphia, 1759 *9973.7 p34*
Radeback, Michael; Philadelphia, 1760 *9973.7 p34*
Rademacher, Carl J.; Washington, 1859-1920 *2872.1 p32*
Rademacher, Gerhard; Illinois, 1889 *5012.40 p25*
Rademacher, Heinerich; Canada, 1783 *9786 p38A*
Rademacher, Herman; Wisconsin, n.d. *9675.7 p199*
Rademacher, John; Wisconsin, n.d. *9675.7 p199*
Rader, Anton; America, 1814 *8582 p23*
Radesivic, Turc; Iowa, 1866-1943 *123.54 p40*
Radez, J. M. 23; America, 1832 *778.5 p447*
Radez, M. 27; America, 1832 *778.5 p447*
Radford, John 17; Pennsylvania, Virginia or Maryland, 1719 *3690.1 p185*
Radford, Richard; Virginia, 1636 *6219 p74*
Radford, Thomas; Virginia, 1647 *6219 p247*
Radford, William 19; Pennsylvania, Virginia or Maryland, 1719 *3690.1 p185*
Radfort, Michael 25; Massachusetts, 1850 *5881.1 p86*
Radicus, William 46; Massachusetts, 1848 *5881.1 p87*
Radigan, Mary 22; Massachusetts, 1848 *5881.1 p85*
Radigois, E. 23; New Orleans, 1826 *778.5 p447*
Radinowitz, Esther 9; New York, NY, 1878 *9253 p47*
Radinowitz, Reisel 9; New York, NY, 1878 *9253 p47*
Radinowitz, Rune 42; New York, NY, 1878 *9253 p47*
Radinowitz, Sara 16; New York, NY, 1878 *9253 p47*
Radish, Jon.; Virginia, 1637 *6219 p113*
Raditch, Andrew; Arkansas, 1918 *95.2 p103*
Radke, Frank Edward; Wisconsin, n.d. *9675.7 p199*
Radley, Richard 37; Virginia, 1700 *2212 p32*
Radloff, Fred; Wisconsin, n.d. *9675.7 p199*
Radloff, Johann; Wisconsin, n.d. *9675.7 p199*
Radosevic, Mijo; Iowa, 1866-1943 *123.54 p40*
Radosevic, Rudolf; Iowa, 1866-1943 *123.54 p75*
Radosevic, Rudolph; Iowa, 1866-1943 *123.54 p40*
Radosevic, Rudolph; Iowa, 1866-1943 *123.54 p41*
Radosevich, Anton; Iowa, 1866-1943 *123.54 p41*
Radosevich, Joe; Iowa, 1866-1943 *123.54 p75*
Radosevich, Josip; Iowa, 1866-1943 *123.54 p75*
Radosevich, Lude; Iowa, 1866-1943 *123.54 p41*
Radosevich, Stepan; Iowa, 1866-1943 *123.54 p41*
Radoszewski, Josef 30; New York, 1912 *9980.29 p72*
Radovich, Christopher J.; Nevada, 1876 *2764.35 p58*
Radovich, David J.; Nevada, 1876 *2764.35 p60*
Radovick, Nickola Chris; Arkansas, 1918 *95.2 p103*
Radtke, Carl; Wisconsin, n.d. *9675.7 p199*
Radtke, Frank; Wisconsin, n.d. *9675.7 p199*
Radu, John; Iowa, 1866-1943 *123.54 p41*
Radway, Isaac; Virginia, 1638 *6219 p145*
Radway, Jane; Virginia, 1636 *6219 p27*
Radway, Wm.; Virginia, 1635 *6219 p27*
Radway, Wm.; Virginia, 1638 *6219 p145*
Radwell, William 22; Jamaica, 1735 *3690.1 p185*
Radye, Robert; Virginia, 1636 *6219 p77*

Radziminski, Karol; New York, 1831 *4606 p176*
Rae, John; Northwest Terr., 1848 *9775.5 p219*
Rae, John; South Carolina, 1743 *1639.20 p265*
Rae, Robert Hancorn; Illinois, 1876 *7857 p6*
Rae, William; Illinois, 1863 *7857 p6*
Raeber, Johann; America, 1840 *8582.3 p53*
Raefs, George; Wisconsin, n.d. *9675.7 p199*
Raefs, John L.; Wisconsin, n.d. *9675.7 p199*
Raes, Pete; Arkansas, 1918 *95.2 p103*
Raetzler, Catharina Dorothea; Port uncertain, 1750-1755 *2444 p169*
Rafert, William; America, 1845 *1450.2 p115A*
Raffel, Frederick; Illinois, 1887 *2896.5 p32*
Raffel, John; Illinois, 1888 *2896.5 p32*
Rafferty, Andrew; Illinois, 1868 *7857 p6*
Rafferty, Ann *SEE* Rafferty, John
Rafferty, Ann; Philadelphia, 1847 *5704.8 p32*
Rafferty, Ann 6; St. John, N.B., 1860 *5704.8 p144*
Rafferty, Ann 40; St. John, N.B., 1860 *5704.8 p144*
Rafferty, Anne 20; Philadelphia, 1859 *5704.8 p142*
Rafferty, Bridget 1; St. John, N.B., 1860 *5704.8 p144*
Rafferty, Catharine 25; Massachusetts, 1847 *5881.1 p83*
Rafferty, Catherine 4; St. John, N.B., 1860 *5704.8 p144*
Rafferty, Cormack; New York, NY, 1837 *8208.4 p55*
Rafferty, Elizabeth 1; St. John, N.B., 1860 *5704.8 p144*
Rafferty, Hugh 11; New York, NY, 1864 *5704.8 p186*
Rafferty, Hugh 18; Massachusetts, 1849 *5881.1 p84*
Rafferty, Hugh 40; St. John, N.B., 1860 *5704.8 p144*
Rafferty, John; America, 1740 *4971 p24*
Rafferty, John; Illinois, 1874 *5012.39 p26*
Rafferty, John; New York, NY, 1811 *2859.11 p18*
Rafferty, John; Philadelphia, 1847 *53.26 p77*
  *Relative:*Ann
Rafferty, John; Philadelphia, 1847 *5704.8 p31*
Rafferty, John 7; St. John, N.B., 1860 *5704.8 p144*
Rafferty, John 39; Arizona, 1890 *2764.35 p59*
Rafferty, Mary; St. John, N.B., 1848 *5704.8 p44*
Rafferty, Mary 9; St. John, N.B., 1860 *5704.8 p144*
Rafferty, Mary Ann 5; Massachusetts, 1847 *5881.1 p85*
Rafferty, Michael 30; Massachusetts, 1849 *5881.1 p86*
Rafferty, Michael 45; Massachusetts, 1848 *5881.1 p85*
Rafferty, Owen 12; Massachusetts, 1849 *5881.1 p86*
Rafferty, Patrick; New York, NY, 1816 *2859.11 p41*
Rafferty, Patrick; St. John, N.B., 1848 *5704.8 p44*
Rafferty, Peter; New York, NY, 1864 *5704.8 p186*
Rafferty, Simeon; New York, NY, 1816 *2859.11 p41*
Rafferty, Stewart; New York, NY, 1816 *2859.11 p41*
Rafferty, William; New York, NY, 1811 *2859.11 p18*
Raffles, Benjamin; Antigua (Antego), 1755 *1219.7 p36*
Raffles, Thomas; Jamaica, 1754 *1219.7 p27*
Raflin, Mr.; Died enroute, 1752-1753 *3689.17 p22*
Raflin, Anna Margareta 5 wks *SEE* Raflin, Eva
Raflin, Eva; South Carolina, 1752-1753 *3689.17 p22*
  *Relative:*Mathias 14
  *Relative:*John Leonard 11
  *Relative:*Margaretha 10
  *Relative:*Eva Marie 3
  *Relative:*Anna Margareta 5 wks
Raflin, Eva Marie 3 *SEE* Raflin, Eva
Raflin, John Leonard 11 *SEE* Raflin, Eva
Raflin, Margaretha 10 *SEE* Raflin, Eva
Raflin, Mathias 14 *SEE* Raflin, Eva
Rafnsdottir, Olof 26; Quebec, 1879 *2557.1 p20*
Rafnsson, Olafur 59; Quebec, 1879 *2557.1 p20*
Rafnsson, Olof 26; Quebec, 1879 *2557.1 p20*
Rafter, Dennis; New York, NY, 1816 *2859.11 p41*
Raftrey, John; New York, NY, 1816 *2859.11 p41*

Ragan, T.; New York, NY, 1816 *2859.11 p41*
Rager, Adalbert; Wisconsin, n.d. *9675.7 p199*
Ragg, Benj.; Virginia, 1635 *6219 p27*
Ragged, Richard; Virginia, 1638 *6219 p125*
Raggen, James 37; St. John, N.B., 1854 *5704.8 p122*
Ragle, Phillip; Illinois, 1860 *2896.5 p32*
Ragnaux, Mr. 40; New Orleans, 1826 *778.5 p447*
Ragnous, Anna Maria 8 *SEE* Ragnous, John
Ragnous, John 12 *SEE* Ragnous, John
Ragnous, John 34; Georgia, 1738 *9332 p334*
  *Wife:*Margaretta 36
  *Son:*John 12
  *Daughter:*Anna Maria 8
Ragnous, Margaretta 36 *SEE* Ragnous, John
Ragon, Adolphe 10; Ohio, 1820 *778.5 p447*
Ragon, Clare 3; Ohio, 1820 *778.5 p447*
Ragon, Cornelius; New York, NY, 1838 *8208.4 p86*
Ragon, Delphine 6; Ohio, 1820 *778.5 p448*
Ragon, Etalide 8; Ohio, 1820 *778.5 p448*
Ragon, Jean Baptiste Marie 38; Ohio, 1820 *778.5 p448*
Ragon, Mathilde 30; Ohio, 1820 *778.5 p448*
Ragona, Andrea; Iowa, 1866-1943 *123.54 p41*
Ragona, Joseph; Iowa, 1866-1943 *123.54 p75*
Ragouzzy, Mme. 26; America, 1839 *778.5 p448*
Ragouzzy, Mariette 8; America, 1839 *778.5 p448*
Ragrosen Gusercratty, Marie 29; Port uncertain, 1837 *778.5 p448*
Raguet, Mme.; Port uncertain, 1839 *778.5 p448*
Raguet, John 22; Philadelphia, 1774 *1219.7 p183*
Raguet, Joseph; Port uncertain, 1839 *778.5 p448*
Rahbuck, John F.; Illinois, 1896 *5012.40 p54*
Rahe, A. M. Elisabeth Vogt *SEE* Rahe, Carl Fr.
Rahe, A. M. W. Caroline *SEE* Rahe, Carl Fr.
Rahe, A.M. Wilhelmine Louise *SEE* Rahe, Carl Fr.
Rahe, Carl Fr. *SEE* Rahe, Carl Fr.
Rahe, Carl Fr.; America, 1881 *4610.10 p152*
  *Wife:*A. M. Elisabeth Vogt
  *Child:*Carl Fr.
  *Child:*A. M. W. Caroline
  *Child:*A.M. Wilhelmine Louise
Rahelly, Charles; America, 1740 *4971 p56*
Rahelly, John; Illinois, 1858 *7857 p6*
Rahily, Catharine 30; Massachusetts, 1849 *5881.1 p83*
Rahind, William 18; Pennsylvania, 1731 *3690.1 p185*
Rahling, William; America, 1847-1849 *1450.2 p117A*
Rahm, Wilhelm; New Orleans, 1848 *8125.8 p438*
  With wife
  With 8 children
Rahn, Fred; Illinois, 1874 *5012.39 p26*
Rahn, George; Illinois, 1884 *2896.5 p32*
Rahrich, Anton; Alberta, n.d. *5262 p58*
Raible, Friedrich; Ohio, 1869-1887 *8582 p23*
Raic, Gabrial; Iowa, 1866-1943 *123.54 p41*
Raid, David 19; Maryland, 1773 *1219.7 p173*
Raigel, Anna; America, 1751 *2444 p201*
Raik, Max; Arkansas, 1918 *95.2 p103*
Raik, Max; Arkansas, 1918 *95.2 p105*
Railey, Thomas; Quebec, 1772 *7603 p79*
Raim, Martin; Wisconsin, n.d. *9675.7 p199*
Raimond, . . .; Canada, 1776-1783 *9786 p31*
Raimondo, Frank; Iowa, 1866-1943 *123.54 p41*
Raimondo, Sam; Arkansas, 1918 *95.2 p103*
Rainaud, Mme. 30; Port uncertain, 1836 *778.5 p448*
Rainaud, Mr. 40; Port uncertain, 1836 *778.5 p448*
Rainaud, Hulas 19; Port uncertain, 1836 *778.5 p448*
Rainbert, Catherine; St. John, N.B., 1847 *5704.8 p33*
Raine, Rowland; Virginia, 1636 *6219 p77*
Rainer, Elizabeth; Wisconsin, n.d. *9675.7 p199*
Rainer, Joe; Wisconsin, n.d. *9675.7 p199*
Rainer, Joseph; Wisconsin, n.d. *9675.7 p199*
Rainer, Sebastian; Wisconsin, n.d. *9675.7 p199*
Raines, Pat.; America, 1742 *4971 p49*
Raines, Patrick; America, 1741 *4971 p48*
Rainey, James; New York, NY, 1815 *2859.11 p41*
Rainey, James; San Francisco, 1866 *3840.3 p8*
Rainey, Robert; Ohio, 1812-1840 *9892.11 p38*
Rainford, Captain; Jamaica, 1774 *1219.7 p205*
  With wife
  With 3 children
Rainhard, Nicho.; Virginia, 1646 *6219 p242*
Rainton, Thomas 16; Pennsylvania, 1728 *3690.1 p186*
Rairnes, A. 40; New Orleans, 1826 *778.5 p448*
Rais, Linka; Iowa, 1866-1943 *123.54 p41*
Raisch, Christina *SEE* Raisch, Conrad
Raisch, Conrad; Pennsylvania, 1749 *2444 p202*
  *Wife:*Christina
  With 4 children
Raisch, Johan Conrad; Pennsylvania, 1750 *2444 p202*
Raisch, Johan Michel; Pennsylvania, 1751 *2444 p202*
Raisch, Michael; America, 1729-1800 *2444 p202*
Raisner, Henry; Indiana, 1880 *5647.5 p31*
  *Wife:*Louise Speck
Raisner, Henry; New Orleans, 1848 *5647.5 p31*

Raisner, Katherine; Indiana, 1848-1850 *5647.5 p31*
Raisner, Louise Speck *SEE* Raisner, Henry
Raison, Francis; Virginia, 1639 *6219 p151*
Raison, Xavier 23; New Orleans, 1838 *778.5 p448*
Raisser, Anna Maria *SEE* Raisser, Jacob
Raisser, Jacob; Pennsylvania, 1752 *2444 p202*
  *Wife:*Anna Maria
  With 6 children
Rajocic, Nikola; Iowa, 1866-1943 *123.54 p41*
Rak, Ivan; Iowa, 1866-1943 *123.54 p41*
Rak, Joseph; Iowa, 1866-1943 *123.54 p41*
Rak, Marko; Iowa, 1866-1943 *123.54 p75*
Rak, Tereza Josefina; Iowa, 1866-1943 *123.54 p75*
Rakela, George; Wisconsin, n.d. *9675.7 p199*
Rakich, Vid; Iowa, 1866-1943 *123.54 p41*
Rakman, . . .; Canada, 1776-1783 *9786 p31*
Ral, Robert; Iowa, 1866-1943 *123.54 p41*
Ralas, Gus; Arkansas, 1918 *95.2 p68*
Ralas, Gus; Arkansas, 1918 *95.2 p103*
Rale, Sebastian; America, 1700-1877 *8582.3 p80*
Raleigh, Walter; Indiana, 1850 *9117 p20*
Ralfe, Margett; Virginia, 1643 *6219 p205*
Rall, Colonel; America, 1775-1781 *8582.3 p75*
Rall, Charles; America, 1855 *6014.1 p3*
Rall, Saml; South Carolina, 1788 *7119 p199*
Ralle, Colonel; America, 1775-1781 *8582.3 p75*
Rallecke, Jean 23; Port uncertain, 1839 *778.5 p448*
Ralleehe, Jean 23; Port uncertain, 1839 *778.5 p448*
Rallestr, Robt; America, 1698 *2212 p10*
Ralley, D. 45; Mexico, 1829 *778.5 p449*
Ralph, John H.; Arkansas, 1918 *95.2 p103*
Ralph, Joseph 27; Boston, 1774 *1219.7 p211*
Ralph, Robert; Illinois, 1863 *5012.38 p98*
Ralston, Andrew 7 *SEE* Ralston, John
Ralston, Anne 2 *SEE* Ralston, Anne
Ralston, Anne 5 *SEE* Ralston, Anne
Ralston, Anne 34; Philadelphia, 1803 *53.26 p77*
  *Relative:*Anne 2
  *Relative:*Robert 19
  *Relative:*David 15
  *Relative:*John 11
  *Relative:*Jane 8
  *Relative:*Anne 5
  *Relative:*Josh 2
Ralston, David 9 *SEE* Ralston, James
Ralston, David 9 *SEE* Ralston, John
Ralston, David 15 *SEE* Ralston, Anne
Ralston, Ellen 3; Philadelphia, 1870 *5704.8 p238*
Ralston, James; Charleston, SC, 1806 *1639.20 p265*
Ralston, James 4; Philadelphia, 1870 *5704.8 p238*
Ralston, James 5 *SEE* Ralston, John
Ralston, James 15 *SEE* Ralston, James
Ralston, James 45; Philadelphia, 1803 *53.26 p78*
  *Relative:*Mary 40
  *Relative:*James 15
  *Relative:*Mary 12
  *Relative:*David 9
  *Relative:*Josh 5
Ralston, Jane 8 *SEE* Ralston, Anne
Ralston, John; Philadelphia, 1870 *5704.8 p238*
Ralston, John 11 *SEE* Ralston, Anne
Ralston, John 40; Philadelphia, 1803 *53.26 p78*
  *Relative:*Sarah 40
  *Relative:*David 9
  *Relative:*Andrew 7
  *Relative:*William 3
  *Relative:*James 5
Ralston, Josh 2 *SEE* Ralston, Anne
Ralston, Josh 5 *SEE* Ralston, James
Ralston, Mary 12 *SEE* Ralston, James
Ralston, Mary 40 *SEE* Ralston, James
Ralston, Mary J. 9 mos; Philadelphia, 1870 *5704.8 p238*
Ralston, Robert; Charleston, SC, 1813 *1639.20 p265*
Ralston, Robert 19 *SEE* Ralston, Anne
Ralston, Sarah 40 *SEE* Ralston, John
Ralston, William 3 *SEE* Ralston, John
Ramanousky, Adam; Wisconsin, n.d. *9675.7 p199*
Rambdt, Agusta 10 *SEE* Rambdt, Fridrik
Rambdt, Fridrik 13 *SEE* Rambdt, Fridrik
Rambdt, Fridrik 57; Quebec, 1879 *2557.1 p21*
  *Wife:*Soly 50
  *Son:*Fridrik 13
  *Son:*Valgerdur 12
  *Daughter:*Agusta 10
Rambdt, Soly 50 *SEE* Rambdt, Fridrik
Rambdt, Valgerdur 12 *SEE* Rambdt, Fridrik
Ramberg, Conrad Albi; Arkansas, 1918 *95.2 p103*
Ramel, Mr. 23; New Orleans, 1822 *778.5 p449*
Ramelo, George; New York, NY, 1835 *8208.4 p37*
Ramen, Francois 40; America, 1837 *778.5 p449*
Ramer, Frederick; Indiana, 1847 *9117 p18*
Ramezay, Commandant de; Quebec, 1759 *9775.5 p197*

Ramish, Robert 29; Maryland or Virginia, 1733 *3690.1 p186*
Ramitz, John; Wisconsin, n.d. *9675.7 p199*
Ramkey, Henry Conrad; Virginia, 1847 *4626.16 p13*
Ramler, . . .; Canada, 1776-1783 *9786 p31*
Ramon, Mr. 22; America, 1820 *778.5 p449*
Ramonawski, Ademas; Wisconsin, n.d. *9675.7 p199*
Rampelberg, Henri; Iowa, 1866-1943 *123.54 p75*
Rampelberg, Henry Victor; Iowa, 1866-1943 *123.54 p75*
Rampelberg, Marie; Iowa, 1866-1943 *123.54 p75*
Rampelberg, Victor Henry; Iowa, 1866-1943 *123.54 p41*
Ramsay, Agnes 31; Philadelphia, 1854 *5704.8 p118*
Ramsay, Charles; America, 1761 *1219.7 p80*
Ramsay, Charles; Philadelphia, 1853 *5704.8 p103*
Ramsay, Elizabeth 11; Quebec, 1847 *5704.8 p8*
Ramsay, Elizabeth 19; Philadelphia, 1857 *5704.8 p132*
Ramsay, Henry 9 mos; Quebec, 1847 *5704.8 p8*
Ramsay, Henry 21; Philadelphia, 1857 *5704.8 p132*
Ramsay, Hugh 20; Quebec, 1858 *5704.8 p138*
Ramsay, Isabella 3; Quebec, 1847 *5704.8 p8*
Ramsay, James; Philadelphia, 1851 *5704.8 p76*
Ramsay, John; Charleston, SC, 1734 *1639.20 p266*
Ramsay, John; Charleston, SC, 1804 *1639.20 p266*
Ramsay, John; Colorado, 1896 *9678.2 p164*
Ramsay, John 13; Quebec, 1847 *5704.8 p8*
Ramsay, John 20; Maryland, 1721 *3690.1 p186*
Ramsay, Mary; Philadelphia, 1851 *5704.8 p76*
Ramsay, Mary; Quebec, 1847 *5704.8 p8*
Ramsay, Mary; St. John, N.B., 1847 *5704.8 p9*
Ramsay, Mary 6; Quebec, 1847 *5704.8 p8*
Ramsay, Mary Jane; Philadelphia, 1852 *5704.8 p84*
Ramsay, Robert; Philadelphia, 1848 *53.26 p78*
Ramsay, Robert; Philadelphia, 1848 *5704.8 p45*
Ramsay, Sally; Philadelphia, 1851 *5704.8 p76*
Ramsay, Sally; Philadelphia, 1853 *5704.8 p88*
Ramsay, Susan; Philadelphia, 1853 *5704.8 p100*
Ramsay, William; Quebec, 1847 *5704.8 p8*
Ramsay, William 22; Virginia, 1774 *1219.7 p239*
Ramsay, William P. 21; Philadelphia, 1864 *5704.8 p157*
Ramsbotten, John; Virginia, 1698 *2212 p14*
Ramsburger, Anna; New York, 1849 *3652 p73*
Ramsden, Jon.; Virginia, 1642 *6219 p196*
Ramsel, John; Kansas, 1872 *5240.1 p35*
Ramsey, Charles; Philadelphia, 1865 *5704.8 p200*
Ramsey, Eliza.; Virginia, 1642 *6219 p192*
Ramsey, George; New York, NY, 1815 *2859.11 p41*
Ramsey, James; New York, NY, 1838 *8208.4 p69*
Ramsey, James 23; Philadelphia, 1857 *5704.8 p133*
Ramsey, John 20; Maryland, 1721 *3690.1 p186*
Ramsey, Joseph 30; St. John, N.B., 1862 *5704.8 p150*
Ramsey, Penelope; Virginia, 1636 *6219 p22*
Ramsey, Robert 20; Jamaica, 1735 *3690.1 p186*
Ramsey, Samuel; Virginia, 1635 *6219 p23*
Ramsey, Thomas 17; Jamaica, 1773 *1219.7 p168*
Ramthun, William; Wisconsin, n.d. *9675.7 p199*
Ran, Michael J.; America, 1879 *5240.1 p35*
Ranar, Max Gustaf; Washington, 1859-1920 *2872.1 p32*
Rance, Mr. 60; New Orleans, 1839 *778.5 p449*
Rance, Edward William 22; Kansas, 1885 *5240.1 p67*
Ranchbaner, Matias; Arkansas, 1918 *95.2 p103*
Rancke, Christian; New York, NY, 1836 *8208.4 p17*
Rand, Asger; Arkansas, 1918 *95.2 p103*
Rand, John 13; Virginia, 1721 *3690.1 p186*
Rand, Thomas 22; Virginia, 1774 *1219.7 p186*
Rand, William 20; Jamaica, 1730 *3690.1 p186*
Randal, Fredc. 22; Port uncertain, 1839 *778.5 p449*
Randal, Robert 21; Maryland, 1774 *1219.7 p222*
Randall, Ann 30 *SEE* Randall, John
Randall, Catharine 45; Massachusetts, 1849 *5881.1 p83*
Randall, Francis 32; Jamaica, 1731 *3690.1 p186*
Randall, John; Virginia, 1639 *6219 p159*
Randall, John 19; Philadelphia, 1774 *1219.7 p217*
Randall, John 23; Philadelphia, 1774 *1219.7 p216*
Randall, John 27; Philadelphia, 1774 *1219.7 p216*
Randall, John 40; Maryland, 1774 *1219.7 p204*
  *Wife:*Ann 30
Randall, Mary 15; Virginia, 1718 *3690.1 p186*
Randall, Tho.; Virginia, 1635 *6219 p16*
Randall, Thomas; Virginia, 1635 *6219 p16*
Randall, William; Washington, 1859-1920 *2872.1 p32*
Randam, Tim.; America, 1736 *4971 p43*
Randam, Timothy; America, 1736 *4971 p45*
Randazzo, Calogero; Arkansas, 1918 *95.2 p103*
Randell, John Davis 29; California, 1867 *3840.3 p8*
Randeris, Christian; Arkansas, 1918 *95.2 p103*
Randers, Christian; Arkansas, 1918 *95.2 p103*
Randolph, Milward; Virginia, 1621 *6219 p24*
Rands, William 33; Maryland, 1775 *1219.7 p253*
Ranel, Albert 32; America, 1838 *778.5 p449*
Raney, Abraham 28; New York, 1774 *1219.7 p218*
Rangais, P. 20; New Orleans, 1839 *778.5 p449*
Rangas, Mathew Anton; Arkansas, 1918 *95.2 p103*
Rangeloff, Evan; Arkansas, 1918 *95.2 p103*

Ranguis, J. 25; New Orleans, 1826 ***778.5*** *p449*
Ranieri, Silvio 16; New York, NY, 1893 ***9026.4*** *p42*
Ranighan, John; New York, NY, 1811 ***2859.11*** *p18*
Ranke, Louis 27; Kansas, 1884 ***5240.1*** *p65*
Ranken, John; South Carolina, 1716 ***1639.20*** *p266*
Ranken, William 18; Jamaica, 1754 ***3690.1*** *p186*
Rankin, Ann; Quebec, 1850 ***5704.8*** *p67*
Rankin, Ann 6; St. John, N.B., 1855 ***5704.8*** *p127*
Rankin, Catherine; St. John, N.B., 1853 ***5704.8*** *p106*
Rankin, Catherine 8; St. John, N.B., 1855 ***5704.8*** *p127*
Rankin, Charles; North Carolina, 1731-1807 ***1639.20*** *p266*
Rankin, David; Quebec, 1847 ***5704.8*** *p28*
Rankin, Duncan; America, 1802 ***1639.20*** *p266*
Rankin, Eliza Jane 19; Quebec, 1855 ***5704.8*** *p126*
Rankin, Francis 20; Philadelphia, 1856 ***5704.8*** *p128*
Rankin, Henry 17; Philadelphia, 1804 ***53.26*** *p78*
Rankin, Hugh 16; Philadelphia, 1833 ***53.26*** *p78*
Rankin, James 4; St. John, N.B., 1855 ***5704.8*** *p127*
Rankin, James 17; Massachusetts, 1849 ***5881.1*** *p84*
Rankin, John; New York, NY, 1834 ***8208.4*** *p42*
Rankin, John; Philadelphia, 1850 ***53.26*** *p78*
Rankin, John; Philadelphia, 1850 ***5704.8*** *p60*
Rankin, John; Virginia, 1858 ***4626.16*** *p17*
Rankin, Joseph; St. John, N.B., 1849 ***5704.8*** *p55*
Rankin, Joseph; St. John, N.B., 1853 ***5704.8*** *p107*
Rankin, Margaret; Quebec, 1847 ***5704.8*** *p27*
Rankin, Margaret; Quebec, 1850 ***5704.8*** *p67*
Rankin, Margaret; St. John, N.B., 1855 ***5704.8*** *p127*
Rankin, Margaret 30; St. John, N.B., 1855 ***5704.8*** *p127*
Rankin, Martha 18; Philadelphia, 1856 ***5704.8*** *p128*
Rankin, Mary Ann 2; Quebec, 1851 ***5704.8*** *p82*
Rankin, Mathew; Quebec, 1849 ***5704.8*** *p51*
Rankin, Richard; Quebec, 1852 ***5704.8*** *p91*
Rankin, Robert; Philadelphia, 1811 ***53.26*** *p78*
Rankin, Robert; Philadelphia, 1811 ***2859.11*** *p18*
Rankin, Robert; Quebec, 1847 ***5704.8*** *p27*
Rankin, Robert 18; Philadelphia, 1853 ***5704.8*** *p112*
Rankin, Robert 25; St. John, N.B., 1860 ***5704.8*** *p144*
Rankin, Sarah; New York, NY, 1816 ***2859.11*** *p41*
Rankin, Steven; St. John, N.B., 1853 ***5704.8*** *p106*
Rankin, Thomas; America, 1864 ***5704.8*** *p169*
Rankin, Thomas 2; Quebec, 1847 ***5704.8*** *p27*
Rankin, William; New York, NY, 1837 ***8208.4*** *p35*
Rankin, William; St. John, N.B., 1853 ***5704.8*** *p106*
Rankin, William 18; Jamaica, 1754 ***1219.7*** *p27*
Rankin, William 18; Jamaica, 1754 ***3690.1*** *p186*
Rankin, William 18; Philadelphia, 1833 ***53.26*** *p78*
Rankin, William 35; St. John, N.B., 1855 ***5704.8*** *p127*
Rankine, John 25; St. John, N.B., 1866 ***5704.8*** *p166*
Rankins, Tho.; Virginia, 1646 ***6219*** *p240*
Rannacher, Franz; America, 1846 ***8582.2*** *p32*
Ranquis, Laurent 21; America, 1837 ***778.5*** *p449*
Ranshaw, Katherine *SEE* Ranshaw, William
Ranshaw, William; Virginia, 1635 ***6219*** *p27*
*Wife:*Katherine
Ranson, E. 38; America, 1827 ***778.5*** *p449*
Ranson, Edward 19; Port uncertain, 1836 ***778.5*** *p449*
Ranson, Emile 20; New Orleans, 1838 ***778.5*** *p449*
Ranson, J. C. 28; America, 1827 ***778.5*** *p450*
Ranson, J. L. 22; Mexico, 1826 ***778.5*** *p450*
Ranson, William 35; Maryland, 1775 ***1219.7*** *p268*
Ransonet, Henri; Louisiana, 1789-1819 ***778.5*** *p556*
Ranssler, Albert; Illinois, 1879 ***2896.5*** *p32*
Rant, John 40; Philadelphia, 1774 ***1219.7*** *p239*
Rantelin, John; Washington, 1859-1920 ***2872.1*** *p32*
Rantelin, Mary; Washington, 1859-1920 ***2872.1*** *p32*
Rantenberg, Josef; Baltimore, 1891 ***1450.2*** *p31B*
Ranto, Nicholas Jansen; New York, NY, 1834 ***8208.4*** *p29*
Ranz, Stephen 32; America, 1853 ***9162.7*** *p15*
Ranzau, Andreas; Wisconsin, n.d. ***9675.7*** *p199*
Raou, Mr. 28; America, 1838 ***778.5*** *p450*
Raoul, Mr. 28; America, 1838 ***778.5*** *p450*
Raoul, J. R. 50; New Orleans, 1827 ***778.5*** *p450*
Rapanelli, Dominico; Washington, 1859-1920 ***2872.1*** *p33*
Rapanelli, John; Washington, 1859-1920 ***2872.1*** *p33*
Rapanelli, Nosita; Washington, 1859-1920 ***2872.1*** *p33*
Rapel, Peter; Wisconsin, n.d. ***9675.7*** *p199*
Raper, Margaretha Schneider *SEE* Raper, Stephan
Raper, Stephan; Pennsylvania, 1727 ***3627*** *p19*
*Wife:*Margaretha Schneider
Raphael, Harry; Arkansas, 1918 ***95.2*** *p103*
Raphaell, Joyner; Virginia, 1639 ***6219*** *p151*
Raphaelson, R.; Washington, 1859-1920 ***2872.1*** *p33*
Raphelson, Charles; Washington, 1859-1920 ***2872.1*** *p33*
Rapley, E. B.; Kansas, 1872 ***5240.1*** *p35*
Raplire, John; Colorado, 1894 ***9678.2*** *p164*
Rapon, George; Wisconsin, n.d. ***9675.7*** *p199*
Raponelli, Dominico; Washington, 1859-1920 ***2872.1*** *p33*
Rapp, . . .; Canada, 1776-1783 ***9786*** *p31*
Rapp, Mr.; Baltimore, 1804 ***8582.2*** *p27*
Rapp, Charles J.; Illinois, 1872 ***5012.39*** *p25*
Rapp, Jacob; America, 1849 ***8582.3*** *p53*
Rapp, Peace; New York, NY, 1832 ***8208.4*** *p49*
Rapp, Peter; Philadelphia, 1760 ***9973.7*** *p34*
Rapp, Valentin; Cincinnati, 1869-1887 ***8582*** *p23*
Rappel, August; Ohio, 1800-1885 ***8582.2*** *p58*
Rappelet, Mr. 32; America, 1839 ***778.5*** *p450*
Rappett, Michael; Wisconsin, n.d. ***9675.7*** *p199*
Rapphold, Gottlob Bernhard; America, 1849 ***8582.3*** *p53*
Rappold, Heinrich; Wisconsin, n.d. ***9675.7*** *p199*
Rappold, Karl; Albany, NY, 1867 ***3702.7*** *p566*
Rappolt, Fredrick; Wisconsin, n.d. ***9675.7*** *p199*
Raprola, John; New Orleans, 1839 ***778.5*** *p450*
Rarick, Anton; Alberta, n.d. ***5262*** *p58*
Rarrot, A. 23; Port uncertain, 1825 ***778.5*** *p450*
Rasall, Richard; Virginia, 1642 ***6219*** *p196*
Rasch, . . .; Canada, 1776-1783 ***9786*** *p31*
Rasche, Mr.; Pennsylvania, 1833-1841 ***8582.2*** *p32*
Rasche, Anna Cath. I. Tempcke *SEE* Rasche, Johann Chr. Fr.
Rasche, Anne Marie; America, 1872 ***4610.10*** *p159*
Rasche, Anne Marie L. Cath. *SEE* Rasche, Johann Chr. Fr.
Rasche, Annemarie W. Engel *SEE* Rasche, Johann Chr. Fr.
Rasche, Heinrich; Baltimore, 1841 ***8582.2*** *p32*
Rasche, Heinrich; Cincinnati, 1830-1849 ***8582*** *p24*
Rasche, Heinrich 24; America, 1872 ***4610.10*** *p124*
Rasche, Johann Chr. Fr.; America, 1844 ***4610.10*** *p134*
*Wife:*Anna Cath. I. Tempcke
*Child:*Louise Cath. Engel
*Child:*Anne Marie L. Cath.
*Child:*Annemarie W. Engel
Rasche, Louise Cath. Engel *SEE* Rasche, Johann Chr. Fr.
Rascher, Henry; Savannah, GA, 1736 ***3652*** *p51*
Raschig, . . .; Cincinnati, 1788-1848 ***8582.3*** *p90*
Raschig, Franz Moritz; Cincinnati, 1788-1848 ***8582.3*** *p89*
Raschig, Franz Moritz 28; Baltimore, 1832 ***8582.1*** *p28*
Rasehorn, . . .; Canada, 1776-1783 ***9786*** *p31*
Rasener, Hermann; America, 1845 ***1450.2*** *p115A*
Rasener, William Frederick; America, 1847 ***1450.2*** *p115A*
Rash, James; South Carolina, 1716 ***1639.20*** *p266*
Rashe, John; Virginia, 1635 ***6219*** *p7*
Rashed, Newman 21; Kansas, 1899 ***5240.1*** *p81*
Rashendorfer, John; Arkansas, 1918 ***95.2*** *p103*
Rashendorfer, Stanely; Arkansas, 1918 ***95.2*** *p103*
Raska, Alex; Washington, 1859-1920 ***2872.1*** *p33*
Raskin, Lonu 29; Kansas, 1906 ***5240.1*** *p84*
Rasman, Charles Emil; America, 1854 ***1450.2*** *p115A*
Rasmussen, Chris 23; Arkansas, 1918 ***95.2*** *p103*
Rasmussen, George Peter 27; Arkansas, 1918 ***95.2*** *p103*
Rasmussen, Harry Emil; Arkansas, 1918 ***95.2*** *p103*
Rasmussen, Iver; Washington, 1859-1920 ***2872.1*** *p33*
Rasmussen, James; New York, NY, 1836 ***8208.4*** *p77*
Rasmussen, Krestin J. 27; Arkansas, 1918 ***95.2*** *p103*
Rasmussen, Kristian; Arkansas, 1918 ***95.2*** *p103*
Rasmussen, Maruis 24; Arkansas, 1918 ***95.2*** *p103*
Rasmussen, Morten; New York, NY, 1904 ***3455.1*** *p53*
*Wife:*Petrea
Rasmussen, Niels C.; New York, 1882 ***1450.2*** *p115A*
Rasmussen, Petrea *SEE* Rasmussen, Morten
Rasmussen, Rasmus; Arkansas, 1918 ***95.2*** *p104*
Rasmussen, Rasmus Anders; Arkansas, 1918 ***95.2*** *p104*
Rasmussen, Rasmus Christian; Arkansas, 1918 ***95.2*** *p104*
Rasoski, Vincenty; Illinois, 1898 ***5012.40*** *p55*
Rasp, Paulus; America, 1836 ***8582.1*** *p28*
Rasp, Paulus; Cincinnati, 1869-1887 ***8582*** *p24*
Raspareil, Felix; America, 1833 ***778.5*** *p476*
Rassel, Nicholas; Wisconsin, n.d. ***9675.7*** *p199*
Rassey, James 24; Maryland, 1774 ***1219.7*** *p179*
Rast, Lenhard; South Carolina, 1788 ***7119*** *p198*
Rastias, Marithe 50; New Orleans, 1826 ***778.5*** *p450*
Rastner, Johann Philipp; America, 1839 ***8582.2*** *p33*
Raston, Thomas; Virginia, 1639 ***6219*** *p154*
Rasuk, Eli Romanowich; Arkansas, 1918 ***95.2*** *p104*
Rasz, Zofia 18; New York, 1912 ***9980.29*** *p71*
Rataj, Stanislawa 11 mos; New York, 1912 ***9980.29*** *p49*
Rataj, Zofia Zaduza 27; New York, 1912 ***9980.29*** *p49*
Ratajewicz, Jan; New York, 1835 ***4606*** *p180*
Ratcliffe, Edward; Virginia, 1641 ***6219*** *p185*
Ratcliffe, J. A.; Washington, 1859-1920 ***2872.1*** *p33*
Ratcliffe, Michaell; Virginia, 1634 ***6219*** *p115*
Ratel, Jose 24; New Orleans, 1825 ***778.5*** *p450*
Ratfoun, Christian; Pennsylvania, 1768 ***9973.8*** *p32*
Rath, . . .; Canada, 1776-1783 ***9786*** *p31*
Rath, Georges; Canada, 1776-1783 ***9786*** *p243*
Rather, Mary; New Brunswick, 1823 ***7603*** *p70*
Rathers, Cathn. 27; New York, NY, 1851 ***9555.10*** *p26*
Rathers, Mary 7 mos; New York, NY, 1851 ***9555.10*** *p26*
Rathers, Morgan 33; New York, NY, 1851 ***9555.10*** *p26*
Rathje, Friedrich; Baltimore, 1832 ***3702.7*** *p97*
Rathke, Christian; Wisconsin, n.d. ***9675.7*** *p199*
Rathke, Frederick; Wisconsin, n.d. ***9675.7*** *p199*
Rathke, William; Wisconsin, n.d. ***9675.7*** *p199*
Rathman, John Henry; Kansas, 1886 ***5240.1*** *p35*
Rathmann, Johann Henrich; Canada, 1780 ***9786*** *p268*
Rathmann, Johann Henrich; New York, 1776 ***9786*** *p268*
Rathropp, Jon.; Virginia, 1643 ***6219*** *p200*
Rathstein, Ethel 9 mos; New York, NY, 1878 ***9253*** *p45*
Rathstein, Friede 23; New York, NY, 1878 ***9253*** *p45*
Rathstein, Zethel 27; New York, NY, 1878 ***9253*** *p45*
Rathwell, John 20; Philadelphia, 1751 ***1219.7*** *p6*
Rathwell, John 20; Philadelphia, 1751 ***3690.1*** *p186*
Ratican, Thomas; Illinois, 1872 ***5012.39*** *p26*
Ratliff, David; Albany, NY, 1830 ***9892.11*** *p38*
Ratliff, Jno; Ohio, 1839 ***9892.11*** *p38*
Ratliff, John; Albany, NY, 1830 ***9892.11*** *p38*
Ratliff, William; Albany, NY, 1830 ***9892.11*** *p38*
Ratner, Irvin Jacob; Arkansas, 1918 ***95.2*** *p104*
Ratsan, Joseph; Wisconsin, n.d. ***9675.7*** *p199*
Ratsch, Carl; Wisconsin, n.d. ***9675.7*** *p199*
Ratsch, Max; America, 1888 ***1450.2*** *p115A*
Ratsham, John; Virginia, 1634 ***6219*** *p84*
Ratt..., Robt 22; Virginia, 1700 ***2212*** *p31*
Rattam, Thomas; Virginia, 1647 ***6219*** *p248*
Rattary, James 15; Antigua (Antego), 1728 ***3690.1*** *p186*
Rattenbury, Thomas 15; Maryland, 1722 ***3690.1*** *p186*
Ratterman, H. A.; America, 1846 ***8582.1*** *p28*
Rattermann, Bernard; America, 1844 ***8582.1*** *p28*
Rattermann, Franz; America, 1835 ***8582.1*** *p28*
Rattie, Frank; Washington, 1859-1920 ***2872.1*** *p33*
Rattner, Isadore; Arkansas, 1918 ***95.2*** *p104*
Rattray, Helen; Charleston, SC, 1782 ***1639.20*** *p266*
Rattray, James 15; Antigua (Antego), 1728 ***3690.1*** *p186*
Rattray, John; Charleston, SC, 1761 ***1639.20*** *p266*
Ratz, Joh. 81; Michigan, 1902 ***1763*** *p48D*
Ratzesberger, Louis; Iroquois Co., IL, 1892 ***3455.1*** *p12*
Ratzmann, . . .; Canada, 1776-1783 ***9786*** *p31*
Rau, Catharina Barbara *SEE* Rau, Johann Jacob
Rau, Heinrich; Wisconsin, n.d. ***9675.7*** *p199*
Rau, Johann Bernhardt; Pennsylvania, 1773 ***4525*** *p233*
Rau, Johann Bernhardt; Pennsylvania, 1773 ***4525*** *p237*
Rau, Johann Jacob; Pennsylvania, 1752 ***2444*** *p202*
*Wife:*Sybilla Lutz
*Child:*Catharina Barbara
With parents
Rau, Michael; America, 1854 ***1450.2*** *p115A*
Rau, Philipp; New England, 1773 ***4525*** *p237*
With wife
With 6 children
Rau, Philipp; New England, 1773 ***4525*** *p250*
Rau, Philipp; Pennsylvania, 1773 ***4525*** *p250*
Rau, Sybilla Lutz *SEE* Rau, Johann Jacob
Raubenheimer, . . .; Canada, 1776-1783 ***9786*** *p31*
Rauber, Oman; Illinois, 1858 ***2896.5*** *p32*
Rauch, . . .; Canada, 1776-1783 ***9786*** *p31*
Rauch, Christian Henry; New York, 1740 ***3652*** *p52*
Rauch, Christian Henry; New York, 1740 ***3652*** *p63*
Rauch, John Henry; New York, 1761 ***3652*** *p88*
Rauch, Thomas; South Carolina, 1788 ***7119*** *p200*
Rauckmann, August; Illinois, 1880 ***2896.5*** *p32*
Rauckmann, Christoph; Illinois, 1879 ***2896.5*** *p32*
Rauckmann, Frank; Illinois, 1877 ***2896.5*** *p32*
Rauckmann, Frederick; Illinois, 1879 ***2896.5*** *p33*
Rauckmann, Henry; Illinois, 1874 ***2896.5*** *p33*
Rauckmann, Henry; Illinois, 1888 ***2896.5*** *p33*
Raudzevicius, Julius; Wisconsin, n.d. ***9675.7*** *p199*
Rauesek, Martin; Wisconsin, n.d. ***9675.7*** *p199*
Raugival, J. 36; Port uncertain, 1839 ***778.5*** *p450*
Raul, . . .; Canada, 1776-1783 ***9786*** *p31*
Raul, Christian; Illinois, 1853 ***7857*** *p6*
Raulber, Challies; South Carolina, 1788 ***7119*** *p202*
Raulstone, Arch.; Philadelphia, 1811 ***2859.11*** *p18*
Raulstone, Archibald; Philadelphia, 1811 ***53.26*** *p78*
Raum, George; Arizona, 1884 ***2764.35*** *p57*
Rauner, Leonard; Georgia, 1739 ***9332*** *p324*
Rauner, Leonard; Georgia, 1739 ***9332*** *p325*
*Wife:*Maria Magdalena
*Son:*Matthias 14
*Daughter:*Maria 7
Rauner, Maria 7 *SEE* Rauner, Leonard
Rauner, Maria Magdalena *SEE* Rauner, Leonard
Rauner, Matthias 14 *SEE* Rauner, Leonard
Rausch, . . .; Canada, 1776-1783 ***9786*** *p31*
Rausch, Vincent 45; Kansas, 1906 ***5240.1*** *p83*
Rauschenberg, . . .; Canada, 1776-1783 ***9786*** *p31*
Rauschenblatt, von; Canada, 1776-1783 ***9786*** *p176*
Rauschenplatt, von; Quebec, 1778 ***9786*** *p167*
Rauschenplatt, von; Quebec, 1778 ***9786*** *p168*
Rauschenplatt, Friedrich von; Quebec, 1778 ***9786*** *p267*
Rauschenplatt, Johann Georg von; Quebec, 1778 ***9786*** *p267*
Rauscher, Barbara; Port uncertain, 1749 ***2444*** *p205*
Rauschert, Julius; America, 1889 ***1450.2*** *p116A*

Rausenberger, Margaretha; Pennsylvania, 1749 ***2444*** *p145*
Rauser, John; America, 1854 ***1450.2*** *p116A*
Raute, Jim; Wisconsin, n.d. ***9675.7*** *p200*
Rautenb..., Magdalena; Pennsylvania, 1751 ***2444*** *p143*
Rauth, Franz; Cincinnati, 1869-1887 ***8582*** *p24*
Rauth, Maria 18; America, 1853 ***9162.7*** *p15*
Rauthe, Philip; Philadelphia, 1779 ***8137*** *p12*
Rauti, Vinanzio; Wisconsin, n.d. ***9675.7*** *p200*
Rautmann, Charles; Wisconsin, n.d. ***9675.7*** *p200*
Rauw, Jacob; Pennsylvania, 1752 ***2444*** *p202*
Rav, Darby; Virginia, 1642 ***6219*** *p193*
Ravain, Jean 29; America, 1836 ***778.5*** *p450*
Ravarino, Joseph; Arkansas, 1918 ***95.2*** *p104*
Ravel, Antoine 35; America, 1839 ***778.5*** *p450*
Raven, Peter; Virginia, 1648 ***6219*** *p241*
Ravenell, Henry 18; Maryland, 1733 ***3690.1*** *p187*
Ravening, Rebecca; Virginia, 1623 ***6219*** *p31*
Ravenstein, Albert 56; Kansas, 1879 ***5240.1*** *p61*
Ravin, Mr. 29; America, 1836 ***778.5*** *p450*
Ravin, Jean B. 31; America, 1838 ***778.5*** *p450*
Ravitis, Charles 32; America, 1837 ***778.5*** *p450*
Raw, Henry; Wisconsin, n.d. ***9675.7*** *p200*
Raw, John; America, 1737 ***4971*** *p12*
Raw, Margarett; Virginia, 1638 ***6219*** *p125*
Rawboord, Mannering; Virginia, 1642 ***6219*** *p196*
Rawers, Henry; America, 1843 ***1450.2*** *p116A*
Rawles, George; Virginia, 1635 ***6219*** *p3*
Rawlings, Christopher; Virginia, 1639 ***6219*** *p159*
Rawlings, John; Virginia, 1642 ***6219*** *p186*
Rawlings, Jon.; Virginia, 1637 ***6219*** *p85*
Rawlings, Robert; St. Christopher, 1775 ***1219.7*** *p263*
With family
Rawlings, William; St. Christopher, 1754 ***1219.7*** *p28*
Rawlings, William; Virginia, 1637 ***6219*** *p114*
Rawlins, Elizabeth 19; Philadelphia, 1774 ***1219.7*** *p182*
Rawlins, Wm.; Virginia, 1635 ***6219*** *p35*
Rawlinson, Joseph; America, 1886 ***1450.2*** *p116A*
Rawlinson, William; Boston, 1835 ***8208.4*** *p50*
Rawski, Vincenty; Illinois, 1898 ***5012.40*** *p55*
Rawson, Thom 14; America, 1702 ***2212*** *p38*
Ray, . . .; Virginia, 1641 ***6219*** *p186*
Ray, A.; America, 1792 ***1639.20*** *p266*
Ray, Alexander 62; North Carolina, 1850 ***1639.20*** *p267*
Ray, Archibald 58 *SEE* Ray, Sarah
Ray, Benj.; Virginia, 1638 ***6219*** *p145*
Ray, Daniel; America, 1792 ***1639.20*** *p267*
Ray, Daniel; North Carolina, 1761 ***1639.20*** *p267*
Ray, Duncan; America, 1791 ***1639.20*** *p267*
Ray, Duncan 55; North Carolina, 1850 ***1639.20*** *p267*
*Relative:*Mary 58
Ray, Duncan 76; North Carolina, 1850 ***1639.20*** *p267*
Ray, Eliza 23; St. John, N.B., 1854 ***5704.8*** *p120*
Ray, Francois 38; America, 1838 ***778.5*** *p451*
Ray, Henry 16; Philadelphia, 1774 ***1219.7*** *p182*
Ray, James; Illinois, 1858 ***5012.39*** *p54*
Ray, John; America, 1792 ***1639.20*** *p268*
Ray, John; North Carolina, 1723-1808 ***1639.20*** *p267*
Ray, John; Virginia, 1642 ***6219*** *p186*
Ray, John 73; North Carolina, 1850 ***1639.20*** *p268*
Ray, John 86; North Carolina, 1850 ***1639.20*** *p268*
Ray, John A.; North Carolina, 1744-1821 ***1639.20*** *p267*
Ray, Margaret; North Carolina, 1719-1809 ***1639.20*** *p268*
Ray, Margaret 45; North Carolina, 1850 ***1639.20*** *p268*
Ray, Margaret McNeill; North Carolina, 1759-1849 ***1639.20*** *p211*
Ray, Mary 19; Massachusetts, 1849 ***5881.1*** *p86*
Ray, Mary 47; North Carolina, 1850 ***1639.20*** *p269*
Ray, Mary 50; North Carolina, 1850 ***1639.20*** *p268*
Ray, Mary 58 *SEE* Ray, Duncan
Ray, Mathew 20; St. John, N.B., 1856 ***5704.8*** *p131*
Ray, Peter 51; North Carolina, 1850 ***1639.20*** *p269*
Ray, Robert 18; Philadelphia, 1834 ***53.26*** *p78*
Ray, Samuel; Quebec, 1824 ***7603*** *p27*
Ray, Sarah 87; North Carolina, 1850 ***1639.20*** *p269*
*Relative:*Archibald 58
Ray, Thomas; New York, NY, 1811 ***2859.11*** *p18*
Ray, Thomas; Virginia, 1642 ***6219*** *p193*
With wife
Ray, William; Illinois, 1858 ***5012.39*** *p54*
Ray, William; New York, NY, 1811 ***2859.11*** *p18*
Rayal, Mrs. 30; America, 1837 ***778.5*** *p451*
Rayal, Ms. 30; Missouri, 1837 ***778.5*** *p451*
Rayal, Auguste 2; America, 1837 ***778.5*** *p451*
Rayal, Eugene 3; America, 1837 ***778.5*** *p451*
Rayano, Mr. 35; New Orleans, 1835 ***778.5*** *p451*
Raye, Henry; Virginia, 1643 ***6219*** *p200*
Rayel, Eugene 27; America, 1838 ***778.5*** *p451*
Raymon, Nicholas; Virginia, 1638 ***6219*** *p125*
Raymond, . . .; Canada, 1776-1783 ***9786*** *p31*
Raymond, Mr.; Quebec, 1815 ***9229.18*** *p81*
Raymond, Mr. 25; America, 1839 ***778.5*** *p451*
Raymond, Arthur; Virginia, 1639 ***6219*** *p162*
Raymond, Carite 20; New Orleans, 1838 ***778.5*** *p451*
Raymond, Charles H.; Colorado, 1897 ***9678.2*** *p164*
Raymond, Margaretha Gratia; Pennsylvania, 1753 ***2444*** *p147*
Raymond, Victor 22; Port uncertain, 1839 ***778.5*** *p451*
Raynal, Peter 36; Port uncertain, 1836 ***778.5*** *p451*
Raynard, Robert; Virginia, 1643 ***6219*** *p204*
Raynaud, Pierre 21; America, 1839 ***778.5*** *p451*
Raynbeare, Nicholas; Virginia, 1624 ***6219*** *p7*
Rayne, Patrick; America, 1742-1743 ***4971*** *p42*
Raynells, Arthur 23; Virginia, 1773 ***1219.7*** *p171*
Rayner, Henry; Virginia, 1652 ***6251*** *p19*
Rayner, Thomas 17; Virginia, 1718 ***3690.1*** *p187*
Rayson, Mathew; Virginia, 1637 ***6219*** *p81*
Razan, Daniel; Iowa, 1866-1943 ***123.54*** *p41*
Razbornick, Anton; Wisconsin, n.d. ***9675.7*** *p200*
Razbornik, John; Wisconsin, n.d. ***9675.7*** *p200*
Razbornink, Johan; Wisconsin, n.d. ***9675.7*** *p200*
Raze, A. 21; New Orleans, 1837 ***778.5*** *p451*
Razin, Fs. Simon 28; Port uncertain, 1836 ***778.5*** *p451*
Razin, Jean 39; Port uncertain, 1836 ***778.5*** *p451*
Razook, Nahoom F.; Kansas, 1899 ***5240.1*** *p35*
Rea, James; Illinois, 1842 ***7857*** *p6*
Rea, John; Philadelphia, 1811 ***53.26*** *p78*
Rea, John; Philadelphia, 1811 ***2859.11*** *p18*
Rea, John 20; Philadelphia, 1833-1834 ***53.26*** *p78*
Rea, Patrick; Philadelphia, 1816 ***2859.11*** *p41*
Rea, William; Illinois, 1844 ***7857*** *p6*
Rea, William; New York, NY, 1811 ***2859.11*** *p18*
With family
Read, Andrew; St. John, N.B., 1849 ***5704.8*** *p49*
Read, Catherine; South Carolina, 1789 ***1639.20*** *p269*
Read, Ellianor; Virginia, 1643 ***6219*** *p201*
Read, Geo.; Virginia, 1643 ***6219*** *p200*
Read, James; New York, NY, 1816 ***2859.11*** *p41*
Read, James 20; Maryland, 1774 ***1219.7*** *p234*
Read, James 23; Philadelphia, 1803 ***53.26*** *p78*
Read, John; St. John, N.B., 1849 ***5704.8*** *p49*
Read, John; Virginia, 1636 ***6219*** *p28*
Read, John; Virginia, 1636 ***6219*** *p75*
Read, John; Virginia, 1648 ***6219*** *p237*
Read, Mary 16; Virginia, 1774 ***1219.7*** *p239*
Read, Patrick; America, 1741 ***4971*** *p33*
Read, Patrick 9; Massachusetts, 1849 ***5881.1*** *p86*
Read, Patrick 22; Massachusetts, 1849 ***5881.1*** *p86*
Read, Robert; St. John, N.B., 1849 ***5704.8*** *p49*
Read, Robert; Virginia, 1637 ***6219*** *p110*
Read, Samuel; St. John, N.B., 1849 ***5704.8*** *p49*
Read, Teragh; St. John, N.B., 1849 ***5704.8*** *p49*
Read, Tho.; Virginia, 1635 ***6219*** *p69*
Read, Tho.; Virginia, 1639 ***6219*** *p153*
Read, Thomas; New York, 1820 ***8208.4*** *p48*
Read, Thomas; New York, NY, 1816 ***2859.11*** *p41*
Read, Thomas; Virginia, 1636 ***6219*** *p78*
Read, Thomas 20; Maryland, 1727 ***3690.1*** *p187*
Read, William; Quebec, 1847 ***5704.8*** *p13*
Read, William; Virginia, 1637 ***6219*** *p82*
Read, William 14; Massachusetts, 1849 ***5881.1*** *p87*
Read, William 15; Maryland, 1774 ***1219.7*** *p236*
Read, William 29; St. Christopher, 1730 ***3690.1*** *p187*
Reade, Joseph 25; Philadelphia, 1774 ***1219.7*** *p216*
Reade, P. M. 39; Kansas, 1888 ***5240.1*** *p72*
Reade, Thomas Edward; Carolina, 1759 ***1219.7*** *p67*
Reader, John 20; Jamaica, 1730 ***3690.1*** *p187*
Reades, Eliza.; Virginia, 1642 ***6219*** *p199*
Readford, John; Virginia, 1628 ***6219*** *p9*
Reading, John 40; Dominica, 1774 ***1219.7*** *p205*
Reading, William 24; Maryland, 1775 ***1219.7*** *p265*
Readman, Andrew 42; Massachusetts, 1860 ***6410.32*** *p99*
Readman, Sarah 30; Massachusetts, 1860 ***6410.32*** *p99*
Readwood, John; Virginia, 1643 ***6219*** *p229*
Ready, Catharine 53; Massachusetts, 1849 ***5881.1*** *p83*
Ready, Cornelius; Ohio, 1852 ***1450.2*** *p116A*
Ready, John; America, 1742 ***4971*** *p53*
Ready, John; Quebec, 1823 ***7603*** *p97*
Ready, John 58; Massachusetts, 1849 ***5881.1*** *p84*
Ready, Mary 27; Massachusetts, 1849 ***5881.1*** *p85*
Ready, Maurice 33; Massachusetts, 1849 ***5881.1*** *p85*
Ready, Michel 28; Kansas, 1879 ***5240.1*** *p60*
Reagan, John; New York, 1841 ***7036*** *p127*
Reagan, Patrick 20; Massachusetts, 1849 ***5881.1*** *p86*
Reagan, Thomas; America, 1739 ***4971*** *p14*
Real, Jesus 68; Arizona, 1921 ***9228.40*** *p25*
Reale, Antionio 35; New York, NY, 1893 ***9026.4*** *p42*
*Relative:*James 6
Reale, James 6 *SEE* Reale, Antionio
Realings, Rebbecca; Montreal, 1739 ***7603*** *p22*
Reaor, Nicholas; Ohio, 1844 ***9892.11*** *p38*
Reaor, Nicholas; Ohio, 1847 ***9892.11*** *p38*
Reaper, Ellen; America, 1737 ***4971*** *p45*
Reardan, Margaret 22; Massachusetts, 1847 ***5881.1*** *p85*
Reardon, Honora 26; Massachusetts, 1850 ***5881.1*** *p84*
Reardon, James; Illinois, 1871 ***5012.39*** *p25*
Reardon, Mary 9; Massachusetts, 1849 ***5881.1*** *p85*
Reardon, Michael 4; Massachusetts, 1850 ***5881.1*** *p86*
Reardon, Pat. 19; Massachusetts, 1849 ***5881.1*** *p86*
Rearodan, Bartholomew 26; Massachusetts, 1850 ***5881.1*** *p83*
Rearodan, Catharine 19; Massachusetts, 1847 ***5881.1*** *p83*
Rearodan, Ellen 24; Massachusetts, 1849 ***5881.1*** *p83*
Rearodan, Ellen 38; Massachusetts, 1849 ***5881.1*** *p83*
Rearodan, Jeremiah 23; Massachusetts, 1847 ***5881.1*** *p84*
Rearodan, Margaret 7; Massachusetts, 1850 ***5881.1*** *p86*
Rearodan, William 20; Massachusetts, 1849 ***5881.1*** *p87*
Reasch, Nicholas; Wisconsin, n.d. ***9675.7*** *p200*
Reason, Henry; Virginia, 1635 ***6219*** *p7*
Reatl, William; Illinois, 1861 ***2896.5*** *p33*
Reaud, Pierre 15; Mobile, AL, 1820 ***778.5*** *p452*
Reaves, Thomas; Virginia, 1638 ***6219*** *p15*
Rebbe, William; Illinois, 1877 ***2896.5*** *p33*
Rebbert, Margaretha Schneider *SEE* Rebbert, Stephan
Rebbert, Stephan; Pennsylvania, 1727 ***3627*** *p19*
*Wife:*Margaretha Schneider
Rebecker, Lucas; Ohio, 1800 ***8582.2*** *p55*
Rebel, Daniel; Ohio, 1839 ***9892.11*** *p38*
Rebell, Wm.; Virginia, 1638 ***6219*** *p124*
Reben, Therese 29; America, 1831 ***778.5*** *p452*
Reber, Gotfried; Washington, 1859-1920 ***2872.1*** *p33*
Rebet, Caroline 26; New Orleans, 1839 ***778.5*** *p452*
Rebis, Nicolas 28; New Orleans, 1838 ***778.5*** *p452*
Rebitsky, Stanley; Arkansas, 1918 ***95.2*** *p104*
Reblin, Jacob; Ohio, 1872-1877 ***9892.11*** *p38*
Rebman, Heinrich; Wisconsin, n.d. ***9675.7*** *p200*
Rebmann, Henry; Wisconsin, n.d. ***9675.7*** *p200*
Reboore, Anth.; Virginia, 1638 ***6219*** *p147*
Rebslock, Albert; Shreveport, LA, 1877 ***7129*** *p45*
Rebslock, Sam; Shreveport, LA, 1877 ***7129*** *p45*
Rebstock, Anna Maria; Nova Scotia, 1752 ***2444*** *p198*
Rebstock, Margaret Catherine; New York, 1749 ***3652*** *p73*
Recard, George; Philadelphia, 1816 ***2859.11*** *p41*
Recard, John; New York, NY, 1815 ***2859.11*** *p41*
With wife
Rech, Antonio; Arkansas, 1918 ***95.2*** *p104*
Rech, Elisabetha 30; America, 1853 ***9162.7*** *p15*
Rech, Mathias; America, 1833 ***1450.2*** *p116A*
Rechel, Adam; Cincinnati, 1840 ***8582.1*** *p28*
Rechil, Patrick; New York, NY, 1816 ***2859.11*** *p41*
Rechtin, Bernard U.; Indiana, 1848 ***9117*** *p17*
Rechtin, Gerhard Heinrich; America, 1837 ***8582.3*** *p53*
Rechtin, John Theodore; Indiana, 1850 ***9117*** *p20*
Reckefuss, Anne Marie Engel *SEE* Reckefuss, Peter Heinrich
Reckefuss, Ernst F. Christoph *SEE* Reckefuss, Peter Heinrich
Reckefuss, Peter Heinrich; America, 1844 ***4610.10*** *p141*
*Wife:*Anne Marie Engel
*Son:*Ernst F. Christoph
Recken, R.; Iroquois Co., IL, 1892 ***3455.1*** *p12*
Recker, Hubert; America, 1853 ***1450.2*** *p116A*
Recker, Johann Caspar; America, 1851 ***8582.3*** *p53*
Recklebe, Herman; Kansas, 1900 ***5240.1*** *p35*
Recklebe, Karl; Kansas, 1900 ***5240.1*** *p35*
Reckrodt, v.; Quebec, 1776 ***9786*** *p105*
Reckrodt, Carl Friederick; Quebec, 1776 ***9786*** *p253*
Recordon, Andre *SEE* Recordon, Marthe
Recordon, Andre; New York, NY, 1913 ***3455.2*** *p80*
*Wife:*Martha
Recordon, Andre; New York, NY, 1913 ***3455.3*** *p78*
*Wife:*Martha
Recordon, Andrew *SEE* Recordon, Marthe
Recordon, Martha *SEE* Recordon, Andre
Recordon, Martha *SEE* Recordon, Andre
Recordon, Marthe; New York, NY, 1913 ***3455.3*** *p81*
*Husband:*Andrew
Recordon, Marthe; New York, NY, 1913 ***3455.4*** *p54*
*Husband:*Andre
Recoulet, J. B. 20; Louisiana, 1820 ***778.5*** *p452*
Rector, Cornelius 27; Massachusetts, 1860 ***6410.32*** *p109*
Recurat, Jean 28; America, 1839 ***778.5*** *p452*
Red, David; Virginia, 1637 ***6219*** *p109*
Red, James 22; St. John, N.B., 1866 ***5704.8*** *p166*
Red, Jeremiah 19; Maryland, 1722 ***3690.1*** *p187*
Redbye, Tho.; Virginia, 1637 ***6219*** *p107*
Redcroft, Elizabeth 45; Massachusetts, 1850 ***5881.1*** *p84*
Redd, Adam; Philadelphia, 1753 ***9973.7*** *p32*
Reddall, Thomas 20; Virginia, 1720 ***3690.1*** *p187*
Reddan, Teddy 21; St. John, N.B., 1859 ***5704.8*** *p140*
Redderberg, Linet; New York, 1752 ***3652*** *p76*
Reddermeyer, Christoph; Canada, 1783 ***9786*** *p38A*
Reddey, James; Virginia, 1636 ***6219*** *p75*
Reddey, Michael; New York, NY, 1840 ***8208.4*** *p104*
Reddin, William S.; New York, 1835 ***8208.4*** *p57*
Redding, Johann Jost; Philadelphia, 1780 ***8137*** *p12*
Redding, John; Virginia, 1698 ***2212*** *p14*
Redding, John 21; Maryland, 1774 ***1219.7*** *p244*

Redding, Margaret 20; Massachusetts, 1849 ***5881.1*** *p86*
Reddinge, Robert; Virginia, 1618 ***6219*** *p200*
Reddington, Patrick; New York, NY, 1816 ***2859.11*** *p41*
Reddington, Patrick 27; Massachusetts, 1847 ***5881.1*** *p86*
Reddington, Thomas L. St. George 28; Kansas, 1892 ***5240.1*** *p35*
Reddish, Hugh 19; Newfoundland, 1699-1700 ***2212*** *p18*
Reddy, Edm.; America, 1739 ***4971*** *p30*
Reddy, Frank; Washington, 1859-1920 ***2872.1*** *p33*
Reddy, John; America, 1738 ***4971*** *p31*
Reddy, Michael; New York, NY, 1838 ***8208.4*** *p76*
Reddy, Thomas; America, 1739 ***4971*** *p30*
Reddy, Thomas; New York, NY, 1839 ***8208.4*** *p92*
Rede, Robert; Virginia, 1645 ***6219*** *p233*
Redecker, Charlotte *SEE* Redecker, Joh. Heinrich
Redecker, Charlotte Frund *SEE* Redecker, Joh. Heinrich
Redecker, Joh. Heinrich; America, 1871 ***4610.10*** *p109*
*Wife:*Charlotte Frund
*Daughter:*Charlotte
Redeken, Friedrich; Quebec, 1776 ***9786*** *p258*
Redeker, Heinrich Johann; Illinois, n.d. ***4610.10*** *p68*
Redemier, Frederick; St. Louis, 1855 ***3840.3*** *p8*
Redez, Frank; America, 1891 ***1450.2*** *p31B*
Redfern, Miss; Quebec, 1815 ***9229.18*** *p77*
Redford, Elizabeth; America, 1742 ***4971*** *p17*
Redgate, Elizabeth 25; Wilmington, DE, 1831 ***6508.3*** *p101*
Redhead, William 27; St. Christopher, 1725 ***3690.1*** *p187*
Redhed, John; Illinois, 1871 ***5012.39*** *p25*
Redicke, John; Virginia, 1643 ***6219*** *p205*
Reding, Andreas; Wisconsin, n.d. ***9675.7*** *p200*
Redington, Thomas L. 22; Kansas, 1892 ***5240.1*** *p76*
Rediz, Frank; America, 1891 ***1450.2*** *p31B*
Redl, Franz; Arkansas, 1918 ***95.2*** *p104*
Redlund, Claus Thoedar; Arkansas, 1918 ***95.2*** *p104*
Redmam, Richard; Virginia, 1639 ***6219*** *p159*
Redman, Andrew; Boston, 1843 ***6410.32*** *p122*
Redman, Harry J.; Washington, 1859-1920 ***2872.1*** *p33*
Redman, John; Illinois, 1858 ***5012.39*** *p54*
Redman, Michael; Virginia, 1856 ***4626.16*** *p16*
Redman, Wm.; Virginia, 1636 ***6219*** *p77*
Redman, Wm.; Virginia, 1642 ***6219*** *p199*
Redmond, Darby; America, 1739 ***4971*** *p33*
Redmond, David; America, 1739 ***4971*** *p33*
Redmond, Hugh; America, 1741 ***4971*** *p16*
Redmond, John; America, 1741 ***4971*** *p9*
Redmond, John; America, 1741 ***4971*** *p94*
Redmond, John 20; Massachusetts, 1850 ***5881.1*** *p85*
Redmond, Joseph 20; Massachusetts, 1847 ***5881.1*** *p84*
Redmond, Moise; Quebec, 1807 ***7603*** *p102*
Redmond, Patrick 21; Maryland, 1773 ***1219.7*** *p172*
Redmond, Thomas; Philadelphia, 1849 ***1450.2*** *p116A*
Redmond, W. J.; Washington, 1859-1920 ***2872.1*** *p33*
Redock, Rich.; Virginia, 1637 ***6219*** *p11*
Redon, Mr. 24; New Orleans, 1821 ***778.5*** *p452*
Redon, Mr. 36; New Orleans, 1839 ***778.5*** *p452*
Redon, Mrs. 40; America, 1838 ***778.5*** *p452*
Redon, Miss Claud 40; America, 1838 ***778.5*** *p452*
Redon, Claudius 53; America, 1838 ***778.5*** *p452*
Redpath, Ellen 7; Quebec, 1857 ***5704.8*** *p136*
Redpath, George 34; Quebec, 1857 ***5704.8*** *p136*
Redpath, Isabella 34; Quebec, 1857 ***5704.8*** *p136*
Redpath, Peter, Jr.; Montreal, 1863 ***9775.5*** *p203*
Redpeth, John 30; Maryland, 1775 ***1219.7*** *p268*
*Wife:*Mary 31
Redpeth, Mary 31 *SEE* Redpeth, John
Reds, Elizabeth; Virginia, 1623-1648 ***6219*** *p252*
Redthouse, Harmaunt; Ohio, 1848 ***8365.27*** *p12*
Redwood, James; Virginia, 1648 ***6219*** *p246*
Redwood, Langford; New York, NY, 1831 ***8208.4*** *p37*
Redzinska, Josefa 45; New York, 1912 ***9980.29*** *p70*
Reeb, Christian; Illinois, 1872 ***5012.39*** *p26*
Reeby, John 24; Baltimore, 1775 ***1219.7*** *p270*
Reece, Thomas 19; Maryland, 1774 ***1219.7*** *p236*
Reece, Thomas 70; North Carolina, 1850 ***1639.20*** *p269*
Reece, William; America, 1868 ***6014.1*** *p3*
Reed, Andrew; Philadelphia, 1851 ***5704.8*** *p71*
Reed, Ann; St. John, N.B., 1850 ***5704.8*** *p67*
Reed, Ann 9 *SEE* Reed, George
Reed, Anne; Philadelphia, 1864 ***5704.8*** *p184*
Reed, Catharine; St. John, N.B., 1847 ***5704.8*** *p32*
Reed, Christopher; Illinois, 1860 ***5012.38*** *p97*
Reed, David; New York, NY, 1811 ***2859.11*** *p18*
Reed, David; Ohio, 1840 ***9892.11*** *p39*
Reed, David; St. John, N.B., 1847 ***5704.8*** *p20*
Reed, David 3; Quebec, 1847 ***5704.8*** *p27*
Reed, Edward; Quebec, 1853 ***5704.8*** *p104*
Reed, Eliza; Quebec, 1853 ***5704.8*** *p104*
Reed, Elizabeth 28 *SEE* Reed, William
Reed, Ellen; Philadelphia, 1847 ***53.26*** *p78*
Reed, Ellen; Philadelphia, 1847 ***5704.8*** *p14*
Reed, George 1 *SEE* Reed, George
Reed, George 8; Quebec, 1847 ***5704.8*** *p27*
Reed, George 16; Maryland, 1774 ***1219.7*** *p207*
Reed, George 16; Pennsylvania, Virginia or Maryland, 1719 ***3690.1*** *p187*
Reed, George 33; North America, 1774 ***1219.7*** *p198*
*Wife:*Hannah 33
*Child:*Ann 9
*Child:*John 6
*Child:*Isabella 4
*Child:*George 1
Reed, Hannah 33 *SEE* Reed, George
Reed, Henry; West Virginia, 1829-1847 ***9788.3*** *p19*
Reed, Hugh; New York, NY, 1811 ***2859.11*** *p18*
Reed, Hugh 23; Virginia, 1774 ***1219.7*** *p239*
Reed, Isaac 30; Virginia, 1774 ***1219.7*** *p178*
Reed, Isabella 4 *SEE* Reed, George
Reed, James; Philadelphia, 1811 ***53.26*** *p78*
Reed, James; Philadelphia, 1811 ***2859.11*** *p18*
Reed, James; St. John, N.B., 1847 ***5704.8*** *p11*
Reed, James 10; Quebec, 1847 ***5704.8*** *p27*
Reed, James 24; Philadelphia, 1813 ***9892.11*** *p39*
Reed, James 27; Jamaica, 1774 ***1219.7*** *p233*
Reed, Jane; Philadelphia, 1847 ***53.26*** *p78*
Reed, Jane; Philadelphia, 1847 ***5704.8*** *p24*
Reed, Jane 5; Massachusetts, 1849 ***5881.1*** *p84*
Reed, John; Philadelphia, 1816 ***2859.11*** *p41*
Reed, John; Quebec, 1847 ***5704.8*** *p27*
Reed, John 6 *SEE* Reed, George
Reed, John 6; Quebec, 1847 ***5704.8*** *p27*
Reed, John 26; North America, 1774 ***1219.7*** *p198*
Reed, John 30; Maryland, 1774 ***1219.7*** *p224*
Reed, John 32; Maryland, 1774 ***1219.7*** *p178*
Reed, Joseph 23; Virginia, 1774 ***1219.7*** *p244*
Reed, Julian; Virginia, 1639 ***6219*** *p161*
Reed, Margaret; New York, NY, 1811 ***2859.11*** *p18*
Reed, Margaret; Philadelphia, 1847 ***53.26*** *p78*
Reed, Margaret; Philadelphia, 1847 ***5704.8*** *p24*
Reed, Margaret 1; New York, 1774 ***1219.7*** *p218*
Reed, Margaret 25; New York, 1774 ***1219.7*** *p218*
Reed, Margaret Ann; Philadelphia, 1847 ***53.26*** *p78*
Reed, Margaret Ann; Philadelphia, 1847 ***5704.8*** *p5*
Reed, Martha; Quebec, 1847 ***5704.8*** *p27*
Reed, Martha 21; Pennsylvania, 1728 ***3690.1*** *p187*
Reed, Martin; New York, NY, 1816 ***2859.11*** *p41*
Reed, Mary; St. John, N.B., 1847 ***5704.8*** *p20*
Reed, Mary 20; Massachusetts, 1849 ***5881.1*** *p85*
Reed, Matilda; Philadelphia, 1851 ***5704.8*** *p71*
Reed, Michael 7; Massachusetts, 1849 ***5881.1*** *p85*
Reed, Nancy; Philadelphia, 1851 ***5704.8*** *p71*
Reed, Robert; Philadelphia, 1864 ***5704.8*** *p184*
Reed, Sarah 20; America, 1705 ***2212*** *p44*
Reed, Thomas 40; Philadelphia, 1775 ***1219.7*** *p274*
Reed, William; Illinois, 1882 ***2896.5*** *p33*
Reed, William; Ohio, 1840 ***9892.11*** *p39*
Reed, William; Ohio, 1848 ***9892.11*** *p39*
Reed, William 12; Quebec, 1847 ***5704.8*** *p27*
Reed, William 14; New York, 1774 ***1219.7*** *p218*
Reed, William 21; Maryland, 1775 ***1219.7*** *p272*
Reed, William 30; Nova Scotia, 1774 ***1219.7*** *p210*
*Sister:*Elizabeth 28
Reed, William 36; New York, 1774 ***1219.7*** *p218*
Reed, William M. 32?; Arizona, 1890 ***2764.35*** *p59*
Reede, J. W.; Washington, 1859-1920 ***2872.1*** *p33*
Reeder, J. W.; Washington, 1859-1920 ***2872.1*** *p33*
Reeder, Jesse; Cincinnati, 1816 ***8582.3*** *p86*
Reeder, Vernon C.; Arkansas, 1918 ***95.2*** *p104*
Reeg, Elisab. 4; America, 1854-1855 ***9162.6*** *p104*
Reeg, Elisab. 4; America, 1854-1855 ***9162.6*** *p105*
Reeg, Mrs. Heinrich 32; America, 1854-1855 ***9162.6*** *p105*
Reeg, Henrich. 32; America, 1854-1855 ***9162.6*** *p104*
Reeg, Johannes 14; America, 1854-1855 ***9162.6*** *p104*
Reeg, Kathr. 10; America, 1854-1855 ***9162.6*** *p104*
Reeg, Margr. 22; America, 1854-1855 ***9162.6*** *p104*
Reeg, Michael 6 mos; America, 1854-1855 ***9162.6*** *p104*
Reeg, Michael 6 mos; America, 1854-1855 ***9162.6*** *p105*
Reegan, Bridget; Montreal, 1822 ***7603*** *p85*
Reeker, Jacob; Pennsylvania, 1751 ***2444*** *p204*
Reeks, Rich.; Virginia, 1638 ***6219*** *p118*
Reel, William; Philadelphia, 1761 ***9973.7*** *p36*
Reemer, Frederick; Philadelphia, 1764 ***9973.7*** *p39*
Reemkus, Alex; Wisconsin, n.d. ***9675.7*** *p200*
Reeny, George; America, 1740 ***4971*** *p15*
Reere, Thomas; Virginia, 1648 ***6219*** *p241*
Reers, Henry 26; Kansas, 1884 ***5240.1*** *p35*
Reers, Henry 26; Kansas, 1884 ***5240.1*** *p66*
Rees, A.P.; Iowa, 1866-1943 ***123.54*** *p41*
Rees, Arizona; Washington, 1859-1920 ***2872.1*** *p33*
Rees, David 22; Virginia, 1774 ***1219.7*** *p227*
Rees, Edward; Virginia, 1847 ***4626.16*** *p13*
Rees, Henry 29; Maryland, 1774 ***1219.7*** *p211*
Rees, James Llewellyn; Washington, 1859-1920 ***2872.1*** *p33*
Rees, John; Kansas, 1872 ***5240.1*** *p35*
Rees, John George; Philadelphia, 1758 ***9973.7*** *p33*
Rees, Lawrence; Philadelphia, 1760 ***9973.7*** *p34*
Rees, Oscar Waldeman; Iowa, 1866-1943 ***123.54*** *p41*
Rees, Oscar Waldemar; Iowa, 1866-1943 ***123.54*** *p41*
Rees, Peter; Pennsylvania, 1753 ***4525*** *p238*
Rees, Virginia Bell; Washington, 1859-1920 ***2872.1*** *p33*
Reese, . . .; Canada, 1776-1783 ***9786*** *p43*
Reese, Mr.; Detroit, 1837 ***8582*** *p24*
Reese, Charles E.; America, 1857 ***1450.2*** *p116A*
Reese, Frank; Washington, 1859-1920 ***2872.1*** *p33*
Reese, Friederich; Cincinnati, 1824-1832 ***8582.1*** *p50*
Reese, Henry; South Carolina, 1788 ***7119*** *p198*
Reese, Henry; Wisconsin, n.d. ***9675.7*** *p200*
Reese, Henry C.; America, 1854 ***1450.2*** *p116A*
Reese, John 55; Kansas, 1888 ***5240.1*** *p72*
Reest, George; Pennsylvania, 1752 ***2444*** *p204*
Reeve, Dennis; Virginia, 1635 ***6219*** *p35*
Reeve, Fr.; Virginia, 1635 ***6219*** *p72*
Reeve, Richard; Virginia, 1625 ***6219*** *p7*
Reeverts, Derk; Illinois, 1863 ***7857*** *p6*
Reeverts, Hagen F.; Illinois, 1863 ***7857*** *p6*
Reeves, Bartholomew 19; Jamaica, 1730 ***3690.1*** *p187*
Reeves, James 19; Maryland, 1733 ***3690.1*** *p187*
Reeves, John; Virginia, 1636 ***6219*** *p36*
Reeves, John; Virginia, 1637 ***6219*** *p113*
Reeves, John; Virginia, 1642 ***6219*** *p196*
Reeves, John 16; Maryland, 1722 ***3690.1*** *p187*
Reeves, Jon.; Virginia, 1642 ***6219*** *p191*
Reeves, Jon.; Virginia, 1642 ***6219*** *p194*
Reeves, Jone; Virginia, 1643 ***6219*** *p229*
Reeves, Joseph; New York, NY, 1839 ***8208.4*** *p94*
Reeves, Joseph 17; Port uncertain, 1774 ***1219.7*** *p176*
Reeves, Joseph 31; Maryland, 1775 ***1219.7*** *p257*
Reeves, Lawrance; Virginia, 1638 ***6219*** *p125*
Reeves, Richard 21; Maryland, 1774 ***1219.7*** *p221*
Reeves, Robert; Virginia, 1635 ***6219*** *p36*
Reeves, Susanna 18; Maryland, 1724 ***3690.1*** *p187*
Reeves, Thomas; New York, NY, 1837 ***8208.4*** *p54*
Reeves, Thomas; Virginia, 1635 ***6219*** *p33*
Refane, Ann 22; Virginia, 1774 ***1219.7*** *p239*
Regal, Edward Bob; Arkansas, 1918 ***95.2*** *p104*
Regalbuto, Alfred; Arkansas, 1918 ***95.2*** *p104*
Regan, Ann 22; Massachusetts, 1849 ***5881.1*** *p82*
Regan, Ann 25; Massachusetts, 1849 ***5881.1*** *p82*
Regan, Catharine 70; Massachusetts, 1848 ***5881.1*** *p83*
Regan, Charles; America, 1741 ***4971*** *p41*
Regan, Charles 40; Massachusetts, 1849 ***5881.1*** *p83*
Regan, Cornelius 7; Massachusetts, 1850 ***5881.1*** *p83*
Regan, Daniel 19; Massachusetts, 1849 ***5881.1*** *p83*
Regan, Edmund 13; Massachusetts, 1850 ***5881.1*** *p84*
Regan, Ellen 9; Massachusetts, 1850 ***5881.1*** *p83*
Regan, James 32; St. John, N.B., 1857 ***5704.8*** *p135*
Regan, Jeremiah 23; Maryland, 1775 ***1219.7*** *p264*
Regan, Jeremiah 52; Massachusetts, 1848 ***5881.1*** *p84*
Regan, Johanna 58; Massachusetts, 1849 ***5881.1*** *p84*
Regan, John; New York, NY, 1838 ***8208.4*** *p64*
Regan, John; New York, NY, 1838 ***8208.4*** *p65*
Regan, John 7; Massachusetts, 1848 ***5881.1*** *p84*
Regan, John 11; Massachusetts, 1850 ***5881.1*** *p84*
Regan, John 60; Massachusetts, 1849 ***5881.1*** *p84*
Regan, Julia 6; Massachusetts, 1848 ***5881.1*** *p84*
Regan, Margaret 25; Massachusetts, 1848 ***5881.1*** *p85*
Regan, Michael; Arkansas, 1918 ***95.2*** *p104*
Regan, Morris; Illinois, 1879 ***2896.5*** *p33*
Regan, Patrick; New York, NY, 1839 ***8208.4*** *p99*
Regan, Peggy 3; Massachusetts, 1848 ***5881.1*** *p86*
Regan, Robert C.; New York, NY, 1838 ***8208.4*** *p83*
Regan, Roger 21; Maryland, 1775 ***1219.7*** *p272*
Regan, Thomas 25; Massachusetts, 1849 ***5881.1*** *p87*
Regan, Thomas 38; Kansas, 1901 ***5240.1*** *p82*
Regan, Timothy; America, 1742-1743 ***4971*** *p42*
Regan, William 21; Massachusetts, 1847 ***5881.1*** *p87*
Regenbogen, . . .; Canada, 1776-1783 ***9786*** *p31*
Regensburger, Paul 21; Kansas, 1890 ***5240.1*** *p74*
Reges, . . .; Canada, 1776-1783 ***9786*** *p31*
Regeuffle, Andre 26; America, 1838 ***778.5*** *p452*
Regier, Abram; Kansas, 1878 ***5240.1*** *p35*
Regier, Bernhard; Kansas, 1878 ***5240.1*** *p36*
Regier, Cornelius; Kansas, 1881 ***5240.1*** *p36*
Regier, Jacob; Kansas, 1878 ***5240.1*** *p36*
Regin, John; New York, NY, 1816 ***2859.11*** *p41*
Regis, Etienne 40; New Orleans, 1825 ***778.5*** *p452*
Regismaret, Antoine 29; America, 1823 ***778.5*** *p452*
Register, Mary 60; North Carolina, 1850 ***1639.20*** *p269*
Reglin, Carl; Wisconsin, n.d. ***9675.7*** *p200*
Regmer, Lorenz; Wisconsin, n.d. ***9675.7*** *p200*
Regnauld, . . .; Halifax, N.S., 1752 ***7074.6*** *p232*
Regnell, Sophia 33; Massachusetts, 1860 ***6410.32*** *p110*
Regnell, Thomas 56; Massachusetts, 1860 ***6410.32*** *p110*
Regnell, Thomas F.; New York, NY, 1854 ***6410.32*** *p124*
Regner, Lorenz; Wisconsin, n.d. ***9675.7*** *p200*
Regnet, J. 29; New Orleans, 1825 ***778.5*** *p452*
Regnier, Francois 30; Port uncertain, 1836 ***778.5*** *p453*

Regula, August; America, 1896 ***1450.2*** *p31B*
Reh, John; Illinois, 1865 ***2896.5*** *p33*
Reh, Joseph; America, 1846 ***8582.3*** *p53*
Rehal, Shikrey George; Arkansas, 1918 ***95.2*** *p104*
Rehbock, Heinrich; America, 1844 ***8582.2*** *p33*
Rehfus, . . .; Ohio, 1831 ***8582.1*** *p28*
Rehfuss, . . .; America, 1836 ***8582.1*** *p39*
Rehfuss, . . .; Cincinnati, 1837-1838 ***8582.1*** *p45*
Rehfuss, Mr.; Cincinnati, 1831 ***8582.1*** *p51*
Rehfuss, Anna Maria *SEE* Rehfuss, Hans Jacob
Rehfuss, Catharina *SEE* Rehfuss, Hans Jacob
Rehfuss, Christina *SEE* Rehfuss, Hans Jacob
Rehfuss, Hans Jacob; Pennsylvania, 1751 ***2444*** *p202*
*Wife:*Catharina
*Child:*Anna Maria
*Child:*Johann Georg
*Child:*Christina
Rehfuss, Johann; America, 1848 ***8582.3*** *p53*
Rehfuss, Johann Georg *SEE* Rehfuss, Hans Jacob
Rehfuss, Ludwig; America, 1833 ***8582*** *p24*
Rehfuss, Ludwig; Cincinnati, 1788-1848 ***8582.3*** *p89*
Rehind, William 18; Pennsylvania, 1731 ***3690.1*** *p185*
Rehind, William 19; Jamaica, 1733 ***3690.1*** *p188*
Rehkob, Daniel; Ohio, 1869-1885 ***8582.2*** *p56*
Rehling, William; America, 1847-1849 ***1450.2*** *p117A*
Rehm, Edmund 20; Kansas, 1884 ***5240.1*** *p65*
Rehm, George; South Carolina, 1788 ***7119*** *p203*
Rehm, Gustav 27; Kansas, 1886 ***5240.1*** *p68*
Rehm, Henry; Wisconsin, n.d. ***9675.7*** *p200*
Rehse, . . .; Canada, 1776-1783 ***9786*** *p31*
Reibe, Ferdinand; Wisconsin, n.d. ***9675.7*** *p200*
Reibel, Anton; Ohio, 1800-1885 ***8582.2*** *p58*
Reibell, Amamd; America, 1852 ***1450.2*** *p117A*
Reibenspis, John; Kansas, 1871 ***5240.1*** *p36*
Reible, Daniel; Ohio, 1848 ***9892.11*** *p39*
Reibold, Johann 28; America, 1853 ***9162.8*** *p37*
Reich, Emanuel A.; Ohio, 1884-1889 ***9892.11*** *p39*
Reich, Johann; Illinois, 1840 ***8582.2*** *p50*
Reich, Peter; Charleston, SC, 1775-1781 ***8582.2*** *p33*
Reich, Stephan; Kentucky, 1810 ***8582.3*** *p97*
Reich, William F.; Illinois, 1890 ***5012.39*** *p53*
Reich, William F.; Illinois, 1900 ***5012.40*** *p77*
Reichard, David; New York, 1743 ***3652*** *p60*
*Wife:*Elizabeth
Reichard, Elizabeth *SEE* Reichard, David
Reichardt, Ernst; Illinois, 1892 ***5012.40*** *p26*
Reichardt, Friederich; Baltimore, 1848-1874 ***8582.3*** *p53*
Reichardt, John; Ohio, 1830 ***8582.1*** *p46*
Reiche, . . .; Canada, 1776-1783 ***9786*** *p31*
Reichel, John B.; Wisconsin, n.d. ***9675.7*** *p200*
Reichen, Emma; New York, NY, 1902 ***3455.1*** *p50*
Reichenbach, . . .; Canada, 1776-1783 ***9786*** *p31*
Reichenbach, Charles; Illinois, 1855 ***7857*** *p6*
Reichenbach, Ernst; Illinois, 1861 ***7857*** *p6*
Reichenback, . . .; Canada, 1776-1783 ***9786*** *p31*
Reichenberg, . . .; Canada, 1776-1783 ***9786*** *p31*
Reichenecker, Catharina *SEE* Reichenecker, Hans Jerg
Reichenecker, Hans Jerg; Port uncertain, 1752 ***2444*** *p202*
*Wife:*Catharina
With 2 children
Reichert, Charles; Wisconsin, n.d. ***9675.7*** *p200*
Reichert, Christian; Kentucky, 1839-1840 ***8582.3*** *p99*
Reichhardt, Friedrich; America, 1849 ***8582.1*** *p28*
Reichl, George; Wisconsin, n.d. ***9675.7*** *p200*
Reichle, Bartholomaeus; Ohio, 1800-1850 ***8582.2*** *p56*
Reichlen, Mrs. Xavier; Milwaukee, 1875 ***4719.30*** *p257*
Reichling, Nicholas; Wisconsin, n.d. ***9675.7*** *p200*
Reichman, Luis; Iroquois Co., IL, 1894 ***3455.1*** *p12*
Reichmann, Carl; Illinois, 1886 ***2896.5*** *p33*
Reichmann, Franz; America, 1852 ***8582.3*** *p53*
Reichmann, Georg; New York, 1900 ***1763*** *p48D*
Reichnauer, Martin; Wisconsin, n.d. ***9675.7*** *p200*
Reichold, August; New York, 1854 ***3702.7*** *p340*
Reichter, August; Wisconsin, n.d. ***9675.7*** *p200*
Reid, Miss 16; Philadelphia, 1833-1834 ***53.26*** *p78*
Reid, Mr.; Quebec, 1815 ***9229.18*** *p78*
Reid, Adam; Baltimore, 1816 ***2859.11*** *p41*
Reid, Agnes 1; Quebec, 1864 ***5704.8*** *p163*
Reid, Alex 24; St. John, N.B., 1864 ***5704.8*** *p158*
Reid, Alexander; New York, NY, 1837 ***8208.4*** *p35*
Reid, Alexander; Philadelphia, 1848 ***53.26*** *p78*
Reid, Alexander; Philadelphia, 1848 ***5704.8*** *p46*
Reid, Ann 55 *SEE* Reid, Robert
Reid, Catharine; New York, NY, 1867 ***5704.8*** *p224*
Reid, Christan 10; St. John, N.B., 1848 ***5704.8*** *p42*
Reid, David; North Carolina, 1825 ***1639.20*** *p269*
Reid, David 22; St. John, N.B., 1859 ***5704.8*** *p140*
Reid, David 83; North Carolina, 1850 ***1639.20*** *p269*
Reid, Elizabeth 12; St. John, N.B., 1848 ***5704.8*** *p42*
Reid, Elizabeth 15; St. John, N.B., 1858 ***5704.8*** *p140*
Reid, Esther 10 *SEE* Reid, Robert
Reid, Esther 25; St. John, N.B., 1867 ***5704.8*** *p167*
Reid, George; New York, NY, 1816 ***2859.11*** *p41*
Reid, George 20; Quebec, 1858 ***5704.8*** *p138*
Reid, Helen 3; Quebec, 1864 ***5704.8*** *p163*
Reid, Henry 24; St. John, N.B., 1867 ***5704.8*** *p167*
Reid, Hugh 20; Philadelphia, 1853 ***5704.8*** *p108*
Reid, Isabella 9; St. John, N.B., 1858 ***5704.8*** *p137*
Reid, Isabella 18; Philadelphia, 1854 ***5704.8*** *p118*
Reid, James; Arkansas, 1918 ***95.2*** *p104*
Reid, James; Charleston, SC, 1680-1830 ***1639.20*** *p269*
Reid, James; Charleston, SC, 1798 ***1639.20*** *p270*
Reid, James; New York, NY, 1815 ***2859.11*** *p41*
Reid, James; New York, NY, 1816 ***2859.11*** *p41*
Reid, James; St. John, N.B., 1852 ***5704.8*** *p95*
Reid, James 3; St. John, N.B., 1848 ***5704.8*** *p42*
Reid, James 9; Quebec, 1864 ***5704.8*** *p163*
Reid, James 25; St. John, N.B., 1855 ***5704.8*** *p127*
Reid, James 30; Quebec, 1864 ***5704.8*** *p163*
Reid, Jane; Philadelphia, 1865 ***5704.8*** *p191*
Reid, Jane 6 mos; St. John, N.B., 1848 ***5704.8*** *p42*
Reid, Jane 5; Quebec, 1864 ***5704.8*** *p163*
Reid, John; Philadelphia, 1851 ***5704.8*** *p76*
Reid, John; Virginia, 1851 ***4626.16*** *p14*
Reid, John 9 mos; Quebec, 1864 ***5704.8*** *p163*
Reid, John 2; St. John, N.B., 1866 ***5704.8*** *p166*
Reid, John 3; Quebec, 1864 ***5704.8*** *p163*
Reid, John 18; Quebec, 1856 ***5704.8*** *p130*
Reid, John 21 *SEE* Reid, Robert
Reid, John 26; St. John, N.B., 1866 ***5704.8*** *p166*
Reid, John 55; Kansas, 1873 ***5240.1*** *p55*
Reid, Joseph; Norfolk, VA, 1801 ***9892.11*** *p39*
Reid, Lesly 21; St. John, N.B., 1864 ***5704.8*** *p158*
Reid, Levy 16 *SEE* Reid, Robert
Reid, M.; New York, NY, 1816 ***2859.11*** *p41*
Reid, Malcolm; South Carolina, 1716 ***1639.20*** *p270*
Reid, Margaret; St. John, N.B., 1850 ***5704.8*** *p61*
Reid, Margaret 11; St. John, N.B., 1858 ***5704.8*** *p137*
Reid, Martha 21; St. John, N.B., 1858 ***5704.8*** *p137*
Reid, Martha 50; St. John, N.B., 1858 ***5704.8*** *p137*
Reid, Mary; St. John, N.B., 1848 ***5704.8*** *p42*
Reid, Mary 28; Quebec, 1864 ***5704.8*** *p163*
Reid, Mary Ann 5; St. John, N.B., 1861 ***5704.8*** *p149*
Reid, Mary Ann 21; Quebec, 1864 ***5704.8*** *p163*
Reid, Mary Ann 41; Philadelphia, 1854 ***5704.8*** *p118*
Reid, Mary J.; St. John, N.B., 1852 ***5704.8*** *p95*
Reid, Mary Jane 18; St. John, N.B., 1858 ***5704.8*** *p137*
Reid, Mary Jane 27; St. John, N.B., 1861 ***5704.8*** *p149*
Reid, Matilda 2; St. John, N.B., 1861 ***5704.8*** *p149*
Reid, Nancy; Philadelphia, 1853 ***5704.8*** *p102*
Reid, Nancy 15; St. John, N.B., 1858 ***5704.8*** *p137*
Reid, Patrick; New York, NY, 1811 ***2859.11*** *p18*
Reid, Rachael; New York, NY, 1816 ***2859.11*** *p41*
Reid, Robert; New York, NY, 1816 ***2859.11*** *p41*
Reid, Robert; New York, NY, 1837 ***8208.4*** *p35*
Reid, Robert; South Carolina, 1767 ***1639.20*** *p270*
Reid, Robert 5; St. John, N.B., 1848 ***5704.8*** *p42*
Reid, Robert 31; Quebec, 1864 ***5704.8*** *p163*
Reid, Robert 60; Philadelphia, 1833-1834 ***53.26*** *p78*
*Relative:*Ann 55
*Relative:*John 21
*Relative:*Esther 10
*Relative:*Sarah 52
*Relative:*Levy 16
Reid, Rose Ann; Quebec, 1850 ***5704.8*** *p70*
Reid, Samuel; St. John, N.B., 1852 ***5704.8*** *p95*
Reid, Samuel 7; St. John, N.B., 1861 ***5704.8*** *p149*
Reid, Samuel 24; Philadelphia, 1860 ***5704.8*** *p144*
Reid, Samuel 26; St. John, N.B., 1866 ***5704.8*** *p166*
Reid, Samuel 50; St. John, N.B., 1858 ***5704.8*** *p137*
Reid, Sarah 20; St. John, N.B., 1866 ***5704.8*** *p166*
Reid, Sarah 52 *SEE* Reid, Robert
Reid, Thomas; New York, 1884 ***1450.2*** *p31B*
Reid, Thomas; New York, NY, 1816 ***2859.11*** *p41*
Reid, William; New York, 1834 ***8894.2*** *p57*
Reid, William; New York, NY, 1811 ***2859.11*** *p18*
Reid, William; Philadelphia, 1853 ***5704.8*** *p102*
Reid, William; St. John, N.B., 1853 ***5704.8*** *p107*
Reid, William 13; St. John, N.B., 1858 ***5704.8*** *p140*
Reid, William John 19; Philadelphia, 1854 ***5704.8*** *p118*
Reid, William John 24; St. John, N.B., 1857 ***5704.8*** *p135*
Reider, Anna *SEE* Reider, Daniel
Reider, Anna Maria *SEE* Reider, Daniel
Reider, Catharina *SEE* Reider, Daniel
Reider, Daniel; Pennsylvania, 1752 ***2444*** *p203*
*Wife:*Anna
*Child:*Catharina
*Child:*Anna Maria
Reideser, Johannes; Lancaster, PA, 1780 ***8137*** *p12*
Reidor, Frederick; Indiana, 1848 ***9117*** *p19*
Reidre, Bernard 27; America, 1837 ***778.5*** *p442*
Reif, Adam; Cincinnati, 1869-1887 ***8582*** *p24*
Reif, Francis, Sr.; Cincinnati, 1869-1887 ***8582*** *p24*
Reif, Gottfried; Ellis Island 1923 ***3455.4*** *p83*
Reif, John 25; Kansas, 1873 ***5240.1*** *p55*
Reiff, Joseph 35; Kansas, 1879 ***5240.1*** *p60*
Reiff, P.; Milwaukee, 1875 ***4719.30*** *p257*
Reiffert, . . .; Canada, 1776-1783 ***9786*** *p31*
Reiffurth, Christ Phil.; Philadelphia, 1779 ***8137*** *p12*
Reifon, George; Wisconsin, n.d. ***9675.7*** *p200*
Reifsteck, Jacob; Illinois, 1894 ***5012.37*** *p63*
Reifsteck, Louis; Illinois, 1888 ***5012.39*** *p122*
Reifsteck, Marie 23; New York, NY, 1922 ***5012.40*** *p78*
Reiger, Jacob; Pennsylvania, 1751 ***2444*** *p204*
Reigher, Jacob; Pennsylvania, 1751 ***2444*** *p204*
Reignier, Jean 22; Port uncertain, 1838 ***778.5*** *p453*
Reihimaki, Leander; Washington, 1859-1920 ***2872.1*** *p33*
Reijonen, John; Washington, 1859-1920 ***2872.1*** *p33*
Reil, John; Wisconsin, n.d. ***9675.7*** *p200*
Reile, William A.; America, 1870 ***6014.1*** *p3*
Reiley, Dennis; Philadelphia, 1852 ***5704.8*** *p89*
Reiley, Eliza; Quebec, 1850 ***5704.8*** *p62*
Reiley, Eliza 5; Quebec, 1850 ***5704.8*** *p63*
Reiley, Fanny 3; Quebec, 1850 ***5704.8*** *p63*
Reiley, Hugh 20; Philadelphia, 1853 ***5704.8*** *p108*
Reiley, James 22; Philadelphia, 1853 ***5704.8*** *p108*
Reiley, Jane; Philadelphia, 1864 ***5704.8*** *p181*
Reiley, John; St. John, N.B., 1848 ***5704.8*** *p43*
Reiley, John 19; New York, 1775 ***1219.7*** *p246*
Reiley, Mary 6 mos; Quebec, 1850 ***5704.8*** *p63*
Reiley, Mary 8; Quebec, 1850 ***5704.8*** *p63*
Reiley, Patrick; America, 1773-1774 ***2859.11*** *p7*
Reiley, Patrick 25; Virginia, 1773 ***1219.7*** *p168*
Reiley, Sarah 6; Quebec, 1850 ***5704.8*** *p63*
Reiley, Thomas; Quebec, 1850 ***5704.8*** *p62*
Reill, . . .; Canada, 1776-1783 ***9786*** *p31*
Reille, Jean 24; America, 1838 ***778.5*** *p453*
Reilley, Margaret; Montreal, 1821 ***7603*** *p60*
Reilley, Thomas; America, 1890 ***1450.2*** *p117A*
Reilly, . . .; New York, NY, 1815 ***2859.11*** *p41*
Reilly, Andy; Quebec, 1853 ***5704.8*** *p104*
Reilly, Ann; Quebec, 1847 ***5704.8*** *p37*
Reilly, Ann; St. John, N.B., 1848 ***5704.8*** *p47*
Reilly, Ann 9 mos; St. John, N.B., 1847 ***5704.8*** *p35*
Reilly, Barnaby; America, 1736 ***4971*** *p83*
Reilly, Bessie; New York, NY, 1867 ***5704.8*** *p224*
Reilly, Biddy; St. John, N.B., 1847 ***5704.8*** *p35*
Reilly, Biddy 2; St. John, N.B., 1847 ***5704.8*** *p35*
Reilly, Biddy 13; St. John, N.B., 1847 ***5704.8*** *p20*
Reilly, Bridget; America, 1743 ***4971*** *p23*
Reilly, Bridget; Quebec, 1822 ***7603*** *p74*
Reilly, Brien; New York, NY, 1811 ***2859.11*** *p18*
Reilly, Bryan; America, 1735-1743 ***4971*** *p78*
Reilly, Catharine 10; St. John, N.B., 1847 ***5704.8*** *p35*
Reilly, Catherine; America, 1740 ***4971*** *p15*
Reilly, Catherine; America, 1742 ***4971*** *p17*
Reilly, Catherine; Maryland, 1740 ***4971*** *p91*
Reilly, Catherine; Philadelphia, 1741 ***4971*** *p92*
Reilly, Catherine; Quebec, 1847 ***5704.8*** *p37*
Reilly, Charles; New York, NY, 1816 ***2859.11*** *p41*
Reilly, Daniel 12; St. John, N.B., 1847 ***5704.8*** *p20*
Reilly, Edward; Quebec, 1847 ***5704.8*** *p37*
Reilly, Francis; New York, NY, 1869 ***5704.8*** *p232*
Reilly, Francis; Quebec, 1847 ***5704.8*** *p37*
Reilly, Fras; New York, NY, 1815 ***2859.11*** *p41*
Reilly, Hugh; America, 1741 ***4971*** *p10*
Reilly, Hugh; Quebec, 1847 ***5704.8*** *p37*
Reilly, Hugh 25; Philadelphia, 1858 ***5704.8*** *p139*
Reilly, James; America, 1741 ***4971*** *p63*
Reilly, James; America, 1742 ***4971*** *p63*
Reilly, James; America, 1840 ***7036*** *p117*
*Wife:*Mary McCabe
Reilly, James; Arizona, 1873 ***2764.35*** *p59*
Reilly, James; New York, NY, 1836 ***8208.4*** *p17*
Reilly, James; New York, NY, 1837 ***8208.4*** *p34*
Reilly, James; New York, NY, 1839 ***8208.4*** *p92*
Reilly, James; Quebec, 1825 ***7603*** *p90*
Reilly, James; Quebec, 1847 ***5704.8*** *p37*
Reilly, James 19; Philadelphia, 1858 ***5704.8*** *p138*
Reilly, Jane; New York, NY, 1871 ***5704.8*** *p240*
Reilly, Jane; Quebec, 1847 ***5704.8*** *p37*
Reilly, John; America, 1735-1743 ***4971*** *p79*
Reilly, John; America, 1738 ***4971*** *p85*
Reilly, John; America, 1738 ***4971*** *p95*
Reilly, John; America, 1739 ***4971*** *p85*
Reilly, John; America, 1739 ***4971*** *p103*
Reilly, John; America, 1742 ***4971*** *p60*
Reilly, John; America, 1743 ***4971*** *p11*
Reilly, John; Montreal, 1824 ***7603*** *p87*
Reilly, John; New York, NY, 1815 ***2859.11*** *p41*
Reilly, John; Quebec, 1820 ***7603*** *p61*
Reilly, John; Quebec, 1820 ***7603*** *p90*
Reilly, John; Quebec, 1847 ***5704.8*** *p37*
Reilly, John; St. John, N.B., 1847 ***5704.8*** *p19*
Reilly, John 26; Maryland, 1774 ***1219.7*** *p230*
Reilly, Judith; Montreal, 1824 ***7603*** *p61*
Reilly, Margaret; Quebec, 1847 ***5704.8*** *p37*
Reilly, Mark; New York, NY, 1832 ***8208.4*** *p29*

Reilly, Mary; America, 1737 ***4971*** *p24*
Reilly, Mary; New York, NY, 1811 ***2859.11*** *p18*
Reilly, Mary; New York, NY, 1866 ***5704.8*** *p212*
Reilly, Mary; Quebec, 1847 ***5704.8*** *p37*
Reilly, Mary; Quebec, 1853 ***5704.8*** *p104*
Reilly, Mary; St. John, N.B., 1847 ***5704.8*** *p19*
Reilly, Mary 12; St. John, N.B., 1847 ***5704.8*** *p35*
Reilly, Mary 20; Philadelphia, 1858 ***5704.8*** *p139*
Reilly, Mary Jane; St. John, N.B., 1848 ***5704.8*** *p47*
Reilly, Mary McCabe *SEE* Reilly, James
Reilly, Mathew; America, 1867 ***5704.8*** *p222*
Reilly, Michael; New York, NY, 1815 ***2859.11*** *p41*
Reilly, Michael; New York, NY, 1840 ***8208.4*** *p112*
Reilly, Michel; Montreal, 1820 ***7603*** *p57*
Reilly, Mick; Quebec, 1847 ***5704.8*** *p37*
Reilly, Mick 13; Quebec, 1847 ***5704.8*** *p38*
Reilly, Miles; America, 1743 ***4971*** *p70*
Reilly, Pat; Quebec, 1847 ***5704.8*** *p37*
Reilly, Patrick; America, 1735-1743 ***4971*** *p8*
Reilly, Patrick; America, 1736 ***4971*** *p12*
Reilly, Patrick; America, 1738 ***4971*** *p24*
Reilly, Patrick; Maryland, 1740 ***4971*** *p91*
Reilly, Patrick; New York, NY, 1815 ***2859.11*** *p41*
Reilly, Patrick; New York, NY, 1867 ***5704.8*** *p224*
Reilly, Patrick; Philadelphia, 1741 ***4971*** *p92*
Reilly, Patrick; Philadelphia, 1867 ***5704.8*** *p220*
Reilly, Patrick 8; St. John, N.B., 1847 ***5704.8*** *p20*
Reilly, Patrick 22; Philadelphia, 1774 ***1219.7*** *p182*
Reilly, Peter; America, 1741 ***4971*** *p10*
Reilly, Peter; America, 1741 ***4971*** *p94*
Reilly, Peter; New York, NY, 1837 ***8208.4*** *p34*
Reilly, Peter 3; St. John, N.B., 1847 ***5704.8*** *p35*
Reilly, Phelim; America, 1740 ***4971*** *p70*
Reilly, Philip S.; Virginia, 1855 ***4626.16*** *p15*
Reilly, Sarah 18; Philadelphia, 1864 ***5704.8*** *p156*
Reilly, Susan; New York, NY, 1867 ***5704.8*** *p224*
Reilly, Susan; Quebec, 1847 ***5704.8*** *p38*
Reilly, Terence; America, 1742 ***4971*** *p30*
Reilly, Terence; Annapolis, MD, 1742 ***4971*** *p93*
Reilly, Thomas; America, 1742 ***4971*** *p37*
Reilly, Thomas; New York, NY, 1811 ***2859.11*** *p18*
Reilly, Thomas; New York, NY, 1816 ***2859.11*** *p41*
Reilly, Thomas; Philadelphia, 1816 ***2859.11*** *p41*
Reilly, Thomas; Philadelphia, 1848 ***53.26*** *p79*
Reilly, Thomas; Philadelphia, 1848 ***5704.8*** *p40*
Reilly, Thomas; Quebec, 1823 ***7603*** *p89*
Reilly, Thomas; Quebec, 1847 ***5704.8*** *p37*
Reilly, William; Philadelphia, 1850 ***5704.8*** *p64*
Reilly, William 35; Philadelphia, 1774 ***1219.7*** *p183*
Reillyn, John; America, 1739 ***4971*** *p9*
Reily, Hugh; America, 1741 ***4971*** *p94*
Reily, John; America, 1736-1743 ***4971*** *p57*
Reily, Margaret; Quebec, 1820 ***7603*** *p74*
Reily, Margaret; Quebec, 1821 ***7603*** *p82*
Reily, Mary; Quebec, 1824 ***7603*** *p83*
Reily, Philip; Philadelphia, 1815 ***2859.11*** *p41*
Reily, Terence; Maryland, 1742 ***4971*** *p106*
Reiman, Joseph; Ohio, 1838 ***9892.11*** *p39*
Reiman, Joseph; Ohio, 1840 ***9892.11*** *p39*
Reiman, Paul Frank; Iowa, 1866-1943 ***123.54*** *p75*
Reimann, William; Washington, 1859-1920 ***2872.1*** *p33*
Reimenschneider, Heinrich; Wisconsin, n.d. ***9675.7*** *p200*
Reimer, Adolph; New York, NY, 1889 ***3455.1*** *p52*
Reimer, Anna 36; New York, NY, 1878 ***9253*** *p46*
Reimer, Catharine 11; New York, NY, 1878 ***9253*** *p46*
Reimer, Christian; America, 1887 ***1450.2*** *p31B*
Reimer, Elisabeth 6; New York, NY, 1878 ***9253*** *p46*
Reimer, Fred Peter; Wisconsin, n.d. ***9675.7*** *p200*
Reimer, Heinrich 7; New York, NY, 1878 ***9253*** *p46*
Reimer, Heinrich 40; New York, NY, 1878 ***9253*** *p46*
Reimer, Johann 8; New York, NY, 1878 ***9253*** *p46*
Reimer, John; Wisconsin, n.d. ***9675.7*** *p200*
Reimer, Margaretha 10; New York, NY, 1878 ***9253*** *p46*
Reimer, Marie Paula; Wisconsin, n.d. ***9675.7*** *p200*
Reimer, Peter; Wisconsin, n.d. ***9675.7*** *p200*
Reimer, Peter 1; New York, NY, 1878 ***9253*** *p46*
Reimer, William; Pennsylvania, 1871 ***5240.1*** *p36*
Reimling, Eva 29; America, 1853 ***9162.7*** *p15*
Reimling, Franz 29; America, 1853 ***9162.7*** *p15*
Reimling, Ludwig 6 mos; America, 1853 ***9162.7*** *p15*
Rein, John; Philadelphia, 1811 ***53.26*** *p79*
Rein, John; Philadelphia, 1811 ***2859.11*** *p18*
Rein, Joseph; Ohio, 1798-1818 ***8582.2*** *p54*
Rein, Rudolf; Washington, 1859-1920 ***2872.1*** *p33*
Reinberger, Lewis; New York, 1835 ***9892.11*** *p39*
Reinberger, Lewis; Ohio, 1839 ***9892.11*** *p39*
Reinboth, . . .; Canada, 1776-1783 ***9786*** *p31*
Reinchenbach, . . .; Canada, 1776-1783 ***9786*** *p31*
Reinchenback, . . .; Canada, 1776-1783 ***9786*** *p31*
Reincke, Abraham; New York, 1744 ***3652*** *p63*
*Wife:*Sarah
Reincke, Sarah *SEE* Reincke, Abraham
Reincking, Lieut.; Quebec, 1776 ***9786*** *p105*
Reineck, . . .; Canada, 1776-1783 ***9786*** *p31*
Reinecke, . . .; Canada, 1776-1783 ***9786*** *p31*
Reinecke, Fr W.; America, 1844 ***8582.1*** *p28*
Reinehl, Henry; Pennsylvania, 1749 ***2444*** *p203*
Reineking, Lt.; Canada, 1776-1783 ***9786*** *p239*
Reiner, Henry; Washington, 1859-1920 ***2872.1*** *p33*
Reiner, Johann Georg; Pennsylvania, 1752 ***4525*** *p237*
Reinerd, George; Pennsylvania, 1772 ***4525*** *p237*
Reinerding, Carl Wilhelm; Quebec, 1776 ***9786*** *p255*
Reinerding, F.; Quebec, 1776 ***9786*** *p105*
Reiners, John; Iroquois Co., IL, 1886 ***3455.1*** *p12*
Reiners, Reiner; Iroquois Co., IL, 1896 ***3455.1*** *p12*
Reinger, John Leopold; Wisconsin, n.d. ***9675.7*** *p200*
Reinges, Siebert 24; Kansas, 1886 ***5240.1*** *p69*
Reinhammer, Peter; Indiana, 1848 ***9117*** *p19*
Reinhard, . . .; Canada, 1776-1783 ***9786*** *p31*
Reinhard, Anna Kath. 19; America, 1853 ***9162.8*** *p37*
Reinhard, Johann Georg; Pennsylvania, 1752 ***4525*** *p237*
Reinhard, Jonas; Philadelphia, 1779 ***8137*** *p12*
Reinhard, Phillip; America, 1848 ***1450.2*** *p117A*
Reinhardt, Christian; America, 1889 ***1450.2*** *p117A*
Reinhardt, Christopher; New York, NY, 1836 ***8208.4*** *p10*
Reinhardt, Ludwig; New York, 1852-1855 ***1450.2*** *p117A*
Reinhart, . . .; Canada, 1776-1783 ***9786*** *p31*
Reinhart, Johann B.; Cincinnati, 1869-1887 ***8582*** *p24*
Reinheimer, Peter; America, 1847 ***5647.5*** *p23*
Reinhert, J. Mark; Shreveport, LA, 1875 ***7129*** *p45*
Reinhold, Christ. Henry; Philadelphia, 1760 ***9973.7*** *p34*
Reinhold, Georg; Philadelphia, 1776 ***8582.3*** *p83*
Reinhold, Max Richard 25; Kansas, 1902 ***5240.1*** *p82*
Reiniger, Gustav; Ohio, 1832 ***8582.1*** *p46*
Reinikka, Carl Clifford; Washington, 1859-1920 ***2872.1*** *p33*
Reinikka, Carl William; Washington, 1859-1920 ***2872.1*** *p33*
Reinikka, Gilbert; Washington, 1859-1920 ***2872.1*** *p33*
Reinikka, Helen Lillian; Washington, 1859-1920 ***2872.1*** *p33*
Reinikka, Hilda; Washington, 1859-1920 ***2872.1*** *p33*
Reinke, Caspar Heinrich August; America, 1856 ***4610.10*** *p149*
Reinke, Mathias; Wisconsin, n.d. ***9675.7*** *p200*
Reinkensmeyer, . . .; Illinois, 1800-1900 ***4610.10*** *p67*
Reinkensmeyer, Miss 27; America, 1853 ***4610.10*** *p148*
Reinkensmeyer, Mr.; Illinois, n.d. ***4610.10*** *p56*
With brother
Reinkensmeyer, Anna Marie L. Christine; America, 1863 ***4610.10*** *p140*
Reinkensmeyer, Caroline; America, 1873 ***4610.10*** *p56*
Reinkensmeyer, Christian F. Wilhelm; America, 1883 ***4610.10*** *p102*
Reinkensmeyer, Ernst; Illinois, 1800-1910 ***4610.10*** *p61*
With brothers
Reinkensmeyer, Ernst Heinrich August; America, 1883 ***4610.10*** *p102*
Reinkensmeyer, Friedrich 15; America, 1872 ***4610.10*** *p100*
Reinkensmeyer, Heinrich F. Gottlieb; America, 1851 ***4610.10*** *p155*
Reinkensmeyer, Heinrich F. Wilhelm; America, 1883 ***4610.10*** *p102*
Reinkensmeyer, Johann F. Wilhelm 59; America, 1853 ***4610.10*** *p156*
*Wife:*Marie Viehe 50
With stepchild
Reinkensmeyer, Marie Louise 26; America, 1850 ***4610.10*** *p138*
Reinkensmeyer, Marie Viehe 50 *SEE* Reinkensmeyer, Johann F. Wilhelm
Reinkensmeyer, Wilhelm; Illinois, 1914 ***4610.10*** *p68*
Reinkensmeyer, Wilhelm; Illinois, 1923 ***4610.10*** *p60*
Reinking, Rittm.; Quebec, 1776 ***9786*** *p104*
Reinking, Carl Friedrich; Quebec, 1776 ***9786*** *p252*
Reinking, Friedrich Carl; Quebec, 1776 ***9786*** *p256*
Reinking, Heinrich Friedrich Wilhelm; America, 1883 ***4610.10*** *p102*
Reinlein, Paul; Cincinnati, 1873 ***8582.3*** *p87*
Reinner, H. D.; Washington, 1859-1920 ***2872.1*** *p33*
Reinoehl, Eva C. Gruenzweig *SEE* Reinoehl, Georg Heinrich
Reinoehl, Georg Heinrich; Pennsylvania, 1749 ***2444*** *p202*
*Wife:*Eva C. Gruenzweig
Reinoeld, Gotthilf Albert; Colorado, 1892 ***9678.2*** *p164*
Reinole, Henry; Pennsylvania, 1749 ***2444*** *p203*
Reinskop, Bernard; Iowa, 1866-1943 ***123.54*** *p41*
Reinthaler, Hans Jerg; Pennsylvania, 1751 ***2444*** *p204*
Reinthalere, Georg; Pennsylvania, 1751 ***2444*** *p204*
Reintz, Jeanette 4; Port uncertain, 1839 ***778.5*** *p453*
Reintz, John; Illinois, 1855 ***7857*** *p6*
Reintz, Julia 7; Port uncertain, 1839 ***778.5*** *p453*
Reintz, Marie 26; Port uncertain, 1839 ***778.5*** *p453*
Reintz, Therese 2; Port uncertain, 1839 ***778.5*** *p453*
Reis, Mr.; Cincinnati, 1843 ***8582.3*** *p16*
Reis, Catharina; Pennsylvania, 1752 ***2444*** *p198*
Reis, David 34; New York, NY, 1851 ***9555.10*** *p26*
Reis, Joseph; Baltimore, 1836 ***8582.3*** *p54*
Reis, Joseph; Ohio, 1869-1887 ***8582*** *p24*
Reisen, Frank; Iroquois Co., IL, 1892 ***3455.1*** *p12*
Reisenwever, John G. 49; West Virginia, 1891 ***9788.3*** *p19*
Reiser, Jacob; Pennsylvania, 1752 ***2444*** *p202*
Reiser, Jacob; Pennsylvania, 1752 ***2444*** *p204*
Reiser, Paul; Philadelphia, 1760 ***9973.7*** *p34*
Reish, Conrad; Pennsylvania, 1749 ***2444*** *p202*
Reish, Johan Conrad; Pennsylvania, 1750 ***2444*** *p202*
Reish, Paul 39; Pennsylvania, 1856 ***1450.2*** *p117A*
Reisheim, Torkel Olai Nilsen; Arkansas, 1918 ***95.2*** *p104*
Reisloh, Heinrich; America, 1851 ***8582.3*** *p54*
Reismeier, Albrecht; Wisconsin, n.d. ***9675.7*** *p200*
Reiss, Franz Joseph; Illinois, 1886 ***2896.5*** *p33*
Reiss, Jacq. 46; Port uncertain, 1839 ***778.5*** *p453*
Reiss, Jakob; Cincinnati, 1826 ***8582.1*** *p51*
Reiss, John M.; Illinois, 1892 ***2896.5*** *p33*
Reiss, Julius Edmond; Illinois, 1886 ***2896.5*** *p33*
Reiss, Philipp; America, 1820 ***8582*** *p24*
Reisser, Anna Maria; Port uncertain, 1725-1800 ***2444*** *p203*
Reisser, Jacob; Pennsylvania, 1752 ***2444*** *p202*
Reissig, . . .; Canada, 1776-1783 ***9786*** *p31*
Reissner, Charlotte 21; America, 1854-1855 ***9162.6*** *p105*
Reissner, Elisab. 23; America, 1854-1855 ***9162.6*** *p105*
Reissner, Franz 29; America, 1854-1855 ***9162.6*** *p105*
Reissner, Gg. Ernst 15; America, 1854-1855 ***9162.6*** *p105*
Reissner, Gg. Jak. 27; America, 1854-1855 ***9162.6*** *p105*
Reissner, Johannes 19; America, 1854-1855 ***9162.6*** *p105*
Reissner, John Gottfried; America, 1851 ***1450.2*** *p117A*
Reissner, Kathr. Elis. 52; America, 1854-1855 ***9162.6*** *p105*
Reissner, Leonh. 53; America, 1854-1855 ***9162.6*** *p105*
Reitem, Peter; New York, NY, 1851 ***2896.5*** *p33*
Reitemeier, A. Cath. C. Wilhelmine *SEE* Reitemeier, Ernst Heinrich
Reitemeier, A. M. W. Schumacher *SEE* Reitemeier, Ernst Heinrich
Reitemeier, Carl Heinrich Fr. *SEE* Reitemeier, Ernst Heinrich
Reitemeier, Ernst Gottlieb *SEE* Reitemeier, Ernst Heinrich
Reitemeier, Ernst Heinrich; America, 1881 ***4610.10*** *p160*
*Wife:*A. M. W. Schumacher
*Child:*Ernst Gottlieb
*Child:*A. Cath. C. Wilhelmine
*Child:*Carl Heinrich Fr.
Reiter, Anna *SEE* Reiter, Daniel
Reiter, Anna Maria *SEE* Reiter, Daniel
Reiter, Catharina *SEE* Reiter, Daniel
Reiter, Daniel; Pennsylvania, 1752 ***2444*** *p203*
*Wife:*Anna
*Child:*Catharina
*Child:*Anna Maria
Reiter, F. W.; Ohio, 1869-1887 ***8582*** *p24*
Reiter, Hans; Georgia, 1738 ***9332*** *p320*
Reiter, Henry; Wisconsin, n.d. ***9675.7*** *p200*
Reiter, John; Wisconsin, n.d. ***9675.7*** *p200*
Reiter, Maria 27; Georgia, 1734 ***9332*** *p327*
Reiter, Michael; Wisconsin, n.d. ***9675.7*** *p200*
Reiter, Nicholas; Wisconsin, n.d. ***9675.7*** *p200*
Reiter, Peter; Georgia, 1738 ***9332*** *p321*
Reiter, Peter; Georgia, 1739 ***9332*** *p323*
Reiter, Peter; Georgia, 1739 ***9332*** *p327*
Reiter, Philip Christian; New York, 1756 ***3652*** *p81*
Reiter, Simon; Georgia, 1739 ***9332*** *p323*
Reiter, Simon; Georgia, 1739 ***9332*** *p325*
Reith, Werner; Philadelphia, 1779-1780 ***8137*** *p12*
Reither, Jacob; Washington, 1859-1920 ***2872.1*** *p33*
Reitmeier, Henry; Illinois, 1898 ***5012.40*** *p55*
Reitmeier, Johann Friedrich 47; Port uncertain, 1854 ***4610.10*** *p157*
With wife
With 4 daughters
Reitmeyer, Anna Marie 19; America, 1881 ***4610.10*** *p160*
Reitober, Ignatz 27; Kansas, 1884 ***5240.1*** *p36*
Reitober, Ignatz 27; Kansas, 1884 ***5240.1*** *p67*
Reittenauer, Philipp 24; Port uncertain, 1839 ***778.5*** *p453*
Reitter, Frederick A.; Illinois, 1899 ***5012.40*** *p55*
Reitter, Frederick A.; Illinois, 1899 ***5012.40*** *p56*
Reitz, . . .; Canada, 1776-1783 ***9786*** *p32*
Reitz, Christoph 26; Kansas, 1885 ***5240.1*** *p68*
Reitz, Christopher 26; Kansas, 1885 ***5240.1*** *p36*
Reitz, Clemens; Indiana, 1847 ***9117*** *p19*
Reitz, Clements; Indiana, 1848 ***9117*** *p18*
Reitz, Johann Caspar; Canada, 1780 ***9786*** *p268*
Reitz, Johann Caspar; New York, 1776 ***9786*** *p268*
Reitzenstein, . . .; Canada, 1776-1783 ***9786*** *p32*
Reitzenstein, v.; Quebec, 1776 ***9786*** *p105*

Reitzenstein, von; Ontario, 1784 ***9786*** *p205*
Reitzenstein, Gottlieb Christian; Quebec, 1776 ***9786*** *p254*
Reive, Eliza; St. John, N.B., 1851 ***5704.8*** *p73*
Reiverts, Jacob; Illinois, 1890 ***5012.37*** *p62*
Reker, Anna Maria Schauwecker *SEE* Reker, Hans Martin
Reker, Georg *SEE* Reker, Hans Martin
Reker, Hans Martin; America, 1766 ***2444*** *p205*
*Wife:*Anna Maria Schauwecker
*Child:*Georg
*Son:*Johann Martin
Reker, Johann Martin *SEE* Reker, Hans Martin
Reker, Michael; Pennsylvania, 1750 ***2444*** *p205*
Relict, William; Virginia, 1698 ***2212*** *p17*
Relihan, P.T.; Nevada, 1882 ***2764.35*** *p60*
Relion, Andre 30; New Orleans, 1825 ***778.5*** *p453*
Rellensmann, Emil Heinrich Wilhelm; America, 1885 ***4610.10*** *p125*
Relsey, John 18; Jamaica, 1752 ***3690.1*** *p132*
Relshaw, Rph.; Virginia, 1698 ***2212*** *p16*
Remann, Frederick 39; Illinois, 1846 ***2896.5*** *p33*
Remarri, Mr. 29; Port uncertain, 1836 ***778.5*** *p453*
Rembold, Sophia Catharina; Pennsylvania, 1753 ***2444*** *p154*
Remer, Frederick; Wisconsin, n.d. ***9675.7*** *p200*
Remerck, . . .; Canada, 1776-1783 ***9786*** *p32*
Remetter, Adam; America, 1880 ***1450.2*** *p117A*
Remetz, Joseph; Wisconsin, n.d. ***9675.7*** *p200*
Remhoff, . . .; Canada, 1776-1783 ***9786*** *p32*
Remi, . . .; Canada, 1776-1783 ***9786*** *p43*
Remic, Anton; Wisconsin, n.d. ***9675.7*** *p200*
Remic, Martin; Wisconsin, n.d. ***9675.7*** *p200*
Remich, John; Wisconsin, n.d. ***9675.7*** *p200*
Remick, John; Arkansas, 1918 ***95.2*** *p104*
Remiker, Henry; Illinois, 1860 ***5012.39*** *p89*
Remington, Jon.; Virginia, 1643 ***6219*** *p200*
Remisch, John; Wisconsin, n.d. ***9675.7*** *p200*
Remitz, Anton; Wisconsin, n.d. ***9675.7*** *p200*
Remitz, Joseph; Wisconsin, n.d. ***9675.7*** *p200*
Remitz, Mary; Wisconsin, n.d. ***9675.7*** *p200*
Remiy, . . .; Canada, 1776-1783 ***9786*** *p43*
Remiz, Joseph; Wisconsin, n.d. ***9675.7*** *p200*
Remkus, Alex; Wisconsin, n.d. ***9675.7*** *p200*
Remkus, Frank; Wisconsin, n.d. ***9675.7*** *p200*
Remkus, John; Wisconsin, n.d. ***9675.7*** *p200*
Remler, . . .; Canada, 1776-1783 ***9786*** *p32*
Remlinger, John C.; Wisconsin, n.d. ***9675.7*** *p200*
Remlinger, John Carl; Wisconsin, n.d. ***9675.7*** *p200*
Remme, H. W.; Cincinnati, 1869-1887 ***8582*** *p24*
Remmeck, . . .; Canada, 1776-1783 ***9786*** *p32*
Remmers, Diedrich 41; Kansas, 1903 ***5240.1*** *p82*
Remmert, Anne M. Catharine Wilhelmine; America, 1857 ***4610.10*** *p136*
Remmert, Carl Heinrich Wilhelm; America, 1857 ***4610.10*** *p136*
Remmert, Caspar Heinrich August; America, 1868 ***4610.10*** *p137*
Remmert, Frederick; Illinois, 1890 ***2896.5*** *p33*
Remmert, William; Illinois, 1888 ***2896.5*** *p33*
Remmy, . . .; Canada, 1776-1783 ***9786*** *p43*
Remnant, John 23; Maryland, 1774 ***1219.7*** *p225*
Remond, Mr. 23; Port uncertain, 1839 ***778.5*** *p453*
Remonda, John 30; Maryland, 1774 ***1219.7*** *p235*
Removich, Alexander; Arkansas, 1918 ***95.2*** *p104*
Remp, Andreas *SEE* Remp, Andreas
Remp, Andreas; America, 1754 ***2444*** *p203*
*Wife:*Anna Eitelbuss
*Child:*Jacob
*Child:*Michel
*Child:*Johannes
*Child:*Johann Martin
*Child:*Andreas
*Child:*Gottlieb
Remp, Anna Eitelbuss *SEE* Remp, Andreas
Remp, Charles 24; America, 1838 ***778.5*** *p453*
Remp, Gottlieb *SEE* Remp, Andreas
Remp, Jacob *SEE* Remp, Andreas
Remp, Johann Martin *SEE* Remp, Andreas
Remp, Johannes *SEE* Remp, Andreas
Remp, Michel *SEE* Remp, Andreas
Rempel, Abraham; Quebec, 1876 ***9980.20*** *p49*
Rempel, Agatha; Quebec, 1878 ***9980.20*** *p49*
Rempel, Anna; Quebec, 1876 ***9980.20*** *p49*
Rempel, Elisabeth; Quebec, 1876 ***9980.20*** *p49*
Rempel, Eva Neufeld; Quebec, 1876 ***9980.20*** *p49*
Rempel, Franz; Quebec, 1876 ***9980.20*** *p49*
Rempel, Gerhard; Quebec, 1876 ***9980.20*** *p49*
Rempel, Johann; Quebec, 1876 ***9980.20*** *p49*
Rempel, Judith; Quebec, 1876 ***9980.20*** *p49*
Rempel, Kathariena; Quebec, 1876 ***9980.20*** *p49*
Rempel, Maria; Quebec, 1876 ***9980.20*** *p49*
Rempel, Sara; Quebec, 1878 ***9980.20*** *p49*
Rempel, Sara Abrams; Quebec, 1878 ***9980.20*** *p49*
Rempel, Sara M.; Quebec, 1878 ***9980.20*** *p49*
Rempel, Susanna; Quebec, 1876 ***9980.20*** *p49*
Rempel, Wilhelm; Quebec, 1878 ***9980.20*** *p49*
Rempp, Andreas *SEE* Rempp, Andreas
Rempp, Andreas; America, 1754 ***2444*** *p203*
*Wife:*Anna Eitelbuss
*Child:*Jacob
*Child:*Michel
*Child:*Johannes
*Child:*Johann Martin
*Child:*Andreas
*Child:*Gottlieb
Rempp, Anna Eitelbuss *SEE* Rempp, Andreas
Rempp, Gottlieb *SEE* Rempp, Andreas
Rempp, Jacob *SEE* Rempp, Andreas
Rempp, Johann Martin *SEE* Rempp, Andreas
Rempp, Johannes *SEE* Rempp, Andreas
Rempp, Michel *SEE* Rempp, Andreas
Remsko, Anton; Wisconsin, n.d. ***9675.7*** *p200*
Remsko, Joseph; Wisconsin, n.d. ***9675.7*** *p200*
Remy, . . .; Canada, 1776-1783 ***9786*** *p43*
Ren, . . .; Canada, 1776-1783 ***9786*** *p32*
Renal, J. 20; New Orleans, 1837 ***778.5*** *p453*
Renall, Randall; Virginia, 1639 ***6219*** *p162*
Renard, Mr. 30; Louisiana, 1821 ***778.5*** *p453*
Renard, Eugene; America, 1854 ***1450.2*** *p117A*
Renard, Ferdynand; New York, 1835 ***4606*** *p180*
Renard, Louis; Arkansas, 1918 ***95.2*** *p104*
Renard, Louis 35; Louisiana, 1820 ***778.5*** *p454*
Renau, Joseph 38; New Orleans, 1826 ***778.5*** *p454*
Renau, Wilhelm; Cincinnati, 1869-1887 ***8582*** *p24*
Renaud, Adolph 21; America, 1836 ***778.5*** *p454*
Renaud, Jean; Quebec, 1710 ***7603*** *p27*
Renaut, Pierre 23; America, 1837 ***778.5*** *p454*
Renberg, Michael; Germantown, PA, 1684 ***2467.7*** *p5*
Rendall, John B.; Wisconsin, n.d. ***9675.7*** *p200*
Rendles, Elizabeth 16 *SEE* Rendles, James
Rendles, James 40; Philadelphia, 1803 ***53.26*** *p79*
*Relative:*John 38
*Relative:*Elizabeth 16
*Relative:*Thomas 12
Rendles, John 38 *SEE* Rendles, James
Rendles, Thomas 12 *SEE* Rendles, James
Rendrick, Edwd.; Virginia, 1644 ***6219*** *p229*
Rene, Pierre 20; Port uncertain, 1830 ***778.5*** *p454*
Renenaugh, James; New York, NY, 1816 ***2859.11*** *p41*
Rener, Catharina *SEE* Rener, Maria Margaret
Rener, Maria Margaret; Pennsylvania, 1700-1746 ***1034.18*** *p18*
*Sister:*Catharina
Renggli, Louis E. 21; Kansas, 1890 ***5240.1*** *p75*
Reniger, John Leopold; Wisconsin, n.d. ***9675.7*** *p200*
Renis, Clement 17; New Orleans, 1838 ***778.5*** *p454*
Renn, Daniel 14; Massachusetts, 1850 ***5881.1*** *p83*
Renn, Michael; America, 1835 ***1450.2*** *p118A*
Rennar, Peter 35; West Virginia, 1900 ***9788.3*** *p19*
Renndle, Margt; Virginia, 1698 ***2212*** *p15*
Rennegabe, Hermann; America, 1880 ***1450.2*** *p118A*
Rennegarbe, Frederick; America, 1892 ***1450.2*** *p118A*
Rennekamp, Anton Louis; America, 1847 ***8582.3*** *p54*
Rennekamp, Carl Heinrich Gottlieb; America, 1885 ***4610.10*** *p160*
Rennekamp, Franz Joseph; America, 1847 ***8582.3*** *p54*
Rennenkamp, Carl Gottlieb *SEE* Rennenkamp, Christian Ludwig
Rennenkamp, Christian Ludwig; America, 1868 ***4610.10*** *p159*
*Wife:*Wilhelmine Charlotte
*Son:*Carl Gottlieb
Rennenkamp, Christian Ludwig; America, 1869 ***4610.10*** *p137*
*Wife:*Wilhelmine Kronenberg
*Son:*Johann Gottlieb
Rennenkamp, Johann Gottlieb *SEE* Rennenkamp, Christian Ludwig
Rennenkamp, Wilhelmine Charlotte *SEE* Rennenkamp, Christian Ludwig
Rennenkamp, Wilhelmine Kronenberg *SEE* Rennenkamp, Christian Ludwig
Renner, Adam; America, 1847 ***8582.2*** *p33*
Renner, Anna Catherine; New York, 1749 ***3652*** *p73*
Renner, Elisabeth; America, 1751 ***2444*** *p229*
Renner, Georg; America, 1852 ***8582.3*** *p54*
Renner, Georg Jacob; America, 1849 ***8582.3*** *p54*
Renner, Jacob; Cincinnati, 1869-1887 ***8582*** *p24*
Renner, John George; New York, 1749 ***3652*** *p72*
Rennert, . . .; Canada, 1776-1783 ***9786*** *p32*
Rennick, Felix; Ohio, 1798 ***8582.2*** *p55*
Rennie, Alexander 4; Quebec, 1850 ***5704.8*** *p63*
Rennie, Betty; Quebec, 1850 ***5704.8*** *p63*
Rennie, Eliza; Philadelphia, 1852 ***5704.8*** *p89*
Rennie, James; Quebec, 1849 ***5704.8*** *p57*
Rennie, James; Quebec, 1850 ***5704.8*** *p63*
Rennie, Jane; Quebec, 1850 ***5704.8*** *p63*
Rennie, Jane 3; Quebec, 1849 ***5704.8*** *p57*
Rennie, John; Quebec, 1850 ***5704.8*** *p63*
Rennie, John 12; Quebec, 1850 ***5704.8*** *p63*
Rennie, John 25; Georgia, 1773 ***1219.7*** *p172*
Rennie, Margaret; Quebec, 1850 ***5704.8*** *p63*
Rennie, Margaret Ann 9 mos; Quebec, 1850 ***5704.8*** *p63*
Rennie, Michael 5; Quebec, 1850 ***5704.8*** *p63*
Rennie, Robert; Quebec, 1850 ***5704.8*** *p63*
Rennie, Robert 35; Kansas, 1888 ***5240.1*** *p72*
Rennie, Sarah; Philadelphia, 1850 ***53.26*** *p79*
Rennie, Sarah; Philadelphia, 1850 ***5704.8*** *p69*
Renoir, Alexandre 40; New Orleans, 1827 ***778.5*** *p454*
Renouf, Philippe; Quebec, 1825 ***7603*** *p49*
Rensch, Lewis; Ohio, 1842 ***8365.25*** *p12*
Renshlar, Mathias 27; Pennsylvania, 1754 ***2444*** *p203*
Renshlar, Mich'l 34; Pennsylvania, 1754 ***2444*** *p203*
Renshler, Mich'l; Pennsylvania, 1754 ***2444*** *p203*
Rensing, Anton; America, 1845 ***8582.1*** *p28*
Rensler, Michael; Pennsylvania, 1754 ***2444*** *p203*
Rensmann, Charles; Illinois, 1882 ***2896.5*** *p33*
Rensmann, Fred; Illinois, 1882 ***2896.5*** *p33*
Rentner, Georg Gottfried Hermann; America, 1852 ***8582.3*** *p54*
Rentsch, Edward; America, 1849 ***1450.2*** *p118A*
Rentsch, Hermann; America, 1853 ***1450.2*** *p118A*
Rentsch, Robert; New York, NY, 1867 ***1450.2*** *p31B*
Rentschler, Michael; Port uncertain, 1754 ***2444*** *p203*
Rentschler, Michael 34; Pennsylvania, 1754 ***2444*** *p203*
Rentz, Anna Catharina *SEE* Rentz, Georg
Rentz, Catharina Majer *SEE* Rentz, Georg
Rentz, Catharina Majer; America, 1742-1800 ***2444*** *p201*
*Husband:*George
Rentz, Christina; Pennsylvania, 1751 ***2444*** *p200*
Rentz, Georg; Pennsylvania, 1751 ***2444*** *p203*
*Wife:*Catharina Majer
*Child:*Johann Georg
*Child:*Anna Catharina
*Child:*Simon
With stepchild
Rentz, George *SEE* Rentz, Catharina Majer
Rentz, Johann Georg *SEE* Rentz, Georg
Rentz, Joseph; New York, NY, 1834 ***8582*** *p24*
Rentz, Sebastian; West Indies, n.d. ***8582.3*** *p79*
Rentz, Simon *SEE* Rentz, Georg
Rentzler, Michael; Pennsylvania, 1754 ***2444*** *p203*
Renwick, Alexander; Ohio, 1801-1802 ***8582.2*** *p55*
Renwick, William; North Carolina, 1823 ***1639.20*** *p270*
Renwood, Thomas 21; Jamaica, 1731 ***3690.1*** *p188*
Renz, . . .; America, 1836 ***8582.1*** *p39*
Renz, August; Cincinnati, 1836 ***8582.1*** *p45*
Repaille, Mme. 34; America, 1829 ***778.5*** *p454*
Repaille, Edward 32; Mexico, 1827 ***778.5*** *p454*
Repaille, Edward 37; America, 1829 ***778.5*** *p454*
Repaille, O. 36; America, 1829 ***778.5*** *p454*
Reph, Frederick 22; America, 1838 ***778.5*** *p454*
Repke, William; Wisconsin, n.d. ***9675.7*** *p200*
Replen, Joseph; Illinois, 1868 ***7857*** *p6*
Replinger, Johan; Wisconsin, n.d. ***9675.7*** *p200*
Repond, Jacob; Illinois, 1888 ***2896.5*** *p33*
Repp, Ester; Washington, 1859-1920 ***2872.1*** *p33*
Repp, Kate; Washington, 1859-1920 ***2872.1*** *p33*
Repp, Ludwig; Washington, 1859-1920 ***2872.1*** *p33*
Repp, Vata; Washington, 1859-1920 ***2872.1*** *p33*
Reppert, Jacob; America, 1776-1781 ***8582.2*** *p33*
Reppert, Jacob; America, 1777-1778 ***8582.2*** *p69*
Reppert, Margaretha Schneider *SEE* Reppert, Stephan
Reppert, Stephan; Pennsylvania, 1727 ***3627*** *p19*
*Wife:*Margaretha Schneider
Repple, Martin; New York, NY, 1838 ***8208.4*** *p67*
Requiniere, Lise 20; New Orleans, 1822 ***778.5*** *p454*
Rerdon, Joseph 25; Maryland, 1733 ***3690.1*** *p188*
Rerhin, Martin; Wisconsin, n.d. ***9675.7*** *p200*
Resaner, Christian Frederick; America, 1836 ***1450.2*** *p118A*
Resburye, John; Virginia, 1637 ***6219*** *p81*
Resch, . . .; Canada, 1776-1783 ***9786*** *p32*
Resch, Joe 71; Arizona, 1917 ***9228.40*** *p21*
Resch, Peter; Wisconsin, n.d. ***9675.7*** *p200*
Resch, Sibylla; Georgia, 1739 ***9332*** *p325*
Resche, . . .; Canada, 1776-1783 ***9786*** *p32*
Rescow, Alexander; Arkansas, 1918 ***95.2*** *p104*
Rese, Friederich; Cincinnati, 1814-1848 ***8582.3*** *p89*
Resener, Charles; Baltimore, 1838 ***1450.2*** *p118A*
Resener, Frederick; America, 1841 ***1450.2*** *p118A*
Resener, Frederick William; America, 1845 ***1450.2*** *p118A*
Reser, Alexander 21; Kansas, 1887 ***5240.1*** *p70*
Resler, Christopher; West Virginia, 1859 ***9788.3*** *p19*
Resner, Christian; America, 1835-1856 ***1450.2*** *p118A*
Resperry, John; Virginia, 1646 ***6219*** *p247*
Ressejac, Louis Simon 27; America, 1838 ***778.5*** *p454*

Ressel, Michael 20; Pennsylvania, 1753 ***2444*** *p205*
Ressing, . . .; Canada, 1776-1783 ***9786*** *p32*
Ressler, Frederick; America, 1866 ***1450.2*** *p119A*
Rest, Georg Adam; South Carolina, 1788 ***7119*** *p198*
Rest, Robert 19; Virginia, 1734 ***3690.1*** *p188*
Restall, Jones 25; Maryland, 1725 ***3690.1*** *p188*
Restley, John 21; Baltimore, 1775 ***1219.7*** *p269*
Reston, Francis C.; North Carolina, 1825 ***1639.20*** *p270*
Reston, John; Wilmington, NC, 1829 ***1639.20*** *p270*
Reston, Jon.; Virginia, 1637 ***6219*** *p113*
Reston, Thomas C.; America, 1811 ***1639.20*** *p270*
Retallack, Simon 22; Maryland, 1774 ***1219.7*** *p224*
Rethorn, Henry; Illinois, 1872 ***2896.5*** *p33*
Rethorn, John; Illinois, 1886 ***2896.5*** *p33*
Retmann, Charles; Wisconsin, n.d. ***9675.7*** *p200*
Retscher, John B.; America, 1847 ***8582.1*** *p29*
Retscher, John B.; Ohio, 1847 ***8582.1*** *p48*
Rettig, Daniel 18; America, 1853 ***9162.7*** *p15*
Rettmann, Albert; Wisconsin, n.d. ***9675.7*** *p200*
Rettmann, Frank H.; Wisconsin, n.d. ***9675.7*** *p200*
Rettmann, Reinhard; Wisconsin, n.d. ***9675.7*** *p200*
Retz, Peter 36; Port uncertain, 1838 ***778.5*** *p455*
Retzlaff, Karl Gottlieb 32; Wisconsin, 1843 ***3702.7*** *p311*
With wife
With 2 children
Retzler, Catharina Dorothea; Port uncertain, 1750-1755 ***2444*** *p169*
Retzolk, Frederick W.; Illinois, 1876 ***5012.39*** *p26*
Reuchlin, Elisabetha; America, 1737-1800 ***2444*** *p209*
Reuffurth, Christoph Philipp; Halifax, N.S., 1780 ***9786*** *p269*
Reuffurth, Christoph Philipp; New York, 1776 ***9786*** *p269*
Reufil, Auguste 25; Port uncertain, 1820 ***778.5*** *p455*
Reuhl, Georg 74; America, 1895 ***1763*** *p40D*
Reunaud, Mr. 26; New Orleans, 1838 ***778.5*** *p455*
Reusch, Georg 26; America, 1854-1855 ***9162.6*** *p104*
Reusch, Joseph; Wisconsin, n.d. ***9675.7*** *p200*
Reusch, Peter 18; America, 1854-1855 ***9162.6*** *p105*
Reuschel, Andreas; Cincinnati, 1839 ***8582*** *p24*
Reuschgott, Simon; Georgia, 1734 ***9332*** *p327*
Reuse, Jakob; Philadelphia, 1781 ***8137*** *p12*
Reuss, Joseph; Cincinnati, 1869-1887 ***8582*** *p24*
Reuss, Magdalene Elizabeth; New York, 1749 ***3652*** *p71*
Reussing, . . .; Canada, 1776-1783 ***9786*** *p32*
Reussner, . . .; Canada, 1776-1783 ***9786*** *p32*
Reuter, Anna *SEE* Reuter, Daniel
Reuter, Anna Maria *SEE* Reuter, Daniel
Reuter, Anton; Illinois, 1894 ***2896.5*** *p33*
Reuter, Catharina *SEE* Reuter, Daniel
Reuter, Daniel; Pennsylvania, 1752 ***2444*** *p203*
*Wife:*Anna
*Child:*Catharina
*Child:*Anna Maria
Reuter, Joseph A.; Wisconsin, n.d. ***9675.7*** *p200*
Reuter, Michael; Philadelphia, 1760 ***9973.7*** *p34*
Reuter, Simon; Georgia, 1738 ***9332*** *p321*
Reuter, Wilhelm; Indiana, 1848 ***9117*** *p17*
Reuter, Wilhelm; Wisconsin, n.d. ***9675.7*** *p200*
Reuth, Louisana 22; Kansas, 1876 ***5240.1*** *p58*
Reuth, Werner; Philadelphia, 1779-1780 ***8137*** *p12*
Reutlinger, Johann Leonhard; Philadelphia, 1754 ***4525*** *p237*
*Wife:*Rosina
Reutlinger, Rosina *SEE* Reutlinger, Johann Leonhard
Reutter, Anna *SEE* Reutter, Daniel
Reutter, Anna Barbara *SEE* Reutter, Matthaeus
Reutter, Anna Barbara Maeurlin *SEE* Reutter, Matthaeus
Reutter, Anna Catharina *SEE* Reutter, Matthaeus
Reutter, Anna Maria *SEE* Reutter, Daniel
Reutter, Catharina *SEE* Reutter, Daniel
Reutter, Clara Sybilla *SEE* Reutter, Matthaeus
Reutter, Daniel; Pennsylvania, 1752 ***2444*** *p202*
Reutter, Daniel; Pennsylvania, 1752 ***2444*** *p203*
*Wife:*Anna
*Child:*Catharina
*Child:*Anna Maria
Reutter, Daniel; Pennsylvania, 1752 ***2444*** *p204*
Reutter, Maria Catharina *SEE* Reutter, Matthaeus
Reutter, Matthaeus; Pennsylvania, 1751 ***2444*** *p204*
*Wife:*Anna Barbara Maeurlin
*Child:*Maria Catharina
*Child:*Anna Catharina
*Child:*Anna Barbara
*Child:*Clara Sybilla
Reutz, Joseph; Cincinnati, 1869-1887 ***8582*** *p24*
Reutz, Magdalen *SEE* Reutz, Matthew
Reutz, Matthew; New York, 1743 ***3652*** *p60*
*Wife:*Magdalen
Reval, . . .; Port uncertain, 1838 ***778.5*** *p455*
Reval, Mme. 30; Port uncertain, 1838 ***778.5*** *p455*
Reval, J. 20; New Orleans, 1837 ***778.5*** *p453*
Reval, J. R. 38; Port uncertain, 1838 ***778.5*** *p455*
Revay, John; Arkansas, 1918 ***95.2*** *p104*
Revell, Eliz.; Virginia, 1637 ***6219*** *p110*
Revely, Edward 32; Dominica, 1774 ***1219.7*** *p205*
Reveran, Mr. 24; New Orleans, 1839 ***778.5*** *p455*
Revillon, J. 25; New Orleans, 1832 ***778.5*** *p455*
Revilly, Etienne 39; America, 1838 ***778.5*** *p455*
Revin, Nancy 40; Massachusetts, 1849 ***5881.1*** *p86*
Revington, Bridget; Albany, NY, 1831-1841 ***7036*** *p125*
Revington, Bridget; Quebec, 1831 ***7036*** *p125*
*Uncle:*Henry
Revington, Henry *SEE* Revington, Bridget
Revington, Henry; Boston, 1831-1841 ***7036*** *p125*
Reviss, Henry 20; Windward Islands, 1722 ***3690.1*** *p188*
Revuella, J. M. 29; Port uncertain, 1836 ***778.5*** *p455*
Rewaldt, Heinrich; Cincinnati, 1869-1887 ***8582*** *p24*
Rewed, Jarvis; Virginia, 1637 ***6219*** *p108*
Rewerts, Henry; Illinois, 1890 ***5012.37*** *p62*
Rex, A. 50; New Orleans, 1830 ***778.5*** *p455*
Rex, De. 12; New Orleans, 1830 ***778.5*** *p455*
Rex, Georg; Ohio, 1816-1817 ***8582.1*** *p48*
Rex, Jane 45; New Orleans, 1830 ***778.5*** *p456*
Rex, M. 10; New Orleans, 1830 ***778.5*** *p456*
Rex, S. 8; New Orleans, 1830 ***778.5*** *p456*
Rexroth, Marie 21; America, 1854-1855 ***9162.6*** *p105*
Rexroth, Marie Luise 27; America, 1854-1855 ***9162.6*** *p104*
Rexroth, Michael 35; America, 1854-1855 ***9162.6*** *p105*
Rexroth, Sophie 23; America, 1854-1855 ***9162.6*** *p105*
Rexwinkel, John W.; Illinois, 1867 ***2896.5*** *p33*
Rey, Mr. 22; America, 1839 ***778.5*** *p456*
Rey, Mr. 29; New Orleans, 1829 ***778.5*** *p456*
Rey, Henry *SEE* Rey, Peter
Rey, Margarett *SEE* Rey, Peter
Rey, Peter; Virginia, 1637 ***6219*** *p29*
*Wife:*Margarett
*Son:*Henry
Reybolt, Jacob 45; Maryland, 1774 ***1219.7*** *p191*
Reyburne, Joseph; Virginia, 1698 ***2212*** *p6*
Reych, William 21; Philadelphia, 1775 ***1219.7*** *p274*
Reycock, Bryan; Virginia, 1637 ***6219*** *p84*
Reydis, Thomas 21; Montreal, 1777 ***7603*** *p97*
Reyes, Feliciano; Iowa, 1866-1943 ***123.54*** *p75*
Reyes, Hilario 26; Arizona, 1890 ***2764.35*** *p60*
Reyes, Santos; Iowa, 1866-1943 ***123.54*** *p75*
Reyet, Eugene 21; America, 1837 ***778.5*** *p456*
Reygert, Barbara 4 *SEE* Reygert, Christopher
Reygert, Christopher; South Carolina, 1752-1753 ***3689.17*** *p22*
With wife
*Relative:*George 20
*Relative:*Jacob 12
*Relative:*Barbara 4
Reygert, George 20 *SEE* Reygert, Christopher
Reygert, Jacob 12 *SEE* Reygert, Christopher
Reyler, Barbara; America, 1752 ***2444*** *p149*
Reyly, Martin; Philadelphia, 1749-1773 ***9973.7*** *p40*
Reymachen, John; Wisconsin, n.d. ***9675.7*** *p200*
Reymond, Tho.; Virginia, 1642 ***6219*** *p197*
Reynard, Mrs. 48; New Orleans, 1822 ***778.5*** *p456*
Reynard, Joan; America, 1740 ***4971*** *p31*
Reynard, Sophie 14; New Orleans, 1822 ***778.5*** *p456*
Reynaud, Mr.; Port uncertain, 1839 ***778.5*** *p456*
Reynaud, Jacques 38; New Orleans, 1822 ***778.5*** *p456*
Reynaud, P. 27; New Orleans, 1832 ***778.5*** *p456*
Reynaud, Simon 14; New Orleans, 1823 ***778.5*** *p456*
Reynior, Simeon 29; New Orleans, 1837 ***778.5*** *p456*
Reyno, . . .; Halifax, N.S., 1752 ***7074.6*** *p232*
Reynold, Alex.; Virginia, 1648 ***6219*** *p246*
Reynolds, Mr.; Quebec, 1815 ***9229.18*** *p76*
Reynolds, Ann 7; Massachusetts, 1849 ***5881.1*** *p82*
Reynolds, Ann 13; Massachusetts, 1848 ***5881.1*** *p82*
Reynolds, Benjamin 4; Massachusetts, 1848 ***5881.1*** *p82*
Reynolds, Bridget 7; St. John, N.B., 1854 ***5704.8*** *p115*
Reynolds, Bridget 9; Massachusetts, 1848 ***5881.1*** *p82*
Reynolds, Catharine 7; Massachusetts, 1848 ***5881.1*** *p83*
Reynolds, Catharine 20; Massachusetts, 1847 ***5881.1*** *p83*
Reynolds, Catharine 21; Philadelphia, 1774 ***1219.7*** *p182*
Reynolds, Catherine; New York, NY, 1816 ***2859.11*** *p41*
Reynolds, Catherine 30; St. John, N.B., 1854 ***5704.8*** *p115*
Reynolds, Edward *SEE* Reynolds, Eliz.
Reynolds, Edward; Virginia, 1629 ***6219*** *p31*
Reynolds, Eliz.; Virginia, 1638 ***6219*** *p147*
*Husband:*Edward
Reynolds, Eliza; New York, NY, 1816 ***2859.11*** *p41*
Reynolds, Francis 22; Maryland, 1775 ***1219.7*** *p251*
Reynolds, Frank; Wisconsin, n.d. ***9675.7*** *p200*
Reynolds, George 17; America, 1699 ***2212*** *p25*
Reynolds, George Graham 10; Quebec, 1849 ***5704.8*** *p52*
Reynolds, Gilbert; Virginia, 1636 ***6219*** *p21*
Reynolds, H. M.; Washington, 1859-1920 ***2872.1*** *p33*
Reynolds, Henry; Illinois, 1856 ***7857*** *p6*
Reynolds, Hugh 10; Quebec, 1850 ***5704.8*** *p63*
Reynolds, James; New York, NY, 1840 ***8208.4*** *p110*
Reynolds, James; New York, NY, 1849 ***6013.19*** *p74*
Reynolds, James; Ohio, 1854-1870 ***9892.11*** *p39*
Reynolds, James 9; Massachusetts, 1850 ***5881.1*** *p84*
Reynolds, Jane 15; St. John, N.B., 1854 ***5704.8*** *p122*
Reynolds, Jane 20; St. John, N.B., 1864 ***5704.8*** *p158*
Reynolds, Jilbert; Virginia, 1642 ***6219*** *p193*
Reynolds, John; Annapolis, MD, 1742 ***4971*** *p92*
Reynolds, John; Iowa, 1866-1943 ***123.54*** *p41*
Reynolds, John; Maryland, 1742 ***4971*** *p106*
Reynolds, John; New Jersey, 1850 ***6013.19*** *p88*
Reynolds, John; Wisconsin, n.d. ***9675.7*** *p200*
Reynolds, John 7; Quebec, 1850 ***5704.8*** *p63*
Reynolds, John 18; Jamaica, 1737 ***3690.1*** *p188*
Reynolds, John 22; Maryland, 1774 ***1219.7*** *p235*
Reynolds, John 22; Massachusetts, 1848 ***5881.1*** *p84*
Reynolds, John 23; Jamaica, 1723 ***3690.1*** *p188*
Reynolds, Jon.; Virginia, 1633 ***6219*** *p32*
Reynolds, Joseph; New York, NY, 1816 ***2859.11*** *p41*
Reynolds, Joseph; Quebec, 1849 ***5704.8*** *p52*
Reynolds, Laurence; New York, NY, 1816 ***2859.11*** *p41*
Reynolds, Margaret 12; Quebec, 1850 ***5704.8*** *p63*
Reynolds, Margaret 16; St. John, N.B., 1854 ***5704.8*** *p122*
Reynolds, Martha 22; Jamaica, 1738 ***3690.1*** *p188*
Reynolds, Martin 6; Massachusetts, 1848 ***5881.1*** *p85*
Reynolds, Mary; Virginia, 1637 ***6219*** *p111*
Reynolds, Mary 5; Massachusetts, 1848 ***5881.1*** *p85*
Reynolds, Mary 45; Massachusetts, 1848 ***5881.1*** *p85*
Reynolds, Mary Ann 6; Quebec, 1849 ***5704.8*** *p52*
Reynolds, Michael 24; St. John, N.B., 1854 ***5704.8*** *p115*
Reynolds, Nancy 45; South Carolina, 1850 ***1639.20*** *p270*
Reynolds, Nich.; Virginia, 1642 ***6219*** *p198*
Reynolds, Patrick; New York, NY, 1816 ***2859.11*** *p41*
Reynolds, Patrick; Virginia, 1858 ***4626.16*** *p17*
Reynolds, Patrick 20; Massachusetts, 1847 ***5881.1*** *p86*
Reynolds, Peter; Virginia, 1856 ***4626.16*** *p16*
Reynolds, Pierre; Montreal, 1816 ***7603*** *p68*
Reynolds, Richard; Virginia, 1637 ***6219*** *p17*
Reynolds, Richard; Virginia, 1638 ***6219*** *p122*
Reynolds, Richard 19; Philadelphia, 1775 ***1219.7*** *p255*
Reynolds, Robert 19; America, 1699 ***2212*** *p25*
Reynolds, Sarah; Quebec, 1849 ***5704.8*** *p52*
Reynolds, Sarah 20; Massachusetts, 1849 ***5881.1*** *p86*
Reynolds, Tho.; Virginia, 1637 ***6219*** *p113*
Reynolds, Thomas 2; St. John, N.B., 1854 ***5704.8*** *p115*
Reynolds, Thomas 11; Massachusetts, 1848 ***5881.1*** *p86*
Reynolds, Thomas 19; Maryland or Virginia, 1737 ***3690.1*** *p188*
Reynolds, Thomas 23; Jamaica, 1730 ***3690.1*** *p188*
Reynolds, Willi.; Virginia, 1637 ***6219*** *p83*
Reynolds, William; New England, 1816 ***2859.11*** *p41*
Reynolds, William; Virginia, 1600-1642 ***6219*** *p199*
Reynolds, William; Virginia, 1638 ***6219*** *p120*
Reynolds, William; Virginia, 1652 ***6251*** *p20*
Reynolds, William 16; America, 1728 ***3690.1*** *p189*
Reynolds, William 16; Pennsylvania, 1728 ***3690.1*** *p189*
Reynolds, Wm.; New York, NY, 1811 ***2859.11*** *p18*
Reynolds, Wm.; Virginia, 1648 ***6219*** *p246*
Reynsbottom, Isaac 16; Maryland, 1775 ***1219.7*** *p268*
Rezer, Johan; Wisconsin, n.d. ***9675.7*** *p200*
Rhea, David; New York, NY, 1811 ***2859.11*** *p18*
Rhea, Seragh; New York, NY, 1811 ***2859.11*** *p18*
Rhein, . . .; Canada, 1776-1783 ***9786*** *p32*
Rheinart, . . .; Canada, 1776-1783 ***9786*** *p32*
Rheingans, Henry; Wisconsin, n.d. ***9675.7*** *p200*
Rheingans, Nicholas; Wisconsin, n.d. ***9675.7*** *p200*
Rheingans, William; Wisconsin, n.d. ***9675.7*** *p200*
Rheinhard, . . .; Canada, 1776-1783 ***9786*** *p32*
Rheinhard, Anna Maria; Pennsylvania, 1732 ***1034.18*** *p5*
Rheintaler, Georg; Pennsylvania, 1751 ***2444*** *p204*
*Wife:*Maria Barbara
*Child:*Georg Immanuel
Rheintaler, Georg Immanuel *SEE* Rheintaler, Georg
Rheintaler, Maria Barbara *SEE* Rheintaler, Georg
Rhenius, Wilhelm Lucas; Quebec, 1776 ***9786*** *p263*
Rhenoh, Janet; Georgia, 1775 ***1219.7*** *p275*
Rheude, George; Illinois, 1888 ***5012.39*** *p122*
Rhien, John Jacob; Philadelphia, 1763 ***9973.7*** *p38*
Rhind, David; Charleston, SC, 1765 ***1639.20*** *p270*
Rhind, Robert; New York, NY, 1836 ***8208.4*** *p16*
Rhine, Jefry; New York, NY, 1836 ***8208.4*** *p17*
Rhinehart, Jacob; Indiana, 1844 ***9117*** *p17*
Rhineheart, Jacob; Indiana, 1844 ***9117*** *p19*
Rhineheart, Sebastian; Ohio, 1838 ***9892.11*** *p39*
Rhoades, Robt.; Virginia, 1638 ***6219*** *p115*
Rhode, Ernest Henry; America, 1840 ***1450.2*** *p119A*
Rhode, Josph; Ohio, 1837 ***9892.11*** *p39*
Rhode, P. 23; Port uncertain, 1838 ***778.5*** *p456*
Rhoden, Mathew; Virginia, 1652 ***6251*** *p19*
Rhodes, Catha'ne 22; Massachusetts, 1849 ***5881.1*** *p83*
Rhodes, John 21; Pennsylvania, Virginia or Maryland, 1699 ***2212*** *p20*
Rhodes, John 22; Maryland, 1774 ***1219.7*** *p208*

Rhodes, John 36; Maryland, 1774 1219.7 p211
Rhodes, Levin Lane 26; Arizona, 1890 2764.35 p59
Rhodes, Mary 17; Massachusetts, 1849 5881.1 p85
Rhorback, Jean 25; America, 1836 778.5 p456
Rhorback, Philippe 21; America, 1836 778.5 p457
Riall, Patrick; New York, NY, 1816 2859.11 p41
Riamas, George H.; Illinois, 1870 5012.38 p99
Rian, Thomas; New York, NY, 1811 2859.11 p18
Rian, Timothy; Ohio, 1838 9892.11 p40
Riaoz, Mr. 38; America, 1829 778.5 p457
Riba, Franziska 2 *SEE* Riba, Josef
Riba, Josef 4; New York, 1912 9980.29 p59
*Relative:*Franziska 2
With cousin
Ribault, Jean; Brazil, 1500-1564 8582.3 p75
Ribault, Jean; South Carolina, 1500-1564 8582.3 p75
Ribble, Richard; Virginia, 1639 6219 p158
Ribbons, Harry W.; Arkansas, 1918 95.2 p104
Ribet, Mr. 20; New Orleans, 1839 778.5 p457
Ribet, Mr. 34; New Orleans, 1839 778.5 p457
Ribet, Alexis 31; America, 1837 778.5 p457
Ribet, J. 29; Port uncertain, 1839 778.5 p457
Ribet, Stephen 29; New Orleans, 1838 778.5 p457
Ribet, Zephirin 34; America, 1838 778.5 p457
Ribiero, Joseph; Virginia, 1846 4626.16 p13
Ribikowski, Wladyslau; Wisconsin, n.d. 9675.7 p200
Ribone, Antho.; Virginia, 1642 6219 p191
Ribot, Jacques 30; New Orleans, 1839 778.5 p457
Ricard, Francis; New England, 1773 1219.7 p163
Ricard, Philippe 32; Port uncertain, 1832 778.5 p457
Ricard, Polin 21; Maryland, 1774 1219.7 p211
Ricau, Mr. 55; America, 1838 778.5 p457
Riccard, Edward; America, 1742 4971 p25
Rice, A. L.; Washington, 1859-1920 2872.1 p33
Rice, Aily; New York, NY, 1811 2859.11 p18
Rice, Alice 24; St. John, N.B., 1861 5704.8 p147
Rice, Ann; New York, NY, 1864 5704.8 p186
Rice, Ann 6; Massachusetts, 1849 5881.1 p82
Rice, Ann 20; Massachusetts, 1847 5881.1 p82
Rice, Ann 20; St. John, N.B., 1863 5704.8 p154
Rice, Benjamin 16; Pennsylvania, 1735 3690.1 p189
Rice, Bennet 18; Virginia, 1727 3690.1 p189
Rice, Canlan; Baltimore, 1816 2859.11 p41
Rice, Christin 44; Massachusetts, 1860 6410.32 p111
Rice, Daniel; Massachusetts, 1850 5881.1 p83
Rice, Daniel 18; St. John, N.B., 1863 5704.8 p154
Rice, Daniel 53; St. John, N.B., 1863 5704.8 p154
Rice, David; Virginia, 1642 6219 p194
Rice, Edward; New York, NY, 1811 2859.11 p18
Rice, Edward 34; Massachusetts, 1860 6410.32 p111
Rice, Edward 40; Massachusetts, 1850 5881.1 p83
Rice, Elizabeth *SEE* Rice, Owen
Rice, Francis-Bourck; Quebec, 1825 7603 p90
Rice, Isabella 75; South Carolina, 1850 1639.20 p271
Rice, James 18; St. John, N.B., 1861 5704.8 p147
Rice, John; Virginia, 1638 6219 p153
Rice, John 22; Pennsylvania, 1733 3690.1 p189
Rice, John 38; Philadelphia, 1804 53.26 p79
Rice, John M.; Illinois, 1892 2896.5 p33
Rice, Joseph; Montreal, 1825 7603 p85
Rice, Joseph; St. John, N.B., 1848 5704.8 p47
Rice, Louis; Indiana, 1848 9117 p17
Rice, Margaret 23; St. John, N.B., 1863 5704.8 p154
Rice, Mary; St. John, N.B., 1848 5704.8 p47
Rice, Mary 8; Massachusetts, 1850 5881.1 p86
Rice, Mary 18; Massachusetts, 1850 5881.1 p86
Rice, Mary 30; Massachusetts, 1850 5881.1 p86
Rice, Mary 50; Massachusetts, 1850 5881.1 p86
Rice, Max; Arkansas, 1918 95.2 p103
Rice, Max; Arkansas, 1918 95.2 p105
Rice, Michael; New York, NY, 1837 8208.4 p39
Rice, Michael 7; Massachusetts, 1850 5881.1 p86
Rice, Michael 13; Massachusetts, 1850 5881.1 p86
Rice, Michael 30; Maryland or Virginia, 1737 3690.1 p189
Rice, Nancy; St. John, N.B., 1848 5704.8 p47
Rice, Nancy 50; St. John, N.B., 1863 5704.8 p154
Rice, Owen; Philadelphia, 1742 3652 p55
*Wife:*Elizabeth
Rice, Owen 8; Massachusetts, 1850 5881.1 p86
Rice, Patrick; America, 1852 1450.2 p119A
Rice, Patrick; Philadelphia, 1816 2859.11 p41
Rice, Patrick 20; St. John, N.B., 1858 5704.8 p137
Rice, Peter; Virginia, 1635 6219 p3
Rice, Peter; Virginia, 1637 6219 p86
Rice, Richard 21; Pennsylvania, 1738 3690.1 p189
Rice, Rose 4; Massachusetts, 1850 5881.1 p86
Rice, Rose 26; St. John, N.B., 1863 5704.8 p154
Rice, Thomas; New York, NY, 1811 2859.11 p18
Rice, Thomas 17; Maryland, 1775 1219.7 p265
Rice, Thomas 18; Massachusetts, 1850 5881.1 p87
Rice, William; Massachusetts, 1849 5881.1 p87
Rice, William 26; Virginia, 1773 1219.7 p168
Rice, William 30; Massachusetts, 1847 5881.1 p87
Rice, William 35; Massachusetts, 1849 5881.1 p87
Rice, Wm.; Virginia, 1636 6219 p13
Ricett, Christo.; Virginia, 1639 6219 p156
Rich, Cutberd; Virginia, 1636 6219 p7
Rich, Frank; Colorado, 1904 9678.2 p165
Rich, Jacob; Philadelphia, 1760 9973.7 p35
Rich, John; Indiana, 1848 9117 p19
Rich, Jos.; Virginia, 1635 6219 p16
Rich, Joseph 18; Philadelphia, 1774 1219.7 p217
Rich, Michael 25; West Virginia, 1897 9788.3 p19
Rich, Michael 27; West Virginia, 1900 9788.3 p19
Rich, Nick Simonetti; Arkansas, 1918 95.2 p105
Richard, Mr. 19; America, 1839 778.5 p457
Richard, Mr. 36; Louisiana, 1820 778.5 p457
Richard, C. Justin 21; America, 1820 778.5 p457
Richard, Cousin 29; Grenada, 1774 1219.7 p231
Richard, F. 24; New Orleans, 1830 778.5 p457
Richard, Francis; America, 1847 1450.2 p119A
Richard, Georg; America, 1834 8582.3 p54
Richard, Jean-Baptiste; Quebec, 1726 7603 p22
Richard, Joachim; Philadelphia, 1779-1780 8137 p12
Richard, John; Cincinnati, 1869-1887 8582 p24
Richard, John 16; Pennsylvania, Virginia or Maryland, 1699 2212 p20
Richard, John 22; Maryland, 1775 1219.7 p254
Richard, Juillet 37; New Orleans, 1826 778.5 p458
Richard, Maude; Virginia, 1642 6219 p199
Richard, Paul 26; Montreal, 1761 7603 p27
Richard, Tho.; Virginia, 1648 6219 p237
Richardon, Cat. Jourdan *SEE* Richardon, Jean
Richardon, Catherine *SEE* Richardon, Jean
Richardon, Etienne *SEE* Richardon, Jean
Richardon, Jean 25; Pennsylvania, 1753 2444 p204
*Wife:*Cat. Jourdan
*Child:*Jean Pierre
*Child:*Catherine
*Child:*Matthieu
*Child:*Etienne
Richardon, Jean Pierre *SEE* Richardon, Jean
Richardon, Matthieu *SEE* Richardon, Jean
Richardot, Frederique-Sybille; Halifax, N.S., 1752 7074.6 p220
Richards, Absalom; Nevada, 1878 2764.35 p58
Richards, Ann; Virginia, 1646 6219 p242
Richards, Arith.; Virginia, 1636 6219 p76
Richards, Benjamin 35; Virginia, 1773 1219.7 p169
Richards, Charles 20; Maryland, 1731 3690.1 p189
Richards, Charles 24; Arkansas, 1918 95.2 p105
Richards, Edward 22; Maryland, 1775 1219.7 p255
*Wife:*Jane 22
Richards, Eliza.; Virginia, 1643 6219 p200
Richards, Eliza.; Virginia, 1647 6219 p244
Richards, Florence; Virginia, 1635 6219 p33
Richards, Francis T.; Baltimore, 1881 2764.35 p58
Richards, Hugh 28; Jamaica, 1724 3690.1 p189
Richards, James 43; West Virginia, 1902 9788.3 p19
Richards, Jane 22 *SEE* Richards, Edward
Richards, Jo.; Virginia, 1648 6219 p246
Richards, John; Virginia, 1638 6219 p125
Richards, John; Virginia, 1639 6219 p161
Richards, John; Virginia, 1645 6219 p233
Richards, John; Virginia, 1648 6219 p246
Richards, John; Virginia, 1765 1219.7 p115
Richards, John 26; Pennsylvania, 1731 3690.1 p189
Richards, John V.; Colorado, 1892 9678.2 p165
Richards, Jon.; Virginia, 1642 6219 p196
Richards, Jon.; Virginia, 1643 6219 p206
Richards, Joseph; Virginia, 1635 6219 p73
Richards, Lewis 29; West Virginia, 1822 9788.3 p19
Richards, Richard; Virginia, 1643 6219 p200
Richards, Robert; New York, NY, 1838 8208.4 p68
Richards, Samuel 16; Maryland, 1775 1219.7 p252
Richards, Tho.; Virginia, 1643 6219 p205
Richards, Thomas 22; Virginia, 1774 1219.7 p186
Richards, Walter 33; America, 1701 2212 p34
Richards, William; Virginia, 1635 6219 p16
Richards, William; Virginia, 1642 6219 p188
Richards, William; Virginia, 1642 6219 p193
Richards, William 31; Kansas, 1880 5240.1 p62
Richards, William L.; Colorado, 1906 9678.2 p165
Richards, Wm.; Virginia, 1636 6219 p21
Richards, Wm.; Virginia, 1637 6219 p13
Richardson, Mr.; Quebec, 1815 9229.18 p74
Richardson, Mr.; St. Kitts, 1774 1219.7 p205
Richardson, Adam; Virginia, 1648 6219 p252
Richardson, Adam 21; Port uncertain, 1774 1219.7 p176
Richardson, Alexander; Montreal, 1818 7603 p38
Richardson, Alexander; Philadelphia, 1867 5704.8 p220
Richardson, Ann; Charleston, SC, 1796 1639.20 p271
Richardson, Ann 20; Maryland or Virginia, 1699 2212 p24
Richardson, Ann 50; Quebec, 1853 5704.8 p105
Richardson, Anne 19; Quebec, 1856 5704.8 p129
Richardson, Charles 20; Jamaica, 1736 3690.1 p189
Richardson, Charles 23; Philadelphia, 1774 1219.7 p190
Richardson, Eliza 15; Quebec, 1853 5704.8 p105
Richardson, Eliza 40; Massachusetts, 1847 5881.1 p83
Richardson, George; New York, NY, 1836 8208.4 p21
Richardson, George; New York, NY, 1838 8208.4 p88
Richardson, George 20; Pennsylvania, 1722 3690.1 p189
Richardson, Helen M. 26; Kansas, 1880 5240.1 p62
Richardson, James; Ohio, 1819-1899 9892.11 p40
Richardson, James; Ohio, 1840 9892.11 p40
Richardson, James; Quebec, 1851 5704.8 p73
Richardson, James 18; St. John, N.B., 1860 5704.8 p143
Richardson, James 20; Quebec, 1854 5704.8 p119
Richardson, James 34; Jamaica, 1730 3690.1 p291
Richardson, Joe; Arkansas, 1918 95.2 p105
Richardson, John; America, 1735-1743 4971 p7
Richardson, John; Charleston, SC, 1765-1818 1639.20 p271
Richardson, John; Northwest Terr., 1848 9775.5 p219
Richardson, John; Quebec, 1815 9229.18 p79
Richardson, John; St. Christopher, 1769 1219.7 p139
Richardson, John; South Carolina, 1716 1639.20 p271
Richardson, John 20; Virginia, 1750 3690.1 p190
Richardson, John 20; Virginia, 1751 1219.7 p3
Richardson, John 24; Virginia, 1775 1219.7 p261
Richardson, John 28; Nova Scotia, 1774 1219.7 p210
Richardson, John 33; Quebec, 1856 5704.8 p129
Richardson, John G.; Cincinnati, 1800-1877 8582.3 p86
Richardson, Joseph; New York, NY, 1865 5704.8 p194
Richardson, Joseph; Philadelphia, 1867 5704.8 p220
Richardson, Joseph 21; Kansas, 1886 5240.1 p69
Richardson, Leonard; Virginia, 1637 6219 p110
Richardson, Leonard; Virginia, 1638 6219 p146
Richardson, Luke; Virginia, 1632 6219 p180
Richardson, Margaret 20; St. John, N.B., 1860 5704.8 p143
Richardson, Mary; Virginia, 1645 6219 p253
Richardson, Matty; Quebec, 1851 5704.8 p73
Richardson, Peter; Virginia, 1638 6219 p159
Richardson, Peter; Virginia, 1647 6219 p249
Richardson, Ralph 35; South Carolina, 1774 1219.7 p234
Richardson, Richard 18; Maryland, 1774 1219.7 p192
Richardson, Robert; South Carolina, 1716 1639.20 p271
Richardson, Robert 20; Jamaica, 1730 3690.1 p190
Richardson, Robert M. 41; Kansas, 1879 5240.1 p60
Richardson, Robt.; Virginia, 1639 6219 p154
Richardson, Samuel; Philadelphia, 1687-1704 4960 p154
With wife & family
Richardson, Samuel 11; Quebec, 1853 5704.8 p105
Richardson, Samuel 22; Maryland, 1774 1219.7 p224
Richardson, Sarah J.; New York, NY, 1865 5704.8 p194
Richardson, Simon; Virginia, 1652 6251 p19
Richardson, Symon; Virginia, 1636 6219 p78
Richardson, Tho.; Virginia, 1638-1700 6219 p150
Richardson, Tho.; Virginia, 1642 6219 p195
Richardson, Tho.; Virginia, 1642 6219 p197
Richardson, Thomas; Charleston, SC, 1792 1639.20 p271
Richardson, Thomas; Virginia, 1643 6219 p206
Richardson, Thomas 15; Maryland, 1751 1219.7 p3
Richardson, Thomas 15; Maryland, 1751 3690.1 p190
Richardson, Thomas 19; Jamaica, 1723 3690.1 p190
Richardson, Thomas 30; Philadelphia, 1774 1219.7 p190
Richardson, Thomas 36; Dominica, 1775 1219.7 p278
Richardson, William; Illinois, 1855 7857 p6
Richardson, William 9; Quebec, 1853 5704.8 p105
Richardson, William 20; Barbados, 1774 1219.7 p212
Richardson, William 22; Maryland, 1774 1219.7 p221
Richardson, Wm.; Virginia, 1637 6219 p11
Richaud, Pierre Alexandre 30; Louisiana, 1820 778.5 p458
Richberg, Konrad; Philadelphia, 1779 8137 p12
Richee, Elizabeth; America, 1863-1871 5704.8 p240
Richer, John 22; Maryland, 1774 1219.7 p213
Richer, Michael; South Carolina, 1752-1753 3689.17 p22
With wife
With mother-in-law
Richerson, Isabell; Virginia, 1642 6219 p198
Riches, George 24; St. Christopher, 1775 1219.7 p279
Riches, John 23; St. Christopher, 1775 1219.7 p279
Richeson, Barnaby; Virginia, 1638 6219 p2
Richett, Francis; Virginia, 1643 6219 p202
Richey, Margaret 20; Quebec, 1864 5704.8 p159
Richey, Susan; Virginia, 1635 6219 p6
Richford, John; Virginia, 1638 6219 p124
Richie, Catherine; New York, NY, 1816 2859.11 p41
Richie, William; New York, NY, 1816 2859.11 p41
Richinson, John; Virginia, 1648 6219 p251
Richl, Ferdinand; Indiana, 1850 9117 p20
Richley, Daniel; New York, NY, 1816 2859.11 p41
Richling, John Henry; New York, 1750 3652 p74

Richmann, Charles; America, 1847 ***1450.2*** *p119A*
Richoney, Andreas; Charleston, SC, 1775-1781 ***8582.2*** *p52*
Richson, Jane 25; America, 1704 ***2212*** *p40*
Richter, . . .; Canada, 1776-1783 ***9786*** *p32*
Richter, Mrs.; America, 1853 ***4610.10*** *p148*
*Child:*Carl Dietrich Gottlieb
*Child:*Christoph Heinrich
*Child:*Ernst F. Gottlieb
*Child:*Anne Marie C. Engel 15
Richter, Amalie 22; New Orleans, 1839 ***9420.2*** *p169*
Richter, Anne Marie C. Engel 15 *SEE* Richter, Mrs.
Richter, August; America, 1853 ***1450.2*** *p119A*
Richter, Carl Dietrich Gottlieb *SEE* Richter, Mrs.
Richter, Carl Ernst Heinrich Wilhelm; America, 1858 ***4610.10*** *p140*
Richter, Carl Gottlieb 32; New Orleans, 1839 ***9420.2*** *p71*
Richter, Carl Heinrich; America, 1854 ***4610.10*** *p144*
Richter, Christ. 53; New Orleans, 1839 ***9420.2*** *p168*
*Wife:*Joh. Sophie 54
Richter, Christ. Doroth. 33; New Orleans, 1839 ***9420.2*** *p169*
Richter, Christina; South Dakota, 1889 ***1641*** *p41*
Richter, Christoph Heinrich *SEE* Richter, Mrs.
Richter, Ernst F. Gottlieb *SEE* Richter, Mrs.
Richter, Ernst Paul; Wisconsin, n.d. ***9675.7*** *p200*
Richter, Frederick; Illinois, 1861 ***5012.38*** *p98*
Richter, Frederick 29 *SEE* Richter, Frederick
Richter, Frederick 63; New Orleans, 1839 ***9420.2*** *p484*
*Wife:*Rachael Rose 63
*Son:*Frederick 29
*Daughter:*Rachael 34
Richter, Heinrich; America, 1852 ***4610.10*** *p148*
Richter, Heinrich Wilhelm August; America, 1858 ***4610.10*** *p140*
Richter, Henry; New Orleans, 1850 ***1450.2*** *p119A*
Richter, J. H.; America, 1850 ***8582.2*** *p33*
Richter, Joh. Sophie 54 *SEE* Richter, Christ.
Richter, Johann Christlieb 25; New Orleans, 1839 ***9420.2*** *p71*
Richter, John; Canada, 1776-1783 ***9786*** *p207A*
Richter, John; New York, 1750 ***3652*** *p74*
Richter, John Christian; New York, 1749 ***3652*** *p72*
Richter, Karl; South Dakota, 1889 ***1641*** *p41*
Richter, Max; Ohio, 1887-1889 ***9892.11*** *p40*
Richter, Peter Heinrich Daniel; America, 1848 ***4610.10*** *p142*
Richter, Rachael 34 *SEE* Richter, Frederick
Richter, Rachael Rose 63 *SEE* Richter, Frederick
Richter, Wilhelm; America, 1852 ***3702.7*** *p322*
Richtmeyer, Daniel; America, 1777-1778 ***8582.2*** *p68*
Richwain, John; America, 1852 ***1450.2*** *p119A*
Richzet, Ewald; Canada, 1776 ***9786*** *p110*
Rick, Charles; Wisconsin, n.d. ***9675.7*** *p200*
Rick, Ferdinand; Wisconsin, n.d. ***9675.7*** *p200*
Rick, Herman; Wisconsin, n.d. ***9675.7*** *p200*
Rick, Josep; Iowa, 1866-1943 ***123.54*** *p41*
Rick, Joseph; Iowa, 1866-1943 ***123.54*** *p41*
Rickard, Henry; New York, 1848 ***1450.2*** *p119A*
Rickards, William 21; Jamaica, 1730 ***3690.1*** *p190*
Rickdahl, Nels; Arkansas, 1918 ***95.2*** *p105*
Ricke, Ludwig 26; Kansas, 1892 ***5240.1*** *p77*
Ricke, William; Illinois, 1898 ***2896.5*** *p34*
Ricker, Anna 47; America, 1831 ***778.5*** *p458*
Ricker, Barbara 6; America, 1831 ***778.5*** *p458*
Ricker, Conrad 21; America, 1831 ***778.5*** *p458*
Ricker, Elizabeth 25; Grenada, 1776 ***1219.7*** *p282*
Ricker, Henry F.; Illinois, 1840 ***8582.2*** *p50*
Ricker, Jacob 12; America, 1831 ***778.5*** *p458*
Ricker, John Peter 30; Grenada, 1776 ***1219.7*** *p282*
Ricker, Marian 15; America, 1831 ***778.5*** *p458*
Ricker, Mathias 10; America, 1831 ***778.5*** *p458*
Ricker, Mathias 48; America, 1831 ***778.5*** *p458*
Rickers, Henry Herman; Illinois, 1901 ***5012.40*** *p79*
Rickert, August 35; Port uncertain, 1839 ***778.5*** *p458*
Rickert, Marie 36; Port uncertain, 1839 ***778.5*** *p458*
Ricket, Jakob; Ohio, 1798-1818 ***8582.2*** *p54*
Rickett, Margaret; Virginia, 1639 ***6219*** *p22*
Ricketts, Edward; Virginia, 1642 ***6219*** *p189*
Ricketts, Edward 18; Maryland, 1721 ***3690.1*** *p190*
Ricketts, James 16; Maryland, 1724 ***3690.1*** *p190*
Ricketts, John; America, 1698 ***2212*** *p10*
Ricketts, John; Virginia, 1698 ***2212*** *p13*
Ricketts, W.H. 19; Jamaica, 1773 ***1219.7*** *p168*
Ricketts, William 25; Maryland, 1725 ***3690.1*** *p190*
Rickey, James 20; Maryland, 1723 ***3690.1*** *p190*
Rickka, Kacpb 30; Harris Co., TX, 1898 ***6254*** *p4*
Rickle, Anchis; New York, 1880 ***1450.2*** *p31B*
Rickman, Charles; Kansas, 1876 ***5240.1*** *p36*
Rickmann, Charles 33; Kansas, 1876 ***5240.1*** *p58*
Ricksle, John 40; New Orleans, 1835 ***778.5*** *p458*
Ricoh, Peter 34; America, 1839 ***778.5*** *p458*
Ricoll, John N. 37; Washington, 1918-1920 ***1728.5*** *p12*
Ricosse, Samuel; Quebec, 1717 ***7603*** *p22*
Ricraft, Silvanas; Virginia, 1645 ***6219*** *p252*
Ricroft, Richard; Virginia, 1640 ***6219*** *p160*
Ricthmann, John; New York, 1848 ***1450.2*** *p119A*
Riddell, John; Washington, 1859-1920 ***2872.1*** *p33*
Riddell, Thomas; New York, NY, 1828 ***8208.4*** *p30*
Riddell, Thomas; Quebec, 1851 ***5704.8*** *p75*
Riddells, Charles 20 *SEE* Riddells, Charles
Riddells, Charles 40; Philadelphia, 1833-1834 ***53.26*** *p79*
*Relative:*Elizabeth 41
*Relative:*Hugh 2
*Relative:*Robert 4
*Relative:*Charles 20
*Relative:*Matty 22
*Relative:*William 12
*Relative:*Matilda 10
*Relative:*Samuel 8
*Relative:*Margaret 6
*Relative:*Mary Ann 60
*Relative:*Robert 64
Riddells, Elizabeth 41 *SEE* Riddells, Charles
Riddells, Hugh 2 *SEE* Riddells, Charles
Riddells, Margaret 6 *SEE* Riddells, Charles
Riddells, Mary Ann 60 *SEE* Riddells, Charles
Riddells, Matilda 10 *SEE* Riddells, Charles
Riddells, Matty 22 *SEE* Riddells, Charles
Riddells, Robert 4 *SEE* Riddells, Charles
Riddells, Robert 64 *SEE* Riddells, Charles
Riddells, Samuel 8 *SEE* Riddells, Charles
Riddells, William 12 *SEE* Riddells, Charles
Ridder, Henry 24; Kansas, 1892 ***5240.1*** *p77*
Riddick, Joseph; Kentucky, 1797 ***8582.3*** *p95*
Riddie, Richard 25; St. Kitts, 1774 ***1219.7*** *p245*
Riddle, Mr.; Quebec, 1815 ***9229.18*** *p82*
Riddle, Archibald 11; Quebec, 1847 ***5704.8*** *p16*
Riddle, Eliza; Quebec, 1847 ***5704.8*** *p7*
Riddle, Elizabeth; Philadelphia, 1849 ***53.26*** *p79*
Riddle, Elizabeth; Philadelphia, 1849 ***5704.8*** *p58*
Riddle, George 13; Quebec, 1847 ***5704.8*** *p16*
Riddle, Henry 10; Quebec, 1847 ***5704.8*** *p7*
Riddle, Hugh 5; Quebec, 1847 ***5704.8*** *p16*
Riddle, Hugh 12; Quebec, 1847 ***5704.8*** *p7*
Riddle, James; Quebec, 1847 ***5704.8*** *p7*
Riddle, James; Quebec, 1847 ***5704.8*** *p16*
Riddle, James; Quebec, 1852 ***5704.8*** *p98*
Riddle, Jane; Quebec, 1847 ***5704.8*** *p16*
Riddle, Janet 4; Quebec, 1847 ***5704.8*** *p7*
Riddle, John; Quebec, 1847 ***5704.8*** *p7*
Riddle, John 9; Quebec, 1847 ***5704.8*** *p16*
Riddle, Margaret; Quebec, 1852 ***5704.8*** *p98*
Riddle, Mary 7; Quebec, 1847 ***5704.8*** *p16*
Riddle, Mary Ann; Philadelphia, 1851 ***5704.8*** *p81*
Riddle, Robert 6 mos; Quebec, 1847 ***5704.8*** *p7*
Riddle, Robert 9 mos; Quebec, 1847 ***5704.8*** *p16*
Riddle, Samuel; New York, NY, 1816 ***2859.11*** *p41*
Riddle, Sarah; Philadelphia, 1851 ***5704.8*** *p81*
Riddle, Susan; Quebec, 1847 ***5704.8*** *p7*
Riddle, William; New York, NY, 1816 ***2859.11*** *p41*
Riddle, William; Quebec, 1847 ***5704.8*** *p7*
Riddle, William; Quebec, 1847 ***5704.8*** *p16*
Riddles, James; Philadelphia, 1852 ***5704.8*** *p88*
Riddles, Margaret 11; Philadelphia, 1852 ***5704.8*** *p88*
Riddles, Mary 20; Philadelphia, 1854 ***5704.8*** *p120*
Riddoller, George; Pennsylvania, 1751 ***2444*** *p204*
Ride, Jean; Quebec, 1714 ***7603*** *p40*
Ridel, Feigel 20; New York, NY, 1878 ***9253*** *p47*
Ridenback, Rudolph; Illinois, 1880 ***2896.5*** *p34*
Rider, Isaac; San Francisco, 1850 ***4914.15*** *p10*
Rider, Sarah; Virginia, 1636 ***6219*** *p22*
Rider, Thomas; America, 1741 ***4971*** *p10*
Rider, Willi.; Virginia, 1637 ***6219*** *p113*
Rider, William; New York, NY, 1816 ***2859.11*** *p41*
Rider, Wm.; Virginia, 1638 ***6219*** *p2*
Rider, Wm.; Virginia, 1647 ***6219*** *p239*
Riderer, Louis; Milwaukee, 1875 ***4719.30*** *p257*
Riderer, Mrs. Louis; Milwaukee, 1875 ***4719.30*** *p257*
With child
Ridgate, Andrew; Philadelphia, 1850 ***5704.8*** *p64*
Ridge, James; New York, NY, 1816 ***2859.11*** *p41*
Ridge, Jonathan 22; Maryland, 1774 ***1219.7*** *p235*
Ridges, Rich.; Virginia, 1637 ***6219*** *p82*
Ridges, Richard; Virginia, 1639 ***6219*** *p156*
Ridges, Richard; Virginia, 1649 ***6219*** *p252*
Ridgway, Mrs.; Milwaukee, 1875 ***4719.30*** *p257*
Ridgway, Mary 29; Maryland, 1775 ***1219.7*** *p265*
Ridican, Owen; America, 1735-1743 ***4971*** *p78*
Ridiere, Mr. 31; Port uncertain, 1838 ***778.5*** *p458*
Riding, Chas. 7; Canada, 1838 ***4535.12*** *p113*
Riding, Henry 9; Canada, 1838 ***4535.12*** *p113*
Riding, Wm. 34; Canada, 1838 ***4535.12*** *p113*
Ridley, Ann; Virginia, 1638 ***6219*** *p147*
Ridley, Drew 22; Maryland, 1774 ***1219.7*** *p192*
Ridley, Gilbert Samuel; Arkansas, 1918 ***95.2*** *p105*
Ridley, Humphrey 26; Pennsylvania, 1728 ***3690.1*** *p190*
Ridley, Thomas; Virginia, 1647 ***6219*** *p245*
Ridley, Wm.; Virginia, 1637 ***6219*** *p113*
Ridley, Wm.; Virginia, 1638 ***6219*** *p2*
Ridly, Ann; Virginia, 1618 ***6219*** *p72*
Ridly, Ann; Virginia, 1634 ***6219*** *p105*
Ridpeth, John 30; Maryland, 1775 ***1219.7*** *p251*
Ridschefsky, . . .; Canada, 1776-1783 ***9786*** *p32*
Riebe, August; Wisconsin, n.d. ***9675.7*** *p200*
Riebe, Fred; Wisconsin, n.d. ***9675.7*** *p200*
Riebe, Otto; Wisconsin, n.d. ***9675.7*** *p200*
Riebel, Barbara 21; America, 1853 ***9162.8*** *p37*
Riebel, Joh. Ad. 33; America, 1853 ***9162.8*** *p37*
Riebel, Katharina 31; America, 1853 ***9162.8*** *p37*
Riebel, Leonh. 11 mos; America, 1853 ***9162.8*** *p37*
Riebell, Amant; America, 1852 ***1450.2*** *p117A*
Rieber, Eva Barbara *SEE* Rieber, Georg Philipp
Rieber, Georg Philipp; Pennsylvania, 1742-1800 ***2444*** *p204*
*Wife:*Margaretha Beck
*Child:*Eva Barbara
Rieber, Jerg Philipp; Pennsylvania, 1749 ***2444*** *p204*
Rieber, Margaretha Beck *SEE* Rieber, Georg Philipp
Riech, . . .; Canada, 1776-1783 ***9786*** *p32*
Riechenmeier, Frederick William; America, 1847 ***1450.2*** *p120A*
Riecher, Gabriel; Philadelphia, 1758 ***9973.7*** *p33*
Riechert, Franz 24; Kansas, 1884 ***5240.1*** *p65*
Rieches, Dietrich; Iroquois Co., IL, 1892 ***3455.1*** *p13*
Rieches, Herman; Iroquois Co., IL, 1892 ***3455.1*** *p13*
Rieches, William; Iroquois Co., IL, 1892 ***3455.1*** *p13*
Riechmann, August 26; America, 1880 ***4610.10*** *p96*
Riecke, Friedrich Wilhelm; Cincinnati, 1869-1887 ***8582*** *p24*
Riecker, Anna Maria *SEE* Riecker, Johann Jacob
Riecker, Georg *SEE* Riecker, Johann Jacob
Riecker, Johann Jacob; America, 1745-1800 ***2444*** *p204*
*Wife:*Anna Maria
*Child:*Georg
Riedel, A. W.; Cincinnati, 1788-1848 ***8582.3*** *p90*
Riedel, Catherine; Savannah, GA, 1736 ***3652*** *p51*
Riedel, David; Wisconsin, n.d. ***9675.7*** *p200*
Riedel, Frederic; Savannah, GA, 1735 ***3652*** *p51*
Riedel, Johann 20; America, 1854-1855 ***9162.6*** *p104*
Riedel, John; Wisconsin, n.d. ***9675.7*** *p200*
Riedelsberger, Maria; Georgia, 1739 ***9332*** *p323*
Riedelsperger, Adam; Georgia, 1734 ***9332*** *p328*
Riedelsperger, Anna *SEE* Riedelsperger, Ruprecht
Riedelsperger, Christ.; Georgia, 1738 ***9332*** *p321*
Riedelsperger, Christian; Georgia, 1739 ***9332*** *p324*
Riedelsperger, Christian; Georgia, 1739 ***9332*** *p326*
Riedelsperger, Nicol.; Georgia, 1734 ***9332*** *p328*
Riedelsperger, Ruprecht; Georgia, 1739 ***9332*** *p326*
*Wife:*Anna
Rieder, Frietz; Colorado, 1893 ***9678.2*** *p165*
Riedesel, Baroness von; Quebec, 1777 ***9786*** *p143*
*Daughter:*Augusta
*Daughter:*Frederika
*Daughter:*Caroline
Riedesel, Augusta *SEE* Riedesel, Baroness von
Riedesel, Caroline *SEE* Riedesel, Baroness von
Riedesel, Frederick Adolphus; Canada, 1776-1783 ***9786*** *p252*
Riedesel, Frederika *SEE* Riedesel, Baroness von
Riedesel, Friederike von 38; Quebec, 1777 ***9786*** *p145*
Riedesel, Friedrich Adolphus von; Quebec, 1776 ***9786*** *p95*
Riedinger, Wilhelm; Ohio, 1869-1885 ***8582.2*** *p56*
Riedy, John; America, 1741 ***4971*** *p83*
Riedy, John; America, 1742 ***4971*** *p83*
Riedy, William; America, 1741 ***4971*** *p83*
Riedy, William; America, 1742 ***4971*** *p83*
Rief, John; Wisconsin, n.d. ***9675.7*** *p200*
Rieff, John; Wisconsin, n.d. ***9675.7*** *p200*
Rieffel, Mr. 30; New Orleans, 1823 ***778.5*** *p458*
Rieffel, J. 28; America, 1836 ***778.5*** *p459*
Riegel, John; New York, NY, 1882 ***1450.2*** *p31B*
Rieger, Anna Maria; Port uncertain, 1752 ***2444*** *p201*
Rieger, Ernest 39; Kansas, 1887 ***5240.1*** *p36*
Rieger, Ernest 39; Kansas, 1887 ***5240.1*** *p70*
Rieger, Jacob; Pennsylvania, 1751 ***2444*** *p204*
Riegler, Christoph; Cincinnati, 1869-1887 ***8582*** *p25*
Riehe, Louis 30; New Orleans, 1838 ***778.5*** *p459*
Riehl, Andreas; America, 1853 ***8582.3*** *p54*
Riehl, Elisabeth 12; America, 1836 ***778.5*** *p459*
Riehl, Emile 18; America, 1836 ***778.5*** *p459*
Riehl, Emilie 22; Illinois, 1836 ***778.5*** *p459*
Riehl, Eugene 19; America, 1836 ***778.5*** *p459*
Riehl, Joseph 9; America, 1836 ***778.5*** *p459*
Riehl, Joseph 59; America, 1836 ***778.5*** *p459*
Riehl, Marie 21; America, 1836 ***778.5*** *p459*
Riehl, Nicolas 25; Illinois, 1836 ***778.5*** *p459*
Riehle, Georg Friedrich; America, 1756 ***2444*** *p207*

Riehle, Jacob Frederick; New York, NY, 1837 *8208.4 p24*
Riehle, Johann Michael; America, 1772 *2444 p207*
Riek, W.; Cincinnati, 1826 *8582.1 p51*
Rieke, Hermann H.; Cincinnati, 1869-1887 *8582 p25*
Rieken, Herro; New York, NY, 1923 *3455.4 p52*
Rieken, Hinrich; New York, NY, 1924 *3455.4 p53*
Rieken, Peter; Illinois, 1871 *7857 p6*
Rieken, Rieke; Iroquois Co., IL, 1894 *3455.1 p13*
Riel, Jean-Baptiste; Sorel, Que., 1704 *7603 p86*
Rieley, John 28; Newfoundland, 1789 *4915.24 p57*
Rielly, Ann 30; Massachusetts, 1849 *5881.1 p82*
Rielly, Daniel 7; Massachusetts, 1849 *5881.1 p83*
Rielly, Eliza; Philadelphia, 1816 *2859.11 p41*
Rielly, Elizabeth; Philadelphia, 1816 *2859.11 p41*
Rielly, James 4; Massachusetts, 1849 *5881.1 p84*
Rielly, James 35; Massachusetts, 1849 *5881.1 p84*
Rielly, John 15; Massachusetts, 1850 *5881.1 p84*
Rielly, John 20; Massachusetts, 1849 *5881.1 p84*
Rielly, Joseph 5; Massachusetts, 1850 *5881.1 p84*
Rielly, Mary 5; Massachusetts, 1849 *5881.1 p86*
Rielly, Mary 17; Massachusetts, 1850 *5881.1 p86*
Rielly, Mary 20; Massachusetts, 1849 *5881.1 p86*
Rielly, Mary 30; Massachusetts, 1849 *5881.1 p85*
Rielly, Michael 9; Massachusetts, 1849 *5881.1 p86*
Rielly, Rose; Philadelphia, 1816 *2859.11 p41*
Rielly, Rose 45; Massachusetts, 1850 *5881.1 p86*
Rielly, Thomas 40; Massachusetts, 1850 *5881.1 p87*
Riely, Francis; New York, NY, 1838 *8208.4 p63*
Riely, Patrick; New York, NY, 1838 *8208.4 p74*
Riely, Thomas; New York, NY, 1837 *8208.4 p51*
Riemann, Henry W.; Baltimore, 1877 *1450.2 p32B*
Riemeier, J. D.; Cincinnati, 1869-1887 *8582 p25*
Riemenschneider, . . .; Canada, 1776-1783 *9786 p32*
Riemenschneider, Friedrich; Philadelphia, 1779 *8137 p12*
Riemenschneider, Heinrich; Wisconsin, n.d. *9675.7 p200*
Riemenschneider, Henry; Canada, 1776-1783 *9786 p242*
Riemer, Carl Friedrich Eduard; America, 1863 *4610.10 p113*
Rientz, Louis 35; Port uncertain, 1839 *778.5 p459*
Riepl, Theresia; Wisconsin, n.d. *9675.7 p200*
Rierdan, Honor; America, 1737 *4971 p52*
Riertz, John; Wisconsin, n.d. *9675.7 p200*
Riery, John; America, 1742 *4971 p54*
Ries, Mr.; Pennsylvania, 1755 *4525 p238*
Ries, Benjamin 14; America, 1835 *778.5 p459*
Ries, Christian; Philadelphia, 1779 *8137 p12*
Ries, Dietrich; Philadelphia, 1776 *8582.3 p84*
Ries, Eckhardt 76; America, 1895 *1763 p48D*
Ries, Elena 54; America, 1835 *778.5 p459*
Ries, Franz; Cincinnati, 1869-1887 *8582 p25*
Ries, Jacob; Ohio, 1869-1887 *8582 p25*
Ries, Jannet 16; America, 1835 *778.5 p459*
Ries, Johann Adam; Pennsylvania, 1785 *4525 p237*
  With wife
  With child
Ries, Johann Peter; Pennsylvania, 1753 *4525 p238*
Ries, Lena 21; America, 1853 *9162.8 p37*
Ries, Louis; Kentucky, 1845 *8582.3 p99*
Ries, M. 59; America, 1835 *778.5 p459*
Ries, Minot 19; America, 1835 *778.5 p460*
Ries, Nanet 25; America, 1835 *778.5 p460*
Ries, Nicholas 43; Kansas, 1894 *5240.1 p79*
Ries, Nicolaus; America, 1840 *8582.3 p54*
Ries, Peter; Wisconsin, n.d. *9675.7 p200*
Ries, Polin 22; America, 1835 *778.5 p460*
Riesenkirch, . . .; Canada, 1776-1783 *9786 p32*
Rieser, Anna Maria; Georgia, 1734 *9332 p328*
Rieser, Anna Maria Steiger SEE Rieser, Michael
Rieser, Balthasar 15 SEE Rieser, Bartholomaus
Rieser, Balthaser SEE Rieser, Bartholomaus
Rieser, Barth.; Georgia, 1738 *9332 p321*
Rieser, Bartholomaus; Georgia, 1739 *9332 p323*
  Wife:Maria Zugeisen
  Relative:Michael
  Relative:Balthaser
  Relative:Georg
Rieser, Bartholomaus; Georgia, 1739 *9332 p326*
  Wife:Maria
  Son:Michael 18
  Son:Balthasar 15
  Son:Georg 13
Rieser, Georg SEE Rieser, Bartholomaus
Rieser, Georg 13 SEE Rieser, Bartholomaus
Rieser, Maria SEE Rieser, Bartholomaus
Rieser, Maria Zugeisen SEE Rieser, Bartholomaus
Rieser, Michael SEE Rieser, Bartholomaus
Rieser, Michael; Georgia, 1739 *9332 p326*
  Wife:Anna Maria Steiger
Rieser, Michael 18 SEE Rieser, Bartholomaus
Riesmeier, Albrecht; Wisconsin, n.d. *9675.7 p200*

Riess, Adam; Pennsylvania, 1785 *4525 p238*
  Relative:Eliz
  Relative:Marg't
  Relative:George
Riess, Eliz SEE Riess, Adam
Riess, George SEE Riess, Adam
Riess, Johann Peter; Pennsylvania, 1753 *4525 p238*
Riess, Marg't SEE Riess, Adam
Riess, Martin; South Carolina, 1788 *7119 p198*
Riesser, Hermann; Charleston, SC, 1775-1781 *8582.2 p52*
Riest, Johannes; Pennsylvania, 1752 *2444 p204*
Riesterer, Joseph; Wisconsin, n.d. *9675.7 p200*
Riethamer, Joseph; Wisconsin, n.d. *9675.7 p200*
Rietmeyer, Henry; Philadelphia, 1758 *9973.7 p33*
Rietz, Albert; Illinois, 1887 *2896.5 p34*
Rietz, Anthony; Philadelphia, 1764 *9973.7 p39*
Rieux, Therese 28; New Orleans, 1821 *778.5 p460*
Riffard, Joseph 35; New Orleans, 1835 *778.5 p460*
Riffe, Maria Elisabeth 30; America, 1836 *778.5 p460*
Riffel, Amalie 11 mos; New York, NY, 1878 *9253 p45*
Riffel, Andreas 40; New York, NY, 1878 *9253 p45*
Riffel, Catharina 9; New York, NY, 1878 *9253 p45*
Riffel, Catharina 15; New York, NY, 1878 *9253 p45*
Riffel, Catharina 40; New York, NY, 1878 *9253 p45*
Riffel, Elisabeth 9 mos; New York, NY, 1878 *9253 p45*
Riffel, Elisabeth 5; New York, NY, 1878 *9253 p45*
Riffel, Georg 7; New York, NY, 1878 *9253 p45*
Riffel, Gottfried 9; New York, NY, 1878 *9253 p45*
Riffel, Gottfried 35; New York, NY, 1878 *9253 p45*
Riffel, Jacob; Kansas, 1892 *5240.1 p36*
Riffel, Jacob 11 mos; New York, NY, 1878 *9253 p45*
Riffel, Johann 5; New York, NY, 1878 *9253 p45*
Riffel, Johann 12; New York, NY, 1878 *9253 p45*
Riffel, Johanne 12; New York, NY, 1878 *9253 p45*
Riffel, Lidia 1 mo; New York, NY, 1878 *9253 p45*
Riffel, Marie 15; New York, NY, 1878 *9253 p45*
Riffel, Marie 34; New York, NY, 1878 *9253 p45*
Riffel, Reinhard 9; New York, NY, 1878 *9253 p45*
Riffel, Susanna 13; New York, NY, 1878 *9253 p45*
Rigan, Bridget; New York, NY, 1811 *2859.11 p18*
Rigarton, Cat. Jourdan SEE Rigarton, Jean
Rigarton, Catherine SEE Rigarton, Jean
Rigarton, Etienne SEE Rigarton, Jean
Rigarton, Jean 25; Pennsylvania, 1753 *2444 p204*
  Wife:Cat. Jourdan
  Child:Jean Pierre
  Child:Catherine
  Child:Matthieu
  Child:Etienne
Rigarton, Jean Pierre SEE Rigarton, Jean
Rigarton, Matthieu SEE Rigarton, Jean
Rigat, L. 70; New Orleans, 1835 *778.5 p460*
Rigaud, J. B.; New Orleans, 1839 *778.5 p460*
Rigby, Nicholas 21; Maryland, 1721 *3690.1 p190*
Rigby, Robert; Virginia, 1642 *6219 p197*
Rigby, Roger 11; America, 1706 *2212 p45*
Rigbye, Dorothy SEE Rigbye, Peter
Rigbye, Peter; Virginia, 1639 *6219 p182*
  Wife:Dorothy
Rigdel, Catharine 22; Maryland, 1775 *1219.7 p257*
Riger, Jacob; Pennsylvania, 1751 *2444 p204*
Rigg, Alexander; Charleston, SC, 1771 *1639.20 p271*
Riggos, Stehos; Arkansas, 1918 *95.2 p105*
Riggs, Brannick 62; Arizona, 1890 *2764.35 p59*
Riggs, James; Illinois, 1892 *5012.39 p53*
Riggs, James; Illinois, 1894 *5012.40 p54*
Riggs, Richard; Virginia, 1645 *6219 p232*
Riggs, Thomas J. 33; Arizona, 1890 *2764.35 p59*
Riggs, William M. 27; Arizona, 1890 *2764.35 p59*
Righi, Amedeo; Wisconsin, n.d. *9675.7 p200*
Righi, Paolo; Wisconsin, n.d. *9675.7 p200*
Right, Giles; Virginia, 1642 *6219 p197*
Right, Jason; Virginia, 1637 *6219 p85*
Right, Jathan; Virginia, 1636 *6219 p79*
Right, John; Virginia, 1638 *6219 p11*
Right, William; Virginia, 1621 *6219 p29*
Right, William 31; Maryland, 1774 *1219.7 p223*
Righting, George 17; Maryland, 1722 *3690.1 p190*
Rightsonne, Ann; Virginia, 1638 *6219 p11*
Riglie, Paul; America, 1698 *2212 p13*
Rigly, Roger; Virginia, 1639 *6219 p150*
Rigney, Edward; America, 1842 *6014.1 p3*
Rigney, James; New York, NY, 1839 *8208.4 p100*
Rigney, John 26; Massachusetts, 1849 *5881.1 p84*
Rigney, Pierre 53; America, 1836 *778.5 p460*
Rigoli, Antonio 49; New York, NY, 1893 *9026.4 p42*
Rigouleau, Anne-Marie SEE Rigouleau, Vernier
Rigouleau, Elisabeth SEE Rigouleau, Vernier
Rigouleau, Jean-Frederic SEE Rigouleau, Vernier
Rigouleau, Jeanne SEE Rigouleau, Vernier
Rigouleau, Suzanne SEE Rigouleau, Vernier

Rigouleau, Vernier 40; Halifax, N.S., 1752 *7074.6 p212*
  Wife:Jeanne
  Child:Anne-Marie
  Child:Jean-Frederic
  Child:Suzanne
  Child:Elisabeth
Rigoulett, Vernier 40; Halifax, N.S., 1752 *7074.6 p207*
  With family of 5
Rigsby, James; Virginia, 1637 *6219 p11*
Rigue, J. 45; New Orleans, 1827 *778.5 p460*
Rihoucq, Pierre 35; America, 1839 *778.5 p460*
Riko, Amalie Friedr. 17; New York, NY, 1857 *9831.14 p153*
Riko, Caroline 43; New York, NY, 1857 *9831.14 p153*
Riko, Ernst 8; New York, NY, 1857 *9831.14 p153*
Riko, Friedr. 6; New York, NY, 1857 *9831.14 p153*
Riko, Johann 40; New York, NY, 1857 *9831.14 p153*
Riks, Johann; Alberta, n.d. *5262 p58*
Rilevard, J. 34; Port uncertain, 1835 *778.5 p435*
Riley, Mrs.; New York, NY, 1811 *2859.11 p18*
Riley, Abraham; New York, 1759 *1219.7 p70*
Riley, Agnes; St. John, N.B., 1852 *5704.8 p83*
Riley, Andrew 38; Massachusetts, 1860 *6410.32 p105*
Riley, Ann 9; Massachusetts, 1849 *5881.1 p82*
Riley, Ann 20; Massachusetts, 1847 *5881.1 p82*
Riley, Ann 45; Massachusetts, 1848 *5881.1 p82*
Riley, Barney 24; Massachusetts, 1847 *5881.1 p82*
Riley, Bartley 28; Massachusetts, 1849 *5881.1 p82*
Riley, Bernard; New York, NY, 1835 *8208.4 p6*
Riley, Betty 14; Massachusetts, 1850 *5881.1 p83*
Riley, Bridget 14; Massachusetts, 1848 *5881.1 p82*
Riley, Bridget 24; Massachusetts, 1850 *5881.1 p82*
Riley, Catharine 1; Massachusetts, 1849 *5881.1 p83*
Riley, Catharine 8; Massachusetts, 1849 *5881.1 p83*
Riley, Catharine 20; Massachusetts, 1848 *5881.1 p83*
Riley, Catharine 21; Massachusetts, 1849 *5881.1 p83*
Riley, Cornelius; Massachusetts, 1847 *5881.1 p83*
Riley, Douglass W.; Maine, 1824-1836 *1450.2 p120A*
Riley, Edmund; Ohio, 1854 *1450.2 p120A*
Riley, Eliza; St. John, N.B., 1849 *5704.8 p48*
Riley, Hugh 14; Massachusetts, 1849 *5881.1 p84*
Riley, Hugh 28; Philadelphia, 1854 *5704.8 p116*
Riley, James; Jamaica, 1763 *1219.7 p97*
Riley, James; St. John, N.B., 1852 *5704.8 p83*
Riley, James 12; Massachusetts, 1849 *5881.1 p84*
Riley, James 28; Newfoundland, 1789 *4915.24 p57*
Riley, Jane 8; Quebec, 1851 *5704.8 p73*
Riley, Jane 24; Massachusetts, 1850 *5881.1 p85*
Riley, Johanna; Massachusetts, 1847 *5881.1 p84*
Riley, John; Shreveport, LA, 1878 *7129 p45*
Riley, John 3 mos; St. John, N.B., 1849 *5704.8 p48*
Riley, John 8; Massachusetts, 1849 *5881.1 p84*
Riley, John 12; Massachusetts, 1850 *5881.1 p84*
Riley, John 13; St. John, N.B., 1852 *5704.8 p83*
Riley, John 19; West Indies, 1722 *3690.1 p190*
Riley, John 21; Jamaica, 1774 *1219.7 p207*
Riley, John 30; Massachusetts, 1849 *5881.1 p84*
Riley, John 40; Massachusetts, 1850 *5881.1 p54*
Riley, John 40; Massachusetts, 1850 *5881.1 p85*
Riley, Jonathan 25; Antigua (Antego), 1737 *3690.1 p191*
Riley, Kate 10; Massachusetts, 1849 *5881.1 p85*
Riley, M. J. 34; Kansas, 1878 *5240.1 p36*
Riley, M. J. 34; Kansas, 1878 *5240.1 p59*
Riley, Marcilia 18; Massachusetts, 1848 *5881.1 p85*
Riley, Margaret; Philadelphia, 1811 *2859.11 p18*
Riley, Margaret 7; Massachusetts, 1849 *5881.1 p85*
Riley, Margaret 7; Massachusetts, 1850 *5881.1 p86*
Riley, Margaret 32; Massachusetts, 1849 *5881.1 p85*
Riley, Mary; Montreal, 1825 *7603 p87*
Riley, Mary 1; Massachusetts, 1848 *5881.1 p85*
Riley, Mary 3; Massachusetts, 1849 *5881.1 p85*
Riley, Mary 11; Massachusetts, 1849 *5881.1 p85*
Riley, Mary 25; Massachusetts, 1847 *5881.1 p85*
Riley, Mary 40; Massachusetts, 1849 *5881.1 p85*
  With child
Riley, Mary 48; Massachusetts, 1848 *5881.1 p85*
Riley, Michael 27; Massachusetts, 1849 *5881.1 p85*
Riley, Nancy; Philadelphia, 1811 *2859.11 p18*
Riley, Owen; New York, NY, 1832 *8208.4 p44*
Riley, Patrick; Illinois, 1870 *7857 p6*
Riley, Patrick; New York, NY, 1835 *8208.4 p5*
Riley, Patrick; New York, NY, 1838 *8208.4 p74*
Riley, Patrick; New York, NY, 1840 *8208.4 p105*
Riley, Patrick 21; Massachusetts, 1849 *5881.1 p86*
Riley, Philip; New York, NY, 1837 *8208.4 p32*
Riley, Philip; New York, NY, 1839 *8208.4 p100*
Riley, Robert; St. John, N.B., 1849 *5704.8 p48*
Riley, Robert; Wisconsin, n.d. *9675.7 p200*
Riley, Rose 16; St. John, N.B., 1853 *5704.8 p110*
Riley, Thomas; Jamaica, 1765 *1219.7 p108*
Riley, Thomas; New York, NY, 1835 *8208.4 p5*
Riley, Thomas; New York, NY, 1838 *8208.4 p88*
Riley, Thomas 2; Massachusetts, 1849 *5881.1 p86*

Riley, Thomas 2; Massachusetts, 1849 ***5881.1*** *p87*
Riley, Thomas 19; Massachusetts, 1849 ***5881.1*** *p87*
Riley, Thomas 32; Kansas, 1887 ***5240.1*** *p70*
Riley, Timothy 10; Massachusetts, 1849 ***5881.1*** *p87*
Riley, William; Illinois, 1864 ***5012.38*** *p98*
Riley, William 30; Massachusetts, 1849 ***5881.1*** *p87*
Rilling, Jacob; New York, NY, 1837 ***8208.4*** *p50*
Rillman, Andrew; New York, 1749 ***3652*** *p72*
Rimas, George H.; Illinois, 1870 ***5012.38*** *p99*
Rime, John; St. Kitts, 1774 ***1219.7*** *p205*
Rimen, Bortolo; Iowa, 1866-1943 ***123.54*** *p41*
Rimer, Edward 25; Philadelphia, 1774 ***1219.7*** *p219*
Rimeri, Bortolo; Iowa, 1866-1943 ***123.54*** *p41*
Rimmington, Thomas; Virginia, 1643 ***6219*** *p204*
Rince, Ann; Quebec, 1852 ***5704.8*** *p91*
Rince, Eliza Jane 7; Quebec, 1852 ***5704.8*** *p91*
Rince, Elizabeth; Quebec, 1852 ***5704.8*** *p91*
Rince, James; Quebec, 1852 ***5704.8*** *p91*
Rince, James 5; Quebec, 1852 ***5704.8*** *p91*
Rince, Robert 3; Quebec, 1852 ***5704.8*** *p91*
Rince, William; Quebec, 1852 ***5704.8*** *p91*
Rince, William 1; Quebec, 1852 ***5704.8*** *p91*
Rindell, Jacques; Quebec, 1787 ***7603*** *p29*
Rindeslie, Maria 25; America, 1838 ***778.5*** *p460*
Rineley, Jason; Virginia, 1636 ***6219*** *p22*
Ring, Ellen 24; Massachusetts, 1849 ***5881.1*** *p83*
Ring, Joh. Matthaus; Pennsylvania, 1717 ***3627*** *p15*
*Wife:*Maria M. Schneider
With stepchild
Ring, John; Montreal, 1824 ***7603*** *p65*
Ring, John 26; Massachusetts, 1849 ***5881.1*** *p84*
Ring, Joseph; Indiana, 1848 ***9117*** *p17*
Ring, Maria M. Schneider *SEE* Ring, Joh. Matthaus
Ring, Philip Henry; New York, 1754 ***3652*** *p80*
Ring, Thomas 11 mos; Massachusetts, 1849 ***5881.1*** *p87*
Ringall, Tho.; Virginia, 1642 ***6219*** *p195*
Ringbom, Hugo; Washington, 1859-1920 ***2872.1*** *p33*
Ringbom, Leo; Washington, 1859-1920 ***2872.1*** *p33*
Ringbom, Lydia Alexandria; Washington, 1859-1920 ***2872.1*** *p33*
Ringbom, Mabel; Washington, 1859-1920 ***2872.1*** *p33*
Ringbom, Marie Lydia; Washington, 1859-1920 ***2872.1*** *p33*
Ringe, . . .; Canada, 1776-1783 ***9786*** *p32*
Ringel, Oscar; America, 1887 ***5240.1*** *p36*
Ringeling, . . .; Canada, 1776-1783 ***9786*** *p32*
Ringer, Joh. Matthias; Pennsylvania, 1717 ***3627*** *p15*
*Wife:*Maria M. Schneider
With stepchild
Ringer, Maria M. Schneider *SEE* Ringer, Joh. Matthias
Ringer, Mathias; Pennsylvania, 1717 ***3627*** *p12*
Ringer, Michael; Pennsylvania, 1765 ***4779.3*** *p14*
Ringer, Robert 27; Maryland, 1774 ***1219.7*** *p208*
Ringgaard, Peter; Washington, 1859-1920 ***2872.1*** *p33*
Ringlund, Nils; Minneapolis, 1882-1887 ***6410.35*** *p65*
Ringma, Adam; Arkansas, 1918 ***95.2*** *p105*
Ringvall, Knut A.; Bangor, ME, 1884-1899 ***6410.22*** *p123*
Ringwall, Knut A.; Maine, 1896 ***6410.22*** *p127*
Ringwood, Thomas 21; Maryland, 1733 ***3690.1*** *p191*
Rinh, Jean 26; America, 1836 ***778.5*** *p460*
Rini, Jean 19; America, 1838 ***778.5*** *p460*
Rinier, . . .; Canada, 1776-1783 ***9786*** *p32*
Rink, John; Milwaukee, 1875 ***4719.30*** *p258*
Rinker, Frederick; Illinois, 1892 ***5012.37*** *p62*
Rinkus, Paul; Arkansas, 1918 ***95.2*** *p105*
Rinn, Jakob 75; America, 1913 ***1763*** *p40D*
Rinne, . . .; Canada, 1776-1783 ***9786*** *p32*
Rinney, Patrick 22; Virginia, 1774 ***1219.7*** *p240*
Rintelmann, Henry; Wisconsin, n.d. ***9675.7*** *p200*
Rintlemann, William H.; Wisconsin, n.d. ***9675.7*** *p200*
Rintoul, William; Toronto, 1848 ***9775.5*** *p216*
Riordan, Bridget 20; Massachusetts, 1850 ***5881.1*** *p82*
Riordan, Catharine 31; Massachusetts, 1847 ***5881.1*** *p83*
Riordan, Coleman; New York, NY, 1816 ***2859.11*** *p41*
Riordan, Denis; New York, NY, 1838 ***8208.4*** *p82*
Riordan, Elizabeth 21; Massachusetts, 1849 ***5881.1*** *p83*
Riordan, Ellen 9; Massachusetts, 1850 ***5881.1*** *p83*
Riordan, James; Illinois, 1871 ***5012.39*** *p25*
Riordan, Johanna 11; Massachusetts, 1850 ***5881.1*** *p84*
Riordan, Kate 46; Massachusetts, 1850 ***5881.1*** *p85*
Riordan, Michel; Quebec, 1798 ***7603*** *p86*
Riordan, Richard; New York, NY, 1850 ***6013.19*** *p88*
Riordau, Dan 61; Arizona, 1902 ***9228.40*** *p8*
Ripley, Henry; America, 1697 ***2212*** *p4*
Ripley, John; Florida, 1773 ***1219.7*** *p166*
Ripley, John; Virginia, 1636 ***6219*** *p76*
Ripley, William 22; Carolina, 1774 ***1219.7*** *p236*
Rippea, Robert; Quebec, 1818 ***7603*** *p25*
Rippel, John Michael; New York, 1756 ***3652*** *p81*
Rippell, Lawrence David; Philadelphia, 1762 ***9973.7*** *p36*
Rippentroph, Eilert; Illinois, 1869 ***7857*** *p6*
Ripper, Robert 21; Maryland, 1725 ***3690.1*** *p191*
Rippin, Christ.; Virginia, 1636 ***6219*** *p74*
Rippin, Christ.; Virginia, 1637 ***6219*** *p108*
Ripple, John; Virginia, 1637 ***6219*** *p81*
Rippon, Ann; Virginia, 1640 ***6219*** *p181*
Rippon, Ellis; Virginia, 1640 ***6219*** *p181*
Rippstein, Michael; Ohio, 1842 ***8365.25*** *p12*
Ris, John; New York, NY, 1836 ***8208.4*** *p78*
Risal, Mr. 16; America, 1837 ***778.5*** *p460*
Risby, Robert; Virginia, 1636 ***6219*** *p28*
Risch, Charles; Wisconsin, n.d. ***9675.7*** *p200*
Rischler, Anton; Cincinnati, 1869-1887 ***8582*** *p25*
Riser, Jacob; Pennsylvania, 1752 ***2444*** *p202*
Riser, Jean 28; New Orleans, 1839 ***778.5*** *p461*
Rish, John 38; Philadelphia, 1774 ***1219.7*** *p216*
Rishtes, Chas 59; Arizona, 1912 ***9228.40*** *p16*
Rising, William 27; Massachusetts, 1860 ***6410.32*** *p118*
Risk, Eliza; Philadelphia, 1851 ***5704.8*** *p80*
Risley, William 19; Jamaica, 1731 ***3690.1*** *p191*
Rissardon, J. C. 30; Mobile, AL, 1837 ***778.5*** *p461*
Risse, Jean Pierre 31; New Orleans, 1838 ***778.5*** *p461*
Risse, Meri; Indianapolis, 1868 ***3702.7*** *p582*
Rissler, Heinrich; Washington, D.C., 1871 ***8582*** *p25*
Rist, Johannes; Pennsylvania, 1752 ***2444*** *p204*
With wife
Ritchey, Margaret 45; St. John, N.B., 1854 ***5704.8*** *p122*
Ritchey, Marmaduke 16; St. John, N.B., 1854 ***5704.8*** *p122*
Ritchey, Robert 13; St. John, N.B., 1854 ***5704.8*** *p122*
Ritchie, Agnes; Charleston, SC, 1817 ***1639.20*** *p88*
Ritchie, Alexander 21; Maryland, 1774 ***1219.7*** *p187*
Ritchie, Alx.; New York, NY, 1811 ***2859.11*** *p18*
Ritchie, Benjamin 23; Maryland, 1774 ***1219.7*** *p208*
Ritchie, Caspar; Cincinnati, 1848 ***8582.1*** *p53*
Ritchie, Caspar; New Orleans, 1834 ***8582.1*** *p29*
Ritchie, Caspar, Sr.; Kentucky, 1869-1887 ***8582*** *p25*
Ritchie, Eliz.; New York, NY, 1811 ***2859.11*** *p19*
Ritchie, Hugues 24; Quebec, 1772 ***7603*** *p38*
Ritchie, Isabella; Massachusetts, 1849 ***5881.1*** *p84*
Ritchie, Isabella; New York, NY, 1864 ***5704.8*** *p187*
Ritchie, Jacques; Ohio, 1869-1887 ***8582*** *p25*
Ritchie, James; Wilmington, NC, 1755-1808 ***1639.20*** *p271*
Ritchie, Jane 3; Massachusetts, 1849 ***5881.1*** *p84*
Ritchie, John; New York, NY, 1816 ***2859.11*** *p41*
Ritchie, Joseph; New York, NY, 1838 ***8208.4*** *p85*
Ritchie, Margaret 18; Massachusetts, 1849 ***5881.1*** *p85*
Ritchie, Robert; Virginia, 1801 ***4778.1*** *p150*
Ritchies, Walter; Illinois, 1874 ***5012.39*** *p26*
Ritchie, William; New York, NY, 1864 ***5704.8*** *p187*
Ritchie, William; North Carolina, 1796 ***1639.20*** *p271*
Ritchie, Wm.; New York, NY, 1816 ***2859.11*** *p41*
Ritchley, Katherine; Virginia, 1698 ***2212*** *p16*
Ritchy, John 12; Philadelphia, 1854 ***5704.8*** *p120*
Rith, Michael; Wisconsin, n.d. ***9675.7*** *p200*
Rithwell, Moses 16; America, 1702 ***2212*** *p36*
Ritner, Mr.; Pennsylvania, 1835-1869 ***8582*** *p25*
Ritschmann, David; Savannah, GA, 1736 ***8582.2*** *p65*
Ritt, Peter; Wisconsin, n.d. ***9675.7*** *p200*
Rittand, Tom; Arkansas, 1918 ***95.2*** *p105*
Rittberg, . . .; Canada, 1776-1783 ***9786*** *p32*
Ritte, Heinrich; America, 1847 ***8582.3*** *p54*
Rittenauer, Anton; Ohio, 1800-1885 ***8582.2*** *p58*
Rittenhaus, David; America, n.d. ***8582.3*** *p79*
Rittenhouse, Claus *SEE* Rittenhouse, Wilhelm
Rittenhouse, Gerhard *SEE* Rittenhouse, Wilhelm
Rittenhouse, Wilhelm; America, 1688 ***8125.8*** *p438*
*Brother:*Claus
*Brother:*Gerhard
Ritter, . . .; Canada, 1776-1783 ***9786*** *p32*
Ritter, Dr.; Cincinnati, 1816 ***8582.3*** *p89*
Ritter, Dr.; Cincinnati, 1831 ***8582.1*** *p51*
Ritter, Mr.; Canada, 1776-1783 ***9786*** *p239*
Ritter, Albert; Illinois, 1892 ***5012.39*** *p53*
Ritter, Antoine 28; America, 1838 ***778.5*** *p461*
Ritter, Anton 2; America, 1838 ***778.5*** *p461*
Ritter, Friederich; Ohio, 1800 ***8582.2*** *p55*
Ritter, Heinrich; America, 1847 ***8582.3*** *p54*
Ritter, Henrich; Halifax, N.S., 1780 ***9786*** *p269*
Ritter, Henrich; New York, 1776 ***9786*** *p269*
Ritter, Henrich; Philadelphia, 1779-1781 ***8137*** *p12*
Ritter, Hermann; Illinois, 1900 ***5012.40*** *p77*
Ritter, Jacob; Missouri, 1871 ***5240.1*** *p36*
Ritter, Johann; Cincinnati, 1830 ***8582.1*** *p51*
Ritter, John; Indiana, 1850 ***9117*** *p20*
Ritter, Joseph; America, 1819 ***8582.1*** *p47*
Ritter, Karl G.; Cincinnati, 1818 ***8582.1*** *p51*
Ritter, Magdalena 25; America, 1838 ***778.5*** *p461*
Ritter, William; Illinois, 1895 ***5012.39*** *p53*
Ritter, William; Illinois, 1897 ***5012.40*** *p55*
Ritter, William; New York, NY, 1840 ***8208.4*** *p108*
Rittig, Louis W.O.; Illinois, 1869 ***5012.38*** *p99*
Rittinghaus, Claus *SEE* Rittinghaus, Wilhelm
Rittinghaus, Gerhard *SEE* Rittinghaus, Wilhelm
Rittinghaus, Wilhelm; America, 1688 ***8125.8*** *p438*
*Brother:*Claus
*Brother:*Gerhard
Rittman, William; Wisconsin, n.d. ***9675.7*** *p200*
Rittweger, Philipp; Cincinnati, 1869-1887 ***8582*** *p25*
Ritz Family ; America, 1820-1833 ***8582*** *p17*
Ritz, Christina; Baltimore, 1833 ***8582*** *p17*
Ritzema, Rudolph von; America, 1777-1778 ***8582.2*** *p67*
Ritzensaler, Johannes 21; Louisiana, 1838 ***778.5*** *p461*
Ritzenthaler, Andre 38; New Orleans, 1839 ***778.5*** *p461*
Ritzer, J. 36; New York, NY, 1875 ***3702.7*** *p410*
Ritzer, Joseph Mathias; America, 1852 ***8582.3*** *p55*
Ritzinger, Frederich; America, 1853 ***1450.2*** *p120A*
Rivard, F. J. 20; New Orleans, 1826 ***778.5*** *p461*
Riveraud, Arnaud 40; Port uncertain, 1838 ***778.5*** *p461*
Rivers, Mr.; Quebec, 1815 ***9229.18*** *p77*
With family
Rivers, James 18; Antigua (Antego), 1728 ***3690.1*** *p191*
Rivet, Jean 32; Port uncertain, 1835 ***778.5*** *p461*
Rivetti, Luigi; Arkansas, 1918 ***95.2*** *p105*
Rivier, J. 44; New Orleans, 1837 ***778.5*** *p461*
Riviere, Mme. 19; New Orleans, 1839 ***778.5*** *p462*
Riviere, Mr. 20; New Orleans, 1823 ***778.5*** *p462*
Riviere, Mr. 23; America, 1839 ***778.5*** *p462*
Riviere, Mr. 26; New Orleans, 1838 ***778.5*** *p462*
Riviere, Mr. 28; New Orleans, 1835 ***778.5*** *p461*
Riviere, Mr. 38; New Orleans, 1839 ***778.5*** *p461*
Riviere, Miss B. 12; New Orleans, 1829 ***778.5*** *p462*
Riviere, Mrs. B. 32; New Orleans, 1829 ***778.5*** *p462*
Riviere, Elizabeth 22; New Orleans, 1839 ***778.5*** *p462*
Riviere, M. 9; New Orleans, 1829 ***778.5*** *p462*
Riviere, Peter 13; New Orleans, 1832 ***778.5*** *p462*
Rivis, Robert 18; Maryland, 1718 ***3690.1*** *p191*
Rivoux, Leopol 30; New Orleans, 1839 ***778.5*** *p462*
Riwarda, Sister M.; Wisconsin, n.d. ***9675.5*** *p264*
Rix, Johann; Alberta, n.d. ***5262*** *p58*
Rixon, John 22; Carolina, 1774 ***1219.7*** *p227*
Rizatto, Alexander; Iowa, 1866-1943 ***123.54*** *p41*
Rizer, Catherine 18; New Orleans, 1839 ***778.5*** *p462*
Rizer, Joseph 2 mos; New Orleans, 1839 ***778.5*** *p462*
Rizos, Michael; Arkansas, 1918 ***95.2*** *p105*
Rizzalo, Domenico; Iowa, 1866-1943 ***123.54*** *p41*
Rizzalo, Eugenio; Iowa, 1866-1943 ***123.54*** *p41*
Rizzie, Deodote; Colorado, 1903 ***9678.2*** *p165*
Rizzotto, Tony 25; Arkansas, 1918 ***95.2*** *p105*
Roach, Bernard 18; Massachusetts, 1849 ***5881.1*** *p82*
Roach, Bridget; Montreal, 1822 ***7603*** *p102*
Roach, Cash; Wisconsin, n.d. ***9675.7*** *p200*
Roach, Catharine 23; Massachusetts, 1850 ***5881.1*** *p83*
Roach, Catharine 50; Massachusetts, 1848 ***5881.1*** *p83*
Roach, Cath'rine 23; Massachusetts, 1850 ***5881.1*** *p53*
Roach, Charles 26; Maryland, 1774 ***1219.7*** *p224*
Roach, David; America, 1735-1743 ***4971*** *p79*
Roach, David 49; Massachusetts, 1848 ***5881.1*** *p83*
Roach, Edward; Montreal, 1824 ***7603*** *p59*
Roach, Ellen 7; Massachusetts, 1849 ***5881.1*** *p83*
Roach, H. 29; America, 1835 ***778.5*** *p462*
Roach, Henry; New York, NY, 1840 ***8208.4*** *p107*
Roach, James 37; Arizona, 1890 ***2764.35*** *p60*
Roach, Jean-Baptiste 24; Montreal, 1779 ***7603*** *p95*
Roach, Johanna 12; Massachusetts, 1849 ***5881.1*** *p84*
Roach, John; New York, NY, 1840 ***8208.4*** *p107*
Roach, John 24; Massachusetts, 1850 ***5881.1*** *p84*
Roach, John 30; Massachusetts, 1849 ***5881.1*** *p84*
Roach, Julia 20; Massachusetts, 1850 ***5881.1*** *p84*
Roach, Margaret 22; Massachusetts, 1849 ***5881.1*** *p85*
Roach, Margaret 25; Massachusetts, 1850 ***5881.1*** *p86*
Roach, Mary; Annapolis, MD, 1742 ***4971*** *p93*
Roach, Mary; Massachusetts, 1849 ***5881.1*** *p85*
Roach, Mary 9; Massachusetts, 1849 ***5881.1*** *p85*
Roach, Mary 17; Massachusetts, 1849 ***5881.1*** *p85*
Roach, Mary 22; Massachusetts, 1850 ***5881.1*** *p86*
Roach, Mary 30; Massachusetts, 1849 ***5881.1*** *p85*
Roach, Michael; Massachusetts, 1850 ***5881.1*** *p55*
Roach, Michael; Massachusetts, 1850 ***5881.1*** *p86*
Roach, Patrick; America, 1736 ***4971*** *p39*
Roach, Patrick 5; Massachusetts, 1848 ***5881.1*** *p86*
Roach, Patrick 8; Massachusetts, 1848 ***5881.1*** *p86*
Roach, Patrick 17; Massachusetts, 1849 ***5881.1*** *p86*
Roach, Redmond 18; Maryland, 1775 ***1219.7*** *p250*
Roach, Thomas 3; Massachusetts, 1849 ***5881.1*** *p87*
Roach, Thomas 54; Massachusetts, 1850 ***5881.1*** *p87*
Roach, William; America, 1739 ***4971*** *p40*
Roach, William; New York, NY, 1833 ***8208.4*** *p34*
Roache, Edmund; America, 1735-1736 ***4971*** *p61*
Roache, Ellenor; America, 1743 ***4971*** *p43*
Roache, John; America, 1741 ***4971*** *p42*
Roache, Mary; Maryland, 1742 ***4971*** *p107*
Road, Patrick; Illinois, 1858 ***7857*** *p7*
Road, William, Jr.; South Carolina, 1788 ***7119*** *p197*
Road, Wm.; South Carolina, 1788 ***7119*** *p197*
Roades, Christopher; Virginia, 1638 ***6219*** *p9*
Roades, Richard; Virginia, 1638 ***6219*** *p15*

Roadly, John 17; New England, 1699 ***2212*** *p19*
Roads, James 15; Maryland, 1775 ***1219.7*** *p264*
Roads, Jon.; Virginia, 1632 ***6219*** *p180*
Roads, William 25; Jamaica, 1736 ***3690.1*** *p191*
Roak, Diana; Montreal, 1820 ***7603*** *p85*
Roalfs, Albert; Illinois, 1888 ***5012.37*** *p61*
Roalfs, Gerd H.; Illinois, 1888 ***5012.37*** *p61*
Roan, Catharine 22; Massachusetts, 1849 ***5881.1*** *p83*
Roan, Christopher 22; Maryland, 1774 ***1219.7*** *p235*
Roaney, Anne; New York, NY, 1816 ***2859.11*** *p41*
Roany, Charles; New York, NY, 1816 ***2859.11*** *p41*
Roark, Jane; Philadelphia, 1864 ***5704.8*** *p178*
Roark, Mary; New York, NY, 1811 ***2859.11*** *p19*
Roark, Patrick 15; Massachusetts, 1847 ***5881.1*** *p86*
Roarke, Elizabeth; Montreal, 1825 ***7603*** *p61*
Roarke, Samuel; Montreal, 1824 ***7603*** *p91*
Roarty, Alexander; Philadelphia, 1865 ***5704.8*** *p199*
Roarty, Hannah; Philadelphia, 1867 ***5704.8*** *p216*
Roarty, Sarah; New York, NY, 1865 ***5704.8*** *p193*
Robar, . . .; Halifax, N.S., 1752 ***7074.6*** *p232*
Robb, Alex; Austin, TX, 1886 ***9777*** *p5*
Robb, Eliza 8 *SEE* Robb, Samuel
Robb, Eliza 8; Philadelphia, 1849 ***5704.8*** *p58*
Robb, Eliza 45; Philadelphia, 1860 ***5704.8*** *p146*
Robb, Elly; Quebec, 1847 ***5704.8*** *p12*
Robb, Hugh; Quebec, 1847 ***5704.8*** *p12*
Robb, Isabella 9; St. John, N.B., 1850 ***5704.8*** *p62*
Robb, J. S.; Washington, 1859-1920 ***2872.1*** *p33*
Robb, James; South Carolina, 1716 ***1639.20*** *p272*
Robb, James 60; Charleston, SC, 1830 ***1639.20*** *p272*
*Relative:*Martha 59
*Relative:*Louisa 25
Robb, Jane 19; St. John, N.B., 1854 ***5704.8*** *p115*
Robb, John; Philadelphia, 1868 ***5704.8*** *p230*
Robb, John; South Carolina, 1716 ***1639.20*** *p272*
Robb, John 6 *SEE* Robb, Samuel
Robb, John 6; Philadelphia, 1849 ***5704.8*** *p58*
Robb, Louisa 25 *SEE* Robb, James
Robb, Margaret 3 *SEE* Robb, Samuel
Robb, Margaret 3; Philadelphia, 1849 ***5704.8*** *p58*
Robb, Martha 59 *SEE* Robb, James
Robb, Mary Jane 9 mos; Quebec, 1847 ***5704.8*** *p12*
Robb, Richard 11 *SEE* Robb, Samuel
Robb, Richard 11; Philadelphia, 1849 ***5704.8*** *p58*
Robb, Robert Alexander; Arkansas, 1918 ***95.2*** *p105*
Robb, Samuel; Philadelphia, 1849 ***53.26*** *p79*
*Relative:*Richard 11
*Relative:*Eliza 8
*Relative:*John 6
*Relative:*Margaret 3
Robb, Samuel; Philadelphia, 1849 ***5704.8*** *p58*
Robb, Samuel; Quebec, 1847 ***5704.8*** *p12*
Robb, Thomas; New York, NY, 1866 ***5704.8*** *p213*
Robb, Thomas; South Carolina, 1716 ***1639.20*** *p272*
Robb, William; Philadelphia, 1868 ***5704.8*** *p225*
Robb, William 22; Philadelphia, 1860 ***5704.8*** *p145*
Robb, William Robert 16; St. John, N.B., 1854 ***5704.8*** *p115*
Robbel, . . .; Canada, 1776-1783 ***9786*** *p32*
Robben, Henry 24; Kansas, 1887 ***5240.1*** *p71*
Robberds, John 17; Jamaica, 1735 ***3690.1*** *p192*
Robberman, Henry; Ohio, 1846 ***9892.11*** *p40*
Robberman, Henry D.; Ohio, 1846 ***9892.11*** *p40*
Robbins, Edward; Virginia, 1646 ***6219*** *p242*
Robbins, John; New York, NY, 1837 ***8208.4*** *p55*
Robbins, John; Virginia, 1625 ***6219*** *p7*
Robbins, John 17; Maryland, 1720 ***3690.1*** *p191*
Robbins, John 27; Maryland, 1739 ***3690.1*** *p191*
Robbins, Robert W.; Washington, 1859-1920 ***2872.1*** *p33*
Robeck, Andrew; Illinois, 1876 ***5012.39*** *p52*
Robel, Lewis Frederick; West Virginia, 1861 ***9788.3*** *p19*
Rober, . . .; Halifax, N.S., 1752 ***7074.6*** *p232*
Roberson, Mr. 29; Port uncertain, 1839 ***778.5*** *p462*
Roberson, Andrew 40; Massachusetts, 1860 ***6410.32*** *p100*
Roberson, Bridgit 32; Massachusetts, 1860 ***6410.32*** *p100*
Roberson, Jacques 25; America, 1838 ***778.5*** *p462*
Roberson, Jane 63; North Carolina, 1850 ***1639.20*** *p272*
Robert, . . .; Canada, 1776-1783 ***9786*** *p43*
Robert, . . .; Halifax, N.S., 1752 ***7074.6*** *p232*
Robert, Mrs. 25; New Orleans, 1837 ***778.5*** *p463*
Robert, Ms. 24; Port uncertain, 1820 ***778.5*** *p463*
Robert, Abraham 30; Halifax, N.S., 1752 ***7074.6*** *p207*
With family of 2
Robert, Abraham 30; Halifax, N.S., 1752 ***7074.6*** *p212*
*Wife:*Elisabeth-Catherine
*Daughter:*Elisabeth
Robert, Adele 25; New Orleans, 1838 ***778.5*** *p463*
Robert, Catherine *SEE* Robert, David-Josue
Robert, Charles-Georges; Quebec, 1816 ***7603*** *p47*
Robert, David-Josue 18; Halifax, N.S., 1752 ***7074.6*** *p212*
*Sister:*Jeanne
*Sister:*Catherine
*Sister:*Elisabeth
Robert, Edward 5; America, 1838 ***778.5*** *p463*
Robert, Elisabeth *SEE* Robert, Abraham
Robert, Elisabeth *SEE* Robert, David-Josue
Robert, Elisabeth-Catherine *SEE* Robert, Abraham
Robert, Francis 29; America, 1831 ***778.5*** *p463*
Robert, Hugh 13; Maryland or Virginia, 1699 ***2212*** *p23*
Robert, Jean 29; Quebec, 1795 ***7603*** *p47*
Robert, Jean 40; New Orleans, 1823 ***778.5*** *p463*
Robert, Jean Marie 35; St. Louis, 1835 ***778.5*** *p463*
Robert, Jeanne *SEE* Robert, David-Josue
Robert, John 12; Virginia, 1700 ***2212*** *p30*
Robert, Joseph 22; America, 1831 ***778.5*** *p463*
Robert, Lucille 31; America, 1838 ***778.5*** *p463*
Robert, M. 50; Louisiana, 1821 ***778.5*** *p463*
Robert, Peter 34; America, 1838 ***778.5*** *p463*
Robertian, Mr. 16; New Orleans, 1837 ***778.5*** *p463*
Roberts Family ; Port uncertain, 1839 ***4535.12*** *p114*
Roberts, Mr.; Quebec, 1815 ***9229.18*** *p75*
With wife
Roberts, Mr. 20; Dominica, 1774 ***1219.7*** *p223*
Roberts, Edward; Virginia, 1637 ***6219*** *p114*
Roberts, Edward; Virginia, 1639 ***6219*** *p158*
Roberts, Edward; Virginia, 1640 ***6219*** *p185*
Roberts, Edward; Virginia, 1643 ***6219*** *p207*
Roberts, Edward 19; Jamaica, 1725 ***3690.1*** *p191*
Roberts, Edward 28; Pennsylvania, 1728 ***3690.1*** *p191*
Roberts, Edward 40; California, 1867 ***3840.3*** *p8*
Roberts, Edward, Jr. 16; West Indies, 1722 ***3690.1*** *p191*
Roberts, Edwd; America, 1697 ***2212*** *p8*
Roberts, Eliz.; America, 1698 ***2212*** *p8*
Roberts, Ellen 14; Massachusetts, 1850 ***5881.1*** *p84*
Roberts, Ellen 19; America, 1705 ***2212*** *p43*
Roberts, Ethel; Iowa, 1866-1943 ***123.54*** *p75*
Roberts, Evan; Virginia, 1643 ***6219*** *p204*
Roberts, Evan 15; Maryland or Virginia, 1699 ***2212*** *p24*
Roberts, Ewen; Virginia, 1643 ***6219*** *p202*
Roberts, Fr.; Virginia, 1637 ***6219*** *p8*
Roberts, Francis; Virginia, 1636 ***6219*** *p115*
Roberts, Fred; Iowa, 1866-1943 ***123.54*** *p75*
Roberts, Frederick William; Iowa, 1866-1943 ***123.54*** *p75*
Roberts, Gabriel; America, 1697 ***2212*** *p8*
Roberts, George; New York, NY, 1811 ***2859.11*** *p19*
Roberts, George; New York, NY, 1837 ***8208.4*** *p34*
Roberts, Griff.; Virginia, 1637 ***6219*** *p8*
Roberts, Henry; Virginia, 1639 ***6219*** *p158*
Roberts, Henry 21; Virginia, 1700 ***2212*** *p30*
Roberts, Hugh; America, 1697 ***2212*** *p4*
Roberts, Humphry; Barbados, 1698 ***2212*** *p5*
Roberts, James; Colorado, 1902 ***9678.2*** *p165*
Roberts, James; New York, 1798-1826 ***1639.20*** *p272*
Roberts, James; New York, NY, 1836 ***8208.4*** *p16*
Roberts, James; Virginia, 1637 ***6219*** *p11*
Roberts, James 22; Maryland, 1775 ***1219.7*** *p252*
Roberts, Jno; America, 1698 ***2212*** *p5*
Roberts, John; Arizona, 1890 ***2764.35*** *p59*
Roberts, John; New York, NY, 1811 ***2859.11*** *p19*
Roberts, John; New York, NY, 1838 ***8208.4*** *p82*
Roberts, John; Virginia, 1638 ***6219*** *p2*
Roberts, John; Virginia, 1638 ***6219*** *p150*
Roberts, John; Virginia, 1639 ***6219*** *p151*
Roberts, John; Virginia, 1642 ***6219*** *p188*
Roberts, John 15; Maryland, 1775 ***1219.7*** *p267*
Roberts, John 17; Jamaica, 1735 ***3690.1*** *p192*
Roberts, John 20; Pennsylvania, 1721 ***3690.1*** *p192*
Roberts, John 22; Maryland, 1774 ***1219.7*** *p184*
Roberts, John 23; Maryland, 1775 ***1219.7*** *p257*
Roberts, John 30; Georgia, 1775 ***1219.7*** *p259*
*Wife:*Margaret 23
Roberts, John 37; Arizona, 1890 ***2764.35*** *p58*
Roberts, John M.; New York, NY, 1816 ***2859.11*** *p41*
Roberts, Jon.; Virginia, 1636 ***6219*** *p76*
Roberts, Jon.; Virginia, 1637 ***6219*** *p11*
Roberts, Jon.; Virginia, 1637 ***6219*** *p114*
Roberts, M.; Quebec, 1815 ***9229.18*** *p81*
Roberts, Margaret 23 *SEE* Roberts, John
Roberts, Margtte; America, 1705 ***2212*** *p45*
Roberts, Mary; Montreal, 1808 ***7603*** *p28*
Roberts, Mary 35; Maryland, 1775 ***1219.7*** *p264*
Roberts, Maurice; Barbados, 1698 ***2212*** *p5*
Roberts, Morgan; Virginia, 1635 ***6219*** *p33*
Roberts, Owen 18; Maryland, 1774 ***1219.7*** *p187*
Roberts, Peter; Virginia, 1642 ***6219*** *p193*
Roberts, Peter; Virginia, 1642 ***6219*** *p199*
Roberts, Philips 56; California, 1873 ***2769.10*** *p5*
Roberts, Ralph; Virginia, 1638 ***6219*** *p150*
Roberts, Richard D.; Iowa, 1866-1943 ***123.54*** *p41*
Roberts, Robert; New York, NY, 1833 ***8208.4*** *p56*
Roberts, Robert W.; Iowa, 1866-1943 ***123.54*** *p41*
Roberts, Samuel 15; Georgia, 1774 ***1219.7*** *p188*
Roberts, Samuel T.; Iowa, 1866-1943 ***123.54*** *p41*
Roberts, Tho; America, 1697 ***2212*** *p8*
Roberts, Thomas; America, 1697 ***2212*** *p8*
Roberts, Thomas; Virginia, 1638 ***6219*** *p125*
Roberts, Thomas; Virginia, 1641 ***6219*** *p185*
Roberts, Thomas 14; Virginia, 1700 ***2212*** *p30*
Roberts, Thomas 30; Philadelphia, 1774 ***1219.7*** *p214*
Roberts, William; Maryland, 1756 ***1219.7*** *p42*
Roberts, William; New York, NY, 1839 ***8208.4*** *p98*
Roberts, William; Quebec, 1824 ***7603*** *p72*
Roberts, William C.; New York, NY, 1834 ***8208.4*** *p4*
Roberts, Wm; America, 1698 ***2212*** *p5*
Roberts, Wm 14; Maryland or Virginia, 1699 ***2212*** *p23*
Roberts, Wm 21; America, 1705 ***2212*** *p43*
Roberts, Wm. 52; Arizona, 1914 ***9228.40*** *p19*
Robertshaw, Tho 21; Virginia, 1699 ***2212*** *p27*
Robertson, Mr.; Quebec, 1815 ***9229.18*** *p79*
With wife
Robertson, A.A. 73; Arizona, 1919 ***9228.40*** *p23*
Robertson, Adam 30; St. John, N.B., 1865 ***5704.8*** *p165*
Robertson, Alec; Austin, TX, 1886 ***9777*** *p5*
Robertson, Andrew; New York, NY, 1843 ***6410.32*** *p122*
Robertson, Betty; New Orleans, 1849 ***5704.8*** *p59*
Robertson, Catharine; New York, NY, 1816 ***2859.11*** *p41*
Robertson, Colin; Manitoba, 1811-1815 ***9775.5*** *p219*
Robertson, D.; New York, NY, 1816 ***2859.11*** *p41*
Robertson, Daniel; Iowa, 1866-1943 ***123.54*** *p41*
Robertson, David 1; St. John, N.B., 1865 ***5704.8*** *p165*
Robertson, David 7; Quebec, 1864 ***5704.8*** *p164*
Robertson, David 20; St. John, N.B., 1866 ***5704.8*** *p166*
Robertson, Donald; America, 1802 ***1639.20*** *p272*
Robertson, Donald; South Carolina, 1716 ***1639.20*** *p272*
Robertson, Donald 19; Massachusetts, 1850 ***5881.1*** *p83*
Robertson, Donald 21; Kansas, 1882 ***5240.1*** *p36*
Robertson, Donald 21; Kansas, 1882 ***5240.1*** *p63*
Robertson, Edward; Austin, TX, 1886 ***9777*** *p5*
Robertson, Edward 31; Kansas, 1878 ***5240.1*** *p59*
Robertson, Eleanor; New York, NY, 1816 ***2859.11*** *p41*
Robertson, Elizabeth 30; Quebec, 1864 ***5704.8*** *p164*
Robertson, Erik Turere; Arkansas, 1918 ***95.2*** *p105*
Robertson, Helen 1; St. John, N.B., 1865 ***5704.8*** *p165*
Robertson, Helen 26; St. John, N.B., 1865 ***5704.8*** *p165*
Robertson, Hugh; America, 1756 ***8894.1*** *p191*
Robertson, Hugh 18; Maryland, 1736 ***3690.1*** *p192*
Robertson, Isaac; Texas, 1836 ***9777*** *p4*
Robertson, James; Charleston, SC, 1823 ***1639.20*** *p273*
Robertson, James; New York, NY, 1704-1804 ***8894.2*** *p56*
Robertson, James 9; Quebec, 1864 ***5704.8*** *p164*
Robertson, James 21; Maryland, 1774 ***1219.7*** *p181*
Robertson, James 27; Kansas, 1879 ***5240.1*** *p60*
Robertson, James 31; Quebec, 1864 ***5704.8*** *p164*
Robertson, James 50; Charleston, SC, 1850 ***1639.20*** *p273*
Robertson, James 60; Charleston, SC, 1850 ***1639.20*** *p273*
Robertson, James Dunn 33; California, 1866 ***3840.3*** *p8*
Robertson, James Scott 26; Kansas, 1886 ***5240.1*** *p69*
Robertson, John; Ontario, 1818 ***9775.5*** *p213*
Robertson, John; Washington, 1859-1920 ***2872.1*** *p33*
Robertson, John 9 mos; Quebec, 1864 ***5704.8*** *p164*
Robertson, John 21; Maryland, 1775 ***1219.7*** *p261*
Robertson, John 24; Maryland, 1774 ***1219.7*** *p183*
Robertson, Mabel Currie *SEE* Robertson, Norman Hay
Robertson, Margaret 3; Quebec, 1864 ***5704.8*** *p164*
Robertson, Margaret Sinclair; Toronto, 1841 ***8893*** *p266*
Robertson, Mary 11; Quebec, 1864 ***5704.8*** *p164*
Robertson, Norman Hay; Buffalo, NY, 1901 ***3455.2*** *p97*
*Wife:*Mabel Currie
Robertson, Peter; Montreal, 1824 ***7603*** *p35*
Robertson, Robert; Austin, TX, 1886 ***9777*** *p5*
Robertson, Robert; Quebec, 1764 ***7603*** *p38*
Robertson, Robert 23; Halifax, N.S., 1774 ***1219.7*** *p213*
Robertson, Robert 25; Maryland, 1775 ***1219.7*** *p267*
Robertson, William; New Orleans, 1849 ***5704.8*** *p59*
Robertson, William; New York, NY, 1838 ***8208.4*** *p86*
Robertson, William 15; North America, 1774 ***1219.7*** *p200*
Robertson, Wm.; Petersburg, VA, 1806 ***4778.2*** *p141*
Robeson, John; New York, NY, 1811 ***2859.11*** *p19*
Robeson, John 20; Maryland, 1737 ***3690.1*** *p193*
Robet, Mr. 24; America, 1838 ***778.5*** *p463*
Robetea, Chas. 10; Port uncertain, 1838 ***778.5*** *p463*
Robetea, Edward 8; Port uncertain, 1838 ***778.5*** *p464*
Robetea, Frances 4; Port uncertain, 1838 ***778.5*** *p464*
Robetea, Maria 37; Port uncertain, 1838 ***778.5*** *p464*
Robetea, Nicolas 36; Port uncertain, 1838 ***778.5*** *p463*
Robey, Thomas; Philadelphia, 1764 ***1219.7*** *p100*
Robieson, Mr.; Quebec, 1815 ***9229.18*** *p74*
Robillard, J.; New Orleans, 1839 ***778.5*** *p464*
Robillon, . . .; America, 1836 ***778.5*** *p464*
Robillon, Mme.; America, 1836 ***778.5*** *p464*
Robillon, Mr. 11; America, 1838 ***778.5*** *p464*

Roche, De La; Nova Scotia, n.d. 8582.3 p75
Roche, Mrs. 63; Louisiana, 1820 778.5 p464
Roche, Cornelius 32; Kansas, 1879 5240.1 p60
Roche, David; New York, NY, 1816 2859.11 p41
Roche, H. 29; America, 1835 778.5 p462
Roche, James; New York, NY, 1816 2859.11 p41
Roche, James; Virginia, 1637 6219 p115
Roche, Jean 37; Port uncertain, 1839 778.5 p464
Roche, John; New York, NY, 1816 2859.11 p41
Roche, John; New York, NY, 1834 8208.4 p78
Roche, Mary; America, 1741 4971 p16
Roche, Philip; Fredericton, N.B., 1817 7603 p79
Roche, Theophile; Colorado, 1904 9678.2 p165
Roche, William; New York, NY, 1816 2859.11 p41
Rochebrun, Miss 2; America, 1829 778.5 p464
Rochebrun, Mrs. 30; America, 1829 778.5 p465
Rochebrun, J. V. 31; America, 1829 778.5 p464
Rocheford, Robert-Jean; Quebec, 1823 7603 p65
Rochefort, P. 50; America, 1825 778.5 p465
Rochenberger, . . .; Canada, 1776-1783 9786 p43
Rochereau, Mr. 25; New Orleans, 1839 778.5 p465
Rochereau, John Albin 20; Port uncertain, 1836 778.5 p465
Rochester, John; Virginia, 1638 6219 p121
Rochette, Peter 23; Kansas, 1872 5240.1 p53
Rochford, Dennis; Pennsylvania, 1682 4961 p164
*Wife:*Mary Heriott
Rochford, Francis; New York, NY, 1816 2859.11 p41
Rochford, Grace 3; Died enroute, 1682 4961 p165
*Sister:*Mary 6 mos
Rochford, John; New York, NY, 1811 2859.11 p19
Rochford, Mary 6 mos *SEE* Rochford, Grace
Rochford, Mary Heriott *SEE* Rochford, Dennis
Rochford, Walter; Philadelphia, 1816 2859.11 p41
Rochon, Batiste 17; New Orleans, 1836 778.5 p436
Rochon, Henri 20 *SEE* Rochon, Pierre
Rochon, Marie *SEE* Rochon, Philippe
Rochon, Marie Talmon *SEE* Rochon, Philippe
Rochon, Philippe; Port uncertain, 1754 2444 p206
*Wife:*Marie Talmon
*Child:*Marie
Rochon, Pierre 22; Pennsylvania, 1753 2444 p206
*Brother:*Henri 20
Rock, Anton; Wisconsin, n.d. 9675.7 p269
Rock, James; New York, NY, 1811 2859.11 p19
Rock, Joe; Iowa, 1866-1943 123.54 p75
Rock, John; Arkansas, 1918 95.2 p105
Rock, Mary; New York, NY, 1811 2859.11 p19
Rock, Palmatz; Wisconsin, n.d. 9675.7 p269
Rock, William 16; Maryland, 1774 1219.7 p187
Rocke, Fra.; Virginia, 1646 6219 p242
Rocke, Fred; Washington, 1859-1920 2872.1 p33
Rocke, John; New York, NY, 1834 8208.4 p78
Rockel, . . .; Quebec, 1777 9786 p143
Rockel, Anton; New York, NY, 1878 1450.2 p32B
Rockel, Joseph; Wisconsin, n.d. 9675.7 p269
Rockenbach, Charles A. 28; Kansas, 1873 5240.1 p55
Rockenbach, Gustav 21; Kansas, 1887 5240.1 p70
Rockenfeld, Abraham; Kentucky, 1810 8582.3 p97
Rockenmire, John; Indiana, 1844 9117 p18
Rockenmire, Nicholas; Indiana, 1843 9117 p18
Rocket, Thomas; Indiana, 1836 9117 p15
Rockett, Thomas; Indiana, 1836 9117 p15
Rockey, John; Ohio, 1851 9892.11 p40
Rockford, Thomas 22; Philadelphia, 1853 5704.8 p112
Rockholt, Joseph; Ohio, 1796 8582.2 p58
Rockite, Thomas; Indiana, 1836 9117 p15
Rockley, George; Virginia, 1753 1219.7 p21
Rockley, George; Virginia, 1753 3690.1 p194
Rocks, Anth.; Virginia, 1643 6219 p200
Rocktreschler, . . .; Canada, 1776-1783 9786 p32
Rockwell, Mr.; Virginia, 1645 6219 p234
Rockwell, John; Washington, 1859-1920 2872.1 p34
Rockwell, Mary *SEE* Rockwell, Robert
Rockwell, Robert; Virginia, 1637 6219 p29
*Wife:*Sarah
*Child:*Mary
*Child:*Thomasin
Rockwell, Sarah *SEE* Rockwell, Robert
Rockwell, Thomas; Virginia, 1639 6219 p157
Rockwell, Thomasin *SEE* Rockwell, Robert
Rockwood, Anth.; Virginia, 1635 6219 p70
Rockwood, Anth.; Virginia, 1638 6219 p116
Roctigan, Mrs. 30; Massachusetts, 1847 5881.1 p85
Roctigan, Catharine 12; Massachusetts, 1847 5881.1 p83
Roctigan, Mary 10; Massachusetts, 1847 5881.1 p85
Roctigan, Peggy 30; Massachusetts, 1847 5881.1 p86
Roctigan, Thomas 3; Massachusetts, 1847 5881.1 p86
Roctigon, John 30; Massachusetts, 1847 5881.1 p84
Rocto, Jon.; Virginia, 1636 6219 p74
Roczelink, Dorota 20; New York, 1912 9980.29 p54
Rodabough, Christian; Pennsylvania, 1739 4779.3 p14
Rodamann, Christopher; America, 1777-1778 8582.2 p69
Rodamber, Christopher; America, 1777-1778 8582.2 p69
Rodamber, Christopher; America, 1778 8582.2 p34
Rodan, Homer; Virginia, 1698 2212 p14
Rodberg, Alfred Peter; Arkansas, 1918 95.2 p105
Rodd, William 20; Philadelphia, 1774 1219.7 p183
Roddan, Bridget; St. John, N.B., 1852 5704.8 p83
Rodden, Ann; New Orleans, 1849 5704.8 p59
Rodden, Bridget 18; Philadelphia, 1854 5704.8 p118
Rodden, Edward; Quebec, 1853 5704.8 p104
Rodden, Elizabeth; St. John, N.B., 1850 5704.8 p65
Rodden, Hannah; New York, NY, 1867 5704.8 p222
Rodden, James; St. John, N.B., 1847 5704.8 p10
Rodden, Manus; Philadelphia, 1849 53.26 p80
Rodden, Manus; Philadelphia, 1849 5704.8 p49
Rodden, Mary; New Orleans, 1849 5704.8 p59
Rodden, Peggy; Philadelphia, 1850 53.26 p80
Rodden, Peggy; Philadelphia, 1850 5704.8 p69
Rodden, Rosey 13; St. John, N.B., 1847 5704.8 p10
Rodden, Susan 20; Philadelphia, 1858 5704.8 p139
Rodden, William 18; Philadelphia, 1859 5704.8 p142
Rodder, Michael; Philadelphia, 1811 53.26 p80
Rodder, Michael; Philadelphia, 1811 2859.11 p19
Roddey, Elizabeth 1; St. John, N.B., 1866 5704.8 p166
Roddey, Elizabeth 22; St. John, N.B., 1866 5704.8 p166
Roddey, John 28; St. John, N.B., 1866 5704.8 p166
Roddick, James 26; Maryland, 1773 1219.7 p172
Roddin, Grace 16; Philadelphia, 1853 5704.8 p111
Roddin, Grace 19; Philadelphia, 1853 5704.8 p111
Roddy, Denis 6 *SEE* Roddy, Hugh
Roddy, Denis 6; Philadelphia, 1850 5704.8 p69
Roddy, Hugh; Philadelphia, 1850 53.26 p80
*Relative:*Jane
*Relative:*James 9
*Relative:*Denis 6
*Relative:*Mary 4
*Relative:*John 1
*Relative:*Patrick 12
Roddy, Hugh; Philadelphia, 1850 5704.8 p69
Roddy, James 9 *SEE* Roddy, Hugh
Roddy, James 9; Philadelphia, 1850 5704.8 p69
Roddy, Jane *SEE* Roddy, Hugh
Roddy, Jane; Philadelphia, 1850 5704.8 p69
Roddy, John; New York, NY, 1837 8208.4 p53
Roddy, John 1 *SEE* Roddy, Hugh
Roddy, John 1; Philadelphia, 1850 5704.8 p69
Roddy, Mary 4 *SEE* Roddy, Hugh
Roddy, Mary 4; Philadelphia, 1850 5704.8 p69
Roddy, Patrick; Wisconsin, n.d. 9675.7 p269
Roddy, Patrick 12 *SEE* Roddy, Hugh
Roddy, Patrick 12; Philadelphia, 1850 5704.8 p69
Roddy, Peter; Quebec, 1847 5704.8 p37
Rode, John; Illinois, 1878 2896.5 p34
Rode, Joseph; Ohio, 1839 9892.11 p39
Rode, Joseph 26; Kansas, 1885 5240.1 p67
Rodeak, William 35; Charleston, SC, 1774 1639.20 p274
Rodebach, Johann Peter; Philadelphia, 1752 8125.6 p23
Rodebagh, Johann Peter; Philadelphia, 1752 8125.6 p23
Rodelbronn, Fred; Wisconsin, n.d. 9675.7 p269
Rodeman, George Henry 46; California, 1868 3840.3 p8
Roden, Alice; America, 1868 5704.8 p227
Roden, Mathias; Wisconsin, n.d. 9675.7 p269
Roden, Michael; Wisconsin, n.d. 9675.7 p269
Roden, Nicholas; Wisconsin, n.d. 9675.7 p269
Roden, Thomas; Arkansas, 1918 95.2 p105
Rodenbach, Christian; Pennsylvania, 1739 4779.3 p14
Rodenbach, Johann Peter; Philadelphia, 1752 8125.6 p23
Rodenbeck, Henry; America, 1885 1450.2 p120A
Rodenberg, Karl Friedrich Wilhelm; America, 1851-1852 4610.10 p112
Rodenburg, Max Joseph; Wisconsin, n.d. 9675.7 p269
Rodenhoure, Paul 22; Kansas, 1873 5240.1 p54
Roder, Adam 24; Kansas, 1885 5240.1 p67
Roder, William; New Orleans, 1837 2896.5 p34
Roderfeld, . . .; Canada, 1776-1783 9786 p32
Rodermill, Christopher; Philadelphia, 1762 9973.7 p37
Rodez, Frank; America, 1891 1450.2 p31B
Rodgemann, Hermann; Cincinnati, 1869-1887 8582 p25
Rodgers, Andrew; Philadelphia, 1850 5704.8 p64
Rodgers, Arthur; America, 1865 5704.8 p194
Rodgers, Bernard; New York, NY, 1864 5704.8 p170
Rodgers, Biddy 21; Philadelphia, 1860 5704.8 p146
Rodgers, Bridget; New York, NY, 1864 5704.8 p176
Rodgers, Bridget; Philadelphia, 1864 5704.8 p180
Rodgers, Catherine; Philadelphia, 1848 53.26 p80
Rodgers, Catherine; Philadelphia, 1848 5704.8 p41
Rodgers, Catherine 20; Philadelphia, 1859 5704.8 p142
Rodgers, Catherine 25; Philadelphia, 1864 5704.8 p161
Rodgers, Cecilia; Philadelphia, 1868 5704.8 p226
Rodgers, Charles; Philadelphia, 1852 5704.8 p89
Rodgers, Cornelius; New York, NY, 1864 5704.8 p177
Rodgers, Daniel 11; Philadelphia, 1867 5704.8 p216
Rodgers, Elleanor *SEE* Rodgers, Francis
Rodgers, Elleanor; Philadelphia, 1849 5704.8 p50
Rodgers, Francis; Philadelphia, 1849 53.26 p80
*Relative:*James
*Relative:*Mary
*Relative:*Elleanor
Rodgers, Francis; Philadelphia, 1849 5704.8 p50
Rodgers, George; America, 1867 5704.8 p217
Rodgers, Grace 12; Philadelphia, 1867 5704.8 p216
Rodgers, James *SEE* Rodgers, Francis
Rodgers, James; America, 1864 5704.8 p186
Rodgers, James; New York, NY, 1834 8208.4 p2
Rodgers, James; Philadelphia, 1849 5704.8 p50
Rodgers, James; Philadelphia, 1849 5704.8 p52
Rodgers, John; Baltimore, 1810 9892.11 p40
Rodgers, John; New York, NY, 1811 2859.11 p19
Rodgers, John; New York, NY, 1864 5704.8 p183
Rodgers, John; Ohio, 1825 9892.11 p40
Rodgers, Joseph; St. John, N.B., 1848 5704.8 p43
Rodgers, Magy 15; Philadelphia, 1853 5704.8 p108
Rodgers, Margaret 23; St. John, N.B., 1854 5704.8 p122
Rodgers, Mary *SEE* Rodgers, Francis
Rodgers, Mary; New York, NY, 1811 2859.11 p19
Rodgers, Mary; New York, NY, 1866 5704.8 p210
Rodgers, Mary; Philadelphia, 1849 5704.8 p50
Rodgers, Mary; Philadelphia, 1850 5704.8 p64
Rodgers, Mary; Philadelphia, 1868 5704.8 p230
Rodgers, Mathew; Philadelphia, 1848 53.26 p80
Rodgers, Mathew; Philadelphia, 1848 5704.8 p40
Rodgers, Michael 23; Philadelphia, 1859 5704.8 p142
Rodgers, Patrick; America, 1864 5704.8 p189
Rodgers, Patrick; New York, NY, 1815 2859.11 p41
Rodgers, Rebecca; New York, NY, 1866 5704.8 p210
Rodgers, Rosanna 21; Philadelphia, 1859 5704.8 p142
Rodgers, Rose; New York, NY, 1864 5704.8 p170
Rodgers, Samuel; Philadelphia, 1811 53.26 p80
Rodgers, Samuel; Philadelphia, 1811 2859.11 p19
Rodgers, Sarah; Philadelphia, 1864 5704.8 p188
Rodgers, Susan *SEE* Rodgers, Thomas
Rodgers, Susan; Philadelphia, 1847 5704.8 p14
Rodgers, Thomas; Philadelphia, 1847 53.26 p80
*Relative:*Susan
Rodgers, Thomas; Philadelphia, 1847 5704.8 p14
Rodgett, Tho.; Virginia, 1642 6219 p199
Rodgison, James; Virginia, 1637 6219 p10
Rodick, James; Charleston, SC, 1799 1639.20 p273
Rodier, Amedee 22; America, 1836 778.5 p465
Rodins, Nicolas; Illinois, 1891 5012.39 p53
Rodius, Nicolas; Illinois, 1891 5012.39 p53
Rodman, Christopher; America, 1777-1778 8582.2 p69
Rodner, Casimir 22; New Orleans, 1836 778.5 p465
Rodney, John 64; Arizona, 1890 2764.35 p59
Rodosevis, Jon; Iowa, 1866-1943 123.54 p41
Rodoski, Peter; Arkansas, 1918 95.2 p105
Rodregues, Marie 53; Arizona, 1924 9228.40 p28
Rodreques, M. 37; Arizona, 1911 9228.40 p16
Rodrigues, Clemente; Arkansas, 1918 95.2 p105
Rodrigues, Jean 20; Port uncertain, 1839 778.5 p465
Rodriguez, Clemente; Arkansas, 1918 95.2 p105
Rodriguez, John 27; Port uncertain, 1838 778.5 p465
Rodstrom, A.P.; Iowa, 1866-1943 123.54 p42
Rodstrom, G.J.; Iowa, 1866-1943 123.54 p42
Rodstrom, Lars; Iowa, 1866-1943 123.54 p42
Rodstrom, O.W.; Iowa, 1866-1943 123.54 p42
Rodziewicz, . . .; New York, 1831 4606 p176
Roe, Ann 35; Maryland, 1775 1219.7 p253
Roe, Charles 11; Port uncertain, 1838 778.5 p465
Roe, Dorothy 43; Port uncertain, 1838 778.5 p465
Roe, Edward; America, 1740 4971 p26
Roe, John; America, 1736 4971 p80
Roe, Jon.; Virginia, 1637 6219 p13
Roe, Jon.; Virginia, 1637 6219 p115
Roe, Joseph 15; Philadelphia, 1774 1219.7 p175
Roe, Mary; Virginia, 1639 6219 p51
Roe, Melchior 44; Port uncertain, 1838 778.5 p465
Roe, Roger 23; Philadelphia, 1775 1219.7 p248
Roe, Thomas; America, 1737 4971 p13
Roe, Willie; Arkansas, 1918 95.2 p105
Roeber, Charles; Wisconsin, n.d. 9675.7 p269
Roebke, Henry; Baltimore, 1881 1450.2 p32B
Roebling, Johann A.; Cincinnati, 1788-1877 8582.3 p80
Roebling, John A.; America, 1831 8582 p25
Roebuck, Jarvis; Philadelphia, 1745 3652 p67
Roecker, Anna Barbara *SEE* Roecker, Michael
Roecker, Anna Maria Schauwecker *SEE* Roecker, Hans Martin
Roecker, Barbara Rauscher *SEE* Roecker, Michael
Roecker, Catharina; Pennsylvania, 1749 2444 p205
Roecker, Christina; Pennsylvania, 1751 2444 p206
Roecker, Georg *SEE* Roecker, Hans Martin
Roecker, Hans Martin; America, 1766 2444 p205
*Wife:*Anna Maria Schauwecker
*Child:*Georg
*Son:*Johann Martin
Roecker, Johann Bernhard *SEE* Roecker, Michael

Roecker, Johann Georg; Pennsylvania, 1749 ***2444*** *p205*
Roecker, Johann Martin *SEE* Roecker, Hans Martin
Roecker, Michael; Port uncertain, 1749 ***2444*** *p205*
*Wife:*Barbara Rauscher
*Child:*Anna Barbara
*Child:*Johann Bernhard
Roedel, Chas. F.; Wisconsin, n.d. ***9675.7*** *p269*
Roedelbronn, Fred; Wisconsin, n.d. ***9675.7*** *p269*
Roedelbronn, Regina; Wisconsin, n.d. ***9675.7*** *p269*
Roeder, John 21; Kansas, 1890 ***5240.1*** *p75*
Roeder, Philip; Philadelphia, 1779 ***8137*** *p13*
Roedingshoefer, A.; Ohio, 1869-1887 ***8582*** *p25*
Roedter, . . .; America, 1836 ***8582.1*** *p39*
Roedter, . . .; Cincinnati, 1837-1838 ***8582.1*** *p45*
Roedter, Mr.; Cincinnati, 1837 ***8582.1*** *p24*
Roedter, Heinrich; Cincinnati, 1788-1848 ***8582.3*** *p89*
Roedter, Heinrich; Cincinnati, 1831 ***8582.1*** *p51*
Roedter, Heinrich; Cincinnati, 1832 ***8582*** *p25*
Roefeld, John 24; Port uncertain, 1838 ***778.5*** *p465*
Roeglin, Carl; Wisconsin, n.d. ***9675.7*** *p269*
Roeglin, William; Wisconsin, n.d. ***9675.7*** *p269*
Roehemeyer, Johann Casp. Heinrich; America, 1843 ***4610.10*** *p133*
With parents
Roehling, . . .; Canada, 1776-1783 ***9786*** *p32*
Roehn, Eugene 19; Port uncertain, 1826 ***778.5*** *p465*
Roehrig, Friedrich Louis Otto; America, 1853 ***8582.1*** *p43*
Roehrle, Andre 48; America, 1838 ***778.5*** *p466*
Roehrle, Christophe 22; America, 1838 ***778.5*** *p466*
Roehrle, Marienne 23; America, 1838 ***778.5*** *p466*
Roeky, Andri; Iowa, 1866-1943 ***123.54*** *p42*
Roelfs, Harm G.; Illinois, 1888 ***5012.39*** *p122*
Roelker, Dr.; Cincinnati, 1837-1838 ***8582.1*** *p45*
Roelker, August; New York, NY, 1825 ***8582*** *p26*
Roelker, Heinrich; Cincinnati, 1869-1887 ***8582*** *p26*
Roeloffon, Mr.; Cincinnati, 1858 ***8582.3*** *p16*
Roelofson, Mr.; Cincinnati, 1858 ***8582.3*** *p16*
Roemelt, Godfrey; New York, 1748 ***3652*** *p68*
Roemer, Dr.; Pennsylvania, 1800-1807 ***8582.3*** *p76*
Roemer, Charles; Wisconsin, n.d. ***9675.7*** *p269*
Roemisch, Anton 36; West Virginia, 1900 ***9788.3*** *p20*
Roen, Andrew Hans; Arkansas, 1918 ***95.2*** *p106*
Roepke, Frederick; Baltimore, 1840 ***1450.2*** *p120A*
Roes, Johannes; Philadelphia, 1779 ***8137*** *p13*
Roesaner, Charles Frederick; America, 1854 ***1450.2*** *p120A*
Roesch, Frank K.; New York, 1880 ***1450.2*** *p32B*
Roesener, Henry; America, 1865 ***1450.2*** *p32B*
Roesler, Godfrey; New York, 1750 ***3652*** *p74*
Roesler, Johann; Illinois, 1853 ***8582.2*** *p50*
Roesner, Mrs.; America, n.d. ***5647.5*** *p3*
*Child:*Peter
*Child:*Henry
*Child:*Sophia
*Child:*Lizzie
*Child:*Louisa
Roesner, Barbara; Indiana, n.d. ***5647.5*** *p3*
Roesner, Barbara; Indiana, 1831-1850 ***5647.5*** *p35*
Roesner, Catharine; Pennsylvania, 1830-1834 ***5647.5*** *p4*
Roesner, Catherine; Pennsylvania, 1834-1835 ***5647.5*** *p37*
Roesner, Christine Bard; America, 1847 ***5647.5*** *p23*
*Child:*Louisa
*Child:*Elizabeth
*Child:*Sophia
*Child:*Peter J.
*Child:*Henry
Roesner, Elizabeth *SEE* Roesner, Christine Bard
Roesner, George; Indiana, 1837 ***5647.5*** *p4*
Roesner, Henry *SEE* Roesner, Mrs.
Roesner, Henry *SEE* Roesner, Christine Bard
Roesner, Henry; America, n.d. ***5647.5*** *p3*
Roesner, Henry; America, 1826-1926 ***5647.5*** *p3*
Roesner, Henry; Indiana, 1880 ***5647.5*** *p31*
*Wife:*Louise Speck
Roesner, Henry; New Orleans, 1848 ***5647.5*** *p31*
Roesner, Kate; America, n.d. ***5647.5*** *p3*
Roesner, Katherine; Indiana, 1848-1850 ***5647.5*** *p31*
Roesner, Lizzie *SEE* Roesner, Mrs.
Roesner, Louisa *SEE* Roesner, Mrs.
Roesner, Louisa *SEE* Roesner, Christine Bard
Roesner, Louise Speck *SEE* Roesner, Henry
Roesner, Peter *SEE* Roesner, Mrs.
Roesner, Peter; Died enroute, n.d. ***5647.5*** *p3*
Roesner, Peter; Died enroute, 1847 ***5647.5*** *p23*
Roesner, Peter J. *SEE* Roesner, Christine Bard
Roesner, Sophia *SEE* Roesner, Mrs.
Roesner, Sophia *SEE* Roesner, Christine Bard
Roesner, William 62; Indiana, 1822 ***5647.5*** *p39*
Roessler, Johann Christoph *SEE* Roessler, Michael
Roessler, Maria Agnes *SEE* Roessler, Michael
Roessler, Maria Barbara *SEE* Roessler, Michael
Roessler, Michael 20; Pennsylvania, 1753 ***2444*** *p205*
*Wife:*Maria Barbara
*Child:*Rosina Barbara
*Child:*Maria Agnes
*Child:*Johann Christoph
Roessler, Regine Katherine; Wisconsin, n.d. ***9675.7*** *p269*
Roessler, Rosina Barbara *SEE* Roessler, Michael
Roessner, Mrs.; America, n.d. ***5647.5*** *p3*
*Child:*Peter
*Child:*Henry
*Child:*Sophia
*Child:*Lizzie
*Child:*Louisa
Roessner, Christine Bard; America, 1847 ***5647.5*** *p23*
*Child:*Louisa
*Child:*Elizabeth
*Child:*Sophia
*Child:*Peter J.
*Child:*Henry
Roessner, Elizabeth *SEE* Roessner, Christine Bard
Roessner, Henry *SEE* Roessner, Mrs.
Roessner, Henry *SEE* Roessner, Christine Bard
Roessner, Henry; America, n.d. ***5647.5*** *p3*
Roessner, Henry; Indiana, 1880 ***5647.5*** *p31*
*Wife:*Louise Speck
Roessner, Henry; New Orleans, 1848 ***5647.5*** *p31*
Roessner, Kate; America, n.d. ***5647.5*** *p3*
Roessner, Katherine; Indiana, 1848-1850 ***5647.5*** *p31*
Roessner, Lizzie *SEE* Roessner, Mrs.
Roessner, Louisa *SEE* Roessner, Mrs.
Roessner, Louisa *SEE* Roessner, Christine Bard
Roessner, Louise Speck *SEE* Roessner, Henry
Roessner, Peter *SEE* Roessner, Mrs.
Roessner, Peter; Died enroute, n.d. ***5647.5*** *p3*
Roessner, Peter; Died enroute, 1847 ***5647.5*** *p23*
Roessner, Peter J. *SEE* Roessner, Christine Bard
Roessner, Sophia *SEE* Roessner, Mrs.
Roessner, Sophia *SEE* Roessner, Christine Bard
Roeszler, Michael 20; Pennsylvania, 1753 ***2444*** *p205*
Roeters, Raymond; Arkansas, 1918 ***95.2*** *p106*
Roether, Philip; Philadelphia, 1779 ***8137*** *p13*
Roethke, August; Illinois, 1902 ***5012.40*** *p79*
Roettger, Wilhelm; America, 1847 ***8582.3*** *p55*
Roewekamp, Heinrich F.; Cincinnati, 1869-1887 ***8582*** *p26*
Roewekamp, William; Colorado, 1894 ***9678.2*** *p165*
Roff, George 30; California, 1867 ***3840.3*** *p8*
Roff, Sabotian; South Carolina, 1788 ***7119*** *p199*
Roffignac, Miss 38; America, 1829 ***778.5*** *p466*
Rofion, Mr. 50; America, 1837 ***778.5*** *p466*
Rogalski, John; Washington, 1859-1920 ***2872.1*** *p34*
Rogan, Ann 7; Massachusetts, 1849 ***5881.1*** *p82*
Rogan, Charles; New York, NY, 1816 ***2859.11*** *p41*
Rogan, Ellen; Philadelphia, 1866 ***5704.8*** *p210*
Rogan, James; Philadelphia, 1851 ***5704.8*** *p80*
Rogan, John; Quebec, 1830 ***4719.7*** *p21*
Rogan, Margaret 7; Massachusetts, 1849 ***5881.1*** *p86*
Rogan, Rose; Massachusetts, 1849 ***5881.1*** *p86*
Roger, Mr. 22; New Orleans, 1825 ***778.5*** *p466*
Roger, Mr. 28; New Orleans, 1839 ***778.5*** *p466*
Roger, Mr. 48; America, 1838 ***778.5*** *p466*
Roger, B. 45; New Orleans, 1831 ***778.5*** *p466*
Roger, Francois 34; Port uncertain, 1823 ***778.5*** *p466*
Roger, Henry 40; Port uncertain, 1839 ***778.5*** *p466*
Roger, Jane 40; America, 1838 ***778.5*** *p466*
Roger, John; Virginia, 1642 ***6219*** *p186*
Roger, Jon.; Virginia, 1643 ***6219*** *p202*
Roger, Paul 32; America, 1838 ***778.5*** *p466*
Roger, Tievre J. 30; America, 1838 ***778.5*** *p466*
Roger, Tievre J., Jr. 1; America, 1838 ***778.5*** *p466*
Roger, Tievre T. 36; America, 1838 ***778.5*** *p467*
Rogers, Alexr.; New York, NY, 1816 ***2859.11*** *p41*
Rogers, Alfred; Arkansas, 1918 ***95.2*** *p106*
Rogers, Ann; New York, NY, 1816 ***2859.11*** *p41*
Rogers, Ann; St. John, N.B., 1849 ***5704.8*** *p49*
Rogers, Anthony; St. John, N.B., 1849 ***5704.8*** *p49*
Rogers, Charles; Virginia, 1635 ***6219*** *p10*
Rogers, Charles; Virginia, 1637 ***6219*** *p10*
Rogers, Charles 15; Maryland, 1724 ***3690.1*** *p194*
Rogers, Christopher; New York, NY, 1837 ***8208.4*** *p35*
Rogers, Edward; Virginia, 1623 ***6219*** *p7*
Rogers, Elianor; Virginia, 1639 ***6219*** *p156*
Rogers, Elizabeth 18; Virginia, 1700 ***2212*** *p31*
Rogers, Ellin; Virginia, 1638 ***6219*** *p116*
Rogers, Francis; Virginia, 1638 ***6219*** *p125*
Rogers, George 19; Pennsylvania, Virginia or Maryland, 1728 ***3690.1*** *p194*
Rogers, H. W.; Washington, 1859-1920 ***2872.1*** *p34*
Rogers, Hugh; New York, NY, 1816 ***2859.11*** *p41*
Rogers, Jacob; New York, 1752 ***3652*** *p76*
Rogers, James; America, 1742 ***4971*** *p23*
Rogers, James; Arkansas, 1918 ***95.2*** *p106*
Rogers, James; Charleston, SC, 1794 ***1639.20*** *p274*
Rogers, James; New York, NY, 1869 ***5704.8*** *p232*
Rogers, James; Philadelphia, 1849 ***53.26*** *p80*
Rogers, James; St. John, N.B., 1849 ***5704.8*** *p49*
Rogers, James 13; Massachusetts, 1847 ***5881.1*** *p84*
Rogers, James 59; Massachusetts, 1848 ***5881.1*** *p84*
Rogers, Jenny 20; Massachusetts, 1850 ***5881.1*** *p85*
Rogers, John; New York, NY, 1815 ***2859.11*** *p41*
Rogers, John; New York, NY, 1816 ***2859.11*** *p41*
Rogers, John; New York, NY, 1816 ***2859.11*** *p41*
With wife
Rogers, John; St. John, N.B., 1849 ***5704.8*** *p49*
Rogers, John; Virginia, 1638 ***6219*** *p159*
Rogers, John 6 mos; St. John, N.B., 1849 ***5704.8*** *p49*
Rogers, John, Family; Nova Scotia, 1767 ***9775.5*** *p206*
Rogers, Joshua 17; Maryland, 1774 ***1219.7*** *p207*
Rogers, Margaret; St. John, N.B., 1849 ***5704.8*** *p49*
Rogers, Mary; New York, NY, 1816 ***2859.11*** *p41*
Rogers, Mary; St. John, N.B., 1849 ***5704.8*** *p49*
Rogers, Mary 7; New York, NY, 1869 ***5704.8*** *p233*
Rogers, Mary Ann; Philadelphia, 1850 ***53.26*** *p80*
Rogers, Mary Ann; Philadelphia, 1850 ***5704.8*** *p68*
Rogers, Mathew 14; Philadelphia, 1853 ***5704.8*** *p111*
Rogers, Matilda; Philadelphia, 1866 ***5704.8*** *p211*
Rogers, Moses 28; Dominica, 1774 ***1219.7*** *p177*
Rogers, Nathan; Philadelphia, 1811 ***53.26*** *p80*
Rogers, Nathan; Philadelphia, 1811 ***2859.11*** *p19*
Rogers, Neil; Philadelphia, 1865 ***5704.8*** *p198*
Rogers, Nicholas; Virginia, 1645 ***6219*** *p233*
Rogers, Nicholas; Virginia, 1647 ***6219*** *p244*
Rogers, Onah; America, 1867 ***5704.8*** *p216*
Rogers, Owen; New York, NY, 1866 ***5704.8*** *p209*
Rogers, Patrick; New York, NY, 1816 ***2859.11*** *p41*
Rogers, Patrick 60; Massachusetts, 1847 ***5881.1*** *p86*
Rogers, Peter 28; New Orleans, 1830 ***778.5*** *p467*
Rogers, Phill.; Virginia, 1648 ***6219*** *p250*
Rogers, Richard; Arizona, 1890 ***2764.35*** *p59*
Rogers, Rose 2; St. John, N.B., 1849 ***5704.8*** *p49*
Rogers, Sarah; Philadelphia, 1865 ***5704.8*** *p198*
Rogers, Stephen; Shreveport, LA, 1877 ***7129*** *p45*
Rogers, Tho.; Virginia, 1637 ***6219*** *p8*
Rogers, Tho.; Virginia, 1637 ***6219*** *p114*
Rogers, Tho.; Virginia, 1639 ***6219*** *p159*
Rogers, Thomas; New York, NY, 1811 ***2859.11*** *p19*
With family
Rogers, Thomas; St. John, N.B., 1849 ***5704.8*** *p49*
Rogers, Thomas 20; Pennsylvania, Virginia or Maryland, 1723 ***3690.1*** *p194*
Rogers, William; New York, NY, 1865 ***5704.8*** *p193*
Rogers, William 21; Maryland, 1775 ***1219.7*** *p266*
Rogers, Wm.; Virginia, 1636 ***6219*** *p80*
Rogers, Wm.; Virginia, 1639 ***6219*** *p161*
Rogerson, Richard 18; America, 1706 ***2212*** *p46*
Rogge, . . .; Canada, 1776-1783 ***9786*** *p32*
Rogge, Johann Heinrich Wilhelm; America, 1850 ***4610.10*** *p139*
Rogge, Karl Heinrich; America, 1853 ***8582.3*** *p55*
Roggenbuck, Herman *SEE* Roggenbuck, Johann
Roggenbuck, Johann; America, 1839 ***3702.7*** *p305*
With wife
*Son:*Herman
With 4 children
Roggie, . . .; Canada, 1776-1783 ***9786*** *p32*
Roggwiller, Elias; Cincinnati, 1848 ***8582.1*** *p53*
Rogne, Olaf Erickson; Arkansas, 1918 ***95.2*** *p106*
Rogowski, Teodor; Boston, 1834 ***4606*** *p179*
Rogues, Miss 3; America, 1838 ***778.5*** *p467*
Rogues, Mme. 30; America, 1838 ***778.5*** *p467*
Rogues, Mr. 40; America, 1838 ***778.5*** *p467*
Rohault, Agathe 33; America, 1838 ***778.5*** *p467*
Rohde, . . .; Canada, 1776-1783 ***9786*** *p32*
Rohde, Johann Carl Friedrich Wilhelm; America, 1852 ***4610.10*** *p144*
Rohde, Lina 18; America, 1882 ***4610.10*** *p150*
Rohde, M. Louise Engel; America, 1881 ***4610.10*** *p150*
Rohe, Heinrich; Cincinnati, 1869-1887 ***8582*** *p26*
Rohenkohl, . . .; Ohio, 1832 ***8582.2*** *p49*
With family
Rohl, Theodor 28; New York, NY, 1862 ***9831.18*** *p16*
Rohl, Therese 29; New York, NY, 1862 ***9831.18*** *p16*
Rohleder, Martin; New York, 1754 ***3652*** *p80*
Rohlfing, Dietrich; Illinois, 1868 ***2896.5*** *p34*
Rohlfs, Anna Margarete; America, 1842 ***4815.7*** *p92*
Rohling, August L. 15; America, 1873 ***1450.2*** *p120A*
Rohling, Friedrich 16; New York, NY, 1867 ***3702.7*** *p571*
Rohmann, . . .; Canada, 1776-1783 ***9786*** *p32*
Rohmann, Friedrich; America, 1841 ***8582.1*** *p29*
Rohn, Elisabeth Langohr 83; America, 1897 ***1763*** *p48D*
Rohr, Caspar Friedrich; Quebec, 1776 ***9786*** *p263*
Rohr, Jacob; New York, NY, 1838 ***8208.4*** *p75*
Rohr, John Frederick; Philadelphia, 1758 ***9973.7*** *p33*
Rohrbach, Adam 17; America, 1853 ***9162.8*** *p37*
Rohre, Frank; Iroquois Co., IL, 1896 ***3455.1*** *p13*
Rohrer, Barbara; Pennsylvania, 1709-1710 ***4480*** *p311*

Rohrer, Catharina; Pennsylvania, 1750 ***2444*** *p173*
Roi, Anton Adolph Heinrich, II; Quebec, 1776 ***9786*** *p258*
Roily, Richard 28; Philadelphia, 1774 ***1219.7*** *p232*
Roin, Francois 40; Louisiana, 1820 ***778.5*** *p467*
Rojecki, . . .; New York, 1831 ***4606*** *p176*
Rokbey, Richard 20; Jamaica, 1721 ***3690.1*** *p194*
Roker, Thomas; Antigua (Antego), 1761 ***1219.7*** *p83*
Rokosz, Jan P.; Arkansas, 1918 ***95.2*** *p106*
Rolan, Juan 30; America, 1835 ***778.5*** *p467*
Roland, Mr. 25; New Orleans, 1822 ***778.5*** *p467*
Roland, Anne; Halifax, N.S., 1752 ***7074.6*** *p216*
Roland, August; Illinois, 1860 ***5012.39*** *p90*
Roland, Herman; Illinois, 1858 ***5012.39*** *p54*
Roland, J. B. 52; New Orleans, 1836 ***778.5*** *p467*
Roland, Jean-Jacques; Halifax, N.S., 1752 ***7074.6*** *p216*
Roland, Jean Jacques 60; Halifax, N.S., 1752 ***7074.6*** *p207*
With family of 4
Roland, Xavier; America, 1851 ***1450.2*** *p121A*
Role, George; Ohio, 1840 ***9892.11*** *p40*
Roles, Robert; Virginia, 1637 ***6219*** *p83*
Rolf oder Reinicke, Heinrich P. August; America, 1846 ***4610.10*** *p150*
Rolfe, John Jacob; Illinois, 1858-1905 ***5012.38*** *p98*
Rolfe, Mary 20; Jamaica, 1775 ***1219.7*** *p265*
Rolfe, Tho.; Virginia, 1635 ***6219*** *p26*
Rolfing, Christian; America, 1849 ***1450.2*** *p121A*
Rolfs, . . .; Canada, 1776-1783 ***9786*** *p32*
Rolfs, John Jacob; Illinois, 1858-1905 ***5012.38*** *p98*
Rolfsmeier, A. M. Louise Wilhelmine; America, 1887 ***4610.10*** *p161*
Rolfsmeier, A. M. Wilhelmine; America, 1887 ***4610.10*** *p161*
Rolfsmeier, Ernst Friedrich Wilhelm; America, 1907 ***4610.10*** *p118*
Rolfsmeier, Johann Heinrich Conrad; America, 1858 ***4610.10*** *p140*
Rolfsmeier, Louise Friederike Johanne; America, 1905 ***4610.10*** *p107*
Rolfsmeyer, Carl Ludwig; America, 1885 ***4610.10*** *p107*
Rolfsmeyer, Caroline Louise Charlotte; America, 1849 ***4610.10*** *p104*
Rolien, Mr. 22; New Orleans, 1832 ***778.5*** *p467*
Rolinck, Friederich; New York, NY, 1867 ***3702.7*** *p579*
Roling, Johann; Ohio, 1801-1802 ***8582.2*** *p55*
Rolings, Mr.; New York, NY, 1867 ***3702.7*** *p585*
Rolker, Johnn Friedrich; Cincinnati, 1869-1887 ***8582*** *p26*
Roll, Allowis; New York, 1853 ***1450.2*** *p121A*
Roll, Gustav 23; Kansas, 1872 ***5240.1*** *p53*
Roll, Henry 23; Kansas, 1892 ***5240.1*** *p77*
Roll, Jacob; South Carolina, 1788 ***7119*** *p200*
Roll, Jacob; South Carolina, 1788 ***7119*** *p201*
Roll, John 22; Maryland, 1774 ***1219.7*** *p214*
Rolland, A. 25; New Orleans, 1830 ***778.5*** *p467*
Rolland, Anne *SEE* Rolland, Jean-Jacques
Rolland, Anne-Catherine *SEE* Rolland, Jean-Jacques
Rolland, Catherine *SEE* Rolland, Jean-Jacques
Rolland, Catherine *SEE* Rolland, Jean-Jacques
Rolland, Faustin 23; New Orleans, 1839 ***778.5*** *p467*
Rolland, Henry; Charleston, SC, 1774 ***1639.20*** *p274*
Rolland, Jean-George *SEE* Rolland, Jean-Jacques
Rolland, Jean-Jacques 60; Halifax, N.S., 1752 ***7074.6*** *p212*
*Wife:*Catherine
*Child:*Jean-George
*Child:*Anne-Catherine
*Child:*Catherine
*Sister:*Anne
Rollando, J. 29; New Orleans, 1839 ***778.5*** *p467*
Roller, Anna Maria; America, 1751-1800 ***2444*** *p150*
Roller, Arnold; Washington, 1859-1920 ***2872.1*** *p34*
Roller, Caroline; Washington, 1859-1920 ***2872.1*** *p34*
Roller, Ed; Washington, 1859-1920 ***2872.1*** *p34*
Roller, Edmund; Washington, 1859-1920 ***2872.1*** *p34*
Roller, Erna; Washington, 1859-1920 ***2872.1*** *p34*
Roller, Ernest; Washington, 1859-1920 ***2872.1*** *p34*
Roller, Ferdinand; Washington, 1859-1920 ***2872.1*** *p34*
Roller, Fred; Washington, 1859-1920 ***2872.1*** *p34*
Roller, Fredrick William; Washington, 1859-1920 ***2872.1*** *p34*
Roller, Friedrick; Washington, 1859-1920 ***2872.1*** *p34*
Roller, Helen; Washington, 1859-1920 ***2872.1*** *p34*
Roller, Hertha; Washington, 1859-1920 ***2872.1*** *p34*
Roller, Jacob; New York, 1854 ***1450.2*** *p121A*
Roller, Jada; Washington, 1859-1920 ***2872.1*** *p34*
Roller, Johan; Washington, 1859-1920 ***2872.1*** *p34*
Roller, Mary; Washington, 1859-1920 ***2872.1*** *p34*
Roller, Mathilda; Washington, 1859-1920 ***2872.1*** *p34*
Roller, Olga; Washington, 1859-1920 ***2872.1*** *p34*
Roller, Otto; Washington, 1859-1920 ***2872.1*** *p34*
Rolles, William; Virginia, 1644 ***6219*** *p229*
Rollet, Louis; America, 1838 ***778.5*** *p468*
Rolliard, Francois 33; Louisiana, 1820 ***778.5*** *p468*
Rolling, Anna 62; America, 1838 ***778.5*** *p468*
Rolling, Charles 4; America, 1838 ***778.5*** *p468*
Rolling, Conrad 12; America, 1838 ***778.5*** *p468*
Rolling, Nicolas 30; America, 1838 ***778.5*** *p468*
Rollins, Eliz; Virginia, 1698 ***2212*** *p12*
Rollwagen, Louis; America, 1851 ***8582.3*** *p55*
Rolnick, George; Wisconsin, n.d. ***9675.7*** *p269*
Rolnicki, Teofil 17; New York, 1912 ***9980.29*** *p54*
Rolot, Mr. 19; New Orleans, 1839 ***778.5*** *p468*
Rolph, John 15; Philadelphia, 1774 ***1219.7*** *p233*
Rolph, Thomas 21; Philadelphia, 1774 ***1219.7*** *p233*
Rolph, William 22; Maryland, 1774 ***1219.7*** *p181*
Rolshaussen, . . .; Canada, 1776-1783 ***9786*** *p32*
Rolston, William; New York, NY, 1866 ***5704.8*** *p207*
Rolun, Mr. 22; New Orleans, 1832 ***778.5*** *p467*
Rom, Frank Joseph; Arkansas, 1918 ***95.2*** *p106*
Romain, Mr. 22; New Orleans, 1821 ***778.5*** *p468*
Romain, Ant. 21; New Orleans, 1839 ***778.5*** *p468*
Romain, J. L. 35; New Orleans, 1827 ***778.5*** *p468*
Roman, . . .; Canada, 1776-1783 ***9786*** *p43*
Romanac, John; New York, NY, 1835 ***8208.4*** *p6*
Romand, M. 47; Port uncertain, 1832 ***778.5*** *p468*
Romani, . . .; New York, 1831 ***4606*** *p176*
Romaniewski, Teodor; New York, 1835 ***4606*** *p180*
Romann, . . .; Canada, 1776-1783 ***9786*** *p43*
Romann, Andreas; Pennsylvania, 1750 ***2444*** *p205*
*Wife:*Maria Barbara Bapp
*Child:*Johann Jacob
*Child:*Elisabetha
*Child:*Johann Friedrich
*Child:*Susanna Margaretha
*Child:*Maria Barbara
Romann, Christoph; Philadelphia, 1779 ***8137*** *p13*
Romann, Elisabetha *SEE* Romann, Andreas
Romann, Johann Friedrich *SEE* Romann, Andreas
Romann, Johann Jacob *SEE* Romann, Andreas
Romann, Maria Barbara *SEE* Romann, Andreas
Romann, Maria Barbara Bapp *SEE* Romann, Andreas
Romann, Susanna Margaretha *SEE* Romann, Andreas
Romano, Joseppe; Arkansas, 1918 ***95.2*** *p106*
Romano, Michael; Colorado, 1899 ***9678.2*** *p165*
Romanovcky, John; America, 1900 ***7137*** *p169*
Romanovsky, Kazimer; Arkansas, 1918 ***95.2*** *p106*
Romanski, Joe; Arkansas, 1918 ***95.2*** *p106*
Rombke, Henry; Baltimore, 1841 ***2896.5*** *p34*
Rombold, Carl David; Kansas, 1888 ***5240.1*** *p36*
Rombold, Gottlob; Philadelphia Co., PA, 1886 ***5240.1*** *p37*
Romby, Peter; South Carolina, 1788 ***7119*** *p203*
Rome, George; Carolina, 1684 ***1639.20*** *p274*
Rome, J. B.; New Orleans, 1839 ***778.5*** *p468*
Romeo, Tony; Colorado, 1904 ***9678.2*** *p165*
Romer, . . .; Canada, 1776-1783 ***9786*** *p43*
Romer, . . .; New York, 1831 ***4606*** *p176*
Romer, Amalie Auguste 2 *SEE* Romer, Ernst Aug. Fr.
Romer, Ernst Aug. Fr. 31; New Orleans, 1839 ***9420.2*** *p168*
*Wife:*Joh. Henriette 27
*Child:*Joh. Emilie 4
*Child:*Amalie Auguste 2
Romer, Joh. Carl David 23; New Orleans, 1839 ***9420.2*** *p168*
Romer, Joh. Emilie 4 *SEE* Romer, Ernst Aug. Fr.
Romer, Joh. Henriette 27 *SEE* Romer, Ernst Aug. Fr.
Romer, Maria; America, 1897 ***1763*** *p40D*
Romerman, . . .; Canada, 1776-1783 ***9786*** *p32*
Romero, Fernando 22; America, 1829 ***778.5*** *p468*
Romero, Jesus M. 27; Arizona, 1890 ***2764.35*** *p59*
Romien, Alexandre 26; America, 1838 ***778.5*** *p468*
Rominger, Christina; Pennsylvania, 1750 ***2444*** *p205*
Romm, . . .; Canada, 1776-1783 ***9786*** *p32*
Rommann, Barbara; Pennsylvania, 1762 ***2444*** *p172*
Rommel, Charles; America, 1890 ***1450.2*** *p32B*
Rommel, Christoph; Port uncertain, 1749 ***2444*** *p205*
Rommel, Karl F., Jr.; New York, 1890 ***1450.2*** *p32B*
Rommell, Charles; Baltimore, 1833 ***1450.2*** *p121A*
Rompel, John F.; Illinois, 1892 ***5012.37*** *p62*
Rompelberg, Adolph; Iowa, 1866-1943 ***123.54*** *p75*
Romrodt, Carl von; Halifax, N.S., 1778 ***9786*** *p270*
Romrodt, Carl von; New York, 1776 ***9786*** *p270*
Romrodt, Wilhelm Ludwig von; Halifax, N.S., 1780 ***9786*** *p269*
Romrodt, Wilhelm Ludwig von; New York, 1776 ***9786*** *p269*
Romweber, Anton; Indiana, 1869-1887 ***8582*** *p26*
Ronald, George; Cape Fear, NC, 1738 ***1639.20*** *p274*
Ronan, John; America, 1742-1743 ***4971*** *p42*
Ronan, Patrick 26; Massachusetts, 1849 ***5881.1*** *p86*
Roncoroni, Giorgio 14; New York, NY, 1893 ***9026.4*** *p42*
Rondel, F. 22; New Orleans, 1822 ***778.5*** *p468*
Rondel, J. 50; America, 1825 ***778.5*** *p469*
Rondio, Michel 28; New Orleans, 1837 ***778.5*** *p469*
Rondot, Pierre Ph. Christophe 35; New Orleans, 1838 ***778.5*** *p469*
Ronell, Richd 20; America, 1703 ***2212*** *p38*
Roney, Catherine; New York, NY, 1816 ***2859.11*** *p41*
Roney, William 19; Philadelphia, 1803 ***53.26*** *p80*
Roney, William 21; Maryland, 1774 ***1219.7*** *p214*
Ronk, Nicholas; Wisconsin, n.d. ***9675.7*** *p269*
Ronk, Paul; Wisconsin, n.d. ***9675.7*** *p269*
Ronnebaum, J. H.; Cincinnati, 1834 ***8582.1*** *p52*
Ronner, John Reinhold; Philadelphia, 1742 ***3652*** *p55*
Ronot, Ana 42; America, 1838 ***778.5*** *p469*
Ronot, Antoine 12; America, 1838 ***778.5*** *p469*
Ronot, Clerre 3; America, 1838 ***778.5*** *p469*
Ronot, Francois 19; America, 1838 ***778.5*** *p469*
Ronot, Jean 5; America, 1838 ***778.5*** *p469*
Ronot, Jean 39; America, 1838 ***778.5*** *p469*
Ronot, Jeanne 5; America, 1838 ***778.5*** *p469*
Ronot, Marie 16; America, 1838 ***778.5*** *p469*
Ronot, Sophine 22; America, 1838 ***778.5*** *p469*
Ronsard, Isidore 17; America, 1836 ***778.5*** *p469*
Ronsheim, Ephraim; America, 1845 ***8582.3*** *p55*
Ronston, Jon.; Virginia, 1642 ***6219*** *p197*
Ronzich, Andro; Iowa, 1866-1943 ***123.54*** *p42*
Ronzo, Martin; Arkansas, 1918 ***95.2*** *p106*
Roob, Jacob; Wisconsin, n.d. ***9675.7*** *p269*
Rood, Joh. Jacob; Pennsylvania, 1717 ***3627*** *p10*
*Wife:*Maria Barbara Weber
*Child:*Johann Conrad
With sister & child
Rood, Johann Conrad *SEE* Rood, Joh. Jacob
Rood, Maria Barbara Weber *SEE* Rood, Joh. Jacob
Rood, Wm.; Virginia, 1642 ***6219*** *p191*
Roof, Joseph; Illinois, 1869 ***5012.38*** *p99*
Roof, Valentine 38; Kansas, 1880 ***5240.1*** *p62*
Rooff, Jacob 21 *SEE* Rooff, Jacob
Rooff, Jacob 48; Georgia, 1738 ***9332*** *p331*
*Son:*Jacob 21
*Daughter:*Margaretta 7
Rooff, Margaretta 7 *SEE* Rooff, Jacob
Rooke, William; Illinois, 1865 ***5012.38*** *p98*
Rookins, Jane Baxter *SEE* Rookins, Wm.
Rookins, Wm.; Virginia, 1636 ***6219*** *p28*
*Wife:*Jane Baxter
Rool, Agatha 22; Ohio, 1837 ***778.5*** *p469*
Rool, Joseph 25; Ohio, 1837 ***778.5*** *p469*
Rooney, Anne 9; Massachusetts, 1849 ***5881.1*** *p82*
Rooney, Catherine 20; Quebec, 1855 ***5704.8*** *p126*
Rooney, Eliza 11; Massachusetts, 1850 ***5881.1*** *p83*
Rooney, Elizabeth; Quebec, 1849 ***5704.8*** *p51*
Rooney, Ellen 45; Massachusetts, 1848 ***5881.1*** *p83*
Rooney, Grace 13; St. John, N.B., 1855 ***5704.8*** *p127*
Rooney, Henry 12; Quebec, 1849 ***5704.8*** *p51*
Rooney, Hugh; New York, NY, 1816 ***2859.11*** *p41*
Rooney, Jane 9; Quebec, 1849 ***5704.8*** *p51*
Rooney, John; America, 1742 ***4971*** *p17*
Rooney, John; Maryland, 1742 ***4971*** *p107*
Rooney, John 20; Philadelphia, 1854 ***5704.8*** *p123*
Rooney, Margaret; America, 1869 ***5704.8*** *p234*
Rooney, Margaret 6; Quebec, 1849 ***5704.8*** *p51*
Rooney, Mary; New York, NY, 1871 ***5704.8*** *p240*
Rooney, Mary; Quebec, 1849 ***5704.8*** *p51*
Rooney, Mary 7; Massachusetts, 1850 ***5881.1*** *p86*
Rooney, Michael; New York, NY, 1816 ***2859.11*** *p41*
Rooney, Owen 25; Quebec, 1855 ***5704.8*** *p126*
Rooney, P.J. 38; Arizona, 1905 ***9228.40*** *p14*
Rooney, Robert; Quebec, 1849 ***5704.8*** *p51*
Rooney, Thomas; America, 1742 ***4971*** *p17*
Rooney, Thomas; Maryland, 1742 ***4971*** *p107*
Rooney, Thomas 9; Quebec, 1849 ***5704.8*** *p51*
Roony, Charles; New York, NY, 1816 ***2859.11*** *p41*
Roony, John; Annapolis, MD, 1742 ***4971*** *p93*
Roony, John; New York, NY, 1816 ***2859.11*** *p41*
Roony, Sarah; New York, NY, 1816 ***2859.11*** *p41*
Roony, Thomas; Annapolis, MD, 1742 ***4971*** *p93*
Roos, Andrew J.; Illinois, 1863 ***7857*** *p7*
Roos, Andrew Peter; Pennsylvania, 1787 ***4525*** *p229*
Roos, Caspar; Pennsylvania, 1752 ***4525*** *p230*
*Relative:*Peter
Roos, Caspar; Pennsylvania, 1752 ***4525*** *p238*
*Brother:*Peter
Roos, Jacob; America, 1854 ***1450.2*** *p121A*
Roos, Joseph 22; West Virginia, 1903 ***9788.3*** *p20*
Roos, Joseph, Sr. 56; West Virginia, 1903 ***9788.3*** *p20*
Roos, Leonhart; Wheeling, WV, 1852 ***8582.3*** *p78*
Roos, Peter *SEE* Roos, Caspar
Roos, Peter *SEE* Roos, Caspar
Rooscher, Michael; Illinois, 1861 ***2896.5*** *p34*
Roose, . . .; Canada, 1776-1783 ***9786*** *p32*
Root, George; New York, NY, 1836 ***8208.4*** *p18*
Root, Louis 28; Kansas, 1895 ***5240.1*** *p80*
Roote, . . .; Virginia, 1641 ***6219*** *p186*
Rooth, . . .; Canada, 1776-1783 ***9786*** *p32*
Rooth, Mistrael 50; New Orleans, 1839 ***9420.2*** *p70*

446 *FOR A COMPLETE EXPLANATION OF ENTRY, SEE "HOW TO READ A CITATION" SECTION*

Ropart, Christian; Wisconsin, n.d. 9675.7 p269
Ropelli, Jan; Iowa, 1866-1943 123.54 p42
Roper, Catharine 32; Virginia, 1774 1219.7 p226
Roper, Phillipp; Virginia, 1618 6219 p200
Roper, Thomas 19; West Indies, 1698-1699 2212 p17
Roper, Wm.; Virginia, 1636 6219 p28
Ropeter, Henrich; Wisconsin, n.d. 9675.7 p269
Ropheds, Mme. 68; America, 1838 778.5 p470
Ropheds, Ms.; America, 1838 778.5 p470
Ropp, . . .; Canada, 1776-1783 9786 p32
Roppert, . . .; Canada, 1776-1783 9786 p32
Roppus, John; Indiana, 1844 9117 p18
Rorback, Frederick; New York, NY, 1839 8208.4 p90
Rorer, . . .; Canada, 1776-1783 9786 p32
Roresten, Mr. 28; New Orleans, 1838 778.5 p470
Rorety, John; St. John, N.B., 1848 5704.8 p44
Rorison, Basil D. 31; Kansas, 1870 5240.1 p51
Rorke, Bridget; Quebec, 1847 5704.8 p37
Rorke, Catherine; Quebec, 1847 5704.8 p37
Rorke, Edward; Quebec, 1847 5704.8 p37
Rorke, James; Quebec, 1847 5704.8 p37
Rorke, John; St. John, N.B., 1847 5704.8 p34
Rorke, Margaret; Quebec, 1847 5704.8 p37
Rorke, Mary; Quebec, 1847 5704.8 p37
Rorke, Mick; Quebec, 1847 5704.8 p37
Rorke, Pat; Quebec, 1847 5704.8 p37
Rorke, Patrick; New York, NY, 1811 2859.11 p19
Rortey, John; New York, NY, 1836 8208.4 p79
Rorthy, Daniel; New Brunswick, 1822 7603 p79
Rorthy, James; New Brunswick, 1824 7603 p79
Rosa, Francois 26; New Orleans, 1826 778.5 p470
Rosa, Peter; Savannah, GA, 1735 3652 p51
Rosander, Aron Albert; Minneapolis, 1880-1881 6410.35 p65
Rosander, Edgar Albert; Arkansas, 1918 95.2 p106
Rosberg, Frank E.; New York, NY, 1892 1450.2 p32B
Rosberg, Iver A.; Arkansas, 1918 95.2 p106
Rosboro, John; Quebec, 1847 5704.8 p36
Rosboro, Keatty; Quebec, 1847 5704.8 p36
Rosboro, Susan; Quebec, 1847 5704.8 p36
Rosborough, John; New York, NY, 1816 2859.11 p41
Rosch, Alexis 33; America, 1838 778.5 p470
Rosch, Charles 43; America, 1838 778.5 p470
Rosch, Delphine 30; America, 1838 778.5 p470
Rosch, Havier; New York, 1864 1450.2 p121A
Roschan, Philip; Pennsylvania, 1754 2444 p206
Rosche, Heinrich Wilhelm; America, 1854 4610.10 p151
Roschon, Philip; Pennsylvania, 1754 2444 p206
Rosdahl, Nels Emil; Arkansas, 1918 95.2 p106
Rose, . . .; Canada, 1776-1783 9786 p32
Rose, Alexander; America, 1738-1755 1639.20 p274
Rose, Babe C.; Arkansas, 1918 95.2 p106
Rose, Charles; Virginia, 1636 6219 p15
Rose, Daniel 14; Maryland, 1719 3690.1 p194
Rose, David; South Carolina, 1743 1639.20 p274
Rose, David 21; Maryland, 1775 1219.7 p250
Rose, Frederick; America, 1894 1450.2 p122A
Rose, Geo.; New York, NY, 1816 2859.11 p41
Rose, Godfried; Canada, 1776-1783 9786 p207A
Rose, Henry; Virginia, 1639 6219 p18
Rose, Henry; Virginia, 1639 6219 p157
Rose, Isadore; Arkansas, 1918 95.2 p106
Rose, Johannes; New Jersey, 1780 8137 p13
Rose, John; America, 1770-1779 8582.2 p34
Rose, John; Antigua (Antego), 1753 1219.7 p19
Rose, John; Montreal, 1863 9775.5 p203
Rose, John; Virginia, 1858 4626.16 p17
Rose, John 21; Jamaica, 1730 3690.1 p194
Rose, John 22; Maryland, 1774 1219.7 p229
Rose, Julius; Wisconsin, n.d. 9675.7 p269
Rose, Louis 36; Harris Co., TX, 1898 6254 p4
Rose, Luke; Carolina, 1772 1219.7 p155
Rose, Mabell; Virginia, 1639 6219 p154
Rose, Maria 26; Canada, 1838 4535.12 p113
Rose, Morice; Virginia, 1636 6219 p80
Rose, Morrice; Virginia, 1639 6219 p161
Rose, Peter; Pennsylvania, 1752 4525 p238
Rose, Robert 20; Carolina, 1774 1219.7 p179
Rose, Stephen; Antigua (Antego), 1755 1219.7 p34
Rose, Stephen 26; Virginia, 1775 1219.7 p261
Rose, Thomas 24; Jamaica, 1738 3690.1 p195
Rose, W. H. H.; Shreveport, LA, 1878 7129 p45
Rose, William 17; Maryland, 1721 3690.1 p194
Rose, Wm.; Virginia, 1637 6219 p113
Rose, Wm. 28; Canada, 1838 4535.12 p113
Rosebach, John; New York, NY, 1834 8208.4 p29
Rosebrock, Herman Henry; America, 1857 1450.2 p122A
Roseen, Anna Margaret SEE Roseen, Sven
Roseen, Sven; Delaware, 1746 3652 p68
  Wife:Anna Margaret
Rosehart, John; Wisconsin, n.d. 9675.7 p269
Roseina, Andrew; Arkansas, 1918 95.2 p106
Roseires, John; Virginia, 1649 6219 p253
Roselius, Henry; Iroquois Co., IL, 1892 3455.1 p13
Rosemann, Meier 18; New York, NY, 1878 9253 p46
Rosemann, Moses 16; New York, NY, 1878 9253 p46
Rosemeyer, . . .; Canada, 1776-1783 9786 p43
Rosemy, Henrich; Philadelphia, 1779 8137 p13
Rosen, Albert; Washington, 1859-1920 2872.1 p34
Rosen, Gust 34; Kansas, 1879 5240.1 p60
Rosen, Hillel 19; New York, NY, 1878 9253 p45
Rosen, Oscar F.; Colorado, 1904 9678.2 p165
Rosen, Patrick; Arkansas, 1918 95.2 p106
Rosenbaum, John; Illinois, 1860 5012.38 p97
Rosenbaum, Josef; Iowa, 1866-1943 123.54 p42
Rosenbaum, Nathan; Iowa, 1866-1943 123.54 p42
Rosenbaum, Sol; Iowa, 1866-1943 123.54 p42
Rosenbaum, William; Illinois, 1860 5012.39 p90
Rosenbeck, Reent; Illinois, 1894 5012.40 p53
Rosenberg, Capit.; Quebec, 1776 9786 p105
Rosenberg, Captain; Canada, 1776-1783 9786 p170
Rosenberg, Alexander; Cincinnati, 1869-1887 8582 p26
Rosenberg, Edna; Washington, 1859-1920 2872.1 p34
Rosenberg, Firve 19; New York, NY, 1878 9253 p47
Rosenberg, Friedrich Albrecht; Quebec, 1776 9786 p254
Rosenberg, H. 40; Harris Co., TX, 1898 6254 p3
Rosenberg, Hirsch 24; New York, NY, 1878 9253 p45
Rosenberg, John William; Washington, 1859-1920 2872.1 p34
Rosenberg, Maurice; Nebraska, 1870 2764.35 p59
Rosenberg, Oswald; Washington, 1859-1920 2872.1 p34
Rosenberg, Pankel 19; New York, NY, 1878 9253 p47
Rosenberg, Sadie Marie; Washington, 1859-1920 2872.1 p34
Rosenberger, . . .; Canada, 1776-1783 9786 p43
Rosenberger, Alois; Wisconsin, n.d. 9675.7 p269
Rosenberger, Hedwig; Wisconsin, n.d. 9675.7 p269
Rosenblad, John A.; Arkansas, 1918 95.2 p106
Rosenbloom, Clary; Kansas, 1887 5240.1 p37
Rosenbloom, Harry; New York, 1885 5240.1 p37
Rosenbrack, George; Kansas, 1916 6013.40 p17
Rosenbrock, Herman Cort; Kansas, 1916 6013.40 p17
Rosenburg, Hirsch 24; New York, NY, 1878 9253 p45
Rosencrantz, . . .; Canada, 1776-1783 9786 p32
Rosener, Anton Heinriah; New York, 1837 1450.2 p122A
Rosenfeld, . . .; New York, 1831 4606 p176
Rosenfeld, Max; New Jersey, 1893 1450.2 p122A
Rosenfeldt, Harry; America, 1882 1450.2 p122A
Rosengarten, O. 24; New York, NY, 1893 9026.4 p42
Rosenhagen, John 21; Kansas, 1892 5240.1 p37
Rosenhagen, John 21; Kansas, 1892 5240.1 p77
Rosenkohl, . . .; Ohio, 1832 8582.2 p49
  With family
Rosenkotter, Anne M. E. Vogelsang SEE Rosenkotter, Herm. Heinrich Caspar
Rosenkotter, Caspar Heinrich Samuel; America, 1844 4610.10 p134
Rosenkotter, Friederike SEE Rosenkotter, Friedrich Adolf
Rosenkotter, Friedrich Adolf; America, 1850 4610.10 p139
  Wife:Louise Homburg
  Child:Louise
  Child:Friederike
Rosenkotter, Herm. Heinrich Caspar; America, 1847 4610.10 p134
  Wife:Anne M. E. Vogelsang
  Child:Joh. Carl Friedrich
Rosenkotter, Joh. Carl Friedrich SEE Rosenkotter, Herm. Heinrich Caspar
Rosenkotter, Louise SEE Rosenkotter, Friedrich Adolf
Rosenkotter, Louise Homburg SEE Rosenkotter, Friedrich Adolf
Rosenlund, John; Iowa, 1866-1943 123.54 p42
Rosenmeier, Adolph; Indiana, 1848 9117 p19
Rosenquist, Erick Gustav 23; Arkansas, 1918 95.2 p106
Rosenstengel, Anne Marie C. Muller; America, 1846 4610.10 p95
  Son:Karl Heinrich L. Ernst
Rosenstengel, Karl Heinrich L. Ernst SEE Rosenstengel, Anne Marie C. Muller
Rosenstengel, Nicholas; Ohio, 1894 1450.2 p33B
Rosenstiel, L. S.; Cincinnati, 1869-1887 8582 p26
Rosenstock, Charles; Wisconsin, n.d. 9675.7 p269
Rosenthal, . . .; Canada, 1776-1783 9786 p32
Rosenthal, Adolph; New York, 1848 1450.2 p122A
Rosenthal, Carl H. Friedrich Wilhelm; America, 1887 4610.10 p103
  Wife:Christine Piepenbrink
  Child:Caroline Wilhelmine
  Child:Caroline F. Charlotte
Rosenthal, Caroline F. Charlotte SEE Rosenthal, Carl H. Friedrich Wilhelm
Rosenthal, Caroline Wilhelmine SEE Rosenthal, Carl H. Friedrich Wilhelm
Rosenthal, Christine Piepenbrink SEE Rosenthal, Carl H. Friedrich Wilhelm
Rosenthal, Christoph; America, 1847 8582.1 p29
Rosenthal, Jacob; Arkansas, 1918 95.2 p106
Rosenthal, Joseph; America, 1854 8582.3 p55
Rosenthal, W.; Wheeling, WV, 1852 8582.3 p78
Rosenthaler, Maurice; Illinois, 1871 5012.39 p25
Rosenthall, August; Baltimore, 1834 1450.2 p122A
Rosenzweig, Joseph; America, 1894 1450.2 p122A
Roseto, Ant. L. 30; New Orleans, 1829 778.5 p470
Rosfeld, Frank; America, 1892 5240.1 p37
Rosfeld, John; America, 1892 5240.1 p37
Rosfeld, Peter; America, 1892 5240.1 p37
Rosfeld, Peter; Kansas, 1893 5240.1 p37
Roshan, Hendrick 20 SEE Roshan, Peter
Roshan, Peter 22; Pennsylvania, 1753 2444 p206
  Brother:Hendrick 20
Roshlacherin, Christina; Georgia, 1738 9332 p320
Roshon, Hendrick 20 SEE Roshon, Peter
Roshon, Peter 22; Pennsylvania, 1753 2444 p206
  Brother:Hendrick 20
Roshong, Hendrick 20 SEE Roshong, Peter
Roshong, Peter 22; Pennsylvania, 1753 2444 p206
  Brother:Hendrick 20
Roshong, Philip; Pennsylvania, 1754 2444 p206
Rosian, Henry; America, 1887 7137 p169
Rosian, Mary A.; America, 1888 7137 p169
Rosie, Elizabeth M.; Wisconsin, n.d. 9675.7 p269
Rosienkiewicz, Marcin; New York, 1831 4606 p176
Rosier, G. 19; New Orleans, 1832 778.5 p470
Rosier, John; Virginia, 1652 6251 p20
Rosier, Morgan; Virginia, 1637 6219 p108
Rosier, Morgin; Virginia, 1636 6219 p74
Rosilia, Mme. 20; America, 1838 778.5 p470
Rosin, Albert; Washington, 1859-1920 2872.1 p34
Rosin, F. W.; Washington, 1859-1920 2872.1 p34
Rosin, Kristin; Maine, 1871-1882 6410.22 p118
Rosindall, Robert; Jamaica, 1765 1219.7 p115
Rosine, Ms. 28; New Orleans, 1839 778.5 p470
Rosinski, John; Arkansas, 1918 95.2 p106
Rosinski, Joseph 21; New York, 1912 9980.29 p52
Roska, George; Wisconsin, n.d. 9675.7 p269
Roska, John; Wisconsin, n.d. 9675.7 p269
Rosman, Christian; America, 1775-1781 8582.3 p77
Rosman, Frank; Arkansas, 1918 95.2 p106
Rosman, Martin; New York, NY, 1816 2859.11 p41
Rosmann, Heinrich; Trenton, NJ, 1775-1781 8582.3 p75
Rosmann, Johann Christoph; America, 1775-1781 8582.3 p77
Rosmenson, Peter; Wisconsin, n.d. 9675.7 p269
Rosnowski, . . .; New York, 1831 4606 p176
Roso, Nick; Arkansas, 1918 95.2 p106
Roson, Ellen 20; America, 1701 2212 p34
Rosowski, Alfred; Wisconsin, n.d. 9675.7 p269
Ross, Mr.; Quebec, 1815 9229.18 p74
Ross, Mr.; Quebec, 1815 9229.18 p82
Ross, A. M.; Washington, 1859-1920 2872.1 p34
Ross, Agnes 21; North Carolina, 1736 1639.20 p274
Ross, Agnes 21; North Carolina, 1736 3690.1 p195
Ross, Alexander; Nova Scotia, 1830 7085.4 p45
  Wife:Anne
  Child:Mary
  Child:John
  Child:Donald
  Child:Bain.
  Child:Flora
Ross, Alexandre; Quebec, 1774 7603 p41
Ross, Andrew; Charleston, SC, 1803 1639.20 p274
Ross, Andrew W.; Iowa, 1866-1943 123.54 p42
Ross, Angus SEE Ross, John
Ross, Anne SEE Ross, Alexander
Ross, Archie SEE Ross, Marion Morrison
Ross, Bain. SEE Ross, Alexander
Ross, Bell SEE Ross, John
Ross, Charles; South Carolina, 1716 1639.20 p275
Ross, Charles 62; North Carolina, 1850 1639.20 p275
Ross, Christy SEE Ross, John
Ross, David; Iowa, 1866-1943 123.54 p42
Ross, David; Philadelphia, 1864 5704.8 p179
Ross, David 16; Massachusetts, 1847 5881.1 p83
Ross, David 24; Philadelphia, 1833-1834 53.26 p80
Ross, David 24; Philadelphia, 1833-1834 53.26 p80
  Relative:Jane 26
Ross, David 27; Jamaica, 1736 3690.1 p195
Ross, David 30; Kansas, 1890 5240.1 p75
Ross, Donald SEE Ross, Alexander
Ross, Donald SEE Ross, William
Ross, Donald; Nova Scotia, 1830 7085.4 p44
  Wife:Ket
  Child:Ket
  Child:Margaret
  Child:Mary
Ross, E. W.; Washington, 1859-1920 2872.1 p34

Ross, Eleanor *SEE* Ross, Joseph
Ross, Eleanor; Philadelphia, 1811 ***2859.11*** *p19*
Ross, Elizabeth 17; Philadelphia, 1853 ***5704.8*** *p112*
Ross, Flora *SEE* Ross, Alexander
Ross, George 31; West Virginia, 1894 ***9788.3*** *p20*
Ross, Guillaume; Quebec, 1764 ***7603*** *p39*
Ross, James; Charleston, SC, 1823 ***1639.20*** *p275*
Ross, James; New York, NY, 1811 ***2859.11*** *p19*
Ross, James; New York, NY, 1816 ***2859.11*** *p41*
Ross, James; Philadelphia, 1819 ***1639.20*** *p275*
Ross, James 16; Wilmington, DE, 1831 ***6508.7*** *p160*
Ross, James 18; Philadelphia, 1853 ***5704.8*** *p108*
Ross, James 40; Charleston, SC, 1850 ***1639.20*** *p275*
Ross, Jane 16; Philadelphia, 1857 ***5704.8*** *p134*
Ross, Jane 21; Nevis, 1774 ***1219.7*** *p237*
Ross, Jane 26 *SEE* Ross, David
Ross, Jane 30; St. John, N.B., 1864 ***5704.8*** *p158*
Ross, Johann Casber; Pennsylvania, 1753 ***4525*** *p238*
Ross, John *SEE* Ross, Alexander
Ross, John; America, 1737 ***4971*** *p77*
Ross, John; Charleston, SC, 1783-1810 ***1639.20*** *p275*
Ross, John; Iowa, 1866-1943 ***123.54*** *p77*
Ross, John; New England, 1770 ***1219.7*** *p147*
Ross, John; Nova Scotia, 1830 ***7085.4*** *p44*
*Wife:*Mary
Ross, John; Nova Scotia, 1830 ***7085.4*** *p45*
*Wife:*Mary
*Child:*Mary
*Child:*Angus
*Child:*Christy
*Child:*Bell
*Child:*Murdo
Ross, John; St. John, N.B., 1848 ***5704.8*** *p44*
Ross, John 18; Philadelphia, 1857 ***5704.8*** *p134*
Ross, John 47; Wilmington, NC, 1774 ***1639.20*** *p275*
With 4 children
With child 20
With child 5
Ross, Joseph; Colorado, 1904 ***9678.2*** *p166*
Ross, Joseph; Philadelphia, 1811 ***53.26*** *p80*
*Relative:*Eleanor
Ross, Joseph; Philadelphia, 1811 ***2859.11*** *p19*
Ross, Katherine; Louisiana, 1849 ***8893*** *p263*
Ross, Ket *SEE* Ross, Donald
Ross, Ket *SEE* Ross, Donald
Ross, Kirsty *SEE* Ross, William
Ross, Margaret *SEE* Ross, Donald
Ross, Margaret *SEE* Ross, William
Ross, Margaret 2; St. John, N.B., 1848 ***5704.8*** *p47*
Ross, Margaret MacDonald *SEE* Ross, William
Ross, Marion Morrison; Quebec, 1886-1889 ***4537.30*** *p37*
*Child:*Archie
*Child:*Peter
*Child:*Mary
*Child:*Mary Ann
*Child:*Sam
Ross, Mary *SEE* Ross, Alexander
Ross, Mary *SEE* Ross, Donald
Ross, Mary *SEE* Ross, John
Ross, Mary *SEE* Ross, John
Ross, Mary *SEE* Ross, John
Ross, Mary *SEE* Ross, Marion Morrison
Ross, Mary; New York, NY, 1811 ***2859.11*** *p19*
Ross, Mary; New York, NY, 1864 ***5704.8*** *p187*
Ross, Mary; New York, NY, 1865 ***5704.8*** *p194*
Ross, Mary; Quebec, 1816 ***7603*** *p88*
Ross, Mary; St. John, N.B., 1848 ***5704.8*** *p47*
Ross, Mary 55 *SEE* Ross, William
Ross, Mary Ann *SEE* Ross, Marion Morrison
Ross, Matty; St. John, N.B., 1848 ***5704.8*** *p47*
Ross, Murdo *SEE* Ross, John
Ross, Nat 12; St. John, N.B., 1848 ***5704.8*** *p47*
Ross, Nathan; Arkansas, 1918 ***95.2*** *p106*
Ross, Patrick 35; Wilmington, NC, 1774 ***1639.20*** *p275*
Ross, Peter *SEE* Ross, Marion Morrison
Ross, Peter; Pennsylvania, 1752 ***4525*** *p238*
Ross, Richard; Philadelphia, 1864 ***5704.8*** *p179*
Ross, Robert; Iowa, 1866-1943 ***123.54*** *p42*
Ross, Robert; Philadelphia, 1849 ***53.26*** *p80*
Ross, Robert 15; Maryland, 1774 ***1219.7*** *p225*
Ross, Sam *SEE* Ross, Marion Morrison
Ross, Sarah 26; South Carolina, 1734 ***3690.1*** *p195*
Ross, Thomas; Iowa, 1866-1943 ***123.54*** *p42*
Ross, Thomas; St. John, N.B., 1848 ***5704.8*** *p47*
Ross, Thomas; South Carolina, 1716 ***1639.20*** *p276*
Ross, Thomas 24; Jamaica, 1738 ***3690.1*** *p195*
Ross, William; Arkansas, 1918 ***95.2*** *p107*
Ross, William; Charleston, SC, 1803 ***1639.20*** *p276*
Ross, William; Iowa, 1866-1943 ***123.54*** *p42*
Ross, William; New York, NY, 1811 ***2859.11*** *p19*
With wife & 4 children
Ross, William; Philadelphia, 1811 ***53.26*** *p80*
Ross, William; Philadelphia, 1811 ***2859.11*** *p19*
Ross, William; Philadelphia, 1867 ***5704.8*** *p220*
Ross, William; Quebec, 1863 ***4537.30*** *p37*
*Wife:*Margaret MacDonald
*Child:*Donald
*Child:*Margaret
*Child:*Kirsty
Ross, William; St. John, N.B., 1848 ***5704.8*** *p39*
Ross, William 18; Jamaica, 1738 ***3690.1*** *p195*
Ross, William 40; Philadelphia, 1774 ***1219.7*** *p216*
Ross, William 60; South Carolina, 1850 ***1639.20*** *p276*
Ross, William 75; South Carolina, 1850 ***1639.20*** *p276*
*Relative:*Mary 55
Ross, William G.; New York, NY, 1849 ***6013.19*** *p73*
Rossan, John; Philadelphia, 1865 ***5704.8*** *p203*
Rossan, Margaret; Philadelphia, 1865 ***5704.8*** *p203*
Rossbacher, Barbara; Georgia, 1739 ***9332*** *p323*
Rosse, James; Virginia, 1642 ***6219*** *p191*
Rosse, Thomas; Virginia, 1642 ***6219*** *p194*
Rosse, Thomas 35; Maryland, 1775 ***1219.7*** *p268*
Rossen, Christian; New York, NY, 1837 ***8208.4*** *p45*
Rosser, Fr.; Virginia, 1643 ***6219*** *p200*
Rosser, John; Colorado, 1894 ***9678.2*** *p166*
Rosseter, James; Georgia, 1766 ***1219.7*** *p117*
Rossetti, Nicola; Arkansas, 1918 ***95.2*** *p107*
Rosshausen, . . .; Canada, 1776-1783 ***9786*** *p32*
Rossi, Antoni; Arizona, 1897 ***9228.30*** *p3*
Rossi, Cheribina 22; New York, NY, 1893 ***9026.4*** *p42*
*Relative:*G.B. 17
Rossi, G.B. 17 *SEE* Rossi, Cheribina
Rossi, Pietro 22; West Virginia, 1904 ***9788.3*** *p20*
Rossier, Mr. 25; Port uncertain, 1836 ***778.5*** *p470*
Rossignol, Antoine 22; Port uncertain, 1839 ***778.5*** *p470*
Rossmann, . . .; Canada, 1776-1783 ***9786*** *p32*
Rossmann, Jakob; America, 1783 ***8582.3*** *p77*
Rossmann, Johannes; America, 1775-1781 ***8582.3*** *p77*
Rossmann, Konrad; America, 1775-1781 ***8582.3*** *p77*
Rossner, Mrs.; America, n.d. ***5647.5*** *p3*
*Child:*Peter
*Child:*Henry
*Child:*Sophia
*Child:*Lizzie
*Child:*Louisa
Rossner, Christine Bard; America, 1847 ***5647.5*** *p23*
*Child:*Louisa
*Child:*Elizabeth
*Child:*Sophia
*Child:*Peter J.
*Child:*Henry
Rossner, Elizabeth *SEE* Rossner, Christine Bard
Rossner, George; Indiana, 1837 ***5647.5*** *p4*
Rossner, Henry *SEE* Rossner, Mrs.
Rossner, Henry *SEE* Rossner, Christine Bard
Rossner, Henry; America, n.d. ***5647.5*** *p3*
Rossner, Kate; America, n.d. ***5647.5*** *p3*
Rossner, Lizzie *SEE* Rossner, Mrs.
Rossner, Louisa *SEE* Rossner, Mrs.
Rossner, Louisa *SEE* Rossner, Christine Bard
Rossner, Peter *SEE* Rossner, Mrs.
Rossner, Peter; Died enroute, n.d. ***5647.5*** *p3*
Rossner, Peter; Died enroute, 1847 ***5647.5*** *p23*
Rossner, Peter J. *SEE* Rossner, Christine Bard
Rossner, Sophia *SEE* Rossner, Mrs.
Rossner, Sophia *SEE* Rossner, Christine Bard
Rost, . . .; Canada, 1776-1783 ***9786*** *p32*
Rost, Mr.; Port uncertain, 1839 ***778.5*** *p470*
Rost, Frederick; New York, 1882 ***1450.2*** *p33B*
Rost, Georg; America, 1840-1845 ***8582*** *p26*
Rostaing, C. 34; America, 1839 ***778.5*** *p471*
Rostainq, Christophe 29; Texas, 1839 ***778.5*** *p471*
Rostello, Felice; Iowa, 1866-1943 ***123.54*** *p42*
Rostello, Leugi; Iowa, 1866-1943 ***123.54*** *p77*
Rostello, Luigi; Iowa, 1866-1943 ***123.54*** *p77*
Rostkowski, Woyciech; New York, 1831 ***4606*** *p176*
Roston, Max; Arkansas, 1918 ***95.2*** *p107*
Rostorah, Margaret 12; St. John, N.B., 1852 ***5704.8*** *p93*
Rostowski, Julius; Wisconsin, n.d. ***9675.7*** *p269*
Rostron, John; New York, NY, 1838 ***8208.4*** *p74*
Roswell, Charles; Washington, 1859-1920 ***2872.1*** *p34*
Roswell, Cora; Washington, 1859-1920 ***2872.1*** *p34*
Roswell, Frank; Washington, 1859-1920 ***2872.1*** *p34*
Roswell, Lillian; Washington, 1859-1920 ***2872.1*** *p34*
Roswell, Melissa; Washington, 1859-1920 ***2872.1*** *p34*
Roswell, Oscar; Washington, 1859-1920 ***2872.1*** *p34*
Roswell, Pearl; Washington, 1859-1920 ***2872.1*** *p34*
Roswinkel, Hermann; America, 1847 ***8582.3*** *p55*
Roszel, Charles; Kansas, 1909 ***6013.40*** *p16*
Rotatore, Ernesto; Wisconsin, n.d. ***9675.7*** *p269*
Rotchford, Dennis; Pennsylvania, 1682 ***4961*** *p165*
*Wife:*Mary Heriott
Rotchford, Grace 3; Died enroute, 1682 ***4961*** *p165*
*Sister:*Mary 6 mos
Rotchford, Mary 6 mos *SEE* Rotchford, Grace
Rotchford, Mary Heriott *SEE* Rotchford, Dennis
Rotchschild, A.; Shreveport, LA, 1878 ***7129*** *p45*
Roteburger, Johan; Philadelphia, 1754 ***2444*** *p206*
Rotelle, Francois 25; Port uncertain, 1836 ***778.5*** *p471*
Rotenbach, Maria Catharina; Port uncertain, 1754 ***2444*** *p160*
Rotenbarger, Michael; Ohio, 1851 ***9892.11*** *p40*
Rotert, Franz Heinrich; America, 1839 ***8582.3*** *p55*
Rotert, Franz Heinrich; Kentucky, 1838 ***8582.3*** *p99*
Roth, . . .; Canada, 1776-1783 ***9786*** *p32*
Roth, . . .; Philadelphia, 1860 ***2691.4*** *p168*
Roth, Jr. 8; Louisiana, 1820 ***778.5*** *p471*
Roth, Mr.; Ohio, 1800-1817 ***8582.3*** *p81*
With wife
Roth, Mr. 45; Louisiana, 1820 ***778.5*** *p471*
Roth, Adam; Philadelphia, 1777-1779 ***8137*** *p13*
Roth, Adam 26; America, 1853 ***9162.8*** *p37*
Roth, Anna Elisabeth; New York, 1717 ***3627*** *p9*
Roth, Anna Marg. 29; America, 1853 ***9162.8*** *p37*
Roth, Anna Maria; New York, 1749 ***3652*** *p73*
Roth, Anna Maria Hoermann *SEE* Roth, Gottlieb
Roth, Balthas; Pennsylvania, 1752 ***2444*** *p206*
*Wife:*Maria Catharina
*Child:*Jerg Friedrich
*Child:*Maria Catharina
Roth, Balthasar; Cincinnati, 1869-1887 ***8582*** *p26*
Roth, Barbara *SEE* Roth, Christian
Roth, Carolina 48; New York, 1881 ***3702.7*** *p464*
Roth, Cath. 73; America, 1895 ***1763*** *p40D*
Roth, Catharina *SEE* Roth, Gottlieb
Roth, Charles; Indiana, 1850 ***9117*** *p20*
Roth, Chris; Kansas, 1904 ***5240.1*** *p37*
Roth, Christian; America, 1739-1799 ***2444*** *p206*
*Wife:*Barbara
*Child:*Margaretha Barbara
*Child:*Johann Georg
*Child:*Johann Michael
Roth, Christian; Pennsylvania, 1753-1800 ***2444*** *p206*
Roth, Elis. 4; America, 1853 ***9162.8*** *p37*
Roth, Elisabetha; America, 1755-1800 ***2444*** *p144*
Roth, Franz; Pittsburgh, 1882 ***3702.7*** *p476*
Roth, Frederick; New York, NY, 1840 ***8208.4*** *p109*
Roth, Gottlieb; Pennsylvania, 1751 ***2444*** *p206*
*Wife:*Anna Maria Hoermann
*Child:*Catharina
Roth, Gregor; Cincinnati, 1869-1887 ***8582*** *p26*
Roth, Heinrich; America, 1847 ***8582.1*** *p29*
Roth, J.; Wheeling, WV, 1852 ***8582.3*** *p78*
Roth, Jacob 25; New Orleans, 1836 ***778.5*** *p471*
Roth, Jacob 48; New Orleans, 1839 ***778.5*** *p471*
Roth, Jakob; Cincinnati, 1829 ***8582.1*** *p51*
Roth, Jakob 19; America, 1850 ***3702.7*** *p465*
Roth, Jerg Friedrich *SEE* Roth, Balthas
Roth, Joh. Jacob; Pennsylvania, 1717 ***3627*** *p10*
*Wife:*Maria Barbara Weber
*Child:*Johann Conrad
With sister & child
Roth, Johann; America, 1869-1885 ***8582.2*** *p69*
Roth, Johann; Illinois, 1838 ***8582.2*** *p50*
Roth, Johann Conrad *SEE* Roth, Joh. Jacob
Roth, Johann Georg *SEE* Roth, Christian
Roth, Johann Georg; Philadelphia, 1782 ***8137*** *p13*
Roth, Johann Michael *SEE* Roth, Christian
Roth, John; Illinois, 1877 ***2896.5*** *p34*
Roth, John; Kansas, 1891 ***5240.1*** *p37*
Roth, John; New York, 1756 ***3652*** *p81*
Roth, John; Philadelphia, 1837 ***8582.2*** *p34*
Roth, John; Washington, 1859-1920 ***2872.1*** *p34*
Roth, Karl 70; New York, NY, 1897 ***1763*** *p40D*
Roth, Margaretha Barbara *SEE* Roth, Christian
Roth, Maria; Pennsylvania, 1751-1800 ***2444*** *p182*
Roth, Maria Barbara Weber *SEE* Roth, Joh. Jacob
Roth, Maria Catharina *SEE* Roth, Balthas
Roth, Maria Catharina *SEE* Roth, Balthas
Roth, Mary 54; America, 1895 ***1763*** *p48D*
Roth, Michael; America, 1741 ***4971*** *p31*
Roth, Sebastian 20; New Orleans, 1835 ***778.5*** *p471*
Roth, Valentin; America, 1849 ***8582.3*** *p55*
Rothacker, W.; Wheeling, WV, 1852 ***8582.3*** *p78*
Rothacker, Wilhelm; Wheeling, WV, 1850-1852 ***8582.1*** *p41*
Rothan, John; Cincinnati, 1869-1887 ***8582*** *p26*
Rothe, Chr. Gottlob; Wisconsin, n.d. ***9675.7*** *p269*
Rothe, Emil; America, 1849 ***8582.2*** *p35*
Rothelem, Wilhelm; Kansas, 1892 ***5240.1*** *p37*
Rothell, Jno; Virginia, 1698 ***2212*** *p15*
Rothenberger, Catharina Piedler *SEE* Rothenberger, Stephan
Rothenberger, Nicol; Georgia, 1738 ***9332*** *p319*
Rothenberger, Stephan; Georgia, 1739 ***9332*** *p324*
*Wife:*Catharina Piedler
Rothenbuchen, Ant. 63; America, 1839 ***778.5*** *p471*
Rothenburger, Johannes; Philadelphia, 1754 ***2444*** *p206*

Rothenhaeuser, Friedr. 15; America, 1854-1855 ***9162.6*** *p105*
Rothenhaeuser, Georg. 38; America, 1854-1855 ***9162.6*** *p105*
Rothenhaeuser, Magdal. 13; America, 1854-1855 ***9162.6*** *p105*
Rothenhaeuser, Marie Elis. 40; America, 1854-1855 ***9162.6*** *p105*
Rothenhoefer, Jacob Friederich; America, 1854 ***8582.3*** *p55*
Rotheram, Geo.; Virginia, 1635 ***6219*** *p3*
Rothermel, Heinr. 86; Canada, 1901 ***1763*** *p48D*
Rothermel, Kath. 18; America, 1853 ***9162.7*** *p15*
Rothermel, Ludwig 16; America, 1853 ***9162.7*** *p15*
Rothert, August; America, 1837 ***8582.3*** *p56*
Rothert, Herman; America, 1837 ***8582.3*** *p56*
Rothert, Johann Heinrich; Cincinnati, 1869-1887 ***8582*** *p26*
Rotherum, Geo.; Virginia, 1637 ***6219*** *p86*
Rothett, John 19; New England, 1699 ***2212*** *p19*
Rothford, Dennis; Pennsylvania, 1682 ***4961*** *p165*
*Wife:*Mary Heriott
Rothford, Grace 3; Died enroute, 1682 ***4961*** *p165*
*Sister:*Mary 6 mos
Rothford, Mary 6 mos *SEE* Rothford, Grace
Rothford, Mary Heriott *SEE* Rothford, Dennis
Rothfuss, Friederich; America, 1850 ***8582.2*** *p35*
Rothhoefer, Johann; Kentucky, 1840-1845 ***8582.3*** *p100*
Rothmann, Miss; America, 1854 ***4610.10*** *p145*
Rothmeyer, Ehrhard; Charleston, SC, 1775-1781 ***8582.2*** *p52*
Rothschild, Jacob 38; New York, NY, 1878 ***9253*** *p45*
Rothweiler, Anna Maria; Pennsylvania, 1753 ***2444*** *p137*
Rotmann, Johann; South Carolina, 1752 ***7829*** *p8*
Rotn, Moli 18; New York, NY, 1878 ***9253*** *p47*
Rotn, Nathan 22; New York, NY, 1878 ***9253*** *p47*
Rott, Barbara; South Dakota, 1889 ***1641*** *p43*
Rottenari, Karolina 59; Kansas, 1887 ***5240.1*** *p71*
Rottenberger, Catharina *SEE* Rottenberger, Stephen
Rottenberger, Stephan; Georgia, 1738 ***9332*** *p321*
Rottenberger, Stephen; Georgia, 1739 ***9332*** *p326*
*Wife:*Catharina
Rottmann, Anne M. L. Wilhelmine 19 *SEE* Rottmann, Johann Ernst H. Gottlieb
Rottmann, Carl Heinrich; America, 1853 ***4610.10*** *p144*
Rottmann, Johann Dietrich; America, 1855 ***4610.10*** *p145*
With wife
With 2 children
Rottmann, Johann E. H. Gottlieb *SEE* Rottmann, Johann Ernst H. Gottlieb
Rottmann, Johann Ernst H. Gottlieb 45; America, 1855 ***4610.10*** *p139*
With wife
*Child:*Anne M. L. Wilhelmine 19
*Child:*Johann E. H. Gottlieb
Rottwilm, Anne M. C. L. Scheidt *SEE* Rottwilm, Johann Diederich
Rottwilm, Carl Ludwig; America, 1854 ***4610.10*** *p121*
Rottwilm, Franz Heinrich August *SEE* Rottwilm, Johann Diederich
Rottwilm, Johann Diederich; America, 1842 ***4610.10*** *p146*
*Wife:*Anne M. C. L. Scheidt
*Son:*Franz Heinrich August
Rotzenborn, F.; Cincinnati, 1869-1887 ***8582*** *p26*
Rotzenborn, Wilhelm; Cincinnati, 1869-1887 ***8582*** *p26*
Rouanick, Pierre 27; America, 1829 ***778.5*** *p471*
Rouch, Richard; Virginia, 1643 ***6219*** *p199*
Rouchard, Mr. 19; New Orleans, 1839 ***778.5*** *p471*
Rouche, . . .; Canada, 1776-1783 ***9786*** *p32*
Rouchon, Henri 20 *SEE* Rouchon, Pierre
Rouchon, Madeleine; Pennsylvania, 1753 ***2444*** *p144*
Rouchon, Marie *SEE* Rouchon, Philippe
Rouchon, Marie Talmon *SEE* Rouchon, Philippe
Rouchon, Philippe; Pennsylvania, 1754 ***2444*** *p206*
Rouchon, Philippe; Port uncertain, 1754 ***2444*** *p206*
*Wife:*Marie Talmon
*Child:*Marie
Rouchon, Pierre 22; Pennsylvania, 1753 ***2444*** *p206*
*Brother:*Henri 20
Roudini, Domenic; Wisconsin, n.d. ***9675.7*** *p269*
Roueche, Henry 30; America, 1839 ***778.5*** *p471*
Roueche, Jean 20; America, 1839 ***778.5*** *p471*
Rouelle, Victor 17; America, 1835 ***778.5*** *p471*
Rouellin, John; Washington, 1859-1920 ***2872.1*** *p34*
Roufe, Symon; Virginia, 1638 ***6219*** *p117*
Roufmann, Emanuel 21; America, 1836 ***778.5*** *p471*
Rougera, Mr. 30; America, 1839 ***778.5*** *p472*
Rougez, Therese 17; New Orleans, 1838 ***778.5*** *p472*
Roughan, John; America, 1849 ***1450.2*** *p121A*
Roughton, Henry; Illinois, 1860 ***5012.39*** *p90*
Roughton, John; Illinois, 1858 ***5012.39*** *p54*
Roughton, Samuel; Illinois, 1860 ***5012.39*** *p90*
Roughton, Thomas; Illinois, 1860 ***5012.39*** *p89*
Rougier, J. 25; America, 1823 ***778.5*** *p472*
Rouig, Antoine 26; Port uncertain, 1838 ***778.5*** *p472*
Rouillier, Mr. 20; America, 1838 ***778.5*** *p472*
Roules, Jean Francois 37; New Orleans, 1838 ***778.5*** *p472*
Roules, Joly 47; New Orleans, 1838 ***778.5*** *p472*
Roulette, Bernard 35; New Orleans, 1821 ***778.5*** *p472*
Roulette, George; New York, NY, 1840 ***8208.4*** *p109*
Roulin, Mr. 35; Louisiana, 1825 ***778.5*** *p472*
Roullet, Mr. 16; New Orleans, 1829 ***778.5*** *p472*
Roulston, David; Philadelphia, 1851 ***5704.8*** *p77*
Roulston, Deborah 22; St. John, N.B., 1856 ***5704.8*** *p131*
Roulston, James; Quebec, 1849 ***5704.8*** *p51*
Roulston, James 3; St. John, N.B., 1853 ***5704.8*** *p106*
Roulston, Jane; Quebec, 1849 ***5704.8*** *p51*
Roulston, John; New York, NY, 1865 ***5704.8*** *p195*
Roulston, John; Philadelphia, 1847 ***5704.8*** *p23*
Roulston, Joseph 2; Quebec, 1849 ***5704.8*** *p51*
Roulston, Margaret; Philadelphia, 1868 ***5704.8*** *p226*
Roulston, Margaret 12; Quebec, 1849 ***5704.8*** *p51*
Roulston, Margaret 50; St. John, N.B., 1856 ***5704.8*** *p131*
Roulston, Mary; St. John, N.B., 1853 ***5704.8*** *p106*
Roulston, Nancy 20; Philadelphia, 1857 ***5704.8*** *p132*
Roulston, Oliver 7; St. John, N.B., 1853 ***5704.8*** *p106*
Roulston, Samuel; St. John, N.B., 1847 ***5704.8*** *p2*
Roulston, William; St. John, N.B., 1853 ***5704.8*** *p106*
Roulston, William 1; St. John, N.B., 1853 ***5704.8*** *p106*
Roulston, William 17; Quebec, 1857 ***5704.8*** *p136*
Roulstone, Anne; Philadelphia, 1849 ***53.26*** *p80*
Roulstone, Anne; Philadelphia, 1849 ***5704.8*** *p54*
Roulstone, Harvey; Philadelphia, 1811 ***53.26*** *p80*
*Relative:*Martha
*Relative:*James
Roulstone, Harvey; Philadelphia, 1811 ***2859.11*** *p19*
Roulstone, James *SEE* Roulstone, Harvey
Roulstone, James; Philadelphia, 1811 ***2859.11*** *p19*
Roulstone, John 20; Quebec, 1858 ***5704.8*** *p137*
Roulstone, Martha *SEE* Roulstone, Harvey
Roulstone, Martha; Philadelphia, 1811 ***2859.11*** *p19*
Roum, Iver Christian; Arkansas, 1918 ***95.2*** *p107*
Roun, Joseph 30; Port uncertain, 1839 ***778.5*** *p472*
Roundtree, Daniel; America, 1866 ***5704.8*** *p207*
Roundtree, John; Philadelphia, 1868 ***5704.8*** *p225*
Roundtree, Kate; Philadelphia, 1864 ***5704.8*** *p187*
Roundtree, Margaret; Philadelphia, 1868 ***5704.8*** *p225*
Roundtree, Owen; Philadelphia, 1816 ***2859.11*** *p41*
With wife
Rounel, Ernest 40; America, 1831 ***778.5*** *p472*
Rourk, James; America, 1737 ***4971*** *p27*
Rourk, James; America, 1738 ***4971*** *p13*
Rourk, John; New York, NY, 1839 ***8208.4*** *p99*
Rourk, Patrick; New York, NY, 1840 ***8208.4*** *p104*
Rourke, Bridget 5; Massachusetts, 1850 ***5881.1*** *p82*
Rourke, Charles; America, 1735-1743 ***4971*** *p8*
Rourke, David 8; Massachusetts, 1850 ***5881.1*** *p83*
Rourke, John 10; Massachusetts, 1849 ***5881.1*** *p84*
Rourke, Julia 31; Massachusetts, 1850 ***5881.1*** *p84*
Rourke, Mary 18; Massachusetts, 1847 ***5881.1*** *p85*
Rourke, Mary 18; Wilmington, DE, 1831 ***6508.3*** *p100*
Rourke, Owen; America, 1735-1743 ***4971*** *p79*
Rourke, Patrick 12; Massachusetts, 1849 ***5881.1*** *p86*
Rourke, Patrick 30; Massachusetts, 1849 ***5881.1*** *p86*
Rourke, Thomas; New York, NY, 1840 ***8208.4*** *p104*
Rourke, William; America, 1741 ***4971*** *p53*
Rous, Lucas; Philadelphia, 1760 ***9973.7*** *p34*
Rousch, Henry; Wisconsin, n.d. ***9675.7*** *p269*
Rouse, Peter 30; America, 1837 ***778.5*** *p473*
Rouse, Thomas; Virginia, 1636 ***6219*** *p12*
Rouse, William 17; Maryland, 1774 ***1219.7*** *p229*
Roush Martyr, Jean Jacques 22; Port uncertain, 1838 ***778.5*** *p473*
Rousille, Mr. 37; New Orleans, 1829 ***778.5*** *p473*
Rouslin, Mr. 29; Port uncertain, 1839 ***778.5*** *p473*
Roussait, Thomas 27; New Orleans, 1836 ***778.5*** *p473*
Roussarie, Mr. 32; America, 1839 ***778.5*** *p473*
Rousse, A. 32; America, 1838 ***778.5*** *p473*
Rousse, Arnold 30; Port uncertain, 1836 ***778.5*** *p473*
Rousse, Gustave 20; Port uncertain, 1836 ***778.5*** *p473*
Rousseau, Mr. 28; New Orleans, 1820 ***778.5*** *p473*
Rousseau, Cadet 45; New Orleans, 1826 ***778.5*** *p473*
Rousseau, Eug. 33; America, 1838 ***778.5*** *p473*
Rousseau, F. 30; New Orleans, 1835 ***778.5*** *p473*
Rousseau, Francois 32; New Orleans, 1835 ***778.5*** *p473*
Rousseau, J. 50; America, 1835 ***778.5*** *p473*
Rousseau, Louis 49; America, 1837 ***778.5*** *p474*
Rousseau, Louis 50; New Orleans, 1838 ***778.5*** *p474*
Rousseau, Martin 25; New Orleans, 1837 ***778.5*** *p474*
Rousseau, N. 32; New Orleans, 1830 ***778.5*** *p474*
Rousseau, Yves 28; America, 1839 ***778.5*** *p474*
Roussel, . . .; Canada, 1776-1783 ***9786*** *p32*
Roussell, . . .; Canada, 1776-1783 ***9786*** *p32*
Rousset, Mr. 20; New Orleans, 1822 ***778.5*** *p474*
Rousset, Mrs. 16; New Orleans, 1822 ***778.5*** *p474*
Roussin, Mr. 33; America, 1838 ***778.5*** *p474*
Roussos, E. G.; Arkansas, 1918 ***95.2*** *p58*
Roussos, Ernest George; Arkansas, 1918 ***95.2*** *p107*
Roussos, James Petros; Arkansas, 1918 ***95.2*** *p107*
Rout, Hugh; Virginia, 1642 ***6219*** *p186*
Rout, James 30; Canada, 1835 ***4535.10*** *p196*
Routh, John 22; Nova Scotia, 1774 ***1219.7*** *p194*
Routlidge, Diana 2 *SEE* Routlidge, William
Routlidge, Joseph 18 mos *SEE* Routlidge, William
Routlidge, Sarah 27 *SEE* Routlidge, William
Routlidge, William 30; Nova Scotia, 1774 ***1219.7*** *p195*
*Wife:*Sarah 27
*Child:*Diana 2
*Child:*Joseph 18 mos
Roux, Amedee 22; New Orleans, 1838 ***778.5*** *p474*
Roux, Emelie Venvealet 27; America, 1837 ***778.5*** *p474*
Roux, Victor A.; Colorado, 1902 ***9678.2*** *p166*
Rov, Lewis; New York, NY, 1869 ***9678.2*** *p166*
Rovan, Eliza 9; Philadelphia, 1864 ***5704.8*** *p178*
Rovan, Mary 7; Philadelphia, 1864 ***5704.8*** *p178*
Rove, Agatino; Iowa, 1866-1943 ***123.54*** *p42*
Rovely, Jason; Virginia, 1648 ***6219*** *p250*
Rover, . . .; Canada, 1776-1783 ***9786*** *p32*
Rover, Rudolph; New York, NY, 1835 ***8208.4*** *p6*
Row, Henry; America, 1838 ***1450.2*** *p122A*
Row, John 21; Philadelphia, 1775 ***1219.7*** *p258*
Row, Robert 19; Maryland, 1719 ***3690.1*** *p195*
Row, Thomas; America, 1698 ***2212*** *p6*
Rowan, George; Washington, 1859-1920 ***2872.1*** *p34*
Rowan, James; Philadelphia, 1816 ***2859.11*** *p41*
Rowan, John; New York, NY, 1816 ***2859.11*** *p41*
Rowan, Margaret; New York, NY, 1816 ***2859.11*** *p41*
Rowan, Margaret; Quebec, 1847 ***5704.8*** *p16*
Rowan, Mary; Iowa, 1866-1943 ***123.54*** *p77*
Rowan, Mary; New York, NY, 1816 ***2859.11*** *p41*
With 4 children
Rowan, Michael 26; Massachusetts, 1847 ***5881.1*** *p85*
Rowan, Thomas 8; Massachusetts, 1849 ***5881.1*** *p87*
Rowand, Andrew; Illinois, 1841 ***7857*** *p7*
Rowand, William; Wilmington, NC, 1774 ***1639.20*** *p276*
Rowden, Elizabeth; Philadelphia, 1676-1684 ***4961*** *p4*
Rowden, Robert; Virginia, 1636 ***6219*** *p32*
Rowden, Thomas 17; Philadelphia, 1774 ***1219.7*** *p197*
Rowe, Charles Ronald; Iowa, 1866-1943 ***123.54*** *p42*
Rowe, Elizabeth 4; Quebec, 1847 ***5704.8*** *p28*
Rowe, Jane; Quebec, 1847 ***5704.8*** *p28*
Rowe, John; Illinois, 1866 ***7857*** *p7*
Rowe, John; Quebec, 1847 ***5704.8*** *p28*
Rowe, Margaret 6; Quebec, 1847 ***5704.8*** *p28*
Rowe, Mary Jane; St. John, N.B., 1848 ***5704.8*** *p45*
Rowe, Michael 20; Jamaica, 1729 ***3690.1*** *p195*
Rowe, Robert 2; Quebec, 1847 ***5704.8*** *p28*
Rowell, Ann 16; Virginia, 1720 ***3690.1*** *p195*
Rowell, Eliz.; Virginia, 1635 ***6219*** *p4*
Rowen, Henry; Virginia, 1628 ***6219*** *p9*
Rowen, Hugh 20; St. John, N.B., 1856 ***5704.8*** *p132*
Rowg, Joseph; Indiana, 1848 ***9117*** *p19*
Rowitzer, Marcus; Milwaukee, 1875 ***4719.30*** *p258*
Rowland, Mrs.; New York, NY, 1815 ***2859.11*** *p41*
With child
Rowland, Charles 21; Maryland, 1774 ***1219.7*** *p224*
Rowland, Charles 23; Virginia, 1774 ***1219.7*** *p244*
Rowland, Ja.; Virginia, 1629 ***6219*** *p8*
Rowland, Jacques; Quebec, 1775 ***7603*** *p47*
Rowland, James 22; Maryland, 1775 ***1219.7*** *p251*
Rowland, Joan; America, 1697 ***2212*** *p4*
Rowland, John; Pennsylvania, 1682 ***4960*** *p158*
*Wife:*Priscilla Shepperd
*Relative:*Thomas
Rowland, John; Pennsylvania, 1682 ***4962*** *p153*
Rowland, John; Pennsylvania, 1682 ***4963*** *p38*
*Wife:*Priscilla Sheppard
Rowland, John 22; Maryland, 1732 ***3690.1*** *p195*
Rowland, Jon.; Virginia, 1635 ***6219*** *p6*
Rowland, Priscilla Sheppard *SEE* Rowland, John
Rowland, Priscilla Shepperd *SEE* Rowland, John
Rowland, Thomas *SEE* Rowland, John
Rowland, Thomas; Pennsylvania, 1682 ***4963*** *p38*
Rowland, Thomas 37; Maryland, 1775 ***1219.7*** *p255*
Rowlands, James 29; New England, 1774 ***1219.7*** *p203*
Rowlands, John 24; America, 1700 ***2212*** *p30*
Rowlands, John M. 28; Kansas, 1872 ***5240.1*** *p53*
Rowlands, Richard 24; Virginia, 1700 ***2212*** *p32*
Rowlandson, Richard 40; New York, 1774 ***1219.7*** *p202*
Rowlatt, James 23; Virginia, 1774 ***1219.7*** *p193*
Rowles, Georg; Virginia, 1637 ***6219*** *p86*
Rowles, John 20; Jamaica, 1720 ***3690.1*** *p195*
Rowlett, Jon.; Virginia, 1635 ***6219*** *p20*
Rowlett, Thomas 21; Maryland or Virginia, 1734 ***3690.1*** *p195*
Rowley, John 29; Virginia, 1774 ***1219.7*** *p241*
Rowley, Thomas 29; Massachusetts, 1850 ***5881.1*** *p87*
Rowley, Truman G. 34; Kansas, 1877 ***5240.1*** *p37*

Rowley, Truman G. 34; Kansas, 1877 **5240.1** *p58*
Rowlington, Edw.; Virginia, 1639 **6219** *p23*
Rowly, William; Virginia, 1638 **6219** *p14*
Rowney, James 20; Jamaica, 1736 **3690.1** *p195*
Rownfifall, Hen.; Virginia, 1642 **6219** *p199*
Rowold, Conrad 48; America, 1888 **4610.10** *p123*
*Wife:*Wilhelmine 52
*Son:*Ernst 14
Rowold, Ernst 14 *SEE* Rowold, Conrad
Rowold, Wilhelmine 52 *SEE* Rowold, Conrad
Roworth, John 21; Baltimore, 1775 **1219.7** *p270*
Rowsell, Wm.; America, 1835 **4535.11** *p52*
With 7 children
With wife
Rowson, Robt.; Virginia, 1635 **6219** *p3*
Roxborough, Rose 17; St. John, N.B., 1858 **5704.8** *p137*
Roxborow, Elizabeth; St. John, N.B., 1847 **5704.8** *p10*
Roxborow, Mary; St. John, N.B., 1847 **5704.8** *p10*
Roxborow, Mary 11; St. John, N.B., 1847 **5704.8** *p10*
Roxborow, Sarah; St. John, N.B., 1847 **5704.8** *p10*
Roxborow, William; St. John, N.B., 1847 **5704.8** *p10*
Roxborow, William 5; St. John, N.B., 1847 **5704.8** *p10*
Roy, Miss 20; New Orleans, 1822 **778.5** *p475*
Roy, Mrs. 45; New Orleans, 1821 **778.5** *p475*
Roy, Mrs. 45; New Orleans, 1822 **778.5** *p475*
Roy, A. 11; New Orleans, 1822 **778.5** *p474*
Roy, Charles 23; New Orleans, 1827 **778.5** *p474*
Roy, Claude 12; New Orleans, 1821 **778.5** *p474*
Roy, E. 30; New Orleans, 1835 **778.5** *p474*
Roy, Elize 10; New Orleans, 1822 **778.5** *p474*
Roy, Etienne 14; New Orleans, 1821 **778.5** *p475*
Roy, Jas. 30; New Orleans, 1839 **778.5** *p475*
Roy, Julie 16; New Orleans, 1821 **778.5** *p475*
Roy, P. 13; New Orleans, 1822 **778.5** *p475*
Roy, Robert; New York, 1824 **8208.4** *p42*
Roy, Samuel; Quebec, 1824 **7603** *p27*
Roy, William 39; Maryland, 1773 **1219.7** *p172*
Royall, Ann *SEE* Royall, Joseph
Royall, Henry *SEE* Royall, Joseph
Royall, Joseph; Virginia, 1637 **6219** *p29*
*Wife:*Ann
*Brother:*Henry
Royall, Thomasin; Virginia, 1637 **6219** *p29*
Royce, William; New York, NY, 1839 **8208.4** *p96*
Royer, M. H.; Washington, 1859-1920 **2872.1** *p34*
Royere, P. 55; New Orleans, 1836 **778.5** *p475*
Royl, Benjamin; Virginia, 1698 **2212** *p17*
Royl, Jinnet 19; America, 1702 **2212** *p38*
Roylie, Robert; St. John, N.B., 1851 **5704.8** *p77*
Royston, John 21; Jamaica, 1730 **3690.1** *p196*
Rozek, Antonio; Arkansas, 1918 **95.2** *p107*
Rozes, Guillaume 25; Port uncertain, 1838 **778.5** *p475*
Rozna, Victoria Tomaszewski 25; New York, 1912 **9980.29** *p68*
Rual, Charles 26; New Orleans, 1838 **778.5** *p475*
Ruan, Jean 20; America, 1838 **778.5** *p475*
Rubb, Jacob 36; New York, NY, 1857 **9831.14** *p86*
Rube, Johannes Hubertus; Washington, 1859-1920 **2872.1** *p35*
Rubel, Johann Kaspar; Philadelphia, 1752 **8125.8** *p438*
Rubel, Wolfgang; Wisconsin, n.d. **9675.7** *p269*
Rubemeyer, Caspar; America, 1844 **4610.10** *p134*
*Wife:*Engel Poppensieker
*Son:*Caspar F. Wilhelm
Rubemeyer, Caspar F. Wilhelm *SEE* Rubemeyer, Caspar
Rubemeyer, Engel Poppensieker *SEE* Rubemeyer, Caspar
Ruben, Girsh; Arkansas, 1918 **95.2** *p107*
Ruben, Joseph; Arkansas, 1918 **95.2** *p107*
Rubenkonig, Henrich Philip; Philadelphia, 1779 **8137** *p13*
Rubenstein, David; Arkansas, 1918 **95.2** *p107*
Rubias, F. 35; Mexico, 1825 **778.5** *p475*
Rubidge, Thomas 37; Maryland, 1774 **1219.7** *p230*
Rubin, Fred; Washington, 1859-1920 **2872.1** *p35*
Rubin, Herman F.; Illinois, 1888 **2896.5** *p34*
Rubin, Jacob; America, 1868 **1450.2** *p122A*
Rubin, Louis; Arkansas, 1918 **95.2** *p107*
Rubin, Ludwig; Illinois, 1866 **2896.5** *p34*
Rubinstein, Joe; Arkansas, 1918 **95.2** *p107*
Rubly, Theodbald; Wisconsin, n.d. **9675.7** *p269*
Rubokof, Aggruan; Wisconsin, n.d. **9675.7** *p269*
Rubokon, Mafady Arlompow; Arkansas, 1918 **95.2** *p107*
Rubsaman, Felix; South Carolina, 1788 **7119** *p203*
Rubsaman, Jacob, Jr.; South Carolina, 1788 **7119** *p203*
Rubseman, Borthlow; South Carolina, 1788 **7119** *p203*
Rubseman, Jacob; South Carolina, 1788 **7119** *p203*
Rubue, Jon.; Virginia, 1638 **6219** *p11*
Ruby, Jr., Mr.; Quebec, 1815 **9229.18** *p76*
Ruby, George 15; Maryland, 1724 **3690.1** *p196*
Ruch, Catherine; New York, 1752 **3652** *p76*
Ruch, Michael; New York, 1756 **3652** *p81*
Ruchert, William; Wisconsin, n.d. **9675.7** *p269*
Ruckaber, Anna Maria; Pennsylvania, 1755-1800 **2444** *p174*
Ruckelshausen, Louis 22; Kansas, 1886 **5240.1** *p68*
Rucker, Christian; South Carolina, 1788 **7119** *p204*
Ruckle, Peter; Kentucky, 1839-1840 **8582.3** *p99*
Ruckles, C. C.; Washington, 1859-1920 **2872.1** *p35*
Ruckwid, Catharina; Carolina, 1770-1809 **2444** *p228*
Rud, Erick; Arkansas, 1918 **95.2** *p107*
Rudd, Abram; Virginia, 1698 **2212** *p14*
Rudd, Amos 25; Philadelphia, 1775 **1219.7** *p255*
Rudd, Grace; New York, NY, 1816 **2859.11** *p41*
Rudd, John; Virginia, 1698 **2212** *p14*
Rudd, John 19; Maryland, 1736 **3690.1** *p196*
Rudd, W.H.; Iowa, 1866-1943 **123.54** *p42*
Ruddack, Robert 30; Antigua (Antego), 1731 **3690.1** *p196*
Rudder, John; New York, NY, 1811 **2859.11** *p19*
Rudder, Patrick; New York, NY, 1811 **2859.11** *p19*
Ruddock, James; New York, NY, 1816 **2859.11** *p41*
Ruddy, Ann; St. John, N.B., 1850 **5704.8** *p61*
Ruddy, Betty; St. John, N.B., 1852 **5704.8** *p92*
Ruddy, Mary; St. John, N.B., 1848 **5704.8** *p38*
Ruddy, Michael; St. John, N.B., 1847 **5704.8** *p5*
Ruddy, Owen; St. John, N.B., 1848 **5704.8** *p38*
Ruddy, Owen; St. John, N.B., 1849 **5704.8** *p49*
Ruddy, Rose; St. John, N.B., 1852 **5704.8** *p92*
Ruddy, Sally; St. John, N.B., 1849 **5704.8** *p49*
Ruddy, Sarah 30; St. John, N.B., 1864 **5704.8** *p159*
Rudesill, Andrew; Philadelphia, 1762 **9973.7** *p36*
Rudg, Edward 28; Jamaica, 1725 **3690.1** *p196*
Rudgalwis, Frank; Wisconsin, n.d. **9675.7** *p269*
Rudibaugh, Christian; Pennsylvania, 1739 **4779.3** *p14*
Rudig, Conrad; Ohio, 1800-1865 **8582.2** *p58*
Rudisilly, Jacob; Philadelphia, 1761 **9973.7** *p35*
Rudisilly, Lewis; Philadelphia, 1768 **9973.7** *p40*
Rudkin, Thomas 28; Virginia, 1774 **1219.7** *p226*
Rudkins, William 22; Kansas, 1873 **5240.1** *p53*
Rudler, Captain; Nicaragua, 1856 **8582.3** *p31*
Rudloff, Catharine 58; Kansas, 1873 **5240.1** *p54*
Rudolf, Miss; Pennsylvania, n.d. **4525** *p239*
Rudolph, Christian; America, 1873 **1450.2** *p123A*
Rudolph, Henrich; Philadelphia, 1779 **8137** *p13*
Rudolphi, . . .; Quebec, 1776 **9786** *p104*
Rudolphi, Otto Heinrich; Quebec, 1776 **9786** *p261*
Rudsdell, Joseph 15; Philadelphia, 1774 **1219.7** *p233*
Rudwig, Johannes; Philadelphia, 1779 **8137** *p13*
Rudy, Edward 28; Jamaica, 1725 **3690.1** *p196*
Rudy, John; America, 1883 **7137** *p170*
Rudy, Joseph; Arkansas, 1918 **95.2** *p107*
Rudy, Julia; America, 1888 **7137** *p170*
Ruege, Fred; Wisconsin, n.d. **9675.7** *p269*
Rueggsegger, Barbara; Pennsylvania, 1709-1710 **4480** *p311*
Ruehe, August H.; Illinois, 1872 **5012.37** *p59*
Ruehle, Christina Roecker *SEE* Ruehle, Johann Michael
Ruehle, Johann Michael; Pennsylvania, 1751 **2444** *p206*
*Wife:*Christina Roecker
Ruella, C. 27; New Orleans, 1832 **778.5** *p475*
Rueller, Jean 62; Port uncertain, 1827 **778.5** *p475*
Ruemelin, . . .; Cincinnati, 1837-1838 **8582.1** *p45*
Ruemelin, Mr.; Cincinnati, 1831 **8582.1** *p51*
Ruemelin, Carl; Cincinnati, 1788-1848 **8582.3** *p89*
Ruemelin, Carl; Ohio, 1869-1887 **8582** *p26*
Ruenger, Daniel; New York, 1750 **3652** *p74*
Ruess, Catharina Bayha *SEE* Ruess, Johann Jacob
Ruess, Hans Georg; Pennsylvania, 1754 **2444** *p207*
*Brother:*Hans Jacob
Ruess, Hans Jacob *SEE* Ruess, Hans Georg
Ruess, Johann Jacob; Pennsylvania, 1754 **2444** *p207*
*Wife:*Catharina Bayha
Ruessele, Jacob; Kentucky, 1797 **8582.3** *p95*
Rueter, Calvin Wilhelm; Cincinnati, 1788-1848 **8582.3** *p89*
Rueter, Martin; Cincinnati, 1824-1831 **8582.3** *p89*
Ruether, August; Wisconsin, n.d. **9675.7** *p269*
Ruff, Mr.; America, 1837 **8582.1** *p55*
Ruff, Mr.; Illinois, 1837 **8582.1** *p55*
Ruff, Jacob 32; Port uncertain, 1838 **778.5** *p475*
Ruff, John; South Carolina, 1788 **7119** *p199*
Ruff, Margaret 22; Port uncertain, 1838 **778.5** *p476*
Ruffe, Jacob; Pennsylvania, 1754 **2444** *p207*
Ruffe, Tim 22; Newport, RI, 1851 **6508.5** *p19*
Ruffenach, Antoine; Colorado, 1888 **9678.2** *p166*
Ruffer, Elisabeth 76; Canada, 1901 **1763** *p40D*
Ruffie, Miss 20; New Orleans, 1821 **778.5** *p476*
Ruffing, William; Wisconsin, n.d. **9675.7** *p269*
Rufner, Mr.; America, 1798 **8582.2** *p55*
With wife
Rugaetti, Zionani; Wisconsin, n.d. **9675.7** *p269*
Ruge, Fred; Wisconsin, n.d. **9675.7** *p269*
Ruger, Frederick William; Washington, 1859-1920 **2872.1** *p35*
Ruger, Maria 27; America, 1838 **778.5** *p476*
Ruger, Thebis; Carolina, 1738 **9898** *p35*
Rugg, Benj.; Virginia, 1643 **6219** *p206*
Rugge, Anna *SEE* Rugge, Heinrich
Rugge, Charlotte Niehus 31 *SEE* Rugge, Heinrich
Rugge, Friederike *SEE* Rugge, Heinrich
Rugge, Heinrich *SEE* Rugge, Heinrich
Rugge, Heinrich 39; America, 1881 **4610.10** *p106*
*Wife:*Charlotte Niehus 31
*Child:*Anna
*Child:*Friederike
*Child:*Heinrich
Rugge, Rudolph; Baltimore, 1853 **1450.2** *p123A*
Ruggier, Pasquale; Arkansas, 1918 **95.2** *p107*
Ruh, Eva 24; America, 1853 **9162.8** *p37*
Ruh, Eva Kath. 11; America, 1853 **9162.8** *p37*
Ruh, Gertraud 25; America, 1853 **9162.8** *p37*
Ruh, Johs. 56; America, 1853 **9162.8** *p37*
Ruh, Katharina 22; America, 1853 **9162.8** *p37*
Ruh, Marg. 46; America, 1853 **9162.8** *p37*
Ruh, Maria 9; America, 1853 **9162.8** *p37*
Ruh, Marie 20; New Orleans, 1839 **778.5** *p476*
Ruhl, Adam; Lancaster, PA, 1780 **8137** *p13*
Ruhl, Valentin; Philadelphia, 1779 **8137** *p13*
Ruhmer, Franz; Wisconsin, n.d. **9675.7** *p269*
Ruhnow, August; Illinois, 1889 **5012.39** *p52*
Ruine, Joseph 33; America, 1839 **778.5** *p476*
Ruitenberg, John; Arkansas, 1918 **95.2** *p107*
Ruiz, Juan 63; Arizona, 1926 **9228.40** *p30*
Ruk, Roy; Arkansas, 1918 **95.2** *p107*
Rukas, Anton; Washington, 1859-1920 **2872.1** *p35*
Rukovino, Marko; Iowa, 1866-1943 **123.54** *p42*
Rukstelis, Anton; Wisconsin, n.d. **9675.7** *p269*
Rukstelis, Frank; Wisconsin, n.d. **9675.7** *p269*
Rule, Dorothy; Virginia, 1639 **6219** *p152*
Rule, Dorothy; Virginia, 1639 **6219** *p158*
Rule, Thomas 27; Maryland, 1773 **1219.7** *p173*
Rulf, Antonie 36; America, 1831 **778.5** *p476*
Rulifson, C. C.; Washington, 1859-1920 **2872.1** *p35*
Rullhaus, Herman; New York, NY, 1840 **8208.4** *p111*
Rullmann, . . .; Canada, 1776-1783 **9786** *p32*
Rullmann, Jean; Canada, 1776-1783 **9786** *p243*
Rum, Franz 25; America, 1839 **778.5** *p476*
Rumanio, Pete; Arkansas, 1918 **95.2** *p107*
Rumback, Nick 27; Kansas, 1893 **5240.1** *p77*
Rumford, William 22; Maryland, 1775 **1219.7** *p259*
Rumier, Victorine 26; America, 1838 **778.5** *p476*
Rumner, N. 26; New Orleans, 1837 **778.5** *p476*
Runberg, Olaf; Colorado, 1904 **9678.2** *p166*
Rundall, Warwick 19; Maryland, 1724 **3690.1** *p196*
Rundle, Warwick 19; Maryland, 1724 **3690.1** *p196*
Rundt, Carl Godfrey; New York, 1752 **3652** *p76*
Runey, Bridget 14; Massachusetts, 1848 **5881.1** *p82*
Runey, Mary 18; Massachusetts, 1848 **5881.1** *p85*
Runge, Albert; Wisconsin, n.d. **9675.7** *p269*
Runge, Ernst; Illinois, 1890 **2896.5** *p34*
Runge, Heinrich; Wisconsin, n.d. **9675.7** *p269*
Rungster, Martin; Ohio, 1798-1818 **8582.2** *p53*
Runies, Arp; New York, NY, 1840 **8208.4** *p106*
Runk, Carl; America, 1849 **8582.3** *p56*
Runk, Friederich; America, 1840 **8582.3** *p56*
Runkel, Johan George; Wisconsin, n.d. **9675.7** *p269*
Runkel, John Philip; Wisconsin, n.d. **9675.7** *p269*
Runkel, John William; Wisconsin, n.d. **9675.7** *p269*
Runnerstrom, Gustav; Wisconsin, n.d. **9675.7** *p269*
Runtz, Georg; Cincinnati, 1869-1887 **8582** *p26*
Ruonelin, J. H.; Washington, 1859-1920 **2872.1** *p35*
Ruos, Catharina Bayha *SEE* Ruos, Johann Jacob
Ruos, Hans Georg; Pennsylvania, 1754 **2444** *p207*
*Brother:*Hans Jacob
Ruos, Hans Jacob *SEE* Ruos, Hans Georg
Ruos, Johann Jacob; Pennsylvania, 1754 **2444** *p207*
*Wife:*Catharina Bayha
Ruoso, Manales Zese; Arkansas, 1918 **95.2** *p107*
Ruoss, Hans Georg; Pennsylvania, 1754 **2444** *p207*
*Brother:*Hans Jacob
Ruoss, Hans Jacob *SEE* Ruoss, Hans Georg
Rupa, Jos.; Iowa, 1866-1943 **123.54** *p42*
Ruple, Biddy 21; Massachusetts, 1849 **5881.1** *p82*
Rupp, Anna Catharina *SEE* Rupp, Christoph
Rupp, Anna Margaretha *SEE* Rupp, Christoph
Rupp, Anna Maria *SEE* Rupp, Christoph
Rupp, Christoph *SEE* Rupp, Christoph
Rupp, Christoph; Pennsylvania, 1737-1770 **2444** *p207*
*Wife:*Anna Margaretha
*Child:*Anna Catharina
*Child:*Anna Maria
*Child:*Christoph
Rupp, Heinrich; Baltimore, 1838 **8582.3** *p56*
Rupp, Henry; Cincinnati, 1869-1887 **8582** *p26*
Rupp, Johannes; Lancaster, PA, 1780 **8137** *p13*
Rupp, Peter; Philadelphia, 1758 **9973.7** *p33*
Ruppe, S. William; Illinois, 1866 **2896.5** *p34*
Ruppel, Heinr. J. 53; America, 1895 **1763** *p40D*

450 *FOR A COMPLETE EXPLANATION OF ENTRY, SEE "HOW TO READ A CITATION" SECTION*

Ruppert, . . .; Canada, 1776-1783 ***9786*** *p32*
Ruppert, Cornelius; Wisconsin, n.d. ***9675.7*** *p269*
Ruppert, Jacob; Philadelphia, 1783 ***8582.2*** *p66*
Ruppert, Michael; Wisconsin, n.d. ***9675.7*** *p269*
Ruppert, William; Wisconsin, n.d. ***9675.7*** *p269*
Rupple, Daniel; Charleston, SC, 1775-1781 ***8582.2*** *p52*
Rupsiris, Kasimir; Wisconsin, n.d. ***9675.7*** *p269*
Rupszis, Kazmer; Wisconsin, n.d. ***9675.7*** *p269*
Rurty, Margery 15; Philadelphia, 1853 ***5704.8*** *p113*
Rurup, Carl 45; America, 1850 ***4610.10*** *p143*
*Child:*Carl Heinrich
*Child:*Friedrich Gottlieb
Rurup, Carl Christoph *SEE* Rurup, Carl Heinrich
Rurup, Carl Friedrich; America, 1849 ***4610.10*** *p142*
Rurup, Carl Heinrich *SEE* Rurup, Carl
Rurup, Carl Heinrich 55; America, 1850 ***4610.10*** *p142*
*Child:*Carl Christoph
*Child:*Louise 19
Rurup, Friedrich Gottlieb *SEE* Rurup, Carl
Rurup, Louise 19 *SEE* Rurup, Carl Heinrich
Rus, John; North Carolina, 1822 ***1639.20*** *p276*
Rusch, Conrad; Wisconsin, n.d. ***9675.7*** *p269*
Rusch, Fridolin; America, 1853 ***1450.2*** *p123A*
Rusch, Josef; Colorado, 1894 ***9678.2*** *p166*
Rusche, Joseph; America, 1847 ***8582.3*** *p56*
Ruschmann, Louis; Illinois, 1873 ***5012.39*** *p26*
Ruschmeier, Louise 36; America, 1865 ***4610.10*** *p105*
Ruschmeyer, Friedrich Wilhelm; America, 1883 ***4610.10*** *p102*
Ruse, Jacob; Pennsylvania, 1754 ***2444*** *p207*
Rusecky, Ludwik; Arkansas, 1918 ***95.2*** *p107*
Rush, Ann Jane 6; St. John, N.B., 1847 ***5704.8*** *p11*
Rush, Francis 11; St. John, N.B., 1847 ***5704.8*** *p11*
Rush, George; Canada, 1776-1783 ***9786*** *p239*
Rush, James 9; St. John, N.B., 1847 ***5704.8*** *p11*
Rush, Jon.; Virginia, 1642 ***6219*** *p194*
Rush, Peter; Philadelphia, 1865 ***5704.8*** *p201*
Rush, Susanna; Philadelphia, 1864 ***5704.8*** *p188*
Rusher, Joseph; New York, 1834 ***8208.4*** *p57*
Rushforth, William; New York, 1832 ***8208.4*** *p47*
Rushhaupt, Henry; Baltimore, 1834 ***1450.2*** *p123A*
Rushton, Ellin 18; Pennsylvania, Virginia or Maryland, 1699 ***2212*** *p20*
Rusk, . . .; Canada, 1776-1783 ***9786*** *p32*
Ruske, Henry Albert; Wisconsin, 1859 ***2896.5*** *p34*
Rusmeyer, Albrecht L.; New York, 1753 ***3652*** *p77*
Ruso, Joe C.; Arkansas, 1918 ***95.2*** *p107*
Ruspareil, Felix; America, 1833 ***778.5*** *p476*
Russ, Mr.; Cincinnati, 1831 ***8582.1*** *p51*
Russ, Anna Barbara Woehrle *SEE* Russ, Johann Jacob
Russ, Jacob; Pennsylvania, 1754 ***2444*** *p207*
Russ, Johann Jacob; Port uncertain, 1740-1800 ***2444*** *p207*
*Wife:*Anna Barbara Woehrle
*Child:*Johannes
Russ, Johannes *SEE* Russ, Johann Jacob
Russe, Wm.; Virginia, 1642 ***6219*** *p195*
Russel, . . .; Canada, 1776-1783 ***9786*** *p32*
Russel, Alexander *SEE* Russel, Mary
Russel, Alexander; Philadelphia, 1848 ***5704.8*** *p40*
Russel, Andrew 24; Maryland, 1774 ***1219.7*** *p236*
Russel, Catherin; Philadelphia, 1847 ***5704.8*** *p23*
Russel, Catherine; Philadelphia, 1847 ***53.26*** *p80*
Russel, David 25; New England, 1774 ***1219.7*** *p191*
Russel, Elizabeth; Philadelphia, 1849 ***53.26*** *p80*
Russel, Elizabeth; Philadelphia, 1849 ***5704.8*** *p50*
Russel, Ellan; Philadelphia, 1848 ***5704.8*** *p40*
Russel, Ellen; Philadelphia, 1848 ***53.26*** *p80*
Russel, Gorie; Ohio, 1824 ***9892.11*** *p40*
Russel, Isaac; Philadelphia, 1815 ***2859.11*** *p41*
Russel, James; Philadelphia, 1847 ***53.26*** *p81*
Russel, James; Philadelphia, 1847 ***5704.8*** *p14*
Russel, James; Philadelphia, 1849 ***53.26*** *p81*
Russel, James 24; Philadelphia, 1775 ***1219.7*** *p258*
Russel, John; Baltimore, 1811 ***2859.11*** *p19*
Russel, John 25; Kansas, 1900 ***5240.1*** *p37*
Russel, Mary *SEE* Russel, Mary
Russel, Mary; Philadelphia, 1848 ***53.26*** *p81*
*Relative:*Mary
*Relative:*Alexander
Russel, Mary; Philadelphia, 1848 ***5704.8*** *p40*
Russel, Mary; Philadelphia, 1850 ***5704.8*** *p64*
Russel, Robert; Quebec, 1795 ***7603*** *p41*
Russel, Thomas 17; Maryland, 1774 ***1219.7*** *p226*
Russel, Wm; Barbados, 1698 ***2212*** *p4*
Russell, Major 35; Antigua (Antego), 1774 ***1219.7*** *p177*
Russell, Alexander; Charleston, SC, 1768 ***1219.7*** *p137*
Russell, Alexander; Philadelphia, 1816 ***2859.11*** *p41*
Russell, Alexander 10; Quebec, 1850 ***5704.8*** *p67*
Russell, Alexander 10; St. John, N.B., 1866 ***5704.8*** *p166*
Russell, Allison 7; St. John, N.B., 1866 ***5704.8*** *p166*
Russell, Andrew; St. John, N.B., 1852 ***5704.8*** *p95*
Russell, Andrew 16; St. John, N.B., 1861 ***5704.8*** *p149*
Russell, Ann; Philadelphia, 1852 ***5704.8*** *p89*
Russell, Ann 20; St. John, N.B., 1861 ***5704.8*** *p149*
Russell, Archy 21; Philadelphia, 1857 ***5704.8*** *p133*
Russell, Catherine; St. John, N.B., 1853 ***5704.8*** *p99*
Russell, Catherine 8; St. John, N.B., 1861 ***5704.8*** *p149*
Russell, Chas.; Virginia, 1637 ***6219*** *p24*
Russell, Dennis; Virginia, 1628 ***6219*** *p31*
Russell, Edward 6; St. John, N.B., 1861 ***5704.8*** *p149*
Russell, Eliza; Quebec, 1848 ***5704.8*** *p42*
Russell, Elizabeth; America, 1740 ***4971*** *p15*
Russell, Elizabeth; Quebec, 1850 ***5704.8*** *p67*
Russell, Elizabeth 9; Philadelphia, 1853 ***5704.8*** *p112*
Russell, Elizabeth 12; Quebec, 1850 ***5704.8*** *p67*
Russell, Elizabeth 21; St. John, N.B., 1860 ***5704.8*** *p144*
Russell, Ellen 14; St. John, N.B., 1861 ***5704.8*** *p149*
Russell, Ester 6; Philadelphia, 1853 ***5704.8*** *p112*
Russell, Felix 4; Quebec, 1847 ***5704.8*** *p27*
Russell, Francis; Philadelphia, 1816 ***2859.11*** *p41*
Russell, Francis 11; Philadelphia, 1853 ***5704.8*** *p112*
Russell, George; Philadelphia, 1853 ***5704.8*** *p103*
Russell, George; St. John, N.B., 1848 ***5704.8*** *p39*
Russell, George 2; Philadelphia, 1854 ***5704.8*** *p120*
Russell, Henry; Jamaica, 1768 ***1219.7*** *p135*
Russell, James; America, 1742 ***4971*** *p17*
Russell, James; New York, NY, 1811 ***2859.11*** *p19*
Russell, James; New York, NY, 1865 ***5704.8*** *p197*
Russell, James; Philadelphia, 1816 ***2859.11*** *p41*
Russell, James; Philadelphia, 1849 ***5704.8*** *p54*
Russell, James; Quebec, 1848 ***5704.8*** *p42*
Russell, James 12; Quebec, 1847 ***5704.8*** *p27*
Russell, James 39; Kansas, 1878 ***5240.1*** *p59*
Russell, Jane; Philadelphia, 1816 ***2859.11*** *p41*
Russell, Jane; Philadelphia, 1853 ***5704.8*** *p101*
Russell, Jane; St. John, N.B., 1866 ***5704.8*** *p166*
Russell, Jane 4; St. John, N.B., 1866 ***5704.8*** *p166*
Russell, Jane 26; St. John, N.B., 1854 ***5704.8*** *p119*
Russell, Jane Eliz.; Philadelphia, 1850 ***53.26*** *p81*
Russell, Jane Eliza; Philadelphia, 1850 ***5704.8*** *p69*
Russell, Jermiah 57; St. John, N.B., 1854 ***5704.8*** *p119*
Russell, Joane; Virginia, 1646 ***6219*** *p235*
Russell, John; America, 1739 ***4971*** *p53*
Russell, John; Jamaica, 1756 ***1219.7*** *p41*
Russell, John; Jamaica, 1756 ***3690.1*** *p196*
Russell, John; Kansas, 1880 ***5240.1*** *p37*
Russell, John; New York, NY, 1816 ***2859.11*** *p41*
Russell, John; New York, NY, 1834 ***8208.4*** *p1*
Russell, John; New York, NY, 1837 ***8208.4*** *p54*
Russell, John; Philadelphia, 1816 ***2859.11*** *p41*
Russell, John; Philadelphia, 1852 ***5704.8*** *p85*
Russell, John 4; St. John, N.B., 1861 ***5704.8*** *p149*
Russell, John 9; Quebec, 1847 ***5704.8*** *p27*
Russell, John 11; St. John, N.B., 1853 ***5704.8*** *p110*
Russell, John 23; Jamaica, 1736 ***3690.1*** *p196*
Russell, John 25; Kansas, 1900 ***5240.1*** *p81*
Russell, Jon.; Virginia, 1635 ***6219*** *p20*
Russell, Margaret; St. John, N.B., 1853 ***5704.8*** *p99*
Russell, Margaret 25; Philadelphia, 1854 ***5704.8*** *p120*
Russell, Margaret Jane 11; St. John, N.B., 1861 ***5704.8*** *p149*
Russell, Martha 10; St. John, N.B., 1861 ***5704.8*** *p149*
Russell, Martin 36; Kansas, 1884 ***5240.1*** *p67*
Russell, Mary; New York, NY, 1811 ***2859.11*** *p19*
Russell, Mary; Philadelphia, 1852 ***5704.8*** *p89*
Russell, Mary; Philadelphia, 1853 ***5704.8*** *p103*
Russell, Mary; Quebec, 1847 ***5704.8*** *p27*
Russell, Mary 18; St. John, N.B., 1861 ***5704.8*** *p149*
Russell, Mary 45; St. John, N.B., 1861 ***5704.8*** *p149*
Russell, Mary 50; Philadelphia, 1853 ***5704.8*** *p112*
Russell, Mary Ann 1; Quebec, 1850 ***5704.8*** *p67*
Russell, Mathew; Philadelphia, 1851 ***5704.8*** *p71*
Russell, Michael; Quebec, 1847 ***5704.8*** *p27*
Russell, Michael; Quebec, 1853 ***5704.8*** *p103*
Russell, Patrick 10; Quebec, 1847 ***5704.8*** *p27*
Russell, Rebecca; Philadelphia, 1865 ***5704.8*** *p199*
Russell, Rebecca 4; Quebec, 1850 ***5704.8*** *p67*
Russell, Richard; Virginia, 1635 ***6219*** *p17*
Russell, Richard; Virginia, 1649 ***6219*** *p252*
Russell, Robert; New York, NY, 1834 ***8208.4*** *p1*
Russell, Robert; Philadelphia, 1851 ***5704.8*** *p71*
Russell, Robert; Philadelphia, 1866 ***5704.8*** *p211*
Russell, Robert 21; Philadelphia, 1853 ***5704.8*** *p109*
Russell, Robert 28; St. John, N.B., 1866 ***5704.8*** *p166*
Russell, Samuel 16; Philadelphia, 1856 ***5704.8*** *p129*
Russell, Sarah 2; Quebec, 1847 ***5704.8*** *p27*
Russell, Thomas; America, 1742 ***4971*** *p23*
Russell, Thomas; New York, NY, 1811 ***2859.11*** *p19*
Russell, Thomas 34; Philadelphia, 1774 ***1219.7*** *p205*
Russell, Thomas Pierce; New York, NY, 1836 ***8208.4*** *p15*
Russell, Thos 28; Philadelphia, 1845 ***6508.6*** *p115*
Russell, William; Charleston, SC, 1804 ***1639.20*** *p276*
Russell, William; New Jersey, 1846 ***3840.3*** *p8*
Russell, William; Philadelphia, 1851 ***5704.8*** *p71*
Russell, William; Quebec, 1850 ***5704.8*** *p67*
Russell, William; Quebec, 1852 ***5704.8*** *p90*
Russell, William; St. John, N.B., 1866 ***5704.8*** *p166*
Russell, William; Virginia, 1648 ***6219*** *p251*
Russell, Wm.; Virginia, 1642 ***6219*** *p208*
Russer, Morgan; Virginia, 1639 ***6219*** *p152*
Russey, Elizabeth; Virginia, 1637 ***6219*** *p86*
Russich, Louis; Iowa, 1866-1943 ***123.54*** *p42*
Russkaup, Bernhard H.; Cincinnati, 1869-1887 ***8582*** *p26*
Russman, Cattrina 30; New York, NY, 1893 ***9026.4*** *p42*
Russman, John E.; Illinois, 1880 ***2896.5*** *p34*
Russo, Frank; Arkansas, 1918 ***95.2*** *p107*
Russo, Gabriele; Iowa, 1866-1943 ***123.54*** *p42*
Russo, Gabrille; Iowa, 1866-1943 ***123.54*** *p42*
Russotto, Guiseppe 45; Harris Co., TX, 1896 ***6254*** *p3*
Rust, . . .; Canada, 1776-1783 ***9786*** *p32*
Rust, Andrew; New York, NY, 1837 ***8208.4*** *p24*
Rust, Hans Georg; Pennsylvania, 1754 ***2444*** *p207*
*Brother:*Hans Jacob
Rust, Hans Jacob *SEE* Rust, Hans Georg
Rust, Hans Jacob; Pennsylvania, 1754 ***2444*** *p207*
Rust, Johann Daniel 37; Halifax, N.S., 1752 ***7074.6*** *p207*
With family of 5
Rust, Johann Peter; Kentucky, 1840 ***8582.3*** *p100*
Rust, Stephen 28; Virginia, 1774 ***1219.7*** *p240*
Rustan, Gustaf; Iowa, 1849-1860 ***2090*** *p613*
Rustede, John W.; Iowa, 1866-1943 ***123.54*** *p42*
Rustedt, Henry 22; Kansas, 1885 ***5240.1*** *p67*
Rustin, Richd 21; Virginia, 1700 ***2212*** *p33*
Ruston, Richard; Indiana, 1836 ***9117*** *p15*
Ruston, Robert; Indiana, 1836 ***9117*** *p15*
Ruston, William; Indiana, 1836 ***9117*** *p15*
Ruszel, Wiktoria 17; New York, 1912 ***9980.29*** *p71*
Ruta, Fortunat; Boston, 1834 ***4606*** *p179*
Rute, Dorothy; Virginia, 1639 ***6219*** *p151*
Rutenop, Hans; New York, NY, 1848 ***6013.19*** *p29*
Ruter, Anne Marie Catharine Charlotte; America, 1858 ***4610.10*** *p99*
Ruter, Calvin Wilhelm; Cincinnati, 1788-1848 ***8582.3*** *p89*
Ruter, Carl E. H. Friedrich *SEE* Ruter, Christian Friedrich
Ruter, Christian Friedrich; America, 1843-1844 ***4610.10*** *p104*
Ruter, Christian Friedrich; America, 1848 ***4610.10*** *p97*
*Wife:*Justine L. C. Oexemann
*Son:*Carl E. H. Friedrich
Ruter, Christian Friedrich; Died enroute, 1844 ***4610.10*** *p104*
Ruter, Elisabeth; America, 1888 ***4610.10*** *p107*
Ruter, Friedrich Heinrich Gottlieb; America, 1893 ***4610.10*** *p103*
Ruter, George; Kansas, 1870 ***5240.1*** *p38*
Ruter, Heinrich Friedrich Wilhelm; America, 1889 ***4610.10*** *p96*
Ruter, Justine L. C. Oexemann *SEE* Ruter, Christian Friedrich
Ruter, Karoline Marie; America, 1905 ***4610.10*** *p103*
Ruter, Louise Caroline; America, 1872 ***4610.10*** *p100*
Ruter, Louise Caroline; America, 1905 ***4610.10*** *p103*
Ruter, Marie Kathrine; America, 1841 ***4610.10*** *p97*
Ruter, Wilhelm Hermann August; America, 1905 ***4610.10*** *p103*
Ruth, E. S.; Washington, 1859-1920 ***2872.1*** *p35*
Ruth, Holt; Virginia, 1621 ***6219*** *p24*
Ruthedge, Margaret; Philadelphia, 1848 ***53.26*** *p81*
Ruthedge, Margaret; Philadelphia, 1848 ***5704.8*** *p46*
Rutheford, Dennis; Pennsylvania, 1682 ***4961*** *p165*
*Wife:*Mary Heriott
Rutheford, Grace 3; Died enroute, 1682 ***4961*** *p165*
*Sister:*Mary 6 mos
Rutheford, Mary 6 mos *SEE* Rutheford, Grace
Rutheford, Mary Heriott *SEE* Rutheford, Dennis
Rutherford, Alexander 2 *SEE* Rutherford, Anten
Rutherford, Alexander 2; Philadelphia, 1848 ***5704.8*** *p40*
Rutherford, Anne; Wilmington, NC, 1766 ***1639.20*** *p276*
Rutherford, Anne; Wilmington, NC, 1767 ***1639.20*** *p280*
Rutherford, Anten; Philadelphia, 1848 ***53.26*** *p81*
*Relative:*Elizabeth
*Relative:*Letitia 3
*Relative:*Alexander 2
Rutherford, Anten; Philadelphia, 1848 ***5704.8*** *p40*
Rutherford, Barbara; Wilmington, NC, 1763 ***1639.20*** *p42*
Rutherford, Barbara; Wilmington, NC, 1763 ***1639.20*** *p276*
Rutherford, C. A. 29; Kansas, 1889 ***5240.1*** *p73*
Rutherford, Charles 22; Boston, 1774 ***1219.7*** *p210*
Rutherford, Dennis; Pennsylvania, 1682 ***4961*** *p165*
*Wife:*Mary Heriott
Rutherford, Elizabeth *SEE* Rutherford, Anten
Rutherford, Elizabeth; Philadelphia, 1848 ***5704.8*** *p40*

Rutherford, Ernest Robinson; Wisconsin, n.d. *9675.7*
p269
Rutherford, Ernst R.; Wisconsin, n.d. *9675.7 p269*
Rutherford, F. P. 43; Kansas, 1890 *5240.1 p74*
Rutherford, Grace 3; Died enroute, 1682 *4961 p165*
*Sister:*Mary 6 mos
Rutherford, James; Charleston, SC, 1751 *1639.20 p277*
Rutherford, James; Philadelphia, 1870 *5704.8 p237*
Rutherford, John; Cape Fear, NC, 1739 *1639.20 p277*
With cousin
Rutherford, John; Philadelphia, 1811 *53.26 p81*
*Relative:*Mary
Rutherford, John; Philadelphia, 1811 *2859.11 p19*
Rutherford, John; Virginia, 1621 *6219 p30*
Rutherford, John 21; Maryland, 1774 *1219.7 p230*
Rutherford, Letitia 3 *SEE* Rutherford, Anten
Rutherford, Letitia 3; Philadelphia, 1848 *5704.8 p40*
Rutherford, Mary *SEE* Rutherford, John
Rutherford, Mary; Philadelphia, 1811 *2859.11 p19*
Rutherford, Mary 6 mos *SEE* Rutherford, Grace
Rutherford, Mary Heriott *SEE* Rutherford, Dennis
Rutherford, Sarah; Philadelphia, 1811 *2859.11 p19*
Rutherford, Thomas Hale; New York, NY, 1832 *8208.4*
p30
Rutherford, Walter; America, 1815 *1639.20 p277*
Rutherford, Walter; North Carolina, 1700-1799 *1639.20*
p277
Rutherford, Walter 53; North Carolina, 1850 *1639.20*
p277
Rutherford, Walter B.; America, 1815 *1639.20 p277*
Ruths, Philipp; America, 1849 *8582.1 p29*
Ruths, Philipp; New York, NY, 1849 *8582.1 p29*
Ruthven, David 58; South Carolina, 1850 *1639.20 p277*
*Relative:*Sarah 58
Ruthven, Sarah 58 *SEE* Ruthven, David
Rutkin, Hen.; Virginia, 1635 *6219 p3*
Rutkowski, Jozef; New York, 1831 *4606 p176*
Rutkowski, Teofil; New York, 1831 *4606 p176*
Rutland, Rich.; Virginia, 1641 *6219 p184*
Rutland, Richard; Jamaica, 1765 *1219.7 p110*
Rutledge, Eliza 8; St. John, N.B., 1854 *5704.8 p122*
Rutledge, John; New York, NY, 1816 *2859.11 p41*
Rutledge, John 19; St. John, N.B., 1865 *5704.8 p165*
Rutledge, William 47; St. John, N.B., 1854 *5704.8 p122*
Rutlidge, Charles 40; St. John, N.B., 1853 *5704.8 p110*
Rutlidge, James; Philadelphia, 1848 *53.26 p81*
Rutlidge, James; Philadelphia, 1848 *5704.8 p45*
Rutlidge, John 24; St. John, N.B., 1853 *5704.8 p110*
Rutlidge, William 22; St. John, N.B., 1864 *5704.8 p159*
Rutolo, Domenico; Colorado, 1903 *9678.2 p166*
Rutt, Jeremiah; Virginia, 1640 *6219 p184*
Rutt, William; Philadelphia, 1760 *9973.7 p35*
Rutter, John; Virginia, 1642 *6219 p189*
Rutter, Thomas; Germantown, PA, 1684 *2467.7 p5*
Rutterly, Thomas; New York, NY, 1836 *8208.4 p76*
Rutz, Edward John; America, 1884 *1450.2 p33B*
Ruude, Peter; Nevada, 1872 *2764.35 p58*
Ruusulehto, Vaino Toivo; Arkansas, 1918 *95.2 p108*
Ruxor, Frederick; Indiana, 1848 *9117 p17*
Ruyland, Thomas; Wisconsin, n.d. *9675.7 p269*
Ruzic, Pyo; Iowa, 1866-1943 *123.54 p42*
Ruzycki, Nicholas; Arkansas, 1918 *95.2 p108*
Ryall, Joseph; Virginia, 1635 *6219 p74*
Ryan, Mr.; New York, NY, 1811 *2859.11 p19*
Ryan, Andrew; America, 1743 *4971 p84*
Ryan, Andrew; America, 1889 *1450.2 p123A*
Ryan, Bessy 39; Massachusetts, 1847 *5881.1 p82*
Ryan, Betsey 13; Massachusetts, 1849 *5881.1 p82*
Ryan, Bridget 13; Massachusetts, 1847 *5881.1 p82*
Ryan, Catharine 3; Massachusetts, 1847 *5881.1 p83*
Ryan, Catharine 8; Massachusetts, 1849 *5881.1 p83*
Ryan, Catharine 10; Massachusetts, 1849 *5881.1 p83*
Ryan, Catharine 20; Massachusetts, 1847 *5881.1 p83*
Ryan, Catherine; America, 1736 *4971 p12*
Ryan, Clement; Montreal, 1822 *7603 p98*
Ryan, Daniel 4; Massachusetts, 1847 *5881.1 p83*
Ryan, Daniel 5; Massachusetts, 1849 *5881.1 p83*
Ryan, Daniel 6; Massachusetts, 1849 *5881.1 p83*
Ryan, Darby; America, 1738 *4971 p31*

Ryan, David; Montreal, 1821 *7603 p98*
Ryan, David; New York, NY, 1811 *2859.11 p19*
Ryan, Dennis *SEE* Ryan, James
Ryan, Dennis; America, 1738 *4971 p31*
Ryan, Dennis; America, 1742 *4971 p29*
Ryan, Dennis; Delaware, 1743 *4971 p105*
Ryan, Dennis 32; Massachusetts, 1847 *5881.1 p83*
Ryan, Dominico 9; Massachusetts, 1849 *5881.1 p83*
Ryan, Dorothy; America, 1738 *4971 p13*
Ryan, Doroty; America, 1738-1743 *4971 p91*
Ryan, Edward 21; Philadelphia, 1774 *1219.7 p228*
Ryan, Elizabeth; America, 1742 *4971 p94*
Ryan, Elizabeth; America, 1743 *4971 p86*
Ryan, Ellen; New York, NY, 1815 *2859.11 p41*
Ryan, Ellen 10; Massachusetts, 1849 *5881.1 p83*
Ryan, Ellen 19; Massachusetts, 1849 *5881.1 p83*
Ryan, Ellen 20; Massachusetts, 1849 *5881.1 p84*
Ryan, Frank 41; Arizona, 1890 *2764.35 p59*
Ryan, George; America, 1841 *1450.2 p123A*
Ryan, George 15; Maryland, 1775 *1219.7 p260*
Ryan, James; New York, NY, 1811 *2859.11 p19*
Ryan, James; New York, NY, 1815 *2859.11 p41*
Ryan, James; Ohio, 1839 *9892.11 p40*
Ryan, James; Plymouth, MA, 1840 *7036 p117*
*Brother:*Dennis
Ryan, James; Quebec, 1786 *7603 p79*
Ryan, James; Quebec, 1820 *7603 p88*
Ryan, James 6; Massachusetts, 1847 *5881.1 p84*
Ryan, James 10; Massachusetts, 1849 *5881.1 p84*
Ryan, Jane; America, 1741 *4971 p16*
Ryan, Jane 13; Massachusetts, 1849 *5881.1 p84*
Ryan, Jean 26; Montreal, 1782 *7603 p94*
Ryan, Jeremiah; New York, NY, 1834 *8208.4 p3*
Ryan, Johanna 30; Massachusetts, 1849 *5881.1 p84*
Ryan, John; America, 1735-1743 *4971 p78*
Ryan, John; America, 1736-1743 *4971 p57*
Ryan, John; America, 1736-1743 *4971 p58*
Ryan, John; America, 1741 *4971 p40*
Ryan, John; America, 1742 *4971 p50*
Ryan, John; America, 1742 *4971 p86*
Ryan, John; America, 1742 *4971 p95*
Ryan, John; Annapolis, MD, 1742 *4971 p92*
Ryan, John; Maryland, 1742 *4971 p107*
Ryan, John 8; Massachusetts, 1849 *5881.1 p84*
Ryan, John 11; Massachusetts, 1849 *5881.1 p84*
Ryan, John 20; Massachusetts, 1849 *5881.1 p84*
Ryan, John 52; Massachusetts, 1849 *5881.1 p84*
Ryan, John H.; Indiana, 1853 *1450.2 p123A*
Ryan, Joseph 22; Harris Co., TX, 1898 *6254 p4*
Ryan, Judy 22; Massachusetts, 1849 *5881.1 p84*
Ryan, Margaret; America, 1739 *4971 p47*
Ryan, Margaret; New York, NY, 1816 *2859.11 p41*
Ryan, Margaret 10 mos; Massachusetts, 1847 *5881.1 p85*
Ryan, Margaret 6; Massachusetts, 1849 *5881.1 p85*
Ryan, Margaret 12; Massachusetts, 1849 *5881.1 p85*
Ryan, Margaret 15; Montreal, 1796 *7603 p70*
Ryan, Martin 25; Newfoundland, 1789 *4915.24 p57*
Ryan, Mary; America, 1738 *4971 p13*
Ryan, Mary; America, 1739 *4971 p47*
Ryan, Mary; America, 1741 *4971 p16*
Ryan, Mary; Massachusetts, 1849 *5881.1 p85*
Ryan, Mary; Montreal, 1823 *7603 p98*
Ryan, Mary; New York, NY, 1811 *2859.11 p19*
Ryan, Mary; New York, NY, 1816 *2859.11 p41*
With child
Ryan, Mary; New York, NY, 1867 *5704.8 p216*
Ryan, Mary 1; Massachusetts, 1848 *5881.1 p85*
Ryan, Mary 21; Montreal, 1796 *7603 p70*
Ryan, Mary 23; Massachusetts, 1849 *5881.1 p85*
Ryan, Mary 30; Massachusetts, 1849 *5881.1 p85*
Ryan, Mary 40; Massachusetts, 1848 *5881.1 p85*
Ryan, Mary 58; Massachusetts, 1849 *5881.1 p85*
Ryan, Mathew 3; Massachusetts, 1849 *5881.1 p85*
Ryan, Mathew 7; Massachusetts, 1849 *5881.1 p85*
Ryan, Mathew 20; Massachusetts, 1849 *5881.1 p86*
Ryan, Matthew; Quebec, 1823 *7603 p59*
Ryan, Michael; New York, NY, 1839 *8208.4 p99*
Ryan, Michael; Quebec, 1830 *7036 p125*
Ryan, Michael 5; Massachusetts, 1849 *5881.1 p85*

Ryan, Michael 13; Massachusetts, 1849 *5881.1 p85*
Ryan, Nelly 11; Massachusetts, 1848 *5881.1 p86*
Ryan, Patrick; America, 1736-1743 *4971 p58*
Ryan, Patrick; America, 1739 *4971 p47*
Ryan, Patrick; Illinois, 1876 *5012.37 p60*
Ryan, Patrick; New York, NY, 1811 *2859.11 p19*
Ryan, Patrick; Quebec, 1823 *7603 p72*
Ryan, Patrick 13; Massachusetts, 1849 *5881.1 p86*
Ryan, Patrick 21; Massachusetts, 1847 *5881.1 p86*
Ryan, Patrick J.; America, 1842 *1450.2 p123A*
Ryan, Richard; New York, NY, 1840 *8208.4 p112*
Ryan, Richard G.; America, 1842 *1450.2 p123A*
Ryan, Robert; New York, NY, 1840 *8208.4 p111*
Ryan, Sally 20; Massachusetts, 1849 *5881.1 p86*
Ryan, Sarah; America, 1739 *4971 p53*
Ryan, Sarah; America, 1741 *4971 p94*
Ryan, Sarah; America, 1742 *4971 p27*
Ryan, Simon 18; Massachusetts, 1850 *5881.1 p86*
Ryan, Thomas; Montreal, 1822 *7603 p98*
Ryan, Thomas; New York, NY, 1811 *2859.11 p19*
Ryan, Thomas; New York, NY, 1834 *8208.4 p50*
Ryan, Thomas 25; Massachusetts, 1849 *5881.1 p87*
Ryan, Thomas 37; Massachusetts, 1849 *5881.1 p87*
Ryan, Thomas D.; Wisconsin, n.d. *9675.7 p269*
Ryan, Timothy; America, 1742-1743 *4971 p62*
Ryan, Timothy; Ohio, 1840 *9892.11 p41*
Ryan, Timothy 32; Massachusetts, 1849 *5881.1 p87*
Ryan, William; America, 1736 *4971 p83*
Ryan, William; America, 1736-1743 *4971 p58*
Ryan, William; America, 1739 *4971 p47*
Ryan, William; Illinois, 1868 *2896.5 p34*
Ryan, William; New York, NY, 1811 *2859.11 p19*
Ryan, William 8; Massachusetts, 1849 *5881.1 p87*
Ryan, Wm.; Virginia, 1858 *4626.16 p17*
Ryans, Catherine; Quebec, 1851 *5704.8 p74*
Rybacki, Antoni 19; New York, 1912 *9980.29 p60*
Rybarczyk, Anton 23; New York, 1912 *9980.29 p70*
Rybicki, Piotr 24; New York, 1912 *9980.29 p55*
Ryburn, John 45; North Carolina, 1850 *1639.20 p277*
Rychlicki, . . .; New York, 1831 *4606 p176*
Rycroft, Joshua 12; America, 1701 *2212 p34*
Rycroft, Wm; America, 1697-1707 *2212 p9*
Ryde, Elizabeth 18; Jamaica, 1774 *1219.7 p223*
Rydecka, Cecylia 18; New York, 1912 *9980.29 p70*
Ryder, Thomas; America, 1741 *4971 p94*
Ryder, William; Florida, 1768 *1219.7 p137*
Ryder, William 25; Maryland, 1775 *1219.7 p250*
Rydholm, J. V. 22; Kansas, 1874 *5240.1 p55*
Rydzekowski, Brony; Arkansas, 1918 *95.2 p108*
Rye, Maria; Philadelphia, 1818 *9892.11 p17*
Ryer, Joe; Wisconsin, n.d. *9675.7 p269*
Ryer, John; New York, NY, 1838 *8208.4 p72*
Ryers, James; New York, NY, 1811 *2859.11 p19*
With wife
Ryglewicz, Cecilia 20; New York, 1912 *9980.29 p51*
Rylance, Jacob 24; America, 1699 *2212 p21*
Ryland, Mr.; Quebec, 1815 *9229.18 p79*
Ryland, John 16; Philadelphia, 1774 *1219.7 p183*
Rylander, Charles 33; Massachusetts, 1860 *6410.32 p108*
Rylander, Mary Ann 24; Massachusetts, 1860 *6410.32 p108*
Ryley, Mr.; Quebec, 1815 *9229.18 p76*
Ryley, Judy 5; Massachusetts, 1849 *5881.1 p84*
Ryley, Mary 22; St. John, N.B., 1856 *5704.8 p132*
Ryley, Mary 23; St. John, N.B., 1854 *5704.8 p122*
Ryley, Thomas 22; Maryland, 1775 *1219.7 p254*
Ryley, William; Barbados, 1761 *1219.7 p83*
Rylie, George; St. John, N.B., 1854 *5704.8 p9*
Ryling, John; Cincinnati, 1869-1887 *8582 p26*
Rymacz, Wojciech 20; New York, 1912 *9980.29 p74*
Ryman, Nicholas; Virginia, 1639 *6219 p155*
Rymecz, Wojciech 20; New York, 1912 *9980.29 p74*
Rymer, James; South Carolina, 1753 *1639.20 p278*
Rys, Stanley P.; Arkansas, 1918 *95.2 p108*
Ryslavy, Ch. John 35; Kansas, 1893 *5240.1 p77*
Rystrom, Chas.; Iowa, 1866-1943 *123.54 p42*
Rythe, Chr.; Virginia, 1645 *6219 p232*
Rytherland, Rich.; Virginia, 1648 *6219 p250*
Rzarzewski, Ludwik; New York, 1831 *4606 p176*

FOR A COMPLETE EXPLANATION OF ENTRY, SEE "HOW TO READ A CITATION" SECTION

S

Saalfeld, Charlotte 59; New Orleans, 1839 *9420.2 p358*
Saalfeld, Fredk. 19; New Orleans, 1839 *9420.2 p358*
Saari, Isaac; Washington, 1859-1920 *2872.1 p35*
Saastamoinen, Alpar; Washington, 1859-1920 *2872.1 p35*
Saastamoinen, Armas; Washington, 1859-1920 *2872.1 p35*
Saastamoinen, Otto; Washington, 1859-1920 *2872.1 p35*
Saathoff, Frank W.; Illinois, 1897 *5012.40 p55*
Saathoff, John; Illinois, 1892 *5012.40 p27*
Saathoff, Klaas; Illinois, 1888 *5012.39 p52*
Saathoff, Reent; Illinois, 1892 *5012.40 p26*
Saatkamp, Rudolph 28; America, 1845 *3702.7 p85*
    With wife
    With 3 children
Saba, Charles; Arkansas, 1918 *95.2 p108*
Saba, Charles Abraham; Arkansas, 1918 *95.2 p108*
Sabalr, Jose 30; Arizona, 1924 *9228.40 p28*
Sabanowitz, Dora 8; New York, NY, 1878 *9253 p47*
Sabanowitz, Emma 29; New York, NY, 1878 *9253 p47*
Sabanowitz, Rosa 6; New York, NY, 1878 *9253 p47*
Sabarien, Miss 43; America, 1837 *778.5 p476*
Sabath, Farmer; America, 1893 *4610.10 p103*
Sabatier, Mr. 21; New Orleans, 1839 *778.5 p476*
Sabatier, Mr. 32; Port uncertain, 1839 *778.5 p476*
Sabatini, Schille; Wisconsin, n.d. *9675.7 p269*
Sabella, Andrew; America, 1892 *7137 p171*
    Wife:Mary
Sabella, Mary *SEE* Sabella, Andrew
Saberton, William; Indiana, 1848 *9117 p18*
Sabin, Ramon 31; New Orleans, 1835 *778.5 p476*
Sabin, Tho.; Virginia, 1648 *6219 p252*
Sabin, Thomas; Virginia, 1642 *6219 p197*
Sabin, Thomas 15; Antigua (Antego), 1774 *1219.7 p241*
Sabine, William; Boston, 1776 *1219.7 p282*
Sabirowsky, Wilhelm Carl Friedrich; America, 1881 *4610.10 p124*
    With son
Sable, Leonard; Philadelphia, 1762 *9973.7 p37*
Sabo, Mike J.; Arkansas, 1918 *95.2 p108*
Sabog, David; Arkansas, 1918 *95.2 p108*
Sabonaitis, Simonas; Wisconsin, n.d. *9675.7 p269*
Sabora, . . .; Canada, 1776-1783 *9786 p32*
Saboulard, Jean M. 24; New Orleans, 1838 *778.5 p477*
Sabouraud, Mrs. 28; New Orleans, 1838 *778.5 p477*
Sabouraud, Modeste 9; New Orleans, 1838 *778.5 p477*
Sabouren, Daniel 21; Virginia, 1774 *1219.7 p238*
Sabourin, J. 39; New Orleans, 1839 *778.5 p477*
Sabrero, Paolo 25; New York, NY, 1893 *9026.4 p42*
Sacalow, Ernest; Arkansas, 1918 *95.2 p108*
Saccaro, Bortalo; Iowa, 1866-1943 *123.54 p42*
Saccaro, Frank; Iowa, 1866-1943 *123.54 p42*
Saccaro, Frank; Iowa, 1866-1943 *123.54 p43*
Saccaro, Victor; Iowa, 1866-1943 *123.54 p77*
Saccaro, Vittore; Iowa, 1866-1943 *123.54 p77*
Saccaro, Vittorio; Iowa, 1866-1943 *123.54 p77*
Sacchi, Celeste; Iowa, 1866-1943 *123.54 p43*
Sacco, Armelia; Iowa, 1866-1943 *123.54 p43*
Sacco, Ernesto Marie; Iowa, 1866-1943 *123.54 p43*
Sacco, Guiseppe; Iowa, 1866-1943 *123.54 p43*
Sacco, James; Iowa, 1866-1943 *123.54 p77*
Sacco, Jasper, Jr.; Iowa, 1866-1943 *123.54 p43*
Sacco, Jenesio; Iowa, 1866-1943 *123.54 p43*
Sacco, Louis; Iowa, 1866-1943 *123.54 p77*
Sacco, Mary; Iowa, 1866-1943 *123.54 p43*
Sacco, Pasquale; Iowa, 1866-1943 *123.54 p43*
Sacco, Ralph; Iowa, 1866-1943 *123.54 p43*

Sacerdotte, Mr. 50; New Orleans, 1829 *778.5 p477*
Sacerdotte, David 28; New Orleans, 1836 *778.5 p477*
Sachan, Christ; Illinois, 1890 *2896.5 p34*
Sacharok, John; Arkansas, 1918 *95.2 p108*
Sachery, Louis; Arkansas, 1918 *95.2 p108*
Sacheveral, William; America, 1739 *4971 p68*
Sachrourtz, Joseph 22; Kansas, 1883 *5240.1 p64*
Sachse, Ernst Maximillian; Ohio, 1879 *1450.2 p124A*
Sachse, Henrich; Philadelphia, 1779 *8137 p13*
Sachsen-Weimar, Bernhard, Herzog von; Cincinnati, 1826 *8582.3 p89*
Sachsteder, Johann P.; Dayton, OH, 1869-1887 *8582 p26*
Sachstetter, Franz; Cincinnati, 1869-1887 *8582 p26*
Sachteleben, Herman; Illinois, 1868 *2896.5 p34*
Sachtelebend, Rudolph; Illinois, 1876 *2896.5 p34*
Sacilouska, Boleslaw; Arkansas, 1918 *95.2 p108*
Sacker, Heinrich; Cincinnati, 1848 *8582.1 p53*
Sacks, Frank; Arkansas, 1918 *95.2 p108*
Sacks, Windelin 39; California, 1872 *2769.8 p6*
Saco, Victor 25; America, 1838 *778.5 p477*
Sacrieuve, Martin 55; Mexico, 1827 *778.5 p477*
Saczek, Emil; Arkansas, 1918 *95.2 p108*
Sadd, Richard; Virginia, 1638 *6219 p119*
Saderdahl, Carl; Iowa, !866-1943 *123.54 p43*
Sadilek, Anton; Washington, 1859-1920 *2872.1 p35*
Sadilek, Eva; Washington, 1859-1920 *2872.1 p35*
Sadilek, Freda; Washington, 1859-1920 *2872.1 p35*
Sadilek, Wilhelmina; Washington, 1859-1920 *2872.1 p35*
Sadine, Erik August 28; Kansas, 1871 *5240.1 p51*
Sadler, Edmund, Jr.; Virginia, 1640 *6219 p183*
Sadler, Edmund, Sr.; Virginia, 1640 *6219 p183*
Sadler, Edward; Virginia, 1637 *6219 p116*
Sadler, Eliz., Jr.; Virginia, 1640 *6219 p183*
Sadler, Eliz., Sr.; Virginia, 1640 *6219 p183*
Sadler, Frances; New York, NY, 1811 *2859.11 p19*
Sadler, George 26; Philadelphia, 1774 *1219.7 p234*
Sadler, Hugh; New York, NY, 1811 *2859.11 p19*
Sadler, Margt.; Virginia, 1640 *6219 p183*
Sadler, Mary; Virginia, 1640 *6219 p183*
Sadler, Samuel 23; America, 1699 *2212 p29*
Sadler, Tho.; Virginia, 1636 *6219 p21*
Sadler, Thomas; Virginia, 1642 *6219 p193*
Sadler, William 21; Maryland, 1775 *1219.7 p262*
Sadlier, Dennis; New York, NY, 1839 *8208.4 p92*
Sadlier, Matthew; Washington, 1859-1920 *2872.1 p35*
Sadlier, William W.; New York, NY, 1833 *8208.4 p78*
Sadlington, Jonas; Virginia, 1635 *6219 p33*
Sadome, Allen; Virginia, 1639 *6219 p155*
Sadowski, Frank; Kansas, 1896 *5240.1 p38*
Sadowski, Jan; New York, 1834 *4606 p179*
Sadowski, Michal; New York, 1831 *4606 p177*
Saeger, Carl; Wisconsin, n.d. *9675.7 p269*
Saesser, S. G.; Indiana, 1844 *9117 p18*
Saflarsky, John; America, 1893 *7137 p170*
Saflarsky, Mary; America, 1895 *7137 p170*
Sagar, Seth; Wisconsin, n.d. *9675.7 p269*
Sagar, William; Wisconsin, n.d. *9675.7 p269*
Sage, Bright; San Francisco, 1908 *9892.11 p41*
Sage, John; Illinois, 1892 *5012.40 p27*
Sagemeier, Korbian; Wisconsin, n.d. *9675.7 p269*
Sager, A.M. Friederike; America, 1856 *4610.10 p112*
Sager, George; Pennsylvania, 1750 *2444 p217*
Sager, Oscar 24; Massachusetts, 1860 *6410.32 p119*
Sages, Isidore; New Orleans, 1839 *778.5 p477*
Sagunsky, Anna Emma; Wisconsin, n.d. *9675.7 p269*
Sagunsky, Julius; Wisconsin, n.d. *9675.7 p269*
Sagus, . . .; Canada, 1776-1783 *9786 p32*

Sahad, Louis John; Arkansas, 1918 *95.2 p108*
Sahki, Luige; Wisconsin, n.d. *9675.7 p269*
Sahler, Peter; Philadelphia, 1762 *9973.7 p37*
Sahli, Gertrude 40; New York, NY, 1889 *7846 p40*
Sahli, Johann 1 mo; New York, NY, 1889 *7846 p40*
Sahli, Sebastian 40; New York, NY, 1889 *7846 p40*
Sahn, Victor 26; Kansas, 1884 *5240.1 p66*
Sahr, Theodore E.; Missouri, 1897 *5240.1 p38*
Saiferne, James; Virginia,· 1647 *6219 p248*
Saifried, Michael; America, 1850 *8582.3 p56*
Sailer, Joseph; Wisconsin, n.d. *9675.7 p269*
Sailer, Karl G.; Arkansas, 1918 *95.2 p108*
Saillant, Mr. 14; America, 1836 *778.5 p477*
Saillie, . . .; Canada, 1776-1783 *9786 p32*
Saillie, Henri; Canada, 1776-1783 *9786 p243*
St. Amand, Mme. 24; America, 1836 *778.5 p477*
St. Amand, C.H.; Nevada, 1876 *2764.35 p62*
St. Antoine, Gabriel 18; America, 1820 *778.5 p477*
St. Arromam, Mr. 35; Port uncertain, 1839 *778.5 p477*
St. Avit, Mr. 24; New Orleans, 1839 *778.5 p477*
St. Clair, S. 35; New Orleans, 1821 *778.5 p478*
Saint-Clair, William; Quebec, 1792 *7603 p38*
St. Diezer, Auguste 42; New Orleans, 1837 *778.5 p478*
St. Dizier, Auguste 42; New Orleans, 1837 *778.5 p478*
St. Esteve, Miss 30; New Orleans, 1821 *778.5 p478*
St. Esteve, J. 33; New Orleans, 1821 *778.5 p478*
St. Germain, Mr. 24; Port uncertain, 1836 *778.5 p478*
Saint-Germain, Charles; Quebec, 1707 *7603 p97*
St. John, Peter; Boston, 1875 *2764.35 p66*
St. John, Thomas 20; Maryland, 1751 *1219.7 p3*
St. John, Thomas 20; Maryland, 1751 *3690.1 p196*
Saint-Joseph, Rene; Quebec, 1712 *4533 p128*
St. Karaces, Dinnitrios; Arkansas, 1918 *95.2 p116*
St. Leger, Anthony; America, 1735-1743 *4971 p78*
St. Leger, Anthony; America, 1742 *4971 p80*
St. Louis, Mrs. 44; Port uncertain, 1838 *778.5 p478*
St. Louis, David; Iroquois Co., IL, 1896 *3455.1 p13*
St. Louis, Louis; Nevada, 1877 *2764.35 p62*
St. Marc, Mr. 22; New Orleans, 1825 *778.5 p478*
St. Martin, Mr. 10; Louisiana, 1820 *778.5 p478*
St. Martin, Auguste 16; Louisiana, 1820 *778.5 p478*
St. Martin, Edmond 13; Louisiana, 1820 *778.5 p478*
St. Martin, F. 46; New Orleans, 1826 *778.5 p478*
St. Martin, J. T. 28; Port uncertain, 1839 *778.5 p478*
St. Martin, P. S. 26; Port uncertain, 1839 *778.5 p479*
St. Moreau, Louis 5; Port uncertain, 1836 *778.5 p479*
St. Moreau, Madelin 36; Port uncertain, 1836 *778.5 p479*
St. Ours, E. 21; New Orleans, 1835 *778.5 p479*
St. Ours, F. 17; New Orleans, 1835 *778.5 p479*
St. Paul de Lechard, Mr. 23; America, 1838 *778.5 p479*
St-Pierre, . . .; Canada, 1776-1783 *9786 p32*
St. Roman, Mme. 32; New Orleans, 1839 *778.5 p479*
St. Roman, Mr. 35; New Orleans, 1839 *778.5 p479*
St. Santis, Mr. 20; New Orleans, 1839 *778.5 p479*
Sainte An de Serchouet, Mr. 25; Port uncertain, 1838 *778.5 p479*
Sainte-Croix, Aubin; Quebec, 1492-1825 *7603 p49*
Sainte-Croix, Guillaume; Quebec, 1803 *7603 p49*
Sakacs, John; Wisconsin, n.d. *9675.7 p269*
Sakalooske, Michael; Wisconsin, n.d. *9675.7 p269*
Sakelins, Andrew; Arkansas, 1918 *95.2 p108*
Sala, Raymond 25; America, 1838 *778.5 p479*
Salaberry, J.B. 28; America, 1835 *778.5 p479*
Salahan, Bridget; Quebec, 1822 *7603 p83*
Salamon, Mr. 29; America, 1839 *778.5 p479*
Salande, John 40; Port uncertain, 1836 *778.5 p479*

Salasar, Rafael 29; California, 1872 ***2769.8*** *p5*
Salavignac, Jean 30; New Orleans, 1825 ***778.5*** *p480*
Salazar, Ignacis 24; California, 1872 ***2769.8*** *p6*
Salback, Jacob; Philadelphia, 1763 ***9973.7*** *p39*
Salber, Anton; Wisconsin, n.d. ***9675.7*** *p269*
Saldana, John Frank; Iowa, 1866-1943 ***123.54*** *p77*
Sale, Eliza.; Virginia, 1639 ***6219*** *p158*
Sale, Joseph 30; Maryland, 1775 ***1219.7*** *p253*
Salem, Collid 22; Kansas, 1901 ***5240.1*** *p82*
Salembher, B. 22; New Orleans, 1827 ***778.5*** *p480*
Sales, Jose 29; New Orleans, 1835 ***778.5*** *p480*
Sales, Thomas 16; Jamaica, 1730 ***3690.1*** *p196*
Salesbury, Eleanor 2; St. John, N.B., 1849 ***5704.8*** *p48*
Salesbury, Elizabeth; St. John, N.B., 1849 ***5704.8*** *p48*
Salesbury, John 9 mos; St. John, N.B., 1849 ***5704.8*** *p48*
Salesbury, Joseph; St. John, N.B., 1849 ***5704.8*** *p48*
Salesbury, Mary Ann 5; St. John, N.B., 1849 ***5704.8*** *p48*
Salford, Sarah; Virginia, 1624 ***6219*** *p30*
Salfried, Michael; America, 1850 ***8582.3*** *p56*
Salge, Henry; America, 1885 ***1450.2*** *p33B*
Salie, Gertrude 40; New York, NY, 1889 ***7846*** *p40*
Salie, Johann 1 mo; New York, NY, 1889 ***7846*** *p40*
Salie, Sebastian 40; New York, NY, 1889 ***7846*** *p40*
Salinas, Manuel 35; Arizona, 1923 ***9228.40*** *p27*
Saliny, Joseph; Arkansas, 1918 ***95.2*** *p108*
Salis, Johann Gaudenz, Graf von; Cincinnati, 1788-1848 ***8582.3*** *p88*
Salis, Julius Ferdinand, Freiherr von; Cincinnati, 1788-1848 ***8582.3*** *p88*
Salisbury, Charles 30; Georgia, 1775 ***1219.7*** *p276*
*Child:*Robert 11
*Child:*Thomas 10
Salisbury, John; Jamaica, 1756 ***1219.7*** *p47*
Salisbury, John; Jamaica, 1756 ***3690.1*** *p196*
Salisbury, Robert; Virginia, 1646 ***6219*** *p238*
Salisbury, Robert 11 *SEE* Salisbury, Charles
Salisbury, Roger; Virginia, 1638 ***6219*** *p117*
Salisbury, Thomas; Virginia, 1652 ***6251*** *p20*
Salisbury, Thomas 10 *SEE* Salisbury, Charles
Salisbury, Thomas 17; Jamaica, 1754 ***1219.7*** *p27*
Salisbury, Thomas 17; Jamaica, 1754 ***3690.1*** *p197*
Salisbury, Thomas 36; Maryland, 1774 ***1219.7*** *p207*
Salisch, Ignatz; Wisconsin, n.d. ***9675.7*** *p269*
Sallar, Ferdinand 20; America, 1835 ***778.5*** *p480*
Sallar, Marc 25; America, 1835 ***778.5*** *p480*
Sallard, John 18; Jamaica, 1730 ***3690.1*** *p197*
Salle, Madame 45; America, 1836 ***778.5*** *p480*
Salle, Mrs. 45; New Orleans, 1827 ***778.5*** *p481*
Salle, Auguste 15; America, 1836 ***778.5*** *p480*
Salle, E. 17; New Orleans, 1827 ***778.5*** *p480*
Salle, Elianor; Virginia, 1642 ***6219*** *p197*
Salle, Henri 30; America, 1836 ***778.5*** *p480*
Salle, John 17; America, 1836 ***778.5*** *p480*
Salle, John 47; America, 1836 ***778.5*** *p480*
Salle, P. 32; America, 1839 ***778.5*** *p480*
Sallenger, Antone 6 mos; America, 1836 ***778.5*** *p481*
Sallenger, Antone 28; America, 1836 ***778.5*** *p481*
Sallenger, Cretienn. 18; America, 1836 ***778.5*** *p481*
Sallenger, Madelena 20; America, 1836 ***778.5*** *p481*
Sallenger, Magellena 32; America, 1836 ***778.5*** *p481*
Salles, Nicolas 22; Port uncertain, 1836 ***778.5*** *p481*
Salles, P. 23; America, 1829 ***778.5*** *p481*
Sallett, Charles; Virginia, 1643 ***6219*** *p204*
Sallett, Gyles; Virginia, 1642 ***6219*** *p192*
Sallettes, Pierre 33; New Orleans, 1838 ***778.5*** *p481*
Salling, Johann; Virginia, 1740-1760 ***8582.3*** *p56*
Sallman, Frank; Iowa, 1866-1943 ***123.54*** *p43*
Sallman, Milcher; Iowa, 1866-1943 ***123.54*** *p43*
Sallmann, Carl 32; America, 1849 ***4610.10*** *p155*
Sallomon, Eberhart 27; Pennsylvania, 1753 ***2444*** *p207*
Sally, Margaret; America, 1742 ***4971*** *p72*
Salm, Carl Philipp 42; Kansas, 1887 ***5240.1*** *p70*
Salmason, John; Washington, 1859-1920 ***2872.1*** *p35*
Salmon, Catherine; Montreal, 1824 ***7603*** *p88*
Salmon, Elizabeth 16; Newfoundland, 1774 ***1219.7*** *p196*
Salmon, John 15; Maryland, 1774 ***1219.7*** *p235*
Salmon, John 16; Maryland, 1775 ***1219.7*** *p264*
Salmon, John 17; Philadelphia, 1774 ***1219.7*** *p216*
Salmon, Leopold; Kansas, 1910 ***6013.40*** *p17*
Salmon, Mathew; New York, NY, 1816 ***2859.11*** *p41*
Salmon, Thomas; New York, NY, 1838 ***8208.4*** *p72*
Salmon, William Bennett 40; California, 1873 ***2769.10*** *p5*
Salmond, Thomas 67; South Carolina, 1850 ***1639.20*** *p278*
Saloman, William; New York, NY, 1840 ***8208.4*** *p113*
Salomon, Eberhard; Port uncertain, 1758 ***2444*** *p207*
With wife
With daughter
Salomon, Louise 28; Port uncertain, 1832 ***778.5*** *p481*
Salorgne, Theodore; New York, NY, 1836 ***8208.4*** *p8*
Saloy, Mr. 25; Port uncertain, 1836 ***778.5*** *p481*
Salsberry, Tho.; Virginia, 1646 ***6219*** *p241*
Salsbury, Edward; Virginia, 1638 ***6219*** *p160*
Salsbury, Humph 19; New England, 1699 ***2212*** *p19*
Salsbury, Robert; Virginia, 1637 ***6219*** *p8*
Salsbury, Robert; Virginia, 1642 ***6219*** *p187*
Salsbury, Wm.; Virginia, 1642 ***6219*** *p191*
Salsido, Manuel 18; Arizona, 1902 ***9228.40*** *p8*
Salter, Edward; Virginia, 1638-1700 ***6219*** *p150*
Salter, Edward; Virginia, 1639 ***6219*** *p152*
Salter, Robert; Virginia, 1639 ***6219*** *p159*
Salter, Robert 21; Virginia, 1774 ***1219.7*** *p238*
Salter, Silas C.; Washington, 1859-1920 ***2872.1*** *p35*
Salter, Thomas; New York, NY, 1815 ***2859.11*** *p41*
Saltinsck, Martin; Wisconsin, n.d. ***9675.7*** *p269*
Salton, William 42; Virginia, 1774 ***1219.7*** *p187*
Saltor, Jacob; Illinois, 1855 ***7857*** *p7*
Saltore, John 25; New Orleans, 1832 ***778.5*** *p481*
Saltrea, John; Virginia, 1642 ***6219*** *p186*
Saltzer, Anna Barbara 6 *SEE* Saltzer, Sebastian
Saltzer, Anna Maria Wolffart *SEE* Saltzer, Christoph
Saltzer, Christoph; America, 1749 ***2444*** *p207*
*Wife:*Anna Maria Wolffart
*Child:*Johann Georg
*Child:*Zacharias
With children
Saltzer, George 10 wks *SEE* Saltzer, Sebastian
Saltzer, Johann Georg *SEE* Saltzer, Christoph
Saltzer, Rosina Barbara 9 *SEE* Saltzer, Sebastian
Saltzer, Sebastian; South Carolina, 1752-1753 ***3689.17*** *p22*
With wife
*Relative:*Rosina Barbara 9
*Relative:*Anna Barbara 6
*Relative:*Sebastian 4
*Relative:*George 10 wks
Saltzer, Sebastian 4 *SEE* Saltzer, Sebastian
Saltzer, Zacharias *SEE* Saltzer, Christoph
Saltzman, Henry; San Francisco, 1880 ***2764.35*** *p60*
Saltzman, Samuel George; Arkansas, 1918 ***95.2*** *p108*
Salucci, Francesco 30; West Virginia, 1904 ***9788.3*** *p20*
Salvage, John 39; Kansas, 1880 ***5240.1*** *p62*
Salvan, Angelo 18 mos *SEE* Salvan, Ceves
Salvan, Ceves 32; New York, NY, 1893 ***9026.4*** *p42*
*Relative:*Teresa 30
*Relative:*Ginseppe 3
*Relative:*Angelo 18 mos
Salvan, Ginseppe 3 *SEE* Salvan, Ceves
Salvan, Teresa 30 *SEE* Salvan, Ceves
Salvatore, Salamone; Iowa, 1866-1943 ***123.54*** *p43*
Salver, Thomas 30; Philadelphia, 1774 ***1219.7*** *p233*
Salvesen, Emma Marie Gustava; Washington, 1859-1920 ***2872.1*** *p35*
Salvesen, Hans; Washington, 1859-1920 ***2872.1*** *p35*
Salvesen, Johan Magnus; Washington, 1859-1920 ***2872.1*** *p35*
Salvesen, Lena; Washington, 1859-1920 ***2872.1*** *p35*
Salvesen, Maylene; Washington, 1859-1920 ***2872.1*** *p35*
Salvesen, Randy Louise; Washington, 1859-1920 ***2872.1*** *p35*
Salvesen, Segward; Washington, 1859-1920 ***2872.1*** *p35*
Salvesen, Stuart; Washington, 1859-1920 ***2872.1*** *p35*
Salvidi, Mike; Arkansas, 1918 ***95.2*** *p108*
Salvonski, Eguaz; Iowa, 1866-1943 ***123.54*** *p43*
Salzer, Anna Maria Wolffart *SEE* Salzer, Christoph
Salzer, Christoph; America, 1749 ***2444*** *p207*
*Wife:*Anna Maria Wolffart
*Child:*Johann Georg
*Child:*Zacharias
With children
Salzer, Johann Georg *SEE* Salzer, Christoph
Salzer, Zacharias *SEE* Salzer, Christoph
Samalionis, Stanislau; Wisconsin, n.d. ***9675.7*** *p269*
Samalonis, Anufras; Wisconsin, n.d. ***9675.7*** *p269*
Samanos, Augustus; New York, NY, 1836 ***8208.4*** *p9*
Sames, Eliz.; Virginia, 1636 ***6219*** *p7*
Samiec, . . .; New York, 1831 ***4606*** *p177*
Samler, Charles 14; Virginia, 1727 ***3690.1*** *p197*
Sammell, Ann 15; Maryland or Virginia, 1699 ***2212*** *p23*
Sammersan, Ellen; Montreal, 1824 ***7603*** *p99*
Sammes, John 42; Savannah, GA, 1733 ***4719.17*** *p312*
Sammonds, Thomas 24; Maryland, 1775 ***1219.7*** *p250*
Sammony, George 16; Philadelphia, 1774 ***1219.7*** *p183*
Samms, Richard 22; Maryland, 1774 ***1219.7*** *p202*
Samon, Joseph; Virginia, 1635 ***6219*** *p73*
Samosjka, Benedict; Wisconsin, n.d. ***9675.7*** *p269*
Sampell, James 32; Virginia, 1775 ***1219.7*** *p261*
Sample, John 20; Massachusetts, 1849 ***5881.1*** *p90*
Sampson, Mr. 40; New Orleans, 1823 ***778.5*** *p481*
Sampson, David; New York, NY, 1815 ***2859.11*** *p41*
Sampson, Edward 16; Maryland, 1737 ***3690.1*** *p197*
Sampson, James; Virginia, 1639 ***6219*** *p150*
Sampson, John; Baltimore, 1816 ***2859.11*** *p41*
Sampson, Rachael 23; Maryland, 1775 ***1219.7*** *p260*
Sampt, George Anthony 19; Jamaica, 1730 ***3690.1*** *p197*
Sams, James; Virginia, 1643 ***6219*** *p229*
Samson, J.; Minneapolis, 1880-1883 ***6410.35*** *p65*
Samson, Jakobson Maland; Wisconsin, n.d. ***9675.7*** *p269*
Samson, John 20; Pennsylvania, 1730 ***3690.1*** *p197*
Samson, S. 26; New Orleans, 1835 ***778.5*** *p481*
Samuel, Gilbert 21; Maryland, 1775 ***1219.7*** *p250*
Samuel, Jeanette 26; America, 1853 ***9162.7*** *p15*
Samuel, Jette 22; America, 1853 ***9162.7*** *p15*
Samuel, John; Arkansas, 1918 ***95.2*** *p108*
Samuel, Robert 22; Philadelphia, 1774 ***1219.7*** *p237*
Samuel, Salomon 33; America, 1836 ***778.5*** *p481*
Samuell, Edw.; Virginia, 1643 ***6219*** *p229*
Samuelson, August; Illinois, 1862 ***5012.38*** *p98*
Samuelson, Charles; Minneapolis, 1866-1879 ***6410.35*** *p65*
Samuelson, Harold V. C.; Washington, 1859-1920 ***2872.1*** *p35*
Samuelson, J. O.; Minneapolis, 1881-1884 ***6410.35*** *p65*
Samuelson, Johannes; Minneapolis, 1880-1883 ***6410.35*** *p65*
Samuelson, Pete; Washington, 1859-1920 ***2872.1*** *p35*
Samuelson, Salomon; Minneapolis, 1881-1883 ***6410.35*** *p65*
Samuelsson, Carl Alfred; Minneapolis, 1866-1879 ***6410.35*** *p65*
Samuelsson, Salomon; Minneapolis, 1881-1883 ***6410.35*** *p65*
Sanbatch, John 13; Grenada, 1774 ***1219.7*** *p237*
Sanbeck, Charles; Colorado, 1903 ***9678.2*** *p166*
Sanches, S. 23; Arizona, 1910 ***9228.40*** *p15*
Sanches, Sediaco 65; Arizona, 1925 ***9228.40*** *p29*
Sanches, William 42; Arizona, 1890 ***2764.35*** *p66*
Sanchez, Daniel; Arkansas, 1918 ***95.2*** *p108*
Sanchez, J. 22; Port uncertain, 1839 ***778.5*** *p482*
Sanchez, Joseph; New York, NY, 1840 ***8208.4*** *p103*
Sand, Nicholas; Wisconsin, n.d. ***9675.7*** *p269*
Sandahl, C. E.; Minneapolis, 1882-1883 ***6410.35*** *p65*
Sandahl, John; Minneapolis, 1873-1888 ***6410.35*** *p65*
Sandal, George Christoffer John; Arkansas, 1918 ***95.2*** *p108*
Sandall, Edward; Virginia, 1636 ***6219*** *p80*
Sandall, Edward; Virginia, 1637 ***6219*** *p112*
Sandalo, Michael; America, 1898 ***7137*** *p170*
Sandanger, Nikolai B.; Washington, 1859-1920 ***2872.1*** *p35*
Sandau, Christian; America, 1847 ***8582.1*** *p29*
Sandberg, Abram; Maine, 1871-1882 ***6410.22*** *p119*
Sandberg, Alfred; Iowa, 1866-1943 ***123.54*** *p43*
Sandberg, Robert; Arkansas, 1918 ***95.2*** *p108*
Sandell, Joseph 20; Maryland, 1718 ***3690.1*** *p197*
Sandell, Michael; America, 1743 ***4971*** *p65*
Sandells, Joseph 20; Maryland, 1718 ***3690.1*** *p197*
Sander, . . .; Canada, 1776-1783 ***9786*** *p32*
Sander, Miss; America, 1853 ***4610.10*** *p144*
Sander, Adam 19; America, 1853 ***9162.8*** *p37*
Sander, Albert 26; New York, 1912 ***9980.29*** *p57*
Sander, Anne C. W. Caroline *SEE* Sander, Carl Ludwig
Sander, Anne M. L. Wilhelmine *SEE* Sander, Carl Ludwig
Sander, Anne M. W. Elisabeth *SEE* Sander, Carl Ludwig
Sander, Anne Marie Louise Wilhelmine; America, 1856 ***4610.10*** *p157*
Sander, Anne Marie W.E. Albert *SEE* Sander, Carl Ludwig
Sander, Barbara 25; America, 1853 ***9162.8*** *p37*
Sander, C.; Quebec, 1776 ***9786*** *p105*
Sander, Carl Friedrich *SEE* Sander, Carl Ludwig
Sander, Carl Heinrich; America, 1856 ***4610.10*** *p157*
With wife
*Son:*Heinrich F. Eduard
Sander, Carl Ludwig 52; America, 1856 ***4610.10*** *p157*
*Child:*Ernst F. Heinrich
*Child:*Anne M. W. Elisabeth
*Child:*Carl Friedrich
*Child:*Charlotte Dorothea
*Child:*Anne C. W. Caroline
*Child:*Friedrich Wilhelm
*Child:*Anne M. L. Wilhelmine
*Wife:*Anne Marie W.E. Albert
Sander, Charlotte Dorothea *SEE* Sander, Carl Ludwig
Sander, Christine; America, 1850 ***4610.10*** *p142*
Sander, Christine Louise Engel 22; America, 1850 ***4610.10*** *p143*
Sander, Christoph Heinrich; America, 1850 ***4610.10*** *p139*
*Wife:*Louise W. Solle
Sander, Conrad; Wisconsin, n.d. ***9675.7*** *p269*
Sander, Engel 19; New York, NY, 1867 ***3702.7*** *p571*
Sander, Ernst F. Heinrich *SEE* Sander, Carl Ludwig
Sander, F. W.; Kansas, 1893 ***5240.1*** *p38*
Sander, Friedrich Wilhelm *SEE* Sander, Carl Ludwig
Sander, Heinerick; Canada, 1783 ***9786*** *p38A*
Sander, Heinrich F. Eduard *SEE* Sander, Carl Heinrich

Sander, Jacob Christian; Quebec, 1776 9786 p254
Sander, Johannes 57; America, 1853 9162.8 p37
Sander, Louise W. Solle SEE Sander, Christoph Heinrich
Sander, Maria 17; America, 1853 9162.8 p37
Sander, Marie 56; America, 1853 9162.8 p37
Sander, Marie Cath. Christine; America, 1850 4610.10 p139
Sander, Mathilde; America, 1850 4610.10 p142
Sander, Zacharias Heinrich; America, 1850 4610.10 p139
Sanderby, Tho.; Virginia, 1642 6219 p189
Sandergard, Holger Peterson; Arkansas, 1918 95.2 p108
Sanders, Mr.; America, 1836-1838 3702.7 p102
Sanders, Daniel 27; Maryland, 1775 1219.7 p253
Sanders, Eliza.; Virginia, 1643 6219 p206
Sanders, Elizabeth; St. John, N.B., 1850 5704.8 p62
Sanders, Henry; Virginia, 1643 6219 p200
Sanders, Isabell; Virginia, 1638 6219 p121
Sanders, James; New York, NY, 1811 2859.11 p19
Sanders, John; Charleston, SC, 1805 1639.20 p278
Sanders, John 15; Virginia, 1774 1219.7 p186
Sanders, John 20; Jamaica, 1731 3690.1 p197
Sanders, John 21; Maryland, 1774 1219.7 p184
Sanders, Jon.; Virginia, 1637 6219 p113
Sanders, Joseph; Bermuda, 1751 1219.7 p6
Sanders, Joseph; Ohio, 1857 6014.2 p7
Sanders, Katherine; Virginia, 1635 6219 p6
Sanders, Margarett; Virginia, 1638 6219 p122
Sanders, Michaell; Virginia, 1642 6219 p189
Sanders, Richard; Virginia, 1639 6219 p151
Sanders, Robert; St. John, N.B., 1849 5704.8 p49
Sanders, Robert; Virginia, 1638 6219 p148
Sanders, Roxana 20; Philadelphia, 1774 1219.7 p212
Sanders, Thomas; Virginia, 1646 6219 p241
Sanders, Thomas 18; Virginia, 1774 1219.7 p201
Sanders, William; Newfoundland, 1774 1219.7 p196
Sanders, William; Virginia, 1639 6219 p151
Sanders, William 22; Maryland, 1775 1219.7 p262
Sanders, William 23; Maryland, 1724 3690.1 p197
Sanderson, Ann; St. John, N.B., 1847 5704.8 p9
Sanderson, Ann J.; New York, NY, 1865 5704.8 p201
Sanderson, Bernard; California, 1863 3840.3 p10
Sanderson, Edward; Virginia, 1639 6219 p155
Sanderson, James; New York, NY, 1865 5704.8 p201
Sanderson, James 12; St. John, N.B., 1847 5704.8 p9
Sanderson, John 5; St. John, N.B., 1847 5704.8 p9
Sanderson, John 45; Carolina, 1774 1219.7 p236
Sanderson, Joseph 20; Maryland, 1720 3690.1 p197
Sanderson, Rebecca 13; St. John, N.B., 1847 5704.8 p9
Sanderson, Robert 10; St. John, N.B., 1847 5704.8 p9
Sanderson, Sally; St. John, N.B., 1847 5704.8 p9
Sanderson, Thomas 22; Philadelphia, 1833-1834 53.26 p81
Sanderson, William; St. John, N.B., 1847 5704.8 p9
Sandes, Mahoudeastus 25; America, 1838 778.5 p482
Sandey, Gus Victor; Washington, 1859-1920 2872.1 p35
Sandford, Charles; New York, NY, 1837 8208.4 p40
Sandford, Elinor; America, 1741 4971 p16
Sandford, John 22; St. John, N.B., 1854 5704.8 p119
Sandford, Mary Eliza 6; Quebec, 1851 5704.8 p74
Sandhagen, . . .; Canada, 1776-1783 9786 p32
Sandhagen, . . .; Canada, 1783 9786 p38A
Sandhop, August; Iroquois Co., IL, 1896 3455.1 p13
Sandin, Edwin; Washington, 1859-1920 2872.1 p35
Sandin, Elsgie; Washington, 1859-1920 2872.1 p35
Sandin, Emma; Washington, 1859-1920 2872.1 p35
Sandin, Oscar; Washington, 1859-1920 2872.1 p35
Sandin, Waldemar; Washington, 1859-1920 2872.1 p35
Sandish, Stephen; Virginia, 1642 6219 p188
Sandlant, William 21; Maryland, 1774 1219.7 p208
Sandler, Morris 21; Kansas, 1903 5240.1 p82
Sandmann, Friederich Heinrich; America, 1844 8582.3 p56
Sandmann, J. H.; Cincinnati, 1869-1887 8582 p26
Sandoz, Marguerite; Port uncertain, 1752 7074.6 p203
Sandrock, Andreas; Halifax, N.S., 1778 9786 p270
Sandrock, Andreas; New York, 1776 9786 p270
Sands, Bernard; New York, NY, 1837 8208.4 p53
Sands, James; Charleston, SC, 1767 1639.20 p278
Sands, Mary; Virginia, 1648 6219 p248
Sands, Wm.; Virginia, 1844 4626.16 p13
Sandstedt, N.P. 33; Massachusetts, 1860 6410.32 p114
Sandstedt, Nils P.; America, 1853 6410.32 p125
Sandstrom, John Fridolf; Washington, 1859-1920 2872.1 p35
Sandstrom, John Peter; Arkansas, 1918 95.2 p109
Sandstrom, Louis; Iroquois Co., IL, 1892 3455.1 p13
Sandulo, Michel; Arkansas, 1918 95.2 p109
Sandusky, Jakob; Kentucky, 1774 8582.3 p96
Brother:Joseph
Sandusky, Johann; America, 1740-1760 8582.3 p96
Sandusky, Joseph SEE Sandusky, Jakob
Sandvick, Peter P.; Arkansas, 1918 95.2 p109
Sandwell, Laurence; Illinois, 1872 5012.37 p59
Sandwell, Martin; Illinois, 1898 5012.40 p55
Sandy, E.; Minneapolis, 1870-1880 6410.35 p65
Sandys, Geo.; Virginia, 1624 6219 p67
Sandys, Georg; Virginia, 1621 6219 p29
Sanem, B.; Wisconsin, n.d. 9675.7 p269
Sanem, Batis; Wisconsin, n.d. 9675.7 p269
Sanem, John; Wisconsin, n.d. 9675.7 p269
Sanford, Eliza 23; St. John, N.B., 1861 5704.8 p147
Sanftleben, Georg; Georgia, 1739 9332 p324
Sanftleben, Georg; Georgia, 1739 9332 p326
Sanger, Stephen 40; Philadelphia, 1774 1219.7 p182
Sangerhausen, . . .; Canada, 1776-1783 9786 p32
Sangerhausen, Anna Margaret SEE Sangerhausen, Christian Jacob
Sangerhausen, Christian Jacob; New York, 1749 3652 p71
Wife:Anna Margaret
Sangster, Guillaume; Quebec, 1782 7603 p35
Sangster, John; Charleston, SC, 1796 1639.20 p278
Sangster, John 21; Virginia, 1773 1219.7 p169
Sangster, William; Charleston, SC, 1797 1639.20 p278
Sangster, William 19; Montserrat, 1774 1219.7 p242
Sanicki, Jozef; New York, 1831 4606 p177
Sanidas, Constantine Stamation; Arkansas, 1918 95.2 p109
Sanidas, Constantine Stamatios; Arkansas, 1918 95.2 p109
Sanin, Robert; Virginia, 1643 6219 p203
Sanios, Gus; Arkansas, 1918 95.2 p109
Saniusa, J. 24; New Orleans, 1827 778.5 p482
Sanne, Jean 23; Port uncertain, 1838 778.5 p482
Sanner, Sarah; Virginia, 1642 6219 p186
Sanning, Johann Hermann; Ohio, 1869-1887 8582 p26
Sannman, Erik; America, 1849 2090 p614
Sannum, Sigvard Peterson; Arkansas, 1918 95.2 p109
Sanot, J. 27; Port uncertain, 1836 778.5 p482
Sansat, Gaudens 36; New Orleans, 1838 778.5 p482
Sansat, Joseph 30; New Orleans, 1839 778.5 p482
Sansate, J. 26; Port uncertain, 1835 778.5 p482
Sanscartier, Pierre; Quebec, 1688 4533 p127
Sansfelt, Anna Maria Henrici; Philadelphia, 1738-1768 4525 p281
Sansom, Benjamin; Indiana, 1845 9117 p18
Sansom, Luke 26; Maryland, 1774 1219.7 p192
Santa Cruz, Jose 28; California, 1867 3840.3 p10
Santache, Nicola; Arkansas, 1918 95.2 p109
Santangelo, Fiora; Wisconsin, n.d. 9675.7 p269
Santer, Anna C. Hindermann SEE Santer, Johann Georg
Santer, Johann Georg; Pennsylvania, 1753 2444 p167
Wife:Anna C. Hindermann
Santerin, Jacobina; Virginia, 1775 1219.7 p275
Santilles, Mr. 22; New Orleans, 1839 778.5 p482
Santo, Filippi; Iowa, 1866-1943 123.54 p43
Santuro, Enrico; Arkansas, 1918 95.2 p109
Saolomon, Eduard; Cincinnati, 1788-1848 8582.3 p90
Saparta, H. 60; Arizona, 1909 9228.40 p14
Sapheir, George; Virginia, 1636 6219 p79
Saphton, William 19; Windward Islands, 1722 3690.1 p197
Sapper, John; Illinois, 1884 2896.5 p34
Sapper, Karl; Illinois, 1884 2896.5 p35
Saquateur, Mr. 55; America, 1838 778.5 p482
Saracco, Josef 15; New York, NY, 1893 9026.4 p42
Relative:Mary 45
Saracco, Mary 45 SEE Saracco, Josef
Saracen, Anne; Philadelphia, 1864 5704.8 p170
Saradet, Jeanne 30; New Orleans, 1836 778.5 p482
Sarem, Jack; Arkansas, 1918 95.2 p109
Sargato, Victor; Arkansas, 1918 95.2 p109
Sargent, Mr. 24; Mexico, 1829 778.5 p482
Sarges, . . .; Canada, 1776-1783 9786 p32
Sargood, John 21; Maryland, 1774 1219.7 p225
Sariat, Mr. 23; Port uncertain, 1836 778.5 p482
Sarignac, Charles 23; New Orleans, 1823 778.5 p482
Sarikaki, Demetrios; Arkansas, 1918 95.2 p109
Sarinsen, Saren; Iowa, 1866-1943 123.54 p43
Sarmer, Lodowick; Philadelphia, 1760 9973.7 p34
Sarnbloom, Augustus 30; Kansas, 1886 5240.1 p68
Sarnecki, Anthony John; Arkansas, 1918 95.2 p109
Sarnighausen, John F. A.; Washington, 1859-1920 2872.1 p35
Saroczka, Matansz; Wisconsin, n.d. 9675.7 p269
Sarodet, Mr. 18; America, 1837 778.5 p482
Sarol, Mrs. 22; New Orleans, 1822 778.5 p483
Sarotte, Pre. 30; New Orleans, 1839 778.5 p483
Sarraailh, August; Arkansas, 1918 95.2 p109
Sarradet, Mr. 21; America, 1839 778.5 p483
Sarradet, Mr. 23; America, 1839 778.5 p483
Sarradet, Jean Bertrand 29; Port uncertain, 1838 778.5 p483
Sarrat, Mr. 23; Port uncertain, 1836 778.5 p482
Sarrat, Antoine 24; New Orleans, 1827 778.5 p483
Sarratt, George 27; Virginia, 1774 1219.7 p244
Sarraute, Louis Jean 21; Port uncertain, 1838 778.5 p483
Sarris, John; Arkansas, 1918 95.2 p109
Sarrot, J. 27; Port uncertain, 1836 778.5 p482
Sarsonn, Wm.; Virginia, 1638 6219 p11
Sarti, Odoardo 32; New York, NY, 1893 9026.4 p42
Relative:Vitto 28
Sarti, Pa. 25; New York, NY, 1893 9026.4 p42
Sarti, Vitto 28 SEE Sarti, Odoardo
Sartonis, John; Iowa, 1866-1943 123.54 p43
Sartor, Valentine; Iowa, 1866-1943 123.54 p43
Sartor, Valentino; Iowa, 1866-1943 123.54 p43
Sartore, Vittorio; Arkansas, 1918 95.2 p109
Sarty, . . .; Halifax, N.S., 1752 7074.6 p232
Sarvent, William 20; Maryland, 1719 3690.1 p197
Sasade, Brounie; Arkansas, 1918 95.2 p109
Sasanelli, Michele; Arkansas, 1918 95.2 p109
Saschiazza, Domenico; Wisconsin, n.d. 9675.7 p269
Saschiazzi, Angelo; Wisconsin, n.d. 9675.7 p269
Sasm, Godfrid; America, 1843 1450.2 p124A
Sass, Jacob; Charleston, SC, 1775-1781 8582.2 p52
Sass, Jakob; Savannah, GA, 1779 8582.2 p52
Sass, John; Illinois, 1868 5012.38 p99
Sasse, . . .; Canada, 1776-1783 9786 p32
Sasse, Charles; Buffalo, NY, 1847 2896.5 p35
Sasse, Frederick; Illinois, 1866 2896.5 p35
Sasse, Gottlieb; Illinois, 1888 2896.5 p35
Sasse, Henry; Kansas, 1896 5240.1 p38
Sasse, Joseph; Wisconsin, n.d. 9675.7 p269
Sasse, Martin; Illinois, 1878 2896.5 p35
Sasse, Michael; Illinois, 1880 2896.5 p35
Sasse, Rudolph; Kansas, 1900 5240.1 p38
Sassell, John; Virginia, 1639 6219 p153
Sassen, Bruno Hopkes; America, 1904 3455.1 p45
Sasson, Albert 38; America, 1838 778.5 p483
Sasson, Clementine 9?; America, 1838 778.5 p483
Sasson, Elizabeth 44; America, 1838 778.5 p483
Sasson, Etienne 11?; America, 1838 778.5 p483
Sasson, Pierre 11?; America, 1838 778.5 p483
Sasucha, Jan 22; New York, 1912 9980.29 p70
Saszkowska, Emilia 25; New York, 1912 9980.29 p54
Satchfield, Elizabeth 24; Savannah, GA, 1733 4719.17 p312
Satchwell, Thomas 17; Maryland, 1775 1219.7 p273
Sater, Andrew A.; New York, NY, 1880 9678.2 p166
Satherley, Arthur E.; Wisconsin, n.d. 9675.7 p269
Satonin, Arkip; Wisconsin, n.d. 9675.7 p269
Satriano, Giovanni; Colorado, 1886 9678.2 p166
Sattinger, Jacob; Illinois, 1894 1450.2 p33B
Sattler, Christine 50; New York, NY, 1889 7846 p40
Sattler, Franz Ignatz 20; America, 1853 9162.8 p37
Sattler, Jacob 24; America, 1854-1855 9162.6 p104
Sattler, Michael 71; New York, NY, 1889 7846 p40
Sattler, Sebastian 30; America, 1853 9162.7 p15
Sattler, Stephan 17; New York, NY, 1889 7846 p40
Sattler, Wilhelm; Ohio, 1798-1818 8582.2 p54
Satums, Robert; Virginia, 1646 6219 p246
Satz, Eduard; Ohio, 1800-1812 8582.2 p57
Sauch, Frank; Wisconsin, n.d. 9675.7 p269
Sauchere, Francois 52; Port uncertain, 1836 778.5 p483
Sauck, Alouis; Wisconsin, n.d. 9675.7 p269
Saudry, Gabriel 18; New Orleans, 1827 778.5 p483
Sauell, Tho.; Virginia, 1638 6219 p11
Sauer, . . .; Canada, 1776-1783 9786 p32
Sauer, Mrs.; Pennsylvania, 1780 4525 p283
Sauer, Adam; America, 1854-1855 9162.6 p105
Sauer, Anna Marg. 20; America, 1853 9162.7 p15
Sauer, Fary; Wisconsin, n.d. 9675.7 p269
Sauer, Ferdinand; Wisconsin, n.d. 9675.7 p270
Sauer, Franc; Illinois, 1854 7857 p7
Sauer, Francis Joseph; New York, NY, 1840 8208.4 p110
Sauer, Fred; Washington, 1859-1920 2872.1 p35
Sauer, Friedrich; Charleston, SC, 1775-1781 8582.2 p52
Sauer, George; Illinois, 1854 7857 p7
Sauer, Gottlieb; Canada, 1783 9786 p38A
Sauer, Hanns Michel; Pennsylvania, 1754 4525 p239
Sauer, Hans Adam; New England, 1754 4525 p239
With wife
With children
Sauer, Hans Adam; Pennsylvania, 1754 4525 p239
Sauer, Henry; Philadelphia, 1760 9973.7 p34
Sauer, Johan Leonhard; Pennsylvania, 1753 4525 p239
Sauer, Johann Adam; Pennsylvania, 1753 4525 p239
Sauer, Johannes; Pennsylvania, 1754 4525 p239
Sauer, John; Wisconsin, n.d. 9675.7 p269
Sauer, Joseph; Wisconsin, n.d. 9675.7 p270
Sauer, Konrad; America, 1842 8582.1 p29
Sauer, Konrad; Trenton, NJ, 1776 8137 p13
Sauer, M.; Cincinnati, 1847 8582.1 p30
Sauer, Martin; New York, NY, 1847 8582.3 p57
Saugher, Elizabeth SEE Saugher, Georg
Saugher, Elizabeth SEE Saugher, Georg

Saugher, Georg; Virginia, 1637 ***6219*** *p111*
*Wife:*Elizabeth
*Daughter:*Elizabeth
*Brother:*Robert
Saugher, Robert *SEE* Saugher, Georg
Saughier, Elizabeth *SEE* Saughier, Georg
Saughier, Elizabeth *SEE* Saughier, Georg
Saughier, Georg; Virginia, 1637 ***6219*** *p111*
*Wife:*Elizabeth
*Daughter:*Elizabeth
*Brother:*Robert
Saughier, Robert *SEE* Saughier, Georg
Saul, John 13 *SEE* Saul, John
Saul, John 37; Virginia, 1774 ***1219.7*** *p243*
*Wife:*Mary 21
*Child:*S.L. 17
*Child:*John 13
Saul, Mary 21 *SEE* Saul, John
Saul, S.L. 17 *SEE* Saul, John
Saulls, Ole Nelson; Wisconsin, n.d. ***9675.7*** *p270*
Saultry, Daniel 29; New York, NY, 1851 ***6013.19*** *p73*
Saultry, William; Montreal, 1818 ***7603*** *p83*
Saunders, Edward; Halifax, N.S., 1833-1840 ***7036*** *p117*
Saunders, Edward; Massachusetts, 1833-1840 ***7036*** *p117*
Saunders, John; Virginia, 1636 ***6219*** *p34*
Saunders, John 42; Virginia, 1773 ***1219.7*** *p168*
Saunders, Jos.; Shreveport, LA, 1877 ***7129*** *p45*
Saunders, Mary 8; St. John, N.B., 1850 ***5704.8*** *p62*
Saunders, Rhoda 6 mos; St. John, N.B., 1850 ***5704.8*** *p62*
Saunders, Richard; Virginia, 1635 ***6219*** *p10*
Saunders, Robert 10; St. John, N.B., 1850 ***5704.8*** *p62*
Saunders, W. H. 23; Kansas, 1876 ***5240.1*** *p57*
Saunders, William; New York, NY, 1839 ***8208.4*** *p96*
Saunders, William; Virginia, 1638 ***6219*** *p153*
Saunderson, Agnes; Quebec, 1852 ***5704.8*** *p98*
Saunderson, Elizabeth; Quebec, 1852 ***5704.8*** *p87*
Saunderson, Elizabeth; Quebec, 1852 ***5704.8*** *p90*
Saunderson, Elizabeth; Quebec, 1852 ***5704.8*** *p98*
Saunderson, Ellan 2; Quebec, 1852 ***5704.8*** *p98*
Saunderson, Henry; New York, NY, 1816 ***2859.11*** *p41*
Saunderson, Isabella 1; Quebec, 1852 ***5704.8*** *p98*
Saunderson, Mary; Quebec, 1852 ***5704.8*** *p98*
Saunderson, Mary 12; Quebec, 1852 ***5704.8*** *p98*
Saunderson, Rachel 5; Quebec, 1852 ***5704.8*** *p98*
Saunderson, Robert; Illinois, 1859 ***7857*** *p7*
Saunderson, Robert 6; Quebec, 1852 ***5704.8*** *p98*
Saunderson, Thomas 7; Quebec, 1852 ***5704.8*** *p98*
Saunderson, William 9; Quebec, 1852 ***5704.8*** *p98*
Saunier, Adele; Port uncertain, 1839 ***778.5*** *p379*
Saupe, . . .; Canada, 1776-1783 ***9786*** *p32*
Saur, Adam; Pennsylvania, 1782 ***4525*** *p273*
With father
Saur, Christoph; Pennsylvania, 1724 ***8582.3*** *p78*
Saurer, Henri; Detroit, 1872 ***1450.2*** *p124A*
Saurin, Antoine E. 20; New Orleans, 1839 ***778.5*** *p484*
Sausey, John; Virginia, 1635 ***6219*** *p70*
Sausseleer, David; Virginia, 1775 ***1219.7*** *p275*
Saust, . . .; Canada, 1776-1783 ***9786*** *p32*
Sautel, Casimir 24; America, 1836 ***778.5*** *p484*
Sauter, . . .; Canada, 1776-1783 ***9786*** *p43*
Sauter, Anna 33 *SEE* Sauter, John George
Sauter, Anna C. Hindermann *SEE* Sauter, Johann Georg
Sauter, Georg; Pennsylvania, 1764 ***2444*** *p208*
Sauter, Johan Jerick 32; Pennsylvania, 1753 ***2444*** *p208*
Sauter, Johann Georg 32; Pennsylvania, 1753 ***2444*** *p207*
*Wife:*Anna C. Hindermann
*Child:*Johann Jacob
Sauter, Johann Jacob *SEE* Sauter, Johann Georg
Sauter, Johannes; Pennsylvania, 1749 ***2444*** *p208*
Sauter, John, Jr.; South Carolina, 1752-1753 ***3689.17*** *p22*
With wife
Sauter, John George; South Carolina, 1752-1753 ***3689.17*** *p22*
*Relative:*Anna 33
*Relative:*Magdalene 31
Sauter, Magdalene 31 *SEE* Sauter, John George
Sauter, Michael; New York, 1750 ***3652*** *p74*
Sautier, Jean 27; New Orleans, 1838 ***778.5*** *p484*
Sautteer, Johan Michale; Virginia, 1775 ***1219.7*** *p275*
Sautter, Adrien 24; Kansas, 1878 ***5240.1*** *p59*
Sautter, Anna *SEE* Sautter, Conrad
Sautter, Anna *SEE* Sautter, Martin
Sautter, Anna Maria *SEE* Sautter, Johannes
Sautter, Catharine Schatz *SEE* Sautter, Martin
Sautter, Conrad; New England, 1746-1756 ***2444*** *p208*
*Wife:*Anna
*Child:*Johannes
Sautter, Georg; Pennsylvania, 1753-1764 ***2444*** *p208*
Sautter, Hans Martin *SEE* Sautter, Johannes
Sautter, Johann Georg 32; Pennsylvania, 1753 ***2444*** *p207*
Sautter, Johannes *SEE* Sautter, Conrad
Sautter, Johannes; Pennsylvania, 1749 ***2444*** *p208*
*Wife:*Anna Maria
*Child:*Hans Martin
Sautter, Martin *SEE* Sautter, Martin
Sautter, Martin; New England, 1749 ***2444*** *p208*
*Wife:*Catharine Schatz
*Child:*Martin
*Child:*Anna
Sautter, Sophie; America, 1905 ***1763*** *p40D*
Sauvage, Helene; Quebec, 1787 ***7603*** *p79*
Sauvage, Juliane 19; New Orleans, 1837 ***778.5*** *p484*
Sauvage, Louis 30; New Orleans, 1837 ***778.5*** *p484*
Sauvage, Pierre 26; America, 1835 ***778.5*** *p484*
Sauvola, Gust; Washington, 1859-1920 ***2872.1*** *p35*
Sauvola, John; Washington, 1859-1920 ***2872.1*** *p35*
Saux, Bertram 22; New Orleans, 1839 ***778.5*** *p484*
Saux, Dominique 17; New Orleans, 1839 ***778.5*** *p484*
Saux, Jean 19; New Orleans, 1839 ***778.5*** *p484*
Saux, Michel 16; New Orleans, 1839 ***778.5*** *p484*
Savadge, Hannah; Virginia, 1621 ***6219*** *p30*
*Husband:*Thomas
Savadge, Thomas *SEE* Savadge, Hannah
Savadge, Willm.; Virginia, 1648 ***6219*** *p251*
Savage, Adele 38; America, 1838 ***778.5*** *p484*
Savage, Andrew; America, 1894 ***7137*** *p170*
Savage, Andrew B.; Illinois, 1870 ***7857*** *p7*
Savage, Anna; America, 1899 ***7137*** *p170*
Savage, Anthony 9 *SEE* Savage, John
Savage, Bartholomew 26; Jamaica, 1750 ***3690.1*** *p197*
Savage, David; Illinois, 1860 ***2896.5*** *p35*
Savage, Elizabeth; Philadelphia, 1866 ***5704.8*** *p215*
Savage, Elizabeth 55 *SEE* Savage, John
Savage, Eugene 3; America, 1838 ***778.5*** *p484*
Savage, Fr.; Virginia, 1635 ***6219*** *p33*
Savage, George; New York, NY, 1834 ***8208.4*** *p45*
Savage, Hugh 19; Philadelphia, 1865 ***5704.8*** *p164*
Savage, James 18; Philadelphia, 1864 ***5704.8*** *p156*
Savage, Jane 16; Philadelphia, 1864 ***5704.8*** *p161*
Savage, John; America, 1735-1743 ***4971*** *p8*
Savage, John; America, 1738-1743 ***4971*** *p91*
Savage, John; Colorado, 1900 ***9678.2*** *p166*
Savage, John 36; Virginia, 1774 ***1219.7*** *p193*
Savage, John 40; North America, 1774 ***1219.7*** *p199*
*Wife:*Elizabeth 55
*Child:*Anthony 9
Savage, John Stephan; Arkansas, 1918 ***95.2*** *p109*
Savage, Jos. 13; America, 1838 ***778.5*** *p484*
Savage, Jos. 33; America, 1838 ***778.5*** *p484*
Savage, Joseph 11; America, 1838 ***778.5*** *p484*
Savage, Joseph 22; Philadelphia, 1774 ***1219.7*** *p232*
Savage, Jules 9; America, 1838 ***778.5*** *p485*
Savage, Louis 6; America, 1838 ***778.5*** *p485*
Savage, Mary; Philadelphia, 1864 ***5704.8*** *p186*
Savage, Paul; Colorado, 1905 ***9678.2*** *p166*
Savage, Rich.; Virginia, 1623-1700 ***6219*** *p182*
Savage, Richard; Virginia, 1638 ***6219*** *p117*
Savage, Tho.; Virginia, 1635 ***6219*** *p12*
Savage, Thomas 33; Maryland, 1775 ***1219.7*** *p260*
Savage, William 18; Maryland, 1774 ***1219.7*** *p181*
Savane, Maurice; America, 1736 ***4971*** *p55*
Savane, Thomas; America, 1736 ***4971*** *p55*
Savani, Harry; Arkansas, 1918 ***95.2*** *p109*
Savarret, Charles 24; New Orleans, 1835 ***778.5*** *p485*
Savary, Mr. 25; New Orleans, 1820 ***778.5*** *p485*
Savary, J. 35; New Orleans, 1827 ***778.5*** *p485*
Savary, William; Virginia, 1637 ***6219*** *p112*
Savas, Mike Frank; Arkansas, 1918 ***95.2*** *p109*
Savaterre, Jn. 32; New Orleans, 1839 ***778.5*** *p485*
Savatier, John 21; Maryland, 1774 ***1219.7*** *p187*
Savenne, J. 32; New Orleans, 1836 ***778.5*** *p485*
Savery, A. 15; New Orleans, 1831 ***778.5*** *p485*
Savic, Andrew; America, 1894 ***7137*** *p170*
Savic, Anna; America, 1899 ***7137*** *p170*
Savickis, Charles; Wisconsin, n.d. ***9675.7*** *p270*
Savicks, Anthony; Wisconsin, n.d. ***9675.7*** *p270*
Savier, Sequin 30; Port uncertain, 1835 ***778.5*** *p485*
Savigny, Elizabeth 21; Philadelphia, 1774 ***1219.7*** *p234*
Savill, Joseph 18; Maryland or Virginia, 1736 ***3690.1*** *p198*
Savill, Robert 19; Jamaica, 1724 ***3690.1*** *p198*
Savin, Charles 24; Maryland, 1774 ***1219.7*** *p235*
Savlon, Louis; Colorado, 1904 ***9678.2*** *p167*
Savo, Henry; Washington, 1859-1920 ***2872.1*** *p35*
Savoy, Mr. 25; Port uncertain, 1836 ***778.5*** *p481*
Savy, Samuel 22; New Orleans, 1837 ***778.5*** *p485*
Savzen, Mike; Wisconsin, n.d. ***9675.7*** *p270*
Sawer, . . .; Canada, 1776-1783 ***9786*** *p32*
Sawers, William; America, 1779-1800 ***1639.20*** *p278*
Sawezka, Matausz; Wisconsin, n.d. ***9675.7*** *p270*
Sawhuk, Zozop; Arkansas, 1918 ***95.2*** *p28*
Sawhuk, Zozop; Arkansas, 1918 ***95.2*** *p109*
Sawicki, . . .; New York, 1831 ***4606*** *p177*
Sawicki, Alex; Arkansas, 1918 ***95.2*** *p109*
Sawickis, John; Wisconsin, n.d. ***9675.7*** *p270*
Sawin, Joseph; Illinois, 1829 ***8582.1*** *p55*
Sawler, John; Philadelphia, 1760 ***9973.7*** *p34*
Sawley, William 28; Jamaica, 1731 ***3690.1*** *p198*
Sawyer, Benjamin; St. Christopher, 1762 ***1219.7*** *p85*
Sawyer, Fra.; Virginia, 1635 ***6219*** *p20*
Sawyer, Frances *SEE* Sawyer, Thomas
Sawyer, Thomas; Virginia, 1637 ***6219*** *p82*
*Wife:*Frances
Sawyer, William; Virginia, 1642 ***6219*** *p195*
Sawyer, William 25; Quebec, 1815 ***9229.18*** *p80*
Sawyer, William 35; Maryland, 1775 ***1219.7*** *p253*
Sawyers, Mary; Philadelphia, 1853 ***5704.8*** *p103*
Sawyers, William 29; Philadelphia, 1854 ***5704.8*** *p116*
Sax, Bassett; Virginia, 1646 ***6219*** *p239*
Sax, Johan Edward; Washington, 1859-1920 ***2872.1*** *p35*
Sax, Newark; Illinois, 1870 ***5012.38*** *p99*
Sax, Thomas; Virginia, 1638 ***6219*** *p125*
Saxon, Den.; America, 1738 ***4971*** *p46*
Saxon, Dennis; America, 1739 ***4971*** *p46*
Saxon, Samuel; New York, 1754 ***3652*** *p80*
Saxton, Edmund 18; Georgia, 1735 ***3690.1*** *p198*
Saxton, Mary 23; Massachusetts, 1849 ***5881.1*** *p92*
Saxton, Patrick 22; Massachusetts, 1849 ***5881.1*** *p93*
Say, John; Virginia, 1639 ***6219*** *p155*
Say, Thomas; Virginia, 1642 ***6219*** *p190*
Saye, John; Virginia, 1637 ***6219*** *p86*
Saye, John; Virginia, 1648 ***6219*** *p245*
Sayer, . . .; Canada, 1776-1783 ***9786*** *p32*
Sayer, John 27; Georgia, 1774 ***1219.7*** *p188*
Sayer, William 27; Maryland, 1775 ***1219.7*** *p267*
Sayers, Mr.; Quebec, 1815 ***9229.18*** *p74*
Sayers, Charles 18; St. John, N.B., 1856 ***5704.8*** *p131*
Sayers, Edward; West Virginia, 1890 ***9788.3*** *p20*
Sayers, Edward 31; West Virginia, 1888 ***9788.3*** *p20*
Sayers, Rabro; Died enroute, 1875 ***4719.30*** *p258*
Sayler, Jacob; South Carolina, 1788 ***7119*** *p199*
Saylor, Arthur; Virginia, 1642 ***6219*** *p194*
Sayol, Prosper 27; America, 1836 ***778.5*** *p485*
Sayre, Joseph; New York, NY, 1840 ***8208.4*** *p113*
Sayron, J. B. 28; New Orleans, 1826 ***778.5*** *p485*
Saysill, John; Virginia, 1645 ***6219*** *p232*
Sayth, John 20; Pennsylvania, Virginia or Maryland, 1719 ***3690.1*** *p198*
Scaccia, Salvatori; Arkansas, 1918 ***95.2*** *p109*
Scaegro, William; Colorado, 1898 ***9678.2*** *p167*
Scahill, Margaret 37; Massachusetts, 1850 ***5881.1*** *p92*
Scaidfield, Luke; New York, NY, 1838 ***8208.4*** *p81*
Scalaipahe, . . .; Canada, 1776-1783 ***9786*** *p32*
Scalapino, Antonio 23; Kansas, 1873 ***5240.1*** *p54*
Scales, Geo.; Virginia, 1636 ***6219*** *p108*
Scalise, Frank Natale; Arkansas, 1918 ***95.2*** *p109*
Scallen, George 9; Quebec, 1853 ***5704.8*** *p103*
Scallen, Hannah; Philadelphia, 1865 ***5704.8*** *p200*
Scallen, Margaret; Quebec, 1853 ***5704.8*** *p103*
Scallen, Mary 11; Quebec, 1853 ***5704.8*** *p103*
Scallen, Thomas 9; Quebec, 1853 ***5704.8*** *p103*
Scalley, James; Quebec, 1825 ***7603*** *p66*
Scallon, Felix; Washington, 1859-1920 ***2872.1*** *p35*
Scallon, Hugh; Quebec, 1823 ***7603*** *p72*
Scallon, John; Philadelphia, 1847 ***53.26*** *p81*
*Relative:*Susan
Scallon, John; Philadelphia, 1847 ***5704.8*** *p23*
Scallon, Owen; St. John, N.B., 1847 ***5704.8*** *p33*
Scallon, Susan *SEE* Scallon, John
Scallon, Susan; Philadelphia, 1847 ***5704.8*** *p23*
Scally, Patrick 23; St. John, N.B., 1864 ***5704.8*** *p159*
Scally, Peter, Jr.; West Virginia, 1856 ***9788.3*** *p20*
Scalzi, Mike; Arkansas, 1918 ***95.2*** *p110*
Scammell, John 66; Massachusetts, 1849 ***5881.1*** *p90*
Scandler, Bryan; New York, NY, 1816 ***2859.11*** *p41*
Scandred, Edward 21; Philadelphia, 1774 ***1219.7*** *p205*
Scanlan, Anne 22; St. John, N.B., 1863 ***5704.8*** *p152*
Scanlan, Bridget 13; Massachusetts, 1848 ***5881.1*** *p87*
Scanlan, Catherine 11; St. John, N.B., 1863 ***5704.8*** *p152*
Scanlan, Cathrine 24; Philadelphia, 1853 ***5704.8*** *p111*
Scanlan, Edmund 27; Massachusetts, 1850 ***5881.1*** *p89*
Scanlan, Ellen 17; St. John, N.B., 1863 ***5704.8*** *p152*
Scanlan, Fanny 9; Massachusetts, 1849 ***5881.1*** *p89*
Scanlan, James 2; Massachusetts, 1849 ***5881.1*** *p90*
Scanlan, James 20; St. John, N.B., 1863 ***5704.8*** *p152*
Scanlan, John; Illinois, 1888 ***5012.37*** *p61*
Scanlan, John; Washington, 1859-1920 ***2872.1*** *p35*
Scanlan, John 6; Massachusetts, 1849 ***5881.1*** *p90*
Scanlan, John 7; Philadelphia, 1853 ***5704.8*** *p111*
Scanlan, John 14; St. John, N.B., 1863 ***5704.8*** *p152*
Scanlan, Joseph Hayes; New York, NY, 1837 ***8208.4*** *p24*
Scanlan, Kate 4; Massachusetts, 1849 ***5881.1*** *p91*
Scanlan, Letitia 4; St. John, N.B., 1863 ***5704.8*** *p153*
Scanlan, Luke 8; St. John, N.B., 1863 ***5704.8*** *p152*
Scanlan, Mary 7; Massachusetts, 1848 ***5881.1*** *p91*
Scanlan, Mary 12; Massachusetts, 1849 ***5881.1*** *p92*

Scanlan, Mary 24; Massachusetts, 1849 5881.1 p91
Scanlan, Pat 10; Philadelphia, 1853 5704.8 p111
Scanlan, Samuel 5; Massachusetts, 1849 5881.1 p93
Scanlan, Susan 40; St. John, N.B., 1863 5704.8 p152
Scanlan, Thomas 6; St. John, N.B., 1863 5704.8 p152
Scanlin, Michael; America, 1834 1450.2 p124A
Scanlon, Connors; America, 1740 4971 p32
Scanlon, Denis 36; Kansas, 1871 5240.1 p52
Scanlon, James; America, 1741 4971 p74
Scanlon, John; New York, NY, 1811 2859.11 p19
Scanlon, Maney; New York, NY, 1816 2859.11 p41
Scanlon, Thomas; America, 1739 4971 p14
Scanlon, Thomas; Washington, 1859-1920 2872.1 p36
Scanlon, William 5; Philadelphia, 1853 5704.8 p111
Scannel, Bridget 30; Massachusetts, 1849 5881.1 p88
Scannel, Catharine 20; Massachusetts, 1849 5881.1 p88
Scannel, Daniel 22; Massachusetts, 1848 5881.1 p88
Scannel, John; America, 1741 4971 p48
Scannell, Daniel; America, 1742-1743 4971 p42
Scannell, Florence; America, 1742 4971 p56
Scannell, Honor; America, 1740 4971 p48
Scannell, John; America, 1741-1742 4971 p60
Scannell, John; America, 1742 4971 p49
Scarano, Angela 8 SEE Scarano, Salvatore
Scarano, Ferdinando 11 SEE Scarano, Salvatore
Scarano, Maria 34 SEE Scarano, Salvatore
Scarano, Salvatore 39; New York, NY, 1893 9026.4 p42
Relative:Maria 34
Relative:Ferdinando 11
Relative:Angela 8
Scarborough, Edmond; Virginia, 1635 6219 p72
Mother:Hannah
Scarborough, Edward; Washington, 1859-1920 2872.1 p36
Scarborough, Hannah SEE Scarborough, Edmond
Scarborough, James 25; Maryland, 1774 1219.7 p235
Scarborough, Math.; Virginia, 1635 6219 p69
Scarborough, Tho.; Virginia, 1639 6219 p151
Scarburgh, Edmund; Virginia, 1640 6219 p160
Wife:Mary
Scarburgh, Mary SEE Scarburgh, Edmund
Scarf, John 34; Maryland, 1775 1219.7 p254
Scarffe, Thomas; America, 1740 4971 p86
Scarlatelli, Carmine 25; West Virginia, 1903 9788.3 p20
Scarlett, John 17; Jamaica, 1733 3690.1 p198
Scarnacacco, Martino 22; Arkansas, 1918 95.2 p110
Scarno, Jery; Colorado, 1904 9678.2 p167
Scarpelli, John; Washington, 1859-1920 2872.1 p36
Scarpelli, Salvatore; Washington, 1859-1920 2872.1 p36
Scarpello, Francesco; Colorado, 1903 9678.2 p167
Scarpula, Joseph; Arkansas, 1918 95.2 p110
Scarr, George 21; Maryland, 1775 1219.7 p261
Scarrott, George 19; Jamaica, 1749 3690.1 p198
Sceale, Walter; America, 1736 4971 p12
Scearle, John; Virginia, 1647 6219 p244
Scellan, Thos.; New York, NY, 1815 2859.11 p42
Schaab, Katharina 20; America, 1853 9162.8 p37
Schaab, Marie 52; America, 1853 9162.7 p15
Schaab, Nicklaus 18; America, 1853 9162.8 p37
Schaad, Martin; Cincinnati, 1788-1848 8582.3 p90
Schaaf, Adam; America, 1888 1450.2 p33B
Schaaf, Anna C. SEE Schaaf, John
Schaaf, Anna Catharina Loze; Pennsylvania, 1743 4525 p239
Husband:Thomas
Schaaf, Jeremiah; New York, 1748 3652 p68
Schaaf, John; New York, 1743 3652 p60
Wife:Anna C.
Schaaf, Thomas SEE Schaaf, Anna Catharina Loze
Schaaf, William; Virginia, 1852 4626.16 p14
Schaal, Anna Margaretha; South Carolina, 1760 2444 p134
Schaap, George Frederick; New York, NY, 1835 8208.4 p78
Schaber, Anna Catharina Schreiner; Pennsylvania, 1711-1783 4525 p247
Schaber, Johann Christof; Pennsylvania, 1752 4525 p239
Schaber, Johann Christoph; Pennsylvania, 1752 4525 p240
With wife
With 2 children
Schaber, Stophel; Died enroute, 1738 9898 p42
Schachel, Christoph; Wisconsin, n.d. 9675.7 p270
Schachel, Christopher; Wisconsin, n.d. 9675.7 p270
Schachman, Carl; Arizona, 1890 2764.35 p67
Schacht, . . .; Canada, 1776-1783 9786 p33
Schacht, Friedrich August von; Quebec, 1776 9786 p265
Schack, Theresia; Ohio, 1842 8582.1 p48
Schad, Anna Barbara SEE Schad, Johann Georg
Schad, George; Wisconsin, n.d. 9675.7 p270
Schad, Johann Georg 27; Pennsylvania, 1748 2444 p208
Wife:Martha
Child:Anna Barbara
Schad, Martha SEE Schad, Johann Georg
Schade, . . .; Canada, 1776-1783 9786 p33
Schade, Kath. Schonholz 23; Michigan, 1902 1763 p48D
Schade, William; Illinois, 1873 5012.39 p26
Schader, Medesch 16; New York, NY, 1878 9253 p46
Schaeber, Henry; Indiana, 1848 9117 p18
Schaefer, . . .; America, 1800-1813 8582.3 p76
Schaefer, Miss; America, 1748-1749 8125.6 p23
Schaefer, Mr.; Cincinnati, 1853 8582.2 p47
Schaefer, Agnes; America, 1730-1800 2444 p208
Schaefer, Andreas SEE Schaefer, Georg
Schaefer, Anna SEE Schaefer, Georg
Schaefer, Barbara SEE Schaefer, Georg
Schaefer, Carl; Savannah, GA, 1779 8582.2 p52
Schaefer, Carl Friedrich Wilhelm; America, 1867 4610.10 p100
Schaefer, Catharina SEE Schaefer, Georg
Schaefer, Charles; America, 1860 5240.1 p38
Schaefer, David; Philadelphia, 1763 9973.7 p38
Schaefer, Dietrich; Philadelphia, 1779 8137 p13
Schaefer, Ernst; Philadelphia, 1869-1887 8582 p26
Schaefer, Ferdinand; Cincinnati, 1830-1849 8582 p26
Schaefer, Frank H. P.; New York, 1883 1450.2 p33B
Schaefer, Georg; New England, 1752 4525 p240
With wife
With 4 children
Schaefer, Georg; Pennsylvania, 1754 4525 p240
Wife:Barbara
Son:Andreas
Son:Joerg
Daughter:Catharina
Daughter:Anna
Schaefer, Georg Wilhelm; Cincinnati, 1819 8582.3 p87
Schaefer, Gottlieb; Illinois, 1866 2896.5 p35
Schaefer, Gottliebin; Port uncertain, 1785 2444 p208
With uncle
Schaefer, Heinrich A.; America, 1842 8582.1 p30
Schaefer, J.; Ohio, 1801-1802 8582.2 p55
Schaefer, Jacob; America, 1830 8582.2 p61
Schaefer, Joerg SEE Schaefer, Georg
Schaefer, Johann Adam; Pennsylvania, 1752 4525 p240
Brother:Peter
Schaefer, John A.; Cincinnati, 1869-1887 8582 p26
Schaefer, Louis; Philadelphia, 1830 8582 p27
With parents
Schaefer, Maria Agnes; America, 1731-1800 2444 p208
Schaefer, Maria Magdalena; Philadelphia, 1785-1791 4525 p198
Schaefer, Peter SEE Schaefer, Johann Adam
Schaefer, Wilh. 15; America, 1854-1855 9162.6 p104
Schaeffer, . . .; Canada, 1776-1783 9786 p33
Schaeffer, Christian SEE Schaeffer, Johanes
Schaeffer, Christina; Alberta, 1909-1950 5262 p58
Schaeffer, Christopher; Canada, 1776-1783 9786 p243
Schaeffer, Dorothea; New England, 1754 2444 p209
Child:Johann Georg
Schaeffer, Godhard; Canada, 1776-1783 9786 p207A
Schaeffer, Hans Adam; Pennsylvania, 1752 4525 p240
Schaeffer, Hans Martin, Jr.; New England, 1742-1800 2444 p209
Wife:Maria Rosina
Child:Johann Jacob
Schaeffer, Hans Martin, Jr.; Pennsylvania, 1749-1754 2444 p209
Schaeffer, Jacob; Cincinnati, 1869-1887 8582 p27
Schaeffer, Johanes; Pennsylvania, 1752 4525 p241
Relative:Christian
Schaeffer, Johann Georg SEE Schaeffer, Dorothea
Schaeffer, Johann Jacob SEE Schaeffer, Hans Martin, Jr.
Schaeffer, Johannes; America, 1854-1855 9162.6 p105
Schaeffer, Joseph 36; Port uncertain, 1839 778.5 p485
Schaeffer, Konrad Henrich; Lancaster, PA, 1780 8137 p13
Schaeffer, Louis; Illinois, 1876 2896.5 p35
Schaeffer, Ludwig; Cincinnati, 1812 8582.1 p51
Schaeffer, Maria Rosina SEE Schaeffer, Hans Martin, Jr.
Schaeffer, Nicholaus; Illinois, 1894 5012.40 p53
Schaeffer, Peter; Cincinnati, 1869-1887 8582 p27
Schaeffer, Vallentin 30; Pennsylvania, 1753 4525 p244
Schaefter, Ullrich; Kentucky, 1839-1840 8582.3 p99
Schaert, Nicholas; Wisconsin, n.d. 9675.7 p270
Schaerthle, Johannes; Pennsylvania, 1752 2444 p210
Schaetzlein, Bartel; New England, 1752 4525 p221
Schaetzlein, Bartel; New England, 1752 4525 p241
With wife
With 7 children
Schaetzlein, Barthel; Pennsylvania, 1752 4525 p241
Schaetzlein, Johann Andreas; New England, 1773 4525 p241
With wife & 2 children
Schaetzlein, Johann Andreas; Pennsylvania, 1773 4525 p241
With wife
With 2 children
Schaeurich, Jacob; Pennsylvania, 1752 4525 p241
Schafer, . . .; Canada, 1776-1783 9786 p33
Schafer, Mr.; America, 1873-1890 4610.10 p161
With son
Schafer, A.M.C.W. Luckenagel SEE Schafer, Heinrich Philipp
Schafer, A. M. Wilhelmine Luise SEE Schafer, Heinrich Philipp
Schafer, Adam 27; America, 1853 9162.7 p15
Schafer, Barb. 16; America, 1853 9162.7 p15
Schafer, Carl Fr. SEE Schafer, Heinrich Philipp
Schafer, Catharina 21; New York, NY, 1889 7846 p40
Schafer, Catharina Maurer; America, 1764 2854 p45
With husband & 4 children
Schafer, Conrad; Wisconsin, n.d. 9675.7 p270
Schafer, Elis. 22; America, 1853 9162.7 p15
Schafer, Ernst August SEE Schafer, Heinrich Philipp
Schafer, Ernst Fr. W.; America, 1890 4610.10 p161
Schafer, Franz 9; New York, NY, 1889 7846 p39
Schafer, Friedr. 69; Wisconsin, 1897 1763 p40D
Schafer, Friedrich W. SEE Schafer, Heinrich Philipp
Schafer, Friedrich Wilhelm; America, 1850 4610.10 p108
Schafer, Friedrich Wilhelm; America, 1854 4610.10 p157
Schafer, George; Virginia, 1844 4626.16 p12
Schafer, Heinrich Philipp; America, 1887 4610.10 p153
Wife:A.M.C.W. Luckenagel
Child:Carl Fr.
Child:Friedrich W.
Child:Hermann Heinrich
Child:Ernst August
Child:A. M. Wilhelmine Luise
Schafer, Herman 24; Harris Co., TX, 1900 6254 p6
Schafer, Hermann Heinrich SEE Schafer, Heinrich Philipp
Schafer, Jacob; America, 1854-1855 9162.6 p104
Schafer, Jacob 16; New York, NY, 1889 7846 p39
Schafer, Jacob 41; New York, NY, 1889 7846 p39
Schafer, Jacob 46; New York, NY, 1889 7846 p39
Schafer, Johannes; Philadelphia, 1756 4525 p261
Schafer, Johannes 7; New York, NY, 1889 7846 p39
Schafer, Josef 22; New York, NY, 1889 7846 p40
Schafer, Joseph; Wisconsin, n.d. 9675.7 p270
Schafer, Katharina 19; America, 1853 9162.7 p15
Schafer, Kunigunde 15; New York, NY, 1889 7846 p39
Schafer, Magdalena 13; New York, NY, 1889 7846 p39
Schafer, Magdalena 44; New York, NY, 1889 7846 p39
Schafer, Maria 49; Pittsburgh, 1912 1763 p40D
Schafer, Marianna 6 mos; New York, NY, 1889 7846 p40
Schafer, Mich. 11 mos; America, 1853 9162.7 p15
Schafer, Mich. 18; America, 1853 9162.7 p15
Schafer, Michel 73; New York, NY, 1889 7846 p39
Schafer, Paul 19; New York, NY, 1889 7846 p39
Schafer, Sebestian 18; New York, NY, 1889 7846 p39
Schafer, Tufilia 6 mos; New York, NY, 1889 7846 p39
Schafers, Theodore 26; Kansas, 1882 5240.1 p64
Schaffalisky, . . .; Canada, 1776-1783 9786 p33
Schaffalisky, Friedrich von; Canada, 1777 9786 p266
Schaffalisky A. Mucadelle, Friedrich; Canada, 1776-1783 9786 p243
Schaffer, . . .; Canada, 1776-1783 9786 p33
Schaffer, Carl Friedrich Wilhelm; America, 1856 4610.10 p157
Schaffer, Carl Heinrich; America, 1884 4610.10 p153
Schaffer, Carl Heinrich Christian; America, 1883 4610.10 p160
Schaffer, Carl Heinrich Fr.; America, 1882 4610.10 p153
Schaffer, David; Philadelphia, 1776 8582.3 p83
Schaffer, Ernst Heinrich Friedrich; America, 1872 4610.10 p101
Schaffer, Henry; New York, NY, 1838 8208.4 p88
Schaffer, John; Illinois, 1854 7857 p7
Schaffer, John; Wisconsin, n.d. 9675.7 p270
Schaffer, Louise 20; America, 1872 4610.10 p101
Schaffer, Wilhelmine 26; America, 1872 4610.10 p159
Schaffmann, Joseph; Wisconsin, n.d. 9675.7 p270
Schafhauser, Michael 48; Indiana, 1906 1450.2 p33B
Schahill, Honora 7; Massachusetts, 1850 5881.1 p89
Schahl, Anna Maria; America, 1766-1816 2444 p209
Schahl, Hans Georg; America, 1766-1816 2444 p209
Schaible, John Baptist; Wisconsin, n.d. 9675.7 p270
Schaich, Peter; Wisconsin, n.d. 9675.7 p270
Schakel, Christian Frederic; America, 1844 1450.2 p124A
Schakel, Gottlieb; New York, 1890 1450.2 p33B
Schaker, Anthony; America, 1845 1450.2 p124A
Schaler, Elisab. 12; Port uncertain, 1839 778.5 p485
Schaler, Elisabeth 19; Port uncertain, 1839 778.5 p485
Schaleste, Michel 16; New Orleans, 1831 778.5 p486
Schalk, Walter E.G.; Wisconsin, n.d. 9675.7 p270

Schallenberger, Hans; Pennsylvania, 1709-1710 ***4480*** *p311*
Schaller, John 32; Kansas, 1879 ***5240.1*** *p60*
Schaller, Joseph; Cincinnati, 1864 ***8582.3*** *p22*
Schaller, Joseph; Ohio, 1869-1887 ***8582*** *p27*
Schaller, Nicklous 27; Kansas, 1879 ***5240.1*** *p59*
Schallern, Ludwig von; Halifax, N.S., 1778 ***9786*** *p270*
Schallern, Ludwig von; New York, 1776 ***9786*** *p270*
Schalleste, Madame 40; New Orleans, 1831 ***778.5*** *p486*
Schalleste, Peter 14; New Orleans, 1831 ***778.5*** *p486*
Schallus, Valentin; Philadelphia, 1776 ***8582.3*** *p83*
Schamehorn, Elias; Ohio, 1869-1885 ***8582.2*** *p56*
Schammel, . . .; Canada, 1776-1783 ***9786*** *p33*
Schampier, Catherine; Washington, 1859-1920 ***2872.1*** *p36*
Schampier, Frank; Washington, 1859-1920 ***2872.1*** *p36*
Schamps, M. P.; Ohio, 1848 ***8582.1*** *p48*
Schanahan, Mary; Colorado, 1891 ***9678.2*** *p168*
Schander, John; New York, NY, 1836 ***8208.4*** *p17*
Schanen, Joseph; Wisconsin, n.d. ***9675.7*** *p270*
Schanen, Nicholas; Wisconsin, n.d. ***9675.7*** *p270*
Schanenwac, John; Indiana, 1848 ***9117*** *p19*
Schanie, Anton 11; Massachusetts, 1849 ***5881.1*** *p87*
Schanie, Carl 14; Massachusetts, 1849 ***5881.1*** *p88*
Schanie, Christina 9; Massachusetts, 1849 ***5881.1*** *p88*
Schanie, Christina 42; Massachusetts, 1849 ***5881.1*** *p88*
Schank, Adam; Indiana, 1844 ***9117*** *p19*
Schano, Mrs.; New York, NY, 1850 ***3702.7*** *p540*
With 2 sons
With daughter
Schano, Franz; New York, NY, 1850 ***3702.7*** *p538*
With father
With brother
Schantz, Blasig; Pennsylvania, 1746-1800 ***2444*** *p209*
*Wife:*Christina
*Child:*Johann Michael
Schantz, Christina *SEE* Schantz, Blasig
Schantz, Johann; Ohio, 1846 ***8582.1*** *p48*
Schantz, Johann Michael *SEE* Schantz, Blasig
Schantz, Joseph; Ohio, 1846 ***8582.1*** *p48*
Schanz, Adam 15; America, 1854-1855 ***9162.6*** *p105*
Schanz, Barbara 42; America, 1854-1855 ***9162.6*** *p104*
Schanz, Michael 16; America, 1854-1855 ***9162.6*** *p104*
Schanzel, Michael 37; Port uncertain, 1839 ***778.5*** *p486*
Schapals, Vincent; Wisconsin, n.d. ***9675.7*** *p270*
Schaper, . . .; Canada, 1776-1783 ***9786*** *p33*
Schaper, Sophie Louise Caroline; America, 1881 ***4610.10*** *p152*
Schapero, Jacob 23; Kansas, 1888 ***5240.1*** *p71*
Schaphardt, . . .; Canada, 1776-1783 ***9786*** *p33*
Schappel, Jeremiah 25; Pennsylvania, 1753 ***2444*** *p145*
Schappel, John 30; Pennsylvania, 1753 ***2444*** *p144*
Schar, Barbara; Philadelphia, 1756 ***4525*** *p261*
Schardt, Peter; Wisconsin, n.d. ***9675.7*** *p270*
Scharf, Frieda; Wisconsin, n.d. ***9675.7*** *p270*
Scharf, Johanna Selma; Wisconsin, n.d. ***9675.7*** *p270*
Scharf, John; Wisconsin, n.d. ***9675.7*** *p270*
Scharf, Joseph 20; America, 1853 ***9162.7*** *p15*
Scharf, Reinhard; Wisconsin, n.d. ***9675.7*** *p270*
Scharf, Selma; Wisconsin, n.d. ***9675.7*** *p270*
Scharf, Teilor Max; New York, NY, 1913 ***3455.3*** *p110*
Scharin, Barbara; Philadelphia, 1756 ***4525*** *p261*
Scharlot, Friedrich; Charleston, SC, 1775-1781 ***8582.2*** *p52*
Scharmann, Elisabeth Schweitzer 71; Pennsylvania, 1897 ***1763*** *p40D*
Scharmann, Johannette 72; America, 1897 ***1763*** *p48D*
Scharp, Abraham; Ohio, 1869-1887 ***8582*** *p27*
Scharringhausen, Karl; St. Louis, 1848 ***8582.1*** *p30*
Schartner, Jacob; Georgia, 1738 ***9332*** *p321*
Schartner, Jacob; Georgia, 1739 ***9332*** *p326*
Schatner, J. Louis; Wisconsin, n.d. ***9675.7*** *p270*
Schats, David; Pennsylvania, 1743 ***2444*** *p209*
Schatz, Catharine; New England, 1749 ***2444*** *p208*
Schatz, David; America, 1737-1800 ***2444*** *p209*
*Wife:*Elisabetha Reuchlin
*Child:*Johann Jacob
Schatz, David; Pennsylvania, 1743 ***2444*** *p209*
Schatz, Elisabetha Reuchlin *SEE* Schatz, David
Schatz, Friedrich; Wisconsin, n.d. ***9675.7*** *p270*
Schatz, Johann Jacob *SEE* Schatz, David
Schatz, John W.; Washington, 1859-1920 ***2872.1*** *p36*
Schatzer, George 27; America, 1831 ***778.5*** *p486*
Schatzmann, Friederich; America, 1830 ***8582.3*** *p57*
Schatzmann, J. J.; Kentucky, 1869-1887 ***8582*** *p27*
Schatzmann, Jacob; America, 1829 ***8582.2*** *p61*
Schatzmann, Jacob; Ohio, 1869-1887 ***8582*** *p27*
Schatzmann, Johann Jakob; America, 1837 ***8582.2*** *p60*
Schau, Hans George; Pennsylvania, 1750 ***4779.3*** *p14A*
Schaub, Divert Mary *SEE* Schaub, John
Schaub, Henry; California, 1855 ***1450.2*** *p124A*
Schaub, John; America, 1853 ***1450.2*** *p125A*
Schaub, John; New York, 1743 ***3652*** *p60*
*Wife:*Divert Mary
Schauble, August; Wisconsin, n.d. ***9675.7*** *p270*
Schauble, Edwin Edward; Washington, 1859-1920 ***2872.1*** *p36*
Schauble, John; Washington, 1859-1920 ***2872.1*** *p36*
Schauble, W. P.; Washington, 1859-1920 ***2872.1*** *p36*
Schauden, Theodor; Cincinnati, 1800-1877 ***8582.3*** *p86*
Schaudt, . . .; Canada, 1776-1783 ***9786*** *p33*
Schauecker, Anna Maria; America, 1766 ***2444*** *p205*
Schauecker, Margaretha; America, 1766 ***2444*** *p209*
Schaueker, Hans Conrad; Pennsylvania, 1749 ***2444*** *p209*
*Brother:*Martin
Schaueker, Martin *SEE* Schaueker, Hans Conrad
Schauer, Georg Peter; Cincinnati, 1869-1887 ***8582*** *p27*
Schauer, George; America, 1893 ***1450.2*** *p125A*
Schaul, George; America, 1850 ***1450.2*** *p125A*
Schaum, . . .; Canada, 1776-1783 ***9786*** *p33*
Schauman, John; Indiana, 1848 ***9117*** *p18*
Schaumloeffel, Johann 66; Ohio, 1872 ***8582*** *p27*
Schaurer, Michel; Cincinnati, 1869-1887 ***8582*** *p27*
Schaus, Frederick; Ohio, 1840 ***9892.11*** *p41*
Schaus, John; Wisconsin, n.d. ***9675.7*** *p270*
Schaus, Philip, Jr.; Ohio, 1840 ***9892.11*** *p41*
Schautt, Barbara *SEE* Schautt, Johannes
Schautt, Claudius *SEE* Schautt, Johannes
Schautt, Jacob *SEE* Schautt, Johannes
Schautt, Johannes *SEE* Schautt, Johannes
Schautt, Johannes; New England, 1746-1756 ***2444*** *p209*
*Wife:*Barbara
*Child:*Johannes
*Child:*Claudius
*Child:*Jacob
Schauwecker, Anna Maria; America, 1766 ***2444*** *p205*
Schauwecker, Hans Cunrad; Pennsylvania, 1749 ***2444*** *p209*
*Brother:*Martin
Schauwecker, Margaretha; America, 1766 ***2444*** *p209*
Schauwecker, Martin *SEE* Schauwecker, Hans Cunrad
Schavas, Nicholas; Philadelphia, 1762 ***9973.7*** *p37*
Schaw, Mary; America, 1815 ***8894.2*** *p56*
Schaw, Robert; North Carolina, 1751 ***1639.20*** *p283*
Schawack, . . .; Canada, 1776-1783 ***9786*** *p33*
Schawe, Johann Heinrich; America, 1849 ***8582.3*** *p57*
Schaz, John George; America, 1859 ***1450.2*** *p125A*
Scheckeler, Philipp; America, 1741-1800 ***2444*** *p210*
Scheckler, Philipp; Pennsylvania, 1768 ***2444*** *p210*
Scheede, . . .; Canada, 1776-1783 ***9786*** *p33*
Scheehy, John; Virginia, 1855 ***4626.16*** *p15*
Scheel, Carl August; Quebec, 1776 ***9786*** *p265*
Scheel, Jane Frederke. 9 *SEE* Scheel, John Frdke.
Scheel, John Frdke. 37; New Orleans, 1839 ***9420.2*** *p485*
*Daughter:*Jane Frederke. 9
Scheer, Barbara *SEE* Scheer, Johann Michael
Scheer, Christina *SEE* Scheer, Johann Michael
Scheer, Daniel *SEE* Scheer, Johann Michael
Scheer, Edward; Pennsylvania, 1896 ***1450.2*** *p34B*
Scheer, Elisabetha *SEE* Scheer, Johann Michael
Scheer, Ferdinand; Wisconsin, n.d. ***9675.7*** *p270*
Scheer, Frederick; Illinois, 1877 ***2896.5*** *p35*
Scheer, Georg Adam *SEE* Scheer, Johann Michael
Scheer, Georg Friedrich *SEE* Scheer, Johann Michael
Scheer, Jadwiga 24; New York, 1912 ***9980.29*** *p66*
*Son:*Rudolf 2
Scheer, Johann Bernhard *SEE* Scheer, Johann Michael
Scheer, Johann Michael *SEE* Scheer, Johann Michael
Scheer, Johann Michael; Pennsylvania, 1752 ***2444*** *p210*
*Wife:*Margaretha Mattheis
*Child:*Christina
*Child:*Daniel
*Child:*Maria Jacobina
*Child:*Margaretha
*Child:*Barbara
*Child:*Johann Bernhard
*Child:*Elisabetha
*Child:*Georg Friedrich
*Child:*Georg Adam
*Child:*Johann Michael
Scheer, Margaretha *SEE* Scheer, Johann Michael
Scheer, Margaretha Mattheis *SEE* Scheer, Johann Michael
Scheer, Maria Jacobina *SEE* Scheer, Johann Michael
Scheer, Math. 50; Kansas, 1885 ***5240.1*** *p68*
Scheer, Michel 48; Kansas, 1885 ***5240.1*** *p68*
Scheer, Nik 21; Kansas, 1893 ***5240.1*** *p78*
Scheer, Nik 23; Kansas, 1893 ***5240.1*** *p78*
Scheer, Rudolf 2 *SEE* Scheer, Jadwiga
Scheerer, Claudius; Wisconsin, n.d. ***9675.7*** *p270*
Scheerer, Henry; Wisconsin, n.d. ***9675.7*** *p270*
Scheerer, Mathias; Wisconsin, n.d. ***9675.7*** *p270*
Schefer, Joh. Geo.; Pennsylvania, 1752 ***4525*** *p240*
Scheffel, Gerog C.; America, 1844 ***8582.1*** *p30*
Scheffer, Andrew J.; Illinois, 1863 ***7857*** *p7*
Scheffer, Christophe 2; America, 1831 ***778.5*** *p486*
Scheffer, Franciscus; Canada, 1780 ***9786*** *p268*
Scheffer, Franciscus; New York, 1776 ***9786*** *p268*
Scheffer, Judith; Pennsylvania, 1752 ***2444*** *p213*
Scheffer, Marie 3; America, 1831 ***778.5*** *p486*
Scheffer, Marie 41; America, 1831 ***778.5*** *p486*
Scheffer, Victor 5; America, 1831 ***778.5*** *p486*
Scheffer, Victor 53; America, 1831 ***778.5*** *p486*
Scheffler, Joh. Carolin 46; New Orleans, 1839 ***9420.2*** *p168*
Schefftgen, Dominic; Wisconsin, n.d. ***9675.7*** *p270*
Schefftgen, John; Wisconsin, n.d. ***9675.7*** *p270*
Scheftall, Levi; Savannah, GA, 1775 ***8582.2*** *p64*
Schehr, Barbara *SEE* Schehr, Johann Michael
Schehr, Christina *SEE* Schehr, Johann Michael
Schehr, Daniel *SEE* Schehr, Johann Michael
Schehr, Elisabetha *SEE* Schehr, Johann Michael
Schehr, Georg Adam *SEE* Schehr, Johann Michael
Schehr, Georg Friedrich *SEE* Schehr, Johann Michael
Schehr, Johann Bernhard *SEE* Schehr, Johann Michael
Schehr, Johann Michael *SEE* Schehr, Johann Michael
Schehr, Johann Michael; Pennsylvania, 1752 ***2444*** *p210*
*Wife:*Margaretha Mattheis
*Child:*Christina
*Child:*Daniel
*Child:*Maria Jacobina
*Child:*Margaretha
*Child:*Barbara
*Child:*Johann Bernhard
*Child:*Elisabetha
*Child:*Georg Friedrich
*Child:*Georg Adam
*Child:*Johann Michael
Schehr, Margaretha *SEE* Schehr, Johann Michael
Schehr, Margaretha Mattheis *SEE* Schehr, Johann Michael
Schehr, Maria Jacobina *SEE* Schehr, Johann Michael
Schehr, Peter; America, 1849 ***8582.3*** *p57*
Scheib, Georg 45; America, 1853 ***9162.8*** *p38*
Scheiber, William; Wisconsin, n.d. ***9675.7*** *p270*
Scheible, Anna Barbara *SEE* Scheible, Johann Michael
Scheible, Anna Ursula; Pennsylvania, 1728-1800 ***2444*** *p210*
Scheible, Johann Michael 29; Philadelphia, 1753 ***2444*** *p210*
*Wife:*Anna Barbara
*Child:*Maria Margaretha
*Child:*Maria Barbara
Scheible, Maria Barbara *SEE* Scheible, Johann Michael
Scheible, Maria Margaretha *SEE* Scheible, Johann Michael
Scheich, Peter; America, 1889 ***1450.2*** *p34B*
Scheid, . . .; Canada, 1776-1783 ***9786*** *p33*
Scheid, Anna Christina; America, 1912 ***1763*** *p40D*
Scheid, Friederika 16; New York, NY, 1889 ***7846*** *p39*
Scheid, Friederike 8 mos; New York, NY, 1889 ***7846*** *p39*
Scheid, Gottlieb 34; New York, NY, 1889 ***7846*** *p39*
Scheid, Marie 4; New York, NY, 1889 ***7846*** *p39*
Scheid, Nicolaus; Cincinnati, 1869-1887 ***8582*** *p27*
Scheid, Susanne 33; New York, NY, 1889 ***7846*** *p39*
Scheid, Valentin; Canada, 1776-1783 ***9786*** *p207A*
Scheidel, Frederick 21; Ohio, 1868 ***6014.1*** *p3*
Scheidler, Georg Valentin; Cincinnati, 1849 ***8582.1*** *p30*
Scheidt, . . .; Canada, 1776-1783 ***9786*** *p33*
Scheidt, Anna Marie; America, 1850 ***4610.10*** *p143*
Scheidt, Anna Marie 5 *SEE* Scheidt, Daniel Friedrich
Scheidt, Anna Marie Engel; America, 1850 ***4610.10*** *p143*
Scheidt, Anne Cath. Engel *SEE* Scheidt, Anne Marie Cath.
Scheidt, Anne Marie Cath.; America, 1850 ***4610.10*** *p147*
*Child:*Anne Cath. Engel
*Child:*Peter Heinrich Samuel
*Child:*Carl Zacharias Daniel
*Child:*Carl Ludwig
*Child:*Johann F. Wilhelm
Scheidt, Anne Marie Christine Louise; America, 1842 ***4610.10*** *p146*
Scheidt, Anne Marie Engel 22 *SEE* Scheidt, Daniel Friedrich
Scheidt, Anne Marie Louise 17 *SEE* Scheidt, Daniel Friedrich
Scheidt, Carl Friedrich August; America, 1850 ***4610.10*** *p143*
Scheidt, Carl Friedrich Christoph; America, 1853 ***4610.10*** *p144*
Scheidt, Carl H. Gottlieb *SEE* Scheidt, Daniel Friedrich
Scheidt, Carl Heinrich Gottlieb; America, 1845 ***4610.10*** *p141*
Scheidt, Carl Heinrich Hartwig; America, 1845 ***4610.10*** *p141*
Scheidt, Carl Ludwig *SEE* Scheidt, Anne Marie Cath.

Schibley, Michael 29; Philadelphia, 1753 **2444** *p210*
*Wife:*Anna Barbara
*Child:*Maria Margaretha
*Child:*Maria Barbara
Schick, v., Cap.; Quebec, 1776 **9786** *p104*
Schick, Adam; Virginia, 1855 **4626.16** *p15*
Schick, Balthasar 3; New York, NY, 1878 **9253** *p45*
Schick, Catharina 3; New York, NY, 1878 **9253** *p45*
Schick, David 11 mos; New York, NY, 1878 **9253** *p45*
Schick, Eva 38; New York, NY, 1878 **9253** *p45*
Schick, Georg 40; New York, NY, 1878 **9253** *p45*
Schick, Gottfried 12; New York, NY, 1878 **9253** *p45*
Schick, Gottlob Dietrich; Quebec, 1776 **9786** *p261*
Schick, Jacob 10 mos; New York, NY, 1878 **9253** *p45*
Schick, Jacob 7; New York, NY, 1878 **9253** *p45*
Schick, Johann 16; New York, NY, 1878 **9253** *p45*
Schick, Susanne 38; New York, NY, 1878 **9253** *p45*
Schickhaus, Caroline; New York, NY, 1840 **8208.4** *p103*
Schickler, Simon; South Carolina, 1788 **7119** *p198*
Schiebel, . . .; Canada, 1776-1783 **9786** *p33*
Schieferstein, Johannette S. 72; America, 1897 **1763** *p48D*
Schiel, Frank; Wisconsin, n.d. **9675.7** *p270*
Schield, Georg; Cincinnati, 1800-1877 **8582.3** *p86*
Schiele, Jacob; New York, 1891 **1450.2** *p34B*
Schienbein, Anna Maria Baeurlin *SEE* Schienbein, Peter
Schienbein, Peter; Pennsylvania, 1751 **2444** *p214*
*Wife:*Anna Maria Baeurlin
*Child:*Susanna Elisabetha
Schienbein, Susanna Elisabetha *SEE* Schienbein, Peter
Schienle, Agnes Barbara; America, 1754 **2444** *p211*
Schienle, Friedrich; America, 1754 **2444** *p211*
Schienle, Jacob F. 22; Kansas, 1884 **5240.1** *p66*
Schier, John; New York, 1885 **1450.2** *p34B*
Schierbecker, Ernst; Illinois, 1883 **4610.10** *p55*
Schierbecker, W.; Illinois, 1800-1900 **4610.10** *p67*
Schierberg, Joseph; Cincinnati, 1869-1887 **8582** *p27*
Schiercher, Simon; Pennsylvania, 1750 **4525** *p247*
Schierenbech, Herman 29; Kansas, 1886 **5240.1** *p69*
Schierenbeck, Hermann 29; Kansas, 1886 **5240.1** *p38*
Schiess, Carl; Cincinnati, 1869-1887 **8582** *p27*
Schiess, Emanuel 24; Kansas, 1870 **5240.1** *p51*
Schiessle, Alphons; Wisconsin, n.d. **9675.7** *p270*
Schietromo, Elvidio; Arkansas, 1918 **95.2** *p110*
Schietromo, Elvidio; Arkansas, 1918 **95.2** *p112*
Schiff, Abraham; Baltimore, 1842 **8582.3** *p57*
Schiff, Abraham; Ohio, 1869-1887 **8582** *p27*
Schiff, Johann; Cincinnati, 1856 **8582.3** *p87*
Schiff, Johann; Cincinnati, 1864 **8582.3** *p22*
Schiff, John; Cincinnati, 1869-1887 **8582** *p27*
Schiffer, . . .; Canada, 1776-1783 **9786** *p33*
Schiffer, Gabriel; New York, NY, 1839 **8208.4** *p96*
Schiflon, John; Wisconsin, n.d. **9675.7** *p270*
Schik, v., Capit.; Quebec, 1776 **9786** *p104*
Schikowvski, August; Illinois, 1888 **5012.39** *p121*
Schilder, Martin; America, 1845 **8582.2** *p36*
Schilder, Martin; Ohio, 1800-1885 **8582.2** *p59*
Schilderink, Johann; America, 1847 **8582.2** *p36*
Schildmeier, Frederick; America, 1842 **1450.2** *p126A*
Schilke, Michael 28; Kansas, 1878 **5240.1** *p59*
Schill, Anna Maria; Pennsylvania, 1751 **2444** *p212*
Schill, Franz; Wisconsin, n.d. **9675.7** *p270*
Schill, Georg; Ohio, 1833 **8582.1** *p47*
Schill, Mathias; Wisconsin, n.d. **9675.7** *p270*
Schill, Mathias, Jr.; Wisconsin, n.d. **9675.7** *p270*
Schiller, . . .; Canada, 1776-1783 **9786** *p33*
Schiller, August; Wisconsin, n.d. **9675.7** *p270*
Schiller, Carl; Wisconsin, n.d. **9675.7** *p270*
Schiller, Charles; Canada, 1776-1783 **9786** *p231*
Schiller, George Emil; Wisconsin, n.d. **9675.7** *p270*
Schiller, Gustav; America, 1848 **8582.3** *p57*
Schiller, Jacob; Illinois, 1896 **2896.5** *p35*
Schiller, Lawrence; Wisconsin, n.d. **9675.7** *p270*
Schiller, Meta; Wisconsin, n.d. **9675.7** *p270*
Schilling, . . .; Canada, 1776-1783 **9786** *p33*
Schilling Family ; America, 1846 **4610.10** *p114*
Schilling, Andrew; New York, NY, 1836 **8208.4** *p12*
Schilling, Anton H. Christoph *SEE* Schilling, Johanne F. Windmeyer
Schilling, Anton Heinrich Wilhelm *SEE* Schilling, Johanne F. Windmeyer
Schilling, Carl Friedrich; America, 1883 **4610.10** *p102*
Schilling, Carl Friedrich; America, 1886 **4610.10** *p102*
Schilling, Carl Friedrich Gottlieb; America, 1883 **4610.10** *p102*
*Wife:*Wilhelmine Stuhmeier
With children
Schilling, Edward; New York, NY, 1848 **2896.5** *p35*
Schilling, Ernst Wilhelm; America, 1885 **4610.10** *p102*
Schilling, Friedrich Ernst Gottlieb; America, 1872 **4610.10** *p101*
Schilling, Heinrich Karl Friedrich; America, 1880 **4610.10** *p101*
Schilling, Henrich Friedrich *SEE* Schilling, Johanne F. Windmeyer
Schilling, Johann Henrich *SEE* Schilling, Johanne F. Windmeyer
Schilling, Johanne F. Windmeyer; America, 1846 **4610.10** *p115*
*Son:*Johann Henrich
*Son:*Anton H. Christoph
*Son:*Anton Heinrich Wilhelm
*Son:*Henrich Friedrich
Schilling, Louise 18; America, 1872 **4610.10** *p101*
Schilling, Maria Magdalena; Port uncertain, 1754 **2444** *p142*
Schilling, Simon Heinrich; America, 1841 **4610.10** *p114*
Schilling, Wilhelmine Stuhmeier *SEE* Schilling, Carl Friedrich Gottlieb
Schilling, William; Canada, 1776-1783 **9786** *p207A*
Schillinger, Johann Martin; Pennsylvania, 1752 **2444** *p211*
Schillinger, Wilhelm; Ohio, 1802 **8582** *p27*
Schillmans, Adrianil; Wisconsin, n.d. **9675.7** *p270*
Schiltmeir, Charles; America, 1834 **1450.2** *p126A*
Schiltz, Peter; Wisconsin, n.d. **9675.7** *p270*
Schimatzak, Thomas; New York, NY, 1834 **8208.4** *p48*
Schimatzek, Thomas; New York, NY, 1834 **8208.4** *p48*
Schimel, Richard; Iroquois Co., IL, 1896 **3455.1** *p13*
Schimmel, Max; Iroquois Co., IL, 1896 **3455.1** *p13*
Schimmelpfennig, Colonel; Pennsylvania, 1861-1865 **8582.3** *p91*
Schimmelpfennig, Berthold Helfrich; Halifax, N.S., 1780 **9786** *p269*
Schimmelpfennig, Berthold Helfrich; New York, 1776 **9786** *p269*
Schimper, William; New York, NY, 1838 **8208.4** *p61*
Schinck, . . .; Canada, 1776-1783 **9786** *p33*
Schincke, Henry; Wisconsin, n.d. **9675.7** *p270*
Schindelberger, Anna Catharina; Pennsylvania, 1747 **2444** *p211*
Schinder, Ignatz 40; Kansas, 1893 **5240.1** *p77*
Schindler, Anton; Ohio, 1840-1845 **8582.1** *p47*
Schindler, Catharine 21; America, 1838 **778.5** *p487*
Schindler, Charles; Illinois, 1860 **5012.39** *p90*
Schindler, George; New York, 1754 **3652** *p80*
Schindler, Simon B., Jr.; New York, NY, 1839 **8208.4** *p97*
Schindler, Wenzel; New York, 1849 **1450.2** *p126A*
Schinell, Melior; South Carolina, 1788 **7119** *p198*
Schininger, F. 30; New Orleans, 1830 **778.5** *p487*
Schinkel, Peter; Kentucky, 1810-1825 **8582.3** *p97*
Schinker, Nicholas; Wisconsin, n.d. **9675.7** *p270*
Schinkewicz, Alexander 23; New York, 1912 **9980.29** *p72*
Schinkunas, Anthony; Arkansas, 1918 **95.2** *p110*
Schiper, Moritz; New York, NY, 1838 **8208.4** *p90*
Schipper, . . .; Canada, 1776-1783 **9786** *p33*
Schipper, Arend 44; New York, NY, 1847 **3377.6** *p13*
Schipper, Dina 8; New York, NY, 1847 **3377.6** *p13*
Schipper, Gebhard Evertz; Iroquois Co., IL, 1892 **3455.1** *p13*
Schipper, Gerritdina 15; New York, NY, 1847 **3377.6** *p13*
Schipper, Janna 20; New York, NY, 1847 **3377.6** *p13*
Schipper, John 23; New York, NY, 1847 **3377.6** *p13*
Schipper, John 55; New York, NY, 1847 **3377.6** *p13*
Schipper, Maria 48; New York, NY, 1847 **3377.6** *p13*
Schipper, Teune 18; New York, NY, 1847 **3377.6** *p13*
Schippert, Carl; Philadelphia, 1893 **3455.3** *p21*
Schirar, Frank; Illinois, 1868 **2896.5** *p35*
Schireman, August; Kansas, 1884 **5240.1** *p38*
Schirff, Charles 37; Harris Co., TX, 1897 **6254** *p3*
Schirmer, Captain; America, 1861-1865 **8582.3** *p92*
Schirmer, Joseph 47; Kansas, 1888 **5240.1** *p38*
Schirmer, Joseph 47; Kansas, 1888 **5240.1** *p73*
Schirmer, Joseph Emil 21; Kansas, 1886 **5240.1** *p69*
Schirmer, Richard; America, 1888 **5240.1** *p38*
Schirner, Edward; Milwaukee, 1875 **4719.30** *p257*
Schirner, Mrs. Edward; Milwaukee, 1875 **4719.30** *p257*
Schissel, Otto; America, 1867 **1450.2** *p126A*
Schisslen, Michel 18; America, 1838 **778.5** *p487*
Schissler, Cecilia; Wisconsin, n.d. **9675.7** *p270*
Schissler, Johann; Wisconsin, n.d. **9675.7** *p270*
Schissler, Maria; Wisconsin, n.d. **9675.7** *p270*
Schissler, Martin; Wisconsin, n.d. **9675.7** *p270*
Schitz, Jerg; Pennsylvania, 1717 **3627** *p11*
*Wife:*Sophia Catharina Klotz
*Child:*Maria Catharina
*Child:*Maria Sophia
*Child:*Joh. Georg
Schitz, Joh. Georg *SEE* Schitz, Jerg
Schitz, Maria Catharina *SEE* Schitz, Jerg
Schitz, Maria Sophia *SEE* Schitz, Jerg
Schitz, Sophia Catharina Klotz *SEE* Schitz, Jerg
Schkolnik, Hesee; Iowa, 1866-1943 **123.54** *p43*
Schlaak, William; Wisconsin, n.d. **9675.7** *p270*
Schlabaum, . . .; Canada, 1776-1783 **9786** *p33*
Schlacke, Flhelm; Indianapolis, 1870 **3702.7** *p586*
Schlaebits, Frederick; New York, 1847 **1450.2** *p126A*
Schlaegel, Charlotte E.; Wisconsin, n.d. **9675.7** *p270*
Schlaeger, E.; Wheeling, WV, 1852 **8582.3** *p78*
Schlafer, Erhart; Cincinnati, 1869-1887 **8582** *p27*
Schlagenteufel, v., Jr.; Quebec, 1776 **9786** *p104*
Schlagenteufel, v., Sr.; Quebec, 1776 **9786** *p104*
Schlagenteuffel, Captain; Canada, 1776-1783 **9786** *p149*
Schlagenteuffel, Adolph, IV; Quebec, 1776 **9786** *p253*
Schlagenteuffel, Carl, III; Quebec, 1776 **9786** *p252*
Schlagenteuffel, Ludewig, I; Quebec, 1776 **9786** *p259*
Schlager, A. Cath. I. Huffmeier *SEE* Schlager, Carl Fr. W.
Schlager, A. Cath. M. Ilsabein *SEE* Schlager, Carl Fr. W.
Schlager, A. M. Ilsabein *SEE* Schlager, Carl Fr. W.
Schlager, Carl Fr. W. *SEE* Schlager, Carl Fr. W.
Schlager, Carl Fr. W.; America, 1888 **4610.10** *p161*
*Wife:*A. Cath. I. Huffmeier
*Child:*Christian Heinrich
*Child:*Carl Fr. W.
*Child:*A. Cath. M. Ilsabein
*Child:*A. M. Ilsabein
Schlager, Christian Heinrich *SEE* Schlager, Carl Fr. W.
Schlagmilch, Henrich; Philadelphia, 1779 **8137** *p13*
Schlaiss, Anna *SEE* Schlaiss, Ulrich
Schlaiss, Anna Catharina *SEE* Schlaiss, Ulrich
Schlaiss, Hans Conrad *SEE* Schlaiss, Ulrich
Schlaiss, Ulrich; Carolina, 1742-1800 **2444** *p211*
*Wife:*Anna
*Child:*Hans Conrad
*Child:*Anna Catharina
Schlamilch, . . .; Canada, 1776-1783 **9786** *p33*
Schlatter, Paul; Charleston, SC, 1775-1781 **8582.2** *p52*
Schlatter, S.F.; Nicaragua, 1856 **8582.3** *p31*
Schlauderbeck, . . .; Canada, 1776-1783 **9786** *p33*
Schlax, Peter; Wisconsin, n.d. **9675.7** *p270*
Schleasman, Nicholas; Pennsylvania, 1752 **4525** *p243*
Schlecht, Anna Barbara *SEE* Schlecht, Daniel
Schlecht, Anna Wollenbehr *SEE* Schlecht, Daniel
Schlecht, Daniel *SEE* Schlecht, Daniel
Schlecht, Daniel; Pennsylvania, 1754-1788 **2444** *p211*
*Wife:*Anna Wollenbehr
*Child:*Hans Jorg
*Child:*Jorg Friedrich
*Child:*Daniel
*Child:*Anna Barbara
*Child:*Johann Jacob
Schlecht, Hans Jorg *SEE* Schlecht, Daniel
Schlecht, Johann Jacob *SEE* Schlecht, Daniel
Schlecht, Jorg Friedrich *SEE* Schlecht, Daniel
Schlechtleitner, . . .; Canada, 1776-1783 **9786** *p33*
Schlegel, Anna Barbara *SEE* Schlegel, Anna Rosina
Schlegel, Anna Rosina; Pennsylvania, 1744 **2444** *p211*
*Sister:*Anna Barbara
Schlegel, Barbara; America, 1897 **1763** *p40C*
Schlegel, Carl August; Wisconsin, n.d. **9675.7** *p270*
Schlegel, Charles; Wisconsin, n.d. **9675.7** *p270*
Schlegel, Christof; South Carolina, 1788 **7119** *p199*
Schlegel, Emanuel; Maryland, 1872 **1450.2** *p34B*
Schlegel, Frederick; New York, 1749 **3652** *p72*
Schlegel, Friedrich; Wisconsin, n.d. **9675.7** *p270*
Schlegel, George Adam; Pennsylvania, 1751 **2444** *p211*
Schlegel, Johann Christoph; Pennsylvania, 1751 **2444** *p211*
Schlegel, John; Wisconsin, n.d. **9675.7** *p270*
Schlegel, Karl August; Wisconsin, n.d. **9675.7** *p270*
Schlegel, Victor Von 31; New Orleans, 1839 **9420.2** *p166*
Schleglin, Miss; Pennsylvania, 1714-1785 **2444** *p176*
Schleglin, Miss; Port uncertain, 1752 **2444** *p176*
Schlegling, Barbara; Philadelphia, 1756 **4525** *p261*
Schleich, Anton; America, 1845 **8582.1** *p30*
Schleich, Philipp; Germantown, PA, 1820-1829 **8582.3** *p98*
Schleicher, Gustav; Texas, 1800-1877 **8582.3** *p92*
Schleicher, Louis; Washington, 1859-1920 **2872.1** *p36*
Schleifer, Christian; Wisconsin, n.d. **9675.7** *p270*
Schleiffer, . . .; Canada, 1776-1783 **9786** *p33*
Schleiter, . . .; Canada, 1776-1783 **9786** *p33*
Schlemer, Nikeland; New York, 1888 **1450.2** *p34B*
Schlemmer, Arnold; Halifax, N.S., 1778 **9786** *p270*
Schlemmer, Arnold; New York, 1776 **9786** *p270*
Schlemmer, Henrich; Lancaster, PA, 1780 **8137** *p13*
Schlensker, Anna Maria Trampe *SEE* Schlensker, Johann Christian Ludwig
Schlensker, Johann Christian Ludwig; America, 1843 **4610.10** *p95*
*Wife:*Anna Maria Trampe
*Son:*Karl Joseph
Schlensker, Karl Joseph *SEE* Schlensker, Johann Christian Ludwig

Schlenvogt, Johann; Wisconsin, n.d. ***9675.7*** *p270*
Schlenvogt, John Henry; Wisconsin, n.d. ***9675.7*** *p270*
Schlenzig, Wilhelm; Wisconsin, n.d. ***9675.7*** *p270*
Schleppe, Albrecht; Pennsylvania, 1751 ***2444*** *p212*
*Wife:*Anna Maria Schill
*Child:*Johannes
*Child:*Maria Magdalena
Schleppe, Anna Maria Schill *SEE* Schleppe, Albrecht
Schleppe, Johannes *SEE* Schleppe, Albrecht
Schleppe, Maria Magdalena *SEE* Schleppe, Albrecht
Schlerett, . . .; Canada, 1776-1783 ***9786*** *p33*
Schlesinger, Louis; Nicaragua, 1856 ***8582.3*** *p31*
Schlesman, Nichs; Pennsylvania, 1752 ***4525*** *p243*
Schlessman, Johannes; Philadelphia, 1753 ***4525*** *p262*
With wife
With children
Schlessmann, Mr.; New England, 1773 ***4525*** *p243*
Schlessmann, Barbara; Pennsylvania, 1752 ***4525*** *p231*
Schlessmann, Barbara; Pennsylvania, 1753 ***4525*** *p241*
With child
Schlessmann, Christof; Pennsylvania, 1753 ***4525*** *p263*
Schlessmann, Hans Christof 18; Pennsylvania, 1752 ***4525*** *p242*
Schlessmann, Hans Paul; New England, 1752 ***4525*** *p242*
Schlessmann, Hans Paul; Pennsylvania, 1752 ***4525*** *p242*
Schlessmann, Heinrich; Philadelphia, 1769 ***4525*** *p265*
Schlessmann, Johann Heinrich; Pennsylvania, 1752 ***4525*** *p242*
Schlessmann, Johannes; Pennsylvania, 1753 ***4525*** *p242*
With wife
With 5 children
Schlessmann, Michael; Pennsylvania, 1773 ***4525*** *p199*
With mother
Schlessmann, Michael; Pennsylvania, 1773 ***4525*** *p243*
Schlessmann, Nicolaus; New England, 1773 ***4525*** *p243*
With wife
With child
With mother
Schlessmann, Nicolaus; Pennsylvania, 1752 ***4525*** *p243*
With wife
Schlessmann, Paul; Pennsylvania, 1753 ***4525*** *p244*
Schlessmann, Paul; Port uncertain, 1752 ***4525*** *p209*
Schlessmann, Paulus; Pennsylvania, 1769 ***4525*** *p265*
Schletz, A.; Wisconsin, n.d. ***9675.7*** *p270*
Schleutker, Gerhard Heinrich; America, 1845 ***8582.3*** *p58*
Schleutker, Heinrich Wilhelm; America, 1845 ***8582.3*** *p58*
Schliachan, Iorgen; Wisconsin, 1872 ***5240.1*** *p38*
Schlichte, Friederich; America, 1852 ***8582.3*** *p58*
Schlicker, Leonard 26; America, 1837 ***778.5*** *p487*
Schliecker, . . .; Canada, 1776-1783 ***9786*** *p33*
Schliefer, Charles; Wisconsin, n.d. ***9675.7*** *p270*
Schlieper Family ; New York, 1765 ***8125.8*** *p436*
Schliephake, . . .; Canada, 1776-1783 ***9786*** *p33*
Schliephuck, Adolf 24; New York, NY, 1878 ***9253*** *p47*
Schliepsiek, C. H.; Missouri, 1848 ***4610.10*** *p72*
Schlierbach, Louis 46; Illinois, 1901 ***1763*** *p40D*
Schlieter, Anton; Canada, 1783 ***9786*** *p38A*
Schlig, R.; Milwaukee, 1875 ***4719.30*** *p257*
Schlim, Nicholas; Wisconsin, n.d. ***9675.7*** *p270*
Schlim, William; Wisconsin, n.d. ***9675.7*** *p270*
Schlimm, Peter; Wisconsin, n.d. ***9675.7*** *p270*
Schlimmer, Jacob; Wisconsin, n.d. ***9675.7*** *p270*
Schlimpert, Amalia 3; New Orleans, 1839 ***9420.1*** *p377*
Schlimpert, Caroline 12; New Orleans, 1839 ***9420.1*** *p377*
Schlimpert, Christiane 32; New Orleans, 1839 ***9420.1*** *p377*
Schlimpert, Ernestine 3; New Orleans, 1839 ***9420.1*** *p377*
Schlimpert, Ernst 1; Died enroute, 1839 ***9420.1*** *p377*
Schlimpert, Ernst 10; New Orleans, 1839 ***9420.1*** *p377*
Schlimpert, Fraugoss 22; New Orleans, 1839 ***9420.1*** *p376*
Schlimpert, Gottfried 35; New Orleans, 1839 ***9420.1*** *p377*
Schlimpert, Gottlob 19; New Orleans, 1839 ***9420.1*** *p377*
Schlimpert, Gottlob 46; New Orleans, 1839 ***9420.1*** *p376*
Schlimpert, Heinrich 5; New Orleans, 1839 ***9420.1*** *p377*
Schlimpert, Julius 12; New Orleans, 1839 ***9420.1*** *p377*
Schlimpert, Rosina 15; New Orleans, 1839 ***9420.1*** *p377*
Schlimpert, Sophia 46; New Orleans, 1839 ***9420.1*** *p376*
Schlimpert, Theresa 7; New Orleans, 1839 ***9420.1*** *p377*
Schlimpert, Wilhelmina 8; New Orleans, 1839 ***9420.1*** *p377*
Schlimpert, William 17; New Orleans, 1839 ***9420.1*** *p377*
Schlingeman, August; Ohio, 1884 ***3702.7*** *p461*
Schliphache, . . .; Canada, 1776-1783 ***9786*** *p33*
Schlippsiek, Anne Marie C. Ilsabein *SEE* Schlippsiek, Carl Ernst Heinrich
Schlippsiek, Carl Ernst Heinrich; America, 1857 ***4610.10*** *p136*
*Wife:*Marie Louise Stucke
*Child:*Carl Heinrich Wilhelm
*Child:*Carl Friedrich Wilhelm
*Child:*Anne Marie C. Ilsabein
Schlippsiek, Carl Friedrich Wilhelm *SEE* Schlippsiek, Carl Ernst Heinrich
Schlippsiek, Carl Heinrich Wilhelm *SEE* Schlippsiek, Carl Ernst Heinrich
Schlippsiek, Marie Louise Stucke *SEE* Schlippsiek, Carl Ernst Heinrich
Schlirff, . . .; Canada, 1776-1783 ***9786*** *p33*
Schlirth, . . .; Canada, 1776-1783 ***9786*** *p33*
Schlitt, Conrad 66; Illinois, 1900 ***1763*** *p48D*
Schlittler, Rudolph; New York, NY, 1835 ***8208.4*** *p26*
Schlitz, Joseph; Milwaukee, 1875 ***4719.30*** *p257*
Schloczmacher, . . .; Canada, 1776-1783 ***9786*** *p33*
Schloczmacher, Michael; Canada, 1776-1783 ***9786*** *p243*
Schloeder, Frank; Wisconsin, n.d. ***9675.7*** *p270*
Schloeder, William; Wisconsin, n.d. ***9675.7*** *p270*
Schloendorn, Christopher; America, 1848 ***8582.1*** *p30*
Schloer, Christian; America, 1845 ***1450.2*** *p126A*
Schloerb, Johann Heinrich; America, 1853 ***3702.7*** *p340*
*Wife:*Margarethe Gisgen
With child 1
With child 4
Schloerb, Margarethe Gisgen *SEE* Schloerb, Johann Heinrich
Schloerke, Wilhelm; Illinois, 1900 ***5012.40*** *p76*
Schloesser, August; New York, 1761 ***3652*** *p88*
Schloessmann, Johann; Pennsylvania, 1753 ***4525*** *p243*
Schloettler, Heinrich; America, 1846 ***8582.3*** *p58*
Schlomann, Anna M. Engel Freimuth *SEE* Schlomann, Ernst Heinrich
Schlomann, Ernst Heinrich; America, 1840-1842 ***4610.10*** *p111*
*Wife:*Anna M. Engel Freimuth
*Son:*Friedrich Karl Wilhelm
Schlomann, Friedrich Karl Wilhelm *SEE* Schlomann, Ernst Heinrich
Schlonecker, Michael; Philadelphia, 1760 ***9973.7*** *p34*
Schlonecker, Michael, Jr.; Philadelphia, 1760 ***9973.7*** *p34*
Schloo, John Henry; New York, NY, 1839 ***8208.4*** *p100*
Schlorf, Charles; Illinois, 1860 ***5012.39*** *p90*
Schlorf, Frederick; Illinois, 1859 ***5012.39*** *p89*
Schlorf, John; Illinois, 1871 ***5012.39*** *p25*
Schlosser, . . .; Ohio, 1881 ***3702.7*** *p431*
Schlosser, Mrs.; Philadelphia, 1872-1874 ***8582.1*** *p30*
Schlosser, Georg; New York, NY, 1751 ***8582.3*** *p85*
Schlosser, Georg; Philadelphia, 1776 ***8582.3*** *p83*
Schlosser, George; Philadelphia, 1759 ***9973.7*** *p33*
Schlosser, Heinrich; Cincinnati, 1870 ***8582.3*** *p62*
Schlosser, Henry; Philadelphia, 1776 ***8582.3*** *p85*
Schlosser, Michael; Alberta, n.d. ***5262*** *p58*
Schlossler, Adolf Adam; Iroquois Co., IL, 1894 ***3455.1*** *p13*
Schlossmacher, . . .; Canada, 1776-1783 ***9786*** *p33*
Schlossmann, Johann Nicolaus; Pennsylvania, 1752 ***4525*** *p242*
Schlossmann, Johann Nicolaus; Pennsylvania, 1752 ***4525*** *p243*
Schlotborn, Henry J.; Indiana, 1848 ***9117*** *p19*
Schlotrer, Anna Barbara; America, 1766 ***2444*** *p166*
Schlotrer, Anna Barbara; Philadelphia Co., PA, 1766-1779 ***2444*** *p166*
Schlotter, Franz; America, 1849 ***8582.3*** *p58*
Schlotter, John; Washington, 1859-1920 ***2872.1*** *p36*
Schlotterbeck, Anna Magdalena; Pennsylvania, 1753 ***2444*** *p164*
Schlotterbecker, Anna Magdalena; Pennsylvania, 1753 ***2444*** *p164*
Schlotterer, . . .; Pennsylvania, 1749 ***2444*** *p209*
Schlotterer, Anna Barbara; America, 1766 ***2444*** *p166*
Schlotterer, Anna Barbara; Philadelphia Co., PA, 1766-1779 ***2444*** *p166*
Schlotterer, Anna Maria; America, 1766 ***2444*** *p212*
Schlotterer, Hans Cunrad; Pennsylvania, 1749 ***2444*** *p212*
Schlotterer, Jacob; Pennsylvania, 1749 ***2444*** *p212*
*Brother:*Martin
Schlotterer, Jacob; Pennsylvania, 1749 ***2444*** *p212*
Schlotterer, Martin *SEE* Schlotterer, Jacob
Schlotterer, Mattheis; Pennsylvania, 1749 ***2444*** *p212*
Schluchter, Margaretha Hermann 81; Ontario, 1908 ***1763*** *p48D*
Schlueter, Heinrich W.; America, 1880 ***4610.10*** *p86*
With 2 brothers
Schlupp, Conrad; Charleston, SC, 1775-1781 ***8582.2*** *p52*
Schluter, . . .; Canada, 1776-1783 ***9786*** *p33*
Schluter, Carl August Johann Ludwig; America, 1876 ***4610.10*** *p122*
Schluter, Heinrich W.; America, 1880 ***4610.10*** *p86*
With 2 brothers
Schmacher, Peter, Jr.; Germantown, PA, 1685 ***2155*** *p2*
Schmahl Family ; Pennsylvania, n.d. ***1034.18*** *p12*
Schmal, Joseph; America, 1851 ***8582.3*** *p58*
Schmale, Carl Heinrich Christian; America, 1863 ***4610.10*** *p113*
Schmalholz, John; New York, 1854 ***1450.2*** *p126A*
Schmaling, William; New York, 1756 ***3652*** *p81*
Schmall, Adam; Philadelphia, 1762 ***9973.7*** *p37*
Schmall, Martin; Indiana, 1836 ***9117*** *p15*
Schmaltzer, John; Wisconsin, n.d. ***9675.7*** *p270*
Schmalz, Johann 19; New York, NY, 1898-1899 ***7846*** *p39*
Schmalzle, Carl; New York, NY, 1837 ***8208.4*** *p51*
Schmantz, Frank; Wisconsin, n.d. ***9675.7*** *p270*
Schmare, Fred; Indiana, 1848 ***9117*** *p18*
Schmatter, Anna Maria; New York, 1749 ***3652*** *p73*
Schmechel, Carl; Wisconsin, n.d. ***9675.7*** *p270*
Schmechel, Emil; Wisconsin, n.d. ***9675.7*** *p270*
Schmedes, Marten; New York, NY, 1836 ***8208.4*** *p10*
Schmegler, Christian Friedrich *SEE* Schmegler, Johann Friedrich
Schmegler, Johann Friedrich; America, 1798 ***2444*** *p215*
*Child:*Christian Friedrich
Schmeichel, Heinrich; Wisconsin, n.d. ***9675.7*** *p270*
Schmeiderberg, Charles F.; Illinois, 1884 ***2896.5*** *p35*
Schmeidle, August; Illinois, 1870 ***2896.5*** *p35*
Schmeiss, Balzer; Philadelphia, 1779 ***8137*** *p13*
Schmeissen, Christ. Constanze 6 mos *SEE* Schmeissen, Joh. Carl Gottl.
Schmeissen, Christiane Sophie 37 *SEE* Schmeissen, Joh. Carl Gottl.
Schmeissen, Emelie Magdal. 7 *SEE* Schmeissen, Joh. Carl Gottl.
Schmeissen, Joh. Carl Gottl. 35; New Orleans, 1839 ***9420.2*** *p170*
*Wife:*Christiane Sophie 37
*Child:*Emelie Magdal. 7
*Child:*Marie Magdal. 5
*Child:*Johanna 4
*Child:*Christ. Constanze 6 mos
Schmeissen, Johanna 4 *SEE* Schmeissen, Joh. Carl Gottl.
Schmeissen, Marie Magdal. 5 *SEE* Schmeissen, Joh. Carl Gottl.
Schmeisser, Wilhelm 29; Kansas, 1872 ***5240.1*** *p38*
Schmeisser, Wilhelm 29; Kansas, 1872 ***5240.1*** *p53*
Schmeissner, Christoph 26; Kansas, 1893 ***5240.1*** *p38*
Schmeissner, Christoph 26; Kansas, 1893 ***5240.1*** *p78*
Schmeling, Gustave; Wisconsin, n.d. ***9675.7*** *p270*
Schmeling, Wilhelmine; Milwaukee, 1843 ***3702.7*** *p311*
Schmeltz, Adam; Lancaster, PA, 1780 ***8137*** *p13*
Schmeltz, Adam; Philadelphia, 1783 ***8137*** *p4*
Schmeltz, Andreas; Lancaster, PA, 1780 ***8137*** *p13*
Schmeltz, Andrew; Philadelphia, 1783 ***8137*** *p4*
Schmeltz, Johannes; Lancaster, PA, 1780 ***8137*** *p13*
Schmeltz, Johannes; Philadelphia, 1783 ***8137*** *p4*
Schmeltzer, Edward; Colorado, 1887 ***9678.2*** *p167*
Schmelz, Christopher; America, 1850 ***8582.3*** *p58*
Schmelzer, . . .; Colorado, 1886 ***9678.2*** *p167*
Schmick, John Jacob; New York, 1751 ***3652*** *p75*
Schmid, Anna *SEE* Schmid, Philipp Karl
Schmid, Anna *SEE* Schmid, Philipp Karl
Schmid, Anna Maria Weber *SEE* Schmid, Martin
Schmid, Augustin 48; New Orleans, 1838 ***778.5*** *p487*
Schmid, Barbara *SEE* Schmid, Johannes
Schmid, Clara 30; New York, NY, 1889 ***7846*** *p40*
Schmid, Georg 32; New York, NY, 1889 ***7846*** *p40*
Schmid, Gottlieb; Wisconsin, n.d. ***9675.7*** *p270*
Schmid, Johann 6; New York, NY, 1889 ***7846*** *p40*
Schmid, Johann Ulrich *SEE* Schmid, Johannes
Schmid, Johannes; Pennsylvania, 1747-1800 ***2444*** *p212*
*Wife:*Margaretha
*Child:*Barbara
*Child:*Johann Ulrich
Schmid, Johannis; Pennsylvania, 1752 ***2444*** *p212*
Schmid, Margaretha *SEE* Schmid, Johannes
Schmid, Margaretha 2; New York, NY, 1889 ***7846*** *p40*
Schmid, Margarotha 4; New York, NY, 1889 ***7846*** *p40*
Schmid, Martin; Pennsylvania, 1752 ***2444*** *p213*
*Wife:*Anna Maria Weber
Schmid, Martin 6 mos; New York, NY, 1889 ***7846*** *p40*
Schmid, Matthaus *SEE* Schmid, Philipp Karl
Schmid, Philipp Karl; Pennsylvania, 1752 ***2444*** *p213*
*Wife:*Anna
*Child:*Matthaus
*Child:*Anna
Schmidlapp, . . .; America, 1869-1885 ***8582.2*** *p36*
Schmidlapp, J. A.; America, 1828 ***8582.2*** *p61*
Schmidlapp, J. A.; Ohio, 1869-1887 ***8582*** *p27*
Schmidler, Jacob; Wisconsin, n.d. ***9675.7*** *p270*
Schmidt, . . .; America, 1800-1813 ***8582.3*** *p76*
Schmidt, . . .; Canada, 1776-1783 ***9786*** *p33*
Schmidt, Dr.; Cincinnati, 1837-1838 ***8582.1*** *p45*
Schmidt, Maj. Gen.; New York, 1776 ***9786*** *p278*
Schmidt, Mr.; Quebec, 1776 ***9786*** *p261*
Schmidt, Adam; New York, NY, 1828 ***8582.1*** *p30*
Schmidt, Adam; Philadelphia, 1779 ***8137*** *p13*

Schmidt, Alexander; Ohio, 1800-1885 ***8582.2*** *p58*
Schmidt, Andreas; Pennsylvania, 1754 ***4525*** *p244*
Schmidt, Andreas; Wisconsin, n.d. ***9675.7*** *p270*
Schmidt, Andrew; Indiana, 1836 ***9117*** *p15*
Schmidt, Andrew; Kansas, 1882 ***5240.1*** *p38*
Schmidt, Andrew J.; Kansas, 1882 ***5240.1*** *p38*
Schmidt, Anthony; Wisconsin, n.d. ***9675.7*** *p270*
Schmidt, Anton Karl; Wisconsin, n.d. ***9675.7*** *p270*
Schmidt, August; America, 1835 ***1450.2*** *p127A*
Schmidt, August; Illinois, 1859 ***5012.39*** *p89*
Schmidt, Augustin 28; New Orleans, 1838 ***778.5*** *p487*
Schmidt, Benedict; New York, NY, 1836 ***8208.4*** *p9*
Schmidt, Bernhard 54; New Orleans, 1839 ***9420.2*** *p358*
Schmidt, C.; Milwaukee, 1875 ***4719.30*** *p257*
Schmidt, Mrs. C.; Milwaukee, 1875 ***4719.30*** *p257*
Schmidt, C. A.; America, 1874 ***5240.1*** *p39*
Schmidt, Carl; America, 1848 ***8582.1*** *p30*
Schmidt, Carl; Cincinnati, 1827 ***8582.1*** *p51*
Schmidt, Carl 76; New York, NY, 1901 ***1763*** *p40D*
Schmidt, Carl Fr. August; America, 1881 ***4610.10*** *p150*
Schmidt, Carl Heinrich Samuel; America, 1850 ***4610.10*** *p143*
Schmidt, Carl L.; America, 1883 ***1450.2*** *p127A*
Schmidt, Catharina *SEE* Schmidt, Hans
Schmidt, Catharina Zehetner *SEE* Schmidt, Hans
Schmidt, Charles; Cincinnati, 1869-1887 ***8582*** *p27*
Schmidt, Charles; Wisconsin, n.d. ***9675.7*** *p270*
Schmidt, Christian; New York, 1748 ***3652*** *p68*
Schmidt, Christian; South Carolina, 1788 ***7119*** *p198*
Schmidt, Clara 46; Port uncertain, 1839 ***778.5*** *p487*
Schmidt, D.; New York, 1754 ***3652*** *p78*
Schmidt, Daniel; America, 1890-1922 ***2691.4*** *p168*
Schmidt, Daniel; Lancaster, PA, 1780 ***8137*** *p13*
Schmidt, Eduard; Wisconsin, n.d. ***9675.7*** *p270*
Schmidt, El. Kath. 27; America, 1853 ***9162.7*** *p15*
Schmidt, Elisa; Washington, 1859-1920 ***2872.1*** *p36*
Schmidt, Elisabeth Dudenhofer; America, 1913 ***1763*** *p40D*
Schmidt, Elisabetha 65; Indiana, 1901 ***1763*** *p40C*
Schmidt, Elisebeth *SEE* Schmidt, Johann
Schmidt, Elisebeth; New York, NY, 1924 ***3455.4*** *p54*
*Husband:*Johann
Schmidt, Elizabetha 22; New York, NY, 1898-1899 ***7846*** *p39*
Schmidt, Emile 29; Harris Co., TX, 1898 ***6254*** *p5*
Schmidt, Erasmus; Lancaster, PA, 1780 ***8137*** *p13*
Schmidt, Ernest P.; Kansas, 1900 ***5240.1*** *p39*
Schmidt, Ernst; Wisconsin, n.d. ***9675.7*** *p270*
Schmidt, Ernst Heinrich; America, 1854 ***4610.10*** *p145*
Schmidt, Eva 61; New Orleans, 1839 ***9420.2*** *p70*
Schmidt, Eva Magdalena 1 *SEE* Schmidt, Joachim
Schmidt, Felde G.; Illinois, 1894 ***5012.39*** *p53*
Schmidt, Felde G.; Illinois, 1898 ***5012.40*** *p55*
Schmidt, Florimand; Illinois, 1870 ***2896.5*** *p35*
Schmidt, Florimond; Illinois, 1868 ***2896.5*** *p35*
Schmidt, Franc. 18; America, 1838 ***778.5*** *p487*
Schmidt, Frank; Wisconsin, n.d. ***9675.7*** *p270*
Schmidt, Frantz; New York, NY, 1840 ***8208.4*** *p109*
Schmidt, Franz 27; Kansas, 1880 ***5240.1*** *p61*
Schmidt, Franz Jos; America, 1828 ***8582.2*** *p61*
Schmidt, Fred; Wisconsin, n.d. ***9675.7*** *p270*
Schmidt, Frederick; New York, 1765 ***3652*** *p89*
With wife
Schmidt, Frederick; New York, 1884 ***1450.2*** *p34B*
Schmidt, Frederick; Wisconsin, n.d. ***9675.7*** *p270*
Schmidt, Frederick W. 52; West Virginia, 1902 ***9788.3*** *p20*
Schmidt, Friderich; Louisville, KY, 1855 ***3702.7*** *p133*
Schmidt, Friedrich; Wisconsin, n.d. ***9675.8*** *p65*
Schmidt, Fritz; Baltimore, 1891 ***1450.2*** *p34B*
Schmidt, Georg; Philadelphia, 1779 ***8137*** *p13*
Schmidt, Georg; Yorktown, VA, 1781 ***8137*** *p13*
Schmidt, Georg 75; America, 1912 ***1763*** *p40D*
Schmidt, Gertude; Wisconsin, n.d. ***9675.8*** *p65*
Schmidt, Gottfreid J.; Milwaukee, 1875 ***4719.30*** *p257*
Schmidt, Gottfried 36; New Orleans, 1839 ***9420.2*** *p69*
Schmidt, Gottlob 30; New Orleans, 1839 ***9420.2*** *p69*
Schmidt, Gottwerth 4 *SEE* Schmidt, Joachim
Schmidt, Gustav Heinrich; America, 1885 ***4610.10*** *p125*
Schmidt, H. P.; Kansas, 1890 ***5240.1*** *p39*
Schmidt, Hans; Georgia, 1739 ***9332*** *p323*
*Wife:*Catharina Zehetner
Schmidt, Hans; Georgia, 1739 ***9332*** *p326*
*Wife:*Catharina
Schmidt, Hans Jacob; New York, 1756 ***3652*** *p81*
Schmidt, Heinrich; Kansas, 1888 ***5240.1*** *p39*
Schmidt, Heinrich; Wisconsin, n.d. ***9675.8*** *p65*
Schmidt, Henrich; Philadelphia, 1779 ***8137*** *p13*
Schmidt, Henry; America, 1890 ***1450.2*** *p34B*
Schmidt, Henry; Arkansas, 1918 ***95.2*** *p110*
Schmidt, Henry; New York, 1847 ***1450.2*** *p127A*
Schmidt, Henry; Wisconsin, n.d. ***9675.8*** *p65*
Schmidt, J. G.; America, 1874 ***5240.1*** *p39*
Schmidt, Jacob; Kansas, 1882 ***5240.1*** *p39*
Schmidt, Jacob; New York, NY, 1912 ***3455.3*** *p26*
Schmidt, Jacob; Washington, 1859-1920 ***2872.1*** *p36*
Schmidt, Jacob; Wisconsin, n.d. ***9675.8*** *p65*
Schmidt, Jacob 34; America, 1831 ***778.5*** *p487*
Schmidt, Jacob H.; America, 1849 ***8582.1*** *p30*
Schmidt, Jacob Henry; Wisconsin, n.d. ***9675.8*** *p65*
Schmidt, Jacob J.; Kansas, 1884 ***5240.1*** *p39*
Schmidt, Jakob; Ohio, 1810 ***8582.1*** *p48*
Schmidt, Jakob; Ohio, 1811 ***8582.1*** *p48*
Schmidt, Jakob; Philadelphia, 1779 ***8137*** *p13*
Schmidt, Jean 19; Port uncertain, 1839 ***778.5*** *p487*
Schmidt, Jean 46; Port uncertain, 1839 ***778.5*** *p487*
Schmidt, Joachim 42; New Orleans, 1839 ***9420.2*** *p358*
*Wife:*Mary 33
*Son:*Gottwerth 4
*Daughter:*Eva Magdalena 1
Schmidt, Joh. 27; America, 1853 ***9162.8*** *p37*
Schmidt, Joh. 77; Wheeling, WV, 1908 ***1763*** *p48D*
Schmidt, Johann *SEE* Schmidt, Elisebeth
Schmidt, Johann; America, 1838 ***8582*** *p27*
Schmidt, Johann; New York, NY, 1924 ***3455.4*** *p53*
*Wife:*Elisebeth
Schmidt, Johann; Ohio, 1842 ***8582.2*** *p59*
Schmidt, Johann; Wisconsin, n.d. ***9675.8*** *p65*
Schmidt, Johann 31; New Orleans, 1839 ***9420.2*** *p70*
Schmidt, Johann 34; New Orleans, 1839 ***9420.2*** *p69*
Schmidt, Johann Friedrich; Germantown, PA, 1776 ***8582.3*** *p85*
Schmidt, Johann Heinrich; America, 1840 ***4610.10*** *p104*
Schmidt, Johannes; Wisconsin, n.d. ***9675.8*** *p65*
Schmidt, Johannes, Jr.; Philadelphia, 1779 ***8137*** *p13*
Schmidt, Johannes, Sr.; Philadelphia, 1779 ***8137*** *p13*
Schmidt, John; America, 1844 ***1450.2*** *p127A*
Schmidt, John; America, 1845 ***8582.1*** *p30*
Schmidt, John; Colorado, 1885 ***9678.2*** *p167*
Schmidt, John; Georgia, 1738 ***9332*** *p321*
Schmidt, John; New York, 1749 ***3652*** *p72*
Schmidt, John; Wisconsin, n.d. ***9675.8*** *p65*
Schmidt, John C.; Wisconsin, n.d. ***9675.8*** *p65*
Schmidt, John Christopher; New York, 1749 ***3652*** *p72*
Schmidt, John Frederick 29; New Orleans, 1839 ***9420.2*** *p485*
Schmidt, John G.; Wisconsin, n.d. ***9675.8*** *p65*
Schmidt, John Martin; New York, 1761 ***3652*** *p88*
Schmidt, John P.; America, 1885 ***1450.2*** *p127A*
Schmidt, Joseph; Kentucky, 1795-1800 ***8582.3*** *p94*
Schmidt, Joseph Konrad; America, 1795 ***8582.2*** *p60*
Schmidt, Josephine 2; New Orleans, 1838 ***778.5*** *p488*
Schmidt, Justine 17; New Orleans, 1839 ***9420.2*** *p70*
Schmidt, Justine 24; New Orleans, 1839 ***9420.2*** *p69*
Schmidt, Kath. 70; New York, NY, 1908 ***1763*** *p40D*
Schmidt, Konrad; Philadelphia, 1779 ***8137*** *p13*
Schmidt, Konrad; Philadelphia, 1779 ***8137*** *p14*
Schmidt, Kurt Henry 22; Kansas, 1904 ***5240.1*** *p83*
Schmidt, Louis; America, 1854 ***1450.2*** *p127A*
Schmidt, Lucien 6; Port uncertain, 1839 ***778.5*** *p488*
Schmidt, Lukas; New Netherland, 1630-1646 ***8582.2*** *p51*
Schmidt, Margaretha 9 mos; New York, NY, 1898-1899 ***7846*** *p39*
Schmidt, Maria 62; New Orleans, 1839 ***9420.2*** *p69*
Schmidt, Marie; Wisconsin, n.d. ***9675.8*** *p65*
Schmidt, Markus 26; New York, NY, 1898-1899 ***7846*** *p39*
Schmidt, Martin; Georgia, 1738 ***9332*** *p320*
Schmidt, Martin; Pennsylvania, 1754 ***2444*** *p213*
Schmidt, Mary 33 *SEE* Schmidt, Joachim
Schmidt, Matheus; Pennsylvania, 1779 ***8137*** *p7*
Schmidt, Mathias; Wisconsin, n.d. ***9675.8*** *p65*
Schmidt, Melchior; New York, 1749 ***3652*** *p72*
Schmidt, Michael 23; New Orleans, 1839 ***9420.2*** *p69*
Schmidt, Mirthe 24; New Orleans, 1838 ***778.5*** *p487*
Schmidt, Nichol 16; America, 1853 ***9162.7*** *p15*
Schmidt, Nicholas; Wisconsin, n.d. ***9675.8*** *p65*
Schmidt, Nicolaus; Wisconsin, n.d. ***9675.8*** *p65*
Schmidt, Ortillie 11; Port uncertain, 1839 ***778.5*** *p488*
Schmidt, Otto; Kansas, 1886 ***5240.1*** *p39*
Schmidt, Peter; New York, NY, 1838 ***8208.4*** *p88*
Schmidt, Peter; Wisconsin, n.d. ***9675.8*** *p65*
Schmidt, Peter A.; Kansas, 1882 ***5240.1*** *p39*
Schmidt, Philippe 17; Port uncertain, 1839 ***778.5*** *p488*
Schmidt, Phillip; Canada, 1776-1783 ***9786*** *p207A*
Schmidt, Rudolph; Wisconsin, n.d. ***9675.8*** *p65*
Schmidt, Rudolph Julius; Arkansas, 1918 ***95.2*** *p110*
Schmidt, Steve; Washington, 1859-1920 ***2872.1*** *p36*
Schmidt, Theodor 32; Cincinnati, 1871 ***8582*** *p27*
Schmidt, Thomas; Arizona, 1898 ***9228.30*** *p9*
Schmidt, Thomas; Georgia, 1738 ***9332*** *p320*
Schmidt, Tolivor A. 44; Harris Co., TX, 1899 ***6254*** *p6*
Schmidt, Ullrich; South America, n.d. ***8582.3*** *p79*
Schmidt, Ulrich; South Carolina, 1788 ***7119*** *p200*
Schmidt, Vinzens 19; New York, NY, 1898-1899 ***7846*** *p39*
Schmidt, Walburga; Wisconsin, n.d. ***9675.8*** *p65*
Schmidt, Wilhelm; Wisconsin, n.d. ***9675.8*** *p65*
Schmidt, Wilhemina 44; Kansas, 1880 ***5240.1*** *p61*
Schmidt, William; New York, 1852 ***1450.2*** *p127A*
Schmidt, William; New York, NY, 1924 ***3455.4*** *p54*
Schmidt, William F.; New York, NY, 1840 ***8208.4*** *p108*
Schmidt-Buergeler, Carl von; Cincinnati, 1788-1848 ***8582.3*** *p90*
Schmidt-Buergeler, Karl, Baron von; Cincinnati, 1846-1875 ***8582.3*** *p90*
Schmidtlapp, . . .; America, 1869-1885 ***8582.2*** *p36*
Schmidtlapp, Miss; Ohio, 1869-1887 ***8582*** *p9*
Schmidtmeier, Friedrick 52; Kansas, 1889 ***5240.1*** *p73*
Schmidtmeyer, . . .; Canada, 1776-1783 ***9786*** *p33*
Schmiedel, . . .; Canada, 1776-1783 ***9786*** *p33*
Schmieder, H.; Ohio, 1869-1887 ***8582*** *p27*
Schmieding, August Heinrich; America, 1846 ***4610.10*** *p134*
*Wife:*Elisabeth Schroder
*Son:*Carl Anton
Schmieding, Carl Anton *SEE* Schmieding, August Heinrich
Schmieding, Elisabeth Schroder *SEE* Schmieding, August Heinrich
Schmieding, Herman; Nevada, 1878 ***2764.35*** *p61*
Schmiehausen, H. A.; Kansas, 1886 ***5240.1*** *p39*
Schmiehauser, Bernard 25; Kansas, 1882 ***5240.1*** *p63*
Schmiehauser, Bernard 26; Kansas, 1882 ***5240.1*** *p39*
Schmierer, William; Wisconsin, n.d. ***9675.8*** *p65*
Schminer, Carl Emil Edward; Wisconsin, n.d. ***9675.8*** *p65*
Schmit, . . .; Canada, 1776-1783 ***9786*** *p33*
Schmit, Andreas; Pennsylvania, 1754 ***4525*** *p244*
Schmit, Andrew; Canada, 1776-1783 ***9786*** *p207A*
Schmit, Gustav; Wisconsin, n.d. ***9675.8*** *p65*
Schmit, Joachem; Wisconsin, n.d. ***9675.8*** *p65*
Schmit, Joh; Charleston, SC, 1775-1781 ***8582.2*** *p52*
Schmit, Johannis; Pennsylvania, 1752 ***2444*** *p212*
Schmit, John; Wisconsin, n.d. ***9675.8*** *p65*
Schmit, Mathias; Wisconsin, n.d. ***9675.8*** *p65*
Schmit, Nicholas; Wisconsin, n.d. ***9675.8*** *p65*
Schmit, Peter; Wisconsin, n.d. ***9675.8*** *p65*
Schmith, . . .; Canada, 1776-1783 ***9786*** *p33*
Schmith, J.M.; Wisconsin, n.d. ***9675.8*** *p65*
Schmitt, . . .; Canada, 1776-1783 ***9786*** *p33*
Schmitt, Ad. 23; America, 1853 ***9162.8*** *p37*
Schmitt, Adam 10; America, 1853 ***9162.8*** *p37*
Schmitt, Andreas; New England, 1754 ***4525*** *p244*
*Wife:*Christine
*Child:*Maria Margaretha
Schmitt, Anna Elis. 9; America, 1853 ***9162.8*** *p37*
Schmitt, Barb. 27; America, 1853 ***9162.8*** *p37*
Schmitt, Christian; America, 1847 ***8582.3*** *p58*
Schmitt, Christina 11 mos; America, 1853 ***9162.8*** *p37*
Schmitt, Christine *SEE* Schmitt, Andreas
Schmitt, Christine *SEE* Schmitt, George
Schmitt, David; Cincinnati, 1869-1887 ***8582*** *p27*
Schmitt, Elisabetha 6; America, 1853 ***9162.8*** *p37*
Schmitt, Elisabetha 11; America, 1853 ***9162.8*** *p37*
Schmitt, Elisabetha 34; America, 1853 ***9162.8*** *p37*
Schmitt, Ferdinand 24; Kansas, 1884 ***5240.1*** *p67*
Schmitt, Franz Joseph; Cincinnati, 1869-1887 ***8582*** *p27*
Schmitt, Fred Joseph; Arkansas, 1918 ***95.2*** *p110*
Schmitt, Georg; South Carolina, 1788 ***7119*** *p198*
Schmitt, Georg; Wisconsin, n.d. ***9675.8*** *p65*
Schmitt, George; New York, NY, 1888 ***3455.2*** *p96*
*Wife:*Christine
Schmitt, Gerhard Bernhard Heinrich; New Orleans, 1846 ***8582.3*** *p58*
Schmitt, Jean Marie; New York, NY, 1837 ***8208.4*** *p31*
Schmitt, John; New York, 1846 ***1450.2*** *p127A*
Schmitt, Kath. 6; America, 1853 ***9162.8*** *p37*
Schmitt, Kath. 36; America, 1853 ***9162.8*** *p37*
Schmitt, Leonh. 23; America, 1853 ***9162.7*** *p15*
Schmitt, Leonhard 8; America, 1853 ***9162.8*** *p37*
Schmitt, Maria Margaretha *SEE* Schmitt, Andreas
Schmitt, Martin; Ohio, 1837 ***8582.1*** *p47*
Schmitt, Martin; Wisconsin, n.d. ***9675.8*** *p65*
Schmitt, Matthias 38; Kansas, 1887 ***5240.1*** *p39*
Schmitt, Matthias 38; Kansas, 1887 ***5240.1*** *p69*
Schmitt, Meger 9; New York, NY, 1878 ***9253*** *p46*
Schmitt, Michael 8; America, 1853 ***9162.8*** *p37*
Schmitt, Michel 53; America, 1853 ***9162.8*** *p37*
Schmitt, Nicolaus; Cincinnati, 1869-1887 ***8582*** *p28*
Schmitt, Nicolaus; New York, NY, 1840 ***8582.1*** *p30*
Schmitt, Nikl. 22; America, 1853 ***9162.8*** *p37*
Schmitt, Peter; Cincinnati, 1869-1887 ***8582*** *p28*
Schmitt, Peter 42; America, 1853 ***9162.8*** *p37*
Schmitt, Schon 17; Port uncertain, 1839 ***778.5*** *p488*
Schmitt, Simon 11 mos; America, 1853 ***9162.8*** *p37*
Schmitt, Simon 18; New York, NY, 1878 ***9253*** *p46*
Schmittag, August; Illinois, 1900 ***5012.40*** *p77*
Schmitte, Erasmus; Lancaster, PA, 1780 ***8137*** *p13*

Schnetzer, Johann Wolfgang; America, 1746-1800 2444 p214
*Wife:*Anna Metzger
*Child:*Catharina Margaretha
*Child:*Maria Magdalena
*Child:*Johanna Rosina
*Child:*Maria Elisabetha
Schnetzer, Johanna Rosina *SEE* Schnetzer, Johann Wolfgang
Schnetzer, Maria Elisabetha *SEE* Schnetzer, Johann Wolfgang
Schnetzer, Maria Magdalena *SEE* Schnetzer, Johann Wolfgang
Schneyer, John L.; Ohio, 1869-1887 8582 p28
Schnichels, Joseph 34; Kansas, 1887 5240.1 p40
Schnichels, Joseph 34; Kansas, 1887 5240.1 p70
Schnickels, John 26; Kansas, 1876 5240.1 p57
Schnider, John; Baltimore, 1834 1450.2 p128A
Schniewind, Gustav A.; New York, 1864 8125.8 p438
Schnippering, Carl; America, 1848 8582.3 p59
Schniring, Agnes *SEE* Schniring, Jerg
Schniring, Catharina *SEE* Schniring, Jerg
Schniring, Jerg; Pennsylvania, 1746 2444 p214
*Wife:*Catharina
*Child:*Agnes
Schnitker, John; New York, NY, 1840 8208.4 p113
Schnitter, . . .; Canada, 1776-1783 9786 p33
Schnittger, John H.; America, 1839 8582.1 p31
Schnittger, Mathilde 21; America, 1881 4610.10 p124
Schnitzemeyer, Heinrich; Illinois, 1840-1890 4610.10 p59
Schnitzemeyer, Wilhelm 6; Illinois, 1812-1912 4610.10 p72
With parents
Schnitzer, Barbara; Wisconsin, n.d. 9675.8 p65
Schnitzer, Mathias; Wisconsin, n.d. 9675.8 p65
Schnitzler, Carl 22; Kansas, 1888 5240.1 p72
Schnitzler, Caroline 62; Kansas, 1893 5240.1 p78
Schnitzler, Charles August 24; Kansas, 1878 5240.1 p59
Schnochel, Julius; Wisconsin, n.d. 9675.8 p65
Schnodler, . . .; Canada, 1776-1783 9786 p33
Schnoerring, Agnes *SEE* Schnoerring, Jerg
Schnoerring, Catharina *SEE* Schnoerring, Jerg
Schnoerring, Jerg; Pennsylvania, 1746 2444 p214
*Wife:*Catharina
*Child:*Agnes
Schnorr, Anton; America, 1853 8582.3 p59
Schnuecker, Henrich; Philadelphia, 1779 8137 p14
Schnull, Friedrich Christian; America, 1841 4610.10 p97
Schnurr, . . .; Canada, 1776-1783 9786 p33
Schoales, Lizzie; New York, NY, 1867 5704.8 p224
Schob, Jacob; Ohio, 1812-1814 8582.2 p59
Schob, Vincent; Ohio, 1812-1814 8582.2 p59
Schober, Andrew; New York, 1743 3652 p60
*Wife:*Hedwig Regina
Schober, Anton; Wisconsin, n.d. 9675.8 p65
Schober, Clemens; Wisconsin, n.d. 9675.8 p65
Schober, Ernst; Wisconsin, n.d. 9675.8 p65
Schober, Gottfried; Cincinnati, 1826 8582.1 p51
Schober, Gottwald; Wisconsin, n.d. 9675.8 p65
Schober, Hedwig Regina *SEE* Schober, Andrew
Schober, Johann Georg; New England, 1773 4525 p244
Schober, Josef 50; Kansas, 1887 5240.1 p70
Schoberlechner, Joseph; New Orleans, 1830-1835 8582.3 p90
Schobloch, Joseph 27; America, 1831 778.5 p489
Schockemoller, Anna Marie I. Schwarze *SEE* Schockemoller, Heinrich Wilhelm
Schockemoller, Anne M. L. Friederike *SEE* Schockemoller, Heinrich Wilhelm
Schockemoller, Anne Marie Dorothea *SEE* Schockemoller, Heinrich Wilhelm
Schockemoller, Christian H. Gottlieb *SEE* Schockemoller, Heinrich Wilhelm
Schockemoller, Heinrich Wilhelm; America, 1857 4610.10 p158
*Wife:*Anna Marie I. Schwarze
*Child:*Anne Marie Dorothea
*Child:*Christian H. Gottlieb
*Child:*Anne M. L. Friederike
Schockemoller, Sophie Louise; America, 1845 4610.10 p97
Schockemuller, Anne M. I. Schwarze *SEE* Schockemuller, Friedrich Wilhelm
Schockemuller, August Heinrich *SEE* Schockemuller, Friedrich Wilhelm
Schockemuller, Friedrich Wilhelm; America, 1856 4610.10 p157
*Wife:*Anne M. I. Schwarze
*Son:*August Heinrich
Schockemuller, Sophie Wilhelmine Marie; America, 1846-1858 4610.10 p99
Schoeben, Nick; Arkansas, 1918 95.2 p110
Schoedinger, G. Jacob; Ohio, 1869-1887 8582 p28
Schoeffer, Georg; Pennsylvania, 1754 4525 p240
Schoeffer, Valt 30; Pennsylvania, 1753 4525 p244
Schoeffler, Moritz; Milwaukee, 1800-1885 8582.2 p69
Schoeffler, Moritz; Milwaukee, 1832-1885 8582.2 p35
Schoeffler, Moritz; New York, NY, 1842 8582.2 p37
Schoeil, . . .; Canada, 1776-1783 9786 p33
Schoel, von; Canada, 1776-1783 9786 p171
Schoell, Friedrich Ludwig von; Quebec, 1776 9786 p265
Schoell, Georg; Pennsylvania, 1751 2444 p209
Schoell, Georg von; Quebec, 1776 9786 p265
Schoemer, Nicolaus; Cincinnati, 1869-1887 8582 p28
Schoen, Charles; Illinois, 1860 7857 p7
Schoen, Henry; New York, 1750 3652 p74
Schoen, Joseph; New York, 1881 1450.2 p35B
Schoen, Sigmond; New York, 1880 1450.2 p35B
Schoenbein, Anna Maria Baeurlin *SEE* Schoenbein, Peter
Schoenbein, Peter; Pennsylvania, 1751 2444 p214
*Wife:*Anna Maria Baeurlin
*Child:*Susanna Elisabetha
Schoenbein, Susanna Elisabetha *SEE* Schoenbein, Peter
Schoenberg, David Dietrich; New York, 1761 3652 p88
Schoene, Jakob; Ohio, 1800-1812 8582.2 p57
Schoeneck, Anna Barbara *SEE* Schoeneck, Hans Jerg
Schoeneck, Georg Friedrich *SEE* Schoeneck, Hans Jerg
Schoeneck, Hans Jerg; America, 1753 2444 p214
*Wife:*Sofia Agatha
*Child:*Johann Michael
*Child:*Anna Barbara
*Child:*Georg Friedrich
Schoeneck, Johann Michael *SEE* Schoeneck, Hans Jerg
Schoeneck, Sofia Agatha *SEE* Schoeneck, Hans Jerg
Schoeneckh, Johann Michel; Pennsylvania, 1753 2444 p214
Schoenenberger, Joseph; America, 1847 8582.1 p31
Schoener, Peter; Ohio, 1808 8582.2 p56
Schoenfeld, Henry 24; Kansas, 1889 5240.1 p39
Schoenfeld, Henry 24; Kansas, 1889 5240.1 p73
Schoeninger, . . .; Cincinnati, 1848 8582.2 p63
Schoenlein, Leonhard; Pennsylvania, 1746-1772 4525 p245
Schoenlein, Michel; Pennsylvania, 1752 4525 p245
With 4 children
Schoepfel, John Ernst; New York, 1761 3652 p88
Schoepner, . . .; Canada, 1776-1783 9786 p33
Schoeppel, Frederich; Kansas, 1885 5240.1 p39
Schoeppel, John; Kansas, 1886 5240.1 p39
Schoeps, Pierre 24; America, 1836 778.5 p489
Schoerger, Jeremias; America, 1754 4525 p245
Schoessler, Moritz; Milwaukee, 1832-1885 8582.2 p35
Schoettle, Johannes; America, 1847 8582.3 p59
Schoettler, Heinrich; Kentucky, 1861 8582.3 p99
Schoetz, Friedrich; Wisconsin, n.d. 9675.8 p65
Schoffel, Andreas 1; Port uncertain, 1839 778.5 p489
Schoffel, Andreas 28; Port uncertain, 1839 778.5 p489
Schoffel, Georg Ging 26; Port uncertain, 1839 778.5 p489
Schoffel, Joseph 18; Port uncertain, 1839 778.5 p489
Schoffel, Magdalena 3; Port uncertain, 1839 778.5 p489
Schoffel, Magdalena 20; Port uncertain, 1839 778.5 p489
Schoffer, Hen.is 26; America, 1837 778.5 p489
Scholar, Hannah 25; Baltimore, 1775 1219.7 p269
Scholl, Agnes Barbara *SEE* Scholl, Hans Jacob
Scholl, Elisabetha *SEE* Scholl, Hans Jacob
Scholl, Hans Jacob; New England, 1730-1800 2444 p214
*Wife:*Elisabetha
*Child:*Agnes Barbara
Scholl, Jacob; Pennsylvania, 1753 2444 p214
Scholl, Jacob; Pennsylvania, 1768 2444 p214
Scholl, Johan T.; Wisconsin, n.d. 9675.8 p65
Scholl, John; Wisconsin, n.d. 9675.8 p65
Scholl, John Theodore; Wisconsin, n.d. 9675.8 p65
Scholl, Marguerite; New York, NY, 1892 3455.2 p75
Scholl, William Joseph; Wisconsin, n.d. 9675.8 p65
Schollhammer, . . .; Canada, 1776-1783 9786 p33
Schollin, William 29; Massachusetts, 1860 6410.32 p115
Scholten, William; Arkansas, 1918 95.2 p110
Scholz, Anna Marie Wilhelmine; America, 1844 4610.10 p133
Scholz, Carl; Washington, 1859-1920 2872.1 p36
Scholz, Friedrick; Washington, 1859-1920 2872.1 p36
Scholz, George; Washington, 1859-1920 2872.1 p36
Schomaker, Bernhard H.; Cincinnati, 1869-1887 8582 p28
Schomaker, Theodor; Cincinnati, 1847 8582.1 p31
Schomberg, . . .; Canada, 1776-1783 9786 p33
Schomberg, Romam 21; Boston, 1774 1219.7 p188
Schomburg, Mrs.; America, 1853 4610.10 p148
*Child:*Carl Dietrich Gottlieb
*Child:*Christoph Heinrich
*Child:*Ernst F. Gottlieb
*Child:*Anne Marie C. Engel 15
Schomburg, Anne Marie C. Engel 15 *SEE* Schomburg, Mrs.
Schomburg, Anne Marie Charlotte; America, 1854 4610.10 p144
Schomburg, Anne Marie Engel 16 *SEE* Schomburg, Johann Friedrich
Schomburg, Carl Daniel Heinrich *SEE* Schomburg, Johann Friedrich
Schomburg, Carl Dietrich Gottlieb *SEE* Schomburg, Mrs.
Schomburg, Carl Heinrich *SEE* Schomburg, Johann Friedrich
Schomburg, Christoph Heinrich *SEE* Schomburg, Mrs.
Schomburg, Engel; America, 1853 4610.10 p144
Schomburg, Ernst F. Gottlieb *SEE* Schomburg, Mrs.
Schomburg, Johann Diedrich *SEE* Schomburg, Johann Friedrich
Schomburg, Johann Friedrich 50; America, 1853 4610.10 p144
With wife
*Child:*Johann Diedrich
*Child:*Carl Heinrich
*Child:*Carl Daniel Heinrich
*Child:*Anne Marie Engel 16
*Child:*Louise 10
Schomburg, Louise 10 *SEE* Schomburg, Johann Friedrich
Schomburg, Ludwig 27; America, 1881 4610.10 p150
Schomen, John A.; New York, NY, 1848 6013.19 p88
Schomer, Gasper; Wisconsin, n.d. 9675.8 p65
Schomer, Lambert; Wisconsin, n.d. 9675.8 p65
Schommers, Johann; Wisconsin, n.d. 9675.8 p65
Schon, Jacob 30; Kansas, 1889 5240.1 p73
Schonberger, G. 22; America, 1854-1855 9162.6 p104
Schonborn, Fr. Aug. 28; New Orleans, 1839 9420.2 p168
Schondorff, . . .; Canada, 1776-1783 9786 p33
Schonebaum, August 28; America, 1881 4610.10 p124
Schoneberg, Auguste 7; New York, NY, 1857 9831.14 p154
Schoneberg, Carl Ludwig 6 mos; New York, NY, 1857 9831.14 p154
Schoneberg, Caroline Louise 36; New York, NY, 1857 9831.14 p154
Schoneberg, Christian 36; New York, NY, 1857 9831.14 p154
Schoneberg, Emilie 4; New York, NY, 1857 9831.14 p154
Schoneberg, Friedr. Wilhelm 9; New York, NY, 1857 9831.14 p154
Schonebohm, Ernst Dietrich; America, 1850 4610.10 p115
Schonebohm, Georg Gustav A. Hermann; America, 1884 4610.10 p123
Schonecker, . . .; Canada, 1776-1783 9786 p33
Schoneman, John; Iroquois Co., IL, 1829 3455.1 p13
Schonemann, William; America, 1851 1450.2 p128A
Schoner, Paulus; Baltimore, 1844 8582.1 p31
Schoner, Paulus; Cincinnati, 1869-1887 8582 p28
Schonewald, C.; Quebec, 1776 9786 p104
Schonewald, Johann Friedrich; Quebec, 1776 9786 p253
Schonholz, Kath. 23; Michigan, 1902 1763 p48D
Schons, Mathias; Baltimore, 1880 9678.2 p167
Schonthal, D. 18; New York, 1865 3702.7 p210
Schoolman, Antje Albers *SEE* Schoolman, John Wilhelm
Schoolman, John Wilhelm; Baltimore, 1900 3455.1 p44
*Wife:*Antje Albers
Schoolman, Kurt; New York, NY, 1923 3455.4 p52
Schoon, Christian; Illinois, 1889 5012.40 p25
Schoon, John G.; Illinois, 1892 5012.37 p63
Schoone, Albert B.; Illinois, 1896 5012.40 p55
Schoone, Lubbe B.; Illinois, 1896 5012.39 p53
Schoonover, George; Washington, 1859-1920 2872.1 p36
Schoonvelt, Henry; Arkansas, 1918 95.2 p110
Schoor, Gust; Kansas, 1891 5240.1 p39
Schopback, Ernest; Arkansas, 1918 95.2 p110
Schoppacher, Gertraud; Georgia, 1739 9332 p323
Schoppacher, Maria; Georgia, 1734 9332 p328
Schoppacher, Ruprecht; Georgia, 1734 9332 p327
Schoppenhorst, . . .; America, 1841 3702.7 p77
Schopperle, Joseph; Illinois, 1829 8582.1 p54
Schoron, John; Philadelphia, 1762 9973.7 p37
Schorr, David; America, 1847 8582.2 p37
Schorr, Georg; America, 1854 8582.3 p59
Schoster, Michel; South Carolina, 1788 7119 p203
Schotrcher, Henrich; Wisconsin, n.d. 9675.8 p65
Schott, Anton; St. Clair Co., IL, 1834 8582 p28
Schott, Bonifazius; Cincinnati, 1869-1887 8582 p28
Schott, John P. 30; St. Kitts, 1774 1219.7 p184
Schott, Joseph; America, 1851 1450.2 p128A
Schott, Ursula Catharina; Pennsylvania, 1742-1800 2444 p182
Schottelius, Maximilian Christoph L.; Quebec, 1776 9786 p262

Schotter, Andreas *SEE* Schotter, Valentin
Schotter, Anna Barbara *SEE* Schotter, Valentin
Schotter, Anna M. Klemmer *SEE* Schotter, Valentin
Schotter, Anna Rosina *SEE* Schotter, Valentin
Schotter, Catharina *SEE* Schotter, Valentin
Schotter, Joh. Hennrich 22 *SEE* Schotter, Valentin
Schotter, Joh. Jacob *SEE* Schotter, Valentin
Schotter, Maria Magdalena *SEE* Schotter, Valentin
Schotter, Valentin 45; Pennsylvania, 1743 *1034.18 p21*
  *Wife:*Anna M. Klemmer
  *Child:*Joh. Hennrich 22
  *Child:*Maria Magdalena
  *Child:*Catharina
  *Child:*Anna Rosina
  *Child:*Andreas
  *Child:*Joh. Jacob
  *Child:*Anna Barbara
Schotz, David; Ohio, 1869-1885 *8582.2 p56*
Schouler, Child; Died enroute, 1754 *2444 p215*
Schouler, Hans; Pennsylvania, 1754 *2444 p215*
Schoultz, George; Indiana, 1847 *9117 p18*
Schouster, Nicholas; Philadelphia, 1763 *9973.7 p38*
Schoute, Andrew; New York, 1754 *3652 p78*
Schoute, Andrew; New York, 1758 *3652 p86*
Schowe, Jacob; America, 1845 *1450.2 p128A*
Schraag, Louis; Kentucky, 1869-1887 *8582 p28*
Schrach, Nicholas 34; Pennsylvania, 1753 *4525 p246*
Schrack, Adam; Pennsylvania, 1753 *4525 p246*
Schrack, Johannes; Philadelphia, 1779 *8137 p14*
Schrade, Anna Margaretha Soenne *SEE* Schrade, Johann Christoph Ehrenreich
Schrade, Anna Margaretha Soenne *SEE* Schrade, Johann Christoph Ehrenreich
Schrade, Dorothea *SEE* Schrade, Georg Friedrich
Schrade, Elisabetha Dorothea *SEE* Schrade, Georg Friedrich
Schrade, Fridrich; Pennsylvania, 1752 *2444 p214*
Schrade, Georg Friedrich; Port uncertain, 1749-1800 *2444 p214*
  *Wife:*Dorothea
  *Child:*Elisabetha Dorothea
Schrade, Johann Christoph Ehrenreich; Pennsylvania, 1752 *2444 p214*
  *Wife:*Anna Margaretha Soenne
  *Child:*Maria Agnes
Schrade, Johann Christoph Ehrenreich; South Carolina, 1752 *2444 p214*
  *Wife:*Anna Margaretha Soenne
  *Child:*Maria Agnes
Schrade, Maria Agnes *SEE* Schrade, Johann Christoph Ehrenreich
Schrade, Maria Agnes *SEE* Schrade, Johann Christoph Ehrenreich
Schrader, . . .; Canada, 1776-1783 *9786 p33*
Schrader, Charlie; Illinois, 1874 *5012.37 p59*
Schrader, Edward Henry; Wisconsin, n.d. *9675.8 p65*
Schrader, Friedrich Wilhelm Conrad; Quebec, 1776 *9786 p255*
Schrader, Hermann; Cincinnati, 1869-1887 *8582 p28*
Schrader, Johann Friedrich; Quebec, 1776 *9786 p261*
Schrader, Maria; Illinois, 1860 *8125.8 p438*
Schrader, Otto C.; America, 1874 *1450.2 p129A*
Schrader, Rudolph; America, 1852 *1450.2 p129A*
Schradin, Anna Margaretha Soenne *SEE* Schradin, Johann Christoph Ehrenreich
Schradin, Anna Margaretha Soenne *SEE* Schradin, Johann Christoph Ehrenreich
Schradin, Johann Christoph Ehrenreich; Pennsylvania, 1752 *2444 p214*
  *Wife:*Anna Margaretha Soenne
  *Child:*Maria Agnes
Schradin, Johann Christoph Ehrenreich; South Carolina, 1752 *2444 p214*
  *Wife:*Anna Margaretha Soenne
  *Child:*Maria Agnes
Schradin, Maria Agnes *SEE* Schradin, Johann Christoph Ehrenreich
Schradin, Maria Agnes *SEE* Schradin, Johann Christoph Ehrenreich
Schraffenberger, Michael; America, 1849 *8582.3 p59*
Schrain, John Nicholas; Philadelphia, 1762 *9973.7 p36*
Schram, George; Philadelphia, 1762 *9973.7 p37*
Schram, Johan Henry; Pennsylvania, 1752 *4779.3 p14A*
Schram, John; Arkansas, 1918 *95.2 p110*
Schramm, Leonhard; New York, NY, 1923 *3455.4 p78*
Schrankemuller, . . .; Canada, 1776-1783 *9786 p33*
Schranz, Peter 49; Kansas, 1898 *5240.1 p40*
Schranz, Peter 49; Kansas, 1898 *5240.1 p81*
Schrape, Paul; Washington, 1859-1920 *2872.1 p36*
Schreck, Adam; Pennsylvania, 1753 *4525 p245*
  With wife
  With 4 children
Schreck, Anna Catharina *SEE* Schreck, Nicolaus

Schreck, Fritz; Kansas, 1900 *5240.1 p40*
Schreck, Hans; Pennsylvania, 1753 *4525 p246*
Schreck, Johannes; Pennsylvania, 1753 *4525 p246*
Schreck, Nicolaus *SEE* Schreck, Nicolaus
Schreck, Nicolaus; Pennsylvania, 1750 *4525 p246*
  *Child:*Anna Catharina
  *Child:*Nicolaus
Schreferderher, Georg Ml 24; New Orleans, 1839 *9420.1 p376*
Schreiber, . . .; Canada, 1776-1783 *9786 p34*
Schreiber, Abraham 9; New York, NY, 1878 *9253 p46*
Schreiber, F. Albin; New York, NY, 1884 *1450.2 p35B*
Schreiber, Francizsca 30; America, 1838 *778.5 p490*
Schreiber, Franz; Philadelphia, 1779 *8137 p14*
Schreiber, Frieda 8; New York, NY, 1878 *9253 p46*
Schreiber, George; Washington, 1859-1920 *2872.1 p36*
Schreiber, Hanne 5; New York, NY, 1878 *9253 p46*
Schreiber, J.W.; New York, 1776 *9786 p277*
Schreiber, Johan F.W.; Wisconsin, n.d. *9675.8 p65*
Schreiber, Johann; Wisconsin, n.d. *9675.8 p65*
Schreiber, John; Illinois, 1867 *5012.38 p98*
Schreiber, John; Philadelphia, 1831 *1450.2 p129A*
Schreiber, Kadisch 11 mos; New York, NY, 1878 *9253 p46*
Schreiber, Lea 40; New York, NY, 1878 *9253 p46*
Schreiber, Leonhard; America, 1849 *8582.1 p31*
Schreiber, Louis 38; America, 1838 *778.5 p490*
Schreiber, Pauline 6; America, 1838 *778.5 p490*
Schreiber, Rahel 9; New York, NY, 1878 *9253 p46*
Schreiber, Reisel 18; New York, NY, 1878 *9253 p46*
Schreier, Anna Catharina *SEE* Schreier, Christian
Schreier, Christian; Pennsylvania, 1727 *1034.18 p15*
  *Wife:*Elisabetha Kroff
  *Child:*Hans Georg
  *Child:*Anna Catharina
  *Child:*Johannes
  *Child:*Joh. Niclas
  *Child:*Jacob
Schreier, Elisabetha Kroff *SEE* Schreier, Christian
Schreier, Hans Georg *SEE* Schreier, Christian
Schreier, Jacob *SEE* Schreier, Christian
Schreier, Joh. Niclas *SEE* Schreier, Christian
Schreier, Johannes *SEE* Schreier, Christian
Schreiner, Anna Catharina; Pennsylvania, 1711-1783 *4525 p247*
Schreiner, Jacob; Philadelphia, 1776 *8582.3 p85*
Schreiner, Peter; Wisconsin, n.d. *9675.8 p65*
Schremer, Benedict; Virginia, 1852 *4626.16 p14*
Schrempf, . . .; Canada, 1776-1783 *9786 p34*
Schreyer, Anna Catharina *SEE* Schreyer, Christian
Schreyer, Christian; Pennsylvania, 1727 *1034.18 p15*
  *Wife:*Elisabetha Kroff
  *Child:*Hans Georg
  *Child:*Anna Catharina
  *Child:*Johannes
  *Child:*Joh. Niclas
  *Child:*Jacob
Schreyer, Elisabetha Kroff *SEE* Schreyer, Christian
Schreyer, Hans Georg *SEE* Schreyer, Christian
Schreyer, Jacob *SEE* Schreyer, Christian
Schreyer, Joh. Niclas *SEE* Schreyer, Christian
Schreyer, Johann Adam; America, 1739 *4349 p48*
Schreyer, Johannes *SEE* Schreyer, Christian
Schrieber, Charles; New York, NY, 1838 *8208.4 p81*
Schriefer, August; Iroquois Co., IL, 1892 *3455.1 p13*
Schriefer, Henry N.; Iroquois Co., IL, 1893 *3455.1 p13*
Schriefer, Herman W.; Iroquois Co., IL, 1892 *3455.1 p13*
Schrieling, John C.; Wisconsin, n.d. *9675.8 p65*
Schriener, Mathias; Wisconsin, n.d. *9675.8 p65*
Schrier, Gottlob; Wisconsin, n.d. *9675.8 p65*
Schrodder, Anna M. M. Engel Meyer *SEE* Schrodder, Johann Carl
Schrodder, Joh. Heinr. Gottlieb *SEE* Schrodder, Johann Carl
Schrodder, Johann Carl; America, 1846 *4610.10 p134*
  *Wife:*Anna M. M. Engel Meyer
  *Son:*Joh. Heinr. Gottlieb
Schrode, Mathias; Wisconsin, n.d. *9675.8 p65*
Schroder, . . .; Canada, 1776-1783 *9786 p34*
Schroder, Anna Sophie *SEE* Schroder, Carl Heinrich
Schroder, Anne Cath. Balsmeyer *SEE* Schroder, Johann Heinrich
Schroder, Anne Marie Engel Meyer *SEE* Schroder, Johann Heinrich
Schroder, Anne Marie Ilsabein *SEE* Schroder, Carl Heinrich
Schroder, Anton Heinrich *SEE* Schroder, Carl Heinrich
Schroder, Carl Friedrich Wilhelm; America, 1853 *4610.10 p116*

Schroder, Carl Heinrich 39; America, 1850 *4610.10 p155*
  *Wife:*Henriette Buschmann
  *Child:*Ernst Wilhelm
  *Child:*Anne Marie Ilsabein
  *Child:*Caspar Heinrich
  *Child:*Anton Heinrich
  *Child:*Anna Sophie
Schroder, Carl Heinrich Wilhelm *SEE* Schroder, Ernst Heinrich
Schroder, Caspar Heinr Friedrich *SEE* Schroder, Johann Heinrich
Schroder, Caspar Heinrich *SEE* Schroder, Carl Heinrich
Schroder, Christine Caroline *SEE* Schroder, Ernst Heinrich
Schroder, Daniel Heinrich Samuel *SEE* Schroder, Ernst Heinrich
Schroder, Elisabeth; America, 1846 *4610.10 p134*
Schroder, Ernst Christian; Quebec, 1776 *9786 p254*
Schroder, Ernst Heinrich; America, 1850 *4610.10 p142*
  *Wife:*Louise Kramer
  *Child:*Carl Heinrich Wilhelm
  *Child:*Daniel Heinrich Samuel
  *Child:*Johanne C. Louise
  *Child:*Christine Caroline
Schroder, Ernst Wilhelm *SEE* Schroder, Carl Heinrich
Schroder, Friedrich Gottlieb; America, 1844 *4610.10 p154*
  *Wife:*Louise C. Vette
  *Son:*Heinrich F. Wilhelm
Schroder, Friedrich H. Gottlieb *SEE* Schroder, Johann Heinrich
Schroder, Fritz; New York, NY, 1853 *4610.10 p34*
Schroder, Hans; Illinois, 1886 *5012.39 p120*
Schroder, Heinrich F. Wilhelm *SEE* Schroder, Friedrich Gottlieb
Schroder, Henriette Buschmann *SEE* Schroder, Carl Heinrich
Schroder, Henry 27; Kansas, 1876 *5240.1 p57*
Schroder, Johann Heinrich; America, 1838 *4610.10 p133*
  *Wife:*Anne Cath. Balsmeyer
  *Son:*Friedrich H. Gottlieb
Schroder, Johann Heinrich; America, 1847 *4610.10 p134*
  *Wife:*Anne Marie Engel Meyer
  *Son:*Caspar Heinr Friedrich
Schroder, Johanne C. Louise *SEE* Schroder, Ernst Heinrich
Schroder, John; Baltimore, 1834 *1450.2 p129A*
Schroder, Lina 22; America, 1881 *4610.10 p146*
Schroder, Louise C. Vette *SEE* Schroder, Friedrich Gottlieb
Schroder, Louise Kramer *SEE* Schroder, Ernst Heinrich
Schroder, Margarete Sophie; America, 1842 *4815.7 p92*
Schroder, William; Illinois, 1858-1905 *5012.39 p25*
Schrodt, . . .; Canada, 1776-1783 *9786 p34*
Schroeder, Lieut.; Quebec, 1776 *9786 p105*
Schroeder, Albert A.; America, 1888 *1450.2 p35B*
Schroeder, Anthony; Ohio, 1841 *8365.25 p12*
Schroeder, Bernard; America, 1842 *8582.3 p59*
Schroeder, Carl; Illinois, 1903 *5012.40 p80*
Schroeder, Ch. Eduard; Wisconsin, n.d. *9675.8 p65*
Schroeder, Charles, Sr.; Iroquois Co., IL, 1892 *3455.1 p13*
Schroeder, Charles L.; Wisconsin, n.d. *9675.8 p65*
Schroeder, Franz F.; America, 1849 *8582.3 p59*
Schroeder, Frederick; Illinois, 1872 *5012.37 p59*
Schroeder, Heinr. Friedr. Ludwig *SEE* Schroeder, Heinrich Ludwig
Schroeder, Heinrich; America, 1849 *8582.3 p59*
Schroeder, Heinrich Anton; Wisconsin, n.d. *9675.8 p65*
Schroeder, Heinrich Ludwig; America, 1840 *4610.10 p119*
  *Father:*Heinr. Friedr. Ludwig
  *Mother:*Martha Elise Fattiger
Schroeder, Hermann; America, 1846 *8582.3 p59*
Schroeder, J. H.; Cincinnati, 1788-1848 *8582.3 p89*
Schroeder, J. H.; Cincinnati, 1788-1848 *8582.3 p90*
Schroeder, J. P.; Kansas, 1904 *5240.1 p40*
Schroeder, Jacob; Baltimore, 1819 *8582 p28*
  *Wife:*Mathilde Messer
Schroeder, Martha Elise Fattiger *SEE* Schroeder, Heinrich Ludwig
Schroeder, Mathilde Messer *SEE* Schroeder, Jacob
Schroeder, P. D.; Kansas, 1877 *5240.1 p40*
Schroeder, Sebastian; Philadelphia, 1779 *8137 p14*
Schroeling, John C.; Wisconsin, n.d. *9675.8 p65*
Schroer, Christine Elisabeth; Cincinnati, 1840 *3702.7 p79*
  With brother
Schroerluecke, Henry; Cincinnati, 1869-1887 *8582 p28*
Schroll, Albert 24; Kansas, 1883 *5240.1 p64*
Schrool, Henry; Canada, 1776-1783 *9786 p207A*

Schroor, Jacob; Arkansas, 1918 95.2 p110
Schroot, . . .; Canada, 1776-1783 9786 p34
Schropp, Anna Margaret SEE Schropp, Matthew
Schropp, Matthew; New York, 1743 3652 p60
Wife: Anna Margaret
Schroter, Otto 29?; Arizona, 1890 2764.35 p64
Schroth, . . .; Canada, 1776-1783 9786 p34
Schroth, Andreas; America, 1847 8582.1 p31
Schrum, John; Iowa, 1866-1943 123.54 p43
Schub, Elisabetha; Port uncertain, 1728-1800 2444 p214
Schubart, . . .; Canada, 1776-1783 9786 p34
Schubart, Johann Michael; Pennsylvania, 1753 4525 p246
Schubart, Johann Nicolaus; Pennsylvania, 1753 4525 p246
Schubart, Michael; Philadelphia, 1764 8582.2 p65
Schubart, Michael; Philadelphia, 1776 8582.3 p84
Schubart, Michael; Philadelphia, 1776 8582.3 p85
Schubarth, Georg. Philp. 29; New Orleans, 1839 9420.2 p169
Schubarth, Johann Nicolaus; Pennsylvania, 1753 4525 p246
With wife
With children
Schuber, Catharina 19; New York, NY, 1878 9253 p45
Schuber, Catharina 25; New York, NY, 1878 9253 p45
Schuber, Christian 3; New York, NY, 1878 9253 p45
Schuber, Conrad 25; America, 1839 778.5 p490
Schuber, David 55; New York, NY, 1878 9253 p45
Schuber, Elisabeth 56; New York, NY, 1878 9253 p45
Schuber, Ferdinand 36; Kansas, 1889 5240.1 p74
Schuber, Georg 25; New York, NY, 1878 9253 p45
Schuber, Johann 17; New York, NY, 1878 9253 p45
Schuber, Marie 5; New York, NY, 1878 9253 p45
Schuber, Reinhard 9 mos; New York, NY, 1878 9253 p45
Schubert, . . .; Canada, 1776-1783 9786 p34
Schubert, Christiane 39; New Orleans, 1839 9420.1 p378
Schubert, F. Wilhelm; Illinois, 1876 2896.5 p36
Schubert, Ferdinand 24; New Orleans, 1839 9420.2 p485
Schubert, Gottleib 35; New Orleans, 1839 9420.1 p378
Schubert, Hans Michel; Philadelphia, 1769 4525 p265
Schubert, Johann Adam; Ohio, 1869-1887 8582 p28
Schubert, Johann Michael; Philadelphia, 1769 4525 p265
Schubert, Johann Nicolaus; Pennsylvania, 1753 4525 p246
Schubert, John; Ohio, 1869-1887 8582 p28
Schubert, John F.; Wisconsin, n.d. 9675.8 p65
Schubert, Julius 13; New Orleans, 1839 9420.1 p378
Schubert, Karl 7; America, 1854-1855 9162.6 p105
Schubert, Kathr. 9; America, 1854-1855 9162.6 p105
Schubert, Lina 23; New Orleans, 1839 9420.2 p483
Schubert, Ludwig 5; America, 1854-1855 9162.6 p105
Schubert, Marie 15; New Orleans, 1839 9420.2 p170
Schubert, Nicolaus; Pennsylvania, 1753 4525 p244
Schubert, Theodor 10; New Orleans, 1839 9420.2 p170
Schubert, Wilhelmina 17; New Orleans, 1839 9420.1 p378
Schuberth, John 33; Kansas, 1877 5240.1 p58
Schuchman, Ernest; Virginia, 1852 4626.16 p14
Schuck, Francis; Ohio, 1851 9892.11 p41
Schuckert, Christine 35; America, 1854-1855 9162.6 p105
Schud, Franz; Ohio, 1869-1887 8582 p29
Schuder, Joseph; Wisconsin, n.d. 9675.8 p65
Schudlett, . . .; Canada, 1776-1783 9786 p34
Schuebner, Gottlieb; Buffalo, NY, 1847 1450.2 p129A
Schuede, Johann Heinrich; America, 1836 8582.1 p31
Schuele, Jacob; America, 1849 8582.1 p31
Schueler, Fred. 37; Kansas, 1884 5240.1 p65
Schuelke, R.; Washington, 1859-1920 2872.1 p36
Schuelke, R. A.; Washington, 1859-1920 2872.1 p36
Schuelke, Reinhard; Washington, 1859-1920 2872.1 p36
Schuells, Gerhard Henry; Ohio, 1843 8365.26 p12
Schueltes, . . .; Canada, 1776-1783 9786 p34
Schuerge, Jeremias; America, 1754 4525 p245
Schuerger, Simon; Pennsylvania, 1750 4525 p247
Schuessele, John Jacob; Missouri, 1860 1450.2 p129A
Schuessler, George 44; Kansas, 1885 5240.1 p40
Schuette, Gerhard; Illinois, 1841 8582.2 p50
Schuette, Joseph; Akron, OH, 1833 8582.1 p49
Schuettelbauer, Eva SEE Schuettelbauer, Johann Georg
Schuettelbauer, Johann Andreas SEE Schuettelbauer, Johann Georg
Schuettelbauer, Johann Georg; America, 1738-1800 2444 p214
Wife: Eva
Child: Johann Andreas
Schuettler, Mr.; America, 1876-1877 8582.3 p59
Schuetz, Jakob; Ohio, 1800-1885 8582.2 p56
Schuetz, Johannes; Philadelphia, 1779 8137 p14
Schuetz, Peter; Boston, 1837 8582.3 p59
Schuetz, Peter; Ohio, 1869-1887 8582 p29
Schuetz, Rudolf; Wisconsin, n.d. 9675.8 p65
Schuffler, Charles C.F.; New York, NY, 1836 8208.4 p10
Schufraham, Mr. 35; New York, NY, 1847 3377.6 p12
Schuh, Augustus; Wisconsin, n.d. 9675.8 p65
Schuh, Henry; New York, NY, 1881 1450.2 p129A
Schuhler, Child; Died enroute, 1754 2444 p215
Schuhler, Hans; Pennsylvania, 1754 2444 p215
Schuhmacher, Adam; America, 1849 8582.1 p31
Schuhmacher, Albrecht; Pennsylvania, 1764 2444 p215
Schuhmacher, Johann Herbert; America, 1750-1752 8125.6 p23
Schuhmacher, Sebastian Topf; Georgia, 1738 9332 p320
Schuhmann, David 6; New Orleans, 1839 9420.1 p378
Schuhmann, Elias 36; New Orleans, 1839 9420.1 p378
Schuhmann, Franz; New Orleans, 1844 8582 p29
Schuhmann, Gottfried 4; New Orleans, 1839 9420.1 p378
Schuhmann, Johanne Christ. 37; New Orleans, 1839 9420.1 p378
Schuhmann, Johanne Rosine 8; New Orleans, 1839 9420.1 p378
Schuhr, Bertha; Milwaukee, 1875 4719.30 p257
Schuhr, Maria; Milwaukee, 1875 4719.30 p257
Schuhrioht, Anne Rosine 56 SEE Schuhrioht, Joh. Glob.
Schuhrioht, Carl Ehregolt 20 SEE Schuhrioht, Joh. Glob.
Schuhrioht, Joh. Furohtegott 15 SEE Schuhrioht, Joh. Glob.
Schuhrioht, Joh. Glob. 49; New Orleans, 1839 9420.2 p169
Wife: Anne Rosine 56
Child: Carl Ehregolt 20
Child: Joh. Traugolt 17
Child: Joha. Rosine 13
Child: Joh. Furohtegott 15
Schuhrioht, Joh. Traugolt 17 SEE Schuhrioht, Joh. Glob.
Schuhrioht, Joha. Rosine 13 SEE Schuhrioht, Joh. Glob.
Schuitzler, Carl 22; Kansas, 1888 5240.1 p40
Schuitzler, Charles August 24; Kansas, 1878 5240.1 p40
Schukar, August; Illinois, 1868 2896.5 p36
Schukar, Carl; Illinois, 1884 2896.5 p36
Schukar, Frederick; Illinois, 1866 2896.5 p36
Schukar, Peter; Wisconsin, 1852 2896.5 p36
Schukar, Wilhelm; Illinois, 1888 2896.5 p36
Schukar, William Carl; Illinois, 1889 2896.5 p36
Schukard, . . .; Canada, 1776-1783 9786 p34
Schukis, Josef; Wisconsin, n.d. 9675.8 p65
Schuldt, Carl; Illinois, 1922 3455.3 p53
Schuldt, Carl; New York, NY, 1889 3455.2 p76
Schuldt, Carl; New York, NY, 1889 3455.3 p51
Schuldt, Carl; New York, NY, 1889-1891 3455.2 p48
Schuldt, William; New York, NY, 1889 3455.3 p23
Schuldt, William; New York, NY, 1889-1891 3455.2 p48
Schulenberg, William; Wisconsin, n.d. 9675.8 p65
Schuler, . . .; Canada, 1776-1783 9786 p34
Schuler, Child; Died enroute, 1754 2444 p215
Schuler, Agnes SEE Schuler, Hans
Schuler, Andreas SEE Schuler, Hans
Schuler, Anna Maria SEE Schuler, Hans
Schuler, Augustin; America, 1847 8582.3 p60
Schuler, Christian SEE Schuler, Hans
Schuler, Hans; Pennsylvania, 1754 2444 p215
Wife: Sybilla
Child: Hans Ludwig
Child: Christian
Child: Anna Maria
Child: Agnes
Child: Andreas
Child: Martin
Schuler, Hans Ludwig SEE Schuler, Hans
Schuler, Ludwig; Colorado, 1892 9678.2 p167
Schuler, Martin SEE Schuler, Hans
Schuler, Sybilla SEE Schuler, Hans
Schuler, Wilhelm; Philadelphia, 1779 8137 p14
Schulhoff, Heinrich; Indiana, 1869-1887 8582 p29
Schuling, Rosina; New York, 1749 3652 p73
Schulman, Charles; Iowa, 1866-1943 123.54 p43
Schulman, Louis; Arkansas, 1918 95.2 p110
Schulman, Ralph; Arkansas, 1918 95.2 p110
Schulmeier, Frederick William; America, 1855 1450.2 p129A
Schulmeier, Peter; America, 1846 1450.2 p129A
Schulmeir, Philip; America, 1851 1450.2 p130A
Schulte, A.M. Friederike Sager SEE Schulte, Carl August Gottlieb
Schulte, Carl August Gottlieb; America, 1856 4610.10 p112
Wife: A.M. Friederike Sager
Son: Carl Friedrich Wilhelm
Schulte, Carl Friedrich; America, 1849 4610.10 p98
Schulte, Carl Friedrich Wilhelm SEE Schulte, Carl August Gottlieb
Schulte, E. H. W.; Cincinnati, 1869-1887 8582 p29
Schulte, Ernst H.W.; Cincinnati, 1843 3702.7 p79
Sister: Karoline
Schulte, Friederike; Cincinnati, 1843 3702.7 p79
Schulte, Gerhard Bernhard; America, 1837 8582.3 p60
Schulte, Heinrich; America, 1842 8582.1 p31
Schulte, Jakob; Ohio, 1798-1818 8582.2 p54
Schulte, Karoline SEE Schulte, Ernst H.W.
Schulte, Peter 24; Kansas, 1875 5240.1 p56
Schulte, Reinhart; Illinois, 1866 2896.5 p36
Schultheis, Anna Catharina; Pennsylvania, 1731 1034.18 p22
Schultheis, Anna Catharina Krahmer SEE Schultheis, Hans Martin
Schultheis, Anna Mara SEE Schultheis, Johannes
Schultheis, Christina SEE Schultheis, Johannes
Schultheis, H. Jacob SEE Schultheis, Johannes
Schultheis, Hans Martin; Pennsylvania, 1731 1034.18 p20
Wife: Anna Catharina Krahmer
Schultheis, Johannes SEE Schultheis, Johannes
Schultheis, Johannes 35; Pennsylvania, 1742 1034.18 p19
Wife: Christina
Child: Anna Mara
Child: H. Jacob
Child: Johannes
Schultheiss, Dietrich; Philadelphia, 1779 8137 p14
Schultheiss, Georg, Sr.; Illinois, 1835 8582.1 p55
Schultheiss, Henrich; Lancaster, PA, 1780 8137 p14
Schultheiss, Johann Georg; America, 1852 8582.3 p60
Schultheiss, John Felix; Kansas, 1914 6013.40 p17
Schultmeir, Charles; America, 1843 1450.2 p130A
Schultz, . . .; Canada, 1776-1783 9786 p34
Schultz, Mr.; America, 1740-1769 8582.2 p56
With wife
Schultz, Mrs.; New York, 1752 3652 p76
Schultz, A.L.A.; Illinois, 1894 5012.40 p53
Schultz, Andreas; Indiana, 1855 2896.5 p36
Schultz, Anna Catharina Krahmer SEE Schultz, Martin
Schultz, Anna Mara SEE Schultz, Johannes
Schultz, Aron 19; New York, NY, 1878 9253 p47
Schultz, Auft Frederick; Washington, 1859-1920 2872.1 p36
Schultz, Carl; Wisconsin, n.d. 9675.8 p65
Schultz, Charles; Illinois, 1902 5012.40 p77
Schultz, Christian; South Carolina, 1788 7119 p200
Schultz, Christina SEE Schultz, Johannes
Schultz, Fred; Washington, 1859-1920 2872.1 p36
Schultz, Fred; Wisconsin, n.d. 9675.8 p65
Schultz, Fred A.; Wisconsin, n.d. 9675.8 p65
Schultz, Frederick; Illinois, 1855 7857 p7
Schultz, Gustav; Wisconsin, n.d. 9675.8 p65
Schultz, H. Jacob SEE Schultz, Johannes
Schultz, Heinrich; America, 1806 8582.2 p38
Schultz, Henrich; Lancaster, PA, 1780 8137 p14
Schultz, Henrich; Saratoga, NY, 1777 8137 p14
Schultz, Henry; Arkansas, 1918 95.2 p110
Schultz, Henry; Wisconsin, n.d. 9675.8 p65
Schultz, Johan; Wisconsin, n.d. 9675.8 p65
Schultz, Johannes SEE Schultz, Johannes
Schultz, Johannes 35; Pennsylvania, 1742 1034.18 p19
Wife: Christina
Child: Anna Mara
Child: H. Jacob
Child: Johannes
Schultz, Johannes Christian; Pennsylvania, 1732 2444 p230
Schultz, John; Illinois, 1860 5012.38 p98
Schultz, John; Wisconsin, n.d. 9675.8 p65
Schultz, John George; Wisconsin, n.d. 9675.8 p65
Schultz, Julius; Illinois, 1880 2896.5 p36
Schultz, Louis; America, 1848 8582.1 p31
Schultz, Martin; Pennsylvania, 1731 1034.18 p20
Wife: Anna Catharina Krahmer
Schultz, Michael; America, 1842 8582.3 p60
Schultz, Peter; New York, NY, 1840 8208.4 p112
Schultz, Peter; Wisconsin, n.d. 9675.8 p65
Schultz, R. Caspers; Illinois, 1870 7857 p7
Schultz, William; Wisconsin, n.d. 9675.8 p65
Schultz, William F.; Illinois, 1896 5012.37 p63
Schultze, . . .; Canada, 1776-1783 9786 p34
Schultze, Albert SEE Schultze, Albert
Schultze, Albert; America, 1905 4610.10 p103
Wife: Karoline Kleine
Child: Anna
Child: Oswald
Child: Helene
Child: Albert
Schultze, Anna SEE Schultze, Albert
Schultze, Anna Maria; New York, 1709 3627 p4
Schultze, Carl; New York, 1749 3652 p72
Schultze, Casper; Canada, 1783 9786 p38A
Schultze, Godfrey; New York, 1749 3652 p72
Schultze, Helene SEE Schultze, Albert

Schultze, John; Canada, 1783 ***9786*** *p38A*
Schultze, Karoline Kleine *SEE* Schultze, Albert
Schultze, Oswald *SEE* Schultze, Albert
Schulz, Mr.; Cincinnati, 1831 ***8582.1*** *p51*
Schulz, Anton Friedrich W. Christian; America, 1886 ***4610.10*** *p125*
Schulz, August Anton Carl Otto; America, 1908 ***4610.10*** *p125*
Schulz, Carl Dietrich *SEE* Schulz, Johann Dietrich
Schulz, Christ Friedrich Wilhelm; America, 1850 ***4610.10*** *p147*
Schulz, Ernst W.; Wisconsin, n.d. ***9675.8*** *p66*
Schulz, Ernst William; Wisconsin, n.d. ***9675.8*** *p66*
Schulz, Fred; Wisconsin, n.d. ***9675.8*** *p66*
Schulz, Friedrich; Cincinnati, 1869-1887 ***8582*** *p29*
Schulz, Friedrich August Ferdinand L.; America, 1893 ***4610.10*** *p125*
Schulz, Friedrich W. Ferdinand *SEE* Schulz, Peter Ludwig Gottlieb
Schulz, Friedrich Wilhelm Ferdinand; America, 1886 ***4610.10*** *p125*
Schulz, Georg; Cincinnati, 1869-1887 ***8582*** *p29*
Schulz, Jacob; Kansas, 1901 ***5240.1*** *p40*
Schulz, Johann Dietrich 55; America, 1852 ***4610.10*** *p148*
*Son:*Carl Dietrich
Schulz, Karl; Wisconsin, n.d. ***9675.8*** *p66*
Schulz, Peter Ludwig Gottlieb; America, 1886 ***4610.10*** *p125*
Schulz, Peter Ludwig Gottlieb; America, 1889 ***4610.10*** *p118*
*Brother:*Friedrich W. Ferdinand
Schulz, William; Wisconsin, n.d. ***9675.8*** *p66*
Schulze, Caspar Ernst Heinrich; America, 1857 ***4610.10*** *p149*
Schulze, Jul. Henriette 27; New Orleans, 1839 ***9420.2*** *p168*
Schulze, Oscar Walter; Fort Wayne, IN, 1883 ***1450.2*** *p35B*
Schumacher, . . .; Ohio, 1812-1814 ***8582.2*** *p59*
Schumacher, A. M. Wilhelmine; America, 1881 ***4610.10*** *p160*
Schumacher, Adam; Port uncertain, 1730-1800 ***2444*** *p215*
*Wife:*Maria Christina
*Child:*Jerg Adam
*Child:*Johann Michael
*Child:*Johann Balthas
Schumacher, Albert; Mexico, 1827 ***8582*** *p29*
Schumacher, Albert; New York, NY, 1826 ***8582*** *p29*
Schumacher, Albrecht; America, 1751 ***2444*** *p215*
Schumacher, Anna *SEE* Schumacher, Hans Jacob
Schumacher, Anna Barbara *SEE* Schumacher, Hans Jacob
Schumacher, Anna Catharina *SEE* Schumacher, Hans Jacob
Schumacher, Anna Margaretha; Pennsylvania, 1749 ***2444*** *p190*
Schumacher, Anna Maria *SEE* Schumacher, Hans Jacob
Schumacher, Anna Marie Engel; America, 1841 ***4610.10*** *p138*
Schumacher, Christian 31; Port uncertain, 1839 ***778.5*** *p490*
Schumacher, Conrad *SEE* Schumacher, Hans Jacob
Schumacher, Dominick; Wisconsin, n.d. ***9675.8*** *p66*
Schumacher, Elisabetha *SEE* Schumacher, Hans Jacob
Schumacher, Ernst Heinrich; America, 1853 ***4610.10*** *p156*
Schumacher, Frank; Wisconsin, n.d. ***9675.8*** *p66*
Schumacher, Hans Jacob; New England, 1749 ***2444*** *p215*
*Wife:*Anna Maria
*Child:*Anna Catharina
*Child:*Conrad
*Child:*Elisabetha
With child
Schumacher, Hans Jacob; Port uncertain, 1754 ***2444*** *p215*
*Wife:*Anna
*Child:*Anna Barbara
*Child:*Helena
*Grandson:*Jacob
Schumacher, Helena *SEE* Schumacher, Hans Jacob
Schumacher, Henry; Wisconsin, n.d. ***9675.8*** *p66*
Schumacher, Herbert; Philadelphia, 1752 ***8125.6*** *p23*
Schumacher, Herman; Wisconsin, n.d. ***9675.8*** *p66*
Schumacher, Jacob *SEE* Schumacher, Hans Jacob
Schumacher, Jacob; Wisconsin, n.d. ***9675.8*** *p66*
Schumacher, Jerg Adam *SEE* Schumacher, Adam
Schumacher, Johan Adam; Philadelphia, 1744 ***8125.6*** *p22*
Schumacher, Johan Atam; Pennsylvania, 1744 ***2444*** *p215*
Schumacher, Johan Thomas; Philadelphia, 1752 ***8125.6*** *p23*
Schumacher, Johann Balthas *SEE* Schumacher, Adam
Schumacher, Johann Frederick; Illinois, 1871 ***5012.39*** *p25*
Schumacher, Johann Michael *SEE* Schumacher, Adam
Schumacher, Johann Peter; Wisconsin, n.d. ***9675.8*** *p66*
Schumacher, John; New York, NY, 1839 ***8208.4*** *p95*
Schumacher, John; Wisconsin, n.d. ***9675.8*** *p66*
Schumacher, Ludwig; Philadelphia, 1779 ***8137*** *p14*
Schumacher, Maria Christina *SEE* Schumacher, Adam
Schumacher, Mathias; Wisconsin, n.d. ***9675.8*** *p66*
Schumacher, Nicholas; Wisconsin, n.d. ***9675.8*** *p66*
Schumacher, Paul; America, 1852 ***8582.3*** *p60*
Schumacher, Peter; Illinois, 1888 ***5012.39*** *p121*
Schumacher, Peter; Wisconsin, n.d. ***9675.8*** *p66*
Schumaker, Fred; Illinois, 1876 ***5012.39*** *p91*
Schuman, George; Wisconsin, n.d. ***9675.8*** *p66*
Schuman, Robert; Wisconsin, n.d. ***9675.8*** *p66*
Schumann, . . .; Canada, 1776-1783 ***9786*** *p34*
Schumann, Franz; Cincinnati, 1869-1887 ***8582*** *p29*
Schumann, Gottlob; Wisconsin, n.d. ***9675.8*** *p66*
Schumann, Johannes; Saratoga, NY, 1777 ***8137*** *p14*
Schumann, John; America, 1887 ***1450.2*** *p130A*
Schumann, William; Washington, 1859-1920 ***2872.1*** *p36*
Schumm, Adam 32; America, 1854-1855 ***9162.6*** *p105*
Schumm, Eva Mgr. 19; America, 1854-1855 ***9162.6*** *p104*
Schumpff, . . .; Canada, 1776-1783 ***9786*** *p34*
Schumpff, Christian; Canada, 1776-1783 ***9786*** *p243*
Schumski, Benjamin 18; New York, NY, 1878 ***9253*** *p46*
Schumski, Lewin 20; New York, NY, 1878 ***9253*** *p46*
Schumski, Rachel 17; New York, NY, 1878 ***9253*** *p46*
Schunamann, August; Wisconsin, n.d. ***9675.8*** *p66*
Schunck, Jacob, Family; Peoria, IL, 1888 ***2691.4*** *p171*
Schunck, Jacob, Jr.; Peoria, IL, 1888 ***2691.4*** *p168*
Schundowiack, Marianne 24; New York, NY, 1862 ***9831.18*** *p16*
Schuneman, Frank 31; Kansas, 1891 ***5240.1*** *p40*
Schuneman, Frank 31; Kansas, 1891 ***5240.1*** *p76*
Schunemann, . . .; Canada, 1776-1783 ***9786*** *p34*
Schuner, John; Wisconsin, n.d. ***9675.8*** *p66*
Schung, Edward J. P.; Ohio, 1885 ***5240.1*** *p40*
Schunke, Oscar; Missouri, 1884 ***5240.1*** *p40*
Schuntlamyer, William; Illinois, 1896 ***5012.40*** *p54*
Schuoter, . . .; Canada, 1776-1783 ***9786*** *p34*
Schuotske, Linacy; Arkansas, 1918 ***95.2*** *p110*
Schupbach, Ernest; Arkansas, 1918 ***95.2*** *p110*
Schupp, Friedrich; America, 1752 ***2444*** *p215*
*Wife:*Margaretha Wetzel
Schupp, H. J.; America, 1880 ***5240.1*** *p40*
Schupp, Margaretha Wetzel *SEE* Schupp, Friedrich
Schur, Bertha; Milwaukee, 1875 ***4719.30*** *p257*
Schur, Ferdinand; Wisconsin, n.d. ***9675.8*** *p66*
Schur, Frederick; Illinois, 1877 ***2896.5*** *p36*
Schur, John George; America, 1848 ***1450.2*** *p130A*
Schur, Maria; Milwaukee, 1875 ***4719.30*** *p257*
Schuricht, Fredr. Wm. 23; New Orleans, 1839 ***9420.2*** *p68*
Schuricht, Joh. Gottleib 26; New Orleans, 1839 ***9420.2*** *p68*
Schuricht, Johann Gottlob 28; New Orleans, 1839 ***9420.2*** *p68*
Schurman, Aleida 33; New York, NY, 1847 ***3377.6*** *p13*
Schurman, Altje 6; New York, NY, 1847 ***3377.6*** *p13*
Schurman, Berendina 8; New York, NY, 1847 ***3377.6*** *p13*
Schurman, Gerrit Jan 3; New York, NY, 1847 ***3377.6*** *p13*
Schurman, Gertie 10; New York, NY, 1847 ***3377.6*** *p13*
Schurman, Jenneken 1; New York, NY, 1847 ***3377.6*** *p13*
Schurman, John 42; New York, NY, 1847 ***3377.6*** *p13*
Schurmann, Gustavus; America, 1855 ***1450.2*** *p130A*
Schurmeier, Friedrich Heinrich; America, 1857 ***4610.10*** *p145*
Schurmeyer, Carl 46; America, 1853 ***4610.10*** *p144*
With wife
*Child:*Carl Friedrich
*Child:*Carl Dietrich Adolph
Schurmeyer, Carl Dietrich Adolph *SEE* Schurmeyer, Carl
Schurmeyer, Carl Friedrich *SEE* Schurmeyer, Carl
Schurr, Leonhard; America, 1854 ***1450.2*** *p130A*
Schurtz, John; Pennsylvania, 1752 ***4779.3*** *p14A*
Schurz, Carl; America, 1776-1877 ***8582.3*** *p80*
Schurz, Carl; America, 1800-1877 ***8582.3*** *p92*
Schurz, Carl; America, 1848-1860 ***3702.7*** *p334*
Schurz, Carl; America, 1861-1865 ***8582.3*** *p92*
Schurz, Christian Gottfried 21; Kansas, 1878 ***5240.1*** *p59*
Schurz, John; Pennsylvania, 1752 ***4779.3*** *p14A*
Schurz, John C.; Kansas, 1872 ***5240.1*** *p40*
Schussler, George 44; Kansas, 1885 ***5240.1*** *p67*
Schuster, . . .; Canada, 1776-1783 ***9786*** *p34*
Schuster, Adam; Wisconsin, n.d. ***9675.8*** *p66*
Schuster, Albert T.; Texas, 1867 ***2764.35*** *p61*
Schuster, August; Canada, 1776-1783 ***9786*** *p207A*
Schuster, Carl Ludwig; America, 1854 ***4610.10*** *p121*
Schuster, Caroline Louise Charlotte; America, 1891 ***4610.10*** *p107*
Schuster, Cen 22; Port uncertain, 1839 ***778.5*** *p490*
Schuster, Elisabetha Zandel *SEE* Schuster, Johannes
Schuster, Felicitas; New York, 1752 ***3652*** *p76*
Schuster, Hans Jerg *SEE* Schuster, Johannes
Schuster, Johannes; Pennsylvania, 1754 ***2444*** *p215*
*Wife:*Elisabetha Zandel
*Child:*Maria Barbara
*Child:*Hans Jerg
Schuster, John; Wisconsin, n.d. ***9675.8*** *p66*
Schuster, Joseph; Wisconsin, n.d. ***9675.8*** *p66*
Schuster, Karoline; America, 1857 ***4610.10*** *p105*
Schuster, Maria Barbara *SEE* Schuster, Johannes
Schut, . . .; Canada, 1776-1783 ***9786*** *p34*
Schutt, . . .; Canada, 1776-1783 ***9786*** *p34*
Schutte, . . .; Illinois, 1800-1900 ***4610.10*** *p67*
Schutte, Miss; America, 1870-1879 ***4610.10*** *p52*
Schutte, A. M. Wilhelmine Ilsabein; America, 1881 ***4610.10*** *p160*
Schutte, Albert; New York, NY, 1896 ***3455.3*** *p18*
Schutte, Andrew; Virginia, 1857 ***4626.16*** *p17*
Schutte, Friederike; America, 1892 ***4610.10*** *p52*
Schutte, Friederike 19; America, 1892 ***4610.10*** *p161*
Schutte, Johan; Wisconsin, n.d. ***9675.8*** *p66*
Schutte, Richard; Virginia, 1855 ***4626.16*** *p15*
Schutte, William; Illinois, 1855 ***7857*** *p7*
Schuttekupf, Christopher; Wisconsin, n.d. ***9675.8*** *p66*
Schutz, . . .; Canada, 1776-1783 ***9786*** *p34*
Schutz, Fred. Wm. Carl; Illinois, 1906 ***5012.37*** *p63*
Schutz, Georg; Pennsylvania, 1717 ***3627*** *p11*
*Wife:*Sophia Catharina Klotz
*Child:*Maria Catharina
*Child:*Maria Sophia
*Child:*Joh. Georg
Schutz, Joh. Georg *SEE* Schutz, Georg
Schutz, Julius 36; New Orleans, 1839 ***9420.2*** *p167*
Schutz, Maria Catharina *SEE* Schutz, Georg
Schutz, Maria Sophia *SEE* Schutz, Georg
Schutz, Mathilde 33; New Orleans, 1839 ***9420.2*** *p166*
Schutz, Michael; Wisconsin, n.d. ***9675.8*** *p66*
Schutz, Sophia Catharina Klotz *SEE* Schutz, Georg
Schutze, Anna Dorothea *SEE* Schutze, Christian
Schutze, Christian; New York, 1743 ***3652*** *p60*
*Wife:*Anna Dorothea
Schutze, Henry; New York, NY, 1836 ***8208.4*** *p9*
Schwaab, . . .; Canada, 1776-1783 ***9786*** *p34*
Schwab, Mr.; America, 1837-1922 ***2691.4*** *p168*
With brother
With 2 sisters
Schwab, Anna 5; New Orleans, 1836 ***778.5*** *p490*
Schwab, Ante Laureny 33; Kansas, 1873 ***5240.1*** *p54*
Schwab, Barbara; America, 1735-1800 ***2444*** *p210*
Schwab, Catherina 2; New Orleans, 1836 ***778.5*** *p490*
Schwab, Fred; Arkansas, 1918 ***95.2*** *p111*
Schwab, Frederick 12; New Orleans, 1836 ***778.5*** *p490*
Schwab, George 18; New Orleans, 1836 ***778.5*** *p490*
Schwab, George 47; New Orleans, 1836 ***778.5*** *p490*
Schwab, George Anton 31; Kansas, 1873 ***5240.1*** *p53*
Schwab, Louise 14; New Orleans, 1836 ***778.5*** *p490*
Schwab, Peter; Philadelphia, 1700-1738 ***9898*** *p35*
Schwab, Philipp 16; New Orleans, 1836 ***778.5*** *p490*
Schwab, Robert 25; Kansas, 1874 ***5240.1*** *p55*
Schwab, Sibylla; Georgia, 1739 ***9332*** *p323*
Schwab, Susanna 40; New Orleans, 1836 ***778.5*** *p490*
Schwab, Wilhelmine 10; New Orleans, 1836 ***778.5*** *p490*
Schwabe, Ernst Christian; Canada, 1780 ***9786*** *p268*
Schwabe, Ernst Christian; New York, 1776 ***9786*** *p268*
Schwack, . . .; Canada, 1776-1783 ***9786*** *p34*
Schwaderer, Christine 2; New York, NY, 1889 ***7846*** *p39*
Schwaderer, Elizabeth 24; New York, NY, 1889 ***7846*** *p39*
Schwaderer, Friedrich 22; New York, NY, 1889 ***7846*** *p39*
Schwaderer, Georg 6 mos; New York, NY, 1889 ***7846*** *p39*
Schwager, Mr.; America, 1842 ***4610.10*** *p99*
With wife
Schwager, Caroline 18; America, 1870 ***4610.10*** *p96*
Schwager, Charles; America, 1869 ***1450.2*** *p131A*
Schwager, Christian Diedrich *SEE* Schwager, Christian Moritz
Schwager, Christian Moritz; America, 1842 ***4610.10*** *p97*
*Wife:*Marie Catharine Frolke
*Son:*Ernst Heinrich Wilhelm
*Son:*Christian Diedrich
*Son:*Diedrich Friedrich R.
Schwager, Diedrich Friedrich R. *SEE* Schwager, Christian Moritz

Schwager, Ernst Heinrich Wilhelm *SEE* Schwager, Christian Moritz
Schwager, Friedrich 22; America, 1870 *4610.10 p96*
Schwager, Heinrich Friedrich Ludwig; America, 1856 *4610.10 p99*
Schwager, Marie Catharine Frolke *SEE* Schwager, Christian Moritz
Schwagerly, Charles A.; Virginia, 1844 *4626.16 p12*
Schwagmeyer, Anne Marie Ilsabein 37; America, 1845 *4610.10 p155*
Schwaiger, George; Georgia, 1738 *9332 p321*
Schwalb, Karl 60; America, 1905 *1763 p40D*
Schwaller, Theresa 24; America, 1838 *778.5 p491*
Schwalm, . . .; Canada, 1776-1783 *9786 p34*
Schwalm, Andreas; Philadelphia, 1779 *8137 p14*
Schwalm, Georg; Lancaster, PA, 1780 *8137 p14*
Schwalm, Henrich; Lancaster, PA, 1780 *8137 p14*
Schwalm, Johann Henrich; Trenton, NJ, 1776 *8137 p14*
Schwalm, Johannes; Philadelphia, 1779 *8137 p14*
Schwalm, Johannes, Sr.; Philadelphia, 1779 *8137 p14*
Schwalm, Johannes, Sr.; Philadelphia, 1783 *8137 p4*
Schwan, . . .; Canada, 1776-1783 *9786 p34*
Schwandrer, Francis 46; Port uncertain, 1836 *778.5 p491*
Schwandrer, William 12; Port uncertain, 1836 *778.5 p491*
Schwandt, August; Wisconsin, n.d. *9675.8 p66*
Schwane, A. W.; Chicago, 1864 *8125.8 p438*
Schwanke, John; Illinois, 1867 *2896.5 p36*
Schwanke, Joseph; New York, NY, 1895 *1450.2 p35B*
Schwanman, John H.; New York, NY, 1840 *8208.4 p107*
Schwantes, August; Wisconsin, n.d. *9675.8 p66*
Schwanz, Anna; Wisconsin, n.d. *9675.8 p66*
Schwanz, Helen M.; Wisconsin, n.d. *9675.8 p66*
Schwanz, Herman G.; Wisconsin, n.d. *9675.8 p66*
Schwanz, Herman Gustave; Wisconsin, n.d. *9675.8 p66*
Schwartz, Captain; Nicaragua, 1856 *8582.3 p31*
Schwartz, Adam 38; Kansas, 1887 *5240.1 p40*
Schwartz, Adam 38; Kansas, 1887 *5240.1 p69*
Schwartz, Charles L.; America, 1865 *1450.2 p131A*
Schwartz, Christian; New York, 1750 *3652 p74*
Schwartz, E. C.; Washington, 1859-1920 *2872.1 p39*
Schwartz, Mrs. E. C.; Washington, 1859-1920 *2872.1 p39*
Schwartz, Emil; New York, 1885 *1450.2 p36B*
Schwartz, Frederick; Illinois, 1868 *2896.5 p36*
Schwartz, Gottfried; New York, 1750 *3652 p74*
Schwartz, Hans Georg; America, 1752 *4349 p47*
Schwartz, Hans Jerg; Philadelphia, 1752 *4349 p47*
Schwartz, Henriette Poppler 71; America, 1911 *1763 p40D*
Schwartz, J.; Washington, 1859-1920 *2872.1 p36*
Schwartz, Jacob; New Jersey, 1854 *1450.2 p131A*
Schwartz, Johannes; America, 1858 *8582.3 p60*
Schwartz, Johannes 21; Pennsylvania, 1753 *2444 p215*
Schwartz, Karl; New York, NY, 1839 *8208.4 p92*
Schwartz, Louis; New York, NY, 1838 *8208.4 p83*
Schwartz, Magdalena; New York, 1749 *3652 p73*
Schwartz, Michael; Charleston, SC, 1775-1781 *8582.2 p52*
Schwartz, Michael; Illinois, 1868 *5012.38 p99*
Schwartz, Paul; Washington, 1859-1920 *2872.1 p36*
Schwartz, Saul; Arkansas, 1918 *95.2 p111*
Schwarz, A. Kath. M. Louise; America, 1893 *4610.10 p153*
Schwarz, Ansel; New York, NY, 1898 *1450.2 p39B*
Schwarz, Celestin; Cincinnati, 1869-1887 *8582 p29*
Schwarz, George; New York, NY, 1835 *8208.4 p41*
Schwarz, Heinrich; America, 1852 *8582.3 p60*
Schwarz, J.; Washington, 1859-1920 *2872.1 p36*
Schwarz, Johann Georg; Pennsylvania, 1749 *7829 p8*
Schwarz, Johannes 21; Pennsylvania, 1753 *2444 p215*
Schwarz, John; Philadelphia, 1890 *1450.2 p36B*
Schwarz, Julius; Cincinnati, 1788-1848 *8582.3 p89*
Schwarz, Julius; Cincinnati, 1788-1848 *8582.3 p90*
Schwarz, Mathias; America, 1850 *8582.3 p60*
Schwarz, Michael; Illinois, 1868 *5012.38 p99*
Schwarz, Paul; Washington, 1859-1920 *2872.1 p36*
Schwarz, Peter; Wisconsin, n.d. *9675.8 p66*
Schwarz, Peter Paul; Ohio, 1869-1887 *8582 p29*
Schwarzburg, C. W. 72; Milwaukee, 1872 *8582 p29*
Schwarze, . . .; Canada, 1776-1783 *9786 p34*
Schwarze, Miss; America, 1854 *4610.10 p156*
Schwarze, Anna Engel; America, 1835-1844 *4610.10 p154*
Schwarze, Anna Marie Ilsabein; America, 1857 *4610.10 p158*
Schwarze, Anne M. E. Isermeyer *SEE* Schwarze, Heinrich Wilhelm
Schwarze, Anne M. Louise Engel *SEE* Schwarze, Carl Diedrich
Schwarze, Anne M. W. Charlotte *SEE* Schwarze, Heinrich Wilhelm

Schwarze, Anne Marie Ilsabein; America, 1856 *4610.10 p157*
Schwarze, Anne Marie L. Detering *SEE* Schwarze, Heinrich Wilhelm
Schwarze, Anne Marie Louise; America, 1853 *4610.10 p156*
Schwarze, Carl Diedrich; America, 1850 *4610.10 p143*
  Wife: Marie Budde
  Child: Carl F. Gottlieb
  Child: Anne M. Louise Engel
Schwarze, Carl Ernst Heinrich; America, 1885 *4610.10 p102*
Schwarze, Carl F. Gottlieb *SEE* Schwarze, Carl Diedrich
Schwarze, Ernst C. Friedrich *SEE* Schwarze, Heinrich Wilhelm
Schwarze, Friederike 20; America, 1883 *4610.10 p106*
Schwarze, Friedrich Christian; America, 1876 *4610.10 p101*
Schwarze, Heinrich F. Wilhelm *SEE* Schwarze, Heinrich Wilhelm
Schwarze, Heinrich Wilhelm; America, 1843 *4610.10 p119*
  Father: Johann Friedrich
  Mother: Anne M. E. Isermeyer
Schwarze, Heinrich Wilhelm; America, 1857 *4610.10 p158*
  Wife: Anne Marie L. Detering
  Child: Anne M. W. Charlotte
  Child: Heinrich F. Wilhelm
  Child: Ernst C. Friedrich
  Son: Hermann C. F. Blobaum
Schwarze, Hermann C. F. Blobaum *SEE* Schwarze, Heinrich Wilhelm
Schwarze, Johann Friedrich *SEE* Schwarze, Heinrich Wilhelm
Schwarze, Marie Budde *SEE* Schwarze, Carl Diedrich
Schwarzenbach, A.; Milwaukee, 1875 *4719.30 p257*
Schwarzenbach, Made. 22; America, 1838 *778.5 p491*
Schwarzmeier, Franz Wilhelm Gustav; America, 1842 *4610.10 p141*
Schwebel, Philipp; Illinois, 1838 *8582.2 p50*
Schwecke, Fred; Wisconsin, n.d. *9675.8 p66*
Schwecke, Frederic; Wisconsin, n.d. *9675.8 p66*
Schwede, Herbert; New York, NY, 1924 *3455.4 p51*
Schweder, August John Martin; Arkansas, 1918 *95.2 p111*
Schwedtmann, Hedwig; Wisconsin, n.d. *9675.8 p66*
Schwegler, Christopher; Washington, 1859-1920 *2872.1 p36*
Schwegmann, Bernhard; Cincinnati, 1869-1887 *8582 p29*
Schwegmann, Franz; Cincinnati, 1830-1849 *8582 p29*
Schwegmann, J. H.; Ohio, 1869-1887 *8582 p29*
Schwehe, John F.; Wisconsin, n.d. *9675.8 p66*
Schweiber, John 26; Kansas, 1899 *5240.1 p81*
Schweichert, Georg Conrad; Pennsylvania, 1751 *2444 p216*
Schweichler, Alexander John; Wisconsin, n.d. *9675.8 p66*
Schweickard, Jacob; Pennsylvania, 1741 *2854 p45*
Schweickart, Eva *SEE* Schweickart, Georg Conrad
Schweickart, Georg Conrad; Pennsylvania, 1751 *2444 p216*
  Wife: Justina C. Bodamer
  Child: Eva
Schweickart, Justina C. Bodamer *SEE* Schweickart, Georg Conrad
Schweickert, Jacob; Pennsylvania, 1751 *2444 p216*
Schweier, Michael; America, 1846 *8582.3 p60*
Schweigart, Christian; South Carolina, 1788 *7119 p200*
Schweigart, Christian; South Carolina, 1788 *7119 p201*
Schweigart, Johannes; South Carolina, 1788 *7119 p200*
Schweigart, Johannes; South Carolina, 1788 *7119 p201*
Schweiger, Anna; Georgia, 1734 *9332 p327*
Schweiger, Eva Regina *SEE* Schweiger, Georg
Schweiger, Eva Regina Unselt *SEE* Schweiger, Georg
Schweiger, Georg; Georgia, 1739 *9332 p324*
  Wife: Eva Regina Unselt
Schweiger, Georg; Georgia, 1739 *9332 p325*
  Wife: Eva Regina
Schweiger, George; New York, 1750 *3652 p74*
Schweiger, Maria; Georgia, 1739 *9332 p323*
Schweigert, Christian; Georgia, 1734 *9332 p327*
Schweigert, Martin; South Carolina, 1788 *7119 p200*
Schweigerts, Johan Christoph; Pennsylvania, 1773 *2444 p216*
Schweighauser, John Conrad; Philadelphia, 1757 *9973.7 p32*
Schweighofer, Margaretha; Georgia, 1739 *9332 p325*
  Daughter: Maria 13
  Son: Thomas 11
  Daughter: Ursula 11
Schweighofer, Maria 13 *SEE* Schweighofer, Margaretha
Schweighofer, Paul; Georgia, 1734 *9332 p327*

Schweighofer, Thomas 11 *SEE* Schweighofer, Margaretha
Schweighofer, Ursula 11 *SEE* Schweighofer, Margaretha
Schweighoffer, Margaretha; Georgia, 1739 *9332 p324*
Schweikart, Sebastian; America, 1772 *2444 p216*
Schweikart, Sebastian; Pennsylvania, 1772 *2444 p216*
Schweikert, Anna Margaretha *SEE* Schweikert, Johann Balthas
Schweikert, Anna Margaretha *SEE* Schweikert, Johann Balthas
Schweikert, Johann Balthas; Pennsylvania, 1748 *2444 p216*
  Wife: Anna Margaretha
  Child: Johannes
  Child: Johann Michael
  Child: Johann Philipp
Schweikert, Johann Balthas; Port uncertain, 1748 *2444 p216*
  Wife: Anna Margaretha
  Child: Johannes
  Child: Johann Michael
  Child: Johann Philipp
Schweikert, Johann Michael *SEE* Schweikert, Johann Balthas
Schweikert, Johann Michael *SEE* Schweikert, Johann Balthas
Schweikert, Johann Philipp *SEE* Schweikert, Johann Balthas
Schweikert, Johann Philipp *SEE* Schweikert, Johann Balthas
Schweikert, Johannes *SEE* Schweikert, Johann Balthas
Schweikert, Johannes *SEE* Schweikert, Johann Balthas
Schweikert, Sebastian; America, 1772 *2444 p216*
Schweikert, Sebastian; Pennsylvania, 1772 *2444 p216*
Schweikhardt, Agnes Maria *SEE* Schweikhardt, Sebastian
Schweikhardt, Agnes Maria *SEE* Schweikhardt, Sebastian
Schweikhardt, Agnes Maria Keller *SEE* Schweikhardt, Sebastian
Schweikhardt, Agnes Maria Keller *SEE* Schweikhardt, Sebastian
Schweikhardt, Anna Barbara *SEE* Schweikhardt, Sebastian
Schweikhardt, Anna Barbara *SEE* Schweikhardt, Sebastian
Schweikhardt, Anna Margaretha *SEE* Schweikhardt, Sebastian
Schweikhardt, Anna Margaretha *SEE* Schweikhardt, Sebastian
Schweikhardt, Felix *SEE* Schweikhardt, Sebastian
Schweikhardt, Felix *SEE* Schweikhardt, Sebastian
Schweikhardt, Sebastian; America, 1772 *2444 p216*
  Wife: Agnes Maria Keller
  Child: Agnes Maria
  Child: Felix
  Child: Anna Margaretha
  Child: Anna Barbara
Schweikhardt, Sebastian; Pennsylvania, 1772 *2444 p216*
  Wife: Agnes Maria Keller
  Child: Agnes Maria
  Child: Felix
  Child: Anna Margaretha
  Child: Anna Barbara
Schweimin, Anthony; Illinois, 1876 *5012.37 p60*
Schwein, Jacob; Cincinnati, 1869-1887 *8582 p29*
Schwein, Julius; Cincinnati, 1847 *8582.1 p31*
Schweinberger, Josef; Colorado, 1904 *9678.2 p167*
Schweinetz, Albert 36; Harris Co., TX, 1899 *6254 p6*
Schweinfuss, Johann H.; America, 1849 *8582.3 p60*
Schweinle, Louis; New York, NY, 1850 *6013.19 p88*
Schweinsberg, Wilhelm; Illinois, 1888 *5012.39 p121*
Schweinsberg, William; Illinois, 1888 *5012.37 p60*
Schweisgut, Michael 54; Kansas, 1890 *5240.1 p75*
Schweissguth, Henry 67; America, 1895 *1763 p48D*
Schweisshaupt, John; New York, 1749 *3652 p72*
Schweiter, Charles 24; Kansas, 1873 *5240.1 p53*
Schweiter, Henry; Kansas, 1869 *5240.1 p40*
Schweitzer, Anna C. Blessing *SEE* Schweitzer, Johannes
Schweitzer, Elisabeth 71; Pennsylvania, 1897 *1763 p40D*
Schweitzer, Jean 16; America, 1838 *778.5 p491*
Schweitzer, Johannes; Pennsylvania, 1750 *2444 p216*
  Wife: Anna C. Blessing
Schweitzer, Michael 45; Kansas, 1883 *5240.1 p64*
Schweizer, Anna Maria; New York, 1754 *2444 p136*
Schweizer, George; Cincinnati, 1869-1887 *8582 p29*
Schweizer, Jakob; Ohio, 1798-1818 *8582.2 p54*
Schweizer, John; Illinois, 1890 *2896.5 p36*
Schweizerhof, Mr.; America, 1872-1874 *8582.1 p39*
Schweizerhof, Mr.; Cincinnati, 1837-1838 *8582.1 p45*
Schweizerhof, Jacob; America, 1832 *8582.1 p39*
  With wife
Schwemin, Andrew; Illinois, 1876 *5012.37 p60*

Schwemin, Anthony; Illinois, 1876 ***5012.37*** *p60*
Schwenckel, Uhllerich; Pennsylvania, 1751 ***2444*** *p216*
Schwenkel, Barbara Schell *SEE* Schwenkel, Ulrich
Schwenkel, Hieronymus *SEE* Schwenkel, Ulrich
Schwenkel, Ulrich; Pennsylvania, 1751 ***2444*** *p216*
*Wife:*Barbara Schell
*Child:*Hieronymus
Schwenker, Friedrich W.; Cincinnati, 1869-1887 ***8582*** *p29*
Schwenkle, Urich; Pennsylvania, 1751 ***2444*** *p216*
Schwenner, John Frank; Wisconsin, n.d. ***9675.8*** *p66*
Schwenniger, Anton; Cincinnati, 1788-1848 ***8582.3*** *p90*
Schwentker, August Ferdinand; America, 1891 ***4610.10*** *p153*
Schwerdfager, John 33; Kansas, 1884 ***5240.1*** *p67*
Schwerdkopf, Johann; New York, NY, 1746-1750 ***8582.3*** *p60*
Schwerdtfeger, Carl Heinrich Ludwig; America, 1836 ***4610.10*** *p114*
Schweri, Gottfried; Illinois, 1866 ***2896.5*** *p36*
Schwerin, William; Wisconsin, n.d. ***9675.8*** *p66*
Schwerin, William Albert H.; Wisconsin, n.d. ***9675.8*** *p66*
Schwermann, Franz Josef; America, 1845 ***8582.3*** *p60*
Schwerte, Gottlieb; Wisconsin, n.d. ***9675.8*** *p66*
Schwerteger, Chas.; Wisconsin, n.d. ***9675.8*** *p66*
Schwertmann, Hermann Heinrich; America, 1856 ***8582.3*** *p60*
Schwertzell, Christian; Philadelphia, 1779 ***8137*** *p14*
Schwibbe, Carl Gottlieb Caspar *SEE* Schwibbe, Johann Zacharias
Schwibbe, Johann Zacharias; America, 1850 ***4610.10*** *p143*
*Child:*Zacharias H. Gottlieb
*Child:*Carl Gottlieb Caspar
Schwibbe, Zacharias H. Gottlieb *SEE* Schwibbe, Johann Zacharias
Schwieger, . . .; Canada, 1776-1783 ***9786*** *p34*
Schwier, Charles; America, 1844 ***1450.2*** *p131A*
Schwier, Christian; America, 1854 ***1450.2*** *p131A*
Schwier, Gottlieb; America, 1854 ***1450.2*** *p143A*
Schwier, Wilhelm; America, 1898 ***1450.2*** *p36B*
Schwigard, J. Martin; South Carolina, 1788 ***7119*** *p201*
Schwigler, Peter; Illinois, 1866 ***2896.5*** *p36*
Schwilke, Jacob; Colorado, 1894 ***9678.2*** *p167*
Schwimmer, . . .; Canada, 1776-1783 ***9786*** *p34*
Schwind, Adam; New York, NY, 1838 ***8208.4*** *p70*
Schwingel, Captain; Nicaragua, 1856 ***8582.3*** *p31*
Schwinn, Max Carl; Arkansas, 1918 ***95.2*** *p111*
Schwint, Johann; Charleston, SC, 1766 ***8582.2*** *p65*
Schwittage, Adam; Illinois, 1890 ***5012.40*** *p25*
Schwitz, Frank; Kansas, 1901 ***5240.1*** *p82*
Schwobel, Barb. 2 mos; America, 1853 ***9162.7*** *p15*
Schwobel, Barb. 34; America, 1853 ***9162.7*** *p15*
Schwobel, Barbara 19; America, 1853 ***9162.8*** *p38*
Schwobel, Elisabetha 27; America, 1853 ***9162.8*** *p38*
Schwobel, Jacob 6; America, 1853 ***9162.7*** *p15*
Schwobel, Joh. 10; America, 1853 ***9162.7*** *p15*
Schwobel, Marg. 8; America, 1853 ***9162.7*** *p15*
Schwobel, Wilh. 36; America, 1853 ***9162.7*** *p15*
Schwomier, Charles; America, 1852 ***1450.2*** *p131A*
Schwomier, Henry; America, 1852 ***1450.2*** *p131A*
Schynlin, Elizabeth; Philadelphia, 1752-1753 ***4525*** *p204*
Sciaccco, Vincenzo; Arkansas, 1918 ***95.2*** *p111*
Scidleir, . . .; Canada, 1776-1783 ***9786*** *p34*
Scilly, Jane; New York, NY, 1816 ***2859.11*** *p42*
Scilly, John; New York, NY, 1816 ***2859.11*** *p42*
Scilly, Margaret; New York, NY, 1816 ***2859.11*** *p42*
Scinlon, Bryan; New York, NY, 1816 ***2859.11*** *p42*
Sciortino, Giuseppe; Arkansas, 1918 ***95.2*** *p111*
Scire, Frank; Illinois, 1904 ***5012.39*** *p53*
Sckans, Michael; Wisconsin, n.d. ***9675.8*** *p66*
Sclore, Isidore; Arkansas, 1918 ***95.2*** *p111*
Scoburne, John; Virginia, 1636 ***6219*** *p36*
Scofen, Jean-Baptiste 31; Montreal, 1722 ***7603*** *p28*
Scoffield, Henry 40; Virginia, 1700 ***2212*** *p32*
Scofield, Isaac 13; America, 1699 ***2212*** *p21*
*Brother:*James 11
Scofield, James 11 *SEE* Scofield, Isaac
Scollard, Catharine 25; Massachusetts, 1849 ***5881.1*** *p88*
Scollay, Samuel; North Carolina, 1751 ***1639.20*** *p278*
Scollen, Ellen 26; Quebec, 1863 ***5704.8*** *p154*
Scollen, James 20; Quebec, 1863 ***5704.8*** *p154*
Scollon, Ann; Quebec, 1847 ***5704.8*** *p29*
Scollon, Catherine; Philadelphia, 1849 ***53.26*** *p81*
Scollon, Catherine; Philadelphia, 1849 ***5704.8*** *p50*
Scollon, Catherine; Quebec, 1847 ***5704.8*** *p29*
Scollon, James 13; Quebec, 1847 ***5704.8*** *p29*
Scollon, John; Quebec, 1847 ***5704.8*** *p29*
Scollon, John 11; Quebec, 1847 ***5704.8*** *p29*
Scollon, Mary; Quebec, 1847 ***5704.8*** *p29*
Scone, Patrick; Illinois, 1858 ***7857*** *p7*
Scory, Robert; Virginia, 1635 ***6219*** *p16*
Scory, William; St. John, N.B., 1848 ***5704.8*** *p44*
Scoryer, Richard 22; Antigua (Antego), 1731 ***3690.1*** *p198*
Scot, Jon.; Virginia, 1635 ***6219*** *p35*
Scot, Thomas; Montreal, 1761-1784 ***9775.5*** *p199*
Scotland, Alexander; Colorado, 1881 ***9678.2*** *p168*
Scotland, James 21; Virginia, 1774 ***1219.7*** *p226*
Scotland, James 37; St. John, N.B., 1864 ***5704.8*** *p159*
Scotland, Lawrence 21; New England, 1699 ***2212*** *p19*
Scotland, Robert 27; Maryland, 1775 ***1219.7*** *p253*
Scotney, Susanna 19; Maryland, 1775 ***1219.7*** *p249*
Scott, Mr.; Quebec, 1815 ***9229.18*** *p75*
With son
Scott, Mr.; Quebec, 1815 ***9229.18*** *p78*
Scott, A.; New York, NY, 1811 ***2859.11*** *p19*
Scott, Agnes 4 *SEE* Scott, John
Scott, Albert; America, 1892 ***1450.2*** *p131A*
Scott, Alex 9 mos; Philadelphia, 1851 ***5704.8*** *p70*
Scott, Alexander; New York, NY, 1811 ***2859.11*** *p19*
Scott, Alexander; New York, NY, 1865 ***5704.8*** *p191*
Scott, Alexander 8; Wilmington, DE, 1831 ***6508.3*** *p101*
Scott, Alexander 18; St. John, N.B., 1857 ***5704.8*** *p136*
Scott, Alexander 21; St. John, N.B., 1855 ***5704.8*** *p126*
Scott, Alexr. 22; Wilmington, DE, 1831 ***6508.7*** *p161*
Scott, Andre; Quebec, 1779 ***7603*** *p99*
Scott, Andrew; North Carolina, 1736 ***1639.20*** *p278*
Scott, Andrew 19; Quebec, 1858 ***5704.8*** *p137*
Scott, Andrew Joseph 4; St. John, N.B., 1866 ***5704.8*** *p167*
Scott, Ann *SEE* Scott, Mary
Scott, Ann; Philadelphia, 1853 ***5704.8*** *p101*
Scott, Ann 27; St. John, N.B., 1866 ***5704.8*** *p167*
Scott, Anne; Philadelphia, 1864 ***5704.8*** *p182*
Scott, Anne 25; Wilmington, DE, 1831 ***6508.3*** *p101*
Scott, Annie; Philadelphia, 1865 ***5704.8*** *p198*
Scott, Archibald 26; Philadelphia, 1804 ***53.26*** *p81*
*Relative:*Elinor 20
Scott, Arthur; Virginia, 1635 ***6219*** *p68*
Scott, Arthur 40; Quebec, 1864 ***5704.8*** *p160*
Scott, Catharine; New York, NY, 1870 ***5704.8*** *p237*
Scott, Catharine 1 *SEE* Scott, Henry
Scott, Catharine A.; New York, NY, 1867 ***5704.8*** *p224*
Scott, Catherine; New York, NY, 1815 ***2859.11*** *p42*
Scott, Catherine; Quebec, 1849 ***5704.8*** *p52*
Scott, Catherine; St. John, N.B., 1853 ***5704.8*** *p106*
Scott, Catherine 17; Quebec, 1858 ***5704.8*** *p137*
Scott, Catherine 28; St. John, N.B., 1857 ***5704.8*** *p136*
Scott, Charles; New York, NY, 1836 ***8208.4*** *p22*
Scott, Chas. W.; Iowa, 1866-1943 ***123.54*** *p43*
Scott, Dan.; Virginia, 1637 ***6219*** *p113*
Scott, Daniell; Virginia, 1638 ***6219*** *p149*
Scott, David; New York, NY, 1811 ***2859.11*** *p19*
Scott, David; Quebec, 1852 ***5704.8*** *p87*
Scott, David; Quebec, 1852 ***5704.8*** *p90*
Scott, David 25; Wilmington, DE, 1831 ***6508.3*** *p101*
Scott, Dorethea; Philadelphia, 1851 ***5704.8*** *p70*
Scott, Edward; Massachusetts, 1888 ***2764.35*** *p63*
Scott, Edward; New York, NY, 1816 ***2859.11*** *p42*
Scott, Edward 12; St. John, N.B., 1857 ***5704.8*** *p136*
Scott, Edward 21; Maryland, 1724 ***3690.1*** *p198*
Scott, Edward H.; Colorado, 1892 ***9678.2*** *p168*
Scott, Elinor 20 *SEE* Scott, Archibald
Scott, Eliza *SEE* Scott, Elizabeth
Scott, Eliza; New York, NY, 1816 ***2859.11*** *p42*
Scott, Eliza; Philadelphia, 1850 ***5704.8*** *p68*
Scott, Eliza; Philadelphia, 1852 ***5704.8*** *p92*
Scott, Eliza 23; St. John, N.B., 1863 ***5704.8*** *p152*
Scott, Elizabeth; Philadelphia, 1850 ***53.26*** *p81*
Scott, Elizabeth; Philadelphia, 1850 ***53.26*** *p81*
*Relative:*Jane
*Relative:*Eliza
Scott, Elizabeth; Philadelphia, 1850 ***5704.8*** *p60*
Scott, Elizabeth; Philadelphia, 1850 ***5704.8*** *p68*
Scott, Elizabeth; Philadelphia, 1864 ***5704.8*** *p182*
Scott, Elizabeth; St. John, N.B., 1850 ***5704.8*** *p67*
Scott, Elizabeth 4; New York, NY, 1867 ***5704.8*** *p221*
Scott, Ellen; St. John, N.B., 1849 ***5704.8*** *p55*
Scott, Ezekle 12; Philadelphia, 1851 ***5704.8*** *p70*
Scott, Francis 40; Savannah, GA, 1733 ***4719.17*** *p312*
Scott, Francis 47; Philadelphia, 1804 ***53.26*** *p81*
Scott, Fras; Ohio, 1840 ***9892.11*** *p41*
Scott, George; North Carolina, 1736 ***1639.20*** *p279*
Scott, Gilbert; Washington, 1859-1920 ***2872.1*** *p36*
Scott, Henry; New York, NY, 1811 ***2859.11*** *p19*
Scott, Henry 3 *SEE* Scott, Henry
Scott, Henry 18; Barbados or Jamaica, 1733 ***3690.1*** *p198*
Scott, Henry 27; North America, 1774 ***1219.7*** *p199*
*Wife:*Mary 29
*Child:*Henry 3
*Child:*Catharine 1
Scott, Henry Albert; Arkansas, 1918 ***95.2*** *p111*
Scott, Henry Peter; California, 1860 ***3840.3*** *p10*
Scott, Hugh; New York, NY, 1815 ***2859.11*** *p42*
Scott, Hugh; North Carolina, 1736 ***1639.20*** *p279*
Scott, Isaac 18; Windward Islands, 1722 ***3690.1*** *p198*
Scott, Isabella; New Orleans, 1849 ***5704.8*** *p59*
Scott, Isabella; St. John, N.B., 1852 ***5704.8*** *p93*
Scott, James *SEE* Scott, John
Scott, James; Baltimore, 1811 ***2859.11*** *p19*
Scott, James; Iowa, 1866-1943 ***123.54*** *p43*
Scott, James; Iroquois Co., IL, 1893 ***3455.1*** *p13*
Scott, James; New York, NY, 1811 ***2859.11*** *p19*
Scott, James; Philadelphia, 1811 ***2859.11*** *p19*
With family
Scott, James; Philadelphia, 1847 ***5704.8*** *p23*
Scott, James; Philadelphia, 1853 ***5704.8*** *p101*
Scott, James; Philadelphia, 1866 ***5704.8*** *p206*
Scott, James; Quebec, 1816 ***7603*** *p38*
Scott, James; Quebec, 1849 ***5704.8*** *p57*
Scott, James; Virginia, 1637 ***6219*** *p109*
Scott, James 10; Philadelphia, 1851 ***5704.8*** *p70*
Scott, James 23; St. John, N.B., 1864 ***5704.8*** *p159*
Scott, James 25; Georgia, 1775 ***1219.7*** *p276*
Scott, James 25; Philadelphia, 1857 ***5704.8*** *p134*
Scott, James 40; New York, 1775 ***1219.7*** *p268*
With wife
With 3 children
Scott, Jane *SEE* Scott, Elizabeth
Scott, Jane; New York, NY, 1815 ***2859.11*** *p42*
Scott, Jane; New York, NY, 1816 ***2859.11*** *p42*
Scott, Jane; New York, NY, 1864 ***5704.8*** *p172*
Scott, Jane; Philadelphia, 1850 ***5704.8*** *p68*
Scott, Jane; Philadelphia, 1867 ***5704.8*** *p218*
Scott, Jane; St. John, N.B., 1853 ***5704.8*** *p107*
Scott, Jane 8; Philadelphia, 1864 ***5704.8*** *p182*
Scott, Jane 19; Philadelphia, 1856 ***5704.8*** *p128*
Scott, Jane 35; Wilmington, DE, 1831 ***6508.3*** *p101*
Scott, John *SEE* Scott, John
Scott, John; New York, NY, 1811 ***2859.11*** *p19*
Scott, John; New York, NY, 1816 ***2859.11*** *p42*
Scott, John; New York, NY, 1840 ***8208.4*** *p112*
Scott, John; New York, NY, 1865 ***5704.8*** *p191*
Scott, John; Ohio, 1812-1840 ***9892.11*** *p41*
Scott, John; Philadelphia, 1847 ***53.26*** *p81*
*Relative:*William
*Relative:*John
*Relative:*James
Scott, John; Philadelphia, 1847 ***5704.8*** *p23*
Scott, John; Philadelphia, 1864 ***5704.8*** *p182*
Scott, John; Philadelphia, 1866 ***5704.8*** *p204*
Scott, John; Washington, 1859-1920 ***2872.1*** *p36*
Scott, John 5; St. John, N.B., 1857 ***5704.8*** *p136*
Scott, John 10 *SEE* Scott, John
Scott, John 22; Maryland, 1774 ***1219.7*** *p193*
Scott, John 22; Maryland, 1774 ***1219.7*** *p196*
Scott, John 23; Wilmington, DE, 1831 ***6508.3*** *p101*
Scott, John 30 *SEE* Scott, Robert
Scott, John 30; Georgia, 1775 ***1219.7*** *p276*
*Wife:*Margaret 35
*Child:*William 13
*Child:*John 10
*Child:*Mary 8
*Child:*Agnes 4
*Child:*Margaret 2
Scott, John H. 23; Kansas, 1873 ***5240.1*** *p54*
Scott, Jon.; Virginia, 1637 ***6219*** *p13*
Scott, Joseph; Quebec, 1847 ***5704.8*** *p12*
Scott, Joseph; St. John, N.B., 1847 ***5704.8*** *p5*
Scott, Joseph 6; Philadelphia, 1851 ***5704.8*** *p70*
Scott, Joseph 18; Maryland, 1774 ***1219.7*** *p180*
Scott, Joseph 21; St. John, N.B., 1864 ***5704.8*** *p159*
Scott, Letitia 9 mos; New Orleans, 1849 ***5704.8*** *p59*
Scott, Margaret; New York, NY, 1811 ***2859.11*** *p19*
Scott, Margaret; New York, NY, 1864 ***5704.8*** *p172*
Scott, Margaret; Philadelphia, 1853 ***5704.8*** *p100*
Scott, Margaret 2 *SEE* Scott, John
Scott, Margaret 2; New York, NY, 1867 ***5704.8*** *p221*
Scott, Margaret 15; St. John, N.B., 1863 ***5704.8*** *p152*
Scott, Margaret 16; North Carolina, 1774 ***1219.7*** *p189*
Scott, Margaret 16; North Carolina, 1774 ***1639.20*** *p279*
Scott, Margaret 19; St. John, N.B., 1864 ***5704.8*** *p159*
Scott, Margaret 22; St. John, N.B., 1866 ***5704.8*** *p167*
Scott, Margaret 35 *SEE* Scott, John
Scott, Margaret 45; St. John, N.B., 1857 ***5704.8*** *p136*
Scott, Margaret Jane 3; St. John, N.B., 1857 ***5704.8*** *p136*
Scott, Martha; Philadelphia, 1864 ***5704.8*** *p182*
Scott, Mary; Philadelphia, 1850 ***53.26*** *p81*
*Relative:*Ann
Scott, Mary; Philadelphia, 1850 ***5704.8*** *p64*
Scott, Mary; Philadelphia, 1851 ***5704.8*** *p79*
Scott, Mary; Quebec, 1847 ***5704.8*** *p13*
Scott, Mary; Quebec, 1850 ***5704.8*** *p69*
Scott, Mary 8 *SEE* Scott, John
Scott, Mary 16; St. John, N.B., 1857 ***5704.8*** *p136*
Scott, Mary 19; Massachusetts, 1850 ***5881.1*** *p92*
Scott, Mary 29 *SEE* Scott, Henry
Scott, Mary Ann; Philadelphia, 1850 ***5704.8*** *p65*

Scott, Mary Ann; St. John, N.B., 1852 ***5704.8*** *p93*
Scott, Mathew; New Orleans, 1852 ***5704.8*** *p98*
Scott, Matilda; Philadelphia, 1852 ***5704.8*** *p92*
Scott, Michael; Quebec, 1852 ***5704.8*** *p90*
Scott, Michael 18; Massachusetts, 1850 ***5881.1*** *p92*
Scott, Nancy; Philadelphia, 1864 ***5704.8*** *p180*
Scott, Nancy; Quebec, 1852 ***5704.8*** *p97*
Scott, Nicholas; New York, NY, 1838 ***8208.4*** *p71*
Scott, Nicholas; Virginia, 1640 ***6219*** *p161*
Scott, Peter 6; Philadelphia, 1864 ***5704.8*** *p182*
Scott, Rachel; St. John, N.B., 1853 ***5704.8*** *p99*
Scott, Robert; Philadelphia, 1853 ***5704.8*** *p100*
Scott, Robert; Quebec, 1847 ***5704.8*** *p12*
Scott, Robert; St. John, N.B., 1847 ***5704.8*** *p5*
Scott, Robert 3; Wilmington, DE, 1831 ***6508.3*** *p101*
Scott, Robert 6; St. John, N.B., 1866 ***5704.8*** *p167*
Scott, Robert 7; St. John, N.B., 1857 ***5704.8*** *p136*
Scott, Robert 10; Philadelphia, 1864 ***5704.8*** *p182*
Scott, Robert 25; New England, 1774 ***1219.7*** *p203*
Scott, Robert 28; Maryland, 1736 ***3690.1*** *p198*
Scott, Robert 32; Philadelphia, 1833-1834 ***53.26*** *p81*
*Relative:*John 30
Scott, Robert 35; Wilmington, DE, 1831 ***6508.3*** *p101*
Scott, Robert S.; Quebec, 1830 ***4719.7*** *p21*
Scott, Roda; New Orleans, 1849 ***5704.8*** *p59*
Scott, Samuel; Barbados, 1775 ***1219.7*** *p280*
Scott, Samuel; Philadelphia, 1851 ***5704.8*** *p70*
Scott, Samuel 8; Philadelphia, 1851 ***5704.8*** *p70*
Scott, Samuel 19; Jamaica, 1730 ***3690.1*** *p198*
Scott, Sarah; New York, NY, 1816 ***2859.11*** *p42*
Scott, Sarah; New York, NY, 1867 ***5704.8*** *p221*
Scott, Sarah; Philadelphia, 1849 ***53.26*** *p81*
Scott, Sarah; Philadelphia, 1849 ***5704.8*** *p54*
Scott, Sarah 28; St. John, N.B., 1864 ***5704.8*** *p158*
Scott, Sarah, Jr. 20; Wilmington, DE, 1831 ***6508.3*** *p101*
Scott, Sarah, Sr. 50; Wilmington, DE, 1831 ***6508.3*** *p101*
Scott, Susan 25; Quebec, 1856 ***5704.8*** *p130*
Scott, Susan Mary 9 mos; St. John, N.B., 1857 ***5704.8*** *p136*
Scott, Thomas; New York, NY, 1811 ***2859.11*** *p19*
Scott, Thomas; Ohio, 1798-1818 ***8582.2*** *p54*
Scott, Thomas; Philadelphia, 1853 ***5704.8*** *p101*
Scott, Thomas 15; Maryland, 1719 ***3690.1*** *p199*
Scott, Thomas 16; Pennsylvania, 1721 ***3690.1*** *p199*
Scott, Thomas 18; Quebec, 1863 ***5704.8*** *p154*
Scott, Thomas 21; Philadelphia, 1853 ***5704.8*** *p108*
Scott, Thomas 23; Philadelphia, 1774 ***1219.7*** *p214*
Scott, Thomas 28; St. John, N.B., 1866 ***5704.8*** *p167*
Scott, Walter; New York, NY, 1816 ***2859.11*** *p42*
Scott, Walter; South Carolina, 1798 ***1639.20*** *p279*
Scott, William *SEE* Scott, John
Scott, William; Charleston, SC, 1765 ***1639.20*** *p279*
Scott, William; Illinois, 1858 ***7857*** *p7*
Scott, William; New York, NY, 1811 ***2859.11*** *p19*
Scott, William; New York, NY, 1815 ***2859.11*** *p42*
Scott, William; Philadelphia, 1847 ***5704.8*** *p23*
Scott, William; Philadelphia, 1852 ***5704.8*** *p92*
Scott, William; Philadelphia, 1864 ***5704.8*** *p182*
Scott, William; Virginia, 1642 ***6219*** *p193*
Scott, William; Virginia, 1698 ***2212*** *p12*
Scott, William 6 mos; Philadelphia, 1853 ***5704.8*** *p101*
Scott, William 13 *SEE* Scott, John
Scott, William 13; Quebec, 1852 ***5704.8*** *p97*
Scott, William 14; America, 1699 ***2212*** *p21*
Scott, William 15; Maryland, 1731 ***3690.1*** *p199*
Scott, William 17; Quebec, 1864 ***5704.8*** *p160*
Scott, William 18; Pennsylvania, Virginia or Maryland, 1728 ***3690.1*** *p199*
Scott, William 18; St. John, N.B., 1856 ***5704.8*** *p131*
Scott, William 20; Philadelphia, 1804 ***53.26*** *p81*
Scott, William 21; North Carolina, 1774 ***1219.7*** *p189*
Scott, William 21; North Carolina, 1774 ***1639.20*** *p279*
Scott, William 22; Philadelphia, 1803 ***53.26*** *p81*
Scott, William 23; New York, 1775 ***1219.7*** *p268*
With wife
Scott, William 24; St. John, N.B., 1858 ***5704.8*** *p137*
Scott, William 25; St. John, N.B., 1866 ***5704.8*** *p167*
Scott, William 28; St. John, N.B., 1855 ***5704.8*** *p126*
Scott, William J.; America, 1864 ***5704.8*** *p186*
Scott, Wm.; Austin, TX, 1886 ***9777*** *p5*
Scott, Wm.; Virginia, 1635 ***6219*** *p33*
Scougle, Alison; Quebec, 1822 ***7603*** *p36*
Scouler, Jasper 30; Carolina, 1774 ***1219.7*** *p234*
Scouler, Thomas; Charleston, SC, 1812 ***1639.20*** *p279*
Scovet, Andrew 29; New Orleans, 1831 ***778.5*** *p491*
Scowden, Theodor; Cincinnati, 1800-1877 ***8582.3*** *p86*
Scowfield, Abram 23; Virginia, 1699 ***2212*** *p26*
Scowfield, Ellis 25; America, 1699 ***2212*** *p28*
Scowne, Humphrey; Virginia, 1636 ***6219*** *p77*
Scragges, William 19; St. Christopher, 1722 ***3690.1*** *p199*
Scrase, Ann Heriott; Philadelphia, 1694-1695 ***4961*** *p164*
Screech, Joseph 15; Philadelphia, 1774 ***1219.7*** *p183*
Scruby, Philip; Wisconsin, n.d. ***9675.8*** *p66*
Scrymgerin, Henry 18; Jamaica, 1774 ***1219.7*** *p178*
Scudder, Jesse 21; Maryland, 1774 ***1219.7*** *p235*
Scull, John; Virginia, 1645 ***6219*** *p235*
Sculler, James; New York, NY, 1816 ***2859.11*** *p42*
Sculley, Philip; New York, NY, 1838 ***8208.4*** *p73*
Scullin, James; Montreal, 1824 ***7603*** *p54*
Scullion, John 16; Philadelphia, 1856 ***5704.8*** *p128*
Scullion, Rose 18; Philadelphia, 1864 ***5704.8*** *p160*
Scully, Barnaby 22; Maryland, 1774 ***1219.7*** *p179*
Scully, Daniel 20; Massachusetts, 1850 ***5881.1*** *p89*
Scully, John; New York, NY, 1811 ***2859.11*** *p19*
Scully, John; Washington, 1859-1920 ***2872.1*** *p36*
Scully, Mary 55; Massachusetts, 1849 ***5881.1*** *p91*
Sculthorpe, John; New York, NY, 1838 ***8208.4*** *p63*
Scunts, Andres 31; New Orleans, 1831 ***778.5*** *p491*
Scurr, Alice 1 *SEE* Scurr, Thomas
Scurr, Charles 5 *SEE* Scurr, Thomas
Scurr, Elizabeth 3 *SEE* Scurr, Thomas
Scurr, Elizabeth 39 *SEE* Scurr, Thomas
Scurr, Thomas 9 *SEE* Scurr, Thomas
Scurr, Thomas 34; North America, 1774 ***1219.7*** *p198*
*Wife:*Elizabeth 39
*Child:*Alice 1
*Child:*Thomas 9
*Child:*William 7
*Child:*Charles 5
*Child:*Elizabeth 3
Scurr, William 7 *SEE* Scurr, Thomas
Scurrier, James 21; Maryland, 1733 ***3690.1*** *p199*
Scurto, Tony; Arkansas, 1918 ***95.2*** *p111*
Scutterling, Joh; Charleston, SC, 1775-1781 ***8582.2*** *p52*
Seaberg, John August; Boston, 1910 ***3455.3*** *p111*
Seabright, Joseph 25; Maryland, 1774 ***1219.7*** *p223*
Seaburn, Mary 22; Philadelphia, 1860 ***5704.8*** *p145*
Seaburne, Nicholas; Virginia, 1636 ***6219*** *p36*
Seacome, James 20; America, 1699 ***2212*** *p25*
Seager, George; Pennsylvania, 1750 ***2444*** *p217*
Seager, Jon.; Virginia, 1643 ***6219*** *p200*
Seagler, Martin; South Carolina, 1752-1753 ***3689.17*** *p22*
With wife
With mother-in-law
*Relative:*Rosine 8 wks
Seagler, Rosine 8 wks *SEE* Seagler, Martin
Seagreen, Charles A.; Illinois, 1872 ***5012.39*** *p26*
Seagrove, William 19; Jamaica, 1731 ***3690.1*** *p199*
Seale, Hen.; Virginia, 1637 ***6219*** *p24*
Seale, John 22; Jamaica, 1736 ***3690.1*** *p199*
Seale, Robert 22; Jamaica, 1736 ***3690.1*** *p199*
Sealey, John 22; Jamaica, 1736 ***3690.1*** *p199*
Sealey, John 26; Massachusetts, 1849 ***5881.1*** *p90*
Sealey, Margaret 30; Massachusetts, 1849 ***5881.1*** *p92*
Sealsfield, Charles; America, 1823-1826 ***8582.1*** *p44*
Sealy, Ann 34; Massachusetts, 1849 ***5881.1*** *p87*
Sealy, Charles 35; Maryland, 1775 ***1219.7*** *p255*
Sealy, James 22; Maryland, 1774 ***1219.7*** *p202*
Seaman, Frank; Iowa, 1866-1943 ***123.54*** *p43*
Seaman, Frederick Edward George; California, 1867 ***2769.8*** *p5*
Seaman, George; Charleston, SC, 1769 ***1639.20*** *p279*
Seaman, William Timothy; Antigua (Antego), 1769 ***1219.7*** *p141*
Seamaty, Jane 24; New Orleans, 1831 ***778.5*** *p491*
Seamaty, John 26; New Orleans, 1831 ***778.5*** *p491*
Seamen, Michael 10; Massachusetts, 1848 ***5881.1*** *p91*
Seamer, Francis; Virginia, 1637 ***6219*** *p108*
Seamer, Owen; Virginia, 1639 ***6219*** *p158*
Seamer, Thomas 24; Jamaica, 1728 ***3690.1*** *p199*
Seane, Ralph; Virginia, 1648 ***6219*** *p252*
Seaner, Peter 28; Pennsylvania, 1741 ***4779.3*** *p14A*
Seanoble, John; Virginia, 1648 ***6219*** *p246*
Seanor, Peter 28; Pennsylvania, 1741 ***4779.3*** *p14A*
Searell, Nich.; Virginia, 1637 ***6219*** *p110*
Searing, John; Pennsylvania, 1753 ***4779.3*** *p13*
Searle, Gabriell; Virginia, 1623-1700 ***6219*** *p182*
Searle, John; Virginia, 1639 ***6219*** *p18*
Searle, Jon.; Virginia, 1618 ***6219*** *p72*
Searle, Jon; Virginia, 1634 ***6219*** *p105*
Searle, Richard; Virginia, 1640 ***6219*** *p185*
Searls, Edward J.; Washington, 1859-1920 ***2872.1*** *p36*
Searne, John; Virginia, 1638 ***6219*** *p147*
Sears, Andrew; America, 1849 ***1450.2*** *p131A*
Season, Judy 34; Massachusetts, 1848 ***5881.1*** *p90*
Seath, Alexander; Iowa, 1866-1943 ***123.54*** *p43*
Seaton, Andrew 22; Grenada, 1774 ***1219.7*** *p206*
Seaton, Jon.; Virginia, 1637 ***6219*** *p8*
Seaton, R. 22; Philadelphia, 1774 ***1219.7*** *p228*
Seaton, Thomas 16; Philadelphia, 1774 ***1219.7*** *p197*
Seave, John; New York, NY, 1811 ***2859.11*** *p19*
With family
Seaver, Hugh; Virginia, 1642 ***6219*** *p186*
Seaverne, Bridgett *SEE* Seaverne, Jno.
Seaverne, Jno.; Virginia, 1646 ***6219*** *p246*
*Wife:*Bridgett
Seaverson, H.A.; Wisconsin, n.d. ***9675.8*** *p66*
Seavey, Frederika 48; Massachusetts, 1860 ***6410.32*** *p120*
Seaward, John; Virginia, 1638 ***6219*** *p117*
Seaward, John; Virginia, 1638 ***6219*** *p150*
Seawell, Jervis; Virginia, 1638 ***6219*** *p11*
Seawell, Mary; Virginia, 1637 ***6219*** *p10*
Seawell, Tho.; Virginia, 1647 ***6219*** *p247*
Seawell, Thomas; Virginia, 1638 ***6219*** *p147*
Seawell, Thomas 26; Virginia, 1730 ***3690.1*** *p199*
Sebanz, John; Wisconsin, n.d. ***9675.8*** *p66*
Sebastian, Joseph; Indiana, 1848 ***9117*** *p18*
Sebastiani, Joseph; America, 1849 ***8582.1*** *p32*
Sebastino, Michele 22; Arkansas, 1918 ***95.2*** *p111*
Sebben, Ambrogio; Iowa, 1866-1943 ***123.54*** *p43*
Sebben, Ambrogio; Iowa, 1866-1943 ***123.54*** *p77*
Sebben, Andrea; Iowa, 1866-1943 ***123.54*** *p43*
Sebben, Andrea; Iowa, 1866-1943 ***123.54*** *p77*
Sebben, Angelo; Iowa, 1866-1943 ***123.54*** *p43*
Sebben, Angelo; Iowa, 1866-1943 ***123.54*** *p77*
Sebben, Anton; Iowa, 1866-1943 ***123.54*** *p43*
Sebben, Antonio; Iowa, 1866-1943 ***123.54*** *p43*
Sebben, Domenico; Iowa, 1866-1943 ***123.54*** *p44*
Sebben, Francesco; Iowa, 1866-1943 ***123.54*** *p44*
Sebben, Giovanni; Iowa, 1866-1943 ***123.54*** *p44*
Sebben, Giuseppe; Iowa, 1866-1943 ***123.54*** *p77*
Sebben, John; Iowa, 1866-1943 ***123.54*** *p44*
Sebben, Lena; Iowa, 1866-1943 ***123.54*** *p44*
Sebben, Maria; Iowa, 1866-1943 ***123.54*** *p77*
Sebben, Tonetta; Iowa, 1866-1943 ***123.54*** *p44*
Sebbon, John; Iowa, 1866-1943 ***123.54*** *p44*
Sebeard, John; Virginia, 1639 ***6219*** *p155*
Seben, Francesco; Iowa, 1866-1943 ***123.54*** *p44*
Seber, Joh. Albrecht; Port uncertain, 1738 ***3627*** *p19*
With wife
With 2 children
Seberry, John; Virginia, 1638 ***6219*** *p147*
Sebert, Josephine 3; America, 1829 ***778.5*** *p491*
Sebert, Mary 32; America, 1829 ***778.5*** *p491*
Sebert, Miette 9; America, 1829 ***778.5*** *p491*
Sebits, Anthony 44; Kansas, 1878 ***5240.1*** *p58*
Sebits, Ernest 42; Kansas, 1887 ***5240.1*** *p70*
Sebits, Martin L. 24; Kansas, 1893 ***5240.1*** *p78*
Secart, Michel; Quebec, 1763 ***7603*** *p23*
Sechene, Jean 24; America, 1838 ***778.5*** *p491*
Seches, David 36; New Orleans, 1838 ***778.5*** *p491*
Sechner, George; South Carolina, 1788 ***7119*** *p203*
Seckelsohn, Jacob; America, 1854 ***1450.2*** *p131A*
Secker, Geo.; Virginia, 1643 ***6219*** *p207*
Secker, Thomas 14; Antigua (Antego), 1774 ***1219.7*** *p241*
Seckinger, Anna Catharina *SEE* Seckinger, Matthias
Seckinger, Christian *SEE* Seckinger, Matthias
Seckinger, Matthias; Pennsylvania, 1749 ***2444*** *p217*
*Wife:*Anna Catharina
*Child:*Christian
Seckinger, Rosina; America, 1751 ***2444*** *p229*
Seckly, Joh; Charleston, SC, 1775-1781 ***8582.2*** *p52*
Second, Ernest Jacques 22; Port uncertain, 1826 ***778.5*** *p492*
Secor, William; Washington, 1859-1920 ***2872.1*** *p36*
Sedado, Valentine; Arizona, 1884 ***2764.35*** *p63*
Sedberry, Peter; Virginia, 1638 ***6219*** *p145*
Sedden, Ellen; America, 1705 ***2212*** *p45*
Sedden, Wm 20; America, 1699 ***2212*** *p29*
Seddon, George 16; Virginia, 1699 ***2212*** *p26*
Seddon, George 25; Philadelphia, 1774 ***1219.7*** *p196*
Seddon, James A.; Iowa, 1866-1943 ***123.54*** *p44*
Seddon, Richard 19; Jamaica, 1723 ***3690.1*** *p199*
Sedel, Bridget 38; Nova Scotia, 1775 ***1219.7*** *p263*
*Child:*Mary 7
*Child:*Frances 6
*Child:*Sarah 1
Sedel, Frances 6 *SEE* Sedel, Bridget
Sedel, Mary 7 *SEE* Sedel, Bridget
Sedel, Sarah 1 *SEE* Sedel, Bridget
Sedgewick, John 39; Nova Scotia, 1774 ***1219.7*** *p194*
Sedgley, Thomas 16; United States or West Indies, 1733 ***3690.1*** *p200*
Sedgwick, Frances 25; Maryland, 1724 ***3690.1*** *p200*
Sedgwick, John; Quebec, 1770 ***1219.7*** *p144*
Sedgwick, Joseph; Virginia, 1634 ***6219*** *p32*
Sedlak, Wladislaw 16; New York, 1912 ***9980.29*** *p63*
Sedler, Wilhelm; America, 1846 ***8582.3*** *p61*
Sedley, Francis 21; Maryland, 1774 ***1219.7*** *p234*
See, Nevin; New York, NY, 1811 ***2859.11*** *p19*
Seeback, Frank; America, 1872 ***6014.1*** *p3*
Seeborg, Steffan; Washington, 1859-1920 ***2872.1*** *p36*
Seeborg, Victor; Washington, 1859-1920 ***2872.1*** *p36*
Seed, Mr.; Quebec, 1815 ***9229.18*** *p75*
Seed, William; Philadelphia, 1811 ***2859.11*** *p19*
Seedon, Jacob 24; Virginia, 1774 ***1219.7*** *p225*
Seeds, William; New York, NY, 1816 ***2859.11*** *p42*
Seegar, Joseph; Virginia, 1775 ***1219.7*** *p275*
Seeger, Emil; Wisconsin, n.d. ***9675.8*** *p66*

Seeger, Ernst Carl Heinrich; America, 1859 4610.10 p122
Seeger, Heinrich; Wisconsin, n.d. 9675.8 p66
Seeger, Johann Georg SEE Seeger, Johann Georg
Seeger, Johann Georg; Pennsylvania, 1750 2444 p217
With wife
Child:Johann Georg
Seeger, William; America, 1869 1450.2 p132A
Seeger, William; Wisconsin, n.d. 9675.8 p66
Seegers, Frederick; Nashville, TN, 1868 1450.2 p132A
Seegmuller, Elisabetha Vogelgesang; North America, 1792-1922 2691.4 p170
Seegmuller, Friedrich, Family; America, 1825-1923 2691.4 p172
Seegmuller, Johann Philipp, Family; America, 1816-1923 2691.4 p172
Seehane, Richard; America, 1740 4971 p47
Seehorn, Gabriel; South Carolina, 1750-1799 8582.1 p55
With parents
Seekamp, Henrich; Chicago, 1866 5240.1 p40
Seel, Anna Maria; America, 1751 2444 p196
Seel, Dorothea; New England, 1752 4525 p247
Son:Hans Joerg
Seel, Hans Joerg SEE Seel, Dorothea
Seelander, . . .; Canada, 1776-1783 9786 p34
Seele, Christian; America, 1850 1450.2 p132A
Seele, Henry; America, 1850 1450.2 p132A
Seelmann, George; Wisconsin, n.d. 9675.8 p66
Seely, John; America, 1740 4971 p67
Seeman, Thomas; New York, NY, 1811 2859.11 p19
Seemann, Joseph; Cincinnati, 1812 8582.1 p51
Seemer, Richard 20; Jamaica, 1731 3690.1 p200
Seenetken, Sjeet; Illinois, 1896 5012.39 p53
Seentken, Sjeet; Illinois, 1896 5012.39 p53
Seestram, Adolph; Arkansas, 1918 95.2 p111
Sefady, Joseph Saleh; Arkansas, 1918 95.2 p111
Sefan, Fred; Kansas, 1900 5240.1 p43
Sefcik, Eva SEE Sefcik, Joseph
Sefcik, Joseph; America, 1890 7137 p170
Wife:Eva
Seffels, Ernest; Wisconsin, n.d. 9675.8 p66
Seffels, Herbert; Wisconsin, n.d. 9675.8 p66
Sefrin, Johan; New York, NY, 1834 8208.4 p25
Sefton, Henry 3; Quebec, 1864 5704.8 p164
Sefton, Margaret 30; Quebec, 1864 5704.8 p164
Sefton, Sarah 11; Quebec, 1864 5704.8 p164
Sefton, William 9 mos; Quebec, 1864 5704.8 p164
Sefton, William 34; Quebec, 1864 5704.8 p164
Segar, Francis; Virginia, 1637 6219 p112
Segarson, William; New York, NY, 1816 2859.11 p42
Seger, Eleonora 15; America, 1835 778.5 p492
Seger, Elizabeth 50; America, 1835 778.5 p492
Segergreen, Selma Louise; Iowa, 1866-1943 123.54 p44
Segermeister, Dave; Wisconsin, n.d. 9675.8 p66
Segerstrom, Charles; Wisconsin, n.d. 9675.8 p66
Seggern, Christian von; Cincinnati, 1869-1887 8582 p29
Segond, Marguerite 26; New Orleans, 1829 778.5 p492
Segreto, Angelo; Arkansas, 1918 95.2 p111
Seguin, Francois; Louisiana, 1789-1819 778.5 p556
Seguin, Francois 20; America, 1838 778.5 p492
Segura, Pedro; Washington, 1859-1920 2872.1 p36
Sehaefes, Hyacinth 33; Kansas, 1892 5240.1 p77
Sehenger, Fanny 40; New Orleans, 1829 778.5 p492
Sehleifer, Joseph; Arkansas, 1918 95.2 p111
Sehlhorst, Theodor; America, 1851 8582.3 p61
Seib, John; Indiana, 1847 9117 p18
Seib, John; Indiana, 1850 9117 p20
Seibel, Gottfried; Indiana, 1869-1887 8582 p29
Seiberlich, Joseph; Wisconsin, n.d. 9675.8 p66
Seiberlich, Lorenz; Wisconsin, n.d. 9675.8 p66
Seibert, . . .; Canada, 1776-1783 9786 p34
Seibert, Adam; Ohio, 1836 8582.1 p47
Seibert, Andreas; Pennsylvania, 1752-1753 4525 p249
Seibert, Anna Catharina Schreiner; Pennsylvania, 1711-1783 4525 p247
Seibert, Jacob; America, 1738 4349 p48
Seibert, Johan Jacob; Philadelphia, 1738 4349 p48
Seibold, Ferdinand David; New York, NY, 1838 8208.4 p83
Seibt, J. F.; New York, NY, 1833 8582.1 p32
Seibt, T. F.; Ohio, 1869-1887 8582 p29
Seidel, Anna; New York, 1761 3652 p88
Seidel, Anna Joh; Pennsylvania, 1752 4525 p248
Seidel, Anna Johanna SEE Seidel, Nathaniel
Seidel, Arthur 3; New Orleans, 1839 9420.1 p376
Seidel, Franz 29; New Orleans, 1839 9420.1 p376
Seidel, John; Philadelphia, 1757 9973.7 p32
Seidel, Juliana; New York, 1749 3652 p73
Seidel, Minna 26; New Orleans, 1839 9420.1 p376
Seidel, Nathaniel; New York, 1761 3652 p87
Wife:Anna Johanna
Seidel, Nathaniel; Philadelphia, 1742 3652 p55
Seidelmaier, Hans Jerg; Pennsylvania, 1754 2444 p217
Wife:Margaretha
Child:Johannes
Seidelmaier, Johannes SEE Seidelmaier, Hans Jerg
Seidelmaier, Margaretha SEE Seidelmaier, Hans Jerg
Seidenstruker, Henry; Wisconsin, n.d. 9675.8 p66
Seidenzahl, . . .; Canada, 1776-1783 9786 p34
Seider, Hans C.; Illinois, 1893 5012.40 p53
Seider, Herman; Illinois, 1892 5012.37 p62
Seider, Jacob; Illinois, 1892 5012.37 p62
Seidla, George; Wisconsin, n.d. 9675.8 p66
Seidler, . . .; Canada, 1776-1783 9786 p34
Seidler, Albert; Wisconsin, n.d. 9675.8 p66
Seidler, Alois; California, 1860 2769.8 p4
Seidler, Ida; Wisconsin, n.d. 9675.8 p66
Seidler, Otto; Wisconsin, n.d. 9675.8 p66
Seidlitz, Elizabeth; New York, 1763 3652 p89
Seidner, Anna Catharina; Pennsylvania, 1723-1785 4525 p247
Seidner, Appollonia SEE Seidner, Philipp
Seidner, Joerg; Pennsylvania, 1752 4525 p230
Seidner, Joerg; Pennsylvania, 1752 4525 p247
Seidner, Johann Michael; Pennsylvania, 1754 4525 p247
With wife
With child
Seidner, Margaret; New York, 1752 3652 p76
Seidner, Margaretha Barbara; Pennsylvania, 1752 4525 p248
Seidner, Martin; Pennsylvania, 1754 4525 p248
With wife
With child
Seidner, Philipp; Pennsylvania, 1754 4525 p248
Sibling:Appollonia
Seifert, Eugene; New York, NY, 1870 1450.2 p36B
Seifert, Franz; America, 1836 8582.2 p38
Seifert, George; New York, 1884 1450.2 p36B
Seifert, Gustave; Wisconsin, n.d. 9675.8 p66
Seifert, Traugott; Wisconsin, n.d. 9675.8 p66
Seiffert, Andrew; New York, 1749 3652 p72
Seifreid, John; New Orleans, 1851 2896.5 p37
Seig, Christian; Baltimore, 1849 2896.5 p37
Seigel, William; Wisconsin, n.d. 9675.8 p66
Seigerist, Jacob; Philadelphia, 1761 9973.7 p36
Seigle, Goliffe; Philadelphia, 1757 9973.7 p32
Seigneur, A. 31; America, 1835 778.5 p492
Seigneur, L. 23; New Orleans, 1825 778.5 p492
Seignouaut, F. 49; America, 1835 778.5 p492
Seiler, Adolph 25; Kansas, 1906 5240.1 p84
Seiler, Alfred 22; Kansas, 1888 5240.1 p71
Seiler, Emil 29; Kansas, 1902 5240.1 p82
Seiler, Ernest 21; Kansas, 1898 5240.1 p40
Seiler, Ernest 21; Kansas, 1898 5240.1 p81
Seiler, Franz 25; America, 1853 9162.8 p37
Seiler, Joseph; New York, 1887 1450.2 p36B
Seiler, Katharina 22; America, 1853 9162.8 p37
Seiler, Wilhelm 6 mos; America, 1853 9162.8 p37
Seim, John; Arkansas, 1918 95.2 p111
Seime, Georg; America, 1781 8582.3 p75
Seimen, Walter; Germantown, PA, 1684 2467.7 p5
Seimens, Jan; Pennsylvania, 1683 2155 p2
Wife:Maria Lucken
Seimens, Maria Lucken SEE Seimens, Jan
Seimens, Wolter; Germantown, PA, 1684 2155 p2
Seinecke, A.; Cincinnati, 1869-1887 8582 p30
Seinier, Peter . 28; Pennsylvania, 1741 4779.3 p14A
Seinsheimer, B.; America, 1843 8582.1 p32
Seinsheimer, Salomon B.; America, 1851 8582.3 p61
Seipel, Johann 24; America, 1872 4610.10 p117
Seise, Fred; America, 1860 2896.5 p37
Seissner, . . .; Canada, 1776-1783 9786 p34
Seitner, Martin; Pennsylvania, 1754 4525 p248
Seittner, Michel; Pennsylvania, 1754 4525 p248
Seitz, . . .; Canada, 1776-1783 9786 p34
Seitz, F.C.E. von; Halifax, N.S., 1778 9786 p269
Seitz, F.C.E. von; New York, 1776 9786 p269
Seitz, Johan Heinrich; South Carolina, 1788 7119 p204
Seitz, Justinus; Philadelphia, 1779 8137 p14
Seiz, . . .; Canada, 1776-1783 9786 p34
Sejnoha, John; Arkansas, 1918 95.2 p111
Sekacs, Anna; Wisconsin, n.d. 9675.8 p66
Sekacs, John; Wisconsin, n.d. 9675.8 p66
Sekander, Charley; Illinois, 1892 5012.37 p62
Sekardi, Andro; Iowa, 1866-1943 123.54 p44
Sekardi, Milivoj; Iowa, 1866-1943 123.54 p44
Sel, J. B. 44; America, 1825 778.5 p492
Selas, Placido 42; Arizona, 1913 9228.40 p17
Selaune, Pierre 24; America, 1838 778.5 p492
Selb, Mathias; New York, 1881 1450.2 p36B
Selbee, Robert; Virginia, 1638 6219 p124
Selbert, Johann; America, 1850 8582.3 p61
Selby, C.I. 27; Maryland, 1775 1219.7 p260
Selby, Georges; Montreal, 1785 7603 p29
Selby, Mary 19; America, 1728 3690.1 p200
Selby, Robert; Virginia, 1635 6219 p17
Selby, Thomas 21; Jamaica, 1724 3690.1 p200
Selden, Richard 31; Philadelphia, 1775 1219.7 p274
Seldome, Wm.; Virginia, 1637 6219 p117
Selfridge, Alexander 2; St. John, N.B., 1847 5704.8 p32
Selfridge, Anne; St. John, N.B., 1847 5704.8 p32
Selfridge, Catherine 9; St. John, N.B., 1847 5704.8 p32
Selfridge, Elizabeth 4; St. John, N.B., 1847 5704.8 p32
Selfridge, John 4; St. John, N.B., 1847 5704.8 p32
Selfridge, Julia 3 mos; St. John, N.B., 1847 5704.8 p32
Selfridge, Margaret 11; St. John, N.B., 1847 5704.8 p32
Selfridge, Margaret Jane; St. John, N.B., 1848 5704.8 p42
Selfridge, Mary 13; St. John, N.B., 1847 5704.8 p32
Selfridge, Robert 29; Wilmington, DE, 1831 6508.3 p101
Selfridge, Thomas; St. John, N.B., 1847 5704.8 p32
Selfridge, William 7; St. John, N.B., 1847 5704.8 p32
Selickowitz, Abraham; Illinois, 1898 5012.40 p55
Selig, Jakob; Ohio, 1798-1818 8582.2 p54
Selinski, John; Illinois, 1867 2896.5 p37
Selkirk, Lord; Manitoba, 1811 9775.5 p219
Selkirk, William; Arkansas, 1918 95.2 p111
Sell, Andreas; Pennsylvania, 1752 4525 p248
With wife
With 7 children
Sell, Andreas; Pennsylvania, 1752 4525 p249
Sell, Andres; Pennsylvania, 1752 4525 p247
Sell, Charles; Minneapolis, 1882-1887 6410.35 p65
Sell, Dorothea; New England, 1752 4525 p247
Son:Hans Joerg
Sell, Hans Joerg SEE Sell, Dorothea
Sell, Hans Jorg; Pennsylvania, 1752 4525 p247
Sell, Hans Jorg; Pennsylvania, 1752 4525 p249
Selle, Auguste 14; New York, NY, 1857 9831.14 p153
Selle, Bertha 16; New York, NY, 1857 9831.14 p153
Selle, Emilie 4; New York, NY, 1857 9831.14 p153
Selle, Friedrich 2; New York, NY, 1857 9831.14 p153
Selle, Gottfried; Wisconsin, n.d. 9675.8 p66
Selle, Gottlieb 43; New York, NY, 1857 9831.14 p153
Selle, Henriette 6; New York, NY, 1857 9831.14 p153
Selle, Henriette 47; New York, NY, 1857 9831.14 p153
Selle, Michel 22; New Orleans, 1838 778.5 p492
Selle, Wilhelm 12; New York, NY, 1857 9831.14 p153
Sellecks, Jacob 27; America, 1835 778.5 p492
Seller, Charles 67; Arizona, 1905 9228.40 p14
Sellers, John A. 26; Kansas, 1885 5240.1 p40
Sellers, John A. 26; Kansas, 1885 5240.1 p67
Sellers, William; Wisconsin, 1869 5240.1 p41
Sellett, Eliza.; Virginia, 1639 6219 p24
Selley, Hugh; Virginia, 1750 3690.1 p200
Selley, Hugh; Virginia, 1751 1219.7 p2
Selley, John 34; Philadelphia, 1775 1219.7 p274
Sellis, Joseph; Wisconsin, n.d. 9675.8 p66
Sellmeier, Johann H.; Indiana, 1869-1887 8582 p30
Sellors, Isabella 24; Virginia, 1700 2212 p31
Selly, Hugh; Virginia, 1750 3690.1 p200
Selly, Johann; New York, 1876-1877 8582.3 p61
Selly, John; Virginia, 1638 6219 p146
Selm, Ferdinand 24; Kansas, 1885 5240.1 p67
Selmes, Matthew R.; New York, NY, 1836 8208.4 p14
Seltvedt, Johannns; Arkansas, 1918 95.2 p111
Seltzer, . . .; Canada, 1776-1783 9786 p43
Selvander, Joseph Henry; New York, NY, 1909 3455.2 p103
Selvian, Max; Arkansas, 1918 95.2 p111
Selwood, William; Antigua (Antego), 1766 1219.7 p124
Selzer, John; New York, 1881 1450.2 p36B
Sem, Marie-Anne 22; Montreal, 1756 7603 p38
Sem, Martin; Wisconsin, n.d. 9675.8 p66
Semanchik, Anna; America, 1895 7137 p170
Semanchik, Anna; Pennsylvania, 1900 7137 p170
Semanchik, George; America, 1883 7137 p170
Semancik, Anna; America, 1895 7137 p170
Semancik, Anna; Pennsylvania, 1900 7137 p170
Semancik, George; America, 1883 7137 p170
Semaster, Hen.; Virginia, 1642 6219 p191
Semel, Martin; Pennsylvania, 1753 4525 p249
Semetkovsky, Anna; America, 1882 7137 p170
Semetkovsky, John; America, 1900 7137 p170
Semetkovsky, Stephen; America, 1898 7137 p170
Semetkovsky, Vasko; America, 1894 7137 p170
Semetosky, Anna; America, 1882 7137 p170
Semetosky, John; America, 1900 7137 p170
Semetosky, Stephen; America, 1898 7137 p170
Semetosky, Vasko; America, 1894 7137 p170
Semisch, Ernst; Wisconsin, n.d. 9675.8 p66
Semisch, Michael 56; Kansas, 1879 5240.1 p61
Semler, . . .; Canada, 1776-1783 9786 p34
Semler, Charles 14; Virginia, 1727 3690.1 p197
Semler, Nikolaus; Philadelphia, 1779 8137 p14
Semmel, Martin; Pennsylvania, 1753 4525 p249
Semmell, Joel 21; Philadelphia, 1774 1219.7 p233

Semmerulle, Anthine 24; Port uncertain, 1836 778.5 p492
Semmiac, Victor 34; Louisiana, 1822 778.5 p493
Semmigen, . . .; Canada, 1776-1783 9786 p34
Semperac, Alexander 45; America, 1829 778.5 p493
Sempf, . . .; Canada, 1776-1783 9786 p34
Semph, Joseph; Quebec, 1776 7603 p22
Sempion, Soule 23; New Orleans, 1829 778.5 p493
Semple, Mrs.; New York, NY, 1864 5704.8 p187
Semple, Biddy 19; Philadelphia, 1853 5704.8 p112
Semple, David; Quebec, 1847 5704.8 p36
Semple, David 5; Quebec, 1847 5704.8 p36
Semple, Eliza 6; New York, NY, 1864 5704.8 p187
Semple, Eliza 10; St. John, N.B., 1850 5704.8 p61
Semple, Elizabeth 7; Quebec, 1847 5704.8 p36
Semple, Hugh 20; Philadelphia, 1853 5704.8 p111
Semple, James 13; Quebec, 1847 5704.8 p36
Semple, James 13; St. John, N.B., 1848 5704.8 p44
Semple, Jane 16; Philadelphia, 1853 5704.8 p112
Semple, John 11; Quebec, 1847 5704.8 p36
Semple, Joseph; St. John, N.B., 1850 5704.8 p61
Semple, Margaret 21; Philadelphia, 1859 5704.8 p142
Semple, Margaret J. 4; New York, NY, 1864 5704.8 p187
Semple, Mary; Quebec, 1847 5704.8 p36
Semple, Mary; St. John, N.B., 1850 5704.8 p61
Semple, Mary 14; Philadelphia, 1859 5704.8 p142
Semple, Mary Ann; Quebec, 1847 5704.8 p36
Semple, Mary J. 14; New York, NY, 1864 5704.8 p187
Semple, Nancy 18; Philadelphia, 1859 5704.8 p142
Semple, Nancy 50; Philadelphia, 1859 5704.8 p142
Semple, Robert; Manitoba, 1816 9775.5 p220
Semple, Robert; New York, NY, 1816 2859.11 p42
Semple, Robert 3; Quebec, 1847 5704.8 p36
Semple, Robert J. 11; New York, NY, 1864 5704.8 p187
Semple, Samuel 16; New York, NY, 1864 5704.8 p187
Semple, Thomas; New York, NY, 1815 2859.11 p42
Semple, William; St. John, N.B., 1848 5704.8 p44
Semple, William 9; Quebec, 1847 5704.8 p36
Semple, William 18; New York, NY, 1864 5704.8 p187
Semsroth, Herman 22; Kansas, 1887 5240.1 p70
Semsroth, Hermann 22; Kansas, 1887 5240.1 p41
Semsroth, Johann 32; Kansas, 1892 5240.1 p41
Semsroth, John 32; Kansas, 1892 5240.1 p77
Sen, Stephen; Virginia, 1642 6219 p189
Senac, Mr. 40; America, 1839 778.5 p493
Senac, Bastien 28; New Orleans, 1838 778.5 p493
Senac, T. A. 22; New Orleans, 1839 778.5 p493
Senat, J. 40; Guadeloupe, 1832 778.5 p493
Senat, Jacob; Illinois, 1796-1872 8582 p30
Senecal, Mr. 34; New Orleans, 1829 778.5 p493
Senecal, A. 30; New Orleans, 1825 778.5 p491
Senecal, A. 30; Port uncertain, 1825 778.5 p493
Senecal, A. 36; New Orleans, 1826 778.5 p493
Seneclose, J. 46; New Orleans, 1832 778.5 p493
Seneff, George; New York, 1756 3652 p81
Seneille, Jean; Quebec, 1674 4533 p131
Senetier, Francois; Louisiana, 1789-1819 778.5 p555
Senette, Antonio 32; New Orleans, 1835 778.5 p493
Senff, Caspar; America, 1773 8582.2 p57
With family
Senfftleber, Hans; Pennsylvania, 1754 4525 p249
Senfleben, Anna Elisabeth *SEE* Senfleben, Hans
Senfleben, Hans; Pennsylvania, 1754 4525 p249
*Wife:*Anna Elisabeth
With 2 daughters
Sengall, John 18; Jamaica, 1730 3690.1 p200
Senger, Damien; Alberta, n.d. 5262 p58
Senger, Ernst 28; Kansas, 1883 5240.1 p64
Senica, Joseph; Wisconsin, n.d. 9675.8 p66
Senior, John; Virginia, 1636 6219 p8
Senior, Sarah; Virginia, 1636 6219 p8
Senn, Mathias D.; South Carolina, 1788 7119 p199
Sennen, Freus; Wisconsin, n.d. 9675.8 p66
Senning, George 22; Kansas, 1893 5240.1 p79
Senor, Peter 28; Pennsylvania, 1741 4779.3 p14A
Senot, Auguste 42; America, 1838 778.5 p493
Senprimosinik, John; Wisconsin, n.d. 9675.8 p66
Senseman, Anna Catherine *SEE* Senseman, Joachim
Senseman, Joachim; Philadelphia, 1742 3652 p55
*Wife:*Anna Catherine
Sensemann, . . .; America, 1700-1877 8582.3 p80
Sensun, L. 50; New Orleans, 1827 778.5 p493
Sentaurus, Heinrich; Akron, OH, 1835 8582.1 p49
Seon, Mr.; Quebec, 1815 9229.18 p75
Seper, Michael; Wisconsin, n.d. 9675.8 p66
Sephor, Jacques 35; New Orleans, 1839 778.5 p493
Sephton, William 19; Windward Islands, 1722 3690.1 p197
Sepp, Anton; America, 1700-1877 8582.3 p80
Sepp, Anton; Buenos Aires, 1693 8582.3 p79
Sepp, Antonius; Paraguay, 1691 8582.3 p86
Sequez, Bernhard 16; America, 1839 778.5 p494
Seragons, Mr. 24; New Orleans, 1837 778.5 p494
Serakman, George; Colorado, 1901 9678.2 p168
Seran, Mr. 21; New Orleans, 1822 778.5 p494
Sereny, . . .; Canada, 1776-1783 9786 p34
Seretes, Nick; Arkansas, 1918 95.2 p111
Sergent, Arthur; Virginia, 1643 6219 p205
Sergent, Arthur W.; Ohio, 1840 1450.2 p132A
Sergent, Arthur W.; Ohio, 1840 9892.11 p41
Sergius, John; Iowa, 1897 1450.2 p132A
Serio, Frank; Arkansas, 1918 95.2 p111
Serjeant, Henry; South Carolina, 1716 1639.20 p279
Serjeant, Wm.; Virginia, 1638 6219 p118
Serle, Ann 19; Maryland, 1738 3690.1 p200
Serne, Suzanne Betfer; Quebec, 1649 7603 p24
Serno, Como; Arkansas, 1918 95.2 p111
Sernrich, Nicholas; Minnesota, 1869 5240.1 p41
Serodino, Hermann; America, 1849 8582.2 p38
Serra, Salvatore; Arkansas, 1918 95.2 p111
Serran, Bernard 30; New Orleans, 1827 778.5 p494
Serre, Henry 33; Port uncertain, 1837 778.5 p494
Serre, Jean Pierre 24; New Orleans, 1836 778.5 p494
Serre, Julia; Montreal, 1825 7603 p65
Serrell, William; New York, NY, 1835 8208.4 p28
Serren, Mr. 32; New Orleans, 1821 778.5 p494
Serridon, Thomas; Virginia, 1642 6219 p186
Sertich, John 35; Arizona, 1921 9228.40 p25
Sertie, Christine *SEE* Sertie, Jean-Urbain
Sertie, Jacques *SEE* Sertie, Jean-Urbain
Sertie, Jean-Urbain 34; Halifax, N.S., 1752 7074.6 p212
*Wife:*Christine
*Son:*Pierre
*Son:*Jacques
Sertie, Pierre *SEE* Sertie, Jean-Urbain
Servant, J. 20; Port uncertain, 1839 778.5 p494
Servant, William 20; Maryland, 1719 3690.1 p197
Servanteau, Joaquin 39; Port uncertain, 1821 778.5 p494
Servanteo, Jose; Arizona, 1925 9228.40 p29
Servat, Laurent 36; New Orleans, 1839 778.5 p494
Serves, Francois 37; America, 1839 778.5 p494
Servical, Amable 32; New Orleans, 1821 778.5 p494
Service, Alexander; New York, NY, 1816 2859.11 p42
Service, Robert; New York, NY, 1811 2859.11 p19
Servoce, Thomas 18; Philadelphia, 1803 53.26 p81
Sessenhofer, Hans; Venezuela, n.d. 8582.3 p79
Session, Judeth; Virginia, 1645 6219 p233
Sesson, Joseph 3; Philadelphia, 1871 5704.8 p241
Sesson, Matilda; Philadelphia, 1871 5704.8 p241
Sesson, Robert; Philadelphia, 1871 5704.8 p241
Sesson, Robert 4; Philadelphia, 1871 5704.8 p241
Sestrunck, Henrich; South Carolina, 1788 7119 p202
Seth, William; Virginia, 1637 6219 p34
Setinsky, Jan; New York, NY, 1907 3455.2 p100
*Wife:*Julia
Setinsky, Julia *SEE* Setinsky, Jan
Setree, Joseph 19; Jamaica, 1751 1219.7 p7
Setree, Joseph 19; Jamaica, 1751 3690.1 p200
Setter, Maurice C.; Chicago, 1888 1450.2 p36B
Settergren, F. G. 24; Kansas, 1888 5240.1 p72
Setzer, Carl; Wisconsin, n.d. 9675.8 p66
Setzer, Charles; Wisconsin, n.d. 9675.8 p66
Setzer, Ernst; Wisconsin, n.d. 9675.8 p66
Setzer, Gottfried; Wisconsin, n.d. 9675.8 p66
Seuban, Mr. 25; New Orleans, 1839 778.5 p495
Seubert, Andreas; Pennsylvania, 1753 4525 p249
Seubert, Hans; Pennsylvania, 1752 4525 p249
Seubert, Michael; Pennsylvania, 1753 4525 p249
Seuberth, Andereas; Pennsylvania, 1752 4525 p249
Seuberth, Andreas; Pennsylvania, 1753 4525 p249
Seuberth, Balsar; Pennsylvania, 1753 4525 p249
Seufferle, Charles 5; Port uncertain, 1839 778.5 p495
Seufferle, Christian; America, 1839 8582.2 p38
Seufferle, Christian; Cincinnati, 1869-1887 8582 p30
Seufferle, Christian 9; Port uncertain, 1839 778.5 p495
Seufferle, Christian 36; Port uncertain, 1839 778.5 p495
Seufferle, Corline 38; Port uncertain, 1839 778.5 p495
Seume, Georg; America, 1781 8582.3 p75
Seume, Johann Gottfield; Quebec, 1776 9786 p79
Sevanson, Iver; Iowa, 1866-1943 123.54 p44
Sevegani, Francisco; Iowa, 1866-1943 123.54 p44
Severied, Peter 25; Arkansas, 1918 95.2 p111
Severin, . . .; Canada, 1776-1783 9786 p34
Severin, Henry; New York, 1849 1450.2 p132A
Severin, Henry C.; New York, NY, 1868 2764.35 p63
Severini, Guglielmo; Arkansas, 1918 95.2 p111
Severn, Samuel 36; Maryland, 1774 1219.7 p220
Severne, Jno., Jr.; Virginia, 1646 6219 p246
Severs, George; Indiana, 1820-1850 9117 p18
Severt, . . .; Canada, 1776-1783 9786 p34
Severt, Joseph; New York, 1832 1450.2 p132A
Severtsen, Iver; Arkansas, 1918 95.2 p112
Sevre, Henry 33; Port uncertain, 1837 778.5 p494
Sewald, Philipp; Ohio, 1833 8582.1 p46
Seward, Samuel C.; Illinois, 1858 5012.39 p54
Sewell, Mr.; Quebec, 1815 9229.18 p79
With family
Sewell, John; Virginia, 1639 6219 p151
Sewell, John 29; Maryland, 1774 1219.7 p192
Sewell, Robert 25; Jamaica, 1776 1219.7 p281
With wife 20
Sewell, Theodore C.; Washington, 1859-1920 2872.1 p36
Sewell, Thomas; Virginia, 1637 6219 p112
Sewell, Thomas 22; Virginia, 1773 1219.7 p168
Sewer, Gottlieb; America, 1848 8582.1 p32
Sewere, John; New York, NY, 1811 2859.11 p19
Sewicki, Frank John; Arkansas, 1918 95.2 p112
Sewthwait, Richard 32; Virginia, 1774 1219.7 p201
Sexton, William; America, 1739 4971 p47
Sexton, William; America, 1741 4971 p49
Sey, Wm.; Virginia, 1642 6219 p199
Seybold, Mr.; Maryland or Virginia, 1732 8582.2 p38
With family
*Son:*Kasper
Seybold, Kasper *SEE* Seybold, Mr.
Seybold, Matthias; Savannah, GA, 1736 3652 p51
Seydler, F. G., Sr.; Texas, 1850 8582 p30
Seyffert, Anton; Savannah, GA, 1735 3652 p51
Seyffert, Charles; Illinois, 1868 5012.37 p59
Seyffert, John; New York, 1748 3652 p68
Seyforette, Christophe 27; America, 1831 778.5 p495
Seyler, Wendel; Cincinnati, 1869-1887 8582 p30
Seyler, Wendel; New Orleans, 1840 8582.3 p61
Seymor, Thomas; Virginia, 1640 6219 p185
Seymore, Alexander 36; Jamaica, 1725 3690.1 p200
Seymour, Christopher 23; Maryland, 1775 1219.7 p272
Seymour, Edward 33; Nevis, 1774 1219.7 p207
Seymour, Fielding; New York, NY, 1839 8208.4 p96
Seymour, George 24; Jamaica, 1733 3690.1 p200
Seymour, John; South Carolina, 1775 1639.20 p280
Seymour, William 27; Virginia, 1774 1219.7 p228
Seys, John 17; Maryland, 1724 3690.1 p201
Seytter, Paul; New York, 1881 1450.2 p37B
Sferruza, Giuseppe; Arkansas, 1918 95.2 p112
Sgobba, Francesco; Arkansas, 1918 95.2 p112
Shabash, . . .; Canada, 1776-1783 9786 p34
Shaber, Christopher; Pennsylvania, 1752 4525 p239
Shackledge, Thomas 19; Pennsylvania, 1730 3690.1 p201
Shaddock, Jon.; Virginia, 1637 6219 p86
Shade, Absolom; Ontario, 1815 9775.5 p214
Shade, Yerrick; Pennsylvania, 1748 2444 p208
Shadecko, Michal 51; New York, 1912 9980.29 p69
Shadeloe, John 23; Maryland, 1725 3690.1 p201
Shadforth, Whitaker 21; Georgia, 1775 1219.7 p276
Shadid, Albert; Arkansas, 1918 95.2 p112
Shadowski, Alexander; Arkansas, 1918 95.2 p112
Shadron, Henry; Pennsylvania, 1769 9973.8 p32
Shady, Patrick 30; Massachusetts, 1849 5881.1 p93
Shaeberger, John; Indiana, 1849 9117 p18
Shaefer, Anton; Ohio, 1842 8365.25 p12
Shafer, Christopher; Illinois, 1858 2896.5 p37
Shafer, Henry; Ohio, 1843 8365.26 p12
Shafer, Jacob; America, 1820 1450.2 p132A
Shafer, Theodore 26; Kansas, 1882 5240.1 p41
Shafers, John 22; Kansas, 1886 5240.1 p69
Shaffer, David; Philadelphia, 1757 9973.7 p32
Shaffer, Lewis; New York, NY, 1836 8208.4 p20
Shafferty, William; New York, NY, 1865 5704.8 p196
Shaffrey, Henry; America, 1742 4971 p23
Shaftin, Rabm 21; Virginia, 1700 2212 p31
Shaggareen, John; America, 1736 4971 p39
Shaghnassy, John; America, 1735-1743 4971 p78
Shaghnassy, Patrick; America, 1735-1743 4971 p78
Shails, Catherine 20; St. John, N.B., 1854 5704.8 p114
Shakemaple, Mary 19; Maryland, 1718 3690.1 p201
Shakespear, William 40; Philadelphia, 1774 1219.7 p200
Shaler, Rosy; Quebec, 1847 5704.8 p29
Shales, . . .; New York, NY, 1815 2859.11 p42
Shallas, Theobald; Philadelphia, 1763 9973.7 p38
Shallcross, Arthur; Iowa, 1866-1943 123.54 p44
Shallock, John; Virginia, 1638 6219 p33
Shallos, Valentine; Philadelphia, 1758 9973.7 p33
Shallow, Margaret; Quebec, 1849 5704.8 p52
Shallow, Mary Ann; Philadelphia, 1852 5704.8 p85
Shallow, Peter; Quebec, 1849 5704.8 p52
Shanaghan, Mary; Philadelphia, 1870 5704.8 p239
Shanahan, Bridget; America, 1735-1743 4971 p51
Shanahan, Cornelius; California, 1861 2764.35 p66
Shanahan, Timothy; Colorado, 1902 9678.2 p168
Shanbacher, Mrs. 36; Georgia, 1738 9332 p331
*Son:*Hans Michael 8
*Son:*Hans George 7
*Daughter:*Magdalena 3
Shanbacher, Hans George 7 *SEE* Shanbacher, Mrs.
Shanbacher, Hans Michael 8 *SEE* Shanbacher, Mrs.
Shanbacher, Magdalena 3 *SEE* Shanbacher, Mrs.
Shancklin, John 18; St. John, N.B., 1854 5704.8 p119
Shandall, Antho.; Virginia, 1646 6219 p242

Shane, Ellen 2; Massachusetts, 1847 ***5881.1*** *p89*
Shane, Margaret 1; Massachusetts, 1847 ***5881.1*** *p91*
Shane, Mary 23; Massachusetts, 1847 ***5881.1*** *p91*
Shanghassy, Michael 12; Massachusetts, 1850 ***5881.1*** *p92*
Shanghy, Michael 27; Massachusetts, 1847 ***5881.1*** *p91*
Shanks, John David; Illinois, 1871 ***5012.39*** *p25*
Shanks, William; New York, NY, 1815 ***2859.11*** *p42*
With wife
Shankster, James; Iowa, 1866-1943 ***123.54*** *p44*
Shannahan, John 18; Massachusetts, 1849 ***5881.1*** *p90*
Shannahan, Julia 35; Massachusetts, 1849 ***5881.1*** *p90*
Shannahane, Mary; America, 1743 ***4971*** *p43*
Shannan, John; New York, NY, 1816 ***2859.11*** *p42*
Shannehan, Thomas 23; Massachusetts, 1849 ***5881.1*** *p93*
Shannon, Ann 20; Massachusetts, 1847 ***5881.1*** *p87*
Shannon, Catharine 50; Massachusetts, 1847 ***5881.1*** *p88*
Shannon, Catherine; New York, NY, 1864 ***5704.8*** *p169*
Shannon, Charles; America, 1742 ***4971*** *p76*
Shannon, Cook; Philadelphia, 1847 ***53.26*** *p81*
Shannon, Cook; Philadelphia, 1847 ***5704.8*** *p31*
Shannon, David; New York, NY, 1815 ***2859.11*** *p42*
Shannon, Eliza; St. John, N.B., 1853 ***5704.8*** *p106*
Shannon, Eliza 18; St. John, N.B., 1854 ***5704.8*** *p115*
Shannon, Francis; New York, NY, 1864 ***5704.8*** *p169*
Shannon, Helen; Quebec, 1822 ***7603*** *p82*
Shannon, Honora 24; Massachusetts, 1850 ***5881.1*** *p89*
With child
Shannon, Hugh; New York, NY, 1815 ***2859.11*** *p42*
With wife
Shannon, Isabella; St. John, N.B., 1853 ***5704.8*** *p106*
Shannon, James; Iowa, 1866-1943 ***123.54*** *p44*
Shannon, James; Philadelphia, 1852 ***5704.8*** *p88*
Shannon, Jane; Philadelphia, 1852 ***5704.8*** *p88*
Shannon, John; Philadelphia, 1847 ***53.26*** *p81*
Shannon, John; Philadelphia, 1847 ***5704.8*** *p31*
Shannon, John 19; Maryland or Virginia, 1734 ***3690.1*** *p201*
Shannon, M.; New York, NY, 1816 ***2859.11*** *p42*
Shannon, Margaret; St. John, N.B., 1853 ***5704.8*** *p106*
Shannon, Martha; St. John, N.B., 1853 ***5704.8*** *p106*
Shannon, Mary; New York, NY, 1864 ***5704.8*** *p175*
Shannon, Mary; St. John, N.B., 1853 ***5704.8*** *p106*
Shannon, Mary 6 mos; Quebec, 1853 ***5704.8*** *p104*
Shannon, Patrick; Philadelphia, 1853 ***5704.8*** *p101*
Shannon, Patrick 20; Philadelphia, 1854 ***5704.8*** *p121*
Shannon, Quinton; New York, NY, 1815 ***2859.11*** *p42*
Shannon, Rebecca; St. John, N.B., 1847 ***5704.8*** *p9*
Shannon, Robert; Philadelphia, 1850 ***5704.8*** *p64*
Shannon, Robert 26; New York, 1774 ***1219.7*** *p218*
Shannon, Rose; Quebec, 1824 ***7603*** *p59*
Shannon, Rosey 6 mos; Quebec, 1853 ***5704.8*** *p104*
Shannon, Samuel 17; Philadelphia, 1854 ***5704.8*** *p116*
Shannon, Sarah; Philadelphia, 1850 ***5704.8*** *p64*
Shannon, Sarah Jane; St. John, N.B., 1853 ***5704.8*** *p106*
Shannon, Terry 17; Massachusetts, 1847 ***5881.1*** *p93*
Shannon, Thomas; New York, NY, 1838 ***8208.4*** *p64*
Shannon, Thomas 22; Quebec, 1855 ***5704.8*** *p125*
Shannon, Thomas 30; Massachusetts, 1850 ***5881.1*** *p93*
Shannon, William 18; St. John, N.B., 1865 ***5704.8*** *p165*
Shanny, Catharine 14; Massachusetts, 1849 ***5881.1*** *p88*
Shanny, Margaret 9; Massachusetts, 1847 ***5881.1*** *p91*
Shanny, Mary 40; Massachusetts, 1847 ***5881.1*** *p91*
Shantler, Mr. 40; New Orleans, 1836 ***778.5*** *p495*
Shanton, Catherine; Quebec, 1823 ***7603*** *p90*
Shantz, Christopher 21; Georgia, 1738 ***9332*** *p329*
*Brother:*William 16
Shantz, William 16 *SEE* Shantz, Christopher
Shantze, Andreas 4 *SEE* Shantze, John Peter
Shantze, Anna Magdalena 18 *SEE* Shantze, John Peter
Shantze, Anna Maria 41 *SEE* Shantze, John Peter
Shantze, Charles 7 *SEE* Shantze, John Peter
Shantze, Hans Adam 12 *SEE* Shantze, John Peter
Shantze, John Peter 42; Georgia, 1738 ***9332*** *p333*
*Wife:*Anna Maria 41
*Daughter:*Anna Magdalena 18
*Son:*Hans Adam 12
*Son:*Charles 7
*Son:*Andreas 4
*Son:*Philip 2
Shantze, Philip 2 *SEE* Shantze, John Peter
Shap, Noah 18; Jamaica, 1736 ***3690.1*** *p201*
Shappel, Eberhard; Pennsylvania, 1751 ***2444*** *p144*
Shappel, Jeremiah 25; Pennsylvania, 1753 ***2444*** *p145*
Shappell, Jeremiah 25; Pennsylvania, 1753 ***2444*** *p145*
Shapwell, William; Virginia, 1638 ***6219*** *p146*
Sharchey, Charles; Arkansas, 1918 ***95.2*** *p112*
Sharcot, James; America, 1736 ***4971*** *p81*
Sharden, Betty 18; Massachusetts, 1850 ***5881.1*** *p88*
Sharden, Patrick 2; Massachusetts, 1850 ***5881.1*** *p93*
Shardia, Julia 22; Massachusetts, 1848 ***5881.1*** *p90*
Sharen, Jacob; Philadelphia, 1759 ***9973.7*** *p33*
Shark, Thomas 30; Philadelphia, 1774 ***1219.7*** *p217*
Sharkey, Ann; St. John, N.B., 1847 ***5704.8*** *p26*
Sharkey, Ann 4; Philadelphia, 1866 ***5704.8*** *p205*
Sharkey, Ann 9; St. John, N.B., 1847 ***5704.8*** *p26*
Sharkey, Catharine 9; Philadelphia, 1867 ***5704.8*** *p193*
Sharkey, Catherine 14; Philadelphia, 1854 ***5704.8*** *p122*
Sharkey, Charles; St. John, N.B., 1847 ***5704.8*** *p26*
Sharkey, Daniel; Philadelphia, 1850 ***5704.8*** *p64*
Sharkey, Dennis; Philadelphia, 1851 ***5704.8*** *p71*
Sharkey, Edward 22; St. John, N.B., 1864 ***5704.8*** *p158*
Sharkey, Ellan; Philadelphia, 1850 ***5704.8*** *p64*
Sharkey, Elleanor; St. John, N.B., 1847 ***5704.8*** *p26*
Sharkey, Ellen 25; Philadelphia, 1857 ***5704.8*** *p134*
Sharkey, Isabella 17; St. John, N.B., 1864 ***5704.8*** *p158*
Sharkey, James; St. John, N.B., 1850 ***5704.8*** *p65*
Sharkey, James 15; St. John, N.B., 1864 ***5704.8*** *p158*
Sharkey, John; Philadelphia, 1847 ***53.26*** *p82*
Sharkey, John; Philadelphia, 1847 ***5704.8*** *p13*
Sharkey, John 9 mos; Philadelphia, 1857 ***5704.8*** *p134*
Sharkey, John 6; Philadelphia, 1866 ***5704.8*** *p205*
Sharkey, John 40; Philadelphia, 1864 ***5704.8*** *p156*
Sharkey, Ludwig; Massachusetts, 1847 ***5881.1*** *p91*
Sharkey, Margery 22; Philadelphia, 1864 ***5704.8*** *p161*
Sharkey, Mary; St. John, N.B., 1847 ***5704.8*** *p10*
Sharkey, Mary; St. John, N.B., 1847 ***5704.8*** *p34*
Sharkey, Mary 2; Philadelphia, 1866 ***5704.8*** *p205*
Sharkey, Mary 12; St. John, N.B., 1847 ***5704.8*** *p26*
Sharkey, Mary 13; Philadelphia, 1857 ***5704.8*** *p134*
Sharkey, Michael 17; Philadelphia, 1853 ***5704.8*** *p108*
Sharkey, Neal; St. John, N.B., 1847 ***5704.8*** *p26*
Sharkey, Niney 14; Philadelphia, 1857 ***5704.8*** *p134*
Sharkey, Patrick; America, 1742 ***4971*** *p25*
Sharkey, Phillip; St. John, N.B., 1847 ***5704.8*** *p15*
Sharkey, Rosanna; St. John, N.B., 1847 ***5704.8*** *p26*
Sharkey, Rosanne; New York, NY, 1869 ***5704.8*** *p234*
Sharkey, Rose 7; Philadelphia, 1867 ***5704.8*** *p193*
Sharkey, Sarah 25; St. John, N.B., 1861 ***5704.8*** *p149*
Sharkey, Thomas; St. John, N.B., 1852 ***5704.8*** *p83*
Sharkey, William; New York, NY, 1816 ***2859.11*** *p42*
Sharkey, William; Philadelphia, 1816 ***2859.11*** *p42*
With sister
Sharkey, William; St. John, N.B., 1852 ***5704.8*** *p83*
Sharkey, William 3; Philadelphia, 1857 ***5704.8*** *p134*
Sharkey, William 50; Philadelphia, 1857 ***5704.8*** *p134*
Sharky, Patrick; America, 1742 ***4971*** *p73*
Sharman, Robert 22; Maryland, 1775 ***1219.7*** *p265*
Sharoff, Nicholas; Arkansas, 1918 ***95.2*** *p112*
Sharp, Ann; Virginia, 1636 ***6219*** *p75*
Sharp, Beatrix; Philadelphia, 1796 ***8894.2*** *p56*
Sharp, Eliz 18; America, 1702 ***2212*** *p39*
Sharp, Elizabeth 11; Quebec, 1864 ***5704.8*** *p162*
Sharp, George 20; St. Christopher, 1722 ***3690.1*** *p201*
Sharp, James; Ohio, 1840 ***9892.11*** *p41*
Sharp, James 14; Quebec, 1864 ***5704.8*** *p162*
Sharp, James 20; Maryland, 1729 ***3690.1*** *p201*
Sharp, James 40; Quebec, 1864 ***5704.8*** *p162*
Sharp, Margaret 9; Quebec, 1864 ***5704.8*** *p162*
Sharp, Mary; Quebec, 1851 ***5704.8*** *p75*
Sharp, Mary 7; Quebec, 1864 ***5704.8*** *p162*
Sharp, Rich.; Virginia, 1636 ***6219*** *p7*
Sharp, Richard; Illinois, 1861 ***5012.38*** *p98*
Sharp, Robert; New York, NY, 1837 ***8208.4*** *p32*
Sharp, Robert; Virginia, 1637 ***6219*** *p108*
Sharp, Robert 17; Jamaica, 1756 ***1219.7*** *p47*
Sharp, Robert 17; Jamaica, 1756 ***3690.1*** *p201*
Sharp, Rosa 38; Quebec, 1864 ***5704.8*** *p162*
Sharp, Thomas; New York, NY, 1868 ***5704.8*** *p229*
Sharp, Thomas; Philadelphia, 1867 ***5704.8*** *p221*
Sharp, Thomas 30; St. Vincent, 1775 ***1219.7*** *p251*
Sharp, William; America, 1737 ***4971*** *p13*
Sharp, William; New York, NY, 1836 ***8208.4*** *p77*
Sharp, William; New York, NY, 1837 ***8208.4*** *p33*
Sharpe, Bella 42; Washington, 1916 ***1728.5*** *p14*
Sharpe, C. W. 51; Washington, 1916 ***1728.5*** *p14*
Sharpe, George 19; Maryland, 1724 ***3690.1*** *p201*
Sharpe, James; North Carolina, 1830 ***1639.20*** *p280*
Sharpe, Jon.; Virginia, 1638 ***6219*** *p123*
Sharpe, Joseph; Quebec, 1852 ***5704.8*** *p97*
Sharpe, Mary; New York, NY, 1864 ***5704.8*** *p174*
Sharpe, Rebecca; Virginia, 1637 ***6219*** *p110*
Sharpe, Robert; Virginia, 1638 ***6219*** *p150*
Sharpe, Robt.; Virginia, 1636 ***6219*** *p180*
Sharpe, Sally; Quebec, 1852 ***5704.8*** *p97*
Sharpe, Thomas 21; Maryland, 1725 ***3690.1*** *p201*
Sharpe, W. D. 28; Kansas, 1890 ***5240.1*** *p74*
Sharpe, William; Virginia, 1641 ***6219*** *p185*
Sharpe, William; Wisconsin, n.d. ***9675.8*** *p66*
Sharples, Eliz.; Virginia, 1639 ***6219*** *p162*
Sharples, Roger; Barbados, 1698 ***2212*** *p4*
Sharples, Thomas; Virginia, 1639 ***6219*** *p161*
Sharples, Wm 25; America, 1706 ***2212*** *p46*
Sharpless, Margt 23; Virginia, 1699 ***2212*** *p26*
Sharrin, Phill.; Virginia, 1635 ***6219*** *p3*
Sharrow, George 26; Nova Scotia, 1774 ***1219.7*** *p209*
Sharwood, Daniel 24; Jamaica, 1738 ***3690.1*** *p202*
Shaser, Alexander; Quebec, 1858 ***5704.8*** *p137*
Shasgreen, Dolly; New York, NY, 1864 ***5704.8*** *p184*
Shatbold, Richard; Virginia, 1637 ***6219*** *p86*
Shatboule, Rich.; Virginia, 1635 ***6219*** *p70*
Shatzler, Charley; Washington, 1859-1920 ***2872.1*** *p36*
Shatzler, Charly; Washington, 1859-1920 ***2872.1*** *p36*
Shaughnessy, John; America, 1742 ***4971*** *p80*
Shaughnessy, John P.; New Haven, CT, 1867 ***2764.35*** *p64*
Shauman, John; Philadelphia, 1762 ***9973.7*** *p37*
Shaver, . . .; Canada, 1776-1783 ***9786*** *p34*
Shaw, Alexander; South Carolina, 1716 ***1639.20*** *p280*
Shaw, Andrew; New York, NY, 1838 ***8208.4*** *p61*
Shaw, Angus; America, 1792 ***1639.20*** *p280*
Shaw, Angus; Montreal, 1792 ***9775.5*** *p202*
Shaw, Angus; Quebec, 1870 ***4537.30*** *p37*
*Wife:*Ann MacDonald
*Child:*Kenneth
*Child:*Donald J.
*Child:*Duncan
Shaw, Ann; Philadelphia, 1816 ***2859.11*** *p42*
Shaw, Ann; Virginia, 1635 ***6219*** *p17*
Shaw, Ann MacDonald *SEE* Shaw, Angus
Shaw, Anne Rutherford; Wilmington, NC, 1767 ***1639.20*** *p280*
Shaw, Archibald; America, 1802 ***1639.20*** *p280*
Shaw, Benjamin; America, 1742 ***4971*** *p34*
Shaw, Benjamin; New York, NY, 1836 ***8208.4*** *p24*
Shaw, Benjamin 50; Massachusetts, 1848 ***5881.1*** *p87*
Shaw, Betty Roberta; Iowa, 1866-1943 ***123.54*** *p77*
Shaw, Colin; North Carolina, 1764 ***1639.20*** *p280*
Shaw, Daniel; America, 1790 ***1639.20*** *p280*
Shaw, Daniel 70; North Carolina, 1850 ***1639.20*** *p280*
Shaw, David 23; Jamaica, 1731 ***3690.1*** *p201*
Shaw, Donald J. *SEE* Shaw, Angus
Shaw, Duncan *SEE* Shaw, Angus
Shaw, Effie 80; North Carolina, 1850 ***1639.20*** *p280*
*Relative:*Flora 78
Shaw, Eliza; Philadelphia, 1847 ***53.26*** *p82*
Shaw, Eliza; Philadelphia, 1847 ***5704.8*** *p1*
Shaw, Elizabeth; America, 1738 ***4971*** *p68*
Shaw, Elizabeth 21; Philadelphia, 1864 ***5704.8*** *p155*
Shaw, Ellen; Quebec, 1853 ***5704.8*** *p104*
Shaw, Flora 56; South Carolina, 1850 ***1639.20*** *p281*
Shaw, Flora 78 *SEE* Shaw, Effie
Shaw, Francis; Virginia, 1643 ***6219*** *p203*
Shaw, Francis 19; Jamaica, 1725 ***3690.1*** *p202*
Shaw, Gilbert 81; North Carolina, 1850 ***1639.20*** *p281*
Shaw, Grizel 80; Raleigh, NC, 1850 ***1639.20*** *p281*
Shaw, Hans George; Pennsylvania, 1750 ***4779.3*** *p14A*
Shaw, Isobel; Charleston, SC, 1715-1734 ***1639.20*** *p281*
Shaw, James; New Bern, NC, 1822 ***1639.20*** *p281*
Shaw, James; New York, NY, 1838 ***8208.4*** *p65*
Shaw, James; New York, NY, 1868 ***5704.8*** *p228*
Shaw, James; North Carolina, 1823 ***1639.20*** *p281*
Shaw, James; Philadelphia, 1816 ***2859.11*** *p42*
Shaw, James; Philadelphia, 1870 ***5704.8*** *p239*
Shaw, James 20; Jamaica, 1731 ***3690.1*** *p202*
Shaw, James 46; New York, 1774 ***1219.7*** *p217*
Shaw, Jane; America, 1739 ***4971*** *p68*
Shaw, Janet 60; North Carolina, 1850 ***1639.20*** *p240*
Shaw, Jno; America, 1698 ***2212*** *p13*
Shaw, Jno; Virginia, 1698 ***2212*** *p15*
Shaw, John; America, 1738 ***4971*** *p66*
Shaw, John; America, 1791 ***1639.20*** *p281*
Shaw, John; Indiana, 1843 ***9117*** *p18*
Shaw, John; New York, NY, 1811 ***2859.11*** *p19*
Shaw, John; New York, NY, 1815 ***2859.11*** *p42*
Shaw, John; North Carolina, 1764 ***1639.20*** *p281*
Shaw, John; Philadelphia, 1816 ***2859.11*** *p42*
Shaw, John; Philadelphia, 1864 ***5704.8*** *p183*
Shaw, John; South Carolina, 1716 ***1639.20*** *p281*
Shaw, John; Virginia, 1642 ***6219*** *p197*
Shaw, John; Washington, 1859-1920 ***2872.1*** *p36*
Shaw, John 6; Massachusetts, 1850 ***5881.1*** *p91*
Shaw, John 19; St. John, N.B., 1866 ***5704.8*** *p167*
Shaw, John 20; Jamaica, 1730 ***3690.1*** *p202*
Shaw, John 22; Baltimore, 1775 ***1219.7*** *p270*
Shaw, Jon.; Virginia, 1638 ***6219*** *p118*
Shaw, Jon.; Virginia, 1642 ***6219*** *p191*
Shaw, Joseph; Indiana, 1849 ***9117*** *p18*
Shaw, Joseph; Philadelphia, 1742 ***3652*** *p56*
Shaw, Kenneth *SEE* Shaw, Angus
Shaw, Kitt; North Carolina, 1764 ***1639.20*** *p282*
Shaw, Lachlan; South Carolina, 1761 ***1639.20*** *p282*
Shaw, Leslie; New York, NY, 1886 ***1450.2*** *p37B*
Shaw, Margaret; New York, NY, 1811 ***2859.11*** *p19*
Shaw, Margaret 8; Quebec, 1853 ***5704.8*** *p105*
Shaw, Marian 74; North Carolina, 1850 ***1639.20*** *p282*
Shaw, Martha 22; Quebec, 1854 ***5704.8*** *p118*
Shaw, Mary; Philadelphia, 1816 ***2859.11*** *p42*
Shaw, Mary; Philadelphia, 1870 ***5704.8*** *p239*

Shaw, Mary 17; Quebec, 1853 ***5704.8*** *p105*
Shaw, Mathew; South Carolina, 1820 ***1639.20*** *p282*
Shaw, Matilda; Quebec, 1851 ***5704.8*** *p82*
Shaw, Matthew; America, 1804 ***1639.20*** *p282*
Shaw, Matthew 51; North Carolina, 1850 ***1639.20*** *p282*
Shaw, Matthew Holfred 22; Maryland, 1773 ***1219.7*** *p172*
Shaw, Nancy 91; North Carolina, 1850 ***1639.20*** *p282*
Shaw, Neil; America, 1802 ***1639.20*** *p282*
Shaw, Nich.; Virginia, 1637 ***6219*** *p108*
Shaw, Owen 21; Philadelphia, 1774 ***1219.7*** *p219*
Shaw, Peter; South Carolina, 1716 ***1639.20*** *p282*
Shaw, Rebecca; Philadelphia, 1870 ***5704.8*** *p239*
Shaw, Rebeccah 20; America, 1706 ***2212*** *p47*
Shaw, Richard; Virginia, 1639 ***6219*** *p154*
Shaw, Richard 21; Maryland or Virginia, 1699 ***2212*** *p24*
Shaw, Richard 22; St. Christopher, 1730 ***3690.1*** *p291*
Shaw, Robert; Philadelphia, 1816 ***2859.11*** *p42*
Shaw, Robert 21; Maryland, 1774 ***1219.7*** *p207*
Shaw, Rose; Philadelphia, 1816 ***2859.11*** *p42*
Shaw, Sarah 54; North Carolina, 1850 ***1639.20*** *p283*
Shaw, Thomas; Philadelphia, 1816 ***2859.11*** *p42*
Shaw, Thomas 19; Maryland, 1736 ***3690.1*** *p202*
Shaw, Thomas 48; North Carolina, 1850 ***1639.20*** *p283*
Shaw, William; America, 1800 ***1639.20*** *p283*
Shaw, William; Baltimore, 1811 ***2859.11*** *p19*
Shaw, William; New York, NY, 1811 ***2859.11*** *p19*
Shaw, William; Raleigh, NC, 1763-1827 ***1639.20*** *p283*
Shaw, William; South Carolina, 1716 ***1639.20*** *p283*
Shaw, William; Virginia, 1643 ***6219*** *p203*
Shaw, William 21; Maryland, 1775 ***1219.7*** *p267*
Shaw, William 65; North Carolina, 1850 ***1639.20*** *p283*
Shaw, Wm.; Philadelphia, 1816 ***2859.11*** *p42*
Shaw, Wm.; Virginia, 1636 ***6219*** *p21*
Shawaker, Conrad; Pennsylvania, 1749 ***2444*** *p209*
*Brother:*Martin
Shawaker, Martin *SEE* Shawaker, Conrad
Shawbooke, Jon.; Virginia, 1635 ***6219*** *p70*
Shawe, Nicho.; Virginia, 1636 ***6219*** *p74*
Shawkling, James; New York, NY, 1811 ***2859.11*** *p19*
Shay, Dennis 1; Massachusetts, 1850 ***5881.1*** *p89*
Shay, James; New York, 1830 ***1450.2*** *p133A*
Shay, Julia 6; Massachusetts, 1850 ***5881.1*** *p91*
Shay, Thomas; Washington Co., MD, 1835 ***1450.2*** *p133A*
Shay, Thomas 40; Kansas, 1880 ***5240.1*** *p61*
Shayler, William; New England, 1764 ***1219.7*** *p98*
Shea, Bridget 20; Massachusetts, 1849 ***5881.1*** *p88*
Shea, Bridget 25; Massachusetts, 1849 ***5881.1*** *p88*
Shea, Catharine 17; Massachusetts, 1850 ***5881.1*** *p88*
Shea, Charles; Washington, 1859-1920 ***2872.1*** *p36*
Shea, Cornelius; America, 1737 ***4971*** *p55*
Shea, Cornelius; New York, 1847 ***1450.2*** *p133A*
Shea, Daniel 21; Massachusetts, 1850 ***5881.1*** *p89*
Shea, Daniel 29; Massachusetts, 1847 ***5881.1*** *p88*
Shea, Dennis; America, 1742 ***4971*** *p56*
Shea, Ellen 26; Massachusetts, 1850 ***5881.1*** *p89*
Shea, Fany; Quebec, 1820 ***7603*** *p81*
Shea, Florence 5; Massachusetts, 1850 ***5881.1*** *p89*
Shea, Gillen; America, 1738 ***4971*** *p52*
Shea, James 20; Massachusetts, 1847 ***5881.1*** *p90*
Shea, James 50; Massachusetts, 1849 ***5881.1*** *p90*
Shea, Johanna 20; Massachusetts, 1849 ***5881.1*** *p91*
Shea, John; Quebec, 1815 ***7603*** *p82*
Shea, John 18; Massachusetts, 1849 ***5881.1*** *p90*
Shea, Kate 19; Massachusetts, 1849 ***5881.1*** *p91*
Shea, Kitty 20; Massachusetts, 1849 ***5881.1*** *p91*
Shea, Margaret 11; Massachusetts, 1850 ***5881.1*** *p92*
Shea, Margaret 20; Massachusetts, 1849 ***5881.1*** *p92*
Shea, Mary; America, 1737 ***4971*** *p13*
Shea, Mary 5; Massachusetts, 1850 ***5881.1*** *p92*
Shea, Mary 25; Massachusetts, 1847 ***5881.1*** *p91*
Shea, Maurice 50; Massachusetts, 1849 ***5881.1*** *p92*
Shea, Michael; Indiana, 1836-1839 ***1450.2*** *p133A*
Shea, Michael; Ohio, 1847 ***1450.2*** *p133A*
Shea, Michael; Quebec, 1825 ***7603*** *p79*
Shea, Michael; Quebec, 1836 ***1450.2*** *p133A*
Shea, Michael 10; Massachusetts, 1850 ***5881.1*** *p92*
Shea, Michael 20; Massachusetts, 1849 ***5881.1*** *p92*
Shea, Murtogh; America, 1742 ***4971*** *p56*
Shea, Patrick; America, 1743 ***4971*** *p54*
Shea, Patrick 18; Massachusetts, 1847 ***5881.1*** *p93*
Shea, Roger; New York, 1847 ***1450.2*** *p133A*
Shea, Thomas 9; Massachusetts, 1849 ***5881.1*** *p93*
Shea, Thomas 12; Massachusetts, 1849 ***5881.1*** *p93*
Shea, Thomas 26; Massachusetts, 1850 ***5881.1*** *p93*
Shea, Thomas 43; Arizona, 1885 ***9228.40*** *p1*
Shea, Thomas R.; America, 1847 ***1450.2*** *p133A*
Shea, Timothy; America, 1738 ***4971*** *p39*
Shea, William 25; Massachusetts, 1850 ***5881.1*** *p93*
Sheaghan, Daniel; America, 1742 ***4971*** *p17*
Sheaghan, Joan; America, 1742 ***4971*** *p53*
Sheaghan, Laurence; America, 1742 ***4971*** *p54*
Sheahan, James; Illinois, 1857 ***2896.5*** *p37*
Sheahan, John; Illinois, 1880 ***2896.5*** *p37*
Sheahan, John; Illinois, 1881 ***2896.5*** *p37*
Sheahan, Thomas; Illinois, 1860 ***2896.5*** *p37*
Sheales, Anne; Quebec, 1849 ***5704.8*** *p52*
Sheals, Rose 18; Philadelphia, 1853 ***5704.8*** *p111*
Shealy, John; America, 1741 ***4971*** *p41*
Shean, Elinor 60; Philadelphia, 1803 ***53.26*** *p82*
Shean, Julia 15; Massachusetts, 1848 ***5881.1*** *p90*
Shean, Patrick; Illinois, 1860 ***2896.5*** *p37*
Shean, Timothy 31; Maryland, 1774 ***1219.7*** *p191*
Shean, Walter; Maryland, 1740 ***4971*** *p91*
Shean, Walter; Philadelphia, 1741 ***4971*** *p92*
Sheapard, Thomas; Virginia, 1652 ***6251*** *p20*
Sheapheard, Wm; Virginia, 1698 ***2212*** *p13*
Shear, Charles; Arkansas, 1918 ***95.2*** *p112*
Shearan, Catherine 40; St. John, N.B., 1854 ***5704.8*** *p119*
Shearan, John 40; St. John, N.B., 1854 ***5704.8*** *p119*
Shearan, Peter 12; St. John, N.B., 1854 ***5704.8*** *p119*
Sheare, Georg; Virginia, 1637 ***6219*** *p82*
Shearer, Donald; Quebec, 1815 ***7603*** *p36*
Shearer, Joseph; St. John, N.B., 1853 ***5704.8*** *p107*
Shearer, Mathew; New York, NY, 1816 ***2859.11*** *p42*
Shearman, Abra.; Virginia, 1648 ***6219*** *p245*
Sheat, George 20; Jamaica, 1730 ***3690.1*** *p202*
Sheate, George 20; Jamaica, 1730 ***3690.1*** *p202*
Shedoran, Jonathan Leonard; Philadelphia, 1762 ***9973.7*** *p36*
Shee, Arthur; New York, NY, 1811 ***2859.11*** *p19*
Sheeban, Walter; America, 1740 ***4971*** *p15*
Sheeham, Dennis 39; Maryland, 1774 ***1219.7*** *p215*
Sheehan, Cornelius; America, 1741 ***4971*** *p49*
Sheehan, Helen; Montreal, 1824 ***7603*** *p98*
Sheehan, Jeremiah; Montreal, 1825 ***7603*** *p65*
Sheehan, John; America, 1741 ***4971*** *p41*
Sheehan, John; Wilmington, DE, 1841 ***7036*** *p123*
Sheehan, John; Wisconsin, n.d. ***9675.8*** *p66*
Sheehan, Micheal; Washington, 1859-1920 ***2872.1*** *p37*
Sheehan, Pat 56; Arizona, 1916 ***9228.40*** *p20*
Sheehan, Patrick; America, 1742-1743 ***4971*** *p42*
Sheehan, Thomas; America, 1741 ***4971*** *p42*
Sheehan, Thomas; Shreveport, LA, 1877 ***7129*** *p45*
Sheehane, Richard; America, 1741 ***4971*** *p49*
Sheehey, Mary; New York, NY, 1816 ***2859.11*** *p42*
Sheehy, Edmond; Quebec, 1825 ***7603*** *p67*
Sheehy, Johanna 30; Newport, RI, 1851 ***6508.5*** *p20*
Sheehy, Michael; Boston, 1831 ***7036*** *p118*
Sheehy, Owen; America, 1737-1738 ***4971*** *p39*
Sheehy, Roger; America, 1736-1743 ***4971*** *p57*
Sheela, Conrad 38; California, 1871 ***2769.8*** *p5*
Sheelan, John; America, 1741 ***4971*** *p42*
Sheelock, Patrick 23; Quebec, 1864 ***5704.8*** *p160*
Sheels, Cormick; St. John, N.B., 1847 ***5704.8*** *p2*
Sheely, Eugene; Boston, 1839 ***7036*** *p121*
Sheen, Nicolaus; Minnesota, 1874 ***5240.1*** *p41*
Sheen, Patrick 21; Maryland, 1775 ***1219.7*** *p259*
Sheen, Thomas; America, 1851 ***6014.1*** *p3*
Sheenan, Cornelius 9; Massachusetts, 1849 ***5881.1*** *p88*
Sheenan, Margaret 11; Massachusetts, 1849 ***5881.1*** *p92*
Sheenan, Margaret 46; Massachusetts, 1849 ***5881.1*** *p92*
Sheerin, Ann *SEE* Sheerin, John
Sheerin, Ann; Philadelphia, 1847 ***5704.8*** *p22*
Sheerin, Ann 6 *SEE* Sheerin, John
Sheerin, Ann 6; Philadelphia, 1847 ***5704.8*** *p22*
Sheerin, Bridget; St. John, N.B., 1847 ***5704.8*** *p11*
Sheerin, Catherine 17; Philadelphia, 1854 ***5704.8*** *p120*
Sheerin, Catherine 50; Philadelphia, 1853 ***5704.8*** *p109*
Sheerin, Daniel 24; Philadelphia, 1804 ***53.26*** *p82*
Sheerin, Eliza 3 *SEE* Sheerin, John
Sheerin, Eliza 3; Philadelphia, 1847 ***5704.8*** *p22*
Sheerin, Ellan; St. John, N.B., 1850 ***5704.8*** *p67*
Sheerin, John; Philadelphia, 1847 ***53.26*** *p82*
*Relative:*Ann
*Relative:*Ann 6
*Relative:*Eliza 3
Sheerin, John; Philadelphia, 1847 ***5704.8*** *p22*
Sheerin, John; Philadelphia, 1852 ***5704.8*** *p96*
Sheering, James 26; St. John, N.B., 1861 ***5704.8*** *p149*
Sheeron, Elizabeth; St. John, N.B., 1851 ***5704.8*** *p77*
Sheers, James; Virginia, 1639 ***6219*** *p161*
Sheers, William; Virginia, 1600-1643 ***6219*** *p200*
Sheffer, Alexander; Philadelphia, 1758 ***9973.7*** *p33*
Sheffer, Andreas; Philadelphia, 1760 ***9973.7*** *p34*
Sheffer, George Jacob; Philadelphia, 1765 ***9973.7*** *p40*
Sheffer, Valentine 30; Pennsylvania, 1753 ***4525*** *p244*
Shefftgen, Dominic; Wisconsin, n.d. ***9675.8*** *p66*
Sheghane, David; America, 1742 ***4971*** *p56*
Shehan, Cornelius H.; New York, NY, 1836 ***8208.4*** *p25*
Shehan, Ellen 1; Massachusetts, 1849 ***5881.1*** *p89*
Shehan, Ellen 20; Massachusetts, 1849 ***5881.1*** *p66*
Shehan, Mary 30; Massachusetts, 1849 ***5881.1*** *p92*
Shehay, Bernard; New York, 1841 ***7036*** *p126*
Shehy, Charles; America, 1698 ***2212*** *p8*
Shehy, Mary Ann 26; Massachusetts, 1849 ***5881.1*** *p91*
Sheil, Cain 10; Philadelphia, 1853 ***5704.8*** *p102*
Sheil, Catharine 2; Massachusetts, 1850 ***5881.1*** *p88*
Sheil, Edward; Philadelphia, 1853 ***5704.8*** *p103*
Sheil, James; Philadelphia, 1853 ***5704.8*** *p102*
Sheil, Mandy 12; Philadelphia, 1853 ***5704.8*** *p102*
Sheil, Mary; Philadelphia, 1853 ***5704.8*** *p102*
Sheil, Paddy; Philadelphia, 1853 ***5704.8*** *p102*
Sheilds, . . . 2 mos; New York, NY, 1864 ***5704.8*** *p169*
Sheilds, Anthony 10; New York, NY, 1864 ***5704.8*** *p169*
Sheilds, Catherine 14; Philadelphia, 1858 ***5704.8*** *p139*
Sheilds, Dorras; New York, NY, 1868 ***5704.8*** *p229*
Sheilds, Eleanor 28; St. John, N.B., 1864 ***5704.8*** *p157*
Sheilds, John; Philadelphia, 1864 ***5704.8*** *p171*
Sheilds, John 12; Quebec, 1852 ***5704.8*** *p90*
Sheilds, John 29; St. John, N.B., 1864 ***5704.8*** *p157*
Sheilds, Margaret; New York, NY, 1868 ***5704.8*** *p229*
Sheilds, Mary; New York, NY, 1864 ***5704.8*** *p169*
Sheilds, Mary 9; Quebec, 1852 ***5704.8*** *p90*
Sheilds, Michael; Philadelphia, 1864 ***5704.8*** *p171*
Sheilds, Samuel; New York, NY, 1868 ***5704.8*** *p229*
Sheilheimer, . . .; Canada, 1776-1783 ***9786*** *p34*
Sheill, Jane; Massachusetts, 1850 ***5881.1*** *p91*
Sheill, Lawrence 10; Massachusetts, 1850 ***5881.1*** *p91*
Sheils, Agnes; Philadelphia, 1869 ***5704.8*** *p234*
Sheils, Andrew; America, 1866 ***5704.8*** *p213*
Sheils, Andrew; New York, NY, 1865 ***5704.8*** *p173*
Sheils, Ann; Philadelphia, 1852 ***5704.8*** *p87*
Sheils, Biddy *SEE* Sheils, Kate
Sheils, Biddy; Philadelphia, 1847 ***5704.8*** *p24*
Sheils, Biddy 7; Philadelphia, 1858 ***5704.8*** *p139*
Sheils, Catherine *SEE* Sheils, Con
Sheils, Catherine; Philadelphia, 1848 ***5704.8*** *p45*
Sheils, Con; Philadelphia, 1848 ***53.26*** *p82*
*Relative:*Catherine
Sheils, Con; Philadelphia, 1848 ***5704.8*** *p45*
Sheils, Elizabeth; Philadelphia, 1852 ***5704.8*** *p85*
Sheils, Elleanor; New Orleans, 1849 ***5704.8*** *p59*
Sheils, Ellen *SEE* Sheils, Michael
Sheils, Ellen; Philadelphia, 1847 ***5704.8*** *p24*
Sheils, Fanny; St. John, N.B., 1850 ***5704.8*** *p61*
Sheils, Hannah 1 *SEE* Sheils, Kate
Sheils, Hannah 1; Philadelphia, 1847 ***5704.8*** *p24*
Sheils, James 16; Philadelphia, 1853 ***5704.8*** *p108*
Sheils, John 20; Philadelphia, 1865 ***5704.8*** *p164*
Sheils, Kate; Philadelphia, 1847 ***53.26*** *p82*
*Relative:*Hannah 1
*Relative:*Biddy
Sheils, Kate; Philadelphia, 1847 ***5704.8*** *p24*
Sheils, Magy *SEE* Sheils, Michael
Sheils, Magy; Philadelphia, 1847 ***5704.8*** *p24*
Sheils, Margaret 7; Philadelphia, 1858 ***5704.8*** *p139*
Sheils, Margaret 16; Philadelphia, 1864 ***5704.8*** *p157*
Sheils, Margaret 18; Philadelphia, 1853 ***5704.8*** *p108*
Sheils, Martin; Philadelphia, 1869 ***5704.8*** *p234*
Sheils, Mary; New York, NY, 1865 ***5704.8*** *p194*
Sheils, Mary 11; Philadelphia, 1852 ***5704.8*** *p92*
Sheils, Mary 20; Philadelphia, 1858 ***5704.8*** *p139*
Sheils, Michael; Philadelphia, 1847 ***53.26*** *p82*
*Relative:*Magy
*Relative:*Ellen
Sheils, Michael; Philadelphia, 1847 ***5704.8*** *p23*
Sheils, Patrick 20; Philadelphia, 1864 ***5704.8*** *p157*
Sheils, Rosanna; New York, NY, 1869 ***5704.8*** *p234*
Sheils, Rose; New York, NY, 1867 ***5704.8*** *p219*
Sheils, Rosey; St. John, N.B., 1850 ***5704.8*** *p65*
Sheils, Shely; Philadelphia, 1852 ***5704.8*** *p92*
Sheils, Susan 18; Philadelphia, 1864 ***5704.8*** *p157*
Sheils, Susan 20; Philadelphia, 1865 ***5704.8*** *p164*
Sheils, Thomas; New Orleans, 1848 ***5704.8*** *p48*
Shein, Jean 47; America, 1836 ***778.5*** *p495*
Shein, John; America, 1835 ***1450.2*** *p133A*
Shelan, Catharine 12; Massachusetts, 1847 ***5881.1*** *p88*
Shelan, Michael 40; Massachusetts, 1847 ***5881.1*** *p91*
Shelburne, Margaret; South Carolina, 1767 ***1639.20*** *p283*
Shelden, Ellen 19; Massachusetts, 1847 ***5881.1*** *p89*
Shelden, Joseph 25; Massachusetts, 1847 ***5881.1*** *p90*
Sheldon, James; Quebec, 1853 ***5704.8*** *p104*
Shelin, Wolfank; South Carolina, 1752-1753 ***3689.17*** *p22*
With wife
With mother
Shell, John; Virginia, 1643 ***6219*** *p203*
Shelley, Patrick S.; Illinois, 1892 ***5012.39*** *p53*
Shelley, Thomas; Virginia, 1642 ***6219*** *p191*
Shellich, Adam; Philadelphia, 1765 ***9973.7*** *p40*
Shellmerdine, John 18; Jamaica, 1725 ***3690.1*** *p202*
Shellom, Peter; Virginia, 1698 ***2212*** *p16*
Shelly, Roger; Virginia, 1637 ***6219*** *p109*
Shelstein, Mr. 24; Port uncertain, 1839 ***778.5*** *p495*
Shelton, Catherine 17; Maryland, 1738 ***3690.1*** *p203*
Shelton, Fr.; Virginia, 1638 ***6219*** *p11*
Shelton, James; New York, NY, 1837 ***8208.4*** *p52*
Shelton, Rich.; Virginia, 1638 ***6219*** *p149*
Shelton, Thomas 28; Jamaica, 1734 ***3690.1*** *p202*
Shenan, Ann; St. John, N.B., 1847 ***5704.8*** *p21*

Shendler, George 16 *SEE* Shendler, Henry
Shendler, Henry; South Carolina, 1752-1753 ***3689.17*** *p22*
With wife
*Relative:*Simon 20
*Relative:*George 16
Shendler, Simon 20 *SEE* Shendler, Henry
Shenirn, Elizabeth 50; Maryland, 1774 ***1219.7*** *p178*
With daughter
Shenk, Louis; Nebraska, 1892 ***5240.1*** *p41*
Shenock, Will 16; Virginia, 1699 ***2212*** *p27*
Shepard, James E.; America, 1851 ***1450.2*** *p134A*
Shepard, Susan; Virginia, 1643 ***6219*** *p206*
Shepardson, B. F.; Washington, 1859-1920 ***2872.1*** *p37*
Shephard, John 23; Virginia, 1775 ***1219.7*** *p261*
Shephard, Roger 27; Maryland, 1775 ***1219.7*** *p262*
Shepherd, Christopher 33; Kansas, 1883 ***5240.1*** *p41*
Shepherd, Christopher 33; Kansas, 1883 ***5240.1*** *p64*
Shepherd, Effie; Virginia, 1790-1863 ***1639.20*** *p284*
Shepherd, Elizabeth 36; New York, 1774 ***1219.7*** *p202*
*Child:*Molly 4
*Child:*John 2
Shepherd, Georg Wilhelm; Cincinnati, 1819 ***8582.3*** *p87*
Shepherd, James; New York, NY, 1811 ***2859.11*** *p19*
Shepherd, Jane; New York, NY, 1816 ***2859.11*** *p42*
Shepherd, John; New York, NY, 1838 ***8208.4*** *p84*
Shepherd, John 2 *SEE* Shepherd, Elizabeth
Shepherd, John 22; Philadelphia, 1774 ***1219.7*** *p182*
Shepherd, John 75; South Carolina, 1850 ***1639.20*** *p284*
Shepherd, Margaret; America, 1735-1743 ***4971*** *p8*
Shepherd, Margaret; New York, NY, 1816 ***2859.11*** *p42*
Shepherd, Molly 4 *SEE* Shepherd, Elizabeth
Shepherd, Richard; New York, NY, 1816 ***2859.11*** *p42*
Shepherd, Samuel 16; Philadelphia, 1774 ***1219.7*** *p197*
Shepherd, Simpson; New York, NY, 1816 ***2859.11*** *p42*
Shepherd, Thomas; America, 1740 ***4971*** *p69*
Shepherd, Thomas R.; Virginia, 1844 ***4626.16*** *p13*
Shepherd, William; Iowa, 1866-1943 ***123.54*** *p44*
Shepherd, William 20; Maryland, 1725 ***3690.1*** *p202*
Shepherd, William 21; Maryland, 1773 ***1219.7*** *p173*
Sheppard, Albert; Arkansas, 1918 ***95.2*** *p112*
Sheppard, Alec; Austin, TX, 1886 ***9777*** *p5*
Sheppard, Ann *SEE* Sheppard, Jon.
Sheppard, Carl; Savannah, GA, 1779 ***8582.2*** *p52*
Sheppard, George G.; New York, NY, 1836 ***8208.4*** *p58*
Sheppard, James; Philadelphia, 1815 ***2859.11*** *p42*
With wife
Sheppard, John; Virginia, 1642 ***6219*** *p187*
Sheppard, Jon.; Virginia, 1638 ***6219*** *p123*
Sheppard, Jon.; Virginia, 1642 ***6219*** *p199*
*Wife:*Ann
Sheppard, Jon.; Virginia, 1643 ***6219*** *p199*
Sheppard, Peter; Philadelphia, 1815 ***2859.11*** *p42*
With wife
Sheppard, Priscilla *SEE* Sheppard, Robert
Sheppard, Priscilla; Pennsylvania, 1682 ***4963*** *p38*
Sheppard, Robert; Virginia, 1635 ***6219*** *p70*
*Wife:*Priscilla
Shepper, Julius; Illinois, 1886 ***5012.39*** *p120*
Shepperd, John; Virginia, 1638 ***6219*** *p160*
Shepperd, Priscilla; Pennsylvania, 1682 ***4960*** *p158*
Shepperd, Richard; Virginia, 1644 ***6219*** *p231*
Shepperd, William; Virginia, 1642 ***6219*** *p195*
Sheppherd, William 20; Maryland, 1725 ***3690.1*** *p202*
Sheran, Andrew; New York, NY, 1816 ***2859.11*** *p42*
Sherbeck, Paul Jansen; New York, 1750 ***3652*** *p74*
Sherbin, Peter 22; Massachusetts, 1850 ***5881.1*** *p93*
Sherborne, James; Virginia, 1642 ***6219*** *p193*
Sherbourne, James; Virginia, 1639 ***6219*** *p161*
Sherdan, Mary 8; St. John, N.B., 1848 ***5704.8*** *p39*
Sherdan, Patrick 10; St. John, N.B., 1848 ***5704.8*** *p39*
Sherdan, Sicily 13; St. John, N.B., 1848 ***5704.8*** *p39*
Sherdan, Susan; St. John, N.B., 1848 ***5704.8*** *p39*
Sherdette, Mr.; Quebec, 1815 ***9229.18*** *p76*
Sherdon, Brigitte; Montreal, 1821 ***7603*** *p88*
Sherdon, Jane; New York, NY, 1815 ***2859.11*** *p42*
Sherdon, Thomas; New York, NY, 1815 ***2859.11*** *p42*
Shere, Strength; Virginia, 1621 ***6219*** *p34*
Sheridan, Ann 20; Massachusetts, 1848 ***5881.1*** *p87*
Sheridan, Barney 17; Massachusetts, 1848 ***5881.1*** *p87*
Sheridan, Bridget; Philadelphia, 1852 ***5704.8*** *p96*
Sheridan, Charles; New York, NY, 1838 ***8208.4*** *p71*
Sheridan, Daniel 20; Massachusetts, 1849 ***5881.1*** *p89*
Sheridan, Edward; New York, NY, 1837 ***8208.4*** *p32*
Sheridan, Edward; New York, NY, 1838 ***8208.4*** *p74*
Sheridan, Eliza 21; Massachusetts, 1847 ***5881.1*** *p89*
Sheridan, James 40; Newfoundland, 1789 ***4915.24*** *p56*
Sheridan, John; America, 1736 ***4971*** *p12*
Sheridan, John; America, 1741 ***4971*** *p70*
Sheridan, John 10; Massachusetts, 1850 ***5881.1*** *p91*
Sheridan, John 50; Massachusetts, 1847 ***5881.1*** *p90*
Sheridan, John 70; Massachusetts, 1847 ***5881.1*** *p90*
Sheridan, Mary 50; Massachusetts, 1849 ***5881.1*** *p92*
Sheridan, Michael; America, 1890 ***1450.2*** *p134A*
Sheridan, Nugent 13; St. John, N.B., 1847 ***5704.8*** *p18*
Sheridan, Patrick; America, 1739 ***4971*** *p85*
Sheridan, Patrick; Illinois, 1858 ***5012.39*** *p54*
Sheridan, Patrick; New York, NY, 1835 ***8208.4*** *p79*
Sheridan, Patrick; New York, NY, 1836 ***8208.4*** *p22*
Sheridan, Patrick 28; Massachusetts, 1849 ***5881.1*** *p93*
Sheridan, Thomas; Arkansas, 1918 ***95.2*** *p112*
Sheridan, Thomas; New York, NY, 1836 ***8208.4*** *p59*
Sheridan, William; West Virginia, 1856 ***9788.3*** *p20*
Sheriffs, Tho.; Virginia, 1649 ***6219*** *p253*
Sherin, Ann; St. John, N.B., 1853 ***5704.8*** *p98*
Sherin, Catherine; St. John, N.B., 1849 ***5704.8*** *p48*
Sherin, Charles 30; Philadelphia, 1861 ***5704.8*** *p148*
Sherin, John; St. John, N.B., 1853 ***5704.8*** *p98*
Sherlacke, John; Virginia, 1643 ***6219*** *p33*
Sherlock, Edward; Ohio, 1844 ***9892.11*** *p41*
Sherlock, John; America, 1742 ***4971*** *p29*
Sherlock, John; Annapolis, MD, 1742 ***4971*** *p93*
Sherlock, John; Maryland, 1742 ***4971*** *p106*
Sherlock, John; Ohio, 1844 ***9892.11*** *p41*
Sherlock, Martin; Ohio, 1844 ***9892.11*** *p41*
Sherlock, Patrick; New York, NY, 1811 ***2859.11*** *p19*
Sherlock, Patrick; Virginia, 1856 ***4626.16*** *p16*
Sherlock, Robert; Philadelphia, 1816 ***2859.11*** *p42*
Sherly, Agnes; Virginia, 1637 ***6219*** *p24*
Sherly, Eliz.; Virginia, 1636 ***6219*** *p21*
Sherman, . . .; Canada, 1776-1783 ***9786*** *p34*
Sherman, Agnes 17; America, 1699 ***2212*** *p28*
Sherman, Elis; Arkansas, 1918 ***95.2*** *p112*
Sherman, Fanny 21; New Orleans, 1835 ***778.5*** *p495*
Sherman, Henry; Washington, 1859-1920 ***2872.1*** *p37*
Sherman, James; Virginia, 1643 ***6219*** *p202*
Shermer, William 71; Virginia, 1774 ***1219.7*** *p206*
Sheron, James; St. John, N.B., 1847 ***5704.8*** *p11*
Sherpin, John 36; Maryland, 1730 ***3690.1*** *p202*
Sherra, John; Philadelphia, 1847 ***53.26*** *p82*
Sherra, John; Philadelphia, 1847 ***5704.8*** *p13*
Sherran, Thomas; New York, NY, 1811 ***2859.11*** *p19*
Sherrard, Catherine 4; Quebec, 1853 ***5704.8*** *p103*
Sherrard, Dorcus; Quebec, 1853 ***5704.8*** *p103*
Sherrard, James; Quebec, 1853 ***5704.8*** *p103*
Sherrard, William 9; Quebec, 1853 ***5704.8*** *p103*
Sherratt, John; West Virginia, 1843-1844 ***9788.3*** *p20*
Sherridan, Christopher; Montreal, 1814 ***7603*** *p91*
Sherridan, Hubert; Quebec, 1822 ***7603*** *p91*
Sherridan, Patrick; New York, NY, 1838 ***8208.4*** *p87*
Sherridan, Rose; Quebec, 1822 ***7603*** *p83*
Sherridan, Sarah; Philadelphia, 1870 ***5704.8*** *p239*
Sherrin, Elizabeth; St. John, N.B., 1847 ***5704.8*** *p11*
Sherrin, Letitia; St. John, N.B., 1849 ***5704.8*** *p48*
Sherry, Dennis; America, 1739 ***4971*** *p63*
Sherry, John; America, 1737 ***4971*** *p12*
Sherry, John; Colorado, 1902 ***9678.2*** *p168*
Sherry, John 34; Philadelphia, 1804 ***53.26*** *p82*
Sherry, Philippe; Quebec, 1822 ***7603*** *p53*
Sherry, Samuel 22; Virginia, 1775 ***1219.7*** *p261*
Sherry, Victor 42?; Arizona, 1890 ***2764.35*** *p64*
Shert, David; Illinois, 1849 ***2896.5*** *p37*
Shert, Frederick David; New Orleans, 1841 ***2896.5*** *p37*
Shertle, John; Pennsylvania, 1752 ***2444*** *p210*
Sherwood, Daniel 24; Jamaica, 1738 ***3690.1*** *p202*
Sherwood, Frederick; New York, NY, 1873 ***9678.2*** *p168*
Sherwood, Henry; New York, NY, 1838 ***8208.4*** *p68*
Sherwood, Hump.; Virginia, 1648 ***6219*** *p250*
Sherwood, Jacob 13; Maryland or Virginia, 1699 ***2212*** *p24*
Sherwood, John; Virginia, 1639 ***6219*** *p155*
Sherwood, John 23; Kansas, 1871 ***5240.1*** *p51*
Sherwood, Reuben 47; Kansas, 1879 ***5240.1*** *p60*
Sherwood, Sarah 17; Virginia, 1699 ***2212*** *p26*
Sherwood, Thomas 17; Maryland, 1723 ***3690.1*** *p202*
Sherwood, William 21; Nova Scotia, 1774 ***1219.7*** *p209*
Sheskran, Catherine 21; Philadelphia, 1853 ***5704.8*** *p113*
Sheston, John 23; Maryland, 1775 ***1219.7*** *p247*
Shetzlein, Barth'a; Pennsylvania, 1752 ***4525*** *p241*
Shetzline, Bartholomew; Pennsylvania, 1752 ***4525*** *p241*
Shevan, Margaret 24; Massachusetts, 1848 ***5881.1*** *p91*
Shevelan, Ann 15; Massachusetts, 1849 ***5881.1*** *p87*
Sheyry, Mathew; Pennsylvania, 1752 ***4525*** *p241*
Sheythe, E. G.; Washington, 1859-1920 ***2872.1*** *p37*
Shibely, Christian; Philadelphia, 1759 ***9973.7*** *p34*
Shick, Martin; South Carolina, 1788 ***7119*** *p201*
Shides, Patrick; Ohio, 1868 ***6014.2*** *p7*
Shiel, Ann 8; Massachusetts, 1850 ***5881.1*** *p87*
Shiel, Betty 9; Massachusetts, 1850 ***5881.1*** *p88*
Shiel, Nancy; America, 1867 ***5704.8*** *p222*
Shiel, Terence; New York, 1834 ***1450.2*** *p134A*
Shiel, Thomas 30; Philadelphia, 1833-1834 ***53.26*** *p82*
Shield, Bridget; America, 1866 ***5704.8*** *p210*
Shield, George; Quebec, 1775 ***1219.7*** *p271*
Shield, Martin 22; Maryland, 1774 ***1219.7*** *p221*
Shield, Michel; Montreal, 1825 ***7603*** *p90*
Shield, Patrick; New York, NY, 1838 ***8208.4*** *p70*
Shield, Thos.; Virginia, 1638 ***6219*** *p2*
Shields, Edward 20; America, 1868 ***5704.8*** *p225*
Shields, Elizabeth 52; South Carolina, 1850 ***1639.20*** *p284*
*Relative:*Jane 45
Shields, Ellen; America, 1868 ***5704.8*** *p231*
Shields, Ellen; Philadelphia, 1864 ***5704.8*** *p177*
Shields, Frindley; New York, NY, 1815 ***2859.11*** *p42*
Shields, George; Philadelphia, 1811 ***2859.11*** *p19*
Shields, Hannah; America, 1868 ***5704.8*** *p231*
Shields, Henry; America, 1803 ***1639.20*** *p284*
Shields, Henry; Ohio, 1839 ***9892.11*** *p41*
Shields, Henry; Ohio, 1841 ***9892.11*** *p41*
Shields, Jane 45 *SEE* Shields, Elizabeth
Shields, John; America, 1865 ***5704.8*** *p204*
Shields, Mary; Philadelphia, 1851 ***5704.8*** *p77*
Shields, Michael; Pennsylvania, 1885 ***5240.1*** *p41*
Shields, Owen; New York, NY, 1835 ***8208.4*** *p4*
Shields, Patrick 50; Ohio, 1865 ***6014.1*** *p3*
Shields, William, Jr.; New York, NY, 1816 ***2859.11*** *p42*
Shields, William, Sr.; New York, NY, 1816 ***2859.11*** *p42*
Shiele, Martin; South Carolina, 1788 ***7119*** *p199*
Shiell, Catharine 4; Massachusetts, 1850 ***5881.1*** *p88*
Shiels, Ambrose; New York, NY, 1864 ***5704.8*** *p176*
Shiels, Daniel 21; Philadelphia, 1774 ***1219.7*** *p228*
Shiels, Ellen; New York, NY, 1865 ***5704.8*** *p191*
Shiels, Ellen; Philadelphia, 1867 ***5704.8*** *p220*
Shiels, John; New York, NY, 1866 ***5704.8*** *p205*
Shiels, John; St. John, N.B., 1853 ***5704.8*** *p107*
Shiels, Kate; Philadelphia, 1867 ***5704.8*** *p217*
Shilawa, Max; Wisconsin, n.d. ***9675.8*** *p66*
Shill, Mary 19; Maryland, 1720 ***3690.1*** *p202*
Shilliam, William; Arizona, 1889 ***2764.35*** *p63*
Shilling, John 17; Jamaica, 1739 ***3690.1*** *p203*
Shillingford, William 18; Jamaica, 1773 ***1219.7*** *p168*
Shillington, James; St. John, N.B., 1847 ***5704.8*** *p18*
Shilton, Catherine 17; Maryland, 1738 ***3690.1*** *p203*
Shimel, William; Philadelphia, 1760 ***9973.7*** *p34*
Shimkus, John; Wisconsin, n.d. ***9675.8*** *p66*
Shimmins, Mary A. 10; New York, NY, 1864 ***5704.8*** *p170*
Shinds, Bridget 20; Philadelphia, 1861 ***5704.8*** *p147*
Shine, Cornelius; America, 1895 ***1450.2*** *p134A*
Shine, John 31; Virginia, 1774 ***1219.7*** *p238*
Shinluig, J.; New York, NY, 1811 ***2859.11*** *p19*
With family
Shinn, Ellen 7; New York, NY, 1865 ***5704.8*** *p193*
Shinnick, James; America, 1742 ***4971*** *p50*
Shinnick, John; America, 1742 ***4971*** *p49*
Shinnick, John; America, 1742 ***4971*** *p50*
Shinnie, Alexander; America, 1751 ***8893*** *p262*
Shinnie, Alexander; Charleston, SC, 1821 ***1639.20*** *p284*
Shipcot, Thomas; Virginia, 1648 ***6219*** *p237*
Shipley, Alfred L.; New York, NY, 1836 ***8208.4*** *p14*
Shipley, Chas 66; Arizona, 1915 ***9228.40*** *p19*
Shipley, Elizabeth 25 *SEE* Shipley, Thomas
Shipley, Frederick W.; New York, NY, 1836 ***8208.4*** *p14*
Shipley, Henry; New York, NY, 1838 ***8208.4*** *p83*
Shipley, Sarah 3 *SEE* Shipley, Thomas
Shipley, Sarah 17; Maryland, 1719 ***3690.1*** *p203*
Shipley, Thomas 1 *SEE* Shipley, Thomas
Shipley, Thomas 31; North America, 1774 ***1219.7*** *p199*
*Wife:*Elizabeth 25
*Child:*Sarah 3
*Child:*Thomas 1
Shippey, Edw.; Virginia, 1637 ***6219*** *p113*
Shippey, Elizabeth; Virginia, 1635 ***6219*** *p72*
Shippey, John; Virginia, 1617 ***6219*** *p11*
Shippey, Thomas; Virginia, 1635 ***6219*** *p72*
Shipton, Thomas 21; Maryland, 1774 ***1219.7*** *p187*
Shira, Nicholas; Pennsylvania, 1768 ***4779.3*** *p14A*
Shire, Nicholas; Pennsylvania, 1768 ***4779.3*** *p14A*
Shirelant, . . .; Canada, 1776-1783 ***9786*** *p34*
Shires, Thomas; Colorado, 1888 ***9678.2*** *p168*
Shires, William 29; Nova Scotia, 1774 ***1219.7*** *p209*
Shirle, Tho.; Virginia, 1643 ***6219*** *p206*
Shirley, G. W.; Washington, 1859-1920 ***2872.1*** *p37*
Shiro, Giovacchino; Iowa, 1866-1943 ***123.54*** *p77*
Shirra, Nicolas; Pennsylvania, 1768 ***4779.3*** *p14A*
Shirras, Alexander; Charleston, SC, 1781 ***1639.20*** *p284*
Shiskey, Bridget; New York, NY, 1864 ***5704.8*** *p175*
Shiskey, Susan; New York, NY, 1864 ***5704.8*** *p175*
Shittleton, William 19; Virginia, 1721 ***3690.1*** *p203*
Shitz, Peter; Philadelphia, 1759 ***9973.7*** *p34*
Shiven, Mrs.; Philadelphia, 1866 ***5704.8*** *p207*
Shiven, James 2; Philadelphia, 1866 ***5704.8*** *p207*
Shiven, John; Philadelphia, 1866 ***5704.8*** *p207*
Shivlen, Catherine 9; St. John, N.B., 1851 ***5704.8*** *p78*
Shivlen, Charles; St. John, N.B., 1851 ***5704.8*** *p78*
Shivlen, John 7; St. John, N.B., 1851 ***5704.8*** *p78*
Shivlen, Mary; St. John, N.B., 1851 ***5704.8*** *p78*
Shivlen, Peter; St. John, N.B., 1851 ***5704.8*** *p78*

Shivlen, Sally; St. John, N.B., 1851 ***5704.8*** *p78*
Shkrubei, Jozep; Wisconsin, n.d. ***9675.8*** *p66*
Shlegel, Christoph; Pennsylvania, 1751 ***2444*** *p211*
Shleis, Conrad; South Carolina, 1788 ***7119*** *p204*
Shleppy, Albrecht; Pennsylvania, 1751 ***2444*** *p144*
Shleppy, Albrecht; Pennsylvania, 1751 ***2444*** *p212*
Shlessman, John; Pennsylvania, 1753 ***4525*** *p242*
Shlogan, A. 41; Arizona, 1901 ***9228.40*** *p8*
Shneider, Jean 29; New Orleans, 1838 ***778.5*** *p495*
Shobrooke, Philip 32; Maryland, 1774 ***1219.7*** *p224*
Shocksti, Frank; Arkansas, 1918 ***95.2*** *p112*
Shoemaker, Mr.; America, 1639-1739 ***9898*** *p46*
With wife
Shoemaker, Frederich; Illinois, 1860 ***5012.38*** *p98*
Shoemaker, Hans Jacob; Pennsylvania, 1749 ***2444*** *p215*
Shoemaker, Henry; Washington, 1859-1920 ***2872.1*** *p37*
Shoemaker, Johann Frederick; Illinois, 1871 ***5012.39*** *p25*
Shoemaker, John Jacob; Philadelphia, 1760 ***9973.7*** *p34*
Shoer, John C.; Wisconsin, n.d. ***9675.8*** *p66*
Shoffel, Catharine 2; Louisiana, 1839 ***778.5*** *p495*
Shoffel, Catharine 25; Louisiana, 1839 ***778.5*** *p495*
Shofin, Andrew Joseph 15; New Orleans, 1838 ***778.5*** *p495*
Shofin, Catherine 13; New Orleans, 1838 ***778.5*** *p495*
Shofin, Nicolas 23; New Orleans, 1838 ***778.5*** *p496*
Sholdt, Carl I.; Colorado, 1906 ***9678.2*** *p168*
Sholl, John; South Carolina, 1788 ***7119*** *p203*
Sholtz, George; Philadelphia, 1760 ***9973.7*** *p35*
Sholtz, Lawrence; Ohio, 1842 ***8365.25*** *p12*
Shonelock, Hen.; Virginia, 1642 ***6219*** *p192*
Shonts, Blanche; Iowa, 1866-1943 ***123.54*** *p77*
Shor, Joe 34; Kansas, 1901 ***5240.1*** *p82*
Shord, John 23; Leeward Islands, 1724 ***3690.1*** *p203*
Shore, James; Virginia, 1636 ***6219*** *p80*
Shore, James; Virginia, 1639 ***6219*** *p161*
Shore, John; Virginia, 1636 ***6219*** *p80*
Shore, John; Virginia, 1639 ***6219*** *p161*
Shore, Kath.; Virginia, 1636 ***6219*** *p80*
Shore, Katherine; Virginia, 1639 ***6219*** *p161*
Shore, Richard 20; Maryland, 1721 ***3690.1*** *p203*
Shorlin, Charles; Arkansas, 1918 ***95.2*** *p112*
Short, Mr.; North Carolina, 1683-1817 ***3702.7*** *p2*
Short, Adam; Pennsylvania, 1682 ***4960*** *p159*
*Sibling:*Miriam
*Sibling:*Ann
Short, Ann *SEE* Short, Adam
Short, Bernard; New York, NY, 1840 ***7036*** *p123*
Short, Charles 35; Massachusetts, 1848 ***5881.1*** *p88*
Short, Dane; Quebec, 1847 ***5704.8*** *p13*
Short, Jane; Philadelphia, 1865 ***5704.8*** *p195*
Short, John; New York, NY, 1838 ***8208.4*** *p69*
Short, John; New York, NY, 1838 ***8208.4*** *p72*
Short, John; Pennsylvania, 1752 ***4779.3*** *p14A*
Short, John 21; Maryland, 1774 ***1219.7*** *p220*
Short, John 33; Philadelphia, 1774 ***1219.7*** *p182*
Short, Margaret 10; Massachusetts, 1847 ***5881.1*** *p91*
Short, Miriam *SEE* Short, Adam
Short, Patrick 12; Massachusetts, 1847 ***5881.1*** *p93*
Short, Robert; Virginia, 1643 ***6219*** *p203*
Short, Samuel 28; Maryland, 1775 ***1219.7*** *p256*
Short, William; Virginia, 1639 ***6219*** *p18*
Short, William; Virginia, 1639 ***6219*** *p155*
Short, Wm.; North America, 1850 ***4535.11*** *p53*
With 8 children
With wife
Short, Wm.; Virginia, 1635 ***6219*** *p26*
Shorte, William; Virginia, 1639 ***6219*** *p157*
Shorten, Hester 7; Massachusetts, 1850 ***5881.1*** *p90*
Shorten, John 9; Massachusetts, 1850 ***5881.1*** *p91*
Shorten, Mary; Virginia, 1636 ***6219*** *p21*
Shorter, John; Virginia, 1638 ***6219*** *p125*
Shortgen, Peter; Wisconsin, n.d. ***9675.8*** *p66*
Shorthell, Robert; America, 1736-1743 ***4971*** *p58*
Shortley, William; America, 1741 ***4971*** *p94*
Shortly, William; America, 1741 ***4971*** *p10*
Shorton, Hannah 7; Massachusetts, 1850 ***5881.1*** *p90*
Shotelier, Mr. 20; New Orleans, 1835 ***778.5*** *p496*
Shotter, . . .; Pennsylvania, n.d. ***1034.18*** *p22*
Shoub, Jacob; Illinois, 1862 ***2896.5*** *p37*
Shoubell, Mr. 16; New Orleans, 1826 ***778.5*** *p496*
Shouldom, Thomas; Quebec, 1716 ***7603*** *p27*
Shous, Frederick; Philadelphia, 1760 ***9973.7*** *p35*
Shout, John; Pennsylvania, 1769 ***2444*** *p209*
Shove, John 29; Maryland, 1775 ***1219.7*** *p264*
Shovlin, Peter; Philadelphia, 1865 ***5704.8*** *p186*
Showland, Daniel; America, 1697 ***2212*** *p4*
Shraden, Margaret; South Carolina, 1752-1753 ***3689.17*** *p22*
Shrader, Julianna; South Carolina, 1752-1753 ***3689.17*** *p23*
Shrater, Florain; Ohio, 1843 ***9892.11*** *p42*
Shrater, Florain; Ohio, 1846 ***9892.11*** *p42*
Shrauber, Christian; Virginia, 1852 ***4626.16*** *p14*
Shreck, Nicholas 34; Pennsylvania, 1753 ***4525*** *p246*
Shreenan, Patrick; Quebec, 1824 ***7603*** *p53*
Shreiber, Adolphe 4; America, 1838 ***778.5*** *p496*
Shreiber, Eliza 1; Died enroute, 1838 ***778.5*** *p496*
Shrenell, . . .; Canada, 1776-1783 ***9786*** *p34*
Shreve, Joseph 35; Jamaica, 1735 ***3690.1*** *p203*
Shreyer, Anna Catharina *SEE* Shreyer, Christian
Shreyer, Christian; Pennsylvania, 1727 ***1034.18*** *p19*
*Wife:*Elisabetha Kroff
*Child:*Hans Georg
*Child:*Anna Catharina
*Child:*Johannes
*Child:*Joh. Niclas
*Child:*Jacob
Shreyer, Elisabetha Kroff *SEE* Shreyer, Christian
Shreyer, Hans Georg *SEE* Shreyer, Christian
Shreyer, Jacob *SEE* Shreyer, Christian
Shreyer, Joh. Niclas *SEE* Shreyer, Christian
Shreyer, Johannes *SEE* Shreyer, Christian
Shriber, Peter; Philadelphia, 1762 ***9973.7*** *p37*
Shrie, Christian; Illinois, 1858 ***5012.39*** *p54*
Shrier, Jacob; Maryland, 1743 ***1034.18*** *p18*
Shrier, John; Maryland, 1743 ***1034.18*** *p18*
Shrier, Nicholas; Maryland, 1743 ***1034.18*** *p18*
Shrior, Daniel; Ohio, 1842 ***9892.11*** *p42*
Shripf, Jacob; New York, NY, 1837 ***8208.4*** *p34*
Shropshire, Robert 26; Maryland, 1774 ***1219.7*** *p191*
Shrubshall, William J. 45; Kansas, 1879 ***5240.1*** *p59*
Shrum, George Barnard; South Carolina, 1788 ***7119*** *p200*
Shrum, John; Pennsylvania, 1752 ***4779.3*** *p14A*
Shubat, Gladys; Iowa, 1866-1943 ***123.54*** *p44*
Shubert, John F.; Wisconsin, n.d. ***9675.8*** *p66*
Shuer, John; New Orleans, 1847 ***1450.2*** *p134A*
Shugart, Mrs.; America, 1843 ***3702.7*** *p242*
Shuggard, Carl; New York, NY, 1837 ***8208.4*** *p46*
Shuham, Henry Guest 30; California, 1873 ***2769.10*** *p5*
Shukis, John; Wisconsin, n.d. ***9675.8*** *p66*
Shulea, Philipp; Washington, 1859-1920 ***2872.1*** *p37*
Shulmeir, Henry; America, 1837 ***1450.2*** *p134A*
Shulte, Peter 24; Kansas, 1875 ***5240.1*** *p41*
Shulte, Reinhart; Illinois, 1866 ***2896.5*** *p36*
Shultsone, Cathrina; Pennsylvania, 1731 ***1034.18*** *p20*
Shultz, Ben 24; Kansas, 1904 ***5240.1*** *p83*
Shultz, George; Philadelphia, 1758 ***9973.7*** *p33*
Shultz, Jacob; Philadelphia, 1762 ***9973.7*** *p37*
Shultz, John; Pennsylvania, 1753 ***1034.18*** *p19*
Shultz, John; Philadelphia, 1753 ***9973.7*** *p32*
Shultz, John; Philadelphia, 1760 ***9973.7*** *p34*
Shultz, John; Philadelphia, 1762 ***9973.7*** *p37*
Shulze, August; Kansas, 1884 ***5240.1*** *p41*
Shuman, William; New York, NY, 1840 ***8208.4*** *p111*
Shumann, . . .; Canada, 1776-1783 ***9786*** *p34*
Shumet, Antoney 20; Port uncertain, 1838 ***778.5*** *p496*
Shunaghane, William; America, 1735-1743 ***4971*** *p78*
Shupek, Sophie; Iowa, 1866-1943 ***123.54*** *p77*
Shupinsky, Frank; New York, 1885 ***1450.2*** *p37B*
Shuring, William 19; Jamaica, 1775 ***1219.7*** *p248*
Shurlock, Richard; New York, NY, 1839 ***8208.4*** *p91*
Shuster, John; Pennsylvania, 1754 ***2444*** *p215*
Shute, Joseph 20; Virginia, 1775 ***1219.7*** *p247*
Shute, Martin; Virginia, 1642 ***6219*** *p199*
Shuter, Mr.; Quebec, 1815 ***9229.18*** *p74*
With wife
Shuter, Ann; Quebec, 1847 ***5704.8*** *p27*
Shuter, Catherine 13; Quebec, 1847 ***5704.8*** *p27*
Shuter, James 7; Quebec, 1847 ***5704.8*** *p27*
Shuter, Jane; Quebec, 1847 ***5704.8*** *p27*
Shuter, John; Quebec, 1847 ***5704.8*** *p27*
Shuter, John 11; Quebec, 1847 ***5704.8*** *p27*
Shuter, Joseph 5; Quebec, 1847 ***5704.8*** *p27*
Shuter, Joseph 9; Quebec, 1847 ***5704.8*** *p27*
Shuter, Mary Ann; Quebec, 1847 ***5704.8*** *p27*
Shuter, Mary Ann 12; Quebec, 1847 ***5704.8*** *p27*
Shuter, Richard; Quebec, 1847 ***5704.8*** *p27*
Shuter, Richard; Virginia, 1638 ***6219*** *p160*
Shuter, Richard 9 mos; Quebec, 1847 ***5704.8*** *p27*
Shuter, Sidney 9 mos; Quebec, 1847 ***5704.8*** *p27*
Shuter, William 6; Quebec, 1847 ***5704.8*** *p27*
Shuter, William 9; Quebec, 1847 ***5704.8*** *p27*
Shutleworth, Jon.; Virginia, 1642 ***6219*** *p192*
Shuttard, Bernard; South Carolina, 1716 ***1639.20*** *p284*
Shutter, Andreas *SEE* Shutter, Valentin
Shutter, Anna Barbara *SEE* Shutter, Valentin
Shutter, Anna M. Klemmer *SEE* Shutter, Valentin
Shutter, Anna Rosina *SEE* Shutter, Valentin
Shutter, Catharina *SEE* Shutter, Valentin
Shutter, Joh. Hennrich 22 *SEE* Shutter, Valentin
Shutter, Joh. Jacob *SEE* Shutter, Valentin
Shutter, Maria Magdalena *SEE* Shutter, Valentin
Shutter, Valentin 45; Pennsylvania, 1743 ***1034.18*** *p21*
*Wife:*Anna M. Klemmer
*Child:*Joh. Hennrich 22
*Child:*Maria Magdalena
*Child:*Catharina
*Child:*Anna Rosina
*Child:*Andreas
*Child:*Joh. Jacob
*Child:*Anna Barbara
Shwartz, Andreas; Philadelphia, 1763 ***9973.7*** *p38*
Shwenkel, Uhllerich; Pennsylvania, 1751 ***2444*** *p144*
Shweyart, Hans Samuel; Pennsylvania, 1751 ***2444*** *p216*
Shyer, Nichs; Pennsylvania, 1765 ***4779.3*** *p14A*
Shylander, Charles 33; Massachusetts, 1860 ***6410.32*** *p118*
Shyne, Eugene Michael; Arkansas, 1918 ***95.2*** *p112*
Siaberg, John; Colorado, 1894 ***9678.2*** *p168*
Siarnaska, Franciska 26; New York, 1912 ***9980.29*** *p73*
Sias, Jesus 37; Arizona, 1890 ***2764.35*** *p67*
Sibbald, E.W.; Colorado, 1904 ***9678.2*** *p168*
Sibert, Mr. 25; Port uncertain, 1838 ***778.5*** *p496*
Sibery, William 17; Virginia, 1774 ***1219.7*** *p186*
Sibley, John; Jamaica, 1763 ***1219.7*** *p91*
Sibut, Mr. 30; New Orleans, 1839 ***778.5*** *p496*
Sicappa, Frank; Arkansas, 1918 ***95.2*** *p112*
Sicard, Mr.; America, 1839 ***778.5*** *p496*
Sichel, Gustavus; New York, NY, 1850 ***6013.19*** *p88*
Sichel, Philip; Illinois, 1849 ***7857*** *p7*
Sicidiano, Santo; Washington, 1859-1920 ***2872.1*** *p37*
Sickich, Anton; Iowa, 1866-1943 ***123.54*** *p77*
Sickich, John; Iowa, 1866-1943 ***123.54*** *p77*
Sickich, Josie; Iowa, 1866-1943 ***123.54*** *p77*
Sicking, Heinrich; Cincinnati, 1869-1887 ***8582*** *p30*
Sickley, Ann; Virginia, 1698 ***2212*** *p13*
Sicler, John; Arkansas, 1918 ***95.2*** *p112*
Siczkus, Stanislau; Wisconsin, n.d. ***9675.8*** *p66*
Siddall, Robert 23; Virginia, 1700 ***2212*** *p32*
Sidell, Ralph 29; North America, 1774 ***1219.7*** *p200*
Sidener, Mich'l; Pennsylvania, 1754 ***4525*** *p248*
Sidney, Eliza.; Virginia, 1643 ***6219*** *p204*
Sidransky, Boruch; Iowa, 1866-1943 ***123.54*** *p44*
Sidransky, Cipa; Iowa, 1866-1943 ***123.54*** *p44*
Siebel, I. E.; America, 1864 ***8125.8*** *p438*
Siebenhaar, . . .; Canada, 1776-1783 ***9786*** *p34*
Sieber, Fred 22; Kansas, 1889 ***5240.1*** *p74*
Siebern, John N.; Ohio, 1869-1887 ***8582*** *p30*
Siebern, Peter Heinrich; New York, NY, 1837 ***8582*** *p30*
Siebern, S. W.; Cincinnati, 1869-1887 ***8582*** *p30*
Sieberns, Reiner F.; Illinois, 1896 ***5012.40*** *p54*
Siebetslie, . . .; Canada, 1776-1783 ***9786*** *p34*
Siebisch, Gustav 36; Kansas, 1879 ***5240.1*** *p60*
Siebrandt, J. R. 22; Kansas, 1894 ***5240.1*** *p41*
Siebrandt, J. R. 22; Kansas, 1894 ***5240.1*** *p79*
Siebrandt, Peter 52; Kansas, 1890 ***5240.1*** *p75*
Siede, Anna Maria 38; New York, NY, 1857 ***9831.14*** *p154*
Siede, Anna Regina 9; New York, NY, 1857 ***9831.14*** *p154*
Siede, Christine 9 mos; New York, NY, 1857 ***9831.14*** *p154*
Siede, Gottfried 3; New York, NY, 1857 ***9831.14*** *p154*
Siede, Maria 6; New York, NY, 1857 ***9831.14*** *p154*
Siede, Michael 40; New York, NY, 1857 ***9831.14*** *p154*
Siedenfaden, Friderika 22; Kansas, 1881 ***5240.1*** *p63*
Siefert, Joseph; Cincinnati, 1869-1887 ***8582*** *p30*
Sieg, Corneleuis; Kansas, 1900 ***5240.1*** *p41*
Sieg, John; Kansas, 1887 ***5240.1*** *p41*
Siegel, Maurice Edward; Arkansas, 1918 ***95.2*** *p112*
Siegel, Morris James; Arkansas, 1918 ***95.2*** *p112*
Sieger, Catharina *SEE* Sieger, Johannes
Sieger, Christian *SEE* Sieger, Johan Georg
Sieger, Clara Sabina *SEE* Sieger, Johannes
Sieger, Johan Georg; Pennsylvania, 1750 ***2444*** *p218*
*Wife:*Margaretha
*Child:*Christian
Sieger, Johann Daniel *SEE* Sieger, Johannes
Sieger, Johannes 29; Pennsylvania, 1753 ***2444*** *p218*
*Wife:*Catharina
*Child:*Johann Daniel
*Child:*Clara Sabina
Sieger, Margaretha *SEE* Sieger, Johan Georg
Siegers, Peter; Iroquois Co., IL, 1896 ***3455.1*** *p13*
Siegert, Johann Friedrich E.; America, 1835 ***8582.1*** *p32*
With family
Siegfried, John Rudolph 25; Kansas, 1892 ***5240.1*** *p41*
Siegfried, John Rudolph 25; Kansas, 1892 ***5240.1*** *p76*
Siegle, Fred; Iroquois Co., IL, 1896 ***3455.1*** *p13*
Siegle, Minnie; New York, NY, 1895 ***3455.3*** *p105*
Siegler, Faitz; South Carolina, 1752-1753 ***3689.17*** *p22*
With wife
*Relative:*John George 21
*Relative:*Nicholas 18
*Relative:*Jacob 13
With 2 children
Siegler, Jacob 13 *SEE* Siegler, Faitz
Siegler, John F.; California, 1869 ***2764.35*** *p63*

Siegler, John George 21 *SEE* Siegler, Faitz
Siegler, Nicholas 18 *SEE* Siegler, Faitz
Siegler, Paul; Illinois, 1890 2896.5 p37
Siegler, Peter; Philadelphia, 1779 8137 p14
Sieglin, John; Pennsylvania, 1753 2444 p217
Siegmann, Henry John; Arkansas, 1918 95.2 p112
Siegmann, Margarete Dorothee; America, 1845 4815.7 p92
Siegmond, Ludwig; Trenton, NJ, 1776 8137 p14
Siegmund, . . .; Canada, 1776-1783 9786 p43
Siegmund, John; Illinois, 1872 5012.39 p26
Siegrest, Chatrine 30; Port uncertain, 1839 778.5 p496
Siegwart, Leo 28; West Virginia, 1905 9788.3 p21
Siek, Carl Heinrich Wilhelm; America, 1839 4610.10 p97
Sieker, Christian Friedrich; America, 1892 4610.10 p161
Siekermann, Carl Ludwig; America, 1865 4610.10 p149
*Wife:*Wilhelmine Borges
With son
Siekermann, Wilhelmine Borges *SEE* Siekermann, Carl Ludwig
Siekmann, Caroline 4 *SEE* Siekmann, Hermann
Siekmann, Engel 43 *SEE* Siekmann, Hermann
Siekmann, Hermann 6 *SEE* Siekmann, Hermann
Siekmann, Hermann 40; America, 1881 4610.10 p140
*Wife:*Engel 43
*Child:*Hermann 6
*Child:*Caroline 4
Siekmeier, Christine Friederike; America, 1847 4610.10 p111
Sielken, Herman; America, 1871 1450.2 p134A
Sieltom, Alvin; Arkansas, 1918 95.2 p110
Sieltom, Alvin; Arkansas, 1918 95.2 p112
Sielungowska, Rosalia 29; New York, 1912 9980.29 p63
Siem, John; Illinois, 1860 5012.38 p98
Siemantel, Georg; America, 1846 8582.2 p39
Siemer, Herman Henry 26; Kansas, 1900 5240.1 p81
Siemers, F.; Shreveport, LA, 1878 7129 p45
Siemes, Walter; Germantown, PA, 1684 2467.7 p5
Siems, Diedrich Gerhard; New York, NY, 1913 3455.3 p86
*Wife:*Mary
Siems, Diedrich Gerhard; New York, NY, 1913 3455.4 p54
Siems, Mary *SEE* Siems, Diedrich Gerhard
Siener, Jacob; America, 1890 1450.2 p134A
Sienicki, Franciszek; New York, 1831 4606 p177
Sienkiewiog, Ignatz; Arkansas, 1918 95.2 p112
Sier, Martin; Pennsylvania, 1749 4525 p252
Sieren, John; Iowa, 1866-1943 123.54 p44
Sierer, Philip; Pennsylvania, 1752 4525 p252
Siergy, Milczislaw; Arkansas, 1918 95.2 p112
Siermann, Anton; America, 1846 8582.1 p32
Siers, Christian; Virginia, 1855 4626.16 p15
Sieston, Toma; Iowa, 1866-1943 123.54 p44
Sieuzat, Josephine 29; New Orleans, 1839 778.5 p496
Sieveking, Carl; New Orleans, 1853 4610.10 p43
Sieven, Tully; New York, NY, 1811 2859.11 p19
With family
Sievers, Herder P.M. 20; Harris Co., TX, 1899 6254 p6
Sievers, John; Wisconsin, n.d. 9675.8 p66
Sievers, Klaus F. 35; Kansas, 1895 5240.1 p80
Sifker, Mrs.; America, 1893 4610.10 p103
Sifrenhouse, Henry; Illinois, 1855 7857 p7
Sig, Gust; Washington, 1859-1920 2872.1 p37
Sigaloff, Samuel; Arkansas, 1918 95.2 p112
Sigel, . . .; America, 1861-1865 8582.3 p92
Sigelman, Sam; New York, NY, 1896 1450.2 p37B
Siger, Johannes 29; Pennsylvania, 1753 2444 p218
Sigle, Johannes; Pennsylvania, 1746 2444 p217
Sigler, Catharina Barbara; Port uncertain, 1699-1800 2444 p217
Sigler, Jacob; South Carolina, 1788 7119 p198
Siglin, Anna *SEE* Siglin, Johannes
Siglin, Anna *SEE* Siglin, Johannes
Siglin, Anna Justina *SEE* Siglin, Johannes
Siglin, Johann Georg *SEE* Siglin, Johannes
Siglin, Johann Jacob; Pennsylvania, 1746 2444 p217
Siglin, Johann Jacob Heinrich *SEE* Siglin, Johannes
Siglin, Johannes *SEE* Siglin, Johannes
Siglin, Johannes; Pennsylvania, 1746 2444 p217
Siglin, Johannes; Pennsylvania, 1753 2444 p217
*Wife:*Anna
*Child:*Johannes
*Child:*Johann Georg
*Child:*Johann Jacob Heinrich
*Child:*Anna
*Child:*Anna Justina
Sigling, John; Pennsylvania, 1753 2444 p217
Sigmar, Rowland; Virginia, 1639 6219 p22
Sigmundsdottir, Margret 23; Quebec, 1879 2557.1 p39A
Sigmundsdottir, Sigundin 62; Quebec, 1879 2557.1 p20
Sigmundsson, Asvaldur 20; Quebec, 1879 2557.1 p37A
Signaigo, Joseph B.; Virginia, 1855 4626.16 p15
Signaire, Cath.rine 5; Port uncertain, 1839 778.5 p496
Signaire, Charles 4; Port uncertain, 1839 778.5 p496
Signaire, Jean 30; Port uncertain, 1839 778.5 p496
Signaire, Marie 37; Port uncertain, 1839 778.5 p497
Signe, G. 18; New Orleans, 1839 778.5 p497
Signett, Balden; Virginia, 1639 6219 p22
Sigrest, Jacques 37; America, 1837 778.5 p497
Sigurbjorn, Sigbjorn 26; Quebec, 1879 2557.1 p21
Sigurbjornsdottir, Halfridur 17; Quebec, 1879 2557.2 p37
Sigurbjornsdottir, Jacobina 2; Quebec, 1879 2557.1 p21
Sigurbjornsdottir, Siguros 6 mos; Quebec, 1879 2557.2 p36
Sigurbjornsson, Benedikt 6 mos; Quebec, 1879 2557.1 p21
Sigurbjornsson, Gisli 4; Quebec, 1879 2557.1 p38
Sigurbjornsson, Magnus 21; Quebec, 1879 2557.2 p37
Sigurdardottir, Johanna 56; Quebec, 1879 2557.1 p39A
Sigurdardottir, Margret 23; Quebec, 1879 2557.1 p39A
Sigurdardottir, Stefania 27; Quebec, 1879 2557.1 p22
Sigurdsdottir, Benedikt 13; Quebec, 1879 2557.1 p39
Sigurdsdottir, Gudrun 21; Quebec, 1879 2557.1 p39
Sigurdsdottir, Ingibjorg 21; Quebec, 1879 2557.1 p21
*Sister:*Sigridur 25
Sigurdsdottir, Jacobina 2; Quebec, 1879 2557.1 p21
Sigurdsdottir, Rannveig 45; Quebec, 1879 2557.1 p39
Sigurdsdottir, Sigridur 25 *SEE* Sigurdsdottir, Ingibjorg
Sigurdsdottir, Sigurbjorg 58; Quebec, 1879 2557.2 p37
Sigurdsdottir, Stefania 6 mos; Quebec, 1879 2557.2 p36
Sigurdsdottir, Thorbjorg 1; Quebec, 1879 2557.1 p21
Sigurdsson, Benedikt 6 mos; Quebec, 1879 2557.1 p21
Sigurdsson, Benj. 28; Quebec, 1879 2557.1 p38A
Sigurdsson, Bjorn 52; Quebec, 1879 2557.1 p22
Sigurdsson, Einar 28; Quebec, 1879 2557.1 p20
Sigurdsson, Fridsteinur 23; Quebec, 1879 2557.2 p36
Sigurdsson, Sigbjorn 26; Quebec, 1879 2557.1 p21
Sigurdsson, Sigurbogi 42; Quebec, 1879 2557.1 p22
Sigurdsson, Sigurdur 6 *SEE* Sigurdsson, Sigvaldi
Sigurdsson, Sigurdur 23; Quebec, 1879 2557.1 p20
Sigurdsson, Sigurdur 33; Quebec, 1879 2557.1 p21
Sigurdsson, Sigurdur 52; Quebec, 1879 2557.1 p20
Sigurdsson, Sigvaldi 14; Quebec, 1879 2557.2 p36
*Brother:*Vilberg 9
*Brother:*Sigurdur 6
Sigurdsson, Stefan 25; Quebec, 1879 2557.1 p38A
Sigurdsson, Thorkell 27; Quebec, 1879 2557.2 p36
Sigurdsson, Vilberg 9 *SEE* Sigurdsson, Sigvaldi
Sigurjonsdottir, Sesselia 28; Quebec, 1879 2557.2 p36
Sigurjonsdottir, Sigurdur 3; Quebec, 1879 2557.2 p36
Sigwart, Andrew 52; West Virginia, 1898 9788.3 p21
Sigwart, Otto Joseph 22; West Virginia, 1898 9788.3 p21
Sihlegel, Ferdinand; America, 1853 1450.2 p134A
Sikardi, Milivoi; Iowa, 1866-1943 123.54 p44
Sikorska, Josefa 20; New York, 1912 9980.29 p54
With sister
With cousin
Sikorski, . . .; Mexico, 1831-1900 4606 p177
Sikorski, . . .; New York, 1831 4606 p177
Silberberg, Chaje 24; New York, NY, 1878 9253 p46
Silberberg, Marie 1 mo; New York, NY, 1878 9253 p46
Silberberg, Temma 11 mos; New York, NY, 1878 9253 p46
Silberdrath, David; Arkansas, 1918 95.2 p112
Silbernagel, Isaac; America, 1847 8582.1 p32
Silbert, John George; Ohio, 1838 9892.11 p42
Siler, Michaell; Virginia, 1636 6219 p75
Siler, Robert; Virginia, 1639 6219 p181
Silk, Edward 23; North Carolina, 1736 3690.1 p203
Silk, James 21; Baltimore, 1775 1219.7 p269
Silk, Joseph 24; Jamaica, 1736 3690.1 p203
Silker, George Phillip; Illinois, 1857 2896.5 p37
Sill, William; Shreveport, LA, 1878 7129 p45
Sillar, Catherine 23 *SEE* Sillar, Hugh
Sillar, Catherine Currie 62 *SEE* Sillar, Hugh
Sillar, Hugh 55; Wilmington, NC, 1774 1639.20 p284
*Wife:*Catherine Currie 62
*Child:*Mary 27
*Child:*Catherine 23
Sillar, Mary 27 *SEE* Sillar, Hugh
Sillery, William; Ohio, 1844 9892.11 p42
Silley, Edward; Virginia, 1638 6219 p146
Sillingat, Dorothy; Virginia, 1648 6219 p246
With daughter
Sillito, Roger; Virginia, 1643 6219 p206
Sillito, Thomas 18; Virginia, 1739 3690.1 p203
Sills, Mr.; Quebec, 1815 9229.18 p77
Sills, William; Virginia, 1750 3690.1 p203
Silva, John; California, 1867 3840.3 p10
Silva, John; New York, NY, 1838 8208.4 p79
Silva, William; Arkansas, 1918 95.2 p113
Silvain, Issom 26; America, 1836 778.5 p497
Silvas, Mrs. Jesus 31; Arizona, 1926 9228.40 p30
Silver, George; Arkansas, 1918 95.2 p113
Silver, James 32; Maryland, 1774 1219.7 p179
Silver, Mary; Virginia, 1643 6219 p202
Silveras, Francisco 65; Arizona, 1924 9228.40 p28
Silverman, Samuel; Arkansas, 1918 95.2 p113
Silvermann, Lion; Wisconsin, n.d. 9675.8 p66
Silvester, Phillipp; Virginia, 1642 6219 p197
Silvester, Phillipp; Virginia, 1643 6219 p206
Silvis, Henry; Arkansas, 1918 95.2 p113
Silvola, Matti; Washington, 1859-1920 2872.1 p37
Silvy, Anthony; New York, NY, 1836 8208.4 p24
Sim, Francis 33; Port uncertain, 1774 1219.7 p176
Sim, Jane 24 *SEE* Sim, William
Sim, Jane 24 *SEE* Sim, William
Sim, William 24; North Carolina, 1774 1219.7 p189
*Wife:*Jane 24
Sim, William 24; North Carolina, 1774 1639.20 p285
*Wife:*Jane 24
Sima, Mary; America, 1890 7137 p170
Sima, Vasco; America, 1884 7137 p170
Simanouskis, Stanislowa; Wisconsin, n.d. 9675.8 p66
Simans, Patrick; New York, NY, 1838 8208.4 p69
Simas, Manuel; Sacramento Co., CA, 1854 2764.35 p63
Simatovich, Andrew; Iowa, 1866-1943 123.54 p77
Simatovich, Dane; Iowa, 1866-1943 123.54 p77
Simatovich, Dane; Iowa, 1866-1943 123.54 p79
Simatovich, Joseph; Iowa, 1866-1943 123.54 p44
Simatovich, Joseph; Iowa, 1866-1943 123.54 p79
Simatovich, Katie; Iowa, 1866-1943 123.54 p79
Simen, John; Wisconsin, n.d. 9675.8 p66
Simeon, Mrs. 28; America, 1835 778.5 p497
Simeon, Nicolas 50; America, 1837 778.5 p497
Simesca, Marin M.; Arkansas, 1918 95.2 p113
Simgren, John; Maine, 1883-1892 6410.22 p120
Similien, J. B. 27; New Orleans, 1829 778.5 p497
Simler, Johannes; New York, NY, 1837 8208.4 p33
Simm, Susan; Philadelphia, 1851 5704.8 p70
Simma, Carl O.; Illinois, 1900 2896.5 p37
Simma, Willibold; Kansas, 1883 2896.5 p37
Simmer, Sarah 22; New York, 1774 1219.7 p203
Simmerlein, Johannes; Cincinnati, 1800-1877 8582.3 p87
Simmey, Peter; Ohio, 1841 9892.11 p42
Simmonds, Henry 22; Maryland, 1774 1219.7 p181
Simmonds, Jane 23; Jamaica, 1738 3690.1 p204
Simmonds, Mary 16; Maryland, 1775 1219.7 p262
Simmons, Christian 60; North Carolina, 1850 1639.20 p285
Simmons, Edward; Nevada, 1874 2764.35 p61
Simmons, Harry; Iowa, 1866-1943 123.54 p44
Simmons, Jane 23; Jamaica, 1738 3690.1 p204
Simmons, Jeremiah; South Carolina, 1767 1639.20 p285
Simmons, John 25; Jamaica, 1730 3690.1 p291
Simmons, John 52; Philadelphia, 1774 1219.7 p228
Simmons, Joseph 22; Maryland, 1774 1219.7 p192
Simmons, Oliver; Virginia, 1638 6219 p118
Simmons, Sampson; California, 1885 2764.35 p61
Simmons, Thomas; Washington, 1859-1920 2872.1 p37
Simmons, Thomas 21; Maryland, 1774 1219.7 p204
Simmons, Thomas 29; Maryland, 1774 1219.7 p202
Simmozheim, Catharina; Pennsylvania, 1754 2444 p221
Simms, Philip 20; Windward Islands, 1722 3690.1 p220
Simnell, John; Virginia, 1624 6219 p14
Simner, Adam 19; Virginia, 1699 2212 p26
Simon, . . .; Canada, 1776-1783 9786 p43
Simon, Miss 22; America, 1837 778.5 p498
Simon, Mme. 37; Mexico, 1829 778.5 p498
Simon, Mr.; New York, 1837 8582.2 p23
Simon, Mr. 43; New Orleans, 1829 778.5 p497
Simon, Mrs. 35; New Orleans, 1836 778.5 p498
Simon, Alexander; Wisconsin, n.d. 9675.8 p66
Simon, Alexander 12; Quebec, 1847 5704.8 p7
Simon, Alice; Iowa, 1866-1943 123.54 p79
Simon, Alphonse Isidore; Iowa, 1866-1943 123.54 p79
Simon, Anna Maria *SEE* Simon, Lorentz
Simon, Benjamin; Cincinnati, 1869-1887 8582 p30
Simon, Benjamin 36; America, 1853 9162.8 p37
Simon, Carl Edward; Wisconsin, n.d. 9675.8 p66
Simon, Charles 2; New Orleans, 1836 778.5 p497
Simon, Chatrine 52; Port uncertain, 1839 778.5 p497
Simon, Christian 60; Pennsylvania, 1736 2444 p217
Simon, Edward; Missouri, 1836 3702.7 p100
Simon, Eliza 4; Quebec, 1847 5704.8 p7
Simon, Franz; Wisconsin, n.d. 9675.8 p66
Simon, Frederick 21; Philadelphia, 1855 1450.2 p134A
Simon, George 18; Port uncertain, 1839 778.5 p497
Simon, Gregoire; Montreal, 1659 4533 p126
Simon, H. 22; New Orleans, 1827 778.5 p497
Simon, Heinrich 27; Kansas, 1877 5240.1 p58
Simon, Henry; Arkansas, 1918 95.2 p113
Simon, Ignast *SEE* Simon, Meri
Simon, Igwast *SEE* Simon, Marie
Simon, Isabella; Quebec, 1847 5704.8 p7
Simon, Isabella 8; Quebec, 1847 5704.8 p7
Simon, Jacob; Philadelphia, 1762 4349 p47

Simon, Jakob; America, 1762 ***4349*** *p47*
Simon, James; Quebec, 1847 ***5704.8*** *p7*
Simon, Jane; Philadelphia, 1811 ***53.26*** *p82*
Simon, Jane; Philadelphia, 1811 ***2859.11*** *p19*
Simon, Jane 10; Quebec, 1847 ***5704.8*** *p7*
Simon, Janet 9 mos; Quebec, 1847 ***5704.8*** *p7*
Simon, Jean 14; Port uncertain, 1839 ***778.5*** *p497*
Simon, Jean-Baptiste; Louisiana, 1789-1819 ***778.5*** *p556*
Simon, Jesse 48; Port uncertain, 1839 ***778.5*** *p497*
Simon, Johannes *SEE* Simon, Lorentz
Simon, John Frank; Wisconsin, n.d. ***9675.8*** *p66*
Simon, John Jacques 30; America, 1825 ***778.5*** *p497*
Simon, John Peter 38; California, 1872 ***2769.8*** *p4*
Simon, Justine 12; Port uncertain, 1839 ***778.5*** *p498*
Simon, Lorance 30; Pennsylvania, 1736 ***2444*** *p217*
Simon, Lorentz; Pennsylvania, 1753 ***2444*** *p217*
*Wife:*Anna Maria
*Child:*Johannes
*Child:*Maria Elisabetha
Simon, Louis; Iowa, 1866-1943 ***123.54*** *p79*
Simon, M. 30; Mexico, 1829 ***778.5*** *p498*
Simon, M. 34; America, 1832 ***778.5*** *p498*
Simon, M. 42; New Orleans, 1836 ***778.5*** *p498*
Simon, Magdalena 25; Port uncertain, 1839 ***778.5*** *p498*
Simon, Maria Elisabetha *SEE* Simon, Lorentz
Simon, Marie; Sault Ste. Marie, 1913 ***3455.3*** *p82*
*Husband:*Igwast
Simon, Martha; Quebec, 1847 ***5704.8*** *p7*
Simon, Mary 6; Quebec, 1847 ***5704.8*** *p7*
Simon, Mary Ann; Quebec, 1847 ***5704.8*** *p7*
Simon, Mathias; Wisconsin, n.d. ***9675.8*** *p66*
Simon, Meri; New York, NY, 1907 ***3455.4*** *p26*
*Husband:*Ignast
Simon, Nancy; Quebec, 1847 ***5704.8*** *p7*
Simon, Nancy; St. John, N.B., 1848 ***5704.8*** *p44*
Simon, Nathan; Arkansas, 1918 ***95.2*** *p113*
Simon, Nicolaus; Wisconsin, n.d. ***9675.8*** *p66*
Simon, Peter Joseph; Wisconsin, n.d. ***9675.8*** *p66*
Simon, Thomas; Quebec, 1847 ***5704.8*** *p7*
Simona, Francois Marie 25; St. Louis, 1835 ***778.5*** *p498*
Simone, Guisseppi; Arkansas, 1918 ***95.2*** *p113*
Simonet, Louis 23; New Orleans, 1838 ***778.5*** *p498*
Simonet, Louis 30; America, 1839 ***778.5*** *p498*
Simonetto, Bertolo; Iowa, 1866-1943 ***123.54*** *p44*
Simonie, . . .; Canada, 1776-1783 ***9786*** *p34*
Simonin, Francois 19; New Orleans, 1838 ***778.5*** *p498*
Simonini, Geno; Iowa, 1866-1943 ***123.54*** *p79*
Simonini, Guiseppe; Iowa, 1866-1943 ***123.54*** *p44*
Simonnet, Mr. 19; America, 1837 ***778.5*** *p498*
Simons, Mr. 42; America, 1836 ***778.5*** *p498*
Simons, Mrs. 36; America, 1836 ***778.5*** *p499*
Simons, John; Pennsylvania, 1683 ***2155*** *p2*
*Wife:*Maria Lucken
Simons, Maria Lucken *SEE* Simons, John
Simons, Paul 18; New York, 1775 ***1219.7*** *p246*
Simons, Richard 21; Virginia, 1700 ***2212*** *p32*
Simons, Thomas; Bangor, ME, 1849-1868 ***6410.22*** *p115*
Simons, Wolter; Germantown, PA, 1684 ***2155*** *p2*
Simonsen, Anton; Wisconsin, n.d. ***9675.8*** *p66*
Simonsen, Anton Christian S.; Kansas, 1884 ***5240.1*** *p65*
Simonsen, Martin; California, 1887 ***1450.2*** *p135A*
Simonsen, Martin Elias 29; Arkansas, 1918 ***95.2*** *p113*
Simonson, Henry; Washington, 1859-1920 ***2872.1*** *p37*
Simonson, Lauritz Martin; California, 1887 ***1450.2*** *p135A*
Simonson, Levin; Washington, 1859-1920 ***2872.1*** *p37*
Simonson, Simon Peter; Arkansas, 1918 ***95.2*** *p113*
Simony, . . .; Canada, 1776-1783 ***9786*** *p34*
Simpcock, Samuel 24; America, 1700 ***2212*** *p30*
Simpkins, Edward; Virginia, 1637 ***6219*** *p83*
Simpkins, Ralph; Virginia, 1636 ***6219*** *p79*
Simpkins, Ralph; Virginia, 1637 ***6219*** *p85*
Simpson, . . .; New York, NY, 1816 ***2859.11*** *p42*
Simpson, Miss; North Carolina, 1826 ***1639.20*** *p286*
Simpson, Mrs.; Philadelphia, 1848 ***53.26*** *p82*
Simpson, Mrs.; Philadelphia, 1848 ***5704.8*** *p40*
Simpson, Mrs.; Quebec, 1815 ***9229.18*** *p78*
With family
Simpson, Andrew 21; Philadelphia, 1855 ***5704.8*** *p124*
Simpson, Ann 24; Philadelphia, 1774 ***1219.7*** *p195*
Simpson, Archibald; South Carolina, 1753 ***1639.20*** *p285*
Simpson, Catharine 23; Virginia, 1774 ***1219.7*** *p240*
Simpson, Catherine; St. John, N.B., 1852 ***5704.8*** *p95*
Simpson, Catherine 10; St. John, N.B., 1852 ***5704.8*** *p95*
Simpson, Charles 10; Philadelphia, 1855 ***5704.8*** *p124*
Simpson, Charles 22; North America, 1774 ***1219.7*** *p198*
Simpson, Christiana; Quebec, 1822 ***7603*** *p38*
Simpson, David 22; Philadelphia, 1861 ***5704.8*** *p148*
Simpson, Ellen 24; Philadelphia, 1854 ***5704.8*** *p120*
Simpson, Francis 22; Virginia, 1774 ***1219.7*** *p185*
Simpson, George; Northwest Terr., 1821 ***9775.5*** *p218*
Simpson, George; St. John, N.B., 1847 ***5704.8*** *p19*
Simpson, George 17; Jamaica, 1749 ***3690.1*** *p204*
Simpson, Henry; Illinois, 1870 ***5012.38*** *p99*
Simpson, Hugh; America, 1792 ***1639.20*** *p285*
Simpson, Isabella; St. John, N.B., 1852 ***5704.8*** *p95*
Simpson, Isobel 64; Wilmington, NC, 1774 ***1639.20*** *p212*
Simpson, Jacob; St. John, N.B., 1849 ***5704.8*** *p55*
Simpson, Jacob; St. John, N.B., 1852 ***5704.8*** *p95*
Simpson, James; Charleston, SC, 1770 ***1639.20*** *p285*
Simpson, James; Colorado, 1897 ***9678.2*** *p168*
Simpson, James; New York, NY, 1816 ***2859.11*** *p42*
Simpson, James; Quebec, 1847 ***5704.8*** *p36*
Simpson, James; St. John, N.B., 1847 ***5704.8*** *p20*
Simpson, James 10; Philadelphia, 1855 ***5704.8*** *p124*
Simpson, James 18; St. John, N.B., 1854 ***5704.8*** *p115*
Simpson, James 34; Maryland, 1775 ***1219.7*** *p250*
Simpson, James M. 55; North Carolina, 1850 ***1639.20*** *p285*
Simpson, Jane 17; Philadelphia, 1855 ***5704.8*** *p124*
Simpson, Jane 49; Philadelphia, 1855 ***5704.8*** *p124*
Simpson, John; Jamaica, 1760 ***1219.7*** *p78*
Simpson, John; New York, NY, 1835 ***8208.4*** *p8*
Simpson, John; North Carolina, 1747-1800 ***1639.20*** *p286*
Simpson, John; North Carolina, 1780-1789 ***1639.20*** *p286*
Simpson, John; Philadelphia, 1864 ***5704.8*** *p186*
Simpson, John; St. John, N.B., 1847 ***5704.8*** *p19*
Simpson, John; South Carolina, 1823 ***1639.20*** *p286*
Simpson, John; Virginia, 1639 ***6219*** *p155*
Simpson, John; Virginia, 1643 ***6219*** *p205*
Simpson, John 22; Baltimore, 1775 ***1219.7*** *p270*
Simpson, John 23; Philadelphia, 1855 ***5704.8*** *p124*
Simpson, John 25; Philadelphia, 1803 ***53.26*** *p82*
Simpson, John 26; Massachusetts, 1849 ***5881.1*** *p90*
Simpson, John 27; Philadelphia, 1774 ***1219.7*** *p228*
Simpson, John H.; Colorado, 1867-1892 ***9678.2*** *p168*
Simpson, Joseph 28; Virginia, 1775 ***1219.7*** *p246*
Simpson, Margaret; St. John, N.B., 1847 ***5704.8*** *p19*
Simpson, Mary; Philadelphia, 1852 ***5704.8*** *p91*
Simpson, Mary 25; North America, 1774 ***1219.7*** *p198*
Simpson, Mary Ann; Quebec, 1852 ***5704.8*** *p97*
Simpson, Mary Ann; St. John, N.B., 1852 ***5704.8*** *p95*
Simpson, Mathew; America, 1853 ***1450.2*** *p135A*
Simpson, Mathew 35; Maryland, 1775 ***1219.7*** *p262*
Simpson, Mathew 48; Maryland, 1774 ***1219.7*** *p235*
Simpson, Mordicai 18; Maryland, 1719-1720 ***3690.1*** *p204*
Simpson, Nath.; Quebec, 1830 ***4719.7*** *p21*
Simpson, Patrick; South Carolina, 1694-1794 ***1639.20*** *p286*
Simpson, Patrick; Virginia, 1639 ***6219*** *p155*
Simpson, Peter 50; Virginia, 1774 ***1219.7*** *p215*
Simpson, Rebecca; St. John, N.B., 1849 ***5704.8*** *p55*
Simpson, Rebecca 14; Philadelphia, 1855 ***5704.8*** *p124*
Simpson, Richard 20; Pennsylvania, Virginia or Maryland, 1723 ***3690.1*** *p204*
Simpson, Robert; America, 1811 ***1639.20*** *p286*
Simpson, Robert; New York, NY, 1816 ***2859.11*** *p42*
Simpson, Robert; New York, NY, 1833 ***8208.4*** *p42*
Simpson, Robert; Virginia, 1637 ***6219*** *p115*
Simpson, Robert 31; Virginia, 1774 ***1219.7*** *p238*
Simpson, Thomas; St. John, N.B., 1847 ***5704.8*** *p19*
Simpson, Thomas 10; St. John, N.B., 1847 ***5704.8*** *p19*
Simpson, Thomas 17; Jamaica, 1736 ***3690.1*** *p204*
Simpson, Thomas 36; Maryland, 1775 ***1219.7*** *p272*
Simpson, Walter 21; Maryland, 1773 ***1219.7*** *p173*
Simpson, William; Iowa, 1866-1943 ***123.54*** *p44*
Simpson, William; New York, NY, 1811 ***2859.11*** *p19*
Simpson, William; Philadelphia, 1847 ***53.26*** *p82*
Simpson, William; Philadelphia, 1847 ***5704.8*** *p1*
Simpson, William; St. John, N.B., 1852 ***5704.8*** *p95*
Simpson, William 11; Philadelphia, 1855 ***5704.8*** *p124*
Simpson, William 19; Barbados, 1719 ***3690.1*** *p204*
Simpson, William 20; St. John, N.B., 1854 ***5704.8*** *p120*
Simpson, William 23; South Carolina, 1774 ***1219.7*** *p205*
Simpson, William 53; Philadelphia, 1855 ***5704.8*** *p124*
Simpson, William, Jr.; New York, NY, 1838 ***8208.4*** *p86*
Simpson, Wm.; New York, NY, 1816 ***2859.11*** *p42*
With wife
Sims, Andrew; Virginia, 1635 ***6219*** *p1*
Sims, James 35; Maryland, 1773 ***1219.7*** *p173*
Sims, L. M.; Washington, 1859-1920 ***2872.1*** *p37*
Sims, Thomas 21; Philadelphia, 1775 ***1219.7*** *p274*
Sims, Thomas 27; Jamaica, 1725 ***3690.1*** *p204*
Simsburg, Georg Antoin Manuel B.; New York, NY, 1838 ***8208.4*** *p70*
Simson, James; South Carolina, 1716 ***1639.20*** *p285*
Simson, Rich.; Virginia, 1643 ***6219*** *p207*
Simson, Thomas; Virginia, 1642 ***6219*** *p198*
Simston, Joseph; Quebec, 1851 ***5704.8*** *p73*
Sinanitto, Egidio; Iowa, 1866-1943 ***123.54*** *p44*
Sinatt, Dominico; Arkansas, 1918 ***95.2*** *p113*
Sinckler, Margarett; Virginia, 1638 ***6219*** *p118*
Sinclair, Alexander; South Carolina, 1735 ***1639.20*** *p286*
Sinclair, Alexander; South Carolina, 1804 ***1639.20*** *p286*
Sinclair, Alexander 36; Wilmington, NC, 1774 ***1639.20*** *p286*
With wife & child
With child 18
With child 2
Sinclair, Ann 19; Philadelphia, 1857 ***5704.8*** *p133*
Sinclair, Ann 65; Wilmington, NC, 1775 ***1639.20*** *p287*
*Daughter:*Margaret 25
Sinclair, Daniel 57; South Carolina, 1850 ***1639.20*** *p287*
*Relative:*Flora 53
Sinclair, Diana 21; Jamaica, 1773 ***1219.7*** *p172*
Sinclair, Duncan 24; Wilmington, NC, 1774 ***1639.20*** *p287*
*Wife:*Isobel McIntyre 24
Sinclair, Effie 25 *SEE* Sinclair, Hugh
Sinclair, Ellan Ann; St. John, N.B., 1848 ***5704.8*** *p45*
Sinclair, Flora 53 *SEE* Sinclair, Daniel
Sinclair, Hugh 14; Philadelphia, 1857 ***5704.8*** *p133*
Sinclair, Hugh 60; North Carolina, 1850 ***1639.20*** *p287*
*Relative:*Margaret 62
*Relative:*John 23
*Relative:*Isabella 19
*Relative:*Effie 25
Sinclair, Isabella 19 *SEE* Sinclair, Hugh
Sinclair, Isobel McIntyre 24 *SEE* Sinclair, Duncan
Sinclair, James; Georgia, 1775 ***1219.7*** *p274*
Sinclair, James; Leeward Islands, 1756 ***3690.1*** *p204*
Sinclair, James; West Indies, 1756 ***1219.7*** *p44*
Sinclair, James 7 *SEE* Sinclair, Nancy
Sinclair, James 7; Philadelphia, 1847 ***5704.8*** *p32*
Sinclair, James 21; Wilmington, NC, 1774 ***1639.20*** *p287*
With wife
Sinclair, John 1; Quebec, 1853 ***5704.8*** *p104*
Sinclair, John 18; Virginia, 1750 ***3690.1*** *p204*
Sinclair, John 18; Virginia, 1751 ***1219.7*** *p2*
Sinclair, John 23 *SEE* Sinclair, Hugh
Sinclair, John 24; Massachusetts, 1849 ***5881.1*** *p90*
Sinclair, John 32; Wilmington, NC, 1774 ***1639.20*** *p287*
*Wife:*Mary 33
Sinclair, John 71; North Carolina, 1850 ***1639.20*** *p287*
Sinclair, Margaret; Toronto, 1841 ***8893*** *p266*
Sinclair, Margaret 25 *SEE* Sinclair, Ann
Sinclair, Margaret 45; Philadelphia, 1857 ***5704.8*** *p133*
Sinclair, Margaret 62 *SEE* Sinclair, Hugh
Sinclair, Mary 33 *SEE* Sinclair, John
Sinclair, Mary 70; North Carolina, 1850 ***1639.20*** *p288*
*Relative:*Nancy 62
Sinclair, Mary Jane; Quebec, 1853 ***5704.8*** *p104*
Sinclair, Nancy 9; Philadelphia, 1847 ***53.26*** *p82*
*Relative:*James 7
Sinclair, Nancy 9; Philadelphia, 1847 ***5704.8*** *p32*
Sinclair, Nancy 62 *SEE* Sinclair, Mary
Sinclair, Neil; Wilmington, NC, 1804 ***1639.20*** *p288*
Sinclair, Patrick; South Carolina, 1716 ***1639.20*** *p288*
Sinclair, Peggy; Brunswick, NC, 1767 ***1639.20*** *p288*
Sinclair, Peggy; Georgia, 1775 ***1219.7*** *p275*
Sinclair, Richard; Charleston, SC, 1733 ***1639.20*** *p288*
Sinclaire, Ame; New York, NY, 1811 ***2859.11*** *p19*
Sinclaire, John; New York, NY, 1811 ***2859.11*** *p19*
Sinclaire, Mary; New York, NY, 1811 ***2859.11*** *p19*
Siner, Peter 28; Pennsylvania, 1741 ***4779.3*** *p14A*
Siney, John; Philadelphia, 1851 ***5704.8*** *p71*
Sing, Catharina Hartmann *SEE* Sing, Johann Georg
Sing, Johann Georg *SEE* Sing, Johann Georg
Sing, Johann Georg; Pennsylvania, 1750 ***2444*** *p218*
*Wife:*Catharina Hartmann
*Child:*Johann Georg
Singbusch, Christian; Illinois, 1872 ***5012.39*** *p90*
Singcleare, Jon.; Virginia, 1635 ***6219*** *p17*
Singer, . . .; Canada, 1776-1783 ***9786*** *p34*
Singer, Mr. 20; New Orleans, 1838 ***778.5*** *p499*
Singer, Frederick L.; Colorado, 1890 ***9678.3*** *p13*
Singer, James; New York, NY, 1816 ***2859.11*** *p42*
Singer, Johann; St. Louis, 1851 ***8582.1*** *p32*
Singer, Joseph; Ohio, 1801-1802 ***8582.2*** *p55*
Singers, John 19; Jamaica, 1725 ***3690.1*** *p204*
Singis, Joseph 29; New Orleans, 1835 ***778.5*** *p499*
Single, William 14; Philadelphia, 1774 ***1219.7*** *p197*
Singleton, Ann 23; New England, 1699 ***2212*** *p19*
Singleton, Charles 30; Maryland, 1775 ***1219.7*** *p254*
Singleton, Deborah 25; Massachusetts, 1850 ***5881.1*** *p89*
Singleton, Dennis 3; Massachusetts, 1850 ***5881.1*** *p89*
Singleton, Henry; Virginia, 1637 ***6219*** *p13*
Singleton, John 31; Maryland or Virginia, 1734 ***3690.1*** *p204*
Singleton, William; Massachusetts, 1849 ***5881.1*** *p93*
Singleton, William 15; Maryland, 1774 ***1219.7*** *p211*
Sinkiwicz, Joseph; Wisconsin, n.d. ***9675.8*** *p66*
Sinkler, Alexdr; Virginia, 1698 ***2212*** *p11*
Sinn, Christian; New York, NY, 1911 ***3455.3*** *p16*
*Wife:*Louise
Sinn, George Christian; Philadelphia, 1760 ***9973.7*** *p34*
Sinn, Louise *SEE* Sinn, Christian

Sinner, Conrad; Washington, 1859-1920 ***2872.1*** *p37*
Sinner, Emma; Washington, 1859-1920 ***2872.1*** *p37*
Sinner, George; Washington, 1859-1920 ***2872.1*** *p37*
Sinner, Henry; Washington, 1859-1920 ***2872.1*** *p37*
Sinner, Lizzie; Washington, 1859-1920 ***2872.1*** *p37*
Sinner, Peter; Washington, 1859-1920 ***2872.1*** *p37*
Sinnering, Anna Marie; South Carolina, 1752-1753 ***3689.17*** *p23*
*Relative:*Hans George 5
Sinnering, Hans George 5 *SEE* Sinnering, Anna Marie
Sinnick, James; America, 1742 ***4971*** *p49*
Sinning, Henry; Illinois, 1876 ***2896.5*** *p37*
Sinnot, Nicholas; New York, NY, 1811 ***2859.11*** *p19*
Sinnot, Richard; New York, NY, 1816 ***2859.11*** *p42*
Sinor, Peter 28; Pennsylvania, 1741 ***4779.3*** *p14A*
Sinot, Patrick; New Orleans, 1850 ***2896.5*** *p37*
Sinowsky, Iwan 22; New York, 1912 ***9980.29*** *p58*
Sinquette, Marie; Pennsylvania, 1752 ***2444*** *p143*
Sinquette, Marie; Port uncertain, 1753 ***2444*** *p143*
Sinsgreen, John 35; Philadelphia, 1774 ***1219.7*** *p182*
Sinskins, Peter H.; Wisconsin, n.d. ***9675.8*** *p121*
Sinton, David; Cincinnati, 1869-1885 ***8582.2*** *p52*
Sinton, Henry; New York, NY, 1815 ***2859.11*** *p42*
Sinton, James; New York, NY, 1815 ***2859.11*** *p42*
Sinton, John; New York, NY, 1815 ***2859.11*** *p42*
Sinton, Joseph; New York, NY, 1815 ***2859.11*** *p42*
Sinton, Mary; New York, NY, 1811 ***2859.11*** *p19*
With family
Sinton, Rebecca; New York, NY, 1815 ***2859.11*** *p42*
Sinton, William 21; North America, 1774 ***1219.7*** *p200*
Sinyard, George *SEE* Sinyard, Johnathan
Sinyard, George; Philadelphia, 1848 ***5704.8*** *p45*
Sinyard, Hannah *SEE* Sinyard, Johnathan
Sinyard, Hannah; Philadelphia, 1848 ***5704.8*** *p45*
Sinyard, Johnathan; Philadelphia, 1848 ***53.26*** *p82*
*Relative:*George
*Relative:*Hannah
Sinyard, Jonathin; Philadelphia, 1848 ***5704.8*** *p45*
Sinz, Charles; Illinois, 1874 ***5012.37*** *p59*
Sioerdts, Kornelius; Germantown, PA, 1684 ***2467.7*** *p5*
Sion, Geehand; Illinois, 1888 ***5240.1*** *p41*
Siorts, Kornelius; Germantown, PA, 1684 ***2467.7*** *p5*
Siovens, Mary 17; Maryland, 1775 ***1219.7*** *p249*
Sipnic, Valentine; America, 1885 ***7137*** *p170*
Sipos, John; New York, NY, 1906 ***9892.11*** *p42*
Sire, . . .; New Orleans, 1839 ***778.5*** *p499*
Sire, Miss; New Orleans, 1839 ***778.5*** *p499*
Sire, Mr. 40; Port uncertain, 1839 ***778.5*** *p499*
Sire, Jean; New Orleans, 1839 ***778.5*** *p499*
Sirger, Catharina *SEE* Sirger, Johannes
Sirger, Christian *SEE* Sirger, Johan Georg
Sirger, Clara Sabina *SEE* Sirger, Johannes
Sirger, Johan Georg; Pennsylvania, 1750 ***2444*** *p218*
*Wife:*Margaretha
*Child:*Christian
Sirger, Johann Daniel *SEE* Sirger, Johannes
Sirger, Johannes 29; Pennsylvania, 1753 ***2444*** *p218*
*Wife:*Catharina
*Child:*Johann Daniel
*Child:*Clara Sabina
Sirger, Margaretha *SEE* Sirger, Johan Georg
Sirnsas, Peter; Wisconsin, n.d. ***9675.8*** *p121*
Sirright, David 20; Jamaica, 1774 ***1219.7*** *p178*
Sirvid, Martion; Arkansas, 1918 ***95.2*** *p113*
Siry, . . .; Canada, 1776-1783 ***9786*** *p34*
Sisa, F. 30; Port uncertain, 1838 ***778.5*** *p499*
Siscil, John; Iowa, 1866-1943 ***123.54*** *p44*
Siscock, Jon.; Virginia, 1637 ***6219*** *p108*
Sisk, William; Quebec, 1825 ***7603*** *p63*
Sison, J. B. 30; Port uncertain, 1839 ***778.5*** *p499*
Sisson, Daniel; Virginia, 1652 ***6251*** *p20*
Sisson, William 21; Maryland, 1774 ***1219.7*** *p235*
Sissons, William; New York, NY, 1837 ***8208.4*** *p24*
Sisul, Jim 25; Arkansas, 1918 ***95.2*** *p113*
Sisul, Margareta; Iowa, 1866-1943 ***123.54*** *p79*
Sisul, Mary Ann; Iowa, 1866-1943 ***123.54*** *p79*
Sisul, Vid; Iowa, 1866-1943 ***123.54*** *p79*
Sithgon, William; New York, NY, 1816 ***2859.11*** *p42*
Sitter, Hermann; Wisconsin, n.d. ***9675.8*** *p121*
Sittler, Johann; Illinois, 1844 ***8582.2*** *p51*
Sittner, Rose 23; New Orleans, 1839 ***9420.2*** *p486*
Sivart, Doro 9; New Orleans, 1839 ***9420.2*** *p166*
Siverts, Kornelius; Germantown, PA, 1684 ***2467.7*** *p5*
Sivon, Mr. 42; America, 1838 ***778.5*** *p499*
Siz, Martin 28; New Orleans, 1831 ***778.5*** *p499*
Size, Bernard; Philadelphia, 1811 ***53.26*** *p82*
*Relative:*Hannah
Size, Bernard; Philadelphia, 1811 ***2859.11*** *p19*
Size, Hannah *SEE* Size, Bernard
Size, Hannah; Philadelphia, 1811 ***2859.11*** *p19*
Size, John H.; Colorado, 1892 ***9678.3*** *p13*
Sjablin, Mathus; Chicago, 1868 ***5240.1*** *p41*
Sjoblom, John; Iowa, 1866-1943 ***123.54*** *p45*
Sjoblorn, Louis; Iowa, 1866-1943 ***123.54*** *p45*
Sjogren, John; Colorado, 1904 ***9678.3*** *p13*
Sjolander, C.; Minneapolis, 1879-1883 ***6410.35*** *p65*
Sjorgren, Adil William; Wisconsin, n.d. ***9675.8*** *p121*
Sjostrom, Alfred Leonard; Arkansas, 1918 ***95.2*** *p113*
Skaale, Bessie; Washington, 1859-1920 ***2872.1*** *p37*
Skaale, Christina; Washington, 1859-1920 ***2872.1*** *p37*
Skaale, John Johnson; Washington, 1859-1920 ***2872.1*** *p37*
Skaale, Martin; Washington, 1859-1920 ***2872.1*** *p37*
Skaale, Torkell; Washington, 1859-1920 ***2872.1*** *p37*
Skaar, Chris; Arkansas, 1918 ***95.2*** *p113*
Skaff, George; Indiana, 1894 ***5240.1*** *p41*
Skakel, Alexander; Montreal, n.d. ***9775.5*** *p202*
Skane, Helena; Quebec, 1803 ***7603*** *p79*
Skans, John W.; Washington, 1859-1920 ***2872.1*** *p37*
Skapka, Jesse Leo; Arkansas, 1918 ***95.2*** *p113*
Skeels, George; Indiana, 1836 ***9117*** *p14*
Skehan, Honora 20; St. John, N.B., 1860 ***5704.8*** *p144*
Skeirstat, Cecilia 27; Massachusetts, 1860 ***6410.32*** *p109*
Skelly, William 29; Maryland, 1775 ***1219.7*** *p261*
Skelton, Ann 18; North America, 1774 ***1219.7*** *p198*
Skelton, Jane 36 *SEE* Skelton, John
Skelton, John 25; Nova Scotia, 1774 ***1219.7*** *p210*
Skelton, John 38; Annapolis, N.S., 1775 ***1219.7*** *p262*
*Wife:*Jane 36
Skelton, Ralph; Jamaica, 1775 ***1219.7*** *p277*
Skelton, Thomas 35; Nova Scotia, 1774 ***1219.7*** *p209*
Skelton, William 18; St. Christopher, 1722 ***3690.1*** *p204*
Skelton, William 20; Jamaica, 1733 ***3690.1*** *p205*
Skene, George; South Carolina, 1766 ***1639.20*** *p288*
Skene, James; Charleston, SC, 1766 ***1639.20*** *p289*
Skene, Thomas; South Carolina, 1760 ***1639.20*** *p289*
Skenonia, Andrew; Virginia, 1852 ***4626.16*** *p14*
Skerak, Micahel; America, 1881 ***7137*** *p170*
Skerak, Susan; America, 1882 ***7137*** *p170*
Skerhutt, Jerome; Wisconsin, n.d. ***9675.8*** *p121*
Skeris, Anton; Wisconsin, n.d. ***9675.8*** *p121*
Skerritt, Catharine 28; Massachusetts, 1849 ***5881.1*** *p88*
Skerritt, Edward 30; Massachusetts, 1849 ***5881.1*** *p89*
Skerritt, Mary 6; Massachusetts, 1849 ***5881.1*** *p91*
Skers, Stanley; Arkansas, 1918 ***95.2*** *p113*
Skevan, Bridget 10; Massachusetts, 1850 ***5881.1*** *p88*
Skevan, Catharine 30; Massachusetts, 1850 ***5881.1*** *p88*
Skevan, Lawrence 6; Massachusetts, 1850 ***5881.1*** *p91*
Skevan, Michael 3; Massachusetts, 1850 ***5881.1*** *p92*
Skewes, Richard; Colorado, 1904 ***9678.3*** *p13*
Skibinski, . . .; New York, 1831 ***4606*** *p177*
Skidmore, Augustine; Virginia, 1638 ***6219*** *p33*
Skiffington, John; New York, NY, 1838 ***8208.4*** *p86*
Skiffington, Mark 21; St. John, N.B., 1854 ***5704.8*** *p121*
Skillen, James; America, 1842 ***1450.2*** *p135A*
Skillorne, Dorothy; Virginia, 1639 ***6219*** *p150*
Skimutis, Charles; Wisconsin, n.d. ***9675.8*** *p121*
Skinner, . . .; Canada, 1776-1783 ***9786*** *p34*
Skinner, Antho.; Virginia, 1635 ***6219*** *p20*
Skinner, Charles 17; Pennsylvania, 1738 ***3690.1*** *p205*
Skinner, Charles 28; Maryland, 1774 ***1219.7*** *p218*
Skinner, Elizabeth 20; Maryland, 1774 ***1219.7*** *p207*
Skinner, James 22; Maryland, 1774 ***1219.7*** *p184*
Skinner, John; Indiana, 1850 ***9117*** *p18*
Skinner, John; Maryland, 1756 ***1219.7*** *p43*
Skinner, John; Maryland, 1756 ***3690.1*** *p205*
Skinner, John; Virginia, 1621 ***6219*** *p25*
Skinner, John 20; Maryland, 1733 ***3690.1*** *p205*
Skinner, John 21; Jamaica, 1736 ***3690.1*** *p205*
Skinner, Jon.; Virginia, 1636 ***6219*** *p115*
Skinner, Martin; Virginia, 1643 ***6219*** *p204*
Skinner, Mathew 40; Maryland, 1775 ***1219.7*** *p247*
Skinner, Michael 18; Maryland, 1736 ***3690.1*** *p205*
Skipper, Mrs.; America, 1700-1800 ***1639.20*** *p68*
Skipper, Carl Marinus Jensen; Arkansas, 1918 ***95.2*** *p113*
Skirrey, William 27; Philadelphia, 1774 ***1219.7*** *p175*
Skirrick, Thomas; Virginia, 1638 ***6219*** *p125*
Sklar, Andrew; Arkansas, 1918 ***95.2*** *p113*
Sklavantes, Michael; Iowa, 1866-1943 ***123.54*** *p45*
Sklenar, Andrew; America, 1890 ***7137*** *p170*
Skocilic, Paul; Iowa, 1866-1943 ***123.54*** *p45*
Skoniecni, John; Arkansas, 1918 ***95.2*** *p113*
Skorupski, Ludwik; New York, 1835 ***4606*** *p180*
Skoryiski, . . .; New York, 1831 ***4606*** *p177*
Skorzynski, . . .; New York, 1831 ***4606*** *p177*
Skotsner, Erik; Colorado, 1905 ***9678.3*** *p13*
Skov, Christian; Boston, 1921 ***3455.4*** *p28*
Skow, Carl Peterson; Arkansas, 1918 ***95.2*** *p113*
Skponvic, Bonna; Iowa, 1866-1943 ***123.54*** *p45*
Skripsick, Joseph; Kansas, 1887 ***5240.1*** *p41*
Skripsik, Michael 22; Kansas, 1880 ***5240.1*** *p62*
Skriver, Rasmus R.; Arkansas, 1918 ***95.2*** *p113*
Skrobek, Frederick; Illinois, 1896 ***5012.40*** *p55*
Skroger, James 16; Port uncertain, 1774 ***1219.7*** *p176*
Skruby, John; Wisconsin, n.d. ***9675.8*** *p121*
Skruby, Philip; Wisconsin, n.d. ***9675.8*** *p121*
Skrzynski, Teoder; New York, 1835 ***4606*** *p180*
Skull, John; Virginia, 1643 ***6219*** *p187*
Skuta, Joseph; Arkansas, 1918 ***95.2*** *p113*
Skutzki, Jan 18; New York, 1912 ***9980.29*** *p54*
With 2 cousins
Skynner, William Augustus; Antigua (Antego), 1763 ***1219.7*** *p96*
Slack, Ann 19; Baltimore, 1775 ***1219.7*** *p271*
Slack, John; New York, NY, 1866 ***5704.8*** *p212*
Slack, Martha J.; New York, NY, 1866 ***5704.8*** *p212*
Slack, Mary; Quebec, 1849 ***5704.8*** *p51*
Slacka, Adam; Iowa, 1866-1943 ***123.54*** *p45*
Slade, Daniel 36; Maryland, 1774 ***1219.7*** *p218*
Slade, John 33; Maryland, 1774 ***1219.7*** *p224*
Slade, Thomas 22; Maryland, 1775 ***1219.7*** *p251*
Sladeck, Mathias; Wisconsin, n.d. ***9675.8*** *p121*
Sladek, Frank; Wisconsin, n.d. ***9675.8*** *p121*
Sladkevich, Vlodyslaw; Arkansas, 1918 ***95.2*** *p113*
Slaffery, Owen; America, 1742 ***4971*** *p26*
Slampa, Joe; Arkansas, 1918 ***95.2*** *p113*
Slan, Branko; Wisconsin, n.d. ***9675.8*** *p121*
Slaney, Mary 22; Massachusetts, 1850 ***5881.1*** *p92*
Slater, Abraham; Illinois, 1854 ***7857*** *p7*
Slater, Belford; Illinois, 1855 ***7857*** *p7*
Slater, Isaac; Illinois, 1856 ***7857*** *p7*
Slater, James 21; Philadelphia, 1861 ***5704.8*** *p148*
Slater, John 19; Virginia, 1719 ***3690.1*** *p205*
Slater, John 20; St. John, N.B., 1854 ***5704.8*** *p115*
Slater, John 27; Maryland, 1775 ***1219.7*** *p252*
Slater, Leonard; Virginia, 1639 ***6219*** *p157*
Slater, Nancy 34; St. John, N.B., 1854 ***5704.8*** *p115*
Slater, Tho 20; America, 1703 ***2212*** *p39*
Slater, Thomas; St. John, N.B., 1851 ***5704.8*** *p72*
Slathers, Andrew 18; Massachusetts, 1849 ***5881.1*** *p87*
Slatinsek, John; Wisconsin, n.d. ***9675.8*** *p121*
Slatisnek, Martin; Wisconsin, n.d. ***9675.8*** *p121*
Slator, Alice 20; America, 1701 ***2212*** *p34*
Slator, Ann 6 mos; St. John, N.B., 1851 ***5704.8*** *p79*
Slator, Eliza 2; St. John, N.B., 1851 ***5704.8*** *p79*
Slator, Elizabeth; St. John, N.B., 1851 ***5704.8*** *p79*
Slator, John; St. John, N.B., 1851 ***5704.8*** *p79*
Slattery, Darby; America, 1736-1743 ***4971*** *p58*
Slattery, James; America, 1736-1743 ***4971*** *p58*
Slattery, James; Quebec, 1820 ***7603*** *p82*
Slattery, John; New York, NY, 1811 ***2859.11*** *p19*
Slattery, John 36; Kansas, 1900 ***5240.1*** *p81*
Slattery, Margaret; New York, NY, 1811 ***2859.11*** *p19*
Slattery, Michael F.; Kansas, 1886 ***5240.1*** *p41*
Slattery, Owen; Maryland, 1742 ***4971*** *p106*
Slattery, Patrick; New York, NY, 1816 ***2859.11*** *p42*
Slattery, Patrick 13; Massachusetts, 1850 ***5881.1*** *p93*
Slattery, Peter; New York, NY, 1811 ***2859.11*** *p19*
Slaughfrwan, August; Illinois, 1876 ***7857*** *p7*
Slaughier, Elizabeth *SEE* Slaughier, Georg
Slaughier, Elizabeth *SEE* Slaughier, Georg
Slaughier, Georg; Virginia, 1637 ***6219*** *p111*
*Wife:*Elizabeth
*Daughter:*Elizabeth
*Brother:*Robert
Slaughier, Robert *SEE* Slaughier, Georg
Slaughter, John; Virginia, 1617 ***6219*** *p18*
Slaughter, John; Virginia, 1635 ***6219*** *p72*
Slaughter, Rebecca; Virginia, 1635 ***6219*** *p69*
Slavar, Stef; Iowa, 1866-1943 ***123.54*** *p45*
Slaven, Hannah; America, 1866 ***5704.8*** *p210*
Slavin, Ann; St. John, N.B., 1847 ***5704.8*** *p33*
Slavin, Anne; New York, NY, 1815 ***2859.11*** *p42*
Slavin, Bernard 8; St. John, N.B., 1848 ***5704.8*** *p47*
Slavin, Bridget; St. John, N.B., 1847 ***5704.8*** *p25*
Slavin, Catherine; New York, NY, 1815 ***2859.11*** *p42*
Slavin, Catherine; St. John, N.B., 1847 ***5704.8*** *p25*
Slavin, Catherine 12; St. John, N.B., 1848 ***5704.8*** *p47*
Slavin, Fanny; St. John, N.B., 1847 ***5704.8*** *p33*
Slavin, Francis; New York, NY, 1870 ***5704.8*** *p239*
Slavin, Hannah; New York, NY, 1870 ***5704.8*** *p239*
Slavin, Henry; America, 1863 ***5704.8*** *p169*
Slavin, Hugh; St. John, N.B., 1847 ***5704.8*** *p35*
Slavin, James; New York, NY, 1815 ***2859.11*** *p42*
Slavin, James 27; Massachusetts, 1850 ***5881.1*** *p91*
Slavin, John; St. John, N.B., 1848 ***5704.8*** *p47*
Slavin, Margaret; St. John, N.B., 1848 ***5704.8*** *p47*
Slavin, Mary 6; St. John, N.B., 1848 ***5704.8*** *p47*
Slavin, Michael; New York, NY, 1815 ***2859.11*** *p42*
Slavin, Michael; St. John, N.B., 1848 ***5704.8*** *p47*
Slavin, Michael 4; St. John, N.B., 1848 ***5704.8*** *p47*
Slavin, Patrick; Quebec, 1849 ***5704.8*** *p57*
Slavin, Peter; Philadelphia, 1851 ***5704.8*** *p71*
Slavin, Rose Ann 3 mos; St. John, N.B., 1848 ***5704.8*** *p47*
Slavin, Sarah 10; St. John, N.B., 1848 ***5704.8*** *p47*
Slavney, Leo M.; Arkansas, 1918 ***95.2*** *p114*
Sleat, Joseph; Virginia, 1857 ***4626.16*** *p17*
Slecht, Anna Barbara *SEE* Slecht, Daniel

Smith, Angus; Quebec, 1852 *4537.30 p39*
  *Wife:*Janet Murray MacDonald
  *Child:*Effie
  *Child:*Margaret
  *Child:*Rachel
  *Child:*Donald
  *Child:*Gormelia
  *Child:*John
  *Child:*Allan
  *Child:*Mary
  *Child:*Ann
  With child & stepchild
Smith, Ann *SEE* Smith, Angus
Smith, Ann *SEE* Smith, Angus
Smith, Ann *SEE* Smith, Angus
Smith, Ann *SEE* Smith, Angus
Smith, Ann *SEE* Smith, Donald
Smith, Ann *SEE* Smith, John
Smith, Ann *SEE* Smith, Murdo
Smith, Ann *SEE* Smith, Thomas
Smith, Ann *SEE* Smith, Thomas
Smith, Ann; Quebec, 1842 *4537.30 p74*
Smith, Ann; Quebec, 1851 *4537.30 p86*
Smith, Ann; Quebec, 1865 *4537.30 p101*
Smith, Ann; Virginia, 1635 *6219 p69*
Smith, Ann 6 wks *SEE* Smith, John
Smith, Ann 3; Massachusetts, 1850 *5881.1 p87*
Smith, Ann 19; Pennsylvania, 1724 *3690.1 p206*
Smith, Ann 21; Maryland, 1775 *1219.7 p266*
Smith, Ann MacKay *SEE* Smith, John
Smith, Ann MacLean *SEE* Smith, John
Smith, Anne; Philadelphia, 1868 *5704.8 p231*
Smith, Anne 3; Philadelphia, 1867 *5704.8 p223*
Smith, Archibald; America, 1802 *1639.20 p289*
Smith, Archibald 18; Quebec, 1864 *5704.8 p162*
Smith, Barbara 21; Philadelphia, 1856 *5704.8 p128*
Smith, Barney; New York, NY, 1838 *8208.4 p65*
Smith, Benjamin; Philadelphia, 1852 *5704.8 p96*
Smith, Benjamin 24; Virginia, 1773 *1219.7 p169*
Smith, Bernard; New York, NY, 1815 *2859.11 p42*
Smith, Bessie 18; Philadelphia, 1859 *5704.8 p142*
Smith, Bridget; Philadelphia, 1868 *5704.8 p226*
Smith, Bryan; Virginia, 1638 *6219 p118*
  With wife
Smith, Casper 35; Jamaica, 1736 *3690.1 p206*
Smith, Catharine; New York, NY, 1816 *2859.11 p42*
Smith, Catharine; Philadelphia, 1867 *5704.8 p223*
Smith, Catharine 3; Massachusetts, 1850 *5881.1 p88*
Smith, Catharine 12; Massachusetts, 1849 *5881.1 p88*
Smith, Catharine 18; Massachusetts, 1849 *5881.1 p88*
Smith, Catharine 28; Massachusetts, 1849 *5881.1 p88*
Smith, Catharine 32; Massachusetts, 1850 *5881.1 p88*
Smith, Catherine *SEE* Smith, Angus
Smith, Catherine *SEE* Smith, John
Smith, Catherine *SEE* Smith, Murdo
Smith, Catherine; Montreal, 1822 *7603 p61*
Smith, Catherine; Philadelphia, 1848 *53.26 p82*
Smith, Catherine; Philadelphia, 1857 *5704.8 p80*
Smith, Catherine; Quebec, 1851 *4537.30 p65*
Smith, Catherine; Quebec, 1851 *4537.30 p70*
Smith, Catherine; Quebec, 1851 *5704.8 p74*
Smith, Catherine; St. John, N.B., 1850 *5704.8 p67*
Smith, Catherine 15; Quebec, 1858 *5704.8 p137*
Smith, Catherine 56 *SEE* Smith, Daniel
Smith, Charles *SEE* Smith, John
Smith, Charles; Bangor, ME, 1835-1856 *6410.22 p115*
Smith, Charles; Colorado, 1894 *9678.3 p13*
Smith, Charles; New York, NY, 1834 *8208.4 p38*
Smith, Charles 15; Philadelphia, 1774 *1219.7 p182*
Smith, Charles 24; Maryland, 1775 *1219.7 p254*
Smith, Charles 24; Pennsylvania, 1730 *3690.1 p291*
Smith, Charles 27; Jamaica, 1774 *1219.7 p179*
Smith, Charles F.; Washington, 1859-1920 *2872.1 p37*
Smith, Charles Lewis; Ohio, 1851 *9892.11 p42*
Smith, Charles P.; Utah, 1872 *2764.35 p66*
Smith, Charleton 36; Baltimore, 1775 *1219.7 p269*
Smith, Charlotte 5 *SEE* Smith, Wm.
Smith, Chas. 17 *SEE* Smith, Wm.
Smith, Chas. J.; Iowa, 1866-1943 *123.54 p45*
Smith, Christopher; America, 1741 *4971 p16*
Smith, Christopher; Annapolis, MD, 1742 *4971 p93*
Smith, Christopher; Maryland, 1742 *4971 p17*
Smith, Christopher; New York, NY, 1838 *8208.4 p74*
Smith, Christopher; San Francisco, 1850 *4914.15 p10*
Smith, Christopher 19; Maryland, 1729 *3690.1 p206*
Smith, Christopher 20; Virginia, 1699 *2212 p27*
Smith, Christopher 49; Carolina, 1774 *1219.7 p242*
  *Wife:*Esther 35
Smith, Christy 21; Kansas, 1876 *5240.1 p58*
Smith, Cornelius; New York, NY, 1811 *2859.11 p19*
Smith, D. 57; North Carolina, 1850 *1639.20 p289*
Smith, D. F. 28; Kansas, 1889 *5240.1 p73*
Smith, Daniel; Philadelphia, 1754 *1219.7 p28*

Smith, Daniel; Philadelphia, 1754 *3690.1 p207*
Smith, Daniel; Philadelphia, 1847 *53.26 p82*
  *Relative:*Jane
  *Relative:*Joseph
  *Relative:*William
  *Relative:*David 13
  *Relative:*Martha 12
Smith, Daniel 21; Maryland, 1774 *1219.7 p204*
Smith, Daniel 30; Maryland, 1774 *1219.7 p179*
Smith, Daniel 38; Maryland, 1774 *1219.7 p235*
Smith, Daniel 61; North Carolina, 1850 *1639.20 p290*
  *Relative:*Catherine 56
  *Relative:*Absalom 66
Smith, David; South Carolina, 1716 *1639.20 p290*
Smith, David 13 *SEE* Smith, Daniel
Smith, David 21; Jamaica, 1774 *1219.7 p237*
Smith, David 23; Virginia, 1774 *1219.7 p201*
Smith, David D.; Colorado, 1880 *9678.3 p13*
Smith, David E. 35; California, 1872 *2769.8 p6*
Smith, Dedrick H.; Iroquois Co., IL, 1896 *3455.1 p13*
Smith, Dominic; Wisconsin, n.d. *9675.8 p121*
Smith, Donald *SEE* Smith, Angus
Smith, Donald *SEE* Smith, Angus
Smith, Donald *SEE* Smith, Angus
Smith, Donald *SEE* Smith, John
Smith, Donald *SEE* Smith, John
Smith, Donald *SEE* Smith, Malcolm
Smith, Donald *SEE* Smith, Murdo
Smith, Donald *SEE* Smith, Murdo
Smith, Donald; Quebec, 1853 *4537.30 p40*
  *Wife:*Mary MacLeod
  *Child:*Malcolm
  *Child:*Ann
  *Child:*Isabella
  *Child:*Effie
  *Child:*Norman Hugh
  *Child:*John
Smith, Donald; South Carolina, 1716 *1639.20 p290*
Smith, Donald A.; Northwest Terr., 1888 *9775.5 p218*
Smith, Donald A.; Ontario, n.d. *9775.5 p216*
Smith, Dorithea 6; Philadelphia, 1856 *5704.8 p128*
Smith, Duncan *SEE* Smith, Malcolm
Smith, Duncan; America, 1786 *1639.20 p290*
Smith, Duncan 90; North Carolina, 1850 *1639.20 p290*
  *Relative:*Margaret 80
Smith, Edw.; Virginia, 1637 *6219 p10*
Smith, Edward; Virginia, 1639 *6219 p151*
Smith, Edward; Virginia, 1643 *6219 p205*
Smith, Edward; Wisconsin, n.d. *9675.8 p121*
Smith, Edward 16; New England, 1721 *3690.1 p207*
Smith, Edward 17; Maryland, 1719 *3690.1 p207*
Smith, Edward 29; Jamaica, 1729 *3690.1 p207*
Smith, Edward 30; Jamaica, 1730 *3690.1 p207*
Smith, Edward 34; Maryland, 1774 *1219.7 p179*
Smith, Effie *SEE* Smith, Angus
Smith, Effie *SEE* Smith, Angus
Smith, Effie *SEE* Smith, Donald
Smith, Effie; Quebec, 1841 *4537.30 p78*
Smith, Effie; Quebec, 1841-1900 *4537.30 p38*
  *Daughter:*Isabella
Smith, Effie; Quebec, 1855 *4537.30 p23*
Smith, Effie MacDonald *SEE* Smith, Angus
Smith, Effie MacDonald *SEE* Smith, John
Smith, Eliz.; Virginia, 1635 *6219 p69*
Smith, Eliz. 11 *SEE* Smith, Wm.
Smith, Eliza *SEE* Smith, Robert
Smith, Eliza; New York, NY, 1811 *2859.11 p19*
  With family
Smith, Eliza; New York, NY, 1816 *2859.11 p42*
Smith, Eliza; Philadelphia, 1847 *5704.8 p31*
Smith, Eliza; Virginia, 1642 *6219 p191*
Smith, Eliza.; Virginia, 1647 *6219 p247*
Smith, Eliza 10; Quebec, 1851 *5704.8 p74*
Smith, Eliza 21; Philadelphia, 1854 *5704.8 p120*
Smith, Eliza 24; Quebec, 1862 *5704.8 p151*
Smith, Eliza A.; Philadelphia, 1867 *5704.8 p218*
Smith, Eliza Jane 17; Philadelphia, 1859 *5704.8 p142*
Smith, Elizabeth; America, 1742 *4971 p17*
Smith, Elizabeth 5; Port uncertain, 1838 *778.5 p500*
Smith, Elizabeth 7 *SEE* Smith, Nathaniel
Smith, Elizabeth 17; Maryland, 1718 *3690.1 p207*
Smith, Elizabeth 18; Philadelphia, 1774 *1219.7 p214*
Smith, Elizabeth 20; Maryland, 1727 *3690.1 p207*
Smith, Elizabeth 20; Maryland or Virginia, 1719 *3690.1 p207*
Smith, Elizabeth 25; Maryland, 1774 *1219.7 p180*
Smith, Elizabeth 52 *SEE* Smith, Nathaniel
Smith, Ellen 20; Virginia, 1699 *2212 p27*
Smith, Ellen 36; Massachusetts, 1849 *5881.1 p89*
Smith, Ellis; Virginia, 1641 *6219 p187*
Smith, Emma; New York, NY, 1881 *3455.2 p43*
Smith, Emma; New York, NY, 1881 *3455.3 p107*
Smith, Esther 16; Maryland, 1774 *1219.7 p207*

Smith, Esther 35 *SEE* Smith, Christopher
Smith, Ethem; Wisconsin, n.d. *9675.8 p121*
Smith, Eva I.; Washington, 1859-1920 *2872.1 p37*
Smith, Fanny; St. John, N.B., 1852 *5704.8 p83*
Smith, Farroll 18; Massachusetts, 1848 *5881.1 p89*
Smith, Ferdinand; Wisconsin, n.d. *9675.8 p121*
Smith, Ferdinand 15; Baltimore, 1835 *1450.2 p135A*
Smith, Flora *SEE* Smith, Angus
Smith, Flora *SEE* Smith, John
Smith, Frances *SEE* Smith, James
Smith, Francis; Philadelphia, 1847 *5704.8 p31*
Smith, Francis; Virginia, 1642 *6219 p193*
Smith, Francis 20; Maryland, 1723 *3690.1 p207*
Smith, Francis 24; Jamaica, 1738 *3690.1 p207*
Smith, Francis 29; Massachusetts, 1849 *5881.1 p89*
Smith, Francois; Quebec, 1825 *7603 p23*
Smith, Frank H.; Illinois, 1903 *2896.5 p38*
Smith, Frank P.; Washington, 1859-1920 *2872.1 p37*
Smith, Frederic K.; Virginia, 1852 *4626.16 p14*
Smith, Frederick; Baltimore, 1831 *1450.2 p135A*
Smith, Frederick; Illinois, 1887 *2896.5 p38*
Smith, Frederick 24; Philadelphia, 1851 *1450.2 p135A*
Smith, Frederick B.; New York, NY, 1838 *8208.4 p88*
Smith, Frederick C.; Arkansas, 1918 *95.2 p114*
Smith, Fredrick C.; Arkansas, 1918 *95.2 p114*
Smith, Fulton 20; Quebec, 1863 *5704.8 p154*
Smith, Gabriel 20; Jamaica, 1725 *3690.1 p207*
Smith, Gabriell; Virginia, 1643 *6219 p205*
Smith, Geo. 7 *SEE* Smith, Wm.
Smith, George; Arkansas, 1918 *95.2 p114*
Smith, George; Austin, TX, 1886 *9777 p5*
Smith, George; New York, 1837 *8893 p264*
Smith, George; New York, NY, 1835 *8208.4 p7*
Smith, George; New York, NY, 1835 *8208.4 p43*
Smith, George; New York, NY, 1837 *8208.4 p56*
Smith, George; New York, NY, 1838 *8208.4 p73*
Smith, George; St. John, N.B., 1848 *5704.8 p47*
Smith, George; South Carolina, 1767 *1639.20 p290*
Smith, George; Virginia, 1639 *6219 p157*
Smith, George; Virginia, 1646 *6219 p238*
Smith, George 2 *SEE* Smith, John
Smith, George 18; Virginia, 1774 *1219.7 p243*
Smith, George 21; Philadelphia, 1774 *1219.7 p233*
Smith, George 23; Maryland, 1775 *1219.7 p254*
Smith, George 30; Port uncertain, 1838 *778.5 p500*
Smith, George 33; Kansas, 1874 *5240.1 p55*
Smith, George 42; Kansas, 1884 *5240.1 p66*
Smith, George 60; North Carolina, 1850 *1639.20 p290*
Smith, George F.; Virginia, 1844 *4626.16 p13*
Smith, George M.; Illinois, 1887 *7857 p7*
Smith, Gerhan; America, 1840 *1450.2 p135A*
Smith, Gert; Illinois, 1892 *5012.40 p26*
Smith, Gormelia *SEE* Smith, Angus
Smith, Grace; Virginia, 1635 *6219 p35*
Smith, Grace; Virginia, 1637 *6219 p114*
Smith, Grace 27; Baltimore, 1775 *1219.7 p271*
Smith, Grace 30; New York, 1774 *1219.7 p217*
Smith, Guillaume; Quebec, 1778 *7603 p65*
Smith, Gustaf; Iowa, 1854 *2090 p612*
Smith, H.; Quebec, 1815 *9229.18 p79*
Smith, Hannah; Philadelphia, 1849 *53.26 p83*
Smith, Hannah 1 *SEE* Smith, Robert
Smith, Hannah 1; Philadelphia, 1847 *5704.8 p31*
Smith, Hans 3; New Orleans, 1831 *778.5 p500*
Smith, Harvold; Washington, 1859-1920 *2872.1 p37*
Smith, Helen; Quebec, 1778 *7603 p79*
Smith, Helena; Montreal, 1823 *7603 p61*
Smith, Hen.; Virginia, 1635 *6219 p10*
Smith, Hen.; Virginia, 1642 *6219 p195*
Smith, Henry; America, 1872 *6014.1 p3*
Smith, Henry; New York, NY, 1835 *8208.4 p45*
Smith, Henry; Ohio, 1846 *9892.11 p42*
Smith, Henry; Ohio, 1849 *9892.11 p42*
Smith, Henry; Philadelphia, 1762 *9973.7 p37*
Smith, Henry; Virginia, 1637 *6219 p10*
Smith, Henry; Virginia, 1639 *6219 p155*
Smith, Henry; Virginia, 1639 *6219 p157*
Smith, Henry; Virginia, 1642 *6219 p188*
  *Wife:*Katherine
Smith, Henry 18; Jamaica, 1729 *3690.1 p207*
Smith, Henry 18; Jamaica, 1730 *3690.1 p207*
Smith, Henry 20; St. John, N.B., 1855 *5704.8 p127*
Smith, Henry 22; Jamaica, 1736 *3690.1 p208*
Smith, Henry 24; Virginia, 1774 *1219.7 p201*
Smith, Henry 30; Maryland, 1774 *1219.7 p192*
Smith, Henry 32; Kansas, 1876 *5240.1 p57*
Smith, Henry 56; Philadelphia, 1864 *5704.8 p161*
Smith, Herman; Illinois, 1892 *2896.5 p38*
Smith, Hester; Virginia, 1645 *6219 p233*
Smith, Honora 10; Massachusetts, 1848 *5881.1 p89*
Smith, Hugh; New York, NY, 1815 *2859.11 p42*
Smith, Hugh; New York, NY, 1838 *8208.4 p84*
Smith, Hugh; Philadelphia, 1816 *2859.11 p42*
Smith, Hugh 28; Philadelphia, 1774 *1219.7 p217*

FOR A COMPLETE EXPLANATION OF ENTRY, SEE "HOW TO READ A CITATION" SECTION

Smith, Margaret Gilchrist; Died enroute, 1680-1736 *1639.20 p291*
Smith, Margtte 16; America, 1706 *2212 p47*
Smith, Maria 10; New Orleans, 1831 *778.5 p500*
Smith, Marianne 15 *SEE* Smith, Wm.
Smith, Marion *SEE* Smith, Angus
Smith, Marion; Quebec, 1865 *4537.30 p55*
Smith, Marion Campbell *SEE* Smith, Malcolm
Smith, Martha; Philadelphia, 1811 *53.26 p83*
Smith, Martha; Virginia, 1638 *6219 p123*
Smith, Martha 12 *SEE* Smith, Daniel
Smith, Martha 15; Maryland, 1775 *1219.7 p249*
Smith, Martha Jane; Philadelphia, 1848 *53.26 p83*
Smith, Martha Jane; Philadelphia, 1848 *5704.8 p46*
Smith, Martin; America, 1738 *4971 p9*
Smith, Martin; Pennsylvania, 1754 *2444 p213*
Smith, Martin A.; Illinois, 1888 *5012.39 p121*
Smith, Mary *SEE* Smith, Angus
Smith, Mary *SEE* Smith, Angus
Smith, Mary *SEE* Smith, Malcolm
Smith, Mary *SEE* Smith, Murdo
Smith, Mary; America, 1698 *2212 p5*
Smith, Mary; America, 1741 *4971 p16*
Smith, Mary; Montreal, 1825 *7603 p61*
Smith, Mary; New York, NY, 1836 *8208.4 p13*
Smith, Mary; Quebec, 1850 *5704.8 p69*
Smith, Mary; Quebec, 1863 *4537.30 p8*
Smith, Mary; Quebec, 1873 *4537.30 p19*
Smith, Mary; Virginia, 1635 *6219 p6*
Smith, Mary; Virginia, 1642 *6219 p192*
Smith, Mary 19 *SEE* Smith, Malcolm
Smith, Mary 19; Maryland, 1725 *3690.1 p209*
Smith, Mary 20; Philadelphia, 1853 *5704.8 p113*
Smith, Mary 22 *SEE* Smith, John
Smith, Mary 22; Massachusetts, 1850 *5881.1 p92*
Smith, Mary 25 *SEE* Smith, John
Smith, Mary 25; Maryland, 1775 *1219.7 p256*
Smith, Mary 26; North America, 1774 *1219.7 p199*
Smith, Mary 44; Massachusetts, 1849 *5881.1 p91*
Smith, Mary Ann; Philadelphia, 1850 *5704.8 p64*
Smith, Mary Ann; Philadelphia, 1866 *5704.8 p208*
Smith, Mary Ann; Philadelphia, 1868 *5704.8 p226*
Smith, Mary Ann 9 mos; Philadelphia, 1856 *5704.8 p128*
Smith, Mary Jane 3 *SEE* Smith, Robert
Smith, Mary Jane 3; Philadelphia, 1847 *5704.8 p31*
Smith, Mary MacLeod *SEE* Smith, Donald
Smith, Mary McAlester 64 *SEE* Smith, Malcolm
Smith, Mathew; Illinois, 1886 *5012.39 p120*
Smith, Mathew; New York, NY, 1866 *5704.8 p212*
Smith, Mathew 4; Philadelphia, 1867 *5704.8 p223*
Smith, Mathew 20; Massachusetts, 1849 *5881.1 p91*
Smith, Matilda; Philadelphia, 1866 *5704.8 p208*
Smith, Matthew; America, 1845 *1450.2 p135A*
Smith, Matthew; North Carolina, 1671-1771 *1639.20 p292*
Smith, Melchior; Philadelphia, 1760 *9973.7 p34*
Smith, Michael; America, 1835 *1450.2 p135A*
Smith, Michael; North Carolina, 1740-1840 *1639.20 p292*
Smith, Michael; Ohio, 1841 *8365.25 p12*
Smith, Michael; Philadelphia, 1815 *2859.11 p42*
Smith, Michael; Wisconsin, n.d. *9675.8 p121*
Smith, Michael 40; Massachusetts, 1849 *5881.1 p92*
Smith, Michel 1; New Orleans, 1831 *778.5 p500*
Smith, Michel 38; New Orleans, 1831 *778.5 p500*
Smith, Murdo *SEE* Smith, Malcolm
Smith, Murdo *SEE* Smith, Murdo
Smith, Murdo *SEE* Smith, Murdo
Smith, Murdo; Quebec, 1851 *4537.30 p42*
  *Wife:*Kirsty MacLean
  *Child:*Donald
  *Child:*Margaret
  *Child:*Catherine
  *Child:*John
  *Child:*Ann
  *Child:*Murdo
Smith, Murdo; Quebec, 1855 *4537.30 p42*
  *Wife:*Jane MacLennan
  *Child:*Mary
  *Child:*Kirsty
  *Child:*Donald
  *Child:*Murdo
  *Child:*John
Smith, N. C.; Illinois, 1864 *5240.1 p42*
Smith, Nathan 24; Jamaica, 1731 *3690.1 p209*
Smith, Nathaniel 22 *SEE* Smith, Nathaniel
Smith, Nathaniel 52; North America, 1774 *1219.7 p198*
  *Wife:*Elizabeth 52
  *Child:*Nathaniel 22
  *Child:*John 18
  *Child:*Robert 9
  *Child:*Elizabeth 7
  *Child:*Rachael 22

Smith, Neal; South Carolina, 1822 *1639.20 p292*
Smith, Neil; America, 1802 *1639.20 p292*
Smith, Nicho.; Virginia, 1647 *6219 p247*
Smith, Nicholas 3; Port uncertain, 1838 *778.5 p500*
Smith, Norman *SEE* Smith, Angus
Smith, Norman *SEE* Smith, John
Smith, Norman *SEE* Smith, John
Smith, Norman *SEE* Smith, John
Smith, Norman Hugh *SEE* Smith, Donald
Smith, Oscar T.; Colorado, 1902 *9678.3 p13*
Smith, Owen; America, 1742 *4971 p70*
Smith, Owen; America, 1866 *5704.8 p208*
Smith, Owen 10; Massachusetts, 1849 *5881.1 p93*
Smith, Owen 14; Massachusetts, 1848 *5881.1 p92*
Smith, Pat; Quebec, 1850 *5704.8 p69*
Smith, Patrick; America, 1743 *4971 p18*
Smith, Patrick; Delaware, 1743 *4971 p105*
Smith, Patrick; Montreal, 1815 *7603 p91*
Smith, Patrick; New York, NY, 1834 *8208.4 p1*
Smith, Patrick; New York, NY, 1838 *8208.4 p84*
Smith, Patrick; South Carolina, 1716 *1639.20 p292*
Smith, Patrick 26; Massachusetts, 1847 *5881.1 p93*
Smith, Paul; New York, NY, 1834 *8208.4 p39*
Smith, Paul 40; Massachusetts, 1849 *5881.1 p93*
Smith, Peter; America, 1849 *1450.2 p136A*
Smith, Peter; Austin, TX, 1886 *9777 p5*
Smith, Peter; Bangor, ME, 1867-1876 *6410.22 p116*
Smith, Peter; Charleston, SC, 1806 *1639.20 p292*
Smith, Peter; New York, NY, 1815 *2859.11 p42*
Smith, Peter; New York, NY, 1816 *2859.11 p42*
Smith, Peter; New York, NY, 1838 *8208.4 p88*
Smith, Peter; Ohio, 1844 *9892.11 p43*
Smith, Peter 23 *SEE* Smith, Malcolm
Smith, Phil.; Virginia, 1648 *6219 p252*
Smith, Philip; Ohio, 1841 *8365.25 p12*
Smith, Phillip; Philadelphia, 1815 *2859.11 p42*
Smith, Phillipp; Virginia, 1628 *6219 p9*
Smith, R. C.; Washington, 1859-1920 *2872.1 p37*
Smith, Rachael 22 *SEE* Smith, Nathaniel
Smith, Rachel *SEE* Smith, Angus
Smith, Ralph 15; Virginia, 1699 *2212 p26*
Smith, Rebecca; Virginia, 1638 *6219 p124*
Smith, Rebecca 28; Massachusetts, 1849 *5881.1 p93*
Smith, Rich.; Virginia, 1636 *6219 p21*
Smith, Rich.; Virginia, 1636 *6219 p77*
Smith, Rich.; Virginia, 1637 *6219 p113*
Smith, Rich.; Virginia, 1648 *6219 p116*
Smith, Richard; America, 1836 *1450.2 p136A*
Smith, Richard; San Francisco, 1850 *4914.15 p10*
Smith, Richard; Virginia, 1637 *6219 p86*
Smith, Richard; Virginia, 1639 *6219 p155*
Smith, Richard; Virginia, 1643 *6219 p204*
Smith, Richard; Virginia, 1646 *6219 p243*
Smith, Richard; Virginia, 1647 *6219 p243*
Smith, Richard; Virginia, 1648 *6219 p246*
Smith, Richard 24; Jamaica, 1724 *3690.1 p210*
Smith, Richard 32; Philadelphia, 1856 *5704.8 p128*
Smith, Richd.; Virginia, 1635 *6219 p3*
Smith, Richd.; Virginia, 1645 *6219 p233*
Smith, Robert; Edenton, NC, 1824 *1639.20 p292*
Smith, Robert; Indiana, 1837 *9117 p15*
Smith, Robert; Jamaica, 1754 *1219.7 p28*
Smith, Robert; New York, NY, 1816 *2859.11 p42*
Smith, Robert; Philadelphia, 1847 *53.26 p83*
  *Relative:*Eliza
  *Relative:*Margaret 13
  *Relative:*Thomas 11
  *Relative:*James 8
  *Relative:*Mary Jane 3
  *Relative:*Hannah 1
Smith, Robert; Philadelphia, 1847 *5704.8 p31*
Smith, Robert; Virginia, 1635 *6219 p69*
Smith, Robert; Virginia, 1652 *6251 p19*
Smith, Robert 9 *SEE* Smith, Nathaniel
Smith, Robert 18; Jamaica, 1729 *3690.1 p210*
Smith, Robert 19; Maryland, 1720 *3690.1 p210*
Smith, Robert 20; Virginia, 1774 *1219.7 p205*
Smith, Robert 23; Philadelphia, 1833-1834 *53.26 p83*
Smith, Robert 24; Baltimore, 1775 *1219.7 p269*
Smith, Robert 24; Jamaica, 1738 *3690.1 p210*
Smith, Robert 24; Philadelphia, 1833-1834 *53.26 p83*
Smith, Robert 29; Kansas, 1876 *5240.1 p57*
Smith, Robert 32; New York, 1774 *1219.7 p217*
Smith, Robt.; Virginia, 1637 *6219 p13*
Smith, Roderick *SEE* Smith, John
Smith, Rose; America, 1740 *4971 p75*
Smith, Rose 70; Massachusetts, 1850 *5881.1 p93*
Smith, Sally; St. John, N.B., 1848 *5704.8 p43*
Smith, Sally; St. John, N.B., 1852 *5704.8 p93*
Smith, Samll.; Virginia, 1642 *6219 p195*
Smith, Samuel; America, 1808 *1639.20 p293*
Smith, Samuel; Jamaica, 1755 *1219.7 p39*
Smith, Samuel; Quebec, 1822 *7603 p79*

Smith, Samuel 13; Jamaica, 1775 *1219.7 p253*
Smith, Samuel 14; Philadelphia, 1864 *5704.8 p161*
Smith, Samuel 20; Philadelphia, 1833-1834 *53.26 p83*
Smith, Samuel 21; Maryland, 1774 *1219.7 p220*
Smith, Samuel 21; St. John, N.B., 1866 *5704.8 p166*
Smith, Samuel 24; Maryland, 1774 *1219.7 p224*
Smith, Samuel 26; Virginia, 1774 *1219.7 p201*
Smith, Sanders; Virginia, 1641 *6219 p187*
Smith, Sara; Montreal, 1823 *7603 p90*
Smith, Sarah *SEE* Smith, Thomas
Smith, Sarah *SEE* Smith, Thomas
Smith, Sarah; Philadelphia, 1850 *53.26 p83*
Smith, Sarah; Philadelphia, 1850 *5704.8 p68*
Smith, Sarah; Quebec, 1853 *5704.8 p104*
Smith, Sarah; Virginia, 1642 *6219 p191*
Smith, Sarah 13 *SEE* Smith, Wm.
Smith, Sarah 21; Baltimore, 1775 *1219.7 p271*
Smith, Sarah Ann; Quebec, 1851 *5704.8 p74*
Smith, Seybert; Illinois, 1855 *7857 p7*
Smith, Silvester; Virginia, 1643 *6219 p200*
Smith, Susan; New York, NY, 1811 *2859.11 p19*
Smith, Susan; Philadelphia, 1868 *5704.8 p221*
Smith, Sy; St. Kitts, 1776 *1219.7 p283*
Smith, Symon; Virginia, 1642 *6219 p187*
Smith, Symon; Virginia, 1646 *6219 p238*
Smith, Terence L.; New York, NY, 1834 *8208.4 p42*
Smith, Tho.; Virginia, 1635 *6219 p10*
Smith, Tho.; Virginia, 1635 *6219 p69*
Smith, Tho.; Virginia, 1635 *6219 p70*
Smith, Tho.; Virginia, 1636 *6219 p75*
Smith, Tho.; Virginia, 1637 *6219 p180*
Smith, Tho.; Virginia, 1638 *6219 p159*
Smith, Tho.; Virginia, 1639 *6219 p151*
Smith, Tho.; Virginia, 1642 *6219 p199*
Smith, Tho.; Virginia, 1643 *6219 p206*
Smith, Tho.; Virginia, 1643 *6219 p208*
Smith, Thomas; Indiana, 1837 *9117 p15*
Smith, Thomas; Maryland, 1751 *1219.7 p3*
Smith, Thomas; Maryland, 1751 *3690.1 p210*
Smith, Thomas; New York, NY, 1834 *8208.4 p62*
Smith, Thomas; New York, NY, 1835 *8208.4 p6*
Smith, Thomas; New York, NY, 1835 *8208.4 p49*
Smith, Thomas; Quebec, 1824 *7603 p79*
Smith, Thomas; St. John, N.B., 1847 *5704.8 p25*
Smith, Thomas; Virginia, 1634 *6219 p32*
Smith, Thomas; Virginia, 1635 *6219 p69*
Smith, Thomas; Virginia, 1635 *6219 p70*
Smith, Thomas; Virginia, 1636 *6219 p76*
  *Wife:*Sarah
  *Daughter:*Ann
Smith, Thomas; Virginia, 1637 *6219 p114*
Smith, Thomas; Virginia, 1638 *6219 p121*
Smith, Thomas; Virginia, 1639 *6219 p157*
  *Wife:*Sarah
  *Daughter:*Ann
Smith, Thomas; Virginia, 1639 *6219 p184*
Smith, Thomas; Virginia, 1643 *6219 p202*
Smith, Thomas 11 *SEE* Smith, Robert
Smith, Thomas 11; Philadelphia, 1847 *5704.8 p31*
Smith, Thomas 15; Jamaica, 1730 *3690.1 p210*
Smith, Thomas 17; Maryland, 1774 *1219.7 p221*
Smith, Thomas 18; Jamaica, 1722 *3690.1 p210*
Smith, Thomas 18; Jamaica, 1725 *3690.1 p210*
Smith, Thomas 18; Jamaica, 1737 *3690.1 p210*
Smith, Thomas 19; Virginia, 1775 *1219.7 p246*
Smith, Thomas 20; Jamaica, 1719 *3690.1 p210*
Smith, Thomas 20; Jamaica, 1727 *3690.1 p210*
Smith, Thomas 21; Maryland, 1775 *1219.7 p256*
Smith, Thomas 22; Grenada, 1775 *1219.7 p280*
Smith, Thomas 22; Maryland, 1773 *1219.7 p173*
Smith, Thomas 22; Maryland, 1774 *1219.7 p207*
Smith, Thomas 22; Virginia, 1774 *1219.7 p201*
Smith, Thomas 23; Maryland, 1775 *1219.7 p264*
Smith, Thomas 24; Maryland, 1775 *1219.7 p254*
Smith, Thomas 25; Maryland, 1730 *3690.1 p210*
Smith, Thomas 25; Maryland, 1775 *1219.7 p267*
Smith, Thomas 26; Maryland, 1775 *1219.7 p254*
Smith, Thomas 29; Maryland, 1775 *1219.7 p181*
Smith, Thomas 57; Arizona, 1890 *2764.35 p62*
Smith, Thomas, Jr.; New York, NY, 1815 *2859.11 p42*
Smith, Thomas Loughton; South Carolina, 1680-1830 *1639.20 p293*
Smith, Thos.; New York, NY, 1815 *2859.11 p42*
  With wife
Smith, Timothy; America, 1742 *4971 p70*
Smith, Timothy 30; Massachusetts, 1850 *5881.1 p93*
Smith, Toby; Virginia, 1640 *6219 p184*
Smith, Toby; Virginia, 1644 *6219 p230*
Smith, Ursula; Virginia, 1637 *6219 p11*
Smith, Uryas; Virginia, 1648 *6219 p246*
Smith, W.J.; Nevada, 1875 *2764.35 p65*
Smith, W. J.; Washington, 1859-1920 *2872.1 p37*
Smith, W. N.; Washington, 1859-1920 *2872.1 p37*

Smith, W. T.; Milwaukee, 1875 ***4719.30*** *p257*
Smith, Wesley; Washington, 1859-1920 ***2872.1*** *p37*
Smith, Whiteford; South Carolina, 1794 ***1639.20*** *p293*
Smith, William *SEE* Smith, Daniel
Smith, William *SEE* Smith, Malcolm
Smith, William; Baltimore, 1831 ***1450.2*** *p136A*
Smith, William; California, 1865 ***3840.3*** *p10*
Smith, William; Charleston, SC, 1784 ***1639.20*** *p293*
Smith, William; Charleston, SC, 1803 ***1639.20*** *p293*
Smith, William; Kansas, 1874 ***5240.1*** *p42*
Smith, William; Kansas, 1886 ***5240.1*** *p42*
Smith, William; New York, NY, 1811 ***2859.11*** *p19*
Smith, William; New York, NY, 1836 ***8208.4*** *p16*
Smith, William; New York, NY, 1837 ***8208.4*** *p51*
Smith, William; New York, NY, 1839 ***8208.4*** *p96*
Smith, William; New York, NY, 1839 ***8208.4*** *p99*
Smith, William; Pennsylvania, 1600-1700 ***4963*** *p40*
Smith, William; Pennsylvania, 1682 ***4960*** *p162*
Smith, William; Philadelphia, 1866 ***5704.8*** *p208*
Smith, William; Quebec, 1784 ***7603*** *p95*
Smith, William; Quebec, 1815 ***9229.18*** *p79*
With wife
With family
Smith, William; Quebec, 1847 ***5704.8*** *p12*
Smith, William; South Carolina, 1799 ***1639.20*** *p293*
Smith, William; Virginia, 1621 ***6219*** *p29*
Smith, William; Washington, 1859-1920 ***2872.1*** *p37*
Smith, William 1 *SEE* Smith, John
Smith, William 4; Philadelphia, 1856 ***5704.8*** *p128*
Smith, William 9; Philadelphia, 1864 ***5704.8*** *p161*
Smith, William 9; Quebec, 1864 ***5704.8*** *p162*
Smith, William 13; New York, 1774 ***1219.7*** *p217*
Smith, William 14; Jamaica, 1736 ***3690.1*** *p211*
Smith, William 15; Maryland, 1774 ***1219.7*** *p208*
Smith, William 16; Philadelphia, 1774 ***1219.7*** *p217*
Smith, William 16; Philadelphia, 1775 ***1219.7*** *p248*
Smith, William 16; St. Christopher, 1730 ***3690.1*** *p211*
Smith, William 18; Jamaica, 1736 ***3690.1*** *p211*
Smith, William 18; Maryland, 1738 ***3690.1*** *p211*
Smith, William 18; Pennsylvania, Virginia or Maryland, 1725 ***3690.1*** *p211*
Smith, William 19; Jamaica, 1731 ***3690.1*** *p211*
Smith, William 20; Maryland, 1775 ***1219.7*** *p249*
Smith, William 20; Virginia, 1774 ***1219.7*** *p193*
Smith, William 21; Maryland, 1774 ***1219.7*** *p220*
Smith, William 21; Maryland, 1774 ***1219.7*** *p221*
Smith, William 21; Philadelphia, 1854 ***5704.8*** *p115*
Smith, William 22; Jamaica, 1738 ***3690.1*** *p211*
Smith, William 23; Jamaica, 1722 ***3690.1*** *p210*
Smith, William 23; Massachusetts, 1849 ***5881.1*** *p93*
Smith, William 25; Maryland, 1774 ***1219.7*** *p220*
Smith, William 25; Virginia, 1774 ***1219.7*** *p193*
Smith, William 26; Maryland, 1775 ***1219.7*** *p251*
Smith, William 26; Virginia, 1774 ***1219.7*** *p239*
Smith, William 27; Jamaica, 1775 ***1219.7*** *p278*
Smith, William 27; Maryland, 1775 ***1219.7*** *p262*
Smith, William 27; St. John, N.B., 1864 ***5704.8*** *p159*
Smith, William 29; Jamaica, 1738 ***3690.1*** *p211*
Smith, William 31; Maryland, 1774 ***1219.7*** *p215*
Smith, William 34; Jamaica, 1730 ***3690.1*** *p211*
Smith, William 34; Maryland, 1774 ***1219.7*** *p181*
Smith, William 36; Dominica, 1774 ***1219.7*** *p223*
Smith, William 39; Quebec, 1864 ***5704.8*** *p162*
Smith, William 42; Virginia, 1773 ***1219.7*** *p168*
Smith, William 44; Baltimore, 1775 ***1219.7*** *p269*
Smith, William B.; Arkansas, 1918 ***95.2*** *p114*
Smith, William H.; Illinois, 1880 ***2896.5*** *p38*
Smith, William J.; Washington, 1859-1920 ***2872.1*** *p37*
Smith, William N.; Illinois, 1857 ***7857*** *p7*
Smith, Willm; America, 1697 ***2212*** *p4*
Smith, Willoughby 19; Virginia, 1773 ***1219.7*** *p171*
Smith, Wm.; Virginia, 1635 ***6219*** *p16*
Smith, Wm.; Virginia, 1637 ***6219*** *p13*
Smith, Wm.; Virginia, 1637 ***6219*** *p82*
Smith, Wm.; Virginia, 1637 ***6219*** *p83*
Smith, Wm.; Virginia, 1643 ***6219*** *p208*
Smith, Wm.; Virginia, 1646 ***6219*** *p241*
Smith, Wm. 43; Montreal, 1840 ***4535.10*** *p195*
With wife 40
*Child:*Chas. 17
*Child:*Marianne 15
*Child:*Sarah 13
*Child:*Eliz. 11
*Child:*Jane 9
*Child:*Geo. 7
*Child:*Charlotte 5
*Child:*Louisa 2
Smithell, William; Virginia, 1642 ***6219*** *p192*
Smithfeild, Hen.; Virginia, 1642 ***6219*** *p192*
Smithing, Francis; New York, NY, 1838 ***8208.4*** *p67*
Smithnest, Edward; Virginia, 1643 ***6219*** *p199*
Smithock, Henry; Virginia, 1635 ***6219*** *p23*
Smithson, Henry L. 23; Kansas, 1885 ***5240.1*** *p42*
Smithson, Henry L. 23; Kansas, 1885 ***5240.1*** *p67*
Smithson, John 30; Virginia, 1774 ***1219.7*** *p225*
Smithson, Wm. S. 24; Kansas, 1887 ***5240.1*** *p42*
Smithson, Wm. S. 24; Kansas, 1887 ***5240.1*** *p70*
Smithurst, Daniel L.; Ohio, 1844 ***9892.11*** *p43*
Smithurst, Daniel L.; Ohio, 1847 ***9892.11*** *p43*
Smithurst, James; Ohio, 1840 ***9892.11*** *p43*
Smithwick, Georgie; Illinois, 1901 ***5012.40*** *p80*
Smithwicke, Hugh; Virginia, 1642 ***6219*** *p186*
Smitmeyer, Henry; Ohio, 1848 ***8365.27*** *p12*
Smitowski, Adolf; New York, 1831 ***4606*** *p177*
Smitt, Baltus; South Carolina, 1752-1753 ***3689.17*** *p23*
With wife
Smitten, Margarita; South Carolina, 1752-1753 ***3689.17*** *p23*
Smitter, Ann 24; Quebec, 1863 ***5704.8*** *p154*
Smitter, Peter 24; Quebec, 1863 ***5704.8*** *p154*
Smitz, Hermann; Kansas, 1890 ***5240.1*** *p42*
Smitzler, Charles 22; Kansas, 1874 ***5240.1*** *p55*
Smock, Andrew; Wisconsin, n.d. ***9675.8*** *p121*
Smodisch, John; Wisconsin, n.d. ***9675.8*** *p121*
Smok, John 43; Kansas, 1893 ***5240.1*** *p79*
Smoke, Andrew; Wisconsin, n.d. ***9675.8*** *p121*
Smolen, Charles; Arkansas, 1918 ***95.2*** *p114*
Smont, O. 20; Louisiana, 1820 ***778.5*** *p500*
Smykaj, Wladislawa 23; New York, 1912 ***9980.29*** *p72*
Smylie, Matthew; Brunswick, NC, 1739 ***1639.20*** *p293*
Smylie, Nathaniel; Brunswick, NC, 1739 ***1639.20*** *p293*
Smyth, . . .; Philadelphia, 1864 ***5704.8*** *p188*
Smyth, Dr.; North Carolina, 1700-1800 ***1639.20*** *p293*
Smyth, Alexander; Quebec, 1848 ***5704.8*** *p41*
Smyth, Andrew; New York, 1852 ***1450.2*** *p136A*
Smyth, Ann; New Orleans, 1848 ***5704.8*** *p48*
Smyth, Ann; Quebec, 1849 ***5704.8*** *p57*
Smyth, Annie; New York, NY, 1865 ***5704.8*** *p193*
Smyth, Catherine; Philadelphia, 1848 ***5704.8*** *p45*
Smyth, Catherine; St. John, N.B., 1847 ***5704.8*** *p3*
Smyth, Daniel; Philadelphia, 1847 ***5704.8*** *p30*
Smyth, David; Philadelphia, 1864 ***5704.8*** *p188*
Smyth, David 5; New Orleans, 1848 ***5704.8*** *p48*
Smyth, David 13; Philadelphia, 1847 ***5704.8*** *p30*
Smyth, Eliza; New York, NY, 1865 ***5704.8*** *p193*
Smyth, Eliza; Philadelphia, 1852 ***5704.8*** *p85*
Smyth, Eliza; Quebec, 1851 ***5704.8*** *p75*
Smyth, Elizabeth 4; New Orleans, 1848 ***5704.8*** *p48*
Smyth, Elizabeth 13; Philadelphia, 1857 ***5704.8*** *p133*
Smyth, Elizabeth 20; Philadelphia, 1853 ***5704.8*** *p111*
Smyth, Ellan; New Orleans, 1852 ***5704.8*** *p98*
Smyth, Elleanor 8 *SEE* Smyth, Hugh
Smyth, Elleanor 8; Philadelphia, 1849 ***5704.8*** *p50*
Smyth, Emma 21; Philadelphia, 1858 ***5704.8*** *p139*
Smyth, Francis; Virginia, 1856 ***4626.16*** *p16*
Smyth, Francis 29; Philadelphia, 1803 ***53.26*** *p83*
Smyth, George; America, 1742 ***4971*** *p23*
Smyth, George; Philadelphia, 1811 ***53.26*** *p83*
Smyth, George; Philadelphia, 1811 ***2859.11*** *p19*
Smyth, George; Quebec, 1848 ***5704.8*** *p41*
Smyth, George 10; Philadelphia, 1852 ***5704.8*** *p96*
Smyth, George 19; St. John, N.B., 1862 ***5704.8*** *p151*
Smyth, Hannah; Philadelphia, 1849 ***5704.8*** *p50*
Smyth, Hugh; Arkansas, 1918 ***95.2*** *p114*
Smyth, Hugh 12; Philadelphia, 1849 ***53.26*** *p83*
*Relative:*Mary 10
*Relative:*Elleanor 8
Smyth, Hugh 12; Philadelphia, 1849 ***5704.8*** *p50*
Smyth, Isaac 4; Quebec, 1847 ***5704.8*** *p7*
Smyth, James; New York, NY, 1811 ***2859.11*** *p19*
Smyth, James; New York, NY, 1837 ***8208.4*** *p56*
Smyth, James; New York, NY, 1838 ***8208.4*** *p86*
Smyth, James; New York, NY, 1865 ***5704.8*** *p193*
Smyth, James; Philadelphia, 1848 ***5704.8*** *p40*
Smyth, James; Philadelphia, 1852 ***5704.8*** *p92*
Smyth, James; Philadelphia, 1852 ***5704.8*** *p96*
Smyth, James; Philadelphia, 1864 ***5704.8*** *p188*
Smyth, James; Quebec, 1849 ***5704.8*** *p57*
Smyth, James; Quebec, 1852 ***5704.8*** *p86*
Smyth, James; Quebec, 1852 ***5704.8*** *p90*
Smyth, James; St. John, N.B., 1847 ***5704.8*** *p35*
Smyth, Jane; New York, NY, 1816 ***2859.11*** *p42*
Smyth, Jane; New York, NY, 1865 ***5704.8*** *p193*
Smyth, Jane; Philadelphia, 1847 ***5704.8*** *p30*
Smyth, Jane; Philadelphia, 1852 ***5704.8*** *p97*
Smyth, Jane; Philadelphia, 1864 ***5704.8*** *p188*
Smyth, Jno.; Virginia, 1643 ***6219*** *p207*
Smyth, John; New York, NY, 1811 ***2859.11*** *p19*
Smyth, John; New York, NY, 1815 ***2859.11*** *p42*
Smyth, John; Philadelphia, 1852 ***5704.8*** *p96*
Smyth, John 3 mos; Quebec, 1847 ***5704.8*** *p7*
Smyth, John 4; Philadelphia, 1852 ***5704.8*** *p89*
Smyth, Jonathan 9 mos; New Orleans, 1848 ***5704.8*** *p48*
Smyth, Joseph; Philadelphia, 1847 ***5704.8*** *p30*
Smyth, Kennedy; Quebec, 1848 ***5704.8*** *p41*
Smyth, Margaret; Philadelphia, 1850 ***5704.8*** *p64*
Smyth, Margaret; St. John, N.B., 1848 ***5704.8*** *p47*
Smyth, Margaret 6; New Orleans, 1848 ***5704.8*** *p48*
Smyth, Margaret 9; Quebec, 1847 ***5704.8*** *p7*
Smyth, Margaret 19; Philadelphia, 1855 ***5704.8*** *p123*
Smyth, Mark; Philadelphia, 1836 ***9892.11*** *p43*
Smyth, Martha; Philadelphia, 1864 ***5704.8*** *p188*
Smyth, Martha; St. John, N.B., 1852 ***5704.8*** *p93*
Smyth, Martha 12; Philadelphia, 1847 ***5704.8*** *p30*
Smyth, Mary; New York, NY, 1865 ***5704.8*** *p193*
Smyth, Mary; New York, NY, 1865 ***5704.8*** *p194*
Smyth, Mary; Philadelphia, 1852 ***5704.8*** *p96*
Smyth, Mary; Philadelphia, 1864 ***5704.8*** *p188*
Smyth, Mary; St. John, N.B., 1850 ***5704.8*** *p66*
Smyth, Mary; St. John, N.B., 1852 ***5704.8*** *p93*
Smyth, Mary 3; Philadelphia, 1852 ***5704.8*** *p89*
Smyth, Mary 10 *SEE* Smyth, Hugh
Smyth, Mary 10; Philadelphia, 1849 ***5704.8*** *p50*
Smyth, Mary 12; Quebec, 1847 ***5704.8*** *p7*
Smyth, Mary 20; Philadelphia, 1853 ***5704.8*** *p113*
Smyth, Mathew; Philadelphia, 1847 ***53.26*** *p83*
Smyth, Mathew; Philadelphia, 1847 ***5704.8*** *p1*
Smyth, Matilda 11; New York, NY, 1865 ***5704.8*** *p193*
Smyth, Michael 18; Philadelphia, 1857 ***5704.8*** *p132*
Smyth, Mitchell 15; Philadelphia, 1853 ***5704.8*** *p113*
Smyth, Neally; Philadelphia, 1852 ***5704.8*** *p89*
Smyth, Patrick; America, 1738 ***4971*** *p22*
Smyth, Patrick; New York, NY, 1816 ***2859.11*** *p42*
Smyth, Patrick; Philadelphia, 1852 ***5704.8*** *p89*
Smyth, Rebecca; Philadelphia, 1852 ***5704.8*** *p88*
Smyth, Robert; New York, NY, 1815 ***2859.11*** *p42*
Smyth, Robert; New York, NY, 1816 ***2859.11*** *p42*
Smyth, Robert 8; Philadelphia, 1852 ***5704.8*** *p96*
Smyth, Rossanna 17; Wilmington, DE, 1831 ***6508.7*** *p160*
Smyth, Sally 24; Philadelphia, 1853 ***5704.8*** *p112*
Smyth, Sally Ann; Philadelphia, 1847 ***53.26*** *p83*
Smyth, Sally Ann; Philadelphia, 1847 ***5704.8*** *p32*
Smyth, Samuel; Philadelphia, 1852 ***5704.8*** *p88*
Smyth, Samuel 48; Quebec, 1857 ***5704.8*** *p136*
Smyth, Susanna 15; Philadelphia, 1853 ***5704.8*** *p113*
Smyth, Thomas; America, 1864 ***5704.8*** *p181*
Smyth, Thomas 16; Philadelphia, 1864 ***5704.8*** *p161*
Smyth, William; New York, NY, 1815 ***2859.11*** *p42*
Smyth, William; Philadelphia, 1847 ***5704.8*** *p30*
Smyth, William; Philadelphia, 1850 ***5704.8*** *p64*
Smyth, William; Quebec, 1847 ***5704.8*** *p7*
Smyth, William; Quebec, 1848 ***5704.8*** *p41*
Smyth, William; Quebec, 1849 ***5704.8*** *p57*
Smyth, William; St. John, N.B., 1853 ***5704.8*** *p106*
Smyth, William 7; Quebec, 1847 ***5704.8*** *p7*
Smythe, Samuell; Virginia, 1652 ***6251*** *p20*
Smythwood, Robert; Virginia, 1647 ***6219*** *p241*
Snabel, John; America, 1850 ***1450.2*** *p136A*
Snackson, Mould; Virginia, 1638 ***6219*** *p119*
Snagnale, Ralph 14; Maryland, 1719 ***3690.1*** *p211*
Snailum, Richd 26; Virginia, 1699 ***2212*** *p27*
Snalshaw, Wm 22; Maryland or Virginia, 1699 ***2212*** *p24*
Snape, Jane; Virginia, 1648 ***6219*** *p251*
Snape, Joseph; Jamaica, 1767 ***1219.7*** *p133*
Snape, Robert 38; Virginia, 1774 ***1219.7*** *p243*
Snaydar, Ivan; Iowa, 1866-1943 ***123.54*** *p45*
Snead, Henry 21; Maryland, 1774 ***1219.7*** *p222*
Snead, Richard; Virginia, 1636 ***6219*** *p27*
Snead, William 18; Philadelphia, 1775 ***1219.7*** *p248*
Sneade, Alice *SEE* Sneade, Samuel
Sneade, Samuel; Virginia, 1635 ***6219*** *p70*
*Wife:*Alice
*Son:*William
Sneade, William *SEE* Sneade, Samuel
Sneal, Thomas 20; Maryland, 1719 ***3690.1*** *p211*
Sneale, Dorothy; Virginia, 1636 ***6219*** *p36*
Sneale, Elizabeth *SEE* Sneale, Henry
Sneale, Henry; Virginia, 1636 ***6219*** *p36*
*Wife:*Elizabeth
Sneale, John; Virginia, 1636 ***6219*** *p36*
Sneale, Mary; Virginia, 1636 ***6219*** *p36*
Sneath, George; Illinois, 1880 ***2896.5*** *p38*
Sneath, William 29; Jamaica, 1722 ***3690.1*** *p211*
Sneddon, John; Iowa, 1866-1943 ***123.54*** *p45*
Snee, Andrew; Philadelphia, 1851 ***5704.8*** *p76*
Snee, Ann 60; Philadelphia, 1853 ***5704.8*** *p108*
Snee, Ellan; Philadelphia, 1851 ***5704.8*** *p76*
Snee, James 18; Philadelphia, 1853 ***5704.8*** *p108*
Snee, John 30; Philadelphia, 1853 ***5704.8*** *p108*
Snee, John 60; Philadelphia, 1853 ***5704.8*** *p108*
Snee, Margaret 16; Philadelphia, 1853 ***5704.8*** *p108*
Snee, Susan; Philadelphia, 1851 ***5704.8*** *p81*
Sneider, Anna 30 *SEE* Sneider, Michael
Sneider, Hans George 12 *SEE* Sneider, Michael
Sneider, John; Philadelphia, 1759 ***9973.7*** *p34*
Sneider, John 6 *SEE* Sneider, Michael
Sneider, John George; Philadelphia, 1760 ***9973.7*** *p34*

484 *FOR A COMPLETE EXPLANATION OF ENTRY, SEE "HOW TO READ A CITATION" SECTION*

Sneider, Michael 40; Georgia, 1738 ***9332*** *p333*
*Wife:*Anna 30
*Son:*Hans George 12
*Son:*John 6
Snelgrove, Thomas; San Francisco, 1850 ***4914.15*** *p10*
Snell, Catharine; New York, NY, 1864 ***5704.8*** *p176*
Snell, Elizabeth 1; New York, 1774 ***1219.7*** *p202*
Snell, Elizabeth 24; New York, 1774 ***1219.7*** *p202*
Snell, Major 36; New York, 1774 ***1219.7*** *p202*
Snell, Richard 16; Philadelphia, 1774 ***1219.7*** *p197*
Snellocke, Jon.; Virginia, 1600-1643 ***6219*** *p200*
Snep, Geo.; Pennsylvania, 1752-1770 ***2444*** *p213*
Snider, John; Ohio, 1861-1867 ***9892.11*** *p41*
Snider, John; Ohio, 1872 ***9892.11*** *p43*
Snider, John M.; Illinois, 1840 ***7857*** *p7*
Snodgrass, James 15; Wilmington, DE, 1831 ***6508.3*** *p101*
Snodgrass, Mary 17; Wilmington, DE, 1831 ***6508.3*** *p101*
Snodgrass, Mary Ann; Philadelphia, 1853 ***5704.8*** *p100*
Snodgrass, Rebecca 20; Philadelphia, 1856 ***5704.8*** *p129*
Snodgrass, Robert; Philadelphia, 1853 ***5704.8*** *p100*
Snodgrass, Thomas; Chicago, 1850 ***6013.19*** *p88*
Snoll, August; Baltimore, 1849 ***1450.2*** *p136A*
Snook, John B.; New York, NY, 1838 ***8208.4*** *p90*
Snook, Joseph 26; Maryland, 1774 ***1219.7*** *p204*
Snow, Anne 16; Quebec, 1855 ***5704.8*** *p125*
Snow, Henry; Virginia, 1636 ***6219*** *p75*
Snow, Henry; Virginia, 1638 ***6219*** *p181*
Snow, John 46; Maryland, 1774 ***1219.7*** *p192*
Snow, Mark 30; Canada, 1838 ***4535.12*** *p113*
Snow, Thomas; New York, NY, 1835 ***8208.4*** *p43*
Snowden, Pickering 23; Nova Scotia, 1774 ***1219.7*** *p195*
Snowden, Ralph 19; New York, 1774 ***1219.7*** *p202*
Snowden, Richard 21; Barbados, 1725 ***3690.1*** *p211*
Snowson, John; Virginia, 1641 ***6219*** *p37*
Snowson, John; Virginia, 1641 ***6219*** *p160*
Snuvre, William 22; Maryland, 1775 ***1219.7*** *p250*
Snyder, Anna Maria Catharina *SEE* Snyder, Maria Helena Nischicker
Snyder, Charles; California, 1855 ***3840.3*** *p10*
Snyder, Charles; Ohio, 1841 ***9892.11*** *p43*
Snyder, Corbenian; Illinois, 1865 ***2896.5*** *p38*
Snyder, Edward Charles; Arkansas, 1918 ***95.2*** *p114*
Snyder, Fred F. 24; Kansas, 1893 ***5240.1*** *p79*
Snyder, Friedrich; Cincinnati, 1869-1887 ***8582*** *p30*
Snyder, Friedrich; New York, NY, 1835 ***8582*** *p28*
Snyder, Irian; Iowa, 1866-1943 ***123.54*** *p45*
Snyder, John G.; New York, NY, 1838 ***8208.4*** *p83*
Snyder, John George; Illinois, 1860 ***5012.39*** *p89*
Snyder, Maria Helena Nischicker; Pennsylvania, 1717 ***3627*** *p15*
*Daughter:*Anna Maria Catharina
With father-in-law
Snyder, Nicholas; Pennsylvania, 1854 ***1450.2*** *p136A*
Snyder, William H.; Kansas, 1900 ***5240.1*** *p42*
Soan, Ann 20; Pennsylvania, 1728 ***3690.1*** *p212*
Soane, William; Virginia, 1621 ***6219*** *p30*
Soaper, Jno.; Virginia, 1646 ***6219*** *p240*
Soare, Richard 18; United States or West Indies, 1735 ***3690.1*** *p212*
Sobbe, Christian; Halifax, N.S., 1780 ***9786*** *p269*
Sobbe, Christian; New York, 1776 ***9786*** *p269*
Sobczuk, Anna 22; New York, 1912 ***9980.29*** *p63*
Sobery, August; Nevada, 1878 ***2764.35*** *p63*
Sobieszczanski, Jan; New York, 1835 ***4606*** *p180*
Sobkowiak, Antoni; Iroquois Co., IL, 1892 ***3455.1*** *p13*
Sobolewski, . . .; New York, 1831 ***4606*** *p176*
Sobota, Jacob; Iowa, 1866-1943 ***123.54*** *p45*
Sochoeki, John; Arkansas, 1918 ***95.2*** *p114*
Sodaro, Giovanna; Iowa, 1866-1943 ***123.54*** *p79*
Sodaro, Giovanna Gagliardo; Iowa, 1866-1943 ***123.54*** *p79*
Sodenberg, Erick M. 37; Massachusetts, 1860 ***6410.32*** *p98*
Sodenberg, Josephine W. 10; Massachusetts, 1860 ***6410.32*** *p98*
Sodenberg, Sarah 32; Massachusetts, 1860 ***6410.32*** *p98*
Soderberg, Erik Magnus; Boston, 1852 ***6410.32*** *p122*
*Wife:*Sara Lena Andersdotter
With child
Soderberg, John Birger; Arkansas, 1918 ***95.2*** *p114*
Soderberg, John Gustav; Arkansas, 1918 ***95.2*** *p114*
Soderberg, Otto; Massachusetts, 1868-1878 ***6410.22*** *p117*
Soderberg, Sara Lena Andersdotter *SEE* Soderberg, Erik Magnus
Soderdren, Peter; Maine, 1879-1885 ***6410.22*** *p118*
Soderer, Walburga; St. Louis, 1841 ***8582.2*** *p43*
Sodergren, Carl Gustafo; Iowa, 1866-1943 ***123.54*** *p45*
Sodergren, Henry; Minneapolis, 1883-1884 ***6410.35*** *p65*
Sodergren, John; Maine, 1879-1882 ***6410.22*** *p119*
Sodergren, Peter; Maine, 1879-1885 ***6410.22*** *p118*
Soderholm, Oscar A.; Iowa, 1866-1943 ***123.54*** *p45*
Soderlund, Emanuel; Washington, 1859-1920 ***2872.1*** *p37*
Soderman, Karl Viktor; Washington, 1859-1920 ***2872.1*** *p37*
Soderman, Mary; Washington, 1859-1920 ***2872.1*** *p37*
Soderman, Peter O.; Washington, 1859-1920 ***2872.1*** *p37*
Soderstrom, A. G. 21; Kansas, 1887 ***5240.1*** *p71*
Soderstrom, Lars P.; New York, NY, 1908 ***3455.2*** *p94*
Soderstrom, Susanna; America, 1825 ***6410.32*** *p125*
Soderstrom, Theodore; Arkansas, 1918 ***95.2*** *p114*
Sodowsky, Jakob; Kentucky, 1774 ***8582.3*** *p96*
*Brother:*Joseph
Sodowsky, Johann; America, 1740-1760 ***8582.3*** *p96*
Sodowsky, Joseph *SEE* Sodowsky, Jakob
Soehngen, Louis; Cincinnati, 1870 ***8582.3*** *p62*
Soelle, George; New York, 1753 ***3652*** *p77*
Soenne, Anna Margaretha; Pennsylvania, 1752 ***2444*** *p214*
Soenne, Anna Margaretha; South Carolina, 1752 ***2444*** *p214*
Soesewitz, Erdmann 20; Harris Co., TX, 1897 ***6254*** *p3*
Soet, A. 30; Port uncertain, 1835 ***778.5*** *p500*
Soeur, Mr. 14 mos; New Orleans, 1821 ***778.5*** *p500*
Soeur, Mrs. 30; New Orleans, 1821 ***778.5*** *p500*
Soffky, Frederick; Illinois, 1892 ***5012.40*** *p26*
Sohn, George; New York, 1890 ***1450.2*** *p37B*
Sohn, Johann Georg; Baltimore, 1842 ***8582.3*** *p62*
Sohn, Johann Wilhelm; Ohio, 1869-1887 ***8582*** *p31*
Sohn, John G.; Cincinnati, 1869-1887 ***8582*** *p31*
Sohn, Joseph; Illinois, 1866 ***2896.5*** *p38*
Sohn, Peter 43; California, 1873 ***2769.10*** *p5*
Sohn, Wilhelm; America, 1817-1842 ***8582.3*** *p62*
Sohnider, John; Baltimore, 1834 ***1450.2*** *p128A*
Sokalski, . . .; New York, 1831 ***4606*** *p177*
Sokolnitzki, Czeslaw 18; New York, 1912 ***9980.29*** *p56*
Solange, A. 25; America, 1838 ***778.5*** *p501*
Solaris, Francisco 30; New Orleans, 1835 ***778.5*** *p501*
Solavan, Cornelius; New York, 1850 ***1450.2*** *p142A*
Soldo, Risto; Arkansas, 1918 ***95.2*** *p114*
Sole, Christian; New York, NY, 1834 ***8208.4*** *p3*
Sole, John 17; Virginia, 1774 ***1219.7*** *p201*
Solem, Lewis; Colorado, 1905 ***9678.3*** *p13*
Soley, Elizabeth 14; Jamaica, 1773 ***1219.7*** *p172*
Soley, Henry 27; Philadelphia, 1774 ***1219.7*** *p175*
Solinos, Bernard 23; New Orleans, 1838 ***778.5*** *p501*
Solis, Estienne 28; New Orleans, 1836 ***778.5*** *p501*
Solito, Manuel 30; New Orleans, 1832 ***778.5*** *p501*
Solk, Georg; Louisville, KY, 1854 ***3702.7*** *p328*
Solle, Louise Wilhelmine; America, 1850 ***4610.10*** *p139*
Sollicoffre, John 17; Philadelphia, 1774 ***1219.7*** *p232*
Sollig, . . .; Canada, 1776-1783 ***9786*** *p34*
Solloman, Jo.; Virginia, 1645 ***6219*** *p233*
Sollos, George; Arkansas, 1918 ***95.2*** *p114*
Sollott, Samuel Solomon; Arkansas, 1918 ***95.2*** *p115*
Solo, Jos. 21; America, 1839 ***778.5*** *p501*
Soloman, Betig 7; New York, NY, 1878 ***9253*** *p45*
Soloman, Hannah 28; New York, NY, 1878 ***9253*** *p45*
Soloman, Israel 46; New York, NY, 1878 ***9253*** *p45*
Soloman, Jane 3; New York, NY, 1878 ***9253*** *p45*
Soloman, Lewis 16; New York, NY, 1878 ***9253*** *p45*
Soloman, Phillip 14; New York, NY, 1878 ***9253*** *p45*
Soloman, Samuel 7; New York, NY, 1878 ***9253*** *p45*
Soloman, Samuel 12; New York, NY, 1878 ***9253*** *p45*
Soloman, Sarah 46; New York, NY, 1878 ***9253*** *p45*
Solomen, Joseph; Iowa, 1866-1943 ***123.54*** *p45*
Solomon, Everhard 27; Pennsylvania, 1753 ***2444*** *p207*
Solomon, Gustave; Arkansas, 1918 ***95.2*** *p115*
Solomon, Joe; Iowa, 1866-1943 ***123.54*** *p45*
Solowej, Frank; Arkansas, 1918 ***95.2*** *p115*
Solstede, Frederick; Illinois, 1862 ***7857*** *p7*
Soltis, Alexander; America, 1895 ***7137*** *p170*
Soltis, Michael; America, 1895 ***7137*** *p170*
Solvasson, Jon 58; Quebec, 1879 ***2557.1*** *p21*
Somers, Alice 9; St. John, N.B., 1855 ***5704.8*** *p126*
Somers, Jane 28; St. John, N.B., 1855 ***5704.8*** *p126*
Somers, William 25; Jamaica, 1738 ***3690.1*** *p212*
Somersal, John 22; Maryland, 1774 ***1219.7*** *p235*
Somersale, Thomas; Virginia, 1636 ***6219*** *p78*
Somerskill, John 26; Maryland, 1774 ***1219.7*** *p206*
Somervill, William; New York, NY, 1837 ***8208.4*** *p33*
Somerville, Ann 25; Massachusetts, 1849 ***5881.1*** *p87*
Somerville, David; South Carolina, 1790 ***1639.20*** *p294*
Somerville, Elizabeth 21; Maryland, 1775 ***1219.7*** *p253*
Somerville, James; Montreal, 1792-1892 ***9775.5*** *p202*
Somerville, Jane; New York, NY, 1816 ***2859.11*** *p42*
Somerville, Margaret 22; Quebec, 1857 ***5704.8*** *p136*
Somerville, Mary; New York, NY, 1816 ***2859.11*** *p42*
Somerville, William 22; Quebec, 1857 ***5704.8*** *p136*
Somes, Marshall; Washington, 1859-1920 ***2872.1*** *p37*
Sommatis, Carli Saseel Francisca; Washington, 1859-1920 ***2872.1*** *p37*
Sommatis, Catrina; Washington, 1859-1920 ***2872.1*** *p37*
Sommatis, Elmar; Washington, 1859-1920 ***2872.1*** *p37*
Sommatis, Joseph; Washington, 1859-1920 ***2872.1*** *p37*
Sommatis, Martin; Washington, 1859-1920 ***2872.1*** *p38*
Sommatis, Minnie; Washington, 1859-1920 ***2872.1*** *p38*
Sommer, . . .; Canada, 1776-1783 ***9786*** *p34*
Sommer, Carl Gottlob; Wisconsin, n.d. ***9675.8*** *p121*
Sommer, Catharina *SEE* Sommer, Joseph
Sommer, Christ. 30; America, 1839 ***778.5*** *p501*
Sommer, Elisabetha *SEE* Sommer, Joseph
Sommer, Georg Philipp *SEE* Sommer, Joseph
Sommer, Hermann; Maryland, 1886 ***1450.2*** *p37B*
Sommer, Jo; South Carolina, 1788 ***7119*** *p197*
Sommer, Joseph; Pennsylvania, 1752 ***2444*** *p218*
*Wife:*Walburga Haussmann
*Child:*Catharina
*Child:*Elisabetha
*Child:*Georg Philipp
*Child:*Maria Magdalena
Sommer, Maria Magdalena *SEE* Sommer, Joseph
Sommer, Michael; Philadelphia, 1762 ***9973.7*** *p37*
Sommer, Richard; Illinois, 1888 ***2896.5*** *p38*
Sommer, Walburga Haussmann *SEE* Sommer, Joseph
Sommereau, E. 35; New Orleans, 1821 ***778.5*** *p501*
Sommereisen, Henrich; New Jersey, 1780 ***8137*** *p14*
Sommerfeld, Christian 55; New York, NY, 1857 ***9831.14*** *p154*
Sommerfeld, Louise 54; New York, NY, 1857 ***9831.14*** *p154*
Sommerlatte, v., Lieut.; Quebec, 1776 ***9786*** *p104*
Sommers, . . .; Canada, 1776-1783 ***9786*** *p34*
Sommers, David; Quebec, 1752 ***7603*** *p36*
Sommers, James; South Carolina, 1713-1753 ***1639.20*** *p294*
Sommers, Levi; Washington, 1859-1920 ***2872.1*** *p38*
Sommerville, James; St. John, N.B., 1852 ***5704.8*** *p95*
Sommerville, Jane 41; Philadelphia, 1864 ***5704.8*** *p161*
Sommerville, Margaret; South Carolina, 1767 ***1639.20*** *p294*
Sommerville, Margaret 22; Quebec, 1864 ***5704.8*** *p161*
Sommerville, William; Iowa, 1866-1943 ***123.54*** *p45*
Sommevialle, Octave 14; America, 1838 ***778.5*** *p501*
Sommoneau, Gabriel 22; Quebec, 1693 ***4533*** *p129*
Sompayrac, Mr. 35; America, 1823 ***778.5*** *p501*
Somsak, Agnes; Washington, 1859-1920 ***2872.1*** *p38*
Somsak, Mary; Washington, 1859-1920 ***2872.1*** *p38*
Somsak, Rosie; Washington, 1859-1920 ***2872.1*** *p38*
Somsak, Steve; Washington, 1859-1920 ***2872.1*** *p38*
Sonalet, Mr. 30; New Orleans, 1822 ***778.5*** *p501*
Sonderagge, Joseph 42; Kansas, 1870 ***5240.1*** *p51*
Sonderegger, Fannie 23; Kansas, 1893 ***5240.1*** *p78*
Sonderegger, Johann 65; Kansas, 1893 ***5240.1*** *p78*
Sondergaard, Christ 25; Arkansas, 1918 ***95.2*** *p115*
Sondermann, Fred.; New York, 1881 ***1450.2*** *p136A*
Sondheim, Emile; Shreveport, LA, 1878 ***7129*** *p45*
Songhurst, Elizabeth *SEE* Songhurst, John
Songhurst, Elizabeth; Pennsylvania, 1682 ***4960*** *p152*
Songhurst, John; Pennsylvania, 1682 ***4961*** *p240*
*Wife:*Mary
*Daughter:*Elizabeth
*Son:*John, Jr.
*Child:*Sarah
With son-in-law
Songhurst, John, Jr. *SEE* Songhurst, John
Songhurst, Mary *SEE* Songhurst, John
Songhurst, Sarah *SEE* Songhurst, John
Songster, Andrew; South Carolina, 1716 ***1639.20*** *p294*
Songuemard, L. 23; New Orleans, 1830 ***778.5*** *p501*
Sonjardien, Mr. 22; New Orleans, 1839 ***778.5*** *p501*
Sonn, George; Philadelphia, 1760 ***9973.7*** *p35*
Sonne, Niels C.; New York, 1871 ***5240.1*** *p42*
Sonnemann, Christian Andreas; Baltimore, 1839 ***2896.5*** *p38*
Sonnemann, John Jacob; New York, NY, 1835 ***2896.5*** *p38*
Sonnerthat, . . .; Canada, 1776-1783 ***9786*** *p34*
Sonntag, Karl; Kentucky, 1840-1845 ***8582.3*** *p100*
Sonogue, Condolado 22; Arizona, 1904 ***9228.40*** *p8*
Sons, Joseph; Ohio, 1884 ***3702.7*** *p459*
Sontag, Louis Karl; New York, NY, 1839 ***8208.4*** *p96*
Soon, John 16; Virginia, 1719 ***3690.1*** *p212*
Soopson, Thomas; Virginia, 1648 ***6219*** *p250*
Soott, John; Buffalo, NY, 1830 ***2896.5*** *p36*
Soper, Greg.; Virginia, 1637 ***6219*** *p115*
Sopton, James; Philadelphia, 1851 ***5704.8*** *p70*
Sorak, Mary; Iowa, 1866-1943 ***123.54*** *p79*
Sorak, Mary Hegedusic; Iowa, 1866-1943 ***123.54*** *p79*
Sorbes, Mr. 14; America, 1837 ***778.5*** *p501*
Sorbet, Jean 32; Port uncertain, 1837 ***778.5*** *p502*
Sordergaard, Tinus Andreas; Arkansas, 1918 ***95.2*** *p115*
Soren, Mr. 25; New Orleans, 1822 ***778.5*** *p502*
Sorensen, Christian; Washington, 1859-1920 ***2872.1*** *p38*
Sorensen, Erhard Suhr; Arkansas, 1918 ***95.2*** *p115*
Sorensen, Fredrik; Washington, 1859-1920 ***2872.1*** *p38*
Sorensen, Hans Hennek; Arkansas, 1918 ***95.2*** *p115*
Sorensen, J. 46; Washington, 1918-1920 ***1728.5*** *p14*
Sorensen, Jans Peter; Arkansas, 1918 ***95.2*** *p115*

Sorensen, Kai Otto Johannes; Arkansas, 1918 95.2 p115
Sorensen, Kai Otto Johnnes; Arkansas, 1918 95.2 p115
Sorensen, Kresten Andreas; Arkansas, 1918 95.2 p115
Sorensen, Mads Christian; Arkansas, 1918 95.2 p115
Sorensen, Marius; Arkansas, 1918 95.2 p115
Sorensen, Nels Chris 26; Arkansas, 1918 95.2 p115
Sorensen, Nels Peter; Arkansas, 1918 95.2 p115
Sorensen, Niels; Arkansas, 1918 95.2 p115
Sorensen, Otto Chris; Arkansas, 1918 95.2 p115
Sorensen, Soren Christian; Arkansas, 1918 95.2 p115
Sorenson, Bessie 32; Washington, 1918-1920 1728.5 p14
Sorenson, Charles A.; Illinois, 1896 5012.39 p53
Sorenson, Charles August; Illinois, 1899 5012.40 p56
Sorenson, Nels Christian; Arkansas, 1918 95.2 p115
Sorg, Heinrich; Cincinnati, 1869-1887 8582 p31
Sorhage, Friedrich Wilhelm; America, 1852 4610.10 p116
Sorlabond, Mr. 25; America, 1839 778.5 p502
Sorlin, Peter; Washington, 1859-1920 2872.1 p38
Sorochan, Parascha 28; New York, 1912 9980.29 p62
Sorreliac, Toussaint 64; New Orleans, 1826 778.5 p502
Sorrell, John; Virginia, 1647 6219 p241
Sorrell, Robert; Virginia, 1647 6219 p241
Sorrell, Robrt; Virginia, 1637 6219 p81
Sorter, Richard; Washington, 1859-1920 2872.1 p38
Sortor, Antonio; Iowa, 1866-1943 123.54 p45
Sorwell, Eliza. *SEE* Sorwell, Wm.
Sorwell, Wm.; Virginia, 1643 6219 p229
*Wife:*Eliza.
Sorzickas, Peter; Arkansas, 1918 95.2 p115
Sosinski, . . .; New York, 1831 4606 p177
Sosnoff, Jake; Arkansas, 1918 95.2 p115
Sosnowski, . . .; America, n.d. 4606 p180
With wife
Sothmann, John Ferdinand 25; Arkansas, 1918 95.2 p115
Sotiller, P. 22; New Orleans, 1830 778.5 p502
Soubiere, Mr. 22; America, 1839 778.5 p502
Souder, Geo.; Pennsylvania, 1753-1764 2444 p208
Souflet, Marie 29; New Orleans, 1839 778.5 p502
Sougert Majeste, J. B. 20; Louisiana, 1827 778.5 p502
Souit, Mr. 30; New Orleans, 1839 778.5 p502
Souith, John; New York, NY, 1838 8208.4 p69
Soul, George; New York, NY, 1840 8208.4 p106
Soul, Samuel 23; Maryland, 1774 1219.7 p215
Soulard, Simon; New York, NY, 1836 8208.4 p17
Soule, Elizabeth; Pennsylvania, 1685 4962 p156
Soule, John; America, 1839 1450.2 p136A
Soulet, Jean 36; New Orleans, 1835 778.5 p502
Soulie, N. 32; New Orleans, 1829 778.5 p502
Soupan, Peter; Iowa, 1866-1943 123.54 p45
Sourd, J. 38; New Orleans, 1827 778.5 p502
Sourdelly, L. J. 36; America, 1839 778.5 p502
Sourri, Pierre 40; America, 1838 778.5 p502
Sourroubille, Jean 18; New Orleans, 1839 778.5 p502
Soussieux, J. Baptiste 30; New Orleans, 1838 778.5 p503
Soustelle, Alfred; Arkansas, 1918 95.2 p115
Soustelle, Alfred Morris; Arkansas, 1918 95.2 p116
Soustelle, Lucien; Arkansas, 1918 95.2 p116
Souter, Henry; Philadelphia, 1760 9973.7 p35
South, Alexander 16; Maryland, 1774 1219.7 p225
South, Christ.; Virginia, 1638 6219 p122
Southam, Robert 23; Philadelphia, 1775 1219.7 p274
Southcombe, Edward; Jamaica, 1769 1219.7 p140
Southerne, Edward; Virginia, 1647 6219 p244
Southerne, Thomas; Virginia, 1635 6219 p5
Southerton, Richard 35; Jamaica, 1725 3690.1 p212
Southerwood, Isaac; Virginia, 1642 6219 p198
Southward, James 24; Maryland, 1774 1219.7 p178
Southward, W.E. 22; Harris Co., TX, 1898 6254 p4
Southwell, Susanna 26; Maryland, 1775 1219.7 p262
Southworth, Robt 16; America, 1699 2212 p28
Soutra, Germain 22; Ohio, 1837 778.5 p503
Soutra, Jean 24; Ohio, 1837 778.5 p503
Souverbie, Jenny 17; New Orleans, 1839 778.5 p503
Sovik, Lars; Arkansas, 1918 95.2 p116
Sowden, John 23; Maryland, 1774 1219.7 p206
Sowell, Thomas; Jamaica, 1751 1219.7 p8
Sowerbutts, Marsh 36; Maryland, 1774 1219.7 p192
Sowersby, William 26; New York, 1774 1219.7 p223
Sowes, George Stephen; Illinois, 1860 7857 p7
Sowny, James; America, 1742 4971 p49
Soy, James; New York, NY, 1837 8208.4 p52
Soye, Sarah 20; Philadelphia, 1859 5704.8 p142
Spaan, Adam; Philadelphia, 1758 9973.7 p33
Spach, Edward; Virginia, 1642 6219 p196
Spackford, Wm.; Virginia, 1638 6219 p116
Spackman, Dorothy *SEE* Spackman, John
Spackman, John; Virginia, 1635 6219 p69
*Wife:*Dorothy
*Child:*Joyce
*Child:*Rosemond
Spackman, Joyce *SEE* Spackman, John
Spackman, Nath.; Virginia, 1637 6219 p24
Spackman, Rich.; Virginia, 1635 6219 p33
Spackman, Rosemond *SEE* Spackman, John
Spackman, Thomas; Jamaica, 1762 1219.7 p90
Spadaccio, Charles 30; West Virginia, 1902 9788.3 p21
Spadaccio, Nicola 29; West Virginia, 1900 9788.3 p21
Spadoccio, Nicola 31; West Virginia, 1903 9788.3 p21
Spaet, Philipp; Cincinnati, 1869-1887 8582 p31
Spaeth, v., Obstl.; Quebec, 1776 9786 p105
Spaeth, Andreas; America, 1736-1800 2444 p218
*Wife:*Anna Catharina
*Child:*Anna Catharina
Spaeth, Anna Catharina *SEE* Spaeth, Andreas
Spaeth, Anna Catharina *SEE* Spaeth, Andreas
Spaeth, Elisabetha; Port uncertain, 1763 2444 p218
With 2 daughters
Spaeth, Philipp Samuel; Pennsylvania, 1743-1767 2444 p218
With wife
With 2 sons
Spaeth, Philipp Samuel; Port uncertain, 1720-1800 2444 p218
With wife
With 2 sons
Spaetnagel, Theodor; Ohio, 1800-1885 8582.2 p59
Spagna, John; Washington, 1859-1920 2872.1 p38
Spahn, . . .; Canada, 1776-1783 9786 p34
Spahn, Anna Catharina Dorothea; Port uncertain, 1701-1800 2444 p218
Spahn, Eva; Port uncertain, 1701-1800 2444 p218
Spahr, John George; Philadelphia, 1762 9973.7 p37
Spaigner, Anna Maria 5 *SEE* Spaigner, John George
Spaigner, Barbara 10 *SEE* Spaigner, John George
Spaigner, Eva Sussana 18 *SEE* Spaigner, John George
Spaigner, George Frederick 13 *SEE* Spaigner, John George
Spaigner, John George; South Carolina, 1752-1753 3689.17 p23
With wife
*Relative:*John Samuel 20
*Relative:*Eva Sussana 18
*Relative:*John George 15
*Relative:*George Frederick 13
*Relative:*Barbara 10
*Relative:*Anna Maria 5
Spaigner, John George 15 *SEE* Spaigner, John George
Spaigner, John Samuel 20 *SEE* Spaigner, John George
Spaine, Thomas; Virginia, 1641 6219 p186
Spalding, Thomas; Virginia, 1754 1219.7 p29
Spalding, Thomas; Virginia, 1754 3690.1 p212
Spallata, Francesco; Arkansas, 1918 95.2 p116
Spaltzcholz, Hellmut Genje; Arkansas, 1918 95.2 p116
Spamer, Jacob; Maryland, 1858 3702.7 p364
Spangenberg, Bishop; New York, 1744 3652 p63
With wife
Spangenberg, Lt.; Canada, 1776-1783 9786 p149
Spangenberg, A. G.; New York, 1754 3652 p78
Spangenberg, Augustus G.; Savannah, GA, 1735 3652 p51
Spangenberg, C.; Ohio, 1869-1887 8582 p31
Spangler, Bolser; Philadelphia, 1752 9973.7 p32
Spanier, Anne M. I. Schwagmeyer 37 *SEE* Spanier, Jurgen Heinrich Friedrich
Spanier, Carl Friedrich Wilhelm *SEE* Spanier, Jurgen Heinrich Friedrich
Spanier, Charlotte S. Amalie *SEE* Spanier, Jurgen Heinrich Friedrich
Spanier, Heinrich F. Gottlieb *SEE* Spanier, Jurgen Heinrich Friedrich
Spanier, Heinrich Wilhelm *SEE* Spanier, Jurgen Heinrich Friedrich
Spanier, Hermann Friedrich *SEE* Spanier, Jurgen Heinrich Friedrich
Spanier, Jurgen Heinrich Friedrich; America, 1845 4610.10 p155
*Wife:*Anne M. I. Schwagmeyer 37
*Child:*Heinrich Wilhelm
*Child:*Charlotte S. Amalie
*Child:*Heinrich F. Gottlieb
*Child:*Marie W. Magdalene
*Child:*Carl Friedrich Wilhelm
*Child:*Hermann Friedrich
Spanier, Marie W. Magdalene *SEE* Spanier, Jurgen Heinrich Friedrich
Spaniola, Anton W.; Illinois, 1902 5012.39 p53
Spaniola, Anton W.; Illinois, 1902 5012.40 p79
Spanjer, Redmer 24; Arkansas, 1918 95.2 p116
Spanknebel, Adam; Philadelphia, 1779 8137 p14
Spankuebel, Elizabeth; Ohio, 1824 8582.1 p46
Spanos, Gusto Spearo; Iowa, 1866-1943 123.54 p79
Spanseiler, George; Philadelphia, 1762 9973.7 p37
Spar, Stephen 16; Maryland, 1720 3690.1 p212
Sparairre, S. M. 21; Port uncertain, 1838 778.5 p503
Sparano, John; Arkansas, 1918 95.2 p116
Sparberg, Harris 23; Kansas, 1886 5240.1 p69
Sparcurre, S. M. 21; Port uncertain, 1838 778.5 p503
Spark, Alexander; Quebec, 1780 9775.5 p202
Spark, Ann; Virginia, 1628 6219 p31
Spark, James; New York, NY, 1815 2859.11 p42
Spark, Johann Bernhard 23; Kansas, 1888 5240.1 p42
Spark, Johann Bernhard 23; Kansas, 1888 5240.1 p72
Spark, John 50; Kansas, 1879 5240.1 p42
Spark, John 50; Kansas, 1879 5240.1 p61
Sparkes, Grace; Virginia, 1635 6219 p69
Sparkes, John; Virginia, 1635 6219 p69
Sparkes, Mary; Virginia, 1635 6219 p69
Sparkowska, Adolfa 24; New York, 1912 9980.29 p54
Sparks, Alexander; New York, NY, 1816 2859.11 p42
Sparks, Eliza; New York, NY, 1816 2859.11 p42
Sparks, Francis; Virginia, 1638 6219 p147
Sparks, Jane 60; South Carolina, 1850 1639.20 p294
Sparks, John; Virginia, 1635 6219 p12
Sparks, Jon.; Virginia, 1635 6219 p26
Sparks, Richard 34; Jamaica, 1734 3690.1 p212
Sparks, Thomas; Virginia, 1638 6219 p146
Sparling, J. L.; Washington, 1859-1920 2872.1 p38
Sparr, George; Pennsylvania, 1765 4779.3 p14A
Sparr, Michael; Pennsylvania, 1769 9973.8 p32
Sparre, John; Colorado, 1904 9678.3 p14
Sparrow, Anthony 24; Maryland, 1724 3690.1 p212
Sparrow, John 17; Jamaica, 1724 3690.1 p212
Sparrow, John 19; Jamaica, 1734 3690.1 p212
Sparrow, Joseph 25; Jamaica, 1724 3690.1 p212
Sparrow, Tho.; Virginia, 1635 6219 p17
Sparrow, William 22; Philadelphia, 1774 1219.7 p232
Sparshott, Edward *SEE* Sparshott, Edward
Sparshott, Edward *SEE* Sparshott, Edward
Sparshott, Edward; Virginia, 1635 6219 p72
*Wife:*Mandolin Canes
Sparshott, Edward; Virginia, 1636 6219 p76
*Son:*Edward
Sparshott, Edward; Virginia, 1638 6219 p180
*Wife:*Madolin Caves
*Son:*Edward
Sparshott, Madolin Caves *SEE* Sparshott, Edward
Sparshott, Mandolin Canes *SEE* Sparshott, Edward
Spasich, Dimitriga; Arkansas, 1918 95.2 p116
Spassafnmo, Masso 38; New York, NY, 1893 9026.4 p42
Spatch, Edward; Virginia, 1646 6219 p236
Spates, Ambron; New York, NY, 1836 8208.4 p10
Spath, . . .; Canada, 1776-1783 9786 p34
Spath, Jean; Canada, 1776-1783 9786 p242
Spath, John; Canada, 1776-1783 9786 p207A
Spath, Peter 29; Jamaica, 1773 1219.7 p170
Spath, Philip; Pennsylvania, 1743-1767 2444 p218
Spath, Philip; Port uncertain, 1720-1800 2444 p218
Spatz, . . .; Canada, 1776-1783 9786 p34
Spaulding, Amos; Washington, 1859-1920 2872.1 p38
Spaulding, Delos; Washington, 1859-1920 2872.1 p38
Spawor, George; Pennsylvania, 1765 4779.3 p14A
Speakman, John 20; Maryland, 1775 1219.7 p273
Speakman, Mary 20; Virginia, 1699 2212 p20
Spear, John 13; Wilmington, DE, 1831 6508.3 p100
Spear, Margaret Jane 19; Philadelphia, 1864 5704.8 p157
Spear, Mary 19; Maryland, 1721 3690.1 p212
Speare, Isabella 30; Philadelphia, 1860 5704.8 p145
Spease, Barbara *SEE* Spease, Henry
Spease, Catherine Roesner *SEE* Spease, Henry
Spease, Henry; Pennsylvania, 1834-1835 5647.5 p37
*Wife:*Catherine Roesner
*Daughter:*Barbara
Specht, . . .; Canada, 1776-1783 9786 p34
Specht, Charles; Washington, 1859-1920 2872.1 p38
Specht, Henry; Washington, 1859-1920 2872.1 p38
Specht, J.F. von; Canada, 1776 9786 p109
Specht, Johann Friedrich; Quebec, 1776 9786 p257
Specht, Johann Julius Anton; Quebec, 1776 9786 p263
Specht, John; Indiana, 1847 9117 p18
Speck, John; Grenada, 1766 1219.7 p117
Speck, Lewis; Illinois, 1896 5012.39 p53
Speck, Lewis; Illinois, 1898 5012.40 p55
Speck, Louise; Indiana, 1880 5647.5 p31
Speckhardts, Johann; Illinois, 1838 8582.2 p50
Speckmann, . . .; Cincinnati, 1826 8582.1 p51
Speckmann, Anne M W Dembergsmeyer *SEE* Speckmann, Johann Heinrich
Speckmann, Carl Friedrich; America, 1845 4610.10 p120
*Wife:*Marie C. F. Bultemeier
*Son:*Carl Friedrich Wilhelm
Speckmann, Carl Friedrich Wilhelm *SEE* Speckmann, Carl Friedrich
Speckmann, Johann F. Wilhelm *SEE* Speckmann, Johann Heinrich

Speckmann, Johann Heinrich; America, 1845 ***4610.10*** *p120*
*Wife:*Anne M W Dembergsmeyer
*Son:*Johann F. Wilhelm
Speckmann, Margarete Dorothee; America, 1845 ***4815.7*** *p92*
Speckmann, Marie C. F. Bultemeier *SEE* Speckmann, Carl Friedrich
Speecher, Henry; Philadelphia, 1761 ***9973.7*** *p35*
Speechly, John; Illinois, 1871 ***5012.39*** *p25*
Speed, Wm.; Virginia, 1633 ***6219*** *p32*
Speer, Andrew; Philadelphia, 1847 ***53.26*** *p83*
Speer, Andrew; Philadelphia, 1847 ***5704.8*** *p13*
Speer, Eliza; St. John, N.B., 1847 ***5704.8*** *p32*
Speer, Elizabeth; Philadelphia, 1847 ***53.26*** *p83*
Speer, Elizabeth; Philadelphia, 1847 ***5704.8*** *p23*
Speer, Hannah; New Orleans, 1848 ***5704.8*** *p48*
Speer, John; New Orleans, 1849 ***5704.8*** *p59*
Speer, John; Quebec, 1847 ***5704.8*** *p28*
Speer, Lenard; New Orleans, 1848 ***5704.8*** *p48*
Speer, Margaret; Quebec, 1848 ***5704.8*** *p42*
Speer, Mary 9 mos; St. John, N.B., 1847 ***5704.8*** *p32*
Speer, Mary J.; New York, NY, 1868 ***5704.8*** *p229*
Speer, Mary Jane; Philadelphia, 1853 ***5704.8*** *p101*
Speer, Matilda 20; Philadelphia, 1858 ***5704.8*** *p139*
Speer, Matty; Quebec, 1852 ***5704.8*** *p91*
Speer, Samuel 13; St. John, N.B., 1847 ***5704.8*** *p32*
Speer, Thomas; St. John, N.B., 1847 ***5704.8*** *p32*
Speer, Thomas Henry; Quebec, 1848 ***5704.8*** *p41*
Speevy, Georg; Virginia, 1643 ***6219*** *p207*
Spehrle, William; Illinois, 1902 ***5012.40*** *p77*
Speice, Kate Roesner; America, n.d. ***5647.5*** *p3*
Speicher, Johann Christoph 25; Pennsylvania, 1748 ***2444*** *p220*
Speichert, Johannes; Philadelphia, 1779 ***8137*** *p14*
Speidel, . . .; Pennsylvania, 1749 ***2444*** *p209*
Speidel, Abraham; Charleston, SC, 1766 ***8582.2*** *p65*
Speidel, Christina *SEE* Speidel, Hans
Speidel, Christina *SEE* Speidel, Hans
Speidel, Hans; Pennsylvania, 1753 ***2444*** *p218*
*Wife:*Christina
*Child:*Christina
Speidel, Hans Jerg; Pennsylvania, 1749 ***2444*** *p219*
Speidel, Johan Georg; Pennsylvania, 1750 ***2444*** *p219*
Speidel, Joseph; Pennsylvania, 1749 ***2444*** *p219*
Speidel, Maximilian; West Indies, 1730-1763 ***2444*** *p219*
Speidel, Maximilianus; Pennsylvania, 1749 ***2444*** *p219*
Speight, Francis; Virginia, 1642 ***6219*** *p186*
Spein, Jean 47; America, 1836 ***778.5*** *p495*
Speir, Alexander 19; Wilmington, NC, 1774 ***1639.20*** *p294*
Speir, Andrew 7 *SEE* Speir, John
Speir, Andrew 7; Philadelphia, 1847 ***5704.8*** *p14*
Speir, Catherine *SEE* Speir, John
Speir, Catherine; Philadelphia, 1847 ***5704.8*** *p13*
Speir, Eliz. *SEE* Speir, John
Speir, Eliza; Philadelphia, 1847 ***5704.8*** *p13*
Speir, Gerred 5 *SEE* Speir, John
Speir, Gerred 5; Philadelphia, 1847 ***5704.8*** *p14*
Speir, Hannah *SEE* Speir, John
Speir, Hannah; Philadelphia, 1847 ***5704.8*** *p13*
Speir, Hannah 5 *SEE* Speir, John
Speir, Hannah 5; Philadelphia, 1847 ***5704.8*** *p14*
Speir, John; Philadelphia, 1847 ***53.26*** *p83*
*Relative:*Hannah
*Relative:*Catherine
*Relative:*Mary
*Relative:*Rebecca
*Relative:*Eliz.
*Relative:*Robert
*Relative:*Margaret 9
*Relative:*Andrew 7
*Relative:*Gerred 5
*Relative:*Hannah 5
Speir, John; Philadelphia, 1847 ***5704.8*** *p13*
Speir, Margaret 9 *SEE* Speir, John
Speir, Margaret 9; Philadelphia, 1847 ***5704.8*** *p14*
Speir, Mary *SEE* Speir, John
Speir, Mary; Philadelphia, 1847 ***5704.8*** *p13*
Speir, Rebecca *SEE* Speir, John
Speir, Rebecca; Philadelphia, 1847 ***5704.8*** *p13*
Speir, Robert *SEE* Speir, John
Speir, Robert; Philadelphia, 1847 ***5704.8*** *p13*
Speird, Louis 30; America, 1839 ***778.5*** *p503*
Speird, Louise 2; America, 1839 ***778.5*** *p503*
Speird, Magdalena 5; America, 1839 ***778.5*** *p503*
Speird, Magdalena 32; America, 1839 ***778.5*** *p503*
Speirs, Elizabeth 22; Virginia, 1774 ***1219.7*** *p244*
Speirs, William; America, 1833 ***1450.2*** *p137A*
Speisel, Joseh; Wisconsin, n.d. ***9675.8*** *p121*
Speiser, Georg 47; Kansas, 1879 ***5240.1*** *p60*
Speke, Thomas; Virginia, 1652 ***6251*** *p19*
Spellesey, Jean; Montreal, 1822 ***7603*** *p62*
Spelman, D.; New York, NY, 1816 ***2859.11*** *p42*
Spence, Alexander; Illinois, 1860 ***5012.38*** *p97*
Spence, Andrew 17; Virginia, 1720 ***3690.1*** *p213*
Spence, Benjamin; Colorado, 1898 ***9678.3*** *p14*
Spence, Bridget 20; Massachusetts, 1847 ***5881.1*** *p87*
Spence, Catherine; Quebec, 1847 ***5704.8*** *p27*
Spence, Catherine 3; Quebec, 1847 ***5704.8*** *p27*
Spence, Eliza 7; Quebec, 1847 ***5704.8*** *p27*
Spence, Eliza 18; Quebec, 1858 ***5704.8*** *p138*
Spence, Elizabeth; America, 1870 ***5704.8*** *p239*
Spence, Elizabeth 16; Virginia, 1774 ***1219.7*** *p226*
Spence, Henry 25; Virginia, 1773 ***1219.7*** *p171*
Spence, James; Savannah, GA, 1774 ***1219.7*** *p227*
Spence, James 41; Virginia, 1775 ***1219.7*** *p261*
Spence, John; North Carolina, 1801 ***1639.20*** *p294*
Spence, John; Savannah, GA, 1774 ***1219.7*** *p227*
Spence, Margaret; Quebec, 1847 ***5704.8*** *p27*
Spence, Mary; Savannah, GA, 1774 ***1219.7*** *p227*
Spence, Mary Ann 9; Quebec, 1847 ***5704.8*** *p27*
Spence, Percy H.; Washington, 1859-1920 ***2872.1*** *p38*
Spence, Philip 14; Antigua (Antego), 1774 ***1219.7*** *p241*
Spence, Rebecca; Philadelphia, 1865 ***5704.8*** *p191*
Spence, Robert 23; Jamaica, 1774 ***1219.7*** *p219*
Spence, Samuel 10; Quebec, 1863 ***5704.8*** *p154*
Spence, Sarah 21; Quebec, 1862 ***5704.8*** *p151*
Spence, Susan; Quebec, 1847 ***5704.8*** *p27*
Spence, Thomas; Quebec, 1823 ***7603*** *p29*
Spence, William; Quebec, 1847 ***5704.8*** *p27*
Spence, William 9 mos; Quebec. 1847 ***5704.8*** *p27*
Spence, William 15; Quebec, 1863 ***5704.8*** *p154*
Spence, William 20; Montserrat, 1699-1700 ***2212*** *p22*
Spence, William 23; Maryland, 1774 ***1219.7*** *p206*
Spence, William 23; Quebec, 1862 ***5704.8*** *p150*
Spence, William 40; Quebec, 1863 ***5704.8*** *p154*
Spencer, Amelia 18 *SEE* Spencer, Geo.
Spencer, Ann 2; Massachusetts, 1850 ***5881.1*** *p87*
Spencer, Benjamin 21; Maryland, 1774 ***1219.7*** *p180*
Spencer, Daniel 20; Massachusetts, 1850 ***5881.1*** *p89*
Spencer, Edward; Virginia, 1648 ***6219*** *p237*
Spencer, Francis; America, 1735-1743 ***4971*** *p78*
Spencer, Francis; Virginia, 1643 ***6219*** *p207*
Spencer, Geo. 53; Canada, 1853 ***4535.11*** *p53*
*Wife:*Mary Ann 50
*Child:*Amelia 18
*Child:*Walter 12
*Child:*Percival 8
Spencer, James 20; Pennsylvania, 1727 ***3690.1*** *p213*
Spencer, James 34; Antigua (Antego), 1775 ***1219.7*** *p256*
Spencer, John; Bermuda, 1760 ***1219.7*** *p79*
Spencer, John; Philadelphia, 1851 ***5704.8*** *p81*
Spencer, Jon.; Virginia, 1638 ***6219*** *p122*
Spencer, Joseph 16; Philadelphia, 1774 ***1219.7*** *p197*
Spencer, Joshua; Virginia, 1698 ***2212*** *p12*
Spencer, Kath.; Virginia, 1643 ***6219*** *p204*
Spencer, Mary 19; Philadelphia, 1774 ***1219.7*** *p195*
Spencer, Mary Ann 6; Massachusetts, 1850 ***5881.1*** *p92*
Spencer, Mary Ann 50 *SEE* Spencer, Geo.
Spencer, Matthew; America, 1735-1743 ***4971*** *p8*
Spencer, Nich.; Virginia, 1637 ***6219*** *p180*
Spencer, Nicho.; Virginia, 1635 ***6219*** *p70*
Spencer, Percival 8 *SEE* Spencer, Geo.
Spencer, Robert; New York, NY, 1815 ***2859.11*** *p42*
Spencer, Samuel; New York, NY, 1816 ***2859.11*** *p42*
Spencer, Samuel; Philadelphia, 1750 ***3690.1*** *p213*
Spencer, Sebstian; Charleston, SC, 1775-1781 ***8582.2*** *p39*
Spencer, Thomas; Philadelphia, 1851 ***5704.8*** *p78*
Spencer, Thomas 18; Virginia, 1750 ***3690.1*** *p213*
Spencer, Thomas 18; Virginia, 1751 ***1219.7*** *p2*
Spencer, Thomas 30; Baltimore, 1775 ***1219.7*** *p270*
Spencer, Walter 12 *SEE* Spencer, Geo.
Spencer, William; Quebec, 1852 ***5704.8*** *p94*
Spencer, William; Virginia, 1624 ***6219*** *p29*
Spencer, William; Virginia, 1638 ***6219*** *p125*
Spencer, William; Virginia, 1642 ***6219*** *p194*
Spencer, William 1; Massachusetts, 1849 ***5881.1*** *p93*
Spencer, William 15; Philadelphia, 1774 ***1219.7*** *p175*
Spencer, William 17; Maryland, 1723 ***3690.1*** *p213*
Spencer, William 25; Maryland, 1775 ***1219.7*** *p262*
Spender, John 22; Jamaica, 1735 ***3690.1*** *p213*
Spendlove, Fredrick Newman Albert 24; Kansas, 1895 ***5240.1*** *p80*
Spendlove, Roger; Boston, 1776 ***1219.7*** *p283*
Spengeler, Johannes; Philadelphia, 1779 ***8137*** *p14*
Spengler, Albert; Wisconsin, n.d. ***9675.8*** *p121*
Spengler, Anna Maria 6; America, 1831 ***778.5*** *p503*
Spengler, Balthasar; Pennsylvania, 1752 ***2444*** *p219*
*Wife:*Rosina Moessner
*Child:*Johann Jacob
*Child:*Christoph Heinrich
*Child:*Catharina Barbara
Spengler, Bernard; Philadelphia, 1762 ***9973.7*** *p37*
Spengler, Catharina Barbara *SEE* Spengler, Balthasar
Spengler, Catharine 14; America, 1831 ***778.5*** *p503*
Spengler, Christoph Heinrich *SEE* Spengler, Balthasar
Spengler, Henry; Philadelphia, 1763 ***9973.7*** *p38*
Spengler, Johann Jacob *SEE* Spengler, Balthasar
Spengler, Magdalena 7; America, 1831 ***778.5*** *p503*
Spengler, Peter 3; America, 1831 ***778.5*** *p503*
Spengler, Peter 43; America, 1831 ***778.5*** *p503*
Spengler, Rosina Moessner *SEE* Spengler, Balthasar
Spenhurakes, Antonio George; Arkansas, 1918 ***95.2*** *p116*
Spenneberg, Heinrich; America, 1853 ***8582.3*** *p62*
Spennso, Francesco 12; New York, NY, 1893 ***9026.4*** *p42*
Spenser, Elizabeth 15; Jamaica, 1730 ***3690.1*** *p213*
Spenzer, Bastian; Charleston, SC, 1775-1781 ***8582.2*** *p52*
Sperbach, Anna; New York, 1752 ***3652*** *p76*
Spering, Joseph; Virginia, 1638 ***6219*** *p122*
Speropoulas, Anthony; Arkansas, 1918 ***95.2*** *p116*
Spert, Jacob; Wisconsin, n.d. ***9675.8*** *p121*
Speth, von; Quebec, 1776 ***9786*** *p106*
Speth, E.L.W. von; Quebec, 1776 ***9786*** *p102*
Speth, Ernst Ludewig Wilhelm; Quebec, 1776 ***9786*** *p256*
Speth, Leopold 24; New Orleans, 1839 ***778.5*** *p504*
Speyer, Barbara Luettich *SEE* Speyer, Johann
Speyer, Johann; Port uncertain, 1751-1800 ***2444*** *p219*
*Wife:*Barbara Luettich
*Child:*Matthaus
*Child:*Johannes
Speyer, Johannes *SEE* Speyer, Johann
Speyer, Johannes; Pennsylvania, 1754 ***2444*** *p174*
Speyer, John; Pennsylvania, 1754 ***2444*** *p219*
Speyer, Matthaus *SEE* Speyer, Johann
Speyr, Anna Catharina *SEE* Speyr, Matthaeus
Speyr, Anna Catharina *SEE* Speyr, Matthaeus
Speyr, Johann Caspar *SEE* Speyr, Matthaeus
Speyr, Matthaeus; Pennsylvania, 1733-1742 ***2444*** *p219*
*Wife:*Anna Catharina
*Child:*Anna Catharina
*Child:*Johann Caspar
Spice, Georg; Virginia, 1638 ***6219*** *p147*
Spice, Joseph; New York, NY, 1838 ***8208.4*** *p72*
Spicer, Edward; Virginia, 1643 ***6219*** *p202*
Spicer, Edward; Virginia, 1645 ***6219*** *p253*
Spicer, James 23; Virginia, 1727 ***3690.1*** *p213*
Spicer, Richard 24; Maryland, 1724 ***3690.1*** *p213*
Spicer, William; Virginia, 1652 ***6251*** *p20*
Spiegel, Georg Carl; Ohio, 1869-1887 ***8582*** *p31*
Spiegel, Wilhelm; America, 1832 ***8582.3*** *p62*
Spiegle, Michael; Philadelphia, 1759 ***9973.7*** *p33*
Spielbiegler, Johann; Georgia, 1739 ***9332*** *p326*
*Mother:*Rosina
Spielbiegler, Rosina *SEE* Spielbiegler, Johann
Spiell, Barbell; Philadelphia, 1756 ***4525*** *p262*
Spiell, Gorg Jacob; Philadelphia, 1756 ***4525*** *p262*
Spielmann, Kath. Schmidt 70; New York, NY, 1908 ***1763*** *p40D*
Spielmann, Leonhard; New England, 1773 ***4525*** *p250*
With 3 children
Spielmann, Leonhard; Pennsylvania, 1773 ***4525*** *p250*
With 3 children
Spier, Anton; Colorado, 1894 ***9678.3*** *p14*
Spiering, August; Wisconsin, n.d. ***9675.8*** *p121*
Spiering, Chas.; Wisconsin, n.d. ***9675.8*** *p121*
Spierring, Albert; Wisconsin, n.d. ***9675.8*** *p121*
Spiers, James; New York, NY, 1811 ***2859.11*** *p19*
Spiers, Mrs. John; New York, NY, 1811 ***2859.11*** *p19*
Spies, . . .; Wisconsin, n.d. ***9675.8*** *p121*
Spies, Barbara *SEE* Spies, Henry
Spies, Barbara *SEE* Spies, Henry
Spies, Catharine Roesner *SEE* Spies, Henry
Spies, Catherine Roesner *SEE* Spies, Henry
Spies, Henry; Pennsylvania, 1830-1834 ***5647.5*** *p4*
*Wife:*Catharine Roesner
*Daughter:*Barbara
Spies, Henry; Pennsylvania, 1834-1835 ***5647.5*** *p37*
*Wife:*Catherine Roesner
*Daughter:*Barbara
Spies, Jacob; Wisconsin, n.d. ***9675.8*** *p121*
Spies, Ludwic; Philadelphia, 1764 ***9973.7*** *p39*
Spiesel, Jacob; Wisconsin, n.d. ***9675.8*** *p121*
Spiesel, Joseph; Wisconsin, n.d. ***9675.8*** *p121*
Spiess, Catharina; New York, NY, 1847 ***8582.2*** *p8*
Spila, Stanley; Arkansas, 1918 ***95.2*** *p116*
Spilbr, Domenic; Iowa, 1866-1943 ***123.54*** *p45*
Spillane, Darby; America, 1736-1743 ***4971*** *p57*
Spillane, Dennis; America, 1741 ***4971*** *p56*
Spillane, Ellen 20; Massachusetts, 1847 ***5881.1*** *p89*
Spillane, Joan 36; Massachusetts, 1849 ***5881.1*** *p90*
Spillane, Maurice; America, 1741 ***4971*** *p42*
Spiller, David; Virginia, 1652 ***6251*** *p20*
Spilli, Frederic; Wisconsin, n.d. ***9675.8*** *p121*
Spilman, Thomas; Virginia, 1624 ***6219*** *p30*
Spiltimber, John; Virginia, 1635 ***6219*** *p69*

Spincke, Tho.; Virginia, 1646 6219 p240
Spindler, Richard; America, 1901 3455.1 p40
Spinelli, Benian.ino 32; New York, NY, 1893 9026.4 p42
Spingen, C. 21; Maryland, 1774 1219.7 p235
Spingler, Rudolph; Philadelphia, 1762 9973.7 p37
Spinhtourokis, Antonios; Arkansas, 1918 95.2 p116
Spinke, Robert; Virginia, 1637 6219 p113
Spiral, L. H. Felipe 20; New Orleans, 1835 778.5 p504
Spiring, John 22; Jamaica, 1738 3690.1 p213
Spitsnagle, Able 21; Port uncertain, 1838 778.5 p504
Spitter, . . .; Canada, 1776-1783 9786 p34
Spittlewood, Sarah; Virginia, 1646 6219 p239
Spitzle, Henry 38; Kansas, 1884 5240.1 p65
Spitzli, Fredrick 47; Kansas, 1878 5240.1 p59
Spiwak, Jake; Arkansas, 1918 95.2 p116
Splaun, John; Newport, RI, 1837 7036 p120
Spoeder, . . .; Canada, 1776-1783 9786 p34
Spohn, Anna Maria SEE Spohn, Johann Matthias
Spohn, Elisabetha; Pennsylvania, 1751 2444 p178
Spohn, Johann Matthias; Pennsylvania, 1750 2444 p219
Wife:Lucia Biezer
Child:Anna Maria
Child:Martin
Spohn, Lucia Biezer SEE Spohn, Johann Matthias
Spohn, Lucia Biezer; Pennsylvania, 1750 2444 p139
Spohn, Martin SEE Spohn, Johann Matthias
Spohr, Konrad; Philadelphia, 1779 8137 p14
Spohr, Wilhelm; Lancaster, PA, 1780 8137 p14
Spon, Anna Maria SEE Spon, Johann Matthias
Spon, Johann Matthias; Pennsylvania, 1750 2444 p219
Wife:Lucia Biezer
Child:Anna Maria
Child:Martin
Spon, Lucia Biezer SEE Spon, Johann Matthias
Spon, Martin SEE Spon, Johann Matthias
Sponct, Blar; Iowa, 1866-1943 123.54 p45
Sponenburk, Oliver 22; Kansas, 1883 5240.1 p64
Sponsel, Thomas; Wisconsin, n.d. 9675.8 p121
Spoo, Angela 28; New York, 1854 3702.7 p367
Spooner, John 32; Virginia, 1700 2212 p30
Spore, Alice; Virginia, 1635 6219 p16
Spore, Harl N. 43; Kansas, 1879 5240.1 p60
Sporer, Anton; Wisconsin, n.d. 9675.8 p121
Sporer, Jakov; Iowa, 1866-1943 123.54 p79
Sporer, Jakov Frank; Iowa, 1866-1943 123.54 p79
Sporer, Valentine; Iowa, 1866-1943 123.54 p45
Sporleder, . . .; Baltimore, 1833 3702.7 p68
Spornberg, Jacob H.; America, 1833 1450.2 p137A
Sportel, Berend; Washington, 1859-1920 2872.1 p38
Spott, John; Arkansas, 1918 95.2 p116
Spracht, Vincent; America, 1886 7137 p170
Spradling, Ann; South Carolina, 1767 1639.20 p294
Spraecher, Johann Christoph; Pennsylvania, 1751 2444 p220
Spraggs, Edward 19; Jamaica, 1723 3690.1 p213
Sprague, John 23; Boston, 1775 1219.7 p258
Sprake, William 19; Pennsylvania, 1728 3690.1 p213
Sprandel, Carl; Cincinnati, 1848 8582.2 p63
Sprandel, George; New York, NY, 1856 1450.2 p137A
Spranger, Gustav; Wisconsin, n.d. 9675.8 p121
Sprason, Wm.; Virginia, 1636 6219 p32
Spratt, Andrew; New York, NY, 1815 2859.11 p42
Spratt, Eliza; Philadelphia, 1853 5704.8 p102
Spratt, Hugh; New York, NY, 1811 2859.11 p19
Spratt, Mary; New York, NY, 1811 2859.11 p19
Spratt, Mary; New York, NY, 1816 2859.11 p42
Spratt, Thomas; New York, NY, 1816 2859.11 p42
Spratt, William; New York, NY, 1811 2859.11 p19
Spraule, Armour; New York, NY, 1816 2859.11 p42
Spray, John 15; Maryland, 1775 1219.7 p272
Spray, Thomas 20; West Indies, 1722 3690.1 p213
Spreadborough, A.; Washington, 1859-1920 2872.1 p38
Spreadborough, Arthur; Washington, 1859-1920 2872.1 p38
Spreadborough, Eli; Washington, 1859-1920 2872.1 p38
Spreadborough, Walter; Washington, 1859-1920 2872.1 p38
Sprecher, Hans Jorg; Pennsylvania, 1751 2444 p220
Sprecher, Jacob; Pennsylvania, 1751 2444 p220
Sprecher, Johann Christoph; Pennsylvania, 1751 2444 p220
Sprecher, Johann Georg; Port uncertain, 1743-1808 2444 p220
Child:Maria Elisabetha
Child:Maria Margaretha
Sprecher, John Christopher 25; Pennsylvania, 1748 2444 p220
Sprecher, Maria Elisabetha SEE Sprecher, Johann Georg
Sprecher, Maria Margaretha SEE Sprecher, Johann Georg
Sprecker, Geo.; Pennsylvania, 1751 2444 p220
Sprecker, Mathias 32; Port uncertain, 1839 778.5 p504
Spreeker, George; Philadelphia, 1758 9973.7 p33
Spreng, Adam; America, 1851 1450.2 p137A
Sprenger, Anna Maria 10; America, 1836 778.5 p504
Sprenger, Henrich; Philadelphia, 1779 8137 p14
Sprenger, Kasper 5; America, 1836 778.5 p504
Sprenger, Susanna 30; America, 1836 778.5 p504
Sprie, James 31; Virginia, 1774 1219.7 p241
Spriegel, William; Iroquois Co., IL, 1895 3455.1 p13
Sprigg, Thomas 20; Antigua (Antego), 1731 3690.1 p214
Spriggs, Thomas 23; Maryland, 1774 1219.7 p211
Sprigmann, Peter Anton; Cincinnati, 1800-1810 8582.3 p81
Spring, J. F.; Shreveport, LA, 1877 7129 p45
Spring, Jos.; Virginia, 1635 6219 p5
Spring, Robert; Virginia, 1634 6219 p32
Spring, William 24; Philadelphia, 1775 1219.7 p255
Springborn, Wilhelm 44; Kansas, 1886 5240.1 p42
Springborn, William 44; Kansas, 1886 5240.1 p68
Springer, . . .; Canada, 1776-1783 9786 p34
Springer, Charles; Illinois, 1888 2896.5 p38
Springer, Christina; New England, 1749 2444 p170
Springer, Fred Carl; Arkansas, 1918 95.2 p116
Springer, Friederic 14; America, 1838 778.5 p504
Springer, Margarethe 21; America, 1838 778.5 p504
Springer, Valentine; Illinois, 1902 5012.40 p77
Springoh, John 38; Kansas, 1873 5240.1 p54
Sprio, Ligor Thomas; Arkansas, 1918 95.2 p116
Sprit, Gorg Jacob; Philadelphia, 1756 4525 p262
Spritz, Hermann; Milwaukee, 1875 4719.30 p257
Spriver, George 30; Jamaica, 1725 3690.1 p214
Sproh, Peter; New York, 1754 3652 p80
Sprott, Henry 24; St. John, N.B., 1861 5704.8 p146
Sproul, James C.; New York, NY, 1811 2859.11 p19
Sproul, John; Baltimore, 1811 2859.11 p19
Sproule, . . . 9 mos; St. John, N.B., 1847 5704.8 p4
Sproule, Adam 45; New England, 1774 1219.7 p196
Sproule, Alexander 2; St. John, N.B., 1851 5704.8 p80
Sproule, Ann; St. John, N.B., 1847 5704.8 p4
Sproule, Beck 7; St. John, N.B., 1847 5704.8 p4
Sproule, Charles; New Orleans, 1849 5704.8 p59
Sproule, Charles 12; St. John, N.B., 1851 5704.8 p79
Sproule, Edmond; St. John, N.B., 1850 5704.8 p67
Sproule, Edward; Iroquois Co., IL, 1894 3455.1 p13
Sproule, Edward 13; St. John, N.B., 1847 5704.8 p4
Sproule, Eleanor; St. John, N.B., 1851 5704.8 p72
Sproule, Eliza; St. John, N.B., 1847 5704.8 p4
Sproule, Harper; St. John, N.B., 1847 5704.8 p4
Sproule, Harper 5; St. John, N.B., 1847 5704.8 p4
Sproule, James 8; St. John, N.B., 1851 5704.8 p80
Sproule, Margaret; St. John, N.B., 1851 5704.8 p79
Sproule, Matty 10; St. John, N.B., 1847 5704.8 p4
Sproule, Phillip 11; St. John, N.B., 1847 5704.8 p4
Sproule, Robert; New Orleans, 1849 5704.8 p59
Sproule, Robert; St. John, N.B., 1849 5704.8 p49
Sproule, Robert; St. John, N.B., 1851 5704.8 p79
Sproule, Robert 6; St. John, N.B., 1851 5704.8 p80
Sproule, Thomas 10; St. John, N.B., 1851 5704.8 p79
Sproule, William 4; St. John, N.B., 1851 5704.8 p80
Sproule, William Knox; America, 1856 1450.2 p137A
Sprouse, Alice; Virginia, 1642 6219 p197
Spruce, John 12; Massachusetts, 1849 5881.1 p90
Spruth, . . .; Illinois, 1897 2896.5 p38
Spry, William; Virginia, 1648 6219 p246
Sprye, Oliver; Virginia, 1639 6219 p158
Spuck, . . .; Canada, 1776-1783 9786 p43
Spuer, Margarett; Virginia, 1643 6219 p204
Spulit, . . .; Canada, 1776-1783 9786 p34
Spunner, Thomas; Philadelphia, 1815 2859.11 p42
Spurjoye, Georg; Virginia, 1639 6219 p159
Spurrier, Michaell; Virginia, 1636 6219 p26
Spurway, John; Virginia, 1637 6219 p37
Sqibbs, Jacob 17; Canada, 1838 4535.12 p113
Squiar, Samuel 21; Maryland, 1775 1219.7 p248
Squire, Edmund; Jamaica, 1768 1219.7 p135
Squire, Henry; Quebec, 1823 7603 p23
Squire, Robt.; Virginia, 1637 6219 p111
Squires, Mr.; Quebec, 1815 9229.18 p76
Squires, George 22; Maryland, 1775 1219.7 p252
Sragel, John; Iowa, 1866-1943 123.54 p45
Sragel, Mike; Iowa, 1866-1943 123.54 p45
Sramel, Math.; Wisconsin, n.d. 9675.8 p121
Sraogle, Tony; Iowa, 1866-1943 123.54 p45
Sreen, Alexander 2 SEE Sreen, Andrew
Sreen, Andrew; Philadelphia, 1847 53.26 p84
Wife:Jane
Relative:Thomas 3
Relative:Alexander 2
Relative:Jane 3 mos
Sreen, Jane SEE Sreen, Andrew
Sreen, Jane 3 mos SEE Sreen, Andrew
Sreen, Thomas 3 SEE Sreen, Andrew
Sroensen, Marius; Arkansas, 1918 95.2 p116
Sroka, Jan 20; New York, 1912 9980.29 p70
Srotten, Samuel 16; Maryland, 1737 3690.1 p214
Srovell, Sarah; Virginia, 1648 6219 p250
Srubek, Charles; Arkansas, 1918 95.2 p116
Staab, Adam; America, 1847 8582.1 p32
Staadt, John W.; Washington, 1859-1920 2872.1 p38
Staal, Christiana 9 SEE Staal, Jacob
Staal, Elizabeth 19 SEE Staal, Jacob
Staal, Jacob; South Carolina, 1752-1753 3689.17 p23
With wife
Relative:Jacoba Anna 21
Relative:Elizabeth 19
Relative:Christiana 9
Staal, Jacoba Anna 21 SEE Staal, Jacob
Staats, Georg W.; Cincinnati, 1855 8582.3 p22
Stabbs, Edward 16; Maryland or Virginia, 1699 2212 p21
Stabbs, Math, Jr. 15; Maryland or Virginia, 1699 2212 p21
Stabbs, Math, Sr. 44; Maryland or Virginia, 1699 2212 p21
Stabile, Sam; Arkansas, 1918 95.2 p116
Stabler, Anna; Washington, 1859-1920 2872.1 p38
Stabler, Frederick David; Washington, 1859-1920 2872.1 p38
Stabler, George David; Washington, 1859-1920 2872.1 p38
Stabler, Luise Fredericka; Washington, 1859-1920 2872.1 p38
Stablia, Carlo Togliac 22; New York, NY, 1893 9026.4 p42
Stabo, Jean Park; South Carolina, 1699-1747 1639.20 p258
Stace, Richard 31; Virginia, 1731 3690.1 p214
Stacey, Jeremiah 19; Virginia, 1774 1219.7 p186
Stacey, Nathaniel 36; Maryland, 1774 1219.7 p244
Stacey, Sarah 24; Philadelphia, 1774 1219.7 p212
Stach, Matthew; New York, 1749 3652 p69
Wife:Rosina
Stach, Matthew; New York, 1749 3652 p71
Wife:Rosina
Stach, Rosina SEE Stach, Matthew
Stach, Rosina SEE Stach, Matthew
Stach, Thomas; New York, 1749 3652 p72
Stachowski, Alexander; New York, 1831 4606 p177
Stachowski, Daniel; New York, 1831 4606 p177
Stachursky, Helena 10; New York, 1912 9980.29 p49
Stachursky, Jusef 57; New York, 1912 9980.29 p49
Stachursky, Kocmira 6; New York, 1912 9980.29 p49
Stachursky, Sofia 16; New York, 1912 9980.29 p49
Stachursky, Stanislawa 8; New York, 1912 9980.29 p49
Stacie, Eliza.; Virginia, 1643 6219 p201
Stacie, Geo.; Virginia, 1642 6219 p199
Stack, James; America, 1737 4971 p55
Stack, John; America, 1741 4971 p56
Stack, John; New York, NY, 1835 8208.4 p7
Stack, Joseph 21; Quebec, 1863 5704.8 p154
Stack, Maurice; America, 1742 4971 p54
Stackhowse, Robert; Virginia, 1636 6219 p21
Stackhowse, Robert; Virginia, 1636 6219 p77
Stackman, Fred; Kansas, 1871 5240.1 p42
Stacks, George 23; Nevis, 1774 1219.7 p197
Staclk, Stephan; Arkansas, 1918 95.2 p116
Stacy, Georg; Virginia, 1636 6219 p77
Stade, Hans; Brazil, 1556 8582.3 p79
Stader, Phillip; Wisconsin, n.d. 9675.8 p121
Stadermann, . . .; Canada, 1776-1783 9786 p34
Stadler, Dominic; Wisconsin, n.d. 9675.8 p121
Stadler, John; Wisconsin, n.d. 9675.8 p121
Stadtmann, August 22; Kansas, 1879 5240.1 p61
Staebler, Anna Catharina Arnold SEE Staebler, Johann Georg
Staebler, Johann Georg; Pennsylvania, 1754 2444 p220
Wife:Anna Catharina Arnold
Staebler, Lucas 28; Port uncertain, 1839 778.5 p504
Staehele, John; New York, 1883 1450.2 p37B
Staehle, William C. 39; Arizona, 1890 2764.35 p60
Staehly, John; New York, 1883 1450.2 p37B
Staelens, Gustaaf; Arkansas, 1918 95.2 p116
Staender, Franz 21; Kansas, 1904 5240.1 p82
Staes, Abraham; New Netherland, 1630-1646 8582.2 p51
Staewen, Robert; Wisconsin, n.d. 9675.8 p121
Staf, John; Washington, 1859-1920 2872.1 p38
Staff, Charles 29; Massachusetts, 1860 6410.32 p113
Staff, Charley Magnus; Iowa, 1850 2090 p609
With wife & 4 children
Staff, Gustave; Arkansas, 1918 95.2 p117
Staffanson, Staffan; Iowa, 1851 2090 p615
Staffieri, Joe; Arkansas, 1918 95.2 p117
Stafford, Catharine; America, 1864-1871 5704.8 p240
Stafford, Christo.; Virginia, 1635 6219 p72
Stafford, Francis; Virginia, 1646 6219 p239
Stafford, James; Quebec, 1822 7603 p79
Stafford, James; St. John, N.B., 1847 5704.8 p26
Stafford, John 15; Maryland, 1774 1219.7 p244

Stafford, Mathew; New York, NY, 1867 ***5704.8*** *p218*
Stafford, Rebecca *SEE* Stafford, William
Stafford, William; Virginia, 1635 ***6219*** *p72*
*Wife:*Rebecca
Stafford, William 17; Virginia, 1700 ***2212*** *p30*
Stagg, Edward 19; Virginia, 1720 ***3690.1*** *p214*
Staggmann, . . .; Canada, 1776-1783 ***9786*** *p34*
Stahan, James 18; Maryland, 1774 ***1219.7*** *p236*
Stahel, Julius; New York, 1861-1865 ***8582.3*** *p91*
Stahl, August; Cincinnati, 1869-1887 ***8582*** *p31*
Stahl, Emil; Wisconsin, n.d. ***9675.8*** *p121*
Stahl, Jacob; Pennsylvania, n.d. ***2444*** *p220*
Stahl, Johann; Cincinnati, 1800-1877 ***8582.3*** *p86*
Stahl, Kal; New York, 1865 ***3702.7*** *p209*
Stahl, Margaretha Widmaier; Pennsylvania, 1752 ***2444*** *p220*
Stahl, Nils Daniel; Minneapolis, 1869-1884 ***6410.35*** *p66*
Stahle, Lieutenant; Nicaragua, 1856 ***8582.3*** *p31*
Stahlhut, Fred; New York, NY, 1888 ***1450.2*** *p37B*
Stahlhut, Karl; New York, NY, 1890 ***1450.2*** *p37B*
Stahlmann, Friedrich H. Christian; America, 1880 ***4610.10*** *p124*
Stahmke, Emil; Wisconsin, n.d. ***9675.8*** *p121*
Stahmke, Ludwig; Wisconsin, n.d. ***9675.8*** *p121*
Staiger, Anna Mgr.; America, 1854-1855 ***9162.6*** *p104*
Staiger, Catharina; America, 1772 ***2444*** *p220*
Staiger, Conrad; Pennsylvania, 1751 ***2444*** *p222*
Staiger, Hans Conrad; Pennsylvania, 1751 ***2444*** *p222*
Staile, Martin; Cincinnati, 1869-1887 ***8582*** *p31*
Stailer, Jacob; Wisconsin, n.d. ***9675.8*** *p121*
Stain, Richard 15; Jamaica, 1730 ***3690.1*** *p291*
Stainback, John; Wisconsin, n.d. ***9675.8*** *p121*
Stainer, Anton; Wisconsin, n.d. ***9675.8*** *p121*
Stainer, Mary 30; Montreal, 1775 ***1219.7*** *p261*
Staines, Mary 27; Maryland, 1775 ***1219.7*** *p253*
Stainger, . . .; Canada, 1776-1783 ***9786*** *p34*
Staining, Crispin 15; Maryland, 1725 ***3690.1*** *p214*
Staisi, John; Arkansas, 1918 ***95.2*** *p117*
Stakorich, Karlo Dragutin; Iowa, 1866-1943 ***123.54*** *p79*
Stalder, Mr.; Ohio, 1823-1826 ***8582.1*** *p39*
With wife & family
Stalder, Elisabeth; America, 1816 ***8582.1*** *p11*
Stalder, Elizabeth; Philadelphia, 1818 ***8582.1*** *p39*
Staley, Ulrick; Philadelphia, 1757 ***9973.7*** *p32*
Stalhammer, Martin Elis; Arkansas, 1918 ***95.2*** *p117*
Stalkamp, Henry; Cincinnati, 1869-1887 ***8582*** *p31*
Stalker, Effie; North Carolina, 1804-1881 ***1639.20*** *p295*
Stalker, John; America, 1824 ***1639.20*** *p295*
Stall, Bernard Georg; America, 1848 ***8582.2*** *p40*
Stall, G. 2; New Orleans, 1830 ***778.5*** *p504*
Stall, G. 30; New Orleans, 1830 ***778.5*** *p504*
Stall, J. 3; New Orleans, 1830 ***778.5*** *p504*
Stall, J. 28; New Orleans, 1830 ***778.5*** *p504*
Stall, John Henry; Cincinnati, 1830-1849 ***8582*** *p31*
Stallard, John 19; Maryland, 1774 ***1219.7*** *p236*
Stallard, John 32; Philadelphia, 1774 ***1219.7*** *p232*
Stalling, Nich.; Virginia, 1635 ***6219*** *p71*
Stallmann, Friederike Wilhelmine; America, 1885 ***4610.10*** *p160*
Stallo, Child; Cincinnati, 1831-1832 ***8582.2*** *p48*
With 4 siblings
Stallo, Franz Joseph; America, 1846 ***8582.3*** *p62*
Stallo, Franz Joseph; Cincinnati, 1788-1848 ***8582.3*** *p89*
Stallo, Franz Joseph; Philadelphia, 1831 ***8582.2*** *p48*
Stallo, Johann Bernard; America, 1839 ***8582.2*** *p40*
Stam, . . .; Canada, 1776-1783 ***9786*** *p34*
Stam, Emil; Illinois, 1885 ***2896.5*** *p38*
Stam, Jacob; Philadelphia, 1762 ***9973.7*** *p37*
Stamatelos, Alexios; Iowa, 1866-1943 ***123.54*** *p45*
Stamatiade, Demetrius; Connecticut, 1833 ***8208.4*** *p44*
Stamatrades, Nickol; Arkansas, 1918 ***95.2*** *p117*
Stambach, Jacob; Philadelphia, 1762 ***9973.7*** *p37*
Stame, Henry; Iroquois Co., IL, 1892 ***3455.1*** *p13*
Stamer, v., G.M.; Quebec, 1776 ***9786*** *p105*
Stamer, Jacob 34; New Orleans, 1838 ***778.5*** *p504*
Stamfel, Antone; Iowa, 1866-1943 ***123.54*** *p45*
Stamin, . . .; Canada, 1776-1783 ***9786*** *p35*
Stamm, G. Wilhelm; Wheeling, WV, 1834 ***8582*** *p31*
Stamm, Johann Georg; Philadelphia, 1779 ***8137*** *p14*
Stammachak, Maryanna 27; New York, 1912 ***9980.29*** *p69*
Stampe, Thomas; Virginia, 1638 ***6219*** *p147*
Stampfel, John; Wisconsin, n.d. ***9675.8*** *p121*
Stampl, John; Iowa, 1866-1943 ***123.54*** *p45*
Stanard, William 17; Windward Islands, 1722 ***3690.1*** *p215*
Stanburey, John 25; Jamaica, 1731 ***3690.1*** *p214*
Stanburg, James; Illinois, 1856 ***7857*** *p7*
Stanbury, George; Illinois, 1857 ***7857*** *p7*
Stanbury, John 44; North Carolina, 1736 ***3690.1*** *p214*
Stanbury, Samuel; Illinois, 1858 ***7857*** *p7*
Stanbye, John; Virginia, 1639 ***6219*** *p153*
Stanch, Colombo; Arkansas, 1918 ***95.2*** *p117*
Stanczak, Jonas; Arkansas, 1918 ***95.2*** *p117*
Standberg, Nels; Colorado, 1903 ***9678.3*** *p15*
Stande, . . .; Canada, 1776-1783 ***9786*** *p43*
Standen, John Hipsley 29; Maryland, 1774 ***1219.7*** *p235*
Standfield, . . . 4 mos; Philadelphia, 1865 ***5704.8*** *p196*
Standfield, John; Philadelphia, 1865 ***5704.8*** *p196*
Standfield, Margaret; Philadelphia, 1865 ***5704.8*** *p196*
Standfield, Patrick; Philadelphia, 1865 ***5704.8*** *p196*
Standfield, Thomas; Philadelphia, 1865 ***5704.8*** *p196*
Standford, Edward; New York, NY, 1816 ***2859.11*** *p42*
Standford, Thomas 22; Maryland, 1729 ***3690.1*** *p214*
Standidge, Thomas 20; Maryland, 1720 ***3690.1*** *p214*
Standish, Dorothy; Virginia, 1635 ***6219*** *p27*
Standish, Dorothy; Virginia, 1638 ***6219*** *p145*
Standish, Georg; Virginia, 1643 ***6219*** *p204*
Standish, Ja.; Virginia, 1646 ***6219*** *p246*
Standish, Mary; Virginia, 1698 ***2212*** *p17*
Standish, Stephen; Virginia, 1637 ***6219*** *p10*
Standy, Hugh; Virginia, 1642 ***6219*** *p191*
Stanfeild, Lawrence; Virginia, 1646 ***6219*** *p242*
Stanfeild, Symond; Virginia, 1634 ***6219*** *p32*
Stanfel, George; Iowa, 1866-1943 ***123.54*** *p45*
Stanfel, Matija; Iowa, 1866-1943 ***123.54*** *p45*
Stanfold, Rev.; America, 1776 ***1219.7*** *p281*
Stanford, Ann; Virginia, 1637 ***6219*** *p113*
Stanford, George Stehn; Jamaica, 1776 ***1219.7*** *p281*
Stanford, Thomas E.; Illinois, 1888 ***5012.39*** *p52*
Stanford, Thomas E.; Illinois, 1892 ***5012.40*** *p27*
Stanford, William 20; Maryland, 1735 ***3690.1*** *p214*
Stange, Fredrick J.; Illinois, 1860 ***5012.38*** *p98*
Stangel, Ancheas; Illinois, 1854 ***7857*** *p7*
Stangel, Franz; New York, NY, 1899 ***1450.2*** *p38B*
Stangell, . . .; Canada, 1776-1783 ***9786*** *p35*
Stangnow, Herman Ludwig; Wisconsin, n.d. ***9675.8*** *p121*
Stanhope, Henry; New York, NY, 1811 ***2859.11*** *p19*
With wife
Stanhope, Thomas 21; Jamaica, 1730 ***3690.1*** *p215*
Staniger, Anna; Iowa, 1866-1943 ***123.54*** *p79*
Staniger, Frank; Iowa, 1866-1943 ***123.54*** *p46*
Stankey, Amelia; Washington, 1859-1920 ***2872.1*** *p38*
Stankey, Ferdinand; Washington, 1859-1920 ***2872.1*** *p38*
Stankey, Fred; Washington, 1859-1920 ***2872.1*** *p38*
Stankey, G. A.; Washington, 1859-1920 ***2872.1*** *p38*
Stankey, Gustave Albert; Washington, 1859-1920 ***2872.1*** *p38*
Stankey, Gustof; Washington, 1859-1920 ***2872.1*** *p38*
Stankey, Henry; Washington, 1859-1920 ***2872.1*** *p38*
Stankey, Joseph; Washington, 1859-1920 ***2872.1*** *p38*
Stankey, Paul; Washington, 1859-1920 ***2872.1*** *p38*
Stankey, Rudolph W.; Washington, 1859-1920 ***2872.1*** *p38*
Stankievicz, Stanislaw; Arkansas, 1918 ***95.2*** *p117*
Stankiewicz, Aniela 18; New York, 1912 ***9980.29*** *p58*
Stankos, Bruno; Arkansas, 1918 ***95.2*** *p117*
Stanks, James; Virginia, 1642 ***6219*** *p189*
Stankus, Kazimer; Arkansas, 1918 ***95.2*** *p117*
Stankus, Stanley Stephen; Arkansas, 1918 ***95.2*** *p117*
Stanley, Elizab 26; America, 1705 ***2212*** *p44*
Stanley, Elizabeth 35 *SEE* Stanley, Joseph
Stanley, F. H.; Washington, 1859-1920 ***2872.1*** *p38*
Stanley, Fred; Washington, 1859-1920 ***2872.1*** *p38*
Stanley, George; America, 1737 ***4971*** *p45*
Stanley, George; America, 1737 ***4971*** *p46*
Stanley, John; Nevis, 1775 ***1219.7*** *p263*
Stanley, John; Virginia, 1639 ***6219*** *p162*
Stanley, John; Virginia, 1652 ***6251*** *p20*
Stanley, John 23; Ontario, 1768 ***7603*** *p24*
Stanley, John 34; St. Kitts, 1774 ***1219.7*** *p203*
Stanley, Joseph 45; Savannah, GA, 1733 ***4719.17*** *p312*
*Wife:*Elizabeth 35
Stanley, Mary 15; Massachusetts, 1849 ***5881.1*** *p92*
Stanley, Mary 17; Maryland, 1775 ***1219.7*** *p272*
Stanley, Patrick 35; Massachusetts, 1849 ***5881.1*** *p93*
Stanley, Peter; New York, NY, 1816 ***2859.11*** *p42*
Stanley, Wm.; New York, NY, 1811 ***2859.11*** *p19*
With family
Stanley, Wm.; Virginia, 1648 ***6219*** *p253*
Stannard, William 17; Windward Islands, 1722 ***3690.1*** *p215*
Stanney, Robert; Virginia, 1636 ***6219*** *p7*
Stannley, Charles H. 24; Quebec, 1859 ***5704.8*** *p143*
Stannor, Richd 17; Maryland or Virginia, 1699 ***2212*** *p23*
Stanny, Joan; Virginia, 1643 ***6219*** *p230*
Stansby, Antho.; Virginia, 1636 ***6219*** *p21*
Stansel, Elizabeth 21; America, 1701 ***2212*** *p34*
Stansell, John 19; Virginia, 1721-1722 ***3690.1*** *p215*
Stansfield, Mr.; Quebec, 1815 ***9229.18*** *p74*
Stansfield, Joseph; New Orleans, 1842 ***6013.19*** *p88*
Stanthrop, Joseph; Virginia, 1698 ***2212*** *p12*
Stanton, Ann; St. John, N.B., 1847 ***5704.8*** *p34*
Stanton, Catharine 35; Massachusetts, 1849 ***5881.1*** *p88*
Stanton, Christopher; Virginia, 1638 ***6219*** *p124*
Stanton, Elizabeth 28; Massachusetts, 1849 ***5881.1*** *p89*
Stanton, Ellen 9 mos; Massachusetts, 1849 ***5881.1*** *p89*
Stanton, John 22; Virginia, 1774 ***1219.7*** *p225*
Stanton, John 25; Maryland, 1735 ***3690.1*** *p215*
Stanton, John J.; America, 1853 ***1450.2*** *p137A*
Stanton, Michael 20; Massachusetts, 1849 ***5881.1*** *p92*
Stanton, Michael Edward 26; California, 1872 ***2769.8*** *p6*
Stanton, Robt.; Virginia, 1642 ***6219*** *p194*
Stanton, Samuel; Sacramento, CA, 1874 ***2764.35*** *p65*
Stanton, Samuel 33; Maryland, 1774 ***1219.7*** *p179*
Stanton, Tho.; Virginia, 1640 ***6219*** *p208*
Stanton, Thomas; Massachusetts, 1847 ***5881.1*** *p93*
Stanton, William 18; Jamaica, 1753 ***1219.7*** *p19*
Stanton, William 18; Jamaica, 1753 ***3690.1*** *p215*
Stanway, David 42; Kansas, 1880 ***5240.1*** *p62*
Stanway, Ralph 23; Jamaica, 1736 ***3690.1*** *p215*
Stanwix, John; Philadelphia, 1756 ***8582.3*** *p95*
Stany, Robert; Virginia, 1642 ***6219*** *p186*
Stanze, . . .; Canada, 1776-1783 ***9786*** *p35*
Stape, Thomas 21; Virginia, 1773 ***1219.7*** *p169*
Stapenhorst, Conrad W.; America, 1833 ***3702.7*** *p68*
Stapenhorst, Florenz; Baltimore, 1832 ***3702.7*** *p68*
Staper, Charles 18; Maryland, 1718 ***3690.1*** *p215*
Stapf, Friederich; Pennsylvania, 1768 ***4525*** *p250*
Stapf, Johann Peter; New England, 1753 ***4525*** *p250*
Stapf, Wilhelm; America, 1848 ***8582.3*** *p63*
Staples, Ann 16; Virginia, 1727 ***3690.1*** *p215*
Staples, Susanna 22; Maryland, 1775 ***1219.7*** *p266*
Staples, Susanna 22; Virginia, 1774 ***1219.7*** *p240*
Staples, William 17; Maryland, 1775 ***1219.7*** *p253*
Stapleton, . . . 30; Nova Scotia, 1774 ***1219.7*** *p210*
Stapleton, Catharine 10; Massachusetts, 1850 ***5881.1*** *p88*
Stapleton, Ellen 12; Massachusetts, 1850 ***5881.1*** *p89*
Stapleton, George 18; Maryland, 1720 ***3690.1*** *p215*
Stapleton, John 2; Massachusetts, 1850 ***5881.1*** *p91*
Stapleton, John 40; Massachusetts, 1850 ***5881.1*** *p91*
Stapleton, Margaret 8; Massachusetts, 1850 ***5881.1*** *p92*
Stapleton, Mary 35; Massachusetts, 1850 ***5881.1*** *p92*
Stapleton, Patrick; Quebec, 1763 ***7603*** *p80*
Stapleton, Richard 6; Massachusetts, 1850 ***5881.1*** *p93*
Stapleton, Susanna 35; Virginia, 1775 ***1219.7*** *p254*
Stapleton, William; Quebec, 1820 ***7603*** *p74*
Stapleton, William 16; Pennsylvania, 1723 ***3690.1*** *p215*
Stapley, William; Illinois, 1860 ***7857*** *p7*
Staplin, John; Antigua (Antego), 1762 ***1219.7*** *p90*
Stappt, John; Indiana, 1848 ***9117*** *p18*
Star, Mr.; Quebec, 1815 ***9229.18*** *p80*
Staras, William; Wisconsin, n.d. ***9675.8*** *p121*
Starcevic, Anton; Iowa, 1866-1943 ***123.54*** *p46*
Starcevic, Jose; Iowa, 1866-1943 ***123.54*** *p46*
Starcevic, Krunoslau; Iowa, 1866-1943 ***123.54*** *p46*
Starcevic, Make; Iowa, 1866-1943 ***123.54*** *p46*
Starcevic, Marko; Iowa, 1866-1943 ***123.54*** *p46*
Starcevic, Met; Iowa, 1866-1943 ***123.54*** *p46*
Starcevic, Mirko; Iowa, 1866-1943 ***123.54*** *p46*
Starcevic, Nik; Iowa, 1866-1943 ***123.54*** *p46*
Starcevic, Takov; Iowa, 1866-1943 ***123.54*** *p46*
Starcevic, Ture; Iowa, 1866-1943 ***123.54*** *p46*
Starcevich, Anton; Iowa, 1866-1943 ***123.54*** *p46*
Starcevich, Frank; Iowa, 1866-1943 ***123.54*** *p79*
Starcevich, Ivan; Iowa, 1866-1943 ***123.54*** *p46*
Starcevich, Vinko; Iowa, 1866-1943 ***123.54*** *p46*
Starch, . . .; Canada, 1776-1783 ***9786*** *p35*
Starch, William; Virginia, 1639 ***6219*** *p158*
Starchavich, Anton; Iowa, 1866-1943 ***123.54*** *p46*
Starchvic, Anton; Iowa, 1866-1943 ***123.54*** *p46*
Starchvic, Matt; Iowa, 1866-1943 ***123.54*** *p46*
Starchvic, Venc; Iowa, 1866-1943 ***123.54*** *p46*
Starcvic, Stipan; Iowa, 1866-1943 ***123.54*** *p46*
Starczevic, George; Iowa, 1866-1943 ***123.54*** *p46*
Starett, Catherine; Quebec, 1847 ***5704.8*** *p16*
Starett, Elizabeth; Quebec, 1847 ***5704.8*** *p16*
Starett, Margaret; Philadelphia, 1848 ***5704.8*** *p46*
Starevic, Bozo; Iowa, 1866-1943 ***123.54*** *p46*
Starford, Margarett; Virginia, 1639 ***6219*** *p181*
Starich, Joseph; Wisconsin, n.d. ***9675.8*** *p121*
Stark, Carl Gustaf; Wisconsin, n.d. ***9675.8*** *p121*
Stark, Charles; Illinois, 1868 ***5012.37*** *p59*
Stark, Charley M.; Washington, 1859-1920 ***2872.1*** *p38*
Stark, George; America, 1889 ***1450.2*** *p38B*
Stark, George; Iowa, 1866-1943 ***123.54*** *p46*
Stark, Gustavus; America, 1843 ***1450.2*** *p137A*
Stark, Jacob; America, 1860 ***6014.1*** *p3*
Stark, John George; New York, 1754 ***3652*** *p80*
Stark, Mary 19; Massachusetts, 1849 ***5881.1*** *p92*
Stark, Reinhold; America, 1889 ***1450.2*** *p137A*
Stark, Sarah; Philadelphia, 1847 ***53.26*** *p84*
Stark, Sarah; Philadelphia, 1847 ***5704.8*** *p1*
Stark, Thomas; New York, NY, 1811 ***2859.11*** *p19*
Starkey, Isabella; Montreal, 1824 ***7603*** *p68*
Starkey, James; New York, NY, 1838 ***8208.4*** *p74*
Starkey, Richard 21; Jamaica, 1736 ***3690.1*** *p215*
Starklauf, Andreas; Philadelphia, 1777-1782 ***8137*** *p14*
Starling, Robert 15; Virginia, 1722 ***3690.1*** *p215*

Starling, Wm.; Virginia, 1647 ***6219*** *p245*
Starndahl, Chas.; Iowa, 1866-1943 ***123.54*** *p46*
Starnell, Richd.; Virginia, 1646 ***6219*** *p245*
Starr, Edward 45; St. John, N.B., 1863 ***5704.8*** *p152*
Starr, Eliz.; Virginia, 1642 ***6219*** *p190*
Starr, Ellen 20; St. John, N.B., 1863 ***5704.8*** *p152*
Starr, Jeremiah; New York, NY, 1811 ***2859.11*** *p19*
Starr, Peter 16; St. John, N.B., 1863 ***5704.8*** *p152*
Starr, Richard 19; Jamaica, 1737 ***3690.1*** *p215*
Starr, Terence 18; St. John, N.B., 1863 ***5704.8*** *p152*
Starrat, Alexander; St. John, N.B., 1850 ***5704.8*** *p62*
Starret, John; Philadelphia, 1852 ***5704.8*** *p92*
Starrett, Mary; New York, NY, 1869 ***5704.8*** *p235*
Starritt, William 33; Quebec, 1863 ***5704.8*** *p154*
Starrs, Anne; Philadelphia, 1864 ***5704.8*** *p184*
Starrs, Edward; Philadelphia, 1847 ***53.26*** *p84*
Starrs, Edward; Philadelphia, 1847 ***5704.8*** *p2*
Starvos, Mike; Arkansas, 1918 ***95.2*** *p117*
Starzewski, Felix; New York, 1835 ***4606*** *p180*
Starzynski, Michal; New York, 1834 ***4606*** *p178*
Stas, August; Indianapolis, 1868 ***3702.7*** *p582*
Stasey, Doritha; Philadelphia, 1816 ***2859.11*** *p42*
Stasey, Eliza; Philadelphia, 1816 ***2859.11*** *p42*
Stasey, John; Philadelphia, 1816 ***2859.11*** *p42*
Stasey, Margaret; Philadelphia, 1816 ***2859.11*** *p42*
Stasey, Sarah; Philadelphia, 1816 ***2859.11*** *p42*
Stasey, Wm.; Philadelphia, 1816 ***2859.11*** *p42*
Stasner, Jacob 34; New Orleans, 1838 ***778.5*** *p504*
Stastney, Chas.; Wisconsin, n.d. ***9675.8*** *p121*
Staszewska, Wladislawa 4 *SEE* Staszewska, Wladislawa
Staszewska, Wladislawa 28; New York, 1912 ***9980.29*** *p51*
*Child:*Wladislawa 4
With mother
With daughter
Staszewski, Jozef; New York, 1834 ***4606*** *p178*
Staszewski, Wladislawa 4 *SEE* Staszewski, Wladislawa
Staszewski, Wladislawa 28; New York, 1912 ***9980.29*** *p51*
*Child:*Wladislawa 4
With mother
With daughter
Stataga, Catherine; Kansas, 1875 ***5240.1*** *p42*
Stataga, Ferdinand; America, 1800-1875 ***5240.1*** *p42*
Statham, Mary 20; America, 1699 ***2212*** *p28*
Stathart, Augustus; Illinois, 1853 ***7857*** *p7*
Stathe, Cyriako Nicola 36; Kansas, 1889 ***5240.1*** *p74*
Stathis, Peter Nicke; Arkansas, 1918 ***95.2*** *p117*
Staton, Anthony; Virginia, 1637 ***6219*** *p109*
Staton, Jno; America, 1698 ***2212*** *p9*
Statson, John Haseotes; Arkansas, 1918 ***95.2*** *p117*
Statson, John Hisotes; Arkansas, 1918 ***95.2*** *p117*
Stauber, . . .; Canada, 1776-1783 ***9786*** *p35*
Stauber, Paul Christian; New York, 1750 ***3652*** *p75*
Stauch, Agnes *SEE* Stauch, Johann Michael
Stauch, Andreas; Port uncertain, 1754 ***2444*** *p220*
Stauch, Andreas 30; Pennsylvania, 1754 ***2444*** *p220*
Stauch, Catharina Simmozheim *SEE* Stauch, Lorentz
Stauch, Eva M. Heldmayer *SEE* Stauch, Hans Jerg
Stauch, Gottfried; Pennsylvania, 1752 ***2444*** *p220*
Stauch, Hans Gerg; Pennsylvania, 1754 ***2444*** *p220*
Stauch, Hans Jacob; Pennsylvania, 1749 ***2444*** *p220*
*Wife:*Sophia
*Child:*Lorentz
Stauch, Hans Jerg *SEE* Stauch, Lorentz
Stauch, Hans Jerg; Pennsylvania, 1749 ***2444*** *p220*
Stauch, Hans Jerg 37; Pennsylvania, 1754 ***2444*** *p221*
*Wife:*Eva M. Heldmayer
Stauch, Jacob *SEE* Stauch, Lorentz
Stauch, Jacob; Pennsylvania, 1749 ***2444*** *p220*
Stauch, Johann Jacob 18; Pennsylvania, 1754 ***2444*** *p220*
Stauch, Johann Jacob 18; Pennsylvania, 1754 ***2444*** *p221*
Stauch, Johann Michael; Pennsylvania, 1754 ***2444*** *p221*
*Wife:*Agnes
*Child:*Maria Catharina
Stauch, Joseph; Pennsylvania, 1766 ***2444*** *p221*
Stauch, Lorentz *SEE* Stauch, Hans Jacob
Stauch, Lorentz; Pennsylvania, 1754 ***2444*** *p221*
*Wife:*Catharina Simmozheim
With 2 children
*Child:*Hans Jerg
*Child:*Jacob
Stauch, Maria Catharina *SEE* Stauch, Johann Michael
Stauch, Maria Elisabetha; Pennsylvania, 1730-1800 ***2444*** *p221*
Stauch, Michael; Port uncertain, 1754 ***2444*** *p220*
Stauch, Michael 18; Pennsylvania, 1754 ***2444*** *p220*
Stauch, Michael 18; Pennsylvania, 1754 ***2444*** *p221*
Stauch, Michael, Sr.; Port uncertain, 1754 ***2444*** *p221*
Stauch, Michel 40; Pennsylvania, 1754 ***2444*** *p220*
Stauch, Sophia *SEE* Stauch, Hans Jacob
Staud, Abraham; America, 1738 ***4349*** *p48*
Staud, Jacob; America, 1738 ***4349*** *p48*
Staud, Johann Michael *SEE* Staud, Johannes
Staud, Johannes; America, 1737-1738 ***4349*** *p48*
*Brother:*Johann Michael
Staud, Margaretha Dorothea; Pennsylvania, 1753 ***2444*** *p159*
Staudenmayer, Anna Catharina; America, 1739-1800 ***2444*** *p168*
Stauffenberg, Justus; Philadelphia, 1779 ***8137*** *p14*
Staughmill, . . .; Canada, 1776-1783 ***9786*** *p35*
Staunton, Edward; America, 1741 ***4971*** *p16*
Staunton, Peter; America, 1737 ***4971*** *p64*
Staus, Gustaf; America, 1853 ***1450.2*** *p137A*
Stauske, Gustave; Wisconsin, n.d. ***9675.8*** *p121*
Stauske, William; Wisconsin, n.d. ***9675.8*** *p121*
Stauss, Peter; Wisconsin, n.d. ***9675.8*** *p121*
Staut, Johann; America, 1848 ***8582.3*** *p63*
Staut, John; Wisconsin, n.d. ***9675.8*** *p121*
Stauter, Peter, Family; America, 1794-1923 ***2691.4*** *p172*
Stautt, Abraham; America, 1738 ***4349*** *p48*
Stautt, Jacob; America, 1738 ***4349*** *p48*
Stautt, Johann Michael *SEE* Stautt, Johannes
Stautt, Johannes; America, 1737-1738 ***4349*** *p48*
*Brother:*Johann Michael
Stav, Ole Johan Olson; New York, NY, 1837 ***8208.4*** *p44*
Stavar, Anton; Iowa, 1866-1943 ***123.54*** *p46*
Stave, Henry; Arizona, 1882 ***2764.35*** *p64*
Stavely, Adam; Virginia, 1635 ***6219*** *p68*
Stavely, Andrew; New York, NY, 1816 ***2859.11*** *p42*
Stavely, Richard 30; Nova Scotia, 1774 ***1219.7*** *p195*
Stavely, Robert 26; Halifax, N.S., 1774 ***1219.7*** *p213*
Stavely, Robert 26; Nova Scotia, 1774 ***1219.7*** *p195*
Staveron, Filpos; Arkansas, 1918 ***95.2*** *p117*
Stavropulas, George; Arkansas, 1918 ***95.2*** *p117*
Stavropulos, George; Arkansas, 1918 ***95.2*** *p117*
Stavros, Mike; Arkansas, 1918 ***95.2*** *p117*
Staworke, Stanley John; Arkansas, 1918 ***95.2*** *p117*
Stay, Peter 50; America, 1853 ***9162.7*** *p15*
Stayle, Rich.; Virginia, 1629 ***6219*** *p8*
Stayther, John Michael; South Carolina, 1752-1753 ***3689.17*** *p23*
With wife
*Relative:*Mary Barbara 12
*Relative:*Margarita 8
Stayther, Margarita 8 *SEE* Stayther, John Michael
Stayther, Mary Barbara 12 *SEE* Stayther, John Michael
Stead, Elizabeth 26; New York, 1774 ***1219.7*** *p224*
Stealy, Baltzer; Pennsylvania, 1749 ***2444*** *p222*
Stean, Edward 20; Maryland, 1753 ***1219.7*** *p19*
Stean, Edward 20; Maryland, 1753 ***3690.1*** *p216*
Steane, John; Virginia, 1844 ***4626.16*** *p12*
Stear, Nicholas 47; Maryland, 1775 ***1219.7*** *p256*
Stearns, Mr.; Quebec, 1815 ***9229.18*** *p77*
With family
Steb, Elias; Pennsylvania, 1749 ***2444*** *p222*
*Brother:*Michael
Steb, Hans Bernhard; America, 1772 ***2444*** *p221*
Steb, Michael *SEE* Steb, Elias
Stebel, Abe; Arkansas, 1918 ***95.2*** *p117*
Stecher, Anna Eva C. Kauffman *SEE* Stecher, Johann Melchior
Stecher, Johann Melchior; Pennsylvania, 1732 ***3627*** *p16*
*Wife:*Anna Eva C. Kauffman
Steck, . . .; America, n.d. ***8582.3*** *p79*
Steck, Anna Margaretha *SEE* Steck, Friedrich
Steck, Anna Margaretha *SEE* Steck, Friedrich
Steck, Anna Maria *SEE* Steck, Friedrich
Steck, Anna Maria *SEE* Steck, Friedrich
Steck, Barbara *SEE* Steck, Johann Georg, Jr.
Steck, Christina *SEE* Steck, Johann Georg, Jr.
Steck, Friedrich *SEE* Steck, Friedrich
Steck, Friedrich *SEE* Steck, Friedrich
Steck, Friedrich; America, 1754 ***2444*** *p222*
*Child:*Anna Margaretha
*Child:*Anna Maria
*Child:*Friedrich
*Child:*Johann Georg
Steck, Friedrich; Pennsylvania, 1754 ***2444*** *p222*
*Child:*Anna Margaretha
*Child:*Anna Maria
*Child:*Friedrich
*Child:*Johann Georg
Steck, Johann Georg *SEE* Steck, Friedrich
Steck, Johann Georg *SEE* Steck, Friedrich
Steck, Johann Georg, Jr.; America, 1754 ***2444*** *p221*
*Child:*Barbara
*Child:*Johann Michael
*Child:*Christina
Steck, Johann Michael *SEE* Steck, Johann Georg, Jr.
Steckhane, . . .; Canada, 1776-1783 ***9786*** *p35*
Steckler, Katharina 10 mos; America, 1853 ***9162.8*** *p37*
Steckler, Marg. 14; America, 1853 ***9162.8*** *p37*
Steckler, Marg. 37; America, 1853 ***9162.8*** *p37*
Steckler, Margaretta 3; America, 1853 ***9162.8*** *p37*
Stedelin, Joseph; Illinois, 1859 ***2896.5*** *p38*
Stedell, Henry 26; Philadelphia, 1774 ***1219.7*** *p185*
Stedenrod, Johannes; Lancaster, PA, 1780 ***8137*** *p14*
Steding, Adam Christoph; Canada, 1780 ***9786*** *p268*
Steding, Adam Christoph; New York, 1776 ***9786*** *p268*
Stedman, John; Virginia, 1698 ***2212*** *p6*
Stedman, John 26; Jamaica, 1738 ***3690.1*** *p216*
Stee, Francis; Virginia, 1642 ***6219*** *p15*
Stee, Francis; Virginia, 1642 ***6219*** *p190*
Steeb, Elias; Pennsylvania, 1749 ***2444*** *p222*
*Brother:*Michael
Steeb, Emil; America, 1883 ***1450.2*** *p137A*
Steeb, Michael *SEE* Steeb, Elias
Steebuer, Wilhelm Alvin; Illinois, 1893 ***5012.40*** *p53*
Steed, Ann 25; America, 1702 ***2212*** *p37*
Steed, Anne 21; America, 1703 ***2212*** *p38*
Steed, Edward 25; Maryland, 1774 ***1219.7*** *p236*
Steed, Jane 18; Quebec, 1856 ***5704.8*** *p130*
Steef, Fred'k; Pennsylvania, 1753 ***2444*** *p222*
Steegler, Gerrard; Philadelphia, 1764 ***9973.7*** *p39*
Steehhan, Louis; New York, 1853 ***1450.2*** *p138A*
Steel, Adal; America, 1742 ***4971*** *p74*
Steel, Alec; Austin, TX, 1886 ***9777*** *p5*
Steel, Alexander; America, 1740 ***4971*** *p66*
Steel, Alexander 26; Maryland, 1774 ***1219.7*** *p196*
Steel, Alice 21; America, 1702 ***2212*** *p37*
Steel, Andrew 13; Quebec, 1847 ***5704.8*** *p29*
Steel, Christopher; Philadelphia, 1767 ***9973.7*** *p40*
Steel, David; South Carolina, 1818 ***1639.20*** *p295*
Steel, David 3; Quebec, 1847 ***5704.8*** *p29*
Steel, Edward 17; Pennsylvania, 1730 ***3690.1*** *p216*
Steel, Elizabeth *SEE* Steel, Joseph
Steel, Elizabeth; Philadelphia, 1811 ***2859.11*** *p19*
Steel, Esther; Quebec, 1847 ***5704.8*** *p29*
Steel, Esther 11; Quebec, 1847 ***5704.8*** *p29*
Steel, George 24; Philadelphia, 1854 ***5704.8*** *p115*
Steel, Henry; Illinois, 1858 ***5012.39*** *p54*
Steel, Henry; Philadelphia, 1760 ***9973.7*** *p34*
Steel, Hugh; Quebec, 1847 ***5704.8*** *p29*
Steel, Isabella *SEE* Steel, Jane
Steel, Isabella; Philadelphia, 1849 ***5704.8*** *p54*
Steel, James; America, 1743 ***4971*** *p64*
Steel, James; New York, NY, 1811 ***2859.11*** *p19*
Steel, James; New York, NY, 1815 ***2859.11*** *p42*
Steel, James; New York, NY, 1864 ***5704.8*** *p177*
Steel, James 20; Philadelphia, 1854 ***5704.8*** *p116*
Steel, James K. 33; Kansas, 1878 ***5240.1*** *p59*
Steel, Jane; Philadelphia, 1849 ***53.26*** *p84*
*Relative:*Isabella
Steel, Jane; Philadelphia, 1849 ***5704.8*** *p54*
Steel, Jane 9; Philadelphia, 1854 ***5704.8*** *p115*
Steel, John; New York, NY, 1864 ***5704.8*** *p176*
Steel, John; Philadelphia, 1852 ***5704.8*** *p85*
Steel, John 1; St. John, N.B., 1854 ***5704.8*** *p114*
Steel, John 25; Philadelphia, 1854 ***5704.8*** *p115*
Steel, John 46; Nova Scotia, 1774 ***1219.7*** *p209*
With son
Steel, Joseph; Philadelphia, 1811 ***53.26*** *p84*
*Relative:*Elizabeth
*Relative:*Sally
Steel, Joseph; Philadelphia, 1811 ***2859.11*** *p19*
Steel, Margaret; Quebec, 1847 ***5704.8*** *p29*
Steel, Martha 27; St. John, N.B., 1854 ***5704.8*** *p114*
Steel, Mary; America, 1697 ***2212*** *p9*
Steel, Mary Ann; Philadelphia, 1852 ***5704.8*** *p96*
Steel, Mary Jane 9; Quebec, 1847 ***5704.8*** *p29*
Steel, Nels; Minneapolis, 1869-1884 ***6410.35*** *p66*
Steel, Sally *SEE* Steel, Joseph
Steel, Sally; Philadelphia, 1811 ***2859.11*** *p19*
Steel, Samuel 35; St. John, N.B., 1854 ***5704.8*** *p114*
Steel, Thomas; America, 1740 ***4971*** *p99*
Steel, Thomas; Quebec, 1847 ***5704.8*** *p28*
Steel, Thomas; South Carolina, 1684 ***1639.20*** *p295*
Steel, Thomas 4; Quebec, 1847 ***5704.8*** *p29*
Steel, William; New York, NY, 1815 ***2859.11*** *p42*
Steel, William; Quebec, 1847 ***5704.8*** *p29*
Steel, William; St. John, N.B., 1847 ***5704.8*** *p25*
Steel, William 9 mos; Quebec, 1847 ***5704.8*** *p29*
Steel, William 20; St. John, N.B., 1854 ***5704.8*** *p114*
Steel, William 30; Philadelphia, 1853 ***5704.8*** *p112*
Steel, William 51; North Carolina, 1850 ***1639.20*** *p295*
Steel, William 55; Philadelphia, 1854 ***5704.8*** *p116*
Steele, Alice; America, 1705 ***2212*** *p45*
Steele, David; Iowa, 1866-1943 ***123.54*** *p46*
Steele, Edwd; America, 1698 ***2212*** *p6*
Steele, Eliza; New York, NY, 1864 ***5704.8*** *p187*
Steele, Eliza; Philadelphia, 1864 ***5704.8*** *p171*
Steele, Gordon; Charleston, SC, 1819 ***1639.20*** *p295*
Steele, Henry; Virginia, 1648 ***6219*** *p252*
Steele, Isabella; New York, NY, 1864 ***5704.8*** *p187*
Steele, James; New York, NY, 1868 ***5704.8*** *p226*
Steele, James K. 33; Kansas, 1878 ***5240.1*** *p42*
Steele, Jeffery; Virginia, 1637 ***6219*** *p113*

Steele, John 30; St. John, N.B., 1861 ***5704.8*** *p149*
Steele, John 34; Kansas, 1888 ***5240.1*** *p42*
Steele, John 34; Kansas, 1888 ***5240.1*** *p71*
Steele, Margaret; Philadelphia, 1851 ***5704.8*** *p81*
Steele, Mary 25; Maryland or Virginia, 1699 ***2212*** *p22*
Steele, Mary Jane 17; Philadelphia, 1853 ***5704.8*** *p112*
Steele, William; New York, NY, 1864 ***5704.8*** *p187*
Steele, William 20; Philadelphia, 1857 ***5704.8*** *p134*
Steemer, Carl; Wisconsin, n.d. ***9675.8*** *p121*
Steen, Alex 16; St. John, N.B., 1864 ***5704.8*** *p159*
Steen, Alexander 2; Philadelphia, 1847 ***5704.8*** *p1*
Steen, Andrew; Philadelphia, 1847 ***5704.8*** *p1*
Steen, George; St. John, N.B., 1852 ***5704.8*** *p83*
Steen, Jane; Philadelphia, 1847 ***5704.8*** *p1*
Steen, Jane 3 mos; Philadelphia, 1847 ***5704.8*** *p1*
Steen, Jane 21; St. John, N.B., 1863 ***5704.8*** *p152*
Steen, John; Quebec, 1850 ***5704.8*** *p62*
Steen, John 19; St. John, N.B., 1864 ***5704.8*** *p158*
Steen, Martha 17; Philadelphia, 1858 ***5704.8*** *p139*
Steen, Mary Ann; New York, NY, 1866 ***5704.8*** *p212*
Steen, Robert; New York, NY, 1815 ***2859.11*** *p42*
Steen, Robert; Quebec, 1850 ***5704.8*** *p62*
Steen, Robert 16; St. John, N.B., 1858 ***5704.8*** *p137*
Steen, Roger 14; Pennsylvania, Virginia or Maryland, 1719-1720 ***3690.1*** *p216*
Steen, Thomas 3; Philadelphia, 1847 ***5704.8*** *p1*
Steenmeyer, John Frederick; Arkansas, 1918 ***95.2*** *p117*
Steers, Henry; New York, NY, 1836 ***8208.4*** *p14*
Steers, James; New York, NY, 1840 ***8208.4*** *p107*
Steers, Robert; Virginia, 1637 ***6219*** *p114*
Stefan, Frank; Kansas, 1900 ***5240.1*** *p42*
Stefan, Joseph; Kansas, 1892 ***5240.1*** *p43*
Stefani, Pete Angelo; Arkansas, 1918 ***95.2*** *p117*
Stefani, Peter Angelo; Arkansas, 1918 ***95.2*** *p117*
Stefania, Helga 6 mos; Quebec, 1879 ***2557.1*** *p39*
Stefaniak, Tony; Arkansas, 1918 ***95.2*** *p117*
Stefanik, Frances *SEE* Stefanik, Peter
Stefanik, Joseph *SEE* Stefanik, Peter
Stefanik, Peter; America, 1885 ***7137*** *p170*
*Wife:*Frances
*Relative:*Joseph
Stefansdottir, Kristbjorg 56; Quebec, 1879 ***2557.1*** *p21*
Stefanski, . . .; New York, 1831 ***4606*** *p177*
Stefansky, Frances *SEE* Stefansky, Peter
Stefansky, Joseph *SEE* Stefansky, Peter
Stefansky, Peter; America, 1885 ***7137*** *p170*
*Wife:*Frances
*Relative:*Joseph
Stefansson, Benedikt 11; Quebec, 1879 ***2557.2*** *p36*
Stefansson, Jon 24; Quebec, 1879 ***2557.1*** *p22*
Steffen, Albert; New York, 1872 ***1450.2*** *p38B*
Steffen, Bernard; Wisconsin, n.d. ***9675.8*** *p121*
Steffen, Carl Christoph Heinrich; America, 1854 ***4610.10*** *p145*
Steffen, Carl Heinrich; America, 1857 ***4610.10*** *p145*
Steffen, Christian 25; Kansas, 1877 ***5240.1*** *p58*
Steffen, Johann Diedrich; America, 1855 ***4610.10*** *p145*
Steffen, Johann Dietrich; America, 1855 ***4610.10*** *p139*
Steffen, Karl Friedrich Wilhelm; America, 1855 ***4610.10*** *p145*
Steffen, Peter; Baltimore, 1837 ***8582*** *p31*
Steffen, Peter; Dayton, OH, 1838 ***8582.2*** *p60*
Steffens, . . .; Cincinnati, 1788-1848 ***8582.3*** *p90*
Steffens, Charles; New York, 1852 ***1450.2*** *p138A*
Steffens, Ernest F.; New York, 1853 ***1450.2*** *p138A*
Steffens, Leonard 40; Kansas, 1881 ***5240.1*** *p43*
Steffens, Leonard 40; Kansas, 1881 ***5240.1*** *p63*
Steffensen, Alfred Borgard; Arkansas, 1918 ***95.2*** *p118*
Stefferton, Francis; Virginia, 1635 ***6219*** *p7*
Stefko, Mike; Wisconsin, n.d. ***9675.8*** *p121*
Stefus, Michael; America, 1899 ***7137*** *p170*
Stege, Otto; Trenton, NJ, 1776 ***8137*** *p14*
Stegemann, . . .; Cincinnati, 1826 ***8582.1*** *p51*
Stegemeier, Carl Friedrich; Cincinnati, 1869-1887 ***8582*** *p31*
Stegemeier, Richard; America, 1891 ***1450.2*** *p138A*
Steger, . . .; Canada, 1776-1783 ***9786*** *p35*
Steger, Leonhard; Wisconsin, n.d. ***9675.8*** *p121*
Steger, Robert; Wisconsin, n.d. ***9675.8*** *p121*
Stegmann, . . .; Cincinnati, 1826-1874 ***8582.1*** *p33*
Stegner, Peter; Ohio, 1798-1818 ***8582.2*** *p54*
Stehben, Jacob; Iroquois Co., IL, 1892 ***3455.1*** *p13*
Stehle, Anna Wezel *SEE* Stehle, Balthasar
Stehle, Balthasar; Pennsylvania, 1749 ***2444*** *p222*
*Wife:*Anna Wezel
Stehle, Martin; New York, NY, 1838 ***8208.4*** *p81*
Stehling, Henrich; Philadelphia, 1779 ***8137*** *p15*
Stehr, Mathias; Pennsylvania, 1772 ***9973.8*** *p33*
Steiert, George; Wisconsin, n.d. ***9675.8*** *p121*
Steifel, Myer; Ohio, 1846 ***9892.11*** *p43*
Steigelmann, Jacob W.; Cincinnati, 1869-1887 ***8582*** *p31*
Steiger, . . .; Canada, 1776-1783 ***9786*** *p35*
Steiger, Adam 6; America, 1853 ***9162.7*** *p15*
Steiger, Adam 10; America, 1853 ***9162.7*** *p15*
Steiger, Adam 24; America, 1854-1855 ***9162.6*** *p104*
Steiger, Adam 27; America, 1854-1855 ***9162.6*** *p105*
Steiger, Agnes *SEE* Steiger, Conrad
Steiger, Agnes *SEE* Steiger, Conrad
Steiger, Anna Maria *SEE* Steiger, Conrad
Steiger, Anna Maria *SEE* Steiger, Conrad
Steiger, Anna Maria *SEE* Steiger, Conrad
Steiger, Anna Maria *SEE* Steiger, Conrad
Steiger, Anna Maria; Georgia, 1739 ***9332*** *p326*
Steiger, Barb. 38; America, 1853 ***9162.7*** *p15*
Steiger, Catharina *SEE* Steiger, Conrad
Steiger, Catharina *SEE* Steiger, Conrad
Steiger, Conrad; America, 1749-1800 ***2444*** *p222*
*Wife:*Anna Maria
*Child:*Agnes
*Child:*Catharina
*Child:*Anna Maria
Steiger, Conrad; Pennsylvania, 1749-1800 ***2444*** *p222*
*Wife:*Anna Maria
*Child:*Agnes
*Child:*Catharina
*Child:*Anna Maria
Steiger, Conrad; Pennsylvania, 1751 ***2444*** *p222*
Steiger, Heinr. 8; America, 1853 ***9162.7*** *p15*
Steiger, Joh. 3; America, 1853 ***9162.7*** *p15*
Steiger, Peter 44; America, 1853 ***9162.7*** *p15*
Steigerwald, Sebastian; America, 1847 ***8582.1*** *p33*
Steigerwald, Sebastian; Cincinnati, 1866 ***8582.1*** *p33*
Steigerwald, Sebastian; Quebec, 1847 ***8582.1*** *p33*
Steigle, Henry William; Philadelphia, 1760 ***9973.7*** *p35*
Steimer, John Adam; Ohio, 1841 ***9892.11*** *p43*
Stein, . . .; Canada, 1776-1783 ***9786*** *p35*
Stein, Mr.; Canada, 1776-1783 ***9786*** *p232*
Stein, von; New York, 1776 ***9786*** *p278*
Stein, Albert; Cincinnati, 1817 ***8582.3*** *p80*
Stein, Albert 84; Cincinnati, 1876 ***8582.3*** *p86*
Stein, Albert, Jr.; Cincinnati, 1877 ***8582.3*** *p86*
Stein, Anton; Illinois, 1894 ***5012.39*** *p53*
Stein, August 24; Kansas, 1885 ***5240.1*** *p68*
Stein, Barb. 11; America, 1853 ***9162.7*** *p15*
Stein, Barb. 15; America, 1853 ***9162.7*** *p15*
Stein, Carl Edward 22; Kansas, 1891 ***5240.1*** *p76*
Stein, Charles; Maryland, 1833 ***8208.4*** *p49*
Stein, Conrad; America, 1852 ***8582.3*** *p63*
Stein, Edward 23; Arkansas, 1918 ***95.2*** *p118*
Stein, Elis. 9 mos; America, 1853 ***9162.8*** *p38*
Stein, Elis. 20; America, 1853 ***9162.7*** *p15*
Stein, Elis. 39; America, 1853 ***9162.8*** *p38*
Stein, Fredrick; Illinois, 1860 ***5012.39*** *p90*
Stein, J. Frederick; America, 1850 ***1450.2*** *p138A*
Stein, Johann Friedrich von; Halifax, N.S., 1780 ***9786*** *p269*
Stein, Johann Friedrich von; New York, 1776 ***9786*** *p269*
Stein, M.; Milwaukee, 1875 ***4719.30*** *p257*
Stein, Marg. 47; America, 1853 ***9162.7*** *p15*
Stein, Maria 10; America, 1853 ***9162.7*** *p15*
Stein, Mich. 4; America, 1853 ***9162.8*** *p38*
Stein, Nicholas 20; America, 1839 ***778.5*** *p505*
Stein, Peter 50; America, 1853 ***9162.7*** *p15*
Stein, Ph. 17; America, 1853 ***9162.7*** *p15*
Stein, Philipp; Philadelphia, 1764 ***8582.3*** *p84*
Stein, Sebastian; Cincinnati, 1847 ***8582.1*** *p33*
Steinaeker, Charles; New York, NY, 1838 ***8208.4*** *p67*
Steinau, Joseph; America, 1837 ***8582.3*** *p63*
Steinbach, Frank; Wisconsin, n.d. ***9675.8*** *p121*
Steinbach, Philipp; Illinois, 1845 ***8582.2*** *p51*
Steinbaugh, John; Colorado, 1904 ***9678.3*** *p14*
Steinbeck, Friederich; Illinois, 1836 ***8582.1*** *p55*
Steinberg, Arved; Iowa, 1866-1943 ***123.54*** *p46*
Steinberg, Carl 27; Kansas, 1906 ***5240.1*** *p84*
Steinberg, Philip; Arkansas, 1918 ***95.2*** *p118*
Steinberg, Victor; Arkansas, 1918 ***95.2*** *p118*
Steinberg, Victor 26; Arkansas, 1918 ***95.2*** *p118*
Steinbery, Nathan; Arkansas, 1918 ***95.2*** *p118*
Steinbicker, J. H.; America, 1844 ***8582.1*** *p33*
Steinbrecher, Adam; Philadelphia, 1779 ***8137*** *p15*
Steinbrecher, Wilhelm; Philadelphia, 1779 ***8137*** *p15*
Steinbrink, Ernst Heinrich; America, 1860 ***4610.10*** *p99*
Steinbrink, Marie Elisabeth Koster; America, 1860-1900 ***4610.10*** *p99*
Steinbuch, Robert; Illinois, 1880 ***2896.5*** *p38*
Steinbuchel, Charles 33; Kansas, 1875 ***5240.1*** *p56*
Steinbuchel, Leopold 25; Kansas, 1885 ***5240.1*** *p43*
Steinbuchel, Leopold 25; Kansas, 1885 ***5240.1*** *p67*
Steinbuchel, Ludwig 36; Kansas, 1883 ***5240.1*** *p43*
Steinbuchel, Ludwig 36; Kansas, 1883 ***5240.1*** *p64*
Steinbuchel, Max 27; Kansas, 1878 ***5240.1*** *p43*
Steinbuchel, Max 27; Kansas, 1878 ***5240.1*** *p59*
Steinbuckel, Charles 33; Kansas, 1875 ***5240.1*** *p43*
Steinbur, Hannah 32; Massachusetts, 1860 ***6410.32*** *p110*
Steine, Peter; Ohio, 1833 ***8582.1*** *p47*
Steineck, . . .; Canada, 1776-1783 ***9786*** *p43*
Steinemann, John H.; Ohio, 1830-1849 ***8582*** *p31*
Steiner, Christian; Georgia, 1734 ***9332*** *p327*
Steiner, Emma Reichen *SEE* Steiner, John
Steiner, Eva 27; America, 1853 ***9162.7*** *p15*
Steiner, Fritz; Kansas, 1890 ***5240.1*** *p43*
Steiner, Gertraud *SEE* Steiner, Simon
Steiner, Gertraud Schoppacher *SEE* Steiner, Simon
Steiner, Heinrich; Ohio, 1814 ***8582.1*** *p47*
Steiner, Jacob; America, 1852 ***1450.2*** *p138A*
Steiner, Jacob 55; Arizona, 1914 ***9228.40*** *p19*
Steiner, Jakob; Ohio, 1814 ***8582.1*** *p47*
Steiner, Jakob 30; America, 1853 ***9162.7*** *p15*
Steiner, Joh. Georg; Philadelphia, 1752 ***7829*** *p8*
Steiner, John; New York, NY, 1902 ***3455.1*** *p50*
*Wife:*Emma Reichen
Steiner, John; Ohio, 1814 ***8582.1*** *p47*
Steiner, John F.; Iroquois Co., IL, 1896 ***3455.1*** *p13*
Steiner, John Isaac; New York, NY, 1912 ***3455.2*** *p73*
Steiner, John Isaac; New York, NY, 1912 ***3455.3*** *p46*
Steiner, Karl 6 mos; America, 1853 ***9162.7*** *p15*
Steiner, Maria *SEE* Steiner, Ruprecht
Steiner, Maria Winter *SEE* Steiner, Ruprecht
Steiner, Melchior; Philadelphia, 1764 ***8582.2*** *p65*
Steiner, Melchior; Philadelphia, 1776 ***8582.3*** *p84*
Steiner, Michael; Illinois, 1837 ***8582.1*** *p55*
Steiner, Michel; Georgia, 1738 ***9332*** *p319*
Steiner, Ruprecht; Georgia, 1738 ***9332*** *p321*
Steiner, Ruprecht; Georgia, 1739 ***9332*** *p324*
*Wife:*Maria Winter
Steiner, Ruprecht; Georgia, 1739 ***9332*** *p326*
*Wife:*Maria
Steiner, Simon; Georgia, 1738 ***9332*** *p321*
Steiner, Simon; Georgia, 1739 ***9332*** *p323*
*Wife:*Gertraud Schoppacher
Steiner, Simon; Georgia, 1739 ***9332*** *p325*
*Wife:*Gertraud
Steingrimsson, Sigmundur 53; Quebec, 1879 ***2557.1*** *p39A*
Steinhardt, Herman; Kansas, 1919 ***6013.40*** *p17*
Steinhauer, Johannes; New York, NY, 1838 ***8208.4*** *p87*
Steinhaur, Frank; Illinois, 1865 ***2896.5*** *p38*
Steinhaur, Michael; New York, NY, 1836 ***2896.5*** *p38*
Steinhausen, Franz Antonius; Philadelphia, 1779 ***8137*** *p15*
Steinhauser, Fritz 33; Kansas, 1880 ***5240.1*** *p62*
Steinimann, Andreas *SEE* Steinimann, Jacob
Steinimann, Jacob; Carolina, 1738 ***9898*** *p35*
*Relative:*Andreas
Steininger, Leopold; Wisconsin, n.d. ***9675.8*** *p121*
Steinkampfer, Christine F. Siekmeier *SEE* Steinkampfer, Johann Friedrich
Steinkampfer, Friedrich Wilhelm *SEE* Steinkampfer, Johann Friedrich
Steinkampfer, Johann Friedrich; America, 1847 ***4610.10*** *p111*
*Wife:*Christine F. Siekmeier
*Son:*Friedrich Wilhelm
Steinke, Edward August; New York, NY, 1903 ***3455.1*** *p42*
Steinke, Henry; Wisconsin, n.d. ***9675.8*** *p121*
Steinkellner, Hans; Washington, 1859-1920 ***2872.1*** *p38*
Steinler, Anna Catharina *SEE* Steinler, Ursula Koempf
Steinler, Ursula Koempf; Pennsylvania, 1751 ***2444*** *p222*
*Child:*Anna Catharina
With child
Steinlin, Anna Catharina *SEE* Steinlin, Ursula Koempf
Steinlin, Ursula Koempf; Pennsylvania, 1751 ***2444*** *p222*
*Child:*Anna Catharina
With child
Steinman, Frederick; California, 1856 ***2769.8*** *p4*
Steinman, Frederick 32; California, 1872 ***2769.8*** *p6*
Steinman, Kaspar 31; California, 1872 ***2769.8*** *p6*
Steinman, Peter; California, 1856 ***2769.8*** *p4*
Steinmann, . . .; Canada, 1776-1783 ***9786*** *p35*
Steinmann, A. Salome; New York, 1763 ***3652*** *p89*
Steinmann, Anna Regina *SEE* Steinmann, Christian Frederick
Steinmann, Anton Heinrich Karl; America, 1844 ***4610.10*** *p95*
*Wife:*Marie F. C. Langeleh
*Son:*Friedrich Gottlieb
Steinmann, Anton Heinrich Karl Wilhelm; America, 1840 ***4610.10*** *p95*
*Son:*Karl Heinrich
*Wife:*Marie F. C. Langeleh
Steinmann, Christian Frederick; New York, 1749 ***3652*** *p71*
*Wife:*Anna Regina
Steinmann, Friedrich Gottlieb *SEE* Steinmann, Anton Heinrich Karl
Steinmann, Heinrich Carl Ernst; America, 1886 ***4610.10*** *p96*
Steinmann, Jacob 30; California, 1872 ***2769.8*** *p5*

Steinmann, John; America, 1849 1450.2 p138A
Steinmann, Karl Heinrich *SEE* Steinmann, Anton Heinrich Karl Wilhel
Steinmann, L.E.; Cincinnati, 1856 8582.3 p45
Steinmann, Louis Edward; Cincinnati, 1869-1887 8582 p31
Steinmann, Marie F. C. Langeleh *SEE* Steinmann, Anton Heinrich Karl
Steinmann, Marie F. C. Langeleh *SEE* Steinmann, Anton Heinrich Karl Wilhel
Steinmann, Sophie Louise; America, 1843 4610.10 p133
Steinmeier, A. M. Cath. Ilsabein *SEE* Steinmeier, Johann Heinrich
Steinmeier, A. M. Ilsabein Koweg *SEE* Steinmeier, Johann Heinrich
Steinmeier, Carl Heinrich *SEE* Steinmeier, Johann Heinrich
Steinmeier, Christ; America, 1838 1450.2 p138A
Steinmeier, Johann Heinrich; America, 1881 4610.10 p153
*Wife:*A. M. Ilsabein Koweg
*Child:*Carl Heinrich
*Child:*A. M. Cath. Ilsabein
Steinmeir, Charles; America, 1838 1450.2 p138A
Steinmeir, Christine; America, 1838 1450.2 p139A
Steinmetz, . . .; Canada, 1776-1783 9786 p35
Steinmetz, Fred; New York, 1882 1450.2 p38B
Steinmetz, Johann; Philadelphia, 1765 8582.3 p84
Steinmetz, Joseph 21; America, 1838 778.5 p505
Steinmetzer, Nicholas; Wisconsin, n.d. 9675.8 p121
Steinmeyer, Ernst Heinrih Christian; America, 1882 4610.10 p106
Steinmuller, Barbara 23; Kansas, 1893 5240.1 p79
Steinmuller, John 25; Kansas, 1887 5240.1 p71
Steinmyer, August; Illinois, 1861 7857 p7
Steinoehl, Georg Heinrich; Pennsylvania, 1749 2444 p203
Steins, Lorenz; Philadelphia, 1780 8137 p15
Steinsiek, Anne M. L. W. Sander *SEE* Steinsiek, Friedrich Wilhelm Gottlieb
Steinsiek, Carl Friedrich *SEE* Steinsiek, Friedrich Wilhelm Gottlieb
Steinsiek, Friedrich Wilhelm Gottlieb; America, 1856 4610.10 p157
*Wife:*Anne M. L. W. Sander
*Son:*Carl Friedrich
Steinsiek, Heinrich Friedrich Wilhelm; America, 1869 4610.10 p152
Steinsson, Sigurdur 51; Quebec, 1879 2557.2 p36
Steinweg, . . .; America, n.d. 8582.3 p79
Steinwehr, Adolph Wilhelm, Baron von; Alabama, 1847 8582.3 p91
Stelinger, Johannes; Ohio, 1798-1818 8582.2 p53
Stellen, Fritz; America, 1884 3702.7 p597
Stelling, Reinhard; Wisconsin, n.d. 9675.8 p121
Stelman, Joseph; Colorado, 1904 9678.3 p14
Stelmaska, Helen; Connecticut, 1912 9980.29 p64
Stelmaska, Janina 9; New York, 1912 9980.29 p64
With aunt
Stelting, Christian; Baltimore, 1834 1450.2 p139A
Stelting, Dederick; America, 1834 1450.2 p139A
Stemann, John; Cincinnati, 1869-1887 8582 p31
Steme, . . .; Canada, 1776-1783 9786 p35
Stempinska, Helena Kowalski 33; New York, 1912 9980.29 p57
With brother
Stempinska, Jan; Pittsburgh, 1912 9980.29 p57
Stempinska, Stefania 8; New York, 1912 9980.29 p57
Stempinski, Helena Kowalski; New York, 1912 9980.29 p57
With brother
Stempinski, Jan; Pittsburgh, 1912 9980.29 p57
Stempinski, Pawel 6 mos; New York, 1912 9980.29 p57
Stenave, Madame 51; America, 1827 778.5 p505
Stenberg, C. E.; Iowa, 1866-1943 123.54 p46
Stenberg, John W.; Iowa, 1866-1943 123.54 p46
Stence, Jacob; Philadelphia, 1762 9973.7 p37
Steneck, Frederick; New York, NY, 1836 8208.4 p14
Stengel, . . .; Canada, 1776-1783 9786 p35
Stengel, Andrew; Colorado, 1904 9678.3 p14
Stengel, Joh. Adam 30; New Orleans, 1839 9420.2 p169
Stengel, Joseph; Colorado, 1890 9678.3 p14
Stengel, Louis; Colorado, 1904 9678.3 p14
Stenger, . . .; Canada, 1776-1783 9786 p35
Stenger, August 25; West Virginia, 1898 9788.3 p21
Stenger, Christiana 2; Port uncertain, 1839 778.5 p505
Stenger, Joseph 41; West Virginia, 1898 9788.3 p21
Stenger, Katherfina 13; Port uncertain, 1839 778.5 p505
Stenger, Katherina 33; Port uncertain, 1839 778.5 p505
Stenger, Margretha 8; Port uncertain, 1839 778.5 p505
Stenger, Peter 4; Port uncertain, 1839 778.5 p505
Stenger, Peter 39; Port uncertain, 1839 778.5 p505
Stenger, Stephen 11; Port uncertain, 1839 778.5 p505
Stenhouse, Andrew; Arkansas, 1918 95.2 p118
Stenke, . . .; Canada, 1776-1783 9786 p35
Stenlund, Lars; New Orleans, 1837 6410.32 p126
Stenquist, Robert John; Washington, 1859-1920 2872.1 p38
Stensby, Antho.; Virginia, 1636 6219 p77
Stensland, John Marshall 30; Arkansas, 1918 95.2 p118
Stenson, Henry; New York, NY, 1865 5704.8 p193
Stenzell, . . .; Canada, 1776-1783 9786 p35
Stepan, Joe; Wisconsin, n.d. 9675.8 p121
Stepannovac, Jrovenka; Iowa, 1866-1943 123.54 p46
Steph, Eso; Washington, 1859-1920 2872.1 p38
Steph, Gabriel; Washington, 1859-1920 2872.1 p38
Steph, George; Washington, 1859-1920 2872.1 p39
Steph, Gertrude; Washington, 1859-1920 2872.1 p39
Steph, Helena; Washington, 1859-1920 2872.1 p39
Steph, Hilda; Washington, 1859-1920 2872.1 p39
Steph, Imbi Tellervo; Washington, 1859-1920 2872.1 p39
Steph, Onni; Washington, 1859-1920 2872.1 p39
Steph, Paul; Washington, 1859-1920 2872.1 p39
Stephan, C. T.; Milwaukee, 1875 4719.30 p257
Stephan, Frank; Washington, 1859-1920 2872.1 p38
Stephan, George S.; New York, NY, 1835 8208.4 p7
Stephan, Joseph; Wisconsin, n.d. 9675.8 p121
Stephan, Ludwig 28; Kansas, 1885 5240.1 p67
Stephan, Martin; St. Louis, 1839 3702.7 p308
Stephan, Martin 16 *SEE* Stephan, Martin
Stephan, Martin 61; New Orleans, 1839 9420.2 p165
*Son:*Martin 16
Stephan, Michael; New Orleans, 1839 9420.1 p373
Stephans, Casper 15; America, 1837 778.5 p505
Stephans, Elnor; New York, NY, 1811 2859.11 p19
Stephans, Thomas; New York, NY, 1811 2859.11 p19
Stephanson, John; New York, NY, 1811 2859.11 p19
Stephen, Alexander; St. John, N.B., 1866 5704.8 p167
Stephen, George; Montreal, 1863 9775.5 p203
Stephen, George; Ontario, n.d. 9775.5 p216
Stephen, James; Charleston, SC, 1766 1639.20 p295
Stephen, Joseph; Wisconsin, n.d. 9675.8 p121
Stephens, Archela; Virginia, 1637 6219 p86
Stephens, Archelane; Virginia, 1638 6219 p115
Stephens, Charles; New Orleans, 1825 1450.2 p139A
Stephens, Dorothy 22 *SEE* Stephens, William
Stephens, Elizabeth; America, 1739 4971 p14
Stephens, George; Jamaica, 1736 3690.1 p216
Stephens, Henry; Virginia, 1638 6219 p122
Stephens, Hugh 22; Maryland, 1775 1219.7 p250
Stephens, J.W.; Arizona, 1897 9228.30 p3
Stephens, Jas.; Quebec, 1830 4719.7 p21
Stephens, Joe 21; Kansas, 1903 5240.1 p82
Stephens, John; New York, NY, 1815 2859.11 p42
Stephens, John; New York, NY, 1816 2859.11 p42
Stephens, John; Virginia, 1635 6219 p27
Stephens, John 24; Philadelphia, 1774 1219.7 p184
Stephens, Jon.; Virginia, 1637 6219 p11
Stephens, Jon.; Virginia, 1637 6219 p114
Stephens, Lewis F.; Colorado, 1904 9678.3 p14
Stephens, Mordecai 18; Jamaica, 1733 3690.1 p216
Stephens, Patrick 24; Maryland, 1775 1219.7 p267
Stephens, Peter; Virginia, 1635 6219 p16
Stephens, Peter; Virginia, 1639 6219 p156
Stephens, Phillipp; Virginia, 1636 6219 p80
Stephens, Rich.; Virginia, 1638 6219 p124
Stephens, Richard; Virginia, 1637 6219 p37
Stephens, Richard; Virginia, 1643 6219 p200
Stephens, Robert 22; Philadelphia, 1774 1219.7 p217
Stephens, Tho.; Virginia, 1638 6219 p145
Stephens, Thomas 26; Philadelphia, 1774 1219.7 p184
Stephens, Thos.; Virginia, 1635 6219 p26
Stephens, Tobias; Virginia, 1646 6219 p240
Stephens, William 22; Virginia, 1774 1219.7 p239
*Wife:*Dorothy 22
Stephens, William 23; Maryland, 1722 3690.1 p216
Stephens, William 23; Pensacola, FL, 1774 1219.7 p227
Stephens, Wm.; Virginia, 1646 6219 p246
Stephenson, Alexander; Philadelphia, 1850 53.26 p84
Stephenson, Alexander; Philadelphia, 1850 5704.8 p65
Stephenson, Ann; Quebec, 1848 5704.8 p41
Stephenson, Ann; Virginia, 1636 6219 p15
Stephenson, Catherine; St. John, N.B., 1847 5704.8 p11
Stephenson, Charles 29; Philadelphia, 1804 53.26 p84
Stephenson, Edward; Quebec, 1848 5704.8 p41
Stephenson, Eliza; Quebec, 1848 5704.8 p41
Stephenson, Eliza 13; Philadelphia, 1851 5704.8 p79
Stephenson, Gastavus; Quebec, 1848 5704.8 p41
Stephenson, George 10; Quebec, 1848 5704.8 p41
Stephenson, Henry; New York, NY, 1811 2859.11 p19
Stephenson, Henry; Quebec, 1848 5704.8 p41
Stephenson, Jane; St. John, N.B., 1852 5704.8 p93
Stephenson, Jane 60; North Carolina, 1850 1639.20 p296
Stephenson, John; Iowa, 1866-1943 123.54 p46
Stephenson, John; Quebec, 1848 5704.8 p41
Stephenson, John 12; Quebec, 1848 5704.8 p41
Stephenson, John 26; Antigua (Antego), 1722 3690.1 p216
Stephenson, John 27; Maryland, 1775 1219.7 p254
Stephenson, John 27; Philadelphia, 1804 53.26 p84
Stephenson, Joseph; Jamaica, 1753 1219.7 p22
Stephenson, Joseph; Jamaica, 1753 3690.1 p216
Stephenson, Margaret 22; Philadelphia, 1804 53.26 p84
Stephenson, Martha; Philadelphia, 1852 5704.8 p89
Stephenson, Mary; Philadelphia, 1852 5704.8 p85
Stephenson, Mary; St. John, N.B., 1847 5704.8 p11
Stephenson, Robert; Ohio, 1845 9892.11 p43
Stephenson, Samuel; New York, NY, 1811 2859.11 p19
Stephenson, Sarah; Philadelphia, 1853 5704.8 p102
Stephenson, Thomas; Philadelphia, 1852 5704.8 p85
Stephenson, Thomas; Quebec, 1848 5704.8 p41
Stephenson, Thomas 22; Port uncertain, 1774 1219.7 p176
Stephenson, Thomas 30; Jamaica, 1774 1219.7 p180
Stephenson, William 20; Philadelphia, 1804 53.26 p84
Stephin, George; Jamaica, 1736 3690.1 p216
Stepien, Maryanna 18; New York, 1912 9980.29 p60
Stepney, James 16; Baltimore, 1775 1219.7 p271
Stepnowski, Pete Francis; Iowa, 1866-1943 123.54 p79
Stepnowski, Peter Francis; Iowa, 1866-1943 123.54 p79
Stepowronski, Irena 3; New York, 1912 9980.29 p59
With uncle
Stepowronski, Tytys; New Jersey, 1912 9980.29 p59
Steppler, Joseph, Jr.; Colorado, 1890 9678.3 p14
Steprowenska, Irena 3; New York, 1912 9980.29 p59
With uncle
Steprowenska, Tytus; New Jersey, 1912 9980.29 p59
Stepukowski, Frank; Arkansas, 1918 95.2 p118
Sterba, John; America, 1886 7137 p170
Sterch, Benctius; Wisconsin, n.d. 9675.8 p121
Stergar, Valentine; America, 1899 1450.2 p38B
Stergis, Ely Thomas; Arkansas, 1918 95.2 p118
Sterkaubarg, Frederick; Illinois, 1851 7857 p7
Sterling, Hugh 18; Quebec, 1864 5704.8 p159
Sterling, James; New York, NY, 1811 2859.11 p19
Sterling, Robert; New York, NY, 1811 2859.11 p19
Sterling, Robert 27; Dominica, 1774 1219.7 p188
Sterling, Sobert; New York, NY, 1815 2859.11 p42
Stern, Adolph; Illinois, 1892 5012.40 p26
Stern, Anna Catharina; Pennsylvania, 1754 2444 p222
Stern, Charles; Wisconsin, n.d. 9675.8 p121
Stern, Henry; Milwaukee, 1875 4719.30 p257
Stern, Henry; Milwaukee, 1875 4719.30 p258
Stern, Ignatz; Illinois, 1871 5012.39 p25
Stern, Johann Marie; Wisconsin, n.d. 9675.8 p121
Stern, John; Ohio, 1840 9892.11 p43
Stern, S.; Milwaukee, 1875 4719.30 p257
Sternall, Richard; Virginia, 1638 6219 p120
Sternberg, F.; Quebec, 1776 9786 p105
Sternberg, Johann Christian; Quebec, 1776 9786 p255
Sterne, . . .; Canada, 1776-1783 9786 p35
Sterne, Johan; Illinois, 1830 8582.1 p55
Sterner, . . .; Canada, 1776-1783 9786 p35
Sterns, William; Illinois, 1861 7857 p7
Sternsnik, John; Wisconsin, n.d. 9675.8 p121
Sternweis, John Henry 29; California, 1872 2769.8 p5
Sterriker, Hannah 12; Nova Scotia, 1774 1219.7 p195
Sterrill, Isabella; Philadelphia, 1864 5704.8 p186
Sterritt, Jermiah; St. John, N.B., 1848 5704.8 p44
Sterritt, Martha 20; St. John, N.B., 1854 5704.8 p121
Stertzel, Hypolis 51; New York, NY, 1878 9253 p46
Stervic, Jas.; Iowa, 1866-1943 123.54 p46
Stetten, Peter V. 24; America, 1853 9162.8 p38
Stettler, Gottfried; New York, 1884 1450.2 p38B
Stettner, John; New York, 1754 3652 p80
Steuart, Thomas 24; Jamaica, 1731 3690.1 p216
Steuft, Christian; Illinois, 1867 2896.5 p39
Steup, Francis; New York, 1750 3652 p75
Steup, Sophia; New York, 1750 3652 p75
Steuven, Marie 72; Kansas, 1876 5240.1 p57
Steven, Christian 23 *SEE* Steven, James
Steven, James 27; North Carolina, 1775 1639.20 p295
*Sister:*Christian 23
*Sister:*Sarah 16
*Brother:*Thomas 11
Steven, Sarah 16 *SEE* Steven, James
Steven, Thomas 11 *SEE* Steven, James
Steven, Wm.; Virginia, 1636 6219 p76
Stevenik, John; Wisconsin, n.d. 9675.8 p121
Stevens, Ann 30 *SEE* Stevens, John
Stevens, Assaf G.; Kansas, 1903 5240.1 p43
Stevens, Bedey 26; Jamaica, 1733 3690.1 p216
Stevens, Charles; Michigan, 1889 2896.5 p39
Stevens, Charles 22; Virginia, 1774 1219.7 p239
Stevens, Chas. 17; Port uncertain, 1849 4535.10 p198
*Relative:*Wm. 16
Stevens, David; Iowa, 1898 5240.1 p43
Stevens, Eliz.; Port uncertain, 1849 4535.10 p198
Stevens, Eliz. 10 *SEE* Stevens, Jas.

Stevens, Emma 24 SEE Stevens, Jas.
Stevens, George; Colorado, 1904 9678.3 p14
Stevens, Harriet 7 SEE Stevens, John
Stevens, Henry; Virginia, 1637 6219 p108
Stevens, Henry 17; Maryland, 1737 3690.1 p217
Stevens, Henry 42; Jamaica, 1734 3690.1 p216
Stevens, J. 44; Arizona, 1904 9228.40 p8
Stevens, James; America, 1798 4778.1 p150
Stevens, James; New York, NY, 1816 2859.11 p42
Stevens, James; North Carolina, 1775 1639.20 p296
Stevens, James 14 SEE Stevens, Jas.
Stevens, James 18; Port uncertain, 1849 4535.10 p198
Relative:John 20
Stevens, James 20; Port uncertain, 1849 4535.10 p198
Relative:Thomas 15
Stevens, James, Jr.; Illinois, 1859 5012.39 p89
Stevens, James, Sr.; Illinois, 1859 5012.39 p89
Stevens, James H.; America, 1893 1450.2 p139A
Stevens, Jas. 51; Port uncertain, 1849 4535.10 p198
Wife:Kezia 45
Child:Emma 24
Child:Sarah 21
Child:Eliz. 10
Child:Kezia 8
Child:John 20
Child:James 14
Child:Jonas 25
Stevens, Joe 21; Kansas, 1903 5240.1 p43
Stevens, John 3 SEE Stevens, John
Stevens, John 20 SEE Stevens, James
Stevens, John 20 SEE Stevens, Jas.
Stevens, John 21; Maryland, 1775 1219.7 p247
Stevens, John 26; Maryland, 1774 1219.7 p179
Stevens, John 28; Jamaica, 1736 3690.1 p217
Stevens, John 36; Port uncertain, 1849 4535.10 p198
Wife:Ann 30
Child:Sophia 8
Child:Harriet 7
Child:Mary Ann 5
Child:John 3
Stevens, John N.; New York, NY, 1839 8208.4 p101
Stevens, Jonas 25 SEE Stevens, Jas.
Stevens, Kezia 8 SEE Stevens, Jas.
Stevens, Kezia 45 SEE Stevens, Jas.
Stevens, Mary Ann 5 SEE Stevens, John
Stevens, Oliver 18; Virginia, 1774 1219.7 p243
Stevens, Richard 29; Kansas, 1887 5240.1 p71
Stevens, Robert; Jamaica, 1774 1219.7 p242
Stevens, Robert 26; Philadelphia, 1774 1219.7 p182
Stevens, Salem; Kansas, 1902 5240.1 p43
Stevens, Sarah 21 SEE Stevens, Jas.
Stevens, Sophia 8 SEE Stevens, John
Stevens, Thomas 15 SEE Stevens, James
Stevens, W. H. 61; Arizona, 1911 9228.40 p15
Stevens, William; Brunswick, NC, 1739 1639.20 p296
Stevens, William; Colorado, 1888 9678.3 p14
Stevens, William; Philadelphia, 1816 2859.11 p42
Stevens, William; Virginia, 1637 6219 p109
Stevens, William George 37; Maryland, 1773 1219.7 p173
Stevens, Wm. 16 SEE Stevens, Chas.
Stevenson, Mrs.; Quebec, 1815 9229.18 p76
Stevenson, Alexander 28; Maryland, 1773 1219.7 p173
Stevenson, Andrew; New York, NY, 1867 5704.8 p219
Stevenson, Ann 9; Quebec, 1864 5704.8 p162
Stevenson, Ann 29; Quebec, 1864 5704.8 p162
Stevenson, Ann 40; St. John, N.B., 1857 5704.8 p134
Stevenson, Archy; Philadelphia, 1852 5704.8 p91
Stevenson, Betty 62; Quebec, 1857 5704.8 p136
Stevenson, Catharine; Philadelphia, 1866 5704.8 p215
Stevenson, Christ.; Virginia, 1637 6219 p86
Stevenson, Crawford; New York, NY, 1865 5704.8 p196
Stevenson, David; America, 1841 1450.2 p139A
Stevenson, David; New York, NY, 1865 5704.8 p196
Stevenson, David; Philadelphia, 1866 5704.8 p215
Stevenson, David; Philadelphia, 1867 5704.8 p218
Stevenson, David 30; Quebec, 1857 5704.8 p136
Stevenson, David 60; Quebec, 1857 5704.8 p136
Stevenson, Eliza 11; St. John, N.B., 1857 5704.8 p134
Stevenson, Elizabeth; Philadelphia, 1864 5704.8 p178
Stevenson, Elizabeth; Philadelphia, 1865 5704.8 p200
Stevenson, Elleanor; Quebec, 1849 5704.8 p51
Stevenson, Ellen Jane 9; Quebec, 1849 5704.8 p51
Stevenson, George; America, 1811 1450.2 p139A
Stevenson, Hugh; New York, NY, 1811 2859.11 p19
Stevenson, Hugh; New York, NY, 1864 5704.8 p171
Stevenson, James; Philadelphia, 1849 53.26 p84
Stevenson, James; Philadelphia, 1849 5704.8 p53
Stevenson, James; Quebec, 1849 5704.8 p51
Stevenson, James; Quebec, 1850 5704.8 p63
Stevenson, James 21; St. John, N.B., 1866 5704.8 p166
Stevenson, Jane SEE Stevenson, Janet
Stevenson, Jane; New York, NY, 1865 5704.8 p196
Stevenson, Jane; Philadelphia, 1849 5704.8 p58
Stevenson, Jane 20; Philadelphia, 1858 5704.8 p139
Stevenson, Janet; Philadelphia, 1849 53.26 p84
Relative:Jane
Relative:Martha 12
Stevenson, Janet; Philadelphia, 1849 5704.8 p58
Stevenson, John; Baltimore, 1811 2859.11 p19
Stevenson, John; New York, NY, 1811 2859.11 p19
Stevenson, John; Philadelphia, 1864 5704.8 p186
Stevenson, John; St. John, N.B., 1866 5704.8 p166
Stevenson, John 6; St. John, N.B., 1857 5704.8 p134
Stevenson, John 19; St. John, N.B., 1864 5704.8 p157
Stevenson, Joseph 25; Virginia, 1773 1219.7 p169
Stevenson, Margaret; Philadelphia, 1864 5704.8 p178
Stevenson, Margaret 1; St. John, N.B., 1857 5704.8 p134
Stevenson, Margaret 20; Quebec, 1857 5704.8 p136
Stevenson, Martha; Baltimore, 1811 2859.11 p19
Stevenson, Martha; Philadelphia, 1865 5704.8 p200
Stevenson, Martha 12 SEE Stevenson, Janet
Stevenson, Martha 12; Philadelphia, 1849 5704.8 p58
Stevenson, Martha 20; Philadelphia, 1854 5704.8 p116
Stevenson, Mary 3; Quebec, 1864 5704.8 p162
Stevenson, Mary 16; Philadelphia, 1860 5704.8 p145
Stevenson, Mary Ann 6 mos; Quebec, 1849 5704.8 p51
Stevenson, Mary Ann 5; Quebec, 1849 5704.8 p51
Stevenson, Mathew 25; Quebec, 1857 5704.8 p136
Stevenson, Robert; New York, NY, 1837 8208.4 p55
Stevenson, Robert 4; Quebec, 1849 5704.8 p51
Stevenson, Robert 9; St. John, N.B., 1857 5704.8 p134
Stevenson, Robert 20; Antigua (Antego), 1728 3690.1 p217
Stevenson, Rosanna 7; Quebec, 1849 5704.8 p51
Stevenson, Samuel 18; Maryland, 1735 3690.1 p217
Stevenson, Thomas; Ohio, 1849 9892.11 p43
Stevenson, Thomas; Ohio, 1851 9892.11 p43
Stevenson, Thomas 21; Philadelphia, 1804 53.26 p84
Stevenson, William; New York, NY, 1811 2859.11 p19
Stevenson, William; Philadelphia, 1865 5704.8 p199
Stevenson, William 20; Maryland or Virginia, 1733 3690.1 p217
Stevenson, William 33; Quebec, 1864 5704.8 p162
Stevenson, Wm.; Petersburg, VA, 1809 4778.2 p141
Steward, Alexander 21; Virginia, 1774 1219.7 p186
Steward, Ann 36 SEE Steward, Thomas
Steward, Benjamin 15; West Indies, 1722 3690.1 p217
Steward, Benjamin 18; Maryland, 1727 3690.1 p217
Steward, Charles; Virginia, 1636 6219 p23
Steward, Charles; Virginia, 1638-1700 6219 p150
Steward, Charles 19; Maryland, 1730 3690.1 p217
Steward, Charles 22; Maryland, 1775 1219.7 p263
Steward, Daniell 15; Virginia, 1700 2212 p31
Steward, Donald 18; Georgia, 1774 1219.7 p188
Steward, Geo.; New York, NY, 1816 2859.11 p42
Steward, George 11 mos SEE Steward, Thomas
Steward, George 25; Philadelphia, 1774 1219.7 p216
Steward, Harriet 6 SEE Steward, Thomas
Steward, Henry 7 SEE Steward, Thomas
Steward, James 13 SEE Steward, Thomas
Steward, Jane 4 SEE Steward, Thomas
Steward, Jno; America, 1697 2212 p4
Steward, John; Virginia, 1639 6219 p22
Steward, John 18 SEE Steward, Thomas
Steward, Martha 11 SEE Steward, Thomas
Steward, Newman; Virginia, 1698 2212 p15
Steward, Richard 19; Philadelphia, 1864 5704.8 p156
Steward, Thomas; America, 1697 2212 p7
Steward, Thomas 42; Port uncertain, 1849 4535.10 p198
Wife:Ann 36
Child:Martha 11
Child:Jane 4
Child:Harriet 6
Child:John 18
Child:James 13
Child:Henry 7
Child:George 11 mos
Child:Wm. 19
Steward, William 24; Maryland, 1774 1219.7 p180
Steward, Wm. 19 SEE Steward, Thomas
Stewardson, Alice; Virginia, 1647 6219 p244
Stewart, . . .; America, 1863-1871 5704.8 p199
Stewart, . . . 3; America, 1863-1871 5704.8 p199
Stewart, . . . 5; America, 1863-1871 5704.8 p199
Stewart, . . . 7; America, 1863-1871 5704.8 p199
Stewart, Mr.; Quebec, 1815 9229.18 p79
Stewart, Mr.; Quebec, 1815 9229.18 p82
Stewart, Adam; New York, NY, 1864 5704.8 p172
Stewart, Agnes 20 SEE Stewart, William
Stewart, Alex SEE Stewart, George
Stewart, Alexan.; New York, NY, 1811 2859.11 p19
Stewart, Alexander; America, 1744 1639.20 p296
Stewart, Alexander; Charleston, SC, 1691-1763 1639.20 p296
Stewart, Alexander; New York, NY, 1815 2859.11 p42
Stewart, Alexander; Philadelphia, 1816 2859.11 p42
Stewart, Alexander; Philadelphia, 1851 5704.8 p79
Stewart, Alexander; Philadelphia, 1853 5704.8 p102
Stewart, Alexander; St. John, N.B., 1847 5704.8 p18
Stewart, Alexander 4 SEE Stewart, Dougald
Stewart, Alexander 9; Quebec, 1864 5704.8 p163
Stewart, Alexander 14 SEE Stewart, Kenneth
Stewart, Alexander 20; Philadelphia, 1803 53.26 p84
Stewart, Alexander 21; Philadelphia, 1803 53.26 p84
Stewart, Alexander 35; Wilmington, NC, 1775 1639.20 p296
Son:Charles 15
Stewart, Alexander 40; Kansas, 1889 5240.1 p74
Stewart, Allan SEE Stewart, Peter
Stewart, Allan; New York, NY, 1816 2859.11 p42
Stewart, Allan 43; Quebec, 1858 5704.8 p138
Stewart, Allan 44; Wilmington, NC, 1775 1639.20 p296
Stewart, Andrew; Iroquois Co., IL, 1892 3455.1 p13
Stewart, Andrew; New York, NY, 1811 2859.11 p19
With wife & child
Stewart, Andrew; New York, NY, 1836 8208.4 p20
Stewart, Andrew; North America, 1819 8894.2 p56
Wife:Frances Thomson
Stewart, Andrew; North Carolina, 1765 1639.20 p297
Stewart, Andrew; Philadelphia, 1850 53.26 p84
Stewart, Andrew; Philadelphia, 1850 5704.8 p60
Stewart, Andrew; St. John, N.B., 1850 5704.8 p61
Stewart, Andrew 20; Philadelphia, 1854 5704.8 p116
Stewart, Andrew 30; Quebec, 1855 5704.8 p126
Stewart, Ann SEE Stewart, George
Stewart, Ann; Philadelphia, 1852 5704.8 p87
Stewart, Ann; Philadelphia, 1865 5704.8 p206
Stewart, Ann; Quebec, 1863 4537.30 p11
Stewart, Ann 13; St. John, N.B., 1847 5704.8 p20
Stewart, Ann 17; St. John, N.B., 1863 5704.8 p152
Stewart, Ann 19; Philadelphia, 1853 5704.8 p113
Stewart, Ann 24 SEE Stewart, William
Stewart, Ann 28; Quebec, 1856 5704.8 p129
Stewart, Ann 30; Quebec, 1863 5704.8 p154
Stewart, Ann Jane; Philadelphia, 1868 5704.8 p228
Stewart, Annabella SEE Stewart, George
Stewart, Anne; New York, NY, 1865 5704.8 p191
Stewart, Anne; Quebec, 1851 5704.8 p74
Stewart, Anne 18; Philadelphia, 1804 53.26 p84
Stewart, Archibald 30; Wilmington, NC, 1775 1639.20 p297
Stewart, Archibald James; New York, NY, 1837 8208.4 p52
Stewart, Arthur; New York, NY, 1834 8208.4 p50
Stewart, Banco 3 SEE Stewart, Kenneth
Stewart, Benj.; New York, NY, 1811 2859.11 p19
Stewart, Benjamin 15; West Indies, 1722 3690.1 p217
Stewart, Bess; Quebec, 1845 4537.30 p117
Stewart, Catharine; America, 1864 5704.8 p178
Stewart, Catherine; Philadelphia, 1851 5704.8 p71
Stewart, Catherine; Philadelphia, 1853 5704.8 p101
Stewart, Catherine; Quebec, 1875 4537.30 p26
Stewart, Catherine 15; St. John, N.B., 1863 5704.8 p152
Stewart, Catherine 20; Philadelphia, 1854 5704.8 p117
Stewart, Catherine 22; Philadelphia, 1854 5704.8 p117
Stewart, Catherine 24; Philadelphia, 1853 5704.8 p113
Stewart, Catherine 25; Philadelphia, 1861 5704.8 p147
Stewart, Charles; New York, NY, 1815 2859.11 p42
Stewart, Charles; New York, NY, 1835 8208.4 p50
Stewart, Charles; North Carolina, 1683-1830 1639.20 p297
Stewart, Charles; St. John, N.B., 1852 5704.8 p95
Stewart, Charles 15 SEE Stewart, Alexander
Stewart, Charles 20; Philadelphia, 1775 1219.7 p248
Stewart, Christian 3 SEE Stewart, Kenneth
Stewart, Christy SEE Stewart, John
Stewart, Daniel; America, 1791 1639.20 p297
Stewart, Daniel; New York, NY, 1816 2859.11 p42
Stewart, Daniel; Philadelphia, 1848 53.26 p85
Relative:Isabella
Relative:William
Stewart, Daniel; Philadelphia, 1848 5704.8 p40
Stewart, Daniel 19; Newfoundland, 1789 4915.24 p57
Stewart, David; New York, NY, 1811 2859.11 p19
Stewart, David; New York, NY, 1816 2859.11 p42
Stewart, David; New York, NY, 1866 5704.8 p212
Stewart, David; Philadelphia, 1848 53.26 p85
Relative:Eleanor
Relative:Eliza
Relative:Nancy
Relative:John 12
Stewart, David; Philadelphia, 1848 5704.8 p45
Stewart, David 21; Virginia, 1774 1219.7 p244
Stewart, Donald SEE Stewart, George
Stewart, Donald; Quebec, 1843 4537.30 p43
Stewart, Donald; South Carolina, 1716 1639.20 p297
Stewart, Donna; St. John, N.B., 1850 5704.8 p61
Stewart, Dougal; North Carolina, 1739 1639.20 p297

Stewart, Dougald 40; Wilmington, NC, 1775 ***1639.20*** *p297*
With wife 40
*Child:*John 16
*Child:*James 10
*Child:*Thomas 6
*Child:*Alexander 4
Stewart, Dugal; Prince Edward Island, 1770 ***9775.5*** *p210*
Stewart, Dugald 69; North Carolina, 1850 ***1639.20*** *p297*
Stewart, Duncan *SEE* Stewart, John
Stewart, Duncan; South Carolina, 1716 ***1639.20*** *p298*
Stewart, Duncan 61; South Carolina, 1850 ***1639.20*** *p298*
Stewart, Edward; St. John, N.B., 1850 ***5704.8*** *p67*
Stewart, Eleanor *SEE* Stewart, David
Stewart, Eleanor; Philadelphia, 1848 ***5704.8*** *p45*
Stewart, Eliz. 6 *SEE* Stewart, John
Stewart, Eliza *SEE* Stewart, David
Stewart, Eliza *SEE* Stewart, John
Stewart, Eliza; Philadelphia, 1848 ***5704.8*** *p45*
Stewart, Eliza; Philadelphia, 1850 ***5704.8*** *p60*
Stewart, Eliza; Philadelphia, 1851 ***5704.8*** *p70*
Stewart, Eliza; Philadelphia, 1851 ***5704.8*** *p76*
Stewart, Eliza; Philadelphia, 1864 ***5704.8*** *p183*
Stewart, Eliza; Quebec, 1847 ***5704.8*** *p6*
Stewart, Eliza 4; Quebec, 1849 ***5704.8*** *p52*
Stewart, Eliza 11 *SEE* Stewart, Jane
Stewart, Eliza 20; Wilmington, DE, 1831 ***6508.3*** *p101*
Stewart, Eliza 30; Kansas, 1874 ***5240.1*** *p56*
Stewart, Eliza Jane; Philadelphia, 1852 ***5704.8*** *p87*
Stewart, Elizabeth 3 *SEE* Stewart, John
Stewart, Elizabeth 14 *SEE* Stewart, John
Stewart, Elizabeth 14; Philadelphia, 1850 ***5704.8*** *p60*
Stewart, Elizabeth 20; St. John, N.B., 1855 ***5704.8*** *p126*
Stewart, Elizabeth 40; Philadelphia, 1856 ***5704.8*** *p128*
Stewart, Elizabeth 46 *SEE* Stewart, John
Stewart, Ellen 2; Quebec, 1857 ***5704.8*** *p135*
Stewart, Ellen 6; Philadelphia, 1860 ***5704.8*** *p145*
Stewart, Ellen 40; Philadelphia, 1860 ***5704.8*** *p145*
Stewart, Ellen J.; America, 1865 ***5704.8*** *p202*
Stewart, Esther 18; Massachusetts, 1849 ***5881.1*** *p89*
Stewart, Fanny 6; Quebec, 1847 ***5704.8*** *p17*
Stewart, Flora 19; St. John, N.B., 1863 ***5704.8*** *p152*
Stewart, Frances Thomson *SEE* Stewart, Andrew
Stewart, Frank 20; St. John, N.B., 1864 ***5704.8*** *p159*
Stewart, George *SEE* Stewart, John
Stewart, George *SEE* Stewart, John
Stewart, George; America, 1737 ***4971*** *p77*
Stewart, George; Ohio, 1848 ***8365.27*** *p12*
Stewart, George; Philadelphia, 1848 ***5704.8*** *p40*
Stewart, George; Quebec, 1847 ***5704.8*** *p17*
Stewart, George; Quebec, 1855 ***4537.30*** *p44*
*Wife:*Margaret Martin
*Child:*Annabella
*Child:*Kirsty
*Child:*Alex
*Child:*Margaret
*Child:*Donald
*Child:*Ann
Stewart, George 3; Quebec, 1847 ***5704.8*** *p17*
Stewart, George 20; Quebec, 1855 ***5704.8*** *p125*
Stewart, Grace 30; St. John, N.B., 1862 ***5704.8*** *p150*
Stewart, H.; New York, NY, 1811 ***2859.11*** *p19*
Stewart, Hamilton 29; Philadelphia, 1853 ***5704.8*** *p109*
Stewart, Hannah; New York, NY, 1866 ***5704.8*** *p211*
Stewart, Harry 18; Philadelphia, 1854 ***5704.8*** *p116*
Stewart, Helene; Quebec, 1824 ***7603*** *p73*
Stewart, Henry; Colorado, 1886 ***9678.3*** *p14*
Stewart, Henry; Philadelphia, 1851 ***5704.8*** *p80*
Stewart, Henry 7; St. John, N.B., 1847 ***5704.8*** *p20*
Stewart, Hugh; South Carolina, 1716 ***1639.20*** *p298*
Stewart, Hugh 8 *SEE* Stewart, John
Stewart, Isabella *SEE* Stewart, Daniel
Stewart, Isabella; Philadelphia, 1848 ***5704.8*** *p40*
Stewart, Isabella; Quebec, 1843 ***4537.30*** *p99*
Stewart, Isabella; Quebec, 1853 ***4537.30*** *p87*
Stewart, Isabella 13; Philadelphia, 1854 ***5704.8*** *p120*
Stewart, Isac 38; Quebec, 1864 ***5704.8*** *p163*
Stewart, Isobel 30 *SEE* Stewart, Kenneth
Stewart, James; America, 1742 ***4971*** *p25*
Stewart, James; Charleston, SC, 1749 ***1639.20*** *p298*
Stewart, James; New York, NY, 1811 ***2859.11*** *p19*
Stewart, James; New York, NY, 1815 ***2859.11*** *p42*
Stewart, James; New York, NY, 1835 ***8208.4*** *p7*
Stewart, James; North Carolina, 1775-1821 ***1639.20*** *p298*
Stewart, James; Philadelphia, 1850 ***5704.8*** *p69*
Stewart, James; Philadelphia, 1853 ***5704.8*** *p100*
Stewart, James; Philadelphia, 1864 ***5704.8*** *p183*
Stewart, James; Philadelphia, 1864 ***5704.8*** *p186*
Stewart, James; Philadelphia, 1865 ***5704.8*** *p193*
Stewart, James; Philadelphia, 1866 ***5704.8*** *p209*
Stewart, James; Quebec, 1852 ***5704.8*** *p86*
Stewart, James; St. John, N.B., 1847 ***5704.8*** *p18*
Stewart, James; St. John, N.B., 1847 ***5704.8*** *p21*
Stewart, James; St. John, N.B., 1852 ***5704.8*** *p95*
Stewart, James 9 mos; Quebec, 1847 ***5704.8*** *p17*
Stewart, James 6; Quebec, 1849 ***5704.8*** *p52*
Stewart, James 10 *SEE* Stewart, Dougald
Stewart, James 10; Philadelphia, 1848 ***53.26*** *p85*
Stewart, James 10; Philadelphia, 1848 ***5704.8*** *p45*
Stewart, James 12; America, 1699 ***2212*** *p28*
Stewart, James 17; Philadelphia, 1854 ***5704.8*** *p117*
Stewart, James 17; Philadelphia, 1864 ***5704.8*** *p157*
Stewart, James 19; Philadelphia, 1833-1834 ***53.26*** *p85*
Stewart, James 19; Quebec, 1856 ***5704.8*** *p130*
Stewart, James 22; Philadelphia, 1774 ***1219.7*** *p234*
Stewart, James 24; Maryland, 1733 ***3690.1*** *p217*
Stewart, James 25; Philadelphia, 1803 ***53.26*** *p85*
Stewart, James 25; St. John, N.B., 1854 ***5704.8*** *p122*
Stewart, James 29; Maryland, 1774 ***1219.7*** *p220*
Stewart, James J.; Ohio, 1874-1879 ***9892.11*** *p43*
Stewart, James William; New York, NY, 1836 ***8208.4*** *p9*
Stewart, Jane *SEE* Stewart, John
Stewart, Jane; New York, NY, 1816 ***2859.11*** *p42*
Stewart, Jane; New York, NY, 1866 ***5704.8*** *p212*
Stewart, Jane; Philadelphia, 1816 ***2859.11*** *p42*
Stewart, Jane; Philadelphia, 1848 ***5704.8*** *p40*
Stewart, Jane; Philadelphia, 1866 ***5704.8*** *p206*
Stewart, Jane; St. John, N.B., 1852 ***5704.8*** *p95*
Stewart, Jane 11; St. John, N.B., 1847 ***5704.8*** *p20*
Stewart, Jane 12; Quebec, 1864 ***5704.8*** *p163*
Stewart, Jane 13; Quebec, 1858 ***5704.8*** *p138*
Stewart, Jane 14; America, 1705 ***2212*** *p42*
Stewart, Jane 35; Maryland, 1775 ***1219.7*** *p249*
*Child:*Eliza 11
Stewart, Jane 36; Quebec, 1864 ***5704.8*** *p163*
Stewart, Jane 40 *SEE* Stewart, John
Stewart, Jane, Jr.; New York, NY, 1811 ***2859.11*** *p19*
Stewart, Jane, Sr.; New York, NY, 1811 ***2859.11*** *p20*
Stewart, Janet 12 *SEE* Stewart, John
Stewart, Jennet *SEE* Stewart, John
Stewart, John; Carolina, 1712 ***1639.20*** *p298*
Stewart, John; Illinois, 1870 ***5240.1*** *p43*
Stewart, John; New York, NY, 1815 ***2859.11*** *p42*
Stewart, John; New York, NY, 1816 ***2859.11*** *p42*
Stewart, John; New York, NY, 1816 ***2859.11*** *p42*
With wife
Stewart, John; North Carolina, 1758 ***1639.20*** *p298*
Stewart, John; Nova Scotia, 1830 ***7085.4*** *p44*
*Wife:*Christy
*Child:*Ket
*Child:*Jennet
Stewart, John; Ohio, 1812-1840 ***9892.11*** *p44*
Stewart, John; Ohio, 1874-1881 ***9892.11*** *p44*
Stewart, John; Ohio, 1884 ***9892.11*** *p44*
Stewart, John; Philadelphia, 1848 ***53.26*** *p85*
*Relative:*Robert
*Relative:*Jane
*Relative:*Mary Anne
*Relative:*George
Stewart, John; Philadelphia, 1848 ***5704.8*** *p40*
Stewart, John; Philadelphia, 1850 ***53.26*** *p85*
*Relative:*Eliza
*Relative:*Martha Jane
*Relative:*Robert
*Relative:*Elizabeth 14
*Relative:*Margaret 12
*Relative:*John 9
Stewart, John; Philadelphia, 1850 ***5704.8*** *p60*
Stewart, John; Philadelphia, 1851 ***5704.8*** *p70*
Stewart, John; Philadelphia, 1851 ***5704.8*** *p71*
Stewart, John; Philadelphia, 1851 ***5704.8*** *p79*
Stewart, John; Philadelphia, 1853 ***5704.8*** *p100*
Stewart, John; Philadelphia, 1866 ***5704.8*** *p207*
Stewart, John; Quebec, 1798 ***7603*** *p27*
Stewart, John; Quebec, 1852 ***5704.8*** *p90*
Stewart, John; Quebec, 1854 ***4537.30*** *p44*
*Wife:*Mary Beaton
*Child:*Duncan
*Child:*Norman
*Child:*George
Stewart, John; South Carolina, 1716 ***1639.20*** *p298*
Stewart, John 3 mos; St. John, N.B., 1850 ***5704.8*** *p67*
Stewart, John 5 *SEE* Stewart, Kenneth
Stewart, John 5; Philadelphia, 1853 ***5704.8*** *p113*
Stewart, John 5; Philadelphia, 1854 ***5704.8*** *p117*
Stewart, John 5; St. John, N.B., 1847 ***5704.8*** *p20*
Stewart, John 9 *SEE* Stewart, John
Stewart, John 9; Philadelphia, 1850 ***5704.8*** *p60*
Stewart, John 12 *SEE* Stewart, David
Stewart, John 12; Philadelphia, 1848 ***5704.8*** *p45*
Stewart, John 14 *SEE* Stewart, John
Stewart, John 15 *SEE* Stewart, John
Stewart, John 16 *SEE* Stewart, Dougald
Stewart, John 18; Pennsylvania, 1723 ***3690.1*** *p217*
Stewart, John 18; Philadelphia, 1833-1834 ***53.26*** *p85*
Stewart, John 19; St. John, N.B., 1865 ***5704.8*** *p165*
Stewart, John 20; Quebec, 1857 ***5704.8*** *p135*
Stewart, John 22; Quebec, 1864 ***5704.8*** *p162*
Stewart, John 25; Massachusetts, 1847 ***5881.1*** *p90*
Stewart, John 25; Philadelphia, 1859 ***5704.8*** *p143*
Stewart, John 34; Philadelphia, 1851 ***5704.8*** *p71*
Stewart, John 40; Philadelphia, 1833-1834 ***53.26*** *p85*
*Relative:*Jane 40
*Relative:*Wiliam 16
*Relative:*John 14
*Relative:*Robert 12
*Relative:*Hugh 8
*Relative:*Eliz. 6
*Relative:*Mary Ann
Stewart, John 48; Wilmington, NC, 1775 ***1639.20*** *p299*
*Wife:*Elizabeth 46
*Child:*John 15
*Child:*Margaret 13
*Child:*Janet 12
*Child:*Patrick 6
*Child:*Elizabeth 3
Stewart, John 50; Philadelphia, 1861 ***5704.8*** *p149*
Stewart, John H.; Philadelphia, 1864 ***5704.8*** *p180*
Stewart, Johnston 23; Quebec, 1864 ***5704.8*** *p162*
Stewart, Kenneth 40; Wilmington, NC, 1775 ***1639.20*** *p299*
*Wife:*Isobel 30
*Child:*Alexander 14
*Child:*John 5
*Child:*Banco 3
*Child:*Christian 3
*Child:*William
Stewart, Ket *SEE* Stewart, John
Stewart, Kirsty *SEE* Stewart, George
Stewart, Letitia; New York, NY, 1815 ***2859.11*** *p42*
Stewart, Mahlon; Ohio, 1817 ***8582.1*** *p48*
Stewart, Malcolm; America, 1791 ***1639.20*** *p299*
Stewart, Manes; Philadelphia, 1850 ***53.26*** *p85*
Stewart, Margaret *SEE* Stewart, George
Stewart, Margaret *SEE* Stewart, Peter
Stewart, Margaret; New York, NY, 1870 ***5704.8*** *p237*
Stewart, Margaret; Philadelphia, 1847 ***53.26*** *p85*
Stewart, Margaret; Philadelphia, 1847 ***5704.8*** *p14*
Stewart, Margaret; Philadelphia, 1851 ***5704.8*** *p78*
Stewart, Margaret; Philadelphia, 1852 ***5704.8*** *p87*
Stewart, Margaret; Quebec, 1851 ***4537.30*** *p32*
Stewart, Margaret 12 *SEE* Stewart, John
Stewart, Margaret 12; Philadelphia, 1850 ***5704.8*** *p60*
Stewart, Margaret 13 *SEE* Stewart, John
Stewart, Margaret 13; Philadelphia, 1853 ***5704.8*** *p112*
Stewart, Margaret 18; Philadelphia, 1860 ***5704.8*** *p146*
Stewart, Margaret 20; Philadelphia, 1860 ***5704.8*** *p145*
Stewart, Margaret 26; Massachusetts, 1847 ***5881.1*** *p91*
Stewart, Margaret 30; Philadelphia, 1833-1834 ***53.26*** *p85*
Stewart, Margaret 38 *SEE* Stewart, William
Stewart, Margaret Martin *SEE* Stewart, George
Stewart, Martha; Philadelphia, 1816 ***2859.11*** *p42*
Stewart, Martha; Quebec, 1856 ***5704.8*** *p129*
Stewart, Martha 14; St. John, N.B., 1861 ***5704.8*** *p146*
Stewart, Martha Ann 19; Philadelphia, 1857 ***5704.8*** *p133*
Stewart, Martha Jane *SEE* Stewart, John
Stewart, Martha Jane; Philadelphia, 1850 ***5704.8*** *p60*
Stewart, Martha Jane; Philadelphia, 1852 ***5704.8*** *p97*
Stewart, Martha Jane; Quebec, 1851 ***5704.8*** *p75*
Stewart, Mary; Philadelphia, 1850 ***53.26*** *p85*
Stewart, Mary; Philadelphia, 1850 ***5704.8*** *p69*
Stewart, Mary; Philadelphia, 1851 ***5704.8*** *p81*
Stewart, Mary; Philadelphia, 1852 ***5704.8*** *p87*
Stewart, Mary; Philadelphia, 1865 ***5704.8*** *p190*
Stewart, Mary; Philadelphia, 1865 ***5704.8*** *p196*
Stewart, Mary; Philadelphia, 1869 ***5704.8*** *p236*
Stewart, Mary; Quebec, 1852 ***5704.8*** *p86*
Stewart, Mary; Quebec, 1852 ***5704.8*** *p90*
Stewart, Mary; St. John, N.B., 1850 ***5704.8*** *p61*
Stewart, Mary 9 mos; St. John, N.B., 1847 ***5704.8*** *p10*
Stewart, Mary 3; St. John, N.B., 1847 ***5704.8*** *p20*
Stewart, Mary 6; Quebec, 1847 ***5704.8*** *p17*
Stewart, Mary 6; Quebec, 1864 ***5704.8*** *p163*
Stewart, Mary 8; Quebec, 1863 ***5704.8*** *p154*
Stewart, Mary 15; Philadelphia, 1858 ***5704.8*** *p139*
Stewart, Mary 20; Philadelphia, 1864 ***5704.8*** *p160*
Stewart, Mary 22; Quebec, 1857 ***5704.8*** *p135*
Stewart, Mary 25; America, 1703 ***2212*** *p40*
Stewart, Mary 45; North Carolina, 1850 ***1639.20*** *p254*
Stewart, Mary 48; Quebec, 1858 ***5704.8*** *p138*
Stewart, Mary 52; St. John, N.B., 1863 ***5704.8*** *p152*
Stewart, Mary 61; North Carolina, 1850 ***1639.20*** *p299*
Stewart, Mary 62; Philadelphia, 1856 ***5704.8*** *p129*
Stewart, Mary A.; Philadelphia, 1869 ***5704.8*** *p235*
Stewart, Mary Ann *SEE* Stewart, John
Stewart, Mary Ann 11; Philadelphia, 1853 ***5704.8*** *p112*
Stewart, Mary Anne *SEE* Stewart, John
Stewart, Mary Anne; Philadelphia, 1848 ***5704.8*** *p40*
Stewart, Mary Beaton *SEE* Stewart, John

Stewart, Mary J.; Philadelphia, 1864 *5704.8 p183*
Stewart, Mary Jane 2; Quebec, 1849 *5704.8 p52*
Stewart, Nancy SEE Stewart, David
Stewart, Nancy; America, 1865 *5704.8 p202*
Stewart, Nancy; Philadelphia, 1848 *5704.8 p45*
Stewart, Nancy; Quebec, 1849 *5704.8 p52*
Stewart, Nancy; Quebec, 1851 *5704.8 p75*
Stewart, Nancy 8; Quebec, 1849 *5704.8 p52*
Stewart, Neil; South Carolina, 1716 *1639.20 p299*
Stewart, Norman SEE Stewart, John
Stewart, Patrick; Cape Fear, NC, 1739 *1639.20 p300*
Stewart, Patrick; North Carolina, 1739 *1639.20 p300*
Stewart, Patrick; South Carolina, 1716 *1639.20 p299*
Stewart, Patrick 6 SEE Stewart, John
Stewart, Patrick 31; St. John, N.B., 1862 *5704.8 p150*
Stewart, Peggy 21; St. John, N.B., 1863 *5704.8 p152*
Stewart, Peter; America, 1811 *1639.20 p300*
Stewart, Peter; Nova Scotia, 1830 *7085.4 p44*
  *Wife:*Margaret
  *Child:*Allan
Stewart, Peter; Philadelphia, 1848 *5704.8 p46*
Stewart, Peter 30; Massachusetts, 1849 *5881.1 p93*
Stewart, Peter D. 48; North Carolina, 1850 *1639.20 p300*
Stewart, Rachael; Quebec, 1851 *5704.8 p75*
Stewart, Rebecca; America, 1863-1871 *5704.8 p199*
Stewart, Rebecca; New York, NY, 1815 *2859.11 p42*
Stewart, Rebecca; Philadelphia, 1848 *53.26 p85*
Stewart, Rebecca; Philadelphia, 1848 *5704.8 p41*
Stewart, Rebecca; Quebec, 1847 *5704.8 p17*
Stewart, Rebecca 2; Philadelphia, 1851 *5704.8 p81*
Stewart, Rebecca 13; Quebec, 1847 *5704.8 p17*
Stewart, Rebecca 15; Philadelphia, 1854 *5704.8 p120*
Stewart, Rebecca Ann; St. John, N.B., 1847 *5704.8 p10*
Stewart, Richard; St. John, N.B., 1847 *5704.8 p18*
Stewart, Richard; St. John, N.B., 1849 *5704.8 p49*
Stewart, Richard 20; Maryland, 1774 *1219.7 p214*
Stewart, Robert SEE Stewart, John
Stewart, Robert SEE Stewart, John
Stewart, Robert; New York, NY, 1864 *5704.8 p169*
Stewart, Robert; Philadelphia, 1816 *2859.11 p42*
Stewart, Robert; Philadelphia, 1848 *5704.8 p40*
Stewart, Robert; Philadelphia, 1850 *5704.8 p60*
Stewart, Robert; Philadelphia, 1851 *5704.8 p79*
Stewart, Robert; Philadelphia, 1858 *5704.8 p87*
Stewart, Robert; St. John, N.B., 1847 *5704.8 p18*
Stewart, Robert; St. John, N.B., 1847 *5704.8 p20*
Stewart, Robert; St. John, N.B., 1852 *5704.8 p95*
Stewart, Robert 3; Philadelphia, 1853 *5704.8 p113*
Stewart, Robert 3; Philadelphia, 1854 *5704.8 p117*
Stewart, Robert 12 SEE Stewart, John
Stewart, Robert 18; Philadelphia, 1859 *5704.8 p141*
Stewart, Robert 75; Philadelphia, 1856 *5704.8 p129*
Stewart, Ronald 54; St. John, N.B., 1863 *5704.8 p152*
Stewart, Rose; New York, NY, 1815 *2859.11 p43*
Stewart, Rose 20; Quebec, 1857 *5704.8 p135*
Stewart, Rose Ann 16; St. John, N.B., 1864 *5704.8 p158*
Stewart, Sally; New York, NY, 1815 *2859.11 p43*
Stewart, Sally; St. John, N.B., 1847 *5704.8 p20*
Stewart, Sally 9; St. John, N.B., 1847 *5704.8 p20*
Stewart, Sally 83; North Carolina, 1850 *1639.20 p300*
Stewart, Samuel; Iowa, 1866-1943 *123.54 p47*
Stewart, Samuel; New York, NY, 1816 *2859.11 p43*
Stewart, Samuel; New York, NY, 1865 *5704.8 p190*
Stewart, Samuel 11; America, 1863-1871 *5704.8 p199*
Stewart, Samuel 31; Kansas, 1872 *5240.1 p53*
Stewart, Sarah; Philadelphia, 1864 *5704.8 p178*
Stewart, Sarah; St. John, N.B., 1852 *5704.8 p95*
Stewart, Sarah 10; Quebec, 1847 *5704.8 p17*
Stewart, Sarah Jane 9; Philadelphia, 1851 *5704.8 p81*
Stewart, Sarah Jane 18; Philadelphia, 1856 *5704.8 p128*
Stewart, Susan 66; Kansas, 1874 *5240.1 p56*
Stewart, Susan 74; Kansas, 1885 *5240.1 p68*
Stewart, Susan Dick SEE Stewart, Thomas
Stewart, Susanna; St. John, N.B., 1847 *5704.8 p26*
Stewart, Susanna; St. John, N.B., 1850 *5704.8 p67*
Stewart, Susannah 18 SEE Stewart, William
Stewart, Thomas; Detroit, 1790 *8894.1 p191*
  *Wife:*Susan Dick
Stewart, Thomas; New York, 1879 *1450.2 p38B*
Stewart, Thomas; New York, NY, 1815 *2859.11 p43*
Stewart, Thomas; New York, NY, 1839 *8208.4 p94*
Stewart, Thomas; Philadelphia, 1866 *5704.8 p208*
Stewart, Thomas; St. John, N.B., 1847 *5704.8 p10*
Stewart, Thomas 6 SEE Stewart, Dougald
Stewart, Thomas 9; St. John, N.B., 1850 *5704.8 p67*
Stewart, Thomas 18; Philadelphia, 1774 *1219.7 p183*
Stewart, Thomas 40; Kansas, 1871 *5240.1 p52*
Stewart, Wiliam 16 SEE Stewart, John
Stewart, William SEE Stewart, Daniel
Stewart, William SEE Stewart, Kenneth
Stewart, William; America, 1739 *4971 p33*
Stewart, William; America, 1830 *1450.2 p139A*
Stewart, William; America, 1863-1871 *5704.8 p199*

Stewart, William; Jamaica, 1775 *1219.7 p277*
Stewart, William; New York, NY, 1811 *2859.11 p20*
Stewart, William; New York, NY, 1816 *2859.11 p43*
Stewart, William; New York, NY, 1838 *8208.4 p72*
Stewart, William; Ontario, 1831 *9775.5 p214*
Stewart, William; Philadelphia, 1848 *5704.8 p40*
Stewart, William; Philadelphia, 1850 *5704.8 p64*
Stewart, William; Philadelphia, 1852 *5704.8 p88*
Stewart, William; Philadelphia, 1864 *5704.8 p182*
Stewart, William; Philadelphia, 1865 *5704.8 p185*
Stewart, William; Quebec, 1849 *5704.8 p52*
Stewart, William; Quebec, 1851 *5704.8 p75*
Stewart, William; Quebec, 1863 *5704.8 p154*
Stewart, William 2; Philadelphia, 1853 *5704.8 p108*
Stewart, William 7; Philadelphia, 1851 *5704.8 p81*
Stewart, William 18; Philadelphia, 1864 *5704.8 p157*
Stewart, William 18; Quebec, 1858 *5704.8 p138*
Stewart, William 24; Georgia, 1775 *1219.7 p276*
Stewart, William 25; Philadelphia, 1803 *53.26 p85*
Stewart, William 25; Philadelphia, 1860 *5704.8 p145*
Stewart, William 35; Kansas, 1870 *5240.1 p51*
Stewart, William 50; Philadelphia, 1803 *53.26 p86*
  *Relative:*Margaret 38
  *Relative:*Ann 24
  *Relative:*Agnes 20
  *Relative:*Susannah 18
Stewart, William John 6 mos; Quebec, 1849 *5704.8 p52*
Stewart, Wm.; Philadelphia, 1816 *2859.11 p43*
Steyer, Tobias, Sr.; Pennsylvania, 1769 *9973.8 p32*
Sthieff, Jurg Fred'k; Pennsylvania, 1753 *2444 p222*
Stibbins, Ralph 40; Nova Scotia, 1774 *1219.7 p209*
  With 3 children
Stibbs, John; Virginia, 1646 *6219 p245*
Stiber, . . .; Canada, 1776-1783 *9786 p35*
Stibler, Ludwig; Wisconsin, n.d. *9675.8 p121*
Stich, Andrew; America, 1896 *7137 p170*
Stich, Anna; America, 1891 *7137 p170*
Stich, Floribert; America, 1854 *1450.2 p139A*
Stich, John; America, 1896 *7137 p170*
Stickdorn, Miss; America, 1853 *4610.10 p144*
Stickdorn, Christian Friedrich Wilhelm; America, 1855 *4610.10 p139*
Stickdorn, Philipp Carl Heinrich; America, 1854 *4610.10 p139*
Stickel, Bartholomeir; Georgia, 1738 *9332 p319*
Sticker, Adam; Philadelphia, 1760 *9973.7 p34*
Stiderick, Robert; Virginia, 1645 *6219 p232*
Stidwell, Tho.; Virginia, 1648 *6219 p245*
Stidwell, Thomas; Virginia, 1636 *6219 p76*
Stie, Ernest; Arkansas, 1918 *95.2 p118*
Stieber, John 40; Kansas, 1881 *5240.1 p63*
Stiechman, Simon; Iowa, 1866-1943 *123.54 p47*
Stief, Gerg Friedrich; Pennsylvania, 1753 *2444 p222*
Stiefel, Joh. Jacob; South Carolina, 1788 *7119 p203*
Stiefel, Johannes; Cincinnati, 1869-1887 *8582 p31*
Stieff, Anna Maria SEE Stieff, Georg Friedrich
Stieff, Catharina Haubensacker SEE Stieff, Georg
  Friedrich
Stieff, Georg Friedrich SEE Stieff, Georg Friedrich
Stieff, Georg Friedrich; Pennsylvania, 1753 *2444 p222*
  *Wife:*Catharina Haubensacker
  *Child:*Regina
  *Child:*Georg Friedrich
  *Child:*Anna Maria
  *Child:*Jacob Friedrich
  *Child:*Maria Catharina
Stieff, Jacob Friedrich SEE Stieff, Georg Friedrich
Stieff, Maria Catharina SEE Stieff, Georg Friedrich
Stieff, Regina SEE Stieff, Georg Friedrich
Stieg, William; Wisconsin, n.d. *9675.8 p121*
Stiegel, Henderick Willem; Pennsylvania, 1750 *2444 p218*
Stiegel, Henderick Willem; Pennsylvania, 1750 *2444 p228*
Stiegemeier, Rudolph H.; New York, 1883 *1450.2 p38B*
Stieger, Stefan; Washington, 1859-1920 *2872.1 p39*
Stiegler, Jane Sophia 37 SEE Stiegler, John George
Stiegler, John Fraugott 12 SEE Stiegler, John George
Stiegler, John George 30; New Orleans, 1839 *9420.2 p486*
  *Wife:*Jane Sophia 37
  *Son:*John Fraugott 12
  *Son:*John Lovegod 4
Stiegler, John Lovegod 4 SEE Stiegler, John George
Stiegmann, Anne Marie Louise; America, 1857 *4610.10 p136*
Stiehle, George; Wisconsin, n.d. *9675.8 p121*
Stiemberger, Frank; Kansas, 1909 *6013.40 p17*
Stiemer, Anton; New York, 1754 *3652 p80*
Stiemer, Christian; New York, 1754 *3652 p80*
Stienkemeyer, Anna M. Caroline Luise; America, 1884 *4610.10 p102*

Stienkemeyer, Anne Marie C. Abke SEE Stienkemeyer, Caspar Heinrich
Stienkemeyer, Carl Friedrich; America, 1884 *4610.10 p102*
Stienkemeyer, Carl Heinrich; America, 1884 *4610.10 p102*
Stienkemeyer, Carl Heinrich Wilhelm SEE Stienkemeyer, Caspar Heinrich
Stienkemeyer, Caspar Heinrich SEE Stienkemeyer, Caspar Heinrich
Stienkemeyer, Caspar Heinrich; America, 1844 *4610.10 p138*
  *Wife:*Anne Marie C. Abke
  *Child:*Caspar Heinrich
  *Child:*Hermann H. Wilhelm
  *Child:*Carl Heinrich Wilhelm
  *Child:*Christiane L. Engel
Stienkemeyer, Christiane L. Engel SEE Stienkemeyer, Caspar Heinrich
Stienkemeyer, Hermann H. Wilhelm SEE Stienkemeyer, Caspar Heinrich
Stiens, Franz; Cincinnati, 1869-1887 *8582 p31*
Stierer, Johann; America, 1852 *8582.3 p63*
Stiern, . . .; Canada, 1776-1783 *9786 p35*
Stiernefelt, Fredrik August; Boston, 1856 *6410.32 p126*
Stiernfelt, Frederick S. 45; Massachusetts, 1860 *6410.32 p119*
Stiever, Andrew; Wisconsin, n.d. *9675.8 p121*
Stifel, Adam; Ohio, 1869-1887 *8582 p31*
Stiff, Dubartus 24; South Carolina, 1730 *3690.1 p217*
Stiger, Elias; Indiana, 1847 *9117 p18*
Stijanovich, Edward; Iowa, 1866-1943 *123.54 p47*
Stile, Hugh; Virginia, 1647 *6219 p243*
Stile, James 22; Baltimore, 1775 *1219.7 p269*
Stile, Joseph; Barbados, 1698 *2212 p4*
Stiles, Mike 25; Massachusetts, 1849 *5881.1 p92*
Stiles, Nathaniell; Virginia, 1639 *6219 p155*
Stiles, Robert; Virginia, 1643 *6219 p203*
Stilet, Thomas; Quebec, 1710 *7603 p22*
Still, James 21; Maryland, 1775 *1219.7 p248*
Stille, . . .; America, 1833-1871 *5704.8 p199*
Stille, Ernst 24; Cincinnati, 1846 *3702.7 p62*
Stille, Ernst 24; New Orleans, 1846 *3702.7 p83*
Stille, Rudolph; America, 1836 *3702.7 p62*
Stille, Wilhelm 32; Ohio, 1833 *3702.7 p9*
Stille, Wilhelmine; Ohio, 1837 *3702.7 p62*
Stiller, Torsten Fredrik; New York, NY, 1919 *3455.2 p78*
Stilling, . . .; Canada, 1776-1783 *9786 p35*
Stilt, John; New York, NY, 1816 *2859.11 p43*
Stiltz, Christian; America, 1852 *1450.2 p140A*
Stimac, Tito; Iowa, 1866-1943 *123.54 p47*
Stimm, John; Ohio, 1855 *9892.11 p44*
Simpson, M. C.; Washington, 1859-1920 *2872.1 p39*
Stindig, Thomas 20; Maryland, 1720 *3690.1 p214*
Stine, Adam; Illinois, 1859 *2896.5 p39*
Stine, Coonrod; Illinois, 1858 *2896.5 p39*
Stine, Fritz; Iowa, 1866-1943 *123.54 p47*
Stinemann, John; Illinois, 1860 *2896.5 p39*
Stinett, Richard; Virginia, 1641 *6219 p187*
Stingel, Johannes; South Carolina, 1788 *7119 p200*
Stinger, Peter; Virginia, 1642 *6219 p199*
Stingsby, Robert; Virginia, 1636 *6219 p11*
Stinness, Adam 53; South Carolina, 1850 *1639.20 p300*
  *Relative:*Elizabeth 55
  *Relative:*Isabella 25
Stinness, Elizabeth 55 SEE Stinness, Adam
Stinness, Isabella 25 SEE Stinness, Adam
Stinson, Ann 32; St. John, N.B., 1854 *5704.8 p122*
Stinson, George; America, 1737 *4971 p75*
Stinson, John 20; Philadelphia, 1833-1834 *53.26 p86*
Stinton, Daniel; New York, NY, 1815 *2859.11 p43*
Stinton, William 26; Jamaica, 1736 *3690.1 p217*
Stipsky, Vincent Michle; Arkansas, 1918 *95.2 p118*
Stipthorpe, Hen.; Virginia, 1648 *6219 p252*
Stirdel, George; New York, 1843 *1450.2 p140A*
Stirk, Johann; Georgia, 1775 *8582.2 p64*
Stirling, Eliza 9 SEE Stirling, Henry
Stirling, Eliza 9; Philadelphia, 1847 *5704.8 p13*
Stirling, Elizabeth SEE Stirling, Henry
Stirling, Elizabeth; Philadelphia, 1847 *5704.8 p13*
Stirling, Esther SEE Stirling, Henry
Stirling, Esther; Philadelphia, 1847 *5704.8 p13*
Stirling, Henry SEE Stirling, Henry
Stirling, Henry; Philadelphia, 1847 *53.26 p86*
  *Relative:*Elizabeth
  *Relative:*James
  *Relative:*Esther
  *Relative:*Henry
  *Relative:*Robert
  *Relative:*Wilson 11
  *Relative:*Eliza 9
Stirling, Henry; Philadelphia, 1847 *5704.8 p13*

Storck, Pauly 23; America, 1838 *778.5 p506*
Storck, Wilhelm; Illinois, 1880 *2896.5 p39*
Stordeur, H.; Cincinnati, 1869-1887 *8582 p32*
Storen, Leonora 32; Texas, 1839 *778.5 p506*
Storen, Lodea 15; Texas, 1839 *778.5 p506*
Storen, Lucy Ann 3 mos; Texas, 1839 *778.5 p506*
Storen, Manuel 3; Texas, 1839 *778.5 p506*
Storey, Ephraim 12; Philadelphia, 1848 *5704.8 p46*
Storey, Jane 11; Philadelphia, 1848 *5704.8 p46*
Storey, Martha; New York, NY, 1870 *5704.8 p238*
Storey, Thomas; Arkansas, 1918 *95.2 p118*
Storie, James; Carolina, 1684 *1639.20 p301*
Stories, John; New York, NY, 1866 *5704.8 p210*
Storl, Johann Gottfried 22; New Orleans, 1839 *9420.2 p68*
Storlin, Johanne 50; New Orleans, 1839 *9420.2 p68*
Storm, Ella; Washington, 1859-1920 *2872.1 p39*
Storm, Giesla; Washington, 1859-1920 *2872.1 p39*
Storm, Jacob; Wisconsin, n.d. *9675.8 p121*
Storm, John; Washington, 1859-1920 *2872.1 p39*
Storm, John George; Pennsylvania, 1771 *9973.8 p33*
Storm, Theodor Hugo; Washington, 1859-1920 *2872.1 p39*
Storni, Toni; Wisconsin, n.d. *9675.8 p121*
Storr, . . .; Canada, 1776-1783 *9786 p35*
Storr, W. M. 36; Kansas, 1893 *5240.1 p78*
Storr, William 36; Kansas, 1893 *5240.1 p43*
Stortz, Eva; Pennsylvania, 1751 *2444 p149*
Stortz, John; New York, 1853 *1450.2 p140A*
Stortz, Lorenz; Philadelphia, 1779 *8137 p15*
Story, Catharine; Philadelphia, 1866 *5704.8 p207*
Story, Eliza; Philadelphia, 1866 *5704.8 p206*
Story, Francis; Virginia, 1648 *6219 p250*
Story, Johann Jacob; Ohio, 1869-1887 *8582 p32*
Story, John 7; Quebec, 1847 *5704.8 p7*
Story, Margaret; Quebec, 1847 *5704.8 p7*
Story, Robert; New York, NY, 1816 *2859.11 p43*
Story, Robert 2; Quebec, 1847 *5704.8 p7*
Story, Samuel; Philadelphia, 1866 *5704.8 p207*
Story, Thomas 12; Quebec, 1847 *5704.8 p7*
Story, William; New York, NY, 1864 *5704.8 p170*
Story, William; Quebec, 1847 *5704.8 p7*
Story, William 6 mos; Quebec, 1847 *5704.8 p7*
Story, Wm.; Virginia, 1645 *6219 p235*
Storzel, Joh. Aug. 25; New Orleans, 1839 *9420.2 p166*
Stosy, Mrs. 53; New York, 1893 *9026.4 p42*
Stote, John Jacob; Ohio, 1840 *9892.11 p44*
Stotesbury, William; New York, NY, 1839 *8208.4 p98*
Stotling, Charlie; Washington, 1859-1920 *2872.1 p39*
Stott, Ann Eliza; Philadelphia, 1851 *5704.8 p71*
Stott, Catherine 6; Philadelphia, 1851 *5704.8 p71*
Stott, Eliza 39; Philadelphia, 1851 *5704.8 p71*
Stott, John 40; Philadelphia, 1851 *5704.8 p71*
Stott, Margaret Jane 8; Philadelphia, 1851 *5704.8 p71*
Stotten, Samuel 16; Maryland, 1737 *3690.1 p214*
Stotz, Anna *SEE* Stotz, Chr
Stotz, Anna Maria *SEE* Stotz, Hans Balthass
Stotz, Anna Maria *SEE* Stotz, Ludwig
Stotz, Catharina Wolfer *SEE* Stotz, Ludwig
Stotz, Chr; Pennsylvania, 1750 *2444 p224*
    *Wife:*Anna
    *Child:*Ludwig
    *Child:*Samuel
Stotz, Christoph *SEE* Stotz, Hans Balthass
Stotz, Hans Balthass; Pennsylvania, 1750 *2444 p224*
    *Wife:*Margaretha
    *Child:*Anna Maria
    *Child:*Lucia
    *Child:*Christoph
    *Child:*Johann Martin
Stotz, Hans Peter; Pennsylvania, 1750 *2444 p224*
Stotz, Johann Jacob *SEE* Stotz, Ludwig
Stotz, Johann Martin *SEE* Stotz, Hans Balthass
Stotz, Lucia *SEE* Stotz, Hans Balthass
Stotz, Ludwig *SEE* Stotz, Chr
Stotz, Ludwig; America, 1750 *2444 p224*
    *Wife:*Catharina Wolfer
    *Child:*Anna Maria
    *Child:*Magdalena
    *Child:*Johann Jacob
Stotz, Magdalena *SEE* Stotz, Ludwig
Stotz, Margaretha *SEE* Stotz, Hans Balthass
Stotz, Samuel *SEE* Stotz, Chr
Stouch, . . .; Pennsylvania, n.d. *2444 p220*
Stouch, Hans Jerg 37; Pennsylvania, 1754 *2444 p221*
Stouck, George 37; Pennsylvania, 1754 *2444 p221*
Stoude, F. 22; Port uncertain, 1839 *778.5 p506*
Stoudemeyer, Stephan; South Carolina, 1788 *7119 p198*
Stoufel, George; Iowa, 1866-1943 *123.54 p47*
Stough, Frederick; Pennsylvania, 1764 *9973.7 p39*
Stough, George; Philadelphia, 1764 *9973.7 p39*
Stough, Godfried; Pennsylvania, 1752 *2444 p220*
Stout, John; New York, NY, 1811 *2859.11 p20*

Stout, John; Newfoundland, 1824 *8893 p263*
Stout, Tho.; Virginia, 1638 *6219 p116*
Stoute, John; Virginia, 1635 *6219 p70*
Stoutz, Phillipp Wilhelm; Illinois, 1873 *5012.39 p26*
Stove, Jacob; Philadelphia, 1760 *9973.7 p35*
Stover, Johann Kaspar; America, 1707-1779 *8125.8 p438*
    *Son:*Johann Kaspar, Jr.
Stover, Johann Kaspar, Jr. *SEE* Stover, Johann Kaspar
Stow, Alexander 26; Maryland, 1733 *3690.1 p218*
Stow, Andreas 30; Pennsylvania, 1754 *2444 p220*
Stow, John Jacob 18; Pennsylvania, 1754 *2444 p221*
Stow, John Jacob 18; Pennsylvania, 1754 *2444 p221*
Stow, Mich'l 18; Pennsylvania, 1754 *2444 p221*
Stow, Nich'ls 18; Pennsylvania, 1754 *2444 p220*
Stowell, Ralph; Virginia, 1641 *6219 p187*
Stowicz, Anton; Wisconsin, n.d. *9675.8 p121*
Stowk, Hans Yerr'k; Pennsylvania, 1754 *2444 p220*
Stowk, Hans Yerr'k 37; Pennsylvania, 1754 *2444 p221*
Stozzel, Joh. Aug. 57; New Orleans, 1839 *9420.2 p166*
Straber, John; Indiana, 1844 *9117 p18*
Strach, Michal 33; New York, 1912 *9980.29 p70*
Strachan, Charles; South Carolina, 1716 *1639.20 p301*
Strachan, James 20; Philadelphia, 1803 *53.26 p86*
Strachan, John; Toronto, n.d. *9775.5 p216*
Strachan, Mary; Philadelphia, 1853 *5704.8 p100*
Strachan, Thomas; South Carolina, 1718-1744 *1639.20 p301*
Strachine, John; Virginia, 1698 *2212 p14*
Strack, George P.F.; America, 1890 *1450.2 p140A*
Strader, Johannes; Kentucky, 1771 *8582.3 p96*
Strader, Richard; Virginia, 1647 *6219 p245*
Straderick, . . .; Canada, 1776-1783 *9786 p35*
Straehle, Rudolph; New York, 1749 *3652 p72*
Straet, Jno; South Carolina, 1788 *7119 p198*
Straeter, Caspar Heinrich; Cincinnati, 1788-1848 *8582.3 p90*
Straeter, Johannes; Kentucky, 1771 *8582.3 p96*
Straf, David; America, 1854 *1450.2 p141A*
Strafford, John 30; Antigua (Antego), 1734 *3690.1 p218*
Strafford, William Henry 26; Arkansas, 1918 *95.2 p118*
Strafsman, . . .; Canada, 1776-1783 *9786 p35*
Straghan, Ann 30; Philadelphia, 1853 *5704.8 p111*
Strahan, William 59; Oregon, 1890 *2764.35 p64*
Strahle, George; Illinois, 1859 *5012.39 p89*
Strahle, Jacob; Illinois, 1859 *5012.39 p89*
Strahm, Martin; Pennsylvania, 1709-1710 *4480 p311*
Straide, Charles; California, 1867 *2769.8 p5*
Strain, Bridget 20; Philadelphia, 1860 *5704.8 p144*
Strain, Cornelius 21; Philadelphia, 1859 *5704.8 p142*
Strain, Grace 22; Philadelphia, 1854 *5704.8 p120*
Strain, Hugh 20; Quebec, 1864 *5704.8 p159*
Strain, John; Illinois, 1861 *7857 p7*
Strain, John; New York, NY, 1866 *5704.8 p210*
Strain, Margaret 16; Philadelphia, 1859 *5704.8 p142*
Strain, Mary; Philadelphia, 1865 *5704.8 p197*
Straing, Wm.; Virginia, 1638 *6219 p145*
Strainger, John 22; Jamaica, 1734 *3690.1 p219*
Strains, Waldemar; Shreveport, LA, 1879 *7129 p46*
Strait, John; Illinois, 1871 *5012.38 p99*
Strait, Richard; Washington, 1859-1920 *2872.1 p39*
Strait, William; Illinois, 1871 *5012.38 p99*
Strak, Vincent; New York, NY, 1863 *2896.5 p39*
Stram, John; New York, NY, 1816 *2859.11 p43*
Stranathan, Samuel; Ohio, 1840 *9892.11 p44*
Stranberg, Peter; Iowa, 1866-1943 *123.54 p47*
Strandberg, Alfred; Washington, 1859-1920 *2872.1 p39*
Strang, Anna Barbara 7 wks *SEE* Strang, John George
Strang, Caleb 30; Philadelphia, 1774 *1219.7 p219*
    *Wife:*Maria 28
Strang, John George; South Carolina, 1752-1753 *3689.17 p23*
    With wife
    *Relative:*Rosina 7
    *Relative:*John George 3
    *Relative:*Anna Barbara 7 wks
Strang, John George 3 *SEE* Strang, John George
Strang, Maria 28 *SEE* Strang, Caleb
Strang, Rosina 7 *SEE* Strang, John George
Strang, William F.; North Carolina, 1825 *1639.20 p301*
Strange, Elizabeth 30; Maryland, 1775 *1219.7 p249*
Strange, William; Virginia, 1641 *6219 p185*
Strange, William F. 45; North Carolina, 1850 *1639.20 p301*
Strange, Wm.; Virginia, 1635 *6219 p27*
Stranger, John 22; Jamaica, 1734 *3690.1 p219*
Stranger, Nicho.; Virginia, 1638 *6219 p147*
Strangmeier, William; New York, NY, 1893 *1450.2 p39B*
Strappazgon, Angelo; Iowa, 1866-1943 *123.54 p47*
Strappazzon, Bartelo; Iowa, 1866-1943 *123.54 p79*
Strappazzon, Bartolo; Iowa, 1866-1943 *123.54 p79*
Strappazzon, Ernesto; Iowa, 1866-1943 *123.54 p79*
Strasburger, Mathias; Colorado, 1893 *9678.3 p15*
Strashun, Louis; New York, 1901 *1450.2 p39B*

Strassburger, Ernst G.; Wisconsin, n.d. *9675.8 p121*
Strassburger, Sophia; Wisconsin, n.d. *9675.8 p121*
Strate, Ann Heriott; Philadelphia, 1694-1695 *4961 p164*
Stratemeyer, Friedrich; America, 1853 *4610.10 p151*
Strater, John; New York, NY, 1840 *8208.4 p106*
Strathmann, Anne M F L H Baumeyer *SEE* Strathmann, Johann Heinrich
Strathmann, Carl Heinrich Eduard; America, 1856 *4610.10 p157*
Strathmann, David Mathias; America, 1844 *4610.10 p97*
Strathmann, Ernst F. Wilhelm *SEE* Strathmann, Johann Heinrich
Strathmann, Ernst Heinrich Wilhelm; America, 1844 *4610.10 p95*
Strathmann, Johann Heinrich; America, 1844 *4610.10 p111*
    *Wife:*Anne M F L H Baumeyer
    *Son:*Ernst F. Wilhelm
Strathmeier, Anne M. Louise Friederike; America, 1857 *4610.10 p136*
Strathmeyer, Heinrich 3 *SEE* Strathmeyer, Heinrich
Strathmeyer, Heinrich 31; America, 1881 *4610.10 p160*
    *Wife:*Wilhelmine 28
    *Child:*Wilhelmine 4
    *Child:*Heinrich 3
    *Child:*Louise 9 mos
Strathmeyer, Louise 9 mos *SEE* Strathmeyer, Heinrich
Strathmeyer, Wilhelmine 4 *SEE* Strathmeyer, Heinrich
Strathmeyer, Wilhelmine 28 *SEE* Strathmeyer, Heinrich
Stratis, Nick Harry; Arkansas, 1918 *95.2 p118*
Stratman, Johann Bernhard; Ohio, 1869-1887 *8582 p32*
Stratmeier, Anne Marie Charlotte; America, 1857 *4610.10 p152*
Strattard, John 27; Maryland, 1775 *1219.7 p262*
Stratton, Andrew; Illinois, 1888 *5012.39 p52*
Stratton, Andrew; Illinois, 1892 *5012.40 p26*
Stratton, Henry; Virginia, 1641 *6219 p184*
Stratton, John; New York, NY, 1836 *8208.4 p13*
Stratton, John 16; Jamaica, 1730 *3690.1 p219*
Stratton, Sisley; Virginia, 1646 *6219 p244*
Stratton, William; Arkansas, 1918 *95.2 p118*
Stratton, Wm P.; Cincinnati, 1807 *8582.3 p81*
Straub, . . .; Canada, 1776-1783 *9786 p35*
Straub, Albert; America, 1847 *1450.2 p141A*
Straub, Anna Catharina *SEE* Straub, Johann Georg
Straub, Cath. 79; Illinois, 1897 *1763 p40D*
Straub, Franz; America, 1847 *8582.1 p33*
Straub, Georg; Ohio, 1799 *8582.2 p54*
Straub, Jakob; Ohio, 1846 *8582.1 p48*
Straub, Johann Georg *SEE* Straub, Johann Georg
Straub, Johann Georg; Pennsylvania, 1751 *2444 p224*
    *Wife:*Anna Catharina
    *Child:*Johann Georg
Straub, Thaddaeus 76; Ohio, 1871 *8582 p32*
Straubert, Andreas; Wisconsin, n.d. *9675.8 p121*
Strauch, Adolph; America, 1851 *8582.3 p64*
Strauss, Moses; America, 1840 *8582.3 p64*
Strauss, Abraham; Cincinnati, 1869-1887 *8582 p32*
Strauss, Abraham; New York, 1750 *3652 p74*
Strauss, Anna Eva; New England, 1753 *4525 p250*
Strauss, Anna Eva; Pennsylvania, 1753 *4525 p250*
Strauss, Carl Albert; Kansas, 1892 *5240.1 p43*
Strauss, Eva *SEE* Strauss, Nicolaus
Strauss, Eva Catharina; New England, 1753 *4525 p252*
Strauss, Mrs. Hans Michel; New England, 1753 *4525 p251*
    With 2 grandchildren
Strauss, Mrs. Hans Michel; Pennsylvania, 1753 *4525 p251*
    With 2 grandchildren
Strauss, Henry; Ohio, 1851 *9892.11 p44*
Strauss, Jacob; Ohio, 1800-1885 *8582.2 p58*
Strauss, Leopold; America, 1865 *1450.2 p141A*
Strauss, Meyer; Pennsylvania, 1856-1878 *8582.3 p64*
Strauss, Mrs. Michel; New England, 1773 *4525 p251*
    With 3 children
Strauss, Mrs. Michel; Pennsylvania, 1773 *4525 p251*
    With 3 children
Strauss, Nicholas; Pennsylvania, 1753 *4525 p251*
Strauss, Nicholas, Jr.; Wisconsin, n.d. *9675.8 p121*
Strauss, Nicolaus; New England, 1752 *4525 p251*
    With wife & child
Strauss, Nicolaus; New England, 1753 *4525 p250*
    *Sister:*Eva
    With wife
Strauss, Nicolaus; Pennsylvania, 1752 *4525 p251*
    With wife
    With child 1
Strauss, Zadok 21; America, 1854-1855 *9162.6 p105*
Strausser, Heinrich; Ohio, 1798-1818 *8582.2 p53*
Strausser, Peter; Ohio, 1798-1818 *8582.2 p53*
Strautman, Henry; Arkansas, 1918 *95.2 p118*
Straw, Nancy; New York, NY, 1865 *5704.8 p193*

Strawbridge, Ellen 40; Philadelphia, 1853 ***5704.8*** *p113*
Strawbridge, James; St. John, N.B., 1848 ***5704.8*** *p39*
Strawbridge, James 14; Philadelphia, 1853 ***5704.8*** *p113*
Strawbridge, John; New York, NY, 1816 ***2859.11*** *p43*
Strawbridge, William; St. John, N.B., 1850 ***5704.8*** *p65*
Stream, Albert T.; Washington, 1859-1920 ***2872.1*** *p39*
Strean, John; New York, NY, 1811 ***2859.11*** *p20*
Strean, John; New York, NY, 1816 ***2859.11*** *p43*
Streat, John 23; Maryland, 1774 ***1219.7*** *p179*
Streate, Antho.; Virginia, 1635 ***6219*** *p70*
Streate, Antho.; Virginia, 1637 ***6219*** *p180*
Strecher, Andr.; Virginia, 1636 ***6219*** *p1*
Strechey, Edmond; Virginia, 1646 ***6219*** *p242*
Strecker, Eneck 33; Kansas, 1874 ***5240.1*** *p56*
Strecker, Otto A.; Virginia, 1844 ***4626.16*** *p12*
Streeper, Jan; Pennsylvania, 1706 ***2155*** *p2*
Streeper, William; Pennsylvania, 1683 ***2155*** *p2*
Street, Frances 23; Canada, 1838 ***4535.12*** *p113*
Street, Garrett; California, 1856 ***2769.8*** *p5*
Street, John; America, 1736 ***4971*** *p39*
Street, Wm. 23; Canada, 1838 ***4535.12*** *p113*
Streete, Ann; Virginia, 1638 ***6219*** *p119*
Streete, James; Virginia, 1698 ***2212*** *p11*
Streete, Tho.; Virginia, 1638 ***6219*** *p181*
Streets, Edward 14; Maryland, 1719 ***3690.1*** *p219*
Stref, Mathias; Wisconsin, n.d. ***9675.8*** *p121*
Streff, J.B.; Wisconsin, n.d. ***9675.8*** *p121*
Streff, Jacob; Wisconsin, n.d. ***9675.8*** *p121*
Streh, . . .; America, 1836 ***778.5*** *p506*
Streh, Mme.; America, 1836 ***778.5*** *p507*
Streh, Jacob 38; America, 1836 ***778.5*** *p507*
Streher, Peter; Philadelphia, 1761 ***9973.7*** *p35*
Strehle, Valentine 30; America, 1838 ***778.5*** *p507*
Streiber, Charles J.; Wisconsin, n.d. ***9675.8*** *p121*
Streiber, Conrad; Philadelphia, 1760 ***9973.7*** *p35*
Streit, A.G.F.; Illinois, 1869-1885 ***8582.2*** *p52*
Streit, John; New York, NY, 1825 ***8208.4*** *p49*
Stremming, Friedrich Heinrich August; America, 1863 ***4610.10*** *p105*
Stremming, Karl Heinrich Wilhelm; America, 1846 ***4610.10*** *p95*
Stremming, Wilhelmine 17; America, 1871 ***4610.10*** *p106*
Strening, Colonel; Illinois, 1838 ***8582.2*** *p50*
Stress, Joseph 17; America, 1835 ***778.5*** *p507*
Stretch, Catherine 17; Philadelphia, 1857 ***5704.8*** *p133*
Stretch, Elizabeth 45; Philadelphia, 1857 ***5704.8*** *p133*
Stretch, George 19; Philadelphia, 1857 ***5704.8*** *p133*
Stretch, Mary Ann 15; Philadelphia, 1857 ***5704.8*** *p133*
Stretchey, Rose; Virginia, 1635 ***6219*** *p23*
Stretz, Bobist; Colorado, 1904 ***9678.3*** *p15*
Streun, Fred; Kansas, 1896 ***5240.1*** *p43*
Strey, Olive; Virginia, 1638 ***6219*** *p121*
Streyper, Agnes; Pennsylvania, 1683 ***2155*** *p1*
Streypers, Jan; Pennsylvania, 1706 ***2155*** *p2*
Streypers, Wilhelm; Pennsylvania, 1683 ***2155*** *p2*
Striber, Emil 34; Kansas, 1885 ***5240.1*** *p67*
Striber, John 40; Kansas, 1881 ***5240.1*** *p44*
Striche, Christian 29; America, 1838 ***778.5*** *p507*
Stricher, Lorenz 30; America, 1835 ***778.5*** *p507*
Stricka, Lorenz 30; America, 1835 ***778.5*** *p507*
Stricker, . . .; Canada, 1776-1783 ***9786*** *p35*
Stricker, Anne Cath. Ilsabein *SEE* Stricker, Joh. Dietrich
Stricker, Anne M. Elisabeth *SEE* Stricker, Joh. Dietrich
Stricker, Anne M. L. Cath. Engel *SEE* Stricker, Joh. Dietrich
Stricker, Anne Marie F. Luise *SEE* Stricker, Joh. Dietrich
Stricker, Caspar Heinrich *SEE* Stricker, Joh. Dietrich
Stricker, Friedrich Wilhelm *SEE* Stricker, Joh. Dietrich
Stricker, Joh. Dietrich; America, 1844 ***4610.10*** *p134*
*Wife:*Anne M. Elisabeth
*Child:*Caspar Heinrich
*Child:*Anne Marie F. Luise
*Child:*Anne M. L. Cath. Engel
*Child:*Anne Cath. Ilsabein
*Child:*Friedrich Wilhelm
Stricker, John 48; Washington, 1918-1920 ***1728.5*** *p14*
Stricker, Peter Heinrich; America, 1865 ***4610.10*** *p136*
Stricklan, Benjamin 15; Virginia, 1775 ***1219.7*** *p261*
Strickland, Catharine Parr; Ontario, 1832 ***9775.5*** *p213*
*Sister:*Susanna
Strickland, Edward 14; Virginia, 1775 ***1219.7*** *p248*
Strickland, John 22; Maryland, 1775 ***1219.7*** *p251*
Strickland, Samuel; Ontario, 1800-1832 ***9775.5*** *p213*
Strickland, Susanna *SEE* Strickland, Catharine Parr
Strickland, William 14; America, 1704 ***2212*** *p40*
Stridla, Anton; Wisconsin, n.d. ***9675.8*** *p122*
Striedinger, Julius H.; New York, NY, 1873 ***2764.35*** *p60*
Striedl, John; Wisconsin, n.d. ***9675.8*** *p122*
Striehtmann, John Friedrich; America, 1848 ***8582.3*** *p64*
Strigel, John; Wisconsin, n.d. ***9675.8*** *p122*
Strimbu, George; Arkansas, 1918 ***95.2*** *p118*
Stringer, Henry 20; Jamaica, 1733 ***3690.1*** *p219*
Stringer, James; Virginia, 1647 ***6219*** *p247*
Stringer, James 21; Jamaica, 1733 ***3690.1*** *p219*
Stringer, Thomas 22; New England, 1699 ***2212*** *p19*
Stringfellow, John 28; Virginia, 1725 ***3690.1*** *p219*
Stripp, Gustav; Illinois, 1863 ***5012.39*** *p90*
Strobel, Adolph 45; Kansas, 1873 ***5240.1*** *p44*
Strobel, Adolph 45; Kansas, 1873 ***5240.1*** *p55*
Strobel, C.; Wheeling, WV, 1852 ***8582.3*** *p78*
Strobel, Daniel; Charleston, SC, 1766 ***8582.2*** *p65*
Strobel, Daniel; Charleston, SC, 1775-1781 ***8582.2*** *p52*
Strobel, Daniel; Savannah, GA, 1779 ***8582.2*** *p52*
Strobel, Johann Wilhelm; Philadelphia, 1753 ***4525*** *p251*
Strobel, John M.; America, 1843 ***8582.1*** *p33*
Strobel, Mathias; America, 1700-1877 ***8582.3*** *p80*
Strobel, Mathias; Wisconsin, n.d. ***9675.8*** *p122*
Strockmann, Frederick; Virginia, 1851 ***4626.16*** *p14*
Strode, Frank; Illinois, 1904 ***5012.37*** *p63*
Strode, George; Illinois, 1892 ***5012.40*** *p27*
Strode, T.W.; Illinois, 1888 ***5012.37*** *p61*
Strodtbeck, Jakob; Cincinnati, 1824 ***8582.1*** *p51*
Stroebel, John; Wisconsin, n.d. ***9675.8*** *p122*
Stroh, Dane; Arkansas, 1918 ***95.2*** *p118*
Stroh, Dave 28; Arkansas, 1918 ***95.2*** *p118*
Stroh, Heinr. 82; Ontario, 1901 ***1763*** *p48D*
Strohmier, John B.; Iowa, 1866-1943 ***123.54*** *p47*
Stroklin, George; Wisconsin, n.d. ***9675.8*** *p122*
Strolde, John 22; New Orleans, 1835 ***778.5*** *p507*
Strollo, Domine; Arkansas, 1918 ***95.2*** *p118*
Strom, Gustaf A.; Illinois, 1897 ***5012.39*** *p53*
Strom, John; Washington, 1859-1920 ***2872.1*** *p39*
Strom, Peter; California, 1849-1867 ***3840.3*** *p10*
Strom, Sten; Washington, 1859-1920 ***2872.1*** *p39*
Strom, Wiljan; Washington, 1859-1920 ***2872.1*** *p39*
Stromberg, Aaron; Colorado, 1906 ***9678.3*** *p15*
Stromberg, Frans Conrad; Boston, 1846 ***6410.32*** *p122*
Stromberg, John Wilhelm; Iowa, 1866-1943 ***123.54*** *p47*
Stromberg, Olof M.; Colorado, 1906 ***9678.3*** *p15*
Stromdal, G. F.; Iowa, 1866-1943 ***123.54*** *p47*
Stronach, William 46; Raleigh, NC, 1850 ***1639.20*** *p301*
Strondberg, Andrew B.; Iowa, 1866-1943 ***123.54*** *p47*
Strong, Alexander; America, 1827 ***9892.11*** *p44*
Strong, Alexander; Canada, 1825 ***9892.11*** *p44*
Strong, Alexander; Ohio, 1840 ***9892.11*** *p44*
Strong, Anna 50; Massachusetts, 1849 ***5881.1*** *p87*
Strong, Archibald 60; Massachusetts, 1849 ***5881.1*** *p87*
Strong, Chr.; New York, NY, 1811 ***2859.11*** *p20*
Strong, David; South Carolina, 1827 ***1639.20*** *p302*
Strong, Edw.; Virginia, 1637 ***6219*** *p113*
Strong, Edward; Virginia, 1635 ***6219*** *p73*
Strong, Hugh; New York, NY, 1811 ***2859.11*** *p20*
Strong, James; Ohio, 1823-1835 ***9892.11*** *p44*
Strong, James; Ohio, 1840 ***9892.11*** *p44*
Strong, James; Virginia, 1642 ***6219*** *p197*
Strong, James 16; Maryland, 1723 ***3690.1*** *p219*
Strong, James 27; Quebec, 1858 ***5704.8*** *p138*
Strong, Jane; Quebec, 1852 ***5704.8*** *p87*
Strong, Jane 2; Quebec, 1852 ***5704.8*** *p90*
Strong, John 14; Massachusetts, 1847 ***5881.1*** *p90*
Strong, John 25; Maryland, 1774 ***1219.7*** *p229*
Strong, Jos.; Canada, 1835 ***4535.10*** *p198*
With child
With wife
Strong, Jos.; New York, 1835 ***4535.10*** *p198*
With child
With wife
Strong, Lawrence; Charleston, SC, 1804 ***1639.20*** *p302*
Strong, Robert; America, 1853 ***2896.5*** *p39*
Strong, Sarah; St. John, N.B., 1848 ***5704.8*** *p39*
Strong, Valentine 39; Virginia, 1774 ***1219.7*** *p244*
Strong, William 20; Maryland, 1719 ***3690.1*** *p219*
Strong, William 20; Quebec, 1856 ***5704.8*** *p130*
Strong, William 36; Jamaica, 1739 ***3690.1*** *p219*
Strongburg, Alfred 14; Massachusetts, 1860 ***6410.32*** *p98*
Strongburg, Frank C. 40; Massachusetts, 1860 ***6410.32*** *p98*
Strongburg, Louisa 40; Massachusetts, 1860 ***6410.32*** *p98*
Strongburgh, F.C. 31; Massachusetts, 1860 ***6410.32*** *p108*
Strongburgh, Louisa 29; Massachusetts, 1860 ***6410.32*** *p108*
Stroot, B. H. 26; Kansas, 1898 ***5240.1*** *p44*
Stroot, B. H. 26; Kansas, 1898 ***5240.1*** *p81*
Stroot, J. B. 66; Kansas, 1898 ***5240.1*** *p44*
Stroot, J. B. 66; Kansas, 1898 ***5240.1*** *p81*
Stroot, J. B., Jr. 21; Kansas, 1898 ***5240.1*** *p81*
Stroska, Charles; Wisconsin, n.d. ***9675.8*** *p122*
Stroska, Heinerich; Wisconsin, n.d. ***9675.8*** *p122*
Strotbeck, Fredrick 21; Kansas, 1888 ***5240.1*** *p71*
Strothnert, Henry; Indiana, 1848 ***9117*** *p19*
Strotz, . . .; Canada, 1776-1783 ***9786*** *p35*
Stroud, William 21; Maryland, 1774 ***1219.7*** *p181*
Strouds, Gilles; Quebec, 1748 ***7603*** *p27*
Stroup, Adam 37; Georgia, 1738 ***9332*** *p329*
Stroup, John; South Carolina, 1788 ***7119*** *p201*
Strous, Nicholas; Pennsylvania, 1753 ***4525*** *p250*
Strouss, Nicholas; Pennsylvania, 1753 ***4525*** *p250*
Strouss, Nicholas; Pennsylvania, 1753 ***4525*** *p252*
Strowd, Thomas; Virginia, 1642 ***6219*** *p196*
Strubbe, Herman Henry; Pittsburgh, 1848 ***1450.2*** *p141A*
Strubinger, George; America, 1854 ***1450.2*** *p141A*
Struck, Herman; Illinois, 1876 ***5012.39*** *p91*
Struckmann, Wilhelm; New York, NY, 1838 ***8208.4*** *p83*
Struckmeier, Carl Friedrich; America, 1868 ***4610.10*** *p95*
Strudwick, Henry 33; Baltimore, 1775 ***1219.7*** *p270*
Struever, Justus; San Francisco, 1871 ***8582*** *p32*
Struewe, Michael; Ohio, 1798-1818 ***8582.2*** *p54*
Struewing, Gerhard; America, 1850 ***8582.2*** *p41*
Struk, Wm.; Illinois, 1866 ***5012.38*** *p98*
Strukton, Wm.; Virginia, 1637 ***6219*** *p11*
Strullmeier, William, Jr.; Illinois, 1888 ***2896.5*** *p39*
Strumberg, Nels O.; Maine, 1877-1882 ***6410.22*** *p116*
Struna, Frank; New York, NY, 1892 ***1450.2*** *p39B*
Strunck, Friedrich; Cincinnati, 1869-1887 ***8582*** *p32*
Strunck, Johann Peter; Philadelphia, 1744 ***8125.6*** *p22*
Strunh, John Joseph 32; Kansas, 1882 ***5240.1*** *p63*
Strunk, Carl Friedrich Ferdinand; America, 1857 ***4610.10*** *p158*
Strunk, Margaret 48; Kansas, 1888 ***5240.1*** *p71*
Strunk, Nick; America, 1888 ***5240.1*** *p44*
Strunk, Peter 35; Kansas, 1876 ***5240.1*** *p44*
Strunk, Peter 35; Kansas, 1876 ***5240.1*** *p57*
Strunk, Peter J.; America, 1888 ***5240.1*** *p44*
Strutton, Wm.; Virginia, 1637 ***6219*** *p114*
Strutz, Wenceslaus; America, 1896 ***7137*** *p170*
Struz, J. 30; America, 1835 ***778.5*** *p507*
Strzelecki, . . .; New York, 1831 ***4606*** *p177*
Stuard, Benjamin 18; Maryland, 1727 ***3690.1*** *p217*
Stuard, James 22; Maryland, 1773 ***1219.7*** *p173*
Stuart, Mr.; Quebec, 1815 ***9229.18*** *p74*
Stuart, Agnes *SEE* Stuart, Alexander
Stuart, Alexander; Nova Scotia, 1830 ***7085.4*** *p44*
*Wife:*Mary
*Child:*Donald
*Child:*Agnes
*Child:*Anne
*Child:*Jannet
*Child:*John
Stuart, Anne *SEE* Stuart, Alexander
Stuart, Antho 34; America, 1700 ***2212*** *p25*
Stuart, Charles; Boston, 1776 ***1219.7*** *p278*
Stuart, Donald *SEE* Stuart, Alexander
Stuart, Francis; South Carolina, 1752 ***1639.20*** *p302*
Stuart, Henry 18; Philadelphia, 1864 ***5704.8*** *p160*
Stuart, James; Philadelphia, 1816 ***2859.11*** *p43*
Stuart, James 51; Arizona, 1909 ***9228.40*** *p14*
Stuart, Jannet *SEE* Stuart, Alexander
Stuart, John *SEE* Stuart, Alexander
Stuart, John; Carolina, 1618-1718 ***1639.20*** *p302*
Stuart, John; Carolina, 1767 ***1639.20*** *p302*
Stuart, John 19; Jamaica, 1731 ***3690.1*** *p219*
Stuart, Mary *SEE* Stuart, Alexander
Stuart, Peter; Quebec, 1764 ***7603*** *p40*
Stuart, Thomas M.; New York, 1873 ***1450.2*** *p141A*
Stuart, William; New York, NY, 1816 ***2859.11*** *p43*
Stuart, William; St. John, N.B., 1847 ***5704.8*** *p25*
Stub, J. F. 60; New Orleans, 1830 ***778.5*** *p507*
Stubbs, Daniel; Virginia, 1637 ***6219*** *p110*
Stubbs, Danll.; Virginia, 1645 ***6219*** *p233*
Stubbs, Hontford; Virginia, 1634 ***6219*** *p84*
Stubbs, Izabell; Virginia, 1636 ***6219*** *p78*
Stube, . . .; Canada, 1776-1783 ***9786*** *p35*
Stubenhauer, . . .; Canada, 1776-1783 ***9786*** *p35*
Stubenitzky, . . .; Canada, 1776-1783 ***9786*** *p35*
Stuber, . . .; Canada, 1776-1783 ***9786*** *p35*
Stuber, Chr Friedrich *SEE* Stuber, Georg Friedrich
Stuber, Georg Friedrich; Philadelphia, 1754 ***2444*** *p224*
*Wife:*Regina Cath. Demmler
*Child:*Chr Friedrich
*Child:*Heinrich J. Friedrich
*Child:*Maria Jacobina
*Child:*Sigmund Friedrich
Stuber, Heinrich J. Friedrich *SEE* Stuber, Georg Friedrich
Stuber, Maria Jacobina *SEE* Stuber, Georg Friedrich
Stuber, Regina Cath. Demmler *SEE* Stuber, Georg Friedrich
Stuber, Sigmund Friedrich *SEE* Stuber, Georg Friedrich
Stubinger, . . .; Canada, 1776-1783 ***9786*** *p35*
Stuchlik, Rudolph; Arkansas, 1918 ***95.2*** *p119*
Stuck, Conrad; Pennsylvania, 1770 ***9973.8*** *p32*
Stuckbury, Edward 19; Jamaica, 1738 ***3690.1*** *p219*
Stucke, Anna M. Louise Engel *SEE* Stucke, Herm. Heinr.

Stucke, Anna Marie C. Kuhlmann SEE Stucke, Herm. Heinr.
Stucke, Anna Marie Louise 34; America, 1843 *4610.10 p133*
Stucke, Anne M. Louise Engel SEE Stucke, Daniel Heinrich
Stucke, Anne Marie Cath. Engel; America, 1860 *4610.10 p136*
Stucke, Anne Marie Ilsabein SEE Stucke, Daniel Heinrich
Stucke, Anne Marie Wilhelmine; America, 1854 *4610.10 p135*
Stucke, Carl Friedrich Wilhelm SEE Stucke, Herm. Heinr.
Stucke, Caroline J. Ellermann 39 SEE Stucke, Daniel Heinrich
Stucke, Catharine Marie Charlotte; America, 1844 *4610.10 p154*
Stucke, Daniel Heinrich; America, 1844 *4610.10 p141*
    Wife:Caroline J. Ellermann 39
    Child:Anne M. Louise Engel
    Child:Anne Marie Ilsabein
    Child:Justine Louise
    Child:Justine C. Ilsabein
    Child:Hermann Heinrich
Stucke, Friedrich Heinrich Wilhelm; America, 1851 *4610.10 p151*
Stucke, Herm. Heinr.; America, 1857 *4610.10 p136*
    Wife:Anna Marie C. Kuhlmann
    Child:Carl Friedrich Wilhelm
    Child:Anna M. Louise Engel
Stucke, Hermann Heinrich SEE Stucke, Daniel Heinrich
Stucke, Johann Christian Diederich; America, 1850 *4610.10 p143*
Stucke, Johann Hermann Heinrich; America, 1850 *4610.10 p142*
Stucke, Justine C. Ilsabein SEE Stucke, Daniel Heinrich
Stucke, Justine Louise SEE Stucke, Daniel Heinrich
Stucke, Marie Louise; America, 1857 *4610.10 p136*
Stuckenberg, August; Illinois, 1856 *7857 p7*
Stuckert, Robert; Arkansas, 1918 *95.2 p119*
Stucki, Johann Georg; Pennsylvania, 1743 *2444 p225*
Stuckinburger, Henry; Illinois, 1853 *7857 p7*
Studebaker, Clark; Washington, 1859-1920 *2872.1 p39*
Studer, Victor; New York, 1882 *1450.2 p39B*
Stuebuer, Otto William V.; Wisconsin, n.d. *9675.8 p122*
Stuecel, Frederick; Illinois, 1880 *2896.5 p39*
Stuetzmann, Conrad; Cincinnati, 1869-1887 *8582 p32*
Stueve, Clemens; Ohio, 1869-1887 *8582 p32*
Stuffira, N. 30; America, 1838 *778.5 p507*
Stuger, Geo. Fred'k; Philadelphia, 1754 *2444 p225*
Stuhde, William 33; Kansas, 1890 *5240.1 p75*
Stuhmeier, Wilhelmine C. Charlotte; America, 1883 *4610.10 p102*
Stuhmeyer, Anne Marie Christine; America, 1846 *4610.10 p111*
Stuhmeyer, Charlotte; America, 1892 *4610.10 p107*
Stuhmeyer, Heinrich Wilhelm August; America, 1882 *4610.10 p106*
Stuhmeyer, Louise; America, 1844 *4610.10 p95*
Stukely, James; Virginia, 1639 *6219 p155*
Stumbra, William; Wisconsin, n.d. *9675.8 p122*
Stumeier, A.M. Louise Justine; America, 1887 *4610.10 p110*
Stumm, C. Wilhelm; Ohio, 1869-1887 *8582 p32*
Stump, Adam; New York, NY, 1838 *8208.4 p66*
Stump, Godlieb; Pennsylvania, 1743-1779 *2444 p225*
Stump, Godlieb; Port uncertain, 1741-1800 *2444 p225*
Stump, Henry; Kansas, 1898 *5240.1 p44*
Stump, Jacob 56; Kansas, 1890 *5240.1 p44*
Stump, Jacob 56; Kansas, 1890 *5240.1 p75*
Stump, John 28; Kansas, 1893 *5240.1 p78*
Stump, Michael; Pennsylvania, 1743 *2444 p225*
Stump, Peter 23; Kansas, 1890 *5240.1 p75*
Stump, Peter 37; Kansas, 1906 *5240.1 p84*
Stumpf, Hs. Michael; Pennsylvania, 1743 *2444 p225*
Stumpf, Mattes; Philadelphia, 1756 *4525 p262*
Stumpf, Michel; Pennsylvania, 1773 *2444 p225*
Stumpf, Nicholas; Indiana, 1848 *9117 p19*
Stumpft, Fr. Traugott Earl 23; New Orleans, 1839 *9420.2 p170*
Stumph, Eva 19; America, 1838 *778.5 p507*
Stumph, George; America, 1839 *1450.2 p141A*
Stumph, John; America, 1850 *1450.2 p141A*
Stumph, John; Baltimore, 1838 *1450.2 p141A*
Stumph, Sibylle 50; America, 1838 *778.5 p507*
Stumph, The.dore 58; America, 1838 *778.5 p507*
Stumpp, Barbara SEE Stumpp, Gottlieb
Stumpp, Barbara SEE Stumpp, Gottlieb
Stumpp, Gottlieb; Pennsylvania, 1743-1779 *2444 p225*
    Wife:Barbara
    Child:Johann Georg

Stumpp, Gottlieb; Port uncertain, 1741-1800 *2444 p225*
    Wife:Barbara
    Child:Johann Georg
Stumpp, Hans Michael; Pennsylvania, 1743 *2444 p225*
    Wife:Maria Catharina
    Child:Maria Catharina
Stumpp, Johann Georg SEE Stumpp, Gottlieb
Stumpp, Johann Georg SEE Stumpp, Gottlieb
Stumpp, Maria Catharina SEE Stumpp, Hans Michael
Stumpp, Maria Catharina SEE Stumpp, Hans Michael
Stundon, Thomas; Baltimore, 1852 *1450.2 p142A*
Stunnerson, Sarah; Virginia, 1643 *6219 p204*
Stunz, Berhard; Halifax, N.S., 1778 *9786 p270*
Stunz, Berhard; New York, 1776 *9786 p270*
Stuokagh, William; America, 1736-1743 *4971 p58*
Stupar, Millie; Arkansas, 1918 *95.2 p119*
Sturchich, George; Iowa, 1866-1943 *123.54 p47*
Sturgeon, Samuel; Iowa, 1866-1943 *123.54 p47*
Sturges, Phillip 22; Jamaica, 1738 *3690.1 p220*
Sturgis, Phillip 22; Jamaica, 1738 *3690.1 p220*
Sturm, John; Wisconsin, n.d. *9675.8 p122*
Sturmfels, Captain; America, 1861-1865 *8582.3 p92*
Sturns, Wm.; Virginia, 1635 *6219 p69*
Sturrupp, Jno.; Virginia, 1646 *6219 p242*
Sturz, Marie 33; Port uncertain, 1839 *778.5 p507*
Stuteville, Charles 22; Maryland, 1774 *1219.7 p228*
Stutt, Ann 20; St. John, N.B., 1857 *5704.8 p135*
Stutz Family ; Port uncertain, 1738 *9898 p36*
    With 3 children
Stutz, John Jacob; Illinois, 1885 *2896.5 p39*
Stutz, Ludwig; America, 1750 *2444 p224*
Stutzback, William; Illinois, 1879 *2896.5 p39*
Stutzer, Johann Balthasar; Quebec, 1776 *9786 p253*
Stutzmann, G. Friedrich, Sr.; Cincinnati, 1869-1887 *8582 p32*
Stutzzer, . . .; Quebec, 1776 *9786 p104*
Stwert, Charles; Wisconsin, n.d. *9675.8 p122*
Styan, Robert; Illinois, 1888 *5012.39 p122*
Styan, William; Illinois, 1892 *5012.40 p27*
Style, Richard 19; Virginia, 1700 *2212 p31*
Styles, Reuben 40; Maryland, 1774 *1219.7 p208*
Styve, Knut; Arkansas, 1918 *95.2 p119*
Suare, Ph. 24; America, 1837 *778.5 p507*
Suarez, Leonardo S.; New York, NY, 1832 *8208.4 p27*
Suarez, Manuel Belarino; Arkansas, 1918 *95.2 p119*
Suart, John; America, 1854 *1450.2 p142A*
Suart, Miles; San Francisco, 1887 *2764.35 p63*
Subacz, Kazimierz; Arkansas, 1918 *95.2 p119*
Subarth, Johan; Wisconsin, n.d. *9675.8 p122*
Subarzycki, . . .; New York, 1831 *4606 p177*
Subat, Andrew; Iowa, 1866-1943 *123.54 p47*
Subat, Drago; Iowa, 1866-1943 *123.54 p47*
Subat, Luko; Iowa, 1866-1943 *123.54 p47*
Subeck, Israel; Arkansas, 1918 *95.2 p119*
Suberkovsky, John; America, 1888 *7137 p170*
Subert, Anton; Iowa, 1866-1943 *123.54 p47*
Suboth, Joseph; Iowa, 1866-1943 *123.54 p47*
Subott, Matt; Iowa, 1866-1943 *123.54 p47*
Such, George 18; Pennsylvania, 1721 *3690.1 p220*
Suchaber, Louis 36; America, 1836 *778.5 p508*
Suchak, . . .; New York, 1831 *4606 p177*
Suchan, Henry; Arkansas, 1918 *95.2 p119*
Suchaud, Eugene 27; Port uncertain, 1836 *778.5 p508*
Suchet, George; Arkansas, 1918 *95.2 p119*
Suchetet, Louis 36; America, 1836 *778.5 p508*
Sud, Mary 22; America, 1838 *778.5 p508*
Sudbrink, Louis; Wisconsin, n.d. *9675.8 p122*
Sudbury, Robert; Virginia, 1638 *6219 p33*
Suder, . . .; Canada, 1776-1783 *9786 p43*
Suder, Christina Mugel SEE Suder, Michael
Suder, Elisabetha SEE Suder, Michael
Suder, Georg SEE Suder, Michael
Suder, Katharina SEE Suder, Michael
Suder, Maria Lisette Susanna; America, 1857 *2691.4 p171*
Suder, Michael SEE Suder, Michael
Suder, Michael; America, 1851-1900 *2691.4 p168*
    Wife:Christina Mugel
    Child:Katharina
    Child:Michael
    Child:Georg
    Child:Elisabetha
Suderman, Marie 85; Kansas, 1906 *5240.1 p84*
Sudewig, John; Wisconsin, n.d. *9675.8 p122*
Sudmeier, Carl Friedrich Gottlieb; America, 1854 *4610.10 p135*
Sudmeyer, Mrs.; America, 1849 *4610.10 p135*
    Child:Carl Heinrich Wilhelm
    Child:Carl August F. Wilhelm
Sudmeyer, Carl August F. Wilhelm SEE Sudmeyer, Mrs.
Sudmeyer, Carl Friedrich Wilhelm; America, 1845 *4610.10 p134*

Sudmeyer, Carl Heinrich Wilhelm SEE Sudmeyer, Mrs.
Sudu, Lucas; America, 1900 *7137 p170*
Sue, Eugen; 1788-1848 *8582.3 p90*
Suehrer, Andreas; New England, 1754 *4525 p251*
Suehrer, Andreas; Pennsylvania, 1754 *4525 p251*
Suehrer, Andreas; Pennsylvania, 1754 *4525 p251*
    With wife
    With 3 children
Suehrer, Anna Eva; Pennsylvania, 1753 *4525 p251*
    With 2 daughters
Suehrer, Eva Catharina Strauss SEE Suehrer, Martin
Suehrer, Johann Adam; New England, 1753 *4525 p252*
Suehrer, Johann Adam; Pennsylvania, 1753 *4525 p252*
Suehrer, Johannes Wilhelm; America, 1752 *4525 p251*
Suehrer, Martin; New England, 1753 *4525 p252*
    Wife:Eva Catharina Strauss
    With child
Suehrer, Martin; Pennsylvania, 1753 *4525 p252*
Suehrer, Philipp; Pennsylvania, 1752 *4525 p252*
    With wife
    With child
Suehrer, Wilhelm; Philadelphia, 1752 *4525 p252*
Suelflohn, August; America, 1839 *3702.7 p316*
Suelflow, Herman; Wisconsin, n.d. *9675.8 p122*
Suelfohn, August; America, 1839 *3702.7 p316*
Suelgreene, Susan; Virginia, 1639 *6219 p24*
Suess, George; Wisconsin, n.d. *9675.8 p122*
Suffrin, George 18; New York, 1775 *1219.7 p246*
Sugars, Thomas; Washington, 1859-1920 *2872.1 p39*
Sugars, William 21; Maryland, 1775 *1219.7 p248*
Sugart, V. 40; New Orleans, 1837 *778.5 p508*
Sugert, Joseph; Wisconsin, n.d. *9675.8 p122*
Suggett, Ann 14 SEE Suggett, Mary
Suggett, Christopher 10 SEE Suggett, Mary
Suggett, John 8 SEE Suggett, Mary
Suggett, Mary 12 SEE Suggett, Mary
Suggett, Mary 40; Nova Scotia, 1774 *1219.7 p195*
    Child:Ann 14
    Child:Mary 12
    Child:John 8
    Child:Christopher 10
Suggett, William 18; Nova Scotia, 1774 *1219.7 p195*
Sugol, Anna SEE Sugol, Paul
Sugol, Paul; America, 1879 *7137 p170*
    Wife:Anna
Suh, . . .; Canada, 1776-1783 *9786 p35*
Suher, Louis 30; Connecticut, 1848 *1450.2 p142A*
Suhm, Jacob 23; Kansas, 1895 *5240.1 p80*
Suhm, Karl 30; Kansas, 1893 *5240.1 p44*
Suhm, Karl 30; Kansas, 1893 *5240.1 p78*
Suhm, William 21; Kansas, 1898 *5240.1 p81*
Suhm, Wm. 21; Kansas, 1898 *5240.1 p44*
Suhr, Albert; America, 1853 *1450.2 p142A*
Suhren, Frederick; Illinois, 1906 *2896.5 p39*
Suidyla, John; Wisconsin, n.d. *9675.8 p122*
Suire, Andre; Louisiana, 1789-1819 *778.5 p556*
Sujkowski, Alexander 20; New York, 1912 *9980.29 p53*
Sukeltz, Mrs. 27; America, 1820 *778.5 p508*
Suldana, Giovanni; Arkansas, 1918 *95.2 p119*
Sulflow, August; America, 1839 *3702.7 p314*
Sulger, Hans Jerg; Pennsylvania, 1752 *2444 p225*
Sulia, D. 27; New Orleans, 1837 *778.5 p508*
Sulik, Anna SEE Sulik, John
Sulik, John; America, 1893 *7137 p170*
    Wife:Anna
Sulimirski, Wincenty; New York, 1831 *4606 p177*
Sulivees, Augustus Ferdinand; Ohio, 1851 *9892.11 p44*
Sulkek, Hermann Friedrich; New York, NY, 1836 *8208.4 p23*
Sullhofer, Carl Heinrich; America, 1856 *4610.10 p99*
Sullhofer, Ernst Heinrich K. Friedrich; America, 1858 *4610.10 p99*
Sullhofer, Sophie W. M. Schockemuller; America, 1846-1858 *4610.10 p99*
Sullinger, Elisabetha; New England, 1749 *2444 p137*
Sullivan, . . . 1; Massachusetts, 1849 *5881.1 p90*
Sullivan, Abby 20; Massachusetts, 1849 *5881.1 p87*
Sullivan, Agnes S. 32; Kansas, 1870 *5240.1 p66*
Sullivan, Anastatia 40; Massachusetts, 1849 *5881.1 p87*
Sullivan, Andrew; America, 1866 *6014.1 p3*
Sullivan, Andrew; New York, NY, 1838 *8208.4 p68*
Sullivan, Ann 2; Massachusetts, 1847 *5881.1 p87*
Sullivan, Ann 16; Massachusetts, 1847 *5881.1 p87*
Sullivan, Ann 33; Massachusetts, 1847 *5881.1 p87*
Sullivan, Annie; Arizona, 1898 *9228.30 p11*
Sullivan, Arthur; Kansas, 1870 *5240.1 p51*
Sullivan, Bartholomew 28; Massachusetts, 1847 *5881.1 p87*
Sullivan, Betty 30; Massachusetts, 1849 *5881.1 p88*
Sullivan, Bridget 6; Massachusetts, 1847 *5881.1 p87*
Sullivan, Bridget 18; Massachusetts, 1850 *5881.1 p88*
Sullivan, Bridget 22; Massachusetts, 1848 *5881.1 p87*
Sullivan, Bridget 22; Massachusetts, 1849 *5881.1 p88*

Sullivan, Bridget 23; Massachusetts, 1849 ***5881.1*** *p88*
Sullivan, Bridget 40; Massachusetts, 1850 ***5881.1*** *p88*
Sullivan, Catharine 7; Massachusetts, 1847 ***5881.1*** *p88*
Sullivan, Catharine 9; Massachusetts, 1849 ***5881.1*** *p88*
Sullivan, Catharine 24; Massachusetts, 1849 ***5881.1*** *p88*
Sullivan, Catharine 28; Massachusetts, 1848 ***5881.1*** *p88*
Sullivan, Catherine; America, 1743 ***4971*** *p43*
Sullivan, Charles; America, 1742 ***4971*** *p49*
Sullivan, Charles; America, 1742 ***4971*** *p50*
Sullivan, Coleman 20; Massachusetts, 1849 ***5881.1*** *p88*
Sullivan, Cornelius; New York, 1850 ***1450.2*** *p142A*
Sullivan, Cornelius; New York, NY, 1836 ***8208.4*** *p21*
Sullivan, Cornelius; Vermont, 1867 ***2764.35*** *p64*
Sullivan, Cornelius 2; Massachusetts, 1849 ***5881.1*** *p88*
Sullivan, Cornelius 5; Massachusetts, 1849 ***5881.1*** *p88*
Sullivan, Cornelius 24; Massachusetts, 1849 ***5881.1*** *p88*
Sullivan, Cyrus; Kansas, 1870 ***5240.1*** *p51*
Sullivan, Daniel; America, 1741 ***4971*** *p41*
Sullivan, Daniel; America, 1853 ***1450.2*** *p142A*
Sullivan, Daniel; Illinois, 1855 ***7857*** *p7*
Sullivan, Daniel; Ohio, 1849-1859 ***1450.2*** *p142A*
Sullivan, Daniel 7; Massachusetts, 1849 ***5881.1*** *p89*
Sullivan, Daniel 8; Massachusetts, 1849 ***5881.1*** *p89*
Sullivan, Daniel 10; Massachusetts, 1849 ***5881.1*** *p89*
Sullivan, Daniel 15; Massachusetts, 1849 ***5881.1*** *p88*
Sullivan, Daniel 23; Massachusetts, 1849 ***5881.1*** *p89*
Sullivan, Daniel 40; Massachusetts, 1850 ***5881.1*** *p89*
Sullivan, Daniel S.; Nevada, 1870 ***2764.35*** *p61*
Sullivan, Darby; America, 1739-1740 ***4971*** *p61*
Sullivan, Darby; America, 1740 ***4971*** *p56*
Sullivan, Darby 40; Massachusetts, 1849 ***5881.1*** *p88*
Sullivan, Dennis; America, 1736 ***4971*** *p39*
Sullivan, Dennis; America, 1741 ***4971*** *p56*
Sullivan, Dennis 6; Massachusetts, 1849 ***5881.1*** *p89*
Sullivan, Dennis 21; Massachusetts, 1849 ***5881.1*** *p89*
Sullivan, Dennis 22; Massachusetts, 1850 ***5881.1*** *p89*
Sullivan, Dennis 26; Maryland, 1775 ***1219.7*** *p259*
Sullivan, Dennis 27; Massachusetts, 1849 ***5881.1*** *p89*
Sullivan, Dennis 40; Massachusetts, 1848 ***5881.1*** *p88*
Sullivan, Dennis 47; Arizona, 1906 ***9228.40*** *p14*
Sullivan, Dennis J.; New York, 1870 ***1450.2*** *p142A*
Sullivan, Edmund 17; Massachusetts, 1849 ***5881.1*** *p89*
Sullivan, Edward 12; Massachusetts, 1850 ***5881.1*** *p89*
Sullivan, Eliza 3; Massachusetts, 1850 ***5881.1*** *p89*
Sullivan, Elizabeth 27; Kansas, 1884 ***5240.1*** *p66*
Sullivan, Ellen 2; Massachusetts, 1849 ***5881.1*** *p89*
Sullivan, Ellen 5; Massachusetts, 1849 ***5881.1*** *p89*
Sullivan, Ellen 7; Massachusetts, 1847 ***5881.1*** *p89*
Sullivan, Ellen 9; Massachusetts, 1849 ***5881.1*** *p89*
Sullivan, Ellen 13; Massachusetts, 1849 ***5881.1*** *p89*
Sullivan, Ellen 19; Massachusetts, 1850 ***5881.1*** *p89*
Sullivan, Ellen 29; Massachusetts, 1849 ***5881.1*** *p89*
Sullivan, Ellenor; America, 1742-1743 ***4971*** *p42*
Sullivan, Eugene; New York, NY, 1836 ***8208.4*** *p18*
Sullivan, Eugene 30; Massachusetts, 1849 ***5881.1*** *p89*
Sullivan, Florah 55; North Carolina, 1850 ***1639.20*** *p302*
Sullivan, George G. 23; Kansas, 1870 ***5240.1*** *p44*
Sullivan, George G. 29; Kansas, 1870 ***5240.1*** *p51*
Sullivan, Georges; Quebec, 1819 ***7603*** *p79*
Sullivan, Henry 21; Kansas, 1872 ***5240.1*** *p52*
Sullivan, Hester Ann 29; Kansas, 1871 ***5240.1*** *p51*
Sullivan, Honora 11; Massachusetts, 1849 ***5881.1*** *p89*
Sullivan, Honora 20; Massachusetts, 1849 ***5881.1*** *p58*
Sullivan, Honora 20; Massachusetts, 1850 ***5881.1*** *p90*
Sullivan, Honora 22; Massachusetts, 1848 ***5881.1*** *p89*
Sullivan, Hugh; Boston, 1841 ***7036*** *p126*
*Brother:*Philip
Sullivan, Hugh; New Brunswick, 1800-1841 ***7036*** *p126*
*Brother:*Philip
*Brother:*John
Sullivan, James; America, 1841 ***7036*** *p127*
Sullivan, James 20; Massachusetts, 1848 ***5881.1*** *p90*
Sullivan, James 50; Arizona, 1907 ***9228.40*** *p14*
Sullivan, James 50; Massachusetts, 1849 ***5881.1*** *p90*
Sullivan, James T. 29; Harris Co., TX, 1898 ***6254*** *p5*
Sullivan, Jeremiah; America, 1833 ***1450.2*** *p142A*
Sullivan, Jeremiah; Illinois, 1854 ***7857*** *p7*
Sullivan, Jeremiah; New York, NY, 1816 ***2859.11*** *p43*
Sullivan, Jeremiah 14; Massachusetts, 1850 ***5881.1*** *p91*
Sullivan, Jerry; Colorado, 1903 ***9678.3*** *p15*
Sullivan, Jerry 8; Massachusetts, 1849 ***5881.1*** *p90*
Sullivan, Jerry 24; Massachusetts, 1849 ***5881.1*** *p90*
Sullivan, Johanna 3; Massachusetts, 1849 ***5881.1*** *p90*
Sullivan, Johanna 13; Massachusetts, 1849 ***5881.1*** *p90*
Sullivan, Johanna 18; Massachusetts, 1849 ***5881.1*** *p90*
Sullivan, Johanna 26; Massachusetts, 1849 ***5881.1*** *p90*
Sullivan, Johanna 60; Massachusetts, 1850 ***5881.1*** *p91*
Sullivan, John *SEE* Sullivan, Hugh
Sullivan, John; America, 1736 ***4971*** *p39*
Sullivan, John; America, 1736 ***4971*** *p45*
Sullivan, John; America, 1741 ***4971*** *p41*
Sullivan, John; America, 1741 ***4971*** *p56*
Sullivan, John; America, 1851 ***1450.2*** *p143A*
Sullivan, John; Boston, 1841 ***7036*** *p126*
Sullivan, John; Illinois, 1858 ***2896.5*** *p39*
Sullivan, John; Illinois, 1858 ***5012.39*** *p54*
Sullivan, John; New York, NY, 1834 ***8208.4*** *p31*
Sullivan, John; New York, NY, 1837 ***8208.4*** *p53*
Sullivan, John; New York, NY, 1838 ***8208.4*** *p68*
Sullivan, John; New York, NY, 1838 ***8208.4*** *p88*
Sullivan, John; New York, NY, 1839 ***8208.4*** *p90*
Sullivan, John; New York, NY, 1840 ***8208.4*** *p111*
Sullivan, John 4; Massachusetts, 1849 ***5881.1*** *p90*
Sullivan, John 12; Massachusetts, 1850 ***5881.1*** *p91*
Sullivan, John 20; Massachusetts, 1849 ***5881.1*** *p90*
Sullivan, John 24; Massachusetts, 1849 ***5881.1*** *p90*
Sullivan, John 25; Massachusetts, 1850 ***5881.1*** *p91*
Sullivan, John 27; Massachusetts, 1848 ***5881.1*** *p90*
Sullivan, John 30; Massachusetts, 1847 ***5881.1*** *p90*
Sullivan, John 35; Massachusetts, 1849 ***5881.1*** *p90*
Sullivan, Judy 8; Massachusetts, 1850 ***5881.1*** *p91*
Sullivan, Julia 1; Massachusetts, 1847 ***5881.1*** *p90*
Sullivan, Julia 15; Massachusetts, 1847 ***5881.1*** *p90*
Sullivan, Julia 22; Massachusetts, 1847 ***5881.1*** *p90*
Sullivan, Julia 28; Massachusetts, 1849 ***5881.1*** *p90*
Sullivan, Julian; America, 1736 ***4971*** *p44*
Sullivan, Julian; America, 1736 ***4971*** *p45*
Sullivan, Letitia 37; Kansas, 1884 ***5240.1*** *p66*
Sullivan, Margaret; America, 1741 ***4971*** *p41*
Sullivan, Margaret 4; Massachusetts, 1850 ***5881.1*** *p92*
Sullivan, Margaret 12; Massachusetts, 1849 ***5881.1*** *p92*
Sullivan, Margaret 30; Massachusetts, 1849 ***5881.1*** *p91*
Sullivan, Margaret 60; Massachusetts, 1849 ***5881.1*** *p92*
Sullivan, Martin; Quebec, 1760 ***7603*** *p68*
Sullivan, Mary; America, 1740 ***4971*** *p53*
Sullivan, Mary 3; Massachusetts, 1849 ***5881.1*** *p92*
Sullivan, Mary 7; Massachusetts, 1849 ***5881.1*** *p92*
Sullivan, Mary 10; Massachusetts, 1847 ***5881.1*** *p91*
Sullivan, Mary 18; Massachusetts, 1849 ***5881.1*** *p91*
Sullivan, Mary 18; Massachusetts, 1849 ***5881.1*** *p92*
Sullivan, Mary 26; Massachusetts, 1849 ***5881.1*** *p92*
Sullivan, Mary 30; Massachusetts, 1849 ***5881.1*** *p92*
Sullivan, Mary 35; Massachusetts, 1850 ***5881.1*** *p92*
Sullivan, Mary 40; Massachusetts, 1849 ***5881.1*** *p92*
Sullivan, Michael; Ohio, 1843 ***8365.26*** *p12*
Sullivan, Michael 5; Massachusetts, 1849 ***5881.1*** *p92*
Sullivan, Michael 11; Massachusetts, 1849 ***5881.1*** *p92*
Sullivan, Michael 12; Massachusetts, 1849 ***5881.1*** *p91*
Sullivan, Michael 18; Newfoundland, 1789 ***4915.24*** *p57*
Sullivan, Michael 20; Massachusetts, 1847 ***5881.1*** *p91*
Sullivan, Michael 24; Massachusetts, 1849 ***5881.1*** *p91*
Sullivan, Michael 25; Kansas, 1880 ***5240.1*** *p61*
Sullivan, Nelly 18; Massachusetts, 1849 ***5881.1*** *p92*
Sullivan, Owen; New York, NY, 1836 ***8208.4*** *p22*
Sullivan, Owen 11; Massachusetts, 1849 ***5881.1*** *p93*
Sullivan, Owen 18; Massachusetts, 1849 ***5881.1*** *p92*
Sullivan, Owen 50; Massachusetts, 1849 ***5881.1*** *p92*
Sullivan, Patrick; America, 1872 ***6014.1*** *p3*
Sullivan, Patrick; Quebec, 1784 ***7603*** *p70*
Sullivan, Patrick 9; Massachusetts, 1849 ***5881.1*** *p93*
Sullivan, Patrick 12; Massachusetts, 1849 ***5881.1*** *p93*
Sullivan, Patrick 21; Massachusetts, 1849 ***5881.1*** *p93*
Sullivan, Patrick 26; Massachusetts, 1849 ***5881.1*** *p93*
Sullivan, Patrick 37; Massachusetts, 1848 ***5881.1*** *p93*
Sullivan, Patrick 40; Massachusetts, 1847 ***5881.1*** *p93*
Sullivan, Patrick 40; Massachusetts, 1849 ***5881.1*** *p93*
Sullivan, Peggy 9; Massachusetts, 1849 ***5881.1*** *p93*
Sullivan, Peter; New York, 1841 ***7036*** *p124*
Sullivan, Philip *SEE* Sullivan, Hugh
Sullivan, Philip *SEE* Sullivan, Hugh
Sullivan, Philip 19; Maryland, 1774 ***1219.7*** *p185*
Sullivan, Rose 9; Massachusetts, 1850 ***5881.1*** *p93*
Sullivan, Sarah 39; Kansas, 1884 ***5240.1*** *p66*
Sullivan, Stephen 20; Massachusetts, 1848 ***5881.1*** *p93*
Sullivan, Terrence 26; Massachusetts, 1849 ***5881.1*** *p93*
Sullivan, Th. 32; New York, NY, 1893 ***9026.4*** *p42*
Sullivan, Thaddeus 7; Massachusetts, 1849 ***5881.1*** *p93*
Sullivan, Thomas; America, 1739 ***4971*** *p14*
Sullivan, Thomas 17; Maryland, 1774 ***1219.7*** *p244*
Sullivan, Thomas 75; Arizona, 1915 ***9228.40*** *p20*
Sullivan, Tim.; America, 1736 ***4971*** *p43*
Sullivan, Timothee; Quebec, 1720 ***7603*** *p95*
Sullivan, Timothy; America, 1736 ***4971*** *p45*
Sullivan, Timothy; America, 1834-1835 ***1450.2*** *p143A*
Sullivan, Timothy 11; Massachusetts, 1849 ***5881.1*** *p93*
Sullivan, Timothy 17; Massachusetts, 1849 ***5881.1*** *p93*
Sullivan, Timothy 19; Massachusetts, 1849 ***5881.1*** *p93*
Sullivan, Timothy 22; Massachusetts, 1847 ***5881.1*** *p93*
Sullivan, William R.; Kansas, 1870 ***5240.1*** *p51*
Sulliward, Jon.; Virginia, 1635 ***6219*** *p20*
Sullmann, Henry; Wisconsin, n.d. ***9675.8*** *p122*
Sullwald, Ernst Heinrich; America, 1910 ***4610.10*** *p123*
Sully, Edward 2; Massachusetts, 1850 ***5881.1*** *p89*
Sully, John 11; Massachusetts, 1850 ***5881.1*** *p91*
Sully, Margaret 6; Massachusetts, 1850 ***5881.1*** *p92*
Sully, Martin 24; Massachusetts, 1850 ***5881.1*** *p92*
Sully, Mary 8; Massachusetts, 1850 ***5881.1*** *p92*
Sully, Mary 20; Massachusetts, 1850 ***5881.1*** *p92*
Sully, Michael 13; Massachusetts, 1850 ***5881.1*** *p92*
Sully, Thomas; Illinois, 1855 ***7857*** *p7*
Sully, Thomas; Virginia, 1624 ***6219*** *p29*
Sully, Thomas 50; Massachusetts, 1850 ***5881.1*** *p93*
Sully, William 21; Maryland, 1774 ***1219.7*** *p184*
Sulsberg, Moritz; Wisconsin, n.d. ***9675.8*** *p122*
Sultemeyer, Friedrich Otto; America, 1881 ***4610.10*** *p124*
Sultenic, Stanislaus Albert; Kansas, 1917 ***6013.40*** *p17*
Sulwees, Augustus Ferdinand; Ohio, 1851 ***9892.11*** *p44*
Sumaghan, Thomas; America, 1735-1743 ***4971*** *p78*
Sumegi, Joseph; America, 1892 ***1450.2*** *p143A*
Sumers, Miles; Virginia, 1637 ***6219*** *p107*
Sumfield, Ann 30; Philadelphia, 1774 ***1219.7*** *p219*
With child
Sumfleth, A. 68; Washington, 1918-1920 ***1728.5*** *p14*
Sumfleth, A. T. 33; Washington, 1918-1920 ***1728.5*** *p14*
Summann, Henry; Illinois, 1888 ***2896.5*** *p39*
Summe, Heinrich; Kentucky, 1844 ***8582.3*** *p101*
Summer, . . .; Canada, 1776-1783 ***9786*** *p35*
Summer, Christian 2; New Orleans, 1836 ***778.5*** *p508*
Summer, Elisabeth 3; New Orleans, 1836 ***778.5*** *p508*
Summer, George 35; New Orleans, 1836 ***778.5*** *p508*
Summer, Jean 1; New Orleans, 1836 ***778.5*** *p508*
Summer, Nanette 23; New Orleans, 1836 ***778.5*** *p508*
Summer, Richard; Virginia, 1638 ***6219*** *p33*
Summer, Samuel; Illinois, 1888 ***2896.5*** *p39*
Summers, Aaron; Virginia, 1698 ***2212*** *p17*
Summers, Alex.; Virginia, 1638 ***6219*** *p117*
Summers, Ellen 17; Philadelphia, 1860 ***5704.8*** *p145*
Summers, John 20; Philadelphia, 1774 ***1219.7*** *p217*
Summers, John 24; Maryland, 1774 ***1219.7*** *p180*
Summers, Levi; Washington, 1859-1920 ***2872.1*** *p39*
Summers, Philip; New York, NY, 1836 ***8208.4*** *p19*
Summers, Robt.; Virginia, 1638 ***6219*** *p17*
Summers, William; Illinois, 1891 ***2896.5*** *p39*
Summers, William 25; Jamaica, 1738 ***3690.1*** *p212*
Summerville, Ann; Philadelphia, 1851 ***5704.8*** *p81*
Summerville, Catherine 15; St. John, N.B., 1853 ***5704.8*** *p110*
Summerville, Elizabeth 50; St. John, N.B., 1853 ***5704.8*** *p110*
Summerville, Garrett; Virginia, 1639 ***6219*** *p152*
Summerville, Margaret 13; St. John, N.B., 1853 ***5704.8*** *p110*
Summerville, Mary Ann; Philadelphia, 1847 ***53.26*** *p86*
Summerville, Mary Ann; Philadelphia, 1847 ***5704.8*** *p24*
Summerville, Summer; Philadelphia, 1851 ***5704.8*** *p81*
Summerville, William; St. John, N.B., 1852 ***5704.8*** *p95*
Sumner, William A.; Illinois, 1850 ***7857*** *p7*
Sumpter, George 19; Virginia, 1721 ***3690.1*** *p220*
Sund, Erik; America, 1849 ***2090*** *p614*
Sundarmire, Ernest; Ohio, 1846 ***9892.11*** *p44*
Sundbeck, August Daniel; Arkansas, 1918 ***95.2*** *p119*
Sundberg, Abram; Maine, 1882 ***6410.22*** *p125*
Sundberg, John Fredrick; Iroquois Co., IL, 1892 ***3455.1*** *p13*
Sundberg, Oscar Sigvard; New York, NY, 1928 ***3455.5*** *p7*
Sunde, Albert John; Arkansas, 1918 ***95.2*** *p119*
Sunde, Andrew Sjurson 26; Arkansas, 1918 ***95.2*** *p119*
Sundelin, John Ulrik; Washington, 1859-1920 ***2872.1*** *p39*
Sunderbruck, August; America, 1849 ***8582.3*** *p64*
Sunderland, Francis; Georgia, 1775 ***1219.7*** *p275*
Sunderland, William; Georgia, 1775 ***1219.7*** *p275*
Sundermann, Aug.; Wisconsin, n.d. ***9675.8*** *p122*
Sundermeier, Anton Friedrich; America, 1853 ***4610.10*** *p116*
*Wife:*Christine F H Lubbing
*Child:*Anton Wilhelm
*Child:*Hermann Emil Friedrich
Sundermeier, Anton Wilhelm *SEE* Sundermeier, Anton Friedrich
Sundermeier, Christian F. Wilhelm *SEE* Sundermeier, Franz Heinrich
Sundermeier, Christine F H Lubbing *SEE* Sundermeier, Anton Friedrich
Sundermeier, Ernst Friedrich Wilhelm; America, 1880 ***4610.10*** *p106*
Sundermeier, Franz Heinrich; America, 1850 ***4610.10*** *p120*
*Brother:*Christian F. Wilhelm
Sundermeier, Hermann Emil Friedrich *SEE* Sundermeier, Anton Friedrich
Sundermeyer, Hermann F. Aug. Ludwig; America, 1883 ***4610.10*** *p106*
Sundin, Andrew; Iowa, 1866-1943 ***123.54*** *p47*
Sundkurist, Albert; Iroquois Co., IL, 1894 ***3455.1*** *p13*
Sundquist, Charles O.; Colorado, 1903 ***9678.3*** *p15*
Sundquist, John; Washington, 1859-1920 ***2872.1*** *p39*
Sundquist, Oscar A.; Washington, 1859-1920 ***2872.1*** *p39*

500 *FOR A COMPLETE EXPLANATION OF ENTRY, SEE "HOW TO READ A CITATION" SECTION*

Sundquist, Richard Emanuel; Boston, 1910 *3455.3* p46
Sundqvist, Johan O.; New York, NY, 1907 *3455.1* p51
Sundstrom, Alfred; Iowa, 1866-1943 *123.54* p47
Sungidard, Hans Peter Meller; Arkansas, 1918 *95.2* p119
Sunmary, John 21; Maryland, 1775 *1219.7* p273
Sunnaghan, James; America, 1736 *4971* p80
Sunquist, Hannah 35; Massachusetts, 1860 *6410.32* p116
Suntken, Sjut; Illinois, 1900 *5012.40* p77
Supervielle, A. 22; New Orleans, 1838 *778.5* p508
Suple, Jan 21; Massachusetts, 1847 *5881.1* p87
Suple, George 26; Massachusetts, 1847 *5881.1* p89
Supon, Joseph; America, 1900 *1450.2* p39B
Suppiger Family ; Illinois, 1824-1827 *8582.1* p54
Suppiger, Adeline; Milwaukee, 1875 *4719.30* p257
Suppiger, John; Milwaukee, 1875 *4719.30* p257
Suppiger, Mrs. John; Milwaukee, 1875 *4719.30* p257
Suppiger, Louis G.; Milwaukee, 1875 *4719.30* p257
Supple, Gottfried; America, 1854 *8582.3* p64
Supple, Patrick; America, 1737-1738 *4971* p59
Supronowski, Jan; New York, 1835 *4606* p180
Surber, Rudolf; Washington, 1859-1920 *2872.1* p39
Surdes, Sam; Arkansas, 1918 *95.2* p119
Sures, Samuell; Virginia, 1645 *6219* p252
Surgeon, John; Philadelphia, 1852 *5704.8* p87
Surgeon, Samuel; Quebec, 1852 *5704.8* p89
Surleau, Pierre 28; Halifax, N.S., 1752 *7074.6* p212
Surley, Andrew M.; Wisconsin, n.d. *9675.8* p122
Surman, Gerhard; Ohio, 1832 *8582.2* p49
  With family
Surmann, Gerhard; Ohio, 1832 *8582.2* p49
  With family
Suronetto, John; Iowa, 1866-1943 *123.54* p47
Surr, George 19; Georgia, 1775 *1219.7* p275
Surredge, Francis 28; Jamaica, 1738 *3690.1* p220
Susagan, Biddy 30; Massachusetts, 1847 *5881.1* p87
Susagan, John; Massachusetts, 1847 *5881.1* p90
Susaine, Stephen; Virginia, 1634 *6219* p32
Susi, Luigi; Wisconsin, n.d. *9675.8* p122
Susich, Frank; Iowa, 1866-1943 *123.54* p79
Susin, Ambrogio 15; New York, NY, 1893 *9026.4* p42
Susin, Angela Luigia; Iowa, 1866-1943 *123.54* p79
Susin, Angelo; Iowa, 1866-1943 *123.54* p47
Susin, Anton; Iowa, 1866-1943 *123.54* p47
Susin, Gabriel; Iowa, 1866-1943 *123.54* p81
Susin, John; Iowa, 1866-1943 *123.54* p47
Susin, Louis; Iowa, 1866-1943 *123.54* p81
Susin, Mary; Iowa, 1866-1943 *123.54* p81
Suskind, Sigmund; Shreveport, LA, 1877 *7129* p46
Susledo, Adaline 8; Louisiana, 1835 *778.5* p508
Susledo, Levis 32; Louisiana, 1835 *778.5* p508
Susledo, Nickenlas 35; Louisiana, 1835 *778.5* p508
Susnik, Frank; Wisconsin, n.d. *9675.8* p122
Susnik, Martin; Wisconsin, n.d. *9675.8* p122
Suss, . . .; Canada, 1776-1783 *9786* p35
Susse, . . .; Canada, 1776-1783 *9786* p35
Sussman, Theodore David; Arkansas, 1918 *95.2* p119
Sussner, . . .; Canada, 1776-1783 *9786* p35
Suter, Francis 20; Maryland, 1774 *1219.7* p207
Suter, George; New Orleans, 1844 *1450.2* p143A
Suter, Johann August; New York, NY, 1834 *8582* p32
Suter, John; New York, NY, 1837 *8208.4* p95
Suthard, John 16; Maryland, 1720 *3690.1* p220
Sutherland, Barbara; South Carolina, 1767 *1639.20* p302
Sutherland, Daniel; North Carolina, 1755-1777 *1639.20* p302
Sutherland, Daniel; Quebec, 1766 *7603* p38
Sutherland, Guillaume; Quebec, 1754 *7603* p42
Sutherland, Harriet F. Ann Medley *SEE* Sutherland, James S.
Sutherland, James; Charleston, SC, 1803 *1639.20* p303
Sutherland, James 18; Virginia, 1774 *1219.7* p185
Sutherland, James S.; Wisconsin, 1852 *8893* p263
  *Wife:*Harriet F. Ann Medley
Sutherland, Jane; Philadelphia, 1853 *5704.8* p103
Sutherland, Jno 15; America, 1699 *2212* p29
Sutherland, John 28; Maryland, 1775 *1219.7* p248
Sutherland, Mary 80; North Carolina, 1850 *1639.20* p303
Sutherland, William 24; Wilmington, NC, 1774 *1639.20* p303
  With wife
Sutherland, William 40; Wilmington, NC, 1774 *1639.20* p303
  With wife
  With 3 children
  With child 19
  With child 9
Sutinen, Jakob; Washington, 1859-1920 *2872.1* p39
Sutkowski, . . .; New York, 1831 *4606* p177
Sutliff, Edward; New York, NY, 1811 *2859.11* p20
Sutliff, Henry; New York, NY, 1811 *2859.11* p20
Sutter, Johann August; New York, NY, 1834 *8582* p32
Sutter, John; Ohio, 1842 *8582.1* p48

Sutter, Samuel; Ohio, 1844 *8582.1* p48
Sutterer, Christ; Illinois, 1860 *5012.39* p90
Sutton, Andrew 21; New York, 1774 *1219.7* p189
Sutton, Annis; Virginia, 1639 *6219* p162
Sutton, Edward 16; Maryland, 1775 *1219.7* p250
Sutton, Francis 29; Jamaica, 1736 *3690.1* p220
Sutton, Georg; Virginia, 1642 *6219* p191
Sutton, James; New York, NY, 1834 *8208.4* p76
Sutton, John; Virginia, 1642 *6219* p189
Sutton, John 19; Philadelphia, 1774 *1219.7* p214
Sutton, John 22; Philadelphia, 1775 *1219.7* p255
Sutton, John 23; Jamaica, 1736 *3690.1* p220
Sutton, John 30; Kansas, 1870 *5240.1* p62
Sutton, John 43; New York, 1775 *1219.7* p268
Sutton, Joseph; Quebec, 1825 *7603* p97
Sutton, Rich.; Virginia, 1637 *6219* p115
Sutton, Richard; Virginia, 1638 *6219* p147
Sutton, Richard; Virginia, 1639 *6219* p151
Sutton, Richard; Virginia, 1639 *6219* p152
Sutton, Robert Henry; West Virginia, 1843-1849 *9788.3* p21
Sutton, Robt.; Virginia, 1636 *6219* p21
Sutton, Samuel 26; Jamaica, 1731 *3690.1* p220
Sutton, Tho.; Virginia, 1643 *6219* p199
Sutton, William; New York, NY, 1811 *2859.11* p20
Sutton, William; Virginia, 1642 *6219* p191
Sutton, Wm.; Virginia, 1635 *6219* p20
Suur, Bernhard; New York, NY, 1925 *3455.4* p92
Suz, Mr. 25; America, 1838 *778.5* p351
Svalin, Arthur Elof; Arkansas, 1918 *95.2* p119
Svanling, Seth; Iroquois Co., IL, 1894 *3455.1* p13
Sveinsson, Arni Metusalem 19; Quebec, 1879 *2557.1* p20
Sveinsson, Jon 54; Quebec, 1879 *2557.1* p20
Sveinsson, Sven 27; Quebec, 1879 *2557.2* p36
Svendsen, Edward Andreas; Arkansas, 1918 *95.2* p119
Svendsen, Einar Gustav; Arkansas, 1918 *95.2* p119
Svendsen, Svend Christian; Arkansas, 1918 *95.2* p119
Svengestol, Got.; Wisconsin, n.d. *9675.8* p122
Svenson, John Peter; Colorado, 1904 *9678.3* p15
Svenson, P.; Minneapolis, 1874-1884 *6410.35* p66
Svenson, S. A. A.; Washington, 1859-1920 *2872.1* p39
Svensson, Abel; Minneapolis, 1870-1879 *6410.35* p59
Svensson, Charlotta; Boston, 1851 *6410.32* p124
  *Daughter:*Sophia Mathilda
Svensson, Frithiof Ferdinand; Minneapolis, 1884-1887 *6410.35* p66
Svensson, Johan Gustaf; Minneapolis, 1878-1883 *6410.35* p66
Svensson, Nils; Minneapolis, 1879-1883 *6410.35* p66
Svensson, Sophia Mathilda *SEE* Svensson, Charlotta
Svensson, Sven August; Minneapolis, 1879-1880 *6410.35* p66
Svob, Anton; Iowa, 1866-1943 *123.54* p47
Svob, Frank; Iowa, 1866-1943 *123.54* p81
Svorcik, Steve; Wisconsin, n.d. *9675.8* p122
Swab, John; Iowa, 1866-1943 *123.54* p47
Swab, Philip; Iowa, 1866-1943 *123.54* p47
Swaeber, Joseph; Wisconsin, n.d. *9675.8* p122
Swaetek, Wenzel; Wisconsin, n.d. *9675.8* p122
Swaetek, Wenzel, Jr.; Wisconsin, n.d. *9675.8* p122
Swain, George W.; New York, NY, 1839 *8208.4* p95
Swain, James; America, 1836 *1450.2* p143A
Swain, John; Kansas, 1870 *5240.1* p51
Swaine, Ann *SEE* Swaine, Tho.
Swaine, John; New York, NY, 1840 *8208.4* p108
Swaine, Tho.; Virginia, 1638 *6219* p124
  *Wife:*Ann
Swalander, Carl 60; Washington, 1918-1920 *1728.5* p12
Swalander, Reinhold 50; Washington, 1918-1920 *1728.5* p12
Swalander, Vera 22; Washington, 1918-1920 *1728.5* p12
Swallow, James 24; Philadelphia, 1774 *1219.7* p224
Swan, Alex 30; Arizona, 1902 *9228.40* p8
Swan, Alexander; Philadelphia, 1816 *2859.11* p43
Swan, Clifford 21; Nova Scotia, 1774 *1219.7* p209
Swan, David; Philadelphia, 1816 *2859.11* p43
Swan, Edw.; Virginia, 1635 *6219* p71
Swan, Elizabeth *SEE* Swan, James
Swan, Elizabeth; Philadelphia, 1850 *5704.8* p68
Swan, Elizabeth; St. John, N.B., 1866 *5704.8* p166
Swan, Elizabeth 10 *SEE* Swan, James
Swan, Elizabeth 10; Philadelphia, 1850 *5704.8* p68
Swan, George *SEE* Swan, James
Swan, George; Philadelphia, 1850 *5704.8* p68
Swan, Hugh; St. John, N.B., 1847 *5704.8* p18
Swan, Isabella *SEE* Swan, Samuel
Swan, Isabella; Philadelphia, 1850 *5704.8* p68
Swan, J. G.; Minneapolis, 1836-1878 *6410.35* p66
Swan, Jacob; Maryland, 1756 *1219.7* p46
Swan, Jacob; Maryland, 1756 *3690.1* p220
Swan, James; Philadelphia, 1850 *53.26* p86
  *Relative:*Elizabeth
  *Relative:*George

  *Relative:*Elizabeth 10
  *Relative:*Jane 6
  *Relative:*James 2
Swan, James; Philadelphia, 1850 *5704.8* p68
Swan, James 2 *SEE* Swan, James
Swan, James 2; Philadelphia, 1850 *5704.8* p68
Swan, James 11; Massachusetts, 1849 *5881.1* p90
Swan, Jane; St. John, N.B., 1847 *5704.8* p18
Swan, Jane 6 *SEE* Swan, James
Swan, Jane 6; Philadelphia, 1850 *5704.8* p68
Swan, Jane 30; St. John, N.B., 1859 *5704.8* p140
Swan, John; Philadelphia, 1816 *2859.11* p43
Swan, John; St. John, N.B., 1866 *5704.8* p166
Swan, John 3 *SEE* Swan, Thomas
Swan, John 3; Philadelphia, 1847 *5704.8* p22
Swan, John 5; St. John, N.B., 1866 *5704.8* p166
Swan, John 27; St. John, N.B., 1864 *5704.8* p159
Swan, Jon.; Virginia, 1635 *6219* p71
Swan, Margaret; Philadelphia, 1816 *2859.11* p43
Swan, Martha *SEE* Swan, Samuel
Swan, Martha; Philadelphia, 1850 *5704.8* p68
Swan, Mary *SEE* Swan, Samuel
Swan, Mary; Philadelphia, 1850 *5704.8* p68
Swan, Matilda *SEE* Swan, Thomas
Swan, Matilda; Philadelphia, 1847 *5704.8* p22
Swan, Michael 1; Massachusetts, 1849 *5881.1* p91
Swan, Paul *SEE* Swan, Samuel
Swan, Paul; Philadelphia, 1850 *5704.8* p68
Swan, Peter 40; Maryland, 1775 *1219.7* p257
Swan, Robert 3; St. John, N.B., 1866 *5704.8* p166
Swan, Samll.; Virginia, 1634 *6219* p84
Swan, Samuel; Philadelphia, 1850 *53.26* p86
  *Relative:*Isabella
  *Relative:*Paul
  *Relative:*Mary
  *Relative:*Martha
  *Relative:*Thomas 12
Swan, Samuel; Philadelphia, 1850 *5704.8* p68
Swan, Samuel 1 *SEE* Swan, Thomas
Swan, Samuel 1; Philadelphia, 1847 *5704.8* p22
Swan, Samuel 58; Arizona, 1898 *9228.40* p3
Swan, Thomas; New York, NY, 1811 *2859.11* p20
Swan, Thomas; Philadelphia, 1847 *53.26* p86
  *Relative:*Matilda
  *Relative:*John 3
  *Relative:*Samuel 1
Swan, Thomas; Philadelphia, 1847 *5704.8* p22
Swan, Thomas 6; Massachusetts, 1849 *5881.1* p93
Swan, Thomas 12 *SEE* Swan, Samuel
Swan, Thomas 12; Philadelphia, 1850 *5704.8* p68
Swanberg, Charles G.T.; Charleston, SC, 1837 *6410.32* p122
Swanberg, Fred W. 64; Massachusetts, 1860 *6410.32* p109
Swanberg, Fredrika Wilhelmina; America, 1848 *6410.32* p124
Swanbergh, Fredrika 64; Massachusetts, 1860 *6410.32* p109
Swanick, Thomas 32; Maryland, 1775 *1219.7* p255
Swann, Martha; Virginia, 1635 *6219* p33
Swann, Richard; Virginia, 1646 *6219* p236
Swansen, Charles 47; Arizona, 1920 *9228.40* p24
Swansen, Otto 29; Arizona, 1890 *2764.35* p64
Swanson, A. L.; Minneapolis, 1870-1887 *6410.35* p66
Swanson, Albert; Iowa, 1866-1943 *123.54* p47
Swanson, Albert; Minneapolis, 1869-1885 *6410.35* p66
Swanson, Andrew; Arkansas, 1918 *95.2* p119
Swanson, August; Colorado, 1904 *9678.3* p15
Swanson, August; Iroquois Co., IL, 1893 *3455.1* p13
Swanson, August P.; Bangor, ME, 1880 *6410.22* p125
Swanson, Augustus; Bangor, ME, 1871-1876 *6410.22* p116
Swanson, Augustus; Bangor, ME, 1876 *6410.22* p124
Swanson, C. E.; Iowa, 1866-1943 *123.54* p47
Swanson, C. N.; Minneapolis, 1870-1880 *6410.35* p66
Swanson, C.S.; Colorado, 1900 *9678.3* p15
Swanson, Carl August 31; Arkansas, 1918 *95.2* p119
Swanson, Carl John; Arkansas, 1918 *95.2* p120
Swanson, Charles Henry; Iroquois Co., IL, 1892 *3455.1* p13
Swanson, Charles J.; Minneapolis, 1869-1887 *6410.35* p66
Swanson, Charles V.; Washington, 1859-1920 *2872.1* p39
Swanson, Elna *SEE* Swanson, Oscar Leonard
Swanson, Evar; Arkansas, 1918 *95.2* p120
Swanson, F. P.; Minneapolis, 1881-1885 *6410.35* p66
Swanson, Frank; Minneapolis, 1884-1887 *6410.35* p66
Swanson, Frank 38; Washington, 1918-1920 *1728.5* p14
Swanson, Gus; Iowa, 1866-1943 *123.54* p48
Swanson, Gus 62; Arizona, 1925 *9228.40* p29
Swanson, Gust; Iowa, 1866-1943 *123.54* p48
Swanson, J. G.; Minneapolis, 1878-1883 *6410.35* p66

T

Taacke, Miss; America, 1849 *4610.10 p135*
Taacke, Bernh. Heinrich Gottlieb; America, 1849 *4610.10 p135*
Taacke, Carl Friedrich Gottlieb; America, 1849 *4610.10 p135*
Taake, Anna Marie Louise *SEE* Taake, Friedrich Wilhelm
Taake, Anne Marie Engel *SEE* Taake, Friedrich Wilhelm
Taake, Elisabeth Hartmann *SEE* Taake, Friedrich Wilhelm
Taake, Friedrich 20; America, 1844 *4610.10 p75*
Taake, Friedrich Wilhelm *SEE* Taake, Friedrich Wilhelm
Taake, Friedrich Wilhelm; America, 1840 *4610.10 p138*
  *Wife:*Elisabeth Hartmann
  *Child:*Anne Marie Engel
  *Child:*Anna Marie Louise
  *Child:*Friedrich Wilhelm
Taake, Peter Friedrich; America, 1885 *4610.10 p14*
Taalbakka, John; Washington, 1859-1920 *2872.1 p40*
Tabaka, Charles; Washington, 1859-1920 *2872.1 p40*
Tabb, Humphry; Virginia, 1642 *6219 p192*
Tabb, Tho.; Virginia, 1643 *6219 p205*
Tabor, John; Virginia, 1639 *6219 p161*
Tabott, Geo.; Virginia, 1637 *6219 p82*
Tachoires, Michel 29; America, 1829 *778.5 p509*
Tacke, Anne Marie Louise Friederike; America, 1856 *4610.10 p135*
Tacke, Carl Friedrich Wilhelm; America, 1851 *4610.10 p135*
Tacke, Christian; America, 1889 *1450.2 p144A*
Tacke, Johanne; America, 1844 *4610.10 p146*
Tacke, Peter Friedrich Gottlieb; America, 1844 *4610.10 p134*
Tacke, Rudolph; Canada, 1783 *9786 p38A*
Tacker, John 39; Philadelphia, 1775 *1219.7 p255*
Tackerman, Mr.; Quebec, 1815 *9229.18 p78*
  With wife
  With family
Tackes, Mathias; Wisconsin, n.d. *9675.8 p122*
Tacquerman, Mathias 20; Port uncertain, 1835 *778.5 p509*
Taddia, Nicola; Arkansas, 1918 *95.2 p120*
Tadej, Juro; Iowa, 1866-1943 *123.54 p81*
Tadz, Pin; Iowa, 1866-1943 *123.54 p48*
Taechel, Gustav. 32; New Orleans, 1839 *9420.2 p165*
Taenzer, Wilhelm; America, 1849 *8582.1 p34*
Taffard de St. Germain, Mr. 36; Port uncertain, 1838 *778.5 p509*
Taft, Joseph 21; Maryland, 1774 *1219.7 p220*
Tag, Mrs. Hans; America, 1752 *4525 p252*
  With 5 children
Tagart, Joseph; Philadelphia, 1811 *53.26 p87*
Tagart, Joseph; Philadelphia, 1811 *2859.11 p20*
Tager, . . .; Canada, 1776-1783 *9786 p35*
Tagg, Joseph 20; America, 1701 *2212 p34*
Taggart, Alexander; America, 1869 *5704.8 p232*
Taggart, Alice; Philadelphia, 1848 *53.26 p87*
Taggart, Alice; Philadelphia, 1848 *5704.8 p46*
Taggart, Arthur, Jr.; Ohio, 1846 *9892.11 p45*
Taggart, Catherine; St. John, N.B., 1852 *5704.8 p95*
Taggart, Daniel; St. John, N.B., 1847 *5704.8 p21*
Taggart, Ellan; Quebec, 1849 *5704.8 p52*
Taggart, James; Ohio, 1839 *9892.11 p45*
Taggart, James; Ohio, 1841 *9892.11 p45*
Taggart, Jane; Philadelphia, 1866 *5704.8 p208*
Taggart, Margaret; Philadelphia, 1866 *5704.8 p208*
Taggart, Martha; St. John, N.B., 1847 *5704.8 p21*

Taggart, Mary; Philadelphia, 1867 *5704.8 p215*
Taggart, Mary; St. John, N.B., 1847 *5704.8 p21*
Taggart, Mary 9; Quebec, 1849 *5704.8 p52*
Taggart, William; New York, NY, 1816 *2859.11 p43*
  With wife
Tagliapietra, Theresa; Iowa, 1866-1943 *123.54 p81*
Tague, Patrick; Philadelphia, 1864 *5704.8 p182*
Tahlitzsch, Jane Gilian 20 *SEE* Tahlitzsch, John Gottl.
Tahlitzsch, John Gottl. 22; New Orleans, 1839 *9420.2 p485*
  *Sister:*Jane Gilian 20
Tahn, Christiane 6; New Orleans, 1839 *9420.2 p70*
Tahn, Dorothea 41; New Orleans, 1839 *9420.2 p70*
Tahn, Friedr. 4; New Orleans, 1839 *9420.2 p70*
Tahn, Gottfried 39; New Orleans, 1839 *9420.2 p70*
Tahn, Justine 14; New Orleans, 1839 *9420.2 p70*
Tahn, Sophie 8; New Orleans, 1839 *9420.2 p70*
Tailfer, Mary *SEE* Tailfer, Patrick
Tailfer, Patrick; Georgia, 1734 *1639.20 p303*
  *Wife:*Mary
Tailor, Bessy; Quebec, 1850 *5704.8 p62*
Tailor, Catherine; Quebec, 1850 *5704.8 p62*
Tailor, Edward; Quebec, 1850 *5704.8 p62*
Tailor, James; Quebec, 1850 *5704.8 p62*
Tailor, John; Quebec, 1850 *5704.8 p62*
Taintre, Mr. 38; New Orleans, 1830 *778.5 p509*
Taintre, Mrs. 24; New Orleans, 1830 *778.5 p509*
Tait, George; Charleston, SC, 1801 *1639.20 p303*
Tait, James; Boston, 1774 *1219.7 p229*
Tait, James 36; Philadelphia, 1803 *53.26 p87*
Tait, Jane; America, 1866 *5704.8 p209*
Tait, John 18; Maryland, 1775 *1219.7 p273*
Tait, Peter; Charleston, SC, 1781-1830 *1639.20 p304*
Tait, Robert M.; Iowa, 1866-1943 *123.54 p48*
Tait, Thomas; Iowa, 1866-1943 *123.54 p48*
Tait, William; Colombia, SC, 1806 *1639.20 p304*
Takacs, Albert; New York, NY, 1909 *9892.11 p45*
Takar, Catharine *SEE* Takar, Jacob
Takar, Jacob; America, 1887 *7137 p170*
  *Wife:*Catharine
  *Relative:*Stanislaus
Takar, Stanislaus *SEE* Takar, Jacob
Talajka, Venzl; Wisconsin, n.d. *9675.8 p122*
Talan, Amanda Johanna; Washington, 1859-1920 *2872.1 p40*
Talan, Arvi Alex; Washington, 1859-1920 *2872.1 p40*
Talan, Axel; Washington, 1859-1920 *2872.1 p40*
Talan, Axel Alexander; Washington, 1859-1920 *2872.1 p40*
Talan, Weikkos Arthur; Washington, 1859-1920 *2872.1 p40*
Talant, Axel; Washington, 1859-1920 *2872.1 p40*
Talarat, Louis 14; New Orleans, 1831 *778.5 p509*
Talbert, John; New York, NY, 1836 *8208.4 p21*
Talbot, Ann; North Carolina, 1777 *1639.20 p213*
Talbot, Eva; Washington, 1859-1920 *2872.1 p40*
Talbot, George; Illinois, 1867 *7857 p7*
Talbot, H. J.; Washington, 1859-1920 *2872.1 p40*
Talbott, Charles C.; New York, NY, 1838 *8208.4 p83*
Talbott, John; Virginia, 1642 *6219 p195*
Talbott, Jon.; Virginia, 1642 *6219 p194*
Talbott, Peter; Virginia, 1642 *6219 p188*
Talciola, Carolina 57; New York, NY, 1893 *9026.4 p42*
Talcott, Pen Anton Jonsson; Arkansas, 1918 *95.2 p120*
Talebury, George 27; Kansas, 1906 *5240.1 p84*
Talien, Mme. 31; New Orleans, 1838 *778.5 p509*
Tallant, Thomas; America, 1738 *4971 p85*

Tallant, Thomas; America, 1738 *4971 p95*
Tallavena, Elisa 24; New York, NY, 1893 *9026.4 p42*
Tallent, Thomas; America, 1743 *4971 p11*
Talley, Eliza.; Virginia, 1638 *6219 p118*
Talling, Patrick; Virginia, 1638 *6219 p18*
Tallock, James; Virginia, 1638 *6219 p33*
Tallon, Andrew; America, 1742 *4971 p24*
Tallon, Hugh; America, 1741 *4971 p59*
Tallon, John A.; Illinois, 1887 *5012.37 p60*
Tally, Dawson Sliza; Virginia, 1636 *6219 p21*
Tally, Elias; Virginia, 1637 *6219 p113*
Talmon, Catharina *SEE* Talmon, Pierre
Talmon, Catharina Mueller *SEE* Talmon, Pierre
Talmon, Frederic *SEE* Talmon, Pierre
Talmon, Jaques; Pennsylvania, 1754 *2444 p225*
Talmon, Jeanne *SEE* Talmon, Pierre
Talmon, Magdalena *SEE* Talmon, Pierre
Talmon, Marie; Port uncertain, 1754 *2444 p206*
Talmon, Pierre; Pennsylvania, 1754 *2444 p225*
  *Wife:*Catharina Mueller
  *Child:*Magdalena
  *Child:*Catharina
  *Child:*Jeanne
  *Child:*Frederic
Talpy, Mary 23; Massachusetts, 1849 *5881.1 p95*
Talty, Margaret 20; Massachusetts, 1849 *5881.1 p95*
Tam, Martin; Virginia, 1638 *6219 p121*
Tamaszaites, Jonas; Wisconsin, n.d. *9675.8 p122*
Tamaszaitis, Joe; Wisconsin, n.d. *9675.8 p122*
Tambaraud, B. 29; New Orleans, 1837 *778.5 p509*
Tamblingson, Nicholas; New York, NY, 1834 *8208.4 p34*
Tamboise, Victor 32; America, 1838 *778.5 p509*
Tamboise, Victoria 22; America, 1838 *778.5 p509*
Tamboli, Ciro; Wisconsin, n.d. *9675.8 p122*
Tamburi, J. 27; New Orleans, 1838 *778.5 p509*
Tame, Edward 21; Maryland, 1774 *1219.7 p196*
Tame, Henry; Virginia, 1642 *6219 p197*
Tamer, Thomas 21; Maryland, 1774 *1219.7 p230*
Tamey, Grace; New York, NY, 1865 *5704.8 p186*
Taming, Johan Olaf; Arkansas, 1918 *95.2 p120*
Tamis, George; Arkansas, 1918 *95.2 p120*
Tamis, Peter; Arkansas, 1918 *95.2 p65*
Tamis, Peter; Arkansas, 1918 *95.2 p121*
Tamlin, William 21; Kansas, 1875 *5240.1 p56*
Tamm, Henry 23; Kansas, 1884 *5240.1 p66*
Tamus, Frank; Arkansas, 1918 *95.2 p121*
Tanbrier, Jean 25; Port uncertain, 1839 *778.5 p510*
Tanch, Joseph 35; Maryland, 1775 *1219.7 p250*
Tancogno, Mr. 28; New Orleans, 1839 *778.5 p510*
Tancrod, John 19; Maryland, 1719 *3690.1 p221*
Tandy, Willi.; Virginia, 1643 *6219 p205*
Tane, Henry; Virginia, 1643 *6219 p205*
Tanesse, Mrs. 40; Louisiana, 1820 *778.5 p510*
Tanesse, J. 45; Louisiana, 1820 *778.5 p510*
Tanesse, Laura 15; Louisiana, 1820 *778.5 p510*
Tangalos, John Peter; Arkansas, 1918 *95.2 p121*
Tangeman, John B.; Cincinnati, 1869-1887 *8582 p32*
Tangen, Karl A.; Washington, 1859-1920 *2872.1 p40*
Tangnay, Dennis; America, 1854 *1450.2 p144A*
Tangreen, John Olaf; Arkansas, 1918 *95.2 p121*
Tankard, William 21; Maryland, 1774 *1219.7 p211*
Tankrod, John 19; Maryland, 1719 *3690.1 p221*
Tanna, Mr. 15; New Orleans, 1823 *778.5 p510*
Tannatt, John; Jamaica, 1762 *1219.7 p85*
Tanneberger, Anna Rosina *SEE* Tanneberger, Michael
Tanneberger, David; New York, 1749 *3652 p72*

Tanneberger, David; Savannah, GA, 1736 ***3652*** *p51*
*Relative:*John
Tanneberger, John *SEE* Tanneberger, David
Tanneberger, John; Georgia, 1736 ***4525*** *p203*
Tanneberger, Michael; Philadelphia, 1742 ***3652*** *p55*
*Wife:*Anna Rosina
Tannenberger, John; Georgia, 1736 ***4525*** *p203*
Tanner, Barbary; Virginia, 1635 ***6219*** *p26*
Tanner, George H.; New York, NY, 1836 ***8208.4*** *p18*
Tanner, John; New York, NY, 1816 ***2859.11*** *p43*
Tanner, John 20; West Indies, 1722 ***3690.1*** *p221*
Tanner, Tobias; Virginia, 1642 ***6219*** *p187*
Tannin, Lazar 28; America, 1838 ***778.5*** *p510*
Tanori, Fermin; Arkansas, 1918 ***95.2*** *p121*
Tanswell, Thomas-Joseph; Quebec, 1791 ***7603*** *p27*
Tanyes, Mr. 25; Port uncertain, 1836 ***778.5*** *p510*
Tapie, Jean 29; Port uncertain, 1837 ***778.5*** *p510*
Tapier, Mr. 17; Port uncertain, 1839 ***778.5*** *p510*
Tapking, Frederick H.; America, 1846 ***1450.2*** *p144A*
Tapley, John 44; Maryland, 1775 ***1219.7*** *p259*
Tapley, Jonath 22; America, 1704 ***2212*** *p41*
Taplin, Isaac 16; Maryland, 1775 ***1219.7*** *p264*
Tapp, Ann 16; Maryland, 1774 ***1219.7*** *p234*
Tapp, Anthony 27; Maryland, 1774 ***1219.7*** *p181*
Tapp, John; Quebec, 1800 ***7603*** *p22*
Tapp, Tho.; Virginia, 1643 ***6219*** *p203*
Tapp, William; New York, 1764 ***1219.7*** *p103*
Tappe, . . .; Canada, 1776-1783 ***9786*** *p35*
Tappey, William 26; Maryland, 1774 ***1219.7*** *p187*
Tappin, Hen.; Virginia, 1642 ***6219*** *p199*
Tapscott, William; New York, NY, 1837 ***8208.4*** *p44*
Tarantola, Joe; Arkansas, 1918 ***95.2*** *p121*
Tarbooke, Robert; Virginia, 1642 ***6219*** *p196*
Tardos, G. 25; New Orleans, 1838 ***778.5*** *p510*
Tarel, C.; New Orleans, 1839 ***778.5*** *p511*
Tareter, Edward 39; New Orleans, 1831 ***778.5*** *p511*
Targowski, Karol; New York, 1834 ***4606*** *p179*
Tarha, Morhige; Kansas, 1901 ***5240.1*** *p44*
Tarke Family ; America, 1885 ***4610.10*** *p76*
Tarke, Frederick 20; America, 1844 ***4610.10*** *p75*
Tarles, P. N.; New Orleans, 1839 ***778.5*** *p511*
Tarling, Richard; Virginia, 1636 ***6219*** *p78*
Tarlossi, Stanley; Arkansas, 1918 ***95.2*** *p121*
Tarlouse, . . .; Canada, 1776-1783 ***9786*** *p35*
Tarmdy, James 21; Maryland, 1775 ***1219.7*** *p267*
Tarminy, Godefroy 28; Ohio, 1837 ***778.5*** *p511*
Tarnapowicz, Jerzy 21; New York, 1912 ***9980.29*** *p63*
Tarresani, Katy; Iowa, 1866-1943 ***123.54*** *p48*
Tarrey, Thomas; Virginia, 1638 ***6219*** *p160*
Tarride, Jean-Baptiste 35; Port uncertain, 1838 ***778.5*** *p511*
Tarride, Jean-Marie 25; New Orleans, 1838 ***778.5*** *p511*
Tarrise, Mr.; Port uncertain, 1839 ***778.5*** *p511*
Tarrus, Mrs. 47; New Orleans, 1821 ***778.5*** *p511*
Tarrus, Charles C. 21; New Orleans, 1821 ***778.5*** *p511*
Tarrus, Marie L. 17; New Orleans, 1821 ***778.5*** *p511*
Tarter, Mr.; Quebec, 1815 ***9229.18*** *p79*
Taslakian, Vartan; Arkansas, 1918 ***95.2*** *p121*
Tassan, J. 28; Port uncertain, 1836 ***778.5*** *p511*
Tasse, Mr. 34; New Orleans, 1838 ***778.5*** *p511*
Tasse, L. 48; Port uncertain, 1839 ***778.5*** *p511*
Tassell, George 15; Maryland, 1718 ***3690.1*** *p221*
Tassell, Robt.; Virginia, 1635 ***6219*** *p16*
Tassemaker, Peter; America, 1671-1690 ***8125.8*** *p438*
Tassha, J. 34; America, 1831 ***778.5*** *p511*
Tassy, Luzane 45; Texas, 1827 ***778.5*** *p511*
Tatczak, Agnes 25; New York, 1912 ***9980.29*** *p57*
Tate, Ann; St. John, N.B., 1849 ***5704.8*** *p48*
Tate, Anne 2; New York, NY, 1868 ***5704.8*** *p231*
Tate, Elizabeth; New York, NY, 1868 ***5704.8*** *p231*
Tate, Elizabeth 20; Maryland, 1775 ***1219.7*** *p252*
Tate, Ellen; St. John, N.B., 1849 ***5704.8*** *p48*
Tate, James; New York, NY, 1811 ***2859.11*** *p20*
Tate, James; St. John, N.B., 1849 ***5704.8*** *p48*
Tate, Jane; St. John, N.B., 1849 ***5704.8*** *p48*
Tate, John; America, 1832 ***1450.2*** *p144A*
Tate, John; Charleston, SC, 1796 ***1639.20*** *p304*
Tate, John 25; Savannah, GA, 1774 ***1219.7*** *p226*
With wife
With 4 children
Tate, Margaret 9; St. John, N.B., 1849 ***5704.8*** *p48*
Tate, Martha 5; St. John, N.B., 1849 ***5704.8*** *p48*
Tate, Mary Ann 7; St. John, N.B., 1849 ***5704.8*** *p48*
Tate, Mary Ann 19; St. John, N.B., 1857 ***5704.8*** *p135*
Tate, Mathew 24; St. John, N.B., 1854 ***5704.8*** *p115*
Tate, Oliver 21; New York, 1775 ***1219.7*** *p246*
Tate, Samuel 13; St. John, N.B., 1849 ***5704.8*** *p48*
Tate, Sarah Jane; St. John, N.B., 1848 ***5704.8*** *p39*
Tate, Sarah Jane 11; St. John, N.B., 1849 ***5704.8*** *p48*
Tate, William; Philadelphia, 1853 ***5704.8*** *p108*
Tatem, Henry; Cincinnati, 1800-1877 ***8582.3*** *p86*
Tatham, John 32; Virginia, 1774 ***1219.7*** *p228*
Tatler, Thomas; Philadelphia, 1765 ***1219.7*** *p112*
Tatlocke, Edwd 22; America, 1702 ***2212*** *p39*
Taton, Samuel 15; Philadelphia, 1774 ***1219.7*** *p185*
Tatteray, Mrs. Jean-George; Died enroute, 1752 ***7074.6*** *p212*
Tatteray, Jean-George 30; Halifax, N.S., 1752 ***7074.6*** *p212*
*Sister:*Jeanne
Tatteray, Jeanne *SEE* Tatteray, Jean-George
Tattrie, . . .; Halifax, N.S., 1752 ***7074.6*** *p232*
Tattrie, George; Halifax, N.S., 1752 ***7074.6*** *p226*
Tatum, Ann *SEE* Tatum, Nathaniell
Tatum, Diana 25; North America, 1774 ***1219.7*** *p200*
Tatum, Mary *SEE* Tatum, Nathaniell
Tatum, Nathaniell; Virginia, 1638 ***6219*** *p122*
*Wife:*Ann
*Daughter:*Mary
Tatum, Ralph; Virginia, 1642 ***6219*** *p194*
Taub, J. W. 46; Harris Co., TX, 1898 ***6254*** *p4*
Taubenheim, Ludewig; Canada, 1783 ***9786*** *p38A*
Tauber, Friedrich; Cincinnati, 1830 ***8582.1*** *p51*
Taubert, Mr. 40; New Orleans, 1839 ***778.5*** *p512*
Taubert, Curt; Illinois, 1901 ***2896.5*** *p40*
Taubner, Fritz; Wisconsin, n.d. ***9675.8*** *p122*
Tauge, . . .; Canada, 1776-1783 ***9786*** *p43*
Taugndin, Toussaint; Port uncertain, 1839 ***778.5*** *p512*
Tauke, . . .; Ohio, 1832 ***8582.2*** *p49*
With family
Tauke, Johann Dietrich; Cincinnati, 1869-1887 ***8582*** *p32*
Tauley, F. 23; Port uncertain, 1838 ***778.5*** *p512*
Taurise, Mme.; Port uncertain, 1839 ***778.5*** *p512*
Taurise, Mr.; Port uncertain, 1839 ***778.5*** *p512*
With brother
Tauschmann, . . .; Canada, 1776-1783 ***9786*** *p35*
Tautwidas, Jonas; Wisconsin, n.d. ***9675.8*** *p122*
Tavelet, Edward 24; New Orleans, 1826 ***778.5*** *p512*
Taven, Andrew 32; Philadelphia, 1774 ***1219.7*** *p197*
Taverne, Francis; Virginia, 1642 ***6219*** *p196*
Taverner, George 21; North Carolina, 1774 ***1219.7*** *p215*
Tavernor, Giles; Virginia, 1639 ***6219*** *p162*
Tavlin, Patrick 23; Maryland, 1774 ***1219.7*** *p221*
Taw, Nicholas; New York, NY, 1838 ***8208.4*** *p64*
Tawney, James 37; Georgia, 1774 ***1219.7*** *p188*
Tawrel, Adam 20; New York, 1912 ***9980.29*** *p69*
Taya, A. 39; New Orleans, 1837 ***778.5*** *p512*
Tayerd, Arricter 3; New Orleans, 1836 ***778.5*** *p512*
Tayerd, Ernest 9; New Orleans, 1836 ***778.5*** *p512*
Tayerd, L. 42; New Orleans, 1836 ***778.5*** *p512*
Tayerd, Victorine 29; New Orleans, 1836 ***778.5*** *p512*
Taylar, Eliza; New York, NY, 1867 ***5704.8*** *p218*
Taylar, James; New York, NY, 1867 ***5704.8*** *p218*
Tayler, Andrew 18; Jamaica, 1730 ***3690.1*** *p291*
Tayler, Charles; Virginia, 1698 ***2212*** *p11*
Tayler, David; Virginia, 1698 ***2212*** *p11*
Tayler, John; Virginia, 1698 ***2212*** *p14*
Tayler, John 17; Jamaica, 1725 ***3690.1*** *p221*
Tayler, John 19; Jamaica, 1722 ***3690.1*** *p221*
Tayler, Mary 22; New England, 1699 ***2212*** *p19*
Tayler, Nathaniel; Virginia, 1698 ***2212*** *p11*
Tayler, Roger; Virginia, 1698 ***2212*** *p12*
Tayler, Tho; Virginia, 1698 ***2212*** *p11*
Tayler, Thomas 15; Virginia, 1720 ***3690.1*** *p221*
Tayler, Thomas 35; Maryland, 1725 ***3690.1*** *p221*
Tayler, William 19; Jamaica, 1730 ***3690.1*** *p221*
Tayler, William 19; Maryland, 1722 ***3690.1*** *p221*
Tayler, William 23; Maryland, 1730 ***3690.1*** *p291*
Tayler, Wm; Virginia, 1698 ***2212*** *p11*
Taylior, Robert; Maryland, 1756 ***3690.1*** *p221*
Taylor, Colonel; Quebec, 1815 ***9229.18*** *p75*
With wife
With 2 daughters
Taylor, Mr.; Wilmington, NC, 1811 ***1639.20*** *p304*
Taylor, Mr. 22; Jamaica, 1775 ***1219.7*** *p260*
Taylor, Abraham 20; Georgia, 1738 ***9332*** *p329*
Taylor, Alexander; Charleston, SC, 1793 ***1639.20*** *p304*
Taylor, Alexander; Charleston, SC, 1797 ***1639.20*** *p304*
Taylor, Alexander P.; New York, NY, 1834 ***8208.4*** *p77*
Taylor, Angus 71; North Carolina, 1850 ***1639.20*** *p304*
Taylor, Ann; America, 1742 ***4971*** *p17*
Taylor, Ann; Raleigh, NC, 1829 ***1639.20*** *p304*
Taylor, Ann 26 *SEE* Taylor, Michael
Taylor, Ann 27 *SEE* Taylor, Solomon
Taylor, Ann 40; Philadelphia, 1775 ***1219.7*** *p257*
Taylor, Anna *SEE* Taylor, Elias
Taylor, Anne; Philadelphia, 1851 ***5704.8*** *p70*
Taylor, Anne; St. John, N.B., 1847 ***5704.8*** *p4*
Taylor, Anne 18; Philadelphia, 1859 ***5704.8*** *p142*
Taylor, Anne J.; New York, NY, 1870 ***5704.8*** *p237*
Taylor, Anthony; Virginia, 1637 ***6219*** *p10*
Taylor, Arthur; Virginia, 1637 ***6219*** *p17*
Taylor, Arthur; Virginia, 1642 ***6219*** *p194*
Taylor, Barbara 40; Wilmington, NC, 1774 ***1639.20*** *p201*
Taylor, Bella 20; Philadelphia, 1853 ***5704.8*** *p113*
Taylor, Benjamin 15; Philadelphia, 1775 ***1219.7*** *p248*
Taylor, Benjamin 21; Maryland, 1774 ***1219.7*** *p179*
Taylor, Betty 3 *SEE* Taylor, William
Taylor, Betty 3; Philadelphia, 1849 ***5704.8*** *p54*
Taylor, Bridget; St. John, N.B., 1847 ***5704.8*** *p25*
Taylor, Catharine 22; Massachusetts, 1849 ***5881.1*** *p94*
Taylor, Charles 41; Virginia, 1773 ***1219.7*** *p168*
Taylor, Christoph; Wisconsin, n.d. ***9675.8*** *p122*
Taylor, Daniel; Philadelphia, 1749-1773 ***9973.7*** *p40*
Taylor, Daniel 18; Pennsylvania, 1723 ***3690.1*** *p221*
Taylor, Daniell 26; Jamaica, 1736 ***3690.1*** *p221*
Taylor, David *SEE* Taylor, William
Taylor, David; Austin, TX, 1886 ***9777*** *p5*
Taylor, David; Philadelphia, 1849 ***5704.8*** *p54*
Taylor, Dean 28; Philadelphia, 1774 ***1219.7*** *p233*
Taylor, Dick; St. John, N.B., 1847 ***5704.8*** *p10*
Taylor, Easy; St. John, N.B., 1847 ***5704.8*** *p10*
Taylor, Edward 19; Maryland, 1774 ***1219.7*** *p204*
Taylor, Edward 45; St. John, N.B., 1856 ***5704.8*** *p131*
Taylor, Eleonore Crowe; Montreal, 1824 ***7603*** *p98*
Taylor, Elias; Virginia, 1640 ***6219*** *p181*
*Wife:*Anna
Taylor, Mrs. Elias; Virginia, 1648 ***6219*** *p246*
With daughter
Taylor, Elias; Virginia, 1648 ***6219*** *p246*
Taylor, Eliz.; Virginia, 1643 ***6219*** *p229*
Taylor, Eliza; Philadelphia, 1867 ***5704.8*** *p216*
Taylor, Eliza 1; Quebec, 1864 ***5704.8*** *p159*
Taylor, Eliza 20; Quebec, 1866 ***5704.8*** *p167*
Taylor, Elizabeth 19; Virginia, 1719 ***3690.1*** *p222*
Taylor, Ellen 19; America, 1705 ***2212*** *p45*
Taylor, Esther J.; St. John, N.B., 1847 ***5704.8*** *p10*
Taylor, Fanny; Philadelphia, 1847 ***53.26*** *p87*
Taylor, Fanny; Philadelphia, 1847 ***5704.8*** *p30*
Taylor, Geo.; Virginia, 1639 ***6219*** *p22*
Taylor, George; Virginia, 1637 ***6219*** *p82*
Taylor, George; Washington, 1859-1920 ***2872.1*** *p40*
Taylor, George 20; Pennsylvania, 1738 ***3690.1*** *p222*
Taylor, George 25; North America, 1774 ***1219.7*** *p198*
Taylor, George 29; Maryland, 1775 ***1219.7*** *p253*
Taylor, George 40; Massachusetts, 1849 ***5881.1*** *p94*
Taylor, George M.; St. John, N.B., 1848 ***5704.8*** *p44*
Taylor, George W.; Washington, 1859-1920 ***2872.1*** *p40*
Taylor, Giles; Virginia, 1638 ***6219*** *p119*
Taylor, Guy; Virginia, 1636 ***6219*** *p108*
Taylor, Henry; Virginia, 1635 ***6219*** *p69*
Taylor, Henry 22; Maryland, 1775 ***1219.7*** *p252*
Taylor, Henry 24; Philadelphia, 1774 ***1219.7*** *p196*
Taylor, Isaac; New Bern, NC, 1762-1846 ***1639.20*** *p304*
Taylor, Isaac; Virginia, 1698 ***2212*** *p14*
Taylor, Isaac 5 *SEE* Taylor, William
Taylor, Isaac 5; Philadelphia, 1849 ***5704.8*** *p54*
Taylor, Isabel; South Carolina, 1767 ***1639.20*** *p304*
Taylor, Isabella; Philadelphia, 1867 ***5704.8*** *p216*
Taylor, James *SEE* Taylor, James
Taylor, James; Austin, TX, 1886 ***9777*** *p5*
Taylor, James; New York, NY, 1811 ***2859.11*** *p20*
Taylor, James; Ohio, 1840 ***9892.11*** *p45*
Taylor, James; Philadelphia, 1847 ***53.26*** *p87*
Taylor, James; Philadelphia, 1847 ***53.26*** *p87*
*Relative:*Martha
*Relative:*James
*Relative:*Stephen
*Relative:*Thomas
Taylor, James; Philadelphia, 1847 ***5704.8*** *p2*
Taylor, James; Philadelphia, 1847 ***5704.8*** *p24*
Taylor, James; Philadelphia, 1850 ***53.26*** *p87*
Taylor, James; Philadelphia, 1850 ***5704.8*** *p60*
Taylor, James; Quebec, 1847 ***5704.8*** *p29*
Taylor, James; Quebec, 1847 ***5704.8*** *p36*
Taylor, James; Virginia, 1638 ***6219*** *p121*
Taylor, James; Virginia, 1643 ***6219*** *p204*
Taylor, James 7; St. John, N.B., 1847 ***5704.8*** *p10*
Taylor, James 15; Maryland, 1775 ***1219.7*** *p272*
Taylor, James 18; Virginia, 1721 ***3690.1*** *p222*
Taylor, James 30; Quebec, 1862 ***5704.8*** *p151*
Taylor, James 32; Port uncertain, 1774 ***1219.7*** *p176*
Taylor, Jane; Philadelphia, 1851 ***5704.8*** *p80*
Taylor, Jane; Virginia, 1643 ***6219*** *p206*
Taylor, Jane 8 *SEE* Taylor, William
Taylor, Jane 8; Philadelphia, 1849 ***5704.8*** *p54*
Taylor, Jane 23; Georgia, 1775 ***1219.7*** *p277*
Taylor, Jane 24; Philadelphia, 1853 ***5704.8*** *p111*
Taylor, Jane 45; Maryland, 1774 ***1219.7*** *p190*
Taylor, Janet Armour *SEE* Taylor, William
Taylor, Jerom 26; America, 1699 ***2212*** *p28*
Taylor, Jno 16; America, 1705 ***2212*** *p43*
Taylor, John; Arkansas, 1918 ***95.2*** *p121*
Taylor, John; Charleston, SC, 1799 ***1639.20*** *p305*
Taylor, John; Illinois, 1888 ***5012.39*** *p121*
Taylor, John; New York, NY, 1838 ***8208.4*** *p65*
Taylor, John; Ohio, 1826 ***9892.11*** *p45*
Taylor, John; Ohio, 1842 ***9892.11*** *p45*
Taylor, John; Ohio, 1844 ***9892.11*** *p45*

Taylor, John; Philadelphia, 1759 ***9973.7*** *p34*
Taylor, John; Philadelphia, 1852 ***5704.8*** *p89*
Taylor, John; Philadelphia, 1864 ***5704.8*** *p185*
Taylor, John; Quebec, 1847 ***5704.8*** *p29*
Taylor, John; Virginia, 1635 ***6219*** *p10*
Taylor, John; Virginia, 1635 ***6219*** *p69*
Taylor, John; Virginia, 1636 ***6219*** *p19*
Taylor, John; Virginia, 1637 ***6219*** *p111*
Taylor, John; Virginia, 1638 ***6219*** *p119*
Taylor, John; Virginia, 1648 ***6219*** *p250*
Taylor, John; Virginia, 1698 ***2212*** *p15*
Taylor, John; West Virginia, 1860 ***9788.3*** *p21*
Taylor, John 4; Quebec, 1864 ***5704.8*** *p159*
Taylor, John 12; St. John, N.B., 1847 ***5704.8*** *p10*
Taylor, John 15; Philadelphia, 1774 ***1219.7*** *p197*
Taylor, John 16; Jamaica, 1754 ***1219.7*** *p27*
Taylor, John 16; Jamaica, 1754 ***3690.1*** *p222*
Taylor, John 18; Barbados, 1720 ***3690.1*** *p222*
Taylor, John 19; Maryland or Virginia, 1735 ***3690.1*** *p222*
Taylor, John 21; Maryland, 1775 ***1219.7*** *p261*
Taylor, John 21; Maryland, 1775 ***1219.7*** *p268*
Taylor, John 21; Virginia, 1774 ***1219.7*** *p243*
Taylor, John 22; Jamaica, 1731 ***3690.1*** *p222*
Taylor, John 33; Maryland, 1774 ***1219.7*** *p229*
Taylor, Joseph; Illinois, 1888 ***5012.37*** *p62*
Taylor, Joshua 22; St. Kitts, 1699 ***2212*** *p25*
Taylor, Lancelot 26; Maryland, 1774 ***1219.7*** *p180*
Taylor, Louisa; New York, NY, 1811 ***2859.11*** *p20*
Taylor, Margaret; New York, NY, 1869 ***5704.8*** *p233*
Taylor, Margaret; Philadelphia, 1852 ***5704.8*** *p96*
Taylor, Margaret 21; Philadelphia, 1853 ***5704.8*** *p113*
Taylor, Margarett *SEE* Taylor, Stephen
Taylor, Margartt 18; America, 1702 ***2212*** *p39*
Taylor, Marguerite; Quebec, 1793 ***7603*** *p66*
Taylor, Marion 21; Wilmington, NC, 1774 ***1639.20*** *p77*
Taylor, Martha *SEE* Taylor, James
Taylor, Martha; Philadelphia, 1847 ***5704.8*** *p2*
Taylor, Martha; Philadelphia, 1851 ***5704.8*** *p80*
Taylor, Mary *SEE* Taylor, Telephore
Taylor, Mary; Philadelphia, 1851 ***5704.8*** *p80*
Taylor, Mary; St. John, N.B., 1847 ***5704.8*** *p4*
Taylor, Mary 4; St. John, N.B., 1847 ***5704.8*** *p4*
Taylor, Mary 9; Quebec, 1864 ***5704.8*** *p159*
Taylor, Mary 16; Philadelphia, 1859 ***5704.8*** *p142*
Taylor, Mary 17; America, 1706 ***2212*** *p46*
Taylor, Mary 18; America, 1701 ***2212*** *p35*
Taylor, Mary 18; Philadelphia, 1854 ***5704.8*** *p117*
Taylor, Mary 34; Maryland or Virginia, 1699 ***2212*** *p23*
Taylor, Mary 40; Quebec, 1864 ***5704.8*** *p159*
Taylor, Mary Ann; St. John, N.B., 1848 ***5704.8*** *p38*
Taylor, Mathew 19; St. John, N.B., 1864 ***5704.8*** *p157*
Taylor, Matilda; New York, NY, 1870 ***5704.8*** *p237*
Taylor, Matthew 24; Jamaica, 1736 ***3690.1*** *p222*
Taylor, Michael; New York, NY, 1816 ***2859.11*** *p43*
Taylor, Michael 23; North America, 1774 ***1219.7*** *p199*
Taylor, Michael 45; North America, 1774 ***1219.7*** *p198*
*Wife:*Ann 26
Taylor, Nancy *SEE* Taylor, William
Taylor, Nancy; Philadelphia, 1849 ***5704.8*** *p54*
Taylor, Neal 22; Quebec, 1855 ***5704.8*** *p126*
Taylor, Patrick; St. John, N.B., 1847 ***5704.8*** *p4*
Taylor, Patrick; St. John, N.B., 1847 ***5704.8*** *p5*
Taylor, Percy 24; Kansas, 1888 ***5240.1*** *p73*
Taylor, Peter; Philadelphia, 1817 ***9892.11*** *p45*
Taylor, Peter; Virginia, 1642 ***6219*** *p192*
Taylor, Phillipp; Virginia, 1637 ***6219*** *p110*
With wife
Taylor, Phillipp, Sr.; Virginia, 1643 ***6219*** *p206*
Taylor, Ralph; Virginia, 1642 ***6219*** *p198*
Taylor, Ralph 33; Jamaica, 1731-1732 ***3690.1*** *p222*
Taylor, Rebecca 27; Philadelphia, 1853 ***5704.8*** *p111*
Taylor, Richard; New York, NY, 1816 ***2859.11*** *p43*
Taylor, Richard; Quebec, 1712 ***7603*** *p24*
Taylor, Richard 18; Virginia, 1720 ***3690.1*** *p222*
Taylor, Richard 25; Philadelphia, 1774 ***1219.7*** *p196*
Taylor, Robert; Maryland, 1756 ***1219.7*** *p47*
Taylor, Robert; New York, NY, 1838 ***8208.4*** *p86*
Taylor, Robert; Ohio, 1870-1888 ***9892.11*** *p45*
Taylor, Robert; Virginia, 1639 ***6219*** *p153*
Taylor, Robert; Virginia, 1642 ***6219*** *p197*
Taylor, Robert; Virginia, 1643 ***6219*** *p204*
Taylor, Robert; Virginia, 1648 ***6219*** *p241*
Taylor, Robert 20; Philadelphia, 1854 ***5704.8*** *p117*
Taylor, Robert 26; Philadelphia, 1774 ***1219.7*** *p183*
Taylor, Robert 28; Nova Scotia, 1774 ***1219.7*** *p210*
Taylor, Samll.; Virginia, 1637 ***6219*** *p82*
Taylor, Samuel; New York, NY, 1864 ***5704.8*** *p173*
Taylor, Samuel; Philadelphia, 1867 ***5704.8*** *p216*
Taylor, Samuel; St. John, N.B., 1847 ***5704.8*** *p10*
Taylor, Samuel 28; Virginia, 1774 ***1219.7*** *p242*
Taylor, Sarah 16; Philadelphia, 1858 ***5704.8*** *p139*
Taylor, Simon 21; Maryland, 1775 ***1219.7*** *p247*
Taylor, Solomon 25; Virginia, 1774 ***1219.7*** *p240*
*Wife:*Ann 27
Taylor, Stephen *SEE* Taylor, James
Taylor, Stephen; Philadelphia, 1847 ***5704.8*** *p2*
Taylor, Stephen; Virginia, 1644 ***6219*** *p229*
*Wife:*Margarett
Taylor, Telephore; New Hampshire, 1891 ***3455.3*** *p108*
*Wife:*Mary
Taylor, Telesphare; New Hampshire, 1891 ***3455.2*** *p49*
Taylor, Tho.; Virginia, 1635 ***6219*** *p17*
Taylor, Tho.; Virginia, 1635 ***6219*** *p20*
Taylor, Tho.; Virginia, 1642 ***6219*** *p195*
Taylor, Tho.; Virginia, 1642 ***6219*** *p197*
Taylor, Thomas *SEE* Taylor, James
Taylor, Thomas; America, 1743 ***4971*** *p69*
Taylor, Thomas; Ohio, 1840 ***9892.11*** *p45*
Taylor, Thomas; Philadelphia, 1847 ***5704.8*** *p2*
Taylor, Thomas; Virginia, 1637 ***6219*** *p83*
Taylor, Thomas; Virginia, 1637 ***6219*** *p107*
Taylor, Thomas; Virginia, 1639 ***6219*** *p152*
Taylor, Thomas; Virginia, 1639 ***6219*** *p158*
Taylor, Thomas; Virginia, 1640 ***6219*** *p181*
Taylor, Thomas 14; America, 1704 ***2212*** *p41*
Taylor, Thomas 17; St. John, N.B., 1856 ***5704.8*** *p131*
Taylor, Thomas 19; Jamaica, 1735 ***3690.1*** *p222*
Taylor, Thomas 20; United States or West Indies, 1721 ***3690.1*** *p222*
Taylor, Thomas 21; Philadelphia, 1774 ***1219.7*** *p232*
Taylor, Thomas 22; Georgia, 1775 ***1219.7*** *p277*
Taylor, William; Illinois, 1866 ***5012.37*** *p59*
Taylor, William; Jamaica, 1754 ***1219.7*** *p30*
Taylor, William; New Bern, NC, 1835 ***1639.20*** *p305*
Taylor, William; New York, NY, 1830 ***8894.2*** *p57*
*Wife:*Janet Armour
Taylor, William; New York, NY, 1838 ***8208.4*** *p67*
Taylor, William; Ohio, 1840 ***9892.11*** *p45*
Taylor, William; Ohio, 1844 ***9892.11*** *p46*
Taylor, William; Philadelphia, 1849 ***53.26*** *p87*
*Relative:*Nancy
*Relative:*Jane 8
*Relative:*Isaac 5
*Relative:*Betty 3
*Relative:*William 3 mos
*Relative:*David
Taylor, William; Philadelphia, 1849 ***5704.8*** *p54*
Taylor, William; South Carolina, 1767 ***1639.20*** *p305*
Taylor, William; Texas, 1880-1889 ***9777*** *p6*
Taylor, William; Virginia, 1638 ***6219*** *p33*
Taylor, William; Virginia, 1638 ***6219*** *p120*
Taylor, William; Virginia, 1638 ***6219*** *p122*
Taylor, William; Virginia, 1640 ***6219*** *p181*
Taylor, William; Virginia, 1648 ***6219*** *p250*
Taylor, William 3 mos *SEE* Taylor, William
Taylor, William 11; Quebec, 1864 ***5704.8*** *p159*
Taylor, William 20; Maryland or Virginia, 1734 ***3690.1*** *p223*
Taylor, William 21; Maryland, 1774 ***1219.7*** *p179*
Taylor, William 24; Jamaica, 1730 ***3690.1*** *p222*
Taylor, William 26; Philadelphia, 1857 ***5704.8*** *p132*
Taylor, William H.; America, 1867 ***5704.8*** *p224*
Taylor, William John 3 mos; Philadelphia, 1849 ***5704.8*** *p54*
Taylor, William O.; America, 1865 ***1450.2*** *p144A*
Taylor, Wm.; Virginia, 1636 ***6219*** *p7*
Taylor, Wm.; Virginia, 1648 ***6219*** *p246*
Taylor, Xtopr.; Virginia, 1645 ***6219*** *p233*
Taylor, Zachariah; Virginia, 1637 ***6219*** *p86*
Taylor, Zachariah; Virginia, 1638 ***6219*** *p123*
Tayton, Dominique 40; New Orleans, 1836 ***778.5*** *p512*
Tayton, Mary 18; St. Kitts, 1774 ***1219.7*** *p245*
Tazbir, Kazimiera Kowalski; Iowa, 1866-1943 ***123.54*** *p81*
Tazin, Jean Pierre 27; Mexico, 1835 ***778.5*** *p512*
Tchokatzoglou, Basil; Arkansas, 1918 ***95.2*** *p121*
Teadley, George; Philadelphia, 1867 ***5704.8*** *p221*
Teague, Bridget 17; Massachusetts, 1849 ***5881.1*** *p94*
Teague, Peter; New York, NY, 1865 ***5704.8*** *p195*
Teal, Christopher; New York, NY, 1836 ***8208.4*** *p18*
Tear, James; Philadelphia, 1852 ***5704.8*** *p97*
Tear, Margaret; Philadelphia, 1853 ***5704.8*** *p100*
Tear, Rebecca; Philadelphia, 1853 ***5704.8*** *p100*
Tear, William 31; New York, 1775 ***1219.7*** *p246*
Tearhan, Daniel 12; Massachusetts, 1850 ***5881.1*** *p94*
Tearhan, Margaret 10; Massachusetts, 1850 ***5881.1*** *p95*
Tearhan, Patrick 14; Massachusetts, 1850 ***5881.1*** *p95*
Tearhan, Patrick 58; Massachusetts, 1850 ***5881.1*** *p95*
Tearnan, Catharine 21; Massachusetts, 1849 ***5881.1*** *p94*
Tearnan, James 27; Massachusetts, 1847 ***5881.1*** *p94*
Tearnan, Mark 5; Massachusetts, 1849 ***5881.1*** *p95*
Tearnan, Mary 3; Massachusetts, 1849 ***5881.1*** *p95*
Tearnan, Matthew; America, 1741 ***4971*** *p94*
Tearnan, Patrick 18; Massachusetts, 1849 ***5881.1*** *p95*
Tearnan, Sally 43; Massachusetts, 1847 ***5881.1*** *p95*
Tearnin, Mark 5; Massachusetts, 1849 ***5881.1*** *p95*
Tearnin, Michael 15; Massachusetts, 1849 ***5881.1*** *p95*
Tearsay, Thomas 19; Massachusetts, 1847 ***5881.1*** *p95*
Teas, Easter; New York, NY, 1811 ***2859.11*** *p20*
Teasdale, John 20; Maryland, 1774 ***1219.7*** *p208*
Tease, John; Philadelphia, 1848 ***53.26*** *p87*
Tease, John; Philadelphia, 1848 ***5704.8*** *p40*
Tease, Margaret *SEE* Tease, Samuel
Tease, Margaret; Philadelphia, 1848 ***5704.8*** *p40*
Tease, Nancy; Philadelphia, 1851 ***5704.8*** *p78*
Tease, Samuel; Philadelphia, 1848 ***53.26*** *p87*
*Relative:*Margaret
Tease, Samuel; Philadelphia, 1848 ***5704.8*** *p40*
Tease, Samuel Sinclair; Washington, 1859-1920 ***2872.1*** *p40*
Teau, Jury 32; New Orleans, 1830 ***778.5*** *p512*
Tebbs, Nathaniell 18; Jamaica, 1736 ***3690.1*** *p223*
Tebelmann, John; Cincinnati, 1869-1887 ***8582*** *p32*
Teber, Michael; Wisconsin, n.d. ***9675.8*** *p122*
Teckenbrock, Christian; America, 1850 ***1450.2*** *p144A*
Teckle, Elizabeth 40 *SEE* Teckle, John
Teckle, John 42; Halifax, N.S., 1774 ***1219.7*** *p213*
*Wife:*Elizabeth 40
Tedford, Isabella; Quebec, 1847 ***5704.8*** *p13*
Tedford, William; Quebec, 1847 ***5704.8*** *p13*
Tedley, Henry; Philadelphia, 1847 ***53.26*** *p88*
Tedley, Henry; Philadelphia, 1847 ***5704.8*** *p23*
Tedmund, Edm.; Virginia, 1648 ***6219*** *p251*
Tee, Richard; New York, NY, 1864 ***5704.8*** *p174*
Teebot, Nathaniel 25; Maryland, 1727 ***3690.1*** *p223*
Teed, Samuel 27; Jamaica, 1723 ***3690.1*** *p226*
Teeds, Bridget 25; Massachusetts, 1847 ***5881.1*** *p94*
Teel, Margaret 26; Philadelphia, 1803 ***53.26*** *p88*
Teem, Frank; Wisconsin, n.d. ***9675.8*** *p122*
Teer, Daniel; Pennsylvania, 1751 ***2444*** *p226*
Teesdale, John; Ohio, 1840 ***9892.11*** *p26*
Teffner, . . .; Canada, 1776-1783 ***9786*** *p35*
Teffner, Georges; Canada, 1776-1783 ***9786*** *p243*
Teffoe, Daniel 24; Philadelphia, 1775 ***1219.7*** *p258*
Tefft, William; Washington, 1859-1920 ***2872.1*** *p40*
Tegel, Catherine 6; America, 1835 ***778.5*** *p513*
Tegel, Dorothea 40; America, 1835 ***778.5*** *p513*
Tegel, George 29; America, 1835 ***778.5*** *p513*
Tegel, Marguerite 9; America, 1835 ***778.5*** *p513*
Tegel, Michel 24; America, 1835 ***778.5*** *p513*
Tegel, Michel 40; America, 1835 ***778.5*** *p513*
Tegeler, Henry; Wisconsin, n.d. ***9675.8*** *p122*
Tegge, Fritz 24; Kansas, 1877 ***5240.1*** *p58*
Tegnnori, J.; Milwaukee, 1875 ***4719.30*** *p258*
Tegtmeyer, Otto E. W.; New York, NY, 1913 ***3455.4*** *p25*
Tegtmeyer, Otto Elmer Wilhelm; New York, NY, 1913 ***3455.3*** *p112*
Tehan, Ann *SEE* Tehan, Patrick
Tehan, Ann; Philadelphia, 1849 ***5704.8*** *p50*
Tehan, Bessy 2 *SEE* Tehan, Patrick
Tehan, Bessy 2; Philadelphia, 1849 ***5704.8*** *p50*
Tehan, Patrick; Philadelphia, 1849 ***53.26*** *p88*
*Relative:*Ann
*Relative:*Bessy 2
Tehan, Patrick; Philadelphia, 1849 ***5704.8*** *p50*
Tehtmeyer, . . .; Canada, 1776-1783 ***9786*** *p35*
Teibe, . . .; Canada, 1783 ***9786*** *p38A*
Teichfuss, William Henry 26; Kansas, 1872 ***5240.1*** *p53*
Teichman, Gottfried 36; New Orleans, 1839 ***9420.2*** *p359*
Teichmoeller, Georg; America, 1853 ***8582.3*** *p64*
Teilkemeier, Carl Heinr. Fr.; America, 1881 ***4610.10*** *p137*
Teilkemeyer, Carl Friedrich Wilhelm; America, 1852 ***4610.10*** *p156*
Teilkemeyer, Carl Heinrich; America, 1844 ***4610.10*** *p154*
Teipel, Peter; America, 1847 ***8582.3*** *p64*
Teirch, John 13; New Orleans, 1827 ***778.5*** *p513*
Teirny, Michael 23; Quebec, 1856 ***5704.8*** *p130*
Teissen, Lijntijen; Pennsylvania, 1683 ***2155*** *p1*
Teissier, J. B. 19; America, 1832 ***778.5*** *p513*
Teisson, Dirck; Pennsylvania, 1683 ***2155*** *p2*
Teisson, Reyneir; Pennsylvania, 1683 ***2155*** *p2*
Tekir, Caroline 40; America, 1838 ***778.5*** *p513*
Tekir, Franc. 26; America, 1838 ***778.5*** *p513*
Telesinska, Wladislawa 31; New York, 1912 ***9980.29*** *p49*
Telfair, Thomas; North Carolina, 1793 ***1639.20*** *p305*
Telford, Henry B.; Michigan, 1895 ***1450.2*** *p39B*
Telford, John 16; Virginia, 1774 ***1219.7*** *p205*
Telford, John 17; Quebec, 1864 ***5704.8*** *p162*
Telford, Thomas 29; Quebec, 1864 ***5704.8*** *p164*
Teliga, . . .; New York, 1831 ***4606*** *p177*
Teline, Nicholas; Wisconsin, n.d. ***9675.8*** *p122*
Tellefson, Jacob A.; Wisconsin, n.d. ***9675.8*** *p122*
Tellier, P. S. 37; Kansas, 1893 ***5240.1*** *p77*
Tellier Velol, Mr. 30?; America, 1838 ***778.5*** *p513*

Telliet, Mme. 45; New Orleans, 1838 ***778.5*** *p513*
Tellotte, Elesine 35; Port uncertain, 1839 ***778.5*** *p513*
Tellotte, Marie 28; Port uncertain, 1839 ***778.5*** *p513*
Telp, George; Philadelphia, 1756 ***9973.7*** *p32*
Telsa, Nicholas; Arkansas, 1918 ***95.2*** *p121*
Telsier, Peter; New York, NY, 1836 ***8208.4*** *p23*
Telson, Elkana; America, 1698 ***2212*** *p5*
Telteng, John 26; Philadelphia, 1774 ***1219.7*** *p185*
Temen, Robert; New York, NY, 1816 ***2859.11*** *p43*
Temes, Joseph 29; Kansas, 1878 ***5240.1*** *p59*
Temke, Anna Marie 52; America, 1850 ***4610.10*** *p135*
*Son:*Gottlieb
Temke, Gottlieb *SEE* Temke, Anna Marie
Temme, . . .; Canada, 1776-1783 ***9786*** *p35*
Temmen, Johann Hermann; America, 1845 ***8582.3*** *p64*
Tempcke, Anna Cath. Ilsabein; America, 1844 ***4610.10*** *p134*
Temperance, John; Virginia, 1642 ***6219*** *p189*
Tempest, Robt.; Virginia, 1635 ***6219*** *p17*
Templar, John 17; Maryland, 1775 ***1219.7*** *p271*
Temple, Andrew 2 *SEE* Temple, Ann
Temple, Andrew 2; Philadelphia, 1847 ***5704.8*** *p14*
Temple, Ann; Philadelphia, 1847 ***53.26*** *p88*
*Relative:*Isabella
*Relative:*James
*Relative:*Mary Ann 11
*Relative:*Hamilton 7
*Relative:*John 4
*Relative:*Andrew 2
Temple, Ann; Philadelphia, 1847 ***5704.8*** *p14*
Temple, Eliza; Philadelphia, 1853 ***5704.8*** *p108*
Temple, Francis; Philadelphia, 1853 ***5704.8*** *p108*
Temple, Hamilton 7 *SEE* Temple, Ann
Temple, Hamilton 7; Philadelphia, 1847 ***5704.8*** *p14*
Temple, Isabella *SEE* Temple, Ann
Temple, Isabella; Philadelphia, 1847 ***5704.8*** *p14*
Temple, James *SEE* Temple, Ann
Temple, James; Philadelphia, 1847 ***5704.8*** *p14*
Temple, John; Washington, 1869 ***2764.35*** *p68*
Temple, John 4 *SEE* Temple, Ann
Temple, John 4; Philadelphia, 1847 ***5704.8*** *p14*
Temple, John 25; Maryland, 1722 ***3690.1*** *p223*
Temple, Mary; Philadelphia, 1853 ***5704.8*** *p108*
Temple, Mary Ann 11 *SEE* Temple, Ann
Temple, Mary Ann 11; Philadelphia, 1847 ***5704.8*** *p14*
Temple, Robert 33; Maryland, 1774 ***1219.7*** *p187*
Templeman, Edward 16; Maryland, 1724 ***3690.1*** *p223*
Templeman, John 17; Maryland, 1729 ***3690.1*** *p223*
Templeman, William 28; Carolina, 1774 ***1219.7*** *p225*
Templemeier, William; America, 1893 ***1450.2*** *p144A*
Templeton, Elizabeth; Philadelphia, 1849 ***53.26*** *p88*
Templeton, Elizabeth; Philadelphia, 1849 ***5704.8*** *p50*
Templeton, James Augustus; Kansas, 1916 ***6013.40*** *p17*
Templeton, William; New York, NY, 1815 ***2859.11*** *p43*
Tenches, Edward; Virginia, 1637 ***6219*** *p83*
Tenerbaum, Sol; Arkansas, 1918 ***95.2*** *p121*
Tenfel, Karl Albert; Arkansas, 1918 ***95.2*** *p121*
Tengesdal, Jargen Larson; Arkansas, 1918 ***95.2*** *p121*
Tengstrom, Gustav 31; Arkansas, 1918 ***95.2*** *p121*
Tenieres, N. 21; New Orleans, 1822 ***778.5*** *p513*
Tenissier, Christian 10; America, 1839 ***778.5*** *p514*
Tenissier, Jean R. 29; America, 1839 ***778.5*** *p514*
Tenissier, Josephine 21; America, 1839 ***778.5*** *p514*
Tenlenden, Henry; Wisconsin, n.d. ***9675.8*** *p122*
Tenman, Robert; Virginia, 1636 ***6219*** *p10*
Tennan, James; Massachusetts, 1847 ***5881.1*** *p94*
Tennant, Betty 16; Virginia, 1774 ***1219.7*** *p215*
Tennant, Christopher; Virginia, 1635 ***6219*** *p69*
Tennant, James; Carolina, 1684 ***1639.20*** *p305*
Tennant, Robert; Charleston, SC, 1787-1813 ***1639.20*** *p305*
Tennant, William; South Carolina, 1734 ***1639.20*** *p305*
Tenner, Benja.; Virginia, 1643 ***6219*** *p229*
Tennessen, John; Wisconsin, n.d. ***9675.8*** *p122*
Tennison, William 20; Jamaica, 1721 ***3690.1*** *p223*
Tennstadt, Albert 62; New Orleans, 1839 ***9420.2*** *p358*
*Wife:*Dorost. Elizab. 64
Tennstadt, Dorost. Elizab. 64 *SEE* Tennstadt, Albert
Tenon, Mr. 22; New Orleans, 1839 ***778.5*** *p514*
Tenpin, Joseph 24; Massachusetts, 1849 ***5881.1*** *p94*
Tentschel, A. S. 48; Kansas, 1873 ***5240.1*** *p53*
TenVoorde, George T.; Indiana, 1848 ***9117*** *p18*
Tenvoorde, John; Indiana, 1847 ***9117*** *p19*
Tenz, Ernst Moritz 31; New Orleans, 1839 ***9420.2*** *p169*
Tenz, Herman; Wisconsin, n.d. ***9675.8*** *p122*
Tepar, Gitil; Arkansas, 1918 ***95.2*** *p121*
Tepe, Fr Wm; America, 1840 ***8582.1*** *p34*
Teper, George; Arkansas, 1918 ***95.2*** *p121*
Teppenhauer, Frederick; America, 1848 ***1450.2*** *p144A*
Teppett, Robt.; Virginia, 1635 ***6219*** *p69*
Tera, Chr Adolph; Cincinnati, 1846 ***8582.1*** *p34*
Terando, Secondino; Iowa, 1866-1943 ***123.54*** *p48*
Teraux, V. 38; America, 1838 ***778.5*** *p514*
Terbacher, Franz; Kentucky, 1839-1840 ***8582.3*** *p99*
Terbe, Johann Wessel; Kentucky, 1843 ***8582.3*** *p100*
Terchfuss, William Henry 26; Kansas, 1872 ***5240.1*** *p45*
Terebeiza, Felix; Wisconsin, n.d. ***9675.8*** *p122*
Terebeiza, Frank; Wisconsin, n.d. ***9675.8*** *p122*
Terkbom, Frank; Wisconsin, n.d. ***9675.8*** *p122*
Terlau, Heinrich; America, 1852 ***8582.3*** *p64*
Termint, Joseph 58; Port uncertain, 1839 ***778.5*** *p514*
Ternan, Elizabeth 13; Quebec, 1849 ***5704.8*** *p57*
Ternan, Gregory 7; Quebec, 1849 ***5704.8*** *p57*
Ternan, Henry; Quebec, 1849 ***5704.8*** *p57*
Ternan, Henry 11; Quebec, 1849 ***5704.8*** *p57*
Ternan, Jane; Quebec, 1849 ***5704.8*** *p57*
Ternan, Jane 3; Quebec, 1849 ***5704.8*** *p57*
Ternan, Matthew; America, 1741 ***4971*** *p10*
Ternan, Rachael; Quebec, 1849 ***5704.8*** *p57*
Ternan, Sarah; Quebec, 1849 ***5704.8*** *p57*
Ternan, William 9; Quebec, 1849 ***5704.8*** *p57*
Ternat, M...e 30; America, 1838 ***778.5*** *p514*
Ternes, August Isidor; Wisconsin, n.d. ***9675.8*** *p122*
Ternes, John; Wisconsin, n.d. ***9675.8*** *p122*
Ternes, John P. 23; Kansas, 1880 ***5240.1*** *p62*
Ternes, Peter 52; Kansas, 1906 ***5240.1*** *p84*
Ternes, Peter Joseph 27; Kansas, 1893 ***5240.1*** *p45*
Ternes, Peter Joseph 27; Kansas, 1893 ***5240.1*** *p79*
Terney, Ann 20; Philadelphia, 1859 ***5704.8*** *p142*
Ternis, L. 27; New Orleans, 1839 ***778.5*** *p514*
Ternoon, Janet; Quebec, 1847 ***5704.8*** *p8*
Terny, Susan 15; Philadelphia, 1860 ***5704.8*** *p144*
Terpack, Mary; America, 1889 ***7137*** *p170*
Terpack, Michael; America, 1884 ***7137*** *p170*
Terpack, Michael; America, 1889 ***7137*** *p170*
Terpin, Mary; America, 1698 ***2212*** *p10*
Terpin, Mary; Virginia, 1698 ***2212*** *p16*
Terran, Ann; Quebec, 1852 ***5704.8*** *p97*
Terrario, Antonio 23; New York, NY, 1893 ***9026.4*** *p42*
Terraud, Mr. 21; America, 1838 ***778.5*** *p514*
Terrell, Tho.; Virginia, 1637 ***6219*** *p81*
Terrell, Thomas; Illinois, 1871 ***5012.39*** *p25*
Terrier, Charles 31; Maryland, 1774 ***1219.7*** *p235*
Terrile, Joseph; New York, 1872 ***1450.2*** *p144A*
Terrill, Ann; America, 1743 ***4971*** *p65*
Terrill, John; America, 1737 ***4971*** *p12*
Terrill, Richard; America, 1740 ***4971*** *p15*
Terro, Pietro 25; New York, NY, 1893 ***9026.4*** *p42*
Terroy, John 23; Virginia, 1699 ***2212*** *p27*
Terry, Clarisse 10; America, 1838 ***778.5*** *p514*
Terry, Clement Michel 39; America, 1838 ***778.5*** *p514*
Terry, Delaure 35; America, 1838 ***778.5*** *p514*
Terry, J. 22; America, 1838 ***778.5*** *p514*
Terry, James; Jamaica, 1773 ***1219.7*** *p161*
Terry, John 24; Philadelphia, 1854 ***5704.8*** *p117*
Terry, Robert 30; Maryland or Virginia, 1734 ***3690.1*** *p223*
Terry, Rodger 28; Philadelphia, 1854 ***5704.8*** *p122*
Terry, William 22; Virginia, 1774 ***1219.7*** *p241*
Terta, Eltone; Iowa, 1866-1943 ***123.54*** *p48*
Terta, Ettore; Iowa, 1866-1943 ***123.54*** *p48*
Tertrou, Francois 22; Louisiana, 1820 ***778.5*** *p514*
Teruchtera, Wladyslaw 20; New York, 1912 ***9980.29*** *p59*
Terzolas, Steve Peter; Arkansas, 1918 ***95.2*** *p121*
Tesche Family ; New York, 1765 ***8125.8*** *p436*
Teschenmacher, Peter; America, 1671-1690 ***8125.8*** *p438*
Tescher, Bartholomaus; Wisconsin, n.d. ***9675.8*** *p122*
Tesdahl, Martin; Arkansas, 1918 ***95.2*** *p121*
Tesier, H.; New Orleans, 1839 ***778.5*** *p514*
Teske, Carl 3; New York, NY, 1862 ***9831.18*** *p16*
Teske, Caroline 29; New York, NY, 1862 ***9831.18*** *p16*
Teske, Dorothea Sophia 43; New York, NY, 1857 ***9831.14*** *p154*
Teske, Ernst David 44; New York, NY, 1857 ***9831.14*** *p154*
Teske, Friedrich 7; New York, NY, 1862 ***9831.18*** *p16*
Teske, John; Wisconsin, n.d. ***9675.8*** *p122*
Teske, Leopold 36; New York, NY, 1862 ***9831.18*** *p16*
Teske, Maria Louise Auguste 15; New York, NY, 1857 ***9831.14*** *p154*
Teske, Mathilde Florentine 13; New York, NY, 1857 ***9831.14*** *p154*
Teske, Paul 6 mos; New York, NY, 1862 ***9831.18*** *p16*
Tesrade, Jean 34; New Orleans, 1838 ***778.5*** *p515*
Tessel, Dr. 40; New Orleans, 1823 ***778.5*** *p207*
Tesselink, Arend 58; New York, NY, 1847 ***3377.6*** *p11*
Tesselink, Gerridina 20; New York, NY, 1847 ***3377.6*** *p11*
Tesselink, Hendrika 55; New York, NY, 1847 ***3377.6*** *p11*
Tesselink, Janna 24; New York, NY, 1847 ***3377.6*** *p11*
Tesselink, John 13; New York, NY, 1847 ***3377.6*** *p11*
Tesselink, Maria 15; New York, NY, 1847 ***3377.6*** *p11*
Tesselink, William 11; New York, NY, 1847 ***3377.6*** *p11*
Tesser, Frederic 43; New Orleans, 1838 ***778.5*** *p515*
Tessfeld, Johann; Wisconsin, n.d. ***9675.8*** *p122*
Tessier, Mr. 50; New Orleans, 1829 ***778.5*** *p515*
Tessier, Auguste 13; America, 1837 ***778.5*** *p515*
Tessier, Auguste 26; Louisiana, 1821 ***778.5*** *p515*
Tessier, G. 17; America, 1829 ***778.5*** *p515*
Tessier, J. B. 35; New Orleans, 1821 ***778.5*** *p515*
Tessier, Jean 37; Montreal, 1724 ***4533*** *p128*
Tessier, Joseph 58; America, 1829 ***778.5*** *p515*
Tessier, Marie Josephine 10; America, 1837 ***778.5*** *p515*
Tessier, Rose 47; America, 1837 ***778.5*** *p515*
Tessitore, Joseph; Arkansas, 1918 ***95.2*** *p121*
Tesson, Amedee 25; Louisiana, 1838 ***778.5*** *p515*
Tesson, Therese 51; Louisiana, 1838 ***778.5*** *p515*
Testain, Mr. 30; New Orleans, 1836 ***778.5*** *p515*
Testard, Charles 24; Kansas, 1893 ***5240.1*** *p45*
Testard, Chas. 24; Kansas, 1893 ***5240.1*** *p77*
Tester, Jane 22 *SEE* Tester, Stephen
Tester, Stephen 22; Maryland, 1775 ***1219.7*** *p250*
*Wife:*Jane 22
Testie, Peter 24; Port uncertain, 1838 ***778.5*** *p515*
Testill, Joshua 27; Maryland, 1774 ***1219.7*** *p211*
Tetterton, Ellen; New York, NY, 1811 ***2859.11*** *p20*
Tetterton, Robert; New York, NY, 1811 ***2859.11*** *p20*
With family
Tetzlaff, August; Wisconsin, n.d. ***9675.8*** *p122*
Tetzlaff, Frederick; Wisconsin, n.d. ***9675.8*** *p122*
Tetzlaff, Michael; Wisconsin, n.d. ***9675.8*** *p122*
Teuerling, Joseph; America, 1851 ***8582.3*** *p64*
Teufel, Anna Wammser *SEE* Teufel, Michel
Teufel, Michel; New England, 1754 ***4525*** *p252*
*Wife:*Anna Wammser
With children
Teufell, Georg; Pennsylvania, 1751 ***2444*** *p225*
Teuffel, Georg; Pennsylvania, 1751 ***2444*** *p225*
Teuffel, Johann Michel; New England, 1754 ***4525*** *p252*
Teuffel, Ludwig; Pennsylvania, 1751 ***2444*** *p225*
Teuk, Johan H.; Illinois, 1844 ***8582.2*** *p51*
Tevrery, Miss 30; America, 1838 ***778.5*** *p515*
Tewan, Bernard; Montreal, 1824 ***7603*** *p61*
Tewes, Caspar Heinrich; Kentucky, 1848 ***8582.3*** *p101*
Tews, August; Wisconsin, n.d. ***9675.8*** *p122*
Teyn, Bernhard; New York, NY, 1840 ***8208.4*** *p108*
Thacker, Hen.; Virginia, 1642 ***6219*** *p198*
Thacker, Henry; New York, NY, 1836 ***8208.4*** *p10*
Thacker, John S.; New York, NY, 1836 ***8208.4*** *p10*
Thaden, Alfred Johannes; Ellis Island 1924 ***3455.4*** *p83*
Thain, Agnes; Canada, 1835 ***8893*** *p264*
Thain, Agnes; New York, 1833 ***8893*** *p264*
Thairjames, Thomas 21; Virginia, 1773 ***1219.7*** *p169*
Thale, Carl 19; Maryland, 1774 ***1219.7*** *p229*
Thalenhorst, Carl Ludwig Theodor; America, 1872 ***4610.10*** *p96*
Thall, John F.; New York, NY, 1837 ***8208.4*** *p36*
Thamnes, Ralph; Virginia, 1644 ***6219*** *p229*
Thanbald, Georg; Cincinnati, 1869-1887 ***8582*** *p32*
Thanweber, . . .; Canada, 1776-1783 ***9786*** *p35*
Thar, E. J.; Iowa, 1866-1943 ***123.54*** *p48*
Tharjer, Fronzo; Iowa, 1866-1943 ***123.54*** *p48*
Tharp, Robert; New York, NY, 1838 ***8208.4*** *p80*
Thatcher, Edward 15; Pennsylvania, 1728 ***3690.1*** *p223*
Thatcher, James 23; Maryland, 1725 ***3690.1*** *p223*
Thatcher, William 19; Maryland, 1719 ***3690.1*** *p223*
Thatmeyer, Artur; California, 1983 ***4610.10*** *p82*
Thaubald, Georg; Cincinnati, 1869-1887 ***8582*** *p32*
Thaubald, Johann; America, 1846 ***8582.3*** *p64*
Thaunisch, Mr. 30; America, 1838 ***778.5*** *p516*
Thayer, G. H.; Washington, 1859-1920 ***2872.1*** *p40*
Thayer, George H.; Washington, 1859-1920 ***2872.1*** *p40*
Theard, Mr. 29; New Orleans, 1829 ***778.5*** *p516*
Thebernice, John; America, 1890 ***1450.2*** *p144A*
Theboult, Clemt.; Virginia, 1643 ***6219*** *p205*
Thecle, Thecle-Cornelius; Quebec, 1670 ***7603*** *p94*
Thedander, Andrew; Boston, 1830-1858 ***6410.32*** *p124*
Thede, Claus; Illinois, 1886 ***5012.39*** *p120*
Thede, John H.; Scott Co., IA, 1859 ***2764.35*** *p69*
Thee, Anne Marie Hedwig Niederlucke; America, 1849 ***4610.10*** *p115*
*Son:*Friedrich Wilhelm
*Son:*Johann Friedrich
Thee, Friedrich Wilhelm *SEE* Thee, Anne Marie Hedwig Niederlucke
Thee, Heinrich Wilhelm; America, 1843 ***4610.10*** *p115*
Thee, Johann Friedrich *SEE* Thee, Anne Marie Hedwig Niederlucke
Thee, Karl Friedrich Wilhelm; America, 1837 ***4610.10*** *p114*
Theesen, Helene; New York, NY, 1925 ***3455.4*** *p55*
Theil, Friedrich; Lancaster, PA, 1780 ***8137*** *p15*
Theil, Konrad; Reading, PA, 1780 ***8137*** *p15*
Theilheimer, . . .; Canada, 1776-1783 ***9786*** *p35*
Theilig, Edward; Wisconsin, n.d. ***9675.8*** *p122*
Theiman, Christian; Indiana, 1848 ***9117*** *p18*
Thein, Joseph; Wisconsin, n.d. ***9675.8*** *p122*

Thomas, Mary 32 *SEE* Thomas, George
Thomas, Michael; Ohio, 1869-1885 ***8582.2*** *p56*
Thomas, Michael; Pennsylvania, 1730 ***2854*** *p45*
With wife & 7 children
Thomas, Mike; Arkansas, 1918 ***95.2*** *p121*
Thomas, Morgan 17; Jamaica, 1734 ***3690.1*** *p224*
Thomas, Nath.; Virginia, 1628 ***6219*** *p9*
Thomas, Nicholos Gustas; Arkansas, 1918 ***95.2*** *p122*
Thomas, Nicolas; Wisconsin, n.d. ***9675.8*** *p122*
Thomas, Patrick 27; Virginia, 1774 ***1219.7*** *p238*
Thomas, Peter; Iowa, 1866-1943 ***123.54*** *p48*
Thomas, Peter; Pennsylvania, 1754 ***4779.3*** *p14A*
Thomas, Peter; Virginia, 1637 ***6219*** *p8*
Thomas, Phillipp; Virginia, 1637 ***6219*** *p108*
Thomas, Reece; Arkansas, 1918 ***95.2*** *p122*
Thomas, Rich.; Virginia, 1642 ***6219*** *p191*
Thomas, Richard; Virginia, 1635 ***6219*** *p6*
Thomas, Richard; Virginia, 1639 ***6219*** *p150*
Thomas, Richard 18; New England, 1699 ***2212*** *p19*
Thomas, Richard 36; Virginia, 1773 ***1219.7*** *p169*
Thomas, Robert; Virginia, 1639 ***6219*** *p153*
Thomas, Robt.; Virginia, 1635 ***6219*** *p20*
Thomas, Robt.; Virginia, 1642 ***6219*** *p194*
Thomas, Rowland; America, 1698 ***2212*** *p9*
Thomas, Rowland 34; Maryland or Virginia, 1699 ***2212*** *p24*
Thomas, Sarah 18; Maryland, 1724 ***3690.1*** *p224*
Thomas, Steph 15; Maryland or Virginia, 1699 ***2212*** *p22*
Thomas, Susan; Quebec, 1853 ***5704.8*** *p103*
Thomas, Sym.; Virginia, 1648 ***6219*** *p250*
Thomas, T.; Quebec, 1815 ***9229.18*** *p74*
Thomas, Terrence 60; Massachusetts, 1850 ***5881.1*** *p95*
Thomas, Thomas; New York, NY, 1835 ***8208.4*** *p49*
Thomas, Thomas; Virginia, 1637 ***6219*** *p82*
Thomas, Thomas 17; Philadelphia, 1774 ***1219.7*** *p197*
Thomas, Timothy; Iowa, 1866-1943 ***123.54*** *p48*
Thomas, Timothy 16; Pennsylvania, Virginia or Maryland, 1718 ***3690.1*** *p224*
Thomas, W. H. 61; Arizona, 1914 ***9228.40*** *p19*
Thomas, Will.; Virginia, 1652 ***6251*** *p19*
Thomas, William; Baltimore, 1903 ***3455.2*** *p43*
Thomas, William; Baltimore, 1903 ***3455.3*** *p106*
Thomas, William; New York, NY, 1816 ***2859.11*** *p43*
Thomas, William; New York, NY, 1834 ***8208.4*** *p3*
Thomas, William; Virginia, 1648 ***6219*** *p251*
Thomas, William; Virginia, 1698 ***2212*** *p13*
Thomas, William 15; Baltimore, 1775 ***1219.7*** *p271*
Thomas, William 17; Windward Islands, 1722 ***3690.1*** *p224*
Thomas, William 20; Jamaica, 1736 ***3690.1*** *p224*
Thomas, William 20; Philadelphia, 1774 ***1219.7*** *p223*
Thomas, William 40; Kansas, 1892 ***5240.1*** *p76*
Thomas, Wm.; Virginia, 1635 ***6219*** *p36*
Thomas, Wm.; Virginia, 1637 ***6219*** *p11*
Thomas, Wm.; Virginia, 1639 ***6219*** *p150*
Thomas, Wm.; Virginia, 1642 ***6219*** *p195*
Thomas, Wm.; Virginia, 1643 ***6219*** *p33*
Thomas, Wm.; Virginia, 1643 ***6219*** *p200*
Thomas, Wm 35; Maryland or Virginia, 1699 ***2212*** *p25*
Thomasin, Marie 25; Louisiana, 1833 ***778.5*** *p405*
Thomayen, Henriette J..nne 30; America, 1838 ***778.5*** *p517*
Thomayen, Jean 28; America, 1838 ***778.5*** *p517*
Thome, Hubert; Wisconsin, n.d. ***9675.8*** *p122*
Thome, John 26; Kansas, 1881 ***5240.1*** *p45*
Thome, John 26; Kansas, 1881 ***5240.1*** *p63*
Thome, Math.; Wisconsin, n.d. ***9675.8*** *p122*
Thome, William; Wisconsin, n.d. ***9675.8*** *p122*
Thomes, Nicholas; Wisconsin, n.d. ***9675.8*** *p122*
Thomkin, Richd.; Virginia, 1648 ***6219*** *p245*
Thomlinson, L. C.; Washington, 1859-1920 ***2872.1*** *p40*
Thommen, William; Wisconsin, n.d. ***9675.8*** *p122*
Thompsen, Throud; Arizona, 1881 ***2764.35*** *p69*
Thompson, Mr.; New York, NY, 1815 ***2859.11*** *p43*
Thompson, Mr.; Quebec, 1815 ***9229.18*** *p79*
Thompson, Mr.; Quebec, 1815 ***9229.18*** *p81*
Thompson, Afemia 55; Quebec, 1862 ***5704.8*** *p151*
Thompson, Alex; New York, NY, 1811 ***2859.11*** *p20*
With family
Thompson, Alexander; Illinois, 1870 ***5012.38*** *p99*
Thompson, Alexander; Philadelphia, 1849 ***53.26*** *p88*
Thompson, Alexander; Philadelphia, 1849 ***5704.8*** *p54*
Thompson, Alexander; Quebec, 1847 ***5704.8*** *p11*
Thompson, Alexander 16; Maryland or Virginia, 1730 ***3690.1*** *p225*
Thompson, Alexander 30; Philadelphia, 1803 ***53.26*** *p88*
Thompson, Andrew 11; Quebec, 1847 ***5704.8*** *p11*
Thompson, Andrew 19; Philadelphia, 1858 ***5704.8*** *p139*
Thompson, Andrew 25 *SEE* Thompson, Samuel
Thompson, Andrew 40; Nova Scotia, 1774 ***1219.7*** *p209*
*Wife:*Mary 32
Thompson, Ann; Philadelphia, 1849 ***53.26*** *p88*
Thompson, Ann; Philadelphia, 1849 ***5704.8*** *p49*
Thompson, Ann; Philadelphia, 1849 ***5704.8*** *p54*
Thompson, Ann; Philadelphia, 1851 ***5704.8*** *p80*
Thompson, Ann Jane 17; St. John, N.B., 1859 ***5704.8*** *p141*
Thompson, Anna 30 *SEE* Thompson, Samuel
Thompson, Anne; Philadelphia, 1867 ***5704.8*** *p221*
Thompson, Anthony; Quebec, 1847 ***5704.8*** *p7*
Thompson, Anthony 20; North America, 1774 ***1219.7*** *p198*
Thompson, Anthony 22; Quebec, 1854 ***5704.8*** *p121*
Thompson, Archibald 21; St. John, N.B., 1861 ***5704.8*** *p147*
Thompson, Arthur; New York, NY, 1816 ***2859.11*** *p43*
Thompson, Augusta 46; Kansas, 1906 ***5240.1*** *p83*
Thompson, Benjamin; Illinois, 1888 ***5012.39*** *p122*
Thompson, Benjamin 27; Virginia, 1774 ***1219.7*** *p186*
Thompson, Biddy 18; Massachusetts, 1849 ***5881.1*** *p94*
Thompson, Cath. 23; Massachusetts, 1860 ***6410.32*** *p114*
Thompson, Catharine; Philadelphia, 1864 ***5704.8*** *p184*
Thompson, Catherine; Quebec, 1852 ***5704.8*** *p94*
Thompson, Catherine; Quebec, 1852 ***5704.8*** *p98*
Thompson, Catherine 2; Quebec, 1852 ***5704.8*** *p94*
Thompson, Charles; California, 1868 ***2769.9*** *p3*
Thompson, Christopher; Illinois, 1890 ***5012.39*** *p53*
Thompson, Christopher; Illinois, 1895 ***5012.40*** *p54*
Thompson, Cornelius 25; Maryland, 1774 ***1219.7*** *p229*
Thompson, Daniel; Wilmington, NC, 1803 ***1639.20*** *p305*
Thompson, David; Philadelphia, 1867 ***5704.8*** *p216*
Thompson, David 25; Quebec, 1857 ***5704.8*** *p135*
Thompson, Donald 34; Quebec, 1858 ***5704.8*** *p138*
Thompson, Dorothea 20; Quebec, 1853 ***5704.8*** *p105*
Thompson, Edward; Quebec, 1847 ***5704.8*** *p29*
Thompson, Edward 8 *SEE* Thompson, Edward
Thompson, Edward 25; Quebec, 1853 ***5704.8*** *p105*
Thompson, Edward 31; Maryland, 1774 ***1219.7*** *p208*
Thompson, Edward 34; Philadelphia, 1804 ***53.26*** *p88*
*Relative:*Edward 8
Thompson, Eldred; Virginia, 1644 ***6219*** *p208*
Thompson, Elias Johannes; Arkansas, 1918 ***95.2*** *p122*
Thompson, Eliza; New York, NY, 1811 ***2859.11*** *p20*
Thompson, Eliza; Philadelphia, 1851 ***5704.8*** *p76*
Thompson, Eliza; Quebec, 1847 ***5704.8*** *p13*
Thompson, Eliza; Quebec, 1851 ***5704.8*** *p73*
Thompson, Eliza 7; Philadelphia, 1865 ***5704.8*** *p165*
Thompson, Eliza 7; Quebec, 1851 ***5704.8*** *p73*
Thompson, Elizabeth; New York, NY, 1836 ***8208.4*** *p16*
Thompson, Elizabeth; Philadelphia, 1867 ***5704.8*** *p220*
Thompson, Elizabeth; Quebec, 1852 ***5704.8*** *p94*
Thompson, Elizabeth; St. John, N.B., 1847 ***5704.8*** *p10*
Thompson, Elizabeth 28; Virginia, 1700 ***2212*** *p31*
Thompson, Esther; Washington, 1859-1920 ***2872.1*** *p40*
Thompson, Fanny Ann; Philadelphia, 1847 ***53.26*** *p88*
Thompson, Fanny Ann; Philadelphia, 1847 ***5704.8*** *p31*
Thompson, Franklin P.; Washington, 1859-1920 ***2872.1*** *p40*
Thompson, Geo.; New York, NY, 1816 ***2859.11*** *p43*
Thompson, George; New York, NY, 1811 ***2859.11*** *p20*
Thompson, George; New York, NY, 1816 ***2859.11*** *p43*
Thompson, George; Pennsylvania, 1682 ***4960*** *p159*
Thompson, George 8; St. John, N.B., 1854 ***5704.8*** *p115*
Thompson, George 27; Maryland, 1733 ***3690.1*** *p225*
Thompson, Guillaume; New Brunswick, 1795 ***7603*** *p79*
Thompson, Guillaume; Quebec, 1787 ***7603*** *p23*
Thompson, Hanna; Washington, 1859-1920 ***2872.1*** *p40*
Thompson, Hannah 19; Maryland, 1775 ***1219.7*** *p260*
Thompson, Hannah 40; Wilmington, DE, 1831 ***6508.3*** *p100*
Thompson, Harry; Washington, 1859-1920 ***2872.1*** *p40*
Thompson, Helene 25; Montreal, 1753 ***7603*** *p38*
Thompson, Henry; Washington, 1859-1920 ***2872.1*** *p40*
Thompson, Hugh 36; Philadelphia, 1804 ***53.26*** *p88*
Thompson, Ja.; Virginia, 1646 ***6219*** *p242*
Thompson, James; Charleston, SC, 1800 ***1639.20*** *p306*
Thompson, James; Illinois, 1869 ***5012.38*** *p99*
Thompson, James; New York, NY, 1811 ***2859.11*** *p20*
Thompson, James; New York, NY, 1816 ***2859.11*** *p43*
Thompson, James; New York, NY, 1864 ***5704.8*** *p175*
Thompson, James; Philadelphia, 1811 ***53.26*** *p88*
Thompson, James; Philadelphia, 1811 ***2859.11*** *p20*
Thompson, James; Quebec, 1851 ***5704.8*** *p73*
Thompson, James 2; Quebec, 1847 ***5704.8*** *p11*
Thompson, James 4; St. John, N.B., 1854 ***5704.8*** *p115*
Thompson, James 6 *SEE* Thompson, Samuel
Thompson, James 9; Philadelphia, 1865 ***5704.8*** *p165*
Thompson, James 12; St. John, N.B., 1853 ***5704.8*** *p106*
Thompson, James 16; Philadelphia, 1861 ***5704.8*** *p148*
Thompson, James 19; New England, 1699 ***2212*** *p18*
Thompson, James 20; Pennsylvania, 1733 ***3690.1*** *p225*
Thompson, James 25; New York, 1774 ***1219.7*** *p189*
Thompson, James 25; Philadelphia, 1803 ***53.26*** *p88*
Thompson, James 30; Maryland, 1775 ***1219.7*** *p267*
Thompson, James 32; New York, 1774 ***1219.7*** *p197*
With wife
With 4 children
Thompson, James 38; Philadelphia, 1774 ***1219.7*** *p219*
Thompson, Jane; New York, NY, 1864 ***5704.8*** *p175*
Thompson, Jane; New York, NY, 1865 ***5704.8*** *p195*
Thompson, Jane; Philadelphia, 1852 ***5704.8*** *p87*
Thompson, Jane; Philadelphia, 1852 ***5704.8*** *p88*
Thompson, Jane; Philadelphia, 1864 ***5704.8*** *p177*
Thompson, Jane 11; New York, NY, 1865 ***5704.8*** *p195*
Thompson, Jane 18; Philadelphia, 1864 ***5704.8*** *p155*
Thompson, Jane 23; Quebec, 1857 ***5704.8*** *p136*
Thompson, John; Charleston, SC, 1790 ***1639.20*** *p307*
Thompson, John; Illinois, 1852 ***7857*** *p7*
Thompson, John; New York, NY, 1811 ***2859.11*** *p20*
Thompson, John; New York, NY, 1811 ***2859.11*** *p20*
With family
Thompson, John; New York, NY, 1815 ***2859.11*** *p43*
Thompson, John; New York, NY, 1816 ***2859.11*** *p43*
Thompson, John; New York, NY, 1834 ***8208.4*** *p1*
Thompson, John; New York, NY, 1864 ***5704.8*** *p175*
Thompson, John; New York, NY, 1866 ***5704.8*** *p208*
Thompson, John; New York, NY, 1913 ***3455.2*** *p43*
Thompson, John; Ohio, 1843 ***9892.11*** *p46*
Thompson, John; Ohio, 1845 ***9892.11*** *p46*
Thompson, John; Ohio, 1848 ***9892.11*** *p46*
Thompson, John; Philadelphia, 1818 ***9892.11*** *p46*
Thompson, John; Philadelphia, 1849 ***53.26*** *p88*
*Relative:*Thomas
Thompson, John; Philadelphia, 1849 ***5704.8*** *p50*
Thompson, John; Philadelphia, 1851 ***5704.8*** *p77*
Thompson, John; Philadelphia, 1852 ***5704.8*** *p87*
Thompson, John; Philadelphia, 1864 ***5704.8*** *p177*
Thompson, John; Philadelphia, 1866 ***5704.8*** *p208*
Thompson, John; St. John, N.B., 1850 ***5704.8*** *p62*
Thompson, John; St. John, N.B., 1851 ***5704.8*** *p72*
Thompson, John; Virginia, 1698 ***2212*** *p14*
Thompson, John; Virginia, 1698 ***2212*** *p17*
Thompson, John; Washington, 1859-1920 ***2872.1*** *p40*
Thompson, John 4; Quebec, 1847 ***5704.8*** *p11*
Thompson, John 13; St. John, N.B., 1853 ***5704.8*** *p106*
Thompson, John 15; Maryland, 1724 ***3690.1*** *p225*
Thompson, John 16; St. John, N.B., 1854 ***5704.8*** *p115*
Thompson, John 17; Jamaica, 1774 ***1219.7*** *p238*
Thompson, John 18; St. John, N.B., 1863 ***5704.8*** *p153*
Thompson, John 20; Philadelphia, 1854 ***5704.8*** *p117*
Thompson, John 21; Charleston, SC, 1734 ***1639.20*** *p306*
Thompson, John 21; Maryland, 1774 ***1219.7*** *p213*
Thompson, John 22; Maryland, 1774 ***1219.7*** *p211*
Thompson, John 24; Kansas, 1904 ***5240.1*** *p83*
Thompson, John 24; Philadelphia, 1804 ***53.26*** *p88*
Thompson, John 25; St. Christopher, 1722 ***3690.1*** *p225*
Thompson, John 26; California, 1872 ***2769.9*** *p4*
Thompson, John 28; Philadelphia, 1803 ***53.26*** *p88*
Thompson, John 32; Maryland, 1774 ***1219.7*** *p204*
Thompson, John 32; North America, 1774 ***1219.7*** *p200*
Thompson, John 32; St. Christopher, 1730 ***3690.1*** *p225*
Thompson, John 33; Jamaica, 1774 ***1219.7*** *p205*
Thompson, John 33; Massachusetts, 1860 ***6410.32*** *p114*
Thompson, John 35; Philadelphia, 1803 ***53.26*** *p88*
Thompson, John 36; Massachusetts, 1860 ***6410.32*** *p114*
Thompson, John 78; Arizona, 1917 ***9228.40*** *p21*
Thompson, John Casper; New York, NY, 1905 ***3455.1*** *p51*
Thompson, John Laurence; Arkansas, 1918 ***95.2*** *p122*
Thompson, Joseph; Iroquois Co., IL, 1896 ***3455.1*** *p13*
Thompson, Joseph; New York, NY, 1811 ***2859.11*** *p20*
Thompson, Joseph; New York, NY, 1815 ***2859.11*** *p43*
Thompson, Joseph; Philadelphia, 1864 ***5704.8*** *p180*
Thompson, Joseph 10; Quebec, 1851 ***5704.8*** *p73*
Thompson, Joseph 26; North America, 1774 ***1219.7*** *p200*
Thompson, Joseph 26; Pennsylvania, 1738 ***3690.1*** *p225*
Thompson, Joseph 30; Virginia, 1774 ***1219.7*** *p244*
Thompson, Joshua 20?; America, 1701 ***2212*** *p35*
Thompson, Kennedy 20; Philadelphia, 1856 ***5704.8*** *p129*
Thompson, Laurence 22; Jamaica, 1735 ***3690.1*** *p225*
Thompson, Lawrence 19; Maryland, 1729 ***3690.1*** *p225*
Thompson, Lawrence 25; Maryland, 1774 ***1219.7*** *p179*
Thompson, Maggie; New York, NY, 1864 ***5704.8*** *p185*
Thompson, Margaret; New York, NY, 1864 ***5704.8*** *p174*
Thompson, Margaret; St. John, N.B., 1849 ***5704.8*** *p56*
Thompson, Margaret; St. John, N.B., 1853 ***5704.8*** *p106*
Thompson, Margaret; Virginia, 1646 ***6219*** *p240*
Thompson, Margaret 30; St. John, N.B., 1859 ***5704.8*** *p140*
Thompson, Marg't; New York, NY, 1811 ***2859.11*** *p20*
Thompson, Maria; New York, NY, 1811 ***2859.11*** *p20*
Thompson, Maria; Philadelphia, 1851 ***5704.8*** *p80*
Thompson, Marie; Quebec, 1752 ***7603*** *p38*
Thompson, Martha; New York, NY, 1864 ***5704.8*** *p175*
Thompson, Martha 8; Quebec, 1847 ***5704.8*** *p11*
Thompson, Martin; Quebec, 1819 ***7603*** *p38*
Thompson, Mary; New York, NY, 1815 ***2859.11*** *p43*

Thompson, Mary; New York, NY, 1867 5704.8 p222
Thompson, Mary; Philadelphia, 1848 53.26 p88
Thompson, Mary; Philadelphia, 1848 5704.8 p46
Thompson, Mary; Quebec, 1847 5704.8 p11
Thompson, Mary 18; St. John, N.B., 1854 5704.8 p115
Thompson, Mary 18; St. John, N.B., 1865 5704.8 p165
Thompson, Mary 22; Philadelphia, 1804 53.26 p88
Thompson, Mary 24; Maryland, 1775 1219.7 p249
Thompson, Mary 26; Maryland, 1774 1219.7 p235
Thompson, Mary 32 *SEE* Thompson, Andrew
Thompson, Mary 59 *SEE* Thompson, Ninian
Thompson, Mary Jane 9 mos; Quebec, 1847 5704.8 p11
Thompson, Mary Jane 3; Quebec, 1852 5704.8 p98
Thompson, Matilda; Philadelphia, 1865 5704.8 p200
Thompson, Matilda J. 6 mos; Quebec, 1847 5704.8 p11
Thompson, Matt; Washington, 1859-1920 2872.1 p40
Thompson, Matthew; Illinois, 1828-1838 2896.5 p40
Thompson, Moses; New York, NY, 1868 5704.8 p228
Thompson, Nancy; Philadelphia, 1853 5704.8 p101
Thompson, Ninian 60; South Carolina, 1850 1639.20 p307
*Relative:*Mary 59
Thompson, R. S.; Washington, 1859-1920 2872.1 p40
Thompson, Rachel 21; Philadelphia, 1864 5704.8 p155
Thompson, Richard 11; Massachusetts, 1849 5881.1 p95
Thompson, Richard 15; Philadelphia, 1774 1219.7 p217
Thompson, Richard 22; Maryland, 1774 1219.7 p180
Thompson, Richard 25; North America, 1774 1219.7 p200
Thompson, Richard 30; Nova Scotia, 1774 1219.7 p194
Thompson, Richard 34; Philadelphia, 1775 1219.7 p274
Thompson, Richard 49; St. John, N.B., 1864 5704.8 p159
Thompson, Robert; New York, NY, 1811 2859.11 p20
With wife
Thompson, Robert; New York, NY, 1864 5704.8 p174
Thompson, Robert; Ohio, 1841 9892.11 p46
Thompson, Robert; Ohio, 1845 9892.11 p46
Thompson, Robert; Philadelphia, 1811 53.26 p88
Thompson, Robert; Philadelphia, 1811 2859.11 p20
Thompson, Robert; Philadelphia, 1851 5704.8 p76
Thompson, Robert; Philadelphia, 1867 5704.8 p220
Thompson, Robert; Quebec, 1847 5704.8 p28
Thompson, Robert; St. John, N.B., 1847 5704.8 p11
Thompson, Robert 5; Quebec, 1852 5704.8 p94
Thompson, Robert 15; Jamaica, 1730 3690.1 p292
Thompson, Robert 17; St. John, N.B., 1864 5704.8 p159
Thompson, Robert 20; Quebec, 1862 5704.8 p151
Thompson, Robert 23; Quebec, 1857 5704.8 p136
Thompson, Robert 34; Kansas, 1887 5240.1 p71
Thompson, Rob't; Baltimore, 1811 2859.11 p20
Thompson, Rob't; New York, NY, 1811 2859.11 p20
Thompson, Rose 35; Philadelphia, 1865 5704.8 p164
Thompson, Roseanna 10; St. John, N.B., 1854 5704.8 p115
Thompson, Sally 30; Philadelphia, 1833-1834 53.26 p88
Thompson, Sally A. 20; Philadelphia, 1857 5704.8 p132
Thompson, Samuel; New York, NY, 1834 8208.4 p40
Thompson, Samuel 21; Philadelphia, 1864 5704.8 p157
Thompson, Samuel 28; Philadelphia, 1803 53.26 p88
*Relative:*Anna 30
*Relative:*Andrew 25
*Relative:*Sarah 22
*Relative:*James 6
Thompson, Sarah; America, 1865 5704.8 p204
Thompson, Sarah; New York, NY, 1811 2859.11 p20
Thompson, Sarah; Philadelphia, 1851 5704.8 p76
Thompson, Sarah; Quebec, 1847 5704.8 p11
Thompson, Sarah; Quebec, 1852 5704.8 p94
Thompson, Sarah 4; Philadelphia, 1865 5704.8 p165
Thompson, Sarah 20; New Orleans, 1858 5704.8 p140
Thompson, Sarah 22 *SEE* Thompson, Samuel
Thompson, Sarah 22; Massachusetts, 1847 5881.1 p95
Thompson, Sarah 22; Philadelphia, 1864 5704.8 p160
Thompson, Sarah 40; St. John, N.B., 1854 5704.8 p115
Thompson, Sarah Ann 4; Quebec, 1847 5704.8 p11
Thompson, Susan 6; St. John, N.B., 1854 5704.8 p115
Thompson, Tho.; Virginia, 1646 6219 p243
Thompson, Thomas *SEE* Thompson, John
Thompson, Thomas; Colorado, 1902 9678.3 p16
Thompson, Thomas; New York, NY, 1815 2859.11 p43
Thompson, Thomas; New York, NY, 1816 2859.11 p43
Thompson, Thomas; New York, NY, 1838 8208.4 p68
Thompson, Thomas; Philadelphia, 1849 5704.8 p50
Thompson, Thomas; Virginia, 1646 6219 p238
Thompson, Thomas; Washington, 1859-1920 2872.1 p40
Thompson, Thomas 11; New York, NY, 1865 5704.8 p195
Thompson, Thomas 13; St. John, N.B., 1854 5704.8 p115
Thompson, Thomas 15; Philadelphia, 1775 1219.7 p259
Thompson, Thomas 16; Jamaica, 1736 3690.1 p225
Thompson, Thomas 23; Jamaica, 1734 3690.1 p225
Thompson, Thomas 23; Maryland, 1775 1219.7 p262
Thompson, Thomas 23; Philadelphia, 1804 53.26 p89
Thompson, Thomas 29; Georgia, 1775 1219.7 p277
Thompson, Thomas 45; St. John, N.B., 1853 5704.8 p110
Thompson, Thomas 46; Massachusetts, 1860 6410.32 p106
Thompson, Thomas B.; Illinois, 1892 5012.37 p62
Thompson, Thomas Peter; Washington, 1859-1920 2872.1 p40
Thompson, Violet 28; St. John, N.B., 1856 5704.8 p132
Thompson, Wilhelmina 38; Massachusetts, 1860 6410.32 p106
Thompson, William; Montreal, 1813 7603 p28
Thompson, William; New York, NY, 1811 2859.11 p20
Thompson, William; New York, NY, 1816 2859.11 p43
Thompson, William; New York, NY, 1867 5704.8 p222
Thompson, William; Philadelphia, 1852 5704.8 p88
Thompson, William; Quebec, 1847 5704.8 p11
Thompson, William; Quebec, 1851 5704.8 p73
Thompson, William; West Virginia, 1859 9788.3 p21
Thompson, William 9 mos; Quebec, 1853 5704.8 p105
Thompson, William 7; Quebec, 1847 5704.8 p11
Thompson, William 10; Quebec, 1852 5704.8 p94
Thompson, William 17; Philadelphia, 1864 5704.8 p156
Thompson, William 18; Maryland, 1720 3690.1 p28A
Thompson, William 19; St. John, N.B., 1856 5704.8 p131
Thompson, William 20; Georgia, 1774 1219.7 p241
Thompson, William 21; Virginia, 1774 1219.7 p241
Thompson, William 22; St. John, N.B., 1854 5704.8 p115
Thompson, William 30; Virginia, 1774 1219.7 p225
Thompson, William 53; Wilmington, NC, 1850 1639.20 p308
*Relative:*William A. 28
Thompson, William 64; Massachusetts, 1848 5881.1 p95
Thompson, William A. 28 *SEE* Thompson, William
Thompson, Wm.; New York, NY, 1811 2859.11 p20
Thompson, Wm 31; America, 1700 2212 p29
Thompson, Wm 31; Montserrat, 1700 2212 p22
Thoms, Ralph; Virginia, 1698 2212 p16
Thoms, William; Wisconsin, n.d. 9675.8 p122
Thomsen, Carl Chris; Arkansas, 1918 95.2 p122
Thomsen, Nels Christian; Arkansas, 1918 95.2 p122
Thomser, William L.; New York, NY, 1834 8208.4 p47
Thomson, Mr.; Quebec, 1815 9229.18 p79
With wife
Thomson, Alexander; Savannah, GA, 1770 8894.2 p56
Thomson, Andrea; Iroquois Co., IL, 1894 3455.1 p13
Thomson, Andrew; North Carolina, 1730-1735 1639.20 p305
Thomson, Ann; Quebec, 1875 4537.30 p72
Thomson, Archibald; Ontario, 1802 9775.5 p216
Thomson, Catherine; Quebec, 1873 4537.30 p90
Thomson, Catherine 36 *SEE* Thomson, John
Thomson, David; North Carolina, 1730-1735 1639.20 p306
Thomson, David; North Carolina, 1749 1639.20 p306
Thomson, David L. 45; South Carolina, 1850 1639.20 p306
Thomson, Frances; North America, 1819 8894.2 p56
Thomson, George; Charleston, SC, 1796 1639.20 p306
Thomson, George; Charleston, SC, 1828 1639.20 p306
Thomson, George; Pennsylvania, 1682 4960 p159
Thomson, Grizel; North Carolina, 1737 1639.20 p306
Thomson, Hugh; America, 1845 1450.2 p145A
Thomson, Isobel; North Carolina, 1737 1639.20 p306
Thomson, James; New York, NY, 1811 2859.11 p20
Thomson, James 32; St. John, N.B., 1862 5704.8 p150
Thomson, James 34; Kansas, 1880 5240.1 p61
Thomson, Jane; New York, NY, 1811 2859.11 p20
Thomson, Jann Harms; Illinois, 1892 2896.5 p40
Thomson, John; Charleston, SC, 1763 1639.20 p307
Thomson, John; Jamaica, 1736 3690.1 p225
Thomson, John; New York, 1715 1639.20 p307
Thomson, John; North Carolina, 1737 1639.20 p307
Thomson, John 18; St. John, N.B., 1866 5704.8 p167
Thomson, John 25; St. Christopher, 1722 3690.1 p225
Thomson, John 40; Charleston, SC, 1850 1639.20 p307
*Relative:*Catherine 36
Thomson, John B.; Charleston, SC, 1827 1639.20 p44
Thomson, John Blane; Charleston, SC, 1827 1639.20 p307
Thomson, Joseph 26; Pennsylvania, 1738 3690.1 p225
Thomson, Margaret; Quebec, 1838-1899 4537.30 p12
Thomson, Mary; North Carolina, 1737 1639.20 p308
Thomson, Mike; Washington, 1859-1920 2872.1 p40
Thomson, Neil 23; Wilmington, NC, 1774 1639.20 p307
Thomson, Peter August; Wisconsin, n.d. 9675.8 p122
Thomson, Richard 21; West Indies, 1734 3690.1 p226
Thomson, Thomas; North Carolina, 1737 1639.20 p308
Thomson, Thomas; South Carolina, 1684 1639.20 p295
Thomson, Thomas; Wisconsin, n.d. 9675.8 p122
Thomson, Thomas 18; Virginia, 1774 1219.7 p238
Thomson, Thomas 38; New York, 1774 1219.7 p203
Thomson, William; North Carolina, 1834 1639.20 p308
Thomson, William; Virginia, 1642 6219 p193
Thomson, William; Virginia, 1775 8894.2 p55
Thomson, William 42; Nova Scotia, 1774 1219.7 p209
Thon, Carrie 9; New York, NY, 1878 9253 p46
Thon, Frieda 4; New York, NY, 1878 9253 p46
Thon, Marg 42; New York, NY, 1878 9253 p46
Thon, Samuel 7; New York, NY, 1878 9253 p46
Thons, William; Wisconsin, n.d. 9675.8 p122
Thorburn, John William; Montreal, 1792 9775.5 p202
Thoresby, John 26; Philadelphia, 1774 1219.7 p183
Thoret, Mme. 28; America, 1825 778.5 p517
Thoret, J. B. 30; America, 1825 778.5 p517
Thorgersen, Charles Einar; Wisconsin, n.d. 9675.8 p122
Thorgrimsdottir, B. 32; Quebec, 1879 2557.2 p37
Thorin, Erick Borge; Washington, 1859-1920 2872.1 p40
Thorin, Grover; Washington, 1859-1920 2872.1 p40
Thorin, Ingrid Margrete; Washington, 1859-1920 2872.1 p40
Thorin, Karin; Washington, 1859-1920 2872.1 p40
Thorin, Karin Ostrud; Washington, 1859-1920 2872.1 p40
Thorin, Per; Washington, 1859-1920 2872.1 p40
Thorkelsen, Christ; Colorado, 1894 9678.3 p16
Thorkelsson, Hallgrimur 13; Quebec, 1879 2557.1 p21
Thorkelsson, Sigurdur 6 mos; Quebec, 1879 2557.2 p37
Thorn, Daniel 32; Jamaica, 1725 3690.1 p226
Thorn, Esther; Quebec, 1850 5704.8 p66
Thorn, Philipp; New York, 1854 5647.5 p89
Thornber, John 35; Virginia, 1773 1219.7 p169
Thornberry, Susan; New York, NY, 1815 2859.11 p43
Thornbury, Rich.; Virginia, 1638 6219 p11
Thorncomb, Wm.; Virginia, 1636 6219 p74
Thorncombe, Wm.; Virginia, 1637 6219 p108
Thorncroft, Edwd; America, 1698 2212 p10
Thorndale, Anthony 25; Maryland, 1774 1219.7 p220
Thorne, Carl Emil Johannes; Arkansas, 1918 95.2 p122
Thorne, Catherine 35; Quebec, 1856 5704.8 p130
Thorne, Frederick; Illinois, 1894 5012.40 p54
Thorne, Henry; Virginia, 1637 6219 p9
Thorne, Henry O. 22; Kansas, 1886 5240.1 p69
Thorne, John; Philadelphia, 1811 53.26 p89
Thorne, John; Philadelphia, 1811 2859.11 p20
Thorne, Jon.; Virginia, 1637 6219 p28
Thorne, Philipp; New York, 1854 5647.5 p89
Thorne, Thomas; Virginia, 1638 6219 p120
Thornecroft, Edward; Virginia, 1640 6219 p181
Thorneford, Saml.; Virginia, 1637 6219 p24
Thorneton, Tho.; Virginia, 1636 6219 p32
Thorneton, W.; Virginia, 1642 6219 p189
Thornicroft, Edwd; Virginia, 1698 2212 p11
Thornley, Aarron 15; America, 1706 2212 p47
Thornley, Thomas 16; Virginia, 1700 2212 p32
Thornley, Thomas 42; Philadelphia, 1774 1219.7 p214
Thornson, Andrew 20; Charleston, SC, 1774 1639.20 p308
Thornton, Bernard; New York, NY, 1837 8208.4 p56
Thornton, Frank M.; Kansas, 1884 5240.1 p46
Thornton, James Albert, Jr.; Arkansas, 1918 95.2 p122
Thornton, John; Philadelphia, 1816 2859.11 p43
Thornton, John 30; Philadelphia, 1774 1219.7 p237
Thornton, John 34; Jamaica, 1731 3690.1 p226
Thornton, Luke; Virginia, 1694 6219 p162
Thornton, Mary 17; America, 1705 2212 p42
Thornton, Mary 18; America, 1705 2212 p45
Thornton, Nicholas; Philadelphia, 1816 2859.11 p43
Thornton, Owen 20; Philadelphia, 1865 5704.8 p164
Thornton, Rich.; Virginia, 1637 6219 p83
Thornton, Robert; New York, NY, 1839 8208.4 p91
Thornton, Thomas; Iowa, 1866-1943 123.54 p48
Thornton, William 8; New York, NY, 1868 5704.8 p227
Thornton, William 31; Maryland, 1723 3690.1 p226
Thorogood, Adam; Virginia, 1628 6219 p31
*Wife:*Sarah
Thorogood, Sarah *SEE* Thorogood, Adam
Thoroughgood, Adam; Virginia, 1634 6219 p32
Thoroughgood, Thos.; Virginia, 1628 6219 p31
Thorowgood, James; Maryland, 1753 1219.7 p26
Thorp, Edward; New York, 1754 3652 p80
Thorp, John 13; Maryland or Virginia, 1699 2212 p22
Thorp, Margaret 20; St. John, N.B., 1862 5704.8 p150
Thorp, Math. 24; Maryland or Virginia, 1699 2212 p22
Thorp, Zephaniah, Jr.; New York, NY, 1838 8208.4 p85
Thorpe, Christ.; Virginia, 1636 6219 p28
Thorpe, Christ.; Virginia, 1637 6219 p28
Thorpe, Daniell; Virginia, 1643 6219 p205
Thorpe, Francis 13; St. John, N.B., 1847 5704.8 p25
Thorpe, Wm.; Virginia, 1643 6219 p203
Thorrogood, Mary; Virginia, 1638 6219 p147
Thorrogood, Thomas; Virginia, 1639 6219 p154

Thorsen, C. 47; Washington, 1918-1920 ***1728.5*** *p14*
Thorsen, Forgus; Wisconsin, n.d. ***9675.8*** *p122*
Thorstein, Halfdan 25; Quebec, 1879 ***2557.2*** *p37*
Thorsteinsdorrir, Anna 7; Quebec, 1879 ***2557.2*** *p36*
Thorsteinsdottir, Anna 28; Quebec, 1879 ***2557.2*** *p36*
Thorsteinsdottir, Jonina 6 mos; Quebec, 1879 ***2557.2*** *p36*
Thorsteinsdottir, Maria 17; Quebec, 1879 ***2557.1*** *p38*
Thorsteinsson, Bjarni 2; Quebec, 1879 ***2557.1*** *p38A*
Thorsteinsson, Halfdan 25; Quebec, 1879 ***2557.2*** *p37*
Thorsteinsson, Magnus 48; Quebec, 1879 ***2557.2*** *p37*
Thorsteinsson, Sigbjorn 30; Quebec, 1879 ***2557.1*** *p38*
Thorsteinsson, Stefan 5; Quebec, 1879 ***2557.1*** *p38A*
Thorsteinsson, Vilborg 4; Quebec, 1879 ***2557.1*** *p38A*
Thorup, Marinus; Arkansas, 1918 ***95.2*** *p122*
Thorwaldsdottir, Ragnhildur 44; Quebec, 1879 ***2557.1*** *p20*
Thorwart, Balthasar; Philadelphia, 1756 ***4525*** *p261*
Thoss, Eduard; Kentucky, 1843 ***8582.3*** *p99*
Thoss, Franz Eduard; America, 1836 ***8582.3*** *p65*
Thoux, Miss 5; America, 1835 ***778.5*** *p517*
Thoux, Miss 7; America, 1835 ***778.5*** *p517*
Thoux, Mme. 32; America, 1835 ***778.5*** *p518*
Thoux, Mr. 9; America, 1835 ***778.5*** *p517*
Thoux, Mr. 34; America, 1835 ***778.5*** *p517*
Thownsend, Edward; Virginia, 1642 ***6219*** *p186*
Thraenle, Innocenz; Cincinnati, 1828 ***8582.1*** *p51*
Thrallop, Timothy; Virginia, 1647 ***6219*** *p245*
Thrane, A. Paulus; New York, 1761 ***3652*** *p88*
Thrant, Anthony; Ohio, 1860 ***6014.2*** *p7*
Threadgold, Sarah 20; Norfolk, VA, 1774 ***1219.7*** *p222*
Threappleton, Arthur 42; West Virginia, 1898 ***9788.3*** *p21*
Threlfell, John; Virginia, 1698 ***2212*** *p11*
Thresher, Isabel; Virginia, 1636 ***6219*** *p32*
*Husband:*Robert
Thresher, Robert *SEE* Thresher, Isabel
Thresher, Robt., Jr.; Virginia, 1636 ***6219*** *p32*
Thrickmorton, Robert; Virginia, 1645 ***6219*** *p239*
Thrift, James; Virginia, 1638 ***6219*** *p158*
Thrift, James; Virginia, 1639 ***6219*** *p158*
Throckmorton, Robert; Virginia, 1637 ***6219*** *p112*
Thromerhaus, Balthasar; Indiana, 1846 ***9117*** *p18*
Thron, Charles; Milwaukee, 1875 ***4719.30*** *p258*
Thron, Conrad; Indiana, 1858 ***5647.5*** *p79*
Thrun, August Gottlieb; Wisconsin, n.d. ***9675.8*** *p122*
Thrun, John; Wisconsin, n.d. ***9675.8*** *p122*
Thrush, Clement; Virginia, 1623 ***6219*** *p20*
Thruston, George 18; Maryland, 1721 ***3690.1*** *p226*
Thuesen, Aksel Christian; Illinois, 1922 ***3455.3*** *p80*
Thuesen, Aksel Christian; New York, NY, 1911 ***3455.3*** *p82*
Thuesen, Sksel Christian; New York, NY, 1911 ***3455.4*** *p55*
Thuillier, Pierre 25; New Orleans, 1838 ***778.5*** *p518*
Thull, Michael; Wisconsin, n.d. ***9675.8*** *p122*
Thull, Peter; Wisconsin, n.d. ***9675.8*** *p122*
Thum, Jacob; Pennsylvania, 1754 ***2444*** *p226*
Thum, Peter; America, 1777-1778 ***8582.2*** *p67*
Thumb, Jacob; Pennsylvania, 1754 ***2444*** *p226*
Thumm, Andreas *SEE* Thumm, Jacob
Thumm, Anna Catharina; Pennsylvania, 1754 ***2444*** *p173*
Thumm, Jacob; Pennsylvania, 1754 ***2444*** *p226*
*Child:*Johann Georg
*Child:*Andreas
Thumm, Johann Georg *SEE* Thumm, Jacob
Thun, . . .; Canada, 1776-1783 ***9786*** *p35*
Thun, Ferdinand; America, 1886 ***8125.8*** *p438*
Thunder, Peter; Virginia, 1642 ***6219*** *p196*
Thunderfeld, v., Cap.; Quebec, 1776 ***9786*** *p105*
Thunel, . . .; Canada, 1776-1783 ***9786*** *p35*
Thungt, Johann Melchior; South Carolina, 1788 ***7119*** *p200*
Thurman, F. U. G. 22; Kansas, 1891 ***5240.1*** *p76*
Thurmauer, Max; Cincinnati, 1869-1887 ***8582*** *p32*
Thuron, Mr. 25; New Orleans, 1825 ***778.5*** *p518*
Thursby, William 28; Nova Scotia, 1774 ***1219.7*** *p195*
Thurston, Tho.; Virginia, 1636 ***6219*** *p32*
Thute, Matthew; New York, NY, 1838 ***8208.4*** *p74*
Thyssen, Cornelius Johannes Jacobus; Washington, 1859-1920 ***2872.1*** *p40*
Tiarks, Fred; Iroquois Co., IL, 1894 ***3455.1*** *p13*
Tibaults, Robert; Virginia, 1643 ***6219*** *p205*
Tibbs, Michaell; Virginia, 1637 ***6219*** *p111*
Tibby, Robert 19; Jamaica, 1725 ***3690.1*** *p226*
Tiberry, Ann Jane; St. John, N.B., 1850 ***5704.8*** *p61*
Tiberry, Charlotte; St. John, N.B., 1850 ***5704.8*** *p61*
Tiberry, Margaret; St. John, N.B., 1850 ***5704.8*** *p61*
Tiberson, Jane 21; Philadelphia, 1774 ***1219.7*** *p234*
Tibor, Michael; Wisconsin, n.d. ***9675.8*** *p122*
Tice, John 24; Maryland, 1774 ***1219.7*** *p214*
Tice, Philip J.; Illinois, 1861 ***7857*** *p7*
Tick, Jacob; Illinois, 1891 ***2896.5*** *p40*
Ticker, Philip 42; Philadelphia, 1774 ***1219.7*** *p217*
Tickle, Peirce 17; New England, 1699 ***2212*** *p19*
Tickner, Isaac 24; Virginia, 1774 ***1219.7*** *p201*
Ticktin, Ascher 11 mos; New York, NY, 1878 ***9253*** *p46*
Ticktin, Isaack 7; New York, NY, 1878 ***9253*** *p46*
Ticktin, Rachel 36; New York, NY, 1878 ***9253*** *p46*
Ticollier, Peter 30; New Orleans, 1836 ***778.5*** *p518*
Tidd, Samuel 27; Jamaica, 1723 ***3690.1*** *p226*
Tidd, William 21; Maryland, 1775 ***1219.7*** *p253*
Tidland, Chas. L. 8; Massachusetts, 1849 ***5881.1*** *p94*
Tidland, Christina M. 10; Massachusetts, 1849 ***5881.1*** *p94*
Tidland, Fred. L. E. 4; Massachusetts, 1849 ***5881.1*** *p94*
Tidland, Jno. A.U. 15; Massachusetts, 1849 ***5881.1*** *p94*
Tidland, John 38; Massachusetts, 1849 ***5881.1*** *p94*
Tidland, Justina 39; Massachusetts, 1849 ***5881.1*** *p94*
Tidwall, Knute 24; Arkansas, 1918 ***95.2*** *p122*
Tie, Timothy 26; Massachusetts, 1850 ***5881.1*** *p95*
Tiebant, Ann 21 *SEE* Tiebant, Peter
Tiebant, Peter 30; Philadelphia, 1774 ***1219.7*** *p182*
*Wife:*Ann 21
Tieckman, . . .; Canada, 1776-1783 ***9786*** *p35*
Tiedemann, Mr.; Charleston, SC, 1777 ***8582.2*** *p42*
Tief, Joachim 40; Kansas, 1884 ***5240.1*** *p45*
Tief, Joachim 40; Kansas, 1884 ***5240.1*** *p65*
Tiegel, Anna Barbara *SEE* Tiegel, Hans Jacob
Tiegel, Hans Jacob; Pennsylvania, 1752 ***2444*** *p148*
*Wife:*Ursula
*Child:*Johann Jacob
*Child:*Anna Barbara
Tiegel, Johann Jacob *SEE* Tiegel, Hans Jacob
Tiegel, Ursula *SEE* Tiegel, Hans Jacob
Tiekemeyer, Mr.; America, 1824-1845 ***4610.10*** *p150*
With wife
Tiekemeyer, Christian Heinrich; America, 1845 ***4610.10*** *p150*
Tielecke, . . .; Canada, 1776-1783 ***9786*** *p35*
Tieleke, . . .; Canada, 1776-1783 ***9786*** *p35*
Tielker, Miss; America, 1854 ***4610.10*** *p135*
Tielker, Heinrich Friedrich; America, 1854 ***4610.10*** *p151*
Tieman, Karl; New York, NY, 1867 ***3702.7*** *p577*
Tiemann, Anne Marie Ilsabein Engel; America, 1845 ***4610.10*** *p141*
Tiemann, August; America, 1829 ***8582.2*** *p61*
Tiemann, August; Baltimore, 1830 ***8582*** *p32*
Tiemann, Catherine F. Moller *SEE* Tiemann, Johann Christoph
Tiemann, Christine L. E. Sander 22 *SEE* Tiemann, Johann Hermann Heinrich
Tiemann, Engel; America, 1844 ***4610.10*** *p141*
Tiemann, Johann Christoph; America, 1842 ***4610.10*** *p119*
*Wife:*Catherine F. Moller
Tiemann, Johann Hermann Heinrich; America, 1850 ***4610.10*** *p143*
*Wife:*Christine L. E. Sander 22
Tiemann, Joseph Ferdinand; America, 1845 ***8582.2*** *p41*
Tiemann, Karl 19; New York, NY, 1867 ***3702.7*** *p571*
Tiemann, Philipp; America, 1845 ***8582.2*** *p42*
Tiemans, Gerritt; Washington, 1859-1920 ***2872.1*** *p40*
Tiemei, Heinerich; Indianapolis, 1867 ***3702.7*** *p578*
Tiemeier, Heinerich; New York, NY, 1867 ***3702.7*** *p579*
Tiemens, William; Washington, 1859-1920 ***2872.1*** *p40*
Tien, Daniel; Pennsylvania, 1751 ***2444*** *p226*
Tien, Jean Henri; Pennsylvania, 1751 ***2444*** *p226*
Tieniger, Fritz 27; Kansas, 1892 ***5240.1*** *p77*
Tienon, Patrick; Ohio, 1867 ***6014.2*** *p7*
Tierer, Michael; Pennsylvania, 1754 ***2444*** *p148*
Tiernay, John; Illinois, 1869 ***5012.38*** *p99*
Tierney, Ann 18; Philadelphia, 1858 ***5704.8*** *p139*
Tierney, Francis; Philadelphia, 1816 ***2859.11*** *p43*
Tierney, John; Colorado, 1894 ***9678.3*** *p16*
Tierney, Joseph; Philadelphia, 1816 ***2859.11*** *p43*
Tierney, Margaret; Philadelphia, 1816 ***2859.11*** *p43*
Tierny, Hugh; Philadelphia, 1816 ***2859.11*** *p43*
Tierny, John; St. John, N.B., 1847 ***5704.8*** *p35*
Tierny, Mary; St. John, N.B., 1847 ***5704.8*** *p35*
Tiers, Catherine *SEE* Tiers, Jean Henri
Tiers, Catherine Chapelle *SEE* Tiers, Jean Henri
Tiers, Daniel *SEE* Tiers, Jean Henri
Tiers, Daniel; Pennsylvania, 1751 ***2444*** *p226*
*Wife:*Marie Conte
*Child:*Matthieu
*Child:*Madeleine
*Child:*Jean Daniel
Tiers, Jean Daniel *SEE* Tiers, Daniel
Tiers, Jean Henri; Pennsylvania, 1751 ***2444*** *p226*
*Wife:*Catherine Chapelle
*Child:*Daniel
*Child:*Catherine
Tiers, Madeleine *SEE* Tiers, Daniel
Tiers, Marie Conte *SEE* Tiers, Daniel
Tiers, Matthieu *SEE* Tiers, Daniel
Tiersch, Paul; New York, 1763 ***3652*** *p89*
Ties, Christine; Kansas, 1885 ***5240.1*** *p45*
Tieske, August; America, 1849 ***1450.2*** *p145A*
Tiesmeier, Ernst Heinrich; America, 1853 ***4610.10*** *p121*
Tiesmeier, Johann Heinrich; America, 1850 ***4610.10*** *p120*
Tieste, Louis; America, 1849 ***1450.2*** *p145A*
Tietz, Anton; Philadelphia, 1892 ***1450.2*** *p39B*
Tiffany, Daniel 24; Philadelphia, 1804 ***53.26*** *p89*
Tiffeney, John; Virginia, 1638 ***6219*** *p146*
Tiffin, William; America, 1738 ***4971*** *p99*
Tiffiney, Jon.; Virginia, 1637 ***6219*** *p110*
Tifford, Michael 23; Massachusetts, 1849 ***5881.1*** *p95*
Tiffords, George 28; Philadelphia, 1803 ***53.26*** *p89*
Tigh, Richard; Montreal, 1822 ***7603*** *p61*
Tighe, John Gustavus; New York, NY, 1839 ***8208.4*** *p92*
Tighe, Joseph W.; Illinois, 1900 ***5012.40*** *p77*
Tighe, Michael; New Brunswick, 1825 ***7603*** *p59*
Tighe, Michael; New York, NY, 1816 ***2859.11*** *p43*
Tigny, Mme. 45; Port uncertain, 1839 ***778.5*** *p518*
Tigny, Maria Renee 7; Port uncertain, 1839 ***778.5*** *p518*
Tigny, Rosalie 4; Port uncertain, 1839 ***778.5*** *p518*
Tigo, Louie; Arkansas, 1918 ***95.2*** *p122*
Tigue, Ann 6; Massachusetts, 1848 ***5881.1*** *p93*
Tigue, Mary 30; Massachusetts, 1848 ***5881.1*** *p94*
Tigut, Matthew; New York, NY, 1816 ***2859.11*** *p43*
Tijan, Ivan; Iowa, 1866-1943 ***123.54*** *p48*
Tikkanen, David; Washington, 1859-1920 ***2872.1*** *p40*
Tikkanen, Edit Ellisi; Washington, 1859-1920 ***2872.1*** *p40*
Tikkanen, Henry; Washington, 1859-1920 ***2872.1*** *p40*
Tikkanen, Miina; Washington, 1859-1920 ***2872.1*** *p40*
Tikkanen, Taavetti Ilmari; Washington, 1859-1920 ***2872.1*** *p40*
Tikkanen, Weikko; Washington, 1859-1920 ***2872.1*** *p40*
Tilcock, William; Virginia, 1642 ***6219*** *p196*
Tilemann, Lubbenns; Illinois, 1895 ***5012.40*** *p54*
Till, Elizabeth *SEE* Till, Jacob
Till, Jacob; New York, 1753 ***3652*** *p77*
*Wife:*Elizabeth
Till, Rebecca *SEE* Till, Susan
Till, Susan; New York, 1753 ***3652*** *p77*
*Relative:*Rebecca
Till, William; Virginia, 1639 ***6219*** *p152*
Tillema, Jan; Arkansas, 1918 ***95.2*** *p122*
Tillert, . . .; Canada, 1776-1783 ***9786*** *p35*
Tillet, John; Virginia, 1648 ***6219*** *p246*
Tilley, D. H.; Washington, 1859-1920 ***2872.1*** *p40*
Tilley, Henry; Washington, 1859-1920 ***2872.1*** *p40*
Tilley, William 21; Virginia, 1774 ***1219.7*** *p240*
Tillford, Eliza 19; Massachusetts, 1847 ***5881.1*** *p94*
Tillig, Alexander; Philadelphia, 1866 ***5704.8*** *p214*
Tillig, Henry; Philadelphia, 1866 ***5704.8*** *p214*
Tillinger, Lodowick; Philadelphia, 1759 ***9973.7*** *p34*
Tillman, George; New York, NY, 1835 ***8208.4*** *p7*
Tillmann, Andrew; Wisconsin, n.d. ***9675.8*** *p122*
Tillney, Symon; Virginia, 1639 ***6219*** *p22*
Tillwood, William 17; Maryland, 1775 ***1219.7*** *p254*
Tilly, Henry; Wisconsin, n.d. ***9675.8*** *p123*
Tilly, James; New York, NY, 1838 ***8208.4*** *p71*
Tilman, Christopher; Virginia, 1638 ***6219*** *p160*
Tilney, Stephen 20; Jamaica, 1731 ***3690.1*** *p226*
Tilsley, Thomas; Virginia, 1638 ***6219*** *p147*
Tilson, Andrew; Illinois, 1888 ***5012.39*** *p121*
Tilson, George; Washington, 1859-1920 ***2872.1*** *p41*
Tilson, Richard; Illinois, 1876 ***5012.37*** *p60*
Tilstra, Peter; Iroquois Co., IL, 1894 ***3455.1*** *p13*
Tilt, John 17; Pennsylvania, 1738 ***3690.1*** *p226*
Timany, Bryan 24; St. John, N.B., 1857 ***5704.8*** *p134*
Timenny, Francis 24; St. John, N.B., 1857 ***5704.8*** *p134*
Timeny, Charles; St. John, N.B., 1847 ***5704.8*** *p3*
Timeny, Ellen; St. John, N.B., 1847 ***5704.8*** *p3*
Timeny, Ellen 10; St. John, N.B., 1847 ***5704.8*** *p3*
Timeny, James; St. John, N.B., 1847 ***5704.8*** *p3*
Timeny, John; St. John, N.B., 1847 ***5704.8*** *p3*
Timeny, Margaret 8; St. John, N.B., 1847 ***5704.8*** *p3*
Timler, Peter; Pennsylvania, 1724-1765 ***2444*** *p150*
Timm, August; Wisconsin, n.d. ***9675.8*** *p123*
Timmerberg, Christine K Friederike *SEE* Timmerberg, Johann Christoph
Timmerberg, Christoph Friedrich *SEE* Timmerberg, Johann Christoph
Timmerberg, Johann Christoph 38; America, 1852 ***4610.10*** *p148*
*Child:*Justine Friederike
*Child:*Christoph Friedrich
*Child:*Karl Friedrich August
*Child:*Christine K Friederike
With wife
Timmerberg, Justine Friederike *SEE* Timmerberg, Johann Christoph
Timmerberg, Karl Friedrich August *SEE* Timmerberg, Johann Christoph

Timmerkamp, H. W. 42; Kansas, 1904 5240.1 p45
Timmerkamp, H. W. 42; Kansas, 1904 5240.1 p83
Timmerkamp, Joseph 25; Kansas, 1896 5240.1 p80
Timmerkamp, William 38; Kansas, 1898 5240.1 p81
Timmerman, Berend 51; New York, NY, 1847 3377.6 p15
Timmerman, H.; Wisconsin, n.d. 9675.8 p123
Timmerman, Hendrik 19; New York, NY, 1847 3377.6 p15
Timmerman, Hendrika 8; New York, NY, 1847 3377.6 p15
Timmerman, Hendrika 22; New York, NY, 1847 3377.6 p15
Timmerman, Hermannus 16; New York, NY, 1847 3377.6 p15
Timmerman, Jenneken 51; New York, NY, 1847 3377.6 p15
Timmerman, Johann G.; Illinois, 1855 7857 p7
Timmerman, John; Illinois, 1839 7857 p7
Timmerman, Petter; South Carolina, 1788 7119 p204
Timmermann, . . .; Cincinnati, 1826 8582.1 p51
Timmins, Luke 22; Massachusetts, 1849 5881.1 p94
Timmins, Sarah 21; Maryland, 1774 1219.7 p230
Timmory, Edward; New York, NY, 1811 2859.11 p20
Timms, Alfred; Iroquois Co., IL, 1894 3455.1 p13
Timms, John 16; Maryland, 1751 1219.7 p3
Timney, Mary; America, 1869 5704.8 p231
Timoly, Mathew 28; Philadelphia, 1803 53.26 p89
Timons, Isabella; New York, NY, 1811 2859.11 p20
Timons, Timothy; New York, NY, 1811 2859.11 p20
Timrod, Heinrich; Charleston, SC, 1775-1781 8582.2 p52
Tims, James; New York, NY, 1839 8208.4 p99
Tims, John 16; Maryland, 1751 3690.1 p226
Timson, George; Iowa, 1866-1943 123.54 p48
Tindall, William; New York, NY, 1815 2859.11 p43
Tiner, Richard; New Brunswick, 1822 7603 p65
Tiney, Thomas; New York, NY, 1816 2859.11 p43
Tingle, William 15; Philadelphia, 1775 1219.7 p271
Tingley, John Henry; Washington, 1859-1920 2872.1 p41
Tingy, Jon.; Virginia, 1636 6219 p34
Tinkler, Edward; New York, NY, 1834 8208.4 p1
Tinkler, William; New York, NY, 1834 8208.4 p2
Tinner, Sylvester; New York, NY, 1840 8208.4 p107
Tinney, John; Philadelphia, 1852 5704.8 p85
Tinney, Margery; Philadelphia, 1865 5704.8 p194
Tinney, Neil; Philadelphia, 1865 5704.8 p173
Tinney, William; New Orleans, 1849 5704.8 p59
Tinsley, William; America, 1851 1450.2 p145A
Tint, Louis 42; Kansas, 1892 5240.1 p77
Tintori, Giovanni; Arkansas, 1918 95.2 p122
Tinwell, John; Virginia, 1637 6219 p24
Tip, . . .; Canada, 1776-1783 9786 p35
Tiplad, Jon.; Virginia, 1642 6219 p198
Tiplady, John; Virginia, 1639 6219 p157
Tiplar, John 19; Jamaica, 1735 3690.1 p226
Tipler, John 19; Jamaica, 1735 3690.1 p226
Tipler, Laurance 19; Maryland, 1718 3690.1 p226
Tippett, James H.; Nevada, 1875 2764.35 p69
Tipping, Dorothy 21; America, 1702 2212 p39
Tipson, Joseph; Barbados, 1751 1219.7 p8
Tireniz, M.-Barbe Nondre; Quebec, 1761 7603 p22
Tiringen, Johann Christoph; Pennsylvania, 1752 2444 p226
Tirmenstein, Anna Maria 12 *SEE* Tirmenstein, Samuel
Tirmenstein, Anna Susanna 2 *SEE* Tirmenstein, Samuel
Tirmenstein, Christ. Concordie 9 *SEE* Tirmenstein, Samuel
Tirmenstein, Christne. Therese 30 *SEE* Tirmenstein, Samuel
Tirmenstein, Elisabeth Juliana 11 *SEE* Tirmenstein, Samuel
Tirmenstein, Esther Therese 7 *SEE* Tirmenstein, Samuel
Tirmenstein, Gustav Adolph 4 *SEE* Tirmenstein, Samuel
Tirmenstein, Martin Paulus 4 mos *SEE* Tirmenstein, Samuel
Tirmenstein, Samuel 44; New Orleans, 1839 9420.2 p169
*Wife:*Christne. Therese 30
*Child:*Anna Maria 12
*Child:*Elisabeth Juliana 11
*Child:*Christ. Concordie 9
*Child:*Samuel Martin 8
*Child:*Esther Therese 7
*Child:*Gustav Adolph 4
*Child:*Anna Susanna 2
*Child:*Martin Paulus 4 mos
Tirmenstein, Samuel Martin 8 *SEE* Tirmenstein, Samuel
Tirney, Fanny 23; Philadelphia, 1858 5704.8 p139
Tirney, Mary 21; Philadelphia, 1858 5704.8 p139
Tirry, William 16; Pennsylvania, 1721 3690.1 p227
Tiry, . . .; Canada, 1776-1783 9786 p35
Tisari, Emel; Washington, 1859-1920 2872.1 p41
Tisciotta, Carmine 40; New York, NY, 1893 9026.4 p42
Tisdale, James 20; Pennsylvania, 1725 3690.1 p227
Tisdale, Thomas Rolph; New Jersey, 1850 6013.19 p89
Tisse, Jean 23; America, 1838 778.5 p518
Tisserand, Mr. 28; Port uncertain, 1838 778.5 p518
Tisserand, Catherine *SEE* Tisserand, Jacques
Tisserand, George *SEE* Tisserand, Jacques
Tisserand, Jacques *SEE* Tisserand, Jacques
Tisserand, Jacques 29; Halifax, N.S., 1752 7074.6 p212
*Wife:*Catherine
*Son:*Pierre
*Son:*George
*Son:*Jacques
Tisserand, Pierre *SEE* Tisserand, Jacques
Titcomb, Thomas 25; Maryland, 1774 1219.7 p235
Tite, James 17; Barbados, 1775 1219.7 p279
Tith, George 19; New Orleans, 1838 778.5 p518
Titlore, Jos.; Virginia, 1636 6219 p21
Titmore, John; Philadelphia, 1759 9973.7 p34
Titon, William; Virginia, 1638 6219 p120
Titting, Friedrich; Cincinnati, 1869-1887 8582 p33
Tittsel, . . .; Canada, 1776-1783 9786 p35
Tixton, John; Virginia, 1641 6219 p187
Tize, Peter; New York, 1831-1832 9892.11 p46
Tjarks, Luppe Jansson; Iroquois Co., IL, 1885 3455.1 p13
Tland, Emile 21; Kansas, 1872 5240.1 p52
Tlgen, N. 27; New Orleans, 1839 9420.2 p169
Toaccea, Ward; Iowa, 1866-1943 123.54 p48
Toady, Ann 18; Massachusetts, 1849 5881.1 p93
Toady, Catharine 50; Massachusetts, 1847 5881.1 p94
Tobaben, Johann; Kansas, 1910 6013.40 p17
Toback, Henry 26; Kansas, 1881 5240.1 p63
Tobalska, Anna 19; New York, 1912 9980.29 p57
Toben, John A. F. 28; Kansas, 1882 5240.1 p63
Tobergh, Magdeline 22; New Orleans, 1836 778.5 p518
Toberman, Charles; Minneapolis, 1867-1884 6410.35 p66
Tobia, Margaret 10; Massachusetts, 1849 5881.1 p95
Tobin, Alexander; Milwaukee, 1875 4719.30 p257
Tobin, Catherine; New York, NY, 1815 2859.11 p43
Tobin, Edward 30; California, 1871 2769.9 p4
Tobin, Ellen 8; Massachusetts, 1848 5881.1 p94
Tobin, James; America, 1741 4971 p60
Tobin, John; America, 1739 4971 p14
Tobin, John; Illinois, 1863 7857 p7
Tobin, Joseph; Quebec, 1814 7603 p59
Tobin, Judy 50; Massachusetts, 1849 5881.1 p94
Tobin, Michael 18; New York, 1775 1219.7 p246
Tobin, Thomas 27; Kansas, 1889 5240.1 p73
Tock, Fred; Iowa, 1866-1943 123.54 p48
Tockhorn, Henry W. 30; Kansas, 1894 5240.1 p46
Tockhorn, Henry W. 30; Kansas, 1894 5240.1 p79
Tockwood, Elizabeth; Virginia, 1643 6219 p207
Todavich, Alice; Iowa, 1866-1943 123.54 p81
Todd, Adam; St. John, N.B., 1848 5704.8 p44
Todd, Adam Gill; St. John, N.B., 1848 5704.8 p44
Todd, Adam Gill 4; St. John, N.B., 1848 5704.8 p44
Todd, Alice; Washington, 1859-1920 2872.1 p41
Todd, Andrew 19; Jamaica, 1731 3690.1 p227
Todd, Arch.d; Petersburg, VA, 1810 4778.2 p142
Todd, Berniece; Washington, 1859-1920 2872.1 p41
Todd, Bessy Ann 2; St. John, N.B., 1848 5704.8 p44
Todd, Earl; Washington, 1859-1920 2872.1 p41
Todd, Elizabeth *SEE* Todd, Thomas
Todd, George 16; Port uncertain, 1774 1219.7 p176
Todd, Hazel; Washington, 1859-1920 2872.1 p41
Todd, Henry; St. John, N.B., 1848 5704.8 p44
Todd, Isaac Ledger 31; Arkansas, 1918 95.2 p122
Todd, Ivy Gale; Washington, 1859-1920 2872.1 p41
Todd, James; Iowa, 1866-1943 123.54 p48
Todd, James; South Carolina, 1734 1639.20 p308
Todd, James 20; Philadelphia, 1803 53.26 p89
Todd, John; New York, NY, 1837 8208.4 p34
Todd, John; New York, NY, 1864 5704.8 p185
Todd, Jonathan 23; Jamaica, 1736 3690.1 p227
Todd, Margaret; St. John, N.B., 1848 5704.8 p44
Todd, Margarett 19; New England, 1699 2212 p19
Todd, Martha; St. John, N.B., 1848 5704.8 p44
Todd, Martha 25; St. John, N.B., 1861 5704.8 p147
Todd, Mary Jane; Philadelphia, 1852 5704.8 p88
Todd, Mathew; Virginia, 1646 6219 p242
Todd, Matilda 1; St. John, N.B., 1848 5704.8 p44
Todd, Oneta; Washington, 1859-1920 2872.1 p41
Todd, P. E.; Washington, 1859-1920 2872.1 p41
Todd, Patrick 20; Philadelphia, 1858 5704.8 p139
Todd, Percy Earle Alonzo; Washington, 1859-1920 2872.1 p41
Todd, Percy Edward; Washington, 1859-1920 2872.1 p41
Todd, Rachael 19; New York, 1774 1219.7 p222
Todd, Rebecca; St. John, N.B., 1848 5704.8 p44
Todd, Rebecca 6; St. John, N.B., 1848 5704.8 p44
Todd, Richard 21; South Carolina, 1775 1219.7 p266
Todd, Robert; Virginia, 1638 6219 p120
Todd, Robert; Virginia, 1647 6219 p239
Todd, Robert 33; Arizona, 1890 2764.35 p69
Todd, Robert 46; Arizona, 1890 2764.35 p68
Todd, Samuel; New York, NY, 1816 2859.11 p43
Todd, Stephen; New York, NY, 1815 2859.11 p43
Todd, Thomas; New York, NY, 1816 2859.11 p43
Todd, Thomas; Virginia, 1637 6219 p33
*Wife:*Elizabeth
Todd, Thomas; Virginia, 1642 6219 p193
Todd, Thomas 24; Wilmington, DE, 1831 6508.3 p101
Todd, William; South Carolina, 1767 1639.20 p308
Todd, Winnefred; Washington, 1859-1920 2872.1 p41
Todd, Winnie; Washington, 1859-1920 2872.1 p41
Todey, George; Iowa, 1866-1943 123.54 p81
Todle, Ann; Quebec, 1749-1750 7603 p86
Tody, Blaz; Iowa, 1866-1943 123.54 p48
Tody, John; Iowa, 1866-1943 123.54 p48
Toelle, . . .; Canada, 1776-1783 9786 p35
Toellner, Christian Frederick; New York, 1753 3652 p77
Toeltschig, John; New York, 1752 3652 p76
Toennessen, Jonas M.; Wisconsin, n.d. 9675.8 p123
Toerner, Gerhard H.; America, 1846 8582.1 p34
Tofield, Charles 31; Jamaica, 1736 3690.1 p227
Toflo, Emilo; Iowa, 1866-1943 123.54 p48
Tofte, Jens Peter; New York, NY, 1840 8208.4 p103
Tofts, William 20; United States or West Indies, 1732 3690.1 p227
Togel, Christian Timotheus; Quebec, 1776 9786 p260
Tognetti, Frank 21; Kansas, 1884 5240.1 p65
Tohbens, Joseph; Montreal, 1823 7603 p99
Tohey, Patrick 30; Massachusetts, 1847 5881.1 p95
Tohill, John; Washington, 1859-1920 2872.1 p41
Tohlis, Mary *SEE* Tohlis, Michael
Tohlis, Michael *SEE* Tohlis, Michael
Tohlis, Michael; America, 1895 7137 p170
*Relative:*Michael
*Wife:*Mary
Toigo, Geo.; Iowa, 1866-1943 123.54 p48
Toigo, John; Iowa, 1866-1943 123.54 p49
Toivrego, Tom; Iowa, 1866-1943 123.54 p49
Toksej, Jurko 39; New York, 1912 9980.29 p63
Toksej, Maria 17; New York, 1912 9980.29 p63
Tolan, Betty; St. John, N.B., 1853 5704.8 p99
Tolan, Brien; Philadelphia, 1849 53.26 p89
Tolan, Brien; Philadelphia, 1849 5704.8 p54
Tolan, Catherine; Philadelphia, 1852 5704.8 p96
Tolan, Catherine 20; Philadelphia, 1853 5704.8 p113
Tolan, Eliza J. 18; Philadelphia, 1853 5704.8 p113
Tolan, Ellen; Philadelphia, 1865 5704.8 p189
Tolan, Ellen; St. John, N.B., 1852 5704.8 p83
Tolan, John 10; Philadelphia, 1852 5704.8 p96
Tolan, John 16; Philadelphia, 1859 5704.8 p141
Tolan, Mary; St. John, N.B., 1849 5704.8 p49
Tolan, Mary 15; Philadelphia, 1859 5704.8 p141
Tolan, Mary 50; Philadelphia, 1859 5704.8 p141
Tolan, Michael; St. John, N.B., 1852 5704.8 p83
Tolan, Sarah 18; Philadelphia, 1859 5704.8 p141
Tolan, William 28; Philadelphia, 1859 5704.8 p141
Toland, Ann 13; St. John, N.B., 1848 5704.8 p43
Toland, Ann 13; St. John, N.B., 1853 5704.8 p109
Toland, Anne 2; St. John, N.B., 1847 5704.8 p4
Toland, Betty; St. John, N.B., 1847 5704.8 p4
Toland, Biddy; St. John, N.B., 1847 5704.8 p4
Toland, Biddy; St. John, N.B., 1847 5704.8 p19
Toland, Biddy 3 mos; St. John, N.B., 1847 5704.8 p3
Toland, Bridget 5; Philadelphia, 1866 5704.8 p209
Toland, Catherine; Philadelphia, 1852 5704.8 p88
Toland, Catherine; St. John, N.B., 1851 5704.8 p78
Toland, Daniel; Philadelphia, 1847 53.26 p89
Toland, Daniel; Philadelphia, 1847 5704.8 p13
Toland, Daniel; Philadelphia, 1849 53.26 p89
Toland, Daniel; Philadelphia, 1849 5704.8 p54
Toland, Dennis 29; Philadelphia, 1854 5704.8 p116
Toland, Edward 1 mo; St. John, N.B., 1852 5704.8 p83
Toland, Edward 12; St. John, N.B., 1853 5704.8 p99
Toland, Ellen; Philadelphia, 1852 5704.8 p88
Toland, Ellen 16; St. John, N.B., 1854 5704.8 p120
Toland, Grace 10; St. John, N.B., 1847 5704.8 p4
Toland, James; Philadelphia, 1852 5704.8 p85
Toland, James; St. John, N.B., 1848 5704.8 p38
Toland, James 3; St. John, N.B., 1847 5704.8 p3
Toland, James 7; Philadelphia, 1852 5704.8 p97
Toland, John; New York, NY, 1816 2859.11 p43
Toland, John; New York, NY, 1864 5704.8 p170
Toland, John; Philadelphia, 1865 5704.8 p201
Toland, John; St. John, N.B., 1848 5704.8 p43
Toland, John; St. John, N.B., 1851 5704.8 p78
Toland, John; St. John, N.B., 1853 5704.8 p99
Toland, John 2; St. John, N.B., 1852 5704.8 p83
Toland, John 50; St. John, N.B., 1853 5704.8 p109
Toland, Kitty 7; St. John, N.B., 1852 5704.8 p83
Toland, Letitia 8; Philadelphia, 1852 5704.8 p97
Toland, Martha 50; St. John, N.B., 1853 5704.8 p109

Toomer, George; Virginia, 1751 1219.7 p1
Toomey, Daniel; Quebec, 1822 7603 p64
Toomey, Denis F.; New York, NY, 1888 1450.2 p40B
Toomey, Frank; Arizona, 1898 9228.30 p6
Toomey, Richard 25; Massachusetts, 1847 5881.1 p95
Toomy, Frances; Montreal, 1822 7603 p65
Toomy, John 27; Baltimore, 1775 1219.7 p270
Tooney, Patrick; Illinois, 1868 2896.5 p40
Toony, George J.; Washington, 1859-1920 2872.1 p41
Toop, Johanna 21; Jamaica, 1730 3690.1 p292
Toope, Johanna 21; Jamaica, 1730 3690.1 p292
Tooth, Joseph 38; Jamaica, 1730 3690.1 p227
Toothacre, Edward 22; Maryland, 1775 1219.7 p265
Topelmann, Edward R.; Wisconsin, n.d. 9675.8 p123
Topham, Richard 29; Nova Scotia, 1774 1219.7 p209
With wife
With child
Topie, Gerh Fried; America, 1841 8582.2 p42
Toporowski, Adam; Arkansas, 1918 95.2 p123
Topos, Jan 20; New York, 1912 9980.29 p66
Topp, Charles; America, 1848 1450.2 p145A
Topp, Charles; America, 1851 1450.2 p145A
Topp, Friederich; America, 1882 3702.7 p450
Topp, William 19; Jamaica, 1731 3690.1 p227
Topper, George 20; Windward Islands, 1722 3690.1 p218
Toppin, Ann *SEE* Toppin, Henry
Toppin, Henry; Virginia, 1636 6219 p13
*Wife:*Ann
Toppin, Henry; Virginia, 1652 6251 p20
Toppin, James 22; America, 1699 2212 p29
Topping, Hugh; America, 1700 2212 p33
Topping, John 23; Philadelphia, 1774 1219.7 p232
Topping, John 38; Philadelphia, 1861 5704.8 p147
Toppitz, Johann Gottlieb 32; New Orleans, 1839 9420.2 p71
Torassin, Catherine 18; Philadelphia, 1860 5704.8 p144
Torell, Charles; Colorado, 1904 9678.3 p16
Torguson, James; Wisconsin, n.d. 9675.8 p123
Torkelson, Job; Illinois, 1892 2896.5 p40
Torkelson, John; Kansas, 1884 5240.1 p46
Torkelson, Nels; Iowa, 1866-1943 123.54 p49
Tormene, Joseph; Arkansas, 1918 95.2 p123
Tornbury, Magaret; America, 1735-1743 4971 p8
Torne, Daniel 24; Pennsylvania, 1740 4779.3 p14A
Torney, William; Illinois, 1875 2896.5 p40
Tornier, . . .; Canada, 1776-1783 9786 p35
Tornquist, John; Maine, 1879-1896 6410.22 p122
Torny, Julien 23; New Orleans, 1835 778.5 p519
Toropila, Anna; America, 1897 7137 p170
Toropila, Ella; Pennsylvania, 1900 7137 p170
Toropila, Frank; America, 1893 7137 p170
Torppa, Oscar; Washington, 1859-1920 2872.1 p41
Torrance, Arthur 11; Quebec, 1864 5704.8 p162
Torrance, Elizabeth 9; Quebec, 1864 5704.8 p162
Torrance, John; Montreal, 1863 9775.5 p203
Torrance, Mary 6; Quebec, 1864 5704.8 p162
Torrance, Mary 45; Quebec, 1864 5704.8 p162
Torre, Agostino 18; New York, NY, 1893 9026.4 p42
Torrens, Ann Jane; Philadelphia, 1853 5704.8 p103
Torrens, Eliza Ann; Philadelphia, 1853 5704.8 p103
Torrens, Francis; Philadelphia, 1853 5704.8 p103
Torrens, Martha 3; Philadelphia, 1853 5704.8 p103
Torrens, Moses; St. John, N.B., 1849 5704.8 p56
Torrens, Wm. 20; Wilmington, DE, 1831 6508.3 p100
Torrers, Ann *SEE* Torrers, Samuel
Torrers, Ann; Philadelphia, 1811 2859.11 p20
Torrers, Ruth *SEE* Torrers, Samuel
Torrers, Ruth; Philadelphia, 1811 2859.11 p20
Torrers, Samuel *SEE* Torrers, Samuel
Torrers, Samuel; Philadelphia, 1811 53.26 p89
*Relative:*Ruth
*Relative:*Samuel
*Relative:*Ann
Torrers, Samuel; Philadelphia, 1811 2859.11 p20
Torres, Epoleto 24; Arizona, 1917 9228.40 p21
Torres, Pedro 58; Arizona, 1925 9228.40 p29
Torres, Romualdo; Arizona, 1848 2764.35 p69
Torrey, Beatrice; North Carolina, 1757-1770 1639.20 p308
Torrey, John; North Carolina, 1744-1820 1639.20 p309
Torry, James; America, 1789 1639.20 p309
Torry, John; Pennsylvania, 1765 1639.20 p309
Torscher, Johann; Alberta, n.d. 5262 p58
Tortorici, Guiseppe; Arkansas, 1918 95.2 p123
Tosch, Fred; Illinois, 1880 2896.5 p40
Tosch, Jacob; Ohio, 1886 5240.1 p46
Tosh, John; Illinois, 1879 2896.5 p40
Tosh, Joseph; St. John, N.B., 1847 5704.8 p18
Tost, . . .; Canada, 1776-1783 9786 p35
Tosti, Louis Mario; Arkansas, 1918 95.2 p123
Tostrik, W.; New Orleans, 1846 3702.7 p84
Totall, Ann; America, 1741 4971 p65
Toteff, Peter Dimitroff; Washington, 1859-1920 2872.1 p41
Totland, Bernhard Kristian Hansen; Arkansas, 1918 95.2 p123
Totnam, Silvester; Virginia, 1635 6219 p69
Toub, Sam; Iowa, 1866-1943 123.54 p49
Touchburn, Margaret 20; Quebec, 1856 5704.8 p130
Tougeot, Pierre 23; New Orleans, 1822 778.5 p519
Tough, Jasper; Quebec, 1815 9229.18 p75
Tougne, Mr. 23; America, 1837 778.5 p519
Touhy, Matthias; America, 1741 4971 p83
Toulakis, Peter William 24; Arkansas, 1918 95.2 p123
Toulson, Georg; Virginia, 1636 6219 p78
Tounau, Mr. 24; Port uncertain, 1836 778.5 p519
Tounau, Mde 23; America, 1836 778.5 p519
Toune, Victor; Iroquois Co., IL, 1896 3455.1 p13
Tounellier, Mr. 35; America, 1838 778.5 p519
Tour, N. 40; Port uncertain, 1838 778.5 p519
Tournait, J. B. 37; America, 1835 778.5 p519
Tournay, Daniel 24; Pennsylvania, 1740 4779.3 p14A
Tourne, Antoine 12; New Orleans, 1835 778.5 p519
Tournier, Claude 28; New Orleans, 1837 778.5 p519
Tournon, Catherine 45; New Orleans, 1838 778.5 p519
Tournon, Jean 35; New Orleans, 1838 778.5 p519
Tournoueur, Francois Xavier 34; New Orleans, 1838 778.5 p520
Tousey, Bazill 20; Maryland, 1729 3690.1 p228
Toussaint, Jean; Canada, 1714 4533 p126
Toussenel, Joseph 26; New Orleans, 1838 778.5 p520
Toussenel, Therese 23; New Orleans, 1838 778.5 p520
Toutain, Margueritte 18; America, 1837 778.5 p520
Toutain, Pierre 28; America, 1837 778.5 p520
Toutfaud, Didie 34; New Orleans, 1826 778.5 p520
Touton, Mr. 22; Louisiana, 1820 778.5 p520
Tovey, George; Arkansas, 1918 95.2 p123
Tow, John 28; Philadelphia, 1774 1219.7 p217
Towel, James 22; Philadelphia, 1803 53.26 p89
Towel, John; America, 1737 4971 p68
Towell, Jon.; Virginia, 1637 6219 p113
Tower, W.P. 21; Harris Co., TX, 1898 6254 p4
Towers, Ann; Quebec, 1848 5704.8 p42
Towers, James; Quebec, 1848 5704.8 p42
Towers, Jane 12; Quebec, 1848 5704.8 p42
Towers, Joseph 1; Quebec, 1848 5704.8 p42
Towers, Samuel 7; Quebec, 1848 5704.8 p42
Towers, Wm.; Virginia, 1637 6219 p11
Towle, George; New York, 1757 1219.7 p58
Towle, Minnie 20; Massachusetts, 1860 6410.32 p110
Towlejevich, John; Iowa, 1866-1943 123.54 p49
Towley, Bart 11; Massachusetts, 1848 5881.1 p94
Towley, Catharine 5; Massachusetts, 1848 5881.1 p94
Towley, David 9; Massachusetts, 1848 5881.1 p94
Towley, Dennis 18; Massachusetts, 1848 5881.1 p94
Towley, James 20; Massachusetts, 1848 5881.1 p94
Towley, Mary 7; Massachusetts, 1848 5881.1 p94
Towley, Mary 13; Massachusetts, 1848 5881.1 p94
Towley, Mary 50; Massachusetts, 1848 5881.1 p94
Town, Christiana 32; Maryland, 1775 1219.7 p262
Town, Thomas 29; Quebec, 1815 9229.18 p80
Townball, Catherine; Quebec, 1815 7603 p38
Towndene, Thomas 15; Maryland, 1719 3690.1 p228
Townesend, Robert; Virginia, 1643 6219 p206
Towney, Catherine; St. John, N.B., 1851 5704.8 p77
Towney, Catherine 1; St. John, N.B., 1851 5704.8 p77
Towning, James 17; America, 1700 2212 p33
Towning, John 19; Pennsylvania, 1734 3690.1 p228
Towning, Tho.; Virginia, 1637 6219 p2
Townley, Henry 18; Maryland, 1775 1219.7 p255
Townsend, Ann Hutchins *SEE* Townsend, Richard
Townsend, David; New Orleans, 1849 5704.8 p58
Townsend, Elizabeth 47 *SEE* Townsend, James
Townsend, Frances; Virginia, 1639 6219 p161
Townsend, George 3; New Orleans, 1849 5704.8 p58
Townsend, Hannah *SEE* Townsend, Richard
Townsend, James *SEE* Townsend, Richard
Townsend, James 5; New Orleans, 1849 5704.8 p58
Townsend, James 10 *SEE* Townsend, James
Townsend, James 24; Port uncertain, 1774 1219.7 p176
Townsend, James 41; St. John Island, 1775 1219.7 p273
*Wife:*Elizabeth 47
*Child:*John 19
*Child:*James 10
*Child:*Lucy 18
*Child:*Richard 13
*Child:*Mary 5
Townsend, Jane; New Orleans, 1849 5704.8 p58
Townsend, John; Ohio, 1863 9892.11 p46
Townsend, John 8; New Orleans, 1849 5704.8 p58
Townsend, John 19 *SEE* Townsend, James
Townsend, Joseph 23; Maryland, 1774 1219.7 p192
Townsend, Lucy 18 *SEE* Townsend, James
Townsend, Martha 1; New Orleans, 1849 5704.8 p58
Townsend, Mary 5 *SEE* Townsend, James
Townsend, Richard; Jamaica, 1751 1219.7 p5
Townsend, Richard; Pennsylvania, 1682 4962 p150
*Wife:*Ann Hutchins
*Daughter:*Hannah
*Son:*James
Townsend, Richard; Virginia, 1639 6219 p161
With wife
Townsend, Richard; Virginia, 1639 6219 p162
With wife
Townsend, Richard 13 *SEE* Townsend, James
Townsend, Simon; Ohio, 1857-1866 9892.11 p46
Townsend, Simon; Ohio, 1868 9892.11 p46
Townsend, William 16; Maryland, 1775 1219.7 p264
Townsend, William 16; Virginia, 1719 3690.1 p228
Townsend, Wm.; Virginia, 1635 6219 p70
Townson, Hen.; Virginia, 1643 6219 p200
Towola, Toivo; Arkansas, 1918 95.2 p123
Tows, Robt.; Virginia, 1644 6219 p229
Towson, John; Virginia, 1645 6219 p233
Toxel, Charles R.; Iroquois Co., IL, 1892 3455.1 p13
Toy, Daniel; New York, NY, 1835 8208.4 p37
Toy, Daniel; Philadelphia, 1867 5704.8 p221
Toy, Dennis; New York, NY, 1837 8208.4 p31
Toy, Eliza 20; Philadelphia, 1858 5704.8 p139
Toy, Ellen; New York, NY, 1869 5704.8 p236
Toy, George; St. John, N.B., 1847 5704.8 p10
Toy, Henry 19; Philadelphia, 1859 5704.8 p141
Toy, James 13; Philadelphia, 1857 5704.8 p132
Toy, John 22; Philadelphia, 1861 5704.8 p149
Toy, Wineford 17; Philadelphia, 1858 5704.8 p139
Tpharraguerau, Peter 35; New Orleans, 1837 778.5 p520
Trabant, . . .; Canada, 1776-1783 9786 p36
Tracey, Ann 3; Quebec, 1854 5704.8 p121
Tracey, Anne; Philadelphia, 1852 5704.8 p88
Tracey, Anne; St. John, N.B., 1852 5704.8 p83
Tracey, Catharine 40; Massachusetts, 1849 5881.1 p94
Tracey, Catherine 5; St. John, N.B., 1852 5704.8 p83
Tracey, Edward 1; Quebec, 1854 5704.8 p121
Tracey, Ellen 5; Quebec, 1854 5704.8 p121
Tracey, Francis 21; Massachusetts, 1847 5881.1 p94
Tracey, Grace 3; Massachusetts, 1849 5881.1 p94
Tracey, Jane; America, 1867 5704.8 p216
Tracey, Jane 28; Quebec, 1854 5704.8 p121
Tracey, John 8; St. John, N.B., 1853 5704.8 p110
Tracey, Margaret 19; St. John, N.B., 1859 5704.8 p143
Tracey, Margaret 21; Massachusetts, 1849 5881.1 p95
Tracey, Marg'et 21; Massachusetts, 1849 5881.1 p21
Tracey, Mary 7; Massachusetts, 1849 5881.1 p95
Tracey, Michael 28; Quebec, 1855 5704.8 p125
Tracey, Nancy 30; St. John, N.B., 1853 5704.8 p110
Tracey, Pat 13; St. John, N.B., 1852 5704.8 p83
Tracey, Peter 11; St. John, N.B., 1852 5704.8 p83
Tracey, Thomas 7; Quebec, 1854 5704.8 p121
Tracey, Thomas 9; St. John, N.B., 1852 5704.8 p83
Tracey, William; New York, NY, 1815 2859.11 p43
Tracey, William 6; St. John, N.B., 1853 5704.8 p110
Tracey, Winfreda 10; St. John, N.B., 1853 5704.8 p110
Trachtenbarg, Louis; Arkansas, 1918 95.2 p123
Trachy, Abraham; Quebec, 1820 7603 p49
Trachy, Edward; Quebec, 1819 7603 p49
Tracy, Andrew 5; Massachusetts, 1849 5881.1 p93
Tracy, Bernard; Philadelphia, 1850 53.26 p89
Tracy, Bernard; Philadelphia, 1850 5704.8 p69
Tracy, Bessy; St. John, N.B., 1853 5704.8 p99
Tracy, Bridget; Massachusetts, 1849 5881.1 p94
Tracy, Catharine; New York, NY, 1816 2859.11 p43
Tracy, Charles; Philadelphia, 1852 5704.8 p92
Tracy, Christopher; Virginia, 1858 4626.16 p17
Tracy, Dennis; New York, NY, 1816 2859.11 p43
Tracy, Farrard; Philadelphia, 1864 5704.8 p180
Tracy, Francis; America, 1742 4971 p53
Tracy, George 59; Kansas, 1875 5240.1 p56
Tracy, Hugh; New York, NY, 1811 2859.11 p20
Tracy, Hugh; Philadelphia, 1851 5704.8 p76
Tracy, James; Kansas, 1884 2764.35 p69
Tracy, John; America, 1853 1450.2 p145A
Tracy, John 45; Arizona, 1902 9228.40 p8
Tracy, Margaret; Philadelphia, 1851 5704.8 p76
Tracy, Mary; New York, NY, 1816 2859.11 p43
Tracy, Mary; Philadelphia, 1865 5704.8 p197
Tracy, Mary 30; Quebec, 1818 7603 p101
Tracy, Mary 50; Massachusetts, 1849 5881.1 p95
Tracy, Patrick; Illinois, 1874 5012.39 p26
Tracy, Rudolph 26; Kansas, 1875 5240.1 p56
Tracy, Susan; Philadelphia, 1851 5704.8 p76
Tracy, Thomas; New York, NY, 1816 2859.11 p43
Trada, Andrew; Iowa, 1866-1943 123.54 p49
Trade, Thomas; Virginia, 1643 6219 p202
Trager, William 53; California, 1873 2769.10 p5
Tragh, Andereas; Pennsylvania, 1752 4525 p211
Trahanes, Serafem N.; Washington, 1859-1920 2872.1 p41

Trahanis, Demetrios Nikolis; Washington, 1859-1920 ***2872.1*** *p41*
Trail, Janet; Georgia, 1775 ***1219.7*** *p274*
Traill, Catharine P Strickland *SEE* Traill, Thomas
Traill, Thomas; Ontario, 1832 ***9775.5*** *p213*
*Wife:*Catharine P Strickland
Train, Margaret 28; Massachusetts, 1849 ***5881.1*** *p95*
Trainer, James 7; Philadelphia, 1864 ***5704.8*** *p171*
Trainer, John; Quebec, 1825 ***7603*** *p73*
Trainer, Margaret; Philadelphia, 1866 ***5704.8*** *p207*
Trainer, Mary 14; Massachusetts, 1850 ***5881.1*** *p95*
Trainer, Mary Ann; New York, NY, 1864 ***5704.8*** *p171*
Trainer, Patrick 21; Massachusetts, 1850 ***5881.1*** *p95*
Trainer, Terrence 20; Massachusetts, 1849 ***5881.1*** *p95*
Trainor, Bernard; Philadelphia, 1864 ***5704.8*** *p183*
Trainor, John; New York, NY, 1838 ***8208.4*** *p73*
Tramel, Marie Elizabeth 32; America, 1835 ***778.5*** *p520*
Tramner, Joseph 32; Nova Scotia, 1774 ***1219.7*** *p209*
With wife
With child
Tramonte, Frank; Arkansas, 1918 ***95.2*** *p123*
Trampe, Anna Maria; America, 1843 ***4610.10*** *p95*
Trampe, Anna Marie Louise; America, 1841 ***4610.10*** *p154*
Trampe, Carl Heinrich; America, 1885 ***4610.10*** *p160*
Trampe, Caroline Louise Lisette; America, 1885 ***4610.10*** *p160*
Trampe, Ernst Heinrich W.; America, 1886 ***4610.10*** *p161*
*Son:*Heinrich Fr. W.
Trampe, Heinrich Fr. W. *SEE* Trampe, Ernst Heinrich W.
Trampe, Heinrich Fr. W.; America, 1886 ***4610.10*** *p161*
Trampe, Heinrich Fr. W.; America, 1892 ***4610.10*** *p161*
Tran, John 20; Virginia, 1774 ***1219.7*** *p186*
Tranar, James; New York, NY, 1811 ***2859.11*** *p20*
Tranchant, Benoit 28; New Orleans, 1835 ***778.5*** *p520*
Tranchaut, Benoit 28; New Orleans, 1835 ***778.5*** *p520*
Traner, Bany; New York, NY, 1811 ***2859.11*** *p20*
Trang, John; Arkansas, 1918 ***95.2*** *p123*
Tranter, Thomas 16; New England, 1724 ***3690.1*** *p228*
Trap, Herman op de; Germantown, PA, 1684 ***2467.7*** *p5*
Trapasso, Vitaliano; Arkansas, 1918 ***95.2*** *p123*
Trasher, Hans George; Pennsylvania, 1746 ***2444*** *p150*
Trassy, Philip; America, 1736-1743 ***4971*** *p58*
Traub, Christ; Iroquois Co., IL, 1894 ***3455.1*** *p13*
Traub, Conrad; America, 1853 ***1450.2*** *p146A*
Traub, John; America, 1851 ***1450.2*** *p146A*
Traub, Lorenz; Akron, OH, 1835 ***8582.1*** *p49*
Traube, Cecilie 2; New York, NY, 1878 ***9253*** *p46*
Traube, Cecilie 22; New York, NY, 1878 ***9253*** *p46*
Traube, Jacob 9 mos; New York, NY, 1878 ***9253*** *p46*
Traudmann, Ernzt; Baltimore, 1865 ***3702.7*** *p209*
Trauscht, J. Peter; Wisconsin, n.d. ***9675.8*** *p123*
Traut, Jacob; Wisconsin, n.d. ***9675.8*** *p123*
Trautarein, William; Wisconsin, n.d. ***9675.8*** *p123*
Trauth, . . .; Canada, 1776-1783 ***9786*** *p36*
Trautner, . . .; Canada, 1776-1783 ***9786*** *p36*
Trautsch, Heinrich; Wisconsin, n.d. ***9675.8*** *p123*
Travagiakis, James; Arkansas, 1918 ***95.2*** *p123*
Traveller, George; Virginia, 1636 ***6219*** *p32*
With wife
Travellor, Alice *SEE* Travellor, Georg
Travellor, Georg; Virginia, 1637 ***6219*** *p180*
*Wife:*Alice
Travers, Bridget; America, 1869 ***5704.8*** *p234*
Travers, Edmund R.; Illinois, 1860 ***7857*** *p7*
Travers, Grace; Philadelphia, 1867 ***5704.8*** *p221*
Travers, John 8; St. John, N.B., 1863 ***5704.8*** *p152*
Travers, John 14; Maryland or Virginia, 1699 ***2212*** *p22*
Travers, Margaret; America, 1869 ***5704.8*** *p234*
Travers, Patrick; New York, NY, 1816 ***2859.11*** *p43*
Travers, Peter; New York, NY, 1889 ***1450.2*** *p40B*
Travers, Reginald 36; New York, NY, 1893 ***9026.4*** *p42*
Traverse, James; Virginia, 1635 ***6219*** *p25*
Traviell, John; Virginia, 1646 ***6219*** *p238*
Travieso, Gus Morales 39; Harris Co., TX, 1900 ***6254*** *p6*
Travis, Edward; Virginia, 1637 ***6219*** *p115*
Travis, John 16; Jamaica, 1729 ***3690.1*** *p228*
Travis, Walter; Virginia, 1637 ***6219*** *p115*
Trawly, John; America, 1740 ***4971*** *p81*
Traxall, Henry 29; America, 1835 ***778.5*** *p520*
Treaner, Margaret; Philadelphia, 1850 ***53.26*** *p89*
Treaner, Margaret; Philadelphia, 1850 ***5704.8*** *p68*
Treanor, Roger; New York, NY, 1838 ***8208.4*** *p69*
Treary, Catherine; St. John, N.B., 1853 ***5704.8*** *p99*
Treasy, Mary 20; St. John, N.B., 1856 ***5704.8*** *p131*
Treat, John; Massachusetts, 1765 ***1219.7*** *p114*
Trebein, Wilhelm; Dayton, OH, 1869-1887 ***8582*** *p33*
Trebert, Kath. 74; America, 1908 ***1763*** *p48D*
Treble, William, Jr.; Virginia, 1640 ***6219*** *p182*
Treble, William, Sr.; Virginia, 1640 ***6219*** *p182*
Treblecock, Frank; Ohio, 1838 ***9892.11*** *p46*
Trebois, Mr. 22; Port uncertain, 1836 ***778.5*** *p520*
Treboul, Mr. 23; Port uncertain, 1836 ***778.5*** *p520*
Trechlen, John; Colorado, 1899 ***9678.3*** *p16*
Tredescant, John; Virginia, 1600-1642 ***6219*** *p192*
Tree, Humph.; Virginia, 1643 ***6219*** *p207*
Tree, Richard; Virginia, 1624 ***6219*** *p31*
Treisch, Marg. 29; America, 1853 ***9162.7*** *p15*
Trelawney, Robert; Virginia, 1643 ***6219*** *p203*
Treller, . . .; Canada, 1776-1783 ***9786*** *p36*
Trembak, Marya; Chicago, 1912 ***9980.29*** *p62*
Tremble, Michael 45; Massachusetts, 1847 ***5881.1*** *p94*
Trencher, Symon; Virginia, 1637 ***6219*** *p24*
Trendall, Paul; Virginia, 1636 ***6219*** *p77*
Trenfield, George 56; Kansas, 1873 ***5240.1*** *p54*
Trenham, James 22; Carolina, 1774 ***1219.7*** *p237*
Trenholm, Richard; Illinois, 1864 ***7857*** *p7*
Trenholm, William; Illinois, 1868 ***7857*** *p7*
Trenker, Max; Arkansas, 1918 ***95.2*** *p123*
Trent, Humphrey; Virginia, 1638 ***6219*** *p123*
Trent, John; Virginia, 1647 ***6219*** *p247*
Trentein, Joannes; Virginia, 1775 ***1219.7*** *p275*
Trentle, Frederick; Virginia, 1775 ***1219.7*** *p275*
Trentle, Peter; Virginia, 1775 ***1219.7*** *p275*
Trento, Pietro 22; Arkansas, 1918 ***95.2*** *p123*
Trenz, Frederick; New York, NY, 1838 ***8208.4*** *p75*
Trepel, John; Wisconsin, n.d. ***9675.8*** *p123*
Trepton, William Herman Otto; Baltimore, 1914 ***3455.2*** *p51*
Trepton, William Hermon Otto; Baltimore, 1914 ***3455.3*** *p110*
Tres, Secildlo 63; Arizona, 1914 ***9228.40*** *p18*
Tresch, Franz; America, 1850 ***8582.3*** *p65*
Treseler, Mary 16; Pennsylvania, 1728 ***3690.1*** *p228*
Tresilian, Kather.; Virginia, 1643 ***6219*** *p200*
Tresom, Alice; Maryland, 1742 ***4971*** *p107*
Tress, Conrad; Pennsylvania, 1746 ***2444*** *p149*
Tresso, Alice; America, 1741 ***4971*** *p16*
Tressuk, Ruben 42; New York, NY, 1878 ***9253*** *p47*
Trestler, . . .; Canada, 1776-1783 ***9786*** *p36*
Tretelski, Isidor; New York, 1875 ***1450.2*** *p146A*
Trettin, Albert 4; New York, NY, 1857 ***9831.14*** *p153*
Trettin, Bertha 9; New York, NY, 1857 ***9831.14*** *p153*
Trettin, Eduard 8 mos; New York, NY, 1857 ***9831.14*** *p153*
Trettin, Ferdinand 39; New York, NY, 1857 ***9831.14*** *p153*
Trettin, Friedrich 5; New York, NY, 1857 ***9831.14*** *p153*
Trettin, Friedrich 59; New York, NY, 1857 ***9831.14*** *p153*
Trettin, Henriette 37; New York, NY, 1857 ***9831.14*** *p153*
Trettin, Hermann 11; New York, NY, 1857 ***9831.14*** *p153*
Trettin, Ulr. Alb. Caroline 40; New York, NY, 1857 ***9831.14*** *p153*
Trettin, Wilhelm 7; New York, NY, 1857 ***9831.14*** *p153*
Tretton, James; New York, 1865 ***1450.2*** *p146A*
Treutlen, Johann Adam *SEE* Treutlen, Peter
Treutlen, Johann Adam; Georgia, 1775 ***8582.2*** *p64*
Treutlen, Peter; Savannah, GA, 1736 ***8582.2*** *p65*
*Son:*Johann Adam
With wife & 2 children
Treutz, . . .; Canada, 1776-1783 ***9786*** *p36*
Treutz, Johann Jacob *SEE* Treutz, Johann Jacob
Treutz, Johann Jacob; America, 1749 ***2444*** *p226*
*Wife:*Magdalena Leyhr
*Child:*Johann Martin
*Child:*Johannes
*Child:*Johann Jacob
*Child:*Johann Martin
With stepchildren
Treutz, Johann Martin *SEE* Treutz, Johann Jacob
Treutz, Johann Martin *SEE* Treutz, Johann Jacob
Treutz, Johannes *SEE* Treutz, Johann Jacob
Treutz, Magdalena Leyhr *SEE* Treutz, Johann Jacob
Trevannion, Thomas; Virginia, 1645 ***6219*** *p234*
Trevar, Patrick; New York, NY, 1811 ***2859.11*** *p20*
Trevell, Eliza.; Virginia, 1642 ***6219*** *p196*
Trevett, George; Virginia, 1640 ***6219*** *p18*
Treville, Mr. 28; Port uncertain, 1836 ***778.5*** *p520*
Trevillian, Frederick 27?; Arizona, 1890 ***2764.35*** *p69*
Trevisol, Frances; Iowa, 1866-1943 ***123.54*** *p81*
Trevisol, John; Iowa, 1866-1943 ***123.54*** *p49*
Trewbey, Christopher; Pennsylvania, 1740 ***4779.3*** *p14A*
Treweeks, George 25; Jamaica, 1734 ***3690.1*** *p228*
Trezona, Richard H. 34; Arizona, 1890 ***2764.35*** *p67*
Triaca, Fredenando 19; West Virginia, 1893 ***9788.3*** *p21*
Triant, Jean 68; America, 1836 ***778.5*** *p521*
Tribal, J. 24; Havana, 1830 ***778.5*** *p521*
Tribelhorn, Carta 48; America, 1838 ***778.5*** *p521*
Tribelhorn, Claude Jn. Baptiste 19; America, 1838 ***778.5*** *p521*
Tribelhorn, Jean-Baptiste 7; America, 1838 ***778.5*** *p521*
Tribelhorn, Joseph 1; America, 1838 ***778.5*** *p521*
Tribelhorn, Marguerite 40; America, 1838 ***778.5*** *p521*
Tribelhorn, Marie 3; America, 1838 ***778.5*** *p521*
Tribelhorn, T. J. 38; America, 1838 ***778.5*** *p521*
Tribet, Simon 20; Pennsylvania, 1728 ***3690.1*** *p228*
Tribolet, Abraham 37; Arizona, 1890 ***2764.35*** *p68*
Tribolet, Godfrey; San Francisco, 1868 ***2764.35*** *p68*
Tribolet, Robert T. 29?; Arizona, 1890 ***2764.35*** *p68*
Tribolet, Sigfried; San Diego, 1878 ***2764.35*** *p68*
Trichard, Mr. 26; America, 1839 ***778.5*** *p521*
Trick, Francis; Virginia, 1638 ***6219*** *p33*
Tricke, Daniel; Canada, 1783 ***9786*** *p38A*
Tricour, Mme. 34; America, 1839 ***778.5*** *p521*
Tricour, Mr. 9; America, 1839 ***778.5*** *p521*
Triebenbach, Christoph; Wisconsin, n.d. ***9675.8*** *p123*
Triebenbach, Michael Christoph; Wisconsin, n.d. ***9675.8*** *p123*
Trienemeyer, Carl Friedrich; America, 1849 ***4610.10*** *p155*
Trier, Charlotta; California, 1837-1922 ***2691.4*** *p169*
Trier, Elisabetha *SEE* Trier, Jacob
Trier, Elisabetha; Iowa, 1881-1922 ***2691.4*** *p170*
Trier, Friedrich; America, 1891 ***2691.4*** *p169*
Trier, Jacob *SEE* Trier, Philipp, Jr.
Trier, Jacob; America, 1821-1922 ***2691.4*** *p169*
Trier, Jacob; California, 1837-1922 ***2691.4*** *p169*
*Sister:*Elisabetha
Trier, Jacob, Family; America, 1820-1923 ***2691.4*** *p172*
Trier, Johann Nikolaus, Family; America, 1798-1923 ***2691.4*** *p172*
Trier, Karolina *SEE* Trier, Philipp, Jr.
Trier, Karolina; America, 1891 ***2691.4*** *p169*
Trier, Katharina; California, 1837-1922 ***2691.4*** *p169*
Trier, Ludwig; California, 1837-1922 ***2691.4*** *p169*
Trier, Luise; California, 1837-1922 ***2691.4*** *p169*
Trier, Magdalena; California, 1837-1922 ***2691.4*** *p169*
Trier, Michael; America, 1891 ***2691.4*** *p169*
Trier, Philipp; Iowa, 1881 ***2691.4*** *p170*
Trier, Philipp, Jr.; Iowa, 1881 ***2691.4*** *p170*
*Child:*Jacob
*Child:*Karolina
Trier, Wilhelm; America, 1848 ***8582.3*** *p65*
Triff, . . .; Canada, 1776-1783 ***9786*** *p36*
Trigg, Ellianor *SEE* Trigg, Samuell
Trigg, Samll.; Virginia, 1635 ***6219*** *p69*
Trigg, Samuell; Virginia, 1639 ***6219*** *p151*
*Wife:*Ellianor
*Brother:*William
Trigg, William *SEE* Trigg, Samuell
Triggs, Ellianor *SEE* Triggs, Samuell
Triggs, Joseph 33; Maryland, 1775 ***1219.7*** *p273*
Triggs, Samuell; Virginia, 1639 ***6219*** *p151*
*Wife:*Ellianor
*Brother:*William
Triggs, William *SEE* Triggs, Samuell
Trim, Eugene 20; Newport, RI, 1851 ***6508.5*** *p20*
Trimble, Eliza 23; New Orleans, 1823 ***778.5*** *p521*
Trimble, William; New York, NY, 1811 ***2859.11*** *p20*
Trimchfeild, Tho.; Virginia, 1635 ***6219*** *p71*
Trimley, Thomas 27; Philadelphia, 1774 ***1219.7*** *p216*
Trimmer, Daniel; Arkansas, 1918 ***95.2*** *p123*
Trimp, John A.; New York, NY, 1836 ***8208.4*** *p9*
Trimpe, Johann Bernard; Baltimore, 1842 ***8582.2*** *p42*
Trimpe, John B.; Ohio, 1869-1887 ***8582*** *p33*
Trinas, B. 29; Port uncertain, 1839 ***778.5*** *p521*
Trinder, George Henry; Arkansas, 1918 ***95.2*** *p123*
Trinder, James; New York, NY, 1835 ***8208.4*** *p46*
Trinis, Andre 27; America, 1839 ***778.5*** *p521*
Trinka, Benedict; Wisconsin, n.d. ***9675.8*** *p123*
Triplet, Joseph; Ohio, 1811 ***8582.1*** *p48*
Tripp, William O.H.; America, 1890 ***1450.2*** *p146A*
Trips, John Peter; New York, NY, 1850 ***1450.2*** *p146A*
Trips, William; New York, 1854 ***1450.2*** *p146A*
Triquet, Margaret Godfrey 45; Montreal, 1777 ***7603*** *p58*
Trischer, Thomas; America, 1777-1778 ***8582.2*** *p67*
Trishman, James; Iowa, 1866-1943 ***123.54*** *p49*
Triska, Anton 24; Kansas, 1872 ***5240.1*** *p52*
Tristram, Robert; New York, NY, 1838 ***8208.4*** *p81*
Trith, . . .; Canada, 1776-1783 ***9786*** *p36*
Triven, John; New York, NY, 1811 ***2859.11*** *p20*
With wife
Trobach, Chritian 26; Massachusetts, 1860 ***6410.32*** *p104*
Trobach, Louisa 21; Massachusetts, 1860 ***6410.32*** *p104*
Troestler, . . .; Canada, 1776-1783 ***9786*** *p36*
Troestler, Jean-Joseph; Canada, 1776-1783 ***9786*** *p236*
Troestler, Jean-Joseph; Canada, 1776-1783 ***9786*** *p239*
Troglia, Battista 34?; Arizona, 1890 ***2764.35*** *p69*
Troha, Giga; Iowa, 1866-1943 ***123.54*** *p49*
Trohamer, Luis 27; Port uncertain, 1836 ***778.5*** *p522*
Troike, August; Illinois, 1872 ***2896.5*** *p40*
Troike, Herman; Illinois, 1880 ***2896.5*** *p40*
Trollock, Jon.; Virginia, 1642 ***6219*** *p192*
Tromp, Henry; New York, NY, 1835 ***8208.4*** *p43*

Tron, Conrad *SEE* Tron, Lorenz
Tron, Conrad; Indiana, 1858 ***5647.5*** *p79*
Tron, Friederich; America, 1817 ***8582.2*** *p60*
Tron, Friederich; Cincinnati, 1817-1877 ***8582.3*** *p86*
Tron, Friedrich; Ohio, 1869-1887 ***8582*** *p33*
Tron, Konrad; Indiana, 1829-1858 ***5647.5*** *p69*
Tron, Lorenz; New York, 1854 ***5647.5*** *p83*
*Brother:*Conrad
*Brother:*Philipp
Tron, Philipp *SEE* Tron, Lorenz
Tron, Philipp; New York, 1854 ***5647.5*** *p89*
Trone, Elizabeth 20 *SEE* Trone, Frederick
Trone, Frederick 59; Indiana, 1850 ***5647.5*** *p129*
*Relative:*Wilhelmina 57
*Relative:*Elizabeth 20
*Relative:*Mary 18
*Relative:*Henry 13
Trone, George; Philadelphia, 1761 ***9973.7*** *p36*
Trone, Henry 13 *SEE* Trone, Frederick
Trone, Mary 18 *SEE* Trone, Frederick
Trone, Wilhelmina 57 *SEE* Trone, Frederick
Tronson, Nels; Wisconsin, n.d. ***9675.8*** *p123*
Trontta, John; Washington, 1859-1920 ***2872.1*** *p41*
Trope, Marcus 24; Halifax, N.S., 1752 ***7074.6*** *p207*
Tros, Auguste 30; Port uncertain, 1838 ***778.5*** *p522*
Trost, Florent; Ohio, 1844 ***9892.11*** *p46*
Trost, Florent; Ohio, 1848 ***9892.11*** *p46*
Trost, Isaac; New York, NY, 1840 ***8582.3*** *p65*
Trost, Ludwig; Wisconsin, n.d. ***9675.8*** *p123*
Trost, Wolf; Baltimore, 1837 ***8582*** *p33*
Trostakinmoen, Einar; Arkansas, 1918 ***95.2*** *p85*
Trostakinmoen, Einar; Arkansas, 1918 ***95.2*** *p123*
Trotman, Samuel 16; Maryland, 1774 ***1219.7*** *p236*
Troton, Nicholas; Virginia, 1638 ***6219*** *p121*
Trott, Lieut.; Quebec, 1776 ***9786*** *p104*
Trott, Christian Wilhelm; Quebec, 1776 ***9786*** *p261*
Trott, Dietrich; Trenton, NJ, 1776 ***8137*** *p15*
Trotter, Charles; New York, NY, 1838 ***8208.4*** *p86*
Trotter, George 20; Quebec, 1859 ***5704.8*** *p143*
Trotter, Henry 26; New York, 1774 ***1219.7*** *p217*
Trotter, Nancy 45; Charlotte, NC, 1850 ***1639.20*** *p309*
Trotter, Tho.; Virginia, 1638 ***6219*** *p122*
Trotter, William; New York, NY, 1816 ***2859.11*** *p43*
Trottmann, . . .; Canada, 1776-1783 ***9786*** *p36*
Troud, Thomas; Iowa, 1866-1943 ***123.54*** *p49*
Trouet, Auguste 9; America, 1838 ***778.5*** *p522*
Trouet, Augustine 13; America, 1838 ***778.5*** *p522*
Trouet, Felix Joseph 3?; America, 1838 ***778.5*** *p522*
Trouet, Francois 11; America, 1838 ***778.5*** *p522*
Trouet, Jean 64; America, 1838 ***778.5*** *p522*
Trouet, Julie 15; America, 1838 ***778.5*** *p522*
Trouet, Marie Anne 6; America, 1838 ***778.5*** *p522*
Trouet, Marie Victoire 35; America, 1838 ***778.5*** *p522*
Trouette, Hypolite 26; New Orleans, 1838 ***778.5*** *p522*
Troughton, Isabel; America, 1697 ***2212*** *p9*
Troughton, James; Ohio, 1841 ***8365.25*** *p12*
Troughweare, Joseph; Maryland or Virginia, 1698 ***2212*** *p6*
Troughweare, Joseph; Virginia, 1698 ***2212*** *p11*
Trounce, Frank W.; Washington, 1859-1920 ***2872.1*** *p41*
Trousil, Fransisek; Iowa, 1866-1943 ***123.54*** *p49*
Troussand, Peter 49; America, 1838 ***778.5*** *p522*
Troussard, Pierre; America, 1839 ***778.5*** *p522*
Troussart, Charles 30; Port uncertain, 1832 ***778.5*** *p522*
Trout, Adam 20; Virginia, 1720 ***3690.1*** *p228*
Troutman, John; Washington, 1859-1920 ***2872.1*** *p41*
Trow, Philipp; New York, 1854 ***5647.5*** *p89*
Trower, Catherine 25; Philadelphia, 1859 ***5704.8*** *p143*
Trower, Margaret 20; Philadelphia, 1859 ***5704.8*** *p143*
Troxel, Fred; Iroquois Co., IL, 1895 ***3455.1*** *p13*
Troxel, Rudolph; Iroquois Co., IL, 1896 ***3455.1*** *p13*
Troy, James; New York, NY, 1834 ***8208.4*** *p25*
Troy, Monah 25; St. John, N.B., 1855 ***5704.8*** *p127*
Trubelle, Js. 25; Port uncertain, 1839 ***778.5*** *p522*
Truby, Christopher; Pennsylvania, 1740 ***4779.3*** *p14A*
Truchan, Alexander; Arkansas, 1918 ***95.2*** *p123*
Trucksess, Frederick; Baltimore, 1835 ***1450.2*** *p146A*
True, John; Iroquois Co., IL, 1892 ***3455.1*** *p13*
Trueman, Joseph A. 4; Quebec, 1857 ***5704.8*** *p136*
Trueman, William; Virginia, 1640 ***6219*** *p185*
Trueman, William 16; Pennsylvania, Virginia or Maryland, 1728 ***3690.1*** *p228*
Truemper, Andreas; Philadelphia, 1779 ***8137*** *p15*
Trugagos, Sotiros; Iowa, 1866-1943 ***123.54*** *p49*
Truherne, John; Virginia, 1638 ***6219*** *p146*
Truille, Mr. 26; America, 1835 ***778.5*** *p523*
Truitt, Jon.; Virginia, 1642 ***6219*** *p191*
Trum, Bernhard; Cincinnati, 1869-1887 ***8582*** *p33*
Truman, Ann 58 *SEE* Truman, William
Truman, William 22 *SEE* Truman, William
Truman, William 52; North America, 1774 ***1219.7*** *p199*
*Wife:*Ann 58
*Son:*William 22
Trumble, Ann; Savannah, GA, 1774 ***1219.7*** *p227*
Trummele, John 37; America, 1835 ***778.5*** *p523*
Trumper, . . .; Canada, 1776-1783 ***9786*** *p36*
Trunley, William 20; Jamaica, 1729 ***3690.1*** *p228*
Trunt, George; Illinois, 1853 ***7857*** *p8*
Truog, Jacob 22; West Virginia, 1898 ***9788.3*** *p21*
Truourt, John J. 27; New Orleans, 1836 ***778.5*** *p523*
Trupe, George 19; Jamaica, 1774 ***1219.7*** *p189*
Truschel, Ludwig; New York, NY, 1838 ***8208.4*** *p64*
Truskett, John S.; Iowa, 1866-1943 ***123.54*** *p49*
Trussell, John; Virginia, 1652 ***6251*** *p19*
Trussell, Jon.; Virginia, 1637 ***6219*** *p113*
Trustall, Robert; Virginia, 1639 ***6219*** *p152*
Trux, Abraham; Ohio, 1816 ***8582.1*** *p47*
Trybulec, John; Arkansas, 1918 ***95.2*** *p123*
Trzaskowski, . . .; New York, 1831 ***4606*** *p177*
Tsangaris, John Stavos; Arkansas, 1918 ***95.2*** *p123*
Tsavinias, George; Arkansas, 1918 ***95.2*** *p123*
Tsavinicis, George; Arkansas, 1918 ***95.2*** *p123*
Tschenhenz, X.; Cincinnati, 1835 ***8582.1*** *p52*
Tschentke, Albert Gothalf; New York, NY, 1910 ***3455.3*** *p16*
Tschopl, Leo 41; Kansas, 1901 ***5240.1*** *p46*
Tschopl, Leo 41; Kansas, 1901 ***5240.1*** *p82*
Tschudy, Johann 90; Ohio, 1871 ***8582*** *p33*
Tschumber, Conrad; South Carolina, 1788 ***7119*** *p199*
Tsenoukos, Jamas; Arkansas, 1918 ***95.2*** *p123*
Tshoudee, Winebert; Philadelphia, 1760 ***9973.7*** *p34*
Tshumber, John; South Carolina, 1788 ***7119*** *p199*
Tshumber, Peter; South Carolina, 1788 ***7119*** *p199*
Tsibrogos, George; Arkansas, 1918 ***95.2*** *p124*
Tskalinas, George; Arkansas, 1918 ***95.2*** *p124*
Tsontsonris, Thomas; Arkansas, 1918 ***95.2*** *p124*
Tubach, Mr.; Cincinnati, 1840 ***8582.1*** *p45*
Tubman, Elizabeth 18; St. John, N.B., 1863 ***5704.8*** *p153*
Tubman, James 20; St. John, N.B., 1863 ***5704.8*** *p153*
Tucci, Tony; Arkansas, 1918 ***95.2*** *p124*
Tuccio, Samuel; Arkansas, 1918 ***95.2*** *p124*
Tucholska, Janina 7; New York, 1912 ***9980.29*** *p54*
Tucholski, Teodor 20; New York, 1912 ***9980.29*** *p56*
Tuchscheer, . . .; Canada, 1776-1783 ***9786*** *p36*
Tuchscher, Johann; Alberta, n.d. ***5262*** *p58*
Tucinelli, G.G. 28; New York, NY, 1893 ***9026.4*** *p42*
Tuck, Woodham; Virginia, 1642 ***6219*** *p191*
Tucke, Heinrich Frederick Wilhelm; Illinois, 1878 ***2896.5*** *p40*
Tucker, Abraham 25; Maryland, 1774 ***1219.7*** *p230*
Tucker, Alex.; Virginia, 1635 ***6219*** *p5*
Tucker, Allen; Virginia, 1636 ***6219*** *p78*
Tucker, Allen; Virginia, 1638 ***6219*** *p119*
Tucker, Ann 21; Maryland, 1774 ***1219.7*** *p228*
Tucker, Barthol; Virginia, 1639 ***6219*** *p22*
Tucker, Henry; Illinois, 1860 ***5012.38*** *p97*
Tucker, Jack; Arkansas, 1918 ***95.2*** *p124*
Tucker, James 20; Newfoundland, 1699-1700 ***2212*** *p18*
Tucker, Jane 20; Maryland, 1775 ***1219.7*** *p252*
Tucker, John; Virginia, 1643 ***6219*** *p204*
Tucker, John 39; Virginia, 1774 ***1219.7*** *p238*
Tucker, Jon.; Virginia, 1642 ***6219*** *p198*
Tucker, Joseph; South Carolina, 1788 ***7119*** *p197*
Tucker, Joseph 23; Maryland, 1733 ***3690.1*** *p229*
Tucker, Patrick 25; Massachusetts, 1847 ***5881.1*** *p95*
Tucker, Thomas 26; Port uncertain, 1774 ***1219.7*** *p176*
Tucker, William 23; Maryland, 1775 ***1219.7*** *p247*
Tuckerbury, Benj.; New York, NY, 1811 ***2859.11*** *p20*
With family
Tuckett, R. H. 27; Kansas, 1888 ***5240.1*** *p72*
Tucks, J. 23; New Orleans, 1831 ***778.5*** *p523*
Tucoo, Martin 22; America, 1838 ***778.5*** *p523*
Tuczynski, Edmund; Arkansas, 1918 ***95.2*** *p124*
Tude, . . .; Canada, 1776-1783 ***9786*** *p36*
Tuder, Robert 18; Virginia, 1773 ***1219.7*** *p169*
Tudhope, William P.; Washington, 1859-1920 ***2872.1*** *p41*
Tue, Mary; America, 1697 ***2212*** *p7*
Tuellmann, Xystus; New York, 1874 ***1450.2*** *p146A*
Tueringer, Johann Christoph; Pennsylvania, 1752 ***2444*** *p226*
Tuffe, William; Antigua (Antego), 1757 ***1219.7*** *p50*
Tugan, Michael 36; New Orleans, 1839 ***9420.2*** *p71*
Tugel, Anne Marie Christine; America, 1837 ***4610.10*** *p138*
Tugen, Georg 38; New Orleans, 1839 ***9420.2*** *p72*
Tugman, Christopher 20; Quebec, 1853 ***5704.8*** *p104*
Tugman, Jane; St. John, N.B., 1849 ***5704.8*** *p48*
Tugman, John 35; Massachusetts, 1849 ***5881.1*** *p94*
Tugman, Margaret 20; Massachusetts, 1849 ***5881.1*** *p95*
Tugman, Margaret 34; Massachusetts, 1849 ***5881.1*** *p95*
Tugman, Mary; St. John, N.B., 1849 ***5704.8*** *p48*
Tuimy, Bridget; Montreal, 1824 ***7603*** *p86*
Tuiska, Isaac; Washington, 1859-1920 ***2872.1*** *p41*
Tuiskee, Isaac; Washington, 1859-1920 ***2872.1*** *p41*
Tuisker, Isaac; Washington, 1859-1920 ***2872.1*** *p41*
Tuisku, Matt; Washington, 1859-1920 ***2872.1*** *p41*
Tuite, Thomas; New York, NY, 1838 ***8208.4*** *p60*
Tuke, John; Charleston, SC, 1768 ***1219.7*** *p137*
Tulhe, Antoine 39; New Orleans, 1838 ***778.5*** *p523*
Tulip, Jane 40 *SEE* Tulip, Thomas
Tulip, Thomas 36; Georgia, 1775 ***1219.7*** *p277*
*Wife:*Jane 40
Tulleken, Friederich; Philadelphia, 1756 ***8582.3*** *p95*
Tullneck, Matthais; Pennsylvania, 1751 ***2444*** *p150*
Tulloch, Charles; America, 1808 ***1639.20*** *p309*
Tulloch, Jacques; Quebec, 1793 ***7603*** *p40*
Tullock, Elizabeth; Georgia, 1775 ***1219.7*** *p274*
Tullock, Janet; Georgia, 1775 ***1219.7*** *p274*
Tullock, John; Georgia, 1775 ***1219.7*** *p274*
Tullock, Magnus; Georgia, 1775 ***1219.7*** *p274*
Tullock, Mary; Georgia, 1775 ***1219.7*** *p274*
Tullock, Samuel; Georgia, 1775 ***1219.7*** *p274*
Tully, Edward 3; Massachusetts, 1849 ***5881.1*** *p94*
Tully, Eliza 2; Massachusetts, 1849 ***5881.1*** *p94*
Tully, James 11; Massachusetts, 1849 ***5881.1*** *p94*
Tully, John 6; Massachusetts, 1849 ***5881.1*** *p94*
Tully, Mary; Montreal, 1822 ***7603*** *p61*
Tully, Mary; Philadelphia, 1848 ***53.26*** *p89*
Tully, Mary 12; Philadelphia, 1848 ***5704.8*** *p46*
Tully, Patrick 9; Massachusetts, 1849 ***5881.1*** *p95*
Tully, Peter 5; Massachusetts, 1849 ***5881.1*** *p95*
Tuma, Martin; Arkansas, 1918 ***95.2*** *p124*
Tumbach, . . .; Alberta, 1909-1950 ***5262*** *p58*
Tumeney, John 22; St. John, N.B., 1854 ***5704.8*** *p115*
Tumulty, Thomas; Montreal, 1821 ***7603*** *p79*
Tunderfeld, v., Cap.; Quebec, 1776 ***9786*** *p105*
Tunderfeld, Carl August Heinrich; Quebec, 1776 ***9786*** *p254*
Tune, William 17; Maryland, 1775 ***1219.7*** *p264*
Tunes, Abraham; Pennsylvania, 1683 ***2155*** *p2*
With wife
Tunkes, Alice 17; Maryland, 1722 ***3690.1*** *p229*
Tunmer, Reuben; New York, NY, 1909 ***3455.4*** *p27*
Tunney, Daniel 24; Pennsylvania, 1740 ***4779.3*** *p14A*
Tunney, Thomas; San Francisco, 1864 ***2764.35*** *p68*
Tunniby, George 40; Philadelphia, 1775 ***1219.7*** *p257*
Tunniby, John 21; Philadelphia, 1775 ***1219.7*** *p257*
Tunnis, Abraham; Pennsylvania, 1683 ***2155*** *p2*
With wife
Tunny, Catherine; St. John, N.B., 1847 ***5704.8*** *p26*
Tunny, George 9 mos; St. John, N.B., 1847 ***5704.8*** *p26*
Tunny, Mary Ann 5; St. John, N.B., 1847 ***5704.8*** *p26*
Tunny, Michael; St. John, N.B., 1847 ***5704.8*** *p26*
Tunny, Patrick 13; St. John, N.B., 1847 ***5704.8*** *p26*
Tunny, Susan 9; St. John, N.B., 1847 ***5704.8*** *p26*
Tunny, Thomas 11; St. John, N.B., 1847 ***5704.8*** *p26*
Tunstall, Josh. 18; America, 1699 ***2212*** *p28*
Tunstall, Robert; Washington, 1859-1920 ***2872.1*** *p41*
Tunstall, Robert E.; Washington, 1859-1920 ***2872.1*** *p41*
Tuohy, Peter Gregory 40; California, 1873 ***2769.10*** *p5*
Tuoly, John 33?; California, 1872 ***2769.9*** *p4*
Tuoncher, Steve; Arkansas, 1918 ***95.2*** *p124*
Tupper, Samuel; Illinois, 1866 ***5012.38*** *p98*
Tuquet, Armand D. 45; Arizona, 1890 ***2764.35*** *p68*
Turanyi, Martone 39; Harris Co., TX, 1897 ***6254*** *p3*
Turba, Wladyslaw 18; New York, 1912 ***9980.29*** *p75*
Turbach, John; New York, NY, 1837 ***8208.4*** *p51*
Turbett, Edward; Philadelphia, 1849 ***53.26*** *p89*
Turbett, Edward; Philadelphia, 1849 ***5704.8*** *p54*
Turbett, James; Philadelphia, 1849 ***5704.8*** *p54*
Turbett, Samuel; Philadelphia, 1850 ***53.26*** *p89*
Turbett, Samuel; Philadelphia, 1850 ***5704.8*** *p69*
Turbett, Thomas 21; Baltimore, 1775 ***1219.7*** *p270*
Turbis, Wladyslaw 18; New York, 1912 ***9980.29*** *p75*
Turbuck, Willi.; Virginia, 1641 ***6219*** *p184*
Turcasse, Mrs. 26; New Orleans, 1829 ***778.5*** *p523*
Turch, Christian; Wisconsin, n.d. ***9675.8*** *p123*
Turdy, George 23; Maryland, 1775 ***1219.7*** *p267*
Turfry, Richard; Virginia, 1642 ***6219*** *p193*
Turinger, Johann Christoph; Pennsylvania, 1752 ***2444*** *p226*
Turk, F.; Shreveport, LA, 1874 ***7129*** *p46*
Turk, Matt; America, 1895 ***1450.2*** *p147A*
Turke, William; Virginia, 1647 ***6219*** *p245*
Turkenton, James; New York, NY, 1811 ***2859.11*** *p20*
Turkenton, Jane; New York, NY, 1811 ***2859.11*** *p20*
Turkenton, John; New York, NY, 1811 ***2859.11*** *p20*
Turkington, Nicholas; New York, NY, 1840 ***8208.4*** *p107*
Turkington, William; Illinois, 1876 ***2896.5*** *p44*
Turkus, Aaron; Arkansas, 1918 ***95.2*** *p124*
Turley, Anne; New York, NY, 1816 ***2859.11*** *p43*
Turley, Eliza; New York, NY, 1816 ***2859.11*** *p43*
Turley, John; New York, NY, 1816 ***2859.11*** *p43*
Turley, Sarah; New York, NY, 1816 ***2859.11*** *p43*
Turnau, . . .; Canada, 1776-1783 ***9786*** *p36*
Turnbull, Andrew; Florida, 1768 ***1639.20*** *p309*

Turnbull, Gavin; Charleston, SC, 1765-1813 *1639.20 p309*
Turnbull, James; Charleston, SC, 1734 *1639.20 p309*
Turnbull, Joseph; South Carolina, 1823 *1639.20 p310*
Turnell, Henry; Illinois, 1881 *5012.39 p52*
Turner, Abraham; Virginia, 1600-1642 *6219 p192*
Turner, Alexander; New York, NY, 1865 *5704.8 p189*
Turner, Ann; Virginia, 1629 *6219 p8*
Turner, Ann 21; Philadelphia, 1774 *1219.7 p183*
Turner, Barnard; America, 1758 *1219.7 p65*
Turner, Bartlett; New York, NY, 1811 *2859.11 p20*
Turner, Charles 22; North America, 1774 *1219.7 p195*
Turner, Charles 53; North America, 1774 *1219.7 p195*
Turner, Daniel 22; Virginia, 1774 *1219.7 p186*
Turner, Elizabeth *SEE* Turner, John
Turner, Elizabeth; America, 1869 *5704.8 p233*
Turner, Fr.; Virginia, 1637 *6219 p83*
Turner, Francis 33; Virginia, 1774 *1219.7 p239*
Turner, Frank; Iowa, 1866-1943 *123.54 p49*
Turner, Garrett; America, 1847 *1450.2 p147A*
Turner, Georg; Virginia, 1642 *6219 p199*
Turner, George; Virginia, 1644 *6219 p229*
Turner, George 19; Antigua (Antego), 1733 *3690.1 p229*
Turner, George 22; Jamaica, 1736 *3690.1 p229*
Turner, Gerhard H.; America, 1846 *8582.1 p34*
Turner, Hannah; America, 1869 *5704.8 p233*
Turner, Harman; Virginia, 1637 *6219 p17*
Turner, Henry; Illinois, 1888 *5012.39 p122*
Turner, Henry 19; Virginia, 1699 *2212 p26*
Turner, Henry 24; Maryland, 1775 *1219.7 p268*
Turner, Isaac; Arkansas, 1918 *95.2 p124*
Turner, Isabel *SEE* Turner, Rober
Turner, James; New York, NY, 1865 *5704.8 p191*
Turner, James; Virginia, 1635 *6219 p19*
Turner, James 1 *SEE* Turner, Mary
Turner, James 1; Philadelphia, 1847 *5704.8 p32*
Turner, James 17; Jamaica, 1723 *3690.1 p229*
Turner, James 21; Jamaica, 1730 *3690.1 p229*
Turner, James 29; Massachusetts, 1850 *5881.1 p94*
Turner, Jane; Philadelphia, 1853 *5704.8 p101*
Turner, Jane 18; Philadelphia, 1857 *5704.8 p134*
Turner, John; Philadelphia, 1742 *3652 p55*
  *Wife:*Elizabeth
Turner, John; Quebec, 1749-1750 *7603 p86*
Turner, John; Virginia, 1637 *6219 p114*
Turner, John; Virginia, 1638 *6219 p24*
Turner, John; Virginia, 1638 *6219 p119*
Turner, John; Virginia, 1638 *6219 p160*
Turner, John; Virginia, 1639 *6219 p151*
Turner, John; Virginia, 1643 *6219 p200*
Turner, John 16; Maryland, 1718 *3690.1 p229*
Turner, John 17; North America, 1774 *1219.7 p195*
Turner, John 18; Jamaica, 1738 *3690.1 p229*
Turner, John 19; Jamaica, 1732 *3690.1 p229*
Turner, John 21; Baltimore, 1775 *1219.7 p270*
Turner, John 21; Maryland, 1774 *1219.7 p222*
Turner, John 22; Maryland, 1774 *1219.7 p235*
Turner, John 25; Virginia, 1773 *1219.7 p168*
Turner, John 27; Virginia, 1774 *1219.7 p186*
Turner, John 48; Wilmington, DE, 1831 *6508.3 p101*
Turner, John H. 22; Kansas, 1898 *5240.1 p46*
Turner, John H. 22; Kansas, 1898 *5240.1 p81*
Turner, Jonas 25; Philadelphia, 1774 *1219.7 p232*
Turner, Joseph; New York, NY, 1837 *8208.4 p48*
Turner, Martin; Virginia, 1621 *6219 p67*
Turner, Mary; Philadelphia, 1847 *53.26 p89*
  *Relative:*Samuel 3
  *Relative:*James 1
Turner, Mary; Philadelphia, 1847 *5704.8 p32*
Turner, Mary; Virginia, 1642 *6219 p195*
Turner, Morris Aaron; Arkansas, 1918 *95.2 p124*
Turner, Patrick 12; Massachusetts, 1849 *5881.1 p95*
Turner, R.P.; Iowa, 1866-1943 *123.54 p49*
Turner, Richard; Virginia, 1639 *6219 p161*
Turner, Richard 21; Maryland, 1774 *1219.7 p206*
Turner, Richard 21; Maryland, 1774 *1219.7 p221*
Turner, Rober; Virginia, 1699 *2212 p27*
  *Daughter:*Isabel
  *Son:*Thomas
Turner, Robert; Virginia, 1637 *6219 p11*

Turner, Robert; Virginia, 1637 *6219 p112*
Turner, Robert 20; Philadelphia, 1857 *5704.8 p133*
Turner, Robert 22; Pennsylvania, 1738 *3690.1 p229*
Turner, Saml.; Virginia, 1635 *6219 p20*
Turner, Samuel 3 *SEE* Turner, Mary
Turner, Samuel 3; Philadelphia, 1847 *5704.8 p32*
Turner, Stephen 24; Maryland, 1775 *1219.7 p273*
Turner, Thomas *SEE* Turner, Rober
Turner, Thomas; Virginia, 1636 *6219 p80*
Turner, Thomas; Virginia, 1645 *6219 p233*
Turner, Thomas; Virginia, 1698 *2212 p12*
Turner, Thomas 19; Pennsylvania, 1730 *3690.1 p229*
Turner, Thomas 22; Maryland, 1733 *3690.1 p229*
Turner, Thomas 22; Maryland, 1774 *1219.7 p222*
Turner, William; New York, NY, 1811 *2859.11 p20*
Turner, William; Virginia, 1639 *6219 p162*
Turner, William; Virginia, 1643 *6219 p206*
Turner, William 16; Maryland, 1775 *1219.7 p255*
Turner, William 17; Philadelphia, 1774 *1219.7 p212*
Turner, William 21; Philadelphia, 1854 *5704.8 p117*
Turner, William 22; Maryland, 1738 *3690.1 p230*
Turner, William 22; Maryland, 1774 *1219.7 p222*
Turner, William 39; Kansas, 1902 *5240.1 p82*
Turner, William 45; Maryland, 1775 *1219.7 p263*
Turner, William 50; Kansas, 1889 *5240.1 p73*
Turner, Zacharias; Virginia, 1635 *6219 p68*
Turnley, John 24; Philadelphia, 1774 *1219.7 p196*
Turny, Ann; Philadelphia, 1852 *5704.8 p87*
Turny, Daniel 24; Pennsylvania, 1740 *4779.3 p14A*
Turowski, Ludwik; New York, 1831 *4606 p177*
Turp, August; Wisconsin, n.d. *9675.8 p123*
Turpeau, Mr. 42; Louisiana, 1821 *778.5 p523*
Turpeinen, John; Washington, 1859-1920 *2872.1 p41*
Turpeinen, John Henry; Washington, 1859-1920 *2872.1 p41*
Turpeinen, Karrta; Washington, 1859-1920 *2872.1 p41*
Turpeinen, Lauri; Washington, 1859-1920 *2872.1 p41*
Turpeinen, Selma Juliana; Washington, 1859-1920 *2872.1 p41*
Turpeinen, Walter Matt; Washington, 1859-1920 *2872.1 p41*
Turpin, Mr. 31; New Orleans, 1825 *778.5 p523*
Turpin, J. 16; Port uncertain, 1832 *778.5 p523*
Turpin, John; Arkansas, 1918 *95.2 p124*
Turpin, John Thomas; Arkansas, 1918 *95.2 p124*
Turquin, Martin; America, 1853 *1450.2 p146A*
Turrell, William; St. Clair Co., IL, 1872 *2896.5 p40*
Turrin, Victor; Iowa, 1866-1943 *123.54 p81*
Turro, Antonio; Iowa, 1866-1943 *123.54 p49*
Tursher, John S.; Illinois, 1860 *5012.39 p90*
Turski, . . .; New York, 1835 *4606 p180*
Turtle, John 23; Virginia, 1774 *1219.7 p242*
Turtle, Thomas 21; Virginia, 1773 *1219.7 p169*
Turtley, Alice Croxon *SEE* Turtley, Avis
Turtley, Avis; Virginia, 1636 *6219 p75*
  *Wife:*Alice Croxon
Turtley, Avis; Virginia, 1638 *6219 p181*
Turton, George; Iowa, 1866-1943 *123.54 p49*
Turton, James 18; Jamaica, 1729 *3690.1 p230*
Turton, Jude; Iowa, 1866-1943 *123.54 p49*
Turull, Alejandro; New York, NY, 1840 *8208.4 p103*
Turvey, John; Virginia, 1637 *6219 p115*
Turvill, John 17; Jamaica, 1729 *3690.1 p230*
Turzanski, . . .; New York, 1831 *4606 p177*
Tusten, Robert 36; Jamaica, 1730 *3690.1 p230*
Tute, J. B.; Quebec, 1815 *9229.18 p78*
Tute, James 19; Virginia, 1774 *1219.7 p193*
Tutton, Henry; Virginia, 1638 *6219 p118*
Tuyes, O. J. 32; America, 1829 *778.5 p523*
Tuyes, P. A. 19; New Orleans, 1831 *778.5 p523*
Tuyes, P. H. 23; Died enroute, 1822 *778.5 p523*
Tuyes, P. H. 29; Died enroute, 1822 *778.5 p523*
Tuyes, P. J. 32; New Orleans, 1830 *778.5 p524*
Tuyes, P. J. 35; Mexico, 1829 *778.5 p523*
Tuyes, P. J. 37; Port uncertain, 1827 *778.5 p222*
Tuzo, Mr.; Quebec, 1815 *9229.18 p78*
Twachtmann, Johann; America, 1848 *8582.2 p42*
Twaddell, Catharine A.; Philadelphia, 1866 *5704.8 p215*
Twaddell, John; New York, NY, 1864 *5704.8 p174*
Twaithe, William 26; Massachusetts, 1850 *5881.1 p95*

Twamley, George; New York, NY, 1816 *2859.11 p43*
Twamley, Jane; New York, NY, 1816 *2859.11 p43*
Twamley, Mary; New York, NY, 1816 *2859.11 p43*
Twarogowcki, Antony; Arkansas, 1918 *95.2 p124*
Twedy, John 28; Baltimore, 1775 *1219.7 p270*
Tweed, Alexander; Carolina, 1683-1830 *1639.20 p310*
Tweed, Mahon 20; Massachusetts, 1848 *5881.1 p94*
Tweedie, William 23; St. John, N.B., 1866 *5704.8 p167*
Tweedy, Effy; New York, NY, 1811 *2859.11 p20*
Tweedy, Patrick; Philadelphia, 1811 *2859.11 p20*
  With family
Twerijonus, Bell; Wisconsin, n.d. *9675.8 p123*
Twiddale, Robert 23; Maryland or Virginia, 1699 *2212 p24*
Twietmeyer, Dora; New York, NY, 1926 *3455.4 p79*
Twietmeyer, Elise; New York, NY, 1925 *3455.4 p92*
Twietmeyer, Fritz Henry; New York, NY, 1922 *3455.4 p24*
Twietmeyer, Heinrich; New York, NY, 1927 *3455.4 p93*
Twig, Alexander; Philadelphia, 1864 *5704.8 p178*
Twigg, William; Iowa, 1866-1943 *123.54 p49*
Twisleton, Richard 25; Jamaica, 1733 *3690.1 p230*
Twitemeyer, Fritz Henry; New York, NY, 1922 *3455.3 p80*
Twohey, Mary 16; Massachusetts, 1850 *5881.1 p95*
Twohey, Norry 30; Massachusetts, 1850 *5881.1 p95*
Twohig, Catharine 22; Massachusetts, 1849 *5881.1 p94*
Twohig, Honora 16; Massachusetts, 1849 *5881.1 p94*
Twohig, Jeremiah 4; Massachusetts, 1849 *5881.1 p94*
Twohig, John 19; Massachusetts, 1849 *5881.1 p94*
Twohig, Margaret 35; Massachusetts, 1849 *5881.1 p95*
Twomay, Jeremiah 25; Massachusetts, 1850 *5881.1 p94*
Twomay, Jerry 25; Massachusetts, 1847 *5881.1 p94*
Twomay, William; America, 1836 *1450.2 p147A*
Twomey, Ellen 15; Massachusetts, 1849 *5881.1 p94*
Twomey, James; America, 1737 *4971 p45*
Twomey, Michael 22; Massachusetts, 1847 *5881.1 p94*
Tydder, Hugh; Virginia, 1637 *6219 p8*
Tydeman, Mr.; Charleston, SC, 1777 *8582.2 p42*
Tye, Richard; Virginia, 1642 *6219 p195*
Tyler, Anth.; Virginia, 1635 *6219 p33*
Tyler, Christopher; Boston, 1770 *1219.7 p142*
Tyler, John 19; Pennsylvania, 1723 *3690.1 p230*
Tyler, Samuel 35; Maryland, 1775 *1219.7 p250*
Tyler, Tho.; Virginia, 1635 *6219 p23*
Tyler, William 19; Maryland, 1774 *1219.7 p192*
Tylior, Robert; Maryland, 1756 *3690.1 p221*
Tylley, John; Virginia, 1623-1700 *6219 p182*
Tyman, Sarah *SEE* Tyman, William
Tyman, William; Virginia, 1642 *6219 p192*
  *Wife:*Sarah
Tynan, Patrick; New York, NY, 1835 *8208.4 p7*
Tyngle, Antho.; Virginia, 1648 *6219 p250*
Tynon, John; America, 1841 *7036 p127*
Typladye, Jno.; Virginia, 1645 *6219 p232*
Tyran, J. B. 17; Port uncertain, 1838 *778.5 p524*
Tyre, John 16; Philadelphia, 1774 *1219.7 p233*
Tyrell, William; America, 1743 *4971 p11*
Tyrer, Xpr. 18; America, 1699 *2212 p28*
Tyrion, Mrs. 28; New Orleans, 1839 *778.5 p524*
Tyrion, Charles 38; New Orleans, 1839 *778.5 p524*
Tyrion, Verginie 10; New Orleans, 1839 *778.5 p524*
Tyror, Alexandr 19; Maryland, 1702 *2212 p36*
Tyrr, Jno 18; America, 1702 *2212 p36*
Tyrrell, Michael; America, 1739 *4971 p24*
Tyrrell, Michael; New York, NY, 1838 *8208.4 p80*
Tyrrell, Richard; America, 1735-1743 *4971 p8*
Tyrrell, Timothy 17; Virginia, 1720 *3690.1 p230*
Tyrrell, William 15; Maryland or Virginia, 1720 *3690.1 p230*
Tysinger, William; Ohio, 1848 *9892.11 p46*
Tysley, Richard; Virginia, 1636 *6219 p12*
Tysoe, Jabez 47; Kansas, 1887 *5240.1 p69*
Tyson, Andrew; California, 1860 *2764.35 p68*
Tyson, Cornelius; Germantown, PA, 1684 *2467.7 p5*
Tyson, Dirck; Pennsylvania, 1683 *2155 p2*
Tyson, George; Virginia, 1642 *6219 p197*
Tyson, Lijntijen; Pennsylvania, 1683 *2155 p1*
Tyson, Ryneir; Pennsylvania, 1683 *2155 p2*
Tyssere, . . .; Canada, 1776-1783 *9786 p36*

U

Upstill, Thomas 19; Pennsylvania, 1738 *3690.1 p231*
Upton, Elizabeth; Virginia, 1698 *2212 p16*
Upton, John; Virginia, 1698 *2212 p16*
Upton, Thomas; America, 1850 *2896.5 p40*
Upton, Thomas; Virginia, 1698 *2212 p16*
Uray, David 12; Massachusetts, 1849 *5881.1 p95*
Uray, Isabella 38; Massachusetts, 1849 *5881.1 p95*
Urban, Anna 24; New York, 1912 *9980.29 p69*
Urban, Isidor; Wisconsin, n.d. *9675.8 p123*
Urban, Joseph; Wisconsin, n.d. *9675.8 p123*
Urban, Mike 22; Kansas, 1894 *5240.1 p79*
Urbane, Nik; Iowa, 1866-1943 *123.54 p50*
Urbani, Joseph A.; Mobile, AL, 1870 *2896.5 p40*
Urbans, George; Iowa, 1866-1943 *123.54 p50*
Urbanski, Wincenty 37; New York, 1912 *9980.29 p52*
Urborn, John 25; Kansas, 1878 *5240.1 p59*
Urbusazasl, Klemansas; Wisconsin, n.d. *9675.8 p123*
Urbuszas, Klemancas; Wisconsin, n.d. *9675.8 p123*
Ure, Alexander; South Carolina, 1684 *1639.20 p310*
Ure, John; South Carolina, 1797 *1639.20 p310*
Ure, William; New York, NY, 1836 *8208.4 p19*
Urinar, Martin; America, 1901 *1450.2 p40B*
Uritte, Eugene 28; America, 1838 *778.5 p524*
Uritte, Joseph 52; America, 1838 *778.5 p524*
Urlich, Adam; Iowa, 1866-1943 *123.54 p50*
Urquhart, Alexander; Wilmington, NC, 1765-1792 *1639.20 p310*
Urquhart, Ann 13; Massachusetts, 1849 *5881.1 p95*
Urquhart, Anna; Wilmington, NC, 1777-1804 *1639.20 p310*

Urquhart, Lennard; South Carolina, 1758 *1639.20 p310*
Urquhart, Malcolm; Austin, TX, 1886 *9777 p5*
Urquhart, Thomas 25; Grenada, 1776 *1219.7 p282*
Urs, Joseph; Illinois, 1876 *2896.5 p40*
Urs, Matthew; Illinois, 1886 *2896.5 p40*
Ursic, Frank; Wisconsin, n.d. *9675.8 p123*
Ursly, John; Virginia, 1636 *6219 p32*
Urstadt, Heinr. 63; America, 1895 *1763 p48D*
Urtubise, Mrs. 25; America, 1838 *778.5 p525*
Urtubise, Louis 20; America, 1838 *778.5 p525*
Urwin, Wm.; Virginia, 1642 *6219 p191*
Urzac, Bertrand 31; Port uncertain, 1827 *778.5 p525*
Usadel, August; Wisconsin, n.d. *9675.8 p123*
Uschisow, Jossel; Wisconsin, n.d. *9675.8 p123*
Uscinowicz, Anton 19; New York, 1912 *9980.29 p52*
Use, Henry 20; Jamaica, 1730 *3690.1 p231*
Uselding, John B.; Wisconsin, n.d. *9675.8 p123*
Useling, Nicholas; Wisconsin, n.d. *9675.8 p123*
Ushart, Mary Jane 20; St. John, N.B., 1863 *5704.8 p153*
Ushart, William John 16; St. John, N.B., 1863 *5704.8 p153*
Usher, Captain; Quebec, 1815 *9229.18 p77*
  With family
Usher, Eliza; Philadelphia, 1864 *5704.8 p179*
Usher, James; Philadelphia, 1864 *5704.8 p179*
Usher, James A. 20; St. John, N.B., 1864 *5704.8 p159*
Usher, Mary; Philadelphia, 1864 *5704.8 p179*
Usher, Robert 14; Maryland, 1719 *3690.1 p231*
Usherwood, Joseph 21; Virginia, 1774 *1219.7 p201*
Usulding, Nicholas; Wisconsin, n.d. *9675.8 p123*

Usus, Jan; Wisconsin, n.d. *9675.8 p123*
Uteley, James; Virginia, 1643 *6219 p201*
Uthe, David Gottfried; Pennsylvania, 1751 *4525 p253*
Uthe, David Gottfried; Pennsylvania, 1752 *4525 p253*
Utley, Richard; New York, 1743 *3652 p60*
  *Wife:*Sarah
Utley, Sarah *SEE* Utley, Richard
Uttenbusch, Wilhelm; Kentucky, 1840 *8582.3 p100*
Utterbridge, Margaret; Quebec, 1825 *7603 p100*
Uttrich, Jacob; Philadelphia, 1776 *8582.3 p83*
Utye, . . .; Virginia, 1642 *6219 p196*
Utye, Mary; Virginia, 1642 *6219 p196*
Utz, Dietrich; South Carolina, 1788 *7119 p204*
Utz, Gottlieb; Pennsylvania, 1750 *4525 p253*
Utz, Peter; South Carolina, 1788 *7119 p203*
Utz, Samuel Gottfried; Pennsylvania, 1752 *4525 p253*
  With wife
  With child
Utz, Thomas; America, 1846 *8582.3 p66*
Uxer, Mary; Virginia, 1647 *6219 p244*
Uxley, Catharine 17; Pennsylvania, 1725 *3690.1 p231*
Uzac, Mr. 15; New Orleans, 1839 *778.5 p525*
Uzae, Mr. 15; New Orleans, 1839 *778.5 p525*
Uzai, John 30; Mexico, 1837 *778.5 p525*
Uzero, P. 22; New Orleans, 1821 *778.5 p525*
Uzireau, Jean 30; New Orleans, 1827 *778.5 p525*
Uzzell, Thomas 17; Maryland, 1773 *1219.7 p173*
Uzzell, William 22; Maryland, 1774 *1219.7 p218*

V

Vaccarezza, Andrew; Arkansas, 1918 **95.2** *p124*
Vache, J. P. 36; New Orleans, 1839 **778.5** *p525*
Vaegly, John 46; Kansas, 1894 **5240.1** *p79*
Vaehr, Cornelius; Quebec, 1876 **9980.20** *p49*
Vaehr, David; Quebec, 1875 **9980.20** *p48*
Vaehr, David; Quebec, 1877 **9980.20** *p49*
Vaehr, David 16; Quebec, 1876 **9980.20** *p49*
Vaehr, Elisabeth Banmann; Quebec, 1875 **9980.20** *p49*
Vaehr, Helena; Quebec, 1875 **9980.20** *p48*
Vaehr, Isak; Quebec, 1875 **9980.20** *p48*
Vaehr, Isak; Quebec, 1875 **9980.20** *p49*
Vaehr, Isak; Quebec, 1876 **9980.20** *p49*
Vaehr, Jacob; Quebec, 1875 **9980.20** *p48*
Vaehr, Jacob; Quebec, 1876 **9980.20** *p49*
Vaehr, Jacob 15; Quebec, 1875 **9980.20** *p48*
Vaehr, Joh. 15; Quebec, 1876 **9980.20** *p49*
Vaehr, Johann; Quebec, 1875 **9980.20** *p48*
Vaehr, Johann; Quebec, 1877 **9980.20** *p49*
Vaehr, Justienna; Quebec, 1875 **9980.20** *p48*
Vaehr, Maria; Quebec, 1875 **9980.20** *p48*
Vaehr, Maria; Quebec, 1876 **9980.20** *p49*
Vaehr, Maria Wiens; Quebec, 1875 **9980.20** *p48*
Vaehr, Maria Wiens; Quebec, 1877 **9980.20** *p49*
Vaehr, Peter; Quebec, 1875 **9980.20** *p48*
Vaehr, Peter; Quebec, 1876 **9980.20** *p49*
Vaes, Emil 39; Arizona, 1918 **9228.40** *p22*
Vaeth, Andreas; Pennsylvania, 1753 **4525** *p253*
Vagenos, Constantine Sam; Arkansas, 1918 **95.2** *p124*
Vagnoni, Nocenzo; Arkansas, 1918 **95.2** *p124*
Vaharty, Miles; Philadelphia, 1816 **2859.11** *p43*
Vahle, Heinrich; New Orleans, 1850 **1450.2** *p149A*
Vahlman, Johannes August; Minneapolis, 1877-1879 **6410.35** *p67*
Vahrenbring, A M Louise Vahrenbrink SEE Vahrenbring, Friedrich Wilhelm
Vahrenbring, Franz Heinrich Wilhelm SEE Vahrenbring, Friedrich Wilhelm
Vahrenbring, Friedrich Wilhelm; America, 1852 **4610.10** *p112*

    *Wife:*A M Louise Vahrenbrink
    *Son:*Franz Heinrich Wilhelm

Vahrenbring, A.M. Louise; America, 1852 **4610.10** *p112*
Vail, William 36; Jamaica, 1750 **3690.1** *p232*
Vaines, M.A. 26; Virginia, 1774 **1219.7** *p244*
Vair, Charles R.; Virginia, 1899 **5240.1** *p46*
Vaira, Sebastian; Iowa, 1866-1943 **123.54** *p50*
Vaisau, Mr. 40; New Orleans, 1839 **778.5** *p525*
Vaith, Andreas; Pennsylvania, 1753 **4525** *p253*
Vakares, Nick; Arkansas, 1918 **95.2** *p124*
Vakas, Steleanos George; Kansas, 1916 **6013.40** *p17*
Vakee, Wilhelm; Wisconsin, n.d. **9675.8** *p123*
Vakendis, Mike George; Arkansas, 1918 **95.2** *p124*
Valantin, Mr. 28; New Orleans, 1835 **778.5** *p525*
Valantin, Mrs. 24; New Orleans, 1835 **778.5** *p525*
Valantine, John 23; Jamaica, 1774 **1219.7** *p178*
Valary, Em. 15; America, 1838 **778.5** *p525*
Valasquez, Anacleto 38; Arizona, 1920 **9228.40** *p24*
Valasse, Adolphe 32; Port uncertain, 1839 **778.5** *p525*
Valasse, Jean 24; Port uncertain, 1839 **778.5** *p525*
Valdarki, Ovidio; Wisconsin, n.d. **9675.8** *p123*
Valdenaire, John J.; New York, 1867 **1450.2** *p40B*
Valdimarsdottir, Johanniner 3; Quebec, 1879 **2557.1** *p20*
Valdimarsson, Valdimar 6 mos; Quebec, 1879 **2557.1** *p20*
Vale, John; New York, NY, 1811 **2859.11** *p20*
Vale, Margaret; New York, NY, 1811 **2859.11** *p20*
Vale, Morris; America, 1830 **1450.2** *p149A*

Valencia, Francisco 48; Arizona, 1926 **9228.40** *p30*
Valencia, Ignacia 77; Arizona, 1920 **9228.40** *p24*
Valencia, Rosa 23; Arizona, 1918 **9228.40** *p22*
Valentin, Mr. 34; Louisiana, 1823 **778.5** *p525*
Valentin, Rasmus; Bangor, ME, 1869-1876 **6410.22** *p115*
Valentina, Frances; Iowa, 1866-1943 **123.54** *p50*
Valentine, Elisa; Virginia, 1698 **2212** *p15*
Valentine, Eliz 21; America, 1702 **2212** *p37*
Valentine, Kaurlaric; Iowa, 1866-1943 **123.54** *p50*
Valentine, Magnus; Arkansas, 1918 **95.2** *p125*
Valentino, Guiseppe; Wisconsin, n.d. **9675.8** *p123*
Valentino, Ponziano; Arkansas, 1918 **95.2** *p125*
Valet, Desir 16; New Orleans, 1839 **778.5** *p526*
Valet, Joseph 22; Jamaica, 1736 **3690.1** *p231*
Valeton, Mr. 22; New Orleans, 1839 **778.5** *p526*
Valeton, A. 19; America, 1838 **778.5** *p526*
Valette, Mr.; Port uncertain, 1839 **778.5** *p526*
Valette, Mr. 23; New Orleans, 1839 **778.5** *p526*
Valette, Mr. 30; America, 1839 **778.5** *p526*
Valette, David SEE Valette, Pierre
Valette, Madeleine SEE Valette, Pierre
Valette, Marie-Louise SEE Valette, Pierre
Valette, Martin 10; America, 1839 **778.5** *p526*
Valette, Pierre 36; Halifax, N.S., 1752 **7074.6** *p213*

    *Wife:*Marie-Louise
    *Child:*Madeleine
    *Child:*David

Valic, Toma; Iowa, 1866-1943 **123.54** *p50*
Valie, Mr. 40; New Orleans, 1830 **778.5** *p526*
Valie, C. 12; New Orleans, 1830 **778.5** *p526*
Valier, Isadore; New York, NY, 1834 **8208.4** *p2*
Valk, John; Arkansas, 1918 **95.2** *p125*
Vallas, James; Arkansas, 1918 **95.2** *p125*
Vallaso, Antoni 45; Arizona, 1921 **9228.40** *p25*
Vallentine, Thore Frederick; Maine, 1896 **6410.22** *p127*
Vallera, Angelo; Wisconsin, n.d. **9675.8** *p123*
Vallet, Eliza 19; Port uncertain, 1838 **778.5** *p526*
Vallett, John; Virginia, 1639 **6219** *p162*
Valley, Mr. 30; Port uncertain, 1839 **778.5** *p526*
Valley, Ann 18; Pennsylvania, 1720 **3690.1** *p231*
Vallie, Peter 22; Jamaica, 1730 **3690.1** *p231*
Vallo, Julian 33; Arizona, 1925 **9228.40** *p29*
Valmont, D. 30; America, 1838 **778.5** *p526*
Valnant, Susanna 22; Maryland, 1775 **1219.7** *p267*
Valot, Jean Baptiste; New York, NY, 1835 **8208.4** *p31*
Van Aken, Reyer; Arkansas, 1918 **95.2** *p125*
Van Asch, Anton; Arkansas, 1918 **95.2** *p125*
Van Blaracom, Isaac; Washington, 1859-1920 **2872.1** *p41*
Van Blaracom, John; Washington, 1859-1920 **2872.1** *p41*
Van Blon, Jacob; America, 1853 **6014.1** *p3*
Van Briouen, Mr. 39; Port uncertain, 1838 **778.5** *p526*
Vance, Allice 7; Quebec, 1854 **5704.8** *p118*
Vance, Allice 38; Quebec, 1854 **5704.8** *p118*
Vance, Andrew; New York, NY, 1864 **5704.8** *p172*
Vance, B. 16; New Orleans, 1830 **778.5** *p526*
Vance, Bell; New York, NY, 1864 **5704.8** *p172*
Vance, Charles; Philadelphia, 1848 **53.26** *p89*
Vance, Charles; Philadelphia, 1848 **5704.8** *p45*
Vance, D.; New York, NY, 1811 **2859.11** *p20*
Vance, Eliza J.; Philadelphia, 1866 **5704.8** *p207*
Vance, Elizabeth; New York, NY, 1864 **5704.8** *p172*
Vance, Elizabeth; Philadelphia, 1848 **53.26** *p89*
Vance, Elizabeth; Philadelphia, 1848 **5704.8** *p46*
Vance, F. 40; New Orleans, 1830 **778.5** *p527*
Vance, Fanny; Philadelphia, 1851 **5704.8** *p80*

Vance, G. 10; New Orleans, 1830 **778.5** *p527*
Vance, George; New York, NY, 1864 **5704.8** *p172*
Vance, Henry; Illinois, 1857 **7857** *p8*
Vance, Isaac; New York, NY, 1811 **2859.11** *p20*
Vance, J. 12; New Orleans, 1830 **778.5** *p527*
Vance, James; New York, NY, 1864 **5704.8** *p186*
Vance, James; Philadelphia, 1847 **53.26** *p89*
Vance, James; Philadelphia, 1847 **5704.8** *p14*
Vance, Jane 11; Quebec, 1854 **5704.8** *p118*
Vance, Jane 40; St. John, N.B., 1863 **5704.8** *p153*
Vance, John; New York, NY, 1864 **5704.8** *p172*
Vance, John; Philadelphia, 1864 **5704.8** *p178*
Vance, John 9; Quebec, 1854 **5704.8** *p118*
Vance, John 21; Philadelphia, 1854 **5704.8** *p118*
Vance, L. 41; New Orleans, 1830 **778.5** *p527*
Vance, Lansht 40; Newfoundland, 1789 **4915.24** *p57*
Vance, Margaret; New York, NY, 1864 **5704.8** *p172*
Vance, Martha 19; Philadelphia, 1858 **5704.8** *p139*
Vance, Patrick 8; St. John, N.B., 1863 **5704.8** *p153*
Vance, R. 8; New Orleans, 1830 **778.5** *p527*
Vance, Robert 11; St. John, N.B., 1863 **5704.8** *p153*
Vance, S. 6; New Orleans, 1830 **778.5** *p527*
Vance, Samuel 5; Quebec, 1854 **5704.8** *p118*
Vance, T. 5; New Orleans, 1830 **778.5** *p527*
Vance, William 42; St. John, N.B., 1863 **5704.8** *p153*
Vance, William John 6; St. John, N.B., 1863 **5704.8** *p153*
Vancik, Michael; America, 1898 **7137** *p170*
Vancik, Stephen; America, 1891 **7137** *p170*
Vancik, Susan; America, 1896 **7137** *p170*
Vanclain, Joseph 43; America, 1838 **778.5** *p527*
Van Corler, John 27; Arkansas, 1918 **95.2** *p125*
Vand, Dorcas; Virginia, 1637 **6219** *p34*
Vandall, Lucy 19; Pennsylvania, Virginia or Maryland, 1719 **3690.1** *p231*
Van Danneker, Jacob; New York, NY, 1834 **8208.4** *p47*
Van De Boom, Gerhard; Wisconsin, n.d. **9675.8** *p123*
VandeBunt, Albertus 22; Arkansas, 1918 **95.2** *p125*
Vande Bunt, Alertus; Arkansas, 1918 **95.2** *p125*
Vandechamp, Joseph 50; New Orleans, 1838 **778.5** *p527*
Van de Hoef, Tennis; Arkansas, 1918 **95.2** *p125*
Vandel, Mr.; New Orleans, 1838 **778.5** *p527*
Vandeleur, William 25; Massachusetts, 1850 **5881.1** *p95*
Van Demann, Johannes; Ohio, 1800 **8582.2** *p58*
Vandenhurck, Anne 18; Pennsylvania, 1739 **3690.1** *p232*
Vanderbergh, Ferdinand; Arkansas, 1918 **95.2** *p125*
Vanderdy, . . . 28; Grenada, 1774 **1219.7** *p185*
Vander Heyden, Canill; Iowa, 1866-1943 **123.54** *p50*
Vander Heyden, Jean; Iowa, 1866-1943 **123.54** *p50*
Vanderlaan, George Fred; Arkansas, 1918 **95.2** *p125*
Vandermann, Johannes; Ohio, 1800 **8582.2** *p58*
Vander Mussele, Michael; Arkansas, 1918 **95.2** *p125*
Vanderville, Emile; Iowa, 1866-1943 **123.54** *p50*
Vanderville, Louie; Iowa, 1866-1943 **123.54** *p50*
Vandervoort, Benjamin, Sr.; New York, NY, 1839 **8208.4** *p94*
Vandery, Francis 18; America, 1705 **2212** *p43*
Van Desand, Utina; Washington, 1859-1920 **2872.1** *p42*
Vandevelde, Ferdinand; Arkansas, 1918 **95.2** *p125*
Van De Ven, George; Iowa, 1866-1943 **123.54** *p81*
Vande Voorde, Julius; Arkansas, 1918 **95.2** *p125*
Vande Walde, Philemon 29; Arkansas, 1918 **95.2** *p125*
Vande Walle, Alidor; Arkansas, 1918 **95.2** *p125*
Vandewyngaerd, Edward F.; Iowa, 1866-1943 **123.54** *p50*
Van Dike, George; Arkansas, 1918 **95.2** *p125*

Van Dorston, Gloudrenus 33; Georgia, 1735 ***3690.1*** *p232*
Vandosme, Abraham 21; Maryland, 1774 ***1219.7*** *p187*
Vandredome, Mrs. 22; New Orleans, 1822 ***778.5*** *p527*
Vandredome, A. 25; New Orleans, 1822 ***778.5*** *p527*
Van Dyk, William; Iroquois Co., IL, 1896 ***3455.1*** *p14*
Vane, George 21; South Carolina, 1732 ***3690.1*** *p232*
Vanelst, Julius; Iowa, 1866-1943 ***123.54*** *p50*
Vanes, Dirk; Washington, 1859-1920 ***2872.1*** *p42*
Vaness, Dirk; Washington, 1859-1920 ***2872.1*** *p42*
Vaness, Guy; Washington, 1859-1920 ***2872.1*** *p42*
Vaness, Joe; Washington, 1859-1920 ***2872.1*** *p42*
Vanetti, Frank 34; West Virginia, 1904 ***9788.3*** *p21*
Van Gelder, Carmiel; Arkansas, 1918 ***95.2*** *p125*
Vangrundy, Joseph; Ohio, 1800-1885 ***8582.2*** *p58*
Vanham, John; Virginia, 1637 ***6219*** *p112*
Vanheddeghem, Alexander 32; New Orleans, 1826 ***778.5*** *p527*
Vanheer, Bartholomew; America, 1777-1778 ***8582.2*** *p68*
Van Heijden, Prosper; Arkansas, 1918 ***95.2*** *p125*
VanHentenryck, Pierre; Arkansas, 1918 ***95.2*** *p125*
Van Hook, Jan; Kentucky, 1810 ***8582.3*** *p97*
Van Huyning, Hendrik; Ohio, 1816 ***8582.1*** *p49*
Vanielle, Zenon 21; Louisiana, 1833 ***778.5*** *p527*
Vanier, J. G. 30; New Orleans, 1823 ***778.5*** *p527*
Vanille, Mme. 28; New Orleans, 1825 ***778.5*** *p528*
Vanille, Ludivine 19; New Orleans, 1825 ***778.5*** *p528*
Van Langen, Herman; Wisconsin, n.d. ***9675.8*** *p123*
Van Langen, Lambert; Wisconsin, n.d. ***9675.8*** *p123*
Van Lanken, George; Illinois, 1886 ***5012.39*** *p120*
Vanlankvelt, John 36; Kansas, 1872 ***5240.1*** *p52*
Van Lienen, Henry; Indiana, 1848 ***9117*** *p18*
Van Name, J. F.; Washington, 1859-1920 ***2872.1*** *p42*
Van Nassau, Jan; Ohio, 1793 ***8582.2*** *p57*
Vanners, Peter; Illinois, 1829 ***8582.1*** *p55*
Van Nevel, Camiel 32; Arkansas, 1918 ***95.2*** *p125*
Vanni, Domenio; Arkansas, 1918 ***95.2*** *p125*
Vanniemoenhuizen, Corneilis; Washington, 1859-1920 ***2872.1*** *p42*
Vannier, Mr. 17; America, 1837 ***778.5*** *p528*
Vannier, Fritz; New York, 1888 ***1450.2*** *p149A*
Vannier, J. B. 30; New Orleans, 1822 ***778.5*** *p528*
Vannier, Jean-Baptiste 28; Louisiana, 1820 ***778.5*** *p528*
Vannier, Pierre Francois 30; New Orleans, 1838 ***778.5*** *p528*
Vanoch, John 26; California, 1869 ***2769.9*** *p4*
Vanoni, Costantino; America, 1842 ***1450.2*** *p149A*
Vanoni, Frederick; Illinois, 1890 ***2896.5*** *p40*
Van Ooteghan, Archiel Joseph; Arkansas, 1918 ***95.2*** *p125*
Van Oy, Franke; Illinois, 1881 ***2896.5*** *p40*
Van Praag, Isaac L.; New York, NY, 1836 ***8208.4*** *p16*
Van Quest, Edith 21; Arizona, 1897 ***9228.40*** *p4*
Vanscheith, Johann; Ohio, 1881 ***3702.7*** *p439*
Van Schoick, Stephan; Ohio, 1819 ***8582.1*** *p47*
Van Sluys, John; Wisconsin, n.d. ***9675.8*** *p123*
Van Sluys, Willemyntje; Wisconsin, n.d. ***9675.8*** *p123*
Vanson, Rich.; Virginia, 1643 ***6219*** *p200*
Vanton, Jacques; Quebec, 1822 ***7603*** *p23*
Van Vlasselaen, Amelie; Iowa, 1866-1943 ***123.54*** *p81*
Van Vlasselaer, Louis; Iowa, 1866-1943 ***123.54*** *p81*
Vapaille, Amante 5; New Orleans, 1829 ***778.5*** *p528*
Vapaille, Eugene 9; New Orleans, 1829 ***778.5*** *p528*
Vapaille, Marie 30; New Orleans, 1829 ***778.5*** *p528*
Vapaille, Noel 35; New Orleans, 1829 ***778.5*** *p528*
Vaque, B. 39; Port uncertain, 1837 ***778.5*** *p528*
Varalli, Raffaele; Arkansas, 1918 ***95.2*** *p125*
Varbler, Joseph 29; America, 1838 ***778.5*** *p528*
Vardaastamio, Nicholis; Arkansas, 1918 ***95.2*** *p126*
Vardale, Richard; Virginia, 1639 ***6219*** *p149*
Vardall, Richard; Virginia, 1639 ***6219*** *p154*
Vardic, P. 17; America, 1831 ***778.5*** *p528*
Vardin, John; America, 1739 ***4971*** *p26*
Varity, Alfred; Iowa, 1866-1943 ***123.54*** *p50*
Varlas, Frank John; Arkansas, 1918 ***95.2*** *p126*
Varley, Margaret 35; New York, 1775 ***1219.7*** *p269*
With 2 children
Varlon, Peter; Virginia, 1635 ***6219*** *p5*
Varney, John 18; Maryland, 1730 ***3690.1*** *p232*
Varnier, Peter 22; Virginia, 1725 ***3690.1*** *p232*
Varnil, S. 35; Port uncertain, 1838 ***778.5*** *p528*
Vartz, Alfred; Iowa, 1866-1943 ***123.54*** *p50*
Vase, Rich.; Virginia, 1636 ***6219*** *p26*
Vase, Rich.; Virginia, 1637 ***6219*** *p86*
Vasey, James 34; Massachusetts, 1850 ***5881.1*** *p95*
Vasey, Maria 4; Massachusetts, 1850 ***5881.1*** *p96*
Vasiq, Lerisa 24; Port uncertain, 1838 ***778.5*** *p529*
Vasler, Elizabeth *SEE* Vasler, John
Vasler, John; Virginia, 1635 ***6219*** *p34*
*Wife:*Elizabeth
Vasnika, Rudi; Wisconsin, n.d. ***9675.8*** *p123*
Vasquez, Joseph 32; Port uncertain, 1838 ***778.5*** *p529*
Vass, Charlotte Johana Macre *SEE* Vass, Edmond Brooke
Vass, Edmond Brooke; Florida, 1830 ***8893*** *p265*
*Wife:*Charlotte Johana Macre
Vassaille, Amante 5; New Orleans, 1829 ***778.5*** *p528*
Vassaille, Eugene 9; New Orleans, 1829 ***778.5*** *p528*
Vassaille, Marie 30; New Orleans, 1829 ***778.5*** *p528*
Vassaille, Noel 35; New Orleans, 1829 ***778.5*** *p528*
Vasse, Guillaume 40; America, 1820 ***778.5*** *p529*
Vasseur, Mr.; Port uncertain, 1839 ***778.5*** *p529*
Vassil, Norman; Arkansas, 1918 ***95.2*** *p126*
Vassins, Charles 36; Havana, 1826 ***778.5*** *p529*
Vater, William; America, 1851 ***1450.2*** *p149A*
Vatinel, T. 30; Port uncertain, 1839 ***778.5*** *p529*
Vatterott, . . .; Canada, 1776-1783 ***9786*** *p36*
Vaudechamp, Mrs. 32; Port uncertain, 1832 ***778.5*** *p529*
Vaudechamp, Adele 4; America, 1835 ***778.5*** *p529*
Vaudechamp, Eugenie 35; America, 1835 ***778.5*** *p529*
Vaudechamp, J. 40; Port uncertain, 1832 ***778.5*** *p529*
Vaudechamp, Jean Joseph 45; America, 1835 ***778.5*** *p529*
Vaudechamp, Joseph 45; Port uncertain, 1836 ***778.5*** *p529*
Vaudry, Marnie 26; America, 1838 ***778.5*** *p529*
Vaughan, Ann; Quebec, 1850 ***5704.8*** *p66*
Vaughan, Ann 18; Quebec, 1863 ***5704.8*** *p153*
Vaughan, Christ.; Virginia, 1642 ***6219*** *p195*
Vaughan, David; Virginia, 1637 ***6219*** *p81*
Vaughan, Dennis 26; Ohio, 1842 ***1450.2*** *p149A*
Vaughan, Edward; Virginia, 1644 ***6219*** *p229*
Vaughan, Enoch; Winchester, VA, 1776-1779 ***4778.2*** *p143*
Vaughan, Francis; Virginia, 1644 ***6219*** *p229*
Vaughan, Geo.; Virginia, 1648 ***6219*** *p252*
Vaughan, Hannah; America, 1698 ***2212*** *p7*
Vaughan, Hugh 28; Virginia, 1774 ***1219.7*** *p244*
Vaughan, James; New York, NY, 1816 ***2859.11*** *p43*
Vaughan, James; Quebec, 1851 ***5704.8*** *p75*
Vaughan, James 10; Quebec, 1863 ***5704.8*** *p153*
Vaughan, Jane 19; Philadelphia, 1774 ***1219.7*** *p182*
Vaughan, Jane 19; Quebec, 1853 ***5704.8*** *p104*
Vaughan, John; America, 1736 ***4971*** *p44*
Vaughan, John; America, 1737 ***4971*** *p46*
Vaughan, John; Virginia, 1622 ***6219*** *p76*
Vaughan, John 23; Maryland, 1774 ***1219.7*** *p196*
Vaughan, John 59; Jamaica, 1774 ***1219.7*** *p223*
Vaughan, Jon.; Virginia, 1638 ***6219*** *p18*
Vaughan, Lewis; Virginia, 1635 ***6219*** *p17*
Vaughan, Margaret 14; Quebec, 1863 ***5704.8*** *p153*
Vaughan, Mary; Quebec, 1850 ***5704.8*** *p70*
Vaughan, Mary; Virginia, 1639 ***6219*** *p155*
Vaughan, Mary 45; Quebec, 1863 ***5704.8*** *p153*
Vaughan, Patrick; Virginia, 1635 ***6219*** *p69*
Vaughan, Patrick; Virginia, 1638 ***6219*** *p33*
Vaughan, Philip 20; Jamaica, 1736 ***3690.1*** *p232*
Vaughan, Rowd.; Virginia, 1636 ***6219*** *p34*
Vaughan, Sarah 11; Quebec, 1863 ***5704.8*** *p153*
Vaughan, Thomas; New York, NY, 1816 ***2859.11*** *p43*
Vaughan, Thos.; Virginia, 1638 ***6219*** *p22*
Vaughan, William 22; Philadelphia, 1775 ***1219.7*** *p248*
Vaughan, William 32; Maryland, 1774 ***1219.7*** *p178*
Vaughan, Y.; New York, NY, 1816 ***2859.11*** *p43*
Vaughn, Edward; Illinois, 1868 ***5012.38*** *p99*
Vaughn, J. A.; Washington, 1859-1920 ***2872.1*** *p42*
Vaughton, George 26; Jamaica, 1736 ***3690.1*** *p232*
Vauginais, J. 17; America, 1829 ***778.5*** *p529*
Vaulotte, James 17; Philadelphia, 1775 ***1219.7*** *p259*
Vaulx, Alice; Virginia, 1640 ***6219*** *p160*
Vaunil, S. 35; Port uncertain, 1838 ***778.5*** *p528*
Vaupel, Johann Nicolaus; Halifax, N.S., 1780 ***9786*** *p269*
Vaupel, Johann Nicolaus; New York, 1776 ***9786*** *p269*
Vauquelin, . . .; Louisiana, 1820 ***778.5*** *p529*
Vauquelin, Mr. 28; Louisiana, 1820 ***778.5*** *p530*
Vauquelin, Mrs.; Louisiana, 1820 ***778.5*** *p530*
Vaus, Jane; South Carolina, 1767 ***1639.20*** *p311*
Vaus, John; Virginia, 1638 ***6219*** *p122*
Vaus, Richard; Virginia, 1637 ***6219*** *p110*
Vausel, Brosard de 41; New Orleans, 1821 ***778.5*** *p530*
Vautier, Daniel 22; Philadelphia, 1774 ***1219.7*** *p182*
Vautsmeyer, Marie Engel; America, 1863 ***4610.10*** *p145*
Vaux, Leonard 19; Maryland or Virginia, 1720 ***3690.1*** *p232*
Vavasor, Ann 23; Virginia, 1699 ***2212*** *p26*
Veal, G. 30; Mexico, 1825 ***778.5*** *p530*
Veal, Joseph 28; America, 1839 ***778.5*** *p530*
Veal, Madeline 30; America, 1839 ***778.5*** *p530*
Veale, Jane; Virginia, 1636 ***6219*** *p26*
Veare, Mary; Virginia, 1642 ***6219*** *p199*
Veasek, Frank; Wisconsin, n.d. ***9675.8*** *p123*
Veatch, James; New York, NY, 1815 ***2859.11*** *p43*
Veaux, Bertrand 23; New Orleans, 1839 ***778.5*** *p530*
Vecchi, Frank Mary 23; Arkansas, 1918 ***95.2*** *p126*
Vecellio, Giovanni; Arkansas, 1918 ***95.2*** *p126*
Veckel, Hannah 20; North America, 1774 ***1219.7*** *p198*
Veckel, Mary 20; North America, 1774 ***1219.7*** *p198*
Vedayes, Gustavo; Arkansas, 1918 ***95.2*** *p126*
Vedder, Heinrich; Cincinnati, 1869-1887 ***8582*** *p33*
Vedder, Joseph; Ohio, 1869-1887 ***8582*** *p2*
Vedder, Joseph; Ohio, 1869-1887 ***8582*** *p33*
Vedovell, Marie; New York, NY, 1886 ***3455.3*** *p79*
Vedrine, Henry 17; Port uncertain, 1838 ***778.5*** *p530*
Vee, John; Washington, 1859-1920 ***2872.1*** *p42*
Veerkamp, Gerhard H.; America, 1846 ***8582.2*** *p43*
Vega, Felipe 75; Arizona, 1901 ***9228.40*** *p9*
Vegilan, Franz Leo 9 mos; New York, NY, 1857 ***9831.14*** *p86*
Vegilan, Jul. Friedr. 29; New York, NY, 1857 ***9831.14*** *p86*
Vegilan, Wilhelmine 32; New York, NY, 1857 ***9831.14*** *p86*
Vehan, Mike; Iowa, 1866-1943 ***123.54*** *p50*
Vehling, Henry W. Christian; America, 1860 ***1450.2*** *p149A*
Vehr, Anna Niessen; Quebec, 1876 ***9980.20*** *p48*
Vehr, Cathariena; Quebec, 1876 ***9980.20*** *p48*
Vehr, Cornelius; Quebec, 1876 ***9980.20*** *p49*
Vehr, David 16; Quebec, 1876 ***9980.20*** *p49*
Vehr, Isak; Quebec, 1876 ***9980.20*** *p49*
Vehr, Jacob; Quebec, 1876 ***9980.20*** *p49*
Vehr, Joh.; Quebec, 1875 ***9980.20*** *p48*
Vehr, Joh. 15; Quebec, 1876 ***9980.20*** *p49*
Vehr, Johann; Quebec, 1876 ***9980.20*** *p48*
Vehr, Maria; Quebec, 1876 ***9980.20*** *p48*
Vehr, Maria; Quebec, 1876 ***9980.20*** *p49*
Vehr, Maria Braun; Quebec, 1876 ***9980.20*** *p49*
Vehr, Peter; Quebec, 1876 ***9980.20*** *p49*
Vehr, Susana; Quebec, 1875 ***9980.20*** *p48*
Vehse, Eduard 32; New Orleans, 1839 ***9420.2*** *p165*
*Child:*Mathilde 9
Vehse, Mathilde 9 *SEE* Vehse, Eduard
Veid, Michael; America, 1847 ***8582.1*** *p34*
Veil, William 36; Jamaica, 1750 ***3690.1*** *p232*
Veinot, Christophe *SEE* Veinot, Leopold
Veinot, George *SEE* Veinot, Leopold
Veinot, Jacques 15 *SEE* Veinot, Leopold
Veinot, Jeanne *SEE* Veinot, Leopold
Veinot, Leopold 48; Halifax, N.S., 1752 ***7074.6*** *p213*
*Wife:*Jeanne
*Son:*Christophe
*Son:*George
*Son:*Jacques 15
Veis, Louis; New York, NY, 1853 ***1450.2*** *p149A*
Veitch, Thomas; New York, NY, 1838 ***8208.4*** *p84*
Veitch, William; Charleston, SC, 1818 ***1639.20*** *p310*
Veitenheimer, Louise; Milwaukee, 1875 ***4719.30*** *p257*
Veith, Charles; Ohio, 1867 ***6014.1*** *p3*
Veith, Michael; Pennsylvania, 1751 ***2444*** *p227*
Veith, Minna 19; America, 1880 ***4610.10*** *p96*
Veitmeir, Frederich; Illinois, 1853 ***7857*** *p8*
Veitmeir, Harmon; Illinois, 1853 ***7857*** *p8*
Veitmeir, William; Illinois, 1853 ***7857*** *p8*
Veitmyre, Frederich; Illinois, 1853 ***7857*** *p8*
Veitmyre, Harmon; Illinois, 1853 ***7857*** *p8*
Veitmyre, William; Illinois, 1853 ***7857*** *p8*
Veito, George; Iowa, 1866-1943 ***123.54*** *p50*
Veizhans, Judith; Pennsylvania, 1766-1782 ***2444*** *p187*
Veizhans, Judith; Port uncertain, 1766 ***2444*** *p187*
Vek, Josep; Iowa, 1866-1943 ***123.54*** *p50*
Velanzula, Marie 35; Arizona, 1920 ***9228.40*** *p23*
Velasco, Mrs. 35; New Orleans, 1839 ***778.5*** *p530*
Velayne, Jeremiah; Virginia, 1642 ***6219*** *p186*
Velden, von den; Canada, 1776-1783 ***9786*** *p185*
Velk, Josep; Iowa, 1866-1943 ***123.54*** *p50*
Velk, Olive; Iowa, 1866-1943 ***123.54*** *p81*
Velke, Fred 73; Washington, 1918-1920 ***1728.5*** *p14*
Velke, Margaret 41; Washington, 1918-1920 ***1728.5*** *p14*
Velke, Margaret 43; Washington, 1918 ***1728.5*** *p14*
Vellion, Enearl 41; Port uncertain, 1836 ***778.5*** *p530*
Vellmier, Jean 25; America, 1838 ***778.5*** *p530*
Vellnagel, Anna Barbara; America, 1754 ***2444*** *p132*
Velsch, Ann 36; Port uncertain, 1839 ***778.5*** *p530*
Velsch, Chatrine 8; Port uncertain, 1839 ***778.5*** *p531*
Velsch, Johann 34; Port uncertain, 1839 ***778.5*** *p531*
Velsch, Joseph 10; Port uncertain, 1839 ***778.5*** *p531*
Velsch, Marie 11; Port uncertain, 1839 ***778.5*** *p531*
Velsch, Pierre 3; Port uncertain, 1839 ***778.5*** *p531*
Velsover, Anna; Pennsylvania, 1731 ***1034.18*** *p22*
Velsover, Katrina; Pennsylvania, 1731 ***1034.18*** *p22*
Velt, Stephen 26; New Orleans, 1837 ***778.5*** *p531*
Velten, Jacob; Pennsylvania, 1745-1800 ***2444*** *p227*
*Wife:*Maria Agnes
*Child:*Josef
Velten, Jacob; Pennsylvania, 1752 ***2444*** *p227*
Velten, Josef *SEE* Velten, Jacob
Velten, Magdalena; Pennsylvania, 1752 ***2444*** *p227*
Velten, Maria Agnes *SEE* Velten, Jacob
Velthuis, Gerrit Hendrik 37; New York, NY, 1847 ***3377.6*** *p11*

Velthuis, Gerritdina 2; New York, NY, 1847 *3377.6 p11*
Velthuis, Johanna 11; New York, NY, 1847 *3377.6 p11*
Velthuis, Mannes 5; New York, NY, 1847 *3377.6 p11*
Velthuis, Zwiertje 35; New York, NY, 1847 *3377.6 p11*
Venable, George; Detroit, 1847-1891 *9678.3 p16*
Venable, Richard; Virginia, 1635 *6219 p70*
Venables, Ralph; America, 1738 *4971 p85*
Venables, Ralph; America, 1738-1743 *4971 p91*
Venamay, John; Boston, 1776 *1219.7 p278*
Vencas, George; Arkansas, 1918 *95.2 p126*
Ven Corler, John; Arkansas, 1918 *95.2 p126*
Venderbosch, Herman; Wisconsin, n.d. *9675.8 p123*
Venditto, Giacomino 25; Arkansas, 1918 *95.2 p126*
Venebles, Ralph; America, 1743 *4971 p11*
Venell, August; Iowa, 1866-1943 *123.54 p50*
Venert, . . .; Canada, 1776-1783 *9786 p36*
Venerucci, Urbano; Wisconsin, n.d. *9675.8 p123*
Venibles, Ann; St. John, N.B., 1848 *5704.8 p44*
Venice, William; Virginia, 1639 *6219 p157*
Venice, Wm.; Virginia, 1642 *6219 p198*
Venille, Caroline 8 mos; New Orleans, 1825 *778.5 p531*
Venken, Heinrich; Kentucky, 1843 *8582.3 p100*
Venkoop, Henrich; Philadelphia, 1776 *8582.3 p83*
Venn, George S.; New York, 1873 *1450.2 p40B*
Venneberg, John 26; Massachusetts, 1860 *6410.32 p101*
Venneberg, Maria 20; Massachusetts, 1860 *6410.32 p101*
Venniman, Joseph; Indiana, 1847 *9117 p18*
Venot, William 40; New Orleans, 1832 *778.5 p531*
Vens, Arthur; Arkansas, 1918 *95.2 p126*
Vensey, Weymouth; Virginia, 1635 *6219 p35*
Venton, John; Quebec, 1798 *7603 p84*
Venus, Philip; Philadelphia, 1763 *9973.7 p38*
Venzi, Vinanzo; Arkansas, 1918 *95.2 p126*
Vera, Felix 19; New Orleans, 1837 *778.5 p531*
Veragut, Mr.; Port uncertain, 1839 *778.5 p531*
Verbonwen, Gustave; Arkansas, 1918 *95.2 p126*
Verbooz, Ladmaz; Arkansas, 1918 *95.2 p126*
Verch, Julius; Wisconsin, n.d. *9675.8 p123*
Verciglio, Sebastiane; Arkansas, 1918 *95.2 p126*
Verdean, Mr. 30; Port uncertain, 1839 *778.5 p531*
Verdier, Mr.; Port uncertain, 1839 *778.5 p531*
Verdier, Mr. 25; Port uncertain, 1827 *778.5 p531*
Verdier, Philippe 30; Port uncertain, 1836 *778.5 p531*
Verdries, . . .; Canada, 1776-1783 *9786 p36*
Veremchuk, Naum; Arkansas, 1918 *95.2 p126*
Verfuerth, Bernhard; Wisconsin, n.d. *9675.8 p123*
Verges, Mr. 17; Port uncertain, 1839 *778.5 p531*
Vergis, Mr. 25; Port uncertain, 1836 *778.5 p532*
Vergis, Paul 26; Port uncertain, 1836 *778.5 p532*
Vergnes, Anna 27; America, 1836 *778.5 p532*
Vergnes, Maurice 36; America, 1836 *778.5 p532*
Verhage, Heinrich; America, 1851 *8582.3 p66*
Verhenne, Gustaaf; Arkansas, 1918 *95.2 p126*
Verhoneck, Vincent; Wisconsin, n.d. *9675.8 p123*
Verhovnik, Anton; Wisconsin, n.d. *9675.8 p123*
Veriker, John 8; Massachusetts, 1849 *5881.1 p95*
Veriker, Michael 5; Massachusetts, 1849 *5881.1 p95*
Veriker, Theophilus 11; Massachusetts, 1849 *5881.1 p95*
Veriker, Tobias 40; Massachusetts, 1849 *5881.1 p95*
Veris, Pierre 24; New Orleans, 1836 *778.5 p532*
Vermedahl, Lars; Arkansas, 1918 *95.2 p126*
Verna, John; Iowa, 1866-1943 *123.54 p50*
Verna, Martin; Iowa, 1866-1943 *123.54 p50*
Vernan, Thomas 22; Carolina, 1774 *1219.7 p179*
Vernau, . . .; Canada, 1776-1783 *9786 p36*
Vernay, Claude 44; America, 1836 *778.5 p532*
Vernay, Francoise 37; America, 1836 *778.5 p532*
Vernay, Jean 6; America, 1836 *778.5 p532*
Verner, . . .; Canada, 1776-1783 *9786 p36*
Verner, Ann 60; St. John, N.B., 1863 *5704.8 p155*
Verner, Frederick; Pennsylvania, 1753 *2444 p233*
Verner, Moore; Philadelphia, 1847 *5704.8 p1*
Verner, Rebecca; Philadelphia, 1847 *5704.8 p1*
Verner, Spjut Ander; Iowa, 1866-1943 *123.54 p50*
Verneri, Paolo; Arkansas, 1918 *95.2 p126*
Vernet, Jeanne 30; Port uncertain, 1836 *778.5 p532*
Verneuil, P. 15; America, 1835 *778.5 p532*
Verneuil, Pierre 21; America, 1823 *778.5 p532*
Vernier, Francois 38; Port uncertain, 1836 *778.5 p532*
Verniere, J. F.; New Orleans, 1839 *778.5 p532*
Verrier, F. 40; Louisiana, 1823 *778.5 p532*
Verrier, F. 45; New Orleans, 1826 *778.5 p532*
Verrier, Francois 13; America, 1838 *778.5 p533*
Verrier, T.; America, 1827 *778.5 p533*
Verrier, V. 18; New Orleans, 1826 *778.5 p533*
Vers, Christoph; Pennsylvania, 1785 *4525 p253*
   With wife
   With 2 children

Verschueren, Paul Mechel; Arkansas, 1918 *95.2 p126*
Verse, Johann; Wisconsin, n.d. *9675.8 p123*
Vertefeuille, Jean-Francois; Quebec, 1722 *7603 p22*
Vertu, Catherine; St. John, N.B., 1849 *5704.8 p55*
Vertu, Elizabeth; St. John, N.B., 1849 *5704.8 p55*
Vertu, John; St. John, N.B., 1849 *5704.8 p55*
Vertu, William; St. John, N.B., 1849 *5704.8 p55*
Verza, Luigi; Arkansas, 1918 *95.2 p126*
Verzier, Francois 50; Port uncertain, 1836 *778.5 p533*
Vesal, Catherine 19; Philadelphia, 1774 *1219.7 p183*
Vesar, Lewis 23; Port uncertain, 1774 *1219.7 p176*
Vesdie, Emma 46; Arizona, 1908 *9228.40 p14*
Vesee, Robert 55; Charleston, SC, 1850 *1639.20 p310*
Vesper, John L.; America, 1891 *1450.2 p40B*
Vessell, Joyce; Virginia, 1645 *6219 p233*
Vessing, Enoch; New York, NY, 1838 *8208.4 p73*
Vester, Andrew Jensen; Arkansas, 1918 *95.2 p126*
Vette, Anne Marie L. W. C. SEE Vette, Johann Friedrich
  Wilhelm
Vette, Carl Friedrich Wilhelm SEE Vette, Johann
  Friedrich Wilhelm
Vette, Friedrich W. Gottlieb SEE Vette, Johann Friedrich
  Wilhelm
Vette, Heinrich E. Wilhelm SEE Vette, Johann Friedrich
  Wilhelm
Vette, Johann Friedrich Wilhelm; America, 1844 *4610.10*
p150
  With father-in-law
  *Wife:*Marie C. F. C. Gerke
  *Child:*Anne Marie L. W. C.
  *Child:*Friedrich W. Gottlieb
  *Child:*Carl Friedrich Wilhelm
  *Child:*Heinrich E. Wilhelm
Vette, Louise Charlotte; America, 1844 *4610.10 p154*
Vette, Marie C. F. C. Gerke SEE Vette, Johann Friedrich
  Wilhelm
Vettenheimer, Louise; Milwaukee, 1875 *4719.30 p257*
Vetter, Albert; Illinois, 1881 *2896.5 p41*
Vetter, William; Wisconsin, n.d. *9675.8 p123*
Vettore, Crestani; Iowa, 1866-1943 *123.54 p81*
Veuilamet, Catherine SEE Veuilamet, Isaac
Veuilamet, Catherine SEE Veuilamet, Isaac
Veuilamet, Isaac 36; Halifax, N.S., 1752 *7074.6 p212*
  *Wife:*Catherine
  *Daughter:*Marguerite
  *Sister:*Catherine
Veuilamet, Leonard 17; Halifax, N.S., 1752 *7074.6 p213*
Veuilamet, Marguerite SEE Veuilamet, Isaac
Veuth, . . .; Canada, 1776-1783 *9786 p36*
Veutilot, Catherine SEE Veutilot, Jean-George
Veutilot, Eleonore SEE Veutilot, Jean-George
Veutilot, Jean-George 36; Halifax, N.S., 1752 *7074.6*
p213
  *Daughter:*Catherine
  *Daughter:*Eleonore
  With wife
  With child
Veuvellier, Junian; Port uncertain, 1839 *778.5 p533*
Vexon, Jane 16; America, 1705 *2212 p44*
Vey, Anna; Wisconsin, n.d. *9675.8 p123*
Vey, Johann Georg; Connecticut, 1858 *3702.7 p362*
Vey, John P.; Wisconsin, n.d. *9675.8 p123*
Vey, Peter; Wisconsin, n.d. *9675.8 p123*
Veyris, P. P. 25; Port uncertain, 1838 *778.5 p533*
Vezin, Nicolas 19; Louisiana, 1820 *778.5 p533*
Vezos, Gainoula P. SEE Vezos, Peter
Vezos, Peter; New York, NY, 1910 *3455.2 p75*
  *Wife:*Gainoula P.
Vezzani, Giovanni 17; New York, NY, 1893 *9026.4 p42*
Viad, Juan 35; America, 1827 *778.5 p533*
Viaene, Emeri Leon; Arkansas, 1918 *95.2 p126*
Vial, . . .; America, 1839 *778.5 p533*
Vial, Mme.; Port uncertain, 1839 *778.5 p533*
Vial, Mr.; Port uncertain, 1839 *778.5 p533*
Vial, Mr. 30; New Orleans, 1821 *778.5 p533*
Viala, Emile 26; Kansas, 1878 *5240.1 p59*
Viala, Pierre 18; New Orleans, 1839 *778.5 p534*
Viall, Charles 19; Grenada, 1774 *1219.7 p206*
Viane, . . .; Canada, 1776-1783 *9786 p44*
Vianne, . . .; Canada, 1776-1783 *9786 p44*
Viano, . . .; Canada, 1776-1783 *9786 p36*
Viaovich, Gasparo 28; New York, NY, 1893 *9026.4 p42*
Vicaire, Victor 40; Port uncertain, 1821 *778.5 p534*
Vicant, Thomas 30; New Orleans, 1820 *778.5 p534*
Vicar, F. Me. 30; America, 1835 *778.5 p534*
Vicard, Wm.; Virginia, 1648 *6219 p252*
Vicario, . . .; Canada, 1776-1783 *9786 p36*
Vicars, John 19; Windward Islands, 1722 *3690.1 p232*
Viccars, Bryan; Virginia, 1639 *6219 p151*
Viccars, Francis; Virginia, 1639 *6219 p155*
Viccars, Mary; Virginia, 1639 *6219 p23*
Vicevic, Fran; Iowa, 1866-1943 *123.54 p50*
Vicevich, Wilma Sylvia; Iowa, 1866-1943 *123.54 p81*

Vichili, Bernard; Wisconsin, n.d. *9675.8 p123*
Vickers, Archibald; America, 1737 *4971 p12*
Vickers, James 30; Massachusetts, 1848 *5881.1 p95*
Vickers, John 19; Windward Islands, 1722 *3690.1 p232*
Vickers, William 20; Jamaica, 1725 *3690.1 p232*
Vickonic, Philip; Iowa, 1866-1943 *123.54 p50*
Victor, Mrs. 36; Georgia, 1738 *9332 p331*
  *Daughter:*Anna 20
  *Daughter:*Annalis 16
  *Son:*Peter 17
  *Son:*Jacob 10
  *Son:*Sule 7
Victor, Amelie 28; America, 1837 *778.5 p534*
Victor, Anna 20 SEE Victor, Mrs.
Victor, Annalis 16 SEE Victor, Mrs.
Victor, Celeste 5; America, 1837 *778.5 p534*
Victor, Eugene 3; America, 1837 *778.5 p534*
Victor, Gioia; Arkansas, 1918 *95.2 p126*
Victor, Henry E.; America, 1884 *1450.2 p41B*
Victor, J. 20; New Orleans, 1830 *778.5 p534*
Victor, Jacob 10 SEE Victor, Mrs.
Victor, Lettelle 53; America, 1837 *778.5 p534*
Victor, Pedro 50; Mexico, 1829 *778.5 p534*
Victor, Peter 17 SEE Victor, Mrs.
Victor, Seline 4 mos; America, 1837 *778.5 p534*
Victor, Sule 7 SEE Victor, Mrs.
Victorine, Ms. 20; New Orleans, 1827 *778.5 p534*
Vidal, Mr. 30; America, 1829 *778.5 p534*
Vidal, Frederick Emeric; Wisconsin, n.d. *9675.8 p123*
Vidal, Gregorio 18; Port uncertain, 1836 *778.5 p534*
Vidal, J. B. 17; America, 1837 *778.5 p534*
Vidal, L. 36; New Orleans, 1830 *778.5 p535*
Vidal, Lewis; Arizona, 1882 *2764.35 p70*
Vidal, Louis 30; Mexico, 1827 *778.5 p534*
Vidal, M. 32; Port uncertain, 1839 *778.5 p535*
Vidal, Maud Ethel; Wisconsin, n.d. *9675.8 p123*
Vidas, Jack; Iowa, 1866-1943 *123.54 p51*
Vidas, Lewis; Iowa, 1866-1943 *123.54 p50*
Videau, . . .; America, 1837 *778.5 p535*
Videau, Mme.; America, 1837 *778.5 p535*
Videau, Mr. 38; America, 1837 *778.5 p535*
Vidian, Louis 36; New Orleans, 1836 *778.5 p535*
Vidler, George James 39; Kansas, 1888 *5240.1 p72*
Vidler, Mary 23; Port uncertain, 1774 *1219.7 p176*
Vidler, Rees Chappel 36; Kansas, 1888 *5240.1 p71*
Vidler, Samuel Walter 28; Kansas, 1888 *5240.1 p72*
Vidmar, George 30; America, 1831 *778.5 p535*
Vidore, Martini; Iowa, 1866-1943 *123.54 p50*
Vidorsky, Stanislaus; Wisconsin, n.d. *9675.8 p123*
Vidrien, Mr. 24; Port uncertain, 1825 *778.5 p535*
Viebrock, Angelus; Illinois, 1873 *3702.7 p261*
Viebrock, Catharina SEE Viebrock, Jakob
Viebrock, Diederich; New York, NY, 1923 *3455.3 p84*
Viebrock, Jakob; New York, NY, 1924 *3455.4 p82*
  *Wife:*Catharina
Viebrock, Klaus; Washington, 1884-1900 *3702.7 p262*
Vieceli, Joseph; Iowa, 1866-1943 *123.54 p50*
Viecelk, Louis; Iowa, 1866-1943 *123.54 p50*
Viecile, Slastelle; Iowa, 1866-1943 *123.54 p50*
Viecill, Bortolo; Iowa, 1866-1943 *123.54 p51*
Viecilli, Louis; Iowa, 1866-1943 *123.54 p51*
Viehe, Anne C. Marie E. Viehe SEE Viehe, Johann
  Hermann Heinrich
Viehe, Anne Catharine Marie Elisabeth; America, 1844
  4610.10 p155
Viehe, Anne Marie W. Justine SEE Viehe, Johann
  Hermann Heinrich
Viehe, Carl F. W. Gottlieb SEE Viehe, Johann Hermann
  Heinrich
Viehe, Caspar Heinrich SEE Viehe, Johann Hermann
  Heinrich
Viehe, Cord Heinrich SEE Viehe, Johann Hermann
  Heinrich
Viehe, Ernst August Wilhelm SEE Viehe, Johann
  Hermann Heinrich
Viehe, Friedrich Wilhelm SEE Viehe, Johann Hermann
  Heinrich
Viehe, Johann Hermann Heinrich; America, 1844
  4610.10 p155
  *Wife:*Anne C. Marie E. Viehe
  *Child:*Cord Heinrich
  *Child:*Friedrich Wilhelm
  *Child:*Anne Marie W. Justine
  *Child:*Caspar Heinrich
  *Child:*Carl F. W. Gottlieb
  *Child:*Marie W. Caroline
  *Child:*Ernst August Wilhelm
  *Child:*Johanne W. Caroline
Viehe, Johanne W. Caroline SEE Viehe, Johann Hermann
  Heinrich
Viehe, Marie 50; America, 1853 *4610.10 p156*
Viehe, Marie W. Caroline SEE Viehe, Johann Hermann
  Heinrich

Vieine, Andrew; Canada, 1783 ***9786*** *p38A*
Viel, Eselaice 25; Port uncertain, 1839 ***778.5*** *p535*
Viel, Jacob 3 mos; Port uncertain, 1839 ***778.5*** *p535*
Viel, M. 30; Port uncertain, 1839 ***778.5*** *p535*
Vieland, Martin; Virginia, 1775 ***1219.7*** *p275*
Vielinillo, Lingio 28; Arkansas, 1918 ***95.2*** *p126*
Vielizevski, Andrzej; Arkansas, 1918 ***95.2*** *p127*
Vienno, Jeanne; Halifax, N.S., 1752 ***7074.6*** *p216*
Vienot, George; Halifax, N.S., 1752 ***7074.6*** *p216*
Vienot, Jeanne; Halifax, N.S., 1752 ***7074.6*** *p216*
Vierermal, Lt.; Quebec, 1778 ***9786*** *p267*
Viering, Anna Marie Ilsabein; America, 1843 ***4610.10*** *p146*
Viering, Friedrich Wilhelm; America, 1850 ***4610.10*** *p143*
Vieschaar, August; California, 1867 ***2769.9*** *p4*
Viesselmann, Henry; Wisconsin, n.d. ***9675.8*** *p123*
Viest, Jacob; Philadelphia, 1761 ***9973.7*** *p36*
Vieth, . . .; Canada, 1776-1783 ***9786*** *p36*
Vieth, Adolph Christoph; Halifax, N.S., 1778 ***9786*** *p270*
Vieth, Adolph Christoph; New York, 1776 ***9786*** *p270*
Vietner, Daniel; Ohio, 1800 ***8582.2*** *p55*
Vieton de Lalanne, Luis; Port uncertain, 1834 ***778.5*** *p535*
Vieux, Mrs. 26; America, 1835 ***778.5*** *p535*
Vieweg, John; Colorado, 1904 ***9678.3*** *p16*
Vigaula, J. B. 33; Louisiana, 1820 ***778.5*** *p535*
Vige, Mme. 40; Port uncertain, 1837 ***778.5*** *p536*
Vige, Mr. 12; Port uncertain, 1837 ***778.5*** *p536*
Vige, Mr. 21; Port uncertain, 1837 ***778.5*** *p536*
Vige, Charles 50; Port uncertain, 1837 ***778.5*** *p536*
Vigens, Frederick; New York, 1881 ***1450.2*** *p149A*
Viger, . . .; Canada, 1776-1783 ***9786*** *p36*
Viger, E.; New Orleans, 1839 ***778.5*** *p536*
Vigetti, Giuseppina; Iowa, 1866-1943 ***123.54*** *p81*
Vigetti, Louis; Iowa, 1866-1943 ***123.54*** *p81*
Vigfusson, Jon 31; Quebec, 1879 ***2557.2*** *p37*
Vigi, Mme. 40; Port uncertain, 1837 ***778.5*** *p536*
Vigi, Mr. 12; Port uncertain, 1837 ***778.5*** *p536*
Vigi, Mr. 21; Port uncertain, 1837 ***778.5*** *p536*
Vigi, Charles 50; Port uncertain, 1837 ***778.5*** *p536*
Vigliano, Caterina 21; New York, NY, 1893 ***9026.4*** *p42*
Vignard, Isaac 36; Port uncertain, 1839 ***778.5*** *p536*
Vignaud, Hippolyte 25; New Orleans, 1826 ***778.5*** *p536*
Vigne, Mrs. 40; New Orleans, 1827 ***778.5*** *p536*
Vigne, Charles 12; New Orleans, 1827 ***778.5*** *p536*
Vigne, Edward 10; New Orleans, 1827 ***778.5*** *p536*
Vigne, Jules 16; New Orleans, 1827 ***778.5*** *p536*
Vigneau, Mr.; Port uncertain, 1839 ***778.5*** *p536*
Vigoroso, P. 41; New Orleans, 1829 ***778.5*** *p536*
Vila, James 30; Massachusetts, 1847 ***5881.1*** *p95*
Vilaine, Maria 24; St. Louis, 1836 ***778.5*** *p536*
Vileer, Jacob 43; America, 1838 ***778.5*** *p537*
Vilk, Ferdinand; Wisconsin, n.d. ***9675.8*** *p123*
Villafranca, Vincent; Arkansas, 1918 ***95.2*** *p127*
Villahe, Jean 64; New Orleans, 1822 ***778.5*** *p537*
Villain, Hubert; New York, 1843 ***1450.2*** *p150A*
Villair, Louis John 24; America, 1831 ***778.5*** *p537*
Villar, Mme. 18; America, 1839 ***778.5*** *p537*
Villar, P. 27; America, 1839 ***778.5*** *p537*
Villard, Henry; New York, 1900 ***2691.4*** *p167*
Villardin, Marguerite; Louisiana, 1789-1819 ***778.5*** *p556*
Ville, Joseph A. B. 39; Louisiana, 1820 ***778.5*** *p537*
Villear, Paul 30; New Orleans, 1838 ***778.5*** *p537*
Villedy, Mr. 22; New Orleans, 1837 ***778.5*** *p404*
Villefranche, Lucien 22; Mexico, 1838 ***778.5*** *p537*
Villemud, Dominique 18; New Orleans, 1839 ***778.5*** *p537*
Villeneuve, C. 20; New Orleans, 1838 ***778.5*** *p537*
Villere, Jean 64; New Orleans, 1822 ***778.5*** *p537*
Villermain, Emile August; New York, NY, 1911 ***3455.3*** *p20*
*Wife:*Madeline
Villermain, Madeline *SEE* Villermain, Emile August
Villion, Eloi Marc 43; Port uncertain, 1839 ***778.5*** *p537*
Villouet, Jean Joseph 35; Louisiana, 1820 ***778.5*** *p537*
Vills, Manuel 45; Arizona, 1912 ***9228.40*** *p17*
Vilmar, Johann Erich; Halifax, N.S., 1778 ***9786*** *p270*
Vilmar, Johann Erich; New York, 1776 ***9786*** *p270*
Viloti, Andrew 27; America, 1825 ***778.5*** *p537*
Vimmo, Charles; New York, NY, 1811 ***2859.11*** *p20*
Vimmo, Eliza; New York, NY, 1811 ***2859.11*** *p20*
Vincelli, Nicola; Arkansas, 1918 ***95.2*** *p127*
Vincent, Mr. 29; New Orleans, 1839 ***778.5*** *p537*
Vincent, Agatha 2; Port uncertain, 1835 ***778.5*** *p537*
Vincent, Charles 54; America, 1838 ***778.5*** *p538*
Vincent, Fedr. 24; America, 1839 ***778.5*** *p538*
Vincent, Henry; Virginia, 1635 ***6219*** *p70*
Vincent, Hugh 12; Quebec, 1847 ***5704.8*** *p27*
Vincent, J. 25; Port uncertain, 1838 ***778.5*** *p538*
Vincent, James; Quebec, 1847 ***5704.8*** *p27*
Vincent, John; Nevada, 1886 ***2764.35*** *p70*
Vincent, John; New York, NY, 1836 ***8208.4*** *p18*
Vincent, John; Quebec, 1847 ***5704.8*** *p27*
Vincent, Joseph; San Francisco, 1854 ***3840.3*** *p10*
Vincent, Joseph 24; America, 1838 ***778.5*** *p538*
Vincent, Joseph 25; New Orleans, 1829 ***778.5*** *p538*
Vincent, Joseph I.; Arizona, 1890 ***2764.35*** *p70*
Vincent, Madeleine; New England, 1753 ***2444*** *p133*
Vincent, Maria Laurisa 22; Port uncertain, 1835 ***778.5*** *p538*
Vincent, Mary; Quebec, 1847 ***5704.8*** *p27*
Vincent, Napoleon 29; Port uncertain, 1835 ***778.5*** *p538*
Vincent, Peggy Ann 10; Quebec, 1847 ***5704.8*** *p27*
Vincent, Richard; Arizona, 1890 ***2764.35*** *p70*
Vincent, Samuel 23; Maryland, 1774 ***1219.7*** *p236*
Vincent, Tho.; Virginia, 1636 ***6219*** *p77*
Vincent, Thomas; Pennsylvania, 1876 ***2764.35*** *p70*
Vincent, William; Virginia, 1652 ***6251*** *p19*
Vincent, William 25; Maryland, 1775 ***1219.7*** *p259*
Vincenti, Hass; Arkansas, 1918 ***95.2*** *p127*
Vincenzo, Leo 22; Arkansas, 1918 ***95.2*** *p127*
Vinceri, Gaetano; Iowa, 1866-1943 ***123.54*** *p51*
Vincint, James; Illinois, 1875 ***7857*** *p8*
Vinconneau, Jean.. 22; New Orleans, 1839 ***778.5*** *p538*
Vinet, Mlle. 17; Port uncertain, 1825 ***778.5*** *p538*
Vinet, Mme. 50; Port uncertain, 1825 ***778.5*** *p538*
Vinet, J. B.; New Orleans, 1839 ***778.5*** *p538*
Viney, C. R.; Kansas, 1900 ***5240.1*** *p46*
Viney, George A. 30; Kansas, 1878 ***5240.1*** *p59*
Viney, W. A. 34; Kansas, 1883 ***5240.1*** *p46*
Viney, William A. 34; Kansas, 1883 ***5240.1*** *p64*
Vinge, John 20; New Orleans, 1835 ***778.5*** *p538*
Vinget, Maria Catharine 32; America, 1831 ***778.5*** *p538*
Vinicombe, John; Antigua (Antego), 1754 ***1219.7*** *p27*
Vining, Jon.; Virginia, 1635 ***6219*** *p70*
Vink, Cornelia G.; Wisconsin, n.d. ***9675.8*** *p123*
Vink, Marinus; Wisconsin, n.d. ***9675.8*** *p123*
Vink, Michael Lambertus; Wisconsin, n.d. ***9675.8*** *p123*
Vinkles, Michael; Virginia, 1637 ***6219*** *p111*
Vinnell, Andrew; Iowa, 1866-1943 ***123.54*** *p51*
Vinnell, George 29; Maryland, 1730 ***3690.1*** *p292*
Vinot, M. 45; America, 1826 ***778.5*** *p538*
Vinot, Philip 39; New Orleans, 1823 ***778.5*** *p538*
Vinsett, Lewis; Wisconsin, n.d. ***9675.8*** *p123*
Vinson, Wm.; Virginia, 1637 ***6219*** *p112*
Vint, John; Antigua (Antego), 1776 ***1219.7*** *p283*
Viol, Andre 27; New Orleans, 1822 ***778.5*** *p539*
Violet, . . . 30; Dominica, 1774 ***1219.7*** *p223*
Vion, L. 18; Port uncertain, 1832 ***778.5*** *p539*
Vionnet, Joseph A. 27; New Orleans, 1829 ***778.5*** *p539*
Vipon, Tho; Virginia, 1639 ***6219*** *p154*
Virga, Guiseppe; Arkansas, 1918 ***95.2*** *p127*
Virgile, Jacques 28; New Orleans, 1826 ***778.5*** *p539*
Virgile, Jacques 35; New Orleans, 1823 ***778.5*** *p539*
Virgin, John 21; Maryland, 1774 ***1219.7*** *p214*
Virgin, Robert; Virginia, 1637 ***6219*** *p112*
Virginie, Miss 6; New Orleans, 1822 ***778.5*** *p539*
Virginie, Charlotte 5; New Orleans, 1822 ***778.5*** *p539*
Virpillot, George *SEE* Virpillot, Pierre
Virpillot, Marguerite *SEE* Virpillot, Pierre
Virpillot, Pierre 40; Halifax, N.S., 1752 ***7074.6*** *p213*
*Wife:*Marguerite
*Son:*George
With child
Virtue, David; New York, NY, 1811 ***2859.11*** *p20*
With family
Virtue, James 20; Quebec, 1854 ***5704.8*** *p119*
Virtue, John J.; St. John, N.B., 1847 ***5704.8*** *p8*
Virtue, Margaret; St. John, N.B., 1847 ***5704.8*** *p9*
Virtue, Mary; St. John, N.B., 1853 ***5704.8*** *p106*
Virtue, Mary; St. John, N.B., 1853 ***5704.8*** *p107*
Virtue, William; Quebec, 1851 ***5704.8*** *p82*
Vischa, Angelo 78; Arizona, 1910 ***9228.40*** *p15*
Visinier, Mr. 18; America, 1829 ***778.5*** *p539*
Visinier, M. 50; America, 1829 ***778.5*** *p539*
Visnier, Ann 45; Port uncertain, 1838 ***778.5*** *p539*
Visnier, Francis 14; Port uncertain, 1838 ***778.5*** *p539*
Vissage, Thomas 20; St. Christopher, 1722 ***3690.1*** *p232*
Visser, Peter; Arkansas, 1918 ***95.2*** *p127*
Vissett, Francis; Virginia, 1636 ***6219*** *p75*
Vitale, Grace Smith; Iowa, 1866-1943 ***123.54*** *p83*
Vitalis, Caroline 3; Port uncertain, 1838 ***778.5*** *p539*
Vitalis, Josephine 28; Port uncertain, 1838 ***778.5*** *p539*
Vitalis, Louis 51; Port uncertain, 1838 ***778.5*** *p539*
Vitalis, Tristen 2 days; New Orleans, 1838 ***778.5*** *p540*
Vitalis, Victorine 21; Port uncertain, 1838 ***778.5*** *p540*
Vito, Gilli; Iowa, 1866-1943 ***123.54*** *p51*
Vitree, Alphonse 18; America, 1837 ***778.5*** *p540*
Vitree, Augustus 18; America, 1837 ***778.5*** *p540*
Vitree, Charles 12; America, 1837 ***778.5*** *p540*
Vitree, Fenique 49; America, 1837 ***778.5*** *p540*
Vitree, Pauline 22; America, 1837 ***778.5*** *p540*
Vittinger, Anna Maria 10 *SEE* Vittinger, George Frederick
Vittinger, Eva Maria 15 *SEE* Vittinger, George Frederick
Vittinger, George Frederick; South Carolina, 1752-1753 ***3689.17*** *p23*
With wife
*Relative:*Eva Maria 15
*Relative:*Sophia Barbara 14
*Relative:*Anna Maria 10
Vittinger, Sophia Barbara 14 *SEE* Vittinger, George Frederick
Vittori, Camillo; Arkansas, 1918 ***95.2*** *p127*
Viviani, Eugeni; America, 1892 ***1450.2*** *p150A*
Vivieu, Mr. 17; Louisiana, 1820 ***778.5*** *p540*
Vizola, John; Arkansas, 1918 ***95.2*** *p127*
Vlahovic, John; Iowa, 1866-1943 ***123.54*** *p51*
Vlassis, George Constantine; Arkansas, 1918 ***95.2*** *p127*
Vlolvic, Tom; Iowa, 1866-1943 ***123.54*** *p51*
Vlsek, Joseph; Arkansas, 1918 ***95.2*** *p127*
Voaux, Campell 30; Dominica, 1774 ***1219.7*** *p207*
Vocasek, Frank 29; Kansas, 1880 ***5240.1*** *p62*
Vochek, John; America, 1890 ***7137*** *p171*
Vochek, Ladislaus; America, 1897 ***7137*** *p171*
Vochek, Mary; America, 1891 ***7137*** *p171*
Vock, Georg 22; America, 1853 ***9162.8*** *p38*
Vocks, Frederick; Wisconsin, n.d. ***9675.8*** *p123*
Voclckers, Christian William; Arkansas, 1918 ***95.2*** *p127*
Vocseen, James; Virginia, 1637 ***6219*** *p110*
Voden, Heinrich; Kentucky, 1798 ***8582.3*** *p94*
Vodine, . . .; Canada, 1776-1783 ***9786*** *p36*
Vodoski, Alex; Arkansas, 1918 ***95.2*** *p127*
Vodoski, Alex; Arkansas, 1918 ***95.2*** *p131*
Voegele, Anna Maria; Philadelphia, 1755-1757 ***2444*** *p227*
Voegele, Jakob; Cincinnati, 1788-1876 ***8582.3*** *p81*
Voegely, Joseph; Minnesota, 1871 ***5240.1*** *p46*
Voeglin, Anna Maria; Port uncertain, 1749-1800 ***2444*** *p133*
Voehr, Carl *SEE* Voehr, Simon
Voehr, Johann Michael *SEE* Voehr, Simon
Voehr, Margaretha *SEE* Voehr, Simon
Voehr, Simon; Port uncertain, 1750-1800 ***2444*** *p227*
*Wife:*Margaretha
*Child:*Carl
*Child:*Johann Michael
Voelcker, Johannes; Philadelphia, 1779 ***8137*** *p15*
Voelckers, Christian William; Arkansas, 1918 ***95.2*** *p127*
Voelger, . . .; Canada, 1776-1783 ***9786*** *p36*
Voelker, August; Wisconsin, n.d. ***9675.8*** *p123*
Voelker, Herman; Wisconsin, n.d. ***9675.8*** *p123*
Voelker, William; Illinois, 1867 ***2896.5*** *p41*
Voelkle, Christian; America, 1871 ***1450.2*** *p150A*
Voeth, Anna Maria *SEE* Voeth, Hans Jerg
Voeth, Anna Maria Zeeb *SEE* Voeth, Hans Jerg
Voeth, Hans Jerg; Philadelphia, 1762-1776 ***2444*** *p227*
*Wife:*Anna Maria Zeeb
*Child:*Hans Stephan
*Child:*Anna Maria
Voeth, Hans Stephan *SEE* Voeth, Hans Jerg
Voeth, Robert; Illinois, 1867 ***8582.2*** *p50*
Vogdt, Catharina C. Winner *SEE* Vogdt, Simon
Vogdt, Simon; New York, 1709 ***3627*** *p6*
*Wife:*Catharina C. Winner
Voge, E.; Washington, 1859-1920 ***2872.1*** *p42*
Voge, Theodore; Washington, 1859-1920 ***2872.1*** *p42*
Voge, William; Wisconsin, n.d. ***9675.8*** *p123*
Vogel, . . .; Canada, 1776-1783 ***9786*** *p36*
Vogel, Carl; America, 1850 ***8582.3*** *p66*
Vogel, Carl Fr.; America, 1883 ***4610.10*** *p160*
Vogel, Caroline Kreutzmuller *SEE* Vogel, Franz Xaver
Vogel, Edwin *SEE* Vogel, Henry
Vogel, Emma *SEE* Vogel, Henry
Vogel, Franz Xaver; America, 1884 ***4610.10*** *p106*
*Wife:*Caroline Kreutzmuller
*Child:*Marie C. Charlotte
*Child:*Franziska Auguste
Vogel, Franziska Auguste *SEE* Vogel, Franz Xaver
Vogel, Friedrich; America, 1890 ***4610.10*** *p14*
*Brother:*Wilhelm
Vogel, Fritz; America, 1883 ***4610.10*** *p55*
Vogel, Hans Henrich; Philadelphia, 1779 ***8137*** *p15*
Vogel, Heinrich 17; America, 1878-1967 ***4610.10*** *p73*
Vogel, Heinrich 17; Illinois, 1895 ***4610.10*** *p58*
Vogel, Heinrich Wilhelm; America, 1891 ***4610.10*** *p161*
Vogel, Henry; America, 1909 ***4610.10*** *p55*
*Son:*Edwin
*Daughter:*Minnie
*Daughter:*Emma
*Son:*Theodore
*Son:*Louis
*Wife:*Marie Gossling
Vogel, Henry William; North America, 1890 ***4610.10*** *p15*
Vogel, Johann Conrad; Illinois, 1874 ***5012.39*** *p26*
Vogel, Johann Michel; Pennsylvania, 1744 ***2444*** *p228*
*Wife:*Maria Margaretha
*Child:*Johann Peter

Vogel, Johann Peter *SEE* Vogel, Johann Michel
Vogel, Joseph; New York, NY, 1838 *8208.4 p63*
Vogel, Karl Heinrich; America, 1895 *4610.10 p161*
Vogel, Louis *SEE* Vogel, Henry
Vogel, Maria Margaretha *SEE* Vogel, Johann Michel
Vogel, Marie C. Charlotte *SEE* Vogel, Franz Xaver
Vogel, Marie Gossling *SEE* Vogel, Henry
Vogel, Michal; Pennsylvania, 1753 *2444 p228*
Vogel, Minnie *SEE* Vogel, Henry
Vogel, Simon; Wisconsin, n.d. *9675.8 p123*
Vogel, Theodore *SEE* Vogel, Henry
Vogel, Wilhelm *SEE* Vogel, Friedrich
Vogel, Wilhelm; America, 1873 *4610.10 p56*
Vogele, Johan 25; Kansas, 1883 *5240.1 p64*
Vogeler, . . .; Canada, 1776-1783 *9786 p36*
Vogeler, Francis; Canada, 1776-1783 *9786 p238*
Vogeler, Johann August Wilhelm; America, 1853 *4610.10 p144*
Vogelgesang, Elisabetha; North America, 1792-1922 *2691.4 p170*
Vogelgesang, Heinrich 88; California, 1910 *2691.4 p170*
Vogelgesang, Jacob; Baltimore, 1814-1922 *2691.4 p170*
With family
Vogeli, Gervais; America, 1882 *1450.2 p150A*
Vogelmann, Georg Friedrich *SEE* Vogelmann, Melchior
Vogelmann, Johann Melchior *SEE* Vogelmann, Melchior
Vogelmann, Johann Philipp *SEE* Vogelmann, Melchior
Vogelmann, Maria Barbara Gramlich *SEE* Vogelmann, Melchior
Vogelmann, Melchior; Pennsylvania, 1749 *2444 p228*
*Wife:*Maria Barbara Gramlich
*Child:*Johann Melchior
*Child:*Johann Philipp
*Child:*Georg Friedrich
Vogelsang, Anne Marie Engel; America, 1847 *4610.10 p134*
Vogelsang, Chatarina; America, n.d. *8125.8 p435*
Vogelsberg, . . .; Canada, 1776-1783 *9786 p36*
Vogelzang, Chatarina; America, n.d. *8125.8 p435*
Voges, . . .; Canada, 1776-1783 *9786 p36*
Vogffft, Catharina C. Winner *SEE* Vogffft, Symeon
Vogffft, Symeon; New York, 1709 *3627 p6*
*Wife:*Catharina C. Winner
Vogler, . . .; Canada, 1776-1783 *9786 p36*
Vogli, Maria; Pennsylvania, 1709-1710 *4480 p311*
Vogt, A.M. Elisabeth; America, 1881 *4610.10 p152*
Vogt, Andreas; Saratoga, NY, 1777 *8137 p15*
Vogt, Anne Marie C. Abke *SEE* Vogt, Caspar Heinrich
Vogt, Anthony Frederick Christian; America, 1838 *1450.2 p150A*
Vogt, Carl Heinrich Wilhelm *SEE* Vogt, Caspar Heinrich
Vogt, Caspar Heinrich *SEE* Vogt, Caspar Heinrich
Vogt, Caspar Heinrich; America, 1844 *4610.10 p138*
*Wife:*Anne Marie C. Abke
*Child:*Caspar Heinrich
*Child:*Hermann H. Wilhelm
*Child:*Carl Heinrich Wilhelm
*Child:*Christiane L. Engel
Vogt, Catharina C. Winner *SEE* Vogt, Simon
Vogt, Charles; New York, 1850 *1450.2 p150A*
Vogt, Christiane L. Engel *SEE* Vogt, Caspar Heinrich
Vogt, Daniel Heinrich; America, 1851 *4610.10 p147*
Vogt, Divert; New York, 1749 *3652 p73*
Vogt, Ernst Christian Heinrich; America, 1848 *4610.10 p97*
Vogt, Ernst Friedrich Wilhelm; America, 1845 *4610.10 p97*
Vogt, Heinrich August; America, 1857 *4610.10 p109*
Vogt, Henry; Lancaster, PA, 1780 *8137 p15*
Vogt, Hermann H. Wilhelm *SEE* Vogt, Caspar Heinrich
Vogt, Jacob B.; Cincinnati, 1869-1887 *8582 p33*
Vogt, John Jacob; Philadelphia, 1764 *9973.7 p39*
Vogt, Karl Diedrich; America, 1848 *4610.10 p97*
Vogt, Peter; Philadelphia, 1777-1779 *8137 p15*
Vogt, Simon; New York, 1709 *3627 p6*
*Wife:*Catharina C. Winner
Vogt, Simon; New York, 1710 *3627 p6*
With children
Vogt, Wilhelm; Iowa, 1816-1873 *8125.8 p438*
Vohlleben, Philippe 30; America, 1838 *778.5 p540*
Vohoric, Anton T.; Iowa, 1866-1943 *123.54 p51*
Vohs, Joseph 37; Kansas, 1884 *5240.1 p66*
Vohsmeier, Caroline Justine Charlotte; America, 1890 *4610.10 p103*
Vohsmeyer, Heinrich Wilhelm Gottlieb; America, 1843 *4610.10 p154*
Voice, Jane; South Carolina, 1767 *1639.20 p311*
Voight, Henry W.; America, 1849 *1450.2 p150A*
Voigt, . . .; Canada, 1776-1783 *9786 p36*
Voigt, Anthony Frederick; America, 1837 *1450.2 p150A*
Voigt, August; Wisconsin, n.d. *9675.8 p123*
Voigt, Louis 23; New York, NY, 1850 *6013.19 p89*
Voigt, Ohris H. 26; Harris Co., TX, 1898 *6254 p5*

Voigt, Richard; Wisconsin, n.d. *9675.8 p123*
Voigt, Wilhelm; Wisconsin, n.d. *9675.8 p123*
Voilein, Mr. 47; America, 1820 *778.5 p540*
Voisain, Francis 30; New Orleans, 1835 *778.5 p540*
Voisin, Josephine 25; America, 1839 *778.5 p540*
Voisin, Theodore 28; New Orleans, 1837 *778.5 p540*
Voisin, Theodore 50; Port uncertain, 1839 *778.5 p540*
Voissen, Peter J.; Wisconsin, n.d. *9675.8 p123*
Voit, Andreas; Pennsylvania, 1753 *4525 p253*
Voit, Charles 43; New Orleans, 1838 *778.5 p540*
Voith, Andreas; Pennsylvania, 1753 *4525 p253*
Voizin, Mr. 24; America, 1838 *778.5 p541*
Vojcekovsky, John; America, 1890 *7137 p171*
Vojcekovsky, Ladislaus; America, 1897 *7137 p171*
Vojcekovsky, Mary; America, 1891 *7137 p171*
Vojcok, John; Arkansas, 1918 *95.2 p127*
Vojna, Anva 27; Arkansas, 1918 *95.2 p127*
Vojno, Onve; Arkansas, 1918 *95.2 p127*
Vojten, Nolken; Pennsylvania, 1683 *2155 p1*
Vola, Bartomoleo; Iowa, 1866-1943 *123.54 p83*
Vola, Madalena; Iowa, 1866-1943 *123.54 p83*
Voland, Carl Gottlob; Wisconsin, n.d. *9675.8 p123*
Voland, Frederick; Wisconsin, n.d. *9675.8 p123*
Volchmann, . . .; Canada, 1776-1783 *9786 p36*
Volckmer, Henry; Kansas, 1916 *6013.40 p17*
Volden, T. O.; Washington, 1859-1920 *2872.1 p42*
Volentinces, Michael; Wisconsin, n.d. *9675.8 p123*
Volk, Jacob 19; America, 1854-1855 *9162.6 p104*
Volk, K. Elizab. 27; America, 1854-1855 *9162.6 p104*
Volk, Philipp 32; Kansas, 1885 *5240.1 p68*
Volker, Louise 22; New Orleans, 1839 *9420.2 p166*
Volkmar, Lieut.; Quebec, 1776 *9786 p105*
Volkmar, Friedrich Wilhelm; Quebec, 1776 *9786 p254*
Volkovich, Dosolina; Iowa, 1866-1943 *123.54 p51*
Voll, Caspar; Baltimore, 1834 *8582 p33*
Volle, Miss; America, 1854 *4610.10 p144*
Volle, Mr.; America, 1868-1887 *4610.10 p107*
Volle, August Friedrich; America, 1862 *4610.10 p110*
Volle, Carl Friedrich; America, 1847-1876 *4610.10 p101*
Volle, Friedrich Carl Wilhelm; America, 1862 *4610.10 p99*
Voller, Georg; Alberta, n.d. *5262 p58*
Vollmann, . . .; Canada, 1776-1783 *9786 p36*
Vollmann, Friedrich; Cincinnati, 1869-1887 *8582 p33*
Vollmar, Catharina *SEE* Vollmar, Johannes
Vollmar, Johann Michael *SEE* Vollmar, Johannes
Vollmar, Johannes; America, 1743-1800 *2444 p228*
*Wife:*Catharina
*Child:*Johann Michael
*Child:*Margaretha
Vollmar, John; Wisconsin, n.d. *9675.8 p123*
Vollmar, Margaretha *SEE* Vollmar, Johannes
Vollmer, Frederick 43; Kansas, 1879 *5240.1 p61*
Vollmer, H. 38; Kansas, 1890 *5240.1 p74*
Vollmer, Johannes; Pennsylvania, 1750 *2444 p228*
Vollmer, Johannes; Pennsylvania, 1770 *2444 p228*
Vollvath, Max Ludwig; Kansas, 1880 *5240.1 p46*
Vollweider, Anna Catharina Bengel *SEE* Vollweider, Heinrich
Vollweider, Heinrich; Port uncertain, 1717 *3627 p15*
*Wife:*Anna Catharina Bengel
*Child:*Maria Catharina O.
*Child:*Maria Margaretha
*Child:*Joh. Jacob
Vollweider, Jacob; Kansas, 1892 *5240.1 p47*
Vollweider, Joh. Jacob *SEE* Vollweider, Heinrich
Vollweider, Maria Catharina O. *SEE* Vollweider, Heinrich
Vollweider, Maria Margaretha *SEE* Vollweider, Heinrich
Volmar, John; Wisconsin, n.d. *9675.8 p123*
Volmer, . . .; Canada, 1776-1783 *9786 p36*
Volmer, Charles; America, 1849 *1450.2 p150A*
Volmer, Frederick; America, 1849 *1450.2 p150A*
Volodka, Scheranti 25; Arkansas, 1918 *95.2 p127*
Volodka, Sherant; Arkansas, 1918 *95.2 p127*
Volovlek, Joseph; Wisconsin, n.d. *9675.8 p123*
Volpe, Charles; Arkansas, 1918 *95.2 p127*
Volquarts, F.B.; Arizona, 1898 *9228.30 p9*
Volsing, Anna Maria 86; Illinois, 1897 *1763 p40D*
Voltan, Miler 26; Port uncertain, 1838 *778.5 p541*
Volthoward, Andrew 49; Georgia, 1738 *9332 p331*
*Wife:*Anna 41
*Son:*Tobias 12
*Son:*Hans George 9
Volthoward, Anna 41 *SEE* Volthoward, Andrew
Volthoward, Barbara 14; Georgia, 1738 *9332 p330*
Volthoward, Hans George 9 *SEE* Volthoward, Andrew
Volthoward, Margaret 19; Savannah, GA, 1738 *9332 p329*
Volthoward, Tobias 12 *SEE* Volthoward, Andrew
Voltmeier, Charles; America, 1837 *1450.2 p151A*
Volz, Jacob; America, 1837 *1450.2 p151A*
Volz, John 30; Kansas, 1884 *5240.1 p66*

Volz, Justus 74; Indiana, 1902 *1763 p40D*
Volz, Karl 14?; New Orleans, 1830 *8582.1 p40*
With mother & stepfather
Volz, Philipp; Cincinnati, 1869-1887 *8582 p33*
Von Axste, Henry; New York, NY, 1840 *8208.4 p112*
von Barner, Friedrich Albrecht; Quebec, 1776 *9786 p262*
Von Behren, Christian; Illinois, 1877 *2896.5 p41*
von Block, Lt. Col.; New York, 1776 *9786 p278*
von Borke, Col.; New York, 1776 *9786 p277*
von Bose, Col.; New York, 1776 *9786 p277*
von Bothmer, Friederich Wilhelm D.; Quebec, 1776 *9786 p253*
Von Brecht, August; America, 1842 *8582 p33*
von Breymann, Heinrich C.; Quebec, 1776 *9786 p261*
Von Buergler, Karl; America, 1846 *8582.2 p66*
With wife
von Buhl, Catharina; Virginia, 1737 *9898 p27*
von Buttlar, Capt.; Quebec, 1776 *9786 p265*
Von Chateaubriand, G. G. 41; Cincinnati, 1871 *8582 p33*
Vondenberg, Joseph; Wisconsin, n.d. *9675.8 p123*
Vondenvelden, . . .; Canada, 1776-1783 *9786 p36*
Vondenvelden, William; Canada, 1776-1783 *9786 p243*
Vonderheide, F.; Cincinnati, 1869-1887 *8582 p33*
Vonderheide, Jos B.; America, 1839 *8582.1 p35*
Vonderheide, Joseph; America, 1850 *8582.3 p66*
Von Der Lippe, Friedrich; Charleston, SC, 1816 *8582.3 p66*
von der Wall, Maria Hornsberger 60; New York, NY, 1897 *1763 p40D*
Von Der Westen, Heinrich; Cincinnati, 1869-1887 *8582 p33*
von Drach, Wilhelm; Philadelphia, 1779 *8137 p7*
von Ehrenkrook, Johann G.; Quebec, 1776 *9786 p259*
von Ehrenkrook, Karl Friedrich; Quebec, 1776 *9786 p257*
von Eiff, Franz 36; America, 1913 *1763 p40C*
Von Eye, John F.; Illinois, 1842 *7857 p8*
von Gall, Wilhelm R.; Quebec, 1776 *9786 p265*
Von Heer, Bartholomaeus; America, 1775-1781 *8582.3 p81*
Von Heer, Bartholomaeus; America, 1777-1778 *8582.2 p67*
Von Hein, Duderich 75; Arizona, 1904 *9228.40 p9*
Vonhof, Joseph; Ohio, 1836 *8582.1 p47*
Von Huben, Daniel; Ohio, 1869-1887 *8582 p33*
von Konig, Edmund Victor; Quebec, 1776 *9786 p255*
von Kreutzbourg, Carl A.; Canada, 1777 *9786 p266*
von Linsingen, Lt. Col.; New York, 1776 *9786 p278*
von Lossberg, Col.; New York, 1776 *9786 p277*
von Lossberg, Col.; New York, 1776 *9786 p278*
Von Lubeken, Ahrendt Dietrich; New York, NY, 1836 *8208.4 p13*
von Luetzow, F.A.L.A.; Philadelphia, 1779 *8137 p11*
von Maibom, Just. Christoph; Quebec, 1776 *9786 p252*
von Marschall, Frederick; New York, 1761 *3652 p87*
*Wife:*Hedwig Elizabeth
von Marschall, Hedwig Elizabeth *SEE* von Marschall, Frederick
von Martels, Charles *SEE* von Martels, Ludwig
von Martels, Gustav *SEE* von Martels, Ludwig
Von Martels, Heinrich; Cincinnati, 1869-1887 *8582 p33*
von Martels, Ludwig; Baltimore, 1832 *3702.7 p108*
*Son:*Charles
*Son:*Gustav
von Mengen, Otto C.A.; Quebec, 1776 *9786 p261*
von Minnegerode, Lt. Col.; New York, 1776 *9786 p278*
von Munchausen, Capt.; Halifax, N.S., 1781-1783 *9786 p270*
Vonnegut, Clemens; America, 1851 *1450.2 p151A*
von Rall, Col.; New York, 1776 *9786 p278*
von Rantzau, Ernst August; Quebec, 1776 *9786 p263*
Von Rene, George William; California, 1877 *2764.35 p70*
von Rhetz, August Wilhelm; Quebec, 1776 *9786 p259*
von Riedesel, Friedrich Adolphus; Quebec, 1776 *9786 p256*
von Rohr, Karl G.H.; America, 1839 *3702.7 p300*
von Schlagenteuffel, George, II; Quebec, 1776 *9786 p258*
von Schlotheim, Emma 32 *SEE* von Schlotheim, Eudard
von Schlotheim, Eudard 43; America, 1870 *4610.10 p123*
*Wife:*Emma 32
Von Schmidt-Buergeler, Karl; America, 1846 *8582.2 p66*
With wife
Von Seggern, Chris; America, 1829 *8582.2 p61*
Von Seggern, Christian; Cincinnati, 1869-1887 *8582 p33*
von Sommerlatte, Otto Arnold; Quebec, 1776 *9786 p253*
von Specht, Johann Friedrich; Quebec, 1776 *9786 p257*
Von Speth, Ernst Ludwig W.; Quebec, 1776 *9786 p256*
von Stammer, Eckhard H.; Quebec, 1776 *9786 p254*

von Watteville, Benigna *SEE* von Watteville, John
von Watteville, John; New York, 1748 *3652 p68*
*Wife:*Benigna
von Wehrt, Catharina; Virginia, 1738-1739 *9898 p39*
von Wittgenstein, Ludwig Carl; Canada, 1777 *9786 p266*
Von Wurml, Maria 8 *SEE* Von Wurml, Wm. John
Von Wurml, Sara 4 *SEE* Von Wurml, Wm. John
Von Wurml, Theobald 6 *SEE* Von Wurml, Wm. John
Von Wurml, Wm. John 35; New Orleans, 1839 *9420.2 p357*
*Daughter:*Maria 8
*Son:*Theobald 6
*Daughter:*Sara 4
Voor Horst, Cornelius 28; New York, NY, 1847 *3377.6 p15*
Voortman, August 26; Kansas, 1884 *5240.1 p66*
Vorbach, Ernest 39; West Virginia, 1897 *9788.3 p21*
Vorbach, Ernest 41; West Virginia, 1900 *9788.3 p22*
Vorbrodt, Chaplain; Quebec, 1776 *9786 p253*
Vorbrodt, Surgeon; Quebec, 1776 *9786 p104*
Vornhelder, Mr.; America, 1851-1854 *4610.10 p151*
Vornhelder, Ernst Heinrich Wilhelm *SEE* Vornhelder, Marie Louise
Vornhelder, Franz Peter H. Wilhelm *SEE* Vornhelder, Marie Louise
Vornhelder, Friedrich Wilhelm *SEE* Vornhelder, Marie Louise
Vornhelder, Heinrich Wilhelm *SEE* Vornhelder, Marie Louise
Vornhelder, Marie Louise; America, 1854 *4610.10 p151*
*Child:*Friedrich Wilhelm
*Child:*Heinrich Wilhelm
*Child:*Ernst Heinrich Wilhelm
*Child:*Franz Peter H. Wilhelm
Vornholt, John F.; Cincinnati, 1869-1887 *8582 p33*
Vornica, Joseph; Arkansas, 1918 *95.2 p127*
Vorre, Oliver; Arkansas, 1918 *95.2 p127*

Vort, Michal; South Carolina, 1788 *7119 p198*
Vortmann, William; Illinois, 1885 *2896.5 p41*
Vos, . . .; Ohio, 1881 *3702.7 p430*
Vosberg, Meinert; Illinois, 1872 *7857 p8*
Voss, . . .; Canada, 1776-1783 *9786 p36*
Voss, August; Iroquois Co., IL, 1892 *3455.1 p14*
Voss, August 31; Kansas, 1892 *5240.1 p77*
Voss, Carl Dietrich Wilhelm; America, 1865 *4610.10 p136*
Voss, Daniel de; Ohio, 1798-1818 *8582.2 p44*
Voss, Erich; Wisconsin, n.d. *9675.8 p124*
Voss, Henry; Illinois, 1877 *2896.5 p41*
Voss, Herta; Wisconsin, n.d. *9675.8 p124*
Voss, Julius; America, 1848 *8582.3 p66*
Voss, Nicholas A.; Wisconsin, n.d. *9675.8 p124*
Voss, T. Henry; New York, NY, 1838 *8208.4 p61*
Vossen, Arnold van; Germantown, PA, 1684 *2467.7 p5*
Vosskoetter, Johann Heinrich; America, 1850 *8582.2 p44*
Votaud, Jacques 39; America, 1838 *778.5 p541*
Voth, J. H.; Kansas, 1888 *5240.1 p46*
Votier, Francois 36; America, 1836 *778.5 p541*
Votsch, Anton 16; New York, NY, 1889 *7846 p40*
Votsch, Johannes 19; New York, NY, 1889 *7846 p40*
Voughan, Eliz 20; America, 1701 *2212 p34*
Voughan, Robt; America, 1698 *2212 p10*
Voukelatos, Angel; Arkansas, 1918 *95.2 p127*
Voulin, Edward; Wisconsin, n.d. *9675.8 p124*
Vourliotis, Spiros; Arkansas, 1918 *95.2 p127*
Vowells, John 22; Maryland, 1774 *1219.7 p181*
Voyce, Elton; Iowa, 1866-1943 *123.54 p51*
Voyce, George; Iowa, 1866-1943 *123.54 p51*
Voyce, Sydney; Iowa, 1866-1943 *123.54 p51*
Vpton, Margarett 18; Virginia, 1700 *2212 p30*
Vpton, Tho; Virginia, 1698 *2212 p11*
Vranich, Martin; Wisconsin, n.d. *9675.8 p124*
Vruwink, Albert 10; New York, NY, 1847 *3377.6 p15*
Vruwink, Henrick 14; New York, NY, 1847 *3377.6 p15*

Vruwink, Jane 22; New York, NY, 1847 *3377.6 p15*
Vruwink, Jane 23; New York, NY, 1847 *3377.6 p15*
Vruwink, Johannah 16; New York, NY, 1847 *3377.6 p15*
Vruwink, John 50; New York, NY, 1847 *3377.6 p15*
Vruwink, Joseph 20; New York, NY, 1847 *3377.6 p15*
Vue, Henry Fois. Benjamin; Port uncertain, 1839 *778.5 p541*
Vuielquie, Pierre 50; Halifax, N.S., 1752 *7074.6 p207*
Vuillaquie, . . .; Halifax, N.S., 1752 *7074.6 p232*
Vuilquet, Baby; Died enroute, 1752 *7074.6 p208*
Vuilquet, Barbe *SEE* Vuilquet, Jean
Vuilquet, Catherine *SEE* Vuilquet, Jean
Vuilquet, Catherine *SEE* Vuilquet, Jean
Vuilquet, Jean 36; Halifax, N.S., 1752 *7074.6 p213*
*Wife:*Catherine
*Child:*Barbe
*Child:*Joseph
*Child:*Catherine
*Child:*Suzette
With child
Vuilquet, Joseph *SEE* Vuilquet, Jean
Vuilquet, Pierre 50; Halifax, N.S., 1752 *7074.6 p213*
Vuilquet, Suzette *SEE* Vuilquet, Jean
Vuilquie, Jean 36; Halifax, N.S., 1752 *7074.6 p207*
With family of 6
Vunier, Michel 51; America, 1831 *778.5 p541*
Vust, Dominiq.e 1; New Orleans, 1836 *778.5 p541*
Vust, Dominiq.e 29; New Orleans, 1836 *778.5 p541*
Vust, Jeannete 3; New Orleans, 1836 *778.5 p541*
Vust, Veronica 26; New Orleans, 1836 *778.5 p541*
Vutokich, Rade; Arkansas, 1918 *95.2 p128*
Vyl, Anna Maria; Pennsylvania, 1754 *2444 p228*
Vyl, Anna Maria; Port uncertain, 1746-1800 *2444 p237*
Vynall, Alice; Virginia, 1646 *6219 p236*
Vyvyan, Henry; New York, NY, 1837 *8208.4 p35*

W

Waagen, Gabriel 29; Arkansas, 1918 **95.2** *p128*
Waagner, William; South Carolina, 1788 **7119** *p203*
Wabben, Gerhard; New York, NY, 1905 **3455.3** *p20*
*Wife:*Helen
Wabben, Helen *SEE* Wabben, Gerhard
Wach, Emil Michael; Wisconsin, n.d. **9675.8** *p124*
Wachner, Bendel 5; New York, NY, 1878 **9253** *p47*
Wachner, Chaie 9; New York, NY, 1878 **9253** *p47*
Wachner, Josef 8; New York, NY, 1878 **9253** *p47*
Wachner, Kraindil 48; New York, NY, 1878 **9253** *p47*
Wachner, Simon 11 mos; New York, NY, 1878 **9253** *p47*
Wachope, John; Charleston, SC, 1739 **1639.20** *p311*
Wachsenmuller, Phil. 20; America, 1854-1855 **9162.6** *p105*
Wachsmut, Pierre 24; Port uncertain, 1836 **778.5** *p541*
Wachtel, John; America, 1893 **1450.2** *p152A*
Wachter, Adam; Wisconsin, n.d. **9675.8** *p124*
Wachter, Anthony; America, 1848 **1450.2** *p152A*
Wachtle, John; Wisconsin, n.d. **9675.8** *p124*
Wachtmann, Ernst Heinrich Daniel; America, 1849 **4610.10** *p142*
Wachtmann, Peter J.H.; Wisconsin, n.d. **9675.8** *p124*
Wachtstetter, Jacob; America, 1856 **1450.2** *p152A*
Wachtstetter, John; America, 1853 **1450.2** *p152A*
Wacinck, Willy; Arkansas, 1918 **95.2** *p128*
Wacker, . . .; Canada, 1776-1783 **9786** *p36*
Wacker, Barbara *SEE* Wacker, Michael
Wacker, Ernst; New York, NY, 1912 **3455.3** *p49*
Wacker, Geoerg; Pennsylvania, 1749 **2444** *p228*
Wacker, Henry; Iroquois Co., IL, 1892 **3455.1** *p14*
Wacker, Maria Barbara *SEE* Wacker, Michael
Wacker, Michael; Port uncertain, 1751 **2444** *p228*
*Wife:*Barbara
*Child:*Maria Barbara
Wacker, Michel; Pennsylvania, 1749 **2444** *p228*
Wackernagel, Ernst; Wisconsin, n.d. **9675.8** *p124*
Wacum, Robert; New England, 1816 **2859.11** *p43*
With wife & child
Waddel, A. K. 53?; Arizona, 1890 **2764.35** *p72*
Waddel, Ralph; New York, NY, 1811 **2859.11** *p20*
Waddell, James; New Brunswick, 1832 **9775.5** *p204*
Waddell, James; North Carolina, 1828 **1639.20** *p311*
Waddell, William 20; Jamaica, 1729 **3690.1** *p240*
Waddilove, Richard; Jamaica, 1756 **1219.7** *p49*
Waddilove, Richard; Jamaica, 1756 **3690.1** *p233*
Waddington, Hanna; Virginia, 1637 **6219** *p85*
Waddington, Hannan; Virginia, 1636 **6219** *p79*
Waddle, Alex; Quebec, 1847 **5704.8** *p12*
Waddle, Ann; Philadelphia, 1853 **5704.8** *p102*
Waddle, Ellen; Quebec, 1847 **5704.8** *p12*
Waddle, Ellen 6; Quebec, 1847 **5704.8** *p12*
Waddle, Henry; Quebec, 1847 **5704.8** *p12*
Waddle, Isabella; Philadelphia, 1853 **5704.8** *p102*
Waddle, Jane; Philadelphia, 1853 **5704.8** *p102*
Waddle, Joseph; Quebec, 1847 **5704.8** *p12*
Waddle, Margaret; Quebec, 1847 **5704.8** *p12*
Waddle, Margaret 4; Quebec, 1847 **5704.8** *p12*
Waddle, Margaret 11; Quebec, 1847 **5704.8** *p12*
Waddle, Mary 4; Quebec, 1847 **5704.8** *p12*
Waddle, Mathew; Quebec, 1847 **5704.8** *p12*
Waddle, Nancy; Quebec, 1847 **5704.8** *p12*
Waddle, Rob 6; Quebec, 1847 **5704.8** *p12*
Waddle, Robert; Quebec, 1847 **5704.8** *p12*
Waddle, William; Quebec, 1847 **5704.8** *p12*
Waddle, William 2; Quebec, 1847 **5704.8** *p12*
Waddle, William 12; Quebec, 1847 **5704.8** *p12*

Waddy, Antho.; Virginia, 1648 **6219** *p246*
Waddy, John; Virginia, 1652 **6251** *p19*
Wade, Albert P.; San Francisco, 1872 **2764.35** *p71*
Wade, Charles 25; Massachusetts, 1849 **5881.1** *p96*
Wade, Edmond; America, 1739 **4971** *p52*
Wade, Edward; Virginia, 1638 **6219** *p124*
Wade, Ellen 50; Massachusetts, 1849 **5881.1** *p96*
Wade, George; New York, NY, 1832 **8208.4** *p43*
Wade, Giles 16; Jamaica, 1734 **3690.1** *p233*
Wade, Isaac; Philadelphia, 1848 **53.26** *p89*
Wade, Isaac; Philadelphia, 1848 **5704.8** *p46*
Wade, Isabella; St. John, N.B., 1847 **5704.8** *p25*
Wade, James; New York, NY, 1816 **2859.11** *p43*
With wife
Wade, James 25; Maryland, 1775 **1219.7** *p250*
Wade, Johanna *SEE* Wade, John
Wade, John; Delaware, 1746 **3652** *p68*
*Wife:*Johanna
Wade, John; New York, NY, 1837 **8208.4** *p34*
Wade, John; Quebec, 1849 **5704.8** *p51*
Wade, John; St. John, N.B., 1853 **5704.8** *p107*
Wade, John; Virginia, 1642 **6219** *p18*
Wade, John; Virginia, 1642 **6219** *p188*
Wade, Margaret; Quebec, 1849 **5704.8** *p51*
Wade, Michael 32; Massachusetts, 1849 **5881.1** *p97*
Wade, Patrick; Illinois, 1872 **5012.39** *p26*
Wade, Phillip; Virginia, 1642 **6219** *p18*
Wade, Phillipp; Virginia, 1642 **6219** *p197*
Wade, Rich.; Virginia, 1642 **6219** *p192*
Wade, Robert; St. John, N.B., 1847 **5704.8** *p11*
Wade, Thomas; Virginia, 1637 **6219** *p8*
Wade, Thomas 16; Philadelphia, 1774 **1219.7** *p183*
Wade, William; Died enroute, 1682 **4962** *p155*
Wade, William; Pennsylvania, 1682 **4960** *p159*
Wade, William 19; Philadelphia, 1774 **1219.7** *p182*
Wadelow, Herbert H.; Illinois, 1894 **2896.5** *p41*
Wader, William; Virginia, 1635 **6219** *p71*
Waderman, Jacob 28; New Orleans, 1831 **778.5** *p541*
Waderman, John 30; New Orleans, 1831 **778.5** *p541*
Wadham, John; St. Christopher, 1752 **1219.7** *p15*
Wadleigh, Charles 34; Arizona, 1890 **2764.35** *p72*
Wadlow, Nicholas; Virginia, 1647 **6219** *p244*
Wadman, John A.; Minneapolis, 1877-1879 **6410.35** *p67*
Wadmer, Egnos; Virginia, 1852 **4626.16** *p14*
Wadsack, Richard 60; Kansas, 1873 **5240.1** *p54*
Wadsworth, Henry; Arkansas, 1918 **95.2** *p128*
Wadsworth, Sarah McSween; North Carolina, 1748-1822 **1639.20** *p227*
Wadsworth, Thomas 19; Maryland, 1733 **3690.1** *p233*
Waecker, Meinrad; Wisconsin, n.d. **9675.8** *p124*
Waegelin, Anna Barbara *SEE* Waegelin, Georg Ludwig
Waegelin, Catharina Ruckwid *SEE* Waegelin, Georg Ludwig
Waegelin, Georg Ludwig; Carolina, 1770-1809 **2444** *p228*
*Wife:*Catharina Ruckwid
*Child:*Anna Barbara
Waeken, Peter C.; Washington, 1859-1920 **2872.1** *p42*
Wael, Catherine; Annapolis, MD, 1742 **4971** *p92*
Waertz, Philip G.; Wisconsin, n.d. **9675.8** *p124*
Waesner, Jacob; Illinois, 1857 **7857** *p8*
Waester, Catharina Groezinger *SEE* Waester, Johann Georg
Waester, Johann Georg; Pennsylvania, 1751 **2444** *p229*
*Wife:*Catharina Groezinger
Wagel, Jacob; Illinois, 1826 **8582.1** *p54*
Wagele, Anna Catharina *SEE* Wagele, Michael

Wagele, Johann Michael *SEE* Wagele, Michael
Wagele, Maria Catharina *SEE* Wagele, Michael
Wagele, Michael; New York, 1709 **3627** *p5*
*Wife:*Anna Catharina
*Child:*Maria Catharina
*Child:*Johann Michael
Wageli, Anna Catharina *SEE* Wageli, Johann Michael
Wageli, Johann Michael *SEE* Wageli, Johann Michael
Wageli, Johann Michael; New York, 1709 **3627** *p5*
*Wife:*Anna Catharina
*Child:*Maria Catharina
*Child:*Johann Michael
Wageli, Maria Catharina *SEE* Wageli, Johann Michael
Wagelin, Anna Catharina *SEE* Wagelin, Michael
Wagelin, Johann Michael *SEE* Wagelin, Michael
Wagelin, Maria Catharina *SEE* Wagelin, Michael
Wagelin, Michael; New York, 1709 **3627** *p5*
*Wife:*Anna Catharina
*Child:*Maria Catharina
*Child:*Johann Michael
Wagemann, . . .; Canada, 1776-1783 **9786** *p36*
Wagener, . . .; Canada, 1776-1783 **9786** *p36*
Wagener, Georg; America, 1842 **8582.3** *p67*
Wagener, Joh. Jacob; Pennsylvania, 1750 **2444** *p229*
Wagener, Johann Andreas 15; America, 1831 **8582.3** *p66*
Wagener, John A.; Charleston, SC, 1833 **8582** *p33*
Wagenerak, Catherina 23 *SEE* Wagenerak, John Clements
Wagenerak, John Clements 48; Georgia, 1738 **9332** *p330*
*Wife:*Catherina 23
Wagenknecht, . . .; Canada, 1776-1783 **9786** *p36*
Wagenseil, John Andrew; New York, 1750 **3652** *p74*
Wager, Thomas 19; Maryland, 1775 **1219.7** *p254*
Waggatt, Thomas; Virginia, 1639 **6219** *p161*
Waggoner, . . .; America, 1869-1885 **8582.2** *p44*
Waggoner, Cornelius; America, 1833 **1450.2** *p152A*
Waggoner, Henry; America, 1833 **1450.2** *p152A*
Waggoner, Henry; Illinois, 1860 **2896.5** *p41*
Waggoner, Johannes; America, 1777-1778 **8582.2** *p68*
Waggoner, Peter; Baltimore, 1833 **1450.2** *p152A*
Wagly, Anna Catharina *SEE* Wagly, Hans Michael
Wagly, Hans Michael; New York, 1709 **3627** *p6*
*Wife:*Anna Catharina
*Child:*Maria Catharina
*Child:*Johann Michael
Wagly, Johann Michael *SEE* Wagly, Hans Michael
Wagly, Maria Catharina *SEE* Wagly, Hans Michael
Wagner, . . .; Canada, 1776-1783 **9786** *p36*
Wagner, A. Nicolaus; Cincinnati, 1832 **8582** *p33*
Wagner, Adam; America, 1849 **8582.3** *p68*
Wagner, Adam 30; Arkansas, 1918 **95.2** *p128*
Wagner, Anna Barbara; Pennsylvania, 1747 **2444** *p232*
Wagner, Anna Haegin *SEE* Wagner, Johann Jacob
Wagner, Anna Magdalena; Pennsylvania, 1751 **2444** *p167*
Wagner, Anna Sophia Berger *SEE* Wagner, Johannes
Wagner, August; Cincinnati, 1869-1887 **8582** *p33*
Wagner, August 32; Kansas, 1878 **5240.1** *p47*
Wagner, August 32; Kansas, 1878 **5240.1** *p59*
Wagner, Balth. 48; America, 1854-1855 **9162.6** *p105*
Wagner, C. G.; Illinois, 1836 **8582.1** *p55*
Wagner, Carolina 6; America, 1838 **778.5** *p541*
Wagner, Catharina 19; America, 1838 **778.5** *p542*
Wagner, Chas. G.; Wisconsin, n.d. **9675.8** *p124*
Wagner, Christian; New York, 1824-1855 **3702.7** *p351*
Wagner, Christina 17; America, 1838 **778.5** *p542*

Wagner, Conrad; Canada, 1776-1783 ***9786*** *p207A*
Wagner, Conrad 67; America, 1895 ***1763*** *p40D*
Wagner, Eliza 43; America, 1838 ***778.5*** *p542*
Wagner, Engelhart; Pennsylvania, 1750 ***2444*** *p229*
Wagner, Ernest; Arkansas, 1918 ***95.2*** *p128*
Wagner, Ferdinand; America, 1843 ***8582.3*** *p68*
Wagner, Franz; New York, NY, 1835 ***8208.4*** *p60*
Wagner, Frederick; Indiana, 1847 ***9117*** *p18*
Wagner, George; Wisconsin, n.d. ***9675.8*** *p124*
Wagner, George 4; America, 1838 ***778.5*** *p542*
Wagner, Henry 8; America, 1838 ***778.5*** *p542*
Wagner, Jacob; America, 1849-1850 ***3702.7*** *p549*
Wagner, Jacob; Illinois, 1838 ***8582.2*** *p50*
Wagner, Jacob; Philadelphia, 1761 ***9973.7*** *p35*
Wagner, Jean Nicolas 43; America, 1838 ***778.5*** *p542*
Wagner, Johann 46; America, 1854-1855 ***9162.6*** *p105*
Wagner, Johann Jacob; New England, 1750 ***2444*** *p229*
*Wife:*Anna Haegin
*Child:*Anna Catharina
Wagner, Johannes; America, 1777-1778 ***8582.2*** *p68*
Wagner, Johannes; Pennsylvania, 1717 ***3627*** *p15*
*Wife:*Anna Sophia Berger
Wagner, John; Wisconsin, n.d. ***9675.8*** *p124*
Wagner, John 66; Massachusetts, 1849 ***5881.1*** *p97*
Wagner, John, Jr.; America, 1862 ***6014.1*** *p3*
Wagner, Joseph; Wisconsin, n.d. ***9675.8*** *p124*
Wagner, Lewis; America, 1861 ***6014.1*** *p3*
Wagner, Louis; Illinois, 1859 ***5012.39*** *p89*
Wagner, Magdalena 15; America, 1838 ***778.5*** *p542*
Wagner, Mathias; Wisconsin, n.d. ***9675.8*** *p124*
Wagner, Michael; Indiana, 1850 ***9117*** *p18*
Wagner, Michael; Wisconsin, n.d. ***9675.8*** *p124*
Wagner, Michel; Wisconsin, n.d. ***9675.8*** *p124*
Wagner, Nicolaus; Ohio, 1869-1887 ***8582*** *p33*
Wagner, Nikolaus; Akron, OH, 1837 ***8582.1*** *p49*
Wagner, Nikolaus; America, 1837 ***8582.1*** *p35*
Wagner, Paul; California, 1863 ***2764.35*** *p73*
Wagner, Paul John; Wisconsin, n.d. ***9675.8*** *p124*
Wagner, Phillip; Canada, 1776-1783 ***9786*** *p207A*
Wagner, Sophia 13; America, 1838 ***778.5*** *p542*
Wagner, Theo; America, 1820 ***8582*** *p33*
Wagner, Theodore A.; America, 1865 ***1450.2*** *p152A*
Wagner, Theodotha 11; America, 1838 ***778.5*** *p542*
Wagner, Valentin; America, 1839 ***8582.1*** *p35*
Wagner, Valentin; Cincinnati, 1869-1887 ***8582*** *p34*
Wagner, Valerius; America, 1754 ***2444*** *p229*
Wagoner, Dominick; Washington, 1859-1920 ***2872.1*** *p42*
Wagoner, Jackson; America, 1833 ***1450.2*** *p152A*
Wagoner, John; America, 1833 ***1450.2*** *p153A*
Wagoner, Thomas; Wisconsin, n.d. ***9675.8*** *p124*
Wagstaff, John 25; Maryland, 1730 ***3690.1*** *p233*
Wagstaff, Thomas; New York, NY, 1837 ***8208.4*** *p28*
Wagstaff, Thomas; New York, NY, 1837 ***8208.4*** *p33*
Wagy, Jacob; Illinois, 1826 ***8582.1*** *p54*
Wahl, . . .; Canada, 1776-1783 ***9786*** *p36*
Wahl, Christian; Iroquois Co., IL, 1892 ***3455.1*** *p14*
Wahl, John; Illinois, 1872 ***5012.39*** *p26*
Wahl, John; Illinois, 1895 ***5012.40*** *p54*
Wahl, John 42; Kansas, 1880 ***5240.1*** *p62*
Wahl, Sebastian; New York, NY, 1834 ***8208.4*** *p25*
Wahlenmaier, John 31; Kansas, 1874 ***5240.1*** *p55*
Wahlgren, John; Colorado, 1904 ***9678.3*** *p16*
Wahlgren, John; Wisconsin, n.d. ***9675.8*** *p124*
Wahlisser, Elisabeth Renner *SEE* Wahlisser, Michael
Wahlisser, Joh. Georg *SEE* Wahlisser, Michael
Wahlisser, Michael; America, 1751 ***2444*** *p229*
*Wife:*Elisabeth Renner
*Child:*Joh. Georg
Wahlstrom, Charles S.; Colorado, 1904 ***9678.3*** *p16*
Wahnert, David; New York, 1749 ***3652*** *p71*
*Wife:*Mary
Wahnert, David; New York, 1752 ***3652*** *p76*
Wahnert, David; New York, 1761 ***3652*** *p88*
Wahnert, David; Philadelphia, 1742 ***3652*** *p55*
*Wife:*Mary Elizabeth
Wahnert, Jacob; New York, 1752 ***3652*** *p76*
Wahnert, Mary *SEE* Wahnert, David
Wahnert, Mary Elizabeth *SEE* Wahnert, David
Waibel, Gottlieb; Iroquois Co., IL, 1896 ***3455.1*** *p14*
Waigand, Franz; Missouri, 1855 ***2896.5*** *p41*
Waigand, Peter; Illinois, 1838-1906 ***2896.5*** *p41*
Waigand, Phillip; Illinois, 1868 ***2896.5*** *p41*
Waight, Ursula; Virginia, 1642 ***6219*** *p199*
Waino, Jacob; Washington, 1859-1920 ***2872.1*** *p42*
Wainscott, Richard 17; Maryland, 1728 ***3690.1*** *p233*
Wainwright, Ann 20; America, 1704 ***2212*** *p41*
Wainwright, Henry 18; America, 1706-1707 ***2212*** *p48*
Wainwright, Jno 11; America, 1699 ***2212*** *p29*
Wainwright, John 25; Savannah, GA, 1775 ***1219.7*** *p274*
Waischmann, Anton; New York, NY, 1839 ***8208.4*** *p95*
Waite, John 50; New York, 1775 ***1219.7*** *p268*
With wife
With 6 children
Waite, Joseph 22; Jamaica, 1730 ***3690.1*** *p233*
Waitekaites, Jozef James; Arkansas, 1918 ***95.2*** *p128*
Waituketys, Charles; Arkansas, 1918 ***95.2*** *p128*
Waity, Andrew; Iroquois Co., IL, 1892 ***3455.1*** *p14*
Wajczekuskis, Simon; Wisconsin, n.d. ***9675.8*** *p124*
Wake, John 15; Philadelphia, 1754 ***1219.7*** *p29*
Wake, John 15; Philadelphia, 1754 ***3690.1*** *p233*
Wakefeild, Jon.; Virginia, 1634 ***6219*** *p32*
Wakefeild, Tho.; Virginia, 1637 ***6219*** *p83*
Wakefield, George 49; Kansas, 1879 ***5240.1*** *p61*
Wakefield, Nathaniel; Ohio, 1844 ***9892.11*** *p47*
Wakeing, Richard; Virginia, 1648 ***6219*** *p246*
Wakeland, Anne; Virginia, 1638 ***6219*** *p186*
Wakeling, W.F.; Iowa, 1866-1943 ***123.54*** *p51*
Wakenham, John 48; West Indies, 1722 ***3690.1*** *p233*
Waker, James 40; Philadelphia, 1804 ***53.26*** *p89*
Wakes, Jonathan; Virginia, 1636 ***6219*** *p19*
Wakins, Edward; Virginia, 1638 ***6219*** *p147*
Wakker, Johann A.; America, 1837 ***8582.2*** *p44*
Walag, Zofia; Iowa, 1866-1943 ***123.54*** *p83*
Walbanck, Henry 24; Virginia, 1700 ***2212*** *p31*
Walber, Dorothy May; Wisconsin, n.d. ***9675.8*** *p124*
Walbert, Johann Christoph; Pennsylvania, 1749 ***4525*** *p257*
Walbridge, John; Virginia, 1639 ***6219*** *p156*
Walburg, Franz; Cincinnati, 1869-1887 ***8582*** *p34*
Walch, . . .; Canada, 1776-1783 ***9786*** *p36*
Walch, Catharine 5; Massachusetts, 1850 ***5881.1*** *p96*
Walch, James 9; Massachusetts, 1850 ***5881.1*** *p97*
Walch, John; Wisconsin, n.d. ***9675.8*** *p124*
Walch, John 7; Massachusetts, 1850 ***5881.1*** *p97*
Walch, Julia 10; Massachusetts, 1847 ***5881.1*** *p97*
Walcke, August; Baltimore, 1832 ***3702.7*** *p97*
Walcke, August; Missouri, 1832-1836 ***3702.7*** *p101*
Walcker, Barbara *SEE* Walcker, Johannes
Walcker, Hans Jerg; Pennsylvania, 1747 ***2444*** *p229*
Walcker, Jacob *SEE* Walcker, Johannes
Walcker, Johannes; Pennsylvania, 1754 ***2444*** *p229*
*Wife:*Barbara
*Child:*Jacob
*Child:*Matthaus
Walcker, Matthaus *SEE* Walcker, Johannes
Walckher, Johannes; Pennsylvania, 1754 ***2444*** *p229*
Walcoke, Robert; Virginia, 1643 ***6219*** *p200*
Wald, Christoph; South Carolina, 1788 ***7119*** *p198*
Wald, Louis; America, 1848 ***8582.3*** *p68*
Waldbeck, Peter; Wisconsin, n.d. ***9675.8*** *p124*
Waldemeier, Anton; Wisconsin, n.d. ***9675.8*** *p124*
Walden, Jacob; Iroquois Co., IL, 1894 ***3455.1*** *p14*
Walden, John 18; Jamaica, 1731 ***3690.1*** *p233*
Walden, Torris; Washington, 1859-1920 ***2872.1*** *p42*
Walder, Henry; Philadelphia, 1763 ***9973.7*** *p38*
Walder, Jacob; Pennsylvania, 1751 ***2444*** *p230*
Waldhauer, Jacob; Georgia, 1775 ***8582.2*** *p64*
Waldhaus, Georg F.; New Orleans, 1837 ***8582.2*** *p50*
Waldhirch, Mathias; Wisconsin, n.d. ***9675.8*** *p124*
Waldhuber, Conrad; Canada, 1763 ***2854*** *p45*
With wife
*Child:*Juliana 15
*Child:*Johann 12
*Child:*Maria Eva 8
*Child:*Jacob 6
*Child:*Michael 1
Waldhuber, Jacob 6 *SEE* Waldhuber, Conrad
Waldhuber, Johann 12 *SEE* Waldhuber, Conrad
Waldhuber, Juliana 15 *SEE* Waldhuber, Conrad
Waldhuber, Maria Eva 8 *SEE* Waldhuber, Conrad
Waldhuber, Michael 1 *SEE* Waldhuber, Conrad
Waldinger, Joseph; Arkansas, 1918 ***95.2*** *p128*
Waldkirch, Matias; Wisconsin, n.d. ***9675.8*** *p124*
Waldkuchn, Frederick; Wisconsin, n.d. ***9675.8*** *p124*
Waldkuchn, Mathe; Wisconsin, n.d. ***9675.8*** *p124*
Waldo, G. F. 21; Kansas, 1890 ***5240.1*** *p75*
Waldren, Walter 24; Massachusetts, 1849 ***5881.1*** *p98*
Waldron, Michael 20; Massachusetts, 1849 ***5881.1*** *p98*
Waldron, Richard Christopher 21; Maryland, 1722 ***3690.1*** *p233*
Waldron, Tho.; Virginia, 1642 ***6219*** *p194*
Waldron, Thomas; Philadelphia, 1816 ***2859.11*** *p43*
Waldschmidt, Christian von; Canada, 1780 ***9786*** *p268*
Waldschmidt, Christian von; New York, 1776 ***9786*** *p268*
Wale, Catherine; Maryland, 1742 ***4971*** *p107*
Wale, Joseph 30; Maryland, 1775 ***1219.7*** *p249*
Wale, Wm.; Virginia, 1636 ***6219*** *p74*
Wale, Wm.; Virginia, 1637 ***6219*** *p108*
Walee, Patrick 19; Newfoundland, 1789 ***4915.24*** *p57*
Walek, Tony; Arkansas, 1918 ***95.2*** *p128*
Walelitsh, Marcus; Illinois, 1870 ***5012.38*** *p99*
Walencik, George; New York, NY, 1908 ***3455.2*** *p51*
Walencip, George; New York, NY, 1908 ***3455.2*** *p79*
Walere, Mrs. A. 24; New Orleans, 1837 ***778.5*** *p542*
Wales, John; Arkansas, 1918 ***95.2*** *p128*
Wales, Reuben T.; Washington, 1859-1920 ***2872.1*** *p42*
Walfer, Julius; Illinois, 1880 ***2896.5*** *p41*
Walicka, John; Arkansas, 1918 ***95.2*** *p128*
Waliser, Michael; Pennsylvania, 1743-1779 ***2444*** *p229*
Waliski, Christ; Illinois, 1896 ***5012.40*** *p54*
Walk, Anton; America, 1853 ***1450.2*** *p153A*
Walk, George 42; Kansas, 1886 ***5240.1*** *p69*
Walk, Louis; America, 1837 ***1450.2*** *p153A*
Walk, Louis; Indianapolis, 1869-1887 ***8582*** *p34*
Walker, . . .; America, 1836 ***8582.1*** *p39*
Walker, . . .; Canada, 1776-1783 ***9786*** *p44*
Walker, . . .; Cincinnati, 1837-1838 ***8582.1*** *p45*
Walker, Mr.; Quebec, 1815 ***9229.18*** *p82*
Walker, Adam; Philadelphia, 1852 ***5704.8*** *p91*
Walker, Alexander; Charleston, SC, 1792 ***1639.20*** *p311*
Walker, Alexander; Quebec, 1847 ***5704.8*** *p8*
Walker, Alexander 18; St. John, N.B., 1865 ***5704.8*** *p165*
Walker, Allen; Sault Ste. Marie, 1881 ***2764.35*** *p71*
Walker, Andrew 18; Quebec, 1853 ***5704.8*** *p105*
Walker, Ann 19; America, 1699 ***2212*** *p28*
Walker, Ann 24; Philadelphia, 1804 ***53.26*** *p90*
Walker, Ann 30 *SEE* Walker, James
Walker, Ann 30 *SEE* Walker, James
Walker, Anne 32 *SEE* Walker, Ralph
Walker, Armstrong; Baltimore, 1811 ***2859.11*** *p20*
Walker, Bartholomew 28; Virginia, 1773 ***1219.7*** *p169*
Walker, Catherine; North Carolina, 1775 ***1639.20*** *p311*
Walker, Constantine; New York, NY, 1816 ***2859.11*** *p43*
Walker, Danll; Virginia, 1698 ***2212*** *p15*
Walker, David; Austin, TX, 1886 ***9777*** *p5*
Walker, David; New York, NY, 1816 ***2859.11*** *p43*
Walker, David; Philadelphia, 1847 ***53.26*** *p90*
Walker, David; Philadelphia, 1847 ***5704.8*** *p13*
Walker, Edward; New York, NY, 1835 ***8208.4*** *p78*
Walker, Edward; Virginia, 1636 ***6219*** *p19*
Walker, Edward 20; Virginia, 1774 ***1219.7*** *p240*
Walker, Edward 32; Virginia, 1775 ***1219.7*** *p246*
Walker, Edwd.; Virginia, 1643 ***6219*** *p229*
Walker, Eliza; New York, NY, 1816 ***2859.11*** *p43*
Walker, Eliza; Philadelphia, 1851 ***5704.8*** *p70*
Walker, Eliza; Quebec, 1850 ***5704.8*** *p63*
Walker, Elizabeth 18 *SEE* Walker, William
Walker, Ellan; St. John, N.B., 1847 ***5704.8*** *p24*
Walker, Francis 9; Quebec, 1851 ***5704.8*** *p74*
Walker, Frederick Henry 43; Harris Co., TX, 1898 ***6254*** *p5*
Walker, Geo.; America, 1837 ***8893*** *p264*
Walker, Georg; Cincinnati, 1788-1848 ***8582.3*** *p89*
Walker, Georg; Cincinnati, 1838 ***8582.1*** *p46*
Walker, Georg; Ohio, 1843 ***8582.1*** *p51*
Walker, George; New Brunswick, 1773 ***9775.5*** *p204*
Walker, George; New York, NY, 1816 ***2859.11*** *p43*
Walker, George; Philadelphia, 1851 ***5704.8*** *p70*
Walker, George 20; Philadelphia, 1803 ***53.26*** *p90*
Walker, Gorg; Pennsylvania, 1751 ***2444*** *p229*
Walker, H.; New York, NY, 1816 ***2859.11*** *p43*
Walker, Hannah; New York, NY, 1866 ***5704.8*** *p213*
Walker, Hen.; Virginia, 1636 ***6219*** *p34*
Walker, Humphrey 27; Maryland, 1730 ***3690.1*** *p233*
Walker, Isabella; Quebec, 1847 ***5704.8*** *p36*
Walker, J.; New York, NY, 1816 ***2859.11*** *p43*
Walker, James; America, 1697 ***2212*** *p4*
Walker, James; New York, NY, 1811 ***2859.11*** *p20*
With family
Walker, James; New York, NY, 1816 ***2859.11*** *p43*
Walker, James; Philadelphia, 1852 ***5704.8*** *p84*
Walker, James; Quebec, 1847 ***5704.8*** *p8*
Walker, James; St. John, N.B., 1849 ***5704.8*** *p55*
Walker, James; St. John, N.B., 1850 ***5704.8*** *p62*
Walker, James; Virginia, 1638 ***6219*** *p121*
Walker, James 11; New York, 1774 ***1219.7*** *p222*
Walker, James 21; Quebec, 1863 ***5704.8*** *p153*
Walker, James 23; Maryland, 1775 ***1219.7*** *p252*
Walker, James 30; Philadelphia, 1774 ***1219.7*** *p200*
*Wife:*Ann 30
Walker, James 32; Philadelphia, 1803 ***53.26*** *p90*
*Relative:*Ann 30
Walker, Jane; New York, NY, 1816 ***2859.11*** *p43*
Walker, Jane 19; St. John, N.B., 1863 ***5704.8*** *p153*
Walker, Jeramiah; Quebec, 1850 ***5704.8*** *p63*
Walker, Jno.; Virginia, 1646 ***6219*** *p241*
Walker, Jno 19; Maryland or Virginia, 1699 ***2212*** *p24*
Walker, Johann Georg; Ohio, 1834 ***8582.3*** *p90*
Walker, John; America, 1698 ***2212*** *p10*
Walker, John; New York, NY, 1811 ***2859.11*** *p20*
With family
Walker, John; New York, NY, 1829 ***8208.4*** *p28*
Walker, John; Pennsylvania, 1754 ***2444*** *p229*
Walker, John; Quebec, 1853 ***5704.8*** *p104*
Walker, John; St. John, N.B., 1849 ***5704.8*** *p55*
Walker, John; Virginia, 1636 ***6219*** *p108*
Walker, John; Virginia, 1694 ***6219*** *p162*
Walker, John; Virginia, 1698 ***2212*** *p11*
Walker, John 8; Quebec, 1855 ***5704.8*** *p125*

Walker, John 12; America, 1706 ***2212*** *p47*
Walker, John 13; Quebec, 1847 ***5704.8*** *p38*
Walker, John 19; Maryland or Virginia, 1733 ***3690.1*** *p234*
Walker, John 19; New England, 1699 ***2212*** *p18*
Walker, John 28; St. John, N.B., 1866 ***5704.8*** *p166*
Walker, John 54; North Carolina, 1850 ***1639.20*** *p311*
Walker, John F.; New York, NY, 1815 ***2859.11*** *p43*
Walker, John-Matthew; Quebec, 1825 ***7603*** *p39*
Walker, Jon.; Virginia, 1636 ***6219*** *p74*
Walker, Jon.; Virginia, 1637 ***6219*** *p108*
Walker, Jone; Virginia, 1637 ***6219*** *p85*
Walker, Joseph; New York, NY, 1816 ***2859.11*** *p43*
Walker, Joseph; New York, NY, 1838 ***8208.4*** *p86*
Walker, Joseph; Philadelphia, 1847 ***53.26*** *p90*
Walker, Joseph; Philadelphia, 1847 ***5704.8*** *p14*
Walker, Joseph 13; St. John, N.B., 1849 ***5704.8*** *p55*
Walker, Joseph 16; Virginia, 1721 ***3690.1*** *p234*
Walker, Joseph 20; Pennsylvania, 1728 ***3690.1*** *p234*
Walker, Joseph 30; Philadelphia, 1774 ***1219.7*** *p200*
*Wife:*Mary 28
Walker, Justice 40; Philadelphia, 1774 ***1219.7*** *p237*
With wife 30
Walker, Lawr.; Virginia, 1637 ***6219*** *p108*
Walker, Lea Josephine; Iowa, 1866-1943 ***123.54*** *p83*
Walker, M.; New York, NY, 1816 ***2859.11*** *p43*
Walker, Maria 19; Philadelphia, 1860 ***5704.8*** *p145*
Walker, Martha; New York, NY, 1816 ***2859.11*** *p43*
Walker, Martin; Quebec, 1847 ***5704.8*** *p36*
Walker, Mary; New York, NY, 1816 ***2859.11*** *p43*
Walker, Mary; Philadelphia, 1852 ***5704.8*** *p84*
Walker, Mary; St. John, N.B., 1847 ***5704.8*** *p24*
Walker, Mary; St. John, N.B., 1849 ***5704.8*** *p55*
Walker, Mary 6; Quebec, 1855 ***5704.8*** *p125*
Walker, Mary 22; America, 1699 ***2212*** *p28*
Walker, Mary 22; Quebec, 1853 ***5704.8*** *p105*
Walker, Mary 28 *SEE* Walker, Joseph
Walker, Mary Ann; St. John, N.B., 1848 ***5704.8*** *p43*
Walker, Mary Ann 20 *SEE* Walker, William
Walker, Mathew 24; Nova Scotia, 1774 ***1219.7*** *p209*
Walker, Michael 19; Jamaica, 1739 ***3690.1*** *p234*
Walker, Morris; Virginia, 1638 ***6219*** *p125*
Walker, Oliver; Virginia, 1637 ***6219*** *p113*
Walker, Patrick 18; Carolina, 1684 ***1639.20*** *p311*
Walker, Peter 21; St. John, N.B., 1866 ***5704.8*** *p165*
Walker, Phillipp; Virginia, 1637 ***6219*** *p113*
Walker, R.; New York, NY, 1816 ***2859.11*** *p43*
Walker, Ralph 36; Philadelphia, 1803 ***53.26*** *p90*
*Relative:*Anne 32
Walker, Rebecca 20; Quebec, 1858 ***5704.8*** *p137*
Walker, Rich.; Virginia, 1652 ***6251*** *p20*
Walker, Richard 15; Jamaica, 1729 ***3690.1*** *p234*
Walker, Richard 38; Nova Scotia, 1774 ***1219.7*** *p210*
Walker, Robert; Philadelphia, 1852 ***5704.8*** *p84*
Walker, Robert; Quebec, 1847 ***5704.8*** *p8*
Walker, Robert; St. John, N.B., 1847 ***5704.8*** *p4*
Walker, Robert 20; Jamaica, 1725 ***3690.1*** *p234*
Walker, Robert D.; Virginia, 1847 ***4626.16*** *p13*
Walker, Robert J.; New York, NY, 1811 ***2859.11*** *p20*
Walker, Robert J.; Philadelphia, 1867 ***5704.8*** *p217*
Walker, Roger; Virginia, 1637 ***6219*** *p13*
Walker, Samll.; Virginia, 1639 ***6219*** *p161*
Walker, Samuel; Philadelphia, 1851 ***5704.8*** *p76*
Walker, Samuel 15; Windward Islands, 1722 ***3690.1*** *p234*
Walker, Sarah 25; Canada, 1838 ***4535.12*** *p113*
Walker, Stephen 27; Maryland, 1775 ***1219.7*** *p254*
Walker, Tho 27; America, 1699 ***2212*** *p28*
Walker, Thomas; America, 1698 ***2212*** *p10*
Walker, Thomas; Charleston, SC, 1796 ***1639.20*** *p311*
Walker, Thomas; St. John, N.B., 1847 ***5704.8*** *p4*
Walker, Thomas; Virginia, 1698 ***2212*** *p11*
Walker, Thomas 2; Quebec, 1847 ***5704.8*** *p36*
Walker, Thomas H.; New York, NY, 1838 ***8208.4*** *p86*
Walker, Timothy; Jamaica, 1775 ***1219.7*** *p277*
Walker, Tristram 27; North America, 1774 ***1219.7*** *p200*
Walker, William; Kansas, 1892 ***5240.1*** *p47*
Walker, William; New York, NY, 1816 ***2859.11*** *p43*
Walker, William; Philadelphia, 1852 ***5704.8*** *p88*
Walker, William; Quebec, 1848 ***5704.8*** *p41*
Walker, William 13; Quebec, 1847 ***5704.8*** *p36*
Walker, William 16; Pennsylvania, 1728 ***3690.1*** *p234*
Walker, William 18; Maryland, 1751 ***1219.7*** *p3*
Walker, William 18; Maryland, 1751 ***3690.1*** *p234*
Walker, William 18; Virginia, 1720 ***3690.1*** *p234*
Walker, William 21; Jamaica, 1724 ***3690.1*** *p234*
Walker, William 22; Quebec, 1858 ***5704.8*** *p137*
Walker, William 24; Maryland, 1775 ***1219.7*** *p251*
Walker, William 26; Jamaica, 1730 ***3690.1*** *p292*
Walker, William 26; St. Vincent, 1775 ***1219.7*** *p251*
Walker, William 30; Philadelphia, 1803 ***53.26*** *p90*
*Relative:*Mary Ann 20
*Relative:*Elizabeth 18
Walker, William 37; South Carolina, 1774 ***1219.7*** *p205*
Walker, William 56; Arizona, 1907 ***9228.40*** *p14*
Walker, William Thos. 40; Kansas, 1884 ***5240.1*** *p67*
Walker, Wm.; Austin, TX, 1886 ***9777*** *p5*
Walkin, Fred; Illinois, 1876 ***5012.37*** *p60*
Walkinshaw, William; New York, NY, 1815 ***2859.11*** *p43*
Walkow, M. B. 22; Kansas, 1902 ***5240.1*** *p82*
Walkow, Max 19; Kansas, 1906 ***5240.1*** *p83*
Wall, Mr.; Philadelphia, 1811 ***2859.11*** *p20*
Wall, Anders; Iowa, 1850 ***2090*** *p609*
With 4 brothers sister & mother
Wall, Andrew 1; Massachusetts, 1847 ***5881.1*** *p96*
Wall, Bennie 29; Kansas, 1906 ***5240.1*** *p84*
Wall, Bridget 20; Philadelphia, 1853 ***5704.8*** *p113*
Wall, Catherine; America, 1742 ***4971*** *p86*
Wall, Catherine; America, 1742 ***4971*** *p95*
Wall, Catherine; America, 1743 ***4971*** *p11*
Wall, Easter; New York, NY, 1811 ***2859.11*** *p20*
Wall, Elizabeth 19; Georgia, 1775 ***1219.7*** *p277*
Wall, Gottlieb 35; Kansas, 1883 ***5240.1*** *p64*
Wall, Henry; America, 1837 ***1450.2*** *p153A*
Wall, James 38; Indiana, 1854 ***1450.2*** *p153A*
Wall, John; New York, NY, 1811 ***2859.11*** *p20*
With family
Wall, John; Philadelphia, 1762 ***9973.7*** *p37*
Wall, John; Virginia, 1636 ***6219*** *p78*
Wall, John 19; Jamaica, 1723 ***3690.1*** *p234*
Wall, John 35; Maryland, 1774 ***1219.7*** *p179*
Wall, Mary 35; Massachusetts, 1847 ***5881.1*** *p97*
Wall, Michael 24; Philadelphia, 1774 ***1219.7*** *p216*
Wall, Richard; Virginia, 1636 ***6219*** *p21*
Wall, Thomas; Bangor, ME, 1875 ***6410.22*** *p124*
Wall, Tobias Janssen; Maine, 1897 ***6410.22*** *p127*
Wall, William; New York, NY, 1838 ***8208.4*** *p69*
Wall, William; Philadelphia, 1865 ***5704.8*** *p194*
Wall, William 23; Maryland, 1774 ***1219.7*** *p225*
Wall, Wm.; Virginia, 1635 ***6219*** *p72*
Wallace, Alexander 7; Quebec, 1849 ***5704.8*** *p51*
Wallace, Andrew 67; South Carolina, 1850 ***1639.20*** *p311*
Wallace, Ann 30; Massachusetts, 1849 ***5881.1*** *p96*
Wallace, Ann 56; St. John, N.B., 1853 ***5704.8*** *p109*
Wallace, Archey 10; Quebec, 1863 ***5704.8*** *p154*
Wallace, Barbara 4; Philadelphia, 1850 ***5704.8*** *p64*
Wallace, Catharine; New York, NY, 1865 ***5704.8*** *p191*
Wallace, Catharine; New York, NY, 1865 ***5704.8*** *p192*
Wallace, D. L.; Washington, 1859-1920 ***2872.1*** *p42*
Wallace, David 16; Philadelphia, 1870 ***5704.8*** *p238*
Wallace, David 60; Massachusetts, 1849 ***5881.1*** *p96*
Wallace, Eliza; Quebec, 1849 ***5704.8*** *p51*
Wallace, Eliza; Quebec, 1849 ***5704.8*** *p57*
Wallace, Eliza 7; Quebec, 1849 ***5704.8*** *p57*
Wallace, Eliza 9; Quebec, 1849 ***5704.8*** *p51*
Wallace, Eliza 11; Quebec, 1863 ***5704.8*** *p154*
Wallace, Elizabeth; Philadelphia, 1852 ***5704.8*** *p92*
Wallace, Elizabeth 6; Philadelphia, 1850 ***5704.8*** *p64*
Wallace, Elizabeth 17; Quebec, 1858 ***5704.8*** *p140*
Wallace, Francis 18; Georgia, 1775 ***1219.7*** *p276*
Wallace, George; New York, NY, 1811 ***2859.11*** *p20*
Wallace, George 10; New York, NY, 1865 ***5704.8*** *p192*
Wallace, George 33; Kansas, 1889 ***5240.1*** *p74*
Wallace, Hannah; New York, NY, 1815 ***2859.11*** *p43*
Wallace, Hugh; New York, NY, 1811 ***2859.11*** *p20*
Wallace, Isabella; St. John, N.B., 1847 ***5704.8*** *p26*
Wallace, Isabella 17; Quebec, 1863 ***5704.8*** *p154*
Wallace, James; America, 1791 ***1639.20*** *p312*
Wallace, James; New York, NY, 1816 ***2859.11*** *p43*
Wallace, James; Philadelphia, 1850 ***53.26*** *p90*
Wallace, James; Philadelphia, 1850 ***5704.8*** *p68*
Wallace, James; Philadelphia, 1870 ***5704.8*** *p238*
Wallace, James; Washington, 1859-1920 ***2872.1*** *p42*
Wallace, James 5; Quebec, 1849 ***5704.8*** *p51*
Wallace, James 8; Quebec, 1863 ***5704.8*** *p154*
Wallace, James 18; Philadelphia, 1870 ***5704.8*** *p238*
Wallace, James 21; Philadelphia, 1857 ***5704.8*** *p132*
Wallace, James 40; Quebec, 1863 ***5704.8*** *p154*
Wallace, Jane; Quebec, 1852 ***5704.8*** *p94*
Wallace, Jane; St. John, N.B., 1850 ***5704.8*** *p67*
Wallace, Jane 9 mos; Quebec, 1849 ***5704.8*** *p51*
Wallace, Jane 5; Quebec, 1858 ***5704.8*** *p140*
Wallace, Jane 45; Quebec, 1858 ***5704.8*** *p140*
Wallace, Jane Mary 8; Philadelphia, 1850 ***5704.8*** *p64*
Wallace, John; Arkansas, 1918 ***95.2*** *p128*
Wallace, John; New York, NY, 1811 ***2859.11*** *p20*
Wallace, John; New York, NY, 1865 ***5704.8*** *p192*
Wallace, John; South Carolina, 1750-1799 ***1639.20*** *p312*
Wallace, John 2; Philadelphia, 1850 ***5704.8*** *p64*
Wallace, John 19; Quebec, 1863 ***5704.8*** *p154*
Wallace, John 22; Virginia, 1775 ***1219.7*** *p248*
Wallace, John 24; Quebec, 1855 ***5704.8*** *p126*
Wallace, John Martin; California, 1869 ***2769.9*** *p5*
Wallace, Joseph; Philadelphia, 1850 ***5704.8*** *p64*
Wallace, Joseph; Philadelphia, 1851 ***5704.8*** *p81*
Wallace, Margaret; New York, NY, 1816 ***2859.11*** *p43*
Wallace, Margaret 1; Philadelphia, 1851 ***5704.8*** *p76*
Wallace, Margaret 20; Philadelphia, 1860 ***5704.8*** *p146*
Wallace, Margaret 20; Quebec, 1858 ***5704.8*** *p140*
Wallace, Martha; Philadelphia, 1850 ***5704.8*** *p64*
Wallace, Martha 17; Philadelphia, 1857 ***5704.8*** *p132*
Wallace, Mary; Philadelphia, 1847 ***5704.8*** *p22*
Wallace, Mary; Philadelphia, 1870 ***5704.8*** *p238*
Wallace, Mary; Quebec, 1850 ***5704.8*** *p66*
Wallace, Mary; St. John, N.B., 1850 ***5704.8*** *p67*
Wallace, Mary 35; Quebec, 1863 ***5704.8*** *p154*
Wallace, Mary 50; North Carolina, 1850 ***1639.20*** *p312*
Wallace, Mary Anne; Quebec, 1849 ***5704.8*** *p51*
Wallace, Mary Anne 15; Quebec, 1863 ***5704.8*** *p154*
Wallace, Mathew; St. John, N.B., 1847 ***5704.8*** *p26*
Wallace, Moses 20; Philadelphia, 1859 ***5704.8*** *p141*
Wallace, P.; Arizona, 1897 ***9228.30*** *p1*
Wallace, Peter; Washington, 1859-1920 ***2872.1*** *p42*
Wallace, Rebecca; Philadelphia, 1851 ***5704.8*** *p76*
Wallace, Richard; New York, NY, 1839 ***8208.4*** *p91*
Wallace, Robert; Quebec, 1849 ***5704.8*** *p51*
Wallace, Robert 6; Quebec, 1863 ***5704.8*** *p154*
Wallace, Robert 11; Quebec, 1849 ***5704.8*** *p51*
Wallace, Robert 12; Philadelphia, 1870 ***5704.8*** *p238*
Wallace, Robert 22; Philadelphia, 1856 ***5704.8*** *p128*
Wallace, S.; New York, NY, 1816 ***2859.11*** *p43*
Wallace, Sam'l; Philadelphia, 1811 ***2859.11*** *p20*
Wallace, Samuel; Boston, 1772 ***1219.7*** *p157*
Wallace, Samuel; Philadelphia, 1811 ***53.26*** *p90*
Wallace, Sarah; Philadelphia, 1850 ***53.26*** *p90*
Wallace, Sarah; Philadelphia, 1850 ***5704.8*** *p68*
Wallace, Thomas; New York, NY, 1815 ***2859.11*** *p43*
Wallace, Thomas; Quebec, 1849 ***5704.8*** *p52*
Wallace, Thomas 3; Quebec, 1863 ***5704.8*** *p154*
Wallace, Walter; South Carolina, 1735 ***1639.20*** *p312*
Wallace, William; Philadelphia, 1850 ***5704.8*** *p64*
Wallace, William 24; Virginia, 1775 ***1219.7*** *p248*
Wallace, William 28; Philadelphia, 1854 ***5704.8*** *p123*
Wallace, William 50; Quebec, 1858 ***5704.8*** *p140*
Wallace, William J.; America, 1817 ***1450.2*** *p153A*
Wallace, William John 12; Quebec, 1849 ***5704.8*** *p51*
Wallach, Abraham; Arkansas, 1918 ***95.2*** *p128*
Wallberg, Frederick August; South Carolina, 1788 ***7119*** *p200*
Wallberg, Fried. August; South Carolina, 1788 ***7119*** *p200*
Wallberg, Oscar; Maine, 1865-1872 ***6410.22*** *p115*
Walle, Anna; Quebec, 1878 ***9980.20*** *p49*
Walle, Cornl.; Quebec, 1877 ***9980.20*** *p49*
Walle, Helena; Quebec, 1878 ***9980.20*** *p49*
Walle, Helena Hilbrand; Quebec, 1878 ***9980.20*** *p49*
Walle, Isak; Quebec, 1878 ***9980.20*** *p49*
Walle, Joh.; Quebec, 1877 ***9980.20*** *p49*
Walle, Johan 23; Quebec, 1878 ***9980.20*** *p49*
Walle, Johann; Quebec, 1878 ***9980.20*** *p49*
Walle, Kornelius 21; Quebec, 1878 ***9980.20*** *p49*
Waller, Ann 19; Virginia, 1699 ***2212*** *p27*
Waller, George; New York, 1881 ***1450.2*** *p41B*
Waller, John 16; Maryland, 1752 ***1219.7*** *p13*
Waller, John 16; Maryland, 1752 ***3690.1*** *p234*
Waller, Piet; Washington, 1859-1920 ***2872.1*** *p42*
Waller, Robert K.; New York, NY, 1836 ***8208.4*** *p18*
Waller, Thomas 22; Jamaica, 1776 ***1219.7*** *p281*
Waller, Thomas 26; Maryland, 1774 ***1219.7*** *p207*
Waller, William; Illinois, 1895 ***5012.39*** *p53*
Waller, William; Illinois, 1899 ***5012.40*** *p56*
Waller, Wm.; Virginia, 1637 ***6219*** *p24*
Walleratts, Peter J.; Wisconsin, n.d. ***9675.8*** *p124*
Wallern, James 21; Tobago, W. Indies, 1775 ***1219.7*** *p251*
Wallers, Alfred; America, 1881 ***1450.2*** *p153A*
Wallestein, Mr. 23; Louisiana, 1820 ***778.5*** *p542*
Wallett, William 27; Pennsylvania, 1750 ***3690.1*** *p235*
Walley, Ambrose 1; Massachusetts, 1850 ***5881.1*** *p96*
Walley, Jane 30; Massachusetts, 1850 ***5881.1*** *p97*
Walley, Mary 22; Virginia, 1738 ***3690.1*** *p235*
Walley, William 18; Massachusetts, 1850 ***5881.1*** *p98*
Wallez, S. 25; America, 1837 ***778.5*** *p542*
Wallford, John; Virginia, 1637 ***6219*** *p10*
Wallgren, John P.; Bangor, ME, 1886 ***6410.22*** *p125*
Wallice, Matt.; Virginia, 1648 ***6219*** *p237*
Wallin, Anth.; Virginia, 1636 ***6219*** *p80*
Wallin, Gustav; Arkansas, 1918 ***95.2*** *p128*
Wallin, Samuel M.F.; Illinois, 1888 ***5012.39*** *p122*
Walling, . . .; Canada, 1776-1783 ***9786*** *p36*
Wallington, Richard 35; Philadelphia, 1774 ***1219.7*** *p205*
Wallington, Samul; Barbados, 1698 ***2212*** *p4*
Wallis, Charles 22; Philadelphia, 1774 ***1219.7*** *p232*
Wallis, Edmund; Virginia, 1628 ***6219*** *p31*
Wallis, Eliz.; Virginia, 1635 ***6219*** *p4*
Wallis, Elizabeth 19; Savannah, GA, 1733 ***4719.17*** *p312*
Wallis, James 23; Maryland, 1774 ***1219.7*** *p204*
Wallis, John; Virginia, 1639 ***6219*** *p162*

Wanberg, Ivan; Wisconsin, n.d. ***9675.8*** *p124*
Wand, Aureus; New York, 1900 ***1450.2*** *p41B*
Wanderbilt, Philip; America, 1880 ***1450.2*** *p153A*
Wandersee, Herman; Baltimore, 1884 ***1450.2*** *p41B*
Wanes, Richard; Virginia, 1636 ***6219*** *p76*
Wangenheim, Julius von; America, 1775-1781 ***8582.3*** *p79*
Wangolis, Joe; Arkansas, 1918 ***95.2*** *p129*
Wangrow, Ferdinand; Illinois, 1885 ***2896.5*** *p41*
Wangrow, Ludwig; Illinois, 1885 ***2896.5*** *p41*
Wank, Johann; Ohio, 1832 ***8582.1*** *p46*
Wank, John George 37; Kansas, 1890 ***5240.1*** *p75*
Wankel, George; Baltimore, 1881 ***1450.2*** *p41B*
Wankelman, Friederich; America, 1849 ***8582.3*** *p68*
Wankelmann, Friederich; America, 1849 ***8582.3*** *p68*
Wanner, Anna Maria; America, 1749 ***2444*** *p235*
Wansell, Thomas 18; Pennsylvania, Virginia or Maryland, 1728 ***3690.1*** *p236*
Wanton, James; Virginia, 1637 ***6219*** *p24*
Wantya, Richmond; New York, NY, 1816 ***2859.11*** *p43*
Wapal, Charles; Wisconsin, n.d. ***9675.8*** *p124*
Wapal, Frederick; Wisconsin, n.d. ***9675.8*** *p124*
Wapler, Esther; New York, 1761 ***3652*** *p88*
Waples, Samuel 21; Virginia, 1775 ***1219.7*** *p261*
Waplett, Thomas; Virginia, 1639 ***6219*** *p152*
Warabeff, Nick; Arkansas, 1918 ***95.2*** *p129*
Waraheff, John; Arkansas, 1918 ***95.2*** *p129*
Waraner, Math.; Virginia, 1637 ***6219*** *p11*
Waraworth, Anastasie 28; America, 1823 ***778.5*** *p542*
Ward, . . .; Virginia, 1637 ***6219*** *p17*
Ward, . . . 7 mos; Philadelphia, 1864 ***5704.8*** *p183*
Ward, Anabella 21; Philadelphia, 1857 ***5704.8*** *p133*
Ward, Anabella 21; Philadelphia, 1864 ***5704.8*** *p157*
Ward, Ann; Philadelphia, 1852 ***5704.8*** *p85*
Ward, Ann; Philadelphia, 1866 ***5704.8*** *p211*
Ward, Ann; Virginia, 1635 ***6219*** *p22*
Ward, Ann; Virginia, 1636 ***6219*** *p21*
Ward, Ann 29; Quebec, 1863 ***5704.8*** *p154*
Ward, Anne; New York, NY, 1816 ***2859.11*** *p43*
Ward, Bernard; New York, NY, 1867 ***5704.8*** *p221*
Ward, Bridget; Philadelphia, 1868 ***5704.8*** *p231*
Ward, Bridget; St. John, N.B., 1847 ***5704.8*** *p19*
Ward, Bridget 17; St. John, N.B., 1853 ***5704.8*** *p110*
Ward, Bridget 45; St. John, N.B., 1864 ***5704.8*** *p159*
Ward, Catherine *SEE* Ward, Margaret
Ward, Catherine; Philadelphia, 1847 ***5704.8*** *p32*
Ward, Catherine; St. John, N.B., 1847 ***5704.8*** *p35*
Ward, Catherine 7; Quebec, 1851 ***5704.8*** *p74*
Ward, Catherine 10; St. John, N.B., 1852 ***5704.8*** *p92*
Ward, Catherine 30; Philadelphia, 1858 ***5704.8*** *p139*
Ward, Catherine 50; St. John, N.B., 1862 ***5704.8*** *p150*
Ward, Chr.; Virginia, 1636 ***6219*** *p34*
Ward, Daniel; Indiana, 1837 ***9117*** *p15*
Ward, Daniel 3; St. John, N.B., 1847 ***5704.8*** *p19*
Ward, Daniel 17; Maryland, 1724 ***3690.1*** *p236*
Ward, David; Indiana, 1833 ***1450.2*** *p153A*
Ward, Dennis 22; St. John, N.B., 1853 ***5704.8*** *p110*
Ward, Eliza; Philadelphia, 1851 ***5704.8*** *p77*
Ward, Eliza; Philadelphia, 1852 ***5704.8*** *p92*
Ward, Elizabeth; Philadelphia, 1864 ***5704.8*** *p183*
Ward, Elizabeth; Virginia, 1623-1636 ***6219*** *p79*
Ward, Elizabeth 13; Quebec, 1851 ***5704.8*** *p75*
Ward, Elizabeth 14; St. John Island, 1775 ***1219.7*** *p273*
Ward, Elizabeth 22 *SEE* Ward, William
Ward, Elizabeth 40; Virginia, 1699 ***2212*** *p26*
Ward, Elleanor 1; St. John, N.B., 1847 ***5704.8*** *p19*
Ward, Ellen; Philadelphia, 1852 ***5704.8*** *p91*
Ward, Ellen; St. John, N.B., 1851 ***5704.8*** *p78*
Ward, Ellen 9; St. John, N.B., 1851 ***5704.8*** *p78*
Ward, Ellen 24; Massachusetts, 1850 ***5881.1*** *p96*
Ward, Ellen 27; St. John, N.B., 1856 ***5704.8*** *p131*
Ward, Farrell; Arkansas, 1918 ***95.2*** *p129*
Ward, Frederick Walter; Arkansas, 1918 ***95.2*** *p129*
Ward, George; Quebec, 1851 ***5704.8*** *p75*
Ward, George 2; Quebec, 1851 ***5704.8*** *p74*
Ward, George 17; Jamaica, 1730 ***3690.1*** *p236*
Ward, George 22; Maryland, 1774 ***1219.7*** *p230*
Ward, Gilee; Philadelphia, 1866 ***5704.8*** *p211*
Ward, Grace *SEE* Ward, John
Ward, Hannah; Philadelphia, 1864 ***5704.8*** *p179*
Ward, Hannah 40; St. John, N.B., 1863 ***5704.8*** *p155*
Ward, Hen.; Virginia, 1637 ***6219*** *p24*
Ward, Henry 36; Maryland, 1774 ***1219.7*** *p187*
Ward, Hugh; Brunswick, NC, 1739 ***1639.20*** *p312*
Ward, Hugh 11; Quebec, 1851 ***5704.8*** *p74*
Ward, Hugh 18; Philadelphia, 1853 ***5704.8*** *p108*
Ward, Hugh 20; Philadelphia, 1860 ***5704.8*** *p145*
Ward, Ignatz; Kentucky, 1839-1840 ***8582.3*** *p99*
Ward, Isabella 7; Philadelphia, 1864 ***5704.8*** *p183*
Ward, James *SEE* Ward, Margaret
Ward, James; New York, NY, 1811 ***2859.11*** *p20*
Ward, James; New York, NY, 1837 ***8208.4*** *p48*
Ward, James; Philadelphia, 1847 ***5704.8*** *p32*
Ward, James; Philadelphia, 1850 ***53.26*** *p90*
*Relative:*Mary
Ward, James; Philadelphia, 1850 ***5704.8*** *p65*
Ward, James 2; St. John, N.B., 1852 ***5704.8*** *p92*
Ward, James 4; Quebec, 1863 ***5704.8*** *p154*
Ward, James 21; Maryland, 1775 ***1219.7*** *p260*
Ward, James 28; Halifax, N.S., 1774 ***1219.7*** *p213*
Ward, Jane; Quebec, 1851 ***5704.8*** *p74*
Ward, Jane 1; St. John, N.B., 1847 ***5704.8*** *p35*
Ward, Jermiah; Philadelphia, 1864 ***5704.8*** *p181*
Ward, John; America, 1737 ***4971*** *p36*
Ward, John; Philadelphia, 1853 ***5704.8*** *p103*
Ward, John; Virginia, 1636 ***6219*** *p79*
*Wife:*Grace
Ward, John; Virginia, 1637 ***6219*** *p23*
Ward, John 9 mos; St. John, N.B., 1848 ***5704.8*** *p39*
Ward, John 2; Quebec, 1863 ***5704.8*** *p154*
Ward, John 3; Philadelphia, 1864 ***5704.8*** *p183*
Ward, John 6; St. John, N.B., 1847 ***5704.8*** *p19*
Ward, John 6; St. John, N.B., 1852 ***5704.8*** *p92*
Ward, John 15; United States or West Indies, 1728 ***3690.1*** *p236*
Ward, John 19; Maryland, 1718 ***3690.1*** *p236*
Ward, John 24; Maryland, 1728 ***3690.1*** *p236*
Ward, John 27; Maryland, 1774 ***1219.7*** *p244*
Ward, John 27; New York, 1774 ***1219.7*** *p217*
Ward, John 66; Massachusetts, 1847 ***5881.1*** *p97*
Ward, John, Jr.; New York, NY, 1838 ***8208.4*** *p88*
Ward, Jon.; Virginia, 1623-1700 ***6219*** *p182*
Ward, Jon.; Virginia, 1636 ***6219*** *p26*
Ward, Jon.; Virginia, 1637 ***6219*** *p86*
Ward, Joseph; Philadelphia, 1865 ***5704.8*** *p195*
Ward, Joseph 34; Massachusetts, 1847 ***5881.1*** *p97*
Ward, Luke 20; Jamaica, 1730 ***3690.1*** *p236*
Ward, Margaret; Philadelphia, 1847 ***53.26*** *p90*
*Relative:*Catherine
*Relative:*Phillip
*Relative:*James
*Relative:*Richard
*Relative:*William
Ward, Margaret; Philadelphia, 1847 ***5704.8*** *p32*
Ward, Margaret 10; St. John, N.B., 1847 ***5704.8*** *p19*
Ward, Martha 10; Philadelphia, 1864 ***5704.8*** *p157*
Ward, Martin; Virginia, 1637 ***6219*** *p85*
Ward, Mary *SEE* Ward, James
Ward, Mary; New York, NY, 1869 ***5704.8*** *p232*
Ward, Mary; Philadelphia, 1850 ***5704.8*** *p65*
Ward, Mary; St. John, N.B., 1847 ***5704.8*** *p35*
Ward, Mary 3; St. John, N.B., 1848 ***5704.8*** *p39*
Ward, Mary 6; Massachusetts, 1847 ***5881.1*** *p97*
Ward, Mary 6; Quebec, 1863 ***5704.8*** *p154*
Ward, Mary 13; St. John, N.B., 1847 ***5704.8*** *p19*
Ward, Mary 20; Massachusetts, 1847 ***5881.1*** *p97*
Ward, Mary 22; St. John, N.B., 1853 ***5704.8*** *p110*
Ward, Mary 30; Massachusetts, 1849 ***5881.1*** *p97*
Ward, Mary 45; Massachusetts, 1849 ***5881.1*** *p97*
Ward, Mary Anne 8; St. John, N.B., 1852 ***5704.8*** *p92*
Ward, Mathew; Virginia, 1639 ***6219*** *p161*
Ward, Michael; New York, NY, 1834 ***8208.4*** *p49*
Ward, Michael; St. John, N.B., 1847 ***5704.8*** *p35*
Ward, Michael 6 mos; Quebec, 1863 ***5704.8*** *p154*
Ward, Michael 7; St. John, N.B., 1847 ***5704.8*** *p19*
Ward, Michael 11; Massachusetts, 1849 ***5881.1*** *p98*
Ward, Michael 12; St. John, N.B., 1852 ***5704.8*** *p92*
Ward, Miles; Brunswick, NC, 1739 ***1639.20*** *p312*
Ward, Moses 18 mos *SEE* Ward, William
Ward, Nancy; St. John, N.B., 1848 ***5704.8*** *p39*
Ward, Neil; St. John, N.B., 1847 ***5704.8*** *p18*
Ward, Patrick; Illinois, 1892 ***5012.40*** *p27*
Ward, Patrick; New York, NY, 1816 ***2859.11*** *p43*
Ward, Patrick; New York, NY, 1840 ***8208.4*** *p111*
Ward, Patrick; Philadelphia, 1852 ***5704.8*** *p85*
Ward, Patrick; St. John, N.B., 1848 ***5704.8*** *p39*
Ward, Patrick 4; St. John, N.B., 1847 ***5704.8*** *p19*
Ward, Patrick 5; St. John, N.B., 1848 ***5704.8*** *p39*
Ward, Patrick 13; Massachusetts, 1849 ***5881.1*** *p98*
Ward, Patrick 25; Philadelphia, 1853 ***5704.8*** *p108*
Ward, Phillip *SEE* Ward, Margaret
Ward, Phillip; Philadelphia, 1847 ***5704.8*** *p32*
Ward, Rich.; Virginia, 1635 ***6219*** *p72*
Ward, Richard *SEE* Ward, Margaret
Ward, Richard; Philadelphia, 1847 ***5704.8*** *p32*
Ward, Richard; Virginia, 1636 ***6219*** *p109*
Ward, Richard; Virginia, 1637 ***6219*** *p84*
Ward, Richard 17; Maryland, 1722 ***3690.1*** *p236*
Ward, Richard 17; Port uncertain, 1757 ***3690.1*** *p236*
Ward, Richard 22; Jamaica, 1736 ***3690.1*** *p236*
Ward, Robert; Virginia, 1637 ***6219*** *p112*
Ward, Robert; Virginia, 1639 ***6219*** *p155*
Ward, Robert; Virginia, 1639 ***6219*** *p161*
Ward, Robert; Virginia, 1642 ***6219*** *p195*
Ward, Robert; Virginia, 1648 ***6219*** *p250*
Ward, Robert 17; Maryland, 1774 ***1219.7*** *p236*
Ward, Robert 21; Philadelphia, 1861 ***5704.8*** *p149*
Ward, Robt; Virginia, 1698 ***2212*** *p17*
Ward, Roger; Virginia, 1634 ***6219*** *p32*
Ward, Rose 9; St. John, N.B., 1847 ***5704.8*** *p19*
Ward, Roseanna; St. John, N.B., 1852 ***5704.8*** *p92*
Ward, Roseanna 4; St. John, N.B., 1852 ***5704.8*** *p92*
Ward, Sam.; Virginia, 1645 ***6219*** *p240*
Ward, Samuel; Quebec, 1851 ***5704.8*** *p75*
Ward, Sarah 21; West Indies, 1731 ***3690.1*** *p236*
Ward, Sarah 56; St. John, N.B., 1856 ***5704.8*** *p131*
Ward, Silvester; Virginia, 1640 ***6219*** *p160*
Ward, Susan; Virginia, 1635 ***6219*** *p10*
Ward, Susan; Virginia, 1637 ***6219*** *p10*
Ward, Tho.; Virginia, 1635 ***6219*** *p69*
Ward, Tho.; Virginia, 1643 ***6219*** *p207*
Ward, Thomas; Virginia, 1637 ***6219*** *p113*
Ward, Thomas 12; St. John, N.B., 1847 ***5704.8*** *p19*
Ward, Thomas 19; Maryland, 1774 ***1219.7*** *p221*
Ward, Thomas 20; Jamaica, 1730 ***3690.1*** *p237*
Ward, Thomas 23; Jamaica, 1736 ***3690.1*** *p237*
Ward, Thomas 30; Quebec, 1863 ***5704.8*** *p154*
Ward, Thomas 39; Philadelphia, 1775 ***1219.7*** *p274*
Ward, William *SEE* Ward, Margaret
Ward, William; Maryland, 1756 ***1219.7*** *p44*
Ward, William; Maryland, 1756 ***3690.1*** *p237*
Ward, William; Maryland, 1773 ***1219.7*** *p163*
Ward, William; New York, NY, 1816 ***2859.11*** *p43*
Ward, William; Philadelphia, 1847 ***5704.8*** *p32*
Ward, William; Virginia, 1637 ***6219*** *p82*
Ward, William 4; Quebec, 1851 ***5704.8*** *p74*
Ward, William 13; Virginia, 1699 ***2212*** *p26*
Ward, William 18; Maryland, 1774 ***1219.7*** *p220*
Ward, William 18; Maryland, 1774 ***1219.7*** *p224*
Ward, William 19; Maryland, 1774 ***1219.7*** *p220*
Ward, William 24; Nova Scotia, 1774 ***1219.7*** *p194*
*Wife:*Elizabeth 22
*Son:*Moses 18 mos
Ward, Wm.; Virginia, 1638 ***6219*** *p2*
Warden, Americus; Cincinnati, 1800-1877 ***8582.3*** *p86*
Warden, Jane; Philadelphia, 1852 ***5704.8*** *p89*
Warden, Jane 27; St. John, N.B., 1854 ***5704.8*** *p122*
Warden, John 21; Philadelphia, 1774 ***1219.7*** *p200*
Warden, Lewis; Cincinnati, 1800-1877 ***8582.3*** *p86*
Warden, Robert; Philadelphia, 1852 ***5704.8*** *p88*
Warden, Tho.; Virginia, 1629 ***6219*** *p8*
Warden, Thomas; Virginia, 1623 ***6219*** *p7*
Warden, William 21; Virginia, 1774 ***1219.7*** *p226*
Warder, Tho.; Virginia, 1635 ***6219*** *p20*
Warder, William; Virginia, 1652 ***6251*** *p20*
Wardlan, Ann J.; America, 1867 ***5704.8*** *p222*
Wardlaw, Charles 21; Quebec, 1857 ***5704.8*** *p136*
Wardlaw, Elizabeth; New York, NY, 1811 ***2859.11*** *p20*
Wardlaw, Mary 18; Philadelphia, 1860 ***5704.8*** *p146*
Wardle, Arthur J.; Colorado, 1905 ***9678.3*** *p17*
Wardle, Charles Henry; Colorado, 1905 ***9678.3*** *p17*
Wardle, James; Colorado, 1905 ***9678.3*** *p17*
Wardle, Jeremiah; New York, NY, 1816 ***2859.11*** *p43*
Wardle, Samuel Ambrose; Arkansas, 1918 ***95.2*** *p129*
Wardler, Hugh; New York, NY, 1816 ***2859.11*** *p43*
Wardrope, David; Charleston, SC, 1804 ***1639.20*** *p312*
Wardzynski, . . .; New York, 1831 ***4606*** *p177*
Ware, Andreas; Cincinnati, 1800-1877 ***8582.3*** *p86*
Ware, Edmond; New York, NY, 1838 ***8208.4*** *p74*
Ware, James; New York, NY, 1815 ***2859.11*** *p43*
Ware, James; Virginia, 1623-1648 ***6219*** *p252*
Ware, John 23; Maryland, 1773 ***1219.7*** *p173*
Ware, Mich.; Virginia, 1648 ***6219*** *p241*
Ware, Robert 15; Jamaica, 1774 ***1219.7*** *p184*
Ware, William; Virginia, 1641 ***6219*** *p185*
Wareham, James 30; Jamaica, 1734 ***3690.1*** *p237*
Wareinberg, Louis; Colorado, 1904 ***9678.3*** *p17*
Wareinburg, August; Colorado, 1904 ***9678.3*** *p17*
Wareinburg, August, Sr.; Colorado, 1904 ***9678.3*** *p17*
Warge, Thomas 27; Jamaica, 1774 ***1219.7*** *p242*
Waring, Alfred; Iowa, 1866-1943 ***123.54*** *p51*
Waring, George; Iowa, 1866-1943 ***123.54*** *p51*
Waring, James; New York, NY, 1838 ***8208.4*** *p74*
Waring, Jonathan; Iowa, 1866-1943 ***123.54*** *p51*
Waring, Margt 22; Virginia, 1699 ***2212*** *p26*
Waring, Nathaniel 37; Maryland or Virginia, 1699 ***2212*** *p24*
Warjelin, John; Arkansas, 1918 ***95.2*** *p129*
Wark, David; Philadelphia, 1848 ***53.26*** *p90*
Wark, David; Philadelphia, 1848 ***5704.8*** *p46*
Wark, Eliza *SEE* Wark, Elizabeth
Wark, Eliza; Philadelphia, 1849 ***5704.8*** *p52*
Wark, Elizabeth; Philadelphia, 1849 ***53.26*** *p90*
*Relative:*Ellen
*Relative:*Eliza
*Relative:*Margaret 11
Wark, Elizabeth; Philadelphia, 1849 ***5704.8*** *p52*
Wark, Ellen *SEE* Wark, Elizabeth
Wark, Ellen; Philadelphia, 1849 ***5704.8*** *p52*

Wark, Isaac 20; Philadelphia, 1834 ***53.26*** *p90*
Wark, James; Quebec, 1852 ***5704.8*** *p87*
Wark, James; Quebec, 1852 ***5704.8*** *p91*
Wark, Jane 7; Quebec, 1853 ***5704.8*** *p105*
Wark, John; Quebec, 1852 ***5704.8*** *p90*
Wark, John 30; Georgia, 1775 ***1219.7*** *p276*
Wark, Margaret; Quebec, 1851 ***5704.8*** *p75*
Wark, Margaret; St. John, N.B., 1847 ***5704.8*** *p18*
Wark, Margaret 11 *SEE* Wark, Elizabeth
Wark, Margaret Jane 11; Philadelphia, 1849 ***5704.8*** *p52*
Wark, Mary 15; Quebec, 1853 ***5704.8*** *p105*
Warke, Ann 13; Quebec, 1858 ***5704.8*** *p137*
Warke, James 18; Quebec, 1858 ***5704.8*** *p137*
Warke, Jane 60; Quebec, 1858 ***5704.8*** *p137*
Warke, John; Quebec, 1852 ***5704.8*** *p87*
Warke, Mary Jane 20; Quebec, 1858 ***5704.8*** *p137*
Warke, William 16; Quebec, 1858 ***5704.8*** *p137*
Warke, William 50; Quebec, 1858 ***5704.8*** *p137*
Warkeham, Grace; Virginia, 1643 ***6219*** *p203*
Warkentin, Henry 25; Kansas, 1879 ***5240.1*** *p61*
Warkin, Mary 22; Massachusetts, 1848 ***5881.1*** *p97*
Warkin, Thomas 24; Massachusetts, 1848 ***5881.1*** *p98*
Warkler, Juliana; New York, 1752 ***3652*** *p76*
Warleck, . . .; Canada, 1776-1783 ***9786*** *p36*
Warley, Jacob; Charleston, SC, 1775-1781 ***8582.2*** *p52*
Warley, Melchior; Charleston, SC, 1766 ***8582.2*** *p65*
Warman, Thomas; Washington, 1859-1920 ***2872.1*** *p42*
Warmbear, Albert; Illinois, 1892 ***5012.40*** *p79*
Warmington, Gibson 31; Kansas, 1872 ***5240.1*** *p53*
Warmington, James 34; Kansas, 1872 ***5240.1*** *p53*
Warne, Thomas; Virginia, 1636 ***6219*** *p26*
Warne, Thomas; Virginia, 1639 ***6219*** *p157*
Warnecke, . . .; Canada, 1776-1783 ***9786*** *p36*
Warnecke, Fred; New York, NY, 1923 ***3455.4*** *p50*
Warnecke, Fred; New York, NY, 1924 ***3455.3*** *p83*
Warnecke, John; Canada, 1783 ***9786*** *p38A*
Warnekros, Paul Bahn; San Francisco, 1872 ***2764.35*** *p74*
Warner, Augustine; Virginia, 1628 ***6219*** *p31*
Warner, Augustine; Virginia, 1638 ***6219*** *p121*
*Wife:*Mary
Warner, Barbara 22 *SEE* Warner, Margarita
Warner, Charles 21; Maryland, 1775 ***1219.7*** *p250*
Warner, David; Virginia, 1634 ***6219*** *p84*
Warner, George; New York, NY, 1839 ***8208.4*** *p95*
Warner, Henry; Virginia, 1636 ***6219*** *p21*
Warner, Henry 24; Jamaica, 1736 ***3690.1*** *p237*
Warner, James 31; Maryland, 1775 ***1219.7*** *p264*
Warner, John 22; Jamaica, 1731 ***3690.1*** *p237*
Warner, John Jacob; South Carolina, 1752-1753 ***3689.17*** *p23*
With wife
Warner, Margarita; South Carolina, 1752-1753 ***3689.17*** *p23*
*Relative:*Barbara 22
Warner, Mary *SEE* Warner, Augustine
Warner, Mary 20; Maryland, 1730 ***3690.1*** *p237*
Warner, Robert; America, 1698 ***2212*** *p8*
Warner, Robert 27; Virginia, 1775 ***1219.7*** *p246*
Warner, Tho.; Virginia, 1643 ***6219*** *p204*
Warner, Thomas; Washington, 1859-1920 ***2872.1*** *p42*
Warner, Thomas 21; Maryland, 1775 ***1219.7*** *p257*
Warner, Wilhelm 19; New York, NY, 1867 ***3702.7*** *p571*
Warnet, Bons. 27; America, 1825 ***778.5*** *p542*
Warnick, R.; New York, NY, 1816 ***2859.11*** *p43*
Warning, Charles J.; Colorado, 1888 ***9678.3*** *p17*
Warnke, Heinrich; America, 1845 ***8582.3*** *p68*
Warnke, Heinrich; America, 1852 ***8582.3*** *p68*
Warnken, Georg; Cincinnati, 1869-1887 ***8582*** *p34*
Warnock, Andrew 70; Kansas, 1884 ***5240.1*** *p65*
Warnock, Betty; Philadelphia, 1852 ***5704.8*** *p96*
Warnock, David 18; St. John, N.B., 1856 ***5704.8*** *p131*
Warnock, Ellen; Philadelphia, 1852 ***5704.8*** *p96*
Warnock, James; New York, NY, 1838 ***8208.4*** *p74*
Warnock, John; New York, NY, 1816 ***2859.11*** *p43*
Warns, Elizabeth *SEE* Warns, George Adolph
Warns, George Adolph; New York, NY, 1909 ***3455.3*** *p24*
*Wife:*Elizabeth
Warnuch, Joseph; Ohio, 1798-1818 ***8582.2*** *p54*
Warr, Eliza; New York, NY, 1816 ***2859.11*** *p44*
Warr, George; New York, NY, 1816 ***2859.11*** *p44*
Warr, Samuel; New York, NY, 1816 ***2859.11*** *p44*
Warrebest, George 22; America, 1831 ***778.5*** *p543*
Warrell, Robert; Virginia, 1637 ***6219*** *p29*
Warren, Amos; Virginia, 1642 ***6219*** *p188*
Warren, Andrew; America, 1736 ***4971*** *p12*
Warren, Ann 19; Philadelphia, 1853 ***5704.8*** *p113*
Warren, Edward; New England, 1816 ***2859.11*** *p44*
Warren, Edward Thonpson; Arkansas, 1918 ***95.2*** *p129*
Warren, Elizabeth 3 *SEE* Warren, John
Warren, Elizabeth 27 *SEE* Warren, John
Warren, George; New York, NY, 1839 ***8208.4*** *p93*
Warren, George 14; Philadelphia, 1775 ***1219.7*** *p258*
Warren, Georgius Marinus 3 wks *SEE* Warren, John
Warren, Henry; Virginia, 1637 ***6219*** *p112*
Warren, Hugh; New York, NY, 1811 ***2859.11*** *p20*
Warren, Jane; New York, NY, 1811 ***2859.11*** *p20*
Warren, Jeremiah; Maine, 1837 ***1450.2*** *p154A*
Warren, John; New England, 1816 ***2859.11*** *p44*
Warren, John; New York, NY, 1834 ***8208.4*** *p31*
Warren, John 2 *SEE* Warren, John
Warren, John 34; Savannah, GA, 1733 ***4719.17*** *p313*
*Wife:*Elizabeth 27
*Daughter:*Elizabeth 3
*Son:*Georgius Marinus 3 wks
*Son:*John 2
*Son:*Richard 4
*Son:*William 6
Warren, Jon.; Virginia, 1638 ***6219*** *p124*
Warren, Josiah; Jamaica, 1753 ***1219.7*** *p18*
Warren, Marie-Madeleine; Montreal, 1693 ***7603*** *p22*
Warren, Marie-Madeleine; New Hampshire, 1685 ***7603*** *p22*
Warren, Richard 4 *SEE* Warren, John
Warren, Tho.; Virginia, 1647 ***6219*** *p243*
Warren, Thomas; Virginia, 1642 ***6219*** *p195*
Warren, Thomas 25; Virginia, 1727 ***3690.1*** *p237*
Warren, Thomas 29; Jamaica, 1731 ***3690.1*** *p237*
Warren, Thomas 31; Maryland, 1774 ***1219.7*** *p230*
Warren, William; Virginia, 1639 ***6219*** *p156*
Warren, William 6 *SEE* Warren, John
Warren, William 23; Jamaica, 1730 ***3690.1*** *p237*
Warren, Wm.; Virginia, 1647 ***6219*** *p239*
Warrendord, Peter; Virginia, 1636 ***6219*** *p21*
Warrick, Thomas 18; Maryland, 1719 ***3690.1*** *p237*
Warrier, George; Philadelphia, 1816 ***2859.11*** *p44*
Warrinet, Fred William; Arkansas, 1918 ***95.2*** *p129*
Warrington, Edwd 27; Maryland or Virginia, 1699 ***2212*** *p24*
Warrnisky, Egnac; Arkansas, 1918 ***95.2*** *p129*
Warsh, Walter; Arkansas, 1918 ***95.2*** *p129*
Warshal, Isaac; Arkansas, 1918 ***95.2*** *p129*
Warshenek, Wladystan; Arkansas, 1918 ***95.2*** *p129*
Warsow, August; Illinois, 1894 ***5012.40*** *p53*
Wartcki, M. A.; Cincinnati, 1869-1887 ***8582*** *p34*
Wartell, G. 27; America, 1838 ***778.5*** *p543*
Wartelle, Mr. 40; New Orleans, 1820 ***778.5*** *p543*
Wartelle, A. 36; New Orleans, 1829 ***778.5*** *p543*
Wartelle, G. 30; America, 1839 ***778.5*** *p543*
Wartelle, J. 39; New Orleans, 1829 ***778.5*** *p543*
Wartendorf, Anna Maria 22; America, 1853 ***9162.8*** *p38*
Warth, Ignatz; Kentucky, 1839-1840 ***8582.3*** *p99*
Warth, Maria Margaretha *SEE* Warth, Philipp Friedrich
Warth, Philipp Friedrich; America, 1753 ***2444*** *p230*
*Wife:*Maria Margaretha
Warth, Philips Fredrick 27; Pennsylvania, 1753 ***2444*** *p230*
Warwall, M.A. 32; Dominica, 1773 ***1219.7*** *p168*
Warweg, Christ; New York, 1849 ***1450.2*** *p154A*
Warweg, Henry; America, 1853 ***1450.2*** *p154A*
Warwick, Edward 24; Jamaica, 1733 ***3690.1*** *p237*
Warwick, John 29; Virginia, 1774 ***1219.7*** *p205*
Warwick, Samuel 31; Jamaica, 1730 ***3690.1*** *p237*
Warworth, Pauline 5; America, 1823 ***778.5*** *p543*
Was, Wm.; Virginia, 1633 ***6219*** *p32*
Wascher, Frederick; Illinois, 1876 ***5012.39*** *p26*
Wascher, John; Illinois, 1876 ***5012.39*** *p26*
Waschke, Anna; Savannah, GA, 1736 ***3652*** *p51*
Waschke, George; Savannah, GA, 1735 ***3652*** *p51*
Washborne, Daniell; Virginia, 1641 ***6219*** *p184*
Washburn, Simeon 47; Arizona, 1890 ***2764.35*** *p72*
Washburn, Simon, Jr. 24; Arizona, 1890 ***2764.35*** *p74*
Washer, Frederick; Illinois, 1876 ***5012.39*** *p26*
Washer, John; Illinois, 1876 ***5012.39*** *p26*
Washington, Richard; Virginia, 1639 ***6219*** *p182*
Washkowski, Felex; Wisconsin, n.d. ***9675.8*** *p124*
Wasilauski, Frank; Arkansas, 1918 ***95.2*** *p129*
Wasilenski, Joseph; Wisconsin, n.d. ***9675.8*** *p124*
Wasilewski, Fryderyk; New York, 1835 ***4606*** *p180*
Wasiolek, Franciszek 25; New York, 1912 ***9980.29*** *p60*
Wasmuth, Philip William; Boston, 1852 ***3840.3*** *p12*
Wason, Anne; St. John, N.B., 1852 ***5704.8*** *p84*
Wason, Archer; Philadelphia, 1811 ***53.26*** *p90*
*Relative:*Jane
Wason, Archer; Philadelphia, 1811 ***2859.11*** *p20*
Wason, Archibald; St. John, N.B., 1848 ***5704.8*** *p48*
Wason, David 10; St. John, N.B., 1852 ***5704.8*** *p84*
Wason, Eliza; St. John, N.B., 1853 ***5704.8*** *p99*
Wason, George; New York, NY, 1811 ***2859.11*** *p20*
Wason, George 9 mos; St. John, N.B., 1853 ***5704.8*** *p99*
Wason, James; Philadelphia, 1853 ***5704.8*** *p100*
Wason, James; St. John, N.B., 1853 ***5704.8*** *p99*
Wason, Jane *SEE* Wason, Archer
Wason, Jane; Philadelphia, 1811 ***2859.11*** *p20*
Wason, John; St. John, N.B., 1852 ***5704.8*** *p84*
Wason, John 9 mos; St. John, N.B., 1852 ***5704.8*** *p84*
Wason, Margaret; New York, NY, 1811 ***2859.11*** *p20*
Wason, Nancy; New York, NY, 1811 ***2859.11*** *p20*
Wass, John; New York, NY, 1816 ***2859.11*** *p44*
Wass, Sarah 20; Jamaica, 1722 ***3690.1*** *p238*
Wassan, Eliza 18; Philadelphia, 1854 ***5704.8*** *p118*
Wassel, George 17; Virginia, 1775 ***1219.7*** *p260*
Wassen, Mary A.; New York, NY, 1866 ***5704.8*** *p214*
Wassenich, Emanuel; America, 1840 ***8582.1*** *p35*
Wassenich, Joseph; Cincinnati, 1869-1887 ***8582*** *p34*
Wasser, Conrad; Illinois, 1880 ***2896.5*** *p41*
Wassermann, Elisabeth; Georgia, 1739 ***9332*** *p323*
Wassermann, M.; Milwaukee, 1875 ***4719.30*** *p257*
Wassermann, Ursula; Georgia, 1739 ***9332*** *p323*
Wassum, Anna Kath. 10; America, 1854-1855 ***9162.6*** *p104*
Wassum, Anna Mgr. 47; America, 1854-1855 ***9162.6*** *p104*
Wassum, Eva Elizab. 10; America, 1854-1855 ***9162.6*** *p104*
Wassum, Leonhard 46; America, 1854-1855 ***9162.6*** *p104*
Wassum, Michael 23; America, 1854-1855 ***9162.6*** *p104*
Wastenays, John 20; Virginia, 1773 ***1219.7*** *p171*
Wasum, Jos.; Wisconsin, n.d. ***9675.8*** *p124*
Water, Thomas 20; Massachusetts, 1849 ***5881.1*** *p98*
Water, William 17; Virginia, 1699 ***2212*** *p26*
Waterhowse, Samll.; Virginia, 1642 ***6219*** *p194*
Waterland, William 44; Savannah, GA, 1733 ***4719.17*** *p313*
Waterman, A.; Milwaukee, 1875 ***4719.30*** *p257*
Waterman, Ann; Virginia, 1622 ***6219*** *p76*
Waterman, Ann; Virginia, 1638 ***6219*** *p145*
Waterman, Georg; Virginia, 1639 ***6219*** *p158*
Watermann, C.D. 42; New York, NY, 1893 ***9026.4*** *p42*
Waters, . . .; New England, 1816 ***2859.11*** *p44*
Waters, Andrew; New York, NY, 1811 ***2859.11*** *p20*
Waters, Ann; Philadelphia, 1849 ***53.26*** *p90*
Waters, Ann; Philadelphia, 1849 ***5704.8*** *p52*
Waters, Ann Jane 16; Philadelphia, 1854 ***5704.8*** *p117*
Waters, Archibald; Philadelphia, 1816 ***2859.11*** *p44*
Waters, Bridget 28; St. John, N.B., 1853 ***5704.8*** *p110*
Waters, Cecilia; Philadelphia, 1867 ***5704.8*** *p221*
Waters, Charles; Philadelphia, 1849 ***53.26*** *p90*
*Relative:*Mary
*Relative:*Michael 6 mos
Waters, Charles; Philadelphia, 1849 ***5704.8*** *p50*
Waters, David; New York, NY, 1864 ***5704.8*** *p171*
Waters, Edward; Virginia, 1647 ***6219*** *p239*
Waters, Eliz.; Virginia, 1647 ***6219*** *p241*
Waters, Eliza; New York, NY, 1869 ***5704.8*** *p233*
Waters, Elizabeth 22; America, 1699 ***2212*** *p28*
Waters, Geo.; Virginia, 1642 ***6219*** *p193*
Waters, George; Illinois, 1856 ***7857*** *p8*
Waters, George; New York, NY, 1838 ***8208.4*** *p84*
Waters, George; Virginia, 1639 ***6219*** *p151*
Waters, Hugh; New York, NY, 1869 ***5704.8*** *p233*
Waters, Hugh; Philadelphia, 1850 ***53.26*** *p90*
Waters, Hugh; Philadelphia, 1850 ***5704.8*** *p68*
Waters, James; Ohio, 1841 ***9892.11*** *p47*
Waters, John; Montreal, 1825 ***7603*** *p65*
Waters, John; New York, NY, 1816 ***2859.11*** *p44*
Waters, John; Philadelphia, 1849 ***53.26*** *p90*
Waters, John; Philadelphia, 1849 ***5704.8*** *p54*
Waters, John; Virginia, 1636 ***6219*** *p7*
Waters, John; Virginia, 1637 ***6219*** *p17*
Waters, John; Virginia, 1639 ***6219*** *p181*
Waters, John C.; America, 1871 ***1450.2*** *p154A*
Waters, Jon.; Virginia, 1628 ***6219*** *p31*
Waters, Letitia 23; Philadelphia, 1774 ***1219.7*** *p182*
Waters, Margaret; Philadelphia, 1864 ***5704.8*** *p180*
Waters, Mary *SEE* Waters, Charles
Waters, Mary; America, 1738 ***4971*** *p13*
Waters, Mary; Philadelphia, 1849 ***5704.8*** *p50*
Waters, Mary; Philadelphia, 1870 ***5704.8*** *p238*
Waters, Mary; Virginia, 1636 ***6219*** *p26*
Waters, Michael 6 mos *SEE* Waters, Charles
Waters, Michael 6 mos; Philadelphia, 1849 ***5704.8*** *p50*
Waters, Michel; Quebec, 1792 ***7603*** *p87*
Waters, Patrick 18; Philadelphia, 1854 ***5704.8*** *p116*
Waters, Rodman; New York, NY, 1838 ***8208.4*** *p84*
Waters, Roger; New York, NY, 1816 ***2859.11*** *p44*
Waters, Roger; Virginia, 1637 ***6219*** *p115*
Waters, Sarah; Philadelphia, 1870 ***5704.8*** *p238*
Waters, Thomas 16; Maryland, 1775 ***1219.7*** *p267*
Waters, Thomas 24; Norfolk, VA, 1774 ***1219.7*** *p222*
Waters, W. H.; Nevada, 1874 ***2764.35*** *p72*
Waters, William; Virginia, 1648 ***6219*** *p241*
Waters, William 35; Jamaica, 1730 ***3690.1*** *p238*
Waters, Winifred; New York, NY, 1815 ***2859.11*** *p44*
Waters, Wm.; Virginia, 1648 ***6219*** *p252*
Waterson, John; New York, NY, 1815 ***2859.11*** *p44*
Waterson, John 18; Quebec, 1855 ***5704.8*** *p126*
Waterson, Mary; Quebec, 1823 ***7603*** *p57*

Waterston, Mary 16; Massachusetts, 1850 ***5881.1*** *p98*
Watersworth, John 33; Nova Scotia, 1774 ***1219.7*** *p194*
Waterworth, George 45; New York, 1774 ***1219.7*** *p227*
Watfield, James 22; New York, 1774 ***1219.7*** *p203*
Watford, John; Virginia, 1639 ***6219*** *p151*
Wathne, Trygre 25; Arkansas, 1918 ***95.2*** *p129*
Watkeyes, Samuell; Virginia, 1638 ***6219*** *p123*
Watkins, Alice; Virginia, 1636 ***6219*** *p75*
Watkins, Alice; Virginia, 1638 ***6219*** *p181*
Watkins, Ame; America, 1697 ***2212*** *p7*
Watkins, Ann; America, 1697 ***2212*** *p8*
Watkins, Charles 48; Massachusetts, 1860 ***6410.32*** *p107*
Watkins, Cornelius; America, 1736 ***4971*** *p12*
Watkins, David 27; Kansas, 1885 ***5240.1*** *p67*
Watkins, Edward; Jamaica, 1754 ***1219.7*** *p31*
Watkins, Edward; Jamaica, 1754 ***3690.1*** *p238*
Watkins, Edward; Virginia, 1642 ***6219*** *p187*
Watkins, Geo.; Virginia, 1638 ***6219*** *p11*
Watkins, John; Montreal, 1818 ***7603*** *p24*
Watkins, John 19; Maryland, 1731 ***3690.1*** *p238*
Watkins, Joseph 17; Jamaica, 1735 ***3690.1*** *p238*
Watkins, Lewis; New York, NY, 1838 ***8208.4*** *p74*
Watkins, Martha 45; Massachusetts, 1860 ***6410.32*** *p107*
Watkins, Morgan; Virginia, 1637 ***6219*** *p84*
Watkins, Nich.; Virginia, 1639 ***6219*** *p151*
Watkins, Richard; Virginia, 1643 ***6219*** *p207*
Watkins, Tho.; Virginia, 1635 ***6219*** *p35*
Watkins, Thomas; Virginia, 1637 ***6219*** *p114*
Watkins, Thomas 21; Philadelphia, 1775 ***1219.7*** *p258*
Watkins, William H.; America, 1876 ***1450.2*** *p154A*
Watkins, Wm.; Virginia, 1643 ***6219*** *p200*
Watkinson, Eliz 27; America, 1704 ***2212*** *p40*
Watkinson, John 18; New York, 1774 ***1219.7*** *p203*
Watley, Joseph 22; Philadelphia, 1774 ***1219.7*** *p233*
Watley, Rebecca; Philadelphia, 1848 ***53.26*** *p90*
Watley, Rebecca; Philadelphia, 1848 ***5704.8*** *p40*
Watry, John P.; Wisconsin, n.d. ***9675.8*** *p124*
Watry, Peter; Wisconsin, n.d. ***9675.8*** *p124*
Watson, A. L.; Washington, 1859-1920 ***2872.1*** *p42*
Watson, Abraham L.; Washington, 1859-1920 ***2872.1*** *p42*
Watson, Alexander; Charleston, SC, 1825 ***1639.20*** *p312*
Watson, Alexander; New York, NY, 1816 ***2859.11*** *p44*
Watson, Alexander; St. John, N.B., 1852 ***5704.8*** *p83*
Watson, Alexander 4; Quebec, 1864 ***5704.8*** *p160*
Watson, Alexander 16; St. John, N.B., 1866 ***5704.8*** *p167*
Watson, Alexander 44; Virginia, 1774 ***1219.7*** *p238*
Watson, Andrew 19; St. John, N.B., 1854 ***5704.8*** *p120*
Watson, Andrew 21; Georgia, 1775 ***1219.7*** *p277*
Watson, Andrew 45; Georgia, 1775 ***1219.7*** *p277*
Watson, Andrew 45; Quebec, 1855 ***5704.8*** *p124*
Watson, Ann 20; Baltimore, 1775 ***1219.7*** *p269*
Watson, Ann 34; St. John, N.B., 1864 ***5704.8*** *p159*
Watson, Anna 45; Massachusetts, 1860 ***6410.32*** *p106*
Watson, Anna Bella 4; Quebec, 1853 ***5704.8*** *p104*
Watson, Anne; Quebec, 1852 ***5704.8*** *p94*
Watson, Anne 2; Quebec, 1849 ***5704.8*** *p51*
Watson, Arthur; Virginia, 1649 ***6219*** *p253*
Watson, Catherine 2; St. John, N.B., 1864 ***5704.8*** *p159*
Watson, Catherine 37; Quebec, 1864 ***5704.8*** *p160*
Watson, Charles 23; Virginia, 1773 ***1219.7*** *p169*
Watson, Charles E.; Colorado, 1888 ***9678.3*** *p17*
Watson, Charles G. 54; Massachusetts, 1860 ***6410.32*** *p106*
Watson, Daniel; America, 1803 ***1639.20*** *p313*
Watson, Daniel 66; North Carolina, 1850 ***1639.20*** *p312*
Watson, David; Charleston, SC, 1732 ***1639.20*** *p313*
Watson, David; North Carolina, 1822 ***1639.20*** *p313*
Watson, David 6; Quebec, 1853 ***5704.8*** *p103*
Watson, David 35; Quebec, 1864 ***5704.8*** *p160*
Watson, Douglas 2 *SEE* Watson, George
Watson, Ebenezer William; New York, NY, 1836 ***8208.4*** *p10*
Watson, Edward; Iowa, 1866-1943 ***123.54*** *p51*
Watson, Edward 34; Quebec, 1864 ***5704.8*** *p162*
Watson, Eliza 12; Quebec, 1849 ***5704.8*** *p51*
Watson, Eliza 12; Quebec, 1853 ***5704.8*** *p103*
Watson, Eliza 14; Massachusetts, 1850 ***5881.1*** *p96*
Watson, Elizabeth *SEE* Watson, John
Watson, Elizabeth; Savannah, GA, 1770 ***1219.7*** *p145*
Watson, Elizabeth 7; Quebec, 1864 ***5704.8*** *p160*
Watson, Elizabeth 13; Pennsylvania, 1736 ***3690.1*** *p238*
Watson, Elona; Philadelphia, 1852 ***5704.8*** *p92*
Watson, Fanny 24; Philadelphia, 1858 ***5704.8*** *p139*
Watson, Francis 18; Annapolis, N.S., 1775 ***1219.7*** *p262*
Watson, Frank L. 28; Kansas, 1897 ***5240.1*** *p47*
Watson, Frank L. 28; Kansas, 1897 ***5240.1*** *p80*
Watson, George; Quebec, 1853 ***5704.8*** *p104*
Watson, George 20; Maryland, 1724 ***3690.1*** *p238*
Watson, George 29; Maryland, 1775 ***1219.7*** *p268*
Watson, George 36; Georgia, 1775 ***1219.7*** *p276*
*Wife:*Mary 33
*Child:*Thomas 12
*Child:*Isabella 10
*Child:*Mary 5
*Child:*Douglas 2
Watson, George Stephen; New York, 1753 ***3652*** *p77*
*Wife:*Susan
Watson, Hamilton 12; Quebec, 1850 ***5704.8*** *p62*
Watson, Helen 2; Quebec, 1864 ***5704.8*** *p162*
Watson, Henry; Virginia, 1645 ***6219*** *p252*
Watson, Hugh; Quebec, 1853 ***5704.8*** *p103*
Watson, Isaac 10; Quebec, 1853 ***5704.8*** *p103*
Watson, Isabella; Quebec, 1853 ***5704.8*** *p104*
Watson, Isabella; Quebec, 1855 ***5704.8*** *p125*
Watson, Isabella 10 *SEE* Watson, George
Watson, J.; South Carolina, 1739 ***1639.20*** *p313*
Watson, Jacob 18; Pennsylvania, 1728 ***3690.1*** *p238*
Watson, James; Baltimore, 1811 ***2859.11*** *p20*
Watson, James; Charleston, SC, 1807 ***1639.20*** *p313*
Watson, James; New York, NY, 1816 ***2859.11*** *p44*
Watson, James; New York, NY, 1838 ***8208.4*** *p61*
Watson, James; Washington, 1859-1920 ***2872.1*** *p42*
Watson, James 6; Quebec, 1853 ***5704.8*** *p104*
Watson, James 9; Quebec, 1864 ***5704.8*** *p160*
Watson, James 50; Charleston, SC, 1850 ***1639.20*** *p313*
Watson, James 50; Quebec, 1855 ***5704.8*** *p124*
Watson, Jane 11; Quebec, 1856 ***5704.8*** *p130*
Watson, Jane 45; Quebec, 1855 ***5704.8*** *p124*
Watson, John; America, 1863 ***5240.1*** *p47*
Watson, John; Charleston, SC, 1782 ***1639.20*** *p313*
Watson, John; Maryland, 1750 ***3690.1*** *p238*
Watson, John; North Carolina, 1809 ***1639.20*** *p313*
Watson, John; Ohio, 1840 ***9892.11*** *p47*
Watson, John; Quebec, 1852 ***5704.8*** *p90*
Watson, John; Quebec, 1852 ***5704.8*** *p94*
Watson, John; Virginia, 1635 ***6219*** *p35*
*Wife:*Elizabeth
Watson, John; Virginia, 1648 ***6219*** *p251*
Watson, John 13; Quebec, 1856 ***5704.8*** *p130*
Watson, John 16; Philadelphia, 1861 ***5704.8*** *p149*
Watson, John 18; Quebec, 1853 ***5704.8*** *p105*
Watson, John 23; Jamaica, 1733 ***3690.1*** *p238*
Watson, John 27; Windward Islands, 1722 ***3690.1*** *p238*
Watson, John 33; North America, 1774 ***1219.7*** *p199*
Watson, John, Jr.; Charleston, SC, 1656-1756 ***1639.20*** *p313*
Watson, John, Jr.; South Carolina, 1748 ***1639.20*** *p313*
Watson, Joseph; Quebec, 1852 ***5704.8*** *p94*
Watson, Joseph 16; Quebec, 1856 ***5704.8*** *p130*
Watson, Joseph 28; Kansas, 1888 ***5240.1*** *p72*
Watson, Lewis R.; Iowa, 1866-1943 ***123.54*** *p51*
Watson, Margaret 4; St. John, N.B., 1864 ***5704.8*** *p159*
Watson, Margaret 24; Massachusetts, 1860 ***6410.32*** *p101*
Watson, Margaret 24; Philadelphia, 1861 ***5704.8*** *p149*
Watson, Margaret 28; Quebec, 1864 ***5704.8*** *p162*
Watson, Martha; Quebec, 1849 ***5704.8*** *p51*
Watson, Mary; New York, NY, 1864 ***5704.8*** *p169*
Watson, Mary; Quebec, 1853 ***5704.8*** *p103*
Watson, Mary 5 *SEE* Watson, George
Watson, Mary 33 *SEE* Watson, George
Watson, Mary Ann 6; St. John, N.B., 1864 ***5704.8*** *p159*
Watson, Nicholas 15; Montreal, 1775 ***1219.7*** *p258*
Watson, Peter 42; Maryland, 1775 ***1219.7*** *p257*
Watson, Prudence; Philadelphia, 1864 ***5704.8*** *p180*
Watson, Rebecca; New York, NY, 1864 ***5704.8*** *p187*
Watson, Rebecca; Philadelphia, 1847 ***53.26*** *p90*
Watson, Rebecca; Philadelphia, 1847 ***5704.8*** *p22*
Watson, Rebecca; Philadelphia, 1851 ***5704.8*** *p71*
Watson, Rebecca 15; Quebec, 1855 ***5704.8*** *p124*
Watson, Robert; Arkansas, 1918 ***95.2*** *p129*
Watson, Robert; Ohio, 1840 ***9892.11*** *p47*
Watson, Robert; Quebec, 1850 ***5704.8*** *p62*
Watson, Robert 8; Quebec, 1849 ***5704.8*** *p51*
Watson, Robert 8; Quebec, 1853 ***5704.8*** *p103*
Watson, Robert 10; Quebec, 1850 ***5704.8*** *p62*
Watson, Robert 12; Quebec, 1855 ***5704.8*** *p124*
Watson, Robert 26; Jamaica, 1731 ***3690.1*** *p239*
Watson, Robert 28; Maryland, 1774 ***1219.7*** *p230*
Watson, Samll.; Virginia, 1635 ***6219*** *p70*
Watson, Samuel; New York, NY, 1838 ***8208.4*** *p61*
Watson, Samuel 6; Quebec, 1849 ***5704.8*** *p51*
Watson, Samuel 17; Quebec, 1855 ***5704.8*** *p125*
Watson, Sarah; Quebec, 1850 ***5704.8*** *p62*
Watson, Sarah Ann; Quebec, 1849 ***5704.8*** *p56*
Watson, Susan *SEE* Watson, George Stephen
Watson, Thomas; America, 1871 ***1450.2*** *p154A*
Watson, Thomas 12 *SEE* Watson, George
Watson, Thomas 28; Massachusetts, 1860 ***6410.32*** *p101*
Watson, Thomas 31; Massachusetts, 1847 ***5881.1*** *p98*
Watson, William; America, 1737 ***4971*** *p71*
Watson, William; Died enroute, 1756 ***1219.7*** *p44*
Watson, William; New York, NY, 1815 ***2859.11*** *p44*
Watson, William; Quebec, 1849 ***5704.8*** *p51*
Watson, William 6; Quebec, 1864 ***5704.8*** *p162*
Watson, William 10; Quebec, 1849 ***5704.8*** *p51*
Watson, William 16; Maryland, 1730 ***3690.1*** *p292*
Watson, William 16; St. John, N.B., 1866 ***5704.8*** *p167*
Watson, William 18; Maryland, 1719 ***3690.1*** *p239*
Watson, William 18; Maryland, 1729 ***3690.1*** *p239*
Watson, William 20; Maryland, 1729 ***3690.1*** *p239*
Watson, William 26; Grenada, 1775 ***1219.7*** *p280*
Watson, Wm; America, 1703 ***2212*** *p39*
Watt, Alexander; Charleston, SC, 1803 ***1639.20*** *p313*
Watt, Alexander 26; Arkansas, 1918 ***95.2*** *p129*
Watt, Arthur; Philadelphia, 1847 ***53.26*** *p90*
*Relative:*Peggy Ann
*Relative:*Betty Ann 2
Watt, Arthur; Philadelphia, 1847 ***5704.8*** *p13*
Watt, Betty Ann 2 *SEE* Watt, Arthur
Watt, Betty Ann 2; Philadelphia, 1847 ***5704.8*** *p13*
Watt, James; Arkansas, 1918 ***95.2*** *p129*
Watt, James; Charleston, SC, 1711-1811 ***1639.20*** *p314*
Watt, James; New York, NY, 1811 ***2859.11*** *p20*
Watt, James; New York, NY, 1816 ***2859.11*** *p44*
Watt, James; Philadelphia, 1847 ***53.26*** *p91*
Watt, James; Philadelphia, 1847 ***5704.8*** *p5*
Watt, James 52; Kansas, 1892 ***5240.1*** *p77*
Watt, Jane; New York, NY, 1811 ***2859.11*** *p20*
Watt, Jane; Philadelphia, 1852 ***5704.8*** *p85*
Watt, Jane; Philadelphia, 1853 ***5704.8*** *p102*
Watt, John; Arizona, 1898 ***9228.30*** *p6*
Watt, John; Arkansas, 1918 ***95.2*** *p129*
Watt, John; Philadelphia, 1811 ***2859.11*** *p20*
With family
Watt, John; Philadelphia, 1865 ***5704.8*** *p198*
Watt, Margaret; New York, NY, 1811 ***2859.11*** *p20*
Watt, Mary; Philadelphia, 1868 ***5704.8*** *p226*
Watt, Mary 25; Massachusetts, 1847 ***5881.1*** *p97*
Watt, Mary 28; Philadelphia, 1861 ***5704.8*** *p148*
Watt, Mary Jane; Philadelphia, 1865 ***5704.8*** *p198*
Watt, Mary Jane 25; St. John, N.B., 1863 ***5704.8*** *p155*
Watt, Peggy Ann *SEE* Watt, Arthur
Watt, Peggy Ann; Philadelphia, 1847 ***5704.8*** *p13*
Watt, Rachel 7; Philadelphia, 1865 ***5704.8*** *p198*
Watt, Robert; Philadelphia, 1849 ***53.26*** *p91*
*Relative:*William
Watt, Robert; Philadelphia, 1849 ***5704.8*** *p52*
Watt, Robert; Quebec, 1850 ***5704.8*** *p63*
Watt, Samuel 17; Philadelphia, 1864 ***5704.8*** *p156*
Watt, Tho.; Virginia, 1636 ***6219*** *p19*
Watt, Thomas; Philadelphia, 1853 ***5704.8*** *p102*
Watt, William *SEE* Watt, Robert
Watt, William; Philadelphia, 1849 ***5704.8*** *p52*
Wattenstron, Peter 55; Kansas, 1874 ***5240.1*** *p55*
Watter, Peter; Virginia, 1641 ***6219*** *p184*
Watters, Mary; Philadelphia, 1853 ***5704.8*** *p101*
Watters, Mary 20; Philadelphia, 1861 ***5704.8*** *p147*
Watters, Patrick; Philadelphia, 1851 ***5704.8*** *p81*
Watterson, John; America, 1743 ***4971*** *p69*
Wattier, Achelle; Iowa, 1866-1943 ***123.54*** *p51*
Wattin, John; Virginia, 1636 ***6219*** *p80*
Wattis, John; Virginia, 1639 ***6219*** *p154*
Wattkins, Phillip; Virginia, 1647 ***6219*** *p245*
Wattkins, Thomas; Virginia, 1647 ***6219*** *p243*
Watton, Thomas; Jamaica, 1756 ***1219.7*** *p46*
Watton, Thomas; Virginia, 1639 ***6219*** *p152*
Watton, Thomas 22; Baltimore, 1775 ***1219.7*** *p270*
Watts, Charles; Philadelphia, 1816 ***2859.11*** *p44*
Watts, Christo., Jr.; Virginia, 1636 ***6219*** *p76*
Watts, Christopher, Sr.; Virginia, 1636 ***6219*** *p76*
Watts, Edward; Virginia, 1640 ***6219*** *p184*
Watts, Elizabeth 19; Virginia, 1727 ***3690.1*** *p238*
Watts, George 41; Kansas, 1884 ***5240.1*** *p65*
Watts, James; Philadelphia, 1816 ***2859.11*** *p44*
Watts, Jane; Philadelphia, 1816 ***2859.11*** *p44*
Watts, Jer.; Virginia, 1638 ***6219*** *p180*
Watts, Jeremiah; Virginia, 1636 ***6219*** *p76*
Watts, John; Arizona, 1897 ***9228.30*** *p3*
Watts, John 22; Philadelphia, 1774 ***1219.7*** *p232*
Watts, Joseph; Philadelphia, 1816 ***2859.11*** *p44*
Watts, Joseph 18; Maryland, 1739 ***3690.1*** *p238*
Watts, Lyddia *SEE* Watts, Thomas
Watts, Margaret; Iowa, 1866-1943 ***123.54*** *p83*
Watts, Margaret; Philadelphia, 1816 ***2859.11*** *p44*
Watts, Mary; Philadelphia, 1816 ***2859.11*** *p44*
Watts, Richard; Virginia, 1642 ***6219*** *p196*
Watts, Tho.; Virginia, 1642 ***6219*** *p199*
Watts, Thomas; Virginia, 1636 ***6219*** *p73*
*Wife:*Lyddia
Watts, William; Virginia, 1638 ***6219*** *p122*
With wife
Watts, William 23; Maryland, 1774 ***1219.7*** *p220*
Watts, William 24; Kansas, 1884 ***5240.1*** *p65*
Watts, William 56; Kansas, 1892 ***5240.1*** *p77*
Watts, William Henry 22; Kansas, 1896 ***5240.1*** *p47*
Watts, Wm.; Virginia, 1638 ***6219*** *p120*
Wattsher, John; New York, NY, 1811 ***2859.11*** *p20*
Wattson, John; Maryland, 1750 ***3690.1*** *p238*

Wattson, Nicholas; Virginia, 1638 ***6219*** *p181*
Wattson, William 18; Maryland, 1729 ***3690.1*** *p239*
Watty, William; Virginia, 1637 ***6219*** *p86*
Wattys, Wm.; Virginia, 1635 ***6219*** *p70*
Watzlauck, Ludwig 38; Kansas, 1896 ***5240.1*** *p47*
Watzlauck, Ludwig 38; Kansas, 1896 ***5240.1*** *p80*
Watzlavek, William 32; Kansas, 1901 ***5240.1*** *p47*
Watzlaw, William 32; Kansas, 1901 ***5240.1*** *p82*
Waugh, Mr.; Quebec, 1815 ***9229.18*** *p75*
Waugh, Elizabeth *SEE* Waugh, Sarah
Waugh, Elizabeth; Philadelphia, 1848 ***5704.8*** *p46*
Waugh, Henry 24; Massachusetts, 1850 ***5881.1*** *p97*
Waugh, James; Quebec, 1851 ***5704.8*** *p73*
Waugh, Mary; St. John, N.B., 1851 ***5704.8*** *p72*
Waugh, Sarah; Philadelphia, 1848 ***53.26*** *p91*
*Relative:*Elizabeth
Waugh, Sarah; Philadelphia, 1848 ***5704.8*** *p46*
Waugh, Wellwood; Prince Edward Island, 1774-1775 ***9775.5*** *p210*
Waugh, William; America, 1738 ***4971*** *p66*
Waus, John; Wisconsin, n.d. ***9675.8*** *p124*
Wauters, Fransisus; Iowa, 1866-1943 ***123.54*** *p51*
Waxell, Tobias; Virginia, 1636 ***6219*** *p22*
Way, Edward; Ohio, 1844 ***9892.11*** *p47*
Way, George; Virginia, 1623-1648 ***6219*** *p252*
Way, John; Virginia, 1636 ***6219*** *p7*
Way, Lawrence; New York, 1836 ***8208.4*** *p60*
Way, Rebecca 20; Jamaica, 1750 ***3690.1*** *p239*
Waydmann, Johann; Philadelphia, 1729 ***2854*** *p43*
Waydmann, Johann; Philadelphia, 1729 ***2854*** *p45*
With wife
With daughter
With son
With daughter 8
Waylett, William 20; Virginia, 1721 ***3690.1*** *p239*
Waymer, John; South Carolina, 1788 ***7119*** *p198*
Wayne, Amy *SEE* Wayne, John
Wayne, John; Virginia, 1638 ***6219*** *p120*
*Wife:*Amy
Wayne, John; Virginia, 1648 ***6219*** *p252*
Wayrerynen, Antti; Washington, 1859-1920 ***2872.1*** *p42*
Wayryn, Alli; Washington, 1859-1920 ***2872.1*** *p42*
Wayryn, Andrew Elmer; Washington, 1859-1920 ***2872.1*** *p42*
Wayryn, Antti; Washington, 1859-1920 ***2872.1*** *p42*
Wayryn, Arne Edward; Washington, 1859-1920 ***2872.1*** *p42*
Wayryn, Eava Tyne; Washington, 1859-1920 ***2872.1*** *p42*
Wayryn, Eeli; Washington, 1859-1920 ***2872.1*** *p42*
Wayryn, Ida; Washington, 1859-1920 ***2872.1*** *p42*
Wayrynen, Eli; Washington, 1859-1920 ***2872.1*** *p42*
Wayrynen, Imbi Wieno; Washington, 1859-1920 ***2872.1*** *p42*
Wayrynen, Sarah; Washington, 1859-1920 ***2872.1*** *p42*
Wazac, Frank; Wisconsin, n.d. ***9675.8*** *p124*
Weaber, Francis, Jr.; Indiana, 1854 ***1450.2*** *p155A*
Weadley, John; Jamaica, 1751 ***1219.7*** *p1*
Wealer, Henry; Philadelphia, 1763 ***9973.7*** *p39*
Wealth, Peter; Charleston, SC, 1775-1781 ***8582.2*** *p52*
Weaner, William; Virginia, 1623 ***6219*** *p30*
Weapher, Ann; New York, NY, 1811 ***2859.11*** *p20*
Weare, Tho.; Virginia, 1637 ***6219*** *p11*
Wearter, John 18; Jamaica, 1730 ***3690.1*** *p239*
Weasel, William; Illinois, 1856 ***7857*** *p8*
Weast, Fisankin 22; New Orleans, 1838 ***778.5*** *p543*
Weast, Theress 26; New Orleans, 1838 ***778.5*** *p543*
Weather, Nich.; Virginia, 1647 ***6219*** *p245*
Weatherfield, John 20; Virginia, 1773 ***1219.7*** *p169*
Weatherley, Thomas 21; Virginia, 1773 ***1219.7*** *p168*
Weathers, Joseph; New York, NY, 1816 ***2859.11*** *p44*
Weatherspoon, David 23; Georgia, 1775 ***1219.7*** *p277*
Weatherton, William 21; Maryland, 1774 ***1219.7*** *p213*
Weaver, Conrad; Philadelphia, 1759 ***9973.7*** *p34*
Weaver, Fred, Sr. 71; Washington, 1918-1920 ***1728.5*** *p16*
Weaver, George 16; Maryland, 1725 ***3690.1*** *p239*
Weaver, Isaac; Virginia, 1652 ***6251*** *p19*
Weaver, Jacob; New York, 1831-1832 ***9892.11*** *p47*
Weaver, Jacob; New York, 1832 ***9892.11*** *p47*
Weaver, John; Philadelphia, 1757 ***9973.7*** *p33*
Weaver, John; Virginia, 1642 ***6219*** *p186*
Weaver, Jon.; Virginia, 1635 ***6219*** *p71*
Weaver, Joseph; Indiana, 1836 ***9117*** *p15*
Weaver, Mary 20; Virginia, 1749 ***3690.1*** *p239*
Weaver, Mathias; Philadelphia, 1760 ***9973.7*** *p34*
Weaver, Peter; Baltimore, 1833 ***9892.11*** *p47*
Weaver, Peter; Ohio, 1839 ***9892.11*** *p48*
Webb, Alice; Virginia, 1639 ***6219*** *p156*
Webb, Alice; Virginia, 1639 ***6219*** *p158*
Webb, Arnold William; Iowa, 1866-1943 ***123.54*** *p51*
Webb, Clare *SEE* Webb, Stephen
Webb, Edmund 16; Maryland, 1724 ***3690.1*** *p239*
Webb, Edward; Virginia, 1647 ***6219*** *p247*
Webb, Eliza; Virginia, 1642 ***6219*** *p197*
Webb, Giles; Virginia, 1646 ***6219*** *p240*
Webb, Henry 55; California, 1873 ***2769.10*** *p6*
Webb, Is. 24; Maryland, 1774 ***1219.7*** *p184*
Webb, Jacob 22; Massachusetts, 1849 ***5881.1*** *p97*
Webb, James Alonzo; California, 1859 ***2769.9*** *p4*
Webb, Job 26; Kansas, 1884 ***5240.1*** *p65*
Webb, John; New York, NY, 1836 ***8208.4*** *p11*
Webb, John 16; Jamaica, 1729 ***3690.1*** *p239*
Webb, John 21; Virginia, 1773 ***1219.7*** *p171*
Webb, Mary; Virginia, 1639 ***6219*** *p157*
Webb, Michael; Virginia, 1646 ***6219*** *p235*
Webb, Peter 39; Maryland, 1774 ***1219.7*** *p196*
Webb, Richard; Virginia, 1643 ***6219*** *p207*
Webb, Richard 20; Jamaica, 1720 ***3690.1*** *p239*
Webb, Richd.; Virginia, 1646 ***6219*** *p243*
Webb, Richd 16; America, 1702 ***2212*** *p37*
Webb, Robert *SEE* Webb, Stephen
Webb, Robert; Jamaica, 1753 ***1219.7*** *p23*
Webb, Robert; Jamaica, 1753 ***3690.1*** *p239*
Webb, Robert; Philadelphia, 1695 ***4960*** *p154*
Webb, Robert Moore 42; California, 1873 ***2769.10*** *p6*
Webb, Samuel; Iowa, 1866-1943 ***123.54*** *p51*
Webb, Samuel, Jr.; Iowa, 1866-1943 ***123.54*** *p51*
Webb, Silas; America, 1847 ***1450.2*** *p154A*
Webb, Stephen; Virginia, 1635 ***6219*** *p35*
Webb, Stephen; Virginia, 1638 ***6219*** *p148*
*Wife:*Clare
*Son:*Robert
Webb, Tho.; Virginia, 1635 ***6219*** *p1*
Webb, Thomas 29; Virginia, 1728 ***3690.1*** *p240*
Webb, William; Virginia, 1642 ***6219*** *p195*
Webb, William; Virginia, 1642 ***6219*** *p197*
Webb, William; Virginia, 1643 ***6219*** *p23*
Webb, William 21; Jamaica, 1730 ***3690.1*** *p292*
Webber, Christian Frederick; America, 1837 ***1450.2*** *p154A*
Webber, Elizabeth 7; Louisiana, 1833 ***778.5*** *p543*
Webber, Elizabeth 46; Louisiana, 1833 ***778.5*** *p543*
Webber, George 21; Maryland, 1774 ***1219.7*** *p204*
Webber, Henry 25; Philadelphia, 1774 ***1219.7*** *p175*
Webber, John; Virginia, 1635 ***6219*** *p27*
Webber, John 21; Philadelphia, 1774 ***1219.7*** *p216*
Webber, Nicolas 27; America, 1836 ***778.5*** *p543*
Webber, Rich.; Virginia, 1635 ***6219*** *p26*
Webelmesser, Charles; Illinois, 1866 ***2896.5*** *p41*
Weber, . . .; America, n.d. ***8582.3*** *p79*
Weber, . . .; Canada, 1776-1783 ***9786*** *p36*
Weber, Captain; Cincinnati, 1816 ***8582.3*** *p89*
Weber, Miss; Pennsylvania, 1748 ***2444*** *p167*
Weber, Albert; Wisconsin, n.d. ***9675.8*** *p124*
Weber, Amalia 12; New Orleans, 1839 ***9420.2*** *p360*
Weber, Andreas; New York, NY, 1838 ***8208.4*** *p68*
Weber, Andrew; New York, 1750 ***3652*** *p74*
Weber, Anna *SEE* Weber, Hans Martin
Weber, Anna Barbara *SEE* Weber, Hans Martin
Weber, Anna Magdalena *SEE* Weber, Hans Martin
Weber, Anna Margaretha Elb *SEE* Weber, Jonas
Weber, Anna Maria *SEE* Weber, Jonas
Weber, Anna Maria; Pennsylvania, 1752 ***2444*** *p213*
Weber, Anna Maria Gajer *SEE* Weber, Hans Martin
Weber, Anthony Frederick; America, 1840 ***1450.2*** *p154A*
Weber, Anton 26; Kansas, 1882 ***5240.1*** *p47*
Weber, Anton 26; Kansas, 1882 ***5240.1*** *p63*
Weber, Arnold; New York, NY, 1891 ***3455.2*** *p97*
Weber, Barbe 25; America, 1839 ***778.5*** *p543*
Weber, Bernhard 30; Kansas, 1882 ***5240.1*** *p47*
Weber, Bernhard 30; Kansas, 1882 ***5240.1*** *p63*
Weber, Burkhard; Wisconsin, n.d. ***9675.8*** *p124*
Weber, Carl; Illinois, 1886 ***2896.5*** *p41*
Weber, Carl Albert; New York, NY, 1897 ***3455.2*** *p74*
Weber, Carl Albert; New York, NY, 1897 ***3455.3*** *p50*
Weber, Chatrine 21; New Orleans, 1838 ***778.5*** *p543*
Weber, Christian 5 *SEE* Weber, John Christoph
Weber, Christiane 17; New Orleans, 1839 ***9420.2*** *p360*
Weber, Christoph; Wisconsin, n.d. ***9675.8*** *p124*
Weber, Conrad; America, 1848 ***8582.3*** *p69*
Weber, Conrad Hieronymus; New York, NY, 1837 ***8208.4*** *p46*
Weber, Daniel; America, 1750 ***4349*** *p48*
*Brother:*Georg
*Brother:*Jacob
Weber, Daniel; Illinois, 1886 ***2896.5*** *p41*
Weber, David; Cincinnati, 1828 ***8582.1*** *p51*
Weber, Dorothea 51 *SEE* Weber, John Christoph
Weber, Edward; Wisconsin, n.d. ***9675.8*** *p124*
Weber, Edward 33; Kansas, 1893 ***5240.1*** *p78*
Weber, Elisabetha *SEE* Weber, Jonas
Weber, Florenz; Akron, OH, 1835 ***8582.1*** *p49*
With parents
Weber, Francis, Jr.; Indiana, 1854 ***1450.2*** *p155A*
Weber, Fredk. Wm. 22; New Orleans, 1839 ***9420.2*** *p360*
Weber, Friederich; America, 1830 ***8582.2*** *p61*
Weber, Friederich; America, 1840 ***8582.3*** *p69*
Weber, Friedrich; Columbus, OH, 1869-1887 ***8582*** *p34*
Weber, Georg *SEE* Weber, Daniel
Weber, Georg; Cincinnati, 1869-1887 ***8582*** *p34*
Weber, Georg Heinrich; New York, NY, 1836 ***8208.4*** *p17*
Weber, George; Canada, 1776-1783 ***9786*** *p207A*
Weber, Gottfried; Cincinnati, 1869-1887 ***8582*** *p34*
Weber, Hans Jerg *SEE* Weber, Jonas
Weber, Hans Martin *SEE* Weber, Hans Martin
Weber, Hans Martin; Pennsylvania, 1749-1773 ***2444*** *p231*
Weber, Hans Martin; Port uncertain, 1748-1800 ***2444*** *p231*
*Wife:*Anna Maria Gajer
*Child:*Hans Martin
*Child:*Anna Barbara
*Child:*Anna Magdalena
*Child:*Anna
Weber, Heinr. 77; New York, NY, 1904 ***1763*** *p40D*
Weber, Heinrich; America, 1851 ***8582.3*** *p69*
Weber, Hermann, Family; New York, 1882 ***3702.7*** *p476*
Weber, Jacob *SEE* Weber, Daniel
Weber, Jacob; Philadelphia, 1749 ***4349*** *p48*
Weber, Jacob 55; Kansas, 1884 ***5240.1*** *p66*
Weber, Jacob P.; Illinois, 1872 ***5012.39*** *p25*
Weber, Joh. 16; New Orleans, 1839 ***9420.2*** *p168*
Weber, Johann; America, 1840 ***8582.3*** *p69*
Weber, Johann; Ohio, 1818 ***8582.1*** *p47*
Weber, Johann Conrad *SEE* Weber, Jonas
Weber, Johann Daniel; Philadelphia, 1749 ***4349*** *p48*
Weber, Johann L.; America, 1843 ***8582.1*** *p35*
Weber, Johann Martin *SEE* Weber, Jonas
Weber, Johannes; Philadelphia, 1749 ***4349*** *p48*
Weber, John; Wisconsin, n.d. ***9675.8*** *p124*
Weber, John 21; Illinois, 1884 ***2896.5*** *p41*
Weber, John 58; Kansas, 1889 ***5240.1*** *p74*
Weber, John Christoph 46; New Orleans, 1839 ***9420.2*** *p358*
*Wife:*Dorothea 51
*Son:*Christian 5
Weber, Jonas; New England, 1753 ***2444*** *p231*
*Wife:*Anna Margaretha Elb
*Child:*Maria Catharina
*Child:*Johann Martin
*Child:*Johann Conrad
*Child:*Anna Maria
*Child:*Elisabetha
*Child:*Hans Jerg
Weber, Joseph; Arkansas, 1918 ***95.2*** *p129*
Weber, Joseph 54; Arizona, 1890 ***2764.35*** *p72*
Weber, Lena *SEE* Weber, Theodore Oscar
Weber, Lena *SEE* Weber, Theodore Oscar
Weber, Louis 15; New Orleans, 1839 ***9420.2*** *p360*
Weber, Ludwig; America, 1735 ***4480*** *p312*
Weber, Maria Barbara; Pennsylvania, 1717 ***3627*** *p10*
Weber, Maria Catharina *SEE* Weber, Jonas
Weber, Maria Hammel 62; America, 1895 ***1763*** *p40D*
Weber, Martin 51; Kansas, 1893 ***5240.1*** *p79*
Weber, Michael; New England, 1766 ***2854*** *p45*
With wife
With 3 children
Weber, Michel 30; America, 1835 ***778.5*** *p543*
Weber, Paul; New York, NY, 1882 ***1450.2*** *p41B*
Weber, Peter; Illinois, 1902 ***5012.40*** *p79*
Weber, Peter; Wisconsin, n.d. ***9675.8*** *p124*
Weber, Peter 40; Kansas, 1900 ***5240.1*** *p81*
Weber, Philip; Philadelphia, 1763 ***9973.7*** *p38*
Weber, Philip; Virginia, 1855 ***4626.16*** *p15*
Weber, Sophia 19; New Orleans, 1839 ***9420.2*** *p360*
Weber, Stephan; Ohio, 1816 ***8582.1*** *p47*
Weber, Theodore Oscar; New York, NY, 1906 ***3455.1*** *p52*
*Wife:*Lena
Weber, Theodore Oscar; New York, NY, 1906 ***3455.3*** *p16*
*Wife:*Lena
Weber, Valentin; Philadelphia, 1749 ***4349*** *p48*
Weber, Wilhelm; Illinois, 1833 ***8582*** *p34*
Weber, Wladislawa Telesinska 31; New York, 1912 ***9980.29*** *p49*
Weblin, Henry; Virginia, 1635 ***6219*** *p68*
Webster, Charles; America, 1697 ***2212*** *p8*
Webster, Charles 36; Quebec, 1774 ***1219.7*** *p226*
*Wife:*Jenna 33
With 3 children
Webster, David; Virginia, 1767 ***1219.7*** *p127*
Webster, Francis; Jamaica, 1756 ***1219.7*** *p43*
Webster, Francis; Jamaica, 1756 ***3690.1*** *p240*
Webster, Francis; Virginia, 1638 ***6219*** *p24*
Webster, Francis; Virginia, 1638 ***6219*** *p119*
Webster, Francis; Virginia, 1639 ***6219*** *p151*
Webster, Georges; Quebec, 1792 ***7603*** *p35*

Webster, Henry C.; Illinois, 1890 *5012.39 p53*
Webster, James 22; Norfolk, VA, 1774 *1219.7 p222*
Webster, Jenna 33 SEE Webster, Charles
Webster, Jno; Maryland or Virginia, 1697-1707 *2212 p3*
Webster, John; South Carolina, 1788 *7119 p199*
Webster, John 25; Nova Scotia, 1774 *1219.7 p194*
Webster, John H.; Illinois, 1905 *5012.39 p53*
Webster, Joseph 19; Philadelphia, 1774 *1219.7 p175*
Webster, Mary 20; Maryland, 1774 *1219.7 p206*
    With 3 children
Webster, Mathew 33; Nova Scotia, 1774 *1219.7 p210*
    With wife
    With 3 children
Webster, Nath.; Virginia, 1642 *6219 p198*
Webster, Nathaniel 20; Jamaica, 1774 *1219.7 p178*
Webster, Richard; Virginia, 1642 *6219 p187*
Webster, Roger; Virginia, 1642 *6219 p196*
Webster, Susan; Virginia, 1642 *6219 p196*
Webster, Susan; Virginia, 1646 *6219 p236*
Webster, Tho.; Virginia, 1642 *6219 p196*
Webster, Thomas; New York, NY, 1815 *2859.11 p44*
Webster, Thomas; Quebec, 1814 *7603 p24*
Webster, Thomas; Quebec, 1815 *9229.18 p80*
    With wife
Webster, Thomas 50; Philadelphia, 1774 *1219.7 p223*
Webster, William 23; Maryland, 1773 *1219.7 p173*
Webster, William 33; Nova Scotia, 1774 *1219.7 p209*
Wechel, Anna Catharina SEE Wechel, Hans Michel
Wechel, Hans Michel; New York, 1709 *3627 p5*
    Wife:Anna Catharina
    Child:Maria Catharina
    Child:Johann Michael
Wechel, Johann Michael SEE Wechel, Hans Michel
Wechel, Maria Catharina SEE Wechel, Hans Michel
Wecholer, Juda; Virginia, 1855 *1450.2 p155A*
Wechsler, Emanuel; Cincinnati, 1869-1887 *8582 p34*
Wechsler, Juda; Virginia, 1855 *1450.2 p155A*
Wecht, Ad. 18; America, 1853 *9162.7 p15*
Wecht, Anna Margaretha 24; America, 1853 *9162.7 p15*
Wecht, Marg. 26; America, 1853 *9162.7 p15*
Wecht, Michael 17; America, 1853 *9162.7 p15*
Weck, John W.; Wisconsin, n.d. *9675.8 p124*
Weck, Theodor; Wisconsin, n.d. *9675.8 p124*
Weckerle, Emanuel Frederick; Philadelphia, 1760 *9973.7 p34*
Weddell, William 20; Jamaica, 1729 *3690.1 p240*
Weddendorf, Mr.; Cincinnati, 1847 *8582.3 p22*
Wedderburn, James; South Carolina, 1733 *1639.20 p314*
Weddig, . . .; Canada, 1776-1783 *9786 p36*
Weddigen, Theodor Julius Ferdinand; America, 1854 *4610.10 p145*
Weddigen, Theodor Julius Wilhelm; America, 1851 *4610.10 p143*
Wedding, . . .; Canada, 1776-1783 *9786 p36*
Weddingen, August Wilhelm Carl; America, 1854 *4610.10 p145*
Wedekind, Julius; Cincinnati, 1869-1887 *8582 p34*
Wedel, Adam 19; New York, NY, 1862 *9831.18 p16*
Wedeward, John; Wisconsin, n.d. *9675.8 p124*
Wedgewood, Mr.; Quebec, 1815 *9229.18 p76*
Wedkowski, Boloslaw; Arkansas, 1918 *95.2 p129*
Wedsted, Christian; New York, 1753 *3652 p77*
Wee, John Edward; Arkansas, 1918 *95.2 p129*
Weeber, Anna SEE Weeber, Hans Martin
Weeber, Anna Barbara SEE Weeber, Hans Martin
Weeber, Anna Magdalena SEE Weeber, Hans Martin
Weeber, Anna Margaretha Elb SEE Weeber, Jonas
Weeber, Anna Maria SEE Weeber, Jonas
Weeber, Anna Maria Gajer SEE Weeber, Hans Martin
Weeber, Elisabetha SEE Weeber, Jonas
Weeber, Hans Jerg SEE Weeber, Jonas
Weeber, Hans Martin SEE Weeber, Hans Martin
Weeber, Hans Martin; Pennsylvania, 1749-1773 *2444 p231*
Weeber, Hans Martin; Port uncertain, 1748-1800 *2444 p231*
    Wife:Anna Maria Gajer
    Child:Hans Martin
    Child:Anna Barbara
    Child:Anna Magdalena
    Child:Anna
Weeber, Johann Conrad SEE Weeber, Jonas
Weeber, Johann Martin SEE Weeber, Jonas
Weeber, Jonas SEE Weeber, Jonas
Weeber, Jonas; New England, 1753 *2444 p231*
    Wife:Anna Margaretha Elb
    Child:Maria Catharina
    Child:Johann Martin
    Child:Johann Conrad
    Child:Anna Maria
    Child:Elisabetha
    Child:Hans Jerg

Weeber, Jonas; New England, 1753 *2444 p231*
    Wife:Maria Catharina Mauch
    Child:Melchior
    Child:Jonas
Weeber, Maria Catharina SEE Weeber, Jonas
Weeber, Maria Catharina Mauch SEE Weeber, Jonas
Weeber, Melchior SEE Weeber, Jonas
Weed, John; South Carolina, 1788 *7119 p201*
Weeden, Joseph 39; Maryland, 1774 *1219.7 p196*
Weedham, John 16; Virginia, 1774 *1219.7 p241*
Weedon, James 20; Maryland, 1718 *3690.1 p240*
Week, William; Wisconsin, n.d. *9675.8 p124*
Weekes, Elizabeth Beardsty SEE Weekes, Thomas
Weekes, Jeremiah 15; Maryland, 1719 *3690.1 p240*
Weekes, Thomas; Virginia, 1637 *6219 p107*
    Wife:Elizabeth Beardsty
Weekes, Walter; Virginia, 1652 *6251 p20*
Weekes, Wm.; Virginia, 1635 *6219 p26*
Weekman, James 25; Maryland, 1774 *1219.7 p207*
Weeks, Caroline; Philadelphia, 1816 *2859.11 p44*
Weeks, Charles; Philadelphia, 1815 *2859.11 p44*
Weeks, Frances; Philadelphia, 1816 *2859.11 p44*
Weeks, James; New Jersey, 1818 *9892.11 p48*
Weeks, Jane; Philadelphia, 1816 *2859.11 p44*
Weeks, John; Washington, 1859-1920 *2872.1 p42*
Weeks, John 22; Philadelphia, 1774 *1219.7 p228*
Weeks, Jon.; Virginia, 1643 *6219 p205*
Weeks, Thos.; Philadelphia, 1816 *2859.11 p44*
Weer, James 26; New Orleans, 1858 *5704.8 p140*
Weer, Thomas 16; Maryland, 1751 *1219.7 p3*
Weer, Thomas 16; Maryland, 1751 *3690.1 p240*
Weetet, Thomas; America, 1793 *8894.1 p192*
Weftermann, Francois 28; Port uncertain, 1839 *778.5 p544*
Weg, Andras; Pennsylvania, 1752 *2444 p231*
Wege, M. Emil Julius Moritz 38; New Orleans, 1839 *9420.2 p165*
Wegele, Johan Michel; New York, 1715 *3627 p5*
Wegelein, . . .; Canada, 1776-1783 *9786 p36*
Wegelin, . . .; Canada, 1776-1783 *9786 p36*
Wegener, . . .; Canada, 1776-1783 *9786 p36*
Wegener, Anna Marie I. Viering SEE Wegener, Johann Friedrich
Wegener, Anna Marie L. Caroline SEE Wegener, Jobst Heinrich
Wegener, Anne M. L. Charlotte SEE Wegener, Jobst Heinrich
Wegener, Anne Marie Wilhelmine SEE Wegener, Jobst Heinrich
Wegener, Caroline W. Charlotte SEE Wegener, Jobst Heinrich
Wegener, Caspar Heinrich; America, 1854 *4610.10 p145*
Wegener, Catharine W. Louise C. SEE Wegener, Jobst Heinrich
Wegener, Christian; Wisconsin, n.d. *9675.8 p124*
Wegener, Engel; America, 1853 *4610.10 p144*
Wegener, Ernst Friedrich SEE Wegener, Johann Friedrich
Wegener, Gothelf; Wisconsin, n.d. *9675.8 p124*
Wegener, Heinrich F. Wilhelm SEE Wegener, Jobst Heinrich
Wegener, Jobst Heinrich; America, 1845 *4610.10 p150*
    Wife:Marie W. Charlotte
    Child:Anne M. L. Charlotte
    Child:Anne Marie Wilhelmine
    Child:Caroline W. Charlotte
    Child:Catharine W. Louise C.
    Child:Anna Marie L. Caroline
    Child:Heinrich F. Wilhelm
Wegener, Johann Friedrich SEE Wegener, Johann Friedrich
Wegener, Johann Friedrich; America, 1843 *4610.10 p146*
    Wife:Anna Marie I. Viering
    Son:Johann Friedrich
Wegener, Johann Friedrich; America, 1844 *4610.10 p146*
    Wife:Johanne Tacke
    Child:Ernst Friedrich
    Child:Karl Friedrich
Wegener, Johanne Tacke SEE Wegener, Johann Friedrich
Wegener, Karl Friedrich SEE Wegener, Johann Friedrich
Wegener, Luise; America, 1852 *4610.10 p148*
Wegener, Marie W. Charlotte SEE Wegener, Jobst Heinrich
Weger, Anna Barbara SEE Weger, Johann Jacob
Weger, Johann Jacob; New York, 1753 *2444 p231*
    Child:Anna Barbara
    Wife:Maria Magdalena
Weger, John 38; Kansas, 1885 *5240.1 p47*
Weger, John 58; Kansas, 1885 *5240.1 p67*
Weger, Maria Magdalena SEE Weger, Johann Jacob
Wegerer, Gabriel; Kansas, 1881 *5240.1 p47*
Weghorst, Henry; America, 1849 *1450.2 p155A*
Weghorst, William; America, 1852 *1450.2 p155A*
Wegierski, August; New York, 1831 *4606 p178*

Wegler, Mme. 24; New Orleans, 1839 *778.5 p544*
Wegner, Casper; Canada, 1783 *9786 p38A*
Wegner, Charles; Wisconsin, n.d. *9675.8 p124*
Wegner, Fred; Wisconsin, n.d. *9675.8 p124*
Wegner, Fredrick; Wisconsin, n.d. *9675.8 p124*
Wegner, Gotthilf; Wisconsin, n.d. *9675.8 p124*
Wegner, Henry 22; Kansas, 1897 *5240.1 p47*
Wegner, Henry 22; Kansas, 1897 *5240.1 p81*
Wegner, Louis C.; Wisconsin, n.d. *9675.8 p124*
Wegner, William; Wisconsin, n.d. *9675.8 p124*
Wegrich, Charles 29; America, 1838 *778.5 p544*
Weh, Anna Catharina; Pennsylvania, 1751 *2444 p231*
Weh, Catharina SEE Weh, Johann Andreas
Weh, Johann Andreas; Pennsylvania, 1752 *2444 p231*
    Wife:Catharina
Weheli, Georges 21; America, 1838 *778.5 p544*
Wehking, Anne Marie C. Louise 9 SEE Wehking, Carl Heinrich
Wehking, Anne Marie Christine 1 SEE Wehking, Carl Heinrich
Wehking, Carl Heinrich; America, 1853 *4610.10 p144*
    Wife:Engel Wegener
    Child:Anne Marie C. Louise 9
    Child:Christine Louise Engel 3
    Child:Anne Marie Christine 1
Wehking, Charles F.; America, 1872 *1450.2 p41B*
Wehking, Christine Louise Engel 3 SEE Wehking, Carl Heinrich
Wehking, Engel Wegener SEE Wehking, Carl Heinrich
Wehking, Heinrich; Illinois, 1865-1951 *4610.10 p66*
Wehle, Lucas; Buffalo, NY, 1854 *1450.2 p155A*
Wehlhof, Catharina 11 mos; New York, NY, 1889 *7846 p39*
Wehlhof, Jacob 29; New York, NY, 1889 *7846 p39*
Wehlhof, Marie 29; New York, NY, 1889 *7846 p39*
Wehling, . . .; Canada, 1776-1783 *9786 p36*
Wehmeier, Anne Marie F.C. Oesker 40 SEE Wehmeier, Johann Friedrich Wilhelm
Wehmeier, Auguste 9 mos SEE Wehmeier, Johann Friedrich Wilhelm
Wehmeier, Caroline SEE Wehmeier, Johann Friedrich Wilhelm
Wehmeier, Friederike 14 SEE Wehmeier, Johann Friedrich Wilhelm
Wehmeier, Henriette 11 SEE Wehmeier, Johann Friedrich Wilhelm
Wehmeier, Johann Friedrich Wilhelm 45; America, 1882 *4610.10 p123*
    Wife:Anne Marie F.C. Oesker 40
    Child:Caroline
    Child:Friederike 14
    Child:Henriette 11
    Child:Louise 7
    Child:Auguste 9 mos
Wehmeier, Louise 7 SEE Wehmeier, Johann Friedrich Wilhelm
Wehmer, John 66; America, 1895 *1763 p48D*
Wehmeyer, . . .; Canada, 1776-1783 *9786 p36*
Wehmeyer, Anna Marie E. Bertha SEE Wehmeyer, Carl Heinrich
Wehmeyer, Anna Marie E. Scheidt SEE Wehmeyer, Carl Heinrich
Wehmeyer, Anne Marie Hedwig; America, 1844 *4610.10 p115*
Wehmeyer, Anne Marie L. F. Tacke SEE Wehmeyer, Joh. Casp. Heinr.
Wehmeyer, August Friedrich; America, 1872 *4610.10 p149*
Wehmeyer, Carl Friedrich Wilhelm SEE Wehmeyer, Joh. Casp. Heinr.
Wehmeyer, Carl Heinrich SEE Wehmeyer, Carl Heinrich
Wehmeyer, Carl Heinrich; America, 1850 *4610.10 p143*
    Wife:Anna Marie E. Scheidt
    Child:Anna Marie E. Bertha
Wehmeyer, Christine Louise; America, 1844 *4610.10 p111*
Wehmeyer, Heinrich Ludwig Wilhelm; America, 1884 *4610.10 p118*
Wehmeyer, Joh. Casp. Heinr.; America, 1856 *4610.10 p135*
    Wife:Anne Marie L. F. Tacke
    Son:Carl Friedrich Wilhelm
Wehmeyer, Johann Heinrich Gottlieb; America, 1852 *4610.10 p144*
Wehmeyer, Justine Conradine; America, 1881 *4610.10 p122*
Wehmeyer, Reinhold Carl Wilhelm Ludwig; America, 1848 *4610.10 p97*
Wehr, . . .; Canada, 1776-1783 *9786 p36*
Wehrle, Henry; Wisconsin, n.d. *9675.8 p124*
Wehrle, William; Wisconsin, n.d. *9675.8 p124*

Wehrmann, Carl Wilhelm August; America, 1884 4610.10 p118
Wehrmann, L. F.; Cincinnati, 1869-1887 8582 p34
Wehrmann, Wilhelm 36; America, 1882 4610.10 p124
Wehrsch, Anna Eulalia Henn SEE Wehrsch, Johann Matthaeus
Wehrsch, Johann Matthaeus; America, 1750-1752 8125.6 p23
  Wife:Anna Eulalia Henn
Weiapk, Henry; New York, 1855 1450.2 p155A
Weib, Hugo 22; Kansas, 1897 5240.1 p81
Weibell, . . .; Canada, 1776-1783 9786 p36
Weiberg, Magnus; Arkansas, 1918 95.2 p129
Weibert, Carl C.; America, 1837 8582.2 p45
Weich, Ludwig; Washington, 1859-1920 2872.1 p42
Weicher, Peter 27; Kansas, 1895 5240.1 p80
Weicht, Peter; New York, 1753 3652 p77
Weicht, Susanna; New York, 1749 3652 p73
Weicker, Nicholas; Wisconsin, n.d. 9675.8 p124
Weickert, Mrs. Georg; Pennsylvania, 1753-1754 4525 p253
Weickert, Hans Dries; Pennsylvania, 1753 4525 p253
Weickert, Johann Georg; Pennsylvania, 1753 4525 p253
Weidelich, Fredk. Pauline 22; New Orleans, 1839 9420.2 p166
Weideman, Martin Simon; Arkansas, 1918 95.2 p130
Weidemann, Frederick; Colorado, 1888 9678.3 p17
Weidemann, Philipp; Philadelphia, 1779 8137 p15
Weidenmeier, Urban; Pennsylvania, 1764 2444 p233
Weider, Jacob; Ohio, 1799 8582.2 p57
Weider, Michael; Philadelphia, 1765 9973.7 p40
Weidig, Emilie 56; America, 1903 1763 p40D
Weidig, Felix; Wisconsin, n.d. 9675.8 p124
Weidler, John; New York, NY, 1780 8137 p15
Weidmeier, Gabriel 39; West Virginia, 1892 9788.3 p22
Weidmer, B. 24; Port uncertain, 1838 778.5 p544
Weidmer, H. 17; Port uncertain, 1838 778.5 p544
Weiest, Jean 20; America, 1838 778.5 p544
Weiffenbach, Henry 73; America, 1893 1763 p48D
Weigand, . . .; Canada, 1776-1783 9786 p36
Weigant, Casper 24; Kansas, 1884 5240.1 p66
Weigel, Anton 7; New York, NY, 1889 7846 p40
Weigel, Franz 2; New York, NY, 1889 7846 p40
Weigel, Jacob 31; New York, NY, 1889 7846 p40
Weigel, Johannes 63; New York, NY, 1889 7846 p40
Weigel, Magdalena 4; New York, NY, 1889 7846 p40
Weigel, Therese 28; New York, NY, 1889 7846 p40
Weigenger, George; Indiana, 1844 9117 p18
Weightman, Robert; America, 1818 1450.2 p155A
Weigold, Andreas SEE Weigold, Hans Jacob
Weigold, Georg; Ohio, 1869-1887 8582 p34
Weigold, Hans Jacob; Pennsylvania, 1752 2444 p231
  Wife:Lucia
  Child:Johannes
  Child:Andreas
Weigold, Johannes SEE Weigold, Hans Jacob
Weigold, Lucia SEE Weigold, Hans Jacob
Weihe, Ernst Ludwig Eduard; America, 1850 4610.10 p155
Weihe, Moritz; Cincinnati, 1846 8582.1 p35
Weihe, Philipp; America, 1860 4610.10 p158
  With brothers
Weihrauch, Anton 60; New York, NY, 1862 9831.18 p16
Weihrauch, Elise 13; New York, NY, 1862 9831.18 p16
Weihrauch, Kunigunde 50; New York, NY, 1862 9831.18 p16
Weihrauch, Louise 24; New York, NY, 1862 9831.18 p16
Weihrauch, Marie 20; New York, NY, 1862 9831.18 p16
Weihte, . . .; Canada, 1776-1783 9786 p36
Weikers, . . .; Pennsylvania, n.d. 4525 p253
Weikert, Georg; Pennsylvania, 1753 4525 p253
Weikert, Mrs. Georg; Pennsylvania, 1753-1754 4525 p253
Weil, Annette 16; America, 1836 778.5 p544
Weil, Charles; America, 1874 1450.2 p155A
Weil, Franz; America, 1849 8582.2 p45
Weil, Frederick; New York, 1884 1450.2 p41B
Weil, Heinr. A.; New York, NY, 1903 1763 p40D
Weil, Henri 26; America, 1835 778.5 p544
Weil, Henry 25; America, 1836 778.5 p544
Weil, Hermann 35; Harris Co., TX, 1900 6254 p6
Weil, Isadore; Shreveport, LA, 1877 7129 p46
Weil, Jean 30; America, 1836 778.5 p544
Weil, Johann; Cincinnati, 1869-1887 8582 p34
Weiland, . . .; Canada, 1776-1783 9786 p36
Weiland, Charles; America, 1852 1450.2 p155A
Weiland, John W.; Wisconsin, n.d. 9675.8 p124
Weiland, Petriem; Philadelphia, 1760 9973.7 p34
Weiler, Anna Catharina Bengel SEE Weiler, Heinrich
Weiler, Georg Frank; America, 1845 8582.1 p35
Weiler, Heinrich; Port uncertain, 1717 3627 p15
  Wife:Anna Catharina Bengel
  Child:Maria Catharina O.
  Child:Maria Margaretha
  Child:Joh. Jacob
Weiler, Joh. Jacob SEE Weiler, Heinrich
Weiler, Johann; America, 1816 8582.1 p47
Weiler, Johann; America, 1844 8582 p34
Weiler, Johann; Ohio, 1819 8582.1 p47
Weiler, Maria Catharina O. SEE Weiler, Heinrich
Weiler, Maria Margaretha SEE Weiler, Heinrich
Weiler, Michael; America, 1834 8582.1 p35
Weiler, Michael; Wisconsin, n.d. 9675.8 p124
Weiler, Nicholas; Wisconsin, n.d. 9675.8 p124
Weiler, Peter; Wisconsin, n.d. 9675.8 p124
Weilmuth, Franz; New York, NY, 1838 8208.4 p60
Weiman, Valentin 29; Kansas, 1906 5240.1 p84
Weimann, Fred; Iroquois Co., IL, 1896 3455.1 p14
Weimann, Jakob; Ohio, 1824 8582.1 p46
Weimar, Louis 50; America, 1895 1763 p40D
Weimer, Georg; Akron, OH, 1847 8582.1 p49
Weimer, Gottfried; Pennsylvania, 1752 4525 p253
Weimer, Jacob; Pennsylvania, 1751 2444 p177
Weimer, Jacob; Pennsylvania, 1751 2444 p230
Weimer, Jacob 25; America, 1831 778.5 p544
Weimer, Michael; Iroquois Co., IL, 1892 3455.1 p14
Wein, Jean 30; America, 1836 778.5 p544
Weinberger, Miss 43; Philadelphia, 1752 4525 p219
Weinberger, Ernest; America, 1849 1450.2 p156A
Weinberger, L. 30; Kansas, 1888 5240.1 p71
Weinberger, Louis; Kansas, 1888 1450.2 p156A
Weinbrecht Brothers ; Illinois, 1841 8582.2 p50
Weinbrenner, Edward; America, 1892 1450.2 p42B
Weinecke, Carl; New York, 1754 3652 p80
Weineg, Peter Joseph; West Virginia, 1859 9788.3 p22
Weinem, . . .; Canada, 1776-1783 9786 p36
Weiner, Wolko; Arkansas, 1918 95.2 p130
Weinert, John Christopher; New York, 1743 3652 p60
  Wife:M. Dorothea
Weinert, M. Dorothea SEE Weinert, John Christopher
Weinerth, Karl; America, 1901 1450.2 p42B
Weingaertner, Georg Nicolaus; Pennsylvania, 1753 4525 p254
Weingaertner, Joh. Michael; Pennsylvania, 1766 4525 p218
Weingaertner, Johann Georg; Pennsylvania, 1753 4525 p254
  With children
Weingaertner, Lorenz; America, 1828 8582.2 p61
Weingardner, Laurenz; Cincinnati, 1869-1887 8582 p34
Weinhage, Joseph; Kentucky, 1839-1840 8582.3 p99
Weinheimer, Amelia; Washington, 1859-1920 2872.1 p42
Weinheimer, Anton; Cincinnati, 1846 8582.1 p35
Weinheimer, Edward; Washington, 1859-1920 2872.1 p42
Weinheimer, Jacob; Washington, 1859-1920 2872.1 p42
Weinheimer, Louisa; Washington, 1859-1920 2872.1 p42
Weinheimer, Rudolf; Washington, 1859-1920 2872.1 p43
Weinheimer, Susana; Washington, 1859-1920 2872.1 p43
Weinhold, Henry 21; New Orleans, 1839 9420.2 p485
Weinkuber, . . .; Canada, 1776-1783 9786 p36
Weinland, John Nicholas; New York, 1749 3652 p72
Weinmann, Karolina Trier; America, 1891 2691.4 p169
Weinmann, Michael; Port uncertain, 1738 3627 p20
  With wife
  With daughter
Weinner, Marie 25; America, 1854-1855 9162.6 p105
Weinrich, Fritz; Illinois, 1884 2896.5 p41
Weinschenk, Xania 49; Kansas, 1880 5240.1 p61
Weinstock, Abraham 18; New York, NY, 1878 9253 p46
Weintriep, Daniel 21; Port uncertain, 1839 778.5 p544
Weinzopflen, Romain; Indiana, 1848 9117 p19
Weipert, . . .; Canada, 1776-1783 9786 p36
Weipert, Hans Melchior; Pennsylvania, 1754 4525 p254
Weipert, Johan Stephan 19; Pennsylvania, 1805 4525 p254
Weippert, Hans Melchior; Pennsylvania, 1754 4525 p254
Weir, Andrew; Philadelphia, 1763 9973.7 p38
Weir, David; Austin, TX, 1886 9777 p5
Weir, James; New Orleans, 1849 5704.8 p59
Weir, James 14; Philadelphia, 1860 5704.8 p145
Weir, Jane; St. John, N.B., 1848 5704.8 p43
Weir, Joan; Philadelphia, 1852 5704.8 p86
Weir, Mary; Philadelphia, 1847 53.26 p91
Weir, Mary; Philadelphia, 1847 5704.8 p24
Weir, Rebecca 18; St. John, N.B., 1854 5704.8 p115
Weir, Robert; St. John, N.B., 1847 5704.8 p10
Weir, Thomas; St. John, N.B., 1850 5704.8 p65
Weir, William; Illinois, 1876 5012.39 p52
Weir, William; New York, NY, 1849 6013.19 p89
Weir, William John; Philadelphia, 1853 5704.8 p101
Weirich, Georg; Ohio, 1801-1802 8582.2 p55
Weirich, Mathias 29; Kansas, 1892 5240.1 p77
Weis, Carl; America, 1847 8582.1 p35
Weis, George; South Carolina, 1788 7119 p200
Weis, Heinrich, Family; America, 1818-1923 2691.4 p172
Weis, John; America, 1850 1450.2 p156A
Weis, John; Arkansas, 1918 95.2 p130
Weis, John; Wisconsin, n.d. 9675.8 p124
Weis, Joseph; Wisconsin, n.d. 9675.8 p124
Weis, Michael; Wisconsin, n.d. 9675.8 p124
Weise, Carolina 26 SEE Weise, Chas. Gottlob
Weise, Chas. Gottlob 24; New Orleans, 1839 9420.2 p359
  Wife:Carolina 26
  Daughter:Christiane 2
  Daughter:Fredr. 3 mos
Weise, Christiane 2 SEE Weise, Chas. Gottlob
Weise, Fredr. 3 mos SEE Weise, Chas. Gottlob
Weise, John G.; New York, NY, 1833 8208.4 p26
Weise, Matheas; Pennsylvania, 1749 2444 p232
Weisenburger, Anna M. 23; New York, NY, 1898-1899 7846 p39
Weisenburn, Frederick; St. Louis, 1850 6013.19 p89
Weiser, Johann 24; America, 1854-1855 9162.6 p105
Weises, Adelheid 6 mos SEE Weises, Christian
Weises, Auguste 34 SEE Weises, Christian
Weises, Christian 34; New Orleans, 1839 9420.2 p359
  Wife:Auguste 34
  Son:Hermann 5
  Son:Oscar 4
  Son:Moritz 3
  Daughter:Adelheid 6 mos
Weises, Hermann 5 SEE Weises, Christian
Weises, Moritz 3 SEE Weises, Christian
Weises, Oscar 4 SEE Weises, Christian
Weishnsen, Carsten; Colorado, 1904 9678.3 p17
Weismann, Anna Barbara Wagner SEE Weismann, Johannes
Weismann, Anna M. Letsch Maute SEE Weismann, Johannes
Weismann, Christina SEE Weismann, Johannes
Weismann, Christine SEE Weismann, Johannes
Weismann, Georg Philipp SEE Weismann, Johannes
Weismann, Johannes; Pennsylvania, 1747 2444 p232
  Wife:Anna Barbara Wagner
  Child:Christine
Weismann, Johannes; Philadelphia, 1751 2444 p232
  Wife:Anna M. Letsch Maute
  With 5 stepchildren
  Child:Georg Philipp
  Child:Christina
Weiss, . . .; Canada, 1776-1783 9786 p36
Weiss, Anna; Pennsylvania, 1748-1800 2444 p138
Weiss, Anna E. Dinckel SEE Weiss, Johann Philipp
Weiss, Anna Magdalena SEE Weiss, Johannes
Weiss, Catherine 8 SEE Weiss, Christopher
Weiss, Christina Heinrica SEE Weiss, Christina Heinrica
Weiss, Christina Heinrica; Pennsylvania, 1749 2444 p232
  Child:Christina Heinrica
  Child:Johann Christoph
Weiss, Christopher; South Carolina, 1752-1753 3689.17 p23
  With wife
  Relative:John George 14
  Relative:Catherine 8
Weiss, Esther SEE Weiss, Johannes
Weiss, Frederick; New York, NY, 1836 8208.4 p15
Weiss, Georg; New England, 1753 4525 p254
  With wife
  With children
Weiss, George 26; Kansas, 1884 5240.1 p65
Weiss, Henry G.; Wisconsin, n.d. 9675.8 p124
Weiss, Jacob; Pennsylvania, 1844 1450.2 p156A
Weiss, Jacob, Sr.; Pennsylvania, 1749 2444 p232
Weiss, Joerg; Pennsylvania, 1753 4525 p254
Weiss, Johann; Pennsylvania, 1738 7829 p8
Weiss, Johann Christoph SEE Weiss, Christina Heinrica
Weiss, Johann Philipp; Pennsylvania, 1753 4525 p254
  Wife:Anna E. Dinckel
Weiss, Johannes; America, 1749-1800 2444 p231
  Wife:Esther
  Child:Anna Magdalena
Weiss, Johannes; Ohio, 1798-1818 8582.2 p54
Weiss, Johannes; Pennsylvania, 1749 2444 p231
Weiss, Johannes; Pennsylvania, 1754 2444 p231
Weiss, Johannes; Pennsylvania, 1764 2444 p231
Weiss, Johannes; Pennsylvania, 1767 2444 p231
Weiss, John; Canada, 1783 9786 p38A
Weiss, John 21; Kansas, 1883 5240.1 p64
Weiss, John C. 28; Kansas, 1875 5240.1 p56
Weiss, John George 14 SEE Weiss, Christopher
Weiss, Joseph 30; Kansas, 1883 5240.1 p47

Welsh, Honor; America, 1740 ***4971*** *p48*
Welsh, Hugh; New York, NY, 1869 ***5704.8*** *p233*
Welsh, J. 49; America, 1838 ***778.5*** *p546*
Welsh, Jacob; Philadelphia, 1762 ***9973.7*** *p37*
Welsh, Jacques; Quebec, 1819 ***7603*** *p100*
Welsh, James; Philadelphia, 1868 ***5704.8*** *p230*
Welsh, Jane 8; Quebec, 1864 ***5704.8*** *p163*
Welsh, John; New York, NY, 1811 ***2859.11*** *p20*
Welsh, John; New York, NY, 1838 ***8208.4*** *p69*
Welsh, John 9; Massachusetts, 1850 ***5881.1*** *p97*
Welsh, John 13; St. John, N.B., 1848 ***5704.8*** *p45*
Welsh, John 21; Jamaica, 1731 ***3690.1*** *p241*
Welsh, Joseph 30; Massachusetts, 1847 ***5881.1*** *p97*
Welsh, Julia 5; Massachusetts, 1849 ***5881.1*** *p97*
Welsh, Lewis; America, 1737-1738 ***4971*** *p59*
Welsh, Louisa; New York, NY, 1811 ***2859.11*** *p20*
Welsh, Mary; Virginia, 1635 ***6219*** *p69*
Welsh, Mary 1; Massachusetts, 1849 ***5881.1*** *p97*
Welsh, Mary 8; St. John, N.B., 1848 ***5704.8*** *p45*
Welsh, Mary 38; Massachusetts, 1850 ***5881.1*** *p98*
Welsh, Michael; Philadelphia, 1762 ***9973.7*** *p37*
Welsh, Michael 20; Quebec, 1856 ***5704.8*** *p130*
Welsh, Patrick 7; Massachusetts, 1849 ***5881.1*** *p98*
Welsh, Patrick 26; Massachusetts, 1849 ***5881.1*** *p98*
Welsh, Rebecca 32; Quebec, 1864 ***5704.8*** *p163*
Welsh, Redmond 40; Massachusetts, 1849 ***5881.1*** *p98*
Welsh, Richard; America, 1735-1743 ***4971*** *p78*
Welsh, Robert 30; Quebec, 1864 ***5704.8*** *p163*
Welsh, Sarah; Quebec, 1852 ***5704.8*** *p86*
Welsh, Sarah; Quebec, 1852 ***5704.8*** *p91*
Welsh, William; Philadelphia, 1868 ***5704.8*** *p230*
Welsh, William; Quebec, 1822 ***7603*** *p81*
Welsh, William 30; Maryland, 1775 ***1219.7*** *p264*
Welshance, Joseph; Philadelphia, 1760 ***9973.7*** *p34*
Welshe, Robt.; Virginia, 1635 ***6219*** *p12*
Welshofer, Anna C. Schultheis *SEE* Welshofer, Jacob
Welshofer, Anna Catharina *SEE* Welshofer, Jacob
Welshofer, Jacob; Pennsylvania, 1731 ***1034.18*** *p23*
*Wife:*Anna C. Schultheis
*Child:*Johann Lorentz
*Child:*Anna Catharina
*Child:*Johan Jacob
Welshofer, Johan Jacob *SEE* Welshofer, Jacob
Welshofer, Johann Lorentz *SEE* Welshofer, Jacob
Welshover, Anna C. Schultheis *SEE* Welshover, Jacob
Welshover, Anna Catharina *SEE* Welshover, Jacob
Welshover, Jacob; Pennsylvania, 1731 ***1034.18*** *p22*
*Wife:*Anna C. Schultheis
*Child:*Johann Lorentz
*Child:*Anna Catharina
*Child:*Johan Jacob
Welshover, Johan Jacob *SEE* Welshover, Jacob
Welshover, Johann Lorentz *SEE* Welshover, Jacob
Welsly, Margarette 19; America, 1701 ***2212*** *p35*
Welson, Mathew; Virginia, 1639 ***6219*** *p155*
Welsonn, Henry; Virginia, 1641 ***6219*** *p184*
Welss, Margaret C. Firnhaber *SEE* Welss, Matthias
Welss, Matthias; America, 1753 ***4525*** *p216*
*Wife:*Margaret C. Firnhaber
Weltch, H.; New York, NY, 1811 ***2859.11*** *p20*
Welter, Christian; Wisconsin, n.d. ***9675.8*** *p124*
Welter, John; Wisconsin, n.d. ***9675.8*** *p124*
Welter, Nic.; Wisconsin, n.d. ***9675.8*** *p124*
Welter, Theodore; Wisconsin, n.d. ***9675.8*** *p124*
Weltz, . . .; Canada, 1776-1783 ***9786*** *p37*
Weltzhoffer, Anna C. Schultheis *SEE* Weltzhoffer, Jacob
Weltzhoffer, Anna Catharina *SEE* Weltzhoffer, Jacob
Weltzhoffer, Jacob; Pennsylvania, 1731 ***1034.18*** *p22*
*Wife:*Anna C. Schultheis
*Child:*Johann Lorentz
*Child:*Anna Catharina
*Child:*Johan Jacob
Weltzhoffer, Johan Jacob *SEE* Weltzhoffer, Jacob
Weltzhoffer, Johann Lorentz *SEE* Weltzhoffer, Jacob
Welz, John B.; New York, 1853 ***1450.2*** *p156A*
Welz, Julius 37; Kansas, 1888 ***5240.1*** *p47*
Welz, Julius 37; Kansas, 1888 ***5240.1*** *p71*
Wemberley, Abraham; South Carolina, 1788 ***7119*** *p199*
Wemhoner, Anna Brakensiek; Illinois, 1815-1879 ***4610.10*** *p67*
Wempe, Clemens August; America, 1848 ***8582.1*** *p36*
Wemyss, Mary *SEE* Wemyss, Peter
Wemyss, Peter; Bahamas, 1793 ***8894.1*** *p192*
*Wife:*Mary
Wen, Mr.; Quebec, 1815 ***9229.18*** *p75*
Wencel, Mathias; Colorado, 1903 ***9678.3*** *p17*
Wenckus, Julius; Wisconsin, n.d. ***9675.8*** *p124*
Wendel, . . .; Canada, 1776-1783 ***9786*** *p37*
Wendel, Dr. A. H. 40; Kansas, 1885 ***5240.1*** *p47*
Wendel, Dr. A. H. 40; Kansas, 1885 ***5240.1*** *p67*
Wendel, Margaretha; Port uncertain, 1751 ***2444*** *p169*
Wendell, Wilhelm; Kentucky, 1840-1845 ***8582.3*** *p100*
Wenderich, . . .; Canada, 1776-1783 ***9786*** *p37*
Wenderoth, Johannes; America, 1853 ***8582.3*** *p69*
Wendlend, Frederick; Wisconsin, n.d. ***9675.8*** *p124*
Wendler, John H.; New York, NY, 1839 ***8208.4*** *p102*
Wendling, Joseph; New York, NY, 1838 ***8208.4*** *p71*
Wendt, Frederick; Illinois, 1869 ***5012.38*** *p99*
Wendt, Heinrich; America, 1845 ***8582.3*** *p69*
Wenger, Georg; Georgia, 1738 ***9332*** *p319*
Wenger, Heinrich; Pennsylvania, 1709-1710 ***4480*** *p311*
Wenger, John; California, 1863 ***3840.3*** *p12*
Wenger, Peter; Wisconsin, n.d. ***9675.8*** *p124*
Wenger, Philip; Georgia, 1738 ***9332*** *p319*
Wenk, Christopher; Illinois, 1876 ***5012.39*** *p26*
Wenk, Ludwig; Wisconsin, n.d. ***9675.8*** *p124*
Wennagel, Eva *SEE* Wennagel, Jacob
Wennagel, Jacob; Pennsylvania, 1748-1800 ***2444*** *p232*
*Wife:*Eva
*Child:*Johann Adam
Wennagel, Johann Adam *SEE* Wennagel, Jacob
Wennberg, John; Colorado, 1894 ***9678.3*** *p17*
Wenner, Jon. Tho.; Virginia, 1635 ***6219*** *p20*
Wennerberg, C. J.; Minneapolis, 1880-1886 ***6410.35*** *p67*
Wennerberg, John E.; Boston, 1853 ***6410.32*** *p122*
Wennerlund, John; Minneapolis, 1882-1883 ***6410.35*** *p67*
Wenning, Dirck; America, 1858 ***1450.2*** *p156A*
Wenning, Wilhelm; Cincinnati, 1846 ***8582.1*** *p36*
Wennington, Joseph 20; Virginia, 1699 ***2212*** *p27*
Wensenkaeler, Nickles; Pennsylvania, 1752 ***4525*** *p256*
Wenslaff, Louis; Illinois, 1889 ***5012.37*** *p62*
Wenslaff, William; Illinois, 1894 ***5012.39*** *p53*
Wenslow, John; Wisconsin, n.d. ***9675.8*** *p124*
Wentherhead, Robert 26; Virginia, 1774 ***1219.7*** *p239*
Wentzel, Catherine; New York, 1749 ***3652*** *p73*
Wentzel, Johann; Philadelphia, 1738 ***9898*** *p43*
Wenz, Anton 13; New York, NY, 1889 ***7846*** *p40*
Wenz, Catharina 46; New York, NY, 1889 ***7846*** *p40*
Wenz, Eva 16; New York, NY, 1889 ***7846*** *p40*
Wenz, Josefa 4; New York, NY, 1889 ***7846*** *p40*
Wenz, Magdalena 7; New York, NY, 1889 ***7846*** *p40*
Wenz, Peter 18; New York, NY, 1889 ***7846*** *p40*
Wenz, Peter 51; New York, NY, 1889 ***7846*** *p40*
Wenzel, Allwin Bruno; Wisconsin, n.d. ***9675.8*** *p124*
Wenzel, Carl; Wisconsin, n.d. ***9675.8*** *p124*
Wenzel, Eldon Wesley; Port Huron, MI, 1922 ***3455.4*** *p83*
Wenzel, Ernst; Wisconsin, n.d. ***9675.8*** *p124*
Wenzel, Godfrey; Arkansas, 1918 ***95.2*** *p130*
Wenzel, Henry; New York, NY, 1837 ***8208.4*** *p54*
Wenzel, Johann Friederich; Baltimore, 1847 ***8582.2*** *p45*
Wenzel, John F.; America, 1847 ***8582.1*** *p36*
Wenzel, Joseph; Illinois, 1836 ***8582.1*** *p55*
Wenzel, Reinhold; Wisconsin, n.d. ***9675.8*** *p124*
Wenzel, Theodore Reinhold; Wisconsin, n.d. ***9675.8*** *p124*
Wenzkus, Frank; Wisconsin, n.d. ***9675.8*** *p124*
Wenzl, John; Maryland, 1877 ***5240.1*** *p47*
Wenzlaff, Charles; Illinois, 1892 ***5012.37*** *p62*
Wenzlaff, Edward; Illinois, 1890 ***5012.37*** *p62*
Wenzlaff, William; Illinois, 1896 ***5012.40*** *p55*
Wenzle, Francis; New York, NY, 1840 ***8208.4*** *p107*
Werbe, Christopher; America, 1834 ***1450.2*** *p156A*
Werbe, Ferdinand Lewis; America, 1836 ***1450.2*** *p156A*
Werbeizki, Bell; Wisconsin, n.d. ***9675.8*** *p124*
Werchert, William; America, 1845 ***1450.2*** *p156A*
Werden, W. S. 35; Kansas, 1892 ***5240.1*** *p76*
Werelberg, A. N.; Kentucky, 1869-1887 ***8582*** *p34*
Wererding, Christian; Indiana, 1850 ***9117*** *p20*
Werkhoven, Andrew Sam 30; Arkansas, 1918 ***95.2*** *p130*
Werkmeister, Carl Christian Ludwig; America, 1882 ***4610.10*** *p101*
Werle, Jacob; Wisconsin, n.d. ***9675.8*** *p124*
Werle, Johan; Wisconsin, n.d. ***9675.8*** *p124*
Werlen, Lewis; America, 1867 ***6014.1*** *p3*
Werndl, Joseph; Kansas, 1913 ***6013.40*** *p17*
Werneke, C. H.; America, 1847 ***8582.2*** *p45*
Werneke, Gustave 26; Kansas, 1874 ***5240.1*** *p55*
Werner, . . .; Canada, 1776-1783 ***9786*** *p37*
Werner, Anna Catharina; Pennsylvania, 1747 ***2444*** *p232*
*Child:*Maria Agnes
Werner, Anton 4; New York, NY, 1898-1899 ***7846*** *p39*
Werner, Axel; Wisconsin, n.d. ***9675.8*** *p124*
Werner, Casper; Virginia, 1855 ***4626.16*** *p15*
Werner, Christian; Philadelphia, 1742 ***3652*** *p56*
Werner, Dietrich; New York, NY, 1924 ***3455.4*** *p51*
Werner, Emil; Kansas, 1871 ***5240.1*** *p48*
Werner, Eva 8; New York, NY, 1898-1899 ***7846*** *p39*
Werner, Heinrich; New York, NY, 1924 ***3455.4*** *p50*
Werner, Johann Conrad; Pennsylvania, 1746 ***2444*** *p232*
Werner, Johann Friderich; Pennsylvania, 1753 ***2444*** *p233*
Werner, Johann Friedrich; America, 1753 ***2444*** *p233*
Werner, Joseph; Washington, 1859-1920 ***2872.1*** *p43*
Werner, Joseph 2; New York, NY, 1898-1899 ***7846*** *p39*
Werner, Lorenz; Wisconsin, n.d. ***9675.8*** *p124*
Werner, Maria Agnes *SEE* Werner, Anna Catharina
Werner, Markus 35; New York, NY, 1898-1899 ***7846*** *p39*
Werner, Max Alfred; Wisconsin, n.d. ***9675.8*** *p125*
Werner, Monika 4; New York, NY, 1898-1899 ***7846*** *p39*
Werner, Philamena 7; New York, NY, 1898-1899 ***7846*** *p39*
Werner, Philip; New York, NY, 1841 ***1450.2*** *p156A*
Werner, Regina 33; New York, NY, 1898-1899 ***7846*** *p39*
Werner, Thomas; Washington, 1859-1920 ***2872.1*** *p42*
Werner, Valentine; Arkansas, 1855 ***3688*** *p7*
Werneri, . . .; Canada, 1776-1783 ***9786*** *p37*
Werneth, Margaretha 20; America, 1839 ***778.5*** *p546*
Wernhamer, Margaret; New York, 1752 ***3652*** *p76*
Werninger, Augustus; West Virginia, 1813 ***9788.3*** *p22*
Wers, Anna Eulalia Henn *SEE* Wers, Johann Matthaeus
Wers, Johann Deis; Philadelphia, 1752 ***8125.6*** *p23*
Wers, Johann Matthaeus; America, 1750-1752 ***8125.6*** *p23*
*Wife:*Anna Eulalia Henn
Wersching, Caspar; Charleston, SC, 1775-1781 ***8582.2*** *p52*
Wersching, Georg; Charleston, SC, 1775-1781 ***8582.2*** *p52*
Wersel, Franz; America, 1847 ***8582.3*** *p69*
Wersnik, Frank; Wisconsin, n.d. ***9675.8*** *p125*
Werss, Anna Eulalia Henn *SEE* Werss, Johann Matthaeus
Werss, Johann Matthaeus; America, 1750-1752 ***8125.6*** *p23*
*Wife:*Anna Eulalia Henn
Wersum, Johannes; Pennsylvania, 1754 ***2444*** *p234*
Wert, Henry; Philadelphia, 1762 ***9973.7*** *p37*
Werton, Richd; America, 1698 ***2212*** *p5*
Wertting, Henry 25; America, 1838 ***778.5*** *p546*
Werwing, Maria Wilhelmina; New York, 1763 ***3652*** *p89*
Wesberg, William A.; Boston, 1857 ***6410.32*** *p123*
Wesby, John; Virginia, 1642 ***6219*** *p189*
Wesche, . . .; Canada, 1776-1783 ***9786*** *p37*
Wescome, Wm.; Virginia, 1636 ***6219*** *p22*
Wesemann, Heinrich; America, 1856 ***8582.3*** *p69*
Wesendonck, Hugo; Philadelphia, 1848 ***8125.8*** *p438*
Wesendorf, Ernst; Wisconsin, n.d. ***9675.8*** *p125*
Wesener, Andereas; Pennsylvania, 1752 ***2444*** *p233*
Wesener, Andereas; Pennsylvania, 1752 ***2444*** *p234*
Weshett, Margaret 28; Quebec, 1774 ***1219.7*** *p226*
Wesir, John 32; Harris Co., TX, 1898 ***6254*** *p5*
Wesley, Ann 44 *SEE* Wesley, Joseph
Wesley, Charles *SEE* Wesley, Johan
Wesley, Charles *SEE* Wesley, John
Wesley, Charles 25; Philadelphia, 1774 ***1219.7*** *p239*
Wesley, Elizabeth 13; Philadelphia, 1774 ***1219.7*** *p239*
Wesley, Johan; Savannah, GA, 1736 ***8582.2*** *p65*
*Brother:*Charles
Wesley, John; Savannah, GA, 1736 ***3652*** *p51*
*Relative:*Charles
Wesley, Joseph 15; Philadelphia, 1774 ***1219.7*** *p239*
*Mother:*Ann 44
Wesley, Mary 22; Philadelphia, 1774 ***1219.7*** *p239*
Wesley, Thomas 26; America, 1724 ***3690.1*** *p241*
Weslike, Ann; Virginia, 1641 ***6219*** *p187*
Wesner, . . .; Pennsylvania, n.d. ***2444*** *p234*
Wesner, Jacob; Pennsylvania, 1752 ***2444*** *p233*
Wesner, Mathes; Pennsylvania, 1752 ***2444*** *p233*
Wesner, Mathes; Pennsylvania, 1752 ***2444*** *p234*
Wesner, Mathias; Pennsylvania, 1732-1785 ***2444*** *p235*
Wesner, Matthias; Pennsylvania, 1752 ***2444*** *p164*
Wesolowski, Ludwik; New York, 1831 ***4606*** *p177*
Wesolowski, Toney; Arkansas, 1918 ***95.2*** *p130*
Wess, Ensign; Quebec, 1815 ***9229.18*** *p79*
With wife
Wessel, . . .; Illinois, 1800-1900 ***4610.10*** *p67*
Wessel, Anna Marie 31 *SEE* Wessel, Friedrich
Wessel, Bernhard; Cincinnati, 1869-1887 ***8582*** *p34*
Wessel, Carl Friedrich Wilhelm; America, 1857 ***4610.10*** *p158*
Wessel, Carl Heinrich; America, 1854 ***4610.10*** *p157*
Wessel, Carl Heinrich; America, 1886 ***4610.10*** *p161*
Wessel, Emilie; America, 1859 ***4610.10*** *p105*
Wessel, Frieder 38; America, 1873 ***4610.10*** *p122*
Wessel, Friedrich 4 *SEE* Wessel, Friedrich
Wessel, Friedrich 33; America, 1881 ***4610.10*** *p160*
*Wife:*Anna Marie 31
*Child:*Friedrich 4
*Child:*Heinrich 3
*Child:*Wilhelm 6 mos
Wessel, Heinrich 3 *SEE* Wessel, Friedrich
Wessel, Wilhelm 6 mos *SEE* Wessel, Friedrich
Wessener, Jacob; Pennsylvania, 1752 ***2444*** *p233*
Wessener, Jacob; Pennsylvania, 1752 ***2444*** *p234*
Wessener, Johannes; Pennsylvania, 1749 ***2444*** *p234*
Wesser, Gottleib 24; New Orleans, 1839 ***9420.2*** *p71*
Wessinger, Michael; South Carolina, 1788 ***7119*** *p201*
Wessler, Henry; Illinois, 1876 ***5012.37*** *p60*

Wesslmann, Bernard; America, 1887 *1450.2 p157A*
Wessner, . . .; Pennsylvania, n.d. *2444 p234*
Wessner, Elisabetha SEE Wessner, Jacob
Wessner, Hans Jerg SEE Wessner, Jacob
Wessner, Jacob; Pennsylvania, 1752 *2444 p233*
  *Wife:*Elisabetha
  *Child:*Hans Jerg
  *Child:*Martin
Wessner, Martin SEE Wessner, Jacob
West, Anne; New York, NY, 1816 *2859.11 p44*
West, Annie; Iowa, 1866-1943 *123.54 p51*
West, Charles H.; Illinois, 1860 *2896.5 p42*
West, David; New York, NY, 1811 *2859.11 p20*
West, Elizabeth 33 SEE West, John
West, George 26; Philadelphia, 1774 *1219.7 p216*
West, George Sydney; Arkansas, 1918 *95.2 p130*
West, Grace; Virginia, 1636 *6219 p36*
West, Henry; Virginia, 1622 *6219 p27*
West, Humphrey; Virginia, 1638 *6219 p115*
West, Humphrey; Virginia, 1642 *6219 p196*
West, James; New York, NY, 1811 *2859.11 p20*
West, Jas.; New York, NY, 1816 *2859.11 p44*
West, John; Philadelphia, 1816 *2859.11 p44*
West, John; Virginia, 1635 *6219 p35*
West, John; Virginia, 1636 *6219 p80*
West, John; Virginia, 1652 *6251 p20*
West, John 24; Jamaica, 1750 *3690.1 p241*
West, John 28; Carolina, 1774 *1219.7 p231*
West, John 33; Savannah, GA, 1733 *4719.17 p313*
  *Wife:*Elizabeth 33
  *Son:*Richard 5
West, John 35; Maryland, 1774 *1219.7 p214*
West, Joseph 21; Maryland, 1774 *1219.7 p192*
West, Joseph 44; Maryland, 1774 *1219.7 p230*
West, Margaret; Philadelphia, 1816 *2859.11 p44*
West, Matthew 30; Pennsylvania, 1739 *3690.1 p241*
West, Peter Andreas; Arkansas, 1918 *95.2 p130*
West, Richard; Virginia, 1635 *6219 p10*
West, Richard; Virginia, 1637 *6219 p10*
West, Richard 5 SEE West, John
West, Robert; Iowa, 1866-1943 *123.54 p51*
West, Robert; Virginia, 1639 *6219 p156*
West, Simon; Colorado, 1894 *9678.3 p17*
West, Thmoas; Philadelphia, 1815 *2859.11 p44*
West, Thomas 16; Maryland, 1724 *3690.1 p241*
West, Thomas W.; Virginia, 1844 *4626.16 p12*
West, William; New York, NY, 1811 *2859.11 p20*
West, William; New York, NY, 1816 *2859.11 p44*
West, William; Ohio, 1840 *9892.11 p48*
West, William 25; Philadelphia, 1775 *1219.7 p271*
West, Wm.; Philadelphia, 1816 *2859.11 p44*
West, Wm.; Virginia, 1642 *6219 p199*
Westake, Jon.; Virginia, 1642 *6219 p191*
Westberg, Alfred; Washington, 1859-1920 *2872.1 p43*
Westberg, Carl A.; Washington, 1859-1920 *2872.1 p43*
Westberg, Oscar; Washington, 1859-1920 *2872.1 p43*
Westberg, William A. 40; Massachusetts, 1860 *6410.32 p104*
Westbery, Richard; Virginia, 1646 *6219 p236*
Weste, Hermine; Milwaukee, 1875 *4719.30 p257*
Weste, Leo; Milwaukee, 1875 *4719.30 p257*
Westein, Henri 19; America, 1837 *778.5 p547*
Westein, Jacques 24; America, 1837 *778.5 p547*
Wester, Catharina Groezinger SEE Wester, Johann Georg
Wester, Henry; Wisconsin, n.d. *9675.8 p125*
Wester, Jacob; Wisconsin, n.d. *9675.8 p125*
Wester, Johann Georg; Pennsylvania, 1751 *2444 p229*
  *Wife:*Catharina Groezinger
Wester, Michael; Wisconsin, n.d. *9675.8 p125*
Westerberg, Ben Gafry 24; Arkansas, 1918 *95.2 p130*
Westerberg, Charles; Massachusetts, 1860 *6410.32 p125*
Westerfield, Jane; Virginia, 1628 *6219 p31*
Westerhoff, Louise Krieger; America, 1893 *4610.10 p103*
Westerhold, Friedrich Wilhelm SEE Westerhold, Hermann Heinrich
Westerhold, Hermann Heinrich; America, 1854 *4610.10 p151*
  With wife
  *Child:*Marie Louise
  *Child:*Friedrich Wilhelm
Westerhold, Marie Louise SEE Westerhold, Hermann Heinrich
Westerholz, Anne Marie Albers SEE Westerholz, Friedrich Wilhelm
Westerholz, Anne Marie Caroline 5 SEE Westerholz, Friedrich Wilhelm
Westerholz, Friedrich Wilhelm 48; America, 1852 *4610.10 p151*
  *Wife:*Anne Marie Albers
  *Child:*Heinrich F. Wilhelm
  *Child:*Anne Marie Caroline 5

Westerholz, Heinrich F. Wilhelm SEE Westerholz, Friedrich Wilhelm
Westerin, Andrew; Virginia, 1645 *6219 p233*
Westerkamp, . . .; Canada, 1776-1783 *9786 p37*
Westerkamp, Heinrich; New Netherland, 1630-1646 *8582.2 p51*
Westerlund, Alfred; Washington, 1859-1920 *2872.1 p43*
Westerlund, Ben; Minneapolis, 1855-1884 *6410.35 p67*
Westerlund, Christine; Washington, 1859-1920 *2872.1 p43*
Westerlund, Edward Johnson; Washington, 1859-1920 *2872.1 p43*
Westerlund, Julius; Washington, 1859-1920 *2872.1 p43*
Westerlund, Myrtle; Washington, 1859-1920 *2872.1 p43*
Westermann, John Eric; Delaware, 1746 *3652 p68*
Westermann, Lambert; America, 1836 *8582.3 p69*
Westermann, Thomas; Virginia, 1855 *4626.16 p15*
Westermeyer, Carl Dietrich Wilhelm; America, 1882 *4610.10 p113*
Westermeyer, Carl Friedrich Wilhelm; America, 1882 *4610.10 p118*
Westermeyer, Caroline Louise Mathilde; America, 1869 *4610.10 p117*
Westermeyer, Friedrich Wilhelm Carl; Illinois, 1881 *4610.10 p118*
Westervelt, Charles; Massachusetts, 1860 *6410.32 p125*
Westervelt, Charles 25; Massachusetts, 1860 *6410.32 p113*
Westfall, James; Indiana, 1837 *9117 p15*
Westhart, Johann; Ohio, 1794 *8582.2 p53*
Westhead, Peter; Virginia, 1647 *6219 p245*
Westhoff, Albert; Wisconsin, n.d. *9675.8 p125*
Westimu, Olga 11 mos; New York, NY, 1878 *9253 p46*
Westimu, Wara 21; New York, NY, 1878 *9253 p46*
Westimu, Wladimir 32; New York, NY, 1878 *9253 p46*
Westing, Fred G.; America, 1893 *1450.2 p157A*
Westlake, Samuel D. 54; Washington, 1918-1920 *1728.5 p16*
Westlake, William 28; Maryland, 1775 *1219.7 p248*
Westley, Ambrose; Charles Town, SC, 1763 *1219.7 p96*
Westley, John 24; Philadelphia, 1833 *53.26 p91*
Westley, John 24; Philadelphia, 1833-1834 *53.26 p91*
Westley, Richard 16; Maryland, 1722 *3690.1 p241*
Westley, William 22; Maryland, 1774 *1219.7 p178*
Westlock, Ann; Virginia, 1640 *6219 p181*
Westly, Ann; Virginia, 1636 *6219 p11*
Westmoreland, Benjamin Welsh; Illinois, 1888 *5012.37 p61*
Westola, Falmar; Washington, 1859-1920 *2872.1 p43*
Weston, Albert; Bangor, ME, 1898-1899 *6410.22 p127*
Weston, Ann 30; Carolina, 1774 *1219.7 p231*
Weston, Christopher; Virginia, 1648 *6219 p250*
Weston, John; Virginia, 1622 *6219 p76*
Weston, John; Virginia, 1635 *6219 p16*
Weston, Phillip; Virginia, 1646 *6219 p246*
Weston, Rich.; Virginia, 1637 *6219 p83*
Weston, Richard; Virginia, 1638 *6219 p122*
Weston, William 21; Jamaica, 1774 *1219.7 p181*
Westover, John; Illinois, 1865 *7857 p8*
Westpahl, John; New York, NY, 1836 *8208.4 p14*
Westphal, . . .; Canada, 1776-1783 *9786 p37*
Westphal, Fred; Washington, 1859-1920 *2872.1 p43*
Westphal, John; New York, NY, 1836 *8208.4 p14*
Westphal, Karl; America, 1850 *8582.3 p69*
Westphal, Peter 24; Virginia, 1773 *1219.7 p169*
Westvold, Rasmus; Arkansas, 1918 *95.2 p130*
Westwell, Robert; Virginia, 1634 *6219 p32*
Westwood, Joseph; New York, NY, 1835 *8208.4 p6*
Westwood, Robert; Virginia, 1643 *6219 p204*
Westwood, William; Virginia, 1639 *6219 p149*
Westwood, Wm.; Virginia, 1634 *6219 p84*
Wetheral, Henry 40; Virginia, 1775 *1219.7 p246*
Wetheral, Thomas 30; Norfolk, VA, 1774 *1219.7 p222*
Wetherall, George; Ohio, 1843 *9892.11 p48*
Wetherall, George; Ohio, 1846 *9892.11 p48*
Wetherall, Joseph; Ohio, 1848 *9892.11 p48*
Wetherall, Robert; Ohio, 1838 *9892.11 p48*
Wetherall, Robert; Philadelphia, 1848 *9892.11 p48*
Wetherbye, Tho.; Virginia, 1637 *6219 p114*
Wetherel, John 15; Philadelphia, 1774 *1219.7 p232*
Wetherell, Joseph; Ohio, 1845 *9892.11 p48*
Wetherell, S. 31; Virginia, 1773 *1219.7 p168*
Wethersby, Tho.; Virginia, 1635 *6219 p35*
Wetjen, Harmen; New York, NY, 1837 *8208.4 p25*
Wetsch, Anton 16; New York, NY, 1889 *7846 p40*
Wetsch, Johannes 19; New York, NY, 1889 *7846 p40*
Wetsell, Frederick; Indiana, 1836 *9117 p15*
Wetta, Jean 18; America, 1838 *778.5 p547*
Wetta, Joseph; Indiana, 1874 *5240.1 p48*
Wetter, . . .; Canada, 1776-1783 *9786 p37*
Wettermann, John; Ohio, 1869-1887 *8582 p34*
Wetteroth, Wilhelm; New York, NY, 1838 *8208.4 p90*
Wetteson, Charles; New York, NY, 1839 *8208.4 p97*

Wettlaufer, Adam 84; Canada, 1901 *1763 p40D*
Wettling, Frederick; New York, NY, 1836 *8208.4 p14*
Wetts, Thomason; Virginia, 1647 *6219 p247*
Wettstein, Theodore; Milwaukee, 1851 *8125.8 p438*
Wetzel, Henry; America, 1866 *1450.2 p157A*
Wetzel, Johann; Pennsylvania, 1800-1874 *8582.1 p56*
Wetzel, Ludwig; Cincinnati, 1788-1885 *8582.2 p52*
Wetzel, Margaretha; America, 1752 *2444 p215*
Wetzel, Marie 37; West Virginia, 1899 *9788.3 p22*
Wetzel, Martin; Pennsylvania, 1743-1767 *2444 p233*
Wetzel, Peter; America, 1850 *1450.2 p157A*
Wetzel, Wilhelm; Philadelphia, 1779 *8137 p15*
Wetzlar, Johann Jost; Philadelphia, 1779 *8137 p15*
Weyan, Jon.; Virginia, 1637 *6219 p24*
Weyand, . . .; Canada, 1776-1783 *9786 p37*
Weyand, Mr.; Cincinnati, 1844-1855 *8582.2 p45*
Weyand, Conrad; Canada, 1776-1783 *9786 p242*
Weyand, Joseph; America, 1852 *8582.3 p69*
Weyand, Nicholas; Canada, 1776-1783 *9786 p207A*
Weyand, Peter; Cincinnati, 1869-1887 *8582 p34*
Weyand, Peter; New Orleans, 1843 *8582.2 p45*
Weyberg, Caspar; Philadelphia, 1776 *8582.3 p85*
Weyden, Jacob von der; Philadelphia, 1738 *9898 p26*
Weydenbach, Christina; America, 1751 *2444 p185*
Weydenmeyer, Johann Georg; Pennsylvania, 1764 *2444 p233*
Weydenmeyer, Melchior; Pennsylvania, 1764 *2444 p233*
Weydenmyer, Eberhardt; Pennsylvania, 1764 *2444 p233*
Weydon, Humphrey; Virginia, 1648 *6219 p252*
Weyel, John; Indiana, 1840 *9117 p18*
Weyer, Mathias; Washington, 1859-1920 *2872.1 p43*
Weyer, Matt; Washington, 1859-1920 *2872.1 p43*
Weyh, Anna; New England, 1749 *2444 p233*
Weyh, Christian; America, 1749 *2444 p233*
Weyinerchirch, Edward; Wisconsin, n.d. *9675.8 p125*
Weyker, John; Wisconsin, n.d. *9675.8 p125*
Weyker, John, Jr.; Wisconsin, n.d. *9675.8 p125*
Weyker, John P.; Wisconsin, n.d. *9675.8 p125*
Weymake, Margaret; Virginia, 1646 *6219 p242*
Weym'ke, Margaret; Virginia, 1646 *6219 p242*
Weyreter, Ernest; New York, 1893 *1450.2 p42B*
Weys, Joh. Mich'l; Pennsylvania, 1785 *2444 p232*
Weys, Mathias; Pennsylvania, 1785 *2444 p232*
Weyse, Hans Jacob; Pennsylvania, 1749 *2444 p232*
Weyse, Julius; Cincinnati, 1788-1848 *8582.3 p89*
Weyse, Julius; Cincinnati, 1788-1848 *8582.3 p90*
Wezel, Anna; Pennsylvania, 1749 *2444 p222*
Wezel, Catharina SEE Wezel, Martin, Jr.
Wezel, Catharina SEE Wezel, Martin, Jr.
Wezel, Martin, Jr.; America, 1742-1800 *2444 p233*
  *Wife:*Catharina
  *Child:*Catharina
Whadsey, Peter; Virginia, 1636 *6219 p26*
Whalen, Bridget 40; Massachusetts, 1850 *5881.1 p96*
Whalen, David 25; Massachusetts, 1847 *5881.1 p96*
Whalen, Mary 23; Massachusetts, 1847 *5881.1 p97*
Whalen, N. P.; Washington, 1859-1920 *2872.1 p43*
Whalen, Thomas; New York, NY, 1816 *2859.11 p44*
Whaley, Betty 2; Massachusetts, 1850 *5881.1 p96*
Whaley, James 4; Massachusetts, 1850 *5881.1 p97*
Whaley, Johanna 24; Massachusetts, 1850 *5881.1 p97*
Whaley, John 17; Jamaica, 1719 *3690.1 p241*
Whaley, Timothy 29; Massachusetts, 1850 *5881.1 p98*
Whaley, William 28; Philadelphia, 1774 *1219.7 p212*
Whaley, William 34; Massachusetts, 1847 *5881.1 p98*
Whalin, Bridget; Massachusetts, 1850 *5881.1 p96*
Whalin, Catharine 3; Massachusetts, 1850 *5881.1 p96*
Whalin, Margaret 20; Massachusetts, 1850 *5881.1 p98*
Whalin, Margaret 21; Massachusetts, 1848 *5881.1 p97*
Whalin, Michael 26; Massachusetts, 1849 *5881.1 p97*
Whaling, Richard 20; Philadelphia, 1774 *1219.7 p182*
Whalley, Ann 23; America, 1706 *2212 p46*
Whalley, Oliver; Virginia, 1698 *2212 p12*
Whalley, Thomas 15; America, 1705 *2212 p43*
Whalon, Thomas; Illinois, 1864 *7857 p8*
Whaly, Timothy 22; Massachusetts, 1847 *5881.1 p98*
Wharton, Anne 17; Virginia, 1700 *2212 p30*
Wharton, Elizabeth 2; Pennsylvania, Virginia or Maryland, 1699 *2212 p20*
Wharton, Geo.; Virginia, 1643 *6219 p205*
Wharton, John 28; Philadelphia, 1774 *1219.7 p216*
Wharton, Joseph; Philadelphia, 1811 *2859.11 p20*
  With family
Wharton, Robert; Philadelphia, 1811 *2859.11 p20*
Wharton, Robert 1; Pennsylvania, Virginia or Maryland, 1719 *3690.1 p242*
Wharton, Thom 19; Virginia, 1703 *2212 p39*
Whealan, Daniel; America, 1742 *4971 p17*
Wheally, John 17; Jamaica, 1719 *3690.1 p241*
Wheatcroft, Richard 18; Jamaica, 1731 *3690.1 p243*
Wheatley, Charles 18; Jamaica, 1739 *3690.1 p242*
Wheatley, David; Virginia, 1645 *6219 p239*
Wheatley, John 19; Jamaica, 1730 *3690.1 p242*

FOR A COMPLETE EXPLANATION OF ENTRY, SEE "HOW TO READ A CITATION" SECTION

White, Jon.; Virginia, 1638 ***6219*** *p11*
White, Joseph; St. John, N.B., 1847 ***5704.8*** *p18*
White, Katherine; Virginia, 1640 ***6219*** *p187*
White, Lawrance; Virginia, 1643 ***6219*** *p206*
White, Lewis; Virginia, 1646 ***6219*** *p239*
White, Lionel 22; Philadelphia, 1774 ***1219.7*** *p182*
White, Margaret *SEE* White, George
White, Margaret; Philadelphia, 1851 ***5704.8*** *p76*
White, Margaret; Quebec, 1852 ***5704.8*** *p94*
White, Margaret; St. John, N.B., 1850 ***5704.8*** *p62*
White, Margaret; St. John, N.B., 1850 ***5704.8*** *p66*
White, Margaret; St. John, N.B., 1852 ***5704.8*** *p92*
White, Margaret 9; St. John, N.B., 1852 ***5704.8*** *p92*
White, Margaret 12; St. John, N.B., 1847 ***5704.8*** *p9*
White, Margaret 20; St. John, N.B., 1860 ***5704.8*** *p144*
White, Margaret 50; St. John, N.B., 1862 ***5704.8*** *p150*
White, Mark; Quebec, 1847 ***5704.8*** *p8*
White, Martha; Quebec, 1849 ***5704.8*** *p57*
White, Martha 21 *SEE* White, Charles
White, Martha 22; Philadelphia, 1854 ***5704.8*** *p123*
White, Mary; New Brunswick, 1821 ***7603*** *p79*
White, Mary; New York, NY, 1866 ***5704.8*** *p212*
White, Mary; New York, NY, 1869 ***5704.8*** *p232*
White, Mary; Quebec, 1847 ***5704.8*** *p12*
White, Mary; Quebec, 1847 ***5704.8*** *p27*
White, Mary; St. John, N.B., 1852 ***5704.8*** *p92*
White, Mary 8 mos *SEE* White, James
White, Mary 20; Nova Scotia, 1774 ***1219.7*** *p209*
White, Mary Ann 8; St. John, N.B., 1850 ***5704.8*** *p61*
White, Mary Ann 17; Philadelphia, 1860 ***5704.8*** *p144*
White, Mary Jane; Philadelphia, 1850 ***53.26*** *p91*
White, Mary Jane; Philadelphia, 1850 ***5704.8*** *p59*
White, Mathew; New York, NY, 1816 ***2859.11*** *p44*
White, Matilda 1; St. John, N.B., 1847 ***5704.8*** *p9*
White, Michael; Philadelphia, 1850 ***53.26*** *p91*
*Relative:*Pat
*Relative:*Biddy
White, Michael; Philadelphia, 1850 ***5704.8*** *p69*
White, Nancy; St. John, N.B., 1847 ***5704.8*** *p9*
White, Nancy 7; St. John, N.B., 1852 ***5704.8*** *p92*
White, Nancy 12; Quebec, 1850 ***5704.8*** *p69*
White, Niccodemus; Virginia, 1635 ***6219*** *p26*
White, Nich.; Virginia, 1636 ***6219*** *p28*
White, Nich.; Virginia, 1638 ***6219*** *p115*
White, Nicho.; Virginia, 1648 ***6219*** *p250*
White, Nicholas; Virginia, 1637 ***6219*** *p28*
White, Noth.; Virginia, 1641 ***6219*** *p184*
White, Oliver; Virginia, 1643 ***6219*** *p187*
White, Pat *SEE* White, Michael
White, Pat; Philadelphia, 1850 ***5704.8*** *p69*
White, Patrick 7; Philadelphia, 1853 ***5704.8*** *p101*
White, Patt 22; St. John, N.B., 1854 ***5704.8*** *p120*
White, Peter; Texas, 1880-1889 ***9777*** *p6*
White, Peter; Virginia, 1635 ***6219*** *p3*
White, Peter; Virginia, 1637 ***6219*** *p86*
White, Peter; Virginia, 1638 ***6219*** *p123*
White, Peter 18; Maryland, 1775 ***1219.7*** *p250*
White, Peter 19; New Orleans, 1839 ***778.5*** *p547*
White, Phillipp; Virginia, 1642 ***6219*** *p191*
White, Rebecca 12; Quebec, 1850 ***5704.8*** *p62*
White, Richard; America, 1847 ***1450.2*** *p157A*
White, Richard; L'Assomption, Que., 1825 ***7603*** *p57*
White, Richard; L'Assomption, Que., 1825 ***7603*** *p80*
White, Richard; New York, NY, 1816 ***2859.11*** *p44*
White, Richard; Virginia, 1639 ***6219*** *p156*
White, Richard; Virginia, 1640 ***6219*** *p181*
White, Richard; Virginia, 1647 ***6219*** *p248*
White, Robert; Illinois, 1848 ***7857*** *p8*
White, Robert; Philadelphia, 1865 ***5704.8*** *p190*
White, Robert; St. John, N.B., 1847 ***5704.8*** *p9*
White, Robert 19; Port uncertain, 1850 ***4535.10*** *p198*
White, Robert 30; Jamaica, 1731 ***3690.1*** *p243*
White, Rosannah 3; St. John, N.B., 1847 ***5704.8*** *p9*
White, Sally; Quebec, 1849 ***5704.8*** *p57*
White, Samuel; Boston, 1835 ***8208.4*** *p58*
White, Samuel; Iowa, 1866-1943 ***123.54*** *p51*
White, Samuel; New York, NY, 1828 ***8208.4*** *p32*
White, Samuel 10; St. John, N.B., 1850 ***5704.8*** *p61*
White, Sarah; Quebec, 1847 ***5704.8*** *p29*
White, Sarah; Quebec, 1851 ***5704.8*** *p73*
White, Sarah 8; St. John, N.B., 1847 ***5704.8*** *p9*
White, Sarah 9 *SEE* White, Thomas
White, Sarah 11; Quebec, 1852 ***5704.8*** *p94*
White, Sarah 56; Carolina, 1774 ***1219.7*** *p221*
White, Solomon 22; Jamaica, 1722 ***3690.1*** *p243*
White, Susan; Philadelphia, 1853 ***5704.8*** *p101*
White, Susan; South Carolina, 1813 ***1639.20*** *p315*
White, Teddy; St. John, N.B., 1853 ***5704.8*** *p107*
White, Tho.; Virginia, 1638 ***6219*** *p116*
White, Tho.; Virginia, 1638 ***6219*** *p117*
White, Thomas; America, 1735-1743 ***4971*** *p78*
White, Thomas; America, 1743 ***4971*** *p80*
White, Thomas; Philadelphia, 1867 ***5704.8*** *p217*
White, Thomas; Virginia, 1648 ***6219*** *p250*
White, Thomas; Virginia, 1760 ***8894.1*** *p191*
White, Thomas 6; St. John, N.B., 1847 ***5704.8*** *p9*
White, Thomas 10; Quebec, 1850 ***5704.8*** *p69*
White, Thomas 12; Quebec, 1849 ***5704.8*** *p51*
White, Thomas 21; Quebec, 1864 ***5704.8*** *p162*
White, Thomas 25; Kansas, 1876 ***5240.1*** *p57*
White, Thomas 25; Massachusetts, 1847 ***5881.1*** *p98*
White, Thomas 42; Massachusetts, 1847 ***5881.1*** *p98*
White, Thomas 42; Virginia, 1775 ***1219.7*** *p246*
White, Thomas 52; Montreal, 1843 ***4535.10*** *p196*
*Wife:*Ann 51
*Child:*Thos., Jr. 22
*Child:*John 18
*Child:*Geo. 18
*Child:*Daniel 15
*Child:*Henry 12
*Child:*Harriet 16
*Child:*Sarah 9
White, Thos. 1 *SEE* White, Wm.
White, Thos., Jr. 22 *SEE* White, Thomas
White, Turns 24; Baltimore, 1775 ***1219.7*** *p269*
White, William; Arkansas, 1918 ***95.2*** *p130*
White, William; Charleston, SC, 1793 ***1639.20*** *p315*
White, William; New York, NY, 1834 ***8208.4*** *p1*
White, William; New York, NY, 1838 ***8208.4*** *p64*
White, William; Philadelphia, 1852 ***5704.8*** *p84*
White, William; Philadelphia, 1853 ***5704.8*** *p101*
White, William; Quebec, 1847 ***5704.8*** *p29*
White, William; Quebec, 1850 ***5704.8*** *p63*
White, William; St. John, N.B., 1847 ***5704.8*** *p19*
White, William; St. John, N.B., 1848 ***5704.8*** *p44*
White, William; Virginia, 1639 ***6219*** *p161*
White, William; Virginia, 1642 ***6219*** *p197*
White, William 5; St. John, N.B., 1852 ***5704.8*** *p92*
White, William 6; St. John, N.B., 1850 ***5704.8*** *p61*
White, William 8; Quebec, 1850 ***5704.8*** *p69*
White, William 9; Philadelphia, 1853 ***5704.8*** *p101*
White, William 14; Philadelphia, 1857 ***5704.8*** *p133*
White, William 16; Barbados, 1774 ***1219.7*** *p212*
White, William 16; Virginia, 1752 ***1219.7*** *p11*
White, William 16; Virginia, 1752 ***3690.1*** *p244*
White, William 18; Philadelphia, 1803 ***53.26*** *p91*
White, William 19; Pennsylvania, 1721 ***3690.1*** *p243*
White, William 24; St. John, N.B., 1862 ***5704.8*** *p150*
White, William 40; Jamaica, 1774 ***1219.7*** *p196*
White, Wm.; Virginia, 1636 ***6219*** *p80*
White, Wm. 3 *SEE* White, Wm.
White, Wm. 28; Montreal, 1843 ***4535.10*** *p196*
*Wife:*Harriet 27
*Child:*Wm. 3
*Child:*Thos. 1
*Child:*Eliz. 6
White, Zachariah; South Carolina, 1753 ***1219.7*** *p23*
Whitechurch, William 20; Jamaica, 1736 ***3690.1*** *p243*
Whitecroft, Robert; Virginia, 1638 ***6219*** *p181*
Whitefield, George; Georgia, 1771 ***1219.7*** *p149*
Whitefoot, Powys 21; Jamaica, 1738 ***3690.1*** *p244*
Whitefoott, John; Jamaica, 1736 ***3690.1*** *p244*
Whiteford, James 29; Maryland, 1730 ***3690.1*** *p244*
Whitehand, Geo.; Virginia, 1628 ***6219*** *p9*
Whitehart, William; Virginia, 1639 ***6219*** *p155*
Whitehead, George; Virginia, 1634 ***6219*** *p32*
Whitehead, J. A. 28; Kansas, 1903 ***5240.1*** *p82*
Whitehead, James; New York, NY, 1838 ***8208.4*** *p87*
Whitehead, James; Virginia, 1638 ***6219*** *p118*
Whitehead, James 27; Virginia, 1773 ***1219.7*** *p169*
Whitehead, Jane 17; Virginia, 1699 ***2212*** *p27*
Whitehead, Job 27; Maryland, 1774 ***1219.7*** *p244*
Whitehead, John 15; America, 1701 ***2212*** *p35*
Whitehead, John 16; Pennsylvania, 1725 ***3690.1*** *p244*
Whitehead, William 21; Kansas, 1892 ***5240.1*** *p77*
Whitehead, William 27; Maryland, 1774 ***1219.7*** *p236*
Whitehouse, Benjamin 19; Jamaica, 1733 ***3690.1*** *p244*
Whiteside, William; New York, NY, 1816 ***2859.11*** *p44*
Whiteside, William 25; Philadelphia, 1774 ***1219.7*** *p231*
Whitethorne, Ann; Virginia, 1635 ***6219*** *p32*
Whitetmost, Wm.; Virginia, 1636 ***6219*** *p34*
Whitewith, William 22; Maryland, 1775 ***1219.7*** *p264*
Whitey, Patrick; America, 1869 ***5704.8*** *p236*
Whitezel, Balthaser; America, 1833 ***1450.2*** *p157A*
Whitfeild, Rich.; Virginia, 1635 ***6219*** *p36*
Whitfeild, Wm.; Virginia, 1632 ***6219*** *p180*
Whitfield, . . .; Virginia, 1637 ***6219*** *p13*
Whitfield, John; Illinois, 1898 ***5012.40*** *p55*
Whitford, William; New York, NY, 1816 ***2859.11*** *p44*
Whitheredge, William; Virginia, 1637 ***6219*** *p33*
Whiting, Albert 50; Kansas, 1906 ***5240.1*** *p83*
Whiting, Ann *SEE* Whiting, James
Whiting, Chris.; Virginia, 1636 ***6219*** *p11*
Whiting, Edmond; Michigan, 1876 ***5240.1*** *p48*
Whiting, Henry George; Michigan, 1876 ***5240.1*** *p48*
Whiting, James; Virginia, 1635 ***6219*** *p17*
Whiting, James; Virginia, 1638 ***6219*** *p122*
Whiting, James; Virginia, 1643 ***6219*** *p201*
*Wife:*Ann
Whiting, Owen; Virginia, 1643 ***6219*** *p203*
Whiting, Rebecca; Virginia, 1635 ***6219*** *p17*
Whiting, Richard; Virginia, 1637 ***6219*** *p84*
Whiting, William 24; Virginia, 1774 ***1219.7*** *p244*
Whitington, Susan *SEE* Whitington, William
Whitington, William; Virginia, 1647 ***6219*** *p244*
*Wife:*Susan
Whitler, Mr.; Quebec, 1815 ***9229.18*** *p76*
Whitley, Mr.; Quebec, 1815 ***9229.18*** *p80*
Whitley, Randall; Virginia, 1638 ***6219*** *p122*
Whitley, Richard; Virginia, 1646 ***6219*** *p241*
Whitley, Roger; South Carolina, 1729 ***1639.20*** *p315*
Whitlisse, Ellen 15; America, 1703 ***2212*** *p40*
Whitlock, Tho.; Virginia, 1638 ***6219*** *p148*
Whitlow, D. W.; Washington, 1859-1920 ***2872.1*** *p43*
Whitmay, Thomas 18; Jamaica, 1724 ***3690.1*** *p244*
Whitmill, Joseph 21; Jamaica, 1730 ***3690.1*** *p244*
Whitmore, Andrew 15; Grenada, 1774 ***1219.7*** *p185*
Whitmore, Mary; Virginia, 1637 ***6219*** *p33*
Whitmore, Samuel 20; Jamaica, 1725 ***3690.1*** *p244*
Whitney, John B.; Charleston, SC, 1803 ***1639.20*** *p315*
Whitpaine, John; Rhode Island, 1692 ***4961*** *p242*
Whitpaine, Patrick; Philadelphia, 1689 ***4961*** *p242*
Whitpaine, Richard; Pennsylvania, 1600-1700 ***4961*** *p242*
Whitpaine, Zachariah; Pennsylvania, 1682 ***4961*** *p241*
Whitpaine, Zechariah; Pennsylvania, 1682 ***4960*** *p159*
Whitsack, . . .; Canada, 1776-1783 ***9786*** *p37*
Whitsell, . . .; Canada, 1776-1783 ***9786*** *p37*
Whitsen, Elizabeth 19; Maryland, 1774 ***1219.7*** *p207*
Whitt, Francis; New York, NY, 1865 ***5704.8*** *p192*
Whitt, John; Illinois, 1861 ***5012.38*** *p98*
Whittaker, . . .; Canada, 1776-1783 ***9786*** *p37*
Whittaker, Dennis; Washington, 1859-1920 ***2872.1*** *p43*
Whittaker, John; New York, NY, 1840 ***8208.4*** *p106*
Whittaker, Sarah; New York, NY, 1866 ***5704.8*** *p207*
Whittekar, John 17; South Carolina, 1733 ***3690.1*** *p243*
Whitten, Edward; Quebec, 1851 ***5704.8*** *p73*
Whitten, James; Quebec, 1851 ***5704.8*** *p73*
Whitten, Mary; Quebec, 1851 ***5704.8*** *p73*
Whitten, Robert; Quebec, 1851 ***5704.8*** *p73*
Whittikar, John 17; Jamaica, 1733 ***3690.1*** *p242*
Whittington, Jas. 19; Canada, 1838 ***4535.12*** *p113*
Whittington, Thomas 16; Maryland, 1774 ***1219.7*** *p185*
Whittle, Nicholas 22; Virginia, 1699 ***2212*** *p27*
Whittle, Richard; Quebec, 1775 ***7603*** *p81*
Whittle, Richard 24; New England, 1774 ***1219.7*** *p203*
Whittle, Robert 38; Maryland, 1774 ***1219.7*** *p179*
Whittle, William 20; Jamaica, 1737 ***3690.1*** *p244*
Whitton, Daniel 29; Maryland, 1775 ***1219.7*** *p260*
Whitton, Samuel 21; Jamaica, 1734 ***3690.1*** *p245*
Wholaghan, Daniel; America, 1742 ***4971*** *p94*
Whomans, Thomas; Illinois, 1886 ***5012.39*** *p120*
Whoorewood, Nich.; Virginia, 1635 ***6219*** *p20*
Whoresky, Bridget 22; Philadelphia, 1861 ***5704.8*** *p148*
Whoresky, Manus 25; Philadelphia, 1861 ***5704.8*** *p148*
Whoresky, Susan 9 mos; Philadelphia, 1861 ***5704.8*** *p148*
Whoriskey, Anne 21; Philadelphia, 1856 ***5704.8*** *p128*
Whoriskey, Charles 8; New York, NY, 1864 ***5704.8*** *p187*
Whoriskey, Ellen; New York, NY, 1864 ***5704.8*** *p187*
Whoriskey, John; Philadelphia, 1868 ***5704.8*** *p225*
Whoriskey, Mary A. 4; New York, NY, 1864 ***5704.8*** *p187*
Whorisky, Charles; Philadelphia, 1852 ***5704.8*** *p97*
Whorsky, Mary; St. John, N.B., 1847 ***5704.8*** *p34*
Whydon, Clement; Virginia, 1636 ***6219*** *p28*
Whyte, Daniel; Charleston, SC, 1813 ***1639.20*** *p314*
Whyte, Laurence; America, 1742 ***4971*** *p37*
Whytford, James 29; Maryland, 1730 ***3690.1*** *p244*
Wiberg, Gustof Adolf; Iowa, 1866-1943 ***123.54*** *p51*
Wiberg, Hans John; Washington, 1859-1920 ***2872.1*** *p43*
Wichl, Kasimir; Colorado, 1887 ***9678.3*** *p18*
Wichman, Henry; Wisconsin, n.d. ***9675.8*** *p125*
Wichmann, Heinrich; Kansas, 1894 ***5240.1*** *p48*
Wichrowski, Stanislaw 16; New York, 1912 ***9980.29*** *p60*
Wick, Alexander 16; Virginia, 1774 ***1219.7*** *p205*
Wickemeyer, Anna Maria Ilsabein; America, 1854 ***4610.10*** *p156*
Wickenkamp, Anton Friedrich; America, 1849 ***4610.10*** *p120*
Wicker, Jane 38; North Carolina, 1850 ***1639.20*** *p315*
Wickers, Michael 35; Virginia, 1775 ***1219.7*** *p261*
Wickers, Minnie; America, 1875 ***1450.2*** *p42B*
Wickert, Johannes; Philadelphia, 1779 ***8137*** *p15*
Wickliff, Joseph 36; St. John, N.B., 1857 ***5704.8*** *p135*
Wicklund, Charles; Minneapolis, 1868-1884 ***6410.35*** *p67*
Wickman, Erick; Maine, 1890-1896 ***6410.22*** *p122*
Wicks, John; Washington, 1859-1920 ***2872.1*** *p43*
Wicks, Perry; Ohio, 1842 ***8365.25*** *p12*
Wickstrom, Edward; Washington, 1859-1920 ***2872.1*** *p43*

Wickstrom, John A. 26; Arizona, 1890 ***2764.35*** *p73*
Widanski, Anna; Wisconsin, n.d. ***9675.8*** *p125*
Widanski, Gerhard; Wisconsin, n.d. ***9675.8*** *p125*
Widas, Jack; Iowa, 1866-1943 ***123.54*** *p51*
Widas, Lew; Iowa, 1866-1943 ***123.54*** *p51*
Widdop, Paul 26; New England, 1699 ***2212*** *p18*
Widdows, John 31; Virginia, 1774 ***1219.7*** *p241*
Widdrington, General; Quebec, 1815 ***9229.18*** *p80*
With 3 daughters
Wideman, . . .; Canada, 1776-1783 ***9786*** *p37*
Widemuth, Cho. 28; Port uncertain, 1839 ***778.5*** *p547*
Widemuth, Chon 2; Port uncertain, 1839 ***778.5*** *p547*
Widemuth, Magdalena 20; Port uncertain, 1839 ***778.5*** *p547*
Widemuth, Nikolaus 3; Port uncertain, 1839 ***778.5*** *p547*
Widemuth, Nikolaus 34; Port uncertain, 1839 ***778.5*** *p547*
Widemuth, Peter 6; Port uncertain, 1839 ***778.5*** *p547*
Widenmajer, Christina Magdalena *SEE* Widenmajer, Hans Jerg
Widenmajer, Eva Catharina *SEE* Widenmajer, Hans Jerg
Widenmajer, Eva Catharina *SEE* Widenmajer, Hans Jerg
Widenmajer, Georg Balthas *SEE* Widenmajer, Hans Jerg
Widenmajer, Hans Jerg; Port uncertain, 1751 ***2444*** *p233*
*Wife:*Eva Catharina
*Child:*Georg Balthas
*Child:*Hans Philipp
*Child:*Johann Christoph
*Child:*Christina Magdalena
*Child:*Johann Gottfried
*Child:*Eva Catharina
Widenmajer, Hans Philipp *SEE* Widenmajer, Hans Jerg
Widenmajer, Johann Christoph *SEE* Widenmajer, Hans Jerg
Widenmajer, Johann Gottfried *SEE* Widenmajer, Hans Jerg
Widenmayer, Anna Maria; Pennsylvania, 1746 ***2444*** *p184*
Widholm, Gustof Adolf; Iroquois Co., IL, 1892 ***3455.1*** *p14*
Widing, Oscar Fredrick; Illinois, 1880 ***5012.39*** *p120*
Widmaier, Margaretha; Pennsylvania, 1752 ***2444*** *p220*
Widmajer, Christina Magdalena *SEE* Widmajer, Hans Jerg
Widmajer, Eva Catharina *SEE* Widmajer, Hans Jerg
Widmajer, Eva Catharina *SEE* Widmajer, Hans Jerg
Widmajer, Georg Balthas *SEE* Widmajer, Hans Jerg
Widmajer, Hans Jerg; Port uncertain, 1751 ***2444*** *p233*
*Wife:*Eva Catharina
*Child:*Georg Balthas
*Child:*Hans Philipp
*Child:*Johann Christoph
*Child:*Christina Magdalena
*Child:*Johann Gottfried
*Child:*Eva Catharina
Widmajer, Hans Philipp *SEE* Widmajer, Hans Jerg
Widmajer, Johann Christoph *SEE* Widmajer, Hans Jerg
Widmajer, Johann Gottfried *SEE* Widmajer, Hans Jerg
Widmajr, Anna Maria *SEE* Widmajr, Martin
Widmajr, Christoph *SEE* Widmajr, Martin
Widmajr, Johann Cunrad *SEE* Widmajr, Martin
Widmajr, Magdalena *SEE* Widmajr, Martin
Widmajr, Margaretha *SEE* Widmajr, Martin
Widmajr, Martin *SEE* Widmajr, Martin
Widmajr, Martin; America, 1751 ***2444*** *p233*
*Wife:*Magdalena
*Child:*Martin
*Child:*Anna Maria
*Child:*Christoph
*Child:*Johann Cunrad
*Child:*Margaretha
Widman, Berger W.; Illinois, 1896 ***5012.40*** *p55*
Widmann, David; Cincinnati, 1788-1848 ***8582.3*** *p89*
Widmar, Cecilia; Iowa, 1866-1943 ***123.54*** *p83*
Widmar, Franjo; Iowa, 1866-1943 ***123.54*** *p51*
Widmar, Franjo; Iowa, 1866-1943 ***123.54*** *p52*
Widmar, Sophia Marie; Iowa, 1866-1943 ***123.54*** *p83*
Widmayer, Catharina; Pennsylvania, 1752 ***2444*** *p135*
Widmayer, George; New York, NY, 1833 ***8208.4*** *p30*
Widmer, Henri 49; America, 1838 ***778.5*** *p547*
Widmeyer, Martin; America, 1751 ***2444*** *p233*
Widmeyr, Anna Maria *SEE* Widmeyr, Martin
Widmeyr, Christoph *SEE* Widmeyr, Martin
Widmeyr, Johann Cunrad *SEE* Widmeyr, Martin
Widmeyr, Magdalena *SEE* Widmeyr, Martin
Widmeyr, Margaretha *SEE* Widmeyr, Martin
Widmeyr, Martin *SEE* Widmeyr, Martin
Widmeyr, Martin; America, 1751 ***2444*** *p233*
*Wife:*Magdalena
*Child:*Martin
*Child:*Anna Maria
*Child:*Christoph
*Child:*Johann Cunrad
*Child:*Margaretha
Widmire, Geo; Pennsylvania, 1764 ***2444*** *p233*
Widop, Tho 17; America, 1699 ***2212*** *p28*
Widrig, Tobias Anton; America, 1845 ***8582.3*** *p70*
Widutis, Gorgis; Wisconsin, n.d. ***9675.8*** *p125*
Wieb, Anna; Quebec, 1877 ***9980.20*** *p48*
Wiebald, Georg; New York, NY, 1839 ***8208.4*** *p98*
Wiebe, Elise; America, 1890 ***5240.1*** *p48*
Wiebe, Henry H.; Kansas, 1891 ***5240.1*** *p48*
Wiebe, John; Kansas, 1900 ***5240.1*** *p48*
Wiebe, John D.; Kansas, 1903 ***5240.1*** *p48*
Wiebe, Wilhelm H.; America, 1851 ***8582.3*** *p70*
Wiebusch, Wilhelmine; New York, NY, 1884 ***3702.7*** *p592*
Wiechelmann, Johann C.; Cincinnati, 1869-1887 ***8582*** *p34*
Wiechers, Anna Catharina Ohe *SEE* Wiechers, Ernst Heinrich Ludwig
Wiechers, Ernst Heinrich Ludwig; America, 1831 ***4815.7*** *p92*
With 4 children
*Wife:*Anna Catharina Ohe
Wiechers, Johann Heinrich; Cincinnati, 1838 ***4815.7*** *p92*
*Wife:*Margarete Lucise Kruse
Wiechers, Margarete Lucise Kruse *SEE* Wiechers, Johann Heinrich
Wiechert, William; America, 1845 ***1450.2*** *p156A*
Wiecheski, Zofia 17; New York, 1912 ***9980.29*** *p64*
Wiechman, Dietrick 31; Kansas, 1906 ***5240.1*** *p84*
Wiechman, Henry; America, 1894 ***5240.1*** *p48*
Wiechman, Herman; America, 1892 ***5240.1*** *p48*
Wiechmann, Anton; America, 1845 ***8582.3*** *p70*
Wied, Jacob; America, 1855 ***3702.7*** *p549*
Wiedau, Anna W. Hakmann *SEE* Wiedau, Christoph Heinrich
Wiedau, Christoph Heinrich; America, 1831 ***4815.7*** *p92*
*Wife:*Anna W. Hakmann
With daughter
Wiedemann, Georg; America, 1854 ***8582.3*** *p70*
Wiedemer, F. X.; Cincinnati, 1869-1887 ***8582*** *p34*
Wiederholdt, Andreas; Philadelphia, 1779 ***8137*** *p15*
Wiederholk, Andreas; Halifax, N.S., 1780 ***9786*** *p269*
Wiederholk, Andreas; New York, 1776 ***9786*** *p269*
Wiederkum, John 23; Philadelphia, 1774 ***1219.7*** *p183*
Wieg, . . .; Canada, 1776-1783 ***9786*** *p37*
Wiegand, Adolph 34; Kansas, 1876 ***5240.1*** *p56*
Wiegand, Henrich; Lancaster, PA, 1780 ***8137*** *p15*
Wiegand, John V.; America, 1842 ***8582.1*** *p36*
Wiegand, Konrad; Philadelphia, 1779 ***8137*** *p15*
Wiegand, Siegesmond; Philadelphia, 1779 ***8137*** *p15*
Wiegman, . . .; Canada, 1776-1783 ***9786*** *p37*
Wiegmann, Christian; America, 1859 ***1450.2*** *p157A*
Wiegmann, Joseph; Cincinnati, 1846 ***8582.1*** *p36*
Wiegmann, N.; Illinois, 1800-1899 ***4610.10*** *p66*
Wiehauss, Heinrich August Ludwig; America, 1865 ***4610.10*** *p117*
Wieke, Caspar 26; Kansas, 1893 ***5240.1*** *p79*
Wieland, John Jacob; Pennsylvania, 1849 ***6013.19*** *p89*
Wieland, Leonhard; Virginia, 1775 ***1219.7*** *p275*
Wieland, Wilhelmine 20; New York, NY, 1862 ***9831.18*** *p16*
Wiele, Caroline Friederike; America, 1881 ***4610.10*** *p117*
Wiele, Ernst Friedrich Wilhelm; America, 1851 ***4610.10*** *p116*
Wiele, Ernst Heinrich Ludwig; America, 1885 ***4610.10*** *p102*
Wieler, Jac.; Quebec, 1875 ***9980.20*** *p48*
Wielert, Heinrich; America, 1851 ***8582.3*** *p70*
Wielgoscon, Marcianna 24; New York, 1912 ***9980.29*** *p49*
Wielking, Henry; New York, 1884 ***1450.2*** *p158A*
Wieman, Herm; America, 1843 ***8582.1*** *p36*
Wiemann, Anton Heinrich; America, 1838 ***4610.10*** *p114*
Wiemann, Herm; America, 1843 ***8582.1*** *p36*
Wienberg, Charles; Detroit, 1861 ***1450.2*** *p158A*
Wienburger, Henry 31; Kansas, 1873 ***5240.1*** *p54*
Wienke, Frederick; Illinois, 1876 ***5012.37*** *p59*
Wiens, Anna; Quebec, 1875 ***9980.20*** *p48*
Wiens, Anna 31; Quebec, 1875 ***9980.20*** *p48*
Wiens, Anna Friesen; Quebec, 1875 ***9980.20*** *p48*
Wiens, Barbara; Quebec, 1875 ***9980.20*** *p48*
Wiens, Cathariena; Quebec, 1875 ***9980.20*** *p48*
Wiens, Franz 14; Quebec, 1875 ***9980.20*** *p48*
Wiens, Hermann; Kansas, 1888 ***5240.1*** *p48*
Wiens, Jacob; Quebec, 1875 ***9980.20*** *p48*
Wiens, Jacob 20; Quebec, 1875 ***9980.20*** *p48*
Wiens, Just.; Quebec, 1875 ***9980.20*** *p48*
Wiens, Maria; Quebec, 1875 ***9980.20*** *p48*
Wiens, Maria; Quebec, 1875 ***9980.20*** *p49*
Wiens, Maria; Quebec, 1877 ***9980.20*** *p49*
Wiens, Peter; Quebec, 1875 ***9980.20*** *p48*
Wiens, Peter; Quebec, 1875 ***9980.20*** *p49*
Wier, Alexander; West Virginia, 1829 ***9788.3*** *p22*
Wier, Alexander; West Virginia, 1836 ***9788.3*** *p22*
Wier, Biddy 18; Massachusetts, 1847 ***5881.1*** *p96*
Wier, George; New York, NY, 1840 ***8208.4*** *p109*
Wier, James 23; Maryland, 1774 ***1219.7*** *p193*
Wier, John 22; Maryland, 1774 ***1219.7*** *p181*
Wier, Mary 50; Massachusetts, 1849 ***5881.1*** *p97*
Wier, Nancy 26; Massachusetts, 1849 ***5881.1*** *p98*
Wiercinski, Bertold; New York, 1831 ***4606*** *p178*
Wierimaa, Emelia; Washington, 1859-1920 ***2872.1*** *p43*
Wierimaa, Jakob; Washington, 1859-1920 ***2872.1*** *p43*
Wierimaa, Witha; Washington, 1859-1920 ***2872.1*** *p43*
Wierimaa, Yorse; Washington, 1859-1920 ***2872.1*** *p43*
Wierimoo, Yakob; Washington, 1859-1920 ***2872.1*** *p43*
Wierimuu, Yakob; Washington, 1859-1920 ***2872.1*** *p43*
Wiersma, Peter 22; Arkansas, 1918 ***95.2*** *p130*
Wierzbicki, Alex; New York, 1831 ***4606*** *p177*
Wierzbicki, Szczesny; New York, 1831 ***4606*** *p178*
Wierzkowski, Antanas 25; New York, 1912 ***9980.29*** *p58*
Wiese, Anthony; America, 1839 ***1450.2*** *p158A*
Wiese, Christian; Illinois, 1884-1954 ***4610.10*** *p66*
Wiese, John; Wisconsin, n.d. ***9675.8*** *p125*
Wiese, John Conrad; America, 1838 ***1450.2*** *p158A*
Wiesell, . . .; Canada, 1776-1783 ***9786*** *p37*
Wiesener, . . .; Canada, 1776-1783 ***9786*** *p37*
Wiesener, . . .; Quebec, 1776 ***9786*** *p105*
Wiesener, Lt.; Canada, 1780 ***9786*** *p181*
Wiesener, Christian Friedrich; Quebec, 1776 ***9786*** *p255*
Wieshmeir, Charles Frederick; America, 1837 ***1450.2*** *p158A*
Wieskirchen, Joseph; Wisconsin, n.d. ***9675.8*** *p125*
Wiesler, Hans Michel; Pennsylvania, 1752 ***4525*** *p255*
With 4 children
Wiesner, . . .; Canada, 1776-1783 ***9786*** *p37*
Wiesner, Chas. T. 44; America, 1897 ***1763*** *p40D*
Wiesner, George; Philadelphia, 1742 ***3652*** *p55*
Wiesner, George; Philadelphia, 1742 ***3652*** *p56*
Wiesner, Hans Michel; Pennsylvania, 1750 ***4525*** *p255*
With wife
With children
Wiesner, Hulda; Washington, 1859-1920 ***2872.1*** *p43*
Wiesner, Julius; Washington, 1859-1920 ***2872.1*** *p43*
Wiesner, Richard Edward; Washington, 1859-1920 ***2872.1*** *p43*
Wiess, Carl; New York, NY, 1894 ***3455.3*** *p26*
*Wife:*Minnie
Wiess, Minnie *SEE* Wiess, Carl
Wiessel, Paul Nicolas 40; Halifax, N.S., 1752 ***7074.6*** *p207*
With family of 6
Wiessler, Nicolaus; Pennsylvania, 1752 ***4525*** *p255*
With wife
With 2 children
Wiessman, Hans; Pennsylvania, 1752 ***4525*** *p255*
Wiessmann, Hans; Pennsylvania, 1752 ***4525*** *p255*
Wiessner, Anna Rosina; New England, 1753 ***4525*** *p223*
Wiest, Carl 6 mos; New York, NY, 1889 ***7846*** *p40*
Wiest, George; Pennsylvania, 1754 ***2444*** *p236*
Wiest, Gottlieb; Cincinnati, 1848 ***8582.2*** *p63*
Wiest, John; America, 1851 ***1450.2*** *p158A*
Wiest, Johnnes; Reading, PA, 1780 ***8137*** *p15*
Wiest, Josef 2; New York, NY, 1889 ***7846*** *p40*
Wiest, Margaretha 30; New York, NY, 1889 ***7846*** *p40*
Wiest, Vincenz 28; New York, NY, 1889 ***7846*** *p40*
Wietersheim, Adolph von; Quebec, 1778 ***9786*** *p267*
Wietersheim, Aug. Van; Wisconsin, n.d. ***9675.8*** *p125*
Wieting, Albert 45; Kansas, 1886 ***5240.1*** *p69*
Wigdor, Henry E.; America, 1884 ***1450.2*** *p41B*
Wigel, Johann; Illinois, 1828 ***8582.1*** *p54*
Wigg, Robert; Virginia, 1638 ***6219*** *p147*
Wigg, William; Virginia, 1638 ***6219*** *p147*
Wiggers, Didrik Laurentius Fog; Colorado, 1897 ***9678.3*** *p18*
Wiggert, Christopher; New York, NY, 1836 ***8208.4*** *p18*
Wiggin, James 26; Maryland, 1774 ***1219.7*** *p204*
Wiggin, Sarah; Massachusetts, 1848 ***5881.1*** *p98*
Wigging, Rachel; Philadelphia, 1816 ***2859.11*** *p44*
Wiggins, Henry; New York, NY, 1816 ***2859.11*** *p44*
Wiggins, Isaac 24; Maryland, 1730 ***3690.1*** *p245*
Wiggins, James; Colorado, 1891 ***9678.3*** *p18*
Wiggins, Thomas J. J. 29; Kansas, 1888 ***5240.1*** *p72*
Wiggmore, John 17; Pennsylvania, 1738 ***3690.1*** *p245*
Wigham, John 23; Virginia, 1773 ***1219.7*** *p171*
Wight, Edward John 17; Maryland, 1735 ***3690.1*** *p243*
Wight, George 32; Philadelphia, 1775 ***1219.7*** *p274*
Wightman, Ann 62 *SEE* Wightman, William
Wightman, Charles 26; Maryland, 1774 ***1219.7*** *p229*
Wightman, William 57; South Carolina, 1850 ***1639.20*** *p315*
*Relative:*Ann 62
Wighton, James 29; St. John, N.B., 1866 ***5704.8*** *p166*
Wighton, Margaret 27; St. John, N.B., 1866 ***5704.8*** *p166*
Wigley, William 23; Virginia, 1774 ***1219.7*** *p241*
Wigmet, Joseph; Kansas, 1912 ***6013.40*** *p17*
Wigmore, Elias; Virginia, 1637 ***6219*** *p113*

Wignall, Alex.; Virginia, 1647 ***6219*** *p245*
Wignall, Thomas; Illinois, 1861 ***2896.5*** *p42*
Wignall, Thomas; Virginia, 1647 ***6219*** *p245*
Wignoll, Margarett; Virginia, 1638 ***6219*** *p121*
Wigold, Johannis; Pennsylvania, 1752 ***2444*** *p231*
Wihl, Carl; Indiana, 1865 ***3702.7*** *p139*
Wike, Alex.; Virginia, 1642 ***6219*** *p189*
Wikers, . . .; Pennsylvania, n.d. ***4525*** *p253*
Wikidal, Martin 19; America, 1869-1887 ***8582*** *p34*
Wiks, William 16; Maryland, 1724 ***3690.1*** *p242*
Wikstedt, John; Colorado, 1904 ***9678.3*** *p18*
Wikstrom, Pehr; Minneapolis, 1869-1876 ***6410.35*** *p63*
Wilber, Henry; Indiana, 1848 ***9117*** *p18*
Wilber, Henry; Indiana, 1848 ***9117*** *p19*
Wilber, William 32; Massachusetts, 1860 ***6410.32*** *p113*
Wilbert, John Jacob; Wisconsin, n.d. ***9675.8*** *p125*
Wilch, Ann; Virginia, 1646 ***6219*** *p241*
Wilchingham, Bartholomew 15; Maryland, 1718 ***3690.1*** *p245*
Wilcke, Johannes; Philadelphia, 1779 ***8137*** *p15*
Wilcken, Conrad; Illinois, 1892 ***5012.40*** *p26*
Wilckening, Mr.; America, 1844 ***4610.10*** *p147*
*Wife:*Dorothee F. Begemann
*Child:*Johann Heinrich
*Child:*Friederike Charlotte
*Child:*Christoph Johann
Wilckening, Christoph Johann *SEE* Wilckening, Mr.
Wilckening, Dorothee F. Begemann *SEE* Wilckening, Mr.
Wilckening, Friederike Charlotte *SEE* Wilckening, Mr.
Wilckening, Johann Heinrich *SEE* Wilckening, Mr.
Wilcock, Georg; Virginia, 1637 ***6219*** *p110*
Wilcocks, John; Virginia, 1636 ***6219*** *p34*
Wilcocks, Thomas 18; Jamaica, 1750 ***3690.1*** *p245*
Wilcox, Mrs.; Philadelphia, 1774 ***1219.7*** *p224*
With 3 children
Wilcox, Grace; Virginia, 1642 ***6219*** *p196*
Wilcox, Michaell; Virginia, 1642 ***6219*** *p196*
Wilcox, Roger; Virginia, 1642 ***6219*** *p195*
Wilcox, Thomas 25; Salem, MA, 1774 ***1219.7*** *p234*
Wilcox, William; Kansas, 1870 ***5240.1*** *p48*
Wilczcwski, Andreas 20; New York, NY, 1878 ***9253*** *p47*
Wild, Abraham; Philadelphia, 1760 ***9973.7*** *p34*
Wild, Anna Eliese; Wisconsin, n.d. ***9675.8*** *p125*
Wild, Elizabeth 30; America, 1837 ***778.5*** *p547*
Wild, Georg Adolphus; New York, NY, 1836 ***8208.4*** *p80*
Wild, George 21; Virginia, 1774 ***1219.7*** *p185*
Wild, George 24; Maryland, 1774 ***1219.7*** *p181*
Wild, Johann Georg; Pennsylvania, 1758 ***4525*** *p256*
Wild, Jonathan 25; Maryland, 1730 ***3690.1*** *p245*
Wild, Nicholas; Philadelphia, 1762 ***9973.7*** *p37*
Wild, Thomas 20; America, 1706 ***2212*** *p47*
Wild, William 19; Philadelphia, 1774 ***1219.7*** *p215*
Wildbahne, Charles Frederick; Philadelphia, 1764 ***9973.7*** *p39*
Wildberg, Louis; Illinois, 1872 ***5012.37*** *p59*
Wilde, Hermann; Wisconsin, n.d. ***9675.8*** *p125*
Wilde, Jacob; Wisconsin, n.d. ***9675.8*** *p125*
Wilde, Jacob 34; Kansas, 1883 ***5240.1*** *p48*
Wilde, Jacob 34; Kansas, 1883 ***5240.1*** *p64*
Wilde, Johann; Wisconsin, n.d. ***9675.8*** *p125*
Wilde, John; Wisconsin, n.d. ***9675.8*** *p125*
Wildeboer, Ben; Arkansas, 1918 ***95.2*** *p130*
Wilden, John 24; Grenada, 1774 ***1219.7*** *p206*
Wildenmuth, Cho. 5; Port uncertain, 1839 ***778.5*** *p547*
Wildenmuth, Christian 17; Port uncertain, 1839 ***778.5*** *p547*
Wildenmuth, Elisabetha 14; Port uncertain, 1839 ***778.5*** *p547*
Wildenmuth, Georg 22; Port uncertain, 1839 ***778.5*** *p548*
Wildenmuth, Georg 43; Port uncertain, 1839 ***778.5*** *p548*
Wildenmuth, Karolina 19; Port uncertain, 1839 ***778.5*** *p548*
Wildenmuth, Magdalena 2; Port uncertain, 1839 ***778.5*** *p548*
Wildenmuth, Marie 42; Port uncertain, 1839 ***778.5*** *p548*
Wildenmuth, Philipp 9; Port uncertain, 1839 ***778.5*** *p548*
Wilder, Angela 3 *SEE* Wilder, John
Wilder, Anna Marie; South Carolina, 1752-1753 ***3689.17*** *p23*
Wilder, Edmund; New York, 1858 ***1450.2*** *p158A*
Wilder, Johannes 6 mos *SEE* Wilder, John
Wilder, John; South Carolina, 1752-1753 ***3689.17*** *p23*
With wife
*Relative:*Angela 3
*Relative:*Johannes 6 mos
Wilder, John 21; Jamaica, 1731 ***3690.1*** *p245*
Wilder, John Godfrey; Arkansas, 1918 ***95.2*** *p130*
Wilder, William 21; Jamaica, 1731 ***3690.1*** *p245*
Wilderich, Captain; America, 1861-1865 ***8582.3*** *p92*
Wildhack, John 81; Illinois, 1911 ***1763*** *p40D*
Wildie, Rebecca 22; Barbados, 1774 ***1219.7*** *p234*
Wildin, Mathew; New York, NY, 1865 ***5704.8*** *p199*
Wilding, Tho; Virginia, 1698 ***2212*** *p11*
Wilding, Thomas; Virginia, 1698 ***2212*** *p10*
Wildman, Richard 23; Maryland, 1775 ***1219.7*** *p273*
Wildman, Thomas; Wisconsin, n.d. ***9675.8*** *p125*
Wildman, Thomas E.; Wisconsin, n.d. ***9675.8*** *p125*
Wildman, William; Wisconsin, n.d. ***9675.8*** *p125*
Wildmann, Heinrich Wilhelm; America, 1845 ***8582.3*** *p70*
Wildmann, John R.; Wisconsin, n.d. ***9675.8*** *p125*
Wildy, William; Virginia, 1642 ***6219*** *p195*
Wile, Joseph; Milwaukee, 1875 ***4719.30*** *p257*
Wiles, John; New York, NY, 1835 ***8208.4*** *p46*
Wiley, Ann; New York, NY, 1816 ***2859.11*** *p44*
Wiley, Elizabeth; New York, NY, 1816 ***2859.11*** *p44*
Wiley, Jane; Philadelphia, 1849 ***53.26*** *p91*
Wiley, Jane; Philadelphia, 1849 ***5704.8*** *p49*
Wiley, Jane 19; Wilmington, DE, 1831 ***6508.3*** *p100*
Wiley, John; New York, NY, 1816 ***2859.11*** *p44*
Wiley, John; Philadelphia, 1866 ***5704.8*** *p206*
Wiley, Mary; New York, NY, 1816 ***2859.11*** *p44*
Wiley, Rebecca; New York, NY, 1867 ***5704.8*** *p220*
Wiley, Samuel; Philadelphia, 1847 ***53.26*** *p91*
*Relative:*Sarah
Wiley, Samuel; Philadelphia, 1847 ***5704.8*** *p31*
Wiley, Sarah *SEE* Wiley, Samuel
Wiley, Sarah; Philadelphia, 1847 ***5704.8*** *p31*
Wiley, Thomas; New York, NY, 1816 ***2859.11*** *p44*
Wilford, Edw.; Virginia, 1635 ***6219*** *p26*
Wilger, Mathias; Wisconsin, n.d. ***9675.8*** *p125*
Wilger, Peter, Jr.; Wisconsin, n.d. ***9675.8*** *p125*
Wilger, Peter, Sr.; Wisconsin, n.d. ***9675.8*** *p125*
Wilgerost, John; Canada, 1783 ***9786*** *p38A*
Wilharm, C. Gotlieb; Baltimore, 1840 ***1450.2*** *p158A*
Wilheim, Marie Berg 55; Pennsylvania, 1909 ***1763*** *p40D*
Wilhelm, . . .; Canada, 1776-1783 ***9786*** *p44*
Wilhelm IX ; Quebec, 1776 ***9786*** *p265*
Wilhelm, Ann Catharina; Philadelphia, 1760 ***9973.7*** *p34*
Wilhelm, Bruno 23; Kansas, 1906 ***5240.1*** *p84*
Wilhelm, Carl; Colorado, 1898 ***9678.3*** *p18*
Wilhelm, Columbian; Cincinnati, 1869-1887 ***8582*** *p34*
Wilhelm, Elis. 28; America, 1853 ***9162.7*** *p15*
Wilhelm, Henrich; Philadelphia, 1779 ***8137*** *p15*
Wilhelm, Jacob; Philadelphia, 1760 ***9973.7*** *p34*
Wilhelm, Johannes; Philadelphia, 1779 ***8137*** *p15*
Wilhelm, Kath. 17; America, 1853 ***9162.7*** *p15*
Wilhelm, Kath. 58; America, 1853 ***9162.7*** *p15*
Wilhelm, Marg. 6; America, 1853 ***9162.7*** *p15*
Wilhelm, Mathias; Illinois, 1893 ***5012.40*** *p53*
Wilhelm, Merchen; Pennsylvania, 1683 ***2155*** *p2*
Wilhelmi, . . .; Canada, 1776-1783 ***9786*** *p37*
Wilhelmi, Christian Ernst Diederich; Canada, 1776-1783 ***9786*** *p15*
Wilhelmi, Ernest D.; Canada, 1776-1783 ***9786*** *p207A*
Wilhelmy, Carl; Wisconsin, n.d. ***9675.8*** *p125*
Wilhelmy, Christian Ernst Diederich; Canada, 1776-1783 ***9786*** *p15*
Wilhem, Elis. 28; America, 1853 ***9162.7*** *p15*
Wilhem, Jean 17; Port uncertain, 1839 ***778.5*** *p548*
Wilhem, Joseph 28; Port uncertain, 1839 ***778.5*** *p548*
Wilhem, Kath. 17; America, 1853 ***9162.7*** *p15*
Wilhem, Kath. 58; America, 1853 ***9162.7*** *p15*
Wilhem, Marg. 6; America, 1853 ***9162.7*** *p15*
Wiliiams, John; Virginia, 1639 ***6219*** *p161*
Wilin, Peter; Arkansas, 1918 ***95.2*** *p130*
Wilis, James; New York, NY, 1816 ***2859.11*** *p44*
Wilke, Carl; Wisconsin, n.d. ***9675.8*** *p125*
Wilke, Christian; Wisconsin, 1842 ***3702.7*** *p307*
Wilke, Frederick; Wisconsin, n.d. ***9675.8*** *p125*
Wilke, Gustave; Wisconsin, n.d. ***9675.8*** *p125*
Wilke, William; Wisconsin, n.d. ***9675.8*** *p125*
Wilken, Fra.; Virginia, 1648 ***6219*** *p246*
Wilken, Frederick; Colorado, 1880 ***9678.3*** *p18*
Wilken, Jacob Matthaus; Washington, 1859-1920 ***2872.1*** *p43*
Wilken, Jakob; Illinois, 1900 ***5012.40*** *p79*
Wilken, Jan Lubben; Iroquois Co., IL, 1892 ***3455.1*** *p14*
Wilken, Kord; Iroquois Co., IL, 1892 ***3455.1*** *p14*
Wilkening, Frederick; America, 1837 ***1450.2*** *p158A*
Wilkening, Karl Diedrich; America, 1843 ***4610.10*** *p115*
Wilkenson, Charles; Philadelphia, 1866 ***5704.8*** *p211*
Wilkenson, John; Philadelphia, 1865 ***5704.8*** *p204*
Wilkerson, John; South Carolina, 1785 ***1639.20*** *p315*
Wilkerson, John 39; Maryland, 1774 ***1219.7*** *p181*
Wilkeson, Jno.; Virginia, 1643 ***6219*** *p207*
Wilkey, Nancy 33; St. John, N.B., 1855 ***5704.8*** *p126*
Wilkey, William 20; Maryland, 1737 ***3690.1*** *p245*
Wilkie, . . .; Halifax, N.S., 1752 ***7074.6*** *p232*
Wilkie, James; South Carolina, 1716 ***1639.20*** *p316*
Wilkie, William; South Carolina, 1832 ***1639.20*** *p316*
Wilkin, Jane 23; Philadelphia, 1864 ***5704.8*** *p155*
Wilkin, Jean; St. John, N.B., 1848 ***5704.8*** *p44*
Wilkin, John; Illinois, 1901 ***5012.40*** *p77*
Wilkin, John; Philadelphia, 1853 ***5704.8*** *p100*
Wilkins, Ann 17 *SEE* Wilkins, Thomas
Wilkins, Anthony 18; Jamaica, 1725 ***3690.1*** *p245*
Wilkins, Edward 39; Maryland, 1773 ***1219.7*** *p173*
Wilkins, Frances 12 *SEE* Wilkins, Thomas
Wilkins, George; New York, NY, 1811 ***2859.11*** *p20*
Wilkins, Humphry; Virginia, 1643 ***6219*** *p202*
Wilkins, Jacob Matlens; Washington, 1859-1920 ***2872.1*** *p43*
Wilkins, James; Charleston, SC, 1797 ***1639.20*** *p316*
Wilkins, James 24; Philadelphia, 1856 ***5704.8*** *p128*
Wilkins, John; Virginia, 1636 ***6219*** *p77*
Wilkins, John; Virginia, 1637 ***6219*** *p81*
Wilkins, John 7 *SEE* Wilkins, Thomas
Wilkins, John 18; Maryland, 1774 ***1219.7*** *p226*
Wilkins, John L.; New York, NY, 1834 ***8208.4*** *p44*
Wilkins, Joseph 14; Philadelphia, 1775 ***1219.7*** *p248*
Wilkins, Katherine; Virginia, 1637 ***6219*** *p115*
Wilkins, Katherine; Virginia, 1639 ***6219*** *p151*
Wilkins, Mary 15 *SEE* Wilkins, Thomas
Wilkins, Temperance 9 *SEE* Wilkins, Thomas
Wilkins, Temperance 46 *SEE* Wilkins, Thomas
Wilkins, Thomas; Virginia, 1644 ***6219*** *p230*
Wilkins, Thomas 21; Maryland, 1775 ***1219.7*** *p253*
Wilkins, Thomas 43; Boston, 1774 ***1219.7*** *p189*
*Wife:*Temperance 46
*Child:*Mary 15
*Child:*Frances 12
*Child:*John 7
*Child:*Temperance 9
*Child:*William 6
*Child:*Ann 17
Wilkins, William; Philadelphia, 1850 ***53.26*** *p91*
Wilkins, William; Philadelphia, 1850 ***5704.8*** *p60*
Wilkins, William 6 *SEE* Wilkins, Thomas
Wilkinson, Abel; New York, NY, 1834 ***8208.4*** *p33*
Wilkinson, Alexander; South Carolina, 1785 ***1639.20*** *p316*
Wilkinson, Angus 40; Kansas, 1881 ***5240.1*** *p63*
Wilkinson, Ann; Philadelphia, 1853 ***5704.8*** *p101*
Wilkinson, Catherine 20; Philadelphia, 1857 ***5704.8*** *p133*
Wilkinson, Charles; Virginia, 1698 ***2212*** *p12*
Wilkinson, Daniel 80; North Carolina, 1850 ***1639.20*** *p316*
Wilkinson, David; Iowa, 1866-1943 ***123.54*** *p52*
Wilkinson, Edward; New York, NY, 1836 ***8208.4*** *p11*
Wilkinson, Eliza; Philadelphia, 1865 ***5704.8*** *p199*
Wilkinson, Elizabeth 26; Virginia, 1774 ***1219.7*** *p193*
Wilkinson, George 18; Maryland, 1775 ***1219.7*** *p264*
Wilkinson, Henry; Philadelphia, 1854 ***5704.8*** *p116*
Wilkinson, James; New York, NY, 1838 ***8208.4*** *p84*
Wilkinson, James; Washington, 1859-1920 ***2872.1*** *p43*
Wilkinson, James 25; Philadelphia, 1859 ***5704.8*** *p141*
Wilkinson, Joane; Virginia, 1639 ***6219*** *p161*
Wilkinson, John; New York, NY, 1815 ***2859.11*** *p44*
Wilkinson, John; Virginia, 1639 ***6219*** *p161*
Wilkinson, John; Virginia, 1643 ***6219*** *p205*
Wilkinson, John 21; Jamaica, 1737 ***3690.1*** *p246*
Wilkinson, John 23; Philadelphia, 1803 ***53.26*** *p91*
Wilkinson, Joseph 28; Pennsylvania, 1730 ***3690.1*** *p246*
Wilkinson, Mary; Virginia, 1645 ***6219*** *p252*
Wilkinson, Mary 19; Maryland, 1773 ***1219.7*** *p173*
Wilkinson, Nancy; Philadelphia, 1850 ***53.26*** *p91*
Wilkinson, Naomy *SEE* Wilkinson, William
Wilkinson, Naomy *SEE* Wilkinson, Wm.
Wilkinson, Naomy; Virginia, 1636 ***6219*** *p180*
Wilkinson, Patrick; Montreal, 1822 ***7603*** *p70*
Wilkinson, Robert; Virginia, 1638 ***6219*** *p160*
Wilkinson, Robert 18; Philadelphia, 1857 ***5704.8*** *p133*
Wilkinson, Robt.; Virginia, 1635 ***6219*** *p72*
Wilkinson, Samuel 15; Maryland, 1723 ***3690.1*** *p246*
Wilkinson, Tho.; Virginia, 1637 ***6219*** *p85*
Wilkinson, Thomas; America, 1741 ***4971*** *p16*
Wilkinson, Thomas; Virginia, 1637 ***6219*** *p115*
Wilkinson, Thomas 21; Maryland, 1775 ***1219.7*** *p254*
Wilkinson, Thomas 23; Nova Scotia, 1774 ***1219.7*** *p209*
With wife
With child
Wilkinson, Thomas 27; Pennsylvania, 1728 ***3690.1*** *p246*
Wilkinson, William; New York, NY, 1815 ***2859.11*** *p44*
Wilkinson, William; Virginia, 1635 ***6219*** *p180*
Wilkinson, William; Virginia, 1637 ***6219*** *p83*
*Wife:*Naomy
Wilkinson, Wm.; Virginia, 1635 ***6219*** *p36*
*Wife:*Naomy
Wilkinson, Wm.; Virginia, 1639 ***6219*** *p154*
Wilkison, Andrew; Philadelphia, 1852 ***5704.8*** *p88*
Wilkison, Andrew 11; Philadelphia, 1852 ***5704.8*** *p88*
Wilkison, Ann; Philadelphia, 1852 ***5704.8*** *p88*
Wilkison, Archy; Philadelphia, 1852 ***5704.8*** *p88*
Wilkison, Jane; Philadelphia, 1852 ***5704.8*** *p88*
Wilkison, Ketty Ann; St. John, N.B., 1847 ***5704.8*** *p33*
Wilkison, Mary; Philadelphia, 1852 ***5704.8*** *p88*
Wilkison, Nancy; Philadelphia, 1850 ***5704.8*** *p60*

Wilkison, Rebecca; Philadelphia, 1852 ***5704.8*** *p88*
Wilkison, Richard 19; Philadelphia, 1854 ***5704.8*** *p117*
Wilkison, William 18; Philadelphia, 1859 ***5704.8*** *p141*
Wilks, James; New York, NY, 1838 ***8208.4*** *p88*
Will, . . .; Canada, 1776-1783 ***9786*** *p37*
Will, Carl; Indiana, 1865 ***3702.7*** *p141*
Will, Fred 36; Kansas, 1892 ***5240.1*** *p48*
Will, Fred 36; Kansas, 1892 ***5240.1*** *p76*
Will, Frederick; Ohio, 1849 ***1450.2*** *p159A*
Will, Friedricka 50; Kansas, 1891 ***5240.1*** *p76*
Will, Philipp; Charleston, SC, 1775-1781 ***8582.2*** *p52*
Willam, George 40; Jamaica, 1774 ***1219.7*** *p189*
Willan, Marie; Quebec, 1770 ***7603*** *p100*
Willan, Patrick; Quebec, 1821 ***7603*** *p69*
Willard, Christian; Pennsylvania, 1749 ***4779.3*** *p14A*
*Relative:*Martin
Willard, Jacob; America, 1741 ***4971*** *p99*
Willard, Martin *SEE* Willard, Christian
Willbourne, William; Virginia, 1636 ***6219*** *p77*
Willdix, Joseph 20; Virginia, 1721 ***3690.1*** *p246*
Wille, Ludwig; Wisconsin, n.d. ***9675.8*** *p125*
Wille, Otto; Wisconsin, n.d. ***9675.8*** *p125*
Wille, William; Wisconsin, n.d. ***9675.8*** *p125*
Willeford, William; Virginia, 1638 ***6219*** *p148*
Willem, Jakob; America, 1845 ***8582.1*** *p36*
Willen, Heinrich; Kentucky, 1843 ***8582.3*** *p100*
Willen, Wilhelm; America, 1835 ***8582.3*** *p70*
Willen, Wilhelm; Kentucky, 1835 ***8582.3*** *p99*
Willenbach, Louis 34; Harris Co., TX, 1898 ***6254*** *p4*
Willenborg, Francis H.; Cincinnati, 1872-1874 ***8582.1*** *p36*
Willenbrink, Bernhardt A.; New Orleans, 1844-1849 ***8582.3*** *p70*
Willerson, Patrick 18; Massachusetts, 1848 ***5881.1*** *p98*
Willes, Joshua; New York, NY, 1816 ***2859.11*** *p44*
Willes, Mary; New York, NY, 1816 ***2859.11*** *p44*
Willesen, Willie H.; Arkansas, 1918 ***95.2*** *p130*
Willet, Charles A. 37; Massachusetts, 1860 ***6410.32*** *p101*
Willet, Jean; Quebec, 1710 ***7603*** *p28*
Willet, Mary J. 30; Massachusetts, 1860 ***6410.32*** *p101*
Willet, Samuel 24; Pennsylvania, 1731 ***3690.1*** *p246*
Willett, Benjamin; Wisconsin, n.d. ***9675.8*** *p125*
Willett, Daniel 27; Virginia, 1773 ***1219.7*** *p171*
Willett, Hen.; Virginia, 1640 ***6219*** *p182*
Willett, James; Virginia, 1636 ***6219*** *p76*
Willett, James 16; Virginia, 1727 ***3690.1*** *p246*
Willett, John; New York, 1751-1767 ***1219.7*** *p126*
Willett, Peter; Virginia, 1638 ***6219*** *p124*
Willey, Fritz N.; Illinois, 1898 ***2896.5*** *p42*
Willey, Robert; Virginia, 1638 ***6219*** *p148*
William, Alice; Quebec, 1822 ***7603*** *p64*
William, Charles; New York, 1854 ***1450.2*** *p159A*
William, David 21; Maryland or Virginia, 1699 ***2212*** *p23*
William, Mrs. E.W.; New York, NY, 1816 ***2859.11*** *p44*
William, Hugh 20; Maryland, 1750 ***3690.1*** *p246*
William, Hugh 20; Maryland, 1751 ***1219.7*** *p2*
Williams, Dr.; Quebec, 1815 ***9229.18*** *p75*
Williams, Miss; Quebec, 1815 ***9229.18*** *p78*
Williams, Mr.; Quebec, 1815 ***9229.18*** *p76*
Williams, Alice; Virginia, 1639 ***6219*** *p150*
Williams, Andrew; Boston, 1858 ***6410.32*** *p122*
Williams, Andrew 27; Massachusetts, 1860 ***6410.32*** *p101*
Williams, Ann; Virginia, 1635 ***6219*** *p4*
Williams, Ann; Virginia, 1647 ***6219*** *p248*
Williams, Ann 20; Port uncertain, 1849 ***4535.10*** *p198*
Williams, Ann 22; Maryland or Virginia, 1699 ***2212*** *p21*
Williams, Ann 23; Maryland, 1775 ***1219.7*** *p265*
Williams, Ann 28; Massachusetts, 1848 ***5881.1*** *p96*
Williams, Anne; St. John, N.B., 1847 ***5704.8*** *p2*
Williams, Anne 9 mos; Philadelphia, 1853 ***5704.8*** *p101*
Williams, Arthur; Boston, 1776 ***1219.7*** *p283*
Williams, Arthur 2 mos; Massachusetts, 1860 ***6410.32*** *p101*
Williams, Ben 38; Arizona, 1890 ***2764.35*** *p73*
Williams, Bohle; Illinois, 1863 ***7857*** *p8*
Williams, Bridgett 27; Massachusetts, 1860 ***6410.32*** *p101*
Williams, Catherine; Quebec, 1847 ***5704.8*** *p6*
Williams, Catherine; St. John, N.B., 1850 ***5704.8*** *p62*
Williams, Catherine Eliza 4; Quebec, 1847 ***5704.8*** *p6*
Williams, Charles; New York, NY, 1841 ***6410.32*** *p122*
Williams, Charles; New York, NY, 1850 ***6013.19*** *p89*
Williams, Charles 2; Philadelphia, 1853 ***5704.8*** *p101*
Williams, Charles 17; Maryland, 1720 ***3690.1*** *p246*
Williams, Charles 23; Maryland, 1774 ***1219.7*** *p229*
Williams, Charles 28; Massachusetts, 1860 ***6410.32*** *p112*
Williams, Charles 32; Massachusetts, 1860 ***6410.32*** *p100*
Williams, Christ.; Virginia, 1638 ***6219*** *p122*
Williams, Corn.; Virginia, 1642 ***6219*** *p191*
Williams, Daniel 50; New York, 1774 ***1219.7*** *p197*
With wife
Williams, Daniell 24; Virginia, 1700 ***2212*** *p33*
Williams, David; Kansas, 1870 ***5240.1*** *p51*
Williams, David 22; Philadelphia, 1858 ***5704.8*** *p139*
Williams, David 35; America, 1700 ***2212*** *p33*
Williams, David Mack; Virginia, 1638 ***6219*** *p121*
Williams, Edmund; Iowa, 1866-1943 ***123.54*** *p52*
Williams, Edw.; Virginia, 1635 ***6219*** *p20*
Williams, Edward; Virginia, 1635 ***6219*** *p73*
Williams, Edward; Virginia, 1637 ***6219*** *p24*
Williams, Edward; Virginia, 1637 ***6219*** *p113*
Williams, Edward; Virginia, 1642 ***6219*** *p186*
Williams, Edward; Virginia, 1642 ***6219*** *p190*
Williams, Edward; Virginia, 1648 ***6219*** *p237*
Williams, Edward; Virginia, 1698 ***2212*** *p15*
Williams, Edward 30; Maryland, 1774 ***1219.7*** *p223*
Williams, Edward 45; Maryland, 1775 ***1219.7*** *p264*
Williams, Eliza; Philadelphia, 1850 ***5704.8*** *p65*
Williams, Eliza; Virginia, 1698 ***2212*** *p14*
Williams, Elizabeth; Philadelphia, 1850 ***53.26*** *p91*
Williams, Elizabeth 10; Philadelphia, 1853 ***5704.8*** *p101*
Williams, Ellen; Illinois, 1894 ***2896.5*** *p42*
Williams, Ellen 21; Massachusetts, 1860 ***6410.32*** *p100*
Williams, Ellin; Virginia, 1635 ***6219*** *p17*
Williams, Evan; Virginia, 1635 ***6219*** *p70*
Williams, Evan; Virginia, 1637 ***6219*** *p180*
Williams, Francis 17; Maryland, 1723 ***3690.1*** *p246*
Williams, Frederick; Illinois, 1888 ***5012.37*** *p61*
Williams, George; Arkansas, 1918 ***95.2*** *p130*
Williams, George; New York, NY, 1838 ***8208.4*** *p75*
Williams, George; Philadelphia, 1811 ***53.26*** *p91*
Williams, George; Philadelphia, 1811 ***2859.11*** *p20*
Williams, George; Washington, 1859-1920 ***2872.1*** *p43*
Williams, George 19; Maryland, 1775 ***1219.7*** *p256*
Williams, Henry; New York, NY, 1811 ***2859.11*** *p20*
Williams, Henry; Virginia, 1623-1642 ***6219*** *p192*
Williams, Henry; Wisconsin, n.d. ***9675.8*** *p125*
Williams, Henry 15; America, 1700 ***2212*** *p30*
Williams, Henry 16; Pennsylvania, Virginia or Maryland, 1719 ***3690.1*** *p246*
Williams, Henry 18; Maryland, 1730 ***3690.1*** *p292*
Williams, Henry 28; Philadelphia, 1803 ***53.26*** *p91*
Williams, Humphrey; Virginia, 1638 ***6219*** *p118*
Williams, James; America, 1741 ***4971*** *p16*
Williams, James; New York, NY, 1838 ***8208.4*** *p82*
Williams, James 18; Jamaica, 1736 ***3690.1*** *p246*
Williams, James 21; Maryland, 1775 ***1219.7*** *p250*
Williams, James 31; Maryland, 1775 ***1219.7*** *p271*
Williams, James 54; Massachusetts, 1860 ***6410.32*** *p102*
Williams, James Parker 42; Kansas, 1871 ***5240.1*** *p52*
Williams, Jane; Virginia, 1645 ***6219*** *p239*
Williams, Jane 9; Philadelphia, 1853 ***5704.8*** *p101*
Williams, Jane 26; Maryland, 1774 ***1219.7*** *p187*
Williams, Jane 29; America, 1706 ***2212*** *p46*
Williams, Janette 37; South Carolina, 1850 ***1639.20*** *p121*
Williams, Jinkin; Virginia, 1638 ***6219*** *p125*
Williams, Jno; America, 1698 ***2212*** *p9*
Williams, Jno; America, 1698 ***2212*** *p13*
Williams, Jno; Virginia, 1698 ***2212*** *p15*
Williams, Jno 12; Maryland or Virginia, 1699 ***2212*** *p23*
Williams, Jno 14; America, 1699 ***2212*** *p28*
Williams, Joan; America, 1697 ***2212*** *p7*
Williams, John; America, 1737 ***4971*** *p13*
Williams, John; America, 1800 ***1639.20*** *p316*
Williams, John; Boston, 1832 ***6410.32*** *p122*
Williams, John; Milwaukee, 1875 ***4719.30*** *p257*
Williams, John; Nevada, 1880 ***2764.35*** *p74*
Williams, John; New York, NY, 1838 ***8208.4*** *p74*
Williams, John; New York, NY, 1839 ***8208.4*** *p96*
Williams, John; Philadelphia, 1756 ***9973.7*** *p32*
Williams, John; Virginia, 1636 ***6219*** *p78*
Williams, John; Virginia, 1637 ***6219*** *p8*
Williams, John; Virginia, 1638 ***6219*** *p2*
Williams, John; Virginia, 1638 ***6219*** *p117*
Williams, John; Virginia, 1638 ***6219*** *p121*
Williams, John; Virginia, 1638 ***6219*** *p150*
Williams, John; Virginia, 1643 ***6219*** *p202*
Williams, John; Virginia, 1643 ***6219*** *p203*
Williams, John; Virginia, 1646 ***6219*** *p236*
Williams, John; Virginia, 1647 ***6219*** *p249*
Williams, John; Virginia, 1648 ***6219*** *p241*
Williams, John; Virginia, 1648 ***6219*** *p250*
Williams, John 5; St. John, N.B., 1850 ***5704.8*** *p62*
Williams, John 7; Philadelphia, 1853 ***5704.8*** *p101*
Williams, John 12; Virginia, 1699 ***2212*** *p27*
Williams, John 15; Maryland, 1719 ***3690.1*** *p246*
Williams, John 15; Maryland, 1724 ***3690.1*** *p247*
Williams, John 18; Maryland, 1729 ***3690.1*** *p247*
Williams, John 18; Maryland, 1774 ***1219.7*** *p236*
Williams, John 18; Pennsylvania, 1721 ***3690.1*** *p247*
Williams, John 18; St. John, N.B., 1858 ***5704.8*** *p137*
Williams, John 18; Virginia, 1720 ***3690.1*** *p247*
Williams, John 19; Maryland, 1723 ***3690.1*** *p247*
Williams, John 19; Philadelphia, 1774 ***1219.7*** *p185*
Williams, John 20; Barbados, 1719 ***3690.1*** *p247*
Williams, John 20; Barbados, 1721 ***3690.1*** *p247*
Williams, John 20; Philadelphia, 1775 ***1219.7*** *p248*
Williams, John 21; Jamaica, 1737 ***3690.1*** *p247*
Williams, John 22; Grenada, 1774 ***1219.7*** *p180*
Williams, John 22; Maryland, 1775 ***1219.7*** *p260*
Williams, John 22; Philadelphia, 1774 ***1219.7*** *p232*
Williams, John 25; Maryland, 1774 ***1219.7*** *p184*
Williams, John 27; Jamaica, 1733 ***3690.1*** *p247*
Williams, John 27; Jamaica, 1774 ***1219.7*** *p184*
Williams, John 27; Virginia, 1774 ***1219.7*** *p186*
Williams, John 29; Baltimore, 1775 ***1219.7*** *p270*
Williams, John 29; New England, 1699 ***2212*** *p19*
Williams, John 30; Carolina, 1774 ***1219.7*** *p179*
Williams, John 30; Maryland, 1774 ***1219.7*** *p221*
Williams, John 30; Maryland, 1775 ***1219.7*** *p271*
Williams, John 31; Jamaica, 1725 ***3690.1*** *p247*
Williams, John 34; Kansas, 1874 ***5240.1*** *p48*
Williams, John 34; Kansas, 1874 ***5240.1*** *p55*
Williams, John 38; Massachusetts, 1860 ***6410.32*** *p117*
Williams, John 40; Maryland, 1774 ***1219.7*** *p230*
Williams, John 50; Philadelphia, 1774 ***1219.7*** *p201*
*Child:*Mary 20
Williams, John 53; Massachusetts, 1860 ***6410.32*** *p100*
Williams, John 70; Wilmington, NC, 1850 ***1639.20*** *p316*
Williams, John Michael; Arkansas, 1918 ***95.2*** *p130*
Williams, John Pawle; New York, 1872 ***1450.2*** *p159A*
Williams, John Reece 29; Kansas, 1875 ***5240.1*** *p56*
Williams, John S.; Arizona, 1882 ***2764.35*** *p72*
Williams, Jon.; Virginia, 1636 ***6219*** *p80*
Williams, Jon.; Virginia, 1642 ***6219*** *p191*
Williams, Jon.; Virginia, 1642 ***6219*** *p198*
Williams, Jon.; Virginia, 1643 ***6219*** *p200*
Williams, Jonas 1; Massachusetts, 1860 ***6410.32*** *p101*
Williams, Jonathan 19; Maryland, 1720 ***3690.1*** *p247*
Williams, Jonathan Hill 35; Kansas, 1870 ***5240.1*** *p51*
Williams, Judeth; Virginia, 1640 ***6219*** *p185*
Williams, Julia 50; New Orleans, 1830 ***778.5*** *p548*
Williams, Kather 18; America, 1702 ***2212*** *p37*
Williams, Katherine; America, 1697 ***2212*** *p9*
Williams, Lew F.; Washington, 1859-1920 ***2872.1*** *p43*
Williams, Lewis; New Haven, CT, 1858 ***2764.35*** *p73*
Williams, Lewis; Quebec, 1847 ***5704.8*** *p6*
Williams, Louis 37; California, 1866 ***3840.3*** *p12*
Williams, Margaret 5; Philadelphia, 1853 ***5704.8*** *p101*
Williams, Margaret 10; Philadelphia, 1853 ***5704.8*** *p100*
Williams, Margery; Philadelphia, 1853 ***5704.8*** *p101*
Williams, Margery; Virginia, 1638 ***6219*** *p146*
Williams, Margtte; America, 1698 ***2212*** *p8*
Williams, Marty; Philadelphia, 1853 ***5704.8*** *p100*
Williams, Mary; America, 1697 ***2212*** *p9*
Williams, Mary 11; Virginia, 1700 ***2212*** *p30*
Williams, Mary 16; America, 1704 ***2212*** *p40*
Williams, Mary 20 *SEE* Williams, John
Williams, Mary 23; Maryland, 1774 ***1219.7*** *p187*
Williams, Mary 55; Massachusetts, 1860 ***6410.32*** *p100*
Williams, Mary 55; Massachusetts, 1860 ***6410.32*** *p102*
Williams, Mary 78; North Carolina, 1850 ***1639.20*** *p316*
Williams, Mary Ann; St. John, N.B., 1850 ***5704.8*** *p62*
Williams, Mary Ann 6; Quebec, 1847 ***5704.8*** *p6*
Williams, Math 26; New England, 1699 ***2212*** *p19*
Williams, Mich.; Virginia, 1639 ***6219*** *p155*
Williams, Morgan; Virginia, 1639 ***6219*** *p154*
Williams, Morgan; Virginia, 1643 ***6219*** *p206*
Williams, Morgan; Virginia, 1647 ***6219*** *p241*
Williams, Moses; Wisconsin, n.d. ***9675.8*** *p125*
Williams, Nancy *SEE* Williams, Patrick
Williams, Nancy; Philadelphia, 1847 ***5704.8*** *p5*
Williams, Nathaniel; America, 1741 ***4971*** *p41*
Williams, Nicholas; Virginia, 1638 ***6219*** *p120*
Williams, Norman; Virginia, 1635 ***6219*** *p20*
Williams, Owen 18; Philadelphia, 1774 ***1219.7*** *p233*
Williams, Patrick; Philadelphia, 1847 ***53.26*** *p91*
*Relative:*Nancy
Williams, Patrick; Philadelphia, 1847 ***5704.8*** *p5*
Williams, Peter; New York, NY, 1827 ***8208.4*** *p57*
Williams, Philip; Maryland, 1740 ***4971*** *p91*
Williams, Philip H.; New York, NY, 1839 ***8208.4*** *p98*
Williams, Philip Ze; Philadelphia, 1741 ***4971*** *p92*
Williams, Rach.; Virginia, 1647 ***6219*** *p243*
Williams, Rees; Iowa, 1866-1943 ***123.54*** *p52*
Williams, Rich.; Virginia, 1636 ***6219*** *p80*
Williams, Rich.; Virginia, 1637 ***6219*** *p108*
Williams, Rich.; Virginia, 1642 ***6219*** *p198*
Williams, Richard; Milwaukee, 1875 ***4719.30*** *p258*
Williams, Richard; Virginia, 1636 ***6219*** *p74*
Williams, Richard; Virginia, 1638 ***6219*** *p2*
Williams, Richard; Virginia, 1642 ***6219*** *p186*
Williams, Richard; Virginia, 1642 ***6219*** *p191*
Williams, Richard; Virginia, 1643 ***6219*** *p200*
Williams, Richard; Virginia, 1646 ***6219*** *p243*
Williams, Richard 20; Jamaica, 1736 ***3690.1*** *p247*
Williams, Richard 20; Philadelphia, 1858 ***5704.8*** *p139*
Williams, Richd 12; Maryland or Virginia, 1699 ***2212*** *p23*
Williams, Robert; Philadelphia, 1853 ***5704.8*** *p100*

544 *FOR A COMPLETE EXPLANATION OF ENTRY, SEE "HOW TO READ A CITATION" SECTION*

Williams, Robert; Virginia, 1639 ***6219*** *p161*
Williams, Robert; Virginia, 1642 ***6219*** *p191*
Williams, Robert; Virginia, 1647 ***6219*** *p243*
Williams, Robert 7; St. John, N.B., 1850 ***5704.8*** *p62*
Williams, Robert 19; Maryland, 1774 ***1219.7*** *p204*
Williams, Robert 22; Maryland, 1774 ***1219.7*** *p187*
Williams, Robert P.; Illinois, 1889 ***5012.39*** *p52*
Williams, Robert P.; Illinois, 1892 ***5012.40*** *p27*
Williams, Robt; America, 1697 ***2212*** *p7*
Williams, Rog.; Virginia, 1642 ***6219*** *p191*
Williams, Roger; Virginia, 1635 ***6219*** *p4*
Williams, Roger; Virginia, 1638 ***6219*** *p33*
Williams, Rowland; Virginia, 1638 ***6219*** *p118*
Williams, S. 22; Philadelphia, 1775 ***1219.7*** *p255*
Williams, Samuel; Quebec, 1847 ***5704.8*** *p6*
Williams, Samuell; Virginia, 1698 ***2212*** *p14*
Williams, Sarah; New York, NY, 1865 ***5704.8*** *p196*
Williams, Sarah; Virginia, 1646 ***6219*** *p239*
Williams, Sarah, Jr. 18; Grenada, 1774 ***1219.7*** *p178*
Williams, Sarah, Sr. 42; Grenada, 1774 ***1219.7*** *p178*
Williams, Tho.; Virginia, 1635 ***6219*** *p3*
Williams, Tho.; Virginia, 1635 ***6219*** *p71*
Williams, Tho.; Virginia, 1637 ***6219*** *p11*
Williams, Tho.; Virginia, 1642 ***6219*** *p193*
Williams, Tho.; Virginia, 1643 ***6219*** *p203*
Williams, Tho.; Virginia, 1648 ***6219*** *p246*
Williams, Tho; Virginia, 1698 ***2212*** *p17*
Williams, Tho 12; America, 1699 ***2212*** *p29*
Williams, Tho 30; America, 1699 ***2212*** *p28*
Williams, Thomas; America, 1742 ***4971*** *p23*
Williams, Thomas; Iowa, 1866-1943 ***123.54*** *p52*
Williams, Thomas; Virginia, 1635 ***6219*** *p1*
Williams, Thomas; Virginia, 1635 ***6219*** *p36*
Williams, Thomas; Virginia, 1638 ***6219*** *p145*
Williams, Thomas; Virginia, 1638 ***6219*** *p153*
Williams, Thomas; Virginia, 1639 ***6219*** *p161*
Williams, Thomas; Virginia, 1648 ***6219*** *p251*
Williams, Thomas; Virginia, 1698 ***2212*** *p14*
Williams, Thomas 3; Massachusetts, 1848 ***5881.1*** *p98*
Williams, Thomas 12; Newfoundland, 1699-1700 ***2212*** *p18*
Williams, Thomas 18; Jamaica, 1730 ***3690.1*** *p248*
Williams, Thomas 19; Pennsylvania, 1721 ***3690.1*** *p247*
Williams, Thomas 20; Jamaica, 1729 ***3690.1*** *p248*
Williams, Thomas 21; North Carolina, 1736 ***3690.1*** *p248*
Williams, Thomas 22; Maryland, 1773 ***1219.7*** *p173*
Williams, Thomas 22; Philadelphia, 1774 ***1219.7*** *p196*
Williams, Thomas 30; Virginia, 1773 ***1219.7*** *p168*
Williams, Thomas 36; Jamaica, 1723 ***3690.1*** *p248*
Williams, Thomas D.; New York, NY, 1839 ***8208.4*** *p102*
Williams, Thomas G.; Washington, 1859-1920 ***2872.1*** *p43*
Williams, W. A.; Washington, 1859-1920 ***2872.1*** *p43*
Williams, Walter; Virginia, 1638 ***6219*** *p117*
Williams, Walter 18; Maryland, 1719 ***3690.1*** *p248*
Williams, William; America, 1737 ***4971*** *p66*
Williams, William; America, 1840 ***1450.2*** *p159A*
Williams, William; New York, NY, 1839 ***8208.4*** *p97*
Williams, William; Philadelphia, 1811 ***53.26*** *p91*
Williams, William; Quebec, 1847 ***5704.8*** *p6*
Williams, William 16; Maryland, 1774 ***1219.7*** *p235*
Williams, William 17; Philadelphia, 1775 ***1219.7*** *p255*
Williams, William 20; Jamaica, 1734 ***3690.1*** *p248*
Williams, William 20; Windward Islands, 1722 ***3690.1*** *p248*
Williams, William 21; Maryland, 1775 ***1219.7*** *p271*
Williams, William 22; Jamaica, 1774 ***1219.7*** *p205*
Williams, William R.; Boston, 1861 ***6410.32*** *p126*
Williams, William R. 42; Massachusetts, 1860 ***6410.32*** *p119*
Williams, Wm.; Philadelphia, 1811 ***2859.11*** *p21*
Williams, Wm.; Virginia, 1638 ***6219*** *p115*
Williams, Wm 14; Maryland or Virginia, 1699 ***2212*** *p23*
Williams, Wm 21; Newfoundland, 1699-1700 ***2212*** *p18*
Williamson, Mr.; Quebec, 1815 ***9229.18*** *p77*
Williamson, Alex; Virginia, 1638 ***6219*** *p115*
Williamson, Andrew; Brunswick, NC, 1775 ***1639.20*** *p317*
With wife & children
Williamson, Angus; New Orleans, 1846 ***6013.19*** *p89*
Williamson, Angus 63; North Carolina, 1850 ***1639.20*** *p317*
Williamson, Ann 30; Quebec, 1857 ***5704.8*** *p136*
Williamson, Anthony; Virginia, 1642 ***6219*** *p193*
Williamson, Catherine Campbell; North Carolina, 1805 ***1639.20*** *p28*
Williamson, Charles; Arizona, 1876 ***2764.35*** *p72*
Williamson, Daniel; Quebec, 1764 ***7603*** *p42*
Williamson, David; Philadelphia, 1848 ***5704.8*** *p45*
Williamson, David; Virginia, 1637 ***6219*** *p108*
Williamson, David; Virginia, 1638 ***6219*** *p153*
Williamson, David 28; Quebec, 1855 ***5704.8*** *p126*
Williamson, Elizabeth; New York, NY, 1811 ***2859.11*** *p21*
Williamson, George; Quebec, 1821 ***7603*** *p25*
Williamson, George 11; Quebec, 1857 ***5704.8*** *p136*
Williamson, George 17; Jamaica, 1731 ***3690.1*** *p248*
Williamson, George 35; Quebec, 1857 ***5704.8*** *p136*
Williamson, George 45; Quebec, 1857 ***5704.8*** *p136*
Williamson, Harrett 18; St. John, N.B., 1857 ***5704.8*** *p134*
Williamson, Henry; New York, NY, 1811 ***2859.11*** *p21*
Williamson, James 5; Quebec, 1857 ***5704.8*** *p136*
Williamson, James 18; Philadelphia, 1854 ***5704.8*** *p117*
Williamson, James 40; Quebec, 1857 ***5704.8*** *p136*
Williamson, James B.; North Carolina, 1825 ***1639.20*** *p317*
Williamson, Jane; New York, NY, 1811 ***2859.11*** *p21*
Williamson, Jane 32; Quebec, 1857 ***5704.8*** *p136*
Williamson, Johan W.; Minneapolis, 1880-1883 ***6410.35*** *p67*
Williamson, John; New York, NY, 1835 ***8208.4*** *p59*
Williamson, John 18; Maryland, 1774 ***1219.7*** *p180*
Williamson, John 21; Virginia, 1774 ***1219.7*** *p238*
Williamson, John 22; Maryland, 1730 ***3690.1*** *p292*
Williamson, John 25; Massachusetts, 1848 ***5881.1*** *p97*
Williamson, John 45; Maryland, 1774 ***1219.7*** *p192*
Williamson, Jon.; Virginia, 1643 ***6219*** *p200*
Williamson, Maria 1; Quebec, 1857 ***5704.8*** *p136*
Williamson, Mary 15; America, 1706 ***2212*** *p48*
Williamson, Mary 17; Maryland, 1775 ***1219.7*** *p256*
Williamson, Mary Ann 7; Quebec, 1857 ***5704.8*** *p136*
Williamson, Mathew; Virginia, 1635 ***6219*** *p10*
Williamson, Mathew 22; Jamaica, 1774 ***1219.7*** *p189*
Williamson, Nancy 7; Quebec, 1857 ***5704.8*** *p136*
Williamson, Richard; Virginia, 1641 ***6219*** *p184*
Williamson, Robert; New York, NY, 1836 ***8208.4*** *p11*
Williamson, Robert; Virginia, 1637 ***6219*** *p113*
Williamson, Sam. 14; America, 1700 ***2212*** *p31*
Williamson, Samuel 20; St. John, N.B., 1857 ***5704.8*** *p134*
Williamson, Stephen 31; Virginia, 1774 ***1219.7*** *p240*
Williamson, Susanna; Virginia, 1635 ***6219*** *p4*
Williamson, Thomas; New York, NY, 1839 ***8208.4*** *p101*
Williamson, Thomas 9; Quebec, 1857 ***5704.8*** *p136*
Williamson, Thomas 18; Leeward Islands, 1739 ***3690.1*** *p248*
Williamson, Thomas 21; Maryland, 1775 ***1219.7*** *p272*
Williamson, Thomas 23; Philadelphia, 1774 ***1219.7*** *p232*
Williamson, W. H.; Washington, 1859-1920 ***2872.1*** *p44*
Williamson, William; New York, NY, 1840 ***8208.4*** *p108*
Williamson, William 9 mos; Quebec, 1857 ***5704.8*** *p136*
Williamson, William 19; Barbados, 1721 ***3690.1*** *p248*
Williamson, William 20; Maryland, 1724 ***3690.1*** *p248*
Williamson, William 21; Virginia, 1774 ***1219.7*** *p238*
Williamson, William 26; Barbados, 1718 ***3690.1*** *p248*
Williarmet, Mr. 27; America, 1838 ***778.5*** *p548*
Willich, August; America, 1853 ***8582.3*** *p70*
Willikin, Mary; New York, NY, 1811 ***2859.11*** *p21*
With family
Willing, George; America, 1849 ***1450.2*** *p159A*
Willingham, John 18; Virginia, 1751 ***1219.7*** *p3*
Willingham, John 18; Virginia, 1751 ***3690.1*** *p248*
Willington, Jane 21; Virginia, 1699 ***2212*** *p26*
Willis, Anne 11; Massachusetts, 1849 ***5881.1*** *p96*
Willis, Edward; Virginia, 1635 ***6219*** *p4*
Willis, Eleanor; New York, NY, 1816 ***2859.11*** *p44*
Willis, Eliz.; Virginia, 1636 ***6219*** *p78*
Willis, Eliza.; Virginia, 1637 ***6219*** *p84*
Willis, Elizabeth 22; Baltimore, 1775 ***1219.7*** *p271*
Willis, Frederick 18; Massachusetts, 1849 ***5881.1*** *p96*
Willis, George 24; Maryland, 1774 ***1219.7*** *p192*
Willis, George Charles; Arizona, 1890 ***2764.35*** *p71*
Willis, Isaac; New York, NY, 1834 ***8208.4*** *p58*
Willis, James; Virginia, 1652 ***6251*** *p20*
Willis, John; Virginia, 1642 ***6219*** *p197*
Willis, Joseph; Virginia, 1639 ***6219*** *p161*
Willis, Joseph 20; Jamaica, 1725 ***3690.1*** *p249*
Willis, Margaret; New York, NY, 1811 ***2859.11*** *p21*
Willis, Mary Ann; New York, NY, 1811 ***2859.11*** *p21*
Willis, Mathew; New York, NY, 1811 ***2859.11*** *p21*
Willis, Richard; New York, NY, 1816 ***2859.11*** *p44*
Willis, Tho.; Virginia, 1637 ***6219*** *p114*
Willis, Thomas; Virginia, 1643 ***6219*** *p206*
Willis, Thomas-Antoine; Quebec, 1817 ***7603*** *p30*
Willis, Thos.; Virginia, 1637 ***6219*** *p110*
Willis, Thos.; Virginia, 1638 ***6219*** *p33*
Willis, Walter; Virginia, 1637 ***6219*** *p109*
Willis, Walter; Virginia, 1638 ***6219*** *p147*
Willis, William; New York, NY, 1811 ***2859.11*** *p21*
Willis, William 17; Jamaica, 1774 ***1219.7*** *p189*
Willison, John 16; Virginia, 1774 ***1219.7*** *p240*
Willison, John 36; Nova Scotia, 1774 ***1219.7*** *p194*
Willkommen, Max; Wisconsin, n.d. ***9675.8*** *p125*
Willman, John 43; New York, 1774 ***1219.7*** *p227*
Willmann, . . .; Cincinnati, 1826 ***8582.1*** *p51*
Willmann, William; America, 1886 ***1450.2*** *p159A*
Willment, George; New York, NY, 1845 ***6013.19*** *p89*
Willmington, Fanny 28; Philadelphia, 1857 ***5704.8*** *p134*
Willms, Claas Siebelts 25; Illinois, 1840 ***2896.5*** *p42*
Willms, Siameke Eils 59; Illinois, 1840 ***2896.5*** *p42*
Willms, Siebeld; Iroquois Co., IL, 1894 ***3455.1*** *p14*
Willms, William; Baltimore, 1884 ***1450.2*** *p42B*
Willmuth, Lewis; New York, NY, 1838 ***8208.4*** *p70*
Willner, . . .; Canada, 1776-1783 ***9786*** *p37*
Willner, Reinhard; Philadelphia, 1779 ***8137*** *p15*
Willos, A. 35; Port uncertain, 1835 ***778.5*** *p548*
Willos, A. 39; Port uncertain, 1835 ***778.5*** *p548*
Willoughan, Mary; Philadelphia, 1848 ***53.26*** *p91*
Willoughan, Mary; Philadelphia, 1848 ***5704.8*** *p40*
Willoughby, A. D.; Washington, 1859-1920 ***2872.1*** *p44*
Willoughby, Peter; Virginia, 1635 ***6219*** *p26*
Willoughby, Richard 24; Philadelphia, 1774 ***1219.7*** *p182*
Willoughby, Tho.; Virginia, 1639 ***6219*** *p22*
Willoughby, W. H. 38; Kansas, 1898 ***5240.1*** *p81*
Willoughby, William 22; Maryland, 1774 ***1219.7*** *p235*
Willow, Merra; Virginia, 1642 ***6219*** *p191*
Willoz, Agustin 30; America, 1830 ***778.5*** *p548*
Wills, Elizabeth; Virginia, 1638 ***6219*** *p122*
Wills, John 17; Philadelphia, 1774 ***1219.7*** *p216*
Wills, John 19; Maryland, 1774 ***1219.7*** *p214*
Wills, John 30; Maryland, 1774 ***1219.7*** *p184*
Wills, Nicholas; Virginia, 1638 ***6219*** *p125*
Wills, Sarah 20; Maryland, 1774 ***1219.7*** *p211*
Wills, Susan 33; Montreal, 1780 ***7603*** *p56*
Wills, Theophilus 25; Virginia, 1725 ***3690.1*** *p249*
Wills, Tho.; Virginia, 1635 ***6219*** *p35*
Willshaw, John; Virginia, 1642 ***6219*** *p192*
Willsher, Edward 15; Maryland, 1719 ***3690.1*** *p249*
Willshire, Thomas 17; Maryland, 1729 ***3690.1*** *p250*
Willskey, F.W.; Illinois, 1892 ***5012.37*** *p63*
Willson, Elizabeth 19; America, 1706 ***2212*** *p47*
Willson, Elizabeth 32; Massachusetts, 1860 ***6410.32*** *p113*
Willson, Francis; Nova Scotia, 1750 ***3690.1*** *p249*
Willson, James 19; Maryland, 1719 ***3690.1*** *p250*
Willson, James 22; Jamaica, 1734 ***3690.1*** *p249*
Willson, John; Barbados, 1775 ***1219.7*** *p280*
Willson, John 17; Jamaica, 1730 ***3690.1*** *p249*
Willson, John 25; Pennsylvania, 1728 ***3690.1*** *p249*
Willson, Joseph 20; Jamaica, 1729 ***3690.1*** *p249*
Willson, Leonard 18; Jamaica, 1728 ***3690.1*** *p250*
Willson, Mary 20; St. Christopher, 1720 ***3690.1*** *p249*
Willson, Robert; Carolina, 1767 ***1639.20*** *p319*
Willson, Robert; Virginia, 1648 ***6219*** *p250*
Willson, Thomas; Virginia, 1646 ***6219*** *p239*
Willson, Thomas 19; Maryland, 1729 ***3690.1*** *p249*
Willson, Thomas 19; Virginia, 1733 ***3690.1*** *p249*
Willson, William; Virginia, 1647 ***6219*** *p247*
Willson, William 26; Jamaica, 1737 ***3690.1*** *p249*
Willy, Joseph; New York, 1754 ***3652*** *p80*
Willyard, Christian; Pennsylvania, 1749 ***4779.3*** *p14A*
*Relative:*Martin
Willyard, Martin *SEE* Willyard, Christian
Wilmes, Theodor; America, 1848 ***8582.1*** *p36*
Wilmore, Letitia 35 *SEE* Wilmore, Thomas
Wilmore, Thomas 32; Maryland, 1775 ***1219.7*** *p250*
*Wife:*Letitia 35
Wilmot, Luke 15; Philadelphia, 1774 ***1219.7*** *p233*
Wilmot, Robert 17; Maryland, 1775 ***1219.7*** *p250*
Wilmot, Thomas; Virginia, 1645 ***6219*** *p252*
Wilmott, Ann 27; Port uncertain, 1774 ***1219.7*** *p176*
Wilmott, Edward; Virginia, 1637 ***6219*** *p180*
Wilmott, Edwd.; Virginia, 1635 ***6219*** *p70*
Wilms, Johann Carl; America, 1848 ***8582.1*** *p36*
Wilms, Johann Karl; America, 1848 ***8125.8*** *p438*
Wilmsmeier, Anton 4 *SEE* Wilmsmeier, Christian Friedrich
Wilmsmeier, August *SEE* Wilmsmeier, Christian Friedrich
Wilmsmeier, Carl Friedrich *SEE* Wilmsmeier, Christian Friedrich
Wilmsmeier, Caroline F. Charlotte *SEE* Wilmsmeier, Christian Friedrich
Wilmsmeier, Caroline Justine *SEE* Wilmsmeier, Christian Friedrich
Wilmsmeier, Christian F. Wilhelm *SEE* Wilmsmeier, Christian Friedrich
Wilmsmeier, Christian Friedrich; America, 1881 ***4610.10*** *p122*
*Wife:*Justine C. Wehmeyer
*Child:*Christian Heinrich
*Child:*Carl Friedrich
*Child:*Friedrich Wilhelm
*Child:*Christian F. Wilhelm
*Child:*Caroline F. Charlotte
*Child:*Ernst C. H. Friedrich
*Child:*August

FOR A COMPLETE EXPLANATION OF ENTRY, SEE "HOW TO READ A CITATION" SECTION

Wilson, Margaret 22; Philadelphia, 1857 ***5704.8*** *p133*
Wilson, Marth 21; America, 1704 ***2212*** *p40*
Wilson, Martha; Philadelphia, 1851 ***5704.8*** *p78*
Wilson, Martha 1; Quebec, 1862 ***5704.8*** *p151*
Wilson, Martha 10 *SEE* Wilson, Anne
Wilson, Martha 10; Philadelphia, 1847 ***5704.8*** *p24*
Wilson, Martha 36; Quebec, 1862 ***5704.8*** *p151*
Wilson, Martha Ann 23; St. John, N.B., 1855 ***5704.8*** *p127*
Wilson, Mary; New York, NY, 1867 ***5704.8*** *p217*
Wilson, Mary; Philadelphia, 1816 ***2859.11*** *p44*
Wilson, Mary; Philadelphia, 1864 ***5704.8*** *p184*
Wilson, Mary; Philadelphia, 1867 ***5704.8*** *p224*
Wilson, Mary; St. John, N.B., 1851 ***5704.8*** *p78*
Wilson, Mary; Virginia, 1647 ***6219*** *p248*
Wilson, Mary 1; Quebec, 1847 ***5704.8*** *p16*
Wilson, Mary 4; Quebec, 1862 ***5704.8*** *p151*
Wilson, Mary 9; Quebec, 1862 ***5704.8*** *p151*
Wilson, Mary 10; Quebec, 1851 ***5704.8*** *p73*
Wilson, Mary 16; Maryland, 1719 ***3690.1*** *p250*
Wilson, Mary 21; Philadelphia, 1864 ***5704.8*** *p160*
Wilson, Mary 22; Baltimore, 1775 ***1219.7*** *p271*
Wilson, Mary 22; Quebec, 1856 ***5704.8*** *p129*
Wilson, Mary 22; Quebec, 1857 ***5704.8*** *p136*
Wilson, Mary 25 *SEE* Wilson, Jasper
Wilson, Mary 28; Quebec, 1851 ***5704.8*** *p73*
Wilson, Mary 45; Massachusetts, 1848 ***5881.1*** *p97*
Wilson, Mary 45; Philadelphia, 1864 ***5704.8*** *p155*
Wilson, Mary 45; Quebec, 1856 ***5704.8*** *p130*
Wilson, Mary Ann *SEE* Wilson, Nancy
Wilson, Mary Ann; Philadelphia, 1847 ***5704.8*** *p30*
Wilson, Mary J. 22; Philadelphia, 1865 ***5704.8*** *p164*
Wilson, Mary Jane 20; Philadelphia, 1860 ***5704.8*** *p146*
Wilson, Mary Jane 22; St. John, N.B., 1861 ***5704.8*** *p147*
Wilson, Mathew; Quebec, 1847 ***5704.8*** *p16*
Wilson, Mathew 11; Quebec, 1847 ***5704.8*** *p16*
Wilson, Matilda 3 *SEE* Wilson, Nancy
Wilson, Matilda 3; Philadelphia, 1847 ***5704.8*** *p30*
Wilson, Matilda 3; Philadelphia, 1864 ***5704.8*** *p184*
Wilson, Matilda 12; Philadelphia, 1851 ***5704.8*** *p78*
Wilson, Matthew; New York, NY, 1816 ***2859.11*** *p44*
Wilson, Nancy; Philadelphia, 1847 ***53.26*** *p92*
*Relative:*John
*Relative:*Mary Ann
*Relative:*Ellen 13
*Relative:*Christianna 8
*Relative:*Samuel 5
*Relative:*Matilda 3
Wilson, Nancy; Philadelphia, 1847 ***5704.8*** *p30*
Wilson, Nancy; Philadelphia, 1865 ***5704.8*** *p196*
Wilson, Nancy 26 *SEE* Wilson, Thomas
Wilson, Nathaniel; New York, NY, 1838 ***8208.4*** *p68*
Wilson, Newson; Iowa, 1866-1943 ***123.54*** *p52*
Wilson, Olof; Washington, 1859-1920 ***2872.1*** *p44*
Wilson, Peter; Philadelphia, 1853 ***5704.8*** *p102*
Wilson, Peter 12; America, 1702 ***2212*** *p38*
Wilson, Pierre-Paul; Quebec, 1752 ***7603*** *p67*
Wilson, Rebecca; New York, NY, 1864 ***5704.8*** *p172*
Wilson, Rebecca 7; Quebec, 1847 ***5704.8*** *p16*
Wilson, Richard 16; New York, 1774 ***1219.7*** *p203*
Wilson, Richard 17; Maryland, 1723 ***3690.1*** *p250*
Wilson, Richard 39; Kansas, 1891 ***5240.1*** *p49*
Wilson, Richard 39; Kansas, 1891 ***5240.1*** *p76*
Wilson, Robert; Charles Town, SC, 1753 ***1219.7*** *p24*
Wilson, Robert; New York, NY, 1811 ***2859.11*** *p21*
With wife & 3 children
Wilson, Robert; New York, NY, 1816 ***2859.11*** *p44*
Wilson, Robert; Ohio, 1840 ***9892.11*** *p48*
Wilson, Robert; Ohio, 1844 ***9892.11*** *p48*
Wilson, Robert; Quebec, 1847 ***5704.8*** *p16*
Wilson, Robert; Quebec, 1852 ***5704.8*** *p90*
Wilson, Robert; South Carolina, 1753 ***1639.20*** *p319*
Wilson, Robert; South Carolina, 1753 ***3690.1*** *p250*
Wilson, Robert 3; Quebec, 1851 ***5704.8*** *p73*
Wilson, Robert 3; Quebec, 1862 ***5704.8*** *p151*
Wilson, Robert 5; St. John, N.B., 1867 ***5704.8*** *p167*
Wilson, Robert 12; Quebec, 1851 ***5704.8*** *p73*
Wilson, Robert 16; New York, 1774 ***1219.7*** *p203*
Wilson, Robert 19; Quebec, 1856 ***5704.8*** *p129*
Wilson, Robert 21; Quebec, 1863 ***5704.8*** *p154*
Wilson, Robert 24; St. John, N.B., 1864 ***5704.8*** *p158*
Wilson, Robert 35; Quebec, 1851 ***5704.8*** *p73*
Wilson, Robert 38; Maryland, 1774 ***1219.7*** *p224*
Wilson, Robert 40; Quebec, 1856 ***5704.8*** *p129*
Wilson, Robert 49; Nova Scotia, 1774 ***1219.7*** *p209*
With wife
With 7 children
Wilson, Robert 50; Quebec, 1855 ***5704.8*** *p126*
Wilson, Robert L.; Kansas, 1876 ***5240.1*** *p49*
Wilson, Roseanna; Philadelphia, 1852 ***5704.8*** *p84*
Wilson, Sam; St. John, N.B., 1852 ***5704.8*** *p92*
Wilson, Samuel; South Carolina, 1819 ***1639.20*** *p319*
Wilson, Samuel 5 *SEE* Wilson, Nancy
Wilson, Samuel 5; Philadelphia, 1847 ***5704.8*** *p30*
Wilson, Samuel 21; Philadelphia, 1774 ***1219.7*** *p212*
Wilson, Samuel 26; Virginia, 1774 ***1219.7*** *p225*
Wilson, Samuel 45 *SEE* Wilson, John
Wilson, Samuel J.; America, 1866 ***1450.2*** *p159A*
Wilson, Sarah; New York, NY, 1816 ***2859.11*** *p44*
Wilson, Sarah; Quebec, 1847 ***5704.8*** *p29*
Wilson, Sarah; Quebec, 1851 ***5704.8*** *p73*
Wilson, Sarah 7; Philadelphia, 1864 ***5704.8*** *p184*
Wilson, Sarah 22; Maryland, 1775 ***1219.7*** *p267*
Wilson, Shem 28; Arizona, 1890 ***2764.35*** *p73*
Wilson, Stafford 32?; New York, 1836 ***7036*** *p120*
Wilson, Susan 2; Quebec, 1862 ***5704.8*** *p151*
Wilson, Susan 25; Quebec, 1862 ***5704.8*** *p151*
Wilson, Susannah 7; Quebec, 1862 ***5704.8*** *p151*
Wilson, Thomas; Baltimore, 1811 ***2859.11*** *p21*
Wilson, Thomas; New York, NY, 1815 ***2859.11*** *p44*
Wilson, Thomas; New York, NY, 1816 ***2859.11*** *p44*
Wilson, Thomas; Philadelphia, 1815 ***2859.11*** *p44*
Wilson, Thomas; Philadelphia, 1853 ***5704.8*** *p102*
Wilson, Thomas; Philadelphia, 1865 ***5704.8*** *p196*
Wilson, Thomas; Quebec, 1793 ***7603*** *p42*
Wilson, Thomas; Quebec, 1847 ***5704.8*** *p12*
Wilson, Thomas; St. John, N.B., 1853 ***5704.8*** *p107*
Wilson, Thomas; St. John, N.B., 1866 ***5704.8*** *p166*
Wilson, Thomas 8; Quebec, 1847 ***5704.8*** *p8*
Wilson, Thomas 18; Maryland, 1774 ***1219.7*** *p179*
Wilson, Thomas 19; Maryland, 1729 ***3690.1*** *p249*
Wilson, Thomas 20; St. John, N.B., 1862 ***5704.8*** *p149*
Wilson, Thomas 22; Philadelphia, 1864 ***5704.8*** *p155*
Wilson, Thomas 23; St. John, N.B., 1855 ***5704.8*** *p127*
Wilson, Thomas 25; Philadelphia, 1803 ***53.26*** *p92*
*Relative:*Nancy 26
Wilson, Thomas 26; Nova Scotia, 1774 ***1219.7*** *p209*
Wilson, Thomas 50; North America, 1774 ***1219.7*** *p200*
Wilson, Thomas James; Arkansas, 1918 ***95.2*** *p130*
Wilson, William; America, 1698 ***2212*** *p5*
Wilson, William; America, 1735-1743 ***4971*** *p78*
Wilson, William; America, 1740 ***4971*** *p64*
Wilson, William; America, 1742 ***4971*** *p80*
Wilson, William; Baltimore, 1822 ***9892.11*** *p48*
Wilson, William; Charleston, SC, 1813 ***1639.20*** *p319*
Wilson, William; Indiana, 1847 ***9117*** *p18*
Wilson, William; New York, NY, 1816 ***2859.11*** *p44*
Wilson, William; New York, NY, 1869 ***5704.8*** *p235*
Wilson, William; North Carolina, 1746-1806 ***1639.20*** *p319*
Wilson, William; Ohio, 1840 ***9892.11*** *p49*
Wilson, William; Philadelphia, 1847 ***53.26*** *p92*
Wilson, William; Philadelphia, 1847 ***5704.8*** *p30*
Wilson, William; Quebec, 1849 ***5704.8*** *p52*
Wilson, William; Quebec, 1851 ***5704.8*** *p75*
Wilson, William; St. John, N.B., 1848 ***5704.8*** *p39*
Wilson, William; St. John, N.B., 1853 ***5704.8*** *p106*
Wilson, William 2 mos; Quebec, 1862 ***5704.8*** *p151*
Wilson, William 10; Quebec, 1847 ***5704.8*** *p16*
Wilson, William 12; Quebec, 1847 ***5704.8*** *p16*
Wilson, William 17; St. Christopher, 1722 ***3690.1*** *p250*
Wilson, William 20; Massachusetts, 1850 ***5881.1*** *p98*
Wilson, William 22; Philadelphia, 1865 ***5704.8*** *p164*
Wilson, William 22; Virginia, 1774 ***1219.7*** *p241*
Wilson, William 23; Nova Scotia, 1774 ***1219.7*** *p209*
Wilson, William 23; Virginia, 1774 ***1219.7*** *p193*
Wilson, William 25; St. John, N.B., 1866 ***5704.8*** *p166*
Wilson, William 29; Maryland, 1775 ***1219.7*** *p251*
Wilson, William 38; Carolina, 1774 ***1219.7*** *p179*
Wilson, William 38; Philadelphia, 1857 ***5704.8*** *p133*
Wilson, William 45; Philadelphia, 1853 ***5704.8*** *p112*
Wilson, William J.; Washington, 1859-1920 ***2872.1*** *p44*
Wilson, William M.; Illinois, 1888 ***5012.39*** *p52*
Wilson, William M.; Illinois, 1892 ***5012.40*** *p26*
Wilson, Wm.; Illinois, 1860 ***5012.38*** *p97*
Wilsonn, Edward; Virginia, 1639 ***6219*** *p151*
Wilsonn, Eliz.; Virginia, 1642 ***6219*** *p195*
Wilsonn, Gabriell; Virginia, 1636 ***6219*** *p75*
Wilsonn, James; Virginia, 1633 ***6219*** *p32*
Wilsonn, John; Virginia, 1635 ***6219*** *p69*
Wilsonn, John; Virginia, 1639 ***6219*** *p158*
Wilsonn, Mary; Virginia, 1635 ***6219*** *p17*
Wilsonn, Nath.; Virginia, 1643 ***6219*** *p205*
Wilsonn, Richard; Virginia, 1636 ***6219*** *p21*
Wilstack, Charles 35; Philadelphia, 1774 ***1219.7*** *p219*
Wilt, Heinrich; Ohio, 1798-1818 ***8582.2*** *p54*
Wiltberger, Heinrich; Philadelphia, 1776 ***8582.3*** *p84*
Wiltgen, John B.; Wisconsin, n.d. ***9675.8*** *p125*
Wiltgen, John Peter; Wisconsin, n.d. ***9675.8*** *p125*
Wiltgen, Michael; Wisconsin, n.d. ***9675.8*** *p125*
Wiltgen, Peter; Wisconsin, n.d. ***9675.8*** *p125*
Wilton, James 20; St. John, N.B., 1866 ***5704.8*** *p166*
Wilton, John; Virginia, 1637 ***6219*** *p113*
Wilts, Wilhelm; Iroquois Co., IL, 1892 ***3455.1*** *p14*
Wiltshire, John 21; Maryland, 1775 ***1219.7*** *p266*
Wiltshire, Thomas 17; Maryland, 1729 ***3690.1*** *p250*
Wiltshire, Wm.; Virginia, 1635 ***6219*** *p10*
Wiltzius, Mathias; Wisconsin, n.d. ***9675.8*** *p125*
Wiltzius, Nicholaus; Wisconsin, n.d. ***9675.8*** *p125*
Wimmer, . . .; Canada, 1776-1783 ***9786*** *p37*
Wimmer, Catharina Christina *SEE* Wimmer, Margaretha Wollauf
Wimmer, George; Canada, 1776-1783 ***9786*** *p207A*
Wimmer, Johannes *SEE* Wimmer, Margaretha Wollauf
Wimmer, Margaretha Wollauf; New York, 1709 ***3627*** *p7*
*Child:*Johannes
*Child:*Catharina Christina
With child
Wimpeney, Edmond 22; Maryland, 1722 ***3690.1*** *p250*
Wimpeny, Edmund 22; Maryland, 1722 ***3690.1*** *p250*
Winard, Tho.; Virginia, 1622 ***6219*** *p76*
Winberg, Samuel Eric; Maine, 1871-1873 ***6410.22*** *p117*
Winblade, Wm. 64; Washington, 1918-1920 ***1728.5*** *p16*
Winchester, Awdrey *SEE* Winchester, John
Winchester, John; Virginia, 1636 ***6219*** *p74*
Winchester, John; Virginia, 1639 ***6219*** *p155*
*Wife:*Awdrey
*Child:*Theodor
Winchester, John Alexander; Arkansas, 1918 ***95.2*** *p130*
Winchester, Jon.; Virginia, 1637 ***6219*** *p83*
Winchester, Theodor *SEE* Winchester, John
Winchester, William 19; Maryland, 1730 ***3690.1*** *p292*
Winckelmann, . . .; Canada, 1776-1783 ***9786*** *p37*
Winckelvoss, . . .; Canada, 1776-1783 ***9786*** *p37*
Winckler, . . .; Canada, 1776-1783 ***9786*** *p37*
Winckler, Johannes 38; America, 1853 ***9162.8*** *p38*
Winckus, Anton; Wisconsin, n.d. ***9675.8*** *p125*
Wincouff, Miller Conrad 23; Arkansas, 1918 ***95.2*** *p130*
Winczewski, Antonina 25; New York, 1912 ***9980.29*** *p74*
Wind, Nicholas; Illinois, 1881 ***2896.5*** *p42*
Windam, Edward; Virginia, 1634 ***6219*** *p32*
Windel, Anton Arnold Theodor; America, 1853 ***4610.10*** *p144*
Windeler, . . .; Cincinnati, 1826 ***8582.1*** *p51*
Windeler, Hermann T.; Cincinnati, 1826 ***8582.1*** *p51*
Windelincx, Flirent 23; Kansas, 1874 ***5240.1*** *p55*
Windels, Gerhard H.; Wisconsin, n.d. ***9675.8*** *p125*
Windelt, Edward; Virginia, 1636 ***6219*** *p13*
Winder, Geo.; Pennsylvania, 1753 ***2444*** *p234*
Winder, Marie-Anne; Quebec, 1708 ***7603*** *p22*
Winderbank, Thomas 15; Maryland, 1775 ***1219.7*** *p251*
Winderlin, Ford 29; Kansas, 1871 ***5240.1*** *p52*
Winders, James; Virginia, 1642 ***6219*** *p190*
Windeth, Fickler; Virginia, 1645 ***6219*** *p233*
Windhurst, Christian; Illinois, 1853 ***7857*** *p8*
Windill, . . .; Canada, 1776-1783 ***9786*** *p37*
Windisch, Conrad; America, 1848 ***8582.1*** *p36*
Windmann, Heinrich Friedrich Wilhelm; America, 1858 ***4610.10*** *p152*
Windmeier, Anton Friedrich; America, 1849 ***4610.10*** *p120*
Windmeyer, Johanne Friederike; America, 1846 ***4610.10*** *p115*
Windnagel, Charles; New York, NY, 1871 ***9678.3*** *p18*
Windoffer, Hienrich B.; Illinois, 1886 ***5240.1*** *p49*
Windon, John 20; Maryland, 1750 ***3690.1*** *p250*
Windsley, Peter; Ohio, 1841 ***9892.11*** *p49*
Windsor, William 18; Pennsylvania, Virginia or Maryland, 1699 ***2212*** *p19*
Wine, Abraham 32; Kansas, 1891 ***5240.1*** *p76*
Wine, Israel 22; Kansas, 1891 ***5240.1*** *p49*
Wine, Israel 22; Kansas, 1891 ***5240.1*** *p76*
Winer, Harry; Arkansas, 1918 ***95.2*** *p130*
Winey, Jacob; Philadelphia, 1765 ***8582.3*** *p84*
Winey, Jacob; Philadelphia, 1776 ***8582.3*** *p83*
Winfield, Mr.; Grenada, 1775 ***1219.7*** *p280*
Winfrye, William; Virginia, 1638 ***6219*** *p150*
Wing, Margaret 22; Massachusetts, 1849 ***5881.1*** *p98*
Wing, Margaret 30; Kansas, 1873 ***5240.1*** *p55*
Wing, Susanna 17; Maryland, 1775 ***1219.7*** *p260*
Wing, Tom 70; Arizona, 1924 ***9228.40*** *p28*
Wingard, Catherine 6 *SEE* Wingard, John Adam
Wingard, George 9 mos *SEE* Wingard, John Adam
Wingard, George Michael 9 *SEE* Wingard, John Adam
Wingard, John Adam; South Carolina, 1752-1753 ***3689.17*** *p21*
*Relative:*John Matthew 18
*Relative:*Mary Margaret 11
*Relative:*George Michael 9
*Relative:*Catherine 6
*Relative:*George 9 mos
Wingard, John Matthew 18 *SEE* Wingard, John Adam
Wingard, Mary Margaret 11 *SEE* Wingard, John Adam
Wingatt, Roger; Virginia, 1648 ***6219*** *p246*
Winger, John Alf; Arkansas, 1918 ***95.2*** *p131*
Wingert, George; South Carolina, 1788 ***7119*** *p199*
Wingert, George Michael; South Carolina, 1788 ***7119*** *p199*
Wingert, Matthias; South Carolina, 1788 ***7119*** *p199*

Winges, Valentine 25; Kansas, 1886 ***5240.1*** *p69*
Wingfeild, Thomas; Virginia, 1636 ***6219*** *p78*
Wingfield, Charles 20; Jamaica, 1725 ***3690.1*** *p250*
Wingfield, William 30; Virginia, 1773 ***1219.7*** *p168*
Winiarska, Maria 24; New York, 1912 ***9980.29*** *p66*
Winifrett, William; Virginia, 1622 ***6219*** *p76*
Winin, Matthis; Albany, NY, 1858 ***2896.5*** *p42*
Wink, Heinrich; New York, 1864 ***8125.8*** *p438*
Winkeford, Jos.; Virginia, 1643 ***6219*** *p200*
Winkeifer, . . .; Canada, 1776-1783 ***9786*** *p37*
Winkel, Jens; Iroquois Co., IL, 1892 ***3455.1*** *p14*
Winkel, Michael; Wisconsin, n.d. ***9675.8*** *p125*
Winkelmann, . . .; Canada, 1776-1783 ***9786*** *p37*
Winkelmeier, Engel 30; New York, 1867 ***3702.7*** *p569*
*Sister:*Margarethe 17
Winkelmeier, Margarethe 17 *SEE* Winkelmeier, Engel
Winkelpost, Andrew; Canada, 1783 ***9786*** *p38A*
Winker, Anton; Illinois, 1836 ***8582.1*** *p55*
Winkhoff, Joseph; Wisconsin, n.d. ***9675.8*** *p125*
Winkle, J.N.; Wheeling, WV, 1852 ***8582.3*** *p78*
Winkleman, Herman; New York, 1884 ***1450.2*** *p159A*
Winklener, William; Auglaize Co., OH, 1854 ***1450.2*** *p160A*
Winkler, Carl William; Wisconsin, n.d. ***9675.8*** *p125*
Winkler, Edward; Wisconsin, n.d. ***9675.8*** *p125*
Winkler, Fredrick A.; Wisconsin, n.d. ***9675.8*** *p125*
Winkler, Fried. Aug.; Wisconsin, n.d. ***9675.8*** *p125*
Winkler, George M.; America, 1881 ***1450.2*** *p160A*
Winkler, John; Colorado, 1889 ***9678.3*** *p18*
Winkler, Simon; Wisconsin, n.d. ***9675.8*** *p125*
Winkler, Willibald; America, 1855-1870 ***8582.1*** *p43*
Winkler, Willibald; Mexico, 1855-1870 ***8582.1*** *p43*
Winley, David; Virginia, 1635 ***6219*** *p69*
Winley, David; Virginia, 1637 ***6219*** *p112*
*Wife:*Jone
Winley, Jone *SEE* Winley, David
Winn, Catharine 40; Massachusetts, 1849 ***5881.1*** *p96*
Winn, Cornelius 40; Massachusetts, 1847 ***5881.1*** *p96*
Winn, David 17; North America, 1774 ***1219.7*** *p200*
Winn, Elizabeth Parr Maude *SEE* Winn, Thomas
Winn, Frederick Charles; Arkansas, 1918 ***95.2*** *p131*
Winn, Joseph 61; Kansas, 1879 ***5240.1*** *p61*
Winn, Michael 23; Massachusetts, 1849 ***5881.1*** *p98*
Winn, Nelly 10; Massachusetts, 1849 ***5881.1*** *p98*
Winn, Rebecca 20; Pennsylvania, 1682 ***4961*** *p5*
Winn, Thomas; Ohio, 1844 ***9892.11*** *p49*
Winn, Thomas; Pennsylvania, 1682 ***4961*** *p5*
*Wife:*Elizabeth Parr Maude
Winn, William; Port uncertain, 1757 ***3690.1*** *p251*
Winn, William 27; North America, 1774 ***1219.7*** *p200*
Winn, William 32; Kansas, 1879 ***5240.1*** *p61*
Winnall, Jon.; Virginia, 1635 ***6219*** *p69*
Winnemuller, Anna; Wisconsin, n.d. ***9675.8*** *p125*
Winner, Catharina Christina *SEE* Winner, Margaretha Wollauf
Winner, Catharina Christina; New York, 1709 ***3627*** *p6*
Winner, Johannes *SEE* Winner, Margaretha Wollauf
Winner, Margaretha Wollauf; New York, 1709 ***3627*** *p7*
*Child:*Johannes
*Child:*Catharina Christina
With child
Winnerhall, John Henry; Antigua (Antego), 1757 ***3690.1*** *p251*
Winnerholt, John Henry; Antigua (Antego), 1757 ***1219.7*** *p50*
Winnick, Max; Arkansas, 1918 ***95.2*** *p131*
Winnicki, Josef 26; New York, 1912 ***9980.29*** *p64*
*Wife:*Katarina 23
Winnicki, Katarina 23 *SEE* Winnicki, Josef
Winning, Alexander 29; Quebec, 1864 ***5704.8*** *p164*
Winole, Thomas; Quebec, 1824 ***7603*** *p61*
Winschel, Frank Peter; Wisconsin, n.d. ***9675.8*** *p125*
Winschum, John; Pennsylvania, 1754 ***2444*** *p234*
Winscill, Robert; Virginia, 1646 ***6219*** *p236*
Winsdoerfer, Joseph 23; America, 1838 ***778.5*** *p548*
Winser, Chas. 30; New Orleans, 1839 ***9420.2*** *p358*
Winship, Thomas 26; North Carolina, 1774 ***1219.7*** *p215*
Winski, Joseph; Arkansas, 1918 ***95.2*** *p131*
Winslow, Alberta; Washington, 1859-1920 ***2872.1*** *p44*
Winslow, Anna; Washington, 1859-1920 ***2872.1*** *p44*
Winslow, Clarence; Washington, 1859-1920 ***2872.1*** *p44*
Winslow, Clyde; Washington, 1859-1920 ***2872.1*** *p44*
Winslow, John; Washington, 1859-1920 ***2872.1*** *p44*
Winslow, Joseph Sidney; Washington, 1859-1920 ***2872.1*** *p44*
Winslow, Marie; Washington, 1859-1920 ***2872.1*** *p44*
Winslow, Richard Bright; Jamaica, 1766 ***1219.7*** *p123*
Winslow, Walter; Washington, 1859-1920 ***2872.1*** *p44*
Winsmore, Elizabeth; America, 1739 ***4971*** *p14*
Winson, Jane Sophia 22; Boston, 1854 ***4535.10*** *p196*
*Brother:*Sam 14
Winson, John; Boston, 1838-1854 ***4535.10*** *p196*
Winson, Sam 14 *SEE* Winson, Jane Sophia
Winsor, John; America, 1851 ***1450.2*** *p160A*
Winstandley, Thomas; Ohio, 1842-1863 ***9892.11*** *p49*
Winstanley, John; New York, NY, 1816 ***2859.11*** *p44*
Winstanley, Mary 17; America, 1705 ***2212*** *p44*
Winstanley, Peter; Virginia, 1698 ***2212*** *p14*
Winstantly, Jn; America, 1698 ***2212*** *p13*
Winstel, Johann; America, 1847 ***8582.1*** *p36*
Wintent, William 22; Maryland, 1774 ***1219.7*** *p235*
Winter, . . .; Canada, 1776-1783 ***9786*** *p44*
Winter, Adolph; Washington, 1859-1920 ***2872.1*** *p44*
Winter, Amie; Washington, 1859-1920 ***2872.1*** *p44*
Winter, Ann; Virginia, 1636 ***6219*** *p74*
Winter, Charles 20; Maryland, 1722 ***3690.1*** *p251*
Winter, Edward; Washington, 1859-1920 ***2872.1*** *p44*
Winter, Elizabeth 19; Philadelphia, 1774 ***1219.7*** *p212*
Winter, Franz; Wisconsin, n.d. ***9675.8*** *p125*
Winter, Fritz; New York, NY, 1924 ***3455.4*** *p52*
Winter, Gottfried; New York, 1869 ***1450.2*** *p42B*
Winter, Gustave; Wisconsin, n.d. ***9675.8*** *p125*
Winter, Henlena; Washington, 1859-1920 ***2872.1*** *p44*
Winter, Hiram O.; America, 1876 ***1450.2*** *p160A*
Winter, Isaac; New York, NY, 1837 ***8208.4*** *p35*
Winter, James 18; Philadelphia, 1859 ***5704.8*** *p142*
Winter, James 21; Philadelphia, 1774 ***1219.7*** *p212*
Winter, Johann; Kentucky, 1832 ***8582.3*** *p100*
Winter, Johann Georg; Pennsylvania, 1751 ***2444*** *p234*
Winter, John; New Orleans, 1851 ***2896.5*** *p42*
Winter, John; Wisconsin, n.d. ***9675.8*** *p125*
Winter, John 28; Maryland, 1774 ***1219.7*** *p208*
Winter, John Charles Henry 46; Kansas, 1878 ***5240.1*** *p59*
Winter, John Charles Henry, Jr. 22; Kansas, 1878 ***5240.1*** *p59*
Winter, Juliana; Washington, 1859-1920 ***2872.1*** *p44*
Winter, Maria; Georgia, 1739 ***9332*** *p324*
Winter, Maria 76; Pennsylvania, 1911 ***1763*** *p40D*
Winter, Philip; Illinois, 1852 ***2896.5*** *p42*
Winter, Rich.; Virginia, 1637 ***6219*** *p112*
Winter, Robert; Quebec, 1798 ***7603*** *p24*
Winter, Rosine 27; New Orleans, 1839 ***9420.2*** *p166*
Winter, Stephen 21; Maryland, 1774 ***1219.7*** *p192*
Winter, Thomas 21; Carolina, 1774 ***1219.7*** *p227*
Winter, Wm.; Virginia, 1635 ***6219*** *p69*
Winterberg, . . .; Canada, 1776-1783 ***9786*** *p37*
Winterbourn, William 20; Jamaica, 1737 ***3690.1*** *p251*
Winterbourne, William 20; Jamaica, 1737 ***3690.1*** *p251*
Winterhalter, Georg; Cincinnati, 1869-1887 ***8582*** *p34*
Winters, Anna; Philadelphia, 1853 ***5704.8*** *p101*
Winters, Edward; New York, NY, 1811 ***2859.11*** *p21*
Winters, Mary; New York, NY, 1811 ***2859.11*** *p21*
Winterschmidt, Gottfried Jul; Quebec, 1776 ***9786*** *p262*
Wintersheim, von; Quebec, 1778 ***9786*** *p168*
Winteschmidt, . . .; Quebec, 1776 ***9786*** *p104*
Winther, Fritz 32; Kansas, 1906 ***5240.1*** *p83*
Winther, Walter 27; Arkansas, 1918 ***95.2*** *p131*
Wintown, John 16; Maryland, 1724 ***3690.1*** *p251*
Wintter, Hans Jerg; Pennsylvania, 1751 ***2444*** *p234*
Wintter, Joh. Jurg; Pennsylvania, 1753 ***2444*** *p234*
Wintter, Johannes; Pennsylvania, 1751 ***2444*** *p234*
Wintzingerode, Ernst Wilhelm von; Canada, 1780 ***9786*** *p268*
Wintzingerode, Ernst Wilhelm von; New York, 1776 ***9786*** *p268*
Winzenheller, Anna Margretha *SEE* Winzenheller, Nicolaus
Winzenheller, Nicolaus; Pennsylvania, 1752 ***4525*** *p256*
*Wife:*Anna Margretha
Winzenhoeller, Nicolaus; New England, 1752 ***4525*** *p256*
With 3 children
Winzer, Ludwig Heinrich Friedrich; America, 1855 ***4610.10*** *p149*
Wippermann, Anne Marie; America, 1850 ***4610.10*** *p142*
Wippermann, Carl Dietrich August; America, 1877 ***4610.10*** *p124*
Wire, John 25; Massachusetts, 1850 ***5881.1*** *p97*
Wirick, Nicholas; South Carolina, 1788 ***7119*** *p203*
Wirkler, Christian 39; Kansas, 1879 ***5240.1*** *p60*
Wirsbinski, John; Wisconsin, n.d. ***9675.8*** *p125*
Wirsum, Johannes; Pennsylvania, 1754 ***2444*** *p234*
Wirsumb, Dorothea *SEE* Wirsumb, Johann Jacob
Wirsumb, Johann Jacob *SEE* Wirsumb, Johann Jacob
Wirsumb, Johann Jacob; Port uncertain, 1740-1800 ***2444*** *p234*
*Wife:*Dorothea
*Child:*Johann Jacob
Wirt, Mr.; Maryland, 1772 ***8582.3*** *p93*
With wife
Wirt, Wilhelm; America, 1776-1877 ***8582.3*** *p80*
Wirth, Auguste 22; New Orleans, 1839 ***9420.2*** *p358*
Wirth, Caroline Sophia 61; New Orleans, 1839 ***9420.2*** *p358*
Wirth, Frederick; Philadelphia, 1760 ***9973.7*** *p34*
Wirth, Jacob; Ohio, 1858 ***9892.11*** *p49*
Wirth, John P.; Wisconsin, n.d. ***9675.8*** *p125*
Wirth, Rudolf; New York, NY, 1904 ***3455.2*** *p71*
Wirth, William 24; New Orleans, 1839 ***9420.2*** *p358*
Wirthlin, Leo; Cincinnati, 1867 ***8582.3*** *p86*
Wirthlin, Nicolaus; Cincinnati, 1800-1877 ***8582.3*** *p86*
Wirthlin, Nicolaus; Cincinnati, 1869-1887 ***8582*** *p35*
Wirtz, Elisabeth 38; New Orleans, 1836 ***778.5*** *p548*
Wirtz, Henry; Ohio, 1840 ***8582.1*** *p48*
Wirtz, Joseph; Wisconsin, n.d. ***9675.8*** *p125*
Wischmeier, Charles F.; America, 1840 ***1450.2*** *p160A*
Wischmeier, Frederick William; Baltimore, 1840 ***1450.2*** *p160A*
Wischmier, Christian F.; America, 1843 ***1450.2*** *p160A*
Wise, Benjamin 18; Maryland, 1775 ***1219.7*** *p260*
Wise, Charles 21; Virginia, 1774 ***1219.7*** *p226*
Wise, Henry James; Illinois, 1870 ***5012.38*** *p99*
Wise, Isaac M.; America, 1846 ***8582.1*** *p36*
Wise, Jane 17; Maryland, 1721 ***3690.1*** *p251*
Wise, John; Virginia, 1652 ***6251*** *p20*
Wise, John 15; Maryland, 1721 ***3690.1*** *p251*
Wise, Lydia 21; Georgia, 1774 ***1219.7*** *p188*
Wise, Thomas 19; Jamaica, 1774 ***1219.7*** *p243*
Wise, William; New York, NY, 1837 ***8208.4*** *p28*
Wiseham, William; New York, 1765 ***1219.7*** *p107*
Wisely, John; Philadelphia, 1847 ***53.26*** *p92*
Wisely, John; Philadelphia, 1847 ***5704.8*** *p13*
Wiseman, Jacques; Quebec, 1783 ***7603*** *p25*
Wiseman, Richard 24; Maryland, 1775 ***1219.7*** *p257*
Wiseman, Robert; Virginia, 1639 ***6219*** *p154*
Wiseman, William Grant; New York, NY, 1907 ***3455.3*** *p109*
Wisenberg, Herman Welvel; Arkansas, 1918 ***95.2*** *p131*
Wiser, Joyce; Virginia, 1643 ***6219*** *p207*
Wisham, Conrad; Pennsylvania, 1770 ***9973.8*** *p32*
Wishart, Dorothy; St. John, N.B., 1852 ***5704.8*** *p93*
Wishart, James 51; Philadelphia, 1804 ***53.26*** *p92*
Wishart, John; St. John, N.B., 1852 ***5704.8*** *p93*
Wishart, Margaret 21; Philadelphia, 1804 ***53.26*** *p92*
Wishart, Patrick; Virginia, 1638 ***6219*** *p121*
Wishart, William; Carolina, 1684 ***1639.20*** *p319*
Wishat, Mary *SEE* Wishat, Robert
Wishat, Mary; Philadelphia, 1811 ***2859.11*** *p21*
Wishat, Robert; Philadelphia, 1811 ***53.26*** *p92*
*Relative:*Sarah
*Relative:*Mary
*Relative:*Ruth
With relative
Wishat, Robert; Philadelphia, 1811 ***2859.11*** *p21*
Wishat, Ruth *SEE* Wishat, Robert
Wishat, Ruth; Philadelphia, 1811 ***2859.11*** *p21*
Wishat, Sarah *SEE* Wishat, Robert
Wishat, Sarah; Philadelphia, 1811 ***2859.11*** *p21*
Wishe, William A. 25; Kansas, 1884 ***5240.1*** *p66*
Wishowski, John; Arkansas, 1918 ***95.2*** *p131*
Wisk, Fred; Arkansas, 1918 ***95.2*** *p131*
Wiske, William A. 25; Kansas, 1884 ***5240.1*** *p49*
Wisler, Hans; Pennsylvania, 1709-1710 ***4480*** *p311*
Wisley, Margaret 45 *SEE* Wisley, Martin
Wisley, Martin 18; Philadelphia, 1833-1834 ***53.26*** *p92*
*Relative:*Margaret 45
Wislicenus, Gustav Adolph; America, 1853 ***8582.2*** *p46*
With family
Wisneiwski, John; Arkansas, 1918 ***95.2*** *p131*
Wisner, Hans Michael; Pennsylvania, 1750 ***2444*** *p234*
Wisner, Hans Michael; Pennsylvania, 1750 ***4525*** *p255*
Wisner, Jacob; Pennsylvania, 1752 ***2444*** *p233*
Wisner, Matthias; Pennsylvania, 1732-1785 ***2444*** *p235*
Wisness, Sigurd; Arkansas, 1918 ***95.2*** *p131*
Wisniewska, Leon 3 *SEE* Wisniewska, Wiktoria Szymczak
Wisniewska, Weronika 11 mos *SEE* Wisniewska, Wiktoria Szymczak
Wisniewska, Wiktoria Szymczak 25; New York, 1912 ***9980.29*** *p61*
*Child:*Leon 3
*Child:*Weronika 11 mos
With nephew
Wisniewski, Leon 3 *SEE* Wisniewski, Wiktoria Szymczak
Wisniewski, Weronika 11 mos *SEE* Wisniewski, Wiktoria Szymczak
Wisniewski, Wiktoria Szymczak 25; New York, 1912 ***9980.29*** *p61*
*Child:*Leon 3
*Child:*Weronika 11 mos
With nephew
Wisnor, . . .; Pennsylvania, n.d. ***2444*** *p234*
Wisocki, Valenti 31; New York, 1912 ***9980.29*** *p57*
With sister
Wisoonik, Frank; Wisconsin, n.d. ***9675.8*** *p125*
Wiss, John; Illinois, 1869 ***2896.5*** *p42*
Wiss, Joseph; Illinois, 1869 ***2896.5*** *p42*
Wisse, Mme. 32; America, 1838 ***778.5*** *p549*

548 *FOR A COMPLETE EXPLANATION OF ENTRY, SEE "HOW TO READ A CITATION" SECTION*

Wohlford, Alfhild V. Augusta SEE Wohlford, Anna Charlotta Hesse
Wohlford, Anna Charlotta Hesse; America, 1850 *6410.32 p123*
  *Child:*Maria Dorothea C.
  *Child:*Lars Hugo
  *Child:*Helena Ulrika Lovisa
  *Child:*Emma Erika Christina
  *Child:*Alfhild V. Augusta
Wohlford, Emma Erika Christina SEE Wohlford, Anna Charlotta Hesse
Wohlford, Helena Ulrika Lovisa SEE Wohlford, Anna Charlotta Hesse
Wohlford, Lars Erik; America, 1848 *6410.32 p123*
Wohlford, Lars Hugo SEE Wohlford, Anna Charlotta Hesse
Wohlford, Maria Dorothea C. SEE Wohlford, Anna Charlotta Hesse
Wohlgemuth, Johannes; Philadelphia, 1779 *8137 p15*
Wohll, Sam 28; Kansas, 1904 *5240.1 p83*
Wohloken, Luhr; New York, NY, 1836 *8208.4 p8*
Wohlrabe, Ernestina Frederika; New York, NY, 1838 *8208.4 p57*
Woillidge, Peter 24; Virginia, 1774 *1219.7 p186*
Woitkiewicz, Felix; Wisconsin, n.d. *9675.8 p125*
Woitkiewicz, Constant; Colorado, 1894 *9678.3 p18*
Wojciechoska, Feliksa 19; New York, 1912 *9980.29 p50*
Wojciechowska, Feliksa 19; New York, 1912 *9980.29 p50*
Wojciechowski, Franciszek 18; New York, 1912 *9980.29 p59*
Wojciechowski, Konstanty 25; New York, 1912 *9980.29 p55*
Wojcik, Antoni 19; New York, 1912 *9980.29 p54*
  *Sister:*Leokadia 17
Wojcik, Leokadia 17 SEE Wojcik, Antoni
Wojnicki, Stanislaw 16; New York, 1912 *9980.29 p56*
Wojtkiewicz, Raymond; Wisconsin, n.d. *9675.8 p125*
Wojtyra, George; Arkansas, 1918 *95.2 p131*
Wolaghan, Daniel; America, 1743 *4971 p86*
Wolberg, Max 24; Kansas, 1893 *5240.1 p78*
Wolbert, Stophel; Pennsylvania, 1749 *4525 p257*
Wolbing, Christoph; Wisconsin, n.d. *9675.8 p125*
Woldmer, Peter H. 34; Kansas, 1879 *5240.1 p61*
Woldorceki, Alexander S.; Arkansas, 1918 *95.2 p127*
Woldorceki, Alexander S.; Arkansas, 1918 *95.2 p131*
Woldridge, John; Virginia, 1646 *6219 p242*
Wolf, . . .; Canada, 1776-1783 *9786 p37*
Wolf, Mr.; Cincinnati, 1831 *8582.1 p51*
  With brother
Wolf, Mr.; Cincinnati, 1840 *8582.1 p8*
Wolf, Agnes 32; New York, 1865 *3702.7 p210*
Wolf, Albert; St. Paul, MN, 1852 *3702.7 p251*
Wolf, Anna Margaretha SEE Wolf, Conrad
Wolf, Anna Maria; Pennsylvania, 1752 *2444 p235*
Wolf, Anna Maria Wanner SEE Wolf, Conrad
Wolf, Anthony; Philadelphia, 1763 *9973.7 p38*
Wolf, Barbara SEE Wolf, Kunigunda
Wolf, Benjamin; Arkansas, 1918 *95.2 p131*
Wolf, Christophe 40; New Orleans, 1838 *778.5 p549*
Wolf, Conrad; America, 1749 *2444 p235*
  *Wife:*Anna Maria Wanner
  *Child:*Elias
  *Child:*Johann Michael
  *Child:*Johann Friedrich
  *Child:*Anna Margaretha
  *Child:*Johann Balthasar
  *Child:*Johann Jonathan
Wolf, Conrad; Pennsylvania, 1749 *2444 p235*
Wolf, Daniel; New York, NY, 1886 *1450.2 p43B*
Wolf, David; Illinois, 1828 *8582.1 p54*
Wolf, Dolly Francis; Washington, 1859-1920 *2872.1 p44*
Wolf, Elias SEE Wolf, Conrad
Wolf, Elisabetha SEE Wolf, Jacob
Wolf, Ernest; Kansas, 1896 *5240.1 p49*
Wolf, Ernest F.; Kansas, 1896 *5240.1 p49*
Wolf, F. Peter; Wisconsin, n.d. *9675.8 p125*
Wolf, Fielieb Jacob; Pennsylvania, 1752 *4525 p256*
Wolf, Frederick; Wisconsin, n.d. *9675.8 p125*
Wolf, Frederick Karl 28; Kansas, 1888 *5240.1 p49*
Wolf, Georg; Illinois, 1822 *8582.1 p54*
Wolf, Georg; New England, 1753 *4525 p256*
  With wife
  With children
Wolf, Georg; Ohio, 1799 *8582.2 p54*
Wolf, George; Philadelphia, 1760 *9973.7 p34*
Wolf, Gottlieb 22; Kansas, 1892 *5240.1 p77*
Wolf, Gottlob; Wisconsin, n.d. *9675.8 p125*
Wolf, Gottwerth; Wisconsin, n.d. *9675.8 p125*
Wolf, Henrick; Philadelphia, 1760 *9973.7 p34*
Wolf, Henry; Michigan, 1898 *1450.2 p161A*
Wolf, Herman Bear; Arkansas, 1918 *95.2 p131*
Wolf, Isaac; Cincinnati, 1869-1887 *8582 p35*

Wolf, Jacob; America, 1857 *2691.4 p171*
  *Wife:*Maria Lisette S. Suder
  *Child:*Elisabetha
  *Child:*Susanna
  *Child:*Katharina
  *Child:*Philippina
  With child
  *Child:*Karolina
  *Child:*Luise
Wolf, Jacob; Cincinnati, 1869-1887 *8582 p35*
Wolf, Jacob; New England, 1752 *4525 p256*
  With wife
  With 3 children
Wolf, Jacob; Pennsylvania, 1752 *4525 p256*
Wolf, Jakob; Kentucky, 1810-1825 *8582.3 p97*
  *Brother:*Karl
Wolf, Johan; Pennsylvania, 1752 *4525 p255*
Wolf, Johann; Ohio, 1817 *8582.1 p47*
Wolf, Johann; Wisconsin, n.d. *9675.8 p125*
Wolf, Johann Balthasar SEE Wolf, Conrad
Wolf, Johann Friedrich SEE Wolf, Conrad
Wolf, Johann Jonathan SEE Wolf, Conrad
Wolf, Johann Michael SEE Wolf, Conrad
Wolf, John; Illinois, 1854 *7857 p8*
Wolf, John; Illinois, 1858 *7857 p8*
Wolf, John; Illinois, 1874 *2896.5 p43*
Wolf, John; Philadelphia, 1760 *9973.7 p34*
Wolf, John; Philadelphia, 1761 *9973.7 p35*
Wolf, Jos. 37; America, 1838 *778.5 p549*
Wolf, Karl SEE Wolf, Jakob
Wolf, Karl; Ohio, 1843 *8582.1 p51*
Wolf, Karl Fredrick 28; Kansas, 1888 *5240.1 p71*
Wolf, Karolina SEE Wolf, Jacob
Wolf, Katharina SEE Wolf, Jacob
Wolf, Kunigunda; Pennsylvania, 1754 *4525 p197*
  With sister
Wolf, Kunigunda; Pennsylvania, 1754 *4525 p257*
  *Sister:*Barbara
Wolf, Louis Leo; New York, NY, 1835 *8208.4 p42*
Wolf, Luise SEE Wolf, Jacob
Wolf, Maria; Pennsylvania, 1753 *4525 p257*
Wolf, Maria Lisette S. Suder SEE Wolf, Jacob
Wolf, Moses; America, 1849 *1450.2 p161A*
Wolf, Moses; Cincinnati, 1869-1887 *8582 p35*
Wolf, Moses 25; Baltimore, 1840 *8582.3 p72*
Wolf, Osmar Kurt; Washington, 1859-1920 *2872.1 p44*
Wolf, Peter; Pennsylvania, 1768 *9973.8 p32*
Wolf, Peter; Wisconsin, n.d. *9675.8 p125*
Wolf, Philipp; America, 1775-1781 *8582.2 p57*
Wolf, Philipp, III; Peoria, IL, 1888 *2691.4 p168*
Wolf, Philipp, III; Peoria, IL, 1888 *2691.4 p171*
Wolf, Philipp Jacob; Pennsylvania, 1752 *4525 p257*
  With wife
  With 2 children
Wolf, Philippina SEE Wolf, Jacob
Wolf, Susanna SEE Wolf, Jacob
Wolf, William; America, 1860 *6014.1 p3*
Wolfart, . . .; Canada, 1776-1783 *9786 p37*
Wolfarth, Peter; Pennsylvania, 1782 *4525 p257*
Wolfarts, Christopher; Pennsylvania, 1749 *4525 p257*
Wolfberg, Harry; America, 1886 *5240.1 p49*
Wolfberg, L.; Allegheny Co., PA, 1886 *5240.1 p49*
Wolfe, . . .; Canada, 1776-1783 *9786 p37*
Wolfe, Ann 11; Massachusetts, 1850 *5881.1 p96*
Wolfe, James; Quebec, 1759 *9786 p108*
Wolfe, James 21; Maryland, 1774 *1219.7 p220*
Wolfe, John; Virginia, 1847 *4626.16 p13*
Wolfe, John Peter; Philadelphia, 1762 *9973.7 p36*
Wolfe, Richard; Virginia, 1646 *6219 p242*
Wolfer, Anna SEE Wolfer, Johannes
Wolfer, Anna; Pennsylvania, 1750 *2444 p145*
Wolfer, Anna; Port uncertain, 1750 *2444 p235*
Wolfer, Anna Maria SEE Wolfer, Johann Martin
Wolfer, Anna Maria SEE Wolfer, Johannes
Wolfer, Catharina; America, 1750 *2444 p224*
Wolfer, Catharina; Port uncertain, 1750 *2444 p235*
Wolfer, Charles F.; Colorado, 1903 *9678.3 p18*
Wolfer, Christina SEE Wolfer, Johann Martin
Wolfer, Christina SEE Wolfer, Johann Martin
Wolfer, Jacob SEE Wolfer, Johann Martin
Wolfer, Johann Martin; Pennsylvania, 1750 *2444 p235*
  *Wife:*Christina
  *Child:*Anna Maria
  *Child:*Jacob
  *Child:*Lucia
  *Child:*Christina
  *Child:*Johann Ulrich
Wolfer, Johann Ulrich SEE Wolfer, Johann Martin
Wolfer, Johannes; Pennsylvania, 1750 *2444 p235*
  *Wife:*Sibylla
  *Child:*Anna Maria
  *Child:*Margaretha
  *Child:*Anna

Wolfer, Johannis; Pennsylvania, 1750 *2444 p177*
Wolfer, Julius; Illinois, 1880 *2896.5 p43*
Wolfer, Lucia SEE Wolfer, Johann Martin
Wolfer, Margaretha SEE Wolfer, Johannes
Wolfer, Sibylla SEE Wolfer, Johannes
Wolfers Family ; New York, 1765 *8125.8 p436*
Wolfert, . . .; Canada, 1776-1783 *9786 p37*
Wolfertson, Jakob; New Netherland, 1630-1646 *8582.2 p51*
Wolff, . . .; Canada, 1776-1783 *9786 p37*
Wolff, Albert; America, 1887 *1450.2 p161A*
Wolff, Albert; St. Paul, MN, 1852 *3702.7 p251*
Wolff, Anna Barbara; Philadelphia, 1754 *4525 p270*
Wolff, Christian SEE Wolff, Wilhelm
Wolff, Conrad; Wisconsin, n.d. *9675.8 p125*
Wolff, D.; Kentucky, 1869-1887 *8582 p35*
Wolff, Daniel SEE Wolff, Wilhelm
Wolff, Daniel; Cincinnati, 1869-1887 *8582 p35*
Wolff, Franz 23; Kansas, 1883 *5240.1 p64*
Wolff, Fred; Colorado, 1901 *5240.1 p49*
Wolff, Frederick; Illinois, 1871 *5012.39 p25*
Wolff, Friedrich Karl; Trenton, NJ, 1776 *8137 p15*
Wolff, Friedrich; Illinois, 1873 *5012.39 p91*
Wolff, Gerg; Pennsylvania, 1753 *4525 p256*
Wolff, Henry 43; Kansas, 1885 *5240.1 p68*
Wolff, Hermann 44; Kansas, 1901 *5240.1 p82*
Wolff, John; Philadelphia, 1762 *9973.7 p36*
Wolff, Karl; New York, NY, 1832-1833 *8582 p35*
Wolff, Louis SEE Wolff, Wilhelm
Wolff, Ludwig; Ohio, 1869-1887 *8582 p35*
Wolff, Mark; Colorado, 1900 *9678.3 p18*
Wolff, Martin; Wisconsin, n.d. *9675.8 p125*
Wolff, Paul; Wisconsin, n.d. *9675.8 p125*
Wolff, Philipp Jacob; Pennsylvania, 1752 *4525 p257*
Wolff, Samuel; Pennsylvania, 1743 *2444 p235*
Wolff, Wilhelm; America, 1802-1833 *8582 p35*
  *Brother:*Christian
  *Brother:*Louis
  *Brother:*Daniel
Wolff, Zacharias Samuel; America, 1743 *2444 p235*
Wolffart, Anna Maria; America, 1749 *2444 p207*
Wolffer, Hans Martin; Pennsylvania, 1750 *2444 p177*
Wolffer, Hans Martin; Pennsylvania, 1750 *2444 p235*
Wolffyramm, Herman; Wisconsin, n.d. *9675.8 p125*
Wolfgram, Robert; Wisconsin, n.d. *9675.8 p125*
Wolfhart, Nicholas; Philadelphia, 1760 *9973.7 p34*
Wolfly, Conrad; Pennsylvania, 1750 *2444 p234*
Wolfman, Abe; Arkansas, 1918 *95.2 p131*
Wolfrom, Charles; Indiana, 1835 *1450.2 p161A*
Wolfs, . . .; Canada, 1776-1783 *9786 p37*
Wolfstein, Nathan; America, 1850 *8582.3 p72*
Wolgart, August Theodore Gottfried, II; Quebec, 1776 *9786 p256*
Wolgart, Johann Friedrich, I; Quebec, 1776 *9786 p254*
Wolgast, Jr.; Quebec, 1776 *9786 p105*
Wolgast, Lieut.; Quebec, 1776 *9786 p105*
Wolken, John D.; Illinois, 1888 *5012.37 p61*
Wolkovinsky, Iradin; Washington, 1859-1920 *2872.1 p44*
Wolkow, Hyman 22; Kansas, 1896 *5240.1 p49*
Wolkow, Hyman 22; Kansas, 1896 *5240.1 p80*
Woll, Johannes; Cincinnati, 1843 *8582.2 p60*
Woll, Johannes; Cincinnati, 1869-1887 *8582 p35*
Woll, Nicolaus; Cincinnati, 1869-1887 *8582 p35*
Woll d'Ossenum, A. 26; New Orleans, 1823 *778.5 p549*
Wollauf, Margaretha; New York, 1709 *3627 p7*
Wollenbehr, Anna; Pennsylvania, 1754-1788 *2444 p211*
Wollenberg, August W. 21; Kansas, 1880 *5240.1 p61*
Wollendorf, . . .; Canada, 1776-1783 *9786 p37*
Wollenking, Wilhelm; Arkansas, 1918 *95.2 p131*
Wollenschlager, Ferd; Illinois, 1883 *2896.5 p43*
Wollenschlager, Gustav; Illinois, 1881 *2896.5 p43*
Wollenschlager, Michael; Illinois, 1884 *2896.5 p43*
Wollenweber, L.A.; Philadelphia, 1837 *8582.2 p34*
Woller, Ernst H. W. 27; Kansas, 1882 *5240.1 p49*
Woller, Ernst H. W. 27; Kansas, 1882 *5240.1 p63*
Wollermann, Theodore; Illinois, 1876 *2896.5 p43*
Wollermann, Theodore; Illinois, 1883 *2896.5 p43*
Wollert, Christian; Illinois, 1888 *5012.39 p122*
Wollford, Charlotte 41; Massachusetts, 1860 *6410.32 p102*
Wollford, Emma E. 14; Massachusetts, 1860 *6410.32 p102*
Wollford, Hilma 16; Massachusetts, 1860 *6410.32 p102*
Wollford, John H. 21; Massachusetts, 1860 *6410.32 p102*
Wollford, Lars 45; Massachusetts, 1860 *6410.32 p102*
Wollford, Lars H. 17; Massachusetts, 1860 *6410.32 p102*
Wollford, Mary C. 19; Massachusetts, 1860 *6410.32 p102*
Wollford, Orfil 12; Massachusetts, 1860 *6410.32 p102*
Wollgast, Albert 26; Kansas, 1887 *5240.1 p49*
Wollgast, Albert 26; Kansas, 1887 *5240.1 p71*
Wollhaf, Catharina 11 mos; New York, NY, 1889 *7846 p39*

Wollhaf, Jacob 29; New York, NY, 1889 *7846 p39*
Wollhaf, Marie 29; New York, NY, 1889 *7846 p39*
Wollin, Ernst; Illinois, 1880 *2896.5 p43*
Wollin, Fred; Illinois, 1868 *2896.5 p43*
Wollin, Friedrich; Illinois, 1880 *2896.5 p43*
Wollmann, . . .; Canada, 1776-1783 *9786 p37*
Wollmar, Jacob; Wisconsin, n.d. *9675.8 p125*
Wollner, Martin; Wisconsin, n.d. *9675.8 p125*
Wollner, Simon; Wisconsin, n.d. *9675.8 p125*
Wollock, Robert; Philadelphia, 1870 *5704.8 p238*
Wollsner, Friedrich 27; New York, NY, 1862 *9831.18 p16*
Wollsner, Friedrich 63; New York, NY, 1862 *9831.18 p16*
Wollsner, Henriette 23; New York, NY, 1862 *9831.18 p16*
Wollsner, Louise 15; New York, NY, 1862 *9831.18 p16*
Wolly, Wm.; Virginia, 1647 *6219 p247*
Wolmand, . . .; Canada, 1776-1783 *9786 p37*
Wolmand, Anthony; Canada, 1776-1783 *9786 p243*
Wolniki, . . .; New York, 1831 *4606 p178*
Woloszczynski, Jan; New York, 1835 *4606 p180*
Wolovlek, Anton; Wisconsin, n.d. *9675.8 p125*
Wolpa, Abe; New York, 1892 *1450.2 p43B*
Wolpers, . . .; Quebec, 1776 *9786 p105*
Wolpers, Paul Gottfried Franz; Quebec, 1776 *9786 p255*
Wolpert, Christoph; Pennsylvania, 1749 *4525 p257*
  With wife
Wolpert, Friedrich; Cincinnati, 1869-1887 *8582 p35*
Wolpert, Peter; New England, 1773 *4525 p257*
  With wife
  With children
Wolsky, Amelia; Washington, 1859-1920 *2872.1 p44*
Wolsky, Leonard Albert; Washington, 1859-1920 *2872.1 p44*
Wolsky, Lou; Washington, 1859-1920 *2872.1 p44*
Wolsky, Olga; Washington, 1859-1920 *2872.1 p44*
Wolsky, William; Washington, 1859-1920 *2872.1 p44*
Wolss, . . .; Canada, 1776-1783 *9786 p37*
Wolstermann, Johann Friedrich; America, 1845 *4815.7 p92*
  Wife:Margarete Dorothee
  With 3 children
Wolstermann, Margarete Dorothee SEE Wolstermann, Johann Friedrich
Wolter, Christian; New York, NY, 1837 *8208.4 p52*
Wolter, Christian; Wisconsin, n.d. *9675.8 p125*
Wolter, Elise 28; Kansas, 1891 *5240.1 p76*
Wolters, Henrick 5; New York, NY, 1847 *3377.6 p14*
Wolters, Henry; New York, NY, 1836 *8208.4 p11*
Wolters, John 14; New York, NY, 1847 *3377.6 p14*
Wolters, John 39; New York, NY, 1847 *3377.6 p14*
Wolters, Joseph 13; New York, NY, 1847 *3377.6 p14*
Wolters, Mary 43; New York, NY, 1847 *3377.6 p14*
Woltmann, G.; Milwaukee, 1875 *4719.30 p257*
Woltring, Engelbert; Wisconsin, n.d. *9675.8 p125*
Woltring, Theodor; Wisconsin, n.d. *9675.8 p125*
Woltz, Anna Elisabeth; Pennsylvania, 1752 *4525 p258*
Wolvert, George; California, 1856 *3840.3 p12*
Wolverton, Roger 17; West Indies, 1722 *3690.1 p253*
Wolz, Anna Elisabeth; Pennsylvania, 1752 *4525 p257*
  With 4 children
Wombwell, Tho.; Virginia, 1648 *6219 p250*
Wombwell, Thomas; Virginia, 1638 *6219 p120*
Wompener, Anton F.; America, 1848 *1450.2 p161A*
Wompener, Henry; America, 1850 *1450.2 p161A*
Wompner, Anthony Frederick; America, 1837 *1450.2 p161A*
Wompner, Christian Henry; America, 1835 *1450.2 p161A*
Wond, Jane; Virginia, 1643 *6219 p203*
Wood, Mr.; Quebec, 1815 *9229.18 p75*
Wood, Abraham 26; Maryland, 1775 *1219.7 p251*
Wood, Adel 26; America, 1835 *778.5 p549*
Wood, Alexander 26; Philadelphia, 1803 *53.26 p92*
  Relative:Mary 20
Wood, Alice; Montreal, 1825 *7603 p101*
Wood, Andrew; South Carolina, 1755 *1639.20 p320*
Wood, Arthur; Virginia, 1635 *6219 p3*
Wood, Bedford; Kansas, 1883 *5240.1 p49*
Wood, Daniel; South Carolina, 1734 *1639.20 p320*
Wood, Daniel 25; Antigua (Antego), 1731 *3690.1 p251*
Wood, David 37; Maryland, 1774 *1219.7 p206*
Wood, Edward; Illinois, 1875 *2896.5 p43*
Wood, Edward; Virginia, 1646 *6219 p240*
Wood, Edward; Virginia, 1647 *6219 p247*
Wood, George 23; Massachusetts, 1847 *5881.1 p96*
Wood, George 23; Maryland, 1774 *1219.7 p230*
Wood, George 35; Maryland, 1775 *1219.7 p252*
Wood, Henry; Virginia, 1621 *6219 p67*
Wood, Henry; Virginia, 1634 *6219 p84*
Wood, Isaac 21; Leeward Islands, 1724 *3690.1 p251*
Wood, J. I.; Washington, 1859-1920 *2872.1 p44*

Wood, James; America, 1837 *1450.2 p162A*
Wood, James 22; Maryland, 1774 *1219.7 p215*
Wood, Jane 22; Maryland, 1775 *1219.7 p260*
Wood, Jno; Virginia, 1698 *2212 p12*
Wood, John; Iowa, 1866-1943 *123.54 p52*
Wood, John; New York, NY, 1838 *8208.4 p86*
Wood, John; Virginia, 1636 *6219 p7*
Wood, John; Virginia, 1636 *6219 p11*
Wood, John; Virginia, 1642 *6219 p189*
Wood, John; Virginia, 1647 *6219 p248*
Wood, John 13; Newfoundland, 1699-1700 *2212 p18*
Wood, John 15; Maryland, 1719 *3690.1 p252*
Wood, John 15; Maryland, 1774 *1219.7 p252*
Wood, John 16; New England, 1723 *3690.1 p252*
Wood, John 18; Maryland, 1774 *1219.7 p196*
Wood, John 20; Barbados, 1718 *3690.1 p252*
Wood, John 20; Jamaica, 1731 *3690.1 p252*
Wood, John 21; Quebec, 1857 *5704.8 p135*
Wood, John 27; Virginia, 1774 *1219.7 p239*
Wood, Jon.; Virginia, 1635 *6219 p35*
Wood, Joseph William; Arkansas, 1918 *95.2 p131*
Wood, Leo.; Virginia, 1639 *6219 p154*
Wood, Margaret 18; Jamaica, 1774 *1219.7 p223*
Wood, Mary 20 SEE Wood, Alexander
Wood, Mary 24; Maryland, 1775 *1219.7 p260*
Wood, Mary 24; Massachusetts, 1849 *5881.1 p98*
Wood, Percival; Washington, 1859-1920 *2872.1 p44*
Wood, Peter; Virginia, 1647 *6219 p248*
Wood, Peter 20; Jamaica, 1738 *3690.1 p252*
Wood, R. W.; Arizona, 1876 *2764.35 p72*
Wood, Ralph; Virginia, 1634 *6219 p84*
Wood, Richard; Illinois, 1846 *7857 p8*
Wood, Richard 26; Maryland, 1775 *1219.7 p254*
Wood, Robert; Virginia, 1642 *6219 p191*
Wood, Seaman T. 30; Kansas, 1874 *5240.1 p55*
Wood, Susan 55; Massachusetts, 1849 *5881.1 p98*
Wood, Thomas; New York, NY, 1815 *5881.1 p44*
Wood, Thomas; Virginia, 1638 *6219 p11*
Wood, Thomas; Virginia, 1638 *6219 p120*
Wood, Thomas 22; Maryland, 1774 *1219.7 p234*
Wood, Thomas 22; Massachusetts, 1847 *5881.1 p98*
Wood, Thomas 23; Virginia, 1773 *1219.7 p169*
Wood, Thomas 24; Philadelphia, 1774 *1219.7 p214*
Wood, Thomas 25; Virginia, 1774 *1219.7 p240*
Wood, Thomas 30; Philadelphia, 1775 *1219.7 p274*
Wood, Walter; Virginia, 1643 *6219 p201*
Wood, William; Colorado, 1894 *9678.3 p18*
Wood, William; Indiana, 1845 *9117 p18*
Wood, William; Jamestown, VA, 1770 *1219.7 p144*
Wood, William; Virginia, 1639 *6219 p155*
Wood, William; Virginia, 1698 *2212 p15*
Wood, William 21; Maryland, 1775 *1219.7 p264*
Wood, Wm.; Virginia, 1638 *6219 p2*
Wood, Wm.; Virginia, 1638 *6219 p11*
Wood, Wm.; Virginia, 1641 *6219 p184*
Woodall, John; Virginia, 1636 *6219 p26*
Woodall, Tho.; Virginia, 1636 *6219 p7*
Woodall, William; Boston, 1772 *1219.7 p153*
Woodards, William; Jamaica, 1766 *1219.7 p123*
Woodason, James; South Potomac, VA, 1752 *1219.7 p9*
Woodaston, Ann 15 SEE Woodaston, Geo.
Woodaston, Esther 35 SEE Woodaston, Geo.
Woodaston, Geo. 10 SEE Woodaston, Geo.
Woodaston, Geo. 44; Port uncertain, 1849 *4535.10 p198*
  Wife:Esther 35
  Child:Ann 15
  Child:Margaret 13
  Child:Jane 11
  Child:Geo. 10
Woodaston, Jane 11 SEE Woodaston, Geo.
Woodaston, Margaret 13 SEE Woodaston, Geo.
Woodbear, Mr. 30; New Orleans, 1835 *778.5 p549*
Woodbear, Mrs. 30; New Orleans, 1835 *778.5 p549*
Woodbridge, Eliza.; Virginia, 1642 *6219 p192*
Woodbridge, John 22; Jamaica, 1731 *3690.1 p252*
Woodburn, John; St. John, N.B., 1847 *5704.8 p25*
Woodburn, Robert 16; Maryland, 1729 *3690.1 p252*
Woodcock, Adela B.; Colorado, 1903 *9678.3 p18*
Woodcock, Georg; Virginia, 1636 *6219 p34*
Woodcock, Jessie 17; Port uncertain, 1859 *4535.11 p54*
Woodcock, John; Virginia, 1639 *6219 p156*
Woodcock, John 33; Philadelphia, 1774 *1219.7 p216*
Woodcock, Thos.; Virginia, 1635 *6219 p68*
Woodcocke, William; Virginia, 1639 *6219 p151*
Woodcocke, Jon.; Virginia, 1637 *6219 p114*
Wooddard, Christopher; Virginia, 1635 *6219 p35*
  With wife
Woodford, Elizabeth 30; Maryland, 1775 *1219.7 p264*
Woodford, George 21; Philadelphia, 1775 *1219.7 p258*
Woodford, Jon.; Virginia, 1638 *6219 p115*
Woodford, Thomas 30; Maryland, 1775 *1219.7 p264*
Woodgate, Wm.; Virginia, 1635 *6219 p27*
Woodgate, Wm.; Virginia, 1638 *6219 p145*

Woodhams, Joseph; New York, NY, 1827 *8208.4 p47*
Woodhead, Edmund 18; Jamaica, 1724 *3690.1 p252*
Woodhead, Sophia 27; Massachusetts, 1849 *5881.1 p98*
Woodhouse, George 22; Virginia, 1775 *1219.7 p261*
Woodhouse, John 36; Virginia, 1774 *1219.7 p242*
Woodhouse, William 18; New England, 1724 *3690.1 p252*
Woodhouse, William 23; Jamaica, 1733 *3690.1 p252*
Woodhowse, Elizabeth SEE Woodhowse, Henry
Woodhowse, Henry; Virginia, 1637 *6219 p82*
  Wife:Mary
  Daughter:Elizabeth
Woodhowse, Mary SEE Woodhowse, Henry
Woodhowse, William; Virginia, 1600-1642 *6219 p193*
Woodier, Kath 24; America, 1704 *2212 p41*
Woodin, John; Jamaica, 1765 *1219.7 p112*
Woodliffe, John; Virginia, 1638 *6219 p122*
Woodny, John 32; Jamaica, 1734 *3690.1 p252*
Woodroffe, George; New York, NY, 1834 *8208.4 p38*
Woodroof, Walter; Illinois, 1888 *5012.37 p61*
Woodroofe, Edith SEE Woodroofe, Thomas
Woodroofe, Edith Pitt SEE Woodroofe, Thomas
Woodroofe, Isaac SEE Woodroofe, Thomas
Woodroofe, John SEE Woodroofe, Thomas
Woodroofe, John Frith; Illinois, 1892 *5012.40 p26*
Woodroofe, Joseph; Pennsylvania, 1682 *4961 p166*
Woodroofe, Mary SEE Woodroofe, Thomas
Woodroofe, Thomas SEE Woodroofe, Thomas
Woodroofe, Thomas; Pennsylvania, 1679 *4961 p167*
  Wife:Edith Pitt
  Child:Thomas
  Child:Edith
  Child:John
  Child:Isaac
  Daughter:Mary
Woodroote, Thomas 19; Jamaica, 1730 *3690.1 p252*
Woodruffe, Richard; Virginia, 1643 *6219 p200*
Woodruffe, Robt.; Virginia, 1647 *6219 p245*
Woods, Adam; Philadelphia, 1811 *53.26 p92*
Woods, Adam; Philadelphia, 1811 *2859.11 p21*
Woods, Ann 11; Quebec, 1862 *5704.8 p151*
Woods, Bridget 20; St. John, N.B., 1858 *5704.8 p137*
Woods, Caelia; Virginia, 1698 *2212 p15*
Woods, Charles; Philadelphia, 1865 *5704.8 p195*
Woods, David; Quebec, 1850 *5704.8 p63*
Woods, Eleanor; Philadelphia, 1851 *5704.8 p71*
Woods, Eliza; New York, NY, 1816 *2859.11 p44*
Woods, Eliza; Quebec, 1850 *5704.8 p63*
Woods, Elizabeth; New York, NY, 1865 *5704.8 p203*
Woods, Elizabeth; Philadelphia, 1865 *5704.8 p195*
Woods, Ellen; New York, NY, 1865 *5704.8 p203*
Woods, Ellen 13; Quebec, 1847 *5704.8 p12*
Woods, George; Quebec, 1847 *5704.8 p29*
Woods, George 10; Quebec, 1849 *5704.8 p57*
Woods, Henry; Quebec, 1851 *5704.8 p82*
Woods, Henry; Virginia, 1698 *2212 p15*
Woods, Henry; Virginia, 1698 *2212 p17*
Woods, James; Baltimore, 1811 *2859.11 p21*
Woods, James; Illinois, 1874 *2764.35 p71*
Woods, James; New York, NY, 1816 *2859.11 p44*
Woods, James; Philadelphia, 1811 *53.26 p92*
Woods, James; Philadelphia, 1811 *2859.11 p21*
Woods, James 12; America, 1705 *2212 p43*
Woods, Jane; St. John, N.B., 1848 *5704.8 p45*
Woods, John; America, 1869 *5704.8 p236*
Woods, John; Philadelphia, 1871 *5704.8 p241*
Woods, John; Quebec, 1847 *5704.8 p12*
Woods, John 11; Quebec, 1852 *5704.8 p93*
Woods, John 16; Maryland, 1775 *1219.7 p267*
Woods, John 19; Antigua (Antego), 1731 *3690.1 p253*
Woods, John 19; Maryland, 1733 *3690.1 p253*
Woods, John 22; St. Kitts, 1699 *2212 p25*
Woods, Lilly 50; Quebec, 1862 *5704.8 p151*
Woods, Malcom 19; Philadelphia, 1854 *5704.8 p117*
Woods, Margaret 9; Quebec, 1852 *5704.8 p93*
Woods, Martha; Quebec, 1850 *5704.8 p63*
Woods, Mary 10; St. John, N.B., 1848 *5704.8 p44*
Woods, Mary 22; America, 1703 *2212 p38*
Woods, Mary 23; America, 1702 *2212 p37*
Woods, Mary Jane 18; Quebec, 1862 *5704.8 p151*
Woods, Matilda; Philadelphia, 1851 *5704.8 p81*
Woods, Michael 40; Massachusetts, 1847 *5881.1 p97*
Woods, Owen 27; Philadelphia, 1858 *5704.8 p139*
Woods, Richd; America, 1698 *2212 p9*
Woods, Robert; Quebec, 1849 *5704.8 p57*
Woods, Robert; Quebec, 1852 *5704.8 p86*
Woods, Robert; Quebec, 1852 *5704.8 p91*
Woods, Robert 14; Virginia, 1699 *2212 p27*
Woods, Ruth; New York, NY, 1815 *2859.11 p44*
Woods, Sally 8; St. John, N.B., 1848 *5704.8 p44*
Woods, Thomas 60; Kansas, 1881 *5240.1 p63*
Woods, William; New York, NY, 1815 *2859.11 p44*
Woods, William; Quebec, 1847 *5704.8 p12*

Woods, Worthy J.; Colorado, 1904 ***9678.3*** *p19*
Woodside, David; New York, NY, 1869 ***5704.8*** *p234*
Woodside, John; New York, NY, 1869 ***5704.8*** *p234*
Woodside, R.; New York, NY, 1816 ***2859.11*** *p44*
Woodside, Rebecca 11; New York, NY, 1869 ***5704.8*** *p234*
Woodside, Robert; New York, NY, 1869 ***5704.8*** *p234*
Woodside, Sarah; New York, NY, 1869 ***5704.8*** *p234*
Woodside, Wm.; New York, NY, 1816 ***2859.11*** *p44*
Woodstock, John 25; Maryland, 1775 ***1219.7*** *p268*
Woodus, John 22; Jamaica, 1737 ***3690.1*** *p253*
Woodville, John; Philadelphia, 1776 ***1219.7*** *p282*
Woodward, Christopher; Virginia, 1636 ***6219*** *p81*
*Wife:*Dorothy
Woodward, Christopher; Virginia, 1637 ***6219*** *p108*
*Wife:*Dorothy
Woodward, Dorothy *SEE* Woodward, Christopher
Woodward, Dorothy *SEE* Woodward, Christopher
Woodward, Elizabeth 26; Massachusetts, 1848 ***5881.1*** *p96*
Woodward, George 19; Jamaica, 1730 ***3690.1*** *p253*
Woodward, Margarett; Virginia, 1636 ***6219*** *p81*
Woodward, Margarett; Virginia, 1637 ***6219*** *p108*
Woodward, Thomas 21; Virginia, 1775 ***1219.7*** *p246*
Woodward, Wm.; Virginia, 1642 ***6219*** *p199*
Woodworth, J. C. 40; Kansas, 1888 ***5240.1*** *p71*
Woodyard, Vincent; Virginia, 1635 ***6219*** *p28*
Woofed, Nich.; Virginia, 1640 ***6219*** *p160*
Woolap, Jacob; Ohio, 1823 ***9892.11*** *p49*
Wooles, Robt.; Virginia, 1635 ***6219*** *p17*
Wooleston, Ann; Virginia, 1639 ***6219*** *p151*
Woolett, Robert 16; Philadelphia, 1774 ***1219.7*** *p217*
Wooley, Benjamin M.; New York, NY, 1834 ***8208.4*** *p44*
Woolf, Moses; America, 1849 ***1450.2*** *p161A*
Woolfe, George; Virginia, 1645 ***6219*** *p233*
Woolfe, Wm.; Virginia, 1636 ***6219*** *p77*
Woolfet, Wm 15; America, 1699 ***2212*** *p28*
Woolgate, Sarah; Virginia, 1639 ***6219*** *p152*
Woolhams, Barton 28; Maryland, 1738 ***3690.1*** *p252*
Woollands, John 35; Arkansas, 1918 ***95.2*** *p131*
Woolley, Cornelius 18; Jamaica, 1739 ***3690.1*** *p253*
Woolley, Mary 26; America, 1704 ***2212*** *p41*
Woolley, William; Virginia, 1636 ***6219*** *p115*
Woolley, William; Virginia, 1637 ***6219*** *p86*
Woolley, Wm.; Virginia, 1636 ***6219*** *p26*
Woollierine, Humphrey; Virginia, 1637 ***6219*** *p109*
Woolly, William; Virginia, 1638 ***6219*** *p145*
Woolner, James 17; Jamaica, 1727 ***3690.1*** *p253*
Woolrich, Mr.; Quebec, 1815 ***9229.18*** *p80*
Woolrich, Joane; Virginia, 1635 ***6219*** *p36*
Woolridge, Tho.; Virginia, 1643 ***6219*** *p201*
Wools, Samuel; Virginia, 1635 ***6219*** *p12*
Woolsey, John Alexander 24; St. John, N.B., 1864 ***5704.8*** *p159*
Woolverton, Roger 17; Pennsylvania, 1722 ***3690.1*** *p253*
Woorgen, Isaac; Virginia, 1636 ***6219*** *p79*
Woorkes, William; Virginia, 1635 ***6219*** *p16*
Woorle, August; Arizona, 1898 ***9228.30*** *p13*
Woosencroft, James 23; Virginia, 1774 ***1219.7*** *p243*
Wootton, Rich.; Virginia, 1642 ***6219*** *p198*
Wootton, Richard; Virginia, 1638 ***6219*** *p121*
Wootton, William; Virginia, 1639 ***6219*** *p155*
Woover, Robert; Virginia, 1638 ***6219*** *p147*
Worbass, Peter; New York, 1753 ***3652*** *p77*
Word, John 26; Maryland, 1775 ***1219.7*** *p255*
Worden, Richd; America, 1698 ***2212*** *p8*
Worke, William; Virginia, 1639 ***6219*** *p156*
Worker, James 23; Maryland, 1774 ***1219.7*** *p230*
Worker, Nathaniel 25; Carolina, 1774 ***1219.7*** *p213*
Working, Nicholas; Philadelphia, 1765 ***9973.7*** *p40*
Workman, George; New York, NY, 1816 ***2859.11*** *p44*
Workman, Henry; Washington, 1859-1920 ***2872.1*** *p44*
Workman, John; St. John, N.B., 1847 ***5704.8*** *p21*
Workman, Richard; Virginia, 1643 ***6219*** *p205*
Workman, Richd.; Virginia, 1646 ***6219*** *p246*
Workman, Thomas 20; Maryland, 1718 ***3690.1*** *p253*
Worlin, George; Quebec, 1847 ***5704.8*** *p15*
Worlin, Margaret; Quebec, 1847 ***5704.8*** *p15*
Wormewell, Mary; Virginia, 1635 ***6219*** *p35*
Worminger, William; Virginia, 1638 ***6219*** *p122*
Wormley, Johannes 21; Pennsylvania, 1753 ***2444*** *p236*
Wormly, John 21; Pennsylvania, 1753 ***2444*** *p236*
Worms, William; Wisconsin, n.d. ***9675.8*** *p125*
Wormser, Louis; New York, NY, 1850 ***6013.19*** *p89*
Wormsley, Roger; Virginia, 1647 ***6219*** *p244*
Wornall, Robert; Virginia, 1638 ***6219*** *p149*
Worner, Martin; Pennsylvania, 1738 ***7829*** *p8*
Worobec, Philip; Arkansas, 1918 ***95.2*** *p131*
Woronecki, Piotr 17; New York, 1912 ***9980.29*** *p68*
Worrall, Mary; America, 1705 ***2212*** *p45*
Worrall, Richard 21; Pennsylvania, Virginia or Maryland, 1699 ***2212*** *p19*
Worrall, Samuel 18; Maryland, 1731 ***3690.1*** *p253*
Worrall, Thomas 20; America, 1700 ***2212*** *p33*
Worrell, John 29; Jamaica, 1731 ***3690.1*** *p253*
Worrhington, John; New York, NY, 1816 ***2859.11*** *p44*
Worrs, Georg.; Maryland or Virginia, 1697 ***2212*** *p3*
Worshin, Edward 30; New York, NY, 1851 ***9555.10*** *p26*
Worshipp, Walter; Virginia, 1639 ***6219*** *p157*
Worster, Richard; Virginia, 1635 ***6219*** *p69*
Worth, George; Indiana, 1848 ***9117*** *p19*
Worthmann, Dietrich; Wisconsin, n.d. ***9675.8*** *p126*
Worthson, Judith 70; Virginia, 1774 ***1219.7*** *p227*
Wortley, William 20; Antigua (Antego), 1739 ***3690.1*** *p253*
Wortman, Ann; Virginia, 1643 ***6219*** *p203*
Wortman, Jon.; Virginia, 1643 ***6219*** *p203*
Wortman, Mary; Virginia, 1643 ***6219*** *p203*
Wortman, Tho.; Virginia, 1643 ***6219*** *p203*
Wortmann, Hermann Friedrich; America, 1852 ***4610.10*** *p144*
Wortmann, Johann Friedrich; America, 1856 ***4610.10*** *p145*
Wortz, Pierre 32; New Orleans, 1836 ***778.5*** *p549*
Wosencroft, Mandelin; Virginia, 1639 ***6219*** *p184*
Wosener, Carl 27; New York, NY, 1857 ***9831.14*** *p153*
Wosener, Caroline 27; New York, NY, 1857 ***9831.14*** *p153*
Wosener, Johann 2; New York, NY, 1857 ***9831.14*** *p153*
Wosener, Joseph 9; New York, NY, 1857 ***9831.14*** *p153*
Wosener, Marie 6; New York, NY, 1857 ***9831.14*** *p153*
Wossatow, Isaac 21; New York, NY, 1878 ***9253*** *p47*
Wostale, Anton; Wisconsin, n.d. ***9675.8*** *p126*
Wotherspoon, Robert; Charleston, SC, 1831 ***1639.20*** *p320*
Wotherspoon, Robert 55; Charleston, SC, 1850 ***1639.20*** *p320*
*Relative:*Sarah 52
Wotherspoon, Sarah 52 *SEE* Wotherspoon, Robert
Wotke, Julius; Illinois, 1882 ***2896.5*** *p43*
Wotke, Michael; Illinois, 1880 ***2896.5*** *p43*
Wottelle, John; Wisconsin, n.d. ***9675.8*** *p126*
Wotter, Eliz.; Virginia, 1643 ***6219*** *p229*
Wouol, Patrice; Quebec, 1824 ***7603*** *p79*
Wowbecz, Philip; Arkansas, 1918 ***95.2*** *p131*
Woyciechowski, . . .; New York, 1831 ***4606*** *p178*
Woytkewicz, Adam; Arkansas, 1918 ***95.2*** *p132*
Wozniak, Stanislaw; Arkansas, 1918 ***95.2*** *p132*
Wragg, Benj.; Virginia, 1642 ***6219*** *p197*
Wragg, Joseph; New York, NY, 1838 ***8208.4*** *p70*
Wragg, Samuel; Charles Town, SC, 1754 ***1219.7*** *p29*
Wray, Ann; Quebec, 1849 ***5704.8*** *p57*
Wray, Ann Jane; Quebec, 1849 ***5704.8*** *p57*
Wray, Arthur; St. John, N.B., 1852 ***5704.8*** *p93*
Wray, Catharine; St. John, N.B., 1850 ***5704.8*** *p61*
Wray, Fanny 4; Quebec, 1849 ***5704.8*** *p57*
Wray, George; Quebec, 1852 ***5704.8*** *p91*
Wray, Hanah 22; St. John, N.B., 1854 ***5704.8*** *p114*
Wray, James; New York, NY, 1815 ***2859.11*** *p44*
Wray, Jon.; Virginia, 1628 ***6219*** *p9*
Wray, Lillie; New York, NY, 1866 ***5704.8*** *p212*
Wray, Lilly; New York, NY, 1867 ***5704.8*** *p220*
Wray, Lucy 19; Philadelphia, 1855 ***5704.8*** *p124*
Wray, Martha 14; Philadelphia, 1868 ***5704.8*** *p225*
Wray, Mary Jane 11; Quebec, 1849 ***5704.8*** *p57*
Wray, Thomas; Virginia, 1636 ***6219*** *p36*
Wray, William; New York, NY, 1815 ***2859.11*** *p44*
Wray, William; St. John, N.B., 1848 ***5704.8*** *p44*
Wreath, Benjamin; St. John, N.B., 1847 ***5704.8*** *p25*
Wreeden, Martin; New York, NY, 1840 ***8208.4*** *p106*
Wreidt, Adolph; America, 1871 ***1450.2*** *p162A*
Wren, Daniel 14; Massachusetts, 1850 ***5881.1*** *p83*
Wren, Ellen 19; Massachusetts, 1849 ***5881.1*** *p96*
Wren, Roger 17; Virginia, 1774 ***1219.7*** *p186*
Wrench, Ann; Virginia, 1641 ***6219*** *p187*
Wrench, Thomas 16; Maryland, 1729 ***3690.1*** *p254*
Wrenn, Ellen; Massachusetts, 1847 ***5881.1*** *p96*
Wrenn, John; Massachusetts, 1847 ***5881.1*** *p97*
Wrenn, Mary 12; Massachusetts, 1849 ***5881.1*** *p98*
Wrenn, Michael 38; Massachusetts, 1847 ***5881.1*** *p97*
Wrenn, Thomas; Virginia, 1638 ***6219*** *p147*
Wriberg, Maria Magdalena; Port uncertain, 1701-1800 ***2444*** *p236*
Wriey, Thomas 21; Maryland, 1774 ***1219.7*** *p206*
Wright, Adolph; America, 1871 ***1450.2*** *p162A*
Wright, Alexander 27; Maryland, 1775 ***1219.7*** *p257*
Wright, Alexander 49; St. John, N.B., 1866 ***5704.8*** *p167*
Wright, Ann; New York, NY, 1811 ***2859.11*** *p21*
Wright, Ann 20; Virginia, 1774 ***1219.7*** *p238*
Wright, Catherine; New York, NY, 1811 ***2859.11*** *p21*
Wright, Charles; San Francisco, 1850 ***4914.15*** *p10*
Wright, Christian; St. John, N.B., 1850 ***5704.8*** *p65*
Wright, Duncan; North Carolina, 1724-1827 ***1639.20*** *p320*
Wright, Edward 18; Virginia, 1721 ***3690.1*** *p254*
Wright, Edward 23; Maryland, 1774 ***1219.7*** *p221*
Wright, Edward 28; Maryland, 1775 ***1219.7*** *p249*
Wright, Edward 28; Maryland, 1775 ***1219.7*** *p252*
Wright, Edward 46; Kansas, 1871 ***5240.1*** *p51*
Wright, Eliz 15; America, 1702 ***2212*** *p38*
Wright, Eliza; New York, NY, 1811 ***2859.11*** *p21*
Wright, Elizabeth; Virginia, 1637 ***6219*** *p84*
Wright, Elizabeth 11 *SEE* Wright, John
Wright, Elizabeth 20; Virginia, 1774 ***1219.7*** *p238*
Wright, Elizabeth 21; America, 1701 ***2212*** *p34*
Wright, Elizabeth 30; Virginia, 1700 ***2212*** *p33*
Wright, Francis 24; Philadelphia, 1775 ***1219.7*** *p273*
Wright, George; Iroquois Co., IL, 1894 ***3455.1*** *p14*
Wright, George; St. John, N.B., 1847 ***5704.8*** *p25*
Wright, George Adams; Arkansas, 1918 ***95.2*** *p132*
Wright, Grace 15; Quebec, 1863 ***5704.8*** *p154*
Wright, Henry; New York, NY, 1816 ***2859.11*** *p44*
Wright, Henry 21; Maryland, 1775 ***1219.7*** *p267*
Wright, Henry H.; New York, NY, 1836 ***8208.4*** *p20*
Wright, Isabella 23; Quebec, 1863 ***5704.8*** *p154*
Wright, Isabella 50; Quebec, 1863 ***5704.8*** *p154*
Wright, Isobel 36; Wilmington, NC, 1774 ***1639.20*** *p146*
Wright, James; New York, NY, 1811 ***2859.11*** *p21*
With wife
Wright, James; New York, NY, 1816 ***2859.11*** *p44*
Wright, James; South Carolina, 1790 ***1639.20*** *p320*
Wright, James 18; Antigua (Antego), 1739 ***3690.1*** *p254*
Wright, James 18; Quebec, 1863 ***5704.8*** *p154*
Wright, James 20; Jamaica, 1724 ***3690.1*** *p254*
Wright, James 22; Virginia, 1774 ***1219.7*** *p239*
Wright, James 24; Philadelphia, 1833-1834 ***53.26*** *p92*
Wright, James 26; Jamaica, 1730 ***3690.1*** *p254*
Wright, James 26; Virginia, 1775 ***1219.7*** *p252*
Wright, James 28; Virginia, 1774 ***1219.7*** *p243*
Wright, James 38; Virginia, 1774 ***1219.7*** *p201*
Wright, Jane; America, 1865 ***5704.8*** *p204*
Wright, Jane; New York, NY, 1816 ***2859.11*** *p44*
Wright, Jane; Virginia, 1637 ***6219*** *p110*
Wright, Jane; Virginia, 1639 ***6219*** *p158*
Wright, Jane; Virginia, 1643 ***6219*** *p202*
Wright, Jane 15; Maryland or Virginia, 1699 ***2212*** *p22*
Wright, Jno.; Virginia, 1646 ***6219*** *p241*
Wright, John; Illinois, 1872 ***5012.39*** *p25*
Wright, John; Illinois, 1874 ***5012.39*** *p91*
Wright, John; Jamaica, 1755 ***1219.7*** *p37*
Wright, John; New York, NY, 1811 ***2859.11*** *p21*
Wright, John; New York, NY, 1816 ***2859.11*** *p44*
Wright, John; New York, NY, 1838 ***8208.4*** *p75*
Wright, John; St. John, N.B., 1847 ***5704.8*** *p25*
Wright, John; Virginia, 1635 ***6219*** *p12*
Wright, John; Virginia, 1636 ***6219*** *p26*
Wright, John; Virginia, 1638 ***6219*** *p124*
Wright, John; Virginia, 1638 ***6219*** *p158*
Wright, John; Virginia, 1640 ***6219*** *p160*
Wright, John; Virginia, 1698 ***2212*** *p11*
Wright, John 22; Port uncertain, 1774 ***1219.7*** *p176*
Wright, John 23; Virginia, 1773 ***1219.7*** *p171*
Wright, John 30; Maryland, 1774 ***1219.7*** *p235*
Wright, John 33; Savannah, GA, 1733 ***4719.17*** *p313*
*Daughter:*Elizabeth 11
*Son:*John Norton 13
*Wife:*Penelope 33
Wright, John 41; New York, 1774 ***1219.7*** *p203*
Wright, John Norton 13 *SEE* Wright, John
Wright, John T. 40; Kansas, 1905 ***5240.1*** *p83*
Wright, Jon.; Virginia, 1642 ***6219*** *p199*
Wright, Joseph; America, 1741 ***4971*** *p65*
Wright, Joseph 16; Philadelphia, 1774 ***1219.7*** *p233*
Wright, Joseph 19; Maryland, 1774 ***1219.7*** *p191*
Wright, Joseph Godell; Illinois, 1871 ***5012.39*** *p25*
Wright, Margret 19; Pennsylvania, 1728 ***3690.1*** *p254*
Wright, Mariam; New York, NY, 1816 ***2859.11*** *p44*
Wright, Mary 22; Jamaica, 1774 ***1219.7*** *p234*
Wright, Mathan; New York, NY, 1816 ***2859.11*** *p44*
Wright, Max; Iowa, 1866-1943 ***123.54*** *p52*
Wright, Michael; New York, NY, 1815 ***2859.11*** *p44*
Wright, Penelope 33 *SEE* Wright, John
Wright, Philomen; Ontario, n.d. ***9775.5*** *p211*
Wright, Richard; Virginia, 1636 ***6219*** *p36*
Wright, Richard; Virginia, 1636 ***6219*** *p78*
Wright, Robert; Illinois, 1861 ***7857*** *p8*
Wright, Robert; Virginia, 1642 ***6219*** *p191*
Wright, Robert 24; Kansas, 1874 ***5240.1*** *p55*
Wright, Robert B.; Colorado, 1896 ***9678.3*** *p19*
Wright, Robert William; New York, NY, 1836 ***8208.4*** *p20*
Wright, Roger; Virginia, 1635 ***6219*** *p73*
Wright, Saml 30; Philadelphia, 1845 ***6508.6*** *p115*
Wright, Samuel; Maryland, 1756 ***1219.7*** *p42*
Wright, Samuel; Maryland, 1756 ***3690.1*** *p254*
Wright, Sarah 20; St. John, N.B., 1860 ***5704.8*** *p143*
Wright, Symon; Virginia, 1637 ***6219*** *p110*
Wright, Tho.; Virginia, 1647 ***6219*** *p247*
Wright, Thomas; America, 1738 ***4971*** *p13*

Wright, Thomas; Maryland, 1775 *1219.7 p265*
Wright, Thomas 16; Maryland, 1735 *3690.1 p254*
Wright, Thomas 22; Virginia, 1774 *1219.7 p243*
Wright, Walter 18; Jamaica, 1736 *3690.1 p254*
Wright, William; Illinois, 1862 *2896.5 p43*
Wright, William; New York, NY, 1815 *2859.11 p44*
Wright, William; New York, NY, 1840 *8208.4 p106*
Wright, William; Virginia, 1639 *6219 p158*
Wright, William; Virginia, 1647 *6219 p244*
Wright, William 18; Maryland, 1774 *1219.7 p221*
Wright, William 18; Pennsylvania, Virginia or Maryland, 1725 *3690.1 p254*
Wright, William 22; Pennsylvania, 1731 *3690.1 p254*
Wright, William 23; Jamaica, 1730 *3690.1 p254*
Wright, William 24; Massachusetts, 1849 *5881.1 p98*
Wright, William 27; Kansas, 1874 *5240.1 p55*
Wright, William 27; Maryland, 1775 *1219.7 p267*
Wright, William 30; Virginia, 1700 *2212 p33*
Wright, William 33; Maryland, 1774 *1219.7 p228*
Wright, Wm.; Virginia, 1637 *6219 p24*
Wright, Wm.; Virginia, 1637 *6219 p110*
Wright, Wm.; Virginia, 1648 *6219 p241*
Wrightson, Elizabeth 20; Nova Scotia, 1774 *1219.7 p194*
Writt, Edward; Virginia, 1636 *6219 p77*
Writt, John; Virginia, 1633 *6219 p31*
Wroblewski, Joseph Antonio; Arkansas, 1918 *95.2 p132*
Wroblewski, Waclaw 24; New York, 1912 *9980.29 p55*
Wronowski, . . .; New York, 1831 *4606 p178*
Wrot, Margaret; America, 1736 *4971 p77*
Wrubel, Bartlomey 22; New York, 1912 *9980.29 p63*
Wry, John 23; Nova Scotia, 1774 *1219.7 p195*
Wryth, Rich.; Virginia, 1635 *6219 p69*
Wttrom, Gust; Iowa, 1866-1943 *123.54 p52*
Wuehle, Henry; Illinois, 1873 *2896.5 p43*
Wuehle, Henry W.; Illinois, 1888 *2896.5 p43*
Wuelfing, Otto; America, 1891 *1450.2 p162A*
Wuermle, Anna Maria *SEE* Wuermle, Johannes
Wuermle, Johannes; America, 1753 *2444 p236*
  *Wife:*Anna Maria
Wuermle, Johannes 21; Pennsylvania, 1753 *2444 p236*
Wuert, Mr. 29; America, 1838 *778.5 p549*
Wuertele, John; New York, 1754 *3652 p80*
Wuerth, Johann; America, 1849 *8582.3 p72*
Wuertz, Mathias; Cincinnati, 1835 *8582.1 p37*
Wuerz, Mathias; Cincinnati, 1835 *8582.1 p52*
Wuest, Adam; Cincinnati, 1869-1887 *8582 p35*
Wuest, Adam; New York, NY, 1846 *8582.1 p37*
Wuest, Anna Elisabetha *SEE* Wuest, Jerg
Wuest, Anna Maria *SEE* Wuest, Jerg
Wuest, Barbara *SEE* Wuest, Bernhard
Wuest, Bernhard; Pennsylvania, 1750 *2444 p236*
  *Wife:*Barbara
  *Child:*Jacob Friedrich
Wuest, Georg; Cincinnati, 1869-1887 *8582 p35*
Wuest, Jacob; Cincinnati, 1869-1887 *8582 p35*
Wuest, Jacob Friedrich *SEE* Wuest, Bernhard
Wuest, Jerg; Pennsylvania, 1754 *2444 p236*
  *Wife:*Anna Maria
  *Child:*Anna Elisabetha
  *Child:*Maria Agnes
Wuest, Maria Agnes *SEE* Wuest, Jerg
Wukmarovich, Joran Rado; Arkansas, 1918 *95.2 p132*
Wulbern, Jacob; New York, NY, 1836 *8208.4 p9*
Wulf, August; Indianapolis, 1870 *3702.7 p586*
Wulf, Heinrich Friedrich Wilhelm; America, 1866 *3702.7 p573*
Wulfeck, Victor; Cincinnati, 1869-1887 *8582 p35*

Wulfeck, Wilhelm Heinrich; America, 1842 *8582.3 p72*
Wulfekoetter, Wilhelm; America, 1849 *8582.3 p72*
Wulff, Burchard; Wisconsin, n.d. *9675.8 p126*
Wulff, John; Wisconsin, n.d. *9675.8 p126*
Wulle, George 21; Ohio, 1870 *1450.2 p162A*
Wuller, Anna Maria 36 *SEE* Wuller, Hans Michael
Wuller, Hans Michael 36; Savannah, GA, 1738 *9332 p330*
  *Wife:*Anna Maria 36
Wullins, Mary 20; Georgia, 1775 *1219.7 p277*
Wullner, Christian Friedrich; America, 1865 *4610.10 p158*
Wullschlager, John 21; Kansas, 1893 *5240.1 p77*
Wullschleger, Otto 23; Kansas, 1893 *5240.1 p77*
Wunder, Johann Georg; Pennsylvania, 1753 *4525 p258*
  With wife
  With 2 children
Wunderlich, Christian 9 *SEE* Wunderlich, John Chas.
Wunderlich, Dorothea 5 *SEE* Wunderlich, John Chas.
Wunderlich, Henrietta 3 *SEE* Wunderlich, John Chas.
Wunderlich, Henry 8 *SEE* Wunderlich, John Chas.
Wunderlich, John Chas. 35; New Orleans, 1839 *9420.2 p359*
  *Wife:*Mary Elizab. 32
  *Son:*Christian 9
  *Son:*Henry 8
  *Daughter:*Dorothea 5
  *Daughter:*Henrietta 3
Wunderlich, Johnnis 75; New Orleans, 1839 *9420.2 p360*
Wunderlich, Mary Elizab. 32 *SEE* Wunderlich, John Chas.
Wunschmann, Paul; Santa Fe, NM, 1904 *3702.7 p121*
Wurfel, . . .; Canada, 1776-1783 *9786 p37*
Wurfel, Carl; Wisconsin, n.d. *9675.8 p126*
Wurmb, von; Canada, 1776-1783 *9786 p200*
Wurmb, Constantin von; Canada, 1780 *9786 p268*
Wurmb, Constantin von; New York, 1776 *9786 p268*
Wurmb, F.W. von; New York, 1776 *9786 p277*
Wursbacher, Wanda 24; New York, 1912 *9980.29 p49*
Wurst, Henry; Wisconsin, n.d. *9675.8 p126*
Wurstbauer, Joseph 45; Kansas, 1887 *5240.1 p70*
Wurstbaurer, John 63; Kansas, 1876 *5240.1 p57*
Wurster, Hans Jacob; Pennsylvania, 1752 *2444 p236*
Wurstner, Andrew; New York, NY, 1852 *1450.2 p162A*
Wurtel, . . .; Canada, 1776-1783 *9786 p37*
Wurth, Georg; Baltimore, 1832 *8582 p35*
Wurthmann, Henry; Wisconsin, n.d. *9675.8 p126*
Wurty, Mathias; New York, NY, 1838 *8208.4 p72*
Wurtz, Catharina 9 mos; New Orleans, 1836 *778.5 p549*
Wurtz, Elisabeth 9 mos; New Orleans, 1836 *778.5 p550*
Wurtz, Elisabeth 20; New Orleans, 1836 *778.5 p550*
Wurtz, George 4; New Orleans, 1836 *778.5 p550*
Wurtz, Mathias 24; New Orleans, 1836 *778.5 p550*
Wurtz, Pierre 8; New Orleans, 1836 *778.5 p550*
Wurz, Ellen Ann; Wisconsin, n.d. *9675.8 p126*
Wuse, George; Wisconsin, n.d. *9675.8 p126*
Wussow, Mr.; Wisconsin, 1842 *3702.7 p307*
Wussow, Wilhelmine 28; America, 1839 *3702.7 p307*
Wust, Carl 6 mos; New York, NY, 1889 *7846 p40*
Wust, Johann Jacob; New York, NY, 1839 *8208.4 p90*
Wust, Josef 2; New York, NY, 1889 *7846 p40*
Wust, Margaretha 30; New York, NY, 1889 *7846 p40*
Wust, Vincenz 28; New York, NY, 1889 *7846 p40*
Wustefeld, Charles; New York, NY, 1838 *8208.4 p87*
Wustholz, Fred; New York, NY, 1893 *3455.2 p72*
  *Wife:*Regiene

Wustholz, Regiene *SEE* Wustholz, Fred
Wuthrich, Jacob; Iroquois Co., IL, 1895 *3455.1 p14*
Wutke, Samuel; New York, 1748 *3652 p68*
Wyant, John; Washington, 1859-1920 *2872.1 p44*
Wyatt, Edwin; Illinois, 1888 *5012.37 p61*
Wyatt, Edwin; Virginia, 1643 *6219 p204*
Wyatt, Francis; Virginia, 1643 *6219 p204*
Wyatt, Joseph 27; Philadelphia, 1774 *1219.7 p232*
Wyatt, Richard; Virginia, 1642 *6219 p198*
Wyatt, Robert; Virginia, 1639 *6219 p152*
Wyatt, Thomas; Maryland, 1756 *1219.7 p48*
Wyatt, Thomas; Virginia, 1642 *6219 p188*
Wyborne, Catharine 37; Baltimore, 1775 *1219.7 p269*
Wyborski, Andrew; Arkansas, 1918 *95.2 p132*
Wybot, William 15; Baltimore, 1775 *1219.7 p271*
Wye, Geo.; Virginia, 1643 *6219 p202*
Wyer, Mathias; Washington, 1859-1920 *2872.1 p27*
Wyer, Mathias; Washington, 1859-1920 *2872.1 p44*
Wyer, Matthew; Washington, 1859-1920 *2872.1 p44*
Wyer, Peter; Quebec, 1823 *7603 p92*
Wyer, William 18; New York, 1775 *1219.7 p246*
Wygant, John Fred.k; Petersburg, VA, 1812 *4778.2 p142*
Wygood, Kather.; Virginia, 1643 *6219 p202*
Wyke, Miss; New York, 1754 *3652 p79*
Wyldryer, Berend 49; New York, NY, 1847 *3377.6 p16*
Wyldryer, Egbert 8; New York, NY, 1847 *3377.6 p16*
Wyldryer, Harm Derk 17; New York, NY, 1847 *3377.6 p16*
Wyldryer, Hendrik 11; New York, NY, 1847 *3377.6 p16*
Wyldryer, Hendrikus 5; New York, NY, 1847 *3377.6 p16*
Wyldryer, Maria 14; New York, NY, 1847 *3377.6 p16*
Wyler, James 20; Newfoundland, 1789 *4915.24 p55*
Wylie, Martha; Philadelphia, 1851 *5704.8 p70*
Wylie, Rachel; New York, NY, 1811 *2859.11 p21*
Wyllie, Hugh; North Carolina, 1787 *1639.20 p320*
Wyman, George; Washington, 1859-1920 *2872.1 p44*
Wymer, Francis; New York, 1832 *9892.11 p49*
Wyne, Jon.; Virginia, 1637 *6219 p110*
Wyner, Mr.; Quebec, 1815 *9229.18 p76*
Wynn, Christopher; Virginia, 1638 *6219 p120*
Wynn, Garrett; Virginia, 1647 *6219 p241*
Wynn, Hugh; Virginia, 1621 *6219 p29*
Wynn, Hugh; Virginia, 1637 *6219 p180*
Wynn, John; America, 1698 *2212 p10*
Wynn, John; Virginia, 1698 *2212 p11*
Wynn, Mathew; Virginia, 1636 *6219 p15*
Wynne, Ambrose 20; America, 1706 *2212 p46*
Wynne, Elizabeth Parr Maude *SEE* Wynne, Thomas
Wynne, Mary; Quebec, 1824 *7603 p84*
Wynne, Patrick; New York, NY, 1816 *2859.11 p44*
Wynne, Rebecca 20; Pennsylvania, 1682 *4961 p5*
Wynne, Thomas; Pennsylvania, 1682 *4961 p4*
  *Wife:*Elizabeth Parr Maude
Wyse, Sam A.; Arkansas, 1918 *95.2 p132*
Wysocki, Constanty William; Arkansas, 1918 *95.2 p132*
Wysocki, Valenti 31; New York, 1912 *9980.29 p57*
  With sister
Wyss, Jacob; America, 1876 *6014.1 p3*
Wyszomirski, . . .; New York, 1831 *4606 p178*
Wyszomirski, Stefan; Boston, 1834 *4606 p179*
Wyszynski, Eustachy; New York, 1831 *4606 p178*
Wyszynski, Karol; New York, 1831 *4606 p177*
Wywell, Wm.; Virginia, 1647 *6219 p239*
Wyyon, Antho.; Virginia, 1636 *6219 p80*

X-Y

X. Kopecki, Eugen; New York, 1834 **4606** *p178*
Xausa, Tiovanni; Iowa, 1866-1943 **123.54** *p52*
Xelander, Ann Maria 28 *SEE* Xelander, Christopher
Xelander, Christopher 22; Philadelphia, 1774 **1219.7** *p182*
    *Wife:*Ann Maria 28
Xiadz, Stasiewicz; New York, 1831 **4606** *p177*
Xinos, Panegeotis Alexandrou; Arkansas, 1918 **95.2** *p132*
Yaakello, Pasqual; Iowa, 1866-1943 **123.54** *p52*
Yaber, Henry; America, 1850 **1450.2** *p163A*
Yabrof, Osip 30; Kansas, 1904 **5240.1** *p83*
Yachwak, Mary *SEE* Yachwak, Nicholas
Yachwak, Nicholas; America, 1898 **7137** *p171*
    *Wife:*Mary
Yacoboui, Lingi; Arkansas, 1918 **95.2** *p132*
Yager, Heinrich; Quebec, 1776 **9786** *p258*
Yahnke, William; Wisconsin, n.d. **9675.8** *p126*
Yaiger, Jacob; Philadelphia, 1759 **9973.7** *p33*
Yaigle, Baltzer; Philadelphia, 1759 **9973.7** *p33*
Yakovac, William; Iowa, 1866-1943 **123.54** *p83*
Yakovich, Albina; Iowa, 1866-1943 **123.54** *p52*
Yakovich, Frank; Iowa, 1866-1943 **123.54** *p83*
Yales, Hannah 20; America, 1701 **2212** *p35*
Yallere, Joseph 19; Maryland, 1733 **3690.1** *p255*
Yanke, Herman; Wisconsin, n.d. **9675.8** *p126*
Yankunas, Bernice; Wisconsin, n.d. **9675.8** *p126*
Yankunas, Stanly; Wisconsin, n.d. **9675.8** *p126*
Yannucci, Guido; Arkansas, 1918 **95.2** *p132*
Yanovitz, Jacob; Arkansas, 1918 **95.2** *p132*
Yanovsky, Benjamin; America, 1886 **1450.2** *p163A*
Yantea, Grovorni; Iowa, 1866-1943 **123.54** *p52*
Yarchow, John; Wisconsin, n.d. **9675.8** *p126*
Yarling, Nicholaus; Wisconsin, n.d. **9675.8** *p126*
Yarner, Ann; Virginia, 1648 **6219** *p246*
Yarrall, William 16; Jamaica, 1735 **3690.1** *p255*
Yarrel, Elizabeth Begbie; Carolina, 1829 **1639.20** *p8*
Yarrell, Anna *SEE* Yarrell, Thomas
Yarrell, Thomas; Philadelphia, 1742 **3652** *p55*
    *Wife:*Anna
Yarrett, William; Virginia, 1641 **6219** *p160*
Yarrett, Wm.; Virginia, 1641 **6219** *p37*
Yass, Herman; Wisconsin, n.d. **9675.8** *p126*
Yate, Thomas 22; Nova Scotia, 1774 **1219.7** *p194*
Yates, Andrew; North Carolina, 1776-1804 **1639.20** *p320*
Yates, Gersham W.; Illinois, 1876 **5012.37** *p59*
Yates, Henry; Virginia, 1635 **6219** *p17*
Yates, James; America, 1698 **2212** *p8*
Yates, Joane; Virginia, 1636 **6219** *p36*
Yates, John; Virginia, 1636 **6219** *p36*
    *Wife:*Jone
Yates, Jon.; Virginia, 1635 **6219** *p27*
Yates, Jon.; Virginia, 1638 **6219** *p145*
Yates, Jone *SEE* Yates, John
Yates, Joseph; Antigua (Antego), 1768 **1219.7** *p135*
Yates, Mary; Virginia, 1636 **6219** *p36*
Yates, Mary; Virginia, 1644 **6219** *p231*
Yates, Richard; Virginia, 1636 **6219** *p36*
Yates, Richard; Virginia, 1638 **6219** *p36*
Yates, Richard 17; Pennsylvania, Virginia or Maryland, 1723 **3690.1** *p255*
Yates, Richard 23; Maryland, 1724 **3690.1** *p255*
Yates, Richard Augustus; New York, 1751 **1219.7** *p8*
Yates, Robt.; Virginia, 1635 **6219** *p27*
Yates, Robt.; Virginia, 1638 **6219** *p145*
Yates, Stephen; Illinois, 1891 **5012.40** *p25*
Yates, Thomas; Charles Town, SC, 1770 **1219.7** *p146*
Yates, Thomas; Virginia, 1698 **2212** *p16*

Yates, Thomas 23; Maryland, 1774 **1219.7** *p210*
Yates, William 18; America, 1703 **2212** *p40*
Yates, Wm. F.; Illinois, 1866-1896 **5012.37** *p59*
Yawnick, Wladyslaw; Wisconsin, n.d. **9675.8** *p126*
Yeager, William; America, 1855 **1450.2** *p163A*
Yeakle, Andrew 38; Kansas, 1879 **5240.1** *p61*
Yeakle, Christopher; Pennsylvania, 1749 **2444** *p171*
Yeakle, Henry; Ohio, 1851 **2896.5** *p44*
Yeakle, Yost; Illinois, 1858 **2896.5** *p44*
Yealke, Thomas; Virginia, 1646 **6219** *p236*
Yeaman, Francis; South Carolina, 1716 **1639.20** *p321*
Yeardley, Argoll; Virginia, 1640 **6219** *p37*
Yeardly, Argoll; Virginia, 1637 **6219** *p114*
    *Wife:*Frances
Yeardly, Frances *SEE* Yeardly, Argoll
Yeargin, Johann; Illinois, 1828 **8582.1** *p54*
Yeaseranes, Petter; Arkansas, 1918 **95.2** *p132*
Yeates, Benjamin 18; Virginia, 1720 **3690.1** *p255*
Yeates, George 42; Kansas, 1884 **5240.1** *p65*
Yeates, John 24; Maryland, 1774 **1219.7** *p221*
Yeates, John 24; Virginia, 1773 **1219.7** *p169*
Yeats, George 16; Jamaica, 1730 **3690.1** *p255*
Yeats, John 26; Baltimore, 1775 **1219.7** *p271*
Yeaveley, Thomas; New York, 1767 **1219.7** *p128*
Yee, Po; Arizona, 1915 **9228.40** *p20*
Yeklin, John 39; Kansas, 1885 **5240.1** *p68*
Yenish, Ignas 22; Kansas, 1905 **5240.1** *p83*
Yenny, Robt.; Virginia, 1646 **6219** *p229*
Yensel, Fred'k; Philadelphia, 1753 **2444** *p171*
Yensel, Michael; Pennsylvania, 1750 **2444** *p171*
Yeo, James 21; Maryland, 1774 **1219.7** *p234*
Yeo, John; Virginia, 1637 **6219** *p24*
Yeoman, Elizabeth 20; America, 1705 **2212** *p44*
Yeoman, Richard 22; Virginia, 1774 **1219.7** *p193*
Yeoman, Tho.; Virginia, 1637 **6219** *p110*
Yeomans, Geo.; Virginia, 1635 **6219** *p71*
Yeorgas, George; Arkansas, 1918 **95.2** *p132*
Yepe, John; Virginia, 1637 **6219** *p24*
Yerian, Alonzo; Washington, 1859-1920 **2872.1** *p44*
Yerkardt, George; Pennsylvania, 1771 **9973.8** *p32*
Yerke, August; Wisconsin, n.d. **9675.8** *p126*
Yerkman, George; Wisconsin, n.d. **9675.8** *p126*
Yerrow, William 36; Baltimore, 1775 **1219.7** *p270*
Yersin, Marc 21; Kansas, 1872 **5240.1** *p52*
Yetman, Rosomae; Virginia, 1636 **6219** *p77*
Yetter, Johannes; Pennsylvania, 1747 **2444** *p171*
Yetter, Johannes; Pennsylvania, 1753 **2444** *p171*
Yffat, Jules 40; Texas, 1826 **778.5** *p550*
Yffla, Jules 38; Mexico, 1831 **778.5** *p550*
Yglecias, Domingo 50; Arizona, 1915 **9228.40** *p19*
Yiatras, Anastassis; Arkansas, 1918 **95.2** *p132*
Yiffard, Joseph 30; Baltimore, 1775 **1219.7** *p270*
Yirner, John; Canada, 1776-1783 **9786** *p207A*
Ykaheimo, Edwin; Washington, 1859-1920 **2872.1** *p44*
Ykaheimo, Fannie Alice; Washington, 1859-1920 **2872.1** *p44*
Ykaheimo, Henry; Washington, 1859-1920 **2872.1** *p44*
Ykaheimo, Hilja; Washington, 1859-1920 **2872.1** *p44*
Ykaheimo, Hugo; Washington, 1859-1920 **2872.1** *p44*
Ykaheimo, Olga; Washington, 1859-1920 **2872.1** *p44*
Yleinig, Godfrey 37; New Orleans, 1839 **9420.2** *p483*
Yngling, Sven Alfred; Minneapolis, 1880-1886 **6410.35** *p54*
Yockell, . . .; Canada, 1776-1783 **9786** *p37*
Yodelis, Anthony Antone; Arkansas, 1918 **95.2** *p132*
Yoder, Peter; Ohio, 1800-1812 **8582.2** *p47*
Yohan, Lars 47; Kansas, 1880 **5240.1** *p62*

Yohansson, Frans O. 24; Kansas, 1884 **5240.1** *p67*
Yokarines, Thomas Pericles; Arkansas, 1918 **95.2** *p132*
Yoke, George; Philadelphia, 1759 **9973.7** *p34*
Yoll, Peter; Indiana, 1846 **9117** *p18*
Yonat, Joseph 23; Kansas, 1872 **5240.1** *p53*
Yoner, Nicholas; Pennsylvania, 1768 **9973.8** *p32*
Yonginger, John; South Carolina, 1788 **7119** *p201*
Yonke, Charles; Wisconsin, n.d. **9675.8** *p126*
Yore, Ann 4; Massachusetts, 1849 **5881.1** *p98*
Yore, Ellen 18; Massachusetts, 1849 **5881.1** *p98*
Yore, Michael 16; Massachusetts, 1849 **5881.1** *p99*
York, Charles; Washington, 1859-1920 **2872.1** *p44*
York, James; San Francisco, 1876 **2764.35** *p75*
York, Mark 14; Maryland, 1723 **3690.1** *p255*
York, Mary 19; Barbados, 1718 **3690.1** *p255*
York, Patience 18; Philadelphia, 1774 **1219.7** *p182*
Yorke, Ann; Virginia, 1639 **6219** *p151*
Yorke, Edw.; Virginia, 1635 **6219** *p3*
Yorke, F. Henry; Illinois, 1898 **5012.40** *p55*
Yorke, Kath.; Virginia, 1637 **6219** *p108*
Yorke, Katherine; Virginia, 1636 **6219** *p74*
Yorocka, Mike; Wisconsin, n.d. **9675.8** *p126*
You, Jean 18; New Orleans, 1826 **778.5** *p550*
You, Tom 61; Arizona, 1922 **9228.40** *p26*
Youl, Thomas; North Carolina, 1813 **1639.20** *p321*
Youle, Thomas; North Carolina, 1814 **1639.20** *p321*
Younen, William 29; Harris Co., TX, 1898 **6254** *p5*
Young, . . .; Canada, 1776-1783 **9786** *p37*
Young, Lt.; Canada, 1776-1783 **9786** *p185*
Young, Mr.; Quebec, 1815 **9229.18** *p79*
Young, A.; Quebec, 1815 **9229.18** *p74*
Young, Adam; Iowa, 1866-1943 **123.54** *p52*
Young, Alex *SEE* Young, Norman
Young, Alexander; New York, NY, 1816 **2859.11** *p44*
Young, Alexander; Philadelphia, 1852 **5704.8** *p85*
Young, Alexander; South Carolina, 1808 **1639.20** *p321*
Young, Alexander 2; St. John, N.B., 1847 **5704.8** *p18*
Young, Alexander 7; St. John, N.B., 1847 **5704.8** *p4*
Young, Alexander 45; Massachusetts, 1849 **5881.1** *p98*
Young, Andrew 13; Quebec, 1847 **5704.8** *p28*
Young, Andrew 22; St. John, N.B., 1863 **5704.8** *p152*
Young, Angus *SEE* Young, Norman
Young, Angus; Quebec, 1851 **4537.30** *p45*
    *Wife:*Mary MacKay
    *Child:*Murdo
    *Child:*John
Young, Ann; Philadelphia, 1850 **5704.8** *p68*
Young, Ann; Quebec, 1848 **5704.8** *p41*
Young, Ann 23; St. John, N.B., 1855 **5704.8** *p126*
Young, Ann 24; Philadelphia, 1774 **1219.7** *p182*
Young, Ann Jane 3; Philadelphia, 1852 **5704.8** *p86*
Young, Ann Morrison *SEE* Young, Norman
Young, Anne; Philadelphia, 1871 **5704.8** *p241*
Young, Anthony; Virginia, 1648 **6219** *p250*
Young, Anton; Wisconsin, n.d. **9675.8** *p126*
Young, Bridget; New York, NY, 1865 **5704.8** *p203*
Young, Catherine; Philadelphia, 1852 **5704.8** *p97*
Young, Charles; St. John, N.B., 1849 **5704.8** *p49*
Young, Charles Allen 31; Kansas, 1872 **5240.1** *p52*
Young, Christo.; Virginia, 1636 **6219** *p26*
Young, Christopher; Virginia, 1638 **6219** *p121*
Young, Ciceley; Virginia, 1643 **6219** *p205*
Young, Clementine Julielle; Iowa, 1866-1943 **123.54** *p83*
Young, D. 28; Kansas, 1873 **5240.1** *p54*
Young, David; New York, NY, 1811 **2859.11** *p21*
Young, David; Tobago, W. Indies, 1775 **1219.7** *p265*
Young, David 12; Philadelphia, 1852 **5704.8** *p85*

FOR A COMPLETE EXPLANATION OF ENTRY, SEE "HOW TO READ A CITATION" SECTION

Z

Zabel, Charles; America, 1851 *1450.2 p163A*
Zabiela, Michal Paul; Arkansas, 1918 *95.2 p132*
Zaccagnino, Camillo; Arkansas, 1918 *95.2 p132*
Zaccanto, Palo; Iowa, 1866-1943 *123.54 p52*
Zaccarelli, Pasquale 24; West Virginia, 1903 *9788.3 p22*
Zach, Margaret; Milwaukee, 1875 *4719.30 p257*
Zach, William; Milwaukee, 1875 *4719.30 p257*
Zach, Mrs. William; Milwaukee, 1875 *4719.30 p257*
Zacharia, . . .; Canada, 1776-1783 *9786 p44*
Zacharzewski, A.; New York, 1831 *4606 p178*
Zacher, Joseph; Wisconsin, n.d. *9675.8 p126*
Zacher, Manus; Virginia, 1635 *6219 p160*
Zadravec, Andrew; Iowa, 1866-1943 *123.54 p83*
Zaduza, Zofia 27; New York, 1912 *9980.29 p49*
Zaeradisnick, Anton; Wisconsin, n.d. *9675.8 p126*
Zaeslein, Joseph; Cincinnati, 1817 *8582.2 p27*
Zaetta, Michele; Iowa, 1866-1943 *123.54 p52*
Zager, Anthony John; Arkansas, 1918 *95.2 p132*
Zaharchuk, Wasily; Arkansas, 1918 *95.2 p132*
Zaharias, Costintinos John; Arkansas, 1918 *95.2 p133*
Zaharis, Frank George; Arkansas, 1918 *95.2 p133*
Zaharoff, George Stavro; Arkansas, 1918 *95.2 p133*
Zahl, Charles; America, 1884 *1450.2 p163A*
Zahle, John; Wisconsin, n.d. *9675.8 p126*
Zahler, Anna *SEE* Zahler, Michael
Zahler, Hans Jacob *SEE* Zahler, Michael
Zahler, Maria Elisabetha *SEE* Zahler, Michael
Zahler, Maria Sara *SEE* Zahler, Michael
Zahler, Michael; Pennsylvania, 1753 *2444 p236*
   *Child:*Maria Elisabetha
   *Child:*Hans Jacob
   *Child:*Maria Sara
   *Child:*Anna
Zahnen, Jacob 34; Kansas, 1884 *5240.1 p49*
Zahnen, Jacob 34; Kansas, 1884 *5240.1 p66*
Zaiaczkowski, . . .; New York, 1831 *4606 p178*
Zaikey, Joseph 28; Port uncertain, 1839 *778.5 p550*
Zaiser, Bernhard; America, 1846 *8582.3 p73*
Zaiz, John; Wisconsin, n.d. *9675.8 p126*
Zakrajseck, Frank; Wisconsin, n.d. *9675.8 p126*
Zakrotchick, Mosha; New York, NY, 1918 *3455.2 p51*
Zakrzewski, Mikolay; New York, 1831 *4606 p178*
Zakszewska, Anna 5 *SEE* Zakszewska, Zofia
Zakszewska, Zofia 26; New York, 1912 *9980.29 p63*
   *Daughter:*Anna 5
Zakusidlo, . . .; New York, 1831 *4606 p178*
Zaleski, Antonino; Arkansas, 1918 *95.2 p133*
Zalewski, Jan; New York, 1831 *4606 p178*
Zalewski, Stanislaw; New York, 1912 *9980.29 p48*
Zalewski, Stanislaw 20; New York, 1912 *9980.29 p74*
Zalewski, Tomasz; New York, 1831 *4606 p178*
Zalewski, Walenti; Detroit, 1912 *9980.29 p74*
Zaller, Hans Jacob; Pennsylvania, 1749 *2444 p236*
Zamminil, Frank 62; Arizona, 1908 *9228.40 p14*
Zamzow, Carl 11; New York, NY, 1862 *9831.18 p16*
Zamzow, Christian 41; New York, NY, 1862 *9831.18 p16*
Zamzow, Gustav 4; New York, NY, 1862 *9831.18 p16*
Zamzow, Henriette 39; New York, NY, 1862 *9831.18 p16*
Zanarini, Fred; Arkansas, 1918 *95.2 p133*
Zandel, Elisabetha; Pennsylvania, 1754 *2444 p215*
Zander, J. William; Philadelphia, 1741 *3652 p52*
Zandler, Emil; Wisconsin, 1896 *5240.1 p49*
Zaning, Angelo; Iowa, 1866-1943 *123.54 p52*
Zankl, Joseph; Wisconsin, n.d. *9675.8 p126*

Zanon, Angelo 28; New York, NY, 1893 *9026.4 p42*
   *Relative:*Costanza 19
Zanon, Costanza 19 *SEE* Zanon, Angelo
Zant, . . .; Georgia, 1738 *9332 p321*
Zant, Barthol.; Georgia, 1739 *9332 p323*
Zant, Bartholomaus; Georgia, 1739 *9332 p326*
Zantow, August; Illinois, 1888 *5012.39 p122*
Zapfe, Christian; Wisconsin, n.d. *9675.8 p126*
Zaputil, Draga; Iowa, 1866-1943 *123.54 p83*
Zaputil, Slavo; Iowa, 1866-1943 *123.54 p83*
Zaragenti, Angelo; Iowa, 1866-1943 *123.54 p52*
Zaragoza, Jose Natividad; Iowa, 1866-1943 *123.54 p83*
Zaraukis, Martin; Wisconsin, n.d. *9675.8 p126*
Zaremba, . . .; New York, 1831 *4606 p178*
Zarembski, John; Arkansas, 1918 *95.2 p133*
Zarling, Carl; Wisconsin, n.d. *9675.8 p126*
Zarling, Henry; Wisconsin, n.d. *9675.8 p126*
Zarling, Stephen; Colorado, 1903 *9678.3 p19*
Zarting, Henry; Wisconsin, n.d. *9675.8 p126*
Zaruba, Frank; Arkansas, 1918 *95.2 p133*
Zarzour, David; Arkansas, 1918 *95.2 p133*
Zasto, James 71; Arizona, 1907 *9228.40 p14*
Zastrow, Otto Carl; Arkansas, 1918 *95.2 p133*
Zatawiecky, Andrew; Arkansas, 1918 *95.2 p133*
Zaun, John; Wisconsin, n.d. *9675.8 p126*
Zausch, William; Wisconsin, n.d. *9675.8 p126*
Zavada, Joseph; Arkansas, 1918 *95.2 p133*
Zawadzki, Jan; New York, 1835 *4606 p180*
Zawatzky, Anthony; America, 1892 *1450.2 p163A*
Zbell, Andrew; America, 1892 *7137 p171*
   *Wife:*Mary
Zbell, Mary *SEE* Zbell, Andrew
Zdaniecki, Malgorzata 18; New York, 1912 *9980.29 p59*
Zdanieczki, Malgorzata 18; New York, 1912 *9980.29 p59*
Zdosinski, Emilia Saszkowska 25; New York, 1912 *9980.29 p54*
   *Daughter:*Irena 11 mos
Zdosinski, Irena 11 mos *SEE* Zdosinski, Emilia Saszkowska
Zdosinski, Leon; Chicago, 1912 *9980.29 p54*
Zdrogewski, Barney J.; Arkansas, 1918 *95.2 p133*
Zdziesinska, Emilia Saszkowska 25; New York, 1912 *9980.29 p54*
   *Daughter:*Irena 11 mos
Zdziesinska, Irena 11 mos *SEE* Zdziesinska, Emilia Saszkowska
Zdziesinska, Leon; Chicago, 1912 *9980.29 p54*
Zear, Ahbram; New York, 1892 *1450.2 p43B*
Zeateff, Jordan Raykoff; Arkansas, 1918 *95.2 p133*
Zechlinzki, Kozemer; Wisconsin, n.d. *9675.8 p126*
Zechmeister, Elizabeth 51; New York, NY, 1889 *7846 p39*
Zechmeister, Georg 14; New York, NY, 1889 *7846 p39*
Zechmeister, Johann 9; New York, NY, 1889 *7846 p39*
Zechmeister, Johann 51; New York, NY, 1889 *7846 p39*
Zedtwitz, Hermann von; America, 1777-1778 *8582.2 p67*
Zeeb, Anna Maria; Philadelphia, 1762-1776 *2444 p227*
Zefferer, Veit; Georgia, 1738 *9332 p320*
Zeheli, John; Wisconsin, n.d. *9675.8 p126*
Zehetner, Catharina; Georgia, 1739 *9332 p323*
Zehlicke, Robert; New York, 1888 *1450.2 p43B*
Zehnert, . . .; Canada, 1776-1783 *9786 p37*
Zehr, Deibolt; New York, NY, 1835 *8208.4 p30*
Zehrer, Johann; Cincinnati, 1869-1887 *8582 p35*
Zehring, Johannes; Pennsylvania, 1753 *4779.3 p13*
Zeibel, Katherina 60; Port uncertain, 1839 *778.5 p550*

Zeidler, Richard; America, 1851 *8582.3 p73*
Zeigler, Jacob; Philadelphia, 1760 *9973.7 p34*
Zeigler, Philip; Philadelphia, 1760 *9973.7 p34*
Zeigler, Wm. F.; Wisconsin, n.d. *9675.8 p126*
Zeillmann, . . .; Canada, 1776-1783 *9786 p37*
Zeininger, E. G. 21; Kansas, 1887 *5240.1 p70*
Zeininger, Ernst G.; America, 1882 *5240.1 p1*
Zeisberger, . . .; America, 1700-1877 *8582.3 p80*
Zeisberger, Anna Dorothea *SEE* Zeisberger, George
Zeisberger, David; New York, 1761 *3652 p88*
Zeisberger, David; Ohio, 1721-1808 *8582 p36*
Zeisberger, David; Savannah, GA, 1736 *3652 p51*
   *Relative:*Rosina
Zeisberger, George; New York, 1743 *3652 p60*
   *Wife:*Anna Dorothea
Zeisberger, Rosina *SEE* Zeisberger, David
Zeising, Albert 9; New Orleans, 1839 *9420.2 p487*
   With stepfather
Zeiss, Christoph; Philadelphia, 1779 *8137 p15*
Zelazowski, . . .; New York, 1831 *4606 p178*
Zelbard, A. 30; New Orleans, 1835 *778.5 p551*
Zelinaki, Peter; Wisconsin, n.d. *9675.8 p126*
Zelinka, Anton; Texas, 1894 *5240.1 p49*
Zelinski, Adolf; Illinois, 1896 *5012.40 p55*
Zelinski, Casimer; Wisconsin, n.d. *9675.8 p126*
Zelko, John; Wisconsin, n.d. *9675.8 p126*
Zell, Georg; Kentucky, 1839-1840 *8582.3 p99*
Zelle, Jacob 34; California, 1872 *2769.10 p3*
Zeller, Anna Margaretha; America, 1746-1800 *2444 p179*
Zeller, August 44; Arizona, 1890 *2764.35 p75*
Zeller, Johann; Philadelphia, 1775-1776 *8582.3 p83*
Zeller, Joseph 33; Port uncertain, 1835 *778.5 p551*
Zellman, Daniel; Canada, 1776-1783 *9786 p207A*
Zellmann, . . .; Canada, 1776-1783 *9786 p37*
Zellmann, Johann Gottl. 28; New York, NY, 1857 *9831.14 p154*
Zellon, John 40; America, 1835 *778.5 p551*
Zelltner, Susanna 23; America, 1854-1855 *9162.6 p104*
Zelmeur, Joseph 15; New Orleans, 1836 *778.5 p551*
Zelmeur, Marianne 43; New Orleans, 1836 *778.5 p551*
Zeltner, Mathias; New York, NY, 1852 *2896.5 p44*
Zembal, Maryanna; Minneapolis, 1912 *9980.29 p62*
Zengen, Henrich Carl von; Canada, 1780 *9786 p268*
Zengen, Henrich Carl von; New York, 1776 *9786 p268*
Zennon, Charles P. 22; America, 1827 *778.5 p551*
Zennon, Pierre 20; America, 1827 *778.5 p551*
Zenzen, Adam 22; Kansas, 1887 *5240.1 p49*
Zenzen, Adam 22; Kansas, 1887 *5240.1 p70*
Zeonic, Joseph; America, 1893 *1450.2 p163A*
Zepka, Stanley Joe; Arkansas, 1918 *95.2 p133*
Zeremer, Adam 26; Kansas, 1882 *5240.1 p63*
Zerener, John; Kansas, 1885 *5240.1 p50*
Zerkmann, Frank; Wisconsin, n.d. *9675.8 p126*
Zernicke, Carl; New York, 1889 *1450.2 p43B*
Zerny, Carl; Wisconsin, n.d. *9675.8 p126*
Zerroglio, Carle; Iowa, 1866-1943 *123.54 p52*
Zervakis, Angelos; Arkansas, 1918 *95.2 p133*
Zervakis, Emanuel; Arkansas, 1918 *95.2 p133*
Zervakis, Nick George; Arkansas, 1918 *95.2 p133*
Zetterland, Albert Edmund; Arkansas, 1918 *95.2 p133*
Zettler, . . .; Georgia, 1738 *9332 p321*
Zettler, Karl Gottlieb; Wisconsin, n.d. *9675.8 p126*
Zettler, Matthias; Georgia, 1739 *9332 p327*
Zeuner, John Henry 50; Arizona, 1890 *2764.35 p75*
Zeuner, Morritz; Wisconsin, n.d. *9675.8 p126*
Zeunert, Wilhelm; Wisconsin, n.d. *9675.8 p126*
Zeuschner, Frank; Illinois, 1879 *2896.5 p44*

Zeuschner, Fred; Illinois, 1879 *2896.5 p44*
Zewatkauski, Wm.; Wisconsin, n.d. *9675.8 p126*
Zezelich, Kuzna; Iowa, 1866-1943 *123.54 p83*
ZeZelich, Mary; Iowa, 1866-1943 *123.54 p52*
Zibart, Peter; Wisconsin, n.d. *9675.8 p126*
Zibel, Hermann 26; America, 1836 *778.5 p551*
Zicarelli, Mike; Arkansas, 1918 *95.2 p133*
Zick, . . .; Canada, 1776-1783 *9786 p37*
Zick, Ludwig; Illinois, 1868 *2896.5 p44*
Ziebig, Carl Aug. 2 SEE Ziebig, Carl Gottl.
Ziebig, Carl Gottl. 28; New Orleans, 1839 *9420.2 p169*
  Wife:Henriette Wme. 25
  *Child:*Carl Aug. 2
  *Child:*Ernst Wilhelm 1
Ziebig, Ernst Wilhelm 1 SEE Ziebig, Carl Gottl.
Ziebig, Henriette Wme. 25 SEE Ziebig, Carl Gottl.
Ziegenfelder, C. F.; Ohio, 1869-1887 *8582 p35*
Ziegenhain, . . .; Canada, 1776-1783 *9786 p37*
Ziegenstiel, . . .; Canada, 1776-1783 *9786 p37*
Ziegler, . . .; Canada, 1776-1783 *9786 p37*
Ziegler, Agatha SEE Ziegler, Philipp
Ziegler, Andrews; Illinois, 1898 *5012.40 p55*
Ziegler, Anna Maria SEE Ziegler, Philipp
Ziegler, Anna Maria Vyl SEE Ziegler, Zacharias
Ziegler, Augusta; Milwaukee, 1875 *4719.30 p257*
  With child
Ziegler, Barbara SEE Ziegler, Philipp
Ziegler, Christian; Cincinnati, 1869-1887 *8582 p35*
Ziegler, Curtius Frederick; New York, 1753 *3652 p77*
Ziegler, David; Cincinnati, 1788-1812 *8582.2 p52*
Ziegler, David; Philadelphia, 1775 *8582 p35*
Ziegler, Dora; Milwaukee, 1875 *4719.30 p257*
Ziegler, Jacob; Ohio, 1869-1887 *8582 p36*
Ziegler, Jacob; South Carolina, 1788 *7119 p198*
Ziegler, Joh Pet; Philadelphia, 1756 *4525 p261*
Ziegler, Johann Jacob SEE Ziegler, Philipp
Ziegler, Johannes SEE Ziegler, Philipp
Ziegler, John; Kansas, 1909 *6013.40 p17*
Ziegler, John George; Illinois, 1873 *2896.5 p44*
Ziegler, Julius; Wisconsin, n.d. *9675.8 p126*
Ziegler, Louis C.; America, 1872 *1450.2 p43B*
Ziegler, Nicolaus SEE Ziegler, Zacharias
Ziegler, Philipp; Baltimore, 1831 *8582 p36*
Ziegler, Philipp; Ohio, 1843 *8582.1 p51*
Ziegler, Philipp; Pennsylvania, 1746 *2444 p236*
  *Wife:*Barbara
  *Child:*Johannes
  *Child:*Johann Jacob
  *Child:*Agatha
  *Child:*Anna Maria
  With child
Ziegler, Phillip; Pennsylvania, 1746 *2444 p184*
Ziegler, Valentin; Ohio, 1843 *8582.1 p51*
Ziegler, Wilhelm; South Carolina, 1788 *7119 p204*
Ziegler, Zacharias; Port uncertain, 1746-1800 *2444 p237*
  *Wife:*Anna Maria Vyl
  *Child:*Nicolaus
Zieglin, Johans; Pennsylvania, 1753 *2444 p217*
Ziegly, Jacob; Pennsylvania, 1746 *2444 p217*
Zielberg, v.; Quebec, 1776 *9786 p105*
Zielberg, von; Canada, 1776-1783 *9786 p169*
Zielberg, George Ernst; Quebec, 1776 *9786 p254*
Zielinski, Franciszek 30; New York, 1912 *9980.29 p53*
Zielinski, Zygmont 22; Arkansas, 1918 *95.2 p133*
Zielschott, Bernhard; Cincinnati, 1869-1887 *8582 p36*
Ziemer, Robert; Wisconsin, n.d. *9675.8 p126*
Zierath, Edward 35; Kansas, 1889 *5240.1 p73*
Zierath, Johan; Wisconsin, n.d. *9675.8 p126*
Ziermann, . . .; Canada, 1776-1783 *9786 p37*
Zieske, William F.; Illinois, 1888 *5012.39 p121*
Ziess, Konrad; Lancaster, PA, 1780 *8137 p15*
Ziethen, Hermann 27; Kansas, 1882 *5240.1 p63*
Zietlow, Charles; Wisconsin, n.d. *9675.8 p126*
Zietz, Abraham; Arkansas, 1918 *95.2 p133*
Ziganek, Gottfried 16; New York, 1912 *9980.29 p61*
Ziganik, Gottfried 16; New York, 1912 *9980.29 p61*
Zigolle, Frank; Wisconsin, n.d. *9675.8 p126*
Zilch, David; Philadelphia, 1779 *8137 p15*
Ziliac, . . .; Canada, 1776-1783 *9786 p37*
Zilig, Jacob; Washington, 1859-1920 *2872.1 p45*
Zilinski, Jozapas; Wisconsin, n.d. *9675.8 p126*
Zill, Carl Friedrich Morritz; Wisconsin, n.d. *9675.8 p126*
Zillig, Jacob; Washington, 1859-1920 *2872.1 p45*
Zillman, Henry; New York, 1754 *3652 p80*
Zillmer, Christopher; Illinois, 1868 *2896.5 p44*
Zima, Anton; Iowa, 1866-1943 *123.54 p83*
Zima, Mary; Iowa, 1866-1943 *123.54 p83*
Zima, Stjepan; Iowa, 1866-1943 *123.54 p52*
Zimer, Ferdinand; America, 1853 *1450.2 p163A*
Zimerman, Henrich; South Carolina, 1788 *7119 p202*
Zimerman, Peter; South Carolina, 1788 *7119 p203*
Zimmer, Mr.; Cincinnati, 1831 *8582.1 p51*
Zimmer, Carl A.; Wisconsin, n.d. *9675.8 p126*

Zimmer, Heinrich; America, 1847 *8582.3 p73*
Zimmer, Henry; New York, NY, 1837 *8208.4 p24*
Zimmer, Henry A. 58; Arizona, 1922 *9228.40 p26*
Zimmer, Herman; Wisconsin, n.d. *9675.8 p126*
Zimmer, Jacob; New York, NY, 1836 *8208.4 p14*
Zimmer, John; Wisconsin, n.d. *9675.8 p126*
Zimmer, Michael; New York, NY, 1838 *8208.4 p85*
Zimmer, Peter; Wisconsin, n.d. *9675.8 p126*
Zimmerling, Pauline; Alberta, 1909-1950 *5262 p58*
Zimmerman, . . .; Canada, 1776-1783 *9786 p44*
Zimmerman, Casper; Baltimore, 1830-1831 *9892.11 p49*
Zimmerman, Conrad; Virginia, 1852 *4626.16 p14*
Zimmerman, Fred 88; Washington, 1918-1920 *1728.5 p16*
Zimmerman, Frederick; Illinois, 1892 *5012.40 p26*
Zimmerman, George; Baltimore, 1830-1831 *9892.11 p49*
Zimmerman, George; Colorado, 1887 *9678.3 p19*
Zimmerman, Henrich; South Carolina, 1788 *7119 p203*
Zimmerman, Henrich Christoph; Halifax, N.S., 1780 *9786 p269*
Zimmerman, Henrich Christoph; New York, 1776 *9786 p269*
Zimmerman, J. F. 28; Kansas, 1889 *5240.1 p50*
Zimmerman, J. F. 28; Kansas, 1889 *5240.1 p74*
Zimmerman, Jacob; South Carolina, 1788 *7119 p203*
Zimmerman, M. 24; America, 1831 *778.5 p551*
Zimmerman, Marie 64; America, 1835 *778.5 p551*
Zimmerman, Otto 32; Kansas, 1902 *5240.1 p82*
Zimmerman, Sebastian; South Carolina, 1788 *7119 p198*
Zimmerman, Wilhelm; Pennsylvania, 1753 *4525 p258*
Zimmerman, Wm. 67; Arizona, 1917 *9228.40 p21*
Zimmerman, Mrs.; Pennsylvania, 1780 *4525 p284*
Zimmermann, Ambrose; Wisconsin, n.d. *9675.8 p126*
Zimmermann, David 11 mos; New York, NY, 1878 *9253 p47*
Zimmermann, Deborah 1 mo; New York, NY, 1878 *9253 p47*
Zimmermann, George; Wisconsin, n.d. *9675.8 p126*
Zimmermann, Hanna 16; New York, NY, 1878 *9253 p47*
Zimmermann, Hermann 8; New York, NY, 1878 *9253 p47*
Zimmermann, Israel 4; New York, NY, 1878 *9253 p47*
Zimmermann, J.; St. Louis, 1851 *8582.1 p37*
Zimmermann, Johann; America, 1848 *8582.1 p37*
Zimmermann, John Gottlieb Frederick; Wisconsin, n.d. *9675.8 p126*
Zimmermann, Marcus 9; New York, NY, 1878 *9253 p47*
Zimmermann, Martin; Wisconsin, n.d. *9675.8 p126*
Zimmermann, Moses 40; New York, NY, 1878 *9253 p47*
Zimmermann, Rebecca 47; New York, NY, 1878 *9253 p47*
Zimmermann, Ruprecht; Georgia, 1738 *9332 p321*
Zimmermann, Ruprecht; Georgia, 1739 *9332 p324*
Zimmermann, Ruprecht; Georgia, 1739 *9332 p326*
Zimmermann, Simon 1 mo; New York, NY, 1878 *9253 p47*
Zimmermann, Teige 6; New York, NY, 1878 *9253 p47*
Zimmermann, W.; Illinois, 1847 *8582.2 p51*
Zimmermann, Wilhelm; Pennsylvania, 1753 *4525 p258*
Zimpelman, George; Wisconsin, n.d. *9675.8 p126*
Zimpelman, Mathias; Wisconsin, n.d. *9675.8 p126*
Zinck, Henrich Friedrich; Halifax, N.S., 1780 *9786 p269*
Zinck, Henrich Friedrich; New York, 1776 *9786 p269*
Zindell, Leopold; Philadelphia, 1779-1780 *8137 p15*
Zinglet, M. 32; Port uncertain, 1836 *778.5 p551*
Zink, Aud.; Quebec, 1776 *9786 p105*
Zink, Anne 5 SEE Zink, Charles
Zink, Cathar. 13; New Orleans, 1839 *9420.2 p362*
Zink, Charles 37; New Orleans, 1839 *9420.2 p487*
  *Child:*Anne 5
  *Child:*Emilie 3
  With stepchild
Zink, Emilie 3 SEE Zink, Charles
Zink, Ferdinand; Arkansas, 1880 *3688 p7*
Zink, Franz; Wisconsin, n.d. *9675.8 p126*
Zink, George Leonhard; Michigan, 1853 *2896.5 p44*
Zink, Georges 26; America, 1835 *778.5 p551*
Zink, John Frederick; Michigan, 1855 *2896.5 p44*
Zink, John M.; Illinois, 1868 *2896.5 p44*
Zinke, Fred; Illinois, 1874 *5012.39 p26*
Zinke, Gottfried; Wisconsin, n.d. *9675.8 p126*
Zinkeisen, Annie; Milwaukee, 1875 *4719.30 p257*
Zinkeisen, Celine; Milwaukee, 1875 *4719.30 p257*
Zinkeisen, Hermann; Milwaukee, 1875 *4719.30 p257*
Zinken, Carl Friedrich Wilhelm; Quebec, 1776 *9786 p257*
Zinmaster, Jacob; New York, 1833 *9892.11 p50*
  *Relative:*Peter 2
Zinmaster, Jacob; Ohio, 1838 *9892.11 p50*
Zinmaster, Peter 2 SEE Zinmaster, Jacob

Zinn, John; Philadelphia, 1761 *9973.7 p35*
Zinn, Philip Jacob; Philadelphia, 1761 *9973.7 p36*
Zinnen, Paul; Wisconsin, n.d. *9675.8 p126*
Zinsmaster, Daniel; New Orleans, 1833 *9892.11 p49*
  *Son:*Michael 14
Zinsmaster, Daniel; Ohio, 1838 *9892.11 p50*
Zinsmaster, Jacob; Ohio, 1838 *9892.11 p50*
  *Relative:*Peter 2
Zinsmaster, Michael 14 SEE Zinsmaster, Daniel
Zinsmaster, Peter; Ohio, 1846 *9892.11 p50*
Zinsmaster, Peter 2 SEE Zinsmaster, Jacob
Zinzendorf, Count; America, 1700-1877 *8582.3 p80*
Zinzendorf, Count; Philadelphia, 1741 *3652 p52*
  *Daughter:*Benigna
Zinzendorf, Benigna SEE Zinzendorf, Count
Ziolkowski, Leon 38; New York, 1912 *9980.29 p52*
Zion, Carl; New York, 1839 *3702.7 p299*
Zipin, Jchel Henry; Arkansas, 1918 *95.2 p133*
Zipoy, Mary SEE Zipoy, Michael
Zipoy, Michael; America, 1892 *7137 p171*
  *Wife:*Mary
Zipp, Elis. 25; America, 1853 *9162.8 p38*
Zipp, Kath. 36; America, 1853 *9162.8 p38*
Zipperlen, Ad; America, 1848 *8582.1 p37*
Zipperlen, Adolph; America, 1848 *8582.3 p73*
Zipperlen, Gustav Adolph Friedrich; New York, NY, 1848 *8582.1 p37*
Zips, . . .; Canada, 1776-1783 *9786 p37*
Zirbes, Heinrich; Wisconsin, n.d. *9675.8 p126*
Zirbis, William; Wisconsin, n.d. *9675.8 p126*
Zirtzlaff, Herman; Wisconsin, n.d. *9675.8 p126*
Zischler, . . .; Canada, 1776-1783 *9786 p37*
Zismer, Paul M.; New York, 1860 *1450.2 p164A*
Ziten, . . .; Canada, 1776-1783 *9786 p37*
Zittrauer, Anna Leihoffer SEE Zittrauer, Ruprecht
Zittrauer, Paul; Georgia, 1738 *9332 p321*
Zittrauer, Paul; Georgia, 1739 *9332 p324*
Zittrauer, Paul; Georgia, 1739 *9332 p326*
Zittrauer, Ruprecht; Georgia, 1739 *9332 p323*
  *Wife:*Anna Leihoffer
Zivackauskis, John; Wisconsin, n.d. *9675.8 p126*
Zivatkaukis, Josef; Wisconsin, n.d. *9675.8 p126*
Zivnes, Angilo; Colorado, 1904 *9678.3 p19*
Ziyn, John Peter; America, 1849 *6013.19 p89*
Zmok, John; America, 1900 *7137 p171*
Zmozynski, Bronislaw; Arkansas, 1918 *95.2 p133*
Znona, Angelo; Iowa, 1866-1943 *123.54 p52*
Zobbe, Carl Friedrick; Baltimore, 1835 *1450.2 p164A*
Zobbe, Christian Frederick; New York, 1837 *1450.2 p164A*
Zobel, Fred 84; Arizona, 1911 *9228.40 p16*
Zobellee, Deni; Wisconsin, n.d. *9675.8 p126*
Zobelo, Kazemer; Wisconsin, n.d. *9675.8 p126*
Zoci, Justina; Virginia, 1775 *1219.7 p275*
Zoeller, Blasius; Cincinnati, 1869-1887 *8582 p36*
Zoeller, Friederich; Ohio, 1825-1829 *8582.1 p46*
Zoeller, Michel 24; New Orleans, 1837 *778.5 p551*
Zoeller, Philipp; America, 1851 *8582.3 p73*
Zoettenet, Caroline 30; New Orleans, 1838 *778.5 p551*
Zoffmann, Rudolf; Illinois, 1890 *1450.2 p164A*
Zogbaum, William; Wisconsin, n.d. *9675.8 p126*
Zoglemann, John; Kansas, 1898 *5240.1 p50*
Zogner, Kath. 71; Cleveland, OH, 1902 *1763 p40D*
Zohorner, Fr. Aug. 38; New Orleans, 1839 *9420.2 p169*
Zolfel, Tadens; Kansas, 1885 *5240.1 p50*
Zolkiewski, . . .; New York, 1831 *4606 p178*
Zoll, Hermann Henrich Georg; Canada, 1780 *9786 p268*
Zoll, Hermann Henrich Georg; New York, 1776 *9786 p268*
Zoll, Jacob Friedrich; Pennsylvania, 1768 *2444 p237*
Zollenger, . . .; Canada, 1776-1783 *9786 p37*
Zoller, Anna; Pennsylvania, 1753 *2444 p184*
Zoller, Henry; Illinois, 1852 *7857 p8*
Zoller, Johann; Cincinnati, 1815-1824 *8582 p7*
  *Daughter:*Maria Eva
Zoller, Maria Eva SEE Zoller, Johann
Zollin, George; Illinois, 1891 *5012.40 p26*
Zollinger, Ulrick; Philadelphia, 1760 *9973.7 p34*
Zollmann, Friedrich; Indiana, 1842-1850 *3702.7 p124*
Zollmann, Johann Philipp; America, 1842 *3702.7 p123*
Zollott, Morris; Arkansas, 1918 *95.2 p133*
Zolna, Anna; America, 1896 *7137 p171*
Zolna, John; America, 1893 *7137 p171*
Zolna, Stanislaus; America, 1900 *7137 p171*
Zolo, Bachisis Raimondo; Arkansas, 1918 *95.2 p133*
Zomok, John; America, 1900 *7137 p171*
Zona, Luigi; Arkansas, 1918 *95.2 p134*
Zongaro, Marco Giovanni; Washington, 1859-1920 *2872.1 p45*
Zonsen, Joseph; Wisconsin, n.d. *9675.8 p126*
Zoo, . . .; Canada, 1776-1783 *9786 p44*
Zoon, John; Canada, 1776-1783 *9786 p207A*
Zorbach, . . .; Canada, 1776-1783 *9786 p44*

FOR A COMPLETE EXPLANATION OF ENTRY, SEE "HOW TO READ A CITATION" SECTION

Zorbas, Alcibiades Fotiou; Arkansas, 1918 *95.2 p134*
Zorbas, Louis F.; Arkansas, 1918 *95.2 p134*
Zorcke, Charles; Arkansas, 1918 *95.2 p134*
Zore, Ivan; Iowa, 1866-1943 *123.54 p52*
Zore, Janez; Wisconsin, n.d. *9675.8 p126*
Zore, Joseph; Wisconsin, n.d. *9675.8 p126*
Zore, Petra; Iowa, 1866-1943 *123.54 p83*
Zorn, . . .; Canada, 1776-1783 *9786 p37*
Zorn, Jacob; South Carolina, 1788 *7119 p197*
Zorn, Nicholas; South Carolina, 1788 *7119 p198*
Zortea, Leopoldo; Iowa, 1866-1943 *123.54 p52*
Zottelmeyer, Kaspar; Philadelphia, 1756 *4525 p261*
Zoutis, Peter; Arkansas, 1918 *95.2 p134*
Zpolor, Gasypar C.; Iowa, 1866-1943 *123.54 p52*
Zrun, Nicolas; Wisconsin, n.d. *9675.8 p126*
Zschech, Justavus; America, 1852 *1450.2 p163A*
Zschommler, Ch. F.E.; Wisconsin, n.d. *9675.8 p126*
Zschucke, Gustave F.; Wisconsin, n.d. *9675.8 p126*
Zubli, Johann Joachim; Savannah, GA, 1775 *8582.2 p64*
Zublin, Ambrosius; Georgia, 1734-1739 *9332 p327*
  *Brother:*Jacob
Zublin, Jacob *SEE* Zublin, Ambrosius
Zucca, Aagelo; Iowa, 1866-1943 *123.54 p52*
Zucca, Matteo; Iowa, 1866-1943 *123.54 p52*
Zuccarello, Sam; Iowa, 1866-1943 *123.54 p83*
Zuccaro, Agostino; Arkansas, 1918 *95.2 p134*
Zucco, Angelo; Iowa, 1866-1943 *123.54 p52*
Zucco, Antonio; Iowa, 1866-1943 *123.54 p53*
Zucco, Frank; Iowa, 1866-1943 *123.54 p53*
Zucco, Joseph; Iowa, 1866-1943 *123.54 p83*
Zuearell, Lui; Wisconsin, n.d. *9675.8 p126*
Zuebelin, Anton; Dayton, OH, 1869-1887 *8582 p36*
Zuehlsdorf, William; Wisconsin, n.d. *9675.8 p126*
Zuendt, Ernst Anton; America, 1857 *8582.1 p38*
  With wife & 2 sons
Zufelt, Fred; Washington, 1859-1920 *2872.1 p45*
Zugeisen, Maria; Georgia, 1739 *9332 p323*
Zugreif, Henrich; Philadelphia, 1779 *8137 p15*
Zuhlsdorf, John; Wisconsin, n.d. *9675.8 p126*
Zuk, Joseph Anton; Arkansas, 1918 *95.2 p134*
Zukaitis, Anna; Wisconsin, n.d. *9675.8 p126*
Zukaitis, Miekalina; Wisconsin, n.d. *9675.8 p126*
Zukaitis, Tony; Wisconsin, n.d. *9675.8 p126*
Zukaitiz, Jonas; Wisconsin, n.d. *9675.8 p126*
Zukajtis, John; Wisconsin, n.d. *9675.8 p126*
Zuke, Pole; Arkansas, 1918 *95.2 p134*

Zukowski, Tomasz; New York, 1831 *4606 p178*
Zulauf, Johannes; Philadelphia, 1779 *8137 p15*
Zulpo, Ernest; Arkansas, 1918 *95.2 p134*
Zulpo, John 24; Arkansas, 1918 *95.2 p134*
Zumbusch, Anton; America, 1839 *8582.2 p60*
Zumbusch, Anton; Baltimore, 1839 *8582.1 p38*
Zumbusch, Anton; Kentucky, 1869-1887 *8582 p36*
Zumbusch, Ferdinand Maria; America, 1848 *8582.2 p47*
Zumbusch, Ferdinand Maria; New York, NY, 1848
  8582.2 p47
Zumdoyle, Christian; Illinois, 1853 *7857 p8*
Zumstag, Martin; Illinois, 1874 *2896.5 p44*
Zumstein, Georg M.; America, 1847 *8582.1 p38*
Zumwalde, Wilhelm; Kentucky, 1839-1840 *8582.3 p99*
Zunich, John; Iowa, 1866-1943 *123.54 p53*
Zunich, Matt; Iowa, 1866-1943 *123.54 p83*
Zunich, Thomas; Iowa, 1866-1943 *123.54 p85*
Zuperko, Joseph; Wisconsin, n.d. *9675.8 p126*
Zurcher, Hans; Pennsylvania, 1709-1710 *4480 p311*
Zurlinden, Friedrich; Iroquois Co., IL, 1892 *3455.1 p14*
Zuro, Desiderio Matij; Iowa, 1866-1943 *123.54 p85*
Zuro, Matt; Iowa, 1866-1943 *123.54 p85*
Zvirn, Michael; Wisconsin, n.d. *9675.8 p126*
Zweck, George; Colorado, 1894 *9678.3 p19*
Zwerens, Barbara *SEE* Zwerens, Johann
Zwerens, Barbara Hemminger *SEE* Zwerens, Johann
Zwerens, Cunrad *SEE* Zwerens, Johann
Zwerens, Johann; Pennsylvania, 1753 *2444 p237*
  *Wife:*Barbara Hemminger
  *Child:*Wilhelm Ludwig Lorenz
  *Child:*Cunrad
  *Child:*Barbara
  *Child:*Regina
  *Child:*Johannes
  *Child:*Rosina
Zwerens, Johannes *SEE* Zwerens, Johann
Zwerens, Regina *SEE* Zwerens, Johann
Zwerens, Rosina *SEE* Zwerens, Johann
Zwerens, Wilhelm Ludwig Lorenz *SEE* Zwerens, Johann
Zwerenz, Barbara *SEE* Zwerenz, Johann
Zwerenz, Barbara Hemminger *SEE* Zwerenz, Johann
Zwerenz, Cunrad *SEE* Zwerenz, Johann
Zwerenz, Johann; Pennsylvania, 1753 *2444 p237*
  *Wife:*Barbara Hemminger
  *Child:*Wilhelm Ludwig Lorenz
  *Child:*Cunrad

  *Child:*Barbara
  *Child:*Regina
  *Child:*Johannes
  *Child:*Rosina
Zwerenz, Johannes *SEE* Zwerenz, Johann
Zwerenz, Regina *SEE* Zwerenz, Johann
Zwerenz, Rosina *SEE* Zwerenz, Johann
Zwerenz, Wilhelm Ludwig Lorenz *SEE* Zwerenz, Johann
Zwerner, Christina Magdalena *SEE* Zwerner, Johann
  Adam
Zwerner, Elisabetha M. Demmler *SEE* Zwerner, Johann
  Adam
Zwerner, Johann Adam 32; Pennsylvania, 1753 *2444*
  p237
  *Wife:*Elisabetha M. Demmler
  *Child:*Christina Magdalena
Zwick, G. A.; America, 1847 *8582.3 p73*
Zwicker, . . .; Canada, 1776-1783 *9786 p37*
Zwiesler, Michael J.; Dayton, OH, 1869-1887 *8582 p36*
Zwifler, Anna Regina; Georgia, 1734 *9332 p328*
Zwilling, Georg; South Carolina, 1788 *7119 p203*
Zwirner, Christina Magdalena *SEE* Zwirner, Johan Adam
Zwirner, Elisabetha M. Demmler *SEE* Zwirner, Johan
  Adam
Zwirner, Johan Adam 32; Pennsylvania, 1753 *2444 p237*
  *Wife:*Elisabetha M. Demmler
  *Child:*Christina Magdalena
Zwoerner, Christina Magdalena *SEE* Zwoerner, Johann
  Adam
Zwoerner, Elisabetha M. Demmler *SEE* Zwoerner,
  Johann Adam
Zwoerner, Johann Adam 32; Pennsylvania, 1753 *2444*
  p237
  *Wife:*Elisabetha M. Demmler
  *Child:*Christina Magdalena
Zygadlo, . . .; New York, 1831 *4606 p178*
Zyglewicz, John; Arkansas, 1918 *95.2 p134*
Zylstra, William; Arkansas, 1918 *95.2 p134*
Zylstra, William 32; Arkansas, 1918 *95.2 p134*
Zyprian, . . .; Canada, 1776-1783 *9786 p37*
Zywicki, . . .; New York, 1831 *4606 p178*
Zywiec, Peter; Arkansas, 1918 *95.2 p134*